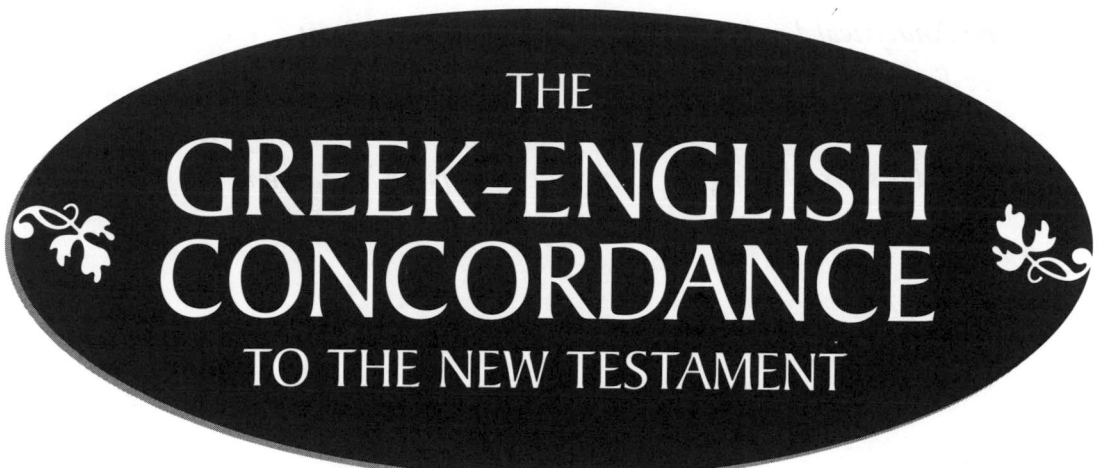

THE GREEK-ENGLISH CONCORDANCE
TO THE NEW TESTAMENT

Zondervan Greek Reference Series

The Analytical Lexicon to the Greek New Testament
The Exhaustive Concordance to the Greek New Testament
The Greek-English Concordance to the Greek New Testament
A Reader's Greek-English Lexicon of the New Testament

·ZONDERVAN GREEK REFERENCE SERIES·

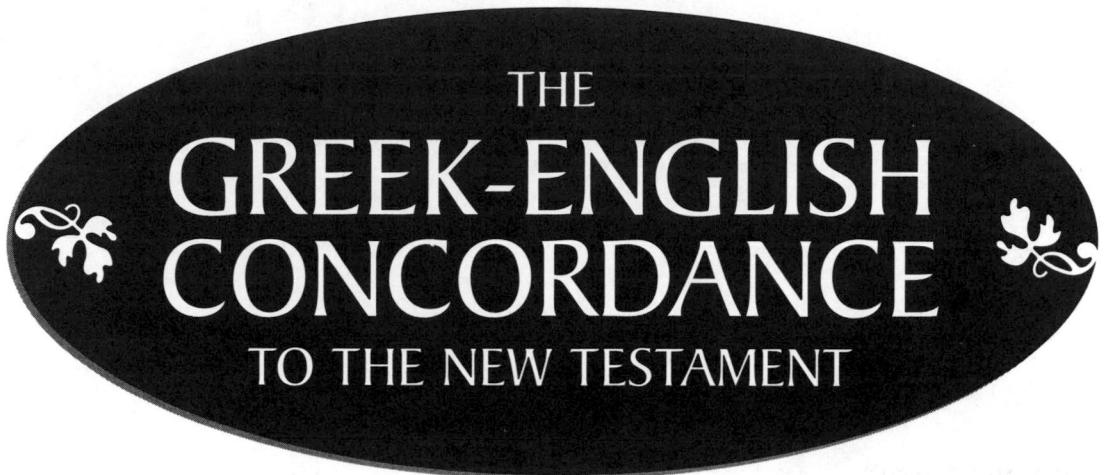

THE GREEK-ENGLISH CONCORDANCE
TO THE NEW TESTAMENT

JOHN R. KOHLENBERGER III

EDWARD W. GOODRICK

JAMES A. SWANSON

ZONDERVAN™

GRAND RAPIDS, MICHIGAN 49530

ZONDERVAN™

The Greek-English Concordance to the New Testament
Copyright © 1997 by John R. Kohlenberger III, Edward W. Goodrick,
James A. Swanson

Requests for information should be addressed to:

Zondervan, *Grand Rapids, Michigan 49530*

Library of Congress Cataloging-in-Publication Data

Kohlenberger, John R.
   The Greek-English concordance to the New Testament / John R. Kohlenberger III, Edward W. Goodrick, James A.
Swanson.
   p. cm.
   ISBN: 0-310-40220-4
   1. Bible. N.T.—Concordances, Greek. 2. Bible. N.T.—Concordances, English—New International.   I. Goodrick,
Edward A., 1913– . II. Swanson, James A. III. Title.
BS2302.K657 1997
225.4'8—dc20   93-32117
                                                   CIP

This edition printed on acid-free paper.

Printed in the United States of America

06 07 /❖ DC/ 10 9 8 7 6

Contents

Acknowledgments

Thanks to Stan Gundry, vice president and editor-in-chief, and Bruce Ryskamp, president of Zondervan Publishing House, for their support and encouragement in permitting us to do this book. Thanks to editors Ed van der Maas and Verlyn Verbrugge for their expert guidance and interaction.

Thanks to Dr. Walter W. Wessel of Bethel Seminary West for interacting with text-critical questions relating to the NIV.

Thanks to Roger Green and Tim Hare of Telios Systems for their work in developing the programing to analyze, sort, and set the contexts for this concordance.

Thanks to Mike and Joan Petersen of Multnomah Graphics for allowing round-the-clock access to their equipment and for their valuable assistance in producing the page proofs.

Editors John R. Kohlenberger III and James A. Swanson acknowledge the significant role of our mentor and friend Edward W. Goodrick, no longer with us but with the Lord. Although Ed was not actively involved in the production of this concordance, he had a crucial role in its design and especially in the development of the database from which it was drawn. Thus he is rightly listed as a co-editor.

Special thanks to our wives and children—Carolyn, Sarah, and Joshua Kohlenberger, and Sandra, Jon, David, and Natanya Lee Swanson—for their loving encouragement and boundless patience.

Introduction

A concordance is an index to a book. It is usually arranged in alphabetical order and shows the location of each word in the book. In addition, it often supplies several words of the context in which each word is found.

The Greek-English Concordance to the New Testament (*GECNT*) is a counterpart to *The Exhaustive Concordance to the Greek New Testament* (*ECGNT*) (Zondervan, 1995), prepared for those who are not fluent in New Testament Greek. Both volumes index the Greek New Testament; however, all headings and contexts in the former volume are in Greek, while in the current volume the headings are also transliterated and the contexts are in the English of the New International Version (NIV). All headings are also numbered according to the Goodrick/Kohlenberger numbering system so that readers can move from the English-oriented *NIV Exhaustive Concordance* (Zondervan, 1990) into this Greek-oriented concordance. Further, the current volume contains a complete listing of NIV NT vocabulary that is indexed to the Greek, so that readers can move directly from the English text into the Greek concordance. Also unique to this volume is a concise Greek-English dictionary that both defines every word in the Greek NT and indexes these words to the standard word study resources.

The Greek-English Concordance to the New Testament provides an exhaustive index to the vocabulary of the Greek New Testament according to *The Greek New Testament*, Fourth Revised Edition (UBS4) edited by Barbara Aland, Kurt Aland, Johannes Karavidopoulos, Carlo M. Martini, and Bruce M. Metzger (Deutsche Bibelgesellschaft / United Bible Societies, 1994), which is identical in text (though not always in format and punctuation) to the 26th edition of the Nestle-Aland *Novum Testamentum Graece* (NA26). In addition, the *GECNT* notes all variant readings between UBS4 and the Greek text that underlies the NIV.[1] Most of the vocabulary is indexed with full contexts; nineteen highly frequent words are indexed by reference only.

The *GECNT* is the first Greek-English concordance that is not based on the King James Version and its underlying text, the so-called *Textus Receptus*. The first Greek-English concordance remains the best known and most widely used. Samuel Bagster and Sons of London first published George V. Wigram's *The Englishman's Greek Concordance of the New Testament* in 1839. The ninth edition of 1903 has been reprinted by several publishers, including Zondervan. Its most popular editions are indexed to Strong's numbering system, but contain no further enhancements or updates. The editors of the *GECNT* have attempted to update and improve on Wigram's pioneering work by including all his well-designed features, including English contexts, a Greek-English vocabulary (dictionary), English-Greek index, and variant readings.

---

1. Because there is no available documentation from the International Bible Society or the Committee on Bible Translation, the Greek text that underlies the NIV has been reconstructed by the editors with the assistance of Dr. Walter W. Wessel of Bethel Seminary West. The variant readings noted in this concordance do not officially represent the International Bible Society or the Committee on Bible Translation, but are the full responsibility of the editors.

Three Greek-English concordances that followed Wigram provide an index to the Greek NT by means of KJV vocabulary; however, none of them include contexts. These are Charles F. Hudson's *A Critical Greek and English Concordance of the New Testament* (Boston: Hosea L. Hastings, 1870), revised by Ezra Abbot in 1892; Jacob Brubaker Smith's still printed *Greek-English Concordance to the New Testament* (Scottsdale: Herald, 1955); and J. Stenega's *The Greek-English Analytical Concordance of the Greek-English New Testament* (Jackson: Hellenes, 1963).

Features of *The Greek-English Concordance to the New Testament*

The *GECNT* expands on the features of these previously published concordances, presenting exhaustive indexes, generous contexts, valuable statistics, and unique features in an affordable and manageable volume. It is divided into four major sections: (1) the Main Concordance, (2) the Index of Articles, Conjunctions, Particles, and Pronouns, (3) the English-Greek Index to the NIV New Testament, and (4) a Concise Greek-English Dictionary to the New Testament.

THE MAIN CONCORDANCE

The following presents elements from a typical entry in the Main Concordance:

> **34** ἄγγελος, **angelos** [175 / 176] [→ *32, 33, 334, 550, 791, 1334, 1972, 2039, 2040, 2041, 2294, 2295, 2296, 2694, 2858, 2859, 4132, 4133, 4600, 4603, 4615; cf. 72*]
>
> ἄγγελος κυρίου (angel of the Lord) [12] Mt 1:20,24; 2:13,19; 28:2; Lk 1:11; 2:9; Ac 5:19; 8:26; 12:7,11,23
>
> angel [86], angels [81], messenger [4], angel's [2], messengers [2], spies [1]
>
> Mt   1:20   an **angel** of the Lord appeared to him in a dream and said,
>
> Lk   1:28   The **angel** [UBS-] went to her and said, "Greetings, you who are

The heading consists of:

(1)   the Goodrick/Kohlenberger (G/K) number: **34**;

(2)   the indexed word in Greek, ἄγγελος, and in transliteration, ***angelos***;

(3)   the frequency count in parentheses, UBS4 first, NIV second: [175 / 176];

(4)   the list of related words in brackets, listed by G/K number, following the arrow: → ;

(5)   the special phrase index, in Greek with simple English translation, including its own frequency count and textual references: ἄγγελος κυρίου (angel of the Lord) [12] Mt 1:20,24;

(6)   the list of NIV translations, in descending order of frequency: angel [86], angels [81], etc.

The context lines consist of:

(1)   the book-chapter-verse reference;

(2)   the context for the indexed word;

(3)   the textual variant flag: [UBS-].

Headings

There are six kinds of headings: (1) Greek word headings, (2) Greek words not in the UBS4 and NIV texts, (3) related words lists, (4) phrase-index subheadings, (5) NIV translations, and (6) "See" references.

(1) *Greek Word Headings*

The Greek NT contains 138,013 words in UBS4 (137,931 in the NIV), with a vocabulary of 5,433 words. The *GECNT* is an exhaustive alphabetical index to every word of the Greek NT.

The simplest heading is a word with its G/K number and its frequency count[2]:

2 'Ααρων, *Aarōn* [5]

The heading presents the word in its lexical form, both in Greek and in English transliteration. Thus the frequency count lists the total number of times the word occurs in the NT, regardless of spelling. If the frequency counts differ between the UBS4 and NIV texts, the UBS4 total is given first:

41 ἅγιος, *hagios* [233 / 234]

In this example, ἅγιος occurs 233 times in UBS4 and 234 times in the NIV. The variant reading itself is noted within the context at Revelation 22:21.

(2) *Greek Words Not in UBS4 and NIV*

As mentioned above, the NT has a vocabulary of 5,433 words. The G/K numbering system, however, accounts for 6,068 words. This vocabulary list was developed by collating the major Greek lexicons—such as those by Bauer, Arndt, Gingrich, and Danker; Louw and Nida; and Thayer—alphabetizing the lists, and then assigning each word a sequential number corresponding to its alphabetical order. The list and its numbering system were developed to replace the useful but dated system developed by James Strong for his *Exhaustive Concordance* of 1890. The G/K numbering system was introduced in *The NIV Exhaustive Concordance*, which also includes two complete indices showing the correspondence of the G/K system to Strong's. The G/K numbering system has also been used in the *Zondervan NIV Nave's Topical Bible* (Zondervan, 1992), the *NIV Compact Nave's Topical Bible* (Zondervan, 1993), the *Zondervan NIV Bible Commentary* (Zondervan, 1994), *The Exhaustive Concordance to the Greek New Testament*, and Zondervan's *BibleSource for Windows* software.

---

2.   Because they are drawn from the same database, the frequency counts of the *ECGNT* and the *GECNT* are identical, with one difference in presentation involving Greek contractions. In the former concordance, the frequency counts for words that appear in contractions did not include the contracted forms; in the current concordance, they do. Thus, for example, in the *ECGNT* the frequency for word *2779 kai* is [9018 / 8997] while in the *GECNT* it is [9161 / 9140]. This is because the latter totals include the contractions *2743 kagō, 2795 kakei, 2796 kakeithen, 2797 kakeinos,* and *2829 kan.* In addition to the frequency counts, the context for these words, or the references in the Index of Articles, Etc., also includes the references to the contractions.

Of the 6,068 total words in the G/K numbering system, 635 words are variant readings or alternate spellings that are not indexed in the *GECNT*:

15 ἀγαθοεργός, *agathoergos* Not used in UBS/NIV

These words are listed without contexts to show that they were not accidentally omitted from the concordance.

(3) *Related Words Lists*

Following most Greek word headings in brackets is a list of words that are related by root or share common elements. For convenience of space, the words are listed by G/K number rather than in Greek:

33 ἀγγέλλω, *angellō* [1] [√ 34]

34 ἄγγελος, *angelos* [175 / 176] [→ 32, 33, 334, 550, 791, 1334, 1972, 2039, 2040, 2041, 2294, 2295, 2296, 2694, 2858, 2859, 4132, 4133, 4600, 4603, 4615; cf. 72]

Rather than listing all related words after each Greek word heading, one word was selected to act as the organizing head. Related words point to the organizing head with a root symbol (√), while the organizing word points to the related word list with an arrow (→). On occasion, the list includes more distantly related words for comparison (cf.). Tentative connections are followed by question marks (?).

Please note that although the root symbol is used as the pointer to the organizing head, this does not mean that the editors understand this word to be the etymological "root" of all related forms. This is true, for example, of the fourteen verbs that are composed of one or two prepositions prefixed to the verb βαίνω (*bainō*). Because *bainō* does not occur in the NT, it could not be used as an organizing head; thus all *bainō* verbs are related to the first such verb in alphabetical order, ἀναβαίνω (*anabainō*). The related words lists are included as pointers to cognate studies; however, the editors do not encourage speculative etymology. Take, for example, the words ἀγγέλλω (*angellō*) and ἄγγελος (*angelos*) cited above. Although these words are related, they do not define each other. Not everyone who brings news is an angel, and not every angel is a messenger.

(4) *Phrase-Index Subheadings*

In addition to indexing all occurrences of every word in the Greek NT, the *GECNT* indexes 2,977 significant and frequent phrases, as well as significant forms of words:

19 ἀγαθός, *agathos* [102]

ἀγαθός ἔργον (good work) [14] Ac 9:36; Ro 2:7; 13:3; 2Co 9:8; Eph 2:10; Php 1:6; Col 1:10; 2Th 2:17; 1Ti 2:10; 5:10; 2Ti 2:21; 3:17; Tit 1:16; 3:1

ἀγαθός συνείδησις (good conscience) [5] Ac 23:1; 1Ti 1:5,19; 1Pe 3:16,21

κακός ... ἀγαθός (evil ... good) [10] Lk 16:25; Ro 3:8; 7:19; 12:21; 13:3,4; 16:19; 1Th 5:15; 1Pe 3:11; 3Jn 1:11

The above example shows fourteen verses where the adjective ἀγαθός (*agathos*) modifies the noun ἔργον (*ergon*). Note that such examples are not suborganized by the specific inflection or by word order, but are simply in biblical order. Note also that there may be intervening words within the Greek phrase. The English translation in parentheses is a simple rendering of the phrase that uses NIV vocabulary, but does not list every way in which the NIV translates the phrase, which includes "do right," "doing good," and "good deed," in addition to "good work" and "good works." Ellipses (...) are used in the third index to indicate verses in which the antonyms κακός (*kakos*) and ἀγαθός (*agathos*) occur, again not suborganized by inflection, word order, or intervening words.

The phrase-index lists are especially useful in identifying highly frequent phrases composed of frequent words. There are, for example, forty phrase-index lists for the word θεός (*theos*), "God," and twenty for κύριος (*kyrios*), "Lord."

(5) *NIV Translations*

The *GECNT* shows the relationship of the Greek NT to the English of the NIV in several ways. In the headings, the list of NIV translations shows every way in which the NIV renders any Greek word. This list is organized in descending order of frequency:

2 'Ααρων, *Aarōn* [5]

> Aaron [4], Aaron's [1]

26 ἀγαπάω, *agapaō* [143] [→ *27, 28*]

> love [74], loved [40], loves [22], love [*+27*] [2], truly love [2], longed for [1], loving [1], showed love [1]

Most proper and place names have only one or two translations: absolute and possessive, as in the case of "Aaron" and "Aaron's." Verbs like ἀγαπάω (*agapaō*) may have several forms, such as "love," "loved," "loves," and "loving," "love." Many words have multiple word translations, such as "longed for" and "showed love." And, if more than one Greek word is translated by an NIV word or phrase, the G/K number of the additional word or words is included in brackets with a plus sign (+), as in "love [+27]." If a word is not directly translated in the NIV, the italicized word "*untranslated*" appears in the list, with the total number of times the word was not translated in brackets. NIV-Greek relationships are also shown in the contexts by means of bold and italic typefaces, G/K numbers, and abbreviations, as detailed below.

(6) *"See" References*

Nineteen words in the Greek NT occur a total of 53,425 times in UBS4 and 53,379 times in the NIV. These words are indexed exhaustively in their own section: the Index of Articles, Conjunctions, Particles, and Pronouns (see p. xv). These words are also represented by headings in the Main Concordance, including NIV translations, with a message referring to the Index of Articles:

899 αὐτός [5601 / 5593] See Index of Articles, Etc.
> [→ *881, 882, 883, 894, 895, 896, 897, 898, 900, 901, 1571, 1831, 1929, 1994, 2070, 4194, 4932, 5437, 5796, 6058*]

> him [1388], his [902], them [814], *untranslated* [639], their [281], ...

Context Lines

The two-column format of the *GECNT* allows for sizeable contexts, often containing complete sentences or even whole verses. The purpose of context lines in a concordance is simply to help the reader locate a specific verse in the Bible. For word study—or any kind of Bible study—the context offered by a concordance is rarely enough, even when an entire verse fits on one line, as do John 1:2 and 11:35.

Taken by themselves, context lines can and do misrepresent the teaching of Scripture by taking statements out the larger biblical context. The words "your faith is futile; you are still in your sins" are taken directly from 1 Corinthians 15:17, but are not statements of fact; these conditions would only exist "if Christ has not been raised." Great care has been taken by the editors and programer of the *GECNT* to create contexts that are informative and accurate. But the reader should always check these limited contexts against the larger text of the English or Greek NT.

(1) *Context Lines: General Format*

The following examples are from the entry for word *41* ἅγιος (*hagios*). The simplest context line presents three items of information. First, the location of the indexed word by book (abbreviated in English), chapter, and verse. (For the few differences between NIV and UBS4 versification, see the list on page xviii.) Second, the context line. Third, within the context line, the NIV translation of the word in bold type. Because the contexts show the relationship of the Greek and the NIV, each occurrence of a word has its own context line:

> Rev 4: 8 "**Holy**, holy, holy is the Lord God Almighty, who was, and is,
>   4: 8 "Holy, **holy**, holy is the Lord God Almighty, who was, and is,
>   4: 8 "Holy, holy, **holy** is the Lord God Almighty, who was, and is,

(2) *Context Lines: Multiple Word Translation*

If more than one NIV word is used to define a Greek word, all the NIV words are bold:

> 1Co 7:34 Her aim is to be **devoted to the Lord** in both body and spirit.
>   16:11 Now about the collection for **God's people**: Do what I told the

If more than one Greek word is translated by an NIV word or phrase, the G/K number of the additional word (or words) is included in brackets in the context, as in the following contexts, which occur under words *41* ἅγιος (*hagios*) and *2813* καλέω (*kaleō*) respectively:

> Lk   2:23 "Every firstborn male *is to be* **consecrated** [*+2813*] to the Lord"),
> Lk   2:23 "Every firstborn male *is to be* **consecrated** [*+41*] to the Lord"),

The preceding contexts also illustrate the italicizing of NIV words that are used to assist in the translation of Greek inflections, such as the tense of verbs and the case of nouns and adjectives. Because these NIV words show the *form* of the Greek word rather than its *definition*, a different typeface is used to show this different relationship. Both defining and assisting words are necessary in translation. In the *GECNT*, as in the *NIV Exhaustive Concordance*, defining words are in bold and assisting words are in italics.

(3) *Context Lines: Abbreviations for Untranslated and Substituted Words*

Under "NIV Translations" on page xi, it was noted that some Greek words are not directly translated in the NIV. This is true of all English Bible translations, because the biblical languages cannot always be translated word for word into understandable English. So for stylistic reasons, the NIV sometimes does not translate repetitive Greek words or translates nouns with pronouns and pronouns with nouns. But even words left untranslated in the NIV are indexed with contexts. These stylistic translation choices are indicated by a system of abbreviations within the context.

Untranslated Words: Not In English (NIE). Most words left untranslated in the NIV, as in the KJV and other English versions, are articles, conjunctions, and prepositions, most of which are not indexed with contexts. Word *2627* ἰδού (*idou*), often "behold" in the KJV, is untranslated in the NIV seventy-five of its two hundred occurrences. These contexts in the *GECNT* contain the abbreviation [**NIE**] to indicate the word is not in English. Note the following contexts with and without direct translation:

> Mt 23:34   Therefore [**NIE**] I am sending you prophets and wise men
> 23:38   **Look**, your house is left to you desolate.

Untranslated Words: Repeated Greek Word (RPG). The NIV sometimes leaves a repeated Greek word untranslated for the sake of English style. These words are included in the *GECNT*, but are marked with the abbreviation [**RPG**]. Matthew 10:13 in the NIV, for example, does not repeat the word "deserving" to translate the second occurrence of *545* ἄξιος (*axios*): "If the home is deserving, let your peace rest on it; if it is not [*deserving*], let your peace return to you." The contexts in the *GECNT* are as follows:

> Mt 10:13   "If the home is **deserving**, let your peace rest on it; if it is not
> 10:13   peace rest on it; if it is not [**RPG**], let your peace return to you."

Because the contexts are in biblical order, the context preceding an RPG context shows the contextual definition of the Greek word that is not translated in the RPG context.

Untranslated Words: Redundant Greek Preposition (RP). Many Greek verbs are composites of simple Greek verbs and prepositions, such as *599* ἀπέρχομαι (*aperchomai*), which prefixes the preposition *608* ἀπό (*apo*) to the verb *2262* ἔρχομαι (*erchomai*). Even though this composite verb has a built-in preposition, the Greek sentence often repeats the preposition independently, as in Matthew 28:8. The first part of this verse would be translated the same with or without the redundant preposition: "So the women hurried away from the tomb." But to show that the preposition is present, even though it is not independently translated, the abbreviation *RP* is prefixed to the G/K number of the preposition in the verb's context and to the G/K number of the verb in the preposition's context, as in the following examples from words *599* and *608*:

> Mt 28: 8   So the women hurried **away** [*RP608*] **from** the tomb, afraid yet
> Mt 28: 8   So the women hurried **away from** [*RP599*] the tomb, afraid yet

Substitute translation (ˢ). Substitute translation occurs in the following example from word *180* ἄκανθα (*akantha*), usually translated "thorns" in the NIV. Mark 4:7 is rendered first word for word and then in the NIV:

> And other fell among the thorns, and the thorns grew up and choked it, and it produced no fruit.
> Other seed fell among thorns, which grew up and choked the plants, so that they did not bear grain.

In this verse, the NIV adds clarifying words and eliminates redundancy, all of which is justified in the context and makes for more readable English. Rather than repeat the word "thorns," the NIV uses the relative pronoun "which." The contexts in the *GECNT* are as follows:

> Mk 4: 7   Other seed fell among **thorns**, which grew up and choked the
> 4: 7   Other seed fell among thorns, **which**ˢ [*+3836*] grew up and choked the

The first context shows the one-to-one relationship of the word ἄκανθα with the NIV "**thorns**." The second context shows the *substitute* translation of "which" for ἄκανθα and the definite article *3836* ὁ ("the thorns" in the word-for-word translation). The substitution is shown by the superscript "s" in both the list of NIV translations and in the context, while the multiple word translation is shown by the additional G/K number in brackets.

(4) *Context Lines: Textual Variants*

The Greek text underlying the NIV varies from UBS4 in three ways: additions, omissions, and differences. Each variant has its own format.

Words Not in UBS4 but in the NIV [UBS-]. When a word occurs in the NIV but not in UBS4, the bolded word is followed by [UBS-], as in the following example from *297* ἀμήν (*amēn*):

Php 4:23 grace of our Lord Jesus Christ be with your spirit. **Amen**. [UBS-]

Words Not in the NIV but in UBS4 [UBS+]. When a word occurs in UBS4 but not in the NIV, the bracketed code [UBS+] is inserted in the appropriate place in the context. Included in the brackets is a translation of the word or phrase in italics, with the indexed word in bold italics, as in the following example from *297* ἀμήν (*amēn*):

1Th 3:13 when our Lord Jesus comes with all his holy ones. [UBS+ *Amen*.]

Words That Differ in Identical Contexts. Contexts in which the indexed word differs between UBS4 and the NIV are flagged with a cross-reference to the variant reading, as in the case of UBS4 word *98* Ἀδμίν (*Admin*) and NIV word *730* Ἀράμ (*Aram*) in Luke 3:33:

Lk   3:33 the son *of* <u>Ram</u>, [UBS *Admin*; NIV *730*] the son of Hezron,
Lk   3:33 the son *of* **Ram**, [UBS *98*] the son of Hezron, the son of Perez,

The first context for the word *98* represents UBS4 but points to the NIV reading, word *730*. Because the word "Ram" represents the NIV text, it is underlined rather than bold. The translation of the UBS4 text is once again within the brackets in bold italics. The second context for word *730* represents the NIV but points to the UBS4 reading, word *98*.

In most cases these variant readings are well documented in the critical apparatus of UBS4. On occasion, an NIV variant is not represented in the apparatus of UBS4, but is in the apparatus of NA26. Note, for example, the appearance of ὁ Ἰησοῦς in Matthew 9:1 of the NIV. All differences between the Greek text underlying the NIV and UBS4 are listed in the apparatus of *The Greek New Testament: UBS4 with NRSV & NIV*, edited by John R. Kohlenberger III (Grand Rapids: Zondervan, 1993). Variants documented in NA26 but not UBS4 are marked with a dagger (†) in the apparatus of that Greek testament.

THE INDEX OF ARTICLES, CONJUNCTIONS, PARTICLES, AND PRONOUNS

The Main Concordance indexes 84,588 UBS4 references and 84,552 NIV references to 5,414 Greek words. The Index of Articles, Conjunctions, Particles, and Pronouns indexes 53,425 UBS4 references and 53,379 NIV references to nineteen highly frequent Greek words.

The format of the Index of Articles, Etc. is simple. Each of the nineteen words has its own heading, followed by a frequency count, UBS4 first, NIV second. Words are followed by an exhaustive index of occurrences. Each book abbreviation and chapter number are in bold print for easier location. Variants between the UBS4 and NIV texts are indicated by [U] and [N] flags:

$$1609 \quad \dot{\epsilon}\gamma\dot{\omega}, \textit{ egō} \quad [2667 / 2669]$$

Mt 1:23; **2:**6, 8, 8, 15; **3:**11, 11, 11, 14, 14, 15, 17; **4:**9, 10[N], 19; **5:**11, 22, 28, 32, 34, 39, 44; **6:**9, 11, 11, 12, 12, 12,

THE ENGLISH-GREEK INDEX TO THE NIV NEW TESTAMENT   _____

The English-Greek Index to the NIV New Testament assists users in moving directly from the NIV NT into the *GECNT*. This index lists every word in the NIV NT in alphabetical order, followed by a complete list of the Greek words translated by any NIV phrase that includes the indexed word:

AGAINST [208]

> against, *2848, kata* [47]
> against, *AIT* [15]
> against, *RPE* [3]
> against, *2093+3836+5111, epi+ho+stēthos* [2]
> rebelling against, *468, anthistēmi* [1]
> pressing [against], *632, apothlibō* [1]

The index of NIV-Greek equivalents is listed in descending order of frequency. Thus, the first line indicates that the Greek word *2848, kata,* is the word most frequently rendered "against" in the NIV. English phrases including the word "against" are also indexed, as in the case of "rebelling against," as are Greek phrases translated "against," such as *2093+3836+5111, epi+ho+stēthos.* Note that in Greek phrases the words are sorted by G/K number, so that every occurrence of a specific phrase can be listed together, regardless of the word order in the original Greek.

The use of brackets in "pressing [against]" indicates that the word "against" does double duty in the NIV translation. This example is taken from Luke 8:45, "Master, the people are crowding and pressing against you." This sentence has two Greek verbs: *5315, synthlibō,* which here is translated "crowding against," and *632, apothlibō,* which here is translated "pressing against." But rather than translating "Master, the people are crowding against and pressing against you," the NIV uses "against" only once in its stylistically correct English. The word "against" is in bold in both contexts in the main concordance to show each word's contextual meaning. In the index, since the word "against" is only used once in this verse in the NIV, it is in brackets with one of the Greek verbs to indicate that it was not counted twice in the total NIV word statistic of 208.

NIV words that do not directly translate the Greek are also listed with statistics and abbreviations. *AIT* is the abbreviation for "assists in translation," referring to NIV words that are used to render Greek tenses, number, and cases (see page xii). Because *AIT* words do not define Greek words, they are not linked to a specific G/K number. The abbreviation *NIG* indicates "not in Greek," and notes words that are supplied for English readability but that do not directly translate any Greek words (compare *NIE* above on page xiii). The abbreviation *RPE*, "repeated English word," is a special category of *NIE*, noting the stylistic repetition of a word that was used to directly translate a Greek word earlier in a context. These statistics are included for the sake of completeness, but cannot be further researched in the *GECNT*. However, *The NIV Exhaustive Concordance* can be consulted to find every *AIT* or *NIG* use of any English word in the entire NIV.

This index also indicates "substitute translation" with a superscript "s," as in Abraham[s], *899, autos* [3] (see pages xiii-xiv).

The English-Greek Index to the NIV New Testament does represent the entire vocabulary of the NIV NT. However, it does not indicate the Greek word that underlies a specific NIV word in a specific context. Again, *The NIV Exhaustive Concordance* is the best resource for determining NIV-Greek relationships within a specific verse.

A CONCISE GREEK-ENGLISH DICTIONARY
TO THE NEW TESTAMENT

The final section of the GECNT offers a concise definition for each word of the Greek NT, including words that do not appear in the NIV and UBS4 Greek texts. In addition, each word is indexed to three standard word study resources for further research.

> *3* Ἀβαδδών, *Abaddōn*, n.pr., "destruction." *Abaddon.* S: *3*, BAGD: 1A, CB: –

> *4* ἀβαρής, *abarēs*, a. *not burdensome.* S: *4*, BAGD: 1B, CB: –

> *5* ἀββά, *abba,* l.[n.]. *father.* S: *5**, BAGD: 1B, CB: 339A

> *735* ἀργύρεος, *argyreos*, a. *(made of) silver.* S: *693*, BAGD: 105A cf. -ους,
>   CB: 343C cf. *-ous*

The first four elements of each entry are always the same: G/K number, Greek word, transliteration, and part of speech. If the word is a proper name that has a meaning in Greek or Hebrew, that meaning follows the part of speech in quotation marks, as in entry *3*, where "Abaddon" means "destruction" in Hebrew. The final four elements are also always the same: the concise definition (in italics), the index to Strong's numbering system (following S:); the index to the Bauer, Arndt, Gingrich, and Danker *Lexicon* (following BAGD:); and the index to Colin Brown's *Theological Dictionary* (following CB:).

The reference to Strong's numbering system keys the *GECNT* to a number of resources that use this standard, but dated system. Note that sometimes the Strong number has an asterisk (*), as in entry *5*, which means that the spelling in the *GECNT* is not exactly the same as Strong's spelling.

A Greek-English Lexicon of the New Testament and Other Early Christian Literature by Bauer, Arndt, Gingrich, and Danker (University of Chicago / Zondervan, 1979) is an indispensable resources to students of the NT. The number in the BAGD index refers to the page; the letter of the alphabet refers to the "quadrant" of the page: A is the upper half of the left column, B is the lower left column, C is upper right, and D is lower right. If an entry word is spelled differently in BAGD or is contained within a different article, this is noted after the page reference, as in entry *735*. Consult this standard resource for more thorough definitions and more specific contextual renderings.

The four volume *New International Dictionary of New Testament Theology*, edited by Colin Brown (Zondervan, 1986), offers more thorough, theologically oriented treatment of key Greek words. It is organized by English articles, but volume four contains several indexes, including the Greek index to which the CB: references point. The three-digit number is the page reference to volume four; the letter of the alphabet refers to the first (A), second (B), or third (C) column. If an entry word is spelled differently in CB, this is noted after the page reference, as in entry *735*. If CB contains no article on the designated word, this is indicated by the dash: CB: –.

ABBREVIATIONS

Books of the New Testament

1Co	1 Corinthians	2Pe	2 Peter	Gal	Galatians	Mt.	Matthew

1Co . . . . 1 Corinthians
1Jn . . . . 1 John
1Pe . . . . 1 Peter
1Th . . . . 1 Thessalonians
1Ti 1Timothy
2Co . . . . 2 Corinthians
2Jn . . . . 2 John

2Pe . . . . 2 Peter
2Th . . . . 2 Thessalonians
2Ti . . . . 2 Timothy
3Jn . . . . 3 John
Ac . . . . Acts
Col. . . . . Colossians
Eph . . . . Ephesians

Gal . . . . Galatians
Heb . . . . Hebrews
Jas . . . . James
Jn . . . . John
Jude . . . . Jude
Lk . . . . Luke
Mk . . . . Mark

Mt. . . . . Matthew
Phm . . . . Philemon
Php . . . . Philippians
Rev . . . . Revelation
Ro. . . . . Romans
Tit. . . . . Titus

Parts of Speech, Translation Codes, and Book Titles

& . . . . and
? . . . . uncertain
+ . . . . plus
a. . . . . adjective
adv. . . . . adverb
adver. . . . . adversative
aff. . . . . affirmative
AIT . . . . . assist in translation
art. . . . . article
BAGD: . . . . Bauer, Arndt,
    Gingrich and Danker,
    Greek-English Lexicon
c. . . . . conjunction
CB: . . . . . . Colin Brown, *New*
    International Dictionary
    of New Testament Theology
comp. . . . . comparative

cond. . . . . conditional
contr. . . . . contraction
demo. . . . . demonstrative
disj. . . . . disjunctive
ECGNT . . . . *Exhaustive*
    Concordance to the Greek
    New Testament
emph. . . . . emphatic
excl. . . . . exclamation
g. . . . . gentilic
GECNT: . *Greek-English Con-*
    cordance to the
    New Testament
imper. . . . . impersonal
indef. . . . . indefinite
infer. . . . . inferential
inten. . . . . intensive

inter. . . . . interrogative
interj. . . . . interjection
l. . . . . loanword
letter . . . . letter of the alphabet
n. . . . . noun
neg. . . . . negative
NIE . . . . not in English
NIG . . . . not in Greek
NIV . . . . . . New International
    Version
num. . . . . numeral
p. . . . . pronoun
pers. . . . . personal
pl. . . . . plural
poss. . . . . possessive
pp. . . . . preposition
pp.* . . . . improper preposition

pr. . . . . proper [noun]
pt. . . . . particle
recip. . . . . reciprocal
reflex. . . . . reflexive
rel. . . . . relative
RP . . . . . redundant preposition
RPG . . . . repeated Greek word
S . . . . . Shorter ending of Mark
S: . . . . Strong's number
super. . . . . superlative
temp. . . . . temporal
trans. . . . . transitional
UBS4 . United Bible Societies'
    Greek New Testament:
    Fourth Edition
v. . . . . verb

GREEK TRANSLITERATION

Α, α . . . .*A, a*
Β, β . . . .*B, b*
Γ, γ . . . .*G, g*
Δ, δ . . . .*D, d*
Ε, ε . . . .*E, e*
Ζ, ζ . . . .*Z, z*
Η, η . . . .*Ē, ē*
Θ, θ . . . .*Th, th*
Ι, ι . . . .*I, i*

Κ, κ . . . .*K, k*
Λ, λ . . . .*L, l*
Μ, μ . . . .*M, m*
Ν, ν . . . .*N, n*
Ξ, ξ . . . .*X, x*
Ο, ο . . . .*O, o*
Π, π . . . .*P, p*
Ρ, ρ . . . .*R, r*

Σ, σ, ς . . . . *S, s, s*
Τ, τ . . . .*T, t*
Υ, υ . . . .*Y, y*
Φ, φ . . . .*Ph, ph*
Χ, χ . . . .*Ch, ch*
Ψ, ψ . . . .*Ps, ps*
Ω, ω . . . .*Ō, ō*
ʽΡ, ῥ. . . . .*Rh, rh*

ʽ . . . .*H, h*
γγ . . . . *ng*
γκ . . . . *nk*
γξ . . . . *nch*
αυ . . . . *au*
ευ . . . . *eu*
ου . . . . *ou*
υι . . . . *yi*

Versification Differences Between the NIV and UBS4

NIV bold text is in . . . . **Greek verse**

Matthew 25:16	. . The man who had received the five talents went **at once**	25:15
Matthew 27:42	. . "He saved others," **they said,** "but he can't save himself!	27:41
Mark 3:8	. . . . . many people came to him **from Judea,** Jerusalem, Idumea,	3:7
Mark 7:21	. . . . evil thoughts, sexual immorality, theft, murder, **adultery**	7:22
Mark 12:15	. . . **Should we pay or shouldn't we?"**	12:14
Mark 12:19	. . . . "Teacher," **they said,** "Moses wrote for us	12:18
Luke 1:25	. . . . . "The Lord has done this for me," **she said.**	1:24
Luke 1:74	. . . . . and **to enable us** to serve him without fear	1:73
Luke 9:31	. . . . appeared in glorious splendor, **talking with Jesus.**	9:30
Luke 18:32	. . . . They will mock him, insult him, spit on him, **flog him and kill him.**	18:33
Luke 19:29	. . . he sent two of his disciples, **saying to them,**	19:30
Luke 20:25	. . . . **"Caesar's," they replied.**	20:24
Luke 21:34	. . . . and that day will close on you unexpectedly **like a trap.**	21:35
John 4:3	. . . . . **When the Lord learned of this,** he left Judea	4:1
John 4:36	. . . . . **Even now** the reaper draws his wages,	4:35
Acts 1:16	. . . . . **and said,** "Brothers, the Scripture had to be fulfilled	1:15
Acts 3:19	. . . . **that times of refreshing may come from the Lord,**	3:20
Acts 5:20	. . . . . "Go, stand in the temple courts," **he said,**	5:19
Acts 5:40	. . . . . **His speech persuaded them.**	5:39
Acts 13:9	. . . . . looked straight at Elymas **and said,**	13:10
Acts 13:39	. . . . . **from everything you could not be justified from by the law of Moses.**	13:38
Acts 19:41	. . . . . **After he had said this, he dismissed the assembly.**	19:40
Acts 22:12	. . . . . "A man named Ananias **came to see me**	22:13
Acts 27:9	. . . . . So Paul warned **them,**	27:10
Acts 28:25	. . . . . **when he said** through Isaiah the prophet:	28:26
Romans 3:25	. . . . because **in his forbearance** he had left the sins committed beforehand	3:26
Romans 7:9	. . . . sin sprang to life **and I died.**	7:10
2Corinthians 1:14	. **you will come to understand fully** that you can boast of us	1:13
2Corinthians 10:5	. **We demolish arguments** and every pretension	10:4
2Corinthians 13:13	**All the saints send their greetings.**	13:12
2 Corinthians 13:14	**May the grace of the Lord Jesus Christ, and the love of God, and the fellowship of the Holy Spirit be with you all.**	13:13
Galatians 2:20	. . . **I have been crucified with Christ** and I no longer live,	2:19
Ephesians 2:15	. . by abolishing **in his flesh** the law with its commandments	2:14
Ephesians 3:18	. . how wide and long and high and deep is **the love of Christ,**	3:19
Philippians 2:8	. . . **And being found in appearance as a man,**	2:7
1Thessalonians 1:3	We **continually** remember before our God and Father	1:2
1Thessalonians 2:6	**As apostles of Christ we could have been a burden to you,**	2:7
2Thessalonians 1:7	when the Lord Jesus is revealed from heaven **in blazing fire**	1:8
1Timothy 3:14	. . . I am writing you these instructions **so that,**	3:15
Hebrews 3:9	. . . . and **for forty years** saw what I did.	3:10
1Peter 3:15	. . . . **But do this with gentleness and respect,**	3:16
1John 2:13	. . . . . **I write to you, dear children, / because you have known the Father.**	2:14
3John 14	. . . . . . **Peace to you. The friends here send their greetings. Greet the friends there by name.**	15
Revelation 2:27	. . **just as I have received authority from my Father.**	2:28
Revelation 13:1	. . **And the dragon stood on the shore of the sea.**	12:18
Revelation 17:10	. **They are also seven kings.**	17:9

THE

GREEK-ENGLISH CONCORDANCE

TO THE

NEW TESTAMENT

KEY FEATURES OF THE MAIN CONCORDANCE

G/K NUMBER
A code that matches the alphabetic order of the Greek words. See the introduction, pages vii-ix.

GREEK WORD
First in Greek letters, then in English transliteration. See the introduction, pages viii-ix.

FREQUENCY
The total number of times this word occurs in the New Testament. See the introduction, pages ix-x.

RELATED WORDS
A list of words related by cognate or common elements. See the introduction, page x.

34 ἄγγελος, *angelos* [175 / 176] [→ 32, 33, 334, 550, 791,

ἄγγελος θεοῦ (angel of God) [7] Lk 12:8,9; 15:10; Jn 1:51;

PHRASE-INDEX
A list of frequent phrases, in Greek and English, with frequency count. See the introduction, pages x-xi.

angel [86], angels [81], messenger [4], angel's [2],

NIV TRANSLATIONS
Every way in which the word is translated in the NIV, with frequency. See the introduction, page xi.

Mt 1:20 an **angel** of the Lord appeared to him in a dream and said,

BOLD TYPE
Bold type highlights the NIV word or phrase that translates the Greek word. See the introduction, pages xii, xiii.

Lk 10:21 **full of joy** through the Holy Spirit, said, "I praise you, Father,

ITALIC TYPE
Italic type highlights NIV words that assist in translating the Greek word inflections. See the introduction, page xii.

ADDITIONAL G/K NUMBERS
When the NIV word or phrase translates more than one Greek word, the additional words are represented by G/K number. See the introduction, page xii.

1Pe 4:13 so that *you may be* **overjoyed** [+5897] when his glory is revealed.

ABBREVIATIONS
Textual variants and untranslated words are indicated by special codes in the context line. See the introduction, pages xii-xiv.

Lk 1:28 The **angel** [UBS-] went to her and said, "Greetings, you who are

The

Greek-English Concordance

to the

New Testament

A, A

1 α, a Not used in UBS/NIV

→ [*270;* 1.1 (negation): *4, 23, 37, 38, 47, 51, 52, 53, 57, 58, 63, 78, 83, 84, 85, 88, 89, 90, 91, 92, 93, 94, 95, 96, 97, 99, 100, 104, 105, 109, 112, 114, 115, 117, 118, 119, 120, 126, 127, 174, 175, 176, 177, 178, 179, 182, 183, 184, 185, 186, 187, 188, 189, 190, 191, 193, 195, 202, 203, 204, 218, 219, 220, 227, 228, 237, 238, 239, 240, 242, 263, 267, 269, 276, 277, 278, 282, 285, 288, 289, 290, 291, 292, 293, 294, 295, 296, 298, 299, 305, 318, 320, 357, 360, 383, 387, 394, 395, 396, 397, 406, 410, 440, 441, 442, 443, 444, 446, 447, 450, 451, 453, 454, 455, 460, 466, 480, 481, 485, 486, 490, 491, 492, 493, 495, 536, 537, 538, 543, 548, 553, 563, 564, 574, 577, 578, 579, 585, 586, 596, 597, 598, 601, 602, 603, 679, 680, 717, 718, 719, 720, 731, 733, 734, 777, 778, 779, 810, 812, 813, 814, 815, 816, 817, 819, 820, 821, 822, 826, 827, 831, 834, 836, 841, 844, 845, 846, 850, 851, 852, 853, 854, 855, 856, 857, 858, 859, 860, 861, 862, 863, 864, 865, 866, 869, 870, 871, 872, 873, 875, 876, 905, 906, 907, 908, 910, 911, 914, 915, 916, 917, 920, 921, 925, 932, 933, 936, 940, 942, 945, 946, 947, 950, 953, 1389, 1989, 2934;* 1.2 (intensity): *12, 867;* 1.3 (commonness): *80, 287?, 1979, 2051, 2887, 4158, 5258, 5788, 5789, 5790, 6012*]

2 Ἀαρών, Aarōn [5]

Aaron [4], Aaron's [1]

Lk   1: 5 of Abijah; his wife Elizabeth was also a descendant *of* **Aaron**.
Ac   7:40 They told **Aaron**, 'Make us gods who will go before us. As for this
Heb 5: 4 honor upon himself; he must be called by God, just as **Aaron** was.
     7:11 one in the order of Melchizedek, not in the order *of* **Aaron**?
     9: 4 **Aaron's** staff that had budded, and the stone tablets of the

3 Ἀβαδδών, Abaddōn [1]

Abaddon [1]

Rev 9:11 whose name in Hebrew is **Abaddon**, and in Greek, Apollyon.

4 ἀβαρής, abarēs [1] [√ *1.1 + 983*]

burden [1]

2Co 11: 9 I have kept myself from being a **burden** to you in any way,

5 ἀββά, abba [3]

Abba [3]

Mk 14:36 "**Abba**, Father," he said, "everything is possible for you. Take this
Ro   8:15 the Spirit of sonship. And by him we cry, "**Abba**, Father."
Gal 4: 6 his Son into our hearts, the Spirit who calls out, "**Abba**, Father."

6 Ἄβελ, Habel [4]

Abel [4]

Mt 23:35 from the blood of righteous **Abel** to the blood of Zechariah son of
Lk 11:51 from the blood *of* **Abel** to the blood of Zechariah, who was killed
Heb 11: 4 By faith **Abel** offered God a better sacrifice than Cain did.
    12:24 sprinkled blood that speaks a better word than the blood of **Abel**.

7 Ἀβιά, Abia [3]

Abijah [3]

Mt   1: 7 Rehoboam the father of **Abijah**, Abijah the father of Asa,
     1: 7 Rehoboam the father of Abijah, **Abijah** the father of Asa,
Lk   1: 5 named Zechariah, who belonged to the priestly division *of* **Abijah**;

8 Ἀβιαθάρ, Abiathar [1]

Abiathar [1]

Mk   2:26 In the days of **Abiathar** the high priest, he entered the house of

9 Ἀβιληνή, Abilēnē [1]

Abilene [1]

Lk   3: 1 of Iturea and Traconitis, and Lysanias tetrarch *of* **Abilene**—

10 Ἀβιούδ, Abioud [2]

Abiud [2]

Mt   1:13 Zerubbabel the father of **Abiud**, Abiud the father of Eliakim,
     1:13 of Abiud, **Abiud** the father of Eliakim, Eliakim the father of Azor,

11 Ἀβραάμ, Abraam [73]

θεός Ἀβραάμ (God of Abraham) [5] Mt 22:32; Mk 12:26; Lk 20:37; Ac 3:13; 7:32

σπέρμα Ἀβραάμ (seed of Abraham) [11] Lk 1:55; Jn 8:33,37; Ac 3:25; Ro 4:13,16; 9:7; 11:1; 2Co 11:22; Gal 3:16; Heb 2:16

υἱός Ἀβραάμ (son of Abraham) [5] Mt 1:1; Lk 19:9; Ac 13:26; Gal 3:7; 4:22

Abraham [64], Abraham's [9]

Mt	1: 1	genealogy of Jesus Christ the son of David, the son *of* **Abraham**:
	1: 2	**Abraham** was the father of Isaac, Isaac the father of Jacob,
	1:17	Thus there were fourteen generations in all from **Abraham** to
	3: 9	you can say to yourselves, 'We have **Abraham** as our father.'
	3: 9	that out of these stones God can raise up children *for* **Abraham**.
	8:11	and will take their places at the feast with **Abraham**, Isaac
	22:32	'I am the God *of* **Abraham**, the God of Isaac, and the God of
Mk	12:26	God said to him, 'I am the God *of* **Abraham**, the God of Isaac,
Lk	1:55	to **Abraham** and his descendants forever, even as he said to our
	1:73	the oath he swore to our father **Abraham**:
	3: 8	not begin to say to yourselves, 'We have **Abraham** as our father.'
	3: 8	that out of these stones God can raise up children *for* **Abraham**.
	3:34	the son of Jacob, the son of Isaac, the son *of* **Abraham**, the son of
	13:16	Then should not this woman, a daughter *of* **Abraham**, whom Satan
	13:28	when you see **Abraham**, Isaac and Jacob and all the prophets in
	16:22	the beggar died and the angels carried him to **Abraham's** side.
	16:23	he looked up and saw **Abraham** far away, with Lazarus by his
	16:24	'Father **Abraham**, have pity on me and send Lazarus to dip the tip
	16:25	"But **Abraham** replied, 'Son, remember that in your lifetime you
	16:29	"**Abraham** replied, 'They have Moses and the Prophets; let them
	16:30	" 'No, father **Abraham**,' he said, 'but if someone from the dead
	19: 9	come to this house, because this man, too, is a son *of* **Abraham**.
	20:37	for he calls the Lord 'the God *of* **Abraham**, and the God of Isaac,
Jn	8:33	"We are **Abraham's** descendants and have never been slaves of
	8:37	I know you are **Abraham's** descendants. Yet you are ready to kill
	8:39	"**Abraham** is our father," they answered. "If you were Abraham's
	8:39	"If you were **Abraham's** children," said Jesus, "then you would do
	8:39	said Jesus, "then you would do the things **Abraham** did.
	8:40	the truth that I heard from God. **Abraham** did not do such things.
	8:52	**Abraham** died and so did the prophets, yet you say that if anyone
	8:53	Are you greater than our father **Abraham**? He died, and so did the
	8:56	Your father **Abraham** rejoiced at the thought of seeing my day;
	8:57	years old," the Jews said to him, "and you have seen **Abraham**!"
	8:58	you the truth," Jesus answered, "before **Abraham** was born, I am!"
Ac	3:13	The God *of* **Abraham**, Isaac and Jacob, the God of our fathers,
	3:25	He said to **Abraham**, 'Through your offspring all peoples on earth
	7: 2	The God of glory appeared to our father **Abraham** while he was
	7:16	and placed in the tomb that **Abraham** had bought from the sons of
	7:17	"As the time drew near for God to fulfill his promise *to* **Abraham**,
	7:32	the God of your fathers, the God *of* **Abraham**, Isaac and Jacob.'
	13:26	"Brothers, children *of* **Abraham**, and you God-fearing Gentiles,
Ro	4: 1	What then shall we say that **Abraham**, our forefather, discovered
	4: 2	If, in fact, **Abraham** was justified by works, he had something to
	4: 3	"**Abraham** believed God, and it was credited to him as
	4: 9	We have been saying that **Abraham's** faith was credited to him as
	4:12	the faith that our father **Abraham** had before he was circumcised.
	4:13	It was not through law that **Abraham** and his offspring received
	4:16	are of the law but also to those who are of the faith *of* **Abraham**.
	9: 7	because they are his descendants are they all **Abraham's** children.
	11: 1	I am an Israelite myself, a descendant of **Abraham**, from the tribe
2Co	11:22	So am I. Are they **Abraham's** descendants? So am I.
Gal	3: 6	Consider **Abraham**: "He believed God, and it was credited to him
	3: 7	Understand, then, that those who believe are children *of* **Abraham**.
	3: 8	by faith, and announced the gospel in advance *to* **Abraham**:
	3: 9	So those who have faith are blessed along with **Abraham**,
	3:14	He redeemed us in order that the blessing *given to* **Abraham**
	3:16	The promises were spoken *to* **Abraham** and to his seed.
	3:18	but God in his grace gave it *to* **Abraham** through a promise.
	3:29	If you belong to Christ, then you are **Abraham's** seed, and heirs
	4:22	For it is written that **Abraham** had two sons, one by the slave
Heb	2:16	For surely it is not angels he helps, but **Abraham's** descendants.
	6:13	When God made his promise *to* **Abraham**, since there was no one
	7: 1	He met **Abraham** returning from the defeat of the kings
	7: 2	and **Abraham** gave him a tenth of everything. First, his name
	7: 4	Even the patriarch **Abraham** gave him a tenth of the plunder!
	7: 5	even though their brothers are descended from **Abraham**.
	7: 6	yet he collected a tenth *from* **Abraham** and blessed him who had
	7: 9	that Levi, who collects the tenth, paid the tenth through **Abraham**,
	11: 8	By faith **Abraham**, when called to go to a place he would later
	11:17	By faith **Abraham**, when God tested him, offered Isaac as a
Jas	2:21	Was not our ancestor **Abraham** considered righteous for what he
	2:23	And the scripture was fulfilled that says, "**Abraham** believed God,

1Pe	3: 6	like Sarah, who obeyed **Abraham** and called him her master.

12 ἄβυσσος, *abyssos* [9] [√ *1.2 + 1113*]

Abyss [8], deep [1]

Lk	8:31	they begged him repeatedly not to order them to go into the **Abyss**.
Ro	10: 7	"or 'Who will descend into the **deep**?' " (that is, to bring Christ up
Rev	9: 1	to the earth. The star was given the key to the shaft *of the* **Abyss**.
	9: 2	When he opened the **Abyss**, smoke rose from it like the smoke
	9:11	They had as king over them the angel *of the* **Abyss**, whose name in
	11: 7	the beast that comes up from the **Abyss** will attack them,
	17: 8	and will come up out of the **Abyss** and go to his destruction.
	20: 1	having the key *to* the **Abyss** and holding in his hand a great chain.
	20: 3	He threw him into the **Abyss**, and locked and sealed it over him,

13 Ἄγαβος, *Hagabos* [2]

Agabus [2]

Ac	11:28	named **Agabus**, stood up and through the Spirit predicted that a
	21:10	number of days, a prophet named **Agabus** came down from Judea.

14 ἀγαθοεργέω, *agathoergeō* [2] [√ *19 + 2240*]

do good [1], shown kindness [1]

Ac	14:17	*He has* **shown kindness** by giving you rain from heaven and crops
1Ti	6:18	Command them *to* **do good**, to be rich in good deeds, and to be

15 ἀγαθοεργός, *agathoergos* Not used in UBS/NIV [√ *19 + 2240*]

16 ἀγαθοποιέω, *agathopoieō* [9] [√ *19 + 4472*]

do good [3], doing good [3], do what is right [1], does what is good [1], good [1]

Lk	6: 9	the Sabbath: *to* **do good** or to do evil, to save life or to destroy it?"
	6:33	And if *you* **do good** to those who are good to you, what credit is
	6:33	And if you do good *to* those *who are* **good** to you, what credit is
	6:35	But love your enemies, **do good** to them, and lend to them without
1Pe	2:15	For it is God's will that *by* **doing good** you should silence the
	2:20	But if you suffer *for* **doing good** and you endure it, this is
	3: 6	You are her daughters if you **do what is right** and do not give way
	3:17	if it is God's will, to suffer *for* **doing good** than for doing evil.
3Jn	1:11	but what is good. Anyone *who* **does what is good** is from God.

17 ἀγαθοποιΐα, *agathopoiia* [1] [√ *19 + 4472*]

do good [1]

1Pe	4:19	themselves to their faithful Creator and continue to **do good**.

18 ἀγαθοποιός, *agathopoios* [1] [√ *19 + 4472*]

do right [1]

1Pe	2:14	punish those who do wrong and to commend *those who* **do right**.

19 ἀγαθός, *agathos* [102] [→ *14, 15, 16, 17, 18, 20, 920, 2817, 5787*]

ἀγαθός ἔργον (good work) [14] Ac 9:36; Ro 2:7; 13:3; 2Co 9:8; Eph 2:10; Php 1:6; Col 1:10; 2Th 2:17; 1Ti 2:10; 5:10; 2Ti 2:21; 3:17; Tit 1:16; 3:1

ἀγαθός συνείδησις (good conscience) [5] Ac 23:1; 1Ti 1:5,19; 1Pe 3:16,21

κακός ... ἀγαθός (evil ... good) [10] Lk 16:25; Ro 3:8; 7:19; 12:21; 13:3,4; 16:19; 1Th 5:15; 1Pe 3:11; 3Jn 1:11

good [89], kind [2], right [2], better [1], clear [1], favor [1], fully [*+4246*] [1], generous [1], goods [1], helpful [1], pleasant [1], useful [1]

Mt	5:45	He causes his sun to rise on the evil and the **good**, and sends rain
	7:11	though you are evil, know how to give **good** gifts to your children,
	7:11	how much more will your Father in heaven give **good** gifts to those

7:17 Likewise every **good** tree bears good fruit, but a bad tree bears bad
7:18 A **good** tree cannot bear bad fruit, and a bad tree cannot bear good
12:34 brood of vipers, how can you who are evil say *anything* **good**?
12:35 The **good** man brings good things out of the good stored up in him,
12:35 The good man brings **good** *things* out of the good stored up in
12:35 The good man brings good things out of the **good** stored up in him,
19:16 and asked, "Teacher, what **good** *thing* must I do to get eternal life?"
19:17 "Why do you ask me about what is **good**?" Jesus replied. "There is
19:17 Jesus replied. "There is only One who is **good**. If you want to enter
20:15 my own money? Or are you envious because I am **generous**?'
22:10 and gathered all the people they could find, both **good** and bad,
25:21 "His master replied, 'Well done, **good** and faithful servant!
25:23 "His master replied, 'Well done, **good** and faithful servant!
Mk 3:4 to do **good** or to do evil, to save life or to kill?" But they remained
10:17 "**Good** teacher," he asked, "what must I do to inherit eternal life?"
10:18 "Why do you call me **good**?" Jesus answered. "No one is good—
10:18 me good?" Jesus answered. "No one is **good**—except God alone.
Lk 1:53 He has filled the hungry *with* **good** *things* but has sent the rich
6:45 The **good** man brings good things out of the good stored up in his
6:45 The good man brings **good** *things* out of the good stored up in his
6:45 The good man brings good things out of the **good** stored up in his
8:8 Still other seed fell on **good** soil. It came up and yielded a crop,
8:15 the seed on good soil stands for those with a noble and **good** heart,
10:42 Mary has chosen what is **better**, and it will not be taken away from
11:13 though you are evil, know how to give **good** gifts to your children,
12:18 build bigger ones, and there I will store all my grain and my **goods**.
12:19 to myself, "You have plenty of **good** *things* laid up for many years.
16:25 remember that in your lifetime you received your **good** *things*,
18:18 A certain ruler asked him, "**Good** teacher, what must I do to
18:19 "Why do you call me **good**?" Jesus answered. "No one is good—
18:19 me good?" Jesus answered. "No one is **good**—except God alone.
19:17 " 'Well done, my **good** servant!' his master replied. 'Because you
23:50 named Joseph, a member of the Council, a **good** and upright man,
Jn 1:46 "Nazareth! Can anything **good** come from there?" Nathanael asked.
5:29 those who have done **good** will rise to live, and those who have
7:12 Some said, "He is a **good** *man*." Others replied, "No, he deceives
Ac 9:36 is Dorcas), who was always doing **good** and helping the poor.
11:24 He was a **good** man, full of the Holy Spirit and faith, and a great
23:1 I have fulfilled my duty to God *in* all **good** conscience to this day."
Ro 2:7 To those who by persistence in doing **good** seek glory, honor
2:10 but glory, honor and peace for everyone who does **good**: first for
3:8 as some claim that we say—"Let us do evil that **good** may result"?
5:7 though for a **good** *man* someone might possibly dare to die.
7:12 the law is holy, and the commandment is holy, righteous and **good**.
7:13 Did that which is **good**, then, become death to me? By no means!
7:13 recognized as sin, it produced death in me through what was **good**,
7:18 I know that nothing **good** lives in me, that is, in my sinful nature.
7:19 For what I do is not the **good** I want to do; no, the evil I do not
8:28 And we know that in all things God works for the **good** of those
9:11 before the twins were born or had done anything **good** or bad—
10:15 "How beautiful are the feet of those who bring **good** news!"
12:2 approve what God's will is—his **good**, pleasing and perfect will.
12:9 Love must be sincere. Hate what is evil; cling *to* what is **good**.
12:21 Do not be overcome by evil, but overcome evil with **good**.
13:3 For rulers hold no terror *for* those who do **right**, but for those who
13:3 one in authority? Then do what is **right** and he will commend you.
13:4 For he is God's servant to do you **good**. But if you do wrong,
14:16 Do not allow what you consider **good** to be spoken of as evil.
15:2 Each of us should please his neighbor for his **good**, to build him
16:19 but I want you to be wise about what is **good**, and innocent about
2Co 5:10 him for the things done while in the body, whether **good** or bad.
9:8 having all that you need, you will abound in every **good** work.
Gal 6:6 in the word must share all **good** *things* with his instructor.
6:10 Therefore, as we have opportunity, let us do **good** to all people,
Eph 2:10 are God's workmanship, created in Christ Jesus to do **good** works,
4:28 but must work, doing something **useful** with his own hands,
4:29 but only what is **helpful** for building others up according to their
6:8 that the Lord will reward everyone for whatever **good** he does,
Php 1:6 that he who began a **good** work in you will carry it on to
Col 1:10 bearing fruit in every **good** work, growing in the knowledge of
1Th 3:6 He has told us that you always have **pleasant** memories of us
5:15 but always try to be **kind** to each other and to everyone else.
2Th 2:16 and by his grace gave us eternal encouragement and **good** hope,
2:17 your hearts and strengthen you in every **good** deed and word.
1Ti 1:5 comes from a pure heart and a **good** conscience and a sincere faith.
1:19 holding on to faith and a **good** conscience. Some have rejected
2:10 but with **good** deeds, appropriate for women who profess to
5:10 those in trouble and devoting herself *to* all kinds of **good** deeds.
2Ti 2:21 made holy, useful to the Master and prepared to do any **good** work.
3:17 the man of God may be thoroughly equipped for every **good** work.
Tit 1:16 They are detestable, disobedient and unfit for doing anything **good**.
2:5 to be self-controlled and pure, to be busy at home, to be **kind**,
2:10 steal from them, but to show that they can be **fully** [*+4246*] trusted,
3:1 and authorities, to be obedient, to be ready to do whatever is **good**,
Phm 1:6 so that you will have a full understanding *of* every **good** *thing* we
1:14 so that any **favor** you do will be spontaneous and not forced.
Heb 9:11 When Christ came as high priest *of* the **good** *things* that are
10:1 The law is only a shadow *of* the **good** *things* that are coming—
13:21 equip you with everything **good** for doing his will, and may he
Jas 1:17 Every **good** and perfect gift is from above, coming down from the
3:17 submissive, full of mercy and **good** fruit, impartial and sincere.
1Pe 2:18 not only *to* those who are **good** and considerate, but also to those
3:10 would love life and see **good** days must keep his tongue from evil
3:11 He must turn from evil and do **good**; he must seek peace
3:13 Who is going to harm you if you are eager to do **good**?
3:16 keeping a **clear** conscience, so that those who speak maliciously
3:16 so that those who speak maliciously against your **good** behavior in
3:21 from the body but the pledge *of* a **good** conscience toward God.
3Jn 1:11 Dear friend, do not imitate what is evil but what is **good**.

20 ἀγαθωσύνη, agathōsynē [4] [√ *19*]

goodness [3], good [1]

Ro 15:14 my brothers, that you yourselves are full *of* **goodness**, complete in
Gal 5:22 is love, joy, peace, patience, kindness, **goodness**, faithfulness,
Eph 5:9 (for the fruit of the light consists in all **goodness**, righteousness
2Th 1:11 and that by his power he may fulfill every **good** purpose of yours

21 ἀγαλλίασις, agalliasis [5] [√ *22*]

joy [2], delight [1], glad [1], great joy [1]

Lk 1:14 He will be a joy and **delight** to you, and many will rejoice
1:44 greeting reached my ears, the baby in my womb leaped for **joy**.
Ac 2:46 bread in their homes and ate together with **glad** and sincere hearts,
Heb 1:9 you above your companions by anointing you with the oil *of* **joy**."
Jude 1:24 you before his glorious presence without fault and with **great joy**—

22 ἀγαλλιάω, agalliaō [11] [→ *21*]

glad [2], rejoices [2], enjoy [1], filled with joy [*+5915*] [1], filled with joy [1], full of joy [1], greatly rejoice [1], overjoyed [*+5897*] [1], rejoiced [1]

Mt 5:12 Rejoice and *be* **glad**, because great is your reward in heaven,
Lk 1:47 and my spirit **rejoices** in God my Savior,
10:21 **full of joy** through the Holy Spirit, said, "I praise you, Father,
Jn 5:35 and gave light, and you chose for a time *to* **enjoy** his light.
8:56 Your father Abraham **rejoiced** at the thought of seeing my day;
Ac 2:26 Therefore my heart is glad and my tongue **rejoices**; my body also
16:34 *he was* **filled with joy** because he had come to believe in God—
1Pe 1:6 In this *you* **greatly rejoice**, though now for a little while you may
1:8 and *are* **filled with** an inexpressible and glorious **joy** [*+5915*],
4:13 so that *you may be* **overjoyed** [*+5897*] when his glory is revealed.
Rev 19:7 *Let us* rejoice and *be* **glad** and give him glory! For the wedding of

23 ἄγαμος, agamos [4] [√ *1.1 + 1141*]

unmarried [4]

1Co 7:8 Now *to* the **unmarried** and the widows I say: It is good for them
7:11 she must remain **unmarried** or else be reconciled to her husband.
7:32 An **unmarried** *man* is concerned about the Lord's affairs—
7:34 An **unmarried** woman or virgin is concerned about the Lord's

24 ἀγανακτέω, aganakteō [7] [→ *25*]

indignant [6], saying indignantly [1]

Mt 20:24 ten heard about this, *they were* **indignant** with the two brothers.
21:15 temple area, "Hosanna to the Son of David," *they were* **indignant**.
26:8 When the disciples saw this, *they were* **indignant**. "Why this
Mk 10:14 When Jesus saw this, *he was* **indignant**. He said to them,

10:41 ten heard about this, they became **indignant** with James and John.
14: 4 Some of those present were **saying indignantly** to one another,
Lk   13:14 **Indignant** because Jesus had healed on the Sabbath, the synagogue

25 ἀγανάκτησις, *aganaktēsis* [1] [√ *24*]

indignation [1]

2Co 7:11 what **indignation**, what alarm, what longing, what concern,

26 ἀγαπάω, *agapaō* [143] [→ *27, 28*]

ἀγαπᾶν, ἀγαπᾶτε ἀλλήλους (love one another) [12] Jn
  13:34; 15:12,17; Ro 13:8; 1Th 4:9; 1Pe 1:22; 1Jn 3:11,23;
  4:7,11,12; 2Jn 1:5

ἀγαπάω κύριον (love the Lord) [4] Mt 22:37; Mk 12:30; Lk
  10:27; Eph 6:24

ἀγαπήσεις πλησίον (love [one's] neighbor) [9] Mt 5:43;
  19:19; 22:39; Mk 12:31,33; Lk 10:27; Ro 13:9; Gal 5:14; Jas 2:8

love [74], loved [40], loves [22], love [+*27*] [2], truly love [2],
longed for [1], loving [1], showed love [1]

Mt   5:43 heard that it was said, 'Love your neighbor and hate your enemy.'
     5:44 **Love** your enemies and pray for those who persecute you,
     5:46 If *you* **love** those who love you, what reward will you get?
     5:46 If you love those *who* **love** you, what reward will you get?
     6:24 Either he will hate the one and love the other, or he will be devoted
    19:19 your father and mother,' and '**love** your neighbor as yourself.' "
    22:37 " '**Love** the Lord your God with all your heart and with all your
    22:39 And the second is like it: '**Love** your neighbor as yourself.'
Mk 10:21 Jesus looked at him and **loved** him. "One thing you lack," he said.
    12:30 **Love** the Lord your God with all your heart and with all your soul
    12:31 The second is this: '**Love** your neighbor as yourself.' There is no
    12:33 *To* **love** him with all your heart, with all your understanding
    12:33 and *to* love your neighbor as yourself is more important than all
Lk   6:27 who hear me: **Love** your enemies, do good to those who hate you,
     6:32 "If *you* **love** those who love you, what credit is that to you?
     6:32 "If you love those *who* **love** you, what credit is that to you?
     6:32 credit is that to you? Even 'sinners' **love** those who love them.
     6:32 credit is that to you? Even 'sinners' love those *who* **love** them.
     6:35 But **love** your enemies, do good to them, and lend to them without
     7: 5 because *he* **loves** our nation and has built our synagogue."
     7:42 the debts of both. Now which of them *will* **love** him more?"
     7:47 I tell you, her many sins have been forgiven—for *she* **loved** much.
     7:47 for she loved much. But he who has been forgiven little **loves** little."
    10:27 " '**Love** the Lord your God with all your heart and with all your
    11:43 because *you* **love** the most important seats in the synagogues
    16:13 Either he will hate the one and **love** the other, or he will be devoted
Jn   3:16 "For God so **loved** the world that he gave his one and only Son,
     3:19 but men **loved** darkness instead of light because their deeds were
     3:35 The Father **loves** the Son and has placed everything in his hands.
     8:42 *you* would **love** me, for I came from God and now am here.
    10:17 The reason my Father **loves** me is that I lay down my life—
    11: 5 Jesus **loved** Martha and her sister and Lazarus.
    12:43 for *they* **loved** praise from men more than praise from God.
    13: 1 *Having* **loved** his own who were in the world, he now showed
    13: 1 were in the world, *he now* **showed** them the full extent of *his* love.
    13:23 Of them, the disciple whom Jesus **loved**, was reclining next to
    13:34 new command I give you: **Love** one another. As I have loved you,
    13:34 new command I give you: Love one another. As *I have* **loved** you,
    13:34 one another. As I have loved you, so you *must* **love** one another.
    14:15 "If *you* **love** me, you will obey what I command.
    14:21 has my commands and obeys them, he is the one *who* **loves** me.
    14:21 one who loves me. He *who* **loves** me will be loved by my Father,
    14:21 one who loves me. He who loves me *will be* **loved** by my Father,
    14:21 by my Father, and I too *will* **love** him and show myself to him."
    14:23 Jesus replied, "If anyone **loves** me, he will obey my teaching.
    14:23 My Father *will* **love** him, and we will come to him and make our
    14:24 He *who does not* **love** me will not obey my teaching. These words
    14:28 If *you* **loved** me, you would be glad that I am going to the Father,
    14:31 but the world must learn that *I* **love** the Father and that I do exactly
    15: 9 "As the Father *has* **loved** me, so have I loved you. Now remain in
    15: 9 As the Father has loved me, so *have* I **loved** you. Now remain in
    15:12 My command is this: **Love** each other as I have loved you.
    15:12 My command is this: Love each other as *I have* **loved** you.

15:17 This is my command: **Love** each other.
17:23 that you sent me and *have* **loved** them even as you have loved me.
17:23 that you sent me and have loved them even as *you have* **loved** me.
17:24 given me because *you* **loved** me before the creation of the world.
17:26 in order that the **love** *you* have [+*27*] for me may be in them
19:26 and the disciple whom *he* **loved** standing nearby, he said to his
21: 7 Then the disciple whom Jesus **loved** said to Peter, "It is the Lord!"
21:15 "Simon son of John, *do you* **truly love** me more than these?"
21:16 Again Jesus said, "Simon son of John, *do you* **truly love** me?"
21:20 and saw that the disciple whom Jesus **loved** was following them.
Ro   8:28 that in all things God works for the good *of* those *who* **love** him,
     8:37 things we are more than conquerors through him *who* **loved** us.
     9:13 Just as it is written: "Jacob *I* **loved**, but Esau I hated."
     9:25 and I will call her 'my **loved** *one*' who is not my loved one,"
     9:25 and I will call her 'my loved one' who is not my **loved** *one*,"
    13: 8 remain outstanding, except the continuing debt *to* **love** one another,
    13: 8 one another, for he *who* **loves** his fellowman has fulfilled the law.
    13: 9 are summed up in this one rule: "**Love** your neighbor as yourself."
1Co 2: 9 no mind has conceived what God has prepared *for* those *who* **love**
     8: 3 But the man who **loves** God is known by God.
2Co 9: 7 or under compulsion, for God **loves** a cheerful giver.
    11:11 Why? Because *I do* not **love** you? God knows I do!
    12:15 expend myself as well. If *I* **love** you more, will you love me less?
    12:15 expend myself as well. If I love you more, *will* you **love** *me* less?
Gal 2:20 by faith in the Son of God, who **loved** me and gave himself for me.
     5:14 up in a single command: "**Love** your neighbor as yourself."
Eph 1: 6 glorious grace, which he has freely given us in the One *he* **loves**.
     2: 4 But because of his great **love** [+*27*] for us, God, who is rich in
     5: 2 just as Christ **loved** us and gave himself up for us as a fragrant
     5:25 Husbands, **love** your wives, just as Christ loved the church
     5:25 just as Christ **loved** the church and gave himself up for her
     5:28 same way, husbands ought *to* **love** their wives as their own bodies.
     5:28 wives as their own bodies. He *who* **loves** his wife loves himself.
     5:28 wives as their own bodies. He who loves his wife **loves** himself.
     5:33 each one of you also *must* **love** his wife as he loves himself,
     6:24 Grace to all who **love** our Lord Jesus Christ with an undying love.
Col 3:12 Therefore, as God's chosen people, holy and dearly **loved**,
     3:19 Husbands, **love** your wives and do not be harsh with them.
1Th 1: 4 For we know, brothers **loved** by God, that he has chosen you,
     4: 9 for you yourselves have been taught by God to **love** each other.
2Th 2:13 we ought always to thank God for you, brothers **loved** by the Lord,
     2:16 who **loved** us and by his grace gave us eternal encouragement
2Ti 4: 8 not only to me, but also *to* all who *have* **longed for** his appearing.
     4:10 for Demas, *because he* **loved** this world, has deserted me and has
Heb 1: 9 *You have* **loved** righteousness and hated wickedness;
    12: 6 because the Lord disciplines those *he* **loves**, and he punishes
Jas 1:12 the crown of life that God has promised *to* those *who* **love** him.
     2: 5 and to inherit the kingdom he promised those *who* **love** him?
     2: 8 in Scripture, "**Love** your neighbor as yourself," you are doing right.
1Pe 1: 8 Though you have not seen him, *you* **love** him; and even though
     1:22 love for your brothers, **love** one another deeply, from the heart.
     2:17 **Love** the brotherhood of believers, fear God, honor the king.
     3:10 "Whoever would **love** life and see good days must keep his tongue
2Pe 2:15 way of Balaam son of Beor, who **loved** the wages of wickedness.
1Jn 2:10 Whoever **loves** his brother lives in the light, and there is nothing in
     2:15 *Do* not **love** the world or anything in the world. If anyone loves
     2:15 If anyone **loves** the world, the love of the Father is not in him.
     3:10 is not a child of God; nor is anyone *who does* not **love** his brother.
     3:11 you heard from the beginning: *We must* **love** one another.
     3:14 we have passed from death to life, because *we* **love** our brothers.
     3:14 we love our brothers. Anyone *who does* not **love** remains in death.
     3:18 *let us* not **love** with words or tongue but with actions and in truth.
     3:23 Jesus Christ, and to **love** one another as he commanded us.
     4: 7 Dear friends, *let us* **love** one another, for love comes from God.
     4: 7 Everyone who **loves** has been born of God and knows God.
     4: 8 Whoever *does* not **love** does not know God, because God is love.
     4:10 not that we **loved** God, but that he loved us and sent his Son as an
     4:10 but that he **loved** us and sent his Son as an atoning sacrifice for our
     4:11 Dear friends, since God so **loved** us, we also ought to love one
     4:11 since God so loved us, we also ought *to* **love** one another.
     4:12 but if *we* **love** one another, God lives in us and his love is made
     4:19 We **love** because he first loved us.
     4:19 We love because he first **loved** us.
     4:20 If anyone says, "*I* **love** God," yet hates his brother, he is a liar.
     4:20 For anyone *who does* not **love** his brother, whom he has seen,
     4:20 whom he has seen, cannot **love** God, whom he has not seen.

	4:21	us this command: Whoever **loves** God must also love his brother.
	4:21	us this command: Whoever *must* also love his brother.
	5:1	and everyone who **loves** the father loves his child as well.
	5:1	and everyone who loves the father **loves** his child as well.
	5:2	This is how we know that *we* **love** the children of God: by loving
	5:2	children of God: by **loving** God and carrying out his commands.
2Jn	1:1	To the chosen lady and her children, whom I **love** in the truth—
	1:5	we have had from the beginning. I ask that *we* **love** one another.
3Jn	1:1	The elder, To my dear friend Gaius, whom I **love** in the truth.
Jude	1:1	who are **loved** by God the Father and kept by Jesus Christ:
Rev	1:5	*To* him *who* **loves** us and has freed us from our sins by his blood,
	3:9	and fall down at your feet and acknowledge that I *have* **loved** you.
	12:11	*they did* not **love** their lives so much as to shrink from death.
	20:9	and surrounded the camp of God's people, the city he **loves**.

27 ἀγάπη, agapē [116] [√ 26]

ἀγάπη τοῦ θεοῦ (love of God) [11] Lk 11:42; Jn 5:42; Ro 5:5;
8:39; 2Co 13:13; 2Th 3:5; 1Jn 2:5; 3:17; 4:9; 5:3; Jude 1:21

ἀγάπη τοῦ Χριστοῦ (love of Christ) [3] Ro 8:35; 2Co 5:14;
Eph 3:19

love [109], love [+2400] [2], love [+26] [2], it's [+3836] [1], love
feasts [1], loves [1]

Mt	24:12	of the increase of wickedness, the **love** of most will grow cold,
Lk	11:42	kinds of garden herbs, but you neglect justice and the **love** of God.
Jn	5:42	I know that you do not have the **love** of God in your hearts.
	13:35	know that you are my disciples, if *you* **love** [+2400] one another."
	15:9	Father has loved me, so have I loved you. Now remain in my **love**.
	15:10	If you obey my commands, you will remain in my **love**, just as I
	15:10	as I have obeyed my Father's commands and remain in his **love**.
	15:13	Greater **love** has no one than this, that he lay down his life for his
	17:26	in order that the **love** [+26] *you have* for me may be in them
Ro	5:5	because God has poured out his **love** into our hearts by the Holy
	5:8	But God demonstrates his own **love** for us in this: While we were
	8:35	Who shall separate us from the **love** of Christ? Shall trouble
	8:39	will be able to separate us from the **love** of God that is in Christ
	12:9	**Love** must be sincere. Hate what is evil; cling to what is good.
	13:10	**Love** does no harm to its neighbor. Therefore love is the
	13:10	harm to its neighbor. Therefore love is the fulfillment of the law.
	14:15	because of what you eat, you are no longer acting in **love**.
	15:30	brothers, by our Lord Jesus Christ and by the **love** of the Spirit,
1Co	4:21	Shall I come to you with a whip, or in **love** and with a gentle spirit?
	8:1	we all possess knowledge. Knowledge puffs up, but love builds up.
	13:1	If I speak in the tongues of men and of angels, but have not **love**,
	13:2	a faith that can move mountains, but have not **love**, I am nothing.
	13:3	surrender my body to the flames, but have not **love**, I gain nothing.
	13:4	**Love** is patient, love is kind. It does not envy, it does not boast,
	13:4	Love is patient, **love** is kind. It does not envy, it does not boast,
	13:4	It does not envy, it's [+3836] does not boast, it is not proud.
	13:8	**Love** never fails. But where there are prophecies, they will cease;
	13:13	And now these three remain: faith, hope and **love**. But the greatest
	13:13	three remain: faith, hope and love. But the greatest of these is **love**.
	14:1	Follow the *way of* **love** and eagerly desire spiritual gifts,
	16:14	Do everything in **love**.
	16:24	My **love** to all of you in Christ Jesus. Amen.
2Co	2:4	not to grieve you but to let you know the depth of my **love** for you.
	2:8	I urge you, therefore, to reaffirm your **love** for him.
	5:14	For Christ's **love** compels us, because we are convinced that one
	6:6	patience and kindness; in the Holy Spirit and in sincere **love**;
	8:7	in knowledge, in complete earnestness and in your **love** for us—
	8:8	but I want to test the sincerity *of* your **love** by comparing it with
	8:24	Therefore show these men the proof *of* your **love** and the reason
	13:11	live in peace. And the God *of* **love** and peace will be with you.
	13:14	May the grace of the Lord Jesus Christ, and the **love** of God,
Gal	5:6	The only thing that counts is faith expressing itself through **love**.
	5:13	to indulge the sinful nature; rather, serve one another in **love**.
	5:22	But the fruit of the Spirit is love, joy, peace, patience, kindness,
Eph	1:4	creation of the world to be holy and blameless in his sight. In **love**
	1:15	about your faith in the Lord Jesus and your **love** for all the saints,
	2:4	But because of his great **love** [+26] for us, God, who is rich in
	3:17	And I pray that you, being rooted and established in **love**,
	3:18	to grasp how wide and long and high and deep is the **love** of Christ,
	4:2	and gentle; be patient, bearing with one another in **love**.
	4:15	Instead, speaking the truth in **love**, we will in all things grow up

	4:16	grows and builds itself up in **love**, as each part does its work.
	5:2	and live a life of **love**, just as Christ loved us and gave himself up
	6:23	and **love** with faith from God the Father and the Lord Jesus Christ.
Php	1:9	that your **love** may abound more and more in knowledge and depth
	1:16	The latter do so in **love**, knowing that I am put here for the defense
	2:1	if any comfort *from* his **love**, if any fellowship with the Spirit,
	2:2	having the same **love**, being one in spirit and purpose.
Col	1:4	faith in Christ Jesus and *of* the **love** you have for all the saints—
	1:8	and who also told us of your **love** in the Spirit.
	1:13	of darkness and brought us into the kingdom of the Son he **loves**,
	2:2	purpose is that they may be encouraged in heart and united in **love**,
	3:14	And over all these virtues put on **love**, which binds them all
1Th	1:3	Father your work produced by faith, your labor *prompted by* **love**,
	3:6	us from you and has brought good news about your faith and **love**.
	3:12	May the Lord make your **love** increase and overflow for each other
	5:8	let us be self-controlled, putting on faith and **love** as a breastplate,
	5:13	Hold them in the highest regard in **love** because of their work.
2Th	1:3	and the **love** every one of you has for each other is increasing.
	2:10	They perish because they refused to **love** the truth and so be saved.
	3:5	May the Lord direct your hearts into God's **love** and Christ's
1Ti	1:5	The goal of this command is **love**, which comes from a pure heart
	1:14	along with the faith and **love** that are in Christ Jesus.
	2:15	if they continue in faith, **love** and holiness with propriety.
	4:12	for the believers in speech, in life, in **love**, in faith and in purity.
	6:11	godliness, faith, **love**, endurance and gentleness.
2Ti	1:7	of timidity, but a spirit of power, *of* **love** and of self-discipline.
	1:13	the pattern of sound teaching, with faith and **love** in Christ Jesus.
	2:22	desires of youth, and pursue righteousness, faith, **love** and peace,
	3:10	my way of life, my purpose, faith, patience, **love**, endurance,
Tit	2:2	self-controlled, and sound in faith, *in* **love** and in endurance.
Phm	1:5	about your faith in the Lord Jesus and your **love** for all the saints.
	1:7	Your **love** has given me great joy and encouragement,
	1:9	yet I appeal to you on the basis of **love**. I then, as Paul—an old man
Heb	6:10	and the **love** you have shown him as you have helped his people
	10:24	And let us consider how we may spur one another on *toward* **love**
1Pe	4:8	Above all, **love** [+2400] each other deeply, because love covers
	4:8	each other deeply, because **love** covers over a multitude of sins.
	5:14	Greet one another with a kiss of **love**. Peace to all of you who are
2Pe	1:7	to godliness, brotherly kindness; and to brotherly kindness, **love**.
1Jn	2:5	anyone obeys his word, God's **love** is truly made complete in him.
	2:15	If anyone loves the world, the **love** of the Father is not in him.
	3:1	How great is the **love** the Father has lavished on us, that we should
	3:16	This is how we know what **love** is: Jesus Christ laid down his life
	3:17	but has no pity on him, how can the **love** of God be in him?
	4:7	Dear friends, let us love one another, for **love** comes from God.
	4:8	Whoever does not love does not know God, because God is **love**.
	4:9	This is how God showed his **love** among us: He sent his one
	4:10	This is **love**: not that we loved God, but that he loved us and sent
	4:12	one another, God lives in us and his **love** is made complete in us.
	4:16	And so we know and rely on the **love** God has for us. God is love.
	4:16	God is **love**. Whoever lives in love lives in God, and God in him.
	4:16	God is love. Whoever lives in **love** lives in God, and God in him.
	4:17	**love** is made complete among us so that we will have confidence
	4:18	There is no fear in **love**. But perfect love drives out fear,
	4:18	But perfect **love** drives out fear, because fear has to do with
	4:18	do with punishment. The one who fears is not made perfect in **love**.
	5:3	This is **love** for God: to obey his commands. And his commands
2Jn	1:3	Jesus Christ, the Father's Son, will be with us in truth and **love**.
	1:6	And this is **love**: that we walk in obedience to his commands.
3Jn	1:6	They have told the church about your **love**. You will do well to
Jude	1:2	Mercy, peace and **love** be yours in abundance.
	1:12	These men are blemishes at your **love feasts**, eating with you
	1:21	Keep yourselves in God's **love** as you wait for the mercy of our
Rev	2:4	Yet I hold this against you: You have forsaken your first **love**.
	2:19	your deeds, your **love** and faith, your service and perseverance,

28 ἀγαπητός, agapētos [61] [√ 26]

ἀδελφός ἀγαπητός (beloved brother) [10] 1Co 15:58; Eph
6:21; Php 4:1; Col 4:7,9; Phm 1:16; Jas 1:16,19; 2:5; 2Pe 3:15

ἀγαπητός τέκνον (beloved child) [4] 1Co 4:14,17; Eph 5:1;
2Ti 1:2

υἱός ἀγαπητός (beloved son) [8] Mt 3:17; 17:5; Mk 1:11; 9:7;
12:6; Lk 3:22; 20:13; 2Pe 1:17

dear friends [22], dear [13], love [11], dear friend [9], loved [3], dearly loved [1], friends [1], so dear [1]

Mt	3:17 And a voice from heaven said, "This is my Son, whom I **love**;
	12:18 my servant whom I have chosen, the one I **love**, in whom I delight;
	17: 5 and a voice from the cloud said, "This is my Son, whom I **love**;
Mk	1:11 "You are my Son, whom I **love**; with you I am well pleased."
	9: 7 from the cloud: "This is my Son, whom I **love**. Listen to him!"
	12: 6 "He had one left to send, a son, whom he **loved**. He sent him last of
Lk	3:22 "You are my Son, whom I **love**; with you I am well pleased."
	20:13 I will send my son, whom I **love**; perhaps they will respect him.'
Ac	15:25 and send them to you with our **dear friends** Barnabas and Paul—
Ro	1: 7 To all in Rome who are **loved** by God and called to be saints:
	11:28 election is concerned, they are **loved** on account of the patriarchs,
	12:19 Do not take revenge, my **friends**, but leave room for God's wrath,
	16: 5 Greet my **dear friend** Epenetus, who was the first convert to
	16: 8 Greet Ampliatus, whom I **love** in the Lord.
	16: 9 our fellow worker in Christ, and my **dear friend** Stachys.
	16:12 Greet my **dear friend** Persis, another woman who has worked very
1Co	4:14 writing this to shame you, but to warn you, as my **dear** children.
	4:17 to you Timothy, my son whom *I* **love**, who is faithful in the Lord.
	10:14 Therefore, my **dear friends**, flee from idolatry.
	15:58 Therefore, my **dear** brothers, stand firm. Let nothing move you.
2Co	7: 1 Since we have these promises, **dear friends**, let us purify ourselves
	12:19 and everything we do, **dear friends**, is for your strengthening.
Eph	5: 1 Be imitators of God, therefore, as **dearly loved** children
	6:21 Tychicus, the **dear** brother and faithful servant in the Lord,
Php	2:12 Therefore, my **dear friends**, as you have always obeyed—
	4: 1 my brothers, you whom I **love** and long for, my joy and crown,
	4: 1 that is how you should stand firm in the Lord, **dear friends**!
Col	1: 7 You learned it from Epaphras, our **dear** fellow servant, who is a
	4: 7 He is a **dear** brother, a faithful minister and fellow servant in the
	4: 9 with Onesimus, our faithful and **dear** brother, who is one of you.
	4:14 Our **dear friend** Luke, the doctor, and Demas send greetings.
1Th	2: 8 but our lives as well, because you had become **so dear** to us.
1Ti	6: 2 who benefit from their service are believers, and **dear** to them.
2Ti	1: 2 *To* Timothy, my **dear** son: Grace, mercy and peace from God the
Phm	1: 1 our brother, *To* Philemon our **dear friend** and fellow worker,
	1:16 no longer as a slave, but better than a slave, as a **dear** brother.
Heb	6: 9 Even though we speak like this, **dear friends**, we are confident of
Jas	1:16 Don't be deceived, my **dear** brothers.
	1:19 My **dear** brothers, take note of this: Everyone should be quick to
	2: 5 Listen, my **dear** brothers: Has not God chosen those who are poor
1Pe	2:11 **Dear friends**, I urge you, as aliens and strangers in the world,
	4:12 **Dear friends**, do not be surprised at the painful trial you are
2Pe	1:17 from the Majestic Glory, saying, "This is my Son, whom I **love**;
	3: 1 **Dear friends**, this is now my second letter to you. I have written
	3: 8 But do not forget this one thing, **dear friends**: With the Lord a day
	3:14 So then, **dear friends**, since you are looking forward to this,
	3:15 just as our **dear** brother Paul also wrote you with the wisdom that
	3:17 Therefore, **dear friends**, since you already know this, be on your
1Jn	2: 7 **Dear friends**, I am not writing you a new command but an old
	3: 2 **Dear friends**, now we are children of God, and what we will be
	3:21 **Dear friends**, if our hearts do not condemn us, we have
	4: 1 **Dear friends**, do not believe every spirit, but test the spirits to see
	4: 7 **Dear friends**, let us love one another, for love comes from God.
	4:11 **Dear friends**, since God so loved us, we also ought to love one
3Jn	1: 1 The elder, *To* my **dear friend** Gaius, whom I love in the truth.
	1: 2 **Dear friend**, I pray that you may enjoy good health and that all
	1: 5 **Dear friend**, you are faithful in what you are doing for the
	1:11 **Dear friend**, do not imitate what is evil but what is good.
Jude	1: 3 **Dear friends**, although I was very eager to write to you about the
	1:17 But, **dear friends**, remember what the apostles of our Lord Jesus
	1:20 But you, **dear friends**, build yourselves up in your most holy faith

29 Ἀγάρ, **Hagar** [2]

Hagar [2]

Gal	4:24 and bears children who are to be slaves: This is **Hagar**.
	4:25 Now **Hagar** stands for Mount Sinai in Arabia and corresponds to

30 ἀγγαρεύω, **angareuō** [3]

forced [2], forces [1]

Mt	5:41 If someone **forces** you to go one mile, go with him two miles.
	27:32 named Simon, and *they* **forced** him to carry the cross.
Mk	15:21 way in from the country, and *they* **forced** him to carry the cross.

31 ἀγγεῖον, **angeion** [1] [√ 35]

jars [1]

Mt	25: 4 The wise, however, took oil in **jars** along with their lamps.

32 ἀγγελία, **angelia** [2] [√ 34]

message [2]

1Jn	1: 5 This is the **message** we have heard from him and declare to you:
	3:11 This is the **message** you heard from the beginning: We should love

33 ἀγγέλλω, **angellō** [1] [√ 34]

with the news [1]

Jn	20:18 Mary Magdalene went to the disciples **with the news**: "I have seen

34 ἄγγελος, **angelos** [175 / 176] [→ 32, 33, 334, 550, 791, 1334, 1972, 2039, 2040, 2041, 2294, 2295, 2296, 2694, 2858, 2859, 4132, 4133, 4600, 4603, 4615; cf. 72]

ἄγγελος θεοῦ (angel of God) [7] Lk 12:8,9; 15:10; Jn 1:51; Ac 10:3; 27:23; Gal 4:14; Heb 1:6; Rev 8:2

ἄγγελος κυρίου (angel of the Lord) [12] Mt 1:20,24; 2:13,19; 28:2; Lk 1:11; 2:9; Ac 5:19; 8:26; 12:7,11,23

angel [86], angels [81], messenger [4], angel's [2], messengers [2], spies [1]

Mt	1:20 an **angel** of the Lord appeared to him in a dream and said,
	1:24 he did what the **angel** of the Lord had commanded him and took
	2:13 they had gone, an **angel** of the Lord appeared to Joseph in a dream.
	2:19 an **angel** of the Lord appeared in a dream to Joseph in Egypt
	4: 6 "'He will command his **angels** concerning you, and they will lift
	4:11 Then the devil left him, and **angels** came and attended him.
	11:10 "'I will send my **messenger** ahead of you, who will prepare your
	13:39 The harvest is the end of the age, and the harvesters are **angels**.
	13:41 The Son of Man will send out his **angels**, and they will weed out of
	13:49 The **angels** will come and separate the wicked from the righteous
	16:27 Son of Man is going to come in his Father's glory with his **angels**,
	18:10 For I tell you that their **angels** in heaven always see the face of my
	22:30 nor be given in marriage; they will be like the **angels** in heaven.
	24:31 And he will send his **angels** with a loud trumpet call, and they will
	24:36 one knows about that day or hour, not even the **angels** in heaven,
	25:31 the Son of Man comes in his glory, and all the **angels** with him,
	25:41 into the eternal fire prepared *for* the devil and his **angels**.
	26:53 will at once put at my disposal more than twelve legions *of* **angels**?
	28: 2 for an **angel** of the Lord came down from heaven and, going to the
	28: 5 The **angel** said to the women, "Do not be afraid, for I know that you
Mk	1: 2 "I will send my **messenger** ahead of you, who will prepare your
	1:13 by Satan. He was with the wild animals, and **angels** attended him.
	8:38 of him when he comes in his Father's glory with the holy **angels**."
	12:25 nor be given in marriage; they will be like the **angels** in heaven.
	13:27 And he will send his **angels** and gather his elect from the four
	13:32 one knows about that day or hour, not even the **angels** in heaven,
Lk	1:11 Then an **angel** of the Lord appeared to him, standing at the right
	1:13 But the **angel** said to him: "Do not be afraid, Zechariah; your prayer
	1:18 Zechariah asked the **angel**, "How can I be sure of this? I am an old
	1:19 The **angel** answered, "I am Gabriel. I stand in the presence of God,
	1:26 God sent the **angel** Gabriel to Nazareth, a town in Galilee,
	1:28 The **angel** [UBS-] went to her and said, "Greetings, you who are
	1:30 But the **angel** said to her, "Do not be afraid, Mary, you have found
	1:34 "How will this be," Mary asked the **angel**, "since I am a virgin?"
	1:35 The **angel** answered, "The Holy Spirit will come upon you,
	1:38 "May it be to me as you have said." Then the **angel** left her.
	2: 9 An **angel** of the Lord appeared to them, and the glory of the Lord
	2:10 But the **angel** said to them, "Do not be afraid. I bring you good
	2:13 a great company of the heavenly host appeared with the **angel**,
	2:15 When the **angels** had left them and gone into heaven,
	2:21 the name the **angel** had given him before he had been conceived.
	4:10 "'He will command his **angels** concerning you to guard you
	7:24 After John's **messengers** left, Jesus began to speak to the crowd

7: 27   " 'I will send my **messenger** ahead of you, who will prepare your
9: 26   in his glory and in the glory of the Father and *of* the holy **angels**.
9: 52   And he sent **messengers** on ahead, who went into a Samaritan
12: 8   the Son of Man will also acknowledge him before the **angels** of
12: 9   me before men will be disowned before the **angels** of God.
15: 10   there is rejoicing in the presence *of* the **angels** of God over one
16: 22   the beggar died and the **angels** carried him to Abraham's side.
22: 43   An **angel** from heaven appeared to him and strengthened him.
24: 23   They came and told us that they had seen a vision *of* **angels**,

Jn   1: 51   and the **angels** of God ascending and descending on the Son of
12: 29   it said it had thundered; others said an **angel** had spoken to him.
20: 12   and saw two **angels** in white, seated where Jesus' body had been,

Ac   5: 19   But during the night an **angel** of the Lord opened the doors of the
6: 15   at Stephen, and they saw that his face was like the face *of* an **angel**.
7: 30   an **angel** appeared to Moses in the flames of a burning bush in the
7: 35   God himself, through the **angel** who appeared to him in the bush.
7: 38   with the **angel** who spoke to him on Mount Sinai, and with our
7: 53   who have received the law that was put into effect through **angels**
8: 26   Now an **angel** of the Lord said to Philip, "Go south to the road—
10: 3   He distinctly saw an **angel** of God, who came to him and said,
10: 7   When the **angel** who spoke to him had gone, Cornelius called two
10: 22   A holy **angel** told him to have you come to his house so that he
11: 13   He told us how he had seen an **angel** appear in his house and say,
12: 7   Suddenly an **angel** of the Lord appeared and a light shone in the
12: 8   Then the **angel** said to him, "Put on your clothes and sandals."
12: 9   but he had no idea that what the **angel** was doing was really
12: 10   had walked the length of one street, suddenly the **angel** left him.
12: 11   "Now I know without a doubt that the Lord sent his **angel**
12: 15   she kept insisting that it was so, they said, "It must be his **angel**."
12: 23   an **angel** of the Lord struck him down, and he was eaten by worms
23: 8   and that there are neither **angels** nor spirits, but the Pharisees
23: 9   they said. "What if a spirit or an **angel** has spoken to him?"
27: 23   Last night an **angel** of the God whose I am and whom I serve

Ro   8: 38   neither **angels** nor demons, neither the present nor the future,
1Co   4: 9   a spectacle to the whole universe, *to* **angels** as well as to men.
6: 3   Do you not know that we will judge **angels**? How much more the
11: 10   For this reason, and because of the **angels**, the woman ought to
13: 1   If I speak in the tongues of men and *of* **angels**, but have not love,
2Co 11: 14   no wonder, for Satan himself masquerades as an **angel** of light.
12: 7   me a thorn in my flesh, a **messenger** of Satan, to torment me.
Gal   1: 8   or an **angel** from heaven should preach a gospel other than the one
3: 19   The law was put into effect through **angels** by a mediator.
4: 14   Instead, you welcomed me as if I were an **angel** of God, as if I
Col   2: 18   and the worship *of* **angels** disqualify you for the prize.
2Th   1: 7   is revealed from heaven in blazing fire with his powerful **angels**.
1Ti   3: 16   in a body, was vindicated by the Spirit, was seen *by* **angels**,
5: 21   in the sight of God and Christ Jesus and the elect **angels**,
Heb   1: 4   So he became as much superior to the **angels** as the name he has
1: 5   For to which *of* the **angels** did God ever say, "You are my Son;
1: 6   into the world, he says, "Let all God's **angels** worship him."
1: 7   In speaking of the **angels** he says, "He makes his angels winds,
1: 7   he says, "He makes his **angels** winds, his servants flames of fire."
1: 13   To which *of* the **angels** did God ever say, "Sit at my right hand until
2: 2   For if the message spoken by **angels** was binding, and every
2: 5   It is not *to* **angels** that he has subjected the world to come,
2: 7   You made him a little lower than the **angels**; you crowned him
2: 9   But we see Jesus, who was made a little lower than the **angels**,
2: 16   For surely it is not **angels** he helps, but Abraham's descendants.
12: 22   You have come to thousands upon thousands *of* **angels** in joyful
13: 2   so doing some people have entertained **angels** without knowing it.
Jas   2: 25   righteous for what she did when she gave lodging to the **spies**
1Pe   1: 12   Spirit sent from heaven. Even **angels** long to look into these things.
3: 22   *with* **angels**, authorities and powers in submission to him.
2Pe   2: 4   For if God did not spare **angels** when they sinned, but sent them to
2: 11   yet even **angels**, although they are stronger and more powerful,
Jude 1: 6   And the **angels** who did not keep their positions of authority
Rev   1: 1   He made it known by sending his **angel** to his servant John,
1: 20   The seven stars are the **angels** of the seven churches, and the seven
2: 1   "*To* the **angel** of the church in Ephesus write: These are the words
2: 8   "*To* the **angel** of the church in Smyrna write: These are the words
2: 12   "*To* the **angel** of the church in Pergamum write: These are
2: 18   "*To* the **angel** of the church in Thyatira write: These are the words
3: 1   "*To* the **angel** of the church in Sardis write: These are the words of
3: 5   but will acknowledge his name before my Father and his **angels**.
3: 7   "*To* the **angel** of the church in Philadelphia write: These are the
3: 14   "*To* the **angel** of the church in Laodicea write: These are the

5: 2   And I saw a mighty **angel** proclaiming in a loud voice, "Who is
5: 11   Then I looked and heard the voice *of* many **angels**, numbering
7: 1   After this I saw four **angels** standing at the four corners of the
7: 2   Then I saw another **angel** coming up from the east, having the seal
7: 2   He called out in a loud voice *to* the four **angels** who had been
7: 11   All the **angels** were standing around the throne and around the
8: 2   And I saw the seven **angels** who stand before God, and to them
8: 3   Another **angel**, who had a golden censer, came and stood at the
8: 4   prayers of the saints, went up before God from the **angel's** hand.
8: 5   Then the **angel** took the censer, filled it with fire from the altar,
8: 6   Then the seven **angels** who had the seven trumpets prepared to
8: 8   The second **angel** sounded his trumpet, and something like a huge
8: 10   The third **angel** sounded his trumpet, and a great star, blazing like
8: 12   The fourth **angel** sounded his trumpet, and a third of the sun was
8: 13   the trumpet blasts about to be sounded by the other three **angels**!"
9: 1   The fifth **angel** sounded his trumpet, and I saw a star that had
9: 11   They had as king over them the **angel** of the Abyss, whose name in
9: 13   The sixth **angel** sounded his trumpet, and I heard a voice coming
9: 14   It said *to* the sixth **angel** who had the trumpet, "Release the four
9: 14   "Release the four **angels** who are bound at the great river
9: 15   And the four **angels** who had been kept ready for this very hour
10: 1   Then I saw another mighty **angel** coming down from heaven.
10: 5   Then the **angel** I had seen standing on the sea and on the land
10: 7   But in the days when the seventh **angel** is about to sound his
10: 8   take the scroll that lies open in the hand *of* the **angel** who is
10: 9   So I went to the **angel** and asked him to give me the little scroll.
10: 10   I took the little scroll from the **angel's** hand and ate it. It tasted as
11: 15   The seventh **angel** sounded his trumpet, and there were loud voices
12: 7   Michael and his **angels** fought against the dragon, and the dragon
12: 7   against the dragon, and the dragon and his **angels** fought back.
12: 9   world astray. He was hurled to the earth, and his **angels** with him.
14: 6   Then I saw another **angel** flying in midair, and he had the eternal
14: 8   A second **angel** followed and said, "Fallen! Fallen is Babylon the
14: 9   A third **angel** followed them and said in a loud voice: "If anyone
14: 10   be tormented with burning sulfur in the presence *of* the holy **angels**
14: 15   Then another **angel** came out of the temple and called in a loud
14: 17   Another **angel** came out of the temple in heaven, and he too had a
14: 18   Still another **angel**, who had charge of the fire, came from the altar
14: 19   The **angel** swung his sickle on the earth, gathered its grapes
15: 1   seven **angels** with the seven last plagues—last, because with them
15: 6   Out of the temple came the seven **angels** with the seven plagues.
15: 7   Then one of the four living creatures gave *to* the seven **angels**
15: 8   temple until the seven plagues *of* the seven **angels** were completed.
16: 1   I heard a loud voice from the temple saying *to* the seven **angels**,
16: 5   Then I heard the **angel** in charge of the waters say: "You are just in
17: 1   One of the seven **angels** who had the seven bowls came and said to
17: 7   Then the **angel** said to me: "Why are you astonished? I will explain
18: 1   After this I saw another **angel** coming down from heaven.
18: 21   Then a mighty **angel** picked up a boulder the size of a large
19: 17   And I saw an **angel** standing in the sun, who cried in a loud voice
20: 1   And I saw an **angel** coming down out of heaven, having the key to
21: 9   One of the seven **angels** who had the seven bowls full of the seven
21: 12   high wall with twelve gates, and with twelve **angels** at the gates.
21: 17   cubits thick, by man's measurement, which the **angel** was using.
22: 6   sent his **angel** to show his servants the things that must soon take
22: 8   I fell down to worship at the feet *of* the **angel** who had been
22: 16   have sent my **angel** to give you this testimony for the churches.

35 ἄγγος, *angos* [1] [→ *31*]

baskets [1]

Mt 13: 48   Then they sat down and collected the good fish in **baskets**,

36 ἀγέλη, *agelē* [7] [√ *72*]

herd [7]

Mt   8: 30   Some distance from them a large **herd** of pigs was feeding.
8: 31   begged Jesus, "If you drive us out, send us into the **herd** of pigs."
8: 32   and the whole **herd** rushed down the steep bank into the lake
Mk   5: 11   A large **herd** of pigs was feeding on the nearby hillside.
5: 13   The **herd**, about two thousand in number, rushed down the steep
Lk   8: 32   A large **herd** of pigs was feeding there on the hillside. The demons
8: 33   and the **herd** rushed down the steep bank into the lake and was

37 ἀγενεαλόγητος, **agenealogētos** [1]

[√ 1.1 + 1181 + 3306]

without genealogy [1]

Heb 7: 3 Without father or mother, **without genealogy**, without beginning

38 ἀγενής, **agenēs** [1] [√ 1.1 + 1181]

lowly [1]

1Co 1: 28 He chose the **lowly** *things* of this world and the despised things—

39 ἀγιάζω, **hagiazō** [28] [√ 41]

sanctified [7], sanctify [4], made holy [3], hallowed [2], make holy [2], makes sacred [2], sanctified [+1639] [2], consecrated [1], holy [1], made holy [+1639] [1], makes holy [1], set apart [1], set apart as very own [1]

Mt 6: 9 you should pray: " 'Our Father in heaven, **hallowed** *be* your name,
23: 17 is greater: the gold, or the temple that **makes** the gold **sacred**?
23: 19 Which is greater: the gift, or the altar that **makes** the gift **sacred**?
Lk 11: 2 say: " 'Father, **hallowed** *be* your name, your kingdom come.
Jn 10: 36 what about the one whom the Father **set apart as** his **very own**
17: 17 **Sanctify** them by the truth; your word is truth.
17: 19 For them I **sanctify** myself, that they too may be truly sanctified.
17: 19 I sanctify myself, that they too *may be* truly **sanctified** [+1639].
Ac 20: 32 and give you an inheritance among all those *who are* **sanctified**.
26: 18 and a place among those *who are* **sanctified** by faith in me.'
Ro 15: 16 an offering acceptable to God, **sanctified** by the Holy Spirit.
1Co 1: 2 to those **sanctified** [+1639] in Christ Jesus and called to be holy,
6: 11 But you were washed, *you were* **sanctified**, you were justified in
7: 14 For the unbelieving husband *has been* **sanctified** through his wife,
7: 14 and the unbelieving wife *has been* **sanctified** through her
Eph 5: 26 to **make** her **holy**, cleansing her by the washing with water through
1Th 5: 23 *May* God himself, the God of peace, **sanctify** you through
1Ti 4: 5 because *it is* **consecrated** by the word of God and prayer.
2Ti 2: 21 **made holy**, useful to the Master and prepared to do any good
Heb 2: 11 Both the one *who* **makes** men **holy** and those who are made holy
2: 11 men holy and those *who are* **made holy** are of the same family.
9: 13 sprinkled on those who are ceremonially unclean **sanctify** them
10: 10 *we have been* **made holy** [+1639] through the sacrifice of the
10: 14 he has made perfect forever those *who are being* **made holy**.
10: 29 as an unholy thing the blood of the covenant that **sanctified** *him*,
13: 12 so Jesus also suffered outside the city gate to **make** the people **holy**
1Pe 3: 15 But in your hearts **set apart** Christ as Lord. Always be prepared to
Rev 22: 11 continue to do right; and *let* him who is holy continue *to be* **holy**."

40 ἀγιασμός, **hagiasmos** [10] [√ 41]

holiness [4], holy [2], sanctifying [2], holy life [1], sanctified [1]

Ro 6: 19 so now offer them in slavery to righteousness leading to **holiness**.
6: 22 the benefit you reap leads to **holiness**, and the result is eternal life.
1Co 1: 30 from God—that is, our righteousness, **holiness** and redemption.
1Th 4: 3 It is God's will that you should be **sanctified**: that you should
4: 4 of you should learn to control his own body in a way that is **holy**
4: 7 For God did not call us to be impure, but to live a **holy life**.
2Th 2: 13 chose you to be saved through the **sanctifying** *work* of the Spirit
1Ti 2: 15 if they continue in faith, love and **holiness** with propriety.
Heb 12: 14 Make every effort to live in peace with all men and to be **holy**;
1Pe 1: 2 through the **sanctifying** work of the Spirit, for obedience to Jesus

41 ἅγιος, **hagios** [233 / 234] [→ 39, 40, 42, 43; cf. 54]

ὁ ἅγιος τοῦ θεοῦ (the holy one of God) [3] Mk 1:24; Lk 4:34; Jn 6:69

πνεῦμα ἅγιος (Holy Spirit) [90] Mt 1:18,20; 3:11; 12:32; 28:19; Mk 1:8; 3:29; 12:36; 13:11; Lk 1:15,35,41,67; 2:25,26; 3:16,22; 4:1; 10:21; 11:13; 12:10,12; Jn 1:33; 14:26; 20:22; Ac 1:2,5,8,16; 2:4,33,38; 4:8,25,31; 5:3,32; 6:5; 7:51,55; 8:15,17,19; 9:17,31; 10:38,44,45,47; 11:15,16,24; 13:2,4,9,52; 15:8,28; 16:6; 19:2,2,6; 20:23,28; 21:11; 28:25; Ro 5:5; 9:1; 14:17; 15:13,16; 1Co 6:19; 12:3; 2Co 6:6; 13:13; Eph 1:13; 4:30; 1Th 1:5,6; 4:8; 2Ti 1:14; Tit 3:5; Heb 2:4; 3:7; 6:4; 9:8; 10:15; 1Pe 1:12; 2Pe 1:21; Jude 1:20

holy [155], saints [45], God's people [8], Most Holy Place [5], sacred [4], sanctuary [3], Most Holy Place [+41] [2], holy people [2], God's holy people [1], Holy One [1], Holy Place [1], believers [1], consecrated [+2813] [1], devoted to the Lord [1], holy ones [1], most holy [1], people [1]

Mt 1: 18 she was found to be with child through the **Holy** Spirit.
1: 20 because what is conceived in her is from the **Holy** Spirit.
3: 11 fit to carry. He will baptize you with the **Holy** Spirit and with fire.
4: 5 Then the devil took him to the **holy** city and had him stand on the
7: 6 "Do not give dogs what is **sacred**; do not throw your pearls to pigs.
12: 32 but anyone who speaks against the **Holy** Spirit will not be
24: 15 "So when you see standing in the **holy** place 'the abomination that
27: 52 and the bodies *of* many **holy people** who had died were raised to
27: 53 and after Jesus' resurrection they went into the **holy** city
28: 19 in the name of the Father and of the Son and of the **Holy** Spirit,
Mk 1: 8 you with water, but he will baptize you with the **Holy** Spirit."
1: 24 come to destroy us? I know who you are—the **Holy** *One* of God!"
3: 29 But whoever blasphemes against the **Holy** Spirit will never be
6: 20 and protected him, knowing him to be a righteous and **holy** man.
8: 38 of him when he comes in his Father's glory with the **holy** angels."
12: 36 David himself, speaking by the **Holy** Spirit, declared: " 'The Lord
13: 11 you at the time, for it is not you speaking, but the **Holy** Spirit.
Lk 1: 15 and he will be filled *with* the **Holy** Spirit even from birth.
1: 35 The angel answered, "The **Holy** Spirit will come upon you,
1: 35 So the **holy** one to be born will be called the Son of God.
1: 41 leaped in her womb, and Elizabeth was filled *with* the **Holy** Spirit.
1: 49 the Mighty One has done great things for me—**holy** is his name.
1: 67 His father Zechariah was filled *with* the **Holy** Spirit
1: 70 (as he said through his **holy** prophets of long ago),
1: 72 to show mercy to our fathers and to remember his **holy** covenant,
2: 23 "Every firstborn male *is to be* **consecrated** [+2813] to the Lord"),
2: 25 for the consolation of Israel, and the **Holy** Spirit was upon him.
2: 26 It had been revealed to him by the **Holy** Spirit that he would not
3: 16 to untie. He will baptize you with the **Holy** Spirit and with fire.
3: 22 and the **Holy** Spirit descended on him in bodily form like a dove.
4: 1 Jesus, full *of* the **Holy** Spirit, returned from the Jordan and was led
4: 34 come to destroy us? I know who you are—the **Holy** *One* of God!"
9: 26 in his glory and in the glory of the Father and *of* the **holy** angels.
10: 21 full of joy through the **Holy** Spirit, said, "I praise you, Father,
11: 13 how much more will your Father in heaven give the **Holy** Spirit to
12: 10 but anyone who blasphemes against the **Holy** Spirit will not be
12: 12 for the **Holy** Spirit will teach you at that time what you should say."
Jn 1: 33 and remain is he who will baptize with the **Holy** Spirit.'
6: 69 We believe and know that you are the **Holy** *One* of God."
14: 26 But the Counselor, the **Holy** Spirit, whom the Father will send in
17: 11 **Holy** Father, protect them by the power of your name—the name
20: 22 with that he breathed on them and said, "Receive the **Holy** Spirit."
Ac 1: 2 after giving instructions through the **Holy** Spirit to the apostles he
1: 5 but in a few days you will be baptized with the **Holy** Spirit."
1: 8 But you will receive power when the **Holy** Spirit comes on you;
1: 16 the Scripture had to be fulfilled which the **Holy** Spirit spoke long
2: 4 All of them were filled *with* the **Holy** Spirit and began to speak in
2: 33 he has received from the Father the promised **Holy** Spirit and has
2: 38 of your sins. And you will receive the gift *of* the **Holy** Spirit.
3: 14 You disowned the **Holy** and Righteous *One* and asked that a
3: 21 as he promised long ago through his **holy** prophets.
4: 8 Then Peter, filled *with* the **Holy** Spirit, said to them: "Rulers
4: 25 You spoke by the **Holy** Spirit through the mouth of your servant,
4: 27 and the people of Israel in this city to conspire against your **holy**
4: 30 and wonders through the name *of* your **holy** servant Jesus."
4: 31 And they were all filled *with* the **Holy** Spirit and spoke the word of
5: 3 Satan has so filled your heart that you have lied to the **Holy** Spirit
5: 32 We are witnesses of these things, and so is the **Holy** Spirit,
6: 5 They chose Stephen, a man full of faith and *of* the **Holy** Spirit;
6: 13 "This fellow never stops speaking against this **holy** place
7: 33 off your sandals; the place where you are standing is **holy** ground.
7: 51 You are just like your fathers: You always resist the **Holy** Spirit!
7: 55 But Stephen, full *of* the **Holy** Spirit, looked up to heaven and saw
8: 15 they prayed for them that they might receive the **Holy** Spirit,
8: 17 John placed their hands on them, and they received the **Holy** Spirit.
8: 19 so that everyone on whom I lay my hands may receive the **Holy**
9: 13 this man and all the harm he has done *to* your **saints** in Jerusalem.
9: 17 so that you may see again and be filled *with* the **Holy** Spirit."
9: 31 and encouraged *by* the **Holy** Spirit, it grew in numbers, living in
9: 32 traveled about the country, he went to visit the **saints** in Lydda.

9:41 Then he called the **believers** and the widows and presented her to
10:22 A **holy** angel told him to have you come to his house so that he
10:38 how God anointed Jesus of Nazareth *with* the **Holy** Spirit
10:44 these words, the **Holy** Spirit came on all who heard the message.
10:45 gift *of* the **Holy** Spirit had been poured out even on the Gentiles.
10:47 with water? They have received the **Holy** Spirit just as we have."
11:15 the **Holy** Spirit came on them as he had come on us at the
11:16 baptized with water, but you will be baptized with the **Holy** Spirit.'
11:24 He was a good man, full *of* the **Holy** Spirit and faith, and a great
13: 2 they were worshiping the Lord and fasting, the **Holy** Spirit said,
13: 4 The two of them, sent on their way by the **Holy** Spirit, went down
13: 9 filled *with* the **Holy** Spirit, looked straight at Elymas and said,
13:52 And the disciples were filled with joy and *with* the **Holy** Spirit.
15: 8 showed that he accepted them by giving the **Holy** Spirit to them,
15:28 It seemed good *to* the **Holy** Spirit and to us not to burden you with
16: 6 having been kept by the **Holy** Spirit from preaching the word in the
19: 2 asked them, "Did you receive the **Holy** Spirit when you believed?"
19: 2 "No, we have not even heard that there is a **Holy** Spirit."
19: 6 the **Holy** Spirit came on them, and they spoke in tongues
20:23 I only know that in every city the **Holy** Spirit warns me that prison
20:28 and all the flock of which the **Holy** Spirit has made you overseers.
21:11 tied his own hands and feet with it and said, "The **Holy** Spirit says,
21:28 brought Greeks into the temple area and defiled this **holy** place."
26:10 On the authority of the chief priests I put many *of* the **saints** in
28:25 "The **Holy** Spirit spoke the truth to your forefathers when he said
Ro   1: 2 promised beforehand through his prophets in the **Holy** Scriptures
     1: 7 To all in Rome who are loved by God and called to be **saints**:
     5: 5 because God has poured out his love into our hearts by the **Holy**
     7:12 So then, the law is **holy**, and the commandment is holy, righteous
     7:12 the law is holy, and the commandment is **holy**, righteous and good.
     8:27 because the Spirit intercedes for the **saints** in accordance with
     9: 1 I am not lying, my conscience confirms it in the **Holy** Spirit—
    11:16 If the part of the dough offered as firstfruits is **holy**, then the whole
    11:16 the whole batch is holy; if the root is **holy**, so are the branches.
    12: 1 to offer your bodies as living sacrifices, **holy** and pleasing to God—
    12:13 Share with **God's people** who are in need. Practice hospitality.
    14:17 but of righteousness, peace and joy in the **Holy** Spirit,
    15:13 so that you may overflow with hope by the power *of* the **Holy**
    15:16 an offering acceptable to God, sanctified by the **Holy** Spirit.
    15:25 I am on my way to Jerusalem in the service of the **saints** there.
    15:26 to make a contribution for the poor *among* the **saints** in Jerusalem.
    15:31 and that my service in Jerusalem may be acceptable *to* the **saints**
    16: 2 I ask you to receive her in the Lord in a way worthy *of* the **saints**
    16:15 Nereus and his sister, and Olympas and all the **saints** with them.
    16:16 Greet one another with a **holy** kiss. All the churches of Christ send
1Co 1: 2 in Corinth, to those sanctified in Christ Jesus and called to be **holy**,
     3:17 destroy him; for God's temple is **sacred**, and you are that temple.
     6: 1 it before the ungodly for judgment instead of before the **saints**?
     6: 2 Do you not know that the **saints** will judge the world? And if you
     6:19 Do you not know that your body is a temple *of* the **Holy** Spirit,
     7:14 your children would be unclean, but as it is, they are **holy**.
     7:34 Her aim is to be **devoted to the Lord** in both body and spirit.
    12: 3 and no one can say, "Jesus is Lord," except by the **Holy** Spirit.
    14:33 of disorder but of peace. As in all the congregations *of* the **saints**,
    16: 1 Now about the collection for **God's people**: Do what I told the
    16:15 and they have devoted themselves to the service *of* the **saints**.
    16:20 here send you greetings. Greet one another with a **holy** kiss.
2Co 1: 1 of God in Corinth, together with all the **saints** throughout Achaia:
     6: 6 patience and kindness; in the **Holy** Spirit and in sincere love;
     8: 4 with us for the privilege of sharing in this service to the **saints**.
     9: 1 is no need for me to write to you about this service to the **saints**.
     9:12 that you perform is not only supplying the needs *of* **God's people**
    13:12 Greet one another with a **holy** kiss.
    13:13 All the **saints** send their greetings.
    13:14 love of God, and the fellowship *of* the **Holy** Spirit be with you all.
Eph 1: 1 will of God, *To* the **saints** in Ephesus, the faithful in Christ Jesus:
     1: 4 For he chose us in him before the creation of the world to be **holy**
     1:13 you were marked in him with a seal, the promised **Holy** Spirit,
     1:15 about your faith in the Lord Jesus and your love for all the **saints**,
     1:18 has called you, the riches of his glorious inheritance in the **saints**,
     2:19 but fellow citizens with **God's people** and members of God's
     2:21 is joined together and rises to become a **holy** temple in the Lord.
     3: 5 as it has now been revealed by the Spirit *to* God's **holy** apostles
     3: 8 Although I am less than the least *of* all **God's people**, this grace
     3:18 may have power, together with all the **saints**, to grasp how wide
     4:12 to prepare **God's people** for works of service, so that the body of

     4:30 And do not grieve the **Holy** Spirit of God, with whom you were
     5: 3 or of greed, because these are improper *for* **God's holy people**.
     5:27 or wrinkle or any other blemish, but **holy** and blameless.
     6:18 this in mind, be alert and always keep on praying for all the **saints**.
Php 1: 1 of Christ Jesus, *To* all the **saints** in Christ Jesus at Philippi,
     4:21 Greet all the **saints** in Christ Jesus. The brothers who are with me
     4:22 All the **saints** send you greetings, especially those who belong to
Col 1: 2 *To* the **holy** and faithful brothers in Christ at Colosse: Grace
     1: 4 faith in Christ Jesus and of the love you have for all the **saints**—
     1:12 who has qualified you to share in the inheritance *of* the **saints** in
     1:22 physical body through death to present you **holy** in his sight,
     1:26 hidden for ages and generations, but is now disclosed *to* the **saints**.
     3:12 Therefore, as God's chosen people, **holy** and dearly loved,
1Th 1: 5 but also with power, with the **Holy** Spirit and with deep conviction.
     1: 6 you welcomed the message with the joy *given by* the **Holy** Spirit.
     3:13 and Father when our Lord Jesus comes with all his **holy** ones.
     4: 8 does not reject man but God, who gives you his **Holy** Spirit.
     5:26 Greet all the brothers with a **holy** kiss.
2Th 1:10 on the day he comes to be glorified in his **holy people** and to be
1Ti 5:10 showing hospitality, washing the feet *of* the **saints**, helping those
2Ti 1: 9 who has saved us and called us *to* a **holy** life—not because of
     1:14 to you—guard it with the help *of* the **Holy** Spirit who lives in us.
Tit 3: 5 us through the washing of rebirth and renewal *by* the **Holy** Spirit,
Phm 1: 5 about your faith in the Lord Jesus and your love for all the **saints**.
     1: 7 because you, brother, have refreshed the hearts *of* the **saints**.
Heb 2: 4 and gifts *of* the **Holy** Spirit distributed according to his will.
     3: 1 Therefore, **holy** brothers, who share in the heavenly calling,
     3: 7 So, as the **Holy** Spirit says: "Today, if you hear his voice,
     6: 4 have tasted the heavenly gift, who have shared in the **Holy** Spirit,
     6:10 and the love you have shown him as you have helped his **people**
     8: 2 and who serves *in* the **sanctuary**, the true tabernacle set up by the
     9: 1 had regulations for worship and also an earthly **sanctuary**.
     9: 2 and the consecrated bread; this was called the **Holy Place**.
     9: 3 the second curtain was a room called the **Most Holy** [+*41*] **Place**,
     9: 3 the second curtain was a room called the **Most Holy Place** [+*41*],
     9: 8 The **Holy** Spirit was showing by this that the way into the Most
     9: 8 *into* the **Most Holy Place** had not yet been disclosed as long as the
     9:12 but he entered the **Most Holy Place** once for all by his own blood,
     9:24 For Christ did not enter a man-made **sanctuary** that was only a
     9:25 the way the high priest enters the **Most Holy Place** every year with
    10:15 The **Holy** Spirit also testifies to us about this. First he says:
    10:19 since we have confidence to enter the **Most Holy Place** by the
    13:11 the blood of animals into the **Most Holy Place** as a sin offering,
    13:24 Greet all your leaders and all **God's people**. Those from Italy send
1Pe 1:12 preached the gospel to you by the **Holy** Spirit sent from heaven.
     1:15 But just as he who called you is **holy**, so be holy in all you do;
     1:15 But just as he who called you is holy, so be **holy** in all you do;
     1:16 for it is written: "Be **holy**, because I am holy."
     1:16 for it is written: "Be holy, because I am **holy**."
     2: 5 are being built into a spiritual house to be a **holy** priesthood,
     2: 9 a royal priesthood, a **holy** nation, a people belonging to God,
     3: 5 For this is the way the **holy** women of the past who put their hope
2Pe 1:18 from heaven when we were with him on the **sacred** mountain.
     1:21 but men spoke from God as they were carried along by the **Holy**
     2:21 then to turn their backs on the **sacred** command that was passed on
     3: 2 I want you to recall the words spoken in the past by the **holy**
     3:11 of people ought you to be? You ought to live **holy** and godly *lives*
1Jn 2:20 But you have an anointing from the **Holy One**, and all of you
Jude 1: 3 to contend for the faith that was once for all entrusted *to* the **saints**.
     1:14 Lord is coming with thousands upon thousands of his **holy ones**
     1:20 build yourselves up *in* your **most holy** faith and pray in the Holy
     1:20 yourselves up in your most holy faith and pray in the **Holy** Spirit.
Rev 3: 7 These are the words of him who is **holy** and true, who holds the
     4: 8 "**Holy**, holy, holy is the Lord God Almighty, who was, and is,
     4: 8 "Holy, **holy**, holy is the Lord God Almighty, who was, and is,
     4: 8 "Holy, holy, **holy** is the Lord God Almighty, who was, and is,
     5: 8 golden bowls full of incense, which are the prayers *of* the **saints**.
     6:10 out in a loud voice, "How long, Sovereign Lord, **holy** and true,
     8: 3 was given much incense to offer, with the prayers *of* all the **saints**,
     8: 4 The smoke of the incense, together with the prayers *of* the **saints**,
    11: 2 to the Gentiles. They will trample on the **holy** city for 42 months.
    11:18 the prophets and your **saints** and those who reverence your name,
    13: 7 He was given power to make war against the **saints** and to conquer
    13:10 for patient endurance and faithfulness *on the part of* the **saints**.
    14:10 be tormented with burning sulfur in the presence *of* the **holy** angels
    14:12 This calls for patient endurance *on the part of* the **saints** who obey

16: 6 for they have shed the blood *of* your **saints** and prophets, and you
17: 6 I saw that the woman was drunk with the blood *of* the **saints**,
18:20 over her, O heaven! Rejoice, **saints** and apostles and prophets!
18:24 In her was found the blood of prophets and *of* the **saints**, and of all
19: 8 her to wear." (Fine linen stands for the righteous acts *of* the **saints**.)
20: 6 Blessed and **holy** are those who have part in the first resurrection.
20: 9 the breadth of the earth and surrounded the camp *of* **God's people**,
21: 2 I saw the **Holy** City, the new Jerusalem, coming down out of
21:10 Spirit to a mountain great and high, and showed me the **Holy** City,
22:11 continue to do right; and let him who is **holy** continue to be holy."
22:19 take away from him his share in the tree of life and in the **holy** city,
22:21 The grace of the Lord Jesus be with **God's people**. [UBS *4246*]

42 ἁγιότης, **hagiotēs** [1 / 2] [√ *41*]

holiness [2]

2Co 1:12 in the **holiness** [UBS *605*] and sincerity that are from God.
Heb 12:10 God disciplines us for our good, that we may share in his **holiness**.

43 ἁγιωσύνη, **hagiōsynē** [3] [√ *41*]

holiness [2], holy [+*1877*] [1]

Ro   1: 4 and who through the Spirit *of* **holiness** was declared with power to
2Co 7: 1 and spirit, perfecting **holiness** out of reverence for God.
1Th 3:13 you will be blameless and **holy** [+*1877*] in the presence of our God

44 ἀγκάλη, **ankalē** [1] [→ *1878*]

arms [1]

Lk   2:28 Simeon took him in his **arms** and praised God, saying:

45 ἄγκιστρον, **ankistron** [1] [√ *46*]

line [1]

Mt 17:27 we may not offend them, go to the lake and throw out your **line**.

46 ἄγκυρα, **ankyra** [4] [→ *45*]

anchors [3], anchor [1]

Ac 27:29 they dropped four **anchors** from the stern and prayed for daylight.
     27:30 pretending they were going to lower *some* **anchors** from the bow.
     27:40 Cutting loose the **anchors**, they left them in the sea and at the same
Heb 6:19 We have this hope as an **anchor** for the soul, firm and secure.

47 ἄγναφος, **agnaphos** [2] [√ *1.1 + 1187*]

unshrunk [2]

Mt   9:16 "No one sews a patch *of* **unshrunk** cloth on an old garment,
Mk   2:21 "No one sews a patch *of* **unshrunk** cloth on an old garment.

48 ἁγνεία, **hagneia** [2] [√ *54*]

purity [2]

1Ti 4:12 for the believers in speech, in life, in love, in faith and in **purity**.
     5: 2 as mothers, and younger women as sisters, with absolute **purity**.

49 ἁγνίζω, **hagnizō** [7] [√ *54*]

purified [2], ceremonial cleansing [1], ceremonially clean [1],
purification rites [1], purifies [1], purify [1]

Jn 11:55 to Jerusalem for their **ceremonial cleansing** before the Passover.
Ac 21:24 these men, join in their **purification rites** and pay their expenses,
     21:26 next day Paul took the men and **purified** *himself* along with them.
     24:18 *I was* **ceremonially clean** when they found me in the temple
Jas 4: 8 Wash your hands, you sinners, and **purify** your hearts,
1Pe 1:22 *Now that you have* **purified** yourselves by obeying the truth
1Jn 3: 3 Everyone who has this hope in him **purifies** himself, just as he is

50 ἁγνισμός, **hagnismos** [1] [√ *54*]

purification [1]

Ac 21:26 to give notice of the date when the days *of* **purification** would end

51 ἀγνοέω, **agnoeō** [22] [√ *1.1 + 1182*]

ignorant [5], not understand [3], unknown [3], not know [2],
unaware [2], don't know [1], ignorance [1], ignored [1], ignores
[1], not realizing [1], not recognize [1], uninformed [1]

Mk   9:32 But they *did* **not understand** what he meant and were afraid to ask
Lk   9:45 But they *did* **not understand** what this meant. It was hidden from
Ac 13:27 The people of Jerusalem and their rulers *did* **not recognize** Jesus,
     17:23 Now what you worship *as something* **unknown** I am going to
Ro   1:13 I do not want you *to be* **unaware**, brothers, that I planned many
     2: 4 **not realizing** that God's kindness leads you toward repentance?
     6: 3 Or **don't** *you* **know** that all of us who were baptized into Christ
     7: 1 *Do you* **not know**, brothers—for I am speaking to men who know
     10: 3 *Since they did* **not know** the righteousness that comes from God
     11:25 I do not want you *to be* **ignorant** of this mystery, brothers,
1Co 10: 1 For I do not want you *to be* **ignorant** of the fact, brothers,
     12: 1 about spiritual gifts, brothers, I do not want you *to be* **ignorant**.
     14:38 If he **ignores** this, he himself will be ignored.
     14:38 If he ignores this, *he himself will be* **ignored**.
2Co 1: 8 We do not want you *to be* **uninformed**, brothers,
     2:11 might not outwit us. For *we are* not **unaware** of his schemes.
     6: 9 known, yet regarded as **unknown**; dying, and yet we live on;
Gal 1:22 I was personally **unknown** to the churches of Judea that are in
1Th 4:13 we do not want you *to be* **ignorant** about those who fall asleep,
1Ti 1:13 I was shown mercy because I acted in **ignorance** and unbelief.
Heb 5: 2 He is able to deal gently *with* those *who are* **ignorant** and are
2Pe 2:12 But these men blaspheme in matters *they do* **not understand**.

52 ἀγνόημα, **agnoēma** [1] [√ *1.1 + 1182*]

sins committed in ignorance [1]

Heb 9: 7 and for the **sins** the people had **committed in ignorance**.

53 ἄγνοια, **agnoia** [4] [√ *1.1 + 1182*]

ignorance [4]

Ac   3:17 "Now, brothers, I know that you acted in **ignorance**, as did your
     17:30 In the past God overlooked such **ignorance**, but now he commands
Eph 4:18 because of the **ignorance** that is in them due to the hardening of
1Pe 1:14 conform to the evil desires you had when you lived in **ignorance**.

54 ἁγνός, **hagnos** [8] [→ *48, 49, 50, 55, 56; cf. 41*]

pure [6], innocent [1], purity [1]

2Co 7:11 At every point you have proved yourselves to be **innocent** in this
     11: 2 to Christ, so that I might present you as a **pure** virgin to him.
Php 4: 8 is true, whatever is noble, whatever is right, whatever is **pure**,
1Ti 5:22 and do not share in the sins of others. Keep yourself **pure**.
Tit 2: 5 to be self-controlled and **pure**, to be busy at home, to be kind,
Jas 3:17 But the wisdom that comes from heaven is first of all **pure**;
1Pe 3: 2 when they see the **purity** and reverence of your lives.
1Jn 3: 3 who has this hope in him purifies himself, just as he is **pure**.

55 ἁγνότης, **hagnotēs** [2] [√ *54*]

pure [1], purity [1]

2Co 6: 6 in **purity**, understanding, patience and kindness; in the Holy Spirit
     11: 3 be led astray from your sincere and **pure** devotion to Christ.

56 ἁγνῶς, **hagnōs** [1] [√ *54*]

sincerely [1]

Php 1:17 The former preach Christ out of selfish ambition, not **sincerely**,

57 ἀγνωσία, *agnōsia* [2] [√ *1.1 + 1182*]

ignorant [2]

1Co 15:34 and stop sinning; for there are some who are **ignorant** of God—
1Pe 2:15 by doing good you should silence the **ignorant** talk of foolish men.

58 ἄγνωστος, *agnōstos* [1] [√ *1.1 + 1182*]

unknown [1]

Ac 17:23 found an altar with this inscription: *TO AN* **UNKNOWN** GOD.

59 ἀγορά, *agora* [11] [√ *60*]

marketplaces [6], marketplace [5]

Mt 11:16 They are like children sitting in the **marketplaces** and calling out
    20: 3 and saw others standing in the **marketplace** doing nothing.
    23: 7 they love to be greeted in the **marketplaces** and to have men call
Mk 6:56 or countryside—they placed the sick in the **marketplaces**.
     7: 4 When they come from the **marketplace** they do not eat unless they
   12:38 walk around in flowing robes and be greeted in the **marketplaces**,
Lk 7:32 They are like children sitting in the **marketplace** and calling out to
   11:43 seats in the synagogues and greetings in the **marketplaces**.
   20:46 in flowing robes and love to be greeted in the **marketplaces**
Ac 16:19 and dragged them into the **marketplace** to face the authorities.
   17:17 as well as in the **marketplace** day by day with those who

60 ἀγοράζω, *agorazō* [30] [→ *59, 61, 251, 1319, 1973; cf. 72*]

buy [13], bought [9], buying [3], purchased [2], buys [1], redeemed [1], spend [1]

Mt 13:44 then in his joy went and sold all he had and **bought** that field.
   13:46 he went away and sold everything he had and **bought** it.
   14:15 so *they can* go to the villages and **buy** themselves some food."
   21:12 temple area and drove out all who *were* **buying** and selling there.
   25: 9 Instead, go to those who sell oil and **buy** some for yourselves.'
   25:10 "But while they were on their way *to* **buy** the oil, the bridegroom
   27: 7 So they decided to use the money to **buy** the potter's field as a
Mk 6:36 and villages and **buy** themselves something to eat."
    6:37 *Are we* to go and **spend** that much *on* bread and give it to them to
   11:15 and began driving out those *who were* **buying** and selling there.
   15:46 So Joseph **bought** some linen cloth, took down the body,
   16: 1 and Salome **bought** spices so that they might go to anoint Jesus'
Lk 9:13 and two fish—unless we go and **buy** food for all this crowd."
   14:18 The first said, '*I have just* **bought** a field, and I must go and see it.
   14:19 'Another said, '*I have just* **bought** five yoke of oxen, and I'm on
   17:28 and drinking, **buying** and selling, planting and building.
   22:36 and if you don't have a sword, sell your cloak and **buy** one.
Jn 4: 8 (His disciples had gone into the town to **buy** food.)
    6: 5 said to Philip, "Where *shall we* **buy** bread for these people to eat?"
   13:29 some thought Jesus was telling him *to* **buy** what was needed for
1Co 6:20 *you* were **bought** at a price. Therefore honor God with your body.
    7:23 *You* were **bought** at a price; do not become slaves of men.
    7:30 those *who* **buy** *something*, as if it were not theirs to keep;
2Pe 2: 1 even denying the sovereign Lord *who* **bought** them—
Rev 3:18 I counsel you *to* **buy** from me gold refined in the fire, so you can
    5: 9 and with your blood *you* **purchased** men for God from every tribe
   13:17 so that no one could **buy** or sell unless he had the mark, which is
   14: 3 song except the 144,000 who *had been* **redeemed** from the earth.
   14: 4 They *were* **purchased** from among men and offered as firstfruits
   18:11 and mourn over her because no one **buys** their cargoes any more—

61 ἀγοραῖος, *agoraios* [2] [√ *60*]

courts [1], marketplace [1]

Ac 17: 5 so they rounded up some bad characters *from* the **marketplace**,
   19:38 against anybody, the **courts** are open and there are proconsuls.

62 ἄγρα, *agra* [2] [→ *65, 70, 71, 2436*]

catch [2]

Lk 5: 4 "Put out into deep water, and let down the nets for a **catch**."
    5: 9 and all his companions were astonished at the **catch** of fish they

63 ἀγράμματος, *agrammatos* [1] [√ *1.1 + 1211*]

unschooled [1]

Ac 4:13 courage of Peter and John and realized that they were **unschooled**,

64 ἀγραυλέω, *agrauleō* [1] [√ *69 + 885*]

living out [1]

Lk 2: 8 And there were shepherds **living out** in the fields nearby, keeping

65 ἀγρεύω, *agreuō* [1] [√ *62*]

catch [1]

Mk 12:13 of the Pharisees and Herodians to Jesus to **catch** him in his words.

66 ἀγριέλαιος, *agrielaios* [2] [√ *69 + 1777*]

olive tree that is wild [1], wild olive shoot [1]

Ro 11:17 and you, though a **wild olive shoot**, have been grafted in among
   11:24 if you were cut out of an **olive tree that is wild** by nature,

67 ἄγριος, *agrios* [3] [√ *69*]

wild [3]

Mt 3: 4 leather belt around his waist. His food was locusts and **wild** honey.
Mk 1: 6 a leather belt around his waist, and he ate locusts and **wild** honey.
Jude 1:13 They are **wild** waves of the sea, foaming up their shame;

68 Ἀγρίππας, *Agrippas* [11] [√ *69 + 2691*]

Agrippa [11]

Ac 25:13 A few days later King **Agrippa** and Bernice arrived at Caesarea to
   25:22 **Agrippa** said to Festus, "I would like to hear this man myself."
   25:23 The next day **Agrippa** and Bernice came with great pomp
   25:24 "King **Agrippa**, and all who are present with us, you see this man!
   25:26 him before all of you, and especially before you, King **Agrippa**,
   26: 1 Then **Agrippa** said to Paul, "You have permission to speak for
   26: 2 "King **Agrippa**, I consider myself fortunate to stand before you
   26:19 "So then, King **Agrippa**, I was not disobedient to the vision from
   26:27 King **Agrippa**, do you believe the prophets? I know you do."
   26:28 Then **Agrippa** said to Paul, "Do you think that in such a short time
   26:32 **Agrippa** said to Festus, "This man could have been set free if he

69 ἀγρός, *agros* [36] [→ *64, 66, 67, 68*]

field [22], countryside [5], fields [5], country [3], its [*+3836*] [1]

Mt 6:28 See how the lilies *of* the **field** grow. They do not labor or spin.
    6:30 If that is how God clothes the grass *of* the **field**, which is here
   13:24 kingdom of heaven is like a man who sowed good seed in his **field**.
   13:27 came to him and said, 'Sir, didn't you sow good seed in your **field**?
   13:31 is like a mustard seed, which a man took and planted in his **field**.
   13:36 and said, "Explain to us the parable of the weeds *in* the **field**."
   13:38 The **field** is the world, and the good seed stands for the sons of the
   13:44 "The kingdom of heaven is like treasure hidden in a **field**. When a
   13:44 then in his joy went and sold all he had and bought that **field**.
   19:29 or **fields** for my sake will receive a hundred times as much
   22: 5 no attention and went off—one to his **field**, another to his business.
   24:18 Let no one in the **field** go back to get his cloak.
   24:40 Two men will be in the **field**; one will be taken and the other left.
   27: 7 So they decided to use the money to buy the potter's **field** as a
   27: 8 That is why it**s** [*+3836*] has been called the Field of Blood to this
   27: 8 That is why it has been called the **Field** of Blood to this day.
   27:10 and they used them to buy the potter's **field**, as the Lord
Mk 5:14 the pigs ran off and reported this in the town and **countryside**,
    6:36 so they can go to the surrounding **countryside** and villages
    6:56 And wherever he went—into villages, towns or **countryside**—
   10:29 or sisters or mother or father or children or **fields** for me
   10:30 present age (homes, brothers, sisters, mothers, children and **fields**—
   11: 8 on the road, while others spread branches they had cut in the **fields**.
   13:16 Let no one in the **field** go back to get his cloak.
   15:21 and Rufus, was passing by on his way in from the **country**,
   16:12 form to two of them while they were walking in the **country**.

Lk   8:34   they ran off and reported this in the town and **countryside**,
     9:12   surrounding villages and **countryside** and find food and lodging,
   12:28   If that is how God clothes the grass of the **field**, which is here
   14:18   The first said, 'I have just bought a **field**, and I must go and see it.
   15:15   to a citizen of that country, who sent him to his **fields** to feed pigs.
   15:25   "Meanwhile, the older son was in the **field**. When he came near the
   17: 7   Would he say to the servant when he comes in from the **field**,
   17:31   Likewise, no one in the **field** should go back for anything.
   23:26   who was on his way in from the **country**, and put the cross on him
Ac   4:37   sold a **field** he owned and brought the money and put it at the

70   ἀγρυπνέω, *agrypneō*   [4]   [√ *62 + 5678*]

alert [1], keep watch [1], on guard [1], on the watch [1]

Mk 13:33   *Be* **on guard**! Be alert! You do not know when that time will
Lk   21:36   *Be* always **on the watch**, and pray that you may be able to escape
Eph⁻   6:18   this in mind, *be* **alert** and always keep on praying for all the saints.
Heb 13:17   They **keep watch** over you as men who must give an account.

71   ἀγρυπνία, *agrypnia*   [2]   [√ *62 + 5678*]

gone without sleep [1], sleepless nights [1]

2Co   6: 5   and riots; in hard work, **sleepless nights** and hunger;
   11:27   I have labored and toiled and have often **gone without sleep**;

72   ἄγω, *agō*   [69]   [→ *36, 73, 343, 442, 552, 795, 1341, 1455, 1456, 1524, 1652, 1687, 1974, 2007, 2042, 2056, 2081, 2190, 2220, 2221, 2448, 2449, 2450, 2451, 2762, 2864, 2989, 3555, 3842, 3843, 4080, 4108, 4135, 4206, 4207, 4219, 4310, 4575, 4605, 4641, 4642, 4643, 5130, 5194, 5251, 5252, 5270, 5632, 5902, 5932, 5933, 5961; cf. 34, 60, 545, 2989*]

brought [21], bring [10], go [6], led [6], brought in [3], bringing [2], listen [2], take [2], took [2], brought home [1], brought to trial [1], for [1], influenced [1], is [1], leads [1], leave [1], led away [1], led off [1], led out [1], open [1], swayed [1], taken [1], took [+4161] [1], took home [1]

Mt 10:18   On my account *you will be* **brought** before governors and kings as
   21: 2   tied there, with her colt by her. Untie them and **bring** them to me.
   21: 7   *They* **brought** the donkey and the colt, placed their cloaks on
   26:46   Rise, *let us* **go**! Here comes my betrayer!"
Mk   1:38   Jesus replied, "*Let us* **go** somewhere else—to the nearby villages—
   13:11   Whenever you are arrested and **brought to trial**, do not worry
   14:42   Rise! *Let us* **go**! Here comes my betrayer!"
Lk   4: 1   returned from the Jordan and *was* **led** by the Spirit in the desert,
   4: 9   The devil **led** him to Jerusalem and had him stand on the highest
   4:29   *They* got up, drove him out of the town, and **took** him to the brow
   4:40   the people **brought** to Jesus all who had various kinds of sickness,
   10:34   man on his own donkey, **took** him to an inn and took care of him.
   18:40   Jesus stopped and ordered the man *to be* **brought** to him.
   19:27   be king over them—**bring** them here and kill them in front of me.' "
   19:30   tied there, which no one has ever ridden. Untie it and **bring** it here.
   19:35   *They* **brought** it to Jesus, threw their cloaks on the colt and put
   22:54   *they* **led** him **away** and took him into the house of the high priest.
   23: 1   Then the whole assembly rose and **led** him **off** to Pilate.
   23:32   both criminals, *were* also **led out** with him to be executed.
   24:21   And what is more, *it* **is** the third day since all this took place.
Jn   1:42   And *he* **brought** him to Jesus. Jesus looked at him and said,
   7:45   and Pharisees, who asked them, "Why didn't *you* **bring** him *in*?"
   8: 3   and the Pharisees **brought in** a woman caught in adultery.
   9:13   *They* **brought** to the Pharisees the man who had been blind.
   10:16   I must **bring** them also. They too will listen to my voice, and there
   11: 7   Then he said to his disciples, "*Let us* **go** back to Judea."
   11:15   glad I was not there, so that you may believe. But *let us* **go** to him."
   11:16   the rest of the disciples, "*Let us* also **go**, that we may die with him."
   14:31   what my Father has commanded me. "Come now; *let us* **leave**.
   18:13   and **brought** him first to Annas, who was the father-in-law of
   18:28   Then the *Jews* **led** Jesus from Caiaphas to the palace of the Roman
   19: 4   *I am* **bringing** him out to you to let you know that I find no basis
   19:13   he **brought** Jesus out and sat down on the judge's seat at a place
Ac   5:21   of the elders of Israel—and sent to the jail **for** the apostles.
   5:26   the captain went with his officers and **brought** the apostles.
   5:27   *Having* **brought** the apostles, they made them appear before the

   6:12   They seized Stephen and **brought** him before the Sanhedrin.
   8:32   "*He was* **led** like a sheep to the slaughter, and as a lamb before the
   9: 2   or women, *he might* **take** them as prisoners to Jerusalem.
   9:21   And hasn't he come here to **take** them as prisoners to the chief
   9:27   But Barnabas took him and **brought** him to the apostles. He told
   11:26   and when he found him, *he* **brought** him to Antioch. So for a
   13:23   "From this man's descendants God *has* **brought** to Israel the Savior
   17:15   The men who escorted Paul **brought** him to Athens and then left
   17:19   Then *they* took him and **brought** him to a meeting of the
   18:12   the Jews made a united attack on Paul and **brought** him into court.
   19:37   *You have* **brought** these men here, though they have neither
   19:38   against anybody, the courts *are* **open** and there are proconsuls.
   20:12   The *people* took the young man **home** alive and were greatly
   21:16   Caesarea accompanied us and **brought** us *to the* **home** of Mnason,
   21:34   of the uproar, he ordered that Paul *be* **taken** into the barracks.
   22: 5   and went there *to* **bring** these people as prisoners to Jerusalem to
   23:10   him away from them by force and **bring** him into the barracks.
   23:18   So he **took** [+*4161*] him to the commander. The centurion said,
   23:18   sent for me and asked me *to* **bring** this young man to you
   23:31   with them during the night and **brought** him as far as Antipatris,
   25: 6   convened the court and ordered that Paul *be* **brought** *before* him.
   25:17   the court the next day and ordered the man *to be* **brought in**.
   25:23   men of the city. At the command of Festus, Paul *was* **brought in**.
Ro   2: 4   not realizing that God's kindness **leads** you toward repentance?
   8:14   because those *who are* **led** by the Spirit of God are sons of God.
1Co 12: 2   somehow or other *you were* **influenced** and led astray to mute
Gal   5:18   But if *you are* **led** by the Spirit, you are not under law.
1Th   4:14   so we believe that God *will* **bring** with Jesus those who have fallen
2Ti   3: 6   loaded down with sins and *are* **swayed** by all kinds of evil desires,
   4:11   Get Mark and **bring** him with you, because he is helpful to me in
Heb 2:10   In **bringing** many sons to glory, it was fitting that God, for whom
Jas   4:13   Now **listen**, you who say, "Today or tomorrow we will go to this
   5: 1   Now **listen**, you rich people, weep and wail because of the misery

73   ἀγωγή, *agōgē*   [1]   [√ *72*]

way of life [1]

2Ti   3:10   my **way of life**, my purpose, faith, patience, love, endurance,

74   ἀγών, *agōn*   [6]   [→ *75, 76, 497, 2043, 2865, 5253*]

fight [2], opposition [1], race [1], struggle [1], struggling [1]

Php   1:30   since you are going through the same **struggle** you saw I had,
Col   2: 1   I want you to know how much I am **struggling** for you and for
1Th   2: 2   God we dared to tell you his gospel in spite of strong **opposition**.
1Ti   6:12   Fight the good **fight** of the faith. Take hold of the eternal life to
2Ti   4: 7   I have fought the good **fight**, I have finished the race, I have kept
Heb 12: 1   and let us run with perseverance the **race** marked out for us.

75   ἀγωνία, *agōnia*   [1]   [√ *74*]

anguish [1]

Lk   22:44   And being in **anguish**, he prayed more earnestly, and his sweat

76   ἀγωνίζομαι, *agōnizomai*   [8]   [√ *74*]

fight [2], competes in the games [1], fought [1], make every effort [1], strive [1], struggling [1], wrestling [1]

Lk   13:24   "**Make every effort** to enter through the narrow door,
Jn   18:36   my servants would **fight** to prevent my arrest by the Jews.
1Co   9:25   Everyone who **competes in the games** goes into strict training.
Col   1:29   **struggling** with all his energy, which so powerfully works in me.
   4:12   *He is* always **wrestling** in prayer for you, that you may stand firm
1Ti   4:10   (and for this we labor and **strive**), that we have put our hope in the
   6:12   **Fight** the good fight of the faith. Take hold of the eternal life to
2Ti   4: 7   *I have* **fought** the good fight, I have finished the race, I have kept

77   Ἀδάμ, *Adam*   [9]

Adam [9]

Lk   3:38   son of Enosh, the son of Seth, the son *of* **Adam**, the son of God.
Ro   5:14   death reigned from the time *of* **Adam** to the time of Moses,
   5:14   a command, as did **Adam**, who was a pattern of the one to come.

1Co 15:22 For as in **Adam** all die, so in Christ all will be made alive.
15:45 "The first man **Adam** became a living being"; the last Adam,
15:45 Adam became a living being"; the last **Adam**, a life-giving spirit.
1Ti 2:13 For **Adam** was formed first, then Eve.
2:14 And **Adam** was not the one deceived; it was the woman who was
Jude 1:14 Enoch, the seventh from **Adam**, prophesied about these men:

78 ἀδάπανος, *adapanos* [1] [√ *1.1 + 1252*]

free of charge [1]

1Co 9:18 that in preaching the gospel I may offer it **free of charge**,

79 ’Αδδί, *Addi* [1]

Addi [1]

Lk 3:28 the son of Melki, the son *of* **Addi**, the son of Cosam, the son of

80 ἀδελφή, *adelphē* [26 / 25] [√ *81 [1.3]*]

sister [15], sisters [8], believing wife [*+1222*] [1], believing woman [1]

Mt 12:50 will of my Father in heaven is my brother and **sister** and mother."
13:56 Aren't all his **sisters** with us? Where then did this man get all these
19:29 has left houses or brothers or **sisters** or father or mother or children
Mk 3:32 "Your mother and brothers [UBS+ *and sisters*] are outside looking
3:35 Whoever does God's will is my brother and **sister** and mother.
6:3 Joseph, Judas and Simon? Aren't his **sisters** here with us?"
10:29 or brothers or **sisters** or mother or father or children or fields for
10:30 present age (homes, brothers, **sisters**, mothers, children and fields—
Lk 10:39 She had a **sister** called Mary, who sat at the Lord's feet listening to
10:40 don't you care that my **sister** has left me to do the work by myself?
14:26 and mother, his wife and children, his brothers and **sisters**—
Jn 11:1 He was from Bethany, the village of Mary and her **sister** Martha.
11:3 So the **sisters** sent word to Jesus, "Lord, the one you love is sick."
11:5 Jesus loved Martha and her **sister** and Lazarus.
11:28 she had said this, she went back and called her **sister** Mary aside.
11:39 "But, Lord," said Martha, the **sister** of the dead man, "by this time
19:25 his mother's **sister**, Mary the wife of Clopas, and Mary
Ac 23:16 But when the son of Paul's **sister** heard of this plot, he went into
Ro 16:1 I commend to you our **sister** Phoebe, a servant of the church in
16:15 Julia, Nereus and his **sister**, and Olympas and all the saints with
1Co 7:15 A **believing** man or woman is not bound in such circumstances;
9:5 Don't we have the right to take a **believing wife** [*+1222*] along
1Ti 5:2 as mothers, and younger women as **sisters**, with absolute purity.
Phm 1:2 *to* Apphia our **sister**, to Archippus our fellow soldier and to the
Jas 2:15 Suppose a brother or **sister** is without clothes and daily food.
2Jn 1:13 The children *of* your chosen **sister** send their greetings.

81 ἀδελφός, *adelphos* [343] [→ *1.3, 80, 82, 5788, 5789, 5790, 6012*]

ἀδελφός ἀγαπητός (beloved brother) [10] 1Co 15:58; Eph 6:21; Php 4:1; Col 4:7,9; Phm 1:16; Jas 1:16,19; 2:5; 2Pe 3:15

brothers of Jesus [21] Mt 12:46,47,48,49; 13:55; 28:10; Mk 3:31,32,33,34,35; Lk 8:19,20,21; Jn 2:12; 7:3,5,10; 20:17; Ac 1:14; 1Co 9:5

ἄνδρες ἀδελφοί (men, brothers) [13] Ac 1:16; 2:29,37; 7:2; 13:15,26,38; 15:7,13; 22:1; 23:1,6; 28:17

brothers [203], brother [104], brothers [*+467*] [13], brother's [8], believers [3], him$ $[*+899+3836*] [2], man [2], own people [2], another$ $[1], believing husband [1], believing man [1], fellow [1], him$ $[*+1609+3836*] [1], people [1]

Mt 1:2 the father of Jacob, Jacob the father of Judah and his **brothers**,
1:11 of Jeconiah and his **brothers** at the time of the exile to Babylon.
4:18 he saw two **brothers**, Simon called Peter and his brother Andrew.
4:18 he saw two brothers, Simon called Peter and his **brother** Andrew.
4:21 Going on from there, he saw two other **brothers**, James son of
4:21 two other brothers, James son of Zebedee and his **brother** John.
5:22 But I tell you that anyone who is angry *with* his **brother** will be
5:22 Again, anyone who says *to* his **brother**, 'Raca,' is answerable to
5:23 and there remember that your **brother** has something against you,
5:24 in front of the altar. First go and be reconciled *to* your **brother**;

5:47 And if you greet only your **brothers**, what are you doing more
7:3 "Why do you look at the speck of sawdust in your **brother's** eye
7:4 How can you say *to* your **brother**, 'Let me take the speck out of
7:5 then you will see clearly to remove the speck from your **brother's**
10:2 and his **brother** Andrew; James son of Zebedee, and his brother
10:2 his brother Andrew; James son of Zebedee, and his **brother** John;
10:21 "**Brother** will betray brother to death, and a father his child;
10:21 "Brother will betray **brother** to death, and a father his child;
12:46 his mother and **brothers** stood outside, wanting to speak to him.
12:47 told him, "Your mother and **brothers** are standing outside,
12:48 He replied to him, "Who is my mother, and who are my **brothers**?"
12:49 to his disciples, he said, "Here are my mother and my **brothers**.
12:50 For whoever does the will of my Father in heaven is my **brother**
13:55 and aren't his **brothers** James, Joseph, Simon and Judas?
14:3 put him in prison because of Herodias, his **brother** Philip's wife,
17:1 Jesus took with him Peter, James and John the **brother** of James,
18:15 "If your **brother** sins against you, go and show him his fault,
18:15 two of you. If he listens to you, you have won your **brother** over.
18:21 how many times shall I forgive my **brother** when he sins against
18:35 treat each of you unless you forgive your **brother** from your heart."
19:29 left houses or **brothers** or sisters or father or mother or children
20:24 ten heard about this, they were indignant with the two **brothers**.
22:24 his **brother** must marry the widow and have children for him.
22:24 must marry the widow and have children *for* him$ $[*+899+3836*].
22:25 Now there were seven **brothers** among us. The first one married
22:25 and since he had no children, he left his wife *to* his **brother**.
23:8 for you have only one Master and you are all **brothers**.
25:40 whatever you did for one of the least *of* these **brothers** of mine,
28:10 Go and tell my **brothers** to go to Galilee; there they will see me."
Mk 1:16 he saw Simon and his **brother** Andrew casting a net into the lake,
1:19 he saw James son of Zebedee and his **brother** John in a boat,
3:17 and his brother John (to them he gave the name Boanerges,
3:31 Then Jesus' mother and **brothers** arrived. Standing outside,
3:32 told him, "Your mother and **brothers** are outside looking for you."
3:33 "Who are my mother and my **brothers**?" he asked.
3:34 circle around him and said, "Here are my mother and my **brothers**!
3:35 Whoever does God's will is my **brother** and sister and mother."
5:37 follow him except Peter, James and John the **brother** of James.
6:3 Isn't this Mary's son and the **brother** of James, Joseph, Judas
6:17 He did this because of Herodias, his **brother** Philip's wife,
6:18 to Herod, "It is not lawful for you to have your **brother's** wife."
10:29 or **brothers** or sisters or mother or father or children or fields for
10:30 age (homes, **brothers**, sisters, mothers, children and fields—
12:19 "Moses wrote for us that if a man's **brother** dies and leaves a wife
12:19 the **man** must marry the widow and have children for his brother.
12:19 the man must marry the widow and have children *for* his **brother**.
12:20 Now there were seven **brothers**. The first one married and died
13:12 "**Brother** will betray brother to death, and a father his child.
13:12 "Brother will betray **brother** to death, and a father his child.
Lk 3:1 of Galilee, his **brother** Philip tetrarch of Iturea and Traconitis,
3:19 Herod the tetrarch because of Herodias, his **brother's** wife,
6:14 his **brother** Andrew, James, John, Philip, Bartholomew,
6:41 "Why do you look at the speck of sawdust in your **brother's** eye
6:42 How can you say *to* your **brother**, 'Brother, let me take the speck
6:42 How can you say to your brother, '**Brother**, let me take the speck
6:42 then you will see clearly to remove the speck from your **brother's**
8:19 Now Jesus' mother and **brothers** came to see him, but they were
8:20 told him, "Your mother and **brothers** are standing outside,
8:21 "My mother and **brothers** are those who hear God's word and put
12:13 "Teacher, tell my **brother** to divide the inheritance with me."
14:12 or dinner, do not invite your friends, your **brothers** or relatives,
14:26 and mother, his wife and children, his **brothers** and sisters—
15:27 'Your **brother** has come,' he replied,
15:32 because this **brother** of yours was dead and is alive again;
16:28 for I have five **brothers**. Let him warn them, so that they will not
17:3 "If your **brother** sins, rebuke him, and if he repents, forgive him.
18:29 "no one who has left home or wife or **brothers** or parents
20:28 "Moses wrote for us that if a man's **brother** dies and leaves a wife
20:28 the **man** must marry the widow and have children for his brother.
20:28 the man must marry the widow and have children *for* his **brother**.
20:29 Now there were seven **brothers**. The first one married a woman
21:16 will be betrayed even by parents, **brothers**, relatives and friends,
22:32 And when you have turned back, strengthen your **brothers**."
Jn 1:40 Andrew, Simon Peter's **brother**, was one of the two who heard
1:41 The first thing Andrew did was to find his **brother** Simon
2:12 to Capernaum with his mother and **brothers** and his disciples.

6: 8 of his disciples, Andrew, Simon Peter's **brother**, spoke up,
7: 3 Jesus' **brothers** said to him, "You ought to leave here and go to
7: 5 For even his own **brothers** did not believe in him.
7: 10 However, after his **brothers** had left for the Feast, he went also,
11: 2 This Mary, whose **brother** Lazarus now lay sick, was the same one
11: 19 to Martha and Mary to comfort them in the loss *of* their **brother**.
11: 21 to Jesus, "if you had been here, my **brother** would not have died.
11: 23 Jesus said to her, "Your **brother** will rise again."
11: 32 "Lord, if you had been here, my **brother** would not have died."
20: 17 Go instead to my **brothers** and tell them, 'I am returning to my
21: 23 the rumor spread among the **brothers** that this disciple would not
Ac 1: 14 the women and Mary the mother of Jesus, and with his **brothers**.
1: 15 In those days Peter stood up among the **believers** (a group
1: 16 and said, "**Brothers** [+*467*], the Scripture had to be fulfilled which
2: 29 "**Brothers** [+*467*], I can tell you confidently that the patriarch
2: 37 and said to Peter and the other apostles, "**Brothers** [+*467*],
3: 17 "Now, **brothers**, I know that you acted in ignorance, as did your
3: 22 raise up for you a prophet like me from among your own **people**;
6: 3 **Brothers**, choose seven men from among you who are known to
7: 2 To this he replied: "**Brothers** [+*467*] and fathers, listen to me!
7: 13 On their second visit, Joseph told his **brothers** who he was,
7: 23 Moses was forty years old, he decided to visit his **fellow** Israelites.
7: 25 Moses thought that his **own people** would realize that God was
7: 26 He tried to reconcile them by saying, 'Men, you are **brothers**;
7: 37 'God will send you a prophet like me from your **own people**.'
9: 17 Placing his hands on Saul, he said, "**Brother** Saul, the Lord—
9: 30 When the **brothers** learned of this, they took him down to
10: 23 out with them, and some *of* the **brothers** from Joppa went along.
11: 1 and the **brothers** throughout Judea heard that the Gentiles also had
11: 12 These six **brothers** also went with me, and we entered the man's
11: 29 decided to provide help *for* the **brothers** living in Judea.
12: 2 He had James, the **brother** of John, put to death with the sword.
12: 17 "Tell James and the **brothers** about this," he said, and then he left
13: 15 the synagogue rulers sent word to them, saying, "**Brothers** [+*467*],
13: 26 "**Brothers** [+*467*], children of Abraham, and you God-fearing
13: 38 "Therefore, my **brothers** [+*467*], I want you to know that through
14: 2 up the Gentiles and poisoned their minds against the **brothers**.
15: 1 came down from Judea to Antioch and were teaching the **brothers**:
15: 3 had been converted. This news made all the **brothers** very glad.
15: 7 Peter got up and addressed them: "**Brothers** [+*467*],
15: 13 they finished, James spoke up: "**Brothers** [+*467*], listen to me.
15: 22 and Silas, two men who were leaders among the **brothers**.
15: 23 The apostles and elders, your **brothers**, To the Gentile believers in
15: 23 *To* the Gentile **believers** in Antioch, Syria and Cilicia:
15: 32 said much to encourage and strengthen the **brothers**.
15: 33 they were sent off by the **brothers** with the blessing of peace to
15: 36 and visit the **brothers** in all the towns where we preached the word
15: 40 and left, commended by the **brothers** to the grace of the Lord.
16: 2 The **brothers** at Lystra and Iconium spoke well of him.
16: 40 where they met with the **brothers** and encouraged them.
17: 6 dragged Jason and some other **brothers** before the city officials,
17: 10 as it was night, the **brothers** sent Paul and Silas away to Berea.
17: 14 The **brothers** immediately sent Paul to the coast, but Silas
18: 18 Then he left the **brothers** and sailed for Syria, accompanied by
18: 27 the **brothers** encouraged him and wrote to the disciples there to
21: 7 where we greeted the **brothers** and stayed with them for a day.
21: 17 When we arrived at Jerusalem, the **brothers** received us warmly.
21: 20 "You see, **brother**, how many thousands of Jews have believed,
22: 1 "**Brothers** [+*467*] and fathers, listen now to my defense."
22: 5 I even obtained letters from them to their **brothers** in Damascus,
22: 13 He stood beside me and said, '**Brother** Saul, receive your sight!'
23: 1 looked straight at the Sanhedrin and said, "My **brothers** [+*467*],
23: 5 Paul replied, "**Brothers**, I did not realize that he was the high
23: 6 called out in the Sanhedrin, "My **brothers** [+*467*], I am a Pharisee.
28: 14 There we found *some* **brothers** who invited us to spend a week
28: 15 The **brothers** there had heard that we were coming, and they
28: 17 "My **brothers** [+*467*], although I have done nothing against our
28: 21 and none *of* the **brothers** who have come from there has reported
Ro 1: 13 I do not want you to be unaware, **brothers**, that I planned many
7: 1 Do you not know, **brothers**—for I am speaking to men who know
7: 4 So, my **brothers**, you also died to the law through the body of
8: 12 Therefore, **brothers**, we have an obligation—but it is not to the
8: 29 of his Son, that he might be the firstborn among many **brothers**.
9: 3 were cursed and cut off from Christ for the sake of my **brothers**,
10: 1 **Brothers**, my heart's desire and prayer to God for the Israelites is
11: 25 of this mystery, **brothers**, so that you may not be conceited:

12: 1 Therefore, I urge you, **brothers**, in view of God's mercy, to offer
14: 10 You, then, why do you judge your **brother**? Or why do you look
14: 10 judge your brother? Or why do you look down on your **brother**?
14: 13 not to put any stumbling block or obstacle in your **brother's** way.
14: 15 If your **brother** is distressed because of what you eat, you are no
14: 21 or to do anything else that will cause your **brother** to fall.
15: 14 I myself am convinced, my **brothers**, that you yourselves are full
15: 30 I urge you, **brothers**, by our Lord Jesus Christ and by the love of
16: 14 Phlegon, Hermes, Patrobas, Hermas and the **brothers** with them.
16: 17 I urge you, **brothers**, to watch out for those who cause divisions
16: 23 of public works, and our **brother** Quartus send you their greetings.
1Co 1: 1 of Christ Jesus by the will of God, and our **brother** Sosthenes,
1: 10 I appeal to you, **brothers**, in the name of our Lord Jesus Christ,
1: 11 My **brothers**, some from Chloe's household have informed me
1: 26 **Brothers**, think of what you were when you were called. Not many
2: 1 When I came to you, **brothers**, I did not come with eloquence
3: 1 **Brothers**, I could not address you as spiritual but as worldly—
4: 6 Now, **brothers**, I have applied these things to myself and Apollos
5: 11 you must not associate with anyone who calls himself a **brother**
6: 5 among you wise enough to judge a dispute between **believers**?
6: 6 But instead, one **brother** goes to law against another—and this in
6: 6 But instead, one brother goes to law against **another**⁵—and this in
6: 8 yourselves cheat and do wrong, and you do this to your **brothers**.
7: 12 If any **brother** has a wife who is not a believer and she is willing
7: 14 wife has been sanctified through her **believing husband**.
7: 15 A **believing man** or woman is not bound in such circumstances;
7: 24 **Brothers**, each man, as responsible to God, should remain in the
7: 29 What I mean, **brothers**, is that the time is short. From now on
8: 11 So this weak **brother**, for whom Christ died, is destroyed by your
8: 12 When you sin against your **brothers** in this way and wound their
8: 13 Therefore, if what I eat causes my **brother** to fall into sin,
8: 13 eat meat again, so that I will not cause him⁵ [+*1609+3836*] to fall.
9: 5 as do the other apostles and the Lord's **brothers** and Cephas?
10: 1 **brothers**, that our forefathers were all under the cloud and that
11: 33 So then, my **brothers**, when you come together to eat, wait for
12: 1 Now about spiritual gifts, **brothers**, I do not want you to be
14: 6 Now, **brothers**, if I come to you and speak in tongues, what good
14: 20 **Brothers**, stop thinking like children. In regard to evil be infants,
14: 26 What then shall we say, **brothers**? When you come together,
14: 39 Therefore, my **brothers**, be eager to prophesy, and do not forbid
15: 1 Now, **brothers**, I want to remind you of the gospel I preached to
15: 6 he appeared *to* more than five hundred of the **brothers** at the same
15: 31 I die every day—I mean that, **brothers**—just as surely as I glory
15: 50 **brothers**, that flesh and blood cannot inherit the kingdom of God,
15: 58 Therefore, my dear **brothers**, stand firm. Let nothing move you.
16: 11 he may return to me. I am expecting him along with the **brothers**.
16: 12 Now about our **brother** Apollos: I strongly urged him to go to you
16: 12 I strongly urged him to go to you with the **brothers**.
16: 15 themselves to the service of the saints. I urge you, **brothers**,
16: 20 All the **brothers** here send you greetings. Greet one another with a
2Co 1: 1 and Timothy our **brother**, To the church of God in Corinth,
1: 8 We do not want you to be uninformed, **brothers**,
2: 13 no peace of mind, because I did not find my **brother** Titus there.
8: 1 And now, **brothers**, we want you to know about the grace that
8: 18 And we are sending along with him the **brother** who is praised by
8: 22 we are sending with them our **brother** who has often proved to us
8: 23 as for our **brothers**, they are representatives of the churches
9: 3 But I am sending the **brothers** in order that our boasting about you
9: 5 So I thought it necessary to urge the **brothers** to visit you in
11: 9 for the **brothers** who came from Macedonia supplied what I
12: 18 I urged Titus to go to you and I sent our **brother** with him.
13: 11 Finally, **brothers**, good-by. Aim for perfection, listen to my
Gal 1: 2 and all the **brothers** with me, To the churches in Galatia:
1: 11 I want you to know, **brothers**, that the gospel I preached is not
1: 19 I saw none of the other apostles—only James, the Lord's **brother**.
3: 15 **Brothers**, let me take an example from everyday life. Just as no
4: 12 I plead with you, **brothers**, become like me, for I became like you.
4: 28 Now you, **brothers**, like Isaac, are children of promise.
4: 31 Therefore, **brothers**, we are not children of the slave woman,
5: 11 **Brothers**, if I am still preaching circumcision, why am I still being
5: 13 You, my **brothers**, were called to be free. But do not use your
6: 1 **Brothers**, if someone is caught in a sin, you who are spiritual
6: 18 The grace of our Lord Jesus Christ be with your spirit, **brothers**.
Eph 6: 21 Tychicus, the dear **brother** and faithful servant in the Lord,
6: 23 Peace *to* the **brothers**, and love with faith from God the Father
Php 1: 12 Now I want you to know, **brothers**, that what has happened to me

1:14 most *of* the **brothers** in the Lord have been encouraged to speak
2:25 my **brother**, fellow worker and fellow soldier, who is also your
3: 1 Finally, my **brothers**, rejoice in the Lord! It is no trouble for me to
3:13 **Brothers**, I do not consider myself yet to have taken hold of it.
3:17 Join with others in following my example, **brothers**, and take note
4: 1 Therefore, my **brothers**, you whom I love and long for, my joy
4: 8 Finally, **brothers**, whatever is true, whatever is noble, whatever is
4:21 in Christ Jesus. The **brothers** who are with me send greetings.
Col 1: 1 of Christ Jesus by the will of God, and Timothy our **brother**,
1: 2 *To* the holy and faithful **brothers** in Christ at Colosse: Grace
4: 7 He is a dear **brother**, a faithful minister and fellow servant in the
4: 9 with Onesimus, our faithful and dear **brother**, who is one of you.
4:15 Give my greetings to the **brothers** at Laodicea, and to Nympha
1Th 1: 4 For we know, **brothers** loved by God, that he has chosen you,
2: 1 You know, **brothers**, that our visit to you was not a failure.
2: 9 Surely you remember, **brothers**, our toil and hardship; we worked
2:14 For you, **brothers**, became imitators of God's churches in Judea,
2:17 But, **brothers**, when we were torn away from you for a short time
3: 2 who is our **brother** and God's fellow worker in spreading the
3: 7 Therefore, **brothers**, in all our distress and persecution we were
4: 1 Finally, **brothers**, we instructed you how to live in order to please
4: 6 and that in this matter no one should wrong his **brother** or take
4:10 And in fact, you do love all the **brothers** throughout Macedonia.
4:10 Yet we urge you, **brothers**, to do so more and more.
4:13 **Brothers**, we do not want you to be ignorant about those who fall
5: 1 Now, **brothers**, about times and dates we do not need to write to
5: 4 But you, **brothers**, are not in darkness so that this day should
5:12 Now we ask you, **brothers**, to respect those who work hard among
5:14 And we urge you, **brothers**, warn those who are idle,
5:25 **Brothers**, pray for us.
5:26 Greet all the **brothers** with a holy kiss.
5:27 you before the Lord to have this letter read *to* all the **brothers**.
2Th 1: 3 We ought always to thank God for you, **brothers**, and rightly so,
2: 1 Jesus Christ and our being gathered to him, we ask you, **brothers**,
2:13 ought always to thank God for you, **brothers** loved by the Lord,
2:15 So then, **brothers**, stand firm and hold to the teachings we passed
3: 1 Finally, **brothers**, pray for us that the message of the Lord may
3: 6 In the name of the Lord Jesus Christ, we command you, **brothers**,
3: 6 to keep away from every **brother** who is idle and does not live
3:13 And as for you, **brothers**, never tire of doing what is right.
3:15 Yet do not regard him as an enemy, but warn him as a **brother**.
1Ti 4: 6 If you point these things out *to* the **brothers**, you will be a good
5: 1 him as if he were your father. Treat younger men as **brothers**,
6: 2 are not to show less respect for them because they are **brothers**,
2Ti 4:21 greets you, and so do Pudens, Linus, Claudia and all the **brothers**.
Phm 1: 1 Paul, a prisoner of Christ Jesus, and Timothy our **brother**,
1: 7 has given me great joy and encouragement, because you, **brother**,
1:16 no longer as a slave, but better than a slave, as a dear **brother**.
1:20 I do wish, **brother**, that I may have some benefit from you in the
Heb 2:11 of the same family. So Jesus is not ashamed to call them **brothers**.
2:12 He says, "I will declare your name *to* my **brothers**; in the presence
2:17 For this reason he had to be made like his **brothers** in every way,
3: 1 Therefore, holy **brothers**, who share in the heavenly calling,
3:12 See to it, **brothers**, that none of you has a sinful, unbelieving heart
7: 5 that is, their **brothers**—even though their brothers are descended
8:11 or a man his **brother**, saying, 'Know the Lord,' because they will
10:19 Therefore, **brothers**, since we have confidence to enter the Most
13:22 **Brothers**, I urge you to bear with my word of exhortation,
13:23 I want you to know that our **brother** Timothy has been released.
Jas 1: 2 Consider it pure joy, my **brothers**, whenever you face trials of
1: 9 The **brother** in humble circumstances ought to take pride in his
1:16 Don't be deceived, my dear **brothers**.
1:19 My dear **brothers**, take note of this: Everyone should be quick to
2: 1 My **brothers**, as believers in our glorious Lord Jesus Christ,
2: 5 Listen, my dear **brothers**: Has not God chosen those who are poor
2:14 What good is it, my **brothers**, if a man claims to have faith
2:15 Suppose a **brother** or sister is without clothes and daily food.
3: 1 Not many of you should presume to be teachers, my **brothers**,
3:10 mouth come praise and cursing. My **brothers**, this should not be.
3:12 My **brothers**, can a fig tree bear olives, or a grapevine bear figs?
4:11 **Brothers**, do not slander one another. Anyone who speaks against
4:11 Anyone who speaks against his **brother** or judges him speaks
4:11 or judges him[s] [+899+3836] speaks against the law and judges it.
5: 7 Be patient, then, **brothers**, until the Lord's coming. See how the
5: 9 Don't grumble against each other, **brothers**, or you will be judged.
5:10 **Brothers**, as an example of patience in the face of suffering,

5:12 Above all, my **brothers**, do not swear—not by heaven or by earth
5:19 My **brothers**, if one of you should wander from the truth
1Pe 5:12 With the help of Silas, whom I regard as a faithful **brother**,
2Pe 1:10 Therefore, my **brothers**, be all the more eager to make your calling
3:15 just as our dear **brother** Paul also wrote you with the wisdom that
1Jn 2: 9 to be in the light but hates his **brother** is still in the darkness.
2:10 Whoever loves his **brother** lives in the light, and there is nothing
2:11 But whoever hates his **brother** is in the darkness and walks around
3:10 is not a child of God; nor is anyone who does not love his **brother**.
3:12 like Cain, who belonged to the evil one and murdered his **brother**.
3:12 his own actions were evil and his **brother's** were righteous.
3:13 Do not be surprised, my **brothers**, if the world hates you.
3:14 we have passed from death to life, because we love our **brothers**.
3:15 Anyone who hates his **brother** is a murderer, and you know that
3:16 life for us. And we ought to lay down our lives for our **brothers**.
3:17 and sees his **brother** in need but has no pity on him,
4:20 If anyone says, "I love God," yet hates his **brother**, he is a liar.
4:20 For anyone who does not love his **brother**, whom he has seen,
4:21 us this command: Whoever loves God must also love his **brother**.
5:16 If anyone sees his **brother** commit a sin that does not lead to
3Jn 1: 3 It gave me great joy to have *some* **brothers** come and tell about
1: 5 you are faithful in what you are doing for the **brothers**,
1:10 Not satisfied with that, he refuses to welcome the **brothers**.
Jude 1: 1 Jude, a servant of Jesus Christ and a **brother** of James, To those
Rev 1: 9 your **brother** and companion in the suffering and kingdom
6:11 and **brothers** who were to be killed as they had been was
12:10 For the accuser *of* our **brothers**, who accuses them before our God
19:10 and with your **brothers** who hold to the testimony of Jesus.
22: 9 am a fellow servant with you and with your **brothers** the prophets

82 ἀδελφότης, *adelphotēs* [2] [√ *81*]

brotherhood of believers [1], brothers [1]

1Pe 2:17 Love the **brotherhood of believers**, fear God, honor the king.
5: 9 because you know that your **brothers** throughout the world are

83 ἄδηλος, *adēlos* [2] [√ *1.1 + 1316*]

not clear [1], unmarked [1]

Lk 11:44 "Woe to you, because you are like **unmarked** graves, which men
1Co 14: 8 Again, if the trumpet does **not** sound a **clear** call, who will get

84 ἀδηλότης, *adēlotēs* [1] [√ *1.1 + 1316*]

uncertain [1]

1Ti 6:17 which is so **uncertain**, but to put their hope in God, who richly

85 ἀδήλως, *adēlōs* [1] [√ *1.1 + 1316*]

aimlessly [1]

1Co 9:26 Therefore I do not run like a man running **aimlessly**; I do not fight

86 ἀδημονέω, *adēmoneō* [3]

troubled [2], distressed [1]

Mt 26:37 along with him, and he began to be sorrowful and **troubled**.
Mk 14:33 along with him, and he began to be deeply distressed and **troubled**.
Php 2:26 For he longs for all of you and *is* **distressed** because you heard he

87 ἄδης, *hadēs* [10]

Hades [5], depths [2], grave [2], hell [1]

Mt 11:23 you be lifted up to the skies? No, you will go down to the **depths**.
16:18 will build my church, and the gates *of* **Hades** will not overcome it.
Lk 10:15 you be lifted up to the skies? No, you will go down to the **depths**.
16:23 In **hell**, where he was in torment, he looked up and saw Abraham
Ac 2:27 because you will not abandon me to the **grave**, nor will you let
2:31 that he was not abandoned to the **grave**, nor did his body see
Rev 1:18 alive for ever and ever! And I hold the keys *of* death and **Hades**.
6: 8 was named Death, and **Hades** was following close behind him.
20:13 in it, and death and **Hades** gave up the dead that were in them,
20:14 Then death and **Hades** were thrown into the lake of fire. The lake

88 ἀδιάκριτος, *adiakritos* [1] [√ *1.1 + 1328 + 3212*]

impartial [1]

Jas   3: 17 submissive, full of mercy and good fruit, **impartial** and sincere.

89 ἀδιάλειπτος, *adialeiptos* [2] [√ *1.1 + 1328 + 3309*]

constantly [1], unceasing [1]

Ro   9: 2 I have great sorrow and **unceasing** anguish in my heart.
2Ti   1: 3 as night and day I **constantly** remember you in my prayers.

90 ἀδιαλείπτως, *adialeiptōs* [4] [√ *1.1 + 1328 + 3309*]

continually [3], constantly [1]

Ro   1: 9 gospel of his Son, is my witness how **constantly** I remember you
1Th   1: 3 We **continually** remember before our God and Father your work
      2: 13 And we also thank God **continually** because, when you received
      5: 17 pray **continually**;

91 ἀδιαφθορία, *adiaphthoria*   Not used in UBS/NIV
[√ *1.1 + 1328 + 5780*]

92 ἀδικέω, *adikeō* [28] [√ *1.1 + 1472*]

harm [5], done wrong [3], do wrong [2], does wrong [2], hurt [2], wronged [2], do harm [1], damage [1], did wrong [1], guilty [1], harm done [1], inflict injury [1], injured [1], mistreated [1], mistreating [1], torment [1], unfair [1], wrong [1]

Mt   20: 13 he answered one of them, 'Friend, *I am* not *being* **unfair** *to* you.
Lk   10: 19 to overcome all the power of the enemy; nothing *will* **harm** you.
Ac   7: 24 He saw one of them *being* **mistreated** by an Egyptian, so he went
      7: 26 'Men, you are brothers; why *do you want to* **hurt** each other?'
      7: 27 "But the man *who was* **mistreating** the other pushed Moses aside
     25: 10 *I have* not **done** any **wrong** to the Jews, as you yourself know very
     25: 11 If, however, *I am* **guilty** of doing anything deserving death,
1Co   6: 7 Why not rather *be* **wronged**? Why not rather be cheated?
      6: 8 Instead, *you* yourselves cheat and **do wrong**, and you do this to
2Co   7: 2 *We have* **wronged** no one, we have corrupted no one, we have
      7: 12 it was not on account *of* the one *who* **did** the **wrong** or of the
      7: 12 on account of the one who did the wrong or of the **injured** party,
Gal   4: 12 like me, for I became like you. *You have* **done** me no **wrong**.
Col   3: 25 Anyone *who* **does wrong** will be repaid for his wrong, and there is
      3: 25 Anyone who does wrong will be repaid for *his* **wrong**, and there is
Phm   1: 18 If *he has* **done** you any **wrong** or owes you anything, charge it to
2Pe   2: 13 They will be paid back with harm for the **harm** *they have* **done**.
Rev   2: 11 He who overcomes *will* not *be* **hurt** at all by the second death.
      6: 6 barley for a day's wages, and *do* not **damage** the oil and the wine!"
      7: 2 to the four angels who had been given power *to* **harm** the land
      7: 3 "Do not **harm** the land or the sea or the trees until we put a seal on
      9: 4 They were told not to **harm** the grass of the earth or any plant
      9: 10 and in their tails they had power *to* **torment** people for five
      9: 19 tails were like snakes, having heads with which *they* **inflict injury**.
     11: 5 If anyone tries *to* **harm** them, fire comes from their mouths
     11: 5 This is how anyone who wants *to* **harm** them must die.
     22: 11 Let him *who* **does wrong** continue to do wrong; let him who is vile
     22: 11 *Let* him who does wrong continue *to* **do wrong**; let him who is

93 ἀδίκημα, *adikēma* [3] [√ *1.1 + 1472*]

crime [1], crimes [1], misdemeanor [1]

Ac   18: 14 "If you Jews were making a complaint about some **misdemeanor**
     24: 20 Or these who are here should state what **crime** they found in me
Rev 18: 5 sins are piled up to heaven, and God has remembered her **crimes**.

94 ἀδικία, *adikia* [25] [√ *1.1 + 1472*]

wickedness [9], evil [4], unjust [2], unrighteousness [2], dishonest [1], evildoers [+2239] [1], harm [1], nothing false [+4024] [1], sin [1], worldly [1], wrong [1], wrongdoing [1]

Lk   13: 27 where you come from. Away from me, all *you* **evildoers** [+2239]!'
     16: 8 "The master commended the **dishonest** manager because he had
     16: 9 I tell you, use **worldly** wealth to gain friends for yourselves,

     18: 6 And the Lord said, "Listen to what the **unjust** judge says.
Jn   7: 18 one who sent him is a man of truth; there is **nothing false** [+4024]
Ac   1: 18 (With the reward he got *for* his **wickedness**, Judas bought a field;
      8: 23 For I see that you are full of bitterness and captive *to* **sin**."
Ro   1: 18 and **wickedness** of men who suppress the truth by their
      1: 18 wickedness of men who suppress the truth by their **wickedness**,
      1: 29 They have become filled with every kind of **wickedness**, evil,
      2: 8 those who are self-seeking and who reject the truth and follow **evil**,
      3: 5 But if our **unrighteousness** brings out God's righteousness more
      6: 13 as instruments of **wickedness**, but rather offer yourselves to God,
      9: 14 What then shall we say? Is God **unjust**? Not at all!
1Co 13: 6 Love does not delight in **evil** but rejoices with the truth.
2Co 12: 13 except that I was never a burden to you? Forgive me this **wrong**!
2Th   2: 10 and in every sort *of* **evil** that deceives those who are perishing.
      2: 12 who have not believed the truth but have delighted *in* **wickedness**.
2Ti   2: 19 confesses the name of the Lord must turn away from **wickedness**."
Heb   8: 12 For I will forgive their **wickedness**, and will remember their sins no
Jas   3: 6 tongue also is a fire, a world *of* **evil** among the parts of the body.
2Pe   2: 13 They will be paid back *with* **harm** for the harm they have done.
      2: 15 way of Balaam son of Beor, who loved the wages *of* **wickedness**.
1Jn   1: 9 will forgive us our sins and purify us from all **unrighteousness**.
      5: 17 All **wrongdoing** is sin, and there is sin that does not lead to death.

95 ἀδικοκρίτης, *adikokritēs*   Not used in UBS/NIV
[√ *1.1 + 1472 + 3212*]

96 ἄδικος, *adikos* [12] [√ *1.1 + 1472*]

unrighteous [3], dishonest [2], unjust [2], wicked [2], evildoers [1], ungodly [1], worldly [1]

Mt   5: 45 and the good, and sends rain on the righteous and the **unrighteous**.
Lk   16: 10 and whoever is **dishonest** with very little will also be dishonest
     16: 10 and whoever is dishonest with very little will also be **dishonest**
     16: 11 So if you have not been trustworthy in handling **worldly** wealth,
     18: 11 robbers, **evildoers**, adulterers—or even like this tax collector.
Ac   24: 15 there will be a resurrection *of* both the righteous and the **wicked**.
Ro   3: 5 what shall we say? That God is **unjust** in bringing his wrath on us?
1Co   6: 1 dare he take it before the **ungodly** for judgment instead of before
      6: 9 Do you not know that the **wicked** will not inherit the kingdom of
Heb   6: 10 God is not **unjust**; he will not forget your work and the love you
1Pe   3: 18 for all, the righteous for the **unrighteous**, to bring you to God.
2Pe   2: 9 from trials and to hold the **unrighteous** for the day of judgment,

97 ἀδίκως, *adikōs* [1] [√ *1.1 + 1472*]

unjust [1]

1Pe   2: 19 For it is commendable if a man bears up under the pain *of* **unjust**

98 Ἀδμίν, *Admin* [1 / 0] [√ *cf. 730*]

Lk   3: 33 the son *of* Ram, [UBS *Admin*; NIV *730*] the son of Hezron,

99 ἀδόκιμος, *adokimos* [8] [√ *1.1 + 1312*]

depraved [1], disqualified [1], fail the test [+1639] [1], failed the test [+1639] [1], rejected [1], to have failed [+1639] [1], unfit [1], worthless [1]

Ro   1: 28 he gave them over to a **depraved** mind, to do what ought not to be
1Co   9: 27 preached to others, I myself will not be **disqualified** *for the prize*.
2Co 13: 5 Jesus is in you—unless, of course, *you* **fail the test** [+1639]?
     13: 6 that you will discover that we *have* not **failed the test** [+1639].
     13: 7 do what is right even though we *may* seem **to have failed** [+1639].
2Ti   3: 8 depraved minds, who, as far as the faith is concerned, are **rejected**.
Tit   1: 16 are detestable, disobedient and **unfit** for doing anything good.
Heb   6: 8 But land that produces thorns and thistles is **worthless** and is in

100 ἄδολος, *adolos* [1] [√ *1.1 + 1515*]

pure [1]

1Pe   2: 2 Like newborn babies, crave **pure** spiritual milk, so that by it you

101 Ἀδραμυττηνός, *Adramyttēnos* [1]

from Adramyttium [1]

Ac 27: 2 We boarded a ship **from Adramyttium** about to sail for ports

102 Ἀδρίας, *Adrias* [1]

Adriatic Sea [1]

Ac 27:27 night we were still being driven across the **Adriatic Sea**,

103 ἀδρότης, *hadrotēs* [1]

liberal [1]

2Co 8:20 to avoid any criticism of the way we administer this **liberal** *gift*.

104 ἀδυνατέω, *adynateō* [2] [√ *1.1 + 1538*]

impossible [2]

Mt 17:20 to there' and it will move. Nothing *will be* **impossible** for you."
Lk 1:37 For nothing *is* **impossible** with God."

105 ἀδύνατος, *adynatos* [10] [√ *1.1 + 1538*]

impossible [7], crippled [1], powerless [1], weak [1]

Mt 19:26 Jesus looked at them and said, "With man this is **impossible**,
Mk 10:27 Jesus looked at them and said, "With man this is **impossible**,
Lk 18:27 Jesus replied, "What is **impossible** with men is possible with God."
Ac 14: 8 In Lystra there sat a man **crippled** in his feet, who was lame from
Ro 8: 3 For what the law was **powerless** to do in that it was weakened by
   15: 1 We who are strong ought to bear with the failings *of* the **weak**
Heb 6: 4 It is **impossible** for those who have once been enlightened,
    6:18 by two unchangeable things in which it is **impossible** for God to
   10: 4 because it is **impossible** for the blood of bulls and goats to take
   11: 6 And without faith it is **impossible** to please God, because anyone

106 ᾄδω, *adō* [5] [√ *6046*]

sang [3], sing [2]

Eph 5:19 and spiritual songs. **Sing** and make music in your heart to the Lord,
Col 3:16 and *as you* **sing** psalms, hymns and spiritual songs with gratitude
Rev 5: 9 And *they* **sang** a new song: "You are worthy to take the scroll
   14: 3 And *they* **sang** a new song before the throne and before the four
   15: 3 and **sang** the song of Moses the servant of God and the song of the

107 ἀεί, *aei* [7] [→ *132*]

always [7]

Ac 7:51 You are just like your fathers: You **always** resist the Holy Spirit!
2Co 4:11 For we who are alive are **always** being given over to death for
    6:10 sorrowful, yet **always** rejoicing; poor, yet making many rich;
Tit 1:12 has said, "Cretans are **always** liars, evil brutes, lazy gluttons."
Heb 3:10 and I said, 'Their hearts are **always** going astray, and they have not
1Pe 3:15 **Always** be prepared to give an answer to everyone who asks you to
2Pe 1:12 So I will **always** remind you of these things, even though you

108 ἀετός, *aetos* [5]

eagle [3], vultures [2]

Mt 24:28 Wherever there is a carcass, there the **vultures** will gather.
Lk 17:37 "Where there is a dead body, there the **vultures** will gather."
Rev 4: 7 the third had a face like a man, the fourth was like a flying **eagle**.
    8:13 I heard an **eagle** that was flying in midair call out in a loud voice:
   12:14 The woman was given the two wings *of* a great **eagle**, so that she

109 ἄζυμος, *azymos* [9] [√ *1.1 + 2434*]

Feast of Unleavened Bread [4], Unleavened Bread [2], Feast of Unleavened Bread [+2465] [1], bread without yeast [1], without yeast [1]

Mt 26:17 On the first day of the **Feast of Unleavened Bread**, the disciples
Mk 14: 1 and the **Feast of Unleavened Bread** were only two days away,

   14:12 On the first day *of* the **Feast of Unleavened Bread**, when it was
Lk 22: 1 Now the Feast *of* **Unleavened Bread**, called the Passover,
   22: 7 Then came the day *of* **Unleavened Bread** on which the Passover
Ac 12: 3 Peter also. This happened during the **Feast of Unleavened Bread**.
   20: 6 sailed from Philippi after the **Feast of Unleavened** [+2465] **Bread**,
1Co 5: 7 rid of the old yeast that you may be a new batch **without yeast**—
    5: 8 the yeast of malice and wickedness, but with **bread without yeast**,

110 Ἀζώρ, *Azōr* [2]

Azor [2]

Mt 1:13 of Abiud, Abiud the father of Eliakim, Eliakim the father of **Azor**,
    1:14 **Azor** the father of Zadok, Zadok the father of Akim, Akim the

111 Ἄζωτος, *Azōtos* [1]

Azotus [1]

Ac 8:40 Philip, however, appeared at **Azotus** and traveled about,

112 ἀηδία, *aēdia* Not used in UBS/NIV [√ *1.1 + 2454*]

113 ἀήρ, *aēr* [7] [→ *874; cf. 150, 885*]

air [6], sky [1]

Ac 22:23 and throwing off their cloaks and flinging dust into the **air**,
1Co 9:26 a man running aimlessly; I do not fight like a man beating the **air**.
   14: 9 know what you are saying? You will just be speaking into the **air**.
Eph 2: 2 the ways of this world and of the ruler of the kingdom *of* the **air**,
1Th 4:17 up together with them in the clouds to meet the Lord in the **air**.
Rev 9: 2 The sun and **sky** were darkened by the smoke from the Abyss.
   16:17 The seventh angel poured out his bowl into the **air**, and out of the

114 ἀθανασία, *athanasia* [3] [√ *1.1 + 2569*]

immortality [2], immortal [1]

1Co 15:53 itself with the imperishable, and the mortal with **immortality**.
   15:54 and the mortal with **immortality**, then the saying that is written
1Ti 6:16 who alone is **immortal** and who lives in unapproachable light,

115 ἀθάνατος, *athanatos* Not used in UBS/NIV
                                  [√ *1.1 + 2569*]

116 ἀθέμιτος, *athemitos* [2]

against law [1], detestable [1]

Ac 10:28 "You are well aware that it is **against** our **law** for a Jew to associate
1Pe 4: 3 lust, drunkenness, orgies, carousing and **detestable** idolatry.

117 ἄθεος, *atheos* [1] [√ *1.1 + 2536*]

without God [1]

Eph 2:12 of the promise, without hope and **without God** in the world.

118 ἄθεσμος, *athesmos* [2] [√ *1.1 + 5502*]

lawless [2]

2Pe 2: 7 who was distressed by the filthy lives *of* **lawless** *men*
    3:17 so that you may not be carried away by the error *of* **lawless** *men*

119 ἀθετέω, *atheteō* [16] [√ *1.1 + 5502*]

rejects [6], reject [2], rejected [2], set aside [2], broken [1], frustrate [1], refuse [1], setting aside [1]

Mk 6:26 of his oaths and his dinner guests, he did not want *to* **refuse** her.
    7: 9 "*You* have a fine way of **setting aside** the commands of God in
Lk 7:30 and experts in the law **rejected** God's purpose for themselves,
   10:16 "He who listens to you listens to me; he *who* **rejects** you rejects me;
   10:16 who listens to you listens to me; he who rejects you **rejects** me;
   10:16 you **rejects** me; but he *who* **rejects** me rejects him who sent me."
   10:16 you rejects me; but he who rejects me **rejects** him who sent me."

Jn   12:48 There is a judge for the one *who* **rejects** me and does not accept
1Co   1:19 of the wise; the intelligence of the intelligent *I will* **frustrate.**"
Gal   2:21 *I do* not **set aside** the grace of God, for if righteousness could be
      3:15 Just as no one *can* **set aside** or add to a human covenant that has
1Th   4: 8 he *who* **rejects** this instruction does not reject man but God,
      4: 8 he who rejects this instruction *does* not **reject** man but God,
1Ti   5:12 on themselves, because *they have* **broken** *their* first pledge.
Heb 10:28 Anyone *who* **rejected** the law of Moses died without mercy on the
Jude 1: 8 their own bodies, **reject** authority and slander celestial beings.

120 ἀθέτησις, athetēsis [2] [√ 1.1 + 5502]

do away [1], set aside [1]

Heb   7:18 The former regulation is **set aside** because it was weak and useless
      9:26 the end of the ages to **do away** with sin by the sacrifice of himself.

121 ’Αθῆναι, Athēnai [4] [→ 122]

Athens [4]

Ac   17:15 The men who escorted Paul brought him to **Athens** and then left
     17:16 While Paul was waiting for them in **Athens**, he was greatly
     18: 1 After this, Paul left **Athens** and went to Corinth.
1Th   3: 1 it no longer, we thought it best to be left by ourselves in **Athens**.

122 ’Αθηναῖος, Athēnaios [2] [√ 121]

Athenians [1], Athens [1]

Ac   17:21 (All the **Athenians** and the foreigners who lived there spent their
     17:22 up in the meeting of the Areopagus and said: "Men *of* **Athens**!

123 ἀθλέω, athleō [2] [→ 124, 5254]

competes [1], competes as an athlete [1]

2Ti   2: 5 Similarly, if anyone **competes as an athlete**, he does not receive
      2: 5 he does not receive the victor's crown unless *he* **competes**

124 ἄθλησις, athlēsis [1] [√ 123]

contest [1]

Heb 10:32 when you stood your ground in a great **contest** in the face of

125 ἀθροίζω, athroizō [1] [→ 2044, 5255; cf. 275, 2577]

assembled together [1]

Lk   24:33 they found the Eleven and those with them, **assembled together**

126 ἀθυμέω, athymeō [1] [√ 1.1 + 2596]

become discouraged [1]

Col   3:21 do not embitter your children, or *they will* **become discouraged**.

127 ἄθῷος, athōos [2] [√ 1.1 + 5502]

innocent [2]

Mt   27: 4 "I have sinned," he said, "for I have betrayed **innocent** blood."
     27:24 "I am **innocent** of this man's blood," he said. "It is your

128 αἴγειος, aigeios [1] [√ 144]

goatskins [+1293] [1]

Heb 11:37 They went about in sheepskins and **goatskins** [+1293], destitute,

129 αἰγιαλός, aigialos [6] [√ 229]

shore [3], beach [2], sandy beach [1]

Mt   13: 2 got into a boat and sat in it, while all the people stood on the **shore**.
     13:48 When it was full, the fishermen pulled it up on the **shore**.
Jn   21: 4 Early in the morning, Jesus stood on the **shore**, but the disciples
Ac   21: 5 us out of the city, and there on the **beach** we knelt to pray.
     27:39 did not recognize the land, but they saw a bay with a **sandy beach**,

27:40 Then they hoisted the foresail to the wind and made for the **beach**.

130 Αἰγύπτιος, Aigyptios [5] [√ 131]

Egyptian [3], Egyptians [2]

Ac   7:22 Moses was educated in all the wisdom *of* the **Egyptians** and was
      7:24 he went to his defense and avenged him by killing the **Egyptian**.
      7:28 Do you want to kill me as you killed the **Egyptian** yesterday?'
     21:38 "Aren't you the **Egyptian** who started a revolt and led four
Heb 11:29 but when the **Egyptians** tried to do so, they were drowned.

131 Αἴγυπτος, Aigyptos [25] [→ 130]

Egypt [20], Egypt [+1178] [5]

Mt   2:13 he said, "take the child and his mother and escape to **Egypt**.
      2:14 took the child and his mother during the night and left for **Egypt**,
      2:15 Lord had said through the prophet: "Out of **Egypt** I called my son."
      2:19 an angel of the Lord appeared in a dream to Joseph in **Egypt**
Ac   2:10 and Pamphylia, **Egypt** and the parts of Libya near Cyrene;
      7: 9 were jealous of Joseph, they sold him as a slave into **Egypt**.
      7:10 and enabled him to gain the goodwill of Pharaoh king *of* **Egypt**;
      7:10 king of Egypt; so he made him ruler over **Egypt** and all his palace.
      7:11 "Then a famine struck all **Egypt** and Canaan, bringing great
      7:12 When Jacob heard that there was grain in **Egypt**, he sent our
      7:15 Then Jacob went down to **Egypt**, where he and our fathers died.
      7:17 to Abraham, the number of our people in **Egypt** greatly increased.
      7:18 who knew nothing about Joseph, became ruler of **Egypt**.
      7:34 I have indeed seen the oppression of my people in **Egypt**.
      7:34 down to set them free. Now come, I will send you back to **Egypt**.'
      7:36 of Egypt and did wonders and miraculous signs in **Egypt** [+1178]
      7:39 they rejected him and in their hearts turned back to **Egypt**.
      7:40 As for this fellow Moses who led us out of **Egypt** [+1178]—
     13:17 he made the people prosper during their stay in **Egypt** [+1178],
Heb   3:16 and rebelled? Were they not all those Moses led out of **Egypt**?
      8: 9 when I took them by the hand to lead them out of **Egypt** [+1178],
     11:26 the sake of Christ as of greater value than the treasures *of* **Egypt**,
     11:27 By faith he left **Egypt**, not fearing the king's anger; he persevered
Jude 1: 5 you that the Lord delivered his people out of **Egypt** [+1178],
Rev 11: 8 which is figuratively called Sodom and **Egypt**, where also their

132 ἀΐδιος, aidios [2] [√ 107]

eternal [1], everlasting [1]

Ro   1:20 his **eternal** power and divine nature—have been clearly seen,
Jude 1: 6 *bound with* **everlasting** chains for judgment on the great Day.

133 αἰδώς, aidōs [1] [→ 357]

decency [1]

1Ti   2: 9 with **decency** and propriety, not with braided hair or gold

134 Αἰθίοψ, Aithiops [2]

Ethiopian [+467] [1], Ethiopians [1]

Ac   8:27 he started out, and on his way he met an **Ethiopian** [+467] eunuch,
      8:27 in charge of all the treasury of Candace, queen *of* the **Ethiopians**.

135 αἷμα, haima [97] [→ 136, 137]

αἷμα [τοῦ] Χριστοῦ (blood [of] Christ) [5] 1Co 10:16; Eph
  2:13; Heb 9:14; 1Pe 1:2,19; cf. Rev 1:5

σάρξ καὶ αἷμα (flesh and blood) [5] Mt 16:17; 1Co 15:50; Gal
  1:16; Eph 6:12; Heb 2:14

blood [86], man [+2779+4922] [2], shedding blood [2], subject to
  bleeding [+1877+4868] [2], bleeding [+3836+4380] [1], bleeding
  [+3836+4868] [1], blood money [+5507] [1], blood red [+6055]
  [1], natural descent [1]

Mt   16:17 of Jonah, for this was not revealed to you *by* **man** [+2779+4922],
     23:30 we would not have taken part with them in **shedding** the **blood** of
     23:35 so upon you will come all the righteous **blood** that has been shed
     23:35 from the **blood** of righteous Abel to the blood of Zechariah son of

23:35   from the blood of righteous Abel to the **blood** of Zechariah son of
26:28   This is my **blood** of the covenant, which is poured out for many for
27: 4   "I have sinned," he said, "for I have betrayed innocent **blood**."
27: 6   law to put this into the treasury, since it is **blood** [+5507] **money**."
27: 8   That is why it has been called the Field *of* **Blood** to this day.
27:24   "I am innocent of this man's **blood**," he said. "It is your
27:25   the people answered, "Let his **blood** be on us and on our children!"
Mk   5:25   who had been **subject to bleeding** [+1877+4868] for twelve years.
    5:29   Immediately her **bleeding** [+3836+4380] stopped and she felt in
  14:24   "This is my **blood** of the covenant, which is poured out for many,"
Lk   8:43   who had been **subject to bleeding** [+1877+4868] for twelve years,
    8:44   of his cloak, and immediately her **bleeding** [+3836+4868] stopped.
  11:50   Therefore this generation will be held responsible for the **blood** of
  11:51   from the **blood** of Abel to the blood of Zechariah, who was killed
  11:51   from the blood of Abel to the **blood** of Zechariah, who was killed
  13: 1   the Galileans whose **blood** Pilate had mixed with their sacrifices.
  22:20   saying, "This cup is the new covenant in my **blood**, which is poured
  22:44   and his sweat was like drops of **blood** falling to the ground.
Jn   1:13   children born not of **natural descent**, nor of human decision
  6:53   unless you eat the flesh of the Son of Man and drink his **blood**,
  6:54   Whoever eats my flesh and drinks my **blood** has eternal life,
  6:55   For my flesh is real food and my **blood** is real drink.
  6:56   Whoever eats my flesh and drinks my **blood** remains in me,
  19:34   Jesus' side with a spear, bringing a sudden *flow of* **blood** and water.
Ac   1:19   that field in their language Akeldama, that is, Field *of* **Blood**.
  2:19   and signs on the earth below, **blood** and fire and billows of smoke.
  2:20   and the moon to **blood** before the coming of the great and glorious
  5:28   and are determined to make us guilty of this man's **blood**."
  15:20   from the meat of strangled animals and from **blood**.
  15:29   *from* **blood**, from the meat of strangled animals and from sexual
  18: 6   in protest and said to them, "Your **blood** be on your own heads!
  20:26   I declare to you today that I am innocent of the **blood** of all men.
  20:28   of the church of God, which he bought with his own **blood**.
  21:25   from **blood**, from the meat of strangled animals and from sexual
  22:20   And when the **blood** of your martyr Stephen was shed, I stood
Ro   3:15   "Their feet are swift *to* shed **blood**;
  3:25   him as a sacrifice of atonement, through faith in his **blood**.
  5: 9   Since we have now been justified by his **blood**, how much more
1Co 10:16   for which we give thanks a participation *in* the **blood** of Christ?
  11:25   took the cup, saying, "This cup is the new covenant in my **blood**;
  11:27   will be guilty of sinning against the body and **blood** of the Lord.
  15:50   brothers, that flesh and **blood** cannot inherit the kingdom of God,
Gal   1:16   him among the Gentiles, I did not consult any **man** [+2779+4922],
Eph   1: 7   In him we have redemption through his **blood**, the forgiveness of
  2:13   were far away have been brought near through the **blood** of Christ.
  6:12   For our struggle is not against flesh and **blood**, but against the
Col   1:20   in heaven, by making peace through his **blood**, shed on the cross.
Heb   2:14   Since the children have flesh and **blood**, he too shared in their
  9: 7   and that only once a year, and never without **blood**, which he
  9:12   He did not enter by means of the **blood** of goats and calves;
  9:12   but he entered the Most Holy Place once for all by his own **blood**,
  9:13   The **blood** of goats and bulls and the ashes of a heifer sprinkled on
  9:14   How much more, then, will the **blood** of Christ, who through the
  9:18   why even the first covenant was not put into effect without **blood**.
  9:19   he took the **blood** of calves, together with water, scarlet wool
  9:20   He said, "This is the **blood** of the covenant, which God has
  9:21   he sprinkled *with* the **blood** both the tabernacle and everything
  9:22   the law requires that nearly everything be cleansed with **blood**,
  9:25   the Most Holy Place every year with **blood** that is not his own.
  10: 4   because it is impossible for the **blood** of bulls and goats to take
  10:19   confidence to enter the Most Holy Place by the **blood** of Jesus,
  10:29   who has treated as an unholy thing the **blood** of the covenant that
  11:28   By faith he kept the Passover and the sprinkling *of* **blood**,
  12: 4   you have not yet resisted to the point of **shedding** your **blood**.
  12:24   and *to* the sprinkled **blood** that speaks a better word than the blood
  13:11   The high priest carries the **blood** of animals into the Most Holy
  13:12   the city gate to make the people holy through his own **blood**.
  13:20   who through the **blood** of the eternal covenant brought back from
1Pe   1: 2   for obedience to Jesus Christ and sprinkling *by* his **blood**:
  1:19   but *with* the precious **blood** of Christ, a lamb without blemish
1Jn   5: 6   This is the one who came by water and **blood**—Jesus Christ.
  5: 6   He did not come by water only, but by water and **blood**.
  5: 8   the Spirit, the water and the **blood**; and the three are in agreement.
Rev   1: 5   To him who loves us and has freed us from our sins by his **blood**,
  5: 9   and with your **blood** you purchased men for God from every tribe

6:10   until you judge the inhabitants of the earth and avenge our **blood**?"
6:12   made of goat hair, the whole moon turned **blood** [+6055] **red**,
7:14   washed their robes and made them white in the **blood** of the Lamb.
8: 7   his trumpet, and there came hail and fire mixed with **blood**,
8: 8   was thrown into the sea. A third of the sea turned into **blood**,
11: 6   and they have power to turn the waters into **blood** and to strike the
12:11   They overcame him by the **blood** of the Lamb and by the word of
14:20   the winepress outside the city, and **blood** flowed out of the press,
16: 3   and it turned into **blood** like that of a dead man, and every living
16: 4   bowl on the rivers and springs of water, and they became **blood**.
16: 6   for they have shed the **blood** of your saints and prophets, and you
16: 6   and you have given them **blood** to drink as they deserve."
17: 6   I saw that the woman was drunk with the **blood** of the saints,
17: 6   blood of the saints, the **blood** of those who bore testimony to Jesus.
18:24   In her was found the **blood** of prophets and of the saints, and of all
19: 2   by her adulteries. He has avenged on her the **blood** of his servants."
19:13   He is dressed in a robe dipped *in* **blood**, and his name is the Word

136 αἱματεκχυσία, *haimatekchysia* [1]
[√ *135 + 1772*]

shedding of blood [1]

Heb   9:22   and without the **shedding of blood** there is no forgiveness.

137 αἱμορροέω, *haimorroeō* [1] [√ *135 + 4835*]
subject to bleeding [1]

Mt   9:20   then a woman *who had been* **subject to bleeding** for twelve years

138 Αἰνέας, *Aineas* [2] [√ *142*]
Aeneas [2]

Ac   9:33   There he found a man named **Aeneas**, a paralytic who had been
  9:34   "**Aeneas**," Peter said to him, "Jesus Christ heals you. Get up

139 αἴνεσις, *ainesis* [1] [√ *142*]
praise [1]

Heb 13:15   therefore, let us continually offer to God a sacrifice *of* **praise**—

140 αἰνέω, *aineō* [8] [√ *142*]
praising [5], praise [3]

Lk   2:13   heavenly host appeared with the angel, **praising** God and saying,
  2:20   and **praising** God for all the things they had heard and seen,
  19:37   the whole crowd of disciples began joyfully *to* **praise** God in loud
Ac   2:47   **praising** God and enjoying the favor of all the people.
  3: 8   into the temple courts, walking and jumping, and **praising** God.
  3: 9   When all the people saw him walking and **praising** God,
Ro 15:11   And again, "**Praise** the Lord, all *you* Gentiles, and sing praises to
Rev 19: 5   "**Praise** our God, all *you* his servants, you who fear him,

141 αἴνιγμα, *ainigma* [1]
poor reflection [1]

1Co 13:12   Now we see but a **poor reflection** as in a mirror;

142 αἶνος, *ainos* [2] [→ *138, 139, 140, 2045, 2046, 2047, 4147*]
praise [1], praised [+*1443*] [1]

Mt 21:16   'From the lips of children and infants you have ordained **praise**'?"
Lk 18:43   When all the people saw it, *they* also **praised** [+*1443*] God.

143 Αἰνών, *Ainōn* [1]
Aenon [1]

Jn   3:23   Now John also was baptizing at **Aenon** near Salim, because there

144 αἴξ, *aix*   Not used in UBS/NIV [→ *128*]

145 αἱρέομαι, **haireomai** [3] [→ 146, 147, 148, 358, 359, 882, 904, 1348, 1349, 1975, 2746, 2747, 4311, 4576]

chose [2], choose [1]

Php 1:22 fruitful labor for me. Yet what *shall I* **choose**? I do not know!
2Th 2:13 because from the beginning God **chose** you to be saved through the
Heb 11:25 *He* **chose** to be mistreated along with the people of God rather than

146 αἵρεσις, **hairesis** [9] [√ 145]

sect [4], party [2], differences [1], factions [1], heresies [1]

Ac   5:17 his associates, who were *members of* the **party** of the Sadducees,
    15: 5 Then some of the believers who belonged to the **party** of the
    24: 5 the Jews all over the world. He is a ringleader *of* the Nazarene **sect**
    24:14 God of our fathers as a follower of the Way, which they call a **sect**.
    26: 5 they are willing, that according to the strictest **sect** of our religion,
    28:22 for we know that people everywhere are talking against this **sect**.”
1Co 11:19 No doubt there have to be **differences** among you to show which
Gal 5:20 jealousy, fits of rage, selfish ambition, dissensions, **factions**
2Pe 2: 1 They will secretly introduce destructive **heresies**, even denying the

147 αἱρετίζω, **hairetizō** [1] [√ 145]

chosen [1]

Mt 12:18 “Here is my servant whom *I have* **chosen**, the one I love, in whom I

148 αἱρετικός, **hairetikos** [1] [√ 145]

divisive [1]

Tit 3:10 Warn a **divisive** person once, and then warn him a second time.

149 αἴρω, **airō** [101] [→ 554, 1976, 2048, 3558, 5256, 5512, 5513, 5643]

take [15], picked up [9], take away [7], pick up [6], taken [6], took [6], get [5], takes away [4], takes away [4], carry [3], take up [3], takes [3], took away [3], away with [2], go [2], lift up [2], pull away [2], raised [2], *untranslated* [1], get out [1], get rid of [1], rid of [+608] [1], called out in a loud voice [+5889] [1], carried [1], cuts off [1], deprived [1], hoisted aboard [1], keep in suspense [+3836+6034] [1], looked [+3836+4057] [1], put [1], removed [1], take out [1], taken down [1], taking out [1], weighed anchor [1]

Mt   4: 6 his angels concerning you, and *they will* **lift** you **up** in their hands,
     9: 6 Then he said to the paralytic, “Get up, **take** your mat and go home.”
     9:16 for the patch *will* **pull away** from the garment, making the tear
    11:29 **Take** my yoke upon you and learn from me, for I am gentle
    13:12 Whoever does not have, even what he has *will be* **taken** from him.
    14:12 John’s disciples came and **took** his body and buried it. Then they
    14:20 and the disciples **picked up** twelve basketfuls of broken pieces that
    15:37 Afterward the disciples **picked up** seven basketfuls of broken
    16:24 he must deny himself and **take up** his cross and follow me.
    17:27 **Take** the first fish you catch; open its mouth and you will find a
    20:14 **Take** your pay and go. I want to give the man who was hired last
    21:21 ‘Go, throw yourself into the sea,’ and it will be done.
    21:43 “Therefore I tell you that the kingdom of God *will be* **taken away**
    24:17 Let no one on the roof of his house go down *to* **take** anything out
    24:18 Let no one in the field go back *to* **get** his cloak.
    24:39 what would happen until the flood came and **took** them all **away**.
    25:28 “ ‘**Take** the talent from him and give it to the one who has the ten
    25:29 Whoever does not have, even what he has *will be* **taken** from him.
    27:32 named Simon, and they forced him to **carry** the cross.
Mk   2: 3 men came, bringing to him a paralytic, **carried** by four of them.
     2: 9 sins are forgiven,’ or to say, ‘Get up, **take** your mat and walk’?
     2:11 “I tell you, get up, **take** your mat and go home.”
     2:12 He got up, **took** his mat and walked out in full view of them all.
     2:21 If he does, the new piece *will* **pull away** from the old, making the
     4:15 Satan comes and **takes away** the word that was sown in them.
     4:25 whoever does not have, even what he has *will be* **taken** from him.”
     6: 8 “**Take** nothing for the journey except a staff—no bread, no bag,
     6:29 John’s disciples came and **took** his body and laid it in a tomb.
     6:43 and the disciples **picked up** twelve basketfuls of broken pieces of
     8: 8 Afterward the disciples **picked up** seven basketfuls of broken
     8:19 five thousand, how many basketfuls of pieces *did you* **pick up**?”

     8:20 four thousand, how many basketfuls of pieces *did you* **pick up**?”
     8:34 he must deny himself and **take up** his cross and follow me.
    11:23 ‘Go, throw yourself into the sea,’ and does not doubt in his heart
    13:15 roof of his house go down or enter the house *to* **take** anything out.
    13:16 Let no one in the field go back *to* **get** his cloak.
    15:21 way in from the country, and they forced him to **carry** the cross.
    15:24 Dividing up his clothes, they cast lots to see what each *would* **get**.
    16:18 *they will* **pick up** snakes with their hands;
Lk   4:11 *they will* **lift** you **up** in their hands, so that you will not strike your
     5:24 the paralyzed man, “I tell you, get up, **take** your mat and go home.”
     5:25 **took** what he had been lying on and went home praising God.
     6:29 *If* someone **takes** your cloak, do not stop him from taking your
     6:30 and if anyone **takes** what belongs to you, do not demand it back.
     8:12 then the devil comes and **takes away** the word from their hearts,
     8:18 does not have, even what he thinks he has *will be* **taken** from him.”
     9: 3 “**Take** nothing for the journey—no staff, no bag, no bread,
     9:17 and the disciples **picked up** twelve basketfuls of broken pieces that
     9:23 he must deny himself and **take up** his cross daily and follow me.
    11:22 *he* **takes away** the armor in which the man trusted and divides up
    11:52 in the law, because *you have* **taken away** the key to knowledge.
    17:13 and **called out in a loud voice** [+5889], “Jesus, Master, have pity
    17:31 of his house, with his goods inside, should go down *to* **get** them.
    19:21 *You* **take out** what you did not put in and reap what you did not
    19:22 did you, that I am a hard man, **taking out** what I did not put in,
    19:24 ‘**Take** his mina **away** from him and give it to the one who has ten
    19:26 for the one who has nothing, even what he has *will be* **taken away**.
    22:36 said to them, “But now if you have a purse, **take** it, and also a bag;
    23:18 With one voice they cried out, “**Away with** this man! Release
Jn   1:29 “Look, the Lamb of God, who **takes away** the sin of the world!
     2:16 To those who sold doves he said, “**Get** these **out** of here! How
     5: 8 Then Jesus said to him, “Get up! **Pick up** your mat and walk.”
     5: 9 At once the man was cured; *he* **picked up** his mat and walked.
     5:10 “It is the Sabbath; the law forbids you to **carry** your mat.”
     5:11 man who made me well said to me, ‘**Pick up** your mat and walk.’ ”
     5:12 “Who is this fellow who told you *to* **pick** it **up** and walk?”
     8:59 At this, *they* **picked up** stones to stone him, but Jesus hid himself,
    10:18 No one **takes** it from me, but I lay it down of my own accord.
    10:24 saying, “How long *will you* **keep** [+3836+6034] us **in suspense**?
    11:39 “**Take away** the stone,” he said. “But, Lord,” said Martha, the sister
    11:41 So *they* **took away** the stone. Then Jesus looked up and said,
    11:41 Then Jesus **looked** [+3836+4057] up and said, “Father, I thank you
    11:48 Romans will come and **take away** both our place and our nation.”
    15: 2 *He* **cuts off** every branch in me that bears no fruit, while every
    16:22 and you will rejoice, and no one *will* **take away** your joy.
    17:15 My prayer is not that *you* **take** them out of the world but that you
    19:15 But they shouted, “**Take** him **away**! Take him away! Crucify him!”
    19:15 But they shouted, “Take him away! **Take** him **away**! Crucify him!”
    19:31 asked Pilate to have the legs broken and the bodies **taken down**.
    19:38 Joseph of Arimathea asked Pilate for **[RPG]** the body of Jesus.
    19:38 With Pilate’s permission, he came and **took** the body **away**.
    20: 1 and saw that the stone *had been* **removed** from the entrance.
    20: 2 Jesus loved, and said, “They have **taken** the Lord out of the tomb,
    20:13 “*They have* **taken** my Lord **away**,” she said, “and I don’t know
    20:15 him away, tell me where you have put him, and I *will* **get** him.”
Ac   4:24 they heard this, *they* **raised** their voices together *in prayer* to God.
     8:33 In his humiliation he *was* **deprived** of justice. Who can speak of
     8:33 speak of his descendants? For his life *was* **taken** from the earth.”
    20: 9 he fell to the ground from the third story and *was* **picked up** dead.
    21:11 *he* **took** Paul’s belt, tied his own hands and feet with it and said,
    21:36 The crowd that followed kept shouting, “**Away with** him!”
    22:22 they raised their voices and shouted, “**Rid** [+608] the earth of him!
    27:13 so they **weighed anchor** and sailed along the shore of Crete.
    27:17 *When* the men had **hoisted** it **aboard**, they passed ropes under the
1Co 5: 2 *put* out of your fellowship the man who did this?
     6:15 Shall I then **take** the members of Christ and unite them with a
Eph 4:31 **Get rid of** all bitterness, rage and anger, brawling and slander,
Col 2:14 that stood opposed to us; *he* **took** it away, nailing it to the cross.
1Jn 3: 5 you know that he appeared so that *he might* **take away** our sins.
Rev 10: 5 standing on the sea and on the land **raised** his right hand to heaven.
    18:21 Then a mighty angel **picked up** a boulder the size of a large

150 αἰσθάνομαι, **aisthanomai** [1] [→ 151, 152; cf. 113]

grasp [1]

Lk   9:45 It was hidden from them, so that *they did* not **grasp** it, and they

151 αἴσθησις, *aisthēsis* [1] [√ *150*]

insight [1]

Php 1: 9 may abound more and more in knowledge and depth of **insight**,

152 αἰσθητήριον, *aisthētērion* [1] [√ *150*]

themselves [1]

Heb 5: 14 who by constant use have trained **themselves** to distinguish good

153 αἰσχροκερδής, *aischrokerdēs* [2] [√ *156 + 3046*]

pursuing dishonest gain [2]

1Ti 3: 8 not indulging in much wine, and not **pursuing dishonest gain**.
Tit 1: 7 given to drunkenness, not violent, not **pursuing dishonest gain**.

154 αἰσχροκερδῶς, *aischrokerdōs* [1] [√ *156 + 3046*]

greedy for money [1]

1Pe 5: 2 as God wants you to be; not **greedy for money**, but eager to serve;

155 αἰσχρολογία, *aischrologia* [1] [√ *156 + 3306*]

filthy language [1]

Col 3: 8 rage, malice, slander, and **filthy language** from your lips.

156 αἰσχρός, *aischros* [4] [→ *153, 154, 155, 157, 158, 159, 454, 2049, 2875*]

disgrace [1], disgraceful [1], dishonest [1], shameful [1]

1Co 11: 6 and if it is a **disgrace** for a woman to have her hair cut or shaved
    14: 35 at home; for it is **disgraceful** for a woman to speak in the church.
Eph 5: 12 For it is **shameful** even to mention what the disobedient do in
Tit 1: 11 they ought not to teach—and that for the sake of **dishonest** gain.

157 αἰσχρότης, *aischrotēs* [1] [√ *156*]

obscenity [1]

Eph 5: 4 Nor should there be **obscenity**, foolish talk or coarse joking,

158 αἰσχύνη, *aischynē* [6] [√ *156*]

shame [3], shameful [2], humiliated [+*3552*] [1]

Lk 14: 9 Then, **humiliated** [+*3552*], you will have to take the least
2Co 4: 2 Rather, we have renounced secret and **shameful** ways; we do not
Php 3: 19 their god is their stomach, and their glory is in their **shame**.
Heb 12: 2 for the joy set before him endured the cross, scorning its **shame**,
Jude 1: 13 They are wild waves of the sea, foaming up their **shame**;
Rev 3: 18 white clothes to wear, so you can cover your **shameful** nakedness;

159 αἰσχύνομαι, *aischynomai* [5] [√ *156*]

ashamed [4], unashamed [+*3590*] [1]

Lk 16: 3 my job. I'm not strong enough to dig, and *I'm* **ashamed** to beg—
2Co 10: 8 you up rather than pulling you down, *I* will not *be* **ashamed** of it.
Php 1: 20 I eagerly expect and hope that *I will* in no way *be* **ashamed**,
1Pe 4: 16 However, if you suffer as a Christian, *do* not *be* **ashamed**,
1Jn 2: 28 be confident and **unashamed** [+*3590*] before him at his coming.

160 αἰτέω, *aiteō* [70] [→ *161, 555, 1977, 2050, 4148, 4644, 4645*]

ask [23], asked for [9], ask for [8], asked [7], asks [6], asks for [4], asking [3], asked [+*161*] [1], asked [+*806*] [1], asked favor [1], beg [+*1797*] [1], called for [1], demand [1], demanded [1], pray [1], request [1], urgently requested [+*4151*] [1]

Mt 5: 42 Give *to* the one *who* **asks** you, and do not turn away from the one
    6: 8 for your Father knows what you need before you **ask** him.
    7: 7 "**Ask** and it will be given to you; seek and you will find; knock
    7: 8 For everyone who **asks** receives; he who seeks finds; and to him
    7: 9 "Which of you, if his son **asks for** bread, will give him a stone?
    7: 10 Or if *he* **asks for** a fish, will give him a snake?
    7: 11 will your Father in heaven give good gifts *to* those *who* **ask** him!
    14: 7 that he promised with an oath to give her whatever *she* **asked**.
    18: 19 you that if two of you on earth agree about anything *you* **ask for**,
    20: 20 to Jesus with her sons and, kneeling down, **asked a favor** of him.
    20: 22 "You don't know what *you are* **asking**," Jesus said to them.
    21: 22 If you believe, you will receive whatever *you* **ask for** in prayer."
    27: 20 and the elders persuaded the crowd to **ask for** Barabbas
    27: 58 Going to Pilate, he **asked for** Jesus' body, and Pilate ordered that it
Mk 6: 22 to the girl, "**Ask** me **for** anything you want, and I'll give it to you."
    6: 23 "Whatever *you* **ask** I will give you, up to half my kingdom."
    6: 24 She went out and said to her mother, "What *shall I* **ask for**?"
    6: 25 At once the girl hurried in to the king with the **request**: "I want you
    10: 35 "Teacher," they said, "we want you to do for us whatever *we* **ask**."
    10: 38 "You don't know what *you are* **asking**," Jesus said. "Can you drink
    11: 24 Therefore I tell you, whatever *you* **ask for** in prayer, believe that
    15: 8 and **asked** [+*806*] Pilate to do for them what he usually did.
    15: 43 kingdom of God, went boldly to Pilate and **asked for** Jesus' body.
Lk 1: 63 *He* **asked for** a writing tablet, and to everyone's astonishment he
    6: 30 Give to everyone *who* **asks** you, and if anyone takes what belongs
    11: 9 **Ask** and it will be given to you; seek and you will find; knock
    11: 10 For everyone who **asks** receives; he who seeks finds; and to him
    11: 11 "Which of you fathers, *if* your son **asks** for a fish, will give him a
    11: 12 Or if *he* **asks for** an egg, will give him a scorpion?
    11: 13 your Father in heaven give the Holy Spirit to those *who* **ask** him!"
    12: 48 one who has been entrusted with much, much more *will be* **asked**.
    23: 23 But with loud shouts they insistently **demanded** that he be
    23: 25 into prison for insurrection and murder, the one *they* **asked for**,
    23: 52 Going to Pilate, he **asked for** Jesus' body.
Jn 4: 9 and I am a Samaritan woman. How *can you* **ask** me **for** a drink?"
    4: 10 you would have **asked** him and he would have given you living
    11: 22 But I know that even now God will give you whatever *you* **ask**."
    14: 13 And I will do whatever *you* **ask** in my name, so that the Son may
    14: 14 *You may* **ask** me **for** anything in my name, and I will do it.
    15: 7 remain in you, **ask** whatever you wish, and it will be given you.
    15: 16 Then the Father will give you whatever *you* **ask** in my name.
    16: 23 the truth, my Father will give you whatever *you* **ask** in my name.
    16: 24 Until now *you have* not **asked for** anything in my name. Ask
    16: 24 my name. **Ask** and you will receive, and your joy will be complete.
    16: 26 In that day *you will* **ask** in my name. I am not saying that I will ask
Ac 3: 2 where he was put every day *to* **beg** [+*1797*] from those going into
    3: 14 and Righteous One and **asked** that a murderer be released to you.
    7: 46 and **asked** that he might provide a dwelling place for the God of
    9: 2 and **asked** him **for** letters to the synagogues in Damascus,
    12: 20 a trusted personal servant of the king, *they* **asked for** peace,
    13: 21 Then the *people* **asked for** a king, and he gave them Saul son of
    13: 28 for a death sentence, *they* **asked** Pilate to have him executed.
    16: 29 The jailer **called for** lights, rushed in and fell trembling before
    25: 3 *They* **urgently requested** [+*4151*] Festus, as a favor to them,
    25: 15 brought charges against him and **asked** that he be condemned.
1Co 1: 22 Jews **demand** miraculous signs and Greeks look for wisdom,
Eph 3: 13 *I* **ask** you, therefore, not to be discouraged because of my
    3: 20 Now to him who is able to do immeasurably more than all *we* **ask**
Col 1: 9 and **asking** God to fill you with the knowledge of his will through
Jas 1: 5 If any of you lacks wisdom, *he should* **ask** God, who gives
    1: 6 But when *he* **asks**, he must believe and not doubt, because he who
    4: 2 and fight. You do not have, because you *do* not **ask** God.
    4: 3 *When you* **ask**, you do not receive, because you ask with wrong
    4: 3 you do not receive, because *you* **ask** with wrong motives,
1Pe 3: 15 Always be prepared to give an answer to everyone who **asks** you
1Jn 3: 22 and receive from him anything *we* **ask**, because we obey his
    5: 14 that if *we* **ask** anything according to his will, he hears us.
    5: 15 And if we know that he hears us—whatever *we* **ask**—we know that
    5: 15 we **ask**—we know that we have what *we* **asked** [+*161*] of him.
    5: 16 does not lead to death, *he should* **pray** and God will give him life.

161 αἴτημα, *aitēma* [3] [√ *160*]

asked [+*160*] [1], demand [1], requests [1]

Lk 23: 24 So Pilate decided to grant their **demand**.
Php 4: 6 and petition, with thanksgiving, present your **requests** to God.
1Jn 5: 15 we ask—we know that we have what *we* **asked** [+*160*] of him.

162 αἰτία, aitia [20] [→ 163, 164, 165, 166, 360, 4577]

basis for a charge [3], reason [3], charge against [2], why [+1328+4005] [2], charge [+5770] [1], charges [1], guilty of crime [1], proper ground [1], situation [1], so [+1328+4005] [1], that is why [+1328+4005] [1], therefore [+1328+4005] [1], why [+3836+5515] [1], why [+1328+3836+4005] [1]

Mt 19: 3 lawful for a man to divorce his wife for any and every **reason**?"
     19:10 "If this is the **situation** between a husband and wife, it is better not
     27:37 Above his head they placed the written **charge against** him:
Mk 15:26 The written notice *of* the **charge against** him read: THE KING OF
Lk   8:47 she told **why** [+1328+4005] she had touched him and how she had
Jn 18:38 to the Jews and said, "I find no **basis for a charge** against him.
     19: 4 you to let you know that I find no **basis for a charge** against him."
     19: 6 crucify him. As for me, I find no **basis for a charge** against him."
Ac 10:21 the one you're looking for. **Why** [+3836+5515] have you come?"
     13:28 Though they found no **proper ground** for a death sentence,
     22:24 and questioned in order to find out **why** [+1328+4005] the people
     23:28 I wanted to know **why** [+1328+3836+4005] they were accusing
     25:18 *they did* not **charge** [+5770] him *with* any of the crimes I had
     25:27 to send on a prisoner without specifying the **charges** against him."
     28:18 because I was not **guilty of** any *crime* deserving death.
     28:20 For this **reason** I have asked to see you and talk with you.
2Ti   1: 6 For this **reason** I remind you to fan into flame the gift of God,
     1:12 **That is why** [+1328+4005] I am suffering as I am. Yet I am not
Tit   1:13 **Therefore** [+1328+4005], rebuke them sharply, so that they will
Heb 2:11 **So** [+1328+4005] Jesus is not ashamed to call them brothers.

163 αἰτίαμα, aitiama Not used in UBS/NIV [√ 162]

164 αἰτιάομαι, aitiaomai Not used in UBS/NIV [√ 162]

165 αἴτιος, aitios [5] [√ 162]

basis [1], basis for a charge [1], grounds for the death penalty [+2505] [1], reason [1], source [1]

Lk 23: 4 and the crowd, "I find no **basis for a charge** against this man."
     23:14 and have found no **basis** for your charges against him.
     23:22 I have found in him no **grounds** [+2505] **for the death penalty**.
Ac 19:40 able to account for this commotion, since there is no **reason** for it."
Heb 5: 9 he became the **source** of eternal salvation for all who obey him

166 αἰτίωμα, aitiōma [1] [√ 162]

charges [1]

Ac 25: 7 bringing many serious **charges** against him, which they could not

167 αἰφνίδιος, aiphnidios [2] [→ 924?, 1978, 1988, 2005]

suddenly [1], unexpectedly [1]

Lk 21:34 of life, and that day will close on you **unexpectedly** like a trap.
1Th 5: 3 "Peace and safety," destruction will come on them **suddenly**,

168 αἰχμαλωσία, aichmalōsia [3] [√ 171]

captivity [2], led captives in his train [+169] [1]

Eph 4: 8 he **led captives in his train** [+169] and gave gifts to men."
Rev 13:10 If anyone is to go into **captivity**, into captivity he will go.
     13:10 If anyone is to go into captivity, into **captivity** he will go.

169 αἰχμαλωτεύω, aichmalōteuō [1] [√ 171]

led captives in his train [+168] [1]

Eph 4: 8 *he* **led captives** [+168] **in his train** and gave gifts to men."

170 αἰχμαλωτίζω, aichmalōtizō [4] [√ 171]

gain control over [1], making a prisoner [1], take captive [1], taken as prisoners [1]

Lk 21:24 fall by the sword and *will be* **taken as prisoners** to all the nations.
Ro   7:23 and **making** me **a prisoner** of the law of sin at work within my
2Co 10: 5 and *we* **take captive** every thought to make it obedient to Christ.
2Ti   3: 6 their way into homes and **gain control over** weak-willed women,

171 αἰχμάλωτος, aichmalōtos [1] [→ 168, 169, 170, 5257; cf. 274]

prisoners [1]

Lk   4:18 He has sent me to proclaim freedom *for* the **prisoners**

172 αἰών, aiōn [122 / 123] [→ 173]

εἰς τὸν αἰῶνα (into the age [forever]) [27] Mt 21:19; Mk 3:29; 11:14; Lk 1:55; Jn 4:14; 6:51,58; 8:35,51,52; 10:28; 11:26; 12:34; 13:8; 14:16; 1Co 8:13; 2Co 9:9; Heb 1:8; 5:6; 6:20; 7:17,21,24,28; 1Pe 1:25; 1Jn 2:17; 2Jn 1:2

εἰς τοὺς αἰῶνας (into the age [forever]) [7] Lk 1:33; Ro 1:25; 9:5; 11:36; 16:27; 2Co 11:31; Heb 13:8

εἰς τοὺς αἰῶνας τῶν αἰώνων (into the age of ages [forever]) [20] Gal 1:5; Php 4:20; 1Ti 1:17; 2Ti 4:18; Heb 1:8; 13:21; 1Pe 4:11; 5:11; Rev 1:6,18; 4:9,10; 5:13; 7:12; 10:6; 11:15; 15:7; 19:3; 20:10; 22:5

ὁ οὗτος αἰών (this age) [11] Mt 12:32; Lk 16:8; 20:34; Ro 12:2; 1Co 1:20; 2:6,6,8; 3:18; 2Co 4:4; Eph 1:21

ever [44], forever [+1650+3836] [23], age [20], ages [6], never [+1650+3590+3836+4024] [5], world [4], eternal [2], life [1], never [+1650+3836+4024] [1], universe [2], *untranslated* [1], again [+1650+3836] [1], ages past [1], ever [+1650+3836] [1], ever [+1666+3836] [1], forever [+1650+2465] [1], forever [+1650] [1], forevermore [+1650+3836+4246] [1], long ago [+608] [1], long ago [1], never again [+1650+3590+3836+4024] [1], time [1], ways [1]

Mt 12:32 Spirit will not be forgiven, either in this **age** or in the age to come.
     13:22 but the worries *of* this **life** and the deceitfulness of wealth choke it,
     13:39 The harvest is the end *of* the **age**, and the harvesters are angels.
     13:40 pulled up and burned in the fire, so it will be at the end *of* the **age**.
     13:49 This is how it will be at the end *of* the **age**. The angels will come
     21:19 he said to it, "May you never bear fruit **again** [+1650+3836]!"
     24: 3 what will be the sign of your coming and of the end *of* the **age**?"
     28:20 And surely I am with you always, to the very end of the **age**."
Mk   3:29 But whoever blasphemes against the Holy Spirit will **never** [+1650+3836+4024] be forgiven; he is guilty of an eternal sin."
     4:19 but the worries *of* this **life**, [UBS; NIV 1050] the deceitfulness of
     10:30 and with them, persecutions) and in the **age** to come, eternal life.
     11:14 tree, "May no one **ever** [+1650+3836] eat fruit from you again."
Lk   1:33 and he will reign over the house of Jacob **forever** [+1650+3836];
     1:55 to Abraham and his descendants **forever** [+1650+3836], even as he
     1:70 (as he said through his holy prophets of **long ago**),
     16: 8 For the people *of* this **world** are more shrewd in dealing with their
     18:30 times as much in this age and, in the **age** to come, eternal life."
     20:34 "The people *of* this **age** marry and are given in marriage.
     20:35 But those who are considered worthy of taking part *in* that **age**
Jn   4:14 but whoever drinks the water I give him will **never** [+1650+3590+3836+4024] thirst. Indeed, the water I give him
     6:51 If anyone eats of this bread, he will live **forever** [+1650+3836].
     6:58 but he who feeds on this bread will live **forever** [+1650+3836]."
     8:35 place in the family, **[RPG]** but a son belongs to it forever.
     8:35 place in the family, but a son belongs to it **forever** [+1650+3836].
     8:51 I tell you the truth, if anyone keeps my word, he will **never** [+1650+3590+3836+4024] see death."
     8:52 and so did the prophets, yet you say that if anyone keeps your word, he will **never** [+1650+3590+3836+4024] taste death.
     9:32 Nobody has **ever** [+1666+3836] heard of opening the eyes of a
     10:28 I give them eternal life, and they shall **never** [+1650+3590+3836+4024] perish; no one can snatch them out of
     11:26 and believes in me will **never** [+1650+3590+3836+4024] die.
     12:34 from the Law that the Christ will remain **forever** [+1650+3836],

13: 8 "No," said Peter, "you shall **never** [+*1650+3836+4024*] wash my feet." Jesus answered, "Unless I wash you, you have no part with

14:16 you another Counselor to be with you **forever** [+*1650+3836*]—

Ac 3:21 as he promised **long ago** [+*608*] through his holy prophets.

15:18 that have been known for **ages**.

Ro 1:25 rather than the Creator—who is **forever** [+*1650+3836*] praised.

9: 5 of Christ, who is God over all, **forever** [+*1650+3836*] praised!

11:36 are all things. To him be the glory **forever** [+*1650+3836*]! Amen.

12: 2 Do not conform any longer to the pattern of this **world**, but be

16:27 to the only wise God be glory **forever** [+*1650+3836*] through Jesus

1Co 1:20 Where is the scholar? Where is the philosopher *of* this **age**?

2: 6 but not the wisdom *of* this **age** or of the rulers of this age,

2: 6 but not the wisdom *of* this age or of the rulers of this **age**,

2: 7 and that God destined for our glory before **time** began.

2: 8 None of the rulers *of* this **age** understood it, for if they had,

3:18 If any one of you thinks he is wise by the standards of this **age**,

8:13 Therefore, if what I eat causes my brother to fall into sin, I will **never** [+*1650+3590+3836+4024*] eat meat **again**,

10:11 as warnings for us, on whom the fulfillment *of* the **ages** has come.

2Co 4: 4 The god *of* this **age** has blinded the minds of unbelievers,

9: 9 his righteousness endures **forever** [+*1650+3836*]."

11:31 who is to be praised **forever** [+*1650+3836*], knows that I am not

Gal 1: 4 gave himself for our sins to rescue us from the present evil **age**,

1: 5 to whom be glory for **ever** and ever. Amen.

1: 5 to whom be glory for ever and **ever**. Amen.

Eph 1:21 be given, not only in the present **age** but also in the one to come.

2: 2 in which you used to live when you followed the **ways** of this

2: 7 in order that in the coming **ages** he might show the incomparable

3: 9 which *for* **ages** past was kept hidden in God, who created all

3:11 according to his **eternal** purpose which he accomplished in Christ

3:21 and in Christ Jesus throughout all *generations, for* **ever** and ever!

3:21 and in Christ Jesus throughout all *generations, for* ever and **ever**!

Php 4:20 To our God and Father be glory for **ever** and ever. Amen.

4:20 To our God and Father be glory for ever and **ever**. Amen.

Col 1:26 the mystery that has been kept hidden for **ages** and generations,

1Ti 1:17 Now to the King **eternal**, immortal, invisible, the only God,

1:17 invisible, the only God, be honor and glory for **ever** and ever.

1:17 invisible, the only God, be honor and glory for ever and **ever**.

6:17 Command those who are rich in this present **world** not to be

2Ti 4:10 for Demas, because he loved this **world**, has deserted me and has

4:18 his heavenly kingdom. To him be glory for **ever** and ever. Amen.

4:18 his heavenly kingdom. To him be glory for ever and **ever**. Amen.

Tit 2:12 to live self-controlled, upright and godly lives in this present **age**,

Heb 1: 2 heir of all things, and through whom he made the **universe**.

1: 8 the Son he says, "Your throne, O God, will last for **ever** and ever,

1: 8 the Son he says, "Your throne, O God, will last for ever and **ever**,

5: 6 "You are a priest **forever** [+*1650+3836*], in the order of

6: 5 goodness of the word of God and the powers of the coming **age**,

6:20 He has become a high priest **forever** [+*1650+3836*], in the order of

7:17 "You are a priest **forever** [+*1650+3836*], in the order of

7:21 not change his mind: 'You are a priest **forever** [+*1650+3836*].' "

7:24 but because Jesus lives **forever** [+*1650+3836*], he has a

7:28 the Son, who has been made perfect **forever** [+*1650+3836*].

9:26 But now he has appeared once for all at the end *of* the **ages** to do

11: 3 By faith we understand that the **universe** was formed at God's

13: 8 Christ is the same yesterday and today and **forever** [+*1650+3836*].

13:21 through Jesus Christ, to whom be glory for **ever** and ever.

13:21 through Jesus Christ, to whom be glory for ever and **ever**.

1Pe 1:25 but the word of the Lord stands **forever** [+*1650+3836*]."

4:11 To him be the glory and the power for **ever** and ever. Amen.

4:11 To him be the glory and the power for ever and **ever**. Amen.

5:11 To him be the power for **ever** and ever. Amen.

5:11 To him be the power for ever and **ever**. [UBS-] Amen.

2Pe 3:18 To him be glory both now and **forever** [+*1650+2465*]! Amen.

1Jn 2:17 but the man who does the will of God lives **forever** [+*1650+3836*].

2Jn 1: 2 which lives in us and will be with us **forever** [+*1650+3836*]:

Jude 1:13 for whom blackest darkness has been reserved **forever** [+*1650*]

1:25 Jesus Christ our Lord, before all **ages**, now and forevermore!

1:25 be glory, majesty, power and authority, through Jesus Christ our Lord, before all ages, now and **forevermore** [+*1650+3836+4246*]!

Rev 1: 6 and Father—to him be glory and power for **ever** and ever!

1: 6 and Father—to him be glory and power for ever and **ever**!

1:18 Living One; I was dead, and behold I am alive for **ever** and ever!

1:18 Living One; I was dead, and behold I am alive for ever and **ever**!

4: 9 to him who sits on the throne and who lives for **ever** and ever,

4: 9 to him who sits on the throne and who lives for ever and **ever**,

4:10 sits on the throne, and worship him who lives for **ever** and ever.

4:10 sits on the throne, and worship him who lives for ever and **ever**.

5:13 Lamb be praise and honor and glory and power, for **ever** and ever!"

5:13 Lamb be praise and honor and glory and power, for ever and **ever**!"

7:12 and honor and power and strength be to our God for **ever** and ever.

7:12 and honor and power and strength be to our God for ever and **ever**.

10: 6 And he swore by him who lives for **ever** and ever, who created the

10: 6 And he swore by him who lives for ever and **ever**, who created the

11:15 of our Lord and of his Christ, and he will reign for **ever** and ever."

11:15 of our Lord and of his Christ, and he will reign for ever and **ever**."

14:11 And the smoke of their torment rises for **ever** and ever. There is no

14:11 And the smoke of their torment rises for ever and **ever**. There is no

15: 3 Just and true are your ways, King *of* the **ages**. [UBS *1620*]

15: 7 bowls filled with the wrath of God, who lives for **ever** and ever.

15: 7 bowls filled with the wrath of God, who lives for ever and **ever**.

19: 3 "Hallelujah! The smoke from her goes up for **ever** and ever."

19: 3 "Hallelujah! The smoke from her goes up for ever and **ever**."

20:10 They will be tormented day and night for **ever** and ever.

20:10 They will be tormented day and night for ever and **ever**.

22: 5 God will give them light. And they will reign for **ever** and ever.

22: 5 God will give them light. And they will reign for ever and **ever**.

173 αἰώνιος, *aiōnios* [71 / 70] [√ *172*]

αἰώνιος πῦρ (eternal fire) [3] Mt 18:8; 25:41; Jude 1:7

ζωὴ αἰώνιος (eternal life) [43] Mt 19:16,29; 25:46; Mk 10:17,30; Lk 10:25; 18:18,30; Jn 3:15,16,36; 4:14,36; 5:24,39; 6:27,40,47,54,68; 10:28; 12:25,50; 17:2,3; Ac 13:46,48; Ro 2:7; 5:21; 6:22,23; Gal 6:8; 1Ti 1:16; 6:12; Tit 1:2; 3:7; 1Jn 1:2; 2:25; 3:15; 5:11,13,20; Jude 1:21

eternal [63], beginning of time [+*5989*] [2], everlasting [2], ages past [1], for good [1], forever [1]

Mt 18: 8 than to have two hands or two feet and be thrown into **eternal** fire.

19:16 asked, "Teacher, what good thing must I do to get **eternal** life?"

19:29 will receive a hundred times as much and will inherit **eternal** life.

25:41 into the **eternal** fire prepared for the devil and his angels.

25:46 "Then they will go away to **eternal** punishment, but the righteous

25:46 go away to eternal punishment, but the righteous to **eternal** life."

Mk 3:29 Holy Spirit will never be forgiven; he is guilty *of* an **eternal** sin."

10:17 "Good teacher," he asked, "what must I do to inherit **eternal** life?"

10:30 and with them, persecutions) and in the age to come, **eternal** life.

16: S [UBS+ *imperishable proclamation of eternal salvation.*]

Lk 10:25 "Teacher," he asked, "what must I do to inherit **eternal** life?"

16: 9 that when it is gone, you will be welcomed into **eternal** dwellings.

18:18 asked him, "Good teacher, what must I do to inherit **eternal** life?"

18:30 times as much in this age and, in the age to come, **eternal** life."

Jn 3:15 that everyone who believes in him may have **eternal** life.

3:16 that whoever believes in him shall not perish but have **eternal** life.

3:36 Whoever believes in the Son has **eternal** life, but whoever rejects

4:14 will become in him a spring of water welling up to **eternal** life."

4:36 even now he harvests the crop for **eternal** life, so that the sower

5:24 hears my word and believes him who sent me has **eternal** life

5:39 because you think that by them you possess **eternal** life.

6:27 work for food that spoils, but for food that endures to **eternal** life,

6:40 who looks to the Son and believes in him shall have **eternal** life,

6:47 I tell you the truth, he who believes has **everlasting** life.

6:54 Whoever eats my flesh and drinks my blood has **eternal** life,

6:68 to whom shall we go? You have the words *of* **eternal** life.

10:28 I give them **eternal** life, and they shall never perish; no one can

12:25 the man who hates his life in this world will keep it for **eternal** life.

12:50 I know that his command leads to **eternal** life. So whatever I say is

17: 2 that he might give **eternal** life to all those you have given him.

17: 3 Now this is **eternal** life: that they may know you, the only true

Ac 13:46 you reject it and do not consider yourselves worthy *of* **eternal** life,

13:48 of the Lord; and all who were appointed for **eternal** life believed.

Ro 2: 7 good seek glory, honor and immortality, he will give **eternal** life.

5:21 so also grace might reign through righteousness to bring **eternal**

6:22 the benefit you reap leads to holiness, and the result is **eternal** life.

6:23 but the gift of God is **eternal** life in Christ Jesus our Lord.

16:25 to the revelation of the mystery hidden *for* long **ages** past,

16:26 the prophetic writings by the command *of* the **eternal** God,

2Co 4:17 and momentary troubles are achieving for us an **eternal** glory that

4:18 For what is seen is temporary, but what is unseen is **eternal**.

5: 1 from God, an **eternal** house in heaven, not built by human hands.

Gal 6: 8 who sows to please the Spirit, from the Spirit will reap **eternal** life.
2Th 1: 9 They will be punished with **everlasting** destruction and shut out
2:16 who loved us and by his grace gave us **eternal** encouragement
1Ti 1:16 for those who would believe on him and receive **eternal** life.
6:12 Take hold *of* the **eternal** life to which you were called when you
6:16 has seen or can see. To him be honor and might **forever**. Amen.
2Ti 1: 9 was given us in Christ Jesus before the **beginning of time** [+*5989*],
2:10 may obtain the salvation that is in Christ Jesus, with **eternal** glory.
Tit 1: 2 a faith and knowledge resting on the hope *of* **eternal** life,
1: 2 who does not lie, promised before the **beginning of time** [+*5989*],
3: 7 his grace, we might become heirs having the hope *of* **eternal** life.
Phm 1:15 you for a little while was that you might have him back **for good**—
Heb 5: 9 he became the source *of* **eternal** salvation for all who obey him
6: 2 on of hands, the resurrection of the dead, and **eternal** judgment.
9:12 once for all by his own blood, having obtained **eternal** redemption.
9:14 who through the **eternal** Spirit offered himself unblemished to
9:15 that those who are called may receive the promised **eternal**
13:20 who through the blood *of* the **eternal** covenant brought back from
1Pe 5:10 the God of all grace, who called you to his **eternal** glory in Christ,
2Pe 1:11 and you will receive a rich welcome into the **eternal** kingdom of
1Jn 1: 2 seen it and testify to it, and we proclaim to you the **eternal** life,
2:25 And this is what he promised us—even **eternal** life.
3:15 a murderer, and you know that no murderer has **eternal** life in him.
5:11 God has given us **eternal** life, and this life is in his Son.
5:13 of the Son of God so that you may know that you have **eternal** life.
5:20 even in his Son Jesus Christ. He is the true God and **eternal** life.
Jude 1: 7 as an example of those who suffer the punishment *of* **eternal** fire.
1:21 for the mercy of our Lord Jesus Christ to bring you to **eternal** life.
Rev 14: 6 and he had the **eternal** gospel to proclaim to those who live on the

174 ἀκαθαρσία, akatharsia [10] [√ *1.1* + *2754*]

impurity [6], impure [2], sexual impurity [1], unclean [1]

Mt 23:27 on the inside are full of dead men's bones and everything **unclean**.
Ro 1:24 **sexual impurity** for the degrading of their bodies with one
6:19 as you used to offer the parts of your body in slavery *to* **impurity**,
2Co 12:21 who have sinned earlier and have not repented of the **impurity**,
Gal 5:19 nature are obvious: sexual immorality, **impurity** and debauchery;
Eph 4:19 over to sensuality so as to indulge in every kind *of* **impurity**,
5: 3 or of any kind of **impurity**, or of greed, because these are improper
Col 3: 5 **impurity**, lust, evil desires and greed, which is idolatry.
1Th 2: 3 the appeal we make does not spring from error or **impure** *motives*,
4: 7 For God did not call us to be **impure**, but to live a holy life.

175 ἀκαθάρτης, akathartēs Not used in UBS/NIV
[√ *1.1* + *2754*]

176 ἀκάθαρτος, akathartos [32 / 31] [√ *1.1* + *2754*]

πνεῦμα ἀκάθαρτος (unclean spirit) [23] Mt 10:1; 12:43; Mk 1:23,26,27; 3:11,30; 5:2,8,13; 6:7; 7:25; 9:25; Lk 4:33,36; 6:18; 8:29; 9:42; 11:24; Ac 5:16; 8:7; Rev 16:13; 18:2

unclean person [3] Ac 10:28; 1Co 7:14; Eph 5:5

unclean food, thing [5] Ac 10:14; 11:8; 2Co 6:17; Rev 17:4; 18:2

evil [23], unclean [6], filth [1], impure [1]

Mt 10: 1 and gave them authority to drive out **evil** spirits and to heal every
12:43 "When an **evil** spirit comes out of a man, it goes through arid places
Mk 1:23 then a man in their synagogue who was possessed by an **evil** spirit
1:26 The **evil** spirit shook the man violently and came out of him with a
1:27 He even gives orders *to* **evil** spirits and they obey him."
3:11 Whenever the **evil** spirits saw him, they fell down before him
3:30 He said this because they were saying, "He has an **evil** spirit."
5: 2 a man with an **evil** spirit came from the tombs to meet him.
5: 8 For Jesus had said to him, "Come out of this man, *you* **evil** spirit!"
5:13 and the **evil** spirits came out and went into the pigs.
6: 7 them out two by two and gave them authority over **evil** spirits.
7:25 a woman whose little daughter was possessed by an **evil** spirit
9:25 that a crowd was running to the scene, he rebuked the **evil** spirit.
Lk 4:33 synagogue there was a man possessed by a demon, an **evil** spirit.
4:36 With authority and power he gives orders *to* **evil** spirits and they
6:18 healed of their diseases. Those troubled by **evil** spirits were cured,
8:29 For Jesus had commanded the **evil** spirit to come out of the man.
9:42 But Jesus rebuked the **evil** spirit, healed the boy and gave him back

11:24 "When an **evil** spirit comes out of a man, it goes through arid places
Ac 5:16 bringing their sick and those tormented by **evil** spirits, and all of
8: 7 With shrieks, **evil** spirits came out of many, and many paralytics
10:14 Peter replied. "I have never eaten anything impure or **unclean**."
10:28 has shown me that I should not call any man impure or **unclean**.
11: 8 Lord! Nothing impure or **unclean** has ever entered my mouth.'
1Co 7:14 Otherwise your children would be **unclean**, but as it is, they are
2Co 6:17 and be separate, says the Lord. Touch no **unclean** *thing*,
Eph 5: 5 No immoral, **impure** or greedy person—such a man is an idolater—
Rev 16:13 Then I saw three **evil** spirits that looked like frogs; they came out
17: 4 filled with abominable things and the **filth** of her adulteries.
18: 2 has become a home for demons and a haunt *for* every **evil** spirit,
18: 2 for every evil spirit, a haunt *for* every **unclean** and detestable bird.
18: 2 [UBS+ *a haunt for every* **unclean** *and detestable beast.*]

177 ἀκαιρέομαι, akaireomai [1] [√ *1.1* + *2789*]

had no opportunity [1]

Php 4:10 you have been concerned, but *you* **had no opportunity** *to show* it.

178 ἀκαίρως, akairōs [1] [√ *1.1* + *2789*]

out of season [1]

2Ti 4: 2 be prepared in season and **out of season**; correct, rebuke

179 ἄκακος, akakos [2] [√ *1.1* + *2805*]

blameless [1], naive [1]

Ro 16:18 smooth talk and flattery they deceive the minds *of* **naive** *people*.
Heb 7:26 one who is holy, **blameless**, pure, set apart from sinners, exalted

180 ἄκανθα, akantha [14] [√ *216*]

thorns [9], thornbushes [2], whichˢ [+*3836*] [3]

Mt 7:16 Do people pick grapes from **thornbushes**, or figs from thistles?
13: 7 Other seed fell among **thorns**, which grew up and choked the
13: 7 Other seed fell among thorns, **which**ˢ [+*3836*] grew up and choked
13:22 The one who received the seed that fell among the **thorns** is the
27:29 and then twisted together a crown of **thorns** and set it on his head.
Mk 4: 7 Other seed fell among **thorns**, which grew up and choked the
4: 7 Other seed fell among thorns, **which**ˢ [+*3836*] grew up and choked
4:18 Still others, like seed sown among **thorns**, hear the word;
Lk 6:44 People do not pick figs from **thornbushes**, or grapes from briers.
8: 7 Other seed fell among **thorns**, which grew up with it and choked
8: 7 **which**ˢ [+*3836*] grew up with it and choked the plants.
8:14 The seed that fell among **thorns** stands for those who hear,
Jn 19: 2 The soldiers twisted together a crown of **thorns** and put it on his
Heb 6: 8 But land that produces **thorns** and thistles is worthless and is in

181 ἀκάνθινος, akanthinos [2] [√ *216*]

of thorns [2]

Mk 15:17 then twisted together a crown **of thorns** and set it on him.
Jn 19: 5 When Jesus came out wearing the crown **of thorns** and the purple

182 ἄκαρπος, akarpos [7] [√ *1.1* + *2843*]

unfruitful [3], unproductive [2], fruitless [1], without fruit [1]

Mt 13:22 and the deceitfulness of wealth choke it, making it **unfruitful**.
Mk 4:19 for other things come in and choke the word, making it **unfruitful**.
1Co 14:14 if I pray in a tongue, my spirit prays, but my mind is **unfruitful**.
Eph 5:11 Have nothing to do with the **fruitless** deeds of darkness, but rather
Tit 3:14 may provide for daily necessities and not live **unproductive** lives.
2Pe 1: 8 and **unproductive** in your knowledge of our Lord Jesus Christ.
Jude 1:12 the wind; autumn trees, **without fruit** and uprooted—twice dead.

183 ἀκατάγνωστος, akatagnōstos [1]
[√ *1.1* + *2848* + *1182*]

cannot be condemned [1]

Tit 2: 8 and soundness of speech *that* **cannot be condemned**, so that those

184 ἀκατακάλυπτος, *akatakalyptos* [2]
[√ *1.1 + 2848 + 2821*]

uncovered [2]

1Co 11: 5   or prophesies *with* her head **uncovered** dishonors her head—
    11: 13   Is it proper for a woman to pray to God with her head **uncovered**?

185 ἀκατάκριτος, *akatakritos* [2] [√ *1.1 + 2848 + 3212*]

hasn't found guilty [1], without a trial [1]

Ac 16: 37   "They beat us publicly **without a trial**, even though we are Roman
    22: 25   you to flog a Roman citizen who **hasn't** even been **found guilty**?"

186 ἀκατάλυτος, *akatalytos* [1] [√ *1.1 + 2848 + 3395*]

indestructible [1]

Heb 7: 16   his ancestry but on the basis of the power *of* an **indestructible** life.

187 ἀκατάπαστος, *akatapastos* Not used in
UBS/NIV [√ *1.1 + 2848 + 4264*]

188 ἀκατάπαυστος, *akatapaustos* [1]
[√ *1.1 + 2848 + 4264*]

never stop [1]

2Pe 2: 14   With eyes full of adultery, they **never stop** sinning; they seduce

189 ἀκαταστασία, *akatastasia* [5]
[√ *1.1 + 2848 + 2705*]

disorder [3], revolutions [1], riots [1]

Lk 21: 9   When you hear *of* wars and **revolutions**, do not be frightened.
1Co 14: 33   For God is not a God *of* **disorder** but of peace. As in all the
2Co 6: 5   in beatings, imprisonments and **riots**; in hard work, sleepless
    12: 20   of anger, factions, slander, gossip, arrogance and **disorder**.
Jas 3: 16   selfish ambition, there you find **disorder** and every evil practice.

190 ἀκατάστατος, *akatastatos* [2]
[√ *1.1 + 2848 + 2705*]

restless [1], unstable [1]

Jas 1: 8   he is a double-minded man, **unstable** in all he does.
    3: 8   man can tame the tongue. It is a **restless** evil, full of deadly poison.

191 ἀκατάσχετος, *akataschetos* Not used in
UBS/NIV [√ *1.1 + 2848 + 2400*]

192 Ἀκελδαμάχ, *Hakeldamach* [1]

Akeldama [1]

Ac 1: 19   so they called that field in their language **Akeldama**, that is,

193 ἀκέραιος, *akeraios* [3] [√ *1.1 + 3042*]

innocent [2], pure [1]

Mt 10: 16   Therefore be as shrewd as snakes and as **innocent** as doves.
Ro 16: 19   to be wise about what is good, and **innocent** about what is evil.
Php 2: 15   so that you may become blameless and **pure**, children of God

194 ἀκηδεμονέω, *akēdemoneō* Not used in UBS/NIV

195 ἀκλινής, *aklinēs* [1] [√ *1.1 + 3111*]

unswervingly [1]

Heb 10: 23   Let us hold **unswervingly** to the hope we profess, for he who

196 ἀκμάζω, *akmazō* [1] [√ *216*]

ripe [1]

Rev 14: 18   of grapes from the earth's vine, because its grapes *are* **ripe**."

197 ἀκμήν, *akmēn* [1] [√ *216*]

still [1]

Mt 15: 16   "Are you **still** so dull?" Jesus asked them.

198 ἀκοή, *akoē* [24] [√ *201*]

ears [4], message [4], heard [3], ever hearing [+*201*] [2], news
[2], rumors [2], what heard [2], ear [1], hearing [1], learn [1],
reports [1], sense of hearing [1]

Mt 4: 24   **News** about him spread all over Syria, and people brought to him
    13: 14   the prophecy of Isaiah: " '*You will be* **ever hearing** [+*201*]
    14: 1   At that time Herod the tetrarch heard the **reports** about Jesus,
    24: 6   You will hear of wars and **rumors** of wars, but see to it that you
Mk 1: 28   **News** about him spread quickly over the whole region of Galilee.
    7: 35   At this, the man's **ears** were opened, his tongue was loosened
    13: 7   When you hear of wars and **rumors** of wars, do not be alarmed.
Lk 7: 1   When Jesus had finished saying all this in the **hearing** of the
Jn 12: 38   who has believed our **message** and to whom has the arm of the
Ac 17: 20   You are bringing some strange ideas to our **ears**, and we want to
    28: 26   "*You will be* **ever hearing** [+*201*] but never understanding;
Ro 10: 16   For Isaiah says, "Lord, who has believed our **message**?"
    10: 17   Consequently, faith comes from hearing the **message**,
    10: 17   the message, and the **message** is heard through the word of Christ.
1Co 12: 17   whole body were an eye, where would the **sense of hearing** be?
    12: 17   If the whole body were an **ear**, where would the sense of smell be?
Gal 3: 2   the Spirit by observing the law, or by believing **what** you **heard**?
    3: 5   you observe the law, or because you believe **what** you **heard**?
1Th 2: 13   when you received the word of God, which you **heard** from us,
2Ti 4: 3   number of teachers to say what their itching **ears** want to hear.
    4: 4   They will turn their **ears** away from the truth and turn aside to
Heb 4: 2   but the message they **heard** was of no value to them, because those
    5: 11   about this, but it is hard to explain because you are slow *to* **learn**.
2Pe 2: 8   in his righteous soul by the lawless deeds he saw and **heard**)—

199 ἀκολουθέω, *akoloutheō* [90] [→ *1.3, 1979, 2051,
2887, 4158, 5258*]

followed [41], follow [32], following [6], accompanied [2], behind
[1], come [1], follow [+*3958*] [1], followed out [+*2002*] [1],
following behind [1], follows [1], is one of us [+*1609+3552*] [1],
one of [1], went with [1]

Mt 4: 20   At once they left their nets and **followed** him.
    4: 22   immediately they left the boat and their father and **followed** him.
    4: 25   Jerusalem, Judea and the region across the Jordan **followed** him.
    8: 1   he came down from the mountainside, large crowds **followed** him.
    8: 10   he was astonished and said *to* those **following** him, "I tell you the
    8: 19   to him and said, "Teacher, *I will* **follow** you wherever you go."
    8: 22   But Jesus told him, "**Follow** me, and let the dead bury their own
    8: 23   Then he got into the boat and his disciples **followed** him.
    9: 9   "**Follow** me," he told him, and Matthew got up and followed him.
    9: 9   "**Follow** me," he told him, and Matthew got up and **followed** him.
    9: 19   Jesus got up and **went with** him, and so did his disciples.
    9: 27   two blind men **followed** him, calling out, "Have mercy on us,
    10: 38   does not take his cross and **follow** [+*3958*] me is not worthy of me.
    12: 15   from that place. Many **followed** him, and he healed all their sick,
    14: 13   Hearing of this, the crowds **followed** him on foot from the towns.
    16: 24   he must deny himself and take up his cross and **follow** me.
    19: 2   Large crowds **followed** him, and he healed them there.
    19: 21   and you will have treasure in heaven. Then come, **follow** me."
    19: 27   Peter answered him, "We have left everything to **follow** you!
    19: 28   you who *have* **followed** me will also sit on twelve thrones,
    20: 29   and his disciples were leaving Jericho, a large crowd **followed** him.
    20: 34   their eyes. Immediately they received their sight and **followed** him.
    21: 9   crowds that went ahead of him and those that **followed** shouted,
    26: 58   But Peter **followed** him at a distance, right up to the courtyard of
    27: 55   They *had* **followed** Jesus from Galilee to care for his needs.
Mk 1: 18   At once *they* left their nets and **followed** him.
    2: 14   "**Follow** me," Jesus told him, and Levi got up and followed him.

    2:14 "Follow me," Jesus told him, and Levi got up and **followed** him.
    2:15 and his disciples, for there were many *who* **followed** him.
    3: 7 his disciples to the lake, and a large crowd from Galilee **followed**.
    5:24 went with him. A large crowd **followed** and pressed around him.
    6: 1 and went to his hometown, **accompanied** *by* his disciples.
    8:34 "If anyone would **come** after me, he must deny himself and take up
    8:34 he must deny himself and take up his cross and **follow** me.
    9:38 your name and we told him to stop, because *he was* not **one of** us."
  10:21 and you will have treasure in heaven. Then come, **follow** me."
  10:28 Peter said to him, "We have left everything *to* **follow** you!"
  10:32 disciples were astonished, while those *who* **followed** were afraid.
  10:52 he received his sight and **followed** Jesus along the road.
  11: 9 who went ahead and those *who* **followed** shouted, "Hosanna!"
  14:13 and a man carrying a jar of water will meet you. **Follow** him.
  14:54 Peter **followed** him at a distance, right into the courtyard of the
  15:41 In Galilee these women had **followed** him and cared for his needs.
Lk   5:11 pulled their boats up on shore, left everything and **followed** him.
    5:27 of Levi sitting at his tax booth. "**Follow** me," Jesus said to him,
    5:28 and Levi got up, left everything and **followed** him.
    7: 9 and turning *to* the crowd **following** him, he said, "I tell you,
    9:11 but the crowds learned about it and **followed** him. He welcomed
    9:23 he must deny himself and take up his cross daily and **follow** me.
    9:49 we tried to stop him, because he **is** not **one of** us [*+1609+3552*]."
    9:57 the road, a man said to him, "*I will* **follow** you wherever you go."
    9:59 He said to another man, "**Follow** me." But the man replied,
    9:61 Still another said, "*I will* **follow** you, Lord; but first let me go back
  18:22 and you will have treasure in heaven. Then come, **follow** me."
  18:28 Peter said to him, "We have left all we had *to* **follow** you!"
  18:43 Immediately he received his sight and **followed** Jesus,
  22:10 jar of water will meet you. **Follow** him to the house that he enters,
  22:39 as usual to the Mount of Olives, and his disciples **followed** him.
  22:54 him into the house of the high priest. Peter **followed** at a distance.
  23:27 A large number of people **followed** him, including women who
Jn   1:37 When the two disciples heard him say this, *they* **followed** Jesus.
    1:38 Turning around, Jesus saw them **following** and asked, "What do
    1:40 two who heard what John had said and who *had* **followed** Jesus.
    1:43 to leave for Galilee. Finding Philip, he said to him, "**Follow** me."
    6: 2 and a great crowd of people **followed** him because they saw the
    8:12 Whoever **follows** me will never walk in darkness, but will have the
  10: 4 of them, and his sheep **follow** him because they know his voice.
  10: 5 But *they will* never **follow** a stranger; in fact, they will run away
  10:27 My sheep listen to my voice; I know them, and *they* **follow** me.
  11:31 noticed how quickly she got up and went out, *they* **followed** her,
  12:26 Whoever serves me *must* **follow** me; and where I am, my servant
  13:36 Jesus replied, "Where I am going, you cannot **follow** now, but you
  13:36 I am going, you cannot follow now, but *you will* **follow** later."
  13:37 Peter asked, "Lord, why can't I **follow** you now? I will lay down
  18:15 Simon Peter and another disciple *were* **following** Jesus.
  20: 6 *who was* **behind** him, arrived and went into the tomb.
  21:19 which Peter would glorify God. Then he said to him, "**Follow** me!"
  21:20 and saw that the disciple whom Jesus loved *was* **following** them.
  21:22 alive until I return, what is that to you? You *must* **follow** me."
Ac 12: 8 "Wrap your cloak around you and **follow** me," the angel told him.
  12: 9 Peter **followed** [*+2002*] him **out** of the prison, but he had no idea
  13:43 and devout converts to Judaism **followed** Paul and Barnabas,
  21:36 The crowd that **followed** kept shouting, "Away with him!"
1Co 10: 4 for they drank from the spiritual rock *that* **accompanied** them,
Rev 6: 8 was named Death, and Hades *was* **following** close **behind** him.
  14: 4 kept themselves pure. They **follow** the Lamb wherever he goes.
  14: 8 A second angel **followed** and said, "Fallen! Fallen is Babylon the
  14: 9 A third angel **followed** them and said in a loud voice: "If anyone
  14:13 "they will rest from their labor, for their deeds *will* **follow** them."
  19:14 The armies of heaven *were* **following** him, riding on white horses

200 ἀκουστός, *akoustos* Not used in UBS/NIV [√ *201*]

201 ἀκούω, *akouō* [428] [→ *198, 200, 1358, 1653, 2052,*
4157, 4159, 4578, 5633, 5634, 5675]

heard [197], hear [99], listen [39], hears [18], hearing [14], heard
about [10], listens [9], listening [8], listened [5], heard of [4], ever
hearing [*+198*] [2], ever hearing [*+201*] [2], understand [2], listen
[*+2627*] [1], accept [1], aware of [1], gets [1], hear [*+1639*] [1],
hear about [1], heard [*+1639*] [1], heard from [1], hearers [1], it
[*+608+794+4005*] [1], learned [1], obey [1], reached [*+1650*] [1],

reported [1], say [*+1666*] [1], told [1], understands [1],
whispered[s] [1], words [1]

Mt 2: 3 **When** King Herod **heard** this he was disturbed, and all Jerusalem
    2: 9 *After* they *had* **heard** the king, they went on their way, and the
    2:18 "A voice *is* **heard** in Ramah, weeping and great mourning,
    2:22 But *when he* **heard** that Archelaus was reigning in Judea in place
    4:12 When Jesus **heard** that John had been put in prison, he returned to
    5:21 "*You have* **heard** that it was said to the people long ago, 'Do not
    5:27 "*You have* **heard** that it was said, 'Do not commit adultery.'
    5:33 "Again, *you have* **heard** that it was said to the people long ago,
    5:38 "*You have* **heard** that it was said, 'Eye for eye, and tooth for
    5:43 "*You have* **heard** that it was said, 'Love your neighbor and hate
    7:24 "Therefore everyone who **hears** these words of mine and puts them
    7:26 But everyone who **hears** these words of mine and does not put
    8:10 When Jesus **heard** this, he was astonished and said to those
    9:12 On **hearing** this, Jesus said, "It is not the healthy who need a
  10:14 If anyone will not welcome you or **listen** *to* your words,
  10:27 what *is* **whispered**[s] in your ear, proclaim from the roofs.
  11: 2 *When* John **heard** in prison what Christ was doing, he sent his
  11: 4 Jesus replied, "Go back and report to John what *you* **hear** and see:
  11: 5 who have leprosy are cured, the deaf **hear**, the dead are raised,
  11:15 He who has ears, *let him* **hear**.
  12:19 will not quarrel or cry out; no one *will* **hear** his voice in the streets.
  12:24 But *when* the Pharisees **heard** this, they said, "It is only by
  12:42 for she came from the ends of the earth *to* **listen** *to* Solomon's
  13: 9 He who has ears, *let him* **hear**."
  13:13 they do not see; *though* **hearing**, they do not hear or understand.
  13:13 they do not see; though hearing, *they do* not **hear** or understand.
  13:14 the prophecy of Isaiah: " '*You will be* ever **hearing** [*+198*]
  13:15 *they* hardly **hear** with their ears, and they have closed their eyes.
  13:15 **hear** with their ears, understand with their hearts and turn,
  13:16 are your eyes because they see, and your ears because *they* **hear**.
  13:17 but did not see it, and *to* **hear** what you hear but did not hear it.
  13:17 but did not see it, and to hear what *you* **hear** but did not hear it.
  13:17 but did not see it, and to hear what you hear but *did* not **hear** it.
  13:18 "**Listen** then *to* what the parable of the sower means:
  13:19 *When* anyone **hears** the message about the kingdom and does not
  13:20 the seed that fell on rocky places is the man *who* **hears** the word
  13:22 the seed that fell among the thorns is the man who **hears** the word,
  13:23 the seed that fell on good soil is the man *who* **hears** the word
  13:43 sun in the kingdom of their Father. He who has ears, *let him* **hear**.
  14: 1 At that time Herod the tetrarch **heard** the reports about Jesus,
  14:13 When Jesus **heard** what had happened, he withdrew by boat
  14:13 **Hearing** of this, the crowds followed him on foot from the towns.
  15:10 Jesus called the crowd to him and said, "**Listen** and understand.
  15:12 "Do you know that the Pharisees were offended *when they* **heard**
  17: 5 my Son, whom I love; with him I am well pleased. **Listen** *to* him!"
  17: 6 *When* the disciples **heard** this, they fell facedown to the ground,
  18:15 two of you. If *he* **listens** *to* you, you have won your brother over.
  18:16 But if *he will* not **listen**, take one or two others along,
  19:22 *When* the young man **heard** this, he went away sad, because he
  19:25 *When* the disciples **heard** this, they were greatly astonished
  20:24 *When* the ten **heard about** this, they were indignant with the two
  20:30 and *when they* **heard** that Jesus was going by, they shouted,
  21:16 "*Do you* **hear** what these children are saying?" they asked him.
  21:33 "**Listen** *to* another parable: There was a landowner who planted a
  21:45 *When* the chief priests and the Pharisees **heard** Jesus' parables,
  22:22 *When they* **heard** this, they were amazed. So they left him
  22:33 When the crowds **heard** this, they were astonished at his teaching.
  22:34 **Hearing** that Jesus had silenced the Sadducees, the Pharisees got
  24: 6 You will **hear** of wars and rumors of wars, but see to it that you
  26:65 any more witnesses? Look, now *you have* **heard** the blasphemy?
  27:13 "Don't *you* **hear** the testimony they are bringing against you?"
  27:47 *When* some of those standing there **heard** this, they said,
  28:14 If this report **gets** to the governor, we will satisfy him and keep you
Mk 2: 1 entered Capernaum, the *people* **heard** that he had come home.
    2:17 *On* **hearing** this, Jesus said to them, "It is not the healthy who need
    3: 8 *When they* **heard** all he was doing, many people came to him
    3:21 *When* his family **heard about** this, they went to take charge of
    4: 3 "**Listen** [*+2627*]! A farmer went out to sow his seed.
    4: 9 Then Jesus said, "He who has ears *to* **hear**, let him hear."
    4: 9 Then Jesus said, "He who has ears to hear, *let him* **hear**."
    4:12 and **ever hearing** [*+201*] but never understanding;
    4:12 and **ever hearing** [*+201*] but never understanding;
    4:15 As soon as *they* **hear** it, Satan comes and takes away the word that

4: 16 on rocky places, **hear** the word and at once receive it with joy.
4: 18 Still others, like seed sown among thorns, **hear** [+*1639*] the word;
4: 20 sown on good soil, **hear** the word, accept it, and produce a crop—
4: 23 If anyone has ears *to* **hear**, let him hear."
4: 23 If anyone has ears to hear, *let him* **hear**."
4: 24 "Consider carefully what *you* **hear**," he continued. "With the
4: 33 Jesus spoke the word to them, as much as they could **understand**.
5: 27 *When she* **heard** about Jesus, she came up behind him in the
6: 2 to teach in the synagogue, and many *who* **heard** him were amazed.
6: 11 And if any place will not welcome you or **listen** *to* you,
6: 14 King Herod **heard about** this, for Jesus' name had become well
6: 16 But *when* Herod **heard** this, he said, "John, the man I beheaded,
6: 20 *When* Herod **heard** John, he was greatly puzzled; yet he liked to
6: 20 heard John, he was greatly puzzled; yet *he* liked *to* **listen** *to* him.
6: 29 *On* **hearing** of this, John's disciples came and took his body
6: 55 and carried the sick on mats to wherever *they* **heard** he was.
7: 14 Again Jesus called the crowd to him and said, "**Listen** *to* me,
7: 25 In fact, as soon as *she* **heard** about him, a woman whose little
7: 37 they said. "He even makes the deaf **hear** and the mute speak."
8: 18 Do you have eyes but fail to see, and ears but fail to **hear**?
9: 7 from the cloud: "This is my Son, whom I love. **Listen** *to* him!"
10: 41 *When* the ten **heard about** this, they became indignant with James
10: 47 *When he* **heard** that it was Jesus of Nazareth, he began to shout,
11: 14 ever eat fruit from you again." And his disciples **heard** him say it.
11: 18 The chief priests and the teachers of the law **heard** this and began
12: 28 One of the teachers of the law came and **heard** them debating.
12: 29 "is this: '**Hear**, O Israel, the Lord our God, the Lord is one.
12: 37 can he be his son?" The large crowd **listened** *to* him with delight.
13: 7 When *you* **hear** of wars and rumors of wars, do not be alarmed.
14: 11 They were delighted *to* **hear** this and promised to give him money.
14: 58 "We **heard** him say, 'I will destroy this man-made temple and in
14: 64 "*You have* **heard** the blasphemy. What do you think?" They all
15: 35 *When* some of those standing near **heard** this, they said, "Listen,
16: 11 *When* they **heard** that Jesus was alive and that she had seen him,

Lk 1: 41 When Elizabeth **heard** Mary's greeting, the baby leaped in her
1: 58 and relatives **heard** that the Lord had shown her great mercy,
1: 66 Everyone who **heard** this wondered about it, asking, "What
2: 18 and all who **heard** it were amazed at what the shepherds said to
2: 20 and praising God for all the things *they had* **heard** and seen,
2: 46 among the teachers, **listening** *to* them and asking them questions.
2: 47 Everyone who **heard** him was amazed at his understanding
4: 23 Do here in your hometown what *we have* **heard** that you did in
4: 28 All the people in the synagogue were furious *when they* **heard**
5: 1 the people crowding around him and **listening** *to* the word of God,
5: 15 so that crowds of people came *to* **hear** him and to be healed of
6: 18 who had come *to* **hear** him and to be healed of their diseases.
6: 27 "But I tell you who **hear** me: Love your enemies, do good to those
6: 47 who comes to me and **hears** my words and puts them into practice.
6: 49 But the one *who* **hears** my words and does not put them into
7: 3 The centurion **heard** of Jesus and sent some elders of the Jews to
7: 9 *When* Jesus **heard** this, he was amazed at him, and turning to the
7: 22 "Go back and report to John what you have seen and **heard**:
7: 22 who have leprosy are cured, the deaf **hear**, the dead are raised,
7: 29 the people, even the tax collectors, *when they* **heard** Jesus' *words*,
8: 8 he said this, he called out, "He who has ears *to* **hear**, let him hear."
8: 8 he said this, he called out, "He who has ears to hear, *let him* **hear**."
8: 10 they may not see; *though* **hearing**, they may not understand.'
8: 12 Those along the path are the ones *who* **hear**, and then the devil
8: 13 rock are the ones who receive the word with joy when *they* **hear** it,
8: 14 The seed that fell among thorns stands for those *who* **hear**,
8: 15 for those with a noble and good heart, *who* **hear** the word, retain it,
8: 18 Therefore consider carefully how *you* **listen**. Whoever has will be
8: 21 "My mother and brothers are those who **hear** God's word and put it
8: 50 **Hearing** this, Jesus said to Jairus, "Don't be afraid; just believe,
9: 7 Now Herod the tetrarch **heard about** all that was going on.
9: 9 "I beheaded John. Who, then, is this *I* **hear** such things about?"
9: 35 saying, "This is my Son, whom I have chosen; **listen** *to* him."
10: 16 "He *who* **listens** *to* you listens to me; he who rejects you rejects me;
10: 16 "He who listens to you **listens** *to* me; he who rejects you rejects me;
10: 24 but did not see it, and *to* **hear** what you hear but did not hear it."
10: 24 but did not see it, and to hear what *you* **hear** but did not hear it."
10: 24 but did not see it, and to hear what you hear but *did* not **hear** it."
10: 39 called Mary, who sat at the Lord's feet **listening** *to* what he said.
11: 28 "Blessed rather are those *who* **hear** the word of God and obey it."
11: 31 for she came from the ends of the earth *to* **listen** *to* Solomon's
12: 3 What you have said in the dark *will be* **heard** in the daylight,

14: 15 *When* one of those at the table with him **heard** this, he said to
14: 35 it is thrown out. "He who has ears *to* **hear**, let him hear."
14: 35 it is thrown out. "He who has ears to hear, *let him* **hear**."
15: 1 tax collectors and "sinners" were all gathering around *to* **hear** him.
15: 25 When he came near the house, *he* **heard** music and dancing.
16: 2 So he called him in and asked him, 'What is this *I* **hear** about you?
16: 14 who loved money, **heard** all this and were sneering at Jesus.
16: 29 'They have Moses and the Prophets; *let them* **listen** *to* them.'
16: 31 "He said to him, 'If *they do* not **listen** *to* Moses and the Prophets,
18: 6 And the Lord said, "**Listen** *to* what the unjust judge says.
18: 22 *When* Jesus **heard** this, he said to him, "You still lack one thing.
18: 23 *When* he **heard** this, he became very sad, because he was a man of
18: 26 Those *who* **heard** this asked, "Who then can be saved?"
18: 36 When *he* **heard** the crowd going by, he asked what was happening.
19: 11 *While* they *were* **listening** *to* this, he went on to tell them a
19: 48 find any way to do it, because all the people hung on his **words**.
20: 16 *When* the *people* **heard** this, they said, "May this never be!"
20: 45 *While* all the people *were* **listening**, Jesus said to his disciples,
21: 9 When *you* **hear** of wars and revolutions, do not be frightened.
21: 38 and all the people came early in the morning *to* **hear** him at the
22: 71 we need any more testimony? We *have* **heard** it from his own lips."
23: 6 *On* **hearing** this, Pilate asked if the man was a Galilean.
23: 8 From what he *had* **heard** about him, he hoped to see him perform

Jn 1: 37 When the two disciples **heard** him say this, they followed Jesus.
1: 40 was one of the two who **heard** what John had said and who had
3: 8 *You* **hear** its sound, but you cannot tell where it comes from
3: 29 The friend who attends the bridegroom waits and **listens** for him,
3: 32 He testifies to what he has seen and **heard**, but no one accepts his
4: 1 The Pharisees **heard** that Jesus was gaining and baptizing more
4: 42 now *we have* **heard** for ourselves, and we know that this man
4: 47 *When* this man **heard** that Jesus had arrived in Galilee from Judea,
5: 24 whoever **hears** my word and believes him who sent me has eternal
5: 25 and has now come when the dead *will* **hear** the voice of the Son of
5: 25 will hear the voice of the Son of God and those *who* **hear** will live.
5: 28 for a time is coming when all who are in their graves *will* **hear** his
5: 30 I judge only as *I* **hear**, and my judgment is just, for I seek not to
5: 37 concerning me. *You* have never **heard** his voice nor seen his form,
6: 45 Everyone who **listens** *to* the Father and learns from him comes to
6: 60 *On* **hearing** it, many of his disciples said, "This is a hard teaching.
6: 60 of his disciples said, "This is a hard teaching. Who can **accept** it?"
7: 32 The Pharisees **heard** the crowd whispering such things about him.
7: 40 *On* **hearing** his words, some of the people said, "Surely this man is
7: 51 "Does our law condemn anyone without first **hearing** him to find
8: 9 At this, those *who* **heard** began to go away one at a time,
8: 26 me is reliable, and what I *have* **heard** from him I tell the world."
8: 38 and you do what *you have* **heard** from your father."
8: 40 to kill me, a man who has told you the truth *that I* **heard** from God.
8: 43 not clear to you? Because you are unable *to* **hear** what I say.
8: 47 He who belongs to God **hears** what God says. The reason you do
8: 47 The reason you *do* not **hear** is that you do not belong to God."
9: 27 He answered, "I have told you already and *you did not* **listen**.
9: 27 and you did not listen. Why do you want *to* **hear** it again?
9: 31 We know that God *does* not **listen** *to* sinners. He listens to the
9: 31 not listen to sinners. *He* **listens** *to* the godly man who does his will.
9: 32 Nobody *has* ever **heard** of opening the eyes of a man born blind.
9: 35 Jesus **heard** that they had thrown him out, and when he found him,
9: 40 Some Pharisees who were with him **heard** him say this and asked,
10: 3 watchman opens the gate for him, and the sheep **listen** *to* his voice.
10: 16 me were thieves and robbers, but the sheep *did* not **listen** *to* them.
10: 16 *They* too *will* **listen** *to* my voice, and there shall be one flock
10: 20 "He is demon-possessed and raving mad. Why **listen** *to* him?"
10: 27 My sheep **listen** *to* my voice; I know them, and they follow me.
11: 4 *When* he **heard** this, Jesus said, "This sickness will not end in
11: 6 Yet when *he* **heard** that Lazarus was sick, he stayed where he was
11: 20 When Martha **heard** that Jesus was coming, she went out to meet
11: 29 When Mary **heard** this, she got up quickly and went to him.
11: 41 looked up and said, "Father, I thank you that *you have* **heard** me.
11: 42 I knew that *you* always **hear** me, but I said this for the benefit of
12: 12 The next day the great crowd that had come for the Feast **heard**
12: 18 because *they had* **heard** that he had given this miraculous sign,
12: 29 The crowd that was there and **heard** it said it had thundered;
12: 34 "We *have* **heard** from the Law that the Christ will remain forever,
12: 47 "As for the person *who* **hears** my words but does not keep them,
14: 24 These words *you* **hear** are not my own; they belong to the Father
14: 28 "*You* **heard** me say, 'I am going away and I am coming back to
15: 15 for everything that *I* **learned** from my Father I have made known

16:13 he will speak only what *he* **hears**, and he will tell you what is yet
18:21 Why question me? Ask those *who* **heard** me. Surely they know
18:37 to testify to the truth. Everyone on the side of truth **listens** *to* me."
19: 8 When Pilate **heard** this, he was even more afraid,
19:13 When Pilate **heard** this, he brought Jesus out and sat down on the
21: 7 *As soon as* Simon Peter **heard** him say, "It is the Lord," he wrapped

Ac   1: 4 gift my Father promised, which *you have* **heard** me speak about.
   2: 6 because each one **heard** them speaking in his own language.
   2: 8 Then how is it that each of us **hears** them in his own native
   2:11 *we* **hear** them declaring the wonders of God in our own tongues!"
   2:22 "Men of Israel, **listen** *to* this: Jesus of Nazareth was a man
   2:33 Holy Spirit and has poured out what you *now* see and **hear**.
   2:37 *When the people* **heard** this, they were cut to the heart and said to
   3:22 your own people; *you must* **listen** to everything he tells you.
   3:23 Anyone who *does* not **listen** *to* him will be completely cut off from
   4: 4 But many who **heard** the message believed, and the number of
   4:19 "Judge for yourselves whether it is right in God's sight *to* **obey** you
   4:20 For we cannot help speaking about what *we have* seen and **heard**."
   4:24 *When they* **heard** this, they raised their voices together in prayer
   5: 5 *When* Ananias **heard** this, he fell down and died. And great fear
   5: 5 and died. And great fear seized all who **heard** what had happened.
   5:11 seized the whole church and all who **heard about** these events.
   5:21 *as they had been* **told**, and began to teach the people.
   5:24 On **hearing** this report, the captain of the temple guard
   5:33 *When they* **heard** this, they were furious and wanted to put them
   6:11 "*We have* **heard** Stephen speak words of blasphemy against
   6:14 For *we have* **heard** him say that this Jesus of Nazareth will destroy
   7: 2 To this he replied: "Brothers and fathers, **listen** *to* me! The God of
   7:12 *When* Jacob **heard** that there was grain in Egypt, he sent our
   7:34 *I have* **heard** their groaning and have come down to set them free.
   7:54 *When they* **heard** this, they were furious and gnashed their teeth
   8: 6 When the crowds **heard** Philip and saw the miraculous signs he
   8:14 *When* the apostles in Jerusalem **heard** that Samaria had accepted
   8:30 ran up to the chariot and **heard** the man reading Isaiah the prophet.
   9: 4 *He* fell to the ground and **heard** a voice say to him, "Saul, Saul,
   9: 7 there speechless; *they* **heard** the sound but did not see anyone.
   9:13 "*I have* **heard** many reports about this man and all the harm he
   9:21 All those *who* **heard** him were astonished and asked, "Isn't he the
   9:38 so *when* the disciples **heard** that Peter was in Lydda, they sent two
 10:22 you come to his house so that he *could* **hear** what you have to say."
 10:33 Now we are all here in the presence of God *to* **listen** *to* everything
 10:44 these words, the Holy Spirit came on all who **heard** the message.
 10:46 For *they* **heard** them speaking in tongues and praising God.
 11: 1 and the brothers throughout Judea **heard** that the Gentiles also had
 11: 7 Then *I* **heard** a voice telling me, 'Get up, Peter. Kill and eat.'
 11:18 *When they* **heard** this, they had no further objections and praised
 11:22 News of this **reached** [+*1650*] the ears of the church at Jerusalem,
 13: 7 for Barnabas and Saul because he wanted *to* **hear** the word of God.
 13:16 "Men of Israel and you Gentiles who worship God, **listen** *to* me!
 13:44 On the next Sabbath almost the whole city gathered *to* **hear** the
 13:48 *When* the Gentiles **heard** this, they were glad and honored the
 14: 9 He **listened** *to* Paul as he was speaking. Paul looked directly at
 14:14 But *when* the apostles Barnabas and Paul **heard** of this, they tore
 15: 7 the Gentiles *might* **hear** from my lips the message of the gospel
 15:12 The whole assembly became silent as *they* **listened** *to* Barnabas
 15:13 When they finished, James spoke up: "Brothers, **listen** *to* me.
 15:24 *We have* **heard** that some went out from us without our
 16:14 One of those **listening** was a woman named Lydia, a dealer in
 16:38 and *when they* **heard** that Paul and Silas were Roman citizens,
 17: 8 *When they* **heard** this, the crowd and the city officials were
 17:21 doing nothing but talking about and **listening** *to* the latest ideas.)
 17:32 *When they* **heard about** the resurrection of the dead, some of
 17:32 but others said, "*We want to* **hear** you again on this subject."
 18: 8 and many of the Corinthians *who* **heard** him believed and were
 18:26 *When* Priscilla and Aquila **heard** him, they invited him to their
 19: 2 "No, *we have* not even **heard** that there is a Holy Spirit."
 19: 5 On **hearing** this, they were baptized into the name of the Lord
 19:10 and Greeks who lived in the province of Asia **heard** the word of
 19:26 And you see and **hear** how this fellow Paul has convinced
 19:28 *When they* **heard** this, they were furious and began shouting:
 21:12 When *we* **heard** this, we and the people there pleaded with Paul
 21:20 *When they* **heard** this, they praised God. Then they said to Paul:
 21:22 What shall we do? *They will* certainly **hear** that you have come,
 22: 1 "Brothers and fathers, **listen** now *to* my defense."
 22: 2 *When they* **heard** him speak to them in Aramaic, they became
 22: 7 I fell to the ground and **heard** a voice say to me, 'Saul! Saul!

22: 9 but *they did* not **understand** the voice of him who was speaking
22:14 and to see the Righteous One and *to* **hear** words from his mouth.
22:15 will be his witness to all men of what *you have* seen and **heard**.
22:22 The crowd **listened** *to* Paul until he said this. Then they raised their
22:26 *When* the centurion **heard** this, he went to the commander
23:16 But *when* the son of Paul's sister **heard of** this plot, he went into
24: 4 I would request that you be kind enough *to* **hear** us briefly.
24:24 and **listened** *to* him as he spoke about faith in Christ Jesus.
25:22 Agrippa said to Festus, "I would like *to* **hear** this man myself."
25:22 hear this man myself." He replied, "Tomorrow *you will* **hear** him."
26: 3 and controversies. Therefore, I beg you *to* **listen** *to* me patiently.
26:14 and *I* **heard** a voice saying to me in Aramaic, 'Saul, Saul,
26:29 but all who *are* **listening** *to* me today may become what I am,
28:15 The brothers there *had* **heard** that we were coming, and they
28:22 But we want *to* **hear** what your views are, for we know that people
28:26 "*You will be* ever **hearing** [+*198*] but never understanding;
28:27 *they* hardly **hear** with their ears, and they have closed their eyes.
28:27 **hear** with their ears, understand with their hearts and turn,
28:28 God's salvation has been sent to the Gentiles, and they *will* **listen**!"

Ro 10:14 how can they believe in the one of whom *they have* not **heard**?
 10:14 And how *can they* **hear** without someone preaching to them?
 10:18 But I ask: *Did they* not **hear**? Of course they did: "Their voice has
 11: 8 so that they could not see and ears so that they *could* not **hear**,
 15:21 about him will see, and those who *have* not **heard** will understand."

1Co 2: 9 "No eye has seen, no ear *has* **heard**, no mind has conceived what
 5: 1 *It is* actually **reported** that there is sexual immorality among you,
 11:18 In the first place, *I* **hear** that when you come together as a church,
 14: 2 Indeed, no one **understands** him; he utters mysteries with his

2Co 12: 4 *He* **heard** inexpressible things, things that man is not permitted to
 12: 6 think more of me than is warranted by what I do or **say** [+*1666*].

Gal 1:13 For *you have* **heard of** my previous way of life in Judaism,
 1:23 *They* only **heard** [+*1639*] the *report*: "The man who formerly
 4:21 want to be under the law, *are you* not **aware of** what the law says?

Eph 1:13 And you also were included in Christ *when* you **heard** the word of
 1:15 *ever since* I **heard about** your faith in the Lord Jesus and your
 3: 2 Surely *you have* **heard about** the administration of God's grace
 4:21 Surely *you* **heard of** him and were taught in him in accordance
 4:29 up according to their needs, that it may benefit those *who* **listen**.

Php 1:27 whether I come and see you or *only* **hear** about you in my absence,
 1:30 the same struggle you saw I had, and now **hear** that I still have.
 2:26 longs for all of you and is distressed because *you* **heard** he was ill.
 4: 9 Whatever you have learned or received or **heard from** me,

Col 1: 4 *because we have* **heard** of your faith in Christ Jesus and of the
 1: 6 just as it has been doing among you since the day *you* **heard** it
 1: 9 For this reason, since the day we **heard about** you, we have not
 1:23 This is the gospel that *you* **heard** and that has been proclaimed to

2Th 3:11 *We* **hear** that some among you are idle. They are not busy;

1Ti 4:16 because if you do, you will save both yourself and your **hearers**.

2Ti 1:13 What *you* **heard** from me, keep as the pattern of sound teaching,
 2: 2 And the things *you have* **heard** me say in the presence of many
 2:14 about words; it is of no value, and only ruins those *who* **listen**.
 4:17 might be fully proclaimed and all the Gentiles *might* **hear** it.

Phm 1: 5 *because* I **hear about** your faith in the Lord Jesus and your love

Heb 2: 1 therefore, to what *we have* **heard**, so that we do not drift away.
 2: 3 by the Lord, was confirmed to us by those *who* **heard** him.
 3: 7 So, as the Holy Spirit says: "Today, if *you* **hear** his voice,
 3:15 "Today, if *you* **hear** his voice, do not harden your hearts as you did
 3:16 Who were *they* who **heard** and rebelled? Were they not all those
 4: 2 to them, because those *who* **heard** did not combine it with faith.
 4: 7 "Today, if *you* **hear** his voice, do not harden your hearts."
 12:19 or to such a voice speaking words that those who **heard** it begged

Jas 1:19 Everyone should be quick to **listen**, slow to speak and slow to
 2: 5 **Listen**, my dear brothers: Has not God chosen those who are poor
 5:11 *You have* **heard of** Job's perseverance and have seen what the

2Pe 1:18 *We* ourselves **heard** this voice that came from heaven when we

1Jn 1: 1 which *we have* **heard**, which we have seen with our eyes,
 1: 3 We proclaim to you what *we have* seen and **heard**, so that you
 1: 5 This is the message *we have* **heard** from him and declare to you:
 2: 7 the beginning. This old command is the message *you have* **heard**.
 2:18 and as *you have* **heard** that the antichrist is coming, even now
 2:24 See that what *you have* **heard** from the beginning remains in you.
 2:24 If it[s] [+*608+794+4005*] does, you also will remain in the Son
 3:11 This is the message *you* **heard** from the beginning: We should
 4: 3 which *you have* **heard** is coming and even now is already in the
 4: 5 from the viewpoint of the world, and the world **listens** *to* them.
 4: 6 We are from God, and whoever knows God **listens** *to* us;

```
4: 6  listens to us; but whoever is not from God does not listen to us.
5:14  that if we ask anything according to his will, he hears us.
5:15  And if we know that he hears us—whatever we ask—we know
2Jn   1: 6  As you have heard from the beginning, his command is that you
3Jn   1: 4  I have no greater joy than to hear that my children are walking in
Rev   1: 3  and blessed are those who hear it and take to heart what is written
      1:10  in the Spirit, and I heard behind me a loud voice like a trumpet,
      2: 7  who has an ear, let him hear what the Spirit says to the churches.
      2:11  who has an ear, let him hear what the Spirit says to the churches.
      2:17  who has an ear, let him hear what the Spirit says to the churches.
      2:29  who has an ear, let him hear what the Spirit says to the churches.
      3: 3  Remember, therefore, what you have received and heard;
      3: 6  who has an ear, let him hear what the Spirit says to the churches.
      3:13  who has an ear, let him hear what the Spirit says to the churches.
      3:20  If anyone hears my voice and opens the door, I will come in
      3:22  who has an ear, let him hear what the Spirit says to the churches."
      4: 1  And the voice I had first heard speaking to me like a trumpet said,
      5:11  Then I looked and heard the voice of many angels, numbering
      5:13  Then I heard every creature in heaven and on earth and under the
      6: 1  Then I heard one of the four living creatures say in a voice like
      6: 3  the second seal, I heard the second living creature say, "Come!"
      6: 5  opened the third seal, I heard the third living creature say, "Come!"
      6: 6  Then I heard what sounded like a voice among the four living
      6: 7  I heard the voice of the fourth living creature say, "Come!"
      7: 4  Then I heard the number of those who were sealed: 144,000 from
      8:13  I heard an eagle that was flying in midair call out in a loud voice:
      9:13  and I heard a voice coming from the horns of the golden altar that
      9:16  mounted troops was two hundred million. I heard their number.
      9:20  bronze, stone and wood—idols that cannot see or hear or walk.
     10: 4  but I heard a voice from heaven say, "Seal up what the seven
     10: 8  Then the voice that I had heard from heaven spoke to me once
     11:12  Then they heard a loud voice from heaven saying to them,
     12:10  Then I heard a loud voice in heaven say: "Now have come the
     13: 9  He who has an ear, let him hear.
     14: 2  And I heard a sound from heaven like the roar of rushing waters.
     14: 2  The sound I heard was like that of harpists playing their harps.
     14:13  Then I heard a voice from heaven say, "Write: Blessed are the dead
     16: 1  Then I heard a loud voice from the temple saying to the seven
     16: 5  Then I heard the angel in charge of the waters say: "You are just in
     16: 7  And I heard the altar respond: "Yes, Lord God Almighty, true
     18: 4  Then I heard another voice from heaven say: "Come out of her,
     18:22  flute players and trumpeters, will never be heard in you again.
     18:22  The sound of a millstone will never be heard in you again.
     18:23  voice of bridegroom and bride will never be heard in you again.
     19: 1  After this I heard what sounded like the roar of a great multitude
     19: 6  Then I heard what sounded like a great multitude, like the roar of
     21: 3  And I heard a loud voice from the throne saying,
     22: 8  I, John, am the one who heard and saw these things. And when I
     22: 8  And when I had heard and seen them, I fell down to worship at
     22:17  and the bride say, "Come!" And let him who hears say, "Come!"
     22:18  I warn everyone who hears the words of the prophecy of this
```

202 ἀκρασία, akrasia [2] [√ 1.1 + 3197]

lack of self-control [1], self-indulgence [1]

```
Mt   23:25  and dish, but inside they are full of greed and self-indulgence.
1Co   7: 5  that Satan will not tempt you because of your lack of self-control.
```

203 ἀκρατής, akratēs [1] [√ 1.1 + 3197]

without self-control [1]

```
2Ti   3: 3  without love, unforgiving, slanderous, without self-control, brutal,
```

204 ἄκρατος, akratos [1] [√ 1.1 + 3042]

full strength [1]

```
Rev  14:10  which has been poured full strength into the cup of his wrath.
```

205 ἀκρίβεια, akribeia [1] [√ 207]

thoroughly [+2848] [1]

```
Ac   22: 3  Under Gamaliel I was thoroughly [+2848] trained in the law of
```

206 ἀκριβέστατος, akribestatos Not used in
UBS/NIV [√ 207]

207 ἀκριβής, akribēs [1] [→ 205, 206, 208, 209]

strictest [1]

```
Ac   26: 5  they are willing, that according to the strictest sect of our religion,
```

208 ἀκριβόω, akriboō [2] [√ 207]

found out exact [1], learned [1]

```
Mt    2: 7  and found out from them the exact time the star had appeared.
      2:16  in accordance with the time he had learned from the Magi.
```

209 ἀκριβῶς, akribōs [9] [√ 207]

more accurate [2], accurately [1], careful [1], carefully [1], more
adequately [1], very careful [1], very well [1], well [1]

```
Mt    2: 8  to Bethlehem and said, "Go and make a careful search for the child.
Lk    1: 3  since I myself have carefully investigated everything from the
Ac   18:25  and he spoke with great fervor and taught about Jesus accurately,
     18:26  and explained to him the way of God more adequately.
     23:15  the pretext of wanting more accurate information about his case.
     23:20  on the pretext of wanting more accurate information about him.
     24:22  Then Felix, who was well acquainted with the Way,
Eph   5:15  Be very careful, then, how you live—not as unwise but as wise,
1Th   5: 2  for you know very well that the day of the Lord will come like a
```

210 ἀκρίς, akris [4]

locusts [4]

```
Mt    3: 4  leather belt around his waist. His food was locusts and wild honey.
Mk    1: 6  a leather belt around his waist, and he ate locusts and wild honey.
Rev   9: 3  And out of the smoke locusts came down upon the earth and were
      9: 7  The locusts looked like horses prepared for battle. On their heads
```

211 ἀκροατήριον, akroatērion [1] [√ 212]

audience room [1]

```
Ac   25:23  and entered the audience room with the high ranking officers
```

212 ἀκροατής, akroatēs [4] [→ 211, 2053]

hear [1], heard [+1181] [1], listen [1], listens [+1639] [1]

```
Ro    2:13  For it is not those who hear the law who are righteous in God's
Jas   1:22  Do not merely listen to the word, and so deceive yourselves.
      1:23  Anyone who listens [+1639] to the word but does not do what it
      1:25  to do this, not forgetting what he has heard [+1181], but doing it—
```

213 ἀκροβυστία, akrobystia [20] [√ 216]

uncircumcised [5], not circumcised [4], uncircumcision [4],
beforeˢ [+1877] [2], before circumcised [+1877] [1], Gentiles [1],
theyˢ [+3836] [1], uncircumcised [+1877] [1], uncircumcised
[+2400] [1]

```
Ac   11: 3  "You went into the house of uncircumcised [+2400] men and ate
Ro    2:25  you have become as though you had not been circumcised.
      2:26  If those who are not circumcised keep the law's requirements,
      2:26  will theyˢ [+3836] not be regarded as though they were
      2:27  The one who is not circumcised physically and yet obeys the law
      3:30  by faith and the uncircumcised through that same faith.
      4: 9  only for the circumcised, or also for the uncircumcised?
      4:10  Was it after he was circumcised, or beforeˢ [+1877]? It was not
      4:10  was circumcised, or before? It was not after, but beforeˢ [+1877]!
      4:11  that he had by faith while he was still uncircumcised.
      4:11  he is the father of all who believe but have not been circumcised,
      4:12  that our father Abraham had before he was circumcised [+1877].
1Co   7:18  Was a man uncircumcised [+1877] when he was called?
      7:19  Circumcision is nothing and uncircumcision is nothing.
Gal   2: 7  entrusted with the task of preaching the gospel to the Gentiles,
      5: 6  For in Christ Jesus neither circumcision nor uncircumcision has
```

6: 15 Neither circumcision nor **uncircumcision** means anything;
Eph 2: 11 and called "**uncircumcised**" by those who call themselves "the
Col 2: 13 dead in your sins and *in* the **uncircumcision** of your sinful nature,
3: 11 Here there is no Greek or Jew, circumcised or **uncircumcised**,

214 ἀκρογωνιαῖος, *akrogōniaios* [2] [√ 216 + 1224]

chief cornerstone [1], cornerstone [1]

Eph 2: 20 and prophets, with Christ Jesus himself as the **chief cornerstone**.
1Pe 2: 6 "See, I lay a stone in Zion, a chosen and precious **cornerstone**,

215 ἀκροθίνιον, *akrothinion* [1] [√ 216]

plunder [1]

Heb 7: 4 Even the patriarch Abraham gave him a tenth of the **plunder**!

216 ἄκρον, *akron* [6] [→ 180, 181, 196, 197, 213, 214, 215, 948, 5644]

ends [2], end [1], other[s] [1], tip [1], top [1]

Mt 24: 31 from the four winds, from *one* **end** of the heavens to the other.
24: 31 from the four winds, from one end of the heavens to the **other**[s].
Mk 13: 27 four winds, from the **ends** of the earth to the ends of the heavens.
13: 27 four winds, from the ends of the earth to the **ends** of the heavens.
Lk 16: 24 pity on me and send Lazarus to dip the **tip** of his finger in water
Heb 11: 21 Joseph's sons, and worshiped as he leaned on the **top** of his staff.

217 'Ακύλας, *Akylas* [6]

Aquila [6]

Ac 18: 2 There he met a Jew named **Aquila**, a native of Pontus, who had
18: 18 and sailed for Syria, accompanied by Priscilla and **Aquila**.
18: 26 When Priscilla and **Aquila** heard him, they invited him to their
Ro 16: 3 Greet Priscilla and **Aquila**, my fellow workers in Christ Jesus.
1Co 16: 19 **Aquila** and Priscilla greet you warmly in the Lord, and so does the
2Ti 4: 19 Greet Priscilla and **Aquila** and the household of Onesiphorus.

218 ἀκυρόω, *akyroō* [3] [√ 1.1 + 3263]

nullify [2], set aside [1]

Mt 15: 6 Thus *you* **nullify** the word of God for the sake of your tradition.
Mk 7: 13 Thus *you* **nullify** the word of God by your tradition that you have
Gal 3: 17 *does* not **set aside** the covenant previously established by God

219 ἀκωλύτως, *akōlytōs* [1] [√ 1.1 + 3266]

without hindrance [1]

Ac 28: 31 Boldly and **without hindrance** he preached the kingdom of God

220 ἄκων, *akōn* [1] [√ 1.1 + 1776]

not voluntarily [1]

1Co 9: 17 if **not voluntarily**, I am simply discharging the trust committed to

221 ἄλα, *hala* Not used in UBS/NIV [√ 229]

222 ἀλάβαστρον, *alabastron* Not used in UBS/NIV [→ 223]

223 ἀλάβαστρος, *alabastros* [4] [√ 222]

alabaster jar [3], jar [1]

Mt 26: 7 a woman came to him with an **alabaster jar** of very expensive
Mk 14: 3 a woman came with an **alabaster jar** of very expensive perfume,
14: 3 pure nard. She broke the **jar** and poured the perfume on his head.
Lk 7: 37 at the Pharisee's house, she brought an **alabaster jar** of perfume,

224 ἀλαζονεία, *alazoneia* [2] [→ 225, 226]

boasting [1], brag [+1877+3836] [1]

Jas 4: 16 As it is, you boast and **brag** [+1877+3836]. All such boasting is
1Jn 2: 16 the lust of his eyes and the **boasting** of what he has and does—

225 ἀλαζών, *alazōn* [2] [√ 224]

boastful [2]

Ro 1: 30 slanderers, God-haters, insolent, arrogant and **boastful**; they invent
2Ti 3: 2 lovers of money, **boastful**, proud, abusive, disobedient to their

226 ἀλαλάζω, *alalazō* [2] [√ 224]

clanging [1], wailing [1]

Mk 5: 38 Jesus saw a commotion, with people crying and **wailing** loudly.
1Co 13: 1 have not love, I am only a resounding gong or a **clanging** cymbal.

227 ἀλάλητος, *alalētos* [1] [√ 1.1 + 3281]

words cannot express [1]

Ro 8: 26 himself intercedes for us with groans *that* **words cannot express**.

228 ἄλαλος, *alalos* [3] [√ 1.1 + 3281]

mute [2], robbed him of speech [1]

Mk 7: 37 they said. "He even makes the deaf hear and the **mute** speak."
9: 17 who is possessed by a spirit that has **robbed him of speech**.
9: 25 "*You* deaf and **mute** spirit," he said, "I command you, come out of

229 ἄλας, *halas* [8] [→ 129, 221, 243, 244, 245, 265, 266, 383, 1879, 4163; cf. 2498]

salt [6], it[s] [+3836] [2]

Mt 5: 13 "You are the **salt** of the earth. But if the salt loses its saltiness,
5: 13 But if the **salt** loses its saltiness, how can it be made salty again?
Mk 9: 50 "**Salt** is good, but if it loses its saltiness, how can you make it salty
9: 50 "Salt is good, but if **it**[s] [+3836] loses its saltiness, how can you
9: 50 Have **salt** in yourselves, and be at peace with each other."
Lk 14: 34 "**Salt** is good, but if it loses its saltiness, how can it be made salty
14: 34 "Salt is good, but if **it**[s] [+3836] loses its saltiness, how can it be
Col 4: 6 Let your conversation be always full of grace, seasoned *with* **salt**,

230 ἀλείφω, *aleiphō* [9] [→ 1981]

poured on [4], anoint [2], anointed [1], put oil on [1], put on [1]

Mt 6: 17 But when you fast, **put oil on** your head and wash your face,
Mk 6: 13 and **anointed** many sick people with oil and healed them.
16: 1 Salome bought spices so that *they might* go to **anoint** Jesus' body.
Lk 7: 38 them with her hair, kissed them and **poured** perfume on them.
7: 46 *You did* not **put** oil **on** my head, but she has poured perfume on
7: 46 not put oil on my head, but she *has* **poured** perfume **on** my feet.
Jn 11: 2 was the same one *who* **poured** perfume **on** the Lord and wiped his
12: 3 *she* **poured** it **on** Jesus' feet and wiped his feet with her hair.
Jas 5: 14 to pray over him and **anoint** him with oil in the name of the Lord.

231 ἀλεκτοροφωνία, *alektorophōnia* [1] [√ 232 + 5889]

when the rooster crows [1]

Mk 13: 35 or at midnight, or **when the rooster crows**, or at dawn.

232 ἀλέκτωρ, *alektōr* [12 / 11] [→ 231]

rooster [11]

Mt 26: 34 Jesus answered, "this very night, before the **rooster** crows,
26: 74 to them, "I don't know the man!" Immediately a **rooster** crowed.
26: 75 "Before the **rooster** crows, you will disown me three times."
Mk 14: 30 before the **rooster** crows twice you yourself will disown me three
14: 68 went out into the entryway [UBS+ *and the* **rooster** *crowed.*]
14: 72 Immediately the **rooster** crowed the second time. Then Peter

14:72 "Before the **rooster** crows twice you will disown me three times."
Lk 22:34 Jesus answered, "I tell you, Peter, before the **rooster** crows today,
22:60 you're talking about!" Just as he was speaking, the **rooster** crowed.
22:61 "Before the **rooster** crows today, you will disown me three times."
Jn 13:38 I tell you the truth, before the **rooster** crows, you will disown me
18:27 Again Peter denied it, and at that moment a **rooster** began to crow.

233 ’Αλεξανδρεύς, *Alexandreus* [2] [√ 235]

of Alexandria [2]

Ac 6:9 Jews **of** Cyrene and **Alexandria** as well as the provinces of Cilicia
18:24 a Jew named Apollos, a native **of Alexandria**, came to Ephesus.

234 ’Αλεξανδρῖνος, *Alexandrinos* [2] [√ 235]

Alexandrian [2]

Ac 27:6 There the centurion found an **Alexandrian** ship sailing for Italy
28:11 It was an **Alexandrian** ship with the figurehead of the twin gods

235 ’Αλέξανδρος, *Alexandros* [6] [→ 233, 234]

Alexander [5], he^s [+3836] [1]

Mk 15:21 man from Cyrene, Simon, the father **of Alexander** and Rufus,
Ac 4:6 John, **Alexander** and the other men of the high priest's family.
19:33 The Jews pushed **Alexander** to the front, and some of the crowd
19:33 **He^s** [+3836] motioned for silence in order to make a defense
1Ti 1:20 Among them are Hymenaeus and **Alexander**, whom I have handed
2Ti 4:14 **Alexander** the metalworker did me a great deal of harm. The Lord

236 ἄλευρον, *aleuron* [2] [√ 241]

flour [2]

Mt 13:33 and mixed into a large amount **of flour** until it worked all through
Lk 13:21 and mixed into a large amount **of flour** until it worked all through

237 ἀλήθεια, *alētheia* [109] [√ 1.1 + 3291]

truth [94], true [5], certainly [+2093] [1], indeed [+1142+2093]
[1], assure [+2093+3306] [1], how true [+2093] [1], right [+2093]
[1], true [+1877] [1], truly [+1877] [1], truthful [1], truthfully [1],
truthfulness [1]

Mt 22:16 and that you teach the way of God in accordance with the **truth**.
Mk 5:33 fell at his feet and, trembling with fear, told him the whole **truth**.
12:14 but you teach the way of God in accordance with the **truth**.
12:32 "You are **right** [+2093] in saying that God is one and there is no
Lk 4:25 *I* **assure** [+2093+3306] you that there were many widows in Israel
20:21 partiality but teach the way of God in accordance with the **truth**.
22:59 About an hour later another asserted, "**Certainly** [+2093] this
Jn 1:14 and Only, who came from the Father, full *of* grace and **truth**.
1:17 given through Moses; grace and **truth** came through Jesus Christ.
3:21 But whoever lives by the **truth** comes into the light, so that it may
4:23 the true worshipers will worship the Father in spirit and **truth**,
4:24 is spirit, and his worshipers must worship in spirit and in **truth**."
5:33 "You have sent to John and he has testified *to* the **truth**.
8:32 Then you will know the **truth**, and the truth will set you free."
8:32 Then you will know the truth, and the **truth** will set you free."
8:40 to kill me, a man who has told you the **truth** that I heard from God.
8:44 the beginning, not holding to the **truth**, for there is no truth in him.
8:44 the beginning, not holding to the truth, for there is no **truth** in him.
8:45 Yet because I tell the **truth**, you do not believe me!
8:46 guilty of sin? If I am telling the **truth**, why don't you believe me?
14:6 Jesus answered, "I am the way and the **truth** and the life. No one
14:17 the Spirit *of* **truth**. The world cannot accept him, because it neither
15:26 the Spirit *of* **truth** who goes out from the Father, he will testify
16:7 But I tell you the **truth**: It is for your good that I am going away.
16:13 But when he, the Spirit *of* **truth**, comes, he will guide you into all
16:13 the Spirit of truth, comes, he will guide you into all **truth**.
17:17 Sanctify them by the **truth**; your word is truth.
17:17 Sanctify them by the truth; your word is **truth**.
17:19 I sanctify myself, that they too may be **truly** [+1877] sanctified.
18:37 was born, and for this I came into the world, to testify *to* the **truth**.
18:37 to testify to the truth. Everyone on the side of **truth** listens to me."
18:38 "What is **truth**?" Pilate asked. With this he went out again to the
Ac 4:27 **Indeed** [+1142+2093] Herod and Pontius Pilate met together with

10:34 "I now realize **how true** [+2093] it is that God does not show
26:25 Paul replied. "What I am saying is **true** and reasonable.
Ro 1:18 and wickedness of men who suppress the **truth** by their
1:25 They exchanged the **truth** of God for a lie, and worshiped
2:2 judgment against those who do such things is based on **truth**.
2:8 who are self-seeking and who reject the **truth** and follow evil,
2:20 you have in the law the embodiment *of* knowledge and **truth**—
3:7 "If my falsehood enhances God's **truthfulness** and so increases his
9:1 I speak the **truth** in Christ—I am not lying, my conscience
15:8 Christ has become a servant of the Jews on behalf of God's **truth**,
1Co 5:8 but with bread without yeast, the bread *of* sincerity and **truth**.
13:6 Love does not delight in evil but rejoices with the **truth**.
2Co 2:2 by setting forth the **truth** plainly we commend ourselves to every
6:7 in **truthful** speech and in the power of God; with weapons of
7:14 But just as everything we said to you was **true** [+1877], so our
7:14 so our boasting about you to Titus has proved to be **true** as well.
11:10 As surely as the **truth** of Christ is in me, nobody in the regions of
12:6 I would not be a fool, because I would be speaking the **truth**.
13:8 For we cannot do anything against the **truth**, but only for the truth.
13:8 For we cannot do anything against the truth, but only for the **truth**.
Gal 2:5 a moment, so that the **truth** of the gospel might remain with you.
2:14 When I saw that they were not acting in line with the **truth** of the
5:7 Who cut in on you and kept you from obeying the **truth**?
Eph 1:13 also were included in Christ when you heard the word *of* **truth**,
4:21 and were taught in him in accordance with the **truth** that is in
4:24 created to be like God in **true** righteousness and holiness.
4:25 of you must put off falsehood and speak **truthfully** to his neighbor,
5:9 fruit of the light consists in all goodness, righteousness and **truth**)
6:14 Stand firm then, with the belt of **truth** buckled around your waist,
Php 1:18 every way, whether from false motives or **true**, Christ is preached.
Col 1:5 and that you have already heard about in the word *of* **truth**,
1:6 the day you heard it and understood God's grace in all its **truth**.
2Th 2:10 They perish because they refused to love the **truth** and so be
2:12 so that all will be condemned who have not believed the **truth**
2:13 the sanctifying work of the Spirit and through belief *in* the **truth**.
1Ti 2:4 all men to be saved and to come to a knowledge *of* the **truth**.
2:7 a herald and an apostle—I am telling the **truth**, I am not lying—
2:7 I am not lying—and a teacher of the **true** faith to the Gentiles.
3:15 the church of the living God, the pillar and foundation *of* the **truth**.
4:3 with thanksgiving by those who believe and who know the **truth**.
6:5 who have been robbed *of* the **truth** and who think that godliness is
2Ti 2:15 need to be ashamed and who correctly handles the word *of* **truth**.
2:18 who have wandered away from the **truth**. They say that the
2:25 grant them repentance leading them to a knowledge *of* the **truth**,
3:7 always learning but never able to acknowledge the **truth**.
3:8 and Jambres opposed Moses, so also these men oppose the **truth**—
4:4 They will turn their ears away from the **truth** and turn aside to
Tit 1:1 and the knowledge of the **truth** that leads to godliness—
1:14 to Jewish myths or to the commands of those who reject the **truth**.
Heb 10:26 keep on sinning after we have received the knowledge *of* the **truth**,
Jas 1:18 He chose to give us birth through the word *of* **truth**, that we might
3:14 ambition in your hearts, do not boast about it or deny the **truth**.
5:19 if one of you should wander from the **truth** and someone should
1Pe 1:22 Now that you have purified yourselves by obeying the **truth**
2Pe 1:12 know them and are firmly established in the **truth** you now have.
2:2 their shameful ways and will bring the way *of* **truth** into disrepute.
1Jn 1:6 him yet walk in the darkness, we lie and do not live by the **truth**.
1:8 to be without sin, we deceive ourselves and the **truth** is not in us.
2:4 not do what he commands is a liar, and the **truth** is not in him.
2:21 I do not write to you because you do not know the **truth**, but
2:21 because you do know it and because no lie comes from the **truth**.
3:18 let us not love with words or tongue but with actions and *in* **truth**.
3:19 This then is how we know that we belong to the **truth**, and how
4:6 This is how we recognize the Spirit *of* **truth** and the spirit of
5:6 And it is the Spirit who testifies, because the Spirit is the **truth**.
2Jn 1:1 To the chosen lady and her children, whom I love in the **truth**—
1:1 love in the truth—and not I only, but also all who know the **truth**—
1:2 because of the **truth**, which lives in us and will be with us forever.
1:3 Jesus Christ, the Father's Son, will be with us in **truth** and love.
1:4 me great joy to find some of your children walking in the **truth**,
3Jn 1:1 The elder, To my dear friend Gaius, whom I love in the **truth**.
1:3 and tell about your faithfulness *to* the **truth** and how you continue
1:3 faithfulness to the truth and how you continue to walk in the **truth**.
1:4 greater joy than to hear that my children are walking in the **truth**.
1:8 to such men so that we may work together *for* the **truth**.
1:12 is well spoken of by everyone—and even by the **truth** itself.

238 ἀληθεύω, *alētheuō* [2] [√ 1.1 + 3291]

speaking truth [1], telling truth [1]

Gal 4:16 Have I now become your enemy *by* **telling** you the **truth**?
Eph 4:15 Instead, **speaking** the **truth** in love, we will in all things grow up

239 ἀληθής, *alēthēs* [26] [√ 1.1 + 3291]

true [9], valid [5], real [3], truth [3], integrity [2], genuine [1], really [1], reliable [1], truthful [1]

Mt 22:16 "we know you are a *man of* **integrity** and that you teach the way of
Mk 12:14 to him and said, "Teacher, we know you are a *man of* **integrity**.
Jn 3:33 The man who has accepted it has certified that God is **truthful**.
4:18 have is not your husband. What you have just said is *quite* **true**."
5:31 "If I testify about myself, my testimony is not **valid**.
5:32 in my favor, and I know that his testimony about me is **valid**.
6:55 For my flesh is **real** food and my blood is real drink.
6:55 For my flesh is real food and my blood is **real** drink.
7:18 works for the honor of the one who sent him is a *man of* **truth**;
8:13 appearing as your own witness; your testimony is not **valid**."
8:14 my testimony is **valid**, for I know where I came from and where I
8:17 your own Law it is written that the testimony of two men is **valid**.
8:26 But he who sent me is **reliable**, and what I have heard from him I
10:41 a miraculous sign, all that John said about this man was **true**."
19:35 He knows that he tells the **truth**, and he testifies so that you also
21:24 and who wrote them down. We know that his testimony is **true**.
Ac 12:9 but he had no idea that what the angel was doing was **really**
Ro 3:4 Not at all! Let God be **true**, and every man a liar. As it is written:
2Co 6:8 bad report and good report; **genuine**, yet regarded as impostors;
Php 4:8 Finally, brothers, whatever is **true**, whatever is noble, whatever is
Tit 1:13 This testimony is **true**. Therefore, rebuke them sharply, so that
1Pe 5:12 encouraging you and testifying that this is the **true** grace of God.
2Pe 2:22 Of them the proverbs are **true**: "A dog returns to its vomit,"
1Jn 2:8 its **truth** is seen in him and you, because the darkness is passing
2:27 anointing teaches you about all things and as that anointing is **real**,
3Jn 1:12 also speak well of him, and you know that our testimony is **true**.

240 ἀληθινός, *alēthinos* [28] [√ 1.1 + 3291]

true [26], right [1], sincere [1]

Lk 16:11 in handling worldly wealth, who will trust you with **true** riches?
Jn 1:9 The **true** light that gives light to every man was coming into the
4:23 and has now come when the **true** worshipers will worship the
4:37 Thus the saying 'One sows and another reaps' is **true**.
6:32 but it is my Father who gives you the **true** bread from heaven.
7:28 I am not here on my own, but he who sent me is **true**. You do not
8:16 But if I do judge, my decisions are **right**, because I am not alone.
15:1 "I am the **true** vine, and my Father is the gardener.
17:3 the only **true** God, and Jesus Christ, whom you have sent.
19:35 man who saw it has given testimony, and his testimony is **true**.
1Th 1:9 you turned to God from idols to serve the living and **true** God,
Heb 8:2 the sanctuary, the **true** tabernacle set up by the Lord, not by man.
9:24 enter a man-made sanctuary that was only a copy *of* the **true** *one*;
10:22 let us draw near to God with a **sincere** heart in full assurance of
1Jn 2:8 the darkness is passing and the **true** light is already shining.
5:20 has given us understanding, so that we may know him who is **true**.
5:20 And we are in him who is **true**—even in his Son Jesus Christ.
5:20 even in his Son Jesus Christ. He is the **true** God and eternal life.
Rev 3:7 These are the words of him who is holy and **true**, who holds the
3:14 the faithful and **true** witness, the ruler of God's creation.
6:10 out in a loud voice, "How long, Sovereign Lord, holy and **true**,
15:3 Lord God Almighty. Just and **true** are your ways, King of the ages.
16:7 "Yes, Lord God Almighty, **true** and just are your judgments.
19:2 for **true** and just are his judgments. He has condemned the great
19:9 of the Lamb!' " And he added, "These are the **true** words of God."
19:11 me was a white horse, whose rider is called Faithful and **True**.
21:5 "Write this down, for these words are trustworthy and **true**."
22:6 The angel said to me, "These words are trustworthy and **true**.

241 ἀλήθω, *alēthō* [2] [→ 236]

grinding [1], grinding grain [1]

Mt 24:41 Two *women will be* **grinding** with a hand mill; one will be taken
Lk 17:35 Two women will be **grinding grain** together; one will be taken

242 ἀληθῶς, *alēthōs* [18] [√ 1.1 + 3291]

surely [6], really [3], truth [3], truly [2], actually [1], true [1], with certainty [1], without a doubt [1]

Mt 14:33 in the boat worshiped him, saying, "**Truly** you are the Son of God."
26:73 there went up to Peter and said, "**Surely** you are one of them,
27:54 were terrified, and exclaimed, "**Surely** he was the Son of God!"
Mk 14:70 said to Peter, "**Surely** you are one of them, for you are a Galilean."
15:39 saw how he died, he said, "**Surely** this man was the Son of God!"
Lk 9:27 I tell you the **truth**, some who are standing here will not taste
12:44 I tell you the **truth**, he will put him in charge of all his possessions.
21:3 "I tell you the **truth**," he said, "this poor widow has put in more
Jn 1:47 he said of him, "Here is a **true** Israelite, in whom there is nothing
4:42 and we know that this man **really** is the Savior of the world."
6:14 "**Surely** this is the Prophet who is to come into the world."
7:26 Have the authorities **really** concluded that he is the Christ?
7:40 some of the people said, "**Surely** this man is the Prophet."
8:31 Jesus said, "If you hold to my teaching, you are **really** my disciples.
17:8 They knew **with certainty** that I came from you, and they believed
Ac 12:11 "Now I know **without a doubt** that the Lord sent his angel
1Th 2:13 but as it **actually** is, the word of God, which is at work in you who
1Jn 2:5 anyone obeys his word, God's love is **truly** made complete in him.

243 ἀλιεύς, *halieus* [5] [√ 229]

fishermen [3], fishers [2]

Mt 4:18 They were casting a net into the lake, for they were **fishermen**.
4:19 follow me," Jesus said, "and I will make you **fishers** of men."
Mk 1:16 Andrew casting a net into the lake, for they were **fishermen**.
1:17 follow me," Jesus said, "and I will make you **fishers** of men."
Lk 5:2 left there by the **fishermen**, who were washing their nets.

244 ἀλιεύω, *halieuō* [1] [√ 229]

fish [1]

Jn 21:3 "I'm going out *to* **fish**," Simon Peter told them, and they said,

245 ἁλίζω, *halizō* [2] [√ 229]

made salty [1], salted [1]

Mt 5:13 But if the salt loses its saltiness, how *can it be* **made salty** again?
Mk 9:49 Everyone *will be* **salted** with fire.

246 ἀλίσγημα, *alisgēma* [1]

polluted [1]

Ac 15:20 telling them to abstain from *food* **polluted** by idols, from sexual

247 ἀλλά, *alla* [638] [√ 257] See Index of Articles, Etc.

but [406], *untranslated* [69], instead [20], yet [15], no [14], rather [11], on the contrary [10], what [7], and [6], but only [6], only [6], in fact [5], indeed [5], nevertheless [4], but rather [4], however [3], now [3], but [+2779] [3], if not [2], so [2], but also [2], again [1], and [+1145+2779] [1], but instead [1], even [+2779] [1], even [1], if [1], in addition [+2779] [1], indeed [+2779] [1], instead [+3437] [1], just [1], on contrary [+1883] [1], on the contrary [+3437+4498] [1], the only thing that counts [1], then [1], though [+1623+2779] [1], what is more [+1254+2779+3667+4024] [1], what is more [+2779+3529] [1], yes [1], although [+2779] [1], and also [+2779] [1], but [+2445] [1], cannot [+2445] [1], certainly [1], even though [1], except [1], except that [1], for [1], instead of [1], more than [1], surely [+1145] [1], though [1], to some extent [+608+3538] [1], what counts [1], what counts [1], yet [+3437] [1]

248 ἀλλάσσω, *allassō* [6] [→ 498, 557, 639, 1367, 2903, 2904, 3563, 4164, 5261; cf. 257]

changed [3], change [2], exchanged [1]

Ac 6:14 this place and **change** the customs Moses handed down to us."
Ro 1:23 and **exchanged** the glory of the immortal God for images made to

1Co 15:51 you a mystery: We will not all sleep, but *we will* all *be* **changed**—
    15:52 the dead will be raised imperishable, and we *will be* **changed**.
Gal 4:20 how I wish I could be with you now and **change** my tone,
Heb 1:12 will roll them up like a robe; like a garment *they will be* **changed**.

249 ἀλλαχόθεν, *allachothen* [1] [√ 257]

other way [1]

Jn 10: 1 the gate, but climbs in by *some* **other way**, is a thief and a robber.

250 ἀλλαχοῦ, *allachou* [1] [√ 257]

somewhere else [1]

Mk 1:38 Jesus replied, "Let us go **somewhere else**—to the nearby villages—

251 ἀλληγορέω, *allēgoreō* [1] [√ 257 + 60]

taken figuratively [1]

Gal 4:24 These things may be **taken figuratively**, for the women represent

252 ἀλληλουϊά, *hallēlouia* [4]

Hallelujah [4]

Rev 19: 1 "**Hallelujah**! Salvation and glory and power belong to our God,
    19: 3 And again they shouted: "**Hallelujah**! The smoke from her goes
    19: 4 was seated on the throne. And they cried: "Amen, **Hallelujah**!"
    19: 6 and like loud peals of thunder, shouting: "**Hallelujah**!

253 ἀλλήλων, *allēlōn* [100] [√ 257]

ἀγαπᾶτε, ἀγαπᾶν ἀλλήλους (love one another) [12] Jn
    13:34; 15:12,17; Ro 13:8; 1Th 4:9; 1Pe 1:22; 1Jn 3:11,23;
    4:7,11,12; 2Jn 1:5

one another [46], each other [32], *untranslated* [4], themselves [3], each other's [2], together [+4639] [2], yourselves [2], all the others [1], argued about [+1363+4639] [1], mutual [1], one another's [1], one body [1], others [1], parted company [+608+714] [1], talked the matter over [+1368+4639] [1], them [1]

Mt 24:10 away from the faith and will betray **[RPG]** and hate each other,
    24:10 will turn away from the faith and will betray and hate **each other**,
    25:32 and he will separate the people **one** from **another** as a shepherd
Mk 4:41 They were terrified and asked **each other**, "Who is this? Even the
    8:16 They discussed this with **one another** and said, "It is because we
    9:34 because on the way *they had* **argued about** [+1363+4639] who
    9:50 Have salt in yourselves, and be at peace with **each other**."
    15:31 and the teachers of the law mocked him among **themselves**.
Lk 2:15 left them and gone into heaven, the shepherds said to **one another**,
    4:36 All the people were amazed and said to **each other**, "What is this
    6:11 and began to discuss with **one another** what they might do to
    7:32 children sitting in the marketplace and calling out *to* **each other**:
    8:25 In fear and amazement they asked **one another**, "Who is this?
    12: 1 so that they were trampling on **one another**, Jesus began to speak
    20:14 the tenants saw him, *they* **talked the matter over** [+1368+4639].
    23:12 Pilate became friends—**[RPG]** before this they had been enemies.
    24:14 They were talking with **each other** about everything that had
    24:17 "What are you discussing **together** [+4639] as you walk along?"
    24:32 They asked **each other**, "Were not our hearts burning within us
Jn 4:33 Then his disciples said to **each other**, "Could someone have
    5:44 How can you believe if you accept praise from **one another**,
    6:43 "Stop grumbling among **yourselves**," Jesus answered.
    6:52 Then the Jews began to argue sharply among **themselves**,
    11:56 and as they stood in the temple area they asked **one another**,
    13:14 have washed your feet, you also should wash **one another's** feet.
    13:22 His disciples stared at **one another**, at a loss to know which of
    13:34 new command I give you: Love **one another**. As I have loved you,
    13:34 one another. As I have loved you, so you must love **one another**.
    13:35 men will know that you are my disciples, if you love **one another**."
    15:12 My command is this: Love **each other** as I have loved you.
    15:17 This is my command: Love **each other**.
    16:17 Some of his disciples said to **one another**, "What does he mean by
    16:19 to them, "Are you asking **one another** what I meant when I said,
    19:24 "Let's not tear it," they said to **one another**. "Let's decide by lot

Ac 4:15 withdraw from the Sanhedrin and then conferred **together** [+4639].
    7:26 'Men, you are brothers; why do you want to hurt **each other**?'
    15:39 such a sharp disagreement that they **parted company** [+608+714].
    19:38 and there are proconsuls. They can press charges. **[RPG]**
    21: 6 After saying good-by to **each other**, we went aboard the ship,
    26:31 They left the room, and while talking with **one another**, they said,
    28: 4 his hand, they said to **each other**, "This man must be a murderer;
    28:25 They disagreed among **themselves** and began to leave after Paul
Ro 1:12 that you and I may be mutually encouraged by **each other's** faith.
    1:27 with women and were inflamed with lust for **one another**.
    2:15 and their thoughts now accusing, now even defending **them**.)
    12: 5 many form one body, and each member *belongs to* **all the others**.
    12:10 Be devoted to **one another** in brotherly love. Honor one another
    12:10 another in brotherly love. Honor **one another** above yourselves.
    12:16 Live in harmony with **one another**. Do not be proud, but be
    13: 8 except the continuing debt to love **one another**,
    14:13 Therefore let us stop passing judgment on **one another**. Instead,
    14:19 every effort to do what leads to peace and to **mutual** edification.
    15: 5 and encouragement give you a spirit of unity among **yourselves** as
    15: 7 Accept **one another**, then, just as Christ accepted you, in order to
    15:14 complete in knowledge and competent to instruct **one another**.
    16:16 Greet **one another** with a holy kiss. All the churches of Christ send
1Co 7: 5 Do not deprive **each other** except by mutual consent and for a
    11:33 my brothers, when you come together to eat, wait for **each other**.
    12:25 but that its parts should have equal concern for **each other**.
    16:20 here send you greetings. Greet **one another** with a holy kiss.
2Co 13:12 Greet **one another** with a holy kiss.
Gal 5:13 to indulge the sinful nature; rather, serve **one another** in love.
    5:15 If you keep on biting and devouring **each other**, watch out
    5:15 each other, watch out or you will be destroyed by **each other**.
    5:17 They are in conflict *with* **each other**, so that you do not do what
    5:26 not become conceited, provoking **[RPG]** and envying each other.
    5:26 Let us not become conceited, provoking and envying **each other**.
    6: 2 Carry **each other's** burdens, and in this way you will fulfill the law
Eph 4: 2 and gentle; be patient, bearing with **one another** in love.
    4:25 truthfully to his neighbor, for we are all members *of* **one body**.
    4:32 Be kind and compassionate to **one another**, forgiving each other,
    5:21 Submit *to* **one another** out of reverence for Christ.
Php 2: 3 but in humility consider **others** better than yourselves.
Col 3: 9 Do not lie to **each other**, since you have taken off your old self
    3:13 Bear with **each other** and forgive whatever grievances you may
1Th 3:12 love increase and overflow for **each other** and for everyone else,
    4: 9 for you yourselves have been taught by God to love **each other**.
    4:18 Therefore encourage **each other** with these words.
    5:11 Therefore encourage **one another** and build each other up,
    5:15 but always try to be kind to **each other** and to everyone else.
2Th 1: 3 and the love every one of you has for **each other** is increasing.
Tit 3: 3 We lived in malice and envy, being hated and hating **one another**.
Heb 10:24 And let us consider how we may spur **one another** on toward love
Jas 4:11 Brothers, do not slander **one another**. Anyone who speaks against
    5: 9 Don't grumble against **each other**, brothers, or you will be judged.
    5:16 Therefore confess your sins *to* **each other** and pray for each other
    5:16 to each other and pray for **each other** so that you may be healed.
1Pe 1:22 love for your brothers, love **one another** deeply, from the heart.
    4: 9 Offer hospitality to **one another** without grumbling.
    5: 5 clothe yourselves with humility *toward* **one another**, because,
    5:14 Greet **one another** with a kiss of love. Peace to all of you who are
1Jn 1: 7 as he is in the light, we have fellowship with **one another**,
    3:11 you heard from the beginning: We should love **one another**.
    3:23 Jesus Christ, and to love **one another** as he commanded us.
    4: 7 Dear friends, let us love **one another**, for love comes from God.
    4:11 since God so loved us, we also ought to love **one another**.
    4:12 but if we love **one another**, God lives in us and his love is made
2Jn 1: 5 we have had from the beginning. I ask that we love **one another**.
Rev 6: 4 to take peace from the earth and to make men slay **each other**.
    11:10 gloat over them and will celebrate by sending **each other** gifts,

254 ἀλλογενής, *allogenēs* [1] [√ 257 + 1181]

foreigner [1]

Lk 17:18 one found to return and give praise to God except this **foreigner**?"

255 ἀλλοιόω, *alloioō* Not used in UBS/NIV [√ 257]

256 ἅλλομαι, hallomai [3] [→ 380, 1880, 1982, 2383; cf. 4888]

jumped up [1], jumping [1], welling up [1]

Jn	4:14	will become in him a spring of water **welling up** to eternal life."
Ac	3: 8	into the temple courts, walking and **jumping**, and praising God.
	14:10	up on your feet!" At that, the *man* **jumped up** and began to walk.

257 ἅλλος, allos [155] [→ 247, 249, 250, 251, 253, 254, 255, 258, 259, 260, 261, 558; cf. 248]

another [35], other [34], others [31], another [+1254] [9], someone else [6], else [5], others [+1254] [5], untranslated [4], more [4], some [4], some [+1254] [2], one another [+257+4639] [2], that one [2], one [1], other [+1254] [1], another [+5516] [1], another's [1], anyone else [1], anything [1], gospel[s] [1], one kind [+3525] [1], one kind [1], other than [1], some more [1], someone [1]

Mt	2:12	go back to Herod, they returned to their country by **another** route.
	4:21	Going on from there, he saw two **other** brothers, James son of
	5:39	someone strikes you on the right cheek, turn to him the **other** also.
	8: 9	this one, 'Go,' and he goes; and **that one**, 'Come,' and he comes.
	12:13	and it was completely restored, just as sound as the **other**.
	13: 5	**Some** [+1254] fell on rocky places, where it did not have much
	13: 7	**Other** [+1254] seed fell among thorns, which grew up and choked
	13: 8	Still **other** seed fell on good soil, where it produced a crop—
	13:24	Jesus told them **another** parable: "The kingdom of heaven is like a
	13:31	He told them **another** parable: "The kingdom of heaven is like a
	13:33	He told them *still* **another** parable: "The kingdom of heaven is like
	16:14	**others** [+1254] say Elijah; and still others, Jeremiah or one of the
	19: 9	and marries **another** *woman* commits adultery."
	20: 3	and saw **others** standing in the marketplace doing nothing.
	20: 6	eleventh hour he went out and found *still* **others** standing around.
	21: 8	while **others** cut branches from the trees and spread them on the
	21:33	"Listen to **another** parable: There was a landowner who planted a
	21:36	Then he sent **other** servants to them, more than the first time,
	21:41	they replied, "and he will rent the vineyard *to* **other** tenants,
	22: 4	"Then he sent **some more** servants and said, 'Tell those who have
	25:16	went at once and put his money to work and gained five **more**.
	25:17	So also, the one with the two talents gained two **more**.
	25:20	The man who had received the five talents brought the **other** five.
	25:20	'you entrusted me with five talents. See, I have gained five **more**.'
	25:22	'you entrusted me with two talents; see, I have gained two **more**.'
	26:71	where **another** *girl* saw him and said to the people there,
	27:42	"He saved **others**," they said, "but he can't save himself! He's the
	27:61	and the **other** Mary were sitting there opposite the tomb.
	28: 1	Mary Magdalene and the **other** Mary went to look at the tomb.
Mk	4: 5	**Some** fell on rocky places, where it did not have much soil.
	4: 7	**Other** seed fell among thorns, which grew up and choked the
	4: 8	Still **other** seed fell on good soil. It came up, grew and produced a
	4:18	Still **others**, like seed sown among thorns, hear the word;
	4:36	just as he was, in the boat. There were also **other** boats with him.
	6:15	**Others** [+1254] said, "He is Elijah." And still others claimed,
	6:15	And *still* **others** claimed, "He is a prophet, like one of the prophets
	7: 4	And they observe many **other** traditions, such as the washing of
	8:28	the Baptist; **others** say Elijah; and still others, one of the prophets."
	8:28	the Baptist; **others** say Elijah; and *still* **others**, one of the prophets."
	10:11	and marries **another** *woman* commits adultery against her.
	10:12	And if she divorces her husband and marries **another** *man*,
	11: 8	the road, while **others** spread branches they had cut in the fields.
	12: 4	Then he sent **another** servant to them; they struck this man on the
	12: 5	He sent *still* **another**,
	12: 5	He sent many **others**; some of them they beat, others they killed.
	12: 9	will come and kill those tenants and give the vineyard *to* **others**."
	12:31	as yourself.' There is no [NIE] commandment greater than these."
	12:32	are right in saying that God is one and there is no **other** but him.
	14:58	this man-made temple and in three days will build **another**,
	15:31	"He saved **others**," they said, "but he can't save himself!
Lk	5:29	Many **other** *women* who had come up with him to Jerusalem were
	5:29	a large crowd of tax collectors and **others** were eating with them.
	6:29	If someone strikes you on one cheek, turn to him the **other** also.
	7: 8	this one, 'Go,' and he goes; and **that one**, 'Come,' and he comes.
	7:19	you the one who was to come, or should we expect **someone else**?"
	7:20	the one who was to come, or should we expect **someone else**?' "

	9: 8	and *still* **others** that one of the prophets of long ago had come back
	9:19	**others** [+1254] say Elijah; and still others, that one of the prophets
	9:19	and *still* **others**, that one of the prophets of long ago has come
	20:16	will come and kill those tenants and give the vineyard *to* **others**."
	22:59	About an hour later **another** [+5516] asserted, "Certainly this
	23:35	They said, "He saved **others**; let him save himself if he is the Christ
Jn	4:37	Thus the saying '**One** sows and another reaps' is true.
	4:37	Thus the saying 'One sows and **another** reaps' is true.
	4:38	**Others** have done the hard work, and you have reaped the benefits
	5: 7	While I am trying to get in, **someone else** goes down ahead of me."
	5:32	There is **another** who testifies in my favor, and I know that his
	5:43	but if **someone else** comes in his own name, you will accept him.
	6:22	of the lake realized that [RPG] only one boat had been there,
	6:23	Then **some** boats from Tiberias landed near the place where the
	7:12	good man." **Others** [+1254] replied, "No, he deceives the people."
	7:41	**Others** said, "He is the Christ." Still others asked, "How can the
	9: 9	**Some** claimed he was. Others said, "No, he only looks like
	9: 9	**Others** said, "No, he only looks like him." But he himself insisted,
	9:16	But **others** asked, "How can a sinner do such miraculous signs?"
	10:16	I have **other** sheep that are not of this sheep pen. I must bring them
	10:21	But **others** said, "These are not the sayings of a man possessed by a
	12:29	it said it had thundered; **others** said an angel had spoken to him.
	14:16	and he will give you **another** Counselor to be with you forever—
	15:24	If I had not done among them what no one **else** did, they would not
	18:15	Simon Peter and **another** disciple were following Jesus.
	18:16	The **other** disciple, who was known to the high priest, came back,
	18:34	your own idea," Jesus asked, "or did **others** talk to you about me?"
	19:18	Here they crucified him, and with him two **others**—one on each
	19:32	who had been crucified with Jesus, and then those *of* the **other**.
	20: 2	So she came running to Simon Peter and the **other** disciple,
	20: 3	So Peter and the **other** disciple started for the tomb.
	20: 4	but the **other** disciple outran Peter and reached the tomb first.
	20: 8	Finally the **other** disciple, who had reached the tomb first,
	20:25	So the **other** disciples told him, "We have seen the Lord!" But he
	20:30	Jesus did many **other** miraculous signs in the presence of his
	21: 2	the sons of Zebedee, and two **other** disciples were together.
	21: 8	The **other** disciples followed in the boat, towing the net full of
	21:18	and **someone else** will dress you and lead you where you do not
	21:25	Jesus did many **other** *things* as well. If every one of them were
Ac	2:12	Amazed and perplexed, they asked **one another** [+257+4639],
	2:12	Amazed and perplexed, they asked **one another** [+257+4639],
	4:12	Salvation is found in no one **else**, for there is no other name under
	15: 2	and Barnabas were appointed, along with some **other** believers,
	19:32	was in confusion: Some were shouting one thing, **some** another.
	19:32	was in confusion: Some were shouting one thing, some **another**.
	21:34	**Some** [+1254] in the crowd shouted one thing and some another,
	21:34	Some in the crowd shouted one thing and some **another**, and since
1Co	1:16	beyond that, I don't remember if I baptized anyone **else**.)
	3:10	foundation as an expert builder, and **someone else** is building on it.
	3:11	For no one can lay any foundation **other** than the one already laid,
	9: 2	Even though I may not be an apostle *to* **others**, surely I am to you!
	9:12	If **others** have this right of support from you, shouldn't we have it
	9:27	and make it my slave so that after I have preached *to* **others**,
	10:29	For why should my freedom be judged by **another's** conscience?
	12: 8	*to* **another** [+1254] the message of knowledge by means of the
	12: 9	same Spirit, *to* **another** [+1254] gifts of healing by that one Spirit,
	12:10	*to* **another** [+1254] miraculous powers, to another prophecy,
	12:10	to another miraculous powers, *to* **another** [+1254] prophecy,
	12:10	*to* **another** [+1254] distinguishing between spirits,
	12:10	and *to still* **another** [+1254] the interpretation of tongues.
	14:19	words to instruct **others** than ten thousand words in a tongue.
	14:29	should speak, and the **others** should weigh carefully what is said.
	14:30	And if a revelation comes *to* **someone** who is sitting down,
	15:39	Men have **one kind** [+3525] of flesh, animals have another,
	15:39	animals have **another** [+1254], birds another and fish another.
	15:39	animals have another, birds **another** [+1254] and fish another.
	15:39	animals have another, birds another and fish **another** [+1254].
	15:41	The sun has **one kind** of splendor, the moon another and the stars
	15:41	has one kind of splendor, the moon **another** and the stars another;
	15:41	has one kind of splendor, the moon another and the stars **another**;
2Co	1:13	For we do not write you **anything** you cannot read or understand.
	8:13	Our desire is not that **others** might be relieved while you are hard
	11: 4	to you and preaches a Jesus **other than** the Jesus we preached,
	11: 8	I robbed **other** churches by receiving support from them so as to
Gal	1: 7	which is really no **gospel**[s] at all. Evidently some people are
	5:10	I am confident in the Lord that you will take no **other** view.

Php 3: 4 If anyone **else** thinks he has reasons to put confidence in the flesh,
1Th 2: 6 not looking for praise from men, not from you or **anyone else**.
Heb 4: 8 them rest, God would not have spoken later about **another** day.
11:35 **Others** [+*1254*] were tortured and refused to be released, so that
Jas 5:12 do not swear—not by heaven or by earth or by anything **else**.
Rev 2:24 so-called deep secrets (I will not impose any **other** burden on you):
6: 4 Then **another** horse came out, a fiery red one. Its rider was given
7: 2 Then I saw **another** angel coming up from the east, having the seal
8: 3 **Another** angel, who had a golden censer, came and stood at the
10: 1 Then I saw **another** mighty angel coming down from heaven.
12: 3 Then **another** sign appeared in heaven: an enormous red dragon
13:11 Then I saw **another** beast, coming out of the earth. He had two
14: 6 Then I saw **another** angel flying in midair, and he had the eternal
14: 8 A [**RPG**] second angel followed and said, "Fallen! Fallen is
14: 9 [**RPG**] A third angel followed them and said in a loud voice:
14:15 Then **another** angel came out of the temple and called in a loud
14:17 **Another** angel came out of the temple in heaven, and he too had a
14:18 Still **another** angel, who had charge of the fire, came from the altar
15: 1 I saw in heaven **another** great and marvelous sign: seven angels
17:10 Five have fallen, one is, the **other** has not yet come; but when he
18: 1 After this I saw **another** angel coming down from heaven.
18: 4 Then I heard **another** voice from heaven say: "Come out of her,
20:12 were opened. **Another** book was opened, which is the book of life.

258 ἀλλοτριεπίσκοπος, *allotriepiskopos* [1]
[√ *257 + 2093 + 5023*]

meddler [1]

1Pe 4:15 or thief or any other kind of criminal, or even as a **meddler**.

259 ἀλλότριος, *allotrios* [14] [√ *257*]

others [4], someone else's [3], stranger [2], another [1], foreign [1], not his own [1], not their own [1], stranger's [1]

Mt 17:25 earth collect duty and taxes—from their own sons or from **others**?"
17:26 "From **others**," Peter answered. "Then the sons are exempt," Jesus
Lk 16:12 if you have not been trustworthy with **someone else's** *property*,
Jn 10: 5 But they will never follow a **stranger**; in fact, they will run away
10: 5 away from him because they do not recognize a **stranger's** voice."
Ac 7: 6 'Your descendants will be strangers in a country **not their own**,
Ro 14: 4 Who are you to judge **someone else's** servant? To his own master
15:20 so that I would not be building on **someone else's** foundation.
2Co 10:15 do we go beyond our limits by boasting of work done by **others**.
10:16 want to boast about work already done in **another** *man's* territory.
1Ti 5:22 in the laying on of hands, and do not share in the sins of **others**.
Heb 9:25 the Most Holy Place every year with blood that is **not his own**.
11: 9 home in the promised land like a **stranger** *in a foreign country*;
11:34 and who became powerful in battle and routed **foreign** armies.

260 ἀλλόφυλος, *allophylos* [1] [√ *257 + 5876*]

Gentile [1]

Ac 10:28 that it is against our law for a Jew to associate with a **Gentile**

261 ἄλλως, *allōs* [1] [√ *257*]

not [1]

1Ti 5:25 deeds are obvious, and even those that are **not** cannot be hidden.

262 ἀλοάω, *aloaō* [3] [→ *272, 3617, 3618, 4254, 4260*]

treading out the grain [2], thresher [1]

1Co 9: 9 Moses: "Do not muzzle an ox *while it is* **treading out the grain**."
9:10 because when the plowman plows and the **thresher** threshes,
1Ti 5:18 "Do not muzzle the ox *while it is* **treading out the grain**,"

263 ἄλογος, *alogos* [3] [√ *1.1 + 3306*]

brute [1], unreasonable [1], unreasoning [1]

Ac 25:27 For I think it is **unreasonable** to send on a prisoner without
2Pe 2:12 They are like **brute** beasts, creatures of instinct, born only to be
Jude 1:10 things they do understand by instinct, like **unreasoning** animals—

264 ἀλόη, *aloē* [1]

aloes [1]

Jn 19:39 Nicodemus brought a mixture *of* myrrh and **aloes**,

265 ἅλς, *hals* Not used in UBS/NIV [√ *229*]

266 ἁλυκός, *halykos* [1] [√ *229*]

salt spring [1]

Jas 3:12 grapevine bear figs? Neither can a **salt spring** produce fresh water.

267 ἄλυπος, *alypos* [1] [√ *1.1 + 3383*]

less anxiety [1]

Php 2:28 you see him again you may be glad and I may have **less anxiety**.

268 ἄλυσις, *halysis* [11]

chains [6], chain [3], chained hand [+*1297*] [1], chained hand [+*1313*] [1]

Mk 5: 3 and no one could bind him any more, not even *with* a **chain**.
5: 4 For he *had* often *been* **chained** [+*1313*] *hand* and foot, but he tore
5: 4 but he tore the **chains** apart and broke the irons on his feet.
Lk 8:29 and *though he was* **chained** [+*1297*] *hand* and foot and kept under
Ac 12: 6 bound *with* two **chains**, and sentries stood guard at the entrance.
12: 7 "Quick, get up!" he said, and the **chains** fell off Peter's wrists.
21:33 and arrested him and ordered him to be bound *with* two **chains**.
28:20 because of the hope of Israel that I am bound with this **chain**."
Eph 6:20 for which I am an ambassador in **chains**. Pray that I may declare it
2Ti 1:16 because he often refreshed me and was not ashamed of my **chains**.
Rev 20: 1 having the key to the Abyss and holding in his hand a great **chain**.

269 ἀλυσιτελής, *alysitelēs* [1] [√ *1.1 + 3395 + 5465*]

no advantage [1]

Heb 13:17 be a joy, not a burden, for that would be of **no advantage** to you.

270 ἄλφα, *alpha* [3] [√ *1*]

Alpha [3]

Rev 1: 8 "I am the **Alpha** and the Omega," says the Lord God, "who is,
21: 6 I am the **Alpha** and the Omega, the Beginning and the End.
22:13 I am the **Alpha** and the Omega, the First and the Last,

271 Ἀλφαῖος, *Halphaios* [5]

Alphaeus [5]

Mt 10: 3 Matthew the tax collector; James son *of* **Alphaeus**, and Thaddaeus;
Mk 2:14 he saw Levi son *of* **Alphaeus** sitting at the tax collector's booth.
3:18 Thomas, James son *of* **Alphaeus**, Thaddaeus,
Lk 6:15 Matthew, Thomas, James *son of* **Alphaeus**, Simon who was called
Ac 1:13 James *son of* **Alphaeus** and Simon the Zealot, and Judas son of

272 ἅλων, *halōn* [2] [√ *262*]

threshing floor [2]

Mt 3:12 and he will clear his **threshing floor**, gathering his wheat into the
Lk 3:17 His winnowing fork is in his hand to clear his **threshing floor**

273 ἀλώπηξ, *alōpēx* [3]

foxes [2], fox [1]

Mt 8:20 Jesus replied, "**Foxes** have holes and birds of the air have nests,
Lk 9:58 Jesus replied, "**Foxes** have holes and birds of the air have nests,
13:32 He replied, "Go tell that **fox**, 'I will drive out demons and heal

274 ἅλωσις, halōsis [1] [→ 379, 384, 2914, 4648, 4649, 5260; cf. 171]

caught [1]

2Pe   2:12   creatures of instinct, born only to be **caught** and destroyed,

275 ἅμα, hama [10] [→ 570, 761; cf. 125, 604]

together [3], at the same time [2], and [1], besides [1], early in the morning [+4745] [1], one thing more [1], with [1]

Mt   13:29   you are pulling the weeds, you may root up the wheat **with** them.
    20: 1   **early in the morning** [+4745] to hire men to work in his vineyard.
Ac   24:26   **At the same time** he was hoping that Paul would offer him a bribe,
    27:40   and **at the same time** untied the ropes that held the rudders.
Ro   3:12   All have turned away, they have **together** become worthless;
Col   4: 3   **And** pray for us, too, that God may open a door for our message,
1Th   4:17   and are left will be caught up **together** with them in the clouds to
    5:10   whether we are awake or asleep, we may live **together** with him.
1Ti   5:13   **Besides**, they get into the habit of being idle and going about from
Phm   1:22   And **one thing more**: Prepare a guest room for me, because I hope

276 ἀμαθής, amathēs [1] [√ 1.1 + 3443]

ignorant [1]

2Pe   3:16   which **ignorant** and unstable people distort, as they do the other

277 ἀμαράντινος, amarantinos [1] [√ 1.1 + 3447]

never fade away [1]

1Pe   5: 4   you will receive the crown of glory that will **never fade away**.

278 ἀμάραντος, amarantos [1] [√ 1.1 + 3447]

that can never fade [1]

1Pe   1: 4   and into an inheritance **that can never** perish, spoil or **fade**—

279 ἁμαρτάνω, hamartanō [43] [→ 280, 281, 283, 387, 4579]

sin [14], sinned [12], sinning [7], sins [5], commit a sin [+281] [1], doing wrong [1], done wrong [1], leave your life of sin [+3600] [1], sinful [1]

Mt   18:15   "If your brother **sins** against you, go and show him his fault,
    18:21   how many times shall I forgive my brother when he **sins** against
    27: 4   "I have **sinned**," he said, "for I have betrayed innocent blood."
Lk   15:18   say to him: Father, I have **sinned** against heaven and against you.
    15:21   said to him, 'Father, I have **sinned** against heaven and against you.
    17: 3   "If your brother **sins**, rebuke him, and if he repents, forgive him.
    17: 4   If he **sins** against you seven times in a day, and seven times comes
Jn   5:14   well again. Stop **sinning** or something worse may happen to you."
    8:11   Jesus declared. "Go now and **leave your life of sin** [+3600]."
    9: 2   who **sinned**, this man or his parents, that he was born blind?"
    9: 3   "Neither this man nor his parents **sinned**," said Jesus, "but this
Ac   25: 8   "I have **done** nothing **wrong** against the law of the Jews or against
Ro   2:12   All who **sin** apart from the law will also perish apart from the law,
    2:12   the law, and all who **sin** under the law will be judged by the law.
    3:23   for all have **sinned** and fall short of the glory of God,
    5:12   and in this way death came to all men, because all **sinned**—
    5:14   even over those who did not **sin** by breaking a command,
    5:16   Again, the gift of God is not like the result of the one man's **sin**:
    6:15   Shall we **sin** because we are not under law but under grace?
1Co   6:18   his body, but he who sins sexually **sins** against his own body.
    7:28   But if you do marry, you have not **sinned**; and if a virgin marries,
    7:28   you have not **sinned**; and if a virgin marries, she has not **sinned**.
    7:36   should do as he wants. He is not **sinning**. They should get married.
    8:12   When you **sin** against your brothers in this way and wound their
    8:12   and wound their weak conscience, you **sin** against Christ.
    15:34   Come back to your senses as you ought, and stop **sinning**;
Eph   4:26   "In your anger do not **sin**": Do not let the sun go down while you
1Ti   5:20   Those who **sin** are to be rebuked publicly, so that the others may
Tit   3:11   You may be sure that such a man is warped and **sinful**; he is
Heb   3:17   Was it not with those who **sinned**, whose bodies fell in the desert?

    10:26   If we deliberately keep on **sinning** after we have received the
1Pe   2:20   how is it to your credit if you receive a beating for **doing wrong**
2Pe   2: 4   For if God did not spare angels when they **sinned**, but sent them to
1Jn   1:10   If we claim we have not **sinned**, we make him out to be a liar
    2: 1   My dear children, I write this to you so that you will not **sin**.
    2: 1   But if anybody does **sin**, we have one who speaks to the Father in
    3: 6   No one who lives in him keeps on **sinning**. No one who continues
    3: 6   No one who continues to **sin** has either seen him or known him.
    3: 8   the devil, because the devil has been **sinning** from the beginning.
    3: 9   he cannot go on **sinning**, because he has been born of God.
    5:16   If anyone sees his brother **commit a sin** [+281] that does not lead
    5:16   give him life. I refer to those whose **sin** does not lead to death.
    5:18   We know that anyone born of God does not continue to **sin**;

280 ἁμάρτημα, hamartēma [4] [√ 279]

sins [3], sin [1]

Mk   3:28   all the **sins** and blasphemies of men will be forgiven them.
    3:29   the Holy Spirit will never be forgiven; he is guilty of an eternal **sin**."
Ro   3:25   because in his forbearance he had left the **sins** committed
1Co   6:18   All other **sins** a man commits are outside his body, but he who sins

281 ἁμαρτία, hamartia [173] √ 279

αἴρω ἁμαρτίαν (take away sin) [2] Jn 1:29; 1Jn 3:5
ἁμαρτία ἀφιέναι (forgive sin) [20] Mt 9:2,5,6; 12:31; Mk 2:5,7,9,10; Lk 5:20,21,23,24; 7:47,48,49; 11:4; Jn 20:23; Jas 5:15; 1Jn 1:9; 2:12
ἄφεσις ἁμαρτίαν (forgiveness of sin) [11] Mt 26:28; Mk 1:4; Lk 1:77; 3:3; 24:47; Ac 2:38; 5:31; 10:43; 13:38; 26:18; Col 1:14
νόμος ... ἁμαρτία (law ... sin) [14] Ro 3:20,20; 5:13; 7:5,7,7,8,9,23,25; 8:2,3; 1Co 15:56; Jas 2:9

sin [75], sins [74], guilty of sin [+2400] [3], sin offering [2], sin offerings [+4309] [2], sinful [2], sinning [2], sins [+3836+4472] [2], commit a sin [+279] [1], guilt [1], promotes sin [+1356] [1], sin [+2237] [1], sin [+4472] [1], sin's [1], sinned [+1639+4472] [1], sins [+1639] [1], what is sinful [1], what sin was [1], without sin [+4024] [1]

Mt   1:21   the name Jesus, because he will save his people from their **sins**."
    3: 6   Confessing their **sins**, they were baptized by him in the Jordan
    9: 2   he said to the paralytic, "Take heart, son; your **sins** are forgiven."
    9: 5   to say, 'Your **sins** are forgiven,' or to say, 'Get up and walk'?
    9: 6   know that the Son of Man has authority on earth to forgive **sins**...."
    12:31   so I tell you, every **sin** and blasphemy will be forgiven men,
    26:28   which is poured out for many for the forgiveness of **sins**.
Mk   1: 4   and preaching a baptism of repentance for the forgiveness of **sins**.
    1: 5   Confessing their **sins**, they were baptized by him in the Jordan
    2: 5   their faith, he said to the paralytic, "Son, your **sins** are forgiven."
    2: 7   like that? He's blaspheming! Who can forgive **sins** but God alone?"
    2: 9   'Your **sins** are forgiven,' or to say, 'Get up, take your mat
    2:10   know that the Son of Man has authority on earth to forgive **sins**...."
Lk   1:77   the knowledge of salvation through the forgiveness of their **sins**,
    3: 3   preaching a baptism of repentance for the forgiveness of **sins**.
    5:20   Jesus saw their faith, he said, "Friend, your **sins** are forgiven."
    5:21   who speaks blasphemy? Who can forgive **sins** but God alone?"
    5:23   Which is easier: to say, 'Your **sins** are forgiven,'
    5:24   know that the Son of Man has authority on earth to forgive **sins**...."
    7:47   Therefore, I tell you, her many **sins** have been forgiven—for she
    7:48   Then Jesus said to her, "Your **sins** are forgiven."
    7:49   to say among themselves, "Who is this who even forgives **sins**?"
    11: 4   Forgive us our **sins**, for we also forgive everyone who sins against
    24:47   and forgiveness of **sins** will be preached in his name to all nations,
Jn   1:29   "Look, the Lamb of God, who takes away the **sin** of the world!
    8:21   going away, and you will look for me, and you will die in your **sin**.
    8:24   I told you that you would die in your **sins**; if you do not believe
    8:24   that I am ⸤the one I claim to be⸥, you will indeed die in your **sins**."
    8:34   you the truth, everyone who **sins** [+3836+4472] is a slave to sin.
    8:34   "I tell you the truth, everyone who sins is a slave to **sin**.
    8:46   Can any of you prove me guilty of **sin**? If I am telling the truth,
    9:34   To this they replied, "You were steeped in **sin** at birth; how dare
    9:41   "If you were blind, you would not be **guilty of sin** [+2400];
    9:41   of sin; but now that you claim you can see, your **guilt** remains.
    15:22   and spoken to them, they would not be **guilty of sin** [+2400].

15: 22   be guilty of sin. Now, however, they have no excuse for their **sin**.
15: 24   what no one else did, *they would* not *be* **guilty of sin** [+*2400*].
16: 8   he will convict the world of guilt in regard to **sin** and righteousness
16: 9   in regard to **sin**, because men do not believe in me;
19: 11   the one who handed me over to you is guilty *of* a greater **sin**."
20: 23   If you forgive anyone his **sins**, they are forgiven; if you do not

Ac   2: 38   in the name of Jesus Christ for the forgiveness *of* your **sins**.
3: 19   then, and turn to God, so that your **sins** may be wiped out,
5: 31   that he might give repentance and forgiveness *of* **sins** to Israel.
7: 60   his knees and cried out, "Lord, do not hold this **sin** against them."
10: 43   who believes in him receives forgiveness *of* **sins** through his name."
13: 38   I want you to know that through Jesus the forgiveness *of* **sins** is
22: 16   Get up, be baptized and wash your **sins** away, calling on his name.'
26: 18   so that they may receive forgiveness *of* **sins** and a place among

Ro   3: 9   made the charge that Jews and Gentiles alike are all under **sin**.
3: 20   the law; rather, through the law we become conscious *of* **sin**.
4: 7   they whose transgressions are forgiven, whose **sins** are covered.
4: 8   Blessed is the man whose **sin** the Lord will never count against
5: 12   Therefore, just as **sin** entered the world through one man,
5: 12   and death through **sin**, and in this way death came to all men,
5: 13   for before the law was given, **sin** was in the world. But sin is not
5: 13   the world. But **sin** is not taken into account when there is no law.
5: 20   But where **sin** increased, grace increased all the more,
5: 21   so that, just as **sin** reigned in death, so also grace might reign
6: 1   then? Shall we go on **sinning** so that grace may increase?
6: 2   By no means! We died *to* **sin**; how can we live in it any longer?
6: 6   with him so that the body *of* **sin** might be done away with,
6: 6   be done away with, that we should no longer be slaves *to* **sin**—
6: 7   because anyone who has died has been freed from **sin**.
6: 10   The death he died, he died *to* **sin** once for all; but the life he lives,
6: 11   count yourselves dead *to* **sin** but alive to God in Christ Jesus.
6: 12   Therefore do not let **sin** reign in your mortal body so that you
6: 13   Do not offer the parts of your body *to* **sin**, as instruments of
6: 14   For **sin** shall not be your master, because you are not under law,
6: 16   whether you are slaves *to* **sin**, which leads to death, or to
6: 17   But thanks be to God that, though you used to be slaves *to* **sin**,
6: 18   You have been set free from **sin** and have become slaves to
6: 20   When you were slaves *to* **sin**, you were free from the control of
6: 22   But now that you have been set free from **sin** and have become
6: 23   For the wages *of* **sin** is death, but the gift of God is eternal life in
7: 5   the **sinful** passions aroused by the law were at work in our bodies,
7: 7   What shall we say, then? Is the law **sin**? Certainly not! Indeed I
7: 7   Indeed I would not have known **what sin was** except through the
7: 8   But **sin**, seizing the opportunity afforded by the commandment,
7: 8   me every kind of covetous desire. For apart from law, **sin** is dead.
7: 9   but when the commandment came, **sin** sprang to life and I died.
7: 11   For **sin**, seizing the opportunity afforded by the commandment,
7: 13   But in order that **sin** might be recognized as **sin**, it produced death
7: 13   But in order that sin might be recognized as **sin**, it produced death
7: 13   so that through the commandment **sin** might become utterly sinful.
7: 14   that the law is spiritual; but I am unspiritual, sold as a slave to **sin**.
7: 17   it is no longer I myself who do it, but it is **sin** living in me.
7: 20   it is no longer I who do it, but it is **sin** living in me that does it.
7: 23   and making me a prisoner of the law *of* **sin** at work within my
7: 25   slave to God's law, but in the sinful nature a slave to the law *of* **sin**.
8: 2   Jesus the law of the Spirit of life set me free from the law *of* **sin**
8: 3   God did by sending his own Son in the likeness *of* **sinful** man to be
8: 3   his own Son in the likeness of sinful man to be a **sin offering**.
8: 3   man to be a sin offering. And so he condemned **sin** in sinful man,
8: 10   your body is dead because of **sin**, yet your spirit is alive because of
11: 27   And this is my covenant with them when I take away their **sins**."
14: 23   not from faith; and everything that does not come from faith is **sin**.

1Co   15: 3   that Christ died for our **sins** according to the Scriptures,
15: 17   has not been raised, your faith is futile; you are still in your **sins**.
15: 56   The sting of death is **sin**,
15: 56   The sting of death is sin, and the power *of* **sin** is the law.

2Co   5: 21   God made him who had no **sin** to be sin for us, so that in him we
5: 21   God made him who had no sin to be **sin** for us, so that in him we
11: 7   Was it a **sin** for me to lower myself in order to elevate you by

Gal   1: 4   who gave himself for our **sins** to rescue us from the present evil
2: 17   are sinners, does that mean that Christ **promotes sin** [+*1356*]?
3: 22   But the Scripture declares that the whole world is a prisoner *of* **sin**,

Eph   2: 1   As for you, you were dead *in* your transgressions and **sins**,

Col   1: 14   in whom we have redemption, the forgiveness *of* **sins**.

1Th   2: 16   be saved. In this way they always heap up their **sins** to the limit.

1Ti   5: 22   in the laying on of hands, and do not share *in* the **sins** of others.

5: 24   The **sins** of some men are obvious, reaching the place of judgment

2Ti   3: 6   who are loaded down *with* **sins** and are swayed by all kinds of evil

Heb   1: 3   After he had provided purification *for* **sins**, he sat down at the right
2: 17   and that he might make atonement for the **sins** of the people.
3: 13   so that none of you may be hardened by **sin's** deceitfulness.
4: 15   been tempted in every way, just as we are—yet was without **sin**.
5: 1   them in matters related to God, to offer gifts and sacrifices for **sins**.
5: 3   This is why he has to offer sacrifices for his own **sins**, as well as
7: 27   after day, first for his own **sins**, and then for the sins of the people.
8: 12   forgive their wickedness and will remember their **sins** no more."
9: 26   the end of the ages to do away *with* **sin** by the sacrifice of himself.
9: 28   so Christ was sacrificed once to take away the **sins** of many
9: 28   and he will appear a second time, not to bear **sin**, but to bring
10: 2   once for all, and would no longer have felt guilty *for* their **sins**.
10: 3   But those sacrifices are an annual reminder *of* **sins**,
10: 4   it is impossible for the blood of bulls and goats to take away **sins**.
10: 6   burnt offerings and **sin** [+*4309*] **offerings** you were not pleased.
10: 8   burnt offerings and **sin** [+*4309*] **offerings** you did not desire,
10: 11   he offers the same sacrifices, which can never take away **sins**.
10: 12   But when this priest had offered for all time one sacrifice for **sins**,
10: 17   he adds: "Their **sins** and lawless acts I will remember no more."
10: 18   these have been forgiven, there is no longer any sacrifice for **sin**.
10: 26   received the knowledge of the truth, no sacrifice for **sins** is left,
11: 25   of God rather than to enjoy the pleasures *of* **sin** for a short time.
12: 1   off everything that hinders and the **sin** that so easily entangles,
12: 4   In your struggle against **sin**, you have not yet resisted to the point
13: 11   the blood of animals into the Most Holy Place as a **sin offering**,

Jas   1: 15   Then, after desire has conceived, it gives birth to **sin**; and sin,
1: 15   birth to sin; and **sin**, when it is full-grown, gives birth to death.
2: 9   *you* **sin** [+*2237*] and are convicted by the law as lawbreakers.
4: 17   knows the good he ought to do and doesn't do it, **sins** [+*1639*].
5: 15   raise him up. If *he has* **sinned** [+*1639+4472*], he will be forgiven.
5: 16   Therefore confess your **sins** to each other and pray for each other
5: 20   way will save him from death and cover over a multitude *of* **sins**.

1Pe   2: 22   "He committed no **sin**, and no deceit was found in his mouth."
2: 24   He himself bore our **sins** in his body on the tree, so that we might
2: 24   on the tree, so that we might die *to* **sins** and live for righteousness;
3: 18   For Christ died for **sins** once for all, the righteous for the
4: 1   because he who has suffered in his body is done with **sin**.
4: 8   each other deeply, because love covers over a multitude *of* **sins**.

2Pe   1: 9   and has forgotten that he has been cleansed *from* his past **sins**.
2: 14   With eyes full of adultery, they never stop **sinning**; they seduce the

1Jn   1: 7   and the blood of Jesus, his Son, purifies us from all **sin**.
1: 8   If we claim to be **without sin** [+*4024*], we deceive ourselves
1: 9   If we confess our **sins**, he is faithful and just and will forgive us
1: 9   he is faithful and just and will forgive us our **sins** and purify us
2: 2   He is the atoning sacrifice for our **sins**, and not only for ours
2: 12   because your **sins** have been forgiven on account of his name.
3: 4   Everyone who **sins** [+*3836+4472*] breaks the law; in fact,
3: 4   Everyone who sins breaks the law; in fact, **sin** is lawlessness.
3: 5   you know that he appeared so that he might take away our **sins**.
3: 5   so that he might take away our sins. And in him is no **sin**.
3: 8   He who does **what is sinful** is of the devil, because the devil has
3: 9   No one who is born of God *will continue to* **sin** [+*4472*],
4: 10   he loved us and sent his Son as an atoning sacrifice for our **sins**.
5: 16   If anyone sees his brother **commit a sin** [+*279*] that does not lead
5: 16   There is a **sin** that leads to death. I am not saying that he should
5: 17   All wrongdoing is **sin**, and there is sin that does not lead to death.
5: 17   All wrongdoing is sin, and there is **sin** that does not lead to death.

Rev   1: 5   To him who loves us and has freed us from our **sins** by his blood,
18: 4   "Come out of her, my people, so that you will not share *in* her **sins**,
18: 5   for her **sins** are piled up to heaven, and God has remembered her

---

282   ἀμάρτυρος, *amartyros* [1]   [√ *1.1* + *3459*]

without testimony [1]

Ac   14: 17   Yet he has not left himself **without testimony**: He has shown

---

283   ἁμαρτωλός, *hamartōlos* [47]   [√ *279*]

sinners [29], sinner [9], sinful [6], sinful life [1], sinner [+*467*] [1], sinner [+*476*] [1]

Mt   9: 10   and "**sinners**" came and ate with him and his disciples.
9: 11   "Why does your teacher eat with tax collectors and '**sinners**'?"

9:13 For I have not come to call the righteous, but **sinners**."
11:19 a friend *of* tax collectors and "**sinners**." ' But wisdom is proved
26:45 and the Son of Man is betrayed into the hands *of* **sinners**.
Mk 2:15 tax collectors and "**sinners**" were eating with him and his disciples,
2:16 of the law who were Pharisees saw him eating with the "**sinners**"
2:16 his disciples: "Why does he eat with tax collectors and '**sinners**'?"
2:17 but the sick. I have not come to call the righteous, but **sinners**."
8:38 of me and my words in this adulterous and **sinful** generation,
14:41 Look, the Son of Man is betrayed into the hands *of* **sinners**.
Lk 5:8 knees and said, "Go away from me, Lord; I am a **sinful** man!"
5:30 "Why do you eat and drink with tax collectors and '**sinners**'?"
5:32 I have not come to call the righteous, but **sinners** to repentance."
6:32 credit is that to you? Even '**sinners**' love those who love them.
6:33 are good to you, what credit is that to you? Even '**sinners**' do that.
6:34 Even '**sinners**' lend to '**sinners**,' expecting to be repaid in full.
6:34 Even '**sinners**' lend *to* '**sinners**,' expecting to be repaid in full.
7:34 a glutton and a drunkard, a friend of tax collectors and "**sinners**." '
7:37 When a woman who had lived a **sinful life** in that town learned
7:39 touching him and what kind of woman she is—that she is a **sinner**."
13:2 "Do you think that these Galileans were worse **sinners** than all the
15:1 tax collectors and "**sinners**" were all gathering around to hear him.
15:2 muttered, "This man welcomes **sinners** and eats with them."
15:7 **sinner** who repents than over ninety-nine righteous persons who
15:10 in the presence of the angels of God over one **sinner** who repents."
18:13 but beat his breast and said, 'God, have mercy on me, a **sinner**.'
19:7 to mutter, "He has gone to be the guest of a '**sinner** [+*467*].' "
24:7 'The Son of Man must be delivered into the hands *of* **sinful** men,
Jn 9:16 others asked, "How can a **sinner** [+*476*] do such miraculous signs?"
9:24 "Give glory to God," they said. "We know this man is a **sinner**."
9:25 He replied, "Whether he is a **sinner** or not, I don't know. One thing
9:31 We know that God does not listen to **sinners**. He listens to the
Ro 3:7 so increases his glory, why am I still condemned as a **sinner**?"
5:8 love for us in this: While we were still **sinners**, Christ died for us.
5:19 the disobedience of the one man the many were made **sinners**,
7:13 so that through the commandment sin might become utterly **sinful**.
Gal 2:15 "We who are Jews by birth and not 'Gentile **sinners**'
2:17 in Christ, it becomes evident that we ourselves are **sinners**,
1Ti 1:9 but *for* lawbreakers and rebels, the ungodly and **sinful**,
1:15 Christ Jesus came into the world to save **sinners**—of whom I am
Heb 7:26 one who is holy, blameless, pure, set apart from **sinners**, exalted
12:3 Consider him who endured such opposition from **sinful** *men*,
Jas 4:8 Wash your hands, *you* **sinners**, and purify your hearts,
5:20 Whoever turns a **sinner** from the error of his way will save him
1Pe 4:18 to be saved, what will become of the ungodly and the **sinner**?"
Jude 1:15 and of all the harsh words ungodly **sinners** have spoken against

284 'Αμασίας, *Amasias*   Not used in UBS/NIV

285 ἄμαχος, *amachos* [2] [√ *1.1* + *3480*]

not quarrelsome [1], peaceable [1]

1Ti 3:3 not violent but gentle, **not quarrelsome**, not a lover of money.
Tit 3:2 to slander no one, to be **peaceable** and considerate, and to show

286 ἀμάω, *amaō* [1]

mowed [1]

Jas 5:4 The wages you failed to pay the workmen who **mowed** your fields

287 ἀμέθυστος, *amethystos* [1] [√ *1.3 [?]* + *3501*]

amethyst [1]

Rev 21:20 tenth chrysoprase, the eleventh jacinth, and the twelfth **amethyst**.

288 ἀμελέω, *ameleō* [4] [√ *1.1* + *3508*]

ignore [1], neglect [1], paid no attention [1], turned away [1]

Mt 22:5 "But they **paid no attention** and went off—one to his field,
1Ti 4:14 *Do* not **neglect** your gift, which was given you through a prophetic
Heb 2:3 how shall we escape *if we* **ignore** such a great salvation?
8:9 to my covenant, and I **turned away** from them, declares the Lord.

289 ἄμεμπτος, *amemptos* [5] [√ *1.1* + *3522*]

blameless [2], blamelessly [1], faultless [+*1181*] [1], nothing wrong with [1]

Lk 1:6 all the Lord's commandments and regulations **blamelessly**.
Php 2:15 so that you may become **blameless** and pure, children of God
3:6 the church; as for legalistic righteousness, **faultless** [+*1181*].
1Th 3:13 May he strengthen your hearts so that you will be **blameless**
Heb 8:7 For if there had been **nothing wrong with** that first covenant,

290 ἀμέμπτως, *amemptōs* [2] [√ *1.1* + *3522*]

blameless [2]

1Th 2:10 righteous and **blameless** we were among you who believed.
5:23 and body be kept **blameless** at the coming of our Lord Jesus

291 ἀμέριμνος, *amerimnos* [2] [√ *1.1* + *3533*]

free from concern [1], out of trouble [1]

Mt 28:14 to the governor, we will satisfy him and keep you **out of trouble**."
1Co 7:32 I would like you to be **free from concern**. An unmarried man is

292 ἀμετάθετος, *ametathetos* [2]
[√ *1.1* + *3552* + *5502*]

unchangeable [1], unchanging [1]

Heb 6:17 Because God wanted to make the **unchanging** *nature* of his
6:18 by two **unchangeable** things in which it is impossible for God to

293 ἀμετακίνητος, *ametakinētos* [1]
[√ *1.1* + *3552* + *3075*]

nothing move [1]

1Co 15:58 Therefore, my dear brothers, stand firm. Let **nothing move** you.

294 ἀμεταμέλητος, *ametamelētos* [2]
[√ *1.1* + *3552* + *3508*]

irrevocable [1], no regret [1]

Ro 11:29 for God's gifts and his call are **irrevocable**.
2Co 7:10 brings repentance that leads to salvation and leaves **no regret**,

295 ἀμετανόητος, *ametanoētos* [1]
[√ *1.1* + *3552* + *3808*]

unrepentant [1]

Ro 2:5 because of your stubbornness and your **unrepentant** heart,

296 ἄμετρος, *ametros* [2] [√ *1.1* + *3586*]

beyond limits [1], limits [1]

2Co 10:13 We, however, will not boast beyond *proper* **limits**, but will
10:15 Neither do we go **beyond** our **limits** by boasting of work done by

297 ἀμήν, *amēn* [129]

ἀμήν ὁ, τό (the amen) [3] 1Co 14:16; 2Co 1:20; Rev 3:14

ἀμήν ἀμήν (amen, amen [truly, truly]) [25] Jn 1:51; 3:3,5,11;
5:19,24,25; 6:26,32,47,53; 8:34,51,58; 10:1,7; 12:24;
13:16,20,21,38; 14:12; 16:20,23; 21:18

end of sentence [25] Ro 1:25; 9:5; 11:36; 15:33; 16:27; 1Co
16:24; Gal 1:5; 6:18; Eph 3:21; Php 4:20,23; 1Th 3:13; 1Ti 1:17;
6:16; 2Ti 4:18; Heb 13:21; 1Pe 4:11; 5:11; 2Pe 3:18; Jude 1:25;
Rev 1:6,7; 7:12; 22:20,21

the truth [74], Amen [30], *untranslated* [25]

Mt 5:18 I tell you **the truth**, until heaven and earth disappear,
5:26 I tell you **the truth**, you will not get out until you have paid the
6:2 I tell you **the truth**, they have received their reward in full.
6:5 I tell you **the truth**, they have received their reward in full.

6:16 I tell you **the truth**, they have received their reward in full.
8:10 and said to those following him, "I tell you **the truth**,
10:15 I tell you **the truth**, it will be more bearable for Sodom
10:23 I tell you **the truth**, you will not finish going through the cities of
10:42 of these little ones because he is my disciple, I tell you **the truth**,
11:11 I tell you **the truth**: Among those born of women there has not
13:17 For I tell you **the truth**, many prophets and righteous men longed
16:28 I tell you **the truth**, some who are standing here will not taste
17:20 I tell you **the truth**, if you have faith as small as a mustard seed,
18: 3 "I tell you **the truth**, unless you change and become like little
18:13 And if he finds it, I tell you **the truth**, he is happier about that one
18:18 "I tell you **the truth**, whatever you bind on earth will be bound in
18:19 I tell you [UBS+ ***the truth***] that if two of you on earth agree
19:23 Then Jesus said to his disciples, "I tell you **the truth**, it is hard for a
19:28 Jesus said to them, "I tell you **the truth**, at the renewal of all things,
21:21 Jesus replied, "I tell you **the truth**, if you have faith and do not
21:31 "I tell you **the truth**, the tax collectors and the prostitutes are
23:36 I tell you **the truth**, all this will come upon this generation.
24: 2 "I tell you **the truth**, not one stone here will be left on another;
24:34 I tell you **the truth**, this generation will certainly not pass away
24:47 I tell you **the truth**, he will put him in charge of all his
25:12 "But he replied, 'I tell you **the truth**, I don't know you.'
25:40 "The King will reply, 'I tell you **the truth**, whatever you did for
25:45 "He will reply, 'I tell you **the truth**, whatever you did not do for
26:13 I tell you **the truth**, wherever this gospel is preached throughout
26:21 he said, "I tell you **the truth**, one of you will betray me."
26:34 "I tell you **the truth**," Jesus answered, "this very night,
Mk 3:28 I tell you **the truth**, all the sins and blasphemies of men will be
8:12 a miraculous sign? I tell you **the truth**, no sign will be given to it."
9: 1 And he said to them, "I tell you **the truth**, some who are standing
9:41 I tell you **the truth**, anyone who gives you a cup of water in my
10:15 I tell you **the truth**, anyone who will not receive the kingdom of
10:29 "I tell you **the truth**," Jesus replied, "no one who has left home
11:23 "I tell you **the truth**, if anyone says to this mountain, 'Go, throw
12:43 Calling his disciples to him, Jesus said, "I tell you **the truth**,
13:30 I tell you **the truth**, this generation will certainly not pass away
14: 9 I tell you **the truth**, wherever the gospel is preached throughout
14:18 he said, "I tell you **the truth**, one of you will betray me—
14:25 "I tell you **the truth**, I will not drink again of the fruit of the vine
14:30 "I tell you **the truth**," Jesus answered, "today—yes, tonight—
16: S [UBS+ *imperishable proclamation of eternal salvation.* ***Amen.***]
Lk 4:24 "I tell you **the truth**," he continued, "no prophet is accepted in his
12:37 I tell you **the truth**, he will dress himself to serve, will have them
18:17 I tell you **the truth**, anyone who will not receive the kingdom of
18:29 "I tell you **the truth**," Jesus said to them, "no one who has left
21:32 "I tell you **the truth**, this generation will certainly not pass away
23:43 Jesus answered him, "I tell you **the truth**, today you will be with
Jn 1:51 He then added, "I tell you **the truth**, you shall see heaven open,
1:51 then added, "I tell you the truth, **[RPG]** you shall see heaven open,
3: 3 In reply Jesus declared, "I tell you **the truth**, no one can see the
3: 3 **[RPG]** no one can see the kingdom of God unless he is born
3: 5 Jesus answered, "I tell you **the truth**, no one can enter the kingdom
3: 5 **[RPG]** no one can enter the kingdom of God unless he is born of
3:11 I tell you **the truth**, we speak of what we know, and we testify to
3:11 I tell you the truth, **[RPG]** we speak of what we know, and we
5:19 "I tell you **the truth**, the Son can do nothing by himself; he can do
5:19 "I tell you the truth, **[RPG]** the Son can do nothing by himself;
5:24 "I tell you **the truth**, whoever hears my word and believes him who
5:24 **[RPG]** whoever hears my word and believes him who sent me has
5:25 I tell you **the truth**, a time is coming and has now come when the
5:25 **[RPG]** a time is coming and has now come when the dead will
6:26 Jesus answered, "I tell you **the truth**, you are looking for me,
6:26 **[RPG]** you are looking for me, not because you saw miraculous
6:32 Jesus said to them, "I tell you **the truth**, it is not Moses who has
6:32 **[RPG]** it is not Moses who has given you the bread from heaven,
6:47 I tell you **the truth**, he who believes has everlasting life.
6:47 I tell you the truth, **[RPG]** he who believes has everlasting life.
6:53 Jesus said to them, "I tell you **the truth**, unless you eat the flesh of
6:53 **[RPG]** unless you eat the flesh of the Son of Man and drink his
8:34 Jesus replied, "I tell you **the truth**, everyone who sins is a slave to
8:34 "I tell you the truth, **[RPG]** everyone who sins is a slave to sin.
8:51 I tell you **the truth**, if anyone keeps my word, he will never see
8:51 I tell you the truth, **[RPG]** if anyone keeps my word, he will never
8:58 "I tell you **the truth**," Jesus answered, "before Abraham was born,
8:58 "I tell you the truth," **[RPG]** Jesus answered, "before Abraham was
10: 1 "I tell you **the truth**, the man who does not enter the sheep pen by
10: 1 **[RPG]** the man who does not enter the sheep pen by the gate,
10: 7 Therefore Jesus said again, "I tell you **the truth**, I am the gate for
10: 7 said again, "I tell you the truth, **[RPG]** I am the gate for the sheep.
12:24 I tell you **the truth**, unless a kernel of wheat falls to the ground
12:24 **[RPG]** unless a kernel of wheat falls to the ground and dies,
13:16 I tell you **the truth**, no servant is greater than his master, nor is a
13:16 I tell you the truth, **[RPG]** no servant is greater than his master,
13:20 I tell you **the truth**, whoever accepts anyone I send accepts me;
13:20 you the truth, **[RPG]** whoever accepts anyone I send accepts me;
13:21 Jesus was troubled in spirit and testified, "I tell you **the truth**,
13:21 "I tell you the truth, **[RPG]** one of you is going to betray me."
13:38 I tell you **the truth**, before the rooster crows, you will disown me
13:38 I tell you the truth, **[RPG]** before the rooster crows, you will
14:12 I tell you **the truth**, anyone who has faith in me will do what I
14:12 **[RPG]** anyone who has faith in me will do what I have been
16:20 I tell you **the truth**, you will weep and mourn while the world
16:20 **[RPG]** you will weep and mourn while the world rejoices.
16:23 I tell you **the truth**, my Father will give you whatever you ask in
16:23 **[RPG]** my Father will give you whatever you ask in my name.
21:18 I tell you **the truth**, when you were younger you dressed yourself
21:18 **[RPG]** when you were younger you dressed yourself and went
Ro 1:25 things rather than the Creator—who is forever praised. **Amen.**
9: 5 ancestry of Christ, who is God over all, forever praised! **Amen.**
11:36 and to him are all things. To him be the glory forever! **Amen.**
15:33 The God of peace be with you all. **Amen.**
16:27 to the only wise God be glory forever through Jesus Christ! **Amen.**
1Co 14:16 those who do not understand say "**Amen**" to your thanksgiving,
16:24 My love to all of you in Christ Jesus. **Amen.** [UBS-]
2Co 1:20 so through him the "**Amen**" is spoken by us to the glory of God.
Gal 1: 5 to whom be glory for ever and ever. **Amen.**
6:18 grace of our Lord Jesus Christ be with your spirit, brothers. **Amen.**
Eph 3:21 Christ Jesus throughout all generations, for ever and ever! **Amen.**
Php 4:20 To our God and Father be glory for ever and ever. **Amen.**
4:23 grace of the Lord Jesus Christ be with your spirit. **Amen.** [UBS-]
1Th 3:13 when our Lord Jesus comes with all his holy ones. [UBS+ ***Amen.***]
1Ti 1:17 the only God, be honor and glory for ever and ever. **Amen.**
6:16 has seen or can see. To him be honor and might forever. **Amen.**
2Ti 4:18 his heavenly kingdom. To him be glory for ever and ever. **Amen.**
Heb 13:21 through Jesus Christ, to whom be glory for ever and ever. **Amen.**
1Pe 4:11 To him be the glory and the power for ever and ever. **Amen.**
5:11 To him be the power for ever and ever. **Amen.**
2Pe 3:18 Savior Jesus Christ. To him be glory both now and forever! **Amen.**
Jude 1:25 Christ our Lord, before all ages, now and forevermore! **Amen.**
Rev 1: 6 and Father—to him be glory and power for ever and ever! **Amen.**
1: 7 of the earth will mourn because of him. So shall it be! **Amen.**
3:14 These are the words of the **Amen**, the faithful and true witness,
5:14 creatures said, "**Amen**," and the elders fell down and worshiped.
7:12 "**Amen**! Praise and glory and wisdom and thanks and honor
7:12 and power and strength be to our God for ever and ever. **Amen**!"
19: 4 who was seated on the throne. And they cried: "**Amen**, Hallelujah!"
22:20 things says, "Yes, I am coming soon." **Amen.** Come, Lord Jesus.
22:21 The grace of the Lord Jesus be with God's people. **Amen.** [UBS-]

298 ἀμήτωρ, *amētōr* [1] [√ *1.1 + 3613*]

without mother [1]

Heb 7: 3 **Without** father or **mother**, without genealogy, without beginning

299 ἀμίαντος, *amiantos* [4] [√ *1.1 + 3620*]

pure [2], faultless [1], that can never spoil [1]

Heb 7:26 one who is holy, blameless, **pure**, set apart from sinners, exalted
13: 4 and the marriage bed kept **pure**, for God will judge the adulterer
Jas 1:27 Religion that God our Father accepts as pure and **faultless** is this:
1Pe 1: 4 and into an inheritance **that can never** perish, **spoil** or fade—

300 'Αμιναδάβ, *Aminadab* [3]

Amminadab [3]

Mt 1: 4 Ram the father of **Amminadab**, Amminadab the father of
1: 4 **Amminadab** the father of Nahshon, Nahshon the father of Salmon,
Lk 3:33 the son *of* **Amminadab**, the son of Ram, the son of Hezron,

301 ἄμμον, **ammon**   Not used in UBS/NIV [√ *302*]

302 ἄμμος, **ammos**   [5]   [→ *301*]

sand [4], shore [1]

Mt   7:26 into practice is like a foolish man who built his house on **sand**.
Ro   9:27 "Though the number of the Israelites be like the **sand** by the sea,
Heb 11:12 as the stars in the sky and as countless as the **sand** on the seashore.
Rev 13: 1 And the dragon stood on the **shore** of the sea. And I saw a beast
      20: 8 them for battle. In number they are like the **sand** on the seashore.

303 ἀμνός, **amnos**   [4]

lamb [4]

Jn   1:29 saw Jesus coming toward him and said, "Look, the **Lamb** of God,
      1:36 When he saw Jesus passing by, he said, "Look, the **Lamb** of God!"
Ac   8:32 and as a **lamb** before the shearer is silent, so he did not open his
1Pe   1:19 the precious blood of Christ, a **lamb** without blemish or defect.

304 ἀμοιβή, **amoibē**   [1]

repaying [+*625*] [1]

1Ti   5: 4 own family and so **repaying** [+*625*] their parents and grandparents,

305 ἄμορφος, **amorphos**   Not used in UBS/NIV
       [√ *1.1 + 3671*]

306 ἄμπελος, **ampelos**   [9]   [→ *307, 308*]

vine [7], grapes [1], grapevine [1]

Mt 26:29 I will not drink of this fruit *of* the **vine** from now on until that day
Mk 14:25 I will not drink again of the fruit *of* the **vine** until that day when I
Lk 22:18 For I tell you I will not drink again of the fruit *of* the **vine** until the
Jn   15: 1 "I am the true **vine**, and my Father is the gardener.
     15: 4 No branch can bear fruit by itself; it must remain in the **vine**.
     15: 5 "I am the **vine**; you are the branches. If a man remains in me
Jas   3:12 My brothers, can a fig tree bear olives, or a **grapevine** bear figs?
Rev 14:18 sharp sickle and gather the clusters of grapes *from* the earth's **vine**,
     14:19 gathered its **grapes** and threw them into the great winepress of

307 ἀμπελουργός, **ampelourgos**   [1]   [√ *306 + 2240*]

took care of the vineyard [1]

Lk   13: 7 So he said to the man who **took care of the vineyard**, 'For three

308 ἀμπελών, **ampelōn**   [23]   [√ *306*]

vineyard [23]

Mt 20: 1 went out early in the morning to hire men to work in his **vineyard**.
     20: 2 to pay them a denarius for the day and sent them into his **vineyard**.
     20: 4 He told them, 'You also go and work in my **vineyard**, and I will
     20: 7 "He said to them, 'You also go and work in my **vineyard**.'
     20: 8 the owner *of* the **vineyard** said to his foreman, 'Call the workers
     21:28 to the first and said, 'Son, go and work today in the **vineyard**.'
     21:33 There was a landowner who planted a **vineyard**. He put a wall
     21:39 they took him and threw him out *of* the **vineyard** and killed him.
     21:40 "Therefore, when the owner *of* the **vineyard** comes, what will he do
     21:41 they replied, "and he will rent the **vineyard** to other tenants,
Mk 12: 1 "A man planted a **vineyard**. He put a wall around it, dug a pit for
     12: 2 the tenants to collect from them some of the fruit *of* the **vineyard**.
     12: 8 they took him and killed him, and threw him out of the **vineyard**.
     12: 9 "What then will the owner *of* the **vineyard** do? He will come
     12: 9 will come and kill those tenants and give the **vineyard** to others.
Lk   13: 6 "A man had a fig tree, planted in his **vineyard**, and he went to look
     20: 9 "A man planted a **vineyard**, rented it to some farmers and went
     20:10 so they would give him some of the fruit *of* the **vineyard**.
     20:13 "Then the owner *of* the **vineyard** said, 'What shall I do? I will send
     20:15 So they threw him out *of* the **vineyard** and killed him. "What
     20:15 killed him. "What then will the owner *of* the **vineyard** do to them?
     20:16 will come and kill those tenants and give the **vineyard** to others."
1Co   9: 7 Who plants a **vineyard** and does not eat of its grapes? Who tends a

309 Ἀμπλιᾶτος, **Ampliatos**   [1]

Ampliatus [1]

Ro 16: 8 Greet **Ampliatus**, whom I love in the Lord.

310 ἀμύνομαι, **amynomai**   [1]

went to defense [1]

Ac   7:24 so he **went to** *his* **defense** and avenged him by killing the

311 ἀμφιβάλλω, **amphiballō**   [1]   [→ *312; cf. 965*]

casting a net [1]

Mk   1:16 he saw Simon and his brother Andrew **casting a net** into the lake,

312 ἀμφίβληστρον, **amphiblēstron**   [1]   [√ *311*]

net [1]

Mt   4:18 They were casting a **net** into the lake, for they were fishermen.

313 ἀμφιέζω, **amphiezō**   [1]   [→ *314; cf. 2667*]

clothes [1]

Lk   12:28 If that is how God **clothes** the grass of the field, which is here

314 ἀμφιέννυμι, **amphiennymi**   [3]   [√ *313*]

dressed [2], clothes [1]

Mt   6:30 If that is how God **clothes** the grass of the field, which is here
     11: 8 A man **dressed** in fine clothes? No, those who wear fine clothes
Lk   7:25 A man **dressed** in fine clothes? No, those who wear expensive

315 Ἀμφίπολις, **Amphipolis**   [1]   [√ *4484*]

Amphipolis [1]

Ac   17: 1 When they had passed through **Amphipolis** and Apollonia,

316 ἄμφοδον, **amphodon**   [1]   [√ *3847*]

street [1]

Mk 11: 4 They went and found a colt outside in the **street**, tied at a doorway.

317 ἀμφότεροι, **amphoteroi**   [14]

both [11], all [2], two [1]

Mt   9:17 they pour new wine into new wineskins, and **both** are preserved."
     13:30 Let **both** grow together until the harvest. At that time I will tell the
     15:14 If a blind man leads a blind man, **both** will fall into a pit."
Lk   1: 6 **Both** of them were upright in the sight of God, observing all the
      1: 7 Elizabeth was barren; and they were **both** well along in years.
      5: 7 and they came and filled **both** boats so full that they began to sink.
      6:39 a blind man lead a blind man? Will they not **both** fall into a pit?
      7:42 had the money to pay him back, so he canceled the debts of **both**.
Ac   8:38 Then **both** Philip and the eunuch went down into the water
     19:16 who had the evil spirit jumped on them and overpowered *them* **all**.
     23: 8 neither angels nor spirits, but the Pharisees acknowledge them **all**.)
Eph   2:14 who has made the **two** one and has destroyed the barrier,
      2:16 and in this one body to reconcile **both** of them to God through the
      2:18 For through him we **both** have access to the Father by one Spirit.

318 ἀμώμητος, **amōmētos**   [1]   [√ *1.1 + 3522*]

blameless [1]

2Pe   3:14 every effort to be found spotless, **blameless** and at peace with him.

319 ἄμωμον, **amōmon**   [1]

spice [1]

Rev 18:13 cargoes of cinnamon and **spice**, of incense, myrrh

320 ἄμωμος, amōmos [8] [√ *1.1 + 3522*]

blameless [3], without blemish [2], without fault [2], unblemished [1]

Eph 1: 4 the creation of the world to be holy and **blameless** in his sight.
5:27 or wrinkle or any other blemish, but holy and **blameless**.
Php 2:15 children of God **without fault** in a crooked and depraved
Col 1:22 you holy in his sight, **without blemish** and free from accusation—
Heb 9:14 who through the eternal Spirit offered himself **unblemished** to
1Pe 1:19 the precious blood of Christ, a lamb **without blemish** or defect.
Jude 1:24 and to present you before his glorious presence **without fault**
Rev 14: 5 No lie was found in their mouths; they are **blameless**.

321 Ἀμών, Amōn [0 / 2]

Amon [2]

Mt 1:10 Manasseh the father of **Amon**, [UBS *322*] Amon the father of
1:10 the father of Amon, **Amon** [UBS *322*] the father of Josiah,

322 Ἀμώς, Amōs [3 / 1]

Amos [1]

Mt 1:10 Manasseh the father of Amon, [UBS *Amos*; NIV *321*]
1:10 Amon [UBS *Amos*; NIV *321*] the father of Josiah,
Lk 3:25 the son *of* Amos, the son of Nahum, the son of Esli, the son of

323 ἄν, an [166 / 167] [→ *1569, 1570, 2054, 2829, 4020, 6056*]

would have [24], whoever [+*4005*] [19], if [17], would [17], until [+*2401*] [14], anyone [+*4005*] [10], whom [+*4005*] [5], *untranslated* [4], before [+*2401*] [4], the one [+*4005*] [2], whatever [+*4005*] [2], so that [+*3968*] [2], that [+*3968*] [2], till [+*2401*] [2], whatever [+*4005+5516*] [2], whatever [+*5516*] [2], when [+*4005*] [2], when [+*6055*] [2], wherever [+*3963*] [2], which [+*5515*] [2], who [+*4005*] [2], whoever [+*4015*] [2], once [+*608+4005*] [1], what [+*1254+1877+4005*] [1], what [+*5515*] [1], when [1], all [+*4012*] [1], all whom [+*4012*] [1], any [+*4005+5516*] [1], any [+*4005*] [1], as [+*2776*] [1], as soon as [+*6055*] [1], before [+*2445+4570*] [1], could have [1], everything [+*4012+4246*] [1], except [+*1623+3614*] [1], had [+*2400*] [1], if any [+*4005*] [1], meaning [+*1639+5515*] [1], might [1], pray [+*2377*] [1], somehow or other [+*6055*] [1], trying to [+*6055*] [1], until [+*948+4005*] [1], what [+*5516*] [1], what going on [+*4047+5515*] [1], whatever [+*4012*] [1], when [+*2471*] [1], whoever [+*3836*] [1]

Mt 2:13 Stay there until [+*2401*] I tell you, for Herod is going to search for
5:18 I tell you the truth, until [+*2401*] heaven and earth disappear,
5:18 will by any means disappear from the Law until [+*2401*]
5:19 but whoever [+*4005*] practices and teaches these commands will
5:21 and anyone [+*4005*] who murders will be subject to judgment.'
5:22 Again, anyone [+*4005*] who says to his brother, 'Raca,'
5:22 to the Sanhedrin. But anyone [+*4005*] who says, 'You fool!'
5:26 you will not get out until [+*2401*] you have paid the last penny.
5:31 'Anyone [+*4005*] who divorces his wife must give her a certificate
10:11 "Whatever [+*4005*] town or village you enter, search for some
10:11 worthy person there and stay at his house until [+*2401*] you leave.
10:14 If anyone will not welcome you or listen to your words,
10:23 will not finish going through the cities of Israel before [+*2401*]
10:33 But whoever [+*4015*] disowns me before men, I will disown him
10:42 And if anyone gives even a cup of cold water to one of these little
11:21 they would have repented long ago in sackcloth and ashes.
11:23 had been performed in Sodom, it would have remained to this day.
12: 7 not sacrifice,' you would not have condemned the innocent.
12:20 wick he will not snuff out, till [+*2401*] he leads justice to victory.
12:32 but anyone [+*4005*] who speaks against the Holy Spirit will not be
12:50 For whoever [+*4015*] does the will of my Father in heaven is my
15: 5 But you say that if a man says to his father or mother,
16:25 will lose it, but whoever [+*4005*] loses his life for me will find it.
16:28 some who are standing here will not taste death before [+*2401*]
18: 6 But if anyone causes one of these little ones who believe in me to
19: 9 I tell you that anyone [+*4005*] who divorces his wife, except for
20:27 and whoever [+*4005*] wants to be first must be your slave—

21:22 If you believe, you will receive whatever you ask for in prayer."
21:44 broken to pieces, but he on whom [+*4005*] it falls will be crushed."
22:44 "Sit at my right hand until [+*2401*] I put your enemies under your
23:16 You say, 'If anyone swears by the temple, it means nothing;
23:16 but if anyone swears by the gold of the temple, he is bound by his
23:18 You also say, 'If anyone swears by the altar, it means nothing;
23:18 but if anyone swears by the gift on it, he is bound by his oath.'
23:30 we would not have taken part with them in shedding the blood of
23:39 For I tell you, you will not see me again until [+*2401*] you say,
24:22 If those days had not been cut short, no one would survive,
24:34 this generation will certainly not pass away until [+*2401*] all these
24:43 he would have kept watch and would not have let his house be
24:43 have kept watch and would not have let his house be broken into.
25:27 so that when I returned I would have received it back with interest.
26:48 signal with them: "The one [+*4005*] I kiss is the man; arrest him."
Mk 3:29 But whoever [+*4005*] blasphemes against the Holy Spirit will
3:35 Whoever [+*4005*] does God's will is my brother and sister
6:10 you enter a house, stay there until [+*2401*] you leave that town.
6:11 And if [+*4005*] any place will not welcome you or listen to you,
6:56 And wherever [+*3963*] he went—into villages, towns
6:56 edge of his cloak, and all [+*4012*] who touched him were healed.
8:35 but whoever [+*4005*] loses his life for me and for the gospel will
9: 1 some who are standing here will not taste death before [+*2401*]
9:37 "Whoever [+*4005*] welcomes one of these little children in my
9:37 and whoever [+*4005*] welcomes me does not welcome me
9:41 anyone [+*4005*] who gives you a cup of water in my name
9:42 "And if anyone causes one of these little ones who believe in me to
10:11 "Anyone [+*4005*] who divorces his wife and marries another
10:15 I tell you the truth, anyone [+*4005*] who will not receive the
10:43 whoever [+*4005*] wants to become great among you must be your
10:44 and whoever [+*4005*] wants to be first must be slave of all.
11:23 "I tell you the truth, If anyone says to this mountain, 'Go, throw
12:36 "Sit at my right hand until [+*2401*] I put your enemies under your
13:20 If the Lord had not cut short those days, no one would survive.
14:44 "The one [+*4005*] I kiss is the man; arrest him and lead him away
Lk 1:62 to his father, to find out what he would like to name the child.
2:26 would not die before [+*2445+4570*] he had seen the Lord's Christ.
2:35 so that [+*3968*] the thoughts of many hearts will be revealed.
6:11 and began to discuss with one another what they might do to Jesus.
7:39 he would know who is touching him and what kind of woman she
8:18 Whoever [+*4005*] has will be given more; whoever does not have,
8:18 whoever [+*4005*] does not have, even what he thinks he has will
9: 4 Whatever [+*4005*] house you enter, stay there until you leave that
9: 5 If people do not welcome you, shake the dust off your feet when
9:24 For whoever [+*4005*] wants to save his life will lose it,
9:24 will lose it, but whoever [+*4005*] loses his life for me will save it.
9:26 If anyone is ashamed of me and my words, the Son of Man will be
9:27 some who are standing here will not taste death before [+*2401*]
9:46 An argument started among the disciples as to which [+*5515*] of
9:48 and whoever [+*4005*] welcomes me welcomes the one who sent
10: 5 "When you enter a house, first say, 'Peace to this house.'
10: 8 "When [+*4005*] you enter a town and are welcomed, eat what is
10:10 But when [+*4005*] you enter a town and are not welcomed,
10:13 performed in Tyre and Sidon, they would have repented long ago,
10:35 I will reimburse you for any [+*4005+5516*] extra expense you may
12: 8 "I tell you, whoever [+*4005*] acknowledges me before men,
12:39 thief was coming, he would not have let his house be broken into.
13:25 Once [+*608+4005*] the owner of the house gets up and closes the
15:26 of the servants and asked him what was going on [+*4047+5515*].
17: 6 you can say [NIE] to this mulberry tree, 'Be uprooted and planted
17: 6 'Be uprooted and planted in the sea,' and it will obey [NIE] you.
17:33 life will lose it, and whoever [+*4005*] loses his life will preserve it.
18:17 anyone [+*4005*] who will not receive the kingdom of God like a
19:23 so that when I came back, I could have collected it with interest?'
20:18 broken to pieces, but he on whom [+*4005*] it falls will be crushed."
20:43 until [+*2401*] I make your enemies a footstool for your feet."'
21:32 this generation will certainly not pass away until [+*2401*] all these
Jn 1:33 'The man on whom [+*4005*] you see the Spirit come down
2: 5 said to the servants, "Do whatever [+*4005+5516*] he tells you."
4:10 you would have asked him and he would have given you living
4:10 would have asked him and he would have given you living water."
4:14 but whoever [+*4005*] drinks the water I give him will never thirst.
5:19 he can do only what [+*5516*] he sees his Father doing,
5:46 believed Moses, you would believe me, for he wrote about me.
8:19 Jesus replied. "If you knew me, you would know my Father also."
8:42 you would love me, for I came from God and now am here.

9:41 Jesus said, "If you were blind, you **would** not be guilty of sin;
11:21 to Jesus, "if you had been here, my brother **would** not **have** died."
11:22 But I know that even now God will give you **whatever** [+*4012*]
11:32 "Lord, if you had been here, my brother **would** not **have** died."
13:20 you the truth, **whoever** [+*3836*] accepts anyone I send accepts me;
13:24 to this disciple and said, "Ask him **which** [+*5515*] one he means."
14: 2 house are many rooms; if it were not so, I **would have** told you.
14: 7 you really knew me, you **would** [UBS-] know my Father as well.
14:13 And I will do **whatever** [+*5516*] you ask in my name, so that the
14:28 If you loved me, you **would** be glad that I am going to the Father,
15:16 Then the Father will give you **whatever** [+*4005+5516*] you ask in
15:19 If you belonged to the world, it **would** love you as its own.
16:23 my Father will give you **whatever** [+*5516*] you ask in my name.
18:30 they replied, "we **would** not **have** handed him over to you."
18:36 my servants **would** fight to prevent my arrest by the Jews.
20:23 **If** you forgive anyone his sins, they are forgiven; if you do not
20:23 are forgiven; **if** you do not forgive them, they are not forgiven."
Ac 2:21 And everyone **who** [+*4005*] calls on the name of the Lord will be
2:35 **until** [+*2401*] I make your enemies a footstool for your feet." '
2:39 who are far off—for **all whom** [+*4012*] the Lord our God will call."
2:45 and goods, they gave to anyone **as** [+*2776*] he had need.
3:19 **that** [+*3968*] times of refreshing may come from the Lord,
3:22 you must listen to **everything** [+*4012+4246*] he tells you.
4:35 and it was distributed to anyone as he **had** [+*2400*] need.
5:24 chief priests were puzzled, wondering what **would** come of this.
7: 3 God said, 'and go to the land [NIE] I will show you.'
8:31 [NIE] "How can I," he said, "unless someone explains it to me?"
10:17 While Peter was wondering about the **meaning** [+*1639+5515*] of
15:17 **that** [+*3968*] the remnant of men may seek the Lord, and all the
17:18 Some of them asked, "**What** [+*5515*] is this babbler trying to say?"
18:14 or serious crime, it **would** be reasonable for me to listen to you.
26:29 I **pray** [+*2377*] God that not only you but all who are listening to
Ro 3: 4 "**So that** [+*3968*] you may be proved right when you speak
9:15 says to Moses, "I will have mercy on **whom** [+*4005*] I have mercy,
9:15 and I will have compassion **on whom** [+*4005*] I have compassion."
9:29 we **would have** become like Sodom, we would have been like
9:29 have become like Sodom, we **would have** been like Gomorrah."
10:13 "Everyone **who** [+*4005*] calls on the name of the Lord will be
15:24 I plan to do so **when** [+*6055*] I go to Spain. I hope to visit you
16: 2 and to give her **any** [+*4005*] help she may need from you,
1Co 2: 8 for if they had, they **would** not **have** crucified the Lord of glory.
4: 5 before the appointed time; wait **till** [+*2401*] the Lord comes.
7: 5 Do not deprive each other **except** [+*1623+3614*] by mutual consent
11:27 **whoever** [+*4005*] eats the bread or drinks the cup of the Lord in an
11:31 But if we judged ourselves, we **would** not come under judgment.
11:34 And **when** [+*6055*] I come I will give further directions.
12: 2 **somehow or other** [+*6055*] you were influenced and led astray to
2Co 3:15 Even to this day **when** [+*2471*] Moses is read, a veil covers their
10: 9 I do not want to seem to be **trying to** [+*6055*] frighten you with my
11:21 **What** [+*1254+1877+4005*] anyone else dares to boast about—
Gal 1:10 I were still trying to please men, I **would** not be a servant of Christ.
3:21 then righteousness **would** certainly **have** come by the law.
Php 2:23 to send him **as soon as** [+*6055*] I see how things go with me.
Heb 1:13 "Sit at my right hand **until** [+*2401*] I make your enemies a footstool
4: 8 them rest, God **would** not **have** spoken later about another day.
8: 4 If he were on earth, he **would** not be a priest, for there are already
8: 7 that first covenant, no place **would have** been sought for another.
10: 2 If it could, **would** they not **have** stopped being offered? For the
11:15 country they had left, they **would have** had opportunity to return.
1Jn 2: 5 But if anyone obeys his word, God's love is truly made complete
2:19 For if they had belonged to us, they **would have** remained with us;
3:17 **If** anyone has material possessions and sees his brother in need
Rev 2:25 Only hold on to what you have **until** [+*948+4005*] I come.
14: 4 They follow the Lamb **wherever** [+*3963*] he goes.

324 ἀνά, ana [13]

[→ *327, 329, 330, 331, 332, 333, 334, 335, 336, 341, 342, 343, 344, 345, 346, 347, 348, 349, 350, 351, 352, 353, 355, 358, 359, 361, 362, 363, 364, 365, 366, 367, 368, 369, 370, 371, 372, 373, 374, 375, 376, 377, 378, 379, 380, 381, 382, 384, 385, 386, 388, 389, 390, 391, 392, 398, 399, 400, 401, 402, 404, 405, 407, 408, 409, 411, 412, 413, 414, 415, 416, 417, 418, 419, 420, 421, 423, 426, 427, 428, 429, 430, 431, 432, 433, 434, 445, 452, 456, 457, 461, 462, 465, 479, 482, 488, 494, 496, 499, 1983, 1985, 2056, 2057,* 2058, 2059, 2060, 2061, 2914, 4646, 4647, 4648, 4649, 4650, 4651, 4652, 5262, 5263, 5264, 5265, 5266; cf. *403, 424, 458, 487, 539*]

each [2], *untranslated* [1], among [+*3545*] [1], at [1], between [+*3545*] [1], each [+*1651+1667*] [1], each one [+*3836*] [1], extra [+*1545*] [1], from [1], into [+*3545*] [1], one at a time [+*3538*] [1], two by two [+*1545+1545*] [1]

Mt 13:25 his enemy came and sowed weeds **among** [+*3545*] the wheat,
20: 9 hired about the eleventh hour came and **each** received a denarius.
20:10 But **each** [+*3836*] **one** of them also received a denarius.
Mk 7:31 to the Sea of Galilee and **into** [+*3545*] the region of the Decapolis.
Lk 9: 3 no staff, no bag, no bread, no money, no **extra** [+*1545*] tunic.
9:14 to his disciples, "Have them sit down in groups of about fifty **each**."
10: 1 and sent them **two by two** [+*1545+1545*] ahead of him to every
Jn 2: 6 ceremonial washing, each holding **from** twenty to thirty gallons.
1Co 6: 5 you wise enough to judge a dispute **between** [+*3545*] believers?
14:27 should speak, **one at a time** [+*3538*], and someone must interpret.
Rev 4: 8 Each of the four living creatures had **[RPG]** six wings and was
7:17 For the Lamb **at** the center of the throne will be their shepherd.
21:21 twelve pearls, **each** [+*1651+1667*] gate made of a single pearl.

325 ἀναβαθμός, anabathmos [2] [√ *326*]

steps [2]

Ac 21:35 When Paul reached the **steps**, the violence of the mob was
21:40 Paul stood on the **steps** and motioned to the crowd.

326 ἀναβαίνω, anabainō [82]

[→ *325, 328, 563, 609, 957, 1000, 1010, 1011, 1012, 1013, 1014, 1037, 1117, 1329, 1331, 1674, 1676, 1832, 1836, 1837, 2094, 2097, 2849, 2853, 2854, 3028, 3553, 4124, 4126, 4127, 4581, 4583, 4584, 4585, 4586, 4646, 5160, 5201, 5204, 5262, 5648*]

went up [23], going up [7], come up [5], go up [4], went [4], ascend [3], ascended [3], came up [3], climbed [3], coming [2], coming up [2], grew up [2], ascending [1], catch [1], climbed aboard [1], climbs in [1], comes up [1], conceived [1], decided [+*2093+2840+3836*], go [1], goes up [1], gone [1], grows [1], left [1], marched [1], reached [1], returned [1], returning [1], rise [1], rises [1], rose [1], went upstairs [1], were up [+*1639*] [1]

Mt 3:16 As soon as Jesus was baptized, *he* **went up** out of the water.
5: 1 he saw the crowds, *he* **went up** on a mountainside and sat down.
13: 7 seed fell among thorns, which **grew up** and choked the plants.
14:23 dismissed them, *he* **went up** on a mountainside by himself to pray.
14:32 And *when* they **climbed** into the boat, the wind died down.
15:29 Sea of Galilee. Then he **went up** on a mountainside and sat down.
17:27 Take the first fish you **catch**; open its mouth and you will find a
20:17 Now *as* Jesus *was* **going up** to Jerusalem, he took the twelve
20:18 "*We are* **going up** to Jerusalem, and the Son of Man will be
Mk 1:10 As Jesus *was* **coming up** out of the water, he saw heaven being
3:13 Jesus **went up** on a mountainside and called to him those he
4: 7 seed fell among thorns, which **grew up** and choked the plants,
4: 8 It **came up**, grew and produced a crop, multiplying thirty,
4:32 *it* **grows** and becomes the largest of all garden plants,
6:51 Then *he* **climbed** into the boat with them, and the wind died down.
10:32 *They* **were** on their way **up** [+*1639*] to Jerusalem, with Jesus
10:33 "*We are* **going up** to Jerusalem," he said, "and the Son of Man will
15: 8 The crowd **came up** and asked Pilate to do for them what he
Lk 2: 4 So Joseph also **went up** from the town of Nazareth in Galilee to
2:42 years old, they **went up** to the Feast, according to the custom.
5:19 *they* **went up** on the roof and lowered him on his mat through the
9:28 and James with him and **went up** onto a mountain to pray.
18:10 "Two men **went up** to the temple to pray, one a Pharisee
18:31 the Twelve aside and told them, "*We are* **going up** to Jerusalem,
19: 4 So he ran ahead and **climbed** a sycamore-fig tree to see him,
19:28 After Jesus had said this, he went on ahead, **going up** to Jerusalem.
24:38 "Why are you troubled, and why *do* doubts **rise** in your minds?
Jn 1:51 and the angels of God **ascending** and descending on the Son of
2:13 almost time for the Jewish Passover, Jesus **went up** to Jerusalem.
3:13 No one *has ever* **gone** into heaven except the one who came from
5: 1 time later, Jesus **went up** to Jerusalem for a feast of the Jews.
6:62 What if you see the Son of Man **ascend** to where he was before!
7: 8 You **go** to the Feast. I am not yet going up to this Feast,

7: 8   I *am* not yet **going up** to this Feast, because for me the right time
7: 10   However, after his brothers *had* **left** for the Feast, he went also,
7: 10   had left for the Feast, he **went** also, not publicly, but in secret.
7: 14   Not until halfway through the Feast *did* Jesus **go up** to the temple
10: 1   the gate, but **climbs in** by some other way, is a thief and a robber.
11: 55   many **went up** from the country to Jerusalem for their ceremonial
12: 20   Now there were some Greeks among those *who* **went up** to
20: 17   "Do not hold on to me, for *I have* not yet **returned** to the Father.
20: 17   '*I am* **returning** to my Father and your Father, to my God
21: 11   Simon Peter **climbed aboard** and dragged the net ashore.

Ac   1: 13   *they* **went** upstairs to the room where they were staying.
2: 34   For David *did* not **ascend** to heaven, and yet he said, " 'The Lord
3: 1   and John *were* **going up** to the temple at the time of prayer—
7: 23   he **decided** [+2093+2840+3836] to visit his fellow Israelites.
8: 31   it to me?" So he invited Philip *to* **come up** and sit with him.
8: 39   When *they* **came up** out of the water, the Spirit of the Lord
10: 4   and gifts to the poor *have* **come up** as a memorial offering before
10: 9   and approaching the city, Peter **went up** on the roof to pray.
11: 2   So when Peter **went up** to Jerusalem, the circumcised believers
15: 2   *to* **go up** to Jerusalem to see the apostles and elders about this
18: 22   he **went up** and greeted the church and then went down to
20: 11   Then *he* **went upstairs** *again* and broke bread and ate. After
21: 6   to each other, *we* **went** aboard the ship, and they returned home.
21: 12   and the people there pleaded with Paul not *to* **go up** to Jerusalem.
21: 15   After this, *we* got ready and **went up** to Jerusalem.
21: 31   news **reached** the commander of the Roman troops that the whole
24: 11   You can easily verify that no more than twelve days ago *I* **went up**
25: 1   in the province, Festus **went up** from Caesarea to Jerusalem,
25: 9   "Are you willing to **go up** to Jerusalem and stand trial before me
Ro   10: 6   'Who *will* **ascend** into heaven?' " (that is, to bring Christ down)
1Co   2: 9   no mind *has* **conceived** what God has prepared for those who love
Gal   2: 1   Fourteen years later *I* **went up** again to Jerusalem, this time with
2: 2   *I* **went** in response to a revelation and set before them the gospel
Eph   4: 8   "When he **ascended** on high, he led captives in his train and gave
4: 9   (What does "*he* **ascended**" mean except that he also descended to
4: 10   He who descended is the very one who **ascended** higher than all
Rev   4: 1   "**Come up** here, and I will show you what must take place after
7: 2   Then I saw another angel **coming up** from the east, having the seal
8: 4   prayers of the saints, **went up** before God from the angel's hand.
9: 2   smoke **rose** from it like the smoke from a gigantic furnace.
11: 7   the beast that **comes up** from the Abyss will attack them,
11: 12   heard a loud voice from heaven saying to them, "**Come up** here."
11: 12   And *they* **went up** to heaven in a cloud, while their enemies
13: 1   And I saw a beast **coming** out of the sea. He had ten horns
13: 11   Then I saw another beast, **coming** out of the earth. He had two
14: 11   And the smoke of their torment **rises** for ever and ever. There is no
17: 8   and will **come up** out of the Abyss and go to his destruction.
19: 3   "Hallelujah! The smoke from her **goes up** for ever and ever."
20: 9   *They* **marched** across the breadth of the earth and surrounded the

327 ἀναβάλλω, *anaballō* [1] [√ 324 + 965]

adjourned the proceedings [1]

Ac   24: 22   was well acquainted with the Way, **adjourned the proceedings**.

328 ἀναβιβάζω, *anabibazō* [1] [√ 326]

pulled up [1]

Mt   13: 48   When it was full, the fishermen **pulled** it **up** on the shore.

329 ἀναβλέπω, *anablepō* [25 / 24] [√ 324 + 1063]

looked up [5], received sight [5], receive sight [4], looking up [3],
see [3], see again [2], able to see [1], restore sight [1]

Mt   11: 5   The blind **receive sight**, the lame walk, those who have leprosy are
14: 19   Taking the five loaves and the two fish and **looking up** to heaven,
20: 34   Immediately *they* **received** *their* **sight** and followed him.
Mk   6: 41   Taking the five loaves and the two fish and **looking up** to heaven,
7: 34   *He* **looked up** to heaven and with a deep sigh said to him,
8: 24   He **looked up** and said, "I see people; they look like trees walking
10: 51   Jesus asked him. The blind man said, "Rabbi, *I* want to **see**."
10: 52   Immediately *he* **received** *his* **sight** and followed Jesus along the
16: 4   But *when* they **looked up**, they saw that the stone, which was very
Lk   7: 22   The blind **receive sight**, the lame walk, those who have leprosy are

9: 16   Taking the five loaves and the two fish and **looking up** to heaven,
18: 41   do you want me to do for you?" "Lord, *I* want to **see**," he replied.
18: 42   Jesus said to him, "**Receive** *your* **sight**; your faith has healed you."
18: 43   Immediately *he* **received** *his* **sight** and followed Jesus,
19: 5   he **looked up** and said to him, "Zacchaeus, come down
21: 1   *As he* **looked up**, Jesus saw the rich putting their gifts into the
Jn   9: 11   to Siloam and wash. So I went and washed, and then *I could* **see**."
9: 15   the Pharisees also asked him how *he had* **received** *his* **sight**.
9: 18   and *had* **received** *his* **sight** until they sent for the man's parents.
9: 18   they sent for the man's [UBS+ *who* **received** *his* **sight**] parents.
Ac   9: 12   Ananias come and place his hands on him to **restore** *his* **sight**."
9: 17   has sent me so that *you may* **see again** and be filled with the Holy
9: 18   like scales fell from Saul's eyes, and *he could* **see again**.
22: 13   He stood beside me and said, 'Brother Saul, **receive** *your* **sight**!'
22: 13   your sight!' And at that very moment I *was* **able to see** him.

330 ἀνάβλεψις, *anablepsis* [1] [√ 324 + 1063]

recovery of sight [1]

Lk   4: 18   freedom for the prisoners and **recovery of sight** for the blind,

331 ἀναβοάω, *anaboaō* [1] [√ 324 + 1068]

cried out [1]

Mt   27: 46   About the ninth hour Jesus **cried out** in a loud voice, "*Eloi,*

332 ἀναβολή, *anabolē* [1] [√ 324 + 965]

delay [+4472] [1]

Ac   25: 17   When they came here with me, *I did* not **delay** [+4472] *the case,*

333 ἀνάγαιον, *anagaion* [2] [√ 324 + 1178]

upper room [2]

Mk   14: 15   He will show you a large **upper room**, furnished and ready.
Lk   22: 12   He will show you a large **upper room**, all furnished.

334 ἀναγγέλλω, *anangellō* [14] [√ 324 + 34]

told [3], reported [2], declare [1], explain [1], make known [1],
making known [1], openly confessed [+2018] [1], preach [1],
proclaim [1], tell [1], told about [1]

Jn   4: 25   "is coming. When he comes, he *will* **explain** everything to us."
5: 15   and **told** the Jews that it was Jesus who had made him well.
16: 13   speak only what he hears, and *he will* **tell** you what is yet to come.
16: 14   to me by taking from what is mine and **making** it **known** to you.
16: 15   the Spirit will take from what is mine and **make** it **known** to you.
Ac   14: 27   *they* gathered the church together and **reported** all that God had
15: 4   to whom *they* **reported** everything God had done through them.
19: 18   believed now came and **openly confessed** [+2018] their evil deeds.
20: 20   You know that I have not hesitated *to* **preach** anything that would
20: 27   For I have not hesitated *to* **proclaim** to you the whole will of God.
Ro   15: 21   "Those who *were* not **told** about him will see, and those who have
2Co   7: 7   *He* **told** us **about** your longing for me, your deep sorrow,
1Pe   1: 12   when they spoke of the things that *have* now *been* **told** you by
1Jn   1: 5   This is the message we have heard from him and **declare** to you:

335 ἀναγεννάω, *anagennaō* [2] [√ 324 + 1181]

born again [1], given new birth [1]

1Pe   1: 3   In his great mercy he *has* **given** us **new birth** into a living hope
1: 23   *For you have been* **born again**, not of perishable seed, but of

336 ἀναγινώσκω, *anaginōskō* [32] [√ 324 + 1182]

read [24], reading [5], reader [2], reads [1]

Mt   12: 3   "Haven't *you* **read** what David did when he and his companions
12: 5   Or haven't *you* **read** in the Law that on the Sabbath the priests
19: 4   "Haven't *you* **read**," he replied, "that at the beginning the Creator
21: 16   "Yes," replied Jesus, "*have you* never **read**, " 'From the lips of
21: 42   Jesus said to them, "*Have you* never **read** in the Scriptures:
22: 31   resurrection of the dead—*have you* not **read** what God said to you,

24:15 spoken of through the prophet Daniel—let the **reader** understand—
Mk 2:25 *"Have you* never **read** what David did when he and his
12:10 Haven't *you* **read** this scripture: " 'The stone the builders rejected
12:26 *have you* not **read** in the book of Moses, in the account of the
13:14 let the **reader** understand—then let those who are in Judea flee to
Lk   4:16 into the synagogue, as was his custom. And he stood up *to* **read**.
6: 3 *"Have you* never **read** what David did when he and his
10:26 "What is written in the Law?" he replied. "How *do you* **read** it?"
Jn 19:20 Many of the Jews **read** this sign, for the place where Jesus was
Ac 8:28 and on his way home was sitting in his chariot **reading** the book of
8:30 ran up to the chariot and heard the man **reading** Isaiah the prophet.
8:30 "Do you understand what *you are* **reading**?" Philip asked.
8:32 The eunuch was **reading** this passage of Scripture: "He was led like
13:27 fulfilled the words of the prophets that *are* **read** every Sabbath.
15:21 the earliest times and *is* **read** in the synagogues on every Sabbath."
15:31 The *people* **read** it and were glad for its encouraging message.
23:34 The governor **read** the *letter* and asked what province he was
2Co 1:13 For we do not write you anything *you* cannot **read** or understand.
3: 2 are our letter, written on our hearts, known and **read** by everybody.
3:15 Even to this day when Moses *is* **read**, a veil covers their hearts.
Eph 3: 4 *In* **reading** this, then, you will be able to understand my insight
Col 4:16 After this letter *has been* **read** to you, see that it is also read in the
4:16 see that *it is* also **read** in the church of the Laodiceans and that you
4:16 the Laodiceans and that you in turn **read** the letter from Laodicea.
1Th 5:27 I charge you before the Lord *to have* this letter **read** to all the
Rev 1: 3 Blessed is the *one who* **reads** the words of this prophecy,

337 ἀναγκάζω, anankazō [9] [√ 340]

compelled [2], force [2], made [2], compel [1], drove to it [1], make [1]

Mt 14:22 Immediately Jesus **made** the disciples get into the boat and go on
Mk 6:45 Immediately Jesus **made** his disciples get into the boat and go on
Lk 14:23 'Go out to the roads and country lanes and **make** them come in,
Ac 26:11 to have them punished, and *I tried to* **force** them to blaspheme.
28:19 when the Jews objected, *I was* **compelled** to appeal to Caesar—
2Co 12:11 I have made a fool of myself, but you **drove me to it**. I ought to
Gal 2: 3 even Titus, who was with me, *was* **compelled** to be circumcised,
2:14 How is it, then, that *you* **force** Gentiles to follow Jewish customs?
6:12 impression outwardly *are trying to* **compel** you to be circumcised.

338 ἀναγκαῖος, anankaios [8] [√ 340]

necessary [2], close [1], daily necessities [+5970] [1], had to [+1639] [1], indispensable [1], more necessary [1], necessary for [1]

Ac 10:24 and had called together his relatives and **close** friends.
13:46 "We **had** [+1639] **to** speak the word of God to you first. Since you
1Co 12:22 those parts of the body that seem to be weaker are **indispensable**,
2Co 9: 5 So I thought it **necessary** to urge the brothers to visit you in
Php 1:24 but it is **more necessary** for you that I remain in the body.
2:25 But I think it is **necessary** to send back to you Epaphroditus,
Tit 3:14 in order that they may provide for **daily necessities** [+5970]
Heb 8: 3 so it was **necessary for** this one also to have something to offer.

339 ἀναγκαστῶς, anankastōs [1] [√ 340]

must [1]

1Pe 5: 2 not *because* you **must**, but because you are willing, as God wants

340 ἀνάγκη, anankē [17] [→ 337, 338, 339, 2055]

necessary [3], compulsion [2], distress [2], hardships [2], must [2], compelled [+2130] [1], crisis [1], forced [+2848] [1], had to [1], must [+2400] [1], need [+2400] [1]

Mt 18: 7 Such things **must** come, but woe to the man through whom they
Lk 14:18 'I have just bought a field, and I **must** [+2400] go and see it.
21:23 There will be great **distress** in the land and wrath against this
Ro 13: 5 it is **necessary** to submit to the authorities, not only because of
1Co 7:26 Because of the present **crisis**, I think that it is good for you to
7:37 who is under no **compulsion** but has control over his own will,
9:16 the gospel, I cannot boast, for I *am* **compelled** [+2130] to preach.
2Co 6: 4 in great endurance; in troubles, **hardships** and distresses;

9: 7 not reluctantly or under **compulsion**, for God loves a cheerful
12:10 in insults, in **hardships**, in persecutions, in difficulties.
1Th 3: 7 in all our **distress** and persecution we were encouraged about you
Phm 1:14 that any favor you do will be spontaneous and not **forced** [+2848].
Heb 7:12 a change of the priesthood, there **must** also be a change of the law.
7:27 he *does* not **need** [+2400] to offer sacrifices day after day,
9:16 of a will, it is **necessary** to prove the death of the one who made it,
9:23 It was **necessary**, then, for the copies of the heavenly things to be
Jude 1: 3 I felt I **had to** write and urge you to contend for the faith that was

341 ἀναγνωρίζω, anagnōrizō [1] [√ 324 + 1182]

told [1]

Ac 7:13 On their second visit, Joseph **told** his brothers *who he was*,

342 ἀνάγνωσις, anagnōsis [3] [√ 324 + 1182]

public reading [1], read [1], reading [1]

Ac 13:15 After the **reading** from the Law and the Prophets, the synagogue
2Co 3:14 to this day the same veil remains when the old covenant *is* **read**.
1Ti 4:13 devote yourself *to* the **public reading** *of Scripture*, to preaching

343 ἀνάγω, anagō [23] [√ 324 + 72]

put out to sea [5], sail [4], brought [2], sailed [2], set sail [2], bring out for trial [1], bring up [1], brought back [1], led [1], led up [1], set out [1], taken upstairs [1], took [1]

Mt 4: 1 Then Jesus *was* **led** by the Spirit into the desert to be tempted by
Lk 2:22 and Mary **took** him to Jerusalem to present him to the Lord
4: 5 The devil **led** him **up** to a high place and showed him in an instant
8:22 to the other side of the lake." So they got into a boat and **set out**.
Ac 7:41 *They* **brought** sacrifices to it and held a celebration in honor of
9:39 and when he arrived *he was* **taken upstairs** to the room.
12: 4 Herod intended *to* **bring** him **out** for public **trial** after the
13:13 Paul and his companions **sailed** to Perga in Pamphylia,
16:11 From Troas we **put out to sea** and sailed straight for Samothrace,
16:34 The jailer **brought** them into his house and set a meal before them;
18:21 will come back if it is God's will." Then *he* **set sail** from Ephesus.
20: 3 Jews made a plot against him just as he was about to **sail** for Syria,
20:13 We went on ahead to the ship and **sailed** for Assos, where we were
21: 1 away from them, we **put out to sea** and sailed straight to Cos.
21: 2 a ship crossing over to Phoenicia, went on board and **set sail**.
27: 2 along the coast of the province of Asia, and *we* **put out to sea**.
27: 4 From there we **put out to sea** *again* and passed to the lee of
27:12 the majority decided that we *should* **sail** on, hoping to reach
27:21 "Men, you should have taken my advice not *to* **sail** from Crete,
28:10 They honored us in many ways and *when we were ready to* **sail**,
28:11 After three months *we* **put out to sea** in a ship that had wintered in
Ro 10: 7 descend into the deep?' " (that is, *to* **bring** Christ **up** from the dead).
Heb 13:20 who through the blood of the eternal covenant **brought back** from

344 ἀναδείκνυμι, anadeiknymi [2] [√ 324 + 1259]

show [1], appointed [1]

Lk 10: 1 After this the Lord **appointed** seventy-two others and sent them
Ac 1:24 everyone's heart. **Show** us which of these two you have chosen

345 ἀνάδειξις, anadeixis [1] [√ 324 + 1259]

appeared publicly [1]

Lk 1:80 and he lived in the desert until he **appeared publicly** to Israel.

346 ἀναδέχομαι, anadechomai [2] [√ 324 + 1312]

received [1], welcomed home [1]

Ac 28: 7 He **welcomed** us *to* his **home** and for three days entertained us
Heb 11:17 He *who had* **received** the promises was about to sacrifice his one

347 ἀναδίδωμι, anadidōmi [1] [√ 324 + 1443]

delivered [1]

Ac 23:33 they **delivered** the letter to the governor and handed Paul over to

348 ἀναζάω, anazaō [2 / 3] [√ *324 + 2409*]

alive again [2], sprang to life [1]

Lk   15:24   For this son of mine was dead and *is* **alive again**; he was lost
     15:32   this brother of yours was dead and *is* **alive again** [UBS 2409];
Ro   7: 9   but when the commandment came, sin **sprang to life** and I died.

349 ἀναζητέω, anazēteō [3] [√ *324 + 2426*]

look for [2], looking for [1]

Lk   2:44   Then *they began* **looking for** him among their relatives
     2:45   they did not find him, they went back to Jerusalem *to* **look for** him.
Ac   11:25   Then Barnabas went to Tarsus *to* **look for** Saul,

350 ἀναζώννυμι, anazōnnymi [1] [√ *324 + 2439*]

prepare for action [*+3836+4019*] [1]

1Pe   1:13   Therefore, **prepare** [*+3836+4019*] your minds **for action**;

351 ἀναζωπυρέω, anazōpyreō [1]
     [√ *324 + 2409 + 4786*]

fan into flame [1]

2Ti   1: 6   For this reason I remind you *to* **fan into flame** the gift of God,

352 ἀναθάλλω, anathallō [1] [√ *324 + 2558*]

renewed [1]

Php   4:10   I rejoice greatly in the Lord that at last *you have* **renewed** your

353 ἀνάθεμα, anathema [6] [→ *354, 356, 2912, 2913; cf.*
     324 + 5502]

cursed [2], eternally condemned [2], curse [1], taken a solemn
oath [*+354*] [1]

Ac   23:14   and said, "*We have* **taken a solemn oath** [*+354*] not to eat
Ro   9: 3   For I could wish that I myself were **cursed** and cut off from Christ
1Co   12: 3   "Jesus be **cursed**," and no one can say, "Jesus is Lord," except by
     16:22   If anyone does not love the Lord—a **curse** be on him. Come,
Gal   1: 8   than the one we preached to you, let him be **eternally condemned**!
     1: 9   other than what you accepted, let him be **eternally condemned**!

354 ἀναθεματίζω, anathematizō [4] [√ *353*]

bound with an oath [1], call down curses [1], taken a solemn oath
[*+353*] [1], taken an oath [1]

Mk   14:71   He began *to* **call down curses** *on* himself, and he swore to them,
Ac   23:12   and **bound** themselves **with an oath** not to eat or drink until they
     23:14   and said, "*We have* **taken a solemn oath** [*+353*] not to eat
     23:21   They *have* **taken an oath** not to eat or drink until they have killed

355 ἀναθεωρέω, anatheōreō [2] [√ *324 + 2555*]

consider [1], looked carefully at [1]

Ac   17:23   I walked around and **looked carefully at** your objects of worship,
Heb   13: 7   **Consider** the outcome of their way of life and imitate their faith.

356 ἀνάθημα, anathēma [1] [√ *353*]

gifts dedicated to God [1]

Lk   21: 5   adorned with beautiful stones and *with* **gifts dedicated to God**.

357 ἀναίδεια, anaideia [1] [√ *1.1 + 133*]

boldness [1]

Lk   11: 8   yet because of the man's **boldness** he will get up and give him as

358 ἀναίρεσις, anairesis [1] [√ *324 + 145*]

death [1]

Ac   8: 1   And Saul was there, giving approval *to* his **death**. On that day a

359 ἀναιρέω, anaireō [24] [√ *324 + 145*]

kill [9], killed [4], put to death [4], executed [2], get rid of [1],
killing [1], overthrow [1], sets aside [1], took [1]

Mt   2:16   and he gave orders *to* **kill** all the boys in Bethlehem and its
Lk   22: 2   teachers of the law were looking for some way *to* **get rid of** Jesus,
     23:32   both criminals, were also led out with him *to be* **executed**.
Ac   2:23   and *you*, with the help of wicked men, **put** him **to death** by nailing
     5:33   heard this, they were furious and wanted *to* **put** them **to death**.
     5:36   He *was* **killed**, all his followers were dispersed, and it all came to
     7:21   Pharaoh's daughter **took** him and brought him up as her own son.
     7:28   Do you want *to* **kill** me as you killed the Egyptian yesterday?'
     7:28   Do you want to kill me as *you* **killed** the Egyptian yesterday?'
     9:23   After many days had gone by, the Jews conspired *to* **kill** him,
     9:24   and night they kept close watch on the city gates in order to **kill**
     9:29   and debated with the Grecian Jews, but they tried *to* **kill** him.
     10:39   and in Jerusalem. *They* **killed** him by hanging him on a tree,
     12: 2   *He had* James, the brother of John, **put to death** with the sword.
     13:28   for a death sentence, they asked Pilate *to have* him **executed**.
     16:27   he drew his sword and was about to **kill** himself because he
     22:20   and guarding the clothes *of* those *who were* **killing** him.'
     23:15   about his case. We are ready *to* **kill** him before he gets here."
     23:21   have taken an oath not to eat or drink until *they have* **killed** him.
     23:27   This man was seized by the Jews and they were about to **kill** him,
     25: 3   for they were preparing an ambush *to* **kill** him along the way.
     26:10   and *when* they *were* **put to death**, I cast my vote against them.
2Th   2: 8   whom the Lord Jesus *will* **overthrow** with the breath of his mouth
Heb   10: 9   to do your will." *He* **sets aside** the first to establish the second.

360 ἀναίτιος, anaitios [2] [√ *1.1 + 162*]

innocent [2]

Mt   12: 5   the priests in the temple desecrate the day and yet are **innocent**?
     12: 7   not sacrifice,' you would not have condemned the **innocent**.

361 ἀνακαθίζω, anakathizō [2] [√ *324 + 2767*]

sat up [2]

Lk   7:15   The dead man **sat up** and began to talk, and Jesus gave him back to
Ac   9:40   "Tabitha, get up." She opened her eyes, and seeing Peter *she* **sat up**.

362 ἀνακαινίζω, anakainizō [1] [√ *324 + 2785*]

brought back [1]

Heb   6: 6   if they fall away, *to be* **brought back** to repentance, because to

363 ἀνακαινόω, anakainoō [2] [√ *324 + 2785*]

renewed [2]

2Co   4:16   are wasting away, yet inwardly we *are being* **renewed** day by day.
Col   3:10   which *is being* **renewed** in knowledge in the image of its Creator.

364 ἀνακαίνωσις, anakainōsis [2] [√ *324 + 2785*]

renewal [1], renewing [1]

Ro   12: 2   of this world, but be transformed *by* the **renewing** of your mind.
Tit   3: 5   us through the washing of rebirth and **renewal** by the Holy Spirit,

365 ἀνακαλύπτω, anakalyptō [2] [√ *324 + 2821*]

removed [1], unveiled [1]

2Co   3:14   *It has* not *been* **removed**, because only in Christ is it taken away.
     3:18   And we, *who with* **unveiled** faces all reflect the Lord's glory,

366 ἀνακάμπτω, anakamptō [4] [√ 324 + 2828]

return [2], come back [1], go back [1]

Mt   2:12 And having been warned in a dream not *to* **go back** to Herod,
Lk 10: 6 is there, your peace will rest on him; if not, *it will* **return** to you.
Ac 18:21 But as he left, he promised, "*I will* **come back** if it is God's will."
Heb 11:15 country they had left, they would have had opportunity *to* **return**.

367 ἀνάκειμαι, anakeimai [14] [√ 324 + 3023]

reclining at the table [4], at the table [2], guests [2], at the meal
[+3836] [1], dinner guests [1], eating [1], having dinner [1],
reclining [1], seated [1]

Mt   9:10 *While Jesus was* **having dinner** at Matthew's house, many tax
    22:10 both good and bad, and the wedding hall was filled *with* **guests**.
    22:11 "But when the king came in to see the **guests**, he noticed a man
    26: 7 which she poured on his head *as he was* **reclining at the table**.
    26:20 evening came, Jesus *was* **reclining at the table** with the Twelve.
Mk   6:26 but because of his oaths and his **dinner guests**, he did not want to
    14:18 *While* they *were* **reclining at the table** eating, he said, "I tell you
    16:14 Later Jesus appeared to the Eleven *as they were* **eating**;
Lk 22:27 who is greater, the one *who is* **at the table** or the one who serves?
    22:27 or the one who serves? Is it not the one *who is* **at the table**?
Jn   6:11 and distributed *to* those *who were* **seated** as much as they wanted.
    12: 2 while Lazarus was among those **reclining at the table** with him.
    13:23 the disciple whom Jesus loved, was **reclining** next to him.
    13:28 but no one **at the meal** [+3836] understood why Jesus said this to

368 ἀνακεφαλαιόω, anakephalaioō [2]
          [√ 324 + 3051]

bring together under one head [1], summed up [1]

Ro 13: 9 commandment there may be, *are* **summed up** in this one rule:
Eph 1:10 *to* **bring** all things in heaven and on earth **together under one
          head,**

369 ἀνακλίνω, anaklinō [6] [√ 324 + 3111]

take places at the feast [2], have recline at the table [1], have sit
down [1], placed [1], sit down [1]

Mt   8:11 and *will* **take** *their* **places at the feast** with Abraham, Isaac
    14:19 And he directed the people *to* **sit down** on the grass.
Mk   6:39 Then Jesus directed them *to* **have** all the people **sit down** in groups
Lk   2: 7 She wrapped him in cloths and **placed** him in a manger,
    12:37 *will* **have** them **recline at the table** and will come and wait on
    13:29 and *will* **take** *their* **places at the feast** in the kingdom of God.

370 ἀνακόπτω, anakoptō Not used in UBS/NIV
          [√ 324 + 3164]

371 ἀνακράζω, anakrazō [5] [√ 324 + 3189]

cried out [5]

Mk   1:23 in their synagogue who was possessed by an evil spirit **cried out**,
     6:49 walking on the lake, they thought he was a ghost. *They* **cried out**,
Lk   4:33 by a demon, an evil spirit. *He* **cried out** at the top of his voice,
     8:28 When he saw Jesus, *he* **cried out** and fell at his feet, shouting at
    23:18 With one voice *they* **cried out**, "Away with this man! Release

372 ἀνακραυγάζω, anakraugazō Not used in
UBS/NIV [√ 324 + 3189]

373 ἀνακρίνω, anakrinō [16] [√ 324 + 3212]

examined [3], judged [2], raising questions [2], called to account
[1], cross-examined [1], discerned [1], examining [1], judge [1],
judges [1], judgment [1], makes judgments about [1], sit in
judgment on [1]

Lk 23:14 I *have* **examined** him in your presence and have found no basis for
Ac   4: 9 If we *are being* **called to account** today for an act of kindness
    12:19 he **cross-examined** the guards and ordered that they be executed.

17:11 and **examined** the Scriptures every day to see if what Paul said
24: 8 *By* **examining** him yourself you will be able to learn the truth
28:18 They **examined** me and wanted to release me,
1Co 2:14 cannot understand them, because *they are* spiritually **discerned**.
     2:15 The spiritual man **makes judgments about** all things, but he
     2:15 all things, but he himself *is* not subject to any man's **judgment**:
     4: 3 I care very little if *I am* **judged** by you or by any human court;
     4: 3 or by any human court; indeed, *I do* not even **judge** myself.
     4: 4 but that does not make me innocent. It is the Lord *who* **judges** me.
     9: 3 This is my defense *to* those *who* **sit in judgment on** me.
    10:25 Eat anything sold in the meat market without **raising questions** of
    10:27 eat whatever is put before you without **raising questions** of
    14:24 *he* will be convinced by all that he is a sinner and *will be* **judged**

374 ἀνάκρισις, anakrisis [1] [√ 324 + 3212]

investigation [1]

Ac 25:26 so that as a result *of* this **investigation** I may have something to

375 ἀνακυλίω, anakyliō Not used in UBS/NIV
          [√ 324 + 3244]

376 ἀνακύπτω, anakyptō [4] [√ 324 + 3252]

straightened up [2], stand up [1], straighten up [1]

Lk 13:11 She was bent over and could not **straighten up** at all.
    21:28 these things begin to take place, **stand up** and lift up your heads,
Jn   8: 7 he **straightened up** and said to them, "If any one of you is without
     8:10 Jesus **straightened up** and asked her, "Woman, where are they?

377 ἀναλαμβάνω, analambanō [13] [√ 324 + 3284]

taken up [4], get [1], lifted up [1], put on [1], take aboard [1], take
up [1], taken [1], taken back [1], took [1], took aboard [1]

Mk 16:19 he was **taken up** into heaven and he sat at the right hand of God.
Ac   1: 2 until the day he was **taken up** *to* heaven, after giving instructions
     1:11 This same Jesus, who *has been* **taken** from you into heaven,
     1:22 from John's baptism to the time when Jesus was **taken up** from us.
     7:43 *You have* **lifted up** the shrine of Molech and the star of your god
    10:16 three times, and immediately the sheet *was* **taken back** to heaven.
    20:13 and sailed for Assos, where we were going to **take** Paul **aboard**.
    20:14 he met us at Assos, we **took** him **aboard** and went on to Mitylene.
    23:31 **took** Paul with them during the night and brought him as far as
Eph 6:13 Therefore **put on** the full armor of God, so that when the day of
     6:16 In addition to all this, **take up** the shield of faith, with which you
1Ti 3:16 the nations, was believed on in the world, *was* **taken up** in glory.
2Ti 4:11 **Get** Mark and bring him with you, because he is helpful to me in

378 ἀνάλημψις, analēmpsis [1] [√ 324 + 3284]

taken up [1]

Lk   9:51 As the time approached for him to be **taken up** *to heaven*,

379 ἀναλίσκω, analiskō Not used in UBS/NIV
          [√ 324 + 274]

380 ἀνάλλομαι, anallomai Not used in UBS/NIV
          [√ 324 + 256]

381 ἀναλογία, analogia [1] [√ 324 + 3306]

proportion [1]

Ro 12: 6 man's gift is prophesying, let him use it in **proportion** to his faith.

382 ἀναλογίζομαι, analogizomai [1] [√ 324 + 3306]

consider [1]

Heb 12: 3 **Consider** him who endured such opposition from sinful men,

383 ἄναλος, analos [1] [√ 1.1 + 229]

loses saltiness [+1181] [1]

Mk   9:50 "Salt is good, but if it **loses** its **saltiness** [+1181], how can you

384 ἀναλόω, analoō [2] [√ 324 + 274]

destroy [1], destroyed [1]

Lk   9:54 do you want us to call fire down from heaven *to* **destroy** them?"
Gal 5:15 each other, watch out or *you will be* **destroyed** by each other.

385 ἀνάλυσις, analysis [1] [√ 324 + 3395]

departure [1]

2Ti 4: 6 out like a drink offering, and the time has come *for* my **departure**.

386 ἀναλύω, analyō [2] [√ 324 + 3395]

depart [1], to return [+4536] [1]

Lk 12:36 like men waiting for their master **to return** [+4536] from a
Php 1:23 I desire to **depart** and be with Christ, which is better by far;

387 ἀναμάρτητος, anamartētos [1] [√ 1.1 + 279]

without sin [1]

Jn   8: 7 straightened up and said to them, "If any one of you is **without sin**,

388 ἀναμένω, anamenō [1] [√ 324 + 3531]

wait for [1]

1Th 1:10 and *to* **wait for** his Son from heaven, whom he raised from the

389 ἀναμιμνῄσκω, anamimnēskō [6] [√ 324 + 3648]

remembered [2], remember [1], remembers [1], remind [1], remind of [1]

Mk 11:21 Peter **remembered** and said to Jesus, "Rabbi, look! The fig tree you
     14:72 Then Peter **remembered** the word Jesus had spoken to him:
1Co 4:17 He *will* **remind** you of my way of life in Christ Jesus, which
2Co 7:15 And his affection for you is all the greater *when he* **remembers**
2Ti 1: 6 For this reason *I* **remind** you to fan into flame the gift of God,
Heb 10:32 **Remember** those earlier days after you had received the light,

390 ἀνάμνησις, anamnēsis [4] [√ 324 + 3648]

remembrance [3], reminder [1]

Lk 22:19 "This is my body given for you; do this in **remembrance** of me."
1Co 11:24 is my body, which is for you; do this in **remembrance** of me."
     11:25 my blood; do this, whenever you drink it, in **remembrance** of me."
Heb 10: 3 But those sacrifices are an annual **reminder** of sins,

391 ἀνανεόομαι, ananeoomai [1] [√ 324 + 3742]

made new [1]

Eph 4:23 *to be* **made new** in the attitude of your minds;

392 ἀνανήφω, ananēphō [1] [√ 324 + 3768]

come to senses [1]

2Ti 2:26 and that *they will* **come to** *their* **senses** and escape from the trap of

393 Ἀνανίας, Hananias [11]

of Jerusalem [3] Ac 5:1,3,5
of Damascus [6] Ac 9:10,10,12,13,17; 22:12
high priest [2] Ac 23:2; 24:1
Ananias [11]

Ac   5: 1 Now a man named **Ananias**, together with his wife Sapphira,
     5: 3 Then Peter said, "**Ananias**, how is it that Satan has so filled your
     5: 5 When **Ananias** heard this, he fell down and died. And great fear
     9:10 In Damascus there was a disciple named **Ananias**. The Lord called
     9:10 The Lord called to him in a vision, "**Ananias**!" "Yes, Lord,"
     9:12 In a vision he has seen a man named **Ananias** come and place his
     9:13 "Lord," **Ananias** answered, "I have heard many reports about this
     9:17 Then **Ananias** went to the house and entered it. Placing his hands
    22:12 "A man named **Ananias** came to see me. He was a devout observer
    23: 2 At this the high priest **Ananias** ordered those standing near Paul to
    24: 1 Five days later the high priest **Ananias** went down to Caesarea

394 ἀναντίρρητος, anantirrētos [1] [√ 1.1 + 505 + 4839]

undeniable [1]

Ac 19:36 Therefore, since these facts are **undeniable**, you ought to be quiet

395 ἀναντιρρήτως, anantirrētōs [1] [√ 1.1 + 505 + 4839]

without raising any objection [1]

Ac 10:29 So when I was sent for, I came **without raising any objection**.

396 ἀνάξιος, anaxios [1] [√ 1.1 + 545]

not competent [1]

1Co 6: 2 to judge the world, are you **not competent** to judge trivial cases?

397 ἀναξίως, anaxiōs [1] [√ 1.1 + 545]

unworthy manner [1]

1Co 11:27 or drinks the cup of the Lord in an **unworthy manner** will be

398 ἀνάπαυσις, anapausis [5] [√ 324 + 4264]

rest [4], stop [+2400] [1]

Mt 11:29 and humble in heart, and you will find **rest** for your souls.
     12:43 it goes through arid places seeking **rest** and does not find it.
Lk 11:24 it goes through arid places seeking **rest** and does not find it.
Rev 4: 8 Day and night *they* never **stop** [+2400] saying: "Holy, holy,
     14:11 There is no **rest** day or night for those who worship the beast

399 ἀναπαύω, anapauō [12] [√ 324 + 4264]

refreshed [3], resting [2], take life easy [1], get rest [1], give rest [1], refresh [1], rest [1], rests [1], wait [1]

Mt 11:28 all you who are weary and burdened, and I *will* **give** you **rest**.
     26:45 the disciples and said to them, "*Are you* still sleeping and **resting**?
Mk   6:31 "Come with me by yourselves to a quiet place and **get** some **rest**."
     14:41 the third time, he said to them, "Are you still sleeping and **resting**?
Lk 12:19 laid up for many years. **Take life easy**; eat, drink and be merry." '
1Co 16:18 For *they* **refreshed** my spirit and yours also. Such men deserve
2Co 7:13 Titus was, because his spirit *has been* **refreshed** by all of you.
Phm 1: 7 because you, brother, *have* **refreshed** the hearts of the saints.
     1:20 some benefit from you in the Lord; **refresh** my heart in Christ.
1Pe 4:14 you are blessed, for the Spirit of glory and of God **rests** on you.
Rev 6:11 and they were told to **wait** a little longer, until the number of their
     14:13 "Yes," says the Spirit, "*they will* **rest** from their labor, for their

400 ἀναπείθω, anapeithō [1] [√ 324 + 4275]

persuading [1]

Ac 18:13 "*is* **persuading** the people to worship God in ways contrary to the

401 ἀνάπειρος, anapeiros [2] [√ 324 + 4386]

crippled [2]

Lk 14:13 give a banquet, invite the poor, the **crippled**, the lame, the blind,
     14:21 and bring in the poor, the **crippled**, the blind and the lame.'

402 ἀναπέμπω, *anapempō* [5] [√ *324 + 4287*]

sent back [2], send [1], sending back [1], sent [1]

Lk 23: 7 *he* **sent** him to Herod, who was also in Jerusalem at that time.
    23:11 Dressing him in an elegant robe, *they* **sent** him **back** to Pilate.
    23:15 Neither has Herod, for *he* **sent** him **back** to us; as you can see,
Ac 25:21 I ordered him held until *I could* **send** him to Caesar."
Phm 1:12 *I am* **sending** him—who is my very heart—**back** to you.

403 ἀναπηδάω, *anapēdaō* [1] [→ *1659, 1737, 324*]

jumped to his feet [1]

Mk 10:50 his cloak aside, he **jumped to his feet** and came to Jesus.

404 ἀναπίπτω, *anapiptō* [12] [√ *324 + 4406*]

sit down [3], reclined at the table [2], sat down [2], leaning back [1], leaned back [1], returned to place [*+4099*] [1], sit down to eat [1], take [*+1650*] [1]

Mt 15:35 He told the crowd *to* **sit down** on the ground.
Mk 6:40 So *they* **sat down** in groups of hundreds and fifties.
    8: 6 He told the crowd *to* **sit down** on the ground. When he had taken
Lk 11:37 him to eat with him; so *he* went in and **reclined at the table**.
    14:10 But when you are invited, **take** [*+1650*] the lowest place, so that
    17: 7 comes in from the field, 'Come along now and **sit down to eat**'?
    22:14 When the hour came, Jesus and his apostles **reclined at the table**.
Jn 6:10 Jesus said, "Have the people **sit down**." There was plenty of grass
    6:10 in that place, and the men **sat down**, about five thousand of them.
    13:12 their feet, he put on his clothes and **returned** [*+4099*] **to** *his* **place**.
    13:25 **Leaning back** against Jesus, he asked him, "Lord, who is it?"
    21:20 (This was the one who *had* **leaned back** against Jesus at the

405 ἀναπληρόω, *anaplēroō* [6] [√ *324 + 4444*]

finds himself [1], fulfill [1], fulfilled [1], heap up to the limit [1], make up for [1], supplied [1]

Mt 13:14 In them *is* **fulfilled** the prophecy of Isaiah: " 'You will be ever
1Co 14:16 how can one *who* **finds himself** among those who do not
    16:17 because they *have* **supplied** what was lacking from you.
Gal 6: 2 other's burdens, and in this way *you will* **fulfill** the law of Christ.
Php 2:30 risking his life to **make up for** the help you could not give me.
1Th 2:16 be saved. In this way they always **heap up** their sins **to the limit**.

406 ἀναπολόγητος, *anapologētos* [2]
    [√ *1.1 + 608 + 3306*]

no excuse [1], without excuse [1]

Ro 1:20 from what has been made, so that men are **without excuse**.
    2: 1 You, therefore, have **no excuse**, you who pass judgment on

407 ἀναπράσσω, *anaprassō*   Not used in UBS/NIV
    [√ *324 + 4556*]

408 ἀναπτύσσω, *anaptyssō* [1] [√ *324 + 4771*]

unrolling [1]

Lk 4:17 handed to him. **Unrolling** it, he found the place where it is written:

409 ἀνάπτω, *anaptō* [2] [√ *324 + 721*]

kindled [1], set on fire [1]

Lk 12:49 to bring fire on the earth, and how I wish *it were* already **kindled**!
Jas 3: 5 Consider what a great forest *is* **set on fire** *by* a small spark.

410 ἀναρίθμητος, *anarithmētos* [1] [√ *1.1 + 750*]

countless [1]

Heb 11:12 as the stars in the sky and as **countless** as the sand on the seashore.

411 ἀνασείω, *anaseiō* [2] [√ *324 + 4940*]

stirred up [1], stirs up [1]

Mk 15:11 But the chief priests **stirred up** the crowd to have Pilate release
Lk 23: 5 "*He* **stirs up** the people all over Judea by his teaching.

412 ἀνασκευάζω, *anaskeuazō* [1] [√ *324 + 5007*]

troubling [1]

Ac 15:24 and disturbed you, **troubling** your minds by what they said.

413 ἀνασπάω, *anaspaō* [2] [√ *324 + 5060*]

pull out [1], pulled up [1]

Lk 14: 5 a well on the Sabbath day, *will you* not immediately **pull** him **out**?"
Ac 11:10 three times, and then *it was* all **pulled up** to heaven again.

414 ἀνάστασις, *anastasis* [42] [√ *324 + 2705*]

ἀνάστασις [ἐκ] νεκροῦ (resurrection from the dead) [15] Mt 22:31; Lk 20:35; Ac 4:2; 17:32; 23:6; 24:21; 26:23; Ro 1:4; 1Co 15:12,13,21,42; Heb 6:2; 11:35; 1Pe 1:3

ἀνάστασις Χριστοῦ (resurrection of Christ) [3] Ac 2:31; 1Pe 1:3; 3:21

ἐν τῇ ἀναστάσει (in the resurrection) [7] Mt 22:28,30; Mk 12:23; Lk 14:14; 20:33; Jn 11:24; Rev 20:6

resurrection [37], rise [3], raised to life again [1], rising [1]

Mt 22:23 who say there is no **resurrection**, came to him with a question.
    22:28 Now then, at the **resurrection**, whose wife will she be of the
    22:30 At the **resurrection** people will neither marry nor be given in
    22:31 But about the **resurrection** of the dead—have you not read what
Mk 12:18 Then the Sadducees, who say there is no **resurrection**, came to
    12:23 At the **resurrection** whose wife will she be, since the seven were
Lk 2:34 child is destined to cause the falling and **rising** of many in Israel,
    14:14 repay you, you will be repaid at the **resurrection** of the righteous."
    20:27 Some of the Sadducees, who say there is no **resurrection**,
    20:33 Now then, at the **resurrection** whose wife will she be,
    20:35 and *in* the **resurrection** from the dead will neither marry nor be
    20:36 are God's children, since they are children *of* the **resurrection**.
Jn 5:29 those who have done good will **rise** to live, and those who have
    5:29 to live, and those who have done evil will **rise** to be condemned.
    11:24 "I know he will rise again in the **resurrection** at the last day."
    11:25 Jesus said to her, "I am the **resurrection** and the life. He who
Ac 1:22 one of these must become a witness with us *of* his **resurrection**."
    2:31 Seeing what was ahead, he spoke of the **resurrection** of the Christ,
    4: 2 the people and proclaiming in Jesus the **resurrection** of the dead.
    4:33 apostles continued to testify to the **resurrection** of the Lord Jesus,
    17:18 was preaching the good news about Jesus and the **resurrection**.
    17:32 When they heard about the **resurrection** of the dead, some of them
    23: 6 stand on trial because of my hope *in* the **resurrection** of the dead."
    23: 8 (The Sadducees say that there is no **resurrection**, and that there
    24:15 that there will be a **resurrection** of both the righteous
    24:21 'It is concerning the **resurrection** of the dead that I am on trial
    26:23 that the Christ would suffer and, as the first to **rise** from the dead,
Ro 1: 4 power to be the Son of God by his **resurrection** from the dead:
    6: 5 we will certainly also be united with him *in* his **resurrection**.
1Co 15:12 how can some of you say that there is no **resurrection** of the dead?
    15:13 If there is no **resurrection** of the dead, then not even Christ has
    15:21 a man, the **resurrection** of the dead comes also through a man.
    15:42 So will it be with the **resurrection** of the dead. The body that is
Php 3:10 I want to know Christ and the power *of* his **resurrection**,
2Ti 2:18 the truth. They say that the **resurrection** has already taken place,
Heb 6: 2 on of hands, the **resurrection** of the dead, and eternal judgment.
    11:35 Women received back their dead, **raised to life again**. Others were
    11:35 to be released, so that they might gain a better **resurrection**.
1Pe 1: 3 hope through the **resurrection** of Jesus Christ from the dead,
    3:21 toward God. It saves you by the **resurrection** of Jesus Christ,
Rev 20: 5 until the thousand years were ended.) This is the first **resurrection**.
    20: 6 and holy are those who have part in the first **resurrection**.

415 ἀναστατόω, **anastatoō** [3] [√ *324 + 2705*]

agitators [1], caused trouble [1], revolt [1]

Ac 17: 6 "These men who *have* **caused trouble** all over the world have now
21:38 "Aren't you the Egyptian who *started* a **revolt** and led four
Gal 5:12 As for those **agitators**, I wish they would go the whole way

416 ἀνασταυρόω, **anastauroō** [1] [√ *324 + 5089*]

crucifying all over again [1]

Heb 6: 6 to their loss *they are* **crucifying** the Son of God **all over again**

417 ἀναστενάζω, **anastenazō** [1] [√ *324 + 5101*]

sighed deeply [+3836+4460] [1]

Mk 8:12 *He* **sighed** [+3836+4460] **deeply** and said, "Why does this

418 ἀναστρέφω, **anastrephō** [9] [√ *324 + 5138*]

live [3], conduct [1], conducted [1], lived [1], return [1], treated [1], went back [1]

Ac 5:22 officers did not find them there. So they **went back** and reported,
15:16 " 'After this *I will* **return** and rebuild David's fallen tent. Its ruins I
2Co 1:12 Our conscience testifies that *we have* **conducted** ourselves in the
Eph 2: 3 All of us also **lived** among them at one time,
1Ti 3:15 you will know how people ought *to* **conduct** *themselves* in God's
Heb 10:33 times you stood side by side *with* those *who were* so **treated**.
13:18 have a clear conscience and desire *to* **live** honorably in every way.
1Pe 1:17 work impartially, **live** your lives as strangers here in reverent fear.
2Pe 2:18 they entice people who are just escaping from those *who* **live** in

419 ἀναστροφή, **anastrophē** [13] [√ *324 + 5138*]

way of life [4], lives [3], behavior [2], life [2], do [1], live [1]

Gal 1:13 For you have heard of my previous **way of life** in Judaism,
Eph 4:22 You were taught, with regard to your former **way of life**, to put off
1Ti 4:12 for the believers in speech, in **life**, in love, in faith and in purity.
Heb 13: 7 Consider the outcome *of* their **way of life** and imitate their faith.
Jas 3:13 Let him show by his good **life**, by deeds done in the humility that
1Pe 1:15 But just as he who called you is holy, so be holy in all you **do**;
1:18 or gold that you were redeemed from the empty **way of life** handed
2:12 Live such good **lives** among the pagans that, though they accuse
3: 1 they may be won over without words by the **behavior** of their
3: 2 when they see the purity and reverence of your **lives**.
3:16 so that those who speak maliciously against your good **behavior** in
2Pe 2: 7 who was distressed by the filthy **lives** of lawless men
3:11 of people ought you to be? You ought to **live** holy and godly lives

420 ἀνασῴζω, **anasōzō** Not used in UBS/NIV
[√ *324 + 5392*]

421 ἀνατάσσομαι, **anatassomai** [1] [√ *324 + 5435*]

draw up [1]

Lk 1: 1 Many have undertaken *to* **draw up** an account of the things that

422 ἀνατέλλω, **anatellō** [9] [√ *424*]

came up [2], rises [2], causes to rise [1], dawned [1], descended [1], just after sunrise [+2463+3836] [1], rising [1]

Mt 4:16 those living in the land of the shadow of death a light *has* **dawned**."
5:45 *He* **causes** his sun **to rise** on the evil and the good, and sends rain
13: 6 But *when* the sun **came up**, the plants were scorched, and they
Mk 4: 6 But *when* the sun **came up**, the plants were scorched, and they
16: 2 **just after sunrise** [+2463+3836], they were on their way to the
Lk 12:54 "When you see a cloud **rising** in the west, immediately you say,
Heb 7:14 For it is clear that our Lord **descended** from Judah, and in regard
Jas 1:11 For the sun **rises** with scorching heat and withers the plant;
2Pe 1:19 until the day dawns and the morning star **rises** in your hearts.

423 ἀνατίθημι, **anatithēmi** [2] [√ *324 + 5502*]

discussed [1], set before [1]

Ac 25:14 many days there, Festus **discussed** Paul's case with the king.
Gal 2: 2 and **set before** them the gospel that I preach among the Gentiles.

424 ἀνατολή, **anatolē** [11 / 10] [→ *422, 425, 1984, 324*]

east [7], east [+2463] [2], rising sun [1]

Mt 2: 1 the time of King Herod, Magi from the **east** came to Jerusalem
2: 2 We saw his star in the **east** and have come to worship him."
2: 9 and the star they had seen in the **east** went ahead of them until it
8:11 I say to you that many will come from the **east** and the west,
24:27 For as lightning that comes from the **east** is visible even in the
Mk 16: S [UBS+ *Jesus himself sent out through them, from* **east** *to west*]
Lk 1:78 of our God, by which the **rising sun** will come to us from heaven
13:29 People will come from **east** and west and north and south,
Rev 7: 2 Then I saw another angel coming up from the **east** [+2463],
16:12 dried up to prepare the way for the kings from the **East** [+2463].
21:13 There were three gates on the **east**, three on the north, three on the

425 ἀνατολικός, **anatolikos** Not used in UBS/NIV
[√ *424*]

426 ἀνατρέπω, **anatrepō** [3] [√ *324 + 5572*]

destroy [1], overturned [1], ruining [1]

Jn 2:15 the coins of the money changers and **overturned** their tables.
2Ti 2:18 has already taken place, and *they* **destroy** the faith of some.
Tit 1:11 *because* they *are* **ruining** whole households by teaching things

427 ἀνατρέφω, **anatrephō** [3] [√ *324 + 5555*]

brought up [2], cared for [1]

Ac 7:20 For three months he *was* **cared for** in his father's house.
7:21 Pharaoh's daughter took him and **brought** him **up** as her own son.
22: 3 "I am a Jew, born in Tarsus of Cilicia, but **brought up** in this city.

428 ἀναφαίνω, **anaphainō** [2] [√ *324 + 5743*]

appear [1], sighting [1]

Lk 19:11 thought that the kingdom of God was going to **appear** at once.
Ac 21: 3 *After* **sighting** Cyprus and passing to the south of it, we sailed on

429 ἀναφέρω, **anapherō** [10] [√ *324 + 5770*]

offer [2], offered [2], bore [1], led [1], led up [1], offering [1], take away [1], taken up [1]

Mt 17: 1 brother of James, and **led** them **up** a high mountain by themselves.
Mk 9: 2 James and John with him and **led** them **up** a high mountain,
Lk 24:51 he was blessing them, he left them and *was* **taken up** into heaven.
Heb 7:27 he does not need *to* **offer** sacrifices day after day, first for his own
7:27 He sacrificed for their sins once for all *when he* **offered** himself.
9:28 so Christ was sacrificed once *to* **take away** the sins of many
13:15 therefore, *let us* continually **offer** to God a sacrifice of praise—
Jas 2:21 for what he did *when he* **offered** his son Isaac on the altar?
1Pe 2: 5 **offering** spiritual sacrifices acceptable to God through Jesus
2:24 He himself **bore** our sins in his body on the tree, so that we might

430 ἀναφωνέω, **anaphōneō** [1] [√ *324 + 5889*]

exclaimed [1]

Lk 1:42 In a loud voice *she* **exclaimed**: "Blessed are you among women,

431 ἀνάχυσις, **anachysis** [1] [√ *1772; cf. 324*]

flood [1]

1Pe 4: 4 you do not plunge with them into the same **flood** of dissipation,

432 ἀναχωρέω, anachōreō [14] [√ 324 + 6003]

withdrew [6], left [3], returned [2], drew [1], go away [1], gone [1]

Mt   2:12 go back to Herod, *they* **returned** to their country by another route.
      2:13 *When they had* **gone**, an angel of the Lord appeared to Joseph in a
      2:14 took the child and his mother during the night and **left** for Egypt,
      2:22 been warned in a dream, *he* **withdrew** to the district of Galilee,
      4:12 heard that John had been put in prison, *he* **returned** to Galilee.
      9:24 he said, "**Go away.** The girl is not dead but asleep." But they
    12:15 Aware of this, Jesus **withdrew** from that place. Many followed
    14:13 had happened, *he* **withdrew** by boat privately to a solitary place.
    15:21 that place, Jesus **withdrew** to the region of Tyre and Sidon.
    27: 5 So Judas threw the money into the temple and **left**. Then he went
Mk   3: 7 Jesus **withdrew** with his disciples to the lake, and a large crowd
Jn   6:15 make him king by force, **withdrew** again to a mountain by himself.
Ac 23:19 **drew** him aside and asked, "What is it you want to tell me?"
    26:31 *They* **left** the *room*, and while talking with one another, they said,

433 ἀνάψυξις, anapsyxis [1] [√ 324 + 6038]

refreshing [1]

Ac   3:19 be wiped out, that times *of* **refreshing** may come from the Lord,

434 ἀναψύχω, anapsychō [1] [√ 324 + 6038]

refreshed [1]

2Ti 1:16 because *he* often **refreshed** me and was not ashamed of my chains.

435 ἀνδραποδιστής, andrapodistēs [1] [√ 467 + 4546]

slave traders [1]

1Ti 1:10 and perverts, *for* **slave traders** and liars and perjurers—

436 'Ανδρέας, Andreas [13] [√ 467]

Andrew [13]

Mt   4:18 he saw two brothers, Simon called Peter and his brother **Andrew**.
    10: 2 and his brother **Andrew**; James son of Zebedee, and his brother
Mk   1:16 he saw Simon and his brother **Andrew** casting a net into the lake,
    1:29 they went with James and John to the home of Simon and **Andrew**.
    3:18 **Andrew**, Philip, Bartholomew, Matthew, Thomas, James son of
    13: 3 the temple, Peter, James, John and **Andrew** asked him privately,
Lk   6:14 his brother **Andrew**, James, John, Philip, Bartholomew,
Jn   1:40 **Andrew**, Simon Peter's brother, was one of the two who heard
    1:44 Philip, like **Andrew** and Peter, was from the town of Bethsaida.
    6: 8 of his disciples, **Andrew**, Simon Peter's brother, spoke up,
    12:22 Philip went to tell **Andrew**; Andrew and Philip in turn told Jesus.
    12:22 Philip went to tell Andrew; **Andrew** and Philip in turn told Jesus.
Ac   1:13 Those present were Peter, John, James and **Andrew**; Philip

437 ἀνδρίζομαι, andrizomai [1] [√ 467]

men of courage [1]

1Co 16:13 your guard; stand firm in the faith; *be* **men of courage**; be strong.

438 'Ανδρόνικος, Andronikos [1] [√ 467 + 3772]

Andronicus [1]

Ro 16: 7 Greet **Andronicus** and Junias, my relatives who have been in

439 ἀνδροφόνος, androphonos [1] [√ 467 + 5840]

murderers [1]

1Ti 1: 9 for those who kill their fathers or mothers, *for* **murderers**,

440 ἀνεγκλησία, anenklēsia Not used in UBS/NIV [√ 1.1 + 1877 + 2813]

441 ἀνέγκλητος, anenklētos [5] [√ 1.1 + 1877 + 2813]

blameless [3], free from accusation [1], nothing against them [1]

1Co 1: 8 so that you will be **blameless** on the day of our Lord Jesus Christ.
Col 1:22 you holy in his sight, without blemish and **free from accusation**—
1Ti 3:10 and then if there is **nothing against them**, let them serve as
Tit 1: 6 An elder must be **blameless**, the husband of but one wife,
    1: 7 an overseer is entrusted with God's work, he must be **blameless**—

442 ἀνεκδιήγητος, anekdiēgētos [1] [√ 1.1 + 1666 + 1328 + 72]

indescribable [1]

2Co 9:15 Thanks be to God for his **indescribable** gift!

443 ἀνεκλάλητος, aneklalētos [1] [√ 1.1 + 1666 + 3281]

inexpressible [1]

1Pe 1: 8 in him and are filled with an **inexpressible** and glorious joy,

444 ἀνέκλειπτος, anekleiptos [1] [√ 1.1 + 1666 + 3309]

not exhausted [1]

Lk 12:33 a treasure in heaven that will **not** be **exhausted**, where no thief

445 ἀνεκτός, anektos [5] [√ 324 + 2400]

more bearable [5]

Mt 10:15 it will be **more bearable** for Sodom and Gomorrah on the day of
    11:22 it will be **more bearable** for Tyre and Sidon on the day of
    11:24 But I tell you that it will be **more bearable** for Sodom on the day
Lk 10:12 it will be **more bearable** on that day for Sodom than for that town.
    10:14 But it will be **more bearable** for Tyre and Sidon at the judgment

446 ἀνελεήμων, aneleēmōn [1] [√ 1.1 + 1799]

ruthless [1]

Ro 1:31 they are senseless, faithless, heartless, **ruthless**.

447 ἀνέλεος, aneleos [1] [√ 1.1 + 1799]

without mercy [1]

Jas 2:13 because judgment **without mercy** will be shown to anyone who

448 ἀνεμίζω, anemizō [1] [√ 449]

blown by the wind [1]

Jas 1: 6 doubts is like a wave of the sea, **blown** and tossed **by the wind**.

449 ἄνεμος, anemos [31] [→ 448]

wind [19], winds [10], squall [+3278] [2]

Mt 7:25 the streams rose, and the **winds** blew and beat against that house;
    7:27 the streams rose, and the **winds** blew and beat against that house,
    8:26 Then he got up and rebuked the **winds** and the waves, and it was
    8:27 kind of man is this? Even the **winds** and the waves obey him!"
    11: 7 did you go out into the desert to see? A reed swayed by the **wind**?
    14:24 from land, buffeted by the waves because the **wind** was against it.
    14:30 But when he saw the **wind**, he was afraid and, beginning to sink,
    14:32 And when they climbed into the boat, the **wind** died down.
    24:31 and they will gather his elect from the four **winds**, from one end of
Mk 4:37 A furious **squall** [+3278] came up, and the waves broke over the
    4:39 He got up, rebuked the **wind** and said to the waves, "Quiet!
    4:39 Be still!" Then the **wind** died down and it was completely calm.
    4:41 each other, "Who is this? Even the **wind** and the waves obey him!"
    6:48 disciples straining at the oars, because the **wind** was against them.
    6:51 Then he climbed into the boat with them, and the **wind** died down.
    13:27 he will send his angels and gather his elect from the four **winds**,
Lk 7:24 did you go out into the desert to see? A reed swayed by the **wind**?

8: 23   A **squall** [+*3278*] came down on the lake, so that the boat was
8: 24   He got up and rebuked the **wind** and the raging waters; the storm
8: 25   He commands even the **winds** and the water, and they obey him."
Jn   6: 18   A strong **wind** was blowing and the waters grew rough.
Ac   27: 4   passed to the lee of Cyprus because the **winds** were against us.
     27: 7   When the **wind** did not allow us to hold our course, we sailed to
     27: 14   a **wind** of hurricane force, called the "northeaster,"
     27: 15   ship was caught by the storm and could not head into the **wind**;
Eph   4: 14   and blown here and there *by* every **wind** of teaching and by the
Jas   3: 4   Although they are so large and are driven by strong **winds**,
Jude   1: 12   They are clouds without rain, blown along by the **wind**;
Rev   6: 13   as late figs drop from a fig tree when shaken by a strong **wind**.
     7: 1   holding back the four **winds** of the earth to prevent any wind from
     7: 1   holding back the four winds of the earth to prevent *any* **wind** from

450   ἀνένδεκτος, *anendektos*   [1]   [√ *1.1 + 1877 + 1312*]

bound to come [+*2262+3590*] [1]

Lk   17: 1   Things that cause people to sin are **bound to come** [+*2262+3590*],

451   ἀνεξεραύνητος, *anexeraunētos*   [1]
[√ *1.1 + 1666 + 2236*]

unsearchable [1]

Ro   11: 33   How **unsearchable** his judgments, and his paths beyond tracing

452   ἀνεξίκακος, *anexikakos*   [1]   [√ *324 + 2400 + 2805*]

not resentful [1]

2Ti   2: 24   he must be kind to everyone, able to teach, **not resentful.**

453   ἀνεξιχνίαστος, *anexichniastos*   [2]
[√ *1.1 + 1666 + 2717*]

beyond tracing out [1], unsearchable [1]

Ro   11: 33   **unsearchable** his judgments, and his paths **beyond tracing out**!
Eph   3: 8   to preach to the Gentiles the **unsearchable** riches of Christ,

454   ἀνεπαίσχυντος, *anepaischyntos*   [1]
[√ *1.1 + 2093 + 156*]

does not need to be ashamed [1]

2Ti   2: 15   a workman *who* **does not need to be ashamed** and who correctly

455   ἀνεπίλημπτος, *anepilēmptos*   [3]
[√ *1.1 + 2093 + 3284*]

above reproach [1], without blame [1], no open to blame [1]

1Ti   3: 2   Now the overseer must be **above reproach**, the husband of
     5: 7   these instructions, too, so that **no** one may be **open to blame**.
     6: 14   **without** spot or **blame** until the appearing of our Lord Jesus Christ,

456   ἀνέρχομαι, *anerchomai*   [3]   [√ *324 + 2262*]

went up [2], go up [1]

Jn   6: 3   Then Jesus **went up** on a mountainside and sat down with his
Gal   1: 17   nor *did I* **go up** to Jerusalem to see those who were apostles before
     1: 18   *I* **went up** to Jerusalem to get acquainted with Peter and stayed

457   ἄνεσις, *anesis*   [5]   [√ *918; cf. 324*]

freedom [1], peace [1], relief [1], relieved [1], rest [1]

Ac   24: 23   but to give him *some* **freedom** and permit his friends to take care
2Co   2: 13   I still had no **peace** of mind,
     7: 5   For when we came into Macedonia, this body of ours had no **rest**,
     8: 13   Our desire is not that others might be **relieved** while you are hard
2Th   1: 7   and give **relief** to you who are troubled, and to us as well.

458   ἀνετάζω, *anetazō*   [2]   [→ *2004; cf. 324*]

question [1], questioned [1]

Ac   22: 24   He directed that he be flogged and **questioned** in order to find out
     22: 29   Those who were about to **question** him withdrew immediately.

459   ἄνευ, *aneu*   [3]

without [2], apart from [1]

Mt   10: 29   Yet not one of them will fall to the ground **apart from** the will of
1Pe   3: 1   they may be won over **without** words by the behavior of their
     4: 9   Offer hospitality to one another **without** grumbling.

460   ἀνεύθετος, *aneuthetos*   [1]   [√ *1.1 + 2292 + 5502*]

unsuitable [1]

Ac   27: 12   Since the harbor was **unsuitable** to winter in, the majority decided

461   ἀνευρίσκω, *aneuriskō*   [2]   [√ *324 + 2351*]

finding [1], found [1]

Lk   2: 16   So they hurried off and **found** Mary and Joseph, and the baby,
Ac   21: 4   **Finding** the disciples there, we stayed with them seven days.

462   ἀνέχομαι, *anechomai*   [15]   [√ *324 + 2400*]

put up with [8], bear with [2], bearing with [1], doings that [1],
endure [1], enduring [1], listen [1]

Mt   17: 17   How long *shall I* **put up with** you? Bring the boy here to me."
Mk   9: 19   How long *shall I* **put up with** you? Bring the boy to me."
Lk   9: 41   Jesus replied, "how long shall I stay with you and **put up with** you?
Ac   18: 14   or serious crime, it would be reasonable for *me to* **listen** *to* you.
1Co   4: 12   we are cursed, we bless; when we are persecuted, *we* **endure** it;
2Co   11: 1   I hope *you will* **put up with** a little of my foolishness; but you are
     11: 1   with a little of my foolishness; but *you are already* **doings** that.
     11: 4   from the one you accepted, *you* **put up with** it easily enough.
     11: 19   *You* gladly **put up with** fools since you are so wise!
     11: 20   *you even* **put up with** anyone who enslaves you or exploits you
Eph   4: 2   and gentle; be patient, **bearing with** one another in love.
Col   3: 13   **Bear with** each other and forgive whatever grievances you may
2Th   1: 4   and faith in all the persecutions and trials *you are* **enduring**.
2Ti   4: 3   For the time will come when *men will* not **put up with** sound
Heb   13: 22   Brothers, I urge you to **bear with** my word of exhortation,

463   ἀνεψιός, *anepsios*   [1]

cousin [1]

Col   4: 10   sends you his greetings, as does Mark, the **cousin** of Barnabas.

464   ἄνηθον, *anēthon*   [1]

dill [1]

Mt   23: 23   You give a tenth of your spices—mint, **dill** and cummin.

465   ἀνήκω, *anēkō*   [3]   [√ *324 + 2457*]

fitting [1], ought to do [1], out of place [+*4024*] [1]

Eph   5: 4   foolish talk or coarse joking, which *are* **out** [+*4024*] **of place**,
Col   3: 18   Wives, submit to your husbands, as *is* **fitting** in the Lord.
Phm   1: 8   Christ I could be bold and order you to do what you **ought to do,**

466   ἀνήμερος, *anēmeros*   [1]   [√ *1.1*]

brutal [1]

2Ti   3: 3   without love, unforgiving, slanderous, without self-control, **brutal,**

467   ἀνήρ, *anēr*   [216]   [→ *435, 436, 437, 438, 439, 3770, 5635, 5791*]

ἄνδρες ἀδελφοί (men, brothers) [13] Ac 1:16; 2:29,37; 7:2; 13:15,26,38; 15:7,13; 22:1; 23:1,6; 28:17

husband [58] Mk 10:2; Lk 16:18; Ro 7:2,3,3; 1Co 7:13; Mt
1:16,19; Mk 10:12; Lk 2:36; Jn 1:13; 4:16,17,17,18,18; Ac 5:9,10;
Ro 7:2,2,3,3; 1Co 7:2,3,3,4,4,10,11,11,13,14,14, 16,16,34,39,39;
14:35; 2Co 11:2; Gal 4:27; Eph 5:22,23,24, 25,28,33; Col 3:18,19;
1Ti 3:2,12; 5:9; Tit 1:6; 2:5; 1Pe 3:1,5,7; Rev 21:2

men [64], man [63], husband [36], brothers [+81] [13], husbands
[12], untranslated [5], husband's [2], Jew [+2681] [2], man's [2], a
[1], am a virgin [+1182+4024] [1], characters [1], divorced
[+608+668] [1], Ethiopian [+134] [1], faithful to her husband
[+1222+1651] [1], he^s [+3836] [1], him^s [+3836] [1], Jews
[+2681] [1], marriage [1], mature [+5455] [1], murderer [+5838]
[1], owner of [+4005] [1], prophet [+4737] [1], sinner [+283] [1],
terrorists [+3836+4974] [1], you [1]

Mt   1:16 the husband of Mary, of whom was born Jesus, who is called
     1:19 Because Joseph her husband was a righteous man and did not
     7:24 and puts them into practice is like a wise man who built his house
     7:26 and does not put them into practice is like a foolish man who built
     12:41 The men of Nineveh will stand up at the judgment with this
     14:21 The number of those who ate was about five thousand men,
     14:35 And when the men of that place recognized Jesus, they sent word
     15:38 who ate was four thousand, [NIE] besides women and children.
Mk   6:20 and protected him, knowing him to be a righteous and holy man.
     6:44 The number of the men who had eaten was five thousand.
     10: 2 tested him by asking, "Is it lawful for a man to divorce his wife?"
     10:12 And if she divorces her husband and marries another man,
Lk   1:27 to a virgin pledged to be married to a man named Joseph,
     1:34 Mary asked the angel, "since I am a virgin [+1182+4024]?"
     2:36 she had lived with her husband seven years after her marriage,
     5: 8 knees and said, "Go away from me, Lord; I am a sinful man!"
     5:12 of the towns, a man came along who was covered with leprosy.
     5:18 Some men came carrying a paralytic on a mat and tried to take him
     6: 8 they were thinking and said to the man with the shriveled hand,
     7:20 When the men came to Jesus, they said, "John the Baptist sent us to
     8:27 he was met by a demon-possessed man from the town.
     8:38 The man from whom the demons had gone out begged to go with
     8:41 Then a man named Jairus, a ruler of the synagogue, came
     9:14 (About five thousand men were there.) But he said to his disciples,
     9:30 Two men, Moses and Elijah,
     9:32 they saw his glory and the two men standing with him.
     9:38 A man in the crowd called out, "Teacher, I beg you to look at my
     11:31 The Queen of the South will rise at the judgment with the men of
     11:32 The men of Nineveh will stand up at the judgment with this
     14:24 not one of those men who were invited will get a taste of my
     16:18 and the man who marries a divorced woman [+608+668] commits
     17:12 As he was going into a village, ten men who had leprosy met him.
     19: 2 A man was there by the name of Zacchaeus; he was a chief tax
     19: 7 to mutter, "He has gone to be the guest of a 'sinner [+283].' "
     22:63 The men who were guarding Jesus began mocking and beating
     23:50 Now there was a man named Joseph, a member of the Council,
     23:50 named Joseph, a member of the Council, a good and upright man,
     24: 4 suddenly two men in clothes that gleamed like lightning stood
     24:19 "He was a prophet [+4737], powerful in word and deed before God
Jn   1:13 nor of human decision or a husband's will, but born of God.
     1:30 'A man who comes after me has surpassed me because he was
     4:16 He told her, "Go, call your husband and come back."
     4:17 "I have no husband," she replied. Jesus said to her, "You are right
     4:17 said to her, "You are right when you say you have no husband.
     4:18 The fact is, you have had five husbands, and the man you now
     4:18 five husbands, and the man you now have is not your husband.
     6:10 in that place, and the men sat down, about five thousand of them.
Ac   1:10 when suddenly two men dressed in white stood beside them.
     1:11 "Men of Galilee," they said, "why do you stand here looking into
     1:16 and said, "Brothers [+81], the Scripture had to be fulfilled which
     1:21 Therefore it is necessary to choose one of the men who have been
     2: 5 Now there were staying in Jerusalem God-fearing Jews [RPG]
     2:14 raised his voice and addressed the crowd: "Fellow Jews [+2681]
     2:22 "Men of Israel, listen to this: Jesus of Nazareth was a man
     2:22 Jesus of Nazareth was a man accredited by God to you by
     2:29 "Brothers [+81], I can tell you confidently that the patriarch
     2:37 and said to Peter and the other apostles, "Brothers [+81],
     3: 2 Now a man crippled from birth was being carried to the temple
     3:12 he said to them: "Men of Israel, why does this surprise you?
     3:14 and asked that a murderer [+5838] be released to you.
     4: 4 and the number of men grew to about five thousand.

5: 1 Now a man named Ananias, together with his wife Sapphira,
5: 9 The feet of the men who buried your husband are at the door,
5:10 her dead, carried her out and buried her beside her husband.
5:14 more and more men and women believed in the Lord and were
5:25 The men you put in jail are standing in the temple courts teaching
5:35 "Men of Israel, consider carefully what you intend to do to these
5:36 to be somebody, and about four hundred men rallied to him.
6: 3 choose seven men from among you who are known to be full of
6: 5 They chose Stephen, a man full of faith and of the Holy Spirit;
6:11 Then they secretly persuaded some men to say, "We have heard
7: 2 To this he replied: "Brothers [+81] and fathers, listen to me!
7:26 He tried to reconcile them by saying, 'Men, you are brothers;
8: 2 Godly men buried Stephen and mourned deeply for him.
8: 3 to house, he dragged off men and women and put them in prison.
8: 9 Now for some time a man named Simon had practiced sorcery in
8:12 name of Jesus Christ, they were baptized, both men and women.
8:27 he started out, and on his way he met an Ethiopian [+134] eunuch,
9: 2 whether men or women, he might take them as prisoners to
9: 7 The men traveling with Saul stood there speechless; they heard the
9:12 In a vision he has seen a man named Ananias come and place his
9:13 "I have heard many reports about this man and all the harm he has
9:38 they sent two men to him and urged him, "Please come at once!"
10: 1 At Caesarea there was a man named Cornelius, a centurion in what
10: 5 Now send men to Joppa to bring back a man named Simon who is
10:17 the men sent by Cornelius found out where Simon's house was
10:19 the Spirit said to him, "Simon, three men are looking for you.
10:21 Peter went down and said to the men, "I'm the one you're looking
10:22 He is a righteous and God-fearing man, who is respected by all the
10:28 "You are well aware that it is against our law for a Jew [+2681] to
10:30 the afternoon. Suddenly a man in shining clothes stood before me
11: 3 went into the house of uncircumcised men and ate with them."
11:11 then three men who had been sent to me from Caesarea stopped at
11:12 six brothers also went with me, and we entered the man's house.
11:20 Some of them, however, men from Cyprus and Cyrene, went to
11:24 He was a good man, full of the Holy Spirit and faith, and a great
13: 6 There they met a Jewish sorcerer and false prophet named
13: 7 The proconsul, an intelligent man, sent for Barnabas and Saul
13:15 the synagogue rulers sent word to them, saying, "Brothers [+81]
13:16 "Men of Israel and you Gentiles who worship God, listen to me!
13:21 of Kish, [RPG] of the tribe of Benjamin, who ruled forty years.
13:22 'I have found David son of Jesse a man after my own heart;
13:26 "Brothers [+81], children of Abraham, and you God-fearing
13:38 "Therefore, my brothers [+81], I want you to know that through
14: 8 In Lystra there sat a man crippled in his feet, who was lame from
14:15 "Men, why are you doing this? We too are only men, human like
15: 7 Peter got up and addressed them: "Brothers [+81],
15:13 they finished, James spoke up: "Brothers [+81], listen to me.
15:22 decided to choose some of their own men and send them to
15:22 and Silas, two men who were leaders among the brothers.
15:25 So we all agreed to choose some men and send them to you with
16: 9 During the night Paul had a vision of a man of Macedonia
17: 5 so they rounded up some bad characters from the marketplace,
17:12 also a number of prominent Greek women and many Greek men.
17:22 up in the meeting of the Areopagus and said: "Men of Athens!
17:31 he will judge the world with justice by the man he has appointed.
17:34 A few men became followers of Paul and believed. Among them
18:24 He was a learned man, with a thorough knowledge of the
19: 7 There were about twelve men in all.
19:25 "Men, you know we receive a good income from this business.
19:35 "Men of Ephesus, doesn't all the world know that the city of
19:37 You have brought these men here, though they have neither robbed
20:30 Even from your own number men will arise and distort the truth in
21:11 'In this way the Jews of Jerusalem will bind the owner [+4005] of
21:23 we tell you. There are four men with us who have made a vow.
21:26 The next day Paul took the men and purified himself along with
21:28 shouting, "Men of Israel, help us! This is the man who teaches all
21:38 and led four thousand terrorists [+3836+4974] out into the desert
22: 1 "Brothers [+81] and fathers, listen now to my defense."
22: 3 "I am a Jew [+2681], born in Tarsus of Cilicia, but brought up in
22: 4 arresting both men and women and throwing them into prison,
22:12 "A man named Ananias came to see me. He was a devout observer
23: 1 Paul looked straight at the Sanhedrin and said, "My brothers [+81],
23: 6 called out in the Sanhedrin, "My brothers [+81], I am a Pharisee.
23:21 because more than [RPG] forty of them are waiting in ambush for
23:27 This man was seized by the Jews and they were about to kill him,
23:30 When I was informed of a plot to be carried out against the man,

24: 5 "We have found this **man** to be a troublemaker, stirring up riots
25: 5 against the man there, if **he**ˢ [+*3836*] has done anything wrong."
25:14 He said: "There is a **man** here whom Felix left as a prisoner.
25:17 the court the next day and ordered the **man** to be brought in.
25:23 with the high ranking officers and the leading **men** of the city.
25:24 "King Agrippa, and all who are present with us, **you** see this man!
27:10 "**Men**, I can see that our voyage is going to be disastrous and bring
27:21 "**Men**, you should have taken my advice not to sail from Crete;
27:25 So keep up your courage, **men**, for I have faith in God that it will
28:17 "My **brothers** [+*81*], although I have done nothing against our
Ro   4: 8 Blessed is the **man** whose sin the Lord will never count against
      7: 2 by law a married woman is bound *to* her **husband** as long as he is
      7: 2 but if her **husband** dies, she is released from the law of marriage.
      7: 2 but if her husband dies, she is released from the law of **marriage**.
      7: 3 if she marries another **man** while her husband is still alive,
      7: 3 if she marries another man while her **husband** is still alive,
      7: 3 But if her **husband** dies, she is released from that law and is not an
      7: 3 and is not an adulteress, even though she marries another **man**.
     11: 4 "I have reserved for myself seven thousand **[NIE]** who have not
1Co   7: 2 should have his own wife, and each woman her own **husband**.
      7: 3 The **husband** should fulfill his marital duty to his wife,
      7: 3 his marital duty to his wife, and likewise the wife *to* her **husband**.
      7: 4 wife's body does not belong to her alone but also to her **husband**.
      7: 4 the **husband's** body does not belong to him alone but also to his
      7:10 but the Lord): A wife must not separate from her **husband**.
      7:11 she must remain unmarried or else be reconciled *to* her **husband**.
      7:11 to her husband. And a **husband** must not divorce his wife.
      7:13 And if a woman has a **husband** who is not a believer and he is
      7:13 he is willing to live with her, she must not divorce **him**ˢ [+*3836*]
      7:14 For the unbelieving **husband** has been sanctified through his wife,
      7:16 How do you know, wife, whether you will save your **husband**?
      7:16 Or, how do you know, **husband**, whether you will save your wife?
      7:34 about the affairs of this world—how she can please her **husband**.
      7:39 A woman is bound *to* her **husband** as long as he lives. But if her
      7:39 But if her **husband** dies, she is free to marry anyone she wishes,
     11: 3 Now I want you to realize that the head *of* every **man** is Christ,
     11: 3 and the head of the woman is **man**, and the head of Christ is God.
     11: 4 Every **man** who prays or prophesies with his head covered
     11: 7 A **man** ought not to cover his head, since he is the image and glory
     11: 7 is the image and glory of God; but the woman is the glory *of* **man**.
     11: 8 For **man** did not come from woman, but woman from man;
     11: 8 For man did not come from woman, but woman from **man**;
     11: 9 neither was **man** created for woman, but woman for man.
     11: 9 neither was man created for woman, but woman for **man**.
     11:11 In the Lord, however, woman is not independent of **man**, nor is
     11:11 is not independent of man, nor is **man** independent of woman.
     11:12 For as woman came from **man**, so also man is born of woman.
     11:12 For as woman came from man, so also **man** is born of woman.
     11:14 Does not the very nature of things teach you that if a **man** has long
     13:11 like a child. When I became a **man**, I put childish ways behind me.
     14:35 about something, they should ask their own **husbands** at home;
2Co 11: 2 I promised you *to* one **husband**, to Christ, so that I might present
Gal   4:27 children of the desolate woman than of her who has a **husband**."
Eph   4:13 in the knowledge of the Son of God and become **mature** [+*5455*],
      5:22 Wives, submit *to* your **husbands** as to the Lord.
      5:23 For the **husband** is the head of the wife as Christ is the head of the
      5:24 so also wives should submit *to* their **husbands** in everything.
      5:25 **Husbands**, love your wives, just as Christ loved the church
      5:28 same way, **husbands** ought to love their wives as their own bodies.
      5:33 wife as he loves himself, and the wife must respect her **husband**.
Col   3:18 Wives, submit *to* your **husbands**, as is fitting in the Lord.
      3:19 **Husbands**, love your wives and do not be harsh with them.
1Ti   2: 8 I want **men** everywhere to lift up holy hands in prayer,
      2:12 I do not permit a woman to teach or to have authority over a **man**;
      3: 2 the **husband** of but one wife, temperate, self-controlled,
      3:12 A deacon must be the **husband** of but one wife and must manage
      5: 9 she is over sixty, has been **faithful to her husband** [+*1222+1651*],
Tit   1: 6 An elder must be blameless, the **husband** of but one wife,
      2: 5 to be busy at home, to be kind, and to be subject *to* their **husbands**,
Jas   1: 8 he is a double-minded **man**, unstable in all he does.
      1:12 Blessed is the **man** who perseveres under trial, because when he
      1:20 for **man's** anger does not bring about the righteous life that God
      1:23 but does not do what it says is like a **man** who looks at his face in
      2: 2 Suppose a **man** comes into your meeting wearing a gold ring
      3: 2 he is a perfect **man**, able to keep his whole body in check.
1Pe   3: 1 Wives, in the same way be submissive *to* your **husbands** so that,

3: 5 They were submissive *to* their own **husbands**,
3: 7 **Husbands**, in the same way be considerate as you live with your
Rev 21: 2 prepared as a bride beautifully dressed *for* her **husband**.

468 ἀνθίστημι, *anthistēmi* [14] [√ *505 + 2705*]

opposed [4], resist [4], do soˢ [1], oppose [1], rebelling against [1], resists [1], stand up against [1], stand your ground [1]

Mt   5:39 But I tell you, *Do* not **resist** an evil person. If someone strikes you
Lk   21:15 and wisdom that none of your adversaries will be able *to* **resist**
Ac   6:10 but they could not **stand up against** his wisdom or the Spirit by
     13: 8 **opposed** them and tried to turn the proconsul from the faith.
Ro   9:19 "Then why does God still blame us? For who **resists** his will?"
     13: 2 he who rebels against the authority *is* **rebelling against** what God
     13: 2 and those *who* **do so**ˢ will bring judgment on themselves.
Gal   2:11 When Peter came to Antioch, *I* **opposed** him to his face,
Eph   6:13 the day of evil comes, you may be able *to* **stand your ground**,
2Ti   3: 8 Just as Jannes and Jambres **opposed** Moses, so also these men
      3: 8 and Jambres opposed Moses, so also these men **oppose** the truth—
      4:15 your guard against him, because *he* strongly **opposed** our message.
Jas   4: 7 then, to God. **Resist** the devil, and he will flee from you.
1Pe   5: 9 **Resist** him, standing firm in the faith, because you know that your

469 ἀνθομολογέομαι, *anthomologeomai* [1]
[√ *505 + 3933*]

gave thanks [1]

Lk   2:38 *she* **gave thanks** to God and spoke about the child to all who were

470 ἄνθος, *anthos* [4]

flowers [2], blossom [1], flower [1]

Jas   1:10 in his low position, because he will pass away like a wild **flower**.
      1:11 and withers the plant; its **blossom** falls and its beauty is destroyed.
1Pe   1:24 are like grass, and all their glory is like the **flowers** of the field;
      1:24 like the flowers of the field; the grass withers and the **flowers** fall,

471 ἀνθρακιά, *anthrakia* [2] [√ *472*]

fire [1], fire of burning coals [1]

Jn   18:18 and officials stood around a **fire** they had made to keep warm.
     21: 9 they saw a **fire of burning coals** there with fish on it, and some

472 ἄνθραξ, *anthrax* [1] [→ *471*]

coals [1]

Ro   12:20 to drink. In doing this, you will heap burning **coals** on his head."

473 ἀνθρωπάρεσκος, *anthrōpareskos* [2]
[√ *476 + 743*]

win favor [2]

Eph   6: 6 Obey them not only to **win** their **favor** when their eye is on you,
Col   3:22 and do it, not only when their eye is on you and to **win** their **favor**,

474 ἀνθρώπινος, *anthrōpinos* [7] [√ *476*]

human [3], among men [1], common to man [1], in human terms [1], man [1]

Ac   17:25 And he is not served by **human** hands, as if he needed anything,
Ro   6:19 I put this **in human terms** because you are weak in your natural
1Co   2:13 not in words taught us *by* **human** wisdom but in words taught by
      4: 3 I care very little if I am judged by you or by any **human** court;
     10:13 No temptation has seized you except what is **common to man**.
Jas   3: 7 creatures of the sea are being tamed and have been tamed *by* **man**,
1Pe   2:13 for the Lord's sake to every authority *instituted* **among men**:

475 ἀνθρωποκτόνος, *anthrōpoktonos* [3]

[√ *476 + 650*]

murderer [3]

Jn   8:44   He was a **murderer** from the beginning, not holding to the truth,
1Jn 3:15   Anyone who hates his brother is a **murderer**, and you know that
     3:15   and you know that no **murderer** has eternal life in him.

476 ἄνθρωπος, *anthrōpos* [550]   [→ *473, 474, 475, 1881, 5792, 5793*]

ὁ υἱὸς τοῦ ἀνθρώπου (the Son of Man)   [82]   Mt 8:20; 9:6;
   10:23; 11:19; 12:8,32,40; 13:37,41; 16:13,27,28; 17:9,12,22;
   19:28; 20:18,28; 24:27,30,30,37,39,44; 25:31; 26:2,24,24,45,64;
   Mk 2:10,28; 8:31,38; 9:9,12,31; 10:33,45; 13:26; 14:21,21,41,62;
   Lk 5:24; 6:5,22; 7:34; 9:22,26,44,58; 11:30; 12:8,10,40;
   17:22,24,26,30; 18:8,31; 19:10; 21:27,36; 22:22,48,69; 24:7; Jn
   1:51; 3:13,14; 6:27,53,62; 8:28; 9:35; 12:23,34,34; 13:31; Ac 7:56

man [277], men [136], people [18], man's [12], human [10],
everyone [*+4246*] [6], himˢ [*+3836*] [5], men's [5], self [4],
untranslated [3], child [3], fellow [3], mankind [3], being [2],
everybody [*+4246*] [2], everyone [2], glutton [*+5741*] [2], heˢ
[*+3836*] [2], king [*+995*] [2], landowner [*+3867*] [2], men
[*+3836+3836+5626*] [2], one [2], others [2], pay attention who
they are [*+1063+4725*] [2], person [2], themˢ [*+3836*] [2], theyˢ
[*+3836*] [2], youˢ [2], all [*+4246*] [1], all the world
[*+1639+4005+5515*] [1], any [*+5515*] [1], anyone [*+3594*] [1],
anyoneˢ [*+3836*] [1], cripple [*+822*] [1], enemy [*+2398*] [1], friend
[1], from everyday life [*+2848*] [1], from human point of view
[*+2848*] [1], hisˢ [*+3836+4047*] [1], human [*+2848*] [1], human
being [*+6034*] [1], husband [1], Jew [*+2681*] [1], judge by
external appearance [*+3284+4725*] [1], merchant [*+1867*] [1],
oneˢ [1], outwardly [*+2032+3836*] [1], owner of a house [*+3867*]
[1], paralytic [*+4168*] [1], people [*+3950*] [1], Roman citizen
[*+4871*] [1], Roman citizens [*+4871*] [1], self [*+2840+3836*] [1],
sinner [*+2848*] [1], someoneˢ [1], something man made up
[*+2848*] [1], suppose one [*+5515*] [1], themˢ [1], thoseˢ [*+3836*]
[1], thoseˢ [1], which [*+5515*] [1], whoˢ [*+3836+4047*] [1], whoˢ
[1]

Mt   4:4   'Man does not live on bread alone, but on every word that comes
     4:19   follow me," Jesus said, "and I will make you fishers of men.
     5:13   good for anything, except to be thrown out and trampled by men.
     5:16   In the same way, let your light shine before men, that they may see
     5:19   and teaches others to do the same will be called least in the
     6:1   "Be careful not to do your 'acts of righteousness' before men,
     6:2   do in the synagogues and on the streets, to be honored by men.
     6:5   in the synagogues and on the street corners to be seen by men.
     6:14   For if you forgive men when they sin against you, your heavenly
     6:15   But if you do not forgive men their sins, your Father will not
     6:16   for they disfigure their faces to show men they are fasting.
     6:18   so that it will not be obvious to men that you are fasting, but only
     7:9   "Which [*+5515*] of you, if his son asks for bread, will give him a
     7:12   do to others what you would have themˢ [*+3836*] do to you,
     8:9   For I myself am a man under authority, with soldiers under me.
     8:20   the air have nests, but the Son of Man has no place to lay his head."
     8:27   The men were amazed and asked, "What kind of man is this?
     9:6   so that you may know that the Son of Man has authority on earth
     9:8   and they praised God, who had given such authority to men.
     9:9   he saw a man named Matthew sitting at the tax collector's booth.
     9:32   a man who was demon-possessed and could not talk was brought
     10:17 "Be on your guard against men; they will hand you over to the local
     10:23 going through the cities of Israel before the Son of Man comes.
     10:32 "Whoever acknowledges me before men, I will also acknowledge
     10:33 But whoever disowns me before men, I will disown him before my
     10:35 For I have come to turn " 'a man against his father, a daughter
     10:36 a man's enemies will be the members of his own household.'
     11:8   A man dressed in fine clothes? No, those who wear fine clothes
     11:19 The Son of Man came eating and drinking, and they say, 'Here is a
     11:19 and they say, 'Here is a glutton [*+5741*] and a drunkard,
     12:8   For the Son of Man is Lord of the Sabbath."
     12:10 and a man with a shriveled hand was there. Looking for a reason
     12:11 "If any [*+5515*] of you has a sheep and it falls into a pit on the
     12:12 How much more valuable is a man than a sheep! Therefore it is

     12:13 Then he said to the man, "Stretch out your hand." So he stretched it
     12:31 so I tell you, every sin and blasphemy will be forgiven men,
     12:32 Anyone who speaks a word against the Son of Man will be
     12:35 The good man brings good things out of the good stored up in him,
     12:35 and the evil man brings evil things out of the evil stored up in him.
     12:36 But I tell you that men will have to give account on the day of
     12:40 so the Son of Man will be three days and three nights in the heart
     12:43 "When an evil spirit comes out of a man, it goes through arid places
     12:45 And the final condition of that man is worse than the first.
     13:24 "The kingdom of heaven is like a man who sowed good seed in his
     13:25 But while everyone was sleeping, his enemy came and sowed
     13:28 " 'An enemy [*+2398*] did this,' he replied. "The servants asked
     13:31 is like a mustard seed, which a man took and planted in his field.
     13:37 "The one who sowed the good seed is the Son of Man.
     13:41 The Son of Man will send out his angels, and they will weed out of
     13:44 When a man found it, he hid it again, and then in his joy went
     13:45 the kingdom of heaven is like a merchant [*+1867*] looking for fine
     13:52 owner of a house [*+3867*] who brings out of his storeroom new
     15:9   worship me in vain; their teachings are but rules taught by men.' "
     15:11 What goes into a man's mouth does not make him 'unclean,'
     15:11 out of his mouth, that is what makes himˢ [*+3836*] 'unclean.' "
     15:18 the mouth come from the heart, and these make a man 'unclean.'
     15:20 These are what make a man 'unclean'; but eating with unwashed
     15:20 but eating with unwashed hands does not make himˢ [*+3836*]
     16:13 he asked his disciples, "Who do people say the Son of Man is?"
     16:13 he asked his disciples, "Who do people say the Son of Man is?"
     16:23 you do not have in mind the things of God, but the things of men."
     16:26 What good will it be for a man if he gains the whole world,
     16:26 forfeits his soul? Or what can a man give in exchange for his soul?
     16:27 For the Son of Man is going to come in his Father's glory with his
     16:28 taste death before they see the Son of Man coming in his kingdom."
     17:9   you have seen, until the Son of Man has been raised from the dead."
     17:12 In the same way the Son of Man is going to suffer at their hands."
     17:14 came to the crowd, a man approached Jesus and knelt before him.
     17:22 "The Son of Man is going to be betrayed into the hands of men.
     17:22 "The Son of Man is going to be betrayed into the hands of men.
     18:7   things must come, but woe to the man through whom they come!
     18:12 If a man owns a hundred sheep, and one of them wanders away,
     18:23 the kingdom of heaven is like a king [*+995*] who wanted to settle
     19:3   it lawful for a man to divorce his wife for any and every reason?"
     19:5   'For this reason a man will leave his father and mother and be
     19:6   Therefore what God has joined together, let man not separate."
     19:10 "If this is the situation between a husband and wife, it is better not
     19:12 they were born that way; others were made that way by men;
     19:26 Jesus looked at them and said, "With man this is impossible,
     19:28 of all things, when the Son of Man sits on his glorious throne,
     20:1   "For the kingdom of heaven is like a landowner [*+3867*] who went
     20:18 and the Son of Man will be betrayed to the chief priests
     20:28 just as the Son of Man did not come to be served, but to serve,
     21:25 where did it come from? Was it from heaven, or from men?"
     21:26 But if we say, 'From men'—we are afraid of the people, for they
     21:28 There was a man who had two sons. He went to the first and said,
     21:33 There was a landowner [*+3867*] who planted a vineyard. He put a
     22:2   "The kingdom of heaven is like a king [*+995*] who prepared a
     22:11 he noticed a man there who was not wearing wedding clothes.
     22:16 because you pay no attention to who they are [*+1063+4725*].
     23:4   They tie up heavy loads and put them on men's shoulders,
     23:5   "Everything they do is done for men to see: They make their
     23:7   be greeted in the marketplaces and to have men call them 'Rabbi.'
     23:13 you hypocrites! You shut the kingdom of heaven in men's faces.
     23:28 on the outside you appear to people as righteous but on the inside
     24:27 visible even in the west, so will be the coming of the Son of Man.
     24:30 "At that time the sign of the Son of Man will appear in the sky,
     24:30 They will see the Son of Man coming on the clouds of the sky,
     24:37 in the days of Noah, so it will be at the coming of the Son of Man.
     24:39 all away. That is how it will be at the coming of the Son of Man.
     24:44 because the Son of Man will come at an hour when you do not
     25:24 "Again, it will be like a man going on a journey, who called his
     25:24 'Master,' he said, 'I knew that you are a hard man,
     25:31 "When the Son of Man comes in his glory, and all the angels with
     26:2   and the Son of Man will be handed over to be crucified."
     26:24 The Son of Man will go just as it is written about him. But woe to
     26:24 But woe to that man who betrays the Son of Man! It would be
     26:24 But woe to that man who betrays the Son of Man! It would be
     26:24 It would be better for him if heˢ [*+3836*] had not been born."
     26:45 is near, and the Son of Man is betrayed into the hands of sinners.

26:64 In the future you will see the Son *of* **Man** sitting at the right hand
26:72 He denied it again, with an oath: "I don't know the **man**!"
26:74 curses on himself and he swore to them, "I don't know the **man**!"
27:32 they were going out, they met a **man** from Cyrene, named Simon,
27:57 there came a rich **man** from Arimathea, named Joseph,

Mk 1:17 follow me," Jesus said, "and I will make you fishers *of* **men**."
1:23 then a **man** in their synagogue who was possessed by an evil spirit
2:10 But that you may know that the Son *of* **Man** has authority on earth
2:27 Then he said to them, "The **Sabbath** was made for **man**, not man for
2:27 "The Sabbath was made for man, not **man** for the Sabbath.
2:28 So the Son *of* **Man** is Lord even of the Sabbath."
3: 1 into the synagogue, and a **man** with a shriveled hand was there.
3: 3 Jesus said *to* the **man** with the shriveled hand, "Stand up in front of
3: 5 at their stubborn hearts, said *to* the **man**, "Stretch out your hand."
3:28 blasphemies *of* **men** [+*3836+3836+5526*] will be forgiven them.
4:26 the kingdom of God is like. A **man** scatters seed on the ground.
5: 2 a **man** with an evil spirit came from the tombs to meet him.
5: 8 For Jesus had said to him, "Come out of this **man**, you evil spirit!"
7: 7 worship me in vain; their teachings are but rules taught *by* **men**.'
7: 8 the commands of God and are holding on to the traditions *of* **men**."
7:11 But you say that if a **man** says to his father or mother:
7:15 Nothing outside a **man** can make him 'unclean' by going into him.
7:15 Rather, it is what comes out of a **man** that makes him 'unclean.' "
7:15 it is what comes out of a man that makes him[s] [+*3836*] 'unclean.' "
7:18 "Don't you see that nothing that enters a **man** from the outside can
7:20 went on: "What comes out of a **man** is what makes him 'unclean.'
7:20 "What comes out of a man is what makes him[s] [+*3836*] 'unclean.'
7:21 For from within, out of **men's** hearts, come evil thoughts,
7:23 All these evils come from inside and make a **man** 'unclean.' "
8:24 He looked up and said, "I see **people**; they look like trees walking
8:27 On the way he asked them, "Who do **people** say I am?"
8:31 then began to teach them that the Son *of* **Man** must suffer many
8:33 do not have in mind the things of God, but the things *of* **men**."
8:36 What good is it for a **man** to gain the whole world, yet forfeit his
8:37 Or what can a **man** give in exchange for his soul?
8:38 the Son *of* **Man** will be ashamed of him when he comes in his
9: 9 what they had seen until the Son *of* **Man** had risen from the dead.
9:12 Why then is it written that the Son *of* **Man** must suffer much
9:31 "The Son *of* **Man** is going to be betrayed into the hands of men.
9:31 "The Son of Man is going to be betrayed into the hands of **men**.
10: 7 'For this reason a **man** will leave his father and mother and be
10: 9 Therefore what God has joined together, let **man** not separate."
10:27 Jesus looked at them and said, "With **man** this is impossible,
10:33 "and the Son *of* **Man** will be betrayed to the chief priests
10:45 For even the Son *of* **Man** did not come to be served, but to serve,
11: 2 you will find a colt tied there, which no **one** has ever ridden.
11:30 John's baptism—was it from heaven, or from **men**? Tell me!"
11:32 But if we say, 'From **men**'...." (They feared the people,
12: 1 "A **man** planted a vineyard. He put a wall around it, dug a pit for
12:14 because *you* **pay** no **attention** to **who they are** [+*1063+4725*];
13:26 "At that time men will see the Son *of* **Man** coming in clouds with
13:34 It's like a **man** going away: He leaves his house and puts his
14:13 "Go into the city, and a **man** carrying a jar of water will meet you.
14:21 The Son *of* **Man** will go just as it is written about him. But woe to
14:21 But woe *to* that **man** who betrays the Son of Man! It would be
14:21 But woe to that man who betrays the Son *of* **Man**! It would be
14:21 It would be better for him if **he**[s] [+*3836*] had not been born."
14:41 Look, the Son *of* **Man** is betrayed into the hands of sinners.
14:62 "And you will see the Son *of* **Man** sitting at the right hand of the
14:71 he swore to them, "I don't know this **man** you're talking about."
15:39 saw how he died, he said, "Surely this **man** was the Son of God!"

Lk 1:25 shown his favor and taken away my disgrace among the **people**."
2:14 in the highest, and on earth peace to **men** on whom his favor rests."
2:25 Now there was a **man** in Jerusalem called Simeon, who was
2:25 there was a man in Jerusalem called Simeon, who[s] [+*3836+4047*]
2:52 Jesus grew in wisdom and stature, and in favor with God and **men**.
4: 4 Jesus answered, "It is written: '**Man** does not live on bread alone.'
4:33 In the synagogue there was a **man** possessed by a demon,
5:10 said to Simon, "Don't be afraid; from now on you will catch **men**."
5:18 Some men came carrying a **paralytic** [+*4168*] on a mat and tried to
5:20 Jesus saw their faith, he said, "**Friend**, your sins are forgiven."
5:24 But that you may know that the Son *of* **Man** has authority on earth
6: 5 Then Jesus said to them, "The Son *of* **Man** is Lord of the Sabbath."
6: 6 and a **man** was there whose right hand was shriveled.
6:22 Blessed are you when **men** hate you, when they exclude you
6:22 and reject your name as evil, because of the Son *of* **Man**.

6:26 Woe to you when all **men** speak well of you, for that is how their
6:31 Do to others as you would have them[s] [+*3836*] do to you.
6:45 The good **man** brings good things out of the good stored up in his
6:48 He is like a **man** building a house, who dug down deep and laid the
6:49 and does not put them into practice is like a **man** who built a house
7: 8 For I myself am a **man** under authority, with soldiers under me.
7:25 A **man** dressed in fine clothes? No, those who wear expensive
7:31 "To what, then, can I compare the **people** of this generation?
7:34 The Son *of* **Man** came eating and drinking, and you say, 'Here is a
7:34 and you say, 'Here is a **glutton** [+*5741*] and a drunkard,
8:29 For Jesus had commanded the evil spirit to come out of the **man**.
8:33 When the demons came out of the **man**, they went into the pigs,
8:35 they found the **man** from whom the demons had gone out,
9:22 "The Son *of* **Man** must suffer many things and be rejected by the
9:25 What good is it for a **man** to gain the whole world, and yet lose
9:26 the Son *of* **Man** will be ashamed of him when he comes in his
9:44 The Son *of* **Man** is going to be betrayed into the hands of men."
9:44 The Son of Man is going to be betrayed into the hands *of* **men**."
9:58 the air have nests, but the Son *of* **Man** has no place to lay his head."
10:30 "A man was going down from Jerusalem to Jericho, when he fell
11:24 "When an evil spirit comes out of a **man**, it goes through arid
11:26 And the final condition *of* that **man** is worse than the first."
11:30 to the Ninevites, so also will the Son *of* **Man** be to this generation.
11:44 like unmarked graves, which **men** walk over without knowing it."
11:46 because you load **people** down with burdens they can hardly carry,
12: 8 "I tell you, whoever acknowledges me before **men**, the Son of Man
12: 8 the Son *of* **Man** will also acknowledge him before the angels of
12: 9 But he who disowns me before **men** will be disowned before the
12:10 And everyone who speaks a word against the Son *of* **Man** will be
12:14 Jesus replied, "**Man**, who appointed me a judge or an arbiter
12:16 "The ground of a certain rich **man** produced a good crop.
12:36 like **men** waiting for their master to return from a wedding
12:40 because the Son *of* **Man** will come at an hour when you do not
13: 4 do you think they were more guilty than all the **others** living in
13:19 is like a mustard seed, which a **man** took and planted in his garden.
14: 2 There in front of him was a **man** suffering from dropsy.
14:16 "A certain **man** was preparing a great banquet and invited many
14:30 saying, 'This **fellow** began to build and was not able to finish.'
15: 4 "**Suppose one** [+*5515*] of you has a hundred sheep and loses one
15:11 Jesus continued: "There was a **man** who had two sons.
16: 1 "There was a rich **man** whose manager was accused of wasting his
16:15 "You are the ones who justify yourselves in the eyes *of* **men**,
16:15 What is highly valued among **men** is detestable in God's sight.
16:19 "There was a rich **man** who was dressed in purple and fine linen
17:22 when you will long to see one of the days of the Son *of* **Man**,
17:24 For the Son *of* **Man** in his day will be like the lightning,
17:26 the days of Noah, so also will it be in the days of the Son *of* **Man**.
17:30 "It will be just like this on the day the Son *of* **Man** is revealed.
18: 2 there was a judge who neither feared God nor cared about **men**.
18: 4 said to himself, 'Even though I don't fear God or care about **men**,
18: 8 However, when the Son *of* **Man** comes, will he find faith on the
18:10 "Two **men** went up to the temple to pray, one a Pharisee
18:11 'God, I thank you that I am not like other **men**—robbers, evildoers,
18:27 Jesus replied, "What is impossible with **men** is possible with God."
18:31 is written by the prophets *about* the Son *of* **Man** will be fulfilled.
19:10 For the Son *of* **Man** came to seek and to save what was lost."
19:12 "A **man** of noble birth went to a distant country to have himself
19:21 I was afraid of you, because you are a hard **man**. You take out
19:22 You knew, did you, that I am a hard **man**, taking out what I did not
19:30 which no one has ever ridden. [**RPG**] Untie it and bring it here.
20: 4 John's baptism—was it from heaven, or from **men**?"
20: 6 But if we say, 'From **men**,' all the people will stone us,
20: 9 "A **man** planted a vineyard, rented it to some farmers and went
21:26 **Men** will faint from terror, apprehensive of what is coming on the
21:27 At that time they will see the Son *of* **Man** coming in a cloud with
21:36 and that you may be able to stand before the Son *of* **Man**."
22:10 "As you enter the city, a **man** carrying a jar of water will meet you.
22:22 The Son *of* **Man** will go as it has been decreed, but woe to that
22:22 go as it has been decreed, but woe *to* that **man** who betrays him."
22:48 asked him, "Judas, are you betraying the Son *of* **Man** with a kiss?"
22:58 said, "You also are one of them." "**Man**, I am not!" Peter replied.
22:60 Peter replied, "**Man**, I don't know what you're talking about!"
22:69 the Son *of* **Man** will be seated at the right hand of the mighty God."
23: 4 and the crowd, "I find no basis for a charge against this **man**."
23: 6 On hearing this, Pilate asked if the **man** was a Galilean.
23:14 "You brought me this **man** as one who was inciting the people to

23:14 I have examined him[s] [+3836] in your presence and have found
23:47 praised God and said, "Surely this was a righteous **man**."
24: 7 'The Son *of* **Man** must be delivered into the hands of sinful men,
24: 7 'The Son of Man must be delivered into the hands *of* sinful **men**,

Jn   1: 4 In him was life, and that life was the light *of* **men**.
1: 6 There came a **man** who was sent from God; his name was John.
1: 9 The true light that gives light to every **man** was coming into the
1:51 the angels of God ascending and descending on the Son *of* **Man**."
2:10 "**Everyone** [+4246] brings out the choice wine first and
2:25 He did not need man's testimony about **man**, for he knew what
2:25 need man's testimony about man, for he knew what was in a **man**.
3: 1 Now there was a **man** of the Pharisees named Nicodemus,
3: 4 "How can a **man** be born when he is old?" Nicodemus asked.
3:13 heaven except the one who came from heaven—the Son *of* **Man**.
3:14 up the snake in the desert, so the Son *of* **Man** must be lifted up,
3:19 but **men** loved darkness instead of light because their deeds were
3:27 "A **man** can receive only what is given him from heaven.
4:28 water jar, the woman went back to the town and said *to* the **people**,
4:29 "Come, see a **man** who told me everything I ever did. Could this be
4:50 Your son will live." The **man** took Jesus at his word and departed.
5: 5 One who[s] was there had been an invalid for thirty-eight years.
5: 7 "I have no one[s] to help me into the pool when the water is stirred.
5: 9 At once the **man** was cured; he picked up his mat and walked.
5:12 "Who is this **fellow** who told you to pick it up and walk?"
5:15 The **man** went away and told the Jews that it was Jesus who had
5:27 he has given him authority to judge because he is the Son *of* **Man**.
5:34 Not that I accept **human** testimony; but I mention it that you may
5:41 "I do not accept praise from **men**,
6:10 Jesus said, "Have the **people** sit down." There was plenty of grass
6:14 After the **people** saw the miraculous sign that Jesus did, they began
6:27 that endures to eternal life, which the Son *of* **Man** will give you.
6:53 unless you eat the flesh of the Son *of* **Man** and drink his blood,
6:62 What if you see the Son *of* **Man** ascend to where he was before!
7:22 but from the patriarchs), you circumcise a **child** on the Sabbath.
7:23 Now if a **child** can be circumcised on the Sabbath so that the law
7:23 why are you angry with me for healing the whole **man** on the
7:46 "No one ever spoke the way this **man** does," the guards declared.
7:51 "Does our law condemn **anyone**[s] [+3836] without first hearing him
8:17 In your own Law it is written that the testimony *of* two **men** is
8:28 So Jesus said, "When you have lifted up the Son *of* **Man**, then you
8:40 to kill me, a **man** who has told you the truth that I heard from God.
9: 1 As he went along, he saw a **man** blind from birth.
9:11 "The **man** they call Jesus made some mud and put it on my eyes.
9:16 Some of the Pharisees said, "This **man** is not from God, for he does
9:16 others asked, "How can a **sinner** [+283] do such miraculous signs?"
9:24 A second time they summoned the **man** who had been blind.
9:24 "Give glory to God," they said. "We know this **man** is a sinner."
9:30 The **man** answered, "Now that is remarkable! You don't know
9:35 when he found him, he said, "Do you believe in the Son *of* **Man**?"
10:33 "but for blasphemy, because you, a *mere* **man**, claim to be God."
11:47 they asked. "Here is this **man** performing many miraculous signs.
11:50 You do not realize that it is better for you that one **man** die for the
12:23 "The hour has come for the Son *of* **Man** to be glorified.
12:34 so how can you say, 'The Son *of* **Man** must be lifted up'?
12:34 'The Son of Man must be lifted up'? Who is this 'Son *of* **Man**'?"
12:43 for they loved praise *from* **men** more than praise from God.
13:31 "Now is the Son *of* **Man** glorified and God is glorified in him.
16:21 the anguish because of her joy that a **child** is born into the world.
17: 6 "I have revealed you *to* those[s] [+3836] whom you gave me out of
18:14 the Jews that it would be good if one **man** died for the people.
18:17 "You are not one of his[s] [+3836+4047] disciples, are you?"
18:29 and asked, "What charges are you bringing against this **man**?"
19: 5 thorns and the purple robe, Pilate said to them, "Here is the **man**!"

Ac   4: 9 to account today for an act of kindness shown to a **cripple** [+822]
4:12 for there is no other name under heaven given to **men** by which we
4:13 ordinary **men**, they were astonished and they took note that these
4:14 But since they could see the **man** who had been healed standing
4:16 "What are we going to do with these **men**?" they asked.
4:17 we must warn these men to speak no longer *to* **anyone** [+3594] in
4:22 For the **man** who was miraculously healed was over forty years
5: 4 think of doing such a thing? You have not lied *to* **men** but to God."
5:28 and are determined to make us guilty of this **man's** blood."
5:29 and the other apostles replied: "We must obey God rather than **men**!
5:34 and ordered that the **men** be put outside for a little while.
5:35 of Israel, consider carefully what you intend to do to these **men**.
5:38 Leave these **men** alone! Let them go! For if their purpose

5:38 For if their purpose or activity is of **human** origin, it will fail.
6:13 "This **fellow** never stops speaking against this holy place
7:56 and the Son *of* **Man** standing at the right hand of God."
9:33 There he found a **man** named Aeneas, a paralytic who had been
10:26 made him get up. "Stand up," he said, "I am *only* a **man** myself."
10:28 But God has shown me that I should not call any **man** impure
12:22 They shouted, "This is the voice of a god, not *of* a **man**."
14:11 "The gods have come down to us *in* **human** form!"
14:15 why are you doing this? We too are *only* **men**, human like you.
15:17 that the remnant *of* **men** may seek the Lord, and all the Gentiles
15:26 **men** who have risked their lives for the name of our Lord Jesus
16:17 rest of us, shouting, "These **men** are servants of the Most High God,
16:20 brought them before the magistrates and said, "These **men** are Jews,
16:35 sent their officers to the jailer with the order: "Release these **men**."
16:37 even though we are **Roman citizens** [+4871], and threw us into
17:26 From one man he made every nation *of* **men**, that they should
17:29 or silver or stone—an image *made by* **man's** design and skill.
17:30 but now he commands all **people** everywhere to repent.
18:13 "is persuading the **people** to worship God in ways contrary to the
19:16 Then the **man** who had the evil spirit jumped on them
19:35 doesn't **all the world** [+1639+4005+5515] know that the city
21:28 This is the **man** who teaches all men everywhere against our
21:39 Paul answered, "I am a **Jew** [+2681], from Tarsus in Cilicia.
22:15 You will be his witness to all **men** of what you have seen
22:25 "Is it legal for you to flog a **Roman citizen** [+4871] who hasn't
22:26 are you going to do?" he asked. "This **man** is a Roman citizen."
23: 9 "We find nothing wrong with this **man**," they said. "What if a spirit
24:16 I strive always to keep my conscience clear before God and **man**.
25:16 "I told them that it is not the Roman custom to hand over any **man**
25:22 Agrippa said to Festus, "I would like to hear this **man** myself."
26:31 "This **man** is not doing anything that deserves death
26:32 "This **man** could have been set free if he had not appealed to
28: 4 his hand, they said to each other, "This **man** must be a murderer;

Ro   1:18 and wickedness *of* **men** who suppress the truth by their
1:23 of the immortal God for images made to look like mortal **man**
2: 1 **You**[s], therefore, have no excuse, you who pass judgment on
2: 3 So when you, a **man**, pass judgment on them and yet do the
2: 9 and distress for every **human** [+6034] *being* who does evil:
2:16 This will take place on the day when God will judge **men's** secrets
2:29 written code. Such a man's praise is not from **men**, but from God.
3: 4 Not at all! Let God be true, and every **man** a liar. As it is written:
3: 5 bringing his wrath on us? (I am using a **human** [+2848] argument.)
3:28 For we maintain that a **man** is justified by faith apart from
4: 6 *of* the **man** to whom God credits righteousness apart from works:
5:12 Therefore, just as sin entered the world through one **man**,
5:12 and death through sin, and in this way death came to all **men**,
5:15 God's grace and the gift that came by the grace *of* the one **man**,
5:18 just as the result of one trespass was condemnation for all **men**,
5:18 act of righteousness was justification that brings life for all **men**.
5:19 For just as through the disobedience *of* the one **man** the many were
6: 6 For we know that our old **self** was crucified with him so that the
7: 1 that the law has authority over a **man** only as long as he lives?
7:22 For in my inner **being** I delight in God's law;
7:24 What a wretched **man** I am! Who will rescue me from this body of
9:20 But who are you, O **man**, to talk back to God? "Shall what is
10: 5 is by the law: "The **man** who does these things will live by them."
12:17 Be careful to do what is right in the eyes *of* **everybody** [+4246].
12:18 as far as it depends on you, live at peace with **everyone** [+4246].
14:18 serves Christ in this way is pleasing to God and approved *by* **men**.
14:20 but it is wrong *for* a **man** to eat anything that causes someone else

1Co   1:25 For the foolishness of God is wiser than **man's** wisdom,
1:25 and the weakness of God is stronger than **man's** strength.
2: 5 so that your faith might not rest on **men's** wisdom, but on God's
2: 9 no mind **[NIE]** has conceived what God has prepared for those
2:11 For who *among* **men** knows the thoughts of a man except the
2:11 For who among men knows the thoughts *of* a **man** except the
2:11 who among men knows the thoughts of a man except the **man's**
2:14 The **man** without the Spirit does not accept the things that come
3: 3 are you not worldly? Are you not acting like *mere* **men**?
3: 4 Paul," and another, "I follow Apollos," are you not *mere* **men**?
3:21 So then, no more boasting about **men**! All things are yours,
4: 1 **men** ought to regard us as servants of Christ and as those entrusted
4: 9 a spectacle to the whole universe, to angels as well as *to* **men**.
6:18 All other sins a **man** commits are outside his body, but he who sins
7: 1 for the matters you wrote about: It is good *for* a **man** not to marry.
7: 7 I wish that all **men** were as I am. But each man has his own gift

7:23 You were bought at a price; do not become slaves *of* **men**.
7:26 present crisis, I think that it is good *for* you*s* to remain as you are.
9: 8 Do I say this merely **from** a **human** [+2848] **point of view**?
11:28 A **man** ought to examine himself before he eats of the bread
13: 1 If I speak in the tongues *of* **men** and of angels, but have not love,
14: 2 For anyone who speaks in a tongue does not speak *to* **men**
14: 3 But everyone who prophesies speaks *to* **men** for their
15:19 life we have hope in Christ, we are to be pitied more than all **men**.
15:21 For since death came through a **man**, the resurrection of the dead
15:21 a man, the resurrection of the dead comes also through a **man**.
15:32 If I fought wild beasts in Ephesus for merely **human** reasons,
15:39 **Men** have one kind of flesh, animals have another, birds another
15:45 "The first **man** Adam became a living being"; the last Adam,
15:47 The first **man** was of the dust of the earth, the second man from
15:47 man was of the dust of the earth, the second **man** from heaven.
2Co 3: 2 written on our hearts, known and read by **everybody** [+4246].
4: 2 commend ourselves to every **man's** conscience in the sight of God.
4:16 Though **outwardly** [+2032+3836] we are wasting away,
5:11 we know what it is to fear the Lord, we try to persuade **men**.
8:21 not only in the eyes of the Lord but also in the eyes *of* **men**.
12: 2 I know a **man** in Christ who fourteen years ago was caught up to
12: 3 And I know that this **man**—whether in the body or apart from the
12: 4 heard inexpressible things, things that **man** is not permitted to tell.
Gal 1: 1 sent not from **men** nor by man, but by Jesus Christ and God the
1: 1 sent not from men nor by **man**, but by Jesus Christ and God the
1:10 Am I now trying to win the approval of **men**, or of God? Or am I
1:10 win the approval of men, or of God? Or am I trying to please **men**?
1:10 If I were still trying to please **men**, I would not be a servant of
1:11 gospel I preached is not **something** that man [+2848] **made up**.
1:12 I did not receive it from any **man**, nor was I taught it; rather,
2: 6 God *does* not **judge by external appearance** [+3284+4725]—
2:16 know that a **man** is not justified by observing the law,
3:15 Brothers, let me take an example **from everyday** [+2848] **life**.
3:15 or add to a **human** covenant that has been duly established,
5: 3 Again I declare *to* every **man** who lets himself be circumcised that
6: 1 Brothers, if **someone**s is caught in a sin, you who are spiritual
6: 7 be deceived: God cannot be mocked. A **man** reaps what he sows.
Eph 2:15 His purpose was to create in himself one new **man** out of the two,
3: 5 which was not made known *to* **men** [+3836+3836+5626] in other
3: 5 generations as it has now been revealed by the Spirit to God's holy
3:16 strengthen you with power through his Spirit in your inner **being**,
4: 8 on high, he led captives in his train and gave gifts *to* **men**."
4:14 by the cunning and craftiness of **men** in their deceitful scheming.
4:22 with regard to your former way of life, to put off your old **self**,
4:24 and to put on the new **self**, created to be like God in true
5:31 "For this reason a **man** will leave his father and mother and be
6: 7 Serve wholeheartedly, as if you were serving the Lord, not **men**,
Php 2: 7 taking the very nature of a servant, being made in **human** likeness.
2: 8 And being found in appearance as a **man**, he humbled himself
4: 5 Let your gentleness be evident to **all** [+4246]. The Lord is near.
Col 1:28 admonishing **[RPG]** and teaching everyone with all wisdom,
1:28 admonishing and teaching **everyone** [+4246] with all wisdom,
1:28 so that we may present **everyone** [+4246] perfect in Christ.
2: 8 which depends on **human** tradition and the basic principles of this
2:22 because they are based on **human** commands and teachings.
3: 9 each other, since you have taken off your old **self** with its practices
3:23 at it with all your heart, as working for the Lord, not *for* **men**,
1Th 2: 4 We are not trying to please **men** but God, who tests our hearts.
2: 6 We were not looking for praise from **men**, not from you or anyone
2:13 you accepted it not as the word *of* **men**, but as it actually is,
2:15 also drove us out. They displease God and are hostile *to* all **men**
4: 8 he who rejects this instruction does not reject **man** but God,
2Th 2: 3 until the rebellion occurs and the **man** of lawlessness is revealed,
3: 2 And pray that we may be delivered from wicked and evil **men**,
1Ti 2: 1 intercession and thanksgiving be made for **everyone** [+4246]—
2: 4 who wants all **men** to be saved and to come to a knowledge of the
2: 5 For there is one God and one mediator between God and **men**,
2: 5 and one mediator between God and men, the **man** Christ Jesus,
4:10 who is the Savior *of* all **men**, and especially of those who believe.
5:24 The sins of some **men** are obvious, reaching the place of judgment
6: 5 and constant friction between **men** of corrupt mind, who have been
6: 9 and harmful desires that plunge **men** into ruin and destruction.
6:11 But you, **man** of God, flee from all this, and pursue righteousness,
6:16 lives in unapproachable light, whom no **one** has seen or can see.
2Ti 2: 2 entrust *to* reliable **men** who will also be qualified to teach others.
3: 2 **People** will be lovers of themselves, lovers of money, boastful,

3: 8 **men** of depraved minds, who, as far as the faith is concerned,
3:13 while evil **men** and impostors will go from bad to worse, deceiving
3:17 so that the **man** of God may be thoroughly equipped for every
Tit 1:14 to Jewish myths or to the commands *of* **those**s who reject the truth.
2:11 For the grace of God that brings salvation has appeared *to* all **men**.
3: 2 and considerate, and to show true humility toward all **men**.
3: 8 is good. These things are excellent and profitable *for* **everyone**.
3:10 Warn a divisive **person** once, and then warn him a second time.
Heb 2: 6 "What is **man** that you are mindful of him, the son of man that you
2: 6 that you are mindful of him, the son *of* **man** that you care for him?
5: 1 Every high priest is selected from among **men** and is appointed to
5: 1 and is appointed to represent **them**s in matters related to God,
6:16 **Men** swear by someone greater than themselves, and the oath
7: 8 In the one case, the tenth is collected by **men** who die; but in the
7:28 For the law appoints as high priests **men** who are weak; but the
8: 2 the sanctuary, the true tabernacle set up by the Lord, not by **man**.
9:27 Just as **man** is destined to die once, and after that to face judgment,
13: 6 Lord is my helper; I will not be afraid. What can **man** do to me?"
Jas 1: 7 That **man** should not think he will receive anything from the Lord;
1:19 **Everyone** [+4246] should be quick to listen, slow to speak
2:20 You foolish **man**, do you want evidence that faith without deeds is
2:24 You see that a **person** is justified by what he does and not by faith
3: 8 but no **man** can tame the tongue. It is a restless evil, full of deadly
3: 9 tongue we praise our Lord and Father, and with it we curse **men**,
5:17 Elijah was a **man** just like us. He prayed earnestly that it would not
1Pe 2: 4 rejected by **men** but chosen by God and precious to him—
2:15 by doing good you should silence the ignorant talk *of* foolish **men**.
3: 4 Instead, it should be that of your inner **self** [+2840+3836],
4: 2 he does not live the rest of his earthly life *for* evil **human** desires,
4: 6 so that they might be judged according to **men** in regard to the
2Pe 1:21 For prophecy never had its origin in the will *of* **man**, but men
1:21 but **men** spoke from God as they were carried along by the Holy
2:16 who spoke with a **man's** voice and restrained the prophet's
3: 7 kept for the day of judgment and destruction *of* ungodly **men**.
1Jn 5: 9 We accept **man's** testimony, but God's testimony is greater
Jude 1: 4 For certain **men** whose condemnation was written about long ago
Rev 1:13 and among the lampstands was someone "like a son *of* **man**,"
4: 7 the second was like an ox, the third had a face like a **man**,
8:11 and many **people** died from the waters that had become bitter.
9: 4 but only those **people** who did not have the seal of God on their
9: 5 was like that of the sting of a scorpion when it strikes a **man**.
9: 6 During those days **men** will seek death, but will not find it;
9: 7 like crowns of gold, and their faces resembled **human** faces.
9:10 and in their tails they had power to torment **people** for five months.
9:15 and month and year were released to kill a third *of* **mankind**.
9:18 A third *of* **mankind** was killed by the three plagues of fire,
9:20 The rest *of* **mankind** that were not killed by these plagues still did
11:13 Seven thousand **people** [+3950] were killed in the earthquake,
13:13 fire to come down from heaven to earth in full view *of* **men**.
13:18 let him calculate the number of the beast, for it is **man's** number.
14: 4 They were purchased from among **men** and offered as firstfruits to
14:14 and seated on the cloud was one "like a son *of* **man**" with a crown
16: 2 and painful sores broke out on the **people** who had the mark of the
16: 8 on the sun, and the sun was given power to scorch **people** with fire.
16: 9 **They**s [+3836] were seared by the intense heat and they cursed the
16:18 No earthquake like it has ever occurred since **man** has been on
16:21 sky huge hailstones of about a hundred pounds each fell upon **men**.
16:21 And **they**s [+3836] cursed God on account of the plague of hail,
18:13 and sheep; horses and carriages; and bodies and souls *of* **men**.
21: 3 "Now the dwelling of God is with **men**, and he will live with them.
21:17 cubits thick, *by* **man's** measurement, which the angel was using.

477 ἀνθυπατεύω, *anthypateuō* Not used in UBS/NIV
[√ *478*]

478 ἀνθύπατος, *anthypatos* [5] [→ *477; cf. 505*]

proconsul [4], proconsuls [1]

Ac 13: 7 who was an attendant of the **proconsul**, Sergius Paulus.
13: 8 opposed them and tried to turn the **proconsul** from the faith.
13:12 When the **proconsul** saw what had happened, he believed,
18:12 While Gallio was **proconsul** of Achaia, the Jews made a united
19:38 against anybody, the courts are open and there are **proconsuls**.

479 ἀνίημι, *aniēmi* [4] [√ 918; cf. 324]

came loose [1], leave [1], not [1], untied [1]

Ac 16:26 all the prison doors flew open, and everybody's chains **came loose**.
    27:40 and at the same time **untied** the ropes that held the rudders.
Eph 6: 9 *Do* **not** threaten them, since you know that he who is both their
Heb 13: 5 with what you have, because God has said, "Never *will I* **leave** you;

480 ἀνίλεως, *anileōs*   Not used in UBS/NIV
[√ 1.1 + 2661]

481 ἄνιπτος, *aniptos* [2] [√ 1.1 + 3782]

unwashed [2]

Mt 15:20 but eating *with* **unwashed** hands does not make him 'unclean.' "
Mk 7: 2 eating food with hands that were "unclean," that is, **unwashed**.

482 ἀνίστημι, *anistēmi* [108 / 107] [√ 324 + 2705]

ἀναστῆναι ἐκ νεκρῶν (to rise from the dead) [11] Mk 9:9,10; 12:25; Lk 16:31; 24:46; Jn 20:9; Ac 10:41; 13:34; 17:3,31; Eph 5:14

got up [15], get up [13], stood up [13], rise [9], *untranslated* [6], raise up [5], rose [5], rise again [4], stand up [3], appeared [2], arise [2], come back to life [2], left [2], opposition arose [1], stand up [+3981] [1], standing up [1], appears [1], came forward [1], come [1], got ready [1], have children [+5065] [1], helped to her feet [1], left [+608] [1], opposes [+2093] [1], raised [1], raised again [1], raised from the dead [1], raised to life [1], raised up [1], raising [1], raising up [1], risen [1], rises [1], rising [1], rose again [1], ruler [1], send [1], set out [1], stood there [1]

Mt 9: 9 "Follow me," he told him, and Matthew **got up** and followed him.
    12:41 The men of Nineveh *will* **stand up** at the judgment with this
    22:24 must marry the widow and **have children** [+5065] for him.
    26:62 Then the high priest **stood up** and said to Jesus, "Are you not going
Mk 1:35 Jesus **got up**, left the house and went off to a solitary place,
    2:14 "Follow me," Jesus told him, and Levi **got up** and followed him.
    3:26 And if Satan **opposes** [+2093] himself and is divided, he cannot
    5:42 Immediately the girl **stood up** and walked around (she was twelve
    7:24 Jesus **left** that place and went to the vicinity of Tyre. He entered a
    8:31 and that he must be killed and after three days **rise again**.
    9: 9 what they had seen until the Son of Man *had* **risen** from the dead.
    9:10 to themselves, discussing what "**rising** from the dead" meant.
    9:27 took him by the hand and lifted him to his feet, and *he* **stood up**.
    9:31 hands of men. They will kill him, and after three days *he will* **rise**."
    10: 1 Jesus then **left** that place and went into the region of Judea
    10:34 spit on him, flog him and kill him. Three days later *he will* **rise**.
    12:23 At the resurrection [UBS+ *when men* **rise** *from the dead*,]
    12:25 When the dead **rise**, they will neither marry nor be given in
    14:57 Then some **stood up** and gave this false testimony against him:
    14:60 Then the high priest **stood up** before them and asked Jesus,
    16: 9 *When* Jesus **rose** early on the first day of the week, he appeared
Lk 1:39 At that time Mary **got ready** and hurried to a town in the hill
    4:16 into the synagogue, as was his custom. And *he* **stood up** to read.
    4:29 They **got up**, drove him out of the town, and took him to the brow
    4:38 Jesus **left** [+608] the synagogue and went to the home of Simon.
    4:39 and it left her. She **got up** at once and began to wait on them.
    5:25 Immediately he **stood up** in front of them, took what he had been
    5:28 and Levi **got up**, left everything and followed him.
    6: 8 and stand in front of everyone." So he **got up** and **stood there**.
    8:55 Her spirit returned, and at once *she* **stood up**. Then Jesus told them
    9: 8 others that one of the prophets of long ago *had* **come back to life**.
    9:19 that one of the prophets of long ago *has* **come back to life**."
    10:25 On one occasion an expert in the law **stood up** to test Jesus.
    11: 7 children are with me in bed. I can't **get up** and give you anything.'
    11: 8 though he will not **get up** and give him the bread because he is his
    11:32 The men of Nineveh *will* **stand up** at the judgment with this
    15:18 I will **set out** and go back to my father and say to him: Father,
    15:20 So he **got up** and went to his father. "But while he was still a long
    16:31 they will not be convinced even if someone **rises** from the dead.' "
    17:19 he said to him, "**Rise** and go; your faith has made you well."
    18:33 On the third day *he will* **rise again**."
    22:45 *When he* **rose** from prayer and went back to the disciples,

    22:46 "**Get up** and pray so that you will not fall into temptation."
    23: 1 Then the whole assembly **rose** and led him off to Pilate.
    24: 7 of sinful men, be crucified and on the third day *be* **raised again**.' "
    24:12 Peter, however, **got up** and ran to the tomb. Bending over,
    24:33 They **got up** and returned at once to Jerusalem. There they found
    24:46 The Christ will suffer and **rise** from the dead on the third day,
Jn 6:39 none of all that he has given me, but **raise** them **up** at the last day.
    6:40 him shall have eternal life, and I *will* **raise** him **up** at the last day."
    6:44 who sent me draws him, and I *will* **raise** him **up** at the last day.
    6:54 my blood has eternal life, and I *will* **raise** him **up** at the last day.
    11:23 Jesus said to her, "Your brother *will* **rise again**."
    11:24 "I know *he will* **rise again** in the resurrection at the last day."
    11:31 comforting her, noticed how quickly she **got up** and went out,
    20: 9 (They still did not understand from Scripture that Jesus had to **rise**
Ac 1:15 In those days Peter **stood up** among the believers (a group
    2:24 But God **raised** him **from the dead**, freeing him from the agony of
    2:32 God *has* **raised** this Jesus **to life**, and we are all witnesses of the
    3:22 'The Lord your God *will* **raise up** for you a prophet like me from
    3:26 *When* God **raised up** his servant, he sent him first to you to bless
    5: 6 Then the young men **came forward**, wrapped up his body,
    5:17 [NIE] Then the high priest and all his associates, who were
    5:34 **stood up** in the Sanhedrin and ordered that the men be put outside
    5:36 Some time ago Theudas **appeared**, claiming to be somebody,
    5:37 Judas the Galilean **appeared** in the days of the census and led a
    6: 9 **Opposition arose**, however, from members of the Synagogue of
    7:18 who knew nothing about Joseph, *became* **ruler** of Egypt.
    7:37 'God *will* **send** you a prophet like me from your own people.'
    8:26 an angel of the Lord said to Philip, [NIE] "Go south to the road—
    8:27 So [NIE] he started out, and on his way he met an Ethiopian
    9: 6 "Now **get up** and go into the city, and you will be told what you
    9:11 [NIE] "Go to the house of Judas on Straight Street and ask for a
    9:18 Saul's eyes, and he could see again. He **got up** and was baptized,
    9:34 to him, "Jesus Christ heals you. **Get up** and take care of your mat."
    9:34 **Get up** and take care of your mat." Immediately Aeneas **got up**.
    9:39 Peter [NIE] went with them, and when he arrived he was taken
    9:40 Turning toward the dead woman, he said, "Tabitha, **get up**."
    9:41 He took her by the hand and **helped** her **to her feet**. Then he called
    10:13 Then a voice told him, "**Get up**, Peter. Kill and eat."
    10:20 So **get up** and go downstairs. Do not hesitate to go with them,
    10:23 The next day Peter [NIE] started out with them, and some of the
    10:26 made him get up. "**Stand up**," he said, "I am only a man myself."
    10:41 by us who ate and drank with him after he **rose** from the dead.
    11: 7 Then I heard a voice telling me, '**Get up**, Peter. Kill and eat.'
    11:28 **stood up** and through the Spirit predicted that a severe famine
    12: 7 "Quick, **get up**!" he said, and the chains fell off Peter's wrists.
    13:16 **Standing up**, Paul motioned with his hand and said: "Men of Israel
    13:33 he has fulfilled for us, their children, *by* **raising** up Jesus.
    13:34 The fact that God **raised** him from the dead, never to decay,
    14:10 and called out, "**Stand** [+3981] **up** on your feet!" At that, the man
    14:20 had gathered around him, he **got up** and went back into the city.
    15: 7 After much discussion, Peter **got up** and addressed them: "Brothers,
    17: 3 and proving that the Christ had to suffer and **rise** from the dead.
    17:31 He has given proof of this to all men *by* **raising** him from the dead."
    20:30 Even from your own number men *will* **arise** and distort the truth in
    22:10 " 'What shall I do, Lord?' I asked. " '**Get up**,' the Lord said,
    22:16 **Get up**, be baptized and wash your sins away, calling on his
    23: 9 and some of the teachers of the law who were Pharisees **stood up**
    26:16 'Now **get up** and stand on your feet. I have appeared to you to
    26:30 The king **rose**, and with him the governor and Bernice and those
Ro 15:12 of Jesse will spring up, one *who will* **arise** to rule over the nations;
1Co 10: 7 sat down to eat and drink and **got up** to indulge in pagan revelry."
Eph 5:14 "Wake up, O sleeper, **rise** from the dead, and Christ will shine on
1Th 4:14 We believe that Jesus died and **rose again** and so we believe that
    4:16 with the trumpet call of God, and the dead in Christ *will* **rise** first.
Heb 7:11 to the people), why was there still need for another priest *to* **come**—
    7:15 said is even more clear if another priest like Melchizedek **appears**,

483 Ἅννα, *Hanna* [1]

Anna [1]

Lk 2:36 a prophetess, **Anna**, the daughter of Phanuel, of the tribe of Asher.

484 Ἅννας, *Hannas* [4]

Annas [4]

Lk 3: 2 during the high priesthood *of* **Annas** and Caiaphas, the word of
Jn 18: 13 and brought him first to **Annas**, who was the father-in-law of
18: 24 Then **Annas** sent him, still bound, to Caiaphas the high priest.
Ac 4: 6 **Annas** the high priest was there, and so were Caiaphas, John,

485 ἀνόητος, *anoētos* [6] [√ *1.1 + 3808*]

foolish [6]

Lk 24: 25 He said to them, "How **foolish** you are, and how slow of heart to
Ro 1: 14 both to Greeks and non-Greeks, both to the wise and the **foolish**.
Gal 3: 1 You **foolish** Galatians! Who has bewitched you? Before your very
3: 3 Are you so **foolish**? After beginning with the Spirit, are you now
1Ti 6: 9 and a trap and into many **foolish** and harmful desires that plunge
Tit 3: 3 At one time we too were **foolish**, disobedient, deceived

486 ἄνοια, *anoia* [2] [√ *1.1 + 3808*]

folly [1], furious [+4398] [1]

Lk 6: 11 But they *were* **furious** [+4398] and began to discuss with one
2Ti 3: 9 as in the case of those men, their **folly** will be clear to everyone.

487 ἀνοίγω, *anoigō* [77] [→ *489, 1380, 1986; cf. 324*]

ἀνοίγω οἱ ὀφθαλμοί (open the eyes) [14] Mt 9:30; 20:33; Jn
9:10,14,17,21,26,30,32; 10:21; 11:37; Ac 9:8,40; 26:18

ἀνοίγω τὸ στόμα (open the mouth) [11] Mt 5:2; 13:35; 17:27;
Lk 1:64; Ac 8:32,35, 10:34; 18:14; 2Co 6:11; Rev 12:16; 13:6

opened [38], open [21], opening [3], opens [3], standing open
[2], *untranslated* [1], began to speak [+3306+3836+5125] [1],
began to teach [+1438+3836+5125] [1], broke open [1], flew
open [1], lay open [1], restored [1], sight [+3836+4057] [1],
speak [+3836+5125] [1], spoken freely [+3836+5125] [1]

Mt 2: 11 Then they **opened** their treasures and presented him with gifts of
3: 16 he went up out of the water. At that moment heaven *was* **opened**,
5: 2 and he **began to teach** [+1438+3836+5125] them, saying:
7: 7 and you will find; knock and the *door will be* **opened** to you.
7: 8 who seeks finds; and to him who knocks, the *door will be* **opened**.
9: 30 and their sight *was* **restored**. Jesus warned them sternly, "See that
13: 35 "I will **open** my mouth in parables, I will utter things hidden since
17: 27 you catch; **open** its mouth and you will find a four-drachma coin.
20: 33 "Lord," they answered, "we want our **sight** [+3836+4057]."
25: 11 the others also came. 'Sir! Sir!' they said. '**Open** the door for us!'
27: 52 The tombs **broke open** and the bodies of many holy people who
Mk 7: 35 At this, the man's ears *were* **opened**, his tongue was loosened
Lk 1: 64 Immediately his mouth *was* **opened** and his tongue was loosed,
3: 21 was baptized too. And as he was praying, heaven *was* **opened**
11: 9 and you will find; knock and the *door will be* **opened** to you.
11: 10 who seeks finds; and to him who knocks, the *door will be* **opened**.
12: 36 and knocks *they can* immediately **open** the *door* for him.
13: 25 stand outside knocking and pleading, 'Sir, **open** the door for us.'
Jn 1: 51 then added, "I tell you the truth, you shall see heaven **open**,
9: 10 "How then *were* your eyes **opened**?" they demanded.
9: 14 had made the mud and **opened** the man's eyes was a Sabbath.
9: 17 It was your eyes he **opened**." The man replied, "He is a prophet."
9: 21 But how he can see now, or who **opened** his eyes, we don't know.
9: 26 asked him, "What did he do to you? How *did he* **open** your eyes?"
9: 30 You don't know where he comes from, yet *he* **opened** my eyes.
9: 32 Nobody has ever heard of **opening** the eyes of a man born blind.
10: 3 The watchman **opens** the gate for him, and the sheep listen to his
10: 21 possessed by a demon. Can a demon **open** the eyes of the blind?"
11: 37 "Could not he who **opened** the eyes of the blind man have kept his
Ac 5: 19 But during the night an angel of the Lord **opened** the doors of the
5: 23 at the doors; but *when we* **opened** them, we found no one inside."
8: 32 a lamb before the shearer is silent, so *he did* not **open** his mouth.
8: 35 Then [RPG] Philip began with that very passage of Scripture
9: 8 the ground, but *when he* **opened** his eyes he could see nothing.
9: 40 "Tabitha, get up." She **opened** her eyes, and seeing Peter she sat up.
10: 11 He saw heaven **opened** and something like a large sheet being let
10: 34 Then Peter **began to speak** [+3306+3836+5125]: "I now realize
12: 10 to the city. It **opened** for them by itself, and they went through it.

12: 14 she was so overjoyed she ran back without **opening** it
12: 16 and *when* they **opened** the door and saw him, they were
14: 27 and how he had **opened** the door of faith to the Gentiles.
16: 26 At once all the prison doors **flew open**, and everybody's chains
16: 27 and when he saw the prison doors **open**, he drew his sword
18: 14 Just as Paul was about to **speak** [+3836+5125], Gallio said to the
26: 18 *to* **open** their eyes and turn them from darkness to light, and from
Ro 3: 13 "Their throats *are* open graves; their tongues practice deceit."
1Co 16: 9 because a great door for effective work *has* **opened** to me,
2Co 2: 12 of Christ and found that the Lord *had* **opened** a door for me,
6: 11 We have **spoken** [+3836+5125] **freely** to you, Corinthians,
Col 4: 3 And pray for us, too, that God *may* **open** a door for our message,
Rev 3: 7 What he **opens** no one can shut, and what he shuts no one can
3: 7 he opens no one can shut, and what he shuts no one *can* **open**.
3: 8 I have placed before you an **open** door that no one can shut.
3: 20 If anyone hears my voice and **opens** the door, I will come in
4: 1 and there before me was a door **standing open** in heaven.
5: 2 loud voice, "Who is worthy *to* break the seals and **open** the scroll?"
5: 3 one in heaven or on earth or under the earth could **open** the scroll
5: 4 because no one was found who was worthy *to* **open** the scroll
5: 5 has triumphed. He *is able to* **open** the scroll and its seven seals."
5: 9 "You are worthy to take the scroll and *to* **open** its seals,
6: 1 I watched as the Lamb **opened** the first of the seven seals.
6: 3 When the Lamb **opened** the second seal, I heard the second living
6: 5 When the Lamb **opened** the third seal, I heard the third living
6: 7 When the Lamb **opened** the fourth seal, I heard the voice of the
6: 9 When he **opened** the fifth seal, I saw under the altar the souls of
6: 12 I watched as he **opened** the sixth seal. There was a great
8: 1 When *he* **opened** the seventh seal, there was silence in heaven for
9: 2 When *he* **opened** the Abyss, smoke rose from it like the smoke
10: 2 He was holding a little scroll, *which* **lay open** in his hand.
10: 8 take the scroll that *lies* **open** in the hand of the angel who is
11: 19 Then God's temple in heaven *was* **opened**, and within his temple
12: 16 But the earth helped the woman *by* **opening** its mouth
13: 6 *He* **opened** his mouth to blaspheme God, and to slander his name
15: 5 the temple, that is, the tabernacle of the Testimony, *was* **opened**.
19: 11 I saw heaven **standing open** and there before me was a white
20: 12 and small, standing before the throne, and books *were* **opened**.
20: 12 were opened. Another book *was* **opened**, which is the book of life.

488 ἀνοικοδομέω, *anoikodomeō* [2]
[√ *324 + 3875 + 1560*]

rebuild [2]

Ac 15: 16 " 'After this I will return and **rebuild** David's fallen tent. Its ruins I
15: 16 David's fallen tent. Its ruins *I will* **rebuild**, and I will restore it,

489 ἀνοιξις, *anoixis* [1] [√ *487*]

open [1]

Eph 6: 19 Pray also for me, that whenever I **open** my mouth, words may be

490 ἀνομία, *anomia* [15] [√ *1.1 + 3795*]

wickedness [5], lawlessness [3], ever-increasing wickedness
[+490+1650+3836] [2], breaks law [+4472] [1], evil [1], evildoers
[+2237+3836] [1], lawless acts [1], transgression [1]

Mt 7: 23 'I never knew you. Away from me, *you* **evildoers** [+2237+3836]!'
13: 41 out of his kingdom everything that causes sin and all who do **evil**.
23: 28 but on the inside you are full *of* hypocrisy and **wickedness**.
24: 12 Because of the increase of **wickedness**, the love of most will grow
Ro 4: 7 "Blessed are they whose **transgressions** are forgiven, whose sins
6: 19 And *to* **ever-increasing wickedness** [+490+1650+3836],
6: 19 and *to* **ever-increasing wickedness** [+490+1650+3836],
2Co 6: 14 For what do righteousness and **wickedness** have in common?
2Th 2: 3 until the rebellion occurs and the man *of* **lawlessness** is revealed,
2: 7 For the secret power *of* **lawlessness** is already at work; but the one
Tit 2: 14 who gave himself for us to redeem us from all **wickedness**
Heb 1: 9 You have loved righteousness and hated **wickedness**;
10: 17 he adds: "Their sins and **lawless acts** I will remember no more."
1Jn 3: 4 Everyone who sins **breaks the law** [+4472]; in fact, sin is
3: 4 Everyone who sins breaks the law; in fact, sin is **lawlessness**.

491 ἄνομος, *anomos* [9] [√ 1.1 + 3795]

not having the law [3], lawless [2], free from law [1], lawbreakers
[1], transgressors [1], wicked [1]

Lk 22:37 'And he was numbered with the **transgressors**'; and I tell you that
Ac 2:23 and you, with the help *of* **wicked** *men*, put him to death by nailing
1Co 9:21 *To* those **not having the law** I became like one not having the law
    9:21 To those not having the law I became like one **not having the law**
    9:21 like one not having the law (though I am not **free from** God's law
    9:21 but am under Christ's law), so as to win those **not having the law**.
2Th 2: 8 And then the **lawless** *one* will be revealed, whom the Lord Jesus
1Ti 1: 9 law is made not for the righteous but *for* **lawbreakers** and rebels,
2Pe 2: 8 was tormented in his righteous soul *by* the **lawless** deeds he saw

492 ἀνόμως, *anomōs* [2] [√ 1.1 + 3795]

apart from the law [2]

Ro 2:12 All who sin **apart from the law** will also perish apart from the
    2:12 who sin apart from the law will also perish **apart from the law**,

493 ἀνόνητος, *anonētos*   Not used in UBS/NIV
[√ 1.1 + 3949]

494 ἀνορθόω, *anorthoō* [3] [√ 324 + 3981]

restore [1], straightened up [1], strengthen [1]

Lk 13:13 on her, and immediately *she* **straightened up** and praised God.
Ac 15:16 David's fallen tent. Its ruins I will rebuild, and *I will* **restore** it,
Heb 12:12 Therefore, **strengthen** your feeble arms and weak knees.

495 ἀνόσιος, *anosios* [2] [√ 1.1 + 4008]

unholy [2]

1Ti 1: 9 but *for* lawbreakers and rebels, the ungodly and sinful, the **unholy**
2Ti 3: 2 proud, abusive, disobedient to their parents, ungrateful, **unholy**,

496 ἀνοχή, *anochē* [2] [√ 324 + 2400]

forbearance [1], tolerance [1]

Ro 2: 4 Or do you show contempt for the riches *of* his kindness, **tolerance**
    3:25 because in his **forbearance** he had left the sins committed

497 ἀνταγωνίζομαι, *antagōnizomai* [1] [√ 505 + 74]

struggle [1]

Heb 12: 4 *In your* **struggle** against sin, you have not yet resisted to the point

498 ἀντάλλαγμα, *antallagma* [2] [√ 505 + 248]

in exchange for [2]

Mt 16:26 forfeits his soul? Or what can a man give **in exchange for** his soul?
Mk 8:37 Or what can a man give **in exchange for** his soul?

499 ἀνταναπληρόω, *antanaplēroō* [1]
[√ 505 + 324 + 4444]

fill up [1]

Col 1:24 and *I* **fill up** in my flesh what is still lacking in regard to Christ's

500 ἀνταποδίδωμι, *antapodidōmi* [7]
[√ 505 + 608 + 1443]

repay [4], in return [1], pay back [1], repaid [1]

Lk 14:14 Although they cannot **repay** you, you will be repaid at the
    14:14 repay you, you *will be* **repaid** at the resurrection of the righteous."
Ro 11:35 "Who has ever given to God, *that* God *should* **repay** him?"
    12:19 for it is written: "It is mine to avenge; I *will* **repay**," says the Lord.
1Th 3: 9 How can we thank God enough for you **in return** for all the joy we
2Th 1: 6 God is just: He *will* **pay back** trouble to those who trouble you
Heb 10:30 avenge; I *will* **repay**," and again, "The Lord will judge his people."

501 ἀνταπόδομα, *antapodoma* [2]
[√ 505 + 608 + 1443]

repaid [1], retribution [1]

Lk 14:12 if you do, they may invite you back and so you will be **repaid**.
Ro 11: 9 a snare and a trap, a stumbling block and a **retribution** for them.

502 ἀνταπόδοσις, *antapodosis* [1]
[√ 505 + 608 + 1443]

reward [1]

Col 3:24 that you will receive an inheritance from the Lord as a **reward**.

503 ἀνταποκρίνομαι, *antapokrinomai* [2]
[√ 505 + 608 + 3212]

say [1], talk back [1]

Lk 14: 6 And they had nothing *to* **say**.
Ro 9:20 But who are you, O man, to **talk back** to God? "Shall what is

504 ἀντέχω, *antechō* [4] [√ 505 + 2400]

devoted to [2], help [1], hold firmly to [1]

Mt 6:24 the other, or *he will be* **devoted to** the one and despise the other.
Lk 16:13 the other, or *he will be* **devoted to** the one and despise the other.
1Th 5:14 warn those who are idle, encourage the timid, **help** the weak,
Tit 1: 9 He must **hold firmly to** the trustworthy message as it has been

505 ἀντί, *anti* [22]

[→ 394, 395, 468, 469, 497, 498, 499, 500, 501, 502, 503, 504, 506,
507, 508, 509, 510, 511, 512, 513, 514, 515, 516, 517, 518, 519,
520, 521, 524, 525, 526, 527, 528, 529, 530, 531, 532, 535, 560,
561, 1882, 2918, 5267, 5268, 5269, 5636, 5637; cf. 478, 1882]

for [9], because [+4005] [4], instead [2], with [2], *untranslated* [1],
after [1], as [1], for this reason [+4047] [1], in place [1]

Mt 2:22 But when he heard that Archelaus was reigning in Judea **in place**
    5:38 "You have heard that it was said, 'Eye **for** eye, and tooth for tooth.'
    5:38 have heard that it was said, 'Eye for eye, and tooth **for** tooth.'
    17:27 Take it and give it to them **for** my tax and yours."
    20:28 be served, but to serve, and to give his life as a ransom **for** many."
Mk 10:45 be served, but to serve, and to give his life as a ransom **for** many.
Lk 1:20 **because** [+4005] you did not believe my words, which will come
    11:11 if your son asks for a fish, will give him a snake **instead**?
    12: 3 **[NIE]** What you have said in the dark will be heard in the
    19:44 **because** [+4005] you did not recognize the time of God's coming
Jn 1:16 of his grace we have all received one blessing **after** another.
Ac 12:23 Immediately, **because** [+4005] Herod did not give praise to God,
Ro 12:17 Do not repay anyone evil **for** evil. Be careful to do what is right in
1Co 11:15 it is her glory? For long hair is given to her **as** a covering.
Eph 5:31 "**For** [+4047] this reason a man will leave his father and mother
1Th 5:15 Make sure that nobody pays back wrong **for** wrong, but always try
2Th 2:10 They perish **because** [+4005] they refused to love the truth and
Heb 12: 2 who **for** the joy set before him endured the cross, scorning its
    12:16 who **for** a single meal sold his inheritance rights as the oldest son.
Jas 4:15 **Instead**, you ought to say, "If it is the Lord's will, we will live
1Pe 3: 9 Do not repay evil **with** evil or insult with insult,
    3: 9 Do not repay evil with evil or insult **with** insult,

506 ἀντιβάλλω, *antiballō* [1] [√ 505 + 965]

discussing [1]

Lk 24:17 asked them, "What *are you* **discussing** together as you walk along?"

507 ἀντιδιατίθημι, *antidiatithēmi* [1]
[√ 505 + 1328 + 5502]

oppose [1]

2Ti 2:25 Those *who* **oppose** him he must gently instruct, in the hope that

508 ἀντίδικος, **antidikos** [5] [√ *505 + 1472*]

adversary [2], adversary is taking to court [1], enemy [1], he^s [+*3836*] [1]

Mt 5:25 matters quickly *with* your **adversary** *who* **is taking** you **to court**.
    5:25 him on the way, or **he**^s [+*3836*] may hand you over to the judge,
Lk 12:58 As you are going with your **adversary** to the magistrate, try hard
   18: 3 to him with the plea, 'Grant me justice against my **adversary**.'
1Pe 5: 8 Your **enemy** the devil prowls around like a roaring lion looking for

509 ἀντίθεσις, **antithesis** [1] [√ *505 + 5502*]

opposing ideas [1]

1Ti 6:20 and the **opposing ideas** of what is falsely called knowledge,

510 ἀντικαθίστημι, **antikathistēmi** [1]
[√ *505 + 2848 + 2705*]

resisted [1]

Heb 12: 4 *you have* not yet **resisted** to the point of shedding your blood.

511 ἀντικαλέω, **antikaleō** [1] [√ *505 + 2813*]

invite back [1]

Lk 14:12 if you do, they *may* **invite** you **back** and so you will be repaid.

512 ἀντίκειμαι, **antikeimai** [8] [√ *505 ı 3023*]

oppose [3], adversaries [1], contrary [1], enemy [1], in conflict [1], opponents [1]

Lk 13:17 When he said this, all his **opponents** were humiliated, but the
   21:15 and wisdom that none of your **adversaries** will be able to resist
1Co 16: 9 work has opened to me, and there are many *who* **oppose** me.
Gal 5:17 They *are* **in conflict** with each other, so that you do not do what
Php 1:28 without being frightened in any way by those *who* **oppose** you.
2Th 2: 4 He *will* **oppose** and will exalt himself over everything that is called
1Ti 1:10 and for whatever else *is* **contrary** to the sound doctrine
     5:14 their homes and to give the **enemy** no opportunity for slander.

513 ἀντικρυς, **antikrys** [1] [√ *505*]

off [1]

Ac 20:15 The next day we set sail from there and arrived **off** Kios. The day

514 ἀντιλαμβάνω, **antilambanō** [3] [√ *505 + 3284*]

benefit [1], help [1], helped [1]

Lk 1:54 *He has* **helped** his servant Israel, remembering to be merciful
Ac 20:35 I showed you that by this kind of hard work we must **help** the
1Ti 6: 2 because those *who* **benefit** from their service are believers,

515 ἀντιλέγω, **antilegō** [11] [√ *505 + 3306*]

say [2], contradict [1], objected [1], obstinate [1], oppose [1], opposes [1], spoken against [1], talk back [1], talked against [1], talking against [1]

Lk 2:34 of many in Israel, and to be a sign *that will be* **spoken against**,
   20:27 Some of the Sadducees, who **say** there is no resurrection, came to
   21:15 that none of your adversaries will be able to resist or **contradict**.
Jn 19:12 friend of Caesar. Anyone who claims to be a king **opposes** Caesar."
Ac 4:14 healed standing there with them, there was nothing they *could* **say**.
   13:45 with jealousy and **talked** abusively **against** what Paul was saying.
   28:19 But *when* the Jews **objected**, I was compelled to appeal to
   28:22 for we know that people everywhere *are* **talking against** this sect."
Ro 10:21 I have held out my hands to a disobedient and **obstinate** people."
Tit 1: 9 others by sound doctrine and refute those *who* **oppose** it.
     2: 9 in everything, to try to please them, not to **talk back** to them,

516 ἀντίλημψις, **antilēmpsis** [1] [√ *505 + 3284*]

those able to help [1]

1Co 12:28 also those having gifts of healing, **those able to help** others,

517 ἀντιλογία, **antilogia** [4] [√ *505 + 3306*]

argument [1], doubt [1], opposition [1], rebellion [1]

Heb 6:16 the oath confirms what is said and puts an end *to* all **argument**.
     7: 7 And without **doubt** the lesser person is blessed by the greater.
    12: 3 Consider him who endured such **opposition** from sinful men,
Jude 1:11 Balaam's error; they have been destroyed in Korah's **rebellion**.

518 ἀντιλοιδορέω, **antiloidoreō** [1] [√ *505 + 3368*]

retaliate [1]

1Pe 2:23 When they hurled their insults at him, *he did* not **retaliate**;

519 ἀντίλυτρον, **antilytron** [1] [√ *505 + 3395*]

ransom [1]

1Ti 2: 6 who gave himself as a **ransom** for all men—the testimony given in

520 ἀντιμετρέω, **antimetreō** [1] [√ *505 + 3586*]

measured [1]

Lk 6:38 For with the measure you use, *it will be* **measured** to you."

521 ἀντιμισθία, **antimisthia** [2] [√ *505 + 3635*]

exchange [1], penalty [1]

Ro 1:27 and received in themselves the due **penalty** for their perversion.
2Co 6:13 As a fair **exchange**—I speak as to my children—open wide your

522 Ἀντιόχεια, **Antiocheia** [18] [→ *523*]

Syrian [14] Ac 11:19,20,22,26,26,27; 13:1; 14:26; 15:22,23,30,35; 18:22; Gal 2:11

Psidian [4] Ac 13:14; 14:19,21; 2Ti 3:11

Antioch [18]

Ac 11:19 Cyprus and **Antioch**, telling the message only to Jews.
   11:20 and Cyrene, went to **Antioch** and began to speak to Greeks also,
   11:22 ears of the church at Jerusalem, and they sent Barnabas to **Antioch**.
   11:26 and when he found him, he brought him to **Antioch**. So for a
   11:26 of people. The disciples were called Christians first at **Antioch**.
   11:27 this time some prophets came down from Jerusalem to **Antioch**.
   13: 1 In the church at **Antioch** there were prophets and teachers:
   13:14 From Perga they went on to Pisidian **Antioch**. On the Sabbath they
   14:19 Then some Jews came from **Antioch** and Iconium and won the
   14:21 of disciples. Then they returned to Lystra, Iconium and **Antioch**,
   14:26 From Attalia they sailed back to **Antioch**, where they had been
   15:22 their own men and send them to **Antioch** with Paul and Barnabas.
   15:23 To the Gentile believers in **Antioch**, Syria and Cilicia.
   15:30 The men were sent off and went down to **Antioch**, where they
   15:35 But Paul and Barnabas remained in **Antioch**, where they
   18:22 he went up and greeted the church and then went down to **Antioch**.
Gal 2:11 When Peter came to **Antioch**, I opposed him to his face,
2Ti 3:11 what kinds of things happened to me in **Antioch**, Iconium

523 Ἀντιοχεύς, **Antiocheus** [1] [√ *522*]

from Antioch [1]

Ac 6: 5 Procorus, Nicanor, Timon, Parmenas, and Nicolas **from Antioch**,

524 ἀντιπαρέρχομαι, **antiparerchomai** [2]
[√ *505 + 4123 + 2262*]

passed by on the other side [2]

Lk 10:31 and when he saw the man, *he* **passed by on the other side**.
   10:32 he came to the place and saw him, **passed by on the other side**.

525 Ἀντιπᾶς, *Antipas* [1] [√ 505 + 4252]

Antipas [1]

Rev 2:13 even in the days *of* **Antipas**, my faithful witness, who was put to

526 Ἀντιπατρίς, *Antipatris* [1] [√ 505 + 4252]

Antipatris [1]

Ac 23:31 with them during the night and brought him as far as **Antipatris**.

527 ἀντιπέρα, *antipera* [1] [√ 505 + 4305]

across the lake [1]

Lk 8:26 the region of the Gerasenes, which is **across the lake** from Galilee.

528 ἀντιπίπτω, *antipiptō* [1] [√ 505 + 4406]

resist [1]

Ac 7:51 You are just like your fathers: You always **resist** the Holy Spirit!

529 ἀντιστρατεύομαι, *antistrateuomai* [1] [√ 505 + 5131]

waging war against [1]

Ro 7:23 **waging war against** the law of my mind and making me a prisoner

530 ἀντιτάσσω, *antitassō* [5] [√ 505 + 5435]

opposes [2], opposed [1], opposing [1], rebels against [1]

Ac 18:6 But *when* the Jews **opposed** Paul and became abusive, he shook
Ro 13:2 he *who* **rebels against** the authority is rebelling against what God
Jas 4:6 "God **opposes** the proud but gives grace to the humble."
 5:6 and murdered innocent men, *who were* not **opposing** you.
1Pe 5:5 because, "God **opposes** the proud but gives grace to the humble."

531 ἀντίτυπος, *antitypos* [2] [√ 505 + 5597]

copy [1], symbolizes [1]

Heb 9:24 enter a man-made sanctuary that was only a **copy** of the true one;
1Pe 3:21 and this water **symbolizes** baptism that now saves you also—

532 ἀντίχριστος, *antichristos* [5] [√ 505 + 5986]

antichrist [4], antichrists [1]

1Jn 2:18 and as you have heard that the **antichrist** is coming, even now
 2:18 the antichrist is coming, even now many **antichrists** have come.
 2:22 Such a man is the **antichrist**—he denies the Father and the Son.
 4:3 This is the spirit *of* the **antichrist**, which you have heard is coming
2Jn 1:7 into the world. Any such person is the deceiver and the **antichrist**.

533 ἀντλέω, *antleō* [4] [√ 534]

draw [1], draw out [1], draw water [1], drawn [1]

Jn 2:8 "Now **draw** some **out** and take it to the master of the banquet."
 2:9 come from, though the servants who *had* **drawn** the water knew.
 4:7 When a Samaritan woman came *to* **draw** water, Jesus said to her,
 4:15 I won't get thirsty and have to keep coming here *to* **draw water**."

534 ἄντλημα, *antlēma* [1] [→ 533]

to draw with [1]

Jn 4:11 woman said, "you have nothing **to draw with** and the well is deep.

535 ἀντοφθαλμέω, *antophthalmeō* [1] [√ 505 + 4057]

head into [1]

Ac 27:15 ship was caught by the storm and could not **head into** the wind;

536 ἄνυδρος, *anydros* [4] [√ 1.1 + 5623]

arid [2], without rain [1], without water [1]

Mt 12:43 it goes through **arid** places seeking rest and does not find it.
Lk 11:24 it goes through **arid** places seeking rest and does not find it.
2Pe 2:17 These men are springs **without water** and mists driven by a storm.
Jude 1:12 They are clouds **without rain**, blown along by the wind;

537 ἀνυπόκριτος, *anypokritos* [6] [√ 1.1 + 5679 + 3212]

sincere [6]

Ro 12:9 Love must be **sincere**. Hate what is evil; cling to what is good.
2Co 6:6 patience and kindness; in the Holy Spirit and in **sincere** love;
1Ti 1:5 comes from a pure heart and a good conscience and a **sincere** faith.
2Ti 1:5 I have been reminded *of* your **sincere** faith, which first lived in
Jas 3:17 submissive, full of mercy and good fruit, impartial and **sincere**.
1Pe 1:22 obeying the truth so that you have **sincere** love for your brothers,

538 ἀνυπότακτος, *anypotaktos* [4] [√ 1.1 + 5679 + 5435]

disobedient [1], not subject [1], rebellious [1], rebels [1]

1Ti 1:9 law is made not for the righteous but *for* lawbreakers and **rebels**.
Tit 1:6 and are not open to the charge of being wild and **disobedient**.
 1:10 For there are many **rebellious** *people*, mere talkers and deceivers,
Heb 2:8 everything under him, God left nothing that is **not subject** to him.

539 ἄνω, *anō* [9] [→ 540, 541, 542, 1382, 2062, 5645; cf. 324]

above [5], up [2], heavenward [1], the brim [1]

Jn 2:7 "Fill the jars with water"; so they filled them to **the brim**.
 8:23 But he continued, "You are from below; I am from **above**. You are
 11:41 Then Jesus looked **up** and said, "Father, I thank you that you have
Ac 2:19 I will show wonders in the heaven above and signs on the earth
Gal 4:26 But the Jerusalem that is **above** is free, and she is our mother.
Php 3:14 prize for which God has called me **heavenward** in Christ Jesus.
Col 3:1 you have been raised with Christ, set your hearts on things **above**,
 3:2 Set your minds on things **above**, not on earthly things.
Heb 12:15 and that no bitter root grows **up** to cause trouble and defile many.

540 ἄνωθεν, *anōthen* [13] [√ 539]

from above [3], top [3], again [2], from heaven [2], all over again [+4099] [1], for a long time [1], from the beginning [1]

Mt 27:51 At that moment the curtain of the temple was torn in two from **top**
Mk 15:38 The curtain of the temple was torn in two from **top** to bottom.
Lk 1:3 myself have carefully investigated everything **from the beginning**,
Jn 3:3 no one can see the kingdom of God unless he is born **again**."
 3:7 should not be surprised at my saying, 'You must be born **again**.'
 3:31 "The one who comes **from above** is above all; the one who is from
 19:11 have no power over me if it were not given to you **from above**.
 19:23 garment was seamless, woven in one piece from **top** to bottom.
Ac 26:5 They have known me **for a long time** and can testify, if they are
Gal 4:9 Do you wish to be enslaved by them **all over again** [+4099]?
Jas 1:17 Every good and perfect gift is **from above**, coming down from the
 3:15 Such "wisdom" does not come down **from heaven** but is earthly,
 3:17 But the wisdom that comes **from heaven** is first of all pure;

541 ἀνωτερικός, *anōterikos* [1] [√ 539]

interior [+3538] [1]

Ac 19:1 Paul took the road through the **interior** [+3538] and arrived at

542 ἀνώτερος, *anōteros* [2] [√ 539]

first [1], up [1]

Lk 14:10 host comes, he will say to you, 'Friend, move **up** to a better place.'
Heb 10:8 **First** he said, "Sacrifices and offerings, burnt offerings and sin

543 ἀνωφελής, *anōphelēs* [2] [√ *1.1 + 6067*]

unprofitable [1], useless [1]

Tit 3: 9 quarrels about the law, because these are **unprofitable** and useless.
Heb 7: 18 The former regulation is set aside because it was weak and **useless**

544 ἀξίνη, *axinē* [2] [√ *2862*]

ax [2]

Mt 3: 10 The **ax** is already at the root of the trees, and every tree that does
Lk 3: 9 The **ax** is already at the root of the trees, and every tree that does

545 ἄξιος, *axios* [41] [→ *396, 397, 546, 547, 2921; cf. 72*]

worthy [17], deserves [5], deserving [4], deserve [+*1639*] [3],
deserve [2], in keeping with [2], worth [2], *untranslated* [1],
advisable [+*1639*] [1], deserved [1], deserves [+*1639*] [1], prove
by [+*4556*] [1], rightly so [+*1639*] [1]

Mt 3: 8 Produce fruit **in keeping with** repentance.
  10: 10 extra tunic, or sandals or a staff; for the worker is **worth** his keep.
  10: 11 search for some **worthy** *person* there and stay at his house until
  10: 13 If the home is **deserving**, let your peace rest on it; if it is not,
  10: 13 peace rest on it; if it is not, [RPG] let your peace return to you.
  10: 37 who loves his father or mother more than me is not **worthy** of me;
  10: 37 who loves his son or daughter more than me is not **worthy** of me;
  10: 38 who does not take his cross and follow me is not **worthy** of me.
  22: 8 is ready, but those I invited *did* not **deserve** [+*1639*] to come.
Lk 3: 8 Produce fruit **in keeping with** repentance. And do not begin to say
  7: 4 with him, "This *man* **deserves** [+*1639*] to have you do this,
  10: 7 whatever they give you, for the worker **deserves** his wages.
  12: 48 and does *things* **deserving** punishment will be beaten with few
  15: 19 I am no longer **worthy** to be called your son; make me like one of
  15: 21 and against you. I am no longer **worthy** to be called your son.'
  23: 15 back to us; as you can see, he has done nothing to **deserve** death.
  23: 41 We are punished justly, for we are getting what our deeds **deserve**.
Jn 1: 27 after me, the thongs of whose sandals I am not **worthy** to untie."
Ac 13: 25 he is coming after me, whose sandals I am not **worthy** to untie.'
  13: 46 you reject it and do not consider yourselves **worthy** of eternal life,
  23: 29 but there was no charge against him that **deserved** death
  25: 11 If, however, I am guilty of doing anything **deserving** death,
  25: 25 I found he had done nothing **deserving** of death, but because he
  26: 20 and turn to God and **prove** their repentance **by** [+*4556*] their deeds.
  26: 31 "This man is not doing anything that **deserves** death
Ro 1: 32 decree that those who do such things **deserve** [+*1639*] death,
  8: 18 I consider that our present sufferings are not **worth** comparing
1Co 16: 4 If *it seems* **advisable** [+*1639*] for me to go also, they will
2Th 1: 3 always to thank God for you, brothers, and **rightly** [+*1639*] **so**,
1Ti 1: 15 Here is a trustworthy saying that **deserves** full acceptance
  4: 9 This is a trustworthy saying that **deserves** full acceptance
  5: 18 it is treading out the grain," and "The worker **deserves** his wages."
  6: 1 of slavery should consider their masters **worthy** of full respect,
Heb 11: 38 the world was not **worthy** of them. They wandered in deserts
Rev 3: 4 They will walk with me, dressed in white, for they are **worthy**.
  4: 11 "You are **worthy**, our Lord and God, to receive glory and honor
  5: 2 loud voice, "Who is **worthy** to break the seals and open the scroll?"
  5: 4 because no one was found who was **worthy** to open the scroll
  5: 9 "You are **worthy** to take the scroll and to open its seals,
  5: 12 "**Worthy** is the Lamb, who was slain, to receive power and wealth
  16: 6 and you have given them blood to drink as *they* **deserve** [+*1639*]."

546 ἀξιόω, *axioō* [7] [√ *545*]

consider worthy [1], count worthy [1], deserves [1], found worthy
of [1], think it wise [1], want [1], worthy [1]

Lk 7: 7 That is why *I* did not even **consider** myself **worthy** to come to
Ac 15: 38 but Paul did not **think it wise** to take him,
  28: 22 But *we* **want** to hear what your views are, for we know that people
2Th 1: 11 pray for you, that our God *may* **count** you **worthy** of his calling,
1Ti 5: 17 The elders who direct the affairs of the church well *are* **worthy** of
Heb 3: 3 Jesus *has been* **found worthy of** greater honor than Moses,
  10: 29 How much more severely do you think a *man* **deserves** to be

547 ἀξίως, *axiōs* [6] [√ *545*]

worthy [3], in a manner worthy [2], in a way worthy [1]

Ro 16: 2 I ask you to receive her in the Lord **in a way worthy** of the saints
Eph 4: 1 I urge you to live a life **worthy** of the calling you have received.
Php 1: 27 conduct yourselves **in a manner worthy** of the gospel of Christ.
Col 1: 10 And we pray this in order that you may live a life **worthy** of the
1Th 2: 12 and urging you to live lives **worthy** of God,
3Jn 1: 6 You will do well to send them on their way **in a manner worthy**

548 ἀόρατος, *aoratos* [5] [√ *1.1 + 3972*]

invisible [5]

Ro 1: 20 For since the creation of the world God's **invisible** *qualities*—
Col 1: 15 He is the image *of* the **invisible** God, the firstborn over all creation.
  1: 16 things in heaven and on earth, visible and **invisible**,
1Ti 1: 17 immortal, **invisible**, the only God, be honor and glory for ever
Heb 11: 27 king's anger; he persevered because he saw him who is **invisible**.

549 Ἀουλία, *Aoulia* Not used in UBS/NIV [√ *2685*]

550 ἀπαγγέλλω, *apangellō* [45] [√ *608 + 34*]

told [13], reported [12], tell [6], report [4], proclaim [3], tell about
[1], confirm [1], declare [1], exclaimed [1], exclaiming [1],
preached [1], said [1]

Mt 2: 8 you find him, **report** to me, so that I too may go and worship him."
  8: 33 tending the pigs ran off, went into the town and **reported** all this,
  11: 4 Jesus replied, "Go back and **report** to John what you hear and see:
  12: 18 put my Spirit on him, and *he* will **proclaim** justice to the nations.
  14: 12 and took his body and buried it. Then *they* went and **told** Jesus.
  28: 8 the tomb, afraid yet filled with joy, and ran *to* **tell** his disciples.
  28: 10 Go and **tell** my brothers to go to Galilee; there they will see me."
  28: 11 and **reported** to the chief priests everything that had happened.
Mk 5: 14 the pigs ran off and **reported** this in the town and countryside,
  5: 19 to your family and **tell** them how much the Lord has done for you,
  6: 30 around Jesus and **reported** to him all they had done and taught.
  16: 10 She went and **told** those who had been with him and who were
  16: 13 These returned and **reported** it to the rest; but they did not believe
Lk 7: 18 John's disciples **told** him about all these things. Calling two of
  7: 22 "Go back and **report** to John what you have seen and heard:
  8: 20 Someone **told** him, "Your mother and brothers are standing outside,
  8: 34 they ran off and **reported** this in the town and countryside,
  8: 36 Those who had seen it **told** the people how the demon-possessed
  8: 47 *she* **told** why she had touched him and how she had been instantly
  9: 36 this to themselves, and **told** no one at that time what they had seen.
  13: 1 Now there were some present at that time *who* **told** Jesus about the
  14: 21 "The servant came back and **reported** this to his master.
  18: 37 *They* **told** him, "Jesus of Nazareth is passing by."
  24: 9 *they* **told** all these things to the Eleven and to all the others.
Jn 16: 25 use this kind of language but *will* **tell** you plainly about my Father.
Ac 4: 23 and **reported** all that the chief priests and elders had said to them.
  5: 22 officers did not find them there. So *they* went back and **reported**,
  5: 25 Then someone came and **said**, "Look! The men you put in jail are
  11: 13 *He* **told** us how he had seen an angel appear in his house and say,
  12: 14 so overjoyed she ran back without opening it and **exclaimed**,
  12: 17 "**Tell** James and the brothers **about** this," he said, and then he left
  15: 27 and Silas *to* **confirm** by word of mouth what we are writing.
  16: 36 The jailer **told** Paul, "The magistrates have ordered that you
  16: 38 The officers **reported** this to the magistrates, and when they heard
  22: 26 centurion heard this, he went to the commander and **reported** it.
  23: 16 sister heard of this plot, he went into the barracks and **told** Paul.
  23: 17 this young man to the commander; he has something *to* **tell** him."
  23: 19 drew him aside and asked, "What is it you want *to* **tell** me?"
  26: 20 *I* **preached** that they should repent and turn to God and prove their
  28: 21 and none of the brothers who have come from there has **reported**
1Co 14: 25 So he will fall down and worship God, **exclaiming**, "God is really
1Th 1: 9 for they themselves **report** what kind of reception you gave us.
Heb 2: 12 He says, "*I will* **declare** your name to my brothers; in the presence
1Jn 1: 2 seen it and testify to it, and *we* **proclaim** to you the eternal life,
  1: 3 *We* **proclaim** to you what we have seen and heard, so that you also

551 ἀπάγχω, *apanchō* [1]

hanged [1]

Mt 27: 5 into the temple and left. Then *he* went away and **hanged** *himself.*

552 ἀπάγω, *apagō* [15] [√ 608 + 72]

led away [4], leads [2], took [2], take [1], brought [1], executed [1], lead away [1], lead out [1], led [1], led astray [1]

Mt 7: 13 For wide is the gate and broad is the road that **leads** to destruction,
7: 14 But small is the gate and narrow the road that **leads** to life,
26: 57 Those who had arrested Jesus **took** him to Caiaphas, the high
27: 2 **led** him **away** and handed him over to Pilate, the governor.
27: 31 his own clothes on him. Then *they* **led** him **away** to crucify him.
Mk 14: 44 one I kiss is the man; arrest him and **lead** him **away** under guard."
14: 53 *They* **took** Jesus to the high priest, and all the chief priests,
15: 16 The soldiers **led** Jesus **away** into the palace (that is,
Lk 13: 15 his ox or donkey from the stall and **lead** it **out** to give it water?
21: 12 and prisons, and *you will be* **brought** before kings and governors,
22: 66 teachers of the law, met together, and Jesus *was* **led** before them.
23: 26 As *they* **led** him **away,** they seized Simon from Cyrene, who was
Ac 12: 19 he cross-examined the guards and ordered that they *be* **executed.**
23: 17 the centurions and said, "**Take** this young man to the commander;
1Co 12: 2 or other you were influenced and **led astray** to mute idols.

553 ἀπαίδευτος, *apaideutos* [1] [√ 1.1 + 4090]

stupid [1]

2Ti 2: 23 Don't have anything to do with foolish and **stupid** arguments,

554 ἀπαίρω, *apairō* [3] [√ 608 + 149]

taken from [RP608] [3]

Mt 9: 15 come when the bridegroom *will be* **taken** [RP608] **from** them;
Mk 2: 20 come when the bridegroom *will be* **taken** [RP608] **from** them,
Lk 5: 35 come when the bridegroom *will be* **taken** [RP608] **from** them;

555 ἀπαιτέω, *apaiteō* [2] [√ 608 + 160]

demand back [RP608] [1], demanded from [RP608] [1]

Lk 6: 30 anyone takes what belongs to you, *do* not **demand** [RP608] it **back.**
12: 20 This very night your life *will be* **demanded** [RP608] **from** you.

556 ἀπαλγέω, *apalgeō* [1]

lost all sensitivity [1]

Eph 4: 19 *Having* **lost all sensitivity,** they have given themselves over to

557 ἀπαλλάσσω, *apallassō* [3] [√ 608 + 248]

cured [RP608] [1], free [1], reconciled to [RP608] [1]

Lk 12: 58 try hard *to be* **reconciled** [RP608] **to** him on the way, or he may
Ac 19: 12 and their illnesses *were* **cured** [RP608] and the evil spirits left
Heb 2: 15 and **free** those who all their lives were held in slavery by their fear

558 ἀπαλλοτριόω, *apallotrioō* [3] [√ 608 + 257]

alienated from [1], excluded [1], separated [1]

Eph 2: 12 **excluded** from citizenship in Israel and foreigners to the covenants
4: 18 in their understanding and **separated** from the life of God
Col 1: 21 Once you were **alienated from** God and were enemies in your

559 ἀπαλός, *hapalos* [2]

tender [2]

Mt 24: 32 As soon as its twigs get **tender** and its leaves come out, you know
Mk 13: 28 As soon as its twigs get **tender** and its leaves come out, you know

560 ἀπαντάω, *apantaō* [2] [√ 608 + 505]

meet [1], met [1]

Mk 14: 13 "Go into the city, and a man carrying a jar of water *will* **meet** you.
Lk 17: 12 As he was going into a village, ten men who had leprosy **met** him.

561 ἀπάντησις, *apantēsis* [3] [√ 608 + 505]

meet [3]

Mt 25: 6 the cry rang out: 'Here's the bridegroom! Come out to **meet** him!'
Ac 28: 15 as far as the Forum of Appius and the Three Taverns to **meet** us.
1Th 4: 17 up together with them in the clouds to **meet** the Lord in the air.

562 ἅπαξ, *hapax* [14] [→ 2384]

once [7], once for all [4], again [2], already [1]

2Co 11: 25 **once** I was stoned, three times I was shipwrecked, I spent a night
Php 4: 16 you sent me aid **again** and again when I was in need.
1Th 2: 18 certainly I, Paul, did, **again** and again—but Satan stopped us.
Heb 6: 4 It is impossible for those who have **once** been enlightened,
9: 7 and that *only* **once** a year, and never without blood, which he
9: 26 But now he has appeared **once for all** at the end of the ages to do
9: 27 Just as man is destined to die **once,** and after that to face judgment,
9: 28 so Christ was sacrificed **once** to take away the sins of many
10: 2 For the worshipers would have been cleansed **once for all,**
12: 26 "**Once** more I will shake not only the earth but also the heavens."
12: 27 The words "**once** more" indicate the removing of what can be
1Pe 3: 18 For Christ died for sins **once for all,** the righteous for the
Jude 1: 3 and urge you to contend for the faith that was **once for all**
1: 5 Though you **already** know all this, I want to remind you that the

563 ἀπαράβατος, *aparabatos* [1] [√ 1.1 + 4123 + 326]

permanent [1]

Heb 7: 24 because Jesus lives forever, he has a **permanent** priesthood.

564 ἀπαρασκεύαστος, *aparaskeuastos* [1] [√ 1.1 + 4123 + 5007]

unprepared [1]

2Co 9: 4 For if any Macedonians come with me and find you **unprepared,**

565 ἀπαρνέομαι, *aparneomai* [11] [√ 608 + 766]

disown [7], deny [3], disowned [1]

Mt 16: 24 he *must* **deny** himself and take up his cross and follow me.
26: 34 before the rooster crows, *you will* **disown** me three times."
26: 35 "Even if I have to die with you, *I will* never **disown** you."
26: 75 "Before the rooster crows, *you will* **disown** me three times."
Mk 8: 34 he *must* **deny** himself and take up his cross and follow me.
14: 30 before the rooster crows twice *you* yourself *will* **disown** me three
14: 31 "Even if I have to die with you, *I will* never **disown** you."
14: 72 "Before the rooster crows twice *you will* **disown** me three times."
Lk 12: 9 But he who disowns me before men *will be* **disowned** before the
22: 34 rooster crows today, *you will* **deny** three times that you know me."
22: 61 "Before the rooster crows today, *you will* **disown** me three times."

566 ἀπαρτί, *aparti*   Not used in UBS/NIV [√ 608 + 785]

567 ἀπάρτι, *aparti*   Not used in UBS/NIV [√ 608 + 785]

568 ἀπαρτισμός, *apartismos* [1] [√ 608 + 785]

complete [1]

Lk 14: 28 and estimate the cost to see if he has enough money to **complete**

569 ἀπαρχή, *aparchē* [9 / 8] [√ 608 + 806]

firstfruits [6], first convert [1], first converts [1]

Ro 8: 23 only so, but we ourselves, who have the **firstfruits** of the Spirit,

11:16   If the *part of the dough offered as* **firstfruits** is holy,
16: 5   who was the **first convert** to Christ in the province of Asia.
1Co 15:20   from the dead, the **firstfruits** of those who have fallen asleep.
15:23   Christ, the **firstfruits**; then, when he comes, those who belong to
16:15   You know that the household of Stephanas were the **first converts**
2Th 2:13   because from the <u>beginning</u> [UBS *as the firstfruits*; NIV *794*] God
       chose you to be saved through the sanctifying work of the Spirit
Jas 1:18   of truth, that we might be a kind of **firstfruits** of all he created.
Rev 14: 4   from among men and *offered as* **firstfruits** to God and the Lamb.

570 ἅπας, hapas [34] [√ 275 + 4246]

all [18], everything [7], whole [3], everyone [2], *untranslated* [1], everybody [1], none [+4024] [1], unlimited [1]

Mt 6:32   and your heavenly Father knows that you need them. **[RPG]**
24:39   what would happen until the flood came and took *them* **all** away.
28:11   and reported to the chief priests **everything** that had happened.
Mk 1:27   The people were **all** so amazed that they asked each other,
8:25   his sight was restored, and he saw **everything** clearly.
11:32   the people, for **everyone** held that John really was a prophet.)
16:15   "Go into **all** the world and preach the good news to all creation.
Lk 3:21   When **all** the people were being baptized, Jesus was baptized too.
4: 6   he said to him, "I will give you **all** their authority and splendor,
4:40   the people brought to Jesus **all** who had various kinds of sickness,
5:26   **Everyone** was amazed and gave praise to God. They were filled
8:37   Then **all** the people of the region of the Gerasenes asked Jesus to
9:15   The disciples did so, and **everybody** sat down.
19:37   the **whole** crowd of disciples began joyfully to praise God in loud
19:48   find any way to do it, because **all** the people hung on his words.
20: 6   But if we say, 'From men,' **all** the people will stone us,
21:15   and wisdom that **none** [+4024] of your adversaries will be able to
23: 1   Then the **whole** assembly rose and led him off to Pilate.
Jn 4:25   "is coming. When he comes, he will explain **everything** to us."
Ac 2: 7   they asked: "Are not **all** these men who are speaking Galileans?
2:44   All the believers were together and had **everything** in common.
4:31   And they were **all** filled with the Holy Spirit and spoke the word of
4:32   his possessions was his own, but they shared **everything** they had.
5:12   And **all** the *believers* used to meet together in Solomon's
5:16   and those tormented by evil spirits, and **all** of them were healed.
10: 8   He told them **everything** that had happened and sent them to
11:10   three times, and then it was **all** pulled up to heaven again.
16: 3   lived in that area, for they **all** knew that his father was a Greek.
16:28   But Paul shouted, "Don't harm yourself! We are **all** here!"
25:24   The **whole** Jewish community has petitioned me about him in
27:33   Just before dawn Paul urged *them* **all** to eat. "For the last fourteen
Eph 6:13   stand your ground, and after you have done **everything**, to stand.
1Ti 1:16   Christ Jesus might display his **unlimited** patience as an example
Jas 3: 2   We **all** stumble in many ways. If anyone is never at fault in what

571 ἀπασπάζομαι, apaspazomai [1] [√ 608 + 832]

saying good-by to [1]

Ac 21: 6   *After* **saying good-by to** each other, we went aboard the ship,

572 ἀπατάω, apataō [3] [√ 573]

deceive [1], deceived [1], deceives [1]

Eph 5: 6   *Let* no one **deceive** you with empty words, for because of such
1Ti 2:14   And Adam *was* not the one **deceived**; it was the woman who was
Jas 1:26   on his tongue, *he* **deceives** himself and his religion is worthless.

573 ἀπάτη, apatē [7] [→ 572, 1987, 5854, 5855]

deceitfulness [3], deceitful [1], deceives [1], deceptive [1], pleasures [1]

Mt 13:22   but the worries of this life and the **deceitfulness** of wealth choke it,
Mk 4:19   the **deceitfulness** of wealth and the desires for other things come in
Eph 4:22   off your old self, which is being corrupted by its **deceitful** desires;
Col 2: 8   one takes you captive through hollow and **deceptive** philosophy,
2Th 2:10   and in every sort of evil that **deceives** those who are perishing.
Heb 3:13   so that none of you may be hardened *by* sin's **deceitfulness**.
2Pe 2:13   reveling in their **pleasures** while they feast with you.

574 ἀπάτωρ, apatōr [1] [√ 1.1 + 4252]

without father [1]

Heb 7: 3   **Without father** or mother, without genealogy, without beginning

575 ἀπαύγασμα, apaugasma [1] [√ 608 + 879]

radiance [1]

Heb 1: 3   The Son is the **radiance** of God's glory and the exact

576 ἀπαφρίζω, apaphrizō Not used in UBS/NIV
    [√ 608 + 931]

577 ἀπείθεια, apeitheia [7 / 6] [√ 1.1 + 4275]

disobedience [4], disobedient [2]

Ro 11:30   to God have now received mercy *as a result of* their **disobedience**,
11:32   For God has bound all men over to **disobedience** so that he may
Eph 2: 2   the spirit who is now at work in those who are **disobedient**.
5: 6   of such things God's wrath comes on those who are **disobedient**.
Col 3: 6   the wrath of God is coming [UBS+ *on those who are disobedient*]
Heb 4: 6   preached to them did not go in, because of their **disobedience**.
4:11   that no one will fall by following their example *of* **disobedience**.

578 ἀπειθέω, apeitheō [14] [√ 1.1 + 4275]

disobedient [4], disobeyed [2], refused to believe [2], disobey [1], do not believe [1], not obey [1], reject [1], rejects [1], unbelievers [1]

Jn 3:36   but whoever **rejects** the Son will not see life, for God's wrath
Ac 14: 2   But the Jews who **refused to believe** stirred up the Gentiles
19: 9   *they* **refused to believe** and publicly maligned the Way.
Ro 2: 8   But *for* those who are self-seeking and *who* **reject** the truth
10:21   "All day long I have held out my hands to a **disobedient**
11:30   Just as you *who were* at one time **disobedient** to God have now
11:31   so they too *have* now *become* **disobedient** in order that they too
15:31   Pray that I may be rescued from the **unbelievers** in Judea
Heb 3:18   that they would never enter his rest if not *to* those *who* **disobeyed**?
11:31   the spies, was not killed with those *who were* **disobedient**.
1Pe 2: 8   They stumble *because they* **disobey** the message—which is also
3: 1   to your husbands so that, if any of them **do not believe** the word,
3:20   *who* **disobeyed** long ago when God waited patiently in the days of
4:17   what will the outcome be *for* those *who do* **not obey** the gospel of

579 ἀπειθής, apeithēs [6] [√ 1.1 + 4275]

disobedient [5], disobey [1]

Lk 1:17   their children and the **disobedient** to the wisdom of the righteous—
Ac 26:19   King Agrippa, I was not **disobedient** to the vision from heaven.
Ro 1:30   they invent ways of doing evil; they **disobey** their parents;
2Ti 3: 2   boastful, proud, abusive, **disobedient** to their parents, ungrateful,
Tit 1:16   are detestable, **disobedient** and unfit for doing anything good.
3: 3   **disobedient**, deceived and enslaved by all kinds of passions

580 ἀπειλέω, apeileō [2] [√ 581]

made threats [1], warn [1]

Ac 4:17   we must **warn** these men to speak no longer to anyone in this
1Pe 2:23   he did not retaliate; when he suffered, *he* **made** no **threats**.

581 ἀπειλή, apeilē [3] [→ 580, 4653]

threats [2], threaten [1]

Ac 4:29   consider their **threats** and enable your servants to speak your word
9: 1   Saul was still breathing out murderous **threats** against the Lord's
Eph 6: 9   Do not **threaten** them, since you know that he who is both their

582 ἄπειμι¹, apeimi¹ [7] [√ 608 + 1639]

absent [3], absent from [1], away [1], in absence [1], not present [1]

1Co   5: 3   Even though I *am* **not** physically **present**, I am with you in spirit.
2Co 10: 1   who am "timid" when face to face with you, but "bold" *when* **away**!
     10: 11   should realize that what we are in our letters *when we are* **absent**,
     13: 2   I now repeat it *while* **absent**: On my return I will not spare those
     13: 10   This is why I write these things *when I am* **absent**, that when I
Php   1: 27   whether I come and see you or only hear about you **in** *my* **absence**,
Col   2: 5   For though *I am* **absent from** you in body, I am present with you

583 ἄπειμι², apeimi² [1] [√ 608 + 1640]

went [1]

Ac   17: 10   to Berea. On arriving there, they **went** to the Jewish synagogue.

584 ἀπεῖπον, apeipon [1] [√ 608 + 3306]

renounced [1]

2Co   4: 2   Rather, *we have* **renounced** secret and shameful ways; we do not

585 ἀπείραστος, apeirastos [1] [√ 1.1 + 4278]

cannot tempted [1]

Jas   1: 13   For God **cannot** be **tempted** by evil, nor does he tempt anyone;

586 ἄπειρος, apeiros [1] [√ 1.1 + 4278]

not acquainted with [1]

Heb   5: 13   an infant, is **not acquainted with** the teaching about righteousness.

587 ἀπεκδέχομαι, apekdechomai [8]
[√ 608 + 1666 + 1312]

eagerly await [1], eagerly await for [1], eagerly wait for [1], wait eagerly for [1], wait for [1], waited [1], waiting for [1], waits [1]

Ro   8: 19   The creation **waits** in eager expectation for the sons of God to be
     8: 23   groan inwardly *as we* **wait eagerly for** our adoption as sons,
     8: 25   if we hope for what we do not yet have, *we* **wait for** it patiently.
1Co   1: 7   you do not lack any spiritual gift *as you* **eagerly wait for**
Gal   5: 5   **eagerly await** through the Spirit the righteousness **for** which we
Php   3: 20   And *we* **eagerly await** a Savior from there, the Lord Jesus Christ,
Heb   9: 28   bear sin, but to bring salvation *to* those *who are* **waiting for** him.
1Pe   3: 20   who disobeyed long ago when God **waited** patiently in the days of

588 ἀπεκδύομαι, apekdyomai [2]
[√ 608 + 1666 + 1544]

disarmed [1], taken off [1]

Col   2: 15   And *having* **disarmed** the powers and authorities, he made a
     3: 9   *since you have* **taken off** your old self with its practices

589 ἀπέκδυσις, apekdysis [1] [√ 608 + 1666 + 1544]

putting off [1]

Col   2: 11   you were also circumcised, in the **putting off** of the sinful nature,

590 ἀπελαύνω, apelaunō [1] [√ 608 + 1785]

ejected from [RP608] [1]

Ac   18: 16   So *he had* them **ejected** [RP608] **from** the court.

591 ἀπελεγμός, apelegmos [1] [√ 608 + 1794]

lose good name [+1650+2262] [1]

Ac   19: 27   not only that our trade *will* **lose** its **good name** [+1650+2262],

592 ἀπελεύθερος, apeleutheros [1] [√ 608 + 1801]

freedman [1]

1Co   7: 22   a slave when he was called by the Lord is the Lord's **freedman**;

593 'Απελλῆς, Apellēs [1]

Apelles [1]

Ro   16: 10   Greet **Apelles**, tested and approved in Christ. Greet those who

594 ἀπελπίζω, apelpizō [1] [√ 608 + 1828]

expecting to get back [1]

Lk   6: 35   and lend to them without **expecting to get** anything **back**.

595 ἀπέναντι, apenanti [5] [√ 608 + 1882]

before [1], defying [+4556] [1], in front of [1], opposite [1], you can see [+5148] [1]

Mt   27: 24   he took water and washed his hands **in front of** the crowd.
     27: 61   and the other Mary were sitting there **opposite** the tomb.
Ac   3: 16   has given this complete healing to him, as **you can** all **see** [+5148].
     17: 7   They *are* all **defying** [+4556] Caesar's decrees, saying that there is
Ro   3: 18   "There is no fear of God **before** their eyes."

596 ἀπέραντος, aperantos [1] [√ 1.1 + 4305]

endless [1]

1Ti   1: 4   nor to devote themselves *to* myths and **endless** genealogies.

597 ἀπερισπάστως, aperispastōs [1]
[√ 1.1 + 4309 + 5060]

undivided [1]

1Co   7: 35   but that you may live in a right way in **undivided** devotion to the

598 ἀπερίτμητος, aperitmētos [1]
[√ 1.1 + 4309 + 5533]

uncircumcised [1]

Ac   7: 51   "You stiff-necked people, with **uncircumcised** hearts and ears!

599 ἀπέρχομαι, aperchomai [117 / 118]
[√ 608 + 2262]

went [24], go [22], went away [18], went back [5], went off [5], left [RP608] [4], go away [3], gone [3], leave [RP608] [3], crossed [2], left [2], passed away [2], returned [2], went out [2], away from [RP608] [1], came [1], cross [1], drew [1], followed [+3958] [1], go on [1], go over [1], goes away [1], going away [1], gone away [1], gone from [RP608] [1], left from [RP608] [1], on their way [1], passed [1], past [1], perversion [+2283+3958+4922] [1], spread [1], turned back [+1650+3836+3958] [1], went up [1], withdraw [1], withdrew [1]

Mt   2: 22   in Judea in place of his father Herod, he was afraid *to* **go** there.
     4: 24   News about him **spread** all over Syria, and people brought to him
     5: 30   lose one part of your body than for your whole body to **go** into hell.
     8: 18   around him, he gave orders *to* **cross** to the other side of the lake.
     8: 19   to him and said, "Teacher, I will follow you wherever *you* **go**."
     8: 21   disciple said to him, "Lord, first let me **go** and bury my father."
     8: 32   So they came out and **went** into the pigs, and the whole herd
     8: 33   tending the pigs ran off, **went** into the town and reported all this,
     9: 7   And the man got up and **went** home.
     10: 5   "*Do* not **go** among the Gentiles or enter any town of the
     13: 25   enemy came and sowed weeds among the wheat, and **went away**.
     13: 28   "The servants asked him, 'Do you want us *to* **go** and pull them up?'
     13: 46   he **went away** and sold everything he had and bought it.
     14: 15   so they can **go** to the villages and buy themselves some food."
     14: 16   Jesus replied, "They do not need *to* **go away**. You give them
     14: 25   During the fourth watch of the night Jesus **went** [UBS 2262] **out**
     16: 4   it except the sign of Jonah." Jesus then left them and **went away**.

	16:21	Jesus began to explain to his disciples that he must **go** to Jerusalem
	18:30	he **went off** and had the man thrown into prison until he could pay
	19:22	man heard this, *he* **went away** sad, because he had great wealth.
	20: 5	So they **went**. "He went out again about the sixth hour and the ninth
	21:29	" 'I will not,' he answered, but later he changed his mind and **went**.
	21:30	said the same thing. He answered, 'I will, sir,' but *he did* not **go**.
	22: 5	"But *they* paid no attention and **went off**—one to his field,
	22:22	heard this, they were amazed. So *they* left him and **went away**.
	25:10	"But *while they were* **on their way** to buy the oil, the bridegroom
	25:18	But the man who had received the one talent **went off**, dug a hole
	25:25	So I was afraid and **went out** and hid your talent in the ground.
	25:46	"Then they *will* **go away** to eternal punishment, but the righteous to
	26:36	and he said to them, "Sit here while I **go** over there and pray."
	26:42	He **went away** a second time and prayed, "My Father, if it is not
	26:44	So he left them and **went away** once more and prayed the third
	27: 5	into the temple and left. Then he **went away** and hanged himself.
	27:60	a big stone in front of the entrance to the tomb and **went away**.
	28: 8	So the women hurried **away** [*RP608*] **from** the tomb, afraid yet
	28:10	Go and tell my brothers to **go** to Galilee; there they will see me."
Mk	1:20	Zebedee in the boat with the hired men and **followed** [+*3958*] him.
	1:35	Jesus got up, left the house and **went off** to a solitary place,
	1:42	Immediately the leprosy **left** [*RP608*] him and he was cured.
	3:13	and called to him those he wanted, and *they* **came** to him.
	5:17	Then the people began to plead with Jesus *to* **leave** [*RP608*] their
	5:20	So the *man* **went away** and began to tell in the Decapolis how
	5:24	So Jesus **went** with him. A large crowd followed and pressed
	6:27	to bring John's head. The *man* **went**, beheaded John in the prison,
	6:32	So *they* **went away** by themselves in a boat to a solitary place.
	6:36	so *they can* **go** to the surrounding countryside and villages
	6:37	Are we to **go** and spend that much on bread and give it to them to
	6:46	After leaving them, *he* **went up** on a mountainside to pray.
	7:24	Jesus left that place and **went** to the vicinity of Tyre. He entered a
	7:30	She **went** home and found her child lying on the bed,
	8:13	he left them, got back into the boat and **crossed** to the other side.
	9:43	It is better for you to enter life maimed than with two hands *to* **go**
	10:22	man's face fell. He **went away** sad, because he had great wealth.
	11: 4	*They* **went** and found a colt outside in the street, tied at a doorway.
	12:12	they were afraid of the crowd; so *they* left him and **went away**.
	14:10	of the Twelve, **went** to the chief priests to betray Jesus to them.
	14:12	"Where do you want us *to* **go** and make preparations for you to eat
	14:39	Once more he **went away** and prayed the same thing.
	16:13	These **returned** and reported it to the rest; but they did not believe
Lk	1:23	When his time of service was completed, *he* **returned** home.
	1:38	be to me as you have said." Then the angel **left** [*RP608*] her.
	2:15	When the angels had **left** [*RP608*] them and gone into heaven,
	5:13	"Be clean!" And immediately the leprosy **left** [*RP608*] him.
	5:14	Then Jesus ordered him, "Don't tell anyone, but **go**, show yourself
	5:25	took what he had been lying on and **went** home praising God.
	7:24	*After* John's messengers **left**, Jesus began to speak to the crowd
	8:31	And they begged him repeatedly not to order them *to* **go** into the
	8:37	of the region of the Gerasenes asked Jesus *to* **leave** [*RP608*] them,
	8:39	So the man **went away** and told all over town how much Jesus had
	9:57	the road, a man said to him, "I will follow you wherever *you* **go**."
	9:59	But the man replied, "Lord, first let me **go** and bury my father."
	9:60	their own dead, but you **go** and proclaim the kingdom of God."
	10:30	him of his clothes, beat him and **went away**, leaving him half dead.
	17:23	'There he is!' or 'Here he is!' *Do* not **go** running off after them.
	19:32	Those who were sent ahead **went** and found it just as he had told
	22: 4	And Judas **went** to the chief priests and the officers of the temple
	22:13	They **left** and found things just as Jesus had told them. So they
	24:12	and he **went away**, wondering to himself what had happened.
	24:24	Then some of our companions **went** to the tomb and found it just
Jn	4: 3	learned of this, he left Judea and **went back** once more to Galilee.
	4: 8	(His disciples *had* **gone** into the town to buy food.)
	4:28	the woman **went back** to the town and said to the people,
	4:47	he **went** to him and begged him to come and heal his son,
	5:15	The man **went away** and told the Jews that it was Jesus who had
	6: 1	Jesus **crossed** to the far shore of the Sea of Galilee (that is,
	6:22	entered it with his disciples, but that they *had* **gone away** alone.
	6:66	From this time many of his disciples **turned** [+*1650+3836+3958*]
		back and no longer followed him.
	6:68	Simon Peter answered him, "Lord, to whom *shall we* **go**? You have
	9: 7	means Sent). So the man **went** and washed, and came home seeing.
	9:11	to Siloam and wash. So *I* **went** and washed, and then I could see."
	10:40	Then Jesus **went back** across the Jordan to the place where John
	11:28	she had said this, *she* **went back** and called her sister Mary aside.

	11:46	But some of them **went** to the Pharisees and told them what Jesus
	11:54	Instead *he* **withdrew** to a region near the desert, to a village called
	12:19	us nowhere. Look how the whole world *has* **gone** after him!"
	12:36	finished speaking, Jesus **left** [*RP608*] and hid himself **from** them.
	16: 7	It is for your good that I *am* **going away**. Unless I go away,
	16: 7	Unless *I* **go away**, the Counselor will not come to you; but if I go,
	18: 6	When Jesus said, "I am he," *they* **drew** back and fell to the ground.
	20:10	Then the disciples **went back** to their homes,
Ac	4:15	So they ordered them *to* **withdraw** from the Sanhedrin and
	5:26	the captain **went** with his officers and brought the apostles.
	9:17	Then Ananias **went** to the house and entered it. Placing his hands
	10: 7	When the angel who spoke to him *had* **gone**, Cornelius called two
	16:39	them from the prison, requesting them to **leave** [*RP608*] the city.
	23:32	The next day they let the cavalry **go on** with him, while they
Ro	15:28	have received this fruit, *I will* **go** to Spain and visit you on the way.
Gal	1:17	but *I* **went** *immediately* into Arabia and later returned to
Jas	1:24	at himself, **goes away** and immediately forgets what he looks like.
Jude	1: 7	Sodom and Gomorrah and the surrounding towns gave themselves
		up to sexual immorality and **perversion** [+*2283+3958+4922*].
Rev	9:12	The first woe *is* **past**; two other woes are yet to come.
	10: 9	So *I* **went** to the angel and asked him to give me the little scroll.
	11:14	The second woe *has* **passed**; the third woe is coming soon.
	12:17	and **went off** to make war against the rest of her offspring—
	16: 2	The first angel **went** and poured out his bowl on the land,
	18:14	will say, 'The fruit you longed for *is* **gone** [*RP608*] **from** you.
	21: 1	new earth, for the first heaven and the first earth *had* **passed away**,
	21: 4	or crying or pain, for the old order of things *has* **passed away**."

600   ἀπέχω, *apechō*   [19]   [√ *608 + 2400*]

abstain from [4], received in full [3], are from [*RP608*] [2], avoid [*RP608*] [2], was from [*RP608*] [2], enough [1], about from [*RP608*] [1], have back [1], received [1], received payment [1], was [1]

Mt	6: 2	I tell you the truth, *they have* **received** their reward **in full**.
	6: 5	I tell you the truth, *they have* **received** their reward **in full**.
	6:16	I tell you the truth, *they have* **received** their reward **in full**.
	14:24	but the boat **was** [*RP608*] already a considerable distance **from**
	15: 8	honor me with their lips, but their hearts **are** [*RP608*] far **from** me.
Mk	7: 6	honor me with their lips, but their hearts **are** [*RP608*] far **from** me.
	14:41	he said to them, "Are you still sleeping and resting? **Enough!**
Lk	6:24	to you who are rich, for *you have already* **received** your comfort.
	7: 6	He **was** [*RP608*] not far **from** the house when the centurion sent
	15:20	"But *while* he **was** still a long way off, his father saw him and was
	24:13	called Emmaus, **about** [*RP608*] seven miles **from** Jerusalem.
Ac	15:20	telling them to **abstain from** food polluted by idols, from sexual
	15:29	You *are to* **abstain from** food sacrificed to idols, from blood,
Php	4:18	*I have* **received** full **payment** and even more; I am amply
1Th	4: 3	be sanctified: that you *should* **avoid** [*RP608*] sexual immorality;
	5:22	**Avoid** [*RP608*] every kind of evil.
1Ti	4: 3	people to marry and order them *to* **abstain from** certain foods,
Phm	1:15	you for a little while was that *you might* **have** him **back** for good—
1Pe	2:11	and strangers in the world, *to* **abstain from** sinful desires,

601   ἀπιστέω, *apisteō*   [8]   [√ *1.1 + 4412*]

not believe [6], faithless [1], not have faith [1]

Mk	16:11	Jesus was alive and that she had seen him, *they did* **not believe** it.
	16:16	will be saved, but whoever *does* **not believe** will be condemned.
Lk	24:11	But *they did* **not believe** the women, because their words seemed
	24:41	And *while* they still *did* **not believe** it because of joy
Ac	28:24	were convinced by what he said, but others *would* **not believe**.
Ro	3: 3	What if some *did* **not have faith**? Will their lack of faith nullify
2Ti	2:13	if *we are* **faithless**, he will remain faithful, for he cannot disown
1Pe	2: 7	But *to those who do* **not believe**, "The stone the builders rejected

602   ἀπιστία, *apistia*   [11]   [√ *1.1 + 4412*]

unbelief [6], lack of faith [4], unbelieving [1]

Mt	13:58	he did not do many miracles there because of their **lack of faith**.
Mk	6: 6	And he was amazed at their **lack of faith**. Then Jesus went around
	9:24	father exclaimed; "I do believe; help me overcome my **unbelief**!"
	16:14	he rebuked them for their **lack of faith** and their stubborn refusal
Ro	3: 3	not have faith? Will their **lack of faith** nullify God's faithfulness?

4:20 Yet he did not waver *through* **unbelief** regarding the promise of
11:20 But they were broken off *because of* **unbelief**, and you stand by
11:23 And if they do not persist in **unbelief**, they will be grafted in,
1Ti 1:13 I was shown mercy because I acted in ignorance and **unbelief**.
Heb 3:12 a sinful, **unbelieving** heart that turns away from the living God.
3:19 we see that they were not able to enter, because of their **unbelief**.

603 ἄπιστος, *apistos* [23] [√ 1.1 + 4412]

unbelievers [7], unbelieving [6], unbeliever [5], not a believer [2], doubting [+1181] [1], incredible [1], not believe [1]

Mt 17:17 "O **unbelieving** and perverse generation," Jesus replied, "how long
Mk 9:19 "O **unbelieving** generation," Jesus replied, "how long shall I stay
Lk 9:41 "O **unbelieving** and perverse generation," Jesus replied, "how long
12:46 will cut him to pieces and assign him a place with the **unbelievers**.
Jn 20:27 and put it into my side. Stop **doubting** [+1181] and believe."
Ac 26: 8 Why should any of you consider it **incredible** that God raises the
1Co 6: 6 goes to law against another—and this in front of **unbelievers**!
7:12 If any brother has a wife who is **not a believer** and she is willing to
7:13 And if a woman has a husband who is **not a believer** and he is
7:14 For the **unbelieving** husband has been sanctified through his wife,
7:14 and the **unbelieving** wife has been sanctified through her believing
7:15 But if the **unbeliever** leaves, let him do so. A believing man
10:27 If some **unbeliever** invites you to a meal and you want to go,
14:22 Tongues, then, are a sign, not for believers but *for* **unbelievers**;
14:22 however, is for believers, not *for* **unbelievers**.
14:23 and some who do not understand or *some* **unbelievers** come in,
14:24 But if an **unbeliever** or someone who does not understand comes
2Co 4: 4 The god of this age has blinded the minds *of* **unbelievers**,
6:14 Do not be yoked together *with* **unbelievers**. For what do
6:15 What does a believer have in common with an **unbeliever**?
1Ti 5: 8 he has denied the faith and is worse than an **unbeliever**.
Tit 1:15 but *to* those who are corrupted and do **not believe**, nothing is pure.
Rev 21: 8 But the cowardly, the **unbelieving**, the vile, the murderers,

604 ἁπλόος, *haploos* Not used in UBS/NIV [→ 605, 606, 607; cf. 275]

605 ἁπλότης, *haplotēs* [8 / 7] [√ 604]

generosity [2], sincerity [2], generous [1], generously [+1877] [1], sincere devotion [1]

Ro 12: 8 to the needs of others, let him give **generously** [+1877];
2Co 1:12 in the holiness [UBS *frankness*; NIV *42*] and sincerity that are
8: 2 and their extreme poverty welled up in rich **generosity**.
9:11 rich in every way so that you can be **generous** on every occasion,
9:13 and *for* your **generosity** in sharing with them and with everyone
11: 3 may somehow be led astray from your **sincere** and pure **devotion**
Eph 6: 5 earthly masters with respect and fear, and with **sincerity** of heart,
Col 3:22 their favor, but with **sincerity** of heart and reverence for the Lord.

606 ἁπλοῦς, *haplous* [2] [√ 604]

good [2]

Mt 6:22 If your eyes are **good**, your whole body will be full of light.
Lk 11:34 When your eyes are **good**, your whole body also is full of light.

607 ἁπλῶς, *haplōs* [1] [√ 604]

generously [1]

Jas 1: 5 should ask God, who gives **generously** to all without finding fault,

608 ἀπό, *apo* [646 / 648]

[→ 406, 500, 501, 502, 503, 550, 552, 554, 555, 557, 558, 560, 561, 565, 566, 567, 568, 569, 571, 575, 576, 582, 583, 584, 587, 588, 589, 590, 591, 592, 594, 595, 599, 600, 609, 610, 611, 612, 613, 614, 615, 616, 617, 618, 619, 620, 621, 622, 623, 624, 625, 626, 627, 628, 629, 630, 631, 632, 633, 634, 635, 636, 637, 638, 639, 640, 641, 642, 643, 644, 645, 646, 647, 648, 649, 652, 653, 654, 655, 656, 657, 658, 659, 660, 661, 664, 665, 666, 667, 668, 669, 670, 671, 672, 673, 674, 675, 676, 677, 678, 681, 682, 683, 684,

685, 686, 687, 688, 689, 690, 691, 694, 695, 696, 697, 698, 699, 700, 701, 702, 703, 704, 705, 706, 707, 708, 709, 710, 711, 712, 713, 714, 715, 724, 904, 909, 919, 922, 923, 926, 927, 928, 929, 934, 935, 3632, 3633, 4467, 4534, 4535, 5270, 5271, 5272; cf. 723, 918]

from [334], *untranslated* [56], of [35], by [23], on [12], in [11], since [11], against [9], for [9], at [7], with [8], because of [5], some [5], away [4], left [RP599] [4], far off [+3427] [3], leave [RP599] [3], left [RP923] [3], out of [3], taken from [RP554] [3], are from [RP600] [2], as for [2], avoid [RP600] [2], belonged to [2], ever since [+4005] [2], in part [+3538] [2], kept hidden for [RP648 + 608] [2], since [+4005] [2], turn away from [RP695] [2], was from [RP600] [2], about from [RP600] [1], after marriage [+4220] [1], again [+3814+3836] [1], again [+785] [1], ago [+4005] [1], ago [1], alike [+1651] [1], as [1], at the hands of [1], away from [RP599] [1], away from [RP713] [1], away from [RP923] [1], because [1], before [+4725] [1], before [1], beyond [1], both [1], cured [RP557] [1], cut off from [1], demand back [RP555] [1], demanded from [RP555] [1], depended on [1], deserted [RP923] [1], deserting [+3572] [1], divorced [+467+668] [1], down from [1], ejected from [RP590] [1], elude [+5771] [1], far away [+3427] [1], for a distance of [1], from [+4725] [1], from among [1], from the time [+4005] [1], given [+2400] [1], gone from [RP599] [1], hidden [RP648] [1], hidden from [RP648] [1], in the future [+785] [1], it [+201+794+4005] [1], leave alone [RP923] [1], leaves [RP713] [1], leaving [+4513] [1], leaving [RP1744] [1], left [+4513+4725] [1], left [+482] [1], left [RP609] [1], left [RP713] [1], left [1], left from [RP599] [1], less than two miles [+1278+5084+6055] [1], long ago [+172] [1], now [+3814+3836] [1], now [+4005] [1], now [+785] [1], once [+323+4005] [1], part [1], parted company [+253+714] [1], receive from [RP655] [1], reconciled to [RP557] [1], rid of [+149] [1], shake off [RP701] [1], some time ago [+792+2465] [1], sound asleep [+2965+3836+5678] [1], take away from [RP923] [1], takes away from [RP904] [1], that had touched [+3836+5999] [1], to [1], to some extent [+247+3538] [1], to turn away from [RP686] [1], took away from [RP655] [1], torn away from [RP682] [1], turn away from [RP923] [1], turning from [RP695] [1], turns away from [RP923] [1], unmarried [+1222+3395] [1], unsettled [+3808+3836+4888] [1], vanished [RP660] [1], wandered from [RP675] [1], with ever-increasing glory [+1518+1518+1650] [1], withdrew [RP923] [1]

Mt 1:17 Thus there were fourteen generations in all **from** Abraham to
1:17 fourteen **from** David to the exile to Babylon, and fourteen **from** the
1:17 to the exile to Babylon, and fourteen **from** the exile to the Christ.
1:21 the name Jesus, because he will save his people **from** their sins."
1:24 [NIE] he did what the angel of the Lord had commanded him
2: 1 the time of King Herod, Magi **from** the east came to Jerusalem
2:16 and its vicinity who were [NIE] two years old and under,
3: 4 John's clothes were made **of** camel's hair, and he had a leather belt
3: 7 brood of vipers! Who warned you to flee **from** the coming wrath?
3:13 Then Jesus came **from** Galilee to the Jordan to be baptized by
3:16 As soon as Jesus was baptized, he went up **out of** the water.
4:17 **From** that time on Jesus began to preach, "Repent, for the kingdom
4:25 Large crowds **from** Galilee, the Decapolis, Jerusalem, Judea
5:18 will by any means disappear **from** the Law until everything is
5:29 If your right eye causes you to sin, gouge it out and throw it **away**.
5:30 if your right hand causes you to sin, cut it off and throw it **away**.
5:42 and do not turn away from the one who wants to borrow **from** you.
6:13 And lead us not into temptation, but deliver us **from** the evil one.'
7:15 "Watch out **for** false prophets. They come to you in sheep's
7:16 **By** their fruit you will recognize them. Do people pick grapes from
7:16 Do people pick grapes **from** thornbushes, or figs from thistles?
7:16 Do people pick grapes from thornbushes, or figs **from** thistles?
7:20 Thus, **by** their fruit you will recognize them.
7:23 'I never knew you. **Away from** [RP713] me, you evildoers!'
8: 1 When he came down **from** the mountainside, large crowds
8:11 I say to you that many will come **from** the east and the west,
8:30 Some distance **from** them a large herd of pigs was feeding.
8:34 they saw him, they pleaded with him to leave [NIE] their region.
9:15 come when the bridegroom *will be* **taken from** [RP554] them;
9:16 for the patch will pull away **from** the garment, making the tear
9:22 has healed you." And the woman was healed **from** that moment.

10: 17 "Be on your guard **against** men; they will hand you over to the
10: 28 Do not be afraid **of** those who kill the body but cannot kill the soul.
11: 12 **From** the days of John the Baptist until now, the kingdom of
11: 19 and "sinners." ' But wisdom is proved right **by** her actions."
11: 25 because you have hidden these things **from** the wise and learned,
11: 29 Take my yoke upon you and learn **from** me, for I am gentle
12: 38 said to him, "Teacher, we want to see a miraculous sign **from** you."
12: 43 "When an evil spirit comes out **of** a man, it goes through arid places
13: 12 Whoever does not have, even what he has will be taken **from** him.
13: 35 I will utter things hidden **since** the creation of the world."
13: 44 and then **in** his joy went and sold all he had and bought that field.
14: 2 attendants, "This is John the Baptist; he has risen **from** the dead!
14: 13 Hearing of this, the crowds followed him on foot **from** the towns.
14: 24 but the boat was already a considerable distance **from** [*RP600*]
14: 26 they were terrified. "It's a ghost," they said, and cried out **in** fear.
14: 29 Then Peter got down **out of** the boat, walked on the water
15: 1 and teachers of the law came to Jesus **from** Jerusalem and asked,
15: 8 honor me with their lips, but their hearts **are** far **from** [*RP600*] me.
15: 22 A Canaanite woman **from** that vicinity came to him, crying out,
15: 27 "but even the dogs eat **[NIE]** the crumbs that fall from their
15: 27 even the dogs eat the crumbs that fall **from** their masters' table."
15: 28 is granted." And her daughter was healed **from** that very hour.
16: 6 "Be on your guard **against** the yeast of the Pharisees
16: 11 But be on your guard **against** the yeast of the Pharisees
16: 12 Then they understood that he was not telling them to guard **against**
16: 12 in bread, but **against** the teaching of the Pharisees and Sadducees.
16: 21 **From** that time on Jesus began to explain to his disciples that he
16: 21 go to Jerusalem and suffer many things **at the hands of** the elders,
17: 18 Jesus rebuked the demon, and it came out **of** the boy, and he was
17: 18 and it came out of the boy, and he was healed **from** that moment.
17: 25 "**From** whom do the kings of the earth collect duty and taxes—
17: 25 earth collect duty and taxes—**from** their own sons or from others?"
17: 25 earth collect duty and taxes—from their own sons or from others?"
17: 26 "**From** others," Peter answered. "Then the sons are exempt,"
18: 7 "Woe to the world **because of** the things that cause people to sin!
18: 8 or your foot causes you to sin, cut it off and throw it **away**.
18: 9 And if your eye causes you to sin, gouge it out and throw it **away**.
18: 35 treat each of you unless you forgive your brother **from** your heart."
19: 1 he left **[NIE]** Galilee and went into the region of Judea to the
19: 4 "that **at** the beginning the Creator 'made them male and female,'
19: 8 your hearts were hard. But it was not this way **from** the beginning.
20: 8 beginning **with** the last ones hired and going on to the first.'
20: 20 to Jesus with her sons and, kneeling down, asked a favor **of** him.
20: 29 As Jesus and his disciples *were* **leaving** [*RP1744*] Jericho,
21: 8 while others cut branches **from** the trees and spread them on the
21: 11 "This is Jesus, the prophet **from** Nazareth in Galilee."
21: 43 I tell you that the kingdom of God will be taken away **from** you
22: 46 and **from** that day on no one dared to ask him any more questions.
23: 33 of vipers! How will you escape **[NIE]** being condemned to hell?
23: 34 you will flog in your synagogues and pursue **from** town to town.
23: 35 **from** the blood of righteous Abel to the blood of Zechariah son of
23: 39 For I tell you, you will not see me **again** [*+785*] until you say,
24: 1 Jesus left **[NIE]** the temple and was walking away when his
24: 21 unequaled **from** the beginning of the world until now—
24: 27 For as lightning that comes **from** the east is visible even in the
24: 29 the stars will fall **from** the sky, and the heavenly bodies will be
24: 31 from the four winds, **from** one end of the heavens to the other.
24: 32 "Now learn this lesson **from** the fig tree: As soon as its twigs get
25: 28 " 'Take the talent **from** him and give it to the one who has the ten
25: 29 Whoever does not have, even what he has will be taken **from** him.
25: 32 and he will separate the people one **from** another as a shepherd
25: 32 one from another as a shepherd separates the sheep **from** the goats.
25: 34 the kingdom prepared for you **since** the creation of the world.
25: 41 will say to those on his left, 'Depart **from** me, you who are cursed,
26: 16 **From** then on Judas watched for an opportunity to hand him over.
26: 29 I will not drink of this fruit of the vine **from** now on until that day
26: 39 "My Father, if it is possible, may this cup be taken **from** me.
26: 47 and clubs, *sent* **from** the chief priests and the elders of the people.
26: 58 But Peter followed him **at** a distance, right up to the courtyard of
26: 64 "But I say to all of you: **In the future** [*+785*] you will see the Son
27: 9 the thirty silver coins, the price set on him **by** the people of Israel,
27: 21 "Which of the two do you want me to release to you?" asked the
27: 24 "I am innocent **of** this man's blood," he said. "It is your
27: 40 Come down **from** the cross, if you are the Son of God!"
27: 42 Let him come down now **from** the cross, and we will believe in
27: 45 **From** the sixth hour until the ninth hour darkness came over all the

27: 51 At that moment the curtain of the temple was torn in two **from** top
27: 55 Many women were there, watching **from** a distance. They had
27: 55 They had followed Jesus **from** Galilee to care for his needs.
27: 57 there came a rich man **from** Arimathea, named Joseph,
27: 64 the body and tell the people that he has been raised **from** the dead.
28: 4 The guards were **[NIE]** so afraid of him that they shook
28: 7 'He has risen **from** the dead and is going ahead of you into Galilee.
28: 8 So the women hurried **away from** [*RP599*] the tomb, afraid yet
Mk 1: 9 At that time Jesus came **from** Nazareth in Galilee and was baptized
1: 42 Immediately the leprosy **left** [*RP599*] him and he was cured.
2: 20 come when the bridegroom *will be* **taken from** [*RP554*] them,
2: 21 If he does, the new piece will pull away **from** the old, making the
3: 7 his disciples to the lake, and a large crowd **from** Galilee followed.
3: 8 many people came to him **from** Judea, Jerusalem, Idumea,
3: 8 **[RPG]** Jerusalem, Idumea, and the regions across the Jordan
3: 8 Jerusalem, **[RPG]** Idumea, and the regions across the Jordan
3: 22 And the teachers of the law who came down **from** Jerusalem said,
4: 25 whoever does not have, even what he has will be taken **from** him."
5: 6 When he saw Jesus **from** a distance, he ran and fell on his knees in
5: 17 Then the people began to plead with Jesus *to* **leave** [*RP599*] their
5: 29 and she felt in her body that she was freed **from** her suffering.
5: 34 has healed you. Go in peace and be freed **from** your suffering."
5: 35 some men came **from** the house of Jairus, the synagogue ruler.
6: 33 and ran on foot **from** all the towns and got there ahead of them.
6: 43 up twelve basketfuls of broken pieces of bread and **[NIE]** fish.
7: 1 and some of the teachers of the law who had come **from** Jerusalem
7: 4 When they come **from** the marketplace they do not eat unless they
7: 6 honor me with their lips, but their hearts **are** far **from** [*RP600*] me.
7: 17 After he had **left** the crowd and entered the house, his disciples
7: 28 even the dogs under the table eat **[NIE]** the children's crumbs."
7: 33 *After he* **took** him aside, **away from** [*RP655*] the crowd,
8: 3 because some of them have come **[NIE]** a long distance."
8: 11 To test him, they asked him for a sign **from** heaven.
8: 15 "Watch out **for** the yeast of the Pharisees and that of Herod."
10: 6 "But **at** the beginning of creation God 'made them male
10: 46 were leaving **[NIE]** the city, a blind man, Bartimaeus (that is,
11: 12 The next day as they were leaving **[NIE]** Bethany, Jesus was
11: 13 Seeing **in** the distance a fig tree in leaf, he went to find out if it had
12: 2 the tenants to collect from them **some** of the fruit of the vineyard.
12: 34 he said to him, "You are not far **from** the kingdom of God."
12: 38 As he taught, Jesus said, "Watch out **for** the teachers of the law.
13: 19 because those will be days of distress unequaled **from** the
13: 27 four winds, **from** the ends of the earth to the ends of the heavens.
13: 28 "Now learn this lesson **from** the fig tree: As soon as its twigs get
14: 35 and prayed that if possible the hour might pass **from** him.
14: 36 Take this cup **from** me. Yet not what I will, but what you will."
14: 54 Peter followed him **at** a distance, right into the courtyard of the
15: 21 and Rufus, was passing by on his way in **from** the country,
15: 30 come down **from** the cross and save yourself!"
15: 32 come down now **from** the cross, that we may see and believe."
15: 38 The curtain of the temple was torn in two **from** top to bottom.
15: 40 Some women were watching **from** a distance. Among them were
15: 43 Joseph **of** Arimathea, a prominent member of the Council,
15: 45 When he learned **from** the centurion that it was so, he gave the
16: 8 and bewildered, the women went out and fled **from** the tomb.
16: S [UBS+ *Jesus himself sent out through them from east to west,*]
Lk 1: 2 just as they were handed down to us by those who **from** the first
1: 26 **[NIE]** God sent the angel Gabriel to Nazareth, a town in Galilee,
1: 38 it be to me as you have said." Then the angel **left** [*RP599*] her.
1: 48 of his servant. **From** now on all generations will call me blessed,
1: 52 He has brought down rulers **from** their thrones but has lifted up the
1: 70 (as he said through his holy prophets **of** long ago),
2: 4 So Joseph also went up from the town **of** Nazareth in Galilee to
2: 15 When the angels *had* **left** [*RP599*] them and gone into heaven,
2: 36 lived with her husband seven years **after** her **marriage** [*+4220*],
3: 7 brood of vipers! Who warned you to flee **from** the coming wrath?
4: 1 returned **from** the Jordan and was led by the Spirit in the desert,
4: 13 all this tempting, *he* **left** [*RP923*] him until an opportune time.
4: 35 "Be quiet!" Jesus said sternly. "Come out **of** him!" Then the demon
4: 35 down before them all and came out **[RPG]** without injuring him.
4: 38 Jesus **left** [*+482*] the synagogue and went to the home of Simon.
4: 41 Moreover, demons came out **of** many people, shouting, "You are
4: 42 where he was, they tried to keep him from **leaving** [*+4513*] them.
5: 2 **left** there **by** [*RP609*] the fishermen, who were washing their nets.
5: 3 belonging to Simon, and asked him to put out a little **from** shore.
5: 8 saw this, he fell at Jesus' knees and said, "Go away **from** me, Lord;

5: 10 said to Simon, "Don't be afraid; **from** now on you will catch men."
5: 13 "Be clean!" And immediately the leprosy **left** [*RP599*] him.
5: 15 of people came to hear him and to be healed **of** their sicknesses.
5: 35 come when the bridegroom *will be* **taken from** [*RP554*] them;
5: 36 "No one tears a patch **from** a new garment and sews it on an old
5: 36 new garment, and the patch **from** the new will not match the old.
6: 13 he called his disciples to him and chose twelve **of** them,
6: 17 was there and a great number of people **from** all over Judea,
6: 18 who had come to hear him and to be healed **of** their diseases.
6: 18 healed of their diseases. Those troubled **by** evil spirits were cured,
6: 29 **[NIE]** If someone takes your cloak, do not stop him from taking
6: 30 takes what belongs to you, *do* not **demand** it **back** [*RP555*].
7: 6 He **was** not far **from** [*RP600*] the house when the centurion sent
7: 21 At that very time Jesus cured many who had **[NIE]** diseases,
7: 35 But wisdom is proved right **by** all her children."
7: 45 give me a kiss, but this woman, **from** [*+4005*] **the time** I entered,
8: 2 and also some women who had been cured **of** evil spirits
8: 2 (called Magdalene) **from** whom seven demons had come out;
8: 12 then the devil comes and takes away the word **from** their hearts,
8: 18 does not have, even what he thinks he has will be taken **from** him."
8: 29 For Jesus had commanded the evil spirit to come out **of** the man.
8: 33 When the demons came out **of** the man, they went into the pigs,
8: 35 they found the man **from** whom the demons had gone out,
8: 37 of the region of the Gerasenes asked Jesus *to* **leave** [*RP599*] them,
8: 38 The man **from** whom the demons had gone out begged to go with
8: 43 And a woman was there who had been subject to bleeding **for**
8: 43 to bleeding for twelve years, but **[NIE]** no one could heal her.
8: 46 "Someone touched me; I know that power has gone out **from** me."
9: 5 **shake** the dust **off** [*RP701*] your feet when you leave their town,
9: 5 shake the dust off your feet when you leave **[NIE]** their town,
9: 22 Son of Man must suffer many things and be rejected **by** the elders,
9: 33 As the men were leaving **[NIE]** Jesus, Peter said to him, "Master,
9: 37 The next day, when they came down **from** the mountain, a large
9: 38 A man **in** the crowd called out, "Teacher, I beg you to look at my
9: 39 *It* scarcely ever **leaves** [*RP713*] him and is destroying him.
9: 45 It was hidden **from** them, so that they did not grasp it, and they
9: 54 do you want us to call fire down **from** heaven to destroy them?"
10: 21 because *you have* **hidden** these things **from** [*RP648*] the wise
10: 30 "A man was going down **from** Jerusalem to Jericho, when he fell
11: 24 "When an evil spirit comes out **of** a man, it goes through arid places
11: 50 the prophets that has been shed **since** the beginning of the world,
11: 50 that has been shed since the beginning of the world, **[RPG]**
11: 51 **from** the blood of Abel to the blood of Zechariah, who was killed
11: 51 I tell you, **[NIE]** this generation will be held responsible for it all.
12: 1 "Be on your guard **against** the yeast of the Pharisees, which is
12: 4 do not be afraid **of** those who kill the body and after that can do no
12: 15 Be on your guard **against** all kinds of greed; a man's life does not
12: 20 This very night your life *will be* **demanded of** [*RP555*] you.
12: 52 **From** now on there will be five in one family divided against each
12: 57 "Why don't you judge **for** yourselves what is right?
12: 58 try hard *to be* **reconciled to** [*RP557*] him on the way, or he may
13: 7 'For three years **now** [*+4005*] I've been coming to look for fruit on
13: 15 his ox or donkey **from** the stall and lead it out to give it water?
13: 16 long years, be set free on the Sabbath day **from** what bound her?"
13: 25 **Once** [*+323+4005*] the owner of the house gets up and closes the
13: 27 you come from. **Away from** [*RP923*] me, all you evildoers!'
13: 29 People will come **from** east and west and north and south,
13: 29 People will come from east and west and **[RPG]** north and south,
14: 18 "But they all **alike** [*+1651*] began to make excuses. The first said,
15: 16 He longed to fill his stomach **with** [UBS *1666*] the pods that the
16: 3 'What shall I do now? My master is taking away **[NIE]** my job.
16: 16 **Since** that time, the good news of the kingdom of God is being
16: 18 and the man who marries a **divorced woman** [*+467+668*] commits
16: 21 and longing to eat **[NIE]** what fell from the rich man's table.
16: 21 and longing to eat what fell **from** the rich man's table. Even the
16: 23 he looked up and saw Abraham **far away** [*+3427*], with Lazarus
16: 30 he said, 'but if someone **from** the dead goes to them, they will
17: 25 first he must suffer many things and be rejected **by** this generation.
17: 29 But the day Lot left **[NIE]** Sodom, fire and sulfur rained down
17: 29 fire and sulfur rained **down from** heaven and destroyed them all.
18: 3 to him with the plea, 'Grant me justice **against** my adversary.'
18: 34 Its meaning was hidden **from** them, and they did not know what he
19: 3 but being a short man he could not, **because of** the crowd.
19: 24 'Take his mina away **from** him and give it to the one who has ten
19: 26 who has, more will be given, but **as for** the one who has nothing,
19: 39 Some of the Pharisees **in** the crowd said to Jesus, "Teacher,

19: 42 what would bring you peace—but now it is hidden **from** your eyes.
20: 10 so they would give him **some** of the fruit of the vineyard.
20: 46 "Beware **of** the teachers of the law. They like to walk around in
21: 11 in various places, and fearful events and great signs **from** heaven.
21: 26 Men will faint **from** terror, apprehensive of what is coming on the
21: 30 you can see **for** yourselves and know that summer is near.
22: 18 For I tell you I will not drink **again** [*+3814+3836*] of the fruit of
22: 18 For I tell you I will not drink again **of** the fruit of the vine until the
22: 41 He withdrew about a stone's throw **beyond** them, knelt down
22: 42 "Father, if you are willing, take this cup **from** me; yet not my will,
22: 43 An angel **from** heaven appeared to him and strengthened him.
22: 45 When he rose **from** prayer and went back to the disciples,
22: 45 to the disciples, he found them asleep, *exhausted* **from** sorrow.
22: 69 But **from** now on, the Son of Man will be seated at the right hand
22: 71 we need any more testimony? We have heard it **from** his own lips."
23: 5 his teaching. He started **in** Galilee and has come all the way here."
23: 26 who was on his way in **from** the country, and put the cross on him
23: 49 including the women who had followed him **from** Galilee,
23: 49 him from Galilee, stood **at** a distance, watching these things.
23: 51 He *came* **from** the Judean town of Arimathea and he was waiting
24: 2 They found the stone rolled away **from** the tomb,
24: 9 When they came back **from** the tomb, they told all these things to
24: 13 called Emmaus, **about** seven miles **from** [*RP600*] Jerusalem.
24: 21 what is more, it is the third day **since** [*+4005*] all this took place.
24: 27 And beginning **with** Moses and all the Prophets, he explained to
24: 27 And beginning with Moses and **[RPG]** all the Prophets,
24: 31 and they recognized him, and he disappeared **from** their *sight.*
24: 41 while they still did not believe it **because of** joy and amazement,
24: 47 will be preached in his name to all nations, beginning **at** Jerusalem.
24: 51 blessing them, he left **[NIE]** them and was taken up into heaven.

Jn 1: 44 Philip, like Andrew and Peter, was from the town **of** Bethsaida.
1: 45 the prophets also wrote—Jesus **of** Nazareth, the son of Joseph."
3: 2 "Rabbi, we know you are a teacher who has come **from** God.
5: 19 "I tell you the truth, the Son can do nothing **by** himself; he can do
5: 30 **By** myself I can do nothing; I judge only as I hear, and my
6: 38 For I have come down from heaven not to do my will but to do the
7: 17 my teaching comes from God or whether I speak **on** my own.
7: 18 He who speaks **on** his own does so to gain honor for himself,
7: 28 I am not here **on** my own, but he who sent me is true. You do not
7: 42 the Christ will come from David's family and from Bethlehem,
8: 9 **[NIE]** the older ones first, until only Jesus was left,
8: 11 Jesus declared. "Go **now** [*+3814+3836*] and leave your life of sin."
8: 28 and that I do nothing **on** my own but speak just what the Father has
8: 42 and now am here. I have not come **on** my own; but he sent me.
8: 44 He was a murderer **from** the beginning, not holding to the truth,
10: 5 they will run away **from** him because they do not recognize a
10: 18 No one takes it **from** me, but I lay it down of my own accord.
10: 18 No one takes it from me, but I lay it down **of** my own accord.
11: 1 He was **from** Bethany, the village of Mary and her sister Martha.
11: 18 Bethany was **less than two miles** [*+1278+5084+6055*] from
        Jerusalem,
11: 51 He did not say this **on** his own, but as high priest that year he
11: 53 So **from** that day on they plotted to take his life.
12: 21 came to Philip, who was **from** Bethsaida in Galilee, with a request.
12: 36 finished speaking, Jesus **left** and hid himself **from** [*RP599*] them.
13: 3 and that he had come **from** God and was returning to God.
13: 19 "I am telling you **now** [*+785*] before it happens, so that when it
14: 7 as well. **From** now on, you do know him and have seen him."
14: 10 The words I say to you are not just **[NIE]** my own. Rather,
15: 4 No branch can bear fruit **by** itself; it must remain in the vine.
15: 27 also must testify, for you have been with me **from** the beginning.
16: 13 He will not speak **on** his own; he will speak only what he hears,
16: 22 and you will rejoice, and no one will take away your **[NIE]** joy.
16: 30 ask you questions. This makes us believe that you came **from** God."
18: 28 Then the Jews led Jesus **from** Caiaphas to the palace of the Roman
18: 34 "Is that **[NIE]** your own idea," Jesus asked, "or did others talk to
19: 27 **From** that time on, this disciple took her into his home.
19: 38 Later, Joseph **of** Arimathea asked Pilate for the body of Jesus.
21: 2 Nathanael **from** Cana in Galilee, the sons of Zebedee,
21: 6 were unable to haul the net in **because of** the large number of fish.
21: 8 of fish, for they were not far **from** shore, about a hundred yards.
21: 8 for they were not far from shore, about a **[NIE]** hundred yards.
21: 10 Jesus said to them, "Bring **some** of the fish you have just caught."

Ac 1: 4 "Do not leave **[NIE]** Jerusalem, but wait for the gift my Father
1: 9 up before their very eyes, and a cloud hid him **from** their sight.
1: 11 This same Jesus, who has been taken **from** you into heaven,

1:12 Then they returned to Jerusalem **from** the hill called the Mount of
1:22 beginning **from** John's baptism to the time when Jesus was taken
1:22 from John's baptism to the time when Jesus was taken up **from** us.
1:25 **[NIE]** which Judas left to go where he belongs."
2: 5 Now there were staying in Jerusalem God-fearing Jews **from** every
2:17 last days, God says, I will pour out **[NIE]** my Spirit on all people.
2:18 and women, I will pour out **[NIE]** my Spirit in those days,
2:22 Jesus of Nazareth was a man accredited **by** God to you by
2:40 pleaded with them, "Save yourselves **from** this corrupt generation."
3:19 that times of refreshing may come **from** [+4725] the Lord,
3:21 as he promised **long ago** [+172] through his holy prophets.
3:24 "Indeed, all the prophets **from** Samuel on, as many as have spoken,
3:26 you by **turning** each of you **from** [RP695] your wicked ways."
4:36 whom **[NIE]** the apostles called Barnabas (which means Son of
5: 2 With his wife's full knowledge he kept back **part** of the money for
5: 3 and have kept for yourself **some** of the money you received for the
5:38 **Leave** these men **alone** [RP923]! Let them go! For if their
5:41 The apostles **left** [+4513+4725] the Sanhedrin, rejoicing
6: 9 and Alexandria as well as **[NIE]** the provinces of Cilicia
7:45 took the land from the nations God drove out **before** [+4725] them.
8:10 and all the people, **both** high and low, gave him their attention
8:22 Repent **of** this wickedness and pray to the Lord. Perhaps he will
8:26 the desert road—that goes down **from** Jerusalem to Gaza."
8:33 speak of his descendants? For his life was taken **from** the earth."
8:35 Then Philip began **with** that very passage of Scripture and told him
9: 8 Saul got up **from** the ground, but when he opened his eyes he
9:13 "I have heard **[NIE]** many reports about this man and all the harm
9:18 Immediately, something like scales fell **from** Saul's eyes,
10:23 out with them, and some of the brothers **from** Joppa went along.
10:30 "Four days **ago** I was in my house praying at this hour, at three in
10:37 beginning **in** Galilee after the baptism that John preached—
10:38 how God anointed Jesus **of** Nazareth with the Holy Spirit
11:11 then three men who had been sent to me **from** Caesarea stopped at
11:19 Now those who had been scattered **by** the persecution in
11:27 During this time some prophets came down **from** Jerusalem to
12: 1 time that King Herod arrested some who **belonged to** the church,
12:10 the length of one street, suddenly the angel **left** [RP923] him.
12:14 she was so **[NIE]** overjoyed she ran back without opening it
12:19 Then Herod went **from** Judea to Caesarea and stayed there a while.
12:20 because they **depended on** the king's country for their food
12:25 they returned **from** [UBS 1650] Jerusalem, taking with them John,
13: 8 opposed them and tried to turn the proconsul **from** the faith.
13:13 **From** Paphos, Paul and his companions sailed to Perga in
13:13 where John **left** [RP713] them to return to Jerusalem.
13:14 **From** Perga they went on to Pisidian Antioch. On the Sabbath they
13:23 "**From** this man's descendants God has brought to Israel the
13:29 they took him down **from** the tree and laid him in a tomb.
13:31 by those who had traveled with him **from** Galilee to Jerusalem.
13:39 Through him everyone who believes is justified **from** everything
13:50 against Paul and Barnabas, and expelled them **from** their region.
14:15 telling you to turn **from** these worthless things to the living God,
14:19 Then some Jews came **from** Antioch and Iconium and won the
15: 1 Some men came down **from** Judea to Antioch and were teaching
15: 4 they were welcomed **by** the church and the apostles and elders,
15: 5 Then some of the believers who **belonged to** the party of the
15: 7 you know that **some time ago** [+792+2465] God made a choice
15:18 that have been known **for** ages.
15:19 that we should not make it difficult for **[NIE]** the Gentiles who
15:33 they were sent off **by** the brothers with the blessing of peace to
15:38 *because he had* **deserted** [RP923] them in Pamphylia and had not
15:38 because he had deserted them **in** Pamphylia and had not continued
15:39 such a sharp disagreement that they **parted company** [+253+714].
16:11 **From** Troas we put out to sea and sailed straight for Samothrace,
16:18 "In the name of Jesus Christ I command you to come out **of** her!"
16:33 of the night the jailer took them and washed **[NIE]** their wounds;
16:39 them from the prison, requesting them *to* **leave** [RP599] the city.
16:40 After Paul and Silas came out of the prison, they went to Lydia's
17: 2 and on three Sabbath days he reasoned with them **from** the
17:13 When the Jews **in** Thessalonica learned that Paul was preaching
17:27 out for him and find him, though he is not far **from** each one of us.
18: 2 who had recently come **from** Italy with his wife Priscilla,
18: 2 because Claudius had ordered all the Jews to leave **[NIE]** Rome.
18: 5 When Silas and Timothy came **from** Macedonia, Paul devoted
18: 6 clear of my responsibility. **From** now on I will go to the Gentiles."
18:16 So *he had* them **ejected from** [RP590] the court.
18:21 will come back if it is God's will." Then he set sail **from** Ephesus.

19: 9 *So* Paul **left** [RP923] them. He took the disciples with him
19:12 and aprons **that had touched** [+3836+5999] him were taken to the
19:12 and their illnesses *were* **cured** [RP557] and the evil spirits left
20: 6 But we sailed **from** Philippi after the Feast of Unleavened Bread,
20: 9 *When he was* **sound asleep** [+2965+3836+5678], he fell to the
20: 9 he fell to the ground **from** the third story and was picked up dead.
20:17 **From** Miletus, Paul sent to Ephesus for the elders of the church.
20:18 I was with you, **from** the first day I came into the province of Asia
20:18 from the first day **[RPG]** I came into the province of Asia.
20:26 I declare to you today that I am innocent **of** the blood of all men.
21: 1 After we had torn ourselves away **from** them, we put out to sea
21: 7 We continued our voyage **from** Tyre and landed at Ptolemais,
21:10 number of days, a prophet named Agabus came down **from** Judea.
21:16 Some of the disciples **from** Caesarea accompanied us and brought
21:21 who live among the Gentiles **to turn away from** [RP686] Moses,
21:27 some Jews **from** the province of Asia saw Paul at the temple.
22:11 into Damascus, **because** the brilliance of the light had blinded me.
22:22 they raised their voices and shouted, "**Rid** the earth **of** [+149] him!
22:29 Those who were about to question him **withdrew** [RP923]
23:21 are ready now, waiting for **[NIE]** your consent to their request."
23:23 and two hundred spearmen to go to Caesarea at nine tonight.
23:34 what province he was from. Learning that he was **from** Cilicia,
24:11 You can easily verify that no more than twelve days **ago** [+4005] I
24:19 But there are some Jews **from** the province of Asia, who ought to
25: 1 in the province, Festus went up **from** Caesarea to Jerusalem,
25: 7 the Jews who had come down **from** Jerusalem stood around him,
26: 4 **from** the beginning of my life in my own country, and also in
26:18 to open their eyes and turn them **from** darkness to light, and from
26:22 But I have had **[NIE]** God's help to this very day,
27:21 "Men, you should have taken my advice not to sail **from** Crete;
27:34 it to survive. Not one of you will lose a single hair **from** his head."
27:44 The rest were to get there on planks or on pieces **of** the ship.
28: 3 as he put it on the fire, a viper, driven out **by** the heat,
28:21 "We have not received any letters **from** Judea concerning you,
28:23 **From** morning till evening he explained and declared to them the
28:23 and tried to convince them about Jesus **from** the Law of Moses
Ro 1: 7 Grace and peace to you **from** God our Father and from the Lord
1:18 The wrath of God is being revealed **from** heaven against all the
1:20 For **since** the creation of the world God's invisible qualities—
5: 9 how much more shall we be saved **from** God's wrath through him!
5:14 death reigned **from** *the time* of Adam to the time of Moses,
6: 7 because anyone who has died has been freed **from** sin.
6:18 You have been set free **from** sin and have become slaves to
6:22 But now that you have been set free **from** sin and have become
7: 2 but if her husband dies, she is released **from** the law of marriage.
7: 3 she is released **from** that law and is not an adulteress,
7: 6 we have been released **from** the law so that we serve in the new
8: 2 Jesus the law of the Spirit of life set me free **from** the law of sin
8:21 that the creation itself will be liberated **from** its bondage to decay
8:35 Who shall separate us **from** the love of Christ? Shall trouble
8:39 will be able to separate us **from** the love of God that is in Christ
9: 3 were cursed and **cut off from** Christ for the sake of my brothers,
11:25 Israel has experienced a hardening **in part** [+3538] until the full
11:26 from Zion; *he will* **turn** godlessness **away from** [RP695] Jacob.
15:15 I have written you quite boldly on **some** points, as if to remind you
15:19 So **from** Jerusalem all the way around to Illyricum, I have fully
15:23 and since I have been longing **for** many years to see you,
15:24 my journey there, after I have enjoyed your company **for** a while.
15:31 Pray that I may be rescued **from** the unbelievers in Judea and that
16:17 contrary to the teaching you have learned. Keep away **from** them.
1Co 1: 3 Grace and peace to you **from** God our Father and the Lord Jesus
1:30 are in Christ Jesus, who has become for us wisdom **from** God—
4: 5 men's hearts. At that time each will receive his praise **from** God.
6:19 Holy Spirit, who is in you, whom you have received **from** God?
7:10 but the Lord): A wife must not separate **from** her husband.
7:27 *Are* you **unmarried** [+1222+3395]? Do not look for a wife.
10:14 Therefore, my dear friends, flee **from** idolatry.
11:23 For I received **from** the Lord what I also passed on to you:
14:36 Did the word of God originate **with** you? Or are you the only
2Co 1: 2 Grace and peace to you **from** God our Father and the Lord Jesus
1:14 as you have understood us **in part** [+3538], you will come to
1:16 my way to Macedonia and to come back to you **from** Macedonia,
2: 3 so that when I came I should not be distressed **by** those who ought
2: 5 me as he has grieved all of you, **to some extent** [+247+3538]—
3: 5 Not that we are competent **in** ourselves to claim anything for
3:18 into his likeness **with ever-increasing glory** [+1518+1518+1650],

3: 18 which *comes* **from** the Lord, who is the Spirit.
5: 6 as long as we are at home in the body we are away **from** the Lord.
5: 16 So **from** now on we regard no one from a worldly point of view.
7: 1 let us purify ourselves **from** everything that contaminates body
7: 13 Titus was, because his spirit has been refreshed **by** all of you.
8: 10 [NIE] Last year you were the first not only to give but also to
9: 2 telling them that **since** last year you in Achaia were ready to give;
11: 3 your minds may somehow be led astray **from** your sincere
11: 9 for the brothers who came **from** Macedonia supplied what I
12: 8 Three times I pleaded with the Lord to **take** it *away* **from** [RP923]

Gal 1: 1 *sent* not **from** men nor by man, but by Jesus Christ and God the
1: 3 Grace and peace to you **from** God our Father and the Lord Jesus
1: 6 I am astonished that *you are* so quickly **deserting** [+3572] the one
2: 6 **As for** those who seemed to be important—whatever they were
2: 12 Before certain men came **from** James, he used to eat with the
3: 2 I would like to learn just one thing **from** you: Did you receive the
4: 24 One covenant is **from** Mount Sinai and bears children who are to
5: 4 You who are trying to be justified by law have been alienated **from**

Eph 1: 2 Grace and peace to you **from** God our Father and the Lord Jesus
3: 9 which for ages past *was kept* **hidden** [RP648] in God,
4: 31 Get rid of [NIE] all bitterness, rage and anger, brawling
6: 23 and love with faith **from** God the Father and the Lord Jesus Christ.

Php 1: 2 Grace and peace to you **from** God our Father and the Lord Jesus
1: 5 because of your partnership in the gospel **from** the first day until
1: 28 will be destroyed, but that you will be saved—and that **by** God.
4: 15 when I set out **from** Macedonia, not one church shared with me in

Col 1: 2 in Christ at Colosse: Grace and peace to you **from** God our Father.
1: 6 just as it has been doing among you **since** [+4005] the day you
1: 7 You learned it **from** Epaphras, our dear fellow servant, who is a
1: 9 For this reason, **since** the day we heard about you, we have not
1: 23 and firm, not moved **from** the hope held out in the gospel.
1: 26 the mystery that *has been* **kept hidden for** [RP648+608] ages and
1: 26 the mystery that *has been* **kept hidden for** [RP648+608] ages and
2: 20 Since you died with Christ **to** the basic principles of this world,
3: 24 since you know that *you will* **receive** an inheritance **from** [RP655]

1Th 1: 8 The Lord's message rang out **from** you not only in Macedonia
1: 9 They tell how you turned to God **from** idols to serve the living
2: 6 not looking for praise from men, not **from** you or anyone else.
2: 6 looking for praise from men, not from you or [RPG] anyone else.
2: 17 *when* we *were* **torn away from** [RP682] you for a short time (in
3: 6 But Timothy has just now come to us **from** you and has brought
4: 3 be sanctified: that you *should* **avoid** [RP600] sexual immorality;
4: 16 For the Lord himself will come down **from** heaven, with a loud
5: 22 **Avoid** [RP600] every kind of evil.

2Th 1: 2 Grace and peace to you **from** God the Father and the Lord Jesus
1: 7 This will happen when the Lord Jesus is revealed **from** heaven in
1: 9 and *shut out* **from** the presence of the Lord and from the majesty
1: 9 from the presence of the Lord and **from** the majesty of his power
2: 2 not *to become* easily **unsettled** [+3808+3836+4888] or alarmed
2: 13 because **from** [UBS-] the beginning God chose you to be saved
3: 2 And pray that we may be delivered **from** wicked and evil men,
3: 3 and he will strengthen and protect you **from** the evil one.
3: 6 to keep away **from** every brother who is idle and does not live

1Ti 1: 2 mercy and peace **from** God the Father and Christ Jesus our Lord.
3: 7 He must also have a good reputation **with** outsiders, so that he will
6: 10 *have* **wandered from** [RP675] the faith and pierced themselves

2Ti 1: 2 mercy and peace **from** God the Father and Christ Jesus our Lord.
1: 3 I thank God, whom I serve, **as** my forefathers did, with a clear
2: 19 the name of the Lord *must* **turn away from** [RP923] wickedness."
2: 21 If a man cleanses himself **from** the latter, he will be an instrument
3: 15 and how **from** infancy you have known the holy Scriptures,
4: 4 *They will* **turn** their ears **away from** [RP695] the truth and turn
4: 18 The Lord will rescue me **from** every evil attack and will bring me

Tit 1: 4 Grace and peace **from** God the Father and Christ Jesus our Savior.
2: 14 who gave himself for us to redeem us **from** all wickedness

Phm 1: 3 Grace to you and peace **from** God our Father and the Lord Jesus

Heb 3: 12 unbelieving heart that **turns away from** [RP923] the living God.
4: 3 And yet his work has been finished **since** the creation of the world.
4: 4 words: "And on the seventh day God rested **from** all his work."
4: 10 for anyone who enters God's rest also rests **from** his own work,
4: 10 God's rest also rests from his own work, just as God did **from** his.
5: 7 from death, and he was heard **because of** his reverent submission.
5: 8 he was a son, he learned obedience **from** what he suffered
6: 1 not laying again the foundation of repentance **from** acts that lead to
6: 7 useful to those for whom it is farmed receives the blessing **of** God.
7: 1 He met Abraham returning **from** the defeat of the kings

7: 2 and Abraham gave him a tenth **of** everything. First, his name
7: 13 and no one **from** that tribe has ever served at the altar.
7: 26 one who is holy, blameless, pure, set apart **from** sinners, exalted
8: 11 they will all know me, **from** the least of them to the greatest.
9: 14 to God, cleanse our consciences **from** acts that lead to death,
9: 26 Then Christ would have had to suffer many times **since** the
10: 22 having our hearts sprinkled to cleanse us **from** a guilty conscience
11: 12 And so **from** this one man, and he as good as dead,
11: 15 If they had been thinking of the country [NIE] they had left,
11: 34 edge of the sword; whose [NIE] weakness was turned to strength;
12: 15 See to it that no one misses [NIE] the grace of God and that no
12: 25 will we, if we turn away from him who warns us **from** heaven?
13: 24 and all God's people. Those **from** Italy send you their greetings.

Jas 1: 13 When tempted, no one should say, [NIE] "God is tempting me."
1: 17 from above, coming down **from** the Father of the heavenly lights,
1: 27 their distress and to keep oneself from being polluted **by** the world.
4: 7 then, to God. Resist the devil, and he will flee **from** you.
5: 4 the workmen who mowed your fields are crying out **against** you.
5: 19 if one of you should wander **from** the truth and someone should

1Pe 1: 12 preached the gospel to you by the Holy Spirit sent **from** heaven.
3: 10 would love life and see good days must keep his tongue **from** evil
3: 11 He must turn **from** evil and do good; he must seek peace
4: 17 For it is time for judgment to begin **with** the family of God;
4: 17 and if it begins **with** us, what will the outcome be for those who do

2Pe 1: 21 but men spoke **from** God as they were carried along by the Holy
3: 4 **Ever since** [+4005] our fathers died, everything goes on as it has
3: 4 everything goes on as it has **since** the beginning of creation."

1Jn 1: 1 That which was **from** the beginning, which we have heard,
1: 5 This is the message we have heard **from** him and declare to you:
1: 7 and the blood of Jesus, his Son, purifies us **from** all sin.
1: 9 and will forgive us our sins and purify us **from** all unrighteousness.
2: 7 but an old one, which you have had **since** the beginning.
2: 13 because you have known him who is **from** the beginning.
2: 14 because you have known him who is **from** the beginning.
2: 20 But you have an anointing **from** the Holy One, and all of you
2: 24 See that what you have heard **from** the beginning remains in you.
2: 24 If it^s [+201+794+4005] does, you also will remain in the Son
2: 27 As for you, the anointing you received **from** him remains in you,
2: 28 we may be confident and unashamed **before** him at his coming.
3: 8 the devil, because the devil has been sinning **from** the beginning.
3: 11 This is the message you heard **from** the beginning: We should love
3: 17 and sees his brother in need but has no pity **on** him,
3: 22 and receive from him anything we ask, because we obey his
4: 21 And he *has* **given us** [+2400] this command: Whoever loves God
5: 15 whatever we ask—we know that we have what we asked **of** him.
5: 21 Dear children, keep yourselves **from** idols.

2Jn 1: 5 you a new command but one we have had **from** the beginning.
1: 6 As you have heard **from** the beginning, his command is that you

3Jn 1: 7 of the Name that they went out, receiving no help **from** the pagans.

Jude 1: 14 Enoch, the seventh **from** Adam, prophesied about these men:
1: 23 with fear—hating even the clothing stained **by** corrupted flesh.

Rev 1: 4 Grace and peace to you **from** him who is, and who was, and who is
1: 4 and who is to come, and **from** the seven spirits before his throne,
1: 5 and **from** Jesus Christ, who is the faithful witness, the firstborn
3: 12 which is coming down out of heaven **from** my God;
6: 16 "Fall on us and hide us **from** the face of him who sits on the throne
6: 16 of him who sits on the throne and **from** the wrath of the Lamb!
7: 2 Then I saw another angel coming up **from** the east, having the seal
9: 6 find it; they will long to die, but death *will* **elude** [+5771] them.
9: 18 A third of mankind was killed **by** the three plagues of fire,
12: 6 The woman fled into the desert to a place prepared for her **by** God,
12: 14 care of for a time, times and half a time, **out of** the serpent's reach.
13: 8 to the Lamb that was slain **from** the creation of the world.
14: 3 song except the 144,000 who had been redeemed **from** the earth.
14: 4 They were purchased **from among** men and offered as firstfruits to
14: 13 Blessed are the dead who die in the Lord **from** now on." "Yes,"
14: 20 rising as high as the horses' bridles **for a distance of** 1,600 stadia.
16: 12 and its water was dried up to prepare the way for the kings **from**
16: 17 and out of the temple came a loud voice **from** the throne, saying,
16: 18 No earthquake like it has **ever** occurred **since** [+4005] man has
17: 8 **from** the creation of the world will be astonished when they see
18: 10 Terrified at her torment, they will stand **far off** [+3427] and cry:
18: 14 will say, 'The fruit you longed for *is* **gone from** [RP599] you.
18: 14 All your riches and splendor *have* **vanished** [RP660], never to be
18: 15 these things and gained their wealth **from** her will stand far off,
18: 15 and gained their wealth from her will stand **far off** [+3427],

18: 17 all who earn their living from the sea, will stand **far off** [+*3427*].
19: 5 Then a voice came **from** the throne, saying: "Praise our God,
20: 11 Earth and sky fled **from** his presence, and there was no place for
21: 2 the new Jerusalem, coming down out of heaven **from** God,
21: 10 the Holy City, Jerusalem, coming down out of heaven **from** God.
21: 13 There were three gates **on** the east, three on the north, three on the
21: 13 three **on** the north, three on the south and three on the west.
21: 13 three on the north, three **on** the south and three on the west.
21: 13 three on the north, three on the south and three **on** the west.
22: 19 And if anyone **takes** words **away from** [*RP904*] this book of
22: 19 God will take away from him his share **in** the tree of life and in the

609 ἀποβαίνω, *apobainō* [4] [√ *608* + *326*]

landed [+*1178*+*1650*+*3836*] [1], left [*RP608*] [1], result [1], turn out [1]

Lk 5: 2 **left** [*RP608*] there *by* the fishermen, who were washing their nets.
    21: 13 *This will* **result** in your being witnesses to them.
Jn 21: 9 When *they* **landed** [+*1178*+*1650*+*3836*], they saw a fire of
Php 1: 19 what has happened to me *will* **turn out** for my deliverance.

610 ἀποβάλλω, *apoballō* [2] [√ *608* + *965*]

throw away [1], throwing aside [1]

Mk 10: 50 **Throwing** his cloak **aside**, he jumped to his feet and came to
Heb 10: 35 So *do* not **throw away** your confidence; it will be richly rewarded.

611 ἀποβλέπω, *apoblepō* [1] [√ *608* + *1063*]

looking ahead [1]

Heb 11: 26 treasures of Egypt, because *he was* **looking ahead** to his reward.

612 ἀπόβλητος, *apoblētos* [1] [√ *608* + *965*]

rejected [1]

1Ti 4: 4 and nothing is to be **rejected** if it is received with thanksgiving,

613 ἀποβολή, *apobolē* [2] [√ *608* + *965*]

lost [1], rejection [1]

Ac 27: 22 you to keep up your courage, because not one of you will be **lost**;
Ro 11: 15 For if their **rejection** is the reconciliation of the world, what will

614 ἀπογίνομαι, *apoginomai* [1] [√ *608* + *1181*]

die [1]

1Pe 2: 24 on the tree, so that we might **die** to sins and live for righteousness;

615 ἀπογραφή, *apographē* [2] [√ *608* + *1211*]

census [2]

Lk 2: 2 (This was the first **census** that took place while Quirinius was
Ac 5: 37 Judas the Galilean appeared in the days *of* the **census** and led a

616 ἀπογράφω, *apographō* [4] [√ *608* + *1211*]

register [2], census be taken of [1], written [1]

Lk 2: 1 a decree that a **census** *should* **be taken of** the entire Roman world.
    2: 3 And everyone went to his own town *to* **register**.
    2: 5 He went there *to* **register** with Mary, who was pledged to be
Heb 12: 23 to the church of the firstborn, *whose names are* **written** in heaven.

617 ἀποδείκνυμι, *apodeiknymi* [4] [√ *608* + *1259*]

accredited [1], proclaiming [1], prove [1], put on display [1]

Ac 2: 22 Jesus of Nazareth was a man **accredited** by God to you by
   25: 7 many serious charges against him, which they could not **prove**.
1Co 4: 9 For it seems to me that God *has* **put** us apostles **on display** at the
2Th 2: 4 sets himself up in God's temple, **proclaiming** himself to be God.

618 ἀπόδειξις, *apodeixis* [1] [√ *608* + *1259*]

demonstration [1]

1Co 2: 4 persuasive words, but with a **demonstration** of the Spirit's power,

619 ἀποδεκατεύω, *apodekateuō*   Not used in UBS/NIV [√ *608* + *1274*]

620 ἀποδεκατόω, *apodekatoō* [4] [√ *608* + *1274*]

give a tenth of [2], collect a tenth from [+*2400*] [1], give God a tenth of [1]

Mt 23: 23 *You* **give a tenth of** your spices—mint, dill and cummin.
Lk 11: 42 because *you* **give God a tenth of** your mint, rue and all other kinds
   18: 12 I fast twice a week and **give a tenth of** all I get.'
Heb 7: 5 who become priests *to* **collect a tenth** [+*2400*] **from** the people—

621 ἀπόδεκτος, *apodektos* [2] [√ *608* + *1312*]

pleases [1], pleasing [1]

1Ti 2: 3 This is good, and **pleases** God our Savior,
    5: 4 their parents and grandparents, for this is **pleasing** to God.

622 ἀποδέχομαι, *apodechomai* [7] [√ *608* + *1312*]

welcomed [3], accepted [1], acknowledge [1], received [1], welcome [1]

Lk 8: 40 Now when Jesus returned, a crowd **welcomed** him, for they were
    9: 11 He **welcomed** them and spoke to them about the kingdom of God,
Ac 2: 41 Those *who* **accepted** his message were baptized, and about three
   18: 27 encouraged him and wrote to the disciples there *to* **welcome** him.
   21: 17 When we arrived at Jerusalem, the brothers **received** us warmly.
   24: 3 excellent Felix, *we* **acknowledge** this with profound gratitude.
   28: 30 in his own rented house and **welcomed** all who came to see him.

623 ἀποδημέω, *apodēmeō* [6] [√ *608* + *1322*]

went away on a journey [2], going on a journey [1], set off [1], went away [1], went on journey [1]

Mt 21: 33 rented the vineyard to some farmers and **went away on a journey**.
   25: 14 "Again, it will be like a man **going on a journey**, who called his
   25: 15 each according to his ability. Then *he* **went on** his **journey**.
Mk 12: 1 rented the vineyard to some farmers and **went away on a journey**.
Lk 15: 13 **set off** for a distant country and there squandered his wealth in
   20: 9 rented it to some farmers and **went away** for a long time.

624 ἀπόδημος, *apodēmos* [1] [√ *608* + *1322*]

going away [1]

Mk 13: 34 It's like a man **going away**: He leaves his house and puts his

625 ἀποδίδωμι, *apodidōmi* [48] [√ *608* + *1443*]

give [9], pay back [6], reward [4], pay [3], repay [3], gave back [2], given [2], paid [2], account [+*3364*] [1], award [1], fulfill [1], give account for [+*3364*] [1], give back [1], give share of [1], got [1], keep [1], pays back [1], produces [1], reimburse [1], repay the debt [1], repaying [+*304*] [1], sold [1], sold as a slave [1], testify to [+*3457*] [1], yielding [1]

Mt 5: 26 the truth, you will not get out until *you have* **paid** the last penny.
    5: 33 break your oath, but **keep** the oaths you have made to the Lord.'
    6: 4 your Father, who sees what is done in secret, *will* **reward** you.
    6: 6 your Father, who sees what is done in secret, *will* **reward** you.
    6: 18 and your Father, who sees what is done in secret, *will* **reward** you.
   12: 36 *will have to* **give** [+*3364*] **account** on the day of judgment for
   16: 27 then *he will* **reward** each person according to what he has done.
   18: 25 Since he was not able *to* **pay**, the master ordered that he and his
   18: 25 and his children and all that he had be sold *to* **repay the debt**.
   18: 26 'Be patient with me,' he begged, 'and *I will* **pay back** everything.'
   18: 28 began to choke him. '**Pay back** what you owe me!' he demanded.
   18: 29 and begged him, 'Be patient with me, and *I will* **pay** you **back**.'

18:30 and had the man thrown into prison until *he could* **pay** the debt.
18:34 to the jailers to be tortured, until *he should* **pay back** all he owed.
20: 8 'Call the workers and **pay** them their wages, beginning with the
21:41 who *will* **give** him *his* **share of** the crop at harvest time."
22:21 Then he said to them, "**Give** to Caesar what is Caesar's, and to
27:58 he asked for Jesus' body, and Pilate ordered that it *be* **given** to him.
Mk 12:17 "**Give** to Caesar what is Caesar's and to God what is God's."
Lk 4:20 he rolled up the scroll, **gave** it **back** to the attendant and sat down.
7:42 Neither of them had the money *to* **pay** him **back**, so he canceled
9:42 the evil spirit, healed the boy and **gave** him **back** to his father.
10:35 I *will* **reimburse** you for any extra expense you may have.'
12:59 I tell you, you will not get out until *you have* **paid** the last penny."
16: 2 **Give** an account of your management, because you cannot be
19: 8 anybody out of anything, *I will* **pay back** four times the *amount*."
20:25 He said to them, "Then **give** to Caesar what is Caesar's, and to God
Ac 4:33 With great power the apostles *continued* to **testify to** [+3457] the
5: 8 "Tell me, is this the price *you* and Ananias **got** for the land?"
7: 9 were jealous of Joseph, *they* **sold** him **as a slave** into Egypt.
19:40 In that case we would not be able *to* **account** [+3364] for this
Ro 2: 6 God "*will* **give** to each person according to what he has done."
12:17 *Do* not **repay** anyone evil for evil. Be careful to do what is right in
13: 7 **Give** everyone what you owe him: If you owe taxes, pay taxes;
1Co 7: 3 The husband *should* **fulfill** his marital duty to his wife,
1Th 5:15 Make sure that nobody **pays back** wrong for wrong, but always try
1Ti 5: 4 own family and so **repaying** [+304] their parents and grandparents,
2Ti 4: 8 the Lord, the righteous Judge, *will* **award** to me on that day—
4:14 great deal of harm. The Lord *will* **repay** him for what he has done.
Heb 12:11 *it* **produces** a harvest of righteousness and peace for those who
12:16 who for a single meal sold his inheritance rights as the oldest son.
13:17 They keep watch over you as *men who must* **give** an account.
1Pe 3: 9 *Do* not **repay** evil with evil or insult with insult,
4: 5 But they *will* have to **give** account to him who is ready to judge the
Rev 18: 6 **Give back** to her as she has given; pay her back double for what
18: 6 Give back to her as she *has* given; pay her back double for what
22: 2 bearing twelve crops of fruit, **yielding** its fruit every month.
22:12 and I *will* **give** to everyone according to what he has done.

626 ἀποδιορίζω, *apodiorizō* [1] [√ 608 + 1328 + 4000]

divide [1]

Jude 1:19 These are the men who **divide** you, who follow mere natural

627 ἀποδοκιμάζω, *apodokimazō* [9] [√ 608 + 1312]

rejected [9]

Mt 21:42 " 'The stone the builders **rejected** has become the capstone;
Mk 8:31 Son of Man must suffer many things and *be* **rejected** by the elders,
12:10 " 'The stone the builders **rejected** has become the capstone;
Lk 9:22 Son of Man must suffer many things and *be* **rejected** by the elders,
17:25 he must suffer many things and *be* **rejected** by this generation.
20:17 " 'The stone the builders **rejected** has become the capstone'?
Heb 12:17 when he wanted to inherit this blessing, *he was* **rejected**.
1Pe 2: 4 **rejected** by men but chosen by God and precious to him—
2: 7 "The stone the builders **rejected** has become the capstone,"

628 ἀποδοχή, *apodochē* [2] [√ 608 + 1312]

acceptance [2]

1Ti 1:15 Here is a trustworthy saying that deserves full **acceptance**:
4: 9 This is a trustworthy saying that deserves full **acceptance**

629 ἀπόθεσις, *apothesis* [2] [√ 608 + 5502]

put aside [+1639] [1], removal from [1]

1Pe 3:21 not the **removal** of dirt **from** the body but the pledge of a good
2Pe 1:14 because I know that *I will* soon **put** [+1639] it **aside**, as our Lord

630 ἀποθήκη, *apothēkē* [6] [√ 608 + 2565]

barn [4], barns [2]

Mt 3:12 gathering his wheat into the **barn** and burning up the chaff with
6:26 they do not sow or reap or store away in **barns**, and yet your
13:30 to be burned; then gather the wheat and bring it into my **barn**.' "

Lk 3:17 to clear his threshing floor and to gather the wheat into his **barn**,
12:18 I will tear down my **barns** and build bigger ones, and there I will
12:24 They do not sow or reap, they have no storeroom or **barn**;

631 ἀποθησαυρίζω, *apothēsaurizō* [1] [√ 608 + 2565]

lay up treasure [1]

1Ti 6:19 In this way *they will* **lay up treasure** for themselves as a firm

632 ἀποθλίβω, *apothlibō* [1] [√ 608 + 2567]

pressing against [1]

Lk 8:45 "Master, the people are crowding and **pressing against** you."

633 ἀποθνῄσκω, *apothnēskō* [111 / 112]
[√ 608 + 2569]

died [49], die [34], dies [11], dead [9], dying [5], death [2],
untranslated [1], put to death [+1877+5840] [1]

Mt 8:32 rushed down the steep bank into the lake and **died** in the water.
9:24 said, "Go away. The girl *is* not **dead** but asleep." But they laughed
22:24 they said, "Moses told us that if a man **dies** without having children,
22:27 Finally, the woman **died**.
26:35 But Peter declared, "Even if I have to **die** with you, I will never
Mk 5:35 of Jairus, the synagogue ruler. "Your daughter *is* **dead**," they said.
5:39 all this commotion and wailing? The child *is* not **dead** but asleep."
9:26 The boy looked so much like a corpse that many said, "*He's* **dead**."
12:19 "Moses wrote for us that if a man's brother **dies** and leaves a wife
12:20 The first one married and **died** without leaving any children.
12:21 second one married the widow, but *he* also **died**, leaving no child.
12:22 of the seven left any children. Last of all, the woman **died** too.
15:44 Summoning the centurion, he asked him if Jesus *had* already **died**.
Lk 8:42 because his only daughter, a girl of about twelve, *was* **dying**.
8:52 for her. "Stop wailing," Jesus said. "*She is* not **dead** but asleep."
8:53 They laughed at him, knowing that *she was* **dead**.
16:22 "The time came when the beggar **died** and the angels carried him to
16:22 him to Abraham's side. The rich man also **died** and was buried.
20:28 "Moses wrote for us that if a man's brother **dies** and leaves a wife
20:29 seven brothers. The first one married a woman and **died** childless.
20:31 and in the same way the seven **died**, leaving no children.
20:32 Finally, the woman **died** too.
20:36 and they can no longer **die**; for they are like the angels. They are
Jn 4:47 and begged him to come and heal his son, who was close to **death**.
4:49 The royal official said, "Sir, come down before my child **dies**."
6:49 Your forefathers ate the manna in the desert, yet *they* **died**.
6:50 that comes down from heaven, which a man may eat and not **die**.
6:58 Your forefathers ate manna and **died**, but he who feeds on this
8:21 going away, and you will look for me, and *you will* **die** in your sin.
8:24 I told you that *you would* **die** in your sins; if you do not believe
8:24 that I am ‪the one I claim to be‪, *you will* indeed **die** in your sins."
8:52 Abraham **died** and so did the prophets, yet you say that if anyone
8:53 He **died**, and so did the prophets. Who do you think you are?"
8:53 and so did the prophets. **[RPG]** Who do you think you are?"
11:14 So then he told them plainly, "Lazarus *is* **dead**,
11:16 the rest of the disciples, "Let us also go, that *we may* **die** with him."
11:21 to Jesus, "if you had been here, my brother would not have **died**.
11:25 and the life. He who believes in me will live, even though *he* **dies**;
11:26 and whoever lives and believes in me *will* never **die**. Do you
11:32 "Lord, if you had been here, my brother would not have **died**."
11:37 opened the eyes of the blind man have kept this man from **dying**?"
11:50 You do not realize that it is better for you that one man **die** for the
11:51 but as high priest that year he prophesied that Jesus would **die** for
12:24 you the truth, unless a kernel of wheat falls to the ground and **dies**,
12:24 it remains only a single seed. But if it **dies**, it produces many seeds.
12:33 He said this to show the kind of **death** he was going to **die**.
18:14 the Jews that it would be good *if* one man **died** for the people.
18:32 indicating the kind of **death** he was going to **die** would be fulfilled.
19: 7 "We have a law, and according to that law he must **die**,
21:23 rumor spread among the brothers that this disciple *would* not **die**.
21:23 But Jesus did not say that *he would* not **die**; he only said, "If I want
Ac 7: 4 After the **death** of his father, God sent him to this land where you
9:37 About that time she became sick and **died**, and her body was
21:13 but also *to* **die** in Jerusalem for the name of the Lord Jesus."
25:11 am guilty of doing anything deserving death, I do not refuse *to* **die**.

Ro 5: 6 when we were still powerless, Christ **died** for the ungodly.
5: 7 Very rarely *will* anyone **die** for a righteous man, though for a good
5: 7 though for a good man someone might possibly dare *to* **die**.
5: 8 love for us in this: While we were still sinners, Christ **died** for us.
5:15 For if the many **died** by the trespass of the one man, how much
6: 2 By no means! We **died** to sin; how can we live in it any longer?
6: 7 because anyone who *has* **died** has been freed from sin.
6: 8 Now if *we* **died** with Christ, we believe that we will also live with
6: 9 that since Christ was raised from the dead, *he* cannot **die** again;
6:10 The death he died, he died to sin once for all; but the life he lives,
6:10 The death he **died**, *he* **died** to sin once for all; but the life he lives,
7: 2 but if her husband **dies**, she is released from the law of marriage.
7: 3 But if her husband **dies**, she is released from that law and is not an
7: 6 But now, *by* **dying** to what once bound us, we have been released
7: 9 but when the commandment came, sin sprang to life and I **died**.
8:13 For if you live according to the sinful nature, you will **die**;
8:34 Christ Jesus, who **died**—more than that, who was raised to life—
14: 7 of us lives to himself alone and none of us **dies** to himself alone.
14: 8 If we live, we live to the Lord; and if *we* **die**, we die to the Lord.
14: 8 If we live, we live to the Lord; and if we die, *we* **die** to the Lord.
14: 8 die to the Lord. So, whether we live or **die**, we belong to the Lord.
14: 9 Christ **died** and returned to life so that he might be the Lord of
14:15 Do not by your eating destroy your brother for whom Christ **died**.
1Co 8:11 So this weak brother, for whom Christ **died**, is destroyed by your
9:15 I *would* rather **die** than have anyone deprive me of this boast.
15: 3 that Christ **died** for our sins according to the Scriptures,
15:22 For as in Adam all **die**, so in Christ all will be made alive.
15:31 *I* **die** every day—I mean that, brothers—just as surely as I glory
15:32 the dead are not raised, "Let us eat and drink, for tomorrow *we* **die**."
15:36 How foolish! What you sow does not come to life unless *it* **dies**.
2Co 5:14 because we are convinced that one **died** for all, and therefore all
5:14 we are convinced that one died for all, and therefore all **died**.
5:15 And *he* **died** for all, that those who live should no longer live for
5:15 but for him *who* **died** for them and was raised again.
6: 9 as unknown; **dying**, and yet we live on; beaten, and yet not killed;
Gal 2:19 For through the law I **died** to the law so that I might live for God.
2:21 could be gained through the law, Christ **died** for nothing!"
Php 1:21 For to me, to live is Christ and *to* **die** is gain.
Col 2:20 Since *you* **died** with Christ to the basic principles of this world,
3: 3 For *you* **died**, and your life is now hidden with Christ in God.
1Th 4:14 We believe that Jesus **died** and rose again and so we believe that
5:10 He **died** for us so that, whether we are awake or asleep, we may
Heb 7: 8 In the one case, the tenth is collected by men *who* **die**; but in the
9:27 Just as man is destined *to* **die** once, and after that to face judgment,
10:28 Anyone who rejected the law of Moses **died** without mercy on the
11: 4 his offerings. And by faith he still speaks, *even though he is* **dead**.
11:13 All these people were still living by faith *when they* **died**.
11:21 By faith Jacob, *when he was* **dying**, blessed each of Joseph's sons,
11:37 in two; *they were* **put to death** [+1877+5840] by the sword.
1Pe 3:18 For Christ **died** [UBS 4248] for sins once for all, the righteous for
Jude 1:12 the wind; autumn trees, without fruit and uprooted—twice **dead**.
Rev 3: 2 Strengthen what remains and is about to **die**, for I have not found
8: 9 a third of the living creatures in the sea **died**, and a third of the
8:11 and many people **died** from the waters that had become bitter.
9: 6 but will not find it; they will long *to* **die**, but death will elude them.
14:13 Blessed are the dead who **die** in the Lord from now on." "Yes,"
16: 3 like that of a dead man, and every living thing in the sea **died**.

634 ἀποκαθιστάνω, *apokathistanō* Not used in
UBS/NIV [√ 608 + 2848 + 2705]

635 ἀποκαθίστημι, *apokathistēmi* [8]
[√ 608 + 2848 + 2705]

completely restored [3], restore [2], restored [2], restores [1]

Mt 12:13 So he stretched it out and it *was* **completely restored**, just as
17:11 Jesus replied, "To be sure, Elijah comes and *will* **restore** all things.
Mk 3: 5 He stretched it out, and his hand *was* **completely restored**.
8:25 Then his eyes were opened, his sight *was* **restored**, and he saw
9:12 "To be sure, Elijah does come first, and **restores** all things.
Lk 6:10 out your hand." He did so, and his hand *was* **completely restored**.
Ac 1: 6 *are you* at this time *going to* **restore** the kingdom to Israel?"
Heb 13:19 urge you to pray so that *I may be* **restored** to you soon.

636 ἀποκαλύπτω, *apokalyptō* [26] [√ 608 + 2821]

revealed [19], reveal [3], disclosed [2], a revelation comes [1], make clear [1]

Mt 10:26 There is nothing concealed that *will* not *be* **disclosed**, or hidden
11:25 *have* hidden these things from the wise and learned, and **revealed**
11:27 except the Son and those to whom the Son chooses *to* **reveal** him.
16:17 Simon son of Jonah, for this *was* not **revealed** to you by man,
Lk 2:35 so that the thoughts of many hearts *will be* **revealed**. And a sword
10:21 from the wise and learned, and **revealed** them to little children.
10:22 except the Son and those to whom the Son chooses *to* **reveal** him."
12: 2 There is nothing concealed that *will* not *be* **disclosed**, or hidden
17:30 "It will be just like this on the day the Son of Man *is* **revealed**.
Jn 12:38 our message and to whom *has* the arm of the Lord *been* **revealed**?"
Ro 1:17 For in the gospel a righteousness from God *is* **revealed**,
1:18 The wrath of God *is being* **revealed** from heaven against all the
8:18 are not worth comparing with the glory that will *be* **revealed** in us.
1Co 2:10 but God *has* **revealed** it to us by his Spirit. The Spirit searches all
3:13 *It will be* **revealed** with fire, and the fire will test the quality of
14:30 And if **a revelation comes** to someone who is sitting down,
Gal 1:16 *to* **reveal** his Son in me so that I might preach him among the
3:23 held prisoners by the law, locked up until faith should *be* **revealed**.
Eph 3: 5 as *it has* now *been* **revealed** by the Spirit to God's holy apostles
Php 3:15 point you think differently, that too God *will* **make clear** to you.
2Th 2: 3 until the rebellion occurs and the man of lawlessness *is* **revealed**,
2: 6 holding him back, so that he *may be* **revealed** at the proper time.
2: 8 And then the lawless one *will be* **revealed**, whom the Lord Jesus
1Pe 1: 5 of the salvation that is ready *to be* **revealed** in the last time.
1:12 *It was* **revealed** to them that they were not serving themselves
5: 1 and one who also will share in the glory to be **revealed**:

637 ἀποκάλυψις, *apokalypsis* [18] [√ 608 + 2821]

revelation [9], revealed [7], revelations [2]

Lk 2:32 a light for **revelation** to the Gentiles and for glory to your people
Ro 2: 5 day of God's wrath, when his righteous judgment will be **revealed**.
8:19 waits in eager expectation for the sons of God to be **revealed**.
16:25 according to the **revelation** of the mystery hidden for long ages
1Co 1: 7 gift as you eagerly wait for our Lord Jesus Christ to be **revealed**.
14: 6 unless I bring you some **revelation** or knowledge or prophecy
14:26 or a word of instruction, a **revelation**, a tongue or an interpretation.
2Co 12: 1 to be gained, I will go on to visions and **revelations** from the Lord.
12: 7 because of these surpassingly great **revelations**,
Gal 1:12 I taught it; rather, I received it by **revelation** from Jesus Christ.
2: 2 I went in response to a **revelation** and set before them the gospel
Eph 1:17 glorious Father, may give you the Spirit *of* wisdom and **revelation**,
3: 3 that is, the mystery made known to me by **revelation**, as I have
2Th 1: 7 This will happen when the Lord Jesus is **revealed** from heaven in
1Pe 1: 7 result in praise, glory and honor when Jesus Christ is **revealed**.
1:13 fully on the grace to be given you when Jesus Christ is **revealed**.
4:13 so that you may be overjoyed when his glory is **revealed**.
Rev 1: 1 The **revelation** of Jesus Christ, which God gave him to show his

638 ἀποκαραδοκία, *apokaradokia* [2]
[√ 608 + 3191 + 1506]

eager expectation for [1], eagerly expect [1]

Ro 8:19 The creation waits in **eager expectation for** the sons of God to be
Php 1:20 I **eagerly expect** and hope that I will in no way be ashamed,

639 ἀποκαταλλάσσω, *apokatallassō* [3]
[√ 608 + 2848 + 248]

reconcile [2], reconciled [1]

Eph 2:16 and in this one body *to* **reconcile** both of them to God through the
Col 1:20 and through him *to* **reconcile** to himself all things, whether things
1:22 But now *he has* **reconciled** you by Christ's physical body through

640 ἀποκατάστασις, *apokatastasis* [1]
[√ 608 + 2848 + 2705]

restore [1]

Ac 3:21 He must remain in heaven until the time comes for God to **restore**

641 ἀπόκειμαι, *apokeimai* [4] [√ 608 + 3023]

destined [1], in store [1], laid away [1], stored up [1]

Lk 19:20 here is your mina; I have kept it **laid away** in a piece of cloth.
Col 1: 5 and love that spring from the hope that is **stored up** for you in
2Ti 4: 8 Now *there is* **in store** for me the crown of righteousness,
Heb 9:27 Just as man *is* **destined** to die once, and after that to face judgment,

642 ἀποκεφαλίζω, *apokephalizō* [4] [√ 608 + 3051]

beheaded [3], had beheaded [+4287] [1]

Mt 14:10 and **had** John **beheaded** [+4287] in the prison.
Mk 6:16 But when Herod heard this, he said, "John, the man I **beheaded**,
     6:27 to bring John's head. The man went, **beheaded** John in the prison,
Lk 9: 9 But Herod said, "I **beheaded** John. Who, then, is this I hear such

643 ἀποκλείω, *apokleiō* [1] [√ 608 + 3091]

closes [1]

Lk 13:25 Once the owner of the house gets up and **closes** the door, you will

644 ἀποκόπτω, *apokoptō* [6] [√ 608 + 3164]

cut off [3], cut [1], cutting off [1], emasculate [1]

Mk 9:43 If your hand causes you to sin, **cut it off**. It is better for you to
     9:45 And if your foot causes you to sin, **cut it off**. It is better for you to
Jn 18:10 and struck the high priest's servant, **cutting off** his right ear.
     18:26 a relative of the man whose ear Peter *had* **cut off**, challenged him,
Ac 27:32 So the soldiers **cut** the ropes that held the lifeboat and let it fall
Gal 5:12 I wish *they would* go the whole way and **emasculate** *themselves*!

645 ἀπόκριμα, *apokrima* [1] [√ 608 + 3212]

sentence [1]

2Co 1: 9 Indeed, in our hearts we felt the **sentence** of death. But this

646 ἀποκρίνομαι, *apokrinomai* [231] [√ 608 + 3212]

answered [80], replied [63], *untranslated* [23], asked [17], said [10], answer [9], gave answer [4], declared [3], spoke up [3], going to answer [2], made reply [2], reply [2], say [2], answers [1], demanded [1], given answer [1], in reply [1], insisted [1], responded [1], retorted [1], say in reply [1], spoke [1], tell [1], told [1]

Mt 3:15 Jesus **replied**, "Let it be so now; it is proper for us to do this to
     4: 4 Jesus **answered**, "It is written: 'Man does not live on bread alone,
     8: 8 The centurion **replied**, "Lord, I do not deserve to have you come
     11: 4 Jesus **replied**, "Go back and report to John what you hear and see:
     11:25 At that time **[RPG]** Jesus said, "I praise you, Father, Lord of
     12:38 some of the Pharisees and teachers of the law **[RPG]** said to him,
     12:39 He **answered**, "A wicked and adulterous generation asks for a
     12:48 He **replied** to him, "Who is my mother, and who are my brothers?"
     13:11 He **replied**, "The knowledge of the secrets of the kingdom of
     13:37 He **answered**, "The one who sowed the good seed is the Son of
     14:28 "Lord, if it's you," Peter **replied**, "tell me to come to you on the
     15: 3 Jesus **replied**, "And why do you break the command of God for the
     15:13 He **replied**, "Every plant that my heavenly Father has not planted
     15:15 Peter **[RPG]** said, "Explain the parable to us."
     15:23 Jesus *did* not **answer** a word. So his disciples came to him
     15:24 He **answered**, "I was sent only to the lost sheep of Israel."
     15:26 He **replied**, "It is not right to take the children's bread and toss it to
     15:28 Then Jesus **answered**, "Woman, you have great faith! Your request
     16: 2 He **replied**, "When evening comes, you say, 'It will be fair weather,
     16:16 Simon Peter **answered**, "You are the Christ, the Son of the living
     16:17 Jesus **replied**, "Blessed are you, Simon son of Jonah, for this was
     17: 4 Peter **[RPG]** said to Jesus, "Lord, it is good for us to be here.
     17:11 Jesus **replied**, "To be sure, Elijah comes and will restore all things.
     17:17 "O unbelieving and perverse generation," Jesus **replied**, "how long
     19: 4 "Haven't you read," he **replied**, "that at the beginning the Creator
     19:27 Peter **answered** him, "We have left everything to follow you!
     20:13 "But he **answered** one of them, 'Friend, I am not being unfair to
     20:22 "You don't know what you are asking," **[RPG]** Jesus said to them.
     21:21 Jesus **replied**, "I tell you the truth, if you have faith and do not

     21:24 Jesus **replied**, "I will also ask you one question. If you answer me,
     21:27 So *they* **answered** Jesus, "We don't know." Then he said, "Neither
     21:29 " 'I will not,' he **answered**,
     21:30 to the other son and said the same thing. He **answered**, 'I will, sir,'
     22: 1 Jesus **[RPG]** spoke to them again in parables, saying:
     22:29 Jesus **replied**, "You are in error because you do not know the
     22:46 No one could **say** a word **in reply**,
     24: 2 **[RPG]** "I tell you the truth, not one stone here will be left on
     24: 4 Jesus **answered**: "Watch out that no one deceives you.
     25: 9 " 'No,' they **replied**, 'there may not be enough for both us and you.
     25:12 "But he **replied**, 'I tell you the truth, I don't know you.'
     25:26 "His master **replied**, 'You wicked, lazy servant! So you knew that I
     25:37 "Then the righteous *will* **answer** him, 'Lord, when did we see you
     25:40 "The King *will* **reply**, 'I tell you the truth, whatever you did for one
     25:44 "They also *will* **answer**, 'Lord, when did we see you hungry
     25:45 "*He will* **reply**, 'I tell you the truth, whatever you did not do for
     26:23 Jesus **replied**, "The one who has dipped his hand into the bowl with
     26:25 the one who would betray him, **[RPG]** said, "Surely not I, Rabbi?"
     26:33 Peter **replied**, "Even if all fall away on account of you, I never
     26:62 priest stood up and said to Jesus, "*Are you* not *going to* **answer**?
     26:66 What do you think?" "He is worthy of death," they **answered**.
     27:12 accused by the chief priests and the elders, *he* **gave** no **answer**.
     27:14 But Jesus **made** no **reply**, not even to a single charge—to the great
     27:21 to release to you?" **asked** the governor. "Barabbas," they answered.
     28: 5 All the people **answered**, "Let his blood be on us and on our
     28: 5 The angel **[RPG]** said to the women, "Do not be afraid, for I know
Mk 3:33 "Who are my mother and my brothers?" *he* **asked**.
     6:37 But *he* **answered**, "You give them something to eat." They said to
     7:28 "Yes, Lord," she **replied**, "but even the dogs under the table eat the
     8: 4 His disciples **answered**, "But where in this remote place can anyone
     8:29 "Who do you say I am?" Peter **answered**, "You are the Christ."
     9: 5 Peter **[RPG]** said to Jesus, "Rabbi, it is good for us to be here.
     9: 6 (He did not know what *to* **say**, they were so frightened.)
     9:17 A man in the crowd **answered**, "Teacher, I brought you my son,
     9:19 "O unbelieving generation," Jesus **replied**, "how long shall I stay
     10: 3 "What did Moses command you?" he **replied**.
     10:24 But Jesus said **[RPG]** again, "Children, how hard it is to enter the
     10:51 Jesus **asked** him. The blind man said, "Rabbi, I want to see."
     11:14 Then he said **[RPG]** to the tree, "May no one ever eat fruit from
     11:22 "Have faith in God," Jesus **answered**.
     11:29 **Answer** me, and I will tell you by what authority I am doing these
     11:30 John's baptism—was it from heaven, or from men? **Tell me!**"
     11:33 So *they* **answered** Jesus, "We don't know." Jesus said, "Neither
     12:28 Noticing that Jesus *had* **given** them a good **answer**, he asked him,
     12:29 "The most important one," **answered** Jesus, "is this: 'Hear,
     12:34 When Jesus saw that *he had* **answered** wisely, he said to him,
     12:35 While Jesus was teaching in the temple courts, **[RPG]** he asked,
     14:40 their eyes were heavy. They did not know what *to* **say** to him.
     14:48 "Am I leading a rebellion," said **[RPG]** Jesus, "that you have come
     14:60 up before them and asked Jesus, "*Are you* not *going to* **answer**?
     14:61 But Jesus remained silent and **gave** no **answer**. Again the high
     15: 2 of the Jews?" asked Pilate. "Yes, it is as you say," Jesus **replied**.
     15: 4 So again Pilate asked him, "Aren't *you* *going to* **answer**? See how
     15: 5 But Jesus still **made** no **reply**,
     15: 9 you want me to release to you the king of the Jews?" **asked** Pilate,
     15:12 with the one you call the king of the Jews?" Pilate **asked** them.
Lk 1:19 The angel **answered**, "I am Gabriel. I stand in the presence of God,
     1:35 The angel **answered**, "The Holy Spirit will come upon you,
     1:60 but his mother **spoke up** and said, "No! He is to be called John."
     3:11 John **answered**, "The man with two tunics should share with him
     3:16 John **answered** them all, "I baptize you with water. But one more
     4: 4 Jesus **answered**, "It is written: 'Man does not live on bread alone.'
     4: 8 Jesus **answered**, "It is written: 'Worship the Lord your God
     4:12 Jesus **answered**, "It says: 'Do not put the Lord your God to the
     5: 5 Simon **answered**, "Master, we've worked hard all night and haven't
     5:22 Jesus knew what they were thinking and **asked**, "Why are you
     5:31 Jesus **answered** them, "It is not the healthy who need a doctor,
     6: 3 Jesus **answered** them, "Have you never read what David did when
     7:22 So *he* **replied** to the messengers, "Go back and report to John what
     7:40 Jesus **answered** him, "Simon, I have something to tell you."
     7:43 Simon **replied**, "I suppose the one who had the bigger debt
     8:21 He **replied**, "My mother and brothers are those who hear God's
     8:50 Hearing this, Jesus **said** to Jairus, "Don't be afraid; just believe,
     9:19 They **replied**, "Some say John the Baptist; others say Elijah;
     9:20 "Who do you say I am?" Peter **answered**, "The Christ of God."
     9:41 "O unbelieving and perverse generation," Jesus **replied**, "how long

9:49 **[RPG]** "we saw a man driving out demons in your name and we
10:27 He **answered**: " 'Love the Lord your God with all your heart
10:28 "You have answered correctly," Jesus **replied**. "Do this and you
10:41 "Martha, Martha," the Lord **answered**, "you are worried and upset
11: 7 "Then the one inside **answers**, 'Don't bother me. The door is
11:45 One of the experts in the law **answered** him, "Teacher, when you
13: 2 Jesus **answered**, "Do you think that these Galileans were worse
13: 8 " 'Sir,' the man **replied**, 'leave it alone for one more year,
13:14 the synagogue ruler said **[RPG]** to the people, "There are six days
13:15 The Lord **answered** him, "You hypocrites! Doesn't each of you on
13:25 "But *he will* **answer**, 'I don't know you or where you come from.'
14: 3 Jesus **asked** the Pharisees and experts in the law, "Is it lawful to
15:29 But he **answered** his father, 'Look! All these years I've been
17:17 Jesus **asked**, "Were not all ten cleansed? Where are the other nine?
17:20 Jesus **replied**, "The kingdom of God does not come with your
17:37 "Where, Lord?" *they* **asked**. He replied, "Where there is a dead
19:40 "I tell you," *he* **replied**, "if they keep quiet, the stones will cry out."
20: 3 *He* **replied**, "I will also ask you a question. Tell me,
20: 7 So *they* **answered**, "We don't know where it was from."
20:39 Some of the teachers of the law **responded**, "Well said, teacher!"
22:51 But Jesus **answered**, "No more of this!" And he touched the man's
22:68 and if I asked you, *you would* not **answer**.
23: 3 you the king of the Jews?" "Yes, it is as you say," Jesus **replied**.
23: 9 He plied him with many questions, but Jesus **gave** him no **answer**.
23:40 But the other criminal **[RPG]** rebuked him. "Don't you fear God,
24:18 One of them, named Cleopas, **asked** him, "Are you only a visitor to
Jn 1:21 He said, "I am not." "Are you the Prophet?" *He* **answered**, "No."
1:26 "I baptize with water," John **replied**, "but among you stands one
1:48 Jesus **answered**, "I saw you while you were still under the fig tree
1:49 Then Nathanael **declared**, "Rabbi, you are the Son of God;
1:50 Jesus **[RPG]** said, "You believe because I told you I saw you under
2:18 Then the Jews **demanded** of him, "What miraculous sign can you
2:19 Jesus **answered** them, "Destroy this temple, and I will raise it again
3: 3 **In reply** Jesus declared, "I tell you the truth, no one can see the
3: 5 Jesus **answered**, "I tell you the truth, no one can enter the kingdom
3: 9 "How can this be?" Nicodemus **asked**.
3:10 "You are Israel's teacher," said **[RPG]** Jesus, "and do you not
3:27 To this John **replied**, "A man can receive only what is given him
4:10 Jesus **answered** her, "If you knew the gift of God and who it is that
4:13 Jesus **answered**, "Everyone who drinks this water will be thirsty
4:17 "I have no husband," she **replied**. Jesus said to her, "You are right
5: 7 "Sir," the invalid **replied**, "I have no one to help me into the pool
5:11 But he **replied**, "The man who made me well said to me, 'Pick up
5:17 Jesus **said** to them, "My Father is always at his work to this very
5:19 Jesus **gave** them this **answer**: "I tell you the truth, the Son can do
6: 7 Philip **answered** him, "Eight months' wages would not buy enough
6:26 Jesus **answered**, "I tell you the truth, you are looking for me,
6:29 Jesus **answered**, "The work of God is this: to believe in the one he
6:43 "Stop grumbling among yourselves," Jesus **answered**.
6:68 Simon Peter **answered** him, "Lord, to whom shall we go?
6:70 Then Jesus **replied**, "Have I not chosen you, the Twelve? Yet one
7:16 Jesus **answered**, "My teaching is not my own. It comes from him
7:20 "You are demon-possessed," the crowd **answered**. "Who is trying
7:21 Jesus said **[RPG]** to them, "I did one miracle, and you are all
7:46 "No one ever spoke the way this man does," the guards **declared**.
7:47 "You mean he has deceived you also?" the Pharisees **retorted**.
7:52 *They* **replied**, "Are you from Galilee, too? Look into it, and you
8:14 Jesus **answered**, "Even if I testify on my own behalf, my testimony
8:19 "You do not know me or my Father," Jesus **replied**. "If you knew
8:33 *They* **answered** him, "We are Abraham's descendants and have
8:34 Jesus **replied**, "I tell you the truth, everyone who sins is a slave to
8:39 "Abraham is our father," *they* **answered**. "If you were Abraham's
8:48 The Jews **answered** him, "Aren't we right in saying that you are a
8:49 a demon," **said** Jesus, "but I honor my Father and you dishonor me.
8:54 Jesus **replied**, "If I glorify myself, my glory means nothing.
9: 3 **said** Jesus, "but this happened so that the work of God might be
9:11 He **replied**, "The man they call Jesus made some mud and put it on
9:20 "We know he is our son," the parents **answered**, "and we know he
9:25 He **replied**, "Whether he is a sinner or not, I don't know. One thing
9:27 *He* **answered**, "I have told you already and you did not listen.
9:30 The man **answered**, "Now that is remarkable! You don't know
9:34 To this *they* **replied**, "You were steeped in sin at birth; how dare
9:36 "Who is he, sir?" the man **asked**. "Tell me so that I may believe in
10:25 Jesus **answered**, "I did tell you, but you do not believe.
10:32 but Jesus **said** to them, "I have shown you many great miracles
10:33 stoning you for any of these," **replied** the Jews, "but for blasphemy,

10:34 Jesus **answered** them, "Is it not written in your Law, 'I have said
11: 9 Jesus **answered**, "Are there not twelve hours of daylight? A man
12:23 Jesus **replied**, "The hour has come for the Son of Man to be
12:30 Jesus **[RPG]** said, "This voice was for your benefit, not mine.
12:34 The crowd **spoke up**, "We have heard from the Law that the Christ
13: 7 Jesus **replied**, "You do not realize now what I am doing, but later
13: 8 Jesus **answered**, "Unless I wash you, you have no part with me."
13:26 Jesus **answered**, "It is the one to whom I will give this piece of
13:36 Jesus **replied**, "Where I am going, you cannot follow now,
13:38 Then Jesus **answered**, "Will you really lay down your life for me?
14:23 Jesus **replied**, "If anyone loves me, he will obey my teaching.
16:31 "You believe at last!" Jesus **answered**.
18: 5 "Jesus of Nazareth," *they* **replied**. "I am he," Jesus said. (And Judas
18: 8 "I told you that I am he," Jesus **answered**. "If you are looking for
18:20 "I have spoken openly to the world," Jesus **replied**. "I always
18:22 "Is this the way *you* **answer** the high priest?" he demanded.
18:23 "If I said something wrong," Jesus **replied**, "testify as to what is
18:30 "If he were not a criminal," *they* **replied**, "we would not have
18:34 "Is that your own idea," Jesus **asked**, "or did others talk to you
18:35 "Am I a Jew?" Pilate **replied**. "It was your people and your chief
18:36 Jesus **said**, "My kingdom is not of this world. If it were, my
18:37 Jesus **answered**, "You are right in saying I am a king. In fact,
19: 7 The Jews **insisted**, "We have a law, and according to that law he
19:11 Jesus **answered**, "You would have no power over me if it were not
19:15 "We have no king but Caesar," the chief priests **answered**.
19:22 Pilate **answered**, "What I have written, I have written."
20:28 Thomas said **[RPG]** to him, "My Lord and my God!"
21: 5 out to them, "Friends, haven't you any fish?" "No," *they* **answered**.
Ac 3:12 When Peter saw this, *he* **said** to them: "Men of Israel, why does this
4:19 Peter and John **replied**, "Judge for yourselves whether it is right
5: 8 Peter **asked** her, "Tell me, is this the price you and Ananias got for
5:29 Peter and the other apostles **replied**: "We must obey God rather
8:24 Then Simon **answered**, "Pray to the Lord for me so that nothing
8:34 The eunuch **asked** Philip, "Tell me, please, who is the prophet
9:13 "Lord," Ananias **answered**, "I have heard many reports about this
10:46 heard them speaking in tongues and praising God. Then Peter **said**,
11: 9 "The voice **spoke** from heaven a second time, 'Do not call anything
15:13 When they finished, James **spoke up**: "Brothers, listen to me.
19:15 ₁One day₂ the evil spirit **answered** them, "Jesus I know, and I know
21:13 Then Paul **answered**, "Why are you weeping and breaking my
22: 8 " 'Who are you, Lord?' I **asked**. " 'I am Jesus of Nazareth,
22:28 Then the commander **said**, "I had to pay a big price for my
24:10 When the governor motioned for him to speak, Paul **replied**:
24:25 to come, Felix was afraid and **said**, "That's enough for now!
25: 4 Festus **answered**, "Paul is being held at Caesarea, and I myself am
25: 9 Festus, wishing to do the Jews a favor, said **[RPG]** to Paul,
25:12 After Festus had conferred with his council, *he* **declared**:
25:16 "*I told* them that it is not the Roman custom to hand over any man
Col 4: 6 with salt, so that you may know how *to* **answer** everyone.
Rev 7:13 Then one of the elders **asked** me, "These in white robes—who are

647 ἀπόκρισις, *apokrisis* [4] [√ 608 + 3212]

answer [3], answers [1]

Lk 2:47 who heard him was amazed at his understanding and his **answers**.
20:26 there in public. And astonished by his **answer**, they became silent.
Jn 1:22 are you? Give us an **answer** to take back to those who sent us.
19: 9 do you come from?" he asked Jesus, but Jesus gave him no **answer**.

648 ἀποκρύπτω, *apokryptō* [4] [√ 608 + 3221]

hidden [*RP608*] [1], hidden [1], hidden from [*RP608*] [1], kept
hidden for [*RP608+608*] [1]

Lk 10:21 because *you have* **hidden** [*RP608*] these things **from** the wise
1Co 2: 7 a wisdom that *has been* **hidden** and that God destined for our
Eph 3: 9 which for ages past *was kept* **hidden** [*RP608*] in God,
Col 1:26 the mystery that *has been* **kept hidden** [*RP608+608*] **for** ages and

649 ἀπόκρυφος, *apokryphos* [3] [√ 608 + 3221]

concealed [2], hidden [1]

Mk 4:22 and whatever is **concealed** is meant to be brought out into the
Lk 8:17 and nothing **concealed** that will not be known or brought out into
Col 2: 3 in whom are **hidden** all the treasures of wisdom and knowledge.

650 ἀποκτείνω, apokteinō [74] [→ 475, 651]

kill [34], killed [26], put to death [4], kills [2], take life [2], *untranslated* [1], die [1], died [1], execute [1], killing [1], strike dead [+1877+2505] [1]

Mt 10:28 Do not be afraid of those *who* **kill** the body but cannot kill the soul.
10:28 Do not be afraid of those who kill the body but cannot **kill** the soul.
14: 5 Herod wanted *to* **kill** John, but he was afraid of the people,
16:21 and that he must *be* **killed** and on the third day be raised to life.
17:23 *They will* **kill** him, and on the third day he will be raised to life."
21:35 "The tenants seized his servants; they beat one, **killed** another,
21:38 'This is the hcir. Come, *let's* **kill** him and take his inheritance.'
21:39 they took him and threw him out of the vineyard and **killed** him.
22: 6 The rest seized his servants, mistreated them and **killed** them.
23:34 Some of them *you will* **kill** and crucify; others you will flog in
23:37 Jerusalem, you *who* **kill** the prophets and stone those sent to you,
24: 9 "Then you will be persecuted and **put to death**,
26: 4 and they plotted to arrest Jesus in some sly way and **kill** him.
Mk 3: 4 to do good or to do evil, to save life or *to* **kill**?" But they remained
6:19 So Herodias nursed a grudge against John and wanted *to* **kill** him.
8:31 the law, and that he must *be* **killed** and after three days rise again.
9:31 hands of men. *They will* **kill** him, and after three days he will rise."
9:31 They will kill him, and **[RPG]** after three days he will rise."
10:34 who will mock him and spit on him, flog him and **kill** him.
12: 5 He sent still another, and that one *they* **killed**. He sent many
12: 5 He sent many others; some of them they beat, others *they* **killed**.
12: 7 is the heir. Come, *let's* **kill** him, and the inheritance will be ours.'
12: 8 So *they* took him and **killed** him, and threw him out of the
14: 1 the law were looking for some sly way to arrest Jesus and **kill** him.
Lk 9:22 and he must *be* **killed** and on the third day be raised to life."
11:47 for the prophets, and it was your forefathers *who* **killed** them.
11:48 forefathers did; they **killed** the prophets, and you build their tombs.
11:49 some of whom *they will* **kill** and others they will persecute.'
12: 4 do not be afraid of those *who* **kill** the body and after that can do no
12: 5 Fear him who, after the **killing** of the body, has power to throw
13: 4 Or those eighteen who **died** when the tower in Siloam fell on
13:31 "Leave this place and go somewhere else. Herod wants *to* **kill** you."
13:34 Jerusalem, you who **kill** the prophets and stone those sent to you,
18:32 They will mock him, insult him, spit on him, flog him and **kill** him.
20:14 they said. 'Let's **kill** him, and the inheritance will be ours.'
20:15 So *they* threw him out of the vineyard and **killed** him. "What
Jn 5:18 For this reason the Jews tried all the harder *to* **kill** him; not only
7: 1 from Judea because the Jews there were waiting *to* **take** his **life**.
7:19 Yet not one of you keeps the law. Why are you trying *to* **kill** me?"
7:20 the crowd answered. "Who is trying *to* **kill** you?"
7:25 Jerusalem began to ask, "Isn't this the man they are trying *to* **kill**?
8:22 This made the Jews ask, "*Will he* **kill** himself? Is that why he says,
8:37 Yet you are ready *to* **kill** me, because you have no room for my
8:40 As it is, you are determined *to* **kill** me, a man who has told you the
11:53 So from that day on they plotted to **take** his **life**.
12:10 So the chief priests made plans to **kill** Lazarus as well,
16: 2 a time is coming when anyone who **kills** you will think he is
18:31 "But we have no right *to* **execute** anyone," the Jews objected.
Ac 3:15 *You* **killed** the author of life, but God raised him from the dead.
7:52 *They* even **killed** those who predicted the coming of the Righteous
21:31 While they were trying *to* **kill** him, news reached the commander
23:12 with an oath not to eat or drink until *they had* **killed** Paul.
23:14 taken a solemn oath not to eat anything until we *have* **killed** Paul.
27:42 The soldiers planned to **kill** the prisoners to prevent any of them
Ro 7:11 deceived me, and through the commandment **put me to death**.
11: 3 *they have* **killed** your prophets and torn down your altars;
2Co 3: 6 but of the Spirit; for the letter **kills**, but the Spirit gives life.
Eph 2:16 to God through the cross, by which he **put to death** their hostility.
1Th 2:15 who **killed** the Lord Jesus and the prophets and also drove us out.
Rev 2:13 my faithful witness, who *was* **put to death** in your city—
2:23 *I will* **strike** her children **dead** [+1877+2505]. Then all the
6: 8 They were given power over a fourth of the earth *to* **kill** by sword,
6:11 and brothers who were to *be* **killed** as they had been was
9: 5 They were not given power to **kill** them, but only to torture them
9:15 and month and year were released to **kill** a third of mankind.
9:18 A third of mankind *was* **killed** by the three plagues of fire,
9:20 The rest of mankind that *were* not **killed** by these plagues still did
11: 5 This is how anyone who wants to harm them must **die**.
11: 7 up from the Abyss will attack them, and overpower and **kill** them.
11:13 Seven thousand people *were* **killed** in the earthquake,

13:10 If anyone *is to be* **killed** with the sword, with the sword he will be
13:10 is to be killed with the sword, with the sword he *will be* **killed**.
13:15 and cause all who refused to worship the image *to be* **killed**.
19:21 The rest of them *were* **killed** with the sword that came out of the

651 ἀποκτέννω, apoktennō   Not used in UBS/NIV
[√ 650]

652 ἀποκυέω, apokyeō [2] [√ 608 + 3246]

give birth [1], gives birth to [1]

Jas 1:15 birth to sin; and sin, when *it is* full-grown, **gives birth to** death.
1:18 He chose *to* **give** us **birth** through the word of truth, that we might

653 ἀποκυλίω, apokyliō [4] [√ 608 + 3244]

rolled away [2], roll away [1], rolled back [1]

Mt 28: 2 heaven and, going to the tomb, **rolled back** the stone and sat on it.
Mk 16: 3 "Who *will* **roll** the stone **away** from the entrance of the tomb?"
16: 4 saw that the stone, which was very large, *had been* **rolled away**.
Lk 24: 2 They found the stone **rolled away** from the tomb,

654 ἀπολαλέω, apolaleō   Not used in UBS/NIV
[√ 608 + 3281]

655 ἀπολαμβάνω, apolambanō [10] [√ 608 + 3284]

receive [2], received [2], getting [1], has back [1], receive from [RP608] [1], repaid [1], rewarded [+3635] [1], took away from [RP608] [1]

Mk 7:33 *After he* **took** [RP608] him aside, **away from** the crowd,
Lk 6:34 Even 'sinners' lend to 'sinners,' expecting *to be* **repaid** in full.
15:27 killed the fattened calf because *he* **has back** safe and sound.'
16:25 remember that in your lifetime *you* **received** your good things,
18:30 *will* fail *to* **receive** many times as much in this age and, in the age
23:41 We are punished justly, for *we are* **getting** what our deeds deserve.
Ro 1:27 and **received** in themselves the due penalty for their perversion.
Gal 4: 5 those under law, that *we might* **receive** the full rights of sons.
Col 3:24 since you know that *you will* **receive** [RP608] an inheritance **from**
2Jn 1: 8 have worked for, but that *you may be* **rewarded** [+3635] fully.

656 ἀπόλαυσις, apolausis [2] [√ 608]

enjoyment [1], pleasures [1]

1Ti 6:17 who richly provides us with everything for our **enjoyment**.
Heb 11:25 of God rather than to enjoy the **pleasures** of sin for a short time.

657 ἀπολείπω, apoleipō [7] [√ 608 + 3309]

left [4], remains [2], abandoned [1]

2Ti 4:13 bring the cloak that *I* **left** with Carpus at Troas, and my scrolls,
4:20 Erastus stayed in Corinth, and *I* **left** Trophimus sick in Miletus.
Tit 1: 5 The reason *I* **left** you in Crete was that you might straighten out
Heb 4: 6 *It still* **remains** that some will enter that rest, and those who
4: 9 *There* **remains**, then, a Sabbath-rest for the people of God;
10:26 received the knowledge of the truth, no sacrifice for sins *is* **left**,
Jude 1: 6 keep their positions of authority but **abandoned** their own home—

658 ἀπολείχω, apoleichō   Not used in UBS/NIV
[√ 608 + 3314]

659 ἀπολιμπάνω, apolimpanō   Not used in UBS/NIV
[√ 608 + 3309]

660 ἀπόλλυμι, apollymi [90] [√ 608 + 3897]

lose [14], lost [12], destroyed [9], perish [9], destroy [8], kill [8], loses [7], killed [4], perishing [4], drown [3], ruined [3], die [2], bring to end [1], executed [1], perishes [1], spoils [1], starving to death [+3350] [1], vanished [RP608] [1], wasted [1]

Mt	2: 13	I tell you, for Herod is going to search for the child *to* **kill** him."
	5: 29	It is better for you to **lose** one part of your body than for your
	5: 30	It is better for you to **lose** one part of your body than for your
	8: 25	and woke him, saying, "Lord, save us! *We're going to* **drown**!"
	9: 17	will burst, the wine will run out and the wineskins *will be* **ruined**.
	10: 6	Go rather to the **lost** sheep of Israel.
	10: 28	be afraid of the One who can **destroy** both soul and body in hell.
	10: 39	Whoever finds his life *will* **lose** it, and whoever loses his life for
	10: 39	life will lose it, and whoever **loses** his life for my sake will find it.
	10: 42	I tell you the truth, *he will* certainly not **lose** his reward."
	12: 14	But the Pharisees went out and plotted how *they might* **kill** Jesus.
	15: 24	He answered, "I was sent only to the **lost** sheep of Israel."
	16: 25	For whoever wants to save his life *will* **lose** it, but whoever loses
	16: 25	his life will lose it, but whoever **loses** his life for me will find it.
	18: 14	in heaven is not willing that any of these little ones *should be* **lost**.
	21: 41	"*He will* **bring** those wretches **to** a wretched **end**," they replied,
	22: 7	*He* sent his army and **destroyed** those murderers and burned their
	26: 52	said to him, "for all who draw the sword *will* **die** by the sword.
	27: 20	the crowd to ask for Barabbas and *to have* Jesus **executed**.
Mk	1: 24	want with us, Jesus of Nazareth? Have you come *to* **destroy** us?
	2: 22	the skins, and both the wine and the wineskins *will be* **ruined**.
	3: 6	and began to plot with the Herodians how *they might* **kill** Jesus.
	4: 38	woke him and said to him, "Teacher, don't you care if *we* **drown**?"
	8: 35	For whoever wants to save his life *will* **lose** it, but whoever loses
	8: 35	but whoever **loses** his life for me and for the gospel will save it.
	9: 22	"It has often thrown him into fire or water to **kill** him. But if you
	9: 41	because you belong to Christ *will* certainly not **lose** his reward.
	11: 18	of the law heard this and began looking for a way *to* **kill** him,
	12: 9	He will come and **kill** those tenants and give the vineyard to others.
Lk	4: 34	want with us, Jesus of Nazareth? Have you come *to* **destroy** us?
	5: 37	the skins, the wine will run out and the wineskins *will be* **ruined**.
	6: 9	the Sabbath: to do good or to do evil, to save life or *to* **destroy** it?"
	8: 24	and woke him, saying, "Master, Master, *we're going to* **drown**!"
	9: 24	For whoever wants to save his life *will* **lose** it, but whoever loses
	9: 24	his life will lose it, but whoever **loses** his life for me will save it.
	9: 25	a man to gain the whole world, and yet **lose** or forfeit his very self?
	11: 51	of Zechariah, who *was* **killed** between the altar and the sanctuary.
	13: 3	I tell you, no! But unless you repent, *you* too *will* all **perish**.
	13: 5	I tell you, no! But unless you repent, *you* too *will* all **perish**."
	13: 33	and the next day—for surely no prophet can **die** outside Jerusalem!
	15: 4	"Suppose one of you has a hundred sheep and **loses** one of them.
	15: 4	in the open country and go after the **lost** sheep until he finds it?
	15: 6	and says, 'Rejoice with me; I have found my **lost** sheep.'
	15: 8	"Or suppose a woman has ten silver coins and **loses** one. Does she
	15: 9	and says, 'Rejoice with me; I have found my **lost** coin.'
	15: 17	men have food to spare, and here I *am* **starving to death** [+3350]!
	15: 24	son of mine was dead and is alive again; he was **lost** and is found.'
	15: 32	of yours was dead and is alive again; he was **lost** and is found.' "
	17: 27	Noah entered the ark. Then the flood came and **destroyed** them all.
	17: 29	and sulfur rained down from heaven and **destroyed** them all.
	17: 33	Whoever tries to keep his life *will* **lose** it, and whoever loses his
	17: 33	keep his life will lose it, and whoever **loses** his life will preserve it.
	19: 10	For the Son of Man came to seek and to save what *was* **lost**."
	19: 47	the law and the leaders among the people were trying *to* **kill** him.
	20: 16	He will come and **kill** those tenants and give the vineyard to others.
	21: 18	But not a hair of your head *will* **perish**.
Jn	3: 16	that whoever believes in him *shall* not **perish** but have eternal life.
	6: 12	"Gather the pieces that are left over. Let nothing *be* **wasted**."
	6: 27	Do not work for food that **spoils**, but for food that endures to
	6: 39	that *I shall* **lose** none of all that he has given me, but raise them up
	10: 10	The thief comes only to steal and kill and **destroy**; I have come
	10: 28	I give them eternal life, and *they shall* never **perish**; no one can
	11: 50	that one man die for the people than that the whole nation **perish**."
	12: 25	The man who loves his life *will* **lose** it, while the man who hates
	17: 12	None *has been* **lost** except the one doomed to destruction
	18: 9	would be fulfilled: "*I have* not **lost** one of those you gave me."
Ac	5: 37	in revolt. He too *was* **killed**, and all his followers were scattered.
	27: 34	it to survive. Not one of you *will* **lose** a single hair from his head."
Ro	2: 12	All who sin apart from the law *will* also **perish** apart from the law,
	14: 15	*Do* not by your eating **destroy** your brother for whom Christ died.
1Co	1: 18	the message of the cross is foolishness *to* those *who are* **perishing**,
	1: 19	"*I will* **destroy** the wisdom of the wise; the intelligence of the
	8: 11	for whom Christ died, *is* **destroyed** by your knowledge.
	10: 9	not test the Lord, as some of them did—and *were* **killed** by snakes.
	10: 10	as some of them did—and *were* **killed** by the destroying angel.
	15: 18	Then those also who have fallen asleep in Christ *are* **lost**.
2Co	2: 15	among those who are being saved and those *who are* **perishing**.
	4: 3	even if our gospel is veiled, it is veiled to those *who are* **perishing**.
	4: 9	persecuted, but not abandoned; struck down, but not **destroyed**.
2Th	2: 10	and in every sort of evil that deceives those *who are* **perishing**.
Heb	1: 11	They *will* **perish**, but you remain; they will all wear out like a
Jas	1: 11	and withers the plant; its blossom falls and its beauty *is* **destroyed**.
	4: 12	one Lawgiver and Judge, the one who is able *to* save and **destroy**.
1Pe	1: 7	worth than gold, which **perishes** even though refined by fire—
2Pe	3: 6	waters also the world of that time *was* deluged and **destroyed**.
	3: 9	He is patient with you, not wanting anyone *to* **perish**, but everyone
2Jn	1: 8	Watch out that *you do* not **lose** what you have worked for,
Jude	1: 5	people out of Egypt, but later **destroyed** those who did not believe.
	1: 11	Balaam's error; *they have been* **destroyed** in Korah's rebellion.
Rev	18: 14	All your riches and splendor *have* **vanished** [RP608], never to be

661 Ἀπολλύων, *Apollyōn* [1] [√ 608 + 3897]

Apollyon [1]

Rev	9: 11	whose name in Hebrew is Abaddon, and in Greek, **Apollyon**.

662 Ἀπολλωνία, *Apollōnia* [1] [√ 663]

Apollonia [1]

Ac	17: 1	When they had passed through Amphipolis and **Apollonia**,

663 Ἀπολλῶς, *Apollōs* [10] [→ 662]

Apollos [10]

Ac	18: 24	Meanwhile a Jew named **Apollos**, a native of Alexandria,
	19: 1	While **Apollos** was at Corinth, Paul took the road through the
1Co	1: 12	another, "I follow **Apollos**"; another, "I follow Cephas";
	3: 4	when one says, "I follow Paul," and another, "I follow **Apollos**,"
	3: 5	What, after all, is **Apollos**? And what is Paul? Only servants,
	3: 6	I planted the seed, **Apollos** watered it, but God made it grow.
	3: 22	whether Paul or **Apollos** or Cephas or the world or life or death
	4: 6	I have applied these things to myself and **Apollos** for your benefit,
	16: 12	Now about our brother **Apollos**: I strongly urged him to go to you
Tit	3: 13	and **Apollos** on their way and see that they have everything they

664 ἀπολογέομαι, *apologeomai* [10] [√ 608 + 3306]

make defense [3], defend [2], defense [2], defending [1], defending ourselves [1], made defense [1]

Lk	12: 11	do not worry about how *you will* **defend** *yourselves* or what you
	21: 14	mind not to worry beforehand how you *will* **defend** *yourselves*.
Ac	19: 33	He motioned for silence in order to **make** a **defense** before the
	24: 10	have been a judge over this nation; so *I* gladly **make** my **defense**.
	25: 8	Then Paul **made** *his* **defense**: "I have done nothing wrong against
	26: 1	So Paul motioned with his hand and *began his* **defense**:
	26: 2	as I **make** my **defense** against all the accusations of the Jews,
	26: 24	At this point Festus interrupted Paul's **defense**. "You are out of
Ro	2: 15	and their thoughts now accusing, now even **defending** them.)
2Co	12: 19	thinking all along that *we have been* **defending ourselves** to you?

665 ἀπολογία, *apologia* [8] [√ 608 + 3306]

defense [4], answer [1], defend [1], defending [1], eagerness to clear [1]

Ac	22: 1	"Brothers and fathers, listen now to my **defense**."
	25: 16	and has had an opportunity to **defend** himself against their charges.
1Co	9: 3	This is my **defense** to those who sit in judgment on me.
2Co	7: 11	what earnestness, what **eagerness to clear** yourselves,
Php	1: 7	for whether I am in chains or **defending** and confirming the
	1: 16	in love, knowing that I am put here for the **defense** of the gospel.
2Ti	4: 16	At my first **defense**, no one came to my support, but everyone
1Pe	3: 15	Always be prepared to give an **answer** to everyone who asks you

666 ἀπολούω, *apolouō* [2] [√ 608 + 3374]

wash away [1], washed [1]

Ac 22:16 Get up, be baptized and **wash** your sins **away**, calling on his
1Co 6:11 But *you were* **washed**, you were sanctified, you were justified in

667 ἀπολύτρωσις, *apolytrōsis* [10] [√ 608 + 3395]

redemption [8], ransom [1], released [1]

Lk 21:28 and lift up your heads, because your **redemption** is drawing near."
Ro 3:24 and are justified freely by his grace through the **redemption** that
   8:23 eagerly for our adoption as sons, the **redemption** of our bodies.
1Co 1:30 from God—that is, our righteousness, holiness and **redemption**.
Eph 1: 7 In him we have **redemption** through his blood, the forgiveness of
   1:14 who is a deposit guaranteeing our inheritance until the **redemption**
   4:30 of God, with whom you were sealed for the day *of* **redemption**.
Col 1:14 in whom we have **redemption**, the forgiveness of sins.
Heb 9:15 now that he has died as a **ransom** *to set* them *free* from the sins
   11:35 Others were tortured and refused to be **released**, so that they might

668 ἀπολύω, *apolyō* [66] [√ 608 + 3395]

ἀπολύω γυναῖκα (divorce [one's] wife) [8] Mt 5:31,32;
   19:3,8,9; Mk 10:2,11; Lk 16:18

release [15], send away [7], divorces [6], let go [6], dismissed
[5], released [5], divorce [4], sent away [4], sent off [3], set free
[3], forgive [1], dismiss [1], divorced [+467+608] [1], divorced
[1], forgiven [1], free [1], leave [1], send [1]

Mt 1:19 her to public disgrace, he had in mind *to* **divorce** her quietly.
   5:31 'Anyone *who* **divorces** his wife must give her a certificate of
   5:32 But I tell you that anyone who **divorces** his wife, except for marital
   5:32 and anyone who marries the **divorced** *woman* commits adultery.
   14:15 **Send** the crowds **away**, so they can go to the villages and buy
   14:22 on ahead of him to the other side, while *he* **dismissed** the crowd.
   14:23 *After he had* **dismissed** them, he went up on a mountainside by
   15:23 So his disciples came to him and urged him, "**Send** her **away**,
   15:32 I do not want *to* **send** them **away** hungry, or they may collapse on
   15:39 *After* Jesus *had* **sent** the crowd **away**, he got into the boat
   18:27 master took pity on him, canceled the debt and **let** him **go**.
   19: 3 lawful for a man *to* **divorce** his wife for any and every reason?"
   19: 7 a man give his wife a certificate of divorce and **send** her **away**?"
   19: 8 "Moses permitted you *to* **divorce** your wives because your hearts
   19: 9 I tell you that anyone *who* **divorces** his wife, except for marital
   27:15 Now it was the governor's custom at the Feast *to* **release** a
   27:17 Pilate asked them, "Which one do you want *me to* **release** to you:
   27:21 "Which of the two do you want *me to* **release** to you?" asked the
   27:26 Then *he* **released** Barabbas to them. But he had Jesus flogged,
Mk 6:36 **Send** the people **away** so they can go to the surrounding
   6:45 go on ahead of him to Bethsaida, while *he* **dismissed** the crowd.
   8: 3 If *I* **send** them home hungry, they will collapse on the way,
   8: 9 four thousand men were present. And *having* **sent** them **away**,
   10: 2 tested him by asking, "Is it lawful for a man *to* **divorce** his wife?"
   10: 4 a man to write a certificate of divorce and **send** her **away**."
   10:11 "Anyone *who* **divorces** his wife and marries another woman
   10:12 And if she **divorces** her husband and marries another man,
   15: 6 Now *it was the custom* at the Feast *to* **release** a prisoner whom
   15: 9 "Do you want *me to* **release** to you the king of the Jews?"
   15:11 But the chief priests stirred up the crowd to *have* Pilate **release**
   15:15 Wanting to satisfy the crowd, Pilate **released** Barabbas to them.
Lk 2:29 as you have promised, *you* now **dismiss** your servant in peace.
   6:37 and you will not be condemned. **Forgive**, and you will be forgiven.
   6:37 you will not be condemned. Forgive, and *you will be* **forgiven**.
   8:38 gone out begged to go with him, but Jesus **sent** him **away**, saying,
   9:12 "**Send** the crowd **away** so they can go to the surrounding villages
   13:12 and said to her, "Woman, you *are* **set free** from your infirmity."
   14: 4 So taking hold of the man, he healed him and **sent** him **away**.
   16:18 "Anyone *who* **divorces** his wife and marries another woman
   16:18 and the man who marries a **divorced** [+467+608] *woman* commits
   23:16 Therefore, *I will* punish him and then **release** him."
   23:18 they cried out, "Away with this man! **Release** Barabbas to us!"
   23:20 Wanting *to* **release** Jesus, Pilate appealed to them again.
   23:22 Therefore I will have him punished and then **release** him."
   23:25 *He* **released** the man who had been thrown into prison for
Jn 18:39 But it is your custom for *me to* **release** to you one prisoner at the

18:39 of the Passover. Do you want *me to* **release** 'the king of the Jews'?"
19:10 "Don't you realize I have power either *to* **free** you or to crucify
19:12 From then on, Pilate tried *to* **set** Jesus **free**, but the Jews kept
19:12 but the Jews kept shouting, "If *you* **let** this man **go**, you are no
Ac 3:13 disowned him before Pilate, though he had decided *to* **let** him **go**.
   4:21 After further threats they **let** them **go**. They could not decide how
   4:23 *On their* **release**, Peter and John went back to their own people
   5:40 ordered them not to speak in the name of Jesus, and **let** them **go**.
   13: 3 and prayed, they placed their hands on them and **sent** them **off**.
   15:30 The men *were* **sent off** and went down to Antioch, where they
   15:33 *they were* **sent off** by the brothers with the blessing of peace to
   16:35 sent their officers to the jailer with the order: "**Release** those men."
   16:36 "The magistrates have ordered that *you* and Silas *be* **released**.
   17: 9 Then they made Jason and the others post bond and **let** them **go**.
   19:41 After he had said this, *he* **dismissed** the assembly.
   23:22 The commander **dismissed** the young man and cautioned him,
   26:32 "This man could have *been* **set free** if he had not appealed to
   28:18 They examined me and wanted *to* **release** me,
   28:25 and *began to* **leave** after Paul had made this final statement:
Heb 13:23 I want you to know that our brother Timothy *has been* **released**.

669 ἀπομάσσω, *apomassō* [1] [√ 608 + 3463]

wipe off against [1]

Lk 10:11 dust of your town that sticks to our feet *we* **wipe off against** you.

670 ἀπομένω, *apomenō* Not used in UBS/NIV
[√ 608 + 3531]

671 ἀπονέμω, *aponemō* [1] [√ 608 + 3795]

treat [1]

1Pe 3: 7 and **treat** them with respect as the weaker partner and as heirs with

672 ἀπονίπτω, *aponiptō* [1] [√ 608 + 3782]

washed [1]

Mt 27:24 *he* took water and **washed** his hands in front of the crowd.

673 ἀποπέμπω, *apopempō* Not used in UBS/NIV
[√ 608 + 4287]

674 ἀποπίπτω, *apopiptō* [1] [√ 608 + 4406]

fell [1]

Ac 9:18 Immediately, something like scales **fell** from Saul's eyes, and he

675 ἀποπλανάω, *apoplanaō* [2] [√ 608 + 4415]

deceive [1], wandered from [RP608] [1]

Mk 13:22 will appear and perform signs and miracles to **deceive** the elect—
1Ti 6:10 *have* **wandered** [RP608] **from** the faith and pierced themselves

676 ἀποπλέω, *apopleō* [4] [√ 608 + 4434]

sail [1], sailed [1], sailed back [1], set sail [1]

Ac 13: 4 went down to Seleucia and **sailed** from there to Cyprus.
   14:26 From Attalia *they* **sailed back** to Antioch, where they had been
   20:15 The next day we **set sail** from there and arrived off Kios. The day
   27: 1 When it was decided that we *would* **sail** for Italy, Paul and some

677 ἀποπλύνω, *apoplynō* Not used in UBS/NIV
[√ 608 + 4459]

678 ἀποπνίγω, *apopnigō* [2] [√ 608 + 4464]

choked [1], drowned [1]

Lk 8: 7 fell among thorns, which grew up with it and **choked** the plants.
   8:33 herd rushed down the steep bank into the lake and *was* **drowned**.

679 ἀπορέω, *aporeō* [6] [√ *1.1 + 4513*]

at a loss [2], perplexed [2], puzzled [1], wondering [1]

Mk 6:20 When Herod heard John, *he was* greatly **puzzled**; yet he liked to
Lk 24: 4 While they *were* **wondering** about this, suddenly two men in
Jn 13:22 stared at one another, **at a loss** to know which of them he meant.
Ac 25:20 I *was* **at a loss** how to investigate such matters; so I asked if he
2Co 4: 8 on every side, but not crushed; **perplexed**, but not in despair;
Gal 4:20 you now and change my tone, because *I am* **perplexed** about you!

680 ἀπορία, *aporia* [1] [√ *1.1 + 4513*]

perplexity [1]

Lk 21:25 be in anguish and **perplexity** at the roaring and tossing of the sea.

681 ἀπορίπτω, *aporiptō* [1] [√ *608 + 4849*]

jump overboard [1]

Ac 27:43 He ordered those who could swim to **jump overboard** first

682 ἀπορφανίζω, *aporphanizō* [1] [√ *608 + 4003*]

torn away from [RP608] [1]

1Th 2:17 *when* we *were* **torn** [RP608] **away from** you for a short time (in

683 ἀποσκευάζω, *aposkeuazō* Not used in UBS/NIV
[√ *608 + 5007*]

684 ἀποσκίασμα, *aposkiasma* [1] [√ *608 + 5014*]

shadows [1]

Jas 1:17 of the heavenly lights, who does not change like shifting **shadows**.

685 ἀποσπάω, *apospaō* [4] [√ *608 + 5060*]

draw away [1], drew out [1], torn away [1], withdrew [1]

Mt 26:51 **drew** it **out** and struck the servant of the high priest, cutting off his
Lk 22:41 He **withdrew** about a stone's throw beyond them, knelt down
Ac 20:30 and distort the truth *in order to* **draw away** disciples after them.
    21: 1 *After* we had **torn** *ourselves* **away** from them, we put out to sea

686 ἀποστασία, *apostasia* [2] [√ *608 + 2705*]

rebellion [1], to turn away from [RP608] [1]

Ac 21:21 who live among the Gentiles **to turn** [RP608] **away from** Moses,
2Th 2: 3 for ˌthat day will not comeˌ until the **rebellion** occurs and the man

687 ἀποστάσιον, *apostasion* [3] [√ *608 + 2705*]

divorce [2], certificate of divorce [1]

Mt 5:31 who divorces his wife must give her a **certificate of divorce**.'
    19: 7 Moses command that a man give his wife a certificate *of* **divorce**
Mk 10: 4 "Moses permitted a man to write a certificate *of* **divorce** and send

688 ἀποστάτης, *apostatēs* Not used in UBS/NIV
[√ *608 + 2705*]

689 ἀποστεγάζω, *apostegazō* [1] [√ *608 + 5095*]

made an opening in [1]

Mk 2: 4 of the crowd, *they* **made an opening in** the roof above Jesus and,

690 ἀποστέλλω, *apostellō* [132] [→ *692, 693, 1990,*
5273, 6013; cf. 608 + 5097]

sent [92], send [15], sending [5], sent out [3], send back [2],
send out [2], sending out [2], sent word [2], gave orders [1],
given orders [1], ordered [1], puts [1], release [+*912+1877*] [1],
sent away [1], sent for [+*3559*] [1], sent message [1], sent out
[+*806*] [1]

Mt 2:16 and he **gave orders** to kill all the boys in Bethlehem and its
     8:31 begged Jesus, "If you drive us out, **send** us into the herd of pigs."
    10: 5 These twelve Jesus **sent out** with the following instructions:
    10:16 I *am* **sending** you **out** like sheep among wolves. Therefore be as
    10:40 and he who receives me receives the one *who* **sent** me.
    11:10 " 'I will **send** my messenger ahead of you, who will prepare your
    13:41 The Son of Man *will* **send out** his angels, and they will weed out
    14:35 recognized Jesus, *they* **sent word** to all the surrounding country.
    15:24 He answered, "I was **sent** only to the lost sheep of Israel."
    20: 2 to pay them a denarius for the day and **sent** them into his vineyard.
    21: 1 to Bethphage on the Mount of Olives, Jesus **sent** two disciples,
    21: 3 him that the Lord needs them, and *he will* **send** them right away."
    21:34 he **sent** his servants to the tenants to collect his fruit.
    21:36 Then *he* **sent** other servants to them, more than the first time,
    21:37 Last of all, *he* **sent** his son to them. 'They will respect my son,'
    22: 3 *He* **sent** his servants to those who had been invited to the banquet
    22: 4 "Then *he* **sent** some more servants and said, 'Tell those who have
    22:16 *They* **sent** their disciples to him along with the Herodians.
    23:34 Therefore I *am* **sending** you prophets and wise men and teachers.
    23:37 Jerusalem, you who kill the prophets and stone those **sent** to you,
    24:31 And *he will* **send** his angels with a loud trumpet call, and they will
    27:19 was sitting on the judge's seat, his wife **sent** him this **message**:
Mk 1: 2 "I will **send** my messenger ahead of you, who will prepare your
     3:14 might be with him and that *he might* **send** them **out** to preach
     3:31 Standing outside, *they* **sent** someone in to call him.
     4:29 As soon as the grain is ripe, *he* **puts** the sickle to it,
     5:10 he begged Jesus again and again not to **send** them out of the area.
     6: 7 Calling the Twelve to him, he **sent** [+*806*] them **out** two by two
     6:17 For Herod himself *had* **given orders** to have John arrested,
     6:27 So he immediately **sent** an executioner with orders to bring John's
     8:26 Jesus **sent** him home, saying, "Don't go into the village."
     9:37 welcomes me does not welcome me but the one *who* **sent** me."
    11: 1 Bethany at the Mount of Olives, Jesus **sent** two of his disciples,
    11: 3 tell him, 'The Lord needs it and *will* **send** it **back** here shortly.' "
    12: 2 At harvest time *he* **sent** a servant to the tenants to collect from
    12: 3 But they seized him, beat him and **sent** him **away** empty-handed.
    12: 4 Then *he* **sent** another servant to them; they struck this man on the
    12: 5 *He* **sent** still another,
    12: 6 *He* **sent** him last of all, saying, 'They will respect my son.'
    12:13 Later *they* **sent** some of the Pharisees and Herodians to Jesus to
    13:27 And *he will* **send** his angels and gather his elect from the four
    14:13 So *he* **sent** two of his disciples, telling them, "Go into the city,
Lk 1:19 and I have been **sent** to speak to you and to tell you this good
     1:26 God **sent** the angel Gabriel to Nazareth, a town in Galilee,
     4:18 He has **sent** me to proclaim freedom for the prisoners and recovery
     4:18 of sight for the blind, *to* **release** [+*912+1877*] the oppressed,
     4:43 of God to the other towns also, because that is why I was **sent**."
     7: 3 centurion heard of Jesus and **sent** some elders of the Jews to him,
     7:20 came to Jesus, they said, "John the Baptist **sent** us to you to ask,
     7:27 " 'I will **send** my messenger ahead of you, who will prepare your
     9: 2 and he **sent** them **out** to preach the kingdom of God and to heal the
     9:48 and whoever welcomes me welcomes the one *who* **sent** me.
     9:52 And *he* **sent** messengers on ahead, who went into a Samaritan
    10: 1 and **sent** them two by two ahead of him to every town and place
    10: 3 Go! I *am* **sending** you **out** like lambs among wolves.
    10:16 you rejects me; but he who rejects me rejects him *who* **sent** me."
    11:49 God in his wisdom said, 'I *will* **send** them prophets and apostles,
    13:34 Jerusalem, you who kill the prophets and stone those **sent** to you,
    14:17 At the time of the banquet he **sent** his servant to tell those who had
    14:32 *he will* **send** a delegation while the other is still a long way off
    19:14 "But his subjects hated him and **sent** a delegation after him to say,
    19:29 the Mount of Olives, *he* **sent** two of his disciples, saying to them,
    19:32 Those *who were* **sent** *ahead* went and found it just as he had told
    20:10 At harvest time *he* **sent** a servant to the tenants so they would give
    20:20 a close watch on him, *they* **sent** spies, who pretended to be honest.
    22: 8 Jesus **sent** Peter and John, saying, "Go and make preparations for
    22:35 "When I **sent** you without purse, bag or sandals, did you lack
    24:49 I *am going to* **send** you what my Father has promised; but stay in
Jn 1: 6 There came a man *who was* **sent** from God; his name was John.
     1:19 Now this was John's testimony when the Jews of Jerusalem **sent**
     1:24 Now some Pharisees who had been **sent**
     3:17 For God *did* not **send** his Son into the world to condemn the
     3:28 testify that I said, 'I am not the Christ but am **sent** ahead of him.'

3:34 For the one whom God *has* **sent** speaks the words of God,
4:38 I **sent** you to reap what you have not worked for. Others have done
5:33 "You *have* **sent** to John and he has testified to the truth.
5:36 and which I am doing, testifies that the Father *has* **sent** me.
5:38 does his word dwell in you, for you do not believe the one he **sent**.
6:29 "The work of God is this: to believe in the one he *has* **sent**."
6:57 Just as the living Father **sent** me and I live because of the Father,
7:29 but I know him because I am from him and he **sent** me."
7:32 the chief priests and the Pharisees **sent** temple guards to arrest him.
8:42 and now am here. I have not come on my own; but he **sent** me.
9: 7 he told him, "wash in the Pool of Siloam" (this word means **Sent**).
10:36 whom the Father set apart as his very own and **sent** into the world?
11: 3 So the sisters **sent** word to Jesus, "Lord, the one you love is sick."
11:42 the people standing here, that they may believe that you **sent** me."
17: 3 the only true God, and Jesus Christ, whom *you have* **sent**.
17: 8 certainty that I came from you, and they believed that you **sent** me.
17:18 As *you* **sent** me into the world, I have sent them into the world.
17:18 As you sent me into the world, I *have* **sent** them into the world.
17:21 also be in us so that the world may believe that you *have* **sent** me.
17:23 brought to complete unity to let the world know that you **sent** me
17:25 not know you, I know you, and they know that you *have* **sent** me.
18:24 Then Annas **sent** him, still bound, to Caiaphas the high priest.
20:21 "Peace be with you! As the Father *has* **sent** me, I am sending you."
Ac   3:20 and that *he may* **send** the Christ, who has been appointed for you—
3:26 *he* **sent** him first to you by turning each of you from
5:21 of the elders of Israel—and **sent** to the jail for the apostles.
7:14 Joseph **sent** for [+3559] his father Jacob and his whole family,
7:34 down to set them free. Now come, *I will* **send** you **back** to Egypt.'
7:35 He *was* **sent** to be their ruler and deliverer by God himself,
8:14 had accepted the word of God, *they* **sent** Peter and John to them.
9:17 *has* **sent** me so that you may see again and be filled with the Holy
9:38 *they* **sent** two men to him and urged him, "Please come at once!"
10: 8 *He* **sent** them everything that had happened and **sent** them to
10:17 the men **sent** by Cornelius found out where Simon's house was
10:20 Do not hesitate to go with them, for I *have* **sent** them."
10:36 You know the message God **sent** to the people of Israel,
11:11 then three men *who had been* **sent** to me from Caesarea stopped at
11:13 in his house and say, '**Send** to Joppa for Simon who is called Peter.
11:30 they did, **sending** their gift to the elders by Barnabas and Saul.
13:15 the synagogue rulers **sent** word to them, saying, "Brothers,
15:27 Therefore *we are* **sending** Judas and Silas to confirm by word of
15:33 with the blessing of peace to return to those *who had* **sent** them.
16:35 the magistrates **sent** their officers to the jailer with the order:
16:36 "The magistrates *have* **ordered** that you and Silas be released.
19:22 *He* **sent** two of his helpers, Timothy and Erastus, to Macedonia,
26:17 your own people and from the Gentiles. I *am* **sending** you to them
28:28 "Therefore I want you to know that God's salvation *has been* **sent**
Ro 10:15 And how can they preach unless *they are* **sent**? As it is written,
1Co 1:17 For Christ *did* not **send** me to baptize, but to preach the gospel—
2Co 12:17 Did I exploit you through any of the men *I* **sent** you?
2Ti 4:12 *I* **sent** Tychicus to Ephesus.
Heb 1:14 Are not all angels ministering spirits **sent** to serve those who will
1Pe 1:12 preached the gospel to you by the Holy Spirit **sent** from heaven.
1Jn 4: 9 He **sent** his one and only Son into the world that we might live
4:10 he loved us and **sent** his Son as an atoning sacrifice for our sins.
4:14 and testify that the Father *has* **sent** his Son to be the Savior of the
Rev 1: 1 He made it known *by* **sending** his angel to his servant John,
5: 6 which are the seven spirits of God **sent out** into all the earth.
22: 6 **sent** his angel to show his servants the things that must soon take

691 ἀποστερέω, *apostereō* [6] [√ 608]

cheat [1], cheated [1], defraud [1], deprive [1], failed to pay [1],
robbed [1]

Mk 10:19 false testimony, *do* not **defraud**, honor your father and mother.' "
1Co 6: 7 Why not rather be wronged? Why not rather *be* **cheated**?
6: 8 Instead, *you* yourselves **cheat** and do wrong, and you do this to
7: 5 *Do* not **deprive** each other except by mutual consent and for a
1Ti 6: 5 *who have been* **robbed** of the truth and who think that godliness is
Jas 5: 4 The wages *you* **failed to pay** the workmen who mowed your fields

692 ἀποστολή, *apostolē* [4] [√ 690]

apostleship [2], apostolic [1], ministry of an apostle [1]

Ac   1:25 to take over this **apostolic** ministry, which Judas left to go where

Ro   1: 5 and **apostleship** to call people from among all the Gentiles to the
1Co 9: 2 I am to you! For you are the seal *of* my **apostleship** in the Lord.
Gal 2: 8 who was at work in the **ministry of** Peter as **an apostle** to the

693 ἀπόστολος, *apostolos* [80] [√ 690]

ἀπόστολοι καὶ πρεσβύτεροι (apostles and elders) [6] Ac
15:2,4,6,22,23; 16:4

ἀπόστολος ... προφήτης (apostle[s] ... prophet[s]) [7] Lk
11:49; 1Co 12:28; Eph 2:20; 3:5; 4:11; 2Pe 3:2; Rev 18:20

ἀπόστολος Χριστοῦ (apostle of Christ) [11] 1Co 1:1; 2Co 1:1;
11:13; Eph 1:1; Col 1:1; 1Th 2:7; 1Ti 1:1; 2Ti 1:1; Tit 1:1; 1Pe 1:1;
2Pe 1:1

δώδεκα ἀπόστολοι (twelve apostles) [2] Mt 10:2; Rev 21:14;
cf. Mk 3:14; Lk 6:13

apostles [56], apostle [19], messenger [2], super-apostles
[+5663] [2], representatives [1]

Mt 10: 2 These are the names *of* the twelve **apostles**: first, Simon (who is
Mk 3:14 He appointed twelve—designating them **apostles**—that they might
6:30 The **apostles** gathered around Jesus and reported to him all they
Lk   6:13 and chose twelve of them, whom he also designated **apostles**:
9:10 When the **apostles** returned, they reported to Jesus what they had
11:49 God in his wisdom said, 'I will send them prophets and **apostles**,
17: 5 The **apostles** said to the Lord, "Increase our faith!"
22:14 When the hour came, Jesus and his **apostles** reclined at the table.
24:10 of James, and the others with them who told this to the **apostles**.
Jn 13:16 his master, nor is a **messenger** greater than the one who sent him.
Ac   1: 2 after giving instructions through the Holy Spirit *to* the **apostles** he
1:26 and the lot fell to Matthias; so he was added to the eleven **apostles**.
2:37 they were cut to the heart and said to Peter and the other **apostles**,
2:42 They devoted themselves to the **apostles**' teaching and to the
2:43 many wonders and miraculous signs were done by the **apostles**.
4:33 With great power the **apostles** continued to testify to the
4:35 and put it at the **apostles**' feet, and it was distributed to anyone as
4:36 whom the **apostles** called Barnabas (which means Son of
4:37 he owned and brought the money and put it at the **apostles**' feet.
5: 2 for himself, but brought the rest and put it at the **apostles**' feet.
5:12 The **apostles** performed many miraculous signs and wonders
5:18 They arrested the **apostles** and put them in the public jail.
5:29 Peter and the other **apostles** replied: "We must obey God rather
5:40 persuaded them. They called the **apostles** in and had them flogged.
6: 6 They presented these men to the **apostles**, who prayed and laid
8: 1 and all except the **apostles** were scattered throughout Judea
8:14 When the **apostles** in Jerusalem heard that Samaria had accepted
8:18 saw that the Spirit was given at the laying on *of* the **apostles**' hands,
9:27 But Barnabas took him and brought him to the **apostles**. He told
11: 1 The **apostles** and the brothers throughout Judea heard that the
14: 4 were divided; some sided with the Jews, others with the **apostles**.
14:14 But when the **apostles** Barnabas and Paul heard of this, they tore
15: 2 to go up to Jerusalem to see the **apostles** and elders about this
15: 4 they were welcomed by the church and the **apostles** and elders,
15: 6 The **apostles** and elders met to consider this question.
15:22 Then the **apostles** and elders, with the whole church, decided to
15:23 The **apostles** and elders, your brothers, To the Gentile believers in
16: 4 they delivered the decisions reached by the **apostles** and elders in
Ro   1: 1 called to be an **apostle** and set apart for the gospel of God—
11:13 Inasmuch as I am the **apostle** to the Gentiles, I make much of my
16: 7 They are outstanding among the **apostles**, and they were in Christ
1Co 1: 1 called to be an **apostle** of Christ Jesus by the will of God,
4: 9 For it seems to me that God has put us **apostles** on display at the
9: 1 Am I not free? Am I not an **apostle**? Have I not seen Jesus our
9: 2 Even though I may not be an **apostle** to others, surely I am to you!
9: 5 as do the other **apostles** and the Lord's brothers and Cephas?
12:28 And in the church God has appointed first of all **apostles**,
12:29 Are all **apostles**? Are all prophets? Are all teachers? Do all work
15: 7 Then he appeared to James, then *to* all the **apostles**,
15: 9 For I am the least *of* the **apostles** and do not even deserve to be
15: 9 of the apostles and do not even deserve to be called an **apostle**,
2Co 1: 1 Paul, an **apostle** of Christ Jesus by the will of God, and Timothy
8:23 they are **representatives** of the churches and an honor to Christ.
11: 5 think I am in the least inferior to those "**super-apostles** [+5663]."
11:13 deceitful workmen, masquerading as **apostles** of Christ.
12:11 for I am not in the least inferior to the "**super-apostles** [+5663],"
12:12 The things that mark an **apostle**—signs, wonders and miracles—

Gal 1: 1 Paul, an **apostle**—sent not from men nor by man, but by Jesus
1:17 nor did I go up to Jerusalem to see those who were **apostles** before
1:19 I saw none *of* the other **apostles**—only James, the Lord's brother.
Eph 1: 1 Paul, an **apostle** of Christ Jesus by the will of God, To the saints in
2:20 built on the foundation *of* the **apostles** and prophets, with Christ
3: 5 as it has now been revealed by the Spirit *to* God's holy **apostles**
4:11 It was he who gave some to be **apostles**, some to be prophets,
Php 2:25 fellow worker and fellow soldier, who is also your **messenger**,
Col 1: 1 Paul, an **apostle** of Christ Jesus by the will of God, and Timothy
1Th 2: 6 As **apostles** of Christ we could have been a burden to you,
1Ti 1: 1 an **apostle** of Christ Jesus by the command of God our Savior
2: 7 And for this purpose I was appointed a herald and an **apostle**—
2Ti 1: 1 Paul, an **apostle** of Christ Jesus by the will of God, according to
1:11 this gospel I was appointed a herald and an **apostle** and a teacher.
Tit 1: 1 of God and an **apostle** of Jesus Christ for the faith of God's elect
Heb 3: 1 thoughts on Jesus, the **apostle** and high priest whom we confess.
1Pe 1: 1 Peter, an **apostle** of Jesus Christ, To God's elect, strangers in the
2Pe 1: 1 Simon Peter, a servant and **apostle** of Jesus Christ, To those who
3: 2 command given by our Lord and Savior *through* your **apostles**.
Jude 1:17 remember what the **apostles** of our Lord Jesus Christ foretold.
Rev 2: 2 that you have tested those who claim to be **apostles** but are not,
18:20 over her, O heaven! Rejoice, saints and **apostles** and prophets!
21:14 and on them were the names *of* the twelve **apostles** of the Lamb.

694 ἀποστοματίζω, *apostomatizō* [1] [√ *608 + 5125*]

besiege with questions [+4309+4498] [1]

Lk 11:53 fiercely and *to* **besiege** him **with questions** [+4309+4498],

695 ἀποστρέφω, *apostrephō* [9] [√ *608 + 5138*]

turn away from [*RP608*] [2], turn away from [2], put back [1],
deserted [1], inciting to rebellion [1], reject [1], turning from
[*RP608*] [1]

Mt 5:42 and *do* not **turn away from** the one who wants to borrow from
26:52 "**Put** your sword **back** in its place," Jesus said to him, "for all who
Lk 23:14 me this man as *one who was* **inciting** the people **to rebellion**.
Ac 3:26 you by **turning** [*RP608*] each of you **from** your wicked ways."
Ro 11:26 from Zion; *he will* **turn** [*RP608*] godlessness **away from** Jacob.
2Ti 1:15 You know that everyone in the province of Asia *has* **deserted** me,
4: 4 *They will* **turn** [*RP608*] their ears **away from** the truth and turn
Tit 1:14 to Jewish myths or to the commands of those *who* **reject** the truth.
Heb 12:25 will we, *if* we **turn away from** him who warns us from heaven?

696 ἀποστυγέω, *apostygeō* [1] [√ *608 + 5144*]

hate [1]

Ro 12: 9 Love must be sincere. **Hate** what is evil; cling to what is good.

697 ἀποσυνάγωγος, *aposynagōgos* [3]
[√ *608 + 5252*]

put out of the synagogue [2], put out of the synagogue [+4472] [1]

Jn 9:22 that Jesus was the Christ would be **put out of the synagogue**.
12:42 their faith for fear they would be **put out of the synagogue**;
16: 2 *They will* **put** you **out of the synagogue** [+4472]; in fact,

698 ἀποτάσσω, *apotassō* [6] [√ *608 + 5435*]

left [2], give up [1], leaving [1], said good-by [1], say good-by [1]

Mk 6:46 *After* **leaving** them, he went up on a mountainside to pray.
Lk 9:61 Lord; but first let me go back and **say good-by** to my family."
14:33 any of you who *does* not **give up** everything he has cannot be my
Ac 18:18 Then he **left** the brothers and sailed for Syria, accompanied by
18:21 But *as* he **left**, he promised, "I will come back if it is God's will."
2Co 2:13 Titus there. So I **said good-by** to them and went on to Macedonia.

699 ἀποτελέω, *apoteleō* [2] [√ *608 + 5465*]

full-grown [1], heal people [+2617] [1]

Lk 13:32 drive out demons and **heal people** [+2617] today and tomorrow,
Jas 1:15 birth to sin; and sin, *when* it is **full-grown**, gives birth to death.

700 ἀποτίθημι, *apotithēmi* [9] [√ *608 + 5502*]

put off [2], rid of [2], get rid of [1], laid [1], put [1], put aside [1],
throw off [1]

Mt 14: 3 and bound him and **put** him in prison because of Herodias,
Ac 7:58 the witnesses **laid** their clothes at the feet of a young man named
Ro 13:12 So *let us* **put aside** the deeds of darkness and put on the armor of
Eph 4:22 with regard to your former way of life, *to* **put off** your old self,
4:25 Therefore each of you *must* **put off** falsehood and speak truthfully
Col 3: 8 But now you *must* **rid** *yourselves* **of** all such things as these:
Heb 12: 1 *let us* **throw off** everything that hinders and the sin that so easily
Jas 1:21 **get rid of** all moral filth and the evil that is so prevalent
1Pe 2: 1 Therefore, **rid** *yourselves* **of** all malice and all deceit, hypocrisy,

701 ἀποτινάσσω, *apotinassō* [2] [√ *1753; cf. 608*]

shake off [*RP608*] [1], shook off [1]

Lk 9: 5 **shake** [*RP608*] the dust **off** your feet when you leave their town,
Ac 28: 5 But Paul **shook** the snake **off** into the fire and suffered no ill

702 ἀποτίνω, *apotinō* [1] [√ *608 + 5514*]

pay back [1]

Phm 1:19 I *will* **pay** it **back**—not to mention that you owe me your very self.

703 ἀποτολμάω, *apotolmaō* [1] [√ *608 + 5528*]

boldly [1]

Ro 10:20 Isaiah **boldly** says, "I was found by those who did not seek me,

704 ἀποτομία, *apotomia* [2] [√ *608 + 5533*]

sternness [2]

Ro 11:22 Consider therefore the kindness and **sternness** of God: sternness to
11:22 **sternness** to those who fell, but kindness to you, provided that you

705 ἀποτόμως, *apotomōs* [2] [√ *608 + 5533*]

harsh [1], sharply [1]

2Co 13:10 that when I come I may not have to be **harsh** in my use of
Tit 1:13 Therefore, rebuke them **sharply**, so that they will be sound in the

706 ἀποτρέπω, *apotrepō* [1] [√ *608 + 5572*]

have nothing to do with [1]

2Ti 3: 5 but denying its power. **Have nothing to do with** them.

707 ἀπουσία, *apousia* [1] [√ *608 + 1639*]

absence [1]

Php 2:12 not only in my presence, but now much more in my **absence**—

708 ἀποφέρω, *apopherō* [6] [√ *608 + 5770*]

carried away [2], carried [1], led away [1], taken [1], with [1]

Mk 15: 1 *They* bound Jesus, **led** him **away** and handed him over to Pilate.
Lk 16:22 the beggar died and the angels **carried** him to Abraham's side.
Ac 19:12 and aprons that had touched him *were* **taken** to the sick,
1Co 16: 3 to the men you approve and send them **with** your gift to Jerusalem.
Rev 17: 3 Then the angel **carried** me **away** in the Spirit into a desert.
21:10 And *he* **carried** me **away** in the Spirit to a mountain great

709 ἀποφεύγω, *apopheugō* [3] [√ *608 + 5771*]

escape [1], escaped [1], escaping from [1]

2Pe 1: 4 and **escape** the corruption in the world caused by evil desires.
2:18 they entice people *who are* just **escaping from** those who live in
2:20 If *they have* **escaped** the corruption of the world by knowing our

710 ἀποφθέγγομαι, *apophthengomai* [3]
[√ 608 + 5779]

addressed [1], enabled [+1443] [1], saying [1]

Ac   2: 4 and began to speak in other tongues as the Spirit **enabled** [+1443]
      2:14 up with the Eleven, raised his voice and **addressed** the crowd:
    26:25 Paul replied. "What *I am* **saying** is true and reasonable.

711 ἀποφορτίζομαι, *apophortizomai* [1]
[√ 608 + 5770]

unload [1]

Ac 21: 3 We landed at Tyre, where our ship was to **unload** its cargo.

712 ἀπόχρησις, *apochrēsis* [1] [√ 608 + 5968]

use [1]

Col 2:22 These are all destined to perish *with* **use**, because they are based

713 ἀποχωρέω, *apochōreō* [3] [√ 608 + 6003]

away from [RP608] [1], leaves [RP608] [1], left [RP608] [1]

Mt   7:23 'I never knew you. **Away** [RP608] **from** me, you evildoers!'
Lk   9:39 It scarcely ever **leaves** [RP608] him and is destroying him.
Ac 13:13 where John **left** [RP608] them to return to Jerusalem.

714 ἀποχωρίζω, *apochōrizō* [2] [√ 608 + 6006]

parted company [+253+608] [1], receded [1]

Ac 15:39 such a sharp disagreement that they **parted** [+253+608] **company**.
Rev 6:14 The sky **receded** like a scroll, rolling up, and every mountain

715 ἀποψύχω, *apopsychō* [1] [√ 608 + 6038]

faint [1]

Lk 21:26 Men *will* **faint** from terror, apprehensive of what is coming on the

716 Ἄππιος, *Appios* [1]

Appius [1]

Ac 28:15 and they traveled as far as the Forum *of* **Appius** and the Three

717 ἀπρόσιτος, *aprositos* [1] [√ 1.1 + 4639 + 1640]

unapproachable [1]

1Ti 6:16 who alone is immortal and who lives in **unapproachable** light,

718 ἀπρόσκοπος, *aproskopos* [3] [√ 1.1 + 4639 + 3164]

blameless [1], clear [1], not cause to stumble [1]

Ac 24:16 So I strive always to keep my conscience **clear** before God
1Co 10:32 Do **not cause** anyone **to stumble**, whether Jews, Greeks
Php 1:10 what is best and may be pure and **blameless** until the day of Christ,

719 ἀπροσωπολήμπτως, *aprosōpolēmptōs* [1]
[√ 1.1 + 4725 + 3284]

impartially [1]

1Pe 1:17 you call on a Father who judges each man's work **impartially**,

720 ἄπταιστος, *aptaistos* [1] [√ 1.1 + 4760]

falling [1]

Jude 1:24 To him who is able to keep you from **falling** and to present you

721 ἅπτω, *haptō* [39] [→ 409, 913, 2750, 4312]

touched [20], touch [10], lights [2], built [1], handle [1], harm [1], hold on to [1], light [1], marry [+1222] [1], touching [1]

Mt   8: 3 Jesus reached out his hand and **touched** the man. "I am willing,"
     8:15 *He* **touched** her hand and the fever left her, and she got up
     9:20 years came up behind him and **touched** the edge of his cloak.
     9:21 She said to herself, "If *I* only **touch** his cloak, I will be healed."
     9:29 Then *he* **touched** their eyes and said, "According to your faith will
   14:36 and begged him to let the sick just **touch** the edge of his cloak,
   14:36 touch the edge of his cloak, and all *who* **touched** him were healed.
   17: 7 But Jesus came and **touched** them. "Get up," he said. "Don't be
   20:34 Jesus had compassion on them and **touched** their eyes.
Mk 1:41 with compassion, Jesus reached out his hand and **touched** the man.
     3:10 so that those with diseases were pushing forward to **touch** him.
     5:27 she came up behind him in the crowd and **touched** his cloak,
     5:28 because she thought, "If *I* just **touch** his clothes, I will be healed."
     5:30 turned around in the crowd and asked, "Who **touched** my clothes?"
     5:31 his disciples answered, "and yet you can ask, 'Who **touched** me?' "
     6:56 They begged him to let *them* **touch** even the edge of his cloak,
     6:56 even the edge of his cloak, and all *who* **touched** him were healed.
     7:33 into the man's ears. Then *he* spit and **touched** the man's tongue.
     8:22 some people brought a blind man and begged Jesus to **touch** him.
   10:13 People were bringing little children to Jesus to *have* him **touch**
Lk   5:13 Jesus reached out his hand and **touched** the man. "I am willing,"
     6:19 and the people all tried *to* **touch** him, because power was coming
     7:14 Then *he* went up and **touched** the coffin, and those carrying it
     7:39 he would know who *is* **touching** him and what kind of woman she
     8:16 "No one **lights** a lamp and hides it in a jar or puts it under a bed.
     8:44 *She* came up behind him and **touched** the edge of his cloak,
     8:45 "Who **touched** me?" Jesus asked. When they all denied it,
     8:46 But Jesus said, "Someone **touched** me; I know that power has gone
     8:47 she told why *she had* **touched** him and how she had been instantly
   11:33 "No one **lights** a lamp and puts it in a place where it will be hidden,
   15: 8 *Does she* not **light** a lamp, sweep the house and search carefully
   18:15 People were also bringing babies to Jesus to *have him* **touch** them.
   22:51 "No more of this!" And he **touched** the man's ear and healed him.
Jn 20:17 Jesus said, "*Do* not **hold on to** me, for I have not yet returned to
Ac 28: 2 They **built** a fire and welcomed us all because it was raining
1Co 7: 1 you wrote about: It is good for a man not *to* **marry** [+1222].
2Co 6:17 from them and be separate, says the Lord. **Touch** no unclean thing,
Col 2:21 "*Do* not **handle**! Do not taste! Do not touch!"?
1Jn 5:18 born of God keeps him safe, and the evil one cannot **harm** him.

722 Ἀπφία, *Apphia* [1]

Apphia [1]

Phm 1: 2 *to* **Apphia** our sister, to Archippus our fellow soldier and to the

723 ἀπωθέω, *apōtheō* [6] [→ 2034; cf. 608]

reject [3], rejected [2], pushed aside [1]

Ac   7:27 "But the man who was mistreating the other **pushed** Moses **aside**
     7:39 *they* **rejected** him and in their hearts turned back to Egypt.
   13:46 Since *you* **reject** it and do not consider yourselves worthy of
Ro 11: 1 I ask then: *Did* God **reject** his people? By no means! I am an
   11: 2 God *did* not **reject** his people, whom he foreknew. Don't you
1Ti 1:19 Some *have* **rejected** these and so have shipwrecked their faith.

724 ἀπώλεια, *apōleia* [18] [√ 608 + 3897]

destruction [10], doomed to destruction [2], destroyed [+1650] [1], destroyed [1], destructive [1], perish [+1639+1650] [1], waste [+1181] [1], waste [1]

Mt   7:13 For wide is the gate and broad is the road that leads to **destruction**,
   26: 8 saw this, they were indignant. "Why this **waste**?" they asked.
Mk 14: 4 indignantly to one another, "Why this **waste** [+1181] of perfume?
Jn 17:12 None has been lost except the one **doomed to destruction**
Ac   8:20 "*May* your money **perish** [+1639+1650] with you, because you
Ro 9:22 great patience the objects of his wrath—prepared for **destruction**?
Php 1:28 This is a sign to them that they will be **destroyed**, but that you will
     3:19 Their destiny is **destruction**, their god is their stomach, and their
2Th 2: 3 man of lawlessness is revealed, the man **doomed to destruction**.
1Ti 6: 9 and harmful desires that plunge men into ruin and **destruction**.

Heb 10:39 we are not of those who shrink back and are **destroyed** [+*1650*],
2Pe 2: 1 They will secretly introduce **destructive** heresies, even denying the
      2: 1 Lord who bought them—bringing swift **destruction** on themselves.
      2: 3 hanging over them, and their **destruction** has not been sleeping.
      3: 7 being kept for the day *of* judgment and **destruction** of ungodly
      3:16 as they do the other Scriptures, to their own **destruction**.
Rev 17: 8 and will come up out of the Abyss and go to his **destruction**.
     17:11 He belongs to the seven and is going to his **destruction**.

725 ἀρά, ara [1] [→ *2063, 2129, 2932, 2933*]

cursing [1]

Ro   3:14 "Their mouths are full *of* **cursing** and bitterness."

726 ἄρα, ara [49]

then [12], *untranslated* [8], so [8], therefore [+*4036*] [5],
consequently [+*4036*] [2], therefore [2], consequently [1], as to
[1], if [+*1623*] [1], if in fact [+*1642*] [1], in that case [+*2075*] [1], in
that case [1], otherwise [+*2075*] [1], perhaps [+*1623*] [1],
perhaps [+*1145+1623*] [1] so then [1], then [+*1145*] [1], thus
[+*1145*] [1]

Mt   7:20 **Thus** [+*1145*], by their fruit you will recognize them.
     12:28 by the Spirit of God, **then** the kingdom of God has come upon you.
     17:26 "**Then** [+*1145*] the sons are exempt," Jesus said to him.
     18: 1 and asked, "Who [NIE] is the greatest in the kingdom of heaven?"
     19:25 they were greatly astonished and asked, "Who **then** can be saved?"
     19:27 have left everything to follow you! What **then** will there be for us?"
     24:45 "Who **then** is the faithful and wise servant, whom the master has
Mk   4:41 They were terrified and asked each other, "Who [NIE] is this?
     11:13 a fig tree in leaf, he went to find out if [+*1623*] it had any fruit.
Lk   1:66 wondered about it, asking, "What **then** is this child going to be?"
      8:25 and amazement they asked one another, "Who [NIE] is this?
     11:20 by the finger of God, **then** the kingdom of God has come to you.
     11:48 **So** you testify that you approve of what your forefathers did;
     12:42 The Lord answered, "Who **then** is the faithful and wise manager,
     22:23 They began to question among themselves which [NIE] of them it
Ac   8:22 **Perhaps** [+*1623*] he will forgive you for having such a thought in
     11:18 they had no further objections and praised God, saying, "**So then,**
     12:18 there was no small commotion among the soldiers **as to** what had
     17:27 and **perhaps** [+*1145+1623*] reach out for him and find him,
     21:38 [NIE] "Aren't you the Egyptian who started a revolt and led four
Ro   5:18 **Consequently** [+*4036*], just as the result of one trespass was
      7: 3 **So then,** if she marries another man while her husband is still alive,
      7:21 **So** I find this law at work: When I want to do good, evil is right
      7:25 **So then,** I myself in my mind am a slave to God's law, but in the
      8: 1 **Therefore,** there is now no condemnation for those who are in
      8:12 **Therefore** [+*4036*], brothers, we have an obligation—but it is not
      9:16 It does not, **therefore** [+*4036*], depend on man's desire or effort,
      9:18 **Therefore** [+*4036*] God has mercy on whom he wants to have
     10:17 **Consequently,** faith comes from hearing the message,
     14:12 **So then,** each of us will give an account of himself to God.
     14:19 **therefore** [+*4036*] make every effort to do what leads to peace
1Co   5:10 **In that case** [+*2075*] you would have to leave this world.
      7:14 **Otherwise** [+*2075*] your children would be unclean, but as it is,
     15:14 been raised, [NIE] our preaching is useless and so is your faith.
     15:15 But he did not raise him **if in fact** [+*1642*] the dead are not raised.
     15:18 **Then** those also who have fallen asleep in Christ are lost.
2Co   1:17 When I planned this, [NIE] did I do it lightly? Or do I make my
      5:14 we are convinced that one died for all, and **therefore** all died.
      7:12 **So** even though I wrote to you, it was not on account of the one
Gal   2:21 could be gained through the law, [NIE] Christ died for nothing!"
      3: 7 Understand, **then,** that those who believe are children of Abraham.
      3:29 If you belong to Christ, **then** you are Abraham's seed, and heirs
      5:11 **In that case** the offense of the cross has been abolished.
      6:10 **Therefore** [+*4036*], as we have opportunity, let us do good to all
Eph   2:19 **Consequently** [+*4036*], you are no longer foreigners and aliens,
1Th   5: 6 **So then,** let us not be like others, who are asleep, but let us be alert
2Th   2:15 **So then,** brothers, stand firm and hold to the teachings we passed
Heb   4: 9 There remains, **then,** a Sabbath-rest for the people of God;
     12: 8 **then** you are illegitimate children and not true sons.

727 ἄρα, ara [3]

untranslated [2], does that mean that [1]

Lk   18: 8 the Son of Man comes, [NIE] will he find faith on the earth?"
Ac   8:30 [NIE] "Do you understand what you are reading?" Philip asked.
Gal   2:17 ourselves are sinners, **does that mean that** Christ promotes sin?

728 Ἀραβία, Arabia [2] [√ *732*]

Arabia [2]

Gal   1:17 but I went immediately into **Arabia** and later returned to
      4:25 Now Hagar stands for Mount Sinai in **Arabia** and corresponds to

729 Ἄραβοι, Araboi Not used in UBS/NIV [√ *732*]

730 Ἀράμ, Aram [2 / 3] [√ *cf. 98, 747, 763, 767*]

Ram [3]

Mt   1: 3 was Tamar, Perez the father of Hezron, Hezron the father of **Ram**,
      1: 4 **Ram** the father of Amminadab, Amminadab the father of Nahshon,
Lk   3:33 the son *of* **Ram**, [UBS *98*] the son of Hezron, the son of Perez,

731 ἄραφος, araphos [1] [√ *1.1 + 4827*]

seamless [1]

Jn   19:23 This garment was **seamless**, woven in one piece from top to

732 Ἄραψ, Araps [1] [→ *728, 729*]

Arabs [1]

Ac   2:11 (both Jews and converts to Judaism); Cretans and **Arabs**—

733 ἀργέω, argeō [1] [√ *1.1 + 2240*]

hanging over [*+4024*] [1]

2Pe   2: 3 Their condemnation *has* long *been* **hanging** [+*4024*] **over** them,

734 ἀργός, argos [8] [√ *1.1 + 2240*]

doing nothing [2], careless [1], idle [1], idlers [1], ineffective [1],
lazy [1], useless [1]

Mt   12:36 on the day of judgment for every **careless** word they have spoken.
     20: 3 and saw others standing in the marketplace **doing nothing**.
     20: 6 'Why have you been standing here all day long **doing nothing**?'
1Ti   5:13 they get into the habit of being **idle** and going about from house to
      5:13 And not only do they become **idlers**, but also gossips
Tit   1:12 has said, "Cretans are always liars, evil brutes, **lazy** gluttons."
Jas   2:20 do you want evidence that faith without deeds is **useless**?
2Pe   1: 8 they will keep you from being **ineffective** and unproductive in

735 ἀργύρεος, argyreos Not used in UBS/NIV [√ *738*]

736 ἀργύριον, argyrion [20] [√ *738*]

money [12], silver [3], silver coins [3], coins [1], drachmas [1]

Mt   25:18 went off, dug a hole in the ground and hid his master's **money**.
     25:27 you should have put my **money** on deposit with the bankers,
     26:15 him over to you?" So they counted out for him thirty **silver coins**.
     27: 3 and returned the thirty **silver coins** to the chief priests
     27: 5 So Judas threw the **money** into the temple and left. Then he went
     27: 6 The chief priests picked up the **coins** and said, "It is against the law
     27: 9 They took the thirty **silver coins**, the price set on him by the people
     28:12 and devised a plan, they gave the soldiers a large sum of **money**,
     28:15 So the soldiers took the **money** and did as they were instructed.
Mk   14:11 They were delighted to hear this and promised to give him **money**.
Lk   9: 3 the journey—no staff, no bag, no bread, no **money**, no extra tunic.
     19:15 Then he sent for the servants to whom he had given the **money**,
     19:23 Why then didn't you put my **money** on deposit,
     22: 5 They were delighted and agreed to give him **money**.
Ac   3: 6 Then Peter said, "**Silver** or gold I do not have, but what I have I
      7:16 from the sons of Hamor at Shechem for a certain sum *of* **money**.

8: 20   "May your **money** perish with you, because you thought you could
19: 19   the value of the scrolls, the total came to fifty thousand **drachmas**.
20: 33   I have not coveted anyone's **silver** or gold or clothing.
1Pe   1: 18   For you know that it was not with perishable things such as **silver**

737 ἀργυροκόπος, *argyrokopos* [1] [√ 738 + 3164]

silversmith [1]

Ac   19: 24   A **silversmith** named Demetrius, who made silver shrines of

738 ἄργυρος, *argyros* [5] [→ 735, 736, 737, 739, 921, 5794, 5795]

silver [5]

Mt   10: 9   Do not take along any gold or **silver** or copper in your belts;
Ac   17: 29   not think that the divine being is like gold or **silver** or stone—
1Co   3: 12   If any man builds on this foundation *using* gold, **silver**,
Jas   5: 3   Your gold and **silver** are corroded. Their corrosion will testify
Rev 18: 12   cargoes of gold, **silver**, precious stones and pearls; fine linen,

739 ἀργυροῦς, *argyrous* [3] [√ 738]

of silver [2], silver [1]

Ac   19: 24   silversmith named Demetrius, who made **silver** shrines of Artemis,
2Ti   2: 20   In a large house there are articles not only **of** gold and **silver**,
Rev   9: 20   and idols **of** gold, **silver**, bronze, stone and wood—

740 Ἄρειος πάγος, *Areios pagos* [2] [√ 4076]

meeting of the Areopagus [2]

Ac   17: 19   they took him and brought him to a **meeting of the Areopagus**,
       17: 22   Paul then stood up in the **meeting of the Areopagus** and said:

741 Ἀρεοπαγίτης, *Areopagitēs* [1] [√ 4076]

member of the Areopagus [1]

Ac   17: 34   Among them was Dionysius, a **member of the Areopagus**,

742 ἀρεσκεία, *areskeia* [1] [√ 743]

please [1]

Col   1: 10   live a life worthy of the Lord and may **please** him in every way:

743 ἀρέσκω, *areskō* [17] [→ 473, 742, 744, 2297, 2298, 2299]

please [10], pleased [3], trying to please [2], displease [+3590] [1], try to please [1]

Mt   14: 6   daughter of Herodias danced for them and **pleased** Herod so much
Mk   6: 22   came in and danced, *she* **pleased** Herod and his dinner guests.
Ac   6: 5   This proposal **pleased** the whole group. They chose Stephen,
Ro   8: 8   Those controlled by the sinful nature cannot **please** God.
       15: 1   bear with the failings of the weak and not *to* **please** ourselves.
       15: 2   Each of us *should* **please** his neighbor for his good, to build him
       15: 3   For even Christ *did* not **please** himself but, as it is written:
1Co   7: 32   concerned about the Lord's affairs—how *he* can **please** the Lord.
        7: 33   about the affairs of this world—how *he* can **please** his wife—
        7: 34   about the affairs of this world—how *she* can **please** her husband.
       10: 33   even as I **try to please** everybody in every way. For I am not
Gal   1: 10   win the approval of men, or of God? Or am I trying *to* **please** men?
        1: 10   If *I were* still **trying to please** men, I would not be a servant of
1Th   2: 4   *We are* not **trying to please** men but God, who tests our hearts.
        2: 15   us out. *They* **displease** [+3590] God and are hostile to all men
        4: 1   brothers, we instructed you how to live in order to **please** God,
2Ti   2: 4   in civilian affairs—he wants *to* **please** his commanding officer.

744 ἀρεστός, *arestos* [4] [√ 743]

pleases [2], pleased [+1639] [1], right [1]

Jn   8: 29   he has not left me alone, for I always do what **pleases** him."
Ac   6: 2   "It would not be **right** for us to neglect the ministry of the word of

12: 3   When he saw that *this* **pleased** [+1639] the Jews, he proceeded to
1Jn   3: 22   because we obey his commands and do what **pleases** him.

745 Ἀρέτας, *Haretas* [1]

Aretas [1]

2Co 11: 32   In Damascus the governor *under* King **Aretas** had the city of the

746 ἀρετή, *aretē* [5]

goodness [3], excellent [1], praises [1]

Php   4: 8   whatever is admirable—if anything is **excellent** or praiseworthy—
1Pe   2: 9   that you may declare the **praises** of him who called you out of
2Pe   1: 3   knowledge of him who called us *by* his own glory and **goodness**.
        1: 5   this very reason, make every effort to add to your faith **goodness**;
        1: 5   effort to add to your faith goodness; and to **goodness**, knowledge;

747 Ἀρηί, *Arēi* Not used in UBS/NIV [√ *cf. 730*]

748 ἀρήν, *arēn* [1] [→ 768]

lambs [1]

Lk   10: 3   Go! I am sending you out like **lambs** among wolves.

749 ἀριθμέω, *arithmeō* [3] [√ 750]

numbered [2], count [1]

Mt   10: 30   And even the very hairs of your head are all **numbered**.
Lk   12: 7   Indeed, the very hairs of your head *are* all **numbered**. Don't be
Rev   7: 9   and there before me was a great multitude that no one could **count**,

750 ἀριθμός, *arithmos* [18] [→ 410, 749, 2935]

number [13], *untranslated* [3], numbering [+1639] [1], numbers [1]

Lk   22: 3   Satan entered Judas, called Iscariot, one of [NIE] the Twelve.
Jn   6: 10   and the men sat down, [NIE] about five thousand of them.
Ac   4: 4   and the **number** of men grew to about five thousand.
        5: 36   be somebody, and about [NIE] four hundred men rallied to him.
        6: 7   The **number** of disciples in Jerusalem increased rapidly, and a
       11: 21   and a great **number** *of people* believed and turned to the Lord.
       16: 5   were strengthened in the faith and grew daily *in* **numbers**.
Ro   9: 27   "Though the **number** of the Israelites be like the sand by the sea,
Rev   5: 11   and heard the voice of many angels, **numbering** [+1639]
        7: 4   Then I heard the **number** of those who were sealed: 144,000 from
        9: 16   mounted troops was two hundred million.
        9: 16   mounted troops was two hundred million. I heard their **number**.
       13: 17   which is the name of the beast or the **number** of his name.
       13: 18   If anyone has insight, let him calculate the **number** of the beast,
       13: 18   let him calculate the **number** of the beast, for it is man's **number**.
       13: 18   number of the beast, for it is man's number. His **number** is 666.
       15: 2   over the beast and his image and over the **number** of his name.
       20: 8   them for battle. *In* **number** they are like the sand on the seashore.

751 Ἀριμαθαία, *Harimathaia* [4]

Arimathea [4]

Mt   27: 57   there came a rich man from **Arimathea**, named Joseph,
Mk   15: 43   Joseph of **Arimathea**, a prominent member of the Council,
Lk   23: 51   He came from the Judean town *of* **Arimathea** and he was waiting
Jn   19: 38   Later, Joseph of **Arimathea** asked Pilate for the body of Jesus.

752 Ἀρίσταρχος, *Aristarchos* [5] [√ 806]

Aristarchus [5]

Ac   19: 29   The people seized Gaius and **Aristarchus**, Paul's traveling
       20: 4   **Aristarchus** and Secundus from Thessalonica, Gaius from Derbe,
       27: 2   **Aristarchus**, a Macedonian from Thessalonica, was with us.
Col   4: 10   My fellow prisoner **Aristarchus** sends you his greetings, as does
Phm   1: 24   And so do Mark, **Aristarchus**, Demas and Luke, my fellow

753 ἀριστάω, *aristaō* [3] [√ *756*]

breakfast [1], eat [1], eating [1]

Lk 11:37 had finished speaking, a Pharisee invited him to **eat** with him;
Jn 21:12 Jesus said to them, "Come and *have* **breakfast**." None of the
     21:15 When *they had finished* **eating**, Jesus said to Simon Peter,

754 ἀριστερός, *aristeros* [4]

left [3], left hand [1]

Mt   6: 3 do not let your **left hand** know what your right hand is doing,
Mk 10:37 one of us sit at your right and the other at your **left** in your glory."
Lk 23:33 along with the criminals—one on his right, the other on his **left**.
2Co 6: 7 with weapons of righteousness in the right hand and *in* the **left**;

755 Ἀριστόβουλος, *Aristoboulos* [1] [√ *1089*]

Aristobulus [1]

Ro 16:10 in Christ. Greet those who belong to the household *of* **Aristobulus**.

756 ἄριστον, *ariston* [3 / 4] [→ *753*]

dinner [1], luncheon [1], meal [1], feast [1]

Mt 22: 4 'Tell those who have been invited that I have prepared my **dinner**:
Lk 11:38 noticing that Jesus did not first wash before the **meal**,
     14:12 "When you give a **luncheon** or dinner, do not invite your friends,
     14:15 "Blessed is the man who will eat at the **feast** [UBS *788*] in the

757 ἀρκετός, *arketos* [3] [√ *758*]

enough [3]

Mt   6:34 will worry about itself. Each day has **enough** trouble of its own.
     10:25 It is **enough** for the student to be like his teacher, and the servant
1Pe 4: 3 For you have spent **enough** time in the past doing what pagans

758 ἀρκέω, *arkeō* [8] [→ *757, 894, 895, 2064*]

content [3], enough [3], satisfied [1], sufficient [1]

Mt 25: 9 they replied, '*there may* not *be* **enough** for both us and you.'
Lk   3:14 and don't accuse people falsely—*be* **content** with your pay."
Jn   6: 7 "Eight months' wages *would* not *buy* **enough** bread for each one to
     14: 8 "Lord, show us the Father and *that will be* **enough** for us."
2Co 12: 9 But he said to me, "My grace *is* **sufficient** for you, for my power is
1Ti 6: 8 But if we have food and clothing, *we will be* **content** with that.
Heb 13: 5 free from the love of money and *be* **content** with what you have,
3Jn 1:10 Not **satisfied** with that, he refuses to welcome the brothers.

759 ἄρκος, *arkos* [1] [→ *760*]

bear [1]

Rev 13: 2 but had feet like those of a **bear** and a mouth like that of a lion.

760 ἄρκτος, *arktos* Not used in UBS/NIV [√ *759*]

761 ἅρμα, *harma* [4] [√ *275*]

chariot [3], chariots [1]

Ac   8:28 and on his way home was sitting in his **chariot** reading the book of
     8:29 The Spirit told Philip, "Go to that **chariot** and stay near it."
     8:38 And he gave orders to stop the **chariot**. Then both Philip
Rev 9: 9 of their wings was like the thundering *of* many horses and **chariots**

762 Ἁρμαγεδών, *Harmagedōn* [1] [√ *cf. 3403*]

Armageddon [1]

Rev 16:16 kings together to the place that in Hebrew is called **Armageddon**.

763 Ἀρμίν, *Armin* Not used in UBS/NIV [√ *cf. 730*]

764 ἁρμόζω, *harmozō* [1] [→ *765, 5274*]

promised [1]

2Co 11: 2 *I* **promised** you to one husband, to Christ, so that I might present

765 ἁρμός, *harmos* [1] [√ *764*]

joints [1]

Heb 4:12 it penetrates even to dividing soul and spirit, **joints** and marrow;

766 ἀρνέομαι, *arneomai* [33] [→ *565*]

denied [10], disown [5], deny [4], denies [3], denying [2], disowned [2], disowns [2], fail [1], refused [1], rejected [1], renounce [1], say no to [1]

Mt 10:33 But whoever **disowns** me before men, I will disown him before my
     10:33 me before men, I *will* **disown** him before my Father in heaven.
     26:70 But he **denied** it before them all. "I don't know what you're talking
     26:72 *He* **denied** it again, with an oath: "I don't know the man!"
Mk 14:68 But he **denied** it. "I don't know or understand what you're talking
     14:70 Again he **denied** it. After a little while, those standing near said to
Lk   8:45 *When they* all **denied** it, Peter said, "Master, the people are
      9:23 he *must* **deny** himself and take up his cross daily and follow me.
     12: 9 But he *who* **disowns** me before men will be disowned before the
     22:57 But he **denied** it. "Woman, I don't know him," he said.
Jn   1:20 did not **fail** to confess, but confessed freely, "I am not the Christ."
     13:38 before the rooster crows, *you will* **disown** me three times!
     18:25 not one of his disciples, are you?" He **denied** it, saying, "I am not."
     18:27 Again Peter **denied** it, and at that moment a rooster began to crow.
Ac   3:13 handed him over to be killed, and *you* **disowned** him before Pilate,
      3:14 You **disowned** the Holy and Righteous One and asked that a
      4:16 they have done an outstanding miracle, and we cannot **deny** it.
      7:35 "This is the same Moses whom *they had* **rejected** with the words,
1Ti 5: 8 he has **denied** the faith and is worse than an unbeliever.
2Ti 2:12 will also reign with him. If *we* **disown** him, he will also disown us;
      2:12 will also reign with him. If we **disown** him, he *will* also disown us;
      2:13 are faithless, he will remain faithful, for he cannot **disown** himself.
      3: 5 having a form of godliness but **denying** its power. Have nothing to
Tit 1:16 They claim to know God, but by their actions *they* **deny** him.
      2:12 It teaches us to **say** "No" **to** ungodliness and worldly passions,
Heb 11:24 grown up, **refused** to be known as the son of Pharaoh's daughter.
2Pe 2: 1 even **denying** the sovereign Lord who bought them—
1Jn 2:22 Who is the liar? It is the *man who* **denies** that Jesus is the Christ.
      2:22 Such a man is the antichrist—he **denies** the Father and the Son.
      2:23 No one *who* **denies** the Son has the Father; whoever acknowledges
Jude 1: 4 for immorality and **deny** Jesus Christ our only Sovereign and Lord.
Rev 2:13 *You did* not **renounce** your faith in me, even in the days of
      3: 8 yet you have kept my word and *have* not **denied** my name.

767 Ἀρνί, *Arni* [1 / 0] [√ *cf. 730*]

Lk   3:33 the son of Amminadab, [UBS+ *the son of Admin, the son of* **Arni**,]

768 ἀρνίον, *arnion* [30] [√ *748*]

lamb [28], lamb's [1], lambs [1]

Jn 21:15 he said, "you know that I love you." Jesus said, "Feed my **lambs**."
Rev 5: 6 Then I saw a **Lamb**, looking as if it had been slain, standing in the
      5: 8 and the twenty-four elders fell down before the **Lamb**.
      5:12 "Worthy is the **Lamb**, who was slain, to receive power and wealth
      5:13 and *to* the **Lamb** be praise and honor and glory and power,
      6: 1 I watched as the **Lamb** opened the first of the seven seals.
      6:16 of him who sits on the throne and from the wrath *of* the **Lamb**!
      7: 9 and language, standing before the throne and in front *of* the **Lamb**.
      7:10 belongs to our God, who sits on the throne, and *to* the **Lamb**."
      7:14 washed their robes and made them white in the blood *of* the **Lamb**.
      7:17 For the **Lamb** at the center of the throne will be their shepherd;
     12:11 They overcame him by the blood *of* the **Lamb** and by the word of
     13: 8 *belonging to* the **Lamb** that was slain from the creation of the
     13:11 He had two horns like a **lamb**, but he spoke like a dragon.
     14: 1 Then I looked, and there before me was the **Lamb**, standing on
     14: 4 kept themselves pure. They follow the **Lamb** wherever he goes.
     14: 4 from among men and offered as firstfruits *to* God and the **Lamb**.
     14:10 burning sulfur in the presence of the holy angels and *of* the **Lamb**.

15: 3 the song of Moses the servant of God and the song *of* the **Lamb**:
17:14 They will make war against the **Lamb**, but the Lamb will
17:14 but the **Lamb** will overcome them because he is Lord of lords
19: 7 For the wedding *of* the **Lamb** has come, and his bride has made
19: 9 are invited to the wedding supper *of* the **Lamb**!' " And he added,
21: 9 to me, "Come, I will show you the bride, the wife *of* the **Lamb**."
21:14 and on them were the names of the twelve apostles *of* the **Lamb**.
21:22 because the Lord God Almighty and the **Lamb** are its temple.
21:23 for the glory of God gives it light, and the **Lamb** is its lamp.
21:27 but only those whose names are written in the **Lamb's** book of life.
22: 1 clear as crystal, flowing from the throne of God and *of* the **Lamb**
22: 3 The throne of God and *of* the **Lamb** will be in the city, and his

769 ἀροτριάω, *arotriaō* [3] [→ 770]

plowing [1], plowman [1], plows [1]

Lk 17: 7 "Suppose one of you had a servant **plowing** or looking after the
1Co 9:10 because when the **plowman** plows and the thresher threshes,
    9:10 because *when* the plowman **plows** and the thresher threshes,

770 ἄροτρον, *arotron* [1] [√ 769]

plow [1]

Lk 9:62 "No one who puts his hand to the **plow** and looks back is fit for

771 ἁρπαγή, *harpagē* [3] [√ 773]

greed [2], confiscation [1]

Mt 23:25 and dish, but inside they are full of **greed** and self-indulgence.
Lk 11:39 and dish, but inside you are full of **greed** and wickedness.
Heb 10:34 in prison and joyfully accepted the **confiscation** of your property,

772 ἁρπαγμός, *harpagmos* [1] [√ 773]

something to be grasped [1]

Php 2: 6 did not consider equality with God **something to be grasped**,

773 ἁρπάζω, *harpazō* [14] [→ 771, 772, 774, 1395, 5275]

caught up [3], snatch [3], attacks [1], carry off [1], force [1], lay hold of [1], snatched up [1], snatches away [1], suddenly took away [1], take by force [1]

Mt 11:12 has been forcefully advancing, and forceful men **lay hold of** it.
    12:29 and **carry off** his possessions unless he first ties up the strong
    13:19 the evil one comes and **snatches away** what was sown in his heart.
Jn   6:15 knowing that they intended to come and make him king by **force**,
    10:12 and runs away. Then the wolf **attacks** the flock and scatters it.
    10:28 they shall never perish; no one *can* **snatch** them out of my hand.
    10:29 greater than all; no one can **snatch** them out of my Father's hand.
Ac   8:39 out of the water, the Spirit of the Lord **suddenly took** Philip **away**,
    23:10 the troops *to* go down and **take** him away from them **by force**
2Co 12: 2 I know a man in Christ *who* fourteen years ago *was* **caught up** to
    12: 4 *was* **caught up** to paradise. He heard inexpressible things,
1Th 4:17 and are left *will be* **caught up** together with them in the clouds to
Jude 1:23 **snatch** others from the fire and save them; to others show mercy,
Rev 12: 5 And her child *was* **snatched up** to God and to his throne.

774 ἅρπαξ, *harpax* [5] [√ 773]

swindlers [2], ferocious [1], robbers [1], swindler [1]

Mt   7:15 to you in sheep's clothing, but inwardly they are **ferocious** wolves.
Lk 18:11 **robbers**, evildoers, adulterers—or even like this tax collector.
1Co 5:10 world who are immoral, or the greedy and **swindlers**, or idolaters.
    5:11 or greedy, an idolater or a slanderer, a drunkard or a **swindler**.
    6:10 nor slanderers nor **swindlers** will inherit the kingdom of God.

775 ἀρραβών, *arrabōn* [3]

deposit guaranteeing what is to come [2], deposit guaranteeing [1]

2Co 1:22 Spirit in our hearts as a **deposit, guaranteeing what is to come**.
    5: 5 given us the Spirit as a **deposit, guaranteeing what is to come**.

Eph 1:14 who is a **deposit guaranteeing** our inheritance until the

776 ἄρρην, *arrēn* Not used in UBS/NIV [√ 781]

777 ἄρρητος, *arrētos* [1] [√ 1.1 + 4839]

inexpressible [1]

2Co 12: 4 He heard **inexpressible** *things*, things that man is not permitted to

778 ἀρρωστέω, *arrōsteō* Not used in UBS/NIV [√ 1.1 + 4874]

779 ἄρρωστος, *arrōstos* [5] [√ 1.1 + 4874]

sick [5]

Mt 14:14 a large crowd, he had compassion on them and healed their **sick**.
Mk   6: 5 except lay his hands on a few **sick** *people* and heal them.
    6:13 and anointed many **sick** *people* with oil and healed them.
    16:18 they will place their hands on **sick** *people*, and they will get well."
1Co 11:30 That is why many among you are weak and **sick**, and a number of

780 ἀρσενοκοίτης, *arsenokoitēs* [2] [√ 781 + 3023]

homosexual offenders [1], perverts [1]

1Co 6: 9 nor adulterers nor male prostitutes nor **homosexual offenders**
1Ti 1:10 *for* adulterers and **perverts**, for slave traders and liars

781 ἄρσην, *arsēn* [9] [→ 776, 780]

male [6], men [3]

Mt 19: 4 "that at the beginning the Creator 'made them **male** and female,'
Mk 10: 6 "But at the beginning of creation God 'made them **male**
Lk   2:23 the Lord, "Every firstborn **male** is to be consecrated to the Lord"),
Ro   1:27 In the same way the **men** also abandoned natural relations with
    1:27 **Men** committed indecent acts with other men, and received in
    1:27 Men committed indecent acts with *other* **men**, and received in
Gal 3:28 There is neither Jew nor Greek, slave nor free, **male** nor female,
Rev 12: 5 She gave birth to a son, a **male** *child*, who will rule all the nations
    12:13 he pursued the woman who had given birth to the **male** *child*.

782 Ἀρτεμᾶς, *Artemas* [1] [√ 783 + 1443]

Artemas [1]

Tit 3:12 As soon as I send **Artemas** or Tychicus to you, do your best to

783 Ἄρτεμις, *Artemis* [5] [→ 782]

Artemis [5]

Ac 19:24 silversmith named Demetrius, who made silver shrines *of* **Artemis**,
    19:27 but also that the temple *of* the great goddess **Artemis** will be
    19:28 and began shouting: "Great is **Artemis** of the Ephesians!"
    19:34 in unison for about two hours: "Great is **Artemis** of the Ephesians!"
    19:35 city of Ephesus is the guardian of the temple *of* the great **Artemis**

784 ἀρτέμων, *artemōn* [1]

foresail [1]

Ac 27:40 Then they hoisted the **foresail** to the wind and made for the beach.

785 ἄρτι, *arti* [36] [→ 566, 567, 568, 786, 787, 1992, 2936, 2937, 2938, 4616]

now [20], now on [3], still [+2401] [3], again [+608] [1], at last [1], at once [1], in the future [+608] [1], just [1], just now [1], now [+608] [1], this moment [1], this very [1], this very day [1]

Mt   3:15 Jesus replied, "Let it be so **now**; it is proper for us to do this to
    9:18 and knelt before him and said, "My daughter has **just** died.
    11:12 From the days of John the Baptist until **now**, the kingdom of
    23:39 For I tell you, you will not see me **again** [+608] until you say,
    26:29 I will not drink of this fruit of the vine from **now on** until that day

26:53 and he will **at once** put at my disposal more than twelve legions of
26:64 "But I say to all of you: **In the future** [+*608*] you will see the Son
Jn   2:10 have had too much to drink; but you have saved the best till **now**."
5:17 said to them, "My Father is always at his work to **this very day**,
9:19 the one you say was born blind? How is it that **now** he can see?"
9:25 I don't know. One thing I do know. I was blind but **now** I see!"
13: 7 Jesus replied, "You do not realize **now** what I am doing, but later
13:19 "I am telling you **now** [+*608*] before it happens, so that when it
13:33 You will look for me, and just as I told the Jews, so I tell you **now**:
13:37 Peter asked, "Lord, why can't I follow you **now**? I will lay down
14: 7 as well. From **now on**, you do know him and have seen him."
16:12 "I have much more to say to you, more than you can **now** bear.
16:24 Until **now** you have not asked for anything in my name. Ask
16:31 "You believe **at last**!" Jesus answered.
1Co   4:11 To **this very** hour we go hungry and thirsty, we are in rags,
4:13 Up to **this moment** we have become the scum of the earth,
8: 7 Some people are **still** [+*2401*] so accustomed to idols that when
13:12 **Now** we see but a poor reflection as in a mirror;
13:12 **Now** I know in part; then I shall know fully, even as I am fully
15: 6 most of whom are **still** [+*2401*] living, though some have fallen
16: 7 I do not want to see you **now** and make only a passing visit;
Gal   1: 9 As we have already said, so **now** I say again: If anybody is
1:10 Am I **now** trying to win the approval of men, or of God? Or am I
4:20 how I wish I could be with you **now** and change my tone,
1Th   3: 6 But Timothy has **just now** come to us from you and has brought
2Th   2: 7 but the one who **now** holds it back will continue to do so till he is
1Pe   1: 6 though **now** for a little while you may have had to suffer grief in
1: 8 and even though you do not see him **now**, you believe in him
1Jn   2: 9 be in the light but hates his brother is **still** [+*2401*] in the darkness.
Rev 12:10 "**Now** have come the salvation and the power and the kingdom of
14:13 Blessed are the dead who die in the Lord from **now on**." "Yes,"

786 ἀρτιγέννητος, *artigennētos* [1] [√ *785* + *1181*]

newborn [1]

1Pe   2: 2 Like **newborn** babies, crave pure spiritual milk, so that by it you

787 ἄρτιος, *artios* [1] [√ *785*]

thoroughly [1]

2Ti   3:17 so that the man of God may be **thoroughly** equipped for every

788 ἄρτος, *artos* [97 / 95]

ὁ ἄρτος ἐκ οὐρανοῦ (bread from heaven) [7] Jn
6:31,32,32,41,50,51,58

λαμβάνω ἄρτος (to take bread) [20] Mt 14:19; 15:26,36; 16:5,7;
26:26; Mk 6:41; 7:27; 8:6,14,14; 14:22; Lk 6:4; 9:16; 22:19; 24:30;
Jn 6:11; 21:13; Ac 27:35; 1Co 11:23

bread [64], loaves [18], food [4], loaf [3], loaves of bread [3],
untranslated [3]

Mt   4: 3 "If you are the Son of God, tell these stones to become **bread**."
4: 4 'Man does not live on **bread** alone, but on every word that comes
6:11 Give us today our daily **bread**.
7: 9 "Which of you, if his son asks for **bread**, will give him a stone?
12: 4 of God, and he and his companions ate the consecrated **bread**—
14:17 "We have here only five **loaves of bread** and two fish," they
14:19 Taking the five **loaves** and the two fish and looking up to heaven,
14:19 and looking up to heaven, he gave thanks and broke the **loaves**.
15: 2 of the elders? They don't wash their hands before they eat!" [NIE]
15:26 "It is not right to take the children's **bread** and toss it to their dogs."
15:33 "Where could we get enough **bread** in this remote place to feed
15:34 "How many **loaves** do you have?" Jesus asked. "Seven," they
15:36 Then he took the seven **loaves** and the fish, and when he had given
16: 5 When they went across the lake, the disciples forgot to take **bread**.
16: 7 and said, "It is because we didn't bring any **bread**."
16: 8 why are you talking among yourselves about having no **bread**?
16: 9 Don't you remember the five **loaves** for the five thousand,
16:10 Or the seven **loaves** for the four thousand, and how many
16:11 it you don't understand that I was not talking to you about **bread**?
16:12 he was not telling them to guard against the yeast *used in* **bread**,
26:26 they were eating, Jesus took **bread**, gave thanks and broke it,

Mk   2:26 he entered the house of God and ate the consecrated **bread**,
3:20 so that he and his disciples were not even able [NIE] to eat.
6: 8 journey except a staff—no **bread**, no bag, no money in your belts.
6:37 Are we to go and spend that much on **bread** and give it to them to
6:38 "How many **loaves** do you have?" he asked. "Go and see."
6:41 Taking the five **loaves** and the two fish and looking up to heaven,
6:41 and looking up to heaven, he gave thanks and broke the **loaves**.
6:44 The number of the men who had eaten [UBS+ *the loaves*]
6:52 for they had not understood about the **loaves**; their hearts were
7: 2 saw some of his disciples eating **food** with hands that were
7: 5 of the elders instead of eating their **food** with 'unclean' hands?"
7:27 "for it is not right to take the children's **bread** and toss it to their
8: 4 "But where in this remote place can anyone get enough **bread** to
8: 5 "How many **loaves** do you have?" Jesus asked. "Seven," they
8: 6 When he had taken the seven **loaves** and given thanks, he broke
8:14 The disciples had forgotten to bring **bread**, except for one loaf
8:14 to bring bread, except for one **loaf** they had with them in the boat.
8:16 this with one another and said, "It is because we have no **bread**."
8:17 Jesus asked them: "Why are you talking about having no **bread**?
8:19 When I broke the five **loaves** for the five thousand, how many
14:22 they were eating, Jesus took **bread**, gave thanks and broke it,
Lk   4: 3 "If you are the Son of God, tell this stone to become **bread**."
4: 4 Jesus answered, "It is written: 'Man does not live on **bread** alone.'
6: 4 He entered the house of God, and taking the consecrated **bread**,
7:33 For John the Baptist came neither eating **bread** nor drinking wine,
9: 3 the journey—no staff, no bag, no **bread**, no money, no extra tunic.
9:13 They answered, "We have only five **loaves of bread** and two fish—
9:16 Taking the five **loaves** and the two fish and looking up to heaven,
11: 3 Give us each day our daily **bread**.
11: 5 him at midnight and says, 'Friend, lend me three **loaves of bread**,
14: 1 when Jesus went to eat [NIE] in the house of a prominent
14:15 "Blessed is the man who will eat at the **feast** [UBS; NIV *756*] in the
15:17 he said, 'How many of my father's hired men have **food** to spare,
22:19 And he took **bread**, gave thanks and broke it, and gave it to them,
24:30 he took **bread**, gave thanks, broke it and began to give it to them.
24:35 and how Jesus was recognized by them when he broke the **bread**.
Jn   6: 5 said to Philip, "Where shall we buy **bread** for these people to eat?"
6: 7 "Eight months' wages would not buy enough **bread** for each one to
6: 9 "Here is a boy with five small barley **loaves** and two small fish,
6:11 Jesus then took the **loaves**, gave thanks, and distributed to those
6:13 and filled twelve baskets with the pieces of the five barley **loaves**
6:23 the people had eaten the **bread** after the Lord had given thanks.
6:26 miraculous signs but because you ate the **loaves** and had your fill.
6:31 as it is written: 'He gave them **bread** from heaven to eat.' "
6:32 it is not Moses who has given you the **bread** from heaven,
6:32 but it is my Father who gives you the true **bread** from heaven.
6:33 For the **bread** of God is he who comes down from heaven
6:34 "Sir," they said, "from now on give us this **bread**."
6:35 Then Jesus declared, "I am the **bread** of life. He who comes to me
6:41 because he said, "I am the **bread** that came down from heaven."
6:48 I am the **bread** of life.
6:50 But here is the **bread** that comes down from heaven, which a man
6:51 I am the living **bread** that came down from heaven. If anyone eats
6:51 If anyone eats of this **bread**, he will live forever. This bread is my
6:51 This **bread** is my flesh, which I will give for the life of the world."
6:58 This is the **bread** that came down from heaven. Your forefathers
6:58 and died, but he who feeds on this **bread** will live forever.'
13:18 'He who shares my **bread** has lifted up his heel against me.'
21: 9 saw a fire of burning coals there with fish on it, and *some* **bread**.
21:13 Jesus came, took the **bread** and gave it to them, and did the same
Ac   2:42 and to the fellowship, to the breaking *of* **bread** and to prayer.
2:46 They broke **bread** in their homes and ate together with glad
20: 7 On the first day of the week we came together to break **bread**.
20:11 Then he went upstairs again and broke **bread** and ate. After talking
27:35 he took *some* **bread** and gave thanks to God in front of them all.
1Co 10:16 And is not the **bread** that we break a participation in the body of
10:17 Because there is one **loaf**, we, who are many, are one body,
10:17 who are many, are one body, for we all partake of the one **loaf**.
11:23 The Lord Jesus, on the night he was betrayed, took **bread**,
11:26 For whenever you eat this **bread** and drink this cup, you proclaim
11:27 whoever eats the **bread** or drinks the cup of the Lord in an
11:28 A man ought to examine himself before he eats of the **bread**
2Co   9:10 and **bread** for food will also supply and increase your store of seed
2Th   3: 8 nor did we eat anyone's **food** without paying for it. On the
3:12 in the Lord Jesus Christ to settle down and earn the **bread** they eat.
Heb   9: 2 room were the lampstand, the table and the consecrated **bread**;

789 ἀρτύω, artyō [3]

made salty [1], make salty [1], seasoned [1]

Mk 9:50 but if it loses its saltiness, how *can you* **make** it **salty** again?
Lk 14:34 but if it loses its saltiness, how *can it be* **made salty** *again*?
Col 4: 6 Let your conversation be always full of grace, **seasoned** with salt,

790 Ἀρφαξάδ, Arphaxad [1]

Arphaxad [1]

Lk 3:36 of Cainan, the son *of* **Arphaxad**, the son of Shem, the son of Noah,

791 ἀρχάγγελος, archangelos [2] [√ 806 + 34]

archangel [2]

1Th 4:16 with the voice *of* the **archangel** and with the trumpet call of God,
Jude 1: 9 But even the **archangel** Michael, when he was disputing with the

792 ἀρχαῖος, archaios [11] [√ 806]

ancient [3], long ago [2], people long ago [2], earliest [1], early [1], old [1], some time ago [+608+2465] [1]

Mt 5:21 "You have heard that it was said *to* the **people long ago**, 'Do not
      5:33 "Again, you have heard that it was said *to* the **people long ago**,
Lk 9: 8 and still others that one of the prophets *of* **long ago** had come back
      9:19 that one of the prophets *of* **long ago** has come back to life."
Ac 15: 7 you know that **some time ago** [+608+2465] God made a choice
      15:21 For Moses has been preached in every city from the **earliest** times
      21:16 He was a man from Cyprus and one of the **early** disciples.
2Co 5:17 he is a new creation; the **old** has gone, the new has come!
2Pe 2: 5 if he did not spare the **ancient** world when he brought the flood on
Rev 12: 9 that **ancient** serpent called the devil, or Satan, who leads the whole
      20: 2 seized the dragon, that **ancient** serpent, who is the devil, or Satan,

793 Ἀρχέλαος, Archelaos [1] [√ 806 + 3295]

Archelaus [1]

Mt 2:22 But when he heard that **Archelaus** was reigning in Judea in place

794 ἀρχή, archē [55 / 56] [√ 806]

beginning [31], first [5], rulers [5], corners [2], power [2], all along [+3836] [1], demons [1], dominion [1], early [1], elementary [1], elementary truths [+3836+5122] [1], it [+201+608+4005] [1], positions of authority [1], powers [1], rule [1], ruler [1]

Mt 19: 4 "that at the **beginning** the Creator 'made them male and female,'
      19: 8 your hearts were hard. But it was not this way from the **beginning**.
      24: 8 All these are the **beginning** of birth pains.
      24:21 unequaled from the **beginning** of the world until now—
Mk 1: 1 The **beginning** of the gospel about Jesus Christ, the Son of God.
      10: 6 "But at the **beginning** of creation God 'made them male
      13: 8 and famines. These are the **beginning** of birth pains.
      13:19 those will be days of distress unequaled from the **beginning**,
Lk 1: 2 just as they were handed down to us by those who from the **first**
      12:11 "When you are brought before synagogues, **rulers** and authorities,
      20:20 so that they might hand him over *to* the **power** and authority of the
Jn 1: 1 In the **beginning** was the Word, and the Word was with God,
      1: 2 He was with God in the **beginning**.
      2:11 This, the **first** of his miraculous signs, Jesus performed at Cana in
      6:64 For Jesus had known from the **beginning** which of them did not
      8:25 "Just what I have been claiming **all along** [+3836]," Jesus replied.
      8:44 He was a murderer from the **beginning**, not holding to the truth,
      15:27 also must testify, for you have been with me from the **beginning**.
      16: 4 I warned you. I did not tell you this at **first** because I was with you.
Ac 10:11 like a large sheet being let down to earth *by* its four **corners**.
      11: 5 like a large sheet being let down from heaven *by* its four **corners**,
      11:15 Holy Spirit came on them as he had come on us at the **beginning**.
      26: 4 from the **beginning** of my life in my own country, and also in
Ro 8:38 neither angels nor **demons**, neither the present nor the future,
1Co 15:24 kingdom to God the Father after he has destroyed all **dominion**,
Eph 1:21 far above all **rule** and authority, power and dominion, and every
      3:10 the manifold wisdom of God should be made known *to* the **rulers**
      6:12 our struggle is not against flesh and blood, but against the **rulers**,

Php 4:15 in the **early** *days* of your acquaintance with the gospel,
Col 1:16 and invisible, whether thrones or powers or **rulers** or authorities;
      1:18 he is the **beginning** and the firstborn from among the dead,
      2:10 fullness in Christ, who is the head *over* every **power** and authority.
      2:15 And having disarmed the **powers** and authorities, he made a public
2Th 2:13 because from the **beginning** [UBS 569] God chose you to be
Tit 3: 1 Remind the people to be subject *to* **rulers** and authorities,
Heb 1:10 He also says, "In the **beginning**, O Lord, you laid the foundations
      2: 3 This salvation, which was **first** announced by the Lord,
      3:14 Christ if we hold firmly till the end the confidence we had at **first**.
      5:12 **elementary truths** [+3836+5122] of God's word all over again.
      6: 1 Therefore let us leave the **elementary** teachings about Christ
      7: 3 without genealogy, without **beginning** of days or end of life,
2Pe 3: 4 everything goes on as it has since the **beginning** of creation."
1Jn 1: 1 That which was from the **beginning**, which we have heard,
      2: 7 but an old one, which you have had since the **beginning**.
      2:13 because you have known him who is from the **beginning**.
      2:14 because you have known him who is from the **beginning**.
      2:24 See that what you have heard from the **beginning** remains in you.
      2:24 If it[s] [+201+608+4005] does, you also will remain in the Son
      3: 8 the devil, because the devil has been sinning from the **beginning**.
      3:11 This is the message you heard from the **beginning**: We should love
2Jn 1: 5 you a new command but one we have had from the **beginning**.
      1: 6 As you have heard from the **beginning**, his command is that you
Jude 1: 6 And the angels who did not keep their **positions of authority**
Rev 3:14 the faithful and true witness, the **ruler** of God's creation.
      21: 6 I am the Alpha and the Omega, the **Beginning** and the End.
      22:13 and the Omega, the First and the Last, the **Beginning** and the End.

795 ἀρχηγός, archēgos [4] [√ 806 + 72]

author [3], Prince [1]

Ac 3:15 You killed the **author** of life, but God raised him from the dead.
      5:31 God exalted him to his own right hand as **Prince** and Savior that he
Heb 2:10 should make the **author** of their salvation perfect through
      12: 2 Let us fix our eyes on Jesus, the **author** and perfecter of our faith,

796 ἀρχιερατικός, archieratikos [1] [√ 806 + 2641]

high priest's [1]

Ac 4: 6 John, Alexander and the other men of the **high priest's** family.

797 ἀρχιερεύς, archiereus [122] [√ 806 + 2641]

οἱ ἀρχιερεῖς καὶ γραμματεῖς (the chief priests and scribes) [22] Mt 2:4; 16:21; 20:18; 21:15; 26:57; Mk 8:31; 10:33; 11:18,27; 14:1,43,53,53; 15:1,31; Lk 9:22; 19:47; 20:1,19; 22:2,66; 23:10

οἱ ἀρχιερεῖς καὶ πρεσβύτεροι (the chief priests and elders) [17] Mt 16:21; 21:23; 26:3,47; 27:1,3,12,20; Mk 8:31; 11:27; 14:43,53; Lk 9:22; 22:52; Ac 4:23; 23:14; 25:15

οἱ ἀρχιερεῖς καὶ Φαρισαῖοι (the chief priests and Pharisees) [7] Mt 21:45; 27:62; Jn 7:32,45; 11:47,57; 18:3

chief priests [64], high priest [51], high priest's [3], high priests [2], chief priest [1], high priesthood [1]

Mt 2: 4 When he had called together all the people's **chief priests**
      16:21 **chief priests** and teachers of the law, and that he must be killed
      20:18 and the Son of Man will be betrayed *to* the **chief priests**
      21:15 But when the **chief priests** and the teachers of the law saw the
      21:23 the **chief priests** and the elders of the people came to him.
      21:45 When the **chief priests** and the Pharisees heard Jesus' parables,
      26: 3 Then the **chief priests** and the elders of the people assembled in
      26: 3 the elders of the people assembled in the palace *of* the **high priest**,
      26:14 the one called Judas Iscariot—went to the **chief priests**
      26:47 and clubs, sent from the **chief priests** and the elders of the people.
      26:51 drew it out and struck the servant *of* the **high priest**, cutting off his
      26:57 the **high priest**, where the teachers of the law and the elders had
      26:58 him at a distance, right up to the courtyard *of* the **high priest**.
      26:59 The **chief priests** and the whole Sanhedrin were looking for false
      26:62 Then the **high priest** stood up and said to Jesus, "Are you not going
      26:63 The **high priest** said to him, "I charge you under oath by the living
      26:65 Then the **high priest** tore his clothes and said, "He has spoken
      27: 1 all the **chief priests** and the elders of the people came to the
      27: 3 and returned the thirty silver coins *to* the **chief priests**

27: 6   The **chief priests** picked up the coins and said, "It is against the law
27:12   When he was accused by the **chief priests** and the elders, he gave
27:20   But the **chief priests** and the elders persuaded the crowd to ask for
27:41   In the same way the **chief priests**, the teachers of the law
27:62   Preparation Day, the **chief priests** and the Pharisees went to Pilate.
28:11   and reported *to* the **chief priests** everything that had happened.
Mk 2:26   In the days of Abiathar the **high priest**, he entered the house of
 8:31   **chief priests** and teachers of the law, and that he must be killed
10:33   "and the Son of Man will be betrayed *to* the **chief priests**
11:18   The **chief priests** and the teachers of the law heard this and began
11:27   the **chief priests**, the teachers of the law and the elders came to
14: 1   and the **chief priests** and the teachers of the law were looking for
14:10   of the Twelve, went to the **chief priests** to betray Jesus to them.
14:43   a crowd armed with swords and clubs, sent from the **chief priests**,
14:47   near drew his sword and struck the servant *of* the **high priest**,
14:53   They took Jesus to the **high priest**, and all the chief priests,
14:53   and all the **chief priests**, elders and teachers of the law came
14:54   him at a distance, right into the courtyard *of* the **high priest**.
14:55   The **chief priests** and the whole Sanhedrin were looking for
14:60   Then the **high priest** stood up before them and asked Jesus,
14:61   Again the **high priest** asked him, "Are you the Christ, the Son of
14:63   The **high priest** tore his clothes. "Why do we need any more
14:66   the courtyard, one of the servant girls *of* the **high priest** came by.
15: 1   the **chief priests**, with the elders, the teachers of the law
15: 3   The **chief priests** accused him of many things.
15:10   knowing it was out of envy that the **chief priests** had handed Jesus
15:11   But the **chief priests** stirred up the crowd to have Pilate release
15:31   In the same way the **chief priests** and the teachers of the law
Lk 3: 2   during the **high priesthood** of Annas and Caiaphas, the word of
 9:22   **chief priests** and teachers of the law, and he must be killed
19:47   But the **chief priests**, the teachers of the law and the leaders among
20: 1   the **chief priests** and the teachers of the law, together with
20:19   and the **chief priests** looked for a way to arrest him immediately,
22: 2   and the **chief priests** and the teachers of the law were looking for
22: 4   And Judas went *to* the **chief priests** and the officers of the temple
22:50   And one of them struck the servant *of* the **high priest**, cutting off
22:52   Then Jesus said to the **chief priests**, the officers of the temple
22:54   they led him away and took him into the house *of* the **high priest**.
22:66   both the **chief priests** and teachers of the law, met together,
23: 4   Then Pilate announced to the **chief priests** and the crowd,
23:10   The **chief priests** and the teachers of the law were standing there,
23:13   Pilate called together the **chief priests**, the rulers and the people,
24:20   The **chief priests** and our rulers handed him over to be sentenced
Jn 7:32   Then the **chief priests** and the Pharisees sent temple guards to
 7:45   Finally the temple guards went back to the **chief priests**
11:47   Then the **chief priests** and the Pharisees called a meeting of the
11:49   named Caiaphas, who was **high priest** that year, spoke up,
11:51   but as **high priest** that year he prophesied that Jesus would die for
11:57   But the **chief priests** and Pharisees had given orders that if anyone
12:10   So the **chief priests** made plans to kill Lazarus as well,
18: 3   of soldiers and some officials from the **chief priests** and Pharisees.
18:10   who had a sword, drew it and struck the **high priest's** servant,
18:13   who was the father-in-law of Caiaphas, the **high priest** that year.
18:15   Because this disciple was known *to* the **high priest**, he went with
18:15   the high priest, he went with Jesus into the **high priest's** courtyard,
18:16   The other disciple, who was known *to* the **high priest**, came back,
18:19   the **high priest** questioned Jesus about his disciples and his
18:22   "Is this the way you answer the **high priest**?" he demanded.
18:24   Then Annas sent him, still bound, to Caiaphas the **high priest**.
18:26   One of the **high priest's** servants, a relative of the man whose ear
18:35   your people and your **chief priests** who handed you over to me.
19: 6   As soon as the **chief priests** and their officials saw him,
19:15   "We have no king but Caesar," the **chief priests** answered.
19:21   The **chief priests** of the Jews protested to Pilate, "Do not write 'The
Ac 4: 6   Annas the **high priest** was there, and so were Caiaphas, John,
 4:23   and reported all that the **chief priests** and elders had said to them.
 5:17   Then the **high priest** and all his associates, who were members of
 5:21   When the **high priest** and his associates arrived, they called
 5:24   the captain of the temple guard and the **chief priests** were puzzled,
 5:27   appear before the Sanhedrin to be questioned by the **high priest**.
 7: 1   Then the **high priest** asked him, "Are these charges true?"
 9: 1   threats against the Lord's disciples. He went to the **high priest**
 9:14   And he has come here with authority from the **chief priests** to
 9:21   hasn't he come here to take them as prisoners to the **chief priests**?"
19:14   Seven sons of Sceva, a Jewish **chief priest**, were doing this.
22: 5   as also the **high priest** and all the Council can testify. I even

22:30   he released him and ordered the **chief priests** and all the Sanhedrin
23: 2   At this the **high priest** Ananias ordered those standing near Paul to
23: 4   standing near Paul said, "You dare to insult God's **high priest**?"
23: 5   Paul replied, "Brothers, I did not realize that he was the **high priest**;
23:14   They went to the **chief priests** and elders and said, "We have taken
24: 1   Five days later the **high priest** Ananias went down to Caesarea
25: 2   where the **chief priests** and Jewish leaders appeared before him
25:15   the **chief priests** and elders of the Jews brought charges against
26:10   On the authority of the **chief priests** I put many of the saints in
26:12   Damascus with the authority and commission *of* the **chief priests**.
Heb 2:17   become a merciful and faithful **high priest** in service to God,
 3: 1   thoughts on Jesus, the apostle and **high priest** whom we confess.
 4:14   since we have a great **high priest** who has gone through the
 4:15   For we do not have a **high priest** who is unable to sympathize with
 5: 1   Every **high priest** is selected from among men and is appointed to
 5: 5   also did not take upon himself the glory of becoming a **high priest**.
 5:10   and was designated by God to be **high priest** in the order of
 6:20   He has become a **high priest** forever, in the order of Melchizedek.
 7:26   Such a **high priest** meets our need—one who is holy, blameless,
 7:27   Unlike the other **high priests**, he does not need to offer sacrifices
 7:28   For the law appoints as **high priests** men who are weak; but the
 8: 1   We do have such a **high priest**, who sat down at the right hand of
 8: 3   Every **high priest** is appointed to offer both gifts and sacrifices,
 9: 7   But only the **high priest** entered the inner room, and that only once
 9:11   When Christ came as **high priest** of the good things that are
 9:25   the way the **high priest** enters the Most Holy Place every year with
13:11   The **high priest** carries the blood of animals into the Most Holy

798 ἀρχιληστής, *archilēstēs*   Not used in UBS/NIV
[√ *806* + *3334*]

799 ἀρχιποίμην, *archipoimēn* [1] [√ *806* + *4478*]

Chief Shepherd [1]

1Pe 5: 4   And when the **Chief Shepherd** appears, you will receive the crown

800 Ἄρχιππος, *Archippos* [2] [√ *806* + *2691*]

Archippus [2]

Col 4:17   Tell **Archippus**: "See to it that you complete the work you have
Phm 1: 2   *to* **Archippus** our fellow soldier and to the church that meets in

801 ἀρχισυνάγωγος, *archisynagōgos* [9]
[√ *806* + *5252*]

synagogue ruler [7], synagogue rulers [2]

Mk 5:22   Then one *of* the **synagogue rulers**, named Jairus, came there.
 5:35   some men came from the house of Jairus, the **synagogue ruler**.
 5:36   what they said, Jesus told the **synagogue ruler**, "Don't be afraid;
 5:38   When they came to the home *of* the **synagogue ruler**, Jesus saw a
Lk 8:49   someone came from the house of Jairus, the **synagogue ruler**.
13:14   the **synagogue ruler** said to the people, "There are six days for
Ac 13:15   the **synagogue rulers** sent word to them, saying, "Brothers,
18: 8   Crispus, the **synagogue ruler**, and his entire household believed in
18:17   Then they all turned on Sosthenes the **synagogue ruler** and beat

802 ἀρχιτέκτων, *architektōn* [1] [√ *806* + *5492*]

builder [1]

1Co 3:10   grace God has given me, I laid a foundation as an expert **builder**,

803 ἀρχιτελώνης, *architelōnēs* [1] [√ *806* + *5467*]

chief tax collector [1]

Lk 19: 2   name of Zacchaeus; he was a **chief tax collector** and was wealthy.

804 ἀρχιτρίκλινος, *architriklinos* [3]
[√ *806* + *5552* + *3111*]

master of the banquet [2], he^s [+*3836*] [1]

Jn 2: 8   "Now draw some out and take it *to* the **master of the banquet**."

2: 9 and the **master of the banquet** tasted the water that had been
2: 9 the water knew. Then he[s] [+3836] called the bridegroom aside

805 ἀρχοστασία, **archostasia** Not used in UBS/NIV

806 ἄρχω, **archō** [86]

[→ 569, 752, 791, 792, 793, 794, 795, 796, 797, 798, 799, 800, 801,
802, 803, 804, 807, 825, 1617, 1672, 1673, 1887, 2065, 2066, 2067,
4256, 4272, 4485, 4599, 4732, 5134, 5135, 5489, 5490, 5638, 5639,
5941]

began [52], beginning [7], will [5], said [+3306] [4], begin [3],
begins [2], became [+160] [1], carried [+4367] [1],
first [1], late in afternoon [+2465+3111] [1], presented case
[+2989] [1], rule over [1], rulers [1], saddened [+3382] [1], sent
out [+690] [1], started [1], told [+3306] [1], went on [1]

Mt 4:17 From that time on Jesus **began** to preach, "Repent, for the kingdom
11: 7 were leaving, Jesus **began** to speak to the crowd about John:
11:20 Then Jesus **began** to denounce the cities in which most of his
12: 1 were hungry and **began** to pick some heads of grain and eat them.
14:30 he was afraid and, **beginning** to sink, cried out, "Lord, save me!"
16:21 From that time on Jesus **began** to explain to his disciples that he
16:22 Peter took him aside and **began** to rebuke him. "Never, Lord!"
18:24 *As* he **began** the settlement, a man who owed him ten thousand
20: 8 **beginning** with the last ones hired and going on to the first.'
24:49 and *he* then **begins** to beat his fellow servants and to eat and drink
26:22 *They* were very sad and **began** to say to him one after the other,
26:37 along with him, and *he* **began** to be sorrowful and troubled.
26:74 Then *he* **began** to call down curses on himself and he swore to
Mk 1:45 Instead *he* went out and **began** to talk freely, spreading the news.
2:23 disciples walked along, *they* **began** to pick some heads of grain.
4: 1 Again Jesus **began** to teach by the lake. The crowd that gathered
5:17 Then the *people* **began** to plead with Jesus to leave their region.
5:20 and **began** to tell in the Decapolis how much Jesus had done for
6: 2 When the Sabbath came, *he* **began** to teach in the synagogue,
6: 7 Calling the Twelve to him, he **sent** them **out** [+690] two by two
6:34 without a shepherd. So *he* **began** teaching them many things.
6:55 and **carried** [+4367] the sick on mats to wherever they heard he
8:11 The Pharisees came and **began** to question Jesus. To test him,
8:31 *He* then **began** to teach them that the Son of Man must suffer
8:32 about this, and Peter took him aside and **began** to rebuke him.
10:28 Peter **said** [+3306] to him, "We have left everything to follow
10:32 Again he took the Twelve aside and **told** [+3306] them what was
10:41 ten heard about this, *they* **became** indignant with James and John.
10:42 "You know that those who are regarded as **rulers** of the Gentiles
10:47 *he* **began** to shout, "Jesus, Son of David, have mercy on me!"
11:15 and **began** driving out those who were buying and selling there.
12: 1 *He* then **began** to speak to them in parables: "A man planted a
13: 5 Jesus **said** [+3306] to them: "Watch out that no one deceives you.
14:19 *They* were **saddened** [+3382], and one by one they said to him,
14:33 along with him, and *he* **began** to be deeply distressed and troubled.
14:65 Then some **began** to spit at him; they blindfolded him, struck him
14:69 he **said** [+3306] again to those standing around, "This fellow is
14:71 He **began** to call down curses on himself, and he swore to them,
15: 8 and **asked** [+160] Pilate to do for them what he usually did.
15:18 And *they* **began** to call out to him, "Hail, king of the Jews!"
Lk 3: 8 And *do not* **begin** to say to yourselves, 'We have Abraham as our
3:23 Now Jesus himself was about thirty years old *when he* **began** his
4:21 and *he* **began** by saying to them, "Today this scripture is fulfilled in
5:21 and the teachers of the law **began** thinking to themselves,
7:15 The dead man sat up and **began** to talk, and Jesus gave him back to
7:24 messengers left, Jesus **began** to speak to the crowd about John:
7:38 him at his feet weeping, *she* **began** to wet his feet with her tears.
7:49 The other guests **began** to say among themselves, "Who is this who
9:12 **Late in the afternoon** [+2465+3111] the Twelve came to him and
11:29 As the crowds increased, Jesus **said** [+3306], "This is a wicked
11:53 and the teachers of the law **began** to oppose him fiercely
12: 1 one another, Jesus **began** to speak first to his disciples, saying:
12:45 and *he* then **begins** to beat the menservants and maidservants
13:25 closes the door, *you* **will** stand outside knocking and pleading, 'Sir,
13:26 "Then *you* **will** say, 'We ate and drank with you, and you taught in
14: 9 humiliated, *you* **will** have to take the least important place.
14:18 "But *they* all alike **began** to make excuses. The first said, 'I have
14:29 and is not able to finish it, everyone who sees it **will** ridicule him,

14:30 saying, 'This fellow **began** to build and was not able to finish.'
15:14 a severe famine in that whole country, and he **began** to be in need.
15:24 alive again; he was lost and is found.' So *they* **began** to celebrate.
19:37 the whole crowd of disciples **began** joyfully to praise God in loud
19:45 the temple area and **began** driving out those who were selling.
20: 9 He **went on** to tell the people this parable: "A man planted a
21:28 *When* these things **begin** to take place, stand up and lift up your
22:23 They **began** to question among themselves which of them it might
23: 2 And *they* **began** to accuse him, saying, "We have found this man
23: 5 his teaching. He **started** in Galilee and has come all the way here."
23:30 Then " '*they* **will** say to the mountains, "Fall on us!" and to the
24:27 And **beginning** with Moses and all the Prophets, he explained to
24:47 be preached in his name to all nations, **beginning** at Jerusalem.
Jn 8: 9 the older ones **first**, until only Jesus was left, with the woman still
13: 5 he poured water into a basin and **began** to wash his disciples' feet,
Ac 1: 1 Theophilus, I wrote about all that Jesus **began** to do and to teach
1:22 **beginning** from John's baptism to the time when Jesus was taken
2: 4 and **began** to speak in other tongues as the Spirit enabled them.
8:35 Then Philip **began** with that very passage of Scripture and told him
10:37 **beginning** in Galilee after the baptism that John preached—
11: 4 Peter **began** and explained everything to them precisely as it had
11:15 "As I **began** to speak, the Holy Spirit came on them as he had come
18:26 He **began** to speak boldly in the synagogue. When Priscilla
24: 2 was called in, Tertullus **presented** his **case** [+2989] before Felix:
27:35 to God in front of them all. Then *he* broke it and **began** to eat.
Ro 15:12 of Jesse will spring up, one who will arise *to* **rule over** the nations;
2Co 3: 1 *Are we* **beginning** to commend ourselves again? Or do we need,
1Pe 4:17 For it is time for judgment *to* **begin** with the family of God;

807 ἄρχων, **archōn** [37] [√ 806]

rulers [12], ruler [9], prince [7], leaders [3], authorities [2],
magistrate [1], prominent [1], ruler's [1], ruling council [1]

Mt 9:18 he was saying this, a **ruler** came and knelt before him and said,
9:23 When Jesus entered the **ruler's** house and saw the flute players
9:34 "It is by the **prince** of demons that he drives out demons."
12:24 they said, "It is only by Beelzebub, the **prince** of demons,
20:25 "You know that the **rulers** of the Gentiles lord it over them,
Mk 3:22 by Beelzebub! By the **prince** of demons he is driving out demons."
Lk 8:41 named Jairus, a **ruler** of the synagogue, came and fell at Jesus' feet,
11:15 But some of them said, "By Beelzebub, the **prince** of demons,
12:58 As you are going with your adversary to the **magistrate**, try hard
14: 1 when Jesus went to eat in the house of a **prominent** Pharisee,
18:18 A certain **ruler** asked him, "Good teacher, what must I do to inherit
23:13 Pilate called together the chief priests, the **rulers** and the people,
23:35 The people stood watching, and the **rulers** even sneered at him.
24:20 and our **rulers** handed him over to be sentenced to death,
Jn 3: 1 named Nicodemus, a *member of* the Jewish **ruling council**.
7:26 Have the **authorities** really concluded that he is the Christ?
7:48 "Has any of the **rulers** or of the Pharisees believed in him?
12:31 on this world; now the **prince** of this world will be driven out.
12:42 Yet at the same time many even among the **leaders** believed in
14:30 with you much longer, for the **prince** of this world is coming.
16:11 because the **prince** of this world now stands condemned.
Ac 3:17 brothers, I know that you acted in ignorance, as did your **leaders**.
4: 5 The next day the **rulers**, elders and teachers of the law met in
4: 8 the Holy Spirit, said to them: "**Rulers** and elders of the people!
4:26 and the **rulers** gather together against the Lord and against his
7:27 Moses aside and said, 'Who made you **ruler** and judge over us?
7:35 had rejected with the words, 'Who made you **ruler** and judge?'
7:35 He was sent *to be* their **ruler** and deliverer by God himself,
13:27 The people of Jerusalem and their **rulers** did not recognize Jesus,
14: 5 afoot among the Gentiles and Jews, together with their **leaders**,
16:19 and dragged them into the marketplace to face the **authorities**.
23: 5 it is written: 'Do not speak evil about the **ruler** of your people.' "
Ro 13: 3 For **rulers** hold no terror for those who do right, but for those who
1Co 2: 6 but not the wisdom of this age or *of* the **rulers** of this age,
2: 8 None *of* the **rulers** of this age understood it, for if they had,
Eph 2: 2 the ways of this world and of the **ruler** of the kingdom of the air,
Rev 1: 5 the firstborn from the dead, and the **ruler** of the kings of the earth.

808 ἄρωμα, **arōma** [4]

spices [4]

Mk 16: 1 and Salome bought **spices** so that they might go to anoint Jesus'

Lk 23:56 Then they went home and prepared **spices** and perfumes. But they
24: 1 the women took the **spices** they had prepared and went to the tomb.
Jn 19:40 the two of them wrapped it, with the **spices**, in strips of linen.

809 Ἀσά, *Asa* [0 / 2] [√ cf. 811]

Asa [2]

Mt 1: 7 the father of Abijah, Abijah the father of **Asa**, [UBS *811*]
1: 8 **Asa** [UBS *811*] the father of Jehoshaphat, Jehoshaphat the father

810 ἀσάλευτος, *asaleutos* [2] [√ 1.1 + 4888]

cannot be shaken [1], not move [+3531] [1]

Ac 27:41 and ran aground. The bow stuck fast and *would* **not move** [+3531],
Heb 12:28 since we are receiving a kingdom that **cannot be shaken**,

811 Ἀσάφ, *Asaph* [2 / 0] [√ cf. 809]

Mt 1: 7 father of Abijah, Abijah the father of Asa, [UBS *Asaph*; NIV *809*]
1: 8 Asa [UBS *Asaph*; NIV *809*] the father of Jehoshaphat,

812 ἄσβεστος, *asbestos* [3] [√ 1.1 + 4931]

unquenchable [2], never goes out [1]

Mt 3:12 into the barn and burning up the chaff *with* **unquenchable** fire."
Mk 9:43 than with two hands to go into hell, where the fire **never goes out**.
Lk 3:17 his barn, but he will burn up the chaff *with* **unquenchable** fire."

813 ἀσέβεια, *asebeia* [6] [√ 1.1 + 4936]

ungodly [3], godlessness [2], ungodliness [1]

Ro 1:18 of God is being revealed from heaven against all the **godlessness**
11:26 will come from Zion; he will turn **godlessness** away from Jacob.
2Ti 2:16 those who indulge in it will become more and more **ungodly**.
Tit 2:12 It teaches us to say "No" to **ungodliness** and worldly passions,
Jude 1:15 and to convict all the ungodly of all the **ungodly** acts they have
1:18 there will be scoffers who will follow their own **ungodly** desires."

814 ἀσεβέω, *asebeō* [1] [√ 1.1 + 4936]

done in ungodly way [1]

Jude 1:15 of all the ungodly acts *they have* **done in** the **ungodly way**,

815 ἀσεβής, *asebēs* [9 / 10] [√ 1.1 + 4936]

ungodly [8], godless [1], wicked [1]

Ro 4: 5 man who does not work but trusts God who justifies the **wicked**,
5: 6 when we were still powerless, Christ died for the **ungodly**.
1Ti 1: 9 but *for* lawbreakers and rebels, the **ungodly** and sinful,
1Pe 4:18 to be saved, what will become of the **ungodly** and the sinner?'
2Pe 2: 5 ancient world when he brought the flood on its **ungodly** people,
2: 6 made them an example of what is going to happen to the **ungodly**;
3: 7 kept for the day of judgment and destruction *of* **ungodly** men.
Jude 1: 4 They are **godless** *men*, who change the grace of our God into a
1:15 and to convict all the **ungodly** [UBS-] of all the ungodly acts they
1:15 and of all the harsh words **ungodly** sinners have spoken against

816 ἀσέλγεια, *aselgeia* [10] [√ 1.1]

debauchery [4], filthy [1], lewdness [1], license for immorality [1], lustful desires [+2123] [1], sensuality [1], shameful [1]

Mk 7:22 greed, malice, deceit, **lewdness**, envy, slander, arrogance and folly.
Ro 13:13 not in sexual immorality and **debauchery**, not in dissension
2Co 12:21 sexual sin and **debauchery** in which they have indulged.
Gal 5:19 nature are obvious: sexual immorality, impurity and **debauchery**;
Eph 4:19 they have given themselves over *to* **sensuality** so as to indulge in
1Pe 4: 3 living in **debauchery**, lust, drunkenness, orgies, carousing
2Pe 2: 2 Many will follow their **shameful** *ways* and will bring the way of
2: 7 who was distressed by the **filthy** lives of lawless men
2:18 to the **lustful desires** [+2123] of sinful human nature, they entice
Jude 1: 4 who change the grace of our God into a **license for immorality**

817 ἄσημος, *asēmos* [1] [√ 1.1 + 4956]

ordinary [1]

Ac 21:39 "I am a Jew, from Tarsus in Cilicia, a citizen of no **ordinary** city."

818 Ἀσήρ, *Asēr* [2]

Asher [2]

Lk 2:36 a prophetess, Anna, the daughter of Phanuel, of the tribe *of* **Asher**.
Rev 7: 6 from the tribe *of* **Asher** 12,000, from the tribe of Naphtali 12,000,

819 ἀσθένεια, *astheneia* [24] [√ 1.1 + 4964]

weakness [8], weaknesses [4], weak [2], crippled [+2400] [1], diseases [1], illness [+3836+4922] [1], illnesses [1], infirmities [1], infirmity [1], invalid [+1877+2400+3836] [1], sick [+2400] [1], sickness [1], sicknesses [1]

Mt 8:17 Isaiah: "He took up our **infirmities** and carried our diseases."
Lk 5:15 of people came to hear him and to be healed of their **sicknesses**.
8: 2 also some women who had been cured of evil spirits and **diseases**:
13:11 and a woman there *who had been* **crippled** [+2400] *by* a
13:12 and said to her, "Woman, you are set free *from* your **infirmity**."
Jn 5: 5 *had been an* **invalid** [+1877+2400+3836] for thirty-eight years.
11: 4 he heard this, Jesus said, "This **sickness** will not end in death.
Ac 28: 9 the rest of the **sick** [+2400] on the island came and were cured.
Ro 6:19 this in human terms because you are **weak** in your natural selves.
8:26 In the same way, the Spirit helps us *in* our **weakness**. We do not
1Co 2: 3 I came to you in **weakness** and fear, and with much trembling.
15:43 it is raised in glory; it is sown in **weakness**, it is raised in power;
2Co 11:30 If I must boast, I will boast of the things that *show* my **weakness**.
12: 5 but I will not boast about myself, except about my **weaknesses**.
12: 9 is sufficient for you, for my power is made perfect in **weakness**."
12: 9 Therefore I will boast all the more gladly about my **weaknesses**,
12:10 I delight in **weaknesses**, in insults, in hardships, in persecutions,
13: 4 For to be sure, he was crucified in **weakness**, yet he lives by God's
Gal 4:13 because of an **illness** [+3836+4922] that I first preached the gospel
1Ti 5:23 a little wine *because* of your stomach and your frequent **illnesses**.
Heb 4:15 a high priest who is unable to sympathize with our **weaknesses**,
5: 2 and are going astray, since he himself is subject to **weakness**.
7:28 For the law appoints as high priests men who are **weak**; but the
11:34 the edge of the sword; whose **weakness** was turned to strength;

820 ἀσθενέω, *astheneō* [33] [√ 1.1 + 4964]

sick [12], weak [11], ill [2], lay sick [2], disabled [1], feel weak [1], invalid [1], sickness [+3798] [1], weakened [1], weakening [1]

Mt 10: 8 Heal the **sick**, raise the dead, cleanse those who have leprosy,
25:36 *I was* **sick** and you looked after me, I was in prison and you came
25:39 When did we see you **sick** or in prison and go to visit you?'
Mk 6:56 towns or countryside—they placed the **sick** in the marketplaces.
Lk 4:40 brought to Jesus all who had various kinds *of* **sickness** [+3798],
Jn 4:46 And there was a certain royal official whose son **lay sick** at
5: 3 Here a great number *of* **disabled** *people* used to lie—the blind,
5: 7 "Sir," the **invalid** replied, "I have no one to help me into the pool
6: 2 they saw the miraculous signs he had performed on the **sick**.
11: 1 Now a man named Lazarus was **sick**. He was from Bethany,
11: 2 This Mary, whose brother Lazarus *now* **lay sick**, was the same one
11: 3 So the sisters sent word to Jesus, "Lord, the one you love *is* **sick**."
11: 6 Yet when he heard that Lazarus *was* **sick**, he stayed where he was
Ac 9:37 About that time she *became* **sick** and died, and her body was
19:12 and aprons that had touched him were taken to the **sick**,
20:35 showed you that by this kind of hard work we must help the **weak**,
Ro 4:19 Without **weakening** in his faith, he faced the fact that his body was
8: 3 For what the law was powerless to do in that *it was* **weakened** by
14: 1 Accept him whose faith *is* **weak**, without passing judgment on
14: 2 but another man, whose faith *is* **weak**, eats only vegetables.
1Co 8:11 So this **weak** brother, for whom Christ died, is destroyed by your
8:12 your brothers in this way and wound their **weak** conscience,
2Co 11:21 To my shame I admit that we *were too* **weak** for that! What
11:29 Who *is* **weak**, and I do not feel weak? Who is led into sin,
11:29 Who is weak, and *I do* not **feel weak**? Who is led into sin,
12:10 in difficulties. For when *I am* **weak**, then I am strong.
13: 3 He *is* not **weak** in dealing with you, but is powerful among you.
13: 4 Likewise, we *are* **weak** in him, yet by God's power we will live

13: 9 We are glad whenever we *are* **weak** but you are strong; and our
Php 2:26 longs for all of you and is distressed because you heard *he was* **ill**.
2:27 Indeed *he was* **ill**, and almost died. But God had mercy on him,
2Ti 4:20 Erastus stayed in Corinth, and I left Trophimus **sick** in Miletus.
Jas 5:14 *Is* any one of you **sick**? He should call the elders of the church to

821 ἀσθένημα, asthenēma [1] [√ 1.1 + 4964]

failings [1]

Ro 15: 1 We who are strong ought to bear with the **failings** of the weak

822 ἀσθενής, asthenēs [26] [√ 1.1 + 4964]

weak [14], sick [6], weaker [2], cripple [+476] [1], powerless [1],
unimpressive [1], weakness [1]

Mt 25:43 clothe me, I was **sick** and in prison and you did not look after me.'
25:44 or thirsty or a stranger or needing clothes or **sick** or in prison,
26:41 not fall into temptation. The spirit is willing, but the body is **weak**."
Mk 14:38 not fall into temptation. The spirit is willing, but the body is **weak**."
Lk 9: 2 sent them out to preach the kingdom of God and to heal the **sick**.
10: 9 Heal the **sick** who are there and tell them, 'The kingdom of God is
Ac 4: 9 to account today for an act of kindness shown to a **cripple** [+476]
5:15 people brought the **sick** into the streets and laid them on beds
5:16 bringing their **sick** and those tormented by evil spirits, and all of
Ro 5: 6 You see, at just the right time, when we were still **powerless**,
1Co 1:25 and the **weakness** of God is stronger than man's strength.
1:27 God chose the **weak** *things* of the world to shame the strong.
4:10 We are **weak**, but you are strong! You are honored, we are
8: 7 to an idol, and since their conscience is **weak**, it is defiled.
8: 9 of your freedom does not become a stumbling block *to* the **weak**.
8:10 For if anyone with a **weak** conscience sees you who have this
9:22 *To* the **weak** I became weak, to win the weak. I have become all
9:22 To the weak I became **weak**, to win the weak. I have become all
9:22 To the weak I became weak, to win the **weak**. I have become all
11:30 That is why many among you are **weak** and sick, and a number of
12:22 those parts of the body that seem to be **weaker** are indispensable,
2Co 10:10 but in person he is **unimpressive** and his speaking amounts to
Gal 4: 9 how is it that you are turning back to those **weak** and miserable
1Th 5:14 warn those who are idle, encourage the timid, help the **weak**,
Heb 7:18 The former regulation is set aside because it was **weak** and useless
1Pe 3: 7 and treat them with respect as the **weaker** partner and as heirs with

823 Ἀσία, Asia [18] [→ 824, 825]

province of Asia [15], Asia [3]

Ac 2: 9 of Mesopotamia, Judea and Cappadocia, Pontus and **Asia**,
6: 9 and Alexandria as well as the provinces of Cilicia and **Asia**.
16: 6 the Holy Spirit from preaching the word in the **province of Asia**.
19:10 and Greeks who lived in the **province of Asia** heard the word of
19:22 while he stayed in the **province of Asia** a little longer.
19:26 here in Ephesus and *in* practically the whole **province of Asia**.
19:27 who is worshiped throughout the **province of Asia** and the world,
20:16 sail past Ephesus to avoid spending time in the **province of Asia**,
20:18 was with you, from the first day I came into the **province of Asia**.
21:27 some Jews from the **province of Asia** saw Paul at the temple.
24:19 But there are some Jews from the **province of Asia**, who ought to
27: 2 about to sail for ports along the coast of the **province of Asia**.
Ro 16: 5 who was the first convert to Christ *in* the **province of Asia**.
1Co 16:19 The churches *in* the **province of Asia** send you greetings.
2Co 1: 8 brothers, about the hardships we suffered in the **province of Asia**.
2Ti 1:15 You know that everyone in the **province of Asia** has deserted me,
1Pe 1: 1 throughout Pontus, Galatia, Cappadocia, **Asia** and Bithynia,
Rev 1: 4 John, To the seven churches in the **province of Asia**: Grace

824 Ἀσιανός, Asianos [1] [√ 823]

from the province of Asia [1]

Ac 20: 4 and Tychicus and Trophimus **from the province of Asia**.

825 Ἀσιάρχης, Asiarchēs [1] [√ 823 + 806]

officials of the province [1]

Ac 19:31 Even some *of* the **officials of the province**, friends of Paul,

826 ἀσιτία, asitia [1] [√ 1.1 + 4992]

without food [1]

Ac 27:21 After the men had gone a long time **without food**, Paul stood up

827 ἄσιτος, asitos [1] [√ 1.1 + 4992]

gone without food [1]

Ac 27:33 "you have been in constant suspense and have **gone without food**—

828 ἀσκέω, askeō [1]

strive [1]

Ac 24:16 So I **strive** always to keep my conscience clear before God

829 ἀσκός, askos [12]

wineskins [9], skins [3]

Mt 9:17 Neither do men pour new wine into old **wineskins**. If they do,
9:17 If they do, the **skins** will burst, the wine will run out
9:17 will burst, the wine will run out and the **wineskins** will be ruined.
9:17 No, they pour new wine into new **wineskins**, and both are
Mk 2:22 And no one pours new wine into old **wineskins**. If he does,
2:22 If he does, the wine will burst the **skins**, and both the wine
2:22 the skins, and both the wine and the **wineskins** will be ruined.
2:22 will be ruined. No, he pours new wine into new **wineskins**."
Lk 5:37 And no one pours new wine into old **wineskins**. If he does,
5:37 If he does, the new wine will burst the **skins**, the wine will run out
5:37 the skins, the wine will run out and the **wineskins** will be ruined.
5:38 No, new wine must be poured into new **wineskins**.

830 ἀσμένως, asmenōs [1] [√ 2454]

warmly [1]

Ac 21:17 When we arrived at Jerusalem, the brothers received us **warmly**.

831 ἄσοφος, asophos [1] [√ 1.1 + 5055]

unwise [1]

Eph 5:15 Be very careful, then, how you live—not as **unwise** but as wise,

832 ἀσπάζομαι, aspazomai [59] [→ 571, 833]

greet [30], send greetings [11], sends greetings [6], greeted [4],
give greetings to [1], call out to [1], give greeting [1], greets [1],
pay respects to [1], said good-by [1], sends greetings to [1],
welcomed [1]

Mt 5:47 And if *you* **greet** only your brothers, what are you doing more than
10:12 As you enter the home, **give** it *your* **greeting**.
Mk 9:15 they were overwhelmed with wonder and ran *to* **greet** him.
15:18 And they began *to* **call out to** him, "Hail, king of the Jews!"
Lk 1:40 where she entered Zechariah's home and **greeted** Elizabeth.
10: 4 a purse or bag or sandals; and *do* not **greet** anyone on the road.
Ac 18:22 he went up and **greeted** the church and then went down to Antioch.
20: 1 after encouraging them, **said good-by** and set out for Macedonia.
21: 7 where *we* **greeted** the brothers and stayed with them for a day.
21:19 Paul **greeted** them and reported in detail what God had done
25:13 and Bernice arrived at Caesarea *to* **pay** *their* **respects to** Festus.
Ro 16: 3 **Greet** Priscilla and Aquila, my fellow workers in Christ Jesus.
16: 5 **Greet** my dear friend Epenetus, who was the first convert to Christ
16: 6 **Greet** Mary, who worked very hard for you.
16: 7 **Greet** Andronicus and Junias, my relatives who have been in
16: 8 **Greet** Ampliatus, whom I love in the Lord.
16: 9 **Greet** Urbanus, our fellow worker in Christ, and my dear friend
16:10 **Greet** Apelles, tested and approved in Christ. Greet those who
16:10 in Christ. **Greet** those who belong to the household of Aristobulus.
16:11 **Greet** Herodion, my relative. Greet those in the household of
16:11 **Greet** those in the household of Narcissus who are in the Lord.
16:12 **Greet** Tryphena and Tryphosa, those women who work hard in the
16:12 **Greet** my dear friend Persis, another woman who has worked very
16:13 **Greet** Rufus, chosen in the Lord, and his mother, who has been a
16:14 **Greet** Asyncritus, Phlegon, Hermes, Patrobas, Hermas

16: 15 **Greet** Philologus, Julia, Nereus and his sister, and Olympas
16: 16 **Greet** one another with a holy kiss. All the churches of Christ send
16: 16 another with a holy kiss. All the churches of Christ **send greetings**.
16: 21 **sends** *his* **greetings to** you, as *do* Lucius, Jason and Sosipater,
16: 22 Tertius, who wrote down this letter, **greet** you in the Lord.
16: 23 and the whole church here enjoy, **sends** you *his* **greetings**.
16: 23 of public works, and our brother Quartus **send** you *their* **greetings**.
1Co 16: 19 The churches in the province of Asia **send** you **greetings**.
16: 19 Aquila and Priscilla **greet** you warmly in the Lord, and so does the
16: 20 All the brothers here **send** you **greetings**. Greet one another with a
16: 20 here send you greetings. **Greet** one another with a holy kiss.
2Co 13: 12 **Greet** one another with a holy kiss.
13: 13 All the saints **send** *their* **greetings**.
Php 4: 21 **Greet** all the saints in Christ Jesus. The brothers who are with me
4: 21 in Christ Jesus. The brothers who are with me **send greetings**.
4: 22 All the saints **send** you **greetings**, especially those who belong to
Col 4: 10 My fellow prisoner Aristarchus **sends** you *his* **greetings**, as does
4: 12 who is one of you and a servant of Christ Jesus, **sends greetings**.
4: 14 Our dear friend Luke, the doctor, and Demas **send greetings**.
4: 15 **Give** my **greetings to** the brothers at Laodicea, and to Nympha
1Th 5: 26 **Greet** all the brothers with a holy kiss.
2Ti 4: 19 **Greet** Priscilla and Aquila and the household of Onesiphorus.
4: 21 Eubulus **greets** you, and so do Pudens, Linus, Claudia and all the
Tit 3: 15 Everyone with me **sends** you **greetings**. Greet those who love us in
3: 15 **Greet** those who love us in the faith. Grace be with you all.
Phm 1: 23 Epaphras, my fellow prisoner in Christ Jesus, **sends** you **greetings**.
Heb 11: 13 *they* only saw them and **welcomed** them from a distance.
13: 24 **Greet** all your leaders and all God's people. Those from Italy send
13: 24 and all God's people. Those from Italy **send** you *their* **greetings**.
1Pe 5: 13 with you, **sends** you *her* **greetings**, and so does my son Mark.
5: 14 **Greet** one another with a kiss of love. Peace to all of you who are
2Jn 1: 13 The children of your chosen sister **send** *their* **greetings**.
3Jn 1: 14 face to face. Peace to you. The friends here **send** *their* **greetings**.
1: 14 friends here send their greetings. **Greet** the friends there by name.

833 ἀσπασμός, *aspasmos* [10] [√ *832*]

greeting [6], greeted [3], greetings [1]

Mt 23: 7 they love to be **greeted** in the marketplaces and to have men call
Mk 12: 38 walk around in flowing robes and be **greeted** in the marketplaces,
Lk 1: 29 at his words and wondered what kind of **greeting** this might be.
1: 41 When Elizabeth heard Mary's **greeting**, the baby leaped in her
1: 44 As soon as the sound of your **greeting** reached my ears, the baby
11: 43 seats in the synagogues and **greetings** in the marketplaces.
20: 46 around in flowing robes and love to be **greeted** in the marketplaces
1Co 16: 21 I, Paul, write this **greeting** in my own hand.
Col 4: 18 I, Paul, write this **greeting** in my own hand. Remember my chains.
2Th 3: 17 I, Paul, write this **greeting** in my own hand, which is the

834 ἄσπιλος, *aspilos* [4] [√ *1.1 + 5070*]

from being polluted [1], spotless [1], without defect [1], without spot [1]

1Ti 6: 14 to keep this command **without spot** or blame until the appearing of
Jas 1: 27 and to keep oneself **from being polluted** by the world.
1Pe 1: 19 the precious blood of Christ, a lamb **without** blemish or **defect**.
2Pe 3: 14 make every effort to be found **spotless**, blameless and at peace

835 ἀσπίς, *aspis* [1] [→ *5646*]

vipers [1]

Ro 3: 13 tongues practice deceit." "The poison *of* **vipers** is on their lips."

836 ἄσπονδος, *aspondos* [1] [√ *1.1 + 5064*]

unforgiving [1]

2Ti 3: 3 without love, **unforgiving**, slanderous, without self-control,

837 ἀσσάριον, *assarion* [2]

pennies [1], penny [1]

Mt 10: 29 Are not two sparrows sold *for* a **penny**? Yet not one of them will
Lk 12: 6 Are not five sparrows sold *for* two **pennies**? Yet not one of them is

838 'Ασσάρων, *Assarōn* Not used in UBS/NIV
[√ cf. *4926*]

839 ἆσσον, *asson* [1]

along the shore [1]

Ac 27: 13 so they weighed anchor and sailed **along the shore** of Crete.

840 ῎Ασσος, *Assos* [2]

Assos [2]

Ac 20: 13 We went on ahead to the ship and sailed for **Assos**, where we were
20: 14 When he met us at **Assos**, we took him aboard and went on to

841 ἀστατέω, *astateō* [1] [√ *1.1 + 2705*]

homeless [1]

1Co 4: 11 we are in rags, we are brutally treated, *we are* **homeless**.

842 ἀστεῖος, *asteios* [2]

no ordinary [+*2536+3836*] [1], no ordinary [1]

Ac 7: 20 Moses was born, and he was **no ordinary** [+*2536+3836*] *child*.
Heb 11: 23 because they saw he was **no ordinary** child, and they were not

843 ἀστήρ, *astēr* [24] [→ *849*]

stars [13], star [11]

Mt 2: 2 We saw his **star** in the east and have come to worship him."
2: 7 and found out from them the exact time the **star** had appeared.
2: 9 and the **star** they had seen in the east went ahead of them until it
2: 10 When they saw the **star**, they were overjoyed.
24: 29 the **stars** will fall from the sky, and the heavenly bodies will be
Mk 13: 25 the **stars** will fall from the sky, and the heavenly bodies will be
1Co 15: 41 has one kind of splendor, the moon another and the **stars** another;
15: 41 and the stars another; and **star** differs from star in splendor.
15: 41 and the stars another; and star differs *from* **star** in splendor.
Jude 1: 13 wandering **stars**, for whom blackest darkness has been reserved
Rev 1: 16 In his right hand he held seven **stars**, and out of his mouth came a
1: 20 The mystery *of* the seven **stars** that you saw in my right hand
1: 20 The seven **stars** are the angels of the seven churches, and the seven
2: 1 These are the words of him who holds the seven **stars** in his right
2: 28 I will also give him the morning **star**.
3: 1 of him who holds the seven spirits of God and the seven **stars**.
6: 13 and the **stars** in the sky fell to earth, as late figs drop from a fig
8: 10 angel sounded his trumpet, and a great **star**, blazing like a torch,
8: 11 the name *of* the **star** is Wormwood. A third of the waters turned
8: 12 of the sun was struck, a third of the moon, and a third *of* the **stars**,
9: 1 and I saw a **star** that had fallen from the sky to the earth.
12: 1 the moon under her feet and a crown *of* twelve **stars** on her head.
12: 4 His tail swept a third *of* the **stars** out of the sky and flung them to
22: 16 the Root and the Offspring of David, and the bright Morning **Star**."

844 ἀστήρικτος, *astēriktos* [2] [√ *1.1 + 5114*]

unstable [+*6034*] [1], unstable [1]

2Pe 2: 14 they never stop sinning; they seduce the **unstable** [+*6034*];
3: 16 which ignorant and **unstable** *people* distort, as they do the other

845 ἄστοργος, *astorgos* [2] [√ *1.1*]

heartless [1], without love [1]

Ro 1: 31 they are senseless, faithless, **heartless**, ruthless.
2Ti 3: 3 **without love**, unforgiving, slanderous, without self-control,

846 ἀστοχέω, *astocheō* [3] [√ *1.1*]

turned [1], wandered [1], wandered away [1]

1Ti 1: 6 have wandered away from these and **turned** to meaningless talk.
6: 21 have professed and in so doing *have* **wandered** from the faith.
2Ti 2: 18 who *have* **wandered away** from the truth. They say that the

847 ἀστραπή, astrapē [9] [→ 848, 1993, 4313]

flashes of lightning [4], lightning [4], light [1]

Mt 24:27 For as **lightning** that comes from the east is visible even in the
28: 3 His appearance was like **lightning**, and his clothes were white as
Lk 10:18 He replied, "I saw Satan fall like **lightning** from heaven.
11:36 be completely lighted, as when the **light** of a lamp shines on you."
17:24 For the Son of Man in his day will be like the **lightning**,
Rev 4: 5 From the throne came **flashes of lightning**, rumblings and peals of
8: 5 of thunder, rumblings, **flashes of lightning** and an earthquake.
11:19 And there came **flashes of lightning**, rumblings, peals of thunder,
16:18 Then there came **flashes of lightning**, rumblings, peals of thunder

848 ἀστράπτω, astraptō [2] [√ 847]

that gleamed like lightning [1], which flashes [1]

Lk 17:24 **which flashes** and lights up the sky from one end to the other.
24: 4 suddenly two men in clothes **that gleamed like lightning** stood

849 ἄστρον, astron [4] [√ 843]

stars [3], star [1]

Lk 21:25 "There will be signs in the sun, moon and **stars**. On the earth,
Ac 7:43 lifted up the shrine of Molech and the **star** of your god Rephan,
27:20 When neither sun nor **stars** appeared for many days and the storm
Heb 11:12 came descendants as numerous as the **stars** in the sky and as

850 Ἀσύγκριτος, Asynkritos [1] [√ 1.1 + 5250 + 3212]

Asyncritus [1]

Ro 16:14 Greet **Asyncritus**, Phlegon, Hermes, Patrobas, Hermas

851 ἀσύμφωνος, asymphōnos [1]
[√ 1.1 + 5250 + 5889]

disagreed [+1639] [1]

Ac 28:25 They **disagreed** [+1639] among themselves and began to leave

852 ἀσύνετος, asynetos [5] [√ 918; cf. 1.1 + 5250]

dull [2], foolish [1], no understanding [1], senseless [1]

Mt 15:16 "Are you still so **dull**?" Jesus asked them.
Mk 7:18 "Are you so **dull**?" he asked. "Don't you see that nothing that
Ro 1:21 their thinking became futile and their **foolish** hearts were darkened.
1:31 they are **senseless**, faithless, heartless, ruthless.
10:19 I will make you angry by a nation that has **no understanding**."

853 ἀσύνθετος, asynthetos [1] [√ 1.1 + 5250 + 5502]

faithless [1]

Ro 1:31 they are senseless, **faithless**, heartless, ruthless.

854 ἀσφάλεια, asphaleia [3] [√ 1.1 + 5378]

certainty [1], safety [1], securely [+1877+4246] [1]

Lk 1: 4 so that you may know the **certainty** of the things you have been
Ac 5:23 "We found the jail **securely** [+1877+4246] locked, with the guards
1Th 5: 3 While people are saying, "Peace and **safety**," destruction will come

855 ἀσφαλής, asphalēs [5] [√ 1.1 + 5378]

definite [1], exactly [1], firm [1], get at truth [+1182] [1],
safeguard [1]

Ac 21:34 and since the commander could not **get at** the **truth** [+1182]
22:30 the commander wanted to find out **exactly** why Paul was
25:26 But I have nothing **definite** to write to His Majesty about him.
Php 3: 1 to write the same things to you again, and it is a **safeguard** for you.
Heb 6:19 We have this hope as an anchor for the soul, **firm** and secure.

856 ἀσφαλίζω, asphalizō [4] [√ 1.1 + 5378]

made secure [2], fastened [1], make secure [1]

Mt 27:64 So give the order for the tomb to be **made secure** until the third
27:65 Pilate answered. "Go, **make** the tomb as **secure** as you know how."
27:66 they went and **made** the tomb **secure** by putting a seal on the stone
Ac 16:24 he put them in the inner cell and **fastened** their feet in the stocks.

857 ἀσφαλῶς, asphalōs [3] [√ 1.1 + 5378]

assured [+1182] [1], carefully [1], under guard [1]

Mk 14:44 one I kiss is the man; arrest him and lead him away **under guard**."
Ac 2:36 "Therefore let all Israel be **assured** [+1182] of this: God has made
16:23 and the jailer was commanded to guard them **carefully**.

858 ἀσχημονέω, aschēmoneō [2] [√ 1.1 + 5386]

acting improperly [1], rude [1]

1Co 7:36 If anyone thinks he is **acting improperly** toward the virgin he is
13: 5 It is not rude, it is not self-seeking, it is not easily angered,

859 ἀσχημοσύνη, aschēmosynē [2] [√ 1.1 + 5386]

indecent acts [1], shamefully [1]

Ro 1:27 Men committed **indecent acts** with other men, and received in
Rev 16:15 with him, so that he may not go naked and be **shamefully** exposed."

860 ἀσχήμων, aschēmōn [1] [√ 1.1 + 5386]

unpresentable [1]

1Co 12:23 And the parts that are **unpresentable** are treated with special

861 ἀσωτία, asōtia [3] [√ 1.1 + 5392]

debauchery [1], dissipation [1], wild [1]

Eph 5:18 Do not get drunk on wine, which leads to **debauchery**. Instead,
Tit 1: 6 and are not open to the charge of being **wild** and disobedient.
1Pe 4: 4 you do not plunge with them into the same flood of **dissipation**,

862 ἀσώτως, asōtōs [1] [√ 1.1 + 5392]

wild [1]

Lk 15:13 a distant country and there squandered his wealth in **wild** living.

863 ἀτακτέω, atakteō [1] [√ 1.1 + 5435]

idle [1]

2Th 3: 7 to follow our example. We were not **idle** when we were with you,

864 ἄτακτος, ataktos [1] [√ 1.1 + 5435]

idle [1]

1Th 5:14 And we urge you, brothers, warn those who are **idle**,

865 ἀτάκτως, ataktōs [2] [√ 1.1 + 5435]

idle [+4344] [1], idle [1]

2Th 3: 6 to keep away from every brother who is **idle** and does not live
3:11 We hear that some among you are **idle** [+4344]. They are not

866 ἄτεκνος, ateknos [2] [√ 1.1 + 5503]

childless [1], no children [1]

Lk 20:28 us that if a man's brother dies and leaves a wife but **no children**,
20:29 seven brothers. The first one married a woman and died **childless**.

867 ἀτενίζω, atenizō [14] [√ 1753 [1.2]]

looked straight [2], fastened [1], gazing [1], look steadily [1],
looked [+2917] [1], looked closely at [1], looked directly at [1],

looked intently [1], looked straight at [1], looked up [1], looking intently up [1], stare at [1], stared at [1]

Lk   4:20 The eyes of everyone in the synagogue were **fastened** on him,
    22:56 She **looked closely at** him and said, "This man was with him."
Ac   1:10 They were **looking intently up** into the sky as he was going,
     3: 4 Peter **looked straight** at him, as did John. Then Peter said,
     3:12 Why *do you* **stare at** us as if by our own power or godliness we
     6:15 All who were sitting in the Sanhedrin **looked intently** at Stephen,
     7:55 of the Holy Spirit, **looked up** to heaven and saw the glory of God,
    10: 4 Cornelius **stared at** him in fear. "What is it, Lord?" he asked.
    11: 6 *I* **looked** [+*2917*] into it and saw four-footed animals of the earth,
    13: 9 filled with the Holy Spirit, **looked straight** at Elymas and said,
    14: 9 Paul **looked directly at** him, saw that he had faith to be healed
    23: 1 Paul **looked straight at** the Sanhedrin and said, "My brothers,
2Co 3: 7 so that the Israelites could not **look steadily** at the face of Moses
     3:13 the Israelites from **gazing** at it while the radiance was fading away.

868 ἄτερ, *ater* [2]

when no was present [1], without [1]

Lk 22: 6 to hand Jesus over to them **when no** crowd **was present**.
    22:35 "When I sent you **without** purse, bag or sandals, did you lack

869 ἀτιμάζω, *atimazō* [7] [√ *1.1 + 5507*]

dishonor [2], treated shamefully [2], degrading of [1], insulted [1], suffering disgrace [1]

Mk 12: 4 they struck this man on the head and **treated** him **shamefully**.
Lk 20:11 but that one also they beat and **treated shamefully** and sent away
Jn   8:49 a demon," said Jesus, "but I honor my Father and you **dishonor** me.
Ac   5:41 because they had been counted worthy of **suffering disgrace** for
Ro   1:24 impurity *for* the **degrading** of their bodies with one another.
     2:23 brag about the law, *do* you **dishonor** God by breaking the law?
Jas   2: 6 But you *have* **insulted** the poor. Is it not the rich who are

870 ἀτιμάω, *atimaō* Not used in UBS/NIV [√ *1.1 + 5507*]

871 ἀτιμία, *atimia* [7] [√ *1.1 + 5507*]

dishonor [2], common use [1], disgrace [1], ignoble [1], shame [1], shameful [1]

Ro   1:26 Because of this, God gave them over to **shameful** lusts. Even their
     9:21 clay some pottery for noble purposes and some for **common use**?
1Co 11:14 things teach you that if a man has long hair, it is a **disgrace** to him,
    15:43 it is sown in **dishonor**, it is raised in glory; it is sown in weakness,
2Co 6: 8 through glory and **dishonor**, bad report and good report; genuine,
    11:21 To my **shame** I admit that we were too weak for that! What anyone
2Ti 2:20 and clay; some are for noble purposes and some for **ignoble**.

872 ἄτιμος, *atimos* [4] [√ *1.1 + 5507*]

without honor [2], dishonored [1], less honorable [1]

Mt 13:57 his hometown and in his own house is a prophet **without honor**."
Mk   6: 4 his relatives and in his own house is a prophet **without honor**."
1Co 4:10 but you are strong! You are honored, we are **dishonored**!
    12:23 and the parts that we think are **less honorable** we treat with special

873 ἀτιμόω, *atimoō* Not used in UBS/NIV [√ *1.1 + 5507*]

874 ἀτμίς, *atmis* [2] [√ *113*]

billows [1], mist [1]

Ac 2:19 and signs on the earth below, blood and fire and **billows** of smoke.
Jas 4:14 You are a **mist** that appears for a little while and then vanishes.

875 ἄτομος, *atomos* [1] [√ *1.1 + 5533*]

flash [1]

1Co 15:52 in a **flash**, in the twinkling of an eye, at the last trumpet.

876 ἄτοπος, *atopos* [4] [√ *1.1 + 5536*]

wrong [2], unusual [1], wicked [1]

Lk 23:41 what our deeds deserve. But this man has done nothing **wrong**."
Ac 25: 5 charges against the man there, if he has done anything **wrong**."
    28: 6 waiting a long time and seeing nothing **unusual** happen to him,
2Th 3: 2 And pray that we may be delivered from **wicked** and evil men,

877 Ἀττάλεια, *Attaleia* [1]

Attalia [1]

Ac 14:25 they had preached the word in Perga, they went down to **Attalia**.

878 αὐγάζω, *augazō* [1] [√ *879*]

see [1]

2Co 4: 4 so that they cannot **see** the light of the gospel of the glory of Christ,

879 αὐγή, *augē* [1] [→ *575, 878, 1315, 1419, 1420, 2964, 5495*]

daylight [1]

Ac 20:11 and broke bread and ate. After talking until **daylight**, he left.

880 Αὔγουστος, *Augoustos* [1]

Augustus [1]

Lk   2: 1 In those days Caesar **Augustus** issued a decree that a census

881 αὐθάδης, *authadēs* [2] [√ *899 + 2454*]

arrogant [1], overbearing [1]

Tit   1: 7 not **overbearing**, not quick-tempered, not given to drunkenness,
2Pe 2:10 Bold and **arrogant**, these men are not afraid to slander celestial

882 αὐθαίρετος, *authairetos* [2] [√ *899 + 145*]

entirely on own [1], on own initiative [1]

2Co 8: 3 were able, and even beyond their ability. **Entirely on** their **own**,
     8:17 is coming to you with much enthusiasm and **on** his **own initiative**.

883 αὐθεντέω, *authenteō* [1] [√ *899*]

have authority over [1]

1Ti 2:12 I do not permit a woman to teach or *to* **have authority over** a man;

884 αὐλέω, *auleō* [3] [√ *888*]

played the flute [2], tune played [+*2445+3068*] [1]

Mt 11:17 " '**We played the flute** for you, and you did not dance; we sang a
Lk   7:32 " '**We played the flute** for you, and you did not dance; we sang a
1Co 14: 7 how will anyone know what **tune** *is being* **played** [+*2445+3068*]

885 αὐλή, *aulē* [12] [→ *64, 2068, 4580; cf. 113, 887*]

courtyard [6], palace [2], court [1], house [1], pen [1], sheep pen [1]

Mt 26: 3 and the elders of the people assembled in the **palace** of the high
    26:58 him at a distance, right up to the **courtyard** of the high priest.
    26:69 Now Peter was sitting out in the **courtyard**, and a servant girl
Mk 14:54 him at a distance, right into the **courtyard** of the high priest.
    14:66 While Peter was below in the **courtyard**, one of the servant girls of
    15:16 The soldiers led Jesus away into the **palace** (that is,
Lk 11:21 "When a strong man, fully armed, guards his own **house**, his
    22:55 But when they had kindled a fire in the middle *of* the **courtyard**
Jn 10: 1 the truth, the man who does not enter the sheep **pen** by the gate,
    10:16 I have other sheep that are not of this **sheep pen**. I must bring them
    18:15 the high priest, he went with Jesus into the high priest's **courtyard**,
Rev 11: 2 But exclude the outer **court**; do not measure it, because it has been

886 αὐλητής, aulētēs [2] [√ 888]

flute players [2]

Mt   9:23 the ruler's house and saw the **flute players** and the noisy crowd,
Rev 18:22 The music of harpists and musicians, **flute players** and trumpeters,

887 αὐλίζομαι, aulizomai [2] [→ 5276; cf. 885]

spend the night [1], spent the night [1]

Mt 21:17 and went out of the city to Bethany, where *he* **spent the night**.
Lk 21:37 and each evening *he* went out to **spend the night** on the hill called

888 αὐλός, aulos [1] [→ 884, 886]

flute [1]

1Co 14: 7 case of lifeless things that make sounds, such as the **flute** or harp,

889 αὐξάνω, auxanō [23] [→ 890, 891, 5277, 5647]

grew [4], grow [4], grow up [2], growing [2], grows [2], become greater [1], enlarge [1], greatly increased [+2779+4437] [1], increase [1], made grow [1], makes grow [1], rises [1], spread [1], spread widely [1]

Mt   6:28 See how the lilies of the field **grow**. They do not labor or spin.
    13:32 yet when *it* **grows**, it is the largest of garden plants and becomes a
Mk   4: 8 It came up, **grew** and produced a crop, multiplying thirty,
Lk   1:80 And the child **grew** and became strong in spirit; and he lived in the
     2:40 And the child **grew** and became strong; he was filled with wisdom,
    12:27 "Consider how the lilies **grow**. They do not labor or spin. Yet I tell
    13:19 *It* **grew** and became a tree, and the birds of the air perched in its
Jn   3:30 He must **become greater**; I must become less.
Ac   6: 7 So the word of God **spread**. The number of disciples in Jerusalem
     7:17 *number* of our people in Egypt **greatly increased** [+2779+4437].
    12:24 But the word of God *continued to* **increase** and spread.
    19:20 In this way the word of the Lord **spread widely** and grew in
1Co 3: 6 I planted the seed, Apollos watered it, but God **made** *it* **grow**.
     3: 7 he who waters is anything, but only God, who **makes** things **grow**.
2Co 9:10 store of seed and *will* **enlarge** the harvest of your righteousness.
    10:15 Our hope is that, *as* your faith *continues to* **grow**, our area of
Eph 2:21 is joined together and **rises** to become a holy temple in the Lord.
     4:15 *we will* in all things **grow up** into him who is the Head, that is,
Col 1: 6 All over the world this gospel is bearing fruit and **growing**,
     1:10 fruit in every good work, **growing** in the knowledge of God,
     2:19 by its ligaments and sinews, **grows** as God causes it to grow.
1Pe 2: 2 spiritual milk, so that by it *you may* **grow up** in your salvation,
2Pe 3:18 But **grow** in the grace and knowledge of our Lord and Savior Jesus

890 αὔξησις, auxēsis [2] [√ 889]

causes to grow [1], grows [+4472] [1]

Eph 4:16 and held together by every supporting ligament, **grows** [+4472]
Col 2:19 by its ligaments and sinews, grows as God **causes** it **to grow**.

891 αὔξω, auxō Not used in UBS/NIV [√ 889]

892 αὔριον, aurion [14] [→ 2069]

tomorrow [11], next day [3]

Mt   6:30 which is here today and **tomorrow** is thrown into the fire,
     6:34 Therefore do not worry about **tomorrow**, for tomorrow will worry
     6:34 not worry about tomorrow, for **tomorrow** will worry about itself.
Lk 10:35 The **next day** he took out two silver coins and gave them to the
    12:28 which is here today, and **tomorrow** is thrown into the fire,
    13:32 'I will drive out demons and heal people today and **tomorrow**,
    13:33 I must keep going today and **tomorrow** and the next day—
Ac   4: 3 because it was evening, they put them in jail until the **next day**.
     4: 5 The **next day** the rulers, elders and teachers of the law met in
    23:20 **tomorrow** on the pretext of wanting more accurate information
    25:22 hear this man myself." He replied, "**Tomorrow** you will hear him."
1Co 15:32 dead are not raised, "Let us eat and drink, for **tomorrow** we die."
Jas 4:13 you who say, "Today or **tomorrow** we will go to this or that city,
     4:14 Why, you do not even know what will happen **tomorrow**.

893 αὐστηρός, austēros [2] [→ 903]

hard [2]

Lk 19:21 I was afraid of you, because you are a **hard** man. You take out
    19:22 You knew, did you, that I am a **hard** man, taking out what I did

894 αὐτάρκεια, autarkeia [2] [√ 899 + 758]

contentment [1], need [1]

2Co 9: 8 so that in all things at all times, having all that you **need**, you will
1Ti 6: 6 But godliness with **contentment** is great gain.

895 αὐτάρκης, autarkēs [1] [√ 899 + 758]

content [1]

Php 4:11 for I have learned to be **content** whatever the circumstances.

896 αὐτοκατάκριτος, autokatakritos [1]
[√ 899 + 2848 + 3212]

self-condemned [1]

Tit 3:11 sure that such a man is warped and sinful; he is **self-condemned**.

897 αὐτόματος, automatos [2] [√ 899]

all by itself [1], by itself [1]

Mk   4:28 **All by itself** the soil produces grain—first the stalk, then the head,
Ac 12:10 to the city. It opened for them **by itself**, and they went through it.

898 αὐτόπτης, autoptēs [1] [√ 899 + 3972]

eyewitnesses [1]

Lk   1: 2 handed down to us by those who from the first were **eyewitnesses**

899 αὐτός, autos [5601 / 5593] [→ 881, 882, 883, 894, 895, 896, 897, 898, 900, 901, 1571, 1831, 1929, 1994, 2070, 4194, 4932, 5437, 5796, 6058] See Index of Articles, Etc.

him [1388], his [902], them [814], *untranslated* [639], their [281], he [221], her [199], it [185], Jesusˢ [156], they [127], its [48], same [38], himself [37], Paulˢ [19], the peopleˢ [17], she [16], the manˢ [15], his own [13], God'sˢ [11], the man'sˢ [10], yourselves [10], Christˢ [9], myself [8], that [8], these [8], those [8], you [8], his disciplesˢ [7], Johnˢ [6], themselves [6], Godˢ [5], home [+3875] [5], the Jewsˢ [5], the cityˢ [5], the disciplesˢ [5], which [5], whose [5], itself [4], others [4], ourselves [4], the apostlesˢ [4], the beastˢ [4], the boyˢ [4], the crowdˢ [4], their own [4], there [+1877] [4], together [+2093+3836] [4], very [4], whom [4], Abrahamˢ [3], I [3], John'sˢ [3], Mosesˢ [3], Peterˢ [3], Peterˢ and John [3], Saulˢ [3], Stephenˢ [3], he himself [3], own [3], that [+3836] [3], the plantsˢ [3], the womenˢ [3], theirs [3], them [+3412+3836] [3], them [+4639] [3], this [3], we [3], who [3], your [3], yourself [3], Jesusˢ and his disciples [2], Josephˢ [2], Lazarusˢ [2], Paulˢ and Barnabas [2], Paulˢ and Silas [2], Peter'sˢ [2], he [+899+1877+3836+4460] [2], here [2], herself [2], him [+81+3836] [2], himself [+2840+3836] [2], his masterˢ [2], home [+3836+3875] [2], its [+3836+4725] [2], loveˢ [+3950] [2], that is how [+2848+3836] [2], that very [2], the Lordˢ [2], the bodyˢ [2], the childˢ [2], the childrenˢ [2], the menˢ [2], the servantˢ [2], the vineyardˢ [2], the young manˢ [2], there [2], they [+899+2779+3412+3836] [2], they themselves [2], a figˢ tree [1], a man'sˢ [1], agree with each other [+3836+5858] [1], agree with one another [+3306+3836] [1], alive [+1877] [1], Ananiasˢ [1], Apollosˢ [1], as I did [+4047] [1], as usual [+2848+3836] [1], at once [+3836+6052] [1], at their hands [+5679] [1], Barnabasˢ and Saul [1], beastsˢ [1], being like-minded [+3836+5858] [1], believersˢ [+1666] [1], both of you [+2779+5148] [1], boy'sˢ [1], by himself [+3668] [1], child'sˢ [1], Christ'sˢ [1], come together [+2093+3836+5302] [1], comes together [+2093+3836+5302] [1], deathˢ [1], Elizabethˢ [1], Elymasˢ [1], equal [+3836] [1], fair [1], faithˢ [1], Festusˢ [1], for the express purpose [+1650+4047]

[1], for this very reason [+*4047*] [1], Galilee^s [1], girl^s [1], governing [+*4047*] [1], he [+*1328+3836+5931*] [1], he [+*3836+4725*] [1], he [+*5679*] [1], he and his disciples [1], he's [+*1639+3836+6034*] [1], he's [1], here [+*1877*] [1], him [+*3836+3950*] [1], him [+*5679*] [1], him [+*6034*] [1], himself [+*2840*] [1], himself [+*3836+3950*] [1], his parents^s [1], his^s [+*3836*] [1], home [+*1650+3836+3875*] [1], I myself [1], immediately [+*1877+3836+6052*] [1], in his sight [+*1967*] [1], in one place [+*2093+3836*] [1], in same way [1], including [+*2779*] [1], Isaac^s [1], Israel^s [1], its [+*1877*] [1], its own [1], Jairus^s [1], James^s [1], Jesus and his disciples^s [1], Jesus^s body [1], Jews^s [1], John's [+*2722*] [1], just as though [+*1651+2779+3836*] [1], just like this [+*2848+3836*] [1], Levi's^s [1], Levi^s [1], lies^s [1], live in harmony [+*3836+5858*] [1], Lydda^s [1], Mary^s [1], men's^s [1], men^s [1], money^s [1], nearby [+*3836*] [1], of the scrolls^s [1], of them [+*5201*] [1], one [+*3836*] [1], one another [1], Paul's^s [1], perfectly united [+*2936+3836*] [1], Pilate^s [1], put on board [+*1650+1837*] [1], same things [1], same way [1], Saul's^s [1], serpent's [+*4058*] [1], she [+*5679*] [1], Simeon^s [1], spirit of unity [+*3836+5858*] [1], such [1], such beings [1], that country^s [1], that one sheep^s [1], that rest^s [1], that same [1], the ark^s [1], the beggar^s [1], the blessing^s [1], the coast^s [1], the commander's^s [1], the commander^s [1], the commandment^s [1], the Council^s [1], the cross^s [1], the disobedient^s [1], the entrance^s [1], the firstborn^s of Israel [1], the flock^s [1], the Gentiles^s [1], the gospel^s [1], the island^s [1], the Israelites^s [1], the kings^s [1], the land^s [1], the messengers^s [1], the money^s [1], the net^s [1], the officers^s [1], the one^s [1], the other [1], the others [1], the perfume^s [1], the pigs^s [1], the prophets^s [1], the same [1], the servants^s [1], the slave girl^s [1], the Son^c [1], the spirit^s [1], the star^s [1], the sun^s [1], the synagogue^s [1], the tongue^s [1], the tree^s [1], the two of you [+*2779+5148*] [1], the two^s [1], the very [1], the very one [1], the widow^s [1], the wine^s [1], their homes^s [1], their own number [1], them [+*3836+4546*] [1], them [+*3836+5284*] [1], themselves [+*2840+3836*] [1], themselves [+*3836+6034*] [1], those men^s [1], these very [1], they [+*1204+3836*] [1], they [+*1328*] [1], they [+*3412+3836*] [1], they [+*3836+4057*] [1], they [+*3836+5125*] [1], they [+*3836+6001*] [1], they [+*4123*] [1], they [+*4639*] [1], they [+*5679*] [1], things [1], this is why [+*1328*] [1], this man^s [1], this perfume^s [1], Timothy^s [1], to their number [+*2093+3836*] [1], too [+*2779+3836*] [1], two Israelites^s [1], what^s we are writing [+*3836*] [1], where [1], whole [1], whose [+*2400*] [1], with this in mind [+*1650*] [1], your slaves^s [1] Zechariah's^s [1],

900 αὐτόφωρος, *autophōros* [1] [√ *899*]

caught in the act [+*2093+2898*] [1]

Jn   8: 4   this woman *was* **caught in the act** [+*2093+2898*] of adultery.

901 αὐτόχειρ, *autocheir* [1] [√ *899 + 5931*]

with own hands [1]

Ac   27:19   they threw the ship's tackle overboard **with** *their* **own hands**.

902 αὐχέω, *aucheō* [1] [→ *3482*]

makes boasts [1]

Jas   3: 5   the tongue is a small part of the body, but *it* **makes** great **boasts**.

903 αὐχμηρός, *auchmēros* [1] [√ *893*]

dark [1]

2Pe   1:19   as to a light shining in a **dark** place, until the day dawns

904 ἀφαιρέω, *aphaireō* [10] [√ *608 + 145*]

cutting off [3], take away [2], take away from [1], taken away [1], taken away from [1], takes away from [RP*608*] [1], taking away [1]

Mt   26:51   and struck the servant of the high priest, **cutting off** his ear.
Mk   14:47   and struck the servant of the high priest, **cutting off** his ear.

Lk   1:25   shown his favor and **taken away** my disgrace among the people."
      10:42   has chosen what is better, and it *will* not *be* **taken away from** her."
      16: 3   'What shall I do now? My master *is* **taking away** my job.
      22:50   them struck the servant of the high priest, **cutting off** his right ear.
Ro   11:27   And this is my covenant with them when *I* **take away** their sins."
Heb 10: 4   it is impossible for the blood of bulls and goats *to* **take away** sins.
Rev 22:19   And if anyone **takes** [RP*608*] words **away from** this book of
      22:19   God *will* **take away from** him his share in the tree of life and in

905 ἀφανής, *aphanēs* [1] [√ *1.1 + 5743*]

hidden from [1]

Heb   4:13   Nothing in all creation is **hidden from** God's sight Everything is

906 ἀφανίζω, *aphanizō* [5] [√ *1.1 + 5743*]

destroy [2], disfigure [1], perish [1], vanishes [1]

Mt   6:16   for *they* **disfigure** their faces to show men they are fasting.
       6:19   where moth and rust **destroy**, and where thieves break in and steal.
       6:20   where moth and rust *do* not **destroy**, and where thieves do not
Ac   13:41   " 'Look, you scoffers, wonder and **perish**, for I am going to do
Jas   4:14   You are a mist that appears for a little while and then **vanishes**.

907 ἀφανισμός, *aphanismos* [1] [√ *1.1 + 5743*]

disappear [1]

Heb   8:13   one obsolete; and what is obsolete and aging *will* soon **disappear**.

908 ἄφαντος, *aphantos* [1] [√ *1.1 + 5743*]

disappeared [+*1181*] [1]

Lk   24:31   they recognized him, and he **disappeared** [+*1181*] from their sight.

909 ἀφεδρών, *aphedrōn* [2] [√ *608 + 1612*]

out of his body [+*1650+1744+3836*] [1], out of the body [+*1650+1675*] [1]

Mt   15:17   goes into the stomach and then **out of the body** [+*1650+1675*]?
Mk   7:19   into his stomach, and then **out of his body** [+*1650+1744+3836*]."

910 ἀφειδία, *apheidia* [1] [√ *1.1 + 5767*]

harsh treatment [1]

Col   2:23   their false humility and their **harsh treatment** of the body,

911 ἀφελότης, *aphelotēs* [1] [√ *1.1*]

sincere [1]

Ac   2:46   bread in their homes and ate together with glad and **sincere** hearts,

912 ἄφεσις, *aphesis* [17] [√ *918*]

ἄφεσις ἁμαρτιῶν (forgiveness of sins) [11] Mt 26:28; Mk 1:4; Lk 1:77; 3:3; 24:47; Ac 2:38; 5:31; 10:43; 13:38; 26:18; Col 1:14

forgiveness [13], forgiven [+*2400*] [1], forgiven [1], freedom [1], release [+*690+1877*] [1]

Mt   26:28   which is poured out for many for the **forgiveness** of sins.
Mk   1: 4   and preaching a baptism of repentance for the **forgiveness** of sins.
       3:29   blasphemes against the Holy Spirit *will* never *be* **forgiven** [+*2400*];
Lk   1:77   the knowledge of salvation through the **forgiveness** of their sins,
       3: 3   preaching a baptism of repentance for the **forgiveness** of sins.
       4:18   He has sent me to proclaim **freedom** for the prisoners and recovery
       4:18   of sight for the blind, *to* **release** [+*690+1877*] the oppressed,
      24:47   and **forgiveness** of sins will be preached in his name to all nations,
Ac   2:38   in the name of Jesus Christ for the **forgiveness** of your sins.
       5:31   that he might give repentance and **forgiveness** of sins to Israel.
      10:43   believes in him receives **forgiveness** of sins through his name."
      13:38   I want you to know that through Jesus the **forgiveness** of sins is
      26:18   so that they may receive **forgiveness** of sins and a place among
Eph   1: 7   the **forgiveness** of sins, in accordance with the riches of God's
Col   1:14   in whom we have redemption, the **forgiveness** of sins.

Heb 9:22 and without the shedding of blood there is no **forgiveness**.
   10:18 And where these have been **forgiven**, there is no longer any

913 ἀφή, *haphē* [2] [√ *721*]

ligament [1], ligaments [1]

Eph 4:16 joined and held together by every supporting **ligament**, grows
Col 2:19 supported and held together by its **ligaments** and sinews,

914 ἀφθαρσία, *aphtharsia* [7] [√ *1.1 + 5780*]

imperishable [3], immortality [2], imperishable [+*1877*] [1], undying [1]

Ro 2:7 good seek glory, honor and **immortality**, he will give eternal life.
1Co 15:42 body that is sown is perishable, it is raised **imperishable** [+*1877*];
   15:50 kingdom of God, nor does the perishable inherit the **imperishable**.
   15:53 For the perishable must clothe itself with the **imperishable**,
   15:54 When the perishable has been clothed with the **imperishable**,
Eph 6:24 Grace to all who love our Lord Jesus Christ with an **undying** love.
2Ti 1:10 and has brought life and **immortality** to light through the gospel.

915 ἄφθαρτος, *aphthartos* [8 / 7] [√ *1.1 + 5780*]

immortal [2], imperishable [2], last forever [1], that can never perish [1], unfading [1]

Mk 16:S [UBS+ *and imperishable proclamation of eternal salvation.*]
Ro 1:23 and exchanged the glory *of* the **immortal** God for images made to
1Co 9:25 that will not last; but we do it to get a crown that will **last forever**.
   15:52 the dead will be raised **imperishable**, and we will be changed.
1Ti 1:17 **immortal**, invisible, the only God, be honor and glory for ever
1Pe 1:4 and into an inheritance **that can never perish**, spoil or fade—
   1:23 but *of* **imperishable**, through the living and enduring word of God.
   3:4 of your inner self, the **unfading** *beauty* of a gentle and quiet spirit,

916 ἀφθονία, *aphthonia* Not used in UBS/NIV
[√ *1.1 + 5784*]

917 ἀφθορία, *aphthoria* [1] [√ *1.1 + 5780*]

integrity [1]

Tit 2:7 doing what is good. In your teaching show **integrity**, seriousness

918 ἀφίημι, *aphiēmi* [143] [→ *457, 479, 852, 912, 1588, 1889, 4217, 4223, 5304, 5305, 5317, 5320; cf. 608*]

ἁμαρτία ἀφιέναι (to forgive sin) [20] Mt 9:2,5,6; 12:31; Mk 2:5,7,9,10; Lk 5:20,21,23,24; 7:47,48,49; 11:4; Jn 20:23; Jas 5:15; 1Jn 1:9; 2:12

left [36], forgive [22], forgiven [22], let [18], leave [8], leave alone [5], leaving [4], divorce [3], canceled [2], deserted [2], let go [2], *untranslated* [1], abandoned [1], abandons [1], allow [1], consented [1], forgives [1], forsaken [1], gave up [1], leaves [1], leaving behind [1], let be [1], let go of [1], let go on [1], let have [1], neglected [1], neglecting [1], refuse [+*4024*] [1], tolerate [1], with[S] [1]

Mt 3:15 Jesus replied, "**Let** it be so now; it is proper for us to do this to
   3:15 for us to do this to fulfill all righteousness." Then John **consented**.
   4:11 Then the devil **left** him, and angels came and attended him.
   4:20 At once they **left** their nets and followed him.
   4:22 and immediately they **left** the boat and their father and followed
   5:24 **leave** your gift there in front of the altar. First go and be reconciled
   5:40 to sue you and take your tunic, **let** him **have** your cloak as well.
   6:12 **Forgive** us our debts, as we also have forgiven our debtors.
   6:12 Forgive us our debts, as we also *have* **forgiven** our debtors.
   6:14 For if *you* **forgive** men when they sin against you, your heavenly
   6:14 when they sin against you, your heavenly Father *will* also **forgive** you.
   6:15 But if *you* **do** not **forgive** men their sins, your Father will not
   6:15 not forgive men their sins, your Father *will* not **forgive** your sins.
   7:4 you say to your brother, '**Let** me take the speck out of your eye,'
   8:15 He touched her hand and the fever **left** her, and she got up
   8:22 Jesus told him, "Follow me, and **let** the dead bury their own dead."

   9:2 he said to the paralytic, "Take heart, son; your sins *are* **forgiven**."
   9:5 to say, 'Your sins *are* **forgiven**,' or to say, 'Get up and walk'?
   9:6 know that the Son of Man has authority on earth *to* **forgive** sins...."
   12:31 so I tell you, every sin and blasphemy *will be* **forgiven** men,
   12:31 but the blasphemy against the Spirit *will* not *be* **forgiven**.
   12:32 who speaks a word against the Son of Man *will be* **forgiven**,
   12:32 anyone who speaks against the Holy Spirit *will* not *be* **forgiven**,
   13:30 **Let** both grow together until the harvest. At that time I will tell the
   13:36 Then he **left** the crowd and went into the house. His disciples came
   15:14 **Leave** them; they are blind guides. If a blind man leads a blind
   18:12 *will he* not **leave** the ninety-nine on the hills and go to look for the
   18:21 how many times *shall I* **forgive** my brother when he sins against
   18:27 master took pity on him, **canceled** the debt and let him go.
   18:32 '*I canceled* all that debt of yours because you begged me to.
   18:35 treat each of you unless *you* **forgive** your brother from your heart."
   19:14 Jesus said, "**Let** the little children come to me, and do not hinder
   19:27 Peter answered him, "We have **left** everything to follow you!
   19:29 And everyone who *has* **left** houses or brothers or sisters or father
   22:22 heard this, they were amazed. So they **left** him and went away.
   22:25 and since he had no children, *he* **left** his wife to his brother.
   23:13 do not enter, nor *will you* **let** those enter who are trying to.
   23:23 But *you have* **neglected** the more important matters of the law—
   23:23 should have practiced the latter, without **neglecting** the former.
   23:38 Look, your house *is* **left** to you desolate.
   24:2 "I tell you the truth, not one stone here *will be* **left** on another;
   24:40 Two men will be in the field; one will be taken and the other **left**.
   24:41 be grinding with a hand mill; one will be taken and the other **left**.
   26:44 So *he* **left** them and went away once more and prayed the third
   26:56 might be fulfilled." Then all the disciples **deserted** him and fled.
   27:49 The rest said, "*Now* **leave** him **alone**. Let's see if Elijah comes to
   27:50 Jesus had cried out again in a loud voice, *he* **gave up** his spirit.

Mk 1:18 At once they **left** their nets and followed him.
   1:20 and *they* **left** their father Zebedee in the boat with the hired men
   1:31 helped her up. The fever **left** her and she began to wait on them.
   1:34 but *he would* not **let** the demons speak because they knew who he
   2:5 their faith, he said to the paralytic, "Son, your sins *are* **forgiven**."
   2:7 like that? He's blaspheming! Who can **forgive** sins but God alone?"
   2:9 'Your sins *are* **forgiven**,' or to say, 'Get up, take your mat
   2:10 know that the Son of Man has authority on earth *to* **forgive** sins...."
   3:28 all the sins and blasphemies of men *will be* **forgiven** them.
   4:12 never understanding; otherwise they might turn and *be* **forgiven**!' "
   4:36 **Leaving** the crowd **behind**, they took him along, just as he was,
   5:19 Jesus *did* not **let** him, but said, "Go home to your family and tell
   5:37 *He did* not **let** anyone follow him except Peter, James and John the
   7:8 *You have* **let go of** the commands of God and are holding on to the
   7:12 then *you* no longer **let** him do anything for his father or mother.
   7:27 "First **let** the children eat all they want," he told her, "for it is not
   8:13 Then he **left** them, got back into the boat and crossed to the other
   10:14 He said to them, "**Let** the little children come to me, and do not
   10:28 Peter said to him, "We *have* **left** everything to follow you!"
   10:29 "no one who *has* **left** home or brothers or sisters or mother
   11:6 answered as Jesus had told them to, and the *people* **let** them **go**.
   11:16 and *would* not **allow** anyone to carry merchandise through the
   11:25 stand praying, if you hold anything against anyone, **forgive** him,
   11:25 so that your Father in heaven *may* **forgive** you your sins."
   12:12 But they were afraid of the crowd; so they **left** him and went away.
   12:19 if a man's brother dies and leaves a wife but **[RPG]** no children,
   12:20 The first one married and died without **leaving** any children.
   12:22 In fact, none of the seven **left** any children. Last of all, the woman
   13:2 "Not one stone here *will be* **left** on another; every one will be
   13:34 He **leaves** his house and puts his servants in charge, each with his
   14:6 "**Leave** her **alone**," said Jesus. "Why are you bothering her?
   14:50 Then everyone **deserted** him and fled.
   15:36 on a stick, and offered it to Jesus to drink. "*Now* **leave** him **alone**.
   15:37 **With**[S] a loud cry, Jesus breathed his last.

Lk 4:39 So he bent over her and rebuked the fever, and *it* **left** her. She got
   5:11 pulled their boats up on shore, **left** everything and followed him.
   5:20 Jesus saw their faith, he said, "Friend, your sins *are* **forgiven**."
   5:21 who speaks blasphemy? Who can **forgive** sins but God alone?"
   5:23 Which is easier: to say, 'Your sins *are* **forgiven**,'
   5:24 know that the Son of Man has authority on earth *to* **forgive** sins...."
   6:42 to your brother, 'Brother, **let** me take the speck out of your eye,'
   7:47 Therefore, I tell you, her many sins *have been* **forgiven**—
   7:47 she loved much. But he who *has been* **forgiven** little loves little."
   7:48 Then Jesus said to her, "Your sins *are* **forgiven**."
   7:49 to say among themselves, "Who is this who even **forgives** sins?"

8: 51   *he did* not **let** anyone go in with him except Peter, John and James,
9: 60   "**Let** the dead bury their own dead, but you go and proclaim the
10: 30   him of his clothes, beat him and went away, **leaving** him half dead.
11: 4   **Forgive** us our sins, for we also forgive everyone who sins against
11: 4   us our sins, for we also **forgive** everyone who sins against us.
12: 10   who speaks a word against the Son of Man *will be* **forgiven**,
12: 10   who blasphemes against the Holy Spirit *will not be* **forgiven**.
12: 39   thief was coming, *he* would not have **let** his house be broken into.
13: 8   " 'Sir,' the man replied, '**leave** it **alone** for one more year,
13: 35   Look, your house *is* **left** to you desolate. I tell you, you will not see
17: 3   "If your brother sins, rebuke him, and if he repents, **forgive** him.
17: 4   seven times comes back to you and says, 'I repent,' **forgive** him."
17: 34   two people will be in one bed; one *will be* taken and the other **left**.
17: 35   be grinding grain together; one will be taken and the other **left**."
18: 16   the children to him and said, "**Let** the little children come to me,
18: 28   Peter said to him, "We *have* **left** all we had to follow you!"
18: 29   "no one who *has* **left** home or wife or brothers or parents
19: 44   within your walls. *They will* not **leave** one stone on another,
21: 6   the time will come when not one stone *will be* **left** on another;
23: 34   Jesus said, "Father, **forgive** them, for they do not know what they
Jn   4: 3   learned of this, *he* **left** Judea and went back once more to Galilee.
4: 28   Then, **leaving** her water jar, the woman went back to the town
4: 52   they said to him, "The fever **left** him yesterday at the seventh hour."
8: 29   *he has* not **left** me alone, for I always do what pleases him."
10: 12   he sees the wolf coming, *he* **abandons** the sheep and runs away.
11: 44   Jesus said to them, "Take off the grave clothes and **let** him go."
11: 48   If *we* **let** him **go on** like this, everyone will believe in him,
12: 7   "**Leave** her **alone**," Jesus replied. "It was intended that she should
14: 18   *I will* not **leave** you as orphans; I will come to you.
14: 27   Peace *I* **leave** with you; my peace I give you. I do not give to you
16: 28   now *I am* **leaving** the world and going back to the Father."
16: 32   *You will* **leave** me all alone. Yet I am not alone, for my Father is
18: 8   Jesus answered. "If you are looking for me, then **let** these men go."
20: 23   If *you* **forgive** anyone his sins, *they are* forgiven; if you do not
20: 23   If you forgive anyone his sins, *they are* **forgiven**; if you do not
Ac   5: 38   **Let** them **go**! For if their purpose or activity is of human origin,
8: 22   Perhaps *he will* **forgive** you for having such a thought in your
14: 17   Yet *he has* not **left** himself without testimony. He has shown
Ro   1: 27   In the same way the men also **abandoned** natural relations with
4: 7   "Blessed are they whose transgressions *are* **forgiven**, whose sins
1Co   7: 11   to her husband. And a husband *must* not **divorce** his wife.
7: 12   and she is willing to live with him, *he* must not **divorce** her.
7: 13   and he is willing to live with her, *she* must not **divorce** him.
Heb   2: 8   everything under him, God **left** nothing that is not subject to him.
6: 1   Therefore let us **leave** the elementary teachings about Christ
Jas   5: 15   the Lord will raise him up. If he has sinned, he *will be* **forgiven**.
1Jn   1: 9   he is faithful and just and *will* **forgive** us our sins and purify us
2: 12   because your sins *have been* **forgiven** on account of his name.
Rev   2: 4   Yet I hold this against you: *You have* **forsaken** your first love.
2: 20   *You* **tolerate** that woman Jezebel, who calls herself a prophetess.
11: 9   nation will gaze on their bodies and **refuse** [+*4024*] them burial.

919 ἀφικνέομαι, *aphikneomai* [1] [√ *608 + 2653*]

heard about [1]

Ro   16: 19   Everyone *has* **heard about** your obedience, so I am full of joy

920 ἀφιλάγαθος, *aphilagathos* [1] [√ *1.1 + 5813 + 19*]

not lovers of good [1]

2Ti   3: 3   slanderous, without self-control, brutal, **not lovers of** the **good**,

921 ἀφιλάργυρος, *aphilargyros* [2]
[√ *1.1 + 5813 + 738*]

free from the love of money [1], not a lover of money [1]

1Ti   3: 3   not violent but gentle, not quarrelsome, **not a lover of money**.
Heb   13: 5   Keep your lives **free from the love of money** and be content with

922 ἄφιξις, *aphixis* [1] [√ *608 + 2653*]

leave [1]

Ac   20: 29   I know that after I **leave**, savage wolves will come in among you

923 ἀφίστημι, *aphistēmi* [14] [√ *608 + 2705*]

left [*RP608*] [3], abandon [1], away from [*RP608*] [1], deserted [*RP608*] [1], fall away [1], leave alone [*RP608*] [1], led in revolt [+*3958*] [1], left [1], take away from [*RP608*] [1], turn away from [*RP608*] [1], turns away from [*RP608*] [1], withdrew [*RP608*] [1]

Lk   2: 37   She never **left** the temple but worshiped night and day, fasting
4: 13   all this tempting, he **left** [*RP608*] him until an opportune time.
8: 13   They believe for a while, but in the time of testing *they* **fall away**.
13: 27   you come from. **Away** [*RP608*] **from** me, all you evildoers!'
Ac   5: 37   the days of the census and **led** a band of people **in revolt** [+*3958*].
5: 38   **Leave** [*RP608*] these men **alone**! Let them go! For if their
12: 10   the length of one street, suddenly the angel **left** [*RP608*] him.
15: 38   *because he had* **deserted** [*RP608*] them in Pamphylia and had not
19: 9   So Paul **left** [*RP608*] them. He took the disciples with him
22: 29   Those who were about to question him **withdrew** [*RP608*]
2Co   12: 8   Three times I pleaded with the Lord to **take** [*RP608*] it **away from**
1Ti   4: 1   The Spirit clearly says that in later times some *will* **abandon** the
2Ti   2: 19   the name of the Lord *must* **turn** [*RP608*] **away from** wickedness."
Heb   3: 12   unbelieving heart that **turns** [*RP608*] **away from** the living God.

924 ἄφνω, *aphnō* [3] [√ *167?*]

suddenly [3]

Ac   2: 2   **Suddenly** a sound like the blowing of a violent wind came from
16: 26   **Suddenly** there was such a violent earthquake that the foundations
28: 6   The people expected him to swell up or **suddenly** fall dead,

925 ἀφόβως, *aphobōs* [4] [√ *1.1 + 5832*]

fearlessly [1], nothing to fear [1], without fear [1], without the slightest qualm [1]

Lk   1: 74   hand of our enemies, and to enable us to serve him **without fear**
1Co   16: 10   see to it that he has **nothing to fear** while he is with you,
Php   1: 14   to speak the word of God more courageously and **fearlessly**.
Jude   1: 12   at your love feasts, eating with you **without the slightest qualm**—

926 ἀφομοιόω, *aphomoioō* [1] [√ *608 + 3927*]

like [1]

Heb   7: 3   or end of life, **like** the Son of God he remains a priest forever.

927 ἀφοράω, *aphoraō* [2] [√ *608 + 3972*]

fix eyes [1], see [1]

Php   2: 23   therefore, to send him as soon as *I* **see** how things go with me.
Heb   12: 2   *Let us* **fix** *our* **eyes** on Jesus, the author and perfecter of our faith,

928 ἀφορίζω, *aphorizō* [10] [√ *608 + 4000*]

separate [4], set apart [3], exclude [1], separates [1], took [1]

Mt   13: 49   The angels will come and **separate** the wicked from the righteous
25: 32   and *he will* **separate** the people one from another as a shepherd
25: 32   from another as a shepherd **separates** the sheep from the goats.
Lk   6: 22   when *they* **exclude** you and insult you and reject your name as
Ac   13: 2   "**Set apart** for me Barnabas and Saul for the work to which I have
19: 9   *He* **took** the disciples *with* him and had discussions daily in the
Ro   1: 1   called to be an apostle and **set apart** for the gospel of God—
2Co   6: 17   "Therefore come out from them and *be* **separate**, says the Lord.
Gal   1: 15   who **set** me **apart** from birth and called me by his grace,
2: 12   *he began to* draw back and **separate** himself *from* the Gentiles

929 ἀφορμή, *aphormē* [7] [√ *608 + 3995*]

opportunity [5], ground [1], indulge [1]

Ro   7: 8   But sin, seizing the **opportunity** afforded by the commandment,
7: 11   For sin, seizing the **opportunity** afforded by the commandment,
2Co   5: 12   to you again, but are giving you an **opportunity** to take pride in us,
11: 12   **ground** from under those who want an opportunity to be
11: 12   **opportunity** to be considered equal with us in the things they boast
Gal   5: 13   But do not use your freedom to **indulge** the sinful nature; rather,
1Ti   5: 14   their homes and to give the enemy no **opportunity** for slander.

930 ἀφρίζω, aphrizō [2] [√ 931]

foaming at the mouth [1], foams at the mouth [1]

Mk   9:18   *He* **foams at the mouth**, gnashes his teeth and becomes rigid.
     9:20   He fell to the ground and rolled around, **foaming at the mouth**.

931 ἀφρός, aphros [1] [→ 576, 930, 2072]

foams at the mouth [1]

Lk   9:39   it throws him into convulsions so that he **foams at the mouth**.

932 ἀφροσύνη, aphrosynē [4] [√ 1.1 + 5856]

as a fool [+1877] [1], folly [1], fool [1], foolishness [1]

Mk   7:22   malice, deceit, lewdness, envy, slander, arrogance and **folly**.
2Co 11: 1   I hope you will put up with a little *of* my **foolishness**; but you are
    11:17   boasting I am not talking as the Lord would, but as a **fool**.
    11:21   I am speaking **as a fool** [+1877]—I also dare to boast about.

933 ἄφρων, aphrōn [11] [√ 1.1 + 5856]

fool [5], foolish [5], fools [1]

Lk 11:40   *You* **foolish** *people*! Did not the one who made the outside make
    12:20   "But God said to him, 'You **fool**! This very night your life will be
Ro   2:20   an instructor *of* the **foolish**, a teacher of infants, because you have
1Co 15:36   *How* **foolish**! What you sow does not come to life unless it dies.
2Co 11:16   I repeat: Let no one take me for a **fool**. But if you do,
    11:16   But if you do, then receive me just as you would a **fool**, so that I
    11:19   You gladly put up with **fools** since you are so wise!
    12: 6   Even if I should choose to boast, I would not be a **fool**, because I
    12:11   I have made a **fool** of myself, but you drove me to it. I ought to
Eph 5:17   Therefore do not be **foolish**, but understand what the Lord's will is.
1Pe 2:15   by doing good you should silence the ignorant talk *of* **foolish** men.

934 ἀφυπνόω, aphypnoō [1] [√ 608 + 5678]

fell asleep [1]

Lk   8:23   As they sailed, *he* **fell asleep**. A squall came down on the lake,

935 ἀφυστερέω, aphystereō Not used in UBS/NIV [√ 608 + 5731]

936 ἄφωνος, aphōnos [4] [√ 1.1 + 5889]

mute [1], silent [1], without meaning [1], without speech [1]

Ac   8:32   and as a lamb before the shearer is **silent**, so he did not open his
1Co 12: 2   or other you were influenced and led astray to **mute** idols.
    14:10   of languages in the world, yet none of them is **without meaning**.
2Pe 2:16   a beast **without speech**—who spoke with a man's voice

937 Ἀχάζ, Achaz [2] [→ 941]

Ahaz [2]

Mt   1: 9   Uzziah the father of Jotham, Jotham the father of **Ahaz**, Ahaz the
     1: 9   of Jotham, Jotham the father of Ahaz, **Ahaz** the father of Hezekiah,

938 Ἀχαΐα, Achaia [10] [→ 939]

Achaia [10]

Ac 18:12   While Gallio was proconsul *of* **Achaia**, the Jews made a united
    18:27   When Apollos wanted to go to **Achaia**, the brothers encouraged
    19:21   to go to Jerusalem, passing through Macedonia and **Achaia**.
Ro 15:26   and **Achaia** were pleased to make a contribution for the poor
1Co 16:15   that the household of Stephanas were the first converts *in* **Achaia**,
2Co 1: 1   *of* God in Corinth, together with all the saints throughout **Achaia**,
     9: 2   telling them that since last year you in **Achaia** were ready to give;
    11:10   nobody in the regions *of* **Achaia** will stop this boasting of mine.
1Th 1: 7   you became a model to all the believers in Macedonia and **Achaia**.
     1: 8   message rang out from you not only in Macedonia and **Achaia**—

939 Ἀχαϊκός, Achaikos [1] [√ 938]

Achaicus [1]

1Co 16:17   I was glad when Stephanas, Fortunatus and **Achaicus** arrived,

940 ἀχάριστος, acharistos [2] [√ 1.1 + 5897]

ungrateful [2]

Lk   6:35   of the Most High, because he is kind to the **ungrateful** and wicked.
2Ti 3: 2   proud, abusive, disobedient to their parents, **ungrateful**, unholy,

941 Ἀχάς, Achas Not used in UBS/NIV [√ 937]

942 ἀχειροποίητος, acheiropoiētos [3] [√ 1.1 + 5931 + 4472]

not built by human hands [1], not done by the hands of men [1], not made by man [1]

Mk 14:58   and in three days will build another, **not made by man**.' "
2Co 5: 1   from God, an eternal house in heaven, **not built by human hands**.
Col 2:11   **not** with a circumcision **done by the hands of men** but with the

943 Ἀχίμ, Achim [2]

Akim [2]

Mt   1:14   of Zadok, Zadok the father of **Akim**, Akim the father of Eliud,
     1:14   of Zadok, Zadok the father of Akim, **Akim** the father of Eliud,

944 ἀχλύς, achlys [1]

mist [1]

Ac 13:11   Immediately **mist** and darkness came over him, and he groped

945 ἀχρεῖος, achreios [2] [√ 1.1 + 5968]

unworthy [1], worthless [1]

Mt 25:30   And throw that **worthless** servant outside, into the darkness,
Lk 17:10   you were told to do, should say, 'We are **unworthy** servants;

946 ἀχρειόω, achreioō [1] [√ 1.1 + 5968]

become worthless [1]

Ro   3:12   All have turned away, *they have* together **become worthless**;

947 ἄχρηστος, achrēstos [1] [√ 1.1 + 5968]

useless [1]

Phm 1:11   Formerly he was **useless** to you, but now he has become useful

948 ἄχρι, achri [49 / 48] [√ 216]

until [16], to [10], until [+4005] [5], as far as [2], up to [2], just before [+4005] [1], then [+4005] [1], as high as [1], as long as [+4005] [1], before [1], even to [1], even to the point of [1], for [1], later [1], right up to [1], so much as [1], to where [1], until [+323+4005] [1]

Mt 24:38   and giving in marriage, **up to** the day Noah entered the ark;
Mk 16: S   [UBS+ *Jesus himself sent out through them, from east to west,*]
Lk   1:20   you will be silent and not able to speak **until** the day this happens,
     4:13   had finished all this tempting, he left him **until** an opportune time.
    17:27   and being given in marriage **up to** the day Noah entered the ark.
    21:24   Jerusalem will be trampled on by the Gentiles **until** [+4005] the
Ac   1: 2   **until** the day he was taken up to heaven, after giving instructions
     2:29   David died and was buried, and his tomb is here **to** this day.
     3:21   He must remain in heaven **until** the time comes for God to restore
     7:18   **Then** [+4005] another king, who knew nothing about Joseph,
    11: 5   from heaven by its four corners, and it came down **to where** I was.
    13: 6   They traveled through the whole island **until** they *came to* Paphos.
    13:11   and **for** a time you will be unable to see the light of the sun."
    20: 6   and five days **later** joined the others at Troas, where we stayed

20:11 and broke bread and ate. After talking **until** daylight, he left.
22: 4 I persecuted the followers of this Way to their death, arresting both
22:22 The crowd listened to Paul **until** he said this. Then they raised their
23: 1 I have fulfilled my duty to God in all good conscience **to** this day.'
26:22 But I have had God's help **to** this very day,
27:33 **Just before** [+4005] dawn Paul urged them all to eat. "For the last
28:15 and they traveled **as far as** the Forum of Appius and the Three
Ro   1:13 to come to you (but have been prevented from doing so **until** now)
5:13 for **before** the law was given, sin was in the world. But sin is not
8:22 groaning as in the pains of childbirth **right up to** the present time.
11:25 Israel has experienced a hardening in part **until** [+4005] the full
1Co 4:11 **To** this very hour we go hungry and thirsty, we are in rags,
11:26 this cup, you proclaim the Lord's death **until** [+4005] he comes.
15:25 For he must reign **until** [+4005] he has put all his enemies under
2Co 3:14 for **to** this day the same veil remains when the old covenant is read.
10:13 to the field God has assigned to us, a field that reaches even **to** you.
10:14 come to you, for we did get **as far as** you with the gospel of Christ.
Gal 3:19 because of transgressions **until** [+4005] the Seed to whom the
4: 2 is subject to guardians and trustees **until** the time set by his father.
Php 1: 5 because of your partnership in the gospel from the first day **until**
1: 6 in you will carry it on to completion **until** the day of Christ Jesus.
Heb 3:13 encourage one another daily, **as long** [+4005] **as** it is called Today,
4:12 it penetrates **even to** dividing soul and spirit, joints and marrow;
6:11 We want each of you to show this same diligence **to** the very end,
Rev 2:10 Be faithful, **even to the point of** death, and I will give you the
2:25 Only hold on to what you have **until** [+323+4005] I come.
2:26 To him who overcomes and does my will **to** the end, I will give
7: 3 or the trees **until** we put a seal on the foreheads of the servants of
12:11 they did not love their lives **so much as** to shrink from death.
14:20 rising **as high as** the horses' bridles for a distance of 1,600 stadia.
15: 8 and no one could enter the temple **until** the seven plagues of the
17:17 give the beast their power to rule, **until** God's words are fulfilled.
18: 5 for her sins are piled up to heaven, and God has remembered her
20: 3 to keep him from deceiving the nations anymore **until** the thousand
20: 5 (The rest of the dead did not come to life **until** the thousand years

949 ἄχυρον, *achyron* [2]

chaff [2]

Mt   3:12 into the barn and burning up the **chaff** with unquenchable fire."
Lk   3:17 into his barn, but he will burn up the **chaff** with unquenchable fire."

950 ἀψευδής, *apseudēs* [1] [√ *1.1 + 6017*]

not lie [1]

Tit   1: 2 which God, who *does* **not lie**, promised before the beginning of

951 ἀψίνθιον, *apsinthion* Not used in UBS/NIV [√ *952*]

952 ἄψινθος, *apsinthos* [2] [→ *951*]

Wormwood [1], bitter [1]

Rev 8:11 the name of the star is **Wormwood**. A third of the waters turned
8:11 A third of the waters turned **bitter**, and many people died from the

953 ἄψυχος, *apsychos* [1] [√ *1.1 + 6038*]

lifeless [1]

1Co 14: 7 Even in the case of **lifeless** *things* that make sounds, such as the

---

B, *B*

954 β, *b* Not used in UBS/NIV

955 Βάαλ, *Baal* [1]

Baal [1]

Ro 11: 4 for myself seven thousand who have not bowed the knee *to* **Baal**."

956 Βαβυλών, *Babylōn* [12]

Babylon [11], *untranslated* [1]

Mt   1:11 of Jeconiah and his brothers at the time of the exile *to* **Babylon**.
1:12 After the exile *to* **Babylon**: Jeconiah was the father of Shealtiel,
1:17 fourteen from David to the exile *to* **Babylon**, and fourteen from the
1:17 exile to Babylon, and fourteen from the exile [RPG] to the Christ.
Ac   7:43 to worship. Therefore I will send you into exile' beyond **Babylon**.
1Pe 5:13 She who is in **Babylon**, chosen together with you, sends her
Rev 14: 8 Fallen is **Babylon** the Great, which made all the nations drink the
16:19 God remembered **Babylon** the Great and gave her the cup filled
17: 5 MYSTERY **BABYLON** THE GREAT THE MOTHER OF
18: 2 a mighty voice he shouted: "Fallen! Fallen is **Babylon** the Great!
18:10 and cry: " 'Woe! Woe, O great city, O **Babylon**, city of power!
18:21 "With such violence the great city of **Babylon** will be thrown

957 βαθμός, *bathmos* [1] [√ *326*]

standing [1]

1Ti 3:13 Those who have served well gain an excellent **standing** and great

958 βάθος, *bathos* [8] [√ *960*]

deep [2], depth [2], shallow [+3590] [2], deep water [1], extreme [+2848] [1]

Mt 13: 5 It sprang up quickly, because the soil was **shallow** [+3590].
Mk   4: 5 It sprang up quickly, because the soil was **shallow** [+3590].
Lk   5: 4 had finished speaking, he said to Simon, "Put out into **deep water**,
Ro   8:39 neither height nor **depth**, nor anything else in all creation,
11:33 the **depth** of the riches of the wisdom and knowledge of God!
1Co 2:10 The Spirit searches all things, even the **deep** *things* of God.
2Co 8: 2 and their **extreme** [+2848] poverty welled up in rich generosity.
Eph 3:18 grasp how wide and long and high and **deep** is the love of Christ,

959 βαθύνω, *bathynō* [1] [√ *960*]

down deep [1]

Lk   6:48 a house, who dug **down deep** and laid the foundation on rock.

960 βαθύς, *bathys* [4] [→ *958, 959*]

deep [3], very early in the morning [+3986] [1]

Lk 24: 1 On the first day of the week, **very early in the morning** [+3986],
Jn   4:11 woman said, "you have nothing to draw with and the well is **deep**.
Ac 20: 9 who was sinking *into* a **deep** sleep as Paul talked on and on.
Rev 2:24 and have not learned Satan's so-called **deep** *secrets* (I will not

961 βάϊον, *baion* [1]

branches [1]

Jn 12:13 They took palm **branches** and went out to meet him, shouting,

962 Βαλαάμ, *Balaam* [3]

Balaam [2], Balaam's [1]

2Pe 2:15 and wandered off to follow the way *of* **Balaam** son of Beor,
Jude 1:11 the way of Cain; they have rushed for profit into **Balaam's** error;
Rev 2:14 You have people there who hold to the teaching *of* **Balaam**,

963 Βαλάκ, *Balak* [1]

Balak [1]

Rev 2:14 who taught **Balak** to entice the Israelites to sin by eating food

964 βαλλάντιον, *ballantion* [4]

purse [3], purses [1]

Lk 10: 4 Do not take a **purse** or bag or sandals; and do not greet anyone on
12:33 Provide **purses** for yourselves that will not wear out, a treasure in
22:35 "When I sent you without **purse**, bag or sandals, did you lack
22:36 said to them, "But now if you have a **purse**, take it, and also a bag;

965 βάλλω, ballō [122] [→ 327, 332, 506, 610, 612, 613, 1017, 1018, 1064, 1074, 1075, 1076, 1286, 1330, 1333, 1675, 1678, 1833, 2095, 2099, 2850, 2856, 3344, 3554, 4125, 4129, 4130, 4212, 4213, 4314, 4316, 4582, 5202, 5560, 5649, 5650, 5651, 5680; cf. 311]

thrown [26], throw [15], put [13], threw [5], hurled [4], put in [4], bring [3], cast [3], casting [3], hurled down [2], lying [2], pour [2], poured [2], pours [2], putting [2], spewed [2], swung [2], toss [2], *untranslated* [1], did^s [1], drives [1], drop [1], entice to sin [+1967+4998] [1], fertilize [+3162] [1], flinging [1], flung [1], gave [+1650] [1], gave [1], help [1], impose [1], jumped [+1571] [1], laid [1], lay [1], let down [1], lies [1], lying in bed [1], others^s [1], planted [1], prompted [+1650+2840+3836] [1], put on deposit [1], scatters [1], stone [+2093] [1], swept [1], threw in [1], throw out [1], thrown down [1]

Mt 3:10 not produce good fruit will be cut down and **thrown** into the fire.
    4: 6 "If you are the Son of God," he said, "**throw** yourself down.
    4:18 *They were* **casting** a net into the lake, for they were fishermen.
    5:13 good for anything, except *to be* **thrown** out and trampled by men.
    5:25 hand you over to the officer, and *you may be* **thrown** into prison.
    5:29 If your right eye causes you to sin, gouge it out and **throw** it away.
    5:29 part of your body than for your whole body *to be* **thrown** into hell.
    5:30 if your right hand causes you to sin, cut it off and **throw** it away.
    6:30 which is here today and tomorrow *is* **thrown** into the fire,
    7: 6 "Do not give dogs what is sacred; *do* not **throw** your pearls to pigs.
    7:19 that does not bear good fruit is cut down and **thrown** into the fire.
    8: 6 "my servant **lies** at home paralyzed and in terrible suffering."
    8:14 he saw Peter's mother-in-law **lying in bed** with a fever.
    9: 2 Some men brought to him a paralytic, **lying** on a mat. When Jesus
    9:17 Neither *do men* **pour** new wine into old wineskins. If they do,
    9:17 No, *they* **pour** new wine into new wineskins, and both are
   10:34 "Do not suppose that I have come *to* **bring** peace to the earth.
   10:34 peace to the earth. I did not come *to* **bring** peace, but a sword.
   13:42 *They will* **throw** them into the fiery furnace, where there will be
   13:47 the kingdom of heaven is like a net that *was* **let down** into the lake
   13:48 and collected the good fish in baskets, but **threw** the bad away.
   13:50 and **throw** them into the fiery furnace, where there will be weeping
   15:26 "It is not right *to* take the children's bread and **toss** it to their dogs."
   17:27 we may not offend them, go to the lake and **throw** out your line.
   18: 8 or your foot causes you to sin, cut it off and **throw** it away.
   18: 8 than to have two hands or two feet and *be* **thrown** into eternal fire.
   18: 9 And if your eye causes you to sin, gouge it out and **throw** it away.
   18: 9 one eye than to have two eyes and *be* **thrown** into the fire of hell.
   18:30 he went off and *had* the man **thrown** into prison until he could pay
   21:21 'Go, **throw** *yourself* into the sea,' and it will be done.
   25:27 you should have **put** my money **on deposit** with the bankers,
   26:12 *When* she **poured** this perfume on my body, she did it to prepare
   27: 6 and said, "It is against the law *to* **put** this into the treasury,
   27:35 they had crucified him, they divided up his clothes *by* **casting** lots.
Mk 2:22 And no one **pours** new wine into old wineskins. If he does,
    4:26 the kingdom of God is like. A man **scatters** seed on the ground.
    7:27 it is not right to take the children's bread and **toss** it to their dogs."
    7:30 She went home and found her child **lying** on the bed,
    7:33 away from the crowd, Jesus **put** his fingers into the man's ears.
    9:22 "*It has* often **thrown** him into fire or water to kill him. But if you
    9:42 it would be better for him *to be* **thrown** into the sea with a large
    9:45 to enter life crippled than to have two feet and *be* **thrown** into hell.
    9:47 God with one eye than to have two eyes and *be* **thrown** into hell,
   11:23 'Go, **throw** *yourself* into the sea,' and does not doubt in his heart
   12:41 and watched the crowd **putting** their money into the temple
   12:41 into the temple treasury. Many rich people **threw in** large amounts.
   12:42 But a poor widow came and **put in** two very small copper coins,
   12:43 this poor widow *has* **put** more into the treasury than all the others.
   12:43 poor widow has put more into the treasury than all the **others**^s.
   12:44 *They* all **gave** out of their wealth;
   12:44 but she, out of her poverty, **put in** everything—all she had to live
   15:24 Dividing up his clothes, they **cast** lots to see what each would get.
Lk 3: 9 not produce good fruit will be cut down and **thrown** into the fire.
    4: 9 you are the Son of God," he said, "**throw** yourself down from here.
    5:37 And no one **pours** new wine into old wineskins. If he does,
   12:28 which is here today, and tomorrow *is* **thrown** into the fire,
   12:49 "I have come *to* **bring** fire on the earth, and how I wish it were
   12:58 turn you over to the officer, and the officer **throw** you into prison.
   13: 8 for one more year, and I'll dig around it and **fertilize** [+3162] it.

13:19 like a mustard seed, which a man took and **planted** in his garden.
14:35 It is fit neither for the soil nor for the manure pile; it *is* **thrown** out.
16:20 At his gate *was* **laid** a beggar named Lazarus, covered with sores
21: 1 Jesus saw the rich **putting** their gifts into the temple treasury.
21: 2 He also saw a poor widow **put** in two very small copper coins.
21: 3 he said, "this poor widow *has* **put in** more than all the others.
21: 4 All these people **gave** [+1650] their gifts out of their wealth;
21: 4 but she out of her poverty **put in** all she had to live on."
23:19 (Barabbas had been **thrown** into prison for an insurrection in the
23:25 He released the man *who had been* **thrown** into prison for
23:34 they are doing." And *they* divided up his clothes *by* **casting** lots.
Jn 3:24 (This was before John was **put** in prison.)
    5: 7 "I have no one *to* **help** me into the pool when the water is stirred.
    8: 7 of you is without sin, *let him* be the first *to* **throw** a stone at her."
    8:59 At this, they picked up stones to **stone** [+2093] him, but Jesus hid
   12: 6 of the money bag, he used to help himself to what *was* **put** *into* it.
   13: 2 meal was being served, and the devil *had* already **prompted** [+1650+2840+3836] Judas Iscariot, son of Simon, to betray Jesus.
   13: 5 *he* **poured** water into a basin and began to wash his disciples' feet,
   15: 6 remain in me, *he is* like a branch that *is* **thrown** away and withers;
   15: 6 such branches are picked up, **thrown** into the fire and burned.
   18:11 Jesus commanded Peter, "**Put** your sword away! Shall I not drink
   19:24 divided my garments among them and **cast** lots for my clothing."
   20:25 the nail marks in his hands and **put** my finger where the nails were,
   20:25 the nails were, and **put** my hand into his side, I will not believe it."
   20:27 see my hands. Reach out your hand and **put** it into my side.
   21: 6 "**Throw** your net on the right side of the boat and you will find
   21: 6 When *they* did^s, they were unable to haul the net in because of the
   21: 7 him (for he had taken it off) and **jumped** [+1571] into the water.
Ac 16:23 they had been severely flogged, they *were* **thrown** into prison,
   16:24 *he* **put** them in the inner cell and fastened their feet in the stocks.
   16:37 even though we are Roman citizens, and **threw** us into prison.
   22:23 *As they were* shouting and throwing off their cloaks and **flinging**
   27:14 called the "northeaster," **swept** down from the island.
Jas 3: 3 When *we* **put** bits into the mouths of horses to make them obey us,
1Jn 4:18 But perfect love **drives** out fear, because fear has to do with
Rev 2:10 I tell you, the devil will **put** some of you in prison to test you,
    2:14 who taught Balak *to* **entice** [+1967+4998] the Israelites **to sin** by
    2:22 So *I will* **cast** her on a bed of suffering, and I will make those who
    2:24 so-called deep secrets (*I will* not **impose** any other burden on you):
    4:10 and ever. *They* **lay** their crowns before the throne and say:
    6:13 as late figs **drop** from a fig tree when shaken by a strong wind.
    8: 5 filled it with fire from the altar, and **hurled** it on the earth;
    8: 7 and fire mixed with blood, and *it was* **hurled** down upon the earth.
    8: 8 like a huge mountain, all ablaze, *was* **thrown** into the sea.
   12: 4 swept a third of the stars out of the sky and **flung** them to the earth.
   12: 9 The great dragon *was* **hurled down**—that ancient serpent called
   12: 9 world astray. *He was* **hurled** to the earth, and his angels with him.
   12: 9 He was hurled to the earth, and his angels with him. **[RPG]**
   12:10 them before our God day and night, *has been* **hurled down**.
   12:13 When the dragon saw that *he had been* **hurled** to the earth,
   12:15 Then from his mouth the serpent **spewed** water like a river,
   12:16 and swallowing the river that the dragon *had* **spewed** out of his
   14:16 So he who was seated on the cloud **swung** his sickle over the earth,
   14:19 The angel **swung** his sickle on the earth, gathered its grapes
   14:19 its grapes and **threw** them into the great winepress of God's wrath.
   18:19 *They will* **throw** dust on their heads, and with weeping
   18:21 up a boulder the size of a large millstone and **threw** it into the sea,
   18:21 such violence the great city of Babylon *will be* **thrown down**,
   19:20 The two of them *were* **thrown** alive into the fiery lake of burning
   20: 3 *He* **threw** him into the Abyss, and locked and sealed it over him,
   20:10 *was* **thrown** into the lake of burning sulfur, where the beast
   20:14 Then death and Hades *were* **thrown** into the lake of fire. The lake
   20:15 written in the book of life, *he was* **thrown** into the lake of fire.

966 βαπτίζω, baptizō [77] [√ 970]

βάπτισμα ... βαπτίζω (baptism ... baptize) [6] Mk 1:4; 10:38,39; Lk 7:29; 12:50; Ac 19:4; cf. Ac 19:3

ἐν βαπτίζω; βαπτίζω ἐν (baptize in) [16] Mt 3:6,11,11; Mk 1:4,5,8; Lk 3:16; Jn 1:26,31,33,33; 3:23; Ac 1:5; 10:48; 11:16; 1Co 10:2

βαπτίζω εἰς; εἰς βαπτίζω (baptize in/into) [13] Mt 3:11; 28:19; Mk 1:9; Ac 8:16; 19:3,5; Ro 6:3,3; 1Co 1:13,15; 10:2; 12:13; Gal 3:27

βαπτίζω ὑπέρ (baptize on behalf of) [2] 1Co 15:29,29

βαπτίζω ὑπό (baptize for) [7] Mt 3:6,13,14; Mk 1:5,9; Lk 3:7;
   7:30

baptized [48], baptize [12], baptizing [8], Baptist [2], wash [2],
baptism [1], baptism receive [1], baptism undergo [+*967*] [1],
baptized [+*5639*] [1], baptized [+*967*] [1]

Mt   3: 6 their sins, *they were* **baptized** by him in the Jordan River.
      3:11 "I **baptize** you with water for repentance. But after me will come
      3:11 fit to carry. He *will* **baptize** you with the Holy Spirit and with fire.
      3:13 Then Jesus came from Galilee to the Jordan *to be* **baptized** by
      3:14 saying, "I need *to be* **baptized** by you, and do you come to me?"
      3:16 As soon as Jesus *was* **baptized**, he went up out of the water.
   28:19 **baptizing** them in the name of the Father and of the Son and of the
Mk   1: 4 **baptizing** in the desert region and preaching a baptism of
      1: 5 their sins, *they were* **baptized** by him in the Jordan River.
      1: 8 I **baptize** you with water, but he will baptize you with the Holy
      1: 8 you with water, but he *will* **baptize** you with the Holy Spirit."
      1: 9 from Nazareth in Galilee and *was* **baptized** by John in the Jordan.
      6:14 were saying, "John the **Baptist** has been raised from the dead,
      6:24 shall I ask for?" "The head *of* John the **Baptist**," she answered.
      7: 4 they come from the marketplace they do not eat unless *they* **wash**.
   10:38 cup I drink or *be* **baptized** *with* the baptism I am baptized with?"
   10:38 cup I drink or be baptized with the baptism I *am* **baptized** *with*?"
   10:39 cup I drink and *be* **baptized** *with* the baptism I am baptized with,
   10:39 cup I drink and be baptized with the baptism I *am* **baptized** *with*,
   16:16 Whoever believes and *is* **baptized** will be saved, but whoever does
Lk   3: 7 John said to the crowds coming out *to be* **baptized** by him,
      3:12 Tax collectors also came *to be* **baptized**. "Teacher," they asked,
      3:16 John answered them all, "I **baptize** you with water. But one more
      3:16 to untie. He *will* **baptize** you with the Holy Spirit and with fire.
      3:21 When all the people *were being* **baptized**, Jesus was baptized too.
      3:21 When all the people were being baptized, Jesus *was* **baptized** too.
      7:29 way was right, *because they had been* **baptized** [+*967*] by John.
      7:30 for themselves, *because they had* not *been* **baptized** by John.)
   11:38 noticing that Jesus *did* not first **wash** before the meal,
   12:50 But I have a **baptism** *to* **undergo** [+*967*],
Jn   1:25 "Why then *do you* **baptize** if you are not the Christ, nor Elijah,
      1:26 "I **baptize** with water," John replied, "but among you stands one
      1:28 on the other side of the Jordan, where John was **baptizing**.
      1:31 but the reason I came **baptizing** with water was that he might be
      1:33 except that the one who sent me *to* **baptize** with water told me,
      1:33 and remain is he who *will* **baptize** with the Holy Spirit.'
      3:22 where he spent some time with them, and **baptized**.
      3:23 Now John also was **baptizing** at Aenon near Salim, because there
      3:23 of water, and people were constantly coming *to be* **baptized**.
      3:26 well, he *is* **baptizing**, and everyone is going to him."
      4: 1 that Jesus was gaining and **baptizing** more disciples than John,
      4: 2 although in fact it was not Jesus *who* **baptized**, but his disciples.
   10:40 to the place where John had been **baptizing** in the early days.
Ac   1: 5 For John **baptized** with water, but in a few days you will be
      1: 5 but in a few days you *will be* **baptized** with the Holy Spirit."
      2:38 Peter replied, "Repent and *be* **baptized**, every one of you,
      2:41 Those who accepted his message *were* **baptized**, and about three
      8:12 name of Jesus Christ, *they were* **baptized**, both men and women.
      8:13 Simon himself believed and was **baptized**. And he followed Philip
      8:16 *they had* simply *been* **baptized** [+*5639*] into the name of the Lord
      8:36 eunuch said, "Look, here is water. Why shouldn't I *be* **baptized**?"
      8:38 and the eunuch went down into the water and Philip **baptized** him.
      9:18 Saul's eyes, and he could see again. *He* got up and *was* **baptized**,
   10:47 "Can anyone keep these people from *being* **baptized** with water?
   10:48 So he ordered that they *be* **baptized** in the name of Jesus Christ.
   11:16 'John **baptized** with water, but you will be baptized with the Holy
   11:16 with water, but you *will be* **baptized** with the Holy Spirit.'
   16:15 When *she* and the members of her household *were* **baptized**,
   16:33 then immediately he and all his family *were* **baptized**.
   18: 8 of the Corinthians who heard him believed and *were* **baptized**.
   19: 3 So Paul asked, "Then what **baptism** *did you* **receive**?" "John's
   19: 4 Paul said, "John's **baptism** was a baptism of repentance. He told
   19: 5 hearing this, *they were* **baptized** into the name of the Lord Jesus.
   22:16 Get up, *be* **baptized** and wash your sins away, calling on his
Ro   6: 3 Or don't you know that all of *us who were* **baptized** into Christ
      6: 3 who were baptized into Christ Jesus *were* **baptized** into his death?
1Co 1:13 Paul crucified for you? *Were you* **baptized** into the name of Paul?
      1:14 I am thankful that *I did* not **baptize** any of you except Crispus

      1:15 so no one can say that *you were* **baptized** into my name.
      1:16 (Yes, *I* also **baptized** the household of Stephanas; beyond that,
      1:16 beyond that, I don't remember if *I* **baptized** anyone else.)
      1:17 For Christ did not send me *to* **baptize**, but to preach the gospel—
   10: 2 *They were* all **baptized** into Moses in the cloud and in the sea.
   12:13 For we *were* all **baptized** by one Spirit into one body—
   15:29 no resurrection, what will those do *who are* **baptized** for the dead?
   15:29 the dead are not raised at all, why *are people* **baptized** for them?
Gal 3:27 for all of you who *were* **baptized** into Christ have clothed

967 βάπτισμα, *baptisma* [19] [√ *970*]

βαπτίζω ... βάπτισμα (to baptize ... baptism) [6] Mk 1:4;
   10:38,39; Lk 7:29; 12:50; Ac 19:4; cf. Ac 19:3

βάπτισμα μετανοίας (baptism of repentance) [4] Mk 1:4; Lk
   3:3; Ac 13:24; 19:4

baptism [16], baptism undergo [+*966*] [1], baptized [+*966*] [1],
baptizing [1]

Mt   3: 7 of the Pharisees and Sadducees coming to where he was **baptizing**,
   21:25 John's **baptism**—where did it come from? Was it from heaven,
Mk   1: 4 and preaching a **baptism** of repentance for the forgiveness of sins.
   10:38 cup I drink or be baptized with the **baptism** I am baptized with?"
   10:39 cup I drink and be baptized with the **baptism** I am baptized with,
   11:30 John's **baptism**—was it from heaven, or from men? Tell me!"
Lk   3: 3 preaching a **baptism** of repentance for the forgiveness of sins.
      7:29 way was right, *because they had been* **baptized** [+*966*] by John.
   12:50 But I have a **baptism** [+*966*] *to* **undergo**,
   20: 4 John's **baptism**—was it from heaven, or from men?"
Ac   1:22 beginning from John's **baptism** to the time when Jesus was taken
   10:37 beginning in Galilee after the **baptism** that John preached
   13:24 John preached repentance and **baptism** to all the people of Israel.
   18:25 about Jesus accurately, though he knew only the **baptism** of John.
   19: 3 what baptism did you receive?" "John's **baptism**," they replied.
   19: 4 Paul said, "John's baptism was a **baptism** of repentance. He told
Ro   6: 4 therefore buried with him through **baptism** into death in order that,
Eph 4: 5 one Lord, one faith, one **baptism**;
1Pe 3:21 and this water symbolizes **baptism** that now saves you also—

968 βαπτισμός, *baptismos* [4] [√ *970*]

baptism [1], baptisms [1], ceremonial washings [1], washing [1]

Mk   7: 4 other traditions, such as the **washing** of cups, pitchers and kettles.)
Col 2:12 having been buried with him in **baptism** and raised with him
Heb 6: 2 instruction *about* **baptisms**, the laying on of hands,
      9:10 a matter of food and drink and various **ceremonial washings**—

969 βαπτιστής, *baptistēs* [12] [√ *970*]

Baptist [12]

Mt   3: 1 In those days John the **Baptist** came, preaching in the Desert of
   11:11 of women there has not risen anyone greater than John the **Baptist**;
   11:12 From the days *of* John the **Baptist** until now, the kingdom of
   14: 2 and he said to his attendants, "This is John the **Baptist**; he has risen
   14: 8 she said, "Give me here on a platter the head *of* John the **Baptist**."
   16:14 They replied, "Some say John the **Baptist**; others say Elijah;
   17:13 understood that he was talking to them about John the **Baptist**.
Mk   6:25 "I want you to give me right now the head *of* John the **Baptist** on a
      8:28 They replied, "Some say John the **Baptist**; others say Elijah;
Lk   7:20 came to Jesus, they said, "John the **Baptist** sent us to you to ask,
      7:33 For John the **Baptist** came neither eating bread nor drinking wine,
      9:19 They replied, "Some say John the **Baptist**; others say Elijah;

970 βάπτω, *baptō* [4] [→ *966, 967, 968, 969, 1834, 1835*]

dipped [2], dip [1], dipping [1]

Lk 16:24 pity on me and send Lazarus to **dip** the tip of his finger in water
Jn 13:26 I will give this piece of bread *when* I *have* **dipped** it *in the dish*."
   13:26 Then, **dipping** the piece of bread, he gave it to Judas Iscariot,
Rev 19:13 He is dressed in a robe **dipped** in blood, and his name is the Word

971 βαρ, *bar*   Not used in UBS/NIV

972 Βαραββᾶς, *Barabbas* [11]

Barabbas [11]

Mt 27:16 At that time they had a notorious prisoner, called **Barabbas**.
27:17 me to release to you: **Barabbas**, or Jesus who is called Christ?"
27:20 and the elders persuaded the crowd to ask for **Barabbas**
27:21 to release to you?" asked the governor. "**Barabbas**," they answered.
27:26 Then he released **Barabbas** to them. But he had Jesus flogged,
Mk 15: 7 A man called **Barabbas** was in prison with the insurrectionists
15:11 stirred up the crowd to have Pilate release **Barabbas** instead.
15:15 Wanting to satisfy the crowd, Pilate released **Barabbas** to them.
Lk 23:18 they cried out, "Away with this man! Release **Barabbas** to us!"
Jn 18:40 They shouted back, "No, not him! Give us **Barabbas**!"
18:40 Give us Barabbas!" Now **Barabbas** had taken part in a rebellion.

973 Βαράκ, *Barak* [1]

Barak [1]

Heb 11:32 **Barak**, Samson, Jephthah, David, Samuel and the prophets,

974 Βαραχίας, *Barachias* [1]

Berekiah [1]

Mt 23:35 blood of righteous Abel to the blood of Zechariah son *of* **Berekiah**,

975 βάρβαρος, *barbaros* [6]

foreigner [2], islanders [2], barbarian [1], non-Greeks [1]

Ac 28: 2 The **islanders** showed us unusual kindness. They built a fire
28: 4 When the **islanders** saw the snake hanging from his hand,
Ro 1:14 I am obligated both to Greeks and **non-Greeks**, both to the wise
1Co 14:11 I am a **foreigner** to the speaker, and he is a foreigner to me.
14:11 I am a foreigner to the speaker, and he is a **foreigner** to me.
Col 3:11 **barbarian**, Scythian, slave or free, but Christ is all, and is in all.

976 βαρέω, *bareō* [6] [√ *983*]

burdened [2], heavy [1], under pressure [1], very sleepy [+*5678*] [1], weighed down [1]

Mt 26:43 he again found them sleeping, because their eyes were **heavy**.
Lk 9:32 Peter and his companions were **very sleepy** [+*5678*], but when
21:34 "Be careful, or your hearts *will be* **weighed down** with dissipation,
2Co 1: 8 We were **under** great **pressure**, far beyond our ability to endure,
5: 4 For while we are in this tent, we groan and are **burdened**,
1Ti 5:16 should help them and not *let* the church *be* **burdened** *with* them,

977 βαρέως, *bareōs* [2] [√ *983*]

hardly [2]

Mt 13:15 they **hardly** hear with their ears, and they have closed their eyes.
Ac 28:27 they **hardly** hear with their ears, and they have closed their eyes.

978 Βαρθολομαῖος, *Bartholomaios* [4]

Bartholomew [4]

Mt 10: 3 Philip and **Bartholomew**; Thomas and Matthew the tax collector;
Mk 3:18 Andrew, Philip, **Bartholomew**, Matthew, Thomas, James son of
Lk 6:14 his brother Andrew, James, John, Philip, **Bartholomew**,
Ac 1:13 and Andrew; Philip and Thomas, **Bartholomew** and Matthew;

979 Βαριησοῦς, *Bariēsous* [1]

Bar-Jesus [1]

Ac 13: 6 they met a Jewish sorcerer and false prophet named **Bar-Jesus**,

980 Βαριωνᾶ, *Bariōna* [1] [→ *981*]

son of Jonah [1]

Mt 16:17 Jesus replied, "Blessed are you, Simon **son of Jonah**, for this was

981 Βαριωνᾶς, *Bariōnas* Not used in UBS/NIV [√ *980*]

982 Βαρναβᾶς, *Barnabas* [28]

Βαρναβᾶς ... Μᾶρκος (Barnabas ... Mark) [4] Ac 12:25; 15:37,39; Col 4:10

Παῦλος ... Βαρναβᾶς (Paul ... Barnabas) [12] Ac 13:43,46,50; 14:12,14; 15:2,2,12,22,25,35,36

Barnabas [28]

Ac 4:36 whom the apostles called **Barnabas** (which means Son of
9:27 But **Barnabas** took him and brought him to the apostles. He told
11:22 of the church at Jerusalem, and they sent **Barnabas** to Antioch.
11:30 they did, sending their gift to the elders by **Barnabas** and Saul.
12:25 When **Barnabas** and Saul had finished their mission, they returned
13: 1 **Barnabas**, Simeon called Niger, Lucius of Cyrene, Manaen (who
13: 2 "Set apart for me **Barnabas** and Saul for the work to which I have
13: 7 sent for **Barnabas** and Saul because he wanted to hear the word of
13:43 and devout converts to Judaism followed Paul and **Barnabas**,
13:46 Then Paul and **Barnabas** answered them boldly: "We had to speak
13:50 They stirred up persecution against Paul and **Barnabas**,
14:12 **Barnabas** they called Zeus, and Paul they called Hermes
14:14 But when the apostles **Barnabas** and Paul heard of this, they tore
14:20 back into the city. The next day he and **Barnabas** left for Derbe.
15: 2 This brought Paul and **Barnabas** into sharp dispute and debate
15: 2 So Paul and **Barnabas** were appointed, along with some other
15:12 The whole assembly became silent as they listened to **Barnabas**
15:22 their own men and send them to Antioch with Paul and **Barnabas**.
15:25 and send them to you with our dear friends **Barnabas** and Paul—
15:35 But Paul and **Barnabas** remained in Antioch, where they
15:36 Some time later Paul said to **Barnabas**, "Let us go back and visit
15:37 **Barnabas** wanted to take John, also called Mark, with them,
15:39 they parted company. **Barnabas** took Mark and sailed for Cyprus,
1Co 9: 6 Or is it only I and **Barnabas** who must work for a living?
Gal 2: 1 years later I went up again to Jerusalem, this time with **Barnabas**.
2: 9 and **Barnabas** the right hand of fellowship when they recognized
2:13 so that by their hypocrisy even **Barnabas** was led astray.
Col 4:10 sends you his greetings, as does Mark, the cousin *of* **Barnabas**.

983 βάρος, *baros* [6] [→ *4*, *976*, *977*, *986*, *987*, *988*, *2096*, *2851*, *2852*]

burden [3], burdens [1], that far outweighs them all [+*1650*+*2848*+*5651*+*5651*] [1], to burden [+*2202*] [1]

Mt 20:12 made them equal to us who have borne the **burden** *of the work*
Ac 15:28 and to us not **to burden** [+*2202*] you *with* anything beyond the
2Co 4:17 light and momentary troubles are achieving for us an eternal glory **that far outweighs** [+*1650*+*2848*+*5651*+*5651*] **them all**.
Gal 6: 2 Carry each other's **burdens**, and in this way you will fulfill the law
1Th 2: 6 As apostles of Christ we could have been a **burden** to you,
Rev 2:24 deep secrets (I will not impose any other **burden** on you):

984 Βαρσαββᾶς, *Barsabbas* [2]

Barsabbas [2]

Ac 1:23 Joseph called **Barsabbas** (also known as Justus) and Matthias.
15:22 They chose Judas (called **Barsabbas**) and Silas, two men who

985 Βαρτιμαῖος, *Bartimaios* [1]

Bartimaeus [1]

Mk 10:46 the city, a blind man, **Bartimaeus** (that is, the Son of Timaeus),

986 βαρύνω, *barynō* Not used in UBS/NIV [√ *983*]

987 βαρύς, *barys* [6] [√ *983*]

burdensome [1], heavy [1], more important matters [1], savage [1], serious [1], weighty [1]

Mt 23: 4 They tie up **heavy** loads and put them on men's shoulders,
23:23 But you have neglected the **more important matters** of the law—
Ac 20:29 **savage** wolves will come in among you and will not spare the

25: 7 bringing many **serious** charges against him, which they could not
2Co 10:10 For some say, "His letters are **weighty** and forceful, but in person
1Jn 5: 3 to obey his commands. And his commands are not **burdensome**,

988 βαρύτιμος, *barytimos* [1] [√ 983 + 5507]

very expensive [1]

Mt 26: 7 a woman came to him with an alabaster jar *of* **very expensive**

989 βασανίζω, *basanizō* [12] [√ 992]

tormented [4], torture [4], buffeted [1], pain [1], straining [1], suffering [1]

Mt 8: 6 "my servant lies at home paralyzed and in terrible **suffering**."
   8:29 "Have you come here *to* **torture** us before the appointed time?"
   14:24 from land, **buffeted** by the waves because the wind was against it.
Mk 5: 7 of the Most High God? Swear to God that *you* won't **torture** me!"
   6:48 He saw the disciples **straining** at the oars, because the wind was
Lk 8:28 Jesus, Son of the Most High God? I beg you, don't **torture** me!"
2Pe 2: 8 *was* **tormented** in his righteous soul by the lawless deeds he saw
Rev 9: 5 given power to kill them, but only to **torture** them for five months.
   11:10 because these two prophets *had* **tormented** those who live on the
   12: 2 was pregnant and cried out *in* **pain** as she was about to give birth.
   14:10 *He will be* **tormented** with burning sulfur in the presence of the
   20:10 *They will be* **tormented** day and night for ever and ever.

990 βασανισμός, *basanismos* [6] [√ 992]

torment [3], agony [1], sting [1], torture [1]

Rev 9: 5 And the **agony** they *suffered* was like that of the sting of a
   9: 5 And the agony they suffered was like that of the **sting** of a scorpion
   14:11 And the smoke *of* their **torment** rises for ever and ever. There is
   18: 7 Give her as much **torture** and grief as the glory and luxury she
   18:10 Terrified *at* her **torment**, they will stand far off and cry: " 'Woe!
   18:15 their wealth from her will stand far off, terrified *at* her **torment**.

991 βασανιστής, *basanistēs* [1] [√ 992]

jailers to be tortured [1]

Mt 18:34 In anger his master turned him over *to* the **jailers to be tortured**,

992 βάσανος, *basanos* [3] [→ 989, 990, 991]

torment [2], severe pain [1]

Mt 4:24 those suffering **severe pain**, the demon-possessed, those having
Lk 16:23 In hell, where he was in **torment**, he looked up and saw Abraham
   16:28 so that they will not also come to this place *of* **torment**.'

993 βασιλεία, *basileia* [162] [√ 995]

βασιλείαν θεοῦ (kingdom of God) [4] 1Co 6:9,10; 15:50; Gal 5:21

βασιλεία τοῦ θεοῦ (kingdom of God) [64] Mt 6:33; 12:28; 19:24; 21:31,43; Mk 1:15; 4:11,26,30; 9:1,47; 10:14,15,23,24,25; 12:34; 14:25; 15:43; Lk 4:43; 6:20; 7:28; 8:1,10; 9:2,11,27,60,62; 10:9,11; 11:20; 13:18,20,28,29; 14:15; 16:16; 17:20,20,21; 18:16,17,24,25,29; 19:11; 21:31; 22:16,18; 23:51; Jn 3:3,5; Ac 1:3; 8:12; 14:22; 19:8; 28:23,31; Ro 14:17; 1Co 4:20; Col 4:11; 2Th 1:5; Rev 12:10

βασιλεία οὐρανῶν (kingdom of heaven) [32] Mt 3:2; 4:17; 5:3,10,19,19,20; 7:21; 8:11; 10:7; 11:11,12; 13:11,24,31,33,44,45,47,52; 16:19; 18:1,3,4,23; 19:12,14,23; 20:1; 22:2; 23:13; 25:1

βασιλεία τοῦ κυρίου (kingdom of the Lord) [2] 2Pe 1:11; Rev 11:15

βασιλεία τοῦ Χριστοῦ (kingdom of Christ) [2] Eph 5:5; Rev 11:15

ἐγγίζω ἡ βασιλεία τοῦ (the kingdom is near) [6] Mt 3:2; 4:17; 10:7; Mk 1:15; Lk 10:9,11

εὐαγγέλιον τῆς βασιλείας (gospel of the kingdom) [3] Mt 4:23; 9:35; 24:14

kingdom [154], kingdoms [3], its [+1847+3836+3836] [1], king [1], made king [+3284+3836] [1], rule [1], rules [+2400] [1]

Mt 3: 2 and saying, "Repent, for the **kingdom** of heaven is near."
   4: 8 and showed him all the **kingdoms** of the world and their splendor.
   4:17 began to preach, "Repent, for the **kingdom** of heaven is near."
   4:23 preaching the good news *of* the **kingdom**, and healing every
   5: 3 "Blessed are the poor in spirit, for theirs is the **kingdom** of heaven.
   5:10 because of righteousness, for theirs is the **kingdom** of heaven.
   5:19 to do the same will be called least in the **kingdom** of heaven,
   5:19 and teaches these commands will be called great in the **kingdom** of
   5:20 of the law, you will certainly not enter the **kingdom** of heaven.
   6:10 your **kingdom** come, your will be done on earth as it is in heaven.
   6:33 But seek first his **kingdom** and his righteousness, and all these
   7:21 who says to me, 'Lord, Lord,' will enter the **kingdom** of heaven,
   8:11 feast with Abraham, Isaac and Jacob in the **kingdom** of heaven.
   8:12 But the subjects *of* the **kingdom** will be thrown outside,
   9:35 preaching the good news *of* the **kingdom** and healing every
   10: 7 As you go, preach this message: 'The **kingdom** of heaven is near.'
   11:11 yet he who is least in the **kingdom** of heaven is greater than he.
   11:12 the **kingdom** of heaven has been forcefully advancing,
   12:25 "Every **kingdom** divided against itself will be ruined, and every
   12:26 he is divided against himself. How then can his **kingdom** stand?
   12:28 by the Spirit of God, then the **kingdom** of God has come upon you.
   13:11 "The knowledge of the secrets *of* the **kingdom** of heaven has been
   13:19 When anyone hears the message *about* the **kingdom** and does not
   13:24 "The **kingdom** of heaven is like a man who sowed good seed in his
   13:31 "The **kingdom** of heaven is like a mustard seed, which a man took
   13:33 "The **kingdom** of heaven is like yeast that a woman took and mixed
   13:38 is the world, and the good seed stands for the sons *of* the **kingdom**.
   13:41 and they will weed out of his **kingdom** everything that causes sin
   13:43 Then the righteous will shine like the sun in the **kingdom** of their
   13:44 "The **kingdom** of heaven is like treasure hidden in a field. When a
   13:45 the **kingdom** of heaven is like a merchant looking for fine pearls.
   13:47 the **kingdom** of heaven is like a net that was let down into the lake
   13:52 *about* the **kingdom** of heaven is like the owner of a house who
   16:19 I will give you the keys *of* the **kingdom** of heaven; whatever you
   16:28 death before they see the Son of Man coming in his **kingdom**."
   18: 1 and asked, "Who is the greatest in the **kingdom** of heaven?"
   18: 3 like little children, you will never enter the **kingdom** of heaven.
   18: 4 himself like this child is the greatest in the **kingdom** of heaven.
   18:23 the **kingdom** of heaven is like a king who wanted to settle
   19:12 have renounced marriage because of the **kingdom** of heaven.
   19:14 hinder them, for the **kingdom** of heaven belongs to such as these."
   19:23 the truth, it is hard for a rich man to enter the **kingdom** of heaven.
   19:24 eye of a needle than for a rich man to enter the **kingdom** of God."
   20: 1 "For the **kingdom** of heaven is like a landowner who went out early
   20:21 may sit at your right and the other at your left in your **kingdom**."
   21:31 and the prostitutes are entering the **kingdom** of God ahead of you.
   21:43 "Therefore I tell you that the **kingdom** of God will be taken away
   22: 2 "The **kingdom** of heaven is like a king who prepared a wedding
   23:13 you hypocrites! You shut the **kingdom** of heaven in men's faces.
   24: 7 Nation will rise against nation, and **kingdom** against kingdom.
   24: 7 Nation will rise against nation, and kingdom against **kingdom**.
   24:14 And this gospel *of* the **kingdom** will be preached in the whole
   25: 1 "At that time the **kingdom** of heaven will be like ten virgins who
   25:34 the **kingdom** prepared for you since the creation of the world.
   26:29 that day when I drink it anew with you in my Father's **kingdom**."
Mk 1:15 "The **kingdom** of God is near. Repent and believe the good news!"
   3:24 If a **kingdom** is divided against itself, that kingdom cannot stand.
   3:24 If a kingdom is divided against itself, that **kingdom** cannot stand.
   4:11 "The secret *of* the **kingdom** of God has been given to you.
   4:26 He also said, "This is what the **kingdom** of God is like. A man
   4:30 Again he said, "What shall we say the **kingdom** of God is like,
   6:23 "Whatever you ask I will give you, up to half my **kingdom**."
   9: 1 taste death before they see the **kingdom** of God come with power."
   9:47 It is better for you to enter the **kingdom** of God with one eye than
   10:14 not hinder them, for the **kingdom** of God belongs to such as these.
   10:15 anyone who will not receive the **kingdom** of God like a little child
   10:23 "How hard it is for the rich to enter the **kingdom** of God!"
   10:24 said again, "Children, how hard it is to enter the **kingdom** of God!
   10:25 eye of a needle than for a rich man to enter the **kingdom** of God."
   11:10 "Blessed is the coming **kingdom** of our father David!" "Hosanna in
   12:34 he said to him, "You are not far from the **kingdom** of God."

13: 8 Nation will rise against nation, and **kingdom** against kingdom.
13: 8 Nation will rise against nation, and kingdom against **kingdom**.
14:25 vine until that day when I drink it anew in the **kingdom** of God."
15:43 who was himself waiting for the **kingdom** of God, went boldly to
Lk   1:33 reign over the house of Jacob forever; his **kingdom** will never end."
     4: 5 and showed him in an instant all the **kingdoms** of the world.
     4:43 "I must preach the good news of the **kingdom** of God to the other
     6:20 "Blessed are you who are poor, for yours is the **kingdom** of God.
     7:28 yet the one who is least in the **kingdom** of God is greater than he."
     8: 1 to another, proclaiming the good news of the **kingdom** of God.
     8:10 "The knowledge of the secrets *of* the **kingdom** of God has been
     9: 2 and he sent them out to preach the **kingdom** of God and to heal the
     9:11 He welcomed them and spoke to them about the **kingdom** of God,
     9:27 here will not taste death before they see the **kingdom** of God."
     9:60 their own dead, but you go and proclaim the **kingdom** of God."
     9:62 the plow and looks back is fit for service *in* the **kingdom** of God."
    10: 9 who are there and tell them, 'The **kingdom** of God is near you.'
    10:11 off against you. Yet be sure of this: The **kingdom** of God is near.'
    11: 2 say: " 'Father, hallowed be your name, your **kingdom** come.
    11:17 "Any **kingdom** divided against itself will be ruined, and a house
    11:18 If Satan is divided against himself, how can his **kingdom** stand?
    11:20 by the finger of God, then the **kingdom** of God has come to you.
    12:31 But seek his **kingdom**, and these things will be given to you as
    12:32 for your Father has been pleased to give you the **kingdom**.
    13:18 Then Jesus asked, "What is the **kingdom** of God like? What shall I
    13:20 Again he asked, "What shall I compare the **kingdom** of God to?
    13:28 Isaac and Jacob and all the prophets in the **kingdom** of God,
    13:29 and will take their places at the feast in the **kingdom** of God.
    14:15 "Blessed is the man who will eat at the feast in the **kingdom** of God
    16:16 that time, the good news of the **kingdom** of God is being preached,
    17:20 having been asked by the Pharisees when the **kingdom** of God
    17:20 The **kingdom** of God does not come with your careful observation,
    17:21 or 'There it is,' because the **kingdom** of God is within you."
    18:16 not hinder them, for the **kingdom** of God belongs to such as these.
    18:17 anyone who will not receive the **kingdom** of God like a little child
    18:24 and said, "How hard it is for the rich to enter the **kingdom** of God!
    18:25 eye of a needle than for a rich man to enter the **kingdom** of God."
    18:29 or parents or children for the sake *of* the **kingdom** of God
    19:11 and the people thought that the **kingdom** of God was going to
    19:12 birth went to a distant country to have himself appointed **king**
    19:15 "He *was* **made king** [+3284+3836], however, and returned home.
    21:10 "Nation will rise against nation, and **kingdom** against kingdom.
    21:10 "Nation will rise against nation, and kingdom against **kingdom**.
    21:31 things happening, you know that the **kingdom** of God is near.
    22:16 I will not eat it again until it finds fulfillment in the **kingdom** of
    22:18 again of the fruit of the vine until the **kingdom** of God comes."
    22:29 And I confer on you a **kingdom**, just as my Father conferred one
    22:30 may eat and drink at my table in my **kingdom** and sit on thrones,
    23:42 he said, "Jesus, remember me when you come into your **kingdom**."
    23:51 town of Arimathea and he was waiting for the **kingdom** of God.
Jn   3: 3 no one can see the **kingdom** of God unless he is born again."
     3: 5 no one can enter the **kingdom** of God unless he is born of water
    18:36 Jesus said, "My **kingdom** is not of this world. If it were, my
    18:36 If it^s [+1847+3836+3836] were, my servants would fight to
    18:36 arrest by the Jews. But now my **kingdom** is from another place."
Ac   1: 3 over a period of forty days and spoke about the **kingdom** of God.
     1: 6 are you at this time going to restore the **kingdom** to Israel?"
     8:12 Philip as he preached the good news of the **kingdom** of God
    14:22 We must go through many hardships to enter the **kingdom** of God,"
    19: 8 for three months, arguing persuasively about the **kingdom** of God
    20:25 I have gone about preaching the **kingdom** will ever see me again.
    28:23 till evening he explained and declared to them the **kingdom** of God
    28:31 Boldly and without hindrance he preached the **kingdom** of God
Ro 14:17 For the **kingdom** of God is not a matter of eating and drinking,
1Co 4:20 For the **kingdom** of God is not a matter of talk but of power.
     6: 9 Do you not know that the wicked will not inherit the **kingdom** of
     6:10 nor slanderers nor swindlers will inherit the **kingdom** of God.
    15:24 when he hands over the **kingdom** to God the Father after he has
    15:50 brothers, that flesh and blood cannot inherit the **kingdom** of God,
Gal 5:21 that those who live like this will not inherit the **kingdom** of God.
Eph 5: 5 has any inheritance in the **kingdom** of Christ and of God.
Col 1:13 of darkness and brought us into the **kingdom** of the Son he loves,
     4:11 are the only Jews among my fellow workers for the **kingdom**
1Th 2:12 lives worthy of God, who calls you into his **kingdom** and glory.
2Th 1: 5 and as a result you will be counted worthy *of* the **kingdom** of God,
2Ti 4: 1 and the dead, and in view of his appearing and his **kingdom**,

     4:18 evil attack and will bring me safely to his heavenly **kingdom**.
Heb 1: 8 and ever, and righteousness will be the scepter *of* your **kingdom**.
    11:33 who through faith conquered **kingdoms**, administered justice,
    12:28 since we are receiving a **kingdom** that cannot be shaken,
Jas 2: 5 and to inherit the **kingdom** he promised those who love him?
2Pe 1:11 will you receive a rich welcome into the eternal **kingdom** of
Rev 1: 6 and has made us to be a **kingdom** and priests to serve his God
     1: 9 your brother and companion in the suffering and **kingdom**
     5:10 You have made them to be a **kingdom** and priests to serve our
    11:15 "The **kingdom** of the world has become the kingdom of our Lord
    12:10 come the salvation and the power and the **kingdom** of our God,
    16:10 throne of the beast, and his **kingdom** was plunged into darkness.
    17:12 horns you saw are ten kings who have not yet received a **kingdom**,
    17:17 his purpose by agreeing to give the beast their power to **rule**,
    17:18 The woman you saw is the great city that **rules** [+2400] over the

994 βασίλειος, *basileios* [2] [√ *995*]

palaces [1], royal [1]

Lk   7:25 who wear expensive clothes and indulge in luxury are in **palaces**.
1Pe 2: 9 a **royal** priesthood, a holy nation, a people belonging to God,

995 βασιλεύς, *basileus* [115] [→ *993, 994, 996, 997, 998, 999, 5203*]

βασιλεῖς τῆς γῆς (king[s] of the world) [10] Mt 17:25; Ac 4:26; Rev 1:5; 6:15; 17:2,18; 18:3,9; 19:19; 21:24

βασιλεύς τῶν αἰώνων (king of the ages) [2] 1Ti 1:17; Rev 15:3[NIV]

βασιλεύς βασιλέων (king of kings) [2] Rev 17:14; 19:16

βασιλεύς τῶν Ἰουδαίων (king of the Jews) [18] Mt 2:2; 27:11,29,37; Mk 15:2,9,12,18,26; Lk 23:3,37,38; Jn 18:33,39; 19:3,19,21,21

βασιλεύς Ἰσραήλ (king of Israel) [4] Mt 27:42; Mk 15:32; Jn 1:49; 12:13

king [82], kings [28], king [+476] [2], king's [2], he^s [+3836] [1]

Mt   1: 6 and Jesse the father of **King** David. David was the father of
     2: 1 during the time *of* **King** Herod, Magi from the east came to
     2: 2 and asked, "Where is the one who has been born **king** of the Jews?
     2: 3 When **King** Herod heard this he was disturbed, and all Jerusalem
     2: 9 After they had heard the **king**, they went on their way, and the star
     5:35 his footstool; or by Jerusalem, for it is the city *of* the Great **King**.
    10:18 and **kings** as witnesses to them and to the Gentiles.
    11: 8 fine clothes? No, those who wear fine clothes are in **kings'** palaces.
    14: 9 The **king** was distressed, but because of his oaths and his dinner
    17:25 "From whom do the **kings** of the earth collect duty and taxes—
    18:23 the kingdom of heaven is like a **king** [+476] who wanted to settle
    21: 5 'See, your **king** comes to you, gentle and riding on a donkey,
    22: 2 "The kingdom of heaven is like a **king** [+476] who prepared a
    22: 7 The **king** was enraged. He sent his army and destroyed those
    22:11 "But when the **king** came in to see the guests, he noticed a man
    22:13 "Then the **king** told the attendants, 'Tie him hand and foot,
    25:34 "Then the **King** will say to those on his right, 'Come, you who are
    25:40 "The **King** will reply, 'I tell you the truth, whatever you did for one
    27:11 and the governor asked him, "Are you the **king** of the Jews?"
    27:29 and mocked him. "Hail, **king** of the Jews!" they said.
    27:37 against him: THIS IS JESUS, THE **KING** OF THE JEWS.
    27:42 they said, "but he can't save himself! He's the **King** of Israel!
Mk   6:14 **King** Herod heard about this, for Jesus' name had become well
     6:22 The **king** said to the girl, "Ask me for anything you want, and I'll
     6:25 At once the girl hurried in to the **king** with the request: "I want you
     6:26 The **king** was greatly distressed, but because of his oaths and his
     6:27 So he^s [+3836] immediately sent an executioner with orders to
    13: 9 you will stand before governors and **kings** as witnesses to them.
    15: 2 you the **king** of the Jews?" asked Pilate. "Yes, it is as you say,"
    15: 9 "Do you want me to release to you the **king** of the Jews?"
    15:12 "What shall I do, then, with the one you call the **king** of the Jews?"
    15:18 And they began to call out to him, "Hail, **king** of the Jews!"
    15:26 of the charge against him read: THE **KING** OF THE JEWS.
    15:32 Let this Christ, this **King** of Israel, come down now from the cross,
Lk   1: 5 In the time of Herod **king** of Judea there was a priest named
    10:24 and **kings** wanted to see what you see but did not see it,
    14:31 "Or suppose a **king** is about to go to war against another king.

14:31 "Or suppose a king is about to go to war *against* another **king**.
19:38 "Blessed is the **king** who comes in the name of the Lord!"
21:12 and prisons, and you will be brought before **kings** and governors,
22:25 Jesus said to them, "The **kings** of the Gentiles lord it over them;
23: 2 payment of taxes to Caesar and claims to be Christ, a **king**."
23: 3 So Pilate asked Jesus, "Are you the **king** of the Jews?" "Yes,
23:37 and said, "If you are the **king** of the Jews, save yourself."
23:38 above him, which read: THIS IS THE **KING** OF THE JEWS.
Jn 1:49 "Rabbi, you are the Son of God; you are the **King** of Israel."
6:15 knowing that they intended to come and make him **king** by force,
12:13 comes in the name of the Lord!" "Blessed is the **King** of Israel!"
12:15 of Zion; see, your **king** is coming, seated on a donkey's colt."
18:33 summoned Jesus and asked him, "Are you the **king** of the Jews?"
18:37 "You are a **king**, then!" said Pilate. Jesus answered, "You are right
18:37 Jesus answered, "You are right in saying I am a **king**. In fact,
18:39 of the Passover. Do you want me to release 'the **king** of the Jews'?"
19: 3 went up to him again and again, saying, "Hail, **king** of the Jews!"
19:12 friend of Caesar. Anyone who claims to be a **king** opposes Caesar."
19:14 about the sixth hour. "Here is your **king**," Pilate said to the Jews.
19:15 him away! Crucify him!" "Shall I crucify your **king**?" Pilate asked.
19:15 "We have no **king** but Caesar," the chief priests answered.
19:19 It read: JESUS OF NAZARETH, THE **KING** OF THE JEWS.
19:21 the Jews protested to Pilate, "Do not write 'The **King** of the Jews,'
19:21 of the Jews,' but that this man claimed to be **king** of the Jews."
Ac 4:26 The **kings** of the earth take their stand and the rulers gather
7:10 and enabled him to gain the goodwill of Pharaoh **king** of Egypt,
7:18 Then another **king**, who knew nothing about Joseph, became ruler
9:15 before the Gentiles and their **kings** and before the people of Israel.
12: 1 It was about this time that **King** Herod arrested some who
12:20 a trusted personal servant *of* the **king**, they asked for peace,
13:21 Then the people asked for a **king**, and he gave them Saul son of
13:22 After removing Saul, he made David their **king**. He testified
17: 7 saying that there is another **king**, one called Jesus."
25:13 A few days later **King** Agrippa and Bernice arrived at Caesarea to
25:14 many days there, Festus discussed Paul's case *with* the **king**.
25:24 "**King** Agrippa, and all who are present with us, you see this man!
25:26 him before all of you, and especially before you, **King** Agrippa.
26: 2 "**King** Agrippa, I consider myself fortunate to stand before you
26: 7 *O* **king**, it is because of this hope that the Jews are accusing me.
26:13 About noon, *O* **king**, as I was on the road, I saw a light from
26:19 "So then, **King** Agrippa, I was not disobedient to the vision from
26:26 The **king** is familiar with these things, and I can speak freely to
26:27 **King** Agrippa, do you believe the prophets? I know you do."
26:30 The **king** rose, and with him the governor and Bernice and those
2Co 11:32 In Damascus the governor *under* **King** Aretas had the city of the
1Ti 1:17 Now *to* the **King** eternal, immortal, invisible, the only God,
2: 2 for **kings** and all those in authority, that we may live peaceful
6:15 the blessed and only Ruler, the **King** of kings and Lord of lords,
Heb 7: 1 This Melchizedek was **king** of Salem and priest of God Most High.
7: 1 He met Abraham returning from the defeat *of* the **kings**
7: 2 tenth of everything. First, his name means "**king** of righteousness";
7: 2 then also, "**king** of Salem" means "king of peace."
7: 2 then also, "**king** of Salem" means "**king** of peace."
11:23 was no ordinary child, and they were not afraid of the **king's** edict.
11:27 By faith he left Egypt, not fearing the **king's** anger; he persevered
1Pe 2:13 among men: whether *to* the **king**, as the supreme authority,
2:17 Love the brotherhood of believers, fear God, honor the **king**.
Rev 1: 5 the firstborn from the dead, and the ruler *of* the **kings** of the earth.
6:15 Then the **kings** of the earth, the princes, the generals, the rich,
9:11 They had as **king** over them the angel of the Abyss, whose name in
10:11 prophesy again about many peoples, nations, languages and **kings**."
15: 3 Lord God Almighty. Just and true are your ways, **King** of the ages.
16:12 and its water was dried up to prepare the way *for* the **kings** from
16:14 miraculous signs, and they go out to the **kings** of the whole world,
17: 2 With her the **kings** of the earth committed adultery
17:10 They are also seven **kings**. Five have fallen, one is, the other has
17:12 "The ten horns you saw are ten **kings** who have not yet received a
17:12 but who for one hour will receive authority as **kings** along with the
17:14 overcome them because he is Lord of lords and **King** of kings—
17:14 overcome them because he is Lord of lords and King *of* **kings**—
17:18 The woman you saw is the great city that rules over the **kings** of
18: 3 The **kings** of the earth committed adultery with her,
18: 9 "When the **kings** of the earth who committed adultery with her
19:16 this name written: **KING** OF KINGS AND LORD OF LORDS.
19:16 this name written: KING *OF* **KINGS** AND LORD OF LORDS.
19:18 so that you may eat the flesh *of* **kings**, generals, and mighty men,

19:19 Then I saw the beast and the **kings** of the earth and their armies
21:24 and the **kings** of the earth will bring their splendor into it.

996 βασιλεύω, *basileuō* [21] [√ *995*]

reign [10], reigned [4], kings [3], king [2], reigning [1], reigns [1]

Mt 2:22 But when he heard that Archelaus *was* **reigning** in Judea in place
Lk 1:33 and *he will* **reign** over the house of Jacob forever; his kingdom
19:14 after him to say, 'We don't want this man *to be* our **king**.'
19:27 But those enemies of mine who did not want me *to be* **king** over
Ro 5:14 death **reigned** from the time of Adam to the time of Moses,
5:17 the trespass of the one man, death **reigned** through that one man,
5:17 and of the gift of righteousness **reign** in life through the one man,
5:21 so that, just as sin **reigned** in death, so also grace might reign
5:21 so also grace *might* **reign** through righteousness to bring eternal
6:12 Therefore *do not let* sin **reign** in your mortal body so that you
1Co 4: 8 have become rich! *You have become* **kings**—and that without us!
4: 8 How I wish that *you* really *had become* **kings** so that we might be
15:25 For he must **reign** until he has put all his enemies under his feet.
1Ti 6:15 the blessed and only Ruler, the King *of* **kings** and Lord of lords,
Rev 5:10 and priests to serve our God, and *they will* **reign** on the earth."
11:15 of our Lord and of his Christ, and *he will* **reign** for ever and ever."
11:17 you have taken your great power and *have begun to* **reign**.
19: 6 shouting: "Hallelujah! For our Lord God Almighty **reigns**.
20: 4 They came to life and **reigned** with Christ a thousand years.
20: 6 and of Christ and *will* **reign** with him for a thousand years.
22: 5 God will give them light. And *they will* **reign** for ever and ever.

997 βασιλικός, *basilikos* [5] [√ *995*]

royal [2], royal official [2], king's country [1]

Jn 4:46 And there was a certain **royal official** whose son lay sick at
4:49 The **royal official** said, "Sir, come down before my child dies."
Ac 12:20 because they depended on the **king's country** for their food
12:21 wearing his **royal** robes, sat on his throne and delivered a public
Jas 2: 8 If you really keep the **royal** law found in Scripture, "Love your

998 βασιλίσκος, *basiliskos*   Not used in UBS/NIV
[√ *995*]

999 βασίλισσα, *basilissa* [4] [√ *995*]

queen [4]

Mt 12:42 The **Queen** of the South will rise at the judgment with this
Lk 11:31 The **Queen** of the South will rise at the judgment with the men of
Ac 8:27 in charge of all the treasury of Candace, **queen** of the Ethiopians.
Rev 18: 7 In her heart she boasts, 'I sit as **queen**; I am not a widow, and I

1000 βάσις, *basis* [1] [√ *326*]

feet [1]

Ac 3: 7 him up, and instantly the man's **feet** and ankles became strong.

1001 βασκαίνω, *baskainō* [1]

bewitched [1]

Gal 3: 1 You foolish Galatians! Who *has* **bewitched** you? Before your very

1002 βαστάζω, *bastazō* [27] [→ *1546*]

carry [5], carrying [4], bear [3], carried [3], bear with [1], borne
[1], carried away [1], endured hardships [1], gave birth [1], help
himself to [1], pay [1], picked up [1], rides [1], support [1], take
[1], tolerate [1]

Mt 3:11 who is more powerful than I, whose sandals I am not fit *to* **carry**.
8:17 "He took up our infirmities and **carried** our diseases."
20:12 'and you have made them equal to us who *have* **borne** the burden
Mk 14:13 "Go into the city, and a man **carrying** a jar of water will meet you.
Lk 7:14 went up and touched the coffin, and those **carrying** it stood still.
10: 4 *Do* not **take** a purse or bag or sandals; and do not greet anyone on

11:27 "Blessed is the mother who **gave** you **birth** and nursed you."
14:27 And anyone *who does* not **carry** his cross and follow me cannot be
22:10 "As you enter the city, a man **carrying** a jar of water will meet you.
Jn   10:31 Again the Jews **picked up** stones to stone him,
12: 6 of the money bag, *he used to* **help himself to** what was put into it.
16:12 "I have much more to say to you, more than you can now **bear**.
19:17 **Carrying** his own cross, he went out to the place of the Skull
20:15 he was the gardener, she said, "Sir, if you *have* **carried** him **away**,
Ac   3: 2 Now a man crippled from birth *was being* **carried** to the temple
9:15 This man is my chosen instrument *to* **carry** my name before the
15:10 a yoke that neither we nor our fathers have been able *to* **bear**?
21:35 of the mob was so great he had to be **carried** by the soldiers.
Ro   11:18 You *do* not **support** the root, but the root supports you.
15: 1 We who are strong ought *to* **bear with** the failings of the weak
Gal   5:10 The one who is throwing you into confusion *will* **pay** the penalty,
6: 2 **Carry** each other's burdens, and in this way you will fulfill the law
6: 5 for each one *should* **carry** his own load.
6:17 one cause me trouble, for I **bear** on my body the marks of Jesus.
Rev   2: 2 I know that you cannot **tolerate** wicked men, that you have tested
2: 3 You have persevered and *have* **endured hardships** for my name,
17: 7 to you the mystery of the woman and *of* the beast she **rides**,

1003 βάτος¹, batos¹ [5]

bush [4], briers [1]

Mk 12:26 in the account *of* the **bush**, how God said to him, 'I am the God of
Lk   6:44 People do not pick figs from thornbushes, or grapes from **briers**.
20:37 But in the account *of* the **bush**, even Moses showed that the dead
Ac   7:30 an angel appeared to Moses in the flames *of* a burning **bush** in the
7:35 God himself, through the angel who appeared to him in the **bush**.

1004 βάτος², batos² [1]

eight hundred gallons [+1669] [1]

Lk   16: 6 " '**Eight hundred gallons** [+1669] of olive oil,' he replied.

1005 βάτραχος, batrachos [1]

frogs [1]

Rev 16:13 Then I saw three evil spirits that looked like **frogs**; they came out

1006 βατταλογέω, battalogeō [1] [√ 3306]

babbling [1]

Mt   6: 7 And when you pray, *do* not *keep on* **babbling** like pagans,

1007 βδέλυγμα, bdelygma [6] [→ 1008, 1009]

abomination [2], abominations [1], abominable [1], detestable [1],
what is shameful [1]

Mt 24:15 "So when you see standing in the holy place 'the **abomination** that
Mk 13:14 "When you see 'the **abomination** that causes desolation' standing
Lk   16:15 What is highly valued among men is **detestable** in God's sight.
Rev 17: 4 filled *with* **abominable** *things* and the filth of her adulteries.
17: 5 AND *OF* THE **ABOMINATIONS** OF THE EARTH.
21:27 enter it, nor will anyone who does **what is shameful** or deceitful,

1008 βδελυκτός, bdelyktos [1] [√ 1007]

detestable [1]

Tit   1:16 They are **detestable**, disobedient and unfit for doing anything

1009 βδελύσσομαι, bdelyssomai [2] [√ 1007]

abhor [1], vile [1]

Ro   2:22 you commit adultery? You *who* **abhor** idols, do you rob temples?
Rev 21: 8 But the cowardly, the unbelieving, the **vile**, the murderers,

1010 βέβαιος, bebaios [8] [√ 326]

binding [1], firm [1], firmly [1], guaranteed [1], in force [1], more
certain [1], secure [1], sure [1]

Ro   4:16 be by grace and may be **guaranteed** to all Abraham's offspring—
2Co   1: 7 And our hope for you is **firm**, because we know that just as you
Heb   2: 2 For if the message spoken by angels was **binding**, and every
3:14 We have come to share in Christ if we hold **firmly** till the end the
6:19 We have this hope as an anchor for the soul, firm and **secure**.
9:17 because a will is **in force** only when somebody has died; it never
2Pe   1:10 be all the more eager to make your calling and election **sure**.
1:19 And we have the word of the prophets made **more certain**,

1011 βεβαιόω, bebaioō [8] [√ 326]

confirmed [3], strengthened [2], confirm [1], keep strong [1],
makes stand firm [1]

Mk 16:20 and **confirmed** his word by the signs that accompanied it.
Ro   15: 8 of God's truth, to **confirm** the promises made to the patriarchs
1Co   1: 6 because our testimony about Christ *was* **confirmed** in you.
1: 8 He *will* **keep** you **strong** to the end, so that you will be blameless
2Co   1:21 Now it is God who **makes** both us and you **stand firm** in Christ.
Col   2: 7 and built up in him, **strengthened** in the faith as you were taught,
Heb   2: 3 by the Lord, *was* **confirmed** to us by those who heard him.
13: 9 It is good for our hearts *to be* **strengthened** by grace, not by

1012 βεβαίωσις, bebaiōsis [2] [√ 326]

confirming [1], confirms [+1650] [1]

Php   1: 7 whether I am in chains or defending and **confirming** the gospel,
Heb   6:16 and the oath **confirms** [+1650] what is said and puts an end to all

1013 βέβηλος, bebēlos [5] [√ 326]

godless [4], irreligious [1]

1Ti   1: 9 and rebels, the ungodly and sinful, the unholy and **irreligious**;
4: 7 Have nothing to do with **godless** myths and old wives' tales;
6:20 Turn away from **godless** chatter and the opposing ideas of what is
2Ti   2:16 Avoid **godless** chatter, because those who indulge in it will become
Heb 12:16 See that no one is sexually immoral, or is **godless** like Esau,

1014 βεβηλόω, bebēloō [2] [√ 326]

desecrate [2]

Mt 12: 5 Law that on the Sabbath the priests in the temple **desecrate** the day
Ac 24: 6 and even tried *to* **desecrate** the temple; so we seized him.

1015 Βεελζεβούλ, Beelzeboul [7]

Beelzebub [7]

Mt 10:25 If the head of the house *has been* called **Beelzebub**, how much
12:24 they said, "It is only by **Beelzebub**, the prince of demons,
12:27 And if I drive out demons by **Beelzebub**, by whom do your people
Mk   3:22 came down from Jerusalem said, "He is possessed by **Beelzebub**!
Lk   11:15 But some of them said, "By **Beelzebub**, the prince of demons,
11:18 because you claim that I drive out demons by **Beelzebub**.
11:19 Now if I drive out demons by **Beelzebub**, by whom do your

1016 Βελιάρ, Beliar [1]

Belial [1]

2Co   6:15 What harmony is there between Christ and **Belial**? What does a

1017 βελόνη, belonē [1] [√ 965]

needle [1]

Lk   18:25 it is easier for a camel to go through the eye *of* a **needle** than for a

1018 βέλος, *belos* [1] [√ *965*]

arrows [1]

Eph   6:16   with which you can extinguish all the flaming **arrows** of the evil

1019 βελτίων, *beltiōn* [1]

very well [1]

2Ti   1:18   You know **very well** in how many ways he helped me in Ephesus.

1020 Βενιαμείν, *Beniamein*   Not used in UBS/NIV
[√ *1021*]

1021 Βενιαμίν, *Beniamin* [4] [→ *1020*]

Benjamin [4]

Ac   13:21   Saul son of Kish, of the tribe *of* **Benjamin**, who ruled forty years.
Ro   11: 1   a descendant of Abraham, from the tribe *of* **Benjamin**.
Php   3: 5   people of Israel, of the tribe *of* **Benjamin**, a Hebrew of Hebrews;
Rev   7: 8   the tribe of Joseph 12,000, from the tribe *of* **Benjamin** 12,000.

1022 Βερνίκη, *Bernikē* [3] [√ *5770* + *3772*]

Bernice [3]

Ac   25:13   and **Bernice** arrived at Caesarea to pay their respects to Festus.
25:23   The next day Agrippa and **Bernice** came with great pomp
26:30   and with him the governor and **Bernice** and those sitting with

1023 Βέροια, *Beroia* [2] [→ *1024*]

Berea [2]

Ac   17:10   as it was night, the brothers sent Paul and Silas away to **Berea**.
17:13   learned that Paul was preaching the word of God at **Berea**,

1024 Βεροιαῖος, *Beroiaios* [1] [√ *1023*]

from Berea [1]

Ac   20: 4   He was accompanied by Sopater son of Pyrrhus **from Berea**,

1025 Βέρος, *Beros*   Not used in UBS/NIV

1026 Βεωρσόρ, *Beōorsor*   Not used in UBS/NIV
[√ *1027*]

1027 Βεώρ, *Beōr* [0 / 1] [→ *1026, 1082*]

Beor [1]

2Pe   2:15   off to follow the way of Balaam son *of* **Beor**, [UBS *1082*]

1028 Βηθαβαρά, *Bēthabara*   Not used in UBS/NIV

1029 Βηθανία, *Bēthania* [12]

Bethany [12]

Mt   21:17   And he left them and went out of the city to **Bethany**, where he
26: 6   While Jesus was in **Bethany** in the home of a man known as
Mk   11: 1   and came to Bethphage and **Bethany** at the Mount of Olives,
11:11   since it was already late, he went out to **Bethany** with the Twelve.
11:12   The next day as they were leaving **Bethany**, Jesus was hungry.
14: 3   While he was in **Bethany**, reclining at the table in the home of a
Lk   19:29   and **Bethany** at the hill called the Mount of Olives,
24:50   When he had led them out to the vicinity of **Bethany**, he lifted up
Jn   1:28   This all happened at **Bethany** on the other side of the Jordan,
11: 1   He was from **Bethany**, the village of Mary and her sister Martha.
11:18   **Bethany** was less than two miles from Jerusalem,
12: 1   the Passover, Jesus arrived at **Bethany**, where Lazarus lived,

1030 Βηθαραβά, *Bētharaba*   Not used in UBS/NIV

1031 Βηθεσδά, *Bēthesda* [0 / 1]

Bethesda [1]

Jn   5: 2   which in Aramaic is called **Bethesda** [UBS *1032*] and which is

1032 Βηθζαθά, *Bēthzatha* [1 / 0]

Jn   5: 2   a pool, which in Aramaic is called Bethesda [UBS *Bethzatha*; NIV
1031] and which is surrounded by five covered colonnades.

1033 Βηθλέεμ, *Bēthleem* [8]

Bethlehem [8]

Mt   2: 1   After Jesus was born in **Bethlehem** in Judea, during the time of
2: 5   "In **Bethlehem** in Judea," they replied, "for this is what the prophet
2: 6   " 'But you, **Bethlehem**, in the land of Judah, are by no means least
2: 8   He sent them to **Bethlehem** and said, "Go and make a careful
2:16   and he gave orders to kill all the boys in **Bethlehem** and its
Lk   2: 4   of Nazareth in Galilee to Judea, to **Bethlehem** the town of David,
2:15   "Let's go to **Bethlehem** and see this thing that has happened,
Jn   7:42   the Christ will come from David's family and from **Bethlehem**,

1034 Βηθσαϊδά, *Bēthsaida* [7]

Bethsaida [7]

Mt   11:21   "Woe to you, Korazin! Woe to you, **Bethsaida**! If the miracles that
Mk   6:45   disciples get into the boat and go on ahead of him to **Bethsaida**,
8:22   They came to **Bethsaida**, and some people brought a blind man
Lk   9:10   and they withdrew by themselves to a town called **Bethsaida**,
10:13   "Woe to you, Korazin! Woe to you, **Bethsaida**! For if the miracles
Jn   1:44   Philip, like Andrew and Peter, was from the town of **Bethsaida**.
12:21   came to Philip, who was from **Bethsaida** in Galilee, with a request.

1035 Βηθσαϊδάν, *Bēthsaidan*   Not used in UBS/NIV

1036 Βηθφαγή, *Bēthphagē* [3]

Bethphage [3]

Mt   21: 1   and came to **Bethphage** on the Mount of Olives,
Mk   11: 1   As they approached Jerusalem and came to **Bethphage**
Lk   19:29   As he approached **Bethphage** and Bethany at the hill called the

1037 βῆμα, *bēma* [12] [√ *326*]

court [4], judge's seat [2], judgment seat [2], convened the court
[+*2093*+*2767*+*3836*] [1], court [+*2093*] [1], foot of ground
[+*4546*] [1], throne [1]

Mt   27:19   While Pilate was sitting on the **judge's seat**, his wife sent him this
Jn   19:13   and sat down on the **judge's seat** at a place known as the Stone
Ac   7: 5   gave him no inheritance here, not even a **foot of ground** [+*4546*].
12:21   sat on his **throne** and delivered a public address to the people.
18:12   the Jews made a united attack on Paul and brought him into **court**.
18:16   So he had them ejected from the **court**.
18:17   Sosthenes the synagogue ruler and beat him in front of the **court**.
25: 6   and the next day he **convened the court** [+*2093*+*2767*+*3836*] and
25:10   "I am now standing before Caesar's **court**, where I ought to be
25:17   but convened the **court** [+*2093*] the next day and ordered the man
Ro   14:10   your brother? For we will all stand before God's **judgment seat**.
2Co   5:10   For we must all appear before the **judgment seat** of Christ,

1038 Βηρεύς, *Bēreus*   Not used in UBS/NIV

1039 βήρυλλος, *bēryllos* [1]

beryl [1]

Rev   21:20   the eighth **beryl**, the ninth topaz, the tenth chrysoprase,

1040 βία, bia [3] [→ 1041, 1042, 1043, 4128]

pounding [1], use force [+3552] [1], violence [1]

Ac   5:26 They did not **use force** [+3552], because they feared that the
     21:35 the **violence** of the mob was so great he had to be carried by the
     27:41 and the stern was broken to pieces by the **pounding** of the surf.

1041 βιάζω, biazō [2] [√ 1040]

forcefully advancing [1], forcing way [1]

Mt 11:12 the kingdom of heaven *has been* **forcefully advancing**,
Lk 16:16 of God is being preached, and everyone *is* **forcing** *his* **way** into it.

1042 βίαιος, biaios [1] [√ 1040]

violent [1]

Ac   2: 2 Suddenly a sound like the blowing of a **violent** wind came from

1043 βιαστής, biastēs [1] [√ 1040]

forceful [1]

Mt 11:12 has been forcefully advancing, and **forceful** *men* lay hold of it.

1044 βιβλαρίδιον, biblaridion [3] [√ 1047]

little scroll [3]

Rev 10: 2 He was holding a **little scroll**, which lay open in his hand.
     10: 9 So I went to the angel and asked him to give me the **little scroll**.
     10:10 I took the **little scroll** from the angel's hand and ate it. It tasted as

1045 βιβλιδάριον, biblidarion Not used in UBS/NIV
[√ 1047]

1046 βιβλίον, biblion [34] [√ 1047]

book [13], scroll [12], books [3], certificate [2], it^s [+3836] [2],
scroll [+3053] [1], scrolls [1]

Mt 19: 7 "did Moses command that a man give his wife a **certificate** of
Mk 10: 4 "Moses permitted a man to write a **certificate** of divorce and send
Lk   4:17 The **scroll** of the prophet Isaiah was handed to him. Unrolling it,
      4:17 Unrolling **it**^s [+3836], he found the place where it is written:
      4:20 Then he rolled up the **scroll**, gave it back to the attendant and sat
Jn 20:30 the presence of his disciples, which are not recorded in this **book**.
     21:25 world would not have room for the **books** that would be written.
Gal 3:10 does not continue to do everything written in the **Book** of the Law."
2Ti 4:13 with Carpus at Troas, and my **scrolls**, especially the parchments.
Heb 9:19 and branches of hyssop, and sprinkled the **scroll** and all the people.
     10: 7 I said, 'Here I am—it is written about me in the **scroll** [+3053]—
Rev 1:11 "Write on a **scroll** what you see and send it to the seven churches:
      5: 1 Then I saw in the right hand of him who sat on the throne a **scroll**
      5: 2 loud voice, "Who is worthy to break the seals and open the **scroll**?"
      5: 3 one in heaven or on earth or under the earth could open the **scroll**
      5: 4 because no one was found who was worthy to open the **scroll**
      5: 5 has triumphed. He is able to open the **scroll** and its seven seals."
      5: 8 And when he had taken **it**^s [+3836], the four living creatures
      5: 9 "You are worthy to take the **scroll** and to open its seals, because
      6:14 The sky receded like a **scroll**, rolling up, and every mountain
     10: 8 take the **scroll** that lies open in the hand of the angel who is
     13: 8 all whose names have not been written in the **book** of life
     17: 8 **book** of life from the creation of the world will be astonished when
     20:12 and small, standing before the throne, and **books** were opened.
     20:12 were opened. Another **book** was opened, which is the book of life.
     20:12 judged according to what they had done as recorded in the **books**.
     21:27 but only those whose names are written in the Lamb's **book** of life.
     22: 7 Blessed is he who keeps the words of the prophecy *in* this **book**."
     22: 9 brothers the prophets and of all who keep the words *of* this **book**.
     22:10 he told me, "Do not seal up the words of the prophecy *of* this **book**,
     22:18 I warn everyone who hears the words of the prophecy *of* this **book**:
     22:18 to them, God will add to him the plagues described in this **book**.
     22:19 And if anyone takes words away from this **book** of prophecy,
     22:19 tree of life and in the holy city, which are described in this **book**.

1047 βίβλος, biblos [10] [→ 1044, 1045, 1046]

book [8], record [1], scrolls [1]

Mt   1: 1 A **record** of the genealogy of Jesus Christ the son of David,
Mk 12:26 have you not read in the **book** of Moses, in the account of the bush,
Lk   3: 4 As is written in the **book** of the words of Isaiah the prophet:
     20:42 David himself declares in the **Book** of Psalms: " 'The Lord said to
Ac   1:20 "For," said Peter, "it is written in the **book** of Psalms, " 'May his
      7:42 This agrees with what is written in the **book** of the prophets:
     19:19 A number who had practiced sorcery brought their **scrolls** together
Php 4: 3 the rest of my fellow workers, whose names are in the **book** of life.
Rev 3: 5 I will never blot out his name from the **book** of life, but will
     20:15 If anyone's name was not found written in the **book** of life,

1048 βιβρώσκω, bibrōskō [1] [→ 1109, 1110, 1111, 4963, 5037]

eaten [1]

Jn   6:13 pieces of the five barley loaves left over *by* those *who had* **eaten**.

1049 Βιθυνία, Bithynia [2]

Bithynia [2]

Ac 16: 7 they came to the border of Mysia, they tried to enter **Bithynia**,
1Pe 1: 1 throughout Pontus, Galatia, Cappadocia, Asia and **Bithynia**,

1050 βίος, bios [10] [→ 1051, 1052, 1053, 4259]

property [2], to live on [2], civilian affairs [+4548] [1], life [1], life's
[1], lives [1], possessions [1], what he has and does [1]

Mk   4:19 but the worries *of* this **life**, [UBS *172*] the deceitfulness of wealth
     12:44 out of her poverty, put in everything—all she had **to live on**."
Lk   8:14 but as they go on their way they are choked by **life's** worries,
      8:43 [UBS+ *though she had spent all her* **possessions** *on physicians*] no
            one could heal her.
     15:12 my share of the estate.' So he divided his **property** between them.
     15:30 But when this son of yours who has squandered your **property**
     21: 4 but she out of her poverty put in all she had **to live on**."
1Ti 2: 2 we may live peaceful and quiet **lives** in all godliness and holiness.
2Ti 2: 4 one serving as a soldier gets involved in **civilian affairs** [+4548]—
1Jn 2:16 the lust of his eyes and the boasting *of* **what he has and does**—
      3:17 If anyone has material **possessions** and sees his brother in need

1051 βιόω, bioō [1] [√ 1050]

live [1]

1Pe 4: 2 he *does* not **live** the rest of his earthly life for evil human desires,

1052 βίωσις, biōsis [1] [√ 1050]

way lived [1]

Ac 26: 4 "The Jews all know the **way** I have **lived** ever since I was a child,

1053 βιωτικός, biōtikos [3] [√ 1050]

of life [1], of this life [1], such^s matters [1]

Lk 21:34 down with dissipation, drunkenness and the anxieties **of life**,
1Co 6: 3 that we will judge angels? How much more the *things* **of this life**!
      6: 4 Therefore, if you have disputes *about* **such**^s **matters**, appoint as

1054 βλαβερός, blaberos [1] [√ 1055]

harmful [1]

1Ti 6: 9 and **harmful** desires that plunge men into ruin and destruction.

1055 βλάπτω, blaptō [2] [→ 1054]

hurt [1], injuring [1]

Mk 16:18 and when they drink deadly poison, *it will* not **hurt** them at all;

Lk   4: 35 the man down before them all and came out without **injuring** him.

1056 βλαστάνω, *blastanō* [4] [→ *1057, 1058, 1677*]

budded [1], produced [1], sprouted [1], sprouts [1]

Mt 13: 26 When the wheat **sprouted** and formed heads, then the weeds also
Mk   4: 27 whether he sleeps or gets up, the seed **sprouts** and grows,
Heb 9: 4 Aaron's staff that *had* **budded**, and the stone tablets of the
Jas 5: 18 and the heavens gave rain, and the earth **produced** its crops.

1057 βλαστάω, *blastaō* Not used in UBS/NIV [√ *1056*]

1058 Βλάστος, *Blastos* [1] [√ *1056*]

Blastus [1]

Ac 12: 20 Having secured the support *of* **Blastus**, a trusted personal servant

1059 βλασφημέω, *blasphēmeō* [34] [→ *1060, 1061;* cf. *5774*]

slander [4], blaspheme [3], cursed [3], hurled insults at [3],
blasphemed [2], blasphemes [2], blaspheming [2], abusive [1],
abusively [1], blasphemies [+*1060*] [1], blasphemy [1], bring into
disrepute [1], denounced [1], heap abuse on [1], insulting [1],
malign [1], slandered [1], slandering [1], slanderously reported
[1], speak abusively against [1], spoken blasphemy [1], spoken
of as evil [1]

Mt   9: 3 of the law said to themselves, "This fellow *is* **blaspheming**!"
    26: 65 high priest tore his clothes and said, "*He has* **spoken blasphemy**!
    27: 39 Those who passed by **hurled insults at** him, shaking their heads
Mk   2: 7 *He's* **blaspheming**! Who can forgive sins but God alone?"
     3: 28 the sins and **blasphemies** [+*1060*] of men will be forgiven them.
     3: 29 But whoever **blasphemes** against the Holy Spirit will never be
    15: 29 Those who passed by **hurled insults at** him, shaking their heads
Lk 12: 10 but anyone *who* **blasphemes** against the Holy Spirit will not be
    22: 65 And they said many other **insulting** things to him.
    23: 39 One of the criminals who hung there **hurled insults at** him:
Jn 10: 36 Why then do you accuse me of **blasphemy** because I said,
Ac 13: 45 with jealousy and talked **abusively** against what Paul was saying.
    18: 6 But when the Jews opposed Paul and *became* **abusive**, he shook
    19: 37 *though* they have neither robbed temples nor **blasphemed** our
    26: 11 to have them punished, and I tried to force them *to* **blaspheme**.
Ro   2: 24 "God's name *is* **blasphemed** among the Gentiles because of you."
     3: 8 as *we are being* **slanderously reported** as saying and as some
    14: 16 *Do* not *allow* what you consider good *to be* **spoken of as evil**.
1Co 10: 30 why *am I* **denounced** because of something I thank God for?
1Ti 1: 20 whom I have handed over to Satan to be taught not *to* **blaspheme**.
     6: 1 so that God's name and our teaching *may* not *be* **slandered**.
Tit 2: 5 to their husbands, so that no *one will* **malign** the word of God.
     3: 2 *to* **slander** no one, to be peaceable and considerate, and to show
Jas 2: 7 Are they not the *ones who are* **slandering** the noble name of him
1Pe 4: 4 into the same flood of dissipation, and *they* **heap abuse on** you.
2Pe 2: 2 shameful ways and *will* **bring** the way of truth **into disrepute**.
     2: 10 and arrogant, these men are not afraid to **slander** celestial beings;
     2: 12 But these men **blaspheme** in matters they do not understand.
Jude 1: 8 their own bodies, reject authority and **slander** celestial beings.
     1: 10 Yet these men **speak abusively against** whatever they do not
Rev 13: 6 and *to* **slander** his name and his dwelling place and those who live
    16: 9 were seared by the intense heat and *they* **cursed** the name of God,
    16: 11 and **cursed** the God of heaven because of their pains and their
    16: 21 And they **cursed** God on account of the plague of hail,

1060 βλασφημία, *blasphēmia* [18] [√ *1059*]

blasphemy [5], slander [5], blasphemous [2], blaspheme [1],
blasphemies [+*1059*] [1], blasphemies [1], blasphemy against
[1], malicious talk [1], slanderous [1]

Mt 12: 31 so I tell you, every sin and **blasphemy** will be forgiven men,
    12: 31 but the **blasphemy against** the Spirit will not be forgiven.
    15: 19 adultery, sexual immorality, theft, false testimony, **slander**.
    26: 65 any more witnesses? Look, now you have heard the **blasphemy**.

Mk   3: 28 the sins and **blasphemies** [+*1059*] of men will be forgiven them.
     7: 22 greed, malice, deceit, lewdness, envy, **slander**, arrogance
    14: 64 "You have heard the **blasphemy**. What do you think?" They all
Lk   5: 21 to themselves, "Who is this fellow who speaks **blasphemy**?
Jn 10: 33 for any of these," replied the Jews, "but for **blasphemy**,
Eph 4: 31 Get rid of all bitterness, rage and anger, brawling and **slander**,
Col 3: 8 anger, rage, malice, **slander**, and filthy language from your lips.
1Ti 6: 4 words that result in envy, strife, **malicious talk**, evil suspicions
Jude 1: 9 did not dare to bring a **slanderous** accusation against him,
Rev 2: 9 I know the **slander** of those who say they are Jews and are not,
    13: 1 ten crowns on his horns, and on each head a **blasphemous** name.
    13: 5 beast was given a mouth to utter proud words and **blasphemies**
    13: 6 He opened his mouth to **blaspheme** God, and to slander his name
    17: 3 on a scarlet beast that was covered with **blasphemous** names

1061 βλάσφημος, *blasphēmos* [4] [√ *1059*]

abusive [1], blasphemer [1], blasphemy [1], slanderous [1]

Ac   6: 11 "We have heard Stephen speak words *of* **blasphemy** against Moses
1Ti 1: 13 Even though I was once a **blasphemer** and a persecutor and a
2Ti 3: 2 lovers of money, boastful, proud, **abusive**, disobedient to their
2Pe 2: 11 do not bring **slanderous** accusations against such beings in the

1062 βλέμμα, *blemma* [1] [√ *1063*]

saw [1]

2Pe 2: 8 was tormented in his righteous soul by the lawless deeds he **saw**

1063 βλέπω, *blepō* [132] [→ *329, 330, 611, 1062, 1332, 1838, 2098, 4315, 4587*]

see [50], saw [8], ever seeing [+*1063*] [6], seen [6], watch out [6],
see to it [5], seeing [5], sees [5], look [3], *untranslated* [2], blind
[+*3590*] [2], careful [2], consider carefully [2], look at [2], pay
attention who they are [+*476+4725*] [2], unseen [+*3590*] [2], alert
[1], be [1], before eyes [1], careful that [1], consider [1], doˢ [1],
exposed [1], facing [1], gaze on [1], hasˢ [1], haveˢ [1], looked in
[1], looking on [1], looks [1], looks at [1], on guard [1], on your
guard [1], saw that [1], sight [1], stared [1], take care [1], think
[1], watch out [+*1571*] [1], watch out for [1]

Mt   5: 28 But I tell you that anyone who **looks at** a woman lustfully has
     6: 4 your Father, who **sees** what is done in secret, will reward you.
     6: 6 your Father, who **sees** what is done in secret, will reward you.
     6: 18 and your Father, who **sees** what is done in secret, will reward you.
     7: 3 "Why *do you* **look** at the speck of sawdust in your brother's eye
    11: 4 Jesus replied, "Go back and report to John what you hear and **see**.
    12: 22 and mute, and Jesus healed him, so that he *could* both talk and **see**.
    13: 13 "*Though* **seeing**, they do not see; though hearing, they do not hear
    13: 13 "Though **seeing**, they *do* not **see**; though hearing, they do not hear
    13: 14 *you will be* **ever seeing** [+*1063*] but never perceiving.
    13: 14 *you will be* **ever seeing** [+*1063*] but never perceiving.
    13: 16 But blessed are your eyes because *they* **see**, and your ears
    13: 17 many prophets and righteous men longed to see what you **see**
    14: 30 But *when he* **saw** the wind, he was afraid and, beginning to sink,
    15: 31 The people were amazed *when they* **saw** the mute speaking,
    15: 31 the crippled made well, the lame walking and the blind **seeing**.
    18: 10 For I tell you that their angels in heaven always **see** the face of my
    22: 16 because *you* **pay** no **attention** [+*476+4725*] to **who they are**.
    24: 2 "*Do you* **see** all these things?" he asked. "I tell you the truth,
    24: 4 Jesus answered: "**Watch out** that no one deceives you.
Mk   4: 12 so that, " '*they may be* **ever seeing** [+*1063*] but never perceiving,
     4: 12 so that, " '*they may be* **ever seeing** [+*1063*] but never perceiving,
     4: 24 "**Consider carefully** what you hear," he continued. "With the
     5: 31 "*You* **see** the people crowding against you," his disciples answered,
     8: 15 "**Watch out** for the yeast of the Pharisees and that of Herod."
     8: 18 *Do you* have eyes but fail to **see**, and ears but fail to hear?
     8: 23 and put his hands on him, Jesus asked, "*Do you* **see** anything?"
     8: 24 He looked up and said, "*I* **see** people; they look like trees walking
    12: 14 because *you* **pay** no **attention** [+*476+4725*] to **who they are**;
    12: 38 As he taught, Jesus said, "**Watch out** for the teachers of the law.
    13: 2 "*Do you* **see** all these great buildings?" replied Jesus. "Not one
    13: 5 Jesus said to them: "**Watch out** that no one deceives you.
    13: 9 "*You* *must be* **on** *your* **guard**. You will be handed over to the local

13:23 So *be* **on your guard**; I have told you everything ahead of time.
13:33 Be on guard! You do not know when that time will
Lk 6:41 "Why *do you* **look at** the speck of sawdust in your brother's eye
6:42 *when you* yourself fail *to* **see** the plank in your own eye?
7:21 sicknesses and evil spirits, and gave **sight** to many who were blind.
7:44 toward the woman and said to Simon, "*Do you* **see** this woman?
8:10 I speak in parables, so that, " '*though* **seeing**, they may not see;
8:10 I speak in parables, so that, " 'though seeing, *they may* not see;
8:16 he puts it on a stand, so that those who come in *can* **see** the light.
8:18 Therefore **consider carefully** how you listen. Whoever has will be
9:62 the plow and **looks** back is fit for service in the kingdom of God."
10:23 and said privately, "Blessed are the eyes that **see** what you see.
10:23 and said privately, "Blessed are the eyes that see what *you* **see**.
10:24 and kings wanted to see what you **see** but did not see it,
11:33 he puts it on its stand, so that those who come in *may* **see** the light.
21: 8 He replied: "**Watch out** that you are not deceived. For many will
21:30 you can **see** for yourselves and know that summer is near.
24:12 Bending over, *he* **saw** the strips of linen lying by themselves,
Jn 1:29 The next day John **saw** Jesus coming toward him and said,
5:19 he can do only what *he* **sees** his Father doing, because whatever the
9: 7 means Sent). So the man went and washed, and came home **seeing**.
9:15 mud on my eyes," the man replied, "and I washed, and *now I* **see**."
9:19 the one you say was born blind? How is it that now *he can* **see**?"
9:21 But how *he can* **see** now, or who opened his eyes, we don't know.
9:25 I don't know. One thing I do know. I was blind but now *I* **see**!"
9:39 so that the **blind** [+*3590*] will see and those who see will become
9:39 so that the blind *will* **see** and those who see will become blind."
9:39 so that the blind will see and those *who* **see** will become blind."
9:41 of sin; but now that you claim *you can* **see**, your guilt remains.
11: 9 walks by day will not stumble, for *he* **sees** by this world's light.
13:22 His disciples **stared** at one another, at a loss to know which of
20: 1 and **saw** that the stone had been removed from the entrance.
20: 5 *He* bent over and **looked in** at the strips of linen lying there
21: 9 *they* **saw** a fire of burning coals there with fish on it, and some
21:20 and **saw that** the disciple whom Jesus loved was following them.
Ac 1: 9 After he said this, he was taken up **before** their *very* **eyes**,
2:33 Holy Spirit and has poured out what you *now* **see** and hear.
3: 4 **looked** straight at him, as did John. Then Peter said, "**Look** at us!"
4:14 But *since they could* **see** the man who had been healed standing
8: 6 the crowds heard Philip and **saw** the miraculous signs he did,
9: 8 the ground, but when he opened his eyes *he could* **see** nothing.
9: 9 For three days he was **blind** [+*3590*], and did not eat or drink
12: 9 doing was really happening; he thought he *was* **seeing** a vision.
13:11 and for a time *you will be* unable *to* **see** the light of the sun."
13:40 **Take care** that what the prophets have said does not happen to
27:12 This was a harbor in Crete, **facing** both southwest and northwest.
28:26 *you will be* **ever seeing** [+*1063*] but never perceiving."
28:26 *you will be* **ever seeing** [+*1063*] but never perceiving."
Ro 7:23 but *I* **see** another law at work in the members of my body,
8:24 in this hope we were saved. But hope *that is* **seen** is no hope at all.
8:24 is seen is no hope at all. Who hopes for what *he already* **has**^{s}?
8:25 But if we hope for what *we do* not yet **have**^{s}, we wait for it
11: 8 eyes so that they *could* not **see** and ears so that they could not hear,
11:10 May their eyes be darkened so they cannot **see**, and their backs be
1Co 1:26 Brothers, **think** of what you were when you were called. Not many
3:10 is building on it. But each one *should be* **careful** how he builds.
8: 9 *Be* **careful**, however, that the exercise of your freedom does not
10:12 if you think you are standing firm, *be* **careful that** you don't fall!
10:18 **Consider** the people of Israel: Do not those who eat the sacrifices
13:12 Now *we* **see** but a poor reflection as in a mirror;
16:10 **see to it** that he has nothing to fear while he is with you,
2Co 4:18 So we fix our eyes not on what *is* **seen**, but on what is unseen.
4:18 fix our eyes not on what is seen, but on what *is* **unseen** [+*3590*].
4:18 For what *is* **seen** is temporary, but what is unseen is eternal.
4:18 what is seen is temporary, but what *is* **unseen** [+*3590*] is eternal.
7: 8 regret it—*I* **see** that my letter hurt you, but only for a little while—
10: 7 *You are* **looking** *only* on the surface of things. If anyone is
12: 6 so no one will think more of me than is warranted by what I **do**^{s}
Gal 5:15 each other, **watch out** or you will be destroyed by each other.
Eph 5:15 *Be* very careful, then, how you live—not as unwise but as wise,
Php 3: 2 **Watch out for** those dogs, those men who do evil, those mutilators
3: 2 Watch out for those dogs, **[RPG]** those men who do evil,
3: 2 those men who do evil, **[RPG]** those mutilators of the flesh.
Col 2: 5 present with you in spirit and delight *to* **see** how orderly you are
2: 8 **See to it** that no one takes you captive through hollow
4:17 "**See to it** that you complete the work you have received in the

Heb 2: 9 But *we* **see** Jesus, who was made a little lower than the angels,
3:12 **See to it**, brothers, that none of you has a sinful, unbelieving heart
3:19 So *we* **see** that they were not able to enter, because of their
10:25 one another—and all the more as *you* **see** the Day approaching.
11: 1 being sure of what we hope for and certain of what *we do* not **see**.
11: 3 so that what *is* **seen** was not made out of what was visible.
11: 7 By faith Noah, when warned about things not yet **seen**, in holy fear
12:25 **See to it** that you do not refuse him who speaks. If they did not
Jas 2:22 *You* **see** that his faith and his actions were working together,
2Jn 1: 8 **Watch** [+*1571*] out that you do not lose what you have worked
Rev 1:11 "Write on a scroll what *you* **see** and send it to the seven churches:
1:12 I turned around *to* **see** the voice that was speaking to me.
3:18 shameful nakedness; and salve to put on your eyes, so *you can* **see**.
5: 3 or under the earth could open the scroll or even **look** *inside* it.
5: 4 one was found who was worthy *to* open the scroll or **look** *inside*.
9:20 bronze, stone and wood—idols that cannot **see** or hear or walk.
11: 9 *men* from every people, tribe, language and nation *will* **gaze on**
16:15 with him, so that he may not go naked and *be* shamefully **exposed**."
17: 8 creation of the world will be astonished *when they* **see** the beast,
18: 9 with her and shared her luxury **see** the smoke of her burning,
18:18 *When they* **see** the smoke of her burning, they will exclaim,
22: 8 I, John, am the one who heard and **saw** these things. And when I
22: 8 And when I had heard and **seen** them, I fell down to worship at the

1064 βλητέος, *blēteos* [1] [√ *965*]

must be poured [1]

Lk 5:38 No, new wine **must be poured** into new wineskins.

1065 Βοανηργές, *Boanērges* [1]

Boanerges [1]

Mk 3:17 and his brother John (to them he gave the name **Boanerges**,

1066 βοάω, *boaō* [12] [√ *1068*]

calling [4], called out [2], shouting [2], cried out [1], cry aloud [1], cry out [1], shrieks [+*3489+5889*] [1]

Mt 3: 3 "A voice *of one* **calling** in the desert, 'Prepare the way for the Lord,
Mk 1: 3 "A voice *of one* **calling** in the desert, 'Prepare the way for the Lord,
15:34 And at the ninth hour Jesus **cried out** in a loud voice, "*Eloi*,
Lk 3: 4 "A voice *of one* **calling** in the desert, 'Prepare the way for the Lord,
9:38 A man in the crowd **called out**, "Teacher, I beg you to look at my
18: 7 justice for his chosen ones, who **cry out** to him day and night?
18:38 *He* **called out**, "Jesus, Son of David, have mercy on me!"
Jn 1:23 "I am the voice *of one* **calling** in the desert, 'Make straight the way
Ac 8: 7 *With* **shrieks** [+*3489+5889*], evil spirits came out of many,
17: 6 and some other brothers before the city officials, **shouting**:
25:24 and here in Caesarea, **shouting** that he ought not to live any longer.
Gal 4:27 break forth and **cry aloud**, you who have no labor pains;

1067 Βόες, *Boes* [2] [→ *1077, 1078*]

Boaz [2]

Mt 1: 5 Salmon the father of **Boaz**, whose mother was Rahab, Boaz the
1: 5 **Boaz** the father of Obed, whose mother was Ruth, Obed the father

1068 βοή, *boē* [1] [→ *331, 1066, 1069, 1070, 1071, 2100, 2855*]

cries [1]

Jas 5: 4 The **cries** of the harvesters have reached the ears of the Lord

1069 βοήθεια, *boētheia* [2] [√ *1068*]

help [1], ropes [1]

Ac 27:17 they passed **ropes** under the ship itself to hold it together.
Heb 4:16 may receive mercy and find grace to **help** us in our time of need.

1070 βοηθέω, *boētheō* [8] [√ *1068*]

help [6], helped [2]

Mt 15:25 The woman came and knelt before him. "Lord, **help** me!" she said.
Mk 9:22 kill him. But if you can do anything, take pity on us and **help** us."
   9:24 father exclaimed, "I do believe; **help** me *overcome* my unbelief!"
Ac 16: 9 and begging him, "Come over to Macedonia and **help** us."
  21:28 shouting, "Men of Israel, **help** us! This is the man who teaches all
2Co 6: 2 of my favor I heard you, and in the day of salvation *I* **helped** you."
Heb 2:18 he was tempted, he is able *to* **help** those who are being tempted.
Rev 12:16 But the earth **helped** the woman by opening its mouth

1071 βοηθός, *boēthos* [1] [√ *1068*]

helper [1]

Heb 13: 6 So we say with confidence, "The Lord is my **helper**; I will not be

1072 βόθρος, *bothros* Not used in UBS/NIV [→ *1073*]

1073 βόθυνος, *bothynos* [3] [√ *1072*]

pit [3]

Mt 12:11 "If any of you has a sheep and it falls into a **pit** on the Sabbath,
  15:14 If a blind man leads a blind man, both will fall into a **pit**."
Lk   6:39 a blind man lead a blind man? Will they not both fall into a **pit**?

1074 βολή, *bolē* [1] [√ *965*]

throw [1]

Lk 22:41 He withdrew about a stone's **throw** beyond them, knelt down

1075 βολίζω, *bolizō* [2] [√ *965*]

took soundings [2]

Ac 27:28 They **took soundings** and found that the water was a hundred
  27:28 A short time later they **took soundings** again and found that it was

1076 βολίς, *bolis* Not used in UBS/NIV [√ *965*]

1077 Βοόζ, *Booz* Not used in UBS/NIV [√ *1067*]

1078 Βόος, *Boos* [1] [√ *1067*]

Boaz [1]

Lk 3:32 the son of Jesse, the son of Obed, the son *of* **Boaz**, the son of

1079 βόρβορος, *borboros* [1]

mud [1]

2Pe 2:22 "A sow that is washed goes back to her wallowing *in* the **mud**."

1080 βορρᾶς, *borras* [2]

north [2]

Lk 13:29 People will come from east and west and **north** and south,
Rev 21:13 three on the **north**, three on the south and three on the west.

1081 βόσκω, *boskō* [9] [→ *1083*]

feed [3], feeding [3], tending [3]

Mt 8:30 Some distance from them a large herd of pigs was **feeding**.
  8:33 Those tending the pigs ran off, went into the town and reported all
Mk 5:11 A large herd of pigs was **feeding** on the nearby hillside.
  5:14 Those **tending** the pigs ran off and reported this in the town
Lk 8:32 A large herd of pigs was **feeding** there on the hillside. The demons
  8:34 When those **tending** the pigs saw what had happened, they ran off
 15:15 to a citizen of that country, who sent him to his fields *to* **feed** pigs.

Jn 21:15 he said, "you know that I love you." Jesus said, "**Feed** my lambs."
 21:17 all things; you know that I love you." Jesus said, "**Feed** my sheep.

1082 Βοσόρ, *Bosor* [1 / 0] [√ *1027*]

2Pe 2:15 to follow the way of Balaam son *of* Beor, [UBS *Bosor*; NIV *1027*]

1083 βοτάνη, *botanē* [1] [√ *1081*]

crop [1]

Heb 6: 7 and that produces a **crop** useful to those for whom it is farmed

1084 βότρυς, *botrys* [1]

clusters of grapes [1]

Rev 14:18 and gather the **clusters of grapes** from the earth's vine,

1085 βουλευτής, *bouleutēs* [2] [√ *1089*]

member of the Council [2]

Mk 15:43 Joseph of Arimathea, a prominent **member of the Council**,
Lk 23:50 named Joseph, a **member of the Council**, a good and upright man,

1086 βουλεύω, *bouleuō* [6] [√ *1089*]

untranslated [1], consider [1], decided [1], made plans [1], make plans [1], plotted [1]

Lk 14:31 *Will he* not first sit down and **consider** whether he is able with ten
Jn 11:53 So from that day on *they* **plotted** to take his life.
 12:10 So the chief priests **made plans** to kill Lazarus as well,
Ac 27:39 where *they* **decided** to run the ship aground if they could.
2Co 1:17 Or **[RPG]** do I make my plans in a worldly manner so that in the
  1:17 Or *do I* **make** *my* **plans** in a worldly manner so that in the same

1087 βουλή, *boulē* [12] [√ *1089*]

βουλή τοῦ θεοῦ (will of God) [4] Lk 7:30; Ac 2:23; 13:36; 20:27

purpose [6], will [2], decided that [*i 5502*] [1], decision [1], motives [1], planned [+*1181*] [1]

Lk 7:30 and experts in the law rejected God's **purpose** for themselves,
 23:51 who had not consented *to* their **decision** and action. He came from
Ac 2:23 This man was handed over to you *by* God's set **purpose**
  4:28 what your power and **will** had decided beforehand should happen.
  5:38 For if their **purpose** or activity is of human origin, it will fail.
 13:36 "For when David had served God's **purpose** in his own generation,
 20:27 For I have not hesitated to proclaim to you the whole **will** of God.
 27:12 the majority **decided** [+*5502*] **that** we should sail on, hoping to
 27:42 The soldiers **planned** [+*1181*] to kill the prisoners to prevent any
1Co 4: 5 is hidden in darkness and will expose the **motives** of men's hearts.
Eph 1:11 works out everything in conformity with the **purpose** of his will,
Heb 6:17 God wanted to make the unchanging nature *of* his **purpose**

1088 βούλημα, *boulēma* [3] [√ *1089*]

choose [1], plan [1], will [1]

Ac 27:43 to spare Paul's life and kept them from carrying out their **plan**.
Ro 9:19 "Then why does God still blame us? For who resists his **will**?"
1Pe 4: 3 spent enough time in the past doing what pagans **choose** to do—

1089 βούλομαι, *boulomai* [37] [→ *755, 1085, 1086,*
1087, 1088, 2101, 2300, 4131, 5205, 5206, 5207]

want [9], wanted [9], chooses [3], planned [2], wanting [2], willing [2], chose [1], counsel [1], determined [1], determines [1], had in mind [1], intended [1], like [1], liked [1], wants [1], will [1]

Mt 1:19 her to public disgrace, *he* **had in mind** to divorce her quietly.
 11:27 except the Son and those to whom the Son **chooses** to reveal him.
Mk 15:15 **Wanting** to satisfy the crowd, Pilate released Barabbas to them.
Lk 10:22 except the Son and those to whom the Son **chooses** to reveal him."

	22:42	"Father, if *you are* **willing**, take this cup from me; yet not my will,
Jn	18:39	of the Passover. *Do you* **want** me to release 'the king of the Jews'?"
Ac	5:28	and *are* **determined** to make us guilty of this man's blood."
	5:33	they heard this, they were furious and **wanted** to put them to death.
	12:4	Herod **intended** to bring him out for public trial after the Passover.
	15:37	Barnabas **wanted** to take John, also called Mark, with them,
	17:20	strange ideas to our ears, and *we* **want** to know what they mean."
	18:15	settle the matter yourselves. I **will** not be a judge of such things."
	18:27	When Apollos **wanted** to go to Achaia, the brothers encouraged
	19:30	Paul **wanted** to appear before the crowd, but the disciples would
	22:30	*since* the commander **wanted** to find out exactly why Paul was
	23:28	*I* **wanted** to know why they were accusing him, so I brought him
	25:20	so I asked if *he would be* **willing** to go to Jerusalem and stand
	25:22	Agrippa said to Festus, "*I would* **like** to hear this man myself."
	27:43	But the centurion **wanted** to spare Paul's life and kept them from
	28:18	They examined me and **wanted** to release me,
1Co	12:11	same Spirit, and he gives them to each one, just as *he* **determines**.
2Co	1:15	*I* **planned** to visit you first so that you might benefit twice.
	1:17	*When I* **planned** this, did I do it lightly? Or do I make my plans in
Php	1:12	Now *I* **want** you to know, brothers, that what has happened to me
1Ti	2:8	*I* **want** men everywhere to lift up holy hands in prayer,
	5:14	So *I* **counsel** younger widows to marry, to have children,
	6:9	People *who* **want** to get rich fall into temptation and a trap
Tit	3:8	And *I* **want** you to stress these things, so that those who have
Phm	1:13	I *would have* **liked** to keep him with me so that he could take your
Heb	6:17	Because God **wanted** to make the unchanging nature of his
Jas	1:18	He **chose** to give us birth through the word of truth, that we might
	3:4	they are steered by a very small rudder wherever the pilot **wants** to
	4:4	Anyone *who* **chooses** to be a friend of the world becomes an
2Pe	3:9	He is patient with you, not **wanting** anyone to perish, but everyone
2Jn	1:12	have much to write to you, but *I do* not **want** to use paper and ink.
3Jn	1:10	He also stops those *who* **want** to do so and puts them out of the
Jude	1:5	*I* **want** to remind you that the Lord delivered his people out of

1090 βουνός, *bounos* [2]

hill [1], hills [1]

Lk	3:5	Every valley shall be filled in, every mountain and **hill** made low.
	23:30	say to the mountains, "Fall on us!" and *to* the **hills**, "Cover us!" '

1091 βοῦς, *bous* [8]

ox [4], cattle [2], oxen [2]

Lk	13:15	Doesn't each of you on the Sabbath untie his **ox** or donkey from
	14:5	of you has a son or an **ox** that falls into a well on the Sabbath day,
	14:19	"Another said, 'I have just bought five yoke *of* **oxen**, and I'm on my
Jn	2:14	In the temple courts he found men selling **cattle**, sheep and doves,
	2:15	and drove all from the temple area, both sheep and **cattle**;
1Co	9:9	of Moses: "Do not muzzle an **ox** while it is treading out the grain."
	9:9	it is treading out the grain." Is it *about* **oxen** that God is concerned?
1Ti	5:18	"Do not muzzle the **ox** while it is treading out the grain,"

1092 βραβεῖον, *brabeion* [2] [√ *1093*]

prize [2]

1Co	9:24	know that in a race all the runners run, but only one gets the **prize**?
Php	3:14	I press on toward the goal to win the **prize** for which God has

1093 βραβεύω, *brabeuō* [1] [→ *1092, 2857*]

rule [1]

Col	3:15	*Let* the peace of Christ **rule** in your hearts, since as members of

1094 βραδύνω, *bradynō* [2] [√ *1096*]

delayed [1], slow [1]

1Ti	3:15	if *I am* **delayed**, you will know how people ought to conduct
2Pe	3:9	The Lord *is* not **slow** in keeping his promise, as some understand

1095 βραδυπλοέω, *bradyploeō* [1] [√ *1096 + 4434*]

made slow headway [1]

Ac	27:7	*We* **made slow headway** for many days and had difficulty arriving

1096 βραδύς, *bradys* [3] [→ *1094, 1095, 1097*]

slow [3]

Lk	24:25	and *how* **slow** of heart to believe all that the prophets have spoken!
Jas	1:19	should be quick to listen, **slow** to speak and slow to become angry,
	1:19	should be quick to listen, slow to speak and **slow** to become angry,

1097 βραδύτης, *bradytēs* [1] [√ *1096*]

slowness [1]

2Pe	3:9	is not slow in keeping his promise, as some understand **slowness**.

1098 βραχίων, *brachiōn* [3] [√ *1099*]

arm [2], power [1]

Lk	1:51	He has performed mighty deeds with his **arm**; he has scattered
Jn	12:38	our message and to whom has the **arm** of the Lord been revealed?"
Ac	13:17	stay in Egypt, with mighty **power** he led them out of that country,

1099 βραχύς, *brachys* [7] [→ *1098*]

little [3], bite [1], for a little while [1], short [+*1328*] [1], short time [1]

Lk	22:58	A **little** later someone else saw him and said, "You also are one of
Jn	6:7	wages would not buy enough bread for each one to have a **bite**!"
Ac	5:34	and ordered that the men be put outside **for a little while**.
	27:28	A **short time** later they took soundings again and found it was
Heb	2:7	You made him a **little** lower than the angels; you crowned him
	2:9	But we see Jesus, who was made a **little** lower than the angels,
	13:22	of exhortation, for I have written you *only* a **short** [+*1328*] letter.

1100 βρέφος, *brephos* [8]

baby [4], babies [2], infancy [1], newborn babies [1]

Lk	1:41	Elizabeth heard Mary's greeting, the **baby** leaped in her womb,
	1:44	greeting reached my ears, the **baby** in my womb leaped for joy.
	2:12	You will find a **baby** wrapped in cloths and lying in a manger.
	2:16	So they hurried off and found Mary and Joseph, and the **baby**,
	18:15	People were also bringing **babies** to Jesus to have him touch them.
Ac	7:19	our forefathers by forcing them to throw out their **newborn babies**
2Ti	3:15	and how from **infancy** you have known the holy Scriptures,
1Pe	2:2	Like newborn **babies**, crave pure spiritual milk, so that by it you

1101 βρέχω, *brechō* [7] [→ *1104*]

rain [3], wet [2], rained [1], sends rain [1]

Mt	5:45	and the good, and **sends rain** on the righteous and the unrighteous.
Lk	7:38	him at his feet weeping, she began *to* **wet** his feet with her tears.
	7:44	but she **wet** my feet with her tears and wiped them with her hair.
	17:29	fire and sulfur **rained** down from heaven and destroyed them all.
Jas	5:17	He prayed earnestly that *it would* not **rain**, and it did not rain on
	5:17	not rain, and *it did* not **rain** on the land for three and a half years.
Rev	11:6	so that it *will* not **rain** during the time they are prophesying;

1102 βριμάομαι, *brimaomai* Not used in UBS/NIV [→ *1839*]

1103 βροντή, *brontē* [12]

peals of thunder [4], thunder [3], thunders [3], peal of thunder [1], thundered [1]

Mk	3:17	he gave the name Boanerges, which means Sons *of* **Thunder**);
Jn	12:29	The crowd that was there and heard it said it had **thundered**;
Rev	4:5	throne came flashes of lightning, rumblings and **peals of thunder**.

6: 1   I heard one of the four living creatures say in a voice like **thunder**,
8: 5   and there came **peals of thunder**, rumblings, flashes of lightning
10: 3   When he shouted, the voices of the seven **thunders** spoke.
10: 4   And when the seven **thunders** spoke, I was about to write;
10: 4   "Seal up what the seven **thunders** have said and do not write it
11: 19 rumblings, **peals of thunder**, an earthquake and a great hailstorm.
14: 2   like the roar of rushing waters and like a loud **peal of thunder**.
16: 18 of lightning, rumblings, **peals of thunder** and a severe earthquake.
19: 6   like the roar of rushing waters and like loud peals *of* **thunder**,

1104 βροχή, *brochē* [2] [√ 1101]

rain [2]

Mt   7: 25 The **rain** came down, the streams rose, and the winds blew
      7: 27 The **rain** came down, the streams rose, and the winds blew

1105 βρόχος, *brochos* [1]

restrict [+2095] [1]

1Co   7: 35 I am saying this for your own good, not to **restrict** [+2095] you,

1106 βρυγμός, *brygmos* [7] [√ 1107]

gnashing [7]

Mt   8: 12 the darkness, where there will be weeping and **gnashing** of teeth."
      13: 42 fiery furnace, where there will be weeping and **gnashing** of teeth.
      13: 50 fiery furnace, where there will be weeping and **gnashing** of teeth.
      22: 13 the darkness, where there will be weeping and **gnashing** of teeth.'
      24: 51 the hypocrites, where there will be weeping and **gnashing** of teeth.
      25: 30 the darkness, where there will be weeping and **gnashing** of teeth.'
Lk   13: 28 and **gnashing** of teeth, when you see Abraham, Isaac and Jacob

1107 βρύχω, *brychō* [1] [→ 1106]

gnashed [1]

Ac   7: 54 they heard this, they were furious and **gnashed** their teeth at him.

1108 βρύω, *bryō* [1]

flow [1]

Jas   3: 11 Can both fresh water and salt water **flow** from the same spring?

1109 βρῶμα, *brōma* [17] [√ 1048]

food [10], foods [3], what eat [2], eating [1], solid food [1]

Mt   14: 15 so they can go to the villages and buy themselves *some* **food**."
Mk   7: 19 out of his body." (In saying this, Jesus declared all **foods** "clean.")
Lk   3: 11 him who has none, and the one who has **food** should do the same."
      9: 13 and two fish—unless we go and buy **food** for all this crowd."
Jn   4: 34 "My **food**," said Jesus, "is to do the will of him who sent me and to
Ro   14: 15 If your brother is distressed because of **what** *you* **eat**, you are no
      14: 15 Do not *by* your **eating** destroy your brother for whom Christ died.
      14: 20 Do not destroy the work of God for the sake *of* **food**. All food is
1Co   3: 2   I gave you milk, not **solid food**, for you were not yet ready for it.
      6: 13 "**Food** for the stomach and the stomach for food"—but God will
      6: 13 "**Food** for the stomach and the stomach *for* **food**"—but God will
      8: 8   But **food** does not bring us near to God; we are no worse if we do
      8: 13 Therefore, if **what** I **eat** causes my brother to fall into sin,
      10: 3 They all ate the same spiritual **food**
1Ti   4: 3   people to marry and order them to abstain from *certain* **foods**,
Heb   9: 10 They are only a matter of **food** and drink and various ceremonial
      13: 9 not *by ceremonial* **foods**, which are of no value to those who eat

1110 βρώσιμος, *brōsimos* [1] [√ 1048]

to eat [1]

Lk   24: 41 amazement, he asked them, "Do you have anything here **to eat**?"

1111 βρῶσις, *brōsis* [11] [√ 1048]

food [6], rust [2], eat [1], eating [1], meal [1]

Mt   6: 19 where moth and **rust** destroy, and where thieves break in and steal.
      6: 20 where moth and **rust** do not destroy, and where thieves do not
Jn   4: 32 he said to them, "I have **food** to eat that you know nothing about."
      6: 27 Do not work for **food** that spoils, but for food that endures to
      6: 27 work for food that spoils, but for **food** that endures to eternal life,
      6: 55 For my flesh is real **food** and my blood is real drink.
Ro   14: 17 For the kingdom of God is not a *matter of* **eating** and drinking,
1Co   8: 4   So then, about *eating* **food** sacrificed to idols: We know that an
2Co   9: 10 and bread for **food** will also supply and increase your store of seed
Col   2: 16 Therefore do not let anyone judge you by what you **eat** or drink,
Heb   12: 16 who for a single **meal** sold his inheritance rights as the oldest son.

1112 βυθίζω, *bythizō* [2] [√ 1113]

plunge [1], sink [1]

Lk   5: 7   and they came and filled both boats so full that they *began to* **sink**.
1Ti   6: 9   and harmful desires that **plunge** men into ruin and destruction.

1113 βυθός, *bythos* [1] [→ 12, 1112]

open sea [1]

2Co   11: 25 times I was shipwrecked, I spent a night and a day in the **open sea**,

1114 βυρσεύς, *byrseus* [3]

tanner [3]

Ac   9: 43 Peter stayed in Joppa for some time with a **tanner** named Simon.
      10: 6   He is staying with Simon the **tanner**, whose house is by the sea."
      10: 32 He is a guest in the home *of* Simon the **tanner**, who lives by the

1115 βύσσινος, *byssinos* [5] [√ 1116]

fine linen [5]

Rev   18: 12 cargoes *of* gold, silver, precious stones and pearls; **fine linen**,
      18: 16 Woe, O great city, dressed in **fine linen**, purple and scarlet,
      19: 8   **Fine linen**, bright and clean, was given her to wear." (Fine linen
      19: 8   her to wear." (**Fine linen** stands for the righteous acts of the saints.)
      19: 14 riding on white horses and dressed in **fine linen**, white and clean.

1116 βύσσος, *byssos* [1] [→ 1115, 3327]

fine linen [1]

Lk   16: 19 was dressed in purple and **fine linen** and lived in luxury every day.

1117 βωμός, *bōmos* [1] [√ 326]

altar [1]

Ac   17: 23 objects of worship, I even found an **altar** with this inscription:

Γ, γ

1118 γ, *g*   Not used in UBS/NIV

1119 Γαββαθᾶ, *Gabbatha* [1]

Gabbatha [1]

Jn   19: 13 known as the Stone Pavement (which in Aramaic is **Gabbatha**).

1120 Γαβριήλ, *Gabriēl* [2]

Gabriel [2]

Lk   1: 19 The angel answered, "I am **Gabriel**. I stand in the presence of God,
      1: 26 God sent the angel **Gabriel** to Nazareth, a town in Galilee,

1121 γάγγραινα, *gangraina* [1]

gangrene [1]

2Ti 2:17 Their teaching will spread like **gangrene**. Among them are

1122 Γάδ, *Gad* [1]

Gad [1]

Rev 7: 5 from the tribe of Reuben 12,000, from the tribe *of* **Gad** 12,000,

1123 Γαδαρηνός, *Gadarēnos* [1]

Gadarenes [1]

Mt 8:28 When he arrived at the other side in the region *of* the **Gadarenes**,

1124 Γάζα[1], *Gaza*[1] [1]

Gaza [1]

Ac 8:26 the desert road—that goes down from Jerusalem to **Gaza**."

1125 γάζα[2], *gaza*[2] [1] [→ 1126]

treasury [1]

Ac 8:27 an important official in charge of all the **treasury** of Candace,

1126 γαζοφυλάκιον, *gazophylakion* [5] [√ 1125 + 5875]

place where the offerings were put [2], temple treasury [2], treasury [1]

Mk 12:41 Jesus sat down opposite the **place where the offerings were put**
    12:41 watched the crowd putting their money into the **temple treasury**.
    12:43 this poor widow has put more into the **treasury** than all the others.
Lk 21: 1 Jesus saw the rich putting their gifts into the **temple treasury**.
Jn   8:20 in the temple area near the **place where the offerings were put**.

1127 Γάϊος, *Gaios* [5] [√ 1178]

Gaius [5]

Ac 19:29 The people seized **Gaius** and Aristarchus, Paul's traveling
    20: 4 **Gaius** from Derbe, Timothy also, and Tychicus and Trophimus
Ro 16:23 **Gaius**, whose hospitality I and the whole church here enjoy,
1Co 1:14 that I did not baptize any of you except Crispus and **Gaius**,
3Jn 1: 1 The elder, *To* my dear friend **Gaius**, whom I love in the truth.

1128 γάλα, *gala* [5]

milk [5]

1Co 3: 2 I gave you **milk**, not solid food, for you were not yet ready for it.
     9: 7 of its grapes? Who tends a flock and does not drink of the **milk**?
Heb 5:12 truths of God's word all over again. You need **milk**, not solid food!
     5:13 Anyone who lives on **milk**, being still an infant, is not acquainted
1Pe 2: 2 Like newborn babies, crave pure spiritual **milk**, so that by it you

1129 Γαλάτης, *Galatēs* [1] [√ 1130]

Galatians [1]

Gal 3: 1 You foolish **Galatians**! Who has bewitched you? Before your very

1130 Γαλατία, *Galatia* [4] [→ 1129, 1131]

Galatia [3], Galatian [1]

1Co 16: 1 for God's people: Do what I told the **Galatian** churches to do.
Gal 1: 2 and all the brothers with me, To the churches *in* **Galatia**:
2Ti 4:10 Crescens has gone to **Galatia**, and Titus to Dalmatia.
1Pe 1: 1 throughout Pontus, **Galatia**, Cappadocia, Asia and Bithynia,

1131 Γαλατικός, *Galatikos* [2] [√ 1130]

Galatia [1], of Galatia [1]

Ac 16: 6 companions traveled throughout the region of Phrygia and **Galatia**,
    18:23 and traveled from place to place throughout the region **of Galatia**

1132 γαλήνη, *galēnē* [3]

calm [3]

Mt 8:26 and rebuked the winds and the waves, and it was completely **calm**.
Mk 4:39 Be still!" Then the wind died down and it was completely **calm**.
Lk 8:24 and the raging waters; the storm subsided, and all was **calm**.

1133 Γαλιλαία, *Galilaia* [61] [→ 1134]

θάλασσα τῆς Γαλιλαίας (Sea of Galilee) [5] Mt 4:18; 15:29; Mk 1:16; 7:31; Jn 6:1

Galilee [61]

Mt 2:22 been warned in a dream, he withdrew to the district *of* **Galilee**,
    3:13 Then Jesus came from **Galilee** to the Jordan to be baptized by
    4:12 heard that John had been put in prison, he returned to **Galilee**.
    4:15 the way to the sea, along the Jordan, **Galilee** of the Gentiles—
    4:18 As Jesus was walking beside the Sea *of* **Galilee**, he saw two
    4:23 Jesus went throughout **Galilee**, teaching in their synagogues,
    4:25 Large crowds from **Galilee**, the Decapolis, Jerusalem, Judea
    15:29 Jesus left there and went along the Sea *of* **Galilee**. Then he went up
    17:22 When they came together in **Galilee**, he said to them, "The Son of
    19: 1 he left **Galilee** and went into the region of Judea to the other side
    21:11 "This is Jesus, the prophet from Nazareth in **Galilee**."
    26:32 But after I have risen, I will go ahead of you into **Galilee**."
    27:55 They had followed Jesus from **Galilee** to care for his needs.
    28: 7 'He has risen from the dead and is going ahead of you into **Galilee**.
    28:10 Go and tell my brothers to go to **Galilee**; there they will see me."
    28:16 Then the eleven disciples went to **Galilee**, to the mountain where
Mk 1: 9 At that time Jesus came from Nazareth *in* **Galilee** and was baptized
    1:14 After John was put in prison, Jesus went into **Galilee**,
    1:16 As Jesus walked beside the Sea *of* **Galilee**, he saw Simon
    1:28 News about him spread quickly over the whole region *of* **Galilee**.
    1:39 So he traveled throughout **Galilee**, preaching in their synagogues
    3: 7 his disciples to the lake, and a large crowd from **Galilee** followed.
    6:21 and military commanders and the leading men *of* **Galilee**.
    7:31 down to the Sea *of* **Galilee** and into the region of the Decapolis.
    9:30 They left that place and passed through **Galilee**. Jesus did not want
    14:28 But after I have risen, I will go ahead of you into **Galilee**."
    15:41 In **Galilee** these women *had* followed him and cared for his needs.
    16: 7 tell his disciples and Peter, 'He is going ahead of you into **Galilee**.
Lk 1:26 God sent the angel Gabriel to Nazareth, a town *in* **Galilee**,
    2: 4 So Joseph also went up from the town of Nazareth *in* **Galilee** to
    2:39 the Lord, they returned to **Galilee** to their own town of Nazareth.
    3: 1 Herod tetrarch *of* **Galilee**, his brother Philip tetrarch of Iturea
    4:14 Jesus returned to **Galilee** in the power of the Spirit, and news about
    4:31 Then he went down to Capernaum, a town *in* **Galilee**, and on the
    5:17 who had come from every village *of* **Galilee** and from Judea
    8:26 the region of the Gerasenes, which is across the lake *from* **Galilee**.
    17:11 Jesus traveled along the border between Samaria and **Galilee**.
    23: 5 his teaching. He started in **Galilee** and has come all the way here."
    23:49 including the women who had followed him from **Galilee**,
    23:55 The women who had come with Jesus from **Galilee** followed
    24: 6 Remember how he told you, while he was still with you in **Galilee**:
Jn 1:43 The next day Jesus decided to leave for **Galilee**. Finding Philip,
    2: 1 On the third day a wedding took place at Cana *in* **Galilee**.
    2:11 first of his miraculous signs, Jesus performed at Cana *in* **Galilee**.
    4: 3 learned of this, he left Judea and went back once more to **Galilee**.
    4:43 After the two days he left for **Galilee**.
    4:45 When he arrived in **Galilee**, the Galileans welcomed him.
    4:46 Once more he visited Cana *in* **Galilee**, where he had turned the
    4:47 When this man heard that Jesus had arrived in **Galilee** from Judea,
    4:54 sign that Jesus performed, having come from Judea to **Galilee**.
    6: 1 Jesus crossed to the far shore of the Sea *of* **Galilee** (that is,
    7: 1 After this, Jesus went around in **Galilee**, purposely staying away
    7: 9 Having said this, he stayed in **Galilee**.
    7:41 Still others asked, "How can the Christ come from **Galilee**?
    7:52 They replied, "Are you from **Galilee**, too? Look into it, and you

7:52 and you will find that a prophet does not come out of **Galilee**."
12:21 came to Philip, who was from Bethsaida *in* **Galilee**, with a request.
21: 2 Nathanael from Cana *in* **Galilee**, the sons of Zebedee,
Ac 9:31 throughout Judea, **Galilee** and Samaria enjoyed a time of peace.
10:37 beginning in **Galilee** after the baptism that John preached—
13:31 by those who had traveled with him from **Galilee** to Jerusalem.

1134 Γαλιλαῖος, *Galilaios* [11] [√ *1133*]

Galileans [5], Galilean [4], Galilee [1], of Galilee [1]

Mt 26:69 girl came to him. "You also were with Jesus **of Galilee**," she said.
Mk 14:70 said to Peter, "Surely you are one of them, for you are a **Galilean**."
Lk 13: 1 the **Galileans** whose blood Pilate had mixed with their sacrifices.
13: 2 "Do you think that these **Galileans** were worse sinners than all the
13: 2 that these **Galileans** were worse sinners than all the other **Galileans**
22:59 "Certainly this fellow was with him, for he is a **Galilean**."
23: 6 On hearing this, Pilate asked if the man was a **Galilean**.
Jn 4:45 When he arrived in Galilee, the **Galileans** welcomed him.
Ac 1:11 "Men *of* **Galilee**," they said, "why do you stand here looking into
2: 7 they asked: "Are not all these men who are speaking **Galileans**?
5:37 Judas the **Galilean** appeared in the days of the census and led a

1135 Γαλλία, *Gallia*   Not used in UBS/NIV

1136 Γαλλίων, *Galliōn* [3]

Gallio [3]

Ac 18:12 While **Gallio** was proconsul of Achaia, the Jews made a united
18:14 Just as Paul was about to speak, **Gallio** said to the Jews, "If you
18:17 him in front of the court. But **Gallio** showed no concern whatever.

1137 Γαμαλιήλ, *Gamaliēl* [2]

Gamaliel [2]

Ac 5:34 But a Pharisee named **Gamaliel**, a teacher of the law, who was
22: 3 Under **Gamaliel** I was thoroughly trained in the law of our fathers

1138 γαμέω, *gameō* [28] [√ *1141*]

marry [12], marries [7], married [5], marrying [2], get married [1],
got married [+*1222*] [1]

Mt 5:32 and anyone *who* **marries** the divorced woman commits adultery.
19: 9 and **marries** another woman commits adultery."
19:10 the situation between a husband and wife, it is better not *to* **marry**."
22:25 The first one **married** and died, and since he had no children,
22:30 At the resurrection *people will* neither **marry** nor be given in
24:38 people were eating and drinking, **marrying** and giving in marriage,
Mk 6:17 of Herodias, his brother Philip's wife, whom *he had* **married**.
10:11 and **marries** another woman commits adultery against her.
10:12 And if she divorces her husband and **marries** another man,
12:25 the dead rise, *they will* neither **marry** nor be given in marriage;
Lk 14:20 "Still another said, '*I* just **got married** [+*1222*],
16:18 divorces his wife and **marries** another woman commits adultery,
16:18 and the man *who* **marries** a divorced woman commits adultery.
17:27 *People were* eating, drinking, **marrying** and being given in
20:34 "The people of this age **marry** and are given in marriage.
20:35 and in the resurrection from the dead *will* neither **marry** nor be
1Co 7: 9 But if they cannot control themselves, *they should* **marry**,
7: 9 should marry, for it is better *to* **marry** than to burn with passion.
7:10 *To* the **married** I give this command (not I, but the Lord):
7:28 But if *you do* **marry**, you have not sinned; and if a virgin marries,
7:28 you have not sinned; and if a virgin **marries**, she has not sinned.
7:33 But a **married** *man* is concerned about the affairs of this world—
7:34 But a **married** *woman* is concerned about the affairs of this
7:36 do as he wants. He is not sinning. *They should* **get married**.
7:39 But if her husband dies, she is free *to* **marry** anyone she wishes,
1Ti 4: 3 They forbid people *to* **marry** and order them to abstain from
5:11 desires overcome their dedication to Christ, they want *to* **marry**.
5:14 So I counsel younger widows *to* **marry**, to have children,

1139 γαμίζω, *gamizō* [7] [√ *1141*]

given in marriage [4], giving in marriage [1], marries [1], marry [1]

Mt 22:30 resurrection *people will* neither marry nor *be* **given in marriage**;
24:38 were eating and drinking, marrying and **giving in marriage**,
Mk 12:25 the dead rise, they will neither marry nor *be* **given in marriage**
Lk 17:27 *were* eating, drinking, marrying and *being* **given in marriage**
20:35 from the dead will neither marry nor *be* **given in marriage**,
1Co 7:38 So then, he *who* **marries** the virgin does right, but he who does not
7:38 virgin does right, but he *who does* not **marry** her does even better.

1140 γαμίσκω, *gamiskō* [1] [√ *1141*]

given in marriage [1]

Lk 20:34 "The people of this age marry and *are* **given in marriage**.

1141 γάμος, *gamos* [16] [→ *23, 1138, 1139, 1140, 1432,* *1433, 1679, 1680, 2102*]

wedding [6], wedding banquet [5], banquet [2], marriage [1],
wedding feast [1], wedding hall [1]

Mt 22: 2 heaven is like a king who prepared a **wedding banquet** for his son.
22: 3 He sent his servants to those who had been invited to the **banquet**
22: 4 and everything is ready. Come to the **wedding banquet**.'
22: 8 "Then he said to his servants, 'The **wedding banquet** is ready,
22: 9 to the street corners and invite to the **banquet** anyone you find.'
22:10 both good and bad, and the **wedding hall** was filled with guests.
22:11 he noticed a man there who was not wearing **wedding** clothes.
22:12 he asked, 'how did you get in here without **wedding** clothes?'
25:10 virgins who were ready went in with him to the **wedding banquet**.
Lk 12:36 men waiting for their master to return from a **wedding banquet**,
14: 8 "When someone invites you to a **wedding feast**, do not take the
Jn 2: 1 On the third day a **wedding** took place at Cana in Galilee.
2: 2 and Jesus and his disciples had also been invited to the **wedding**.
Heb 13: 4 **Marriage** should be honored by all, and the marriage bed kept
Rev 19: 7 For the **wedding** of the Lamb has come, and his bride has made
19: 9 'Blessed are those who are invited to the **wedding** supper of the

1142 γάρ, *gar* [1041 / 1040]   See Index of Articles, Etc. [→ *5521*]

for [501], *untranslated* [378], because [85], but [11], and [9], now
[7], indeed [5], in fact [4], since [4], after all [3], why [3], as [2], as
for [2], so [2], yes [2], again [1], because of [1], even though
[+*3525*] [1], for [+*3525*] [1], for [+*3590*] [1], for example [1], for to
be sure [1], how [+*3590*] [1], if [1], in [1], in fact [+*2779*] [1],
indeed [+*237+2093*] [1], moreover [1], no [1], no doubt [1], or [1],
rather [1], surely [1], the fact is [1], though [1], yet [1], you see [1]

1143 γαστήρ, *gastēr* [9]

pregnant women [+*1877+2400*] [3], with child [+*1877+2400*] [2],
gluttons [1], pregnant [+*1877+2400*] [1], pregnant woman
[+*1877+2400*] [1], with child [+*1877+5197*] [1]

Mt 1:18 she was found *to be* **with child** [+*1877+2400*] through the Holy
1:23 "The virgin *will be* **with child** [+*1877+2400*] and will give birth to
24:19 it will be in those days *for* **pregnant** [+*1877+2400*] **women**
Mk 13:17 it will be in those days *for* **pregnant** [+*1877+2400*] **women**
Lk 1:31 You *will be* **with child** [+*1877+5197*] and give birth to a son,
21:23 it will be in those days *for* **pregnant** [+*1877+2400*] **women**
1Th 5: 3 as labor pains *on a* **pregnant** [+*1877+2400*] **woman**, and they will
Tit 1:12 has said, "Cretans are always liars, evil brutes, lazy **gluttons**."
Rev 12: 2 *She was* **pregnant** [+*1877+2400*] and cried out in pain as she was

1144 Γαύδη, *Gaudē*   Not used in UBS/NIV [√ *cf. 3007*]

1145 γέ, *ge* [25] [→ *2301, 2781, 2793, 3529, 3591, 3615,* *4007, 5522*]

untranslated [4], do [+*3590*] [3], surely [+*1623*] [2], does [+*3590*]
[2], really [2], yet [2], and [+*247+2779*] [1], because

[+1623+2779] [1], even [+2779] [1], if [+1623] [1], perhaps [+726+1623] [1], surely [+247] [1], then [1], then [+726] [1], though [+2779] [1], thus [+726] [1]

Mt   6: 1 If you do^s [+3590], you will have no reward from your Father in
    7:20 **Thus** [+726], by their fruit you will recognize them.
    9:17 If they do^s [+3590], the skins will burst, the wine will run out
  17:26 **"Then** [+726] the sons are exempt," Jesus said to him.
Lk   5:36 If he does^s [+3590], he will have torn the new garment,
    5:37 If he does^s [+3590], the new wine will burst the skins, the wine
  10: 6 your peace will rest on him; if not, **[NIE]** it will return to you.
  11: 8 **yet** because of the man's boldness he will get up and give him as
  13: 9 If it bears fruit next year, fine! If not, **then** cut it down.' "
  14:32 If he is not **[NIE]** able, he will send a delegation while the other is
  18: 5 **yet** because this widow keeps bothering me, I will see that she gets
  24:21 **And** [+247+2779] what is more, it is the third day since all this
Ac   2:18 **Even** [+2779] on my servants, both men and women, I will pour
  8:30 **[NIE]** "Do you understand what you are reading?" Philip asked.
  17:27 and **perhaps** [+726+1623] reach out for him and find him,
  17:27 and find him, **though** [+2779] he is not far from each one of us.
Ro   8:32 He who **[NIE]** did not spare his own Son, but gave him up for us
1Co   4: 8 How I wish that you **really** had become kings so that we might be
  9: 2 I may not be an apostle to others, **surely** [+247] I am to you!
2Co   5: 3 **because** [+1623+2779] when we are clothed, we will not be found
  11:16 I repeat: Let no one take me for a fool. But if you do^s [+3590],
Gal   3: 4 you suffered so much for nothing—if it **really** was for nothing?
Eph   3: 2 **Surely** [+1623] you have heard about the administration of God's
  4:21 **Surely** [+1623] you heard of him and were taught in him in
Col   1:23 **if** [+1623] you continue in your faith, established and firm,

1146 Γεδεών, Gedeōn [1]

Gideon [1]

Heb 11:32 I do not have time to tell about **Gideon**, Barak, Samson, Jephthah,

1147 γέεννα, geenna [12]

hell [12]

Mt   5:22 anyone who says, 'You fool!' will be in danger of the fire of **hell**.
  5:29 part of your body than for your whole body to be thrown into **hell**.
  5:30 one part of your body than for your whole body to go into **hell**.
  10:28 be afraid of the One who can destroy both soul and body in **hell**.
  18: 9 one eye than to have two eyes and be thrown into the fire *of* **hell**.
  23:15 you make him twice as much a son *of* **hell** as you are.
  23:33 brood of vipers! How will you escape being condemned *to* **hell**?
Mk   9:43 for you to enter life maimed than with two hands to go into **hell**,
  9:45 to enter life crippled than to have two feet and be thrown into **hell**.
  9:47 of God with one eye than to have two eyes and be thrown into **hell**,
Lk   12: 5 after the killing of the body, has power to throw you into **hell**.
Jas   3: 6 the whole course of his life on fire, and is itself set on fire by **hell**.

1148 Γεθσημανῆ, Gethsēmanē Not used in
UBS/NIV [√ cf. 1149]

1149 Γεθσημανί, Gethsēmani [2] [√ cf. 1148]

Gethsemane [2]

Mt 26:36 Then Jesus went with his disciples to a place called **Gethsemane**,
Mk 14:32 They went to a place called **Gethsemane**, and Jesus said to his

1150 γείτων, geitōn [4]

neighbors [4]

Lk 14:12 your friends, your brothers or relatives, or your rich **neighbors**;
  15: 6 Then he calls his friends and **neighbors** together and says,
  15: 9 she calls her friends and **neighbors** together and says,
Jn   9: 8 His **neighbors** and those who had formerly seen him begging

1151 γελάω, gelaō [2] [→ 1152, 2860]

laugh [2]

Lk   6:21 be satisfied. Blessed are you who weep now, for *you will* **laugh**.
  6:25 Woe to you who **laugh** now, for you will mourn and weep.

1152 γέλως, gelōs [1] [√ 1151]

laughter [1]

Jas   4: 9 Change your **laughter** to mourning and your joy to gloom.

1153 γεμίζω, gemizō [8 / 9] [√ 1154]

filled [5], fill [2], full [1], swamped [1]

Mk   4:37 and the waves broke over the boat, so that it *was* nearly **swamped**.
  15:36 One man ran, **filled** a sponge with wine vinegar, put it on a stick,
Lk   14:23 and make them come in, so that my house *will be* **full**.
  15:16 He longed *to* **fill** [UBS 5963] his stomach with the pods that the
Jn   2: 7 Jesus said to the servants, "**Fill** the jars with water"; so they filled
  2: 7 "Fill the jars with water"; so *they* **filled** them to the brim.
  6:13 and **filled** twelve baskets with the pieces of the five barley loaves
Rev   8: 5 **filled** it with fire from the altar, and hurled it on the earth;
  15: 8 And the temple *was* **filled** with smoke from the glory of God

1154 γέμω, gemō [11] [→ 1153, 1203]

full [5], covered with [3], filled [2], full of [1]

Mt 23:25 and dish, but inside *they are* **full** of greed and self-indulgence.
  23:27 but on the inside *are* **full** of dead men's bones and everything
Lk 11:39 and dish, but inside you *are* **full of** greed and wickedness.
Ro   3:14 "Their mouths *are* **full** of cursing and bitterness."
Rev   4: 6 and *they were* **covered with** eyes, in front and in back.
  4: 8 creatures had six wings and *was* **covered with** eyes all around,
  5: 8 one had a harp and they were holding golden bowls **full** of incense,
  15: 7 the seven angels seven golden bowls **filled** with the wrath of God,
  17: 3 on a scarlet beast that *was* **covered with** blasphemous names
  17: 4 **filled** with abominable things and the filth of her adulteries.
  21: 9 One of the seven angels who had the seven bowls **full** of the seven

1155 γενεά, genea [43] [√ 1181]

generation [29], generations [5], *untranslated* [4], descendants [1], it^s [+3836+4047] [1], kind [1], past [+4233] [1], times [1]

Mt   1:17 Thus there were fourteen **generations** in all from Abraham to
  1:17 **[RPG]** fourteen from David to the exile to Babylon, and fourteen
  1:17 fourteen **[RPG]** from David to the exile to Babylon, and fourteen
  1:17 exile to Babylon, and **[RPG]** fourteen from the exile to the Christ.
  11:16 "To what can I compare this **generation**? They are like children
  12:39 "A wicked and adulterous **generation** asks for a miraculous sign!
  12:41 men of Nineveh will stand up at the judgment with this **generation**
  12:42 Queen of the South will rise at the judgment with this **generation**
  12:45 than the first. That is how it will be *with* this wicked **generation**."
  16: 4 A wicked and adulterous **generation** looks for a miraculous sign,
  17:17 "O unbelieving and perverse **generation**," Jesus replied, "how long
  23:36 I tell you the truth, all this will come upon this **generation**.
  24:34 this **generation** will certainly not pass away until all these things
Mk   8:12 and said, "Why does this **generation** ask for a miraculous sign?
  8:12 I tell you the truth, no sign will be given *to* **it**^{s} [+3836+4047]."
  8:38 of me and my words in this adulterous and sinful **generation**,
  9:19 "O unbelieving **generation**," Jesus replied, "how long shall I stay
  13:30 this **generation** will certainly not pass away until all these things
Lk   1:48 of his servant. From now on all **generations** will call me blessed,
  1:50 extends to those who fear him, from **generation** to generation.
  1:50 extends to those who fear him, from generation to **generation**.
  7:31 "To what, then, can I compare the people *of* this **generation**?
  9:41 "O unbelieving and perverse **generation**," Jesus replied, "how long
  11:29 crowds increased, Jesus said, "This **[RPG]** is a wicked generation.
  11:29 As the crowds increased, Jesus said, "This is a wicked **generation**.
  11:30 to the Ninevites, so also will the Son of Man be *to* this **generation**.
  11:31 the South will rise at the judgment with the men *of* this **generation**
  11:32 men of Nineveh will stand up at the judgment with this **generation**
  11:50 Therefore this **generation** will be held responsible for the blood of
  11:51 I tell you, this **generation** will be held responsible for it all.
  16: 8 in dealing with their own **kind** than are the people of the light.
  17:25 he must suffer many things and be rejected by this **generation**.
  21:32 this **generation** will certainly not pass away until all these things
Ac   2:40 pleaded with them, "Save yourselves from this corrupt **generation**."
  8:33 Who can speak of his **descendants**? For his life was taken from the
  13:36 "For when David had served God's purpose *in* his own **generation**,
  14:16 In the **past** [+4233], he let all nations go their own way.

15:21 For Moses has been preached in every city from the earliest **times**
Eph 3: 5 which was not made known to men *in* other **generations** as it has
     3:21 glory in the church and in Christ Jesus throughout all **generations**,
Php 2:15 of God without fault in a crooked and depraved **generation**,
Col 1:26 the mystery that has been kept hidden for ages and **generations**,
Heb 3:10 That is why I was angry *with* that **generation**, and I said,

1156 γενεαλογέω, *genealogeō* [1] [√ *1181* + *3306*]

trace descent [1]

Heb 7: 6 This man, however, *did* not **trace** *his* **descent** from Levi, yet he

1157 γενεαλογία, *genealogia* [2] [√ *1181* + *3306*]

genealogies [2]

1Ti 1: 4 nor to devote themselves *to* myths and endless **genealogies**.
Tit 3: 9 and **genealogies** and arguments and quarrels about the law,

1158 γενέθλια, *genethlia*   Not used in UBS/NIV [√ *1181*]

1159 γενέθλιος, *genethlios*   Not used in UBS/NIV [√ *1181*]

1160 γενέσια, *genesia* [2] [√ *1181*]

birthday [2]

Mt 14: 6 On Herod's **birthday** the daughter of Herodias danced for them
Mk 6:21 *On* his **birthday** Herod gave a banquet for his high officials

1161 γένεσις, *genesis* [5] [√ *1181*]

birth [2], *untranslated* [1], genealogy [1], life [1]

Mt 1: 1 A record *of* the **genealogy** of Jesus Christ the son of David,
     1:18 This is how the **birth** of Jesus Christ came about: His mother Mary
Lk 1:14 and delight to you, and many will rejoice because of his **birth**,
Jas 1:23 what it says is like a man who looks at his face [NIE] in a mirror
     3: 6 corrupts the whole person, sets the whole course *of* his **life** on fire,

1162 γενετή, *genetē* [1] [√ *1181*]

birth [1]

Jn 9: 1 As he went along, he saw a man blind from **birth**.

1163 γένημα, *genēma* [4] [√ *1181*]

fruit [3], harvest [1]

Mt 26:29 I will not drink of this **fruit** of the vine from now on until that day
Mk 14:25 I will not drink again of the **fruit** of the vine until that day when I
Lk 22:18 For I tell you I will not drink again of the **fruit** of the vine until the
2Co 9:10 store of seed and will enlarge the **harvest** of your righteousness.

1164 γεννάω, *gennaō* [97] [√ *1181*]

father [40], born [37], become father [3], gives birth to [2], bear [1], bears children [1], became father [1], became son^s [1], became the father of [1], birth [1], bore [1], came descendants [1], child [1], conceived [1], gave birth to [1], had [1], illegitimate children [+*1666*+*4518*] [1], native [+*1877*+*4005*] [1], produce [1]

Mt 1: 2 Abraham *was the* **father** *of* Isaac, Isaac the father of Jacob,
     1: 2 Isaac *the* **father** *of* Jacob, Jacob the father of Judah and his
     1: 2 the father of Jacob, Jacob *the* **father** *of* Judah and his brothers,
     1: 3 Judah *the* **father** *of* Perez and Zerah, whose mother was Tamar,
     1: 3 was Tamar, Perez *the* **father** *of* Hezron, Hezron the father of Ram,
     1: 3 was Tamar, Perez the father of Hezron, Hezron *the* **father** *of* Ram,
     1: 4 Ram *the* **father** *of* Amminadab, Amminadab the father of
     1: 4 Amminadab *the* **father** *of* Nahshon, Nahshon the father of Salmon,
     1: 4 Amminadab the father of Nahshon, Nahshon *the* **father** *of* Salmon,
     1: 5 Salmon *the* **father** *of* Boaz, whose mother was Rahab, Boaz the

1: 5 Boaz *the* **father** *of* Obed, whose mother was Ruth, Obed the father
1: 5 father of Obed, whose mother was Ruth, Obed *the* **father** *of* Jesse,
1: 6 and Jesse *the* **father** *of* King David. David was the father of
1: 6 David *was the* **father** *of* Solomon, whose mother had been Uriah's
1: 7 Solomon *the* **father** *of* Rehoboam, Rehoboam the father of Abijah,
1: 7 Rehoboam *the* **father** *of* Abijah, Abijah the father of Asa,
1: 7 Rehoboam the father of Abijah, Abijah *the* **father** *of* Asa,
1: 8 Asa *the* **father** *of* Jehoshaphat, Jehoshaphat the father of Jehoram,
1: 8 Jehoshaphat *the* **father** *of* Jehoram, Jehoram the father of Uzziah,
1: 8 Jehoshaphat the father of Jehoram, Jehoram *the* **father** *of* Uzziah,
1: 9 Uzziah *the* **father** *of* Jotham, Jotham the father of Ahaz, Ahaz the
1: 9 Uzziah the father of Jotham, Jotham *the* **father** *of* Ahaz, Ahaz the
1: 9 Jotham the father of Ahaz, Ahaz *the* **father** *of* Hezekiah,
1:10 Hezekiah *the* **father** *of* Manasseh, Manasseh the father of Amon,
1:10 Manasseh *the* **father** *of* Amon, Amon the father of Josiah,
1:10 Manasseh the father of Amon, Amon *the* **father** *of* Josiah,
1:11 and Josiah *the* **father** *of* Jeconiah and his brothers at the time of
1:12 Jeconiah *was the* **father** *of* Shealtiel, Shealtiel the father of
1:12 was the father of Shealtiel, Shealtiel *the* **father** *of* Zerubbabel,
1:13 Zerubbabel *the* **father** *of* Abiud, Abiud the father of Eliakim,
1:13 of Abiud, Abiud *the* **father** *of* Eliakim, Eliakim the father of Azor,
1:13 of Abiud, Abiud the father of Eliakim, Eliakim *the* **father** *of* Azor,
1:14 Azor *the* **father** *of* Zadok, Zadok the father of Akim, Akim the
1:14 of Zadok, Zadok *the* **father** *of* Akim, Akim the father of Eliud,
1:14 of Zadok, Zadok the father of Akim, Akim *the* **father** *of* Eliud,
1:15 Eliud *the* **father** *of* Eleazar, Eleazar the father of Matthan,
1:15 Eliud the father of Eleazar, Eleazar *the* **father** *of* Matthan,
1:15 Eleazar the father of Matthan, Matthan *the* **father** *of* Jacob,
1:16 and Jacob *the* **father** *of* Joseph, the husband of Mary, of whom
1:16 husband of Mary, of whom *was* **born** Jesus, who is called Christ.
1:20 because what *is* **conceived** in her is from the Holy Spirit.
2: 1 *After* Jesus *was* **born** in Bethlehem in Judea, during the time of
2: 4 of the law, he asked them where the Christ *was to be* **born**.
19:12 For some are eunuchs *because they were* **born** that way;
26:24 Son of Man! It would be better for him if he *had* not *been* **born**."
Mk 14:21 Son of Man! It would be better for him if he *had* not *been* **born**."
Lk 1:13 Your wife Elizabeth *will* **bear** you a son, and you are to give him
     1:35 So the holy one *to be* **born** will be called the Son of God.
     1:57 it was time for Elizabeth to have her baby, *she* **gave birth to** a son.
     23:29 the wombs that never **bore** and the breasts that never nursed!'
Jn 1:13 children **born** not of natural descent, nor of human decision
     3: 3 no one can see the kingdom of God unless he *is* **born** again."
     3: 4 "How can a man *be* **born** when he is old?" Nicodemus asked.
     3: 4 he cannot enter a second time into his mother's womb *to be* **born**!"
     3: 5 no one can enter the kingdom of God unless he *is* **born** of water
     3: 6 Flesh **gives birth to** flesh, but the Spirit gives birth to
     3: 6 Flesh gives birth to flesh, but the Spirit **gives birth to** spirit.
     3: 7 should not be surprised at my saying, 'You must *be* **born** again.'
     3: 8 or where it is going. So it is with everyone **born** of the Spirit."
     8:41 "We *are* not **illegitimate children** [+*1666*+*4518*]," they protested.
     9: 2 who sinned, this man or his parents, that *he was* **born** blind?"
     9:19 this your son?" they asked. "Is this the one you say *was* **born** blind?
     9:20 our son," the parents answered, "and we know he was **born** blind.
     9:32 Nobody has ever heard of opening the eyes *of a man* **born** blind.
     9:34 To this they replied, "You *were* steeped in sin *at* **birth**; how dare
     16:21 but when her baby *is* **born** she forgets the anguish because of her
     16:21 the anguish because of her joy that a child *is* **born** into the world.
     18:37 In fact, for this reason *I was* **born**, and for this I came into the
Ac 2: 8 each of us hears them in his own **native** [+*1877*+*4005*] language?
     7: 8 And Abraham **became the father of** Isaac and circumcised him
     7:20 "At that time Moses *was* **born**, and he was no ordinary child.
     7:29 fled to Midian, where he settled as a foreigner and **had** two sons.
     13:33 " 'You are my Son; today I *have* **become** your **Father**.'
     22: 3 "I am a Jew, **born** in Tarsus of Cilicia, but brought up in this city.
     22:28 price for my citizenship." "But I *was* **born** a citizen," Paul replied.
Ro 9:11 before the **twins** *were* **born** or had done anything good or bad—
1Co 4:15 for in Christ Jesus I **became** your **father** through the gospel.
Gal 4:23 His son by the slave woman *was* **born** in the ordinary way;
     4:24 is from Mount Sinai and **bears children** who are to be slaves:
     4:29 At that time the son **born** in the ordinary way persecuted the son
2Ti 2:23 and stupid arguments, because you know *they* **produce** quarrels.
Phm 1:10 my son Onesimus, who **became** *my* **son**^{s} while I was in chains.
Heb 1: 5 ever say, "You are my Son; today I *have* **become** your **Father**"?
     5: 5 said to him, "You are my Son; today I *have* **become** your **Father**."
     11:12 **came descendants** as numerous as the stars in the sky and as
     11:23 faith Moses' parents hid him for three months *after he was* **born**,

2Pe 2:12 creatures of instinct, **born** only to be caught and destroyed,
1Jn 2:29 you know that everyone who does what is right *has been* **born** of
     3: 9 No one who *is* **born** of God will continue to sin, because God's
     3: 9 he cannot go on sinning, because *he has been* **born** of God.
     4: 7 Everyone who loves *has been* **born** of God and knows God.
     5: 1 Everyone who believes that Jesus is the Christ *is* **born** of God,
     5: 1 and everyone who loves the **father** loves his child as well.
     5: 1 and everyone who loves the father loves his **child** as well.
     5: 4 for everyone **born** of God overcomes the world. This is the victory
     5:18 We know that anyone **born** of God does not continue to sin;
     5:18 the *one who was* **born** of God keeps him safe, and the evil one

1165 γέννημα, *gennēma* [4] [√ *1181*]

brood [4]

Mt   3: 7 to where he was baptizing, he said to them: "*You* **brood** of vipers!
    12:34 *You* **brood** of vipers, how can you who are evil say anything
    23:33 "You snakes! *You* **brood** of vipers! How will you escape being
Lk   3: 7 crowds coming out to be baptized by him, "*You* **brood** of vipers!

1166 Γεννησαρέτ, *Gennēsaret* [3]

Gennesaret [3]

Mt 14:34 When they had crossed over, they landed at **Gennesaret**.
Mk   6:53 had crossed over, they landed at **Gennesaret** and anchored there.
Lk   5: 1 One day as Jesus was standing by the Lake *of* **Gennesaret**,

1167 γέννησις, *gennēsis* Not used in UBS/NIV [√ *1181*]

1168 γεννητός, *gennētos* [2] [√ *1181*]

born [2]

Mt 11:11 Among *those* **born** of women there has not risen anyone greater
Lk   7:28 among *those* **born** of women there is no one greater than John;

1169 γένος, *genos* [20] [√ *1181*]

offspring [3], people [3], different kinds [2], family [2], native [2], *untranslated* [1], Jews [+*1609*+*1877*+*3836*] [1], born [1], children [+*5626*] [1], countrymen [1], kind [1], kinds [1], sorts [1]

Mt 13:47 a net that was let down into the lake and caught all **kinds** *of fish*.
Mk   7:26 The woman was a Greek, **born** in Syrian Phoenicia. She begged
     9:29 He replied, "This **kind** can come out only by prayer."
Ac   4: 6 John, Alexander and the other men of the high priest's **family**.
     4:36 [NIE] whom the apostles called Barnabas (which means Son of
     7:13 brothers who he was, and Pharaoh learned about Joseph's **family**.
     7:19 He dealt treacherously with our **people** and oppressed our
    13:26 "Brothers, **children** [+*5626*] of Abraham, and you God-fearing
    17:28 As some of your own poets have said, 'We are his **offspring**.'
    17:29 "Therefore since we are God's **offspring**, we should not think that
    18: 2 There he met a Jew named Aquila, a **native** of Pontus, who had
    18:24 a Jew named Apollos, a **native** of Alexandria, came to Ephesus.
1Co 12:10 between spirits, to another speaking in **different kinds** of tongues,
    12:28 and those speaking in **different kinds** of tongues.
    14:10 Undoubtedly there are all **sorts** of languages in the world,
2Co 11:26 in danger from bandits, in danger from my own **countrymen**,
Gal 1:14 I was advancing in Judaism beyond many **Jews** [+*1609*+*1877*+*3836*] of my own age and was extremely zealous
Php 3: 5 *of* the **people** of Israel, of the tribe of Benjamin, a Hebrew of
1Pe 2: 9 But you are a chosen **people**, a royal priesthood, a holy nation,
Rev 22:16 I am the Root and the **Offspring** of David, and the bright Morning

1170 Γερασηνός, *Gerasēnos* [3] [√ *cf. 1171*]

Gerasenes [3]

Mk   5: 1 They went across the lake to the region *of* the **Gerasenes**.
Lk   8:26 They sailed to the region *of* the **Gerasenes**, which is across the
     8:37 Then all the people of the region *of* the **Gerasenes** asked Jesus to

1171 Γεργεσηνός, *Gergesēnos* Not used in UBS/NIV [√ *cf. 1170*]

1172 γερουσία, *gerousia* [1] [√ *1173*]

assembly of elders [1]

Ac   5:21 the full **assembly of** the **elders** of Israel—and sent to the jail for

1173 γέρων, *gerōn* [1] [→ *1172; cf. 1179*]

old [1]

Jn   3: 4 "How can a man be born when he is **old**?" Nicodemus asked.

1174 γεύομαι, *geuomai* [15]

taste [6], tasted [4], eat [2], ate [1], get a taste [1], tasting [1]

Mt 16:28 some who are standing here *will* not **taste** death before they see the
    27:34 mixed with gall; but *after* **tasting** it, he refused to drink it.
Mk   9: 1 some who are standing here *will* not **taste** death before they see the
Lk   9:27 some who are standing here *will* not **taste** death before they see the
    14:24 not one of those men who were invited *will* **get a taste** of my
Jn   2: 9 and the master of the banquet **tasted** the water that had been turned
     8:52 you say that if anyone keeps your word, *he will* never **taste** death.
Ac 10:10 He became hungry and wanted something *to* **eat**, and while the
    20:11 Then *he* went upstairs again and broke bread and **ate**. After talking
    23:14 "We have taken a solemn oath not *to* **eat** anything until we have
Col 2:21 "Do not handle! *Do* not **taste**! Do not touch!"?
Heb 2: 9 so that by the grace of God *he might* **taste** death for everyone.
     6: 4 who *have* **tasted** the heavenly gift, who have shared in the Holy
     6: 5 who *have* **tasted** the goodness of the word of God and the powers
1Pe 2: 3 now that *you have* **tasted** that the Lord is good.

1175 γεωργέω, *geōrgeō* [1] [√ *1178* + *2240*]

farmed [1]

Heb 6: 7 and that produces a crop useful to those for whom *it is* **farmed**

1176 γεώργιον, *geōrgion* [1] [√ *1178* + *2240*]

field [1]

1Co 3: 9 we are God's fellow workers; you are God's **field**, God's building.

1177 γεωργός, *geōrgos* [19] [√ *1178* + *2240*]

tenants [12], farmers [3], farmer [2], gardener [1], them[s] [+*3836*] [1]

Mt 21:33 Then he rented the vineyard *to some* **farmers** and went away on a
    21:34 he sent his servants to the **tenants** to collect his fruit.
    21:35 "The **tenants** seized his servants; they beat one, killed another,
    21:38 "But when the **tenants** saw the son, they said to each other,
    21:40 the owner of the vineyard comes, what will he do *to* those **tenants**?"
    21:41 they replied, "and he will rent the vineyard to other **tenants**,
Mk 12: 1 Then he rented the vineyard *to some* **farmers** and went away on a
    12: 2 At harvest time he sent a servant to the **tenants** to collect from
    12: 2 to collect from them[s] [+*3836*] some of the fruit of the vineyard.
    12: 7 "But the **tenants** said to one another, 'This is the heir. Come,
    12: 9 He will come and kill those **tenants** and give the vineyard to
Lk 20: 9 rented it *to some* **farmers** and went away for a long time.
    20:10 At harvest time he sent a servant to the **tenants** so they would give
    20:10 But the **tenants** beat him and sent him away empty-handed.
    20:14 "But when the **tenants** saw him, they talked the matter over.
    20:16 He will come and kill those **tenants** and give the vineyard to
Jn 15: 1 "I am the true vine, and my Father is the **gardener**.
2Ti 2: 6 The hardworking **farmer** should be the first to receive a share of
Jas 5: 7 See how the **farmer** waits for the land to yield its valuable crop

1178 γῆ, *gē* [250] [→ *333, 1127, 1175, 1176, 1177, 2103*]

βασιλεῖς τῆς γῆς (kings of the earth) [10] Mt 17:25; Ac 4:26; Rev 1:5; 6:15; 17:2,18; 18:3,9; 19:19; 21:24

καινός γῆ (new earth) [2] 2Pe 3:13; Rev 21:1

οὐρανὸς ... γῆ (heaven ... earth) [57] Mt 5:18; 6:10; 11:25;
16:19; 18:18,19; 24:30,35; 28:18; Mk 13:27,31; Lk 4:25; 10:21;
12:56; 16:17; 21:33; Jn 3:31; Ac 2:19; 4:24; 7:49; 10:11,12; 11:6;
14:15; 17:24; 1Co 8:5; 15:47; Eph 1:10; 3:15; Col 1:16,20; Heb
1:10; 12:25,26; Jas 5:12,18; 2Pe 3:5,7,10,13; Rev 5:3,13; 6:13;
9:1; 10:5,6,8; 11:6; 12:4,12; 13:13; 14:7; 18:1; 20:9,11; 21:1,1

earth [151], land [31], ground [20], soil [13], Egypt [+*131*] [5],
shore [5], *untranslated* [2], Sodom [+*5047*] [2], country [2],
earthly [+*2093+3836*] [2], landed [+*2093+2262+3836*] [2], region
[2], world [2], Canaan [+*5913*] [1], Midian [+*3409*] [1], ashore
[+*1650+3836*] [1], ashore [+*2093*] [1], countryside [1], earth's [1],
earthly [1], its^s [+*3836*] [1], landed [+*609+1650+3836*] [1], them
[+*2093+2997+3836+3836*] [1], world's [1]

Mt 2: 6 " 'But you, Bethlehem, in the **land** of Judah, are by no means least
2:20 "Get up, take the child and his mother and go to the **land** of Israel.
2:21 took the child and his mother and went to the **land** of Israel.
4:15 "**Land** of Zebulun and land of Naphtali, the way to the sea,
4:15 "Land of Zebulun and **land** of Naphtali, the way to the sea,
5: 5 Blessed are the meek, for they will inherit the **earth**.
5:13 "You are the salt *of* the **earth**. But if the salt loses its saltiness,
5:18 I tell you the truth, until heaven and **earth** disappear,
5:35 or by the **earth**, for it is his footstool;
6:10 your kingdom come, your will be done on **earth** as it is in heaven.
6:19 "Do not store up for yourselves treasures on **earth**, where moth
9: 6 so that you may know that the Son of Man has authority on **earth**
9:26 News of this spread through all that **region**.
9:31 they went out and spread the news about him all over that **region**.
10:15 it will be more bearable *for* **Sodom** [+*5047*] and Gomorrah on the
10:29 Yet not one of them will fall to the **ground** apart from the will of
10:34 "Do not suppose that I have come to bring peace to the **earth**.
11:24 But I tell you that it will be more bearable *for* **Sodom** [+*5047*] on
11:25 time Jesus said, "I praise you, Father, Lord of heaven and **earth**,
12:40 of Man will be three days and three nights in the heart *of* the **earth**.
12:42 for she came from the ends *of* the **earth** to listen to Solomon's
13: 5 Some fell on rocky places, where it did not have much **soil**.
13: 5 have much soil. It sprang up quickly, because the **soil** was shallow.
13: 8 Still other seed fell on good **soil**, where it produced a crop—
13:23 But the one who received the seed that fell on good **soil** is the man
14:24 but the boat was already a considerable distance from **land**,
14:34 had crossed over, *they* **landed** [+*2093+2262+3836*] at Gennesaret.
15:35 He told the crowd to sit down on the **ground**.
16:19 whatever you bind on **earth** will be bound in heaven, and whatever
16:19 and whatever you loose on **earth** will be loosed in heaven."
17:25 "From whom do the kings *of* the **earth** collect duty and taxes—
18:18 you the truth, whatever you bind on **earth** will be bound in heaven,
18:18 and whatever you loose on **earth** will be loosed in heaven.
18:19 I tell you that if two of you on **earth** agree about anything you ask
23: 9 And do not call anyone on **earth** 'father,' for you have one Father,
23:35 you will come all the righteous blood that has been shed on **earth**,
24:30 will appear in the sky, and all the nations *of* the **earth** will mourn.
24:35 Heaven and **earth** will pass away, but my words will never pass
25:18 went off, dug a hole in the **ground** and hid his master's money.
25:25 So I was afraid and went out and hid your talent in the **ground**.
27:45 the sixth hour until the ninth hour darkness came over all the **land**.
27:51 in two from top to bottom. The **earth** shook and the rocks split.
28:18 "All authority in heaven and on **earth** has been given to me.

Mk 2:10 But that you may know that the Son of Man has authority on **earth**
4: 1 while all the people were along the **shore** at the water's edge.
4: 5 Some fell on rocky places, where it did not have much **soil**.
4: 5 have much soil. It sprang up quickly, because the **soil** was shallow.
4: 8 Still other seed fell on good **soil**. It came up, grew and produced a
4:20 Others, like seed sown on good **soil**, hear the word, accept it,
4:26 the kingdom of God is like. A man scatters seed on the **ground**.
4:28 All by itself the **soil** produces grain—first the stalk, then the head,
4:31 which is the smallest seed [**RPG**] you plant in the ground.
4:31 a mustard seed, which is the smallest seed you plant in the **ground**.
6:47 the boat was in the middle of the lake, and he was alone on **land**.
6:53 had crossed over, *they* **landed** [+*2093+2262+3836*] at Gennesaret
8: 6 He told the crowd to sit down on the **ground**. When he had taken
9: 3 whiter than anyone in the **world** could bleach them.
9:20 He fell to the **ground** and rolled around, foaming at the mouth.
13:27 four winds, from the ends *of* the **earth** to the ends of the heavens.
13:31 Heaven and **earth** will pass away, but my words will never pass

14:35 he fell to the **ground** and prayed that if possible the hour might
15:33 At the sixth hour darkness came over the whole **land** until the

Lk 2:14 in the highest, and on **earth** peace to men on whom his favor rests."
4:25 a half years and there was a severe famine throughout the **land**.
5: 3 belonging to Simon, and asked him to put out a little from **shore**.
5:11 So they pulled their boats up on **shore**, left everything
5:24 But that you may know that the Son of Man has authority on **earth**
6:49 like a man who built a house on the **ground** without a foundation.
8: 8 Still other seed fell on good **soil**. It came up and yielded a crop,
8:15 But the seed on good **soil** stands for those with a noble and good
8:27 When Jesus stepped **ashore** [+*2093*], he was met by a
10:21 Holy Spirit, said, "I praise you, Father, Lord of heaven and **earth**,
11:31 for she came from the ends *of* the **earth** to listen to Solomon's
12:49 "I have come to bring fire on the **earth**, and how I wish it were
12:51 Do you think I came to bring peace on **earth**? No, I tell you,
12:56 You know how to interpret the appearance *of* the **earth**
13: 7 haven't found any. Cut it down! Why should it use up the **soil**?'
14:35 It is fit neither for the **soil** nor for the manure pile; it is thrown out.
16:17 It is easier *for* heaven and **earth** to disappear than for the least
18: 8 when the Son of Man comes, will he find faith on the **earth**?"
21:23 There will be great distress in the **land** and wrath against this
21:25 On the **earth**, nations will be in anguish and perplexity at the
21:33 Heaven and **earth** will pass away, but my words will never pass
21:35 it will come upon all those who live on the face *of* the whole **earth**.
22:44 and his sweat was like drops of blood falling to the **ground**.
23:44 and darkness came over the whole **land** until the ninth hour,
24: 5 their fright the women bowed down with their faces to the **ground**,

Jn 3:22 Jesus and his disciples went out into the Judean **countryside**.
3:31 the one who is from the **earth** belongs to the earth, and speaks as
3:31 the one who is from the earth belongs to the **earth**, and speaks as
3:31 the **earth** belongs to the earth, and speaks as one from the earth.
6:21 and immediately the boat reached the **shore** where they were
8: 6 Jesus bent down and started to write on the **ground** with his finger.
8: 8 Again he stooped down and wrote on the **ground**.
12:24 you the truth, unless a kernel of wheat falls to the **ground** and dies,
12:32 But I, when I am lifted up from the **earth**, will draw all men to
17: 4 I have brought you glory on **earth** by completing the work you
21: 8 of fish, for they were not far from **shore**, about a hundred yards.
21: 9 When *they* **landed** [+*609+1650+3836*], they saw a fire of burning
coals there with fish on it, and some bread.
21:11 Peter climbed aboard and dragged the net **ashore** [+*1650+3836*].

Ac 1: 8 and in all Judea and Samaria, and to the ends *of* the **earth**."
2:19 show wonders in the heaven above and signs on the **earth** below,
3:25 'Through your offspring all peoples *on* **earth** will be blessed.'
4:24 they said, "you made the heaven and the **earth** and the sea,
4:26 The kings *of* the **earth** take their stand and the rulers gather
7: 3 'Leave your **country** and your people,' God said,
7: 3 and your people,' God said, 'and go to the **land** I will show you.'
7: 4 "So he left the **land** of the Chaldeans and settled in Haran. After the
7: 4 of his father, God sent him to this **land** where you are now living.
7: 6 'Your descendants will be strangers in a **country** not their own,
7:29 When Moses heard this, he fled to **Midian** [+*3409*], where he
7:33 off your sandals; the place where you are standing is holy **ground**.
7:36 of Egypt and did wonders and miraculous signs in **Egypt** [+*131*],
7:40 As for this fellow Moses who led us out of **Egypt** [+*131*]—
7:49 " 'Heaven is my throne, and the **earth** is my footstool. What kind of
8:33 speak of his descendants? For his life was taken from the **earth**."
9: 4 He fell to the **ground** and heard a voice say to him, "Saul, Saul,
9: 8 Saul got up from the **ground**, but when he opened his eyes he
10:11 and something like a large sheet being let down to **earth** by its four
10:12 as well as reptiles *of* the **earth** and birds of the air.
11: 6 I looked into it and saw four-footed animals *of* the **earth**, wild
13:17 he made the people prosper during their stay in **Egypt** [+*131*],
13:19 he overthrew seven nations in **Canaan** [+*5913*] and gave their land
13:19 in Canaan and gave their **land** to his people as their inheritance.
13:47 that you may bring salvation to the ends *of* the **earth**.' "
14:15 who made heaven and **earth** and sea and everything in them.
17:24 the world and everything in it is the Lord *of* heaven and **earth**
17:26 every nation of men, that they should inhabit the whole **earth**;
22:22 Then they raised their voices and shouted, "Rid the **earth** of him!
26:14 We all fell to the **ground**, and I heard a voice saying to me in
27:39 When daylight came, they did not recognize the **land**, but they saw
27:43 those who could swim to jump overboard first and get to **land**.
27:44 on pieces of the ship. In this way everyone reached **land** in safety.

Ro 9:17 in you and that my name might be proclaimed in all the **earth**."
9:28 For the Lord will carry out his sentence on **earth** with speed

10:18 "Their voice has gone out into all the **earth**, their words to the ends
1Co 8: 5 or on **earth** (as indeed there are many "gods" and many "lords"),
    10:26 for, "The **earth** is the Lord's, and everything in it."
    15:47 The first man was of the dust of the **earth**, the second man from
Eph 1:10 to bring all things in heaven and on **earth** together under one head,
     3:15 whom his whole family in heaven and on **earth** derives its name.
     4: 9 mean except that he also descended to the lower, **earthly** regions?
     6: 3 go well with you and that you may enjoy long life on the **earth**."
Col 1:16 things in heaven and on **earth**, visible and invisible,
     1:20 whether things on **earth** or things in heaven, by making peace
     3: 2 your minds on things above, not on **earthly** [*+2093+3836*] things.
     3: 5 therefore, whatever belongs to your **earthly** [*+2093+3836*] nature:
Heb 1:10 "In the beginning, O Lord, you laid the foundations of the **earth**,
     6: 7 **Land** that drinks in the rain often falling on it and that produces a
     8: 4 If he were on **earth**, he would not be a priest, for there are already
     8: 9 when I took them by the hand to lead them out of **Egypt** [*+131*],
    11: 9 By faith he made his home in the promised **land** like a stranger in a
    11:13 And they admitted that they were aliens and strangers on **earth**.
    11:29 By faith the people passed through the Red Sea as on dry **land**;
    11:38 in deserts and mountains, and in caves and holes *in* the **ground**.
    12:25 did not escape when they refused him who warned them on **earth**,
    12:26 At that time his voice shook the **earth**, but now he has promised,
    12:26 "Once more I will shake not only the **earth** but also the heavens."
Jas 5: 5 You have lived on **earth** in luxury and self-indulgence. You have
     5: 7 See how the farmer waits for the **land** to yield its valuable crop
     5:12 do not swear—not by heaven or by **earth** or by anything else.
     5:17 not rain, and it did not rain on the **land** for three and a half years.
     5:18 and the heavens gave rain, and the **earth** produced its crops.
2Pe 3: 5 and the **earth** was formed out of water and by water.
     3: 7 the same word the present heavens and **earth** are reserved for fire,
     3:10 by fire, and the **earth** and everything in it will be laid bare.
     3:13 promise we are looking forward to a new heaven and a new **earth**,
Jude 1: 5 remind you that the Lord delivered his people out of **Egypt** [*+131*],
Rev 1: 5 the firstborn from the dead, and the ruler of the kings *of* the **earth**.
     1: 7 and all the peoples *of* the **earth** will mourn because of him.
     3:10 to come upon the whole world to test those who live on the **earth**.
     5: 3 But no one in heaven or on **earth** or under the earth could open the
     5: 3 one in heaven or on earth or under the **earth** could open the scroll
     5: 6 which are the seven spirits of God sent out into all the **earth**.
     5:10 and priests to serve our God, and they will reign on the **earth**."
     5:13 creature in heaven and on **earth** and under the earth and on the sea,
     5:13 creature in heaven and on earth and under the **earth** and on the sea,
     6: 4 Its rider was given power to take peace from the **earth** and to make
     6: 8 They were given power over a fourth *of* the **earth** to kill by sword,
     6: 8 by sword, famine and plague, and by the wild beasts *of* the **earth**.
     6:10 until you judge the inhabitants of the **earth** and avenge our blood?"
     6:13 and the stars in the sky fell to **earth**, as late figs drop from a fig
     6:15 Then the kings *of* the **earth**, the princes, the generals, the rich,
     7: 1 this I saw four angels standing at the four corners *of* the **earth**,
     7: 1 holding back the four winds of the **earth** to prevent any wind from
     7: 1 winds of the earth to prevent any wind from blowing on the **land**
     7: 2 to the four angels who had been given power to harm the **land**
     7: 3 "Do not harm the **land** or the sea or the trees until we put a seal on
     8: 5 filled it with fire from the altar, and hurled it on the **earth**;
     8: 7 and fire mixed with blood, and it was hurled down upon the **earth**.
     8: 7 A third *of* the **earth** was burned up, a third of the trees were burned
     8:13 Woe to the inhabitants of the **earth**, because of the trumpet blasts
     9: 1 and I saw a star that had fallen from the sky to the **earth**.
     9: 3 And out of the smoke locusts came down upon the **earth** and were
     9: 3 the earth and were given power like that of scorpions *of* the **earth**.
     9: 4 They were told not to harm the grass *of* the **earth** or any plant
    10: 2 He planted his right foot on the sea and his left foot on the **land**,
    10: 5 standing on the sea and on the **land** raised his right hand to heaven.
    10: 6 the **earth** and all that is in it, and the sea and all that is in it,
    10: 8 the hand of the angel who is standing on the sea and on the **land**."
    11: 4 and the two lampstands that stand before the Lord *of* the **earth**.
    11: 6 and to strike the **earth** with every kind of plague as often as they
    11:10 The inhabitants of the **earth** will gloat over them and will celebrate
    11:10 these two prophets had tormented those who live on the **earth**.
    11:18 and great—and for destroying those who destroy the **earth**."
    12: 4 a third of the stars out of the sky and flung them to the **earth**.
    12: 9 world astray. He was hurled to the **earth**, and his angels with him.
    12:12 But woe *to* the **earth** and the sea, because the devil has gone down
    12:13 When the dragon saw that he had been hurled to the **earth**,
    12:16 But the **earth** helped the woman by opening its mouth
    12:16 But the earth helped the woman by **[RPG]** opening its mouth

13: 3 The whole **world** was astonished and followed the beast.
13: 8 All inhabitants of the **earth** will worship the beast—all whose
13:11 Then I saw another beast, coming out of the **earth**. He had two
13:12 and made the **earth** and its inhabitants worship the first beast,
13:13 even causing fire to come down from heaven to **earth** in full view
13:14 behalf of the first beast, he deceived the inhabitants of the **earth**.
13:14 He ordered them^s [*+2093+2997+3836+3836*] to set up an image
14: 3 song except the 144,000 who had been redeemed from the **earth**.
14: 6 had the eternal gospel to proclaim to those who live on the **earth**—
14: 7 who made the heavens, the **earth**, the sea and the springs of water."
14:15 the time to reap has come, for the harvest *of* the **earth** is ripe."
14:16 he who was seated on the cloud swung his sickle over the **earth**,
14:16 cloud swung his sickle over the earth, and the **earth** was harvested.
14:18 and gather the clusters of grapes *from* the **earth's** vine,
14:19 The angel swung his sickle on the **earth**, gathered its grapes
14:19 gathered its^s [*+3836*] grapes and threw them into the great
16: 1 "Go, pour out the seven bowls of God's wrath on the **earth**."
16: 2 The first angel went and poured out his bowl on the **land**,
16:18 earthquake like it has ever occurred since man has been on **earth**,
17: 2 With her the kings *of* the **earth** committed adultery
17: 2 and the inhabitants of the **earth** were intoxicated with the wine of
17: 5 AND OF THE ABOMINATIONS *OF* THE **EARTH**.
17: 8 The inhabitants of the **earth** whose names have not been written in
17:18 you saw is the great city that rules over the kings *of* the **earth**."
18: 1 I had great authority, and the **earth** was illuminated by his splendor.
18: 3 The kings *of* the **earth** committed adultery with her,
18: 3 and the merchants *of* the **earth** grew rich from her excessive
18: 9 "When the kings *of* the **earth** who committed adultery with her
18:11 "The merchants *of* the **earth** will weep and mourn over her
18:23 heard in you again. Your merchants were the **world's** great men.
18:24 and of the saints, and of all who have been killed on the **earth**."
19: 2 He has condemned the great prostitute who corrupted the **earth** by
19:19 Then I saw the beast and the kings *of* the **earth** and their armies
20: 8 will go out to deceive the nations in the four corners *of* the **earth**—
20: 9 They marched across the breadth *of* the **earth** and surrounded the
20:11 **Earth** and sky fled from his presence, and there was no place for
21: 1 Then I saw a new heaven and a new **earth**, for the first heaven
21: 1 new earth, for the first heaven and the first **earth** had passed away,
21:24 and the kings *of* the **earth** will bring their splendor into it.

1179 γῆρας, *gēras* [1] [→ *1180; cf. 1173*]

old age [1]

Lk   1:36 Elizabeth your relative is going to have a child in her **old age**,

1180 γηράσκω, *gērasko* [2] [√ *1179*]

aging [1], old [1]

Jn 21:18 but when *you are* **old** you will stretch out your hands,
Heb 8:13 one obsolete; and what is obsolete and **aging** will soon disappear.

1181 γίνομαι, *ginomai* [669 / 668] [→ *37, 38, 254, 335,*
614, 786, 1155, 1156, 1157, 1158, 1159, 1160, 1161, 1162,
1163, 1164, 1165, 1167, 1168, 1169, 1188, 1189, 1204, 1335,
1681, 2104, 2302, 2441, 3666, 4098, 4100, 4134, 4588, 4591,
5149, 5150, 5151, 5219, 5449, 5450]

untranslated [62], was [54], be [48], become [45], came [41],
happened [28], became [25], were [20], done [13], happen [13],
is [13], made [11], been [10], take place [8], performed [7],
become [*+1650*] [6], come [6], are [5], do [5], took place [5], by
no means [*+3590*] [4], not at all [*+3590*] [4], be done [4], get [4],
making [4], appeared [3], approached [3], becomes [3], born [3],
broke out [3], comes [3], happening [3], happens [3], absolutely
not [*+3590*] [2], arrived [2], became [*+1650*] [2], becoming [2],
been [*+1639*] [2], being [2], brought [2], came up [2], certainly
not [*+3590*] [2], had [2], lived [2], marries [2], occurred [2], once
[*+1254*] [2], perform [2], promised [*+2039*] [2], reached [*+2093*]
[2], seized [*+2093*] [2], served [2], share [*+5171*] [2], stood [2],
surpassed [*+1869*] [2], taken place [2], turned [2], turned into [2],
went [2], accomplished [1], after [1], agreed [*+3924*] [1], am [1],
and [*+2779*] [1], approaching [*+1584*] [1], arose [*+1254*] [1],
arose [1], arriving [1], at daybreak [*+2002+2465*] [1], at hour

[+6052] [1], bear [1], became [+1639] [1], become of [1], been [+1650] [1], been turned into [1], belong [1], betrayed [+4595] [1], brought about [1], came about [1], changed [+2283] [1], come of [1], come true [1], complained [+1198] [1], dawn [+2465+3516] [1], daybreak [+2465] [1], decided [+1191] [1], developed [1], did [1], died [+2505] [1], died [+3738] [1], disappeared [+908] [1], do [+4475] [1], does [1], does⁵ [+4048] [1], doing [1], doubting [+603] [1], early in the morning [+4746] [1], entered [+1656] [1], equaled [1], experienced [1], faultless [+289] [1], fell [1], fell headlong [+4568] [1], fell into trance [+1749+2093] [1], finds [+2351] [1], finished [1], follow example [+3629] [1], fright [+1873] [1], gain freedom [+1801] [1], given [1], go [1], grant [1], granted [1], grew [1], grown up [+3489] [1], happened [+1639] [1], has [1], have [1], heard [+212] [1], heard about [+1196] [1], heard sound [+5889] [1], heard⁵ [1], held accountable [+5688] [1], imitate [+3629] [1], in fear [+1873] [1], in the morning [+2465] [1], in unison [+1651+5889] [1], introduced [1], join with others following example [+5213] [1], learned about [+5745] [1], look somber [+5034] [1], looked so much like [+6059] [1], loses saltiness [+383] [1], make [1], man-made [+1328+5931] [1], may never [+3590] [1], moths have eaten [+4963] [1], neared [+1581] [1], need [+2400+5970] [1], never [+3590] [1], now [+2779] [1], obey [+5675] [1], on [1], once [+2779] [1], one day [+1254] [1], one day [+2779] [1], owns [1], participate in [+3128] [1], performed [+1328+3836+5931] [1], planned [+1087] [1], plunged into [1], praying [+4666] [1], proved [1], proved to be [1], rang out [1], reach [+1650] [1], reached [1], reaching [+2093] [1], receive [1], result [1], result in [+1666] [1], revealed [+1871] [1], rewards [+3633] [1], set [1], settled [1], shared in [+3581] [1], show [+5745] [1], so [+1254] [1], spending time [+5990] [1], spent [1], split [1], spoken [1], stand firm [+1612] [1], starting [1], suffered [1], suffering [1], supply [1], take charge of [+2062] [1], taken [1], that are [1], that evening [+4068] [1], the next morning [+2465] [1], the time came when [+1254] [1], thinking like [+3836+5856] [1], to marry [+4048] [1], told [+4639] [1], trembled with fear [+1958] [1], trembling [+1958] [1], turn [1], turned [+1650] [1], turned out [1], undergoes [+3581] [1], unequaled [+3888+4024+5525] [1], unequaled [+3888+4024] [1], used [1], visit [+4639] [1], wake up [+1213] [1], was [+1639] [1], was filled with [1], was going on [1], waste [+724] [1], went on [1], wept [+2653+3088] [1], woke up [+2031] [1], work together [+5301] [1]

Mt 1:22 All this **took place** to fulfill what the Lord had said through the
4: 3 "If you are the Son of God, tell these stones *to* **become** bread."
5:18 means disappear from the Law until everything *is* **accomplished**.
5:45 that *you may* **be** sons of your Father in heaven. He causes his sun
6:10 your kingdom come, your will **be done** on earth as it is in heaven.
6:16 "When you fast, *do* not **look somber** [+5034] as the hypocrites do,
7:28 **[NIE]** When Jesus had finished saying these things, the crowds
8:13 the centurion, "Go! *It will* **be done** just as you believed it would."
8:16 *When* evening **came**, many who were demon-possessed were
8:24 Without warning, a furious storm **came up** on the lake, so that the
8:26 and rebuked the winds and the waves, and *it* **was** completely calm.
9:10 **[NIE]** While Jesus was having dinner at Matthew's house,
9:16 the patch will pull away from the garment, **making** the tear worse.
9:29 eyes and said, "According to your faith *will it* **be done** to you";
10:16 Therefore **be** as shrewd as snakes and as innocent as doves.
10:25 It is enough for the student to **be** like his teacher, and the servant
11: 1 **[NIE]** After Jesus had finished instructing his twelve disciples,
11:20 the cities in which most of his miracles *had been* **performed**,
11:21 If the miracles that *were* **performed** in you had been performed in
11:21 If the miracles that were performed in you *had been* **performed** in
11:23 If the miracles that *were* **performed** in you had been performed in
11:23 If the miracles that were performed in you *had been* **performed** in
11:26 Yes, Father, for this **was** your good pleasure.
12:45 And the final condition of that man **is** worse than the first.
13:21 *When* trouble or persecution **comes** because of the word,
13:22 and the deceitfulness of wealth choke it, **making** it unfruitful.
13:32 when it grows, it is the largest of garden plants, and **becomes** a tree,
13:53 **[NIE]** When Jesus had finished saying these parables, he moved on from
14: 6 **On** Herod's birthday the daughter of Herodias danced for them
14:15 *As* evening **approached**, the disciples came to him and said,
14:23 by himself to pray. *When* evening **came**, he was there alone,

15:28 "Woman, you have great faith! Your request *is* **granted**."
16: 2 He replied, "*When* evening **comes**, you say, 'It will be fair
17: 2 shone like the sun, and his clothes **became** as white as the light.
18: 3 you the truth, unless you change and **become** like little children,
18:12 If a man **owns** a hundred sheep, and one of them wanders away,
18:13 And if he **finds** [+2351] it, I tell you the truth, he is happier about
18:19 you ask for, *it will be* **done** for you by my Father in heaven.
18:31 When the other servants saw what *had* **happened**, they were
18:31 and went and told their master everything that *had* **happened**.
19: 1 **[NIE]** When Jesus had finished saying these things, he left
19: 8 your hearts were hard. But *it* **was** not this way from the beginning.
20: 8 "*When* evening **came**, the owner of the vineyard said to his
20:26 whoever wants *to* **become** great among you must be your servant,
21: 4 This **took place** to fulfill what was spoken through the prophet:
21:19 Then he said to it, "*May* you never **bear** fruit again!" Immediately
21:21 'Go, throw yourself into the sea,' *and it will* **be done**.
21:42 'The stone the builders rejected *has* **become** [+1650] the capstone;
21:42 the Lord *has* **done** this, and it is marvelous in our eyes'?
23:15 and sea to win a single convert, and when *he* **becomes** one,
23:26 inside of the cup and dish, and then the outside *also will* **be** clean.
24: 6 not alarmed. Such things must **happen**, but the end is still to come.
24:20 Pray that your flight *will* not **take place** in winter or on the
24:21 great distress, **unequaled** [+3888+4024] from the beginning of the
24:21 beginning of the world until now—and never *to be* **equaled** again.
24:32 As soon as its twigs **get** tender and its leaves come out, you know
24:34 will certainly not pass away until all these things *have* **happened**.
24:44 So you also *must* **be** ready, because the Son of Man will come at
25: 6 "At midnight the cry **rang out**: 'Here's the bridegroom! Come out
26: 1 **[NIE]** When Jesus had finished saying all these things, he said to
26: 2 you know, the Passover **is** two days away—and the Son of Man
26: 5 the Feast," they said, "or *there may* **be** a riot among the people."
26: 6 *While* Jesus **was** in Bethany in the home of a man known as Simon
26:20 *When* evening **came**, Jesus was reclining at the table with the
26:42 this cup to be taken away unless I drink it, *may* your will *be* **done**."
26:54 then would the Scriptures be fulfilled that say it must **happen** in
26:56 But this *has* all **taken place** that the writings of the prophets might
27: 1 and the elders of the people **came** to the decision to put Jesus to
27:24 but that instead an uproar *was* **starting**, he took water and washed
27:45 From the sixth hour until the ninth hour darkness **came** over all the
27:54 guarding Jesus saw the earthquake and all that *had* **happened**,
27:57 *As* evening **approached**, there came a rich man from Arimathea,
28: 2 *There* **was** a violent earthquake, for an angel of the Lord came
28: 4 so afraid of him that *they* shook and **became** like dead men.
28:11 and reported to the chief priests everything that *had* **happened**.

Mk 1: 4 And so John **came**, baptizing in the desert region and preaching a
1: 9 **[NIE]** At that time Jesus came from Nazareth in Galilee and was
1:11 And a voice **came** from heaven: "You are my Son, whom I love;
1:17 follow me," Jesus said, "and I will make you **[NIE]** fishers of men."
1:32 **That evening** [+4068] after sunset the people brought to Jesus all
2:15 While Jesus **was** having dinner at Levi's house, many tax
2:21 the new piece will pull away from the old, **making** the tear worse.
2:23 **[NIE]** One Sabbath Jesus was going through the grainfields,
2:27 Then he said to them, "The Sabbath *was* **made** for man, not man for
4: 4 **[NIE]** As he was scattering the seed, some fell along the path,
4:10 *When he* **was** alone, the Twelve and the others around him asked
4:11 to you. But to those on the outside everything **is** said in parables
4:17 When trouble or persecution **comes** because of the word,
4:19 for other things come in and choke the word, **making** it unfruitful.
4:22 and whatever **is** concealed is meant to be brought out into the open.
4:32 it grows and **becomes** the largest of all garden plants,
4:35 That day *when* evening **came**, he said to his disciples, "Let us go
4:37 A furious squall **came up**, and the waves broke over the boat,
4:39 Be still!" Then the wind died down and *it* **was** completely calm.
5:14 and the people went out to see what *had* **happened** [+1639].
5:16 Those who had seen it told the people what *had* **happened** to the
5:33 knowing what *had* **happened** to her, came and fell at his feet and,
6: 2 *When* the Sabbath **came**, he began to teach in the synagogue,
6: 2 this wisdom that has been given him, that he even **does** miracles!
6:14 Herod heard about this, for Jesus' name *had* **become** well known.
6:21 Finally the opportune time **came**. On his birthday Herod gave a
6:26 The king **was** greatly distressed, but because of his oaths and his
6:35 By this time *it* **was** late in the day, so his disciples came to him.
6:47 *When* evening **came**, the boat was in the middle of the lake,
9: 3 His clothes **became** dazzling white, whiter than anyone in the
9: 6 (He did not know what to say, *they* **were** so frightened.)
9: 7 Then a cloud **appeared** and enveloped them, and a voice came

9: 7 and enveloped them, and a voice **came** from the cloud:
9: 21 asked the boy's father, "How long *has* he **been** [+*1639*] like this?"
9: 26 The boy **looked so much like** [+*6059*] a corpse that many said,
9: 33 *When* he **was** in the house, he asked them, "What were you arguing
9: 50 "Salt is good, but if it **loses** its **saltiness** [+*383*], how can you make
10: 43 whoever wants *to* **become** great among you must be your servant,
11: 19 When evening **came**, they went out of the city.
11: 23 not doubt in his heart but believes that what he says *will* **happen**,
12: 10 'The stone the builders rejected *has* **become** [+*1650*] the capstone;
12: 11 the Lord *has* **done** this, and it is marvelous in our eyes'?"
13: 7 be alarmed. Such things must **happen**, but the end is still to come.
13: 18 Pray that *this will* not **take place** in winter,
13: 19 days of distress **unequaled** [+*3888*+*4024*+*5525*] from the
13: 19 God created the world, until now—and never *to* be equaled again.
13: 28 As soon as its twigs **get** tender and its leaves come out, you know
13: 29 Even so, when you see these things **happening**, you know that it is
13: 30 will certainly not pass away until all these things *have* **happened**.
14: 4 indignantly to one another, "Why this **waste** [+*724*] of perfume?
14: 17 *When* evening **came**, Jesus arrived with the Twelve.
15: 33 **At** the sixth **hour** [+*6052*] darkness came over the whole land until
15: 33 At the sixth hour darkness **came** over the whole land until the ninth
15: 42 (that is, the day before the Sabbath). So as evening **approached**,
16: 10 She went and told those *who* had **been** with him and who were

Lk   1: 2 handed down to us by those who from the first *were* eyewitnesses
1: 5 In the time of Herod king of Judea *there* **was** a priest named
1: 8 **Once** [+*1254*] when Zechariah's division was on duty and he was
1: 20 you will be silent and not able to speak until the day this **happens**,
1: 23 [NIE] When his time of service was completed, he returned
1: 38 Mary answered. "*May it* **be** to me as you have said."
1: 41 [NIE] When Elizabeth heard Mary's greeting, the baby leaped in
1: 44 As soon as the sound of your greeting **reached** my ears, the baby
1: 59 [NIE] On the eighth day they came to circumcise the child,
1: 65 The neighbors **were** all *filled with* awe, and throughout the hill
2: 1 [NIE] In those days Caesar Augustus issued a decree that a
2: 2 (This **was** the first census that took place while Quirinius was
2: 6 [NIE] While they were there, the time came for the baby to be
2: 13 Suddenly a great company of the heavenly host **appeared** with the
2: 15 [NIE] When the angels had left them and gone into heaven,
2: 15 "Let's go to Bethlehem and see this thing that *has* **happened**,
2: 42 When *he* **was** twelve years old, they went up to the Feast,
2: 46 [NIE] After three days they found him in the temple courts,
3: 2 the word of God **came** to John son of Zechariah in the desert.
3: 21 [NIE] When all the people were being baptized, Jesus was
3: 22 And a voice **came** from heaven: "You are my Son, whom I love;
4: 3 "If you are the Son of God, tell this stone to **become** bread."
4: 23 Do here in your hometown what we have heard that you **did** in
4: 25 a half years and *there* **was** a severe famine throughout the land.
4: 36 All the people **were** amazed and said to each other, "What is this
4: 42 **At daybreak** [+*2002*+*2465*] Jesus went out to a solitary place.
5: 1 **One** [+*1254*] **day** as Jesus was standing by the Lake of Gennesaret,
5: 12 [NIE] While Jesus was in one of the towns, a man came along
5: 17 [NIE] One day as he was teaching, Pharisees and teachers of the
6: 1 [NIE] One Sabbath Jesus was going through the grainfields,
6: 6 [NIE] On another Sabbath he went into the synagogue and was
6: 12 [NIE] One of those days Jesus went out to a mountainside to
6: 13 When morning **came**, he called his disciples to him and chose
6: 16 Judas son of James, and Judas Iscariot, who **became** a traitor.
6: 36 **Be** merciful, just as your Father is merciful.
6: 48 *When* a flood **came**, the torrent struck that house but could not
6: 49 struck that house, it collapsed and its destruction **was** complete."
7: 11 [NIE] Soon afterward, Jesus went to a town called Nain,
8: 1 [NIE] After this, Jesus traveled about from one town and village
8: 17 For there is nothing hidden that *will* not **be** disclosed, and nothing
8: 22 [NIE] One day Jesus said to his disciples, "Let's go over to the
8: 24 and the raging waters; the storm subsided, and *all* **was** calm.
8: 34 When those tending the pigs saw what *had* **happened**, they ran off
8: 35 and the people went out to see what *had* **happened**. When they
8: 56 but he ordered them not to tell anyone what *had* **happened**.
9: 7 Now Herod the tetrarch heard about all that **was going on**.
9: 18 **Once** [+*2779*] when Jesus was praying in private and his disciples
9: 28 [NIE] About eight days after Jesus said this, he took Peter,
9: 29 As he was praying, the appearance of his face **changed** [+*2283*],
9: 33 [NIE] As the men were leaving Jesus, Peter said to him, "Master,
9: 34 While he was speaking, a cloud **appeared** and enveloped them,
9: 35 A voice **came** from the cloud, saying, "This is my Son, whom I
9: 36 When the voice *had* **spoken**, they found that Jesus was alone.

9: 37 [NIE] The next day, when they came down from the mountain,
9: 51 [NIE] As the time approached for him to be taken up to heaven,
10: 13 For if the miracles that *were* **performed** in you had been
10: 13 miracles that were performed in you *had been* **performed** in Tyre
10: 21 to little children. Yes, Father, for this **was** your good pleasure.
10: 32 So too, a Levite, *when* he **came** to the place and saw him,
10: 36 "Which of these three do you think **was** a neighbor to the man who
11: 1 **One** [+*2779*] **day** Jesus was praying in a certain place. When he
11: 14 [NIE] When the demon left, the man who had been mute spoke,
11: 26 And the final condition of that man **is** worse than the first."
11: 27 [NIE] As Jesus was saying these things, a woman in the crowd
11: 30 For as Jonah **was** a sign to the Ninevites, so also will the Son of
12: 40 You also *must* **be** ready, because the Son of Man will come at an
12: 54 immediately you say, 'It's going to rain,' and it **does**[s] [+*4048*].
12: 55 the south wind blows, you say, 'It's going to be hot,' and *it* **is**.
13: 2 "Do you think that these Galileans **were** worse sinners than all the
13: 4 do you think they **were** more guilty than all the others living in
13: 17 people were delighted with all the wonderful things he *was* **doing**.
13: 19 It grew and **became** [+*1650*] a tree, and the birds of the air perched
14: 1 [NIE] One Sabbath, when Jesus went to eat in the house of a
14: 12 if you do, they may invite you back and so you *will* **be** repaid.
14: 22 " 'Sir,' the servant said, 'what you ordered *has* **been done**, but there
15: 10 *there* **is** rejoicing in the presence of the angels of God over one
15: 14 *there* **was** a severe famine in that whole country, and he began to
16: 11 So if *you have* not **been** trustworthy in handling worldly wealth,
16: 12 And if *you have* not **been** trustworthy with someone else's
16: 22 "**The time** [+*1254*] **came** when the beggar died and the angels
17: 11 **Now** [+*2779*] on his way to Jerusalem, Jesus traveled along the
17: 14 to the priests." **And** [+*2779*] as they went, they were cleansed.
17: 26 "Just as *it* **was** in the days of Noah, so also will it be in the days of
17: 28 "*It* **was** the same in the days of Lot. People were eating
18: 23 When he heard this, *he* **became** very sad, because he was a man of
18: 24 Jesus looked at him [UBS+ **becoming** *very sad*] and said, "How
18: 35 [NIE] As Jesus approached Jericho, a blind man was sitting by
19: 9 Jesus said to him, "Today salvation *has* **come** to this house,
19: 15 [NIE] "He was made king, however, and returned home. Then he
19: 17 'Because *you have* **been** trustworthy in a very small matter,
19: 19 "His master answered, 'You **take charge of** [+*2062*] five cities.'
19: 29 [NIE] As he approached Bethphage and Bethany at the hill called
20: 1 [NIE] One day as he was teaching the people in the temple courts
20: 14 they said. 'Let's kill him, and the inheritance *will* **be** ours.'
20: 16 When the people heard this, they said, "May this never **be**!"
20: 17 " 'The stone the builders rejected *has* **become** [+*1650*] the
20: 33 Now then, at the resurrection whose wife *will* she **be**,
21: 7 And what will be the sign that they are about to **take place**?"
21: 9 These things must **happen** first, but the end will not come right
21: 28 When these things begin *to* **take place**, stand up and lift up your
21: 31 Even so, when you see these things **happening**, you know that
21: 32 will certainly not pass away until all these things *have* **happened**.
21: 36 pray that you may be able to escape all that is about to **happen**,
22: 14 When the hour **came**, Jesus and his apostles reclined at the table.
22: 24 Also a dispute **arose** among them as to which of them was
22: 26 Instead, the greatest among you *should* **be** like the youngest,
22: 40 *On* **reaching** [+*2093*] the place, he said to them, "Pray that you will
22: 42 take this cup from me; yet not my will, but yours *be* **done**."
22: 44 And *being* in anguish, he prayed more earnestly, and his sweat was
22: 44 and his sweat **was** like drops of blood falling to the ground.
22: 66 At **daybreak** [+*2465*] the council of the elders of the people,
23: 8 had heard about him, he hoped to see him **perform** some miracle.
23: 12 That day Herod and Pilate **became** friends—before this they had
23: 19 (Barabbas had been thrown into prison for an insurrection [NIE]
23: 24 So Pilate decided *to* **grant** their demand.
23: 31 things when the tree is green, what *will* **happen** when it is dry?"
23: 44 and darkness **came** over the whole land until the ninth hour,
23: 47 The centurion, seeing what *had* **happened**, praised God and said,
23: 48 who had gathered to witness this sight saw what **took place**,
24: 4 [NIE] While they were wondering about this, suddenly two men
24: 5 *In* their **fright** [+*1873*] the women bowed down with their faces to
24: 12 and he went away, wondering to himself what *had* **happened**.
24: 15 [NIE] As they talked and discussed these things with each other,
24: 18 and do not know the things *that have* **happened** there in these
24: 19 "He **was** a prophet, powerful in word and deed before God
24: 21 And what is more, it is the third day since all this **took place**.
24: 22 our women amazed us. *They* **went** to the tomb early this morning
24: 30 [NIE] When he was at the table with them, he took bread,
24: 31 they recognized him, and he **disappeared** [+*908*] from their sight.

24: 37 They **were** startled and frightened, thinking they saw a ghost.
24: 51 **[NIE]** While he was blessing them, he left them and was taken up

Jn   1: 3 Through him all things *were* **made**; without him nothing was made
    1: 3 were made; without him nothing *was* **made** that has been made.
    1: 3 were made; without him nothing was made that *has been* **made**.
    1: 6 *There* **came** a man who was sent from God; his name was John.
  1: 10 He was in the world, and though the world *was* **made** through him,
  1: 12 in his name, he gave the right *to* **become** children of God—
  1: 14 The Word **became** flesh and made his dwelling among us.
  1: 15 'He who comes after me *has* **surpassed** [+*1869*] me because he
  1: 17 given through Moses; grace and truth **came** through Jesus Christ.
  1: 28 This all **happened** at Bethany on the other side of the Jordan,
  1: 30 'A man who comes after me *has* **surpassed** [+*1869*] me
  2: 1 On the third day a wedding **took place** at Cana in Galilee.
  2: 9 of the banquet tasted the water *that had* **been turned into** wine.
  3: 9 "How can this **be**?" Nicodemus asked.
  3: 25 An argument **developed** between some of John's disciples
  4: 14 the water I give him *will* **become** in him a spring of water welling
  5: 6 condition for a long time, he asked him, "Do you want *to* **get** well?"
  5: 9 At once the man **was** cured; he picked up his mat and walked.
  5: 14 found him at the temple and said to him, "See, *you* are well *again*.
  5: 14 well again. Stop sinning or something worse *may* **happen** to you."
  6: 16 When evening **came**, his disciples went down to the lake,
  6: 17 By now *it* **was** dark, and Jesus had not yet joined them.
  6: 19 and a half miles, they saw Jesus **approaching** [+*1584*] the boat,
  6: 21 and immediately the boat **reached** [+*2093*] the shore where they
  6: 25 side of the lake, they asked him, "Rabbi, when *did you* **get** here?"
  7: 43 Thus the people **were** divided because of Jesus.
  8: 33 been slaves of anyone. How can you say that *we shall* **be** set free?"
  8: 58 you the truth," Jesus answered, "before Abraham *was* **born**, I am!"
  9: 22 that Jesus was the Christ *would* **be** put out of the synagogue.
  9: 27 want to hear it again? Do you want *to* **become** his disciples, too?"
  9: 39 so that the blind will see and those who see *will* **become** blind."
  10: 16 listen to my voice, and *there shall* **be** one flock and one shepherd.
  10: 19 At these words the Jews **were** again divided.
  10: 22 Then **came** the Feast of Dedication at Jerusalem. It was winter,
  10: 35 If he called them 'gods,' to whom the word of God **came**—
  12: 29 The crowd that was there and heard it said it **had** thundered;
  12: 30 Jesus said, "This voice **was** for your benefit, not mine.
  12: 36 the light while you have it, so that *you may* **become** sons of light."
  12: 42 confess their faith for fear *they would* **be** put out of the synagogue;
  13: 2 The evening meal *was being* **served**, and the devil had already
  13: 19 "I am telling you now before it **happens**, so that when it does
  13: 19 so that when *it does* **happen** you will believe that I am He.
  14: 22 why **[NIE]** do you intend to show yourself to us and not to the
  14: 29 I have told you now before *it* **happens**, so that when it does
  14: 29 before it happens, so that when *it does* **happen** you will believe.
  15: 7 remain in you, ask whatever you wish, and *it will be* **given** you.
  15: 8 that you bear much fruit, *showing yourselves to* **be** my disciples.
  16: 20 the world rejoices. You will grieve, but your grief *will* **turn** to joy.
  19: 36 These things **happened** so that the scripture would be fulfilled:
  20: 27 and put it into my side. Stop **doubting** [+*603*] and believe."
  21: 4 **Early in the morning** [+*4746*], Jesus stood on the shore,

Ac 1: 16 who **served** as guide for those who arrested Jesus—
  1: 18 there *he* **fell headlong** [+*4568*], his body burst open and all his
  1: 19 Everyone in Jerusalem **heard about** [+*1196*] this, so they called
  1: 20 "it is written in the book of Psalms, " '*May* his place **be** deserted;
  1: 22 For one of these *must* **become** a witness with us of his
  2: 2 Suddenly a sound like the blowing of a violent wind **came** from
  2: 6 When they **heard** this **sound** [+*5889*], a crowd came together in
  2: 43 Everyone **was filled with** awe, and many wonders and miraculous
  2: 43 many wonders and miraculous signs *were* **done** by the apostles.
  4: 4 and the number of men **grew** to about five thousand.
  4: 5 **[NIE]** The next day the rulers, elders and teachers of the law met
  4: 11 you builders rejected, which *has* **become** [+*1650*] the capstone.'
  4: 16 "Everybody living in Jerusalem knows they *have* **done** an
  4: 21 because all the people were praising God for what *had* **happened**.
  4: 22 For the man who **was** miraculously healed was over forty years
  4: 28 what your power and will had decided beforehand *should* **happen**.
  4: 30 Stretch out your hand to heal and **perform** miraculous signs
  5: 5 And great fear **seized** [+*2093*] all who heard what had happened.
  5: 7 **[NIE]** About three hours later his wife came in, not knowing what
  5: 7 hours later his wife came in, not knowing what *had* **happened**.
  5: 11 Great fear **seized** [+*2093*] the whole church and all who heard
  5: 12 The apostles **performed** [+*1328+3836+5931*] many miraculous
  5: 24 chief priests were puzzled, wondering what would **come of** this.

5: 36 all his followers were dispersed, and *it all* **came** to nothing.
6: 1 the Grecian Jews among them **complained** [+*1198*] against the
7: 13 who he was, and Pharaoh **learned about** [+*5745*] Joseph's family.
7: 29 fled to Midian, where *he* **settled** as a foreigner and had two sons.
7: 31 As he went over to look more closely, *he* **heard**[ˢ] the Lord's voice:
7: 32 Moses **trembled with fear** [+*1958*] and did not dare to look.
7: 38 He **was** [+*1639*] in the assembly in the desert, with the angel who
7: 39 "But our fathers refused *to* **obey** [+*5675*] him. Instead, they rejected
7: 40 led us out of Egypt—we don't know what *has* **happened** to him!'
7: 52 And now you *have* **betrayed** [+*4595*] and murdered him—
8: 1 On that day a great persecution **broke out** against the church at
8: 8 So *there* **was** great joy in that city.
8: 13 astonished by the great **[NIE]** signs and miracles he saw.
9: 3 As he **neared** [+*1581*] Damascus on his journey, suddenly a light
9: 19 Saul **spent** several days with the disciples in Damascus.
9: 32 **[NIE]** As Peter traveled about the country, he went to visit the
9: 37 **[NIE]** About that time she became sick and died, and her body
9: 42 *This* **became** known all over Joppa, and many people believed in
9: 43 **[NIE]** Peter stayed in Joppa for some time with a tanner named
10: 4 Cornelius stared at him **in fear** [+*1873*]. "What is it, Lord?"
10: 10 *He* **became** hungry and wanted something to eat, and while the
10: 10 the meal was being prepared, he **fell into** a **trance** [+*1749+2093*].
10: 13 Then a voice **told** [+*4639*] him, "Get up, Peter. Kill and eat."
10: 16 This **happened** three times, and immediately the sheet was taken
10: 25 As Peter **entered** the **house** [+*1656*], Cornelius met him and fell at
10: 37 You know what *has* **happened** throughout Judea, beginning in
10: 40 him from the dead on the third day and caused him *to* **be** seen.
11: 10 This **happened** three times, and then it was all pulled up to heaven
11: 19 Now those who had been scattered by the persecution **[NIE]** in
11: 26 **So** [+*1254*] for a whole year Barnabas and Saul met with the
11: 28 Roman world. (This **happened** during the reign of Claudius.)
12: 5 but the church was earnestly **praying** [+*4666*] to God for him.
12: 9 had no idea that what the angel was doing was really **happening**;
12: 11 Then Peter **came** to himself and said, "Now I know without a doubt
12: 18 **In the morning** [+*2465*], there was no small commotion among
12: 18 commotion among the soldiers as to what *had* **become of** Peter.
12: 23 of the Lord struck him down, and *he* **was** eaten by worms and died.
13: 5 *When they* **arrived** at Salamis, they proclaimed the word of God
13: 12 When the proconsul saw what *had* **happened**, he believed,
13: 32 tell you the good news: What God **promised** [+*2039*] our fathers
14: 1 **[NIE]** At Iconium Paul and Barnabas went as usual into the
14: 3 who confirmed the message of his grace by enabling them *to* **do**
14: 5 *There* **was** a plot afoot among the Gentiles and Jews, together with
15: 2 This **brought** Paul and Barnabas *into* sharp dispute and debate
15: 7 **After** much discussion, Peter got up and addressed them: "Brothers,
15: 25 So we all **agreed** [+*3924*] to choose some men and send them to
15: 39 *They* **had** such a sharp disagreement that they parted company.
16: 16 **Once** [+*1254*] when we were going to the place of prayer,
16: 26 Suddenly *there* **was** such a violent earthquake that the foundations
16: 27 The jailer **woke up** [+*2031*], and when he saw the prison doors
16: 29 rushed in and fell **trembling** [+*1958*] before Paul and Silas.
16: 35 *When it* **was** daylight, the magistrates sent their officers to the
19: 1 **[NIE]** While Apollos was at Corinth, Paul took the road through
19: 10 This **went on** for two years, so that all the Jews and Greeks who
19: 17 When this **became** known to the Jews and Greeks living in
19: 21 "After I *have* **been** there," he said, "I must visit Rome also."
19: 23 About that time *there* **arose** [+*1254*] a great disturbance about the
19: 26 He says that **man-made** [+*1328+5931*] gods are no gods at all.
19: 28 When they heard this, *they* **were** furious and began shouting:
19: 34 they all shouted **in unison** [+*1651+5889*] for about two hours:
20: 3 *Because* the Jews **made** a plot against him just as he was about to
20: 3 sail for Syria, *he* **decided** [+*1191*] to go back through Macedonia.
20: 16 Ephesus to avoid **spending time** [+*5990*] in the province of Asia,
20: 16 for he was in a hurry *to* **reach** [+*1650*] Jerusalem, if possible,
20: 18 "You know how *I* **lived** the whole time I was with you,
20: 37 *They* all **wept** [+*2653+3088*] as they embraced him and kissed
21: 1 **[NIE]** After we had torn ourselves away from them, we put out to
21: 5 But when our time **was** up, we left and continued on our way.
21: 14 not be dissuaded, we gave up and said, "The Lord's will *be* **done**."
21: 17 *When we* **arrived** at Jerusalem, the brothers received us warmly.
21: 30 city was aroused, and the people **came** running from all directions.
21: 35 When Paul **reached** [+*2093*] the steps, the violence of the mob was
21: 40 the crowd. *When they* **were** all silent, he said to them in Aramaic:
22: 6 **[NIE]** "About noon as I came near Damascus, suddenly a bright
22: 17 **[NIE]** "When I returned to Jerusalem and was praying at the
22: 17 to Jerusalem and was praying at the temple, I **fell** into a trance

23: 7 a dispute **broke out** between the Pharisees and the Sadducees,
23: 9 *There* **was** a great uproar, and some of the teachers of the law who
23:10 The dispute **became** so violent that the commander was afraid Paul
23:12 **The next morning** [*+2465*] the Jews formed a conspiracy
24: 2 and your foresight *has* **brought about** reforms in this nation.
24:25 to come, Felix **was** afraid and said, "That's enough for now!
25:15 *When* I **went** to Jerusalem, the chief priests and elders of the Jews
25:26 so that *as* a **result** of this investigation I may have something to
26: 4 [NIE] from the beginning of my life in my own country,
26: 6 because of my hope in what God *has* **promised** [*+2039*] our
26:19 King Agrippa, *I* **was** not disobedient to the vision from heaven.
26:22 nothing beyond what the prophets and Moses said would **happen**—
26:29 but all who are listening to me today *may* **become** what I am,
27: 7 headway for many days and had difficulty **arriving** off Cnidus.
27:16 called Cauda, we were hardly able *to* **make** the lifeboat secure.
27:27 On the fourteenth night we **were** still being driven across the
27:29 four anchors from the stern and prayed for [NIE] daylight.
27:33 Just before **dawn** [*+2465+3516*] Paul urged them all to eat.
27:36 They **were** all encouraged and ate some food themselves.
27:39 When daylight **came**, they did not recognize the land, but they saw
27:42 The soldiers **planned** [*+1087*] to kill the prisoners to prevent any
27:44 of the ship. In this way [NIE] everyone reached land in safety.
28: 6 waiting a long time and seeing nothing unusual **happen** to him,
28: 8 [NIE] His father was sick in bed, suffering from fever
28: 9 *When* this *had* **happened**, the rest of the sick on the island came
28:17 [NIE] Three days later he called together the leaders of the Jews.

Ro 1: 3 his Son, who as to his human nature **was** a descendant of David,
2:25 you *have* **become** as though you had not been circumcised.
3: 4 **Not at all** [*+3590*]! Let God be true, and every man a liar.
3: 4 Not at all! *Let* God **be** true, and every man a liar. As it is written:
3: 6 **Certainly not** [*+3590*]! If that were so, how could God judge the
3:19 and the whole world **held accountable** [*+5688*] to God.
3:31 law by this faith? **Not at all** [*+3590*]! Rather, we uphold the law.
4:18 in hope believed and so **became** the father of many nations,
6: 2 **By no means** [*+3590*]! We died to sin; how can we live in it any
6: 5 If *we have* **been** united with him like this in his death, we will
6:15 we are not under law but under grace? **By no means** [*+3590*]!
7: 3 if *she* **marries** another man while her husband is still alive,
7: 3 and is not an adulteress, *even though she* **marries** another man.
7: 4 that you *might* **belong** to another, to him who was raised from the
7: 7 What shall we say, then? Is the law sin? **Certainly not** [*+3590*]!
7:13 *Did* that which is good, then, **become** death to me? By no means!
7:13 which is good, then, become death to me? **By no means** [*+3590*]!
7:13 so that through the commandment sin *might* **become** utterly sinful.
9:14 What then shall we say? Is God unjust? **Not at all** [*+3590*]!
9:29 *we* would have **become** like Sodom, we would have been like
10:20 *I* **revealed myself** [*+1871*] to those who did not ask for me."
11: 1 **By no means** [*+3590*]! I am an Israelite myself, a descendant of
11: 5 So too, at the present time *there* **is** a remnant chosen by grace.
11: 6 is no longer by works; if it were, grace *would* no longer **be** grace.
11: 9 "*May* their table **become** [*+1650*] a snare and a trap, a stumbling
11:11 **Not at all** [*+3590*]! Rather, because of their transgression,
11:17 and now **share** [*+5171*] in the nourishing sap from the olive root,
11:25 Israel *has* **experienced** a hardening in part until the full number of
11:34 *has* known the mind of the Lord? Or who *has* **been** his counselor?"
12:16 to associate with people of low position. *Do* not **be** conceited.
15: 8 For I tell you that Christ *has* **become** a servant of the Jews on
15:16 so that the Gentiles *might* **become** an offering acceptable to God,
15:31 and that my service in Jerusalem *may* **be** acceptable to the saints
16: 2 for she *has* **been** a great help to many people, including me.
16: 7 among the apostles, and they **were** in Christ before I was.

1Co 1:30 are in Christ Jesus, who *has* **become** for us wisdom from God—
2: 3 I **came** to you in weakness and fear, and with much trembling.
3:13 his work *will* **be** shown for what it is, because the Day will bring it
3:18 of this age, *he should* **become** a "fool" so that he may become wise.
3:18 of this age, he should become a "fool" so that *he may* **become** wise.
4: 5 men's hearts. At that time each *will* **receive** his praise from God.
4: 9 *We have been* **made** a spectacle to the whole universe, to angels
4:13 Up to this moment *we have* **become** the scum of the earth,
4:16 Therefore I urge you to **imitate** [*+3629*] me.
6:15 of Christ and unite them with a prostitute? **Never** [*+3590*]!
7:21 although if you can **gain** *your* **freedom** [*+1801*], do so.
7:23 You were bought at a price; *do* not **become** slaves of men.
7:36 is getting along in years and he feels he ought **to marry**ˢ [*+4048*],
8: 9 that the exercise of your freedom *does* not **become** a stumbling
9:15 And I am not writing this in the hope that you *will* **do** such things

9:20 To the Jews *I* **became** like a Jew, to win the Jews. To those under
9:22 To the weak *I* **became** weak, to win the weak. I have become all
9:22 *I have* **become** all things to all men so that by all possible means I
9:23 the sake of the gospel, that *I may* **share** *in* its **blessings** [*+5171*].
9:27 preached to others, I myself *will* not **be** disqualified for the prize.
10: 6 Now these things **occurred** as examples to keep us from setting
10: 7 *Do* not **be** idolaters, as some of them were; as it is written:
10:20 not to God, and I do not want you *to* **be** participants with demons.
10:32 **Do** not cause anyone to stumble, whether Jews, Greeks
11: 1 **Follow** my **example** [*+3629*], as I follow the example of Christ.
11:19 No doubt there have to be differences among you to **show** [*+5745*]
13: 1 I have not love, *I* **am** only a resounding gong or a clanging cymbal.
13:11 like a child. When *I* **became** a man, I put childish ways behind me.
14:20 Brothers, stop **thinking like** [*+3836+5856*] children. In regard to
14:20 In regard to evil be infants, but in your thinking **be** adults.
14:25 and the secrets of his heart *will* **be** laid bare. So he will fall down
14:26 All of these *must be* **done** for the strengthening of the church.
14:40 But everything *should be* **done** in a fitting and orderly way.
15:10 of God I am what I am, and his grace to me **was** not without effect.
15:37 you sow, you do not plant the body that *will* **be**, but just a seed,
15:45 "The first man Adam **became** [*+1650*] a living being"; the last
15:54 with immortality, then the saying that is written *will* **come true**:
15:58 Therefore, my dear brothers, **stand firm** [*+1612*]. Let nothing
16: 2 so that when I come no collections *will have to be* **made**.
16:10 see to it that *he* **has** nothing to fear while he is with you,
16:14 **Do** everything in love.

2Co 1: 8 brothers, about the hardships we **suffered** in the province of Asia.
1:19 among you by me and Silas and Timothy, **was** not "Yes" and "No,"
1:19 was not "Yes" and "No," but in him *it has always* **been** "Yes."
3: 7 which was engraved in letters on stone, **came** with glory,
5:17 he is a new creation; the old has gone, the new *has* **come**!
5:21 so that in him we *might* **become** the righteousness of God.
6:14 *Do* not **be** yoked together with unbelievers. For what do
7:14 so our boasting about you to Titus *has* **proved to be** true as well.
8:14 At the present time your plenty *will* **supply** what they need,
8:14 plenty will supply what you need. Then *there will* **be** equality,
12:11 *I have* **made** a fool of myself, but you drove me to it. I ought to

Gal 2:17 does that mean that Christ promotes sin? **Absolutely not** [*+3590*]!
3:13 Christ redeemed us from the curse of the law *by* **becoming** a curse
3:14 to Abraham *might* **come** to the Gentiles through Christ Jesus,
3:17 The law, **introduced** 430 years later, does not set aside the
3:21 opposed to the promises of God? **Absolutely not** [*+3590*]!
3:24 So the law **was** put in charge to lead us to Christ that we might be
4: 4 fully come, God sent his Son, **born** of a woman, born under law,
4: 4 fully come, God sent his Son, born of a woman, **born** under law,
4:12 I plead with you, brothers, **become** like me, for I became like you.
4:16 *Have I* now **become** your enemy by telling you the truth?
5:26 *Let us* not **become** conceited, provoking and envying each other.
6:14 **May** I **never** [*+3590*] boast except in the cross of our Lord Jesus

Eph 2:13 far away *have been* **brought** near through the blood of Christ.
3: 7 I **became** a servant of this gospel by the gift of God's grace given
4:32 **Be** kind and compassionate to one another, forgiving each other,
5: 1 **Be** imitators of God, therefore, as dearly loved children
5: 7 Therefore *do* not **be** partners with them.
5:12 For it is shameful even to mention what the disobedient **do** in
5:17 Therefore *do* not **be** foolish, but understand what the Lord's will is.
6: 3 "that *it may* **go** well with you and that you may enjoy long life on

Php 1:13 it *has* **become** clear throughout the whole palace guard and to
2: 7 taking the very nature of a servant, *being* **made** in human likeness.
2: 8 as a man, he humbled himself and **became** obedient to death—
2:15 so that *you may* **become** blameless and pure, children of God
3: 6 the church; as for legalistic righteousness, **faultless** [*+289*].
3:17 **Join with others** in **following** my **example** [*+5213*], brothers,

Col 1:18 the dead, so that in everything he *might* **have** the supremacy.
1:23 under heaven, and of which I, Paul, *have* **become** a servant.
1:25 I *have* **become** its servant by the commission God gave me to
3:15 members of one body you were called to peace. And **be** thankful.
4:11 for the kingdom of God, and *they have* **proved** a comfort to me.

1Th 1: 5 because our gospel **came** to you not simply with words, but also
1: 5 You know how *we* **lived** among you for your sake.
1: 6 You **became** imitators of us and of the Lord; in spite of severe
1: 7 And so you **became** a model to all the believers in Macedonia
2: 1 You know, brothers, that our visit to you **was** not a failure.
2: 5 You know *we* never **used** flattery, nor did we put on a mask to
2: 7 but *we* **were** gentle among you, like a mother caring for her little
2: 8 but our lives as well, because *you had* **become** so dear to us.

2:10 righteous and blameless *we* **were** among you who believed.
2:14 For you, brothers, **became** imitators of God's churches in Judea,
3: 4 be persecuted. And *it* **turned out** that way, as you well know.
3: 5 tempted you and our efforts *might have* **been** [+*1650*] useless.
2Th 2: 7 holds it back will continue to do so till *he is* **taken** out of the way.
1Ti 2:14 it was the woman who was deceived and **became** a sinner.
4:12 but **set** an example for the believers in speech, in life, in love,
5: 9 No widow may be put on the list of widows unless *she* **is** over
6: 4 and quarrels about words that **result** [+*1666*] **in** envy,
2Ti 1:17 On the contrary, *when he* **was** in Rome, he searched hard for me
2:18 the truth. They say that the resurrection *has* already **taken place**,
3: 9 the case of those men, their **[NIE]** folly will be clear to everyone.
3:11 what kinds of things **happened** to me in Antioch, Iconium
Tit 3: 7 his grace, *we might* **become** heirs having the hope of eternal life.
Phm 1: 6 I pray that you *may* **be** active in sharing your faith, so that you will
Heb 1: 4 So *he* **became** as much superior to the angels as the name he has
2: 2 For if the message spoken by angels **was** binding, and every
2:17 in order that *he might* **become** a merciful and faithful high priest
3:14 *We have* **come** to share in Christ if we hold firmly till the end the
4: 3 yet his work *has been* **finished** since the creation of the world.
5: 5 So Christ also did not take upon himself the glory *of* **becoming** a
5: 9 *he* **became** the source of eternal salvation for all who obey him
5:11 about this, but it is hard to explain because *you* **are** slow to learn.
5:12 word all over again. *You* **need** [+*2400+5970*] milk, not solid food!
6: 4 the heavenly gift, who *have* **shared in** [+*3581*] the Holy Spirit,
6:12 We do not want *you to* **become** lazy, but to imitate those who
6:20 *He has* **become** a high priest forever, in the order of Melchizedek.
7:12 a change of the priesthood, there must also **be** a change of the law.
7:16 one who *has* **become** a priest not on the basis of a regulation as to
7:18 The former regulation **is** set aside because it was weak and useless
7:20 without an oath! Others **became** [+*1639*] priests without any oath,
7:22 of this oath, Jesus *has* **become** the guarantee of a better covenant.
7:23 Now *there have* **been** [+*1639*] many of those priests, since death
7:26 *one who* **is** holy, blameless, pure, set apart from sinners, exalted
9:11 came as high priest *of* the good things **that are** *already here*,
9:15 *now that he has* **died** [+*2505*] as a ransom to set them free from
9:22 and without the shedding of blood *there* **is** no forgiveness.
10:33 at other times *you* **stood** side by side with those who were
11: 3 so that what is seen **was** not made out of what was visible.
11: 6 and that *he* **rewards** [+*3633*] those who earnestly seek him.
11: 7 and **became** heir of the righteousness that comes by faith.
11:24 By faith Moses, *when he had* **grown up** [+*3489*], refused to be
11:34 and who **became** powerful in battle and routed foreign armies.
12: 8 are not disciplined (and everyone **undergoes** [+*3581*] discipline),
Jas 1:12 who perseveres under trial, because *when he has* **stood** the test,
1:22 to the word, and so deceive yourselves. **Do** [+*4475*] what it says.
1:25 to do this, not forgetting *what he has* **heard** [+*212*], but doing it—
2: 4 among yourselves and **become** judges with evil thoughts?
2:10 and yet stumbles at just one point **is** guilty of breaking all of it.
2:11 but do commit murder, *you have* **become** a lawbreaker.
3: 1 Not many of *you should presume to* **be** teachers, my brothers,
3: 9 and with it we curse men, who *have been* **made** in God's likeness.
3:10 mouth come praise and cursing. My brothers, this should not **be**.
5: 2 wealth has rotted, and **moths have eaten** [+*4963*] your clothes.
1Pe 1:15 But just as he who called you is holy, so **be** holy in all you do;
2: 7 stone the builders rejected *has* **become** [+*1650*] the capstone,"
3: 6 *You* **are** her daughters if you do what is right and do not give way
3:13 Who is going to harm you if *you* **are** eager to do good?
4:12 do not be surprised at the painful trial you *are* **suffering**,
5: 3 it over those entrusted to you, but **being** examples to the flock.
2Pe 1: 4 so that through them *you may* **participate in** [+*3128*] the divine
1:16 of our Lord Jesus Christ, but *we* **were** eyewitnesses of his majesty.
1:20 you must understand that no prophecy of Scripture **came about** by
2: 1 But *there* **were** also false prophets among the people, just as there
2:20 they **are** worse off at the end than they were at the beginning.
1Jn 2:18 the antichrist is coming, even now many antichrists *have* **come**.
2Jn 1:12 I hope *to* **visit** [+*4639*] you and talk with you face to face,
3Jn 1: 8 to such men so that *we may* **work together** [+*5301*] for the truth.
Rev 1: 1 God gave him to show his servants what must soon **take place**.
1: 9 **was** on the island of Patmos because of the word of God
1:10 On the Lord's Day *I* **was** in the Spirit, and I heard behind me a
1:18 Living One; *I* **was** dead, and behold I am alive for ever and ever!
1:19 what you have seen, what is now and what will **take place** later.
2: 8 is the First and the Last, who **died** [+*3738*] and came to life again.
2:10 **Be** faithful, even to the point of death, and I will give you the
3: 2 **Wake up** [+*1213*]! Strengthen what remains and is about to die,
4: 1 up here, and I will show you what must **take place** after this."
4: 2 At once *I* **was** in the Spirit, and there before me was a throne in
6:12 watched as he opened the sixth seal. *There* **was** a great earthquake.
6:12 The sun **turned** black like sackcloth made of goat hair, the whole
6:12 sackcloth made of goat hair, the whole moon **turned** blood red,
8: 1 seventh seal, *there* **was** silence in heaven for about half an hour.
8: 5 and *there* **came** peals of thunder, rumblings, flashes of lightning
8: 7 his trumpet, and *there* **came** hail and fire mixed with blood,
8: 8 was thrown into the sea. A third of the sea **turned into** blood,
8:11 A third of the waters **turned** [+*1650*] bitter, and many people died
11:13 At that very hour *there* **was** a severe earthquake and a tenth of the
11:13 and the survivors **were** terrified and gave glory to the God of
11:15 his trumpet, and *there* **were** loud voices in heaven, which said:
11:15 "The kingdom of the world *has* **become** the kingdom of our Lord
11:19 And *there* **came** flashes of lightning, rumblings, peals of thunder,
12: 7 And *there* **was** war in heaven. Michael and his angels fought
12:10 "Now *have* **come** the salvation and the power and the kingdom of
16: 2 and painful sores **broke out** on the people who had the mark of the
16: 3 and *it* **turned into** blood like that of a dead man, and every living
16: 4 bowl on the rivers and springs of water, and *they* **became** blood.
16:10 throne of the beast, and his kingdom *was* **plunged into** darkness.
16:17 the temple came a loud voice from the throne, saying, "*It is* **done**!"
16:18 Then *there* **came** flashes of lightning, rumblings, peals of thunder
16:18 **[RPG]** No earthquake like it has ever occurred since man has
16:18 No earthquake like it *has* ever **occurred** since man has been on
16:18 No earthquake like it has ever occurred since man *has* **been** on
16:19 The great city **split** into three parts, and the cities of the nations
18: 2 *She has* **become** a home for demons and a haunt for every evil
21: 6 He said to me: "*It is* **done**. I am the Alpha and the Omega,
22: 6 angel to show his servants the things that must soon **take place**."

1182 γινώσκω, *ginōskō* [222 / 221] [→ *51, 52, 53, 57, 58, 183, 336, 341, 342, 1191, 1192, 1193, 1194, 1195, 1196, 1336, 1337, 1338, 2105, 2106, 2841, 2861, 4589, 4590, 5152*]

know [90], understand [17], known [15], knows [12], knew [11], learned [6], find out [5], aware [4], knowing [4], recognize [4], recognized [4], found out [3], aware of [2], know that [2], knowledge [2], made known [2], sure of [2], understood [2], acknowledge [1], am a virgin [*+467+4024*] [1], assured [*+857*] [1], concluded [1], discover [1], do[s] so [1], evidence [1], evident [1], felt [1], find out about [1], get at truth [*+855*] [1], had [1], had[s] [1], keep in mind [1], knew about [1], know about [1], know how [1], knows about [1], knows thoughts [1], learn [1], learned about [1], mark [1], not clear [*+4024*] [1], realize [1], realized [1], receive news [1], regarded [1], remember [1], saw [1], see if [1], speak [1], sure [*+3857*] [1], unaware [*+4024*] [1], union with [1]

Mt 1:25 But *he had* no **union with** her until she gave birth to a son.
6: 3 *do* not *let* your left hand **know** what your right hand is doing,
7:23 Then I will tell them plainly, '*I* never **knew** you. Away from me,
9:30 Jesus warned them sternly, "See that no one **knows about** this."
10:26 that will not be disclosed, or hidden that *will* not *be* **made known**.
12: 7 If *you had* **known** what these words mean, 'I desire mercy,
12:15 **Aware** of this, Jesus withdrew from that place. Many followed
12:33 and its fruit will be bad, for a tree *is* **recognized** by its fruit.
13:11 "The **knowledge** of the secrets of the kingdom of heaven has been
16: 3 *You* **know how** to interpret the appearance of the sky, but you
16: 8 **Aware** of their discussion, Jesus asked, "You of little faith,
21:45 heard Jesus' parables, *they* **knew** he was talking about them.
22:18 But Jesus, **knowing** their evil intent, said, "You hypocrites,
24:32 get tender and its leaves come out, *you* **know** that summer is near.
24:33 you see all these things, you **know** that it is near, right at the door.
24:39 and *they* **knew** nothing **about** what would happen until the flood
24:43 But **understand** this: If the owner of the house had known at what
24:50 when he does not expect him and at an hour he is not **aware of**.
25:24 'Master,' he said, '*I* **knew** that you are a hard man,
26:10 **Aware** of this, Jesus said to them, "Why are you bothering this
Mk 4:13 this parable? How then *will you* **understand** any parable?
5:29 and *she* **felt** in her body that she was freed from her suffering.
5:43 He gave strict orders not to let anyone **know about** this, and told
6:38 and see." *When they* **found out**, they said, "Five—and two fish."
7:24 He entered a house and did not want anyone *to* **know** it; yet he
8:17 **Aware** of their discussion, Jesus asked them: "Why are you talking
9:30 Jesus did not want anyone to **know** where they were,

12:12 because *they* **knew** he had spoken the parable against them.
13:28 get tender and its leaves come out, *you* **know** that summer is near.
13:29 these things happening, *you* **know** that it is near, right at the door.
15:10 **knowing** it was out of envy that the chief priests had handed Jesus
15:45 *When he* **learned** from the centurion that it was so, he gave the

Lk 1:18 Zechariah asked the angel, "How *can* I *be* **sure of** this? I am an old
1:34 Mary asked the angel, "since *I* **am a virgin** [+467+4024]?"
2:43 stayed behind in Jerusalem, but they were **unaware** [+4024] of it.
6:44 Each tree *is* **recognized** by its own fruit. People do not pick figs
7:39 he would **know** who is touching him and what kind of woman she
8:10 "The **knowledge** of the secrets of the kingdom of God has been
8:17 and nothing concealed that *will* not *be* **known** or brought out into
8:46 "Someone touched me; I **know that** power has gone out from me."
9:11 but the crowds **learned about** it and followed him. He welcomed
10:11 off against you. Yet *be* **sure** of this: The kingdom of God is near.'
10:22 No one **knows** who the Son is except the Father, and no one knows
12: 2 that will not be disclosed, or hidden that *will* not *be* **made known**.
12:39 But **understand** this: If the owner of the house had known at what
12:46 when he does not expect him and at an hour *he* is not **aware of**.
12:47 "That servant who **knows** his master's will and does not get ready
12:48 But the one *who does* not **know** and does things deserving
16: 4 *I* **know** what I'll do so that, when I lose my job here, people will
16:15 justify yourselves in the eyes of men, but God **knows** your hearts.
18:34 from them, and *they did* not **know** what he was talking about.
19:15 given the money, in order to **find out** what they had gained with it.
19:42 "If *you*, even you, *had only* **known** on this day what would bring
19:44 because *you did* not **recognize** the time of God's coming to you."
20:19 because *they* **knew** he had spoken this parable against them.
21:20 surrounded by armies, *you will* **know** that its desolation is near.
21:30 *you can* see for yourselves and **know** that summer is near.
21:31 these things happening, *you* **know** that the kingdom of God is near.
24:18 and *do* not **know** the things that have happened there in these
24:35 and how Jesus *was* **recognized** by them when he broke the bread.

Jn 1:10 the world was made through him, the world *did* not **recognize** him.
1:48 "How *do you* **know** me?" Nathanael asked. Jesus answered,
2:24 But Jesus would not entrust himself to them, for he **knew** all men.
2:25 need man's testimony about man, for he **knew** what was in a man.
3:10 said Jesus, "and *do you* not **understand** these things?
4: 3 When the Lord **learned** of this, he left Judea and went back once
4:53 Then the father **realized** that this was the exact time at which Jesus
5: 6 and **learned** that he had been in this condition for a long time,
5:42 but *I* **know** you. I know that you do not have the love of God in
6:15 **knowing** that they intended to come and make him king by force,
6:69 We believe and **know** that you are the Holy One of God."
7:17 he will **find out** whether my teaching comes from God or whether
7:26 *Have* the authorities really **concluded** that he is the Christ?
7:27 when the Christ comes, no one *will* **know** where he is from."
7:49 But this mob that **knows** nothing of the law—there is a curse on
7:51 anyone without first hearing him *to* **find out** what he is doing?"
8:27 *They did* not **understand** that he was telling them about his
8:28 then *you will* **know** that I am ˌthe one I claim to beˌ and that I do
8:32 Then *you will* **know** the truth, and the truth will set you free."
8:43 Why *is* my language **not clear** [+4024] to you? Because you are
8:52 the Jews exclaimed, "Now *we* **know** that you are demon-possessed!
8:55 Though *you do* not **know** him, I know him. If I said I did not,
10: 6 of speech, but they *did* not **understand** what he was telling them.
10:14 am the good shepherd; *I* **know** my sheep and my sheep know me—
10:14 am the good shepherd; I know my sheep and my sheep **know** me—
10:15 just as the Father **knows** me and I know the Father—and I lay
10:15 just as the Father knows me and I **know** the Father—and I lay
10:27 My sheep listen to my voice; I **know** them, and they follow me.
10:38 that *you may* **know** and understand that the Father is in me,
10:38 that you may know and **understand** that the Father is in me,
11:57 and Pharisees had given orders that if anyone **found out** where
12: 9 Meanwhile a large crowd of Jews **found out** that Jesus was there
12:16 At first his disciples *did* not **understand** all this. Only after Jesus
13: 7 do not realize now what I am doing, but later *you will* **understand**."
13:12 "*Do you* **understand** what I have done for you?" he asked them.
13:28 but no one at the meal **understood** why Jesus said this to him.
13:35 By this all men *will* **know** that you are my disciples, if you love
14: 7 If *you really* **knew** me, you would know my Father as well.
14: 7 *you* would <u>know</u> [UBS *you will* **know**; NIV 3857] my Father
14: 7 as well. From now on, *you do* **know** him and have seen him."
14: 9 "Don't *you* **know** me, Philip, even after I have been among you
14:17 cannot accept him, because it neither sees him nor **knows** him.
14:17 But you **know** him, for he lives with you and will be in you.

14:20 On that day you *will* **realize** that I am in my Father, and you are in
14:31 but the world *must* **learn** that I love the Father and that I do
15:18 "If the world hates you, **keep in mind** that it hated me first.
16: 3 do such things because *they have* not **known** the Father or me.
16:19 Jesus **saw** that they wanted to ask him about this, so he said to
17: 3 that *they may* **know** you, the only true God, and Jesus Christ,
17: 7 Now *they* **know** that everything you have given me comes from
17: 8 *They* **knew** with certainty that I came from you, and they believed
17:23 May they be brought to complete unity to let the world **know** that
17:25 though the world *does* not **know** you, I know you,
17:25 though the world *does* not know you, I **know** you,
17:25 not know you, I know you, and they **know** that you have sent me.
19: 4 I am bringing him out to you to let *you* **know** that I find no basis
21:17 He said, "Lord, you know all things; you **know** that I love you."

Ac 1: 7 "It is not for you *to* **know** the times or dates the Father has set by
2:36 "Therefore *let* all Israel *be* **assured** [+857] of this: God has made
8:30 "*Do you* **understand** what you are reading?" Philip asked.
9:24 but Saul **learned** of their plan. Day and night they kept close watch
17:13 When the Jews in Thessalonica **learned** that Paul was preaching
17:19 "May we **know** what this new teaching is that you are presenting?
17:20 strange ideas to our ears, and we want *to* **know** what they mean."
19:15 "Jesus *I* **know**, and I know about Paul, but who are you?"
19:35 doesn't all the world **know that** the city of Ephesus is the guardian
20:34 *You* yourselves **know** that these hands of mine have supplied my
21:24 Then everybody *will* **know** there is no truth in these reports about
21:34 and since the commander could not **get at** the **truth** [+855]
21:37 "May I say something to you?" "*Do you* **speak** Greek?" he replied.
22:14 'The God of our fathers has chosen *you to* **know** his will and to see
22:30 since the commander wanted *to* **find out** exactly why Paul was
23: 6 **knowing** that some of them were Sadducees and the others

Ro 1:21 For *although they* **knew** God, they neither glorified him as God
2:18 if *you* **know** his will and approve of what is superior because you
3:17 and the way of peace *they do* not **know**."
6: 6 For *we* **know** that our old self was crucified with him so that the
7: 1 brothers—for I am speaking *to men who* **know** the law—
7: 7 Indeed *I would* not *have* **known** what sin was except through the
7:15 *I do* not **understand** what I do. For what I want to do I do not do,
10:19 *Did* Israel not **understand**? First, Moses says, "I will make you
11:34 "Who *has* **known** the mind of the Lord? Or who has been his

1Co 1:21 wisdom of God the world through its wisdom *did* not **know** him,
2: 8 None of the rulers of this age **understood** it, for if they had,
2: 8 None of the rulers of this age understood it, for if *they* **had**ˢ,
2:11 In the same way no one **knows** the **thoughts** of God except the
2:14 for they are foolishness to him, and he cannot **understand** them,
2:16 "For who *has* **known** the mind of the Lord that he may instruct
3:20 again, "The Lord **knows** that the thoughts of the wise are futile."
4:19 then *I will* **find out** not only how these arrogant people are talking,
8: 2 The man who thinks he **knows** something does not yet know as he
8: 2 The man who thinks he knows something *does* not yet **know** as he
8: 2 he knows something does not yet know as he ought *to* **know**.
8: 3 But the man who loves God *is* **known** by God.
13: 9 For *we* **know** in part and we prophesy in part,
13:12 Now *I* **know** in part; then I shall know fully, even as I am fully
14: 7 how *will anyone* **know** what tune is being played unless there is a
14: 9 with your tongue, how *will anyone* **know** what you are saying?

2Co 2: 4 not to grieve you but to let *you* **know** the depth of my love for you.
2: 9 The reason I wrote you was to **see if** you would stand the test
3: 2 are our letter, written on our hearts, **known** and read by everybody.
5:16 Though *we once* **regarded** Christ in this way, we do so no longer.
5:16 Though *we* once regarded Christ in this way, *we* **do**ˢ so no longer.
5:21 God made him *who* **had** no sin to be sin for us, so that in him we
8: 9 For *you* **know** the grace of our Lord Jesus Christ, that though he
13: 6 And I trust that *you will* **discover** that we have not failed the test.

Gal 2: 9 and Barnabas the right hand of fellowship *when they* **recognized**
3: 7 **Understand**, then, that those who believe are children of
4: 9 But now *that you* **know** God—or rather are known by God—
4: 9 But now that you know God—or rather *are* **known** by God—

Eph 3:19 and *to* **know** this love that surpasses knowledge—that you may be
5: 5 For of this *you can be* **sure** [+3857]: No immoral, impure
6:22 that *you may* **know** how we are, and that he may encourage you.

Php 1:12 Now I want you *to* **know**, brothers, that what has happened to me
2:19 that I also may be cheered *when I* **receive news** about you.
2:22 But *you* **know** that Timothy has proved himself, because as a son
3:10 I *want to* **know** Christ and the power of his resurrection
4: 5 *Let* your gentleness *be* **evident** to all. The Lord is near.

Col 4: 8 the express purpose that *you may* **know** about our circumstances

1Th 3: 5 when I could stand it no longer, I sent to **find out about** your faith.
2Ti 1:18 You **know** very well in how many ways he helped me in Ephesus.
     2:19 "The Lord **knows** those who are his," and, "Everyone who
     3: 1 But **mark** this: There will be terrible times in the last days.
Heb 3:10 are always going astray, and they *have* not **known** my ways.'
     8:11 or a man his brother, saying, '**Know** the Lord,' because they will
    10:34 *because you* **knew** that you yourselves had better and lasting
    13:23 I *want you to* **know** that our brother Timothy has been released.
Jas 1: 3 *because you* **know** that the testing of your faith develops
     2:20 do you want **evidence** that faith without deeds is useless?
     5:20 **remember** this: Whoever turns a sinner from the error of his way
2Pe 1:20 you *must* **understand** that no prophecy of Scripture came about
     3: 3 *you must* **understand** that in the last days scoffers will come,
1Jn 2: 3 *We* **know** that we have come to know him if we obey his
     2: 3 We know that *we have come to* **know** him if we obey his
     2: 4 The man who says, "*I* **know** him," but does not do what he
     2: 5 truly made complete in him. This is how *we* **know** we are in him:
     2:13 because *you have* **known** him who is from the beginning.
     2:13 I write to you, dear children, because *you have* **known** the Father.
     2:14 because *you have* **known** him who is from the beginning.
     2:18 antichrists have come. This is how *we* **know** it is the last hour.
     2:29 *you* **know** that everyone who does what is right has been born of
     3: 1 The reason the world *does* not **know** us is that it did not know him.
     3: 1 The reason the world does not know us is that *it did* not **know** us.
     3: 6 No one who continues to sin has either seen him or **known** him.
     3:16 This is how *we* **know** what love is: Jesus Christ laid down his life
     3:19 This then is how *we* **know** that we belong to the truth, and how we
     3:20 For God is greater than our hearts, and *he* **knows** everything.
     3:24 and he in them. And this is how *we* **know** that he lives in us:
     4: 2 This is how *you can* **recognize** the Spirit of God: Every spirit that
     4: 6 We are from God, and whoever **knows** God listens to us;
     4: 6 This is how *we* **recognize** the Spirit of truth and the spirit of
     4: 7 Everyone who loves has been born of God and **knows** God.
     4: 8 Whoever does not love *does* not **know** God, because God is love.
     4:13 *We* **know** that we live in him and he in us, because he has given us
     4:16 And so we **know** and rely on the love God has for us. God is love.
     5: 2 This is how *we* **know** that we love the children of God: by loving
     5:20 has given us understanding, so that *we may* **know** him who is true.
2Jn 1: 1 love in the truth—and not I only, but also all who **know** the truth—
Rev 2:23 Then all the churches *will* **know** that I am he who searches hearts
     2:24 and *have* not **learned** Satan's so-called deep secrets (I will not
     3: 3 like a thief, and *you will* not **know** at what time I will come to you.
     3: 9 and fall down at your feet and **acknowledge** that I have loved you.

1183 γλεῦκος, **gleukos** [1] [√ *1184*]

wine [1]

Ac 2:13 made fun of them and said, "They have had too much **wine**."

1184 γλυκύς, **glykys** [4] [→ *1183*]

sweet [2], fresh [1], fresh water [1]

Jas 3:11 Can both **fresh water** and salt water flow from the same spring?
     3:12 grapevine bear figs? Neither can a salt spring produce **fresh** water.
Rev 10: 9 your stomach sour, but in your mouth it will be as **sweet** as honey."
    10:10 It tasted as **sweet** as honey in my mouth, but when I had eaten it,

1185 γλῶσσα, **glōssa** [50] [→ *1186, 2280, 2303*]

λαλεῖν γλώσσαι (to speak in tongues) [17] Mk 16:17; Ac
2:4,11; 10:46; 19:6; 1Co 12:30; 13:1; 14:2,4,5,5,6,13,18,23,27,39

tongue [21], tongues [19], language [5], languages [2], speaking
in tongues [2], *untranslated* [1]

Mk 7:33 into the man's ears. Then he spit and touched the man's **tongue**.
     7:35 his **tongue** was loosened and he began to speak plainly.
    16:17 name they will drive out demons; they will speak *in* new **tongues**;
Lk 1:64 Immediately his mouth was opened and his **tongue** was loosed,
    16:24 Lazarus to dip the tip of his finger in water and cool my **tongue**,
Ac 2: 3 They saw what seemed to be **tongues** of fire that separated
     2: 4 and began to speak *in* other **tongues** as the Spirit enabled them.
     2:11 we hear them declaring the wonders of God *in* our own **tongues**!"
     2:26 Therefore my heart is glad and my **tongue** rejoices; my body also
    10:46 For they heard them speaking *in* **tongues** and praising God.

     19: 6 Spirit came on them, and they spoke *in* **tongues** and prophesied.
Ro   3:13 "Their throats are open graves; their **tongues** practice deceit."
    14:11 knee will bow before me; every **tongue** will confess to God.' "
1Co 12:10 between spirits, to another **speaking in** different kinds of **tongues**,
    12:10 kinds of tongues, and to still another the interpretation *of* **tongues**.
    12:28 and *those* **speaking in** different kinds *of* **tongues**.
    12:30 all have gifts of healing? Do all speak *in* **tongues**? Do all interpret?
    13: 1 If I speak *in* the **tongues** of men and of angels, but have not love,
    13: 8 they will cease; where there are **tongues**, they will be stilled;
    14: 2 For anyone who speaks *in* a **tongue** does not speak to men
    14: 4 He who speaks *in* a **tongue** edifies himself, but he who prophesies
    14: 5 I would like every one of you to speak *in* **tongues**, but I would
    14: 5 He who prophesies is greater than one who speaks *in* **tongues**,
    14: 6 Now, brothers, if I come to you and speak *in* **tongues**, what good
    14: 9 Unless you speak intelligible words with your **tongue**, how will
    14:13 For this reason anyone who speaks *in* a **tongue** should pray that he
    14:14 For if I pray *in* a **tongue**, my spirit prays, but my mind is
    14:18 I thank God that I speak *in* **tongues** more than all of you.
    14:19 words to instruct others than ten thousand words in a **tongue**.
    14:22 **Tongues**, then, are a sign, not for believers but for unbelievers;
    14:23 the whole church comes together and everyone speaks *in* **tongues**,
    14:26 or a word of instruction, a revelation, a **tongue** or an interpretation.
    14:27 If anyone speaks *in* a **tongue**, two—or at the most three—
    14:39 be eager to prophesy, and do not forbid speaking *in* **tongues**.
Php 2:11 and every **tongue** confess that Jesus Christ is Lord, to the glory of
Jas 1:26 himself religious and yet does not keep a tight rein on his **tongue**,
     3: 5 Likewise the **tongue** is a small part of the body, but it makes great
     3: 6 The **tongue** also is a fire, a world of evil among the parts of the
     3: 6 also is a fire, a world of evil **[RPG]** among the parts of the body.
     3: 8 but no man can tame the **tongue**. It is a restless evil, full of deadly
1Pe 3:10 would love life and see good days must keep his **tongue** from evil
1Jn 3:18 let us not love *with* words or **tongue** but with actions and in truth.
Rev 5: 9 men for God from every tribe and **language** and people and nation.
     7: 9 from every nation, tribe, people and **language**, standing before the
    10:11 prophesy again about many peoples, nations, **languages** and kings."
    11: 9 **language** and nation will gaze on their bodies and refuse them
    13: 7 was given authority over every tribe, people, **language** and nation.
    14: 6 who live on the earth—to every nation, tribe, **language** and people.
    16:10 was plunged into darkness. Men gnawed their **tongues** in agony
    17:15 the prostitute sits, are peoples, multitudes, nations and **languages**.

1186 γλωσσόκομον, **glōssokomon** [2] [√ *1185 + 3180*]

money [1], money bag [1]

Jn 12: 6 as keeper *of* the **money bag**, he used to help himself to what was
    13:29 Since Judas had charge of the **money**, some thought Jesus was

1187 γναφεύς, **gnapheus** [1] [→ *47*; cf. *3117*]

anyone[s] [1]

Mk 9: 3 whiter than **anyone**[s] in the world could bleach them.

1188 γνήσιος, **gnēsios** [4] [√ *1181*]

true [2], loyal [1], sincerity [1]

2Co 8: 8 but I want to test the **sincerity** of your love by comparing it with
Php 4: 3 Yes, and I ask you, loyal yokefellow, help these women who have
1Ti 1: 2 To Timothy my **true** son in the faith: Grace, mercy and peace from
Tit 1: 4 To Titus, my **true** son in our common faith: Grace and peace from

1189 γνησίως, **gnēsiōs** [1] [√ *1181*]

genuine [1]

Php 2:20 no one else like him, who takes a **genuine** interest in your welfare.

1190 γνόφος, **gnophos** [1]

darkness [1]

Heb 12:18 and that is burning with fire; *to* **darkness**, gloom and storm;

1191 γνώμη, *gnōmē* [9] [√ *1182*]

judgment [2], purpose [2], advice [1], agreeing [*+1651+4472*] [1], consent [1], decided [*+1181*] [1], thought [1]

Ac 20: 3 sail for Syria, *he* **decided** [*+1181*] to go back through Macedonia.
1Co 1:10 and that you may be perfectly united in mind and **thought**.
      7:25 but I give a **judgment** as one who by the Lord's mercy is
      7:40 In my **judgment**, she is happier if she stays as she is—and I think
2Co 8:10 And here is my **advice** about what is best for you in this matter:
Phm 1:14 But I did not want to do anything without your **consent**, so that any
Rev 17:13 They have one **purpose** and will give their power and authority to
     17:17 For God has put it into their hearts to accomplish his **purpose** by
     17:17 *by* **agreeing** [*+1651+4472*] to give the beast their power to rule,

1192 γνωρίζω, *gnōrizō* [25] [√ *1182*]

made known [8], make known [5], tell [4], know [2], told about [2], know about [1], present [1], remind of [1], spread [1]

Lk   2:15 this thing that has happened, which the Lord *has* **told** us **about**."
     2:17 *they* **spread** the word concerning what had been told them about
Jn 15:15 for everything that I learned from my Father *I have* **made known**
    17:26 *I have* **made** you **known** to them, and will continue to make you
    17:26 and *will continue to* **make** you **known** in order that the love you
Ac   2:28 *You have* **made known** to me the paths of life; you will fill me
Ro   9:22 if God, choosing to show his wrath and **make** his power **known**,
     9:23 What if he did this to **make** the riches of his glory **known** to the
    16:26 and **made known** through the prophetic writings by the command
1Co 12: 3 Therefore *I* **tell** you that no one who is speaking by the Spirit of
     15: 1 brothers, *I want to* **remind** you *of* the gospel I preached to you,
2Co 8: 1 *we want* you *to* **know about** the grace that God has given the
Gal 1:11 *I want* you *to* **know**, brothers, that the gospel I preached is not
Eph 1: 9 And he **made known** to us the mystery of his will according to his
     3: 3 that is, the mystery **made known** to me by revelation, as I have
     3: 5 which *was* not **made known** to men in other generations as it has
     3:10 the manifold wisdom of God *should be* **made known** to the rulers
     6:19 so that I *will* fearlessly **make known** the mystery of the gospel,
     6:21 and faithful servant in the Lord, *will* **tell** you everything,
Php 1:22 fruitful labor for me. Yet what shall I choose? *I do* not **know**!
     4: 6 and petition, with thanksgiving, **present** your requests to God.
Col 1:27 To them God has chosen *to* **make known** among the Gentiles the
     4: 7 Tychicus *will* **tell** you all the news about me. He is a dear brother,
     4: 9 is one of you. *They will* **tell** you everything that is happening here.
2Pe 1:16 cleverly invented stories *when we* **told** you **about** the power

1193 γνώριμος, *gnōrimos* Not used in UBS/NIV [√ *1182*]

1194 γνῶσις, *gnōsis* [29] [√ *1182*]

knowledge [25], considerate [*+2848*] [1], knowing [1], knows [1], understanding [1]

Lk   1:77 to give his people the **knowledge** of salvation through the
    11:52 in the law, because you have taken away the key *to* **knowledge**.
Ro   2:20 because you have in the law the embodiment *of* **knowledge**
    11:33 the depth of the riches of the wisdom and **knowledge** of God!
    15:14 complete *in* **knowledge** and competent to instruct one another.
1Co 1: 5 in every way—in all your speaking and in all your **knowledge**—
     8: 1 We know that we all possess **knowledge**. Knowledge puffs up,
     8: 1 all possess knowledge. **Knowledge** puffs up, but love builds up.
     8: 7 But not everyone **knows** this. Some people are still so accustomed
     8:10 sees you who have this **knowledge** eating in an idol's temple,
     8:11 for whom Christ died, is destroyed by your **knowledge**.
    12: 8 to another the message *of* **knowledge** by means of the same Spirit,
    13: 2 gift of prophecy and can fathom all mysteries and all **knowledge**,
    13: 8 they will be stilled; where there is **knowledge**, it will pass away.
    14: 6 some revelation or **knowledge** or prophecy or word of instruction?
2Co 2:14 and through us spreads everywhere the fragrance *of* the **knowledge**
     4: 6 light *of* the **knowledge** of the glory of God in the face of Christ.
     6: 6 in purity, **understanding**, patience and kindness; in the Holy Spirit
     8: 7 in faith, in speech, *in* **knowledge**, in complete earnestness
    10: 5 and every pretension that sets itself up against the **knowledge** of
    11: 6 I may not be a trained speaker, but I do have **knowledge**. We have
Eph 3:19 and to know this love that surpasses **knowledge**—that you may be

Php 3: 8 to the surpassing greatness *of* **knowing** Christ Jesus my Lord,
Col 2: 3 in whom are hidden all the treasures *of* wisdom and **knowledge**.
1Ti 6:20 and the opposing ideas *of* what is falsely called **knowledge**,
1Pe 3: 7 in the same way be **considerate** [*+2848*] as you live with your
2Pe 1: 5 effort to add to your faith goodness; and to goodness, **knowledge**;
     1: 6 and to **knowledge**, self-control; and to self-control, perseverance;
     3:18 But grow in the grace and **knowledge** of our Lord and Savior Jesus

1195 γνώστης, *gnōstēs* [1] [√ *1182*]

well acquainted with [1]

Ac 26: 3 because you are **well acquainted with** all the Jewish customs

1196 γνωστός, *gnōstos* [15] [√ *1182*]

known [6], know [*+1639*] [2], know [2], explain [*+1639*] [1], friends [1], heard about [*+1181*] [1], knew [1], outstanding [1]

Lk   2:44 they began looking for him among their relatives and **friends**.
    23:49 But all those who **knew** him, including the women who had
Jn 18:15 Because this disciple was **known** to the high priest, he went with
    18:16 The other disciple, who was **known** to the high priest, came back,
Ac   1:19 Everyone in Jerusalem **heard** [*+1181*] **about** this, so they called
     2:14 of you who live in Jerusalem, *let* me **explain** [*+1639*] this to you;
     4:10 then **know** *this*, you and all the people of Israel: It is by the name
     4:16 living in Jerusalem knows they have done an **outstanding** miracle.
     9:42 This became **known** all over Joppa, and many people believed in
    13:38 I want you to **know** that through Jesus the forgiveness of sins is
    15:18 *that have been* **known** for ages.
    19:17 When this became **known** to the Jews and Greeks living in
    28:22 for we **know** [*+1639*] that people everywhere are talking against
    28:28 "Therefore *I want* you *to* **know** [*+1639*] that God's salvation has
Ro   1:19 since what may be **known** about God is plain to them,

1197 γογγύζω, *gongyzō* [8] [→ *1198, 1199, 1339*]

grumble [3], grumbling [2], complained [1], did[s] [1], whispering [1]

Mt 20:11 they received it, *they began to* **grumble** against the landowner.
Lk   5:30 and the teachers of the law who belonged to their sect **complained**
Jn   6:41 At this the Jews *began to* **grumble** about him because he said,
     6:43 "Stop **grumbling** among yourselves," Jesus answered.
     6:61 Aware that his disciples *were* **grumbling** about this, Jesus said to
     7:32 The Pharisees heard the crowd **whispering** such things about him.
1Co 10:10 And *do* not **grumble**, as some of them did—and were killed by the
    10:10 And do not grumble, as some of them **did**[s]—and were killed by

1198 γογγυσμός, *gongysmos* [4] [√ *1197*]

complained [*+1181*] [1], complaining [1], grumbling [1], whispering [1]

Jn   7:12 Among the crowds there was widespread **whispering** about him.
Ac   6: 1 the Grecian Jews among them **complained** [*+1181*] against the
Php 2:14 Do everything without **complaining** or arguing,
1Pe 4: 9 Offer hospitality to one another without **grumbling**.

1199 γογγυστής, *gongystēs* [1] [√ *1197*]

grumblers [1]

Jude 1:16 These men are **grumblers** and faultfinders; they follow their own

1200 γόης, *goēs* [1]

impostors [1]

2Ti 3:13 while evil men and **impostors** will go from bad to worse,

1201 Γολγοθᾶ, *Golgotha* [3]

Golgotha [3]

Mt 27:33 They came to a place called **Golgotha** (which means The Place of
Mk 15:22 They brought Jesus to the place called **Golgotha** (which means

Jn 19:17 to the place of the Skull (which in Aramaic is called **Golgotha**).

1202 Γόμορρα, *Gomorra* [4]

Gomorrah [4]

Mt 10:15 it will be more bearable *for* Sodom and **Gomorrah** on the day of
Ro 9:29 have become like Sodom, we would have been like **Gomorrah**."
2Pe 2: 6 if he condemned the cities *of* Sodom and **Gomorrah** by burning
Jude 1: 7 Sodom and **Gomorrah** and the surrounding towns gave

1203 γόμος, *gomos* [3] [√ *1154*]

cargo [1], cargoes [2]

Ac 21: 3 We landed at Tyre, where our ship was to unload its **cargo**.
Rev 18:11 and mourn over her because no one buys their **cargoes** any more—
18:12 **cargoes** of gold, silver, precious stones and pearls; fine linen,

1204 γονεύς, *goneus* [20] [√ *1181*]

parents [19], they[s] [*+899+3836*] [1]

Mt 10:21 children will rebel against their **parents** and have them put to
Mk 13:12 Children will rebel against their **parents** and have them put to
Lk 2:27 When the **parents** brought in the child Jesus to do for him what the
2:41 Every year his **parents** went to Jerusalem for the Feast of the
2:43 behind in Jerusalem, but they[s] [*+899+3836*] were unaware of it.
8:56 Her **parents** were astonished,
18:29 "no one who has left home or wife or brothers or **parents**
21:16 You will be betrayed even by **parents**, brothers, relatives
Jn 9: 2 "Rabbi, who sinned, this man or his **parents**, that he was born
9: 3 "Neither this man nor his **parents** sinned," said Jesus, "but this
9:18 and had received his sight until they sent for the man's **parents**.
9:20 "We know he is our son," the **parents** answered, "and we know he
9:22 His **parents** said this because they were afraid of the Jews,
9:23 That was why his **parents** said, "He is of age; ask him."
Ro 1:30 they invent ways of doing evil; they disobey their **parents**;
2Co 12:14 After all, children should not have to save up *for* their **parents**,
12:14 not have to save up for their parents, but **parents** for their children.
Eph 6: 1 Children, obey your **parents** in the Lord, for this is right.
Col 3:20 Children, obey your **parents** in everything, for this pleases the
2Ti 3: 2 boastful, proud, abusive, disobedient *to* their **parents**, ungrateful,

1205 γόνυ, *gony* [12] [→ *1206*]

knees [5], knee [3], knelt down [*+3836+5502*] [2], kneel
[*+2828+3836*] [1], knelt [*+3836+5502*] [1]

Mk 15:19 and spit on him. Falling on their **knees**, they paid homage to him.
Lk 5: 8 saw this, he fell at Jesus' **knees** and said, "Go away from me, Lord;
22:41 about a stone's throw beyond them, **knelt** [*+3836+5502*] **down**
Ac 7:60 Then he fell on his **knees** and cried out, "Lord, do not hold this sin
9:40 all out of the room; then he got down *on* his **knees** and prayed.
20:36 When he had said this, he **knelt** [*+3836+5502*] **down** with all of
21: 5 of the city, and there on the beach *we* **knelt** [*+3836+5502*] to pray.
Ro 11: 4 for myself seven thousand who have not bowed the **knee** to Baal."
14:11 surely as I live,' says the Lord, 'every **knee** will bow before me;
Eph 3:14 For this reason *I* **kneel** [*+2828+3836*] before the Father,
Php 2:10 that at the name of Jesus every **knee** should bow, in heaven
Heb 12:12 Therefore, strengthen your feeble arms and weak **knees**.

1206 γονυπετέω, *gonypeteō* [4] [√ *1205 + 4406*]

fell on knees before [1], knelt [1], knelt before [1], on knees [1]

Mt 17:14 came to the crowd, a man approached Jesus and **knelt before** him.
27:29 a staff in his right hand and **knelt** in front of him and mocked him.
Mk 1:40 A man with leprosy came to him and begged him **on** his **knees**,
10:17 on his way, a man ran up to him and **fell on** his **knees before** him.

1207 γράμμα, *gramma* [14] [√ *1211*]

letters [3], written code [3], bill [2], letter [2], Scriptures [1], get
learning [*+3857*] [1], learning [1], wrote [1]

Lk 16: 6 "The manager told him, 'Take your **bill**, sit down quickly,
16: 7 "He told him, 'Take your **bill** and make it eight hundred.'

Jn 5:47 But since you do not believe what he **wrote**, how are you going to
7:15 "How *did* this man **get** *such* **learning** [*+3857*] without having
Ac 26:24 Paul!" he shouted. "Your great **learning** is driving you insane."
28:21 "We have not received any **letters** from Judea concerning you,
Ro 2:27 even though you have the **written code** and circumcision,
2:29 is circumcision of the heart, by the Spirit, not *by* the **written code**.
7: 6 new way of the Spirit, and not in the old way of the **written code**.
2Co 3: 6 not *of* the **letter** but of the Spirit; for the letter kills, but the Spirit
3: 6 but of the Spirit; for the **letter** kills, but the Spirit gives life.
3: 7 which was engraved in **letters** on stone, came with glory,
Gal 6:11 See what large **letters** I use as I write to you with my own hand!
2Ti 3:15 and how from infancy you have known the holy **Scriptures**,

1208 γραμματεύς, *grammateus* [63] [√ *1211*]

ἀρχιερεῖς καὶ γραμματεῖς (chief priests and teachers of the
law) [22] Mt 2:4; 16:21; 20:18; 21:15; 26:57; Mk 8:31; 10:33;
11:18,27; 14:1,43,53,53; 15:1,31; Lk 9:22; 19:47; 20:1,19; 22:2,66;
23:10

γραμματεῖς καὶ πρεσβύτεροι (teachers of the law and
elders) [12] Mt 16:21; 26:57; 27:41; Mk 8:31; 11:27; 14:43,53;
15:1; Lk 9:22; 20:1; Ac 4:5; 6:12

γραμματεῖς καὶ Φαρισαῖοι (teachers of the law and
Pharisees) [19] Mt 5:20; 12:38; 15:1; 23:2,13,15,23,25,27,29; Mk
2:16; 7:1; Lk 5:21,30; 6:7; 11:53; 15:2; Jn 8:3; Ac 23:9

teachers of the law [57], teacher of the law [2], city clerk [1], man[s]
[1], scholar [1], teachers [1]

Mt 2: 4 together all the people's chief priests and **teachers of the law**,
5:20 surpasses that *of* the Pharisees and the **teachers of the law**,
7:29 as one who had authority, and not as their **teachers of the law**.
8:19 Then a **teacher of the law** came to him and said, "Teacher,
9: 3 At this, some *of* the **teachers of the law** said to themselves,
12:38 Then some of the Pharisees and **teachers of the law** said to him,
13:52 "Therefore every **teacher of the law** who has been instructed about
15: 1 and teachers of the law came to Jesus from Jerusalem and asked,
16:21 chief priests and **teachers of the law**, and that he must be killed
17:10 then do the **teachers of the law** say that Elijah must come first?"
20:18 will be betrayed *to* the chief priests and the **teachers of the law**.
21:15 and the **teachers of the law** saw the wonderful things he did
23: 2 "The **teachers of the law** and the Pharisees sit in Moses' seat.
23:13 "Woe to you, **teachers of the law** and Pharisees, you hypocrites!
23:15 "Woe to you, **teachers of the law** and Pharisees, you hypocrites!
23:23 "Woe to you, **teachers of the law** and Pharisees, you hypocrites!
23:25 "Woe to you, **teachers of the law** and Pharisees, you hypocrites!
23:27 "Woe to you, **teachers of the law** and Pharisees, you hypocrites!
23:29 "Woe to you, **teachers of the law** and Pharisees, you hypocrites!
23:34 Therefore I am sending you prophets and wise men and **teachers**.
26:57 where the **teachers of the law** and the elders had assembled.
27:41 chief priests, the **teachers of the law** and the elders mocked him.
Mk 1:22 them as one who had authority, not as the **teachers of the law**.
2: 6 Now some **teachers of the law** were sitting there, thinking to
2:16 When the **teachers of the law** who were Pharisees saw him eating
3:22 And the **teachers of the law** who came down from Jerusalem said,
7: 1 and some *of* the **teachers of the law** who had come from
7: 5 So the Pharisees and **teachers of the law** asked Jesus, "Why don't
8:31 chief priests and **teachers of the law**, and that he must be killed
9:11 "Why do the **teachers of the law** say that Elijah must come first?"
9:14 crowd around them and the **teachers of the law** arguing with them.
10:33 Man will be betrayed *to* the chief priests and **teachers of the law**.
11:18 The chief priests and the **teachers of the law** heard this and began
11:27 chief priests, the **teachers of the law** and the elders came to him.
12:28 One *of* the **teachers of the law** came and heard them debating,
12:32 "Well said, teacher," the **man**[s] replied. "You are right in saying that
12:35 "How is it that the **teachers of the law** say that the Christ is the son
12:38 As he taught, Jesus said, "Watch out for the **teachers of the law**.
14: 1 and the **teachers of the law** were looking for some sly way to
14:43 sent from the chief priests, the **teachers of the law**, and the elders.
14:53 all the chief priests, elders and **teachers of the law** came together.
15: 1 with the elders, the **teachers of the law** and the whole Sanhedrin,
15:31 and the **teachers of the law** mocked him among themselves.
Lk 5:21 and the **teachers of the law** began thinking to themselves,
5:30 and the **teachers of the law** who belonged to their sect complained
6: 7 and the **teachers of the law** were looking for a reason to accuse

9:22 chief priests and **teachers of the law**, and he must be killed
11:53 and the **teachers of the law** began to oppose him fiercely
15: 2 But the Pharisees and the **teachers of the law** muttered, "This man
19:47 the **teachers of the law** and the leaders among the people were
20: 1 the chief priests and the **teachers of the law**, together with the
20:19 The **teachers of the law** and the chief priests looked for a way to
20:39 Some of the **teachers of the law** responded, "Well said, teacher!"
20:46 "Beware of the **teachers of the law**. They like to walk around in
22: 2 and the **teachers of the law** were looking for some way to get rid
22:66 both the chief priests and **teachers of the law**, met together,
23:10 The chief priests and the **teachers of the law** were standing there,
Jn 8: 3 The **teachers of the law** and the Pharisees brought in a woman
Ac 4: 5 day the rulers, elders and **teachers of the law** met in Jerusalem.
6:12 stirred up the people and the elders and the **teachers of the law**.
19:35 The **city clerk** quieted the crowd and said: "Men of Ephesus,
23: 9 and some of the **teachers of the law** who were Pharisees stood up
1Co 1:20 Where is the wise man? Where is the **scholar**? Where is the

1209 γραπτός, *graptos* [1] [√ *1211*]

written [1]

Ro 2:15 since they show that the requirements of the law are **written** on

1210 γραφή, *graphē* [50] [√ *1211*]

scripture [30], Scriptures [18], writings [2]

Mt 21:42 Jesus said to them, "Have you never read in the **Scriptures**:
22:29 "You are in error because you do not know the **Scriptures**
26:54 then would the **Scriptures** be fulfilled that say it must happen in
26:56 But this has all taken place that the **writings** of the prophets might
Mk 12:10 Haven't you read this **scripture**: " 'The stone the builders rejected
12:24 "Are you not in error because you do not know the **Scriptures**
14:49 and you did not arrest me. But the **Scriptures** must be fulfilled."
Lk 4:21 saying to them, "Today this **scripture** is fulfilled in your hearing."
24:27 he explained to them what was said in all the **Scriptures**
24:32 he talked with us on the road and opened the **Scriptures** to us?"
24:45 he opened their minds so they could understand the **Scriptures**.
Jn 2:22 Then they believed the **Scripture** and the words that Jesus had
5:39 You diligently study the **Scriptures** because you think that by
7:38 Whoever believes in me, as the **Scripture** has said, streams of
7:42 Does not the **Scripture** say that the Christ will come from David's
10:35 the word of God came—and the **Scripture** cannot be broken—
13:18 I know those I have chosen. But this is to fulfill the **scripture**:
17:12 the one doomed to destruction so that **Scripture** would be fulfilled.
19:24 This happened that the **scripture** might be fulfilled which said,
19:28 and so that the **Scripture** would be fulfilled, Jesus said, "I am
19:36 These things happened so that the **scripture** would be fulfilled:
19:37 and, as another **scripture** says, "They will look on the one they
20: 9 (They still did not understand from **Scripture** that Jesus had to rise
Ac 1:16 the **Scripture** had to be fulfilled which the Holy Spirit spoke long
8:32 The eunuch was reading this passage of **Scripture**: "He was led like
8:35 Then Philip began with that very passage of **Scripture** and told
17: 2 on three Sabbath days he reasoned with them from the **Scriptures**,
17:11 and examined the **Scriptures** every day to see if what Paul said
18:24 was a learned man, with a thorough knowledge of the **Scriptures**.
18:28 proving from the **Scriptures** that Jesus was the Christ.
Ro 1: 2 promised beforehand through his prophets in the Holy **Scriptures**
4: 3 What does the **Scripture** say? "Abraham believed God, and it was
9:17 For the **Scripture** says to Pharaoh: "I raised you up for this very
10:11 As the **Scripture** says, "Anyone who trusts in him will never be put
11: 2 Don't you know what the **Scripture** says in the passage about
15: 4 and the encouragement of the **Scriptures** we might have hope.
16:26 and made known through the prophetic **writings** by the command
1Co 15: 3 that Christ died for our sins according to the **Scriptures**,
15: 4 that he was raised on the third day according to the **Scriptures**,
Gal 3: 8 The **Scripture** foresaw that God would justify the Gentiles by
3:22 But the **Scripture** declares that the whole world is a prisoner of
4:30 But what does the **Scripture** say? "Get rid of the slave woman
1Ti 5:18 For the **Scripture** says, "Do not muzzle the ox while it is treading
2Ti 3:16 All **Scripture** is God-breathed and is useful for teaching, rebuking,
Jas 2: 8 If you really keep the royal law found in **Scripture**, "Love your
2:23 And the **scripture** was fulfilled that says, "Abraham believed God,
4: 5 Or do you think **Scripture** says without reason that the spirit he
1Pe 2: 6 For in **Scripture** it says: "See, I lay a stone in Zion, a chosen

2Pe 1:20 you must understand that no prophecy of **Scripture** came about by
3:16 as they do the other **Scriptures**, to their own destruction.

1211 γράφω, *graphō* [191] [→ *63, 615, 616, 1207, 1208,*
1209, 1210, 1582, 2107, 2108, 2863, 4592, 5681, 5934]

καθώς γέγραπται, γεγραμμένος (as it is written) [28] Mt
26:24; Mk 1:2; 9:13; 14:21; Lk 2:23; Jn 6:31; 12:14; Ac 7:42;
15:15; Ro 1:17; 2:24; 3:4,10; 4:17; 8:36; 9:13,33; 10:15; 11:8,26;
15:3,9,21; 1Co 1:31; 2:9; 10:7; 2Co 8:15; 9:9; 2Pe 3:15

Μωϋσῆς ... ἔγραψεν (Moses ... wrote) [5] Mk 12:19; Lk 20:28;
Jn 1:45; 5:46; cf. Mk 10:5

written [105], write [40], wrote [15], writing [11], described [2],
make it [2], recorded [2], write down [2], written down [2], wrote
down [2], describes [1], doˢ so [1], had a notice prepared
[+*5518*] [1], read [+*1639*] [1], sent the letter [1], with writing [1],
write an account [1], wrote about [1]

Mt 2: 5 in Judea," they replied, "for this is what the prophet has **written**:
4: 4 Jesus answered, "*It is* **written**: 'Man does not live on bread alone,
4: 6 the Son of God," he said, "throw yourself down. For it is **written**:
4: 7 Jesus answered him, "*It is* also **written**: 'Do not put the Lord your
4:10 Jesus said to him, "Away from me, Satan! For it is **written**:
11:10 This is the one about whom it is **written**: " 'I will send my
21:13 "*It is* **written**," he said to them, " 'My house will be called a house
26:24 The Son of Man will go just as it is **written** about him. But woe to
26:31 night you will all fall away on account of me, for it is **written**:
27:37 Above his head they placed the **written** charge against him:
Mk 1: 2 *It is* **written** in Isaiah the prophet: "I will send my messenger ahead
7: 6 right when he prophesied about you hypocrites; as it is **written**:
9:12 Why then is it **written** that the Son of Man must suffer much
9:13 to him everything they wished, just as it is **written** about him."
10: 4 "Moses permitted a man to **write** a certificate of divorce and send
10: 5 because your hearts were hard that Moses **wrote** you this law,"
11:17 And as he taught them, he said, "*Is it* not **written**: " 'My house will
12:19 "Moses **wrote** for us that if a man's brother dies and leaves a wife
14:21 The Son of Man will go just as it is **written** about him. But woe to
14:27 "You will all fall away," Jesus told them, "for it is **written**: " 'I will
Lk 1: 3 it seemed good also to me to **write** an orderly **account** for you,
1:63 and to everyone's astonishment he **wrote**, "His name is John."
2:23 (as it is **written** in the Law of the Lord, "Every firstborn male is to
3: 4 As is **written** in the book of the words of Isaiah the prophet:
4: 4 Jesus answered, "*It is* **written**: 'Man does not live on bread
4: 8 Jesus answered, "*It is* **written**: 'Worship the Lord your God
4:10 For it is **written**: " 'He will command his angels concerning you to
4:17 handed to him. Unrolling it, he found the place where it is **written**:
7:27 This is the one about whom it is **written**: " 'I will send my
10:26 "What is **written** in the Law?" he replied. "How do you read it?"
16: 6 'Take your bill, sit down quickly, and **make it** four hundred.'
16: 7 "He told him, 'Take your bill and **make it** eight hundred.'
18:31 and everything that is **written** by the prophets about the Son of
19:46 "*It is* **written**," he said to them, " 'My house will be a house of
20:17 and asked, "Then what is the meaning of that which is **written**:
20:28 "Moses **wrote** for us that if a man's brother dies and leaves a wife
21:22 the time of punishment in fulfillment of all that has been **written**.
22:37 It is **written**: 'And he was numbered with the transgressors';
24:44 Everything must be fulfilled that is **written** about me in the Law of
24:46 He told them, "This is what is **written**: The Christ will suffer
Jn 1:45 told him, "We have found the one Moses **wrote about** in the Law,
2:17 His disciples remembered that it is **written**: "Zeal for your house
5:46 believed Moses, you would believe me, for he **wrote** about me.
6:31 Our forefathers ate the manna in the desert; as it is **written**:
6:45 It is **written** in the Prophets: 'They will all be taught by God.'
8: 8 Again he stooped down and **wrote** on the ground.
8:17 In your own Law it is **written** that the testimony of two men is
10:34 Jesus answered them, "Is it not **written** in your Law, 'I have said
12:14 Jesus found a young donkey and sat upon it, as it is **written**,
12:16 did they realize that these things had been **written** about him
15:25 But this is to fulfill what is **written** in their Law: 'They hated me
19:19 Pilate **had a notice prepared** [+*5518*] and fastened to the cross.
19:19 had a notice prepared and fastened to the cross. *It* read [+*1639*]:
19:20 the city, and the sign was **written** in Aramaic, Latin and Greek.
19:21 the Jews protested to Pilate, "*Do* not **write** 'The King of the Jews,'
19:22 Pilate answered, "What I have **written**, I have written."

     19:22 Pilate answered, "What I have written, *I have* **written**."
     20:30 the presence of his disciples, which are not **recorded** in this book.
     20:31 But these *are* **written** that you may believe that Jesus is the Christ,
     21:24 disciple who testifies to these things and who **wrote** them **down**.
     21:25 If every one of them *were* **written down**, I suppose that even the
     21:25 world would not have room for the books that *would be* **written**.
Ac 1:20 "For," said Peter, "*it is* **written** in the book of Psalms, " 'May his
     7:42 This agrees with *what is* **written** in the book of the prophets:
   13:29 When they had carried out all that *was* **written** about him,
   13:33 As *it is* **written** in the second Psalm: " 'You are my Son; today I
   15:15 words of the prophets are in agreement with this, as *it is* **written**:
   15:23 With them *they* **sent** *the following* **letter**: The apostles and elders,
   18:27 encouraged him and **wrote** to the disciples there to welcome him.
   23: 5 I did not realize that he was the high priest; for *it is* **written**:
   23:25 He **wrote** a letter as follows:
   24:14 that agrees with the Law and that *is* **written** in the Prophets,
   25:26 But I have nothing definite *to* **write** to His Majesty about him.
   25:26 that as a result of this investigation I may have something *to* **write**.
Ro 1:17 righteousness that is by faith from first to last, just as *it is* **written**:
   2:24 As *it is* **written**: "God's name is blasphemed among the Gentiles
   3: 4 Not at all! Let God be true, and every man a liar. As *it is* **written**:
   3:10 As *it is* **written**: "There is no one righteous, not even one;
   4:17 As *it is* **written**: "I have made you a father of many nations."
   4:23 The *words* "it was credited to him" *were* **written** not for him alone,
   8:36 As *it is* **written**: "For your sake we face death all day long;
   9:13 Just as *it is* **written**: "Jacob I loved, but Esau I hated."
   9:33 As *it is* **written**: "See, I lay in Zion a stone that causes men to
  10: 5 Moses **describes** in this way the righteousness that is by the law:
  10:15 As *it is* **written**, "How beautiful are the feet of those who bring
  11: 8 as *it is* **written**: "God gave them a spirit of stupor, eyes so that they
  11:26 And so all Israel will be saved, as *it is* **written**: "The deliverer will
  12:19 my friends, but leave room for God's wrath, for *it is* **written**:
  14:11 It *is* **written**: " 'As surely as I live,' says the Lord, 'every knee will
  15: 3 For even Christ did not please himself but, as *it is* **written**:
  15: 4 For everything that was written in the past *was* **written** to teach us,
  15: 9 so that the Gentiles may glorify God for his mercy, as *it is* **written**:
  15:15 *I have* **written** you quite boldly on some points, as if to remind
  15:21 Rather, as *it is* **written**: "Those who were not told about him will
  16:22 I, Tertius, who **wrote down** this letter, greet you in the Lord.
1Co 1:19 For *it is* **written**: "I will destroy the wisdom of the wise;
   1:31 Therefore, as *it is* **written**: "Let him who boasts boast in the Lord."
   2: 9 However, as *it is* **written**: "No eye has seen, no ear has heard,
   3:19 As *it is* **written**: "He catches the wise in their craftiness";
   4: 6 us the meaning of the saying, "Do not go beyond what *is* **written**."
   4:14 *I am* not **writing** this to shame you, but to warn you, as my dear
   5: 9 *I have* **written** you in my letter not to associate with sexually
   5:11 But now *I am* **writing** you that you must not associate with anyone
   7: 1 Now for the matters *you* **wrote** about: It is good for a man not to
   9: 9 For *it is* **written** in the Law of Moses: "Do not muzzle an ox while
   9:10 Yes, *this was* **written** for us, because when the plowman plows
   9:15 And *I am* not **writing** this in the hope that you will do such things
  10: 7 Do not be idolaters, as some of them were; as *it is* **written**:
  10:11 to them as examples and *were* **written down** as warnings for us,
  14:21 In the Law *it is* **written**: "Through men of strange tongues
  14:37 let him acknowledge that what *I am* **writing** to you is the Lord's
  15:45 So *it is* **written**: "The first man Adam became a living being";
  15:54 with immortality, then the saying that *is* **written** will come true:
2Co 1:13 For *we do* not **write** you anything you cannot read or understand.
   2: 3 *I* **wrote** as I did so that when I came I should not be distressed by
   2: 4 For *I* **wrote** you out of great distress and anguish of heart and with
   2: 9 The reason *I* **wrote** you was to see if you would stand the test
   4:13 It *is* **written**: "I believed; therefore I have spoken." With that same
   7:12 So even though *I* **wrote** to you, it was not on account of the one
   8:15 as *it is* **written**: "He who gathered much did not have too much,
   9: 1 There is no need for me *to* **write** to you about this service to the
   9: 9 As *it is* **written**: "He has scattered abroad his gifts to the poor;
  13:10 This is why *I* **write** these things when I am absent, that when I
Gal 1:20 I assure you before God that what *I am* **writing** you is no lie.
   3:10 who rely on observing the law are under a curse, for *it is* **written**:
   3:10 not continue to do everything **written** in the Book of the Law."
   3:13 the curse of the law by becoming a curse for us, for *it is* **written**:
   4:22 For *it is* **written** that Abraham had two sons, one by the slave
   4:27 For *it is* **written**: "Be glad, O barren woman, who bears no
   6:11 See what large letters I use as *I* **write** to you with my own hand!
Php 3: 1 It is no trouble for me *to* **write** the same things to you again,
1Th 4: 9 Now about brotherly love we do not need *to* **write** to you,

   5: 1 brothers, about times and dates we do not need *to* **write** to you,
2Th 3:17 I, Paul, **write** this greeting in my own hand, which is the
1Ti 3:14 to come to you soon, *I am* **writing** you these instructions so that,
Phm 1:19 I, Paul, *am* **writing** this with my own hand. I will pay it back—
   1:21 Confident of your obedience, *I* **write** to you, knowing that you will
Heb 10: 7 Then I said, 'Here I am—*it is* **written** about me in the scroll—
1Pe 1:16 for *it is* **written**: "Be holy, because I am holy."
   5:12 *I have* **written** to you briefly, encouraging you and testifying that
2Pe 3: 1 *I have* **written** both of them as reminders to stimulate you to
   3:15 just as our dear brother Paul also **wrote** you with the wisdom that
1Jn 1: 4 We **write** this to make our joy complete.
   2: 1 My dear children, *I* **write** this to you so that you will not sin.
   2: 7 *I am* not **writing** you a new command but an old one,
   2: 8 Yet *I am* **writing** you a new command; its truth is seen in him
   2:12 *I* **write** to you, dear children, because your sins have been forgiven
   2:13 *I* **write** to you, fathers, because you have known him who is from
   2:13 *I* **write** to you, young men, because you have overcome the evil
   2:13 *I* **write** to you, dear children, because you have known the Father.
   2:14 *I* **write** to you, fathers, because you have known him who is from
   2:14 *I* **write** to you, young men, because you are strong, and the word
   2:21 *I do* not **write** to you because you do not know the truth, but
   2:26 *I am* **writing** these things to you about those who are trying to lead
   5:13 *I* **write** these things to you who believe in the name of the Son of
2Jn 1: 5 *I am* not **writing** you a new command but one we have had from
   1:12 I have much *to* **write** to you, but I do not want to use paper
3Jn 1: 9 *I* **wrote** to the church, but Diotrephes, who loves to be first,
   1:13 I have much *to* **write** you, but I do not want to do so with pen
   1:13 much to write you, but I do not want *to* **do**ˢ so with pen and ink.
Jude 1: 3 although I was very eager *to* **write** to you about the salvation we
   1: 3 I felt I had to **write** and urge you to contend for the faith that was
Rev 1: 3 blessed are those who hear it and take to heart what *is* **written** in it,
   1:11 "**Write** on a scroll what you see and send it to the seven churches:
   1:19 "**Write**, therefore, what you have seen, what is now and what will
   2: 1 "To the angel of the church in Ephesus **write**: These are the words
   2: 8 "To the angel of the church in Smyrna **write**: These are the words
   2:12 "To the angel of the church in Pergamum **write**: These are the
   2:17 I will also give him a white stone with a new name **written** on it,
   2:18 "To the angel of the church in Thyatira **write**: These are the words
   3: 1 "To the angel of the church in Sardis **write**: These are the words of
   3: 7 "To the angel of the church in Philadelphia **write**: These are the
   3:12 *I will* **write** on him the name of my God and the name of the city
   3:14 "To the angel of the church in Laodicea **write**: These are the words
   5: 1 of him who sat on the throne a scroll **with writing** on both sides
  10: 4 And when the seven thunders spoke, I was about to **write**;
  10: 4 up what the seven thunders have said and *do* not **write** it **down**."
  13: 8 all whose names *have* not *been* **written** in the book of life
  14: 1 had his name and his Father's name **written** on their foreheads.
  14:13 Then I heard a voice from heaven say, "**Write**: Blessed are the
  17: 5 This title *was* **written** on her forehead: MYSTERY BABYLON
  17: 8 The inhabitants of the earth whose names *have* not *been* **written** in
  19: 9 Then the angel said to me, "**Write**: 'Blessed are those who are
  19:12 He has a name **written** *on* him that no one knows but he himself.
  19:16 On his robe and on his thigh he has this name **written**: KING OF
  20:12 judged according to what they had done as **recorded** in the books.
  20:15 If anyone's name was not found **written** in the book of life,
  21: 5 Then he said, "**Write** this **down**, for these words are trustworthy
  21:27 but only those whose names *are* **written** in the Lamb's book of
  22:18 to them, God will add to him the plagues **described** in this book.
  22:19 tree of life and in the holy city, which *are* **described** in this book.

1212 γραώδης, *graōdēs* [1] [√ *1626*]

old wives tales [1]

1Ti 4: 7 Have nothing to do with godless myths and **old wives' tales**;

1213 γρηγορέω, *grēgoreō* [22] [√ *1586*]

keep watch [8], watch [3], alert [2], on guard [2], awake [1], kept watch [1], stays awake [1], wake up [1], wake up [+*1181*] [1], watchful [1], watching [1]

Mt 24:42 "Therefore **keep watch**, because you do not know on what day
  24:43 he would have **kept watch** and would not have let his house be
  25:13 "Therefore **keep watch**, because you do not know the day
  26:38 sorrow to the point of death. Stay here and **keep watch** with me."

26:40 "Could you men not **keep watch** with me for one hour?" he asked
26:41 "**Watch** and pray so that you will not fall into temptation.
Mk 13:34 with his assigned task, and tells the one at the door to **keep watch**.
13:35 "Therefore **keep watch** because you do not know when the owner
13:37 What I say to you, I say to everyone: '**Watch!**'"
14:34 to the point of death," he said to them. "Stay here and **keep watch**."
14:37 to Peter, "are you asleep? Could you not **keep watch** for one hour?
14:38 **Watch** and pray so that you will not fall into temptation. The spirit
Lk 12:37 those servants whose master finds them **watching** when he comes.
Ac 20:31 So *be* on *your* **guard**! Remember that for three years I never
1Co 16:13 *Be* on *your* **guard**; stand firm in the faith; be men of courage;
Col 4: 2 Devote yourselves to prayer, *being* **watchful** and thankful.
1Th 5: 6 like others, who are asleep, but *let us be* **alert** and self-controlled.
5:10 He died for us so that, whether *we are* **awake** or asleep, we may
1Pe 5: 8 *Be* self-controlled and **alert**. Your enemy the devil prowls around
Rev 3: 2 **Wake** [*+1181*] **up!** Strengthen what remains and is about to die,
3: 3 But if *you do* not **wake up**, I will come like a thief, and you will
16:15 Blessed is he *who* **stays awake** and keeps his clothes with him,

1214 γυμνάζω, *gymnazō* [4] [√ *1218*]

experts [*+2840*] [1], train [1], trained [*+2400*] [1], trained [1]

1Ti 4: 7 and old wives' tales; rather, **train** yourself to be godly.
Heb 5:14 who by constant use *have* **trained** [*+2400*] themselves to
12:11 of righteousness and peace *for* those *who have been* **trained** by it.
2Pe 2:14 they are **experts** [*+2840*] in greed—an accursed brood!

1215 γυμνασία, *gymnasia* [1] [√ *1218*]

training [1]

1Ti 4: 8 For physical **training** is of some value, but godliness has value for

1216 γυμνητεύω, *gymnēteuō* Not used in UBS/NIV
[√ *1218*]

1217 γυμνιτεύω, *gymniteuō* [1] [√ *1218*]

in rags [1]

1Co 4:11 To this very hour we go hungry and thirsty, *we are* **in rags**,

1218 γυμνός, *gymnos* [15] [→ *1214, 1215, 1216, 1217, 1219*]

naked [6], needed clothes [2], needing clothes [2], just [1],
taken it off [1], uncovered [1], wearing nothing [*+2093+4314*] [1],
without clothes [1]

Mt 25:36 I **needed clothes** and you clothed me, I was sick and you looked
25:38 a stranger and invite you in, or **needing clothes** and clothe you?
25:43 I **needed clothes** and you did not clothe me, I was sick and in
25:44 or thirsty or a stranger or **needing clothes** or sick or in prison,
Mk 14:51 young man, **wearing nothing** [*+2093+4314*] but a linen garment,
14:52 he fled **naked**, leaving his garment behind.
Jn 21: 7 he wrapped his outer garment around him (for he had **taken it off**)
Ac 19:16 He gave them such a beating that they ran out of the house **naked**
1Co 15:37 will be, but **just** a seed, perhaps of wheat or of something else.
2Co 5: 3 because when we are clothed, we will not be found **naked**.
Heb 4:13 in all creation is hidden from God's sight Everything is **uncovered**
Jas 2:15 Suppose a brother or sister is **without clothes** and daily food.
Rev 3:17 do not realize that you are wretched, pitiful, poor, blind and **naked**.
16:15 with him, so that he may not go **naked** and be shamefully exposed."
17:16 They will bring her to ruin and leave her **naked**; they will eat her

1219 γυμνότης, *gymnotēs* [3] [√ *1218*]

nakedness [2], naked [1]

Ro 8:35 or persecution or famine or **nakedness** or danger or sword?
2Co 11:27 and have often gone without food; I have been cold and **naked**.
Rev 3:18 white clothes to wear, so you can cover your shameful **nakedness**;

1220 γυναικάριον, *gynaikarion* [1] [√ *1222*]

weak-willed women [1]

2Ti 3: 6 their way into homes and gain control over **weak-willed women**,

1221 γυναικεῖος, *gynaikeios* [1] [√ *1222*]

wives [1]

1Pe 3: 7 in the same way be considerate as you live with your **wives**,

1222 γυνή, *gynē* [215] [→ *1220, 1221*]

ἀπολύειν γυναῖκα (to divorce a wife) [8] Mt 5:31,32; 19:3,8,9;
 Mk 10:2,11; Lk 16:18

ἔχω γυναῖκα (to have a wife) [8] Mk 6:18; 12:23; Lk 20:28,33;
 1Co 5:1; 7:2,12,29

λαμβάνω γυναῖκα (to take a wife) [4] Mk 12:19,20; Lk 20:28,29

παραλαμβάνω τὴν γυναῖκα [2] Mt 1:20,24 (to take a wife)

woman [91], wife [59], women [30], wives [12], widow [3], dear
woman [2], wife's [2], *untranslated* [1], believing wife [*+80*] [1],
bride [1], faithful to her husband [*+467+1651*] [1], got married
[*+1138*] [1], married [*+1313*] [1], married [*+3284*] [1], married to
[1], marry [*+721*] [1], mother [1], she [*+3836*] [1], she [1],
unmarried [*+608+3395*] [1], widow [*+5939*] [1], woman's [1],
women's [1]

Mt 1:20 son of David, do not be afraid to take Mary home as your **wife**,
1:24 of the Lord had commanded him and took Mary home as his **wife**.
5:28 But I tell you that anyone who looks at a **woman** lustfully has
5:31 'Anyone who divorces his **wife** must give her a certificate of
5:32 But I tell you that anyone who divorces his **wife**, except for marital
9:20 then a **woman** who had been subject to bleeding for twelve years
9:22 has healed you." And the **woman** was healed from that moment.
11:11 Among those born *of* **women** there has not risen anyone greater
13:33 "The kingdom of heaven is like yeast that a **woman** took and mixed
14: 3 put him in prison because of Herodias, his brother Philip's **wife**,
14:21 ate was about five thousand men, besides **women** and children.
15:22 A Canaanite **woman** from that vicinity came to him, crying out,
15:28 Then Jesus answered, "**Woman**, you have great faith!
15:38 of those who ate was four thousand, besides **women** and children.
18:25 the master ordered that he and his **wife** and his children and all that
19: 3 lawful for a man to divorce his **wife** for any and every reason?"
19: 5 a man will leave his father and mother and be united to his **wife**,
19: 8 "Moses permitted you to divorce your **wives** because your hearts
19: 9 I tell you that anyone who divorces his **wife**, except for marital
19:10 "If this is the situation between a husband and **wife**, it is better not
22:24 his brother must marry the **widow** and have children for him.
22:25 and since he had no children, he left his **wife** to his brother.
22:27 Finally, the **woman** died.
22:28 Now then, at the resurrection, whose **wife** will she be of the seven,
26: 7 a **woman** came to him with an alabaster jar of very expensive
26:10 of this, Jesus said to them, "Why are you bothering this **woman**?
27:19 was sitting on the judge's seat, his **wife** sent him this message:
27:55 Many **women** were there, watching from a distance. They had
28: 5 The angel said *to* the **women**, "Do not be afraid, for I know that you
Mk 5:25 And a **woman** was there who had been subject to bleeding for
5:33 Then the **woman**, knowing what had happened to her, came
6:17 He did this because of Herodias, his brother Philip's **wife**,
6:18 to Herod, "It is not lawful for you to have your brother's **wife**."
7:25 a **woman** whose little daughter was possessed by an evil spirit
7:26 The **woman** was a Greek, born in Syrian Phoenicia. She begged
10: 2 tested him by asking, "Is it lawful for a man to divorce his **wife**?"
10: 7 a man will leave his father and mother and be united to his **wife**,
10:11 "Anyone who divorces his **wife** and marries another woman
12:19 for us that if a man's brother dies and leaves a **wife** but no children,
12:19 the man must marry the **widow** and have children for his brother.
12:20 The first one **married** [*+3284*] and died without leaving any
12:22 of the seven left any children. Last of all, the **woman** died too.
12:23 At the resurrection whose **wife** will she be, since the seven were
12:23 wife will she be, since the seven were married to her?" **[RPG]**
14: 3 a **woman** came with an alabaster jar of very expensive perfume,
15:40 *Some* **women** were watching from a distance. Among them were
Lk 1: 5 of Abijah; his **wife** Elizabeth was also a descendant of Aaron.

1:13   Your **wife** Elizabeth will bear you a son, and you are to give him
1:18   sure of this? I am an old man and my **wife** is well along in years."
1:24   After this his **wife** Elizabeth became pregnant and for five months
1:42   "Blessed are you among **women**, and blessed is the child you will
3:19   rebuked Herod the tetrarch because of Herodias, his brother's **wife**,
4:26   but to a **widow** [+*5939*] in Zarephath in the region of Sidon.
7:28   among those born *of* **women** there is no one greater than John;
7:37   When a **woman** who had lived a sinful life in that town learned
7:39   would know who is touching him and what kind of **woman** she is
7:44   Then he turned toward the **woman** and said to Simon, "Do you see
7:44   toward the woman and said to Simon, "Do you see this **woman**?
7:50   Jesus said to the **woman**, "Your faith has saved you; go in peace."
8: 2   and also some **women** who had been cured of evil spirits
8: 3   Joanna the **wife** of Cuza, the manager of Herod's household;
8:43   And a **woman** was there who had been subject to bleeding for
8:47   Then the **woman**, seeing that she could not go unnoticed,
10:38 he came to a village where a **woman** named Martha opened her
11:27 Jesus was saying these things, a **woman** in the crowd called out,
13:11 and a **woman** was there who had been crippled by a spirit for
13:12 Jesus saw her, he called her forward and said to her, "**Woman**,
13:21 It is like yeast that a **woman** took and mixed into a large amount of
14:20 "Still another said, '*I* just **got married** [+*1138*],
14:26 and mother, his **wife** and children, his brothers and sisters—
15: 8 "Or suppose a **woman** has ten silver coins and loses one. Does she
16:18 "Anyone who divorces his **wife** and marries another woman
17:32 Remember Lot's **wife**!
18:29 "no one who has left home or **wife** or brothers or parents
20:28 for us that if a man's brother dies and leaves a **wife** but no children,
20:28 the man must marry the **widow** and have children for his brother.
20:29 seven brothers. The first one married a **woman** and died childless.
20:32 Finally, the **woman** died too.
20:33 Now then, at the resurrection whose **wife** will she be,
20:33 Now then, at the resurrection whose wife will **she**ˢ be,
20:33 whose wife will she be, since the seven were **married to** her?"
22:57 But he denied it. "**Woman**, I don't know him," he said.
23:27 followed him, including **women** who mourned and wailed for him.
23:49 including the **women** who had followed him from Galilee,
23:55 The **women** who had come with Jesus from Galilee followed
24:22 In addition, some of our **women** amazed us. They went to the
24:24 went to the tomb and found it just as the **women** had said,
Jn   2: 4 "**Dear woman**, why do you involve me?" Jesus replied. "My time
4: 7   When a Samaritan **woman** came to draw water, Jesus said to her,
4: 9   The Samaritan **woman** said to him, "You are a Jew and I am a
4: 9   woman said to him, "You are a Jew and I am a Samaritan **woman**.
4:11   "Sir," the **woman** said, "you have nothing to draw with and the
4:15   The **woman** said to him, "Sir, give me this water so that I won't get
4:17   "I have no husband," **she**ˢ [+*3836*] replied. Jesus said to her,
4:19   "Sir," the **woman** said, "I can see that you are a prophet.
4:21   Jesus declared, "Believe me, **woman**, a time is coming when you
4:25   The **woman** said, "I know that Messiah" (called Christ) "is coming.
4:27   and were surprised to find him talking with a **woman**.
4:28   water jar, the **woman** went back to the town and said to the people,
4:39   from that town believed in him because of the **woman's** testimony,
4:42   They said *to* the **woman**, "We no longer believe just because of
8: 3   and the Pharisees brought in a **woman** caught in adultery.
8: 4   to Jesus, "Teacher, this **woman** was caught in the act of adultery.
8: 9   until only Jesus was left, with the **woman** still standing there.
8:10   Jesus straightened up and asked her, "**Woman**, where are they?
16:21 A **woman** giving birth to a child has pain because her time has
19:26 he said to his mother, "**Dear woman**, here is your son,"
20:13 They asked her, "**Woman**, why are you crying?" "They have taken
20:15 "**Woman**," he said, "why are you crying? Who is it you are looking
Ac   1:14 along with the **women** and Mary the mother of Jesus, and with his
5: 1   Now a man named Ananias, together with his **wife** Sapphira,
5: 2   With his **wife's** full knowledge he kept back part of the money for
5: 7   About three hours later his **wife** came in, not knowing what had
5:14   more and more men and **women** believed in the Lord and were
8: 3   to house, he dragged off men and **women** and put them in prison.
8:12   name of Jesus Christ, they were baptized, both men and **women**.
9: 2   whether men or **women**, he might take them as prisoners to
13:50 But the Jews incited the God-fearing **women** of high standing
16: 1 whose **mother** was a Jewess and a believer, but whose father was a
16:13 and began to speak *to* the **women** who had gathered there.
16:14 One of those listening was a **woman** named Lydia, a dealer in
17: 4 number of God-fearing Greeks and not a few prominent **women**.
17:12 as did also a number of prominent Greek **women** and many Greek

17:34 also a **woman** named Damaris, and a number of others.
18: 2 who had recently come from Italy with his **wife** Priscilla,
21: 5 All the disciples and their **wives** and children accompanied us out
22: 4 arresting both men and **women** and throwing them into prison,
24:24 Several days later Felix came with his **wife** Drusilla, who was a
Ro   7: 2 by law a married **woman** is bound to her husband as long as he is
1Co 5: 1 does not occur even among pagans: A man has his father's **wife**.
7: 1   matters you wrote about: It is good for a man not *to* **marry** [+*721*].
7: 2   so much immorality, each man should have his own **wife**,
7: 3   The husband should fulfill his marital duty *to* his **wife**,
7: 3   his marital duty to his wife, and likewise the **wife** to her husband.
7: 4   The **wife's** body does not belong to her alone but also to her
7: 4   husband's body does not belong to him alone but also to his **wife**.
7:10   but the Lord): A **wife** must not separate from her husband.
7:11   to her husband. And a husband must not divorce his **wife**.
7:12   If any brother has a **wife** who is not a believer and she is willing to
7:13   And if a **woman** has a husband who is not a believer and he is
7:14   For the unbelieving husband has been sanctified through his **wife**,
7:14   and the unbelieving **wife** has been sanctified through her believing
7:16   How do you know, **wife**, whether you will save your husband?
7:16   how do you know, husband, whether you will save your **wife**?
7:27   *Are you* **married** [+*1313*]? Do not seek a divorce. Are you
7:27   *Are* you **unmarried** [+*608+3395*]? Do not look for a wife.
7:27   Do not seek a divorce. Are you unmarried? Do not look for a **wife**.
7:29   From now on those who have **wives** should live as if they had
7:33   about the affairs of this world—how he can please his **wife**—
7:34   An unmarried **woman** or virgin is concerned about the Lord's
7:39   A **woman** is bound to her husband as long as he lives. But if her
9: 5   Don't we have the right to take a **believing wife** [+*80*] along with
11: 3 and the head *of* the **woman** is man, and the head of Christ is God.
11: 5 And every **woman** who prays or prophesies with her head
11: 6 If a **woman** does not cover her head, she should have her hair cut
11: 6 and if it is a disgrace *for* a **woman** to have her hair cut or shaved
11: 7 is the image and glory of God; but the **woman** is the glory of man.
11: 8 For man did not come from **woman**, but woman from man;
11: 8 For man did not come from woman, but **woman** from man;
11: 9 neither was man created for **woman**, but woman for man.
11: 9 neither was man created for woman, but **woman** for man.
11:10 the **woman** ought to have a sign of authority on her head.
11:11 In the Lord, however, **woman** is not independent of man, nor is
11:11 is not independent of man, nor is man independent of **woman**.
11:12 For as **woman** came from man, so also man is born of woman.
11:12 For as woman came from man, so also man is born of **woman**.
11:13 Is it proper for a **woman** to pray to God with her head uncovered?
11:15 but that if a **woman** has long hair, it is her glory? For long hair is
14:34 **women** should remain silent in the churches. They are not allowed
14:35 at home; for it is disgraceful *for* a **woman** to speak in the church.
Gal 4: 4 fully come, God sent his Son, born of a **woman**, born under law,
Eph 5:22 **Wives**, submit to your husbands as to the Lord.
5:23   For the husband is the head *of* the **wife** as Christ is the head of the
5:24   so also **wives** should submit to their husbands in everything.
5:25   Husbands, love your **wives**, just as Christ loved the church
5:28   same way, husbands ought to love their **wives** as their own bodies.
5:28   wives as their own bodies. He who loves his **wife** loves himself.
5:31   a man will leave his father and mother and be united to his **wife**,
5:33   each one of you also must love his **wife** as he loves himself,
5:33   wife as he loves himself, and the **wife** must respect her husband.
Col 3:18 **Wives**, submit to your husbands, as is fitting in the Lord.
3:19   Husbands, love your **wives** and do not be harsh with them.
1Ti 2: 1 I also want **women** to dress modestly, with decency and propriety,
2:10   good deeds, appropriate *for* **women** who profess to worship God.
2:11   A **woman** should learn in quietness and full submission.
2:12   I do not permit a **woman** to teach or to have authority over a man;
2:14   it was the **woman** who was deceived and became a sinner.
3: 2   the husband *of* but one **wife**, temperate, self-controlled,
3:11   In the same way, their **wives** are to be women worthy of respect,
3:12   A deacon must be the husband *of* but one **wife** and must manage
5: 9   she is over sixty, has been **faithful to her husband** [+*467+1651*],
Tit 1: 6 An elder must be blameless, the husband *of* but one **wife**, a man
Heb 11:35 **Women** received back their dead, raised to life again. Others were
1Pe 3: 1 **Wives**, in the same way be submissive to your husbands so that,
3: 1   may be won over without words by the behavior of their **wives**,
3: 5   For this is the way the holy **women** of the past who put their hope
Rev 2:20 You tolerate that **woman** Jezebel, who calls herself a prophetess.
9: 8   Their hair was like **women's** hair, and their teeth were like lions'
12: 1 a **woman** clothed with the sun, with the moon under her feet

12: 4 The dragon stood in front *of* the **woman** who was about to give
12: 6 The **woman** fled into the desert to a place prepared for her by God,
12:13 he pursued the **woman** who had given birth to the male child.
12:14 The **woman** was given the two wings of a great eagle, so that she
12:15 to overtake the **woman** and sweep her away with the torrent.
12:16 But the earth helped the **woman** by opening its mouth
12:17 Then the dragon was enraged at the **woman** and went off to make
14: 4 These are those who did not defile themselves with **women**,
17: 3 There I saw a **woman** sitting on a scarlet beast that was covered
17: 4 The **woman** was dressed in purple and scarlet, and was glittering
17: 6 I saw that the **woman** was drunk with the blood of the saints,
17: 7 I will explain to you the mystery *of* the **woman** and of the beast
17: 9 The seven heads are seven hills on which the **woman** sits.
17:18 The **woman** you saw is the great city that rules over the kings of
19: 7 of the Lamb has come, and his **bride** has made herself ready.
21: 9 to me, "Come, I will show you the bride, the **wife** of the Lamb."

1223 Γώγ, *Gōg* [1]

Gog [1]

Rev 20: 8 corners of the earth—**Gog** and Magog—to gather them for battle.

1224 γωνία, *gōnia* [9] [→ *214, 5481*]

capstone [*+3051*] [5], corners [3], corner [1]

Mt 6: 5 in the synagogues and on the street **corners** to be seen by men.
  21:42 'The stone the builders rejected has become the **capstone** [*+3051*];
Mk 12:10 'The stone the builders rejected has become the **capstone** [*+3051*];
Lk 20:17 stone the builders rejected has become the **capstone**' [*+3051*]?
Ac 4:11 you builders rejected, which has become the **capstone** [*+3051*].'
  26:26 of this has escaped his notice, because it was not done in a **corner**.
1Pe 2: 7 stone the builders rejected has become the **capstone** [*+3051*],"
Rev 7: 1 After this I saw four angels standing at the four **corners** of the
  20: 8 and will go out to deceive the nations in the four **corners** of the

D, d

1225 δ, *d* Not used in UBS/NIV

1226 Δαβίδ, *Dabid* Not used in UBS/NIV [√ *1253*]

1227 δαιμονίζομαι, *daimonizomai* [13] [√ *1228*]

demon-possessed [10], possessed by a demon [1], possessed by demons [1], suffering from demon-possession [1]

Mt 4:24 the **demon-possessed**, those having seizures, and the paralyzed,
  8:16 many *who were* **demon-possessed** were brought to him,
  8:28 two **demon-possessed** *men* coming from the tombs met him.
  8:33 including what had happened to the **demon-possessed** *men*.
  9:32 a man *who was* **demon-possessed** and could not talk was brought
  12:22 Then they brought him a **demon-possessed** *man who* was blind
  15:22 My daughter *is* **suffering** terribly **from demon-possession**."
Mk 1:32 the people brought to Jesus all the sick and **demon-possessed**.
  5:15 saw the man who *had been* **possessed by** the legion of **demons**,
  5:16 told the people what had happened *to* the **demon-possessed** *man*—
  5:18 the man *who had been* **demon-possessed** begged to go with him.
Lk 8:36 it told the people how the **demon-possessed** *man* had been cured.
Jn 10:21 "These are not the sayings *of* a *man* **possessed by a demon**.

1228 δαιμόνιον, *daimonion* [63] [→ *1227, 1229, 1230, 1272, 1273*]

ἄρχων δαιμονίων (ruler of demons) [4] Mt 9:34; 12:24; Mk 3:22; Lk 11:15

ἐκβάλλω δαιμόνιον (cast out a demon) [24] Mt 7:22; 9:33, 34; 10:8; 12:24,27,28; Mk 1:34,39; 3:15,22; 6:13; 7:26; 9:38; 16:9,17; Lk 9:49; 11:14,15,18,19,20; 13:32

ἔχω δαιμόνιον (have a demon) [9] Mt 11:18; Lk 4:33; 7:33; 8:27; Jn 7:20; 8:48,49,52; 10:20

demons [42], demon [15], demon-possessed [*+2400*] [5], gods [1]

Mt 7:22 and in your name drive out **demons** and perform many miracles?'
  9:33 And when the **demon** was driven out, the man who had been mute
  9:34 "It is by the prince *of* **demons** that he drives out demons."
  9:34 "It is by the prince of demons that he drives out **demons**."
  10: 8 raise the dead, cleanse those who have leprosy, drive out **demons**.
  11:18 came neither eating nor drinking, and they say, 'He has a **demon**.'
  12:24 they said, "It is only by Beelzebub, the prince *of* **demons**,
  12:24 the prince of demons, that this fellow drives out **demons**."
  12:27 And if I drive out **demons** by Beelzebub, by whom do your people
  12:28 But if I drive out **demons** by the Spirit of God, then the kingdom
  17:18 Jesus rebuked the **demon**, and it came out of the boy, and he was
Mk 1:34 He also drove out many **demons**, but he would not let the demons
  1:34 but he would not let the **demons** speak because they knew who he
  1:39 preaching in their synagogues and driving out **demons**.
  3:15 and to have authority to drive out **demons**.
  3:22 by Beelzebub! By the prince *of* **demons** he is driving out demons."
  3:22 by Beelzebub! By the prince of demons he is driving out **demons**."
  6:13 They drove out many **demons** and anointed many sick people with
  7:26 She begged Jesus to drive the **demon** out of her daughter.
  7:29 "For such a reply, you may go; the **demon** has left your daughter."
  7:30 and found her child lying on the bed, and the **demon** gone.
  9:38 "we saw a man driving out **demons** in your name and we told him
  16: 9 to Mary Magdalene, out of whom he had driven seven **demons**.
  16:17 In my name they will drive out **demons**; they will speak in new
Lk 4:33 In the synagogue there was a man possessed by a **demon**,
  4:35 Then the **demon** threw the man down before them all and came out
  4:41 Moreover, **demons** came out of many people, shouting, "You are
  7:33 eating bread nor drinking wine, and you say, 'He has a **demon**.'
  8: 2 (called Magdalene) from whom seven **demons** had come out;
  8:27 he was met by a **demon-possessed** [*+2400*] man from the town.
  8:29 his chains and had been driven by the **demon** into solitary places.
  8:30 "Legion," he replied, because many **demons** had gone into him.
  8:33 When the **demons** came out of the man, they went into the pigs,
  8:35 they found the man from whom the **demons** had gone out,
  8:38 The man from whom the **demons** had gone out begged to go with
  9: 1 he gave them power and authority to drive out all **demons**
  9:42 was coming, the **demon** threw him to the ground in a convulsion.
  9:49 "we saw a man driving out **demons** in your name and we tried to
  10:17 and said, "Lord, even the **demons** submit to us in your name."
  11:14 Jesus was driving out a **demon** that was mute. When the demon
  11:14 When the **demon** left, the man who had been mute spoke,
  11:15 But some of them said, "By Beelzebub, the prince *of* **demons**,
  11:15 "By Beelzebub, the prince of demons, he is driving out **demons**."
  11:18 because you claim that I drive out **demons** by Beelzebub.
  11:19 Now if I drive out **demons** by Beelzebub, by whom do your
  11:20 But if I drive out **demons** by the finger of God, then the kingdom
  13:32 'I will drive out **demons** and heal people today and tomorrow,
Jn 7:20 "*You are* **demon-possessed** [*+2400*]," the crowd answered.
  8:48 saying that you are a Samaritan and **demon-possessed** [*+2400*]?"
  8:49 "I am not possessed by a **demon**," said Jesus, "but I honor my
  8:52 "Now we know that *you are* **demon-possessed** [*+2400*]!
  10:20 Many of them said, "*He is* **demon-possessed** [*+2400*] and raving
  10:21 possessed by a demon. Can a **demon** open the eyes of the blind?"
Ac 17:18 Others remarked, "He seems to be advocating foreign **gods**."
1Co 10:20 No, but the sacrifices of pagans are offered *to* **demons**, not to God,
  10:20 not to God, and I do not want you to be participants *with* **demons**.
  10:21 You cannot drink the cup of the Lord and the cup *of* **demons** too;
  10:21 have a part in both the Lord's table and the table *of* **demons**.
1Ti 4: 1 and follow deceiving spirits and things taught *by* **demons**.
Jas 2:19 is one God. Good! Even the **demons** believe that—and shudder.
Rev 9:20 they did not stop worshiping **demons**, and idols of gold, silver,
  16:14 They are spirits *of* **demons** performing miraculous signs, and they
  18: 2 She has become a home *for* **demons** and a haunt for every evil

1229 δαιμονιώδης, *daimoniōdēs* [1] [√ *1228 + 1626*]

of the devil [1]

Jas 3:15 come down from heaven but is earthly, unspiritual, **of the devil**.

1230 δαίμων, **daimōn** [1] [√ *1228*]

demons [1]

Mt   8:31 The **demons** begged Jesus, "If you drive us out, send us into the

1231 δάκνω, **daknō** [1]

biting [1]

Gal   5:15 If *you keep on* **biting** and devouring each other, watch out

1232 δάκρυον, **dakryon** [10] [→ *1233*]

tears [8], tear [2]

Lk   7:38 him at his feet weeping, she began to wet his feet *with* her **tears**.
       7:44 but she wet my feet *with* her **tears** and wiped them with her hair.
Ac   20:19 I served the Lord with great humility and with **tears**, although I
     20:31 I never stopped warning each of you night and day with **tears**.
2Co   2: 4 you out of great distress and anguish of heart and with many **tears**,
2Ti   1: 4 Recalling your **tears**, I long to see you, so that I may be filled with
Heb   5: 7 loud cries and **tears** to the one who could save him from death,
     12:17 about no change of mind, though he sought the blessing with **tears**.
Rev   7:17 living water. And God will wipe away every **tear** from their eyes."
     21: 4 He will wipe every **tear** from their eyes. There will be no more

1233 δακρύω, **dakryō** [1] [√ *1232*]

wept [1]

Jn   11:35 Jesus **wept**.

1234 δακτύλιος, **daktylios** [1] [√ *1235*]

ring [1]

Lk   15:22 and put it on him. Put a **ring** on his finger and sandals on his feet.

1235 δάκτυλος, **daktylos** [8] [→ *1234, 5993; cf. 1259*]

finger [6], fingers [1], lift a finger [1]

Mt   23: 4 but they themselves are not willing to **lift a finger** to move them.
Mk   7:33 away from the crowd, Jesus put his **fingers** into the man's ears.
Lk   11:20 But if I drive out demons by the **finger** of God, then the kingdom
     11:46 and you yourselves will not lift one **finger** to help them.
     16:24 pity on me and send Lazarus to dip the tip *of* his **finger** in water
Jn   8: 6 Jesus bent down and started to write on the ground *with* his **finger**.
     20:25 the nail marks in his hands and put my **finger** where the nails were,
     20:27 Then he said to Thomas, "Put your **finger** here; see my hands.

1236 Δαλμανουθά, **Dalmanoutha** [1]

Dalmanutha [1]

Mk   8:10 the boat with his disciples and went to the region *of* **Dalmanutha**.

1237 Δαλματία, **Dalmatia** [1]

Dalmatia [1]

2Ti   4:10 Crescens has gone to Galatia, and Titus to **Dalmatia**.

1238 δαμάζω, **damazō** [4] [→ *1239*]

tamed [2], subdue [1], tame [1]

Mk   5: 4 the irons on his feet. No one was strong enough *to* **subdue** him.
Jas   3: 7 reptiles and creatures of the sea *are being* **tamed** and have been
       3: 7 creatures of the sea are being tamed and *have been* **tamed** by man,
       3: 8 but no man can **tame** the tongue. It is a restless evil, full of deadly

1239 δάμαλις, **damalis** [1] [√ *1238*]

heifer [1]

Heb   9:13 and the ashes *of* a **heifer** sprinkled on those who are ceremonially

1240 Δάμαρις, **Damaris** [1]

Damaris [1]

Ac   17:34 also a woman named **Damaris**, and a number of others.

1241 Δαμασκηνός, **Damaskēnos** [1] [√ *1242*]

the Damascenes [1]

2Co 11:32 had the city *of* **the Damascenes** guarded in order to arrest me.

1242 Δαμασκός, **Damaskos** [15] [→ *1241*]

Damascus [15]

Ac   9: 2 and asked him for letters to the synagogues in **Damascus**,
       9: 3 As he neared **Damascus** on his journey, suddenly a light from
       9: 8 he could see nothing. So they led him by the hand into **Damascus**.
       9:10 In **Damascus** there was a disciple named Ananias. The Lord called
       9:19 Saul spent several days with the disciples in **Damascus**.
       9:22 and baffled the Jews living in **Damascus** by proving that Jesus is
       9:27 and how in **Damascus** he had preached fearlessly in the name of
     22: 5 I even obtained letters from them to their brothers in **Damascus**,
     22: 6 "About noon *as* I came near **Damascus**, suddenly a bright light
     22:10 Lord?' I asked. " 'Get up,' the Lord said, 'and go into **Damascus**.
     22:11 My companions led me by the hand into **Damascus**,
     26:12 "On one of these journeys I was going to **Damascus** with the
     26:20 First to those in **Damascus**, then to those in Jerusalem and in all
2Co 11:32 In **Damascus** the governor under King Aretas had the city of the
Gal   1:17 I went immediately into Arabia and later returned to **Damascus**.

1243 Δάν, **Dan**   Not used in UBS/NIV

1244 δανείζω, **daneizō**   Not used in UBS/NIV [√ *1249*]

1245 δάνειον, **daneion** [1] [√ *1249*]

debt [1]

Mt   18:27 master took pity on him, canceled the **debt** and let him go.

1246 δανειστής, **daneistēs**   Not used in UBS/NIV
          [√ *1249*]

1247 δανίζω, **danizō** [4] [√ *1249*]

lend [3], borrow [1]

Mt   5:42 and do not turn away from the one who wants *to* **borrow** from
Lk   6:34 And if *you* **lend** to those from whom you expect repayment,
       6:34 Even 'sinners' **lend** to 'sinners,' expecting to be repaid in full.
       6:35 to them, and **lend** to them without expecting to get anything back.

1248 Δανιήλ, **Daniēl** [1]

Daniel [1]

Mt   24:15 that causes desolation,' spoken of through the prophet **Daniel**—

1249 δάνιον, **danion**   Not used in UBS/NIV [→ *1244,
          1245, 1246, 1247, 1250*]

1250 δανιστής, **danistēs** [1] [√ *1249*]

moneylender [1]

Lk   7:41 "Two men owed money to a certain **moneylender**. One owed him

1251 δαπανάω, **dapanaō** [5] [√ *1252*]

spent [2], pay expenses [1], spend [1], spend everything [1]

Mk   5:26 deal under the care of many doctors and *had* **spent** all she had,
Lk   15:14 *After* he *had* **spent** everything, there was a severe famine in that

Ac 21:24 these men, join in their purification rites and **pay** their **expenses,**
2Co 12:15 So I *will* very gladly **spend** for you **everything** *I have* and expend
Jas   4: 3 that *you may* **spend** what you get on your pleasures.

1252 δαπάνη, *dapanē* [1] [→ *78, 1251, 1682, 4655*]

cost [1]

Lk 14:28 and estimate the **cost** to see if he has enough money to complete it?

1253 Δαυίδ, *Dauid* [59] [→ *1226*]

οἶκος Δαυίδ (house of David) [3] Lk 1:27,69; 2·4

σπέρμα Δαυίδ (seed of David) [3] Jn 7:42; Ro 1:3; 2Ti 2:8

υἱὸς Δαυίδ (son of David) [15] Mt 1:1,20; 9:27; 12:23; 15:22;
   20:30,31; 21:9,15; Mk 10:47,48; 12:35; Lk 18:38,39; 20:41; cf. Mt
   22:42

David [57], David's [2]

Mt 1: 1 A record of the genealogy of Jesus Christ the son *of* **David,**
   1: 6 and Jesse the father of King **David.** David was the father of
   1: 6 **David** was the father of Solomon, whose mother had been Uriah's
   1:17 there were fourteen generations in all from Abraham to **David,**
   1:17 fourteen from **David** to the exile to Babylon, and fourteen from the
   1:20 Lord appeared to him in a dream and said, "Joseph son *of* **David,**
   9:27 men followed him, calling out, "Have mercy on us, Son *of* **David!"**
  12: 3 "Haven't you read what **David** did when he and his companions
  12:23 people were astonished and said, "Could this be the Son *of* **David**?"
  15:22 came to him, crying out, "Lord, Son *of* **David,** have mercy on me!
  20:30 going by, they shouted, "Lord, Son *of* **David,** have mercy on us!"
  20:31 shouted all the louder, "Lord, Son *of* **David,** have mercy on us!"
  21: 9 and those that followed shouted, "Hosanna to the Son *of* **David!"**
  21:15 temple area, "Hosanna to the Son *of* **David,"** they were indignant.
  22:42 the Christ? Whose son is he?" "The son *of* **David,"** they replied.
  22:43 He said to them, "How is it then that **David,** speaking by the Spirit,
  22:45 If then **David** calls him 'Lord,' how can he be his son?"
Mk 2:25 "Have you never read what **David** did when he and his companions
  10:47 he began to shout, "Jesus, Son *of* **David,** have mercy on me!"
  10:48 but he shouted all the more, "Son *of* **David,** have mercy on me!"
  11:10 "Blessed is the coming kingdom *of* our father **David!"** "Hosanna in
  12:35 that the teachers of the law say that the Christ is the son *of* **David**?
  12:36 **David** himself, speaking by the Holy Spirit, declared: " 'The Lord
  12:37 **David** himself calls him 'Lord.' How then can he be his son?"
Lk 1:27 to be married to a man named Joseph, a descendant *of* **David.**
  1:32 The Lord God will give him the throne of his father **David,**
  1:69 up a horn of salvation for us in the house *of* his servant **David**
  2: 4 of Nazareth in Galilee to Judea, to Bethlehem the town *of* **David,**
  2: 4 of David, because he belonged to the house and line *of* **David.**
  2:11 Today in the town *of* **David** a Savior has been born to you;
  3:31 the son of Mattatha, the son of Nathan, the son *of* **David,**
  6: 3 "Have you never read what **David** did when he and his companions
  18:38 He called out, "Jesus, Son *of* **David,** have mercy on me!"
  18:39 but he shouted all the more, "Son *of* **David,** have mercy on me!"
  20:41 to them, "How is it that they say the Christ is the Son *of* **David**?
  20:42 **David** himself declares in the Book of Psalms: " 'The Lord said to
  20:44 **David** calls him 'Lord.' How then can he be his son?"
Jn 7:42 Does not the Scripture say that the Christ will come from **David's**
  7:42 David's family and from Bethlehem, the town where **David** lived?"
Ac 1:16 spoke long ago through the mouth *of* **David** concerning Judas,
  2:25 **David** said about him: " 'I saw the Lord always before me.
  2:29 I can tell you confidently that the patriarch **David** died and was
  2:34 For **David** did not ascend to heaven, and yet he said, " 'The Lord
  4:25 Holy Spirit through the mouth of your servant, our father **David:**
  7:45 out before them. It remained in the land until the time *of* **David,**
  13:22 After removing Saul, he made **David** their king. He testified
  13:22 'I have found **David** son of Jesse a man after my own heart;
  13:34 " 'I will give you the holy and sure blessings promised to **David.'**
  13:36 "For when **David** had served God's purpose in his own generation,
  15:16 " 'After this I will return and rebuild **David's** fallen tent. Its ruins I
Ro 1: 3 his Son, who as to his human nature was a descendant *of* **David,**
  4: 6 **David** says the same thing when he speaks of the blessedness of
  11: 9 And **David** says: "May their table become a snare and a trap,
2Ti 2: 8 Jesus Christ, raised from the dead, descended from **David.**
Heb 4: 7 calling it Today, when a long time later he spoke through **David,**
  11:32 Barak, Samson, Jephthah, **David,** Samuel and the prophets,

---

Rev 3: 7 words of him who is holy and true, who holds the key *of* **David.**
  5: 5 the Lion of the tribe of Judah, the Root *of* **David,** has triumphed.
  22:16 I am the Root and the Offspring *of* **David,** and the bright Morning

1254 δέ, *de* [2792 / 2789] See Index of Articles, Etc.

[→ *2022, 2023, 2024, 2025, 3592, 3593, 3594, 3595, 3596, 3598, 3599, 4027, 4028, 4029, 4030, 4031, 4032*]

untranslated [1284], but [665], and [254], then [89], now [82], he [+3836] [70], they [+3836] [49], so [36], Jesus [+3836] [25], however [23], yet [17], when [12], another [+257] [9], she [+3836] [8], while [8], another [+4005] [6], instead [6], meanwhile [5], others [+257] [5], the man [+3836] [4], also [3], and yet [3], as it is [+3814] [3], at this [3], even [3], others [+3836] [3], others [+4005] [3], those [+3836] [3], as [2], and some [+4005] [2], another [2], but when [2], for [2], if he does [+1623+3590] [2], moreover [2], nevertheless [2], once [+1181] [2], or [+4005] [2], or [2], rather [+3437] [2], rather [2], some [2], some [+257] [2], still [2], that [2], the disciples [+3836] [2], the men [+3836] [2], the other [+4005] [2], though [2], where [2], after this [1], again [1], and even [1], and now [1], as for [1], as it is [+3815] [1], as it is [+4022] [1], at this point [+4047] [1], because [1], but even [1], by [1], by now [1], Cornelius [+3836] [1], finally [1], if [1], in addition [+2093] [1], in addition [1], instead [+3814] [1], Jesus followers [+3836] [1], just [1], just as [1], Mary [+3836] [1], and some [1], another [+3836] [1], arose [+1181] [1], at other times [+4047] [1], but [+1883+3836] [1], but [+3437] [1], but as far as [1], but in the other case [+1695] [1], especially [+3437] [1], even though [1], former [1], more than that [+3437] [1], nor anyone [+4029] [1], not until [+2453] [1], now that [1], on [1], once [1], one day [+1181] [1], other [+257] [1], or at least [+1623+3590] [1], others [+5516] [1], otherwise [+1623+3590] [1], Pilate [+3836] [1], remember this [+4047] [1], similarly [1], simply [1], so [+1181] [1], so he [+3836] [1], so they [+3836] [1], still another [1], still others [+3836] [1], the expert in the law [+3836] [1], the father [+3836] [1], the man's [+3836] [1], the manager [+3836] [1], the people [+3836] [1], the rioters [+3836] [1], the time came when [+1181] [1], what [+323+1877+4005] [1], what is more [+247+2779+3667+4024] [1], which [1], yes [1]

1255 δέησις, *deēsis* [18] [√ *1289*]

prayers [6], prayer [4], pray [+4472] [2], praying [2], requests [2], ask God for help [1], petition [1]

Lk 1:13 to him: "Do not be afraid, Zechariah; your **prayer** has been heard.
  2:37 left the temple but worshiped night and day, fasting and **praying.**
  5:33 "John's disciples often fast and **pray** [+4472], and so do the
Ro 10: 1 and **prayer** to God for the Israelites is that they may be saved.
2Co 1:11 as you help us *by* your **prayers.** Then many will give thanks on
  9:14 And *in* their **prayers** for you their hearts will go out to you,
Eph 6:18 the Spirit on all occasions with all kinds of prayers and **requests.**
  6:18 this in mind, be alert and always keep on **praying** for all the saints.
Php 1: 4 In all my **prayers** for all of you, I always pray with joy
  1: 4 In all my prayers for all of you, I always **pray** [+4472] with joy
  1:19 for I know that through your **prayers** and the help given by the
  4: 6 but in everything, by prayer and **petition,** with thanksgiving,
1Ti 2: 1 I urge, then, first of all, that **requests,** prayers, intercession
  5: 5 and continues night and day to pray and to **ask God for help.**
2Ti 1: 3 as night and day I constantly remember you in my **prayers.**
Heb 5: 7 he offered up **prayers** and petitions with loud cries and tears to the
Jas 5:16 The **prayer** of a righteous man is powerful and effective.
1Pe 3:12 Lord are on the righteous and his ears are attentive to their **prayer,**

1256 δεῖ, *dei* [101] [√ *1313*]

δεῖ γενέσθαι (it must happen) [7] Mt 24:6; 26:54; Mk 13:7; Lk 21:9; Rev 1:1; 4:1; 22:6

δεῖ παθεῖν (it is necessary to suffer) [8] Mt 16:21; Mk 8:31; Lk 9:22; 17:25; 24:26; Ac 9:16; 17:3; Heb 9:26

must [57], ought [13], had to [8], should [5], have to [4], should have [4], *untranslated* [2], belong [1], due [1], for work

[*+1877+2237+4005*] [1], had to [*+1639*] [1], necessary [1], ought to [1], should be [1], shouldn't have [*+4024*] [1]

Mt 16:21 Jesus began to explain to his disciples that he **must** go to Jerusalem
17:10 then do the teachers of the law say that Elijah **must** come first?"
18:33 **Shouldn't** [*+4024*] you **have** had mercy on your fellow servant
23:23 You **should have** practiced the latter, without neglecting the
24: 6 not alarmed. Such things **must** happen, but the end is still to come.
25:27 you **should have** put my money on deposit with the bankers,
26:35 But Peter declared, "Even if I **have to** die with you, I will never
26:54 then would the Scriptures be fulfilled that say *it* **must** happen in
Mk 8:31 then began to teach them that the Son of Man **must** suffer many
9:11 "Why do the teachers of the law say that Elijah **must** come first?"
13: 7 be alarmed. Such things **must** happen, but the end is still to come.
13:10 And the gospel **must** first be preached to all nations.
13:14 that causes desolation' standing where *it does* not **belong**—
14:31 "Even if I **have to** die with you, I will never disown you."
Lk 2:49 he asked. "Didn't you know I **had to** be in my Father's house?"
4:43 "I **must** preach the good news of the kingdom of God to the other
9:22 "The Son of Man **must** suffer many things and be rejected by the
11:42 You **should have** practiced the latter without leaving the former
12:12 the Holy Spirit will teach you at that time what you **should** say."
13:14 to the people, "There are six days **for work** [*+1877+2237+4005*].
13:16 Then **should** not this woman, a daughter of Abraham, whom Satan
13:33 I **must** keep going today and tomorrow and the next day—
15:32 But *we* **had to** celebrate and be glad, because this brother of yours
17:25 But first he **must** suffer many things and be rejected by this
18: 1 his disciples a parable to show them that they **should** always pray
19: 5 come down immediately. I **must** stay at your house today."
21: 9 These things **must** happen first, but the end will not come right
22: 7 Bread on which the Passover lamb **had to** be sacrificed.
22:37 the transgressors'; and I tell you that this **must** be fulfilled in me.
24: 7 'The Son of Man **must** be delivered into the hands of sinful men,
24:26 *Did* not the Christ **have to** suffer these things and then enter his
24:44 Everything **must** be fulfilled that is written about me in the Law of
Jn 3: 7 should not be surprised at my saying, 'You **must** be born again.'
3:14 up the snake in the desert, so the Son of Man **must** be lifted up,
3:30 He **must** become greater; I must become less.
4: 4 Now he **had to** go through Samaria.
4:20 but you Jews claim that the place where we **must** worship is in
4:24 is spirit, and his worshipers **must** worship in spirit and in truth."
9: 4 As long as it is day, we **must** do the work of him who sent me.
10:16 I **must** listen to my voice, and there
12:34 so how can you say, 'The Son of Man **must** be lifted up'?
20: 9 (They still did not understand from Scripture that Jesus **had to** rise
Ac 1:16 the Scripture **had to** be fulfilled which the Holy Spirit spoke long
1:21 Therefore *it is* **necessary** *to choose* one of the men who have been
3:21 He **must** remain in heaven until the time comes for God to restore
4:12 name under heaven given to men by which we **must** be saved."
5:29 the other apostles replied: "We **must** obey God rather than men!
9: 6 and go into the city, and you will be told what you **must** do."
9:16 I will show him how much he **must** suffer for my name."
14:22 We **must** go through many hardships to enter the kingdom of God,"
15: 5 "The Gentiles **must** be circumcised and required to obey the law of
16:30 brought them out and asked, "Sirs, what **must** I do to be saved?"
17: 3 explaining and proving that the Christ **had to** suffer and rise from
19:21 "After I have been there," he said, "I **must** visit Rome also."
19:36 are undeniable, you **ought** to be quiet and not do anything rash.
20:35 I showed you that by this kind of hard work we **must** help the
23:11 testified about me in Jerusalem, so you **must** also testify in Rome."
24:19 who **ought** to be here before you and bring charges if they have
25:10 am now standing before Caesar's court, where I **ought** to be tried.
25:24 and here in Caesarea, shouting that he **ought** not to live any longer.
26: 9 "I too was convinced that *I* **ought** to do all that was possible to
27:21 "Men, you **should have** taken my advice not to sail from Crete;
27:24 You **must** stand trial before Caesar; and God has graciously given
27:26 Nevertheless, we **must** run aground on some island."
Ro 1:27 and received in themselves the **due** penalty for their perversion.
8:26 We do not know what we **ought** to pray for, but the Spirit himself
12: 3 one of you: Do not think of yourself more highly than *you* **ought**,
1Co 8: 2 he knows something does not yet know as he **ought** to know.
11:19 No doubt *there* **have to** be differences among you to show which
15:25 For he **must** reign until he has put all his enemies under his feet.
15:53 For the perishable **must** clothe itself with the imperishable,
2Co 2: 3 so that when I came I should not be distressed by those who **ought**
5:10 For we **must** all appear before the judgment seat of Christ,

11:30 If *I* **must** boast, I will boast of the things that show my weakness.
12: 1 *I* **must** go on boasting. Although there is nothing to be gained,
Eph 6:20 in chains. Pray that I may declare it fearlessly, as *I* **should**.
Col 4: 4 Pray that I may proclaim it clearly, as I **should**.
4: 6 with salt, so that you may know how **[NIE]** to answer everyone.
1Th 4: 1 we instructed you how **[NIE]** to live in order to please God,
2Th 3: 7 For you yourselves know how *you* **ought** to follow our example.
1Ti 3: 2 Now the overseer **must** be above reproach, the husband of
3: 7 He **must** also have a good reputation with outsiders, so that he will
3:15 you will know how *people* **ought** to conduct themselves in God's
5:13 but also gossips and busybodies, saying things *they* **ought** not **to**.
2Ti 2: 6 The hardworking farmer **should be** the first to receive a share of
2:24 And the Lord's servant **must** not quarrel; instead, he must be kind
Tit 1: 7 an overseer is entrusted with God's work, *he* **must** be blameless—
1:11 They **must** be silenced, because they are ruining whole households
1:11 whole households by teaching things they **ought** not to teach—
Heb 2: 1 We **must** pay more careful attention, therefore, to what we have
9:26 Then Christ *would have* **had to** suffer many times since the
11: 6 because anyone who comes to him **must** believe that he exists
1Pe 1: 6 though now for a little while you *may have had* [*+1639*] **to** suffer
2Pe 3:11 be destroyed in this way, what kind of people **ought** you to be?
Rev 1: 1 which God gave him to show his servants what **must** soon take
4: 1 up here, and I will show you what **must** take place after this."
10:11 "You **must** prophesy again about many peoples, nations, languages
11: 5 This is how anyone who wants to harm them **must** die.
17:10 but when he does come, he **must** remain for a little while.
20: 3 years were ended. After that, he **must** be set free for a short time.
22: 6 sent his angel to show his servants the things that **must** soon take

1257 δεῖγμα, *deigma* [1] [→ *1258, 1891, 4136, 5682; cf. 1259*]

example [1]

Jude 1: 7 They serve as an **example** of those who suffer the punishment of

1258 δειγματίζω, *deigmatizō* [2] [√ *1257*]

expose to public disgrace [1], made a spectacle [1]

Mt 1:19 righteous man and did not want *to* **expose** her **to public disgrace**,
Col 2:15 the powers and authorities, he **made a** public **spectacle** of them,

1259 δείκνυμι, *deiknymi* [33] [→ *344, 345, 617, 618, 1260, 1892, 1893, 2109, 5683, 5684; cf. 1235, 1257*]

show [19], showed [6], shown [3], bring about [1], explain [1], show to prove [1], showing [1], shows [1]

Mt 4: 8 and **showed** him all the kingdoms of the world and their splendor.
8: 4 **show** yourself to the priest and offer the gift Moses commanded,
16:21 From that time on Jesus began *to* **explain** to his disciples that he
Mk 1:44 **show** yourself to the priest and offer the sacrifices that Moses
14:15 He *will* **show** you a large upper room, furnished and ready.
Lk 4: 5 and **showed** him in an instant all the kingdoms of the world.
5:14 **show** yourself to the priest and offer the sacrifices that Moses
20:24 "**Show** me a denarius. Whose portrait and inscription are on it?"
22:12 He *will* **show** you a large upper room, all furnished.
24:40 When he had said this, *he* **showed** them his hands and feet.
Jn 2:18 "What miraculous sign *can you* **show** us **to prove** your *authority* to
5:20 For the Father loves the Son and **shows** him all he does. Yes,
5:20 to your amazement *he will* **show** him even greater things than
10:32 "*I have* **shown** you many great miracles from the Father.
14: 8 "Lord, **show** us the Father and that will be enough for us."
14: 9 me has seen the Father. How can you say, '**Show** us the Father'?
20:20 After he said this, *he* **showed** them his hands and side. The
Ac 7: 3 and your people,' God said, 'and go to the land *I will* **show** you.'
10:28 But God *has* **shown** me that I should not call any man impure
1Co 12:31 the greater gifts. And now *I will* **show** you the most excellent way.
1Ti 6:15 which God *will* **bring about** in his own time—God, the blessed
Heb 8: 5 "See to it that you make everything according to the pattern **shown**
Jas 2:18 "You have faith; I have deeds." **Show** me your faith without deeds,
2:18 faith without deeds, and *I will* **show** you my faith by what I do.
3:13 *Let him* **show** it by his good life, by deeds done in the humility
Rev 1: 1 which God gave him *to* **show** his servants what must soon take
4: 1 up here, and *I will* **show** you what must take place after this."
17: 1 "Come, *I will* **show** you the punishment of the great prostitute,

21: 9 last plagues came and said to me, "Come, *I will* **show** you the bride,
21: 10 away in the Spirit to a mountain great and high, and **showed**
22: 1 Then the angel **showed** me the river of the water of life, as clear as
22: 6 sent his angel *to* **show** his servants the things that must soon take
22: 8 at the feet of the angel who *had been* **showing** them to me.

1260 δείκνύω, *deiknyō* Not used in UBS/NIV [√ *1259*]

1261 δειλία, *deilia* [1] [√ *1290*]

timidity [1]

2Ti 1: 7 For God did not give us a spirit *of* **timidity**, but a spirit of power,

1262 δειλιάω, *deiliaō* [1] [√ *1290*]

afraid [1]

Jn 14: 27 Do not let your hearts be troubled and *do* not *be* **afraid**.

1263 δειλινός, *deilinos* Not used in UBS/NIV

1264 δειλός, *deilos* [3] [√ *1290*]

afraid [1], cowardly [1], so afraid [1]

Mt 8: 26 He replied, "You of little faith, why are you **so afraid**?"
Mk 4: 40 He said to his disciples, "Why are you *so* **afraid**? Do you still have
Rev 21: 8 But the **cowardly**, the unbelieving, the vile, the murderers,

1265 δεῖνα, *deina* [1]

certain [1]

Mt 26: 18 He replied, "Go into the city to a **certain** *man* and tell him,

1266 δεινός, *deinos* Not used in UBS/NIV [√ *1290*]

1267 δεινῶς, *deinōs* [2] [√ *1290*]

fiercely [1], terrible [1]

Mt 8: 6 "my servant lies at home paralyzed and in **terrible** suffering."
Lk 11: 53 and the teachers of the law began to oppose him **fiercely**

1268 δειπνέω, *deipneō* [4] [√ *1270*]

supper [2], eat [1], my supper [+*5515*] [1]

Lk 17: 8 'Prepare **my supper** [+*5515*], get yourself ready and wait on me
22: 20 In the same way, after the **supper** he took the cup, saying,
1Co 11: 25 In the same way, after **supper** he took the cup, saying, "This cup is
Rev 3: 20 opens the door, I will come in and **eat** with him, and he with me.

1269 δειπνοκλήτωρ, *deipnoklētōr* Not used in UBS/NIV [√ *1270 + 2813*]

1270 δεῖπνον, *deipnon* [16] [→ *1268, 1269, 1271*]

banquet [4], supper [4], banquets [3], dinner [2], *untranslated* [1], evening meal [1], meal [1]

Mt 23: 6 they love the place of honor at **banquets** and the most important
Mk 6: 21 On his birthday Herod gave a **banquet** for his high officials
12: 39 seats in the synagogues and the places of honor at **banquets**.
Lk 14: 12 "When you give a luncheon or **dinner**, do not invite your friends,
14: 16 "A certain man was preparing a great **banquet** and invited many
14: 17 At the time *of* the **banquet** he sent his servant to tell those who had
14: 24 of those men who were invited will get a taste *of* my **banquet**.' "
20: 46 seats in the synagogues and the places of honor at **banquets**.
Jn 12: 2 Here a **dinner** was given in Jesus' honor. Martha served,
13: 2 The **evening meal** was being served, and the devil had already
13: 4 so he got up from the **meal**, took off his outer clothing,
21: 20 (This was the one who had leaned back against Jesus at the **supper**

1Co 11: 20 When you come together, it is not the Lord's **Supper** you eat,
11: 21 each of you **[RPG]** goes ahead without waiting for anybody else.
Rev 19: 9 'Blessed are those who are invited to the wedding **supper** of the
19: 17 in midair, "Come, gather together for the great **supper** of God,

1271 δεῖπνος, *deipnos* Not used in UBS/NIV [√ *1270*]

1272 δεισιδαιμονία, *deisidaimonia* [1] [√ *1290 + 1228*]

religion [1]

Ac 25: 19 they had some points of dispute with him about their own **religion**

1273 δεισιδαίμων, *deisidaimōn* [1] [√ *1290 + 1228*]

very religious [1]

Ac 17: 22 "Men of Athens! I see that in every way you are **very religious**.

1274 δέκα, *deka* [25] [→ *619, 620, 1275, 1276, 1277, 1278, 1279, 1280, 1281, 1282, 1557, 1558, 1559, 1894, 1895, 4298, 5476*]

ten [24], eighteen [+*2779+3893*] [1]

Mt 20: 24 When the **ten** heard about this, they were indignant with the two
25: 1 "At that time the kingdom of heaven will be like **ten** virgins who
25: 28 the talent from him and give it to the one who has the **ten** talents.
Mk 10: 41 When the **ten** heard about this, they became indignant with James
Lk 13: 16 whom Satan has kept bound *for* **eighteen** [+*2779+3893*] long
14: 31 and consider whether he is able with **ten** thousand men to oppose
15: 8 "Or suppose a woman has **ten** silver coins and loses one. Does she
17: 12 As he was going into a village, **ten** men who had leprosy met him.
17: 17 Jesus asked, "Were not all **ten** cleansed? Where are the other nine?
19: 13 So he called **ten** of his servants and gave them ten minas. 'Put this
19: 13 So he called ten of his servants and gave them **ten** minas. 'Put this
19: 16 "The first one came and said, 'Sir, your mina has earned **ten** more.'
19: 17 been trustworthy in a very small matter, take charge of **ten** cities.'
19: 24 his mina away from him and give it to the one who has **ten** minas.'
19: 25 " 'Sir,' they said, 'he already has **ten**!'
Ac 25: 6 After spending eight or **ten** days with them, he went down to
Rev 2: 10 in prison to test you, and you will suffer persecution *for* **ten** days.
12: 3 with seven heads and **ten** horns and seven crowns on his heads.
13: 1 He had **ten** horns and seven heads, with ten crowns on his horns,
13: 1 He had ten horns and seven heads, with **ten** crowns on his horns,
17: 3 with blasphemous names and had seven heads and **ten** horns.
17: 7 of the beast she rides, which has the seven heads and **ten** horns.
17: 12 "The **ten** horns you saw are ten kings who have not yet received a
17: 12 "The ten horns you saw are **ten** kings who have not yet received a
17: 16 The beast and the **ten** horns you saw will hate the prostitute.

1275 δεκαδύο, *dekadyo* Not used in UBS/NIV [√ *1274 + 1545*]

1276 δεκαέξ, *dekaex* Not used in UBS/NIV [√ *1274 + 1971*]

1277 δεκαοκτώ, *dekaoktō* [2] [√ *1274 + 3893*]

eighteen [2]

Lk 13: 4 Or those **eighteen** who died when the tower in Siloam fell on
13: 11 was there who had been crippled by a spirit *for* **eighteen** years.

1278 δεκαπέντε, *dekapente* [3] [√ *1274 + 4297*]

fifteen [1], less than two miles [+*608+5084+6055*] [1], ninety feet deep [+*3976*] [1]

Jn 11: 18 Bethany was **less than two miles** [+*608+5084+6055*] from Jerusalem,
Ac 27: 28 took soundings again and found it was **ninety feet deep** [+*3976*].
Gal 1: 18 to get acquainted with Peter and stayed with him **fifteen** days.

1279 Δεκάπολις, *Dekapolis* [3] [√ 1274 + 4484]

Decapolis [3]

Mt	4:25	the **Decapolis**, Jerusalem, Judea and the region across the Jordan
Mk	5:20	and began to tell in the **Decapolis** how much Jesus had done for
	7:31	down to the Sea of Galilee and into the region *of* the **Decapolis**.

1280 δεκατέσσαρες, *dekatessares* [5]
[√ 1274 + 5475]

fourteen [5]

Mt	1:17	Thus there were **fourteen** generations in all from Abraham to
	1:17	**fourteen** from David to the exile to Babylon, and fourteen from
	1:17	to the exile to Babylon, and **fourteen** from the exile to the Christ.
2Co	12:2	I know a man in Christ who **fourteen** years ago was caught up to
Gal	2:1	**Fourteen** years later I went up again to Jerusalem, this time with

1281 δέκατος, *dekatos* [7] [√ 1274]

tenth [7]

Jn	1:39	and spent that day with him. It was about the **tenth** hour.
Heb	7:2	and Abraham gave him a **tenth** of everything. First, his name
	7:4	Even the patriarch Abraham gave him a **tenth** of the plunder!
	7:8	In the one case, the **tenth** is collected by men who die; but in the
	7:9	One might even say that Levi, who collects the **tenth**,
Rev	11:13	there was a severe earthquake and a **tenth** of the city collapsed.
	21:20	the eighth beryl, the ninth topaz, the **tenth** chrysoprase,

1282 δεκατόω, *dekatoō* [2] [√ 1274]

collected a tenth [1], paid the tenth [1]

Heb	7:6	yet *he* **collected a tenth** from Abraham and blessed him who had
	7:9	that Levi, who collects the tenth, **paid the tenth** through Abraham,

1283 δεκτός, *dektos* [5] [√ 1312]

favor [2], acceptable [1], accepted [1], accepts [+1639] [1]

Lk	4:19	to proclaim the year of the Lord's **favor**."
	4:24	the truth," he continued, "no prophet is **accepted** in his hometown.
Ac	10:35	but **accepts** [+1639] men from every nation who fear him
2Co	6:2	For he says, "*In* the time of my **favor** I heard you, and in the day
Php	4:18	are a fragrant offering, an **acceptable** sacrifice, pleasing to God.

1284 δελεάζω, *deleazō* [3] [√ 1515]

entice [1], enticed [1], seduce [1]

Jas	1:14	*when*, by his own evil desire, *he is* dragged away and **enticed**.
2Pe	2:14	full of adultery, they never stop sinning; *they* **seduce** the unstable;
	2:18	*they* **entice** people who are just escaping from those who live in

1285 δένδρον, *dendron* [25]

tree [17], trees [8]

Mt	3:10	The ax is already at the root *of* the **trees**, and every tree that does
	3:10	and every **tree** that does not produce good fruit will be cut down
	7:17	Likewise every good **tree** bears good fruit, but a bad tree bears bad
	7:17	every good tree bears good fruit, but a bad **tree** bears bad fruit.
	7:18	A good **tree** cannot bear bad fruit, and a bad tree cannot bear good
	7:18	tree cannot bear bad fruit, and a bad **tree** cannot bear good fruit.
	7:19	Every **tree** that does not bear good fruit is cut down and thrown
	12:33	"Make a **tree** good and its fruit will be good, or make a tree bad
	12:33	its fruit will be good, or make a **tree** bad and its fruit will be bad,
	12:33	and its fruit will be bad, for a **tree** is recognized by its fruit.
	13:32	when it grows, it is the largest of garden plants and becomes a **tree**,
	21:8	while others cut branches from the **trees** and spread them on the
Mk	8:24	and said, "I see people; they look like **trees** walking around."
Lk	3:9	The ax is already at the root *of* the **trees**, and every tree that does
	3:9	and every **tree** that does not produce good fruit will be cut down
	6:43	"No good **tree** bears bad fruit, nor does a bad tree bear good fruit.
	6:43	"No good tree bears bad fruit, nor does a bad **tree** bear good fruit.
	6:44	Each **tree** is recognized by its own fruit. People do not pick figs
	13:19	It grew and became a **tree**, and the birds of the air perched in its

	21:29	He told them this parable: "Look at the fig tree and all the **trees**.
Jude	1:12	the wind; autumn **trees**, without fruit and uprooted—twice dead.
Rev	7:1	any wind from blowing on the land or on the sea or on any **tree**.
	7:3	or the **trees** until we put a seal on the foreheads of the servants of
	8:7	of the earth was burned up, a third *of* the **trees** were burned up,
	9:4	were told not to harm the grass of the earth or any plant or **tree**,

1286 δεξιοβόλος, *dexiobolos*   Not used in UBS/NIV
[√ 1288 + 965]

1287 δεξιολάβος, *dexiolabos* [1] [√ 1288 + 3284]

spearmen [1]

Ac	23:23	and two hundred **spearmen** to go to Caesarea at nine tonight.

1288 δεξιός, *dexios* [54] [→ 1286, 1287]

δεξιός χείρ (right hand) [6] Mt 5:30; Lk 6:6; Ac 3:7; Rev 1:16; 10:5; 13:16

ἐκ δεξιᾶς (from the right) [1] Rev 5:7

ἐκ δεξιῶν (from/at the right) [22] Mt 20:21,23; 22:44; 25:33,34; 26:64; 27:38; Mk 10:37,40; 12:36; 14:62; 15:27; 16:19; Lk 1:11; 20:42; 22:69; 23:33; Ac 2:25,34; 7:55,56; Heb 1:13

ἐν δεξιᾷ, δεξιοῖς (on/at the right) [12] Mt 27:29; Mk 16:5; Ro 8:34; Eph 1:20; Col 3:1; Heb 1:3; 8:1; 10:12; 12:2; 1Pe 3:22; Rev 1:16; 2:1

right hand [31], right [21], right side [2]

Mt	5:29	If your **right** eye causes you to sin, gouge it out and throw it away.
	5:30	And if your **right** hand causes you to sin, cut it off and throw it
	5:39	If someone strikes you on the **right** cheek, turn to him the other
	6:3	do not let your left hand know what your **right hand** is doing,
	20:21	"Grant that one of these two sons of mine may sit at your **right**
	20:23	from my cup, but to sit at my **right** or left is not for me to grant.
	22:44	"Sit at my **right hand** until I put your enemies under your feet." '
	25:33	He will put the sheep on his **right** and the goats on his left.
	25:34	"Then the King will say to those on his **right**, 'Come, you who are
	26:64	In the future you will see the Son of Man sitting at the **right hand**
	27:29	They put a staff in his **right hand** and knelt in front of him
	27:38	were crucified with him, one on his **right** and one on his left.
Mk	10:37	"Let one of us sit at your **right** and the other at your left in your
	10:40	but to sit at my **right** or left is not for me to grant. These places
	12:36	"Sit at my **right hand** until I put your enemies under your feet." '
	14:62	"And you will see the Son of Man sitting at the **right hand** of the
	15:27	two robbers with him, one on his **right** and one on his left.
	16:5	saw a young man dressed in a white robe sitting on the **right side**
	16:19	he was taken up into heaven and he sat at the **right hand** of God.
Lk	1:11	appeared to him, standing at the **right side** of the altar of incense.
	6:6	and a man was there whose **right** hand was shriveled.
	20:42	Psalms: " 'The Lord said to my Lord: "Sit at my **right hand**
	22:50	them struck the servant of the high priest, cutting off his **right** ear.
	22:69	Son of Man will be seated at the **right hand** of the mighty God."
	23:33	along with the criminals—one on his **right**, the other on his left.
Jn	18:10	and struck the high priest's servant, cutting off his **right** ear.
	21:6	"Throw your net on the **right** side of the boat and you will find
Ac	2:25	before me. Because he is at my **right** hand, I will not be shaken.
	2:33	Exalted *to* the **right hand** of God, he has received from the Father
	2:34	and yet he said, " 'The Lord said to my Lord: "Sit at my **right hand**
	3:7	Taking him *by* the **right** hand, he helped him up, and instantly the
	5:31	God exalted him *to* his own **right hand** as Prince and Savior that
	7:55	saw the glory of God, and Jesus standing at the **right hand** of God.
	7:56	and the Son of Man standing at the **right hand** of God."
Ro	8:34	to life—is at the **right hand** of God and is also interceding for us.
2Co	6:7	with weapons of righteousness *in* the **right hand** and in the left;
Gal	2:9	and Barnabas the **right hand** of fellowship when they recognized
Eph	1:20	the dead and seated him at his **right hand** in the heavenly realms,
Col	3:1	on things above, where Christ is seated at the **right hand** of God.
Heb	1:3	for sins, he sat down at the **right hand** of the Majesty in heaven.
	1:13	"Sit at my **right hand** until I make your enemies a footstool for
	8:1	who sat down at the **right hand** of the throne of the Majesty in
	10:12	time one sacrifice for sins, he sat down at the **right hand** of God.
	12:2	its shame, and sat down at the **right hand** of the throne of God.
1Pe	3:22	who has gone into heaven and is at God's **right hand**—

Rev 1:16 In his **right** hand he held seven stars, and out of his mouth came a
     1:17 Then he placed his **right hand** on me and said: "Do not be afraid.
     1:20 The mystery of the seven stars that you saw in my **right hand**
     2: 1 are the words of him who holds the seven stars in his **right hand**
     5: 1 Then I saw in the **right hand** of him who sat on the throne a scroll
     5: 7 and took the scroll from the **right hand** of him who sat on the
    10: 2 He planted his **right** foot on the sea and his left foot on the land,
    10: 5 standing on the sea and on the land raised his **right** hand to heaven.
    13:16 and slave, to receive a mark on his **right** hand or on his forehead,

1289 δέομαι, deomai [22] [→ 1255, 1890, 4656]

pray [5], beg [4], begged [3], ask [2], please [+5148] [2], prayed
[2], implore [1], plead [1], pleaded with [1], prayed to [1]

Mt   9:38 **Ask** the Lord of the harvest, therefore, to send out workers into his
Lk   5:12 he fell with his face to the ground and **begged** him, "Lord, if you
     8:28 Jesus, Son of the Most High God? I **beg** you, don't torture me!"
     8:38 The man from whom the demons had gone out **begged** to go with
     9:38 "Teacher, I **beg** you to look at my son, for he is my only child.
     9:40 I **begged** your disciples to drive it out, but they could not."
    10: 2 **Ask** the Lord of the harvest, therefore, to send out workers into his
    21:36 and **pray** that you may be able to escape all that is about to happen,
    22:32 But I *have* **prayed** for you, Simon, that your faith may not fail.
Ac   4:31 *After* they **prayed**, the place where they were meeting was shaken.
     8:22 Repent of this wickedness and **pray** to the Lord. Perhaps he will
     8:24 "**Pray** to the Lord for me so that nothing you have said may
     8:34 The eunuch asked Philip, "Tell me, **please** [+5148], who is the
    10: 2 he gave generously to those in need and **prayed to** God regularly.
    21:39 of no ordinary city. **Please** [+5148] let me speak to the people."
    26: 3 and controversies. Therefore, I **beg** you to listen to me patiently.
Ro   1:10 and I **pray** that now at last by God's will the way may be opened
2Co 5:20 We **implore** you on Christ's behalf: Be reconciled to God.
     8: 4 *they* urgently **pleaded with** us for the privilege of sharing in this
    10: 2 I **beg** you that when I come I may not have to be as bold as I
Gal 4:12 I **plead** with you, brothers, become like me, for I became like you.
1Th 3:10 and day *we* **pray** most earnestly that we may see you again

1290 δέος, deos [1] [→ 1261, 1262, 1264, 1266, 1267, 1272, 1273]

awe [1]

Heb 12:28 and so worship God acceptably with reverence and **awe**,

1291 Δερβαῖος, Derbaios [1] [√ 1292]

from Derbe [1]

Ac 20: 4 Gaius **from Derbe**, Timothy also, and Tychicus and Trophimus

1292 Δέρβη, Derbē [3] [→ 1291, 1523]

Derbe [3]

Ac 14: 6 cities of Lystra and **Derbe** and to the surrounding country,
    14:20 back into the city. The next day he and Barnabas left for **Derbe**.
    16: 1 He came to **Derbe** and then to Lystra, where a disciple named

1293 δέρμα, derma [1] [√ 1296]

goatskins [+128] [1]

Heb 11:37 They went about in sheepskins and **goatskins** [+128], destitute,

1294 δερμάτινος, dermatinos [2] [√ 1296]

leather [2]

Mt   3: 4 made of camel's hair, and he had a **leather** belt around his waist.
Mk   1: 6 with a **leather** belt around his waist, and he ate locusts and wild

1295 δέρρις, derris Not used in UBS/NIV [√ 1296]

1296 δέρω, derō [15] [→ 1293, 1294, 1295]

beat [7], beaten with blows [2], beating [2], flogged [2], slaps [1],
strike [1]

Mt 21:35 "The tenants seized his servants; *they* **beat** one, killed another,
Mk 12: 3 But *they* seized him, **beat** him and sent him away empty-handed.
    12: 5 He sent many others; some of them *they* **beat**, others they killed.
    13: 9 handed over to the local councils and **flogged** in the synagogues.
Lk 12:47 not do what his master wants *will be* **beaten with** many **blows**.
    12:48 does things deserving punishment *will be* **beaten with** few **blows**.
    20:10 But the tenants **beat** him and sent him away empty-handed.
    20:11 but that one also they **beat** and treated shamefully and sent away
    22:63 men who were guarding Jesus began mocking and **beating** him.
Jn 18:23 to what is wrong. But if I spoke the truth, why *did you* **strike** me?"
Ac   5:40 They called the apostles in and *had them* **flogged**.
    16:37 "*They* **beat** us publicly without a trial, even though we are Roman
    22:19 that I went from one synagogue to another *to* imprison and **beat**
1Co 9:26 a man running aimlessly; I do not fight like a *man* **beating** the air.
2Co 11:20 of you or pushes himself forward or **slaps** you in the face.

1297 δεσμεύω, desmeuō [3] [√ 1313]

arresting [1], chained hand [+268] [1], tie up [1]

Mt 23: 4 They **tie up** heavy loads and put them on men's shoulders,
Lk   8:29 and *though he was* **chained hand** [+268] and foot and kept under
Ac 22: 4 **arresting** both men and women and throwing them into prison,

1298 δεσμέω, desmeō Not used in UBS/NIV [√ 1313]

1299 δέσμη, desmē [1] [√ 1313]

bundles [1]

Mt 13:30 First collect the weeds and tie them in **bundles** to be burned;

1300 δέσμιος, desmios [16] [√ 1313]

prisoner [11], in prison [2], prisoners [2], arrested [1]

Mt 27:15 it was the governor's custom at the Feast to release a **prisoner**
    27:16 At that time they had a notorious **prisoner**, called Barabbas.
Mk 15: 6 Now it was the custom at the Feast to release a **prisoner** whom the
Ac 16:25 hymns to God, and the other **prisoners** were listening to them.
    16:27 to kill himself because he thought the **prisoners** had escaped.
    23:18 "Paul, the **prisoner**, sent for me and asked me to bring this young
    25:14 He said: "There is a man here whom Felix left as a **prisoner**.
    25:27 For I think it is unreasonable to send on a **prisoner** without
    28:17 I was **arrested** in Jerusalem and handed over to the Romans.
Eph 3: 1 the **prisoner** of Christ Jesus for the sake of you Gentiles—
     4: 1 As a **prisoner** for the Lord, then, I urge you to live a life worthy of
2Ti 1: 8 ashamed to testify about our Lord, or ashamed of me his **prisoner**.
Phm 1: 1 Paul, a **prisoner** of Christ Jesus, and Timothy our brother,
     1: 9 as Paul—an old man and now also a **prisoner** of Christ Jesus—
Heb 10:34 You sympathized with those **in prison** and joyfully accepted the
    13: 3 Remember those **in prison** as if you were their fellow prisoners,

1301 δεσμός, desmos [18] [√ 1313]

chains [11], chained [2], imprisonment [2], *untranslated* [1],
bound [1], prison [1]

Mk   7:35 **[NIE]** his tongue was loosened and he began to speak plainly.
Lk   8:29 he had broken his **chains** and had been driven by the demon into
    13:16 long years, be set free on the Sabbath day from what **bound** her?"
Ac 16:26 all the prison doors flew open, and everybody's **chains** came loose.
    20:23 I only know that in every city the Holy Spirit warns me that **prison**
    23:29 was no charge against him that deserved death or **imprisonment**.
    26:29 to me today may become what I am, except for these **chains**."
    26:31 man is not doing anything that deserves death or **imprisonment**."
Php 1: 7 for whether I am in **chains** or defending and confirming the gospel,
     1:13 palace guard and to everyone else that I am in **chains** for Christ.
     1:14 *Because of* my **chains**, most of the brothers in the Lord have been
     1:17 supposing that they can stir up trouble for me while I am *in* **chains**.
Col 4:18 in my own hand. Remember my **chains**. Grace be with you.
2Ti 2: 9 for which I am suffering even to the point of *being* **chained** like a

Phm 1:10 for my son Onesimus, who became my son while I was in **chains**.
1:13 so that he could take your place in helping me while I am in **chains**
Heb 11:36 and flogging, while still others were **chained** and put in prison.
Jude 1: 6 *bound with* everlasting **chains** for judgment on the great Day.

1302 δεσμοφύλαξ, *desmophylax* [3] [√ *1313* + *5875*]

jailer [3]

Ac 16:23 and the **jailer** was commanded to guard them carefully.
16:27 The **jailer** woke up, and when he saw the prison doors open,
16:36 The **jailer** told Paul, "The magistrates have ordered that you

1303 δεσμωτήριον, *desmōtērion* [4] [√ *1313*]

jail [2], prison [2]

Mt 11: 2 When John heard in **prison** what Christ was doing, he sent his
Ac 5:21 of the elders of Israel—and sent to the **jail** for the apostles.
5:23 "We found the **jail** securely locked, with the guards standing at the
16:26 violent earthquake that the foundations *of* the **prison** were shaken.

1304 δεσμώτης, *desmōtēs* [2] [√ *1313*]

prisoners [2]

Ac 27: 1 and some other **prisoners** were handed over to a centurion named
27:42 The soldiers planned to kill the **prisoners** to prevent any of them

1305 δεσπότης, *despotēs* [10] [→ *3866, 3867*; cf. *1313*]

masters [4], sovereign Lord [4], Master [1], Sovereign [1]

Lk 2:29 "**Sovereign Lord**, as you have promised, you now dismiss your
Ac 4:24 "**Sovereign Lord**," they said, "you made the heaven and the earth
1Ti 6: 1 of slavery should consider their **masters** worthy of full respect,
6: 2 Those who have believing **masters** are not to show less respect for
2Ti 2:21 useful *to* the **Master** and prepared to do any good work.
Tit 2: 9 Teach slaves to be subject to their **masters** in everything, to try to
1Pe 2:18 Slaves, submit yourselves *to* your **masters** with all respect,
2Pe 2: 1 even denying the **sovereign Lord** who bought them—
Jude 1: 4 for immorality and deny Jesus Christ our only **Sovereign** and Lord.
Rev 6:10 out in a loud voice, "How long, **Sovereign Lord**, holy and true,

1306 δεῦρο, *deuro* [9] [→ *1307*]

come [7], go [1], now [1]

Mt 19:21 and you will have treasure in heaven. Then **come**, follow me."
Mk 10:21 and you will have treasure in heaven. Then **come**, follow me."
Lk 18:22 and you will have treasure in heaven. Then **come**, follow me."
Jn 11:43 he had said this, Jesus called in a loud voice, "Lazarus, **come** out!"
Ac 7: 3 and your people,' God said, 'and **go** to the land I will show you.'
7:34 down to set them free. Now **come**, I will send you back to Egypt.'
Ro 1:13 to come to you (but have been prevented from doing so until **now**)
Rev 17: 1 angels who had the seven bowls came and said to me, "**Come**,
21: 9 bowls full of the seven last plagues came and said to me, "**Come**,

1307 δεῦτε, *deute* [12] [√ *1306*]

come [12]

Mt 4:19 "**Come**, follow me," Jesus said, "and I will make you fishers of
11:28 "**Come** to me, all *you* who are weary and burdened,
21:38 'This is the heir. **Come**, let's kill him and take his inheritance.'
22: 4 and everything is ready. **Come** to the wedding banquet.'
25:34 to those on his right, '**Come**, you who are blessed by my Father;
28: 6 he has risen, just as he said. **Come** and see the place where he lay.
Mk 1:17 "**Come**, follow me," Jesus said, "and I will make you fishers of
6:31 "**Come** *with* me by yourselves to a quiet place and get some rest."
12: 7 is the heir. **Come**, let's kill him, and the inheritance will be ours.'
Jn 4:29 "**Come**, see a man who told me everything I ever did. Could this
21:12 Jesus said to them, "**Come** and have breakfast." None of the
Rev 19:17 in midair, "**Come**, gather together for the great supper of God,

1308 δευτεραῖος, *deuteraios* [1] [√ *1545*]

on the following day [1]

Ac 28:13 south wind came up, and **on the following day** we reached Puteoli.

1309 δεύτερον, *deuteron* [6] [√ *1545*]

second time [2], again [1], again [+*4099*] [1], later [1], second [1]

Jn 3: 4 "Surely he cannot enter a **second time** into his mother's womb to
21:16 **Again** [+*4099*] Jesus said, "Simon son of John, do you truly love
1Co 12:28 **second** prophets, third teachers, then workers of miracles,
2Co 13: 2 already gave you a warning when I was with you the **second time**.
Jude 1: 5 people out of Egypt, but **later** destroyed those who did not believe.
Rev 19: 3 And **again** they shouted: "Hallelujah! The smoke from her goes up

1310 δευτερόπρωτος, *deuteroprōtos* Not used in UBS/NIV [√ *1545* + *4755*]

1311 δεύτερος, *deuteros* [37] [√ *1545*]

θάνατος δεύτερος (second death) [4] Rev 2:11; 20:6,14; 21:8

second [27], second time [+*1666*] [6], another [1], inner [1], second time [1], twice [1]

Mt 22:26 The same thing happened to the **second** and third brother,
22:39 And the **second** is like it: 'Love your neighbor as yourself.'
26:42 He went away a **second** [+*1666*] **time** and prayed, "My Father,
Mk 12:21 The **second** one married the widow, but he also died, leaving no
12:31 The **second** is this: 'Love your neighbor as yourself.' There is no
14:72 Immediately the rooster crowed the **second** [+*1666*] **time**.
Lk 12:38 even if he comes in the **second** or third watch of the night.
19:18 "The **second** came and said, 'Sir, your mina has earned five more.'
20:30 The **second**
Jn 4:54 This was the **second** miraculous sign that Jesus performed,
9:24 A **second** [+*1666*] **time** they summoned the man who had been
Ac 7:13 On their **second** visit, Joseph told his brothers who he was,
10:15 The voice spoke to him a **second** [+*1666*] **time**, "Do not call
11: 9 "The voice spoke from heaven a **second** [+*1666*] **time**, 'Do not call
12:10 They passed the first and **second** guards and came to the iron gate
13:33 As it is written in the **second** Psalm: " 'You are my Son; today I
1Co 15:47 first man was of the dust of the earth, the **second** man from heaven.
2Co 1:15 I planned to visit you first so that you might benefit **twice**.
Tit 3:10 Warn a divisive person once, and then warn him a **second time**.
Heb 8: 7 that first covenant, no place would have been sought for **another**.
9: 3 Behind the **second** curtain was a room called the Most Holy Place,
9: 7 But only the high priest entered the **inner** *room*, and that only once
9:28 and he will appear a **second** [+*1666*] **time**, not to bear sin,
10: 9 to do your will." He sets aside the first to establish the **second**.
2Pe 3: 1 Dear friends, this is now my **second** letter to you. I have written
Rev 2:11 He who overcomes will not be hurt at all by the **second** death.
4: 7 the **second** was an ox, the third had a face like a man,
6: 3 When the Lamb opened the **second** seal, I heard the second living
6: 3 the second seal, I heard the **second** living creature say, "Come!"
8: 8 The **second** angel sounded his trumpet, and something like a huge
11:14 The **second** woe has passed; the third woe is coming soon.
14: 8 A **second** angel followed and said, "Fallen! Fallen is Babylon the
16: 3 The **second** angel poured out his bowl on the sea, and it turned into
20: 6 The **second** death has no power over them, but they will be priests
20:14 thrown into the lake of fire. The lake of fire is the **second** death.
21: 8 will be in the fiery lake of burning sulfur. This is the **second** death."
21:19 the **second** sapphire, the third chalcedony, the fourth emerald,

1312 δέχομαι, *dechomai* [56] [→ *99, 346, 450, 587, 621, 622, 627, 628, 1283, 1342, 1345, 1507, 1508, 1509, 1510, 1511, 1531, 1654, 1683, 1693, 1896, 2110, 2347, 2839, 3827, 4104, 4105, 4106, 4107, 4138, 4657, 5685*]

welcomes [9], welcome [7], welcomed [7], receive [6], receives [6], received [5], accept [3], accepted [3], take [3], obtained [1], receiving [1], refused [+*4024*] [1], remain [1], taking [1], took [1], welcomed [+*1645*+*3552*] [1]

Mt 10:14 If anyone *will* not **welcome** you or listen to your words,

10:40 "He who **receives** you receives me, and he who receives me
10:40 "He who receives you **receives** me, and he who receives me
10:40 and he who **receives** me receives the one who sent me.
10:40 and he who receives me **receives** the one who sent me.
10:41 Anyone who **receives** a prophet because he is a prophet will
10:41 and anyone who **receives** a righteous man because he is a
11:14 And if you are willing *to* **accept** it, he is the Elijah who was to
18: 5 "And whoever **welcomes** a little child like this in my name
18: 5 welcomes a little child like this in my name **welcomes** me.
Mk   6:11 And if any place *will* not **welcome** you or listen to you,
9:37 "Whoever **welcomes** one of these little children in my name
9:37 welcomes one of these little children in my name **welcomes** me;
9:37 and whoever **welcomes** me does not welcome me but the one who
9:37 and whoever welcomes mc *does* not **welcome** me but the one who
10:15 anyone *who will* not **receive** the kingdom of God like a little child
Lk   2:28 Simeon **took** him in his arms and praised God, saying:
8:13 Those on the rock are the ones *who* **receive** the word with joy
9: 5 If people *do* not **welcome** you, shake the dust off your feet when
9:48 "Whoever **welcomes** this little child in my name welcomes me;
9:48 "Whoever welcomes this little child in my name **welcomes** me;
9:48 and whoever **welcomes** me welcomes the one who sent me.
9:48 and whoever welcomes me **welcomes** the one who sent me.
9:53 but the *people* there *did* not **welcome** him, because he was heading
10: 8 "When you enter a town and *are* **welcomed**, eat what is set before
10:10 But when you enter a town and *are* not **welcomed**, go into its
16: 4 I lose my job here, *people will* **welcome** me into their houses.'
16: 6 "The manager told him, '**Take** your bill, sit down quickly,
16: 7 "He told him, '**Take** your bill and make it eight hundred.'
16: 9 that when it is gone, you *will be* **welcomed** into eternal dwellings.
18:17 anyone *who will* not **receive** the kingdom of God like a little child
22:17 *After* **taking** the cup, he gave thanks and said, "Take this
Jn   4:45 When he arrived in Galilee, the Galileans **welcomed** him.
Ac   3:21 He must **remain** in heaven until the time comes for God to restore
7:38 and with our fathers; and he **received** living words to pass on to us.
7:59 were stoning him, Stephen prayed, "Lord Jesus, **receive** my spirit."
8:14 When the apostles in Jerusalem heard that Samaria *had* **accepted**
11: 1 Judea heard that the Gentiles also *had* **received** the word of God.
17:11 for they **received** the message with great eagerness and examined
22: 5 *I* even **obtained** letters from them to their brothers in Damascus,
28:21 "We *have* not **received** any letters from Judea concerning you,
1Co 2:14 The man without the Spirit *does* not **accept** the things that come
2Co 6: 1 As God's fellow workers we urge you not *to* **receive** God's grace
7:15 that you were all obedient, **receiving** him with fear and trembling.
8:17 For Titus not only **welcomed** our appeal, but he is coming to you
11: 4 or a different gospel from the one *you* **accepted**, you put up with it
11:16 But if you do, then **receive** me just as you would a fool, so that I
Gal 4:14 Instead, *you* **welcomed** me as if I were an angel of God, as if I
Eph 6:17 **Take** the helmet of salvation and the sword of the Spirit, which is
Php 4:18 now that I *have* **received** from Epaphroditus the gifts you sent.
Col 4:10 instructions about him; if he comes to you, **welcome** him.)
1Th 1: 6 *you* **welcomed** the message with the joy given by the Holy Spirit.
2:13 *you* **accepted** it not as the word of men, but as it actually is,
2Th 2:10 They perish because *they* **refused** [+4024] to love the truth and
Heb 11:31 prostitute Rahab, *because she* **welcomed** [+1645+3552] the spies,
Jas 1:21 that is so prevalent and humbly **accept** the word planted in you,

Mk   3:27 and carry off his possessions unless *he* first **ties up** the strong man.
5: 3 and no one could **bind** him any more, not even with a chain.
5: 4 For he *had* often *been* **chained hand** [+268] and foot, but he tore
6:17 to have John arrested, and *he* had him **bound** and put in prison.
11: 2 and just as you enter it, you will find a colt **tied** there, which no
11: 4 They went and found a colt outside in the street, **tied** at a doorway.
15: 1 They **bound** Jesus, led him away and handed him over to Pilate.
15: 7 A man called Barabbas was **in prison** with the insurrectionists who
Lk 13:16 of Abraham, whom Satan *has kept* **bound** for eighteen long years,
19:30 and as you enter it, you will find a colt **tied** there, which no one has
Jn 11:44 man came out, his hands and feet **wrapped** with strips of linen,
18:12 and the Jewish officials arrested Jesus. *They* **bound** him
18:24 Then Annas sent him, *still* **bound**, to Caiaphas the high priest.
19:40 the two of *them* **wrapped** it, with the spices, in strips of linen.
Ac   9: 2 or women, he might take them as **prisoners** to Jerusalem.
9:14 from the chief priests *to* **arrest** all who call on your name."
9:21 And hasn't he come here to take them *as* **prisoners** to the chief
12: 6 **bound** with two chains, and sentries stood guard at the entrance.
20:22 "And now, **compelled** by the Spirit, I am going to Jerusalem,
21:11 he took Paul's belt, **tied** his own hands and feet *with* it and said,
21:11 'In this way the Jews of Jerusalem *will* **bind** the owner of this belt
21:13 I am ready not only *to be* **bound**, but also to die in Jerusalem for
21:33 and arrested him and ordered him *to be* **bound** with two chains.
22: 5 and went there to bring these people as **prisoners** [+1639] to
22:29 realized that *he had* **put** Paul, a Roman citizen, **in chains** [+1639].
24:27 Felix wanted to grant a favor to the Jews, he left Paul **in prison**.
Ro   7: 2 by law a married woman *is* **bound** to her husband as long as he is
1Co 7:27 *Are you* **married** [+1222]? Do not seek a divorce. Are you
7:39 A woman *is* **bound** to her husband as long as he lives. But if her
Col 4: 3 we may proclaim the mystery of Christ, for which *I am* **in chains**.
2Ti 2: 9 of being **chained** like a criminal. But God's word *is* not **chained**.
Rev 9:14 "Release the four angels who *are* **bound** at the great river
20: 2 who is the devil, or Satan, and **bound** him for a thousand years.

1314 δή, dē [5] [→ *1325, 1326, 1327, 2076, 2077, 3889*]

untranslated [4], therefore [1]

Mt 13:23 He **[NIE]** produces a crop, yielding a hundred, sixty or thirty
Lk   2:15 "Let's go **[NIE]** to Bethlehem and see this thing that has happened,
Ac 13: 2 **[NIE]** "Set apart for me Barnabas and Saul for the work to which I
15:36 **[NIE]** "Let us go back and visit the brothers in all the towns where
1Co 6:20 you were bought at a price. **Therefore** honor God with your body.

1315 δηλαυγῶς, dēlaugōs Not used in UBS/NIV [√ *879*]

1316 δῆλος, dēlos [3] [→ *83, 84, 85, 1317, 1684, 2867, 4593*]

clear [1], clearly [1], gives away [+4472] [1]

Mt 26:73 you are one of them, for your accent **gives** you **away** [+4472]."
1Co 15:27 it is **clear** that this does not include God himself, who put
Gal 3:11 **Clearly** no one is justified before God by the law, because,

1317 δηλόω, dēloō [7] [√ *1316*]

bring to light [1], indicate [1], informed [1], made clear [1], pointing [1], showing [1], told of [1]

1Co 1:11 some from Chloe's household *have* **informed** me that there are
3:13 will be shown for what it is, because the Day *will* **bring** it **to light**.
Col 1: 8 and who also **told us of** your love in the Spirit.
Heb 9: 8 The Holy Spirit *was* **showing** by this that the way into the Most
12:27 The words "once more" **indicate** the removing of what can be
1Pe 1:11 in them *was* **pointing** when he predicted the sufferings of Christ
2Pe 1:14 soon put it aside, as our Lord Jesus Christ *has* **made clear** to me.

1318 Δημᾶς, Dēmas [3] [√ *1322 (or) 1320*]

Demas [3]

Col 4:14 Our dear friend Luke, the doctor, and **Demas** send greetings.
2Ti 4:10 for **Demas**, because he loved this world, has deserted me and has
Phm 1:24 And so do Mark, Aristarchus, **Demas** and Luke, my fellow

1313 δέω, deō [43] [→ *1256, 1297, 1298, 1299, 1300, 1301, 1302, 1303, 1304, 1343, 2866, 4317, 5278, 5279, 5686, 5687; cf. 1305*]

bound [16], tied [5], bind [4], in prison [2], prisoners [2], tie [2], ties up [2], wrapped [2], arrest [1], chained [1], chained hand [+268] [1], compelled [1], in chains [1], married [+1222] [1], prisoners [+1639] [1], put in chains [+1639] [1]

Mt 12:29 and carry off his possessions unless *he* first **ties up** the strong
13:30 First collect the weeds and **tie** them in bundles to be burned;
14: 3 and **bound** him and put him in prison because of Herodias,
16:19 whatever *you* **bind** on earth will be bound in heaven, and whatever
16:19 whatever you bind on earth will be **bound** in heaven, and whatever
18:18 you the truth, whatever *you* **bind** on earth will be bound in heaven,
18:18 you the truth, whatever you bind on earth will be **bound** in heaven,
21: 2 and at once you will find a donkey **tied** there, with her colt by her.
22:13 'Tie him hand and foot, and throw him outside, into the darkness,
27: 2 They **bound** him, led him away and handed him over to Pilate,

1319 δημηγορέω, dēmēgoreō [1] [√ 1322 + 60]

delivered a public address [1]

Ac 12:21 sat on his throne and **delivered a public address** to the people.

1320 Δημήτριος, Dēmētrios [3] [→ 1318?]

Demetrius [3]

Ac 19:24 A silversmith named **Demetrius**, who made silver shrines of
19:38 **Demetrius** and his fellow craftsmen have a grievance against
3Jn 1:12 **Demetrius** is well spoken of by everyone—and even by the truth

1321 δημιουργός, dēmiourgos [1] [√ 1322 + 2240]

builder [1]

Heb 11:10 to the city with foundations, whose architect and **builder** is God.

1322 δῆμος, dēmos [4] [→ 623, 624, 1318?, 1319, 1321, 1323, 1685, 1897, 2111, 3773, 4215, 5292]

crowd [2], people [1], they^s [+3836] [1]

Ac 12:22 They^s [+3836] shouted, "This is the voice of a god, not of a man."
17: 5 in search of Paul and Silas in order to bring them out to the **crowd**.
19:30 Paul wanted to appear before the **crowd**, but the disciples would
19:33 motioned for silence in order to make a defense *before* the **people**.

1323 δημόσιος, dēmosios [4] [√ 1322]

public [2], publicly [2]

Ac 5:18 They arrested the apostles and put them in the **public** jail.
16:37 "They beat us **publicly** without a trial, even though we are Roman
18:28 For he vigorously refuted the Jews *in* **public** *debate*, proving from
20:20 to you but have taught you **publicly** and from house to house.

1324 δηνάριον, dēnarion [16]

denarius [7], a day's wages [2], denarii [2], a year's wages [+5559] [1], eight months of a man's wages [+1357] [1], eight months wages [+1357] [1], silver coins [1], the money worth a year's wages [+5559] [1]

Mt 18:28 found one of his fellow servants who owed him a hundred **denarii**.
20: 2 He agreed to pay them a **denarius** for the day and sent them into
20: 9 hired about the eleventh hour came and each received a **denarius**.
20:10 to receive more. But each one of them also received a **denarius**.
20:13 not being unfair to you. Didn't you agree to work for a **denarius**?
22:19 me the coin used for paying the tax." They brought him a **denarius**,
Mk 6:37 "That would take **eight months of a man's wages** [+1357]!
12:15 to trap me?" he asked. "Bring me a **denarius** and let me look at it."
14: 5 It could have been sold for more than **a year's wages** [+5559]
Lk 7:41 One owed him five hundred **denarii**, and the other fifty.
10:35 The next day he took out two **silver coins** and gave them to the
20:24 "Show me a **denarius**. Whose portrait and inscription are on it?"
Jn 6: 7 Philip answered him, "**Eight months' wages** [+1357] would not
12: 5 **the money** [+5559] given to the poor? It was **worth a year's wages**."
Rev 6: 6 saying, "A quart of wheat *for* **a day's wages**, and three quarts of
6: 6 and three quarts of barley *for* **a day's wages**, and do not damage

1325 δήποτε, dēpote Not used in UBS/NIV [√ 1314 + 4544]

1326 δηποτοῦν, dēpotoun Not used in UBS/NIV [√ 1314 + 4544 + 4036]

1327 δήπου, dēpou [1] [√ 1314 + 4544]

surely [1]

Heb 2:16 For **surely** it is not angels he helps, but Abraham's descendants.

1328 διά, dia [667 / 665]

[→ 88, 89, 90, 91, 442, 507, 626, 1329, 1330, 1331, 1332, 1333, 1334, 1335, 1336, 1337, 1338, 1339, 1340, 1341, 1342, 1343, 1344, 1345, 1346, 1347, 1348, 1349, 1350, 1351, 1352, 1353, 1358, 1359, 1360, 1361, 1362, 1363, 1364, 1365, 1366, 1367, 1368, 1369, 1370, 1371, 1372, 1373, 1374, 1375, 1376, 1377, 1378, 1379, 1380, 1381, 1382, 1383, 1384, 1385, 1386, 1387, 1388, 1389, 1390, 1391, 1392, 1393, 1394, 1395, 1396, 1397, 1398, 1399, 1400, 1401, 1402, 1403, 1404, 1405, 1406, 1407, 1408, 1409, 1410, 1411, 1412, 1413, 1414, 1415, 1416, 1417, 1418, 1419, 1420, 1421, 1422, 1423, 1424, 1425, 1426, 1427, 1428, 1429, 1430, 1431, 1444, 1445, 1446, 1447, 1448, 1449, 1450, 1451, 1452, 1455, 1456, 1457, 1459, 1460, 1461, 1462, 1475, 1476, 1478, 1480, 1481, 1482, 1484, 1494, 1687, 2112, 2114, 4139]

διὰ θελήματος θεοῦ (through/by the will of God) [7] Ro 15:32; 1Co 1:1; 2Co 1:1; 8:5; Eph 1:1; Col 1:1; 2Ti 1:1; cf. Rev 4:11

διὰ ['Ιησοῦ] Χριστοῦ (through/by [Jesus] Christ) [18] Jn 1:17; Ac 10:36; Ro 1:8; 2:16; 5:21; 7:25; 16:27; 2Co 1:5; 3:4; 5:18; Gal 1:1; Eph 1:5; Php 1:11; Tit 3:6; Heb 13:21; 1Pe 2:5; 4:11; Jude 1:25

διὰ του προφήτου, -τῶν (through/by the prophet[s]) [18] Mt 1:22; 2:5,15,17,23; 3:3; 4:14; 8:17; 12:17; 13:35; 21:4; 24:15; 27:9; Lk 1:70; 18:31; Ac 2:16; 28:25; Ro 1:2

διὰ τοῦτο (therefore) [65] Mt 6:25; 12:27,31; 13:13,52; 14:2; 18:23; 21:43; 23:34; 24:44; Mk 6:14; 11:24; 12:24; Lk 11:19,49; 12:22; 14:20; Jn 1:31; 5:16,18; 6:65; 7:22; 8:47; 9:23; 10:17; 12:18,27,39; 13:11; 15:19; 16:15; 19:11; Ac 2:26; Ro 1:26; 4:16; 5:12; 13:6; 15:9; 1Co 4:17; 11:10,10,30; 2Co 4:1; 7:13; 13:10; Eph 1:15; 5:17; 6:13; Col 1:9; 1Th 2:13; 3:5,7; 2Th 2:11; 1Ti 1:16; 2Ti 2:10; Phm 1:15; Heb 1:9; 2:1; 9:15; 1Jn 3:1; 4:5; 3Jn 1:10; Rev 7:15; 12:12; 18:8

διὰ χειρῶν (through/by hands) [11] Mk 6:2; Ac 2:23; 5:12; 7:25; 8:18; 11:30; 14:3; 15:23; 19:11,26, 2Ti 1:6

through [176], by [79], because of [65], *untranslated* [39], for [29], therefore [+4047] [23], why [+5515] [23], because [+3836] [21], with [14], in [13], because [12], for this reason [+4047] [9], for sake [8], for the sake of [8], from [7], that is why [+4047] [5], the reason [+4047] [5], at [4], out of [4], so [+4047] [4], this is why [+4047] [4], always [+4246] [3], because [+4047] [3], during [3], for benefit [3], go through [RP1451] [3], how is it that [+5515] [3], on [3], on account of [3], the result of [3], through [+5125] [3], afforded by [2], continually [+4246] [2], for [+3836] [2], goes through [RP1451] [2], in answer to [2], regularly [+4246] [2], since [+3836] [2], so then [+4047] [2], that was why [+4047] [2], who [+4005] [2], why [+162+4005] [2], a few days later [+2465] [1], after [1], as the result of [1], briefly [+3900] [1], bring about [1], by [+5931] [1], by all this [+4047] [1], by comparing with [1], by means of [1], by the authority of [1], causes [1], compared to [1], due to [1], enabling [+1443+3836+5931] [1], for sakes [1], for that very reason [+4047] [1], for the benefit of [1], for this very reason [+4047] [1], forever [+4246] [1], give [1], go through [1], going through [RP1388] [1], he [+899+3836+5931] [1], in keeping with [1], in the presence of [1], in view of [1], man-made [+1181+5931] [1], night [+3816+4246] [1], of [1], on account [1], on the basis of [1], on the evidence of [1], over a period [1], passed through [RP1451] [1], patiently [+5705] [1], performed [+1181+3836+5931] [1], reaching more and more [+3836+4429+4498] [1], saved through [RP1407] [1], short [+1099] [1], since [1], so [+4005] [1], so [+162+4005] [1], terrified [+5832] [1], that is why [+162+4005] [1], therefore [+162+4005] [1], they [+899] [1], this is why [+899] [1], through [+3836+5931] [1], to bottom [+3910] [1], traveled about [RP1451] [1], traveled along [RP1451] [1], under [1], use [1], using [+5931] [1], visit on the way [1], visit on way [RP1451] [1], walked right through [+1451+3545] [1], when [1], why [+162+3836+4005] [1], with [+5931] [1], with the help of [1]

Mt 1:22 All this took place to fulfill what the Lord had said **through** the
2: 5 they replied, "for this is what **[NIE]** the prophet has written:

2:12 go back to Herod, they returned to their country **by** another route.
2:15 so was fulfilled what the Lord had said **through** the prophet:
2:17 Then what was said **through** the prophet Jeremiah was fulfilled:
2:23 So was fulfilled what was said **through** the prophets: "He will be
3: 3 This is he who was spoken of **through** the prophet Isaiah:
4: 4 but on every word that comes **from** the mouth of God.' "
4:14 to fulfill what was said **through** the prophet Isaiah:
6:25 "**Therefore** [+4047] I tell you, do not worry about your life,
7:13 "Enter **through** the narrow gate. For wide is the gate and broad is
7:13 is the road that leads to destruction, and many enter **through** it.
8:17 This was to fulfill what was spoken **through** the prophet Isaiah:
8:28 They were so violent that no one could pass **[NIE]** that way.
9:11 they asked his disciples, "**Why** [+5515] does your teacher eat with
9:14 and asked him, "**How is it that** [+5515] we and the Pharisees fast,
10:22 All men will hate you **because of** me, but he who stands firm to the
11: 2 in prison what Christ was doing, he sent **[NIE]** his disciples
12: 1 At that time Jesus went **through** the grainfields on the Sabbath.
12:17 This was to fulfill what was spoken **through** the prophet Isaiah:
12:27 people drive them out? **So then** [+4047], they will be your judges.
12:31 And **so** [+4047] I tell you, every sin and blasphemy will be
12:43 it **goes through** [RP1451] arid places seeking rest and does not
13: 5 It sprang up quickly, **because** [+3836] the soil was shallow.
13: 6 and they withered **because** [+3836] they had no root.
13:10 and asked, "**Why** [+5515] do you speak to the people in parables?"
13:13 **This is why** [+4047] I speak to them in parables: "Though seeing,
13:21 When trouble or persecution comes **because of** the word,
13:35 So was fulfilled what was spoken **through** the prophet: "I will open
13:52 "**Therefore** [+4047] every teacher of the law who has been
13:58 he did not do many miracles there **because of** their lack of faith.
14: 2 **That is why** [+4047] miraculous powers are at work in him."
14: 3 and bound him and put him in prison **because of** Herodias,
14: 9 king was distressed, but **because of** his oaths and his dinner guests,
15: 2 "**Why** [+5515] do your disciples break the tradition of the elders?"
15: 3 "And **why** [+5515] do you break the command of God for the sake
15: 3 "And why do you break the command of God **for the sake of** your
15: 6 Thus you nullify the word of God **for the sake of** your tradition.
17:19 in private and asked, "**Why** [+5515] couldn't we drive it out?"
17:20 He replied, "**Because** you have so little faith. I tell you the truth,
18: 7 things must come, but woe to the man **through** whom they come!
18:10 For I tell you that their angels in heaven **always** [+4246] see the
18:23 "**Therefore** [+4047], the kingdom of heaven is like a king who
19:12 have renounced marriage **because of** the kingdom of heaven.
19:24 it is easier for a camel *to* **go through** [RP1451] the eye of a needle
21: 4 This took place to fulfill what was spoken **through** the prophet:
21:25 he will ask, 'Then **why** [+5515] didn't you believe him?'
21:43 "**Therefore** [+4047] I tell you that the kingdom of God will be
23:34 **Therefore** [+4047] I am sending you prophets and wise men
24: 9 put to death, and you will be hated by all nations **because of** me.
24:12 **Because of** the increase of wickedness, the love of most will grow
24:15 that causes desolation,' spoken of **through** the prophet Daniel—
24:22 but **for the sake of** the elect those days will be shortened.
24:44 **So** [+4047] you also must be ready, because the Son of Man will
26:24 But woe to that man **who** [+4005] betrays the Son of Man!
26:61 am able to destroy the temple of God and rebuild it **in** three days.' "
27: 9 Then what was spoken **by** Jeremiah the prophet was fulfilled:
27:18 For he knew it was **out of** envy that they had handed Jesus over to
27:19 for I have suffered a great deal today in a dream **because of** him."

Mk 2: 1 **A few days later** [+2465], when Jesus again entered Capernaum,
2: 4 Since they could not get him to Jesus **because of** the crowd,
2:18 and asked Jesus, "**How is it that** [+5515] John's disciples
2:23 One Sabbath Jesus was going **through** the grainfields, and as his
2:27 Then he said to them, "The Sabbath was made **for** man, not man for
2:27 "The Sabbath was made for man, not man **for** the Sabbath.
3: 9 **Because of** the crowd he told his disciples to have a small boat
4: 5 It sprang up quickly, **because** [+3836] the soil was shallow.
4: 6 and they withered **because** [+3836] they had no root.
4:17 When trouble or persecution comes **because of** the word,
5: 4 **For** he had often been chained hand and foot, but he tore the
5: 5 **Night** [+3816+4246] and day among the tombs and in the hills he
6: 2 been given him, that **he** [+899+3836+5931] even does miracles!
6: 6 And he was amazed at their lack of faith. Then Jesus went around
6:14 and **that is why** [+4047] miraculous powers are at work in him."
6:17 He did this **because of** Herodias, his brother Philip's wife,
6:26 but **because of** his oaths and his dinner guests, he did not want to
7: 5 and teachers of the law asked Jesus, "**Why** [+5515] don't your
7:29 Then he told her, "**For** such a reply, you may go; the demon has

7:31 Then Jesus left the vicinity of Tyre and went **through** Sidon,
9:30 They left that place and passed **through** Galilee. Jesus did not
10:25 It is easier for a camel *to* **go through** [RP1451] the eye of a needle
11:16 and would not allow anyone to carry merchandise **through** the
11:24 **Therefore** [+4047] I tell you, whatever you ask for in prayer,
11:31 he will ask, 'Then **why** [+5515] didn't you believe him?'
12:24 you not in error **because** [+4047] you do not know the Scriptures
13:13 All men will hate you **because of** me, but he who stands firm to the
13:20 But **for the sake of** the elect, whom he has chosen, he has
14:21 But woe to that man **[NIE]** who betrays the Son of Man!
14:58 destroy this man-made temple and **in** three days will build another,
15:10 knowing it was **out of** envy that the chief priests had handed Jesus
16:20 and confirmed his word **by** the signs that accompanied it.
16: S [UBS+ *And after these things Jesus himself sent out* **through** *them*]

Lk 1:70 (as he said **through** [+5125] his holy prophets of long ago),
1:78 **because of** the tender mercy of our God, by which the rising sun
2: 4 **because** [+3836] he belonged to the house and line of David.
4:30 But he **walked right through** [+1451+3545] the crowd and went
5: 5 we've worked hard **[NIE]** all night and haven't caught anything.
5:19 When they could not find a way to do this **because of** the crowd,
5:19 and lowered him on his mat **through** the tiles into the middle of
5:30 belonged to their sect complained to his disciples, "**Why** [+5515]
6: 1 One Sabbath Jesus *was* **going through** [RP1388] the grainfields,
6:48 but could not shake it, **because** [+3836] it was well built.
8: 4 coming to Jesus from town after town, he told this **[NIE]** parable:
8: 6 the plants withered **because** [+3836] they had no moisture.
8:19 but they were not able to get near him **because of** the crowd,
8:47 she told why [+162+4005] she had touched him and how she had
9: 7 **because** [+3836] some were saying that John had been raised from
11: 8 get up and give him the bread **because** [+3836] he is his friend,
11: 8 yet **because of** the man's boldness he will get up and give him as
11:19 drive them out? **So** [+4047] **then**, they will be your judges.
11:24 it **goes through** [RP1451] arid places seeking rest and does not
11:49 **Because of** this, God in his wisdom said, 'I will send them
12:22 "**Therefore** [+4047] I tell you, do not worry about your life,
13:24 "Make every effort to enter **through** the narrow door,
14:20 "Still another said, 'I just got married, **so** [+4047] I can't come.'
17: 1 bound to come, but woe to that person **through** whom they come.
17:11 Jesus **traveled along** [RP1451] the border between Samaria
18: 5 yet **because** [+3836] this widow keeps bothering me, I will see that
18:25 it is easier for a camel to **go through** [RP1451] the eye of a needle than for a
18:31 and everything that is written **by** the prophets about the Son of
19:11 **because** [+3836] he was near Jerusalem and the people thought
19:23 **Why** [+5515] then didn't you put my money on deposit,
19:31 If anyone asks you, '**Why** [+5515] are you untying it?' tell him,
20: 5 he will ask, '**Why** [+5515] didn't you believe him?'
21:17 All men will hate you **because of** me.
22:22 it has been decreed, but woe to that man **who** [+4005] betrays him."
23: 8 **From** what he had heard about him, he hoped to see him perform
23:19 (Barabbas had been thrown into prison **for** an insurrection in the
23:25 He released the man who had been thrown into prison **for**
24:38 are you troubled, and **why** [+5515] do doubts rise in your minds?
24:53 And they stayed **continually** [+4246] at the temple, praising God.

Jn 1: 3 **Through** him all things were made; without him nothing was
1: 7 concerning that light, so that **through** him all men might believe.
1:10 was in the world, and though the world was made **through** him,
1:17 For the law was given **through** Moses; grace and truth came
1:17 given through Moses; grace and truth came **through** Jesus Christ.
1:31 but **the reason** [+4047] I came baptizing with water was that he
2:24 would not entrust himself to them, **for** [+3836] he knew all men.
3:17 world to condemn the world, but to save the world **through** him.
3:29 and is full of joy when he hears **[NIE]** the bridegroom's voice.
4: 4 Now he had to **go through** [RP1451] Samaria.
4:39 from that town believed in him **because of** the woman's testimony.
4:41 And **because** of his words many more became believers.
4:42 the woman, "We no longer believe just **because of** what you said;
5:16 **because** [+4047] Jesus was doing these things on the Sabbath.
5:18 **For** [+4047] **this reason** the Jews tried all the harder to kill him;
6:57 Just as the living Father sent me and I live **because of** the Father,
6:57 of the Father, so the one who feeds on me will live **because of** me.
6:65 "**This is why** [+4047] I told you that no one can come to me unless
7:13 But no one would say anything publicly about him **for** fear of the
7:22 **because** [+4047] Moses gave you circumcision (though actually it
7:43 Thus the people were divided **because of** Jesus.
7:45 who asked them, "**Why** [+5515] didn't you bring him in?"
8:43 **Why** [+5515] is my language not clear to you? Because you are

8:46 If I am telling the truth, **why** [+5515] don't you believe me?
8:47 **The reason** [+4047] you do not hear is that you do not belong to
9:23 **That was why** [+4047] his parents said, "He is of age; ask him."
10: 1 the truth, the man who does not enter the sheep pen **by** the gate,
10: 2 The man who enters **by** the gate is the shepherd of his sheep.
10: 9 I am the gate; whoever enters **through** me will be saved. He will
10:17 **The reason** [+4047] my Father loves me is that I lay down my
10:19 **At** these words the Jews were again divided.
10:32 miracles from the Father. **For** which of these do you stone me?"
11: 4 for God's glory so that God's Son may be glorified **through** it."
11:15 and **for** your **sake** I am glad I was not there, so that you may
11:42 but I said this **for the benefit of** the people standing here,
12: 5 "**Why** [+5515] wasn't this perfume sold and the money given to
12: 9 and came, not only **because of** him but also to see Lazarus,
12:11 for **on account of** him many of the Jews were going over to Jesus
12:18 [NIE] Many people, because they had heard that he had given this
12:27 No, it was **for** [+4047] **this very reason** I came to this hour.
12:30 Jesus said, "This voice was **for** your **benefit**, not mine.
12:30 Jesus said, "This voice was for your benefit, not [RPG] mine.
12:39 **For** [+4047] **this reason** they could not believe, because, as Isaiah
12:42 **because of** the Pharisees they would not confess their faith for fear
13:11 and **that was why** [+4047] he said not every one was clean.
13:37 Peter asked, "Lord, **why** [+5515] can't I follow you now? I will lay
14: 6 and the life. No one comes to the Father except **through** me.
14:11 or at least believe **on the evidence of** the miracles themselves.
15: 3 You are already clean **because of** the word I have spoken to you.
15:19 you out of the world. **That is why** [+4047] the world hates you.
15:21 They will treat you this way **because of** my name, for they do not
16:15 **That is why** [+4047] I said the Spirit will take from what is mine
16:21 the anguish **because of** her joy that a child is born into the world.
17:20 I pray also for those who will believe in me **through** their
19:11 **Therefore** [+4047] the one who handed me over to you is guilty of
19:23 was seamless, woven in one piece from top **to** [+3910] **bottom**.
19:38 was a disciple of Jesus, but secretly **because** he feared the Jews.
19:42 **Because** it was the Jewish day of Preparation and since the tomb
20:19 with the doors locked **for** fear of the Jews, Jesus came and stood

Ac 1: 2 after giving instructions **through** the Holy Spirit to the apostles he
1: 3 He appeared to them **over a period** of forty days and spoke about
1:16 spoke long ago **through** the mouth of David concerning Judas,
2:16 No, this is what was spoken **by** the prophet Joel:
2:22 wonders and signs, which God did among you **through** him,
2:23 and you, **with** the help of wicked men, put him to death by nailing
2:25 David said about him: " 'I saw the Lord **always** [+4246] before me.
2:26 **Therefore** [+4047] my heart is glad and my tongue rejoices;
2:43 many wonders and miraculous signs were done **by** the apostles.
3:16 and the faith that *comes* **through** him that has given this complete
3:18 fulfilled what he had foretold **through** [+5125] all the prophets,
3:21 as he promised long ago **through** [+5125] his holy prophets.
4: 2 **because** [+3836] the apostles were teaching the people
4:16 "Everybody living in Jerusalem knows **they** [+899] have done an
4:21 **because** all the people were praising God for what had happened.
4:25 You spoke **by** the Holy Spirit through the mouth of your servant,
4:30 and wonders **through** the name of your holy servant Jesus."
5: 3 "Ananias, **how is it that** [+5515] Satan has so filled your heart that
5:12 The apostles **performed** [+1181+3836+5931] many miraculous
     signs and wonders among the people.
5:19 But **during** the night an angel of the Lord opened the doors of the
7:25 would realize that God was **using** [+5931] him to rescue them,
8:11 **because** [+3836] he had amazed them for a long time with his
8:18 When Simon saw that the Spirit was given **at** the laying on of the
8:20 because you thought you could buy the gift of God **with** money!
9:25 and lowered him in a basket **through** *an opening* in the wall.
9:32 *As* Peter **traveled about** [RP1451] the country, he went to visit the
10: 2 generously to those in need and prayed to God **regularly** [+4246].
10:21 "I'm the one you're looking for. Why [NIE] have you come?"
10:36 telling the good news of peace **through** Jesus Christ, who is Lord
10:43 believes in him receives forgiveness of sins **through** his name."
11:28 and **through** the Spirit predicted that a severe famine would spread
11:30 sending their gift to the elders **by** [+5931] Barnabas and Saul.
12: 9 but he had no idea that what [NIE] the angel was doing was really
12:20 **because** they depended on the king's country for their food supply.
13:38 I want you to know that **through** Jesus the forgiveness of sins is
13:49 The word of the Lord spread **through** the whole region.
14: 3 **by** enabling [+1443+3836+5931] them to do miraculous signs and
14:22 must **go through** many hardships to enter the kingdom of God,"
15: 7 the Gentiles might hear **from** my lips the message of the gospel

15:11 We believe it is **through** the grace of our Lord Jesus that we are
15:12 and wonders God had done among the Gentiles **through** them.
15:23 **With** [+5931] them they sent the following letter: The apostles
15:27 and Silas to confirm **by** word of mouth what we are writing.
15:32 [NIE] said much to encourage and strengthen the brothers.
16: 3 so he circumcised him **because of** the Jews who lived in that area,
16: 9 **During** the night Paul had a vision of a man of Macedonia
17:10 As soon as it was [NIE] night, the brothers sent Paul and Silas
18: 2 **because** [+3836] Claudius had ordered all the Jews to leave Rome.
18: 3 and **because** [+3836] he was a tentmaker as they were, he stayed
18: 9 One night the Lord spoke to Paul **in** a vision: "Do not be afraid;
18:27 he was a great help to those who **by** grace had believed.
18:28 proving **from** the Scriptures that Jesus was the Christ.
19:11 God did extraordinary miracles **through** [+3836+5931] Paul,
19:26 He says that **man-made** [+1181+5931] gods are no gods at all.
20: 3 about to sail for Syria, he decided to go back **through** Macedonia.
20:28 of the church of God, which he bought **with** his own blood.
21: 4 **Through** the Spirit they urged Paul not to go on to Jerusalem.
21:19 what God had done among the Gentiles **through** his ministry.
21:34 the commander could not get at the truth **because of** the uproar,
21:35 [NIE] the violence of the mob was so great he had to be carried
22:24 and questioned in order to find out **why** [+162+4005] the people
23:28 I wanted to know **why** [+162+3836+4005] they were accusing
23:31 took Paul with them **during** the night and brought him as far as
24: 2 "We have enjoyed a long period of peace **under** you, and your
24: 2 and [NIE] your foresight has brought about reforms in this nation.
24:16 So I strive **always** [+4246] to keep my conscience clear before God
24:17 "**After** an absence of several years, I came to Jerusalem to bring
27: 4 to the lee of Cyprus **because** [+3836] the winds were against us.
27: 9 become dangerous **because** [+3836] by now it was after the Fast.
28: 2 built a fire and welcomed us all **because** it was raining and cold.
28: 2 and welcomed us all because it was raining and [RPG] cold.
28:18 **because** [+3836] I was not guilty of any crime deserving death.
28:20 **For** this reason I have asked to see you and talk with you.
28:25 truth to your forefathers when he said **through** Isaiah the prophet:

Ro 1: 2 the gospel he promised beforehand **through** his prophets in
1: 5 **Through** him and for his name's sake, we received grace
1: 8 First, I thank my God **through** Jesus Christ for all of you,
1:12 and I may be mutually encouraged by each other's [NIE] faith.
1:26 **Because** of this, God gave them over to shameful lusts. Even their
2:12 the law, and all who sin under the law will be judged **by** the law.
2:16 the day when God will judge men's secrets **through** Jesus Christ,
2:23 who brag about the law, **do** you dishonor God **by** breaking the law?
2:24 "God's name is blasphemed among the Gentiles **because of** you."
2:27 even though you have [NIE] the written code and circumcision,
3:20 the law; rather, **through** the law we become conscious of sin.
3:22 This righteousness from God *comes* **through** faith in Jesus Christ
3:24 and are justified freely by his grace **through** the redemption that
3:25 him as a sacrifice of atonement, **through** faith in his blood.
3:25 **because** in his forbearance he had left the sins committed
3:27 Where, then, is boasting? It is excluded. **On** what principle?
3:27 On that of observing the law? No, but **on** that of faith.
3:30 by faith and the uncircumcised **through** that same faith.
3:31 Do we, then, nullify the law **by** this faith? Not at all! Rather,
4:11 father of all who believe but have [NIE] not been circumcised,
4:13 It was not **through** law that Abraham and his offspring received
4:13 of the world, but **through** the righteousness that comes by faith.
4:16 **Therefore** [+4047], the promise comes by faith, so that it may be
4:23 The words "it was credited to him" were written not **for** him alone,
4:24 but also **for** us, to whom God will credit righteousness—for us who
4:25 He was delivered over to death **for** our sins and was raised to life
4:25 to death for our sins and was raised to life **for** our justification.
5: 1 we have peace with God **through** our Lord Jesus Christ,
5: 2 **through** whom we have gained access by faith into this grace in
5: 5 because God has poured out his love into our hearts **by** the Holy
5: 9 how much more shall we be saved from God's wrath **through** him!
5:10 we were reconciled to him **through** the death of his Son,
5:11 but we also rejoice in God **through** our Lord Jesus Christ,
5:11 Jesus Christ, **through** whom we have now received reconciliation.
5:12 **Therefore** [+4047], just as sin entered the world through one man,
5:12 Therefore, just as sin entered the world **through** one man,
5:12 and death **through** sin, and in this way death came to all men,
5:16 the gift of God is not like **the result of** the one man's sin:
5:17 the trespass of the one man, death reigned **through** that one man,
5:17 and of the gift of righteousness reign in life **through** the one man,
5:18 just as **the result of** one trespass was condemnation for all men,

5: 18 so also **the result of** one act of righteousness was justification that
5: 19 For just as **through** the disobedience of the one man the many
5: 19 so also **through** the obedience of the one man the many will be
5: 21 so also grace might reign **through** righteousness to bring eternal
5: 21 righteousness to bring eternal life **through** Jesus Christ our Lord.
6: 4 therefore buried with him **through** baptism into death in order that,
6: 4 just as Christ was raised from the dead **through** the glory of the
6: 19 this in human terms **because** you are weak in your natural selves.
7: 4 my brothers, you also died to the law **through** the body of Christ,
7: 5 the sinful passions *aroused* **by** the law were at work in our bodies,
7: 7 Indeed I would not have known what sin was except **through** the
7: 8 But sin, seizing the opportunity **afforded by** the commandment,
7: 11 For sin, seizing the opportunity **afforded by** the commandment,
7: 11 deceived me, and **through** the commandment put me to death.
7: 13 recognized as sin, it produced death in me **through** what was good,
7: 13 so that **through** the commandment sin might become utterly sinful.
7: 25 Thanks be to God—**through** Jesus Christ our Lord! So then,
8: 3 For what the law was powerless to do in that it was weakened **by**
8: 10 your body is dead **because of** sin, yet your spirit is alive because of
8: 10 because of sin, yet your spirit is alive **because of** righteousness.
8: 11 dead will also give life to your mortal bodies **through** his Spirit,
8: 20 its own choice, but **by** the will of the one who subjected it, in hope
8: 25 hope for what we do not yet have, we wait for it **patiently** [+5705].
8: 37 in all these things we are more than conquerors **through** him who
9: 32 **Why** [+5515] not? Because they pursued it not by faith but as if it
10: 17 the message, and the message is heard **through** the word of Christ.
11: 10 so they cannot see, and their backs be bent **forever** [+4246]."
11: 28 far as the gospel is concerned, they are enemies **on** your **account;**
11: 28 election is concerned, they are loved **on account of** the patriarchs,
11: 36 For from him and **through** him and to him are all things. To him
12: 1 Therefore, I urge you, brothers, **in view of** God's mercy, to offer
12: 3 For **by** the grace given me I say to every one of you: Do not think
13: 5 not only **because of** possible punishment but also because of
13: 5 because of possible punishment but also **because of** conscience.
13: 6 **This is** also **why** [+4047] you pay taxes, for the authorities are
14: 14 Lord Jesus, I am fully convinced that no food is unclean **in** itself.
14: 15 If your brother is distressed **because of** what you eat, you are no
14: 20 but it is wrong for a man to eat anything that **causes** someone else
15: 4 so that **through** endurance and the encouragement of the
15: 4 and **[RPG]** the encouragement of the Scriptures we might have
15: 9 "**Therefore** [+4047] I will praise you among the Gentiles;
15: 15 if to remind you of them again, **because of** the grace God gave me
15: 18 **through** me in leading the Gentiles to obey God by what I have
15: 28 received this fruit, I will go to Spain and **visit** you **on the way.**
15: 30 brothers, **by** our Lord Jesus Christ and by the love of the Spirit,
15: 30 brothers, by our Lord Jesus Christ and **by** the love of the Spirit,
15: 32 so that **by** God's will I may come to you with joy and together with
16: 18 **By** smooth talk and flattery they deceive the minds of naive
16: 26 and made known **through** the prophetic writings by the command
16: 27 to the only wise God be glory forever **through** Jesus Christ!
1Co 1: 1 Paul, called to be an apostle of Christ Jesus **by** the will of God,
1: 9 **[NIE]** who has called you into fellowship with his Son Jesus
1: 10 I appeal to you, brothers, **in** the name of our Lord Jesus Christ,
1: 21 For since in the wisdom of God the world **through** its wisdom did
1: 21 God was pleased **through** the foolishness of what was preached to
2: 10 but God has revealed it to us **by** his Spirit. The Spirit searches all
3: 5 Only servants, **through** whom you came to believe—as the Lord
3: 15 will be saved, but only as one *escaping* **through** the flames.
4: 6 I have applied these things to myself and Apollos for your **benefit,**
4: 10 We are fools **for** Christ, but you are so wise in Christ! We are
4: 15 for in Christ Jesus I became your father **through** the gospel.
4: 17 **For** [+4047] **this reason** I am sending to you Timothy, my son
6: 7 **Why** [+5515] not rather be wronged? Why not rather be cheated?
6: 7 Why not rather be wronged? **Why** [+5515] not rather be cheated?
6: 14 **By** his power God raised the Lord from the dead, and he will raise
7: 2 But **since** there is so much immorality, each man should have his
7: 5 that Satan will not tempt you **because of** your lack of self-control.
7: 26 **Because of** the present crisis, I think that it is good for you to
8: 6 **through** whom all things *came* and through whom we live.
8: 6 through whom all things came and **through** whom we live.
8: 11 So this weak brother, **for** whom Christ died, is destroyed by your
9: 10 Surely he says this **for** us, doesn't he? Yes, this was written for us,
9: 10 Yes, this was written **for** us, because when the plowman plows
9: 23 I do all this **for the sake of** the gospel, that I may share in its
10: 1 the cloud and that *they* all **passed through** [RP1451] the sea.
10: 25 in the meat market without raising questions **[NIE]** of conscience,

10: 27 eat whatever is put before you without raising questions **[NIE]** of
10: 28 both **for the sake of** the man who told you and for conscience'
11: 9 neither was man created **for** woman, but woman for man.
11: 9 neither was man created for woman, but woman **for** man.
11: 10 **For** [+4047] **this reason,**
11: 10 For this reason, and **because of** the angels, the woman ought to
11: 12 For as woman came from man, so also man is *born* **of** woman.
11: 30 **That is why** [+4047] many among you are weak and sick,
12: 8 To one there is given **through** the Spirit the message of wisdom,
13: 12 Now we see but a poor reflection as **in** a mirror;
14: 9 Unless you speak intelligible words **with** your tongue, how will
15: 2 **By** this gospel you are saved, if you hold firmly to the word I
15: 21 For since death *came* **through** a man, the resurrection of the dead
15: 21 a man, the resurrection of the dead *comes* also **through** a man.
15: 57 be to God! He gives us the victory **through** our Lord Jesus Christ.
16: 3 I will **give** letters of introduction to the men you approve and send
2Co 1: 1 Paul, an apostle of Christ Jesus **by** the will of God, and Timothy
1: 4 so that we can comfort those in any trouble **with** the comfort we
1: 5 over into our lives, so also **through** Christ our comfort overflows.
1: 11 for the gracious favor granted us **in answer to** the prayers of many.
1: 16 I planned *to* **visit** you *on my* **way** [RP1451] to Macedonia
1: 19 who was preached among you **[NIE]** by me and Silas
1: 19 who was preached among you **by** me and Silas and Timothy,
1: 20 so **through** him the "Amen" is spoken by us to the glory of God.
1: 20 so through him the "Amen" is *spoken* **by** us to the glory of God.
2: 4 you out of great distress and anguish of heart and **with** many tears,
2: 10 to forgive—I have forgiven in the sight of Christ **for** your **sake,**
2: 14 and **through** us spreads everywhere the fragrance of the
3: 4 Such confidence as this is ours **through** Christ before God.
3: 7 could not look steadily at the face of Moses **because of** its glory,
3: 11 And if what was fading away *came* **with** glory, how much greater
4: 1 **Therefore** [+4047], since through God's mercy we have this
4: 5 Jesus Christ as Lord, and ourselves as your servants **for** Jesus' **sake.**
4: 11 who are alive are always being given over to death **for** Jesus' **sake,**
4: 15 All this is **for** your **benefit,** so that the grace that is reaching more
4: 15 so that the grace that *is* **reaching more and more people**
  [+3836+4429+4498] may cause thanksgiving to overflow
5: 7 We live **by** faith, not by sight.
5: 7 We live by faith, not **by** sight.
5: 10 may receive what is due him for the things done *while* **in** the body,
5: 18 who reconciled us to himself **through** Christ and gave us the
5: 20 as though God were making his appeal **through** us.
6: 7 **with** weapons of righteousness in the right hand and in the left;
6: 8 **through** glory and dishonor, bad report and good report; genuine,
6: 8 through glory and dishonor, **[RPG]** bad report and good report;
7: 13 **By** [+4047] **all this** we are encouraged. In addition to our own
8: 5 first to the Lord and then to us **in keeping with** God's will.
8: 8 but I want to test the sincerity of your love **by comparing** it with
8: 9 that though he was rich, yet **for** your **sakes** he became poor,
8: 18 And we are sending along with him the brother who is praised **by**
9: 11 and **through** us your generosity will result in thanksgiving to God.
9: 12 but is also overflowing **in** many expressions of thanks to God.
9: 13 **Because of** the service by which you have proved yourselves,
9: 14 go out to you, **because of** the surpassing grace God has given you.
10: 1 **By** the meekness and gentleness of Christ, I appeal to you—
10: 9 I do not want to seem to be trying to frighten you **with** my letters.
10: 11 Such people should realize that what we are **in** our letters when we
11: 11 **Why** [+5515]? Because I do not love you? God knows I do!
11: 33 But I was lowered in a basket **from** a window in the wall
11: 33 But I was lowered in a basket **from** a window in the wall
12: 17 Did I exploit you **through** any of the men I sent you?
13: 10 **This is why** [+4047] I write these things when I am absent,
Gal 1: 1 sent not from men nor **by** man, but by Jesus Christ and God the
1: 1 not from men nor by man, but **by** Jesus Christ and God the Father,
1: 12 was I taught it; rather, I received it **by** revelation from Jesus Christ.
1: 15 who set me apart from birth and called me **by** his grace,
2: 1 **[NIE]** Fourteen years later I went up again to Jerusalem,
2: 4 **because** some false brothers had infiltrated our ranks to spy on the
2: 16 is not justified by observing the law, but **by** faith in Jesus Christ.
2: 19 For **through** the law I died to the law so that I might live for God.
2: 21 for if righteousness could be *gained* **through** the law, Christ died
3: 14 so that **by** faith we might receive the promise of the Spirit.
3: 18 but God in his grace gave it to Abraham **through** a promise.
3: 19 The law was put into effect **through** angels by a mediator.
3: 26 You are all sons of God **through** faith in Christ Jesus,
4: 7 and since you are a son, **[NIE]** God has made you also an heir.

4: 13 **because of** an illness that I first preached the gospel to you.
4: 23 but his son by the free woman was born **as the result of** a promise.
5: 6 The only thing that counts is faith expressing itself **through** love.
5: 13 to indulge the sinful nature; rather, serve one another **in** love.
6: 14 Jesus Christ, **through** which the world has been crucified to me,

Eph 1: 1 Paul, an apostle of Christ Jesus **by** the will of God, To the saints in
    1: 5 he predestined us to be adopted as his sons **through** Jesus Christ,
    1: 7 In him we have redemption **through** his blood, the forgiveness of
    1: 15 **For** [+4047] **this reason**, ever since I heard about your faith in the
    2: 4 But **because of** his great love for us, God, who is rich in mercy,
    2: 8 For it is by grace you have been saved, **through** faith—and this not
    2: 16 and in this one body to reconcile both of them to God **through** the
    2: 18 For **through** him we both have access to the Father by one Spirit.
    3: 6 This mystery is that **through** the gospel the Gentiles are heirs
    3: 10 His intent was that now, **through** the church, the manifold wisdom
    3: 12 and **through** faith in him we may approach God with freedom
    3: 16 strengthen you with power **through** his Spirit in your inner being,
    3: 17 so that Christ may dwell in your hearts **through** faith. And I pray
    4: 6 and Father of all, who is over all and **through** all and in all.
    4: 16 joined and held together **by** every supporting ligament, grows
    4: 18 **because of** the ignorance that is in them due to the hardening of
    4: 18 because of the ignorance that is in them **due to** the hardening of
    5: 6 **because of** such things God's wrath comes on those who are
    5: 17 **Therefore** [+4047] do not be foolish, but understand what the
    6: 13 **Therefore** [+4047] put on the full armor of God, so that when the
    6: 18 And pray in the Spirit on all occasions **with** all kinds of prayers

Php 1: 7 this way about all of you, **since** [+3836] I have you in my heart;
    1: 11 filled with the fruit of righteousness that *comes* **through** Jesus
    1: 15 It is true that some preach Christ **out of** envy and rivalry,
    1: 15 preach Christ out of envy and rivalry, but others **out of** goodwill.
    1: 19 for I know that **through** your prayers and the help given by the
    1: 20 Christ will be exalted in my body, whether **by** life or by death.
    1: 20 Christ will be exalted in my body, whether by life or **by** death.
    1: 24 but it is more necessary **for** you that I remain in the body.
    1: 26 so that **through** my being with you again your joy in Christ Jesus
    2: 30 because he almost died **for** the work of Christ, risking his life to
    3: 7 But whatever was to my profit I now consider loss **for the sake of**
    3: 8 I consider everything a loss **compared to** the surpassing greatness
    3: 8 Christ Jesus my Lord, **for** whose **sake** I have lost all things.
    3: 9 that comes from the law, but that which is **through** faith in Christ—

Col 1: 1 Paul, an apostle of Christ Jesus **by** the will of God, and Timothy
    1: 5 and love that *spring* **from** the hope that is stored up for you in
    1: 9 **For** [+4047] **this reason**, since the day we heard about you,
    1: 16 or authorities; all things were created **by** him and for him.
    1: 20 and **through** him to reconcile to himself all things, whether things
    1: 20 in heaven, by making peace **through** his blood, shed on the cross.
    1: 20 through his blood, shed on the cross, [UBS+ ***through*** *him*]
    1: 22 But now he has reconciled you by Christ's physical body **through**
    2: 8 See to it that no one takes you captive **through** hollow
    2: 12 and raised with him **through** your faith in the power of God,
    2: 19 supported and held together **by** its ligaments and sinews,
    3: 6 **Because of** these, the wrath of God is coming.
    3: 17 of the Lord Jesus, giving thanks to God the Father **through** him.
    4: 3 we may proclaim the mystery of Christ, **for** which I am in chains.

1Th 1: 5 You know how we lived among you **for** your sake.
    2: 13 And [NIE] we also thank God continually because, when you
    3: 5 **For** [+4047] **this reason**, when I could stand it no longer,
    3: 7 **Therefore** [+4047], brothers, in all our distress and persecution we
    3: 7 persecution we were encouraged about you **because of** your faith.
    3: 9 for all the joy we have in the presence of our God **because of** you?
    4: 2 For you know what instructions we gave you **by the authority of**
    4: 14 that God will bring with Jesus those who have fallen asleep **in** him.
    5: 9 but to receive salvation **through** our Lord Jesus Christ.
    5: 13 Hold them in the highest regard in love **because of** their work.

2Th 2: 2 not to become easily unsettled or alarmed **by** some prophecy,
    2: 2 [NIE] report or letter supposed to have come from us,
    2: 2 report or [NIE] letter supposed to have come from us,
    2: 2 by some prophecy, report or letter supposed to have *come* **from** us,
    2: 11 **For** [+4047] **this reason** God sends them a powerful delusion
    2: 14 He called you to this **through** our gospel, that you might share in
    2: 15 we passed on to you, whether **by** word of mouth or by letter.
    2: 15 we passed on to you, whether by word of mouth or **by** letter.
    3: 14 If anyone does not obey our instruction **in** this letter, take special
    3: 16 Now may the Lord of peace himself give you peace **at** all times

1Ti 1: 16 But **for** [+4047] **that very reason** I was shown mercy so that in
    2: 10 but **with** good deeds, appropriate for women who profess to

    2: 15 But women will be saved **through** childbearing—if they continue
    4: 5 because it is consecrated **by** the word of God and prayer.
    4: 14 which was given you **through** a prophetic message when the body
    5: 23 and use a little wine **because of** your stomach and your frequent

2Ti 1: 1 Paul, an apostle of Christ Jesus **by** the will of God, according to the
    1: 6 **For** this reason I remind you to fan into flame the gift of God,
    1: 6 gift of God, which is in you **through** the laying on of my hands.
    1: 10 but it has now been revealed **through** the appearing of our Savior,
    1: 10 and has brought life and immortality to light **through** the gospel.
    1: 12 **That is why** [+162+4005] I am suffering as I am. Yet I am not
    1: 14 to you—guard it **with** *the help* of the Holy Spirit who lives in us.
    2: 2 And the things you have heard me say **in the presence of** many
    2: 10 **Therefore** [+4047] I endure everything for the sake of the elect,
    2: 10 Therefore I endure everything **for the sake of** the elect, that they
    3: 15 which are able to make you wise for salvation **through** faith in
    4: 17 so that **through** me the message might be fully proclaimed

Tit 1: 13 **Therefore** [+162+4005], rebuke them sharply, so that they will be
    3: 5 He saved us **through** the washing of rebirth and renewal by the
    3: 6 whom he poured out on us generously **through** Jesus Christ our

Phm 1: 7 has given me great joy and encouragement, **because** you, brother,
    1: 9 yet I appeal to you **on the basis of** love. I then, as Paul—an old
    1: 15 Perhaps **the reason** [+4047] he was separated from you for a little
    1: 22 because I hope to be restored to you **in answer to** your prayers.

Heb 1: 2 heir of all things, and **through** whom he made the universe.
    1: 9 **therefore** [+4047] God, your God, has set you above your
    1: 14 Are not all angels ministering spirits sent to serve [NIE] those
    2: 1 **therefore** [+4047], to what we have heard, so that we do not drift
    2: 2 For if the message spoken **by** angels was binding, and every
    2: 3 This salvation, which was first announced **by** the Lord,
    2: 9 now crowned with glory and honor **because** he suffered death,
    2: 10 fitting that God, **for** whom and through whom everything exists,
    2: 10 fitting that God, for whom and **through** whom everything exists,
    2: 10 should make the author of their salvation perfect **through**
    2: 11 **So** [+162+4005] Jesus is not ashamed to call them brothers.
    2: 14 so that **by** his death he might destroy him who holds the power of
    2: 15 and free those who [NIE] all their lives were held in slavery by
    3: 16 Were they not all those [NIE] Moses led out of Egypt?
    3: 19 we see that they were not able to enter, **because of** their unbelief.
    4: 6 preached to them did not go in, **because of** their disobedience.
    5: 3 **This is why** [+899] he has to offer sacrifices for his own sins,
    5: 12 In fact, though **by** this time you ought to be teachers, you need
    5: 14 who **by** constant use have trained themselves to distinguish good
    6: 7 and that produces a crop useful to those **for** whom it is farmed
    6: 12 but to imitate those who **through** faith and patience inherit what
    6: 18 **by** two unchangeable things in which it is impossible for God to
    7: 9 that Levi, who collects the tenth, paid the tenth **through** Abraham,
    7: 11 If perfection could have been attained **through** the Levitical
    7: 18 regulation is set aside **because** [+3836] it was weak and useless
    7: 19 and a better hope is introduced, **by** which we draw near to God.
    7: 21 but he became a priest with an oath **when** God said to him:
    7: 23 **since** [+3836] death prevented them from continuing in office;
    7: 24 but **because** [+3836] Jesus lives forever, he has a permanent
    7: 25 he is able to save completely those who come to God **through** him,
    9: 6 the priests entered **regularly** [+4246] into the outer room to carry
    9: 11 he *went* **through** the greater and more perfect tabernacle that is not
    9: 12 He did not enter **by means of** the blood of goats and calves;
    9: 12 but he entered the Most Holy Place once for all **by** his own blood,
    9: 14 who **through** the eternal Spirit offered himself unblemished to
    9: 15 **For** [+4047] **this reason** Christ is the mediator of a new covenant,
    9: 26 the end of the ages to do away with sin **by** the sacrifice of himself.
    10: 2 **For** [+3836] the worshipers would have been cleansed once for all,
    10: 10 we have been made holy **through** the sacrifice of the body of Jesus
    10: 20 by a new and living way opened for us **through** the curtain,
    11: 4 **By** faith he was commended as a righteous man, when God spoke
    11: 4 his offerings. And **by** faith he still speaks, even though he is dead.
    11: 7 **By** his faith he condemned the world and became heir of the
    11: 29 **By** faith the people passed through the Red Sea as **on** dry land;
    11: 33 who **through** faith conquered kingdoms, administered justice,
    11: 39 These were all commended **for** their faith, yet none of them
    12: 1 and let us run **with** perseverance the race marked out for us.
    12: 11 of righteousness and peace for those who have been trained **by** it.
    12: 15 no bitter root grows up to cause trouble and defile many. [NIE]
    12: 28 and **so** [+4005] worship God acceptably with reverence and awe,
    13: 2 for **by** so doing some people have entertained angels without
    13: 11 [NIE] The high priest carries the blood of animals into the Most
    13: 12 the city gate to make the people holy **through** his own blood.

13:15 **Through** Jesus, therefore, let us continually offer to God a
13:15 let us **continually** [+4246] offer to God a sacrifice of praise—
13:21 **through** Jesus Christ, to whom be glory for ever and ever.
13:22 of exhortation, for I have written you *only* a **short** [+1099] letter.
Jas 2:12 and act as those who are going to be judged **by** the law that gives
4: 2 and fight. You do not have, **because** [+3836] you do not ask God.
1Pe 1: 3 living hope **through** the resurrection of Jesus Christ from the dead,
1: 5 who **through** faith are shielded by God's power until the coming
1: 7 worth than gold, which perishes even though refined **by** fire—
1:12 when they spoke of the things that have now been told you **by**
1:20 of the world, but was revealed in these last times **for** your **sake**.
1:21 **Through** him you believe in God, who raised him from the dead
1:23 but of imperishable, **through** the living and enduring word of God.
2: 5 offering spiritual sacrifices acceptable to God **through** Jesus
2:13 Submit yourselves **for** the Lord's **sake** to every authority instituted
2:14 who are sent **by** him to punish those who do wrong and to
2:19 under the pain of unjust suffering **because** he is conscious of God.
3: 1 they may be won over without words **by** the behavior of their
3:14 But even if you should suffer **for** what is right, you are blessed.
3:20 a few people, eight in all, *were* **saved through** [RP1407] water,
3:21 toward God. It saves you **by** the resurrection of Jesus Christ,
4:11 so that in all things God may be praised **through** Jesus Christ.
5:12 **With the help of** Silas, whom I regard as a faithful brother,
5:12 I have written to you **briefly** [+3900], encouraging you
2Pe 1: 3 and godliness **through** our knowledge of him who called us by his
1: 4 **Through** these he has given us his very great and precious
1: 4 so that **through** them you may participate in the divine nature
2: 2 and [NIE] will bring the way of truth into disrepute.
3: 5 and the earth was formed out of water and **by** water.
3: 6 **By** these waters also the world of that time was deluged
3:12 That day will **bring about** the destruction of the heavens by fire,
1Jn 2:12 because your sins have been forgiven **on account of** his name.
3: 1 **The reason** [+4047] the world does not know us is that it did not
4: 5 **therefore** [+4047] speak from the viewpoint of the world,
4: 9 and only Son into the world that we might live **through** him.
5: 6 This is the one who came **by** water and blood—Jesus Christ.
2Jn 1: 2 **because of** the truth, which lives in us and will be with us forever.
1:12 I have much to write to you, but I do not want to **use** paper and ink.
3Jn 1:10 So [+4047] if I come, I will call attention to what he is doing,
1:13 much to write you, but I do not want to do so **with** pen and ink.
Jude 1:25 majesty, power and authority, **through** Jesus Christ our Lord,
Rev 1: 1 He made it known by sending [NIE] his angel to his servant John,
1: 9 of Patmos **because of** the word of God and the testimony of Jesus.
2: 3 You have persevered and have endured hardships **for** my name,
4:11 all things, and **by** your will they were created and have their being."
6: 9 **because of** the word of God and the testimony they had
6: 9 the word of God and [RPG] the testimony they had maintained.
7:15 **Therefore** [+4047], "they are before the throne of God and serve
12:11 They overcame him **by** the blood of the Lamb and by the word of
12:11 him by the blood of the Lamb and **by** the word of their testimony;
12:12 **Therefore** [+4047] rejoice, you heavens and you who dwell in
13:14 **Because of** the signs he was given power to do on behalf of the
17: 7 Then the angel said to me: "**Why** [+5515] are you astonished?
18: 8 **Therefore** [+4047] in one day her plagues will overtake her:
18:10 [NIE] Terrified at her torment, they will stand far off and cry:
18:15 gained their wealth from her will stand far off, **terrified** [+5832]
20: 4 **because of** their testimony for Jesus and because of the word of
20: 4 of their testimony for God and **because of** the word of God.
21:24 The nations will walk **by** its light, and the kings of the earth will

---

1329 διαβαίνω, *diabainō* [3] [√ *1328 + 326*]

come over [1], go [1], passed through [1]

Lk 16:26 been fixed, so that those who want *to* **go** from here to you cannot,
Ac 16: 9 and begging him, "**Come over** to Macedonia and help us."
Heb 11:29 By faith the *people* **passed through** the Red Sea as on dry land;

1330 διαβάλλω, *diaballō* [1] [√ *1328 + 965*]

accused [1]

Lk 16: 1 "There was a rich man whose manager *was* **accused** of wasting his

---

1331 διαβεβαιόομαι, *diabebaioomai* [2]

[√ *1328 + 326*]

confidently affirm [1], stress [1]

1Ti 1: 7 what they are talking about or what *they* so **confidently affirm**.
Tit 3: 8 And I want you *to* **stress** these things, so that those who have

---

1332 διαβλέπω, *diablepō* [3] [√ *1328 + 1063*]

see clearly [2], eyes opened [1]

Mt 7: 5 then *you will* **see clearly** to remove the speck from your brother's
Mk 8:25 Then *his* **eyes** *were* **opened**, his sight was restored, and he saw
Lk 6:42 then *you will* **see clearly** to remove the speck from your brother's

---

1333 διάβολος, *diabolos* [37 / 38] [√ *1328 + 965*]

devil [31], devil's [3], he^s [+3836] [1], malicious talkers [1],
slanderers [1], slanderous [1]

Mt 4: 1 was led by the Spirit into the desert to be tempted by the **devil**.
4: 5 Then the **devil** took him to the holy city and had him stand on the
4: 8 the **devil** took him to a very high mountain and showed him all the
4:11 Then the **devil** left him, and angels came and attended him.
13:39 and the enemy who sows them is the **devil**. The harvest is the end
25:41 into the eternal fire prepared *for* the **devil** and his angels.
Lk 4: 2 where for forty days he was tempted by the **devil**. He ate nothing
4: 3 The **devil** said to him, "If you are the Son of God, tell this stone to
4: 5 The **devil** [UBS-] led him up to a high place and showed him in
4: 6 And he^s [+3836] said to him, "I will give you all their authority
4:13 When the **devil** had finished all this tempting, he left him until an
8:12 and then the **devil** comes and takes away the word from their
Jn 6:70 "Have I not chosen you, the Twelve? Yet one of you is a **devil**!"
8:44 You belong to your father, the **devil**, and you want to carry out
13: 2 and the **devil** had already prompted Judas Iscariot, son of Simon,
Ac 10:38 doing good and healing all who were under the power of the **devil**,
13:10 "You are a child *of* the **devil** and an enemy of everything that is
Eph 4:27 and do not give the **devil** a foothold.
6:11 so that you can take your stand against the **devil's** schemes.
1Ti 3: 6 become conceited and fall under the same judgment *as* the **devil**.
3: 7 so that he will not fall into disgrace and into the **devil's** trap.
3:11 not **malicious talkers** but temperate and trustworthy in everything.
2Ti 2:26 will come to their senses and escape from the trap *of* the **devil**,
3: 3 without love, unforgiving, **slanderous**, without self-control,
Tit 2: 3 not to be **slanderers** or addicted to much wine, but to teach what is
Heb 2:14 destroy him who holds the power of death—that is, the **devil**—
Jas 4: 7 then, to God. Resist the **devil**, and he will flee from you.
1Pe 5: 8 Your enemy the **devil** prowls around like a roaring lion looking for
1Jn 3: 8 He who does what is sinful is of the **devil**, because the devil has
3: 8 the devil, because the **devil** has been sinning from the beginning.
3: 8 The reason the Son of God appeared was to destroy the **devil's**
3:10 who the children of God are and who the children *of* the **devil** are:
Jude 1: 9 when he was disputing *with* the **devil** about the body of Moses,
Rev 2:10 I tell you, the **devil** will put some of you in prison to test you,
12: 9 that ancient serpent called the **devil**, or Satan, who leads the whole
12:12 to the earth and the sea, because the **devil** has gone down to you!
20: 2 seized the dragon, that ancient serpent, who is the **devil**, or Satan,
20:10 And the **devil**, who deceived them, was thrown into the lake of

---

1334 διαγγέλλω, *diangellō* [3] [√ *1328 + 34*]

give notice of [1], proclaim [1], proclaimed [1]

Lk 9:60 their own dead, but you go and **proclaim** the kingdom of God."
Ac 21:26 Then he went to the temple *to* **give notice of** the date when the
Ro 9:17 in you and that my name *might be* **proclaimed** in all the earth."

1335 διαγίνομαι, *diaginomai* [3] [√ *1328 + 1181*]

later [1], lost [1], was over [1]

Mk 16: 1 *When* the Sabbath **was over**, Mary Magdalene, Mary the mother
Ac 25:13 A few days **later** King Agrippa and Bernice arrived at Caesarea to
27: 9 Much time *had been* **lost**, and sailing had already become

1336 διαγινώσκω, *diaginōskō* [2] [√ 1328 + 1182]

decide [1], information [1]

Ac　23:15　the pretext of wanting more accurate **information** about his case.
　　24:22　Lysias the commander comes," he said, "*I will* **decide** your case."

1337 διαγνωρίζω, *diagnōrizō* Not used in UBS/NIV
[√ 1328 + 1182]

1338 διάγνωσις, *diagnōsis* [1] [√ 1328 + 1182]

decision [1]

Ac　25:21　Paul made his appeal to be held over for the Emperor's **decision**,

1339 διαγογγύζω, *diagongyzō* [2] [√ 1328 + 1197]

mutter [1], muttered [1]

Lk　15: 2　But the Pharisees and the teachers of the law **muttered**, "This man
　　19: 7　All the people saw this and *began to* **mutter**, "He has gone to be

1340 διαγρηγορέω, *diagrēgoreō* [1] [√ 1328 + 1586]

fully awake [1]

Lk　9:32　but *when they became* **fully awake**, they saw his glory

1341 διάγω, *diagō* [2] [√ 1328 + 72]

live [1], lived [1]

1Ti　2: 2　that *we may* **live** peaceful and quiet lives in all godliness
Tit　3: 3　*We* **lived** in malice and envy, being hated and hating one another.

1342 διαδέχομαι, *diadechomai* [1] [√ 1328 + 1312]

received [1]

Ac　7:45　*Having* **received** the tabernacle, our fathers under Joshua brought

1343 διάδημα, *diadēma* [3] [√ 1328 + 1313]

crowns [3]

Rev　12: 3　with seven heads and ten horns and seven **crowns** on his heads.
　　13: 1　He had ten horns and seven heads, with ten **crowns** on his horns,
　　19:12　His eyes are like blazing fire, and on his head are many **crowns**.

1344 διαδίδωμι, *diadidōmi* [4] [√ 1328 + 1443]

distributed [2], divides up [1], give [1]

Lk　11:22　away the armor in which the man trusted and **divides up** the spoils.
　　18:22　Sell everything you have and **give** to the poor, and you will have
Jn　6:11　and **distributed** to those who were seated as much as they wanted.
Ac　4:35　the apostles' feet, and *it was* **distributed** to anyone as he had need.

1345 διάδοχος, *diadochos* [1] [√ 1328 + 1312]

succeeded [+3284] [1]

Ac　24:27　Felix *was* **succeeded** [+3284] *by* Porcius Festus, but because Felix

1346 διαζώννυμι, *diazōnnymi* [3] [√ 1328 + 2439]

wrapped around [2], wrapped around waist [+3284] [1]

Jn　13: 4　outer clothing, and **wrapped** [+3284] a towel **around** his **waist**.
　　13: 5　drying them with the towel that was **wrapped around** *him*.
　　21: 7　he **wrapped** his outer garment **around** *him* (for he had taken it

1347 διαθήκη, *diathēkē* [33] [√ 1328 + 5502]

διαθήκη ... αἷμα (covenant ... blood) [8] Mt 26:28; Mk 14:24;
　　Lk 22:20; 1Co 11:25; Heb 9:20; 10:29; 12:24; 13:20

καινός διαθήκη (new covenant) [5] Lk 22:20; 1Co 11:25; 2Co
　　3:6; Heb 8:8; 9:15

κρείττων διαθήκη (better covenant) [2] Heb 7:22; 8:6

covenant [25], covenants [3], covenant make [+1416] [2], will [2],
covenant made [+1416] [1]

Mt　26:28　This is my blood *of* the **covenant**, which is poured out for many
Mk　14:24　"This is my blood *of* the **covenant**, which is poured out for many,"
Lk　1:72　to show mercy to our fathers and to remember his holy **covenant**,
　　22:20　"This cup is the new **covenant** in my blood, which is poured
Ac　3:25　and *of* the **covenant** [+1416] God **made** with your fathers.
　　7: 8　Then he gave Abraham the **covenant** of circumcision.
Ro　9: 4　theirs the divine glory, the **covenants**, the receiving of the law,
　　11:27　And this is my **covenant** with them when I take away their sins."
1Co　11:25　took the cup, saying, "This cup is the new **covenant** in my blood;
2Co　3: 6　He has made us competent as ministers *of* a new **covenant**—
　　3:14　for to this day the same veil remains when the old **covenant** is
Gal　3:15　or add to a human **covenant** that has been duly established,
　　3:17　does not set aside the **covenant** previously established by God
　　4:24　may be taken figuratively, for the women represent two **covenants**.
Eph　2:12　in Israel and foreigners *to* the **covenants** of the promise,
Heb　7:22　of this oath, Jesus has become the guarantee of a better **covenant**.
　　8: 6　as the **covenant** of which he is mediator is superior to the old one,
　　8: 8　when I will make a new **covenant** with the house of Israel
　　8: 9　It will not be like the **covenant** I made with their forefathers when
　　8: 9　out of Egypt, because they did not remain faithful to my **covenant**,
　　8:10　This is the **covenant** [+1416] *I will* **make** with the house of Israel
　　9: 4　golden altar of incense and the gold-covered ark *of* the **covenant**.
　　9: 4　staff that had budded, and the stone tablets *of* the **covenant**.
　　9:15　For this reason Christ is the mediator *of* a new **covenant**, that those
　　9:15　to set them free from the sins committed under the first **covenant**.
　　9:16　In the case of a **will**, it is necessary to prove the death of the one
　　9:17　because a **will** is in force only when somebody has died; it never
　　9:20　He said, "This is the blood *of* the **covenant**, which God has
　　10:16　"This is the **covenant** [+1416] *I will* **make** with them after that
　　10:29　who has treated as an unholy thing the blood *of* the **covenant** that
　　12:24　to Jesus the mediator *of* a new **covenant**, and to the sprinkled
　　13:20　who through the blood *of* the eternal **covenant** brought back from
Rev　11:19　and within his temple was seen the ark of his **covenant**

1348 διαίρεσις, *diairesis* [3] [√ 1328 + 145]

different kinds [3]

1Co　12: 4　There are **different kinds** of gifts, but the same Spirit.
　　12: 5　There are **different kinds** of service, but the same Lord.
　　12: 6　There are **different kinds** of working, but the same God works all

1349 διαιρέω, *diaireō* [2] [√ 1328 + 145]

divided between [1], gives [1]

Lk　15:12　my share of the estate.' So he **divided** his property **between** them.
1Co　12:11　work of one and the same Spirit, and *he* **gives** them to each one,

1350 διακαθαίρω, *diakathairō* [1] [√ 1328 + 2754]

clear [1]

Lk　3:17　His winnowing fork is in his hand *to* **clear** his threshing floor

1351 διακαθαρίζω, *diakatharizō* [1] [√ 1328 + 2754]

clear [1]

Mt　3:12　and *he will* **clear** his threshing floor, gathering his wheat into the

1352 διακατελέγχομαι, *diakatelenchomai* [1]
[√ 1328 + 2848 + 1794]

refuted [1]

Ac　18:28　For *he* vigorously **refuted** the Jews in public debate, proving from

1353 διακελεύω, *diakeleuō* Not used in UBS/NIV
[√ 1328 + 3027]

1354 διακονέω, *diakoneō* [37] [√ 1356]

serves [6], wait on [6], served [4], serve [3], administer [2], attended [2], help [2], helped [2], care for needs [1], cared for needs [1], do the work [1], helpers [1], helping [1], helping to support [1], in the service of [1], ministry [1], serve as deacons [1], serving [1]

Mt 4: 11 Then the devil left him, and angels came and **attended** him.
    8: 15 and the fever left her, and she got up and *began to* **wait on** him.
    20: 28 just as the Son of Man did not come *to be* **served**, but to serve,
    20: 28 be served, but *to* **serve**, and to give his life as a ransom for many."
    25: 44 or needing clothes or sick or in prison, and *did* not **help** you?'
    27: 55 They had followed Jesus from Galilee *to* **care for** his **needs**.
Mk 1: 13 by Satan. He was with the wild animals, and angels **attended** him.
    1: 31 **helped** her up. The fever left her and *she began to* **wait on** them.
    10: 45 For even the Son of Man did not come *to be* **served**, but to serve,
    10: 45 be served, but *to* **serve**, and to give his life as a ransom for many."
    15: 41 In Galilee these women had followed him and **cared for** his **needs**.
Lk 4: 39 and it left her. *She* got up at once and *began to* **wait on** them.
    8: 3 These women *were* **helping to support** them out of their own
    10: 40 don't you care that my sister has left me *to* **do the work** by
    12: 37 have them recline at the table and *will* come and **wait on** them.
    17: 8 get yourself ready and **wait on** me while I eat and drink;
    22: 26 like the youngest, and the one who rules like the one *who* **serves**
    22: 27 who is greater, the one who is at the table or the one *who* **serves**?
    22: 27 one who is at the table? But I am among you as one *who* **serves**.
Jn 12: 2 Martha **served**, while Lazarus was among those reclining at the
    12: 26 Whoever **serves** me must follow me; and where I am, my servant
    12: 26 servant also will be. My Father will honor the one who **serves** me.
Ac 6: 2 neglect the ministry of the word of God *in order to* **wait on** tables.
    19: 22 He sent two *of* his **helpers**, Timothy and Erastus, to Macedonia,
Ro 15: 25 I am on my way to Jerusalem **in the service of** the saints there.
2Co 3: 3 the result of our **ministry**, written not with ink but with the Spirit
    8: 19 which we **administer** in order to honor the Lord himself and to
    8: 20 We want to avoid any criticism of the way we **administer** this
1Ti 3: 10 then if there is nothing against them, *let them* **serve as deacons**.
    3: 13 Those *who have* **served** well gain an excellent standing and great
2Ti 1: 18 You know very well in how many ways *he* **helped** me in Ephesus.
Phm 1: 13 so that *he could* take your place in **helping** me while I am in
Heb 6: 10 and the love you have shown him *as you have* **helped** his people
    6: 10 him as you have helped his people and *continue to* **help** them.
1Pe 1: 12 It was revealed to them that *they were* not **serving** themselves
    4: 10 Each one *should use* whatever gift he has received *to* **serve** others,
    4: 11 If anyone **serves**, he should do it with the strength God provides,

1355 διακονία, *diakonia* [34] [√ 1356]

ministry [14], service [9], serve [3], distribution [1], help [1], mission [1], preparations to be made [1], service that perform [+3311+3836+4047] [1], serving [1], task [1], work [1]

Lk 10: 40 was distracted by all the **preparations** that had **to be made**.
Ac 1: 17 he was one of our number and shared *in* this **ministry**."
    1: 25 to take over this apostolic **ministry**, which Judas left to go where
    6: 1 widows were being overlooked in the daily **distribution** *of food*.
    6: 4 and will give our attention to prayer and the **ministry** of the word."
    11: 29 his ability, decided to provide **help** for the brothers living in Judea.
    12: 25 When Barnabas and Saul had finished their **mission**, they returned
    20: 24 finish the race and complete the **task** the Lord Jesus has given me—
    21: 19 what God had done among the Gentiles through his **ministry**.
Ro 11: 13 as I am the apostle to the Gentiles, I make much of my **ministry**
    12: 7 If it is **serving**, let him serve; if it is teaching, let him teach;
    12: 7 If it is serving, let him **serve**; if it is teaching, let him teach;
    15: 31 and that my **service** in Jerusalem may be acceptable to the saints
1Co 12: 5 There are different kinds *of* **service**, but the same Lord.
    16: 15 and they have devoted themselves to the **service** of the saints.
2Co 3: 7 Now if the **ministry** that brought death, which was engraved in
    3: 8 will not the **ministry** of the Spirit be even more glorious?
    3: 9 If the **ministry** that condemns men is glorious, how much more
    3: 9 how much more glorious is the **ministry** that brings righteousness!
    4: 1 Therefore, since through God's mercy we have this **ministry**,
    5: 18 himself through Christ and gave us the **ministry** of reconciliation;
    6: 3 in anyone's path, so that our **ministry** will not be discredited.
    8: 4 with us for the privilege of sharing *in* this **service** to the saints.
    9: 1 There is no need for me to write to you about this **service** to the

9: 12 This **service** [+3311+3836+4047] **that** *you* **perform** is not only supplying the needs of God's people but is also overflowing
9: 13 Because of the **service** by which you have proved yourselves,
11: 8 other churches by receiving support from them so as to **serve** you.
Eph 4: 12 to prepare God's people for works *of* **service**, so that the body of
Col 4: 17 "See to it that you complete the **work** you have received in the
1Ti 1: 12 that he considered me faithful, appointing me to his **service**.
2Ti 4: 5 work of an evangelist, discharge all the duties of your **ministry**.
    4: 11 bring him with you, because he is helpful to me in my **ministry**.
Heb 1: 14 Are not all angels ministering spirits sent to **serve** those who will
Rev 2: 19 your deeds, your love and faith, your **service** and perseverance,

1356 διάκονος, *diakonos* [29] [→ 1354, 1355]

servant [13], servants [7], minister [3], deacons [2], attendants [1], deacon [1], ministers [1], promotes sin [+281] [1]

Mt 20: 26 whoever wants to become great among you must be your **servant**,
    22: 13 "Then the king told the **attendants**, 'Tie him hand and foot,
    23: 11 The greatest among you will be your **servant**.
Mk 9: 35 wants to be first, he must be the very last, and the **servant** of all."
    10: 43 whoever wants to become great among you must be your **servant**,
Jn 2: 5 His mother said *to* the **servants**, "Do whatever he tells you."
    2: 9 come from, though the **servants** who had drawn the water knew.
    12: 26 me must follow me; and where I am, my **servant** also will be.
Ro 13: 4 For he is God's **servant** to do you good. But if you do wrong,
    13: 4 He is God's **servant**, an agent of wrath to bring punishment on the
    15: 8 For I tell you that Christ has become a **servant** of the Jews on
    16: 1 to you our sister Phoebe, a **servant** of the church in Cenchrea.
1Co 3: 5 *Only* **servants**, through whom you came to believe—as the Lord
2Co 3: 6 He has made us competent as **ministers** of a new covenant—
    6: 4 as **servants** of God we commend ourselves in every way:
    11: 15 then, if his **servants** masquerade as servants of righteousness.
    11: 15 then, if his servants masquerade as **servants** of righteousness.
    11: 23 Are they **servants** of Christ? (I am out of my mind to talk like
Gal 2: 17 are sinners, does that mean that Christ **promotes sin** [+281]?
Eph 3: 7 I became a **servant** of this gospel by the gift of God's grace given
    6: 21 Tychicus, the dear brother and faithful **servant** in the Lord,
Php 1: 1 Christ Jesus at Philippi, together with the overseers and **deacons**:
Col 1: 7 fellow servant, who is a faithful **minister** of Christ on our behalf,
    1: 23 under heaven, and of which I, Paul, have become a **servant**.
    1: 25 I have become its **servant** by the commission God gave me to
    4: 7 is a dear brother, a faithful **minister** and fellow servant in the Lord.
1Ti 3: 8 **Deacons**, likewise, are to be men worthy of respect, sincere,
    3: 12 A **deacon** must be the husband of but one wife and must manage
    4: 6 you will be a good **minister** of Christ Jesus, brought up in the

1357 διακόσιοι, *diakosioi* [8] [√ 1545]

1 [+2008+5943] [2], two hundred [2], 276 [+1573+1971] [1], eight months of a man's wages [+1324] [1], eight months wages [+1324] [1], hundred yards [+4388] [1]

Mk 6: 37 "That would take **eight months of a man's wages** [+1324]!
Jn 6: 7 Philip answered him, "**Eight months' wages** [+1324] would not
    21: 8 for they were not far from shore, about a **hundred yards** [+4388].
Ac 23: 23 "Get ready a detachment of **two hundred** soldiers, seventy
    23: 23 and **two hundred** spearmen to go to Caesarea at nine tonight.
    27: 37 Altogether there were **276** [+1573+1971] of us on board.
Rev 11: 3 and they will prophesy for **1** [+2008+5943],260 days, clothed in
    12: 6 where she might be taken care of *for* **1** [+2008+5943],260 days.

1358 διακούω, *diakouō* [1] [√ 1328 + 201]

hear case [1]

Ac 23: 35 he said, "*I will* **hear** your **case** when your accusers get here."

1359 διακρίνω, *diakrinō* [19] [√ 1328 + 3212]

doubt [4], doubts [2], criticized [1], discriminated [1], disputing [+1363] [1], hesitate [1], hesitation [1], interpret [1], judge a dispute [1], judged [1], made distinction [1], makes different [1], recognizing [1], waver [1], weigh carefully [1]

Mt 16: 3 You know how *to* **interpret** the appearance of the sky, but you

21:21 "I tell you the truth, if you have faith and *do* not **doubt**,
Mk 11:23 and *does* not **doubt** in his heart but believes that what he says will
Ac 10:20 *Do* not **hesitate** to go with them, for I have sent them."
11: 2 went up to Jerusalem, the circumcised believers **criticized** him
11:12 The Spirit told me to *have* no **hesitation** *about* going with them.
15: 9 *He* made no **distinction** between us and them, for he purified their
Ro 4:20 Yet *he did* not **waver** through unbelief regarding the promise of
14:23 But the man who has **doubts** is condemned if he eats, because his
1Co 4: 7 For who **makes** you **different** *from* anyone else? What do you
6: 5 among you wise enough *to* **judge a dispute** between believers?
11:29 who eats and drinks without **recognizing** the body of the Lord eats
11:31 But if *we* **judged** ourselves, we would not come under judgment.
14:29 should speak, and the others *should* **weigh carefully** what is said.
Jas 1: 6 But when he asks, he must believe and not **doubt**, because he who
1: 6 because he who **doubts** is like a wave of the sea, blown and tossed
2: 4 *have you* not **discriminated** among yourselves and become judges
Jude 1: 9 when *he was* **disputing** [+*1363*] with the devil about the body of
1:22 Be merciful to those *who* **doubt**;

1360 διάκρισις, *diakrisis* [3] [√ *1328 + 3212*]

distinguish from [1], distinguishing between [1], passing judgment [1]

Ro 14: 1 faith is weak, without **passing judgment** on disputable matters.
1Co 12:10 to another prophecy, to another **distinguishing between** spirits,
Heb 5:14 use have trained themselves to **distinguish** good **from** evil.

1361 διακωλύω, *diakōlyō* [1] [√ *1328 + 3266*]

deter [1]

Mt 3:14 But John *tried to* **deter** him, saying, "I need to be baptized by you,

1362 διαλαλέω, *dialaleō* [2] [√ *1328 + 3281*]

discuss [1], talking about [1]

Lk 1:65 hill country of Judea *people were* **talking about** all these things.
6:11 and *began to* **discuss** with one another what they might do to

1363 διαλέγομαι, *dialegomai* [13] [√ *1328 + 3306*]

reasoned [4], arguing [2], addresses [1], argued about [+*253+4639*] [1], discoursed [1], disputing [+*1359*] [1], had discussions [1], spoke to [1], talked [1]

Mk 9:34 because on the way *they had* **argued** [+*253+4639*] **about** who was
Ac 17: 2 and on three Sabbath days he **reasoned** with them from the
17:17 So he **reasoned** in the synagogue with the Jews
18: 4 Every Sabbath he **reasoned** in the synagogue, trying to persuade
18:19 He himself went into the synagogue and **reasoned** with the Jews.
19: 8 for three months, **arguing** persuasively about the kingdom of God.
19: 9 and **had discussions** daily in the lecture hall of Tyrannus.
20: 7 Paul **spoke to** the people and, because he intended to leave the next
20: 9 who was sinking into a deep sleep *as* Paul **talked** on and on.
24:12 My accusers did not find me **arguing** with anyone at the temple,
24:25 *As* Paul **discoursed** on righteousness, self-control
Heb 12: 5 forgotten that word of encouragement that **addresses** you as sons:
Jude 1: 9 when *he was* **disputing** [+*1359*] with the devil about the body of

1364 διαλείπω, *dialeipō* [1] [√ *1328 + 3309*]

stopped [1]

Lk 7:45 from the time I entered, *has* not **stopped** kissing my feet.

1365 διάλεκτος, *dialektos* [6] [√ *1328 + 3306*]

in Aramaic [+*1579*] [3], language [3]

Ac 1:19 so they called that field *in* their **language** Akeldama, that is,
2: 6 because each one heard them speaking *in* his own **language**.
2: 8 how is it that each of us hears them *in* his own native **language**?
21:40 When they were all silent, he said to them **in Aramaic** [+*1579*]:
22: 2 When they heard him speak to them **in Aramaic** [+*1579*],
26:14 and I heard a voice saying to me **in Aramaic** [+*1579*], 'Saul,

1366 διαλιμπάνω, *dialimpanō* Not used in UBS/NIV
[√ *1328 + 3309*]

1367 διαλλάσσομαι, *diallassomai* [1] [√ *1328 + 248*]

reconciled [1]

Mt 5:24 in front of the altar. First go and *be* **reconciled** to your brother;

1368 διαλογίζομαι, *dialogizomai* [16] [√ *1328 + 3306*]

thinking [5], discussed [4], arguing about [1], talked the matter over [+*253+4639*] [1], talking [1], talking about [1], thought [1], wondered [1], wondering [1]

Mt 16: 7 They **discussed** this among themselves and said, "It is because we
16: 8 why *are you* **talking** among yourselves about having no bread?
21:25 They **discussed** it among themselves and said, "If we say,
Mk 2: 6 teachers of the law were sitting there, **thinking** to themselves,
2: 8 in his spirit that this was what *they were* **thinking** in their hearts,
2: 8 and he said to them, "Why *are you* **thinking** these things?
8:16 *They* **discussed** this with one another and said, "It is because we
8:17 Jesus asked them: "Why *are you* **talking about** having no bread?
9:33 he asked them, "What *were you* **arguing about** on the road?"
11:31 *They* **discussed** it among themselves and said, "If we say,
Lk 1:29 at his words and **wondered** what kind of greeting this might be.
3:15 and *were* all **wondering** in their hearts if John might possibly be
5:21 and the teachers of the law began **thinking** to themselves,
5:22 and asked, "Why *are you* **thinking** these things in your hearts?
12:17 *He* **thought** to himself, 'What shall I do? I have no place to store
20:14 the tenants saw him, *they* **talked** [+*253+4639*] **the matter over**.

1369 διαλογισμός, *dialogismos* [14] [√ *1328 + 3306*]

thoughts [5], thinking [3], arguing [1], argument [1], disputable [1], disputing [1], doubts [1], thoughts [+*2840+3836*] [1]

Mt 15:19 For out of the heart come evil **thoughts**, murder, adultery,
Mk 7:21 come evil **thoughts**, sexual immorality, theft, murder, adultery,
Lk 2:35 so that the **thoughts** of many hearts will be revealed. And a sword
5:22 Jesus knew what they were **thinking** and asked, "Why are you
6: 8 But Jesus knew what they were **thinking** and said to the man with
9:46 An **argument** started among the disciples as to which of them
9:47 Jesus, knowing their **thoughts** [+*2840+3836*], took a little child
24:38 "Why are you troubled, and why do **doubts** rise in your minds?
Ro 1:21 but their **thinking** became futile and their foolish hearts were
14: 1 faith is weak, without passing judgment *on* **disputable** *matters*.
1Co 3:20 again, "The Lord knows that the **thoughts** of the wise are futile."
Php 2:14 Do everything without complaining or **arguing**,
1Ti 2: 8 to lift up holy hands in prayer, without anger or **disputing**.
Jas 2: 4 among yourselves and become judges *with* evil **thoughts**?

1370 διαλύω, *dialyō* [1] [√ *1328 + 3395*]

dispersed [1]

Ac 5:36 He was killed, all his followers *were* **dispersed**, and it all came to

1371 διαμαρτύρομαι, *diamartyromai* [15] [√ *1328 + 3459*]

testified [3], declared [2], warn [2], warned [2], charge [1], give charge [1], testify [1], testifying [1], testifying to [1], warns [1]

Lk 16:28 Let *him* **warn** them, so that they will not also come to this place of
Ac 2:40 With many other words he **warned** them; and he pleaded with
8:25 When *they had* **testified** and proclaimed the word of the Lord,
10:42 and *to* **testify** that he is the one whom God appointed as judge of
18: 5 to preaching, **testifying** to the Jews that Jesus was the Christ.
20:21 *I have* **declared** to both Jews and Greeks that they must turn to
20:23 I only know that in every city the Holy Spirit **warns** me that prison
20:24 has given me—the task of **testifying to** the gospel of God's grace.
23:11 As *you have* **testified** about me in Jerusalem, so you must also
28:23 evening he explained and **declared** to them the kingdom of God
1Th 4: 6 for all such sins, as we have already told you and **warned** you.

1Ti 5:21 *I* **charge** you, in the sight of God and Christ Jesus and the elect
2Ti 2:14 **Warn** them before God against quarreling about words; it is of no
    4: 1 in view of his appearing and his kingdom, *I* **give** you this **charge**:
Heb 2: 6 But there is a place where someone *has* **testified**: "What is man that

1372 διαμάχομαι, *diamachomai* [1] [√ *1328 + 3480*]

argued vigorously [1]

Ac 23: 9 of the law who were Pharisees stood up and **argued vigorously**.'

1373 διαμένω, *diamenō* [5] [√ *1328 + 3531*]

remain [2], goes on [1], remained [1], stood [1]

Lk 1:22 for he kept making signs to them but **remained** unable to speak.
    22:28 You are those *who have* **stood** by me in my trials.
Gal 2: 5 a moment, so that the truth of the gospel *might* **remain** with you.
Heb 1:11 They will perish, but you **remain**; they will all wear out like a
2Pe 3: 4 everything **goes on** as it has since the beginning of creation."

1374 διαμερίζω, *diamerizō* [11] [√ *1328 + 3538*]

divided [4], divided up [2], divide [1], divided among [1], dividing up [1], gave [1], separated [1]

Mt 27:35 they had crucified him, *they* **divided up** his clothes by casting lots.
Mk 15:24 **Dividing up** his clothes, they cast lots to see what each would get.
Lk 11:17 "Any kingdom **divided** against itself will be ruined, and a house
    11:18 If Satan *is* **divided** against himself, how can his kingdom stand?
    12:52 From now on there will be five in one family **divided** *against* each
    12:53 *They will be* **divided**, father against son and son against father,
    22:17 he gave thanks and said, "Take this and **divide** it among you.
    23:34 they are doing." And they **divided up** his clothes by casting lots.
Jn 19:24 *"They* **divided** my garments **among** them and cast lots for my
Ac 2: 3 They saw what seemed to be tongues of fire *that* **separated**
    2:45 their possessions and goods, *they* **gave** to anyone as he had need.

1375 διαμερισμός, *diamerismos* [1] [√ *1328 + 3538*]

division [1]

Lk 12:51 think I came to bring peace on earth? No, I tell you, but **division**.

1376 διανέμω, *dianemō* [1] [√ *1328 + 3795*]

spreading [1]

Ac 4:17 But to stop *this thing* from **spreading** any further among the

1377 διανεύω, *dianeuō* [1] [√ *1328 + 3748*]

making signs [1]

Lk 1:22 for he kept **making signs** to them but remained unable to speak.

1378 διανόημα, *dianoēma* [1] [√ *1328 + 3808*]

thoughts [1]

Lk 11:17 Jesus knew their **thoughts** and said to them: "Any kingdom divided

1379 διάνοια, *dianoia* [12] [√ *1328 + 3808*]

minds [4], mind [3], thoughts [2], understanding [2], thinking [1]

Mt 22:37 with all your heart and with all your soul and with all your **mind**.'
Mk 12:30 and with all your soul and with all your **mind** and with all your
Lk 1:51 he has scattered those who are proud *in* their inmost **thoughts**.
    10:27 all your soul and with all your strength and with all your **mind**';
Eph 2: 3 of our sinful nature and following its desires and **thoughts**.
    4:18 They are darkened *in* their **understanding** and separated from the
Col 1:21 and were enemies *in* your **minds** because of your evil behavior.
Heb 8:10 I will put my laws in their **minds** and write them on their hearts.
    10:16 put my laws in their hearts, and I will write them on their **minds**."
1Pe 1:13 Therefore, prepare your **minds** for action; be self-controlled;
2Pe 3: 1 of them as reminders to stimulate you to wholesome **thinking**.
1Jn 5:20 that the Son of God has come and has given us **understanding**,

1380 διανοίγω, *dianoigō* [8] [√ *487; cf. 1328*]

opened [5], explaining [1], firstborn [*+3616*] [1], open [1]

Mk 7:34 deep sigh said to him, "*Ephphatha!*" (which means, "*Be* **opened!**").
Lk 2:23 "Every **firstborn** [*+3616*] male is to be consecrated to the Lord"),
    24:31 Then their eyes *were* **opened** and they recognized him, and he
    24:32 he talked with us on the road and **opened** the Scriptures to us?"
    24:45 Then *he* **opened** their minds so they could understand the
Ac 7:56 "I see heaven **open** and the Son of Man standing at the right hand of
    16:14 of God. The Lord **opened** her heart to respond to Paul's message.
    17: 3 **explaining** and proving that the Christ had to suffer and rise from

1381 διανυκτερεύω, *dianyktereuō* [1] [√ *1328 + 3816*]

spent the night [*+1639*] [1]

Lk 6:12 mountainside to pray, and **spent the night** [*+1639*] praying to God.

1382 διανύω, *dianyō* [1] [√ *1328 + 539*]

continued [1]

Ac 21: 7 We **continued** our voyage from Tyre and landed at Ptolemais,

1383 διαπαντός, *diapantos* Not used in UBS/NIV [√ *1328 + 4246*]

1384 διαπαρατριβή, *diaparatribē* [1] [√ *1328 + 4123 + 5561*]

constant friction between [1]

1Ti 6: 5 and **constant friction between** men of corrupt mind, who have

1385 διαπεράω, *diaperaō* [6] [√ *1328 + 4305*]

crossed over [4], cross over [1], crossing over [1]

Mt 9: 1 Jesus stepped into a boat, **crossed over** and came to his own town.
    14:34 *When they had* **crossed over**, they landed at Gennesaret.
Mk 5:21 *When* Jesus *had* again **crossed over** by boat to the other side of
    6:53 *When they had* **crossed over**, they landed at Gennesaret
Lk 16:26 here to you cannot, nor *can anyone* **cross over** from there to us.'
Ac 21: 2 We found a ship **crossing over** to Phoenicia, went on board

1386 διαπλέω, *diapleō* [1] [√ *1328 + 4434*]

sailed across [1]

Ac 27: 5 *When we had* **sailed across** the open sea off the coast of Cilicia

1387 διαπονέομαι, *diaponeomai* [2] [√ *1328 + 4506*]

greatly disturbed [1], troubled [1]

Ac 4: 2 *They were* **greatly disturbed** because the apostles were teaching
    16:18 Finally Paul *became* so **troubled** that he turned around and said to

1388 διαπορεύομαι, *diaporeuomai* [5] [√ *1328 + 4513*]

going by [1], going through [*RP1328*] [1], passing through [1], traveled [1], went through [1]

Lk 6: 1 One Sabbath Jesus *was* **going** [*RP1328*] **through** the grainfields,
    13:22 Then Jesus **went through** the towns and villages, teaching as he
    18:36 When he heard the crowd **going by**, he asked what was happening.
Ac 16: 4 As *they* **traveled** from town to town, they delivered the decisions
Ro 15:24 I hope to visit you *while* **passing through** and to have you assist

1389 διαπορέω, *diaporeō* [4] [√ *1328 + 1.1 + 4513*]

perplexed [2], puzzled [1], wondering about [*+1571+1877*] [1]

Lk 9: 7 And *he was* **perplexed**, because some were saying that John had

Ac   2:12 Amazed and **perplexed**, they asked one another, "What does this
     5:24 the captain of the temple guard and the chief priests *were* **puzzled**,
     10:17 While Peter *was* **wondering** [*+1571+1877*] **about** the meaning of

1390 διαπραγματεύομαι, *diapragmateuomai* [1]
[√ *1328 + 4556*]

gained [1]

Lk   19:15 given the money, in order to find out what *they had* **gained** with it.

1391 διαπρίω, *diapriō* [2] [√ *1328 + 4573*]

furious [*+2840+3836*] [1], furious [1]

Ac   5:33 heard this, *they were* **furious** and wanted to put them to death.
     7:54 they *were* **furious** [*+2840+3836*] and gnashed their teeth at him.

1392 διαρήγνυμι, *diarēgnymi* Not used in UBS/NIV
[√ *1328 + 4838*]

1393 διαρήσσω, *diarēssō* Not used in UBS/NIV
[√ *1328 + 4838*]

1394 διαρθρόω, *diarthroō* Not used in UBS/NIV
[√ *1328*]

1395 διαρπάζω, *diarpazō* [3] [√ *1328 + 773*]

rob [2], carry off [1]

Mt   12:29 unless he first ties up the strong man? Then *he can* **rob** his house.
Mk   3:27 and **carry off** his possessions unless he first ties up the strong man.
     3:27 unless he first ties up the strong man. Then *he can* **rob** his house.

1396 διαρρήγνυμι, *diarrēgnymi* [5] [√ *1328 + 4838*]

tore [3], break [1], broken [1]

Mt   26:65 Then the high priest **tore** his clothes and said, "He has spoken
Mk   14:63 The high priest **tore** his clothes. "Why do we need any more
Lk   5: 6 caught such a large number of fish that their nets *began to* **break**.
     8:29 he had **broken** his chains and had been driven by the demon into
Ac   14:14 they **tore** their clothes and rushed out into the crowd, shouting:

1397 διασαφέω, *diasapheō* [2] [√ *1328*]

explain [1], told [1]

Mt   13:36 and said, "**Explain** to us the parable of the weeds in the field."
     18:31 and went and **told** their master everything that had happened.

1398 διασείω, *diaseiō* [1] [√ *1328 + 4940*]

extort money [1]

Lk   3:14 He replied, "Don't **extort money** and don't accuse people falsely—

1399 διασκορπίζω, *diaskorpizō* [9] [√ *1328 + 5025*]

scattered [5], scattered seed [2], squandered [1], wasting [1]

Mt   25:24 have not sown and gathering where *you have* not **scattered seed**.
     25:26 I have not sown and gather where *I have* not **scattered seed**?
     26:31 strike the shepherd, and the sheep of the flock *will be* **scattered**.'
Mk   14:27 " 'I will strike the shepherd, and the sheep *will be* **scattered**.'
Lk   1:51 he has **scattered** those who are proud in their inmost thoughts.
     15:13 a distant country and there **squandered** his wealth in wild living.
     16: 1 "There was a rich man whose manager was accused of **wasting** his
Jn   11:52 not only for that nation but also for the **scattered** children of God,
Ac   5:37 in revolt. He too was killed, and all his followers *were* **scattered**.

1400 διασπάω, *diaspaō* [2] [√ *1328 + 5060*]

tore apart [1], torn to pieces [1]

Mk   5: 4 but he **tore** the chains **apart** and broke the irons on his feet.
Ac   23:10 the commander was afraid Paul *would be* **torn to pieces** by them.

1401 διασπείρω, *diaspeirō* [3] [√ *1328 + 5062*]

scattered [3]

Ac   8: 1 and all except the apostles *were* **scattered** throughout Judea
     8: 4 Those *who had been* **scattered** preached the word wherever they
     11:19 Now those *who had been* **scattered** by the persecution in

1402 διασπορά, *diaspora* [3] [√ *1328 + 5062*]

people live scattered among [*+3836*] [1], scattered among the
nations [1], scattered throughout [1]

Jn   7:35 Will he go where our **people live scattered** [*+3836*] **among** the
Jas   1: 1 Jesus Christ, To the twelve tribes **scattered among the nations**:
1Pe   1: 1 **scattered throughout** Pontus, Galatia, Cappadocia, Asia

1403 διαστέλλω, *diastellō* [8 / 7] [√ *1328 + 5097*]

commanded [2], gave orders [2], warned [1], authorization [1],
did^s so [1]

Mt   16:20 Then he warned [UBS **gave orders**; NIV *2203*] his disciples not to
Mk   5:43 *He* **gave** strict **orders** not to let anyone know about this, and told
     7:36 Jesus **commanded** them not to tell anyone. But the more he did so,
     7:36 But the more *he* **did^s so**, the more they kept talking about it.
     8:15 "Be careful," Jesus **warned** them. "Watch out for the yeast of the
     9: 9 Jesus **gave** them **orders** not to tell anyone what they had seen until
Ac   15:24 have heard that some went out from us without our **authorization**
Heb 12:20 because they could not bear what *was* **commanded**: "If even an

1404 διάστημα, *diastēma* [1] [√ *1328 + 2705*]

later [1]

Ac   5: 7 About three hours **later** his wife came in, not knowing what had

1405 διαστολή, *diastolē* [3] [√ *1328 + 5097*]

difference [2], distinction [1]

Ro   3:22 faith in Jesus Christ to all who believe. There is no **difference**,
     10:12 For there is no **difference** between Jew and Gentile—the same
1Co 14: 7 what tune is being played unless there is a **distinction** in the notes?

1406 διαστρέφω, *diastrephō* [7] [√ *1328 + 5138*]

perverse [2], depraved [1], distort the truth [*+3281*] [1],
perverting [1], subverting [1], turn [1]

Mt   17:17 "O unbelieving and **perverse** generation," Jesus replied, "how long
Lk   9:41 "O unbelieving and **perverse** generation," Jesus replied, "how long
     23: 2 saying, "We have found this man **subverting** our nation.
Ac   13: 8 opposed them and tried *to* **turn** the proconsul from the faith.
     13:10 Will you never stop **perverting** the right ways of the Lord?
     20:30 and **distort** [*+3281*] **the truth** in order to draw away disciples after
Php   2:15 of God without fault in a crooked and **depraved** generation,

1407 διασῴζω, *diasōzō* [8] [√ *1328 + 5392*]

safely [2], escaped [1], heal [1], healed [1], in safety [1], saved
through [*RP1328*] [1], spare life [1]

Mt   14:36 touch the edge of his cloak, and all who touched him *were* **healed**.
Lk   7: 3 elders of the Jews to him, asking him to come and **heal** his servant.
Ac   23:24 mounts for Paul so that *he may be* taken **safely** to Governor Felix."
     27:43 But the centurion wanted *to* **spare** Paul's **life** and kept them from
     27:44 on pieces of the ship. In this way everyone reached land **in safety**.
     28: 1 Once **safely** on shore, we found out that the island was called
     28: 4 for *though he* **escaped** from the sea, Justice has not allowed him to
1Pe   3:20 a few people, eight in all, *were* **saved** [*RP1328*] **through** water,

1408 διαταγή, *diatagē* [2] [√ *1328 + 5435*]

instituted [1], put into effect [1]

Ac 7:53 you who have received the law that was **put into effect** through
Ro 13: 2 against the authority is rebelling against what God has **instituted**,

1409 διάταγμα, *diatagma* [1] [√ *1328 + 5435*]

edict [1]

Heb 11:23 was no ordinary child, and they were not afraid of the king's **edict**.

1410 διαταράσσω, *diatarassō* [1] [√ *1328 + 5429*]

greatly troubled [1]

Lk 1:29 Mary *was* **greatly troubled** at his words and wondered what kind

1411 διατάσσω, *diatassō* [16] [√ *1328 + 5435*]

told to do [3], directed [2], ordered [2], commanded [1], give
directions [1], instructing [1], made arrangement [1], orders [1],
put into effect [1], required [1], the rule lay down [1], told [1]

Mt 11: 1 After Jesus had finished **instructing** his twelve disciples, he went
Lk 3:13 "Don't collect any more than you *are* **required** to," he told them.
    8:55 she stood up. Then Jesus **told** her to give her something to eat.
    17: 9 he thank the servant because he did what *he was* **told to do**?
    17:10 when you have done everything you *were* **told to do**, should say,
Ac 7:44 It had been made as God **directed** Moses, according to the pattern
    18: 2 because Claudius *had* **ordered** all the Jews to leave Rome.
    20:13 *He had* **made** this **arrangement** because he was going there on
    23:31 So the soldiers, carrying out their **orders**, took Paul with them
    24:23 *He* **ordered** the centurion to keep Paul under guard but to give him
1Co 7:17 has called him. This is **the rule** *I* **lay down** in all the churches.
    9:14 the Lord *has* **commanded** that those who preach the gospel should
    11:34 result in judgment. And when I come *I will* **give** further **directions**.
    16: 1 for God's people: Do what *I* **told** the Galatian churches **to do**.
Gal 3:19 The law *was* **put into effect** through angels by a mediator.
Tit 1: 5 left unfinished and appoint elders in every town, as I **directed** you.

1412 διατελέω, *diateleō* [1] [√ *1328 + 5465*]

last [1]

Ac 27:33 "For the **last** fourteen days," he said, "you have been in constant

1413 διατηρέω, *diatēreō* [2] [√ *1328 + 5498*]

avoid [1], treasured [1]

Lk 2:51 to them. But his mother **treasured** all these things in her heart.
Ac 15:29 You will do well *to* **avoid** these things. Farewell.

1414 διατί, *diati* Not used in UBS/NIV [√ *1328 + 5515*]

1415 διατίθεμαι, *diatithemai* Not used in UBS/NIV
[√ *1328 + 5502*]

1416 διατίθημι, *diatithēmi* [7] [√ *1328 + 5502*]

covenant make [+*1347*] [2], made [2], confer [1], conferred [1],
covenant made [+*1347*] [1]

Lk 22:29 And I **confer** on you a kingdom, just as my Father conferred one
    22:29 confer on you a kingdom, just as my Father **conferred** one on me,
Ac 3:25 and *of* the **covenant** God **made** [+*1347*] with your fathers.
Heb 8:10 This is the **covenant** *I will* **make** [+*1347*] with the house of Israel
    9:16 of a will, it is necessary to prove the death *of* the one *who* **made**,
    9:17 has died; it never takes effect while the one *who* **made** it is living.
    10:16 "This is the **covenant** *I will* **make** [+*1347*] with them after that

1417 διατρίβω, *diatribō* [9] [√ *1328 + 5561*]

spending [2], stayed [2], remained [1], spent [1], spent some
time [1], stayed [+*1639*] [1], stayed a while [1]

Jn 3:22 where *he* **spent some time** with them, and baptized.
Ac 12:19 Herod went from Judea to Caesarea and **stayed** there a while.
    14: 3 So Paul and Barnabas **spent** considerable time there,
    14:28 And *they* **stayed** there a long time with the disciples.
    15:35 But Paul and Barnabas **remained** in Antioch, where they
    16:12 district of Macedonia. And *we* **stayed** [+*1639*] there several days.
    20: 6 days later joined the others at Troas, where *we* **stayed** seven days.
    25: 6 *After* **spending** eight or ten days with them, he went down to
    25:14 Since *they were* **spending** many days there, Festus discussed

1418 διατροφή, *diatrophē* [1] [√ *1328 + 5555*]

food [1]

1Ti 6: 8 But if we have **food** and clothing, we will be content with that.

1419 διαυγάζω, *diaugazō* [1] [√ *1328 + 879*]

dawns [1]

2Pe 1:19 until the day **dawns** and the morning star rises in your hearts.

1420 διαυγής, *diaugēs* [1] [√ *1328 + 879*]

transparent [1]

Rev 21:21 great street of the city was of pure gold, like **transparent** glass.

1421 διαφανής, *diaphanēs* Not used in UBS/NIV
[√ *1328 + 5743*]

1422 διαφέρω, *diapherō* [13] [√ *1328 + 5770*]

worth more than [2], best [1], carry [1], different from [1], differs
[1], driven [1], makes difference [1], more valuable than [1],
spread [1], superior [1], valuable [1], valuable than [1]

Mt 6:26 Father feeds them. *Are* you not much **more valuable than** they?
    10:31 So don't be afraid; you *are* **worth more than** many sparrows.
    12:12 How much more **valuable** *is* a man **than** a sheep! Therefore it is
Mk 11:16 and would not allow anyone *to* **carry** merchandise through the
Lk 12: 7 Don't be afraid; *you are* **worth more than** many sparrows.
    12:24 feeds them. And how much more **valuable** you *are* than birds!
Ac 13:49 The word of the Lord **spread** through the whole region.
    27:27 On the fourteenth night we were *still being* **driven** across the
Ro 2:18 if you know his will and approve of what *is* **superior** because you
1Co 15:41 and the stars another; and star **differs** from star in splendor.
Gal 2: 6 to be important—whatever they were **makes** no **difference** to me;
    4: 1 he is no **different from** a slave, although he owns the whole estate.
Php 1:10 so that you may be able to discern what *is* **best** and may be pure

1423 διαφεύγω, *diapheugō* [1] [√ *1328 + 5771*]

escaping [1]

Ac 27:42 to prevent any of them from swimming away and **escaping**.

1424 διαφημίζω, *diaphēmizō* [3] [√ *1328 + 5774*]

spread the news about [1], spreading [1], widely circulated [1]

Mt 9:31 they went out and **spread the news about** him all over that region.
    28:15 And this story *has been* **widely circulated** among the Jews to this
Mk 1:45 Instead he went out and began to talk freely, **spreading** the news.

1425 διαφθείρω, *diaphtheirō* [6] [√ *1328 + 5780*]

corrupt [1], destroy [1], destroyed [1], destroying [1], destroys
[1], wasting away [1]

Lk 12:33 be exhausted, where no thief comes near and no moth **destroys**.
2Co 4:16 Though outwardly we *are* **wasting away**, yet inwardly we are

1Ti   6: 5 and constant friction between men *of* **corrupt** mind, who have
Rev   8: 9 creatures in the sea died, and a third of the ships *were* **destroyed.**
     11:18 and great—and *for* **destroying** those who destroy the earth."
     11:18 and great—and for destroying those *who* **destroy** the earth."

1426 διαφθορά, *diaphthora* [6] [√ 1328 + 5780]

decay [4], body decayed [+3972] [1], decay [+1650+5715] [1]

Ac   2:27 me to the grave, nor will you let your Holy One see **decay.**
      2:31 he was not abandoned to the grave, nor did his body see **decay.**
     13:34 the dead, never *to* **decay** [+1650+5715], is stated in these words:
     13:35 it is stated elsewhere: " 'You will not let your Holy One see **decay.'**
     13:36 he was buried with his fathers and *his* **body decayed** [+3972].
     13:37 But the one whom God raised from the dead did not see **decay.**

1427 διάφορος, *diaphoros* [4] [√ 1328 + 5770]

superior [2], different [1], various [1]

Ro   12: 6 We have **different** gifts, according to the grace given us. If a
Heb   1: 4 to the angels as the name he has inherited is **superior** to theirs.
      8: 6 But the ministry Jesus has received is *as* **superior** *to* theirs as the
      9:10 only a matter of food and drink and **various** ceremonial washings—

1428 διαφυλάσσω, *diaphylassō* [1] [√ 1328 + 5875]

guard carefully [1]

Lk   4:10 will command his angels concerning you *to* **guard** you **carefully;**

1429 διαχειρίζω, *diacheirizō* [2] [√ 1328 + 5931]

kill [1], killed [1]

Ac   5:30 from the dead—whom you *had* **killed** by hanging him on a tree.
     26:21 is why the Jews seized me in the temple courts and tried *to* **kill** me.

1430 διαχλευάζω, *diachleuazō* [1] [√ 1328 + 5949]

made fun of [1]

Ac   2:13 Some, however, **made fun of** them and said, "They have had too

1431 διαχωρίζω, *diachōrizō* [1] [√ 1328 + 6006]

leaving [1]

Lk   9:33 As the men *were* **leaving** Jesus, Peter said to him, "Master,

1432 διγαμία, *digamia* Not used in UBS/NIV
[√ 1545 + 1141]

1433 δίγαμος, *digamos* Not used in UBS/NIV
[√ 1545 + 1141]

1434 διδακτικός, *didaktikos* [2] [√ 1438]

able to teach [2]

1Ti   3: 2 temperate, self-controlled, respectable, hospitable, **able to teach,**
2Ti   2:24 instead, he must be kind to everyone, **able to teach,** not resentful.

1435 διδακτός, *didaktos* [3] [√ 1438]

taught [3]

Jn   6:45 It is written in the Prophets: 'They will all be **taught** by God.'
1Co   2:13 not in words **taught** us by human wisdom but in words taught by
      2:13 taught us by human wisdom but in words **taught** by the Spirit,

1436 διδασκαλία, *didaskalia* [21] [√ 1438]

teaching [10], doctrine [5], teach [2], teachings [+1438] [2],
teachings [1], things taught [1]

Mt   15: 9 me in vain; their **teachings** [+1438] are but rules taught by men.' "
Mk   7: 7 me in vain; their **teachings** [+1438] are but rules taught by men.'
Ro   12: 7 If it is serving, let him serve; if it is teaching, let him **teach;**
     15: 4 For everything that was written in the past was written to **teach** us,
Eph   4:14 and blown here and there by every wind *of* **teaching** and by the
Col   2:22 because they are based on human commands and **teachings.**
1Ti   1:10 and for whatever else is contrary *to* the sound **doctrine.**
      4: 1 and follow deceiving spirits and **things taught** by demons.
      4: 6 truths of the faith and *of* the good **teaching** that you have followed.
      4:13 to the public reading of Scripture, to preaching and *to* **teaching.**
      4:16 Watch your life and **doctrine** closely. Persevere in them,
      5:17 especially those whose work is preaching and **teaching.**
      6: 1 so that God's name and our **teaching** may not be slandered.
      6: 3 sound instruction of our Lord Jesus Christ and *to* godly **teaching,**
2Ti   3:10 You, however, know all about my **teaching,** my way of life,
      3:16 All Scripture is God-breathed and is useful for **teaching,** rebuking,
      4: 3 a time will come when men will not put up with sound **doctrine.**
Tit   1: 9 so that he can encourage others by sound **doctrine** and refute those
      2: 1 You must teach what is in accord *with* sound **doctrine.**
      2: 7 doing what is good. In your **teaching** show integrity, seriousness
      2:10 so that in every way they will make the **teaching** about God our

1437 διδάσκαλος, *didaskalos* [59] [√ 1438]

teacher [50], teachers [8], Master [1]

Mt   8:19 Then a teacher of the law came to him and said, "**Teacher,**
      9:11 "Why does your **teacher** eat with tax collectors and 'sinners'?"
     10:24 "A student is not above his **teacher,** nor a servant above his master.
     10:25 It is enough for the student to be like his **teacher,** and the servant
     12:38 of the Pharisees and teachers of the law said to him, "**Teacher,**
     17:24 to Peter and asked, "Doesn't your **teacher** pay the temple tax?"
     19:16 Now a man came up to Jesus and asked, "**Teacher,** what good
     22:16 "**Teacher,**" they said, "we know you are a man of integrity and that
     22:24 "**Teacher,**" they said, "Moses told us that if a man dies without
     22:36 "**Teacher,** which is the greatest commandment in the Law?"
     23: 8 for you have only one **Master** and you are all brothers.
     26:18 "Go into the city to a certain man and tell him, 'The **Teacher** says:
Mk   4:38 The disciples woke him and said to him, "**Teacher,** don't you care
      5:35 daughter is dead," they said. "Why bother the **teacher** any more?"
      9:17 A man in the crowd answered, "**Teacher,** I brought you my son,
      9:38 "**Teacher,**" said John, "we saw a man driving out demons in your
     10:17 "Good **teacher,**" he asked, "what must I do to inherit eternal life?"
     10:20 "**Teacher,**" he declared, "all these I have kept since I was a boy."
     10:35 "**Teacher,**" they said, "we want you to do for us whatever we ask."
     12:14 They came to him and said, "**Teacher,** we know you are a man of
     12:19 "**Teacher,**" they said, "Moses wrote for us that if a man's brother
     12:32 "Well said, **teacher,**" the man replied. "You are right in saying that
     13: 1 the temple, one of his disciples said to him, "Look, **Teacher!**
     14:14 Say to the owner of the house he enters, 'The **Teacher** asks:
Lk   2:46 sitting among the **teachers,** listening to them and asking them
      3:12 came to be baptized. "**Teacher,**" they asked, "what should we do?"
      6:40 A student is not above his **teacher,** but everyone who is fully
      6:40 but everyone who is fully trained will be like his **teacher.**
      7:40 "Simon, I have something to tell you." "Tell me, **teacher,**" he said.
      8:49 daughter is dead," he said. "Don't bother the **teacher** any more."
      9:38 "**Teacher,** I beg you to look at my son, for he is my only child.
     10:25 "**Teacher,**" he asked, "what must I do to inherit eternal life?"
     11:45 "**Teacher,** when you say these things, you insult us also."
     12:13 Someone in the crowd said to him, "**Teacher,** tell my brother to
     18:18 A certain ruler asked him, "Good **teacher,** what must I do to inherit
     19:39 in the crowd said to Jesus, "**Teacher,** rebuke your disciples!"
     20:21 "**Teacher,** we know that you speak and teach what is right,
     20:28 "**Teacher,**" they said, "Moses wrote for us that if a man's brother
     20:39 Some of the teachers of the law responded, "Well said, **teacher!**"
     21: 7 "**Teacher,**" they asked, "when will these things happen? And what
     22:11 and say to the owner of the house, 'The **Teacher** asks: Where is
Jn   1:38 said, "Rabbi" (which means **Teacher),** "where are you staying?"
      3: 2 "Rabbi, we know you are a **teacher** who has come from God.
      3:10 "You are Israel's **teacher,**" said Jesus, "and do you not understand
      8: 4 and said to Jesus, "**Teacher,** this woman was caught in the act of
     11:28 "The **Teacher** is here," she said, "and is asking for you."

13:13 "You call me **'Teacher'** and 'Lord,' and rightly so, for that is what I
13:14 Now that I, your Lord and **Teacher**, have washed your feet,
20:16 and cried out in Aramaic, "Rabboni!" (which means **Teacher**).
Ac 13: 1 In the church at Antioch there were prophets and **teachers**:
Ro 2:20 an instructor of the foolish, a **teacher** of infants, because you have
1Co 12:28 second prophets, third **teachers**, then workers of miracles,
12:29 Are all apostles? Are all prophets? Are all **teachers**? Do all work
Eph 4:11 some to be evangelists, and some to be pastors and **teachers**,
1Ti 2: 7 I am not lying—and a **teacher** of the true faith to the Gentiles.
2Ti 1:11 this gospel I was appointed a herald and an apostle and a **teacher**.
4: 3 they will gather around them a great number of **teachers** to say
Heb 5:12 In fact, though by this time you ought to be **teachers**, you need
Jas 3: 1 Not many of you should presume to be **teachers**, my brothers,

1438 διδάσκω, *didaskō* [97] [→ 1434, 1435, 1436, 1437, 1439, 2281, 2531, 2815, 3791, 6015]

teach [34], teaching [31], taught [20], teaches [4], taught [+*1639*] [2], teachings [+*1436*] [2], began to teach [+*487*+*3836*+*5125*] [1], instructed [1], lecture [1], passed on [1]

Mt 4:23 Jesus went throughout Galilee, **teaching** in their synagogues,
5: 2 and he **began to teach** [+*487*+*3836*+*5125*] them, saying:
5:19 and **teaches** others to do the same will be called least in the
5:19 and **teaches** these commands will be called great in the kingdom of
7:29 because he **taught** [+*1639*] as one who had authority, and not as
9:35 through all the towns and villages, **teaching** in their synagogues,
11: 1 he went on from there to **teach** and preach in the towns of Galilee.
13:54 he began **teaching** the people in their synagogue, and they were
15: 9 me in vain; their **teachings** [+*1436*] are but rules taught by men.' "
21:23 and, *while* he was **teaching**, the chief priests and the elders of the
22:16 and that *you* **teach** the way of God in accordance with the truth.
26:55 Every day I sat in the temple courts **teaching**, and you did not
28:15 So the soldiers took the money and did as *they were* **instructed**.
28:20 and **teaching** them to obey everything I have commanded you.
Mk 1:21 Sabbath came, Jesus went into the synagogue and *began to* **teach**.
1:22 because he **taught** [+*1639*] them as one who had authority,
2:13 A large crowd came to him, and *he began to* **teach** them.
4: 1 Again Jesus began to **teach** by the lake. The crowd that gathered
4: 2 He **taught** them many things by parables, and in his teaching said:
6: 2 When the Sabbath came, he began to **teach** in the synagogue,
6: 6 of faith. Then Jesus went around **teaching** from village to village.
6:30 around Jesus and reported to him all they had done and **taught**.
6:34 without a shepherd. So he began **teaching** them many things.
7: 7 me in vain; their **teachings** [+*1436*] are but rules taught by men.'
8:31 then began to **teach** them that the Son of Man must suffer many
9:31 because *he was* **teaching** his disciples. He said to them, "The Son
10: 1 of people came to him, and as was his custom, *he* **taught** them.
11:17 And as *he* **taught** them, he said, "Is it not written: " 'My house will
12:14 but *you* **teach** the way of God in accordance with the truth.
12:35 *While* Jesus *was* **teaching** in the temple courts, he asked,
14:49 with you, **teaching** in the temple courts, and you did not arrest me.
Lk 4:15 He **taught** in their synagogues, and everyone praised him.
4:31 a town in Galilee, and on the Sabbath began *to* **teach** the people.
5: 3 from shore. Then *he* sat down and **taught** the people from the boat.
5:17 One day as he was **teaching**, Pharisees and teachers of the law,
6: 6 On another Sabbath he went into the synagogue and *was* **teaching**,
11: 1 he finished, one of his disciples said to him, "Lord, **teach** us to pray,
11: 1 to him, "Lord, teach us to pray, just as John **taught** his disciples."
12:12 for the Holy Spirit *will* **teach** you at that time what you should say."
13:10 On a Sabbath Jesus was **teaching** in one of the synagogues,
13:22 the towns and villages, **teaching** as he made his way to Jerusalem.
13:26 'We ate and drank with you, and *you* **taught** in our streets.'
19:47 Every day he was **teaching** at the temple. But the chief priests,
20: 1 One day *as he was* **teaching** the people in the temple courts
20:21 "Teacher, we know that *you* speak and **teach** what is right,
20:21 partiality but **teach** the way of God in accordance with the truth.
21:37 Each day Jesus was **teaching** at the temple, and each evening he
23: 5 they insisted, "He stirs up the people all over Judea *by his* **teaching**.
Jn 6:59 He said this *while* **teaching** in the synagogue in Capernaum.
7:14 the Feast did Jesus go up to the temple courts and *begin to* **teach**.
7:28 Then Jesus, *still* **teaching** in the temple courts, cried out, "Yes,
7:35 our people live scattered among the Greeks, and **teach** the Greeks?
8: 2 all the people gathered around him, and he sat down *to* **teach** them.
8:20 He spoke these words *while* **teaching** in the temple area near the
8:28 nothing on my own but speak just what the Father *has* **taught** me.

9:34 "You were steeped in sin at birth; *how dare* you **lecture** us!"
14:26 *will* **teach** you all things and will remind you of everything I have
18:20 "I always **taught** in synagogues or at the temple, where all the Jews
Ac 1: 1 Theophilus, I wrote about all that Jesus began to do and *to* **teach**
4: 2 greatly disturbed because the apostles *were* **teaching** the people
4:18 and commanded them not *to* speak or **teach** at all in the name of
5:21 as they had been told, and *began to* **teach** the people.
5:25 The men you put in jail are standing in the temple courts **teaching**
5:28 "We gave you strict orders not *to* **teach** in this name," he said.
5:42 they never stopped **teaching** and proclaiming the good news that
11:26 and Saul met with the church and **taught** great numbers of people.
15: 1 came down from Judea to Antioch and *were* **teaching** the brothers:
15:35 where they and many others **taught** and preached the word of the
18:11 Paul stayed for a year and a half, **teaching** them the word of God.
18:25 and he spoke with great fervor and **taught** about Jesus accurately,
20:20 to you but *have* **taught** you publicly and from house to house.
21:21 They have been informed that *you* **teach** all the Jews who live
21:28 This is the man who **teaches** all men everywhere against our
28:31 the kingdom of God and **taught** about the Lord Jesus Christ.
Ro 2:21 you, then, *who* **teach** others, do you not teach yourself? You who
2:21 you, then, who teach others, *do you* not **teach** yourself? You who
12: 7 If it is serving, let him serve; if it is **teaching**, let him teach;
1Co 4:17 which agrees with what *I* **teach** everywhere in every church.
11:14 *Does* not the very nature of things **teach** you that if a man has long
Gal 1:12 I did not receive it from any man, nor *was I* **taught** it; rather,
Eph 4:21 and *were* **taught** in him in accordance with the truth that is in
Col 1:28 admonishing and **teaching** everyone with all wisdom,
2: 7 and built up in him, strengthened in the faith as *you were* **taught**,
3:16 Let the word of Christ dwell in you richly *as you* **teach**
2Th 2:15 stand firm and hold to the teachings we **passed on** to you,
1Ti 2:12 I do not permit a woman *to* **teach** or to have authority over a man;
4:11 Command and **teach** these things.
6: 2 to them. These are the things *you are to* **teach** and urge on them.
2Ti 2: 2 entrust to reliable men who will also be qualified *to* **teach** others.
Tit 1:11 because they are ruining whole households *by* **teaching** things they
Heb 5:12 you need someone *to* **teach** you the elementary truths of God's
8:11 No longer *will* a man **teach** his neighbor, or a man his brother,
1Jn 2:27 him remains in you, and you do not need anyone *to* **teach** you.
2:27 But as his anointing **teaches** you about all things and as that
2:27 not counterfeit—just as *it has* **taught** you, remain in him.
Rev 2:14 who **taught** Balak to entice the Israelites to sin by eating food
2:20 *By her* **teaching** she misleads my servants into sexual immorality

1439 διδαχή, *didachē* [30] [√ 1438]

teaching [23], taught [2], word of instruction [2], careful instruction [1], instruction [1], teachings [1]

Mt 7:28 saying these things, the crowds were amazed at his **teaching**,
16:12 in bread, but against the **teaching** of the Pharisees and Sadducees.
22:33 When the crowds heard this, they were astonished at his **teaching**.
Mk 1:22 The people were amazed at his **teaching**, because he taught them
1:27 each other, "What is this? A new **teaching**—and with authority!
4: 2 He taught them many things by parables, and in his **teaching** said:
11:18 feared him, because the whole crowd was amazed at his **teaching**.
12:38 As he **taught**, Jesus said, "Watch out for the teachers of the law.
Lk 4:32 They were amazed at his **teaching**, because his message had
Jn 7:16 Jesus answered, "My **teaching** is not my own. It comes from him
7:17 he will find out whether my **teaching** comes from God or whether
18:19 high priest questioned Jesus about his disciples and his **teaching**.
Ac 2:42 They devoted themselves to the apostles' **teaching** and to the
5:28 "Yet you have filled Jerusalem *with* your **teaching** and are
13:12 he believed, for he was amazed at the **teaching** about the Lord.
17:19 "May we know what this new **teaching** is that you are presenting?
Ro 6:17 you wholeheartedly obeyed the form *of* **teaching** to which you
16:17 and put obstacles in your way that are contrary to the **teaching** you
1Co 14: 6 or knowledge or prophecy or **word of instruction**?
14:26 or a **word of instruction**, a revelation, a tongue or an
2Ti 4: 2 and encourage—with great patience and **careful instruction**.
Tit 1: 9 must hold firmly to the trustworthy message as it has been **taught**,
Heb 6: 2 **instruction** about baptisms, the laying on of hands,
13: 9 Do not be carried away by all kinds of strange **teachings**. It is good
2Jn 1: 9 and does not continue in the **teaching** of Christ does not have God;
1: 9 whoever continues in the **teaching** has both the Father and the Son.
1:10 If anyone comes to you and does not bring this **teaching**, do not
Rev 2:14 You have people there who hold to the **teaching** of Balaam,

2: 15 Likewise you also have those who hold to the **teaching** of the
2: 24 to you who do not hold to her **teaching** and have not learned

1440 δίδραχμον, *didrachmon* [2] [√ *1545* + *1533*]

temple tax [1], two-drachma [1]

Mt 17: 24 the collectors of the **two-drachma** tax came to Peter and asked,
17: 24 to Peter and asked, "Doesn't your teacher pay the **temple tax**?"

1441 Δίδυμος, *Didymos* [3] [√ *1545*]

Didymus [3]

Jn 11: 16 Then Thomas (called **Didymus**) said to the rest of the disciples,
20: 24 Now Thomas (called **Didymus**), one of the Twelve, was not with
21: 2 Simon Peter, Thomas (called **Didymus**), Nathanael from Cana in

1442 διδῶ, *didō* [1] [√ *1443*]

make [1]

Rev 3: 9 *I will* **make** those who are of the synagogue of Satan, who claim to

1443 δίδωμι, *didōmi* [414 / 415] [→ *347, 500, 501, 502, 625, 782, 1344, 1442, 1517, 1521, 1522, 1561, 1562, 1563, 1564, 1566, 1686, 1692, 2113, 2331, 2882, 3556, 3632, 3633, 4140, 4142, 4261, 4594, 4595, 4658; cf. 1565*]

give [115], given [106], gave [74], gives [13], put [9], *untranslated* [5], pay [5], grant [4], granted [4], offered [4], giving [3], let [3], offer [3], arranged [2], commanded [+*1953*] [2], enable [2], gave up [2], give the right [2], give to the poor [+*1797*] [2], is^s [2], make [2], perform [2], placed [2], produced [2], show [2], struck in the face [+*4825*] [2], appointed [1], assigned [1], bear [1], benefit [+*5921*] [1], bring [1], buy [1], cast [1], caused [1], does [1], enabled [+*1639*] [1], enabled [+*710*] [1], enabling [+*1328*+*3836*+*593 1*] [1], entrusted [1], gifts [1], given [+*1639*] [1], given authority [1], glorified [+*1518*] [1], glorify [+*1518*] [1], hinder [+*1600*] [1], lavished [1], leave [1], pass on [1], payment [1], plot [+*5206*] [1], poured [1], praised [+*142*] [1], presented [1], punish [+*1689*] [1], puts [1], receive [1], repay [1], rescue [+*5401*] [1], rewarding [+*3635*+*3836*] [1], set [1], sound [1], speak [1], strengthen [+*3194*] [1], take back [1], took [1], try hard [+*2238*] [1], venture [+*1571*] [1]

Mt 4: 9 "All this *I will* **give** you," he said, "if you will bow down and
5: 31 'Anyone who divorces his wife *must* **give** her a certificate of
5: 42 **Give** to the one who asks you, and do not turn away from the one
6: 11 **Give** us today our daily bread.
7: 6 "*Do* not **give** dogs what is sacred; do not throw your pearls to pigs.
7: 7 "Ask and *it will be* **given** to you; seek and you will find; knock
7: 11 though you are evil, know how *to* **give** good gifts to your children,
7: 11 how much more *will* your Father in heaven **give** good gifts to those
9: 8 and they praised God, who *had* **given** such authority to men.
10: 1 and **gave** them authority to drive out evil spirits and to heal every
10: 8 drive out demons. Freely you have received, freely **give**.
10: 19 or how to say it. At that time you *will be* **given** what to say,
12: 39 But none *will be* **given** it except the sign of the prophet Jonah.
13: 8 Still other seed fell on good soil, where *it* **produced** a crop—
13: 11 of the secrets of the kingdom of heaven *has been* **given** to you,
13: 11 kingdom of heaven has been given to you, but not [RPG] to them.
13: 12 Whoever has *will be* **given** more,
14: 7 that he promised with an oath *to* **give** her whatever she asked.
14: 8 she said, "**Give** me here on a platter the head of John the Baptist."
14: 9 and his dinner guests, he ordered that her request *be* **granted**
14: 11 His head was brought in on a platter and **given** to the girl,
14: 16 "They do not need to go away. You **give** them something to eat."
14: 19 Then *he* **gave** them to the disciples, and the disciples gave them to
15: 36 he broke them and **gave** them to the disciples, and they in turn to
16: 4 miraculous sign, but none *will be* **given** it except the sign of Jonah."
16: 19 *I will* **give** you the keys of the kingdom of heaven; whatever you
16: 26 forfeits his soul? Or what *can* a man **give** in exchange for his soul?
17: 27 Take it and **give** it to them for my tax and yours."
19: 7 "did Moses command that a man **give** his wife a certificate of
19: 11 can accept this word, but only those to whom *it has been* **given**.

19: 21 want to be perfect, go, sell your possessions and **give** to the poor,
20: 4 and work in my vineyard, and *I will* **pay** you whatever is right.'
20: 14 I want *to* **give** the man who was hired last the same as I gave you.
20: 23 from my cup, but to sit at my right or left is not for me *to* **grant**.
20: 28 be served, but to serve, and *to* **give** his life as a ransom for many."
21: 23 these things?" they asked. "And who **gave** you this authority?"
21: 43 away from you and **given** to a people who will produce its fruit.
22: 17 what is your opinion? Is it right *to* **pay** taxes to Caesar or not?"
24: 24 and false prophets will appear and **perform** great signs
24: 29 " 'the sun will be darkened, and the moon *will* not **give** its light;
24: 45 in his household *to* **give** them their food at the proper time?
25: 8 The foolish ones said to the wise, '**Give** us some of your oil;
25: 15 To one *he* **gave** five talents of money, to another two talents,
25: 28 the talent from him and **give** it to the one who has the ten talents.
25: 29 For everyone who has *will be* **given** more, and he will have an
25: 35 For I was hungry and *you* **gave** me something to eat, I was thirsty
25: 42 For I was hungry and *you* **gave** me nothing to eat, I was thirsty
26: 9 have been sold at a high price and the money **given** to the poor."
26: 15 "What are you willing *to* **give** me if I hand him over to you?"
26: 26 and broke it, and **gave** it to his disciples, saying, "Take and eat;
26: 27 Then *he* took the cup, gave thanks and **offered** it to them,
26: 48 Now the betrayer *had* **arranged** a signal with them: "The one I kiss
27: 10 and *they* used them to **buy** the potter's field, as the Lord
27: 34 There *they* **offered** Jesus wine to drink, mixed with gall; but after
28: 12 and devised a plan, *they* **gave** the soldiers a large sum of money,
28: 18 "All authority in heaven and on earth *has been* **given** to me.

Mk 2: 26 only for priests to eat. And *he* also **gave** some to his companions."
3: 6 and *began to* **plot** [+*5206*] with the Herodians how they might kill
4: 7 grew up and choked the plants, so that *they did* not **bear** grain.
4: 8 *It* came up, grew and **produced** a crop, multiplying thirty,
4: 11 "The secret of the kingdom of God *has been* **given** to you.
4: 25 Whoever has *will be* **given** more; whoever does not have,
5: 43 know about this, and told them *to* **give** her something to eat.
6: 2 "What's this wisdom that *has been* **given** him, that he even does
6: 7 them out two by two and **gave** them authority over evil spirits.
6: 22 to the girl, "Ask me for anything you want, and *I'll* **give** it to you."
6: 23 "Whatever you ask *I will* **give** you, up to half my kingdom."
6: 25 "I want *you to* **give** me right now the head of John the Baptist on a
6: 28 a platter. *He* **presented** it to the girl, and she gave it to her mother.
6: 28 a platter. He presented it to the girl, and she **gave** it to her mother.
6: 37 But he answered, "You **give** them something to eat." They said to
6: 37 we to go and spend that much on bread and **give** it to them to eat?"
6: 41 Then *he* **gave** them to his disciples to set before the people.
8: 6 broke them and **gave** them to his disciples to set before the people,
8: 12 a miraculous sign? I tell you the truth, no sign *will be* **given** to it."
8: 37 Or what *can* a man **give** in exchange for his soul?
10: 21 "Go, sell everything you have and **give** to the poor, and you will
10: 37 "**Let** one of us sit at your right and the other at your left in your
10: 40 but to sit at my right or left is not for me *to* **grant**. These places
10: 45 be served, but to serve, and *to* **give** his life as a ransom for many."
11: 28 things?" they asked. "And who **gave** you authority to do this?"
12: 9 He will come and kill those tenants and **give** the vineyard to others.
12: 14 accordance with the truth. Is it right *to* **pay** taxes to Caesar or not?
12: 15 *Should we* **pay** or shouldn't we?" But Jesus knew their hypocrisy.
12: 15 or shouldn't we?" [RPG] But Jesus knew their hypocrisy.
13: 11 Just say whatever *is* **given** you at the time, for it is not you
13: 22 For false Christs and false prophets will appear and **perform** signs
13: 24 " 'the sun will be darkened, and the moon *will* not **give** its light;
13: 34 He leaves his house and **puts** his servants in charge, each with his
14: 5 for more than a year's wages and the money **given** to the poor."
14: 11 They were delighted to hear this and promised *to* **give** him money.
14: 22 and broke it, and **gave** it to his disciples, saying, "Take it;
14: 23 Then *he* took the cup, gave thanks and **offered** it to them,
14: 44 Now the betrayer *had* **arranged** a signal with them: "The one I kiss
15: 23 Then *they* **offered** him wine mixed with myrrh, but he did not take

Lk 1: 32 The Lord God *will* **give** him the throne of his father David,
1: 74 hand of our enemies, and *to* **enable** us to serve him without fear
1: 77 *to* **give** his people the knowledge of salvation through the
2: 24 and *to* **offer** a sacrifice in keeping with what is said in the Law of
4: 6 he said to him, "*I will* **give** you all their authority and splendor,
4: 6 for it has been given to me, and *I can* **give** it to anyone I want to.
6: 4 only for priests to eat. And *he* also **gave** some to his companions."
6: 30 **Give** to everyone who asks you, and if anyone takes what belongs
6: 38 **Give**, and it will be given to you. A good measure, pressed down,
6: 38 **Give**, and *it will be* **given** to you. A good measure, pressed down,
6: 38 shaken together and running over, *will be* **poured** into your lap.

7:15 and began to talk, and Jesus **gave** him *back* to his mother.
7:44 *You did* not **give** me any water for my feet, but she wet my feet
7:45 *You did* not **give** me a kiss, but this woman, from the time I
8:10 of the secrets of the kingdom of God *has been* **given** to you,
8:18 Whoever has *will be* **given** more; whoever does not have,
8:55 she stood up. Then Jesus told them *to* **give** her something to eat.
9: 1 he **gave** them power and authority to drive out all demons
9:13 He replied, "You **give** them something to eat." They answered,
9:16 Then *he* **gave** them to the disciples to set before the people.
10:19 *I have* **given** you authority to trample on snakes and scorpions
10:35 The next day *he* took out two silver coins and **gave** them to the
11: 3 **Give** us each day our daily bread.
11: 7 children are with me in bed. I can't get up and **give** you *anything.*'
11: 8 though *he will* not get up and **give** him the bread because he is his
11: 8 because of the man's boldness *he will* get up and **give** him as much
11: 9 Ask and *it will be* **given** to you; seek and you will find; knock
11:13 though you are evil, know how *to* **give** good gifts to your children,
11:13 how much more *will* your Father in heaven **give** the Holy Spirit to
11:29 miraculous sign, but none *will be* **given** it except the sign of Jonah.
11:41 But **give** [*+1797*] what is inside ⸤the dish⸥ **to the poor,**
12:32 for your Father has been pleased *to* **give** you the kingdom.
12:33 Sell your possessions and **give** [*+1797*] **to the poor.** Provide purses
12:42 whom the master puts in charge of his servants *to* **give** them their
12:48 From everyone who *has been* **given** much, much will be
12:51 Do you think I came *to* **bring** peace on earth? No, I tell you,
12:58 **try** [*+2238*] **hard** to be reconciled to him on the way, or he may
14: 9 both of you will come and say to you, '**Give** this man your seat.'
15:12 one said to his father, 'Father, **give** me my share of the estate.'
15:16 the pods that the pigs were eating, but no one **gave** him *anything.*
15:22 and put it on him. **Put** a ring on his finger and sandals on his feet.
15:29 Yet *you* never **gave** me even a young goat so I could celebrate with
16:12 someone else's property, who *will* **give** you property of your own?
17:18 Was no one found *to* return and **give** praise to God except this
18:43 When all the people saw it, *they* also **praised** [*+142*] God.
19: 8 Here and *now* I **give** half of my possessions to the poor, and if I
19:13 So *he* called ten of his servants and **gave** them ten minas. 'Put this
19:15 Then he sent for the servants to whom *he had* **given** the money,
19:23 Why then didn't *you* **put** my money on deposit,
19:24 his mina away from him and **give** it to the one who has ten minas.'
19:26 who has, more *will be* **given,** but as for the one who has nothing,
20: 2 are doing these things," they said. "Who **gave** you this authority?"
20:10 so *they would* **give** him some of the fruit of the vineyard.
20:16 He will come and kill those tenants and **give** the vineyard to others."
20:22 Is it right for us *to* **pay** taxes to Caesar or not?"
21:15 For I *will* **give** you words and wisdom that none of your
22: 5 They were delighted and agreed *to* **give** him money.
22:19 took bread, gave thanks and broke it, and **gave** it to them, saying,
22:19 and gave it to them, saying, "This is my body **given** for you;
23: 2 He opposes **payment** of taxes to Caesar and claims to be Christ,

Jn 1:12 in his name, *he* **gave** the right to become children of God—
1:17 For the law *was* **given** through Moses; grace and truth came
1:22 are you? Give us an answer to **take back** to those who sent us.
3:16 "For God so loved the world that *he* **gave** his one and only Son,
3:27 "A man can receive only what is **given** him from heaven.
3:34 speaks the words of God, for God **gives** the Spirit without limit.
3:35 The Father loves the Son and *has* **placed** everything in his hands.
4: 5 near the plot of ground Jacob *had* **given** to his son Joseph.
4: 7 came to draw water, Jesus said to her, "*Will you* **give** me a drink?"
4:10 the gift of God and who it is that asks you for **[RPG]** a drink,
4:10 would have asked him and *he* would have **given** you living water."
4:12 who **gave** us the well and drank from it himself, as did also his
4:14 but whoever drinks the water I **give** him will never thirst. Indeed,
4:14 the water *I* **give** him will become in him a spring of water welling
4:15 **give** me this water so that I won't get thirsty and have to keep
5:22 Father judges no one, but *has* **entrusted** all judgment to the Son,
5:26 life in himself, so *he has* **granted** the Son to have life in himself.
5:27 And *he has* **given** him authority to judge because he is the Son of
5:36 of John. For the very work that the Father *has* **given** me to finish,
6:27 that endures to eternal life, which the Son of Man *will* **give** you.
6:31 as it is written: '*He* **gave** them bread from heaven to eat.' "
6:32 it is not Moses *who has* **given** you the bread from heaven,
6:32 but it is my Father *who* **gives** you the true bread from heaven.
6:33 is he who comes down from heaven and **gives** life to the world."
6:34 "Sir," they said, "from now on **give** us this bread."
6:37 All that the Father **gives** me will come to me, and whoever comes
6:39 that I shall lose none of all that *he has* **given** me, but raise them up

6:51 This bread is my flesh, which I *will* **give** for the life of the world."
6:52 among themselves, "How can this man **give** us his flesh to eat?"
6:65 one can come to me unless the Father *has* **enabled** [*+1639*] him."
7:19 *Has* not Moses **given** you the law? Yet not one of you keeps the
7:22 because Moses **gave** you circumcision (though actually it did not
7:39 Up to that time the Spirit *had* not *been* **given** [*+1639*], [UBS-]
9:24 "**Give** glory to God," they said. "We know this man is a sinner."
10:28 I **give** them eternal life, and they shall never perish; no one can
10:29 My Father, who *has* **given** them to me, is greater than all;
11:22 But I know that even now God *will* **give** you whatever you ask.
11:57 and Pharisees *had* **given** orders that if anyone found out where
12: 5 "Why wasn't this perfume sold and the money **given** to the poor?
12:49 but the Father who sent me **commanded** [*+1953*] me what to say
13: 3 Jesus knew that the Father *had* **put** all things under his power,
13:15 *I have* **set** you an example that you should do as I have done for
13:26 "It is the one to whom *I will* **give** this piece of bread when I have
13:26 the piece of bread, *he* **gave** it to Judas Iscariot, son of Simon.
13:29 what was needed for the Feast, or to **give** something to the poor.
13:34 "A new command *I* **give** you: Love one another. As I have loved
14:16 and *he will* **give** you another Counselor to be with you forever—
14:27 Peace I leave with you; my peace *I* **give** you. I do not give to you
14:27 my peace I give you. I *do* not **give** to you as the world gives.
14:27 my peace I give you. I do not give to you as the world **gives.**
15:16 Then the Father *will* **give** you whatever you ask in my name.
16:23 the truth, my Father *will* **give** you whatever you ask in my name.
17: 2 For *you* **granted** him authority over all people that he might give
17: 2 For you granted him authority over all people that *he might* **give**
17: 2 that he might give eternal life to all those *you have* **given** him.
17: 4 you glory on earth by completing the work *you* **gave** me to do.
17: 6 "I have revealed you to those whom *you* **gave** me out of the world.
17: 6 were yours; *you* **gave** them to me and they have obeyed your word.
17: 7 Now they know that everything *you have* **given** me comes from
17: 8 For *I* **gave** them the words you gave me and they accepted them.
17: 8 For I gave them the words *you* **gave** me and they accepted them.
17: 9 for the world, but for those *you have* **given** me, for they are yours.
17:11 the name *you* **gave** me—so that they may be one as we are one.
17:12 I protected them and kept them safe by that name *you* **gave** me.
17:14 *I have* **given** them your word and the world has hated them,
17:22 *I have* **given** them the glory that you gave me, that they may be
17:22 I have given them the glory that *you* **gave** me, that they may be
17:24 I want those *you have* **given** me to be with me where I am,
17:24 the glory *you have* **given** me because you loved me before the
18: 9 would be fulfilled: "I have not lost one of those *you* **gave** me."
18:11 sword away! Shall I not drink the cup the Father *has* **given** me?"
18:22 one of the officials nearby **struck** him **in the face** [*+4825*].
19: 3 king of the Jews!" And *they* **struck** him **in the face** [*+4825*].
19: 9 do you come from?" he asked Jesus, but Jesus **gave** him no answer.
19:11 "You would have no power over me if it were not **given** to you
21:13 Jesus came, took the bread and **gave** it to them, and did the same

Ac 1:26 Then *they* **cast** lots,
2: 4 and began to speak in other tongues as the Spirit **enabled** [*+710*]
2:19 *I will* **show** wonders in the heaven above and signs on the earth
2:27 me to the grave, nor *will you* **let** your Holy One see decay.
3: 6 Peter said, "Silver or gold I do not have, but what I have *I* **give** you.
3:16 and the faith that comes through him that *has* **given** this complete
4:12 for there is no other name under heaven **given** to men by which we
4:29 and **enable** your servants to speak your word with great boldness.
5:31 and Savior that he *might* **give** repentance and forgiveness of sins to
5:32 so is the Holy Spirit, whom God *has* **given** to those who obey him."
7: 5 *He* **gave** him no inheritance here, not even a foot of ground.
7: 5 But God promised **[RPG]** him that he and his descendants after
7: 8 Then *he* **gave** Abraham the covenant of circumcision.
7:10 *He* **gave** Joseph wisdom and enabled him to gain the goodwill of
7:25 would realize that God was using him to **rescue** [*+5401*] them,
7:38 and with our fathers; and he received living words *to* **pass on** to us.
8:18 When Simon saw that the Spirit *was* **given** at the laying on of the
8:19 "**Give** me also this ability so that everyone on whom I lay my
9:41 *He* **took** her by the hand and helped her to her feet. Then he called
10:40 him from the dead on the third day and **caused** him to be seen.
11:17 So if God **gave** them the same gift as he gave us, who believed in
11:18 "So then, God *has* **granted** even the Gentiles repentance unto life."
12:23 Immediately, because Herod *did* not **give** praise to God, an angel
13:20 God **gave** them judges until the time of Samuel the prophet.
13:21 and he **gave** them Saul son of Kish, of the tribe of Benjamin,
13:34 " '*I will* **give** you the holy and sure blessings promised to David.'
13:35 is stated elsewhere: " '*You will* not **let** your Holy One see decay.'

14: 3 for the Lord, who confirmed the message of his grace *by* **enabling** [+*1328*+*3836*+*5931*] them to do miraculous signs and wonders.
14:17 He has shown kindness *by* **giving** you rain from heaven and crops
15: 8 showed that he accepted them *by* **giving** the Holy Spirit to them,
17:25 *because he* himself **gives** all men life and breath and everything
19:31 sent him a message begging him not *to* **venture** [+*1571*] into the
20:32 and **give** you an inheritance among all those who are sanctified.
20:35 Jesus himself said: 'It is more blessed *to* **give** than to receive.' "
24:26 At the same time he was hoping that Paul *would* **offer** him a bribe,

Ro 4:20 of God, but was strengthened in his faith and **gave** glory to God,
5: 5 his love into our hearts by the Holy Spirit, whom *he* has **given** us.
11: 8 "God **gave** them a spirit of stupor, eyes so that they could not see
12: 3 For by the grace **given** me I say to every one of you: Do not think
12: 6 We have different gifts, according to the grace **given** us. If a man's
12:19 my friends, but **leave** room for God's wrath, for it is written:
14:12 So then, each of us *will* **give** an account of himself to God.
15: 5 *May* the God who gives endurance and encouragement **give** you a
15:15 if to remind you of them again, because of the grace **gave** me

1Co 1: 4 thank God for you because of his grace **given** you in Christ Jesus.
3: 5 you came to believe—as the Lord *has* **assigned** to each his *task*.
3:10 By the grace God *has* **given** me, I laid a foundation as an expert
7:25 but *I* **give** a judgment as one who by the Lord's mercy is
9:12 we put up with anything rather than **hinder** [+*1600*] the gospel of
11:15 it is her glory? For long hair *is* **given** to her as a covering.
12: 7 Now to each one the manifestation of the Spirit *is* **given** for the
12: 8 To one *there is* **given** through the Spirit the message of wisdom,
12:24 of the body and *has* **given** greater honor to the parts that lacked it,
14: 7 Even in the case of lifeless things *that* **make** sounds, such as the
14: 7 how will anyone know what tune is being played unless *there* **is**s a
14: 8 Again, if the trumpet *does* not **sound** a clear call, who will get
14: 9 Unless *you* **speak** intelligibly words with your tongue, how will
15.38 But God **gives** it a body as he has determined, and to each kind of
15:57 be to God! He **gives** us the victory through our Lord Jesus Christ.

2Co 1:22 and **put** his Spirit in our hearts as a deposit, guaranteeing what is to
5: 5 us for this very purpose and *has* **given** us the Spirit as a deposit,
5:12 to you again, but *are* **giving** you an opportunity to take pride in us,
5:18 himself through Christ and **gave** us the ministry of reconciliation.
6: 3 We **put** no stumbling block in anyone's path, so that our ministry
8: 1 we want you to know about the grace that God *has* **given** the
8: 5 but *they* **gave** themselves first to the Lord and then to us in
8:10 And *here* **is**s my advice about what is best for you in this matter:
8:16 who **put** into the heart of Titus the same concern I have for you.
9: 9 "He has scattered abroad his **gifts** to the poor; his righteousness
10: 8 the Lord **gave** us for building you up rather than pulling you down,
12: 7 *there was* **given** me a thorn in my flesh, a messenger of Satan,
13:10 the authority the Lord **gave** me for building you up, not for tearing

Gal 1: 4 who **gave** himself for our sins to rescue us from the present evil
2: 9 **gave** me and Barnabas the right hand of fellowship when they
2: 9 hand of fellowship when they recognized the grace **given** to me.
3:21 For if a law *had been* **given** that could impart life,
3:22 through faith in Jesus Christ, *might be* **given** to those who believe.
4:15 you *would have* torn out your eyes and **given** them to me.

Eph 1:17 glorious Father, *may* **give** you the Spirit of wisdom and revelation,
1:22 and **appointed** him *to be* head over everything for the church,
3: 2 the administration of God's grace that *was* **given** to me for you,
3: 7 I became a servant of this gospel by the gift of God's grace **given**
3: 8 am less than the least of all God's people, this grace *was* **given** me:
3:16 I pray that out of his glorious riches *he may* **strengthen** [+*3194*]
4: 7 But to each one of us grace *has been* **given** as Christ apportioned
4: 8 on high, he led captives in his train and **gave** gifts to men."
4:11 It was he *who* **gave** some to be apostles, some to be prophets,
4:27 and *do* not **give** the devil a foothold.
4:29 to their needs, that *it may* **benefit** [+*5921*] those who listen.
6:19 words *may he* **given** me so that I will fearlessly make known the

Col 1:25 I have become its servant by the commission God **gave** me to

1Th 4: 2 For you know what instructions *we* **gave** you by the authority of
4: 8 does not reject man but God, who **gives** you his Holy Spirit.

2Th 1: 8 *He will* **punish** [+*1689*] those who do not know God and do not
2:16 who loved us and by his grace **gave** us eternal encouragement
3: 9 but in order to **make** ourselves a model for you to follow.
3:16 Now *may* the Lord of peace himself **give** you peace at all times

1Ti 2: 6 who **gave** himself as a ransom for all men—the testimony given in
4:14 which *was* **given** you through a prophetic message when the body
5:14 their homes and *to* **give** the enemy no opportunity for slander.

2Ti 1: 7 For God *did* not **give** us a spirit of timidity, but a spirit of power,
1: 9 This grace *was* **given** us in Christ Jesus before the beginning of

1:16 *May* the Lord **show** mercy to the household of Onesiphorus,
1:18 *May* the Lord **grant** that he will find mercy from the Lord on that
2: 7 on what I am saying, for the Lord *will* **give** you insight into all this.
2:25 in the hope that God *will* **grant** them repentance leading them to a

Tit 2:14 who **gave** himself for us to redeem us from all wickedness
Heb 2:13 again he says, "Here am I, and the children God *has* **given** me."
7: 4 Even the patriarch Abraham **gave** him a tenth of the plunder!
8:10 *I will* **put** my laws in their minds and write them on their hearts.
10:16 *I will* **put** my laws in their hearts, and I will write them on their

Jas 1: 5 should ask God, who **gives** generously to all without finding fault,
1: 5 generously to all without finding fault, and *it will be* **given** to him.
2:16 and well fed," but **does** nothing about his physical needs,
4: 6 But *he* **gives** us more grace. That is why Scripture says: "God
4: 6 "God opposes the proud but **gives** grace to the humble."
5:18 Again he prayed, and the heavens **gave** rain, and the earth

1Pe 1:21 who raised him from the dead and **glorified** [+*1518*] him,
5: 5 because, "God opposes the proud but **gives** grace to the humble."

2Pe 3:15 brother Paul also wrote you with the wisdom that God **gave** him.

1Jn 3: 1 How great is the love the Father *has* **lavished** on us, that we should
3:23 and to love one another as *he* **commanded** [+*1953*] us.
3:24 we know that he lives in us: We know it by the Spirit *he* **gave** us.
4:13 we live in him and he in us, because *he has* **given** us of his Spirit.
5:11 God *has* **given** us eternal life, and this life is in his Son.
5:16 does not lead to death, he should pray and God *will* **give** him life.
5:20 also that the Son of God has come and *has* **given** us understanding,

Rev 1: 1 which God **gave** him to show his servants what must soon take
2: 7 who overcomes, *I will* **give the right** to eat from the tree of life,
2:10 even to the point of death, and *I will* **give** you the crown of life.
2:17 To him who overcomes, *I will* **give** some of the hidden manna.
2:17 *I will* also **give** him a white stone with a new name written on it,
2:21 *I have* **given** her time to repent of her immorality, but she is
2:23 and minds, and *I will* **repay** each of you according to your deeds.
2:26 and does my will to the end, *I will* **give** authority over the nations—
2:28 *I will* also **give** him the morning star.
3: 8 *I have* **placed** before you an open door that no one can shut.
3:21 *I will* **give the right** to sit with me on my throne, just as I
4: 9 Whenever the living creatures **give** glory, honor and thanks to him
6: 2 Its rider held a bow, and he. *was* **given** a crown, and he rode out as
6: 4 Its rider *was* **given** power to take peace from the earth and to make
6: 4 and to make men slay each other. To him *was* **given** a large sword.
6: 8 They *were* **given** power over a fourth of the earth to kill by sword,
6:11 Then each of them *was* **given** a white robe, and they were told to
7: 2 to the four angels who *had been* **given** power to harm the land
8: 2 who stand before God, and to them *were* **given** seven trumpets.
8: 3 He *was* **given** much incense to offer, with the prayers of all the
8: 3 He was given much incense to **offer**, with the prayers of all the
9: 1 to the earth. The star *was* **given** the key to the shaft of the Abyss.
9: 3 the earth and *were* **given** power like that of scorpions of the earth.
9: 5 They *were* not **given** power to kill them, but only to torture them
10: 9 So I went to the angel and asked him *to* **give** me the little scroll.
11: 1 I *was* **given** a reed like a measuring rod and was told, "Go
11: 2 do not measure it, because *it has been* **given** to the Gentiles.
11: 3 And *I will* **give** power to my two witnesses, and they will prophesy
11:13 the survivors were terrified and **gave** glory to the God of heaven.
11:18 and *for* **rewarding** [+*3635*+*3836*] your servants the prophets
12:14 The woman *was* **given** the two wings of a great eagle, so that she
13: 2 The dragon **gave** the beast his power and his throne and great
13: 4 worshiped the dragon because *he had* **given** authority to the beast,
13: 5 The beast *was* **given** a mouth to utter proud words
13: 5 was given a mouth to utter proud words and blasphemies **[RPG]**
13: 7 He *was* **given** power to make war against the saints and to conquer
13: 7 And he *was* **given** authority over every tribe, people, language
13:14 Because of the signs he *was* **given** power to do on behalf of the
13:15 He *was* **given** power to give breath to the image of the first beast,
13:15 He was given power *to* **give** breath to the image of the first beast,
13:16 and slave, to **receive** a mark on his right hand or on his forehead,
14: 7 He said in a loud voice, "Fear God and **give** him glory,
15: 7 Then one of the four living creatures **gave** to the seven angels
16: 6 and *you have* **given** them blood to drink as they deserve."
16: 8 on the sun, and the sun *was* **given** power to scorch people with fire.
16: 9 these plagues, but they refused to repent and **glorify** [+*1518*] him.
16:19 and **gave** her the cup filled with the wine of the fury of his wrath.
17:13 They have one purpose and *will* **give** their power and authority to
17:17 For God *has* **put** it into their hearts to accomplish his purpose by
17:17 his purpose by agreeing *to* **give** the beast their power to rule,
18: 7 **Give** her as much torture and grief as the glory and luxury she gave

19: 7 *Let us* rejoice and be glad and **give** him glory! For the wedding of
19: 8 Fine linen, bright and clean, *was* **given** her to wear." (Fine linen
20: 4 which were seated *those* who *had been* **given authority** to judge.
20:13 The sea **gave up** the dead that were in it, and death and Hades gave
20:13 in it, and death and Hades **gave up** the dead that were in them,
21: 6 To him who is thirsty I *will* **give** *to drink* without cost from the

1444 διεγείρω, *diegeirō* [6] [√ 1328 + 1586]

got up [2], refresh [1], rough [1], stimulate to [1], woke [1]

Mk 4:39 He **got up**, rebuked the wind and said to the waves, "Quiet!
Lk 8:24 The disciples went and **woke** him, saying, "Master, Master,
    8:24 He **got up** and rebuked the wind and the raging waters; the storm
Jn 6:18 A strong wind was blowing and the waters *grew* **rough**.
2Pe 1:13 I think it is right *to* **refresh** your memory as long as I live in the
    3: 1 I have written both of them as reminders *to* **stimulate** you **to**

1445 διενθυμέομαι, *dienthymeomai* [1]
[√ 1328 + 1877 + 2596]

thinking [1]

Ac 10:19 *While* Peter *was still* **thinking** about the vision, the Spirit said to

1446 διεξέρχομαι, *diexerchomai*   Not used in UBS/NIV [√ 1328 + 1666 + 2262]

1447 διέξοδος, *diexodos* [1] [√ 1328 + 1666 + 3847]

corners [1]

Mt 22: 9 Go to the street **corners** and invite to the banquet anyone you

1448 διερμηνεία, *diermēneia*   Not used in UBS/NIV [√ 1328 + 2257]

1449 διερμηνευτής, *diermēneutēs* [1]
[√ 1328 + 2257]

interpreter [1]

1Co 14:28 If there is no **interpreter**, the speaker should keep quiet in the

1450 διερμηνεύω, *diermēneuō* [6] [√ 1328 + 2257]

interpret [3], explained what said [1], interprets [1], translated [1]

Lk 24:27 he **explained** to them **what** *was* **said** in all the Scriptures
Ac 9:36 *when* **translated**, is Dorcas), who was always doing good
1Co 12:30 have gifts of healing? Do all speak in tongues? Do all **interpret**?
    14: 5 in tongues, unless *he* **interprets**, so that the church may be edified.
    14:13 in a tongue should pray that *he may* **interpret** what he says.
    14:27 should speak, one at a time, and someone *must* **interpret**.

1451 διέρχομαι, *dierchomai* [43 / 42] [√ 1328 + 2262]

go through [RP1328] [3], traveled through [3], coming [2], go [2], go over [2], goes through [RP1328] [2], going through [2], passing through [2], traveled throughout [2], went [2], came [1], come [1], go through [1], gone about [1], gone through [1], passed [1], passed through [RP1328] [1], pierce [1], spread [1], took the road through [1], traveled [1], traveled about [RP1328] [1], traveled about [1], traveled along [RP1328] [1], visit on way [RP1328] [1], walked around [1], walked right through [+1328+3545] [1], went around [1], went on [+4134] [1], went through [1]

Mt 12:43 *it goes* [RP1328] **through** arid places seeking rest and does not
    19:24 it is easier for a camel *to* **go** [RP1328] **through** the eye of a needle
Mk 4:35 he said to his disciples, "*Let us* **go over** to the other side."
    10:25 It is easier for a camel *to* **go** [RP1328] **through** the eye of a needle
Lk 2:15 "*Let's* **go** to Bethlehem and see this thing that has happened,
    2:35 will be revealed. And a sword *will* **pierce** your own soul too."
    4:30 But he **walked** [+1328+3545] **right through** the crowd and went

    5:15 Yet the news about him **spread** all the more, so that crowds of
    8:22 said to his disciples, "*Let's* **go over** to the other side of the lake."
    9: 6 So *they* set out and **went** from village to village,
    11:24 *it goes* [RP1328] **through** arid places seeking rest and does not
    17:11 Jesus **traveled** [RP1328] **along** the border between Samaria
    19: 1 Jesus entered Jericho and *was* **passing through**.
    19: 4 a sycamore-fig tree to see him, since Jesus was **coming** that way.
Jn 4: 4 Now he had to **go** [RP1328] **through** Samaria.
    4:15 I won't get thirsty and *have to keep* **coming** here to draw water."
Ac 8: 4 who had been scattered preached the word wherever *they* **went**.
    8:40 Philip, however, appeared at Azotus and **traveled about**,
    9:32 *As* Peter **traveled** [RP1328] **about** the country, he went to visit the
    9:38 they sent two men to him and urged him, "Please **come** *at once!*"
    10:38 and how he **went around** doing good and healing all who were
    11:19 in connection with Stephen **traveled** as far as Phoenicia,
    11:22 and they sent Barnabas [UBS+ *to go through*] to Antioch.
    12:10 *They* **passed** the first and second guards and came to the iron gate
    13: 6 *They* **traveled through** the whole island until they came to
    13:14 From Perga they **went** [+4134] **on** to Pisidian Antioch. On the
    14:24 *After* **going through** Pisidia, they came into Pamphylia,
    15: 3 their way, and as they **traveled through** Phoenicia and Samaria,
    15:41 *He* **went through** Syria and Cilicia, strengthening the churches.
    16: 6 and his companions **traveled throughout** the region of Phrygia
    17:23 For *as I* **walked around** and looked carefully at your objects of
    18:23 and **traveled** from place to place **throughout** the region of Galatia
    18:27 When Apollos wanted *to* **go** to Achaia, the brothers encouraged
    19: 1 Paul **took the road through** the interior and arrived at Ephesus.
    19:21 to go to Jerusalem, **passing through** Macedonia and Achaia.
    20: 2 *He* **traveled through** that area, speaking many words of
    20:25 "Now I know that none of you among whom *I have* **gone about**
Ro 5:12 and death through sin, and in this way death **came** to all men,
1Co 10: 1 the cloud and that *they* all **passed** [RP1328] **through** the sea.
    16: 5 After *I* **go through** Macedonia, I will come to you—for I will be
    16: 5 I will come to you—for *I will be* **going through** Macedonia.
2Co 1:16 I planned *to* **visit** [RP1328] you **on** *my* **way** to Macedonia
Heb 4:14 since we have a great high priest *who has* **gone through** the

1452 διερωτάω, *dierōtaō* [1] [√ 1328 + 2263]

found out [1]

Ac 10:17 the men sent by Cornelius **found out** where Simon's house was

1453 διετής, *dietēs* [1] [√ 1545 + 2291]

two years old [1]

Mt 2:16 in Bethlehem and its vicinity who were **two years old** and under,

1454 διετία, *dietia* [2] [√ 1545 + 2291]

two years [2]

Ac 24:27 When **two years** had passed, Felix was succeeded by Porcius
    28:30 For **two** whole **years** Paul stayed there in his own rented house

1455 διηγέομαι, *diēgeomai* [8] [√ 1328 + 72]

tell [3], told [2], described [1], reported [1], speak of [1]

Mk 5:16 Those who had seen it **told** the people what had happened to the
    9: 9 Jesus gave them orders not to **tell** anyone what they had seen until
Lk 8:39 "Return home and **tell** how much God has done for you."
    9:10 the apostles returned, *they* **reported** to Jesus what they had done.
Ac 8:33 Who *can* **speak of** his descendants? For his life was taken from the
    9:27 *He* **told** them how Saul on his journey had seen the Lord and that
    12:17 and **described** how the Lord had brought him out of prison.
Heb 11:32 I do not have time *to* **tell** about Gideon, Barak, Samson, Jephthah,

1456 διήγησις, *diēgēsis* [1] [√ 1328 + 72]

account [1]

Lk 1: 1 Many have undertaken to draw up an **account** of the things that

1457 διηνεκής, *diēnekēs* [4] [√ *1328 + 5770*]

forever [+*1650+3836*] [2], endlessly [+*1650+3836*] [1], for all time [+*1650+3836*] [1]

Heb 7: 3 like the Son of God he remains a priest **forever** [+*1650+3836*].
     10: 1 by the same sacrifices repeated **endlessly** [+*1650+3836*] year after
    10: 12 But when this priest had offered **for all time** [+*1650+3836*] one
    10: 14 perfect **forever** [+*1650+3836*] those who are being made holy.

1458 διθάλασσος, *dithalassos* [1] [√ *1545 + 2498*]

sandbar [+*5536*] [1]

Ac 27: 41 But the ship struck a **sandbar** [+*5536*] and ran aground. The bow

1459 διϊκνέομαι, *diikneomai* [1] [√ *1328 + 2653*]

penetrates [1]

Heb 4: 12 it **penetrates** even to dividing soul and spirit, joints and marrow;

1460 διΐστημι, *diistēmi* [3] [√ *1328 + 2705*]

later [2], left [1]

Lk 22: 59 About an hour **later** another asserted, "Certainly this fellow was
    24: 51 he was blessing them, *he* **left** them and was taken up into heaven.
Ac 27: 28 A short time **later** they took soundings again and found it was

1461 διϊστορέω, *diistoreō*   Not used in UBS/NIV [√ *1328 + 2707*]

1462 διϊσχυρίζομαι, *diischyrizomai* [2] [√ *1328 + 2709*]

asserted [1], insisting that [1]

Lk 22: 59 About an hour later another **asserted**, "Certainly this fellow was
Ac 12: 15 *When* she *kept* **insisting that** it was so, they said, "It must be his

1463 δικάζω, *dikazō*   Not used in UBS/NIV [√ *1472*]

1464 δικαιοκρισία, *dikaiokrisia* [1] [√ *1472 + 3212*]

righteous judgment [1]

Ro 2: 5 of God's wrath, when his **righteous judgment** will be revealed.

1465 δίκαιος, *dikaios* [79] [√ *1472*]

righteous [53], right [11], just [8], upright [3], innocent [2], honest [1], righteousness [1]

Mt 1: 19 Because Joseph her husband was a **righteous** *man* and did not
    5: 45 and the good, and sends rain on the **righteous** and the unrighteous.
    9: 13 For I have not come to call the **righteous**, but sinners."
    10: 41 and anyone who receives a **righteous** *man* because he is a
    10: 41 because he is a **righteous** *man* will receive a righteous man's
    10: 41 because he is a righteous man will receive a **righteous** *man's*
    13: 17 many prophets and **righteous** *men* longed to see what you see
    13: 43 Then the **righteous** will shine like the sun in the kingdom of their
    13: 49 The angels will come and separate the wicked from the **righteous**
    20: 4 and work in my vineyard, and I will pay you whatever is **right**.'
    23: 28 on the outside you appear to people as **righteous** but on the inside
    23: 29 tombs for the prophets and decorate the graves *of* the **righteous**.
    23: 35 so upon you will come all the **righteous** blood that has been shed
    23: 35 from the blood *of* **righteous** Abel to the blood of Zechariah son of
    25: 37 "Then the **righteous** will answer him, 'Lord, when did we see you
    25: 46 go away to eternal punishment, but the **righteous** to eternal life."
    27: 19 "Don't have anything to do *with* that **innocent** *man*, for I have
Mk 2: 17 but the sick. I have not come to call the **righteous**, but sinners."
    6: 20 and protected him, knowing him to be a **righteous** and holy man.
Lk 1: 6 Both of them were **upright** in the sight of God, observing all the
    1: 17 their children and the disobedient to the wisdom *of* the **righteous**—
    2: 25 a man in Jerusalem called Simeon, who was **righteous** and devout.

    5: 32 I have not come to call the **righteous**, but sinners to repentance."
    12: 57 "Why don't you judge for yourselves what is **right**?
    14: 14 repay you, you will be repaid at the resurrection *of* the **righteous**."
    15: 7 over ninety-nine **righteous** *persons* who do not need to repent.
    18: 9 To some who were confident of their own **righteousness**
    20: 20 a close watch on him, they sent spies, who pretended to be **honest**.
    23: 47 praised God and said, "Surely this was a **righteous** man."
    23: 50 named Joseph, a member of the Council, a good and **upright** man,
Jn 5: 30 I judge only as I hear, and my judgment is **just**, for I seek not to
    7: 24 Stop judging by mere appearances, and make a **right** judgment."
    17: 25 "**Righteous** Father, though the world does not know you,
Ac 3: 14 You disowned the Holy and **Righteous** *One* and asked that a
    4: 19 "Judge for yourselves whether it is **right** in God's sight to obey you
    7: 52 even killed those who predicted the coming *of* the **Righteous** One.
    10: 22 He is a **righteous** and God-fearing man, who is respected by all the
    22: 14 and to see the **Righteous** *One* and to hear words from his mouth.
    24: 15 that there will be a resurrection *of* both the **righteous**
Ro 1: 17 first to last, just as it is written: "The **righteous** will live by faith."
    2: 13 For it is not those who hear the law who are **righteous** in God's
    3: 10 As it is written: "There is no *one* **righteous**, not even one;
    3: 26 so as to be **just** and the one who justifies those who have faith in
    5: 7 Very rarely will anyone die for a **righteous** *man*, though for a
    5: 19 the obedience of the one man the many will be made **righteous**.
    7: 12 law is holy, and the commandment is holy, **righteous** and good.
Gal 3: 11 before God by the law, because, "The **righteous** will live by faith."
Eph 6: 1 Children, obey your parents in the Lord, for this is **right**.
Php 1: 7 It is **right** for me to feel this way about all of you, since I have you
    4: 8 is true, whatever is noble, whatever is **right**, whatever is pure,
Col 4: 1 Masters, provide your slaves with what is **right** and fair,
2Th 1: 5 All this is evidence that God's judgment is **right**, and as a result
    1: 6 God is **just**: He will pay back trouble to those who trouble you
1Ti 1: 9 We also know that law is made not *for* the **righteous** but for
2Ti 4: 8 which the Lord, the **righteous** Judge, will award to me on that
Tit 1: 8 what is good, who is self-controlled, **upright**, holy and disciplined.
Heb 10: 38 But my **righteous** *one* will live by faith. And if he shrinks back,
    11: 4 By faith he was commended as a **righteous** man, when God spoke
    12: 23 the judge of all men, to the spirits *of* **righteous** men made perfect,
Jas 5: 6 You have condemned and murdered **innocent** men, who were not
    5: 16 The prayer *of* a **righteous** *man* is powerful and effective.
1Pe 3: 12 For the eyes of the Lord are on the **righteous** and his ears are
    3: 18 once for all, the **righteous** for the unrighteous, to bring you to God.
    4: 18 And, "If it is hard for the **righteous** to be saved, what will become
2Pe 1: 13 I think it is **right** to refresh your memory as long as I live in the
    2: 7 and if he rescued Lot, a **righteous** *man*, who was distressed by the
    2: 8 (for that **righteous** *man*, living among them day after day,
    2: 8 was tormented in his **righteous** soul by the lawless deeds he saw
1Jn 1: 9 he is faithful and **just** and will forgive us our sins and purify us
    2: 1 to the Father in our defense—Jesus Christ, the **Righteous** One.
    2: 29 If you know that he is **righteous**, you know that everyone who
    3: 7 He who does what is right is **righteous**, just as he is righteous.
    3: 7 He who does what is right is righteous, just as he is **righteous**.
    3: 12 his own actions were evil and his brother's were **righteous**.
Rev 15: 3 Lord God Almighty. **Just** and true are your ways, King of the ages.
    16: 5 "You are **just** *in* these *judgments*, you who are and who were,
    16: 7 "Yes, Lord God Almighty, true and **just** are your judgments."
    19: 2 for true and **just** are his judgments. He has condemned the great
    22: 11 continue to be vile; let him who does **right** continue to do right;

1466 δικαιοσύνη, *dikaiosynē* [92] [√ *1472*]

δικαιοσύνη θεοῦ (righteousness of God) [10] Ro 1:17;
3:5,21,22; 10:3,3; 2Co 5:21; Php 3:9; Jas 1:20; 2Pe 1:1

δικαιοσύνη πιστέως (righteousness of faith) [6] Ro 4:11,13;
9:30; 10:6; Gal 5:5; Php 3:9

νόμος ... δικαιοσύνη (law ... righteousness) [8] Ro 3:21; 9:31;
10:4,5; Gal 2:21; 3:21; Php 3:6,9

righteousness [74], justice [5], what is right [5], right [2],
untranslated [1], acts of righteousness [1], it[s] [1], justified [+*1650*]
[1], righteous [+*1877*] [1], righteous life [1]

Mt 3: 15 so now; it is proper for us to do this to fulfill all **righteousness**."
    5: 6 Blessed are those who hunger and thirst for **righteousness**,
    5: 10 Blessed are those who are persecuted because *of* **righteousness**,
    5: 20 For I tell you that unless your **righteousness** surpasses that of the

6: 1 "Be careful not to do your 'acts of righteousness' before men,
6:33 But seek first his kingdom and his righteousness, and all these
21:32 For John came to you to show you the way of righteousness.
Lk   1:75 in holiness and righteousness before him all our days.
Jn   16: 8 the world of guilt in regard to sin and righteousness and judgment:
16:10 in regard to righteousness, because I am going to the Father,
Ac   10:35 accepts men from every nation who fear him and do what is right.
13:10 are a child of the devil and an enemy of everything that is right!
17:31 For he has set a day when he will judge the world with justice by
24:25 As Paul discoursed on righteousness, self-control
Ro   1:17 For in the gospel a righteousness from God is revealed,
3: 5 But if our unrighteousness brings out God's righteousness more
3:21 But now a righteousness from God, apart from law, has been
3:22 This righteousness from God comes through faith in Jesus Christ
3:25 He did this to demonstrate his justice, because in his forbearance
3:26 he did it to demonstrate his justice at the present time, so as to be
4: 3 believed God, and it was credited to him as righteousness."
4: 5 who justifies the wicked, his faith is credited as righteousness.
4: 6 of the man to whom God credits righteousness apart from works:
4: 9 saying that Abraham's faith was credited to him as righteousness.
4:11 a seal of the righteousness that he had by faith while he was still
4:11 in order that righteousness might be credited to them.
4:13 of the world, but through the righteousness that comes by faith.
4:22 This is why "it was credited to him as righteousness."
5:17 and of the gift of righteousness reign in life through the one man,
5:21 so also grace might reign through righteousness to bring eternal
6:13 the parts of your body to him as instruments of righteousness.
6:16 leads to death, or to obedience, which leads to righteousness?
6:18 been set free from sin and have become slaves to righteousness.
6:19 so now offer them in slavery to righteousness leading to holiness.
6:20 slaves to sin, you were free from the control of righteousness.
8:10 because of sin, yet your spirit is alive because of righteousness.
9:30 the Gentiles, who did not pursue righteousness, have obtained it,
9:30 have obtained it^s, a righteousness that is by faith;
9:30 have obtained it, a righteousness that is by faith;
9:31 but Israel, who pursued a law of righteousness, has not attained it.
10: 3 Since they did not know the righteousness that comes from God
10: 3 their own, [RPG] they did not submit to God's righteousness.
10: 3 to establish their own, they did not submit to God's righteousness.
10: 4 so that there may be righteousness for everyone who believes.
10: 5 Moses describes in this way the righteousness that is by the law:
10: 6 But the righteousness that is by faith says: "Do not say in your
10:10 For it is with your heart that you believe and are justified [+1650],
14:17 but of righteousness, peace and joy in the Holy Spirit,
1Co   1:30 from God—that is, our righteousness, holiness and redemption.
2Co   3: 9 much more glorious is the ministry that brings righteousness!
5:21 so that in him we might become the righteousness of God.
6: 7 with weapons of righteousness in the right hand and in the left;
6:14 For what do righteousness and wickedness have in common?
9: 9 abroad his gifts to the poor; his righteousness endures forever."
9:10 store of seed and will enlarge the harvest of your righteousness.
11:15 then, if his servants masquerade as servants of righteousness.
Gal   2:21 for if righteousness could be gained through the law, Christ died
3: 6 "He believed God, and it was credited to him as righteousness."
3:21 then righteousness would certainly have come by the law.
5: 5 But by faith we eagerly await through the Spirit the righteousness
Eph   4:24 created to be like God in true righteousness and holiness.
5: 9 fruit of the light consists in all goodness, righteousness and truth)
6:14 around your waist, with the breastplate of righteousness in place,
Php   1:11 filled with the fruit of righteousness that comes through Jesus
3: 6 persecuting the church; as for legalistic righteousness, faultless.
3: 9 not having a righteousness of my own that comes from the law,
3: 9 in Christ—the righteousness that comes from God and is by faith.
1Ti   6:11 and pursue righteousness, godliness, faith, love, endurance
2Ti   2:22 desires of youth, and pursue righteousness, faith, love and peace,
3:16 for teaching, rebuking, correcting and training in righteousness,
4: 8 Now there is in store for me the crown of righteousness,
Tit   3: 5 not because of righteous [+1877] things we had done, but
Heb   1: 9 You have loved righteousness and hated wickedness;
5:13 an infant, is not acquainted with the teaching about righteousness.
7: 2 tenth of everything. First, his name means "king of righteousness";
11: 7 and became heir of the righteousness that comes by faith.
11:33 administered justice, and gained what was promised;
12:11 it produces a harvest of righteousness and peace for those who
Jas   1:20 for man's anger does not bring about the righteous life that God
2:23 believed God, and it was credited to him as righteousness,"

3:18 Peacemakers who sow in peace raise a harvest of righteousness.
1Pe   2:24 on the tree, so that we might die to sins and live for righteousness;
3:14 But even if you should suffer for what is right, you are blessed.
2Pe   1: 1 To those who through the righteousness of our God and Savior
2: 5 but protected Noah, a preacher of righteousness, and seven others;
2:21 been better for them not to have known the way of righteousness,
3:13 to a new heaven and a new earth, the home of righteousness.
1Jn   2:29 you know that everyone who does what is right has been born of
3: 7 He who does what is right is righteous, just as he is righteous.
3:10 Anyone who does not do what is right is not a child of God;
Rev   19:11 is called Faithful and True. With justice he judges and makes war.
22:11 continue to be vile; let him who does right continue to do right;

1467 δικαιόω, dikaioō [39] [√ 1472]

justified [19], justify [4], justifies [3], proved right [3], considered righteous [2], declared righteous [2], acknowledged that right [1], acquitted [1], freed [1], justified before God [1], make innocent [1], vindicated [1]

Mt   11:19 and "sinners." ' But wisdom is proved right by her actions."
12:37 For by your words you will be acquitted, and by your words you
Lk   7:29 they heard Jesus' words, acknowledged that God's way was right,
7:35 But wisdom is proved right by all her children."
10:29 But he wanted to justify himself, so he asked Jesus, "And who is
16:15 "You are the ones who justify yourselves in the eyes of men,
18:14 this man, rather than the other, went home justified before God.
Ac   13:39 Through him everyone who believes is justified from everything
13:39 everything you could not be justified from by the law of Moses.
Ro   2:13 but it is those who obey the law who will be declared righteous.
3: 4 "So that you may be proved right when you speak and prevail
3:20 Therefore no one will be declared righteous in his sight by
3:24 and are justified freely by his grace through the redemption that
3:26 to be just and the one who justifies those who have faith in Jesus.
3:28 For we maintain that a man is justified by faith apart from
3:30 who will justify the circumcised by faith and the uncircumcised
4: 2 If, in fact, Abraham was justified by works, he had something to
4: 5 man who does not work but trusts God who justifies the wicked,
5: 1 Therefore, since we have been justified through faith, we have
5: 9 Since we have now been justified by his blood, how much more
6: 7 because anyone who has died has been freed from sin.
8:30 he predestined, he also called; those he called, he also justified;
8:30 he called, he also justified; those he justified, he also glorified.
8:33 against those whom God has chosen? It is God who justifies.
1Co   4: 4 My conscience is clear, but that does not make me innocent.
6:11 you were justified in the name of the Lord Jesus Christ and by the
Gal   2:16 know that a man is not justified by observing the law,
2:16 have put our faith in Christ Jesus that we may be justified by faith
2:16 the law, because by observing the law no one will be justified.
2:17 "If, while we seek to be justified in Christ, it becomes evident that
3: 8 The Scripture foresaw that God would justify the Gentiles by
3:11 Clearly no one is justified before God by the law, because,
3:24 in charge to lead us to Christ that we might be justified by faith.
5: 4 You who are trying to be justified by law have been alienated
1Ti   3:16 in a body, was vindicated by the Spirit, was seen by angels,
Tit   3: 7 so that, having been justified by his grace, we might become heirs
Jas   2:21 Was not our ancestor Abraham considered righteous for what he
2:24 You see that a person is justified by what he does and not by faith
2:25 was not even Rahab the prostitute considered righteous for what

1468 δικαίωμα, dikaiōma [10] [√ 1472]

regulations [3], righteous acts [2], act of righteousness [1], justification [1], requirements [1], righteous decree [1], righteous requirements [1]

Lk   1: 6 all the Lord's commandments and regulations blamelessly.
Ro   1:32 Although they know God's righteous decree that those who do
2:26 If those who are not circumcised keep the law's requirements,
5:16 but the gift followed many trespasses and brought justification.
5:18 so also the result of one act of righteousness was justification that
8: 4 in order that the righteous requirements of the law might be fully
Heb   9: 1 Now the first covenant had regulations for worship and also an
9:10 external regulations applying until the time of the new order.
Rev   15: 4 worship before you, for your righteous acts have been revealed."
19: 8 her to wear." (Fine linen stands for the righteous acts of the saints.)

1469 δικαίως, *dikaiōs* [5] [√ *1472*]

justly [2], as ought [1], righteous [1], upright [1]

Lk 23:41 We are punished **justly**, for we are getting what our deeds deserve.
1Co 15:34 Come back to your senses **as** you **ought**, and stop sinning;
1Th 2:10 **righteous** and blameless we were among you who believed.
Tit 2:12 to live self-controlled, **upright** and godly *lives* in this present age,
1Pe 2:23 no threats. Instead, he entrusted himself to him who judges **justly**.

1470 δικαίωσις, *dikaiōsis* [2] [√ *1472*]

justification [2]

Ro 4:25 to death for our sins and was raised to life for our **justification**.
5:18 so also the result of one act of righteousness was **justification** that

1471 δικαστής, *dikastēs* [2] [√ *1472*]

judge [2]

Ac 7:27 Moses aside and said, 'Who made you ruler and **judge** over us?
7:35 had rejected with the words, 'Who made you ruler and **judge**?'

1472 δίκη, *dikē* [3] [→ *92, 93, 94, 95, 96, 97, 508, 1463,
1464, 1465, 1466, 1467, 1468, 1469, 1470, 1471, 1688, 1689,
1690, 1899, 2868, 2869, 3293, 3294, 5688*]

Justice [1], punished [+*5514*] [1], punishment [1]

Ac 28: 4 he escaped from the sea, **Justice** has not allowed him to live."
2Th 1: 9 They *will be* **punished** [+*5514*] with everlasting destruction
Jude 1: 7 They serve as an example of those who suffer the **punishment** of

1473 δίκτυον, *diktyon* [12]

nets [8], net [4]

Mt 4:20 At once they left their **nets** and followed him.
4:21 They were in a boat with their father Zebedee, preparing their **nets**.
Mk 1:18 At once they left their **nets** and followed him.
1:19 son of Zebedee and his brother John in a boat, preparing their **nets**.
Lk 5: 2 left there by the fishermen, who were washing their **nets**.
5: 4 "Put out into deep water, and let down the **nets** for a catch."
5: 5 caught anything. But because you say so, I will let down the **nets**."
5: 6 they caught such a large number of fish that their **nets** began to
Jn 21: 6 "Throw your **net** on the right side of the boat and you will find
21: 8 towing the **net** full of fish, for they were not far from shore,
21:11 Simon Peter climbed aboard and dragged the **net** ashore. It was full
21:11 full of large fish, 153, but even with so many the **net** was not torn.

1474 δίλογος, *dilogos* [1] [√ *1545 + 3306*]

sincere [+*3590*] [1]

1Ti 3: 8 likewise, are to be men worthy of respect, **sincere** [+*3590*],

1475 διό, *dio* [53] [√ *1328 + 4005*]

therefore [27], so [11], that is why [5], this is why [4], *untranslated*
[1], and so [1], for this reason [1], now [1], so then [1], then [1]

Mt 27: 8 **That is why** it has been called the Field of Blood to this day.
Lk 1:35 **So** the holy one to be born will be called the Son of God.
7: 7 **That is why** I did not even consider myself worthy to come to you.
Ac 10:29 **So** when I was sent for, I came without raising any objection.
15:19 "It is my judgment, **therefore**, that we should not make it difficult
20:31 **So** be on your guard! Remember that for three years I never
24:26 him a bribe, **so** he sent for him frequently and talked with him.
25:26 **Therefore** I have brought him before all of you, and especially
26: 3 and controversies. **Therefore**, I beg you to listen to me patiently.
27:25 **So** keep up your courage, men, for I have faith in God that it will
27:34 Now I urge you to take some food. You need it to survive.
Ro 1:24 **Therefore** God gave them over in the sinful desires of their hearts
2: 1 You, **therefore**, have no excuse, you who pass judgment on
4:22 **This is why** "it was credited to him as righteousness."
13: 5 **Therefore**, it is necessary to submit to the authorities, not only
15: 7 Accept one another, **then**, just as Christ accepted you, in order to

15:22 **This is why** I have often been hindered from coming to you.
1Co 12: 3 **Therefore** I tell you that no one who is speaking by the Spirit of
14:13 **For this reason** anyone who speaks in a tongue should pray that
2Co 1:20 **so** through him the "Amen" is spoken by us to the glory of God.
2: 8 I urge you, **therefore**, to reaffirm your love for him.
4:13 It is written: "I believed; **therefore** I have spoken." With that same
4:13 With that same spirit of faith we also believe and **therefore** speak,
4:16 **Therefore** we do not lose heart. Though outwardly we are wasting
5: 9 **So** we make it our goal to please him, whether we are at home in
6:17 "**Therefore** come out from them and be separate, says the Lord.
12: 7 [NIE] To keep me from becoming conceited because of these
12:10 **That is why**, for Christ's sake, I delight in weaknesses, in insults,
Gal 4:31 **Therefore**, brothers, we are not children of the slave woman,
Eph 2:11 **Therefore**, remember that formerly you who are Gentiles by birth
3:13 I ask you, **therefore**, not to be discouraged because of my
4: 8 **This is why** it says: "When he ascended on high, he led captives in
4:25 **Therefore** each of you must put off falsehood and speak truthfully
5:14 **This is why** it is said: "Wake up, O sleeper, rise from the dead,
Php 2: 9 **Therefore** God exalted him to the highest place and gave him the
1Th 3: 1 **So** when we could stand it no longer, we thought it best to be left
5:11 **Therefore** encourage one another and build each other up,
Phm 1: 8 **Therefore**, although in Christ I could be bold and order you to do
Heb 3: 7 **So**, as the Holy Spirit says: "Today, if you hear his voice,
3:10 **That is why** I was angry with that generation, and I said,
6: 1 **Therefore** let us leave the elementary teachings about Christ
10: 5 **Therefore**, when Christ came into the world, he said: "Sacrifice
11:12 And **so** from this one man, and he as good as dead,
11:16 **Therefore** God is not ashamed to be called their God, for he has
12:12 **Therefore**, strengthen your feeble arms and weak knees.
12:28 **Therefore**, since we are receiving a kingdom that cannot be
13:12 And **so** Jesus also suffered outside the city gate to make the people
Jas 1:21 **Therefore**, get rid of all moral filth and the evil that is so prevalent
4: 6 **That is why** Scripture says: "God opposes the proud but gives
1Pe 1:13 **Therefore**, prepare your minds for action; be self-controlled;
2Pe 1:10 **Therefore**, my brothers, be all the more eager to make your calling
1:12 **So** I will always remind you of these things, even though you know
3:14 **So then**, dear friends, since you are looking forward to this,

1476 διοδεύω, *diodeuō* [2] [√ *1328 + 3847*]

passed through [1], traveled about [1]

Lk 8: 1 Jesus **traveled about** from one town and village to another,
Ac 17: 1 *When they had* **passed through** Amphipolis and Apollonia,

1477 Διονύσιος, *Dionysios* [1]

Dionysius [1]

Ac 17:34 Among them was **Dionysius**, a member of the Areopagus,

1478 διόπερ, *dioper* [2] [√ *1328 + 4005 + 4302*]

therefore [2]

1Co 8:13 **Therefore**, if what I eat causes my brother to fall into sin,
10:14 **Therefore**, my dear friends, flee from idolatry.

1479 διοπετής, *diopetēs* [1] [√ *2416 + 4406*]

image which fell from heaven [1]

Ac 19:35 of the great Artemis and *of* her **image, which fell from heaven**?

1480 διόρθωμα, *diorthōma* [1] [√ *1328 + 3981*]

reforms [1]

Ac 24: 2 and your foresight has brought about **reforms** in this nation.

1481 διόρθωσις, *diorthōsis* [1] [√ *1328 + 3981*]

the new order [1]

Heb 9:10 external regulations applying until the time *of* **the new order**.

1482 διορύσσω, *dioryssō* [4] [√ *1328 + 4002*]

break in [2], broken into [2]

Mt 6: 19 where moth and rust destroy, and where thieves **break in** and steal.
     6: 20 rust do not destroy, and where thieves *do* not **break in** and steal.
    24: 43 have kept watch and would not have let his house *be* **broken into**.
Lk 12: 39 thief was coming, he would not have let his house *be* **broken into**.

1483 Διόσκουροι, *Dioskouroi* [1] [√ *2416 + 3025*]

twin gods Castor and Pollux [1]

Ac 28: 11 ship with the figurehead of the **twin gods Castor and Pollux**.

1484 διότι, *dioti* [23] [√ *1328 + 4005 + 5515*]

because [10], for [6], *untranslated* [3], therefore [2], since [1], so [1]

Lk   1: 13 "Do not be afraid, Zechariah; **[NIE]** your prayer has been heard.
     2: 7 him in a manger, **because** there was no room for them in the inn.
    21: 28 and lift up your heads, **because** your redemption is drawing near."
Ac 13: 35 **So** it is stated elsewhere: " 'You will not let your Holy One see
    18: 10 **For** I am with you, and no one is going to attack and harm you,
    18: 10 to attack and harm you, **because** I have many people in this city."
    20: 26 **Therefore**, I declare to you today that I am innocent of the blood
    22: 18 **because** they will not accept your testimony about me.'
Ro   1: 19 **since** what may be known about God is plain to them, because God
     1: 21 **For** although they knew God, they neither glorified him as God
     3: 20 **Therefore** no one will be declared righteous in his sight by
     8: 7 **[NIE]** the sinful mind is hostile to God. It does not submit to
1Co 15: 9 to be called an apostle, **because** I persecuted the church of God.
Php 2: 26 longs for all of you and is distressed **because** you heard he was ill.
1Th 2: 8 but our lives as well, **because** you had become so dear to us.
     2: 18 **For** we wanted to come to you—certainly I, Paul, did, again
     4: 6 **[NIE]** The Lord will punish men for all such sins, as we have
Heb 11: 5 he could not be found, **because** God had taken him away.
    11: 23 **because** they saw he was no ordinary child, and they were not
Jas 4: 3 you do not receive, **because** you ask with wrong motives,
1Pe 1: 16 **for** it is written: "Be holy, because I am holy."
     1: 24 **For**, "All men are like grass, and all their glory is like the flowers of
     2: 6 **For** in Scripture it says: "See, I lay a stone in Zion, a chosen

1485 Διοτρέφης, *Diotrephēs* [1] [√ *2416 + 5555*]

Diotrephes [1]

3Jn 1: 9 I wrote to the church, but **Diotrephes**, who loves to be first,

1486 διπλόος, *diploos* Not used in UBS/NIV [√ *1545*]

1487 διπλοῦς, *diplous* [4] [√ *1545*]

double [2], pay back double [+*1488*] [1], twice as much [1]

Mt 23: 15 you make him **twice as much** a son of hell *as* you are.
1Ti 5: 17 direct the affairs of the church well are worthy *of* **double** honor,
Rev 18: 6 has given; **pay** her **back double** [+*1488*] for what she has done.
    18: 6 what she has done. Mix her a **double** *portion* from her own cup.

1488 διπλόω, *diploō* [1] [√ *1545*]

pay back double [+*1487*] [1]

Rev 18: 6 has given; **pay** her **back double** [+*1487*] for what she has done.

1489 δίς, *dis* [6] [√ *1545*]

twice [4], again [2]

Mk 14: 30 before the rooster crows **twice** you yourself will disown me three
    14: 72 "Before the rooster crows **twice** you will disown me three times."
Lk 18: 12 I fast **twice** a week and give a tenth of all I get.'
Php 4: 16 you sent me aid again and **again** when I was in need.
1Th 2: 18 certainly I, Paul, did, again and **again**—but Satan stopped us.
Jude 1: 12 by the wind; autumn trees, without fruit and uprooted—**twice** dead.

1490 δισμυριάς, *dismyrias* [1] [√ *1545 + 3692*]

two hundred million [+*3689*] [1]

Rev 9: 16 number of the mounted troops was **two hundred million** [+*3689*].

1491 διστάζω, *distazō* [2] [√ *1545*]

doubt [1], doubted [1]

Mt 14: 31 and caught him. "You of little faith," he said, "why *did you* **doubt**?"
    28: 17 When they saw him, they worshiped him; but some **doubted**.

1492 δίστομος, *distomos* [3] [√ *1545 + 5125*]

double-edged [3]

Heb 4: 12 Sharper than any **double-edged** sword, it penetrates even to
Rev 1: 16 and out of his mouth came a sharp **double-edged** sword.
     2: 12 are the words of him who has the sharp, **double-edged** sword.

1493 δισχίλιοι, *dischilioi* [1] [√ *1545 + 5943*]

two thousand [1]

Mk   5: 13 The herd, about **two thousand** *in number*, rushed down the steep

1494 διϋλίζω, *diylizō* [1] [√ *1328 + 5627*]

strain out [1]

Mt 23: 24 You blind guides! You **strain out** a gnat but swallow a camel.

1495 διχάζω, *dichazō* [1] [√ *1545*]

turn [1]

Mt 10: 35 For I have come *to* **turn** " 'a man against his father, a daughter

1496 διχοστασία, *dichostasia* [2] [√ *1545 + 2705*]

dissensions [1], divisions [1]

Ro 16: 17 to watch out for those who cause **divisions** and put obstacles in
Gal 5: 20 jealousy, fits of rage, selfish ambition, **dissensions**, factions

1497 διχοτομέω, *dichotomeō* [2] [√ *1545 + 5533*]

cut to pieces [2]

Mt 24: 51 *He will* **cut** him **to pieces** and assign him a place with the
Lk 12: 46 *He will* **cut** him **to pieces** and assign him a place with the

1498 διψάω, *dipsaō* [16] [→ *1499*]

thirsty [13], thirst [2], thirst for [1]

Mt   5: 6 Blessed are those who hunger and **thirst for** righteousness,
    25: 35 *I was* **thirsty** and you gave me something to drink, I was a stranger
    25: 37 and feed you, or **thirsty** and give you something to drink?
    25: 42 me nothing to eat, *I was* **thirsty** and you gave me nothing to drink,
    25: 44 or **thirsty** or a stranger or needing clothes or sick or in prison,
Jn   4: 13 "Everyone who drinks this water *will be* **thirsty** again,
     4: 14 but whoever drinks the water I give him *will* never **thirst**.
     4: 15 give me this water so that *I* won't *get* **thirsty** and have to keep
     6: 35 never go hungry, and he who believes in me *will* never *be* **thirsty**.
     7: 37 in a loud voice, "If anyone *is* **thirsty**, let him come to me and drink.
    19: 28 so that the Scripture would be fulfilled, Jesus said, "*I am* **thirsty**."
Ro 12: 20 is hungry, feed him; if *he is* **thirsty**, give him something to drink.
1Co 4: 11 To this very hour *we* go hungry and **thirsty**, we are in rags,
Rev 7: 16 Never again will they hunger; never again *will they* **thirst**.
    21: 6 *To* him *who is* **thirsty** I will give to drink without cost from the
    22: 17 Whoever *is* **thirsty**, let him come; and whoever wishes, let him

1499 δίψος, *dipsos* [1] [√ *1498*]

thirst [1]

2Co 11: 27 I have known hunger and **thirst** and have often gone without food;

1500 δίψυχος, *dipsychos* [2] [√ *1545 + 6038*]

double-minded [2]

Jas 1: 8 he is a **double-minded** man, unstable in all he does.
     4: 8 you sinners, and purify your hearts, you **double-minded**.

1501 διωγμός, *diōgmos* [10] [√ *1503*]

persecution [5], persecutions [5]

Mt 13:21 When trouble or **persecution** comes because of the word,
Mk   4:17 When trouble or **persecution** comes because of the word,
    10:30 mothers, children and fields—and with them, **persecutions**)
Ac   8: 1 On that day a great **persecution** broke out against the church at
    13:50 They stirred up **persecution** against Paul and Barnabas,
Ro   8:35 Shall trouble or hardship or **persecution** or famine or nakedness
2Co 12:10 in insults, in hardships, in **persecutions**, in difficulties.
2Th 1: 4 and faith in all the **persecutions** and trials you are enduring.
2Ti 3:11 **persecutions**, sufferings—what kinds of things happened to me in
     3:11 to me in Antioch, Iconium and Lystra, the **persecutions** I endured.

1502 διώκτης, *diōktēs* [1] [√ *1503*]

persecutor [1]

1Ti 1:13 I was once a blasphemer and a **persecutor** and a violent man,

1503 διώκω, *diōkō* [45] [→ *1501, 1502, 1691, 2870*]

persecuted [15], persecute [11], pursue [5], persecuting [4],
make every effort [2], press on [2], pursued [2], follow [1],
practice [1], running off after [1], try [1]

Mt   5:10 Blessed are those *who are* **persecuted** because of righteousness,
     5:11 **persecute** you and falsely say all kinds of evil against you
     5:12 for in the same way *they* **persecuted** the prophets who were before
     5:44 Love your enemies and pray for those *who* **persecute** you,
    10:23 When you *are* **persecuted** in one place, flee to another. I tell you
    23:34 others *you will* flog in your synagogues and **pursue** from town to
Lk 11:49 some of whom they will kill and others *they will* **persecute**.'
    17:23 'There he is!' or 'Here he is!' Do not go **running off after** them.
    21:12 "But before all this, they will lay hands on you and **persecute** you.
Jn   5:16 was doing these things on the Sabbath, the Jews **persecuted** him.
    15:20 If *they* **persecuted** me, they will persecute you also. If they obeyed
    15:20 If they persecuted me, *they* will **persecute** you also. If they obeyed
Ac   7:52 Was there ever a prophet your fathers *did* not **persecute**?
     9: 4 heard a voice say to him, "Saul, Saul, why *do you* **persecute** me?"
     9: 5 Saul asked. "I am Jesus, whom you *are* **persecuting**," he replied.
    22: 4 I **persecuted** the followers of this Way to their death,
    22: 7 heard a voice say to me, 'Saul! Saul! Why *do you* **persecute** me?'
    22: 8 " 'I am Jesus of Nazareth, whom you *are* **persecuting**,' he replied.
    26:11 against them, I even went to foreign cities *to* **persecute** them.
    26:14 saying to me in Aramaic, 'Saul, Saul, why *do you* **persecute** me?
    26:15 " 'I am Jesus, whom you *are* **persecuting**,' the Lord replied.
Ro   9:30 the Gentiles, who *did* not **pursue** righteousness, have obtained it,
     9:31 but Israel, who **pursued** a law of righteousness, has not attained it.
    12:13 Share with God's people who are in need. **Practice** hospitality.
    12:14 Bless those *who* **persecute** you; bless and do not curse.
    14:19 *Let us* therefore **make every effort** to do what leads to peace
1Co 4:12 we are cursed, we bless; *when we are* **persecuted**, we endure it;
    14: 1 **Follow** the way of love and eagerly desire spiritual gifts,
    15: 9 to be called an apostle, because *I* **persecuted** the church of God.
2Co 4: 9 **persecuted**, but not abandoned; struck down, but not destroyed.
Gal 1:13 how intensely *I* **persecuted** the church of God and tried to destroy
     1:23 "The man *who* formerly **persecuted** us is now preaching the faith
     4:29 At that time the son born in the ordinary way **persecuted** the son
     5:11 am still preaching circumcision, why *am I* still *being* **persecuted**?
     6:12 The only reason they do this is to avoid *being* **persecuted** for
Php 3: 6 as for zeal, **persecuting** the church; as for legalistic righteousness,
     3:12 but *I* **press on** to take hold of that for which Christ Jesus took hold
     3:14 *I* **press on** toward the goal to win the prize for which God has
1Th 5:15 but always *try* to be kind to each other and to everyone else.
1Ti 6:11 and **pursue** righteousness, godliness, faith, love, endurance
2Ti 2:22 desires of youth, and **pursue** righteousness, faith, love and peace,
     3:12 who wants to live a godly life in Christ Jesus *will be* **persecuted**,
Heb 12:14 **Make every effort** *to live* in peace with all men and to be holy;

1Pe 3:11 turn from evil and do good; he must seek peace and **pursue** it.
Rev 12:13 *he* **pursued** the woman who had given birth to the male child.

1504 δόγμα, *dogma* [5] [√ *1506*]

regulations [2], decisions [1], decree [1], decrees [1]

Lk   2: 1 In those days Caesar Augustus issued a **decree** that a census should
Ac 16: 4 they delivered the **decisions** reached by the apostles and elders in
    17: 7 They are all defying Caesar's **decrees**, saying that there is another
Eph 2:15 in his flesh the law with its commandments and **regulations**.
Col 2:14 *with* its **regulations**, that was against us and that stood opposed to

1505 δογματίζω, *dogmatizō* [1] [√ *1506*]

submit to rules [1]

Col 2:20 as though you still belonged to it, *do you* **submit to** its **rules**:

1506 δοκέω, *dokeō* [62] [→ *638, 1504, 1505, 2305, 2306, 4659, 4660, 5306; cf. 1518*]

think [20], thought [7], thinks [6], seems [3], thinking [3], expect
[2], seem [2], seemed good [2], think that [2], considered [1],
considers himself [1], convinced [+*1831*] [1], decided [1], found
[1], men[s] [1], opinion [1], regarded [1], reputed [1], seemed [1],
seemed to be leaders [1], so[s] [1], supposing [1], take for [+*1639*]
[1], wants [1]

Mt   3: 9 And *do* not **think** you can say to yourselves, 'We have Abraham as
     6: 7 for *they* **think** they will be heard because of their many words.
    17:25 Jesus was the first to speak. "What *do* you **think**, Simon?"
    18:12 "What *do* you **think**? If a man owns a hundred sheep, and one of
    21:28 "What *do* you **think**? There was a man who had two sons. He went
    22:17 Tell us then, what *is* your **opinion**? Is it right to pay taxes to Caesar
    22:42 "What *do* you **think** about the Christ? Whose son is he?"
    24:44 the Son of Man will come at an hour *when you do* not **expect** him.
    26:53 *Do you* **think** I cannot call on my Father, and he will at once put at
    26:66 What *do* you **think**?" "He is worthy of death," they answered.
Mk   6:49 they saw him walking on the lake, *they* **thought** he was a ghost.
    10:42 "You know that those *who are* **regarded** as rulers of the Gentiles
Lk   1: 3 *it* **seemed good** also to me to write an orderly account for you,
     8:18 does not have, even what *he* **thinks** he has will be taken from him."
    10:36 "Which of these three *do* you **think** was a neighbor to the man who
    12:40 the Son of Man will come at an hour *when you do* not **expect** him."
    12:51 *Do you* **think** I came to bring peace on earth? No, I tell you,
    13: 2 "*Do you* **think** that these Galileans were worse sinners than all the
    13: 4 *do you* **think** they were more guilty than all the others living in
    19:11 and the people **thought** that the kingdom of God was going to
    22:24 among them as to which of them *was* **considered** to be greatest.
    24:37 *They* were startled and frightened, **thinking** they saw a ghost.
Jn   5:39 because you **think that** by them you possess eternal life.
     5:45 "But *do* not **think** I will accuse you before the Father. Your accuser
    11:13 of his death, but his disciples **thought** he meant natural sleep.
    11:31 followed her, **supposing** she was going to the tomb to mourn there.
    11:56 in the temple area they asked one another, "What *do you* **think**?
    13:29 some **thought** Jesus was telling him to buy what was needed for
    16: 2 a time is coming when anyone who kills you *will* **think** he is
    20:15 **Thinking** he was the gardener, she said, "Sir, if you have carried
Ac 12: 9 doing was really happening; *he* **thought** he was seeing a vision.
    15:22 **decided** to choose some of their own men and send them to
    15:25 So[s] we all agreed to choose some men and send them to you with
    15:28 *It* **seemed good** to the Holy Spirit and to us not to burden you with
    17:18 Others remarked, "*He* **seems** to be advocating foreign gods."
    25:27 For *I* **think** it is unreasonable to send on a prisoner without
    26: 9 "I too *was* **convinced** [+*1831*] that I ought to do all that was
    27:13 began to blow, *they* **thought** they had obtained what they wanted;
1Co 3:18 If any one of you **thinks** he is wise by the standards of this age,
     4: 9 For *it* **seems** *to* me that God has put us apostles on display at the
     7:40 if she stays as she is—and *I* **think that** I too have the Spirit of God.
     8: 2 The man who **thinks** he knows something does not yet know as he
    10:12 So, *if you* **think** you are standing firm, be careful that you don't
    11:16 If anyone **wants** to be contentious about this, we have no other
    12:22 those parts of the body that **seem** to be weaker are indispensable,
    12:23 and the parts that *we* **think** are less honorable we treat with special
    14:37 If anybody **thinks** he is a prophet or spiritually gifted, let him

2Co 10: 9 *I do* not want *to* **seem** to be trying to frighten you with my letters.
    11:16 I repeat: *Let* no one **take** [+*1639*] me **for** a fool. But if you do,
    12:19 *Have you been* **thinking** all along that we have been defending
Gal 2: 2 But I did this privately *to* those *who* **seemed to be leaders,**
     2: 6 As for those *who* **seemed** to be important—whatever they were
     2: 6 external appearance—those men^s added nothing to my message.
     2: 9 those **reputed** to be pillars, gave me and Barnabas the right hand
     6: 3 If anyone **thinks** he is something when he is nothing, he deceives
Php 3: 4 If anyone else **thinks** *he has reasons* to put confidence in the
Heb 4: 1 let us be careful that none of you *be* **found** to have fallen short of
    10:29 How much more severely *do you* **think** a man deserves to be
    12:10 Our fathers disciplined us for a little while as they **thought** *best*;
    12:11 No discipline **seems** pleasant at the time, but painful. Later on,
Jas 1:26 If anyone **considers himself** religious and yet does not keep a tight
     4: 5 Or *do you* **think** Scripture says without reason that the spirit he

1507 δοκιμάζω, *dokimazō* [22] [√ *1312*]

test [6], approve [2], interpret [2], approved [1], approves [1], discern [1], examine [1], find out [1], proved [1], refined [1], test and approve [1], tested [1], tests [1], think it worthwhile [1], try out [1]

Lk 12:56 You know how *to* **interpret** the appearance of the earth
    12:56 How is it that you don't know how *to* **interpret** this present time?
    14:19 just bought five yoke of oxen, and I'm on my way *to* **try** them **out**.
Ro   1:28 since *they did* not **think it worthwhile** to retain the knowledge of
     2:18 if you know his will and **approve** of what is superior because you
    12: 2 Then you will be able *to* **test and approve** what God's will is—
    14:22 is the man who does not condemn himself by what *he* **approves**.
1Co 3:13 with fire, and the fire *will* **test** the quality of each man's work.
    11:28 A man *ought to* **examine** himself before he eats of the bread
    16: 3 I will give letters of introduction to the men *you* **approve**
2Co 8: 8 but *I want to* **test** the sincerity of your love by comparing it with
     8:22 we are sending with them our brother who *has* often **proved** *to us*
    13: 5 yourselves to see whether you are in the faith; **test** yourselves.
Gal 6: 4 Each one *should* **test** his own actions. Then he can take pride in
Eph 5:10 and **find out** what pleases the Lord.
Php 1:10 so that you *may be able to* **discern** what is best and may be pure
1Th 2: 4 we speak as men **approved** by God to be entrusted with the gospel.
     2: 4 We are not trying to please men but God, who **tests** our hearts.
     5:21 **Test** everything. Hold on to the good.
1Ti 3:10 They *must* first *be* **tested**; and then if there is nothing against
1Pe 1: 7 worth than gold, which perishes even *though* **refined** by fire—
1Jn 4: 1 every spirit, but **test** the spirits to see whether they are from God,

1508 δοκιμασία, *dokimasia* [1] [√ *1312*]

tried [1]

Heb 3: 9 where your fathers tested and **tried** me and for forty years saw

1509 δοκιμή, *dokimē* [7] [√ *1312*]

character [2], proved [2], proof [1], severe trial [+*2568*] [1], would stand the test [1]

Ro   5: 4 perseverance, **character**; and character, hope.
     5: 4 perseverance, character; and **character**, hope.
2Co 2: 9 The reason I wrote you was to see if you **would stand the test**
     8: 2 Out of the most **severe trial** [+*2568*], their overflowing joy
     9:13 Because of the service by which you have **proved** yourselves,
    13: 3 since you are demanding **proof** that Christ is speaking through me.
Php 2:22 But you know that Timothy has **proved** himself, because as a son

1510 δοκίμιον, *dokimion* [2] [√ *1312*]

proved genuine [1], testing [1]

Jas 1: 3 because you know that the **testing** of your faith develops
1Pe 1: 7 may be **proved genuine** and may result in praise, glory and honor

1511 δόκιμος, *dokimos* [7] [√ *1312*]

approved [3], approval [1], stood the test [1], test [1], tested and approved [1]

Ro 14:18 serves Christ in this way is pleasing to God and **approved** by men.
    16:10 Greet Apelles, **tested and approved** in Christ. Greet those who
1Co 11:19 among you to show which of you have God's **approval**.
2Co 10:18 For it is not the one who commends himself who is **approved**,
    13: 7 Not that people will see that we have **stood the test** but that you
2Ti 2:15 Do your best to present yourself to God as one **approved**,
Jas 1:12 who perseveres under trial, because when he has stood the **test**,

1512 δοκός, *dokos* [6]

plank [6]

Mt   7: 3 brother's eye and pay no attention to the **plank** in your own eye?
     7: 4 of your eye,' when all the time there is a **plank** in your own eye?
     7: 5 first take the **plank** out of your own eye, and then you will see
Lk   6:41 brother's eye and pay no attention to the **plank** in your own eye?
     6:42 when you yourself fail to see the **plank** in your own eye?
     6:42 first take the **plank** out of your eye, and then you will see clearly to

1513 δόλιος, *dolios* [1] [√ *1515*]

deceitful [1]

2Co 11:13 For such men are false apostles, **deceitful** workmen,

1514 δολιόω, *dolioō* [1] [√ *1515*]

practice deceit [1]

Ro   3:13 "Their throats are open graves; their tongues **practice deceit**."

1515 δόλος, *dolos* [11] [→ *100, 1284, 1513, 1514, 1516*]

deceit [5], deceitful [1], false [1], sly [+*1877*] [1], sly way [1], trick [1], trickery [1]

Mt 26: 4 and they plotted to arrest Jesus *in some* **sly way** and kill him.
Mk   7:22 greed, malice, **deceit**, lewdness, envy, slander, arrogance and folly.
    14: 1 and the teachers of the law were looking for some **sly** [+*1877*] way
Jn   1:47 of him, "Here is a true Israelite, in whom there is nothing **false**."
Ac 13:10 that is right! You are full of all kinds of **deceit** and trickery.
Ro   1:29 They are full *of* envy, murder, strife, **deceit** and malice.
2Co 12:16 to you. Yet, crafty fellow that I am, I caught you *by* **trickery**!
1Th 2: 3 from error or impure motives, nor are we trying to **trick** you.
1Pe 2: 1 Therefore, rid yourselves of all malice and all **deceit**, hypocrisy,
     2:22 "He committed no sin, and no **deceit** was found in his mouth."
     3:10 must keep his tongue from evil and his lips from **deceitful** speech.

1516 δολόω, *doloō* [1] [√ *1515*]

distort [1]

2Co 4: 2 we do not use deception, nor *do we* **distort** the word of God.

1517 δόμα, *doma* [4] [√ *1443*]

gifts [3], gift [1]

Mt   7:11 though you are evil, know how to give good **gifts** to your children,
Lk 11:13 though you are evil, know how to give good **gifts** to your children,
Eph 4: 8 on high, he led captives in his train and gave **gifts** to men."
Php 4:17 Not that I am looking for a **gift**, but I am looking for what may be

1518 δόξα, *doxa* [166] [→ *1519, 1901, 1902, 3029, 3030, 4141, 5280; cf. 1506*]

δόξα ἐν ὑψίστοις (glory in the highest) [2] Lk 2:14; 19:38

δόξα καὶ τιμή; τιμή καὶ δόξα (glory and honor; honor and glory) [12] Ro 2:7,10; 1Ti 1:17; Heb 2:7,9; 1Pe 1:7; 2Pe 1:17; Rev 4:9,11; 5:12,13; 21:26

δόξα [τοῦ] θεοῦ (glory of God) [22] Jn 11:4,40; 12:43; Ac 7:55; Ro 1:23; 3:7,23; 5:2; 15:7; 1Co 10:31; 11:7; 2Co 4:6,15; Php 1:11; 2:11; 1Ti 1:11; Tit 2:13; 1Pe 4:14; Rev 15:8; 19:1; 21:11,23

δόξα τῷ θεῷ (glory to God) [6] Lk 2:14; 17:18; Jn 9:24; Ac 12:23; Ro 4:20; Rev 11:13

δόξα [τοῦ] κυρίου (glory of the Lord) [5] Lk 2:9; 2Co 3:18; 8:19; 2Th 2:14; Jas 2:1

δόξα [του] Χριστοῦ (glory of Christ) [3] 2Co 4:4; 8:23; 2Th 2:14; cf. 1Pe 4:13

glory [112], glorious [15], praise [9], splendor [9], honor [5], *untranslated* [2], celestial beings [2], with ever-increasing glory [+608+1518+1650] [2], brilliance [1], divine glory [1], glories [1], glorified [+1443] [1], glorify [+1443] [1], glorious [+1877] [1], glorious presence [1], glorious splendor [1], honored [1], majesty [1]

Mt	4: 8 and showed him all the kingdoms of the world and their **splendor**.
	6:29 Yet I tell you that not even Solomon in all his **splendor** was
	16:27 For the Son of Man is going to come in his Father's **glory** with his
	19:28 of all things, when the Son of Man sits on his **glorious** throne,
	24:30 Man coming on the clouds of the sky, with power and great **glory**.
	25:31 "When the Son of Man comes in his **glory**, and all the angels with
	25:31 all the angels with him, he will sit on his throne in *heavenly* **glory**.
Mk	8:38 of him when he comes in his Father's **glory** with the holy angels."
	10:37 one of us sit at your right and the other at your left in your **glory**."
	13:26 see the Son of Man coming in clouds with great power and **glory**.
Lk	2: 9 and the **glory** of the Lord shone around them, and they were
	2:14 "**Glory** to God in the highest, and on earth peace to men on whom
	2:32 for revelation to the Gentiles and for **glory** to your people Israel."
	4: 6 he said to him, "I will give you all their authority and **splendor**,
	9:26 Son of Man will be ashamed of him when he comes in his **glory**
	9:31 appeared in **glorious splendor**, talking with Jesus. They spoke
	9:32 they saw his **glory** and the two men standing with him.
	12:27 not even Solomon in all his **splendor** was dressed like one of
	14:10 Then you will be **honored** in the presence of all your fellow
	17:18 one found to return and give **praise** to God except this foreigner?"
	19.38 the name of the Lord!" "Peace in heaven and **glory** in the highest!"
	21:27 see the Son of Man coming in a cloud with power and great **glory**.
	24:26 not the Christ have to suffer these things and then enter his **glory**?"
Jn	1:14 We have seen his **glory**, the glory of the One and Only, who came
	1:14 We have seen his glory, the **glory** of the One and Only, who came
	2:11 He thus revealed his **glory**, and his disciples put their faith in him.
	5:41 "I do not accept **praise** from men,
	5:44 How can you believe if you accept **praise** from one another,
	5:44 yet make no effort to obtain the **praise** that comes from the only
	7:18 He who speaks on his own does so to gain **honor** for himself,
	7:18 but he who works for the **honor** of the one who sent him is a man
	8:50 I am not seeking **glory** for myself; but there is one who seeks it,
	8:54 Jesus replied, "If I glorify myself, my **glory** means nothing.
	9:24 "Give **glory** to God," they said. "We know this man is a sinner."
	11: 4 it is for God's **glory** so that God's Son may be glorified through it."
	11:40 tell you that if you believed, you would see the **glory** of God?"
	12:41 Isaiah said this because he saw Jesus' **glory** and spoke about him.
	12:43 for they loved **praise** from men more than praise from God.
	12:43 for they loved praise from men more than **praise** from God.
	17: 5 glorify me in your presence *with* the **glory** I had with you before
	17:22 I have given them the **glory** that you gave me, that they may be
	17:24 and to see my **glory**, the glory you have given me because you
Ac	7: 2 The God *of* **glory** appeared to our father Abraham while he was
	7:55 of the Holy Spirit, looked up to heaven and saw the **glory** of God,
	12:23 Immediately, because Herod did not give **praise** to God, an angel
	22:11 into Damascus, because the **brilliance** of the light had blinded me.
Ro	1:23 and exchanged the **glory** of the immortal God for images made to
	2: 7 To those who by persistence in doing good seek **glory**, honor
	2:10 but **glory**, honor and peace for everyone who does good: first for
	3: 7 falsehood enhances God's truthfulness and so increases his **glory**,
	3:23 for all have sinned and fall short of the **glory** of God,
	4:20 of God, but was strengthened in his faith and gave **glory** to God,
	5: 2 we now stand. And we rejoice in the hope *of* the **glory** of God.
	6: 4 just as Christ was raised from the dead through the **glory** of the
	8:18 are not worth comparing with the **glory** that will be revealed in us.
	8:21 and brought into the **glorious** freedom of the children of God.
	9: 4 theirs the **divine glory**, the covenants, the receiving of the law,
	9:23 What if he did this to make the riches *of* his **glory** known to the

	9:23 the objects of his mercy, whom he prepared in advance for **glory**—
	11:36 and to him are all things. To him be the **glory** forever! Amen.
	15: 7 just as Christ accepted you, in order to bring **praise** to God.
	16:27 to the only wise God be **glory** forever through Jesus Christ!
1Co	2: 7 and that God destined for our **glory** before time began.
	2: 8 for if they had, they would not have crucified the Lord *of* **glory**.
	10:31 or drink or whatever you do, do it all for the **glory** of God.
	11: 7 not to cover his head, since he is the image and **glory** of God;
	11: 7 is the image and glory of God; but the woman is the **glory** of man.
	11:15 but that if a woman has long hair, it is her **glory**? For long hair is
	15:40 but the **splendor** of the heavenly bodies is one kind,
	15:41 The sun has one kind of **splendor**, the moon another and the stars
	15:41 kind of splendor, the moon another **[RPG]** and the stars another;
	15:41 the stars another; **[RPG]** and star differs from star in splendor.
	15:41 and the stars another; and star differs from star in **splendor**.
	15:43 it is sown in dishonor, it is raised in **glory**; it is sown in weakness,
2Co	1:20 so through him the "Amen" is spoken by us to the **glory** of God.
	3: 7 which was engraved in letters on stone, came with **glory**,
	3: 7 could not look steadily at the face of Moses because of its **glory**,
	3: 8 will not the ministry of the Spirit be even more **glorious** [+1877]?
	3: 9 If the ministry that condemns men is **glorious**, how much more
	3: 9 how much more **glorious** is the ministry that brings righteousness!
	3:10 has no glory now in comparison with the surpassing **glory**.
	3:11 And if what was fading away came with **glory**, how much greater
	3:11 came with glory, how much greater is the **glory** of that which lasts!
	3:18 And we, who with unveiled faces all reflect the Lord's **glory**,
	3:18 are being transformed into his likeness **with ever-increasing glory** [+608+1518+1650], which comes from the Lord, who is the Spirit.
	3:18 are being transformed into his likeness **with ever-increasing glory** [+608+1518+1650], which comes from the Lord, who is the Spirit.
	4: 4 so that they cannot see the light of the gospel *of* the **glory** of
	4: 6 the light of the knowledge *of* the **glory** of God in the face of Christ.
	4:15 and more people may cause thanksgiving to overflow to the **glory**
	4:17 and momentary troubles are achieving for us an eternal **glory** that
	6: 8 through **glory** and dishonor, bad report and good report; genuine,
	8:19 which we administer in order to **honor** the Lord himself and to
	8:23 they are representatives of the churches and an **honor** to Christ.
Gal	1: 5 to whom be **glory** for ever and ever. Amen.
Eph	1: 6 to the praise *of* his **glorious** grace, which he has freely given us in
	1:12 were the first to hope in Christ, might be for the praise *of* his **glory**.
	1:14 of those who are God's possession—to the praise *of* his **glory**.
	1:17 the **glorious** Father, may give you the Spirit of wisdom
	1:18 has called you, the riches *of* his **glorious** inheritance in the saints,
	3:13 because of my sufferings for you, which are your **glory**.
	3:16 I pray that out of his **glorious** riches he may strengthen you with
	3:21 to him be **glory** in the church and in Christ Jesus throughout all
Php	1:11 that comes through Jesus Christ—to the **glory** and praise of God.
	2:11 confess that Jesus Christ is Lord, to the **glory** of God the Father.
	3:19 their god is their stomach, and their **glory** is in their shame.
	3:21 our lowly bodies so that they will be like his **glorious** body.
	4:19 And my God will meet all your needs according to his **glorious**
	4:20 To our God and Father be **glory** for ever and ever. Amen.
Col	1:11 being strengthened with all power according to his **glorious** might
	1:27 known among the Gentiles the **glorious** riches of this mystery,
	1:27 riches of this mystery, which is Christ in you, the hope *of* **glory**.
	3: 4 is your life, appears, then you also will appear with him in **glory**.
1Th	2: 6 We were not looking for **praise** from men, not from you or anyone
	2:12 lives worthy of God, who calls you into his kingdom and **glory**.
	2:20 Indeed, you are our **glory** and joy.
2Th	1: 9 from the presence of the Lord and from the **majesty** of his power
	2:14 that you might share *in* the **glory** of our Lord Jesus Christ.
1Ti	1:11 that conforms to the **glorious** gospel of the blessed God, which he
	1:17 invisible, the only God, be honor and **glory** for ever and ever.
	3:16 the nations, was believed on in the world, was taken up in **glory**.
2Ti	2:10 may obtain the salvation that is in Christ Jesus, with eternal **glory**.
	4:18 his heavenly kingdom. To him be **glory** for ever and ever. Amen.
Tit	2:13 glorious appearing of our great God and Savior, Jesus Christ,
Heb	1: 3 The Son is the radiance *of* God's **glory** and the exact
	2: 7 lower than the angels; you crowned him *with* **glory** and honor
	2: 9 now crowned *with* **glory** and honor because he suffered death,
	2:10 In bringing many sons to **glory**, it was fitting that God, for whom
	3: 3 Jesus has been found worthy of greater **honor** than Moses,
	9: 5 Above the ark were the cherubim *of* the **Glory**,
	13:21 through Jesus Christ, to whom be **glory** for ever and ever.
Jas	2: 1 My brothers, as believers *in* our **glorious** Lord Jesus Christ,
1Pe	1: 7 result in praise, **glory** and honor when Jesus Christ is revealed.

1:11 the sufferings of Christ and the **glories** that would follow.
1:21 who raised him from the dead and **glorified** [+*1443*] him,
1:24 are like grass, and all their **glory** is like the flowers of the field;
4:11 To him be the **glory** and the power for ever and ever. Amen.
4:13 of Christ, so that you may be overjoyed when his **glory** is revealed.
4:14 you are blessed, for the Spirit *of* **glory** and of God rests on you.
5:1 and one who also will share *in* the **glory** to be revealed:
5:4 you will receive the crown *of* **glory** that will never fade away.
5:10 the God of all grace, who called you to his eternal **glory** in Christ,
2Pe 1:3 through our knowledge of him who called us *by* his own **glory**
1:17 and **glory** from God the Father when the voice came to him from
1:17 the Father when the voice came to him from the Majestic **Glory**,
2:10 and arrogant, these men are not afraid to slander **celestial beings**;
3:18 Savior Jesus Christ. To him be **glory** both now and forever! Amen.
Jude 1:8 their own bodies, reject authority and slander **celestial beings**.
1:24 and to present you before his **glorious presence** without fault
1:25 to the only God our Savior be **glory**, majesty, power and authority,
Rev 1:6 and Father—to him be **glory** and power for ever and ever!
4:9 Whenever the living creatures give **glory**, honor and thanks to him
4:11 our Lord and God, to receive **glory** and honor and power,
5:12 and wisdom and strength and honor and **glory** and praise!"
5:13 and to the Lamb be praise and honor and **glory** and power,
7:12 Praise and **glory** and wisdom and thanks and honor and power
11:13 the survivors were terrified and gave **glory** to the God of heaven.
14:7 He said in a loud voice, "Fear God and give him **glory**,
15:8 And the temple was filled with smoke from the **glory** of God
16:9 these plagues, but they refused to repent and **glorify** [+*1443*] him.
18:1 had great authority, and the earth was illuminated by his **splendor**.
19:1 "Hallelujah! Salvation and **glory** and power belong to our God,
19:7 Let us rejoice and be glad and give him **glory**! For the wedding of
21:11 It shone with the **glory** of God, and its brilliance was like that of a
21:23 for the **glory** of God gives it light, and the Lamb is its lamp.
21:24 and the kings of the earth will bring their **splendor** into it.
21:26 The **glory** and honor of the nations will be brought into it.

1519 δοξάζω, doxazō [61] [√ *1518*]

glorify [12], glorified [11], praised [11], honored [4], praising [4],
bring glory to [3], praise [3], glorious [2], brought glory [1], gave
praise to [1], glorifies [1], glorifying [1], glory [1], glory come to
[1], glory gave [1], has glory [1], honor [1], make much of [1],
take glory [1]

Mt 5:16 they may see your good deeds and **praise** your Father in heaven.
6:2 do in the synagogues and on the streets, to *be* **honored** by men.
9:8 and *they* **praised** God, who had given such authority to men.
15:31 and the blind seeing. And *they* **praised** the God of Israel.
Mk 2:12 This amazed everyone and they **praised** God, saying, "We have
Lk 2:20 **glorifying** and praising God for all the things they had heard
4:15 He taught in their synagogues, and everyone **praised** *him*.
5:25 took what he had been lying on and went home **praising** God.
5:26 Everyone was amazed and **gave praise** to God. They were filled
7:16 They were all filled with awe and **praised** God. "A great prophet
13:13 on her, and immediately she straightened up and **praised** God.
17:15 he saw he was healed, came back, **praising** God in a loud voice.
18:43 received his sight and followed Jesus, **praising** God.
23:47 The centurion, seeing what had happened, **praised** God and said,
Jn 7:39 Spirit had not been given, since Jesus *had* not yet *been* **glorified**.
8:54 Jesus replied, "If I **glorify** myself, my glory means nothing.
8:54 whom you claim as your God, is the one *who* **glorifies** me.
11:4 it is for God's glory so that God's Son *may be* **glorified** through it."
12:16 Only after Jesus *was* **glorified** did they realize that these things had
12:23 "The hour has come for the Son of Man *to be* **glorified**.
12:28 Father, **glorify** your name!" Then a voice came from heaven,
12:28 came from heaven, "*I* have **glorified** it, and will glorify it again."
12:28 came from heaven, "*I* have **glorified** it, and *will* **glorify** it again."
13:31 "Now *is* the Son of Man **glorified** and God is glorified in him.
13:31 "Now is the Son of Man glorified and God *is* **glorified** in him.
13:32 If God *is* **glorified** in him, God will glorify the Son in himself,
13:32 If God is glorified in him, God *will* **glorify** the Son in himself,
13:32 God will glorify the Son in himself, and *will* **glorify** him at once.
14:13 ask in my name, so that the Son *may* **bring glory to** the Father.
15:8 This *is to* my Father's **glory**, that you bear much fruit, showing
16:14 He *will* **bring glory to** me by taking from what is mine
17:1 time has come. **Glorify** your Son, that your Son may glorify you.
17:1 time has come. Glorify your Son, that your Son *may* **glorify** you.

17:4 I *have* **brought** you **glory** on earth by completing the work you
17:5 **glorify** me in your presence with the glory I had with you before
17:10 all you have is mine. And **glory** *has* **come to** me through them.
21:19 to indicate the kind of death by which Peter *would* **glorify** God.
Ac 3:13 and Jacob, the God of our fathers, *has* **glorified** his servant Jesus.
4:21 because all the people *were* **praising** God for what had happened.
11:18 they had no further objections and **praised** God, saying, "So then,
13:48 heard this, they were glad and **honored** the word of the Lord;
21:20 When they heard *this*, *they* **praised** God. Then they said to Paul,
Ro 1:21 *they* neither **glorified** him as God nor gave thanks to him,
8:30 he called, he also justified; those he justified, *he* also **glorified**.
11:13 as I am the apostle to the Gentiles, *I* **make much of** my ministry
15:6 so that with one heart and mouth *you may* **glorify** the God
15:9 so that the Gentiles *may* **glorify** God for his mercy, as it is written:
1Co 6:20 you were bought at a price. Therefore **honor** God with your body.
12:26 suffers with it; if one part *is* **honored**, every part rejoices with it.
2Co 3:10 For what *was* **glorious** has no glory now in comparison with the
3:10 For what was glorious *has* no **glory** now in comparison with the
9:13 *men will* **praise** God for the obedience that accompanies your
Gal 1:24 And *they* **praised** God because of me.
2Th 3:1 that the message of the Lord may spread rapidly and *be* **honored**,
Heb 5:5 So Christ also *did* not **take** upon himself the **glory** of becoming a
1Pe 1:8 in him and are filled with an inexpressible and **glorious** joy,
2:12 *they may* see your good deeds and **glorify** God on the day he visits
4:11 so that in all things God *may be* **praised** through Jesus Christ.
4:16 do not be ashamed, but **praise** God that you bear that name.
Rev 15:4 Who will not fear you, O Lord, and **bring glory to** your name?
18:7 as much torture and grief as the **glory** and luxury *she* **gave** herself.

1520 Δορκάς, Dorkas [2]

Dorcas [2]

Ac 9:36 when translated, is **Dorcas**), who was always doing good
9:39 and other clothing that **Dorcas** had made while she was still with

1521 δόσις, dosis [2] [√ *1443*]

untranslated [1], giving [1]

Php 4:15 not one church shared with me in the matter *of* **giving**
Jas 1:17 Every good **[RPG]** and perfect gift is from above, coming down

1522 δότης, dotēs [1] [√ *1443*]

giver [1]

2Co 9:7 or under compulsion, for God loves a cheerful **giver**.

1523 Δουβέριος, Douberios Not used in UBS/NIV [√ *1292*]

1524 δουλαγωγέω, doulagōgeō [1] [√ *1528 + 72*]

make slave [1]

1Co 9:27 I beat my body and **make** it my **slave** so that after I have preached

1525 δουλεία, douleia [5] [√ *1528*]

slavery [2], bondage [1], makes a slave [1], slaves [1]

Ro 8:15 For you did not receive a spirit that **makes** you **a slave** again to
8:21 that the creation itself will be liberated from its **bondage** to decay
Gal 4:24 is from Mount Sinai and bears children who are to be **slaves**:
5:1 and do not let yourselves be burdened again by a yoke *of* **slavery**.
Heb 2:15 and free those who all their lives were held *in* **slavery** by their fear

1526 δουλεύω, douleuō [25] [√ *1528*]

serve [10], serving [3], slaves [3], enslaved [2], served [2], in
slavery [1], serve as slaves [1], serves [1], slave [1], slaving [1]

Mt 6:24 "No one can **serve** two masters. Either he will hate the one
6:24 and despise the other. You cannot **serve** both God and Money.
Lk 15:29 All these years *I've been* **slaving** for you and never disobeyed

16: 13 "No servant can **serve** two masters. Either he will hate the one
16: 13 and despise the other. You cannot **serve** both God and Money."
Jn 8: 33 are Abraham's descendants and *have* never *been* **slaves** of anyone.
Ac 7: 7 But I will punish the nation *they* **serve as slaves**,' God said,
20: 19 *I* **served** the Lord with great humility and with tears, although I
Ro 6: 6 be done away with, that we *should* no longer *be* **slaves** to sin—
7: 6 released from the law so that we **serve** in the new way of the Spirit,
7: 25 So then, I myself in my mind *am* a **slave** to God's law, but in the
9: 12 him who calls—she was told, "The older *will* **serve** the younger."
12: 11 be lacking in zeal, but keep your spiritual fervor, **serving** the Lord.
14: 18 because anyone *who* **serves** Christ in this way is pleasing to God
16: 18 For such people *are* not **serving** our Lord Christ, but their own
Gal 4: 8 know God, *you were* **slaves** to those who by nature are not gods.
4: 9 Do you wish *to be* **enslaved** by them all over again?
4: 25 city of Jerusalem, because *she is* **in slavery** with her children.
5: 13 to indulge the sinful nature; rather, **serve** one another in love.
Eph 6: 7 **Serve** wholeheartedly, as if you were serving the Lord, not men,
Php 2: 22 because as a son with his father *he has* **served** with me in the work
Col 3: 24 from the Lord as a reward. It is the Lord Christ *you are* **serving**.
1Th 1: 9 They tell how you turned to God from idols *to* **serve** the living
1Ti 6: 2 Instead, *they are to* **serve** them even better, because those who
Tit 3: 3 deceived and **enslaved** by all kinds of passions and pleasures.

1527 δούλη, *doulē* [3] [√ *1528*]

servant [2], servants women [1]

Lk 1: 38 "I am the Lord's **servant**," Mary answered. "May it be to me as you
1: 48 for he has been mindful of the humble state *of* his **servant**.
Ac 2: 18 Even on my **servants**, both men and **women**, I will pour out my

1528 δοῦλος[1], *doulos*[1] [124] [→ *1524, 1525, 1526, 1527, 1529, 1530, 2871, 4056, 5281*]

δοῦλος τῆς ἁμαρτίας (slave to sin) [3] Jn 8:34; Ro 6:17,20

δοῦλος ... ἐλεύθερος (slave ... free) [12] Ro 6:20; 1Co 7:21,22,22; 12:13; Gal 3:28; Eph 6:8; Col 3:11; 1Pe 2:16; Rev 6:15; 13:16; 19:18

δοῦλος θεοῦ (slave of God) [6] Ac 16:17; Tit 1:1; Jas 1:1; 1Pe 2:16; Rev 7:3; 15:3

δοῦλος κυρίου (slave of the Lord) [2] 2Ti 2:24; Jas 1:1

δοῦλος Χριστοῦ (slave of Christ) [9] Ro 1:1; 1Co 7:22; Gal 1:10; Eph 6:6; Php 1:1; Col 4:12; Jas 1:1; 2Pe 1:1; Jude 1:1

servant [54], servants [37], slave [18], slaves [11], servant's [2], servants men [1], slavery [1]

Mt 8: 9 and he comes. I say *to* my **servant**, 'Do this,' and he does it."
10: 24 "A student is not above his teacher, nor a **servant** above his master.
10: 25 the student to be like his teacher, and the **servant** like his master.
13: 27 "The owner's **servants** came to him and said, 'Sir, didn't you sow
13: 28 "The **servants** asked him, 'Do you want us to go and pull them
18: 23 is like a king who wanted to settle accounts with his **servants**.
18: 26 "The **servant** fell on his knees before him. 'Be patient with me,'
18: 27 The **servant's** master took pity on him, canceled the debt
18: 28 "But when that **servant** went out, he found one of his fellow
18: 32 '*You* wicked **servant**,' he said, 'I canceled all that debt of yours
20: 27 and whoever wants to be first must be your **slave**—
21: 34 he sent his **servants** to the tenants to collect his fruit.
21: 35 "The tenants seized his **servants**; they beat one, killed another,
21: 36 Then he sent other **servants** to them, more than the first time,
22: 3 He sent his **servants** to those who had been invited to the banquet
22: 4 "Then he sent some more **servants** and said, 'Tell those who have
22: 6 The rest seized his **servants**, mistreated them and killed them.
22: 8 "Then he said *to* his **servants**, 'The wedding banquet is ready,
22: 10 So the **servants** went out into the streets and gathered all the
24: 45 "Who then is the faithful and wise **servant**, whom the master has
24: 46 It will be good for that **servant** whose master finds him doing
24: 48 But suppose that **servant** is wicked and says to himself,
24: 50 The master *of* that **servant** will come on a day when he does not
25: 14 who called his **servants** and entrusted his property to them.
25: 19 "After a long time the master *of* those **servants** returned and settled
25: 21 "His master replied, 'Well done, good and faithful **servant**!
25: 23 "His master replied, 'Well done, good and faithful **servant**!
25: 26 "His master replied, '*You* wicked, lazy **servant**! So you knew that I
25: 30 And throw that worthless **servant** outside, into the darkness,
26: 51 drew it out and struck the **servant** of the high priest, cutting off his
Mk 10: 44 and whoever wants to be first must be **slave** of all.
12: 2 At harvest time he sent a **servant** to the tenants to collect from
12: 4 Then he sent another **servant** to them; they struck this man on the
13: 34 He leaves his house and puts his **servants** in charge, each with his
14: 47 near drew his sword and struck the **servant** of the high priest,
Lk 2: 29 as you have promised, you now dismiss your **servant** in peace.
7: 2 There a centurion's **servant**, whom his master valued highly,
7: 3 elders of the Jews to him, asking him to come and heal his **servant**.
7: 8 and he comes. I say *to* my **servant**, 'Do this,' and he does it."
7: 10 had been sent returned to the house and found the **servant** well.
12: 37 It will be good for those **servants** whose master finds them
12: 43 It will be good for that **servant** whom the master finds doing
12: 45 But suppose the **servant** says to himself, 'My master is taking a
12: 46 The master *of* that **servant** will come on a day when he does not
12: 47 "That **servant** who knows his master's will and does not get ready
14: 17 At the time of the banquet he sent his **servant** to tell those who had
14: 21 "The **servant** came back and reported this to his master.
14: 21 the owner of the house became angry and ordered his **servant**,
14: 22 " 'Sir,' the **servant** said, 'what you ordered has been done, but there
14: 23 "Then the master told his **servant**, 'Go out to the roads and country
15: 22 "But the father said to his **servants**, 'Quick! Bring the best robe
17: 7 "Suppose one of you had a **servant** plowing or looking after the
17: 9 Would he thank the **servant** because he did what he was told to
17: 10 you were told to do, should say, 'We are unworthy **servants**;
19: 13 So he called ten of his **servants** and gave them ten minas.
19: 15 Then he sent for the **servants** to whom he had given the money,
19: 17 " 'Well done, my good **servant**!' his master replied. 'Because you
19: 22 'I will judge you by your own words, *you* wicked **servant**!
20: 10 At harvest time he sent a **servant** to the tenants so they would give
20: 11 He sent another **servant**,
22: 50 And one of them struck the **servant** of the high priest, cutting off
Jn 4: 51 his **servants** met him with the news that his boy was living.
8: 34 "I tell you the truth, everyone who sins is a **slave** to sin.
8: 35 Now a **slave** has no permanent place in the family,
13: 16 I tell you the truth, no **servant** is greater than his master, nor is a
15: 15 I no longer call you **servants**, because a servant does not know his
15: 15 because a **servant** does not know his master's business.
15: 20 'No **servant** is greater than his master.' If they persecuted me,
18: 10 who had a sword, drew it and struck the high priest's **servant**,
18: 10 cutting off his right ear. (The **servant's** name was Malchus.)
18: 18 and the **servants** and officials stood around a fire they had made to
18: 26 One of the high priest's **servants**, a relative of the man whose ear
Ac 2: 18 Even on my **servants**, both **men** and women, I will pour out my
4: 29 and enable your **servants** to speak your word with great boldness.
16: 17 of us, shouting, "These men are **servants** of the Most High God,
Ro 1: 1 Paul, a **servant** of Christ Jesus, called to be an apostle and set apart
6: 16 that when you offer yourselves to someone to obey him as **slaves**,
6: 16 to obey him as slaves, you are **slaves** to the one whom you obey—
6: 17 But thanks be to God that, though you used to be **slaves** to sin,
6: 20 When you were **slaves** to sin, you were free from the control of
1Co 7: 21 Were you a **slave** when you were called? Don't let it trouble you—
7: 22 For he who was a **slave** when he was called by the Lord is the
7: 22 he who was a free man when he was called is Christ's **slave**.
7: 23 You were bought at a price; do not become **slaves** of men.
12: 13 whether Jews or Greeks, **slave** or free—and we were all given the
2Co 4: 5 Christ as Lord, and ourselves as your **servants** for Jesus' sake.
Gal 1: 10 were still trying to please men, I would not be a **servant** of Christ.
3: 28 There is neither Jew nor Greek, **slave** nor free, male nor female,
4: 1 he is no different from a **slave**, although he owns the whole estate.
4: 7 So you are no longer a **slave**, but a son; and since you are a son,
Eph 6: 5 **Slaves**, obey your earthly masters with respect and fear, and with
6: 6 but like **slaves** of Christ, doing the will of God from your heart.
6: 8 everyone for whatever good he does, whether he is **slave** or free.
Php 1: 1 Paul and Timothy, **servants** of Christ Jesus, To all the saints in
2: 7 but made himself nothing, taking the very nature *of* a **servant**,
Col 3: 11 barbarian, Scythian, **slave** or free, but Christ is all, and is in all.
3: 22 **Slaves**, obey your earthly masters in everything; and do it,
4: 1 Masters, provide your **slaves** with what is right and fair,
4: 12 Epaphras, who is one of you and a **servant** of Christ Jesus,
1Ti 6: 1 All who are under the yoke of **slavery** should consider their
2Ti 2: 24 And the Lord's **servant** must not quarrel; instead, he must be kind
Tit 1: 1 a **servant** of God and an apostle of Jesus Christ for the faith of
2: 9 Teach **slaves** to be subject to their masters in everything, to try to
Phm 1: 16 no longer as a **slave**, but better than a slave, as a dear brother.

1:16 no longer as a slave, but better than a **slave**, as a dear brother.
Jas 1: 1 James, a **servant** of God and of the Lord Jesus Christ,
1Pe 2:16 use your freedom as a cover-up for evil; live as **servants** of God.
2Pe 1: 1 Simon Peter, a **servant** and apostle of Jesus Christ, To those who
     2:19 them freedom, while they themselves are **slaves** of depravity—
Jude 1: 1 Jude, a **servant** of Jesus Christ and a brother of James, To those
Rev 1: 1 which God gave him to show his **servants** what must soon take
     1: 1 He made it known by sending his angel *to* his **servant** John,
     2:20 By her teaching she misleads my **servants** into sexual immorality
     6:15 and every **slave** and every free man hid in caves and among the
     7: 3 or the trees until we put a seal on the foreheads of the **servants** of
    10: 7 just as he announced *to* his **servants** the prophets.”
    11:18 and for rewarding your **servants** the prophets and your saints
    13:16 forced everyone, small and great, rich and poor, free and **slave**,
    15: 3 and sang the song of Moses the **servant** of God and the song of the
    19: 2 by her adulteries. He has avenged on her the blood *of* his **servants**.”
    19: 5 “Praise our God, all you his **servants**, you who fear him, both small
    19:18 and the flesh *of* all people, free and **slave**, small and great.”
    22: 3 of the Lamb will be in the city, and his **servants** will serve him.
    22: 6 sent his angel to show his **servants** the things that must soon take

1529 δοῦλος², *doulos²* [2] [√ *1528*]

in slavery [2]

Ro 6:19 Just as you used to offer the parts of your body **in slavery** to
    6:19 so now offer them **in slavery** to righteousness leading to holiness.

1530 δουλόω, *douloō* [8] [√ *1528*]

become slaves [2], addicted [1], bound [1], enslaved [1], in
slavery [1], make a slave [1], slave [1]

Ac 7: 6 and *they will be* **enslaved** and mistreated four hundred years.
Ro 6:18 been set free from sin and *have* **become slaves** to righteousness.
    6:22 you have been set free from sin and *have* **become slaves** to God,
1Co 7:15 A believing man or woman *is* not **bound** in such circumstances;
    9:19 and belong to no man, *I* **make** myself **a slave** to everyone,
Gal 4: 3 we were **in slavery** under the basic principles of the world.
Tit 2: 3 not to be slanderers or **addicted** to much wine, but to teach what is
2Pe 2:19 of depravity—for a man *is a* **slave** to whatever has mastered him.

1531 δοχή, *dochē* [2] [√ *1312*]

banquet [2]

Lk 5:29 Then Levi held a great **banquet** for Jesus at his house, and a large
   14:13 But when you give a **banquet**, invite the poor, the crippled,

1532 δράκων, *drakōn* [13]

dragon [13]

Rev 12: 3 an enormous red **dragon** with seven heads and ten horns and seven
   12: 4 The **dragon** stood in front of the woman who was about to give
   12: 7 Michael and his angels fought against the **dragon**, and the dragon
   12: 7 against the dragon, and the **dragon** and his angels fought back.
   12: 9 The great **dragon** was hurled down—that ancient serpent called the
   12:13 When the **dragon** saw that he had been hurled to the earth,
   12:16 and swallowing the river that the **dragon** had spewed out of his
   12:17 Then the **dragon** was enraged at the woman and went off to make
   13: 2 The **dragon** gave the beast his power and his throne and great
   13: 4 Men worshiped the **dragon** because he had given authority to the
   13:11 He had two horns like a lamb, but he spoke like a **dragon**.
   16:13 they came out of the mouth *of* the **dragon**, out of the mouth of the
   20: 2 He seized the **dragon**, that ancient serpent, who is the devil,

1533 δράσσομαι, *drassomai* [1] [→ *1440, 1534*]

catches [1]

1Co 3:19 As it is written: “He **catches** the wise in their craftiness”;

1534 δραχμή, *drachmē* [3] [√ *1533*]

untranslated [1], coin [1], silver coins [1]

Lk 15: 8 “Or suppose a woman has ten **silver coins** and loses one. Does she
   15: 8 **[RPG]** Does she not light a lamp, sweep the house and search
   15: 9 and says, ‘Rejoice with me; I have found my lost **coin**.’

1535 δρέπανον, *drepanon* [8]

sickle [8]

Mk 4:29 As soon as the grain is ripe, he puts the **sickle** to it,
Rev 14:14 with a crown of gold on his head and a sharp **sickle** in his hand.
   14:15 “Take your **sickle** and reap, because the time to reap has come,
   14:16 So he who was seated on the cloud swung his **sickle** over the earth,
   14:17 came out of the temple in heaven, and he too had a sharp **sickle**.
   14:18 and called in a loud voice to him who had the sharp **sickle**,
   14:18 “Take your sharp **sickle** and gather the clusters of grapes from the
   14:19 The angel swung his **sickle** on the earth, gathered its grapes

1536 δρόμος, *dromos* [3] [√ *5556*]

race [2], work [1]

Ac 13:25 As John was completing his **work**, he said: ‘Who do you think I
   20:24 if only I may finish the **race** and complete the task the Lord Jesus
2Ti 4: 7 the good fight, I have finished the **race**, I have kept the faith.

1537 Δρούσιλλα, *Drousilla* [1]

Drusilla [1]

Ac 24:24 Several days later Felix came with his wife **Drusilla**, who was a

1538 δύναμαι, *dynamai* [210] [→ *104, 105, 1539, 1540,* *1541, 1542, 1543, 1904, 2872*]

can [84], cannot [+*4024*] [40], could [31], able [24], can't [+*4024*]
[5], could have [4], cannot [+*3590*] [3], couldn't [+*4024*] [2],
ready [2], and cannot [+*4028*] [1], bear [1], can do [1], cannot
[+*4046*] [1], cannot do [+*4024*] [1], cannot do [+*4028*] [1],
competent [1], enables [1], enough [1], has the right [1], hoping
[+*1623*+*4803*] [1], may [1], possible [1], unable [+*3590*] [1],
unable [+*4024*] [1]

Mt 3: 9 I tell you that out of these stones God **can** raise up children for
     5:14 the light of the world. A city on a hill **cannot** [+*4024*] be hidden.
     5:36 for you **cannot** [+*4024*] make even one hair white or black.
     6:24 “No one **can** serve two masters. Either he will hate the one
     6:24 despise the other. *You* **cannot** [+*4024*] serve both God and Money.
     6:27 Who of you by worrying **can** add a single hour to his life?
     7:18 A good tree **cannot** [+*4024*] bear bad fruit, and a bad tree cannot
     8: 2 and said, “Lord, if you are willing, you **can** make me clean.”
     9:15 “How **can** the guests of the bridegroom mourn while he is with
     9:28 and he asked them, “Do you believe that *I am* **able** to do this?”
    10:28 afraid of those who kill the body but cannot [+*3590*] kill the soul.
    10:28 be afraid of the One *who* **can** destroy both soul and body in hell.
    12:29 how **can** anyone enter a strong man's house and carry off his
    12:34 brood of vipers, how **can** you who are evil say anything good?
    16: 3 of the sky, but you **cannot** [+*4024*] interpret the signs of the times.
    17:16 I brought him to your disciples, but *they* **could** not heal him.”
    17:19 in private and asked, “Why **couldn't** [+*4024*] we drive it out?”
    19:12 kingdom of heaven. The one *who* **can** accept this should accept it.”
    19:25 they were greatly astonished and asked, “Who then **can** be saved?”
    20:22 “**Can** *you* drink the cup I am going to drink?” “We can,”
    20:22 you drink the cup I am going to drink?” “*We* **can**,” they answered.
    22:46 No one **could** say a word in reply,
    26: 9 “This perfume **could have** been sold at a high price and the money
    26:42 if *it is* not **possible** for this cup to be taken away unless I drink it,
    26:53 Do you think *I* **cannot** [+*4024*] call on my Father, and he will at
    26:61 ‘*I am* **able** to destroy the temple of God and rebuild it in three
    27:42 “He saved others,” they said, “but *he* **can't** [+*4024*] save himself!
Mk 1:40 him on his knees, “If you are willing, you **can** make me clean.”
     1:45 Jesus **could** no longer enter a town openly but stayed outside in
     2: 4 *Since they* **could** not get him to Jesus because of the crowd,
     2: 7 like that? He's blaspheming! Who **can** forgive sins but God alone?”

2: 19 "How **can** the guests of the bridegroom fast while he is with them?
2: 19 the bridegroom fast while he is with them? *They* **cannot** [*+4024*],
3: 20 so that he and his disciples *were* not even **able** to eat.
3: 23 and spoke to them in parables: "How **can** Satan drive out Satan?
3: 24 is divided against itself, that kingdom **cannot** [*+4024*] stand.
3: 25 a house is divided against itself, that house **cannot** [*+4024*] stand.
3: 26 if Satan opposes himself and is divided, *he* **cannot** [*+4024*] stand;
3: 27 no one **can** enter a strong man's house and carry off his
4: 32 with such big branches that the birds of the air **can** perch in its
4: 33 Jesus spoke the word to them, as much as *they* **could** understand.
5: 3 and no one **could** bind him any more, not even with a chain.
6: 5 *He* **could** not do any miracles there, except lay his hands on a few
6: 19 against John and wanted to kill him. But *she was* not **able** to,
7: 15 Nothing outside a man **can** make him 'unclean' by going into him.
7: 18 "Don't you see that nothing that enters a man from the outside **can**
7: 24 want anyone to know it; yet *he* **could** not keep his presence secret.
8: 4 "But where in this remote place **can** anyone get enough bread to
9: 3 whiter than anyone in the world **could** bleach them.
9: 22 kill him. But if *you* **can do** anything, take pity on us and help us."
9: 23 " 'If *you* **can**'?" said Jesus. "Everything is possible for him who
9: 28 asked him privately, "Why **couldn't** [*+4024*] we drive it out?"
9: 29 He replied, "This kind **can** come out only by prayer."
9: 39 "No one who does a miracle in my name **can** in the next moment
10: 26 more amazed, and said to each other, "Who then **can** be saved?"
10: 38 "**Can** you drink the cup I drink or be baptized with the baptism I
10: 39 "*We* **can**," they answered. Jesus said to them, "You will drink the
14: 5 It **could have** been sold for more than a year's wages
14: 7 always have with you, and *you* **can** help them any time you want.
15: 31 "He saved others," they said, "but *he* **can't** [*+4024*] save himself!

Lk 1: 20 you will be silent and not **able** to speak until the day this happens,
1: 22 When he came out, *he* **could** not speak to them. They realized he
3: 8 For I tell you that out of these stones God **can** raise up children for
5: 12 begged him, "Lord, if you are willing, you **can** make me clean."
5: 21 who speaks blasphemy? Who **can** forgive sins but God alone?"
5: 34 "**Can** you make the guests of the bridegroom fast while he is with
6: 39 also told them this parable: "**Can** a blind man lead a blind man?
6: 42 How **can** you say to your brother, 'Brother, let me take the speck
8: 19 but *they were* not **able** to get near him because of the crowd.
9: 40 I begged your disciples to drive it out, but *they* **could** not."
11: 7 are with me in bed. *I* **can't** [*+4024*] get up and give you anything.'
12: 25 Who of you by worrying **can** add a single hour to his life?
12: 26 Since *you* **cannot** [*+4028*] do this very little thing, why do you
13: 11 She was bent over and **could** not straighten up at all.
14: 20 "Still another said, 'I just got married, so *I* **can't** [*+4024*] come.'
14: 26 yes, even his own life—*he* **cannot** [*+4024*] be my disciple.
14: 27 not carry his cross and follow me **cannot** [*+4024*] be my disciple.
14: 33 any of you who does not give up everything he has **cannot** [*+4024*] be
16: 2 because *you* **cannot** [*+4024*] be manager any longer.'
16: 13 "No servant **can** serve two masters. Either he will hate the one
16: 13 the other. You **cannot** [*+4024*] serve both God and Money."
16: 26 so that those who want to go from here to you **cannot** [*+3590*],
18: 26 Those who heard this asked, "Who then **can** be saved?"
19: 3 but being a short man *he* **could** not, because of the crowd.
20: 36 and *they* **can** no longer die; for they are like the angels. They are
21: 15 and wisdom that none of your adversaries *will be* **able** to resist

Jn 1: 46 "Nazareth! **Can** anything good come from there?" Nathanael asked.
3: 2 For no one **could** perform the miraculous signs you are doing if
3: 3 no *one* **can** see the kingdom of God unless he is born again."
3: 4 "How **can** a man be born when he is old?" Nicodemus asked.
3: 4 "Surely *he* **cannot** [*+3590*] enter a second time into his mother's
3: 5 no *one* **can** enter the kingdom of God unless he is born of water
3: 9 "How **can** this be?" Nicodemus asked.
3: 27 "A man **can** receive only what is given him from heaven.
5: 19 "I tell you the truth, the Son **can** do nothing by himself; he can do
5: 30 By myself I **can** do nothing; I judge only as I hear, and my
5: 44 How **can** you believe if you accept praise from one another,
6: 44 "No one **can** come to me unless the Father who sent him draws him,
6: 52 among themselves, "How **can** this man give us his flesh to eat?"
6: 60 of his disciples said, "This is a hard teaching. Who **can** accept it?"
6: 65 "This is why I told you that no one **can** come to me unless the
7: 7 The world **cannot** [*+4024*] hate you, but it hates me because I
7: 34 you will not find me; and where I am, you **cannot** [*+4024*] come."
7: 36 will not find me,' and 'Where I am, you **cannot** [*+4024*] come'?"
8: 21 you will die in your sin. Where I go, you **cannot** [*+4024*] come."
8: 22 Is that why he says, 'Where I go, you **cannot** [*+4024*] come'?"
8: 43 clear to you? Because *you are* **unable** [*+4024*] to hear what I say.

9: 4 of him who sent me. Night is coming, when no one **can** work.
9: 16 But others asked, "How **can** a sinner do such miraculous signs?"
9: 33 If this man were not from God, *he* **could** do nothing."
10: 21 possessed by a demon. **Can** a demon open the eyes of the blind?"
10: 29 greater than all; no one **can** snatch them out of my Father's hand.
10: 35 word of God came—and the Scripture **cannot** [*+4024*] be broken—
11: 37 "**Could** not he who opened the eyes of the blind man have kept
12: 39 For this reason *they* **could** not believe, because, as Isaiah says
13: 33 so I tell you now: Where I am going, you **cannot** [*+4024*] come.
13: 36 Jesus replied, "Where I am going, you **cannot** [*+4024*] follow now,
13: 37 Peter asked, "Lord, why **can't** [*+4024*] I follow you now? I will lay
14: 5 don't know where you are going, so how **can** we know the way?"
14: 17 The world **cannot** [*+4024*] accept him, because it neither sees him
15: 4 No branch **can** bear fruit by itself; it must remain in the vine.
15: 5 he will bear much fruit; apart from me *you* **can** do nothing.
16: 12 "I have much more to say to you, more than *you* **can** now bear.

Ac 4: 16 have done an outstanding miracle, and *we* **cannot** [*+4024*] deny it.
4: 20 For we **cannot** [*+4024*] help speaking about what we have seen
5: 39 But if it is from God, *you* will not *be* **able** to stop these men;
8: 31 "How can *I*," he said, "unless someone explains it to me?" So he
10: 47 "**Can** anyone keep these people from being baptized with water?
13: 39 everything *you* **could** not be justified from by the law of Moses.
15: 1 according to the custom taught by Moses, *you* **cannot** [*+4024*] be
17: 19 "**May** we know what this new teaching is that you are presenting?
19: 40 In that case *we would* not *be* **able** to account for this commotion,
20: 32 which **can** build you up and give you an inheritance among all
21: 34 and *since* the commander **could** not get at the truth because of the
24: 8 By examining him yourself *you will be* **able** to learn the truth
24: 11 You **can** easily verify that no more than twelve days ago I went up
24: 13 **And** *they* **cannot** [*+4028*] prove to you the charges they are now
25: 11 Jews are not true, no one **has the right** to hand me over to them.
26: 32 "This man **could have** been set free if he had not appealed to
27: 12 sail on, **hoping** [*+1623+4803*] to reach Phoenix and winter there.
27: 15 ship was caught by the storm and **could** not head into the wind;
27: 31 these men stay with the ship, you **cannot** [*+4024*] be saved."
27: 39 where they decided to run the ship aground if *they* **could**.
27: 43 He ordered those *who* **could** swim to jump overboard first

Ro 8: 7 is hostile to God. It does not submit to God's law, nor **can** it do so.
8: 8 Those controlled by the sinful nature **cannot** [*+4024*] please God.
8: 39 *will be* **able** to separate us from the love of God that is in Christ
15: 14 complete in knowledge and **competent** to instruct one another.
16: 25 Now to him *who is* **able** to establish you by my gospel

1Co 2: 14 are foolishness to him, and *he* **cannot** [*+4024*] understand them,
3: 1 Brothers, I **could** not address you as spiritual but as worldly—
3: 2 I gave you milk, not solid food, for *you were* not yet **ready** for it.
3: 2 for you were not yet ready for it. Indeed, *you are* still not **ready**.
3: 11 For no one **can** lay any foundation other than the one already laid,
6: 5 Is it possible that there is nobody among you wise **enough** to judge
7: 21 let it trouble you—although if you **can** gain your freedom, do so.
10: 13 he will not let you be tempted beyond what *you can* **bear**.
10: 13 he will also provide a way out so that you **can** stand up under it.
10: 21 *You* **cannot** [*+4024*] drink the cup of the Lord and the cup of
10: 21 *you* **cannot** [*+4024*] have a part in both the Lord's table
12: 3 "Jesus be cursed," and no one **can** say, "Jesus is Lord," except by
12: 21 The eye **cannot** [*+4024*] say to the hand, "I don't need you!"
14: 31 For *you* **can** all prophesy in turn so that everyone may be
15: 50 that flesh and blood **cannot** [*+4024*] inherit the kingdom of God,

2Co 1: 4 so that we **can** comfort those in any trouble with the comfort we
3: 7 so that the Israelites **could** not look steadily at the face of Moses
13: 8 For *we* **cannot** [*+4024*] do anything against the truth, but only for

Gal 3: 21 For if a law had been given that **could** impart life,

Eph 3: 4 *you will be* **able** to understand my insight into the mystery of
3: 20 Now to him *who is* **able** to do immeasurably more than all we ask
6: 11 so that you **can** take your stand against the devil's schemes.
6: 13 the day of evil comes, *you may be* **able** to stand your ground,
6: 16 with which you **can** extinguish all the flaming arrows of the evil

Php 3: 21 by the power that **enables** him to bring everything under his

1Th 2: 6 As apostles of Christ we **could have** been a burden to you,
3: 9 How *can* we thank God enough for you in return for all the joy we

1Ti 5: 25 are obvious, and even those that are not **cannot** [*+4024*] be hidden.
6: 7 brought nothing into the world, and *we* **can** take nothing out of it.
6: 16 lives in unapproachable light, whom no one has seen or **can** see.

2Ti 2: 13 he will remain faithful, for *he* **cannot** [*+4024*] disown himself.
3: 7 always learning but never **able** to acknowledge the truth.
3: 15 which *are* **able** to make you wise for salvation through faith in

Heb 2: 18 he was tempted, *he is* **able** to help those who are being tempted.

3:19 So we see that *they were* not **able** to enter, because of their
4:15 For we do not have a high priest *who is* **unable** [+3590] to
5: 2 *He is* **able** to deal gently with those who are ignorant and are going
5: 7 loud cries and tears to the one *who* **could** save him from death,
7:25 Therefore *he is* **able** to save completely those who come to God
9: 9 and sacrifices being offered *were* not **able** to clear the conscience
10: 1 For this reason *it* **can** never, by the same sacrifices repeated
10:11 he offers the same sacrifices, which **can** never take away sins.

Jas   1:21 and humbly accept the word planted in you, which **can** save you.
2:14 claims to have faith but has no deeds? **Can** such faith save him?
3: 8 but no man **can** tame the tongue. It is a restless evil, full of deadly
3:12 My brothers, **can** a fig tree bear olives, or a grapevine bear figs?
4: 2 You kill and covet, but *you* **cannot** [+4024] have what you want.
4:12 one Lawgiver and Judge, the one *who is* **able** to save and destroy.

1Jn   3: 9 *he* **cannot** [+4024] go on sinning, because he has been born of
4:20 whom he has seen, **cannot** [+4024] love God, whom he has not

Jude   1:24 *To* him *who is* **able** to keep you from falling and to present you

Rev   2: 2 I know that *you* **cannot** [+4024] tolerate wicked men, that you
3: 8 I have placed before you an open door that no one **can** shut.
5: 3 one in heaven or on earth or under the earth **could** open the scroll
6:17 For the great day of their wrath has come, and who **can** stand?"
7: 9 and there before me was a great multitude that no one **could** count,
9:20 and wood—idols that **cannot** [+4046] see or hear or walk.
13: 4 asked, "Who is like the beast? Who **can** make war against him?"
13:17 so that no one **could** buy or sell unless he had the mark, which is
14: 3 No one **could** learn the song except the 144,000 who had been
15: 8 and no one **could** enter the temple until the seven plagues of the

1539 δύναμις, *dynamis* [119] [√ 1538]

δύναμις [τοῦ ἁγίου] πνεύματος (power of the [Holy] Spirit) [4] Lk 4:14; Ac 1:8; Ro 15:13,19

δύναμις [τοῦ] θεοῦ (power of God) [18] Mt 22:29; Mk 12:24; Lk 22:69; Ac 8:10; Ro 1:16; 15:19; 1Co 1:18,24; 2:5; 2Co 4:7; 6:7; 13:4,4; Eph 3:7; 2Ti 1:8; 1Pe 1:5; Rev 12:10; 19:1

δύναμις [τοῦ] κυρίου (power of the Lord) [3] Lk 5:17; 1Co 5:4; 2Pe 1:16

δύναμις Χριστοῦ (power of Christ) [1] 2Co 12:9

πνεῦμα [ἅγιος] καὶ δύναμις ([Holy] Spirit and power) [4] Lk 1:17; Ac 10:38; 1Co 2:4; Gal 3:5

power [73], miracles [16], ability [3], bodies [3], miraculous powers [3], powerful [3], powers [3], mighty [2], Mighty One [1], as much as were able [+2848] [1], brilliance [1], enabled [1], excessive [1], fury [1], grasp the meaning [+3836+3857] [1], miracle [1], miraculous powers [+1920] [1], so powerfully [+1877] [1], strength [1], work miracles [1], workers of miracles [1]

Mt   7:22 and in your name drive out demons and perform many **miracles**?'
11:20 the cities in which most *of* his **miracles** had been performed,
11:21 If the **miracles** that were performed in you had been performed in
11:23 If the **miracles** that were performed in you had been performed in
13:54 did this man get this wisdom and these **miraculous powers**?"
13:58 And he did not do many **miracles** there because of their lack of
14: 2 the dead! That is why **miraculous powers** are at work in him."
22:29 because you do not know the Scriptures or the **power** of God.
24:29 will fall from the sky, and the heavenly **bodies** will be shaken.'
24:30 Man coming on the clouds of the sky, with **power** and great glory.
25:15 two talents, and to another one talent, each according to his **ability**.
26:64 will see the Son of Man sitting at the right hand *of* the **Mighty** *One*

Mk   5:30 At once Jesus realized that **power** had gone out from him.
6: 2 this wisdom that has been given him, that he even does **miracles**!
6: 5 He could not do any **miracles** there, except lay his hands on a few
6:14 the dead, and that is why **miraculous powers** are at work in him."
9: 1 taste death before they see the kingdom of God come with **power**.
9:39 "No one who does a **miracle** in my name can in the next moment
12:24 because you do not know the Scriptures or the **power** of God?
13:25 will fall from the sky, and the heavenly **bodies** will be shaken.'
13:26 men will see the Son of Man coming in clouds with great **power**
14:62 will see the Son of Man sitting at the right hand *of* the **Mighty One**

Lk   1:17 he will go on before the Lord, in the spirit and **power** of Elijah,
1:35 upon you, and the **power** of the Most High will overshadow you.
4:14 Jesus returned to Galilee in the **power** of the Spirit, and news about
4:36 With authority and **power** he gives orders to evil spirits and they

5:17 And the **power** of the Lord was present for him to heal the sick.
6:19 because **power** was coming from him and healing them all.
8:46 "Someone touched me; I know that **power** has gone out from me."
9: 1 he gave them **power** and authority to drive out all demons
10:13 For if the **miracles** that were performed in you had been performed
10:19 and scorpions and to overcome all the **power** of the enemy;
19:37 to praise God in loud voices for all the **miracles** they had seen:
21:26 is coming on the world, for the heavenly **bodies** will be shaken.
21:27 time they will see the Son of Man coming in a cloud with **power**
22:69 the Son of Man will be seated at the right hand *of* the **mighty** God."
24:49 but stay in the city until you have been clothed with **power** from

Ac   1: 8 But you will receive **power** when the Holy Spirit comes on you;
2:22 of Nazareth was a man accredited by God to you *by* **miracles**,
3:12 Why do you stare at us as if *by* our own **power** or godliness we
4: 7 to question them: "By what **power** or what name did you do this?"
4:33 *With* great **power** the apostles continued to testify to the
6: 8 Now Stephen, a man full of *God's* grace and **power**, did great
8:10 "This man is the divine **power** known as the Great Power."
8:13 astonished *by* the great signs and **miracles** he saw.
10:38 God anointed Jesus of Nazareth with the Holy Spirit and **power**,
19:11 God did extraordinary **miracles** through Paul,

Ro   1: 4 and who through the Spirit of holiness was declared with **power** to
1:16 because it is the **power** of God for the salvation of everyone who
1:20 his eternal **power** and divine nature—have been clearly seen,
8:38 nor demons, neither the present nor the future, nor any **powers**,
9:17 that I might display my **power** in you and that my name might be
15:13 so that you may overflow with hope by the **power** of the Holy
15:19 by the **power** of signs and miracles, through the power of the
15:19 the power of signs and miracles, through the **power** of the Spirit.

1Co   1:18 are perishing, but to us who are being saved it is the **power** of God.
1:24 and Greeks, Christ the **power** of God and the wisdom of God.
2: 4 persuasive words, but with a demonstration *of* the Spirit's **power**,
2: 5 your faith might not rest on men's wisdom, but on God's **power**.
4:19 how these arrogant people are talking, but what **power** they have.
4:20 For the kingdom of God is not a matter of talk but of **power**.
5: 4 I am with you in spirit, and the **power** of our Lord Jesus is present,
6:14 By his **power** God raised the Lord from the dead, and he will raise
12:10 to another **miraculous powers** [+1920], to another prophecy,
12:28 second prophets, third teachers, then **workers of miracles**,
12:29 Are all prophets? Are all teachers? Do all **work miracles**?
14:11 then *I do* not **grasp the meaning** [+3836+3857] of what someone
15:24 Father after he has destroyed all dominion, authority and **power**.
15:43 it is raised in glory; it is sown in weakness, it is raised in **power**;
15:56 The sting of death is sin, and the **power** of sin is the law.

2Co   1: 8 We were under great pressure, far beyond our **ability** *to endure*,
4: 7 in jars of clay to show that this all-surpassing **power** is from God
6: 7 in truthful speech and in the **power** of God; with weapons of
8: 3 For I testify that they gave **as much as** they were able [+2848],
8: 3 gave as much as they were able, and even beyond their **ability**.
12: 9 is sufficient for you, for my **power** is made perfect in weakness."
12: 9 about my weaknesses, so that Christ's **power** may rest on me.
12: 9 The things that mark an apostle—signs, wonders and **miracles**—
13: 4 he was crucified in weakness, yet he lives by God's **power**.
13: 4 in him, yet by God's **power** we will live with him to serve you.

Gal   3: 5 Does God give you his Spirit and work **miracles** among you

Eph   1:19 and his incomparably great **power** for us who believe. That power
1:21 far above all rule and authority, **power** and dominion, and every
3: 7 gift of God's grace given me through the working of his **power**.
3:16 strengthen you *with* **power** through his Spirit in your inner being,
3:20 or imagine, according to his **power** that is at work within us,

Php   3:10 I want to know Christ and the **power** of his resurrection

Col   1:11 being strengthened with all **power** according to his glorious might
1:29 with all his energy, which **so powerfully** [+1877] works in me.

1Th   1: 5 but also with **power**, with the Holy Spirit and with deep

2Th   1: 7 is revealed from heaven in blazing fire with his **powerful** angels.
1:11 and that by his **power** he may fulfil every good purpose of yours
2: 9 the work of Satan displayed in all kinds of counterfeit **miracles**,

2Ti   1: 7 of timidity, but a spirit *of* **power**, of love and of self-discipline.
1: 8 But join with me in suffering for the gospel, by the **power** of God,
3: 5 having a form of godliness but denying its **power**. Have nothing to

Heb   1: 3 of his being, sustaining all things by his **powerful** word.
2: 4 God also testified to it *by* signs, wonders and various **miracles**,
6: 5 goodness of the word of God and the **powers** of the coming age,
7:16 his ancestry but on the basis of the **power** of an indestructible life.
11:11 was **enabled** to become a father because he considered him faithful
11:34 quenched the **fury** of the flames, and escaped the edge of the

1Pe 1: 5 who through faith are shielded by God's **power** until the coming of
3:22 *with* angels, authorities and **powers** in submission to him.
2Pe 1: 3 His divine **power** has given us everything we need for life
1:16 follow cleverly invented stories when we told you about the **power**
2:11 yet even angels, although they are stronger and more **powerful**,
Rev 1:16 His face was like the sun shining in all its **brilliance**.
3: 8 I know that you have little **strength**, yet you have kept my word
4:11 our Lord and God, to receive glory and honor and **power**,
5:12 to receive **power** and wealth and wisdom and strength and honor
7:12 Praise and glory and wisdom and thanks and honor and **power**
11:17 because you have taken your great **power** and have begun to reign.
12:10 come the salvation and the **power** and the kingdom of our God,
13: 2 The dragon gave the beast his **power** and his throne and great
15: 8 was filled with smoke from the glory of God and from his **power**,
17:13 They have one purpose and will give their **power** and authority to
18: 3 and the merchants of the earth grew rich from her **excessive**
19: 1 "Hallelujah! Salvation and glory and **power** belong to our God,

1540 δυναμόω, *dynamoō* [2] [√ *1538*]

strengthened [1], turned to strength [1]

Col 1:11 *being* **strengthened** with all power according to his glorious might
Heb 11:34 the edge of the sword; whose weakness *was* **turned to strength**;

1541 δυνάστης, *dynastēs* [3] [√ *1538*]

important official [1], Ruler [1], rulers [1]

Lk 1:52 He has brought down **rulers** from their thrones but has lifted up
Ac 8:27 an **important official** in charge of all the treasury of Candace,
1Ti 6:15 God, the blessed and only **Ruler**, the King of kings and Lord of

1542 δυνατέω, *dynateō* [3] [√ *1538*]

able [2], powerful [1]

Ro 14: 4 And he will stand, for the Lord *is* **able** to make him stand.
2Co 9: 8 And God *is* **able** to make all grace abound to you, so that in all
13: 3 He is not weak in dealing with you, but *is* **powerful** among you.

1543 δυνατός, *dynatos* [32] [√ *1538*]

possible [10], able [4], power [3], strong [3], could [2], powerful
[2], can [+*1639*] [1], could have done so [1], impossible [+*4024*]
[1], influential [1], leaders [1], mighty [1], possible [+*1639*] [1],
thorough knowledge [1]

Mt 19:26 "With man this is impossible, but with God all things are **possible**."
24:24 and miracles to deceive even the elect—if that were **possible**.
26:39 with his face to the ground and prayed, "My Father, if it is **possible**,
Mk 9:23 said Jesus. "Everything is **possible** for him who believes."
10:27 is impossible, but not with God; all things are **possible** with God."
13:22 and miracles to deceive the elect—if that were **possible**.
14:35 and prayed that if **possible** [+*1639*] the hour might pass from him.
14:36 "*Abba*, Father," he said, "everything is **possible** for you. Take this
Lk 1:49 for the **Mighty** *One* has done great things for me—holy is his
14:31 and consider whether he is **able** with ten thousand men to oppose
18:27 Jesus replied, "What is impossible with men is **possible** with God."
24:19 **powerful** in word and deed before God and all the people.
Ac 2:24 because it was **impossible** [+*4024*] for death to keep its hold on
7:22 wisdom of the Egyptians and was **powerful** in speech and action.
11:17 the Lord Jesus Christ, who was I to think that I **could** oppose God?"
18:24 was a learned man, with a **thorough knowledge** of the Scriptures.
20:16 in a hurry to reach Jerusalem, if **possible**, by the day of Pentecost.
25: 5 Let some of your **leaders** come with me and press charges against
Ro 4:21 being fully persuaded that God had **power** to do what he had
9:22 if God, choosing to show his wrath and make his **power** known,
11:23 they will be grafted in, for God is **able** to graft them in again.
12:18 If it is **possible**, as far as it depends on you, live at peace with
15: 1 We who are **strong** ought to bear with the failings of the weak
1Co 1:26 not many were **influential**; not many were of noble birth.
2Co 10: 4 On the contrary, they have divine **power** to demolish strongholds.
12:10 in difficulties. For when I am weak, then I am **strong**.
13: 9 We are glad whenever we are weak but you are **strong**; and our
Gal 4:15 I can testify that, if you **could have done so**, you would have torn

2Ti 1:12 and am convinced that he is **able** to guard what I have entrusted to
Tit 1: 9 so that *he can* [+*1639*] encourage others by sound doctrine
Heb 11:19 Abraham reasoned that God **could** raise the dead, and figuratively
Jas 3: 2 he is a perfect man, **able** to keep his whole body in check.

1544 δύνω, *dynō* [2] [→ *588, 589, 1550, 1553, 1694, 1898, 1903, 1905, 1906, 1907, 2086, 2087, 2115, 4208*]

setting [1], sunset [+*2463*] [1]

Mk 1:32 That evening after **sunset** [+*2463*] the people brought to Jesus all
Lk 4:40 *When* the sun *was* **setting**, the people brought to Jesus all who had

1545 δύο, *dyo* [135] [→ *1275, 1308, 1309, 1310, 1311, 1357, 1432, 1433, 1440, 1441, 1453, 1454, 1458, 1474, 1486, 1487, 1488, 1489, 1490, 1491, 1492, 1493, 1495, 1496, 1497, 1500, 1557, 1558, 1559*]

two [122], extra [2], seventy-two [+*1573*] [2], two by two [+*1545*]
[2], two by two [+*324+1545*] [2], 42 [+*2779+5477*] [1], both
[+*3836+3938*] [1], extra [+*324*] [1], forty-two [+*2779+5477*] [1],
twenty to thirty gallons [+*2445+3583+5552*] [1]

Mt 4:18 he saw **two** brothers, Simon called Peter and his brother Andrew.
4:21 Going on from there, he saw **two** other brothers, James son of
5:41 If someone forces you to go one mile, go with him **two** miles.
6:24 "No one can serve **two** masters. Either he will hate the one
8:28 **two** demon-possessed men coming from the tombs met him.
9:27 **two** blind men followed him, calling out, "Have mercy on us,
10:10 take no bag for the journey, or **extra** tunic, or sandals or a staff;
10:29 Are not **two** sparrows sold for a penny? Yet not one of them will
14:17 "We have here only five loaves of bread and **two** fish," they
14:19 Taking the five loaves and the **two** fish and looking up to heaven,
18: 8 or crippled than to have **two** hands or two feet and be thrown into
18: 8 than to have two hands or **two** feet and be thrown into eternal fire.
18: 9 It is better for you to enter life with one eye than to have **two** eyes
18:16 But if he will not listen, take one or **two** *others* along,
18:16 so that 'every matter may be established by the testimony *of* **two**
18:19 I tell you that if **two** of you on earth agree about anything you ask
18:20 For where **two** or three come together in my name, there am I with
19: 5 and be united to his wife, and the **two** will become one flesh'?
19: 6 So they are no longer **two**, but one. Therefore what God has joined
20:21 "Grant that one of these **two** sons of mine may sit at your right
20:24 the ten heard about this, they were indignant with the **two** brothers.
20:30 **Two** blind men were sitting by the roadside, and when they heard
21: 1 to Bethphage on the Mount of Olives, Jesus sent **two** disciples,
21:28 There was a man who had **two** sons. He went to the first and said,
21:31 "Which of the **two** did what his father wanted?" "The first,"
22:40 All the Law and the Prophets hang on these **two** commandments."
24:40 **Two** *men* will be in the field; one will be taken and the other left.
24:41 **Two** women will be grinding with a hand mill; one will be taken
25:15 to another **two** talents, and to another one talent, each according to
25:17 So also, the one with the **two** talents gained two more.
25:17 So also, the one with the two talents gained **two** more.
25:22 "The man with the **two** talents also came. 'Master,' he said,
25:22 'Master,' he said, 'you entrusted me with **two** talents; see,
25:22 'you entrusted me with two talents; see, I have gained **two** more.'
26: 2 you know, the Passover is **two** days away—and the Son of Man
26:37 He took Peter and the **two** sons of Zebedee along with him,
26:60 many false witnesses came forward. Finally **two** came forward
27:21 "Which of the **two** do you want me to release to you?" asked the
27:38 **Two** robbers were crucified with him, one on his right and one on
27:51 At that moment the curtain of the temple was torn in **two** from top
Mk 6: 7 he sent them out **two by two** [+*1545*] and gave them authority
6: 7 he sent them out **two by two** [+*1545*] and gave them authority
6: 9 Wear sandals but not an **extra** tunic.
6:38 and see." When they found out, they said, "Five—and **two** fish."
6:41 Taking the five loaves and the **two** fish and looking up to heaven,
6:41 set before the people. He also divided the **two** fish among them all.
9:43 It is better for you to enter life maimed than with **two** hands to go
9:45 It is better for you to enter life crippled than to have **two** feet
9:47 to enter the kingdom of God with one eye than to have **two** eyes
10: 8 and the **two** will become one flesh.' So they are no longer two,
10: 8 the two will become one flesh.' So they are no longer **two**, but one.
11: 1 Bethany at the Mount of Olives, Jesus sent **two** of his disciples,

12:42 But a poor widow came and put in **two** very small copper coins,
14: 1 and the Feast of Unleavened Bread were *only* **two** days away,
14:13 So he sent **two** of his disciples, telling them, "Go into the city,
15:27 They crucified **two** robbers with him, one on his right and one on
15:38 The curtain of the temple was torn in **two** from top to bottom.
16:12 Afterward Jesus appeared in a different form *to* **two** of them while

Lk   2:24 in the Law of the Lord: "a pair of doves or **two** young pigeons."
3:11 "The man with **two** tunics should share with him who has none,
5: 2 he saw at the water's edge **two** boats, left there by the fishermen,
7:18 disciples told him about all these things. Calling **two** of them,
7:41 "**Two** *men* owed money to a certain moneylender. One owed him
9: 3 no staff, no bag, no bread, no money, no **extra** [+*324*] tunic.
9:13 They answered, "We have only five loaves of bread and **two** fish—
9:16 Taking the five loaves and the **two** fish and looking up to heaven,
9:30 **Two** men, Moses and Elijah,
9:32 they saw his glory and the **two** men standing with him.
10: 1 After this the Lord appointed **seventy-two** [+*1573*] others
10: 1 and sent them **two** [+*324+1545*] **by two** ahead of him to every
10: 1 and sent them **two by two** [+*324+1545*] ahead of him to every
10:17 The **seventy-two** [+*1573*] returned with joy and said, "Lord,
10:35 The next day he took out **two** silver coins and gave them to the
12: 6 Are not five sparrows sold *for* **two** pennies? Yet not one of them is
12:52 divided against each other, three against **two** and two against three.
12:52 divided against each other, three against two and **two** against three.
15:11 Jesus continued: "There was a man who had **two** sons.
16:13 "No servant can serve **two** masters. Either he will hate the one
17:34 I tell you, on that night **two** *people* will be in one bed; one will be
17:35 **Two** *women* will be grinding grain together; one will be taken
18:10 "**Two** men went up to the temple to pray, one a Pharisee
19:29 the Mount of Olives, he sent **two** of his disciples, saying to them,
21: 2 He also saw a poor widow put in **two** very small copper coins,
22:38 The disciples said, "See, Lord, here are **two** swords."
23:32 **Two** other men, both criminals, were also led out with him to be
24: 4 suddenly **two** men in clothes that gleamed like lightning stood
24:13 Now that same day **two** of them were going to a village called

Jn   1:35 The next day John was there again with **two** of his disciples.
1:37 When the **two** disciples heard him say this, they followed Jesus.
1:40 was one of the **two** who heard what John had said and who had
2: 6 stone water jars, the kind used by the Jews for ceremonial washing,
          each holding from **twenty to thirty gallons** [+*2445+3583+5552*].
4:40 they urged him to stay with them, and he stayed **two** days.
4:43 After the **two** days he left for Galilee.
6: 9 "Here is a boy with five small barley loaves and **two** small fish,
8:17 In your own Law it is written that the testimony *of* **two** men is
11: 6 that Lazarus was sick, he stayed where he was **two** *more* days.
19:18 Here they crucified him, and with him **two** others—one on each
20: 4 **Both** [+*3836+3938*] were running, but the other disciple outran
20:12 and saw **two** angels in white, seated where Jesus' body had been,
21: 2 the sons of Zebedee, and **two** other disciples were together.

Ac   1:10 when suddenly **two** men dressed in white stood beside them.
1:23 So they proposed **two** *men*: Joseph called Barsabbas (also known
1:24 everyone's heart. Show us which of these **two** you have chosen
7:29 fled to Midian, where he settled as a foreigner and had **two** sons.
9:38 they sent **two** men to him and urged him, "Please come at once!"
10: 7 Cornelius called **two** of his servants and a devout soldier who was
12: 6 Peter was sleeping between **two** soldiers, bound with two chains,
12: 6 bound *with* **two** chains, and sentries stood guard at the entrance.
19:10 This went on for **two** years, so that all the Jews and Greeks who
19:22 He sent **two** of his helpers, Timothy and Erastus, to Macedonia,
19:34 he was a Jew, they all shouted in unison for about **two** hours:
21:33 and arrested him and ordered him to be bound *with* **two** chains.
23:23 Then he called **two** of his centurions and ordered them, "Get ready a

1Co 6:16 with her in body? For it is said, "The **two** will become one flesh."
14:27 If anyone speaks in a tongue, **two**—or at the most three—
14:29 **Two** or three prophets should speak, and the others should weigh
2Co 13: 1 "Every matter must be established by the testimony of **two**
Gal 4:22 For it is written that Abraham had **two** sons, one by the slave
4:24 may be taken figuratively, for the women represent **two** covenants.
Eph 2:15 His purpose was to create in himself one new man out of the **two**,
5:31 and be united to his wife, and the **two** will become one flesh."
Php 1:23 I am torn between the **two**: I desire to depart and be with Christ,
1Ti 5:19 entertain an accusation against an elder unless it is brought by **two**
Heb 6:18 by **two** unchangeable things in which it is impossible for God to
10:28 the law of Moses died without mercy on the testimony of **two**
Rev 9:12 The first woe is past; **two** other woes are yet to come.
11: 2 They will trample on the holy city *for* **42** [+*2779+5477*] months.

11: 3 And I will give power *to* my **two** witnesses, and they will prophesy
11: 4 These are the **two** olive trees and the two lampstands that stand
11: 4 and the **two** lampstands that stand before the Lord of the earth.
11:10 because these **two** prophets had tormented those who live on the
12:14 The woman was given the **two** wings of a great eagle, so that she
13: 5 and to exercise his authority *for* **forty-two** [+*2779+5477*] months.
13:11 He had **two** horns like a lamb, but he spoke like a dragon.
19:20 The **two** of them were thrown alive into the fiery lake of burning

1546 δυσβάστακτος, *dysbastaktos* [2 / 1] [√ *1002*]

hardly carry [1]

Mt 23: 4 They tie up heavy loads [UBS+ *they can* **hardly carry**] and put them
Lk 11:46 you load people down with burdens *they can* **hardly carry**,

1547 δυσεντερία, *dysenteria* Not used in UBS/NIV
[→ *1548; cf. 1877*]

1548 δυσεντέριον, *dysenterion* [1] [√ *1547*]

dysentery [1]

Ac 28: 8 His father was sick in bed, suffering from fever and **dysentery**.

1549 δυσερμήνευτος, *dysermēneutos* [1] [√ *2257*]

hard to explain [1]

Heb 5:11 about this, but it is **hard to explain** because you are slow to learn.

1550 δύσις, *dysis* [1 / 0] [√ *1544*]

Mk 16: S [UBS+ *Jesus himself sent out through them, from east to* **west**,]

1551 δύσκολος, *dyskolos* [1] [→ *1552; cf. 3266*]

hard [1]

Mk 10:24 said again, "Children, how **hard** it is to enter the kingdom of God!

1552 δυσκόλως, *dyskolōs* [3] [√ *1551*]

hard [3]

Mt 19:23 the truth, it is **hard** for a rich man to enter the kingdom of heaven.
Mk 10:23 "How **hard** it is for the rich to enter the kingdom of God!"
Lk 18:24 and said, "How **hard** it is for the rich to enter the kingdom of God!"

1553 δυσμή, *dysmē* [5] [√ *1544*]

west [5]

Mt   8:11 I say to you that many will come from the east and the **west**,
24:27 as lightning that comes from the east is visible even in the **west**,
Lk 12:54 "When you see a cloud rising in the **west**, immediately you say,
13:29 People will come from east and **west** and north and south,
Rev 21:13 three on the north, three on the south and three on the **west**.

1554 δυσνόητος, *dysnoētos* [1] [√ *3808*]

hard to understand [1]

2Pe 3:16 His letters contain some things that are **hard to understand**,

1555 δυσφημέω, *dysphēmeō* [1] [→ *1556; cf. 5774*]

slandered [1]

1Co 4:13 *when we are* **slandered**, we answer kindly. Up to this moment we

1556 δυσφημία, *dysphēmia* [1] [√ *1555*]

bad report [1]

2Co 6: 8 through glory and dishonor, **bad report** and good report; genuine,

1557 δώδεκα, *dōdeka* [75] [√ *1545 + 1274*]

οἱ δώδεκα (the twelve) [27] Mt 10:5; 26:14,20,47; Mk 3:16; 4:10; 6:7; 9:35; 10:32; 11:11; 14:10,17,20,43; Lk 6:13; 8:1; 9:1,12; 18:31; 22:3,47; Jn 6:67,70,71; 20:24; Ac 6:2; 1Co 15:5

δώδεκα ἀπόστολοι (twelve apostles) [2] Mt 10:2; Rev 21:14; cf. Mk 3:14; Lk 6:13

δώδεκα μαθηταί (twelve disciples) [3] Mt 10:1; 11:1; 20:17

twelve [60], 12 [+*5942*] [13], *untranslated* [1], twelve [+*2291*] [1]

Mt	9:20	then a woman who had been subject to bleeding *for* **twelve** years
	10: 1	He called his **twelve** disciples to him and gave them authority to
	10: 2	These are the names *of* the **twelve** apostles: first, Simon (who is
	10: 5	These **twelve** Jesus sent out with the following instructions:
	11: 1	After Jesus had finished instructing his **twelve** disciples, he went
	14:20	and the disciples picked up **twelve** basketfuls of broken pieces that
	19:28	you who have followed me will also sit on **twelve** thrones,
	19:28	will also sit on twelve thrones, judging the **twelve** tribes of Israel.
	20:17	to Jerusalem, he took the **twelve** disciples aside and said to them,
	26:14	Then *one of* the **Twelve**—the one called Judas Iscariot—went to
	26:20	evening came, Jesus was reclining at the table with the **Twelve**.
	26:47	While he was still speaking, Judas, one *of* the **Twelve**, arrived.
	26:53	and he will at once put at my disposal more than **twelve** legions of
Mk	3:14	He appointed **twelve**—designating them apostles—that they might
	3:16	These are the **twelve** he appointed: Simon (to whom he gave the
	4:10	the **Twelve** and the others around him asked him about the
	5:25	was there who had been subject to bleeding *for* **twelve** years.
	5:42	the girl stood up and walked around (she was **twelve** years old).
	6: 7	Calling the **Twelve** to him, he sent them out two by two and gave
	6:43	and the disciples picked up **twelve** basketfuls of broken pieces of
	8:19	basketfuls of pieces did you pick up?" "**Twelve**," they replied.
	9:35	Sitting down, Jesus called the **Twelve** and said, "If anyone wants to
	10:32	Again he took the **Twelve** aside and told them what was going to
	11:11	since it was already late, he went out to Bethany with the **Twelve**.
	14:10	Then Judas Iscariot, one *of* the **Twelve**, went to the chief priests to
	14:17	When evening came, Jesus arrived with the **Twelve**.
	14:20	"It is one *of* the **Twelve**," he replied, "one who dips bread into the
	14:43	Just as he was speaking, Judas, one *of* the **Twelve**, appeared.
Lk	2:42	When he was **twelve** years old, they went up to the Feast,
	6:13	he called his disciples to him and chose **twelve** of them,
	8: 1	the good news of the kingdom of God. The **Twelve** were with him,
	8:42	his only daughter, a girl *of* about **twelve** [+*2291*], was dying.
	8:43	was there who had been subject to bleeding for **twelve** years,
	9: 1	When Jesus had called the **Twelve** together, he gave them power
	9:12	Late in the afternoon the **Twelve** came to him and said,
	9:17	and the disciples picked up **twelve** basketfuls of broken pieces that
	18:31	Jesus took the **Twelve** aside and told them, "We are going up to
	22: 3	Then Satan entered Judas, called Iscariot, one *of* the **Twelve**.
	22:30	my kingdom and sit on thrones, judging the **twelve** tribes of Israel.
	22:47	man who was called Judas, one *of* the **Twelve**, was leading them.
Jn	6:13	and filled **twelve** baskets with the pieces of the five barley loaves
	6:67	"You do not want to leave too, do you?" Jesus asked the **Twelve**.
	6:70	Then Jesus replied, "Have I not chosen you, the **Twelve**? Yet one
	6:71	who, though one of the **Twelve**, was later to betray him.)
	11: 9	Jesus answered, "Are there not **twelve** hours of daylight? A man
	20:24	Now Thomas (called Didymus), one of the **Twelve**, was not with
Ac	6: 2	So the **Twelve** gathered all the disciples together and said,
	7: 8	of Jacob, and Jacob became the father of the **twelve** patriarchs.
	19: 7	There were about **twelve** men in all.
	24:11	You can easily verify that no more than **twelve** days ago I went up
1Co	15: 5	and that he appeared to Peter, and then *to* the **Twelve**.
Jas	1: 1	Jesus Christ, *To* the **twelve** tribes scattered among the nations:
Rev	7: 5	From the tribe of Judah **12** [+*5942*],000 were sealed, from the tribe
	7: 5	from the tribe of Reuben **12** [+*5942*],000, from the tribe of Gad
	7: 5	the tribe of Reuben 12,000, from the tribe of Gad **12** [+*5942*],000,
	7: 6	from the tribe of Asher **12** [+*5942*],000, from the tribe of Naphtali
	7: 6	tribe of Asher 12,000, from the tribe of Naphtali **12** [+*5942*],000,
	7: 6	of Naphtali 12,000, from the tribe of Manasseh **12** [+*5942*],000,
	7: 7	from the tribe of Simeon **12** [+*5942*],000, from the tribe of Levi
	7: 7	tribe of Simeon 12,000, from the tribe of Levi **12** [+*5942*],000,
	7: 7	the tribe of Levi 12,000, from the tribe of Issachar **12** [+*5942*],000,
	7: 8	from the tribe of Zebulun **12** [+*5942*],000, from the tribe of Joseph
	7: 8	tribe of Zebulun 12,000, from the tribe of Joseph **12** [+*5942*],000,
	7: 8	tribe of Joseph 12,000, from the tribe of Benjamin **12** [+*5942*],000.
	12: 1	the moon under her feet and a crown *of* **twelve** stars on her head.
	21:12	It had a great, high wall with **twelve** gates, and with twelve angels
	21:12	high wall with twelve gates, and with **twelve** angels at the gates.
	21:12	On the gates were written the names *of* the **twelve** tribes of Israel.
	21:14	The wall of the city had **twelve** foundations, and on them were the
	21:14	and on them were the **[RPG]** names of the twelve apostles of the
	21:14	and on them were the names *of* the **twelve** apostles of the Lamb.
	21:16	city with the rod and found it to be **12** [+*5942*],000 stadia in length,
	21:21	The **twelve** gates were twelve pearls, each gate made of a single
	21:21	The twelve gates were **twelve** pearls, each gate made of a single
	22: 2	bearing **twelve** *crops* of fruit, yielding its fruit every month.

1558 δωδέκατος, *dōdekatos* [1] [√ *1545 + 1274*]

twelfth [1]

Rev	21:20	tenth chrysoprase, the eleventh jacinth, and the **twelfth** amethyst.

1559 δωδεκάφυλον, *dōdekaphylon* [1] [√ *1545 + 1274 + 5876*]

twelve tribes [1]

Ac	26: 7	This is the promise our **twelve tribes** are hoping to see fulfilled as

1560 δῶμα, *dōma* [7] [→ *488, 1900, 1908, 2224, 3868, 3869, 3870, 3871, 5325*]

roof [4], roofs [2], roof of house [1]

Mt	10:27	what is whispered in your ear, proclaim from the **roofs**.
	24:17	Let no one on the **roof** of his house go down to take anything out
Mk	13:15	Let no one on the **roof** of his house go down or enter the house to
Lk	5:19	they went up on the **roof** and lowered him on his mat through the
	12: 3	in the ear in the inner rooms will be proclaimed from the **roofs**.
	17:31	On that day no one who is on the **roof** of his house, with his goods
Ac	10: 9	and approaching the city, Peter went up on the **roof** to pray.

1561 δωρεά, *dōrea* [11] [√ *1443*]

gift [10], it^s [+*3836*] [1]

Jn	4:10	"If you knew the **gift** of God and who it is that asks you for a drink,
Ac	2:38	of your sins. And you will receive the **gift** of the Holy Spirit.
	8:20	because you thought you could buy the **gift** of God with money!
	10:45	**gift** of the Holy Spirit had been poured out even on the Gentiles.
	11:17	So if God gave them the same **gift** as he gave us, who believed in
Ro	5:15	did God's grace and the **gift** that came by the grace of the one man,
	5:17	and *of* the **gift** of righteousness reign in life through the one man,
2Co	9:15	Thanks be to God for his indescribable **gift**!
Eph	3: 7	I became a servant of this gospel by the **gift** of God's grace given
	4: 7	one of us grace has been given as Christ apportioned **it**^{s} [+*3836*].
Heb	6: 4	who have tasted the heavenly **gift**, who have shared in the Holy

1562 δωρεάν, *dōrean* [9] [√ *1443*]

freely [3], for nothing [1], free gift [1], free of charge [1], without cost [1], without paying for it [1], without reason [1]

Mt	10: 8	drive out demons. **Freely** you have received, freely give.
	10: 8	drive out demons. Freely you have received, **freely** give.
Jn	15:25	what is written in their Law: 'They hated me **without reason**.'
Ro	3:24	and are justified **freely** by his grace through the redemption that
2Co	11: 7	elevate you by preaching the gospel of God to you **free of charge**?
Gal	2:21	could be gained through the law, Christ died **for nothing**!"
2Th	3: 8	nor did we eat anyone's food **without paying for it**. On the
Rev	21: 6	To him who is thirsty I will give to drink **without cost** from the
	22:17	and whoever wishes, let him take the **free gift** of the water of life.

1563 δωρέομαι, *dōreomai* [3] [√ *1443*]

given [2], gave [1]

Mk	15:45	from the centurion that it was so, *he* **gave** the body to Joseph.
2Pe	1: 3	His divine power *has* **given** us everything we need for life
	1: 4	Through these *he has* **given** us his very great and precious

1564 δώρημα, *dōrēma* [2] [√ *1443*]

gift [2]

Ro 5:16 Again, the **gift** of God is not like the result of the one man's sin:
Jas 1:17 Every good and perfect **gift** is from above, coming down from the

1565 δῶρον, *dōron* [19] [→ *2554; cf. 1443*]

gift [8], gifts [8], gift devoted to God [1], help [1], offerings [1]

Mt   2:11 and presented him with **gifts** of gold and of incense and of myrrh.
     5:23 if you are offering your **gift** at the altar and there remember that
     5:24 leave your **gift** there in front of the altar. First go and be reconciled
     5:24 and be reconciled to your brother; then come and offer your **gift**,
     8: 4 show yourself to the priest and offer the **gift** Moses commanded,
    15: 5 'Whatever **help** you might otherwise have received from me is a
    23:18 but if anyone swears by the **gift** on it, he is bound by his oath.'
    23:19 Which is greater: the **gift**, or the altar that makes the gift sacred?
    23:19 Which is greater: the gift, or the altar that makes the **gift** sacred?
Mk   7:11 have received from me is Corban' (that is, a **gift devoted to God**),
Lk 21: 1 Jesus saw the rich putting their **gifts** into the temple treasury.
    21: 4 All these people gave their **gifts** out of their wealth; but she out of
Eph 2: 8 through faith—and this not from yourselves, it is the **gift** of God—
Heb 5: 1 them in matters related to God, to offer **gifts** and sacrifices for sins.
     8: 3 Every high priest is appointed to offer both **gifts** and sacrifices,
     8: 3 for there are already men who offer the **gifts** prescribed by the law.
     9: 9 indicating that the **gifts** and sacrifices being offered were not able
    11: 4 as a righteous man, when God spoke well of his **offerings**.
Rev 11:10 will gloat over them and will celebrate by sending each other **gifts**,

1566 δωροφορία, *dōrophoria*   Not used in UBS/NIV
[√ *1443 + 5770*]

E, ε

1567 ε, *e*   Not used in UBS/NIV

1568 ἔα, *ea* [1]

Ha [1]

Lk   4:34 "**Ha**! What do you want with us, Jesus of Nazareth? Have you

1569 ἐάν, *ean* [350 / 351] [√ *1623 + 323*]

if [205], unless [+*3590*] [31], *untranslated* [16], whatever [+*4005*]
[11], whoever [+*4005*] [6], anyone [+*4005*] [5], suppose [5], when
[5], wherever [+*3963*] [5], what [+*4005*] [4], though [3], whatever
[+*5516*] [3], anyone [+*5516*] [2], anything [+*4005*] [2], even if [2],
whatever [+*4012*] [2], whenever [+*3963*] [2], whenever [+*4006*]
[2], whoever [+*5516*] [2], all who [+*4012*] [1], anyone [+*4012*] [1],
anything [+*5516*] [1], as for [1], as often as [+*4006*] [1], at least
[+*2779*] [1], but [+*3590*] [1], even [+*2779*] [1], even though [1],
everyone [1], everything [+*4012+4246*] [1], fail [+*3590*] [1], in
keeping with income [+*2338+4005+5516*] [1], just [+*2779*] [1],
like [+*6055*] [1], man [+*4005*] [1], on [1], only [+*3590*] [1],
provided that [1], since [1], the man [+*4005*] [1], the men [+*4005*]
[1], those whom [+*4005*] [1], those whom [+*4012*] [1], until
[+*3590+4754*] [1], what [+*4012*] [1], whatever [1], whatever
[+*4005+5516*] [1], whenever [+*2471*] [1], whenever [1], wherever
[+*4023*] [1], whether [1], who [+*4015*] [1], who [+*5516*] [1],
whoever [+*4015*] [1], whom [+*4005*] [1], without [+*3590*] [1],
would [1]

Mt   4: 9 I will give you," he said, "**if** you will bow down and worship me."
     5:13 But **if** the salt loses its saltiness, how can it be made salty again?
     5:19 **Anyone** [+*4005*] who breaks one of the least of these
     5:20 For I tell you that **unless** [+*3590*] your righteousness surpasses that
     5:23 **if** you are offering your gift at the altar and there remember that
     5:32 and **anyone** [+*4005*] who marries the divorced woman commits
     5:46 **If** you love those who love you, what reward will you get?
     5:47 And **if** you greet only your brothers, what are you doing more than

6:14 For **if** you forgive men when they sin against you, your heavenly
6:15 But **if** you do not forgive men their sins, your Father will not
6:22 **If** your eyes are good, your whole body will be full of light.
6:23 But **if** your eyes are bad, your whole body will be full of darkness.
7: 9 "Which of you, **if** [UBS-] his son asks for bread, will give him a
7:12 do to others **what** [+*4012*] you would have them do to you,
8: 2 and knelt before him and said, "Lord, **if** you are willing,
8:19 and said, "Teacher, I will follow you **wherever** [+*3963*] you go."
9:21 She said to herself, "**If** I only touch his cloak, I will be healed."
10:13 **If** the home is deserving, let your peace rest on it; if it is not,
10:13 let your peace rest on it; **if** it is not, let your peace return to you.
11: 6 Blessed is the **man** [+*4005*] who does not fall away on account of
11:27 and **those** *to* **whom** [+*4005*] the Son chooses to reveal him.
12:11 "**If** any of you has a sheep and it falls into a pit on the Sabbath,
12:29 and carry off his possessions **unless** [+*3590*] he first ties up the
12:32 **Anyone** [+*4005*] who speaks a word against the Son of Man will
14: 7 that he promised with an oath to give her **whatever** [+*4005*] she
15: 5 **Whatever** [+*4005*] help you might otherwise have received from
15:14 **If** a blind man leads a blind man, both will fall into a pit."
16:19 **whatever** [+*4005*] you bind on earth will be bound in heaven,
16:19 **whatever** [+*4005*] you loose on earth will be loosed in heaven."
16:25 For **whoever** [+*4005*] wants to save his life will lose it,
16:26 What good will it be for a man **if** he gains the whole world,
17:20 I tell you the truth, **if** you have faith as small as a mustard seed,
18: 3 **unless** [+*3590*] you change and become like little children,
18: 5 "And **whoever** [+*4005*] welcomes a little child like this in my name
18:12 **If** a man owns a hundred sheep, and one of them wanders away,
18:13 And **if** he finds it, I tell you the truth, he is happier about that one
18:15 "**If** your brother sins against you, go and show him his fault,
18:15 two of you. **If** he listens to you, you have won your brother over.
18:16 But **if** he will not listen, take one or two others along,
18:17 **If** he refuses to listen to them, tell it to the church; and if he refuses
18:17 and **if** he refuses to listen even to the church, treat him as you
18:18 **whatever** [+*4012*] you bind on earth will be bound in heaven,
18:18 and **whatever** [+*4012*] you loose on earth will be loosed in heaven.
18:19 I tell you that **if** two of you on earth agree about anything you ask
18:19 I tell you that **if** two of you on earth agree about anything **[RPG]**
18:35 of you **unless** [+*3590*] you forgive your brother from your heart."
20: 4 in my vineyard, and I will pay you **whatever** [+*4005*] is right.'
20:26 **whoever** [+*4005*] wants to become great among you must be your
21: 3 **If** anyone says anything to you, tell him that the Lord needs them,
21:21 "I tell you the truth, **if** you have faith and do not doubt,
21:21 but also **[NIE]** you can say to this mountain, 'Go, throw yourself
21:24 **If** you answer me, I will tell you by what authority I am doing
21:25 They discussed it among themselves and said, "**If** we say,
21:26 But **if** we say, 'From men'—we are afraid of the people, for they
22: 9 street corners and invite to the banquet **anyone** [+*4012*] you find.'
22:24 they said, "Moses told us that **if** a man dies without having children,
23: 3 So you must obey them and do **everything** [+*4012+4246*] they tell
24:23 At that time **if** anyone says to you, 'Look, here is the Christ!'
24:26 "So **if** anyone tells you, 'There he is, out in the desert,' do not go
24:28 **Wherever** [+*3963*] there is a carcass, there the vultures will gather.
24:48 But **suppose** that servant is wicked and says to himself,
26:13 **wherever** [+*3963*] this gospel is preached throughout the world,
26:35 But Peter declared, "Even **if** I have to die with you, I will never
26:42 if it is not possible for this cup to be taken away **unless** [+*3590*] I
28:14 **If** this report gets to the governor, we will satisfy him and keep you
Mk   1:40 him on his knees, "**If** you are willing, you can make me clean."
     3:24 **If** a kingdom is divided against itself, that kingdom cannot stand.
     3:25 **If** a house is divided against itself, that house cannot stand.
     3:27 and carry off his possessions **unless** [+*3590*] he first ties up the
     3:28 the sins and blasphemies of men will be forgiven them. **[RPG]**
     4:22 For **whatever** is hidden is meant to be disclosed, and whatever is
     5:28 because she thought, "**If** I just touch his clothes, I will be healed."
     5:28 she thought, "If I **just** [+*2779*] touch his clothes, I will be healed."
     6:10 **Whenever** [+*3963*] you enter a house, stay there until you leave
     6:22 "Ask me for **anything** [+*4005*] you want, and I'll give it to you."
     6:23 "**Whatever** [+*4005+5516*] you ask I will give you, up to half my
     6:56 They begged him to let them touch **even** [+*2779*] the edge of his
     7: 3 and all the Jews do not eat **unless** [+*3590*] they give their hands a
     7: 4 from the marketplace they do not eat **unless** [+*3590*] they wash.
     7:11 But you say that **if** a man says to his father or mother:
     7:11 '**Whatever** [+*4005*] help you might otherwise have received from
     8: 3 **If** I send them home hungry, they will collapse on the way,
     8:35 For **whoever** [+*4005*] wants to save his life will lose it,
     8:38 **If** anyone is ashamed of me and my words in this adulterous

9: 18 **Whenever** [+*3963*] it seizes him, it throws him to the ground.
9: 43 **If** your hand causes you to sin, cut it off. It is better for you to enter
9: 45 And **if** your foot causes you to sin, cut it off. It is better for you to
9: 47 And **if** your eye causes you to sin, pluck it out. It is better for you
9: 50 "Salt is good, but **if** it loses its saltiness, how can you make it salty
10: 12 And **if** she divorces her husband and marries another man,
10: 30 will **fail** [+*3590*] to receive a hundred times as much in this present
10: 35 they said, "we want you to do for us **whatever** [+*4005*] we ask."
11: 3 **If** anyone asks you, 'Why are you doing this?' tell him, 'The Lord
11: 31 They discussed it among themselves and said, "**If** we say,
12: 19 "Moses wrote for us that **if** a man's brother dies and leaves a wife
13: 11 Just say **whatever** [+*4005*] is given you at the time, for it is not
13: 21 At that time **if** anyone says to you, 'Look, here is the Christ!'
14: 9 **wherever** [+*3963*] the gospel is preached throughout the world,
14: 14 Say to the owner of the house **[NIE]** he enters, 'The Teacher asks:
14: 31 "**Even if** I have to die with you, I will never disown you."
16: 18 they will pick up snakes with their hands; and **when** they drink
Lk 4: 6 been given to me, and I can give it *to* **anyone** [+*4005*] I want to.
4: 7 So **if** you worship me, it will all be yours."
5: 12 his face to the ground and begged him, "Lord, **if** you are willing,
6: 33 And **if** you do good to those who are good to you, what credit is
6: 34 And **if** you lend to those from whom you expect repayment,
7: 23 Blessed is **the man**[s] [+*4005*] who does not fall away on account of
9: 48 "**Whoever** [+*4005*] welcomes this little child in my name
9: 57 a man said to him, "I will follow you **wherever** [+*3963*] you go."
10: 6 **If** a man of peace is there, your peace will rest on him; if not,
10: 22 and those *to* **whom** [+*4005*] the Son chooses to reveal him."
12: 38 be good for those servants whose master finds them ready, even **if**
12: 38 even if he comes in the second or **[RPG]** third watch of the night.
12: 45 But **suppose** the servant says to himself, 'My master is taking a
13: 3 no! But **unless** [+*3590*] you repent, you too will all perish.
13: 5 no! But **unless** [+*3590*] you repent, you too will all perish."
13: 9 **If** it bears fruit next year, fine! If not, then cut it down.' "
14: 34 "Salt is good, but **if** it loses its saltiness, how can it be made salty
15: 8 "Or **suppose** a woman has ten silver coins and loses one. Does she
16: 30 he said, 'but **if** someone from the dead goes to them, they will
16: 31 they will not be convinced even **if** someone rises from the dead.' "
17: 3 "**If** your brother sins, rebuke him, and if he repents, forgive him.
17: 3 "If your brother sins, rebuke him, and **if** he repents, forgive him.
17: 4 **If** he sins against you seven times in a day, and seven times comes
17: 33 **Whoever** [+*4005*] tries to keep his life will lose it, and whoever
19: 31 **If** anyone asks you, 'Why are you untying it?' tell him, 'The Lord
19: 40 "I tell you," he replied, "**if** they keep quiet, the stones will cry out."
20: 5 They discussed it among themselves and said, "**If** we say,
20: 6 But **if** we say, 'From men,' all the people will stone us,
20: 28 "Moses wrote for us that **if** a man's brother dies and leaves a wife
22: 67 "tell us." Jesus answered, "**If** I tell you, you will not believe me,
22: 68 and **if** I asked you, you would not answer.
Jn 3: 2 For no one could perform the miraculous signs you are doing **if**
3: 3 no one can see the kingdom of God **unless** [+*3590*] he is born
3: 5 no one can enter the kingdom of God **unless** [+*3590*] he is born of
3: 12 how then will you believe **if** I speak of heavenly things?
3: 27 "A man can receive only **[NIE]** what is given him from heaven.
4: 48 "**Unless** [+*3590*] you people see miraculous signs and wonders,"
5: 19 he can do **only** [+*3590*] what he sees his Father doing,
5: 31 "**If** I testify about myself, my testimony is not valid.
5: 43 but **if** someone else comes in his own name, you will accept him.
6: 44 "No one can come to me **unless** [+*3590*] the Father who sent me
6: 51 **If** anyone eats of this bread, he will live forever. This bread is my
6: 53 **unless** [+*3590*] you eat the flesh of the Son of Man and drink his
6: 62 What **if** you see the Son of Man ascend to where he was before!
6: 65 "This is why I told you that no one can come to me **unless** [+*3590*]
7: 17 **If** anyone chooses to do God's will, he will find out whether my
7: 37 a loud voice, "**If** anyone is thirsty, let him come to me and drink.
7: 51 "Does our law condemn anyone **without** [+*3590*] first hearing him
8: 14 Jesus answered, "Even **if** I testify on my own behalf, my testimony
8: 16 But **if** I do judge, my decisions are right, because I am not alone.
8: 24 **if** you do not believe that I am ⌞the one I claim to be⌟, you will
8: 31 Jesus said, "**If** you hold to my teaching, you are really my
8: 36 So **if** the Son sets you free, you will be free indeed.
8: 51 I tell you the truth, **if** anyone keeps my word, he will never see
8: 52 so did the prophets, yet you say that **if** anyone keeps your word,
8: 54 Jesus replied, "**If** I glorify myself, my glory means nothing.
8: 55 I know him. **If** I said I did not, I would be a liar like you, but I do
9: 22 for already the Jews had decided that **anyone** [+*5516*] who
9: 31 to sinners. He listens to the **[NIE]** godly man who does his will.
10: 9 I am the gate; **whoever** [+*5516*] enters through me will be saved.
10: 38 But if I do it, even **though** you do not believe me,
11: 9 **[NIE]** A man who walks by day will not stumble, for he sees by
11: 10 **[NIE]** It is when he walks by night that he stumbles, for he has no
11: 25 and the life. He who believes in me will live, even **though** he dies;
11: 40 Then Jesus said, "Did I not tell you that **if** you believed, you would
11: 48 **If** we let him go on like this, everyone will believe in him,
11: 57 and Pharisees had given orders that **if** anyone found out where
12: 24 **unless** [+*3590*] a kernel of wheat falls to the ground and dies,
12: 24 it remains only a single seed. But **if** it dies, it produces many seeds.
12: 26 **Whoever** [+*5516*] serves me must follow me; and where I am,
12: 26 also will be. My Father will honor the one **who** [+*5516*] serves me.
12: 32 But I, **when** I am lifted up from the earth, will draw all men to
12: 47 "**As for** the person who hears my words but does not keep them,
13: 8 Jesus answered, "**Unless** [+*3590*] I wash you, you have no part
13: 17 that you know these things, you will be blessed **if** you do them.
13: 35 men will know that you are my disciples, **if** you love one another."
14: 3 And **if** I go and prepare a place for you, I will come back and take
14: 14 You may ask me for **anything** [+*5516*] in my name, and I will do
14: 15 "**If** you love me, you will obey what I command.
14: 23 Jesus replied, "**If** anyone loves me, he will obey my teaching.
15: 4 branch can bear fruit by itself; **[NIE]** it must remain in the vine.
15: 4 Neither can you bear fruit **unless** [+*3590*] you remain in me.
15: 6 **If** anyone does not remain in me, he is like a branch that is thrown
15: 7 **If** you remain in me and my words remain in you, ask whatever
15: 7 ask **whatever** [+*4005*] you wish, and it will be given you.
15: 10 **If** you obey my commands, you will remain in my love, just as I
15: 14 You are my friends **if** you do what I command.
16: 7 **Unless** [+*3590*] I go away, the Counselor will not come to you;
16: 7 Counselor will not come to you; but **if** I go, I will send him to you.
19: 12 but the Jews kept shouting, "**If** you let this man go, you are no
20: 25 "**Unless** [+*3590*] I see the nail marks in his hands and put my
21: 22 Jesus answered, "**If** I want him to remain alive until I return,
21: 23 he only said, "**If** I want him to remain alive until I return,
21: 25 **If** every one of them were written down, I suppose that even the
Ac 3: 23 Anyone **who** [+*4015*] does not listen to him will be completely cut
5: 15 so that **at least** [+*2779*] Peter's shadow might fall on some of them
5: 38 For **if** their purpose or activity is of human origin, it will fail.
7: 7 But I will punish the nation **[NIE]** they serve as slaves,' God said,
8: 19 so that **everyone** on whom I lay my hands may receive the Holy
8: 31 "How can I," he said, "**unless** [+*3590*] someone explains it to me?"
9: 2 so that **if** he found any there who belonged to the Way,
13: 41 days that you would never believe, even **if** someone told you.' "
15: 1 "**Unless** [+*3590*] you are circumcised, according to the custom
26: 5 have known me for a long time and can testify, **if** they are willing,
27: 31 and the soldiers, "**Unless** [+*3590*] these men stay with the ship,
Ro 2: 25 Circumcision has value **if** you observe the law, but if you break the
2: 25 has value if you observe the law, but **if** you break the law,
2: 26 **If** those who are not circumcised keep the law's requirements,
7: 2 but **if** her husband dies, she is released from the law of marriage.
7: 3 **if** she marries another man while her husband is still alive,
7: 3 But **if** her husband dies, she is released from that law and is not an
9: 27 "**Though** the number of the Israelites be like the sand by the sea,
10: 9 That **if** you confess with your mouth, "Jesus is Lord," and believe
10: 15 And how can they preach **unless** [+*3590*] they are sent? As it is
11: 22 but kindness to you, **provided that** you continue in his kindness.
11: 23 And **if** they do not persist in unbelief, they will be grafted in,
12: 20 "**If** your enemy is hungry, feed him; if he is thirsty, give him
12: 20 is hungry, feed him; **if** he is thirsty, give him something to drink.
13: 4 But **if** you do wrong, be afraid, for he does not bear the sword for
14: 8 **If** we live, we live to the Lord; and if we die, we die to the Lord.
14: 8 If we live, we live to the Lord; and **if** we die, we die to the Lord.
14: 8 die to the Lord. So, **whether** we live or die, we belong to the Lord.
14: 8 So, whether we live or **[RPG]** die, we belong to the Lord.
14: 23 But the man who has doubts is condemned **if** he eats, because his
15: 24 **[NIE]** after I have enjoyed your company for a while.
1Co 4: 15 **Even though** you have ten thousand guardians in Christ, you do
4: 19 **if** the Lord is willing, and then I will find out not only how these
5: 11 not associate with **anyone** [+*5516*] who calls himself a brother
6: 4 Therefore, **if** you have disputes about such matters, appoint as
6: 18 All other sins **[NIE]** a man commits are outside his body,
7: 8 I say: It is good for them **[NIE]** to stay unmarried, as I am.
7: 11 But **if** she does, she must remain unmarried or else be reconciled to
7: 28 But **if** you do marry, you have not sinned; and if a virgin marries,
7: 28 you have not sinned; and **if** a virgin marries, she has not sinned.
7: 36 and **if** she is getting along in years and he feels he ought to marry,

7: 39 But **if** her husband dies, she is free to marry anyone she wishes,
7: 40 In my judgment, she is happier **if** she stays as she is—and I think
8: 8 to God; we are no worse **if** we do not eat, and no better if we do.
8: 8 to God; we are no worse if we do not eat, and no better **if** we do.
8: 10 For **if** anyone with a weak conscience sees you who have this
9: 16 Yet **when** I preach the gospel, I cannot boast, for I am compelled
9: 16 I am compelled to preach. Woe to me **if** I do not preach the gospel!
10: 28 But **if** anyone says to you, "This has been offered in sacrifice,"
11: 14 Does not the very nature of things teach you that **if** a man has long
11: 15 but that **if** a woman has long hair, it is her glory? For long hair is
11: 25 do this, **whenever** [+4006] you drink it, in remembrance of me."
11: 26 For **whenever** [+4006] you eat this bread and drink this cup,
12: 15 **If** the foot should say, "Because I am not a hand, I do not belong to
12: 16 And **if** the ear should say, "Because I am not an eye, I do not belong
13: 1 **If** I speak in the tongues of men and of angels, but have not love,
13: 2 **If** I have the gift of prophecy and can fathom all mysteries
13: 2 and **if** I have a faith that can move mountains, but have not love,
13: 3 **If** I give all I possess to the poor and surrender my body to the
13: 3 I possess to the poor and **[RPG]** surrender my body to the flames,
14: 6 Now, brothers, **if** I come to you and speak in tongues, what good
14: 6 **unless** [+3590] I bring you some revelation or knowledge
14: 7 how will anyone know what tune is being played **unless** [+3590]
14: 8 Again, **if** the trumpet does not sound a clear call, who will get
14: 9 **Unless** [+3590] you speak intelligible words with your tongue,
14: 11 **If** then I do not grasp the meaning of what someone is saying,
14: 14 For **if** I pray in a tongue, my spirit prays, but my mind is unfruitful.
14: 16 **If** you are praising God with your spirit, how can one who finds
14: 23 So **if** the whole church comes together and everyone speaks in
14: 24 But **if** an unbeliever or someone who does not understand comes in
14: 28 **If** there is no interpreter, the speaker should keep quiet in the
14: 30 And **if** a revelation comes to someone who is sitting down,
15: 36 What you sow does not come to life **unless** [+3590] it dies.
16: 2 a sum of money **in keeping with** *his* **income** [+2338+4005+5516],
16: 3 I will give letters of introduction to **the men**ˢ [+4005] you approve
16: 4 **If** it seems advisable for me to go also, they will accompany me.
16: 6 so that you can help me on my journey, **wherever** [+4023] I go.
16: 7 I hope to spend some time with you, **if** the Lord permits.
16: 10 **If** Timothy comes, see to it that he has nothing to fear while he is
2Co 3: 16 But **whenever** [+2471] anyone turns to the Lord, the veil is taken
5: 1 Now we know that **if** the earthly tent we live in is destroyed,
8: 12 is there, the gift is acceptable according to **what** [+4005] one has,
9: 4 For **if** any Macedonians come with me and find you unprepared,
10: 8 For even **if** I boast somewhat freely about the authority the Lord
11: 16 But if you do, then receive me just as you **would** a fool, so that I
12: 6 **Even if** I should choose to boast, I would not be a fool, because I
13: 2 **On** my return I will not spare those who sinned earlier or any of
Gal 1: 8 But even **if** we or an angel from heaven should preach a gospel
2: 16 know that a man is not justified by observing the law, **but** [+3590]
5: 2 I, Paul, tell you that **if** you let yourselves be circumcised,
5: 10 into confusion will pay the penalty, **whoever** [+4015] he may be.
5: 17 with each other, so that you do not do **what** [+4005] you want.
6: 1 Brothers, **if** someone is caught in a sin, you who are spiritual
6: 7 God cannot be mocked. A man reaps **what** [+4005] he sows.
Eph 6: 8 the Lord will reward everyone for **whatever** [+5516] good he does,
Col 3: 13 and forgive **whatever** [+5516] grievances you may have against
3: 17 And **whatever** [+5516] you do, whether in word or deed, do it all
3: 23 **Whatever** [+4005] you do, work at it with all your heart,
4: 10 received instructions about him; **if** he comes to you, welcome him.)
1Th 2: 7 among you, **like** [+6055] a mother caring for her little children.
3: 8 For now we really live, **since** you are standing firm in the Lord.
2Th 2: 3 for ₜthat day will not come₎ **until** [+3590+4754] the rebellion
1Ti 1: 8 We know that the law is good **if** one uses it properly.
2: 15 **if** they continue in faith, love and holiness with propriety.
3: 15 **if** I am delayed, you will know how people ought to conduct
2Ti 2: 5 Similarly, **if** anyone competes as an athlete, he does not receive the
2: 5 he does not receive the victor's crown **unless** [+3590] he competes
2: 21 **If** a man cleanses himself from the latter, he will be an instrument
Heb 3: 7 So, as the Holy Spirit says: "Today, **if** you hear his voice,
3: 15 "Today, **if** you hear his voice, do not harden your hearts as you did
4: 7 "Today, **if** you hear his voice, do not harden your hearts."
10: 38 by faith. And **if** he shrinks back, I will not be pleased with him."
12: 20 because they could not bear what was commanded: "**If** even an
13: 23 been released. **If** he arrives soon, I will come with him to see you.
Jas 2: 2 **Suppose** a man comes into your meeting wearing a gold ring
2: 14 my brothers, **if** a man claims to have faith but has no deeds?
2: 15 **Suppose** a brother or sister is without clothes and daily food.

2: 17 faith by itself, **if** it is not accompanied by action, is dead.
4: 4 **Anyone** [+4005] who chooses to be a friend of the world becomes
4: 15 to say, "**If** it is the Lord's will, we will live and do this or that."
5: 15 the Lord will raise him up. **If** he has sinned, he will be forgiven.
5: 19 **if** one of you should wander from the truth and someone should
1Pe 3: 13 Who is going to harm you **if** you are eager to do good?
1Jn 1: 6 **If** we claim to have fellowship with him yet walk in the darkness,
1: 7 But **if** we walk in the light, as he is in the light, we have fellowship
1: 8 **If** we claim to be without sin, we deceive ourselves and the truth is
1: 9 **If** we confess our sins, he is faithful and just and will forgive us
1: 10 **If** we claim we have not sinned, we make him out to be a liar
2: 1 But **if** anybody does sin, we have one who speaks to the Father in
2: 3 We know that we have come to know him **if** we obey his
2: 15 **If** anyone loves the world, the love of the Father is not in him.
2: 24 **If** it does, you also will remain in the Son and in the Father.
2: 28 so that **when** he appears we may be confident and unashamed
2: 29 **If** you know that he is righteous, you know that everyone who does
3: 2 But we know that **when** he appears, we shall be like him, for we
3: 20 **whenever** our hearts condemn us. For God is greater than our
3: 21 Dear friends, **if** our hearts do not condemn us, we have confidence
3: 22 and receive from him **anything** [+4005] we ask, because we obey
4: 12 but **if** we love one another, God lives in us and his love is made
4: 15 **If** anyone acknowledges that Jesus is the Son of God, God lives in
4: 20 **If** anyone says, "I love God," yet hates his brother, he is a liar.
5: 14 that **if** we ask anything according to his will, he hears us.
5: 15 And **if** we know that he hears us—whatever we ask—we know that
5: 15 And if we know that he hears us—**whatever** [+4005] we ask—
5: 16 **If** anyone sees his brother commit a sin that does not lead to death,
3Jn 1: 5 you are faithful *in* **what** [+4005] you are doing for the brothers,
1: 10 So **if** I come, I will call attention to what he is doing,
Rev 2: 5 **If** you do not repent, I will come to you and remove your
2: 22 with her suffer intensely, **unless** [+3590] they repent of her ways.
3: 3 But **if** you do not wake up, I will come like a thief, and you will
3: 19 **Those whom** [+4012] I love I rebuke and discipline. So be earnest,
3: 20 **If** anyone hears my voice and opens the door, I will come in
11: 6 the earth with every kind of plague **as often as** [+4006] they want.
13: 15 and cause **all who** [+4012] refused to worship the image to be
22: 18 **If** anyone adds anything to them, God will add to him the plagues
22: 19 And **if** anyone takes words away from this book of prophecy,

1570 ἐάνπερ, *eanper* [3] [√ 1623 + 323 + 4302]

if [2], *untranslated* [1]

Heb 3: 6 **if** we hold on to our courage and the hope of which we boast.
3: 14 We have come to share in Christ **if** we hold firmly till the end the
6: 3 And God permitting, we will do so. **[NIE]**

1571 ἑαυτοῦ, *heautou* [319 / 320] [√ 899]

first person [22] Ac 23:14; 25:4; Ro 8:23; 15:1; 1Co 11:31; 2Co
1:9,9; 3:1,5,5; 4:2,5,5; 5:12; 6:4; 7:1; 10:12,14; 1Th 2:8; 2Th 3:9;
Heb 10:25; 1Jn 1:8

second person [51] Mt 3:9; 16:8; 23:31; 25:9; 26:11; Mk 9:50;
12:33; 13:9; 14:7; Lk 3:8; 12:1,33,57; 16:9,15; 17:3,14; 21:30,34;
22:17; 23:28; Jn 5:42; 6:53; 12:8; Ac 5:35; 13:46; 15:29; 20:28; Ro
6:11,13,16; 11:25; 12:16,19; 1Co 3:18; 6:19; 10:29; 2Co 7:11;
13:5,5,5; Php 2:3,4,12; Heb 10:34; Jas 1:22; 2:4; 1Jn 5:21; 2Jn
1:8; Jude 1:20, 21

reciprocal [20] Mt 21:38; Mk 1:27; 10:26; 11:31; 12:7; 14:4; 16:3;
Lk 20:5; 22:23; Jn 7:35; 12:19; 1Co 6:7; Eph 4:32; 5:19; Col
3:13,16; 1Th 5:13; Heb 3:13; 1Pe 4:8,10

himself [77], themselves [30], yourselves [30], *untranslated* [24],
his own [17], ourselves [15], his [14], itself [12], their [12], their
own [9], each other [7], one another [7], you [7], them [6], he [3],
herself [3], claim [+3306] [2], conceited [+4123+5861] [2], her
[2], our [2], they [2], your [2], your own [2], appeared [+5746] [1],
bringing [+2400+3552] [1], claimed to be [+4472] [1], claiming
[+3306] [1], claims [+3306] [1], claims to be [+4472] [1], her own
[1], him [1], his heart [1], his senses [1], his very self [1], in
seclusion [+4332] [1], inwardly [+1877] [1], it [1], jumped [+965]
[1], myself [1], oneself [1], others [1], our hearts [1], proper [1],
renounced marriage [+2335+2336] [1], self-seeking

[+2426+3836] [1], set aside [+4123+5502] [1], take revenge
[+1688] [1], their hearts [1], to himself [+1877] [1], venture
[+1443] [1], watch out [+1063] [1], we [1], wondering about
[+1389+1877] [1], your hearts [1], yours [1], yourself [1]

Mt 3: 9 And do not think you can say to **yourselves**, 'We have Abraham as
   6:34 not worry about tomorrow, for tomorrow will worry about **itself**.
   8:22 Jesus told him, "Follow me, and let the dead bury **their own** dead."
   9: 3 At this, some of the teachers of the law said to **themselves**,
   9:21 She said to **herself**, "If I only touch his cloak, I will be healed."
   12:25 "Every kingdom divided against **itself** will be ruined, and every city
   12:25 and every city or household divided against **itself** will not stand.
   12:26 If Satan drives out Satan, he is divided against **himself**. How
   12:45 and takes with **it** seven other spirits more wicked than itself,
   12:45 and takes with it seven other spirits more wicked than **itself**,
   13:21 But since he has no root, [NIE] he lasts only a short time.
   14:15 so they can go to the villages and buy **themselves** some food."
   15:30 **bringing** [+2400+3552] the lame, the blind, the crippled, the mute
   16: 7 They discussed this among **themselves** and said, "It is because we
   16: 8 why are you talking among **yourselves** about having no bread?
   16:24 he must deny **himself** and take up his cross and follow me.
   18: 4 whoever humbles **himself** like this child is the greatest in the
   18:31 and went and told **their** master everything that had happened.
   19:12 and others *have* **renounced marriage** [+2335+2336] because of
   21: 8 A very large crowd spread **their** cloaks on the road, while others
   21:25 They discussed it among **themselves** and said, "If we say,
   21:38 the tenants saw the son, they said to **each other**, 'This is the heir.
   23:12 For whoever exalts **himself** will be humbled, and whoever
   23:12 will be humbled, and whoever humbles **himself** will be exalted.
   23:31 So you testify *against* **yourselves** that you are the descendants of
   25: 1 kingdom of heaven will be like ten virgins who took **their** lamps
   25: 3 foolish ones took their lamps but did not take any oil with **them**.
   25: 4 The wise, however, took oil in jars along with **their** lamps.
   25: 7 "Then all the virgins woke up and trimmed **their** lamps.
   25: 9 Instead, go to those who sell oil and buy some *for* **yourselves**.'
   26:11 The poor you will always have with **you**, but you will not always
   27:42 "He saved others," they said, "but he can't save **himself**! He's the

Mk 1:27 The people were all so amazed that they asked **each other**,
   2: 8 in his spirit that this was what they were thinking in **their hearts**,
   3:24 If a kingdom is divided against **itself**, that kingdom cannot stand.
   3:25 If a house is divided against **itself**, that house cannot stand.
   3:26 And if Satan opposes **himself** and is divided, he cannot stand;
   4:17 But since they have no root, [RPG] they last only a short time.
   5: 5 and in the hills he would cry out and cut **himself** with stones.
   5:30 At once Jesus realized that [RPG] power had gone out from him.
   6:36 and villages and buy **themselves** something to eat."
   6:51 and the wind died down. [RPG] They were completely amazed,
   8:14 to bring bread, except for one loaf they had with **them** in the boat.
   8:34 he must deny **himself** and take up his cross and follow me.
   9: 8 looked around, they no longer saw anyone with **them** except Jesus.
   9:10 They kept the matter to **themselves**, discussing what "rising from
   9:50 Have salt in **yourselves**, and be at peace with each other."
   10:26 more amazed, and said to **each other**, "Who then can be saved?"
   11:31 They discussed it among **themselves** and said, "If we say,
   12: 7 "But the tenants said to **one another**, 'This is the heir. Come,
   12:33 and to love your neighbor as **yourself** is more important than all
   13: 9 You will be [RPG] handed over to the local councils and flogged
   14: 4 Some of those present were saying indignantly to **one another**,
   14: 7 The poor you will always have with **you**, and you can help them
   15:31 "He saved others," they said, "but he can't save **himself**!
   16: 3 and they asked **each other**, "Who will roll the stone away from the

Lk 1:24 and for five months *remained* in seclusion [+4332].
   2: 3 And everyone went to **his own** town to register.
   2:39 the Lord, they returned to Galilee to **their own** town of Nazareth.
   3: 8 And do not begin to say to **yourselves**, 'We have Abraham as our
   7:30 and experts in the law rejected God's purpose for **themselves**,
   7:39 he said to **himself**, "If this man were a prophet, he would know
   7:49 The other guests began to say among **themselves**, "Who is this who
   9:23 he must deny **himself** and take up his cross daily and follow me.
   9:25 a man to gain the whole world, and yet lose or forfeit **his very self**?
   9:47 their thoughts, took a little child and had him stand beside **him**.
   9:60 "Let the dead bury **their own** dead, but you go and proclaim the
   10:29 But he wanted to justify **himself**, so he asked Jesus, "And who is
   11:17 "Any kingdom divided against **itself** will be ruined, and a house
   11:18 If Satan is divided against **himself**, how can his kingdom stand?
   11:21 "When a strong man, fully armed, guards **his own** house, his

   11:26 Then it goes and takes seven other spirits more wicked than **itself**,
   12: 1 "Be on **your** guard against the yeast of the Pharisees, which is
   12:17 He thought to **himself**, 'What shall I do? I have no place to store
   12:21 This is how it will be with anyone who stores up things *for* **himself**
   12:33 Provide purses *for* **yourselves** that will not wear out, a treasure in
   12:36 like men waiting for **their** master to return from a wedding
   12:57 "Why don't you judge for **yourselves** what is right?
   13:19 is like a mustard seed, which a man took and planted in **his** garden.
   13:34 as a hen gathers **her** chicks under her wings, but you were not
   14:11 For everyone who exalts **himself** will be humbled, and he who
   14:11 will be humbled, and he who humbles **himself** will be exalted."
   14:26 "If anyone comes to me and does not hate **his** father and mother,
   14:26 and children, his brothers and sisters—yes, even **his own** life—
   14:27 And anyone who does not carry **his** cross and follow me cannot be
   14:33 any of you who does not give up everything **he** has cannot be my
   15:17 "When he came to **his** senses, he said, 'How many of my father's
   15:20 So he got up and went to **his** father. "But while he was still a long
   16: 3 "The manager said **to himself** [+1877], 'What shall I do now?
   16: 5 "So he called in each one of **his** master's debtors. He asked the first,
   16: 8 in dealing with **their own** kind than are the people of the light.
   16: 9 I tell you, use worldly wealth to gain friends *for* **yourselves**,
   16:15 "You are the ones who justify **yourselves** in the eyes of men,
   17: 3 So watch **yourselves**. "If your brother sins, rebuke him, and if he
   17:14 When he saw them, he said, "Go, show **yourselves** to the priests."
   18: 4 But finally he said to **himself**, 'Even though I don't fear God
   18: 9 To some who were confident of **their own** righteousness
   18:11 The Pharisee stood up and prayed about **himself**: 'God, I thank you
   18:14 For everyone who exalts **himself** will be humbled, and he who
   18:14 will be humbled, and he who humbles **himself** will be exalted."
   19:12 "A man of noble birth went to a distant country to have **himself**
   19:13 So he called ten *of* **his** servants and gave them ten minas. 'Put this
   20: 5 They discussed it among **themselves** and said, "If we say,
   20:20 watch on him, they sent spies, who pretended [RPG] to be honest.
   21:30 you can see for **yourselves** and know that summer is near.
   21:34 [RPG] or your hearts will be weighed down with dissipation,
   22:17 he gave thanks and said, "Take this and divide it among **you**.
   22:23 They began to question among **themselves** which of them it might
   23: 2 payment of taxes to Caesar and **claims** [+3306] to be Christ,
   23:28 do not weep for me; weep for **yourselves** and for your children.
   23:35 let him save **himself** if he is the Christ of God, the Chosen One."
   24:12 and he went away, wondering to **himself** what had happened.
   24:27 to them what was said in all the Scriptures concerning **himself**.

Jn 5:18 even calling God his own Father, making **himself** equal with God.
   5:19 "I tell you the truth, the Son can do nothing by **himself**; he can do
   5:26 For as the Father has life in **himself**, so he has granted the Son to
   5:26 life in himself, so he has granted the Son to have life in **himself**.
   5:42 I know that you do not have the love of God in **your hearts**.
   6:53 of the Son of Man and drink his blood, you have no life in **you**.
   6:61 Aware [RPG] that his disciples were grumbling about this,
   7:18 He who speaks on **his own** does so to gain honor for himself,
   7:35 The Jews said to **one another**, "Where does this man intend to go
   8:22 This made the Jews ask, "Will he kill **himself**? Is that why he says,
   9:21 we don't know. Ask him. He is of age; he will speak for **himself**."
   11:33 also weeping, he was deeply moved in spirit and troubled. [RPG]
   11:38 Jesus, once more deeply moved, [RPG] came to the tomb.
   11:51 He did not say this on **his own**, but as high priest that year he
   11:55 many went up from the country to Jerusalem for **their** ceremonial
   12: 8 You will always have the poor among **you**, but you will not always
   12:19 So the Pharisees said to **one another**, "See, this is getting us
   13: 4 took off his outer clothing, and wrapped a towel around **his** waist.
   15: 4 No branch can bear fruit by **itself**; it must remain in the vine.
   16:13 He will not speak on **his own**; he will speak only what he hears,
   17:13 so that they may have the full measure of my joy within **them**.
   19: 7 he must die, because *he* **claimed to be** [+4472] the Son of God."
   19:12 Anyone who **claims to be** [+4472] a king opposes Caesar."
   19:17 Carrying **his own** cross, he went out to the place of the Skull
   19:24 "They divided my garments among **them** and cast lots for my
   21: 1 Afterward Jesus **appeared** [+5746] again to his disciples,
   21: 7 him (for he had taken it off) and **jumped** [+965] into the water.

Ac 1: 3 he showed **himself** to these men and gave many convincing proofs
   5:35 consider carefully what you intend [RPG] to do to these men.
   5:36 time ago Theudas appeared, **claiming** [+3306] to be somebody,
   7:21 Pharaoh's daughter took him and brought him up as **her own** son.
   8: 9 all the people of Samaria. He boasted that **he** was someone great,
   8:34 who is the prophet talking about, **himself** or someone else?"
   10:17 While Peter *was* **wondering about** [+1389+1877] the meaning of

12:11 Then Peter came to **himself** and said, "Now I know without a doubt
13:46 you reject it and do not consider **yourselves** worthy of eternal life,
15:29 **You** will do well to avoid these things. Farewell.
16:27 he drew his sword and was about to kill **himself** because he
19:31 sent him a message begging him not *to* **venture** [+*1443*] into the
20:28 Keep watch over **yourselves** and all the flock of which the Holy
21:11 he took Paul's belt, tied **his own** hands and feet with it and said,
21:23 There are four men with us who have made a vow. **[RPG]**
23:12 and bound **themselves** with an oath not to eat or drink until they
23:14 "We have taken a solemn oath not to eat anything until **we** have
23:21 They have taken an oath **[RPG]** not to eat or drink until they have
25: 4 "Paul is being held at Caesarea, and *I* **myself** am going there soon.
28:16 When we got to Rome, Paul was allowed to live by **himself**,
Ro 1:27 and received in **themselves** the due penalty for their perversion.
2:14 they are a law *for* **themselves**, even though they do not have the
4:19 in his faith, he faced the fact that **his** body was as good as dead—
5: 8 But God demonstrates **his own** love for us in this: While we were
6:11 count **yourselves** dead to sin but alive to God in Christ Jesus.
6:13 as instruments of wickedness, but rather offer **yourselves** to God,
6:16 Don't you know that when you offer **yourselves** to someone to
8: 3 God did by sending **his own** Son in the likeness of sinful man to be
8:23 groan **inwardly** [+*1877*] as we wait eagerly for our adoption as
11:25 so that you may not be **conceited** [+*4123+5861*]: Israel has
12:16 with people of low position. Do not be **conceited** [+*4123+5861*].
12:19 *Do* not **take revenge** [+*1688*], my friends, but leave room for
13: 2 and those who do so will bring judgment *on* **themselves**.
14: 7 For none of us lives *to* **himself** alone and none of us dies to
14: 7 of us lives to himself alone and none of us dies *to* **himself** alone.
14:12 So then, each of us will give an account of **himself** to God.
14:14 Lord Jesus, I am fully convinced that no food is unclean in **itself**.
14:22 Blessed is the man who does not condemn **himself** by what he
15: 1 to bear with the failings of the weak and not to please **ourselves**.
15: 3 For even Christ did not please **himself** but, as it is written:
16: 4 They risked **their** lives for me. Not only I but all the churches of
16:18 people are not serving our Lord Christ, but **their own** appetites.
1Co 3:18 Do not deceive **yourselves**. If any one of you thinks he is wise by
6: 7 The very fact that you have lawsuits among **you** means you have
6:19 whom you have received from God? You are not **your own**;
7: 2 so much immorality, each man should have **his own** wife,
7:37 and who has made up his mind not to marry the **[RPG]** virgin—
7:38 So then, he who marries the **[RPG]** virgin does right, but he who
10:24 Nobody should seek **his own** *good*, but the good of others.
10:29 the other man's conscience, I mean, not **yours**. For why should my
11:28 A man ought to examine **himself** before he eats of the bread
11:29 the body of the Lord eats and drinks judgment *on* **himself**.
11:31 But if we judged **ourselves**, we would not come under judgment.
13: 5 It is not rude, *it is* not **self-seeking** [+*2426+3836*], it is not easily
14: 4 He who speaks in a tongue edifies **himself**, but he who prophesies
14:28 should keep quiet in the church and speak *to* **himself** and God.
16: 2 each one of you *should* **set aside** [+*4123+5502*] a sum of money in
16:15 and they have devoted **themselves** to the service of the saints.
2Co 1: 9 Indeed, in **our hearts** we felt the sentence of death. But this
1: 9 But this happened that we might not rely on **ourselves** but on God,
3: 1 Are we beginning to commend **ourselves** again? Or do we need,
3: 5 Not that we are competent in **ourselves** to claim anything for
3: 5 that we are competent in ourselves to claim anything for **ourselves**,
4: 2 by setting forth the truth plainly we commend **ourselves** to every
4: 5 For we do not preach **ourselves**, but Jesus Christ as Lord,
4: 5 Jesus Christ as Lord, and **ourselves** as your servants for Jesus' sake.
5:12 We are not trying to commend **ourselves** to you again, but are
5:15 that those who live should no longer live *for* **themselves** but for
5:18 who reconciled us *to* **himself** through Christ and gave us the
5:19 that God was reconciling the world *to* **himself** in Christ,
6: 4 Rather, as servants of God we commend **ourselves** in every way:
7: 1 let us purify **ourselves** from everything that contaminates body
7:11 At every point you have proved **yourselves** to be innocent in this
8: 5 but they gave **themselves** first to the Lord and then to us in
10: 7 If anyone is confident that **he** belongs to Christ, he should consider
10: 7 he should consider again **[RPG]** that we belong to Christ just as
10:12 or compare **ourselves** with some who commend themselves.
10:12 or compare ourselves with some who commend **themselves**.
10:12 When they measure **themselves** by themselves and compare
10:12 When they measure themselves by **themselves** and compare
10:12 by themselves and compare **themselves** with themselves,
10:12 by themselves and compare themselves *with* **themselves**,
10:14 We are not going too far in **our** boasting, as would be the case if
10:18 For it is not the one who commends **himself** who is approved,
13: 5 Examine **yourselves** to see whether you are in the faith;
13: 5 yourselves to see whether you are in the faith; test **yourselves**.
13: 5 Do you not realize **[RPG]** that Christ Jesus is in you—unless,
Gal 1: 4 who gave **himself** for our sins to rescue us from the present evil
2:12 he began to draw back and separate **himself** from the Gentiles
2:20 by faith in the Son of God, who loved me and gave **himself** for me.
6: 3 thinks he is something when he is nothing, he deceives **himself**.
6: 4 Each one should test **his own** actions. Then he can take pride in
6: 4 Then he can take pride in **himself**, without comparing himself to
6: 8 The one who sows to please **his** sinful nature, from that nature will
Eph 2:15 His purpose was to create in **himself** [UBS *899*] one new man out
4:16 grows and builds **itself** up in love, as each part does its work.
4:19 they have given **themselves** over to sensuality so as to indulge in
4:32 forgiving **each other**, just as in Christ God forgave you.
5: 2 and gave **himself** up for us as a fragrant offering and sacrifice to
5:19 Speak *to* **one another** with psalms, hymns and spiritual songs.
5:25 just as Christ loved the church and gave **himself** up for her
5:27 and to present her *to* **himself** as a radiant church, without stain
5:28 same way, husbands ought to love **their** wives as their own bodies.
5:28 same way, husbands ought to love their wives as **their own** bodies.
5:28 wives as their own bodies. He who loves **his** wife loves himself.
5:28 wives as their own bodies. He who loves his wife loves **himself**.
5:29 After all, no one ever hated **his own** body, but he feeds and cares
5:33 each one of you also must love **his** wife as he loves himself,
5:33 each one of you also must love his wife as he loves **himself**,
Php 2: 3 but in humility consider others better than **yourselves**.
2: 4 Each of you should look not only to **your own** interests, but also to
2: 7 but made **himself** nothing, taking the very nature of a servant,
2: 8 as a man, he humbled **himself** and became obedient to death—
2:12 continue to work out **your** salvation with fear and trembling,
2:21 For everyone looks out for **his own** interests, not those of Jesus
Col 3:13 and forgive **[RPG]** whatever grievances you may have against
3:16 richly as you teach and admonish **one another** with all wisdom,
1Th 2: 7 were gentle among you, like a mother caring for **her** little children.
2: 8 to share with you not only the gospel of God but **our** lives as well,
2:11 we dealt with each of you as a father deals with **his own** children,
2:12 lives worthy of God, who calls you into **his** kingdom and glory.
4: 4 that each of you should learn to control **his own** body in a way that
5:13 in love because of their work. Live in peace with **each other**.
2Th 2: 4 he sets himself up in God's temple, proclaiming **himself** to be God.
2: 6 holding him back, so that he may be revealed at the **proper** time.
3: 9 but in order to make **ourselves** a model for you to follow.
3:12 in the Lord Jesus Christ to settle down and earn the bread **they** eat.
1Ti 2: 6 who gave **himself** as a ransom for all men—the testimony given in
2: 9 I also want women to dress **[RPG]** modestly, with decency
3:13 Those who have served well gain an excellent standing **[RPG]**
6:10 wandered from the faith and pierced **themselves** with many griefs.
6:19 In this way they will lay up treasure *for* **themselves** as a firm
2Ti 2:13 are faithless, he will remain faithful, for he cannot disown **himself**.
2:21 If a man cleanses **himself** from the latter, he will be an instrument
4: 3 they will gather *around* **them** a great number of teachers to say
Tit 2:14 who gave **himself** for us to redeem us from all wickedness
2:14 and to purify *for* **himself** a people that are his very own,
Heb 3:13 But encourage **one another** daily, as long as it is called Today,
5: 4 No one takes this honor *upon* **himself**; he must be called by God,
5: 5 So Christ also did not take *upon* **himself** the glory of becoming a
6: 6 because *to* **their** *loss* they are crucifying the Son of God all over
6:13 there was no one greater for him to swear by, he swore by **himself**,
7:27 He sacrificed for their sins once for all when he offered **himself**.
9: 7 which he offered for **himself** and for the sins the people had
9:14 who through the eternal Spirit offered **himself** unblemished to
9:25 Nor did he enter heaven to offer **himself** again and again, the way
10:25 **[RPG]** as some are in the habit of doing, but let us encourage one
10:34 because you knew that you **yourselves** had better and lasting
12: 3 sinful men, **[RPG]** so that you will not grow weary and lose heart.
12:16 who for a single meal sold **his** inheritance rights as the oldest son.
Jas 1:22 Do not merely listen to the word, and so deceive **yourselves**.
1:24 and, after looking at **himself**, goes away and immediately forgets
1:27 their distress and to keep **oneself** from being polluted by the world.
2: 4 have you not discriminated among **yourselves** and become judges
2:17 In the same way, faith by **itself**, if it is not accompanied by action,
1Pe 1:12 It was revealed to them that they were not serving **themselves**
3: 5 past who put their hope in God used to make **themselves** beautiful.
4: 8 Above all, love **each other** deeply, because love covers over a
4:10 Each one should use whatever gift he has received to serve **others**,

2Pe   2: 1 Lord who bought them—bringing swift destruction on **themselves**.
1Jn   1: 8 to be without sin, we deceive **ourselves** and the truth is not in us.
      3: 3 Everyone who has this hope in him purifies **himself**, just as he is
      5:10 who believes in the Son of God has this testimony in **his heart**.
      5:21 Dear children, keep **yourselves** from idols.
2Jn   1: 8 **Watch out** [+*1063*] that you do not lose what you have worked
Jude 1: 6 And the angels who did not keep **their** positions of authority
      1:12 without the slightest qualm—shepherds who feed *only* **themselves**.
      1:13 They are wild waves of the sea, foaming up **their** shame;
      1:16 are grumblers and faultfinders; they follow **their own** evil desires;
      1:18 "In the last times there will be scoffers who will follow **their own**
      1:20 build **yourselves** up in your most holy faith and pray in the Holy
      1:21 Keep **yourselves** in God's love as you wait for the mercy of our
Rev   2: 2 that you have tested those *who* **claim** [+*3306*] to be apostles
      2: 9 I know the slander of those who say **they** are Jews and are not,
      2:20 You tolerate that woman Jezebel, who calls **herself** a prophetess.
      3: 9 who **claim** [+*3306*] to be Jews though they are not, but are liars—
      6:15 and every slave and every free man hid **[RPG]** in caves
     10: 4 When he shouted, the **[RPG]** voices of the seven thunders spoke.
     10: 7 accomplished, just as he announced to **his** servants the prophets."
     19: 7 of the Lamb has come, and his bride has made **herself** ready.

1572 ἐάω, eaō [11] [→ *4661*]

let [6], allow [2], allowed [1], left [1], no more [+*2401*] [1]

Mt 24:43 have kept watch and would not have **let** his house be broken into.
Lk   4:41 But *he* rebuked them and *would* not **allow** them to speak,
    22:51 But Jesus answered, "**No more** [+*2401*] of this!" And he touched
Ac 14:16 In the past, he **let** all nations go their own way.
    16: 7 to enter Bithynia, but the Spirit of Jesus *would* not **allow** them to.
    19:30 to appear before the crowd, but the disciples *would* not **let** him.
    23:32 The next day *they* **let** the cavalry go on with him, while they
    27:32 the soldiers cut the ropes that held the lifeboat and **let** it fall away.
    27:40 *they* **left** them in the sea and at the same time untied the ropes that
    28: 4 he escaped from the sea, Justice *has* not **allowed** him to live."
1Co 10:13 he *will* not **let** you be tempted beyond what you can bear.

1573 ἑβδομήκοντα, hebdomēkonta [5] [√ *2231*]

seventy-two [+*1545*] [2], 276 [+*1357*+*1971*] [1], seventy [1],
seventy-five [+*4297*] [1]

Lk 10: 1 After this the Lord appointed **seventy-two** [+*1545*] others
    10:17 The **seventy-two** [+*1545*] returned with joy and said, "Lord,
Ac   7:14 his father Jacob and his whole family, **seventy-five** [+*4297*] in all.
    23:23 **seventy** horsemen and two hundred spearmen to go to Caesarea at
    27:37 Altogether there were **276** [+*1357*+*1971*] of us on board.

1574 ἑβδομηκοντάκις, hebdomēkontakis [1]
[√ *2231*]

seventy-seven times [+*2231*] [1]

Mt 18:22 "I tell you, not seven times, but **seventy-seven** [+*2231*] **times**.

1575 ἕβδομος, hebdomos [9] [√ *2231*]

seventh [9]

Jn   4:52 said to him, "The fever left him yesterday at the **seventh** hour."
Heb 4: 4 For somewhere he has spoken about the **seventh** day in these
     4: 4 words: "And on the **seventh** day God rested from all his work."
Jude 1:14 Enoch, the **seventh** from Adam, prophesied about these men:
Rev 8: 1 When he opened the **seventh** seal, there was silence in heaven for
    10: 7 But in the days when the **seventh** angel is about to sound his
    11:15 The **seventh** angel sounded his trumpet, and there were loud voices
    16:17 The **seventh** angel poured out his bowl into the air, and out of the
    21:20 the **seventh** chrysolite, the eighth beryl, the ninth topaz,

1576 Ἔβερ, Eber [1]

Eber [1]

Lk   3:35 the son of Serug, the son of Reu, the son of Peleg, the son *of* **Eber**,

1577 Ἑβραϊκός, Hebraikos Not used in UBS/NIV
[√ *1578*]

1578 Ἑβραῖος, Hebraios [4] [→ *1577, 1579, 1580*]

Hebrews [2], Hebraic Jews [1], Hebrew [1]

Ac   6: 1 Grecian Jews among them complained against the **Hebraic Jews**
2Co 11:22 Are they **Hebrews**? So am I. Are they Israelites? So am I.
Php 3: 5 people of Israel, of the tribe of Benjamin, a **Hebrew** of Hebrews;
     3: 5 people of Israel, of the tribe of Benjamin, a Hebrew of **Hebrews**;

1579 Ἑβραΐς, Hebrais [3] [√ *1578*]

in Aramaic [+*1365*] [3]

Ac 21:40 When they were all silent, he said to them **in Aramaic** [+*1365*]:
    22: 2 When they heard him speak to them **in Aramaic** [+*1365*],
    26:14 and I heard a voice saying to me **in Aramaic** [+*1365*], 'Saul,

1580 Ἑβραϊστί, Hebraisti [7] [√ *1578*]

in Aramaic [5], in Hebrew [2]

Jn   5: 2 which **in Aramaic** is called Bethesda and which is surrounded by
    19:13 known as the Stone Pavement (which **in Aramaic** is Gabbatha).
    19:17 he went out to the place of the Skull (which **in Aramaic** is called
    19:20 the city, and the sign was written **in Aramaic**, Latin and Greek.
    20:16 She turned toward him and cried out **in Aramaic**, "Rabboni!"
Rev 9:11 whose name **in Hebrew** is Abaddon, and in Greek, Apollyon.
    16:16 Then they gathered the kings together to the place that **in Hebrew**

1581 ἐγγίζω, engizō [42] [√ *1584*]

near [12], approached [9], approaching [3], came near [2], came
up [2], come near [2], comes [2], almost [1], almost here [1],
comes near [1], draw near [1], drawing near [1], drew near [1],
gathering around [1], gets here [1], near [+*2093*] [1], neared
[+*1181*] [1]

Mt   3: 2 and saying, "Repent, for the kingdom of heaven *is* **near**."
     4:17 began to preach, "Repent, for the kingdom of heaven *is* **near**."
    10: 7 As you go, preach this message: 'The kingdom of heaven *is* **near**.'
    21: 1 As *they* **approached** Jerusalem and came to Bethphage on the
    21:34 When the harvest time **approached**, he sent his servants to the
    26:45 Look, the hour *is* **near**, and the Son of Man is betrayed into the
    26:46 Rise, let us go! Here **comes** my betrayer!"
Mk   1:15 "The kingdom of God *is* **near**. Repent and believe the good news!"
    11: 1 As *they* **approached** Jerusalem and came to Bethphage
    14:42 Rise! Let us go! Here **comes** my betrayer!"
Lk   7:12 As *he* **approached** the town gate, a dead person was being carried
    10: 9 and tell them, 'The kingdom of God *is* **near** [+*2093*] you.'
    10:11 off against you. Yet be sure of this: The kingdom of God *is* **near**.'
    12:33 be exhausted, where no thief **comes near** and no moth destroys.
    15: 1 tax collectors and "sinners" were all **gathering around** to hear him.
    15:25 When *he* came **near** the house, he heard music and dancing.
    18:35 As Jesus **approached** Jericho, a blind man was sitting by the
    18:40 man to be brought to him. *When* he **came near**, Jesus asked him,
    19:29 As *he* **approached** Bethphage and Bethany at the hill called the
    19:37 *When* he **came near** the place where the road goes down the
    19:41 As *he* **approached** Jerusalem and saw the city, he wept over it
    21: 8 come in my name, claiming, 'I am he,' and, 'The time *is* **near**.'
    21:20 surrounded by armies, you will know that its desolation *is* **near**.
    21:28 and lift up your heads, because your redemption *is* **drawing near**."
    22: 1 Feast of Unleavened Bread, called the Passover, *was* **approaching**,
    22:47 the Twelve, was leading them. *He* **approached** Jesus to kiss him,
    24:15 each other, Jesus himself **came up** and walked along with them;
    24:28 As *they* **approached** the village to which they were going,
Ac   7:17 "As the time **drew near** for God to fulfill his promise to Abraham,
     9: 3 As he **neared** [+*1181*] Damascus on his journey, suddenly a light
    10: 9 day as they were on their journey and **approaching** the city,
    21:33 The commander **came up** and arrested him and ordered him to be
    22: 6 "About noon *as* I came **near** Damascus, suddenly a bright light
    23:15 about his case. We are ready to kill him before he **gets here**."
Ro 13:12 The night is nearly over; the day *is* **almost here**. So let us put aside
Php 2:30 because *he* **almost** died for the work of Christ, risking his life to

Heb 7:19 and a better hope is introduced, by which *we* **draw near** to God.
10:25 one another—and all the more as you see the Day **approaching**.
Jas 4: 8 **Come near** to God and he will come near to you. Wash your
4: 8 Come near to God and *he will* **come near** to you. Wash your
5: 8 be patient and stand firm, because the Lord's coming *is* **near**.
1Pe 4: 7 The end of all things *is* **near**. Therefore be clear minded

1582 ἐγγράφω, engraphō [3] [√ 1877 + 1211]

written [1], written in [RP1877] [1], written on [RP1877] [1]

Lk 10:20 but rejoice that your names *are* **written** [RP1877] **in** heaven."
2Co 3: 2 **written** [RP1877] **on** our hearts, known and read by everybody.
3: 3 **written** not with ink but with the Spirit of the living God,

1583 ἔγγυος, engyos [1]

guarantee [1]

Heb 7:22 of this oath, Jesus has become the **guarantee** of a better covenant.

1584 ἐγγύς, engys [31] [→ 1581, 1585, 4662]

near [22], almost time [2], approaching [+1181] [1], from [1], in danger of [1], nearby [1], nearer [1], Sabbath day's walk from [+2400+3847+4879] [1], soon [1]

Mt 24:32 get tender and its leaves come out, you know that summer is **near**.
24:33 you see all these things, you know that it is **near**, right at the door.
26:18 and tell him, 'The Teacher says: My appointed time is **near**.
Mk 13:28 get tender and its leaves come out, you know that summer is **near**.
13:29 these things happening, you know that it is **near**, right at the door.
Lk 19:11 because he was **near** Jerusalem and the people thought that the
21:30 you can see for yourselves and know that summer is **near**.
21:31 things happening, you know that the kingdom of God is **near**.
Jn 2:13 When it was **almost time** for the Jewish Passover, Jesus went up to
3:23 Now John also was baptizing at Aenon **near** Salim, because there
6: 4 The Jewish Passover Feast was **near**.
6:19 and a half miles, they saw Jesus **approaching** [+1181] the boat,
6:23 Then some boats from Tiberias landed **near** the place where the
7: 2 But when the Jewish Feast of Tabernacles was **near**,
11:18 Bethany was less than two miles **from** Jerusalem,
11:54 Instead he withdrew to a region **near** the desert, to a village called
11:55 When it was **almost time** for the Jewish Passover, many went up
19:20 for the place where Jesus was crucified was **near** the city,
19:42 was the Jewish day of Preparation and since the tomb was **nearby**,
Ac 1:12 Olives, a **Sabbath day's walk from** [+2400+3847+4879] the city.
9:38 Lydda was **near** Joppa; so when the disciples heard that Peter was
27: 8 and came to a place called Fair Havens, **near** the town of Lasea.
Ro 10: 8 "The word is **near** you; it is in your mouth and in your heart,"
13:11 because our salvation is **nearer** now than when we first believed.
Eph 2:13 were far away have been brought **near** through the blood of Christ.
2:17 to you who were far away and peace to those who were **near**.
Php 4: 5 Let your gentleness be evident to all. The Lord is **near**.
Heb 6: 8 and thistles is worthless and is **in danger of** being cursed.
8:13 one obsolete; and what is obsolete and aging will **soon** disappear.
Rev 1: 3 and take to heart what is written in it, because the time is **near**.
22:10 the words of the prophecy of this book, because the time is **near**.

1585 ἐγγύτερον, engyteron Not used in UBS/NIV
[√ 1584]

1586 ἐγείρω, egeirō [144 / 143] [→ 1213, 1340, 1444, 1587, 1995, 2074, 5283]

raised [45], get up [15], got up [11], risen [10], rise [8], raised to life [7], raised from the dead [6], raise [5], appear [3], raise up [3], raises [3], woke up [3], come [2], gets up [2], helped up [2], wake up [2], woke [2], appeared [1], go [1], lift out [1], lifted to his feet [1], made [1], made get up [1], on your feet [1], raise again [1], raised again [1], raised up [1], rise again [1], rising [1], stand up [1], stir up [1]

Mt 1:24 *When* Joseph **woke up**, he did what the angel of the Lord had
2:13 "**Get up**," he said, "take the child and his mother and escape to

2:14 So he **got up**, took the child and his mother during the night
2:20 and said, "**Get up**, take the child and his mother and go to the land
2:21 So he **got up**, took the child and his mother and went to the land of
3: 9 I tell you that out of these stones God can **raise up** children for
8:15 and the fever left her, and *she* **got up** and began to wait on him.
8:25 The disciples went and **woke** him, saying, "Lord, save us!
8:26 Then he **got up** and rebuked the winds and the waves, and it was
9: 5 to say, 'Your sins are forgiven,' or to say, '**Get up** and walk'?
9: 6 Then he said to the paralytic, "**Get up**, take your mat and go home."
9: 7 And the man **got up** and went home.
9:19 Jesus **got up** and went with him, and so did his disciples.
9:25 he went in and took the girl by the hand, and *she* **got up**.
10: 8 Heal the sick, **raise** the dead, cleanse those who have leprosy,
11: 5 who have leprosy are cured, the deaf hear, the dead *are* **raised**,
11:11 Among those born of women *there has* not **risen** anyone greater
12:11 into a pit on the Sabbath, will you not take hold of it and **lift** it **out**?
12:42 The Queen of the South *will* **rise** at the judgment with this
14: 2 his attendants, "This is John the Baptist; he *has* **risen** from the dead!
16:21 and that he must be killed and on the third day *be* **raised to life**.
17: 7 Jesus came and touched them. "**Get up**," he said. "Don't be afraid."
17: 9 have seen, until the Son of Man *has been* **raised** from the dead."
17:23 They will kill him, and on the third day *he will be* **raised to life**."
20:19 and crucified. On the third day *he will be* **raised to life**!"
24: 7 Nation *will* **rise** against nation, and kingdom against kingdom.
24:11 and many false prophets *will* **appear** and deceive many people.
24:24 For false Christs and false prophets *will* **appear** and perform great
25: 7 "Then all the virgins **woke up** and trimmed their lamps.
26:32 But after I *have* **risen**, I will go ahead of you into Galilee."
26:46 **Rise**, let us go! Here comes my betrayer!"
27:52 the bodies of many holy people who had died *were* **raised to life**.
27:63 still alive that deceiver said, 'After three days *I will* **rise again**.'
27:64 and tell the people that *he has been* **raised** from the dead.
28: 6 He is not here; he *has* **risen**, just as he said. Come and see the
28: 7 '*He has* **risen** from the dead and is going ahead of you into
Mk 1:31 So he went to her, took her hand and **helped** her **up**. The fever left
2: 9 sins are forgiven,' or to say, '**Get up**, take your mat and walk'?
2:11 "I tell you, **get up**, take your mat and go home."
2:12 *He* **got up**, took his mat and walked out in full view of them all.
3: 3 the man with the shriveled hand, "**Stand up** in front of everyone."
4:27 Night and day, whether he sleeps or **gets up**, the seed sprouts
4:38 The disciples **woke** him and said to him, "Teacher, don't you care if
5:41 "*Talitha koum!*" (which means, "Little girl, I say to you, **get up!**").
6:14 were saying, "John the Baptist *has been* **raised** from the dead,
6:16 "John, the man I beheaded, *has been* **raised** from the dead!"
9:27 But Jesus took him by the hand and **lifted** him **to his feet**,
10:49 So they called to the blind man, "Cheer up! **On your feet!**
12:26 Now about the dead **rising**—have you not read in the book of
13: 8 Nation *will* **rise** against nation, and kingdom against kingdom.
13:22 For false Christs and false prophets *will* **appear** and perform signs
14:28 But after I *have* **risen**, I will go ahead of you into Galilee."
14:42 **Rise!** Let us go! Here comes my betrayer!"
16: 6 the Nazarene, who was crucified. *He has* **risen!** He is not here.
16:14 refusal to believe those who had seen him *after he had* **risen**.
Lk 1:69 *He has* **raised up** a horn of salvation for us in the house of his
3: 8 For I tell you that out of these stones God can **raise up** children for
5:23 to say, 'Your sins are forgiven,' or to say, '**Get up** and walk'?
5:24 the paralyzed man, "I tell you, **get up**, take your mat and go home."
6: 8 with the shriveled hand, "**Get up** and stand in front of everyone."
7:14 carrying it stood still. He said, "Young man, I say to you, **get up!**"
7:16 praised God. "A great prophet *has* **appeared** among us," they said.
7:22 who have leprosy are cured, the deaf hear, the dead *are* **raised**,
8:54 But he took her by the hand and said, "My child, **get up!**"
9: 7 because some were saying that John *had been* **raised** from the
9:22 and he must be killed and on the third day *be* **raised to life**."
11: 8 yet because of the man's boldness he will **get up** and give him as
11:31 The Queen of the South *will* **rise** at the judgment with the men of
13:25 Once the owner of the house **gets up** and closes the door, you will
20:37 in the account of the bush, even Moses showed that the dead **rise**,
21:10 "Nation *will* **rise** against nation, and kingdom against kingdom.
24: 6 He is not here; he *has* **risen!** Remember how he told you,
24:34 "It is true! The Lord *has* **risen** and has appeared to Simon."
Jn 2:19 "Destroy this temple, and *I will* **raise** it **again** in three days."
2:20 to build this temple, and you *are going to* **raise** it in three days?"
2:22 After *he was* **raised** from the dead, his disciples recalled what he
5: 8 Then Jesus said to him, "**Get up!** Pick up your mat and walk."
5:21 For just as the Father **raises** the dead and gives them life, even

7:52 and you will find that a prophet *does* not **come** out of Galilee."
11:29 When Mary heard this, *she* **got up** quickly and went to him.
12: 1 where Lazarus lived, whom Jesus *had* **raised** from the dead.
12: 9 but also to see Lazarus, whom *he had* **raised** from the dead.
12:17 and **raised** him from the dead continued to spread the word.
13: 4 so *he* **got up** from the meal, took off his outer clothing,
14:31 what my Father has commanded me. "**Come** *now*; let us leave."
21:14 Jesus appeared to his disciples *after he was* **raised** from the dead.
Ac   3: 6 In the name of Jesus Christ of Nazareth, [UBS+ *get up and*] walk."
     3: 7 *he* **helped** him **up**, and instantly the man's feet and ankles became
     3:15 You killed the author of life, but God **raised** him from the dead.
     4:10 whom you crucified but whom God **raised** from the dead,
     5:30 The God of our fathers **raised** Jesus **from the dead**—whom you
     9: 8 Saul **got up** from the ground, but when he opened his eyes he
    10:26 But Peter **made** him **get up**. "Stand up," he said, "I am only a man
    10:40 but God **raised** him **from the dead** on the third day and caused
    12: 7 *He* struck Peter on the side and **woke** him **up**. "Quick, get up!"
    13:22 After removing Saul, *he* **made** David their king. He testified
    13:30 But God **raised** him from the dead,
    13:37 But the one whom God **raised from the dead** did not see decay.
    26: 8 Why should any of you consider it incredible that God **raises** the
Ro   4:24 for us who believe in him *who* **raised** Jesus our Lord from the
     4:25 to death for our sins and *was* **raised to life** for our justification.
     6: 4 just as Christ *was* **raised** from the dead through the glory of the
     6: 9 For we know that *since* Christ *was* **raised** from the dead, he cannot
     7: 4 might belong to another, *to* him *who was* **raised** from the dead,
     8:11 And if the Spirit *of* him *who* **raised** Jesus from the dead is living in
     8:11 he *who* **raised** Christ from the dead will also give life to your
     8:34 Christ Jesus, who died—more than that, *who was* **raised to life**—
    10: 9 and believe in your heart that God **raised** him from the dead,
    13:11 The hour has come for you *to* **wake up** from your slumber,
1Co 6:14 By his power God **raised** the Lord **from the dead**, and he will
    15: 4 that *he was* **raised** on the third day according to the Scriptures,
    15:12 But if it is preached that Christ *has been* **raised** from the dead,
    15:13 no resurrection of the dead, then not even Christ *has been* **raised**.
    15:14 And if Christ *has* not *been* **raised**, our preaching is useless
    15:15 we have testified about God that *he* **raised** Christ **from the dead**.
    15:15 But *he did* not **raise** him if in fact the dead are not raised.
    15:15 But he did not raise him if in fact the dead *are* not **raised**.
    15:16 For if the dead *are* not **raised**, then Christ has not been raised
    15:16 if the dead are not raised, then Christ *has* not *been* **raised** either.
    15:17 And if Christ *has* not *been* **raised**, your faith is futile; you are still
    15:20 But Christ *has* indeed *been* **raised** from the dead, the firstfruits of
    15:29 If the dead *are* not **raised** at all, why are people baptized for them?
    15:32 If the dead *are* not **raised**, "Let us eat and drink, for tomorrow we
    15:35 But someone may ask, "How *are* the dead **raised**? With what kind
    15:42 The body that is sown is perishable, *it is* **raised** imperishable;
    15:43 it is sown in dishonor, *it is* **raised** in glory; it is sown in weakness,
    15:43 it is raised in glory; it is sown in weakness, *it is* **raised** in power;
    15:44 it is sown a natural body, *it is* **raised** a spiritual body. If there is a
    15:52 the dead *will be* **raised** imperishable, and we will be changed.
2Co 1: 9 we might not rely on ourselves but on God, who **raises** the dead.
     4:14 *who* **raised** the Lord Jesus **from the dead** will also raise us with
     4:14 raised the Lord Jesus from the dead *will* also **raise** us with Jesus
     5:15 but for him who died for them and was **raised again**.
Gal 1: 1 Jesus Christ and God the Father, who **raised** him from the dead—
Eph 1:20 which he exerted in Christ *when he* **raised** him from the dead
     5:14 "**Wake up**, O sleeper, rise from the dead, and Christ will shine on
Php 1:17 supposing that they *can* **stir up** trouble for me while I am in
Col 2:12 your faith in the power of God, who **raised** him from the dead.
1Th 1:10 to wait for his Son from heaven, whom *he* **raised** from the dead—
2Ti 2: 8 Jesus Christ, **raised** from the dead, descended from David.
Heb 11:19 Abraham reasoned that God could **raise** the dead, and figuratively
Jas 5:15 in faith will make the sick person well; the Lord *will* **raise** him **up**.
1Pe 1:21 who **raised** him from the dead and glorified him, and so your faith
Rev 11: 1 and was told, "**Go** and measure the temple of God and the altar,

---

1587 ἔγερσις, *egersis* [1] [√ *1586*]

resurrection [1]

Mt 27:53 and after Jesus' **resurrection** they went into the holy city

---

1588 ἐγκάθετος, *enkathetos* [1] [√ *918;*
    cf. 1877 + 2848]

spies [1]

Lk 20:20 a close watch on him, they sent **spies**, who pretended to be honest.

1589 ἐγκαίνια, *enkainia* [1] [√ *1877 + 2785*]

Feast of Dedication [1]

Jn 10:22 Then came the **Feast of Dedication** at Jerusalem. It was winter,

---

1590 ἐγκαινίζω, *enkainizō* [2] [√ *1877 + 2785*]

opened [1], put into effect [1]

Heb 9:18 This is why even the first covenant *was* not **put into effect** without
    10:20 by a new and living way **opened** for us through the curtain,

---

1591 ἐγκακέω, *enkakeō* [6] [√ *1877 + 2805*]

lose heart [2], become weary [1], discouraged [1], give up [1],
tire of [1]

Lk 18: 1 to show them that they should always pray and not **give up**.
2Co 4: 1 through God's mercy we have this ministry, *we do* not **lose heart**.
     4:16 Therefore *we do* not **lose heart**. Though outwardly we are wasting
Gal 6: 9 *Let us* not **become weary** in doing good, for at the proper time we
Eph 3:13 therefore, not *to be* **discouraged** because of my sufferings for you,
2Th 3:13 And as for you, brothers, never **tire of** doing what is right.

1592 ἐγκαλέω, *enkaleō* [7] [√ *1877 + 2813*]

accusing [2], accusation [1], accusations [1], bring any charge
[1], charged with [1], press charges [1]

Ac 19:38 courts are open and there are proconsuls. *They can* **press charges**.
    19:40 we are in danger of *being* **charged with** rioting because of today's
    23:28 I wanted to know why *they were* **accusing** him, so I brought him
    23:29 I found that the **accusation** had to do with questions about their
    26: 2 as I make my defense against all the **accusations** of the Jews,
    26: 7 O king, it is because of this hope that the Jews *are* **accusing** me.
Ro 8:33 Who *will* **bring any charge** against those whom God has chosen?

1593 ἐγκαταλείπω, *enkataleipō* [10]
    [√ *1877 + 2848 + 3309*]

abandoned [2], deserted [2], forsaken [2], abandon [1], forsake
[1], give up [1], left [1]

Mt 27:46 which means, "My God, my God, why *have you* **forsaken** me?"
Mk 15:34 which means, "My God, my God, why *have you* **forsaken** me?"
Ac 2:27 because *you will* not **abandon** me to the grave, nor will you let
     2:31 that *he was* not **abandoned** to the grave, nor did his body see
Ro 9:29 "Unless the Lord Almighty *had* **left** us descendants, we would have
2Co 4: 9 persecuted, but not **abandoned**; struck down, but not destroyed.
2Ti 4:10 loved this world, *has* **deserted** me and has gone to Thessalonica.
     4:16 no one came to my support, but everyone **deserted** me.
Heb 10:25 *Let us* not **give up** meeting together, as some are in the habit of
    13: 5 God has said, "Never will I leave you; never *will I* **forsake** you."

1594 ἐγκατοικέω, *enkatoikeō* [1]
    [√ *1877 + 2848 + 3875*]

living among [*RP1877*] [1]

2Pe 2: 8 that righteous man, **living** [*RP1877*] **among** them day after day,

---

1595 ἐγκαυχάομαι, *enkauchaomai* [1]
    [√ *1877 + 3016*]

boast [1]

2Th 1: 4 among God's churches we **boast** about your perseverance

1596 ἐγκεντρίζω, *enkentrizō* [6] [√ *1877 + 3034*]

grafted in [2], graft in [1], grafted [1], grafted in among [*RP1877*] [1], grafted into [1]

Ro 11: 17 *have been* grafted [*RP1877*] in among the others and now share
11: 19 say then, "Branches were broken off so that I *could be* grafted in."
11: 23 And if they do not persist in unbelief, *they will be* grafted in,
11: 23 they will be grafted in, for God is able *to* graft them in again.
11: 24 and contrary to nature *were* grafted into a cultivated olive tree,
11: 24 much more readily *will* these, the natural branches, *be* grafted into

1597 ἐγκλείω, *enkleiō*   Not used in UBS/NIV
[√ *1877 + 3091*]

1598 ἔγκλημα, *enklēma* [2] [√ *1877 + 2813*]

charge [1], charges [1]

Ac 23: 29 but there was no charge *against* him that deserved death
25: 16 and has had an opportunity to defend himself against their charges.

1599 ἐγκομβόομαι, *enkomboomai* [1] [√ *1877*]

clothe with [1]

1Pe 5: 5 All of *you*, clothe *yourselves* with humility toward one another,

1600 ἐγκοπή, *enkopē* [1] [√ *1877 + 3164*]

hinder [*+1443*] [1]

1Co 9: 12 we put up with anything rather than hinder [*+1443*] the gospel of

1601 ἐγκόπτω, *enkoptō* [5] [√ *1877 + 3164*]

cut in on [1], hinder [1], hindered from [1], stopped [1], weary [1]

Ac 24: 4 But in order not to weary you further, I would request that you be
Ro 15: 22 This is why *I have* often *been* hindered from coming to you.
Gal 5: 7 Who cut in on you and kept you from obeying the truth?
1Th 2: 18 certainly I, Paul, did, again and again—but Satan stopped us.
1Pe 3: 7 the gracious gift of life, so that nothing *will* hinder your prayers.

1602 ἐγκράτεια, *enkrateia* [4] [√ *1877 + 3197*]

self-control [4]

Ac 24: 25 self-control and the judgment to come, Felix was afraid and said,
Gal 5: 23 gentleness and self-control. Against such things there is no law.
2Pe 1: 6 and to knowledge, self-control; and to self-control, perseverance;
1: 6 and to knowledge, self-control; and to self-control, perseverance;

1603 ἐγκρατεύομαι, *enkrateuomai* [2]
[√ *1877 + 3197*]

control [1], goes into training [1]

1Co 7: 9 But if *they* cannot control *themselves*, they should marry,
9: 25 Everyone who competes in the games goes into strict training.

1604 ἐγκρατής, *enkratēs* [1] [√ *1877 + 3197*]

disciplined [1]

Tit 1: 8 what is good, who is self-controlled, upright, holy and disciplined.

1605 ἐγκρίνω, *enkrinō* [1] [√ *1877 + 3212*]

classify [1]

2Co 10: 12 We do not dare *to* classify or compare ourselves with some who

1606 ἐγκρύπτω, *enkryptō* [2] [√ *1877 + 3221*]

mixed [2]

Mt 13: 33 and mixed into a large amount of flour until it worked all through

Lk 13: 21 and mixed into a large amount of flour until it worked all through

1607 ἔγκυος, *enkyos* [1] [√ *1877 + 3246*]

expecting a child [1]

Lk 2: 5 who was pledged to be married to him and was expecting a child.

1608 ἐγχρίω, *enchriō* [1] [√ *1877 + 5987*]

put on [1]

Rev 3: 18 and salve *to* put on your eyes, so you can see.

1609 ἐγώ, *egō* [2667 / 2669]   See Index of Articles, Etc.
[→ *1831, 1847, 2466, 2743, 3592, 3598, 5652*]

ἐγώ εἰμί (I am) [48] Mt 14:27; 22:32; 24:5; 26:22,25; Mk 6:50; 13:6; 14:62; Lk 1:19; 21:8; 22:70; 24:39; Jn 4:26; 6:20,35,41,48,51; 8:12,18,24,28,58; 9:9; 10:7,9,11,14; 11:25; 13:19; 14:6; 15:1,5; 18:5,6,8; Ac 9:5; 10:21; 18:10; 22:3,8; 26:15,29; Rev 1:8,17; 2:23; 21:6; 22:16

εἰμί ἐγώ (I am) [11] Jn 1:27; 3:28; 7:34,36; 12:26; 14:3; 17:24; Ac 13:25; 27:23; Ro 11:13; 1Ti 1:15

me [743], I [508], my [478], us [365], our [290], we [177], *untranslated* [47], mine [11], I myself [7], ours [6], my own [5], me [*+3836+3950*] [4], me [*+3836+4725*] [2], our own [2], your [2], as surely as I live [*+2409*] [1], here [*+1877*] [1], him [*+81+3836*] [1], I [*+3836+6034*] [1], I [*+6034*] [1], I'm [*+1639*] [1], is one of us [*+199+3552*] [1], Jews [*+1169+1877+3836*] [1], me [*+3836+5889*] [1], me [*+3836+6034*] [1], me [*+6034*] [1], me say [*+4123*] [1], my [*+3836+3950*] [1], myself [*+6034*] [1], myself [1], of mine [*+1650*] [1], ourselves [1], them [*+3836+4252*] [1], we are [1], we'll [1], what business is it of mine [*+5515*] [1], yes [*+2627*] [1]

1610 ἐδαφίζω, *edaphizō* [1] [√ *1611*]

dash to the ground [1]

Lk 19: 44 *They will* dash you to the ground, you and the children within

1611 ἔδαφος, *edaphos* [1] [→ *1610*]

ground [1]

Ac 22: 7 I fell to the ground and heard a voice say to me, 'Saul! Saul!

1612 ἑδραῖος, *hedraios* [3] [→ *909, 1613, 1909, 1910, 1911, 2339, 2348, 2757, 4204, 4663, 5284, 5285, 5286; cf. 2757*]

firm [1], settled the matter [*+2705*] [1], stand firm [*+1181*] [1]

1Co 7: 37 But the man *who has* settled [*+2705*] the matter in his own mind,
15: 58 Therefore, my dear brothers, stand firm [*+1181*]. Let nothing
Col 1: 23 if you continue in your faith, established and firm, not moved from

1613 ἑδραίωμα, *hedraiōma* [1] [√ *1612*]

foundation [1]

1Ti 3: 15 the church of the living God, the pillar and foundation of the truth.

1614 Ἐζεκίας, *Hezekias* [2]

Hezekiah [2]

Mt 1: 9 Jotham the father of Ahaz, Ahaz the father of Hezekiah,
1: 10 Hezekiah the father of Manasseh, Manasseh the father of Amon,

1615 ἐθελοθρησκία, *ethelothrēskia* [1]

[√ *2527 + 2580*]

self-imposed worship [1]

Col   2:23   with their **self-imposed worship**, their false humility and their

1616 ἐθίζω, *ethizō* [1] [√ *1621*]

custom [1]

Lk   2:27   the child Jesus to do for him what the **custom** of the Law required,

1617 ἐθνάρχης, *ethnarchēs* [1] [√ *1620 + 806*]

governor [1]

2Co 11:32   In Damascus the **governor** under King Aretas had the city of the

1618 ἐθνικός, *ethnikos* [4] [√ *1620*]

pagans [3], pagan [1]

Mt   5:47   what are you doing more than others? Do not even **pagans** do that?
      6: 7   And when you pray, do not keep on babbling like **pagans**,
      18:17   to the church, treat him as you would a **pagan** or a tax collector.
3Jn   1: 7   of the Name that they went out, receiving no help from the **pagans**.

1619 ἐθνικῶς, *ethnikōs* [1] [√ *1620*]

like a Gentile [1]

Gal   2:14   "You are a Jew, yet you live **like a Gentile** and not like a Jew.

1620 ἔθνος, *ethnos* [162] [→ *1617, 1618, 1619*]

τὰ ἔθνη (the Gentiles) [93] Mt 4:15; 6:32; 10:18; 12:18;
20:19,25; 24:9,14; 25:32; 28:19; Mk 10:33,42; 11:17; 13:10; Lk
12:30; 18:32; 21:24; 22:25, 24:47; Ac 7:45; 10:45; 11:1,18;
13:46,48; 14:2,5,16,27; 15:3,7,12,17,19; 18:6; 21:19,21,25;
26:17,20,23; 28:28; Ro 1:5,13; 2:24; 11:11,13,25;
15:9,11,16,16,27; 16:4,26; 1Co 5:1; 10:20; Gal 1:16;
2:2,8,9,12,14; 3:8,8,14; Eph 2:11; 3:1,6,8; 4:17; Col 1:27; 1Th
2:16; 4:5; 2Ti 4:17; 1Pe 2:12; 4:3; Rev 2:26; 11:2,18; 12:5, 14:8;
15:3,4; 16:19; 18:3,23; 19:15; 20:3,8; 21:24,26; 22:2

Gentiles [81], nations [37], nation [26], pagans [6], people [6],
Gentile [2], Gentile [+ *1666*] [1], country [1], heathen [1], pagan [1]

Mt   4:15   the way to the sea, along the Jordan, Galilee of the **Gentiles**—
      6:32   For the **pagans** run after all these things, and your heavenly Father
      10: 5   not go among the **Gentiles** or enter any town of the Samaritans.
      10:18   and kings as witnesses to them and to the **Gentiles**.
      12:18   put my Spirit on him, and he will proclaim justice to the **nations**.
      12:21   In his name the **nations** will put their hope."
      20:19   and will turn him over to the **Gentiles** to be mocked and flogged
      20:25   "You know that the rulers of the **Gentiles** lord it over them,
      21:43   away from you and given to a **people** who will produce its fruit.
      24: 7   **Nation** will rise against nation, and kingdom against kingdom.
      24: 7   Nation will rise against **nation**, and kingdom against kingdom.
      24: 9   put to death, and you will be hated by all **nations** because of me.
      24:14   will be preached in the whole world as a testimony to all **nations**,
      25:32   All the **nations** will be gathered before him, and he will separate
      28:19   Therefore go and make disciples of all **nations**, baptizing them in
Mk   10:33   will condemn him to death and will hand him over to the **Gentiles**,
      10:42   "You know that those who are regarded as rulers of the **Gentiles**
      11:17   " 'My house will be called a house of prayer for all **nations**'?
      13: 8   **Nation** will rise against nation, and kingdom against kingdom.
      13: 8   Nation will rise against **nation**, and kingdom against kingdom.
      13:10   And the gospel must first be preached to all **nations**.
Lk   2:32   a light for revelation to the **Gentiles** and for glory to your people
      7: 5   because he loves our **nation** and has built our synagogue."
      12:30   For the **pagan** world runs after all such things, and your Father
      18:32   He will be handed over to the **Gentiles**. They will mock him,
      21:10   "**Nation** will rise against nation, and kingdom against kingdom.
      21:10   "Nation will rise against **nation**, and kingdom against kingdom.
      21:24   fall by the sword and will be taken as prisoners to all the **nations**.
      21:24   Jerusalem will be trampled on by the **Gentiles** until the times of

      21:24   on by the Gentiles until the times of the **Gentiles** are fulfilled.
      21:25   **nations** will be in anguish and perplexity at the roaring and tossing
      22:25   Jesus said to them, "The kings of the **Gentiles** lord it over them;
      23: 2   saying, "We have found this man subverting our **nation**.
      24:47   and forgiveness of sins will be preached in his name to all **nations**,
Jn   11:48   Romans will come and take away both our place and our **nation**."
      11:50   that one man die for the people than that the whole **nation** perish."
      11:51   that year he prophesied that Jesus would die for the *Jewish* **nation**,
      11:52   and not only for that **nation** but also for the scattered children of
      18:35   "It was your **people** and your chief priests who handed you over to
Ac   2: 5   in Jerusalem God-fearing Jews from every **nation** under heaven.
      4:25   " 'Why do the **nations** rage and the peoples plot in vain?'
      4:27   Indeed Herod and Pontius Pilate met together with the **Gentiles**
      7: 7   But I will punish the **nation** they serve as slaves,' God said,
      7:45   they took the land from the **nations** God drove out before them.
      8: 9   practiced sorcery in the city and amazed all the **people** of Samaria.
      9:15   man is my chosen instrument to carry my name before the **Gentiles**
      10:22   and God-fearing man, who is respected by all the Jewish **people**.
      10:35   but accepts men from every **nation** who fear him and do what is
      10:45   gift of the Holy Spirit had been poured out even on the **Gentiles**.
      11: 1   and the brothers throughout Judea heard that the **Gentiles** also had
      11:18   "So then, God has granted even the **Gentiles** repentance unto life."
      13:19   he overthrew seven **nations** in Canaan and gave their land to his
      13:46   yourselves worthy of eternal life, we now turn to the **Gentiles**.
      13:47   " 'I have made you a light for the **Gentiles**, that you may bring
      13:48   When the **Gentiles** heard this, they were glad and honored the
      14: 2   But the Jews who refused to believe stirred up the **Gentiles**
      14: 5   There was a plot afoot among the **Gentiles** and Jews, together with
      14:16   In the past, he let all **nations** go their own way.
      14:27   and how he had opened the door of faith to the **Gentiles**.
      15: 3   and Samaria, they told how the **Gentiles** had been converted.
      15: 7   the **Gentiles** might hear from my lips the message of the gospel
      15:12   and wonders God had done among the **Gentiles** through them.
      15:14   his concern by taking from the **Gentiles** a people for himself.
      15:17   and all the **Gentiles** who bear my name, says the Lord, who does
      15:19   that we should not make it difficult for the **Gentiles** who are
      15:23   To the **Gentile** [+ *1666*] believers in Antioch, Syria and Cilicia:
      17:26   From one man he made every **nation** of men, that they should
      18: 6   clear of my responsibility. From now on I will go to the **Gentiles**."
      21:11   the owner of this belt and will hand him over to the **Gentiles**.' "
      21:19   and reported in detail what God had done among the **Gentiles**
      21:21   the Jews who live among the **Gentiles** to turn away from Moses,
      21:25   As for the **Gentile** believers, we have written to them our decision
      22:21   Lord said to me, 'Go; I will send you far away to the **Gentiles**.' "
      24: 2   and your foresight has brought about reforms in this **nation**.
      24:10   that for a number of years you have been a judge over this **nation**;
      24:17   I came to Jerusalem to bring my **people** gifts for the poor and to
      26: 4   from the beginning of my life in my own **country**, and also in
      26:17   I will rescue you from your own people and from the **Gentiles**.
      26:20   to those in Jerusalem and in all Judea, and to the **Gentiles** also,
      26:23   would proclaim light to his own people and to the **Gentiles**."
      28:19   not that I had any charge to bring against my own **people**.
      28:28   you to know that God's salvation has been sent to the **Gentiles**,
Ro   1: 5   and apostleship to call people from among all the **Gentiles** to the
      1:13   a harvest among you, just as I have had among the other **Gentiles**.
      2:14   (Indeed, when **Gentiles**, who do not have the law, do by nature
      2:24   "God's name is blasphemed among the **Gentiles** because of you."
      3:29   Jews only? Is he not the God of **Gentiles** too? Yes, of Gentiles too,
      3:29   Jews only? Is he not the God of Gentiles too? Yes, of **Gentiles** too,
      4:17   As it is written: "I have made you a father of many **nations**."
      4:18   in hope believed and so became the father of many **nations**,
      9:24   he also called, not only from the Jews but also from the **Gentiles**?
      9:30   That the **Gentiles**, who did not pursue righteousness, have obtained
      10:19   "I will make you envious by those who are not a **nation**;
      10:19   I will make you angry by a **nation** that has no understanding."
      11:11   salvation has come to the **Gentiles** to make Israel envious.
      11:12   and their loss means riches for the **Gentiles**, how much greater
      11:13   I am talking to you **Gentiles**. Inasmuch as I am the apostle to the
      11:13   Inasmuch as I am the apostle to the **Gentiles**, I make much of my
      11:25   hardening in part until the full number of the **Gentiles** has come in.
      15: 9   so that the **Gentiles** may glorify God for his mercy, as it is written:
      15: 9   "Therefore I will praise you among the **Gentiles**; I will sing hymns
      15:10   Again, it says, "Rejoice, O **Gentiles**, with his people."
      15:11   And again, "Praise the Lord, all you **Gentiles**, and sing praises to
      15:12   of Jesse will spring up, one who will arise to rule over the **nations**;
      15:12   will arise to rule over the nations; the **Gentiles** will hope in him."

15:16 to be a minister of Christ Jesus to the **Gentiles** with the priestly
15:16 so that the **Gentiles** might become an offering acceptable to God,
15:18 me in leading the **Gentiles** to obey God by what I have said
15:27 For if the **Gentiles** have shared in the Jews' spiritual blessings,
16: 4 Not only I but all the churches *of* the **Gentiles** are grateful to them.
16:26 the eternal God, so that all **nations** might believe and obey him—
1Co 1:23 a stumbling block to Jews and foolishness *to* **Gentiles**,
5: 1 among you, and of a kind that does not occur even among **pagans**:
10:20 but the sacrifices of **pagans** [UBS-] are offered to demons,
12: 2 You know that when you were **pagans**, somehow or other you
2Co 11:26 in danger from my own countrymen, in danger from **Gentiles**;
Gal 1:16 his Son in me so that I might preach him among the **Gentiles**.
2: 2 and set before them the gospel that I preach among the **Gentiles**.
2: 8 was also at work in my ministry as an apostle to the **Gentiles**.
2: 9 They agreed that we should go to the **Gentiles**, and they to the
2:12 certain men came from James, he used to eat with the **Gentiles**.
2:14 How is it, then, that you force **Gentiles** to follow Jewish customs?
2:15 "We who are Jews by birth and not 'Gentile sinners'
3: 8 The Scripture foresaw that God would justify the **Gentiles** by faith,
3: 8 in advance to Abraham: "All **nations** will be blessed through you."
3:14 to Abraham might come to the **Gentiles** through Christ Jesus,
Eph 2:11 remember that formerly you who are **Gentiles** by birth and called
3: 1 the prisoner of Christ Jesus for the sake of you **Gentiles**—
3: 6 This mystery is that through the gospel the **Gentiles** are heirs
3: 8 to preach *to* the **Gentiles** the unsearchable riches of Christ,
4:17 on it in the Lord, that you must no longer live as the **Gentiles** do,
Col 1:27 To them God has chosen to make known among the **Gentiles** the
1Th 2:16 in their effort to keep us from speaking *to* the **Gentiles** so that they
4: 5 not in passionate lust like the **heathen**, who do not know God;
1Ti 2: 7 I am not lying—and a teacher of the true faith *to* the **Gentiles**.
3:16 the Spirit, was seen by angels, was preached among the **nations**,
2Ti 4:17 might be fully proclaimed and all the **Gentiles** might hear it.
1Pe 2: 9 a royal priesthood, a holy **nation**, a people belonging to God,
2:12 Live such good lives among the **pagans** that, though they accuse
4: 3 For you have spent enough time in the past doing what **pagans**
Rev 2:26 does my will to the end, I will give authority over the **nations**—
5: 9 men for God from every tribe and language and people and **nation**.
7: 9 from every **nation**, tribe, people and language, standing before the
10:11 prophesy again about many peoples, **nations**, languages and kings."
11: 2 do not measure it, because it has been given *to* the **Gentiles**.
11: 9 language and **nation** will gaze on their bodies and refuse them
11:18 The **nations** were angry; and your wrath has come. The time has
12: 5 a male child, who will rule all the **nations** with an iron scepter.
13: 7 was given authority over every tribe, people, language and **nation**.
14: 6 who live on the earth—to every **nation**, tribe, language and people.
14: 8 which made all the **nations** drink the maddening wine of her
15: 3 true are your ways, King *of* the ages. [UBS *nations*; NIV *172*]
15: 4 All **nations** will come and worship before you, for your righteous
16:19 city split into three parts, and the cities *of* the **nations** collapsed.
17:15 the prostitute sits, are peoples, multitudes, **nations** and languages.
18: 3 For all the **nations** have drunk the maddening wine of her
18:23 great men. By your magic spell all the **nations** were led astray.
19:15 mouth comes a sharp sword with which to strike down the **nations**.
20: 3 to keep him from deceiving the **nations** anymore until the
20: 8 and will go out to deceive the **nations** in the four corners of the
21:24 The **nations** will walk by its light, and the kings of the earth will
21:26 The glory and honor *of* the **nations** will be brought into it.
22: 2 And the leaves of the tree are for the healing *of* the **nations**.

1621 ἔθος, *ethos* [12] [→ *1616, 1622, 1665, 2456, 2799,* *5311*]

customs [6], custom [4], as usual [*+2848+3836*] [1], in the habit of [1]

Lk 1: 9 he was chosen by lot, according to the **custom** of the priesthood,
2:42 years old, they went up to the Feast, according to the **custom**.
22:39 Jesus went out **as usual** [*+2848+3836*] to the Mount of Olives,
Jn 19:40 strips of linen. This was in accordance with Jewish burial **customs**.
Ac 6:14 this place and change the **customs** Moses handed down to us."
15: 1 *according to* the **custom** taught by Moses, you cannot be saved."
16:21 by advocating **customs** unlawful for us Romans to accept
21:21 not to circumcise their children or live *according to* our **customs**.
25:16 "I told them that it is not the Roman **custom** to hand over any man

26: 3 because you are well acquainted with all the Jewish **customs**
28:17 nothing against our people or against the **customs** of our ancestors,
Heb 10:25 as some are **in the habit of** doing, but let us encourage one

1622 ἔθω, *ethō*   Not used in UBS/NIV [√ *1621*]

1623 εἰ, *ei* [502] [→ *1569, 1570, 1638, 1642, 1643, 1664,* *2829, 6059, 6062*]

if [303], *untranslated* [39], except [*+3590*] [36], but [*+3590*] [11], since [10], only [*+3590*] [8], if [*+3525*] [7], that [6], whether [6], only [*+3590+4024*] [5], though [5], or [4], though [*+2779*] [4], but only [*+3590*] [3], never [3], if he does [*+1254+3590*] [2], only [2], surely [*+1145*] [2], unless [*+1760+3590*] [2], unless [*+3590*] [2], unless [*+3614*] [2], whatever [*+5516*] [2], when [2], and [1], because [*+1145+2779*] [1], but if [*+3590*] [1], but only [*+2779*] [1], even though [1], evidently [*+3590*] [1], except [*+323+3614*] [1], except for [*+3590*] [1], hoping [*+1538+4803*] [1], if [*+1145*] [1], if [*+726*] [1], in the hope that [1], nevertheless [*+3590*] [1], no [1], now that [1], only [*+3590+3667*] [1], only [*+3590+3668*] [1], only to [*+3590+4029*] [1], or at least [*+1254+3590*] [1], otherwise [*+1254+3590*] [1], otherwise [*+1760+3590*] [1], perhaps [*+726*] [1], perhaps [*+5593*] [1], perhaps [*+726+1145*] [1], somehow [*+4803*] [1], such as [1], surely [*+3605*] [1], that [*+4803*] [1], though [*+247+2779*] [1], to see if [1], undoubtedly [*+5593*] [1], unless [*+4024*] [1], until [*+3590+4020*] [1], what [*+5516*] [1], what if [1], whether or not [1]

Mt 4: 3 The tempter came to him and said, "**If** you are the Son of God,
4: 6 "**If** you are the Son of God," he said, "throw yourself down.
5:13 **except** [*+3590*] to be thrown out and trampled by men.
5:29 **If** your right eye causes you to sin, gouge it out and throw it away.
5:30 And **if** your right hand causes you to sin, cut it off and throw it
6: 1 "**If** you do, you will have no reward from your Father in heaven.
6:23 **If** then the light within you is darkness, how great is that darkness!
6:30 **If** that is how God clothes the grass of the field, which is here
7:11 **If** you, then, though you are evil, know how to give good gifts to
8:31 The demons begged Jesus, "**If** you drive us out, send us into the
9:17 **If** they do, the skins will burst, the wine will run out
10:25 **If** the head of the house has been called Beelzebub, how much
11:14 And **if** you are willing to accept it, he is the Elijah who was to
11:21 **If** the miracles that were performed in you had been performed in
11:23 **If** the miracles that were performed in you had been performed in
11:27 No one knows the Son **except** [*+3590*] the Father, and no one
11:27 and no one knows the Father **except** [*+3590*] the Son and those to
12: 4 was not lawful for them to do, **but** [*+3590*] only for the priests.
12: 7 **If** you had known what these words mean, 'I desire mercy,
12:10 they asked him, [NIE] "Is it lawful to heal on the Sabbath?"
12:24 they said, "It is **only** [*+3590*] by Beelzebub, the prince of demons,
12:26 **If** Satan drives out Satan, he is divided against himself. How
12:27 And **if** I drive out demons by Beelzebub, by whom do your people
12:28 But **if** I drive out demons by the Spirit of God, then the kingdom of
12:39 But none will be given it **except** [*+3590*] the sign of the prophet
13:57 "**Only** [*+3590*] in his hometown and in his own house is a prophet
14:17 "We have here **only** [*+3590+4024*] five loaves of bread and two
14:28 "Lord, **if** it's you," Peter replied, "tell me to come to you on the
15:24 "I was sent **only** [*+3590+4024*] to the lost sheep of Israel."
16: 4 but none will be given it **except** [*+3590*] the sign of Jonah."
16:24 "**If** anyone would come after me, he must deny himself and take
17: 4 **If** you wish, I will put up three shelters—one for you, one for
17: 8 When they looked up, they saw no one **except** [*+3590*] Jesus.
18: 8 **If** your hand or your foot causes you to sin, cut it off and throw it
18: 9 And **if** your eye causes you to sin, gouge it out and throw it away.
18:28 choke him. 'Pay back **what** [*+5516*] you owe me!' he demanded.
19: 3 [NIE] "Is it lawful for a man to divorce his wife for any and every
19:10 "**If** this is the situation between a husband and wife, it is better not
19:17 who is good. **If** you want to enter life, obey the commandments."
19:21 Jesus answered, "**If** you want to be perfect, go, sell your
21:19 he went up to it but found nothing on it **except** [*+3590*] leaves.
22:45 **If** then David calls him 'Lord,' how can he be his son?"
23:30 And you say, '**If** we had lived in the days of our forefathers,
24:22 **If** those days had not been cut short, no one would survive,
24:24 and miracles to deceive even the elect—**if** that were possible.
24:36 the angels in heaven, nor the Son, **but** [*+3590*] only the Father.

24:43 If the owner of the house had known at what time of night the thief
26:24 the Son of Man! It would be better for him if he had not been born."
26:33 Peter replied, "Even if all fall away on account of you, I never
26:39 with his face to the ground and prayed, "My Father, if it is possible,
26:42 if it is not possible for this cup to be taken away unless I drink it,
26:63 by the living God: Tell us if you are the Christ, the Son of God."
27:40 Come down from the cross, if you are the Son of God!"
27:43 Let God rescue him now if he wants him, for he said, 'I am the
27:49 "Now leave him alone. Let's see if Elijah comes to save him."
Mk 2: 7 He's blaspheming! Who can forgive sins but [+3590] God alone?"
2:21 If [+1254+3590] he does, the new piece will pull away from the
2:22 If [+1254+3590] he does, the wine will burst the skins, and both
2:26 consecrated bread, which is lawful only [+3590] for priests to eat.
3: 2 so they watched him closely to see if he would heal him on the
3:26 And if Satan opposes himself and is divided, he cannot stand;
4:23 If anyone has ears to hear, let him hear."
5:37 He did not let anyone follow him except [+3590] Peter, James
6: 4 Jesus said to them, "Only [+3590+4024] in his hometown,
6: 5 except [+3590] lay his hands on a few sick people and heal them.
6: 8 "Take nothing for the journey except [+3590] a staff—no bread,
8:12 a miraculous sign? I tell you the truth, no sign will be given to it."
8:14 except [+3590] for one loaf they had with them in the boat.
8:23 put his hands on him, Jesus asked, [NIE] "Do you see anything?"
8:34 "If anyone would come after me, he must deny himself and take
9: 9 seen until [+3590+4020] the Son of Man had risen from the dead.
9:22 to kill him. But if you can do anything, take pity on us and help us."
9:23 " 'If you can'?" said Jesus. "Everything is possible for him who
9:29 He replied, "This kind can come out only [+3590] by prayer."
9:35 Jesus called the Twelve and said, "If anyone wants to be first,
9:42 it would be better for him [NIE] to be thrown into the sea with a
10: 2 him by asking, [NIE] "Is it lawful for a man to divorce his wife?"
10:18 Jesus answered. "No one is good—except [+3590] God alone.
11:13 a fig tree in leaf, he went to find out if [+726] it had any fruit.
11:13 When he reached it, he found nothing but [+3590] leaves,
11:25 stand praying, if you hold anything against anyone, forgive him,
13:20 If the Lord had not cut short those days, no one would survive.
13:22 and miracles to deceive the elect—if that were possible.
13:32 the angels in heaven, nor the Son, but only [+3590] the Father.
14:21 the Son of Man! It would be better for him if he had not been born."
14:29 Peter declared, "Even if all fall away, I will not."
14:35 and prayed that if possible the hour might pass from him.
15:36 him alone. Let's see if Elijah comes to take him down," he said.
15:44 Pilate was surprised to hear that he was already dead. Summoning
15:44 Summoning the centurion, he asked him if Jesus had already died.
Lk 4: 3 The devil said to him, "If you are the Son of God, tell this stone to
4: 9 "If you are the Son of God," he said, "throw yourself down from
4:26 but [+3590] to a widow in Zarephath in the region of Sidon.
4:27 not one of them was cleansed—only [+3590] Naaman the Syrian."
5:21 speaks blasphemy? Who can forgive sins but [+3590] God alone?"
5:36 If he does, he will have torn the new garment, and the patch from
5:37 If he does, the new wine will burst the skins, the wine will run out
6: 4 he ate what is lawful only [+3590+3668] for priests to eat.
6: 7 so they watched him closely to see if he would heal on the
6: 9 said to them, "I ask you, which [NIE] is lawful on the Sabbath:
6:32 "If you love those who love you, what credit is that to you?
7:39 he said to himself, "If this man were a prophet, he would know
8:51 he did not let anyone go in with him except [+3590] Peter,
9:13 two fish—unless [+3614] we go and buy food for all this crowd."
9:23 "If anyone would come after me, he must deny himself and take
10: 6 is there, your peace will rest on him; if not, it will return to you.
10:13 For if the miracles that were performed in you had been performed
10:22 No one knows who the Son is except [+3590] the Father, and no
10:22 and no one knows who the Father is except [+3590] the Son
11: 8 though [+2779] he will not get up and give him the bread
11:13 If you then, though you are evil, know how to give good gifts to
11:18 If Satan is divided against himself, how can his kingdom stand?
11:19 Now if I drive out demons by Beelzebub, by whom do your
11:20 But if I drive out demons by the finger of God, then the kingdom
11:29 but none will be given it except [+3590] the sign of Jonah.
11:36 Therefore, if your whole body is full of light, and no part of it dark,
12:26 Since you cannot do this very little thing, why do you worry about
12:28 If that is how God clothes the grass of the field, which is here
12:39 If the owner of the house had known at what hour the thief was
12:49 fire on the earth, and how I wish [NIE] it were already kindled!
13: 9 If it bears fruit next year, fine! If not, then cut it down.' "
13:23 asked him, "Lord, are only a few people going to be saved?"

14:26 "If anyone comes to me and does not hate his father and mother,
14:28 and estimate the cost to see if he has enough money to complete it?
14:31 and consider whether he is able with ten thousand men to oppose
14:32 If he is not able, he will send a delegation while the other is still a
16:11 So if you have not been trustworthy in handling worldly wealth,
16:12 And if you have not been trustworthy with someone else's
16:31 "He said to him, 'If they do not listen to Moses and the Prophets,
17: 2 It would be better for him [NIE] to be thrown into the sea with a
17: 6 He replied, "If you have faith as small as a mustard seed, you can
17:18 to return and give praise to God except [+3590] this foreigner?"
18: 4 said to himself, 'Even though I don't fear God or care about men,
18:19 Jesus answered. "No one is good—except [+3590] God alone.
19: 8 and if I have cheated anybody out of anything, I will pay back four
19:42 and said, "If you, even you, had only known on this day what
22:42 "Father, if you are willing, take this cup from me; yet not my will,
22:49 they said, "Lord, [NIE] should we strike with our swords?"
22:67 "If you are the Christ," they said, "tell us." Jesus answered, "If I tell
23: 6 On hearing this, Pilate asked if the man was a Galilean.
23:31 For if men do these things when the tree is green, what will happen
23:35 let him save himself if he is the Christ of God, the Chosen One."
23:37 and said, "If you are the king of the Jews, save yourself."
Jn 1:25 "Why then do you baptize if you are not the Christ, nor Elijah,
3:12 [NIE] I have spoken to you of earthly things and you do not
3:13 No one has ever gone into heaven except [+3590] the one who
4:10 "If you knew the gift of God and who it is that asks you for a
5:46 If you believed Moses, you would believe me, for he wrote about
5:47 But since you do not believe what he wrote, how are you going to
6:22 of the lake realized that only [+3590] one boat had been there,
6:46 No one has seen the Father except [+3590] the one who is from
7: 4 Since you are doing these things, show yourself to the world."
7:23 Now if a child can be circumcised on the Sabbath so that the law of
8:19 Jesus replied. "If you knew me, you would know my Father also."
8:39 "If you were Abraham's children," said Jesus, "then you would do
8:42 Jesus said to them, "If God were your Father, you would love me,
8:46 guilty of sin? If I am telling the truth, why don't you believe me?
9:25 He replied, "Whether he is a sinner or not, I don't know.
9:33 If this man were not from God, he could do nothing."
9:41 Jesus said, "If you were blind, you would not be guilty of sin;
10:10 The thief comes only [+3590+4024] to steal and kill and destroy;
10:24 will you keep us in suspense? If you are the Christ, tell us plainly."
10:35 If he called them 'gods,' to whom the word of God came—
10:37 Do not believe me unless [+4024] I do what my Father does.
10:38 But if I do it, even though you do not believe me,
11:12 His disciples replied, "Lord, if he sleeps, he will get better."
11:21 "Lord," Martha said to Jesus, "if you had been here, my brother
11:32 saw him, she fell at his feet and said, "Lord, if you had been here,
13:10 "A person who has had a bath needs only [+3590+4024] to wash
13:14 Now that I, your Lord and Teacher, have washed your feet,
13:17 Now that you know these things, you will be blessed if you do
13:32 If God is glorified in him, God will glorify the Son in himself,
14: 2 house are many rooms; if it were not so, I would have told you.
14: 6 the life. No one comes to the Father except [+3590] through me.
14: 7 If you really knew me, you would know my Father as well.
14:11 or [+1254+3590] at least believe on the evidence of the miracles
14:28 If you loved me, you would be glad that I am going to the Father,
15:18 "If the world hates you, keep in mind that it hated me first.
15:19 If you belonged to the world, it would love you as its own.
15:20 If they persecuted me, they will persecute you also. If they obeyed
15:20 you also. If they obeyed my teaching, they will obey yours also.
15:22 If I had not come and spoken to them, they would not be guilty of
15:24 If I had not done among them what no one else did, they would not
17:12 None has been lost except [+3590] the one doomed to destruction
18: 8 Jesus answered. "If you are looking for me, then let these men go."
18:23 "If I said something wrong," Jesus replied, "testify as to what is
18:23 to what is wrong. But if I spoke the truth, why did you strike me?"
18:30 "If he were not a criminal," they replied, "we would not have
18:36 If it were, my servants would fight to prevent my arrest by the
19:11 "You would have no power over me if it were not given to you
19:15 "We have no king but [+3590] Caesar," the chief priests answered.
20:15 he was the gardener, she said, "Sir, if you have carried him away,
Ac 1: 6 [NIE] are you at this time going to restore the kingdom to Israel?"
4: 9 If we are being called to account today for an act of kindness
4:19 "Judge for yourselves whether it is right in God's sight to obey you
5: 8 [NIE] is this the price you and Ananias got for the land?"
5:39 But if it is from God, you will not be able to stop these men;
7: 1 Then the high priest asked him, [NIE] "Are these charges true?"

8: 22 **Perhaps** [*+726*] he will forgive you for having such a thought in
10: 18 asking **if** Simon who was known as Peter was staying there.
11: 17 So **if** God gave them the same gift as he gave us, who believed in
11: 19 and Antioch, telling the message **only** [*+3590+3667*] to Jews.
13: 15 "Brothers, **if** you have a message of encouragement for the people,
16: 15 "**If** you consider me a believer in the Lord," she said, "come
17: 11 and examined the Scriptures every day to see **if** what Paul said was
17: 27 and **perhaps** [*+726+1145*] reach out for him and find him,
18: 14 "**If** [*+3525*] you Jews were making a complaint about some
18: 15 But **since** it involves questions about words and names and your
19: 2 **[NIE]** "Did you receive the Holy Spirit when you believed?"
19: 2 "No, we have not even heard **that** there is a Holy Spirit."
19: 38 **If** [*+3525*], then, Demetrius and his fellow craftsmen have a
19: 39 **If** there is anything further you want to bring up, it must be settled
20: 16 in a hurry to reach Jerusalem, **if** possible, by the day of Pentecost.
21: 37 he asked the commander, **[NIE]** "May I say something to you?"
22: 25 **[NIE]** "Is it legal for you to flog a Roman citizen who hasn't even
23: 9 they said. "**What if** a spirit or an angel has spoken to him?"
24: 19 before you and bring charges **if** they have anything against me.
25: 5 charges against the man there, **if** he has done anything wrong."
25: 11 **If** [*+3525*], however, I am guilty of doing anything deserving
25: 11 But **if** the charges brought against me by these Jews are not true,
25: 20 so I asked **if** he would be willing to go to Jerusalem and stand trial
26: 8 Why should any of you consider it incredible **that** God raises the
26: 23 **that** the Christ would suffer and, as the first to rise from the dead,
26: 23 Christ would suffer and, **[RPG]** as the first to rise from the dead,
26: 32 man could have been set free **if** he had not appealed to Caesar."
27: 12 sail on, **hoping** [*+1538+4803*] to reach Phoenix and winter there.
27: 39 where they decided to run the ship aground **if** they could.
Ro 1: 10 and I pray **that** [*+4803*] now at last by God's will the way may be
2: 17 Now you, **if** you call yourself a Jew; if you rely on the law
3: 3 What **if** some did not have faith? Will their lack of faith nullify
3: 5 But **if** our unrighteousness brings out God's righteousness more
3: 7 "**If** my falsehood enhances God's truthfulness and so increases his
4: 2 **If**, in fact, Abraham was justified by works, he had something to
4: 14 For **if** those who live by law are heirs, faith has no value
5: 10 For **if**, when we were God's enemies, we were reconciled to him
5: 15 For **if** the many died by the trespass of the one man, how much
5: 17 For **if**, by the trespass of the one man, death reigned through that
6: 5 **If** we have been united with him like this in his death, we will
6: 8 Now **if** we died with Christ, we believe that we will also live with
7: 7 Indeed I would not have known what sin was **except** [*+3590*]
7: 7 For I would not have known what coveting really was **if** the law
7: 16 And **if** I do what I do not want to do, I agree that the law is good.
7: 20 Now **if** I do what I do not want to do, it is no longer I who do it,
8: 9 And **if** anyone does not have the Spirit of Christ, he does not
8: 10 But **if** Christ is in you, your body is dead because of sin, yet your
8: 11 And **if** the Spirit of him who raised Jesus from the dead is living in
8: 13 For **if** you live according to the sinful nature, you will die;
8: 13 but **if** by the Spirit you put to death the misdeeds of the body,
8: 17 Now **if** we are children, then we are heirs—heirs of God
8: 25 But **if** we hope for what we do not yet have, we wait for it
8: 31 we say in response to this? **If** God is for us, who can be against us?
9: 22 What **if** God, choosing to show his wrath and make his power
9: 29 "**Unless** [*+3590*] the Lord Almighty had left us descendants,
11: 6 And **if** by grace, then it is no longer by works; if it were, grace
11: 12 But **if** their transgression means riches for the world, and their loss
11: 14 **in the hope that** I may somehow arouse my own people to envy
11: 15 For **if** their rejection is the reconciliation of the world, what will
11: 15 what will their acceptance be **but** [*+3590*] life from the dead?
11: 16 **If** the part of the dough offered as firstfruits is holy, then the whole
11: 16 the whole batch is holy; **if** the root is holy, so are the branches.
11: 17 **If** some of the branches have been broken off, and you, though a
11: 18 **If** you do, consider this: You do not support the root, but the root
11: 21 For **if** God did not spare the natural branches, he will not spare you
11: 24 After all, **if** you were cut out of an olive tree that is wild by nature,
12: 18 **If** it is possible, as far as it depends on you, live at peace with
13: 1 for there is no authority **except** [*+3590*] that which God has
13: 8 **except** [*+3590*] the continuing debt to love one another,
13: 9 and **whatever** [*+5516*] other commandment there may be,
14: 14 But **if** [*+3590*] anyone regards something as unclean, then for him
14: 15 **If** your brother is distressed because of what you eat, you are no
15: 27 For **if** the Gentiles have shared in the Jews' spiritual blessings,
1Co 1: 14 I am thankful that I did not baptize any of you **except** [*+3590*]
1: 16 beyond that, I don't remember **if** I baptized anyone else.)
2: 2 to know nothing while I was with you **except** [*+3590*] Jesus Christ

2: 8 None of the rulers of this age understood it, for **if** they had,
2: 11 For who among men knows the thoughts of a man **except** [*+3590*]
2: 11 In the same way no one knows the thoughts of God **except** [*+3590*]
3: 12 **If** any man builds on this foundation using gold, silver,
3: 14 **If** what he has built survives, he will receive his reward.
3: 15 **If** it is burned up, he will suffer loss; he himself will be saved,
3: 17 **If** anyone destroys God's temple, God will destroy him; for God's
3: 18 **If** any one of you thinks he is wise by the standards of this age,
4: 7 And **if** you did receive it, why do you boast as though you did not?
6: 2 And **if** you are to judge the world, are you not competent to judge
7: 5 Do not deprive each other **except** [*+323+3614*] by mutual consent
7: 9 But **if** they cannot control themselves, they should marry,
7: 12 **If** any brother has a wife who is not a believer and she is willing to
7: 13 And **if** a woman has a husband who is not a believer and he is
7: 15 But **if** the unbeliever leaves, let him do so. A believing man
7: 16 How do you know, wife, **whether** you will save your husband?
7: 16 how do you know, husband, **whether** you will save your wife?
7: 17 **Nevertheless** [*+3590*], each one should retain the place in life that
7: 21 let it trouble you—although **if** you can gain your freedom, do so.
7: 36 **If** anyone thinks he is acting improperly toward the virgin he is
8: 2 **[NIE]** The man who thinks he knows something does not yet
8: 3 **[NIE]** But the man who loves God is known by God.
8: 4 at all in the world and that there is no **but** [*+3590*] one.
8: 13 Therefore, **if** what I eat causes my brother to fall into sin, I will
9: 2 **Even though** I may not be an apostle to others, surely I am to you!
9: 11 **If** we have sown spiritual seed among you, is it too much if we
9: 11 among you, is it too much **if** we reap a material harvest from you?
9: 12 **If** others have this right of support from you, shouldn't we have it
9: 17 **If** I preach voluntarily, I have a reward; if not voluntarily,
9: 17 **if** not voluntarily, I am simply discharging the trust committed to
10: 13 No temptation has seized you **except** [*+3590*] what is common to
10: 27 **If** some unbeliever invites you to a meal and you want to go,
10: 30 **If** I take part in the meal with thankfulness, why am I denounced
11: 6 **If** a woman does not cover her head, she should have her hair cut
11: 6 and **if** it is a disgrace for a woman to have her hair cut or shaved
11: 16 **If** anyone wants to be contentious about this, we have no other
11: 31 But **if** we judged ourselves, we would not come under judgment.
11: 34 **If** anyone is hungry, he should eat at home, so that when you meet
12: 3 no one can say, "Jesus is Lord," **except** [*+3590*] by the Holy Spirit.
12: 17 **If** the whole body were an eye, where would the sense of hearing
12: 17 **If** the whole body were an ear, where would the sense of smell be?
12: 19 **If** they were all one part, where would the body be?
14: 5 **unless** [*+1760+3590*] he interprets, so that the church may be
14: 10 **Undoubtedly** [*+5593*] there are all sorts of languages in the world,
14: 35 **If** they want to inquire about something, they should ask their own
14: 37 **If** anybody thinks he is a prophet or spiritually gifted, let him
14: 38 **If** he ignores this, he himself will be ignored.
15: 2 you are saved, **if** you hold firmly to the word I preached to you.
15: 2 **Otherwise** [*+1760+3590*], you have believed in vain.
15: 12 But **if** it is preached that Christ has been raised from the dead,
15: 13 **If** there is no resurrection of the dead, then not even Christ has
15: 14 And **if** Christ has not been raised, our preaching is useless
15: 16 For **if** the dead are not raised, then Christ has not been raised
15: 17 And **if** Christ has not been raised, your faith is futile; you are still
15: 19 **If** only for this life we have hope in Christ, we are to be pitied
15: 29 **If** the dead are not raised at all, why are people baptized for them?
15: 32 **If** I fought wild beasts in Ephesus for merely human reasons,
15: 32 **If** the dead are not raised, "Let us eat and drink, for tomorrow we
15: 37 but just a seed, **perhaps** [*+5593*] of wheat or of something else.
15: 44 **If** there is a natural body, there is also a spiritual body.
16: 22 **If** anyone does not love the Lord—a curse be on him. Come,
2Co 2: 2 For **if** I grieve you, who is left to make me glad but you whom I
2: 2 is left to make me glad **but** [*+3590*] you whom I have grieved?
2: 5 **If** anyone has caused grief, he has not so much grieved me as he
2: 9 if you would stand the test and **[NIE]** be obedient in everything.
2: 10 And what I have forgiven—**if** there was anything to forgive—
3: 7 Now **if** the ministry that brought death, which was engraved in
3: 9 **If** the ministry that condemns men is glorious, how much more
3: 11 And **if** what was fading away came with glory, how much greater
4: 3 And even **if** our gospel is veiled, it is veiled to those who are
4: 16 **Though** [*+247+2779*] outwardly we are wasting away,
5: 3 **because** [*+1145+2779*] when we are clothed, we will not be found
5: 16 **Though** [*+2779*] we once regarded Christ in this way, we do
5: 17 Therefore, **if** anyone is in Christ, he is a new creation; the old has
7: 8 Even **if** I caused you sorrow by my letter, I do not regret it.
7: 8 **Though** [*+2779*] I did regret it—I see that my letter hurt you,

7: 8 I see that my letter hurt you, **but only** [+*2779*] for a little while—
7:12 So even **though** I wrote to you, it was not on account of the one
7:14 **[NIE]** I had boasted to him about you, and you have not
8:12 For **if** the willingness is there, the gift is acceptable according to
10: 7 **If** anyone is confident that he belongs to Christ, he should consider
11: 4 For **if** [+*3525*] someone comes to you and preaches a Jesus other
11: 6 **[NIE]** I may not be a trained speaker, but I do have knowledge.
11:15 then, **if** his servants masquerade as servants of righteousness.
11:16 I repeat: Let no one take me for a fool. But **if** you do,
11:20 you even put up with **[NIE]** anyone who enslaves you or exploits
11:20 **or** exploits you or takes advantage of you or pushes himself
11:20 or exploits you **or** takes advantage of you or pushes himself
11:20 of you **or** pushes himself forward or slaps you in the face.
11:20 of you or pushes himself forward **or** slaps you in the face.
11:30 **If** I must boast, I will boast of the things that show my weakness.
12: 5 will not boast about myself, **except** [+*3590*] about my weaknesses.
12:11 the least inferior to the "super-apostles," even **though** I am nothing.
12:13 other churches, **except** [+*3590*] that I was never a burden to you?
12:15 expend myself as well. **If** I love you more, will you love me less?
13: 5 Examine yourselves to see **whether** you are in the faith;
13: 5 Christ Jesus is in you—**unless** [+*3614*], of course, you fail the test?
Gal 1: 7 **Evidently** [+*3590*] some people are throwing you into confusion
1: 9 **If** anybody is preaching to you a gospel other than what you
1:10 **If** I were still trying to please men, I would not be a servant of
1:19 of the other apostles—**only** [+*3590*] James, the Lord's brother.
2:14 "You **[NIE]** are a Jew, yet you live like a Gentile and not like a
2:17 "**If**, while we seek to be justified in Christ, it becomes evident that
2:18 **If** I rebuild what I destroyed, I prove that I am a lawbreaker.
2:21 for **if** righteousness could be gained through the law, Christ died
3: 4 you suffered so much for nothing—**if** it really was for nothing?
3:18 For **if** the inheritance depends on the law, then it no longer depends
3:21 For **if** a law had been given that could impart life,
3:29 **If** you belong to Christ, then you are Abraham's seed, and heirs
4: 7 but a son; and **since** you are a son, God has made you also an heir.
4:15 I can testify that, **if** you could have done so, you would have torn
5:11 Brothers, **if** I am still preaching circumcision, why am I still being
5:15 **If** you keep on biting and devouring each other, watch out
5:18 But **if** you are led by the Spirit, you are not under law.
5:25 **Since** we live by the Spirit, let us keep in step with the Spirit.
6: 3 **If** anyone thinks he is something when he is nothing, he deceives
6:14 May I never boast **except** [+*3590*] in the cross of our Lord Jesus
Eph 3: 2 **Surely** [+*1145*] you have heard about the administration of God's
4: 9 (What does "he ascended" mean **except** [+*3590*] that he also
4:21 **Surely** [+*1145*] you heard of him and were taught in him in
4:29 but **only** what is helpful for building others up according to their
Php 1:22 **If** I am to go on living in the body, this will mean fruitful labor for
2: 1 **If** you have any encouragement from being united with Christ,
2: 1 **if** any comfort from his love, if any fellowship with the Spirit,
2: 1 **if** any fellowship with the Spirit, if any tenderness and compassion,
2: 1 if any fellowship with the Spirit, **if** any tenderness and compassion,
2:17 But even **if** I am being poured out like a drink offering on the
3: 4 **If** anyone else thinks he has reasons to put confidence in the flesh,
3:11 and so, **somehow** [+*4803*], to attain to the resurrection from the
3:12 but **[NIE]** I press on to take hold of that for which Christ Jesus
3:15 And **if** on some point you think differently, that too God will make
4: 8 whatever is admirable—**if** anything is excellent or praiseworthy—
4: 8 is admirable—if anything is excellent or **[RPG]** praiseworthy—
4:15 me in the matter of giving and receiving, **except** [+*3590*] you only;
Col 1:23 **if** [+*1145*] you continue in your faith, established and firm,
2: 5 For **though** [+*2779*] I am absent from you in body, I am present
2:20 **Since** you died with Christ to the basic principles of this world,
3: 1 **Since**, then, you have been raised with Christ, set your hearts on
1Th 4:14 **[NIE]** We believe that Jesus died and rose again and so we
2Th 3:10 we gave you this rule: "**If** a man will not work, he shall not eat."
3:14 **If** anyone does not obey our instruction in this letter, take special
1Ti 1:10 and for **whatever** [+*5516*] else is contrary to the sound doctrine
3: 1 **If** anyone sets his heart on being an overseer, he desires a noble
3: 5 (**If** anyone does not know how to manage his own family,
5: 4 But **if** a widow has children or grandchildren, these should learn
5: 8 **If** anyone does not provide for his relatives, and especially for his
5:10 **such as** bringing up children, showing hospitality, washing the feet
5:10 such as bringing up children, **[RPG]** showing hospitality,
5:10 showing hospitality, **[RPG]** washing the feet of the saints,
5:10 **[RPG]** helping those in trouble and devoting herself to all kinds
5:10 those in trouble **and** devoting herself to all kinds of good deeds.
5:16 **If** any woman who is a believer has widows in her family,
5:19 against an elder **unless** [+*1760+3590*] it is brought by two
6: 3 **If** anyone teaches false doctrines and does not agree to the sound
2Ti 2:11 **If** we died with him, we will also live with him;
2:12 **if** we endure, we will also reign with him. If we disown him,
2:12 will also reign with him. **If** we disown him, he will also disown us;
2:13 **if** we are faithless, he will remain faithful, for he cannot disown
Tit 1: 6 **[NIE]** An elder must be blameless, the husband of but one wife,
Phm 1:17 So **if** you consider me a partner, welcome him as you would
1:18 **If** he has done you any wrong or owes you anything, charge it to
Heb 2: 2 For **if** the message spoken by angels was binding, and every
3:11 I declared on oath in my anger, 'They shall **never** enter my rest.' "
3:18 And to whom did God swear that they would never enter his rest **if**
4: 3 'They shall **never** enter my rest.' " And yet his work has been
4: 5 in the passage above he says, "They shall **never** enter my rest."
4: 8 For **if** Joshua had given them rest, God would not have spoken
6: 9 Even **though** we speak like this, dear friends, we are confident of
6:14 "I will **surely** [+*3605*] bless you and give you many descendants."
7:11 **If** [+*3525*] perfection could have been attained through the
7:15 And what we have said is even more clear **if** another priest like
8: 4 **If** [+*3525*] he were on earth, he would not be a priest, for there are
8: 7 For **if** there had been nothing wrong with that first covenant,
9:13 **[NIE]** The blood of goats and bulls and the ashes of a heifer
11:15 **If** [+*3525*] they had been thinking of the country they had left,
12: 8 **If** you are not disciplined (and everyone undergoes discipline),
12:25 **If** they did not escape when they refused him who warned them on
Jas 1: 5 **If** any of you lacks wisdom, he should ask God, who gives
1:23 **[NIE]** Anyone who listens to the word but does not do what it
1:26 **If** anyone considers himself religious and yet does not keep a tight
2: 8 **If** you really keep the royal law found in Scripture, "Love your
2: 9 But **if** you show favoritism, you sin and are convicted by the law as
2:11 **If** you do not commit adultery but do commit murder, you have
3: 2 **If** anyone is never at fault in what he says, he is a perfect man,
3: 3 **When** we put bits into the mouths of horses to make them obey us,
3:14 But **if** you harbor bitter envy and selfish ambition in your hearts,
4:11 **When** you judge the law, you are not keeping it, but sitting in
1Pe 1: 6 **though** now for a little while you may have had to suffer grief in
1:17 **Since** you call on a Father who judges each man's work
2: 3 **now that** you have tasted that the Lord is good.
2:19 For it is commendable **if** a man bears up under the pain of unjust
2:20 But how is it to your credit **if** you receive a beating for doing
2:20 But **if** you suffer for doing good and you endure it, this is
3: 1 to your husbands so that, **if** any of them do not believe the word,
3:14 But even **if** you should suffer for what is right, you are blessed.
3:17 It is better, **if** it is God's will, to suffer for doing good than for
4:11 **If** anyone speaks, he should do it as one speaking the very words
4:11 **If** anyone serves, he should do it with the strength God provides,
4:14 **If** you are insulted because of the name of Christ, you are blessed,
4:16 However, **if** you suffer as a Christian, do not be ashamed,
4:17 and **if** it begins with us, what will the outcome be for those who do
4:18 And, "**If** it is hard for the righteous to be saved, what will become
2Pe 2: 4 For **if** God did not spare angels when they sinned, but sent them to
2:20 **If** they have escaped the corruption of the world by knowing our
1Jn 2:19 For **if** they had belonged to us, they would have remained with us;
2:22 is the liar? **[NIE]** It is the man who denies that Jesus is the Christ.
3:13 Do not be surprised, my brothers, **if** the world hates you.
4: 1 every spirit, but test the spirits to see **whether** they are from God,
4:11 Dear friends, **since** God so loved us, we also ought to love one
5: 5 **Only** [+*3590*] he who believes that Jesus is the Son of God.
5: 9 **[NIE]** We accept man's testimony, but God's testimony is greater
2Jn 1:10 **If** anyone comes to you and does not bring this teaching, do not
Rev 2: 5 **[RPG]** If you do not repent, I will come to you and remove your
2:16 Repent therefore! **Otherwise** [+*1254+3590*], I will soon come to
2:17 written on it, known **only to** [+*3590+4029*] him who receives it.
9: 4 **but only** [+*3590*] those people who did not have the seal of God on
11: 5 **If** anyone tries to harm them, fire comes from their mouths
11: 5 This is how **[NIE]** anyone who wants to harm them must die.
13: 9 **[NIE]** He who has an ear, let him hear.
13:10 **If** anyone is to go into captivity, into captivity he will go. If anyone
13:10 **If** anyone is to be killed with the sword, with the sword he will be
13:17 so that no one could buy or sell **unless** [+*3590*] he had the mark,
14: 3 No one could learn the song **except** [+*3590*] the 144,000 who had
14: 9 "**If** anyone worships the beast and his image and receives his mark
14:11 or for **[NIE]** anyone who receives the mark of his name."
19:12 He has a name written on him that no one knows **but** [+*3590*] he
20:15 **If** anyone's name was not found written in the book of life,
21:27 **but only** [+*3590*] those whose names are written in the Lamb's

1624 εἰδέα, *eidea* [1] [√ *1626*]

appearance [1]

Mt 28: 3 His **appearance** was like lightning, and his clothes were white as

1625 εἶδον, *eidon* Not used in UBS/NIV [√ *1626*]

1626 εἶδος, *eidos* [5] [→ *1212, 1229, 1624, 1625, 2078, 2623, 2624, 2627, 4378, 5653; cf. 1631*]

form [2], appearance [1], kind [1], sight [1]

Lk   3:22 and the Holy Spirit descended on him in bodily **form** like a dove.
      9:29 As he was praying, the **appearance** of his face changed, and his
Jn   5:37 concerning me. You have never heard his voice nor seen his **form**,
2Co 5: 7 We live by faith, not by **sight**.
1Th 5:22 Avoid every **kind** of evil.

1627 εἰδωλεῖον, *eidōleion* [1] [√ *1631*]

idol's temple [1]

1Co 8:10 sees you who have this knowledge eating in an **idol's temple**,

1628 εἰδωλόθυτος, *eidōlothytos* [9] [√ *1631 + 2604*]

food sacrificed to idols [5], sacrificed to idols [2], food sacrificed to an idol [1], sacrifice offered to an idol [1]

Ac 15:29 You are to abstain from **food sacrificed to idols**, from blood,
   21:25 our decision that they should abstain from **food sacrificed to idols**,
1Co 8: 1 Now about **food sacrificed to idols**: We know that we all possess
    8: 4 So then, about eating food **sacrificed to idols**: We know that an
    8: 7 eat such **food** they think of it as having been **sacrificed to an idol**,
    8:10 won't he be emboldened to eat what *has been* **sacrificed to idols**?
   10:19 Do I mean then that a **sacrifice offered to an idol** is anything,
Rev 2:14 to entice the Israelites to sin by eating **food sacrificed to idols**
    2:20 into sexual immorality and the eating of **food sacrificed to idols**.

1629 εἰδωλολάτρης, *eidōlolatrēs* [7] [√ *1631 + 3301*]

idolaters [5], idolater [2]

1Co 5:10 world who are immoral, or the greedy and swindlers, or **idolaters**.
    5:11 but is sexually immoral or greedy, an **idolater** or a slanderer,
    6: 9 Neither the sexually immoral nor **idolaters** nor adulterers nor
   10: 7 Do not be **idolaters**, as some of them were; as it is written:
Eph 5: 5 No immoral, impure or greedy person—such a man is an **idolater**—
Rev 21: 8 those who practice magic arts, the **idolaters** and all liars—
   22:15 the **idolaters** and everyone who loves and practices falsehood.

1630 εἰδωλολατρία, *eidōlolatria* [4] [√ *1631 + 3301*]

idolatry [4]

1Co 10:14 Therefore, my dear friends, flee from **idolatry**.
Gal 5:20 **idolatry** and witchcraft; hatred, discord, jealousy, fits of rage,
Col 3: 5 impurity, lust, evil desires and greed, which is **idolatry**.
1Pe 4: 3 lust, drunkenness, orgies, carousing and detestable **idolatry**.

1631 εἴδωλον, *eidōlon* [11] [→ *1627, 1628, 1629, 1630, 2977; cf. 1626*]

idols [8], idol [2], it^s [+3836] [1]

Ac 7:41 They brought sacrifices *to* it^s [+3836] and held a celebration in
   15:20 telling them to abstain from food polluted *by* **idols**, from sexual
Ro 2:22 you commit adultery? You who abhor **idols**, do you rob temples?
1Co 8: 4 We know that an **idol** is nothing at all in the world and that there is
    8: 7 so accustomed to **idols** that when they eat such food they think of it
   10:19 sacrifice offered to an idol is anything, or that an **idol** is anything?
   12: 2 or other you were influenced and led astray to mute **idols**.
2Co 6:16 What agreement is there between the temple of God and **idols**?
1Th 1: 9 They tell how you turned to God from **idols** to serve the living

1Jn 5:21 Dear children, keep yourselves from **idols**.
Rev 9:20 and **idols** of gold, silver, bronze, stone and wood—

1632 εἰκῆ, *eikē* [6]

for nothing [3], in vain [1], wasted [1], with idle notions [1]

Ro 13: 4 do wrong, be afraid, for he does not bear the sword **for nothing**.
1Co 15: 2 the word I preached to you. Otherwise, you have believed **in vain**.
Gal 3: 4 Have you suffered so much **for nothing**—if it really was for
    3: 4 you suffered so much for nothing—if it really was **for nothing**?
    4:11 I fear for you, that somehow I have **wasted** my efforts on you.
Col 2:18 has seen, and his unspiritual mind puffs him up **with idle notions**.

1633 εἴκοσι, *eikosi* [11]

twenty-four [+5475] [6], twenty [2], a hundred and twenty feet deep [+3976] [1], three or three and a half miles [+2445+4297+5084+5558] [1], twenty-three [+5552] [1]

Lk 14:31 men to oppose the one coming against him with **twenty** thousand?
Jn 6:19 When they had rowed **three or three and a half miles** [+2445+4297+5084+5558], they saw Jesus approaching the boat,
Ac 1:15 the believers (a group numbering about a hundred and **twenty**)
   27:28 that the *water* was **a hundred and twenty feet deep** [+3976].
1Co 10: 8 and in one day **twenty-three** [+5552] thousand of them died.
Rev 4: 4 Surrounding the throne were **twenty-four** [+5475] other thrones,
    4: 4 and seated on them were **twenty-four** [+5475] elders.
    4:10 the **twenty-four** [+5475] elders fall down before him who sits on
    5: 8 and the **twenty-four** [+5475] elders fell down before the Lamb.
   11:16 And the **twenty-four** [+5475] elders, who were seated on their
   19: 4 The **twenty-four** [+5475] elders and the four living creatures fell

1634 εἴκω, *eikō* [1] [→ *5640*]

give in [+3836+5717] [1]

Gal 2: 5 *We did* not **give** [+3836+5717] **in** to them for a moment, so that

1635 εἰκών, *eikōn* [23] [√ *2036*]

image [13], likeness [4], portrait [3], images [1], it^s [+2563+3836+3836] [1], realities [+3836+4547] [1]

Mt 22:20 and he asked them, "Whose **portrait** is this? And whose
Mk 12:16 They brought the coin, and he asked them, "Whose **portrait** is this?
Lk 20:24 "Show me a denarius. Whose **portrait** and inscription are on it?"
Ro 1:23 and exchanged the glory of the immortal God for **images** made to
    8:29 he also predestined to be conformed *to* the **likeness** of his Son,
1Co 11: 7 not to cover his head, since he is the **image** and glory of God;
   15:49 And just as we have borne the **likeness** of the earthly man,
   15:49 earthly man, so shall we bear the **likeness** of the man from heaven.
2Co 3:18 are being transformed into his **likeness** with ever-increasing glory,
    4: 4 light of the gospel of the glory of Christ, who is the **image** of God.
Col 1:15 He is the **image** of the invisible God, the firstborn over all creation.
    3:10 which is being renewed in knowledge in the **image** of its Creator.
Heb 10: 1 that are coming—not the **realities** [+3836+4547] themselves.
Rev 13:14 He ordered them to set up an **image** in honor of the beast who was
   13:15 He was given power to give breath *to* the **image** of the first beast,
   13:15 so that it^s [+2563+3836+3836] could speak and cause all who
   13:15 and cause all who refused to worship the **image** to be killed.
   14: 9 "If anyone worships the beast and his **image** and receives his mark
   14:11 no rest day or night for those who worship the beast and his **image**,
   15: 2 over the beast and his **image** and over the number of his name.
   16: 2 the people who had the mark of the beast and worshiped his **image**.
   19:20 who had received the mark of the beast and worshiped his **image**.
   20: 4 They had not worshiped the beast or his **image** and had not

1636 εἰλικρίνεια, *eilikrineia* [3] [√ *1637*]

sincerity [3]

1Co 5: 8 but with bread without yeast, the bread *of* **sincerity** and truth.
2Co 1:12 relations with you, in the holiness and **sincerity** that are from God.
    2:17 On the contrary, in Christ we speak before God with **sincerity**,

1637 εἰλικρινής, *eilikrinēs* [2]
[→ *1636*; cf. *2463* + *3212*]

pure [1], wholesome [1]

Php 1:10 what is best and may be **pure** and blameless until the day of Christ,
2Pe 3:1 both of them as reminders to stimulate you to **wholesome** thinking.

1638 εἰ μήν, *ei mēn*   Not used in UBS/NIV
[√ *1623* + *3605*]

1639 εἰμί, *eimi* [2462] [→ *582, 707, 1913, 1928, 1930, 1997, 2003, 2026, 2157, 3953, 4045, 4205, 4242, 4342, 5223, 5289, 5542; cf. 2026*]

ἐγώ εἰμί (I am) [48] Mt 14:27; 22:32; 24:5; 26:22,25; Mk 6:50; 13:6; 14:62; Lk 1:19; 21:8; 22:70; 24:39; Jn 4:26; 6:20,35,41,48,51; 8:12,18,24,28,58; 9:9; 10:7,9,11,14; 11:25; 13:19; 14:6; 15:1,5; 18:5,6,8; Ac 9:5; 10:21; 18:10; 22:3,8; 26:15,29; Rev 1:8,17; 2:23; 21:6; 22:16

εἰμὶ ἐγώ (I am) [11] Jn 1:27; 3:28; 7:34,36; 12:26; 14:3; 17:24; Ac 13:25; 27:23; Ro 11:13; 1Ti 1:15

is [702], are [369], was [300], be [262], am [130], were [129], *untranslated* [105], been [35], have [16], come [15], had [10], means [10], comes [8], happen [7], be [+*1650*] [6], lived [6], as [5], belong to [+*1666*] [5], belong to [5], do [5], isn't [+*4024*] [5], mean [5], means [+*3493*] [5], stands for [5], become [+*1650*] [4], belonged to [+*1666*] [4], has [4], live [4], stay [4], stayed [4], with [4], become [3], belongs to [+*1666*] [3], belongs to [3], calls for [3], deserve [+*545*] [3], hate [+*3631*] [3], it's [3], remain [3], aren't [+*4024*] [2], aren't [+*4049*] [2], been [+*1181*] [2], began [2], being [2], cannot [+*4024*] [2], cease to be [+*4024*] [2], companions [+*3552*+*3836*] [2], companions [+*3836*+*5250*] [2], controlled [2], deserve [+*2653*] [2], did [2], done [2], follow [2], form [2], get [2], go [2], had [+*1877*] [2], had [+*2400*] [2], have being [2], hit [+*4091*] [2], kept [2], know [+*1196*] [2], leads to [2], moan [+*2527*] [2], meaning [2], meant [2], pleases [+*2298*] [2], represent [2], sanctified [+*39*] [2], saved [+*5392*] [2], taught [+*1438*] [2], though [2], accepts [+*1283*] [1], advisable [+*545*] [1], all the world [+*476*+*4005*+*5515*] [1], am present [1], are [+*1650*] [1], at work [1], attained [1], be diligent [1], be that as it may [1], bears [+*4472*] [1], became [+*1181*] [1], because are [1], before this been [+*4732*] [1], believe [+*4409*] [1], belonged to [1], belonging to [1], belongs [1], betray [+*4140*] [1], binds together [+*5278*] [1], boast [+*3017*] [1], break [+*4127*] [1], bring [+*1650*] [1], came about [1], can [+*1543*] [1], care very little [+*1650*+*1788*] [1], carried out [1], catch [+*2436*] [1], come [+*2262*] [1], come together [+*5251*] [1], come upon [RP21582093] [1], come with [+*5302*] [1], consented [+*5163*] [1], consist [1], continued [1], cured [+*2543*] [1], cut [+*3300*] [1], deserves [+*545*] [1], devoted to [+*4674*] [1], disagreed [+*851*] [1], done [+*2237*] [1], done [+*4472*] [1], done [+*4556*] [1], enabled [+*1443*] [1], end [+*4639*] [1], enjoy [1], enter [+*1656*] [1], envious [+*3836*+*4057*+*4505*] [1], equality [+*2698*+*3836*] [1], exist [1], existed [1], exists [1], explain [+*1196*] [1], fail the test [+*99*] [1], failed the test [+*99*] [1], fall [+*4406*] [1], find [+*2351*] [1], find [1], forgive [+*2664*] [1], found [1], gathered [+*2190*] [1], gathered [1], given [1], given fullness [+*4444*] [1], gives life [+*2443*] [1], had taken part in a rebellion [+*3334*] [1], had to [+*1256*] [1], had to [+*338*] [1], had too much [+*3551*] [1], happened [+*1181*] [1], happened [1], have all you want [+*3170*] [1], have hope [+*1827*] [1], have such a place [1], he's [+*899*+*3836*+*6034*] [1], he's [1], hear [+*201*] [1], heard [+*201*] [1], hold [1], how far will they go [+*4047*+*5515*] [1], I'm [+*1609*] [1], in all [+*4047*] [1], in charge of [+*2093*] [1], in other words [+*4047*] [1], including [+*4005*] [1], involves [1], is [+*3493*] [1], is now [1], isn't [+*4049*] [1], Jesus [1], joined constantly [+*4674*] [1], keep [1], kept on [1], know [+*5745*] [1], last [1], lasts [1], leaders [+*4755*] [1], listens [+*212*] [1], lived [+*1695*] [1], longs for [+*2160*] [1], looks [1], looks like [1], made [1], made holy [+*39*] [1], made up of [1], make complete [+*4444*] [1], making a complaints about [1], marveled [+*2513*] [1], may [1], meaning [+*323*+*5515*] [1], means [+*3306*] [1], meet [1], numbering [+*750*] [1], numbering

[1], on the evening [+*4068*] [1], on the side [1], on way home [+*5715*] [1], one [1], one of [+*1666*] [1], owe [+*4050*] [1], owed money to [+*5971*] [1], owns [+*2625*] [1], owns [+*3261*] [1], paralytic [+*4168*] [1], participate [+*3128*] [1], perish [+*724*+*1650*] [1], place [1], please [+*2298*] [1], pleased [+*744*] [1], possible [+*1543*] [1], present [1], previously seen [+*4632*] [1], prisoners [+*1313*] [1], put aside [+*1650*] [1], put in chains [+*1313*] [1], put trust [+*4275*] [1], read [+*1211*] [1], read [+*2108*] [1], receive [1], rely [+*4275*] [1], rely on [+*1666*] [1], resembled [+*3927*] [1], rest [1], rightly so [+*545*] [1], riot [+*2573*] [1], sat [+*5153*] [1], say [+*4123*] [1], say [1], settle matters [+*2333*] [1], share [+*3128*] [1], share [1], share with [+*5171*] [1], show favoritism [+*4720*] [1], show favoritism [+*4721*] [1], sided [1], sinned [+*281*+*4472*] [1], sins [+*281*] [1], spent the night [+*1381*] [1], spread [1], spring up [1], standing [+*2705*] [1], standing [1], stood [+*1417*] [1], stood [+*2705*] [1], stood [+*3023*] [1], stood opposed [+*5641*] [1], stood there [+*2392*] [1], sums up [1], take [+*2400*] [1], take for [+*1506*] [1], taken part [+*3128*] [1], takes captive [+*5194*] [1], tasted [1], testify [+*3457*] [1], testify [+*3459*] [1], to [1], to have failed [+*99*] [1], treat [1], try [1], using [1], valued highly [+*1952*] [1], want [1], was [+*1181*] [1], was present [1], went [1], were [+*4537*] [1], were up [+*326*] [1], what shall we do [+*4036*+*5515*] [1], while [+*1877*+*3836*] [1], will [1], withdrew [+*5723*] [1], wore clothing [+*1907*] [1], work with [+*5301*] [1], worth [+*4005*] [1], would [1]

Mt 1:18 This is how the birth of Jesus Christ **came about**: His mother Mary
   1:19 *Because* Joseph her husband **was** a righteous man and did not want
   1:20 because what is conceived in her **is** from the Holy Spirit.
   1:23 will call him Immanuel"—which **means** [+*3493*], "God with us."
   2: 2 and asked, "Where **is** the one who has been born king of the Jews?
   2: 6 land of Judah, **are** by no means least among the rulers of Judah;
   2: 9 ahead of them until it stopped over the place where the child **was**.
   2:13 **Stay** there until I tell you, for Herod is going to search for the child
   2:15 where *he* **stayed** until the death of Herod. And so was fulfilled
   2:18 and refusing to be comforted, because *they* **are** no more."
   3: 3 This **is** he who was spoken of through the prophet Isaiah: "A voice
   3: 4 leather belt around his waist. His food **was** locusts and wild honey.
   3:11 But after me will come one *who* **is** more powerful than I,
   3:11 who is more powerful than I, whose sandals *I* **am** not fit to carry.
   3:15 so now; *it* **is** proper for us to do this to fulfill all righteousness."
   3:17 And a voice from heaven said, "This **is** my Son, whom I love;
   4: 3 The tempter came to him and said, "If you **are** the Son of God,
   4: 6 "If *you* **are** the Son of God," he said, "throw yourself down.
   4:18 They were casting a net into the lake, for *they* **were** fishermen.
   5: 3 "Blessed are the poor in spirit, for theirs **is** the kingdom of heaven.
   5:10 because of righteousness, for theirs **is** the kingdom of heaven.
   5:11 "Blessed **are** *you* when people insult you, persecute you and falsely
   5:13 "You **are** the salt of the earth. But if the salt loses its saltiness,
   5:14 "You **are** the light of the world. A city on a hill cannot be hidden.'
   5:21 not murder, and anyone who murders *will* **be** subject to judgment.'
   5:22 But I tell you that anyone who is angry with his brother *will* **be**
   5:22 who says to his brother, 'Raca,' **is** answerable to the Sanhedrin.
   5:22 anyone who says, 'You fool!' *will* **be** in danger of the fire of hell.
   5:25 "**Settle matters** [+*2333*] quickly with your adversary who is
   5:25 Do it while *you* **are** still with him on the way, or he may hand you
   5:34 Do not swear at all: either by heaven, for *it* **is** God's throne;
   5:35 or by the earth, for it **is** his footstool;
   5:35 his footstool; or by Jerusalem, for *it* **is** the city of the Great King.
   5:37 Simply *let* your 'Yes' **be** 'Yes,' and your 'No,' 'No'; anything
   5:37 your 'No,' 'No'; anything beyond this **comes** from the evil one.
   5:48 **Be** perfect, therefore, as your heavenly Father is perfect.
   5:48 **Be** perfect, therefore, as your heavenly Father is perfect.
   6: 4 so that your giving *may* **be** in secret. Then your Father, who sees
   6: 5 "And when you pray, *do* not **be** like the hypocrites, for they love to
   6:21 For where your treasure **is**, there your heart will be also.
   6:21 For where your treasure **is**, there your heart *will* **be** also.
   6:22 "The eye **is** the lamp of the body. If your eyes are good, your whole
   6:22 If your eyes **are** good, your whole body will be full of light.
   6:22 If your eyes are good, your whole body *will* **be** full of light.
   6:23 But if your eyes **are** bad, your whole body will be full of darkness.
   6:23 But if your eyes are bad, your whole body *will* **be** full of darkness.
   6:23 If then the light within you **is** darkness, how great is that darkness!
   6:25 **Is** not life more important than food, and the body more important
   6:30 *which* **is** *here* today and tomorrow is thrown into the fire,
   7: 9 "Which **[NIE]** of you, if his son asks for bread, will give him a

7: 11 If you, then, *though* you **are** evil, know how to give good gifts to
7: 12 have them do to you, for this **sums up** the Law and the Prophets.
7: 13 road that leads to destruction, and many **enter** [+*1656*] through it.
7: 14 narrow the road that leads to life, and only a few **find** [+*2351*] it.
7: 15 to you in sheep's clothing, but inwardly *they* **are** ferocious wolves.
7: 27 and beat against that house, and it fell **with** a great crash."
7: 29 because *he* **taught** [+*1438*] as one who had authority, and not as
8: 8 *I do* not **deserve** [+*2653*] to have you come under my roof.
8: 9 For I myself **am** a man under authority, with soldiers under me.
8: 12 the darkness, where *there will* **be** weeping and gnashing of teeth."
8: 26 He replied, "You of little faith, why **are** *you* so afraid?" Then he got
8: 27 The men were amazed and asked, "What kind of man **is** this?
8: 30 Some distance from them a large herd of pigs **was** feeding.
9: 5 Which **is** easier: to say, 'Your sins are forgiven,' or to say,
9: 13 But go and learn what *this* **means**: 'I desire mercy, not sacrifice.'
9: 15 "How can the guests of the bridegroom mourn while he **is** with
9: 36 compassion on them, because *they* **were** harassed and helpless,
10: 2 These **are** the names of the twelve apostles: first, Simon (who is
10: 11 search for some worthy person **[NIE]** and there stay at his house
10: 13 If the home **is** deserving, let your peace rest on it; if it is not,
10: 13 let your peace rest on it; if *it* is not, let your peace return to you.
10: 15 *it will* **be** more bearable for Sodom and Gomorrah on the day of
10: 20 for it *will* not **be** you speaking, but the Spirit of your Father
10: 22 All men *will* **hate you** [+*3631*] because of me, but he who stands
10: 24 "A student **is** not above his teacher, nor a servant above his master.
10: 26 *There* **is** nothing concealed that will not be disclosed, or hidden
10: 30 And even the very hairs of your head **are** all numbered.
10: 37 who loves his father or mother more than me **is** not worthy of me;
10: 37 who loves his son or daughter more than me **is** not worthy of me;
10: 38 who does not take his cross and follow me **is** not worthy of me.
11: 3 to ask him, "**Are** you the one who was to come, or should we
11: 6 Blessed **is** the man who does not fall away on account of me."
11: 8 fine clothes? No, those who wear fine clothes **are** in kings' palaces.
11: 10 This **is** the one about whom it is written: " 'I will send my
11: 11 yet he who is least in the kingdom of heaven **is** greater than he.
11: 14 if you are willing to accept it, *he* **is** the Elijah who was to come.
11: 16 *They* **are** like children sitting in the marketplaces and calling out
11: 22 *it will* **be** more bearable for Tyre and Sidon on the day of judgment
11: 24 But I tell you that *it will* **be** more bearable for Sodom on the day of
11: 29 upon you and learn from me, for *I* **am** gentle and humble in heart,
11: 30 For my yoke **is** easy and my burden is light."
12: 4 ate the consecrated bread—which **was** not lawful for them to do,
12: 5 the priests in the temple desecrate the day and yet **are** innocent?
12: 6 I tell you that one greater than the temple **is** here.
12: 7 If you had known what *these words* **mean**, 'I desire mercy,
12: 8 For the Son of Man **is** Lord of the Sabbath."
12: 11 "If any **[NIE]** of you has a sheep and it falls into a pit on the
12: 23 people were astonished and said, "Could this **be** the Son of David?"
12: 27 do your people drive them out? So then, they *will* **be** your judges.
12: 30 "He *who* **is** not with me is against me, and he who does not gather
12: 30 "He who is not with me is against me, and he who does not gather
12: 34 brood of vipers, how can you *who* **are** evil say anything good?
12: 40 For as Jonah **was** three days and three nights in the belly of a huge
12: 40 so the Son of Man *will* **be** three days and three nights in the heart
12: 45 than the first. That is how *it will* **be** with this wicked generation."
12: 48 He replied to him, "Who **is** my mother, and who are my brothers?"
12: 48 He replied to him, "Who is my mother, and who **are** my brothers?"
12: 50 For whoever does the will of my Father in heaven **is** my brother
13: 19 what was sown in his heart. This **is** the seed sown along the path.
13: 20 The one who received the seed that fell on rocky places **is** the man
13: 21 But since he has no root, *he* **lasts** only a short time. When trouble
13: 22 The one who received the seed that fell among the thorns **is** the
13: 23 But the one who received the seed that fell on good soil **is** the man
13: 31 "The kingdom of heaven **is** like a mustard seed, which a man took
13: 32 Though it **is** the smallest of all your seeds, yet when it grows,
13: 32 when it grows, *it* **is** the largest of garden plants and becomes a tree,
13: 33 "The kingdom of heaven **is** like yeast that a woman took and mixed
13: 37 "The one who sowed the good seed **is** the Son of Man.
13: 38 The field **is** the world, and the good seed stands for the sons of the
13: 38 **is** the world, and the good seed **stands for** the sons of the kingdom.
13: 38 the sons of the kingdom. The weeds **are** the sons of the evil one,
13: 39 and the enemy who sows them **is** the devil. The harvest is the end
13: 39 The harvest **is** the end of the age, and the harvesters are angels.
13: 39 The harvest is the end of the age, and the harvesters **are** angels.
13: 40 pulled up and burned in the fire, so *it will* **be** at the end of the age.
13: 42 fiery furnace, where *there will* **be** weeping and gnashing of teeth.

13: 44 "The kingdom of heaven **is** like treasure hidden in a field. When a
13: 45 the kingdom of heaven **is** like a merchant looking for fine pearls.
13: 47 the kingdom of heaven **is** like a net that was let down into the lake
13: 49 This is how *it will* **be** at the end of the age. The angels will come
13: 50 fiery furnace, where *there will* **be** weeping and gnashing of teeth.
13: 52 **is** like the owner of a house who brings out of his storeroom new
13: 55 "**Isn't** [+*4024*] this the carpenter's son? Isn't his mother's name
13: 56 **Aren't** [+*4049*] all his sisters with us? Where then did this man get
13: 57 in his hometown and in his own house **is** a prophet without honor."
14: 2 and he said to his attendants, "This **is** John the Baptist; he has risen
14: 15 the disciples came to him and said, "This **is** a remote place,
14: 21 The number of those who ate **was** about five thousand men,
14: 23 by himself to pray. When evening came, *he* **was** there alone,
14: 24 from land, buffeted by the waves because the wind **was** against it.
14: 26 walking on the lake, they were terrified. "**It's** a ghost," they said,
14: 27 immediately said to them: "Take courage! *It* **is** I. Don't be afraid."
14: 28 "Lord, if *it's* you," Peter replied, "tell me to come to you on the
14: 33 in the boat worshiped him, saying, "Truly *you* **are** the Son of God."
15: 14 Leave them; *they* **are** blind guides. If a blind man leads a blind
15: 16 "**Are** you still so dull?" Jesus asked them.
15: 20 These **are** what make a man 'unclean'; but eating with unwashed
15: 26 "*It* **is** not right to take the children's bread and toss it to their dogs."
15: 38 The number of those who ate **was** four thousand, besides women
16: 13 he asked his disciples, "Who do people say the Son of Man **is**?"
16: 15 "But what about you?" he asked. "Who do you say I **am**?"
16: 16 Simon Peter answered, "You **are** the Christ, the Son of the living
16: 17 Jesus replied, "Blessed **are** *you*, Simon son of Jonah, for this was
16: 18 And I tell you that you **are** Peter, and on this rock I will build my
16: 19 whatever you bind on earth *will* **be** bound in heaven, and whatever
16: 19 and whatever you loose on earth *will* **be** loosed in heaven."
16: 20 Then he warned his disciples not to tell anyone that he **was** the
16: 22 "Never, Lord!" he said. "This *shall* never **happen** to you!"
16: 23 *You* **are** a stumbling block to me; you do not have in mind the
16: 28 some who **are** standing here will not taste death before they see the
17: 4 Peter said to Jesus, "Lord, *it* **is** good for us to be here. If you wish,
17: 4 Peter said to Jesus, "Lord, it is good for us *to* **be** here. If you wish,
17: 5 and a voice from the cloud said, "This **is** my Son, whom I love;
17: 17 generation," Jesus replied, "how long *shall I* **stay** with you?
17: 26 Peter answered. "Then the sons **are** exempt," Jesus said to him.
18: 1 and asked, "Who **is** the greatest in the kingdom of heaven?"
18: 4 whoever humbles himself like this child **is** the greatest in the
18: 8 *It* **is** better for you to enter life maimed or crippled than to have
18: 9 *It* **is** better for you to enter life with one eye than to have two eyes
18: 14 In the same way your Father in heaven **is** not willing that any of
18: 17 to the church, **treat** him as you would a pagan or a tax collector.
18: 18 you the truth, whatever you bind on earth *will* **be** bound in heaven,
18: 18 and whatever you loose on earth *will* **be** loosed in heaven.
18: 20 For where two or three **come together** [+*5251*] in my name,
18: 20 or three come together in my name, there **am** *I* with them."
19: 5 be united to his wife, and the two *will* **become** [+*1650*] one flesh'?
19: 6 So *they* **are** no longer two, but one. Therefore what God has joined
19: 10 "If this **is** the situation between a husband and wife, it is better not
19: 12 For some **are** eunuchs because they were born that way; others
19: 12 were born that way; **[RPG]** others were made that way by men;
19: 12 and **[RPG]** others have renounced marriage because of the
19: 14 hinder them, for the kingdom of heaven **belongs to** such as these."
19: 17 Jesus replied. "*There* **is** only One who is good. If you want to
19: 21 Jesus answered, "If you want *to* **be** perfect, go, sell your possessions
19: 22 he went away sad, because *he* **had** [+*2400*] great wealth.
19: 24 *it* **is** easier for a camel to go through the eye of a needle than for a
19: 26 Jesus looked at them and said, "With man this **is** impossible,
19: 27 have left everything to follow you! What then *will there* **be** for us?"
19: 30 But many who are first *will* **be** last, and many who are last will be
20: 1 "For the kingdom of heaven **is** like a landowner who went out early
20: 4 and work in my vineyard, and I will pay you whatever **is** right.'
20: 15 Or are you **envious** [+*3836*+*4057*+*4505*] because I am generous?'
20: 15 my own money? Or are you envious because I **am** generous?'
20: 16 "So the last *will* **be** first, and the first will be last."
20: 23 from my cup, but to sit at my right or left **is** not for me to grant.
20: 26 Not so **[NIE]** with you. Instead, whoever wants to become great
20: 26 whoever wants to become great among you *must* **be** your servant,
20: 27 and whoever wants *to* **be** first must be your slave—
20: 27 and whoever wants to be first *must* **be** your slave—
21: 10 the whole city was stirred and asked, "Who **is** this?"
21: 11 The crowds answered, "This **is** Jesus, the prophet from Nazareth in
21: 25 where did it come from? **Was** *it* from heaven, or from men?"

21:33 *There* **was** a landowner who planted a vineyard. He put a wall
21:38 the tenants saw the son, they said to each other, 'This **is** the heir.
21:42 the Lord has done this, and *it* **is** marvelous in our eyes'?
22: 8 "Then he said to his servants, 'The wedding banquet **is** ready,
22: 8 is ready, but those I invited *did* not **deserve** [*+545*] to come.
22:13 the darkness, where *there* will **be** weeping and gnashing of teeth.'
22:14 "For many **are** invited, but few are chosen."
22:16 "we know *you* **are** a man of integrity and that you teach the way of
22:23 who say *there* **is** no resurrection, came to him with a question.
22:25 Now *there* **were** seven brothers among us. The first one married
22:28 Now then, at the resurrection, whose wife *will she* **be** of the seven,
22:30 nor be given in marriage; *they will* **be** like the angels in heaven.
22:32 'I **am** the God of Abraham, the God of Isaac, and the God of
22:32 the God of Jacob'? *He* **is** not the God of the dead but of the living."
22:38 This **is** the first and greatest commandment.
22:42 the Christ? Whose son **is** *he*?" "The son of David," they replied.
22:45 If then David calls him 'Lord,' how *can he* **be** his son?"
23: 8 for you **have** only one Master and you are all brothers.
23: 8 for you have only one Master and you **are** all brothers.
23: 9 on earth 'father,' for you **have** one Father, and he is in heaven.
23:10 you to be called 'teacher,' for you **have** one Teacher, the Christ.
23:11 The greatest among you *will* **be** your servant.
23:16 You say, 'If anyone swears by the temple, *it* **means** nothing;
23:17 Which **is** greater: the gold, or the temple that makes the gold
23:18 You also say, 'If anyone swears by the altar, *it* **means** nothing;
23:28 but on the inside *you* **are** full of hypocrisy and wickedness.
23:30 And you say, 'If *we had* **lived** in the days of our forefathers,
23:30 *we* would not have **taken part** [*+3128*] with them in shedding the
23:31 So you testify against yourselves that *you* **are** the descendants of
24: 3 "Tell us," they said, "when *will* this **happen**, and what will be the
24: 5 in my name, claiming, 'I **am** the Christ,' and will deceive many.
24: 6 not alarmed. Such things must happen, but the end **is** still to come.
24: 7 *There* will **be** famines and earthquakes in various places.
24: 9 put to death, and *you will* **be** hated by all nations because of me.
24:21 For then *there will* **be** great distress, unequaled from the beginning
24:26 if anyone tells you, 'There he **is**, out in the desert,' do not go out;
24:27 visible even in the west, so *will* **be** the coming of the Son of Man.
24:28 Wherever *there* **is** a carcass, there the vultures will gather.
24:33 you see all these things, you know that *it* **is** near, right at the door.
24:37 in the days of Noah, so *it will* **be** at the coming of the Son of Man.
24:38 *people* **were** eating and drinking, marrying and giving in marriage,
24:39 all away. That is how *it will* **be** at the coming of the Son of Man.
24:40 Two men *will* **be** in the field; one will be taken and the other left.
24:45 "Who then **is** the faithful and wise servant, whom the master has
24:51 the hypocrites, where *there will* **be** weeping and gnashing of teeth.
25: 2 Five of them **were** foolish and five were wise.
25:21 *You have* **been** faithful with a few things; I will put you in charge
25:23 *You have* **been** faithful with a few things; I will put you in charge
25:24 'Master,' he said, 'I knew that you **are** a hard man,
25:30 the darkness, where *there will* **be** weeping and gnashing of teeth.'
25:35 me something to drink, *I* **was** a stranger and you invited me in,
25:36 you looked after me, *I* **was** in prison and you came to visit me.'
25:43 *I* **was** a stranger and you did not invite me in, I needed clothes
26:18 and tell him, 'The Teacher says: My appointed time **is** near.
26:22 began to say to him one after the other, "Surely **[NIE]** not I, Lord?"
26:24 Son of Man! *It would* **be** better for him if he had not been born."
26:25 the one who would betray him, said, "Surely not **[NIE]** I, Rabbi?"
26:26 and gave it to his disciples, saying, "Take and eat; this **is** my body."
26:28 This **is** my blood of the covenant, which is poured out for many for
26:38 "My soul **is** overwhelmed with sorrow to the point of death.
26:39 with his face to the ground and prayed, "My Father, if *it* **is** possible,
26:43 he again found them sleeping, because their eyes **were** heavy.
26:48 arranged a signal with them: "The one I kiss **is** the man; arrest him."
26:63 by the living God: Tell us if you **are** the Christ, the Son of God."
26:66 What do you think?" "*He* **is** worthy of death," they answered.
26:68 and said, "Prophesy to us, Christ. Who **hit** [*+4091*] you?"
26:69 girl came to him. "You also **were** with Jesus of Galilee," she said.
26:71 said to the people there, "This fellow **was** with Jesus of Nazareth."
26:73 there went up to Peter and said, "Surely you **are** one of them,
27: 6 the law to put this into the treasury, since *it* **is** blood money."
27:11 and the governor asked him, "**Are** you the king of the Jews?"
27:24 "*I* **am** innocent of this man's blood," he said. "It is your
27:33 They came to a place called Golgotha (which **means** [*+3306*] The
27:37 against him: THIS **IS** JESUS, THE KING OF THE JEWS.
27:40 Come down from the cross, if *you* **are** the Son of God!"
27:42 they said, "but he can't save himself! **He's** King of Israel!

27:43 him now if he wants him, for he said, '*I* **am** the Son of God.' "
27:46 which **means**, "My God, my God, why have you forsaken me?"
27:54 were terrified, and exclaimed, "Surely he **was** the Son of God!"
27:55 Many women **were** there, watching from a distance. They had
27:56 Among them **were** Mary Magdalene, Mary the mother of James
27:61 and the other Mary **were** sitting there opposite the tomb.
27:62 The next day, the one *[NIE]* after Preparation Day, the chief
27:64 from the dead. This last deception *will* **be** worse than the first."
28: 3 His appearance **was** like lightning, and his clothes were white as
28: 6 *He* **is** not here; he has risen, just as he said. Come and see the place
28:20 And surely I **am** with you always, to the very end of the age."

Mk 1: 6 John **wore** clothing [*+1907*] made of camel's hair, with a leather
1: 7 the thongs of whose sandals *I* **am** not worthy to stoop down
1:11 "You **are** my Son, whom I love; with you I am well pleased."
1:13 and he **was** in the desert forty days, being tempted by Satan.
1:13 by Satan. *He* **was** with the wild animals, and angels attended him.
1:16 Andrew casting a net into the lake, for *they* **were** fishermen.
1:22 because *he* **taught** [*+1438*] them as one who had authority,
1:23 then **[NIE]** a man in their synagogue who was possessed by an
1:24 come to destroy us? I know who *you* **are**—the Holy One of God!"
1:27 were all so amazed that they asked each other, "What **is** this?
1:33 The whole town **gathered** [*+2190*] at the door,
1:45 no longer enter a town openly but **stayed** outside in lonely places.
2: 1 entered Capernaum, the people heard that *he had* **come** home.
2: 4 of the crowd, they made an opening in the roof above **Jesus** and,
2: 6 Now some teachers of the law **were** sitting there, thinking to
2: 9 Which **is** easier: to say to the paralytic, 'Your sins are forgiven,'
2:15 and his disciples, for *there* **were** many who followed him.
2:18 Now John's disciples and the Pharisees **were** fasting. Some people
2:19 "How can the guests of the bridegroom fast while he **is** with them?
2:26 And he also gave some *to* his **companions** [*+3836+5250*]."
2:28 So the Son of Man **is** Lord even of the Sabbath."
3: 1 into the synagogue, and a man with a shriveled hand **was** there.
3:11 they fell down before him and cried out, "You **are** the Son of God."
3:14 that *they might* **be** with him and that he might send them out to
3:17 he gave the name Boanerges, which **means** Sons of Thunder);
3:29 will never be forgiven; *he* **is** guilty of an eternal sin."
3:33 "Who **are** my mother and my brothers?" he asked.
3:35 Whoever does God's will **is** my brother and sister and mother."
4: 1 while all the people **were** along the shore at the water's edge.
4:15 Some people **are** like seed along the path, where the word is sown.
4:16 Others, **[RPG]** like seed sown on rocky places, hear the word
4:17 But since they have no root, *they* **last** only a short time.
4:18 Still others, **[RPG]** like seed sown among thorns, hear the word;
4:18 Still others, like seed sown among thorns, **hear** [*+201*] the word;
4:20 Others, **[RPG]** like seed sown on good soil, hear the word,
4:22 For whatever **is** hidden is meant to be disclosed, and whatever is
4:26 He also said, "This is what the kingdom of God **is** like. A man
4:31 a mustard seed, which **is** the smallest seed you plant in the ground.
4:36 the crowd behind, they took him along, just as *he* **was**, in the boat.
4:36 just as he was, in the boat. *There* **were** also other boats with him.
4:38 Jesus **was** in the stern, sleeping on a cushion. The disciples woke
4:40 He said to his disciples, "Why **are** *you* so afraid? Do you still have
4:41 They were terrified and asked each other, "Who **is** this? Even the
5: 5 and day among the tombs and in the hills he *would* **cry** out
5: 9 your name?" "My name is Legion," he replied, "for *we* **are** many."
5:11 A large herd of pigs **was** feeding on the nearby hillside.
5:14 and the people went out to see what *had* **happened** [*+1181*].
5:18 the man who had been demon-possessed begged to **go** with him.
5:21 a large crowd gathered around him while he **was** by the lake.
5:25 And a woman **was** there who had been subject to bleeding for
5:34 has healed you. Go in peace and **be** freed from your suffering."
5:40 the disciples who were with him, and went in where the child **was**.
5:41 (which **means** [*+3493*], "Little girl, I say to you, get up!").
5:42 the girl stood up and walked around (*she* **was** twelve years old).
6: 3 **Isn't** [*+4024*] this the carpenter? Isn't this Mary's son
6: 3 Judas and Simon? **Aren't** [*+4024*] his sisters here with us?"
6: 4 his relatives and in his own house **is** a prophet without honor."
6:15 Others said, "*He* **is** Elijah." And still others claimed, "He is a
6:31 because so many people **were** coming and going that they did not
6:34 on them, because *they* **were** like sheep without a shepherd.
6:35 "*This* **is** a remote place," they said, "and it's already very late.
6:44 The number of the men who had eaten **was** five thousand.
6:47 When evening came, the boat **was** in the middle of the lake,
6:48 disciples straining at the oars, because the wind **was** against them.
6:49 they saw him walking on the lake, they thought *he* **was** a ghost.

6:50 Immediately he spoke to them and said, "Take courage! *It* **is** I.
6:52 had not understood about the loaves; their hearts **were** hardened.
6:55 and carried the sick on mats to wherever they heard *he* **was**.
7: 2 eating food with hands that were "unclean," that **is**, unwashed.
7: 4 And **[NIE]** they observe many other traditions, such as the
7:11 you might otherwise have received from me is Corban" (that **is**,
7:15 **[NIE]** Nothing outside a man can make him 'unclean' by going
7:15 Rather, *it* **is** what comes out of a man that makes him 'unclean.' "
7:18 "**Are** you so dull?" he asked. "Don't you see that nothing that enters
7:26 The woman **was** a Greek, born in Syrian Phoenicia. She begged
7:27 "for *it* **is** not right to take the children's bread and toss it to their
7:34 deep sigh said to him, "*Ephphatha!*" (which **means**, "Be opened!").
8: 1 During those days another large crowd **gathered**. Since they had
8: 9 About four thousand men *were* **present**. And having sent them
8:27 On the way he asked them, "Who do people say I **am**?"
8:29 he asked. "Who do you say I **am**?" Peter answered, "You are the
8:29 "Who do you say I am?" Peter answered, "You **are** the Christ."
9: 1 some who **are** standing here will not taste death before they see the
9: 4 before them Elijah and Moses, *who* **were** talking with Jesus.
9: 5 Peter said to Jesus, "Rabbi, *it* **is** good for us to be here. Let us put up
9: 5 Peter said to Jesus, "Rabbi, it is good for us *to* **be** here. Let us put up
9: 7 from the cloud: "This **is** my Son, whom I love. Listen to him!"
9:10 to themselves, discussing what "rising from the dead" **meant**.
9:19 Jesus replied, "how long *shall I* **stay** with you?
9:21 asked the boy's father, "How long *has* he **been** [+*1181*] like this?"
9:35 Jesus called the Twelve and said, "If anyone wants *to* **be** first,
9:35 wants to be first, *he must* **be** the very last, and the servant of all."
9:39 "No one **[NIE]** who does a miracle in my name can in the next
9:40 for whoever **is** not against us is for us.
9:40 for whoever is not against us **is** for us.
9:41 because *you* **belong to** Christ will certainly not lose his reward.
9:42 *it would* **be** better for him to be thrown into the sea with a large
9:43 *It* **is** better for you to enter life maimed than with two hands to go
9:45 *It* **is** better for you to enter life crippled than to have two feet
9:47 *It* **is** better for you to enter the kingdom of God with one eye than
10: 8 and the two *will* **become** [+*1650*] one flesh.' So they are no longer
10: 8 two will become one flesh.' So *they* **are** no longer two, but one.
10:14 not hinder them, for the kingdom of God **belongs to** such as these.
10:22 face fell. He went away sad, because *he* **had** [+*2400*] great wealth.
10:24 said again, "Children, how hard *it* **is** to enter the kingdom of God!
10:25 *It* **is** easier for a camel to go through the eye of a needle than for a
10:29 "no one **[NIE]** who has left home or brothers or sisters or mother
10:31 But many who are first *will* **be** last, and the last first."
10:32 *They* **were** [+*326*] on their way *up* to Jerusalem, with Jesus
10:32 **[NIE]** with Jesus leading the way, and the disciples were
10:40 but to sit at my right or left **is** not for me to grant. These places
10:43 Not so **[NIE]** with you. Instead, whoever wants to become great
10:43 whoever wants to become great among you *must* **be** your servant,
10:44 and whoever wants *to* **be** first must be slave of all.
10:44 and whoever wants to be first *must* **be** slave of all.
10:47 When he heard that *it* **was** Jesus of Nazareth, he began to shout,
11:11 He looked around at everything, but *since* it **was** already late,
11:13 he found nothing but leaves, because *it* **was** not the season for figs.
11:23 but believes that what he says will happen, *it will be* **done** for him.
11:24 in prayer, believe that you have received it, and *it will* **be** yours.
11:30 John's baptism—**was** *it* from heaven, or from men? Tell me!"
11:32 the people, for everyone held that John really **was** a prophet.)
12: 7 "But the tenants said to one another, 'This **is** the heir. Come,
12: 7 is the heir. Come, let's kill him, and the inheritance *will* **be** ours.'
12:11 the Lord has done this, and *it* **is** marvelous in our eyes'?"
12:14 to him and said, "Teacher, we know *you* **are** a man of integrity.
12:18 Then the Sadducees, who say *there* **is** no resurrection, came to him
12:20 Now *there* **were** seven brothers. The first one married and died
12:23 At the resurrection whose wife *will she* **be**, since the seven were
12:25 nor be given in marriage; *they will* **be** like the angels in heaven.
12:27 *He* **is** not the God of the dead, but of the living. You are badly
12:28 "Of all the commandments, which **is** the most important?"
12:29 "The most important one," answered Jesus, "**is** this: 'Hear, O Israel,
12:29 "is this: 'Hear, O Israel, the Lord our God, the Lord **is** one.
12:31 as yourself.' *There* **is** no commandment greater than these."
12:32 "You are right in saying that God **is** one and there is no other
12:32 are right in saying that God is one and *there* **is** no other but him.
12:33 and to love your neighbor as yourself **is** more important than all
12:34 he said to him, "*You* **are** not far from the kingdom of God."
12:35 "How is it that the teachers of the law say that the Christ **is** the son
12:37 David himself calls him 'Lord.' How then *can* he **be** his son?"

12:42 and put in two very small copper coins, **worth** [+*4005*] *only* a
13: 4 "Tell us, when *will* these things **happen**? And what will be the sign
13: 6 will come in my name, claiming, 'I **am** he,' and will deceive many.
13: 8 *There will* **be** earthquakes in various places, and famines.
13: 8 There will be earthquakes in various places, and **[RPG]** famines.
13:11 you at the time, for *it* **is** not you speaking, but the Holy Spirit.
13:13 All men *will* **hate you** [+*3631*] because of me, but he who stands
13:19 because those *will* **be** days of distress unequaled from the
13:25 the stars *will* **fall** [+*4406*] from the sky, and the heavenly bodies
13:28 get tender and its leaves come out, you know that summer **is** near.
13:29 these things happening, you know that *it* **is** near, right at the door.
13:33 Be on guard! Be alert! You do not know when that time *will* **come**.
14: 1 and the Feast of Unleavened Bread **were** only two days away,
14: 2 not during the Feast," they said, "or the people *may* **riot** [+*2573*]."
14: 3 *While* he **was** in Bethany, reclining at the table in the home of a
14: 4 Some of *those present* **were** saying indignantly to one another,
14:14 Where *is* my guest room, where I may eat the Passover with my
14:22 and gave it to his disciples, saying, "Take it; this **is** my body."
14:24 "This **is** my blood of the covenant, which is poured out for many,"
14:34 "My soul **is** overwhelmed with sorrow to the point of death,"
14:35 and prayed that if **possible** [+*1543*] the hour might pass from him.
14:40 he again found them sleeping, because their eyes **were** heavy.
14:44 "The one I kiss **is** the man; arrest him and lead him away under
14:49 Every day *I* **was** with you, teaching in the temple courts, and you
14:54 There *he* **sat** [+*5153*] with the guards and warmed himself at the
14:56 testified falsely against him, but their statements **did** not agree.
14:59 Yet even then their testimony **did** not agree.
14:61 priest asked him, "**Are** you the Christ, the Son of the Blessed One?"
14:62 "I **am**," said Jesus. "And you will see the Son of Man sitting at the
14:64 What do you think?" They all condemned him **as** worthy of death.
14:66 *While* Peter **was** below in the courtyard, one of the servant girls of
14:67 closely at him. "You also **were** with that Nazarene, Jesus," she said.
14:69 said again to those standing around, "This fellow **is** one of them."
14:70 said to Peter, "Surely *you* **are** one of them, for you are a Galilean."
14:70 said to Peter, "Surely you are one of them, for *you* **are** a Galilean."
15: 2 "**Are** you the king of the Jews?" asked Pilate. "Yes, it is as you
15: 7 A man called Barabbas was in prison with the insurrectionists who
15:16 The soldiers led Jesus away into the palace (that **is**, the Praetorium)
15:22 called Golgotha (which **means** [+*3493*] The Place of the Skull).
15:25 *It* **was** the third hour when they crucified him.
15:26 The written notice of the charge against him **read** [+*2108*]:
15:34 which **means** [+*3493*], "My God, my God, why have you forsaken
15:39 saw how he died, he said, "Surely this man **was** the Son of God!"
15:40 Some women **were** watching from a distance. Among them were
15:41 **[NIE]** In Galilee these women had followed him and cared for his
15:42 *It* **was** Preparation Day (that is, the day before the Sabbath).
15:42 It was Preparation Day (that **is**, the day before the Sabbath).
15:43 who **was** himself waiting for the kingdom of God, went boldly to
15:46 it in the linen, and placed it in a tomb **cut** [+*3300*] out of rock.
16: 4 saw that the stone, *which* **was** very large, had been rolled away.
16: 6 the Nazarene, who was crucified. He has risen! *He* **is** not here.
Lk 1: 6 Both of them **were** upright in the sight of God, observing all the
1: 7 But they **had** no children, because Elizabeth was barren; and they
1: 7 But they had no children, because Elizabeth **was** barren; and they
1: 7 Elizabeth was barren; and *they* **were** both well along in years.
1:10 incense came, all the assembled worshipers **were** praying outside.
1:14 *He will* **be** a joy and delight to you, and many will rejoice
1:15 for *he will* **be** great in the sight of the Lord. He is never to take
1:18 sure of this? *I* **am** an old man and my wife is well along in years."
1:19 The angel answered, "I **am** Gabriel. I stand in the presence of God,
1:20 And now *you will* **be** silent and not able to speak until the day this
1:21 the people **were** waiting for Zechariah and wondering why he
1:22 for he **kept** making signs to them but remained unable to speak.
1:29 at his words and wondered what kind of greeting this *might* **be**.
1:32 He *will* **be** great and will be called the Son of the Most High.
1:33 reign over the house of Jacob forever; his kingdom *will* never end."
1:34 "How *will* this **be**," Mary asked the angel, "since I am a virgin?"
1:36 old age, and she who was said to be barren **is** in her sixth month.
1:45 believed that what the Lord has said to her *will* **be** accomplished!"
1:61 "*There* **is** no one among your relatives who has that name."
1:63 and to everyone's astonishment he wrote, "His name **is** John."
1:66 wondered about it, asking, "What then *is* this child *going to* **be**?"
1:66 then is this child going to be?" For the Lord's hand **was** with him.
1:80 and *he* **lived** in the desert until he appeared publicly to Israel.
2: 4 because he **belonged** [+*1666*] **to** the house and line of David.
2: 5 who was pledged to be married to him and **was** expecting a child.

2: 6 **While** [*+1877+3836*] they were there, the time came for the baby
2: 7 him in a manger, because *there* **was** no room for them in the inn.
2: 8 And *there* **were** shepherds living out in the fields nearby,
2:10 I bring you good news of great joy that *will* **be** for all the people.
2:11 town of David a Savior has been born to you; he **is** Christ the Lord.
2:25 Now *there* **was** a man in Jerusalem called Simeon, who was
2:25 for the consolation of Israel, and the Holy Spirit **was** upon him.
2:26 *It had* **been** revealed to him by the Holy Spirit that he would not
2:33 and mother **marveled** [*+2513*] at what was said about him.
2:36 *There* **was** also a prophetess, Anna, the daughter of Phanuel,
2:40 he was filled with wisdom, and the grace of God **was** upon him.
2:44 Thinking he **was** in their company, they traveled on for a day.
2:49 he asked. "Didn't you know I had to **be** in my Father's house?"
2:51 he went down to Nazareth with them and **was** obedient to them.
3: 5 The crooked roads *shall* **become** straight, the rough ways smooth.
3:15 and were all wondering in their hearts if John *might possibly* **be**
3:16 I will come, the thongs of whose sandals *I* **am** not worthy to untie.
3:22 "You **are** my Son, whom I love; with you I am well pleased."
3:23 Now Jesus himself **was** about thirty years old when he began his
3:23 *He* **was** the son, so it was thought, of Joseph, the son of Heli,
4: 3 The devil said to him, "If *you* **are** the Son of God, tell this stone to
4: 7 So if you worship me, *it will* **be** all yours."
4: 9 "If *you* **are** the Son of God," he said, "throw yourself down from
4:16 He went to Nazareth, where *he had* **been** brought up, and on the
4:17 handed to him. Unrolling it, he found the place where *it* **is** written:
4:20 The eyes of everyone in the synagogue **were** fastened on him,
4:22 came from his lips. "**Isn't** [*+4049*] this Joseph's son?" they asked.
4:24 the truth," he continued, "no prophet **is** accepted in his hometown.
4:25 I assure you that *there* **were** many widows in Israel in Elijah's
4:27 And *there* **were** many in Israel with leprosy in the time of Elisha
4:31 a town in Galilee, and on the Sabbath **began** to teach the people.
4:32 at his teaching, because his message **had** [*+1877*] authority.
4:33 In the synagogue *there* **was** a man possessed by a demon,
4:34 come to destroy us? I know who *you* **are**—the Holy One of God!"
4:38 Now Simon's mother-in-law **was** suffering from a high fever,
4:41 came out of many people, shouting, "You **are** the Son of God!"
4:41 not allow them to speak, because they knew he **was** the Christ.
4:44 and *he* **kept** on preaching in the synagogues of Judea.
5: 1 One day *as* Jesus **was** standing by the Lake of Gennesaret,
5: 3 He got into one of the boats, the one **belonging to** Simon,
5: 8 knees and said, "Go away from me, Lord; *I* **am** a sinful man!"
5:10 and John, the sons of Zebedee, **[NIE]** Simon's partners.
5:10 "Don't be afraid; from now on *you will* **catch** [*+2436*] men."
5:12 While Jesus **was** in one of the towns, a man came along who was
5:16 But Jesus *often* **withdrew** [*+5723*] to lonely places and prayed.
5:17 One day as he **was** teaching, Pharisees and teachers of the law,
5:17 who *had* **come** [*+2262*] from every village of Galilee and from
5:17 of Galilee and from Judea and Jerusalem, **were** sitting there.
5:17 And the power of the Lord **was** **present** for him to heal the sick.
5:18 Some men came carrying **[NIE]** a paralytic on a mat and tried to
5:21 thinking to themselves, "Who **is** this fellow who speaks blasphemy?
5:23 Which **is** easier: to say, 'Your sins are forgiven,'
5:29 and **[RPG]** a large crowd of tax collectors and others were eating
5:29 a large crowd of tax collectors and others **were** eating with them.
5:34 "Can you make the guests of the bridegroom fast while he **is** with
5:39 drinking old wine wants the new, for he says, 'The old **is** better.' "
6: 3 did when he and his **companions** [*+3552+3836*] were hungry?
6: 5 Then Jesus said to them, "The Son of Man **is** Lord of the Sabbath."
6: 6 was teaching, and a man **was** there whose right hand was shriveled.
6: 6 was teaching, and a man was there whose right hand **was** shriveled.
6:12 mountainside to pray, **spent the night** [*+1381*] praying to God.
6:20 "Blessed are you who are poor, for yours **is** the kingdom of God.
6:22 Blessed **are** *you* when men hate you, when they exclude you
6:32 "If you love those who love you, what credit **is** that to you?
6:33 do good to those who are good to you, what credit **is** that to you?
6:34 those from whom you expect repayment, what credit **is** that to you?
6:35 Then your reward *will* **be** great, and you will be sons of the Most
6:35 your reward will be great, and *you will* **be** sons of the Most High,
6:35 of the Most High, because he **is** kind to the ungrateful and wicked.
6:36 Be merciful, just as your Father **is** merciful.
6:40 A student **is** not above his teacher, but everyone who is fully
6:40 but everyone who is fully trained *will* **be** like his teacher.
6:43 "No good tree **bears** [*+4472*] bad fruit, nor does a bad tree bear
6:47 I will show you what *he* **is** like who comes to me and hears my
6:48 *He* **is** like a man building a house, who dug down deep and laid the
6:49 and does not put them into practice **is** like a man who built a house

7: 2 whom his master **valued highly** [*+1952*], was sick and about to
7: 4 earnestly with him, "This *man* **deserves** [*+545*] to have you do this,
7: 6 for *I do* not **deserve** [*+2653*] to have you come under my roof.
7: 8 For I myself **am** a man under authority, with soldiers under me.
7:12 carried out—the only son of his mother, and she **was** a widow.
7:12 she was a widow. And a large crowd from the town **was** with her.
7:19 sent them to the Lord to ask, "**Are** you the one who was to come,
7:20 '**Are** you the one who was to come, or should we expect someone
7:23 Blessed **is** the man who does not fall away on account of me."
7:25 who wear expensive clothes and indulge in luxury **are** in palaces.
7:27 This **is** the one about whom it is written: " 'I will send my
7:28 among those born of women *there* **is** no one greater than John;
7:28 yet the one who is least in the kingdom of God **is** greater than he."
7:31 can I compare the people of this generation? What **are** *they* like?
7:32 *They* **are** like children sitting in the marketplace and calling out to
7:37 When a woman *who had* **lived** a sinful life in that town learned
7:39 he said to himself, "If this man **were** a prophet, he would know
7:39 touching him and what kind of woman she is—that *she* **is** a sinner."
7:41 "Two men **owed money to** [*+5971*] a certain moneylender.
7:49 to say among themselves, "Who **is** this who even forgives sins?"
8: 2 and also some women who *had been* **cured** [*+2543*] of evil spirits
8: 9 His disciples asked him what this parable **meant**.
8:11 "This *is the* **meaning** of the parable: The seed is the word of God.
8:11 "This is the meaning of the parable: The seed **is** the word of God.
8:12 Those along the path **are** the ones who hear, and then the devil
8:14 The seed that fell among thorns **stands for** those who hear,
8:15 But the seed on good soil **stands for** those with a noble and good
8:17 For *there* **is** nothing hidden that will not be disclosed, and nothing
8:21 "My mother and brothers **are** those who hear God's word and put it
8:25 In fear and amazement they asked one another, "Who **is** this?
8:26 the region of the Gerasenes, which **is** across the lake from Galilee.
8:30 Jesus asked him, "What **is** your name?" "Legion," he replied,
8:32 A large herd of pigs **was** feeding there on the hillside. The demons
8:38 The man from whom the demons had gone out begged *to* **go** with
8:40 a crowd welcomed him, for *they* **were** all expecting him.
8:42 because **[NIE]** his only daughter, a girl of about twelve, was
8:43 And a woman was there *who had* **been** subject to bleeding for
9: 9 "I beheaded John Who, then, **is** this I hear such things about?"
9:12 and find food and lodging, because *we* **are** in a remote place here."
9:13 They answered, "We **have** only five loaves of bread and two fish—
9:14 (About five thousand men **were** there.) But he said to his disciples,
9:18 Once when Jesus was praying in private and his disciples
9:18 were with him, he asked them, "Who do the crowds say I **am**?"
9:20 he asked. "Who do you say I **am**?" Peter answered, "The Christ of
9:27 some who **are** standing here will not taste death before they see the
9:30 Two men, **[NIE]** Moses and Elijah,
9:32 Peter and his companions **were** very sleepy, but when they became
9:33 Peter said to him, "Master, *it* **is** good for us to be here.
9:33 Peter said to him, "Master, it is good *for us to* **be** here.
9:35 from the cloud, saying, "This **is** my Son, whom I have chosen;
9:38 "Teacher, I beg you to look at my son, for *he* **is** my only child.
9:41 Jesus replied, "how long *shall I* **stay** with you and put up with you?
9:45 *It* was hidden from them, so that they did not grasp it, and they
9:46 among the disciples as to which of them *would* **be** the greatest.
9:48 sent me. For he who is least among you all—he **is** the greatest."
9:50 stop him," Jesus said, "for whoever **is** not against you is for you."
9:50 stop him," Jesus said, "for whoever is not against you is for you."
9:53 there did not welcome him, because he **was** heading for Jerusalem.
9:62 the plow and looks back **is** fit for service in the kingdom of God."
10: 6 If a man of peace **is** there, your peace will rest on him; if not,
10:12 *it will* **be** more bearable on that day for Sodom than for that town.
10:14 But *it will* **be** more bearable for Tyre and Sidon at the judgment
10:22 No one knows who the Son **is** except the Father, and no one knows
10:22 and no one knows who the Father **is** except the Son and those to
10:29 to justify himself, so he asked Jesus, "And who **is** my neighbor?"
10:39 She **had** a sister called Mary, who sat at the Lord's feet listening to
10:42 but only one thing **is** needed. Mary has chosen what is better,
11: 1 One day Jesus **was** praying in a certain place. When he finished,
11: 7 The door is already locked, and my children **are** with me in bed.
11: 8 he will not get up and give him the bread because he **is** his friend,
11:14 Jesus **was** driving out a demon that was mute. When the demon
11:14 Jesus was driving out a demon that **was** mute. When the demon
11:19 your followers drive them out? So then, they *will* **be** your judges.
11:21 fully armed, guards his own house, his possessions **are** safe.
11:23 "He *who* **is** not with me is against me, and he who does not gather
11:23 "He who is not with me **is** against me, and he who does not gather

11: 29   As the crowds increased, Jesus said, "This **is** a wicked generation.
11: 30   to the Ninevites, so also *will* the Son of Man **be** to this generation.
11: 34   Your eye **is** the lamp of your body. When your eyes are good,
11: 34   When your eyes **are** good, your whole body also is full of light.
11: 34   When your eyes are good, your whole body also **is** full of light.
11: 34   But when *they* **are** bad, your body also is full of darkness.
11: 35   See to it, then, that the light within you **is** not darkness.
11: 36   is full of light, and no part of it dark, *it will* **be** completely lighted,
11: 41   inside ιthe dishι to the poor, and everything *will* **be** clean for you.
11: 44   "Woe to you, because *you* **are** like unmarked graves, which men
11: 48   So *you* **testify** [+3459] that you approve of what your forefathers
12: 1   your guard against the yeast of the Pharisees, which **is** hypocrisy.
12: 2   *There* **is** nothing concealed that will not be disclosed, or hidden
12: 6   sold for two pennies? Yet not one of them **is** forgotten by God.
12: 15   a man's life *does* not **consist** in the abundance of his possessions."
12: 20   Then who *will* **get** what you have prepared for yourself?'
12: 23   Life **is** more than food, and the body more than clothes.
12: 24   They do not sow or reap, they **have** no storeroom or barn;
12: 28   *which* **is** *here* today, and tomorrow is thrown into the fire,
12: 34   For where your treasure **is**, there your heart will be also.
12: 34   For where your treasure is, there your heart *will* **be** also.
12: 35   "**Be** dressed ready for service and keep your lamps burning,
12: 38   *It will* **be** good for those servants whose master finds them ready,
12: 42   The Lord answered, "Who then **is** the faithful and wise manager,
12: 52   From now on *there will* **be** five in one family divided against each
12: 55   the south wind blows, you say, '*It's going to* **be** hot,' and it is.
13: 10   On a Sabbath Jesus **was** teaching in one of the synagogues,
13: 11   *She* **was** bent over and could not straighten up at all.
13: 14   synagogue ruler said to the people, "*There* **are** six days for work.
13: 16   Then should not this woman, **[NIE]** a daughter of Abraham,
13: 18   Then Jesus asked, "What **is** the kingdom of God like? What shall I
13: 19   *It* **is** like a mustard seed, which a man took and planted in his
13: 21   *It* **is** like yeast that a woman took and mixed into a large amount of
13: 25   "But he will answer, 'I don't know you or where *you* **come** from.'
13: 27   "But he will reply, 'I don't know you or where *you* **come** from.
13: 28   "*There will* **be** weeping there, and gnashing of teeth, when you
13: 30   Indeed *there* **are** those who are last who will be first, and first who
13: 30   Indeed there are those who are last who *will* **be** first, and first who
13: 30   who are last who will be first, and **[RPG]** first who will be last."
13: 30   are those who are last who will be first, and first who *will* **be** last."
14: 1   the house of a prominent Pharisee, he **was** being carefully watched.
14: 2   There in front of him **was** a man suffering from dropsy.
14: 8   for a person more distinguished than you *may have* **been** invited.
14: 10   Then you *will* **be** honored in the presence of all your fellow guests.
14: 14   and *you will* **be** blessed. Although they cannot repay you,
14: 17   those who had been invited, 'Come, for everything **is** now ready.'
14: 22   'what you ordered has been done, but *there* **is** still room.'
14: 26   and sisters—yes, even his own life—he cannot **be** my disciple.
14: 27   who does not carry his cross and follow me cannot **be** my disciple.
14: 31   and consider whether *he* **is** able with ten thousand men to oppose
14: 32   he will send a delegation *while* the other **is** still a long way off
14: 33   any of you who does not give up everything he has cannot **be** my
14: 35   *It* **is** fit neither for the soil nor for the manure pile; it is thrown out.
15: 1   tax collectors and "sinners" **were** all gathering around to hear him.
15: 7   I tell you that in the same way *there will* **be** more rejoicing in
15: 19   *I* **am** no longer worthy to be called your son; make me like one of
15: 21   and against you. *I* **am** no longer worthy to be called your son.'
15: 24   For this son of mine *was* dead and is alive again; he was lost
15: 24   son of mine was dead and is alive again; *he* **was** lost and is found.'
15: 25   "Meanwhile, the older son **was** in the field. When he came near the
15: 26   So he called one of the servants and asked him what **was** going on.
15: 31   " 'My son,' the father said, 'you **are** always with me,
15: 31   'you are always with me, and everything I have **is** yours.
15: 32   because this brother of yours **was** dead and is alive again;
16: 1   "*There* **was** a rich man whose manager was accused of wasting his
16: 8   For the people of this world **are** more shrewd in dealing with their
16: 10   **[RPG]** and whoever is dishonest with very little will also be
16: 10   and whoever is dishonest with very little *will* also **be** dishonest
16: 15   "You **are** the ones who justify yourselves in the eyes of men,
16: 17   *It* **is** easier for heaven and earth to disappear than for the least
16: 19   "*There* **was** a rich man who was dressed in purple and fine linen
17: 1   "Things that cause people to sin **are** bound to come, but woe to that
17: 10   you were told to do, should say, '*We* **are** unworthy servants';
17: 16   himself at Jesus' feet and thanked him—and he **was** a Samaritan.
17: 21   or 'There it is,' because the kingdom of God **is** within you."
17: 24   For the Son of Man in his day *will* **be** like the lightning,

17: 26   the days of Noah, so also *will it* **be** in the days of the Son of Man.
17: 30   "*It will* **be** just like this on the day the Son of Man is revealed.
17: 31   On that day no one who **is** on the roof of his house, with his goods
17: 34   I tell you, on that night two people *will* **be** in one bed; one will be
17: 35   Two women *will* **be** grinding grain together; one will be taken
18: 2   "In a certain town *there* **was** a judge who neither feared God nor
18: 3   And *there* **was** a widow in that town who kept coming to him with
18: 9   To some who were confident of their own **[NIE]** righteousness
18: 11   'God, I thank you that *I* **am** not like other men—robbers, evildoers,
18: 16   not hinder them, for the kingdom of God **belongs to** such as these.
18: 23   he became very sad, because *he* **was** a man of great wealth.
18: 25   *it* **is** easier for a camel to go through the eye of a needle than for a
18: 27   Jesus replied, "What is impossible with men **is** possible with God."
18: 29   "no one **[NIE]** who has left home or wife or brothers or parents
18: 34   Its meaning **was** hidden from them, and they did not know what he
18: 36   When he heard the crowd going by, he asked what **was** happening.
19: 2   name of Zacchaeus; he **was** a chief tax collector and was wealthy.
19: 3   He wanted to see who Jesus **was**, but being a short man he could
19: 3   but *being* a short man he could not, because of the crowd.
19: 9   has come to this house, because this man, too, **is** a son of Abraham.
19: 11   because he **was** near Jerusalem and the people thought that the
19: 17   you have been trustworthy in a very small matter, **take** [+2400]
19: 21   I was afraid of you, because *you* **are** a hard man. You take out
19: 22   You knew, did you, that I **am** a hard man, taking out what I did not
19: 46   written," he said to them, " 'My house *will* **be** a house of prayer';
19: 47   Every day he **was** teaching at the temple. But the chief priests,
20: 2   these things," they said. "Who **[NIE]** gave you this authority?"
20: 4   John's baptism—**was** *it* from heaven, or from men?"
20: 6   will stone us, because *they* **are** persuaded that John was a prophet."
20: 6   will stone us, because they are persuaded that John **was** a prophet."
20: 14   'This **is** the heir,' they said. 'Let's kill him, and the inheritance will
20: 17   and asked, "Then what *is the* **meaning** *of* that which is written:
20: 20   a close watch on him, they sent spies, who pretended *to* **be** honest.
20: 27   Some of the Sadducees, who say *there* **is** no resurrection,
20: 28   **[NIE]** the man must marry the widow and have children for his
20: 29   Now *there* **were** seven brothers. The first one married a woman
20: 36   and they can no longer die; for *they* **are** like the angels. They are
20: 36   *They* **are** God's children, since they are children of the
20: 36   are God's children, *since they* **are** children of the resurrection.
20: 38   *He* **is** not the God of the dead, but of the living, for to him all are
20: 41   said to them, "How is it that they say the Christ **is** the Son of David?
20: 44   David calls him 'Lord.' How then *can he* **be** his son?"
21: 7   "Teacher," they asked, "when *will* these things **happen**? And what
21: 8   come in my name, claiming, 'I **am** he,' and, 'The time is near.'
21: 11   *There will* **be** great earthquakes, famines and pestilences in
21: 11   and fearful events and great signs from heaven. **[RPG]**
21: 17   All men *will* **hate you** [+3631] because of me.
21: 22   For this **is** the time of punishment in fulfillment of all that has been
21: 23   *There will* **be** great distress in the land and wrath against this
21: 24   Jerusalem *will* **be** trampled on by the Gentiles until the times of the
21: 25   "*There will* **be** signs in the sun, moon and stars. On the earth,
21: 30   you can see for yourselves and know that summer **is** near.
21: 31   these things happening, you know that the kingdom of God **is** near.
21: 37   Each day Jesus **was** teaching at the temple, and each evening he
22: 3   Then Satan entered Judas, called Iscariot, **one** of the Twelve.
22: 11   Where **is** the guest room, where I may eat the Passover with my
22: 19   and gave it to them, saying, "This **is** my body given for you;
22: 23   among themselves which of them *it might* **be** who would do this.
22: 24   among them as to which of them was considered *to* **be** greatest.
22: 27   one who is at the table? But I **am** among you as one who serves.
22: 28   You **are** those who have stood by me in my trials.
22: 33   replied, "Lord, *I* **am** ready to go with you to prison and to death."
22: 38   "See, Lord, here are two swords." "*That* **is** enough," he replied.
22: 49   When Jesus' followers saw what *was going to* **happen**, they said,
22: 53   Every day I **was** with you in the temple courts, and you did not lay
22: 53   not lay a hand on me. But this **is** your hour—when darkness reigns."
22: 56   She looked closely at him and said, "This man **was** with him."
22: 58   later someone else saw him and said, "You also **are** one of them."
22: 58   said, "You also are one of them." "Man, *I* **am** not!" Peter replied.
22: 59   "Certainly this fellow **was** with him, for he is a Galilean."
22: 59   "Certainly this fellow was with him, for *he* **is** a Galilean."
22: 64   blindfolded him and demanded, "Prophesy! Who **hit** [+4091] you?"
22: 67   "If you **are** the Christ," they said, "tell us." Jesus answered, "If I tell
22: 69   the Son of Man *will* **be** seated at the right hand of the mighty God."
22: 70   They all asked, "**Are** you then the Son of God?" He replied,
22: 70   then the Son of God?" He replied, "You are right in saying I **am**."

23: 2 He opposes payment of taxes to Caesar and claims *to* be Christ,
23: 3 So Pilate asked Jesus, "**Are** you the king of the Jews?" "Yes,
23: 6 On hearing this, Pilate asked if the man **was** a Galilean.
23: 7 When he learned that Jesus **was** under Herod's jurisdiction,
23: 7 he sent him to Herod, who **was** also in Jerusalem at that time.
23: 8 because for a long time *he had* **been** wanting to see him.
23:12 became friends—**before this** *they had* **been** [+4732] enemies.
23:15 as you can see, he *has* **done** [+4556] nothing to deserve death.
23:19 (Barabbas *had* **been** thrown into prison for an insurrection in the
23:35 let him save himself if he **is** the Christ of God, the Chosen One."
23:37 and said, "If you **are** the king of the Jews, save yourself."
23:38 *There* **was** a written notice above him, which read: THIS IS THE
23:39 at him: "**Aren't** [+4049] you the Christ? Save yourself and us!"
23:40 you fear God," he said, "since *you* **are** under the same sentence?
23:43 "I tell you the truth, today *you will* **be** with me in paradise."
23:44 *It* **was** now about the sixth hour, and darkness came over the whole
23:47 praised God and said, "Surely this **was** a righteous man."
23:51 who *had* not **consented** [+5163] to their decision and action.
23:53 it in a tomb cut in the rock, one in which no one *had* yet **been** laid.
23:54 *It* **was** Preparation Day, and the Sabbath was about to begin.
23:55 The women who *had* **come with** [+5302] Jesus from Galilee
24: 6 *He* **is** not here; he has risen! Remember how he told you, while he
24: 6 Remember how he told you, *while he* **was** still with you in Galilee:
24:10 *It* **was** Mary Magdalene, Joanna, Mary the mother of James,
24:13 Now that same day two of them **were** going to a village called
24:21 but we had hoped that he **was** the one who was going to redeem
24:29 But they urged him strongly, "Stay with us, for *it* **is** nearly evening;
24:32 "**Were** not our hearts burning within us while he talked with us on
24:38 He said to them, "Why **are** *you* troubled, and why do doubts rise in
24:39 *It* **is** I myself! Touch me and see; a ghost does not have flesh
24:44 He said to them, "This is what I told you *while I* **was** still with you:
24:53 And *they* **stayed** continually at the temple, praising God.

Jn 1: 1 In the beginning **was** the Word, and the Word was with God,
1: 1 the Word, and the Word **was** with God, and the Word was God.
1: 1 the Word, and the Word **was** with God, and the Word was God.
1: 2 He **was** with God in the beginning.
1: 4 In him **was** life, and that life was the light of men.
1: 4 In him **was** life, and that life **was** the light of men.
1: 8 He himself **was** not the light; he came only as a witness to the
1: 9 The true light that gives light to every man **was** coming into the
1:10 *He* **was** in the world, and though the world was made through him,
1:15 He cries out, saying, "This **was** he of whom I said, 'He who comes
1:15 who comes after me has surpassed me because *he* **was** before me.' "
1:18 but God the One and Only, who **is** at the Father's side, has made
1:19 Now this **was** John's testimony when the Jews of Jerusalem sent
1:19 Jews of Jerusalem sent priests and Levites to ask him who he **was**.
1:20 did not fail to confess, but confessed freely, "I **am** not the Christ."
1:21 him, "Then who are you? **Are** *you* Elijah?" He said, "I am not."
1:21 him, "Then who are you? Are *you* Elijah?" He said, "*I* **am** not."
1:21 him, "I am not." "**Are** you the Prophet?" He answered, "No."
1:22 Finally they said, "Who **are** *you*? Give us an answer to take back to
1:24 Now some Pharisees *who had* **been** sent
1:25 "Why then do you baptize if you **are** not the Christ, nor Elijah,
1:27 after me, the thongs of whose sandals I **am** not worthy to untie."
1:28 Bethany on the other side of the Jordan, where John **was** baptizing.
1:30 This **is** the one I meant when I said, 'A man who comes after me
1:30 who comes after me has surpassed me because *he* **was** before me.'
1:33 and remain is he who will baptize with the Holy Spirit.'
1:34 I have seen and I testify that this **is** the Son of God."
1:39 and spent that day with him. *It* **was** about the tenth hour.
1:40 **was** one of the two who heard what John had said and who had
1:41 tell him, "We have found the Messiah" (that **is** [+3493], the Christ).
1:42 Jesus looked at him and said, "You **are** Simon son of John.
1:44 Philip, like Andrew and Peter, **was** from the town of Bethsaida.
1:46 "Nazareth! Can anything good **come** from there?" Nathanael asked.
1:47 of him, "Here is a true Israelite, in whom *there* **is** nothing false."
1:48 "I saw you *while you* **were** still under the fig tree before Philip
1:49 Then Nathanael declared, "Rabbi, you **are** the Son of God;
1:49 "Rabbi, you are the Son of God; you **are** the King of Israel."
2: 1 a wedding took place at Cana in Galilee. Jesus' mother **was** there,
2: 6 Nearby **stood** [+3023] six stone water jars, the kind used by the
2: 9 He did not realize where *it had* **come** from, though the servants
2:13 When *it* **was** almost time for the Jewish Passover, Jesus went up to
2:17 His disciples remembered that *it* **is** written: "Zeal for your house
2:23 Now while *he* **was** in Jerusalem at the Passover Feast,
2:25 need man's testimony about man, for he knew what **was** in a man.

3: 1 Now *there* **was** a man of the Pharisees named Nicodemus,
3: 2 the miraculous signs you are doing if God **were** not with him."
3: 4 "How can a man be born *when he* **is** old?" Nicodemus asked.
3: 6 Flesh gives birth to flesh, [**NIE**] but the Spirit gives birth to spirit.
3: 6 gives birth to flesh, but the Spirit gives birth to spirit. [**NIE**]
3: 8 or where it is going. So *it* **is** with everyone born of the Spirit."
3:10 "You **are** Israel's teacher," said Jesus, "and do you not understand
3:19 This **is** the verdict: Light has come into the world, but men loved
3:19 men loved darkness instead of light because their deeds **were** evil.
3:21 that what he has done *has been* **done** [+2237] through God."
3:23 Now John also **was** baptizing at Aenon near Salim, because there
3:23 baptizing at Aenon near Salim, because *there* **was** plenty of water,
3:24 (This was before John **was** put in prison.)
3:26 that man who **was** with you on the other side of the Jordan—
3:27 "A man can receive only *what* **is** given him from heaven.
3:28 testify that I said, 'I **am** not the Christ but am sent ahead of him.'
3:28 testify that I said, 'I am not the Christ but **am** sent ahead of him.'
3:29 The bride [**NIE**] belongs to the bridegroom. The friend who
3:31 "The one who comes from above **is** above all; the one who is from
3:31 the one *who* **is** from the earth belongs to the earth, and speaks as
3:31 the one who is from the earth **belongs** [+1666] **to** the earth,
3:31 one from the earth. The one who comes from heaven **is** above all.
3:33 The man who has accepted it has certified that God **is** truthful.
4: 6 Jacob's well **was** there, and Jesus, tired as he was from the journey,
4: 6 the journey, sat down by the well. *It* **was** about the sixth hour.
4: 9 woman said to him, "You **are** a Jew and I am a Samaritan woman.
4: 9 woman said to him, "You are a Jew and I **am** a Samaritan woman.
4:10 "If you knew the gift of God and who *it* **is** that asks you for a drink,
4:11 woman said, "you have nothing to draw with and the well **is** deep.
4:12 **Are** you greater than our father Jacob, who gave us the well
4:18 had five husbands, and the man you now have **is** not your husband.
4:19 "Sir," the woman said, "I can see that you **are** a prophet.
4:20 but you Jews claim that the place where we must worship **is** in
4:22 we worship what we do know, for salvation **is** from the Jews.
4:23 and *has* now **come** when the true worshipers will worship the
4:26 Then Jesus declared, "I who speak to you **am** he."
4:29 a man who told me everything I ever did. Could this **be** the Christ?"
4:34 "**is** to do the will of him who sent me and to finish his work.
4:35 Do you not say, [**NIE**] 'Four months more and then the harvest'?
4:35 open your eyes and look at the fields! *They* **are** ripe for harvest.
4:37 Thus the saying 'One [**RPG**] sows and another reaps' is true.
4:37 Thus the saying 'One sows and another reaps' **is** true.
4:42 and we know that this man really **is** the Savior of the world."
4:46 And *there* **was** a certain royal official whose son lay sick at
5: 1 Jesus went up to Jerusalem for [**NIE**] a feast of the Jews.
5: 2 Now *there* **is** in Jerusalem near the Sheep Gate a pool, which in
5: 5 One who **was** there had been an invalid for thirty-eight years.
5: 9 and walked. The day on which this took place **was** a Sabbath,
5:10 the Jews said to the man who had been healed, "*It* **is** the Sabbath;
5:12 him, "Who **is** this fellow who told you to pick it up and walk?"
5:13 The man who was healed had no idea who *it* **was**, for Jesus had
5:13 it was, for Jesus had slipped away into the crowd that **was** there.
5:15 and told the Jews that *it* **was** Jesus who had made him well.
5:25 and *has* now **come** when the dead will hear the voice of the Son of
5:27 he has given him authority to judge because *he* **is** the Son of Man.
5:30 I judge only as I hear, and my judgment **is** just, for I seek not to
5:31 "If I testify about myself, my testimony **is** not valid.
5:32 *There* **is** another who testifies in my favor, and I know that his
5:32 in my favor, and I know that his testimony about me **is** valid.
5:35 John **was** a lamp that burned and gave light, and you chose for a
5:39 possess eternal life. These **are** the Scriptures that testify about me,
5:45 the Father. Your accuser **is** Moses, on whom your hopes are set.
6: 4 The Jewish Passover Feast **was** near.
6: 9 "Here **is** a boy with five small barley loaves and two small fish,
6: 9 but **how far will they go** [+4047+5515] among so many?"
6:10 *There* **was** plenty of grass in that place, and the men sat down,
6:14 to say, "Surely this **is** the Prophet who is to come into the world."
6:20 But he said to them, "*It* **is** I; don't be afraid."
6:22 shore of the lake realized that only one boat *had* **been** there,
6:24 Once the crowd realized that neither Jesus nor his disciples **were**
6:29 Jesus answered, "The work of God **is** this: to believe in the one he
6:31 Our forefathers ate the manna in the desert; as it **is** written:
6:33 For the bread of God **is** he who comes down from heaven
6:35 Then Jesus declared, "I **am** the bread of life. He who comes to me
6:39 And this **is** the will of him who sent me, that I shall lose none of all
6:40 For my Father's will **is** that everyone who looks to the Son

6:41 because he said, "I **am** the bread that came down from heaven."
6:42 They said, "**Is** this not Jesus, the son of Joseph, whose father
6:45 *It* **is** written in the Prophets: 'They will all be taught by God.'
6:45 It is written in the Prophets: '*They will* all **be** taught by God.'
6:46 No one has seen the Father except the one *who* **is** from God;
6:48 I **am** the bread of life.
6:50 But here **is** the bread that comes down from heaven, which a man
6:51 I **am** the living bread that came down from heaven. If anyone eats
6:51 This bread **is** my flesh, which I will give for the life of the world."
6:55 For my flesh **is** real food and my blood is real drink.
6:55 For my flesh is real food and my blood **is** real drink.
6:58 This **is** the bread that came down from heaven. Your forefathers
6:60 On hearing it, many of his disciples said, "This **is** a hard teaching.
6:62 What if you see the Son of Man ascend to where *he* **was** before!
6:63 The Spirit gives **life** [+*2443*]; the flesh counts for nothing.
6:63 The words I have spoken to you **are** spirit and they are life.
6:63 The words I have spoken to you are spirit and *they* **are** life.
6:64 Yet *there* **are** some of you who do not believe." For Jesus had
6:64 known from the beginning which of them *did* not **believe** [+*4409*]
6:64 of them did not believe and who *would* **betray** [+*4140*] him.
6:65 one can come to me unless the Father *has* **enabled** [+*1443*] him."
6:69 We believe and know that you **are** the Holy One of God."
6:70 "Have I not chosen you, the Twelve? Yet one of you **is** a devil!"
6:71 who, **though** [UBS-] one of the Twelve, was later to betray him.)
7: 2 But *when* the Jewish Feast of Tabernacles **was** near,
7: 4 No one who wants *to* **become** a public figure acts in secret.
7: 6 "The right time for me has not yet come; for you any time **is** right.
7: 7 hate you, but it hates me because I testify that what it does **is** evil.
7:11 the Jews were watching for him and asking, "Where **is** that man?"
7:12 Among the crowds *there* **was** widespread whispering about him.
7:12 Some said, "*He* **is** a good man." Others replied, "No, he deceives
7:16 Jesus answered, "My teaching **is** not my own. It comes from him
7:17 he will find out whether my teaching **comes** from God or whether I
7:18 but he who works for the honor of the one who sent him **is** a man
7:18 who sent him is a man of truth; *there* **is** nothing false about him.
7:22 you circumcision (though actually *it did* not **come** from Moses,
7:25 began to ask, "**Isn't** [+*4024*] this the man they are trying to kill?
7:26 Have the authorities really concluded that he **is** the Christ?
7:27 But we know where this man **is** from; when the Christ comes,
7:27 when the Christ comes, no one will know where *he* **is** from."
7:28 cried out, "Yes, you know me, and you know where *I* **am** from.
7:28 I am not here on my own, but he who sent me **is** true. You do not
7:29 but I know him because *I* **am** from him and he sent me."
7:33 "*I* **am** with you for only a short time, and then I go to the one who
7:34 but you will not find me; and where *I* **am**, you cannot come."
7:36 What *did* he **mean** when he said, 'You will look for me, but you
7:36 but you will not find me,' and 'Where *I* **am**, you cannot come'?"
7:39 Up to that time the Spirit *had* not **been given**, since Jesus had not
7:40 words, some of the people said, "Surely this man **is** the Prophet."
7:41 Others said, "He **is** the Christ." Still others asked, "How can the
7:42 David's family and from Bethlehem, the town where David **lived**?"
7:49 this mob that knows nothing of the law—*there* **is** a curse on them."
7:50 had gone to Jesus earlier and *who* **was** one of their own number,
7:52 They replied, "**Are** you from Galilee, too? Look into it, and you
8: 9 until only Jesus was left, with the woman *still* **standing** there.
8:10 Jesus straightened up and asked her, "Woman, where **are** *they*?
8:12 spoke again to the people, he said, "I **am** the light of the world."
8:13 appearing as your own witness; your testimony **is** not valid."
8:14 my testimony **is** valid, for I know where I came from and where I
8:16 But if I do judge, my decisions **are** right, because I am not alone.
8:16 But if I do judge, my decisions are right, because *I* **am** not alone.
8:17 In your own Law it is written that the testimony of two men **is**
8:18 I **am** one who testifies for myself; my other witness is the Father,
8:19 Then they asked him, "Where **is** your father?" "You do not know
8:23 But he continued, "You **are** from below; I am from above.
8:23 But he continued, "You are from below; I **am** from above. You are
8:23 I am from above. You **are** of this world; I am not of this world.
8:23 I am from above. You are of this world; I **am** not of this world.
8:24 if you do not believe that I **am** ₁the one I claim to be₎, you will
8:25 "Who **are** you?" they asked. "Just what I have been claiming all
8:26 But he who sent me **is** reliable, and what I have heard from him I
8:28 then you will know that I **am** ₁the one I claim to be₎ and that I do
8:29 The one who sent me **is** with me; he has not left me alone,
8:31 Jesus said, "If you hold to my teaching, *you* **are** really my disciples.
8:33 "*We* **are** Abraham's descendants and have never been slaves of
8:34 "I tell you the truth, everyone who sins **is** a slave to sin.

8:36 So if the Son sets you free, *you will* **be** free indeed.
8:37 I know *you* **are** Abraham's descendants. Yet you are ready to kill
8:39 "Abraham **is** our father," they answered. "If you were Abraham's
8:39 "If *you were* Abraham's children," said Jesus, "then you would do
8:42 Jesus said to them, "If God **were** your Father, you would love me,
8:44 You **belong** [+*1666*] **to** your father, the devil, and you want to
8:44 He **was** a murderer from the beginning, not holding to the truth,
8:44 the beginning, not holding to the truth, for *there* **is** no truth in him.
8:44 he speaks his native language, for *he* **is** a liar and the father of lies.
8:47 He *who* **belongs** [+*1666*] **to** God hears what God says. The reason
8:47 The reason you do not hear is that *you do* not **belong** [+*1666*] **to**
8:48 "Aren't we right in saying that you **are** a Samaritan
8:50 glory for myself; but *there* **is** one who seeks it, and he is the judge.
8:53 **Are** you greater than our father Abraham? He died, and so did the
8:54 Jesus replied, "If I glorify myself, my glory **means** nothing.
8:54 My Father, whom you claim as **[NIE]** your God, is the one who
8:54 whom you claim as your God, **is** the one who glorifies me.
8:55 If I said I did not, *I would* **be** a liar like you, but I do know him
8:58 you the truth," Jesus answered, "before Abraham was born, I **am**!"
9: 4 As long as *it* **is** day, we must do the work of him who sent me.
9: 5 While *I* **am** in the world, I am the light of the world."
9: 5 While I am in the world, *I* **am** the light of the world."
9: 8 and those who had formerly seen him **[NIE]** begging asked,
9: 8 "**Isn't** [+*4024*] this the same man who used to sit and beg?"
9: 9 Some claimed that he **was**. Others said, "No, he only looks like
9: 9 Others said, "No, *he* only **looks** like him." But he himself insisted,
9: 9 he only looks like him." But he himself insisted, "I **am** the man."
9:12 "Where **is** this man?" they asked him. "I don't know," he said.
9:14 Jesus had made the mud and opened the man's eyes **was** a Sabbath.
9:16 Some of the Pharisees said, "This man **is** not from God, for he does
9:16 can a sinner do such miraculous signs?" So they **were** divided.
9:17 It was your eyes he opened." The man replied, "*He* **is** a prophet."
9:18 The Jews still did not believe that *he had* **been** blind and had
9:19 "Is this your son?" they asked. "Is this the one you say was born
9:20 "We know he **is** our son," the parents answered, "and we know he
9:24 A second time they summoned the man who *had* **been** blind.
9:24 "Give glory to God," they said. "We know this man **is** a sinner."
9:25 He replied, "Whether he **is** a sinner or not, I don't know. One thing
9:25 I don't know. One thing I do know. *I* **was** blind but now I see!"
9:28 they hurled insults at him and said, "You **are** this fellow's disciple!
9:28 "You are this fellow's disciple! We **are** disciples of Moses!
9:29 but as for this fellow, we don't even know where *he* **comes** from."
9:30 The man answered, "Now that **is** remarkable! You don't know
9:30 You don't know where *he* **comes** from, yet he opened my eyes.
9:31 to sinners. He listens to the **[NIE]** godly man who does his will.
9:33 If this man **were** not from God, he could do nothing."
9:36 "Who **is** he, sir?" the man asked. "Tell me so that I may believe in
9:37 "You have now seen him; in fact, he **is** the one speaking with you."
9:40 Some Pharisees *who* **were** with him heard him say this and asked,
9:40 with him heard him say this and asked, "What? **Are** we blind too?"
9:41 Jesus said, "If *you* **were** blind, you would not be guilty of sin;
10: 1 the gate, but climbs in by some other way, **is** a thief and a robber.
10: 2 The man who enters by the gate **is** the shepherd of his sheep.
10: 6 of speech, but they did not understand what *he* **was** telling them.
10: 7 Jesus said again, "I tell you the truth, I **am** the gate for the sheep.
10: 8 All who ever came before me **were** thieves and robbers,
10: 9 I **am** the gate; whoever enters through me will be saved. He will
10:11 "I **am** the good shepherd. The good shepherd lays down his life for
10:12 The hired hand **is** not the shepherd who owns the sheep. So when
10:12 The hired hand is not the shepherd who **owns** [+*2625*] the sheep.
10:13 The man runs away because *he* **is** a hired hand and cares nothing
10:14 "I **am** the good shepherd; I know my sheep and my sheep know
10:16 I have other sheep that **are** not of this sheep pen. I must bring them
10:21 "These **are** not the sayings of a man possessed by a demon.
10:22 Then came the Feast of Dedication at Jerusalem. *It* **was** winter,
10:24 will you keep us in suspense? If you **are** the Christ, tell us plainly."
10:26 but you do not believe because *you* **are** not my sheep.
10:29 My Father, who has given them to me, **is** greater than all; no one
10:30 I and the Father **are** one."
10:33 for blasphemy, because you, **[NIE]** a mere man, claim to be God."
10:34 Jesus answered them, "**Is** *it* not written in your Law, 'I have said
10:34 "Is it not written in your Law, 'I have said *you* **are** gods'?
10:36 do you accuse me of blasphemy because I said, '*I* **am** God's Son'?
10:40 to the place where John *had* **been** baptizing in the early days.
10:41 a miraculous sign, all that John said about this man **was** true."
11: 1 Now a man named Lazarus **was** sick. He was from Bethany,

11: 2 **was** the same one who poured perfume on the Lord and wiped his
11: 4 heard this, Jesus said, "This sickness *will* not **end in** [+*4639*] death.
11: 6 that Lazarus was sick, he stayed where he **was** two more days.
11: 9 Jesus answered, "**Are** *there* not twelve hours of daylight?
11:10 It is when he walks by night that he stumbles, for he **has** no light."
11:15 and for your sake I am glad *I* **was** not there, so that you may
11:18 Bethany **was** less than two miles from Jerusalem,
11:21 "Lord," Martha said to Jesus, "if *you* had **been** here, my brother
11:25 Jesus said to her, "**I am** the resurrection and the life. He who
11:27 "Yes, Lord," she told him, "I believe that you **are** the Christ,
11:30 the village, but **was** still at the place where Martha had met him.
11:31 When the Jews who *had* **been** with Mary in the house, comforting
11:32 When Mary reached the place where Jesus **was** and saw him,
11:32 saw him, she fell at his feet and said, "Lord, if *you* had **been** here,
11:38 to the tomb. *It* **was** a cave with a stone laid across the entrance.
11:39 "by this time there is a bad odor, for *he* has **been** there four days."
11:49 named Caiaphas, *who* **was** high priest that year,
11:51 but **as** high priest that year he prophesied that Jesus would die for
11:55 When *it* **was** almost time for the Jewish Passover, many went up
11:57 had given orders that if anyone found out where Jesus **was**,
12: 1 before the Passover, Jesus arrived at Bethany, where Lazarus **lived**,
12: 2 while Lazarus **was** among those reclining at the table with him.
12: 6 because he cared about the poor but because he **was** a thief;
12: 9 Meanwhile a large crowd of Jews found out that Jesus **was** there
12:14 Jesus found a young donkey and sat upon it, as *it* **is** written,
12:16 did they realize that these things *had* **been** written about him
12:17 Now the crowd that **was** with him when he called Lazarus from the
12:20 Now *there* **were** some Greeks among those who went up to
12:26 me must follow me; and where **I am**, my servant also will be.
12:26 me must follow me; and where I am, my servant also *will* **be**.
12:31 Now **is** the time for judgment on this world; now the prince of this
12:34 'The Son of Man must be lifted up'? Who **is** this 'Son of Man'?"
12:35 "You *are going to* **have** the light just a little while longer.
12:50 I know that his command **leads to** eternal life. So whatever I say is
13: 5 drying them with the towel that **was** wrapped around him.
13:10 has had a bath needs only to wash his feet; his whole body **is** clean.
13:10 body is clean. And you are **clean**, though not every one of you."
13:11 to betray him, and that was why he said not every one **was** clean.
13:13 call me 'Teacher' and 'Lord,' and rightly so, for that is what *I* **am**.
13:16 I tell you the truth, no servant **is** greater than his master, nor is a
13:17 that you know these things, *you will* **be** blessed if you do them.
13:19 so that when it does happen you will believe that I **am** He.
13:23 the disciple whom Jesus loved, **was** reclining next to him.
13:24 to this disciple and said, "Ask him which **[NIE]** one he means."
13:25 Leaning back against Jesus, he asked him, "Lord, who **is** *it*?"
13:26 "*It* **is** the one to whom I will give this piece of bread when I have
13:30 soon as Judas had taken the bread, he went out. And *it* **was** night.
13:33 "My children, *I will* **be** with you only a little longer. You will look
13:35 By this all men will know that *you* **are** my disciples, if you love
14: 2 In my Father's house **are** many rooms; if it were not so, I would
14: 3 and take you to be with me that you also *may* **be** where I am.
14: 3 and take you to be with me that you also *may* **be** where I **am**.
14: 6 Jesus answered, "I **am** the way and the truth and the life. No one
14: 9 Philip, even *after I have* **been** among you such a long time?
14:10 you believe that I am in the Father, and that the Father **is** in me?
14:16 and he will give you another Counselor to **be** with you forever—
14:17 But you know him, for he lives with you and *will* **be** in you.
14:21 has my commands and obeys them, he **is** the one who loves me.
14:24 These words you hear **are** not my own; they belong to the Father
14:28 glad that I am going to the Father, for the Father **is** greater than I.
15: 1 "I **am** the true vine, and my Father is the gardener.
15: 1 "I **am** the true vine, and my Father **is** the gardener.
15: 3 You **are** already clean because of the word I have spoken to you.
15: 5 "I **am** the vine; you are the branches. If a man remains in me
15:11 I have told you this so that my joy *may* **be** in you and that your joy
15:12 My command **is** this: Love each other as I have loved you.
15:14 You **are** my friends if you do what I command.
15:19 If *you* **belonged** [+*1666*] **to** the world, it would love you as its
15:19 As it is, *you do* not **belong** [+*1666*] **to** the world, but I have chosen
15:20 'No servant **is** greater than his master.' If they persecuted me,
15:27 also must testify, for *you have* **been** with me from the beginning.
16: 4 I warned you. I did not tell you this at first because *I* **was** with you.
16:15 All that belongs to the Father **is** mine. That is why I said the Spirit
16:17 of his disciples said to one another, "What *does he* **mean** by saying,
16:18 They kept asking, "What *does he* **mean** by 'a little while'?
16:24 my name. Ask and you will receive, and your joy *will* **be** complete.

16:32 leave me all alone. Yet *I* **am** not alone, for my Father is with me.
16:32 leave me all alone. Yet I am not alone, for my Father **is** with me.
17: 3 Now this **is** eternal life: that they may know you, the only true
17: 5 presence with the glory I had with you before the world **began**.
17: 6 *They* **were** yours; you gave them to me and they have obeyed your
17: 7 Now they know that everything you have given me **comes** from
17: 9 for the world, but for those you have given me, for *they* **are** yours.
17:10 All I have **is** yours, and all you have is mine. And glory has come
17:11 *I will* **remain** in the world no longer, but they are still in the world,
17:11 I will remain in the world no longer, but they **are** *still* in the world,
17:11 the name you gave me—so that *they may* **be** one as we are one.
17:12 While *I* **was** with them, I protected them and kept them safe by
17:14 for *they* **are** not of the world any more than I am of the world.
17:14 for they are not of the world any more than I **am** of the world.
17:16 *They* **are** not of the world, even as I am not of it.
17:16 They are not of the world, even as I **am** not of it.
17:17 Sanctify them by the truth; your word **is** truth.
17:19 them I sanctify myself, that they too *may be* truly **sanctified** [+*39*].
17:21 that all of them *may* **be** one, Father, just as you are in me
17:21 *May* they also **be** in us so that the world may believe that you have
17:22 the glory that you gave me, that *they may* **be** one as we are one:
17:23 *May they* **be** brought to complete unity to let the world know that
17:24 I want those you have given me to **be** with me where I am,
17:24 I want those you have given me to be with me where I **am**,
17:26 you known in order that the love you have for me *may* **be** in them
18: 1 On the other side *there* **was** an olive grove, and he and his
18: 5 "Jesus of Nazareth," they replied. "I **am** he," Jesus said.
18: 6 When Jesus said, "I **am** he," they drew back and fell to the ground.
18: 8 "I told you that I **am** he," Jesus answered. "If you are looking for
18:10 cutting off his right ear. (The servant's name **was** Malchus.)
18:13 *who* **was** the father-in-law of Caiaphas, the high priest that year.
18:13 the father-in-law of Caiaphas, **[RPG]** the high priest that year.
18:14 Caiaphas **was** the one who had advised the Jews that it would be
18:15 Because this disciple **was** known to the high priest, he went with
18:17 "*You* **are** not one of his disciples, are you?" the girl at the door
18:17 are you?" the girl at the door asked Peter. He replied, "*I* **am** not."
18:18 *It* **was** cold, and the servants and officials stood around a fire they
18:18 keep warm. Peter also **was** standing with them, warming himself.
18:25 As Simon Peter **stood** [+*2705*] warming himself, he was asked,
18:25 he was asked, "*You* **are** not one of his disciples, are you?"
18:25 not one of his disciples, are you?" He denied it, saying, "*I* **am** not."
18:26 **[NIE]** a relative of the man whose ear Peter had cut off,
18:28 By now *it* **was** early morning, and to avoid ceremonial uncleanness
18:30 "If he **were** not a criminal," they replied, "we would not have
18:33 summoned Jesus and asked him, "**Are** you the king of the Jews?"
18:35 "**Am** I a Jew?" Pilate replied. "It was your people and your chief
18:36 Jesus said, "My kingdom **is** not of this world. If it were,
18:36 If it **were**, my servants would fight to prevent my arrest by the
18:36 arrest by the Jews. But now my kingdom **is** from another place."
18:37 "*You* **are** a king, then!" said Pilate. Jesus answered, "You are right
18:37 Jesus answered, "You are right in saying I **am** a king. In fact,
18:37 to testify to the truth. Everyone **on the side** of truth listens to me."
18:38 "What **is** truth?" Pilate asked. With this he went out again to the
18:39 But *it* **is** your custom for me to release to you one prisoner at the
18:40 Now Barabbas **had taken part in a rebellion** [+*3334*].
19: 9 "Where *do you* **come** from?" he asked Jesus, but Jesus gave him no
19:11 "You would have no power over me if *it* **were** not given to you
19:12 kept shouting, "If you let this man go, *you* **are** no friend of Caesar.
19:14 *It* **was** the day of Preparation of Passover Week, about the sixth
19:14 day of Preparation of Passover Week, **[NIE]** about the sixth hour.
19:19 had a notice prepared and fastened to the cross. *It* **read** [+*1211*]:
19:20 this sign, for the place where Jesus was crucified **was** near the city,
19:20 the city, and the sign was written in Aramaic, Latin and Greek.
19:21 of the Jews,' but that this man claimed *to* **be** king of the Jews."
19:23 This garment **was** seamless, woven in one piece from top to
19:24 they said to one another. "Let's decide by lot who *will* **get** it."
19:31 Now *it* **was** the day of Preparation, and the next day was to be a
19:31 day of Preparation, and the next day **was** to be a special Sabbath.
19:35 The man who saw it has given testimony, and his testimony **is** true.
19:38 *Now* Joseph **was** a disciple of Jesus, but secretly because he feared
19:40 strips of linen. *This* **was** in accordance with Jewish burial customs.
19:41 *there* **was** a garden, and in the garden a new tomb, in which no one
19:41 and in the garden a new tomb, in which no one *had* ever **been** laid.
19:42 was the Jewish day of Preparation and since the tomb **was** nearby,
20: 1 Early on the first day of the week, *while it* **was** still dark,
20: 7 as well as the burial cloth that *had* **been** around Jesus' head.

20: 14 saw Jesus standing there, but she did not realize that *it* was Jesus.
20: 15 Thinking *he* was the gardener, she said, "Sir, if you have carried
20: 19 **On the evening** [+4068] of that first day of the week,
20: 19 *when* the disciples were together, with the doors locked for fear of
20: 24 one of the Twelve, was not with the disciples when Jesus came.
20: 26 A week later his disciples were in the house again, and Thomas
20: 30 the presence of his disciples, which **are** not recorded in this book.
20: 31 But these are written that you may believe that Jesus **is** the Christ,
21: 2 the sons of Zebedee, and two other disciples were together.
21: 4 on the shore, but the disciples did not realize that *it* was Jesus.
21: 7 Then the disciple whom Jesus loved said to Peter, "*It* is the Lord!"
21: 7 As soon as Simon Peter heard him say, "*It* is the Lord," he wrapped
21: 7 he wrapped his outer garment around him (for *he* **had** taken it off)
21: 8 of fish, for *they* were not far from shore, about a hundred yards.
21: 11 full of large fish, 153, but even **with** so many the net was not torn.
21: 12 None of the disciples dared ask him, "Who **are** you?"
21: 12 dared ask him, "Who are you?" They knew *it* was the Lord.
21: 18 when *you* were younger you dressed yourself and went where you
21: 20 at the supper and had said, "Lord, who **is** going to betray you?")
21: 24 This is the disciple who testifies to these things and who wrote
21: 24 and who wrote them down. We know that his testimony **is** true.
21: 25 [NIE] Jesus did many other things as well. If every one of them
Ac   1: 7 "*It* **is** not for you to know the times or dates the Father has set by
1: 8 and *you will* **be** my witnesses in Jerusalem, and in all Judea
1: 10 *They* were looking intently up into the sky as he was going,
1: 12 the Mount of Olives, [NIE] a Sabbath day's walk from the city.
1: 13 they went upstairs to the room where they were staying.
1: 14 They all **joined** together **constantly** [+4674] in prayer, along with
1: 15 stood up among the believers (a group **numbering** about a hundred
1: 17 *he* was one of our number and shared in this ministry."
1: 19 that field in their language Akeldama, that **is**, Field of Blood.)
1: 20 *let there* **be** no one to dwell in it,' and, " 'May another take his place
2: 1 the day of Pentecost came, *they* were all together in one place.
2: 2 from heaven and filled the whole house where *they* were sitting.
2: 5 Now *there* were staying in Jerusalem God-fearing Jews from
2: 7 they asked: "**Are** not all these men who are speaking Galileans?
2: 12 they asked one another, "What *does* this **mean** [+2527]?"
2: 13 fun of them and said, "*They* **have** **had too much** [+3551] wine."
2: 14 of you who live in Jerusalem, *let* me **explain** [+1196] this to you;
2: 15 men are not drunk, as you suppose. **It's** only nine in the morning!
2: 16 No, this **is** what was spoken by the prophet Joel:
2: 17 [NIE] " 'In the last days, God says, I will pour out my Spirit on all
2: 21 And [NIE] everyone who calls on the name of the Lord will be
2: 24 because *it* was impossible for death to keep its hold on him.
2: 25 before me. Because *he* **is** at my right hand, I will not be shaken.
2: 29 David died and was buried, and his tomb **is** here to this day.
2: 32 has raised this Jesus to life, and we **are** all witnesses of the fact.
2: 39 The promise **is** for you and your children and for all who are far
2: 42 *They* **devoted** *themselves* **to** [+4674] the apostles' teaching
2: 44 All the believers were together and had everything in common.
3: 10 they recognized him as [NIE] the same man who used to sit
3: 15 but God raised him from the dead. We **are** witnesses of this.
3: 23 [NIE] Anyone who does not listen to him will be completely cut
3: 25 And you **are** heirs of the prophets and of the covenant God made
4: 3 They seized Peter and John, and because *it* was evening, they put
4: 6 Alexander and the other men [NIE] of the high priest's family.
4: 10 then know [RPG] this, you and all the people of Israel: It is by the
4: 11 He **is** " 'the stone you builders rejected, which has become the
4: 12 Salvation *is* **found** in no one else, for there is no other name under
4: 12 for *there* **is** no other name under heaven given to men by which we
4: 13 courage of Peter and John and realized that *they* were unschooled,
4: 13 and they took note that *these men had* **been** with Jesus.
4: 19 "Judge for yourselves whether *it* **is** right in God's sight to obey you
4: 22 For the man who was miraculously healed was over forty years
4: 31 After they prayed, the place where *they* were meeting was shaken.
4: 32 All the believers were one in heart and mind. No one claimed that
4: 32 No one claimed that any of his possessions was his own, but they
4: 32 his possessions was his own, but they shared everything they **had**.
4: 33 resurrection of the Lord Jesus, and much grace was upon them all.
4: 34 *There* were no needy persons among them. For from time to time
4: 36 whom the apostles called Barnabas (which **means** [+3493] Son of
5: 12 And all the believers *used to* **meet** together in Solomon's
5: 17 his associates, who were members of the party of the Sadducees,
5: 25 The men you put in jail **are** standing in the temple courts teaching
5: 32 We **are** witnesses of these things, and so is the Holy Spirit,
5: 36 Some time ago Theudas appeared, claiming *to* **be** somebody,

5: 38 For if their purpose or activity **is** of human origin, it will fail.
5: 39 But if *it* **is** from God, you will not be able to stop these men;
6: 2 "*It would* not **be** right for us to neglect the ministry of the word of
7: 2 to our father Abraham *while he* was *still* in Mesopotamia,
7: 5 possess the land, *even though at that time* Abraham **had** no child.
7: 6 'Your descendants *will* **be** strangers in a country not their own,
7: 9 they sold him as a slave into Egypt. But God was with him
7: 12 When Jacob heard that *there* was grain in Egypt, he sent our
7: 20 At that time Moses was born, and *he* was no ordinary child.
7: 22 wisdom of the Egyptians and was powerful in speech and action.
7: 26 He tried to reconcile them by saying, 'Men, *you* **are** brothers;
7: 33 off your sandals; the place where you are standing **is** holy ground.
7: 37 "This is that Moses who told the Israelites, 'God will send you a
7: 38 He was [+1181] in the assembly in the desert, with the angel who
7: 44 "Our forefathers **had** the tabernacle of the Testimony with them in
8: 1 And Saul was there, giving approval to his death. On that day a
8: 9 all the people of Samaria. He boasted that he was someone great,
8: 10 "This man **is** the divine power known as the Great Power."
8: 13 Simon himself believed and was baptized. And he followed Philip
8: 16 because the Holy Spirit **had** not yet **come upon** [RP21582093]
8: 20 "*May* your money **perish** [+724+1650] with you, because you
8: 21 You **have** no part or share in this ministry, because your heart is
8: 21 share in this ministry, because your heart **is** not right before God.
8: 23 For I see that you **are** full of bitterness and captive to sin."
8: 26 Lord said to Philip, "Go south to the road—[NIE] the desert road—
8: 27 an important official **in charge of** [+2093] all the treasury of
8: 28 and on *his* **way home** [+5715] was sitting in his chariot reading the
8: 32 The eunuch was reading this passage of Scripture: "He was led like
9: 2 so that if he found any there *who* **belonged to** the Way,
9: 5 "Who **are** you, Lord?" Saul asked. "I am Jesus, whom you are
9: 5 Saul asked. "I **am** Jesus, whom you are persecuting," he replied.
9: 9 For three days *he* was blind, and did not eat or drink anything.
9: 10 In Damascus *there* was a disciple named Ananias. The Lord called
9: 15 This man **is** my chosen instrument to carry my name before the
9: 20 At once he began to preach in the synagogues that Jesus **is** the Son
9: 21 "**Isn't** [+4024] he the man who raised havoc in Jerusalem among
9: 22 and baffled the Jews living in Damascus by proving that Jesus **is**
9: 26 were all afraid of him, not believing that *he* *really* was a disciple.
9: 28 So Saul **stayed** with them and moved about freely in Jerusalem,
9: 33 There he found a man named Aeneas, a **paralytic** [+4168] who
9: 36 In Joppa *there* was a disciple named Tabitha (which,
9: 36 is Dorcas), who was always doing good and helping the poor.
9: 38 Lydda was near Joppa; so when the disciples heard that Peter was
9: 38 so when the disciples heard that Peter was in Lydda, they sent two
9: 39 and other clothing that Dorcas had made *while she* was *still* with
10: 4 "What **is** it, Lord?" he asked. The angel answered, "Your prayers
10: 6 He is staying with Simon the tanner, whose house **is** by the sea."
10: 17 While Peter was wondering about the **meaning** [+323+5515] of
10: 21 and said to the men, "**I'm** [+1609] the one you're looking for.
10: 24 Cornelius was expecting them and had called together his relatives
10: 26 made him get up. "Stand up," he said, "I **am** only a man myself."
10: 28 "You are well aware that *it* **is** against our law for a Jew to associate
10: 30 "Four days ago *I* was in my house praying at this hour, at three in
10: 34 realize how true it is that God *does* not **show favoritism** [+4720]
10: 35 but **accepts** [+1283] men from every nation who fear him
10: 36 the good news of peace through Jesus Christ, who **is** Lord of all.
10: 38 were under the power of the devil, because God was with him.
10: 42 and to testify that he **is** the one whom God appointed as judge of
11: 1 and the brothers [NIE] throughout Judea heard that the Gentiles
11: 5 "I was in the city of Joppa praying, and in a trance I saw a vision.
11: 11 to me from Caesarea stopped at the house where *I* was *staying*.
11: 17 the Lord Jesus Christ, who was I to think that I could oppose God?"
11: 20 Some of them, however, [NIE] men from Cyprus and Cyrene,
11: 21 The Lord's hand was with them, and a great number of people
11: 22 News of this reached the ears of the church [NIE] at Jerusalem,
11: 24 *He* was a good man, full of the Holy Spirit and faith, and a great
11: 28 and through the Spirit predicted that a severe famine would **spread**
12: 3 When he saw that *this* **pleased** [+744] the Jews, he proceeded to
12: 3 Peter also. *This* **happened** during the Feast of Unleavened Bread.
12: 5 in prison, but the church was earnestly praying to God for him.
12: 9 but he had no idea that what the angel was doing was really
12: 12 called Mark, where many people **had** gathered and were praying.
12: 15 she kept insisting that it was so, they said, "*It must* **be** his angel."
12: 18 *there* was no small commotion among the soldiers as to what had
12: 20 *He had* **been** quarreling with the people of Tyre and Sidon;

13: 1   In the [NIE] church at Antioch there were prophets and teachers:
13: 1   In the church at Antioch *there* were prophets and teachers:
13: 7   who **was** an attendant of the proconsul, Sergius Paulus.
13:11   *You are going to* **be** blind, and for a time you will be unable to see
13:15   "Brothers, if you **have** a message of encouragement for the people,
13:25   John was completing his work, he said: 'Who do you think **I am**?
13:25   I **am** not that one. No, but he is coming after me, whose sandals I
13:25   he is coming after me, whose sandals *I* **am** not worthy to untie.'
13:31   Galilee to Jerusalem. They **are** now his witnesses to our people.
13:33   " 'You **are** my Son; today I have become your Father.'
13:38   *I* **want** you to know that through Jesus the forgiveness of sins is
13:46   "We **had to** [+338] speak the word of God to you first. Since you
13:47   *that* you *may* **bring** [+1650] salvation to the ends of the earth.' "
13:48   of the Lord; and all *who* **were** appointed for eternal life believed.
14: 4   were divided; some **sided** with the Jews, others with the apostles.
14: 7   where *they* **continued** to preach the good news.
14:12   and Paul they called Hermes because he **was** the chief speaker.
14:13   whose temple **was** just outside the city, brought bulls and wreaths
14:15   why are you doing this? We too **are** only men, human like you.
14:26   where *they had* **been** committed to the grace of God for the work
15:32   Judas and Silas, *who* themselves **were** prophets, said much to
16: 1   then to Lystra, where a disciple named Timothy **lived** [+1695],
16: 3   so he circumcised him because of the Jews who **lived** in that area,
16: 9   night Paul had a vision of a man of Macedonia **standing** [+2705]
16:12   [NIE] a Roman colony and the leading city of that district of
16:12   district of Macedonia. And *we* **stayed** [+1417] there several days.
16:13   city gate to the river, where we expected *to* **find** a place of prayer.
16:15   "If you consider me [NIE] a believer in the Lord," she said,
16:17   of us, shouting, "These men **are** servants of the Most High God,
16:21   by advocating customs unlawful for us [NIE] Romans to accept
16:28   But Paul shouted, "Don't harm yourself! *We* **are** all here!"
16:38   and when they heard that Paul and Silas **were** Roman citizens,
17: 1   they came to Thessalonica, where *there* **was** a Jewish synagogue.
17: 3   "This Jesus I am proclaiming to you **is** the Christ," he said.
17: 7   saying that *there* **is** another king, one called Jesus."
17:11   Now the Bereans **were** of more noble character than the
17:16   he was greatly distressed to see that the city **was** full of idols.
17:18   Others remarked, "He seems *to* **be** advocating foreign gods."
17:20   ideas to our ears, and we want to know what they **mean** [+2527]."
17:28   'For in him we live and move and **have** *our* **being**.' As some of
17:28   As some of your own poets have said, '*We* **are** his offspring.'
17:29   we should not think that the divine being **is** like gold or silver
18: 3   and because he **was** a tentmaker as they were, he stayed
18: 3   and because he was a tentmaker as *they* **were**, he stayed
18: 5   to preaching, testifying to the Jews that Jesus **was** the Christ.
18: 7   door to the house of Titius Justus, a worshiper of God. [NIE]
18:10   For **I am** with you, and no one is going to attack and harm you,
18:10   to attack and harm you, because I **have** many people in this city."
18:12   *While* Gallio **was** proconsul of Achaia, the Jews made a united
18:14   "If you Jews *were* **making a complaint**[s] **about** some misdemeanor
18:15   But since *it* involves questions about words and names and your
18:15   settle the matter yourselves. I will not **be** a judge of such things."
18:24   was a learned man, **with** a thorough knowledge of the Scriptures.
18:25   He *had* **been** instructed in the way of the Lord, and he spoke with
18:28   proving from the Scriptures that Jesus **was** the Christ.
19: 1   While Apollos **was** at Corinth, Paul took the road through the
19: 2   "No, we have not even heard that *there* **is** a Holy Spirit."
19: 4   the people to believe in the one coming after him, that **is**, in Jesus."
19: 7   *There* **were** about twelve men in all.
19:14   Seven sons of Sceva, a Jewish chief priest, **were** doing this.
19:15   "Jesus I know, and I know about Paul, but who **are** you?"
19:16   Then the man who **had** [+1877] the evil spirit jumped on them
19:25   "Men, you know we **receive** a good income from this business.
19:26   province of Asia. He says that man-made gods **are** no gods at all.
19:31   Even some of the officials of the province, [NIE] friends of Paul,
19:32   The assembly **was** in confusion: Some were shouting one thing,
19:34   But when they realized *he* **was** a Jew, they all shouted in unison
19:35   doesn't **all the world** [+476+4005+5515] know that the city of
19:35   doesn't all the world know that the city of Ephesus **is** the guardian
19:36   Therefore, *since* these facts **are** undeniable, you ought to be quiet
19:36   [NIE] you ought to be quiet and not do anything rash.
19:38   against anybody, the courts are open and *there* **are** proconsuls.
20: 8   *There* **were** many lamps in the upstairs room where we were
20: 8   There were many lamps in the upstairs room where *we* **were**
20:10   "Don't be alarmed," he said. "**He's** [+899+3836+6034] alive!"
20:13   He had made this arrangement because he **was** going there on foot.

20:16   to reach Jerusalem, if possible, [NIE] by the day of Pentecost.
20:26   I declare to you today that *I* **am** innocent of the blood of all men.
20:34   my own needs and the needs of my **companions** [+3552+3836].
20:35   Jesus himself said: '*It* **is** more blessed to give than to receive.' "
21: 3   We landed at Tyre, where our ship **was** to unload its cargo.
21: 8   and stayed at the house of Philip the evangelist, **one of** [+1666] the
21: 9   He **had** four unmarried daughters who prophesied.
21:11   'In this way the Jews of Jerusalem will bind [NIE] the owner of
21:20   brother, how many thousands [NIE] of Jews have believed,
21:22   **What shall we do** [+4036+5515]? They will certainly hear that
21:23   we tell you. *There* **are** four men with us who have made a vow.
21:24   Then everybody will know *there* **is** no truth in these reports about
21:28   This is the man who teaches all men everywhere against our people
21:29   (*They had* **previously seen** [+4632] Trophimus the Ephesian in
21:33   with two chains. Then he asked who he **was** and what he had done.
21:33   Then he asked who he was and what *he had* **done** [+4472].
21:38   "**Aren't** [+4024] you the Egyptian who started a revolt and led
21:39   Paul answered, "I **am** a Jew, from Tarsus in Cilicia, a citizen of no
22: 3   "I **am** a Jew, born in Tarsus of Cilicia, but brought up in this city.
22: 3   and was just as zealous for God as any of you **are** today.
22: 5   and went there to bring these people as **prisoners** [+1313] to
22: 8   " 'Who **are** *you*, Lord?' I asked. " 'I am Jesus of Nazareth,
22: 8   " 'I **am** Jesus of Nazareth, whom you are persecuting,' he replied.
22: 9   My **companions** [+3836+5250] saw the light, but they did not
22:15   *You will* **be** his witness to all men of what you have seen
22:19   'these men know that I **went** from one synagogue to another to
22:20   I **stood there** [+2392] giving my approval and guarding the clothes
22:26   are you going to do?" he asked. "This man **is** a Roman citizen."
22:27   went to Paul and asked, "Tell me, **are** you a Roman citizen?"
22:29   realized that *he had* **put** Paul, a Roman citizen, **in chains** [+1313].
22:29   he realized that he had put Paul, [NIE] a Roman citizen, in chains.
23: 5   Paul replied, "Brothers, I did not realize that *he* **was** the high priest;
23: 6   knowing that some of them **were** Sadducees and the others
23: 6   the Sanhedrin, "My brothers, I **am** a Pharisee, the son of a Pharisee.
23: 8   (The Sadducees say that *there* **is** no resurrection, and that there are
23:13   More than forty men were involved in this plot.
23:15   about his case. We **are** ready to kill him before he gets here."
23:19   drew him aside and asked, "What **is** *it* you want to tell me?"
23:21   *They* **are** ready now, waiting for your consent to their request."
23:27   and rescued him, for I had learned that *he* **is** a Roman citizen.
23:30   When I was informed of a plot *to be* **carried out** against the man,
23:34   The governor read the letter and asked what province *he* **was** from.
24:10   "I know that for a number of years you *have* **been** a judge over this
24:11   You can easily verify that [NIE] no more than twelve days ago I
24:15   that *there* will **be** a resurrection of both the righteous
24:24   days later Felix came with his wife Drusilla, *who* **was** a Jewess.
25: 5   charges against the man there, if he *has* **done** anything wrong."
25:10   "*I* **am** now standing before Caesar's court, where I ought to be
25:11   But if the charges brought against me by these Jews **are** not true,
25:14   He said: "*There* **is** a man *here* whom Felix left as a prisoner.
25:16   "I told them that *it* **is** not the Roman custom to hand over any man
26: 3   **because** you **are** well acquainted with all the Jewish customs
26:15   "Then I asked, 'Who **are** *you*, Lord?' " 'I am Jesus, whom you are
26:15   " 'I **am** Jesus, whom you are persecuting,' the Lord replied.
26:21   That is why the Jews seized me [NIE] in the temple courts
26:26   of this has escaped his notice, because it **was** not done in a corner.
26:29   but all who are listening to me today may become what **I am**,
27: 2   Aristarchus, a Macedonian from Thessalonica, **was** with us.
27: 4   passed to the lee of Cyprus because the winds **were** against us.
27: 8   came to a place called Fair Havens, [NIE] near the town of Lasea.
27: 9   and sailing *had* already **become** dangerous because by now it was
27:10   I can see that our voyage is going to **be** disastrous and bring great
27:22   you to keep up your courage, because not one of you *will* **be** lost;
27:23   Last night an angel of the God whose *I* **am** and whom I serve
27:25   for I have faith in God that *it will* **happen** just as he told me.
27:37   Altogether *there* **were** 276 of us on board.
28: 4   his hand, they said to each other, "This man must **be** a murderer;
28: 6   happen to him, they changed their minds and said he **was** a god.
28:17   Three days later he called together the **leaders** [+4755] of the
28:22   for we **know** [+1196] that people everywhere are talking against
28:25   *They* **disagreed** [+851] among themselves and began to leave after
28:28   "Therefore *I want* you *to* **know** [+1196] that God's salvation has
Ro 1: 6   And you also **are** among those who are called to belong to Jesus
1: 7   To all in Rome who **are** loved by God and called to be saints:
1: 9   gospel of his Son, **is** my witness how constantly I remember you
1:12   that **is**, that you and I may be mutually encouraged by each other's

1: 14 *I am* obligated both to Greeks and non-Greeks, both to the wise
1: 16 because *it* is the power of God for the salvation of everyone who
1: 19 since what may be known about God **is** plain to them, because God
1: 20 from what has been made, so that men **are** without excuse.
1: 22 Although they claimed *to* **be** wise, they became fools
1: 25 created things rather than the Creator—who **is** forever praised.
1: 32 decree that those who do such things **deserve** [+545] death,
2: 1 You, therefore, **have** no excuse, you who pass judgment on
2: 2 God's judgment against those who do such things **is** based on truth.
2: 11 For God *does* not **show favoritism** [+4721].
2: 14 they **are** a law for themselves, even though they do not have the
2: 19 if you are convinced that you **are** a guide for the blind, a light for
2: 25 has value if you observe the law, but if *you* **break** [+4127] the law,
2: 28 A *man* **is** not a Jew if he is only one outwardly, nor is circumcision
3: 8 us do evil that good may result"? Their condemnation **is** deserved.
3: 9 made the charge that Jews and Gentiles alike **are** all under sin.
3: 10 As it is written: "*There* **is** no one righteous, not even one;
3: 11 *there* **is** no one who understands, no one who seeks God.
3: 11 there **is** no one who understands, **[RPG]** no one who seeks God.
3: 12 become worthless; *there* **is** no one who does good, not even one."
3: 12 there **is** no one who does good, **[RPG]** not even one."
3: 18 "*There* **is** no fear of God before their eyes."
3: 22 faith in Jesus Christ to all who believe. *There* **is** no difference,
3: 26 so as *to* **be** just and the one who justifies those who have faith in
4: 10 Was it after *he* **was** circumcised, or before? It was not after,
4: 11 he **is** the father of all who believe but have not been circumcised,
4: 13 and his offspring received the promise that he *would* **be** heir of the
4: 15 brings wrath. And where *there* **is** no law there is no transgression.
4: 16 be by grace and *may* **be** guaranteed to all Abraham's offspring—
4: 16 to those who are of the faith of Abraham. He **is** the father of us all.
4: 17 life to the dead and calls things that **are** not as though they were.
4: 17 life to the dead and calls things that are not as though *they* **were**.
4: 18 just as it had been said to him, "So *shall* your offspring **be**."
4: 21 being fully persuaded that God **had** power to do what he had
5: 6 You see, at just the right time, *when* we **were** still powerless,
5: 8 love for us in this: *While* we **were** still sinners, Christ died for us.
5: 10 For if, *when* we **were** God's enemies, we were reconciled to him
5: 13 for before the law was given, sin **was** in the world. But sin is not
5: 13 the world. But sin is not taken into account *when there* **is** no law.
5: 14 a command, as did Adam, who **was** a pattern of the one to come.
6: 5 we *will* certainly also **be** united with him in his resurrection.
6: 11 count yourselves [UBS+ *to* **be**] dead to sin but alive to God
6: 14 be your master, because *you* **are** not under law, but under grace.
6: 15 Shall we sin because *we* **are** not under law but under grace?
6: 16 to obey him as slaves, *you* **are** slaves to the one whom you obey—
6: 17 But thanks be to God that, *though you used to* **be** slaves to sin,
6: 20 When *you* **were** slaves to sin, you were free from the control of
6: 20 were slaves to sin, *you* **were** free from the control of righteousness.
7: 3 husband dies, *she* **is** released from that law and is not an adulteress,
7: 3 husband dies, she is released from that law and **is** not an adulteress,
7: 5 For when *we* **were** controlled by the sinful nature, the sinful
7: 14 We know that the law **is** spiritual; but I am unspiritual, sold as a
7: 14 that the law is spiritual; but I **am** unspiritual, sold as a slave to sin.
7: 18 I know that nothing good lives in me, that **is**, in my sinful nature.
7: 23 and making me a prisoner of the law of sin **at work** within my
8: 5 Those *who* **live** according to the sinful nature have their minds set
8: 8 Those **controlled** by the sinful nature cannot please God.
8: 9 however, *are* **controlled** not by the sinful nature but by the Spirit,
8: 9 does not have the Spirit of Christ, he *does* not **belong to** Christ.
8: 12 Therefore, brothers, *we* **have** an obligation—but it is not to the
8: 14 because those who are led by the Spirit of God **are** sons of God.
8: 16 The Spirit himself testifies with our spirit that *we* **are** God's
8: 24 in this hope we were saved. But hope that is seen **is** no hope at all.
8: 28 who love him, who *have* **been** called according to his purpose.
8: 29 of his Son, that he *might* **be** the firstborn among many brothers.
8: 34 to life—**is** at the right hand of God and is also interceding for us.
9: 2 I **have** great sorrow and unceasing anguish in my heart.
9: 3 For I could wish that I myself **were** cursed and cut off from Christ
9: 4 the people **[NIE]** of Israel. Theirs is the adoption as sons;
9: 5 the human ancestry of Christ, who **is** God over all, forever praised!
9: 7 because *they* **are** his descendants are they all Abraham's children.
9: 8 **In other words** [+4047], it is not the natural children who are
9: 9 "At the appointed time I will return, and Sarah *will* **have** a son."
9: 20 But who **are** you, O man, to talk back to God? "Shall what is
9: 26 "*It will* **happen** that in the very place where it was said to them,
9: 27 "Though the number of the Israelites **be** like the sand by the sea,

10: 6 'Who will ascend into heaven?' " (that **is**, to bring Christ down)
10: 7 "or 'Who will descend into the deep?' " (that **is**, to bring Christ up
10: 8 "The word **is** near you; it is in your mouth and in your heart,"
10: 8 it is in your mouth and in your heart," that **is**, the word of faith we
10: 12 For *there* **is** no difference between Jew and Gentile—the same
11: 1 I **am** an Israelite myself, a descendant of Abraham, from the tribe
11: 13 Inasmuch as I **am** the apostle to the Gentiles, I make much of my
11: 17 and you, **though** a wild olive shoot, have been grafted in among
11: 23 they will be grafted in, for God **is** able to graft them in again.
11: 25 of this mystery, brothers, so that *you may* not **be** conceited:
12: 3 For by the grace given me I say to every one **[NIE]** of you:
12: 5 so in Christ *we* who are many **form** one body, and each member
13: 1 for *there* **is** no authority except that which God has established.
13: 1 The authorities *that* **exist** have been established by God.
13: 1 The authorities that exist *have* **been** established by God.
13: 3 For rulers **hold** no terror for those who do right, but for those who
13: 4 For *he* **is** God's servant to do you good. But if you do wrong,
13: 4 *He* **is** God's servant, an agent of wrath to bring punishment on the
13: 6 is also why you pay taxes, for the authorities **are** God's servants,
14: 4 Who **are** you to judge someone else's servant? To his own master
14: 8 die to the Lord. So, whether we live or die, *we* **belong to** the Lord.
14: 14 But if anyone regards something *as* unclean, then for him it is
14: 17 For the kingdom of God **is** not a matter of eating and drinking,
14: 23 not from faith; and everything that does not come from faith **is** sin.
15: 12 And again, Isaiah says, "The Root of Jesse *will* **spring up**,
15: 14 my brothers, that *you* yourselves **are** full of goodness, complete in
15: 16 *to* **be** a minister of Christ Jesus to the Gentiles with the priestly
15: 27 were pleased to do it, and indeed *they* **owe** [+4050] it to them.
16: 1 you our sister Phoebe, **[NIE]** a servant of the church in Cenchrea.
16: 5 who **was** the first convert to Christ in the province of Asia.
16: 7 They **are** outstanding among the apostles, and they were in Christ
16: 11 Greet those in the household of Narcissus who **are** in the Lord.
16: 19 but I want *you to* **be** wise about what is good, and innocent about
1Co 1: 2 to those **sanctified** [+39] in Christ Jesus and called to be holy,
1: 10 with one another so that *there may* **be** no divisions among you
1: 10 and that *you may* **be** perfectly united in mind and thought.
1: 11 some from Chloe's household have informed me that *there* **are**
1: 12 One of you says, "**I follow** Paul"; another, "I follow Apollos";
1: 18 For the message of the cross **is** foolishness to those who are
1: 18 are perishing, but to us who are being saved *it* **is** the power of God.
1: 25 For the foolishness of God **is** wiser than man's wisdom,
1: 28 of this world and the despised things—and the things *that* **are** not—
1: 28 and the things that are not—to nullify the things *that* **are**,
1: 30 It is because of him that *you* **are** in Christ Jesus, who has become
2: 5 so that your faith *might* not **rest** on men's wisdom, but on God's
2: 14 for *they* **are** foolishness to him, and he cannot understand them,
3: 3 *You* **are** still worldly. For since there is jealousy and quarreling
3: 3 there is jealousy and quarreling among you, **are** *you* not worldly?
3: 4 when one says, "I **follow** Paul," and another, "I follow Apollos,"
3: 4 Paul," and another, "I follow Apollos," **are** *you* not mere men?
3: 5 What, after all, **is** Apollos? And what is Paul? Only servants,
3: 5 What, after all, is Apollos? And what **is** Paul? Only servants,
3: 7 So neither he who plants nor he who waters **is** anything, but only
3: 8 The man who plants and the man who waters **have** one purpose,
3: 9 For *we* **are** God's fellow workers; you are God's field,
3: 9 we are God's fellow workers; *you* **are** God's field, God's building.
3: 11 foundation other than the one already laid, which **is** Jesus Christ.
3: 13 and the fire will test the quality **[NIE]** of each man's work.
3: 16 Don't you know that *you yourselves* **are** God's temple and that
3: 17 destroy him; for God's temple **is** sacred, and you are that temple.
3: 17 destroy him; for God's temple is sacred, and you **are** that temple.
3: 18 If any one of you thinks he **is** wise by the standards of this age,
3: 19 For the wisdom of this world **is** foolishness in God's sight.
3: 20 again, "The Lord knows that the thoughts of the wise **are** futile."
3: 21 So then, no more boasting about men! All things **are** yours,
4: 3 I **care very little** [+1650+1788] if I am judged by you or by any
4: 4 but that does not make me innocent. *It* **is** the Lord who judges me.
4: 8 Already *you* **have all you want** [+3170]! Already you have
4: 17 to you Timothy, my son whom I love, who **is** faithful in the Lord.
5: 2 And you **are** proud! Shouldn't you rather have been filled with
5: 7 Get rid of the old yeast that *you may* **be** a new batch without
5: 7 that you may be a new batch without yeast—as *you really* **are**.
5: 11 who calls himself a brother but **is** sexually immoral or greedy,
6: 2 to judge the world, **are** *you* not competent to judge trivial cases?
6: 7 The very fact that you have lawsuits among you **means** you have
6: 11 And that is what some of *you* **were**. But you were washed,

6: 15 Do you not know that your bodies **are** members of Christ himself?
6: 16 Do you not know that he who unites himself with a prostitute **is**
6: 16 in body? For it is said, "The two *will* **become** [+*1650*] one flesh."
6: 17 But he who unites himself with the Lord **is** one with him in spirit.
6: 18 All other sins a man commits **are** outside his body, but he who sins
6: 19 Do you not know that your body **is** a temple of the Holy Spirit,
6: 19 whom you have received from God? *You* **are** not your own;
7: 5 Then **come** together again so that Satan will not tempt you
7: 7 I wish that all men **were** as I am. But each man has his own gift
7: 9 should marry, for *it* **is** better to marry than to burn with passion.
7: 14 Otherwise your children *would* **be** unclean, but as it is, they are
7: 14 your children would be unclean, but as it is, *they* **are** holy.
7: 19 Circumcision **is** nothing and uncircumcision **is** nothing.
7: 19 Circumcision **is** nothing and uncircumcision **is** nothing.
7: 22 For he who was a slave when he was called by the Lord **is** the
7: 22 he who was a free man when he was called **is** Christ's slave.
7: 25 but I give a judgment as *one who* by the Lord's mercy **is**
7: 26 present crisis, I think that it is good for you *to* **remain** as you are.
7: 29 What I mean, brothers, is that the time **is** short. From now on those
7: 29 From now on those who have wives *should* **live** as if they had
7: 32 I would like you *to* **be** free from concern. An unmarried man is
7: 34 Her aim is to **be** devoted to the Lord in both body and spirit.
7: 36 and if *she* **is** getting along in years and he feels he ought to marry,
7: 39 But if her husband dies, *she* **is** free to marry anyone she wishes,
7: 40 In my judgment, *she* **is** happier if she stays as she is—and I think
8: 5 For even if *there* **are** so-called gods, whether in heaven or on earth
8: 5 or on earth (as indeed *there* **are** many "gods" and many "lords"),
8: 7 to an idol, and *since* their conscience **is** weak, it is defiled.
8: 10 For if anyone **with** a weak conscience sees you who have this
9: 1 **Am** *I* not free? Am I not an apostle? Have I not seen Jesus our
9: 1 Am I not free? **Am** *I* not an apostle? Have I not seen Jesus our
9: 1 Jesus our Lord? **Are** you not the result of my work in the Lord?
9: 2 Even though *I may* not **be** an apostle to others, surely I am to you!
9: 2 Even though I may not **be** an apostle to others, surely *I* **am** to you!
9: 2 I am to you! For you **are** the seal of my apostleship in the Lord.
9: 3 This **is** my defense to those who sit in judgment on me.
9: 16 the gospel, I **cannot** [+*4024*] boast, for I am compelled to preach.
9: 16 to preach. Woe **[NIE]** to me if I do not preach the gospel!
9: 18 What then **is** my reward? Just this: that in preaching the gospel I
9: 19 *Though I* **am** free and belong to no man, I make myself a slave to
9: 20 like one under the law (*though I* myself **am** not under the law),
9: 21 like one not having the law (*though I* **am** not free from God's law
10: 1 that our forefathers **were** all under the cloud and that they all
10: 4 the spiritual rock that accompanied them, and that rock **was** Christ.
10: 6 Now these things occurred as examples to **keep** us from setting our
10: 16 **Is** not the cup of thanksgiving for which we give thanks a
10: 16 And **is** not the bread that we break a participation in the body of
10: 17 Because there is one loaf, *we*, who are many, **are** one body,
10: 18 *Do* not those who eat the sacrifices **participate** [+*3128*] in the
10: 19 Do I mean then that a sacrifice offered to an idol **is** anything,
10: 19 sacrifice offered to an idol is anything, or that an idol **is** anything?
10: 22 we trying to arouse the Lord's jealousy? **Are** *we* stronger than he?
10: 28 says to you, "This *has* **been** offered in sacrifice," then do not eat it,
11: 3 Now I want you to realize that the head of every man **is** Christ,
11: 5 dishonors her head—*it* **is** just as though her head were shaved.
11: 7 is the image and glory of God; but the woman **is** the glory of man.
11: 8 For man *did* not **come** from woman, but woman from man;
11: 13 **Is** it proper for a woman to pray to God with her head uncovered?
11: 14 things teach you that if a man has long hair, *it* **is** a disgrace to him,
11: 15 but that if a woman has long hair, *it* **is** her glory? For long hair is
11: 16 If anyone wants *to* **be** contentious about this, we have no other
11: 19 No doubt there have to **be** differences among you to show which of
11: 20 When you come together, *it* **is** not the Lord's Supper you eat,
11: 24 he broke it and said, "This **is** my body, which is for you;
11: 25 he took the cup, saying, "This cup **is** the new covenant in my blood;
11: 27 or drinks the cup of the Lord in an unworthy manner *will* **be** guilty
12: 2 You know that when *you* **were** pagans, somehow or other you
12: 4 *There* **are** different kinds of gifts, but the same Spirit.
12: 5 *There* **are** different kinds of service, but the same Lord.
12: 6 *There* **are** different kinds of working, but the same God works all
12: 12 The body **is** a unit, though it is made up of many parts; and though
12: 12 many parts; and *though* all its parts **are** many, they form one body.
12: 12 many parts; and though all its parts are many, *they* **form** one body.
12: 14 Now the body *is* not **made up** of one part but of many.
12: 15 If the foot should say, "Because *I* **am** not a hand, I do not belong to
12: 15 should say, "Because I am not a hand, *I* **do** not belong to the body,"

12: 15 *it would* not for that reason **cease to be** [+*4024*] part of the body.
12: 16 if the ear should say, "Because *I* **am** not an eye, I do not belong
12: 16 should say, "Because I am not an eye, *I* **do** not belong to the body,"
12: 16 *it would* not for that reason **cease to be** [+*4024*] part of the body.
12: 19 If *they* **were** all one part, where would the body be?
12: 22 those parts of the body that seem to be weaker **are** indispensable,
12: 23 and the parts that we think **are** less honorable we treat with special
12: 25 so that *there should* **be** no division in the body, but that its parts
12: 27 Now you **are** the body of Christ, and each one of you is a part of it.
13: 2 a faith that can move mountains, but have not love, *I* **am** nothing.
13: 11 When *I was* a child, I talked like a child, I thought like a child,
14: 9 know what you are saying? *You will* just **be** speaking into the air.
14: 10 Undoubtedly *there* **are** all sorts of languages in the world,
14: 11 *I* **am** a foreigner to the speaker, and he is a foreigner to me.
14: 12 Since *you* **are** eager to have spiritual gifts, try to excel in gifts that
14: 14 For if I pray in a tongue, my spirit prays, but my mind **is** unfruitful.
14: 15 So what *shall I* **do**? I will pray with my spirit, but I will also pray
14: 22 Tongues, then, **are** [+*1650*] a sign, not for believers but for
14: 25 down and worship God, exclaiming, "God **is** really among you!"
14: 26 What then *shall we* **say**, brothers? When *you* come together,
14: 28 If *there* **is** no interpreter, the speaker should keep quiet in the
14: 33 For God **is** not a God of disorder but of peace. As in all the
14: 35 at home; for *it* **is** disgraceful for a woman to speak in the church.
14: 37 If anybody thinks he **is** a prophet or spiritually gifted, let him
14: 37 let him acknowledge that what I am writing to you **is** the Lord's
15: 9 For *I* **am** the least of the apostles and do not even deserve to be
15: 9 of the apostles and **do** not even deserve to be called an apostle,
15: 10 But by the grace of God *I* **am** what I am, and his grace to me was
15: 10 But by the grace of God I am what *I* **am**, and his grace to me was
15: 12 how can some of you say that *there* **is** no resurrection of the dead?
15: 13 If *there* **is** no resurrection of the dead, then not even Christ has
15: 17 has not been raised, your faith is futile; *you* **are** still in your sins.
15: 19 If only for this life *we* **have** hope [+*1827*] in Christ, we are to be
15: 19 life we have hope in Christ, *we* **are** to be pitied more than all men.
15: 28 him who put everything under him, so that God *may* **be** all in all.
15: 44 If *there* **is** a natural body, there is also a spiritual body.
15: 44 If there is a natural body, *there* **is** also a spiritual body.
15: 58 because you know that your labor in the Lord **is** not in vain.
16: 4 If *it seems* **advisable** [+*545*] for me to go also, they will
16: 12 He **was** quite unwilling to go now, but he will go when he has the
16: 15 You know that the household of Stephanas **were** the first converts
16: 22 If anyone does not love the Lord—a curse **be** *on him*. Come,
2Co 1: 1 and Timothy our brother, To the church of God **[NIE]** in Corinth,
1: 1 in Corinth, together with all the saints **[NIE]** throughout Achaia:
1: 7 because we know that just as *you* **share** [+*3128*] in our sufferings,
1: 9 But this happened that *we might* not **rely** [+*4275*] on ourselves
1: 12 Now this **is** our boast: Our conscience testifies that we have
1: 14 just as *we will* **boast** [+*3017*] of you in the day of the Lord Jesus.
1: 17 in a worldly manner so that *in the same breath* I **say** [+*4123*],
1: 18 surely as God is faithful, our message to you **is** not "Yes" and "No."
1: 24 lord it over your faith, but *we* **work with** [+*5301*] you for your joy,
2: 3 I had confidence in all of you, that you *would* all **share** my joy.
2: 9 to see if you would stand the test and **be** obedient in everything.
2: 15 For *we* **are** to God the aroma of Christ among those who are being
2: 17 Unlike so many, *we* **do** not peddle the word of God for profit.
3: 2 *You* yourselves **are** our letter, written on our hearts, known
3: 3 You show that *you* **are** a letter from Christ, the result of our
3: 5 Not that *we* **are** competent in ourselves to claim anything for
3: 8 *will* not the ministry of the Spirit **be** even more glorious?
3: 17 Now the Lord **is** the Spirit, and where the Spirit of the Lord is,
4: 3 And even if our gospel **is** veiled, it is veiled to those who are
4: 3 even if our gospel is veiled, *it* **is** veiled to those who are perishing.
4: 4 light of the gospel of the glory of Christ, who **is** the image of God.
4: 7 in jars of clay to show that this all-surpassing power **is** from God
5: 4 For *while* we **are** in this tent, we groan and are burdened,
5: 9 So we make it our goal *to* **please** [+*2298*] him, whether we are at
5: 19 that God **was** reconciling the world to himself in Christ,
6: 16 temple of God and idols? For *we* **are** the temple of the living God.
6: 16 will live with them and walk among them, and *I* **will** **be** their God,
6: 16 among them, and I will be their God, and they *will* **be** my people."
6: 18 "I *will* **be** [+*1650*] a Father to you, and you will be my sons
6: 18 and you *will* **be** [+*1650*] my sons and daughters, says the Lord
7: 3 I have said before that *you* **have such a place** in our hearts that we
7: 11 At every point you have proved yourselves *to* **be** innocent in this
7: 15 And his affection for you **is** all the greater when he remembers that
8: 9 that *though he* **was** rich, yet for your sakes he became poor,

8:22 who has often proved to us in many ways that *he* **is** zealous,
9: 1 *There* **is** no need for me to write to you about this service to the
9: 3 prove hollow, but that *you may* **be** ready, as I said you would be.
9: 5 Then it *will* **be** ready as a generous gift, not as one grudgingly
9:12 This service that you perform **is** not only supplying the needs of
10: 7 If anyone is confident that he **belongs** to Christ, he should consider
10:11 Such people should realize that what *we* **are** in our letters when we
10:18 For it is not the one who commends himself who **is** approved,
11:10 As surely as the truth of Christ **is** in me, nobody in the regions of
11:15 of righteousness. Their end *will* **be** what their actions deserve.
11:16 I repeat: *Let* no one **take** me for [+1506] a fool. But if you do,
11:19 You gladly put up with fools *since you* **are** so wise!
11:22 **Are** *they* Hebrews? So am I. Are they Israelites? So am I.
11:22 Are *they* Hebrews? So am I. **Are** *they* Israelites? So am I.
11:22 So am I. **Are** *they* Abraham's descendants? So am I.
11:23 **Are** *they* servants of Christ? (I am out of my mind to talk like
11:31 who **is** *to be* praised forever, knows that I am not lying.
12: 6 Even if I should choose to boast, *I would* not **be** a fool, because I
12:10 in difficulties. For when I am weak, then *I* **am** strong.
12:11 the least inferior to the "super-apostles," even though *I* **am** nothing.
12:13 How **were** you inferior to the other churches, except that I was
12:16 **Be** that as it may, I have not been a burden to you. Yet,
13: 5 Examine yourselves to see whether *you* **are** in the faith;
13: 5 Christ Jesus is in you—unless, of course, *you* **fail the test** [+99]?
13: 6 I trust that you will discover that we *have* not **failed the test** [+99].
13: 7 do what is right even though we *may* seem **to have failed** [+99].
13: 9 We are glad whenever we are weak but you **are** strong; and our
13:11 live in peace. And the God of love and peace *will* **be** with you.

Gal 1: 7 which **is** *really* no gospel at all. Evidently some people are
1: 7 Evidently some people **are** throwing you into confusion and are
1: 8 than the one we preached to you, *let him* **be** eternally condemned!
1: 9 other than what you accepted, *let him* **be** eternally condemned!
1:10 I were still trying to please men, *I* would not **be** a servant of Christ.
1:11 that the gospel I preached **is** not something that man made up.
1:22 *I* **was** personally unknown to the churches of Judea that are in
1:23 *They* only **heard** the **report** [+201]: "The man who formerly
2: 3 was compelled to be circumcised, *even though he* **was** a Greek.
2: 6 As for those who seemed *to* **be** important—whatever they were
2: 6 whatever *they* **were** [+4537] makes no difference to me;
2: 9 those reputed *to* **be** pillars, gave me and Barnabas the right hand of
2:11 I opposed him to his face, because *he* **was** clearly in the wrong.
3: 3 **Are** *you* so foolish? After beginning with the Spirit, are you now
3: 7 Understand, then, that those who believe **are** children of Abraham.
3:10 All who **rely** [+1666] **on** observing the law are under a curse,
3:10 All who rely on observing the law **are** under a curse, for it is
3:12 The law **is** not based on faith; on the contrary, "The man who does
3:16 but "and to your seed," meaning one person, who **is** Christ.
3:20 A mediator, however, *does* not **represent** just one party; but God
3:20 however, does not represent just one party; but God **is** one.
3:21 then righteousness would certainly have **come** by the law.
3:25 faith has come, *we* **are** no longer under the supervision of the law.
3:26 *You* **are** all sons of God through faith in Christ Jesus,
3:28 slave nor free, male nor female, for you **are** all one in Christ Jesus.
3:29 If you belong to Christ, then *you* **are** Abraham's seed, and heirs
4: 1 What I am saying is that as long as the heir **is** a child, he is no
4: 1 different from a slave, *although he* **owns** [+3261] the whole estate.
4: 2 *He* **is** subject to guardians and trustees until the time set by his
4: 3 So also, when we **were** children, we were in slavery under the
4: 3 *we* **were** in slavery under the basic principles of the world.
4: 6 Because *you* **are** sons, God sent the Spirit of his Son into our
4: 7 So *you* **are** no longer a slave, but a son; and since you are a son,
4: 8 know God, you were slaves *to* those *who* by nature **are** not gods.
4:21 Tell me, you who want *to* **be** under the law, are you not aware of
4:24 These things *may* **be** taken figuratively, for the women represent
4:24 be taken figuratively, for the women **represent** two covenants.
4:24 and bears children who are to be slaves: This **is** Hagar.
4:25 Now Hagar **stands for** Mount Sinai in Arabia and corresponds to
4:26 But the Jerusalem that is above **is** free, and she is our mother.
4:26 But the Jerusalem that is above is free, and she **is** our mother.
4:28 Now you, brothers, like Isaac, **are** children of promise.
4:31 Therefore, brothers, *we* **are** not children of the slave woman,
5: 3 himself be circumcised that *he* **is** obligated to obey the whole law.
5:10 you into confusion will pay the penalty, whoever *he may* **be**.
5:18 But if you are led by the Spirit, *you* **are** not under law.
5:19 The acts of the sinful nature **are** obvious: sexual immorality,
5:19 are obvious: [RPG] sexual immorality, impurity and debauchery;

5:22 But the fruit of the Spirit **is** love, joy, peace, patience, kindness,
5:23 gentleness and self-control. Against such things *there* **is** no law.
6: 3 If anyone thinks he **is** something when he is nothing, he deceives
6: 3 If anyone thinks he is something *when he* **is** nothing, he deceives
6:15 Neither circumcision nor uncircumcision **means** anything;

Eph 1: 1 To the saints [NIE] in Ephesus, the faithful in Christ Jesus:
1: 4 For he chose us in him before the creation of the world *to* **be** holy
1:12 the first to hope in Christ, *might* **be** for the praise of his glory.
1:14 who **is** a deposit guaranteeing our inheritance until the redemption
1:18 that you may know [NIE] the hope to which he has called you,
1:23 which **is** his body, the fullness of him who fills everything in every
2: 1 As for you, you **were** dead in your transgressions and sins,
2: 3 and thoughts. Like the rest, *we* **were** by nature objects of wrath.
2: 4 because of his great love for us, God, *who* **is** rich in mercy,
2: 5 made us alive with Christ even *when* we **were** dead in
2: 5 in transgressions—it is by grace *you have been* **saved** [+5392].
2: 8 For it is by grace *you have been* **saved** [+5392], through faith—
2:10 For *we* **are** God's workmanship, created in Christ Jesus to do good
2:12 remember that at that time *you* **were** separate from Christ,
2:13 But now in Christ Jesus you who once **were** far away have been
2:14 For he himself **is** our peace, who has made the two one and has
2:19 Consequently, *you* **are** no longer foreigners and aliens, but fellow
2:19 but [RPG] fellow citizens with God's people and members of
2:20 and prophets, with Christ Jesus himself **as** the chief cornerstone.
3: 6 This mystery is that through the gospel the Gentiles **are** heirs
3:13 because of my sufferings for you, which **are** your glory.
4: 9 (What *does* "he ascended" **mean** except that he also descended to
4:10 He who descended **is** the very one who ascended higher than all
4:14 Then *we will* no longer **be** infants, tossed back and forth by the
4:15 we will in all things grow up into him who **is** the Head, that is,
4:18 *They* **are** darkened in their understanding and separated from the
4:18 because of the ignorance that **is** in them due to the hardening of
4:21 and were taught in him in accordance with the truth that **is** in Jesus.
4:25 truthfully to his neighbor, for *we* **are** all members of one body.
5: 5 No immoral, impure or greedy person—such a man **is** an idolater—
5: 8 For *you* **were** once darkness, but now you are light in the Lord.
5:10 and find out what **pleases** [+2298] the Lord.
5:12 For *it* **is** shameful even to mention what the disobedient do in
5:14 for *it* **is** light that makes everything visible. This is why it is said:
5:16 making the most of every opportunity, because the days **are** evil.
5:18 Do not get drunk on wine, which **leads to** debauchery. Instead,
5:23 For the husband **is** the head of the wife as Christ is the head of the
5:27 or wrinkle or any other blemish, but [NIE] holy and blameless.
5:30 for *we* **are** members of his body.
5:31 be united to his wife, and the two *will* **become** [+1650] one flesh."
5:32 This **is** a profound mystery—but I am talking about Christ
6: 1 Children, obey your parents in the Lord, for this **is** right.
6: 2 and mother"—which **is** the first commandment with a promise—
6: 3 go well with you and that *you may* **enjoy** long life on the earth."
6: 9 you know that he who is both their Master and yours **is** in heaven,
6: 9 and yours is in heaven, and *there* **is** no favoritism with him.
6:12 For our struggle **is** not against flesh and blood, but against the
6:17 of salvation and the sword of the Spirit, which **is** the word of God.

Php 1: 1 of Christ Jesus, To all the saints in Christ Jesus [NIE] at Philippi,
1: 7 *It* **is** right for me to feel this way about all of you, since I have you
1: 7 the gospel, all of you **share** in God's grace **with** [+5171] me.
1:10 what is best and *may* **be** pure and blameless until the day of Christ,
1:23 I desire to depart and **be** with Christ, which is better by far;
1:28 This **is** a sign to them that they will be destroyed, but that you will
2: 6 did not consider **equality** [+2698+3836] with God something to be
2:13 for *it* **is** God who works in you to will and to act according to his
2:26 For *he* **longs for** [+2160] all of you and is distressed because you
2:28 you see him again you may be glad and I *may* **have** less anxiety.
3: 3 For it is we who **are** the circumcision, we who worship by the
3: 7 But whatever **was** to my profit I now consider loss for the sake of
3: 8 I consider everything [NIE] a loss compared to the surpassing
4: 8 Finally, brothers, whatever **is** true, whatever is noble, whatever is
4: 9 put it into practice. And the God of peace *will* **be** with you.
4:11 for I have learned *to* **be** content whatever the circumstances.
4:11 I have learned to be content whatever the circumstances. [NIE]

Col 1: 6 All over the world this gospel **is** bearing fruit and growing,
1: 7 fellow servant, who **is** a faithful minister of Christ on our behalf,
1:15 He **is** the image of the invisible God, the firstborn over all creation.
1:17 He **is** before all things, and in him all things hold together.
1:18 And he **is** the head of the body, the church; he is the beginning
1:18 he **is** the beginning and the firstborn from among the dead,

1:21 Once you **were** alienated from God and were enemies in your
1:24 to Christ's afflictions, for the sake of his body, which **is** the church.
1:27 riches of this mystery, which **is** Christ in you, the hope of glory.
2: 3 in whom **are** hidden all the treasures of wisdom and knowledge.
2: 5 *I* **am** present with you in spirit and delight to see how orderly you
2: 8 See to it that no one **takes** you **captive** [+5194] through hollow
2:10 and *you have been* **given fullness** [+4444] in Christ, who is the
2:10 fullness in Christ, who **is** the head over every power and authority.
2:13 *When* you **were** dead in your sins and in the uncircumcision of
2:14 that was against us and that **stood opposed** [+5641] to us;
2:17 These **are** a shadow of the things that were to come; the reality,
2:22 These **are** all destined to perish with use, because they are based
2:23 Such regulations indeed **[RPG]** have an appearance of wisdom,
3: 1 on things above, where Christ **is** seated at the right hand of God.
3: 5 impurity, lust, evil desires and greed, which **is** idolatry.
3:14 on love, which **binds** them all **together** [+5278] in perfect unity.
3:20 obey your parents in everything, for this **pleases** [+2298] the Lord.
3:25 wrong will be repaid for his wrong, and *there* **is** no favoritism.
4: 9 with Onesimus, our faithful and dear brother, who **is** one of you.
4:11 These **are** the only Jews among my fellow workers for the

1Th 2: 6 As apostles of Christ we could have **been** a burden to you,
2:13 but as *it* actually **is**, the word of God, which is at work in you who
2:14 imitators of God's churches in Judea, which **are** in Christ Jesus:
2:20 Indeed, you **are** our glory and joy.
3: 4 In fact, when *we* **were** with you, we kept telling you that we would
4: 3 It **is** God's will that you should be sanctified: that you should avoid
4: 9 for you yourselves *have* **been** taught by God to love each other.
4:17 meet the Lord in the air. And so *we will* **be** with the Lord forever.
5: 4 **are** not in darkness so that this day should surprise you like a thief.
5: 5 You **are** all sons of the light and sons of the day. We do not belong
5: 5 sons of the day. *We do* not **belong to** the night or to the darkness.
5: 8 But *since* we **belong to** the day, let us be self-controlled.

2Th 1: 3 always to thank God for you, brothers, and **rightly so** [+545],
2: 4 he sets himself up in God's temple, proclaiming himself *to* **be** God.
2: 5 Don't you remember that *when I* **was** with you I used to tell you
2: 9 The coming of the lawless one *will* **be** in accordance with the work
3: 3 But the Lord **is** faithful, and he will strengthen and protect you
3:10 For even when *we* **were** with you, we gave you this rule: "If a man
3:17 in my own hand, which **is** the distinguishing mark in all my letters.

1Ti 1: 5 The goal of this command **is** love, which comes from a pure heart
1: 7 They want *to* **be** teachers of the law, but they do not know what
1:13 *Even though I* **was** once a blasphemer and a persecutor and a
1:15 came into the world to save sinners—of whom I **am** the worst.
1:20 Among them **are** Hymenaeus and Alexander, whom I have handed
2: 2 for kings and all those **[NIE]** in authority, that we may live
2:12 to teach or to have authority over a man; she *must* **be** silent.
3: 2 Now the overseer must **be** above reproach, the husband of
3:10 and then *if there* **is** nothing against them, let them serve as
3:12 A deacon *must* **be** the husband of but one wife and must manage
3:15 which **is** the church of the living God, the pillar and foundation of
3:16 Beyond all question, the mystery of godliness is great: He appeared
4: 6 *you will* **be** a good minister of Christ Jesus, brought up in the
4: 8 For physical training **is** of some value, but godliness has value for
4: 8 training is of some value, but godliness **has** value for all things,
4:10 who **is** the Savior of all men, and especially of those who believe.
4:15 **Be diligent** in these matters; give yourself wholly to them,
4:15 yourself wholly to them, so that everyone **may** see your progress.
5: 4 repaying their parents and grandparents, for this **is** pleasing to God.
5: 7 these instructions, too, so that no one *may* **be** open to blame.
5: 8 he has denied the faith and **is** worse than an unbeliever.
5:24 The sins of some men **are** obvious, reaching the place of judgment
6: 1 All *who* **are** under the yoke of slavery should consider their
6: 2 are not to show less respect for them because *they* **are** brothers.
6: 2 because those who benefit from their service **are** believers,
6: 5 the truth and who think that godliness **is** a means to financial gain.
6: 6 But godliness with contentment **is** great gain.
6:10 For the love of money **is** a root of all kinds of evil. Some people,
6:18 to be rich in good deeds, and *to* **be** generous and willing to share.

2Ti 1: 6 the gift of God, which **is** in you through the laying on of my hands.
1:12 and am convinced that *he* **is** able to guard what I have entrusted to
1:15 has deserted me, **including** [+4005] Phygelus and Hermogenes.
2: 2 entrust to reliable men who *will* also **be** qualified to teach others.
2:17 spread like gangrene. Among them **are** Hymenaeus and Philetus,
2:19 "The Lord knows those *who* **are** his," and, "Everyone who
2:20 In a large house *there* **are** articles not only of gold and silver,
2:21 *he will* **be** an instrument for noble purposes, made holy, useful to

2:24 instead, he *must* **be** kind to everyone, able to teach, not resentful.
3: 2 People *will* **be** lovers of themselves, lovers of money, boastful,
3: 6 They **are** the kind who worm their way into homes and gain
3: 9 as in the case of those men, their folly *will* **be** clear to everyone.
3:17 so that the man of God *may* **be** thoroughly equipped for every
4: 3 For the time *will* **come** when men will not put up with sound
4:11 Only Luke **is** with me. Get Mark and bring him with you,
4:11 bring him with you, because *he* **is** helpful to me in my ministry.

Tit 1: 6 An elder *must* **be** blameless, the husband of but one wife,
1: 7 an overseer is entrusted with God's work, he must **be** blameless—
1: 9 so that *he* **can** [+1543] encourage others by sound doctrine
1:10 For *there* **are** many rebellious people, mere talkers and deceivers,
1:13 This testimony **is** true. Therefore, rebuke them sharply, so that
1:16 *They* **are** detestable, disobedient and unfit for doing anything
2: 2 Teach the older men *to* **be** temperate, worthy of respect,
2: 4 Then they can train the younger women *to* love their husbands
2: 9 in everything, *to* **try** to please them, not to talk back to them,
3: 1 and authorities, to be obedient, *to* **be** ready to do whatever is good,
3: 2 to slander no one, *to* **be** peaceable and considerate, and to show
3: 3 At one time we too **were** foolish, disobedient, deceived
3: 8 is good. These things **are** excellent and profitable for everyone.
3: 9 quarrels about the law, because *these* **are** unprofitable and useless.
3:11 be sure that such a man is warped and sinful; *he* **is** self-condemned.
3:14 may provide for daily necessities and not **live** unproductive lives.

Phm 1: 9 I then, **[NIE]** as Paul—an old man and now also a prisoner of
1:12 I am sending him—who **is** my very heart—back to you.
1:14 so that any favor you do *will* **be** spontaneous and not forced.

Heb 1: 3 The Son **is** the radiance of God's glory and the exact representation
1: 5 For to which of the angels did God ever say, "You **are** my Son;
1: 5 Or again, "I *will* **be** [+1650] his Father, and he will be my Son"?
1: 5 Or again, "I will be his Father, and he *will* **be** [+1650] my Son"?
1:10 of the earth, and the heavens **are** the work of your hands.
1:12 But you **remain** the same, and your years will never end."
1:14 **Are** not all angels ministering spirits sent to serve those who will
2: 6 "What **is** man that you are mindful of him, the son of man that you
2:13 And again, "I *will* **put my trust** [+4275] in him." And again he
2:14 destroy him who holds the power of death—that **is**, the devil—
2:15 and free those who all their lives **were** held in slavery by their fear
3: 2 *He* **was** faithful to the one who appointed him, just as Moses was
3: 6 And we **are** his house, if we hold on to our courage and the hope
3:12 See to it, brothers, that none of you **has** a sinful, unbelieving heart
4: 2 For *we* also *have* **had** the gospel preached to us, just as they did;
4:13 Nothing in all creation **is** hidden from God's sight Everything is
5: 5 But God said to him, "You **are** my Son; today I have become your
5: 8 Although *he* **was** a son, he learned obedience from what he
5:12 In fact, though by this time you ought *to* **be** teachers, you need
5:13 Anyone who lives on milk, **being** *still* an infant, is not acquainted
5:14 But solid food **is** for the mature, who by constant use have trained
7: 2 righteousness"; then also, "king of Salem" **means** "king of peace."
7: 5 that **is**, their brothers—even though their brothers are descended
7:10 met Abraham, Levi was still in the body of his ancestor.
7:11 If perfection *could have* **been** **attained** through the Levitical
7:15 And what we have said **is** even more clear if another priest like
7:20 without an oath! Others **became** [+1181] priests without any oath,
7:23 Now *there have* **been** [+1181] many of those priests, since death
8: 4 If *he* **were** on earth, he would not be a priest, for there are already
8: 4 If he were on earth, *he* would not **be** a priest, for there are already
8: 4 *for there* **are** *already* men who offer the gifts prescribed by the
8: 6 as the covenant of which he is mediator **is** superior to the old one,
8: 7 For if *there had* **been** nothing wrong with that first covenant,
8:10 *I will* **be** [+1650] their God, and they will be my people.
8:10 I will be their God, and they *will* **be** [+1650] my people.
8:12 For *I will* **forgive** [+2664] their wickedness and will remember
9: 5 But we **cannot** [+4024] discuss these things in detail now.
9:11 that is not man-made, that **is** to say, not a part of this creation.
9:15 For this reason Christ **is** the mediator of a new covenant, that those
10:10 *we have been* **made holy** [+39] through the sacrifice of the body
10:20 and living way opened for us through the curtain, that **is**, his body,
10:39 But we **are** not of those who shrink back and are destroyed,
11: 1 Now faith **is** being sure of what we hope for and certain of what we
11: 4 By faith he was commended **as** a righteous man, when God spoke
11: 6 because anyone who comes to him must believe that *he* **exists**
11:13 And they admitted that *they* **were** aliens and strangers on earth.
11:16 they were longing for a better country—**[NIE]** a heavenly one.
11:38 the world **was** not worthy of them. They wandered in deserts
12: 8 If *you* **are** not disciplined (and everyone undergoes discipline),

12: 8 then *you* **are** illegitimate children and not true sons.
12:11 No discipline seems **[NIE]** pleasant at the time, but painful.
12:21 The sight **was** so terrifying that Moses said, "I am trembling with
12:21 sight was so terrifying that Moses said, "*I* **am** trembling with fear."
13: 3 and those who are mistreated as if *you* yourselves **were** suffering.
13:15 a sacrifice of praise—**[NIE]** the fruit of lips that confess his name.
Jas 1: 4 must finish its work so that *you may* **be** mature and complete,
1:13 For God cannot **be** tempted by evil, nor does he tempt anyone;
1:17 Every good and perfect gift **is** from above, coming down from the
1:18 of truth, that we *might* **be** a kind of firstfruits of all he created.
1:19 Everyone *should* **be** quick to listen, slow to speak and slow to
1:23 Anyone *who* **listens to** [+212] the word but does not do what it
1:24 at himself, goes away and immediately forgets what *he* **looks like.**
1:25 he has heard, but doing it—he *will* **be** blessed in what he does,
1:26 If anyone considers himself **[NIE]** religious and yet does not keep
1:27 Religion that God our Father accepts as pure and faultless **is** this:
2:17 faith by itself, if it is not accompanied by action, **is** dead.
2:19 You believe that *there* **is** one God. Good! Even the demons believe
2:20 do you want evidence that faith without deeds **is** useless?
2:26 As the body without the spirit **is** dead, so faith without deeds is
2:26 the body without the spirit is dead, so faith without deeds **is** dead.
3: 4 *Although they* **are** so large and are driven by strong winds,
3: 5 Likewise the tongue **is** a small part of the body, but it makes great
3:15 **[NIE]** Such "wisdom" does not come down from heaven but is
3:17 But the wisdom that comes from heaven **is** first of all pure;
4: 4 don't you know that friendship with the world **is** hatred toward
4: 4 Anyone who chooses *to* **be** a friend of the world becomes an
4:11 When you judge the law, *you* **are** not keeping it, but sitting in
4:12 *There* **is** only one Lawgiver and Judge, the one who is able to save
4:12 and destroy. But you—who **are** *you* to judge your neighbor?
4:14 *You* **are** a mist that appears for a little while and then vanishes.
4:16 As it is, you boast and brag. All such boasting **is** evil.
4:17 who knows the good he ought to do and doesn't do it, **sins** [+281].
5: 3 Their corrosion *will* **testify** [+3457] against you and eat your flesh
5:11 finally brought about. The Lord **is** full of compassion and mercy.
5:12 *Let* your "Yes" **be** yes, and your "No," no, or you will be
5:15 raise him up. If *he has* **sinned** [+281+4472], he will be forgiven.
5:17 Elijah **was** a man just like us. He prayed earnestly that it would not
1Pe 1: 6 though now for a little while you *may have* **had to** [+1256] suffer
1:16 for it is written: "**Be** holy, because I am holy."
1:16 for it is written: "Be holy, because I **am** holy."
1:21 the dead and glorified him, and so your faith and hope **are** in God.
1:25 Lord stands forever." And this **is** the word that was preached to you.
2:15 For *it is* God's will that by doing good you should silence the
2:25 For *you* **were** like sheep going astray, but now you have returned
3: 3 Your beauty *should* not **come** from outward adornment, such as
3: 4 of a gentle and quiet spirit, which **is** of great worth in God's sight.
3:20 In it only a few people, eight **in all** [+4047], were saved through
3:22 who has gone into heaven and **is** at God's right hand—with angels,
4:11 To him **be** the glory and the power for ever and ever. Amen.
5:12 encouraging you and testifying that this **is** the true grace of God.
2Pe 1: 9 But if anyone does not have them, *he* **is** nearsighted and blind,
1:13 I think it is right to refresh your memory as long as *I* **live** in the
1:14 because I know that *I will* soon **put** it **aside** [+629], as our Lord
1:17 from the Majestic Glory, saying, "This **is** my Son, whom I love;
1:18 from heaven *when we* **were** with him on the sacred mountain.
2: 1 among the people, just as *there will* **be** false teachers among you.
2:11 yet even angels, *although they* **are** stronger and more powerful,
2:17 These men **are** springs without water and mists driven by a storm.
2:21 *It would have* **been** better for them not to have known the way of
3: 4 They will say, "Where **is** this 'coming' he promised? Ever since our
3: 5 forget that long ago by God's word the heavens **existed**
3: 7 the same word the present heavens and earth **are** reserved for fire,
3:16 His letters contain some things *that* **are** hard to understand,
1Jn 1: 1 That which **was** from the beginning, which we have heard,
1: 2 the eternal life, which **was** with the Father and has appeared to us.
1: 4 We write this to **make** our joy **complete** [+4444].
1: 5 This **is** the message we have heard from him and declare to you:
1: 5 and declare to you: God **is** light; in him there is no darkness at all.
1: 5 and declare to you: God **is** light; in him *there* **is** no darkness at all.
1: 7 But if we walk in the light, as he **is** in the light, we have fellowship
1: 8 to be without sin, we deceive ourselves and the truth **is** not in us.
1: 9 *he* **is** faithful and just and will forgive us our sins and purify us
1:10 make him out to be a liar and his word *has* no **place** in our lives.
2: 2 He **is** the atoning sacrifice for our sins, and not only for ours
2: 4 says, "I know him," but does not do what he commands **is** a liar,

2: 4 does not do what he commands is a liar, and the truth **is** not in him.
2: 5 truly made complete in him. This is how we know *we* **are** in him:
2: 7 the beginning. This old command **is** the message you have heard.
2: 8 its truth **is** seen in him and you, because the darkness is passing
2: 9 Anyone who claims *to* **be** in the light but hates his brother is still in
2: 9 claims to be in the light but hates his brother **is** still in the darkness.
2:10 lives in the light, and *there* **is** nothing in him to make him stumble.
2:11 But whoever hates his brother **is** in the darkness and walks around
2:14 I write to you, young men, because *you* **are** strong, and the word
2:15 If anyone loves the world, the love of the Father **is** not in him.
2:16 and does—**comes** not from the Father but from the world.
2:16 and does—comes not from the Father but **[RPG]** from the world.
2:18 Dear children, *this* **is** the last hour; and as you have heard that the
2:18 antichrists have come. This is how we know *it* **is** the last hour.
2:19 went out from us, but *they did* not *really* **belong** [+1666] **to** us.
2:19 For if *they had* **belonged** [+1666] **to** us, they would have
2:19 but their going showed that none of them **belonged** [+1666] **to** us.
2:21 because you do know it and because no lie **comes** from the truth.
2:22 Who **is** the liar? It is the man who denies that Jesus is the Christ.
2:22 Who is the liar? It is the man who denies that Jesus **is** the Christ.
2:22 Such a man **is** the antichrist—he denies the Father and the Son.
2:25 And this **is** what he promised us—even eternal life.
2:27 anointing teaches you about all things and as that anointing **is** real,
2:27 all things and as that anointing is real, **[RPG]** not counterfeit—
2:29 If you know that *he* **is** righteous, you know that everyone who does
3: 1 that we should be called children of God! And that is what *we* **are!**
3: 2 Dear friends, now *we* **are** children of God, and what we will be has
3: 2 of God, and what *we will* **be** has not yet been made known.
3: 2 he appears, *we shall* **be** like him, for we shall see him as he is.
3: 2 he appears, we shall be like him, for we shall see him as *he* **is.**
3: 3 who has this hope in him purifies himself, just as he **is** pure.
3: 4 Everyone who sins breaks the law; in fact, sin **is** lawlessness.
3: 5 so that he might take away our sins. And in him **is** no sin.
3: 7 He who does what is right **is** righteous, just as he is righteous.
3: 7 He who does what is right is righteous, just as he **is** righteous.
3: 8 He who does what is sinful **is** of the devil, because the devil has
3:10 This is how we **know** [+5745] who the children of God are
3:10 Anyone who does not do what is right **is** not a child of God;
3:11 This **is** the message you heard from the beginning: We should love
3:12 who belonged to **[NIE]** the evil one and murdered his brother.
3:12 Because his own actions **were** evil and his brother's were
3:15 Anyone who hates his brother **is** a murderer, and you know that no
3:19 then is how we know that *we* **belong** [+1666] **to** the truth,
3:20 For God is greater than our hearts, and he knows everything.
3:23 And this **is** his command: to believe in the name of his Son,
4: 1 every spirit, but test the spirits to see whether *they* **are** from God,
4: 2 acknowledges that Jesus Christ has come in the flesh **is** from God,
4: 3 but every spirit that does not acknowledge Jesus **is** not from God.
4: 3 This **is** the spirit of the antichrist, which you have heard is coming
4: 3 you have heard is coming and even now **is** already in the world.
4: 4 You, dear children, **are** from God and have overcome them,
4: 4 because the one who is in you is greater than the one who is in the
4: 5 They **are** from the world and therefore speak from the viewpoint
4: 6 We **are** from God, and whoever knows God listens to us;
4: 6 listens to us; but whoever **is** not from God does not listen to us.
4: 7 Dear friends, let us love one another, for love **comes** from God.
4: 8 Whoever does not love does not know God, because God **is** love.
4:10 This **is** love: not that we loved God, but that he loved us and sent
4:12 one another, God lives in us and his love **is** made complete in us.
4:15 If anyone acknowledges that Jesus **is** the Son of God, God lives in
4:16 God **is** love. Whoever lives in love lives in God, and God in him.
4:17 on the day of judgment, because in this world we **are** like him.
4:17 day of judgment, because in this world we are like him. **[RPG]**
4:18 *There* **is** no fear in love. But perfect love drives out fear,
4:20 If anyone says, "I love God," yet hates his brother, *he* **is** a liar.
5: 1 Everyone who believes that Jesus **is** the Christ is born of God,
5: 3 This **is** love for God: to obey his commands. And his commands
5: 3 to obey his commands. And his commands **are** not burdensome,
5: 4 This **is** the victory that has overcome the world, even our faith.
5: 5 Who **is** it that overcomes the world? Only he who believes that
5: 5 the world? Only he who believes that Jesus **is** the Son of God.
5: 6 This **is** the one who came by water and blood—Jesus Christ.
5: 6 And *it* **is** the Spirit who testifies, because the Spirit is the truth.
5: 6 And it is the Spirit who testifies, because the Spirit **is** the truth.
5: 7 For *there* **are** three that testify:
5: 8 the Spirit, the water and the blood; and the three **are** in agreement.

5: 9 but God's testimony **is** greater because it is the testimony of God,
5: 9 but God's testimony **is** greater because it is the testimony of God,
5: 11 And this **is** the testimony: God has given us eternal life, and this
5: 11 God has given us eternal life, and this life **is** in his Son.
5: 14 This **is** the confidence we have in approaching God: that if we ask
5: 16 *There* is a sin that leads to death. I am not saying that he should
5: 17 All wrongdoing **is** sin, and there is sin that does not lead to death.
5: 17 All wrongdoing is sin, and *there* **is** sin that does not lead to death.
5: 19 We know that *we* **are** children of God, and that the whole world is
5: 20 And *we* **are** in him who is true—even in his Son Jesus Christ.
5: 20 even in his Son Jesus Christ. He **is** the true God and eternal life.

2Jn 1: 2 because of the truth, which lives in us and *will* **be** with us forever:
1: 3 Jesus Christ, the Father's Son, *will* **be** with us in truth and love.
1: 6 And this **is** love: that we walk in obedience to his commands.
1: 6 heard from the beginning, his command **is** that you walk in love.
1: 7 into the world. Any such person **is** the deceiver and the antichrist.
1: 12 and talk with you face to face, so that our joy *may* **be** complete.

3Jn 1: 11 but what is good. Anyone who does what is good **is** from God.
1: 12 also speak well of him, and you know that our testimony **is** true.

Jude 1: 12 These men **are** blemishes at your love feasts, eating with you
1: 16 These men **are** grumblers and faultfinders; they follow their own
1: 18 "In the last times *there* *will* **be** scoffers who will follow their own
1: 19 These **are** the men who divide you, who follow mere natural

Rev 1: 4 Grace and peace to you from him *who* **is**, and who was, and who is
1: 4 peace to you from him who is, and who **was**, and who is to come,
1: 8 "I **am** the Alpha and the Omega," says the Lord God, "who is,
1: 8 and the Omega," says the Lord God, "who **is**, and who was,
1: 8 and the Omega," says the Lord God, "who is, and who **was**,
1: 17 hand on me and said: "Do not be afraid. I **am** the First and the Last.
1: 18 Living One; I was dead, and behold *I* **am** alive for ever and ever!
1: 19 what you have seen, what **is** *now* and what will take place later.
1: 20 The seven stars **are** the angels of the seven churches, and the seven
1: 20 seven churches, and the seven lampstands **are** the seven churches.
2: 2 that you have tested those who claim to be apostles but **are** not,
2: 7 right to eat from the tree of life, which **is** in the paradise of God.
2: 9 I know your afflictions and your poverty—yet *you* **are** rich!
2: 9 I know the slander of those who say they **are** Jews and are not,
2: 9 I know the slander of those who say they are Jews and **are** not,
2: 23 Then all the churches will know that I **am** he who searches hearts
3: 1 your deeds; you have a reputation of being alive, but *you* **are** dead.
3: 4 They will walk with me, dressed in white, for *they* **are** worthy.
3: 9 of Satan, who claim *to* **be** Jews though they are not, but are liars—
3: 9 of Satan, who claim to be Jews though *they* **are** not, but are liars—
3: 15 I know your deeds, that *you* **are** neither cold nor hot. I wish you
3: 15 are neither cold nor hot. I wish *you* **were** either one or the other!
3: 16 So, because *you* **are** lukewarm—neither hot nor cold—I am about
3: 17 You say, '*I* **am** rich; I have acquired wealth and do not need a
3: 17 But you do not realize that you are wretched, pitiful, poor,
4: 5 seven lamps were blazing. These **are** the seven spirits of God.
4: 8 holy is the Lord God Almighty, who **was**, and is, and is to come."
4: 8 holy is the Lord God Almighty, who was, and **is**, and is to come."
4: 11 "*You* **are** worthy, our Lord and God, to receive glory and honor
4: 11 and by your will they were created and **have** *their* **being**."
5: 6 which **are** the seven spirits of God sent out into all the earth.
5: 8 golden bowls full of incense, which **are** the prayers of the saints.
5: 9 "*You* **are** worthy to take the scroll and to open its seals,
5: 11 and heard the voice of many angels, **numbering** [*+750*] thousands
5: 12 "Worthy **is** the Lamb, who was slain, to receive power and wealth
7: 13 in white robes—who **are** *they*, and where did they come from?"
7: 14 "These **are** they who have come out of the great tribulation;
7: 15 "*they* **are** before the throne of God and serve him day and night in
9: 8 hair was like women's hair, and their teeth **were** like lions' teeth.
9: 19 The power of the horses **was** in their mouths and in their tails;
10: 6 and all that is in it, and said, "*There* *will* **be** no more delay!
10: 9 your stomach sour, but in your mouth *it* *will* **be** as sweet as honey."
10: 10 *It* **tasted** as sweet as honey in my mouth, but when I had eaten it,
11: 4 These **are** the two olive trees and the two lampstands that stand
11: 17 thanks to you, Lord God Almighty, the *One who* **is** and who was,
11: 17 thanks to you, Lord God Almighty, the One who is and who **was**,
13: 2 The beast I saw **resembled** [*+3927*] a leopard, but had feet like
13: 10 This **calls for** patient endurance and faithfulness on the part of the
13: 18 This **calls for** wisdom. If anyone has insight, let him calculate the
13: 18 let him calculate the number of the beast, for *it* **is** man's number.
14: 4 These **are** those who did not defile themselves with women,
14: 4 not defile themselves with women, for they **kept** *themselves* pure.
14: 5 No lie was found in their mouths; *they* **are** blameless.

14: 12 This **calls for** patient endurance on the part of the saints who obey
16: 5 "*You* **are** just in these judgments, you who are and who were,
16: 5 you who **are** and who were, the Holy One, because you have
16: 5 you who are and who **were**, the Holy One, because you have
16: 6 and you have given them blood to drink as *they* **deserve** [*+545*]."
16: 14 *They* **are** spirits of demons performing miraculous signs, and they
16: 21 account of the plague of hail, because the plague **was** so terrible.
17: 4 The woman **was** dressed in purple and scarlet, and was glittering
17: 8 The beast, which you saw, *once* **was**, now is not, and will come up
17: 8 The beast, which you saw, once was, now **is** not, and will come up
17: 8 see the beast, because *he* *once* **was**, now is not, and yet will come.
17: 8 see the beast, because he once was, *now* **is** not, and yet will come.
17: 9 The seven heads **are** seven hills on which the woman sits.
17: 10 *They* **are** also seven kings. Five have fallen, one is, the other has
17: 10 Five have fallen, one **is**, the other has not yet come; but when he
17: 11 The beast who *once* **was**, and now is not, is an eighth king.
17: 11 The beast who once was, and now **is** not, is an eighth king.
17: 11 The beast who once was, and now is not, **is** an eighth king.
17: 11 *He* **belongs** [*+1666*] **to** the seven and is going to his destruction.
17: 12 "The ten horns you saw **are** ten kings who have not yet received a
17: 14 overcome them because *he* **is** Lord of lords and King of kings—
17: 15 the prostitute sits, **are** peoples, multitudes, nations and languages.
17: 18 The woman you saw **is** the great city that rules over the kings of
18: 7 'I sit as queen; *I* **am** not a widow, and I will never mourn.'
18: 23 heard in you again. Your merchants **were** the world's great men.
19: 8 her to wear." (Fine linen **stands for** the righteous acts of the saints.)
19: 9 of the Lamb!' " And he added, "These **are** the true words of God."
19: 10 *I* **am** a fellow servant with you and with your brothers who hold to
19: 10 Worship God! For the testimony of Jesus **is** the spirit of prophecy."
20: 2 seized the dragon, that ancient serpent, who **is** the devil, or Satan,
20: 6 but *they* *will* **be** priests of God and of Christ and will reign with
20: 12 were opened. Another book was opened, which **is** the book of life.
20: 14 thrown into the lake of fire. The lake of fire **is** the second death.
21: 1 the first earth had passed away, and *there* **was** no longer any sea.
21: 3 They *will* **be** his people, and God himself will be with them
21: 3 be his people, and God himself *will* **be** with them and be their God.
21: 4 *There* *will* **be** no more death or mourning or crying or pain,
21: 4 or pain, **[RPG]** for the old order of things has passed away."
21: 5 "Write this down, for these words **are** trustworthy and true."
21: 6 I am the Alpha and the Omega, the Beginning and the End.
21: 7 will inherit all this, and *I* *will* **be** his God and he will be my son.
21: 7 will inherit all this, and I will be his God and he *will* **be** my son.
21: 8 will be in the fiery lake of burning sulfur. This **is** the second death."
21: 12 On the gates were written the names **[NIE]** of the twelve tribes of
21: 16 it to be 12,000 stadia in length, and as wide and high as it **is** long.
21: 17 cubits thick, by man's measurement, which the angel *was* **using**.
21: 21 twelve gates were twelve pearls, each gate **made** of a single pearl.
21: 22 because the Lord God Almighty and the Lamb **are** its temple.
21: 25 no day will its gates ever be shut, for *there* *will* **be** no night there.
22: 3 No longer *will* *there* **be** any curse. The throne of God and of the
22: 3 The throne of God and of the Lamb *will* **be** in the city, and his
22: 5 *There* *will* **be** no more night. They will not need the light of a
22: 9 *I* **am** a fellow servant with you and with your brothers the prophets
22: 10 up the words of the prophecy of this book, because the time **is** near.
22: 12 and I will give to everyone according to what he **has** done.
22: 14 that they *may* **have** the right to the tree of life and may go through
22: 16 I **am** the Root and the Offspring of David, and the bright Morning

1640 εἶμι, *eimi* Not used in UBS/NIV [→ *583, 717, 1655,*
1996, 2079, 2768, 5290]

1641 εἵνεκεν, *heineken* [2] [√ *1914*]

because [*+4005*] [1], in comparison with
[*+1877+3538+3836+1017*] [1]

Lk 4: 18 "The Spirit of the Lord is on me, **because** [*+4005*] he has anointed
2Co 3: 10 For what was glorious has no glory now **in comparison with**
[*+1877+3538+3836+4047*] the surpassing glory.

1642 εἴπερ, *eiper* [6] [√ *1623 + 4302*]

if [2], *untranslated* [1], in fact [*+726*] [1], if indeed [1], since [1]

Ro 3: 30 **since** there is only one God, who will justify the circumcised by
8: 9 the sinful nature but by the Spirit, **if** the Spirit of God lives in you.
8: 17 **if indeed** we share in his sufferings in order that we may also share

1Co 8: 5 For even **if** there are so-called gods, whether in heaven or on earth
   15: 15 But he did not raise him **if** [*+726*] **in fact** the dead are not raised.
2Th 1: 6 [**NIE**] God is just: He will pay back trouble to those who trouble

1643 εἴπως, *eipōs* Not used in UBS/NIV [√ *1623* + *4544*]

1644 εἰρηνεύω, *eirēneuō* [4] [√ *1645*]

live in peace [2], be at peace [1], live at peace [1]

Mk   9: 50 Have salt in yourselves, and **be at peace** with each other."
Ro 12: 18 as far as it depends on you, **live at peace** with everyone.
2Co 13: 11 for perfection, listen to my appeal, be of one mind, **live in peace**.
1Th 5: 13 in love because of their work. **Live in peace** with each other.

1645 εἰρήνη, *eirēnē* [92] [→ *1644, 1646, 1647, 1648*]

εἰρήνη ἀπὸ θεοῦ (peace from God) [12] Ro 1:7; 1Co 1:3; 2Co
  1:2; Gal 1:3; Eph 1:2; Php 1:2; Col 1:2; 2Th 1:2; 1Ti 1:2; 2Ti 1:2;
  Tit 1:4; Phm 1:3

ὁ θεὸς [τῆς] εἰρήνης (the God of peace) [7] Ro 15:33; 16:20;
  1Co 14:33; 2Co 13:11; Php 4:9; 1Th 5:23; Heb 13:20

πορεύω εἰς [ἐν] εἰρήνη (go in peace) [3] Lk 7:50; 8:48; Ac
  16:36

ὑπάγω εἰς [ἐν] εἰρήνη (go in peace) [2] Mk 5:34; Jas 2:16

χάρις καὶ εἰρήνη (grace and peace) [17] Ro 1:7; 1Co 1:3; 2Co
  1:2; Gal 1:3; Eph 1:2; Php 1:2; Col 1:2; 1Th 1:1; 2Th 1:2; 1Ti 1:2;
  2Ti 1:2; Tit 1:4; Phm 1:3; 1Pe 1:2; 2Pe 1:2; 2Jn 1:3; Rev 1:4

peace [82], peace be with [4], blessing of peace [1],
peacemakers [*+4472*] [1], reconcile [*+1650+5261*] [1], safe
[*+1877*] [1], welcomed [*+1312+3552*] [1], wish well [*+1877*] [1]

Mt 10: 13 If the home is deserving, let your **peace** rest on it; if it is not,
    10: 13 let your peace rest on it; if it is not, let your **peace** return to you.
    10: 34 "Do not suppose that I have come to bring **peace** to the earth.
    10: 34 peace to the earth. I did not come to bring **peace**, but a sword.
Mk   5: 34 faith has healed you. Go in **peace** and be freed from your suffering."
Lk   1: 79 in the shadow of death, to guide our feet into the path *of* **peace**."
     2: 14 in the highest, and on earth **peace** to men on whom his favor rests."
     2: 29 as you have promised, you now dismiss your servant in **peace**.
     7: 50 Jesus said to the woman, "Your faith has saved you; go in **peace**."
     8: 48 he said to her, "Daughter, your faith has healed you. Go in **peace**."
    10: 5 "When you enter a house, first say, '**Peace** to this house.'
    10: 6 If a man *of* **peace** is there, your peace will rest on him; if not,
    10: 6 If a man of peace is there, your **peace** will rest on him; if not,
    11: 21 guards his own house, his possessions are **safe** [*+1877*].
    12: 51 Do you think I came to bring **peace** on earth? No, I tell you,
    14: 32 the other is still a long way off and will ask for terms of **peace**.
    19: 38 the name of the Lord!" "**Peace** in heaven and glory in the highest!"
    19: 42 had only known on this day what would bring you **peace**—
    24: 36 himself stood among them and said to them, "**Peace be with** you."
Jn 14: 27 **Peace** I leave with you; my peace I give you. I do not give to you
    14: 27 Peace I leave with you; my **peace** I give you. I do not give to you
    16: 33 I have told you these things, so that in me you may have **peace**.
    20: 19 Jesus came and stood among them and said, "**Peace be with** you!"
    20: 21 Again Jesus said, "**Peace be with** you! As the Father has sent me,
    20: 26 Jesus came and stood among them and said, "**Peace be with** you!"
Ac   7: 26 *He tried to* **reconcile** [*+1650+5261*] them by saying, 'Men,
     9: 31 throughout Judea, Galilee and Samaria enjoyed a *time of* **peace**.
    10: 36 telling the good news *of* **peace** through Jesus Christ, who is Lord
    12: 20 a trusted personal servant of the king, they asked for **peace**,
    15: 33 they were sent off by the brothers with the **blessing of peace** to
    16: 36 that you and Silas be released. Now you can leave. Go in **peace**."
    24: 2 "We have enjoyed a long period *of* **peace** under you, and your
Ro   1: 7 Grace and **peace** to you from God our Father and from the Lord
     2: 10 but glory, honor and **peace** for everyone who does good: first for
     3: 17 and the way *of* **peace** they do not know."
     5: 1 we have **peace** with God through our Lord Jesus Christ,
     8: 6 is death, but the mind controlled by the Spirit is life and **peace**;
    14: 17 but *of* righteousness, **peace** and joy in the Holy Spirit,
    14: 19 Let us therefore make every effort to do what *leads to* **peace**
    15: 13 the God of hope fill you with all joy and **peace** as you trust in him,
    15: 33 The God *of* **peace** be with you all. Amen.
    16: 20 The God *of* **peace** will soon crush Satan under your feet. The grace

1Co 1: 3 Grace and **peace** to you from God our Father and the Lord Jesus
     7: 15 bound in such circumstances; God has called us to live in **peace**.
    14: 33 For God is not a God of disorder but *of* **peace**. As in all the
    16: 11 Send him on his way in **peace** so that he may return to me.
2Co 1: 2 Grace and **peace** to you from God our Father and the Lord Jesus
    13: 11 live in peace. And the God *of* love and **peace** will be with you.
Gal 1: 3 Grace and **peace** to you from God our Father and the Lord Jesus
     5: 22 is love, joy, **peace**, patience, kindness, goodness, faithfulness,
     6: 16 **Peace** and mercy to all who follow this rule, even to the Israel of
Eph 1: 2 Grace and **peace** to you from God our Father and the Lord Jesus
     2: 14 For he himself is our **peace**, who has made the two one and has
     2: 15 create in himself one new man out of the two, thus making **peace**,
     2: 17 He came and preached **peace** to you who were far away and peace
     2: 17 to you who were far away and **peace** to those who were near.
     4: 3 effort to keep the unity of the Spirit through the bond *of* **peace**.
     6: 15 feet fitted with the readiness that comes from the gospel *of* **peace**.
     6: 23 **Peace** to the brothers, and love with faith from God the Father
Php 1: 2 Grace and **peace** to you from God our Father and the Lord Jesus
     4: 7 And the **peace** of God, which transcends all understanding,
     4: 9 put it into practice. And the God *of* **peace** will be with you.
Col 1: 2 in Christ at Colosse: Grace and **peace** to you from God our Father.
     3: 15 Let the **peace** of Christ rule in your hearts, since as members of
1Th 1: 1 God the Father and the Lord Jesus Christ: Grace and **peace** to you.
     5: 3 While people are saying, "**Peace** and safety," destruction will come
     5: 23 May God himself, the God *of* **peace**, sanctify you through
2Th 1: 2 Grace and **peace** to you from God the Father and the Lord Jesus
     3: 16 Now may the Lord *of* **peace** himself give you peace at all times
     3: 16 Now may the Lord of peace himself give you **peace** at all times
1Ti 1: 2 mercy and **peace** from God the Father and Christ Jesus our Lord.
2Ti 1: 2 mercy and **peace** from God the Father and Christ Jesus our Lord.
     2: 22 desires of youth, and pursue righteousness, faith, love and **peace**,
Tit 1: 4 Grace and **peace** from God the Father and Christ Jesus our Savior.
Phm 1: 3 Grace to you and **peace** from God our Father and the Lord Jesus
Heb 7: 2 righteousness"; then also, "king of Salem" means "king *of* **peace**."
    11: 31 By faith the prostitute Rahab, *because she* **welcomed**
            [*+1312+3552*] the spies, was not killed with those who were
    12: 14 Make every effort to live *in* **peace** with all men and to be holy;
    13: 20 May the God *of* **peace**, who through the blood of the eternal
Jas   2: 16 If one of you says to him, "Go, I **wish** you **well** [*+1877*]; keep
     3: 18 **Peacemakers** [*+4472*] who sow in peace raise a harvest of
     3: 18 Peacemakers who sow in **peace** raise a harvest of righteousness.
1Pe 1: 2 sprinkling by his blood: Grace and **peace** be yours in abundance.
     3: 11 must turn from evil and do good; he must seek **peace** and pursue it.
     5: 14 another with a kiss of love. **Peace** to all of you who are in Christ.
2Pe 1: 2 and **peace** be yours in abundance through the knowledge of God
     3: 14 every effort to be found spotless, blameless and at **peace** with him.
2Jn 1: 3 mercy and **peace** from God the Father and from Jesus Christ,
3Jn 1: 14 I hope to see you soon, and we will talk face to face. **Peace** to you.
Jude 1: 2 Mercy, **peace** and love be yours in abundance.
Rev 1: 4 Grace and **peace** to you from him who is, and who was, and who is
     6: 4 Its rider was given power to take **peace** from the earth and to make

1646 εἰρηνικός, *eirēnikos* [2] [√ *1645*]

peace [1], peace-loving [1]

Heb 12: 11 of righteousness and **peace** for those who have been trained by it.
Jas   3: 17 then **peace-loving**, considerate, submissive, full of mercy

1647 εἰρηνοποιέω, *eirēnopoieō* [1] [√ *1645* + *4472*]

making peace [1]

Col 1: 20 in heaven, *by* **making peace** through his blood, shed on the cross.

1648 εἰρηνοποιός, *eirēnopoios* [1] [√ *1645* + *4472*]

peacemakers [1]

Mt   5: 9 Blessed are the **peacemakers**, for they will be called sons of God.

1649 εἴρω, *eirō* Not used in UBS/NIV [→ *4694, 4937*]

1650 εἰς, eis [1767 / 1766] [→ 1652, 1653, 1654, 1655, 1656, 1657, 1658, 1659, 1660, 1661, 1662, 2081, 2082, 2269, 2276, 2277, 2278, 4206, 4207, 4208, 4209, 4210, 5291]

εἰς τὸν αἰῶνα (into the age; forever) [27] Mt 21:19; Mk 3:29; 11:14; Lk 1:55; Jn 4:14; 6:51,58; 8:35,51,52; 10:28; 11:26; 12:34; 13:8; 14:16; 1Co 8:13; 2Co 9:9; Heb 1:8; 5:6; 6:20; 7:17,21,24,28; 1Pe 1:25; 1Jn 2:17; 2Jn 1:2

εἰς τοὺς αἰῶνας (into the ages; forever) [7] Lk 1:33; Ro 1:25; 9:5; 11:36; 16:27; 2Co 11:31; Heb 13:8

εἰς τοὺς αἰῶνας τῶν αἰώνων (into the ages of ages; forever) [21] Gal 1:5; Php 4:20; Eph 3:21; 1Ti 1:17; 2Ti 4:18; Heb 1:8; 13:21; 1Pe 4:11; 5:11; Rev 1:6,18; 4:9,10; 5:13; 7:12; 10:6; 11:15; 15:7; 19:3; 20:10; 22:5

to [462], into [248], in [165], for [143], untranslated [106], on [48], enter [RP1656] [46], at [36], as [26], entered [RP1656] [26], forever [+172+3836] [23], to [+3836] [21], against [17], so that [+3836] [15], went into [RP1656] [14], among [11], so that [10], that [+3836] [7], about [6], be [+1639] [6], become [+1181] [6], go into [RP1656] [6], of [6], with [6], before [5], entered [+2262] [5], never [+172+3590+3836+4024] [5], until [5], back [+3836+3958] [4], become [+1639] [4], for purpose [4], leads to [4], reached [+2262] [4], toward [4], went to [RP1656] [4], why [+5515] [4], and so [+3836] [3], because he is [+3950] [3], brought [3], enters [RP1656] [3], enters [RP1660] [3], fall into [RP1656] [3], in order that [+3836] [3], leading to [3], went inside [RP1656] [3], where [+4005] [3], among [+3545+3836] [2], arrived in [RP1656] [2], became [+1181] [2], brought into [RP1652] [2], came into [RP1656] [2], come and share [RP1656] [2], down upon [2], enter [RP16561650] [2], enter [RP1660] [2], for [+3836] [2], forever [+1457+3836] [2], go into [RP16601650] [2], going into [RP1660] [2], home [+3836+3875+5148] [2], lead into [RP1662] [2], never [+172+3836+4024] [2], on to [2], over [2], saved [+5401] [2], that [2], the reason [+4047] [2], through [2], throughout [+3910] [2], to bring [2], to do [2], aboard [1], across [+3836+4305] [1], across the lake [+3836+4305] [1], again [+172+3836] [1], all over [+3910] [1], among [+3847] [1], and thus [+3836] [1], appear before [RP1656] [1], are [+1639] [1], arrived [+2262] [1], arrived [RP1656] [1], as a result [+3836] [1], as far as [1], ashore [+1178+3836] [1], at [RP1656] [1], at all [+3836+4117] [1], attaining to [1], aways [+2557+3836] [1], become [1], been [+1181] [1], before [+3545+3836] [1], before them [+3545] [1], belonging to God [+4348] [1], beyond [1], bring [+1639] [1], bring into [1], bring to [1], bringing to [RP1662] [1], brings into [RP1652] [1], brought into [RP1662] [1], burial [+3645+5502] [1], by [1], by itself [+1651+3023+5536+6006] [1], came to [RP1656] [1], care very little [+1639+1788] [1], come at [RP1656] [1], come in among [RP1656] [1], come to [RP1656] [1], comes into [RP1656] [1], completely [+3836+4117] [1], condemned [+2262+3213] [1], confirms [+1012] [1], decay [+1426+5715] [1], destroyed [+724] [1], discredited [+3357+4029] [1], dos [1], doing [1], endlessly [+1457+3836] [1], enter [+4513] [1], enter [RP1658] [1], enter into [RP1656] [1], entered [RP5291] [1], entered into [RP1655] [1], entered into [RP1656] [1], entering [RP1656] [1], eventually [+5465] [1], ever [+172+3836] [1], ever-increasing wickedness [+490+490+3836] [1], faith from first to last [+4411+4411] [1], far off [+3426] [1], for all time [+1457+3836] [1], for the express purpose [+899+4047] [1], for this reason [+4047] [1], forever [+172+2465] [1], forever [+172] [1], forevermore [+172+3836+4246] [1], from [1], full of [1], gave [+965] [1], go through into [RP1656] [1], gos [1], goes into [RP1656] [1], going into [RP1656] [1], gone into [RP1656] [1], got to [RP1656] [1], granted [1], greatly [+4353] [1], grew [+2262+3836] [1], hand over to [+4140+5931] [1], has enough [+2400] [1], home [+899+3836+3875] [1], how to gratify [1], in agreement [+1651+3836] [1], in dealing with [1], in order that [1], in order to bring [1], in regard to [1], in this way [+3836] [1], increases [1], indoors [+3836+3864] [1], indoors [+3875] [1], intended to bring [1], it [+3795] [1], justified [+1466] [1], landed [+609+1178+3836] [1], led into [RP1652] [1], led to [1], listen carefully [+3836+4044+5148+5148+5502] [1], lose good name [+591+2262] [1], make [1], never again

[+172+3590+3836+4024] [1], next [+3516+3836] [1], of mine [+1609] [1], onto [1], out of his body [+909+1744+3836] [1], out of the body [+909+1675] [1], perish [+724+1639] [1], possess [+2959] [1], prompted [+965+2840+3836] [1], put on board [+899+1837] [1], reach [+1181] [1], reached [+201] [1], reached [RP1656] [1], reaching [+2262] [1], reaped the benefits of [RP1656] [1], receive [1], reconcile [+1645+5261] [1], regarding [1], result [+3836] [1], result in [1], return [+2262+3836+4099] [1], return [+5715] [1], right into [+2276+2401] [1], saved [+4348+6034] [1], so [+3836] [1], so as [+3836] [1], so as to [1], so then [+3836] [1], spur on [+4237] [1], supply [1], take [+2884] [1], take [+404] [1], take into [RP1652] [1], taken into [RP1652] [1], that far outweighs them all [+983+2848+5651+5651] [1], that is why [+4047] [1], the full extent of [+5465] [1], the places of [1], then will be able [+3836] [1], there [+2038+3836] [1], this is the reason [+4047] [1], this very reason [+4047] [1], throughout [+4246] [1], throughout [1], till [1], to [+4047] [1], to cause [1], to serve [1], to this end [+4005] [1], took into [RP1652] [1], treat [+4472] [1], turned [+1181] [1], turned around [+3836+3958+5138] [1], turned back [+599+3836+3958] [1], under [1], under power [+5931] [1], unto [1], up [1], visit [+4601] [1], visited [+2262] [1], welcome into [RP1658] [1], went back into [RP1656] [1], went into [RP1660] [1], went to [RP1655] [1], went to [RP1660] [1], went with into [RP5291] [1], what [+5515] [1], where [+3836+5536] [1], where [+3836+5596] [1], where [1], with [+3836] [1], with ever-increasing glory [+608+1518+1518] [1], with this in mind [+899] [1], without [+3590] [1]

Mt	2: 1	the time of King Herod, Magi from the east came **to** Jerusalem
	2: 8	He sent them **to** Bethlehem and said, "Go and make a careful search
	2:11	On coming **to** the house, they saw the child with his mother Mary,
	2:12	go back to Herod, they returned **to** their country by another route.
	2:13	he said, "take the child and his mother and escape **to** Egypt.
	2:14	took the child and his mother during the night and left **for** Egypt,
	2:20	"Get up, take the child and his mother and go **to** the land of Israel,
	2:21	the child and his mother and **went to** [RP1656] the land of Israel.
	2:22	been warned in a dream, he withdrew **to** the district of Galilee,
	2:23	and he went and lived **in** a town called Nazareth. So was fulfilled
	3:10	not produce good fruit will be cut down and thrown **into** the fire.
	3:11	"I baptize you with water **for** repentance. But after me will come
	3:12	gathering his wheat **into** the barn and burning up the chaff with
	4: 1	Then Jesus was led by the Spirit **into** the desert to be tempted by
	4: 5	Then the devil took him **to** the holy city and had him stand on the
	4: 8	the devil took him **to** a very high mountain and showed him all the
	4:12	heard that John had been put in prison, he returned **to** Galilee.
	4:13	Leaving Nazareth, he went and lived **in** Capernaum, which was by
	4:18	They were casting a net **into** the lake, for they were fishermen.
	4:24	News about him spread **all over** [+3910] Syria, and people brought
	5: 1	he saw the crowds, he went up **on** a mountainside and sat down.
	5:13	It is no longer good **for** anything, except to be thrown out
	5:20	*you will* certainly not **enter** [RP1656] the kingdom of heaven,
	5:22	who says, 'You fool!' will be in danger of the fire **[NIE]** of hell.
	5:25	hand you over to the officer, and you may be thrown **into** prison.
	5:29	part of your body than for your whole body to be thrown **into** hell.
	5:30	one part of your body than for your whole body to go **into** hell.
	5:35	his footstool; or **by** Jerusalem, for it is the city of the Great King.
	5:39	If someone strikes you on the right cheek, turn to him the other
	6: 6	**go into** [RP1656] your room, close the door and pray to your
	6:13	And **lead** us not **into** [RP1662] temptation, but deliver us from the
	6:26	Look at **[NIE]** the birds of the air; they do not sow or reap
	6:26	they do not sow or reap or store away **in** barns, and yet your
	6:30	which is here today and tomorrow is thrown **into** the fire, will he
	6:34	Therefore do not worry **about** tomorrow, for tomorrow will worry
	7:13	For wide is the gate and broad is the road that leads **to** destruction,
	7:14	But small is the gate and narrow the road that leads **to** life,
	7:19	that does not bear good fruit is cut down and thrown **into** the fire.
	7:21	'Lord, Lord,' *will* **enter** [RP1656] the kingdom of heaven,
	8: 4	and offer the gift Moses commanded, **as** a testimony to them."
	8: 5	*When* Jesus *had* **entered** [RP1656] Capernaum, a centurion came
	8:12	**into** the darkness, where there will be weeping and gnashing of
	8:14	When Jesus came **into** Peter's house, he saw Peter's mother-in-law
	8:18	around him, he gave orders to cross **to** the other side of the lake.
	8:23	Then he got **into** the boat and his disciples followed him.
	8:28	When he arrived **at** the other side in the region of the Gadarenes,
	8:28	When he arrived at the other side **in** the region of the Gadarenes,

8:31 begged Jesus, "If you drive us out, send us **into** the herd of pigs."
8:32 So they came out and went **into** the pigs, and the whole herd
8:32 and the whole herd rushed down the steep bank **into** the lake
8:33 tending the pigs ran off, went **into** the town and reported all this,
8:34 Then the whole town went out **to** meet Jesus. And when they saw
9: 1 Jesus stepped **into** a boat, crossed over and came to his own town.
9: 1 Jesus stepped into a boat, crossed over and came **to** his own town.
9: 6 said to the paralytic, "Get up, take your mat and go **[NIE]** home."
9: 7 And the man got up and went **[NIE]** home.
9:17 Neither do men pour new wine **into** old wineskins. If they do,
9:17 No, they pour new wine **into** new wineskins, and both are
9:23 *When* Jesus **entered** [+2262] the ruler's house and saw the flute
9:26 News of this spread **through** all that region.
9:28 When he had gone **indoors** [+3836+3864], the blind men came to
9:38 of the harvest, therefore, to send out workers **into** his harvest field."
10: 5 "Do not go **among** [+3847] the Gentiles or enter any town of the
10: 5 among the Gentiles or **enter** [RP1656] any town of the Samaritans.
10: 9 Do not take along any gold or silver or copper **in** your belts;
10:10 take no bag **for** the journey, or extra tunic, or sandals or a staff;
10:11 "Whatever town or village *you* **enter** [RP1656], search for some
10:12 *As you* **enter** [RP1656] the home, give it your greeting.
10:17 they will hand you over **to** the local councils and flog you in their
10:18 and kings **as** witnesses to them and to the Gentiles.
10:21 "Brother will betray brother **to** death, and a father his child;
10:22 because of me, but he who stands firm **to** the end will be saved.
10:23 When you are persecuted in one place, flee **to** another. I tell you
10:27 what is whispered **in** your ear, proclaim from the roofs.
10:41 Anyone who receives a prophet **because he**s **is** [+3950] a prophet
10:41 and anyone who receives a righteous man **because he**s **is** [+3950]
10:42 of cold water to one of these little ones **because he**s **is** [+3950]
11: 7 "What did you go out **into** the desert to see? A reed swayed by the
12: 4 *He* **entered** [RP1656] the house of God, and he and his
12: 9 Going on from that place, he went **into** their synagogue,
12:11 "If any of you has a sheep and it falls **into** a pit on the Sabbath,
12:18 my servant whom I have chosen, the one I love, **in** whom I delight;
12:20 wick he will not snuff out, till he leads justice **to** victory.
12:29 how can anyone **enter** [RP1656] a strong man's house and carry
12:41 for they repented **at** the preaching of Jonah, and now one greater
12:44 Then it says, 'I will return **to** the house I left.' When it arrives,
13: 2 Such large crowds gathered around him that he got **into** a boat
13:22 The one who received the seed that fell **among** the thorns is the
13:30 First collect the weeds and tie them **in** bundles to be burned;
13:30 to be burned; then gather the wheat and **bring** it **into** my barn.' "
13:33 and mixed **into** a large amount of flour until it worked all through
13:36 Then he left the crowd and went **into** the house. His disciples came
13:42 They will throw them **into** the fiery furnace, where there will be
13:47 the kingdom of heaven is like a net that was let down **into** the lake
13:48 Then they sat down and collected the good fish **in** baskets,
13:50 and throw them **into** the fiery furnace, where there will be weeping
13:54 Coming to his hometown, he began teaching the people in their
14:13 had happened, he withdrew by boat privately **to** a solitary place.
14:15 so they can go **to** the villages and buy themselves some food."
14:19 Taking the five loaves and the two fish and looking up **to** heaven,
14:22 Immediately Jesus made the disciples get **into** the boat and go on
14:22 disciples get into the boat and go on ahead of him **to** the other side,
14:23 dismissed them, he went up **on** a mountainside by himself to pray.
14:31 "You of little faith," he said, "**why** [+5515] did you doubt?"
14:32 And when they climbed **into** the boat, the wind died down.
14:34 When they had crossed over, they landed **at** Gennesaret.
14:35 recognized Jesus, they sent word **to** all the surrounding country.
15:11 What **goes into** [RP1656] a man's mouth does not make him
15:14 If a blind man leads a blind man, both will fall **into** a pit."
15:17 "Don't you see that whatever **enters** [RP1660] the mouth goes into
15:17 "Don't you see that whatever enters the mouth goes **into** the
15:17 goes into the stomach and then **out of the body** [+909+1675]?
15:21 that place, Jesus withdrew **to** the region of Tyre and Sidon.
15:24 He answered, "I was sent only **to** the lost sheep of Israel."
15:29 Sea of Galilee. Then he went up **on** a mountainside and sat down.
15:39 he got into **[RPG]** the boat and went to the vicinity of Magadan.
15:39 he got into the boat and went **to** the vicinity of Magadan.
16: 5 When they went **across the lake** [+3836+4305], the disciples
16:13 When Jesus came **to** the region of Caesarea Philippi, he asked his
16:21 Jesus began to explain to his disciples that he must go **to** Jerusalem
17: 1 of James, and led them up **[NIE]** a high mountain by themselves.
17:15 is suffering greatly. He often falls **into** the fire or into the water.
17:15 is suffering greatly. He often falls into the fire or **into** the water.

17:22 "The Son of Man is going to be betrayed **into** the hands of men.
17:24 After Jesus and his disciples arrived **in** Capernaum, the collectors
17:25 When Peter came **into** the house, Jesus was the first to speak.
17:27 we may not offend them, go **to** the lake and throw out your line.
18: 3 *you will* never **enter** [RP1656] the kingdom of heaven.
18: 6 But if anyone causes one of these little ones who believe **in** me to
18: 8 It is better for you *to* **enter** [RP1656] life maimed or crippled than
18: 8 than to have two hands or two feet and be thrown **into** eternal fire.
18: 9 It is better for you *to* **enter** [RP1656] life with one eye than to
18: 9 one eye than to have two eyes and be thrown **into** the fire of hell.
18:15 "If your brother sins **against** you, go and show him his fault,
18:20 For where two or three come together **in** my name, there am I with
18:21 how many times shall I forgive my brother when he sins **against**
18:30 and had the man thrown **into** prison until he could pay the debt.
19: 1 and went **into** the region of Judea to the other side of the Jordan.
19: 5 be united to his wife, and the two *will* **become** [+1639] one flesh'?
19:17 If you want *to* **enter** [RP1656] life, obey the commandments."
19:23 it is hard for a rich man *to* **enter** [RP1656] the kingdom of heaven.
19:24 needle than for a rich man *to* **enter** [RP1656] the kingdom of God."
20: 1 went out early in the morning to hire men to work **in** his vineyard.
20: 2 to pay them a denarius for the day and sent them **into** his vineyard.
20: 4 He told them, 'You also go and work **in** my vineyard, and I will
20: 7 "He said to them, 'You also go and work **in** my vineyard.'
20:17 Now as Jesus was going up **to** Jerusalem, he took the twelve
20:18 "We are going up **to** Jerusalem, and the Son of Man will be
20:19 and will turn him over to the Gentiles **to** [+3836] be mocked
21: 1 As they approached **[RPG]** Jerusalem and came to Bethphage on
21: 1 and came **to** Bethphage on the Mount of Olives,
21: 1 and came to Bethphage **on** the Mount of Olives,
21: 2 saying to them, "Go **to** the village ahead of you, and at once you
21:10 *When* Jesus **entered** [RP1656] Jerusalem, the whole city was
21:12 Jesus **entered** [RP1656] the temple area and drove out all who
21:17 And he left them and went out of the city **to** Bethany, where he
21:18 the morning, as he was on his way back **to** the city, he was hungry.
21:19 Then he said to it, "May you never bear fruit **again** [+172+3836]!"
21:21 'Go, throw yourself **into** the sea,' and it will be done.
21:23 Jesus **entered** [+2262] the temple courts, and, while he was
21:31 and the prostitutes are entering **[NIE]** the kingdom of God ahead
21:42 'The stone the builders rejected *has* **become** [+1181] the capstone;
21:46 of the crowd because the people held that he was a **[NIE]** prophet.
22: 3 He sent his servants to those who had been invited **to** the banquet
22: 4 and everything is ready. Come **to** the wedding banquet.'
22: 5 no attention and went off—one **to** his field, another to his business.
22: 9 Go to the street corners and invite **to** the banquet anyone you find.'
22:10 So the servants went out **into** the streets and gathered all the people
22:13 'Tie him hand and foot, and throw him outside, **into** the darkness,
22:16 swayed by men, because you pay no attention **to** who they are.
23:34 you will flog in your synagogues and pursue from town **to** town.
24: 9 "Then you will be handed over **to** be persecuted and put to death,
24:13 but he who stands firm **to** the end will be saved.
24:14 will be preached in the whole world **as** a testimony to all nations,
24:16 then let those who are in Judea flee **to** the mountains.
24:38 giving in marriage, up to the day Noah **entered** [RP1656] the ark;
25: 1 virgins who took their lamps and went out **to** meet the bridegroom.
25: 6 the cry rang out: 'Here's the bridegroom! Come out **to** meet him!'
25:10 The virgins who were ready went in with him **to** the wedding
25:21 **Come and share** [RP1656] your master's happiness!'
25:23 **Come and share** [RP1656] your master's happiness!'
25:30 **into** the darkness, where there will be weeping and gnashing of
25:41 **into** the eternal fire prepared for the devil and his angels.
25:46 "Then they will go away **to** eternal punishment, but the righteous to
25:46 go away to eternal punishment, but the righteous **to** eternal life."
26: 2 and the Son of Man will be handed over **to** [+3836] be crucified."
26: 3 and the elders of the people assembled **in** the palace of the high
26: 8 they were indignant. "**Why** [+5515] this waste?" they asked.
26:10 you bothering this woman? She has done a beautiful thing **to** me.
26:13 the world, what she has done will also be told, **in** memory of her."
26:18 He replied, "Go **into** the city to a certain man and tell him,
26:28 which is poured out for many **for** the forgiveness of sins.
26:30 When they had sung a hymn, they went out **to** the Mount of Olives.
26:32 But after I have risen, I will go ahead of you **into** Galilee."
26:36 Then Jesus went with his disciples **to** a place called Gethsemane,
26:41 and pray so that *you will* not **fall into** [RP1656] temptation.
26:45 is near, and the Son of Man is betrayed **into** the hands of sinners.
26:52 "Put your sword back **in** its place," Jesus said to him, "for all who
26:67 Then they spit **in** his face and struck him with their fists.

26: 71   Then he went out **to** the gateway, where another girl saw him
27:   5   So Judas threw the money **into** the temple and left. Then he went
27:   6   the coins and said, "It is against the law to put this **into** the treasury,
27:   7   So they decided to use the money to buy the potter's field **as** a
27: 10   and they used them to buy **[NIE]** the potter's field, as the Lord
27: 27   Then the governor's soldiers took Jesus **into** the Praetorium
27: 30   They spit **on** him, and took the staff and struck him on the head
27: 30   and took the staff and struck him **on** the head again and again.
27: 31   clothes on him. Then they led him away **to** [*+3836*] crucify him.
27: 33   They came **to** a place called Golgotha (which means The Place of
27: 51   At that moment the curtain of the temple was torn **in** two from top
27: 53   and after Jesus' resurrection *they* **went into** [*RP1656*] the holy city
28:   1   at dawn **on** the first day of the week, Mary Magdalene
28:   7   'He has risen from the dead and is going ahead of you **into** Galilee.
28: 10   Go and tell my brothers to go **to** Galilee; there they will see me."
28: 11   some of the guards **went into** the city and reported to the chief
28: 16   Then the eleven disciples went **to** Galilee, to the mountain where
28: 16   went to Galilee, **to** the mountain where Jesus had told them to go.
28: 19   baptizing them **in** the name of the Father and of the Son and of the
Mk   1:   4   and preaching a baptism of repentance **for** the forgiveness of sins.
1:   9   from Nazareth in Galilee and was baptized by John **in** the Jordan.
1: 10   being torn open and the Spirit descending **on** him like a dove.
1: 12   At once the Spirit sent him out **into** the desert,
1: 14   After John was put in prison, Jesus went **into** Galilee,
1: 21   *They* **went to** [*RP1660*] Capernaum, and when the Sabbath came,
1: 21   Jesus **went into** [*RP1656*] the synagogue and began to teach.
1: 28   News about him spread quickly **over** the whole region of Galilee.
1: 29   they went with James and John **to** the home of Simon and Andrew.
1: 35   Jesus got up, left the house and went off **to** a solitary place,
1: 38   **to** the nearby villages—so I can preach there also.
1: 38   so I can preach there also. **That is why** [*+4047*] I have come."
1: 39   So he traveled **throughout** [*+3910*] Galilee, preaching in their
1: 39   preaching **in** their synagogues and driving out demons.
1: 44   that Moses commanded for your cleansing, **as** a testimony to them."
1: 45   Jesus could no longer **enter** [*RP1656*] a town openly but stayed
2:   1   A few days later, when Jesus again **entered** [*RP1656*] Capernaum,
2: 11   get up, take your mat and go **home** [*+3836+3875+5148*]."
2: 22   And no one pours new wine **into** old wineskins. If he does,
2: 22   will be ruined. No, he pours new wine **into** new wineskins."
2: 26   *he* **entered** [*RP1656*] the house of God and ate the consecrated
3:   1   Another time *he* **went into** [*RP1656*] the synagogue, and a man
3:   3   to the man with the shriveled hand, "Stand up **in** front of everyone."
3: 13   Jesus went up **on** a mountainside and called to him those he
3: 20   Then Jesus **entered** [*+2262*] a house, and again a crowd gathered,
3: 27   no one can **enter** [*RP1656*] a strong man's house and carry off his
3: 29   But whoever blasphemes **against** the Holy Spirit will never be
3: 29   But whoever blasphemes against the Holy Spirit will **never**
         [*+172+3836+4024*] be forgiven; he is guilty of an eternal sin."
4:   1   so large that he got **into** a boat and sat in it out on the lake,
4:   7   Other seed fell **among** thorns, which grew up and choked the
4:   8   Still other seed fell **on** good soil. It came up, grew and produced a
4: 15   Satan comes and takes away the word that was sown **in** them.
4: 18   Still others, like seed sown **among** thorns, hear the word;
4: 22   and whatever is concealed is meant to be brought out **into** the
4: 35   he said to his disciples, "Let us go over to the other side."
4: 37   A furious squall came up, and the waves broke **over** the boat,
5:   1   They went **across** [*+3836+4305*] the lake to the region of the
5:   1   They went across the lake **to** the region of the Gerasenes.
5: 12   The demons begged Jesus, "Send us **among** the pigs; allow us to go
5: 12   "Send us among the pigs; allow *us to* **go into** [*RP1656*] them."
5: 13   and the evil spirits came out and **went into** [*RP1656*] the pigs.
5: 13   rushed down the steep bank **into** the lake and were drowned.
5: 14   the pigs ran off and reported this **in** the town and countryside,
5: 14   pigs ran off and reported this in the town and **[RPG]** countryside,
5: 18   As Jesus was getting **into** the boat, the man who had been
5: 19   "Go **[NIE]** home to your family and tell them how much the Lord
5: 21   When Jesus had again crossed over by boat **to** the other side of the
5: 26   yet instead of getting better *she* **grew** [*+2262+3836*] worse.
5: 34   has healed you. Go **in** peace and be freed from your suffering."
5: 38   When they came **to** the home of the synagogue ruler, Jesus saw a
6:   1   Jesus left there and went **to** his hometown, accompanied by his
6:   8   "Take nothing **for** the journey except a staff—no bread, no bag,
6:   8   journey except a staff—no bread, no bag, no money **in** your belts.
6: 10   Whenever *you* **enter** [*RP1656*] a house, stay there until you leave
6: 11   the dust off your feet when you leave, **as** a testimony against them."
6: 31   "Come with me by yourselves **to** a quiet place and get some rest."

6: 32   So they went away by themselves in a boat **to** a solitary place.
6: 36   so they can go **to** the surrounding countryside and villages
6: 41   Taking the five loaves and the two fish and looking up **to** heaven,
6: 45   Immediately Jesus made his disciples get **into** the boat and go on
6: 45   and go on ahead of him [UBS+ *to the other side*] to Bethsaida,
6: 46   After leaving them, he went up **on** a mountainside to pray.
6: 51   Then he climbed **into** the boat with them, and the wind died down.
6: 53   had crossed over, they landed **at** Gennesaret and anchored there.
6: 56   And wherever *he* **went—into** [*RP1660*] villages, towns
6: 56   wherever he went—into villages, **[RPG]** towns or countryside—
6: 56   wherever he went—into villages, towns or **[RPG]** countryside—
7: 15   a man can make him 'unclean' *by* **going into** [*RP1660*] him.
7: 17   After *he had* left the crowd and **entered** [*RP1656*] the house,
7: 18   "Don't you see that nothing that **enters** [*RP1660*] a man from the
7: 19   For *it* doesn't **go into** [*RP16601650*] his heart but into his
7: 19   For *it* doesn't **go into** [*RP16601650*] his heart but into his
7: 19   into his stomach, and then **out of his body** [*+909+1744+3836*]."
7: 24   Jesus left that place and went **to** the vicinity of Tyre. He entered a
7: 24   He **entered** [*RP1656*] a house and did not want anyone to know it;
7: 30   She went **[NIE]** home and found her child lying on the bed,
7: 31   *down* **to** the Sea of Galilee and into the region of the Decapolis.
7: 33   away from the crowd, Jesus put his fingers **into** the man's ears.
7: 34   He looked up **to** heaven and with a deep sigh said to him,
8:   3   If I send them **[NIE]** home hungry, they will collapse on the way,
8: 10   he got **into** the boat with his disciples and went to the region of
8: 10   the boat with his disciples and went **to** the region of Dalmanutha.
8: 13   got back **into** [UBS-] the boat and crossed to the other side.
8: 13   he left then, got back into the boat and crossed **to** the other side.
8: 19   When I broke the five loaves **for** the five thousand, how many
8: 20   "And when I broke the seven loaves **for** the four thousand,
8: 22   They came **to** Bethsaida, and some people brought a blind man
8: 23   When he had spit **on** the man's eyes and put his hands on him,
8: 26   Jesus sent him **[NIE]** home, saying, "Don't go into the village."
8: 26   Jesus sent him home, saying, "Don't **go into** [*RP1656*] the village."
8: 27   and his disciples went on **to** the villages around Caesarea Philippi.
9:   2   James and John with him and led them **up** a high mountain,
9: 22   "It has often thrown him **into** fire or water to kill him. But if you
9: 22   "It has often thrown him into fire or **[RPG]** water to kill him.
9: 25   come out of him and never **enter** [*RP1656*] him again."
9: 28   After Jesus had gone **indoors** [*+3875*], his disciples asked him
9: 31   "The Son of Man is going to be betrayed **into** the hands of men.
9: 33   They came **to** Capernaum. When he was in the house, he asked
9: 42   "And if anyone causes one of these little ones who believe **in** me to
9: 42   it would be better for him to be thrown **into** the sea with a large
9: 43   It is better for you *to* **enter** [*RP1656*] life maimed than with two
9: 43   for you to enter life maimed than with two hands to go **into** hell,
9: 43   two hands to go into hell, **[RPG]** where the fire never goes out.
9: 45   It is better for you *to* **enter** [*RP1656*] life crippled than to have two
9: 45   to enter life crippled than to have two feet and be thrown **into** hell.
9: 47   It is better for you *to* **enter** [*RP1656*] the kingdom of God with
9: 47   of God with one eye than to have two eyes and be thrown **into** hell,
10:   1   Jesus then left that place and went **into** the region of Judea
10:   8   and the two *will* **become** [*+1639*] one flesh.' So they are no longer
10: 10   When they were **in** the house again, the disciples asked Jesus about
10: 15   the kingdom of God like a little child *will* never **enter** [*RP1656*] it."
10: 17   As Jesus started **on** his way, a man ran up to him and fell on his
10: 23   hard it is for the rich *to* **enter** [*RP1656*] the kingdom of God!"
10: 24   "Children, how hard it is *to* **enter** [*RP1656*] the kingdom of God!
10: 25   needle than for a rich man *to* **enter** [*RP1656*] the kingdom of God."
10: 32   They were on their way up **to** Jerusalem, with Jesus leading the
10: 33   "We are going up **to** Jerusalem," he said, "and the Son of Man will
10: 46   Then they came **to** Jericho. As Jesus and his disciples,
11:   1   As they approached **[RPG]** Jerusalem and came to Bethphage
11:   1   As they approached Jerusalem and came **to** Bethphage
11:   2   saying to them, "Go **to** the village ahead of you, and just as you
11:   2   and just as *you* **enter** [*RP1660*] it, you will find a colt tied there,
11:   8   Many people spread their cloaks **on** the road, while others spread
11: 11   Jesus **entered** [*RP1656*] Jerusalem and went to the temple.
11: 11   Jesus entered Jerusalem and went **to** the temple. He looked around
11: 11   since it was already late, he went out **to** Bethany with the Twelve.
11: 14   the tree, "May no one **ever** [*+172+3836*] eat fruit from you again."
11: 15   On **reaching** [*+2262*] Jerusalem, Jesus entered the temple area
11: 15   Jesus **entered** [*RP1656*] the temple area and began driving out
11: 23   'Go, throw yourself **into** the sea,' and does not doubt in his heart
11: 27   *They* **arrived** [*+2262*] again in Jerusalem, and while Jesus was
12: 10   'The stone the builders rejected *has* **become** [*+1181*] the capstone;

12:14 swayed by men, because you pay no attention **to** who they are;
12:41 and watched the crowd putting their money **into** the temple
12:43 this poor widow has put more **into** the treasury than all the others.
13: 3 As Jesus was sitting **on** the Mount of Olives opposite the temple,
13: 9 You will be handed over **to** the local councils and flogged in the
13: 9 handed over to the local councils and flogged **in** the synagogues.
13: 9 you will stand before governors and kings **as** witnesses to them.
13:10 And the gospel must first be preached **to** all nations.
13:12 "Brother will betray brother **to** death, and a father his child.
13:13 because of me, but he who stands firm **to** the end will be saved.
13:14 then let those who are in Judea flee **to** the mountains.
13:16 Let no one **in** the field go back to get his cloak.
13:16 Let no one in the field go **back** [+3836+3958] to get his cloak.
14: 4 present were saying indignantly to one another, "**Why** [↑5515]
14: 8 She poured perfume on my body beforehand to prepare **for** my
14: 9 wherever the gospel is preached **throughout** [+3910] the world,
14: 9 the world, what she has done will also be told, **in** memory of her."
14:13 So he sent two of his disciples, telling them, "Go **into** the city,
14:16 went **into** the city and found things just as Jesus had told them.
14:20 Twelve," he replied, "one who dips bread **into** the bowl with me.
14:26 When they had sung a hymn, they went out **to** the Mount of Olives.
14:28 But after I have risen, I will go ahead of you **into** Galilee."
14:32 They went **to** a place called Gethsemane, and Jesus said to his
14:38 Watch and pray so that you will not fall **into** temptation. The spirit
14:41 Look, the Son of Man is betrayed **into** the hands of sinners.
14:54 Peter followed him at a distance, **right into** [+2276+2401] the
14:55 against Jesus so that [+3836] they could put him to death,
14:60 Then the high priest stood up **before** [+3545] **them** and asked
14:68 what you're talking about," he said, and went out **into** the entryway.
15:34 "My God, my God, why [+5515] have you forsaken me?"
15:38 The curtain of the temple was torn **in** two from top to bottom.
15:41 Many other women who had come up with him **to** Jerusalem were
16: 5 *As* they **entered** [RP1656] the tomb, they saw a young man
16: 7 tell his disciples and Peter, 'He is going ahead of you **into** Galilee.'
16:12 form to two of them while they were walking **in** the country.
16:15 "Go **into** all the world and preach the good news to all creation.
16:19 he was taken up **into** heaven and he sat at the right hand of God.
Lk 1: 9 to **go into** [RP1656] the temple of the Lord and burn incense.
1:20 not believe my words, which will come true **at** their proper time."
1:23 his time of service was completed, he returned [NIE] home.
1:26 God sent the angel Gabriel **to** Nazareth, a town in Galilee,
1:33 and he will reign over the house of Jacob **forever** [+172+3836];
1:39 Mary got ready and hurried **to** a town in the hill country of Judea,
1:39 Mary got ready and hurried to a town **in** the hill country of Judea,
1:40 where *she* **entered** [RP1656] Zechariah's home and greeted
1:44 As soon as the sound of your greeting reached my [NIE] ears,
1:50 extends to those who fear him, **from** generation to generation.
1:55 to Abraham and his descendants **forever** [+172+3836], even as he
1:56 Elizabeth for about three months and then returned [NIE] home.
1:79 in the shadow of death, to guide our feet **into** the path of peace."
2: 3 And everyone went **to** his own town to register.
2: 4 So Joseph also went up from the town of Nazareth in Galilee **to**
2: 4 of Nazareth in Galilee to Judea, **to** Bethlehem the town of David,
2:15 When the angels had left them and gone **into** heaven,
2:22 and Mary took him **to** Jerusalem to present him to the Lord
2:27 Moved by the Spirit, he went **into** the temple courts. When the
2:28 Simeon took him **in** his arms and praised God, saying:
2:32 a light **for** revelation to the Gentiles and for glory to your people
2:34 "This child is destined **to** cause the falling and rising of many in
2:34 of many in Israel, and **to** be a sign that will be spoken against,
2:39 the Lord, they returned **to** Galilee to their own town of Nazareth.
2:39 the Lord, they returned to Galilee **to** their own town of Nazareth.
2:41 Every year his parents went **to** Jerusalem for the Feast of the
2:45 they did not find him, they went back **to** Jerusalem to look for him.
2:51 Then he went down **to** Nazareth with them and was obedient to
3: 3 He went **into** all the country around the Jordan, preaching a
3: 3 preaching a baptism of repentance **for** the forgiveness of sins.
3: 5 The crooked roads shall become [NIE] straight, the rough ways
3: 5 roads shall become straight, the rough [NIE] ways smooth.
3: 9 not produce good fruit will be cut down and thrown **into** the fire."
3:17 to clear his threshing floor and to gather the wheat **into** his barn,
4: 5 The devil led him up **to** [UBS-] a high place and showed him in
4: 9 The devil led him **to** Jerusalem and had him stand on the highest
4:14 Jesus returned **to** Galilee in the power of the Spirit, and news about
4:16 He went **to** Nazareth, where he had been brought up, and on the
4:16 and on the Sabbath day *he* **went into** [RP1656] the synagogue,

4:23 Do here in your hometown what we have heard that you did **in**
4:26 to any of them, but to a widow **in** Zarephath in the region of Sidon.
4:31 Then he went down **to** Capernaum, a town in Galilee, and on the
4:35 Then the demon threw the man down **before** [+3545+3836] them
4:37 And the news about him spread **throughout** [+4246] the
4:38 left the synagogue and **went to** [RP1656] the home of Simon.
4:42 At daybreak Jesus went out **to** a solitary place. The people were
4:44 And he kept on preaching **in** the synagogues of Judea.
5: 3 He got **into** one of the boats, the one belonging to Simon,
5: 4 had finished speaking, he said to Simon, "Put out **into** deep water,
5: 4 "Put out into deep water, and let down the nets **for** a catch."
5:14 that Moses commanded for your cleansing, **as** a testimony to them."
5:17 And the power of the Lord was present **for** [+3836] him to heal the
5:19 and lowered him on his mat through the tiles **into** the middle of the
5:24 tell you, get up, take your mat and go **home** [+3836+3875+5148]."
5:25 been lying on and went **home** [+899+3836+3875] praising God.
5:32 I have not come to call the righteous, but sinners **to** repentance."
5:37 And no one pours new wine **into** old wineskins. If he does,
5:38 No, new wine must be poured **into** new wineskins.
6: 4 *He* **entered** [RP1656] the house of God, and taking the
6: 6 On another Sabbath he **went into** [RP1656] the synagogue
6: 8 with the shriveled hand, "Get up and stand **in** front of everyone."
6:12 One of those days Jesus went out **to** a mountainside to pray,
6:20 Looking **at** his disciples, he said: "Blessed are you who are poor,
6:38 shaken together and running over, will be poured **into** your lap.
6:39 a blind man lead a blind man? Will they not both fall **into** a pit?
7: 1 When Jesus had finished saying all this **in** the hearing of the
7: 1 this in the hearing of the people, *he* **entered** [RP1656] Capernaum.
7:10 Then the men who had been sent returned **to** the house and found
7:11 Soon afterward, Jesus went **to** a town called Nain, and his disciples
7:24 "What did you go out **into** the desert to see? A reed swayed by the
7:30 and experts in the law rejected God's purpose **for** themselves,
7:36 so *he* **went to** [RP1656] the Pharisee's house and reclined at the
7:44 "Do you see this woman? *I* **came into** [RP1656] your house.
7:50 Jesus said to the woman, "Your faith has saved you; go **in** peace."
8: 8 Still other seed fell **on** good soil. It came up and yielded a crop,
8:14 The seed that fell **among** thorns stands for those who hear,
8:17 concealed that will not be known or brought out **into** the open.
8:22 said to his disciples, "Let's go over **to** the other side of the lake."
8:22 to the other side of the lake." So they got **into** a boat and set out.
8:23 A squall came down **on** the lake, so that the boat was being
8:26 They sailed **to** the region of the Gerasenes, which is across the lake
8:29 his chains and had been driven by the demon **into** solitary places.
8:30 he replied, because many demons *had* **gone into** [RP1656] him.
8:31 And they begged him repeatedly not to order them to go **into** the
8:32 The demons begged Jesus to let them **go into** [RP1656] them,
8:33 demons came out of the man, *they* **went into** [RP1656] the pigs,
8:33 and the herd rushed down the steep bank **into** the lake and was
8:34 they ran off and reported this **in** the town and countryside,
8:34 they ran off and reported this in the town and [RPG] countryside,
8:37 they were overcome with fear. So he got **into** the boat and left.
8:39 "**Return** [+5715] home and tell how much God has done for you."
8:41 at Jesus' feet, pleading with him *to* **come to** [RP1656] his house
8:48 he said to her, "Daughter, your faith has healed you. Go **in** peace."
8:51 When he arrived **at** the house of Jairus, he did not let anyone go in
9: 3 "Take nothing **for** the journey—no staff, no bag, no bread,
9: 4 Whatever house *you* **enter** [RP1656], stay there until you leave
9: 5 your feet when you leave their town, **as** a testimony against them."
9:10 and they withdrew by themselves **to** a town called Bethsaida,
9:12 so they can go **to** the surrounding villages and countryside
9:13 and two fish—unless we go and buy food **for** all this crowd."
9:16 Taking the five loaves and the two fish and looking up **to** heaven,
9:28 and James with him and went up **onto** a mountain to pray.
9:34 and they were afraid as they **entered** [RP1656] the cloud.
9:44 "**Listen carefully to** [+3836+4044+5148+5148+5502] what I am
9:44 The Son of Man is going to be betrayed **into** the hands of men."
9:51 to be taken up to heaven, Jesus resolutely set out **for** Jerusalem.
9:52 *who* **went into** [RP1656] a Samaritan village to get things ready
9:53 there did not welcome him, because he was heading **for** Jerusalem.
9:56 and they went **to** another village.
9:61 Lord; but first let me go back and say good-by **to** my family."
9:62 and looks **back** [+3836+3958] is fit for service in the kingdom of
10: 1 and sent them two by two ahead of him **to** every town and place
10: 2 of the harvest, therefore, to send out workers **into** his harvest field.
10: 5 "When *you* **enter** [RP1656] a house, first say, 'Peace to this house.'
10: 7 deserves his wages. Do not move around from house **to** house.

10: 8 "When *you* **enter** [*RP1656*] a town and are welcomed, eat what is
10:10 But when *you* **enter** [*RP1656*] a town and are not welcomed,
10:10 you enter a town and are not welcomed, go **into** its streets and say,
10:11 'Even the dust of your town that sticks **to** our feet we wipe off
10:30 "A man was going down from Jerusalem **to** Jericho, when he fell
10:34 man on his own donkey, took him **to** an inn and took care of him.
10:36 was a neighbor to the man who fell **into** the *hands* of robbers?"
10:38 he **came to** [*RP1656*] a village where a woman named Martha
11: 4 who sins against us. And **lead** us not **into** [*RP1662*] temptation.' "
11: 7 The door is already locked, and my children are with me **in** bed.
11:24 and does not find it. Then it says, 'I will return **to** the house I left.'
11:32 for they repented **at** the preaching of Jonah, and now one greater
11:33 "No one lights a lamp and puts it **in** a place where it will be hidden,
11:49 in his wisdom said, 'I will send **[NIE]** them prophets and apostles,
12: 5 after the killing of the body, has power to throw you **into** hell.
12:10 And everyone who speaks a word **against** the Son of Man will be
12:10 but anyone who blasphemes **against** the Holy Spirit will not be
12:19 to myself, "You have plenty of good things laid up **for** many years.
12:21 who stores up things for himself but is not rich **toward** God."
12:28 which is here today, and tomorrow is thrown **into** the fire,
12:58 turn you over to the officer, and the officer throw you **into** prison.
13: 9 If it bears fruit **next** [*+3516+3836*] year, fine! If not, then cut it
13:11 was bent over and could not straighten up **at** [*+3836+4117*] **all**.
13:19 is like a mustard seed, which a man took and planted **in** his garden.
13:19 It grew and **became** [*+1181*] a tree, and the birds of the air perched
13:21 and mixed **into** a large amount of flour until it worked all through
13:22 the towns and villages, teaching as he made his way **to** Jerusalem.
14: 1 when Jesus went to eat **in** the house of a prominent Pharisee.
14: 5 of you has a son or an ox that falls **into** a well on the Sabbath day,
14: 8 "When someone invites you **to** a wedding feast, do not take the
14: 8 you to a wedding feast, *do* not **take** [*+2884*] the place of honor,
14:10 But when you are invited, **take** [*+404*] the lowest place, so that
14:21 'Go out quickly **into** the streets and alleys of the town and bring in
14:23 'Go out **to** the roads and country lanes and make them come in,
14:28 and estimate the cost to see if *he* **has enough** [*+2400*] money to
14:31 "Or suppose a king is about to go **to** war against another king.
14:35 It is fit neither **for** the soil nor for the manure pile; it is thrown out.
14:35 It is fit neither for the soil nor **for** the manure pile; it is thrown out.
15: 6 and goes **[NIE]** home. Then he calls his friends and neighbors
15:13 set off **for** a distant country and there squandered his wealth in
15:15 to a citizen of that country, who sent him **to** his fields to feed pigs.
15:17 "When he came **to** his senses, he said, 'How many of my father's
15:18 say to him: Father, I have sinned **against** heaven and against you.
15:21 said to him, 'Father, I have sinned **against** heaven and against you.
15:22 and put it on him. Put a ring **on** his finger and sandals on his feet.
15:22 and put it on him. Put a ring on his finger and sandals **on** his feet.
16: 4 I lose my job here, people will welcome me **into** their houses.'
16: 8 For the people of this world are more shrewd **in** *dealing with* their
16: 9 that when it is gone, you will be welcomed **into** eternal dwellings.
16:16 of God is being preached, and everyone is forcing his way **into** it.
16:22 the beggar died and the angels carried him **to** Abraham's side.
16:27 'Then I beg you, father, send Lazarus **to** my father's house,
16:28 so that they will not also come **to** this place of torment.'
17: 2 It would be better for him to be thrown **into** the sea with a
17: 4 If he sins **against** you seven times in a day, and seven times comes
17:11 Now on his way **to** Jerusalem, Jesus traveled along the border
17:12 *As* he *was* **going into** [*RP1656*] a village, ten men who had
17:24 which flashes and lights up the sky from one end **to** the other.
17:27 and being given in marriage up to the day Noah **entered** [*RP1656*]
17:31 no one in the field should go **back** [*+3836+3958*] for anything.
18: 5 so that she won't **eventually** [*+5465*] wear me out with her
18:10 "Two men went up **to** the temple to pray, one a Pharisee
18:13 He would not even look up **to** heaven, but beat his breast and said,
18:14 rather than the other, went **[NIE]** home justified before God.
18:17 the kingdom of God like a little child *will* never **enter** [*RP1656*] it."
18:24 "How hard it is for the rich *to* **enter** [*RP1660*] the kingdom of God!
18:25 needle than for a rich man *to* **enter** [*RP1656*] the kingdom of God."
18:31 the Twelve aside and told them, "We are going up **to** Jerusalem,
18:35 As Jesus approached **[NIE]** Jericho, a blind man was sitting by
19: 4 So he ran **[NIE]** ahead and climbed a sycamore-fig tree to see
19:12 "A man of noble birth went **to** a distant country to have himself
19:28 After Jesus had said this, he went on ahead, going up **to** Jerusalem.
19:29 As he approached **[NIE]** Bethphage and Bethany at the hill called
19:30 "Go **to** the village ahead of you, and as you enter it, you will find a
19:45 Then *he* **entered** [*RP1656*] the temple area and began driving out
20:17 " 'The stone the builders rejected *has* **become** [*+1181*] the

21: 1 Jesus saw the rich putting their gifts **into** the temple treasury.
21: 4 All these people **gave** [*+965*] their gifts out of their wealth;
21:12 They will deliver you **to** synagogues and prisons, and you will be
21:13 This will result **in** your being witnesses to them.
21:21 Then let those who are in Judea flee **to** the mountains, let those in
21:21 get out, and *let* those in the country not **enter** [*RP1656*] the city.
21:24 fall by the sword and will be taken as prisoners **to** all the nations.
21:37 and each evening he went out to spend the night **on** the hill called
22: 3 Then Satan **entered** [*RP1656*] Judas, called Iscariot, one of the
22:10 He replied, "*As* you **enter** [*RP1656*] the city, a man carrying a jar
22:10 jar of water will meet you. Follow him **to** the house that he enters,
22:10 will meet you. Follow him to the house that *he* **enters** [*RP1660*],
22:17 he gave thanks and said, "Take this and divide it **among** you.
22:19 "This is my body given for you; do this **in** remembrance of me."
22:33 replied, "Lord, I am ready to go with you **to** prison and to death."
22:33 replied, "Lord, I am ready to go with you to prison and **to** death."
22:39 Jesus went out as usual **to** the Mount of Olives, and his disciples
22:40 to them, "Pray that you *will* not **fall into** [*RP1656*] temptation."
22:46 and pray so that *you will* not **fall into** [*RP1656*] temptation."
22:54 and **took** him **into** [*RP1652*] the house of the high priest.
22:65 And they said many other insulting things **to** him.
22:66 teachers of the law, met together, and Jesus was led **before** them.
23:25 He released the man who had been thrown **into** prison for
23:42 he said, "Jesus, remember me when you come **into** your kingdom."
23:46 out with a loud voice, "Father, **into** your hands I commit my spirit."
24: 5 In their fright the women bowed down with their faces **to** the
24: 7 'The Son of Man must be delivered **into** the hands of sinful men,
24:13 Now that same day two of them were going **to** a village called
24:20 and our rulers handed him over **to** be sentenced to death,
24:26 have to suffer these things and then **enter** [*RP1656*] his glory?"
24:28 As they approached **[NIE]** the village to which they were going,
24:33 They got up and returned at once **to** Jerusalem. There they found
24:47 **and** [UBS ***unto***; NIV *2779*] forgiveness of sins will be preached in
24:47 and forgiveness of sins will be preached in his name **to** all nations,
24:51 he was blessing them, he left them and was taken up **into** heaven.
24:52 Then they worshiped him and returned **to** Jerusalem with great joy.
Jn 1: 7 He came **as** a witness to testify concerning that light, so that
1: 9 The true light that gives light to every man was coming **into** the
1:11 He came **to** that which was his own, but his own did not receive
1:12 Yet to all who received him, to those who believed **in** his name,
1:18 but God the One and Only, who is **at** the Father's side, has made
1:43 The next day Jesus decided to leave **for** Galilee. Finding Philip,
2: 2 and Jesus and his disciples had also been invited **to** the wedding.
2:11 He thus revealed his glory, and his disciples put their faith **in** him.
2:12 After this he went down **to** Capernaum with his mother
2:13 almost time for the Jewish Passover, Jesus went up **to** Jerusalem.
2:23 saw the miraculous signs he was doing and believed **in** his name.
3: 4 "Surely he cannot **enter** a second time **into** [*RP1656*] his mother's
3: 5 no one can **enter** [*RP1656*] the kingdom of God unless he is born
3:13 No one has ever gone **into** heaven except the one who came from
3:16 that whoever believes **in** him shall not perish but have eternal life.
3:17 For God did not send his Son **into** the world to condemn the world,
3:18 Whoever believes **in** him is not condemned, but whoever does not
3:18 because he has not believed **in** the name of God's one and only
3:19 Light has come **into** the world, but men loved darkness instead of
3:22 Jesus and his disciples went out **into** the Judean countryside,
3:24 (This was before John was put **in** prison.)
3:36 Whoever believes **in** the Son has eternal life, but whoever rejects
4: 3 learned of this, he left Judea and went back once more **to** Galilee.
4: 5 So he came **to** a town in Samaria called Sychar, near the plot of
4: 8 (His disciples had gone **into** the town to buy food.)
4:14 the water I give him will never [*+172+3590+3836+4024*] thirst.
4:14 will become in him a spring of water welling up **to** eternal life."
4:28 water jar, the woman went back **to** the town and said to the people,
4:36 even now he harvests the crop **for** eternal life, so that the sower
4:38 and you *have* **reaped the benefits** of [*RP1656*] their labor."
4:39 Many of the Samaritans from that town believed **in** him because of
4:43 After the two days he left **for** Galilee.
4:45 When he arrived **in** Galilee, the Galileans welcomed him.
4:45 at the Passover Feast, for they also had been **there**[s] [*+2038+3836*].
4:46 Once more *he* **visited** [*+2262*] Cana in Galilee, where he had
4:47 When this man heard that Jesus had arrived **in** Galilee from Judea,
4:54 sign that Jesus performed, having come from Judea **to** Galilee.
5: 1 Some time later, Jesus went up **to** Jerusalem for a feast of the Jews.
5: 7 "I have no one to help me **into** the pool when the water is stirred.
5:24 has eternal life and *will* not *be* **condemned** [*+2262+3213*];

5: 24 and will not be condemned; he has crossed over from death **to** life.
5: 29 those who have done good will **[NIE]** rise to live, and those who
5: 29 and those who have done evil will **[NIE]** rise to be condemned.
5: 45 the Father. Your accuser is Moses, **on** whom your hopes are set.
6: 3 Then Jesus went up **on** a mountainside and sat down with his
6: 9 and two small fish, but how far will they go **among** so many?"
6: 14 to say, "Surely this is the Prophet who is to come **into** the world."
6: 15 make him king by force, withdrew again **to** a mountain by himself.
6: 17 where they got **into** a boat and set off across the lake for
6: 17 they got into a boat and set off across the lake **for** Capernaum.
6: 21 Then they were willing to take him **into** the boat, and immediately
6: 21 and immediately the boat reached the shore **where** [+4005] they
6: 22 and that Jesus *had* not **entered** [RP5291] it with his disciples,
6: 24 they got **into** the boats and went to Capernaum in search of Jesus.
6: 24 they got into the boats and went **to** Capernaum in search of Jesus.
6: 27 work for food that spoils, but for food that endures to eternal life,
6: 29 "The work of God is this: to believe **in** the one he has sent."
6: 35 never go hungry, and he who believes **in** me will never be thirsty.
6: 40 who looks to the Son and believes **in** him shall have eternal life,
6: 51 If anyone eats of this bread, he will live **forever** [+172+3836].
6: 58 but he who feeds on this bread will live **forever** [+172+3836]."
6: 66 this time many of his disciples **turned back** [+599+3836+3958]
7: 3 brothers said to him, "You ought to leave here and go **to** Judea,
7: 5 For even his own brothers did not believe **in** him.
7: 8 You go **to** the Feast. I am not yet going up to this Feast,
7: 8 I am not yet going up **to** this Feast, because for me the right time
7: 10 However, after his brothers had left **for** the Feast, he went also,
7: 14 Not until halfway through the Feast did Jesus go up **to** the temple
7: 31 Still, many in the crowd put their faith **in** him. They said,
7: 35 Will he go **where** our people live scattered among the Greeks,
7: 38 Whoever believes **in** me, as the Scripture has said, streams of
7: 39 the Spirit, whom those who believed **in** him were later to receive.
7: 48 "Has any of the rulers or of the Pharisees believed **in** him?
7: 53 Then each went **to** his own home.
8: 1 But Jesus went **to** the Mount of Olives.
8: 2 At dawn he appeared again **in** the temple courts, where all the
8: 6 Jesus bent down and started to write **on** the ground with his finger.
8: 8 Again he stooped down and wrote **on** the ground.
8: 26 is reliable, and what I have heard from him I tell **[NIE]** the world."
8: 30 Even as he spoke, many put their faith **in** him.
8: 35 place in the family, **[RPG]** but a son belongs to it forever.
8: 35 place in the family, but a son belongs to it **forever** [+172+3836].
8: 51 my word, he will **never** [+172+3590+3836+4024] see death."
8: 52 your word, he will **never** [+172+3590+3836+4024] taste death.
9: 7 he told him, "wash **in** the Pool of Siloam" (this word means Sent).
9: 11 He told me to go to Siloam and wash. So I went and washed,
9: 35 when he found him, he said, "Do you believe **in** the Son of Man?"
9: 36 is he, sir?" the man asked. "Tell me so that I may believe **in** him."
9: 39 Jesus said, "**For** judgment I have come into this world, so that the
9: 39 Jesus said, "For judgment I have come **into** this world, so that the
10: 1 the man *who does* not **enter** [RP1656] the sheep pen by the gate,
10: 28 eternal life, and they shall **never** [+172+3590+3836+4024] perish;
10: 36 whom the Father set apart as his very own and sent **into** the world?
10: 40 Then Jesus went back across the Jordan **to** the place where John
10: 42 And in that place many believed **in** Jesus.
11: 7 Then he said to his disciples, "Let us go back **to** Judea."
11: 25 and the life. He who believes **in** me will live, even though he dies;
11: 26 and whoever lives and believes **in** me will never die. Do you
11: 26 believes in me will **never** [+172+3590+3836+4024] die.
11: 27 are the Christ, the Son of God, who was to come **into** the world."
11: 30 Now Jesus *had* not yet **entered** [+2262] the village, but was still at
11: 31 followed her, supposing she was going to the tomb to mourn there.
11: 38 Jesus, once more deeply moved, came **to** the tomb. It was a cave
11: 45 to visit Mary, and had seen what Jesus did, put their faith **in** him.
11: 48 everyone will believe **in** him, and then the Romans will come
11: 52 children of God, to bring them together and **make** them one.
11: 54 Instead he withdrew **to** a region near the desert, to a village called
11: 54 **to** a village called Ephraim, where he stayed with his disciples.
11: 55 many went up from the country **to** Jerusalem for their ceremonial
11: 56 "What do you think? Isn't he coming **to** the Feast at all?"
12: 1 the Passover, Jesus arrived **at** Bethany, where Lazarus lived,
12: 7 "⸤It was intended⸥ that she should save this perfume **for** the day of
12: 11 for on account of him many of the Jews were going over **to** Jesus
12: 12 The next day the great crowd that had come **for** the Feast heard
12: 12 come for the Feast heard that Jesus was on his way **to** Jerusalem.
12: 13 They took palm branches and went out **to** meet him, shouting,

12: 24 you the truth, unless a kernel of wheat falls **to** the ground and dies,
12: 25 while the man who hates his life in this world will keep it **for**
12: 27 from this hour'? No, it was for this very reason I came **to** this hour.
12: 34 from the Law that the Christ will remain **forever** [+172+3836],
12: 36 Put your trust **in** the light while you have it, so that you may
12: 37 signs in their presence, they still would not believe **in** him.
12: 42 Yet at the same time many even among the leaders believed **in**
12: 44 Then Jesus cried out, "When a man believes **in** me, he does not
12: 44 he does not believe **in** me only, but in the one who sent me.
12: 44 he does not believe in me only, but **in** the one who sent me.
12: 46 I have come **into** the world as a light, so that no one who believes
12: 46 so that no one who believes **in** me should stay in darkness.
13: 1 he now showed them the **full extent of** [+5465] his love.
13: 2 devil *had* already **prompted** [+965+2840+3836] Judas Iscariot,
13: 3 knew that the Father had put all things **under** his **power** [+5931],
13: 5 he poured water **into** a basin and began to wash his disciples' feet,
13: 8 said Peter, "you shall **never** [+172+3836+4024] wash my feet."
13: 22 His disciples stared **at** one another, at a loss to know which of
13: 27 soon as Judas took the bread, Satan **entered into** [RP1656] him.
13: 29 some thought Jesus was telling him to buy what was needed **for**
14: 1 "Do not let your hearts be troubled. Trust **in** God; trust also in me.
14: 1 "Do not let your hearts be troubled. Trust in God; trust also **in** me.
14: 12 anyone who has faith **in** me will do what I have been doing.
14: 16 give you another Counselor to be with you **forever** [+172+3836]—
15: 6 such branches are picked up, thrown **into** the fire and burned.
15: 21 *They will* **treat** [+4472] you this way because of my name,
16: 9 in regard to sin, because men do not believe **in** me;
16: 20 the world rejoices. You will grieve, but your grief will turn **to** joy.
16: 21 the anguish because of her joy that a child is born **into** the world.
16: 28 I came from the Father and **entered** [+2262] the world; now I am
16: 32 and has come, when you will be scattered, each **to** his own home.
17: 1 After Jesus said this, he looked **toward** heaven and prayed:
17: 18 As you sent me **into** the world, I have sent them into the world.
17: 18 As you sent me into the world, I have sent them **into** the world.
17: 20 I pray also for those who will believe **in** me through their message,
17: 23 May they be **brought** to complete unity to let the world know that
18: 1 an olive grove, and he and his disciples **went into** [RP1656] it.
18: 6 "I am he," they drew **back** [+3836+3958] and fell to the ground.
18: 11 Jesus commanded Peter, "Put your sword **away**ˢ [+2557+3836]!
18: 15 *he* went with Jesus **into** [RP5291] the high priest's courtyard,
18: 28 Then the Jews led Jesus from Caiaphas **to** the palace of the Roman
18: 28 uncleanness the Jews *did* not **enter** [RP1656] the palace;
18: 33 Pilate then went back **inside** [RP1656] the palace, summoned
18: 37 In fact, **for** [+4047] **this reason** I was born, and for this I came into
18: 37 was born, and **for** this I came into the world, to testify to the truth.
18: 37 was born, and for this I came **into** the world, to testify to the truth.
19: 9 and *he* went back **inside** [RP1656] the palace. "Where do you come
19: 13 and sat down on the judge's seat **at** a place known as the Stone
19: 17 he went out **to** the place of the Skull (which in Aramaic is called
19: 27 From that time on, this disciple took her **into** his home.
19: 37 scripture says, "They will look **on** the one they have pierced."
20: 1 Mary Magdalene went **to** the tomb and saw that the stone had been
20: 3 So Peter and the other disciple started **for** the tomb.
20: 4 the other disciple outran Peter and **reached** [+2262] the tomb first.
20: 6 who was behind him, arrived and **went into** [RP1656] the tomb.
20: 7 The cloth was folded up **by itself** [+1651+3023+5536+6006],
20: 8 who had reached the tomb first, also **went inside** [RP1656].
20: 11 the tomb crying. As she wept, she bent over to look **into** the tomb
20: 14 At this, *she* **turned around** [+3836+3958+5138] and saw Jesus
20: 19 Jesus came and stood **among** [+3545+3836] them and said,
20: 25 his hands and put my finger **where**ˢ [+3836+5596] the nails were,
20: 25 the nails were, and put my hand **into** his side, I will not believe it."
20: 26 Jesus came and stood **among** [+3545+3836] them and said,
20: 27 see my hands. Reach out your hand and put it **into** my side,
21: 3 So they went out and got into **[NIE]** the boat, but that night they
21: 4 Early in the morning, Jesus stood **on** the shore, but the disciples
21: 6 "Throw your net **on** the right side of the boat and you will find
21: 7 around him (for he had taken it off) and jumped **into** the water.
21: 9 When *they* **landed** [+609+1178+3836], they saw a fire of burning
21: 11 Peter climbed aboard and dragged the net **ashore** [+1178+3836].
21: 23 the rumor spread **among** the brothers that this disciple would not

Ac 1: 10 They were looking intently up **into** the sky as he was going,
1: 11 of Galilee," they said, "why do you stand here looking **into** the sky?
1: 11 This same Jesus, who has been taken from you **into** heaven,
1: 11 will come back in the same way you have seen him go **into**
1: 12 Then they returned **to** Jerusalem from the hill called the Mount of

1:13 When *they* **arrived** [*RP1656*], they went upstairs to the room
1:25 which Judas left to go **where** [*+3836+5536*] he belongs."
2: 5 Now there were staying **in** Jerusalem God-fearing Jews from every
2:20 The sun will be turned **to** darkness and the moon to blood before
2:20 and the moon **to** blood before the coming of the great and glorious
2:22 Jesus of Nazareth was a man accredited by God **to** you by
2:25 David said **about** him: " 'I saw the Lord always before me.
2:27 because you will not abandon me **to** the grave, nor will you let
2:31 that he was not abandoned **to** the grave, nor did his body see decay.
2:34 For David did not ascend **to** heaven, and yet he said, " 'The Lord
2:38 in the name of Jesus Christ **for** the forgiveness of your sins.
2:39 is for you and your children and for all who are **far off** [*+3426*]—
3: 1 and John were going up **to** the temple at the time of prayer—
3: 2 day to beg from those **going into** [*RP1660*] the temple courts.
3: 3 and John about to enter, **[RPG]** he asked them for money.
3: 4 Peter looked straight **at** him, as did John. Then Peter said,
3: 4 looked straight **at** him, as did John. Then Peter said, "Look **at** us!"
3: 8 Then *he* **went** with them **into** [*RP1656*] the temple courts,
3:19 and turn to God, **so that** [*+3836*] your sins may be wiped out,
4: 3 because it was evening, they put them **in** jail until the next day.
4: 3 because it was evening, they put them in jail **until** the next day.
4:11 you builders rejected, which *has* **become** [*+1181*] the capstone.'
4:17 But to stop this thing from spreading any further **among** the
4:30 Stretch out your hand **to** heal and perform miraculous signs
5:15 people brought the sick **into** the streets and laid them on beds
5:21 At daybreak *they* **entered** [*RP1656*] the temple courts, as they had
5:21 of the elders of Israel—and sent **to** the jail for the apostles.
5:36 all his followers were dispersed, and it all came **to** nothing.
6:11 "We have heard Stephen speak words of blasphemy **against** Moses
6:12 They seized Stephen and brought him **before** the Sanhedrin.
6:15 All who were sitting in the Sanhedrin looked intently **at** Stephen,
7: 3 and your people,' God said, 'and go **to** the land I will show you.'
7: 4 of his father, God sent him **to** this land where you are now living.
7: 4 God sent him to this land **where** [*+4005*] you are now living.
7: 5 and his descendants after him *would* **possess** [*+2959*] the land,
7: 9 were jealous of Joseph, they sold him as a slave **into** Egypt.
7:12 When Jacob heard that there was grain **in** Egypt, he sent our
7:15 Then Jacob went down **to** Egypt, where he and our fathers died.
7:16 Their bodies were brought back **to** Shechem and placed in the
7:19 to throw out their newborn babies **so that** [*+3836*] they would die.
7:21 Pharaoh's daughter took him and brought him up **as** her own son.
7:26 *He tried to* **reconcile** [*+1645+5261*] them by saying, 'Men,
7:34 down to set them free. Now come, I will send you back **to** Egypt.'
7:39 they rejected him and in their hearts turned back **to** Egypt.
7:53 you who have received the law that was put into effect **through**
7:55 of the Holy Spirit, looked up **to** heaven and saw the glory of God,
8: 3 to house, he dragged off men and women and put them **in** prison.
8: 5 Philip went down **to** a city in Samaria and proclaimed the Christ
8:16 they had simply been baptized **into** the name of the Lord Jesus.
8:20 *"May* your money **perish** [*+724+1639*] with you, because you
8:23 For I see that you are **full of** bitterness and captive to sin."
8:25 the word of the Lord, Peter and John returned **to** Jerusalem,
8:26 the desert road—that goes down from Jerusalem **to** Gaza."
8:27 of the Ethiopians. This man had gone **to** Jerusalem to worship,
8:38 Then both Philip and the eunuch went down **into** the water
8:40 Philip, however, appeared **at** Azotus and traveled about,
8:40 preaching the gospel in all the towns until he **reached** [*+2262*]
9: 1 Saul was still breathing out murderous threats **against** the Lord's
9: 2 and asked him for letters to the synagogues **in** Damascus,
9: 2 or women, he might take them as prisoners **to** Jerusalem.
9: 6 "Now get up and **go into** [*RP1656*] the city, and you will be told
9: 8 So *they* **led** him by the hand **into** [*RP1652*] Damascus.
9:17 Then Ananias went **to** the house and entered it. Placing his hands
9:21 "Isn't he the man who raised havoc **in** Jerusalem among those who
9:21 And hasn't he come here **[NIE]** to take them as prisoners to the
9:26 When he came **to** Jerusalem, he tried to join the disciples,
9:28 So Saul stayed with them and moved about freely **in** Jerusalem,
9:30 they took him down **to** Caesarea and sent him off to Tarsus.
9:30 they took him down to Caesarea and sent him off **to** Tarsus.
9:39 with them, and when he arrived he was taken upstairs **to** the room.
10: 4 and gifts to the poor have come up **as** a memorial offering before
10: 5 Now send men **to** Joppa to bring back a man named Simon who is
10: 8 He told them everything that had happened and sent them **to** Joppa.
10:16 three times, and immediately the sheet was taken back **to** heaven.
10:22 A holy angel told him to have you come **to** his house so that he
10:24 The following day *he* **arrived in** [*RP1656*] Caesarea. Cornelius

10:32 Send **to** Joppa for Simon who is called Peter. He is a guest in the
10:43 All the prophets testify about him that everyone who believes **in**
11: 2 So when Peter went up **to** Jerusalem, the circumcised believers
11: 6 I looked **into** it and saw four-footed animals of the earth, wild
11: 8 or unclean *has* ever **entered** [*RP1656*] my mouth.'
11:10 three times, and then it was all pulled up **to** heaven again.
11:12 also went with me, and *we* **entered** [*RP1656*] the man's house.
11:13 in his house and say, 'Send **to** Joppa for Simon who is called Peter.
11:18 "So then, God has granted even the Gentiles repentance **unto** life."
11:20 and Cyrene, went **to** Antioch and began to speak to Greeks also,
11:22 News of this **reached** [*+201*] the ears of the church at Jerusalem,
11:25 Then Barnabas went **to** Tarsus to look for Saul,
11:26 and when he found him, he brought him **to** Antioch. So for a whole
11:27 During this time some prophets came down from Jerusalem **to**
11:29 decided to provide **[NIE]** help for the brothers living in Judea.
12: 4 After arresting him, he put him **in** prison, handing him over to be
12:10 and second guards and came to the iron gate leading **to** the city.
12:17 the brothers about this," he said, and then he left **for** another place.
12:19 Then Herod went from Judea **to** Caesarea and stayed there a while.
12:25 they returned *from* [UBS *to*; NIV *608*] Jerusalem, taking with them
13: 2 me Barnabas and Saul **for** the work to which I have called them."
13: 4 went down **to** Seleucia and sailed from there to Cyprus.
13: 4 went down to Seleucia and sailed from there **to** Cyprus.
13: 9 filled with the Holy Spirit, looked straight **at** Elymas and said,
13:13 Paul and his companions sailed **to** Perga in Pamphylia,
13:13 to Perga in Pamphylia, where John left them to return **to** Jerusalem.
13:14 From Perga they went on **to** Pisidian Antioch. On the Sabbath they
13:14 On the Sabbath they **entered** [*RP1656*] the synagogue and sat
13:22 After removing Saul, he made David **[NIE]** their king. He
13:29 they took him down from the tree and laid him **in** a tomb.
13:31 by those who had traveled with him from Galilee **to** Jerusalem.
13:34 the dead, never *to* **decay** [*+1426+5715*], is stated in these words:
13:42 the people invited them to speak further about these things **on** the
13:46 yourselves worthy of eternal life, we now turn **to** the Gentiles.
13:47 " 'I have made you **[NIE]** a light for the Gentiles, that you may
13:47 *that* you *may* **bring** [*+1639*] salvation to the ends of the earth.' "
13:48 of the Lord; and all who were appointed **for** eternal life believed.
13:51 dust from their feet in protest against them and went **to** Iconium.
14: 1 and Barnabas **went** as usual **into** [*RP1656*] the Jewish synagogue.
14: 6 out about it and fled **to** the Lycaonian cities of Lystra and Derbe
14:14 they tore their clothes and rushed out **into** the crowd, shouting:
14:20 around him, *he* got up and **went back into** [*RP1656*] the city.
14:20 back into the city. The next day he and Barnabas left **for** Derbe.
14:21 of disciples. Then they returned **to** Lystra, Iconium and Antioch,
14:21 Then they returned to Lystra, **[RPG]** Iconium and Antioch,
14:21 Then they returned to Lystra, Iconium and **[RPG]** Antioch,
14:22 "We must go through many hardships *to* **enter** [*RP1656*] the
14:23 committed them to the Lord, **in** whom they had put their trust.
14:24 After going through Pisidia, they came **into** Pamphylia,
14:25 they had preached the word in Perga, they went down **to** Attalia.
14:26 From Attalia they sailed back **to** Antioch, where they had been
14:26 where they had been committed to the grace of God **for** the work
15: 2 to go up **to** Jerusalem to see the apostles and elders about this
15: 4 When they came **to** Jerusalem, they were welcomed by the church
15:22 their own men and send them **to** Antioch with Paul and Barnabas.
15:30 The men were sent off and went down **to** Antioch, where they
15:38 them in Pamphylia and had not continued with them **in** the work.
15:39 they parted company. Barnabas took Mark and sailed **for** Cyprus,
16: 1 He came **to** Derbe and then to Lystra, where a disciple named
16: 1 He came to Derbe and then **to** Lystra, where a disciple named
16: 7 came to the border of Mysia, they tried *to* **enter** [*+4513*] Bithynia,
16: 8 So they passed by Mysia and went down **to** Troas.
16: 9 and begging him, "Come over **to** Macedonia and help us."
16:10 had seen the vision, we got ready at once to leave **for** Macedonia,
16:11 From Troas we put out to sea and sailed straight **for** Samothrace,
16:11 sailed straight for Samothrace, and the next day **on to** Neapolis.
16:12 From there we *traveled* **to** Philippi, a Roman colony
16:15 in the Lord," she said, "**come** and stay **at** [*RP1656*] my house."
16:16 Once when we were going **to** the place of prayer, we were met by a
16:19 and dragged them **into** the marketplace to face the authorities.
16:23 they had been severely flogged, they were thrown **into** prison,
16:24 he put them **in** the inner cell and fastened their feet in the stocks.
16:24 he put them in the inner cell and fastened their feet **in** the stocks.
16:34 The jailer brought them **into** his house and set a meal before them;
16:37 even though we are Roman citizens, and threw us **into** prison.
17: 1 through Amphipolis and Apollonia, they came **to** Thessalonica,

17: 5 in search of Paul and Silas in order to bring them out **to** the crowd.
17: 10 as it was night, the brothers sent Paul and Silas away **to** Berea.
17: 10 to Berea. On arriving there, they went **to** the Jewish synagogue.
17: 20 *You are* **bringing** some strange ideas **to** [*RP1662*] our ears,
17: 21 and the foreigners who lived there spent their time **doing** nothing
18: 1 After this, Paul left Athens and went **to** Corinth.
18: 6 clear of my responsibility. From now on I will go **to** the Gentiles."
18: 7 and **went** next door **to** [*RP1656*] the house of Titius Justus,
18: 18 Then he left the brothers and sailed **for** Syria, accompanied by
18: 19 They arrived **at** Ephesus, where Paul left Priscilla and Aquila.
18: 19 *He* himself **went into** [*RP1656*] the synagogue and reasoned with
18: 22 When he landed **at** Caesarea, he went up and greeted the church
18: 22 he went up and greeted the church and then went down **to** Antioch.
18: 24 a Jew named Apollos, a native of Alexandria, came **to** Ephesus.
18: 27 When Apollos wanted to go **to** Achaia, the brothers encouraged
19: 1 Paul took the road through the interior and arrived **at** Ephesus.
19: 3 So Paul asked, "Then what [*+5515*] baptism did you receive?"
19: 3 baptism did you receive?" **[NIE]** "John's baptism," they replied.
19: 4 He told the people to believe **in** the one coming after him,
19: 4 the people to believe in the one coming after him, that is, **in** Jesus."
19: 5 hearing this, they were baptized **into** the name of the Lord Jesus.
19: 8 Paul **entered** [*RP1656*] the synagogue and spoke boldly there for
19: 21 Paul decided to go **to** Jerusalem, passing through Macedonia
19: 22 He sent two of his helpers, Timothy and Erastus, **to** Macedonia,
19: 22 while he stayed **in** the province of Asia a little longer.
19: 27 not only that our trade *will* **lose** its **good name** [*+591+2262*],
19: 27 of the great goddess Artemis *will be* **discredited** [*+3357+4029*],
19: 29 from Macedonia, and rushed as one man **into** the theater.
19: 30 Paul wanted *to* **appear before** [*RP1656*] the crowd,
19: 31 sent him a message begging him not to venture **into** the theater.
20: 1 after encouraging them, said good-by and set out **for** Macedonia.
20: 2 of encouragement to the people, and finally arrived **in** Greece,
20: 3 Jews made a plot against him just as he was about to sail **for** Syria,
20: 6 and five days later joined the others **at** Troas, where we stayed
20: 14 When he met us **at** Assos, we took him aboard and went on to
20: 14 he met us at Assos, we took him aboard and went on **to** Mitylene.
20: 15 The day after that we crossed over **to** Samos, and on the following
20: 15 over to Samos, and on the following day arrived **at** Miletus.
20: 16 for he was in a hurry *to* **reach** [*+1181*] Jerusalem, if possible,
20: 17 From Miletus, Paul sent **to** Ephesus for the elders of the church.
20: 18 I was with you, from the first day I came **into** the province of Asia.
20: 21 to both Jews and Greeks that they must turn **to** God in repentance
20: 21 must turn to God in repentance and have faith **in** our Lord Jesus.
20: 22 "And now, compelled by the Spirit, I am going **to** Jerusalem,
20: 29 savage wolves *will* **come in among** [*RP1656*] you and will not
20: 38 never see his face again. Then they accompanied him **to** the ship.
21: 1 away from them, we put out to sea and sailed straight **to** Cos.
21: 1 The next day we went **to** Rhodes and from there to Patara.
21: 1 The next day we went to Rhodes and from there **to** Patara.
21: 2 We found a ship crossing over **to** Phoenicia, went on board
21: 3 and passing to the south of it, we sailed *on* **to** Syria.
21: 3 We landed **at** Tyre, where our ship was to unload its cargo.
21: 4 Through the Spirit they urged Paul not to go on **to** Jerusalem.
21: 6 to each other, we went **aboard** the ship, and they returned home.
21: 6 we went aboard the ship, and they returned **[NIE]** home.
21: 7 We continued our voyage from Tyre and landed **at** Ptolemais,
21: 8 *we* **reached** [*+2262*] Caesarea and stayed at the house of Philip the
21: 8 stayed **at** [*RP1656*] the house of Philip the evangelist,
21: 11 this belt and *will* **hand** him **over to** [*+4140+5931*] the Gentiles.' "
21: 12 and the people there pleaded with Paul not to go up **to** Jerusalem.
21: 13 but also to die **in** Jerusalem for the name of the Lord Jesus."
21: 15 After this, we got ready and went up **to** Jerusalem.
21: 17 When we arrived **at** Jerusalem, the brothers received us warmly.
21: 26 Then *he* **went to** [*RP1655*] the temple to give notice of the date
21: 28 *he has* **brought** Greeks **into** [*RP1652*] the temple area and defiled
21: 29 and assumed that Paul *had* **brought** him **into** [*RP1652*] the temple
21: 34 of the uproar, he ordered that Paul be taken **into** the barracks.
21: 37 As the soldiers were about to **take** Paul **into** [*RP1652*] the
21: 38 and led four thousand terrorists out **into** the desert some time ago?"
22: 4 arresting both men and women and throwing them **into** prison,
22: 5 I even obtained letters from them to their brothers **in** Damascus,
22: 5 and went there to bring these people as prisoners **to** Jerusalem to
22: 7 I fell **to** the ground and heard a voice say to me, 'Saul! Saul!
22: 10 Lord?' I asked. " 'Get up,' the Lord said, 'and go **into** Damascus.
22: 11 My companions led me by the hand **into** Damascus,
22: 13 your sight!' And at that very moment I was able to see **[NIE]** him.

22: 17 "When I returned **to** Jerusalem and was praying at the temple,
22: 21 Lord said to me, 'Go; I will send you far away **to** the Gentiles.' "
22: 23 and throwing off their cloaks and flinging dust **into** the air,
22: 24 the commander ordered Paul *to be* **taken into** [*RP1652*] the
22: 30 to assemble. Then he brought Paul and had him stand **before** them.
23: 10 take him away from them by force and bring him **into** the barracks.
23: 11 As you have testified about me **in** Jerusalem, so you must also
23: 11 testified about me in Jerusalem, so you must also testify **in** Rome."
23: 15 and the Sanhedrin petition the commander to bring him **before** you
23: 16 of this plot, *he* **went into** [*RP1656*] the barracks and told Paul.
23: 20 "The Jews have agreed to ask you to bring Paul **before** the
23: 28 why they were accusing him, so I brought him **to** their Sanhedrin.
23: 30 When I was informed of a plot to be carried out **against** the man,
23: 31 with them during the night and brought him **as far as** Antipatris.
23: 32 let the cavalry go on with him, while they returned **to** the barracks.
23: 33 *When* the cavalry **arrived in** [*RP1656*] Caesarea, they delivered
24: 11 no more than twelve days ago I went up **to** Jerusalem to worship.
24: 15 and I have the same hope **in** God as these men, that there will be a
24: 17 bring my people gifts for the poor and to present offerings. **[NIE]**
24: 24 and listened to him as he spoke about faith **in** Christ Jesus.
25: 1 in the province, Festus went up from Caesarea **to** Jerusalem,
25: 3 as a favor to them, to have Paul transferred **to** Jerusalem,
25: 4 Festus answered, "Paul is being held **at** Caesarea, and I myself am
25: 6 spending eight or ten days with them, he went down **to** Caesarea,
25: 8 "I have done nothing wrong **against** the law of the Jews or against
25: 8 against the law of the Jews or **against** the temple or against Caesar."
25: 8 against the law of the Jews or against the temple or **against** Caesar."
25: 9 "Are you willing to go up **to** Jerusalem and stand trial before me
25: 13 and Bernice arrived **at** Caesarea to pay their respects to Festus.
25: 15 When I went **to** Jerusalem, the chief priests and elders of the Jews
25: 20 so I asked if he would be willing to go **to** Jerusalem and stand trial
25: 21 When Paul made his appeal to be held over **for** the Emperor's
25: 23 and **entered** [*RP1656*] the audience room with the high ranking
26: 6 because of my hope in what God has promised **[NIE]** our fathers
26: 7 This is **[NIE]** the promise our twelve tribes are hoping to see
26: 11 against them, I even went to foreign cities to persecute them.
26: 12 "On one of these journeys I was going **to** Damascus with the
26: 14 We all fell **to** the ground, and I heard a voice saying to me in
26: 16 I have appeared to you to [*+4047*] appoint you as a servant
26: 17 your own people and from the Gentiles. I am sending you **to** them
26: 18 to open their eyes and turn them from darkness **to** light, and from
26: 18 and a place among those who are sanctified by faith **in** me.'
26: 24 he shouted. "Your great learning is driving you **[NIE]** insane."
27: 1 When it was decided that we would sail **for** Italy, Paul and some
27: 2 We boarded a ship from Adramyttium about to sail **for** ports along
27: 3 The next day we landed **at** Sidon; and Julius, in kindness to Paul,
27: 5 the coast of Cilicia and Pamphylia, we landed **at** Myra in Lycia.
27: 6 There the centurion found an Alexandrian ship sailing **for** Italy
27: 6 ship sailing for Italy and **put** us **on board** [*+899+1837*].
27: 8 the coast with difficulty and came **to** a place called Fair Havens,
27: 12 should sail on, hoping to reach **[NIE]** Phoenix and winter there.
27: 17 Fearing that they would run aground **on** the sandbars of Syrtis,
27: 26 Nevertheless, we must run aground **on** some island."
27: 30 escape from the ship, the sailors let the lifeboat down **into** the sea,
27: 38 they lightened the ship by throwing the grain **into** the sea.
27: 39 but they saw a bay with a sandy beach, **where** [*+4005*] they
27: 40 they left them **in** the sea and at the same time untied the ropes that
27: 40 Then they hoisted the foresail to the wind and made **for** the beach.
27: 41 But the ship struck **[NIE]** a sandbar and ran aground. The bow
28: 5 But Paul shook the snake off **into** the fire and suffered no ill
28: 6 waiting a long time and seeing nothing unusual happen **to** him,
28: 12 We put in **at** Syracuse and stayed there three days.
28: 13 From there we set sail and arrived **at** Rhegium. The next day
28: 13 came up, and on the following day *we* **reached** [*+2262*] Puteoli.
28: 14 invited us to spend a week with them. And so we came **to** Rome.
28: 15 as far as the Forum of Appius and the Three Taverns **to** meet us.
28: 16 When *we* **got to** [*RP1656*] Rome, Paul was allowed to live by
28: 17 I was arrested in Jerusalem and handed over **to** the Romans.
28: 23 and came in even larger numbers **to** the place where he was
Ro 1: 1 called to be an apostle and set apart **for** the gospel of God—
1: 5 and apostleship **to** *call* people from among all the Gentiles to the
1: 11 so that I may impart to you some spiritual gift **to** [*+3836*] make
1: 16 because it is the power of God **for** the salvation of everyone who
1: 17 a righteousness that is by **faith from first to last** [*+4411+4411*],
1: 20 what has been made, **so that** [*+3836*] men are without excuse.
1: 24 God gave them over in the sinful desires of their hearts **to**

1:25 rather than the Creator—who is **forever** [+172+3836] praised.
1:26 Because of this, God gave them over **to** shameful lusts. Even their
1:26 Even their women exchanged natural relations **for** unnatural ones.
1:27 relations with women and were inflamed with lust **for** one another.
1:28 he gave them over **to** a depraved mind, to do what ought not to be
2: 4 not realizing that God's kindness leads you **toward** repentance?
2:26 will they not be regarded **as** *though* they were circumcised?
3: 7 falsehood enhances God's truthfulness and so **increases** his glory,
3:22 from God comes through faith in Jesus Christ **to** all who believe.
3:25 He did this **to** demonstrate his justice, because in his forbearance
3:26 **so** [+3836] **as** to be just and the one who justifies those who have
4: 3 believed God, and it was credited to him **as** righteousness."
4: 5 God who justifies the wicked, his faith is credited **as** righteousness.
4: 9 We have been saying that Abraham's faith was credited to him **as**
4:11 **So** [+3836] **then**, he is the father of all who believe but have not
4:11 **in order that** [+3836] righteousness might be credited to them.
4:16 and [NIE] may be guaranteed to all Abraham's offspring—
4:18 hope believed **and so** [+3836] became the father of many nations,
4:20 Yet he did not waver through unbelief **regarding** the promise of
4:22 This is why "it was credited to him **as** righteousness."
5: 2 through whom we have gained access by faith **into** this grace in
5: 8 But God demonstrates his own love **for** us in this: While we were
5:12 just as sin **entered** [RP1656] the world through one man,
5:12 and death through sin, and in this way death came to all men,
5:15 by the grace of the one man, Jesus Christ, overflow **to** the many!
5:16 The judgment followed one sin and **brought** condemnation,
5:16 but the gift followed many trespasses and **brought** justification.
5:18 just as the result of one trespass was [NIE] condemnation for all
5:18 just as the result of one trespass was condemnation **for** all men,
5:18 so also the result of one act of righteousness was [NIE]
5:18 act of righteousness was justification that brings life for all men.
5:21 so also grace might reign through righteousness **to bring** eternal
6: 3 Or don't you know that all of us who were baptized **into** Christ
6: 3 who were baptized into Christ Jesus were baptized **into** his death?
6: 4 therefore buried with him through baptism **into** death in order that,
6:12 in your mortal body **so that** [+3836] you obey its evil desires.
6:16 Don't you know that when you offer yourselves to someone **to**
6:16 you are slaves to sin, which **leads to** death, or to obedience,
6:16 leads to death, or to obedience, which **leads to** righteousness?
6:17 you wholeheartedly obeyed the form of teaching **to** which you
6:19 impurity and *to* **ever-increasing wickedness** [+490+490+3836],
6:19 so now offer them in slavery to righteousness **leading to** holiness.
6:22 the benefit you reap **leads to** holiness, and the result is eternal life.
7: 4 **that** [+3836] you might belong to another, to him who was raised
7: 5 at work in our bodies, **so that** [+3836] we bore fruit for death.
7:10 I found that the very commandment that was **intended to bring**
7:10 that was intended to bring life actually **brought** death.
8: 7 the sinful mind is hostile **to** God. It does not submit to God's law,
8:15 For you did not receive a spirit that makes you a slave again **to**
8:18 are not worth comparing with the glory that will be revealed in us.
8:21 and *brought* **into** the glorious freedom of the children of God.
8:28 And we know that in all things God works **for** the good of those
8:29 **that** [+3836] he might be the firstborn among many brothers.
9: 5 of Christ, who is God over all, **forever** [+172+3836] praised!
9: 8 but it is the children of the promise who are regarded **as**
9:17 "I raised you up **for** this very **purpose**, that I might display my
9:21 out of the same lump of clay some pottery **for** noble purposes
9:21 clay some pottery for noble purposes and some **for** common use?
9:22 great patience the objects of his wrath—prepared **for** destruction?
9:23 the objects of his mercy, whom he prepared in advance **for** glory—
9:31 who pursued a law of righteousness, has not attained it⁵ [+3795].
10: 1 prayer to God for the Israelites is that they may be **saved** [+5401].
10: 4 **so that** there may be righteousness for everyone who believes.
10: 6 'Who will ascend **into** heaven?' " (that is, to bring Christ down)
10: 7 "or 'Who will descend **into** the deep?' " (that is, to bring Christ up
10:10 For it is with your heart that you believe and are **justified** [+1466],
10:10 and it is with your mouth that you confess and are **saved** [+5401].
10:12 Lord is Lord of all and richly blesses [NIE] all who call on him,
10:14 How, then, can they call on the one they have not believed in?
10:18 "Their voice has gone out **into** all the earth, their words to the ends
10:18 gone out into all the earth, their words **to** the ends of the world."
11: 9 "*May* their table **become** [+1181] a snare and a trap, a stumbling
11: 9 "May their table become a snare and **[RPG]** a trap, a stumbling
11: 9 and a trap, **[RPG]** a stumbling block and a retribution for them.
11: 9 and a trap, a stumbling block and **[RPG]** a retribution for them.
11:11 salvation has come to the Gentiles **to** [+3836] make Israel envious.

11:24 and contrary to nature were grafted **into** a cultivated olive tree,
11:32 For God has bound all men over **to** disobedience so that he may
11:36 For from him and through him and **to** him are all things. To him be
11:36 are all things. To him be the glory **forever** [+172+3836]! Amen.
12: 2 **Then** [+3836] you **will be able** to test and approve what God's
12: 3 but rather think of yourself **with** [+3836] sober judgment,
12:10 Be devoted **to** one another in brotherly love. Honor one another
12:16 Live in harmony **with** one another. Do not be proud, but be willing
13: 4 For he is God's servant **to** do you good. But if you do wrong,
13: 4 an agent **of** wrath to bring punishment on the wrongdoer.
13: 6 are God's servants, who give their full time **to** governing.
13:14 and do not think about **how to gratify** the desires of the sinful
14: 1 Accept him whose faith is weak, **without** [+3590] passing
14: 9 For **this very reason** [+4047], Christ died and returned to life
14:19 every effort to do what leads to peace and **to** mutual edification.
15: 2 Each of us should please his neighbor **for** his good, to build him
15: 4 For everything that was written in the past was written **to** teach us,
15: 7 just as Christ accepted you, **in order to bring** praise to God.
15: 8 **to** [+3836] confirm the promises made to the patriarchs
15:13 **so that** [+3836] you may overflow with hope by the power of the
15:16 [NIE] to be a minister of Christ Jesus to the Gentiles with the
15:16 to be a minister of Christ Jesus **to** the Gentiles with the priestly
15:18 me in **leading** the Gentiles **to** obey God by what I have said
15:24 I plan to do so when I go **to** Spain. I hope to visit you while
15:25 I am on my way **to** Jerusalem in the service of the saints there.
15:26 and Achaia were pleased to make a contribution **for** the poor
15:28 have received this fruit, I will go **to** Spain and visit you on the way.
15:31 and that my service **in** Jerusalem may be acceptable to the saints
16: 5 who was the first convert **to** Christ in the province of Asia.
16: 6 Greet Mary, who worked very hard **for** you.
16:19 [NIE] Everyone has heard about your obedience, so I am full of
16:19 but I want you to be wise **about** what is good, and innocent about
16:19 to be wise about what is good, and innocent **about** what is evil.
16:26 the eternal God, **so that** all nations might believe and obey him—
16:26 so that [NIE] all nations might believe and obey him—
16:27 to the only wise God be glory **forever** [+172+3836] through Jesus
1Co 1: 9 who has called you **into** fellowship with his Son Jesus Christ our
1:13 Paul crucified for you? Were you baptized **into** the name of Paul?
1:15 so no one can say that you were baptized **into** my name.
2: 7 and that God destined **for** our glory before time began.
4: 3 I **care very little** [+1639+1788] if I am judged by you or by any
4: 6 I have applied these things **to** myself and Apollos for your benefit,
5: 5 **so that** the sinful nature may be destroyed and his spirit saved on
6:16 in body? For it is said, "The two *will* **become** [+1639] one flesh."
6:18 his body, but he who sins sexually sins **against** his own body.
8: 6 the Father, from whom all things came and **for** whom we live;
8:10 won't he be emboldened **to** [+3836] eat what has been sacrificed to
8:12 When you sin **against** your brothers in this way and wound their
8:12 and wound their weak conscience, you sin **against** Christ.
8:13 into sin, I will **never** eat meat **again** [+172+3590+3836+4024],
9:18 **and so** [+3836] not make use of my rights in preaching it.
10: 2 They were all baptized **into** Moses in the cloud and in the sea.
10: 6 Now these things occurred as examples **to** [+3836] keep us from
10:11 as warnings for us, **on** whom the fulfillment of the ages has come.
10:31 or drink or whatever you do, do it all **for** the glory of God.
11:17 no praise for you, for your meetings do⁵ more harm than good.
11:17 praise for you, for your meetings do more harm than **[RPG]** good.
11:22 Don't you have homes **to** [+3836] eat and drink in? Or do you
11:24 "This is my body, which is for you; do this **in** remembrance of me."
11:25 my blood; do this, whenever you drink it, **in** remembrance of me."
11:33 So then, my brothers, when you come together **to** [+3836] eat,
11:34 so that when you meet together it may not **result in** judgment.
12:13 For we were all baptized by one Spirit **into** one body—
14: 8 trumpet does not sound a clear call, who will get ready **for** battle?
14: 9 know what you are saying? You will just be speaking **into** the air.
14:22 Tongues, then, **are** [+1639] a sign, not for believers but for
14:36 with you? Or are [NIE] you the only people it has reached?
15:10 of God I am what I am, and his grace **to** me was not without effect.
15:45 "The first man Adam **became** [+1181] a living being"; the last
15:45 became a living being"; the last Adam, **[RPG]** a life-giving spirit.
15:54 written will come true: "Death has been swallowed up **in** victory."
16: 1 Now about the collection **for** God's people: Do what I told the
16: 3 to the men you approve and send them with your gift **to** Jerusalem.
16:15 and they have devoted themselves **to** the service of the saints.
2Co 1: 4 **so that** [+3836] we can comfort those in any trouble with the
1: 5 For just as the sufferings of Christ flow over **into** our lives,

1:10 **On** him we have set our hope that he will continue to deliver us,
1:11 for the gracious favor **granted** us in answer to the prayers of many.
1:16 I planned to visit you on my way **to** Macedonia and to come back
1:16 and then to have you send me on my way **to** Judea.
1:21 Now it is God who makes both us and you stand firm **in** Christ.
1:23 that it was in order to spare you that I did not return **to** Corinth.
2: 4 not to grieve you but to let you know the depth of my love **for** you.
2: 8 I urge you, therefore, to reaffirm your love **for** him.
2: 9 **The reason** [+4047] I wrote you was to see if you would stand the
2: 9 to see if you would stand the test and be obedient **in** everything.
2:12 Now when I went to Troas to preach the gospel of Christ
2:12 Now when I went to Troas **to** preach the gospel of Christ
2:13 Titus there. So I said good-by to them and went on **to** Macedonia.
2:16 we are the smell of death; **[NIE]** to the other, the fragrance of life.
2:16 the fragrance of life. **[NIE]** And who is equal to such a task?
3: 7 so that the Israelites could not look steadily **at** the face of Moses
3:13 the Israelites from gazing **at** it while the radiance was fading away.
3:18 into his likeness **with ever-increasing glory** [+608+1518+1518],
4: 4 **so that** [+3836] they cannot see the light of the gospel of the glory
4:11 For we who are alive are always being given over **to** death for
4:15 and more people may cause thanksgiving to overflow **to** the glory
4:17 glory **that far outweighs them all** [+983+2848+5651+5651].
5: 5 Now it is God who has made us **for** this very **purpose** and has
6: 1 fellow workers we urge you not to receive God's grace **in** vain.
6:18 "*I will* **be** [+1639] a Father to you, and you will be my sons
6:18 and you *will* **be** [+1639] my sons and daughters, says the Lord
7: 3 you have such a place in our hearts **that** [+3836] we would live
7: 5 For when we came **into** Macedonia, this body of ours had no rest,
7: 9 were made sorry, but because your sorrow **led** you **to** repentance.
7:10 Godly sorrow brings repentance that **leads** to salvation and leaves
7:15 And his affection **for** you is all the greater when he remembers that
8: 2 and their extreme poverty welled up **in** rich generosity.
8: 4 with us for the privilege of sharing in this service **to** the saints.
8: 6 **So** [+3836] we urged Titus, since he had earlier made a beginning,
8: 6 to bring also to completion this act of grace **on** your *part.*
8:14 At the present time your plenty will supply what **[NIE]** they need,
8:14 they need, so that in turn their plenty will **supply** what you need.
8:22 and now even more so because of his great confidence in **you.**
8:23 As for Titus, he is my partner and fellow worker **among** you;
8:24 Therefore show **[NIE]** these men the proof of your love
8:24 and the reason for our pride in you, **so that** the churches can see it.
9: 1 There is no need for me to write to you about this service **to** the
9: 5 So I thought it necessary to urge the brothers to **visit** [+4601] you
9: 8 And God is able to make all grace abound **to** you, so that in all
9: 8 having all that you need, you will abound **in** every good work.
9: 9 gifts to the poor; his righteousness endures **forever** [+172+3836]."
9:10 and bread **for** food will also supply and increase your store of seed
9:11 rich in every way **so that** you can be generous on every occasion,
9:13 that accompanies your confession **of** the gospel of Christ,
9:13 and for your generosity in sharing **with** them and with everyone
9:13 for your generosity in sharing with them and **with** everyone else.
10: 1 "timid" when face to face with you, but "bold" **[NIE]** when away!
10: 5 and we take captive every thought **to** *make* it obedient to Christ.
10: 8 the Lord gave us **for** building you up rather than pulling you down,
10: 8 gave us for building you up rather than **[RPG]** pulling you down,
10:13 We, however, will not boast **beyond** proper limits, but will confine
10:14 in our boasting, as would be the case if we had not come to you,
10:15 Neither do we **go**ˢ beyond our limits by boasting of work done by
10:15 our area of activity among you will **greatly** [+4353] expand,
10:16 so that we can preach the gospel **in** the regions beyond you.
10:16 For we do not want to boast **about** work already done in another
11: 3 be led astray from your sincere and pure devotion **to** Christ.
11: 6 We have made this perfectly clear **to** you in every way.
11:10 in the regions of Achaia will stop this boasting **of mine** [+1609].
11:13 deceitful workmen, masquerading **as** apostles of Christ.
11:14 no wonder, for Satan himself masquerades **as** an angel of light.
11:20 of you or pushes himself forward or slaps you **in** the face.
11:31 who is to be praised **forever** [+172+3836], knows that I am not
12: 1 to be gained, I will go **on to** visions and revelations from the Lord.
12: 4 was caught up **to** paradise. He heard inexpressible things,
12: 6 so no one will think more **of** me than is warranted by what I do
13: 2 On *my* **return** [+2262+3836+4099] I will not spare those who
13: 3 He is not weak **in dealing with** you, but is powerful among you.
13: 4 in him, yet by God's power we will live with him **to serve** you.
13:10 the authority the Lord gave me **for** building you up, not for tearing
13:10 the Lord gave me for building you up, not **for** tearing you down.

Gal 1: 5 to whom be glory **for** ever and ever. Amen.
1: 6 you by the grace of Christ and are *turning* **to** a different gospel—
1:17 nor did I go up **to** Jerusalem to see those who were apostles before
1:17 but I went immediately **into** Arabia and later returned to
1:17 I went immediately into Arabia and later returned **to** Damascus.
1:18 I went up **to** Jerusalem to get acquainted with Peter and stayed
1:21 Later I went **to** Syria and Cilicia.
2: 1 Fourteen years later I went up again **to** Jerusalem, this time with
2: 2 be leaders, for fear that I was running or had run my race **in** vain.
2: 8 who was at work in the ministry of Peter **as** an apostle to the Jews,
2: 8 was also at work in my ministry as an apostle **to** the Gentiles.
2: 9 They agreed that we should *go* **to** the Gentiles, and they to the
2: 9 agreed that we should go to the Gentiles, and they **to** the Jews.
2:11 When Peter came **to** Antioch, I opposed him to his face,
2:16 have put our faith **in** Christ Jesus that we may be justified by faith
3: 6 "He believed God, and it was credited to him **as** righteousness."
3:14 given to Abraham might come **to** the Gentiles through Christ Jesus,
3:17 established by God **and thus** [+3836] do away with the promise.
3:23 held prisoners by the law, locked up **until** faith should be revealed.
3:24 So the law was put in charge to lead us **to** Christ that we might be
3:27 for all of you who were baptized **into** Christ have clothed
4: 6 you are sons, God sent the Spirit of his Son **into** our hearts,
4:11 I fear for you, that somehow I have wasted my efforts **on** you.
4:24 is from Mount Sinai and bears children who are **to** be slaves:
5:10 I am confident in the Lord **[NIE]** that you will take no other view.
5:13 But do not use your freedom **to** indulge the sinful nature; rather,
6: 1 Then he can take pride in himself, without comparing himself to
6: 4 pride in himself, without *comparing* himself **to** somebody else,
6: 8 The one who sows **to** *please* his sinful nature, from that nature will
6: 8 the one who sows **to** *please* the Spirit, from the Spirit will reap

Eph 1: 5 he predestined us **to** be adopted as his sons through Jesus Christ,
1: 5 Jesus Christ, **[NIE]** in accordance with his pleasure and will—
1: 6 **to** the praise of his glorious grace, which he has freely given us in
1: 8 that he lavished **on** us with all wisdom and understanding.
1:10 **to** be put into effect *when* the times will have reached their
1:12 **in order that** [+3836] we, who were the first to hope in Christ,
1:12 were the first to hope in Christ, might be **for** the praise of his glory.
1:14 who is a deposit guaranteeing our inheritance **until** the redemption
1:14 of those who are God's possession—**to** the praise of his glory.
1:15 about your faith in the Lord Jesus and your love **for** all the saints,
1:18 **in order that** [+3836] you may know the hope to which he has
1:19 and his incomparably great power **for** us who believe. That power
2:15 His purpose was to create in himself **[NIE]** one new man out of
2:21 is joined together and rises **to** become a holy temple in the Lord.
2:22 And in him you too are being built together **to** become a dwelling
3: 2 the administration of God's grace that was given to me **for** you,
3:16 strengthen you with power through his Spirit **in** your inner being,
3:19 that you may be filled **to** the measure of all the fullness of God.
3:21 glory in the church and in Christ Jesus **throughout** all generations,
4: 8 "When he ascended **on** high, he led captives in his train and gave
4: 9 (What does "he ascended" mean except that he also descended **to**
4:12 to prepare God's people **for** works of service, so that the body of
4:12 for works of service, **so that** the body of Christ may be built up
4:13 until we all reach **[NIE]** unity in the faith and in the knowledge of
4:13 and in the knowledge of the Son of God and **become** mature,
4:13 **attaining to** the whole measure of the fullness of Christ.
4:15 we will in all things grow up **into** him who is the Head, that is,
4:16 grows and **[NIE]** builds itself up in love, as each part does its
4:19 over to sensuality **so as to** indulge in every kind of impurity,
4:30 of God, with whom you were sealed **for** the day of redemption.
4:32 Be kind and compassionate **to** one another, forgiving each other,
5: 2 and gave himself up for us as a **[NIE]** fragrant offering
5:31 be united to his wife, and the two *will* **become** [+1639] one flesh."
5:32 a profound mystery—but I am talking **about** Christ and the church.
5:32 but I am talking about Christ and **[RPG]** the church.
6:18 with all kinds of prayers and requests. **With this in mind** [+899],
6:22 I am sending him to you **for** this very **purpose**, that you may know

Php 1: 5 because of your partnership **in** the gospel from the first day until
1:10 **so that** [+3836] you may be able to discern what is best and may
1:10 what is best and may be pure and blameless **until** the day of Christ,
1:11 that comes through Jesus Christ—**to** the glory and praise of God.
1:12 that what has happened to me has really served **to** advance the
1:16 in love, knowing that I am put here **for** the defense of the gospel.
1:19 what has happened to me will turn out **for** my deliverance.
1:23 I desire **to** [+3836] depart and be with Christ, which is better by
1:25 and I will continue with all of you **for** your progress and joy in the

1:29 been granted to you on behalf of Christ not only to believe **on** him,
2:11 confess that Jesus Christ is Lord, **to** the glory of God the Father.
2:16 *in order* **that** I may boast on the day of Christ that I did not run
2:16 in order that I may boast **on** the day of Christ that I did not run
2:16 boast on the day of Christ that I did not run or labor **for** nothing.
2:16 on the day of Christ that I did not run or labor for nothing. **[RPG]**
2:22 because as a son with his father he has served with me **in** the work
3:11 and so, somehow, to attain **to** the resurrection from the dead.
3:14 I press on toward the goal **to** *win* the prize for which God has
3:16 Only let us live up **to** what we have already attained.
4:15 not one church shared with me **in** the matter of giving
4:16 you sent me aid again and again when I was **in** need.
4:17 but I am looking for what may be credited **to** your account.
4:20 To our God and Father be glory **for** ever and ever. Amen.
Col 1: 4 faith in Christ Jesus and of the love you have **for** all the saints—
1: 6 that has come **to** you. All over the world this gospel is bearing fruit
1:10 live a life worthy of the Lord and may please him **in** every way:
1:11 glorious might **so that** you may have great endurance and patience,
1:12 who has qualified you **to** share in the inheritance of the saints in
1:13 of darkness and brought us **into** the kingdom of the Son he loves,
1:16 or authorities; all things were created by him and **for** him.
1:20 and through him to reconcile **to** himself all things, whether things
1:25 God gave me to present **to** you the word of God in its fullness—
1:29 **To** [+*4005*] **this end** I labor, struggling with all his energy,
2: 2 **so that** they may have the full riches of complete understanding,
2: 2 **in order that** they may know the mystery of God, namely,
2: 5 to see how orderly you are and how firm your faith **in** Christ is.
2:22 These are all *destined* **to** perish with use, because they are based
3: 9 Do not lie **to** each other, since you have taken off your old self
3:10 which is being renewed **in** knowledge in the image of its Creator.
3:15 since as members of one body you were called **to** peace.
4: 8 I am sending him to you **for** [+*899+4047*] **the express purpose**
4:11 These are the only Jews among my fellow workers **for** the
1Th 1: 5 because our gospel came **to** you not simply with words, but also
2: 9 a burden to anyone while we preached the gospel of God **to** you.
2:12 comforting and urging you **to** [+*3836*] live lives worthy of God,
2:12 lives worthy of God, who calls you **into** his kingdom and glory.
2:16 **In** [+*3836*] **this way** they always heap up their sins to the limit.
2:16 sins to the limit. The wrath of God has come upon them **at** last.
3: 2 of Christ, **to** [+*3836*] strengthen and encourage you in your faith,
3: 3 these trials. You know quite well that we were destined **for** them.
3: 5 could stand it no longer, I sent **to** [+*3836*] find out about your faith.
3: 5 tempted you and our efforts *might have* **been** [+*1181*] useless.
3:10 and day we pray most earnestly **that** [+*3836*] we may see you
3:12 love increase and overflow **for** each other and for everyone else,
3:12 love increase and overflow for each other and **for** everyone else,
3:12 for each other and for everyone else, just as ours does **for** you.
3:13 May he **[NIE]** strengthen your hearts so that you will be
4: 8 not reject man but God, who gives **[NIE]** you his Holy Spirit.
4: 9 for you yourselves have been taught by God **to** [+*3836*] love each
4:10 you do love **[NIE]** all the brothers throughout Macedonia.
4:15 that we who are still alive, who are left **till** the coming of the Lord,
4:17 and are left will be caught up together with them in the clouds **to**
4:17 up together with them in the clouds to meet the Lord **in** the air.
5: 9 For God did not appoint us **to** *suffer* wrath but to receive salvation
5: 9 suffer wrath but **to** receive salvation through our Lord Jesus Christ.
5:15 but always try to be kind **to** each other and to everyone else.
5:15 but always try to be kind to each other and **to** everyone else.
5:18 in all circumstances, for this is God's will **for** you in Christ Jesus.
2Th 1: 3 and the love every one of you has **for** each other is increasing.
1: 5 and as a **result** [+*3836*] you will be counted worthy of the kingdom
1:11 **With** this *in mind*, we constantly pray for you, that our God may
2: 2 **[NIE]** not to become easily unsettled or alarmed by some
2: 4 or is worshiped, so that he sets himself up **in** God's temple,
2: 6 him back, **so that** [+*3836*] he may be revealed at the proper time.
2:10 because they refused to love the truth **and so** [+*3836*] be saved.
2:11 them a powerful delusion **so that** [+*3836*] they will believe the lie
2:13 because from the beginning God chose you **to** be saved through the
2:14 He called you **to** this through our gospel, that you might share in
2:14 **that** you might share in the glory of our Lord Jesus Christ.
3: 5 May the Lord direct your hearts **into** God's love and Christ's
3: 5 your hearts into God's love and **[RPG]** Christ's perseverance.
3: 9 but in order to make ourselves a model for you **to** [+*3836*] follow.
1Ti 1: 3 As I urged you when I went **into** Macedonia, stay there in Ephesus
1: 6 have wandered away from these and turned **to** meaningless talk.
1:12 that he considered me faithful, appointing me **to** his service.
1:15 Christ Jesus came **into** the world to save sinners—of whom I am
1:16 for those who would believe on him and **receive** eternal life.
1:17 invisible, the only God, be honor and glory **for** ever and ever.
2: 4 wants all men to be saved and to come **to** a knowledge of the truth.
2: 7 And **for** this **purpose** I was appointed a herald and an apostle—
3: 6 become conceited and fall **under** the same judgment as the devil.
3: 7 so that he will not fall **into** disgrace and into the devil's trap.
4: 3 which God created **to** be received with thanksgiving by those who
4:10 (and **for** this we labor and strive), that we have put our hope in the
5:24 men are obvious, reaching **the place**[s] **of** judgment ahead of them;
6: 7 For *we* **brought** nothing **into** [*RP1662*] the world,
6: 9 People who want to get rich fall **into** temptation and a trap
6: 9 and harmful desires that plunge men **into** ruin and destruction.
6:12 Take hold of the eternal life **to** which you were called when you
6:17 who richly provides us with everything **for** our enjoyment.
6:19 up treasure for themselves as a firm foundation **for** the coming age,
2Ti 1:11 And **of** this gospel I was appointed a herald and an apostle
1:12 that he is able to guard what I have entrusted to him **for** that day.
2:20 and clay; some are **for** noble purposes and some for ignoble.
2:20 and clay; some are for noble purposes and some **for** ignoble.
2:21 he will be an instrument **for** noble purposes, made holy, useful to
2:21 made holy, useful to the Master and prepared **to do** any good work.
2:25 in the hope that God will grant them repentance **leading** them **to** a
2:26 the trap of the devil, who has taken them captive **to do** his will.
3: 6 They are the kind who worm their way **into** homes and gain
3: 7 always learning but never able **[NIE]** to acknowledge the truth.
3:15 which are able to make you wise **for** salvation through faith in
4:10 he loved this world, has deserted me and has gone **to** Thessalonica.
4:10 Crescens has gone **to** Galatia, and Titus to Dalmatia.
4:10 Crescens has gone to Galatia, and Titus **to** Dalmatia.
4:11 bring him with you, because he is helpful to me **in** my ministry.
4:12 I sent Tychicus **to** Ephesus.
4:18 every evil attack and will bring me safely **to** his heavenly kingdom.
4:18 his heavenly kingdom. To him be glory **for** ever and ever. Amen.
Tit 3:12 or Tychicus to you, do your best to come to me **at** Nicopolis,
3:14 in order that they may *provide* **for** daily necessities and not live
Phm 1: 5 about your faith in the Lord Jesus and your love **for** all the saints.
1: 6 have a full understanding of every good thing we have **in** Christ.
Heb 1: 5 Or again, "I *will* **be** [+*1639*] his Father, and he will be my Son"?
1: 5 Or again, "I will be his Father, and he *will* **be** [+*1639*] my Son"?
1: 6 when God **brings** his firstborn **into** [*RP1652*] the world, he says,
1: 8 the Son he says, "Your throne, O God, will last **for** ever and ever,
1:14 Are not all angels ministering spirits sent **to** serve those who will
2: 3 by the Lord, was confirmed **to** us by those who heard him.
2:10 In bringing many sons **to** glory, it was fitting that God, for whom
2:17 and **that** [+*3836*] he might make atonement for the sins of the
3: 5 God's house, **[NIE]** testifying to what would be said in the future.
3:11 on oath in my anger, '*They shall* never **enter** [*RP1656*] my rest.' "
3:18 *would* never **enter** [*RP1656*] his rest if not to those who
4: 1 since the promise *of* **entering** [*RP1656*] his rest still stands,
4: 3 Now *we* who have believed **enter** [*RP1656*] that rest, just as God
4: 3 '*They shall* never **enter** [*RP1656*] my rest.' " And yet his work has
4: 5 above he says, "*They shall* never **enter** [*RP1656*] my rest."
4: 6 It still remains that some *will* **enter** [*RP1656*] that rest, and those
4:10 for anyone *who* **enters** [*RP1656*] God's rest also rests from his
4:11 Let us, therefore, make every effort *to* **enter** [*RP1656*] that rest,
4:16 may receive mercy and find grace to help us **in** our time of need.
5: 6 "You are a priest **forever** [+*172+3836*], in the order of
6: 6 if they fall away, to be brought back **to** repentance, because to their
6: 8 is in danger of being cursed. In the end it will be **[NIE]** burned.
6:10 and the love you have shown **[NIE]** him as you have helped his
6:16 and the oath **confirms** [+*1012*] what is said and puts an end to all
6:19 *It* **enters** [*RP1656*] the inner sanctuary behind the curtain,
6:20 He has become a high priest **forever** [+*172+3836*], in the order of
7: 3 like the Son of God he remains a priest **forever** [+*1457+3836*].
7:14 and **in regard to** that tribe Moses said nothing about priests.
7:17 "You are a priest **forever** [+*172+3836*], in the order of
7:21 not change his mind: 'You are a priest **forever** [+*172+3836*].' "
7:24 but because Jesus lives **forever** [+*172+3836*], he has a permanent
7:25 Therefore he is able to save **completely** [+*3836+4117*] those who
7:25 because he always lives **to** [+*3836*] intercede for them.
7:28 the Son, who has been made perfect **forever** [+*172+3836*].
8: 3 Every high priest is appointed **to** [+*3836*] offer both gifts
8:10 I will put my laws **in** their minds and write them on their hearts.
8:10 *I will* **be** [+*1639*] their God, and they will be my people.
8:10 I will be their God, and they *will* **be** [+*1639*] my people.

9: 6 the priests **entered** regularly **into** [*RP1655*] the outer room to
9: 7 But only the high priest entered **[RPG]** the inner room, and that
9: 9 This is an illustration **for** the present time, indicating that the gifts
9: 12 *He did* not **enter** [*RP1656*] by means of the blood of goats
9: 14 that lead to death, **so that** [*+3836*] we may serve the living God!
9: 15 now that he has died **as** a ransom to set them free from the sins
9: 24 For Christ *did* not **enter** [*RP16561650*] a man-made sanctuary that
9: 24 For Christ *did* not **enter** [*RP16561650*] a man-made sanctuary that
9: 25 the way the high priest **enters** [*RP1656*] the Most Holy Place
9: 26 But now he has appeared once for all at the end of the ages **to** do
9: 28 so Christ was sacrificed once to take away the sins **of** many people;
9: 28 to bear sin, but **to bring** salvation to those who are waiting for him.
10: 1 by the same sacrifices repeated **endlessly** [*+1457+3836*] year after
10: 5 Therefore, *when* Christ **came into** [*RP1656*] the world, he said:
10: 12 But when this priest had offered **for all time** [*+1457+3836*] one
10: 14 perfect **forever** [*+1457+3836*] those who are being made holy.
10: 19 since we have confidence to **enter** [*RP1658*] the Most Holy Place
10: 24 And let us consider how we may **spur** one another on [*+4237*]
10: 31 It is a dreadful thing to fall **into** the hands of the living God.
10: 39 But we are not of those who shrink back and are **destroyed** [*+724*],
10: 39 but of those who believe and are **saved** [*+4348+6034*].
11: 3 **so that** [*+3836*] what is seen was not made out of what was visible.
11: 7 things not yet seen, in holy fear built an ark **to** save his family.
11: 8 when called to go **to** a place he would later receive **as** his
11: 8 when called to go **to** a place he would later receive **as** his
11: 9 By faith he made his home **in** the promised land like a stranger in a
11: 11 was enabled **to** become a father because he considered him faithful
11: 26 treasures of Egypt, because he was looking ahead **to** his reward.
12: 2 Let us fix our eyes **on** Jesus, the author and perfecter of our faith,
12: 3 sinful men, **[NIE]** so that you will not grow weary and lose heart.
12: 7 Endure hardship **as** discipline; God is treating you as sons.
12: 10 us for our good, **that** [*+3836*] we may share in his holiness.
13: 8 Christ is the same yesterday and today and **forever** [*+172+3836*].
13: 11 The high priest carries the blood of animals into the Most Holy
13: 21 equip you with everything good **for** [*+3836*] doing his will,
13: 21 through Jesus Christ, to whom be glory **for** ever and ever.
Jas 1: 18 **that** [*+3836*] we might be a kind of firstfruits of all he created.
1: 19 Everyone should be quick **to** [*+3836*] listen, slow to speak
1: 19 quick to listen, slow **to** [*+3836*] speak and slow to become angry,
1: 19 should be quick to listen, slow to speak and slow **to** become angry,
1: 25 But the man who looks intently **into** the perfect law that gives
2: 2 Suppose a man **comes into** [*RP1656*] your meeting wearing a gold
2: 6 Are they not the ones who are dragging you **into** court?
2: 23 believed God, and it was credited to him **as** righteousness,"
3: 3 When we put bits **into** the mouths of horses to make them obey us,
3: 3 When we put bits into the mouths of horses **to** [*+3836*] make them
4: 9 Change your laughter **to** mourning and your joy to gloom.
4: 9 Change your laughter to mourning and your joy **to** gloom.
4: 13 you who say, "Today or tomorrow we will go **to** this or that city,
5: 3 Their corrosion **[NIE]** will testify against you and eat your flesh
5: 4 The cries of the harvesters *have* **reached** [*RP1656*] the ears of the
1Pe 1: 2 **for** obedience to Jesus Christ and sprinkling by his blood:
1: 3 In his great mercy he has given us new birth **into** a living hope
1: 4 and **into** an inheritance that can never perish, spoil or fade—
1: 4 that can never perish, spoil or fade—kept in heaven **for** you,
1: 5 who through faith are shielded by God's power **until** the coming of
1: 7 may be proved genuine and may result **in** praise, glory and honor
1: 8 and even though you do not see **[NIE]** him now, you believe in
1: 10 the prophets, who spoke of the grace that was to *come* **to** you,
1: 11 and circumstances **to** which the Spirit of Christ in them was
1: 11 in them was pointing when he predicted the sufferings **of** Christ
1: 12 Spirit sent from heaven. Even angels long to look **into** these things.
1: 21 Through him you believe **in** God, who raised him from the dead
1: 21 the dead and glorified him, and so your faith and hope are **in** God.
1: 22 obeying the truth **so that** you have sincere love for your brothers,
1: 25 but the word of the Lord stands **forever** [*+172+3836*]." And this is
1: 25 Lord stands forever." And this is the word that was preached **to** you.
2: 2 spiritual milk, so that by it you may grow up **in** your salvation,
2: 5 are being built into a spiritual house to be a holy priesthood,
2: 7 "The stone the builders rejected *has* **become** [*+1181*] the capstone,"
2: 8 disobey the message—which is also what they were destined **for**.
2: 9 a holy nation, a people **belonging to** God [*+4348*],
2: 9 of him who called you out of darkness **into** his wonderful light.
2: 14 who are sent by him **to** punish those who do wrong and to
2: 21 **To** this you were called, because Christ suffered for you,
3: 5 past who put their hope **in** God used to make themselves beautiful.

3: 7 gift of life, **so that** [*+3836*] nothing will hinder your prayers.
3: 9 because **to** this you were called so that you may inherit a blessing.
3: 12 Lord are on the righteous and his ears are *attentive* **to** their prayer,
3: 20 **In** it only a few people, eight in all, were saved through water,
3: 21 from the body but the pledge of a good conscience **toward** God.
3: 22 who has gone **into** heaven and is at God's right hand—with angels,
4: 2 **As a result** [*+3836*], he does not live the rest of his earthly life for
4: 4 They think it strange that you do not plunge with them **into** the
4: 6 For **this is the reason** [*+4047*] the gospel was preached even to
4: 7 be clear minded and self-controlled **so that** you can pray.
4: 8 Above all, love **[NIE]** each other deeply, because love covers
4: 9 *Offer* hospitality **to** one another without grumbling.
4: 10 Each one should use whatever gift he has received to serve **[NIE]**
4: 11 To him be the glory and the power **for** ever and ever. Amen.
5: 10 the God of all grace, who called you **to** his eternal glory in Christ,
5: 11 To him be the power **for** ever and ever. Amen.
5: 12 and testifying that this is the true grace of God. Stand fast **in** it.
2Pe 1: 8 and unproductive **in** your knowledge of our Lord Jesus Christ.
1: 11 and you will receive a rich **welcome into** [*RP1658*] the eternal
1: 17 "This is my Son, whom I love; **with** him I am well pleased."
2: 4 putting them into gloomy dungeons to be held **for** judgment;
2: 9 from trials and to hold the unrighteous **for** the day of judgment,
2: 12 creatures of instinct, born only **to** be caught and destroyed,
2: 22 "A sow that is washed *goes back* **to** her wallowing in the mud."
3: 7 being kept **for** the day of judgment and destruction of ungodly
3: 9 He is patient **with** you, not wanting anyone to perish, but everyone
3: 9 not wanting anyone to perish, but everyone to come **to** repentance.
3: 18 To him be glory both now and **forever** [*+172+2465*]! Amen.
1Jn 2: 17 but the man who does the will of God lives **forever** [*+172+3836*].
3: 8 **The reason** [*+4047*] the Son of God appeared was to destroy the
3: 14 We know that we have passed from death **to** life, because we love
4: 1 because many false prophets have gone out **into** the world.
4: 9 and only Son **into** the world that we might live through him.
5: 8 water and the blood; and the three are **in agreement** [*+1651+3836*].
5: 10 Anyone who believes **in** the Son of God has this testimony in his
5: 10 because he has not believed **[NIE]** the testimony God has given
5: 13 I write these things to you who believe **in** the name of the Son of
2Jn 1: 2 which lives in us and will be with us **forever** [*+172+3836*]:
1: 7 Jesus Christ as coming in the flesh, have gone out **into** the world.
1: 10 this teaching, do not take him **into** your house or welcome him.
3Jn 1: 5 Dear friend, you are faithful in what you are doing **for** the brothers,
Jude 1: 4 For certain men whose **[NIE]** condemnation was written about
1: 4 who change the grace of our God **into** a license for immorality
1: 6 bound with everlasting chains **for** judgment on the great Day.
1: 13 for whom blackest darkness has been reserved **forever** [*+172*].
1: 21 for the mercy of our Lord Jesus Christ to **bring** you to eternal life.
1: 25 Lord, before all ages, now and **forevermore** [*+172+3836+4246*]!
Rev 1: 6 and Father—to him be glory and power **for** ever and ever!
1: 11 "Write **on** a scroll what you see and send it to the seven churches:
1: 11 **to** Ephesus, Smyrna, Pergamum, Thyatira, Sardis, Philadelphia
1: 11 to Ephesus, Smyrna, **[RPG]** Smyrna, Pergamum, Thyatira, Sardis,
1: 11 to Ephesus, Smyrna, Pergamum, **[RPG]** Pergamum, Thyatira, Sardis,
1: 11 to Ephesus, Smyrna, Pergamum, Thyatira, **[RPG]** Thyatira, Sardis,
1: 11 to Ephesus, Smyrna, Pergamum, Thyatira, Sardis, **[RPG]** Sardis,
1: 11 Pergamum, Thyatira, Sardis, **[RPG]** Philadelphia and Laodicea."
1: 11 Pergamum, Thyatira, Sardis, Philadelphia and **[RPG]** Laodicea."
1: 18 Living One; I was dead, and behold I am alive **for** ever and ever!
2: 10 I tell you, the devil will put some of you **in** prison to test you,
2: 22 So I will cast her **on** a bed of suffering, and I will make those who
2: 22 and I will make those who commit adultery with her **[NIE]** suffer
4: 9 to him who sits on the throne and who lives **for** ever and ever,
4: 10 sits on the throne, and worship him who lives **for** ever and ever.
5: 6 which are the seven spirits of God sent out **into** all the earth.
5: 13 Lamb be praise and honor and glory and power, **for** ever and ever!"
6: 13 and the stars in the sky fell **to** earth, as late figs drop from a fig tree
6: 15 and every slave and every free man hid **in** caves and among the
6: 15 every free man hid in caves and **among** the rocks of the mountains.
7: 12 and honor and power and strength be to our God **for** ever and ever.
8: 5 filled it with fire from the altar, and hurled it **on** the earth;
8: 7 and fire mixed with blood, and it was hurled **down upon** the earth.
8: 8 like a huge mountain, all ablaze, was thrown **into** the sea.
8: 11 A third of the waters **turned** [*+1181*] bitter, and many people died
9: 1 and I saw a star that had fallen from the sky **to** the earth.
9: 3 And out of the smoke locusts came **down upon** the earth and were
9: 7 The locusts looked like horses prepared **for** battle. On their heads
9: 9 like the thundering of many horses and chariots rushing **into** battle.

9: 15 And the four angels who had been kept ready **for** this very hour
10: 5 standing on the sea and on the land raised his right hand **to** heaven.
10: 6 And he swore by him who lives **for** ever and ever, who created the
11: 6 and they have power to turn the waters **into** blood and to strike the
11: 9 will gaze on their bodies and refuse them **burial** [+3645+5502].
11: 12 And they went up **to** heaven in a cloud, while their enemies looked
11: 15 of our Lord and of his Christ, and he will reign **for** ever and ever."
12: 4 swept a third of the stars out of the sky and flung them **to** the earth.
12: 6 The woman fled **into** the desert to a place prepared for her by God,
12: 9 world astray. He was hurled **to** the earth, and his angels with him.
12: 13 When the dragon saw that he had been hurled **to** the earth,
12: 14 so that she might fly **to** the place prepared for her in the desert,
12: 14 so that she might fly **to** the place prepared for her in the desert,
13: 3 One of the heads of the beast seemed to have had a **[NIE]** fatal
13: 6 He opened his mouth **to** blaspheme God, and to slander his name
13: 10 If anyone is to go **into** captivity, into captivity he will go. If anyone
13: 10 If anyone is to go **into** captivity, into captivity he will go. If anyone
13: 13 even causing fire to come down from heaven **to** earth in full view
14: 11 And the smoke of their torment rises **for** ever and ever. There is no
14: 19 The angel swung his sickle **on** the earth, gathered its grapes
14: 19 its grapes and threw them **into** the great winepress of God's wrath.
15: 7 bowls filled with the wrath of God, who lives **for** ever and ever.
15: 8 and no one could **enter** [RP1656] the temple until the seven
16: 1 "Go, pour out the seven bowls of God's wrath **on** the earth."
16: 2 The first angel went and poured out his bowl **on** the land, and ugly
16: 3 The second angel poured out his bowl **on** the sea, and it turned into
16: 4 The third angel poured out his bowl **on** the rivers and springs of
16: 14 to gather them **for** the battle on the great day of God Almighty.
16: 16 Then they gathered the kings together **to** the place that in Hebrew
16: 19 The great city split **into** three parts, and the cities of the nations
17: 3 Then the angel carried me away in the Spirit **into** a desert.
17: 8 and will come up out of the Abyss and go **to** his destruction.
17: 11 He belongs to the seven and is going **to** his destruction.
17: 17 For God has put it **into** their hearts to accomplish his purpose by
18: 21 up a boulder the size of a large millstone and threw it **into** the sea,
19: 3 "Hallelujah! The smoke from her goes up **for** ever and ever."
19: 9 'Blessed are those who are invited **to** the wedding supper of the
19: 17 In midair, "Come, gather together **for** the great supper of God,
19: 20 The two of them were thrown alive **into** the fiery lake of burning
20: 3 He threw him **into** the Abyss, and locked and sealed it over him,
20: 8 corners of the earth—Gog and Magog—to gather them **for** battle.
20: 10 was thrown **into** the lake of burning sulfur, where the beast
20: 10 They will be tormented day and night **for** ever and ever.
20: 14 Then death and Hades were thrown **into** the lake of fire. The lake
20: 15 written in the book of life, he was thrown **into** the lake of fire.
21: 24 and the kings of the earth will bring their splendor **into** it.
21: 26 The glory and honor of the nations will be brought **into** it.
21: 27 Nothing impure will ever **enter** [RP1656] it, nor will anyone who
22: 2 And the leaves of the tree are **for** the healing of the nations.
22: 5 God will give them light. And they will reign **for** ever and ever.
22: 14 tree of life and may **go through** the gates **into** [RP1656] the city.

1651 εἰς, heis [345 / 346] [→ 1894, 1895, 1942, 2022, 2023, 2024, 2025, 2758, 3594, 3599, 4029, 4032]

one [243], a [17], first [9], *untranslated* [7], a single [7], the other^s [6], each [+1667] [5], man [4], alone [3], an [3], one [+5516] [3], the [3], each [+1651+2848] [2], each other [+1651+3836] [2], one at a time [+1651+2848] [2], a unit [1], agreeing [+1191+4472] [1], alike [+608] [1], among [+1666] [1], another [1], any [1], by itself [+1650+3023+5536+6006] [1], detail [+1667] [1], each [+324+1667] [1], each [1], everyone [+1667] [1], faithful to her husband [+467+1222] [1], final statement [+4839] [1], in agreement [+1650+3836] [1], in turn [+2848] [1], in unison [+1181+5889] [1], just as though [+899+2779+3836] [1], nothing [+4028] [1], once [1], one [+3836] [1], one after the other [+1667] [1], one and the same [1], only [+4028] [1], some [+3538+3836] [1], someone [1], the next day [+2465+3552] [1], the one [1], the only [1], the same [1], unity [1]

Mt 5: 18 the truth, until heaven and earth disappear, not **the** smallest letter,
    5: 18 earth disappear, not **the** smallest letter, not **the** least stroke of a pen,
    5: 19 Anyone who breaks **one** of the least of these commandments
    5: 29 It is better for you to lose **one** part of your body than for your
    5: 30 It is better for you to lose **one** part of your body than for your

5: 36 by your head, for you cannot make *even* **one** hair white or black.
5: 41 If someone forces you to go **one** mile, go with him two miles.
6: 24 Either he will hate the **one** and love the other, or he will be devoted
6: 24 the other, or he will be devoted to the **one** and despise the other.
6: 27 Who of you by worrying can add **a single** hour to his life?
6: 29 not even Solomon in all his splendor was dressed like **one** of these.
8: 19 Then **a** teacher of the law came to him and said, "Teacher, I will
9: 18 he was saying this, **a** ruler came and knelt before him and said,
10: 29 Yet not **one** of them will fall to the ground apart from the will of
10: 42 And if anyone gives even a cup of cold water to **one** of these little
12: 11 "If any of you has **a** sheep and it falls into a pit on the Sabbath,
13: 46 When he found **one** of great value, he went away and sold
16: 14 others say Elijah; and still others, Jeremiah or **one** of the prophets."
17: 4 up three shelters—**one** for you, one for Moses and one for Elijah."
17: 4 up three shelters—one for you, **one** for Moses and one for Elijah."
17: 4 up three shelters—one for you, one for Moses and **one** for Elijah."
18: 5 "And whoever welcomes **a** little child like this in my name
18: 6 But if anyone causes **one** of these little ones who believe in me to
18: 10 "See that you do not look down on **one** of these little ones.
18: 12 If a man owns a hundred sheep, and **one** of them wanders away,
18: 14 In the same way your Father in heaven is not willing that **any** of
18: 16 But if he will not listen, take **one** or two others along,
18: 24 a **man** who owed him ten thousand talents was brought to him.
18: 28 he found **one** of his fellow servants who owed him a hundred
19: 5 and be united to his wife, and the two will become **one** flesh'?
19: 6 So they are no longer two, but **one**. Therefore what God has joined
19: 16 Now a **man** came up to Jesus and asked, "Teacher, what good thing
19: 17 Jesus replied. "There is *only* **One** who is good. If you want to enter
20: 12 'These men who were hired last worked *only* **one** hour,' they said,
20: 13 "But he answered **one** of them, 'Friend, I am not being unfair to
20: 21 "Grant that one of these two sons of mine may sit **[RPG]** at your
20: 21 may sit at your right and **the other**^s at your left in your kingdom."
21: 19 Seeing a fig tree by the road, he went up to it but found nothing on
21: 24 Jesus replied, "I will also ask you **one** question. If you answer me,
22: 35 **One** of them, an expert in the law, tested him with this question:
23: 8 for you have *only* **one** Master and you are all brothers.
23: 9 on earth 'father,' for you have **one** Father, and he is in heaven.
23: 10 you to be called 'teacher,' for you have **one** Teacher, the Christ.
23: 15 You travel over land and sea to win **a single** convert, and when he
24: 40 Two men will be in the field; **one** will be taken and the other
24: 40 Two men will be in the field; one will be taken and **the other**^s left.
24: 41 be grinding with a hand mill; **one** will be taken and the other left.
24: 41 be grinding with a hand mill; one will be taken and **the other**^s left.
25: 15 to another two talents, and to another **one** talent, each according to
25: 18 But the man who had received the **one** talent went off, dug a hole
25: 24 "Then the man who had received the **one** talent came. 'Master,'
25: 40 whatever you did *for* **one** of the least of these brothers of mine,
25: 45 you the truth, whatever you did not do *for* **one** of the least of these,
26: 14 Then **one** of the Twelve—the one called Judas Iscariot—went to
26: 21 eating, he said, "I tell you the truth, **one** of you will betray me."
26: 22 very sad and began to say to him **one** [+1667] **after the other**,
26: 40 "Could you men not keep watch with me *for* **one** hour?" he asked
26: 47 While he was still speaking, Judas, **one** of the Twelve, arrived.
26: 51 With that, **one** of Jesus' companions reached for his sword,
26: 69 was sitting out in the courtyard, and **a** servant girl came to him.
27: 14 But Jesus made no reply, not even to **a single** charge—to the great
27: 15 Now it was the governor's custom at the Feast to release **a** prisoner
27: 38 were crucified with him, **one** on his right and one on his left.
27: 38 were crucified with him, one on his right and **one** on his left.
27: 48 Immediately **one** of them ran and got a sponge. He filled it with
28: 1 at dawn on the **first** *day* of the week, Mary Magdalene

Mk 2: 7 like that? He's blaspheming! Who can forgive sins but God **alone**?"
    4: 8 grew and produced a crop, multiplying **[RPG]** thirty, sixty,
    4: 8 grew and produced a crop, multiplying thirty, **[RPG]** sixty,
    4: 8 a crop, multiplying thirty, sixty, or even **a** hundred times."
    4: 20 **[RPG]** thirty, sixty or even a hundred times what was sown."
    4: 20 thirty, **[RPG]** sixty or even a hundred times what was sown."
    4: 20 a crop—thirty, sixty or even **a** hundred times what was sown."
    5: 22 Then **one** of the synagogue rulers, named Jairus, came there.
    6: 15 "He is a prophet, like **one** of the prophets of long ago."
    8: 14 to bring bread, except for **one** loaf they had with them in the boat.
    8: 28 the Baptist; others say Elijah; and still others, **one** of the prophets."
    9: 5 up three shelters—**one** for you, one for Moses and one for Elijah."
    9: 5 up three shelters—one for you, **one** for Moses and one for Elijah."
    9: 5 up three shelters—one for you, one for Moses and **one** for Elijah."
    9: 17 A **man** in the crowd answered, "Teacher, I brought you my son,

9:37 "Whoever welcomes **one** of these little children in my name
9:42 "And if anyone causes **one** of these little ones who believe in me to
10: 8 and the two will become **one** flesh.' So they are no longer two,
10: 8 the two will become **one** flesh.' So they are no longer two, but **one**.
10:17 on his way, a **man** ran up to him and fell on his knees before him.
10:18 me good?" Jesus answered. "No one is good—except God **alone**.
10:21 "**One** *thing* you lack," he said. "Go, sell everything you have
10:37 "Let **one** of us sit at your right and the other at your left in your
10:37 one of us sit at your right and **the other**ˢ at your left in your glory."
11:29 Jesus replied, "I will ask you **one** question. Answer me, and I will
12: 6 "He had **one** left to send, a son, whom he loved. He sent him last of
12:28 **One** of the teachers of the law came and heard them debating.
12:29 "is this: 'Hear, O Israel, the Lord our God, the Lord is **one**.
12:32 "You are right in saying that God is **one** and there is no other
12:42 But **a** poor widow came and put in two very small copper coins,
13: 1 the temple, one of his disciples said to him, "Look, Teacher!
14:10 Then Judas Iscariot, **one** of the Twelve, went to the chief priests to
14:18 he said, "I tell you the truth, **one** of you will betray me—
14:19 were saddened, and **one** by one they said to him, "Surely not I?"
14:19 were saddened, and one by **one** they said to him, "Surely not I?"
14:20 "It is **one** of the Twelve," he replied, "one who dips bread into the
14:37 to Peter, "are you asleep? Could you not keep watch *for* **one** hour?
14:43 Just as he was speaking, Judas, **one** of the Twelve, appeared.
14:47 Then **one** [+5516] of those standing near drew his sword
14:66 in the courtyard, **one** of the servant girls of the high priest came by.
15: 6 Now it was the custom at the Feast to release **a** prisoner whom the
15:27 two robbers with him, **one** on his right and one on his left.
15:27 two robbers with him, one on his right and **one** on his left.
16: 2 Very early *on* the **first** *day* of the week, just after sunrise,

Lk   4:40 of sickness, and laying his hands on each **one**, he healed them.
   5: 3 He got into **one** of the boats, the one belonging to Simon,
   5:12 While Jesus was in **one** of the towns, a man came along who was
   5:17 **One** day as he was teaching, Pharisees and teachers of the law,
   7:41 **One** owed him five hundred denarii, and the other fifty.
   8:22 **One** day Jesus said to his disciples, "Let's go over to the other side
   9:33 up three shelters—**one** for you, one for Moses and one for Elijah."
   9:33 up three shelters—one for you, **one** for Moses and one for Elijah."
   9:33 up three shelters—one for you, one for Moses and **one** for Elijah."
  10:42 but *only* **one** *thing* is needed. Mary has chosen what is better,
  11:46 and you yourselves will not lift **one** finger to help them.
  12: 6 sold for two pennies? Yet not **one** of them is forgotten by God.
  12:25 Who of you by worrying can add a **single** [UBS-] hour to his life?
  12:27 not even Solomon in all his splendor was dressed like **one** of these.
  12:52 From now on there will be five in **one** family divided against each
  13:10 On a Sabbath Jesus was teaching in **one** of the synagogues,
  14:18 "But they all **alike** [+608] began to make excuses. The first said,
  15: 4 "Suppose one of you has a hundred sheep and loses **one** of them.
  15: 7 **one** sinner who repents than over ninety-nine righteous persons
  15: 8 "Or suppose a woman has ten silver coins and loses **one**. Does she
  15:10 there is rejoicing in the presence of the angels of God over **one**
  15:15 So he went and hired himself out to **a** citizen of that country,
  15:19 to be called your son; make me like **one** of your hired men.'
  15:26 So he called **one** of the servants and asked him what was going on.
  16: 5 "So he called in each **one** of his master's debtors. He asked the first,
  16:13 Either he will hate the **one** and love the other, or he will be devoted
  16:13 the other, or he will be devoted to **the one** and despise the other.
  16:17 and earth to disappear than *for* **the** least stroke of a pen to drop out
  17: 2 around his neck than for him to cause **one** of these little ones to sin.
  17:15 **One** of them, when he saw he was healed, came back,
  17:22 "The time is coming when you will long to see **one** of the days of
  17:34 I tell you, on that night two people will be in **one** bed; one will be
  17:34 two people will be in one bed; **one** will be taken and the other left.
  17:35 will be grinding grain together; **one** will be taken and the other left."
  18:10 to the temple to pray, **one** a Pharisee and the other a tax collector.
  18:19 me good?" Jesus answered. "No one is good—except God **alone**.
  18:22 When Jesus heard this, he said to him, "You still lack **one** *thing*.
  20: 1 **One** day as he was teaching the people in the temple courts
  22:47 man who was called Judas, **one** of the Twelve, was leading them.
  22:50 And **one** [+5516] of them struck the servant of the high priest,
  22:59 About **an** hour later another asserted, "Certainly this fellow was
  23:39 **One** of the criminals who hung there hurled insults at him:
  24: 1 *On* the **first** *day* of the week, very early in the morning,
  24:18 one of them, named Cleopas, asked him, "Are you only a visitor to

Jn   1: 3 without him **nothing** [+4028] was made that has been made.
   1:40 was **one** of the two who heard what John had said and who had
   3:27 "A man can receive **only** [+4028] what is given him from heaven.

   6: 8 **Another** of his disciples, Andrew, Simon Peter's brother,
   6:22 shore of the lake realized that only **one** boat had been there,
   6:70 "Have I not chosen you, the Twelve? Yet **one** of you is a devil!"
   6:71 who, though **one** of the Twelve, was later to betray him.)
   7:21 Jesus said to them, "I did **one** miracle, and you are all astonished.
   7:50 had gone to Jesus earlier and who was **one** of their own number,
   8: 9 those who heard began to go away one [+1651+2848] **at a time**,
   8: 9 those who heard began to go away **one at a time** [+1651+2848],
   8:41 they protested. "**The** only Father we have is God himself."
   9:25 I don't know. **One** *thing* I do know. I was blind but now I see!"
  10:16 listen to my voice, and there shall be **one** flock and one shepherd.
  10:16 listen to my voice, and there shall be one flock and **one** shepherd.
  10:30 I and the Father are **one**."
  11:49 Then **one** [+5516] of them, named Caiaphas, who was high priest
  11:50 You do not realize that it is better for you that **one** man die for the
  11:52 children of God, to bring them together and make them **one**.
  12: 2 while Lazarus was **among** [+1666] those reclining at the table with
  12: 4 But **one** of his disciples, Judas Iscariot, who was later to betray
  13:21 and testified, "I tell you the truth, **one** of you is going to betray me."
  13:23 **One** of them, the disciple whom Jesus loved, was reclining next to
  17:11 the name you gave me—so that they may be **one** as we are one.
  17:21 that all of them may be **one**, Father, just as you are in me
  17:22 the glory that you gave me, that they may be **one** as we are one:
  17:22 the glory that you gave me, that they may be one as we are **one**:
  17:23 May they be brought to complete **unity** to let the world know that
  18:14 the Jews that it would be good if **one** man died for the people.
  18:22 Jesus said this, **one** of the officials nearby struck him in the face.
  18:26 **One** of the high priest's servants, a relative of the man whose ear
  18:39 But it is your custom for me to release to you **one** *prisoner* at the
  19:34 Instead, **one** of the soldiers pierced Jesus' side with a spear,
  20: 1 Early *on* the **first** *day* of the week, while it was still dark,
  20: 7 The cloth was folded up **by itself** [+1650+3023+5536+6006],
  20:12 Jesus' body had been, **one** at the head and the other at the foot.
  20:12 Jesus' body had been, one at the head and **the other**ˢ at the foot.
  20:19 On the evening *of* that **first** day of the week, when the disciples
  20:24 Now Thomas (called Didymus), **one** of the Twelve, was not with
  21:25 If every **one** of them were written down, I suppose that even the

Ac   1:22 For **one** of these must become a witness with us of his resurrection."
   1:24 Show us which [RPG] of these two you have chosen
   2: 3 of fire that separated and came to rest on **each** [+1667] of them.
   2: 6 because each **one** heard them speaking in his own language.
   4:32 All the believers were **one** in heart and mind. No one claimed that
   4:32 No **one** claimed that any of his possessions was his own, but they
  11:28 **One** of them, named Agabus, stood up and through the Spirit
  12:10 When they had walked the *length of* **one** street, suddenly the angel
  17:26 From **one** *man* he made every nation of men, that they should
  17:27 out for him and find him, though he is not far from each **one** of us.
  19:34 they all shouted **in unison** [+1181+5889] for about two hours:
  20: 7 On the **first** *day* of the week we came together to break bread.
  20:31 for three years I never stopped warning **each** [+1667] of you night
  21: 7 where we greeted the brothers and stayed with them *for* **a** day.
  21:19 and reported in **detail** [+1667] what God had done among the
  21:26 and the offering would be made for **each** [+1667] of them.
  23: 6 knowing that **some** [+3538+3836] of them were Sadducees
  23:17 Then Paul called **one** of the centurions and said, "Take this young
  24:21 unless it was this **one** thing I shouted as I stood in their presence:
  28:13 **The next day** [+2465+3552] the south wind came up, and on the
  28:25 began to leave *after* Paul had made this **final statement** [+4839]:

Ro   3:10 As it is written: "There is no one righteous, not even **one**;
   3:12 become worthless; there is no one who does good, not even **one**."
   3:30 since there is *only* **one** God, who will justify the circumcised by
   5:12 Therefore, just as sin entered the world through **one** man,
   5:15 For if the many died by the trespass *of* the **one** *man*, how much
   5:15 did God's grace and the gift that came by the grace *of* the **one** man,
   5:16 Again, the gift of God is not like the result of the **one** *man's* sin:
   5:16 The judgment followed **one** sin and brought condemnation,
   5:17 For if, by the trespass *of* the **one** *man*, death reigned through that
   5:17 the trespass of the one man, death reigned through that **one** *man*,
   5:17 and of the gift of righteousness reign in life through the **one** *man*,
   5:18 just as the result of **one** trespass was condemnation for all men,
   5:18 so also the result of **one** act of righteousness was justification that
   5:19 For just as through the disobedience *of* the **one** man the many were
   5:19 so also through the obedience *of* the **one** *man* the many will be
   9:10 only that, but Rebekah's children had **one and the same** father,
  12: 4 Just as each of us has **one** body with many members, and these
  12: 5 so in Christ we who are many form **one** body, and each member

12: 5 many form one body, and **each** member belongs to all the others.
15: 6 so that with **one** heart and mouth you may glorify the God
1Co 3: 8 The man who plants and the man who waters have **one** *purpose*,
4: 6 Then **[RPG]** you will not take pride in one man over against
4: 6 Then you will not take pride in **one** [*+3836*] *man* over against
6:16 he who unites himself with a prostitute is **one** with her in body?
6:16 with her in body? For it is said, "The two will become **one** flesh."
6:17 But he who unites himself with the Lord is **one** with him in spirit.
8: 4 idol is nothing at all in the world and that there is no God but **one**.
8: 6 yet for us there is but **one** God, the Father, from whom all things
8: 6 and there is but **one** Lord, Jesus Christ, through whom all things
9:24 know that in a race all the runners run, but *only* **one** gets the prize?
10: 8 of them did—and *in* **one** day twenty-three thousand of them died.
10:17 Because there is **one** loaf, we, who are many, are one body,
10:17 Because there is one loaf, we, who are many, are **one** body,
10:17 who are many, are one body, for we all partake of the **one** loaf.
11: 5 it is **just as though** [*+899+2779+3836*] her head were shaved.
12: 9 by the same Spirit, to another gifts of healing by that **one** Spirit,
12:11 All these are the work of **one** and the same Spirit, and he gives
12:12 The body is **a unit**, though it is made up of many parts; and though
12:12 many parts; and though all its parts are many, they form **one** body.
12:13 For we were all baptized by **one** Spirit into one body—
12:13 For we were all baptized by one Spirit into **one** body—
12:13 slave or free—and we were all given the **one** Spirit to drink.
12:14 Now the body is not made up of **one** part but of many.
12:18 parts in the body, every **one** of them, just as he wanted them to be.
12:19 If they were all **one** part, where would the body be?
12:20 As it is, there are many parts, but **one** body.
12:26 If **one** part suffers, every part suffers with it; if one part is honored,
12:26 suffers with it; if **one** part is honored, every part rejoices with it.
14:27 should speak, one at a time, and **someone** must interpret.
14:31 For you can all prophesy **in turn** [*+2848*] so that everyone may be
16: 2 *On the* **first** *day* of every week, each one of you should set aside a
2Co 5:14 because we are convinced that **one** died for all, and therefore all
11: 2 I promised you *to* **one** husband, to Christ, so that I might present
11:24 Five times I received from the Jews the forty lashes minus **one**.
Gal 3:16 but "and to your seed," meaning **one** *person*, who is Christ.
3:20 A mediator, however, does not represent *just* **one** *party*, but God
3:20 however, does not represent just one party; but God is **one**.
3:28 slave nor free, male nor female, for you are all **one** in Christ Jesus.
4:22 **one** by the slave woman and the other by the free woman.
4:22 one by the slave woman and **the other**ˢ by the free woman.
4:24 **One** covenant is from Mount Sinai and bears children who are to
5:14 The entire law is summed up in **a single** command: "Love your
Eph 2:14 who has made the two **one** and has destroyed the barrier,
2:15 His purpose was to create in himself **one** new man out of the two,
2:16 and in this **one** body to reconcile both of them to God through the
2:18 For through him we both have access to the Father by **one** Spirit.
4: 4 There is **one** body and one Spirit—just as you were called to one
4: 4 There is one body and **one** Spirit—just as you were called to one
4: 4 just as you were called to **one** hope when you were called—
4: 5 **one** Lord, one faith, one baptism;
4: 5 one Lord, **one** faith, one baptism;
4: 5 one Lord, one faith, **one** baptism;
4: 6 **one** God and Father of all, who is over all and through all
4: 7 But to each **one** of us grace has been given as Christ apportioned it.
4:16 and builds itself up in love, as **each** [*+1667*] part does its work.
5:31 and be united to his wife, and the two will become **one** flesh."
5:33 each **one** of you also must love his wife as he loves himself,
Php 1:27 you in my absence, I will know that you stand firm in **one** spirit,
1:27 in one spirit, contending as **one** man for the faith of the gospel
2: 2 having the same love, being **one** in spirit and purpose.
3:13 But **one** *thing* I do: Forgetting what is behind and straining toward
Col 3:15 since as members of **one** body you were called to peace.
4: 6 with salt, so that you may know how to answer **everyone** [*+1667*].
1Th 2:11 For you know that we dealt with **each** [*+1667*] of you as a father
5:11 encourage one another and build **each other** [*+1651+3836*] up,
5:11 encourage one another and build **each other** [*+1651+3836*] up,
2Th 1: 3 and the love every **one** of you has for each other is increasing.
1Ti 2: 5 For there is **one** God and one mediator between God and men,
2: 5 For there is one God and **one** mediator between God and men,
3: 2 the husband *of* but **one** wife, temperate, self-controlled,
3:12 A deacon must be the husband *of* but **one** wife and must manage
5: 9 she is over sixty, has been **faithful to her husband** [*+467+1222*],
Tit 1: 6 An elder must be blameless, the husband *of* but **one** wife,
3:10 Warn a divisive person **once**, and then warn him a second time.

Heb 2:11 men holy and those who are made holy are of **the same** *family*.
10:12 But when this priest had offered for all time **one** sacrifice for sins,
10:14 because *by* **one** sacrifice he has made perfect forever those who are
11:12 And so from this **one** *man*, and he as good as dead,
12:16 who for **a single** meal sold his inheritance rights as the oldest son.
Jas 2:10 and yet stumbles at just **one** *point* is guilty of breaking all of it.
2:19 You believe that there is **one** God. Good! Even the demons believe
4:12 There is *only* **one** Lawgiver and Judge, the one who is able to save
2Pe 3: 8 But do not forget this **one** *thing*, dear friends: With the Lord a day
3: 8 With the Lord **a** day is like a thousand years, and a thousand years
3: 8 a day is like a thousand years, and a thousand years are like **a** day.
1Jn 5: 8 and the blood; and the three are **in agreement** [*+1650+3836*].
Rev 4: 8 **Each** [*+1651+2848*] of the four living creatures had six wings
4: 8 **Each** [*+1651+2848*] of the four living creatures had six wings
5: 5 Then **one** of the elders said to me, "Do not weep! See, the Lion of
6: 1 I watched as the Lamb opened the **first** of the seven seals.
6: 1 Then I heard **one** of the four living creatures say in a voice like
7:13 Then **one** of the elders asked me, "These in white robes—who are
8:13 I heard **an** eagle that was flying in midair call out in a loud voice:
9:12 The **first** woe is past; two other woes are yet to come.
9:13 and I heard **a** voice coming from the horns of the golden altar that
13: 3 **One** of the heads of the beast seemed to have had a fatal wound,
15: 7 Then **one** of the four living creatures gave to the seven angels
17: 1 **One** of the seven angels who had the seven bowls came and said to
17:10 Five have fallen, **one** is, the other has not yet come; but when he
17:12 but who *for* **one** hour will receive authority as kings along with the
17:13 They have **one** purpose and will give their power and authority to
17:17 *by* **agreeing** [*+1191+4472*] to give the beast their power to rule,
18: 8 Therefore in **one** day her plagues will overtake her: death,
18:10 O Babylon, city of power! *In* **one** hour your doom has come!'
18:17 *In* **one** hour such great wealth has been brought to ruin!' "Every sea
18:19 rich through her wealth! *In* **one** hour she has been brought to ruin!
18:21 Then **a** mighty angel picked up a boulder the size of a large
19:17 And I saw **an** angel standing in the sun, who cried in a loud voice
21: 9 **One** of the seven angels who had the seven bowls full of the seven
21:21 were twelve pearls, **each** [*+324+1667*] gate made of a single pearl.
21:21 twelve gates were twelve pearls, each gate made of **a single** pearl.

1652 εἰσάγω, *eisagō* [11] [√ *1650 + 72*]

brought in [2], brought into [*RP1650*] [2], bring in [1], brings into
[*RP1650*] [1], brought [1], led into [*RP1650*] [1], take into
[*RP1650*] [1], taken into [*RP1650*] [1], took into [*RP1650*] [1]

Lk   2:27 When the parents **brought in** the child Jesus to do for him what the
14:21 into the streets and alleys of the town and **bring in** the poor,
22:54 and **took** [*RP1650*] him into the house of the high priest.
Jn 18:16 came back, spoke to the girl on duty there and **brought** Peter **in**.
Ac   7:45 our fathers under Joshua **brought** it *with* them when they took the
9: 8 So *they* **led** [*RP1650*] him by the hand **into** Damascus.
21:28 *he has* **brought** [*RP1650*] Greeks **into** the temple area and defiled
21:29 and assumed that Paul *had* **brought** [*RP1650*] him **into** the temple
21:37 As the soldiers were about to **take** [*RP1650*] Paul **into** the
22:24 the commander ordered Paul *to be* **taken** [*RP1650*] **into** the
Heb 1: 6 when God **brings** [*RP1650*] his firstborn **into** the world, he says,

1653 εἰσακούω, *eisakouō* [5] [√ *1650 + 201*]

heard [4], listen [1]

Mt   6: 7 for they think *they will be* **heard** because of their many words.
Lk   1:13 "Do not be afraid, Zechariah; your prayer *has been* **heard**.
Ac 10:31 God *has* **heard** your prayer and remembered your gifts to the poor.
1Co 14:21 this people, but even then *they will* not **listen** *to* me," says the Lord.
Heb 5: 7 from death, and *he was* **heard** because of his reverent submission.

1654 εἰσδέχομαι, *eisdechomai* [1] [√ *1650 + 1312*]

receive [1]

2Co 6:17 says the Lord. Touch no unclean thing, and I *will* **receive** you."

1655 εἴσειμι, *eiseimi* [4] [√ *1650 + 1640*]

enter [1], entered into [*RP1650*] [1], went [1], went to [*RP1650*] [1]

Ac   3: 3 When he saw Peter and John about to **enter**, he asked them for

21:18 The next day Paul and the rest of us **went** to see James, and all the
21:26 Then *he* **went** [*RP1650*] **to** the temple to give notice of the date
Heb 9: 6 the priests **entered** [*RP1650*] regularly **into** the outer room to

1656 εἰσέρχομαι, *eiserchomai* [194] [√ *1650 + 2262*]

enter [*RP1650*] [46], entered [*RP1650*] [26], went into [*RP1650*] [14], entered [8], enter [7], went in [7], go in [6], go into [*RP1650*] [6], come in [5], came in [4], went to [*RP1650*] [4], come [3], comes in [3], enters [*RP1650*] [3], enters [3], fall into [*RP1650*] [3], went [3], went inside [*RP1650*] [3], arrived in [*RP1650*] [2], came into [*RP1650*] [2], come and share [*RP1650*] [2], gone [2], went into [2], appear before [*RP1650*] [1], arrived [*RP1650*] [1], at [*RP1650*] [1], came [1], came to [*RP1650*] [1], come at [*RP1650*] [1], come in among [*RP1650*] [1], come to [*RP1650*] [1], comes into [*RP1650*] [1], enter [*+1639*] [1], enter [*RP16501650*] [1], enter into [*RP1650*] [1], entered [*+1181*] [1], entered into [*RP1650*] [1], entering [*RP1650*] [1], entering [1], get in [1], go [1], go through into [*RP1650*] [1], goes into [*RP1650*] [1], going into [*RP1650*] [1], gone into [*RP1650*] [1], got to [*RP1650*] [1], in [1], reached [*RP1650*] [1], reaped the benefits of [*RP1650*] [1], started [1], trying[s] to [1], went back into [*RP1650*] [1], went inside [1]

Mt 2:21 the child and his mother and **went** [*RP1650*] **to** the land of Israel.
5:20 *you* will certainly not **enter** [*RP1650*] the kingdom of heaven.
6: 6 **go** [*RP1650*] **into** your room, close the door and pray to your
7:13 "**Enter** through the narrow gate. For wide is the gate and broad is
7:13 road that leads to destruction, and many **enter** [*+1639*] through it.
7:21 'Lord, Lord,' *will* **enter** [*RP1650*] the kingdom of heaven,
8: 5 When Jesus had **entered** [*RP1650*] Capernaum, a centurion came
8: 8 "Lord, I do not deserve to *have you* **come** under my roof.
9:25 had been put outside, he **went in** and took the girl by the hand,
10: 5 among the Gentiles or **enter** [*RP1650*] any town of the Samaritans.
10:11 "Whatever town or village *you* **enter** [*RP1650*], search for some
10:12 *As you* **enter** [*RP1650*] the home, give it your greeting.
12: 4 *He* **entered** [*RP1650*] the house of God, and he and his
12:29 how can anyone **enter** [*RP1650*] a strong man's house and carry
12:45 other spirits more wicked than itself, and *they* **go in** and live there.
15:11 What **goes** [*RP1650*] **into** a man's mouth does not make him
18: 3 *you* will never **enter** [*RP1650*] the kingdom of heaven.
18: 8 It is better for you *to* **enter** [*RP1650*] life maimed or crippled than
18: 9 It is better for you *to* **enter** [*RP1650*] life with one eye than to
19:17 If you want *to* **enter** [*RP1650*] life, obey the commandments."
19:23 it is hard for a rich man *to* **enter** [*RP1650*] the kingdom of heaven.
19:24 needle than for a rich man *to* **enter** [*RP1650*] the kingdom of God."
21:10 *When* Jesus **entered** [*RP1650*] Jerusalem, the whole city was
21:12 Jesus **entered** [*RP1650*] the temple area and drove out all who
22:11 "But *when* the king **came in** to see the guests, he noticed a man
22:12 he asked, 'how *did you* **get in** here without wedding clothes?'
23:13 *You* yourselves *do* not **enter**, nor will you let those enter who are
23:13 do not enter, nor will you let those **enter** who are trying to.
23:13 do not enter, nor will you let those enter who *are* **trying**[s] **to**.
24:38 giving in marriage, up to the day Noah **entered** [*RP1650*] the ark;
25:10 The virgins who were ready **went in** with him to the wedding
25:21 **Come** [*RP1650*] **and share** your master's happiness!'
25:23 **Come** [*RP1650*] **and share** your master's happiness!'
26:41 and pray so that *you* will not **fall** [*RP1650*] **into** temptation.
26:58 He **entered** and sat down with the guards to see the outcome.
27:53 and after Jesus' resurrection *they* **went** [*RP1650*] **into** the holy city
Mk 1:21 Jesus **went** [*RP1650*] **into** the synagogue and began to teach.
1:45 Jesus could no longer **enter** [*RP1650*] a town openly but stayed
2: 1 A few days later, *when* Jesus again **entered** [*RP1650*] Capernaum,
2:26 he **entered** [*RP1650*] the house of God and ate the consecrated
3: 1 Another time *he* **went** [*RP1650*] **into** the synagogue, and a man
3:27 no one can **enter** [*RP1650*] a strong man's house and carry off his
5:12 "Send us among the pigs; allow *us to* **go** [*RP1650*] **into** them."
5:13 and the evil spirits came out and **went** [*RP1650*] **into** the pigs.
5:39 He **went in** and said to them, "Why all this commotion and
6:10 Whenever *you* **enter** [*RP1650*] a house, stay there until you leave
6:22 *When* the daughter of Herodias **came in** and danced, she pleased
6:25 At once the girl hurried **in** to the king with the request: "I want you
7:17 After *he had* left the crowd and **entered** [*RP1650*] the house,
7:24 He **entered** [*RP1650*] a house and did not want anyone to know it;
8:26 Jesus sent him home, saying, "Don't **go** [*RP1650*] **into** the village."
9:25 come out of him and never **enter** [*RP1650*] him again."

9:28 *After* Jesus *had* **gone** indoors, his disciples asked him privately,
9:43 It is better for you *to* **enter** [*RP1650*] life maimed than with two
9:45 It is better for you *to* **enter** [*RP1650*] life crippled than to have two
9:47 It is better for you *to* **enter** [*RP1650*] the kingdom of God with
10:15 the kingdom of God like a little child *will* never **enter** [*RP1650*] it."
10:23 hard it is for the rich *to* **enter** [*RP1650*] the kingdom of God!"
10:24 "Children, how hard it is *to* **enter** [*RP1650*] the kingdom of God!
10:25 needle than for a rich man *to* **enter** [*RP1650*] the kingdom of God."
11:11 Jesus **entered** [*RP1650*] Jerusalem and went to the temple.
11:15 Jesus **entered** [*RP1650*] the temple area and began driving out
13:15 roof of his house go down or **enter** the house to take anything out.
14:14 Say to the owner of the house *he* **enters**, 'The Teacher asks:
15:43 kingdom of God, **went** boldly to Pilate and *asked* for Jesus' body.
16: 5 *As* they **entered** [*RP1650*] the tomb, they saw a young man
Lk 1: 9 to **go** [*RP1650*] **into** the temple of the Lord and burn incense.
1:28 The angel **went** to her and said, "Greetings, you who are highly
1:40 where *she* **entered** [*RP1650*] Zechariah's home and greeted
4:16 and on the Sabbath day *he* **went** [*RP1650*] **into** the synagogue,
4:38 left the synagogue and **went** [*RP1650*] **to** the home of Simon.
6: 4 *He* **entered** [*RP1650*] the house of God, and taking the
6: 6 On another Sabbath he **went** [*RP1650*] **into** the synagogue
7: 1 this in the hearing of the people, *he* **entered** [*RP1650*] Capernaum.
7: 6 for I do not deserve to *have you* **come** under my roof.
7:36 so *he* **went** [*RP1650*] to the Pharisee's house and reclined at the
7:44 "Do you see this woman? *I* **came** [*RP1650*] **into** your house.
7:45 did not give me a kiss, but this woman, from the time *I* **entered**,
8:30 he replied, because many demons *had* **gone** [*RP1650*] **into** him.
8:32 The demons begged Jesus to let them **go** [*RP1650*] **into** them,
8:33 demons came out of the man, *they* **went** [*RP1650*] **into** the pigs,
8:41 at Jesus' feet, pleading with him *to* **come** [*RP1650*] **to** his house
8:51 he did not let anyone **go in** with him except Peter, John and James,
9: 4 Whatever house *you* **enter** [*RP1650*], stay there until you leave
9:34 and they were afraid as they **entered** [*RP1650*] the cloud.
9:46 An argument **started** among the disciples as to which of them
9:52 who **went** [*RP1650*] **into** a Samaritan village to get things ready
10: 5 "When *you* **enter** [*RP1650*] a house, first say, 'Peace to this house.'
10: 8 "When *you* **enter** [*RP1650*] a town and are welcomed, eat what is
10:10 But when *you* **enter** [*RP1650*] a town and are not welcomed,
10:38 he **came** [*RP1650*] **to** a village where a woman named Martha
11:26 other spirits more wicked than itself, and they **go in** and live there.
11:37 invited him to eat with him; so he **went in** and reclined at the table.
11:52 *You* yourselves *have* not **entered**, and you have hindered those
11:52 have not entered, and you have hindered those *who were* **entering**."
13:24 "Make every effort *to* **enter** through the narrow door,
13:24 because many, I tell you, will try *to* **enter** and will not be able to.
14:23 'Go out to the roads and country lanes and make them **come in**,
15:28 "The older brother became angry and refused *to* **go in**. So his father
17: 7 Would he say to the servant *when* he **comes in** from the field,
17:12 *As he was* **going** [*RP1650*] **into** a village, ten men who had
17:27 and being given in marriage up to the day Noah **entered** [*RP1650*]
18:17 the kingdom of God like a little child *will* never **enter** [*RP1650*] it."
18:25 it is easier for a camel *to* **go** through the eye of a needle than for a
18:25 needle than for a rich man *to* **enter** [*RP1650*] the kingdom of God."
19: 1 Jesus **entered** Jericho and was passing through.
19: 7 and began to mutter, "*He has* **gone** to be the guest of a 'sinner.' "
19:45 Then *he* **entered** [*RP1650*] the temple area and began driving out
21:21 get out, and *let* those in the country not **enter** [*RP1650*] the city.
22: 3 Then Satan **entered** [*RP1650*] Judas, called Iscariot, one of the
22:10 He replied, "*As you* **enter** [*RP1650*] the city, a man carrying a jar
22:40 said to them, "Pray that you *will* not **fall** [*RP1650*] **into** temptation."
22:46 and pray so that *you* will not **fall** [*RP1650*] **into** temptation."
24: 3 but *when* they **entered**, they did not find the body of the Lord
24:26 have to suffer these things and then **enter** [*RP1650*] his glory?"
24:29 the day is almost over." So *he* **went in** to stay with them.
Jn 3: 4 "Surely he cannot **enter** [*RP1650*] a second time **into** his mother's
3: 5 no one can **enter** [*RP1650*] the kingdom of God unless he is born
4:38 and you *have* **reaped** [*RP1650*] **the benefits** of their labor."
10: 1 the man *who does* not **enter** [*RP1650*] the sheep pen by the gate,
10: 2 The man *who* **enters** by the gate is the shepherd of his sheep.
10: 9 I am the gate; whoever **enters** through me will be saved. He will
10: 9 me will be saved. *He will* **come in** and go out, and find pasture.
13:27 soon as Judas took the bread, Satan **entered** [*RP1650*] **into** him.
18: 1 an olive grove, and he and his disciples **went** [*RP1650*] **into** it.
18:28 uncleanness the Jews *did* not **enter** [*RP1650*] the palace;
18:33 Pilate then **went** [*RP1650*] back **inside** the palace, summoned
19: 9 and *he* **went** [*RP1650*] back **inside** the palace. "Where do you come

20: 5 and looked in at the strips of linen lying there but *did* not **go in**.
20: 6 who was behind him, arrived and **went** [*RP1650*] **into** the tomb.
20: 8 who had reached the tomb first, also **went** [*RP1650*] **inside**.
Ac 1:13 When *they* **arrived** [*RP1650*], they went upstairs to the room
1:21 men who have been with us the whole time the Lord Jesus **went in**
3: 8 Then *he* **went** [*RP1650*] with them into the temple courts,
5: 7 About three hours later his wife **came in**, not knowing what had
5:10 Then the young men **came in** and, finding her dead, carried her out
5:21 At daybreak *they* **entered** [*RP1650*] the temple courts, as they had
9: 6 "Now get up and **go** [*RP1650*] **into** the city, and you will be told
9:12 In a vision he has seen a man named Ananias **come** and place his
9:17 Then Ananias went to the house and **entered** it. Placing his hands
10: 3 saw an angel of God, *who* **came** to him and said, "Cornelius!"
10:24 The following day *he* **arrived** [*RP1650*] **in** Caesarea. Cornelius
10:25 As Peter **entered** [*+1181*] the *house*, Cornelius met him and fell at
10:27 with him, Peter **went inside** and found a large gathering of people.
11: 3 "*You* **went into** the house of uncircumcised men and ate with
11: 8 or unclean *has* ever **entered** [*RP1650*] my mouth.'
11:12 also went with me, and *we* **entered** [*RP1650*] the man's house.
13:14 On the Sabbath they **entered** [*RP1650*] the synagogue and sat
14: 1 and Barnabas **went** [*RP1650*] as usual **into** the Jewish synagogue.
14:20 around him, *he* got up and **went** [*RP1650*] **back into** the city.
14:22 "We must go through many hardships *to* **enter** [*RP1650*] the
16:15 in the Lord," she said, "**come** [*RP1650*] and stay **at** my house."
16:40 As his custom was, Paul **went into** the synagogue, and on three
17: 2 As his custom was, Paul **went into** the synagogue, and on three
18: 7 and **went** [*RP1650*] next door **to** the house of Titius Justus,
18:19 He himself **went** [*RP1650*] **into** the synagogue and reasoned with
19: 8 Paul **entered** [*RP1650*] the synagogue and spoke boldly there for
19:30 Paul wanted *to* **appear** [*RP1650*] **before** the crowd,
20:29 savage wolves *will* **come** [*RP1650*] **in among** you and will not
21: 8 and stayed **at** [*RP1650*] the house of Philip the evangelist,
23:16 of this plot, *he* **went** [*RP1650*] into the barracks and told Paul.
23:33 *When* the cavalry **arrived** [*RP1650*] **in** Caesarea, they delivered
25:23 and **entered** [*RP1650*] the audience room with the high ranking
28: 8 Paul **went in** to see him and, after prayer, placed his hands on him
28:16 When *we* **got** [*RP1650*] **to** Rome, Paul was allowed to live by
Ro 5:12 just as sin **entered** [*RP1650*] the world through one man,
11:25 hardening in part until the full number of the Gentiles *has* **come in**.
1Co 14:23 and some who do not understand or some unbelievers **come in**,
14:24 or someone who does not understand **comes in** while everybody is
Heb 3:11 on oath in my anger, 'They shall never **enter** [*RP1650*] my rest.' "
3:18 *would* never **enter** [*RP1650*] his rest if not to those who
3:19 So we see that they were not able *to* **enter**, because of their
4: 1 since the promise *of* **entering** [*RP1650*] his rest still stands,
4: 3 Now we who have believed **enter** [*RP1650*] that rest, just as God
4: 3 'They shall never **enter** [*RP1650*] my rest.' " And yet his work has
4: 5 above he says, "They shall never **enter** [*RP1650*] my rest."
4: 6 It still remains that some *will* **enter** [*RP1650*] that rest, and those
4: 6 those who formerly had the gospel preached to them *did* not **go in**,
4:10 for anyone *who* **enters** [*RP1650*] God's rest also rests from his
4:11 Let us, therefore, make every effort *to* **enter** [*RP1650*] that rest,
6:19 It **enters** [*RP1650*] the inner sanctuary behind the curtain,
6:20 where Jesus, who went before us, *has* **entered** on our behalf.
9:12 *He did* not **enter** [*RP1650*] by means of the blood of goats
9:24 For Christ *did* not **enter** [*RP1650*] a man-made sanctuary that
9:25 the way the high priest **enters** [*RP1650*] the Most Holy Place
10: 5 Therefore, *when* Christ **came** [*RP1650*] **into** the world, he said:
Jas 2: 2 Suppose a man **comes** [*RP1650*] **into** your meeting wearing a gold
2: 2 and fine clothes, and a poor man in shabby clothes also **comes in**.
5: 4 The cries of the harvesters *have* **reached** [*RP1650*] the ears of the
Rev 3:20 opens the door, *I* will **come in** and eat with him, and he with me.
11:11 the three and a half days a breath of life from God **entered** them,
15: 8 and no one could **enter** [*RP1650*] the temple until the seven
21:27 Nothing impure *will* ever **enter** [*RP1650*] it, nor will anyone who
22:14 tree of life and *may* **go** [*RP1650*] **through** the gates **into** the city.

1657 εἰσκαλέομαι, *eiskaleomai* [1] [√ *1650 + 2813*]

invited into [1]

Ac 10:23 Then Peter **invited** the men **into** the house to be his guests.

1658 εἴσοδος, *eisodos* [5] [√ *1650 + 3847*]

coming [1], enter [*RP1650*] [1], reception [1], visit [1], welcome into [*RP1650*] [1]

Ac 13:24 Before the **coming** of Jesus, John preached repentance and baptism
1Th 1: 9 for they themselves report what kind of **reception** you gave us.
2: 1 You know, brothers, that our **visit** to you was not a failure.
Heb 10:19 since we have confidence to **enter** [*RP1650*] the Most Holy Place
2Pe 1:11 and you will receive a rich **welcome** [*RP1650*] **into** the eternal

---

1659 εἰσπηδάω, *eispēdaō* [1] [√ *403; cf. 1650*]

rushed in [1]

Ac 16:29 for lights, **rushed in** and fell trembling before Paul and Silas.

1660 εἰσπορεύομαι, *eisporeuomai* [18]
[√ *1650 + 4513*]

come in [3], enters [*RP1650*] [3], enter [*RP1650*] [2], going into [*RP1650*] [2], came [1], enter [1], go into [*RP16501650*] [1], going [1], moved about freely [*+1744+2779*] [1], went in [1], went into [*RP1650*] [1], went to [*RP1650*] [1]

Mt 15:17 "Don't you see that whatever **enters** [*RP1650*] the mouth goes into
Mk 1:21 They **went** [*RP1650*] **to** Capernaum, and when the Sabbath came,
4:19 and the desires for other things **come in** and choke the word,
5:40 the disciples who were with him, and **went in** where the child was.
6:56 And wherever *he* **went** [*RP1650*]—**into** villages, towns
7:15 a man can make him 'unclean' *by* **going** [*RP1650*] **into** him.
7:18 "Don't you see that nothing that **enters** [*RP1650*] a man from the
7:19 For *it* doesn't **go** [*RP16501650*] **into** his heart but into his
11: 2 and just as *you* **enter** [*RP1650*] it, you will find a colt tied there,
Lk 8:16 he puts it on a stand, so that those *who* **come in** can see the light.
11:33 he puts it on its stand, so that those *who* **come in** may see the light.
18:24 "How hard it is for the rich *to* **enter** [*RP1650*] the kingdom of God!
19:30 and *as you* **enter** it, you will find a colt tied there, which no one
22:10 will meet you. Follow him to the house that *he* **enters** [*RP1650*],
Ac 3: 2 day to beg from those **going** [*RP1650*] **into** the temple courts.
8: 3 **Going** from house to house, he dragged off men and women
9:28 with them and **moved** [*+1744+2779*] **about freely** in Jerusalem,
28:30 in his own rented house and welcomed all who **came** to see him.

1661 εἰστρέχω, *eistrechō* [1] [√ *1650 + 5556*]

ran back [1]

Ac 12:14 she was so overjoyed *she* **ran back** without opening it

---

1662 εἰσφέρω, *eispherō* [8] [√ *1650 + 5770*]

lead into [*RP1650*] [2], bringing to [*RP1650*] [1], brought [1], brought into [*RP1650*] [1], carries [1], do^s this [1], take into [1]

Mt 6:13 And **lead** [*RP1650*] us not **into** temptation, but deliver us from the
Lk 5:18 and tried *to* **take** him **into** the *house* to lay him before Jesus.
5:19 When they could not find a way *to* **do^s this** because of the crowd,
11: 4 who sins against us. And **lead** [*RP1650*] us not **into** temptation.' "
12:11 "When you *are* **brought** before synagogues, rulers and authorities,
Ac 17:20 *You are* **bringing** [*RP1650*] some strange ideas **to** our ears,
1Ti 6: 7 For *we* **brought** [*RP1650*] nothing **into** the world,
Heb 13:11 The high priest **carries** the blood of animals into the Most Holy

---

1663 εἶτα, *eita* [15] [→ *2083, 3575*]

then [10], *untranslated* [1], after that [1], and [1], moreover [*+3525*] [1], when [1]

Mk 4:17 **When** trouble or persecution comes because of the word,
4:28 first the stalk, **then** the head, then the full kernel in the head.
4:28 first the stalk, then the head, **then** the full kernel in the head.
8:25 [NIE] Once more Jesus put his hands on the man's eyes,
Lk 8:12 and **then** the devil comes and takes away the word from their
Jn 13: 5 **After that**, he poured water into a basin and began to wash his
19:27 **and** to the disciple, "Here is your mother." From that time on,
20:27 **Then** he said to Thomas, "Put your finger here; see my hands.
1Co 15: 5 and that he appeared to Peter, and **then** to the Twelve.

    15: 7 Then he appeared to James, **then** to all the apostles,
    15:24 **Then** the end will come, when he hands over the kingdom to God
1Ti 2:13 For Adam was formed first, **then** Eve.
    3:10 and **then** if there is nothing against them, let them serve as
Heb 12: 9 **Moreover** [+3525], we have all had human fathers who disciplined
Jas 1:15 **Then**, after desire has conceived, it gives birth to sin; and sin,

1664 εἴτε, eite [65] [√ 1623 + 5445]

or [29], whether [18], if [11], where [3], *untranslated* [1], as for [1], as for [+5642] [1], such as [1]

Ro 12: 6 **If** a man's gift is prophesying, let him use it in proportion to his
   12: 7 **If** it is serving, let it serve, if it is teaching, let him teach;
   12: 7 If it is serving, let him serve; **if** it is teaching, let him teach;
   12: 8 **if** it is encouraging, let him encourage; if it is contributing to the
1Co 3:22 **whether** Paul or Apollos or Cephas or the world or life or death
    3:22 whether Paul **or** Apollos or Cephas or the world or life or death
    3:22 whether Paul or Apollos **or** Cephas or the world or life or death
    3:22 whether Paul or Apollos or Cephas **or** the world or life or death
    3:22 whether Paul or Apollos or Cephas or the world **or** life or death
    3:22 whether Paul or Apollos or Cephas or the world or life **or** death
    3:22 or Apollos or Cephas or the world or life or death **or** the present
    3:22 or Cephas or the world or life or death or the present **or** the future—
    8: 5 **whether** in heaven or on earth (as indeed there are many "gods"
    8: 5 **or** on earth (as indeed there are many "gods" and many "lords"),
  10:31 So **whether** you eat or drink or whatever you do, do it all for the
  10:31 So whether you eat **or** drink or whatever you do, do it all for the
  10:31 So whether you eat or drink **or** whatever you do, do it all for the
  12:13 **whether** Jews or Greeks, slave or free—and we were all given the
  12:13 whether Jews **or** Greeks, slave or free—and we were all given the
  12:13 whether Jews or Greeks, **[RPG]** slave or free—and we were all
  12:13 whether Jews or Greeks, slave **or** free—and we were all given the
  12:26 **If** one part suffers, every part suffers with it; if one part is honored,
  12:26 suffers with it; **if** one part is honored, every part rejoices with it.
  13: 8 But **where** there are prophecies, they will cease; where there are
  13: 8 they will cease; **where** there are tongues, they will be stilled;
  13: 8 they will be stilled; **where** there is knowledge, it will pass away.
  14: 7 case of lifeless things that make sounds, **such as** the flute or harp,
  14: 7 case of lifeless things that make sounds, such as the flute **or** harp,
  14:27 **If** anyone speaks in a tongue, two—or at the most three—
  15:11 **Whether**, then, it was I or they, this is what we preach, and this is
  15:11 Whether, then, it was I **or** they, this is what we preach, and this is
2Co 1: 6 **If** we are distressed, it is for your comfort and salvation; if we are
    1: 6 **if** we are comforted, it is for your comfort, which produces in you
    5: 9 please him, **whether** we are at home in the body or away from it.
    5: 9 to please him, whether we are at home in the body **or** away from it.
    5:10 him for the things done while in the body, **whether** good or bad.
    5:10 him for the things done while in the body, whether good **or** bad.
    5:13 **If** we are out of our mind, it is for the sake of God; if we are in our
    5:13 it is for the sake of God; **if** we are in our right mind, it is for you.
    8:23 **As for** [+5642] Titus, he is my partner and fellow worker among
    8:23 **as for** our brothers, they are representatives of the churches
  12: 2 **Whether** it was in the body or out of the body I do not know—
  12: 2 Whether it was in the body **or** out of the body I do not know—
  12: 3 **whether** in the body or apart from the body I do not know,
  12: 3 whether in the body **or** apart from the body I do not know,
Eph 6: 8 everyone for whatever good he does, **whether** he is slave or free.
    6: 8 everyone for whatever good he does, whether he is slave **or** free.
Php 1:18 every way, **whether** from false motives or true, Christ is preached.
    1:18 every way, whether from false motives **or** true, Christ is preached.
    1:20 Christ will be exalted in my body, **whether** by life or by death.
    1:20 Christ will be exalted in my body, whether by life **or** by death.
    1:27 **whether** I come and see you or only hear about you in my absence,
    1:27 whether I come and see you **or** only hear about you in my absence,
Col 1:16 and invisible, **whether** thrones or powers or rulers or authorities;
    1:16 and invisible, whether thrones **or** powers or rulers or authorities;
    1:16 and invisible, whether thrones or powers **or** rulers or authorities;
    1:16 and invisible, whether thrones or powers or rulers **or** authorities;
    1:20 **whether** things on earth or things in heaven, by making peace
    1:20 whether things on earth **or** things in heaven, by making peace
1Th 5:10 He died for us so that, **whether** we are awake or asleep, we may
    5:10 He died for us so that, whether we are awake **or** asleep, we may
2Th 2:15 we passed on to you, **whether** by word of mouth or by letter.
    2:15 we passed on to you, whether by word of mouth **or** by letter.
1Pe 2:13 among men: **whether** to the king, as the supreme authority,

    2:14 **or** to governors, who are sent by him to punish those who do

1665 εἴωθα, eiōtha [4] [√ 1621]

custom [4]

Mt 27:15 Now *it was* the governor's **custom** at the Feast to release a
Mk 10: 1 of people came to him, and as *was* his **custom**, he taught them.
Lk   4:16 on the Sabbath day he went into the synagogue, as was his **custom**.
Ac 17: 2 As his **custom** was, Paul went into the synagogue, and on three

1666 ἐκ, ek [914 / 916]

[→ 442, 443, 444, 451, 453, 587, 588, 589, 1446, 1447, 1674, 1675, 1676, 1677, 1678, 1679, 1680, 1681, 1682, 1683, 1684, 1685, 1686, 1687, 1688, 1689, 1690, 1691, 1692, 1693, 1694, 1699, 1700, 1701, 1702, 1703, 1704, 1705, 1706, 1707, 1708, 1709, 1710, 1711, 1712, 1713, 1714, 1715, 1716, 1717, 1718, 1719, 1720, 1721, 1722, 1723, 1724, 1725, 1726, 1727, 1728, 1729, 1732, 1733, 1734, 1735, 1736, 1737, 1738, 1739, 1740, 1741, 1742, 1743, 1744, 1745, 1746, 1747, 1748, 1749, 1750, 1751, 1752, 1754, 1758, 1760, 1762, 1763, 1764, 1765, 1766, 1767, 1768, 1769, 1770, 1771, 1774, 1775, 1972, 1973, 1974, 1975, 1976, 1977, 1978, 1979, 1981, 1982, 1983, 1984, 1985, 1986, 1987, 1988, 1989, 1990, 1992, 1993, 1994, 1995, 1996, 1997, 1998, 1999, 2000, 2001, 2002, 2003, 2004, 2005, 2006, 2007, 2010, 2012, 2013, 2014, 2015, 2016, 2017, 2018, 2019, 2020, 2021, 2022, 2023, 2024, 2025, 2026, 2029, 2030, 2031, 2032, 2033, 2034, 2035, 2274, 2275, 4211, 5292, 5293, 5294, 5655, 5656, 5658; cf. 1753, 1772]

from [313], of [160], *untranslated* [57], by [53], out of [49], at [20], with [18], in [17], on [12], some of [10], one of [9], came out of [RP2002] [6], for [6], second time [+1311] [6], belong to [+1639] [5], from among [5], left [RP2002] [5], belong to [4], belonged to [+1639] [4], come out of [RP2002] [4], through [4], among [3], because of [3], belonged to [3], belongs to [+1639] [3], brings out of [RP1675] [3], circumcised [+4364] [3], comes out of [RP1744] [3], depends on [3], out of came [RP2002] [3], out of come [RP2002] [3], since [3], whose mother was [3], because [2], come out of [RP1744] [2], followed [2], got out of [RP2002] [2], have faith [+4411] [2], leave [RP2002] [2], leave [RP2002+1666] [2], out of came [RP1744] [2], over [2], part of [2], take out [RP1675] [2], under [2], went out from [RP2002] [2], according to [+3836] [2], after [1], among [+1651] [1], as [1], away [+3545+3836] [1], away from [+3545] [1], away from [RP1685] [1], back [1], based on [1], believe [+4411] [1], believers [+899] [1], between [1], blot out from [RP1981] [1], brought out of [RP1974] [1], came from [RP1744] [1], came from [RP2002] [1], came out of [RP1744] [1], come from [RP2002] [1], come out [RP2002] [1], comes from [RP1744] [1], coming from [RP2002] [1], completely [+3336+4356] [1], completely cut off from [RP2017] [1], cut out of [RP1716] [1], descendant [+2588+3836] [1], descendant [+3875] [1], descended from [+2002+3836+4019] [1], descended from [+5065] [1], descended from [1], drive out [RP1675] [1], drove from [RP1675] [1], escaped [RP2002] [1], ever [+172+3836] [1], father [+3130] [1], fell off [RP1738] [1], flowed out of [RP2002] [1], flowing from [RP1744] [1], free and belong to no man [+1801+4246] [1], from [+3545] [1], from came [RP1744] [1], from then on [+4047] [1], Gentile [+1620] [1], gone out from [RP2002] [1], heavenly [+4041] [1], his native language [+2625+3836] [1], illegitimate children [+1164+4518] [1], imperfect [+3538] [1], in front of [+1885] [1], Jews [+4364] [1], lead out of [RP1974] [1], leaving [RP1744] [1], leaving [RP1996] [1], led out of [RP2002] [1], lose [+3496] [1], on [+5931] [1], on a journey [+3847] [1], on account of [1], one of [+1639] [1], oppose [+1885] [1], out [1], out of come [RP1744] [1], out of comes [RP1744] [1], physically [+5882] [1], puts out of [RP1675] [1], ran out of [RP1767] [1], redeemed from [RP1973] [1], reluctantly [+3383] [1], rely on [+1639] [1], remove from [RP1675] [1], result in [+1181] [1], say [+201] [1], say [+3836+5125] [1], slipping away from [RP2002] [1], some [1], take out of [RP1675] [1], the kings [1], third time [+5569] [1], this is how [+4047] [1], to pay [1], use [1], wholeheartedly [*+2840*] [1], whose mother [1], wipe away from [*RP1981*] [1], wipe from [*RP1981*] [1], without [*+4024*] [1]

Mt   1: 3 Judah the father of Perez and Zerah, **whose mother was** Tamar,
     1: 5 **whose mother was** Rahab, Boaz the father of Obed, whose mother
     1: 5 father of Obed, **whose mother was** Ruth, Obed the father of Jesse,
     1: 6 was the father of Solomon, **whose mother** had been Uriah's wife,
     1:16 husband of Mary, **of** whom was born Jesus, who is called Christ.
     1:18 she was found to be with child **through** the Holy Spirit.
     1:20 because what is conceived in her is **from** the Holy Spirit.
     2: 6 for **out of** you *will* come [*RP2002*] a ruler who will be the
     2:15 Lord had said through the prophet: "**Out of** Egypt I called my son."
     3: 9 I tell you that **out of** these stones God can raise up children for
     3:17 And a voice **from** heaven said, "This is my Son, whom I love;
     5:37 your 'No,' 'No'; anything beyond this comes **from** the evil one.
     6:27 Who of you by worrying can add a single hour to his life?
     7: 4 your brother, 'Let *me* **take** the speck out [*RP1675*] of your eye,'
     7: 5 first **take** the plank **out** [*RP1675*] of your own eye, and then you
     7: 5 then you will see clearly *to* **remove** the speck **from** [*RP1675*] your
     7: 9 "Which **of** you, if his son asks for bread, will give him a stone?
     8:28 two demon-possessed men **coming from** [*RP2002*] the tombs met
   10:29 Yet not one **of** them will fall to the ground apart from the will of
   12:11 "If any **of** you has a sheep and it falls into a pit on the Sabbath,
   12:33 and its fruit will be bad, for a tree is recognized **by** its fruit.
   12:34 For **out of** the overflow of the heart the mouth speaks.
   12:35 The good man **brings** good things **out of** [*RP1675*] the good
   12:35 and the evil man **brings** evil things **out of** [*RP1675*] the evil stored
   12:37 For **by** your words you will be acquitted, and by your words you
   12:37 you will be acquitted, and **by** your words you will be condemned."
   12:42 for she came **from** the ends of the earth to listen to Solomon's
   13:41 and they will weed **out of** his kingdom everything that causes sin
   13:47 that was let down into the lake and caught [**NIE**] all kinds of fish.
   13:49 will come and separate the wicked **from** [*+3545*] the righteous
   13:52 **brings out of** [*RP1675*] his storeroom new treasures as well as
   15: 5 'Whatever help you might otherwise have received **from** me is a
   15:11 but what **comes out of** [*RP1744*] his mouth, that is what makes
   15:18 But the things that **come out of** [*RP1744*] the mouth come from
   15:18 But the things that come out of the mouth **come from** [*RP2002*]
   15:19 For **out of** the heart come [*RP2002*] evil thoughts, murder,
   16: 1 and tested him by asking him to show them a sign **from** heaven.
   17: 5 and a voice **from** the cloud said, "This is my Son, whom I love;
   17: 9 As they were coming down [**NIE**] the mountain, Jesus instructed
   17: 9 have seen, until the Son of Man has been raised **from** the dead."
   18:12 If a man owns a hundred sheep, and one **of** them wanders away,
   18:19 I tell you that if two **of** you on earth agree about anything you ask
   19:12 For some are eunuchs [**NIE**] because they were born that way;
   20: 2 He agreed **to pay** them a denarius for the day and sent them into
   20:21 "Grant that one of these two sons of mine may sit **at** your right
   20:21 may sit at your right and the other **at** your left in your kingdom."
   20:23 from my cup, but to sit **at** my right or left is not for me to grant.
   20:23 but to sit at my right or [**RPG**] left is not for me to grant.
   21:16 " '**From** the lips of children and infants you have ordained
   21:19 Then he said to it, "May [**NIE**] you never bear fruit again!"
   21:25 where did it come from? Was it **from** heaven, or from men?"
   21:25 where did it come from? Was it from heaven, or **from** men?"
   21:25 among themselves and said, "If we say, '**From** heaven,'
   21:26 But if we say, '**From** men'—we are afraid of the people, for they
   21:31 "Which **of** the two did what his father wanted?" "The first,"
   22:35 One of them, an expert in the law, tested him with this question:
   22:44 "Sit **at** my right hand until I put your enemies under your feet." '
   23:25 and dish, but inside they are full **of** greed and self-indulgence.
   23:34 **Some of** them you will kill and crucify; others you will flog in
   23:34 [**RPG**] others you will flog in your synagogues and pursue from
   24:17 on the roof of his house go down to take anything **out of** the house.
   24:31 and they will gather his elect **from** the four winds, from one end of
   25: 2 Five **of** them were foolish and five were wise.
   25: 8 The foolish ones said to the wise, 'Give us **some of** your oil;
   25:33 He will put the sheep **on** his right and the goats on his left.
   25:33 He will put the sheep on his right and the goats **on** his left.
   25:34 "Then the King will say to those **on** his right, 'Come, you who are
   25:41 "Then he will say to those **on** his left, 'Depart from me, you who
   26:21 eating, he said, "I tell you the truth, one **of** you will betray me."
   26:27 and offered it to them, saying, "Drink **from** it, all of you.
   26:29 I will not drink **of** this fruit of the vine from now on until that day
   26:42 He went away a **second time** [*+1311*] and prayed, "My Father,
   26:44 and went away once more and prayed the **third time** [*+5569*],

   26:64 In the future you will see the Son of Man sitting **at** the right hand
   26:73 there went up to Peter and said, "Surely you are **one** of them,
   27: 7 So they decided to use the [**NIE**] money to buy the potter's field
   27:29 and then twisted together a crown **of** thorns and set it on his head.
   27:38 were crucified with him, one **on** his right and one on his left.
   27:38 were crucified with him, one on his right and one **on** his left.
   27:48 Immediately one **of** them ran and got a sponge. He filled it with
   27:53 *They* **came out of** [*RP2002*] the tombs, and after Jesus'
   28: 2 for an angel of the Lord came down **from** heaven and, going to the
Mk   1:10 As Jesus was coming up **out of** the water, he saw heaven being
     1:11 And a voice came **from** heaven: "You are my Son, whom I love;
     1:25 "Be quiet!" said Jesus sternly. "**Come out of** [*RP2002*] him!"
     1:26 the man violently and **came out of** [*RP2002*] him with a shriek.
     1:29 As soon as *they* **left** [*RP2002*] the synagogue, they went with
     5: 2 *When* Jesus **got out of** [*RP2002*] the boat, a man with an evil
     5: 2 a man with an evil spirit *came* **from** the tombs to meet him.
     5: 8 had said to him, "**Come out of** [*RP2002*] this man, you evil spirit!"
     5:30 At once Jesus realized that power *had* **gone out from** [*RP2002*]
     6:14 Some were saying, "John the Baptist has been raised **from** the dead,
     6:16 the man I beheaded, has been raised **from** [UBS-] the dead!"
     6:51 wind died down. They were **completely** [*+3336+4356*] amazed,
     6:54 As soon as they **got out of** [*RP2002*] the boat, people recognized
     7:11 'Whatever help you might otherwise have received **from** me is
     7:15 it is what **comes out of** [*RP1744*] a man that makes him
     7:20 "What **comes out of** [*RP1744*] a man is what makes him 'unclean.'
     7:21 For from within, **out of** [*RP1744*] men's hearts, come [*RP1744*] evil
     7:26 She begged Jesus to **drive** the demon **out** [*RP1675*] of her
     7:29 you may go; the demon *has* **left** [*RP2002*] your daughter."
     7:31 Then Jesus **left** [*RP2002*] the vicinity of Tyre and went through
     9: 7 and enveloped them, and a voice came **from** the cloud:
     9: 9 As they were coming down [**NIE**] the mountain, Jesus gave them
     9: 9 what they had seen until the Son of Man had risen **from** the dead.
     9:10 to themselves, discussing what "rising **from** the dead" meant.
     9:17 A man in the crowd answered, "Teacher, I brought you my son,
     9:21 "How long has he been like this?" "**From** childhood," he answered.
     9:25 **come out of** [*RP2002*] him and never enter him again."
   10:20 "Teacher," he declared, "all these I have kept **since** I was a boy."
   10:37 "Let one of us sit **at** your right and the other at your left in your
   10:37 one of us sit at your right and the other **at** your left in your glory."
   10:40 but to sit **at** my right or left is not for me to grant. These places
   10:40 but to sit at my right or [**RPG**] left is not for me to grant.
   11: 8 on the road, while others spread branches they had cut **in** the fields.
   11:14 he said to the tree, "May no one ever eat fruit **from** you again."
   11:20 as they went along, they saw the fig tree withered **from** the roots.
   11:30 John's baptism—was it **from** heaven, or from men? Tell me!"
   11:30 John's baptism—was it from heaven, or **from** men? Tell me!"
   11:31 among themselves and said, "If we say, '**From** heaven,'
   11:32 But if we say, '**From** men'...." (They feared the people, for
   12:25 When the [**NIE**] dead rise, they will neither marry nor be given in
   12:30 Love the Lord your God **with** all your heart and with all your soul
   12:30 and **with** all your soul and with all your mind and with all your
   12:30 and with all your soul and **with** all your mind and with all your
   12:30 all your soul and with all your mind and **with** all your strength.'
   12:33 To love him **with** all your heart, with all your understanding
   12:33 your heart, **with** all your understanding and with all your strength,
   12:33 your heart, with all your understanding and **with** all your strength,
   12:36 "Sit **at** my right hand until I put your enemies under your feet." '
   12:44 They all gave **out of** their wealth;
   12:44 but she, **out of** her poverty, put in everything—all she had to live
   13: 1 As he was *leaving* [*RP1744*] the temple, one of his disciples said
   13:15 roof of his house go down or enter the house to take anything **out**.
   13:25 the stars will fall **from** the sky, and the heavenly bodies will be
   13:27 he will send his angels and gather his elect **from** the four winds,
   14:18 he said, "I tell you the truth, one **of** you will betray me—
   14:23 gave thanks and offered it to them, and they all drank **from** it.
   14:25 I will not drink again **of** the fruit of the vine until that day when I
   14:62 "And you will see the Son of Man sitting **at** the right hand of the
   14:69 said again to those standing around, "This fellow is **one** of them."
   14:70 said to Peter, "Surely you are **one** of them, for you are a Galilean."
   14:72 Immediately the rooster crowed the **second time** [*+1311*].
   15:27 two robbers with him, one **on** his right and one on his left.
   15:27 two robbers with him, one on his right and one **on** his left.
   15:39 who stood there **in front of** [*+1885*] Jesus, heard his cry and saw
   15:46 wrapped it in the linen, and placed it in a tomb cut **out of** rock.
   16: 3 "Who will roll the stone away **from** the entrance of the tomb?"
   16:12 Afterward Jesus appeared in a different form to two **of** them while

Lk 16:19 he was taken up into heaven and he sat **at** the right hand of God.
    1: 5 named Zechariah, who **belonged to** the priestly division of Abijah;
    1: 5 his wife Elizabeth was also a **descendant** [*+2588+3836*] of Aaron.
    1:11 appeared to him, standing **at** the right side of the altar of incense.
    1:15 and he will be filled with the Holy Spirit even **from** birth.
    1:27 married to a man named Joseph, a **descendant** [*+3875*] of David.
    1:61 "There is no one **among** your relatives who has that name."
    1:71 salvation **from** our enemies and from the hand of all who hate us—
    1:71 salvation from our enemies and **from** the hand of all who hate us—
    1:74 to rescue us **from** the hand of our enemies, and to enable us to
    1:78 of our God, by which the rising sun will come to us **from** heaven
    2: 4 So Joseph also went up **from** the town of Nazareth in Galilee to
    2: 4 because he **belonged to** [*+1639*] the house and line of David.
    2:35 so that the thoughts **of** many hearts will be revealed. And a sword
    2:36 a prophetess, Anna, the daughter of Phanuel, **of** the tribe of Asher.
    3: 8 For I tell you that **out of** these stones God can raise up children for
    3:22 And a voice came **from** heaven: "You are my Son, whom I love;
    4:22 and were amazed at the gracious words that **came from** [*RP1744*]
    5: 3 from shore. Then he sat down and taught the people **from** the boat.
    5:17 who had come **from** every village of Galilee and from Judea
    6:42 first **take** the plank **out of** [*RP1675*] your eye, and then you will
    6:44 Each tree is recognized **by** its own fruit. People do not pick figs
    6:44 People do not pick figs **from** thornbushes, or grapes from briers.
    6:44 People do not pick figs from thornbushes, or grapes **from** briers.
    6:45 The good man brings good things **out of** the good stored up in his
    6:45 and the evil man brings evil things **out of** the evil stored up in his
    6:45 in his heart. For **out of** the overflow of his heart his mouth speaks.
    8: 3 These women were helping to support them **out of** their own
    8:27 he was met by a demon-possessed man **from** the town.
    9: 7 because some were saying that John had been raised **from** the
    9:35 A voice came **from** the cloud, saying, "This is my Son, whom I
  10: 7 deserves his wages. Do not move around **from** house to house.
  10:11 'Even the dust **of** your town that sticks to our feet we wipe off
  10:18 He replied, "I saw Satan fall like lightning **from** heaven.
  10:27 'Love the Lord your God **with** all your heart and with all your soul
  11: 5 Then he said to them, "Suppose one **of** you has a friend, and he goes
  11: 6 because a friend of mine **on a journey** [*+3847*] has come to me,
  11:11 "Which **of** you fathers, if your son asks for a fish, will give him a
  11:13 how much more will your Father **in** heaven give the Holy Spirit to
  11:15 But some **of** them said, "By Beelzebub, the prince of demons,
  11:16 Others tested him by asking for a sign **from** heaven.
  11:27 As Jesus was saying these things, a woman **in** the crowd called out,
  11:31 for she came **from** the ends of the earth to listen to Solomon's
  11:49 some **of** whom they will kill and others they will persecute.'
  11:54 waiting to catch him in something he might **say** [*+3836+5125*].
  12: 6 sold for two pennies? Yet not one **of** them is forgotten by God.
  12:13 Someone **in** the crowd said to him, "Teacher, tell my brother to
  12:15 a man's life does not consist in the abundance **of** his possessions."
  12:25 Who **of** you by worrying can add a single hour to his life?
  12:36 like men waiting for their master to return **from** a wedding
  14:28 "Suppose one **of** you wants to build a tower. Will he not first sit
  14:33 any **of** you who does not give up everything he has cannot be my
  15: 4 "Suppose one **of** you has a hundred sheep and loses one of them.
  15: 4 "Suppose one of you has a hundred sheep and loses one **of** them.
  15:16 He longed to fill his stomach **with** [UBS *from*; NIV *608*] the pods
  16: 4 I know what I'll do so that, when *I* **lose** [*+3496*] my job here,
  16: 9 I tell you, **use** worldly wealth to gain friends for yourselves,
  16:31 they will not be convinced even if someone rises **from** the dead.' "
  17: 7 "Suppose one **of** you had a servant plowing or looking after the
  17: 7 Would he say to the servant when he comes in **from** the field,
  17:15 One **of** them, when he saw he was healed, came back, praising God
  17:24 which flashes and lights up the sky **from** *one end* to the other.
  18:21 "All these I have kept **since** I was a boy," he said.
  19:22 "His master replied, 'I will judge you **by** your own words,
  20: 4 John's baptism—was it **from** heaven, or from men?"
  20: 4 John's baptism—was it from heaven, or **from** men?"
  20: 5 discussed it among themselves and said, "If we say, '**From** heaven,'
  20: 6 But if we say, '**From** men,' all the people will stone us,
  20:35 and in the resurrection **from** the dead will neither marry nor be
  20:42 Book of Psalms: " 'The Lord said to my Lord: "Sit **at** my right hand
  21: 4 All these people gave their gifts **out of** their wealth; but she out of
  21: 4 but she **out of** her poverty put in all she had to live on."
  21:16 relatives and friends, and they will put **some of** you to death.
  21:18 But not a hair **of** your head will perish.
  22: 3 Then Satan entered Judas, called Iscariot, one **of** the Twelve.
  22:23 They began to question among themselves which **of** them it might

  22:50 And one **of** them struck the servant of the high priest, cutting off
  22:58 later someone else saw him and said, "You also are **one of** them."
  22:69 the Son of Man will be seated **at** the right hand of the mighty God."
  23: 7 When he learned that Jesus was **under** Herod's jurisdiction,
  23: 8 because **for** a long time he had been wanting to see him.
  23:33 along with the criminals—one **on** his right, the other on his left.
  23:33 along with the criminals—one on his right, the other **on** his left.
  23:55 The women who had come with Jesus **from** Galilee followed
  24:13 Now that same day two **of** them were going to a village called
  24:18 One **of** [UBS-] them, named Cleopas, asked him, "Are you only a
  24:22 In addition, some **of** our women amazed us. They went to the
  24:46 The Christ will suffer and rise **from** the dead on the third day,
  24:49 but stay in the city until you have been clothed with power **from**

Jn   1:13 children born not **of** natural descent, nor of human decision
   1:13 nor **of** human decision or a husband's will, but born of God.
   1:13 nor of human decision or [RPG] a husband's will, but born of God.
   1:13 nor of human decision or a husband's will, but born **of** God.
   1:16 **From** the fullness of his grace we have all received one blessing
   1:19 Now this was John's testimony when the Jews **of** Jerusalem sent
   1:24 Now some Pharisees who had been sent
   1:32 "I saw the Spirit come down **from** heaven as a dove and remain on
   1:35 The next day John was there again with two **of** his disciples.
   1:40 was one **of** the two who heard what John had said and who had
   1:44 Philip, like Andrew and Peter, was **from** the town of Bethsaida.
   1:46 "Nazareth! Can anything good come **from** there?" Nathanael asked.
   2:15 So he made a whip **out of** cords, and drove all from the temple
   2:15 and **drove** all **from** [*RP1675*] the temple area, both sheep
   2:22 After he was raised **from** the dead, his disciples recalled what he
   3: 1 Now there was a man **of** the Pharisees named Nicodemus,
   3: 5 no one can enter the kingdom of God unless he is born **of** water
   3: 6 [NIE] Flesh gives birth to flesh,
   3: 6 gives birth to flesh, but [NIE] the Spirit gives birth to spirit.
   3: 8 or where it is going. So it is with everyone born **of** the Spirit."
   3:13 No one has ever gone into heaven except the one who came **from**
   3:25 An argument developed between **some of** John's disciples
   3:27 "A man can receive only what is given him **from** heaven.
   3:31 the one who is **from** the earth belongs to the earth, and speaks as
   3:31 the one who is from the earth **belongs to** [*+1639*] the earth,
   3:31 the earth belongs to the earth, and speaks as one **from** the earth.
   3:31 one from the earth. The one who comes **from** heaven is above all.
   3:34 the words of God, for God gives the Spirit **without** [*+4024*] limit.
   4: 6 and Jesus, tired as he was **from** the journey, sat down by the well.
   4: 7 When a [NIE] Samaritan woman came to draw water, Jesus said
   4:12 who gave us the well and drank **from** it himself, as did also his
   4:13 "Everyone who drinks [NIE] this water will be thirsty again,
   4:14 but whoever drinks [NIE] the water I give him will never thirst.
   4:22 we worship what we do know, for salvation is **from** the Jews.
   4:30 *They* **came out of** [*RP2002*] the town and made their way toward
   4:39 Many of the Samaritans **from** that town believed in him because of
   4:47 When this man heard that Jesus had arrived in Galilee **from** Judea,
   4:54 sign that Jesus performed, having come **from** Judea to Galilee.
   5:24 and will not be condemned; he has crossed over **from** death to life.
   6: 8 Another **of** his disciples, Andrew, Simon Peter's brother, spoke up,
   6:11 were seated as much as they wanted. He did the same **with** the fish.
   6:13 and filled twelve baskets with the pieces **of** the five barley loaves
   6:23 Then some boats **from** Tiberias landed near the place where the
   6:26 but because you ate [NIE] the loaves and had your fill.
   6:31 as it is written: 'He gave them bread **from** heaven to eat.' "
   6:32 it is not Moses who has given you the bread **from** heaven,
   6:32 but it is my Father who gives you the true bread **from** heaven.
   6:33 For the bread of God is he who comes down **from** heaven
   6:39 that I shall lose none of all that he has given me, but raise them up
   6:41 because he said, "I am the bread that came down **from** heaven."
   6:42 we know? How can he now say, 'I came down **from** heaven'?"
   6:50 But here is the bread that comes down **from** heaven, which a man
   6:50 down from heaven, which a man may eat [NIE] and not die.
   6:51 I am the living bread that came down **from** heaven. If anyone eats
   6:51 If anyone eats **of** this bread, he will live forever. This bread is my
   6:58 This is the bread that came down **from** heaven. Your forefathers
   6:60 On hearing it, many of his disciples said, "This is a hard teaching.
   6:64 Yet there are some **of** you who do not believe." For Jesus had
   6:64 For Jesus had known **from** the beginning which of them did not
   6:65 "This is why I told you that no one can come to me unless [NIE]
   6:66 **From** this time many of his disciples turned back and no longer
   6:66 From this time many **of** his disciples turned back and no longer
   6:70 "Have I not chosen you, the Twelve? Yet one **of** you is a devil!"

6: 71 who, though one **of** the Twelve, was later to betray him.)
7: 17 he will find out whether my teaching comes **from** God or whether
7: 19 Yet not one **of** you keeps the law. Why are you trying to kill me?"
7: 22 you circumcision (though actually it did not come **from** Moses,
7: 22 but **from** the patriarchs), you circumcise a child on the Sabbath.
7: 25 At that point some **of** the people of Jerusalem began to ask,
7: 31 Still, many **in** the crowd put their faith in him. They said,
7: 38 has said, streams of living water will flow **from** within him."
7: 40 On hearing his words, **some of** the people said, "Surely this man is
7: 41 Still others asked, "How can the Christ come **from** Galilee?
7: 42 Does not the Scripture say that the Christ will come **from** David's
7: 44 Some [NIE] wanted to seize him, but no one laid a hand on him.
7: 48 "Has any **of** the rulers or of the Pharisees believed in him?
7: 48 "Has any of the rulers or **of** the Pharisees believed in him?
7: 50 had gone to Jesus earlier and who was one **of** their own number,
7: 52 They replied, "Are you **from** Galilee, too? Look into it, and you
7: 52 and you will find that a prophet does not come **out of** Galilee."
8: 23 But he continued, "You are **from** below; I am from above.
8: 23 But he continued, "You are from below; I am **from** above.
8: 23 I am from above. You are **of** this world; I am not of this world.
8: 23 I am from above. You are of this world; I am not **of** this world.
8: 41 "We *are* not **illegitimate children** [+1164+4518]," they protested.
8: 42 would love me, for I **came from** [RP2002] God and now am here.
8: 44 You **belong to** [+1639] your father, the devil, and you want to
8: 44 When he lies, he speaks **his native language** [+2625+3836], for
8: 46 Can any **of** you prove me guilty of sin? If I am telling the truth,
8: 47 He *who* **belongs to** [+1639] God hears what God says. The reason
8: 47 The reason you do not hear is that *you do* not **belong to** [+1639]
8: 59 hid himself, **slipping away from** [RP2002] the temple grounds.
9: 1 As he went along, he saw a man blind **from** birth.
9: 6 said this, he spit on the ground, made some mud **with** the saliva,
9: 16 Some **of** the Pharisees said, "This man is not from God, for he does
9: 24 A **second time** [+1311] they summoned the man who had been
9: 32 Nobody has **ever** [+172+3836] heard of opening the eyes of a man
9: 40 Some [NIE] Pharisees who were with him heard him say this
10: 16 I have other sheep that are not **of** this sheep pen. I must bring them
10: 20 Many of them said, "He is demon-possessed and raving mad.
10: 26 but you do not believe because you are not [NIE] my sheep.
10: 28 they shall never perish; no one can snatch them **out of** my hand.
10: 29 greater than all; no one can snatch them **out of** my Father's hand.
10: 32 to them, "I have shown you many great miracles **from** the Father.
10: 39 they tried to seize him, but *he* **escaped** [RP2002] their grasp.
11: 1 from Bethany, [NIE] the village of Mary and her sister Martha.
11: 19 and many [NIE] Jews had come to Martha and Mary to comfort
11: 37 But some **of** them said, "Could not he who opened the eyes of the
11: 45 Therefore many **of** the Jews who had come to visit Mary, and had
11: 46 But some **of** them went to the Pharisees and told them what Jesus
11: 49 Then one of them, named Caiaphas, who was high priest that year,
11: 55 many went up **from** the country to Jerusalem for their ceremonial
12: 1 where Lazarus lived, whom Jesus had raised **from** the dead.
12: 2 while Lazarus was **among** [+1651] those reclining at the table with
12: 3 And the house was filled **with** the fragrance of the perfume.
12: 4 But one **of** his disciples, Judas Iscariot, who was later to betray
12: 9 Meanwhile a large crowd **of** Jews found out that Jesus was there
12: 9 but also to see Lazarus, whom he had raised **from** the dead.
12: 17 Now the crowd that was with him when he called Lazarus **from**
12: 17 and raised him **from** the dead continued to spread the word.
12: 20 Now there were some Greeks **among** those who went up to
12: 27 'Father, save me **from** this hour'? No, it was for this very reason I
12: 28 Then a voice came **from** heaven, "I have glorified it, and will
12: 32 But I, when I am lifted up **from** the earth, will draw all men to
12: 34 "We have heard **from** the Law that the Christ will remain forever,
12: 42 Yet at the same time many even **among** the leaders believed in
12: 49 For I did not speak **of** my own accord, but the Father who sent me
13: 1 Jesus knew that the time had come for him to leave [NIE] this
13: 4 so he got up **from** the meal, took off his outer clothing,
13: 21 and testified, "I tell you the truth, one **of** you is going to betray me."
13: 23 One of them, the disciple whom Jesus loved, was reclining next to
15: 19 If *you* **belonged to** [+1639] the world, it would love you as its
15: 19 As it is, *you do* not **belong to** [+1639] the world, but I have chosen
15: 19 do not belong to the world, but I have chosen you **out of** the world.
16: 4 I warned you. I did not tell you this **at** first because I was with you.
16: 5 who sent me, yet none **of** you asks me, 'Where are you going?'
16: 14 He will bring glory to me by taking **from** what is mine and making
16: 15 That is why I said the Spirit will take **from** what is mine and make
16: 17 **Some of** his disciples said to one another, "What does he mean by

17: 6 "I have revealed you to those whom you gave me **out of** the world.
17: 12 None [NIE] has been lost except the one doomed to destruction
17: 14 for they are not **of** the world any more than I am of the world.
17: 14 for they are not of the world any more than I am **of** the world.
17: 15 My prayer is not that you take them **out of** the world but that you
17: 15 them out of the world but that you protect them **from** the evil one.
17: 16 They are not **of** the world, even as I am not of it.
17: 16 They are not of the world, even as I am not **of** it.
18: 3 of soldiers and some officials **from** the chief priests and Pharisees.
18: 3 and some officials from the chief priests and [RPG] Pharisees.
18: 9 would be fulfilled: "I have not lost one **of** those you gave me."
18: 17 "You are not **one of** his disciples, are you?" the girl at the door
18: 25 he was asked, "You are not **one of** his disciples, are you?"
18: 26 One of the high priest's servants, a relative of the man whose ear
18: 36 Jesus said, "My kingdom is not **of** this world. If it were,
18: 36 [RPG] my servants would fight to prevent my arrest by the Jews.
18: 37 to testify to the truth. Everyone on the side **of** truth listens to me."
19: 2 The soldiers twisted together a crown **of** thorns and put it on his
19: 12 **From** [+4047] **then on**, Pilate tried to set Jesus free, but the Jews
19: 23 garment was seamless, woven in one piece **from** top to bottom.
20: 1 and saw that the stone had been removed **from** the entrance.
20: 2 Jesus loved, and said, "They have taken the Lord **out of** the tomb,
20: 9 understand from Scripture that Jesus had to rise **from** the dead.)
20: 24 Now Thomas (called Didymus), one **of** the Twelve, was not with
21: 2 the sons of Zebedee, and two other [NIE] disciples were together.
21: 14 Jesus appeared to his disciples after he was raised **from** the dead.

Ac 1: 18 (With the reward he got for his wickedness, Judas bought a field;
1: 24 everyone's heart. Show us which **of** these two you have chosen
2: 2 Suddenly a sound like the blowing of a violent wind came **from**
2: 25 before me. Because he is **at** my right hand, I will not be shaken.
2: 30 on oath that he would place **one of** his descendants on his throne.
2: 34 and yet he said, " 'The Lord said to my Lord: "Sit **at** my right hand
3: 2 Now a man crippled **from** birth was being carried to the temple
3: 15 You killed the author of life, but God raised him **from** the dead.
3: 22 raise up for you a prophet like me **from among** your own people;
3: 23 *will be* **completely cut off from among** [RP2017] his people.'
4: 2 the people and proclaiming in Jesus the resurrection of the dead.
4: 6 John, Alexander and the other men **of** the high priest's family.
4: 10 whom you crucified but whom God raised **from** the dead,
5: 38 For if their purpose or activity is **of** human *origin*, it will fail.
5: 39 But if it is **from** God, you will not be able to stop these men;
6: 3 choose seven men **from among** you who are known to be full of
6: 9 from members **of** the Synagogue of the Freedmen (as it was
7: 3 '**Leave** [RP2002+1666] your country and your people,' God said,
7: 3 '**Leave** [RP2002+1666] your country and your people,' God said,
7: 4 "So *he* **left** [RP2002] the land of the Chaldeans and settled in
7: 10 and rescued him **from** all his troubles. He gave Joseph wisdom
7: 37 'God will send you a prophet like me **from** your own people.'
7: 40 As for this fellow Moses who **led** us **out of** [RP1974] Egypt—
7: 55 saw the glory of God, and Jesus standing **at** the right hand of God.
7: 56 open and the Son of Man standing **at** the right hand of God."
8: 39 When they came up **out of** the water, the Spirit of the Lord
9: 3 on his journey, suddenly a light **from** heaven flashed around him.
9: 33 named Aeneas, a paralytic who had been bedridden **for** eight years.
10: 1 a centurion in what was known as the Italian [NIE] Regiment.
10: 15 The voice spoke to him a **second time** [+1311], "Do not call
10: 41 by us who ate and drank with him after he rose **from** the dead.
10: 45 The **circumcised** [+4364] believers who had come with Peter were
11: 2 up to Jerusalem, the **circumcised believers** [+4364] criticized him
11: 5 I saw something like a large sheet being let down **from** heaven by
11: 9 "The voice spoke **from** heaven a second time, 'Do not call anything
11: 9 "The voice spoke from heaven a **second time** [+1311], 'Do not call
11: 20 Some **of** them, however, men from Cyprus and Cyrene, went to
11: 28 One of them, named Agabus, stood up and through the Spirit
12: 7 get up!" he said, and the chains **fell off** [RP1738] Peter's wrists.
12: 11 that the Lord sent his angel and rescued me **from** Herod's clutches
12: 17 and described how the Lord *had* **brought** him **out of** [RP1974]
13: 17 with mighty power *he* **led** them **out of** [RP1974] that country,
13: 21 Saul son of Kish, **of** the tribe of Benjamin, who ruled forty years.
13: 30 But God raised him **from** the dead,
13: 34 The fact that God raised him **from** the dead, never to decay,
13: 42 *As* Paul and Barnabas *were* **leaving** [RP1996] the synagogue,
14: 8 in his feet, who was lame **from** birth and had never walked.
15: 2 were appointed, along with some other **believers**ˢ [+899],
15: 14 his concern by taking **from** the Gentiles a people for himself.
15: 21 For Moses has been preached in every city **from** the earliest times

15:22 decided to choose **some of** their own men and send them to
15:23 To the **Gentile** [*+1620*] believers in Antioch, Syria and Cilicia:
15:24 We have heard that some **went out from** [*RP2002*] us without our
15:29 You will do well to avoid **[NIE]** these things. Farewell.
17: 3 and proving that the Christ had to suffer and rise **from** the dead.
17: 4 Some **of** the Jews were persuaded and joined Paul and Silas,
17:12 Many **of** the Jews believed, as did also a number of prominent
17:26 **From** one man he made every nation of men, that they should
17:31 He has given proof of this to all men by raising him **from** the dead."
17:33 At that, Paul **left** [*RP2002*] the Council.
18: 1 After this, Paul left **[NIE]** Athens and went to Corinth.
19:16 He gave them such a beating that *they* **ran out of** [*RP1767*] the
19:25 "Men, you know we receive a good income **from** this business.
19:33 to the front, and **some of** the crowd shouted instructions to him.
19:34 was a Jew, they **[NIE]** all shouted in unison for about two hours:
20:30 Even **from** your own number men will arise and distort the truth in
21: 8 and stayed at the house of Philip the evangelist, **one of** [*+1639*] the
22: 6 suddenly a bright light **from** heaven flashed around me.
22:14 and to see the Righteous One and to hear words **from** his mouth.
22:18 '**Leave** [*RP2002*] Jerusalem immediately, because they will not
23:10 and take him **away** [*+3545*] **from** them by force and bring him into
23:21 because more than forty **of** them are waiting in ambush for him.
23:34 The governor read the letter and asked what province he was **from**.
24:10 "I know that **for** a number of years you have been a judge over this
26: 4 "The Jews all know the way I have lived *ever* **since** I was a child,
26:17 I will rescue you **from** your own people and from the Gentiles.
26:17 I will rescue you from your own people and **from** the Gentiles.
26:23 Christ would suffer and, as the first to **[NIE]** rise from the dead,
27:22 you to keep up your courage, because not one **of** you will be lost;
27:29 they dropped four anchors **from** the stern and prayed for daylight.
27:30 In an attempt to escape **from** the ship, the sailors let the lifeboat
27:30 pretending they were going to lower some anchors **from** the bow.
28: 4 When the islanders saw the snake hanging **from** his hand,
28: 4 for though he escaped **from** the sea, Justice has not allowed him to
28:17 I was arrested **in** Jerusalem and handed over to the Romans.

Ro   1: 3 his Son, who as to his human nature was a descendant **of** David,
1: 4 with power to be the Son of God **by** his resurrection from the dead:
1:17 a righteousness that is **by** faith from first to last, just as it is written:
1:17 first to last, just as it is written: "The righteous will live **by** faith."
2: 8 But for those who are **[NIE]** self-seeking and who reject the truth
2:18 approve of what is superior because you are instructed **by** the law;
2:27 The one who is not circumcised **physically** [*+5882*] and yet obeys
2:29 written code. Such a man's praise is not **from** men, but from God.
2:29 written code. Such a man's praise is not from men, but **from** God.
3:20 Therefore no one will be declared righteous in his sight **by**
3:26 and the one who justifies those *who* **have faith** [*+4411*] in Jesus.
3:30 who will justify the circumcised **by** faith and the uncircumcised
4: 2 If, in fact, Abraham was justified **by** works, he had something to
4:12 father of the circumcised who not only are **circumcised** [*+4364*]
4:14 For if those who *live* **by** law are heirs, faith has no value
4:16 Therefore, the promise comes **by** faith, so that it may be by grace
4:16 not only to those who are **of** the law but also to those who are of
4:16 are of the law but also to those who are **of** the faith of Abraham.
4:24 for us who believe in him who raised Jesus our Lord **from** the
5: 1 Therefore, since we have been justified **through** faith, we have
5:16 The judgment **followed** one sin and brought condemnation,
5:16 but the gift **followed** many trespasses and brought justification.
6: 4 just as Christ was raised **from** the dead through the glory of the
6: 9 For we know that since Christ was raised **from** the dead, he cannot
6:13 to God, as those who have been brought **from** death to life;
6:17 you **wholeheartedly** [*+2840*] obeyed the form of teaching to which
7: 4 might belong to another, to him who was raised **from** the dead,
7:24 wretched man I am! Who will rescue me **from** this body of death?
8:11 And if the Spirit of him who raised Jesus **from** the dead is living in
8:11 he who raised Christ **from** the dead will also give life to your
9: 5 and **from** them is traced the human ancestry of Christ, who is God
9: 6 had failed. For not all who are **descended** from Israel are Israel.
9:10 but Rebekah's children had one and the same **father**ˢ [*+3130*],
9:12 not **by** works but by him who calls—she was told, "The older will
9:12 not by works but **by** him who calls—she was told, "The older will
9:21 Does not the potter have the right to make **out of** the same lump of
9:24 he also called, not only **from** the Jews but also from the Gentiles?
9:24 he also called, not only from the Jews but also **from** the Gentiles?
9:30 have obtained it, a righteousness that is **by** faith;
9:32 Because they pursued it not **by** faith but as if it were by works.
9:32 Because they pursued it not by faith but as if it were **by** works.

10: 5 Moses describes in this way the righteousness that is **by** the law:
10: 6 But the righteousness that is **by** faith says: "Do not say in your
10: 7 descend into the deep?' " (that is, to bring Christ up **from** the dead).
10: 9 and believe in your heart that God raised him **from** the dead,
10:17 Consequently, faith *comes* **from** hearing the message,
11: 1 I am an Israelite myself, a descendant **of** Abraham, from the tribe
11: 6 And if by grace, then it is no longer **by** works; if it were, grace
11:14 somehow arouse my own people to envy and save some **of** them.
11:15 of the world, what will their acceptance be but life **from** the dead?
11:24 if you *were* **cut out of** [*RP1716*] an olive tree that is wild by
11:26 "The deliverer will come **from** Zion; he will turn godlessness away
11:36 For **from** him and through him and to him are all things. To him be
12:18 If it is possible, *as far as* it **depends** on you, live at peace with
13: 3 Then do what is right and **[NIE]** he will commend you.
13:11 The hour has come for you to wake up **from** your slumber,
14:23 is condemned if he eats, because his eating is not **from** faith;
14:23 not from faith; and everything that does not *come* **from** faith is sin.
16:10 in Christ. Greet those who **belong to** the household of Aristobulus.
16:11 Greet those **in** the household of Narcissus who are in the Lord.

1Co   1:30 It is **because of** him that you are in Christ Jesus, who has become
2:12 not received the spirit of the world but the Spirit who is **from** God,
5: 2 and have put **out of** your fellowship the man who did this?
5:10 In that case you would have to **leave** [*RP2002*] this world.
5:13 will judge those outside. "Expel the wicked man **from among** you."
7: 5 Do not deprive each other except **by** mutual consent and for a time,
7: 7 But each man has his own gift **from** God; one has this gift,
8: 6 the Father, **from** whom all things *came* and for whom we live;
9: 7 of its grapes? Who tends a flock and does not drink **of** the milk?
9:13 that those who work in the temple get their food **from** the temple,
9:14 who preach the gospel should receive their living **from** the gospel.
9:19 Though I am **free and belong to no man** [*+1801+4246*], I make
10: 4 for they drank **from** the spiritual rock that accompanied them,
10:17 who are many, are one body, for we all partake **of** the one loaf.
11: 8 For man did not come **from** woman, but woman from man;
11: 8 For man did not come from woman, but woman **from** man;
11:12 For as woman *came* **from** man, so also man is born of woman.
11:12 so also man is born of woman. But everything *comes* **from** God.
11:28 A man ought to examine himself before he eats **of** the bread
11:28 examine himself before he eats **of** the bread and drinks **of** the cup.
12:15 should say, "Because I am not a hand, I do not **belong to** the body,"
12:15 the body," it would not for that reason cease to be **part of** the body.
12:16 should say, "Because I am not an eye, I do not **belong to** the body,"
12:16 the body," it would not for that reason cease to be **part of** the body.
12:27 Now you are the body of Christ, and each one of you is a part **of** it.
13: 9 For we know **in** part and we prophesy in part,
13: 9 For we know in part and we prophesy **in** part,
13:10 but when perfection comes, the **imperfect** [*+3538*] disappears.
13:12 Now I know **in** part; then I shall know fully, even as I am fully
15: 6 most **of** whom are still living, though some have fallen asleep.
15:12 But if it is preached that Christ has been raised **from** the dead,
15:20 But Christ has indeed been raised **from** the dead, the firstfruits of
15:47 The first man was of the dust **of** the earth, the second man from
15:47 man was of the dust of the earth, the second man **from** heaven.

2Co   1:10 He has delivered us **from** such a deadly peril, and he will deliver
1:11 Then **[NIE]** many will give thanks on our behalf for the gracious
2: 2 who is left to make me glad but you whom **[NIE]** I have grieved?
2: 4 For I wrote you **out of** great distress and anguish of heart and with
2:16 To the one we are the smell **of** death; to the other, the fragrance of
2:16 the one we are the smell of death; to the other, the fragrance **of** life.
2:17 On the contrary, in Christ we speak before God **with** sincerity,
2:17 we speak before God with sincerity, like men *sent* **from** God.
3: 1 like some people, letters of recommendation to you or **from** you?
3: 5 Not that we are competent in ourselves to claim anything **for**
3: 5 anything for ourselves, but our competence *comes* **from** God.
4: 6 For God, who said, "Let light shine **out of** darkness," made his light
4: 7 show that this all-surpassing power is from God and not **from** us.
5: 1 we have a building **from** God, an eternal house in heaven,
5: 2 longing to be clothed with our **heavenly** [*+4041*] dwelling,
5: 8 and would prefer *to be* **away from** [*RP1685*] the body and at
5:18 All this is **from** God, who reconciled us to himself through Christ
6:17 "Therefore **come out** [*RP2002*] from them and be separate,
7: 9 as God intended and so were not harmed in any way **by** us.
8: 7 in knowledge, in complete earnestness and **in** your love for us—
8:11 by your completion of it, **according** [*+3836*] **to** your means.
8:13 you are hard pressed, but that there might be **[NIE]** equality.
9: 7 not **reluctantly** [*+3383*] or under compulsion, for God loves a

9: 7 not reluctantly or **under** compulsion, for God loves a cheerful
11:26 in danger from bandits, in danger **from** my own countrymen,
11:26 in danger from my own countrymen, in danger **from** Gentiles;
12: 6 think more of me than is warranted by what I do or say [+201].
13: 4 For to be sure, he was crucified **in** weakness, yet he lives by God's
13: 4 he was crucified in weakness, yet he lives **by** God's power.
13: 4 in him, yet **by** God's power we will live with him to serve you.

Gal 1: 1 Jesus Christ and God the Father, who raised him **from** the dead—
1: 4 who gave himself for our sins to rescue us **from** the present evil
1: 8 or an angel **from** heaven should preach a gospel other than the one
1:15 who set me apart **from** birth and called me by his grace,
2:12 because he was afraid of those who **belonged to** the circumcision
2:15 "We who are Jews by birth and not [NIE] 'Gentile sinners'
2:16 know that a man is not justified **by** observing the law,
2:16 have put our faith in Christ Jesus that we may be justified **by** faith
2:16 may be justified by faith in Christ and not **by** observing the law,
2:16 the law, because **by** observing the law no one will be justified.
3: 2 Did you receive the Spirit **by** observing the law, or by believing
3: 2 the Spirit by observing the law, or **by** believing what you heard?
3: 5 and work miracles among you **because** you observe the law,
3: 5 you observe the law, or **because** you believe what you heard?
3: 7 then, that those who **believe** [+4411] are children of Abraham.
3: 8 The Scripture foresaw that God would justify the Gentiles **by** faith,
3: 9 So those who **have faith** [+4411] are blessed along with Abraham,
3:10 All who **rely on** [+1639] observing the law are under a curse,
3:11 before God by the law, because, "The righteous will live **by** faith."
3:12 The law is not **based on** faith; on the contrary, "The man who does
3:13 Christ **redeemed** us from [RP1973] the curse of the law by
3:18 For if the inheritance **depends on** the law, then it no longer
3:18 depends on the law, then it no longer **depends on** a promise;
3:21 then righteousness would certainly have come **by** the law.
3:22 that what was promised, being given **through** faith in Jesus Christ,
3:24 in charge to lead us to Christ that we might be justified **by** faith.
4: 4 fully come, God sent his Son, born of a woman, born under law,
4:22 one **by** the slave woman and the other by the free woman.
4:22 one by the slave woman and the other **by** the free woman.
4:23 His son **by** the slave woman was born in the ordinary way;
4:23 but his son **by** the free woman was born as the result of a promise.
5: 5 But **by** faith we eagerly await through the Spirit the righteousness
5: 8 That kind of persuasion does not *come* **from** the one who calls
6: 8 to please his sinful nature, **from** that nature will reap destruction;
6: 8 who sows to please the Spirit, **from** the Spirit will reap eternal life.

Eph 1:20 which he exerted in Christ when he raised him **from** the dead
2: 8 through faith—and this not **from** yourselves, it is the gift of God—
2: 9 not **by** works, so that no one can boast.
3:15 **from** whom his whole family in heaven and on earth derives its
4:16 **From** him the whole body, joined and held together by every
4:29 *Do* not *let* any unwholesome talk **come out of** [RP1744] your
5:14 "Wake up, O sleeper, rise **from** the dead, and Christ will shine on
6: 6 but like slaves of Christ, doing the will of God **from** your heart.

Php 1:16 The latter do so **in** love, knowing that I am put here for the defense
1:17 The former preach Christ **out of** selfish ambition, not sincerely,
1:23 I am torn **between** the two: I desire to depart and be with Christ,
3: 5 people of Israel, **of** the tribe of Benjamin, a Hebrew of Hebrews;
3: 5 people of Israel, of the tribe of Benjamin, a Hebrew **of** Hebrews;
3: 9 not having a righteousness of my own that *comes* **from** the law,
3: 9 in Christ—the righteousness that *comes* **from** God and is by faith.
3:11 and so, somehow, to attain to the resurrection **from** the dead.
3:20 And we eagerly await a Savior **from** there, the Lord Jesus Christ,
4:22 you greetings, especially those who **belong to** Caesar's household.

Col 1:13 For he has rescued us **from** the dominion of darkness and brought
1:18 he is the beginning and the firstborn **from among** the dead,
2:12 your faith in the power of God, who raised him **from** the dead.
2:14 to us; he took it **away** [+3545+3836], nailing it to the cross.
2:19 **from** whom the whole body, supported and held together by its
3: 8 anger, rage, malice, slander, and filthy language **from** your lips.
3:23 Whatever you do, work at it **with** all your heart, as working for the
4: 9 with Onesimus, our faithful and dear brother, who is **one of** you.
4:11 These are the only Jews [+4364] among my fellow workers for the
4:12 Epaphras, who is **one of** you and a servant of Christ Jesus,
4:16 the Laodiceans and that you in turn read the letter **from** Laodicea.

1Th 1:10 and to wait for his Son **from** heaven, whom he raised from the
1:10 to wait for his Son from heaven, whom he raised **from** the dead—
1:10 from the dead—Jesus, who rescues us **from** the coming wrath.
2: 3 For the appeal we make does not *spring* **from** error or impure
2: 3 we make does not spring from error or [RPG] impure motives,

2: 6 We were not looking for praise **from** men, not from you or anyone
2Th 2: 7 holds it back will continue to do so till he is taken **out of** the way.
1Ti 1: 5 which *comes* **from** a pure heart and a good conscience and a
6: 4 and quarrels about words that **result in** [+1181] envy,
2Ti 2: 8 Jesus Christ, raised **from** the dead, descended from David.
2: 8 raised from the dead, **descended from** [+5065] David.
2:22 along with those who call on the Lord **out of** a pure heart.
2:26 will come to their senses and *escape* **from** the trap of the devil,
3: 6 They are **the kind**ˢ who worm their way into homes and gain
3:11 persecutions I endured. Yet the Lord rescued me **from** all of them.
4:17 Gentiles might hear it. And I was delivered **from** the lion's mouth.
Tit 1:10 and deceivers, especially those **of** the circumcision group.
1:12 Even one **of** their own prophets has said, "Cretans are always liars,
2: 8 so that those who **oppose** [+1885] you may be ashamed
3: 5 not **because of** righteous things we had done, but because of his
Heb 1:13 "Sit **at** my right hand until I make your enemies a footstool for your
2:11 men holy and those who are made holy are **of** the same family.
3:13 so that none **of** you may be hardened by sin's deceitfulness.
3:16 Were they not all those Moses **led out of** [RP2002] Egypt?
4: 1 let us be careful that none **of** you be found to have fallen short of it.
5: 1 Every high priest is selected **from among** men and is appointed to
5: 7 loud cries and tears to the one who could save him **from** death,
7: 4 Even the patriarch Abraham gave him a tenth **of** the plunder!
7: 5 Now the law requires the descendants **of** Levi who become priests
7: 5 their brothers *are* **descended from** [+2002+3836+4019] Abraham.
7: 6 This man, however, did not trace his descent **from** Levi, yet he
7:12 of the priesthood, there [NIE] must also be a change of the law.
7:14 For it is clear that our Lord descended **from** Judah, and in regard to
8: 9 I took them by the hand *to* **lead** them **out of** [RP1974] Egypt,
9:28 and he will appear a **second time** [+1311], not to bear sin,
10:38 But my righteous one will live **by** faith. And if he shrinks back,
11: 3 so that what is seen was not *made* **out of** what was visible.
11:19 Abraham reasoned that God could raise the [NIE] dead,
11:35 Women received **back** their dead, raised to life again. Others were
13:10 We have an altar **from** which those who minister at the tabernacle
13:20 who through the blood of the eternal covenant brought back **from**
Jas 2:16 If one **of** you says to him, "Go, I wish you well; keep warm
2:18 faith without deeds, and I will show you my faith **by** what I do.
2:21 Was not our ancestor Abraham considered righteous **for** what he
2:22 working together, and his faith was made complete **by** what he did.
2:24 You see that a person is justified **by** what he does and not by faith
2:24 that a person is justified by what he does and not **by** faith alone.
2:25 was not even Rahab the prostitute considered righteous **for** what
3:10 **Out of** the same mouth *come* [RP2002] praise and cursing.
3:11 Can both fresh water and salt water flow **from** the same spring?
3:13 Let him show it **by** his good life, by deeds done in the humility that
4: 1 Don't they come from [RPG] your desires that battle within you?
5:20 Whoever turns a sinner **from** the error of his way will save him
5:20 turns a sinner from the error of his way will save him **from** death
1Pe 1: 3 living hope through the resurrection of Jesus Christ **from** the dead,
1:18 or gold that you were redeemed **from** the empty way of life handed
1:21 who raised him **from** the dead and glorified him, and so your faith
1:22 love for your brothers, love one another deeply, **from** the heart.
1:23 not **of** perishable seed, but of imperishable, through the living
2: 9 that you may declare the praises of him who called you **out of**
2:12 they may see [NIE] your good deeds and glorify God on the day
4:11 If anyone serves, he should do it **with** the strength God provides,
2Pe 1:18 We ourselves heard this voice that came **from** heaven when we
2: 8 (for that righteous man, living among them day **after** day,
2: 9 then the Lord knows how to rescue godly men from trials
2:21 then to turn their backs **on** the sacred command that was passed on
3: 5 and the earth was formed **out of** water and by water.
1Jn 2:16 and does—comes not from the Father but from the world.
2:16 and does—comes not from the Father but **from** the world.
2:19 *They* **went out from** [RP2002] us, but they did not really belong
2:19 went out from us, but *they did* not *really* **belong to** [+1639] us.
2:19 For if *they had* **belonged to** [+1639] us, they would have
2:19 but their going showed that none of them **belonged to** [+1639] us.
2:21 because you do know it and because no lie comes **from** the truth.
2:29 you know that everyone who does what is right has been born **of**
3: 8 He who does what is sinful is **of** the devil, because the devil has
3: 9 No one who is born **of** God will continue to sin, because God's
3: 9 he cannot go on sinning, because he has been born **of** God.
3:10 Anyone who does not do what is right is not a child **of** God;
3:12 like Cain, who **belonged to** the evil one and murdered his brother.
3:14 We know that we have passed **from** death to life, because we love

3: 19   then is how we know that *we* **belong to** [+*1639*] the truth,
3: 24   we know that he lives in us: We know it **by** the Spirit he gave us.
4: 1   every spirit, but test the spirits to see whether they are **from** God,
4: 2   acknowledges that Jesus Christ has come in the flesh is **from** God,
4: 3   but every spirit that does not acknowledge Jesus is not **from** God.
4: 4   You, dear children, are **from** God and have overcome them,
4: 5   They are **from** the world and therefore speak from the viewpoint
4: 5   the world and therefore speak **from** *the viewpoint* of the world,
4: 6   We are **from** God, and whoever knows God listens to us;
4: 6   listens to us; but whoever is not **from** God does not listen to us.
4: 6   **This is how** [+*4047*] we recognize the Spirit of truth and the spirit
4: 7   Dear friends, let us love one another, for love comes **from** God.
4: 7   Everyone who loves has been born **of** God and knows God.
4: 13   we live in him and he in us, because he has given us **of** his Spirit.
5: 1   Everyone who believes that Jesus is the Christ is born **of** God,
5: 1   and everyone who loves the father loves **[NIE]** his child as well.
5: 4   for everyone born **of** God overcomes the world. This is the victory
5: 18   We know that anyone born **of** God does not continue to sin;
5: 18   the one who was born **of** God keeps him safe, and the evil one
5: 19   We know that we are *children* **of** God, and that the whole world is
2Jn 1: 4   It has given me great joy to find **some of** your children walking in
3Jn 1: 10   who want to do so and **puts** them out of [*RP1675*] the church.
1: 11   but what is good. Anyone who does what is good is **from** God.
Jude 1: 5   I want to remind you that the Lord delivered his people **out of**
1: 23   snatch others **from** the fire and save them; to others show mercy,
Rév 1: 5   To him who loves us and has freed us **from** our sins by his blood,
1: 16   and **out of** his mouth came [*RP1744*] a sharp double-edged sword.
2: 5   I will come to you and remove your lampstand **from** its place.
2: 7   who overcomes, I will give the right to eat **from** the tree of life,
2: 9   I know the slander **of** those who say they are Jews and are not,
2: 10   I tell you, the devil will put **some of** you in prison to test you,
2: 11   He who overcomes will not be hurt at all **by** the second death.
2: 21   I have given her time to repent **of** her immorality, but she is
2: 22   adultery with her suffer intensely, unless they repent **of** her ways.
3: 5   *I will* never **blot out** his name **from** [*RP1981*] the book of life,
3: 9   I will make those who are **of** the synagogue of Satan, who claim to
3: 10   I will also keep you **from** the hour of trial that is going to come
3: 12   which is coming down **out of** heaven from my God;
3: 16   neither hot nor cold—I am about to spit you **out of** my mouth.
3: 18   I counsel you to buy from me gold refined **in** the fire, so you can
4: 5   **From** the throne came [*RP1744*] flashes of lightning, rumblings
5: 5   Then one **of** the elders said to me, "Do not weep! See, the Lion of
5: 5   See, the Lion **of** the tribe of Judah, the Root of David,
5: 7   and took the scroll **from** the right hand of him who sat on the
5: 9   and with your blood you purchased men for God **from** every tribe
6: 1   I watched as the Lamb opened the first **of** the seven seals.
6: 1   Then I heard one **of** the four living creatures say in a voice like
6: 4   Its rider was given power to take peace **from** the earth and to make
6: 10   until you judge **[NIE]** the inhabitants of the earth and avenge our
6: 14   and every mountain and island was removed **from** its place.
7: 4   of those who were sealed: 144,000 **from** all the tribes of Israel.
7: 5   **From** the tribe of Judah 12,000 were sealed, from the tribe of
7: 5   **from** the tribe of Reuben 12,000, from the tribe of Gad 12,000,
7: 5   from the tribe of Reuben 12,000, **from** the tribe of Gad 12,000,
7: 6   **from** the tribe of Asher 12,000, from the tribe of Naphtali 12,000,
7: 6   from the tribe of Asher 12,000, **from** the tribe of Naphtali 12,000,
7: 6   the tribe of Naphtali 12,000, **from** the tribe of Manasseh 12,000,
7: 7   **from** the tribe of Simeon 12,000, from the tribe of Levi 12,000,
7: 7   from the tribe of Simeon 12,000, **from** the tribe of Levi 12,000,
7: 7   from the tribe of Levi 12,000, **from** the tribe of Issachar 12,000,
7: 8   **from** the tribe of Zebulun 12,000, from the tribe of Joseph 12,000,
7: 8   from the tribe of Zebulun 12,000, **from** the tribe of Joseph 12,000,
7: 8   the tribe of Joseph 12,000, **from** the tribe of Benjamin 12,000.
7: 9   **from** every nation, tribe, people and language, standing before the
7: 13   Then one **of** the elders asked me, "These in white robes—who are
7: 14   "These are they who have come **out of** the great tribulation;
7: 17   And God *will* **wipe away** every tear **from** [*RP1981*] their eyes."
8: 4   prayers of the saints, went up before God **from** the angel's hand.
8: 5   filled it **with** fire from the altar, and hurled it on the earth;
8: 10   fell **from** the sky on a third of the rivers and on the springs of
8: 11   and many people died **from** the waters that had become bitter.
8: 13   because of the trumpet blasts about to be sounded **by** the other
9: 1   and I saw a star that had fallen **from** the sky to the earth.
9: 2   smoke rose **from** it like the smoke from a gigantic furnace.
9: 2   The sun and sky were darkened **by** the smoke from the Abyss.
9: 3   And **out of** the smoke locusts came [*RP2002*] down upon the earth

9: 13   and I heard a voice *coming* **from** the horns of the golden altar that
9: 17   and **out of** their mouths came [*RP1744*] fire, smoke and sulfur.
9: 18   A third of mankind was killed by the three plagues **of** fire,
9: 18   smoke and sulfur that **came out of** [*RP1744*] their mouths.
9: 20   by these plagues still did not repent **of** the work of their hands;
9: 21   Nor did they repent **of** their murders, their magic arts, their sexual
9: 21   **[NIE]** their magic arts, their sexual immorality or their thefts.
9: 21   their magic arts, their **[NIE]** sexual immorality or their thefts.
9: 21   their magic arts, their sexual immorality or **[NIE]** their thefts.
10: 1   Then I saw another mighty angel coming down **from** heaven.
10: 4   but I heard a voice **from** heaven say, "Seal up what the seven
10: 8   Then the voice that I had heard **from** heaven spoke to me once
10: 10   I took the little scroll **from** the angel's hand and ate it. It tasted as
11: 5   fire **comes from** [*RP1744*] their mouths and devours their
11: 7   the beast that comes up **from** the Abyss will attack them,
11: 9   For three and a half days men **from** every people, tribe, language
11: 11   the three and a half days a breath of life **from** God entered them,
11: 12   Then they heard a loud voice **from** heaven saying to them,
12: 15   Then **from** his mouth the serpent spewed water like a river,
12: 16   and swallowing the river that the dragon had spewed **out of** his
13: 1   And I saw a beast coming **out of** the sea. He had ten horns
13: 3   One **of** the heads of the beast seemed to have had a fatal wound,
13: 11   Then I saw another beast, coming **out of** the earth. He had two
13: 13   even causing fire to come down **from** heaven to earth in full view
14: 2   And I heard a sound **from** heaven like the roar of rushing waters
14: 8   which made all the nations drink the maddening **[NIE]** wine of
14: 10   he, too, will drink **of** the wine of God's fury, which has been
14: 13   Then I heard a voice **from** heaven say, "Write: Blessed are the dead
14: 13   "Yes," says the Spirit, "they will rest **from** their labor, for their
14: 15   Then another angel **came out of** [*RP2002*] the temple and called in
14: 17   Another angel **came out of** [*RP2002*] the temple in heaven,
14: 18   came **from** the altar and called in a loud voice to him who had the
14: 20   outside the city, and blood **flowed out of** [*RP2002*] the press,
15: 2   those who had been victorious **over** the beast and his image
15: 2   the beast and **[RPG]** his image and over the number of his name.
15: 2   over the beast and his image and **over** the number of his name.
15: 6   **Out of** the temple came [*RP2002*] the seven angels with the seven
15: 7   Then one **of** the four living creatures gave to the seven angels
15: 8   And the temple was filled with smoke **from** the glory of God
15: 8   was filled with smoke from the glory of God and **from** his power,
16: 1   Then I heard a loud voice **from** the temple saying to the seven
16: 10   was plunged into darkness. Men gnawed their tongues **in** agony
16: 11   cursed the God of heaven **because of** their pains and their sores,
16: 11   the God of heaven because of their pains and **[RPG]** their sores,
16: 11   and their sores, but they refused to repent **of** what they had done.
16: 13   they *came* **out of** the mouth of the dragon, out of the mouth of the
16: 13   **out of** the mouth of the beast and out of the mouth of the false
16: 13   of the mouth of the beast and **out of** the mouth of the false prophet.
16: 17   and **out of** the temple came [*RP2002*] a loud voice from the
16: 21   **From** the sky huge hailstones of about a hundred pounds each fell
16: 21   And they cursed God **on account of** the plague of hail,
17: 1   One **of** the seven angels who had the seven bowls came and said to
17: 2   and the inhabitants of the earth were intoxicated **with** the wine of
17: 6   I saw that the woman was drunk **with** the blood of the saints,
17: 6   the saints, **[RPG]** the blood of those who bore testimony to Jesus.
17: 8   and will come up **out of** the Abyss and go to his destruction.
17: 11   *He* **belongs to** [+*1639*] the seven and is going to his destruction.
18: 1   After this I saw another angel coming down **from** heaven.
18: 1   had great authority, and the earth was illuminated **by** his splendor.
18: 3   For all the nations have drunk **[NIE]** the maddening wine of her
18: 3   and the merchants of the earth grew rich **from** her excessive
18: 4   Then I heard another voice **from** heaven say: "Come out of her,
18: 4   "**Come out of** [*RP2002*] her, my people, so that you will not share
18: 4   share in her sins, so that you will not receive any **of** her plagues;
18: 12   kind made of ivory, **NIE** costly wood, bronze, iron and marble;
18: 19   where all who had ships on the sea became rich **through** her
18: 20   God has judged her for the way **[NIE]** she treated you.' "
19: 2   He has avenged **on** [+*5931*] her the blood of his servants."
19: 15   **Out of** his mouth comes [*RP1744*] a sharp sword with which to
19: 21   that **came out of** [*RP2002*] the mouth of the rider on the horse,
19: 21   on the horse, and all the birds gorged themselves **on** their flesh.
20: 1   And I saw an angel coming down **out of** heaven, having the key to
20: 7   the thousand years are over, Satan will be released **from** his prison
20: 9   he loves. But fire came down **from** heaven and devoured them.
20: 12   The dead were judged according to what they had done **as** recorded
21: 2   the new Jerusalem, coming down **out of** heaven from God,

21: 3   And I heard a loud voice **from** the throne saying,
21: 4   *He will* **wipe** every tear **from** [*RP1981*] their eyes. There will be
21: 6   To him who is thirsty I will give to drink without cost **from** the
21: 9   One **of** the seven angels who had the seven bowls full of the seven
21:10   the Holy City, Jerusalem, coming down **out of** heaven from God.
21:21   twelve gates were twelve pearls, each gate made **of** a single pearl.
22: 1   **flowing from** [*RP1744*] the throne of God and of the Lamb
22:19   take away from him his share in the tree of life and **in** the holy city,

1667 ἕκαστος, *hekastos* [82] [→ *1668*]

each [55], each [+*1651*] [5], every [3], everyone [3], a man⁵ [2], *untranslated* [1], anyone [1], daily [+*2465+2848*] [1], detail [+*1651*] [1], each [+*324+1651*] [1], each of [1], every one [1], everyone [+*1651*] [1], everyone [+*4246*] [1], him [1], his [1], one [1], one after the other [+*1651*] [1], yourself [1]

Mt 16:27   then he will reward **each** *person* according to what he has done.
    18:35   "This is how my heavenly Father will treat **each** of you unless you
    25:15   two talents, and to another one talent, **each** according to his ability.
    26:22   very sad and began to say to him **one after the other** [+*1651*],
Mk 13:34   and puts his servants in charge, **each** with his assigned task,
Lk   2: 3   And **everyone** [+*4246*] went to his own town to register.
     4:40   of sickness, and laying his hands on **each** one, he healed them.
     6:44   **Each** tree is recognized by its own fruit. People do not pick figs
    13:15   Doesn't **each** of you on the Sabbath untie his ox or donkey from
    16: 5   "So he called in **each** one of his master's debtors. He asked the
Jn   6: 7   "Eight months' wages would not buy enough bread for **each** *one* to
     7:53   Then **each** went to his own home.
    16:32   and has come, when you will be scattered, **each** to his own home.
    19:23   his clothes, dividing them into four shares, one *for* **each** of them,
Ac   2: 3   of fire that separated and came to rest on **each** [+*1651*] of them.
     2: 6   because **each** one heard them speaking in his own language.
     2: 8   Then how is it that **each** of us hears them in his own native
     2:38   Peter replied, "Repent and be baptized, **every one** of you,
     3:26   he sent him first to you to bless you by turning **each** of you from
     4:35   the apostles' feet, and it was distributed *to* **anyone** as he had need.
    11:29   The disciples, **each** according to his ability, decided to provide
    17:27   out for him and find him, though he is not far from **each** one of us.
    20:31   for three years I never stopped warning **each** [+*1651*] of you night
    21:19   and reported in **detail** [+*1651*] what God had done among the
    21:26   and the offering would be made for **each** [+*1651*] of them.
Ro   2: 6   God "will give *to* **each** *person* according to what he has done."
    12: 3   than you ought, but rather think *of* **yourself** with sober judgment,
    14: 5   day alike. **Each** *one* should be fully convinced in his own mind.
    14:12   So then, **each** of us will give an account of himself to God.
    15: 2   **Each** of us should please his neighbor for his good, to build him
1Co 1:12   **One** of you says, "I follow Paul"; another, "I follow Apollos";
     3: 5   you came to believe—as the Lord has assigned *to* **each** his task.
     3: 8   and **each** will be rewarded according to his own labor.
     3:10   is building on it. But **each** *one* should be careful how he builds.
     3:13   **his** work will be shown for what it is, because the Day will bring it
     3:13   with fire, and the fire will test the quality *of* **each** *man's* work.
     4: 5   men's hearts. At that time **each** will receive his praise from God.
     7: 2   so much immorality, **each** *man* should have his own wife,
     7: 2   man should have his own wife, and **each** *woman* her own husband.
     7: 7   But **each** *man* has his own gift from God; one has this gift,
     7:17   **each** *one* should retain the place in life that the Lord assigned to
     7:17   that the Lord assigned to him and to which God has called **him**.
     7:20   **Each** *one* should remain in the situation which he was in when
     7:24   Brothers, **each** *man*, as responsible to God, should remain in the
    11:21   **each** of you goes ahead without waiting for anybody else.
    12: 7   Now *to* **each** *one* the manifestation of the Spirit is given for the
    12:11   work of one and the same Spirit, and he gives them *to* **each** *one*,
    12:18   parts in the body, **every** one of them, just as he wanted them to be.
    14:26   **everyone** has a hymn, or a word of instruction, a revelation,
    15:23   But **each** in his own turn: Christ, the firstfruits; then, when he
    15:38   he has determined, and *to* **each** *kind* of seed he gives its own body.
    16: 2   **each** *one* of you should set aside a sum of money in keeping with
2Co 5:10   that **each** *one* may receive what is due him for the things done
     9: 7   **Each** man should give what he has decided in his heart to give,
Gal 6: 4   **Each** *one* should test his own actions. Then he can take pride in
     6: 5   for **each** *one* should carry his own load.
Eph 4: 7   But *to* **each** one of us grace has been given as Christ apportioned
     4:16   and builds itself up in love, as **each** [+*1651*] part does its work.
     4:25   Therefore **each of** you must put off falsehood and speak truthfully

5:33   **each** one of you also must love his wife as he loves himself,
6: 8   because you know that the Lord will reward **everyone** for
Php 2: 4   **Each** of you should look not only to your own interests, but also to
     2: 4   to your own interests, but also to **[RPG]** the interests of others.
Col 4: 6   with salt, so that you may know how to answer **everyone** [+*1651*].
1Th 2:11   For you know that we dealt with **each** [+*1651*] of you as a father
     4: 4   that **each** of you should learn to control his own body in a way that
2Th 1: 3   and the love **every** one of you has for each other is increasing.
Heb 3:13   But encourage one another **daily** [+*2465+2848*], as long as it is
     6:11   We want **each** of you to show this same diligence to the very end,
     8:11   No longer will **a man**⁵ teach his neighbor, or a man his brother,
     8:11   or **a man**⁵ his brother, saying, 'Know the Lord,' because they will
    11:21   By faith Jacob, when he was dying, blessed **each** of Joseph's sons,
Jas 1:14   but **each** *one* is tempted when, by his own evil desire, he is
1Pe 1:17   Since you call on a Father who judges **each** *man's* work
     4:10   **Each** *one* should use whatever gift he has received to serve others,
Rev 2:23   and minds, and I will repay **each** of you according to your deeds.
     5: 8   **Each** *one* had a harp and they were holding golden bowls full of
     6:11   Then **each** of them was given a white robe, and they were told to
    20:13   and **each** *person* was judged according to what he had done.
    21:21   were twelve pearls, **each** [+*324+1651*] gate made of a single pearl.
    22: 2   bearing twelve crops of fruit, yielding its fruit **every** month.
    22:12   and I will give *to* **everyone** according to what he has done.

1668 ἑκάστοτε, *hekastote* [1] [√ *1667 + 4005 + 5445*]

always [1]

2Pe 1:15   my departure you may **always** be able to remember these things.

1669 ἑκατόν, *hekaton* [17] [→ *1670, 1671, 1672, 1673*]

hundred [8], 144 [+*5475+5477+5942*] [3], 144 [+*5475+5477*] [1], 153 [+*4299+5552*] [1], eight hundred gallons [+*1004*] [1], hundreds [1], seventy-five pounds [+*3354*] [1], thousand bushels [+*3174*] [1]

Mt 13: 8   a crop—**a hundred**, sixty or thirty *times* what was sown.
    13:23   yielding **a hundred**, sixty or thirty *times* what was sown."
    18:12   If a man owns **a hundred** sheep, and one of them wanders away,
    18:28   he found one of his fellow servants who owed him **a hundred**
Mk   4: 8   a crop, multiplying thirty, sixty, or even **a hundred** *times*."
     4:20   a crop—thirty, sixty or even **a hundred** *times* what was sown."
     6:40   So they sat down in groups of **hundreds** and fifties.
Lk 15: 4   "Suppose one of you has **a hundred** sheep and loses one of them.
    16: 6   " 'Eight **hundred gallons** [+*1004*] of olive oil,' he replied.
    16: 7   'And how much do you owe?' " 'A **thousand bushels** [+*3174*] of
Jn 19:39   a mixture of myrrh and aloes, about **seventy-five pounds** [+*3354*].
    21:11   dragged the net ashore. It was full of large fish, **153** [+*4299+5552*],
Ac   1:15   stood up among the **believers** (a group numbering about **a hundred**
Rev 7: 4   who were sealed: **144,000** [+*5475+5477+5942*] from all the tribes
    14: 1   and with him **144,000** [+*5475+5477+5942*] who had his name and
    14: 3   one could learn the song except the **144,000** [+*5475+5477+5942*]
    21:17   He measured its wall and it was **144** [+*5475+5477*] cubits thick,

1670 ἑκατονταετής, *hekatontaetēs* [1] [√ *1669 + 2291*]

hundred years old [1]

Ro   4:19   since he was about a **hundred years old**—and that Sarah's womb

1671 ἑκατονταπλασίων, *hekatontaplasiōn* [3] [√ *1669*]

hundred times [3]

Mt 19:29   or fields for my sake will receive a **hundred times** as much
Mk 10:30   will fail to receive a **hundred times** *as much* in this present age
Lk   8: 8   and yielded a crop, a **hundred times** *more* than was sown."

1672 ἑκατοντάρχης, *hekatontarchēs* [20] [√ *1669 + 806*]

centurion [16], centurions [2], centurion's [1], officers [1]

Mt   8: 5   had entered Capernaum, a **centurion** came to him, asking for help.

8: 8 The **centurion** replied, "Lord, I do not deserve to have you come
8: 13 Then Jesus said *to* the **centurion**, "Go! It will be done just as you
27: 54 When the **centurion** and those with him who were guarding Jesus
Lk 7: 2 There a **centurion's** servant, whom his master valued highly,
    7: 6 He was not far from the house when the **centurion** sent friends to
23: 47 The **centurion**, seeing what had happened, praised God and said,
Ac 10: 1 a **centurion** in what was known as the Italian Regiment.
10: 22 The men replied, "We have come from Cornelius the **centurion**.
21: 32 He at once took *some* **officers** and soldiers and ran down to the
22: 25 him out to flog him, Paul said to the **centurion** standing there,
22: 26 When the **centurion** heard this, he went to the commander
23: 17 Then Paul called one *of* the **centurions** and said, "Take this young
23: 23 Then he called two *of* his **centurions** and ordered them, "Get ready
24: 23 He ordered the **centurion** to keep Paul under guard but to give him
27: 1 and some other prisoners were handed over *to* a **centurion** named
27: 6 There the **centurion** found an Alexandrian ship sailing for Italy
27: 11 But the **centurion**, instead of listening to what Paul said,
27: 31 Then Paul said *to* the **centurion** and the soldiers, "Unless these men
27: 43 But the **centurion** wanted to spare Paul's life and kept them from

1673 ἑκατόνταρχος, *hekatontarchos* Not used in UBS/NIV [√ *1669 + 806*]

1674 ἐκβαίνω, *ekbainō* [1] [√ *1666 + 326*]

left [1]

Heb 11: 15 If they had been thinking of the country *they had* **left**, they would

1675 ἐκβάλλω, *ekballō* [81] [√ *1666 + 965*]

ἐκβάλλω δαιμόνιον (cast out a demon) [24] Mt 7:22; 9:33,34; 10:8; 12:24,24,27,28; Mk 1:34,39; 3:15,22; 6:13; 7:26; 9:38; 16:9,17; Lk 9:49; 11:14,15,18,19,20; 13:32

drive out [19], driving out [8], drove out [5], brings out of [*RP1666*] [3], drives out [3], threw [3], thrown [3], driven [2], get rid of [2], send out [2], take out [*RP1666*] [2], threw out [2], throw [2], brought out [1], dragged [1], drive [1], drive out [*RP1666*] [1], driven out [1], drove from [*RP1666*] [1], exclude [1], expelled [1], leads [1], out of the body [*+909+1650*] [1], pluck out [1], put out [1], put outside [1], puts out of [*RP1666*] [1], reject [1], remove from [*RP1666*] [1], remove from [1], sent [1], sent away [1], sent off [1], sent out [1], take out of [*RP1666*] [1], take out of [1], throwing [1], took out [1]

Mt 7: 4 your brother, 'Let *me* **take** [*RP1666*] the speck **out** of your eye,'
    7: 5 first **take** [*RP1666*] the plank **out** of your own eye, and then you
    7: 5 then you will see clearly *to* **remove** [*RP1666*] the speck **from** your
    7: 22 and in your name **drive out** demons and perform many miracles?'
    8: 12 But the subjects of the kingdom *will be* **thrown** outside,
    8: 16 and *he* **drove out** the spirits with a word and healed all the sick.
    8: 31 The demons begged Jesus, "If *you* **drive** us **out**, send us into the
    9: 25 After the crowd *had been* **put outside**, he went in and took the girl
    9: 33 And *when* the demon *was* **driven out**, the man who had been mute
    9: 34 "It is by the prince of demons that *he* **drives out** demons."
    9: 38 of the harvest, therefore, to **send out** workers into his harvest field."
10: 1 and gave them authority to **drive out** evil spirits and to heal every
10: 8 raise the dead, cleanse those who have leprosy, **drive out** demons.
12: 20 wick he will not snuff out, till *he* **leads** justice to victory.
12: 24 the prince of demons, that this fellow **drives out** demons."
12: 26 If Satan **drives out** Satan, he is divided against himself. How
12: 27 And if I **drive out** demons by whom do your people
12: 27 demons by Beelzebub, by whom *do* your people **drive** them **out**?
12: 28 But if I **drive out** demons by the Spirit of God, then the kingdom
12: 35 The good man **brings** [*RP1666*] good things **out of** the good
12: 35 and the evil man **brings** [*RP1666*] evil things **out of** the evil stored
13: 52 **brings** [*RP1666*] **out of** his storeroom new treasures as well as
15: 17 goes into the stomach and then **out** [*+909+1650*] **of the body**?
17: 19 to Jesus in private and asked, "Why couldn't we **drive** it **out**?"
21: 12 temple area and **drove out** all who were buying and selling there.
21: 39 So *they* took him and **threw** him **out** of the vineyard and killed
22: 13 'Tie him hand and foot, and **throw** him outside, into the darkness,
25: 30 And **throw** that worthless servant outside, into the darkness,
Mk 1: 12 At once the Spirit **sent** him **out** into the desert,
    1: 34 *He* also **drove out** many demons, but he would not let the demons

1: 39 preaching in their synagogues and **driving out** demons.
1: 43 Jesus **sent** him **away** at once with a strong warning:
3: 15 and to have authority *to* **drive out** demons.
3: 22 by Beelzebub! By the prince of demons *he is* **driving out** demons."
3: 23 and spoke to them in parables: "How can Satan **drive out** Satan?
5: 40 *After* he **put** them all **out**, he took the child's father and mother
6: 13 *They* **drove out** many demons and anointed many sick people with
7: 26 She begged Jesus to **drive** [*RP1666*] the demon **out** of her
9: 18 I asked your disciples to **drive out** the spirit, but they could not."
9: 28 his disciples asked him privately, "Why couldn't we **drive** it **out**?"
9: 38 "we saw a man **driving out** demons in your name and we told him
9: 47 And if your eye causes you to sin, **pluck** it **out**. It is better for you
11: 15 and began **driving out** those who were buying and selling there.
12: 8 they took him and killed him, and **threw** him out of the vineyard.
16: 9 to Mary Magdalene, out of whom *he had* **driven** seven demons.
16: 17 In my name *they will* **drive out** demons; they will speak in new
Lk 4: 29 *They* got up, **drove** him **out** of the town, and took him to the brow
    6: 22 they exclude you and insult you and **reject** your name as evil,
    6: 42 to your brother, 'Brother, let *me* **take** the speck **out of** your eye,'
    6: 42 first **take** [*RP1666*] the plank **out of** your eye, and then you will
    6: 42 then you will see clearly *to* **remove** the speck **from** your brother's
    9: 40 I begged your disciples to **drive** it **out**, but they could not."
    9: 49 "we saw a man **driving out** demons in your name and we tried to
10: 2 of the harvest, therefore, to **send out** workers into his harvest field.
10: 35 The next day he **took out** two silver coins and gave them to the
11: 14 Jesus was **driving out** a demon that was mute. When the demon
11: 15 "By Beelzebub, the prince of demons, *he is* **driving out** demons."
11: 18 because you claim that I **drive out** demons by Beelzebub.
11: 19 Now if I **drive out** demons by Beelzebub, by whom do your
11: 19 by Beelzebub, by whom *do* your followers **drive** them **out**?
11: 20 But if I **drive out** demons by the finger of God, then the kingdom
13: 28 prophets in the kingdom of God, but *you* yourselves **thrown** out.
13: 32 '*I will* **drive out** demons and heal people today and tomorrow,
19: 45 the temple area and began **driving out** those who were selling.
20: 12 He sent still a third, and they wounded him and **threw** him **out**.
20: 15 So they **threw** him **out** of the vineyard and killed him. "What
Jn 2: 15 and **drove** [*RP1666*] all **from** the temple area, both sheep
    6: 37 come to me, and whoever comes to me I *will* never **drive** away.
    9: 34 in sin at birth; how dare you lecture us!" And *they* **threw** him out.
    9: 35 Jesus heard that *they had* **thrown** him out, and when he found
10: 4 When *he has* **brought out** all his own, he goes on ahead of them,
12: 31 on this world; now the prince of this world *will be* **driven** out.
Ac 7: 58 **dragged** him out of the city and began to stone him. Meanwhile,
    9: 40 Peter **sent** them all out of the room; then he got down on his knees
13: 50 against Paul and Barnabas, and **expelled** them from their region.
16: 37 us into prison. And now *do they want to* **get rid of** us quietly? No!
27: 38 they lightened the ship *by* **throwing** the grain into the sea.
Gal 4: 30 "**Get rid of** the slave woman and her son, for the slave woman's
Jas 2: 25 gave lodging to the spies and **sent** them **off** in a different direction?
3Jn 1: 10 who want to do so and **puts** [*RP1666*] them **out of** the church.
Rev 11: 2 But **exclude** the outer court; do not measure it, because it has been

1676 ἔκβασις, *ekbasis* [2] [√ *1666 + 326*]

outcome [1], way out [1]

1Co 10: 13 he will also provide a **way out** so that you can stand up under it.
Heb 13: 7 Consider the **outcome** of their way of life and imitate their faith.

1677 ἐκβλαστάνω, *ekblastanō* Not used in UBS/NIV [√ *1666 + 1056*]

1678 ἐκβολή, *ekbolē* [1] [√ *1666 + 965*]

throw the cargo overboard [1]

Ac 27: 18 storm that the next day they began to **throw the cargo overboard**.

1679 ἐκγαμίζω, *ekgamizō* Not used in UBS/NIV [√ *1666 + 1141*]

1680 ἐκγαμίσκω, *ekgamiskō* Not used in UBS/NIV [√ *1666 + 1141*]

1681 ἔκγονος, **ekgonos** [1] [√ 1666 + 1181]

grandchildren [1]

1Ti   5: 4   But if a widow has children or **grandchildren**, these should learn

1682 ἐκδαπανάω, **ekdapanaō** [1] [√ 1666 + 1252]

expend [1]

2Co 12:15   gladly spend for you everything I have and **expend** *myself* as well.

1683 ἐκδέχομαι, **ekdechomai** [6] [√ 1666 + 1312]

expecting [1], looking forward to [1], wait for [1], waiting for [1], waits [1], waits for [1]

Ac 17:16   *While* Paul *was* **waiting for** them in Athens, he was greatly
1Co 11:33   my brothers, when you come together to eat, **wait for** each other.
      16:11   he may return to me. *I am* **expecting** him along with the brothers.
Heb 10:13   Since that time *he* **waits** for his enemies to be made his footstool,
      11:10   For *he was* **looking forward to** the city with foundations,
Jas   5: 7   See how the farmer **waits for** the land to yield its valuable crop

1684 ἔκδηλος, **ekdēlos** [1] [√ 1666 + 1316]

clear [1]

2Ti   3: 9   as in the case of those men, their folly will be **clear** to everyone.

1685 ἐκδημέω, **ekdēmeō** [3] [√ 1666 + 1322]

away [1], away from [RP1666] [1], away from [1]

2Co   5: 6   and know that as long as we are at home in the body *we are* **away**
      5: 8   and would prefer *to be* **away** [RP1666] **from** the body and at
      5: 9   please him, whether we are at home in the body or **away from** it.

1686 ἐκδίδωμι, **ekdidōmi** [4] [√ 1666 + 1443]

rented [3], rent [1]

Mt 21:33   Then *he* **rented** the vineyard to some farmers and went away on a
      21:41   they replied, "and *he will* **rent** the vineyard to other tenants,
Mk 12: 1   Then *he* **rented** the vineyard to some farmers and went away on a
Lk 20: 9   **rented** it to some farmers and went away for a long time.

1687 ἐκδιηγέομαι, **ekdiēgeomai** [2] [√ 1666 + 1328 + 72]

told [1], told how [1]

Ac 13:41   days that you would never believe, even if someone **told** you.' "
      15: 3   and Samaria, *they* **told how** the Gentiles had been converted.

1688 ἐκδικέω, **ekdikeō** [6] [√ 1666 + 1472]

avenge [1], avenged [1], justice [1], punish [1], see that gets justice [1], take revenge [+1571] [1]

Lk 18: 3   to him with the plea, 'Grant me **justice** against my adversary.'
      18: 5   this widow keeps bothering me, *I will* **see that** she **gets justice**,
Ro 12:19   *Do* not **take revenge** [+1571], my friends, but leave room for
2Co 10: 6   And we will be ready *to* **punish** every act of disobedience,
Rev   6:10   until you judge the inhabitants of the earth and **avenge** our blood?"
      19: 2   by her adulteries. He has **avenged** on her the blood of his servants."

1689 ἐκδίκησις, **ekdikēsis** [9] [√ 1666 + 1472]

avenge [2], justice [2], avenged [+4472] [1], punish [+1443] [1], punish [1], punishment [1], readiness to see justice done [1]

Lk 18: 7   And will not God bring about **justice** for his chosen ones,
      18: 8   I tell you, he will see that they get **justice**, and quickly. However,
      21:22   For this is the time *of* **punishment** in fulfillment of all that has
Ac   7:24   so *he* went to his defense and **avenged** [+4472] him by killing the
Ro 12:19   for it is written: "It is mine *to* **avenge**; I will repay," says the Lord.

2Co   7:11   what longing, what concern, what **readiness to see justice done**.
2Th   1: 8   *He will* **punish** [+1443] those who do not know God and do not
Heb 10:30   For we know him who said, "It is mine to **avenge**; I will repay,"
1Pe   2:14   who are sent by him to **punish** those who do wrong and to

1690 ἔκδικος, **ekdikos** [2] [√ 1666 + 1472]

agent to bring punishment [1], punish [1]

Ro 13: 4   an **agent** of wrath **to bring punishment** on the wrongdoer.
1Th   4: 6   The Lord will **punish** men for all such sins, as we have already

1691 ἐκδιώκω, **ekdiōkō** [1] [√ 1666 + 1503]

drove out [1]

1Th   2:15   who killed the Lord Jesus and the prophets and also **drove** us **out**.

1692 ἔκδοτος, **ekdotos** [1] [√ 1666 + 1443]

handed over [1]

Ac   2:23   This man was **handed over** to you by God's set purpose

1693 ἐκδοχή, **ekdochē** [1] [√ 1666 + 1312]

expectation [1]

Heb 10:27   but only a fearful **expectation** of judgment and of raging fire that

1694 ἐκδύω, **ekdyō** [6 / 5] [√ 1666 + 1544]

took off [2], stripped [1], stripped of clothes [1], unclothed [1]

Mt 27:28   They **stripped** him and put a scarlet robe on him,
      27:31   *they* **took off** the robe and put his own clothes on him.
Mk 15:20   *they* **took off** the purple robe and put his own clothes on him.
Lk 10:30   They **stripped** him **of** his **clothes**, beat him and went away,
2Co   5: 3   because *when we are* **clothed**, [UBS *unclothed*; NIV *1907*] we will
      5: 4   because we do not wish *to be* **unclothed** but to be clothed with

1695 ἐκεῖ, **ekei** [105] [→ 1696, 1697, 1698, 2084, 2795, 2796, 2797, 5654]

there [72], where [12], *untranslated* [9], here [2], nearby [2], at Bereaˢ [1], at his house [1], but in the other case [+1254] [1], in [1], in that place [1], lived [+1639] [1], stayed [+3531] [1], to the groveˢ [1]

Mt   2:13   Stay **there** until I tell you, for Herod is going to search for the child
      2:15   **where** he stayed until the death of Herod. And so was fulfilled
      2:22   in Judea in place of his father Herod, he was afraid to go **there**.
      5:23   if you are offering your gift at the altar and **there** remember that
      5:24   leave your gift **there** in front of the altar. First go and be reconciled
      6:21   For where your treasure is, **there** your heart will be also.
      8:12   the darkness, **where** there will be weeping and gnashing of teeth."
     10:11   search for some worthy person there and stay **at his house** until
     12:45   other spirits more wicked than itself, and they go in and live **there**.
     13:42   fiery furnace, **where** there will be weeping and gnashing of teeth.
     13:50   fiery furnace, **where** there will be weeping and gnashing of teeth.
     13:58   And he did not do many miracles **there** because of their lack of
     14:23   by himself to pray. When evening came, he was **there** alone,
     15:29   Then he went up on a mountainside and sat down. [RPG]
     17:20   say to this mountain, 'Move from here to **there**' and it will move.
     18:20   or three come together in my name, **there** am I with them."
     19: 2   Large crowds followed him, and he healed them **there**.
     21:17   and went out of the city to Bethany, **where** he spent the night.
     22:11   he noticed a man **there** who was not wearing wedding clothes.
     22:13   the darkness, **where** there will be weeping and gnashing of teeth.'
     24:28   Wherever there is a carcass, **there** the vultures will gather.
     24:51   the hypocrites, **where** there will be weeping and gnashing of teeth.
     25:30   the darkness, **where** there will be weeping and gnashing of teeth.'
     26:36   and he said to them, "Sit here while I go over **there** and pray."
     26:71   where another girl saw him and said to the people **there**,
     27:36   And sitting down, they kept watch over him **there**.
     27:47   When some of those standing **there** heard this, they said, "He's
     27:55   Many women were **there**, watching from a distance. They had
     27:61   and the other Mary were sitting **there** opposite the tomb.

28: 7 of you into Galilee. **There** you will see him.' Now I have told you."
28: 10 and tell my brothers to go to Galilee; **there** they will see me."
Mk 1: 35 left the house and went off to a solitary place, **where** he prayed.
1: 38 to the nearby villages—so I can preach **there** also.
2: 6 Now some teachers of the law were sitting **there**, thinking to
3: 1 into the synagogue, and a man with a shriveled hand was **there**.
5: 11 A large herd of pigs was feeding on the **nearby** hillside.
6: 5 He could not do any miracles **there**, except lay his hands on a few
6: 10 Whenever you enter a house, stay **there** until you leave that town.
6: 33 and ran **[RPG]** on foot from all the towns and got there ahead of
11: 5 some people standing **there** asked, "What are you doing,
13: 21 here is the Christ!' or, 'Look, **there** he is!' do not believe it.
14: 15 upper room, furnished and ready. Make preparations for us **there**."
16: 7 of you into Galilee. **There** you will see him, just as he told you.' "
Lk 2: 6 While they were **there**, the time came for the baby to be born,
6: 6 and a man was **there** whose right hand was shriveled.
8: 32 A large herd of pigs was feeding **there** on the hillside. The demons
9: 4 Whatever house you enter, stay **there** until you leave that town.
10: 6 If a man of peace is **there**, your peace will rest on him; if not,
11: 26 other spirits more wicked than itself, and they go in and live **there**.
12: 18 bigger ones, and **there** I will store all my grain and my goods.
12: 34 For where your treasure is, **there** your heart will be also.
13: 28 "There will be weeping **there**, and gnashing of teeth, when you see
15: 13 a distant country and **there** squandered his wealth in wild living.
17: 21 nor will people say, 'Here it is,' or '**There** it is,'
17: 23 Men will tell you, '**There** he is!' or 'Here he is!' Do not go
17: 37 "Where there is a dead body, **there** the vultures will gather."
21: 2 He also saw a poor widow put in two very small copper coins.
22: 12 you a large upper room, all furnished. Make preparations **there**."
23: 33 the Skull, **there** they crucified him, along with the criminals—
Jn 2: 1 a wedding took place at Cana in Galilee. Jesus' mother was **there**,
2: 6 **Nearby** stood six stone water jars, the kind used by the Jews for
2: 12 and brothers and his disciples. **There** they stayed for a few days.
3: 22 **where** he spent some time with them, and baptized.
3: 23 **[RPG]** and people were constantly coming to be baptized.
4: 6 Jacob's well was **there**, and Jesus, tired as he was from the
4: 40 they urged him to stay with them, and *he* **stayed** [+3531] two days.
5: 5 One who was **there** had been an invalid for thirty-eight years.
6: 3 up on a mountainside and sat down **[RPG]** with his disciples.
6: 22 shore of the lake realized that only one boat had been **there**,
6: 24 the crowd realized that neither Jesus nor his disciples were **there**,
10: 40 where John had been baptizing in the early days. **Here** he stayed
10: 42 And **in that place** many believed in Jesus.
11: 8 ago the Jews tried to stone you, and yet you are going back **there**?"
11: 15 and for your sake I am glad I was not **there**, so that you may
11: 31 followed her, supposing she was going to the tomb to mourn **there**.
11: 54 to a village called Ephraim, **where** he stayed with his disciples.
12: 2 **Here** a dinner was given in Jesus' honor. Martha served,
12: 9 Meanwhile a large crowd of Jews found out that Jesus was **there**
12: 26 also will be. **[RPG]** My Father will honor the one who serves me.
18: 2 the place, because Jesus had often met **there** with his disciples.
18: 3 So Judas came **to the grove**s, guiding a detachment of soldiers
19: 42 and since the tomb was nearby, they laid Jesus **there**.
Ac 9: 33 **There** he found a man named Aeneas, a paralytic who had been
14: 7 **where** they continued to preach the good news.
16: 1 then to Lystra, where a disciple named Timothy **lived** [+1639],
17: 13 they went **there** too, agitating the crowds and stirring them up.
17: 14 sent Paul to the coast, but Silas and Timothy stayed **at Berea**s.
19: 21 "After I have been **there**," he said, "I must visit Rome also."
22: 10 'and go into Damascus. **There** you will be told all that you have
25: 9 up to Jerusalem and stand trial before me **there** on these charges?"
25: 14 Since they were spending many days **there**, Festus discussed
25: 20 if he would be willing to go to Jerusalem and stand trial **there**
27: 6 **There** the centurion found an Alexandrian ship sailing for Italy
Ro 9: 26 my people,' **[RPG]** they will be called 'sons of the living God.' "
15: 24 passing through and to have you assist me on my journey **there**,
Tit 3: 12 come to me at Nicopolis, because I have decided to winter **there**.
Heb 7: 8 **but in the other case** [+1254], by him who is declared to be living.
Jas 2: 3 to the poor man, "You stand **there**" or "Sit on the floor by my feet,"
3: 16 selfish ambition, **there** you find disorder and every evil practice.
4: 13 or tomorrow we will go to this or that city, spend a year **there**.
Rev 2: 14 You have people **there** who hold to the teaching of Balaam,
12: 6 The woman fled into the desert to **[RPG]** a place prepared for her
12: 6 by God, where **[RPG]** she might be taken care of for 1,260 days.
12: 14 where she would be taken care of **[RPG]** for a time, times
21: 25 no day will its gates ever be shut, for there will be no night **there**.

1696 ἐκεῖθεν, *ekeithen* [37] [√ *1695*]

from there [12], *untranslated* [8], that place [4], there [4], from that place [2], that town [2], from [1], on [1], on each side [+*1949*+*2779*] [1], then [+*2779*] [1], where [1]

Mt 4: 21 Going on **from there**, he saw two other brothers, James son of
5: 26 you will not get out **[RPG]** until you have paid the last penny.
9: 9 As Jesus went on **from there**, he saw a man named Matthew
9: 27 As Jesus went on **from there**, two blind men followed him,
11: 1 he went on **from there** to teach and preach in the towns of Galilee.
12: 9 Going on **from that place**, he went into their synagogue,
12: 15 Aware of this, Jesus withdrew **from that place**. Many followed
13: 53 When Jesus had finished these parables, he moved on **from there**.
14: 13 he withdrew **[RPG]** by boat privately to a solitary place.
15: 21 Leaving **that place**, Jesus withdrew to the region of Tyre
15: 29 Jesus left **there** and went along the Sea of Galilee. Then he went
19: 15 When he had placed his hands on them, he went on **from there**.
Mk 6: 1 Jesus left **there** and went to his hometown, accompanied by his
6: 10 Whenever you enter a house, stay there until you leave **that town**.
6: 11 off your feet when you leave, **[RPG]** as a testimony against them."
7: 24 Jesus left **that place** and went to the vicinity of Tyre. He entered a
9: 30 They left **that place** and passed through Galilee. Jesus did not
10: 1 Jesus then left **that place** and went into the region of Judea
Lk 9: 4 Whatever house you enter, stay there until you leave **that town**.
11: 53 When Jesus left **there**, the Pharisees and the teachers of the law
12: 59 you will not get out **[RPG]** until you have paid the last penny."
16: 26 here to you cannot, nor can anyone cross over **from there** to us.'
Jn 4: 43 After the two days he left **[RPG]** for Galilee.
11: 54 Instead he withdrew **[RPG]** to a region near the desert, to a
Ac 7: 4 and settled in Haran. **[RPG]** After the death of his father,
13: 4 went down to Seleucia and sailed **from there** to Cyprus.
13: 21 **Then** [+*2779*] the people asked for a king, and he gave them Saul
14: 26 **From** Attalia they sailed back to Antioch, where they had been
16: 12 **From there** we traveled to Philippi, a Roman colony
18: 7 Then Paul left **[RPG]** the synagogue and went next door to the
20: 13 and sailed for Assos, **where** we were going to take Paul aboard.
20: 15 The next day we set sail **from there** and arrived off Kios.
21: 1 The next day we went to Rhodes and **from there** to Patara.
27: 4 **From there** we put out to sea again and passed to the lee of
27: 12 the majority decided that we should sail **on**, hoping to reach
28: 15 The brothers **there** had heard that we were coming, and they
Rev 22: 2 **On each side** [+*1949*+*2779*] of the river stood the tree of life,

1697 ἐκεῖνος, *ekeinos* [265 / 264]   See Index of Articles

[√ *1695*]

ἐκεῖνος ἡμέρα (that day) [49] Mt 3:1; 7:22; 13:1; 22:23,46; 24:19,22,22,29,36; 26:29; Mk 1:9; 2:20; 4:35; 8:1; 13:17,19,24,32; 14:25; Lk 2:1; 4:2; 5:35; 6:23; 9:36; 10:12; 17:31; 21:23,34; Jn 1:39; 5:9; 11:53; 14:20; 16:23,26; 19:31; 20:19; Ac 2:18,41; 7:41; 8:1; 9:37; 2Th 1:10; 2Ti 1:12,18; 4:8; Heb 8:10; 10:16; Rev 9:6

ἐκεῖνος καιρός (that time) [6] Mt 11:25; 12:1; 14:1; Ac 12:1; 19:23; Eph 2:12

ἐκεῖνος ὥρα (that hour) [13] Mt 8:13; 9:22; 10:19; 15:28; 17:18; 18:1; 26:55; Mk 13:11; Lk 7:21; Jn 4:53; 19:27; Ac 16:33; Rev 11:13

ὁ ἄνθρωπος ἐκεῖνος (that person) [9] Mt 12:45; 26:24,24; Mk 14:21,21; Lk 11:26; 22:22; Ac 16:35; Jas 1:7

that [97], he [29], those [28], *untranslated* [23], they [15], this [9], them [7], him [6], that very [5], his [3], she [3], these [3], he himself [2], the [2], that same [2], the former's [2], the man's [2], the one [2], their [2], who [2], himself [1], his disciples's [1], it [1], Jesus's Christ [1], Jesus's [1], John's [1], Judas's [1], Mary's [1], next [1], others [1], Priscilla's and Aquila [1], same [1], that was the time [+*1877*+*2465*+*3836*] [1], the Father's [1], the country's [1], the disciples's [1], the other [1], what [1], which [1], your brother's [1]

1698 ἐκεῖσε, *ekeise* [2] [√ *1695*]

there [1], where [1]

Ac 21: 3 We landed at Tyre, **where** our ship was to unload its cargo.

22: 5 and went **there** to bring these people as prisoners to Jerusalem to

1699 ἐκζητέω, *ekzēteō* [7] [√ *1666 + 2426*]

held responsible for [2], earnestly seek [1], searched intently and with the greatest care [*+2001+2779*] [1], seek [1], seeks [1], sought [1]

Lk 11: 50 Therefore this generation *will be* **held responsible for** the blood of
    11: 51 I tell you, this generation *will be* **held responsible for** it all.
Ac 15: 17 that the remnant of men *may* **seek** the Lord, and all the Gentiles
Ro   3: 11 there is no one who understands, no one *who* **seeks** God.
Heb 11: 6 that he exists and that he rewards those *who* **earnestly seek** him.
    12: 17 about no change of mind, though *he* **sought** the blessing with tears.
1Pe 1: 10 **searched intently and with the greatest care** [*+2001+2779*],

1700 ἐκζήτησις, *ekzētēsis* [1] [√ *1666 + 2426*]

controversies [1]

1Ti 1: 4 These promote **controversies** rather than God's work—which is by

1701 ἐκθαμβέω, *ekthambeō* [4] [√ *1666 + 2502*]

alarmed [2], deeply distressed [1], overwhelmed with wonder [1]

Mk 9: 15 *they were* **overwhelmed with wonder** and ran to greet him.
    14: 33 with him, and he began *to be* **deeply distressed** and troubled.
    16: 5 in a white robe sitting on the right side, and *they were* **alarmed**.
    16: 6 "Don't *be* **alarmed**," he said. "You are looking for Jesus the

1702 ἔκθαμβος, *ekthambos* [1] [√ *1666 + 2502*]

astonished [1]

Ac   3: 11 all the people were **astonished** and came running to them in the

1703 ἐκθαυμάζω, *ekthaumazō* [1] [√ *1666 + 2513*]

amazed [1]

Mk 12: 17 and to God what is God's." And *they were* **amazed** at him.

1704 ἔκθετος, *ekthetos* [1] [√ *1666 + 5502*]

throw out [1]

Ac   7: 19 and oppressed our forefathers by forcing them *to* **throw out** their

1705 ἐκκαθαίρω, *ekkathairō* [2] [√ *1666 + 2754*]

cleanses [1], get rid of [1]

1Co 5: 7 **Get rid of** the old yeast that you may be a new batch without
2Ti 2: 21 If a man **cleanses** himself from the latter, he will be an instrument

1706 ἐκκαίω, *ekkaiō* [1] [√ *1666 + 2794*]

inflamed [1]

Ro   1: 27 relations with women and *were* **inflamed** with lust for one another.

1707 ἐκκακέω, *ekkakeō* Not used in UBS/NIV
    [√ *1666 + 2805*]

1708 ἐκκεντέω, *ekkenteō* [2] [√ *1666 + 3034*]

pierced [2]

Jn 19: 37 scripture says, "They will look on the one *they have* **pierced**."
Rev 1: 7 and every eye will see him, even those *who* **pierced** him;

1709 ἐκκλάω, *ekklaō* [3] [√ *1666 + 3089*]

broken off [3]

Ro 11: 17 If some of the branches *have been* **broken off**, and you, though a

11: 19 say then, "Branches *were* **broken off** so that I could be grafted in."
11: 20 But *they were* **broken off** because of unbelief, and you stand by

1710 ἐκκλείω, *ekkleiō* [2] [√ *1666 + 3091*]

alienate [1], excluded [1]

Ro   3: 27 Where, then, is boasting? *It is* **excluded**. On what principle?
Gal 4: 17 What they want *is to* **alienate** you ⌊from us⌋, so that you may be

1711 ἐκκλησία, *ekklēsia* [114] [√ *1666 + 2813*]

with a proper name (city or area) [24] Ac 8:1; 9:31; 11:22; 13:1; Ro 16:1; 1Co 1:2; 16:1,19; 2Co 1:1; 8:1; Gal 1:2,22; Col 4:16; 1Th 1:1; 2:14; 2Ti 1:1; Rev 1:4; 2:1,8,12,18; 3:1,7,14

ἐκκλησία θεοῦ (church of God) [12] Ac 20:28; 1Co 1:2; 10:32; 11:16,22; 15:9; 2Co 1:1; Gal 1:13; 1Th 2:14; 2Th 1:4; 1Ti 3:5,15

ἐκκλησίαι Χριστοῦ (churches of Christ) [1] Ro 16:16

church [74], churches [34], assembly [4], congregation [1], congregations [1]

Mt 16: 18 tell you that you are Peter, and on this rock I will build my **church**,
    18: 17 If he refuses to listen to them, tell it *to* the **church**; and if he
    18: 17 and if he refuses to listen even to the **church**, treat him as you
Ac   5: 11 Great fear seized the whole **church** and all who heard about these
    7: 38 He was in the **assembly** in the desert, with the angel who spoke to
    8: 1 On that day a great persecution broke out against the **church** at
    8: 3 But Saul began to destroy the **church**. Going from house to house,
    9: 31 Then the **church** throughout Judea, Galilee and Samaria enjoyed a
   11: 22 News of this reached the ears *of* the **church** at Jerusalem,
   11: 26 So for a whole year Barnabas and Saul met with the **church**
   12: 1 time that King Herod arrested some who belonged to the **church**,
   12: 5 in prison, but the **church** was earnestly praying to God for him.
   13: 1 In the **church** at Antioch there were prophets and teachers:
   14: 23 and Barnabas appointed elders for them in each **church** and,
   14: 27 they gathered the **church** together and reported all that God had
   15: 3 The **church** sent them on their way, and as they traveled through
   15: 4 they were welcomed by the **church** and the apostles and elders,
   15: 22 Then the apostles and elders, with the whole **church**, decided to
   15: 41 He went through Syria and Cilicia, strengthening the **churches**.
   16: 5 So the **churches** were strengthened in the faith and grew daily in
   18: 22 he went up and greeted the **church** and then went down to
   19: 32 The **assembly** was in confusion: Some were shouting one thing,
   19: 39 further you want to bring up, it must be settled in a legal **assembly**.
   19: 41 After he had said this, he dismissed the **assembly**.
   20: 17 From Miletus, Paul sent to Ephesus for the elders *of* the **church**.
   20: 28 Be shepherds of the **church** of God, which he bought with his own
Ro 16: 1 to you our sister Phoebe, a servant *of* the **church** in Cenchrea.
   16: 4 Not only I but all the **churches** of the Gentiles are grateful to them.
   16: 5 Greet also the **church** that meets at their house. Greet my dear
   16: 16 another with a holy kiss. All the **churches** of Christ send greetings.
   16: 23 Gaius, whose hospitality I and the whole **church** here enjoy,
1Co 1: 2 *To* the **church** of God in Corinth, to those sanctified in Christ
   4: 17 which agrees with what I teach everywhere in every **church**.
   6: 4 appoint as judges even men of little account in the **church**!
   7: 17 God has called him. This is the rule I lay down in all the **churches**.
  10: 32 anyone to stumble, whether Jews, Greeks or the **church** of God—
  11: 16 we have no other practice—nor do the **churches** of God.
  11: 18 In the first place, I hear that when you come together as a **church**,
  11: 22 Or do you despise the **church** of God and humiliate those who
  12: 28 And in the **church** God has appointed first of all apostles,
  14: 4 a tongue edifies himself, but he who prophesies edifies the **church**.
  14: 5 in tongues, unless he interprets, so that the **church** may be edified.
  14: 12 to have spiritual gifts, try to excel in gifts that build up the **church**.
  14: 19 But in the **church** I would rather speak five intelligible words to
  14: 23 So if the whole **church** comes together and everyone speaks in
  14: 28 the speaker should keep quiet in the **church** and speak to himself
  14: 33 of disorder but of peace. As in all the **congregations** of the saints,
  14: 34 women should remain silent in the **churches**. They are not allowed
  14: 35 at home; for it is disgraceful for a woman to speak in the **church**.
  15: 9 to be called an apostle, because I persecuted the **church** of God.
  16: 1 for God's people: Do what I told the Galatian **churches** to do.
  16: 19 The **churches** in the province of Asia send you greetings.
  16: 19 in the Lord, and so does the **church** that meets at their house.
2Co 1: 1 and Timothy our brother, *To* the **church** of God in Corinth,

8: 1 about the grace that God has given the Macedonian **churches**.
8:18 who is praised by all the **churches** for his service to the gospel.
8:19 he was chosen by the **churches** to accompany us as we carry the
8:23 they are representatives *of* the **churches** and an honor to Christ.
8:24 and the reason for our pride in you, so that the **churches** can see it.
11: 8 I robbed other **churches** by receiving support from them so as to
11:28 I face daily the pressure of my concern *for* all the **churches**.
12:13 How were you inferior to the other **churches**, except that I was
Gal 1: 2 and all the brothers with me, *To* the **churches** in Galatia,
1:13 how intensely I persecuted the **church** of God and tried to destroy
1:22 I was personally unknown *to* the **churches** of Judea that are in
Eph 1:22 and appointed him to be head over everything *for* the **church**,
3:10 His intent was that now, through the **church**, the manifold wisdom
3:21 to him be glory in the **church** and in Christ Jesus throughout all
5:23 husband is the head of the wife as Christ is the head *of* the **church**,
5:24 Now as the **church** submits to Christ, so also wives should submit
5:25 just as Christ loved the **church** and gave himself up for her
5:27 and to present her to himself as a radiant **church**, without stain
5:29 but he feeds and cares for it, just as Christ does the **church**—
5:32 a profound mystery—but I am talking about Christ and the **church**.
Php 3: 6 as for zeal, persecuting the **church**; as for legalistic righteousness,
4:15 not one **church** shared with me in the matter of giving
Col 1:18 And he is the head of the body, the **church**; he is the beginning
1:24 Christ's afflictions, for the sake of his body, which is the **church**.
4:15 brothers at Laodicea, and to Nympha and the **church** in her house.
4:16 see that it is also read in the **church** of the Laodiceans and that you
1Th 1: 1 *To* the **church** of the Thessalonians in God the Father and the Lord
2:14 For you, brothers, became imitators of God's **churches** in Judea,
2Th 1: 1 *To* the **church** of the Thessalonians in God our Father
1: 4 among God's **churches** we boast about your perseverance
1Ti 3: 5 manage his own family, how can he take care of God's **church**?)
3:15 which is the **church** of the living God, the pillar and foundation of
5:16 should help them and not let the **church** be burdened with them,
Phm 1: 2 our fellow soldier and *to* the **church** that meets in your home:
Heb 2:12 in the presence *of* the **congregation** I will sing your praises."
12:23 *to* the **church** of the firstborn, whose names are written in heaven.
Jas 5:14 He should call the elders *of* the **church** to pray over him and anoint
3Jn 1: 6 They have told the **church** about your love. You will do well to
1: 9 I wrote *to* the **church**, but Diotrephes, who loves to be first,
1:10 stops those who want to do so and puts them out of the **church**.
Rev 1: 4 John, *To* the seven **churches** in the province of Asia: Grace
1:11 "Write on a scroll what you see and send it *to* the seven **churches**:
1:20 The seven stars are the angels *of* the seven **churches**, and the seven
1:20 seven churches, and the seven lampstands are the seven **churches**.
2: 1 "To the angel *of* the **church** in Ephesus write: These are the words
2: 7 who has an ear, let him hear what the Spirit says *to* the **churches**.
2: 8 "To the angel *of* the **church** in Smyrna write: These are the words
2:11 who has an ear, let him hear what the Spirit says *to* the **churches**.
2:12 "To the angel *of* the **church** in Pergamum write: These are the
2:17 who has an ear, let him hear what the Spirit says *to* the **churches**.
2:18 "To the angel *of* the **church** in Thyatira write: These are the words
2:23 Then all the **churches** will know that I am he who searches hearts
2:29 who has an ear, let him hear what the Spirit says *to* the **churches**.
3: 1 "To the angel *of* the **church** in Sardis write: These are the words of
3: 6 who has an ear, let him hear what the Spirit says *to* the **churches**.
3: 7 "To the angel *of* the **church** in Philadelphia write: These are the
3:13 who has an ear, let him hear what the Spirit says *to* the **churches**.
3:14 "To the angel *of* the **church** in Laodicea write: These are the words
3:22 who has an ear, let him hear what the Spirit says *to* the **churches**."
22:16 have sent my angel to give you this testimony for the **churches**.

1712 ἐκκλίνω, ekklinō [3] [√ 1666 + 3111]

away [1], turn [1], turned away [1]

Ro   3:12 All *have* **turned away**, they have together become worthless;
16:17 contrary to the teaching you have learned. *Keep* **away** from them.
1Pe   3:11 *He must* **turn** from evil and do good; he must seek peace

1713 ἐκκολυμβάω, ekkolymbaō [1] [√ 1666 + 3147]

swimming away [1]

Ac   27:42 to kill the prisoners to prevent any of them *from* **swimming away**

1714 ἐκκομίζω, ekkomizō [1] [√ 1666 + 3180]

carried out [1]

Lk   7:12 approached the town gate, a dead person *was being* **carried out**—

1715 ἐκκοπή, ekkopē   Not used in UBS/NIV [√ 1666 + 3164]

1716 ἐκκόπτω, ekkoptō [10] [√ 1666 + 3164]

cut down [5], cut off [3], cut from under [1], cut out of [*RP1666*] [1]

Mt   3:10 and every tree that does not produce good fruit *will be* **cut down**
5:30 if your right hand causes you to sin, **cut** it **off** and throw it away.
7:19 Every tree that does not bear good fruit *is* **cut down** and thrown
18: 8 or your foot causes you to sin, **cut** it **off** and throw it away.
Lk   3: 9 and every tree that does not produce good fruit *will be* **cut down**
13: 7 look for fruit on this fig tree and haven't found any. **Cut** it **down**!
13: 9 If it bears fruit next year, fine! If not, then **cut** it **down**.' "
Ro 11:22 you continue in his kindness. Otherwise, you also *will be* **cut off**.
11:24 if you *were* **cut** [*RP1666*] **out of** an olive tree that is wild by
2Co 11:12 **cut** the ground **from under** those who want an opportunity to be

1717 ἐκκρεμάννυμι, ekkremannymi [1] [√ 1666 + 3203]

hung on [1]

Lk   19:48 find any way to do it, because all the people **hung on** his words.

1718 ἐκλαλέω, eklaleō [1] [√ 1666 + 3281]

tell [1]

Ac   23:22 him, "Don't **tell** anyone that you have reported this to me."

1719 ἐκλάμπω, eklampō [1] [√ 1666 + 3290]

shine [1]

Mt   13:43 Then the righteous *will* **shine** like the sun in the kingdom of their

1720 ἐκλανθάνομαι, eklanthanomai [1] [√ 1666 + 3291]

forgotten [1]

Heb 12: 5 And *you have* **forgotten** that word of encouragement that

1721 ἐκλέγομαι, eklegomai [22] [√ 1666 + 3306]

chosen [9], chose [8], choose [3], made a choice [1], picked [1]

Mk 13:20 the sake of the elect, whom *he has* **chosen**, he has shortened them.
Lk   6:13 he called his disciples to him and **chose** twelve of them,
9:35 from the cloud, saying, "This is my Son, whom *I have* **chosen**;
10:42 Mary *has* **chosen** what is better, and it will not be taken away from
14: 7 When he noticed how the guests **picked** the places of honor at the
Jn   6:70 Then Jesus replied, "*Have* I not **chosen** you, the Twelve?
13:18 "I am not referring to all of you; I know those *I have* **chosen**.
15:16 You *did* not **choose** me, but I chose you and appointed you to go
15:16 but I **chose** you and appointed you to go and bear fruit—
15:19 do not belong to the world, but I *have* **chosen** you out of the world.
Ac   1: 2 instructions through the Holy Spirit to the apostles *he had* **chosen**.
1:24 everyone's heart. Show us which of these two *you have* **chosen**
6: 5 *They* **chose** Stephen, a man full of faith and of the Holy Spirit;
13:17 The God of the people of Israel **chose** our fathers; he made the
15: 7 you know that some time ago God **made a choice** among you that
15:22 decided *to* **choose** some of their own men and send them to
15:25 So we all agreed *to* **choose** some men and send them to you with
1Co 1:27 But God **chose** the foolish things of the world to shame the wise;
1:27 God **chose** the weak things of the world to shame the strong.
1:28 He **chose** the lowly things of this world and the despised things—
Eph 1: 4 For *he* **chose** us in him before the creation of the world to be holy
Jas 2: 5 *Has* not God **chosen** those who are poor in the eyes of the world to

1722 ἐκλείπω, ekleipō [4] [√ 1666 + 3309]

end [1], fail [1], gone [1], stopped shining [1]

Lk 16: 9 so that when *it is* **gone,** you will be welcomed into eternal
    22:32 But I have prayed for you, Simon, that your faith *may* not **fail.**
    23:45 for the sun **stopped shining.** And the curtain of the temple was
Heb 1:12 But you remain the same, and your years *will* never **end.**"

1723 ἐκλεκτός, eklektos [22] [√ 1666 + 3306]

chosen [12], elect [9], God's elect [1]

Mt 22:14 "For many are invited, but few are **chosen.**"
    24:22 but for the sake of the **elect** those days will be shortened.
    24:24 and perform great signs and miracles to deceive even the **elect**—
    24:31 and they will gather his **elect** from the four winds, from one end of
Mk 13:20 But for the sake of the **elect,** whom he has chosen, he has
    13:22 will appear and perform signs and miracles to deceive the **elect**—
    13:27 he will send his angels and gather his **elect** from the four winds,
Lk 18: 7 And will not God bring about justice *for* his **chosen** ones,
    23:35 let him save himself if he is the Christ of God, the **Chosen** *One.*"
Ro   8:33 Who will bring any charge against those whom God has **chosen**?
    16:13 Greet Rufus, **chosen** in the Lord, and his mother, who has been a
Col 3:12 Therefore, as God's **chosen** *people,* holy and dearly loved,
1Ti 5:21 in the sight of God and Christ Jesus and the **elect** angels,
2Ti 2:10 Therefore I endure everything for the sake of the **elect,** that they
Tit 1: 1 of God and an apostle of Jesus Christ for the faith of God's **elect**
1Pe 1: 1 an apostle of Jesus Christ, *To* God's **elect,** strangers in the world,
     2: 4 rejected by men but **chosen** by God and precious to him—
     2: 6 "See, I lay a stone in Zion, a **chosen** and precious cornerstone,
     2: 9 But you are a **chosen** people, a royal priesthood, a holy nation,
2Jn 1: 1 The elder, *To* the **chosen** lady and her children, whom I love in the
     1:13 The children *of* your **chosen** sister send their greetings.
Rev 17:14 and with him will be his called, **chosen** and faithful followers."

1724 ἐκλογή, eklogē [7] [√ 1666 + 3306]

chosen [3], election [3], elect [1]

Ac   9:15 This man is my **chosen** instrument to carry my name before the
Ro   9:11 or bad—in order that God's purpose in **election** might stand:
    11: 5 So too, at the present time there is a remnant **chosen** by grace.
    11: 7 What Israel sought so earnestly it did not obtain, but the **elect** did.
    11:28 but as far as **election** is concerned, they are loved on account of the
1Th 1: 4 For we know, brothers loved by God, that he has **chosen** you,
2Pe 1:10 be all the more eager to make your calling and **election** sure.

1725 ἐκλύω, eklyō [5] [√ 1666 + 3395]

collapse [2], give up [1], lose [1], lose heart [1]

Mt 15:32 want to send them away hungry, or *they may* **collapse** on the way."
Mk   8: 3 If I send them home hungry, *they will* **collapse** on the way,
Gal 6: 9 for at the proper time we will reap a harvest *if we do* not **give up.**
Heb 12: 3 from sinful men, so that you will not grow weary and **lose** heart.
    12: 5 the Lord's discipline, and *do* not **lose heart** when he rebukes you,

1726 ἐκμάσσω, ekmassō [5] [√ 1666 + 3463]

wiped [4], drying [1]

Lk   7:38 Then *she* **wiped** them with her hair, kissed them and poured
     7:44 but she wet my feet with her tears and **wiped** them with her hair.
Jn 11: 2 who poured perfume on the Lord and **wiped** his feet with her hair.
    12: 3 she poured it on Jesus' feet and **wiped** his feet with her hair.
    13: 5 **drying** them with the towel that was wrapped around him.

1727 ἐκμυκτηρίζω, ekmyktērizō [2] [√ 1666 + 3682]

sneered at [1], sneering at [1]

Lk 16:14 who loved money, heard all this and *were* **sneering at** Jesus.
    23:35 The people stood watching, and the rulers even **sneered at** him.

1728 ἐκνεύω, ekneuō [1] [√ 1666 + 3748]

slipped away [1]

Jn   5:13 for Jesus *had* **slipped away** into the crowd that was there.

1729 ἐκνήφω, eknēphō [1] [√ 1666 + 3768]

come back to senses [1]

1Co 15:34 **Come back to** *your* **senses** as you ought, and stop sinning;

1730 ἑκούσιος, hekousios [1] [√ 1776]

spontaneous [+2848] [1]

Phm 1:14 so that any favor you do will be **spontaneous** [+2848] and not

1731 ἑκουσίως, hekousiōs [2] [√ 1776]

deliberately [1], willing [1]

Heb 10:26 If we **deliberately** keep on sinning after we have received the
1Pe 5: 2 not because you must, but *because* you are **willing,** as God wants

1732 ἔκπαλαι, ekpalai [2] [√ 1666 + 4093]

long [1], long ago [1]

2Pe 2: 3 Their condemnation has **long** been hanging over them, and their
     3: 5 But they deliberately forget that **long ago** by God's word the

1733 ἐκπειράζω, ekpeirazō [4] [√ 1666 + 4278]

put to the test [2], test [2]

Mt   4: 7 "It is also written: '*Do* not **put** the Lord your God **to the test.**' "
Lk   4:12 "It says: '*Do* not **put** the Lord your God **to the test.**' "
    10:25 On one occasion an expert in the law stood up *to* **test** Jesus.
1Co 10: 9 *We should* not **test** the Lord, as some of them did—and were

1734 ἐκπέμπω, ekpempō [2] [√ 1666 + 4287]

sent away [1], sent on way [1]

Ac 13: 4 The two of them, **sent on** *their* **way** by the Holy Spirit, went down
    17:10 as it was night, the brothers **sent** Paul and Silas **away** to Berea.

1735 ἐκπερισσῶς, ekperissōs [1] [√ 1666 + 4356]

emphatically [1]

Mk 14:31 But Peter insisted **emphatically,** "Even if I have to die with you,

1736 ἐκπετάννυμι, ekpetannymi [1] [√ 1666 + 4375]

held out [1]

Ro 10:21 "All day long *I have* **held out** my hands to a disobedient

1737 ἐκπηδάω, ekpēdaō [1] [√ 403; cf. 1666]

rushed out [1]

Ac 14:14 *they* tore their clothes and **rushed out** into the crowd, shouting:

1738 ἐκπίπτω, ekpiptō [10] [√ 1666 + 4406]

run aground [2], dashed [1], failed [1], fall [1], fall away [1], fall from [1], fallen away from [1], falls [1], fell off [RP1666] [1]

Ac 12: 7 get up!" he said, and the chains **fell** [RP1666] **off** Peter's wrists.
    27:17 Fearing that *they would* **run aground** on the sandbars of Syrtis,
    27:26 Nevertheless, we must **run aground** on some island."
    27:29 Fearing that *we would be* **dashed** against the rocks, they dropped
    27:32 the soldiers cut the ropes that held the lifeboat and let it **fall away.**
Ro   9: 6 It is not as though God's word *had* **failed.** For not all who are
Gal 5: 4 been alienated from Christ; *you have* **fallen away from** grace.
Jas 1:11 and withers the plant; its blossom **falls** and its beauty is destroyed.
1Pe 1:24 like the flowers of the field; the grass withers and the flowers **fall,**
2Pe 3:17 *may* not be carried away by the error of lawless men and **fall from**

1739 ἐκπλέω, *ekpleō* [3] [√ *1666 + 4434*]

sailed [3]

Ac 15:39 they parted company. Barnabas took Mark and **sailed** for Cyprus,
18:18 Then *he* left the brothers and **sailed** for Syria, accompanied by
20: 6 But we **sailed** from Philippi after the Feast of Unleavened Bread,

1740 ἐκπληρόω, *ekplēroō* [1] [√ *1666 + 4444*]

fulfilled [1]

Ac 13:33 he *has* **fulfilled** for us, their children, by raising up Jesus. As it is

1741 ἐκπλήρωσις, *ekplērōsis* [1] [√ *1666 + 4444*]

end [1]

Ac 21:26 to give notice of the date when the days of purification *would* **end**

1742 ἐκπλήσσω, *ekplēssō* [13] [√ *1666 + 4448*]

amazed [9], astonished [3], overwhelmed with amazement
[+*5669*] [1]

Mt 7:28 saying these things, the crowds *were* **amazed** at his teaching,
13:54 teaching the people in their synagogue, and they *were* **amazed**.
19:25 *they were* greatly **astonished** and asked, "Who then can be saved?"
22:33 When the crowds heard this, *they were* **astonished** at his teaching.
Mk 1:22 The *people were* **amazed** at his teaching, because he taught them
6: 2 to teach in the synagogue, and many who heard him *were* **amazed**.
7:37 *People were* **overwhelmed** [+*5669*] **with amazement**. "He has
10:26 The disciples *were* even more **amazed**, and said to each other,
11:18 feared him, because the whole crowd *was* **amazed** at his teaching.
Lk 2:48 When his parents saw his way, *they were* **astonished**. His mother said
4:32 *They were* **amazed** at his teaching, because his message had
9:43 And *they were* all **amazed** at the greatness of God. While
Ac 13:12 he believed, *for he was* **amazed** at the teaching about the Lord.

1743 ἐκπνέω, *ekpneō* [3] [√ *1666 + 4463*]

breathed last [2], died [1]

Mk 15:37 With a loud cry, Jesus **breathed** *his* **last**.
15:39 there in front of Jesus, heard his cry and saw how *he* **died**, he said,
Lk 23:46 I commit my spirit." When he had said this, *he* **breathed** *his* **last**.

1744 ἐκπορεύομαι, *ekporeuomai* [33]
[√ *1666 + 4513*]

comes out of [*RP1666*] [3], come out of [*RP1666*] [2], out of came
[*RP1666*] [2], came from [*RP1666*] [1], came out of [*RP1666*] [1],
come [1], come out [1], comes [1], comes from [*RP1666*] [1],
coming out [1], flowing from [*RP1666*] [1], from came [*RP1666*]
[1], go out [1], goes out [1], going [1], leave [1], leaving [*RP1666*]
[1], leaving [*RP608*] [1], leaving [1], left [1], moved about freely
[+*1660+2779*] [1], out of come [*RP1666*] [1], out of comes
[*RP1666*] [1], out of his body [+*909+1650+3836*] [1], spread [1],
started [1], went [1], went out [1], went out from [1]

Mt 3: 5 *People* **went out** to him **from** Jerusalem and all Judea
4: 4 but on every word that **comes** from the mouth of God.' "
15:11 but what **comes** [*RP1666*] **out of** his mouth, that is what makes
15:18 But the things that **come** [*RP1666*] **out of** the mouth come from
20:29 As Jesus and his disciples *were* **leaving** [*RP608*] Jericho,
Mk 1: 5 and all the people of Jerusalem **went out** to him.
6:11 or listen to you, shake the dust off your feet *when you* **leave**,
7:15 it is what **comes** [*RP1666*] **out of** a man that makes him
7:19 into his stomach, and then out [+*909+1650+3836*] **of his body**."
7:20 "What **comes** [*RP1666*] **out of** a man is what makes him 'unclean.'
7:21 For from within, **out of** men's hearts, **come** [*RP1666*] evil
7:23 All these evils **come** from inside and make a man 'unclean.' "
10:17 As Jesus **started** on his way, a man ran up to him and fell on his
10:46 *were* **leaving** the city, a blind man, Bartimaeus (that is, the Son of
11:19 When evening came, *they* **went** out of the city.
13: 1 *As he was* **leaving** [*RP1666*] the temple, one of his disciples said
Lk 3: 7 John said *to* the crowds **coming out** to be baptized by him,
4:22 and were amazed at the gracious words that **came** [*RP1666*] **from**

4:37 And the news about him **spread** throughout the surrounding area.
Jn 5:29 and **come out**—those who have done good will rise to live,
15:26 the Spirit of truth who **goes out** from the Father, he will testify
Ac 9:28 with them and **moved about freely** [+*1660+2779*] in Jerusalem,
19:12 and their illnesses were cured and the evil spirits **left** them.
25: 4 "Paul is being held at Caesarea, and I myself am **going** there soon.
Eph 4:29 *Do not let* any unwholesome talk **come** [*RP1666*] **out of** your
Rev 1:16 and **out of** his mouth **came** [*RP1666*] a sharp double-edged sword.
4: 5 **From** the throne **came** [*RP1666*] flashes of lightning, rumblings
9:17 and **out of** their mouths **came** [*RP1666*] fire, smoke and sulfur.
9:18 smoke and sulfur that **came** [*RP1666*] **out of** their mouths.
11: 5 fire **comes** [*RP1666*] **from** their mouths and devours their
16:14 miraculous signs, and they **go out** to the kings of the whole world,
19:15 **Out of** his mouth **comes** [*RP1666*] a sharp sword with which to
22: 1 **flowing** [*RP1666*] **from** the throne of God and of the Lamb

1745 ἐκπορνεύω, *ekporneuō* [1] [√ *1666 + 4520*]

gave up to sexual immorality [1]

Jude 1: 7 the surrounding towns **gave** themselves **up to sexual immorality**

1746 ἐκπτύω, *ekptyō* [1] [√ *1666 + 4772*]

treat with scorn [1]

Gal 4:14 was a trial to you, *you did* not **treat** me **with** contempt or **scorn**.

1747 ἐκπυρόω, *ekpyroō* Not used in UBS/NIV
[√ *1666 + 4786*]

1748 ἐκριζόω, *ekrizoō* [4] [√ *1666 + 4844*]

uprooted [2], pulled up by the roots [1], root up [1]

Mt 13:29 you are pulling the weeds, *you may* **root up** the wheat with them.
15:13 heavenly Father has not planted *will be* **pulled up by the roots**.
Lk 17: 6 '*Be* **uprooted** and planted in the sea,' and it will obey you.
Jude 1:12 the wind; autumn trees, without fruit and **uprooted**—twice dead.

1749 ἔκστασις, *ekstasis* [7] [√ *1666 + 2705*]

trance [2], amazed [+*3284*] [1], amazement [1], astonished
[+*2014*] [1], bewildered [1], fell into trance [+*1181+2093*] [1]

Mk 5:42 years old). At this *they were* completely **astonished** [+*2014*].
16: 8 Trembling and **bewildered**, the women went out and fled from the
Lk 5:26 Everyone *was* **amazed** [+*3284*] and gave praise to God. They
Ac 3:10 filled with wonder and **amazement** at what had happened to him.
10:10 the meal was being prepared, he **fell into** a **trance** [+*1181+2093*].
11: 5 "I was in the city of Joppa praying, and in a **trance** I saw a vision.
22:17 to Jerusalem and was praying at the temple, I **fell into** a **trance**

1750 ἐκστρέφω, *ekstrephō* [1] [√ *1666 + 5138*]

warped [1]

Tit 3:11 You may be sure that such a man *is* **warped** and sinful; he is

1751 ἐκσῴζω, *eksōzō* Not used in UBS/NIV
[√ *1666 + 5392*]

1752 ἐκταράσσω, *ektarassō* [1] [√ *1666 + 5429*]

throwing into an uproar [1]

Ac 16:20 "These men are Jews, and *are* **throwing** our city **into an uproar**

1753 ἐκτείνω, *ekteinō* [16] [→ *701, 867, 1755, 1756,
1757, 1759, 2085, 2364, 4189, 4727, 4742, 5657, 5936; cf.
1666*]

ἐκτείνω χεῖρα (stretch out a hand) [14] Mt 8:3; 12:13,49;
14:31; 26:51; Mk 1:41; 3:5,5; Lk 5:13; 6:10; 22:53; Jn 21:18; Ac
4:30; 26:1

stretch out [5], reached out [4], stretched out [2], lay [1], lower [1], motioned with [1], pointing [*+3836+5931*] [1], reached for [*+3836+5931*] [1]

Mt 8: 3 Jesus **reached out** his hand and touched the man. "I am willing,"
12:13 Then he said to the man, "**Stretch out** your hand." So he stretched
12:13 So he **stretched** it **out** and it was completely restored, just as
12:49 **Pointing** [*+3836+5931*] to his disciples, he said, "Here are my
14:31 Immediately Jesus **reached out** his hand and caught him. "You of
26:51 one of Jesus' companions **reached** [*+3836+5931*] **for** his sword,
Mk 1:41 Jesus **reached out** his hand and touched the man.
3: 5 at their stubborn hearts, said to the man, "**Stretch out** your hand."
3: 5 *He* **stretched** it **out**, and his hand was completely restored.
Lk 5:13 Jesus **reached out** his hand and touched the man. "I am willing,"
6:10 at them all, and then said to the man, "**Stretch out** your hand."
22:53 with you in the temple courts, and *you did* not **lay** a hand on me.
Jn 21:18 but when you are old *you will* **stretch out** your hands,
Ac 4:30 **Stretch out** your hand to heal and perform miraculous signs
26: 1 So Paul **motioned with** his hand and began his defense:
27:30 pretending they were going to **lower** some anchors from the bow.

1754 ἐκτελέω, *ekteleō* [2] [√ *1666 + 5465*]

finish [2]

Lk 14:29 For if he lays the foundation and is not able *to* **finish** it,
14:30 saying, 'This fellow began to build and was not able *to* **finish**.'

1755 ἐκτένεια, *ekteneia* [1] [√ *1753*]

earnestly [*+1877*] [1]

Ac 26: 7 are hoping to see fulfilled as they **earnestly** [*+1877*] serve God day

1756 ἐκτενής, *ektenēs* [1] [√ *1753*]

deeply [1]

1Pe 4: 8 Above all, love each other **deeply**, because love covers over a

1757 ἐκτενῶς, *ektenōs* [3] [√ *1753*]

deeply [1], earnestly [1], more earnestly [1]

Lk 22:44 And being in anguish, he prayed **more earnestly**, and his sweat
Ac 12: 5 in prison, but the church was **earnestly** praying to God for him.
1Pe 1:22 love for your brothers, love one another **deeply**, from the heart.

1758 ἐκτίθημι, *ektithēmi* [4] [√ *1666 + 5502*]

explained [3], placed outside [1]

Ac 7:21 When he *was* **placed outside**, Pharaoh's daughter took him
11: 4 and **explained** everything to them precisely as it had happened:
18:26 their home and **explained** to him the way of God more adequately.
28:23 From morning till evening he **explained** and declared to them the

1759 ἐκτινάσσω, *ektinassō* [4] [√ *1753*]

shake off [2], shook from [1], shook out [1]

Mt 10:14 **shake** the dust **off** your feet when you leave that home or town.
Mk 6:11 or listen to you, **shake** the dust **off** your feet when you leave,
Ac 13:51 So they **shook** the dust **from** their feet *in protest* against them
18: 6 he **shook out** his clothes *in protest* and said to them,

1760 ἐκτός, *ektos* [8] [√ *1666*]

outside [2], unless [*+1623+3590*] [2], beyond [1], not include [1], otherwise [*+1623+3590*] [1], out of [1]

Mt 23:26 inside of the cup and dish, and then the **outside** also will be clean.
Ac 26:22 I am saying nothing **beyond** what the prophets and Moses said
1Co 6:18 All other sins a man commits are **outside** his body, but he who sins
14: 5 **unless** [*+1623+3590*] he interprets, so that the church may be
15: 2 **Otherwise** [*+1623+3590*], you have believed in vain.
15:27 it is clear that this does **not include** God himself, who put
2Co 12: 2 Whether it was in the body or **out of** the body I do not know—
1Ti 5:19 against an elder **unless** [*+1623+3590*] it is brought by two

1761 ἕκτος, *hektos* [14] [√ *1971*]

sixth [13], noon [*+6052*] [1]

Mt 20: 5 "He went out again about the **sixth** hour and the ninth hour
27:45 From the **sixth** hour until the ninth hour darkness came over all the
Mk 15:33 At the **sixth** hour darkness came over the whole land until the ninth
Lk 1:26 In the **sixth** month, God sent the angel Gabriel to Nazareth.
1:36 old age, and she who was said to be barren is in her **sixth** month.
23:44 It was now about the **sixth** hour, and darkness came over the whole
Jn 4: 6 from the journey, sat down by the well. It was about the **sixth** hour.
19:14 was the day of Preparation of Passover Week, about the **sixth** hour.
Ac 10: 9 About **noon** [*+6052*] the following day as they were on their
Rev 6:12 I watched as he opened the **sixth** seal. There was a great
9:13 The **sixth** angel sounded his trumpet, and I heard a voice coming
9:14 It said *to* the **sixth** angel who had the trumpet, "Release the four
16:12 The **sixth** angel poured out his bowl on the great river Euphrates,
21:20 the fifth sardonyx, the **sixth** carnelian, the seventh chrysolite,

1762 ἐκτρέπω, *ektrepō* [5] [√ *1666 + 5572*]

disabled [1], turn aside [1], turn away from [1], turned away [1], wandered away from [1]

1Ti 1: 6 Some *have* **wandered away from** these and turned to meaningless
5:15 Some *have* in fact already **turned away** to follow Satan.
6:20 **Turn away from** godless chatter and the opposing ideas of what is
2Ti 4: 4 will turn their ears away from the truth and **turn aside** to myths.
Heb 12:13 your feet," so that the lame *may* not *be* **disabled**, but rather healed.

1763 ἐκτρέφω, *ektrephō* [2] [√ *1666 + 5555*]

bring up [1], feeds [1]

Eph 5:29 but he **feeds** and cares for it, just as Christ does the church—
6: 4 **bring** them **up** in the training and instruction of the Lord.

1764 ἔκτρομος, *ektromos*   Not used in UBS/NIV [√ *1666 + 5554*]

1765 ἔκτρωμα, *ektrōma* [1] [√ *1666 + 5546*]

abnormally born [1]

1Co 15: 8 and last of all he appeared to me also, as to one **abnormally born**.

1766 ἐκφέρω, *ekpherō* [8] [√ *1666 + 5770*]

carried out [2], bring [1], brought [1], carry out [1], led [1], produces [1], take out of [1]

Mk 8:23 He took the blind man by the hand and **led** him outside the village.
Lk 15:22 said to his servants, 'Quick! **Bring** the best robe and put it on him.
Ac 5: 6 wrapped up his body, and **carried** him **out** and buried him.
5: 9 your husband are at the door, and *they will* **carry** you **out** also."
5:10 her dead, **carried** her **out** and buried her beside her husband.
5:15 *people* **brought** the sick into the streets and laid them on beds
1Ti 6: 7 brought nothing into the world, and we can **take** nothing **out of** it.
Heb 6: 8 But land that **produces** thorns and thistles is worthless and is in

1767 ἐκφεύγω, *ekpheugō* [8] [√ *1666 + 5771*]

escape [5], escaped [1], ran out of [*RP1666*] [1], slipped through [1]

Lk 21:36 and pray that you may be able *to* **escape** all that is about to happen,
Ac 16:27 to kill himself because he thought the prisoners *had* **escaped**.
19:16 He gave them such a beating that *they* **ran** [*RP1666*] **out of** the
Ro 2: 3 do the same things, do you think you *will* **escape** God's judgment?
2Co 11:33 a basket from a window in the wall and **slipped through** his hands.
1Th 5: 3 as labor pains on a pregnant woman, and *they will* not **escape**.
Heb 2: 3 how *shall* we **escape** if we ignore such a great salvation?
12:25 If they *did* not **escape** when they refused him who warned them on

1768 ἐκφοβέω, *ekphobeō* [1] [√ *1666 + 5832*]

frighten [1]

2Co 10: 9 I do not want to seem to be trying to **frighten** you with my letters.

1769 ἔκφοβος, *ekphobos* [2] [√ *1666 + 5832*]

so frightened [1], with fear [1]

Mk   9: 6 (He did not know what to say, they were **so frightened**.)
Heb 12:21 sight was so terrifying that Moses said, "I am trembling **with fear**."

1770 ἐκφύω, *ekphyō* [2] [√ *1666 + 5886*]

come out [2]

Mt 24:32 As soon as its twigs get tender and its leaves **come out**, you know
Mk 13:28 As soon as its twigs get tender and its leaves **come out**, you know

1771 ἐκφωνέω, *ekphōneō* Not used in UBS/NIV
[√ *1666 + 5889*]

1772 ἐκχέω, *ekcheō* [22] [→ *136, 431, 1773, 2219, 2972, 4717, 5177, 5179, 5180, 5658, 5954, 5959, 5967; cf. 1666*]

poured out [11], pour out [3], shed [3], run out [2], rushed [1], scattered [1], spilled out [1]

Mt   9:17 will burst, the wine *will* **run out** and the wineskins will be ruined.
Lk   5:37 the skins, the wine *will* **run out** and the wineskins will be ruined.
      11:50 the prophets that *has been* **shed** since the beginning of the world,
Jn   2:15 he **scattered** the coins of the money changers and overturned their
Ac   1:18 fell headlong, his body burst open and all his intestines **spilled out**.
       2:17 " 'In the last days, God says, *I will* **pour out** my Spirit on all
       2:18 both men and women, *I will* **pour out** my Spirit in those days,
       2:33 Holy Spirit and *has* **poured out** what you now see and hear.
      10:45 gift of the Holy Spirit *had been* **poured out** even on the Gentiles.
Ro   3:15 "Their feet are swift to **shed** blood;
       5: 5 because God *has* **poured out** his love into our hearts by the Holy
Tit   3: 6 whom *he* **poured out** on us generously through Jesus Christ our
Jude   1:11 the way of Cain; *they have* **rushed** for profit into Balaam's error;
Rev   16: 1 "Go, **pour out** the seven bowls of God's wrath on the earth."
      16: 2 The first angel went and **poured out** his bowl on the land,
      16: 3 The second angel **poured out** his bowl on the sea, and it turned
      16: 4 The third angel **poured out** his bowl on the rivers and springs of
      16: 6 for *they have* **shed** the blood of your saints and prophets,
      16: 8 The fourth angel **poured out** his bowl on the sun, and the sun was
      16:10 The fifth angel **poured out** his bowl on the throne of the beast,
      16:12 The sixth angel **poured out** his bowl on the great river Euphrates,
      16:17 The seventh angel **poured out** his bowl into the air, and out of the

1773 ἐκχύννομαι, *ekchynnomai* [5] [√ *1772*]

poured out [3], shed [2]

Mt 23:35 so upon you will come all the righteous blood *that has been* **shed**
   26:28 which *is* **poured out** for many for the forgiveness of sins.
Mk 14:24 of the covenant, which *is* **poured out** for many," he said to them.
Lk 22:20 cup is the new covenant in my blood, which *is* **poured out** for you.
Ac 22:20 And when the blood of your martyr Stephen *was* **shed**, I stood

1774 ἐκχωρέω, *ekchōreō* [1] [√ *1666 + 6003*]

get out [1]

Lk 21:21 *let* those in the city **get out**, and let those in the country not enter

1775 ἐκψύχω, *ekpsychō* [3] [√ *1666 + 6038*]

died [3]

Ac   5: 5 When Ananias heard this, *he* fell down and **died**. And great fear
     5:10 At that moment she fell down at his feet and **died**. Then the young
    12:23 of the Lord struck him down, and he was eaten by worms and **died**.

1776 ἑκών, *hekōn* [2] [→ *220, 1730, 1731*]

by its own choice [1], voluntarily [1]

Ro   8:20 not **by its own choice**, but by the will of the one who subjected it,
1Co 9:17 If I preach **voluntarily**, I have a reward; if not voluntarily,

1777 ἐλαία, *elaia* [13] [→ *66, 1778, 1779, 2814*]

olives [10], olive [1], olive tree [1], olive trees [1]

Mt 21: 1 and came to Bethphage on the Mount *of* **Olives**,
   24: 3 As Jesus was sitting on the Mount *of* **Olives**, the disciples came to
   26:30 When they had sung a hymn, they went out to the Mount *of* **Olives**.
Mk 11: 1 and came to Bethphage and Bethany at the Mount *of* **Olives**,
   13: 3 As Jesus was sitting on the Mount *of* **Olives** opposite the temple,
   14:26 When they had sung a hymn, they went out to the Mount *of* **Olives**.
Lk 19:37 near the place where the road goes down the Mount *of* **Olives**,
   22:39 Jesus went out as usual to the Mount *of* **Olives**, and his disciples
Jn 8: 1 But Jesus went to the Mount *of* **Olives**.
Ro 11:17 the others and now share in the nourishing sap *from* the **olive** root,
   11:24 the natural branches, be grafted into their own **olive tree**!
Jas 3:12 My brothers, can a fig tree bear **olives**, or a grapevine bear figs?
Rev 11: 4 These are the two **olive trees** and the two lampstands that stand

1778 ἔλαιον, *elaion* [11] [√ *1777*]

oil [9], olive oil [2]

Mt 25: 3 foolish ones took their lamps but did not take any **oil** with them.
   25: 4 The wise, however, took **oil** in jars along with their lamps.
   25: 8 The foolish ones said to the wise, 'Give us some of your **oil**;
Mk 6:13 and anointed many sick people *with* **oil** and healed them.
Lk   7:46 You did not put **oil** on my head, but she has poured perfume on my
   10:34 went to him and bandaged his wounds, pouring on **oil** and wine.
   16: 6 " 'Eight hundred gallons *of* **olive oil**,' he replied. "The manager told
Heb 1: 9 has set you above your companions by anointing you with the **oil**
Jas 5:14 to pray over him and anoint him *with* **oil** in the name of the Lord.
Rev 6: 6 barley for a day's wages, and do not damage the **oil** and the wine!"
   18:13 and frankincense, of wine and **olive oil**, of fine flour and wheat;

1779 ἐλαιών, *elaiōn* [3] [√ *1777*]

Mount of Olives [3]

Lk 19:29 and Bethany at the hill called the **Mount of Olives**,
   21:37 went out to spend the night on the hill called the **Mount of Olives**,
Ac 1:12 returned to Jerusalem from the hill called the **Mount of Olives**,

1780 Ἐλαμίτης, *Elamitēs* [1]

Elamites [1]

Ac 2: 9 Parthians, Medes and **Elamites**; residents of Mesopotamia,

1781 ἐλάσσων, *elassōn* [4] [→ *1782, 1783, 1784, 1788*]

cheaper [1], lesser [1], unless over [1], younger [1]

Jn 2:10 then the **cheaper** wine after the guests have had too much to drink;
Ro 9:12 him who calls—she was told, "The older will serve the **younger**."
1Ti 5: 9 No widow may be put on the list of widows **unless** she is **over**
Heb 7: 7 And without doubt the **lesser** *person* is blessed by the greater.

1782 ἐλαττονέω, *elattoneō* [1] [√ *1781*]

have too little [1]

2Co 8:15 have too much, and he who gathered little *did* not **have too little**."

1783 ἐλαττόω, *elattoō* [3] [√ *1781*]

made lower [2], less [1]

Jn   3:30 He must become greater; I must *become* **less**.
Heb 2: 7 *You* **made** him a little **lower** than the angels; you crowned him
     2: 9 But we see Jesus, *who was* **made** a little **lower** than the angels,

1784 ἐλάττων, *elattōn* Not used in UBS/NIV [√ *1781*]

1785 ἐλαύνω, elaunō [5] [→ 590, 5295]

driven [3], rowed [1], the oars[s] [1]

Mk 6:48 He saw the disciples straining at **the oars**[s], because the wind was
Lk 8:29 his chains and *had been* **driven** by the demon into solitary places.
Jn 6:19 When *they had* **rowed** three or three and a half miles, they saw
Jas 3: 4 Although they are so large and *are* **driven** by strong winds,
2Pe 2:17 These men are springs without water and mists **driven** by a storm.

1786 ἐλαφρία, elaphria [1] [√ 1787]

lightly [1]

2Co 1:17 When I planned this, did I do it **lightly**? Or do I make my plans in

1787 ἐλαφρός, elaphros [2] [→ 1786]

light [2]

Mt 11:30 For my yoke is easy and my burden is **light**."
2Co 4:17 For our **light** and momentary troubles are achieving for us an

1788 ἐλάχιστος, elachistos [14] [√ 1781]

least [7], very little [3], very small [2], care very little
[+1639+1650] [1], trivial [1]

Mt 2: 6 the land of Judah, are by no means **least** among the rulers of Judah;
    5:19 Anyone who breaks one *of* the **least** of these commandments
    5:19 and teaches others to do the same will be called **least** in the
    25:40 whatever you did for one *of* the **least** of these brothers of mine,
    25:45 you the truth, whatever you did not do for one *of* the **least** of these,
Lk 12:26 Since you cannot do this **very little** *thing*, why do you worry about
    16:10 "Whoever can be trusted with **very little** can also be trusted with
    16:10 and whoever is dishonest with **very little** will also be dishonest
    19:17 'Because you have been trustworthy in a **very small** *matter*,
1Co 4: 3 I **care very little** [+1639+1650] if I am judged by you or by any
    6: 2 to judge the world, are you not competent to judge **trivial** cases?
    15: 9 For I am the **least** of the apostles and do not even deserve to be
Eph 3: 8 Although I am *less than* the **least** of all God's people, this grace
Jas 3: 4 they are steered by a **very small** rudder wherever the pilot wants to

1789 Ἐλεάζαρ, Eleazar [2]

Eleazar [2]

Mt 1:15 Eliud the father of **Eleazar**, Eleazar the father of Matthan,
    1:15 Eliud the father of Eleazar, **Eleazar** the father of Matthan,

1790 ἐλεάω, eleaō [3] [√ 1799]

merciful to [1], mercy [1], to show mercy [1]

Ro 9:16 therefore, depend on man's desire or effort, but *on* God's **mercy**.
Jude 1:22 *Be* **merciful to** those who doubt;
    1:23 the fire and save them; *to* others **show mercy**, mixed with fear—

1791 ἐλεγμός, elegmos [1] [√ 1794]

rebuking [1]

2Ti 3:16 for teaching, **rebuking**, correcting and training in righteousness,

1792 ἔλεγξις, elenxis [1] [√ 1794]

rebuked [1]

2Pe 2:16 But he was **rebuked** for his wrongdoing by a donkey—a beast

1793 ἔλεγχος, elenchos [1] [√ 1794]

certain [1]

Heb 11: 1 being sure of what we hope for and **certain** of what we do not see.

1794 ἐλέγχω, elenchō [17] [→ 591, 1352, 1791, 1792, 1793, 1998]

rebuke [3], exposed [2], rebuked [2], convict [1], convict of guilt
[1], convicted [1], convinced that is a sinner [1], correct [1],
expose [1], prove guilty [1], rebukes [1], refute [1], show fault [1]

Mt 18:15 go and **show** him his **fault**, just between the two of you.
Lk 3:19 But *when* John **rebuked** Herod the tetrarch because of Herodias,
Jn 3:20 will not come into the light for fear that his deeds *will be* **exposed**.
    8:46 Can any of you **prove** me **guilty** of sin? If I am telling the truth,
    16: 8 he will **convict** the world **of guilt** in regard to sin
1Co 14:24 he will *be* **convinced** by all that *he* **is a sinner** and will be judged
Eph 5:11 to do with the fruitless deeds of darkness, but rather **expose** them.
    5:13 But everything **exposed** by the light becomes visible,
1Ti 5:20 Those who sin *are to be* **rebuked** publicly, so that the others may
2Ti 4: 2 in season and out of season; **correct**, rebuke and encourage—
Tit 1: 9 others by sound doctrine and **refute** those who oppose it.
    1:13 Therefore, **rebuke** them sharply, so that they will be sound in the
    2:15 Encourage and **rebuke** with all authority. Do not let anyone
Heb 12: 5 the Lord's discipline, and do not lose heart *when* he **rebukes** you,
Jas 2: 9 you sin and *are* **convicted** by the law as lawbreakers.
Jude 1:15 and *to* **convict** all the ungodly of all the ungodly acts they have
Rev 3:19 Those whom I love *I* **rebuke** and discipline. So be earnest,

1795 ἐλεεινός, eleeinos [2] [√ 1799]

pitied more than [1], pitiful [1]

1Co 15:19 life we have hope in Christ, we are to be **pitied more than** all men.
Rev 3:17 do not realize that you are wretched, **pitiful**, poor, blind and naked.

1796 ἐλεέω, eleeō [29] [√ 1799]

have mercy on [11], had mercy on [3], mercy [3], received mercy
[3], shown mercy [3], have pity [2], had[s] [1], has mercy on [1],
receive mercy [1], showing mercy [1]

Mt 5: 7 Blessed are the merciful, for they *will be* **shown mercy**.
    9:27 men followed him, calling out, "**Have mercy on** us, Son of David!"
    15:22 came to him, crying out, "Lord, Son of David, **have mercy on** me!
    17:15 "Lord, **have mercy on** my son," he said. "He has seizures and is
    18:33 Shouldn't you have **had mercy on** your fellow servant just as I had
    18:33 you have had mercy on your fellow servant just as I **had**[s] on you?'
    20:30 going by, they shouted, "Lord, Son of David, **have mercy on** us!"
    20:31 shouted all the louder, "Lord, Son of David, **have mercy on** us!"
Mk 5:19 the Lord has done for you, and how he has **had mercy on** you."
    10:47 he began to shout, "Jesus, Son of David, **have mercy on** me!"
    10:48 but he shouted all the more, "Son of David, **have mercy on** me!"
Lk 16:24 **have pity** on me and send Lazarus to dip the tip of his finger in
    17:13 and called out in a loud voice, "Jesus, Master, **have pity** on us!"
    18:38 He called out, "Jesus, Son of David, **have mercy on** me!"
    18:39 but he shouted all the more, "Son of David, **have mercy on** me!"
Ro 9:15 For he says to Moses, "*I will* **have mercy on** whom I have mercy,
    9:15 For he says to Moses, "I will have mercy on whom *I have* **mercy**,
    9:18 Therefore God **has mercy on** whom he wants to have mercy,
    11:30 to God have now **received mercy** as a result of their disobedience,
    11:31 too *may* now **receive mercy** as a result of God's mercy to you.
    11:32 men over to disobedience so that *he may* **have mercy on** them all.
    12: 8 govern diligently; if it is **showing mercy**, let him do it cheerfully.
1Co 7:25 but I give a judgment as one who by the Lord's **mercy** is
2Co 4: 1 Therefore, since through God's **mercy** we have this ministry,
Php 2:27 But God **had mercy on** him, and not on him only but also on me,
1Ti 1:13 *I was* **shown mercy** because I acted in ignorance and unbelief.
    1:16 But for that very reason *I was* **shown mercy** so that in me,
1Pe 2:10 once you *had* not **received mercy**, but now you have received
    2:10 you had not received mercy, but now *you* **have received mercy**.

1797 ἐλεημοσύνη, eleēmosynē [13] [√ 1799]

gifts to the poor [2], give to the needy [+4472] [2], give to the
poor [+1443] [2], beg [+160] [1], begging [+3836+4639] [1],
gave to in need [+4472] [1], gifts for the poor [1], giving [1],
helping the poor [+4472] [1], money [1]

Mt 6: 2 "So when *you* **give to the needy** [+4472], do not announce it with
    6: 3 But *when* you **give to the needy** [+4472], do not let your left hand

6: 4 so that your **giving** may be in secret. Then your Father, who sees
Lk 11:41 But **give** what is inside ɩthe dishɩ **to the poor** [+*1443*],
12:33 Sell your possessions and **give to the poor**. Provide purses
Ac 3: 2 where he was put every day *to* **beg** [+*160*] from those going into
3: 3 he saw Peter and John about to enter, he asked them for **money**.
3:10 to sit **begging** [+*3836+4639*] at the temple gate called Beautiful,
9:36 who was always doing good and **helping** [+*4472*] **the poor**.
10: 2 *he* **gave** generously to those **in need** [+*4472*] and prayed to God
10: 4 and **gifts to the poor** have come up as a memorial offering before
10:31 God has heard your prayer and remembered your **gifts to the poor**.
24:17 I came to Jerusalem to bring my people **gifts for the poor**

1798 ἐλεήμων, *eleēmōn* [2] [√ *1799*]

merciful [2]

Mt 5: 7 Blessed are the **merciful**, for they will be shown mercy.
Heb 2:17 in order that he might become a **merciful** and faithful high priest in

1799 ἔλεος, *eleos* [27] [→ *446, 447, 1790, 1795, 1796, 1797, 1798*]

mercy [24], merciful [2], tender mercy [+*5073*] [1]

Mt 9:13 and learn what this means: 'I desire **mercy**, not sacrifice.'
12: 7 had known what these words mean, 'I desire **mercy**, not sacrifice,'
23:23 important matters of the law—justice, **mercy** and faithfulness.
Lk 1:50 His **mercy** extends to those who fear him, from generation to
1:54 He has helped his servant Israel, remembering to be **merciful**
1:58 and relatives heard that the Lord had shown her great **mercy**,
1:72 to show **mercy** to our fathers and to remember his holy covenant,
1:78 because of the **tender mercy** [+*5073*] of our God, by which the
10:37 The expert in the law replied, "The one who had **mercy** on him."
Ro 9:23 to make the riches of his glory known to the objects *of* his **mercy**,
11:31 too may now receive mercy as a result of God's **mercy** to you.
15: 9 so that the Gentiles may glorify God for his **mercy**, as it is written:
Gal 6:16 Peace and **mercy** to all who follow this rule, even to the Israel of
Eph 2: 4 because of his great love for us, God, who is rich in **mercy**,
1Ti 1: 2 **mercy** and peace from God the Father and Christ Jesus our Lord.
2Ti 1: 2 **mercy** and peace from God the Father and Christ Jesus our Lord.
1:16 May the Lord show **mercy** to the household of Onesiphorus,
1:18 May the Lord grant that he will find **mercy** from the Lord on that
Tit 3: 5 of righteous things we had done, but because of his **mercy**.
Heb 4:16 so that we may receive **mercy** and find grace to help us in our time
Jas 2:13 mercy will be shown to anyone who has not been **merciful**.
2:13 who has not been merciful. **Mercy** triumphs over judgment!
3:17 submissive, full *of* **mercy** and good fruit, impartial and sincere.
1Pe 1: 3 In his great **mercy** he has given us new birth into a living hope
2Jn 1: 3 **mercy** and peace from God the Father and from Jesus Christ,
Jude 1: 2 **Mercy**, peace and love be yours in abundance.
1:21 Keep yourselves in God's love as you wait for the **mercy** of our

1800 ἐλευθερία, *eleutheria* [11] [√ *1801*]

freedom [10], free [1]

Ro 8:21 and brought into the glorious **freedom** of the children of God.
1Co 10:29 For why should my **freedom** be judged by another's conscience?
2Co 3:17 is the Spirit, and where the Spirit of the Lord is, there is **freedom**.
Gal 2: 4 infiltrated our ranks to spy on the **freedom** we have in Christ Jesus
5: 1 It is *for* **freedom** that Christ has set us free. Stand firm, then,
5:13 You, my brothers, were called to be **free**. But do not use your
5:13 But do not use your **freedom** to indulge the sinful nature;
Jas 1:25 man who looks intently into the perfect law that *gives* **freedom**,
2:12 as those who are going to be judged by the law that *gives* **freedom**,
1Pe 2:16 as free men, but do not use your **freedom** as a cover-up for evil;
2Pe 2:19 They promise them **freedom**, while they themselves are slaves of

1801 ἐλεύθερος, *eleutheros* [23] [→ *592, 1800, 1802*]

δοῦλος ... ἐλεύθερος (slave ... free) [12] Ro 6:20; 1Co
7:21,22,22; 12:13; Gal 3:28; Eph 6:8; Col 3:11; 1Pe 2:16; Rev
6:15; 13:16; 19:18

free [18], exempt [1], free and belong to no man [+*1666+4246*]
[1], gain freedom [+*1181*] [1], released [1], set free [1]

Mt 17:26 Peter answered. "Then the sons are **exempt**," Jesus said to him.

Jn 8:33 been slaves of anyone. How can you say that we shall be **set free**?"
8:36 So if the Son sets you free, you will be **free** indeed.
Ro 6:20 were slaves to sin, you were **free** from the control of righteousness.
7: 3 she is **released** from that law and is not an adulteress,
1Co 7:21 although if you can **gain** *your* **freedom** [+*1181*], do so.
7:22 he who was a **free** *man* when he was called is Christ's slave.
7:39 But if her husband dies, she is **free** to marry anyone she wishes,
9: 1 Am I not **free**? Am I not an apostle? Have I not seen Jesus our
9:19 Though I am **free** [+*1666+4246*] **and belong to no man**, I make
12:13 whether Jews or Greeks, slave or **free**—and we were all given the
Gal 3:28 There is neither Jew nor Greek, slave nor **free**, male nor female,
4:22 one by the slave woman and the other by the **free** *woman*.
4:23 but his son by the **free** *woman* was born as the result of a promise.
4:26 But the Jerusalem that is above is **free**, and she is our mother.
4:30 son will never share in the inheritance with the **free** *woman's* son."
4:31 we are not children of the slave woman, but *of* the **free** *woman*.
Eph 6: 8 everyone for whatever good he does, whether he is slave or **free**.
Col 3:11 barbarian, Scythian, slave or **free**, but Christ is all, and is in all.
1Pe 2:16 Live as **free** men, but do not use your freedom as a cover-up for
Rev 6:15 and every slave and every **free** *man* hid in caves and among the
13:16 forced everyone, small and great, rich and poor, **free** and slave,
19:18 and the flesh *of* all people, **free** and slave, small and great."

1802 ἐλευθερόω, *eleutheroō* [7] [√ *1801*]

set free [5], liberated [1], sets free [1]

Jn 8:32 Then you will know the truth, and the truth *will* **set** you **free**."
8:36 So if the Son **sets** you **free**, you will be free indeed.
Ro 6:18 *You have been* **set free** from sin and have become slaves to
6:22 But now *that you have been* **set free** from sin and have become
8: 2 through Christ Jesus the law of the Spirit of life **set** me **free**
8:21 that the creation itself *will be* **liberated** from its bondage to decay
Gal 5: 1 It is for freedom that Christ *has* **set** us **free**. Stand firm, then,

1803 ἔλευσις, *eleusis* [1] [√ *2262*]

coming [1]

Ac 7:52 They even killed those who predicted the **coming** of the Righteous

1804 ἐλεφάντινος, *elephantinos* [1]

made of ivory [1]

Rev 18:12 and articles of every kind **made of ivory**, costly wood, bronze, iron

1805 Ἐλιακείμ, *Eliakeim* Not used in UBS/NIV
[√ cf. *1806*]

1806 Ἐλιακίμ, *Eliakim* [3] [√ cf. *1805*]

Eliakim [3]

Mt 1:13 of Abiud, Abiud the father of **Eliakim**, Eliakim the father of Azor,
1:13 of Abiud, Abiud the father of Eliakim, **Eliakim** the father of Azor,
Lk 3:30 of Judah, the son of Joseph, the son of Jonam, the son *of* **Eliakim**,

1807 ἔλιγμα, *heligma* Not used in UBS/NIV [√ *1813*]

1808 Ἐλιέζερ, *Eliezer* [1]

Eliezer [1]

Lk 3:29 the son of Joshua, the son *of* **Eliezer**, the son of Jorim, the son of

1809 Ἐλιούδ, *Elioud* [2]

Eliud [2]

Mt 1:14 of Zadok, Zadok the father of Akim, Akim the father of **Eliud**,
1:15 **Eliud** the father of Eleazar, Eleazar the father of Matthan,

1810 Ἐλισάβετ, *Elisabet* [9]

Elizabeth [9]

Lk	1: 5	of Abijah; his wife **Elizabeth** was also a descendant of Aaron.
	1: 7	But they had no children, because **Elizabeth** was barren; and they
	1:13	Your wife **Elizabeth** will bear you a son, and you are to give him
	1:24	After this his wife **Elizabeth** became pregnant and for five months
	1:36	Even **Elizabeth** your relative is going to have a child in her old
	1:40	where she entered Zechariah's home and greeted **Elizabeth**.
	1:41	When **Elizabeth** heard Mary's greeting, the baby leaped in her
	1:41	leaped in her womb, and **Elizabeth** was filled with the Holy Spirit.
	1:57	When it was time *for* **Elizabeth** to have her baby, she gave birth to

1811 Ἐλισαῖος, *Elisaios* [1] [→ *1812*]

Elisha [1]

Lk	4:27	And there were many in Israel with leprosy in the time of **Elisha**

1812 Ἐλισσαῖος, *Elissaios* Not used in UBS/NIV [√ *1811*]

1813 ἑλίσσω, *helissō* [2] [→ *1807*]

roll up [1], rolling up [1]

Heb	1:12	*You* will **roll** them **up** like a robe; like a garment they will be
Rev	6:14	**rolling up**, and every mountain and island was removed from its

1814 ἕλκος, *helkos* [3] [→ *1815*]

sores [3]

Lk	16:21	the rich man's table. Even the dogs came and licked his **sores**.
Rev	16: 2	and painful **sores** broke out on the people who had the mark of the
	16:11	cursed the God of heaven because of their pains and their **sores**,

1815 ἑλκόω, *helkoō* [1] [√ *1814*]

covered with sores [1]

Lk	16:20	At his gate was laid a beggar named Lazarus, **covered with sores**

1816 ἑλκύω, *helkyō* [8] [→ *1999*]

dragged [3], dragging [1], draw [1], draws [1], drew [1], haul in [1]

Jn	6:44	"No one can come to me unless the Father who sent me **draws** him,
	12:32	when *I* am lifted up from the earth, *will* **draw** all men to myself."
	18:10	who had a sword, **drew** it and struck the high priest's servant,
	21: 6	they were unable *to* **haul** the net **in** because of the large number of
	21:11	Simon Peter climbed aboard and **dragged** the net ashore. It was
Ac	16:19	*they* seized Paul and Silas and **dragged** them into the marketplace
	21:30	Seizing Paul, *they* **dragged** him from the temple, and immediately
Jas	2: 6	Are they not the *ones who are* **dragging** you into court?

1817 Ἑλλάς, *Hellas* [1] [√ *1818*]

Greece [1]

Ac	20: 2	of encouragement to the people, and finally arrived in **Greece**,

1818 Ἕλλην, *Hellēn* [25 / 26] [→ *1817, 1819, 1820, 1821, 1822*]

Greeks [15], Greek [5], Gentile [4], Gentiles [2]

Jn	7:35	Will he go where our people live scattered among the **Greeks**,
	7:35	our people live scattered among the Greeks, and teach the **Greeks**?
	12:20	Now there were some **Greeks** among those who went up to
Ac	11:20	went to Antioch and began to speak to **Greeks** [UBS *1821*] also,
	14: 1	so effectively that a great number *of* Jews and **Gentiles** believed.
	16: 1	was a Jewess and a believer, but whose father was a **Greek**.
	16: 3	lived in that area, for they all knew that his father was a **Greek**.
	17: 4	as did a large number of God-fearing **Greeks** and not a few
	18: 4	he reasoned in the synagogue, trying to persuade Jews and **Greeks**.
	19:10	and **Greeks** who lived in the province of Asia heard the word of

	19:17	When this became known *to* the Jews and **Greeks** living in
	20:21	I have declared *to* both Jews and **Greeks** that they must turn to
	21:28	he has brought **Greeks** into the temple area and defiled this holy
Ro	1:14	I am obligated both *to* **Greeks** and non-Greeks, both to the wise
	1:16	of everyone who believes: first for the Jew, then *for* the **Gentile**.
	2: 9	human being who does evil: first for the Jew, then for the **Gentile**;
	2:10	for everyone who does good: first for the Jew, then for the **Gentile**.
	3: 9	made the charge that Jews and **Gentiles** alike are all under sin.
	10:12	For there is no difference between Jew and **Gentile**—the same
1Co	1:22	Jews demand miraculous signs and **Greeks** look for wisdom,
	1:24	both Jews and **Greeks**, Christ the power of God and the wisdom of
	10:32	anyone to stumble, whether Jews, **Greeks** or the church of God—
	12:13	whether Jews or **Greeks**, slave or free—and we were all given the
Gal	2: 3	was compelled to be circumcised, even though he was a **Greek**.
	3:28	There is neither Jew nor **Greek**, slave nor free, male nor female,
Col	3:11	Here there is no **Greek** or Jew, circumcised or uncircumcised,

1819 Ἑλληνικός, *Hellēnikos* [1] [√ *1818*]

Greek [1]

Rev	9:11	whose name in Hebrew is Abaddon, and in **Greek**, Apollyon.

1820 Ἑλληνίς, *Hellēnis* [2] [√ *1818*]

Greek [2]

Mk	7:26	The woman was a **Greek**, born in Syrian Phoenicia. She begged
Ac	17:12	as did also a number of prominent **Greek** women and many Greek

1821 Ἑλληνιστής, *Hellēnistēs* [3 / 2] [√ *1818*]

Grecian Jews [2]

Ac	6: 1	the **Grecian Jews** among them complained against the Hebraic
	9:29	He talked and debated with the **Grecian Jews**,
	11:20	and began to speak to Greeks [UBS *Grecian Jews*; NIV *1818*] also,

1822 Ἑλληνιστί, *Hellēnisti* [2] [√ *1818*]

Greek [1], in Greek [1]

Jn	19:20	the city, and the sign was written in Aramaic, Latin and **Greek**.
Ac	21:37	"May I say something to you?" "Do you speak **Greek**?" he replied.

1823 ἐλλογάω, *ellogaō* [1] [√ *1877 + 3306*]

charge [1]

Phm	1:18	he has done you any wrong or owes you anything, **charge** it to me.

1824 ἐλλογέω, *ellogeō* [1] [√ *1877 + 3306*]

taken into account [1]

Ro	5:13	the world. But sin *is* not **taken into account** when there is no law.

1825 Ἐλμαδάμ, *Elmadam* [1] [→ *1826*]

Elmadam [1]

Lk	3:28	son of Addi, the son of Cosam, the son *of* **Elmadam**, the son of Er,

1826 Ἐλμωδάμ, *Elmōdam* Not used in UBS/NIV [√ *1825*]

1827 ἐλπίζω, *elpizō* [31] [√ *1828*]

hope [11], put hope [4], hope for [2], hoped [2], hoping [2], set hope [2], expect [1], expected [1], have hope [+ *1639*] [1], hopes [1], hopes are set [1], hopes for [1], puts hope [1], trust [1]

Mt	12:21	In his name the nations *will* **put** *their* **hope**."
Lk	6:34	And if you lend to those from whom *you* **expect** repayment,
	23: 8	had heard about him, *he* **hoped** to see him perform some miracle.
	24:21	but *we* *had* **hoped** that he was the one who was going to redeem
Jn	5:45	the Father. Your accuser is Moses, on whom your **hopes are set**.
Ac	24:26	At the same time *he was* **hoping** that Paul would offer him a bribe,

	26: 7	This is the promise our twelve tribes *are* **hoping** to see fulfilled as
Ro	8:24	that is seen is no hope at all. Who **hopes for** what he already has?
	8:25	But if *we* **hope for** what we do not yet have, we wait for it
	15:12	will arise to rule over the nations; the Gentiles *will* **hope** in him."
	15:24	*I* **hope** to visit you while passing through and to have you assist me
1Co	13: 7	It always protects, always trusts, always **hopes**, always perseveres.
	15:19	If only for this life we **have hope** [+*1639*] in Christ, we are to be
	16: 7	I **hope** to spend some time with you, if the Lord permits.
2Co	1:10	On him *we* **have** set *our* **hope** that he will continue to deliver us,
	1:13	you anything you cannot read or understand. And *I* **hope** that,
	5:11	are is plain to God, and *I* **hope** it is also plain to your conscience.
	8: 5	And they did not do as *we* **expected**, but they gave themselves first
	13: 6	And *I* **trust** that you will discover that we have not failed the test.
Php	2:19	*I* **hope** in the Lord Jesus to send Timothy to you soon, that I also
	2:23	*I* **hope**, therefore, to send him as soon as I see how things go with
1Ti	3:14	Although *I* **hope** to come to you soon, I am writing you these
	4:10	we labor and strive), that *we* have **put** *our* **hope** in the living God,
	5: 5	and left all alone **puts** *her* **hope** in God and continues night
	6:17	present world not to be arrogant nor *to* **put** their **hope** in wealth,
Phm	1:22	because *I* **hope** to be restored to you in answer to your prayers.
Heb	11: 1	Now faith is being sure *of what* we **hope for** and certain of what
1Pe	1:13	**set** *your* **hope** fully on the grace to be given you when Jesus Christ
	3: 5	For this is the way the holy women of the past who **put** their **hope**
2Jn	1:12	Instead, *I* **hope** to visit you and talk with you face to face,
3Jn	1:14	*I* **hope** to see you soon, and we will talk face to face. Peace to you.

1828 ἐλπίς, *elpis* [53] [→ *594, 1827, 4598*]

ἐλπίς ἔχειν (to have hope) [7] Ac 24:15; Ro 15:4; 2Co 3:12; 10:15; Eph 2:12; 1Th 4:13; 1Jn 3:3

ὁ θεὸς τῆς ἐλπίδος (the God of hope) [1] Ro 15:13

hope [51], *untranslated* [1], all hope [1]

Ac	2:26	is glad and my tongue rejoices; my body also will live in **hope**,
	16:19	When the owners of the slave girl realized that their **hope** of
	23: 6	I stand on trial because *of* my **hope** in the resurrection of the dead."
	24:15	and I have the same **hope** in God as these men, that there will be a
	26: 6	because of my **hope** in what God has promised our fathers that I
	26: 7	O king, it is because *of* this **hope** that the Jews are accusing me.
	27:20	continued raging, we finally gave up all **hope** of being saved.
	28:20	because *of* the **hope** of Israel that I am bound with this chain."
Ro	4:18	Against **all hope**, Abraham in hope believed and so became the
	4:18	Abraham in **hope** believed and so became the father of many
	5: 2	we now stand. And we rejoice in the **hope** of the glory of God.
	5: 4	perseverance, character; and character, **hope**.
	5: 5	And **hope** does not disappoint us, because God has poured out his
	8:20	its own choice, but by the will of the one who subjected it, in **hope**
	8:24	For *in* this **hope** we were saved. But hope that is seen is no hope at
	8:24	in this **hope** we were saved. But **hope** that is seen is no hope at all.
	8:24	in this hope we were saved. But hope that is seen is no **hope** at all.
	12:12	Be joyful *in* **hope**, patient in affliction, faithful in prayer.
	15: 4	and the encouragement of the Scriptures we might have **hope**.
	15:13	May the God *of* **hope** fill you with all joy and peace as you trust in
	15:13	so that you may overflow with **hope** by the power of the Holy
1Co	9:10	they ought to do so in the **hope** of sharing in the harvest.
	9:10	they ought to do so in the hope **[RPG]** of sharing in the harvest.
	13:13	And now these three remain: faith, **hope** and love. But the greatest
2Co	1: 7	And our **hope** for you is firm, because we know that just as you
	3:12	Therefore, since we have such a **hope**, we are very bold.
	10:15	Our **hope** is that, as your faith continues to grow, our area of
Gal	5: 5	await through the Spirit the righteousness for which we **hope**.
Eph	1:18	in order that you may know the **hope** to which he has called you,
	2:12	of the promise, without **hope** and without God in the world.
	4: 4	just as you were called to one **hope** when you were called—
Php	1:20	I eagerly expect and **hope** that I will in no way be ashamed,
Col	1: 5	Lord because of the **hope** that is stored up for you in
	1:23	and firm, not moved from the **hope** held out in the gospel.
	1:27	riches of this mystery, which is Christ in you, the **hope** of glory.
1Th	1: 3	and your endurance *inspired by* **hope** in our Lord Jesus Christ.
	2:19	For what is our **hope**, our joy, or the crown in which we will glory
	4:13	fall asleep, or to grieve like the rest of men, who have no **hope**.
	5: 8	and love as a breastplate, and the **hope** of salvation as a helmet.
2Th	2:16	and by his grace gave us eternal encouragement and good **hope**,
1Ti	1: 1	by the command of God our Savior and *of* Christ Jesus our **hope**,
Tit	1: 2	a faith and knowledge resting on the **hope** of eternal life,

	2:13	while we wait for the blessed **hope**—the glorious appearing of our
	3: 7	his grace, we might become heirs having the **hope** of eternal life.
Heb	3: 6	if we hold on to our courage and the **hope** of which we boast.
	6:11	same diligence to the very end, in order to make your **hope** sure.
	6:18	we who have fled to take hold *of* the **hope** offered to us may be
	7:19	and a better **hope** is introduced, by which we draw near to God.
	10:23	Let us hold unswervingly to the **hope** we profess, for he who
1Pe	1: 3	In his great mercy he has given us new birth into a living **hope**
	1:21	the dead and glorified him, and so your faith and **hope** are in God.
	3:15	who asks you to give the reason for the **hope** that you have.
1Jn	3: 3	Everyone who has this **hope** in him purifies himself, just as he is

1829 Ἐλύμας, *Elymas* [1] [√ *cf. 2287*]

Elymas [1]

|Ac | 13: 8 | But **Elymas** the sorcerer (for that is what his name means) |

1830 ἐλωΐ, *elōi* [2 / 4] [√ *cf. 2458*]

eloi [4]

Mt	27:46	loud voice, "**Eloi**, [UBS *2458*] *Eloi, lama sabachthani?*"—
	27:46	a loud voice, "*Eloi, Eloi,* [UBS *2458*] *lama sabachthani?*"—
Mk	15:34	cried out in a loud voice, "**Eloi**, *Eloi, lama sabachthani?*"—
	15:34	cried out in a loud voice, "*Eloi,* **Eloi**, *lama sabachthani?*"—

1831 ἐμαυτοῦ, *emautou* [37] [√ *1609 + 899*]

myself [17], my own [7], me [4], my [3], I [2], my own accord [2], convinced [+*1506*] [1], my [+*3836+4309*] [1]

Mt	8: 9	For I myself am a man under authority, with soldiers under **me**.
Lk	7: 7	That is why I did not even consider **myself** worthy to come to you.
	7: 8	For I myself am a man under authority, with soldiers under **me**.
Jn	5:30	By **myself** I can do nothing; I judge only as I hear, and my
	5:31	"If I testify about **myself**, my testimony is not valid.
	7:17	my teaching comes from God or whether I speak on **my own**.
	7:28	I am not here on **my own**, but he who sent me is true. You do not
	8:14	Jesus answered, "Even if I testify on **my own** behalf, my testimony
	8:18	I am one who testifies for **myself**; my other witness is the Father,
	8:28	and that I do nothing on **my own** but speak just what the Father has
	8:42	and now am here. I have not come on **my own**; but he sent me.
	8:54	Jesus replied, "If I glorify **myself**, my glory means nothing.
	10:18	No·one takes it from me, but I lay it down of **my own accord**.
	12:32	when I am lifted up from the earth, will draw all men to **myself**."
	12:49	For I did not speak of **my own accord**, but the Father who sent me
	14: 3	and take you to be with **me** that you also may be where I am.
	14:10	The words I say to you are not just **my own**. Rather, it is the
	14:21	by my Father, and I too will love him and show **myself** to him."
	17:19	For them I sanctify **myself**, that they too may be truly sanctified."
Ac	20:24	However, I consider **my** life worth nothing to me, if only I may
	24:10	over this nation; so I gladly make **my** [+*3836+4309*] defense.
	26: 2	I consider **myself** fortunate to stand before you today as I make my
	26: 9	"I too *was* **convinced** [+*1506*] that I ought to do all that was
Ro	11: 4	"I have reserved *for* **myself** seven thousand who have not bowed
1Co	4: 3	or by any human court; indeed, I do not even judge **myself**.
	4: 4	**My** conscience is clear, but that does not make me innocent.
	4: 6	I have applied these things to **myself** and Apollos for your benefit,
	7: 7	I wish that all men were as **I** am. But each man has his own gift
	9:19	and belong to no man, I make **myself** a slave to everyone,
	10:33	For I am not seeking **my own** good but the good of many,
2Co	2: 1	So I made up **my** mind that I would not make another painful visit
	11: 7	Was it a sin for me to lower **myself** in order to elevate you by
	11: 9	I have kept **myself** from being a burden to you in any way,
	12: 5	but I will not boast about **myself**, except about my weaknesses.
Gal	2:18	If I rebuild what I destroyed, I prove that **I** am a lawbreaker.
Php	3:13	Brothers, I do not consider **myself** yet to have taken hold of it.
Phm	1:13	I would have liked to keep him with **me** so that he could take your

1832 ἐμβαίνω, *embainō* [16] [√ *1877 + 326*]

got [10], get [2], got into [2], getting [1], stepped [1]

Mt	8:23	Then he **got** into the boat and his disciples followed him.
	9: 1	Jesus **stepped** into a boat, crossed over and came to his own town.
	13: 2	Such large crowds gathered around him that he **got** into a boat

14:22 Immediately Jesus made the disciples **get** into the boat and go on
15:39 *he* **got into** the boat and went to the vicinity of Magadan.
Mk 4: 1 so large that he **got** into a boat and sat in it out on the lake,
     5:18 *As* Jesus *was* **getting** into the boat, the man who had been
     6:45 Immediately Jesus made his disciples **get** into the boat and go on
     8:10 *he* **got** into the boat with his disciples and went to the region of
     8:13 he left them, **got** back into the boat and crossed to the other side.
Lk   5: 3 *He* **got** into one of the boats, the one belonging to Simon,
     8:22 to the other side of the lake." So they **got** into a boat and set out.
     8:37 they were overcome with fear. So he **got** into the boat and left.
Jn   6:17 where *they* **got** into a boat and set off across the lake for
     6:24 they **got** into the boats and went to Capernaum in search of Jesus.
    21: 3 So they went out and **got into** the boat, but that night they caught

1833 ἐμβάλλω, *emballō* [1] [√ *1877 + 965*]

throw [1]

Lk 12: 5 after the killing of the body, has power *to* **throw** you into hell.

1834 ἐμβαπτίζω, *embaptizō*   Not used in UBS/NIV
[√ *1877 + 970*]

1835 ἐμβάπτω, *embaptō* [2] [√ *1877 + 970*]

dipped [1], dips [1]

Mt 26:23 "The one *who has* **dipped** his hand into the bowl with me will
Mk 14:20 the Twelve," he replied, "one who **dips** bread into the bowl with
               me.

1836 ἐμβατεύω, *embateuō* [1] [√ *1877 + 326*]

goes into great detail about [1]

Col 2:18 Such a person **goes into great detail about** what he has seen,

1837 ἐμβιβάζω, *embibazō* [1] [√ *1877 + 326*]

put on board [*+899+1650*] [1]

Ac 27: 6 ship sailing for Italy and **put** us **on board** [*+899+1650*].

1838 ἐμβλέπω, *emblepō* [12] [√ *1877 + 1063*]

looked at [4], saw [2], blinded [*+4024*] [1], look at [1], looked
closely at [1], looked directly at [1], looked straight at [1], looking
[1]

Mt   6:26 **Look at** the birds of the air; they do not sow or reap or store away
    19:26 Jesus **looked at** them and said, "With man this is impossible,
Mk   8:25 were opened, his sight was restored, and *he* **saw** everything clearly.
    10:21 Jesus **looked at** him and loved him. "One thing you lack," he said.
    10:27 Jesus **looked at** them and said, "With man this is impossible,
    14:67 When she saw Peter warming himself, *she* **looked closely at** him.
Lk 20:17 Jesus **looked directly at** them and asked, "Then what is the
    22:61 The Lord turned and **looked straight at** Peter. Then Peter
Jn   1:36 *When he* **saw** Jesus passing by, he said, "Look, the Lamb of God!"
     1:42 Jesus **looked at** him and said, "You are Simon son of John.
Ac   1:11 of Galilee," they said, "why do you stand here **looking** into the sky?
    22:11 because the brilliance of the light *had* **blinded** [*+4024*] me.

1839 ἐμβριμάομαι, *embrimaomai* [5]
[√ *1877 + 1102*]

deeply moved [2], rebuked harshly [1], strong warning [1],
warned sternly [1]

Mt   9:30 Jesus **warned** them **sternly**, "See that no one knows about this."
Mk   1:43 Jesus sent him away at once *with* a **strong warning**:
    14: 5 and the money given to the poor." And *they* **rebuked** her **harshly**.
Jn 11:33 her also weeping, *he was* **deeply moved** in spirit and troubled.
    11:38 Jesus, once more **deeply moved**, came to the tomb. It was a cave

1840 ἐμέω, *emeō* [1]

spit [1]

Rev 3:16 neither hot nor cold—I am about to **spit** you out of my mouth.

1841 ἐμμαίνομαι, *emmainomai* [1] [√ *1877 + 3419*]

obsession [*+4360*] [1]

Ac 26:11 *In my* **obsession** [*+4360*] *against* them, I even went to foreign

1842 Ἐμμανουήλ, *Emmanouēl* [1]

Immanuel [1]

Mt   1:23 and will give birth to a son, and they will call him **Immanuel**"—

1843 Ἐμμαοῦς, *Emmaous* [1] [√ *cf. 4035*]

Emmaus [1]

Lk 24:13 that same day two of them were going to a village called **Emmaus**,

1844 ἐμμένω, *emmenō* [4] [√ *1877 + 3531*]

continue [1], remain faithful to [*RP1877*] [1], remain true to [1],
stayed in [*RP1877*] [1]

Ac 14:22 the disciples and encouraging them *to* **remain true** to the faith.
    28:30 For two whole years Paul **stayed** [*RP1877*] there **in** his own rented
Gal 3:10 "Cursed is everyone who *does* not **continue** to do everything
Heb 8: 9 because they *did* not **remain** [*RP1877*] **faithful to** my covenant,

1845 ἐμμέσω, *emmesō*   Not used in UBS/NIV
[√ *1877 + 3545*]

1846 Ἐμμώρ, *Hemmōr* [1]

Hamor [1]

Ac   7:16 from the sons *of* **Hamor** at Shechem for a certain sum of money.

1847 ἐμός, *emos* [75] [√ *1609*]

my [44], my own [9], mine [5], I [4], me [4], for me [3], I have
[*+3836*] [2], it [*+993+3836+3836*] [1], it^s [*+3836*] [1], my [*+6034*]
[1], myself [1]

Mt 18:20 For where two or three come together in **my** name, there am I with
    20:15 Don't I have the right to do what I want with **my own** money?
    20:23 from my cup, but to sit at my right or left is not **for me** to grant.
    25:27 so that when I returned I would have received it^s [*+3836*] back
Mk   8:38 of me and **my** words in this adulterous and sinful generation,
    10:40 but to sit at my right or left is not **for me** to grant. These places
Lk   9:26 If anyone is ashamed of me and **my** words, the Son of Man will be
    15:31 'you are always with me, and everything **I** [*+3836*] **have** is yours.
    22:19 "This is my body given for you; do this in remembrance of **me**."
Jn   3:29 the bridegroom's voice. That joy is **mine**, and it is now complete.
     4:34 "**My** food," said Jesus, "is to do the will of him who sent me
     5:30 I judge only as I hear, and **my** judgment is just, for I seek not to
     5:30 is just, for I seek not to please **myself** but him who sent me.
     5:47 believe what he wrote, how are you going to believe what **I** say?"
     6:38 For I have come down from heaven not to do **my** will but to do the
     7: 6 Therefore Jesus told them, "The right time for **me** has not yet come;
     7: 8 up to this Feast, because **for me** the right time has not yet come."
     7:16 Jesus answered, "**My** teaching is not my own. It comes from him
     7:16 Jesus answered, "My teaching is not **my own**. It comes from him
     8:16 But if I do judge, **my** decisions are right, because I am not alone.
     8:31 Jesus said, "If you hold to **my** teaching, you are really my disciples.
     8:37 you are ready to kill me, because you have no room for **my** word.
     8:43 Why is **my** language not clear to you? Because you are unable to
     8:43 not clear to you? Because you are unable to hear what **I** say.
     8:51 I tell you the truth, if anyone keeps **my** word, he will never see
     8:56 Your father Abraham rejoiced at the thought of seeing **my** day;
    10:14 am the good shepherd; I know **my** *sheep* and my sheep know me—
    10:14 am the good shepherd; I know my sheep and **my** *sheep* know me—
    10:26 but you do not believe because you are not **my** sheep.

10:27 **My** sheep listen to my voice; I know them, and they follow me.
12:26 me must follow me; and where I am, **my** servant also will be.
13:35 By this all men will know that you are **my** disciples, if you love
14:15 "If you love me, you will obey what **I** command.
14:24 These words you hear are not **my** own; they belong to the Father
14:27 Peace I leave with you; **my** peace I give you. I do not give to you
15: 9 Father has loved me, so have I loved you. Now remain in **my** love.
15:11 I have told you this so that **my** joy may be in you and that your joy
15:12 **My** command is this: Love each other as I have loved you.
16:14 He will bring glory to me by taking from what is **mine** and making
16:15 All that belongs to the Father is **mine**. That is why I said the Spirit
16:15 That is why I said the Spirit will take from what is **mine** and make
17:10 All **I have** [+3836] is yours, and all you have is mine. And glory
17:10 All I have is yours, and all you have is **mine**. And glory has come
17:13 so that they may have the full measure of **my** joy within them.
17:24 and to see **my** glory, the glory you have given me because you
18:36 Jesus said, "**My** kingdom is not of this world. If it were, my
18:36 If it* [+993+3836+3836] were, my servants would fight to prevent
18:36 **my** servants would fight to prevent my arrest by the Jews.
18:36 my arrest by the Jews. But now **my** kingdom is from another place."
Ro   3: 7 "If **my** falsehood enhances God's truthfulness and so increases his
10: 1 **my** heart's desire and prayer to God for the Israelites is that they
1Co   1:15 so no one can say that you were baptized into **my** name.
5: 4 in the name of our Lord Jesus and **I** am with you in spirit,
7:40 In **my** judgment, she is happier if she stays as she is—and I think
9: 3 This is **my** defense to those who sit in judgment on me.
11:24 "This is my body, which is for you; do this in remembrance of **me**."
11:25 he took the cup, saying, "This cup is the new covenant in **my** blood;
11:25 my blood; do this, whenever you drink it, in remembrance of **me**."
16:18 For they refreshed **my** spirit and yours also. Such men deserve
16:21 I, Paul, write this greeting *in* **my own** hand.
2Co   1:23 I call God as **my** [+6034] witness that it was in order to spare you
2: 3 I had confidence in all of you, that you would all share **my** joy.
8:23 As for Titus, he is **my** partner and fellow worker among you;
Gal   1:13 For you have heard of **my** previous way of life in Judaism,
6:11 See what large letters I use as I write to you *with* **my own** hand!
Php   1:26 so that through **my** being with you again your joy in Christ Jesus
3: 9 not having a righteousness of **my own** that comes from the law,
Col   4:18 I, Paul, write this greeting *in* **my own** hand. Remember my chains.
2Th   3:17 I, Paul, write this greeting *in* **my own** hand, which is the
Phm   1:10 I appeal to you for **my** son Onesimus, who became my son while I
1:12 I am sending him—who is **my** very heart—back to you.
1:19 I, Paul, am writing this *with* **my own** hand. I will pay it back—
2Pe   1:15 And I will make every effort to see that after **my** departure you will
3Jn   1: 4 I have no greater joy than to hear that **my** children are walking in
Rev   2:20 By her teaching she misleads **my** servants into sexual immorality

1848 ἐμπαιγμονή, *empaigmonē* [1] [√ 1877 + 4089]

scoffing [1]

2Pe   3: 3 scoffers will come, **scoffing** and following their own evil desires.

1849 ἐμπαιγμός, *empaigmos* [1] [√ 1877 + 4089]

jeers [1]

Heb 11:36 Some faced **jeers** and flogging, while still others were chained

1850 ἐμπαίζω, *empaizō* [13] [√ 1877 + 4089]

mocked [8], mock [2], mocking [1], outwitted [1], ridicule [1]

Mt   2:16 When Herod realized that *he had been* **outwitted** by the Magi,
20:19 and will turn him over to the Gentiles to *be* **mocked** and flogged
27:29 a staff in his right hand and knelt in front of him and **mocked** him.
27:31 After *they had* **mocked** him, they took off the robe and put his
27:41 chief priests, the teachers of the law and the elders **mocked** him.
Mk   10:34 who will **mock** him and spit on him, flog him and kill him.
15:20 And when *they had* **mocked** him, they took off the purple robe
15:31 and the teachers of the law **mocked** him among themselves.
Lk   14:29 and is not able to finish it, everyone who sees it will **ridicule** him,
18:32 They *will* **mock** *him*, insult him, spit on him, flog him and kill
22:63 The men who were guarding Jesus *began* **mocking** and beating
23:11 Then Herod and his soldiers ridiculed and **mocked** him.
23:36 The soldiers also came up and **mocked** him. They offered him

1851 ἐμπαίκτης, *empaiktēs* [2] [√ 1877 + 4089]

scoffers [2]

2Pe   3: 3 you must understand that in the last days **scoffers** will come,
Jude 1:18 "In the last times there will be **scoffers** who will follow their own

1852 ἐμπέμπω, *empempō* Not used in UBS/NIV [√ 1877 + 4287]

1853 ἐμπεριπατέω, *emperipateō* [1] [√ 1877 + 4309 + 4251]

walk among [1]

2Co   6:16 "I will live with them and **walk among** them, and I will be their

1854 ἐμπιμπλάω, *empimplaō* Not used in UBS/NIV [√ 1877 + 4398]

1855 ἐμπίμπλημι, *empimplēmi* [5] [√ 1877 + 4398]

enjoyed company [1], filled [1], had enough [1], provides with plenty [1], well fed [1]

Lk   1:53 He has **filled** the hungry with good things but has sent the rich
6:25 Woe to you who *are* **well fed** now, for you will go hungry.
Jn   6:12 When *they had all* **had enough** *to eat*, he said to his disciples,
Ac   14:17 he **provides** you **with plenty** of food and fills your hearts with joy."
Ro   15:24 my journey there, after *I have* **enjoyed** your **company** for a while.

1856 ἐμπίμπρημι, *empimprēmi* [1] [√ 1877 + 4399]

burned [1]

Mt   22: 7 sent his army and destroyed those murderers and **burned** their city.

1857 ἐμπιπλάω, *empiplaō* Not used in UBS/NIV [√ 1877 + 4398]

1858 ἐμπίπλημι, *empiplēmi* Not used in UBS/NIV [√ 1877 + 4398]

1859 ἐμπίπρημι, *empiprēmi* Not used in UBS/NIV [√ 1877 + 4399]

1860 ἐμπίπτω, *empiptō* [7] [√ 1877 + 4406]

fall [5], falls [1], fell [1]

Mt   12:11 "If any of you has a sheep and it **falls** into a pit on the Sabbath,
Lk   6:39 a blind man lead a blind man? *Will they* not both **fall** into a pit?
10:36 was a neighbor to the man *who* **fell** into the hands of robbers?"
1Ti   3: 6 become conceited and **fall** under the same judgment as the devil.
3: 7 so that *he will* not **fall** into disgrace and into the devil's trap.
6: 9 People who want to get rich **fall** into temptation and a trap
Heb 10:31 It is a dreadful thing *to* **fall** into the hands of the living God.

1861 ἐμπλέκω, *emplekō* [2] [√ 1877 + 4428]

entangled in [1], involved in [1]

2Ti   2: 4 No one serving as a soldier *gets* **involved in** civilian affairs—
2Pe   2:20 Savior Jesus Christ and *are* again **entangled in** it and overcome,

1862 ἐμπλοκή, *emplokē* [1] [√ 1877 + 4428]

braided [1]

1Pe   3: 3 such as **braided** hair and the wearing of gold jewelry and fine

1863 ἐμπνέω, *empneō* [1] [√ 1877 + 4463]

breathing out [1]

Ac   9: 1 Saul *was* still **breathing out** murderous threats against the Lord's

1864 ἐμπορεύομαι, *emporeuomai* [2]
[√ *1877 + 4513*]

carry on business [1], exploit [1]

Jas 4:13 that city, spend a year there, **carry on business** and make money.”
2Pe 2: 3 In their greed *these* teachers *will* **exploit** you with stories they have

1865 ἐμπορία, *emporia* [1] [√ *1877 + 4513*]

business [1]

Mt 22: 5 no attention and went off—one to his field, another to his **business**.

1866 ἐμπόριον, *emporion* [1] [√ *1877 + 4513*]

market [+*3875*] [1]

Jn 2:16 How dare you turn my Father's house into a **market** [+*3875*]!”

1867 ἔμπορος, *emporos* [5] [√ *1877 + 4513*]

merchants [4], merchant [+*476*] [1]

Mt 13:45 the kingdom of heaven is like a **merchant** [+*476*] looking for fine
Rev 18: 3 and the **merchants** of the earth grew rich from her excessive
    18:11 “The **merchants** of the earth will weep and mourn over her
    18:15 The **merchants** who sold these things and gained their wealth from
    18:23 heard in you again. Your **merchants** were the world's great men.

1868 ἐμπρήθω, *emprēthō* Not used in UBS/NIV
[√ *1877 + 4399*]

1869 ἔμπροσθεν, *emprosthen* [48 / 47]
[√ *1877 + 4639*]

before [19], in front of [7], ahead [4], *untranslated* [3], in the
presence [3], at [2], in presence [2], surpassed [+*1181*] [2], in
faces [1], in front [1], in full view of [1], on ahead [1], to [1]

Mt 5:16 In the same way, let your light shine **before** men, that they may see
    5:24 leave your gift there **in front of** the altar. First go and be
    6: 1 “Be careful not to do your 'acts of righteousness' **before** men,
    6: 2 [NIE] as the hypocrites do in the synagogues and on the streets,
    7: 6 “Do not give dogs what is sacred; do not throw your pearls **to** pigs.
   10:32 “Whoever acknowledges me **before** men, I will also acknowledge
   10:32 I will also acknowledge him **before** my Father in heaven.
   10:33 But whoever disowns me **before** men, I will disown him before my
   10:33 me before men, I will disown him **before** my Father in heaven.
   11:10 messenger ahead of you, who will prepare your way **before** you.'
   11:26 Yes, Father, for this was [NIE] your good pleasure.
   17: 2 There he was transfigured **before** them. His face shone like the
   18:14 your Father in heaven is not willing [UBS+ *is not the will before*
        your Father]
   23:13 you hypocrites! You shut the kingdom of heaven **in** men's **faces**.
   25:32 All the nations will be gathered **before** him, and he will separate
   26:70 But he denied it **before** them all. “I don't know what you're talking
   27:11 Meanwhile Jesus stood **before** the governor, and the governor
   27:29 a staff in his right hand and knelt **in front of** him and mocked him.
Mk 2:12 He got up, took his mat and walked out **in full view of** them all.
    9: 2 where they were all alone. There he was transfigured **before** them.
Lk 5:19 the tiles into the middle of the crowd, *right* **in front of** Jesus.
    7:27 messenger ahead of you, who will prepare your way **before** you.'
   10:21 little children. Yes, Father, for this was [NIE] your good pleasure.
   12: 8 “I tell you, whoever acknowledges me **before** men, the Son of Man
   12: 8 the Son of Man will also acknowledge him **before** the angels of
   14: 2 There **in front of** him was a man suffering from dropsy.
   19: 4 So he ran **ahead** and climbed a sycamore-fig tree to see him,
   19:27 king over them—bring them here and kill them **in front of** me.' ”
   19:28 After Jesus had said this, he went on **ahead**, going up to Jerusalem.
   21:36 and that you may be able to stand **before** the Son of Man.”
Jn 1:15 'He who comes after me *has* **surpassed** [+*1181*] me because he
    1:30 'A man who comes after me *has* **surpassed** [+*1181*] me
    3:28 testify that I said, 'I am not the Christ but am sent **ahead** of him.'
   10: 4 he goes **on ahead** of them, and his sheep follow him because they
   12:37 after Jesus had done all these miraculous signs **in** their **presence**,
Ac 10: 4 and gifts to the poor have come up as a memorial offering **before**

   18:17 Sosthenes the synagogue ruler and beat him **in front of** the court.
2Co 5:10 For we must all appear **before** the judgment seat of Christ,
Gal 2:14 I said to Peter **in front of** them all, “You are a Jew, yet you live like
Php 3:13 Forgetting what is behind and straining toward what is **ahead**,
1Th 1: 3 We continually remember **before** our God and Father your work
    2:19 or the crown in which we will glory **in the presence** of our Lord
    3: 9 you in return for all the joy we have **in the presence** of our God
    3:13 so that you will be blameless and holy **in the presence** of our God
1Jn 3:19 to the truth, and how we set our hearts at rest **in his presence**
Rev 4: 6 and they were covered with eyes, **in front** and in back.
   19:10 At this I fell **at** his feet to worship him. But he said to me,
   22: 8 I fell down to worship **at** the feet of the angel who had been

1870 ἐμπτύω, *emptyō* [6] [√ *1877 + 4772*]

spit on [3], spit [2], spit at [1]

Mt 26:67 Then *they* **spit** in his face and struck him with their fists. Others
   27:30 *They* **spit** on him, and took the staff and struck him on the head
Mk 10:34 who will mock him and **spit** on him, flog him and kill him.
   14:65 Then some began *to* **spit at** him; they blindfolded him, struck him
   15:19 *Again and again they* struck him on the head with a staff and **spit on**
Lk 18:32 will mock him, insult him, **spit on** *him*, flog him and kill him.

1871 ἐμφανής, *emphanēs* [2] [√ *1877 + 5743*]

revealed [+*1181*] [1], seen [1]

Ac 10:40 him from the dead on the third day and caused him to be **seen**.
Ro 10:20 *I* **revealed** [+*1181*] *myself* to those who did not ask for me.”

1872 ἐμφανίζω, *emphanizō* [10] [√ *1877 + 5743*]

show [3], brought charges [2], appear [1], appeared [1],
appeared and presented the charges [1], petition [1], reported [1]

Mt 27:53 they went into the holy city and **appeared** to many people.
Jn 14:21 by my Father, and I too will love him and **show** myself to him.”
   14:22 why do you intend to **show** yourself to us and not to the world?”
Ac 23:15 and the Sanhedrin **petition** the commander to bring him before you
   23:22 “Don't tell anyone that *you have* **reported** this to me.”
   24: 1 and they **brought** their **charges** against Paul before the governor.
   25: 2 Jewish leaders **appeared** before him **and presented the charges**
   25:15 chief priests and elders of the Jews **brought charges** against him
Heb 9:24 he entered heaven itself, now *to* **appear** for us in God's presence.
   11:14 People who say such things **show** that they are looking for a

1873 ἔμφοβος, *emphobos* [5] [√ *1877 + 5832*]

afraid [1], fright [+*1181*] [1], frightened [1], in fear [+*1181*] [1],
terrified [1]

Lk 24: 5 *In* their **fright** [+*1181*] the women bowed down with their faces to
   24:37 They were startled and **frightened**, thinking they saw a ghost.
Ac 10: 4 Cornelius stared at him **in fear** [+*1181*]. “What is it, Lord?”
   24:25 to come, Felix was **afraid** and said, “That's enough for now!
Rev 11:13 and the survivors were **terrified** and gave glory to the God of

1874 ἐμφυσάω, *emphysaō* [1] [√ *1877 + 5886*]

breathed on [1]

Jn 20:22 And with that *he* **breathed on** them and said, “Receive the Holy

1875 ἔμφυτος, *emphytos* [1] [√ *1877 + 5886*]

planted in [1]

Jas 1:21 so prevalent and humbly accept the word **planted in** you,

1876 ἐμφωνέω, *emphōneō* Not used in UBS/NIV
[√ *1877 + 5889*]

1877 ἐν, en [2752 / 2749]

[→ *440, 441, 450, 1445, 1582, 1588, 1589, 1590, 1591, 1592, 1593,
1594, 1595, 1596, 1597, 1598, 1599, 1600, 1601, 1602, 1603, 1604,*

1605, 1606, 1607, 1608, 1823, 1824, 1832, 1833, 1834, 1835, 1836, 1837, 1838, 1839, 1841, 1844, 1845, 1848, 1849, 1850, 1851, 1852, 1853, 1854, 1855, 1856, 1857, 1858, 1859, 1860, 1861, 1862, 1863, 1864, 1865, 1866, 1867, 1868, 1869, 1870, 1871, 1872, 1873, 1874, 1875, 1876, 1878, 1879, 1880, 1881, 1882, 1887, 1889, 1890, 1891, 1892, 1893, 1896, 1897, 1898, 1899, 1900, 1901, 1902, 1903, 1904, 1905, 1906, 1907, 1908, 1909, 1910, 1911, 1912, 1913, 1918, 1919, 1920, 1921, 1922, 1923, 1924, 1925, 1926, 1927, 1928, 1930, 1931, 1932, 1935, 1936, 1937, 1938, 1939, 1940, 1941, 1943, 1944, 1946, 1947, 1949, 1950, 1951, 1952, 1954, 1955, 1956, 1957, 1958, 1959, 1960, 1961, 1962, 1963, 1964, 1965, 1966, 1967, 1969, 2086, 2087, 2979, 3028, 4212, 4213, 4214, 4599, 5659; cf. 1547, 1953]

ἐν ἡμέραις (in the days [of]) [48] Mt 2:1, 3:1; 23:30; 24:19,38; 27:40; Mk 1:9; 8:1; 13:17,24; 15:29; Lk 1:5,7,18,25,39; 2:1,36; 4:2,25; 5:35; 6:12; 9:36; 17:26,26,28; 21:23; 23:7; 24:18; Jn 2:19,20; Ac 1:15; 2:17,18; 5:37; 6:1; 7:41; 9:37; 11:27; 13:41; 27:7; 2Ti 3:1; Heb 5:7; Jas 5:3; 1Pe 3:20; Rev 2:13; 9:6; 10:7

ἐν σαρκί (in the flesh) [26] Ro 2:28; 7:5,18; 8:3,8,9; 2Co 10:3; Gal 2:20; 4:14; 6:12,13; Eph 2:11,11,14; Php 1:22,24; 3:3,4,4; Col 1:24; 2:1; 1Ti 3:16; Phm 1:16; 1Pe 4:2; 1Jn 4:2; 2Jn 1:7

ἐν [τῷ] Χριστῷ (in Christ) [84] Ro 3:24; 6:11,23; 8:1,2,39; 9:1; 12:5; 15:17; 16:3,7,9,10; 1Co 1:2,4,30; 3:1; 4:10,15,15,17; 15:18,19,22,31; 16:24; 2Co 2:14,17; 3:14; 5:17,19; 12:2,19; Gal 1:22; 2:4,17; 3:14,26,28; 5:6; Eph 1:1,3,10,12,20; 2:6,7,10,13; 3:6,11,21; 4:32; Php 1:1,13,26; 2:1,5; 3:3,14; 4:7,19,21; Col 1:2,4,28; 1Th 2:14; 4:16; 5:18; 1Ti 1:14; 3:13; 2Ti 1:1,9,13; 2:1,10; 3:12,15; Phm 1:8,20,23; 1Pe 3:16; 5:10,14

in [1412], untranslated [207], with [150], by [139], at [133], on [92], among [86], to [39], through [34], of [26], as [+3836] [17], for [16], when [+3836] [15], when [15], among [+3545] [14], during [10], into [10], about [8], within [8], when [+4005] [7], at work in [RP1919] [6], because of [6], this is how [+4047] [6], throughout [+3910] [6], while [+3836] [6], on account of [5], soon [+5443] [5], under [5], against [4], from [4], have [4], how [+5515] [4], out of [4], there [+899] [4], where [+4005] [4], according to [3], as [3], everywhere [+4246+5536] [3], pregnant women [+1143+2400] [3], while [+4005] [3], while in [3], along [2], before [+213] [2], by [+3836] [2], had [+1639] [2], had [2], how [2], in [+3545] [2], in spite of [2], lives in [RP1940] [2], on [+3836] [2], over [2], subject to bleeding [+135+4868] [2], there [+2639+3836] [2], throughout [2], while [2], with child [+1143+2400] [2], works in [RP1919] [2], a public figure [+4244] [1], across [1], after [+4364] [1], after [1], after this [+2759+3836] [1], alive [+899] [1], always [+2789+4246] [1], and [+3836] [1], as a fool [+932] [1], as a man [+4922] [1], as members of [1], as of first importance [+4755] [1], at [+3836] [1], at the time of [1], at work within [RP1919] [1], bear [1], because [+4005] [1], before [+3545+3836] [1], before [+3545] [1], before [1], before circumcised [+213] [1], before the group [+3545] [1], believe [+4409] [1], belong to [1], besides [1], blessed through [RP1922] [1], both of them [+4005] [1], brag [+224+3836] [1], briefly [+3900] [1], by [+5931] [1], by the power of [1], caused by [1], cheerfully [+2660] [1], clearly [+4244] [1], complete [+4246] [1], conceived [+3120+3836+5197] [1], contain [1], contained [+2400] [1], contained [+5639] [1], continue [1], decided [+3836+4460+5502] [1], diligently [+5082] [1], does [+3531+5148] [1], done by [1], down [1], dwell in [RP1940] [1], earnestly [+1755] [1], earthly [+4922] [1], elsewhere [+2283] [1], encircled by [+3545] [1], enemies [+2397] [1], exerted in [RP1919] [1], fearlessly [+4244] [1], figuratively [+4231] [1], figuratively speaking [+4130] [1], following [1], for [+3545+3836] [1], for work [+1256+2237+4005] [1], from among [1], full of [1], gaveˢ [1], generously [+605] [1], gently [+4460+4559] [1], gently [+4559] [1], given a trust [+3874] [1], glorious [+1518] [1], grafted in among [RP1596] [1], gratifyingˢ [1], he [+899+899+3836+4460] [1], heavenly [+3836+4041] [1], heavenly things [+3836+4041] [1], here [+1609] [1], here [+899] [1], here [+4047] [1], holy [+43] [1], humbly [+4559] [1], immediately [+5443] [1], immediately [+899+3836+6052] [1], imperishable [+914] [1], in accordance with [1], in addition [1], in comparison with [+1641+3538+3836+4047] [1], in presence [1],

in the cause of [1], inside [1], invalid [+819+2400+3836] [1], inwardly [+1571] [1], inwardly [+3220+3836] [1], its [+899] [1], Jews [+1169+1609+3836] [1], legalistic [+3795] [1], live [1], live with [RP1940] [1], lived in [RP1940] [1], living among [RP1594] [1], made think [+2840+3836+5502] [1], make up mind [+2840+3836+5502] [1], makeˢ [1], mark [1], meanwhile [+3568+3836] [1], meanwhile [+4005] [1], meanwhile [+4047] [1], modestly [+2950+3177] [1], native [+1164+4005] [1], near [1], next to [+3146+3836] [1], observing [+4513] [1], old [+2465+4581] [1], on board [+3836+4450] [1], on duty [+3836+5423] [1], one Sabbath [+3836+4879] [1], one Sabbath [+4879] [1], open to [1], outward [+3836+5745] [1], outwardly [+3836+5745] [1], outwardly [+4922] [1], painful [+3383] [1], perfectly [+4246] [1], perishable [+5785] [1], personally [+4922] [1], physical [+4922] [1], preaching [+3364] [1], pregnant [+1143+2400] [1], pregnant woman [+1143+2400] [1], produces in [RP1919] [1], purpose [1], put on [1], put to death [+633+5840] [1], quick [+5443] [1], quickly [+5443] [1], relationship to [1], release [+690+912] [1], remain faithful to [RP1844] [1], righteous [+1466] [1], safe [+1645] [1], secret [+3696] [1], securely [+854+4246] [1], show favoritism [+4721] [1], sly [+1515] [1], so powerfully [+1539] [1], soon afterward [+2009+3836] [1], stayed in [RP1844] [1], staying away from [+4024+4344] [1], strike dead [+650+2505] [1], such [+4922] [1], suffering [+5393] [1], that [+3836] [1], that was the time [+1697+2465+3836] [1], there [+3545] [1], there [+3836+4047+4484] [1], there [+3836+5536] [1], Thessalonians [+2553] [1], this kind of [+4231] [1], this makes [+4047] [1], thus [+4047] [1], to himself [+1571] [1], to show [1], true [+237] [1], truly [+237] [1], trying to [1], uncircumcised [+213] [1], united with [1], unseen [+3220+3836] [1], unseen [+3224+3836] [1], until [+4005] [1], use [+4344] [1], wear [1], what [+5515] [1], what [+323+1254+4005] [1], when [+2465] [1], whenever [1], where [+4005+5536] [1], while [+1639+3836] [1], while with [1], wish well [+1645] [1], with [+3545] [1], with [+3836] [1], with child [+1143+5197] [1], with regard to [+3538] [1], with the help of [1], within [+3517+3836] [1], wondered about [+2840+3836+5502] [1], wondering about [+1389+1571] [1], work among [RP1919] [1], written in [RP1582] [1], written on [RP1582] [1]

Mt 1:18 she was found *to be* **with child** [+1143+2400] through the Holy
1:20 because what is conceived **in** her is from the Holy Spirit.
1:23 "The virgin *will be* **with child** [+1143+2400] and will give birth to
2: 1 After Jesus was born **in** Bethlehem in Judea, during the time of
2: 1 **during** the time of King Herod, Magi from the east came to
2: 2 We saw his star **in** the east and have come to worship him."
2: 5 "**In** Bethlehem in Judea," they replied, "for this is what the prophet
2: 6 land of Judah, are by no means least **among** the rulers of Judah;
2: 9 and the star they had seen **in** the east went ahead of them until it
2:16 and he gave orders to kill all the boys **in** Bethlehem and its
2:16 and **[RPG]** its vicinity who were two years old and under,
2:18 "A voice is heard **in** Ramah, weeping and great mourning,
2:19 an angel of the Lord appeared in a dream to Joseph **in** Egypt
3: 1 **In** those days John the Baptist came, preaching in the Desert of
3: 1 those days John the Baptist came, preaching **in** the Desert of Judea
3: 3 "A voice of one calling **in** the desert, 'Prepare the way for the Lord,
3: 6 their sins, they were baptized by him **in** the Jordan River.
3: 9 And do not think you can say **to** yourselves, 'We have Abraham as
3:11 "I baptize you **with** water for repentance. But after me will come
3:11 fit to carry. He will baptize you **with** the Holy Spirit and with fire.
3:12 His winnowing fork is **in** his hand, and he will clear his threshing
3:17 "This is my Son, whom I love; **with** him I am well pleased."
4:13 which was by the lake in the area of Zebulun and Naphtali—
4:16 the people living **in** darkness have seen a great light; on those
4:16 on those living **in** the land of the shadow of death a light has
4:21 They were **in** a boat with their father Zebedee, preparing their nets.
4:23 Jesus went **throughout** [+3910] Galilee, teaching in their
4:23 Jesus went throughout Galilee, teaching **in** their synagogues,
4:23 and healing every disease and sickness **among** the people.
5:12 Rejoice and be glad, because great is your reward **in** heaven,
5:13 But if the salt loses its saltiness, **how** [+5515] can it be made salty
5:15 they put it on its stand, and it gives light to everyone **in** the house.
5:16 they may see your good deeds and praise your Father **in** heaven.
5:19 and teaches others to do the same will be called least **in** the
5:19 and teaches these commands will be called great **in** the kingdom of

5:25 Do it while you are still with him **on** the way, or he may hand you
5:28 lustfully has already committed adultery with her **in** his heart.
5:34 Do not swear at all: either **by** heaven, for it is God's throne;
5:35 or **by** the earth, for it is his footstool;
5:36 And do not swear **by** your head, for you cannot make even one hair
5:45 that you may be sons of your Father **in** heaven. He causes his sun
6: 1 If you do, you will have no reward from your Father **in** heaven.
6: 2 as the hypocrites do **in** the synagogues and on the streets, to be
6: 2 as the hypocrites do **in** the synagogues and on the streets, to be
6: 4 so that your giving may be **in** secret. Then your Father, who sees
6: 4 your Father, who sees what is done **in** secret, will reward you.
6: 5 for they love to pray standing **in** the synagogues and on the street
6: 5 in the synagogues and **on** the street corners to be seen by men.
6: 6 the door and pray to your Father, who is **unseen** [+3220+3836].
6: 6 your Father, who sees what is done **in** secret, will reward you.
6: 7 for they think they will be heard **because of** their many words.
6: 9 you should pray: " 'Our Father **in** heaven, hallowed be your name,
6:10 your kingdom come, your will be done on earth as it is **in** heaven.
6:18 are fasting, but only to your Father, who is **unseen** [+3224+3836];
6:18 and your Father, who sees what is done **in** secret, will reward you.
6:20 But store up for yourselves treasures **in** heaven, where moth
6:23 If then the light **within** you is darkness, how great is that darkness!
6:29 Yet I tell you that not even Solomon **in** all his splendor was
7: 2 For **in** the same way you judge others, you will be judged,
7: 2 you will be judged, and **with** the measure you use, it will be
7: 3 "Why do you look at the speck of sawdust **in** your brother's eye
7: 3 brother's eye and pay no attention to the plank **in** your own eye?
7: 4 of your eye,' when all the time there is a plank **in** your own eye?
7: 6 they may trample them **under** their feet, and then turn and tear you
7:11 how much more will your Father **in** heaven give good gifts to those
7:15 They come to you **in** sheep's clothing, but inwardly they are
7:21 but only he who does the will of my Father who is **in** heaven.
7:22 Many will say to me **on** that day, 'Lord, Lord, did we not prophesy
8: 6 "my servant lies **at** home paralyzed and in terrible suffering."
8:10 the truth, I have not found anyone **in** Israel with such great faith.
8:11 the feast with Abraham, Isaac and Jacob **in** the kingdom of heaven.
8:13 believed it would." And his servant was healed **at** that very hour.
8:24 Without warning, a furious storm came up **on** the lake, so that the
8:32 rushed down the steep bank into the lake and died **in** the water.
9: 3 At this, some of the teachers of the law said **to** themselves,
9: 4 Jesus said, "Why do you entertain evil thoughts **in** your hearts?
9:10 While Jesus was having dinner **at** Matthew's house, many tax
9:21 She said **to** herself, "If I only touch his cloak, I will be healed."
9:31 and spread the news about him **[NIE]** all over that town.
9:33 and said, "Nothing like this has ever been seen **in** Israel."
9:34 "It is **by** the prince of demons that he drives out demons."
9:35 through all the towns and villages, teaching **in** their synagogues,
10:11 search for some worthy person **[NIE]** there and stay at his house
10:15 and Gomorrah **on** the day of judgment than for that town.
10:16 I am sending you out like sheep **among** [+3545] wolves.
10:17 you over to the local councils and flog you **in** their synagogues.
10:19 or how to say it. **At** that time you will be given what to say,
10:20 you speaking, but the Spirit of your Father speaking **through** you.
10:23 When you are persecuted **in** one place, flee to another. I tell you
10:27 What I tell you **in** the dark, speak in the daylight; what is
10:27 What I tell you in the dark, speak **in** the daylight; what is
10:28 be afraid of the One who can destroy both soul and body **in** hell.
10:32 "Whoever acknowledges **[NIE]** me before men, I will also
10:32 I will also acknowledge **[NIE]** him before my Father in heaven.
10:32 I will also acknowledge him before my Father **in** heaven.
10:33 me before men, I will disown him before my Father **in** heaven.
11: 1 he went on from there to teach and preach **in** the towns of Galilee.
11: 2 When John heard **in** prison what Christ was doing, he sent his
11: 6 Blessed is the man who does not fall away **on account of** me."
11: 8 A man dressed **in** fine clothes? No, those who wear fine clothes are
11: 8 fine clothes? No, those who wear fine clothes are **in** kings' palaces.
11:11 **Among** those born of women there has not risen anyone greater
11:11 yet he who is least **in** the kingdom of heaven is greater than he.
11:16 They are like children sitting **in** the marketplaces and calling out
11:20 Then Jesus began to denounce the cities **in** which most of his
11:21 If the miracles that were performed **in** you had been performed in
11:21 If the miracles that were performed in you had been performed **in**
11:21 they would have repented long ago **in** sackcloth and ashes.
11:22 bearable for Tyre and Sidon **on** the day of judgment than for you.
11:23 If the miracles that were performed **in** you had been performed in
11:23 If the miracles that were performed in you had been performed **in**

11:24 But I tell you that it will be more bearable for Sodom **on** the day of
11:25 **At** that time Jesus said, "I praise you, Father, Lord of heaven
12: 1 **At** that time Jesus went through the grainfields on the Sabbath.
12: 2 Your disciples are doing what is unlawful **on** the Sabbath."
12: 5 Or haven't you read in the Law that on the Sabbath the priests **in**
12: 5 Or haven't you read in the Law that on the Sabbath the priests **in**
12:19 will not quarrel or cry out; no one will hear his voice **in** the streets.
12:24 this, they said, "It is only **by** Beelzebub, the prince of demons,
12:27 And if I drive out demons **by** Beelzebub, by whom do your people
12:27 demons by Beelzebub, **by** whom do your people drive them out?
12:28 But if I drive out demons **by** the Spirit of God, then the kingdom of
12:32 Spirit will not be forgiven, either **in** this age or in the age to come.
12:32 Spirit will not be forgiven, either in this age or in the age to come.
12:36 But I tell you that men will have to give account **on** the day of
12:40 as Jonah was three days and three nights **in** the belly of a huge fish,
12:40 of Man will be three days and three nights **in** the heart of the earth.
12:41 The men of Nineveh will stand up **at** the judgment with this
12:42 The Queen of the South will rise **at** the judgment with this
12:50 For whoever does the will of my Father **in** heaven is my brother
13: 1 **[NIE]** That same day Jesus went out of the house and sat by the
13: 3 Then he told them many things **in** parables, saying: "A farmer went
13: 4 **As** [+3836] he was scattering the seed, some fell along the path,
13:10 to him and asked, "Why do you speak to the people **in** parables?"
13:13 This is why I speak to them **in** parables: "Though seeing, they do
13:19 the evil one comes and snatches away what was sown **in** his heart.
13:21 But since he has no root, **[NIE]** he lasts only a short time.
13:24 "The kingdom of heaven is like a man who sowed good seed **in** his
13:25 But **while** [+3836] everyone was sleeping, his enemy came
13:27 came to him and said, 'Sir, didn't you sow good seed **in** your field?
13:30 **At** that time I will tell the harvesters: First collect the weeds
13:31 is like a mustard seed, which a man took and planted **in** his field.
13:32 so that the birds of the air come and perch **in** its branches."
13:34 Jesus spoke all these things to the crowd **in** parables; he did not say
13:35 "I will open my mouth **in** parables, I will utter things hidden since
13:40 pulled up and burned in the fire, so it will be **at** the end of the age.
13:43 Then the righteous will shine like the sun **in** the kingdom of their
13:44 "The kingdom of heaven is like treasure hidden **in** a field. When a
13:49 This is how it will be **at** the end of the age. The angels will come
13:54 he began teaching the people **in** their synagogue, and they were
13:57 And they took offense **at** him. But Jesus said to them, "Only in his
13:57 "Only **in** his hometown and in his own house is a prophet without
13:57 in his hometown and **in** his own house is a prophet without honor."
14: 1 **At** that time Herod the tetrarch heard the reports about Jesus,
14: 2 That is why miraculous powers *are* **at** work in [*RP1919*] him."
14: 3 and bound him and put him **in** prison because of Herodias,
14: 6 birthday the daughter of Herodias danced **for** [+3545+3836] them
14:10 and had John beheaded **in** the prison.
14:13 had happened, he withdrew **by** boat privately to a solitary place.
14:33 Then those who were **in** the boat worshiped him, saying, "Truly
15:32 want to send them away hungry, or they may collapse **on** the way."
15:33 "Where could we get enough bread **in** this remote place to feed
16: 7 They discussed this **among** themselves and said, "It is because we
16: 8 why are you talking **among** yourselves about having no bread?
16:17 this was not revealed to you by man, but by my Father **in** heaven.
16:19 whatever you bind on earth will be bound **in** heaven, and whatever
16:19 and whatever you loose on earth will be loosed **in** heaven."
16:27 For the Son of Man is going to come **in** his Father's glory with his
16:28 taste death before they see the Son of Man coming **in** his kingdom."
17: 5 "This is my Son, whom I love; **with** [+3545] him I am well pleased.
17:12 not recognize him, but have done **to** him everything they wished.
17:22 When they came together **in** Galilee, he said to them, "The Son of
18: 1 **At** that time the disciples came to Jesus and asked, "Who is the
18: 1 and asked, "Who is the greatest **in** the kingdom of heaven?"
18: 2 He called a little child and had him stand **among** [+3545] them.
18: 4 whoever humbles himself like this child is the greatest **in** the
18: 6 hung around his neck and to be drowned **in** the depths of the sea.
18:10 For I tell you that their angels **in** heaven always see the face of my
18:10 their angels in heaven always see the face of my Father **in** heaven.
18:14 In the same way your Father **in** heaven is not willing that any of
18:18 you the truth, whatever you bind on earth will be bound **in** heaven,
18:18 and whatever you loose on earth will be loosed **in** heaven."
18:19 you ask for, it will be done for you by my Father **in** heaven.
18:20 or three come together in my name, there am I **with** [+3545] them."
19:21 and give to the poor, and you will have treasure **in** heaven.
19:28 Jesus said to them, "I tell you the truth, **at** the renewal of all things,
20: 3 and saw others standing **in** the marketplace doing nothing.

20:15 Don't I have the right to do what I want **with** my own money?
20:17 took the twelve disciples aside and said to them, [UBS+ *on the way*]
20:21 may sit at your right and the other at your left **in** your kingdom."
20:26 Not so **with** you. Instead, whoever wants to become great among
20:26 whoever wants to become great **among** you must be your servant,
20:27 and whoever wants [NIE] to be first must be your slave—
21: 8 A very large crowd spread their cloaks **on** the road, while others
21: 8 others cut branches from the trees and spread them **on** the road.
21: 9 "Blessed is he who comes **in** the name of the Lord!" "Hosanna in
21: 9 he who comes in the name of the Lord!" "Hosanna **in** the highest!"
21:12 drove out all who were buying and selling **there**ˢ [+2639+3836].
21:14 The blind and the lame came to him **at** the temple, and he healed
21:15 things he did and the children shouting **in** the temple area,
21:19 by the road, he went up to it but found nothing **on** it except leaves.
21:22 If you believe, you will receive whatever you ask for **in** prayer."
21:23 "**By** what authority are you doing these things?" they asked.
21:24 I will tell you **by** what authority I am doing these things.
21:25 They discussed it **among** themselves and said, "If we say,
21:27 "Neither will I tell you **by** what authority I am doing these things.
21:28 to the first and said, 'Son, go and work today **in** the vineyard.'
21:32 For John came to you **to show** you the way of righteousness,
21:33 put a wall around it, dug a winepress **in** it and built a watchtower.
21:38 the tenants saw the son, they said **to** each other, 'This is the heir.
21:41 who will give him his share of the crop **at** harvest time."
21:42 Jesus said to them, "Have you never read **in** the Scriptures:
21:42 the Lord has done this, and it is marvelous **in** our eyes'?
22: 1 Jesus spoke to them again in parables, saying:
22:15 the Pharisees went out and laid plans to trap him **in** his words.
22:16 and that you teach the way of God **in accordance with** the truth.
22:23 [NIE] That same day the Sadducees, who say there is no
22:28 Now then, **at** the resurrection, whose wife will she be of the seven,
22:30 **At** the resurrection people will neither marry nor be given in
22:30 nor be given in marriage; they will be like the angels **in** heaven.
22:36 "Teacher, which is the greatest commandment **in** the Law?"
22:37 " 'Love the Lord your God **with** all your heart and with all your
22:37 with all your heart and **with** all your soul and with all your mind.'
22:37 with all your heart and with all your soul and **with** all your mind.'
22:40 All the Law and the Prophets hang **on** these two commandments."
22:43 He said to them, "How is it then that David, speaking **by** the Spirit,
23: 6 they love the place of honor **at** banquets and the most important
23: 6 honor at banquets and the most important seats **in** the synagogues;
23: 7 they love to be greeted **in** the marketplaces and to have men call
23:16 You say, 'If anyone swears **by** the temple, it means nothing;
23:16 but if anyone swears **by** the gold of the temple, he is bound by his
23:18 You also say, 'If anyone swears **by** the altar, it means nothing;
23:18 but if anyone swears **by** the gift on it, he is bound by his oath.'
23:20 he who swears **by** the altar swears by it and by everything on it.
23:20 he who swears by the altar swears **by** it and by everything on it.
23:20 he who swears by the altar swears by it and **by** everything on it.
23:21 And he who swears **by** the temple swears by it and by the one who
23:21 And he who swears by the temple swears **by** it and by the one who
23:21 swears by the temple swears by it and **by** the one who dwells in it.
23:22 And he who swears **by** heaven swears by God's throne and by the
23:22 And he who swears by heaven swears **by** God's throne and by the
23:22 by heaven swears by God's throne and **by** the one who sits on it.
23:30 And you say, 'If we had lived **in** the days of our forefathers,
23:30 we would not have taken part with them **in** shedding the blood of
23:34 others you will flog **in** your synagogues and pursue from town to
23:39 until you say, 'Blessed is he who comes **in** the name of the Lord.' "
24:14 And this gospel of the kingdom will be preached **in** the whole
24:15 "So when you see standing **in** the holy place 'the abomination that
24:16 then let those who are **in** Judea flee to the mountains.
24:18 Let no one **in** the field go back to get his cloak.
24:19 How dreadful it will be **in** those days for pregnant women
24:19 it will be in those days *for* **pregnant women** [+1143+2400]
24:26 if anyone tells you, 'There he is, out **in** the desert,' do not go out;
24:26 do not go out; or, 'Here he is, **in** the inner rooms,' do not believe it.
24:30 "At that time the sign of the Son of Man will appear **in** the sky,
24:38 For **in** the days before the flood, people were eating and drinking,
24:40 Two men will be **in** the field; one will be taken and the other left.
24:41 Two women will be grinding **with** a hand mill; one will be taken
24:45 in his household to give them their food **at** the proper time?
24:48 But suppose that servant is wicked and says **to** himself, 'My master
24:50 The master of that servant will come **on** a day when he does not
24:50 day when he does not expect him and **at** an hour he is not aware of.
25: 4 The wise, however, took oil **in** jars along with their lamps.

25:16 at once and put his [NIE] money to work and gained five more.
25:25 So I was afraid and went out and hid your talent **in** the ground.
25:31 "When the Son of Man comes **in** his glory, and all the angels with
25:36 you looked after me, I was **in** prison and you came to visit me.'
25:39 When did we see you sick or **in** prison and go to visit you?'
25:43 clothe me, I was sick and **in** prison and you did not look after me.'
25:44 or thirsty or a stranger or needing clothes or sick or **in** prison,
26: 5 "But not **during** the Feast," they said, "or there may be a riot among
26: 5 the Feast," they said, "or there may be a riot **among** the people."
26: 6 While Jesus was **in** Bethany in the home of a man known as Simon
26: 6 While Jesus was in Bethany **in** the home of a man known as Simon
26:13 wherever this gospel is preached **throughout** [+3910] the world,
26:23 "The one who has dipped his hand **into** the bowl with me will
26:29 that day when I drink it anew with you **in** my Father's kingdom."
26:31 [NIE] "This very night you will all fall away on account of me,
26:31 "This very night you will all fall away **on account of** me, for it is
26:33 Peter replied, "Even if all fall away **on account of** you, I never
26:34 "I tell you the truth," Jesus answered, [NIE] "this very night,
26:52 said to him, "for all who draw the sword will die **by** the sword.
26:55 **At** that time Jesus said to the crowd, "Am I leading a rebellion,
26:55 Every day I sat **in** the temple courts teaching, and you did not
26:69 Now Peter was sitting out **in** the courtyard, and a servant girl came
27:12 **When** [+3836] he was accused by the chief priests and the elders,
27:29 They put a staff **in** his right hand and knelt in front of him
27:40 "You who are going to destroy the temple and build it **in** three days,
27:56 **Among** them were Mary Magdalene, Mary the mother of James
27:59 Joseph took the body, wrapped it **in** a clean linen cloth,
27:60 and placed it **in** his own new tomb that he had cut out of the rock.
27:60 and placed it in his own new tomb that he had cut out **of** the rock.
28:18 "All authority **in** heaven and on earth has been given to me.
Mk 1: 2 It is written **in** Isaiah the prophet: "I will send my messenger ahead
1: 3 "a voice of one calling **in** the desert, 'Prepare the way for the Lord,
1: 4 baptizing **in** the desert region and preaching a baptism of
1: 5 their sins, they were baptized by him **in** the Jordan River.
1: 8 you with water, but he will baptize you **with** the Holy Spirit."
1: 9 **At** that time Jesus came from Nazareth in Galilee and was baptized
1:11 "You are my Son, whom I love; **with** you I am well pleased."
1:13 and he was **in** the desert forty days, being tempted by Satan.
1:15 of God is near. Repent and **believe** [+4409] the good news!"
1:16 he saw Simon and his brother Andrew casting a net **into** the lake,
1:19 he saw James son of Zebedee and his brother John **in** a boat,
1:20 and they left their father Zebedee **in** the boat with the hired men
1:23 then a man **in** their synagogue who was possessed by an evil spirit
1:23 then a man in their synagogue who was *possessed* **by** an evil spirit
2: 1 the people heard that he had come [NIE] home.
2: 6 some teachers of the law were sitting there, thinking **to** themselves,
2: 8 in his spirit that this was what they were thinking **in** their hearts,
2: 8 and he said to them, "Why are you thinking these things? [RPG]
2:15 While Jesus was having dinner **at** Levi's house, many tax
2:19 "How can the guests of the bridegroom fast **while** [+4005] he is
2:20 bridegroom will be taken from them, and **on** that day they will fast.
2:23 **One Sabbath** [+3836+4879] Jesus was going through the
3:22 by Beelzebub! **By** the prince of demons he is driving out demons."
3:23 So Jesus called them and spoke to them **in** parables: "How can
4: 1 so large that he got into a boat and sat **in** it out on the lake,
4: 2 He taught them many things **by** parables, and in his teaching said:
4: 2 He taught them many things by parables, and **in** his teaching said:
4: 4 **As** [+3836] he was scattering the seed, some fell along the path,
4:11 to you. But to those on the outside everything is said **in** parables
4:17 But since they have no root, [NIE] they last only a short time.
4:24 "**With** the measure you use, it will be measured to you—
4:28 first the stalk, then the head, then the full kernel **in** the head.
4:30 of God is like, or **what** [+5515] parable shall we use to describe it?
4:35 [NIE] That day when evening came, he said to his disciples,
4:36 the crowd behind, they took him along, just as he was, **in** the boat.
4:38 Jesus was **in** the stern, sleeping on a cushion. The disciples woke
5: 2 a man **with** an evil spirit came from the tombs to meet him.
5: 3 This man lived **in** the tombs, and no one could bind him any more,
5: 5 Night and day **among** the tombs and in the hills he would cry out
5: 5 and day among the tombs and **in** the hills he would cry out
5:13 down the steep bank into the lake and were drowned. [RPG]
5:20 and began to tell **in** the Decapolis how much Jesus had done for
5:21 When Jesus had again crossed over **by** boat to the other side of the
5:25 who had been **subject to bleeding** [+135+4868] for twelve years.
5:27 she came up behind him **in** the crowd and touched his cloak,
5:30 At once Jesus realized that [NIE] power had gone out from him.

5: 30 He turned around **in** the crowd and asked, "Who touched my
6: 2 When the Sabbath came, he began to teach **in** the synagogue,
6: 3 Aren't his sisters here with us?" And they took offense **at** him.
6: 4 Jesus said to them, "Only **in** his hometown, among his relatives
6: 4 **among** his relatives and in his own house is a prophet without
6: 4 his relatives and **in** his own house is a prophet without honor."
6: 14 and that is why miraculous powers *are* **at work in** [*RP1919*] him."
6: 17 to have John arrested, and he had him bound and put **in** prison.
6: 27 to bring John's head. The man went, beheaded John **in** the prison,
6: 29 John's disciples came and took his body and laid it **in** a tomb.
6: 32 So they went away by themselves **in** a boat to a solitary place.
6: 47 When evening came, the boat was **in** the middle of the lake,
6: 48 He saw the disciples straining **at** [*+3836*] the oars,
6: 51 and the wind died down. **[NIE]** They were completely amazed,
6: 56 towns or countryside—they placed the sick **in** the marketplaces.
8: 1 **During** those days another large crowd gathered. Since they had
8: 3 If I send them home hungry, they will collapse **on** the way,
8: 14 to bring bread, except for one loaf they had with them **in** the boat.
8: 27 **On** the way he asked them, "Who do people say I am?"
8: 38 of me and my words **in** this adulterous and sinful generation,
8: 38 the Son of Man will be ashamed of him when he comes **in** his
9: 1 taste death before they see the kingdom of God come **with** power."
9: 29 He replied, "This kind **[NIE]** can come out only by prayer."
9: 29 He replied, "This kind can come out only **by** prayer."
9: 33 When he was **in** the house, he asked them, "What were you arguing
9: 33 he asked them, "What were you arguing about **on** the road?"
9: 34 because **on** the way they had argued about who was the greatest.
9: 36 He took a little child and had him stand **among** [*+3545*] them.
9: 38 "we saw a man driving out demons **in** your name and we told him
9: 41 anyone who gives you a cup of water **in** my name because you
9: 50 but if it loses its saltiness, **how** [*+5515*] can you make it salty
9: 50 Have salt **in** yourselves, and be at peace with each other."
9: 50 Have salt in yourselves, and be **at** peace with each other."
10: 21 and give to the poor, and you will have treasure **in** heaven.
10: 30 will fail to receive a hundred times as much **in** this present age
10: 30 and with them, persecutions) and **in** the age to come, eternal life.
10: 32 They were on their way up to Jerusalem, with Jesus leading the
10: 37 one of us sit at your right and the other at your left **in** your glory."
10: 43 Not so **with** you. Instead, whoever wants to become great among
10: 43 whoever wants to become great **among** you must be your servant,
10: 44 and whoever wants to be first **[RPG]** must be slave of all.
10: 52 he received his sight and followed Jesus **along** the road.
11: 9 "Hosanna!" "Blessed is he who comes **in** the name of the Lord!"
11: 10 coming kingdom of our father David!" "Hosanna **in** the highest!"
11: 13 a fig tree in leaf, he went to find out if **[NIE]** it had any fruit.
11: 15 out those who were buying and selling **there**ˢ [*+2639+3836*].
11: 23 and does not doubt **in** his heart but believes that what he says will
11: 25 so that your Father in heaven may forgive you your sins."
11: 27 and while Jesus was walking **in** the temple courts, the chief priests,
11: 28 "**By** what authority are you doing these things?" they asked.
11: 29 and I will tell you **by** what authority I am doing these things.
11: 33 "Neither will I tell you **by** what authority I am doing these things."
12: 1 He then began to speak to them **in** parables: "A man planted a
12: 11 the Lord has done this, and it is marvelous **in** our eyes'?"
12: 23 **At** the resurrection whose wife will she be, since the seven were
12: 25 nor be given in marriage; they will be like the angels **in** heaven.
12: 26 have you not read **in** the book of Moses, in the account of the bush,
12: 35 While Jesus was teaching **in** the temple courts, he asked, "How is it
12: 36 David himself, speaking **by** the Holy Spirit, declared: " 'The Lord
12: 38 **As** he taught, Jesus said, "Watch out for the teachers of the law.
12: 38 They like to walk around **in** flowing robes and be greeted in the
12: 38 walk around in flowing robes and be greeted **in** the marketplaces,
12: 39 and have the most important seats **in** the synagogues and the places
12: 39 seats in the synagogues and the places of honor **at** banquets.
13: 11 Just say whatever is given you **at** the time, for it is not you
13: 14 then let those who are **in** Judea flee to the mountains.
13: 17 How dreadful it will be **in** those days for pregnant women
13: 17 it will be in those days *for* **pregnant women** [*+1143+2400*]
13: 24 "But **in** those days, following that distress, " 'the sun will be
13: 25 the sky, and the **heavenly** [*+3836+4041*] bodies will be shaken.'
13: 26 "At that time men will see the Son of Man coming **in** clouds with
13: 32 one knows about that day or hour, not even the angels **in** heaven,
14: 1 and the teachers of the law were looking for some **sly** [*+1515*] way
14: 2 "But not **during** the Feast," they said, "or the people may riot."
14: 3 While he was **in** Bethany, reclining at the table in the home of a
14: 3 reclining at the table **in** the home of a man known as Simon the

14: 6 "Why are you bothering her? She has done a beautiful thing **to** me.
14: 25 vine until that day when I drink it anew **in** the kingdom of God."
14: 49 with you, teaching **in** the temple courts, and you did not arrest me.
14: 66 While Peter was below **in** the courtyard, one of the servant girls of
15: 7 the insurrectionists who had committed murder **in** the uprising.
15: 29 You who are going to destroy the temple and build it **in** three days,
15: 40 **Among** them were Mary Magdalene, Mary the mother of James
15: 41 **In** Galilee these women had followed him and cared for his needs.
15: 46 wrapped it in the linen, and placed it **in** a tomb cut out of rock.
16: 5 they saw a young man dressed in a white robe sitting **on** the right
16: 12 Afterward Jesus appeared **in** a different form to two of them while
16: 17 **In** my name they will drive out demons; they will speak in new
16: 18 they will pick up snakes **with** their hands;

Lk   1: 1 up an account of the things that have been fulfilled **among** us,
1: 5 **In** the time of Herod king of Judea there was a priest named
1: 6 **observing** [*+4513*] all the Lord's commandments and regulations
1: 7 Elizabeth was barren; and they were both well along **in** years.
1: 8 Once **when** Zechariah's division was on duty and he was serving
1: 8 Once when Zechariah's division was **on duty** [*+3836+5423*]
1: 17 he will go on before the Lord, **in** the spirit and power of Elijah,
1: 17 their children and the disobedient **to** the wisdom of the righteous—
1: 18 sure of this? I am an old man and my wife is well along **in** years."
1: 21 and wondering why he **[NIE]** stayed so long in the temple.
1: 21 for Zechariah and wondering why he stayed so long **in** the temple.
1: 22 They realized he had seen a vision **in** the temple, for he kept
1: 25 "**In** these days he has shown his favor and taken away my disgrace
1: 25 shown his favor and taken away my disgrace **among** the people."
1: 26 **In** the sixth month, God sent the angel Gabriel to Nazareth,
1: 31 *You will be* **with child** [*+1143+5197*] and give birth to a son,
1: 36 Even Elizabeth your relative is going to have a child **in** her old age,
1: 39 **At** that time Mary got ready and hurried to a town in the hill
1: 41 Elizabeth heard Mary's greeting, the baby leaped **in** her womb,
1: 42 "Blessed are you **among** women, and blessed is the child you will
1: 44 greeting reached my ears, the baby **in** my womb leaped for joy.
1: 44 greeting reached my ears, the baby in my womb leaped **for** joy.
1: 51 He has performed mighty deeds **with** his arm; he has scattered
1: 59 **On** the eighth day they came to circumcise the child, and they were
1: 65 and **throughout** [*+3910*] the hill country of Judea people were
1: 66 Everyone who heard this **wondered about** [*+2840+3836 | 5502*] it,
1: 69 He has raised up a horn of salvation for us **in** the house of his
1: 75 **in** holiness and righteousness before him all our days.
1: 77 to give his people the knowledge of salvation **through** the
1: 78 of our God, **by** which the rising sun will come to us from heaven
1: 79 to shine on those living **in** darkness and in the shadow of death,
1: 80 and he lived **in** the desert until he appeared publicly to Israel.
2: 1 **In** those days Caesar Augustus issued a decree that a census should
2: 6 **While** [*+1639+3836*] they were there, the time came for the baby
2: 7 She wrapped him in cloths and placed him **in** a manger,
2: 7 him in a manger, because there was no room for them **in** the inn.
2: 8 And there were shepherds living out **in** the fields nearby, keeping
2: 11 Today **in** the town of David a Savior has been born to you;
2: 12 You will find a baby wrapped in cloths and lying **in** a manger."
2: 14 "Glory to God **in** the highest, and on earth peace to men on whom
2: 14 in the highest, and on earth peace **to** men on whom his favor rests."
2: 16 and Joseph, and the baby, who was lying **in** the manger.
2: 19 Mary treasured up all these things and pondered them **in** her heart.
2: 21 had given him before he *had been* **conceived** [*+3120+3836+5197*].
2: 23 (as it is written **in** the Law of the Lord, "Every firstborn male is to
2: 24 and to offer a sacrifice in keeping with what is said **in** the Law of
2: 25 Now there was a man **in** Jerusalem called Simeon, who was
2: 27 **Moved** by the Spirit, he went into the temple courts. When the
2: 27 **When** [*+3836*] the parents brought in the child Jesus to do for him
2: 29 as you have promised, you now dismiss your servant **in** peace.
2: 34 child is destined to cause the falling and rising of many **in** Israel,
2: 36 She *was* very **old** [*+2465+4581*]; she had lived with her husband
2: 43 Feast was over, **while** [*+3836*] his parents were returning home,
2: 43 the boy Jesus stayed behind **in** Jerusalem, but they were unaware
2: 44 Thinking he was **in** their company, they traveled on for a day.
2: 44 Then they began looking for him **among** their relatives and friends.
2: 46 After three days they found him **in** the temple courts, sitting among
2: 46 sitting **among** [*+3545*] the teachers, listening to them and asking
2: 49 he asked. "Didn't you know I had to be **in** my Father's house?"
2: 51 to them. But his mother treasured all these things **in** her heart.
2: 52 And Jesus grew in **[UBS+** *in***]** wisdom and stature,
3: 1 **In** the fifteenth year of the reign of Tiberius Caesar—when Pontius
3: 2 the word of God came to John son of Zechariah **in** the desert.

3: 4   As is written **in** the book of the words of Isaiah the prophet:
3: 4   "A voice of one calling **in** the desert, 'Prepare the way for the Lord,
3: 8   And do not begin to say **to** yourselves, 'We have Abraham as our
3: 15 and were all wondering **in** their hearts if John might possibly be
3: 16 to untie. He will baptize you **with** the Holy Spirit and with fire.
3: 17 His winnowing fork is **in** his hand to clear his threshing floor
3: 20 Herod added this to them all: He locked John up **in** prison.
3: 21 **When** [+3836] all the people were being baptized, Jesus was
3: 22 "You are my Son, whom I love; **with** you I am well pleased."
4: 1   returned from the Jordan and was led **by** the Spirit in the desert,
4: 1   returned from the Jordan and was led by the Spirit **in** the desert,
4: 2   He ate nothing **during** those days, and at the end of them he was
4: 5   and showed him **in** an instant all the kingdoms of the world.
4: 14 Jesus returned to Galilee **in** the power of the Spirit, and news about
4: 15 He taught **in** their synagogues, and everyone praised him.
4: 16 and on the Sabbath day he went into the synagogue, as was his
4: 18 of sight for the blind, *to* **release** [+690+912] the oppressed,
4: 20 The eyes of everyone **in** the synagogue were fastened on him,
4: 21 saying to them, "Today this scripture is fulfilled **in** your hearing."
4: 23 Do here **in** your hometown what we have heard that you did in
4: 24 the truth," he continued, "no prophet is accepted **in** his hometown.
4: 25 I assure you that there were many widows **in** Israel in Elijah's
4: 25 I assure you that there were many widows in Israel **in** Elijah's
4: 27 And there were many **in** Israel with leprosy in the time of Elisha
4: 28 All the people **in** the synagogue were furious when they heard this.
4: 31 a town in Galilee, and **on** the Sabbath began to teach the people.
4: 32 at his teaching, because his message **had** [+1639] authority.
4: 33 **In** the synagogue there was a man possessed by a demon,
4: 36 **With** authority and power he gives orders to evil spirits and they
5: 1   **with** [+3836] the people crowding around him and listening to the
5: 7   So they signaled their partners **in** the other boat to come and help
5: 12 **While** [+3836] Jesus was in one of the towns, a man came along
5: 12 While Jesus was **in** one of the towns, a man came along who was
5: 16 But Jesus often withdrew **to** lonely places and prayed.
5: 17 [NIE] One day as he was teaching, Pharisees and teachers of the
5: 22 and asked, "Why are you thinking these things **in** your hearts?
5: 29 Then Levi held a great banquet for Jesus **at** his house, and a large
5: 34 "Can you make the guests of the bridegroom fast **while** [+4005] he
5: 35 bridegroom will be taken from them; **in** those days they will fast."
6: 1   **One Sabbath** [+4879] Jesus was going through the grainfields,
6: 6   **On** another Sabbath he went into the synagogue and was teaching,
6: 7   so they watched him closely to see if he would heal **on** the
6: 12 One **of** those days Jesus went out to a mountainside to pray,
6: 12 a mountainside to pray, and spent the night [NIE] praying to God.
6: 23 "Rejoice **in** that day and leap for joy,
6: 23 that day and leap for joy, because great is your reward **in** heaven.
6: 41 "Why do you look at the speck of sawdust **in** your brother's eye
6: 41 brother's eye and pay no attention to the plank **in** your own eye?
6: 42 'Brother, let me take the speck out of [NIE] your eye,'
6: 42 when you yourself fail to see the plank **in** your own eye?
6: 42 then you will see clearly to remove the speck from [NIE] your
7: 9   "I tell you, I have not found such great faith even **in** Israel."
7: 11 **Soon afterward** [+2009+3836], Jesus went to a town called Nain,
7: 16 praised God. "A great prophet has appeared **among** us," they said.
7: 17 This news about Jesus spread **throughout** [+3910] Judea and the
7: 21 **At** that very time Jesus cured many who had diseases, sicknesses
7: 23 Blessed is the man who does not fall away **on account of** me."
7: 25 A man dressed **in** fine clothes? No, those who wear expensive
7: 25 those who **wear** expensive clothes and indulge in luxury are in
7: 25 who wear expensive clothes and indulge in luxury are **in** palaces.
7: 28 **among** those born of women there is no one greater than John;
7: 28 yet the one who is least **in** the kingdom of God is greater than he."
7: 32 They are like children sitting **in** the marketplace and calling out to
7: 37 When a woman who had lived a sinful life **in** that town learned that
7: 37 in that town learned that Jesus was eating **at** the Pharisee's house,
7: 39 he said to himself, "If this man were a prophet, he would know who
7: 49 The other guests began to say **among** themselves, "Who is this who
8: 1   **After this** [+2759+3836], Jesus traveled about from one town
8: 5   **As** [+3836] he was scattering the seed, some fell along the path;
8: 7   Other seed fell **among** [+3545] thorns, which grew up with it
8: 10 but to others I speak **in** parables, so that, " 'though seeing, they may
8: 13 They believe for a while, but **in** the time of testing they fall away.
8: 15 But the seed **on** good soil stands for those with a noble and good
8: 15 But the seed on good soil stands for those **with** a noble and good
8: 15 who hear the word, retain it, and **by** persevering produce a crop.
8: 22 [NIE] One day Jesus said to his disciples, "Let's go over to the

8: 27 For a long time this man had not worn clothes or lived **in** a house,
8: 27 not worn clothes or lived in a house, but had lived **in** the tombs.
8: 32 A large herd of pigs was feeding there **on** the hillside. The demons
8: 40 Now **when** [+3836] Jesus returned, a crowd welcomed him,
8: 42 **As** [+3836] Jesus was on his way, the crowds almost crushed him.
8: 43 who had been **subject to bleeding** [+135+4868] for twelve years,
9: 12 and find food and lodging, because we are **in** a remote place here."
9: 18 Once **when** [+3836] Jesus was praying in private and his disciples
9: 26 the Son of Man will be ashamed of him when he comes **in** his
9: 29 **As** [+3836] he was praying, the appearance of his face changed,
9: 31 appeared **in** glorious splendor, talking with Jesus. They spoke
9: 31 which he was about to bring to fulfillment **at** Jerusalem.
9: 33 **As** [+3836] the men were leaving Jesus, Peter said to him,
9: 34 and they were afraid **as** [+3836] they entered the cloud.
9: 36 **When** [+3836] the voice had spoken, they found that Jesus was
9: 36 this to themselves, and told no one **at** that time what they had seen.
9: 46 An argument started **among** the disciples as to which of them
9: 48 sent me. For he who is least **among** you all—he is the greatest."
9: 49 "we saw a man driving out demons **in** your name and we tried to
9: 51 **As** [+3836] the time approached for him to be taken up to heaven,
9: 57 As they were walking **along** the road, a man said to him, "I will
10: 3 Go! I am sending you out like lambs **among** [+3545] wolves.
10: 7 Stay **in** that house, eating and drinking whatever they give you,
10: 9 Heal the sick who are **there** [+899] and tell them, 'The kingdom
10: 12 it will be more bearable **on** that day for Sodom than for that town.
10: 13 For if the miracles that were performed **in** you had been performed
10: 13 miracles that were performed in you had been performed **in** Tyre
10: 13 they would have repented long ago, sitting **in** sackcloth and ashes.
10: 14 be more bearable for Tyre and Sidon **at** the judgment than for you.
10: 17 and said, "Lord, even the demons submit to us **in** your name."
10: 20 to you, but [NIE] rejoice that your names are written in heaven."
10: 20 but rejoice that your names *are* **written in** [RP1582] heaven."
10: 21 **At** that time Jesus, full of joy through the Holy Spirit, said,
10: 21 full of joy **through** the Holy Spirit, said, "I praise you, Father,
10: 26 "What is written **in** the Law?" he replied. "How do you read it?"
10: 27 and **with** all your soul and with all your strength and with all your
10: 27 and with all your soul and **with** all your strength and with all your
10: 27 all your soul and with all your strength and **with** all your mind';
10: 31 A priest happened to be going down [NIE] the same road,
10: 35 'Look after him,' he said, 'and **when** [+3836] I return, I will
10: 38 **As** [+3836] Jesus and his disciples were on their way, he came to a
11: 1 One day Jesus [NIE] was praying in a certain place. When he
11: 1 One day Jesus was praying **in** a certain place. When he finished,
11: 15 But some of them said, "**By** Beelzebub, the prince of demons,
11: 18 I say this because you claim that I drive out demons **by** Beelzebub.
11: 19 Now if I drive out demons **by** Beelzebub, by whom do your
11: 19 demons by Beelzebub, **by** whom do your followers drive them out?
11: 20 But if I drive out demons **by** the finger of God, then the kingdom
11: 21 guards his own house, his possessions are **safe** [+1645].
11: 27 **As** [+3836] Jesus was saying these things, a woman in the crowd
11: 31 The Queen of the South will rise **at** the judgment with the men of
11: 32 The men of Nineveh will stand up **at** the judgment with this
11: 35 See to it, then, that the light **within** you is not darkness.
11: 37 **When** [+3836] Jesus had finished speaking, a Pharisee invited him
11: 43 because you love the most important seats **in** the synagogues
11: 43 seats in the synagogues and greetings **in** the marketplaces.
12: 1 **Meanwhile** [+4005], when a crowd of many thousands had
12: 3 What you have said **in** the dark will be heard in the daylight,
12: 3 What you have said in the dark will be heard **in** the daylight,
12: 3 and what you have whispered in the ear **in** the inner rooms will be
12: 8 "I tell you, whoever acknowledges [NIE] me before men,
12: 8 the Son of Man will also acknowledge [NIE] him before the
12: 12 for the Holy Spirit will teach you **at** that time what you should say."
12: 15 a man's life does not consist **in** the abundance of his possessions."
12: 17 He thought **to** himself, 'What shall I do? I have no place to store
12: 27 not even Solomon **in** all his splendor was dressed like one of these.
12: 28 If that is how God clothes the grass of the field, which is here
12: 33 a treasure **in** heaven that will not be exhausted, where no thief
12: 38 even if he comes **in** the second or third watch of the night.
12: 38 even if he comes in the second or [RPG] third watch of the night.
12: 42 his servants to give them their food allowance **at** the proper time?
12: 45 But suppose the servant says **to** himself, 'My master is taking a
12: 46 The master of that servant will come **on** a day when he does not
12: 46 day when he does not expect him and **at** an hour he is not aware of.
12: 51 Do you think I came to bring peace **on** earth? No, I tell you,
12: 52 From now on there will be five **in** one family divided against each

12:58 try hard to be reconciled to him **on** the way, or he may drag you off
13: 1 Now there were some present **at** that time who told Jesus about the
13: 4 Or those eighteen who died when the tower **in** Siloam fell on
13: 6 "A man had a fig tree, planted **in** his vineyard, and he went to look
13: 6 and he went to look for fruit **on** it, but did not find any.
13: 7 'For three years now I've been coming to look for fruit **on** this fig
13:10 **On** a Sabbath Jesus was teaching in one of the synagogues,
13:10 On a Sabbath Jesus was teaching **in** one of the synagogues,
13:14 to the people, "There are six days **for work** [+1256+2237+4005].
13:14 So come and be healed **on** those days, not on the Sabbath."
13:19 and became a tree, and the birds of the air perched **in** its branches."
13:26 'We ate and drank with you, and you taught **in** our streets.'
13:28 Isaac and Jacob and all the prophets **in** the kingdom of God,
13:29 and will take their places at the feast **in** the kingdom of God.
13:31 **At** that time some Pharisees came to Jesus and said to him,
13:35 until you say, 'Blessed is he who comes **in** the name of the Lord.' "
14: 1 **when** [+3836] Jesus went to eat in the house of a prominent
14: 5 of you has a son or an ox that falls into a well **on** the Sabbath day,
14:14 repay you, you will be repaid **at** the resurrection of the righteous."
14:15 is the man who will eat at the feast **in** the kingdom of God."
14:31 and consider whether he is able **with** ten thousand men to oppose
14:34 but if it loses its saltiness, **how** [+5515] can it be made salty again?
15: 4 Does he not leave the ninety-nine **in** the open country and go after
15: 7 I tell you that in the same way there will be more rejoicing **in**
15:25 "Meanwhile, the older son was **in** the field. When he came near the
16: 3 "The manager said **to himself** [+1571], 'What shall I do now?
16:10 "Whoever can be trusted **with** very little can also be trusted with
16:10 "Whoever can be trusted with very little can also be trusted **with**
16:10 and whoever is dishonest **with** very little will also be dishonest
16:10 is dishonest with very little will also be dishonest **with** much.
16:11 So if you have not been trustworthy **in** *handling* worldly wealth,
16:12 And if you have not been trustworthy **with** someone else's
16:15 What is highly valued **among** men is detestable in God's sight.
16:23 **In** hell, where he was in torment, he looked up and saw Abraham
16:23 In hell, where he was **in** torment, he looked up and saw Abraham
16:23 he looked up and saw Abraham far away, with Lazarus **by** his side.
16:24 in water and cool my tongue, because I am in agony **in** this fire.'
16:25 remember that **in** your lifetime you received your good things,
16:26 And **besides** all this, between us and you a great chasm has been
17: 6 'Be uprooted and planted **in** the sea,' and it will obey you.
17:11 Now **on** [+3836] his way to Jerusalem, Jesus traveled along the
17:14 to the priests." And **as** [+3836] they went, they were cleansed.
17:24 For the Son of Man **in** his day will be like the lightning,
17:26 "Just as it was **in** the days of Noah, so also will it be in the days of
17:26 the days of Noah, so also will it be **in** the days of the Son of Man.
17:28 "It was the same **in** the days of Lot. People were eating
17:31 **On** that day no one who is on the roof of his house, with his goods
17:31 of his house, with his goods **inside**, should go down to get them.
17:31 Likewise, no one **in** the field should go back for anything.
18: 2 "**In** a certain town there was a judge who neither feared God nor
18: 3 And there was a widow **in** that town who kept coming to him with
18: 4 But finally he said **to** himself, 'Even though I don't fear God
18: 8 I tell you, he will see that they get justice, and **quickly** [+5443].
18:22 and give to the poor, and you will have treasure **in** heaven.
18:30 will fail to receive many times as much **in** this age and, in the age
18:30 times as much in this age and, **in** the age to come, eternal life."
18:35 **As** [+3836] Jesus approached Jericho, a blind man was sitting by
19: 5 come down immediately. I must stay **at** your house today."
19:13 'Put this money to work,' he said, '**until** [+4005] I come back.'
19:15 "He was made king, however, **and** [+3836] returned home.
19:17 'Because you have been trustworthy **in** a very small matter,
19:20 here is your mina; I have kept it laid away **in** a piece of cloth.
19:30 and as you enter **[NIE]** it, you will find a colt tied there, which no
19:36 As he went along, people spread their cloaks **on** the road.
19:38 "Blessed is the king who comes **in** the name of the Lord!" "Peace in
19:38 the name of the Lord!" "Peace **in** heaven and glory in the highest!"
19:38 the name of the Lord!" "Peace in heaven and glory **in** the highest!"
19:42 had only known **on** this day what would bring you peace—
19:44 dash you to the ground, you and the children **within** your *walls*.
19:44 **[NIE]** because you did not recognize the time of God's coming
19:47 Every day he was teaching **at** the temple. But the chief priests,
20: 1 **[NIE]** One day as he was teaching the people in the temple courts
20: 1 One day as he was teaching the people **in** the temple courts
20: 2 "Tell us **by** what authority you are doing these things," they said.
20: 8 "Neither will I tell you **by** what authority I am doing these things."
20:19 looked for a way to arrest him **immediately** [+899+3836+6052],

20:33 Now then, **at** the resurrection whose wife will she be,
20:42 David himself declares **in** the Book of Psalms: " 'The Lord said to
20:46 They like to walk around **in** flowing robes and love to be greeted in
20:46 around in flowing robes and love to be greeted **in** the marketplaces
20:46 and have the most important seats **in** the synagogues and the places
20:46 seats in the synagogues and the places of honor **at** banquets.
21: 6 the time will come **when** [+4005] not one stone will be left on
21:14 But **make up** your **mind** [+2840+3836+5502] not to worry
21:19 **By** standing firm you will gain life.
21:21 Then let those who are **in** Judea flee to the mountains, let those in
21:21 let those **in** [+3545] the city get out, and let those in the country not
21:21 in the city get out, and let those **in** the country not enter the city.
21:23 How dreadful it will be **in** those days for pregnant women
21:23 it will be in those days for **pregnant women** [+1143+2400]
21:25 "There will be signs **in** the sun, moon and stars. On the earth,
21:25 nations will be **in** anguish and perplexity at the roaring and tossing
21:27 At that time they will see the Son of Man coming **in** a cloud with
21:34 "Be careful, or your hearts will be weighed down **with** dissipation,
21:36 Be **always** [+2789+4246] on the watch, and pray that you may be
21:37 Each day Jesus was teaching **at** the temple, and each evening he
21:38 and all the people came early in the morning to hear him **at** the
22: 7 the day of Unleavened Bread **on** which the Passover
22:16 I will not eat it again until it finds fulfillment **in** the kingdom of
22:20 saying, "This cup is the new covenant **in** my blood, which is poured
22:24 Also a dispute arose **among** them as to which of them was
22:26 Instead, the greatest **among** you should be like the youngest,
22:27 is at the table? But I am **among** [+3545] you as one who serves.
22:28 You are those who have stood by me **in** my trials.
22:30 may eat and drink at my table **in** my kingdom and sit on thrones,
22:37 the transgressors'; and I tell you that this must be fulfilled **in** me.
22:44 And being **in** anguish, he prayed more earnestly, and his sweat was
22:49 to happen, they said, "Lord, should we strike **with** our swords?"
22:53 Every day I was with you **in** the temple courts, and you did not lay
22:55 But when they had kindled a fire **in** the middle of the courtyard
23: 4 and the crowd, "I find no basis for a charge **against** this man."
23: 7 he sent him to Herod, who was also **in** Jerusalem at that time.
23: 7 he sent him to Herod, who was also in Jerusalem **at** that time.
23: 9 He plied him **with** many questions, but Jesus gave him no answer.
23:12 **[NIE]** That day Herod and Pilate became friends—before this
23:12 Pilate became friends—before this they had been **enemies** [+2397].
23:14 I have examined **[NIE]** him in your presence and have found no
23:19 (Barabbas had been thrown **into** prison for an insurrection in the
23:19 (Barabbas had been thrown into prison for an insurrection **in** the
23:22 I have found **in** him no grounds for the death penalty. Therefore I
23:29 For the time will come **when** [+4005] you will say, 'Blessed are
23:31 For if men do these things **when** the tree is green, what will happen
23:31 things when the tree is green, what will happen **when** it is dry?'"
23:40 you fear God," he said, "since you are **under** the same sentence?
23:43 "I tell you the truth, today you will be with me **in** paradise."
23:53 wrapped it in linen cloth and placed it **in** a tomb cut in the rock,
24: 4 **While** [+3836] they were wondering about this, suddenly two men
24: 4 suddenly two men **in** clothes that gleamed like lightning stood
24: 6 Remember how he told you, while he was still with you **in** Galilee:
24:13 Now **[NIE]** that same day two of them were going to a village
24:15 **As** [+3836] they talked and discussed these things with each other,
24:18 and do not know the things that have happened **there** [+899] in
24:18 do not know the things that have happened there **in** these days?"
24:19 powerful **in** word and deed before God and all the people.
24:27 he explained to them what was said **in** all the Scriptures concerning
24:30 **When** [+3836] he was at the table with them, he took bread,
24:32 "Were not our hearts burning **within** us while he talked with us on
24:32 "Were not our hearts burning within us while he talked with us **on**
24:35 Then the two told what had happened **on** the way, and how Jesus
24:35 and how Jesus was recognized by them **when** he broke the bread.
24:36 Jesus himself stood **among** [+3545] them and said to them,
24:38 "Why are you troubled, and why do doubts rise **in** your minds?
24:44 Everything must be fulfilled that is written about me **in** the Law of
24:49 but stay **in** the city until you have been clothed with power from on
24:51 **While** [+3836] he was blessing them, he left them and was taken
24:53 And they stayed continually **at** the temple, praising God.

Jn 1: 1 **In** the beginning was the Word, and the Word was with God,
1: 2 He was with God **in** the beginning.
1: 4 **In** him was life, and that life was the light of men.
1: 5 The light shines **in** the darkness, but the darkness has not
1:10 He was **in** the world, and though the world was made through him,
1:14 The Word became flesh and made his dwelling **among** us.

1:23 "I am the voice of one calling **in** the desert, 'Make straight the way
1:26 "I baptize **with** water," John replied, "but among you stands one
1:28 This all happened **at** Bethany on the other side of the Jordan,
1:31 but the reason I came baptizing **with** water was that he might be
1:33 except that the one who sent me to baptize **with** water told me,
1:33 and remain is he who will baptize **with** the Holy Spirit.'
1:45 told him, "We have found the one Moses wrote about **in** the Law,
1:47 of him, "Here is a true Israelite, **in** whom there is nothing false."
2: 1 On the third day a wedding took place **at** Cana in Galilee.
2:11 first of his miraculous signs, Jesus performed **at** Cana in Galilee.
2:14 **In** the temple courts he found men selling cattle, sheep and doves,
2:19 "Destroy this temple, and I will raise it again **in** three days."
2:20 to build this temple, and you are going to raise it **in** three days?"
2:23 Now while he was **in** Jerusalem at the Passover Feast, many people
2:23 Now while he was in Jerusalem **at** the Passover Feast,
2:23 Now while he was in Jerusalem at the Passover **[RPG]** Feast,
2:25 need man's testimony about man, for he knew what was **in** a man.
3:14 Just as Moses lifted up the snake **in** the desert, so the Son of Man
3:15 that everyone who believes **in** him may have eternal life.
3:21 be seen plainly that what he has done has been done **through** God."
3:23 Now John also was baptizing **at** Aenon near Salim, because there
3:35 The Father loves the Son and has placed everything **in** his hands.
4:14 the water I give him will become **in** him a spring of water welling
4:20 Our fathers worshiped **on** this mountain, but you Jews claim that
4:20 but you Jews claim that the place where we must worship is **in**
4:21 a time is coming when you will worship the Father neither **on** this
4:21 will worship the Father neither on this mountain nor **in** Jerusalem.
4:23 come when the true worshipers will worship the Father **in** spirit
4:24 is spirit, and his worshipers must worship **in** spirit and in truth."
4:31 **Meanwhile** [+3568+3836] his disciples urged him, "Rabbi, eat
4:37 **Thus** [+4047] the saying 'One sows and another reaps' is true.
4:44 (Now Jesus himself had pointed out that a prophet has no honor **in**
4:45 They had seen all that he had done **in** Jerusalem at the Passover
4:45 They had seen all that he had done in Jerusalem **at** the Passover
4:46 And there was a certain royal official whose son lay sick **at**
4:52 When he inquired as to the time **when** [+4005] his son got better,
4:53 Then the father realized that **[NIE]** this was the exact time at
4:53 Then the father realized that this was the exact time **at** which Jesus
5: 2 Now there is **in** Jerusalem near the Sheep Gate a pool, which in
5: 3 **Here** [+4047] a great number of disabled people used to lie—
5: 5 *had been an* **invalid** [+819+2400+3836] for thirty-eight years.
5: 7 **While** [+4005] I am trying to get in, someone else goes down
5: 9 and walked. The day **on** which this took place was a Sabbath,
5:13 had slipped away into the crowd that was **there** [+3836+5536].
5:14 Later Jesus found him **at** the temple and said to him, "See, you are
5:16 So, because Jesus was doing these things **on** the Sabbath, the Jews
5:26 For as the Father has life **in** himself, so he has granted the Son to
5:26 life in himself, so he has granted the Son to have life **in** himself.
5:28 for a time is coming **when** [+4005] all who are in their graves will
5:28 for a time is coming when all who are **in** their graves will hear his
5:35 and gave light, and you chose for a time to enjoy **[NIE]** his light.
5:38 nor does his word dwell **in** you, for you do not believe the one he
5:39 because you think that **by** them you possess eternal life.
5:42 I know that you do not have the love of God **in** your hearts.
5:43 I have come **in** my Father's name, and you do not accept me;
5:43 but if someone else comes **in** his own name, you will accept him.
6:10 There was plenty of grass **in** that place, and the men sat down,
6:31 Our forefathers ate the manna **in** the desert; as it is written:
6:39 none of all that he has given me, but raise them up **at** the last day.
6:40 him shall have eternal life, and I will raise him up **at** the last day."
6:44 who sent me draws him, and I will raise him up **at** the last day.
6:45 It is written **in** the Prophets: 'They will all be taught by God.'
6:49 Your forefathers ate the manna **in** the desert, yet they died.
6:53 of the Son of Man and drink his blood, you have no life **in** you.
6:56 Whoever eats my flesh and drinks my blood remains **in** me,
6:56 eats my flesh and drinks my blood remains in me, and I **in** him.
6:59 He said this while teaching **in** the synagogue in Capernaum.
6:59 He said this while teaching in the synagogue **in** Capernaum.
6:61 Aware **[NIE]** that his disciples were grumbling about this,
7: 1 After this, Jesus went around **in** Galilee, purposely staying away
7: 1 purposely **staying away from** [+4024+4344] Judea
7: 4 No one who wants to become **a public figure** [+4244] acts in
7: 4 No one who wants to become a public figure acts **in** secret.
7: 9 Having said this, he stayed **in** Galilee.
7:10 had left for the Feast, he went also, not publicly, but **in** secret.
7:11 Now **at** the Feast the Jews were watching for him and asking,

7:12 **Among** the crowds there was widespread whispering about him.
7:18 who sent him is a man of truth; there is nothing false **about** him.
7:22 but from the patriarchs), you circumcise a child **on** the Sabbath.
7:23 Now if a child can be circumcised **on** the Sabbath so that the law
7:23 why are you angry with me for healing the whole man **on** the
7:28 Then Jesus, still teaching **in** the temple courts, cried out, "Yes,
7:37 **On** the last and greatest day of the Feast, Jesus stood and said in a
7:43 Thus **[NIE]** the people were divided because of Jesus.
8: 3 in adultery. They made her stand **before the group** [+3545]
8: 5 **In** the Law Moses commanded us to stone such women. Now what
8: 9 only Jesus was left, with the woman still standing **there** [+3545].
8:12 Whoever follows me will never walk **in** darkness, but will have the
8:17 **In** your own Law it is written that the testimony of two men is
8:20 He spoke these words while teaching **in** the temple area near the
8:20 He spoke these words while teaching in the temple area **near** the
8:21 going away, and you will look for me, and you will die **in** your sin.
8:24 I told you that you would die **in** your sins; if you do not believe
8:24 that I am ‚the one I claim to be‚, you will indeed die **in** your sins."
8:31 Jesus said, "If you hold **to** my teaching, you are really my disciples.
8:35 Now a slave has no permanent place **in** the family,
8:37 ready to kill me, because **[NIE]** you have no room for my word.
8:44 the beginning, not holding **to** the truth, for there is no truth in him.
8:44 the beginning, not holding to the truth, for there is no truth **in** him.
9: 3 so that the work of God might be displayed **in** his life.
9: 5 While I am **in** the world, I am the light of the world."
9:14 Now the day **on** which Jesus had made the mud and opened the
9:16 a sinner do such miraculous signs?" So **[NIE]** they were divided.
9:30 The man answered, "Now **[NIE]** that is remarkable! You don't
9:34 To this they replied, "You were steeped **in** sin at birth; how dare
10:19 At these words **[NIE]** the Jews were again divided.
10:22 Then came the Feast of Dedication **at** Jerusalem. It was winter,
10:23 and Jesus was **in** the temple area walking in Solomon's Colonnade.
10:23 and Jesus was in the temple area walking **in** Solomon's Colonnade.
10:25 not believe. The miracles I do **in** my Father's name speak for me,
10:34 Jesus answered them, "Is it not written **in** your Law, 'I have said
10:38 that you may know and understand that the Father is **in** me,
10:38 and understand that the Father is in me, and I **in** the Father."
11: 6 was sick, he stayed **where** [+4005+5536] he was two more days.
11: 9 A man who walks **by** day will not stumble, for he sees by this
11:10 It is when he walks **by** night that he stumbles, for he has no light."
11:10 he walks by night that he stumbles, for **[NIE]** he has no light."
11:17 Jesus found that Lazarus had already been **in** the tomb for four
11:20 was coming, she went out to meet him, but Mary stayed **at** home.
11:24 "I know he will rise again **in** the resurrection at the last day."
11:24 "I know he will rise again in the resurrection **at** the last day."
11:30 the village, but was still **at** the place where Martha had met him.
11:31 When the Jews who had been with Mary **in** the house, comforting
11:38 Jesus, once more deeply moved, **[NIE]** came to the tomb.
11:54 Therefore Jesus no longer moved about publicly **among** the Jews.
11:56 and as they stood **in** the temple area they asked one another,
12:13 "Hosanna!" "Blessed is he who comes **in** the name of the Lord!"
12:20 some Greeks among those who went up to worship **at** the Feast.
12:25 while the man who hates his life **in** this world will keep it for
12:35 **[NIE]** "You are going to have the light just a little while longer.
12:35 The man who walks **in** the dark does not know where he is going.
12:46 so that no one who believes in me should stay **in** darkness.
12:48 that very word which I spoke will condemn him **at** the last day.
13: 1 Having loved his own who were **in** the world, he now showed
13:23 whom Jesus loved, was reclining **next** [+3146+3836] to him.
13:31 "Now is the Son of Man glorified and God is glorified **in** him.
13:32 If God is glorified **in** him, God will glorify the Son in himself,
13:32 If God is glorified in him, God will glorify the Son **in** himself,
13:35 **By** this all men will know that you are my disciples, if you love
13:35 know that you are my disciples, if you love **[NIE]** one another."
14: 2 **In** my Father's house are many rooms; if it were not so, I would
14:10 Don't you believe that I am **in** the Father, and that the Father is in
14:10 you believe that I am in the Father, and that the Father is **in** me?
14:10 Rather, it is the Father, living **in** me, who is doing his work.
14:11 Believe me when I say that I am **in** the Father and the Father is in
14:11 me when I say that I am in the Father and the Father is **in** me;
14:13 And I will do whatever you ask **in** my name, so that the Son may
14:13 in my name, so that **[NIE]** the Son may bring glory to the Father.
14:14 You may ask me for anything **in** my name, and I will do it.
14:17 But you know him, for he lives with you and will be **in** you.
14:20 **On** that day you will realize that I am in my Father, and you are in
14:20 On that day you will realize that I am **in** my Father, and you are in

14:20 that day you will realize that I am in my Father, and you are **in** me,
14:20 realize that I am in my Father, and you are in me, and I am **in** you.
14:26 the Holy Spirit, whom the Father will send **in** my name,
14:30 for the prince of this world is coming. He has no hold **on** me,
15: 2 He cuts off every branch **in** me that bears no fruit, while every
15: 4 Remain **in** me, and I will remain in you. No branch can bear fruit
15: 4 Remain in me, and I will remain **in** you. No branch can bear fruit
15: 4 No branch can bear fruit by itself; it must remain **in** the vine.
15: 4 in the vine. Neither can you bear fruit unless you remain **in** me.
15: 5 If a man remains **in** me and I in him, he will bear much fruit;
15: 5 If a man remains in me and I **in** him, he will bear much fruit;
15: 6 If anyone does not remain **in** me, he is like a branch that is thrown
15: 7 If you remain **in** me and my words remain in you, ask whatever
15: 7 If you remain in me and my words remain **in** you, ask whatever
15: 8 **[NIE]** This is to my Father's glory, that you bear much fruit,
15: 9 Father has loved me, so have I loved you. Now remain **in** my love.
15:10 If you obey my commands, you will remain **in** my love, just as I
15:10 as I have obeyed my Father's commands and remain **in** his love.
15:11 I have told you this so that my joy may be **in** you and that your joy
15:16 Then the Father will give you whatever you ask **in** my name.
15:24 If I had not done **among** them what no one else did, they would not
15:25 But this is to fulfill what is written in their Law: 'They hated me
16:13 the Spirit of truth, comes, he will guide you **into** all truth.
16:23 **In** that day you will no longer ask me anything. I tell you the truth,
16:23 the truth, my Father will give you whatever you ask **in** my name.
16:24 Until now you have not asked for anything **in** my name. Ask
16:25 "Though I have been speaking **figuratively** [*+4231*], a time is
16:25 a time coming when I will no longer use **this**ˢ kind of [*+4231*]
16:26 **In** that day you will ask in my name. I am not saying that I will ask
16:26 In that day you will ask **in** my name. I am not saying that I will ask
16:29 "Now you are speaking **clearly** [*+4244*] and without figures of
16:30 **This makes** [*+4047*] us believe that you came from God."
16:33 "I have told you these things, so that **in** me you may have peace.
16:33 **In** this world you will have trouble. But take heart! I have
17:10 and all you have is mine. And glory has come to me **through** them.
17:11 I will remain **in** the world no longer, but they are still in the world,
17:11 I will remain in the world no longer, but they are still **in** the world,
17:11 Holy Father, protect them **by the power of** your name—the name
17:12 I protected them and kept them safe **by** that name you gave me.
17:13 to you now, but I say these things **while** I am *still* in the world,
17:13 so that they may have the full measure of my joy **within** them.
17:17 Sanctify them **by** the truth; your word is truth.
17:19 I sanctify myself, that they too may be **truly** [*+237*] sanctified.
17:21 of them may be one, Father, just as you are **in** me and I am in you.
17:21 of them may be one, Father, just as you are in me and I am **in** you.
17:21 May they also be **in** us so that the world may believe that you have
17:23 I **in** them and you in me. May they be brought to complete unity to
17:23 I in them and you **in** me. May they be brought to complete unity to
17:26 you known in order that the love you have for me may be **in** them
17:26 you have for me may be in them and that I myself may be **in** them."
18:20 "I always taught **in** synagogues or at the temple, where all the Jews
18:20 "I always taught in synagogues or at the temple, where all the Jews
18:20 where all the Jews come together. I said nothing **in** secret.
18:26 challenged him, "Didn't I see you with him **in** the olive grove?"
18:38 to the Jews and said, "I find no basis for a charge **against** him.
18:39 for me to release to you one prisoner **at the time of** the Passover.
19: 4 you to let you know that I find no basis for a charge **against** him."
19: 6 crucify him. As for me, I find no basis for a charge **against** him."
19:31 did not want the bodies left on the crosses **during** the Sabbath,
19:41 **At** the place where Jesus was crucified, there was a garden,
19:41 there was a garden, and **in** the garden a new tomb, in which no one
19:41 and in the garden a new tomb, **in** which no one had ever been laid.
20:12 and saw two angels in white, seated where Jesus' body had been,
20:25 "Unless I see the nail marks **in** his hands and put my finger where
20:30 the presence of his disciples, which are not recorded **in** this book.
20:31 Son of God, and that by believing you may have life **in** his name.
21: 3 and got into the boat, but **[NIE]** that night they caught nothing.
21:20 (This was the one who had leaned back against Jesus **at** the supper
Ac 1: 3 to these men and **gave**ˢ many convincing proofs that he was alive.
1: 5 but in a few days you will be baptized **with** the Holy Spirit."
1: 6 are you **at** this time going to restore the kingdom to Israel?"
1: 7 to know the times or dates the Father has set **by** his own authority.
1: 8 and you will be my witnesses **in** Jerusalem, and in all Judea
1: 8 and **in** all Judea and Samaria, and to the ends of the earth."
1:10 when suddenly two men dressed **in** white stood beside them.
1:15 **In** those days Peter stood up among the believers (a group

1:15 In those days Peter stood up **among** [*+3545*] the believers (a group
1:17 he was one **of** our number and shared in this ministry."
1:20 said Peter, "it is written **in** the book of Psalms, " 'May his place
1:20 there be no one to dwell **in** it,' and, " 'May another take his place
1:21 have been with us **[NIE]** the whole time the Lord Jesus went in
2: 1 **When** [*+3836*] the day of Pentecost came, they were all together in
2: 8 each of us hears them in his own **native** [*+1164+4005*] language?
2:17 " '**In** the last days, God says, I will pour out my Spirit on all
2:18 both men and women, I will pour out my Spirit **in** those days,
2:19 I will show wonders **in** the heaven above and signs on the earth
2:22 and signs, which God did **among** [*+3545*] you through him,
2:29 and was buried, and his tomb is **here** [*+1609*] to this day.
2:41 and about three thousand were added to their number **[NIE]** that
2:46 Every day they continued to meet together **in** the temple courts.
2:46 bread in their homes and ate together **with** glad and sincere hearts,
3: 6 I have I give you. **In** the name of Jesus Christ of Nazareth, walk."
3:25 'Through your offspring all peoples on earth will be blessed.'
3:26 he sent him first to you to bless you **by** [*+3836*] turning each of
4: 2 the people and proclaiming **in** Jesus the resurrection of the dead.
4: 5 day the rulers, elders and teachers of the law met **in** Jerusalem.
4: 7 They had Peter and John brought **before** [*+3545+3836*] them
4: 7 to question them: "**By** what power or what name did you do this?"
4: 7 "By what power or **[RPG]** what name did you do this?"
4: 9 shown to a cripple and are asked **how** [*+5515*] he was healed,
4:10 It is **by** the name of Jesus Christ of Nazareth, whom you crucified
4:10 from the dead, that **[RPG]** this man stands before you healed.
4:12 Salvation is found **in** no one else, for there is no other name under
4:12 for there is no other name under heaven given **to** men by which we
4:12 for there is no other name under heaven given to men **by** which we
4:24 made the heaven and the earth and the sea, and everything **in** them.
4:27 and the people of Israel **in** this city to conspire against your holy
4:30 **[NIE]** Stretch out your hand to heal and perform miraculous signs
4:31 the place **where** [*+4005*] they were meeting was shaken.
4:34 There were no needy persons **among** them. For from time to time
5: 4 And after it was sold, wasn't the money **at** your disposal?
5: 4 What **made** you **think** [*+2840+3836+5502*] of doing such a thing?
5:12 performed many miraculous signs and wonders **among** the people.
5:12 And all the believers used to meet together **in** Solomon's
5:18 They arrested the apostles and put them **in** the public jail.
5:20 "Go, stand **in** the temple courts," he said, "and tell the people the
5:22 But on arriving **at** the jail, the officers did not find them there.
5:23 "We found the jail **securely** [*+854+4246*] locked, with the guards
5:25 The men you put **in** jail are standing in the temple courts teaching
5:25 The men you put in jail are standing **in** the temple courts teaching
5:27 they made them appear **before** the Sanhedrin to be questioned by
5:34 stood up **in** the Sanhedrin and ordered that the men be put outside
5:37 Judas the Galilean appeared **in** the days of the census and led a
5:42 Day after day, **in** the temple courts and from house to house,
6: 1 **In** those days when the number of disciples was increasing,
6: 1 because their widows were being overlooked **in** the daily
6: 7 The number of disciples **in** Jerusalem increased rapidly, and a large
6: 8 did great wonders and miraculous signs **among** the people.
6:15 All who were sitting **in** the Sanhedrin looked intently at Stephen,
7: 2 appeared to our father Abraham while he was still **in** Mesopotamia,
7: 2 while he was still in Mesopotamia, before he lived in Haran.
7: 4 "So he left the land of the Chaldeans and settled in Haran. After the
7: 5 He gave him no inheritance **here** [*+899*], not even a foot of
7: 6 'Your descendants will be strangers **in** a country not their own,
7: 7 they will come out of that country and worship me **in** this place.'
7:13 **On** their second visit, Joseph told his brothers who he was,
7:14 sent for his father Jacob and his whole family, seventy-five **in** all.
7:16 and placed **in** the tomb that Abraham had bought from the sons of
7:16 from the sons of Hamor **at** Shechem for a certain sum of money.
7:17 to Abraham, the number of our people **in** Egypt greatly increased.
7:20 "**At** that time Moses was born, and he was no ordinary child.
7:20 For three months he was cared for **in** his father's house.
7:22 Moses was educated **in** all the wisdom of the Egyptians and was
7:22 wisdom of the Egyptians and was powerful **in** speech and action.
7:29 **When** Moses heard this, he fled to Midian, where he settled as a
7:29 When Moses heard this, he fled **to** Midian, where he settled as a
7:30 an angel appeared to Moses **in** the flames of a burning bush, a
7:30 an angel appeared to Moses in the flames of a burning bush **in** the
7:34 I have indeed seen the oppression of my people **in** Egypt. I have
7:35 God himself, through the angel who appeared to him **in** the bush.
7:36 them out of Egypt and did wonders and miraculous signs **in** Egypt,
7:36 signs in Egypt, **at** the Red Sea and for forty years in the desert.

7:36 signs in Egypt, at the Red Sea and for forty years **in** the desert.
7:38 He was **in** the assembly in the desert, with the angel who spoke to
7:38 He was in the assembly **in** the desert, with the angel who spoke to
7:38 with the angel who spoke to him **on** Mount Sinai, and with our
7:39 they rejected him and in their hearts turned back to Egypt.
7:41 **That was the time** [+1697+2465+3836] they made an idol in the
7:41 and held a celebration **in** honor of what their hands had made.
7:42 This agrees with what is written **in** the book of the prophets:
7:42 'Did you bring me sacrifices and offerings forty years **in** the desert,
7:44 "Our forefathers had the tabernacle of the Testimony with them **in**
7:45 our fathers under Joshua brought it with them **when** they took the
7:48 "However, the Most High does not live **in** houses made by men.
8: 1 **On** that day a great persecution broke out against the church at
8: 1 On that day a great persecution broke out against the church **at**
8: 6 **When** [+3836] the crowds heard Philip and saw the miraculous
8: 8 So there was great joy **in** that city.
8: 9 Now for some time a man named Simon had practiced sorcery **in**
8:14 When the apostles **in** Jerusalem heard that Samaria had accepted
8:21 You have no part or share **in** this ministry, because your heart is
8:33 **In** his humiliation he was deprived of justice. Who can speak of his
9: 3 As he neared Damascus **on** [+3836] his journey, suddenly a light
9:10 **In** Damascus there was a disciple named Ananias. The Lord called
9:10 The Lord called to him **in** a vision, "Ananias!" "Yes, Lord," he
9:11 "Go **to** the house of Judas on Straight Street and ask for a man from
9:12 **In** a vision he has seen a man named Ananias come and place his
9:13 this man and all the harm he has done to your saints **in** Jerusalem.
9:17 who appeared to you **on** the road as you were coming here—
9:19 Saul spent several days with the disciples **in** Damascus.
9:20 At once he began to preach **in** the synagogues that Jesus is the Son
9:22 and baffled the Jews living **in** Damascus by proving that Jesus is
9:25 and lowered him in a basket through an opening in the wall.
9:27 He told them how Saul **on** his journey had seen the Lord and that
9:27 and how **in** Damascus he had preached fearlessly in the name of
9:27 and how in Damascus he had preached fearlessly **in** the name of
9:28 about freely in Jerusalem, speaking boldly **in** the name of the Lord.
9:36 **In** Joppa there was a disciple named Tabitha (which,
9:37 **About** that time she became sick and died, and her body was
9:37 and her body was washed and placed **in** an upstairs room.
9:38 so when the disciples heard that Peter was **in** Lydda, they sent two
9:43 Peter stayed **in** Joppa for some time with a tanner named Simon.
10: 1 **At** Caesarea there was a man named Cornelius, a centurion in what
10: 3 One day at about three in the afternoon he **had** a vision.
10:12 It **contained** [+5639] all kinds of four-footed animals, as well as
10:17 While Peter *was* **wondering about** [+1389+1571] the meaning of
10:30 "Four days ago I was **in** my house praying at this hour, at three in
10:30 the afternoon. Suddenly a man **in** shining clothes stood before me
10:32 He is a guest in the home of Simon the tanner, who lives by the
10:35 but accepts men **from** every nation who fear him and do what is
10:39 "We are witnesses of everything he did **in** the country of the Jews
10:39 of everything he did in the country of the Jews and **in** Jerusalem.
10:40 but God raised him from the dead **on** the third day and caused him
10:48 So he ordered that they be baptized **in** the name of Jesus Christ.
11: 5 "I was **in** the city of Joppa praying, and in a trance I saw a vision.
11: 5 "I was in the city of Joppa praying, and **in** a trance I saw a vision.
11:11 from Caesarea stopped at the house **where** [+4005] I was staying.
11:13 He told us how he had seen an angel appear **in** his house and say,
11:14 He will bring you a message **through** which you and all your
11:15 "As [+3836] I began to speak, the Holy Spirit came on them as he
11:15 the Holy Spirit came on them as he had come on us **at** the
11:16 baptized with water, but you will be baptized **with** the Holy Spirit.'
11:22 News of this reached the ears of the church **at** Jerusalem, and they
11:26 So for a whole year Barnabas and Saul met **with** the church
11:26 of people. The disciples were called Christians first **at** Antioch.
11:27 **During** this time some prophets came down from Jerusalem to
11:29 his ability, decided to provide help for the brothers living **in** Judea.
12: 5 So Peter was kept in prison, but the church was earnestly praying
12: 7 an angel of the Lord appeared and a light shone **in** the cell.
12: 7 "**Quick** [+5443], get up!" he said, and the chains fell off Peter's
12:11 Then Peter came **to** himself and said, "Now I know without a doubt
12:18 there was no small commotion **among** the soldiers as to what had
13: 1 In the church **at** Antioch there were prophets and teachers:
13: 5 When they arrived **at** Salamis, they proclaimed the word of God in
13: 5 they proclaimed the word of God in the Jewish synagogues.
13:15 if [NIE] you have a message of encouragement for the people,
13:17 he made the people prosper **during** their stay in Egypt, with
13:17 he made the people prosper during their stay **in** Egypt, with mighty

13:18 he endured their conduct for about forty years **in** the desert,
13:19 he overthrew seven nations **in** Canaan and gave their land to his
13:26 children of Abraham, and [NIE] you God-fearing Gentiles,
13:27 The people **of** Jerusalem and their rulers did not recognize Jesus,
13:33 As it is written **in** the second Psalm: " 'You are my Son; today I
13:35 it is stated **elsewhere** [+2283]: " 'You will not let your Holy One
13:39 **Through** him everyone who believes is justified from everything
13:39 everything you could not be justified from **by** the law of Moses.
13:40 Take care that what [NIE] the prophets have said does not happen
13:41 for I am going to do something **in** your days that you would never
14: 1 **At** Iconium Paul and Barnabas went as usual into the Jewish
14: 8 **In** Lystra there sat a man crippled in his feet, who was lame from
14:15 who made heaven and earth and sea and everything **in** them.
14:16 **In** the past, he let all nations go their own way.
14:25 and when they had preached the word **in** Perga, they went down to
15: 7 you know that some time ago God made a choice **among** you that
15:12 and wonders God had done **among** the Gentiles through them.
15:21 the earliest times and is read **in** the synagogues on every Sabbath."
15:22 and Silas, two men who were leaders **among** the brothers.
15:35 But Paul and Barnabas remained in Antioch, where they and many
15:36 and visit the brothers in all the towns **where** [+4005] we preached
16: 2 The brothers **at** Lystra and Iconium spoke well of him.
16: 3 so he circumcised him because of the Jews who lived **in** that area,
16: 4 by the apostles and elders **in** Jerusalem for the people to obey.
16: 6 having been kept by the Holy Spirit from preaching the word **in** the
16:12 And we stayed **there**ˢ [+3836+4047+4484] several days.
16:18 "**In** the name of Jesus Christ I command you to come out of her!"
16:32 the word of the Lord to him and to all the others **in** his house.
16:33 **At** that hour of the night the jailer took them and washed their
16:36 that you and Silas be released. Now you can leave. Go **in** peace."
17:11 were of more noble character than the **Thessalonians** [+2553],
17:13 learned that Paul was preaching the word of God **at** Berea,
17:16 While Paul was waiting for them **in** Athens, he was greatly
17:16 he ˢ [+899+899+3836+4460] was greatly distressed to see that the
17:17 So he reasoned **in** the synagogue with the Jews
17:17 as well as **in** the marketplace day by day with those who happened
17:22 Paul then stood up **in** [+3545] the meeting of the Areopagus
17:23 your objects of worship, I even found an altar **with** this inscription:
17:24 made the world and everything **in** it is the Lord of heaven and earth
17:24 of heaven and earth and does not live **in** temples built by hands.
17:28 'For **in** him we live and move and have our being.' As some of
17:31 For he has set a day **when** [+4005] he will judge the world with
17:31 For he has set a day when he will judge the world with justice by
17:31 For he has set a day when he will judge the world with justice **by**
17:34 **Among** them was Dionysius, a member of the Areopagus,
18: 4 Every Sabbath he reasoned **in** the synagogue, trying to persuade
18: 9 One [NIE] night the Lord spoke to Paul in a vision: "Do not be
18:10 to attack and harm you, because I have many people **in** this city."
18:11 for a year and a half, teaching [NIE] them the word of God.
18:18 he had his hair cut off **at** Cenchrea because of a vow he had taken.
18:24 was a learned man, with a thorough knowledge **of** the Scriptures.
18:26 He began to speak boldly **in** the synagogue. When Priscilla
19: 1 **While** [+3836] Apollos was at Corinth, Paul took the road through
19: 1 While Apollos was **at** Corinth, Paul took the road through the
19: 9 with him and had discussions daily **in** the lecture hall of Tyrannus
19:16 Then the man who **had** [+1639] the evil spirit jumped on them
19:21 Paul **decided** [+3836+4460+5502] to go to Jerusalem, passing
19:39 further you want to bring up, it must be settled **in** a legal assembly.
20: 5 These men went on ahead and waited for us **at** Troas.
20: 7 **On** the first day of the week we came together to break bread.
20: 8 There were many lamps **in** the upstairs room where we were
20:10 arms around him. "Don't be alarmed," he said. "He's **alive** [+899]!"
20:16 Paul had decided to sail past Ephesus to avoid spending time **in** the
20:19 with tears, although I was severely tested **by** the plots of the Jews.
20:22 to Jerusalem, not knowing what will happen to me **there** [+899].
20:25 "Now I know that none of you **among** whom I have gone about
20:26 I declare to you [NIE] today that I am innocent of the blood of all
20:28 and all the flock **of** which the Holy Spirit has made you overseers.
20:32 and give you an inheritance **among** all those who are sanctified.
21: 1 'In this way the Jews **of** Jerusalem will bind the owner of this belt
21:19 and reported in detail what God had done **among** the Gentiles
21:20 "You see, brother, how many thousands **of** Jews have believed,
21:27 some Jews from the province of Asia saw Paul **at** the temple.
21:29 (They had previously seen Trophimus the Ephesian **in** the city with
21:34 Some **in** the crowd shouted one thing and some another, and since
22: 3 "I am a Jew, born **in** Tarsus of Cilicia, but brought up in this city.

22: 3 "I am a Jew, born in Tarsus of Cilicia, but brought up **in** this city.
22: 17 "When I returned to Jerusalem and was praying **at** the temple,
22: 17 to Jerusalem and was praying at the temple, I fell **into** a trance
22: 18 'Leave Jerusalem **immediately** [*+5443*], because they will not
23: 6 called out **in** the Sanhedrin, "My brothers, I am a Pharisee,
23: 9 "We find nothing wrong **with** this man," they said. "What if a spirit
23: 35 Then he ordered that Paul be kept under guard **in** Herod's palace.
24: 12 My accusers did not find me arguing with anyone **at** the temple,
24: 12 or stirring up a crowd **in** the synagogues or anywhere else in the
24: 14 that agrees with the Law and that is written **in** the Prophets,
24: 16 **[NIE]** So I strive always to keep my conscience clear before God
24: 18 I was ceremonially clean **when** [*+4005*] they found me in the
24: 18 I was ceremonially clean when they found me **in** the temple courts
24: 21 unless it was this one thing I shouted as I stood **in** their **presence**:
25: 4 being held at Caesarea, and I myself am going there **soon** [*+5443*].
25: 5 Let some **of** your leaders come with me and press charges against
25: 5 against the man there, if **[NIE]** he has done anything wrong."
25: 6 After spending eight or ten days **with** them, he went down to
25: 24 The whole Jewish community has petitioned me about him **in**
26: 4 from the beginning of my life **in** my own country, and also in
26: 4 the beginning of my life in my own country, and also **in** Jerusalem.
26: 7 are hoping to see fulfilled as they **earnestly** [*+1755*] serve God day
26: 10 And that is just what I did **in** Jerusalem. On the authority of the
26: 10 On the authority of the chief priests I put many of the saints **in**
26: 12 "**On** one of these journeys I was going to Damascus with the
26: 18 and a place **among** those who are sanctified by faith in me.'
26: 20 First to those **in** Damascus, then to those in Jerusalem and in all
26: 21 That is why the Jews seized me **in** the temple courts and tried to
26: 26 of this has escaped his notice, because it was not done **in** a corner.
26: 28 "Do you think that **in** such a short time you can persuade me to be a
26: 29 Paul replied, **[NIE]** "Short time or long—I pray God that not only
26: 29 Paul replied, "Short time or **[NIE]** long—I pray God that not only
27: 7 We made slow headway **for** many days and had difficulty arriving
27: 21 time without food, Paul stood up **before** [*+3545*] them and said:
27: 27 On the fourteenth night we were still being driven **across** the
27: 31 centurion and the soldiers, "Unless these men stay **with** the ship,
27: 37 Altogether there were 276 of us **on board** [*+3836+4450*].
28: 7 **[NIE]** There was an estate nearby that belonged to Publius,
28: 9 the rest of the sick **on** the island came and were cured.
28: 11 After three months we put out to sea **in** a ship that had wintered in
28: 11 After three months we put out to sea in a ship that had wintered **in**
28: 18 because **[NIE]** I was not guilty of any crime deserving death.
28: 30 For two whole years Paul **stayed** there in [*RP1844*] his own rented

Ro 1: 2 the gospel he promised beforehand through his prophets in the
1: 4 and who through the Spirit of holiness was declared **with** power to
1: 5 and apostleship to call people **from among** all the Gentiles to the
1: 6 And you also are **among** those who are called to belong to Jesus
1: 7 To all **in** Rome who are loved by God and called to be saints:
1: 8 all of you, because your faith is being reported all **over** the world.
1: 9 whom I serve **with** my whole heart in preaching the gospel of his
1: 9 whom I serve with my whole heart in preaching the gospel of his
1: 10 and I pray that now at last **by** God's will the way may be opened
1: 12 that you and I may be mutually encouraged **by** each other's faith.
1: 12 and I may be mutually encouraged by each other's faith. **[NIE]**
1: 13 in order that I might have a harvest **among** you, just as I have had
1: 13 a harvest among you, just as I have had **among** the other Gentiles.
1: 15 so eager to preach the gospel also to you who are **at** Rome.
1: 17 For **in** the gospel a righteousness from God is revealed,
1: 18 and wickedness of men who suppress the truth **by** their
1: 19 since what may be known about God is plain **to** them, because God
1: 21 but their **[NIE]** thinking became futile and their foolish hearts
1: 23 the immortal God for images made to **[NIE]** look like mortal man
1: 24 Therefore God gave them over **in** the sinful desires of their hearts
1: 24 sexual impurity for the degrading of their bodies **with** one another.
1: 25 They exchanged the truth of God **for** a lie, and worshiped
1: 27 relations with women and were inflamed **with** lust for one another.
1: 27 Men committed indecent acts **with** other men, and received in
1: 27 and received **in** themselves the due penalty for their perversion.
1: 28 since they did not think it worthwhile to retain the **[NIE]**
2: 1 for **at** whatever point you judge the other, you are condemning
2: 5 you are storing up wrath against yourself **for** the day of God's
2: 12 the law, and all who sin **under** the law will be judged by the law.
2: 15 since they show that the requirements of the law are written **on**
2: 16 This will take place **on** the day when God will judge men's secrets
2: 17 if you rely on the law and brag about your **relationship to** God;
2: 19 you are a guide for the blind, a light for those who are **in** the dark,

2: 20 because you have **in** the law the embodiment of knowledge
2: 23 You who brag **about** the law, do you dishonor God by breaking the
2: 24 "God's name is blasphemed **among** the Gentiles because of you."
2: 28 A man is not a Jew if he is only one **outwardly** [*+3836+5745*],
2: 28 nor is circumcision merely **outward** [*+3836+5745*] and physical.
2: 28 nor is circumcision merely outward and **physical** [*+4922*].
2: 29 No, a man is a Jew if he is one **inwardly** [*+3220+3836*]; and
2: 29 is circumcision of the heart, **by** the Spirit, not by the written code.
3: 4 "So that you may be proved right **when** you speak and prevail when
3: 4 right when you speak and prevail **when** [*+3836*] you judge."
3: 7 "If my **[NIE]** falsehood enhances God's truthfulness and
3: 16 ruin and misery **mark** their ways,
3: 19 it says to those who are **under** the law, so that every mouth may be
3: 24 by his grace through the redemption that came **by** Christ Jesus.
3: 25 him as a sacrifice of atonement, through faith **in** his blood.
3: 25 because **in** his forbearance he had left the sins committed
3: 26 he did it to demonstrate his justice **at** the present time, so as to be
4: 10 Was it **after** he was circumcised, or before? It was not after,
4: 10 Was it after he was circumcised, or **before**[s] [*+213*]? It was not
4: 10 was circumcised, or before? It was not **after**[s] [*+4364*], but before!
4: 10 was circumcised, or before? It was not after, but **before**[s] [*+213*]!
4: 11 a seal of the righteousness that he had by faith **while** he was *still*
4: 12 that our father Abraham had **before** he was **circumcised** [*+213*].
5: 2 through whom we have gained access by faith into this grace **in**
5: 3 Not only so, but we also rejoice **in** our sufferings, because we
5: 5 because God has poured out his love **into** our hearts by the Holy
5: 9 Since we have now been justified **by** his blood, how much more
5: 10 having been reconciled, shall we be saved **through** his life!
5: 11 but we also rejoice **in** God through our Lord Jesus Christ,
5: 13 for before the law was given, sin was **in** the world. But sin is not
5: 15 God's grace and the gift that *came* **by** the grace of the one man,
5: 17 abundant provision of grace and of the gift of righteousness reign **in**
5: 21 so that, just as sin reigned **in** death, so also grace might reign
6: 2 By no means! We died to sin; how can we live **in** it any longer?
6: 4 through the glory of the Father, we too may live **[NIE]** a new life.
6: 11 count yourselves dead to sin but alive to God **in** Christ Jesus.
6: 12 Therefore do not let sin reign **in** your mortal body so that you
6: 23 but the gift of God is eternal life **in** Christ Jesus our Lord.
7: 5 For when we were *controlled* **by** the sinful nature, the sinful
7: 5 the sinful passions aroused by the law *were* **at** work in [*RP1919*]
7: 6 But now, by dying **to** what once bound us, we have been released
7: 6 released from the law so that we serve **in** the new way of the Spirit,
7: 8 the commandment, produced **in** me every kind of covetous desire.
7: 17 it is no longer I myself who do it, but it is sin living **in** me.
7: 18 I know that nothing good lives **in** me, that is, in my sinful nature.
7: 18 I know that nothing good lives in me, that is, **in** my sinful nature.
7: 20 it is no longer I who do it, but it is sin living **in** me that does it.
7: 23 but I see another law at work **in** the members of my body,
7: 23 and making me a prisoner **of** the law of sin at work within my
7: 23 and making me a prisoner of the law of sin at work **within** my
8: 1 there is now no condemnation for those who are **in** Christ Jesus,
8: 2 because **through** Christ Jesus the law of the Spirit of life set me
8: 3 For what the law was powerless to do **in** that it was weakened by
8: 3 God did by sending his own Son **in** the likeness of sinful man to be
8: 3 man to be a sin offering. And so he condemned sin **in** sinful man,
8: 4 that the righteous requirements of the law might be fully met **in** us,
8: 8 Those controlled **by** the sinful nature cannot please God.
8: 9 however, are controlled not **by** the sinful nature but by the Spirit,
8: 9 however, are controlled not by the sinful nature but by the Spirit,
8: 9 the sinful nature but by the Spirit, if the Spirit of God lives **in** you.
8: 10 But if Christ is **in** you, your body is dead because of sin, yet your
8: 11 And if the Spirit of him who raised Jesus from the dead is living **in**
8: 11 your mortal bodies through his Spirit, who **lives in** [*RP1940*] you.
8: 15 received the Spirit of sonship. And **by** him we cry, "*Abba*, Father."
8: 23 groan **inwardly** [*+1571*] as we wait eagerly for our adoption as
8: 29 of his Son, that he might be the firstborn **among** many brothers.
8: 34 to life—is **at** the right hand of God and is also interceding for us.
8: 37 **in** all these things we are more than conquerors through him who
8: 39 will be able to separate us from the love of God that is **in** Christ
9: 1 I speak the truth **in** Christ—I am not lying, my conscience confirms
9: 1 I am not lying, my conscience confirms it **in** the Holy Spirit—
9: 7 "It is **through** Isaac that your offspring will be reckoned."
9: 17 that I might display my power **in** you and that my name might be
9: 17 in you and that my name might be proclaimed **in** all the earth."
9: 22 power known, bore **with** great patience the objects of his wrath—
9: 25 As he says **in** Hosea: "I will call them 'my people' who are not my

9:26 "It will happen that **in** the very place where it was said to them,
9:33 I lay **in** Zion a stone that causes men to stumble and a rock that
10: 5 is by the law: "The man who does these things will live **by** them."
10: 6 "Do not say **in** your heart, 'Who will ascend into heaven?' " (that is,
10: 8 it is **in** your mouth and in your heart," that is, the word of faith we
10: 8 it is in your mouth and **in** your heart," that is, the word of faith we
10: 9 That if you confess **with** your mouth, "Jesus is Lord," and believe
10: 9 and believe **in** your heart that God raised him from the dead,
10:20 And Isaiah boldly says, "I was found **by** those who did not seek me;
11: 2 Don't you know what the Scripture says **in** the passage about
11: 5 So too, **at** the present time there is a remnant chosen by grace.
11:17 *have been* **grafted in among** [*RP1596*] the others and now share
12: 3 For by the grace given me I say to every one **of** you: Do not think
12: 4 Just as each of us has **[NIE]** one body with many members,
12: 5 so **in** Christ we who are many form one body, and each member
12: 7 If it is serving, let him **[NIE]** serve; if it is teaching, let him teach;
12: 7 If it is serving, let him serve; if it is teaching, let him **[NIE]** teach;
12: 8 if it is encouraging, let him **[NIE]** encourage; if it is contributing
12: 8 to the needs of others, let him give **generously** [*+605*];
12: 8 if it is leadership, let him govern **diligently** [*+5082*]; if it is
12: 8 if it is showing mercy, let him do it **cheerfully** [*+2660*].
12:21 Do not be overcome by evil, but overcome evil **with** good.
13: 9 other commandment there may be, are summed up **in** this one rule:
13: 9 in this one rule: [UBS+ **RPG**] "Love your neighbor as yourself."
13:13 behave decently, as **in** the daytime, not in orgies and drunkenness,
14: 5 day alike. Each one should be fully convinced **in** his own mind.
14:14 As one who is **in** the Lord Jesus, I am fully convinced that no food
14:17 but of righteousness, peace and joy **in** the Holy Spirit,
14:18 because anyone who serves Christ **in** this way is pleasing to God
14:21 or to do anything else **[NIE]** that will cause your brother to fall.
14:22 Blessed is the man who does not condemn himself **by** what he
15: 5 and encouragement give you a spirit of unity **among** yourselves as
15: 6 so that **with** one heart and mouth you may glorify the God
15: 9 "Therefore I will praise you **among** the Gentiles; I will sing hymns
15:13 of hope fill you with all joy and peace **as** [*+3836*] you trust in him,
15:13 so that you may overflow **with** hope by the power of the Holy
15:13 so that you may overflow with hope **by** the power of the Holy
15:16 an offering acceptable to God, sanctified **by** the Holy Spirit.
15:17 Therefore I glory **in** Christ Jesus in my service to God.
15:19 **by** the power of signs and miracles, through the power of the
15:19 the power of signs and miracles, **through** the power of the Spirit.
15:23 But now that there is no more place for me to *work* **in** these
15:26 to make a contribution for the poor among the saints **in** Jerusalem.
15:27 they owe it to the Jews to share with them **[NIE]** their material
15:29 to you, I will come **in** the full measure of the blessing of Christ.
15:30 of the Spirit, to join me in my struggle **by** praying to God for me.
15:31 Pray that I may be rescued from the unbelievers **in** Judea and that
15:32 so that by God's will I may come to you **with** joy and together
16: 1 to you our sister Phoebe, a servant of the church **in** Cenchrea.
16: 2 I ask you to receive her **in** the Lord in a way worthy of the saints
16: 2 the saints and to give her **[NIE]** any help she may need from you,
16: 3 Greet Priscilla and Aquila, my fellow workers **in** Christ Jesus.
16: 7 They are outstanding **among** the apostles, and they were in Christ
16: 7 among the apostles, and they were **in** Christ before I was.
16: 8 Greet Ampliatus, whom I love **in** the Lord.
16: 9 Greet Urbanus, our fellow worker **in** Christ, and my dear friend
16:10 Greet Apelles, tested and approved **in** Christ. Greet those who
16:11 Greet those in the household of Narcissus who are **in** the Lord.
16:12 and Tryphosa, those women who work hard **in** the Lord.
16:12 another woman who has worked very hard **in** the Lord.
16:13 Greet Rufus, chosen **in** the Lord, and his mother, who has been a
16:16 Greet one another with a holy kiss. All the churches of Christ send
16:20 The God of peace will **soon** [*+5443*] crush Satan under your feet.
16:22 Tertius, who wrote down this letter, greet you **in** the Lord.
1Co 1: 2 To the church of God **in** Corinth, to those sanctified in Christ Jesus
1: 2 in Corinth, to those sanctified **in** Christ Jesus and called to be holy,
1: 2 together with all those **[NIE]** everywhere who call on the name of
1: 4 thank God for you because of his grace given you **in** Christ Jesus.
1: 5 For **in** him you have been enriched in every way—in all your
1: 5 For in him you have been enriched **in** every way—in all your
1: 5 in every way—**in** all your speaking and in all your knowledge—
1: 6 because our testimony about Christ was confirmed **in** you.
1: 7 Therefore you do not lack **[NIE]** any spiritual gift as you eagerly
1: 8 so that you will be blameless **on** the day of our Lord Jesus Christ.
1:10 with one another so that there may be no divisions **among** you
1:10 and that you may be perfectly united **in** mind and thought.

1:10 and that you may be perfectly united in mind and **[RPG]** thought.
1:11 household have informed me that there are quarrels **among** you.
1:17 not **with** words of human wisdom, lest the cross of Christ be
1:21 For since **in** the wisdom of God the world through its wisdom did
1:30 It is because of him that you are **in** Christ Jesus, who has become
1:31 Therefore, as it is written: "Let him who boasts boast **in** the Lord."
2: 2 For I resolved to know nothing **while** I was with you except Jesus
2: 3 I came to you in weakness and fear, and with much trembling.
2: 3 I came to you in weakness and **[RPG]** fear, and with much
2: 3 I came to you in weakness and fear, and **with** much trembling.
2: 4 My message and my preaching were not **with** wise and persuasive
2: 4 persuasive words, but **with** a demonstration of the Spirit's power,
2: 5 so that your faith might not rest **on** men's wisdom, but on God's
2: 5 your faith might not rest on men's wisdom, but **on** God's power.
2: 6 We do, however, speak a message of wisdom **among** the mature,
2: 7 No, we speak of God's **secret** [*+3696*] wisdom, a wisdom that has
2:11 knows the thoughts of a man except the man's spirit **within** him?
2:13 not **in** words taught us by human wisdom but in words taught by
2:13 taught us by human wisdom but **in** words taught by the Spirit,
3: 1 not address you as spiritual but as worldly—mere infants **in** Christ.
3: 3 For since there is jealousy and quarreling **among** you, are you not
3:13 It will be revealed **with** fire, and the fire will test the quality of
3:16 yourselves are God's temple and that God's Spirit lives **in** you?
3:18 If any one **of** you thinks he is wise by the standards of this age,
3:18 If any one of you thinks he is wise **by** *the standards of* this age,
3:19 As it is written: "He catches the wise **in** their craftiness";
3:21 So then, no more boasting **about** men! All things are yours,
4: 2 Now it is required that those who have been **given a trust** [*+3874*]
4: 4 conscience is clear, but **[NIE]** that does not make me innocent.
4: 6 so that you may learn **from** us the meaning of the saying,
4:10 We are fools for Christ, but you are so wise **in** Christ! We are
4:15 Even though you have ten thousand guardians **in** Christ, you do not
4:15 for **in** Christ Jesus I became your father through the gospel.
4:17 to you Timothy, my son whom I love, who is faithful **in** the Lord.
4:17 He will remind you of my way of life **in** Christ Jesus, which agrees
4:17 which agrees with what I teach everywhere **in** every church.
4:20 For the kingdom of God is not a matter **of** talk but of power.
4:20 For the kingdom of God is not a matter of talk but **of** power.
4:21 Shall I come to you **with** a whip, or in love and with a gentle
4:21 I come to you with a whip, or **in** love and with a gentle spirit?
5: 1 It is actually reported that there is sexual immorality **among** you,
5: 1 among you, and of a kind that does not occur even **among** pagans:
5: 4 When you are assembled in the name of our Lord Jesus and I am
5: 5 may be destroyed and his spirit saved **on** the day of the Lord.
5: 8 not **with** the old yeast, the yeast of malice and wickedness,
5: 8 not with the old yeast, **[RPG]** the yeast of malice and wickedness,
5: 8 the yeast of malice and wickedness, but **with** bread without yeast,
5: 9 I have written you **in** my letter not to associate with sexually
6: 2 And if **[NIE]** you are to judge the world, are you not competent to
6: 4 appoint as judges even men of little account **in** the church!
6: 5 Is it possible that there is nobody **among** you wise enough to judge
6:11 you were justified **in** the name of the Lord Jesus Christ and by the
6:11 in the name of the Lord Jesus Christ and **by** the Spirit of our God.
6:19 Holy Spirit, who is **in** you, whom you have received from God?
6:20 you were bought at a price. Therefore honor God **with** your body.
7:14 For the unbelieving husband has been sanctified **through** his wife,
7:14 and the unbelieving wife has been sanctified **through** her believing
7:15 A believing man or woman is not bound **in** such circumstances;
7:15 bound in such circumstances; God has called us to *live* **in** peace.
7:17 God has called him. This is the rule I lay down **in** all the churches.
7:18 *Was* a man **uncircumcised** [*+213*] when he was called? He should
7:20 Each one should remain **in** the situation which he was in when God
7:20 Each one should remain in the situation which he was **in** when God
7:22 For he who was a slave when he was called **by** the Lord is the
7:24 to God, should remain **in** the situation God called him to.
7:24 should remain in the situation **[RPG]** God called him to.
7:37 But the man who has settled the matter **in** his own mind, who is
7:37 and who has made up **[NIE]** his mind not to marry the virgin—
7:39 free to marry anyone she wishes, but he must **belong to** the Lord.
8: 4 We know that an idol is nothing at all **in** the world and that there is
8: 5 whether **in** heaven or on earth (as indeed there are many "gods"
8: 7 But not **[NIE]** everyone knows this. Some people are still
8:10 sees you who have this knowledge eating **in** an idol's temple,
8:11 for whom Christ died, is destroyed **by** your knowledge.
9: 1 Jesus our Lord? Are you not the result of my work **in** the Lord?
9: 2 I am to you! For you are the seal of my apostleship **in** the Lord.

9: 9 For it is written **in** the Law of Moses: "Do not muzzle an ox while it
9: 15 am not writing this in the hope that you will do such things **for** me.
9: 18 it free of charge, and so not make use of my rights **in** preaching it.
9: 24 Do you not know that **in** a race all the runners run, but only one
10: 2 They were all baptized into Moses **in** the cloud and in the sea.
10: 2 They were all baptized into Moses in the cloud and **in** the sea.
10: 5 Nevertheless, God was not pleased **with** most of them; their bodies
10: 5 with most of them; their bodies were scattered **over** the desert.
10: 25 Eat anything sold **in** the meat market without raising questions of
11: 11 **In** the Lord, however, woman is not independent of man, nor is
11: 13 Judge **for** yourselves: Is it proper for a woman to pray to God with
11: 18 **In** the first place, I hear that when you come together **as** a church,
11: 18 there are divisions **among** you, and to some extent I believe it.
11: 19 No doubt there have to be differences **among** you to show which
11: 19 No doubt there have to be differences among you to show which **of**
11: 21 for **as** [+3836] you eat, each of you goes ahead without waiting for
11: 22 What shall I say to you? Shall I praise you **for** this? Certainly not!
11: 23 The Lord Jesus, **on** the night he was betrayed, took bread,
11: 25 he took the cup, saying, "This cup is the new covenant **in** my blood;
11: 30 That is why many **among** you are weak and sick, and a number of
11: 34 If anyone is hungry, he should eat **at** home, so that when you meet
12: 3 Therefore I tell you that no one who is speaking **by** the Spirit of
12: 3 and no one can say, "Jesus is Lord," except **by** the Holy Spirit.
12: 6 kinds of working, but the same God works all of them **in** all men.
12: 9 to another faith **by** the same Spirit, to another gifts of healing by
12: 9 by the same Spirit, to another gifts of healing **by** that one Spirit,
12: 13 For we were all baptized **by** one Spirit into one body—
12: 18 But in fact God has arranged the parts **in** the body, every one of
12: 25 so that there should be no division **in** the body, but that its parts
12: 28 And **in** the church God has appointed first of all apostles,
13: 12 Now we see but a **[NIE]** poor reflection as in a mirror;
14: 6 unless I bring you some **[NIE]** revelation or knowledge
14: 6 or **[NIE]** knowledge or prophecy or word of instruction?
14: 6 or knowledge or **[NIE]** prophecy or word of instruction?
14: 6 or knowledge or prophecy or **[NIE]** word of instruction?
14: 10 Undoubtedly there are all sorts of languages in the world,
14: 11 I am a foreigner to the speaker, and he is a foreigner **to** me.
14: 16 If you are praising God **with** your spirit, how can one who finds
14: 19 But **in** the church I would rather speak five intelligible words to
14: 19 words to instruct others than ten thousand words **in** a tongue.
14: 21 **In** the Law it is written: "Through men of strange tongues
14: 21 "**Through** men of strange tongues and through the lips of
14: 21 and **through** the lips of foreigners I will speak to this people,
14: 25 down and worship God, exclaiming, "God is really **among** you!"
14: 28 the speaker should keep quiet **in** the church and speak to himself
14: 33 of disorder but of peace. As **in** all the congregations of the saints,
14: 34 women should remain silent **in** the churches. They are not allowed
14: 35 about something, they should ask their own husbands **at** home;
14: 35 at home; for it is disgraceful for a woman to speak **in** the church.
15: 1 which you received and **on** which you have taken your stand.
15: 3 what I received I passed on to you **as** of first importance [+4755]:
15: 12 how can some **of** you say that there is no resurrection of the dead?
15: 17 has not been raised, your faith is futile; you are still **in** your sins.
15: 18 Then those also who have fallen asleep **in** Christ are lost.
15: 19 If only **for** this life we have hope in Christ, we are to be pitied
15: 19 If only for this life we have hope **in** Christ, we are to be pitied
15: 22 For as **in** Adam all die, so in Christ all will be made alive.
15: 22 For as in Adam all die, so **in** Christ all will be made alive.
15: 23 But each in his own turn: Christ, the firstfruits; then, when he
15: 23 the firstfruits; then, **when** he comes, those who belong to him.
15: 28 him who put everything under him, so that God may be all **in** all.
15: 31 just as surely as I glory over you **in** Christ Jesus our Lord.
15: 32 If I fought wild beasts in Ephesus for merely human reasons,
15: 41 and the stars another; and star differs from star **in** splendor.
15: 42 The body that is sown is **perishable** [+5785], it is raised
15: 42 body that is sown is perishable, it is raised **imperishable** [+914];
15: 43 it is sown **in** dishonor, it is raised in glory; it is sown in weakness,
15: 43 it is sown in dishonor, it is raised **in** glory; it is sown in weakness,
15: 43 it is raised in glory; it is sown **in** weakness, it is raised in power;
15: 43 it is raised in glory; it is sown in weakness, it is raised **in** power;
15: 52 **in** a flash, in the twinkling of an eye, at the last trumpet.
15: 52 in a flash, **in** the twinkling of an eye, at the last trumpet.
15: 52 in a flash, in the twinkling of an eye, **at** the last trumpet.
15: 58 Always give yourselves fully **to** the work of the Lord, because you
15: 58 because you know that your labor **in** the Lord is not in vain.
16: 7 I do not want to see you now and **make**ˢ only a passing visit;

16: 8 But I will stay on **at** Ephesus until Pentecost,
16: 11 Send him on his way **in** peace so that he may return to me.
16: 13 Be on your guard; stand firm **in** the faith; be men of courage;
16: 14 Do everything **in** love.
16: 19 Aquila and Priscilla greet you warmly **in** the Lord, and so does the
16: 20 here send you greetings. Greet one another **with** a holy kiss.
16: 24 My love to all of you **in** Christ Jesus. Amen.
2Co 1: 1 and Timothy our brother, To the church of God **in** Corinth,
1: 1 together with all the saints **throughout** [+3910] Achaia:
1: 4 so that we can comfort those **in** any trouble with the comfort we
1: 6 which **produces in** [RP1919] you patient endurance of the same
1: 8 brothers, about the hardships we suffered **in** the province of Asia.
1: 9 Indeed, in our hearts we felt the sentence of death. But this
1: 12 Our conscience testifies that we have conducted ourselves **in** the
1: 12 relations with you, **in** the holiness and sincerity that are from God.
1: 12 We have done so not **according to** worldly wisdom but according
1: 12 so not according to worldly wisdom but **according to** God's grace.
1: 14 of us just as we will boast of you **in** the day of the Lord Jesus.
1: 19 who was preached **among** you by me and Silas and Timothy,
1: 19 was not "Yes" and "No," but **in** him it has always been "Yes."
1: 20 matter how many promises God has made, they are "Yes" **in** Christ.
1: 22 and put his Spirit **in** our hearts as a deposit, guaranteeing what is to
2: 1 mind that I would not make another **painful** [+3383] visit to you.
2: 10 to forgive—I have forgiven **in** the sight of Christ for your sake,
2: 12 and found that the **[NIE]** Lord had opened a door for me,
2: 14 who always leads us in triumphal procession **in** Christ and through
2: 14 through us spreads **everywhere** [+4246+5536] the fragrance of the
2: 15 For we are to God the aroma of Christ **among** those who are being
2: 15 those who are being saved and **[RPG]** those who are perishing.
2: 17 On the contrary, **in** Christ we speak before God with sincerity,
3: 2 **written on** [RP1582] our hearts, known and read by everybody.
3: 3 living God, not **on** tablets of stone but on tablets of human hearts.
3: 3 living God, not on tablets of stone but **on** tablets of human hearts.
3: 7 which was engraved **in** letters on stone, came with glory,
3: 7 which was engraved in letters on stone, came **with** glory,
3: 8 will not the ministry of the Spirit be even more **glorious** [+1518]?
3: 10 has no glory now **in comparison with** [+1641+3538+3836+4047]
3: 11 how much greater is the **[NIE]** glory of that which lasts!
3: 14 It has not been removed, because only **in** Christ is it taken away.
4: 2 we do not **use** [+4344] deception, nor do we distort the word of
4: 3 even if our gospel is veiled, it is veiled **to** those who are perishing.
4: 4 The god of this age has blinded **[NIE]** the minds of unbelievers,
4: 6 made his light shine **in** our hearts to give us the light of the
4: 6 the light of the knowledge of the glory of God **in** the face of Christ.
4: 7 But we have this treasure **in** jars of clay to show that this
4: 8 We are hard pressed **on** every side, but not crushed; perplexed,
4: 10 We always carry around **in** our body the death of Jesus, so that the
4: 10 of Jesus, so that the life of Jesus may also be revealed **in** our body.
4: 11 for Jesus' sake, so that his life may be revealed **in** our mortal body.
4: 12 So then, death *is* **at work in** [RP1919] us, but life is at work in
4: 12 So then, death is at work in us, but life is at work **in** you.
5: 1 from God, an eternal house in heaven, not built by human hands.
5: 2 **Meanwhile** [+4047] we groan, longing to be clothed with our
5: 4 For while we are **in** this tent, we groan and are burdened,
5: 6 and know that as long as we are at home **in** the body we are away
5: 11 are is plain to God, and I hope it is also plain **to** your conscience.
5: 12 so that you can answer those who take pride **in** what is seen rather
5: 12 who take pride in what is seen rather than in what is **in** the heart.
5: 17 Therefore, if anyone is **in** Christ, he is a new creation; the old has
5: 19 that God was reconciling the world to himself **in** Christ,
5: 19 And he has committed **to** us the message of reconciliation.
5: 21 so that **in** him we might become the righteousness of God.
6: 2 of my favor I heard you, and **in** the day of salvation I helped you."
6: 3 We put no stumbling block **in** anyone's *path*, so that our ministry
6: 4 Rather, as servants of God we commend ourselves **in** every way:
6: 4 **in** great endurance; in troubles, hardships and distresses;
6: 4 in great endurance; **in** troubles, hardships and distresses;
6: 4 in great endurance; in troubles, **[RPG]** hardships and distresses;
6: 4 in great endurance; in troubles, hardships and **[RPG]** distresses;
6: 5 **in** beatings, imprisonments and riots; in hard work, sleepless nights
6: 5 in beatings, **[RPG]** imprisonments and riots; in hard work,
6: 5 in beatings, imprisonments and **[RPG]** riots; in hard work,
6: 5 and riots; **in** hard work, sleepless nights and hunger;
6: 5 and riots; in hard work, **[RPG]** sleepless nights and hunger;
6: 5 and riots; in hard work, sleepless nights and **[RPG]** hunger;
6: 6 **in** purity, understanding, patience and kindness; in the Holy Spirit

6: 6 in purity, [RPG] understanding, patience and kindness;
6: 6 in purity, understanding, [RPG] patience and kindness;
6: 6 in purity, understanding, patience and [RPG] kindness;
6: 6 patience and kindness; in the Holy Spirit and in sincere love;
6: 6 patience and kindness; in the Holy Spirit and in sincere love;
6: 7 in truthful speech and in the power of God; with weapons of
6: 7 in truthful speech and in the power of God; with weapons of
6: 12 [NIE] We are not withholding our affection from you, but you are
6: 12 We are not withholding our [NIE] affection from you, but you are
6: 16 "I will live with [RP1940] them and walk among them, and I will
7: 1 and spirit, perfecting holiness out of reverence for God.
7: 3 I have said before that you have such a place in our hearts that we
7: 5 this body of ours had no rest, but we were harassed at every turn—
7: 6 who comforts the downcast, comforted us by the coming of Titus,
7: 7 and not only by his coming but also by the comfort you had given
7: 7 not only by his coming but also by the comfort you had given him.
7: 8 Even if I caused you sorrow by my letter, I do not regret it.
7: 9 as God intended and so were not harmed in any way by us.
7: 11 At every point you have proved yourselves to be innocent in this
7: 14 But just as everything we said to you was true [+237], so our
7: 16 I am glad I can have complete [+4246] confidence in you.
7: 16 I am glad I can have complete confidence in you.
8: 1 we want you to know about the grace that God has given [NIE]
8: 2 Out of the most severe trial, their overflowing joy and their
8: 7 But just as you excel in everything—in faith, in speech, in
8: 7 in knowledge, in complete earnestness and in your love for us—
8: 7 in your love for us—see that you also excel in this grace of giving.
8: 10 And here is my advice about what is best for you in this matter:
8: 14 At the present time your plenty will supply what they need,
8: 16 who put into the heart of Titus the same concern I have for you.
8: 18 who is praised by all the churches for his service to the gospel.
8: 20 We want to avoid any criticism of the way we administer [NIE]
8: 22 who has often proved to us in many ways that he is zealous,
9: 3 that our boasting about you in this matter should not prove hollow,
9: 4 would be ashamed of having been so [NIE] confident.
9: 8 so that in all things at all times, having all that you need, you will
9: 11 You will be made rich in every way so that you can be generous on
10: 1 I, Paul, who am "timid" when face to face with you, but "bold"
10: 3 For though we live in the world, we do not wage war as the world
10: 6 And we will be [NIE] ready to punish every act of disobedience,
10: 12 When they measure themselves by themselves and compare
10: 14 come to you, for we did get as far as you with the gospel of Christ.
10: 15 Neither do we go beyond our limits by boasting of work done by
10: 15 to grow, our area of activity among you will greatly expand,
10: 16 For we do not want to boast about work already done in another
10: 17 But, "Let him who boasts boast in the Lord."
11: 3 But I am afraid that just as Eve was deceived by the serpent's
11: 6 We have made this perfectly [+4246] clear to you in every way.
11: 6 We have made this perfectly clear to you in every way.
11: 9 I have kept myself from being a burden to you in any way,
11: 10 As surely as the truth of Christ is in me, nobody in the regions of
11: 10 nobody in the regions of Achaia will stop this boasting of mine.
11: 12 to be considered equal with us in the things they boast about.
11: 17 In this self-confident boasting I am not talking as the Lord would,
11: 17 boasting I am not talking as the Lord would, but as [NIE] a fool.
11: 21 What [+323+1254+4005] anyone else dares to boast about—I am
11: 21 I am speaking as a fool [+932]—I also dare to boast about.
11: 23 I have [NIE] worked much harder, been in prison more
11: 23 I have worked much harder, been in prison more frequently,
11: 23 in prison more frequently, been [NIE] flogged more severely,
11: 23 more severely, and been [NIE] exposed to death again and again.
11: 25 times I was shipwrecked, I spent a night and a day in the open sea,
11: 26 in danger in the city, in danger in the country, in danger at sea;
11: 26 in danger in the city, in danger in the country, in danger at sea;
11: 26 in danger in the city, in danger in the country, in danger at sea;
11: 26 in the country, in danger at sea; and in danger from false brothers.
11: 27 have labored and toiled and have often [NIE] gone without sleep;
11: 27 I have known [NIE] hunger and thirst and have often gone
11: 27 known hunger and thirst and have often [NIE] gone without food;
11: 27 have often gone without food; I have been [NIE] cold and naked.
11: 32 In Damascus the governor under King Aretas had the city of the
11: 33 But I was lowered in a basket from a window in the wall
12: 2 I know a man in Christ who fourteen years ago was caught up to
12: 2 Whether it was in the body or out of the body I do not know—
12: 3 whether in the body or apart from the body I do not know,
12: 5 but I will not boast about myself, except about my weaknesses.

12: 9 is sufficient for you, for my power is made perfect in weakness."
12: 9 Therefore I will boast all the more gladly about my weaknesses,
12: 10 I delight in weaknesses, in insults, in hardships, in persecutions,
12: 10 in insults, in hardships, in persecutions, in difficulties.
12: 10 in insults, in hardships, in persecutions, in difficulties.
12: 10 in insults, in hardships, in persecutions, in difficulties.
12: 12 and miracles—were done among you with great perseverance.
12: 12 and miracles—were done among you with great perseverance.
12: 19 We have been speaking in the sight of God as those in Christ;
13: 3 since you are demanding proof that Christ is speaking through me.
13: 3 He is not weak in dealing with you, but is powerful among you.
13: 4 Likewise, we are weak in him, yet by God's power we will live
13: 5 Examine yourselves to see whether you are in the faith;
13: 5 Do you not realize that Christ Jesus is in you—unless, of course,
13: 12 Greet one another with a holy kiss.

Gal 1: 6 so quickly deserting the one who called you by the grace of Christ
    1: 13 For you have heard of my previous way of life in Judaism,
    1: 14 I was advancing in Judaism beyond many Jews of my own age
    1: 14 beyond many Jews [+1169+1609+3836] of my own age and was
    1: 16 to reveal his Son in me so that I might preach him among the
    1: 16 his Son in me so that I might preach him among the Gentiles,
    1: 22 I was personally unknown to the churches of Judea that are in
    1: 24 And they praised God because of me.
    2: 2 and set before them the gospel that I preach among the Gentiles.
    2: 4 infiltrated our ranks to spy on the freedom we have in Christ Jesus
    2: 17 "If, while we seek to be justified in Christ, it becomes evident that
    2: 20 crucified with Christ and I no longer live, but Christ lives in me.
    2: 20 The life I live in the body, I live by faith in the Son of God,
    2: 20 I live by faith in the Son of God, who loved me and gave himself
    3: 5 God give you his Spirit and work miracles among [RP1919] you
    3: 8 to Abraham: "All nations will be blessed through [RP1922] you."
    3: 10 does not continue to do everything written in the Book of the Law."
    3: 11 Clearly no one is justified before God by the law, because,
    3: 12 on the contrary, "The man who does these things will live by them."
    3: 14 to Abraham might come to the Gentiles through Christ Jesus,
    3: 19 The law was put into effect through angels by [+5931] a mediator.
    3: 26 You are all sons of God through faith in Christ Jesus,
    3: 28 slave nor free, male nor female, for you are all one in Christ Jesus.
    4: 14 Even though my illness [NIE] was a trial to you, you did not treat
    4: 18 provided the purpose is good, and to be so always and not just
    4: 18 and to be so always and not just when [+3836] I am with you.
    4: 19 I am again in the pains of childbirth until Christ is formed in you,
    4: 20 you now and change my tone, because I am perplexed about you!
    4: 25 Now Hagar stands for Mount Sinai in Arabia and corresponds to
    5: 4 You who are trying to be justified by law have been alienated from
    5: 6 For in Christ Jesus neither circumcision nor uncircumcision has
    5: 10 I am confident in the Lord that you will take no other view.
    5: 14 The entire law is summed up in a single command: "Love your
    5: 14 up in a single command: [RPG] "Love your neighbor as yourself."
    6: 1 Brothers, if someone is caught in a sin, you who are spiritual
    6: 1 you who are spiritual should restore him gently [+4460+4559].
    6: 6 Anyone who receives instruction in the word must share [NIE] all
    6: 12 Those who want to make a good impression outwardly [+4922]
    6: 13 yet they want you to be circumcised that they may boast about
    6: 14 May I never boast except in the cross of our Lord Jesus Christ,
    6: 17 no one cause me trouble, for I bear on my body the marks of Jesus.
Eph 1: 1 will of God, To the saints in Ephesus, the faithful in Christ Jesus:
    1: 1 will of God, To the saints in Ephesus, the faithful in Christ Jesus:
    1: 3 who has blessed us in the heavenly realms with every spiritual
    1: 3 who has blessed us in the heavenly realms with every spiritual
    1: 3 us in the heavenly realms with every spiritual blessing in Christ.
    1: 4 For he chose us in him before the creation of the world to be holy
    1: 4 creation of the world to be holy and blameless in his sight. In love
    1: 6 glorious grace, which he has freely given us in the One he loves.
    1: 7 In him we have redemption through his blood, the forgiveness of
    1: 8 that he lavished on us with all wisdom and understanding.
    1: 9 will according to his good pleasure, which he purposed in Christ,
    1: 10 and on earth together under one head, even [NIE] Christ.
    1: 10 and on earth together under one head, even Christ. [RPG]
    1: 11 In him we were also chosen, having been predestined according to
    1: 12 in order that we, who were the first to hope in Christ, might be for
    1: 13 And you also were included in Christ when you heard the word of
    1: 13 Having believed, you were marked in him with a seal,
    1: 15 ever since I heard about your faith in the Lord Jesus and your love
    1: 17 and revelation, so that you may [NIE] know him better.
    1: 18 has called you, the riches of his glorious inheritance in the saints,

1:20 which *he* **exerted in** [*RP1919*] Christ when he raised him from the
1:20 the dead and seated him **at** his right hand in the heavenly realms,
1:20 the dead and seated him at his right hand **in** the heavenly realms,
1:21 be given, not only **in** the present age but also in the one to come.
1:21 be given, not only in the present age but also **in** the one to come.
1:23 is his body, the fullness of him who fills everything **in** every way.
2: 2 **in** which you used to live when you followed the ways of this
2: 2 the spirit who *is* now **at work in** [*RP1919*] those who are
2: 3 All of us also lived **among** them at one time,
2: 3 **gratifying**ˢ the cravings of our sinful nature and following its
2: 4 because of his great love for us, God, who is rich **in** mercy,
2: 6 and seated us with him **in** the heavenly realms in Christ Jesus,
2: 6 and seated us with him in the heavenly realms **in** Christ Jesus,
2: 7 in order that **in** the coming ages he might show the incomparable
2: 7 riches of his grace, *expressed* **in** his kindness to us in Christ Jesus.
2: 7 riches of his grace, expressed in his kindness to us **in** Christ Jesus.
2:10 are God's workmanship, created **in** Christ Jesus to do good works,
2:10 good works, which God prepared in advance for **[NIE]** us to do.
2:11 remember that formerly you who are Gentiles **by** birth and called
2:11 "the circumcision" (that done **in** the body by the hands of men)—
2:12 of the promise, without hope and without God **in** the world.
2:13 But now **in** Christ Jesus you who once were far away have been
2:13 were far away have been brought near **through** the blood of Christ.
2:15 by abolishing **in** his flesh the law with its commandments
2:15 his flesh the law with its commandments and **[NIE]** regulations.
2:15 His purpose was to create **in** himself one new man out of the two,
2:16 and **in** this one body to reconcile both of them to God through the
2:16 to God through the cross, **by** which he put to death their hostility.
2:18 For through him we both have access to the Father **by** one Spirit.
2:21 **In** him the whole building is joined together and rises to become a
2:21 is joined together and rises to become a holy temple **in** the Lord.
2:22 And **in** him you too are being built together to become a dwelling
2:22 together to become a dwelling in which God *lives* **by** his Spirit.
3: 3 to me by revelation, as I have already written **briefly** [*+3900*].
3: 4 you will be able to understand my insight **into** the mystery of
3: 5 as it has now been revealed **by** the Spirit to God's holy apostles
3: 6 of one body, and sharers together in the promise **in** Christ Jesus.
3: 9 which for ages past was kept hidden **in** God, who created all
3:10 made known to the rulers and authorities **in** the heavenly realms,
3:11 according to his eternal purpose which he accomplished **in** Christ
3:12 **In** him and through faith in him we may approach God with
3:12 and through faith in him we may approach God **with** freedom
3:13 therefore, not to be discouraged **because of** my sufferings for you,
3:15 from whom his whole family **in** heaven and on earth derives its
3:17 so that Christ may dwell **in** your hearts through faith. And I pray
3:17 And I pray that you, being rooted and established **in** love,
3:20 according to his power that *is* **at work within** [*RP1919*] us,
3:21 to him be glory in the church and in Christ Jesus throughout all
3:21 glory in the church and **in** Christ Jesus throughout all generations,
4: 1 As a prisoner **for** the Lord, then, I urge you to live a life worthy of
4: 2 and gentle; be patient, bearing with one another **in** love.
4: 3 Make every effort to keep the unity of the Spirit **through** the bond
4: 4 just as you were called **to** one hope when you were called—
4: 6 and Father of all, who is over all and through all and **in** all.
4:14 and there by every wind of teaching and **by** the cunning
4:14 and **[NIE]** craftiness of men in their deceitful scheming.
4:15 Instead, speaking the truth **in** love, we will in all things grow up
4:16 grows and builds itself up **in** love, as each part does its work.
4:16 and builds itself up in love, as each part **[NIE]** does its work.
4:17 So I tell you this, and insist on it **in** the Lord, that you must no
4:17 no longer live as the Gentiles do, **in** the futility of their thinking.
4:18 because of the ignorance that is **in** them due to the hardening of
4:19 indulge in every kind of impurity, **with** a *continual* lust for more.
4:21 and were taught **in** him in accordance with the truth that is in Jesus.
4:21 and were taught in him in accordance with the truth that is **in** Jesus.
4:24 new self, created to be like God **in** true righteousness and holiness.
4:30 of God, **with** whom you were sealed for the day of redemption.
4:32 forgiving each other, just as **in** Christ God forgave you.
5: 2 and live a life **of** love, just as Christ loved us and gave himself up
5: 3 But **among** you there must not be even a hint of sexual immorality,
5: 5 has any inheritance **in** the kingdom of Christ and of God.
5: 8 For you were once darkness, but now you are light **in** the Lord.
5: 9 (for the fruit of the light *consists* **in** all goodness, righteousness
5:18 Do not get drunk on wine, **[NIE]** which leads to debauchery.
5:18 which leads to debauchery. Instead, be filled **with** the Spirit.
5:19 Speak to one another **with** psalms, hymns and spiritual songs.

5:20 the Father for everything, **in** the name of our Lord Jesus Christ.
5:21 Submit to one another **out of** reverence for Christ.
5:24 so also wives should submit to their husbands **in** everything.
5:26 cleansing her by the washing with water **through** the word,
6: 1 Children, obey your parents **in** the Lord, for this is right.
6: 2 and mother"—which is the first commandment **with** a promise—
6: 4 instead, bring them up **in** the training and instruction of the Lord.
6: 5 earthly masters with respect and fear, and **with** sincerity of heart,
6: 9 you know that he who is both their Master and yours is **in** heaven,
6:10 Finally, be strong **in** the Lord and in his mighty power.
6:10 Finally, be strong in the Lord and **in** his mighty power.
6:12 and against the spiritual forces of evil **in** the heavenly realms.
6:13 so that **when** the day of evil *comes*, you may be able to stand your
6:14 Stand firm then, with the belt **of** truth buckled around your waist,
6:15 and with your feet fitted **with** the readiness that comes from the
6:16 **In addition** to all this, take up the shield of faith, with which you
6:16 **with** which you can extinguish all the flaming arrows of the evil
6:18 And pray **in** the Spirit on all occasions with all kinds of prayers
6:18 And pray in the Spirit **on** all occasions with all kinds of prayers
6:18 be alert and **[NIE]** always keep on praying for all the saints.
6:19 Pray also for me, that **whenever** I open my mouth, words may be
6:19 so that I will **fearlessly** [*+4244*] make known the mystery of the
6:20 for which I am an ambassador **in** chains. Pray that I may declare it
6:20 in chains. Pray that I may declare **[NIE]** it fearlessly, as I should.
6:21 Tychicus, the dear brother and faithful servant **in** the Lord,
6:24 Grace to all who love our Lord Jesus Christ **with** an undying love.
Php 1: 1 of Christ Jesus, To all the saints **in** Christ Jesus at Philippi,
1: 1 of Christ Jesus, To all the saints in Christ Jesus **at** Philippi,
1: 4 **In** all my prayers for all of you, I always pray with joy
1: 6 that he who began a good work **in** you will carry it on to
1: 7 me to feel this way about all of you, since I have you **in** my heart;
1: 7 for whether I am in chains or defending and confirming the gospel,
1: 7 for whether I am in chains or **[NIE]** defending and confirming the
1: 8 God can testify how I long for all of you **with** the affection of
1: 9 may abound more and more **in** knowledge and depth of insight,
1:13 it has become clear **throughout** the whole palace guard and to
1:13 palace guard and to everyone else that I am in chains **for** Christ.
1:14 most of the brothers **in** the Lord have been encouraged to speak the
1:18 And **because of** this I rejoice. Yes, and I will continue to rejoice,
1:20 I eagerly expect and hope that I will **in** no way be ashamed,
1:20 but will **have** sufficient courage so that now as always Christ will
1:20 so that now as always Christ will be exalted **in** my body,
1:22 If I am to go on living **in** the body, this will mean fruitful labor for
1:24 but it is more necessary for you that I remain **in** the body.
1:26 so that through my being with you again your joy **in** Christ Jesus
1:26 you again your joy in Christ Jesus will overflow **on account of** me.
1:27 you in my absence, I will know that you stand firm **in** one spirit,
1:28 without being frightened **in** any way by those who oppose you.
1:30 since you are going through the same struggle you saw I **had**,
1:30 the same struggle you saw I had, and now hear that I still **have**.
2: 1 If you have any encouragement from being **united with** Christ,
2: 5 **[NIE]** Your attitude should be the same as that of Christ Jesus:
2: 5 Your attitude should be the same as that **of** Christ Jesus:
2: 6 Who, being **in** very nature God, did not consider equality with God
2: 7 taking the very nature of a servant, being made **in** human likeness.
2:10 that **at** the name of Jesus every knee should bow, in heaven
2:12 not only **in** my presence, but now much more in my absence—
2:12 not only in my presence, but now much more **in** my absence—
2:13 for it is God who **works in** [*RP1919*] you to will and to act
2:15 depraved generation, **in** which you shine like stars in the universe
2:15 depraved generation, in which you shine like stars **in** the universe
2:19 I hope in the Lord Jesus to send Timothy to you soon, that I also
2:24 And I am confident **in** the Lord that I myself will come soon.
2:29 Welcome him **in** the Lord with great joy, and honor men like him,
3: 1 Finally, my brothers, rejoice **in** the Lord! It is no trouble for me to
3: 3 we who worship by the Spirit of God, who glory **in** Christ Jesus,
3: 3 who glory in Christ Jesus, and who put no confidence **in** the flesh—
3: 4 though I myself have reasons for **such**ˢ [*+4922*] confidence.
3: 4 If anyone else thinks he has reasons to put confidence **in** the flesh,
3: 6 the church; as for **legalistic** [*+3795*] righteousness, faultless.
3: 9 and be found **in** him, not having a righteousness of my own that
3:14 the prize for which God has called me heavenward **in** Christ Jesus.
3:19 their god is their stomach, and their glory is **in** their shame.
3:20 But our citizenship is **in** heaven. And we eagerly await a Savior
4: 1 and crown, that is how you should stand firm **in** the Lord,
4: 2 and I plead with Syntyche to agree with each other **in** the Lord.

4: 3 help these women who have contended at my side **in the cause of**
4: 3 the rest of my fellow workers, whose names are **in** the book of life.
4: 4 Rejoice **in** the Lord always. I will say it again: Rejoice!
4: 6 but **in** everything, by prayer and petition, with thanksgiving,
4: 7 will guard your hearts and your minds **in** Christ Jesus.
4: 9 you have learned or received or heard from me, or seen **in** me—
4: 10 I rejoice greatly **in** the Lord that at last you have renewed your
4: 11 for I have learned to be content **[NIE]** whatever the
4: 12 I have learned the secret of being content **in** any and every
4: 12 the secret of being content in any and **[RPG]** every situation,
4: 13 I can do everything **through** him who gives me strength.
4: 15 **in** the early days of your acquaintance with the gospel,
4: 16 for even when I was **in** Thessalonica, you sent me aid again
4: 19 And my God will meet all your needs according to his **[NIE]**
4: 19 meet all your needs according to his glorious riches **in** Christ Jesus.
4: 21 Greet all the saints **in** Christ Jesus. The brothers who are with me

Col 1: 2 To the holy and faithful brothers **in** Christ at Colosse: Grace
1: 2 To the holy and faithful brothers in Christ **at** Colosse: Grace
1: 4 because we have heard of your faith **in** Christ Jesus and of the love
1: 5 and love that spring from the hope that is stored up for you **in**
1: 5 and that you have already heard about **in** the word of truth,
1: 6 **[NIE]** All over the world this gospel is bearing fruit and growing,
1: 6 just as it has been doing **among** you since the day you heard it
1: 6 the day you heard it and understood God's grace **in** all its truth.
1: 8 and who also told us of your love **in** the Spirit.
1: 9 and asking God to fill you with the knowledge of his will **through**
1: 10 bearing fruit **in** every good work, growing in the knowledge of
1: 11 being strengthened **with** all power according to his glorious might
1: 12 who has qualified you to share in the inheritance of the saints **in**
1: 14 in whom we have redemption, the forgiveness of sins.
1: 16 For **by** him all things were created: things in heaven and on earth,
1: 16 things **in** heaven and on earth, visible and invisible,
1: 17 He is before all things, and **in** him all things hold together.
1: 18 the dead, so that **in** everything he might have the supremacy.
1: 19 For God was pleased to have all his fullness dwell **in** him,
1: 20 whether things on earth or things **in** heaven, by making peace
1: 21 and were enemies in your minds **because of** your evil behavior.
1: 22 But now he has reconciled you **by** Christ's physical body through
1: 23 and that has been proclaimed **to** every creature under heaven,
1: 24 Now I rejoice **in** what was suffered for you, and I fill up in my
1: 24 and I fill up **in** my flesh what is still lacking in regard to Christ's
1: 27 To them God has chosen to make known **among** the Gentiles the
1: 27 riches of this mystery, which is Christ **in** you, the hope of glory.
1: 28 admonishing and teaching everyone **with** all wisdom,
1: 28 all wisdom, so that we may present everyone perfect **in** Christ.
1: 29 with all his energy, which **so powerfully** [+1539] works in me.
1: 29 with all his energy, which so powerfully **works in** [RP1919] me.
2: 1 know how much I am struggling for you and for those **at** Laodicea,
2: 1 at Laodicea, and for all who have not met me **personally** [+4922].
2: 2 purpose is that they may be encouraged in heart and united **in** love,
2: 3 **in** whom are hidden all the treasures of wisdom and knowledge.
2: 4 so that no one may deceive you **by** fine-sounding arguments.
2: 6 just as you received Christ Jesus as Lord, continue to live **in** him,
2: 7 rooted and built up **in** him, strengthened in the faith as you were
2: 7 in the faith as you were taught, and overflowing **with** thankfulness.
2: 9 For **in** Christ all the fullness of the Deity lives in bodily form,
2: 10 and you have been given fullness **in** Christ, who is the head over
2: 11 **In** him you were also circumcised, in the putting off of the sinful
2: 11 you were also circumcised, **in** the putting off of the sinful nature,
2: 11 by the hands of men but **with** the circumcision done by Christ,
2: 12 having been buried with him **in** baptism and raised with him
2: 12 and raised **with** him through your faith in the power of God,
2: 13 When you were dead **in** your sins and in the uncircumcision of
2: 15 and authorities, he made **[NIE]** a public spectacle of them,
2: 15 a public spectacle of them, triumphing over them **by** the cross.
2: 16 Therefore do not let anyone judge you **by** what you eat or drink,
2: 16 do not let anyone judge you by what you eat or **[RPG]** drink,
2: 16 you eat or drink, or **with regard to** [+3538] a religious festival,
2: 18 Do not let anyone who delights **in** false humility and the worship
2: 20 why, as though you still belonged **to** it, do you submit to its rules:
2: 23 **with** their self-imposed worship, their false humility and their
2: 23 but they lack **[NIE]** any value in restraining sensual indulgence.
3: 1 on things above, where Christ is seated **at** the right hand of God.
3: 3 For you died, and your life is now hidden with Christ **in** God.
3: 4 is your life, appears, then you also will appear with him **In** glory.
3: 7 You used to walk **in** these ways, in the life you once lived.

3: 7 You used to walk in these ways, **in** the life you once lived.
3: 11 barbarian, Scythian, slave or free, but Christ is all, and is **in** all.
3: 15 Let the peace of Christ rule **in** your hearts, since as members of
3: 15 since **as members of** one body you were called to peace.
3: 16 *Let* the word of Christ **dwell in** [RP1940] you richly as you teach
3: 16 richly as you teach and admonish one another **with** all wisdom,
3: 16 hymns and spiritual songs **with** gratitude in your hearts to God.
3: 16 hymns and spiritual songs with gratitude **in** your hearts to God.
3: 17 And whatever you do, whether **in** word or deed, do it all in the
3: 17 And whatever you do, whether in word or **[RPG]** deed, do it all in
3: 17 whether in word or deed, do it all **in** the name of the Lord Jesus,
3: 18 Wives, submit to your husbands, as is fitting **in** the Lord.
3: 20 obey your parents in everything, for this pleases **[NIE]** the Lord.
3: 22 and do it, not only **when** their eye is on you and to win their favor,
3: 22 their favor, but **with** sincerity of heart and reverence for the Lord.
4: 1 because you know that you also have a Master **in** heaven.
4: 2 Devote yourselves to prayer, being watchful and **[NIE]** thankful.
4: 2 Devote yourselves to prayer, being watchful and **[NIE]** thankful.
4: 5 Be **[NIE]** wise in the way you act toward outsiders;
4: 6 Let your conversation be always **full of** grace, seasoned with salt,
4: 7 is a dear brother, a faithful minister and fellow servant **in** the Lord.
4: 12 He is always wrestling **in** prayer for you, that you may stand firm
4: 12 that you may stand firm **in** all the will of God, mature and fully
4: 13 is working hard for you and for those **at** Laodicea and Hierapolis.
4: 13 hard for you and for those at Laodicea and **[RPG]** Hierapolis.
4: 15 Give my greetings to the brothers **at** Laodicea, and to Nympha
4: 16 see that it is also read **in** the church of the Laodiceans and that you
4: 17 that you complete the work you have received **in** the Lord."

1Th 1: 1 To the church of the Thessalonians **in** God the Father and the Lord
1: 5 because our gospel came to you not simply **with** words, but also
1: 5 but also **with** power, with the Holy Spirit and with deep
1: 5 also with power, **with** the Holy Spirit and with deep conviction.
1: 5 also with power, with the Holy Spirit and **with** deep conviction.
1: 5 You know how we lived **among** you for your sake.
1: 6 **in spite of** severe suffering, you welcomed the message with the
1: 7 And so you became a model to all the believers **in** Macedonia
1: 7 a model to all the believers in Macedonia and **[RPG]** Achaia.
1: 8 The Lord's message rang out from you not only **in** Macedonia
1: 8 rang out from you not only in Macedonia and **[RPG]** Achaia—
1: 8 your faith in God has become known **everywhere** [+4246+5536].
2: 2 We had previously suffered and been insulted **in** Philippi,
2: 2 but **with the help of** our God we dared to tell you his gospel in
2: 2 God we dared to tell you his gospel **in spite of** strong opposition.
2: 3 from error or impure motives, nor are we **trying to** trick you.
2: 5 You know we never used **[NIE]** flattery, nor did we put on a
2: 5 never used flattery, nor did we **put on** a mask to cover up greed—
2: 6 As apostles of Christ we could have been a **[NIE]** burden to you,
2: 7 but we were gentle **among** [+3545] you, like a mother caring for
2: 13 the word of God, which *is* **at work in** [RP1919] you who believe.
2: 14 For you, brothers, became imitators of God's churches **in** Judea,
2: 14 imitators of God's churches in Judea, which are **in** Christ Jesus:
2: 17 **out of** our intense longing we made every effort to see you.
2: 19 glory in the presence of our Lord Jesus **when** [+3836] he comes?
3: 1 it no longer, we thought it best to be left by ourselves **in** Athens.
3: 2 and God's fellow worker **in** spreading the gospel of Christ,
3: 3 so that no one would be unsettled **by** these trials. You know quite
3: 8 For now we really live, since you are standing firm **in** the Lord.
3: 13 you will be blameless and **holy** [+43] in the presence of our God
3: 13 and Father **when** our Lord Jesus comes with all his holy ones.
4: 1 ask you and urge you **in** the Lord Jesus to do this more and more.
4: 4 that each of you should learn to control his own body **in** *a way* that
4: 5 not **in** passionate lust like the heathen, who do not know God;
4: 6 and that **in** this matter no one should wrong his brother or take
4: 7 For God did not call us to be impure, but *to* **live** a holy life.
4: 10 you do love all the brothers **throughout** [+3910] Macedonia.
4: 15 **According** to the Lord's own word, we tell you that we who are
4: 16 **with** a loud command, with the voice of the archangel and with the
4: 16 **with** the voice of the archangel and with the trumpet call of God,
4: 16 with the voice of the archangel and **with** the trumpet call of God,
4: 16 with the trumpet call of God, and the dead **in** Christ will rise first.
4: 17 and are left will be caught up together with them **in** the clouds to
4: 18 Therefore encourage each other **with** these words.
5: 2 well that the day of the Lord will come like a thief **in** the night.
5: 3 as labor pains *on* a **pregnant woman** [+1143+2400], and they will
5: 4 are not **in** darkness so that this day should surprise you like a thief.
5: 12 we ask you, brothers, to respect those who work hard **among** you,

5:12 among you, who are over you **in** the Lord and who admonish you.
5:13 Hold them in the highest regard **in** love because of their work.
5:13 in love because of their work. Live in peace **with** each other.
5:18 give thanks **in** all circumstances, for this is God's will for you in
5:18 in all circumstances, for this is God's will for you **in** Christ Jesus.
5:23 and body be kept blameless **at** the coming of our Lord Jesus Christ.
5:26 Greet all the brothers **with** a holy kiss.
2Th 1:1 To the church of the Thessalonians **in** God our Father and the Lord
1:4 **among** God's churches we boast about your perseverance
1:4 among God's churches we boast [NIE] about your perseverance
1:4 and faith **in** all the persecutions and trials you are enduring.
1:7 This will happen **when** the Lord Jesus is revealed from heaven in
1:7 This will happen when the Lord Jesus is revealed from heaven **in**
1:10 **on** the day he comes to be glorified in his holy people and to be
1:10 on the day he comes to be glorified **in** his holy people and to be
1:10 and to be marveled at **among** all those who have believed.
1:11 and that **by** his power he may fulfill every good purpose of yours
1:12 so that the name of our Lord Jesus may be glorified **in** you,
1:12 and you **in** him, according to the grace of our God and the Lord
2:6 is holding him back, so that he may be revealed **at** the proper time.
2:9 the work of Satan *displayed* **in** all kinds of counterfeit miracles,
2:10 and **in** every sort of evil that deceives those who are perishing.
2:13 because from the beginning God chose you to be saved **through**
2:16 who loved us and **by** his grace gave us eternal encouragement
2:17 your hearts and strengthen you **in** every good deed and word.
3:4 We have confidence **in** the Lord that you are doing and will
3:6 **In** the name of the Lord Jesus Christ, we command you, brothers,
3:7 to follow our example. We were not idle *when* we were **with** you,
3:8 [NIE] laboring and toiling so that we would not be a burden to
3:11 We hear that some **among** you are idle. They are not busy;
3:12 we command and urge **in** the Lord Jesus Christ to settle down
3:16 of peace himself give you peace at all times and **in** every way.
3:17 in my own hand, which is the distinguishing mark **in** all my letters.
1Ti 1:2 To Timothy my true son **in** the faith: Grace, mercy and peace from
1:3 stay there **in** Ephesus so that you may command certain men not
1:4 promote controversies rather than God's work—which is **by** faith.
1:13 I was shown mercy because I acted **in** ignorance and unbelief.
1:14 along with the faith and love that are **in** Christ Jesus.
1:16 But for that very reason I was shown mercy so that **in** me,
1:18 about you, so that **by** *following* them you may fight the good fight,
2:2 for kings and all those **in** authority, that we may live peaceful
2:2 we may live peaceful and quiet lives **in** all godliness and holiness.
2:7 I am not lying—and a teacher **of** the true faith to the Gentiles.
2:8 I want men **everywhere** [+4246+5536] to lift up holy hands in
2:9 I also want women to dress **modestly** [+2950+3177], with
2:9 not **with** braided hair or gold or pearls or expensive clothes,
2:11 A woman should learn **in** quietness and full submission.
2:11 A woman should learn in quietness and [RPG] full submission.
2:12 or to have authority over a man; she must be [NIE] silent.
2:14 it was the woman who was deceived and became a [NIE] sinner.
2:15 if they continue in faith, love and holiness with propriety.
3:4 and see that his children [NIE] obey him with proper respect.
3:9 They must keep hold of the deep truths of the faith **with** a clear
3:11 not malicious talkers but temperate and trustworthy **in** everything.
3:13 standing and great assurance **in** their faith in Christ Jesus.
3:13 standing and great assurance in their faith **in** Christ Jesus.
3:14 Although I hope to come to you **soon** [+5443], I am writing you
3:15 you will know how people ought to conduct themselves **in** God's
3:16 He appeared in a body, was vindicated **by** the Spirit, was seen by
3:16 in a body, was vindicated **by** the Spirit, was seen by angels,
3:16 by the Spirit, was seen by angels, was preached **among** the nations,
3:16 the nations, was believed on **in** the world, was taken up in glory.
3:16 the nations, was believed on in the world, was taken up **in** glory.
4:1 The Spirit clearly says that **in** later times some will abandon the
4:2 Such teachings *come* **through** hypocritical liars,
4:12 but set an example for the believers **in** speech, in life, in love,
4:12 for the believers in speech, **in** life, in love, in faith and in purity.
4:12 for the believers in speech, in life, **in** love, in faith and in purity.
4:12 for the believers in speech, in life, in love, **in** faith and in purity.
4:12 for the believers in speech, in life, in love, in faith and **in** purity.
4:14 Do not neglect [NIE] your gift, which was given you **through** a
4:15 Be diligent **in** these matters; give yourself wholly to them,
5:2 as mothers, and younger women as sisters, **with** absolute purity.
5:10 and is well known **for** her good deeds, such as bringing up
5:17 especially those whose work is **preaching** [+3364] and teaching.
6:17 Command those who are rich **in** this present world not to be

6:18 to be rich **in** good deeds, and to be generous and willing to share.
2Ti 1:1 will of God, according to the promise of life that is **in** Christ Jesus,
1:3 **with** a clear conscience, as night and day I constantly remember
1:3 as night and day I constantly remember you **in** my prayers.
1:5 I have been reminded [NIE] of your sincere faith, which first
1:5 which first **lived in** [RP1940] your grandmother Lois and in your
1:5 in your mother Eunice and, I am persuaded, now lives **in** you also.
1:6 the gift of God, which is **in** you through the laying on of my hands.
1:9 This grace was given us **in** Christ Jesus before the beginning of
1:13 the pattern of sound teaching, **with** faith and love in Christ Jesus.
1:13 the pattern of sound teaching, with faith and love **in** Christ Jesus.
1:14 guard it with the help **of** the Holy Spirit who **lives in** [RP1940] us.
1:15 You know that everyone **in** the province of Asia has deserted me,
1:17 On the contrary, when he was **in** Rome, he searched hard for me
1:18 May the Lord grant that he will find mercy from the Lord **on** that
1:18 You know very well in how many ways he helped me **in** Ephesus.
2:1 You then, my son, be strong **in** the grace that is in Christ Jesus.
2:1 You then, my son, be strong in the grace that is **in** Christ Jesus.
2:7 what I am saying, for the Lord will give you insight **into** all this.
2:9 **for** which I am suffering even to the point of being chained like a
2:10 that they too may obtain the salvation that is **in** Christ Jesus,
2:20 **In** a large house there are articles not only of gold and silver,
2:25 Those who oppose him he must **gently** [+4559] instruct,
3:1 But mark this: There will be terrible times in the last days.
3:11 what kinds of things happened to me **in** Antioch, Iconium
3:11 [RPG] Iconium and Lystra, the persecutions I endured.
3:11 Iconium and [RPG] Lystra, the persecutions I endured.
3:12 everyone who wants to live a godly life **in** Christ Jesus will be
3:14 continue **in** what you have learned and have become convinced of,
3:15 which are able to make you wise for salvation through faith **in**
3:16 for teaching, rebuking, correcting and training **in** righteousness,
4:2 and encourage—**with** great patience and careful instruction.
4:5 But you, keep your head **in** all situations, endure hardship,
4:8 the Lord, the righteous Judge, will award to me **on** that day—
4:13 bring the cloak that I left with Carpus **at** Troas, and my scrolls,
4:16 **At** my first defense, no one came to my support, but everyone
4:20 Erastus stayed **in** Corinth, and I left Trophimus sick in Miletus.
4:20 Erastus stayed in Corinth, and I left Trophimus sick **in** Miletus.
Tit 1:3 and at his appointed season he brought his word to light **through**
1:5 The reason I left you **in** Crete was that you might straighten out
1:6 and are not **open to** the charge of being wild and disobedient.
1:9 so that he can encourage others **by** sound doctrine and refute those
1:13 rebuke them sharply, so that they will be sound **in** the faith
2:3 teach the older women to be reverent in the way they live,
2:7 doing what is good. **In** your teaching show integrity, seriousness
2:9 Teach slaves to be subject to their masters **in** everything, to try to
2:10 so that in every way they will make the teaching about God our
2:12 to live self-controlled, upright and godly lives **in** this present age,
3:3 We lived **in** malice and envy, being hated and hating one another.
3:5 not because of **righteous** [+1466] things we had done, but
3:15 Greet those who love us **in** the faith. Grace be with you all.
Phm 1:6 so that you will have a full understanding of every good thing we
1:6 a full understanding of every good thing [NIE] we have in Christ.
1:8 although **in** Christ I could be bold and order you to do what you
1:10 for my son Onesimus, who became my son **while** I was in chains.
1:13 so that he could take your place in helping me **while** I am in chains
1:16 dearer to you, both **as a man** [+4922] and as a brother in the Lord.
1:16 but even dearer to you, both as a man and as a brother **in** the Lord.
1:20 brother, that I may have some benefit from you **in** the Lord;
1:20 have some benefit from you in the Lord; refresh my heart **in** Christ.
1:23 Epaphras, my fellow prisoner **in** Christ Jesus, sends you greetings.
Heb 1:1 In the past God spoke to our forefathers **through** the prophets at
1:2 but in these last days he has spoken to us **by** his Son, whom he
1:3 for sins, he sat down **at** the right hand of the Majesty in heaven.
1:3 for sins, he sat down at the right hand of the Majesty **in** heaven.
2:8 **In** putting everything under him, God left nothing that is not
2:12 **in** the presence of the congregation I will sing your praises."
2:18 Because [NIE] he himself suffered when he was tempted,
3:2 who appointed him, just as Moses was faithful **in** all God's house.
3:5 Moses was faithful as a servant **in** all God's house, testifying to
3:8 do not harden your hearts as you did **in** the rebellion,
3:8 as you did in the rebellion, during the time of testing **in** the desert,
3:9 where your fathers tested [NIE] and tried me and for forty years
3:11 So I declared on oath **in** my anger, 'They shall never enter my
3:12 See to it, brothers, that [NIE] none of you has a sinful,
3:12 unbelieving heart **that** [+3836] turns away from the living God.

3: 15 **As** [+*3836*] has just been said: "Today, if you hear his voice,
3: 15 his voice, do not harden your hearts as you did **in** the rebellion."
3: 17 Was it not with those who sinned, whose bodies fell **in** the desert?
4: 3 that rest, just as God has said, "So I declared on oath **in** my anger,
4: 4 words: "And **on** the seventh day God rested from all his work."
4: 5 And again **in** the passage above he says, "They shall never enter my
4: 7 calling it Today, when a long time later he spoke **through** David,
4: 11 so that no one will fail *by* **following** their example of disobedience.
5: 6 And he says **in** another place, "You are a priest forever, in the order
5: 7 **During** the days of Jesus' life on earth, he offered up prayers
6: 17 **Because** [+*4005*] God wanted to make the unchanging nature of
6: 18 by two unchangeable things **in** which it is impossible for God to
7: 10 met Abraham, Levi was still **in** the body of his ancestor.
8: 1 who sat down **at** the right hand of the throne of the Majesty in
8: 1 who sat down at the right hand of the throne of the Majesty **in**
8: 5 everything according to the pattern shown you **on** the mountain."
8: 9 **when** [+*2465*] I took them by the hand to lead them out of Egypt,
8: 9 because they *did* not **remain faithful to** [*RP1844*] my covenant,
8: 13 **By** [+*3836*] calling this covenant "new," he has made the first one
9: 2 **In** its first room were the lampstand, the table and the consecrated
9: 4 This ark **contained** [+*2400*] the gold jar of manna, Aaron's staff
9: 22 the law requires that nearly everything be cleansed **with** blood,
9: 23 for the copies of the **heavenly things** [+*3836+4041*] to be purified
9: 25 the way the high priest enters the Most Holy Place every year **with**
10: 3 But [**NIE**] those sacrifices are an annual reminder of sins,
10: 7 Then I said, 'Here I am—it is written about me **in** the scroll—
10: 10 And **by** that will, we have been made holy through the sacrifice of
10: 12 time one sacrifice for sins, he sat down **at** the right hand of God.
10: 19 since we have confidence to enter the Most Holy Place **by**
10: 22 let us draw near to God with a sincere heart **in** full assurance of
10: 29 unholy thing the blood of the covenant [**NIE**] that sanctified him,
10: 32 **when** [+*4005*] you stood your ground in a great contest in the face
10: 38 by faith. And if he shrinks back, I will not be pleased **with** him."
11: 2 This is what the ancients were commended **for**.
11: 9 he lived in tents, as did Isaac and Jacob, who were heirs with him
11: 18 to him, "It is **through** Isaac that your offspring will be reckoned."
11: 19 and **figuratively speaking** [+*4130*], he did receive Isaac back from
11: 34 and who became powerful **in** battle and routed foreign armies.
11: 37 sawed in two; *they were* **put to death** [+*633+5840*] by the sword.
11: 37 They went about **in** sheepskins and goatskins, destitute, persecuted
11: 37 They went about in sheepskins and [**NIE**] goatskins, destitute,
12: 2 its shame, and sat down **at** the right hand of the throne of God.
12: 23 to the church of the firstborn, whose names are written **in** heaven.
13: 3 who are mistreated as if you yourselves were **suffering**ˢ [+*5393*].
13: 4 Marriage should be honored **by** all, and the marriage bed kept pure,
13: 9 [**NIE**] which are of no value to those who eat them.
13: 18 have a clear conscience and desire to live honorably **in** every way.
13: 20 who **through** the blood of the eternal covenant brought back from
13: 21 equip you **with** everything good for doing his will, and may he
13: 21 and may he work **in** us what is pleasing to him, through Jesus

Jas 1: 1 To the twelve tribes [**NIE**] scattered among the nations:
1: 4 you may be mature and complete, not lacking [**NIE**] anything.
1: 6 But when he asks, [**NIE**] he must believe and not doubt,
1: 8 he is a double-minded man, unstable **in** all he does.
1: 9 The brother in humble circumstances ought to take pride **in** his
1: 10 But the one who is rich should take pride **in** his low position,
1: 11 the rich man will fade away *even* **while** he goes about his business.
1: 21 so prevalent and **humbly** [+*4559*] accept the word planted in you,
1: 23 but does not do what it says is like a man who looks at his face **in**
1: 25 he has heard, but doing it—he will be blessed **in** what he does.
1: 27 to look after orphans and widows **in** their distress and to keep
2: 1 in our glorious Lord Jesus Christ, don't **show favoritism** [+*4721*].
2: 2 into your meeting wearing a gold ring and [**NIE**] fine clothes,
2: 2 and fine clothes, and a poor man **in** shabby clothes also comes in.
2: 4 have you not discriminated **among** yourselves and become judges
2: 5 those who are poor in the eyes of the world to be rich **in** faith
2: 10 and yet stumbles **at** just one point is guilty of breaking all of it.
2: 16 one of you says to him, "Go, I **wish** you well [+*1645*]; keep warm
3: 2 If anyone is never at fault **in** what he says, he is a perfect man,
3: 6 tongue also is a fire, a world of evil **among** the parts of the body.
3: 9 **With** the tongue we praise our Lord and Father, and with it we
3: 9 tongue we praise our Lord and Father, and **with** it we curse men,
3: 13 Who is wise and understanding **among** you? Let him show it by
3: 13 good life, by deeds done **in** the humility that comes from wisdom.
3: 14 But if you harbor bitter envy and selfish ambition **in** your hearts,
3: 18 Peacemakers who sow **in** peace raise a harvest of righteousness.

4: 1 What causes fights and quarrels **among** you? Don't they come
4: 1 they come from your desires that battle **within** [+*3517+3836*] you?
4: 3 that you may spend what you get **on** your pleasures.
4: 5 reason that the spirit he caused to live **in** us envies intensely?
4: 16 As it is, you boast and **brag** [+*224+3836*]. All such boasting is
5: 3 eat your flesh like fire. You have hoarded wealth **in** the last days.
5: 5 You have fattened yourselves **in** the day of slaughter.
5: 10 of suffering, take the prophets who spoke **in** the name of the Lord.
5: 13 Is any one **of** you in trouble? He should pray. Is anyone happy?
5: 14 Is any one **of** you sick? He should call the elders of the church to
5: 14 to pray over him and anoint him with oil **in** the name of the Lord.
5: 19 if one **of** you should wander from the truth and someone should

1Pe 1: 2 **through** the sanctifying work of the Spirit, for obedience to Jesus
1: 4 that can never perish, spoil or fade—kept **in** heaven for you,
1: 5 who through faith are shielded **by** God's power until the coming of
1: 5 coming of the salvation that is ready to be revealed **in** the last time.
1: 6 **In** this you greatly rejoice, though now for a little while you may
1: 6 though now for a little while you may have had to suffer grief **in**
1: 7 result in praise, glory and honor **when** Jesus Christ is revealed.
1: 11 and circumstances to which the Spirit of Christ **in** them was
1: 12 preached the gospel to you **by** the Holy Spirit sent from heaven.
1: 13 set your hope fully on the grace to be given you **when** Jesus Christ
1: 14 do not conform to the evil desires you had when you *lived* **in**
1: 15 But just as he who called you is holy, so be holy **in** all you do;
1: 17 work impartially, live your lives as strangers here **in** reverent fear.
1: 22 Now that you have purified yourselves **by** obeying the truth
2: 2 spiritual milk, so that **by** it you may grow up in your salvation,
2: 6 For **in** Scripture it says: "See, I lay a stone in Zion, a chosen
2: 6 "See, I lay a stone **in** Zion, a chosen and precious cornerstone,
2: 12 Live such good lives **among** the pagans that, though they accuse
2: 12 [**NIE**] though they accuse you of doing wrong, they may see your
2: 12 may see your good deeds and glorify God **on** the day he visits us.
2: 18 Slaves, submit yourselves to your masters **with** all respect,
2: 22 "He committed no sin, and no deceit was found **in** his mouth."
2: 24 He himself bore our sins **in** his body on the tree, so that we might
3: 2 when they see the purity and [**NIE**] reverence of your lives.
3: 4 inner self, [**NIE**] the unfading beauty of a gentle and quiet spirit,
3: 15 But **in** your hearts set apart Christ as Lord. Always be prepared to
3: 15 who asks you to give the reason for the hope that you **have**.
3: 16 so that those who speak maliciously against your good behavior **in**
3: 16 good behavior in Christ may be ashamed of their [**NIE**] slander.
3: 19 **through** whom also he went and preached to the spirits in prison
3: 19 through whom also he went and preached to the spirits **in** prison
3: 20 who disobeyed long ago when God waited patiently **in** the days of
3: 22 who has gone into heaven and is **at** God's right hand—with angels,
4: 2 he does not live the rest of his **earthly** [+*4922*] life for evil human
4: 3 living in debauchery, lust, drunkenness, orgies, carousing
4: 4 They think it strange that you [**NIE**] do not plunge with them into
4: 11 so that **in** all things God may be praised through Jesus Christ.
4: 12 do not be surprised at the painful trial [**NIE**] you are suffering,
4: 13 of Christ, so that you may be overjoyed **when** his glory is revealed.
4: 14 If you are insulted **because of** the name of Christ, you are blessed,
4: 16 do not be ashamed, but praise God that you **bear** that name.
4: 19 themselves to their faithful Creator and **continue** to do good.
5: 1 To the elders **among** you, I appeal as a fellow elder, a witness of
5: 2 Be shepherds of God's flock that is **under** your *care*, serving as
5: 6 under God's mighty hand, that he may lift you up **in** due time.
5: 9 because you know that your brothers **throughout** the world are
5: 10 the God of all grace, who called you to his eternal glory **in** Christ,
5: 13 She who is **in** Babylon, chosen together with you, sends you her
5: 14 Greet one another **with** a kiss of love. Peace to all of you who are
5: 14 another with a kiss of love. Peace to all of you who are **in** Christ.

2Pe 1: 1 To those who **through** the righteousness of our God and Savior
1: 2 and peace be yours in abundance **through** the knowledge of God
1: 4 and escape the corruption **in** the world caused by evil desires.
1: 4 and escape the corruption in the world **caused by** evil desires.
1: 5 this very reason, make every effort to add **to** your faith goodness;
1: 5 effort to add to your faith goodness; and **to** goodness, knowledge;
1: 6 and **to** knowledge, self-control; and to self-control, perseverance;
1: 6 and to knowledge, self-control; and **to** self-control, perseverance,
1: 6 and to self-control, perseverance; and **to** perseverance, godliness;
1: 7 and **to** godliness, brotherly kindness; and to brotherly kindness,
1: 7 to godliness, brotherly kindness; and **to** brotherly kindness, love.
1: 12 know them and are firmly established **in** the truth you now have.
1: 13 I think it is right to refresh your [**NIE**] memory as long as I live in
1: 13 I think it is right to refresh your memory as long as I live **in** the

1:18 from heaven when we were with him **on** the sacred mountain.
1:19 as to a light shining **in** a dark place, until the day dawns
1:19 until the day dawns and the morning star rises **in** your hearts.
2: 1 But there were also false prophets **among** the people, just as there
2: 1 among the people, just as there will be false teachers **among** you.
2: 3 **In** their greed these teachers will exploit you with stories they have
2: 7 who was distressed by the **[NIE]** filthy lives of lawless men
2: 8 that righteous man, **living among** [*RP1594*] them day after day,
2:10 This is especially true of those who follow **[NIE]** the corrupt
2:12 But these men blaspheme **in** matters they do not understand.
2:12 and destroyed, and **[NIE]** like beasts they too will perish.
2:13 Their idea of pleasure is to carouse **in** broad daylight. They are
2:13 reveling **in** their pleasures while they feast with you.
2:16 who spoke **with** a man's voice and restrained the prophet's
2:18 **by** *appealing* to the lustful desires of sinful human nature,
2:18 they entice people who are just escaping from those who live **in**
2:20 If they have escaped the corruption of the world **by** knowing our
3: 1 I have written **both of them** [*+4005*] as reminders to stimulate you
3: 1 I have written both of them **as** reminders to stimulate you to
3: 3 will come, **[NIE]** scoffing and following their own evil desires.
3:10 **[NIE]** The heavens will disappear with a roar; the elements will
3:10 by fire, and the earth and everything **in** it will be laid bare.
3:11 ought you to be? You ought to live **[NIE]** holy and godly lives
3:13 a new heaven and a new earth, the **[NIE]** home of righteousness.
3:14 every effort to be found spotless, blameless and **at** peace with him.
3:16 He writes the same way **in** all his letters, speaking in them of these
3:16 the same way in all his letters, speaking **in** them of these matters.
3:16 His letters **contain** some things that are hard to understand,
3:18 But grow **in** the grace and knowledge of our Lord and Savior Jesus

1Jn 1: 5 and declare to you: God is light; **in** him there is no darkness at all.
1: 6 If we claim to have fellowship with him yet walk **in** the darkness,
1: 7 But if we walk **in** the light, as he is in the light, we have fellowship
1: 7 But if we walk in the light, as he is **in** the light, we have fellowship
1: 8 to be without sin, we deceive ourselves and the truth is not **in** us.
1:10 make him out to be a liar and his word has no place **in** our lives.
2: 3 **[NIE]** We know that we have come to know him if we obey his
2: 4 does not do what he commands is a liar, and the truth is not **in** him.
2: 5 anyone obeys his word, God's love is truly made complete **in** him.
2: 5 complete **in** him. **This is how** [*+4047*] we know we are in him.
2: 5 truly made complete in him. This is how we know we are **in** him:
2: 6 Whoever claims to live **in** him must walk as Jesus did.
2: 8 its truth is *seen* **in** him and you, because the darkness is passing
2: 8 its truth is seen in him and **[RPG]** you, because the darkness is
2: 9 Anyone who claims to be **in** the light but hates his brother is still in
2: 9 claims to be in the light but hates his brother is still **in** the darkness.
2:10 Whoever loves his brother lives **in** the light, and there is nothing in
2:10 lives in the light, and there is nothing **in** him to make him stumble.
2:11 But whoever hates his brother is **in** the darkness and walks around
2:11 his brother is in the darkness and walks around **in** the darkness;
2:14 because you are strong, and the word of God lives **in** you,
2:15 Do not love the world or anything **in** the world. If anyone loves the
2:15 If anyone loves the world, the love of the Father is not **in** him.
2:16 For everything **in** the world—the cravings of sinful man, the lust of
2:24 See that what you have heard from the beginning remains **in** you.
2:24 If it **does**ˢ [*+3531+5148*], you also will remain in the Son
2:24 If it does, you also will remain **in** the Son and in the Father.
2:24 If it does, you also will remain in the Son and **in** the Father.
2:27 As for you, the anointing you received from him remains **in** you,
2:27 is real, not counterfeit—just as it has taught you, remain **in** him.
2:28 And now, dear children, continue **in** him, so that when he appears
2:28 we may be confident and unashamed before him **at** his coming.
3: 5 so that he might take away our sins. And **in** him is no sin.
3: 6 No one who lives **in** him keeps on sinning. No one who continues
3: 9 of God will continue to sin, because God's seed remains **in** him;
3:10 **This is how** [*+4047*] we know who the children of God are
3:14 we love our brothers. Anyone who does not love remains **in** death.
3:15 a murderer, and you know that no murderer has eternal life **in** him.
3:16 **This is how** [*+4047*] we know what love is: Jesus Christ laid down
3:17 but has no pity on him, how can the love of God be **in** him?
3:18 let us not love with words or tongue but **with** actions and in truth.
3:19 This then is **how** we know that we belong to the truth, and how we
3:24 Those who obey his commands live **in** him, and he in them.
3:24 Those who obey his commands live in him, and he **in** them.
3:24 and he in them. And this is **how** we know that he lives in us:
3:24 and he in them. And this is how we know that he lives **in** us:
4: 2 **This is how** [*+4047*] you can recognize the Spirit of God:

4: 2 Every spirit that acknowledges that Jesus Christ has come **in** the
4: 3 you have heard is coming and even now is already **in** the world.
4: 4 because the one who is **in** you is greater than the one who is in the
4: 4 because the one who is in you is greater than the one who is **in** the
4: 9 **This is how** [*+4047*] God showed his love among us: He sent his
4: 9 This is how God showed his love **among** us: He sent his one
4:10 **[NIE]** This is love: not that we loved God, but that he loved us
4:12 one another, God lives **in** us and his love is made complete in us.
4:12 one another, God lives in us and his love is made complete **in** us.
4:13 **[NIE]** We know that we live in him and he in us, because he has
4:13 We know that we live **in** him and he in us, because he has given us
4:13 We know that we live in him and he **in** us, because he has given us
4:15 that Jesus is the Son of God, God lives **in** him and he in God.
4:15 that Jesus is the Son of God, God lives in him and he **in** God.
4:16 And so we know and rely on the love God has **for** us. God is love.
4:16 God is love. Whoever lives **in** love lives in God, and God in him.
4:16 God is love. Whoever lives in love lives **in** God, and God in him.
4:16 God is love. Whoever lives in love lives in God, and God **in** him.
4:17 **In** this way, love is made complete among us so that we will have
4:17 among us so that we will have confidence **on** the day of judgment,
4:17 on the day of judgment, because **in** this world we are like him.
4:18 There is no fear **in** love. But perfect love drives out fear,
4:18 with punishment. The one who fears is not made perfect **in** love.
5: 2 **This is how** [*+4047*] we know that we love the children of God:
5: 6 He did not *come* **by** water only, but by water and blood.
5: 6 He did not come by water only, but **by** water and blood.
5: 6 He did not come by water only, but by water and **[RPG]** blood.
5:10 Anyone who believes in the Son of God has this testimony **in** his
5:11 God has given us eternal life, and this life is **in** his Son.
5:19 and that the whole world is under the control **of** the evil one.
5:20 And we are **in** him who is true—even in his Son Jesus Christ.
5:20 And we are in him who is true—even **in** his Son Jesus Christ.

2Jn 1: 1 To the chosen lady and her children, whom I love **in** the truth—
1: 2 because of the truth, which lives **in** us and will be with us forever:
1: 3 Jesus Christ, the Father's Son, will be with us **in** truth and love.
1: 4 It has given me great joy to find some of your children walking **in**
1: 6 heard from the beginning, his command is that you walk **in** love.
1: 7 who do not acknowledge Jesus Christ as coming **in** the flesh,
1: 9 and does not continue **in** the teaching of Christ does not have God;
1: 9 whoever continues **in** the teaching has both the Father and the Son.

3Jn 1: 1 The elder, To my dear friend Gaius, whom I love **in** the truth.
1: 3 faithfulness to the truth and how you continue to walk **in** the truth.
1: 4 I have no greater joy than to hear that my children are walking **in**

Jude 1: 1 who are loved **by** God the Father and kept by Jesus Christ:
1:10 **[NIE]** these are the very things that destroy them.
1:12 These men are blemishes **at** your love feasts, eating with you
1:14 the Lord is coming **with** thousands upon thousands of his holy
1:20 yourselves up in your most holy faith and pray **in** the Holy Spirit.
1:21 Keep yourselves **in** God's love as you wait for the mercy of our
1:23 the fire and save them; to others show mercy, *mixed* **with** fear—
1:24 you before his glorious presence without fault and **with** great joy—

Rev 1: 1 which God gave him to show his servants what must **soon** [*+5443*]
1: 3 blessed are those who hear it and take to heart what is written in it,
1: 4 John, To the seven churches **in** the province of Asia: Grace
1: 5 To him who loves us and has freed us from our sins **by** his blood,
1: 9 your brother and companion in the suffering and kingdom
1: 9 and kingdom and patient endurance that are ours **in** Jesus,
1: 9 was **on** the island of Patmos because of the word of God
1:10 **On** the Lord's Day I was in the Spirit, and I heard behind me a
1:10 On the Lord's Day I was in the Spirit, and I heard behind me a
1:13 and **among** [*+3545*] the lampstands was someone "like a son of
1:15 His feet were like bronze glowing **in** a furnace, and his voice was
1:16 **In** his right hand he held seven stars, and out of his mouth came a
1:16 His face was like the sun shining **in** all its brilliance.
2: 1 "To the angel of the church **in** Ephesus write: These are the words
2: 1 These are the words of him who holds the seven stars **in** his right
2: 1 right hand and walks **among** [*+3545*] the seven golden lampstands:
2: 7 right to eat from the tree of life, which is **in** the paradise of God.
2: 8 "To the angel of the church **in** Smyrna write: These are the words
2:12 "To the angel of the church **in** Pergamum write: These are the
2:13 even **in** the days of Antipas, my faithful witness, who was put to
2:16 to you and will fight against them **with** the sword of my mouth.
2:18 "To the angel of the church **in** Thyatira write: These are the words
2:23 *I will* **strike** her children **dead** [*+650+2505*]. Then all the churches
2:24 Now I say to the rest of you **in** Thyatira, to you who do not hold to
2:27 'He will rule them **with** an iron scepter; he will dash them to pieces

3: 1 "To the angel of the church **in** Sardis write: These are the words of
3: 4 Yet you have a few people **in** Sardis who have not soiled their
3: 4 They will walk with me, *dressed* **in** white, for they are worthy.
3: 5 He who overcomes will, like them, be dressed **in** white. I will
3: 7 "To the angel of the church **in** Philadelphia write: These are the
3: 12 Him who overcomes I will make a pillar **in** the temple of my God.
3: 14 "To the angel of the church **in** Laodicea write: These are the words
3: 21 I will give the right to sit with me **on** my throne, just as I overcame
3: 21 just as I overcame and sat down with my Father **on** his throne.
4: 1 I looked, and there before me was a door standing open **in** heaven.
4: 2 At once I was **in** the Spirit, and there before me was a throne in
4: 2 and there before me was a throne **in** heaven with someone sitting
4: 4 They were dressed **in** white and had crowns of gold on their heads.
4: 6 **In** the center, around the throne, were four living creatures.
5: 2 And I saw a mighty angel proclaiming **in** a loud voice, "Who is
5: 3 But no one in heaven or on earth or under the earth could open the
5: 6 looking as if it had been slain, standing **in** the center of the throne,
5: 6 standing in the center of the throne, **encircled**^{s} **by** [+*3545*] the
5: 9 and **with** your blood you purchased men for God from every tribe
5: 13 Then I heard every creature **in** heaven and on earth and under the
5: 13 and under the earth and on the sea, and all that is **in** them, singing:
6: 5 a black horse! Its rider was holding a pair of scales **in** his hand.
6: 6 Then I heard what sounded like a voice **among** [+*3545*] the four
6: 8 They were given power over a fourth of the earth to kill **by** sword,
6: 8 **[RPG]** famine and plague, and by the wild beasts of the earth.
6: 8 famine and **[RPG]** plague, and by the wild beasts of the earth.
7: 9 white robes and were *holding* palm branches **in** their hands.
7: 14 washed their robes and made them white **in** the blood of the Lamb.
7: 15 the throne of God and serve him day and night **in** his temple;
8: 1 seventh seal, there was silence **in** heaven for about half an hour.
8: 7 his trumpet, and there came hail and fire mixed **with** blood,
8: 9 a third of the living creatures **in** the sea died, and a third of the
8: 13 I heard an eagle that was flying **in** midair call out in a loud voice:
9: 6 **During** those days men will seek death, but will not find it;
9: 10 and **in** their tails they had power to torment people for five months.
9: 11 whose name in Hebrew is Abaddon, and **in** Greek, Apollyon.
9: 17 The horses and riders I saw **in** my vision looked like this:
9: 19 The power of the horses was **in** their mouths and in their tails;
9: 19 The power of the horses was in their mouths and **in** their tails;
9: 19 tails were like snakes, having heads **with** which they inflict injury.
9: 20 The rest of mankind that were not killed **by** these plagues still did
10: 2 He was holding a little scroll, which lay open **in** his hand.
10: 6 And he swore **by** him who lives for ever and ever, who created the
10: 6 who created the heavens and all that is **in** them, the earth and all
10: 6 the earth and all that is **in** it, and the sea and all that is in it,
10: 6 and all that is in it, and the sea and all that is **in** it, and said,
10: 7 But **in** the days when the seventh angel is about to sound his
10: 8 take the scroll that lies open **in** the hand of the angel who is
10: 9 your stomach sour, but **in** your mouth it will be as sweet as honey."
10: 10 It tasted as sweet as honey **in** my mouth, but when I had eaten it,
11: 1 of God and the altar, and count the worshipers **there** [+*899*].
11: 6 and to strike the earth **with** every kind of plague as often as they
11: 11 and a half days a breath of life from God entered **[NIE]** them,
11: 12 And they went up to heaven **in** a cloud, while their enemies looked
11: 13 **At** that very hour there was a severe earthquake and a tenth of the
11: 13 Seven thousand people were killed **in** the earthquake,
11: 15 his trumpet, and there were loud voices **in** heaven, which said:
11: 19 Then God's temple **in** heaven was opened, and within his temple
11: 19 and **within** his temple was seen the ark of his covenant.
12: 1 A great and wondrous sign appeared **in** heaven: a woman clothed
12: 2 *She was* **pregnant** [+*1143*+*2400*] and cried out in pain as she was
12: 3 Then another sign appeared **in** heaven: an enormous red dragon
12: 5 a male child, who will rule all the nations **with** an iron scepter.
12: 7 And there was war **in** heaven. Michael and his angels fought
12: 8 But he was not strong enough, and they lost their place **in** heaven.
12: 10 Then I heard a loud voice **in** heaven say: "Now have come the
12: 12 Therefore rejoice, you heavens and you who dwell **in** them!
13: 6 his name and his dwelling place and those who live **in** heaven.
13: 8 all whose names have not been written **in** the book of life
13: 10 If anyone is to be killed **with** the sword, with the sword he will be
13: 10 is to be killed with the sword, **with** the sword he will be killed.
13: 12 made the earth and **its** [+*899*] inhabitants worship the first beast,
14: 2 The sound I heard was like that of harpists playing **[NIE]** their
14: 5 No lie was found in their mouths; they are blameless.
14: 6 Then I saw another angel flying **in** midair, and he had the eternal
14: 7 He said **in** a loud voice, "Fear God and give him glory,

14: 9 A third angel followed them and said **in** a loud voice: "If anyone
14: 10 which has been poured full strength **into** the cup of his wrath.
14: 10 He will be tormented **with** burning sulfur in the presence of the
14: 13 Blessed are the dead who die **in** the Lord from now on." "Yes,"
14: 14 with a crown of gold on his head and a sharp sickle **in** his hand.
14: 15 and called **in** a loud voice to him who was sitting on the cloud,
14: 17 Another angel came out of the temple **in** heaven, and he too had a
15: 1 I saw **in** heaven another great and marvelous sign: seven angels
15: 1 last plagues—last, because **with** them God's wrath is completed.
15: 5 After this I looked and **in** heaven the temple, that is, the tabernacle
16: 3 like that of a dead man, and every living thing **in** the sea died.
16: 8 on the sun, and the sun was given power to scorch people **with** fire.
17: 3 Then the angel carried me away **in** the Spirit into a desert.
17: 4 She held a golden cup **in** her hand, filled with abominable things
17: 16 and leave her naked; they will eat her flesh and burn her **with** fire.
18: 2 **With** a mighty voice he shouted: "Fallen! Fallen is Babylon the
18: 6 for what she has done. Mix her a double portion **from** her own cup.
18: 7 **In** her heart she boasts, 'I sit as queen; I am not a widow, and I will
18: 8 Therefore **in** one day her plagues will overtake her: death,
18: 8 She will be consumed **by** fire, for mighty is the Lord God who
18: 16 purple and scarlet, and glittering **with** gold, precious stones
18: 19 O great city, **where** [+*4005*] all who had ships on the sea became
18: 19 where all who had ships **on** the sea became rich through her
18: 22 flute players and trumpeters, will never be heard **in** you again.
18: 22 No workman of any trade will ever be found **in** you again.
18: 22 The sound of a millstone will never be heard **in** you again.
18: 23 The light of a lamp will never shine **in** you again. The voice of
18: 23 voice of bridegroom and bride will never be heard **in** you again.
18: 23 great men. **By** your magic spell all the nations were led astray.
18: 24 **In** her was found the blood of prophets and of the saints, and of all
19: 1 After this I heard what sounded like the roar of a great multitude **in**
19: 2 He has condemned the great prostitute who corrupted the earth **by**
19: 11 is called Faithful and True. **With** justice he judges and makes war.
19: 14 The armies **of** heaven were following him, riding on white horses
19: 15 Out of his mouth comes a sharp sword **with** which to strike down
19: 15 "He will rule them **with** an iron scepter." He treads the winepress of
19: 17 And I saw an angel standing **in** the sun, who cried in a loud voice
19: 17 who cried **in** a loud voice to all the birds flying in midair, "Come,
19: 17 who cried in a loud voice to all the birds flying **in** midair, "Come,
19: 20 **With** these signs he had deluded those who had received the mark
19: 20 were thrown alive into the fiery lake of burning **[NIE]** sulfur.
19: 21 The rest of them were killed **with** the sword that came out of the
20: 6 Blessed and holy are those who have part **in** the first resurrection.
20: 8 and will go out to deceive the nations **in** the four corners of the
20: 12 judged according to what they had done as recorded **in** the books.
20: 13 The sea gave up the dead that were **in** it, and death and Hades gave
20: 13 in it, and death and Hades gave up the dead that were **in** them,
20: 15 If anyone's name was not found written **in** the book of life,
21: 8 and all liars—their place will be **in** the fiery lake of burning sulfur.
21: 10 And he carried me away **in** the Spirit to a mountain great and high,
21: 22 I did not see a temple **in** the city, because the Lord God Almighty
21: 27 but only those whose names are written **in** the Lamb's book of life.
22: 2 **down** the middle of the great street of the city. On each side of the
22: 3 The throne of God and of the Lamb will be **in** the city, and his
22: 6 to show his servants the things that must **soon** [+*5443*] take place."
22: 18 to them, God will add to him the plagues described **in** this book.
22: 19 tree of life and in the holy city, which are described **in** this book.

1878 ἐναγκαλίζομαι, *enankalizomai* [2]

[√ *1877* + *44*]

taking in his arms [1], took in arms [1]

Mk 9: 36 him stand among them. **Taking** him **in his arms**, he said to them,
   10: 16 And *he* **took** the children **in** his **arms**, put his hands on them

1879 ἐνάλιος, *enalios* [1] [√ *1877* + *229*]

creatures of sea [1]

Jas 3: 7 All kinds *of* animals, birds, reptiles and **creatures of** the **sea** are

1880 ἐνάλλομαι, *enallomai* Not used in UBS/NIV

[√ *1877* + *256*]

1881 ἐνανθρωπέω, **enanthrōpeō**   Not used in UBS/NIV [√ *1877 + 476*]

1882 ἔναντι, **enanti**   [2] [→ *595, 1883, 1884, 1885, 2978, 5539, 5641; cf. 1877 + 505*]

before [2]

Lk   1: 8   division was on duty and he was serving as priest **before** God,
Ac   8:21   share in this ministry, because your heart is not right **before** God.

1883 ἐναντίον, **enantion**   [8] [√ *1882*]

before [2], *untranslated* [1], but [*+1254+3836*] [1], in public [*+3295+3836*] [1], in the sight [1], instead [*+3437+3836*] [1], on contrary [*+247*] [1]

Lk   1: 6   Both of them were upright **in the sight** of God, observing all the
     20:26   to trap him in what he had said there **in public** [*+3295+3836*].
     24:19   powerful in word and deed **before** God and all the people.
Ac   7:10   and enabled him to gain the goodwill **[NIE]** of Pharaoh king of
     8:32   and as a lamb **before** the shearer is silent, so he did not open his
2Co 2: 7   Now **instead** [*+3437+3836*], you ought to forgive and comfort
Gal 2: 7   **On the contrary** [*+247*], they saw that I had been entrusted with
1Pe 3: 9   with evil or insult with insult, **but** [*+1254+3836*] with blessing,

1884 ἐναντιόομαι, **enantioomai**   Not used in UBS/NIV [√ *1882*]

1885 ἐναντίος, **enantios**   [8] [√ *1882*]

against [4], hostile [1], in front of [*+1666*] [1], oppose [*+1666*] [1], oppose [1]

Mt 14:24   from land, buffeted by the waves because the wind was **against** it.
Mk   6:48   disciples straining at the oars, because the wind was **against** them.
     15:39   who stood there **in front** [*+1666*] **of** Jesus, heard his cry and saw
Ac 26: 9   do all that was possible to **oppose** the name of Jesus of Nazareth.
     27: 4   passed to the lee of Cyprus because the winds were **against** us.
     28:17   although I have done nothing **against** our people or against the
1Th 2:15   also drove us out. They displease God and are **hostile** to all men
Tit 2: 8   so that those who **oppose** [*+1666*] you may be ashamed

1886 ἐναργής, **enargēs**   Not used in UBS/NIV

1887 ἐνάρχομαι, **enarchomai**   [2] [√ *1877 + 806*]

began [1], beginning [1]

Gal 3: 3   *After* **beginning** with the Spirit, are you now trying to attain your
Php 1: 6   that he *who* **began** a good work in you will carry it on to

1888 ἔνατος, **enatos**   [10] [√ *1933*]

ninth [7], three in the afternoon [2], three in the afternoon [*+2465+3836+6052*] [1]

Mt 20: 5   about the sixth hour and the **ninth** hour and did the same thing.
     27:45   From the sixth hour until the **ninth** hour darkness came over all the
     27:46   About the **ninth** hour Jesus cried out in a loud voice, "*Eloi,*
Mk 15:33   sixth hour darkness came over the whole land until the **ninth** hour.
     15:34   And *at* the **ninth** hour Jesus cried out in a loud voice, "*Eloi,*
Lk 23:44   and darkness came over the whole land until the **ninth** hour,
Ac   3: 1   up to the temple at the time of prayer—at **three in the afternoon**.
     10: 3   One day at about **three** [*+2465+3836+6052*] **in the afternoon** he
            had a vision. He distinctly saw an angel of God, who came to him
     10:30   I was in my house praying at this hour, at **three in the afternoon**.
Rev 21:20   the eighth beryl, the **ninth** topaz, the tenth chrysoprase,

1889 ἐναφίημι, **enaphiēmi**   Not used in UBS/NIV [√ *918; cf. 1877*]

1890 ἐνδεής, **endeēs**   [1] [√ *1877 + 1289*]

needy [1]

Ac   4:34   There were no **needy** persons among them. For from time to time

1891 ἔνδειγμα, **endeigma**   [1] [√ *1877 + 1257*]

evidence [1]

2Th 1: 5   All this is **evidence** that God's judgment is right, and as a result

1892 ἐνδείκνυμι, **endeiknymi**   [11] [√ *1877 + 1259*]

show [5], display [2], show that [2], did [1], shown [1]

Ro   2:15   *since* they **show that** the requirements of the law are written on
      9:17   that *I might* **display** my power in you and that my name might be
      9:22   if God, choosing *to* **show** his wrath and make his power known,
2Co 8:24   Therefore **show** these men the proof of your love and the reason
Eph 2: 7   in order that in the coming ages *he might* **show** the incomparable
1Ti 1:16   Christ Jesus *might* **display** his unlimited patience as an example
2Ti 4:14   Alexander the metalworker **did** me a great deal of harm. The Lord
Tit 2:10   not to steal from them, but to **show that** they can be fully trusted,
      3: 2   and considerate, and to **show** true humility toward all men.
Heb 6:10   and the love *you have* **shown** him as you have helped his people
      6:11   We want each of you *to* **show** this same diligence to the very end,

1893 ἔνδειξις, **endeixis**   [4] [√ *1877 + 1259*]

demonstrate [2], proof [1], sign [1]

Ro   3:25   He did this to **demonstrate** his justice, because in his forbearance
      3:26   he did it to **demonstrate** his justice at the present time, so as to be
2Co 8:24   Therefore show these men the **proof** of your love and the reason
Php 1:28   This is a **sign** to them that they will be destroyed, but that you will

1894 ἔνδεκα, **hendeka**   [6] [√ *1651 + 1274*]

eleven [6]

Mt 28:16   Then the **eleven** disciples went to Galilee, to the mountain where
Mk 16:14   Later Jesus appeared *to* the **Eleven** as they were eating; he rebuked
Lk 24: 9   they told all these things *to* the **Eleven** and to all the others.
     24:33   There they found the **Eleven** and those with them,
Ac   1:26   and the lot fell to Matthias; so he was added to the **eleven** apostles.
      2:14   Then Peter stood up with the **Eleven**, raised his voice

1895 ἐνδέκατος, **hendekatos**   [3] [√ *1651 + 1274*]

eleventh [3]

Mt 20: 6   About the **eleventh** hour he went out and found still others
     20: 9   "The workers who were hired about the **eleventh** hour came
Rev 21:20   the ninth topaz, the tenth chrysoprase, the **eleventh** jacinth,

1896 ἐνδέχομαι, **endechomai**   [1] [√ *1877 + 1312*]

can [1]

Lk 13:33   and the next day—for surely no prophet **can** die outside Jerusalem!

1897 ἐνδημέω, **endēmeō**   [3] [√ *1877 + 1322*]

at home [3]

2Co 5: 6   and know that *as long as we are* **at home** in the body we are away
      5: 8   would prefer to be away from the body and **at home** with the Lord.
      5: 9   please him, whether *we are* **at home** in the body or away from it.

1898 ἐνδιδύσκω, **endidyskō**   [2] [√ *1877 + 1544*]

dressed in [1], put on [1]

Mk 15:17   *They* **put** a purple robe **on** him, then twisted together a crown of
Lk 16:19   "There was a rich man *who was* **dressed in** purple and fine linen

1899 ἔνδικος, **endikos** [2] [√ *1877 + 1472*]

deserved [1], just [1]

Ro   3: 8 us do evil that good may result"? Their condemnation is **deserved**.
Heb 2: 2 and every violation and disobedience received its **just** punishment,

1900 ἐνδόμησις, **endomēsis** Not used in UBS/NIV
[√ *1877 + 1560*]

1901 ἐνδοξάζομαι, **endoxazomai** [2] [√ *1877 + 1518*]

glorified [2]

2Th 1: 10 on the day he comes *to be* **glorified** in his holy people and to be
     1: 12 so that the name of our Lord Jesus *may be* **glorified** in you,

1902 ἔνδοξος, **endoxos** [4] [√ *1877 + 1518*]

expensive [1], honored [1], radiant [1], wonderful [1]

Lk   7: 25 those who wear **expensive** clothes and indulge in luxury are in
     13: 17 but the people were delighted with all the **wonderful** *things* he
1Co 4: 10 but you are strong! You are **honored**, we are dishonored!
Eph 5: 27 and to present her to himself as a **radiant** church, without stain

1903 ἔνδυμα, **endyma** [8] [√ *1877 + 1544*]

clothes [7], clothing [1]

Mt   3: 4 John's **clothes** were made of camel's hair, and he had a leather belt
     6: 25 important than food, and the body more important than **clothes**?
     6: 28 "And why do you worry about **clothes**? See how the lilies of the
     7: 15 They come to you in sheep's **clothing**, but inwardly they are
     22: 11 he noticed a man there who was not wearing wedding **clothes**.
     22: 12 he asked, 'how did you get in here without wedding **clothes**?'
     28: 3 appearance was like lightning, and his **clothes** were white as snow.
Lk   12: 23 Life is more than food, and the body more than **clothes**.

1904 ἐνδυναμόω, **endynamoō** [7] [√ *1877 + 1538*]

strong [2], gave strength [1], given strength [1], gives strength
[1], powerful [1], strengthened [1]

Ac   9: 22 Yet Saul *grew* more and more **powerful** and baffled the Jews
Ro   4: 20 of God, but *was* **strengthened** in his faith and gave glory to God,
Eph 6: 10 Finally, *be* **strong** in the Lord and in his mighty power.
Php 4: 13 I can do everything through him *who* **gives** me **strength**.
1Ti 1: 12 I thank Christ Jesus our Lord, who *has* **given** me **strength**,
2Ti 2: 1 You then, my son, *be* **strong** in the grace that is in Christ Jesus.
     4: 17 But the Lord stood at my side and **gave** me **strength**, so that

1905 ἐνδύνω, **endynō** [1] [√ *1877 + 1544*]

worm way [1]

2Ti 3: 6 They are the kind who **worm** *their* **way** into homes and gain

1906 ἔνδυσις, **endysis** [1] [√ *1877 + 1544*]

fine clothes [+*2668*] [1]

1Pe 3: 3 and the wearing of gold jewelry and **fine clothes** [+*2668*].

1907 ἐνδύω, **endyō** [27 / 28] [√ *1877 + 1544*]

put on [7], clothe with [3], clothed with [3], dressed in [3], wear
[2], wearing [2], with^s [2], *untranslated* [1], in place [1], putting on
[1], wore clothing [+*1639*] [1], worn [1], clothed [1]

Mt   6: 25 you will eat or drink; or about your body, what *you will* **wear**.
     22: 11 he noticed a man there *who was* not **wearing** wedding clothes.
     27: 31 they took off the robe and **put** his own clothes **on** him.
Mk   1: 6 John **wore** [+*1639*] **clothing** made of camel's hair, with a leather
     6: 9 Wear sandals but not [RPG] an extra tunic.
     15: 20 they took off the purple robe and **put** his own clothes **on** him.
Lk   8: 27 For a long time this man *had* not **worn** clothes or lived in a house,
     12: 22 what you will eat; or about your body, what *you will* **wear**.
     15: 22 said to his servants, 'Quick! Bring the best robe and **put** it **on** him.

     24: 49 but stay in the city until *you have been* **clothed with** power from
Ac   12: 21 **wearing** his royal robes, sat on his throne and delivered a public
Ro   13: 12 So *let us* put aside the deeds of darkness and **put on** the armor of
     13: 14 Rather, **clothe** *yourselves* **with** the Lord Jesus Christ, and do not
1Co 15: 53 For the perishable must **clothe** itself **with** the imperishable,
     15: 53 itself with the imperishable, and the mortal **with^s** immortality.
     15: 54 When the perishable *has been* **clothed with** the imperishable,
     15: 54 and the mortal **with^s** immortality, then the saying that is written
2Co 5: 3 because *when we are* **clothed**, [UBS *1694*] we will not be found
Gal 3: 27 were baptized into Christ *have* **clothed** *yourselves* **with** Christ.
Eph 4: 24 and *to* **put on** the new self, created to be like God in true
     6: 11 **Put on** the full armor of God so that you can take your stand
     6: 14 around your waist, with the breastplate of righteousness **in place**,
Col 3: 10 and *have* **put on** the new self, which is being renewed in
     3: 12 **clothe** *yourselves* **with** compassion, kindness, humility, gentleness
1Th 5: 8 let us be self-controlled, **putting on** faith and love as a breastplate,
Rev 1: 13 **dressed in** a robe reaching down to his feet and with a golden sash
     15: 6 *They were* **dressed in** clean, shining linen and wore golden sashes
     19: 14 riding on white horses and **dressed in** fine linen, white and clean.

1908 ἐνδώμησις, **endōmēsis** [1] [√ *1877 + 1560*]

made of [1]

Rev 21: 18 The wall was **made of** jasper, and the city of pure gold, as pure as

1909 ἐνέδρα, **enedra** [2] [√ *1877 + 1612*]

ambush [1], plot [1]

Ac   23: 16 But when the son of Paul's sister heard of this **plot**, he went into
     25: 3 for they were preparing an **ambush** to kill him along the way.

1910 ἐνεδρεύω, **enedreuō** [2] [√ *1877 + 1612*]

waiting [1], waiting in ambush for [1]

Lk   11: 54 **waiting** to catch him in something he might say.
Ac   23: 21 because more than forty of them *are* **waiting in ambush for** him.

1911 ἔνεδρον, **enedron** Not used in UBS/NIV
[√ *1877 + 1612*]

1912 ἐνειλέω, **eneileō** [1] [√ *1877*]

wrapped in [1]

Mk   15: 46 some linen cloth, took down the body, **wrapped** it **in** the linen,

1913 ἔνειμι, **eneimi** [1] [√ *1877 + 1639*]

inside [1]

Lk   11: 41 But give what *is* **inside** ˌthe dishˌ to the poor, and everything will

1914 ἕνεκα, **heneka** Not used in UBS/NIV [→ *1641*,
1915]

1915 ἕνεκεν, **heneken** [24] [√ *1914*]

because [4], for [4], on account [4], for reason [2], for the sake
[2], sake [2], *untranslated* [1], for sake [1], of [1], that [1], why
[+*5515*] [1], why [1]

Mt   5: 10 Blessed are those who are persecuted **because** of righteousness,
     5: 11 and falsely say all kinds of evil against you **because** of me.
     10: 18 **On** my **account** you will be brought before governors and kings as
     10: 39 life will lose it, and whoever loses his life **for** my **sake** will find it.
     16: 25 his life will lose it, but whoever loses his life **for** me will find it.
     19: 5 'For this **reason** a man will leave his father and mother and be
     19: 29 or fields *for* my **sake** will receive a hundred times as much
Mk   8: 35 but whoever loses his life **for** me and for the gospel will save it.
     10: 7 'For this **reason** a man will leave his father and mother and be
     10: 29 or sisters or mother or father or children or fields **for** me
     10: 29 or father or children or fields for me and [RPG] the gospel
     13: 9 **On account** of me you will stand before governors and kings as
Lk   6: 22 and reject your name as evil, **because** of the Son of Man.

```
      9:24  his life will lose it, but whoever loses his life for me will save it.
     18:29  or parents or children for the sake of the kingdom of God
     21:12  before kings and governors, and all on account of my name.
Ac   19:32  Most of the people did not even know why [+5515] they were
     26:21  That is why the Jews seized me in the temple courts and tried to
     28:20  because of the hope of Israel that I am bound with this chain."
Ro    8:36  "For your sake we face death all day long; we are considered as
     14:20  Do not destroy the work of God for the sake of food. All food is
2Co   7:12  it was not on account of the one who did the wrong or of the
      7:12  on account of the one who did the wrong or of the injured party,
      7:12  but rather that before God you could see for yourselves how
```

1916 ἐνενήκοντα, *enenēkonta* [4] [√ *1933*]

ninety-nine [+*1933*] [4]

```
Mt   18:12  will he not leave the ninety-nine [+1933] on the hills and go to
     18:13  sheep than about the ninety-nine [+1933] that did not wander off.
Lk   15: 4  Does he not leave the ninety-nine [+1933] in the open country
     15: 7  ninety-nine [+1933] righteous persons who do not need to repent.
```

1917 ἐνεός, *eneos* [1] [→ *1934*]

speechless [1]

```
Ac    9: 7  The men traveling with Saul stood there speechless; they heard the
```

1918 ἐνέργεια, *energeia* [8] [√ *1877* + *2240*]

power [2], work [2], working [2], energy [1], powerful [1]

```
Eph   1:19  That power is like the working of his mighty strength,
      3: 7  gift of God's grace given me through the working of his power.
      4:16  grows and builds itself up in love, as each part does its work.
Php   3:21  by the power that enables him to bring everything under his
Col   1:29  struggling with all his energy, which so powerfully works in me.
      2:12  and raised with him through your faith in the power of God,
2Th   2: 9  The coming of the lawless one will be in accordance with the work
      2:11  For this reason God sends them a powerful delusion so that they
```

1919 ἐνεργέω, *energeō* [21] [√ *1877* + *2240*]

at work in [*RP1877*] [6], at work in [2], works in [*RP1877*] [2], act
[1], at work [1], at work within [*RP1877*] [1], effective [1], exerted
in [*RP1877*] [1], expressing [1], produces in [*RP1877*] [1], work
[1], work among [*RP1877*] [1], works [1], works out [1]

```
Mt   14: 2  That is why miraculous powers are at work [RP1877] in him."
Mk    6:14  and that is why miraculous powers are at work [RP1877] in him."
Ro    7: 5  The sinful passions aroused by the law were at work [RP1877] in
1Co  12: 6  kinds of working, but the same God works all of them in all men.
     12:11  All these are the work of one and the same Spirit, and he gives
2Co   1: 6  which produces [RP1877] in you patient endurance of the same
      4:12  So then, death is at work [RP1877] in us, but life is at work in
Gal   2: 8  who was at work in the ministry of Peter as an apostle to the Jews,
      2: 8  was also at work in my ministry as an apostle to the Gentiles.
      3: 5  God give you his Spirit and work [RP1877] miracles among you
      5: 6  The only thing that counts is faith expressing itself through love.
Eph   1:11  of him who works out everything in conformity with the purpose
      1:20  which he exerted [RP1877] in Christ when he raised him from the
      2: 2  the spirit who is now at work [RP1877] in those who are
      3:20  according to his power that is at work [RP1877] within us,
Php   2:13  for it is God who works [RP1877] in you to will and to act
      2:13  who works in you to will and to act according to his good purpose.
Col   1:29  with all his energy, which so powerfully works [RP1877] in me.
1Th   2:13  the word of God, which is at work [RP1877] in you who believe.
2Th   2: 7  For the secret power of lawlessness is already at work; but the one
Jas   5:16  The prayer of a righteous man is powerful and effective.
```

1920 ἐνέργημα, *energēma* [2] [√ *1877* + *2240*]

miraculous powers [+*1539*] [1], working [1]

```
1Co  12: 6  There are different kinds of working, but the same God works all
     12:10  to another miraculous powers [+1539], to another prophecy,
```

1921 ἐνεργής, *energēs* [3] [√ *1877* + *2240*]

active [2], effective work [1]

```
1Co  16: 9  because a great door for effective work has opened to me,
Phm   1: 6  I pray that you may be active in sharing your faith, so that you will
Heb   4:12  For the word of God is living and active. Sharper than any
```

1922 ἐνευλογέω, *eneulogeō* [2] [√ *1877* + *2292* + *3306*]

blessed [1], blessed through [*RP1877*] [1]

```
Ac    3:25  'Through your offspring all peoples on earth will be blessed.'
Gal   3: 8  to Abraham: "All nations will be blessed [RP1877] through you."
```

1923 ἐνέχω, *enechō* [3] [√ *1877* + *2400*]

burdened [1], nursed a grudge against [1], oppose [1]

```
Mk    6:19  So Herodias nursed a grudge against John and wanted to kill
Lk   11:53  and the teachers of the law began to oppose him fiercely
Gal   5: 1  and do not let yourselves be burdened again by a yoke of slavery.
```

1924 ἐνθάδε, *enthade* [8] [√ *1877*]

here [6], back [1], there [1]

```
Lk   24:41  amazement, he asked them, "Do you have anything here to eat?"
Jn    4:15  I won't get thirsty and have to keep coming here to draw water."
      4:16  He told her, "Go, call your husband and come back."
Ac   10:18  asking if Simon who was known as Peter was staying there.
     16:28  But Paul shouted, "Don't harm yourself! We are all here!"
     17: 6  who have caused trouble all over the world have now come here,
     25:17  When they came here with me, I did not delay the case,
     25:24  has petitioned me about him in Jerusalem and here in Caesarea,
```

1925 ἔνθεν, *enthen* [2] [√ *1877*]

from here [2]

```
Mt   17.20  say to this mountain, 'Move from here to there' and it will move.
Lk   16:26  been fixed, so that those who want to go from here to you cannot,
```

1926 ἐνθυμέομαι, *enthymeomai* [2] [√ *1877* + *2596*]

considered [1], entertain thoughts [1]

```
Mt    1:20  But after he had considered this, an angel of the Lord appeared to
      9: 4  Jesus said, "Why do you entertain evil thoughts in your hearts?
```

1927 ἐνθύμησις, *enthymēsis* [4] [√ *1877* + *2596*]

thoughts [3], design [1]

```
Mt    9: 4  Knowing their thoughts, Jesus said, "Why do you entertain evil
     12:25  Jesus knew their thoughts and said to them, "Every kingdom
Ac   17:29  or silver or stone—an image made by man's design and skill.
Heb   4:12  and marrow; it judges the thoughts and attitudes of the heart.
```

1928 ἔνι, *eni* [6] [√ *1877* + *1639*]

is [3], *untranslated* [2], does [1]

```
1Co   6: 5  Is it possible that there is nobody among you wise enough to judge
Gal   3:28  There is neither Jew nor Greek, slave nor free, male nor female,
      3:28  is neither Jew nor Greek, [RPG] slave nor free, male nor female,
      3:28  is neither Jew nor Greek, slave nor free, [RPG] male nor female,
Col   3:11  Here there is no Greek or Jew, circumcised or uncircumcised,
Jas   1:17  of the heavenly lights, who does not change like shifting shadows.
```

1929 ἐνιαυτός, *eniautos* [14] [√ *899*]

year [10], years [2], annual [+*2848*] [1], year after year [+*2848*] [1]

```
Lk    4:19  to proclaim the year of the Lord's favor."
Jn   11:49  named Caiaphas, who was high priest that year, spoke up,
     11:51  but as high priest that year he prophesied that Jesus would die for
     18:13  who was the father-in-law of Caiaphas, the high priest that year.
Ac   11:26  So for a whole year Barnabas and Saul met with the church
     18:11  So Paul stayed for a year and a half, teaching them the word of
```

Gal   4:10   are observing *special* days and months and seasons and **years**!
Heb   9: 7   and that only once a **year**, and never without blood, which he
     9:25   the way the high priest enters the Most Holy Place every **year** with
    10: 1   by the same sacrifices repeated endlessly **year** [*+2848*] **after year**,
    10: 3   But those sacrifices are an **annual** [*+2848*] reminder of sins,
Jas   4:13   or tomorrow we will go to this or that city, spend a **year** there,
    5:17   not rain, and it did not rain on the land *for* three and a half **years**.
Rev   9:15   and month and **year** were released to kill a third of mankind.

1930 ἐνίοτε, **eniote**   Not used in UBS/NIV
[√ *1639 + 1877 + 4005*]

1931 ἐνίστημι, **enistēmi** [7] [√ *1877 + 2705*]

present [3], the present [2], be [1], come [1]

Ro   8:38   nor demons, neither **the present** nor the future, nor any powers,
1Co   3:22   or Apollos or Cephas or the world or life or death or **the present**
    7:26   Because of the **present** crisis, I think that it is good for you to
Gal   1: 4   who gave himself for our sins to rescue us from the **present** evil
2Th   2: 2   come from us, saying that the day of the Lord *has already* **come**.
2Ti   3: 1   But mark this: *There will* **be** terrible times in the last days.
Heb   9: 9   This is an illustration for the **present** time, indicating that the gifts

1932 ἐνισχύω, **enischyō** [2] [√ *1877 + 2709*]

regained strength [1], strengthened [1]

Lk   22:43   An angel from heaven appeared to him and **strengthened** him.
Ac   9:19   and after taking some food, *he* **regained** his **strength**. Saul spent

1933 ἐννέα, **ennea** [5] [→ *1888, 1916*]

ninety-nine [*+1916*] [4], nine [1]

Mt   18:12   will he not leave the **ninety-nine** [*+1916*] on the hills and go to
   18:13   sheep than about the **ninety-nine** [*+1916*] that did not wander off.
Lk   15: 4   Does he not leave the **ninety-nine** [*+1916*] in the open country
   15: 7   **ninety-nine** [*+1916*] righteous persons who do not need to repent.
   17:17   Jesus asked, "Were not all ten cleansed? Where are the other **nine**?

1934 ἐννεός, **enneos**   Not used in UBS/NIV [√ *1917*]

1935 ἐννεύω, **enneuō** [1] [√ *1877 + 3748*]

made signs [1]

Lk   1:62   Then *they* **made signs** to his father, to find out what he would like

1936 ἔννοια, **ennoia** [2] [√ *1877 + 3808*]

attitude [1], attitudes [1]

Heb   4:12   and marrow; it judges the thoughts and **attitudes** of the heart.
1Pe   4: 1   suffered in his body, arm yourselves also with the same **attitude**,

1937 ἔννομος, **ennomos** [2] [√ *1877 + 3795*]

legal [1], under law [1]

Ac   19:39   further you want to bring up, it must be settled in a **legal** assembly.
1Co   9:21   (though I am not free from God's law but am **under** Christ's **law**),

1938 ἐννόμως, **ennomōs**   Not used in UBS/NIV
[√ *1877 + 3795*]

1939 ἔννυχος, **ennychos** [1] [√ *1877 + 3816*]

while it was still dark [1]

Mk   1:35   **while it was still dark**, Jesus got up, left the house and went off to

1940 ἐνοικέω, **enoikeō** [5] [√ *1877 + 3875*]

lives in [*RP1877*] [2], dwell in [*RP1877*] [1], live with [*RP1877*] [1], lived in [*RP1877*] [1]

Ro   8:11   your mortal bodies through his Spirit, who **lives** [*RP1877*] **in** you.
2Co   6:16   "*I will* **live** [*RP1877*] **with** them and walk among them, and I will
Col   3:16   *Let* the word of Christ **dwell** [*RP1877*] **in** you richly as you teach
2Ti   1: 5   which first **lived** [*RP1877*] **in** your grandmother Lois and in your
   1:14   guard it with the help *of* the Holy Spirit who **lives** [*RP1877*] **in** us.

1941 ἐνορκίζω, **enorkizo** [1] [√ *1877 + 3992*]

charge before [1]

1Th   5:27   *I* **charge** you **before** the Lord to have this letter read to all the

1942 ἑνότης, **henotēs** [2] [√ *1651*]

unity [2]

Eph   4: 3   Make every effort to keep the **unity** of the Spirit through the bond
   4:13   until we all reach **unity** in the faith and in the knowledge of the

1943 ἐνοχλέω, **enochleō** [2] [√ *1877 + 4063*]

cause trouble [1], troubled [1]

Lk   6:18   healed of their diseases. Those **troubled** by evil spirits were cured,
Heb   12:15   and that no bitter root grows up to **cause trouble** and defile many.

1944 ἔνοχος, **enochos** [10] [√ *1877 + 2400*]

guilty [2], subject [2], worthy [2], answerable [1], guilty of sinning against [1], held [1], in danger [1]

Mt   5:21   not murder, and anyone who murders will be **subject** to judgment.'
   5:22   anyone who is angry with his brother will be **subject** to judgment.
   5:22   who says to his brother, 'Raca,' is **answerable** to the Sanhedrin.
   5:22   anyone who says, 'You fool!' will be **in danger** of the fire of hell.
   26:66   What do you think?" "He is **worthy** of death," they answered.
Mk   3:29   Holy Spirit will never be forgiven; he is **guilty** of an eternal sin."
   14:64   What do you think?" They all condemned him as **worthy** of death.
1Co   11:27   in an unworthy manner will be **guilty of sinning against** the body
Heb   2:15   and free those who all their lives were **held** in slavery by their fear
Jas   2:10   and yet stumbles at just one point is **guilty** of breaking all of it.

1945 ἔνταλμα, **entalma** [3] [√ *1953*]

rules [2], commands [1]

Mt   15: 9   worship me in vain; their teachings are but **rules** taught by men.' "
Mk   7: 7   worship me in vain; their teachings are but **rules** taught by men.'
Col   2:22   because they are based on human **commands** and teachings.

1946 ἐνταφιάζω, **entaphiazō** [2] [√ *1877 + 5439*]

burial [1], prepare for burial [1]

Mt   26:12   this perfume on my body, she did it to **prepare** me **for burial**.
Jn   19:40   strips of linen. This was in accordance with Jewish **burial** customs.

1947 ἐνταφιασμός, **entaphiasmos** [2]
[√ *1877 + 5439*]

burial [2]

Mk   14: 8   poured perfume on my body beforehand to prepare for my **burial**.
Jn   12: 7   that she should save this perfume for the day *of* my **burial**.

1948 ἐντέλλω, **entellō** [15] [√ *1953*]

command [6], commanded [4], commanded to keep [1], gave instructions [1], giving instructions [1], instructed [1], tells [1]

Mt   4: 6   " '*He will* **command** his angels concerning you, and they will lift
   17: 9   Jesus **instructed** them, "Don't tell anyone what you have seen,
   19: 7   "*did* Moses **command** that a man give his wife a certificate of
   28:20   and teaching them to obey everything *I have* **commanded** you.
Mk   10: 3   "What *did* Moses **command** you?" he replied.

13:34 with his assigned task, and **tells** the one at the door to keep watch.
Lk 4:10 " '*He will* **command** his angels concerning you to guard you
Jn 8: 5 In the Law Moses **commanded** us to stone such women.
14:31 and that I do exactly what my Father *has* **commanded** me.
15:14 You are my friends if you do what I **command**.
15:17 This *is my* **command**: Love each other.
Ac 1: 2 *after* **giving instructions** through the Holy Spirit to the apostles he
13:47 For this is what the Lord *has* **commanded** us: " 'I have made you a
Heb 9:20 blood of the covenant, which God *has* **commanded** you **to keep**."
11:22 of the Israelites from Egypt and **gave instructions** about his bones.

1949 ἐντεῦθεν, *enteuthen* [10] [√ *1877*]

one on each side [*+1949+2779*] [2], *untranslated* [1], from [1], from another place [1], from here [1], here [1], of here [1], on each side [*+1696+2779*] [1], this place [1]

Lk 4: 9 you are the Son of God," he said, "throw yourself down **from here**.
13:31 and said to him, "Leave **this place** and go somewhere else.
Jn 2:16 To those who sold doves he said, "Get these out **of here**! How dare
7: 3 brothers said to him, "You ought to leave **here** and go to Judea,
14:31 my Father has commanded me. "Come now; let us leave. **[RPG]**
18:36 arrest by the Jews. But now my kingdom is **from another place**."
19:18 **one on each side** [*+1949+2779*] and Jesus in the middle.
19:18 **one on each side** [*+1949+2779*] and Jesus in the middle.
Jas 4: 1 Don't they *come* **from** your desires that battle within you?
Rev 22: 2 **On each side** [*+1696+2779*] of the river stood the tree of life,

1950 ἔντευξις, *enteuxis* [2] [√ *1877 + 5593*]

intercession [1], prayer [1]

1Ti 2: 1 prayers, **intercession** and thanksgiving be made for everyone—
4: 5 because it is consecrated by the word of God and **prayer**.

1951 ἐντίθημι, *entithēmi* Not used in UBS/NIV [√ *1877 + 5502*]

1952 ἔντιμος, *entimos* [5] [√ *1877 + 5507*]

precious [2], honor [*+2400*] [1], person more distinguished [1], valued highly [*+1639*] [1]

Lk 7: 2 whom his master **valued** [*+1639*] **highly**, was sick and about to
14: 8 for a **person more distinguished** *than* you may have been invited.
Php 2:29 him in the Lord with great joy, and **honor** [*+2400*] men like him,
1Pe 2: 4 rejected by men but chosen by God and **precious** to him—
2: 6 "See, I lay a stone in Zion, a chosen and **precious** cornerstone,

1953 ἐντολή, *entolē* [67] [→ *1945, 1948; cf. 1877*]

ἐντολή [τοῦ] θεοῦ (command of God) [6] Mt 15:3; Mk 7:8,9; 1Co 7:19; Rev 12:17; 14:12

ἐντολή [τοῦ] κυρίου (command of the Lord) [3] Lk 1:6; 1Co 14:37; 2Pe 3:2

καινός ἐντολή (new commandment) [4] Jn 13:34; 1Jn 2:7,8; 2Jn 1:5

μέγας ἐντολή (great commandment) [2] Mt 22:36,38

τηρέω ἐντολάς (to keep commandments) [13] Mt 19:17; Jn 14:15,21; 15:10,10; 1Ti 6:14; 1Jn 2:3,4; 3:22,24; 5:3; Rev 12:17; 14:12

command [17], commands [15], commandment [13], commandments [10], commanded [*+1443*] [2], orders [2], commanded [*+3284*] [1], instructions [1], law [1], ones [1], regulation [*+3795*] [1], regulation [1], requires [1], with instructions [*+3284*] [1]

Mt 5:19 Anyone who breaks one of the least *of* these **commandments**
15: 3 "And why do you break the **command** of God for the sake of your
19:17 who is good. If you want to enter life, obey the **commandments**."
22:36 "Teacher, which is the greatest **commandment** in the Law?"
22:38 This is the first and greatest **commandment**.
22:40 All the Law and the Prophets hang on these two **commandments**."
Mk 7: 8 You have let go of the **commands** of God and are holding on to
7: 9 "You have a fine way of setting aside the **commands** of God in
10: 5 because your hearts were hard that Moses wrote you this **law**,"
10:19 You know the **commandments**: 'Do not murder, do not commit

12:28 he asked him, "Of all the **commandments**, which is the most
12:31 as yourself.' There is no **commandment** greater than these."
Lk 1: 6 observing all the Lord's **commandments** and regulations
15:29 years I've been slaving for you and never disobeyed your **orders**.
18:20 You know the **commandments**: 'Do not commit adultery,
23:56 But they rested on the Sabbath in obedience to the **commandment**.
Jn 10:18 to take it up again. This **command** I received from my Father."
11:57 and Pharisees had given **orders** that if anyone found out where
12:49 but the Father who sent me **commanded** [*+1443*] me what to say
12:50 I know that his **command** leads to eternal life. So whatever I say is
13:34 "A new **command** I give you: Love one another. As I have loved
14:15 "If you love me, you will obey what I **command**.
14:21 Whoever has my **commands** and obeys them, he is the one who
15:10 If you obey my **commands**, you will remain in my love, just as I
15:10 just as I have obeyed my Father's **commands** and remain in his
15:12 My **command** is this: Love each other as I have loved you.
Ac 17:15 and then left **with instructions** [*+3284*] for Silas and Timothy to
Ro 7: 8 But sin, seizing the opportunity afforded by the **commandment**,
7: 9 but when the **commandment** came, sin sprang to life and I died.
7:10 I found that the very **commandment** that was intended to bring life
7:11 For sin, seizing the opportunity afforded by the **commandment**,
7:12 law is holy, and the **commandment** is holy, righteous and good.
7:13 so that through the **commandment** sin might become utterly
13: "Do not covet," and whatever other **commandment** there may be,
1Co 7:19 is nothing. Keeping God's **commands** is what counts.
14:37 that what I am writing to you is the Lord's **command**.
Eph 2:15 by abolishing in his flesh the law *with* its **commandments**
6: 2 and mother"—which is the first **commandment** with a promise—
Col 4:10 (You have received **instructions** about him; if he comes to you,
1Ti 6:14 to keep this **command** without spot or blame until the appearing of
Tit 1:14 to Jewish myths or *to* the **commands** of those who reject the truth.
Heb 7: 5 Now the law **requires** the descendants of Levi who become priests
7:16 a priest not on the basis of a **regulation** [*+3795*] as to his ancestry
7:18 The former **regulation** is set aside because it was weak
9:19 When Moses had proclaimed every **commandment** of the law to
2Pe 2:21 then to turn their backs on the sacred **command** that was passed on
3: 2 and the **command** given by our Lord and Savior through your
1Jn 2: 3 know that we have come to know him if we obey his **commands**.
2: 4 "I know him," but does not do what he **commands** is a liar,
2: 7 Dear friends, I am not writing you a new **command** but an old one,
2: 7 I am not writing you a new command but an old ones,
2: 7 the beginning. This old **command** is the message you have heard.
2: 8 Yet I am writing you a new **command**; its truth is seen in him
3:22 because we obey his **commands** and do what pleases him.
3:23 And this is his **command**: to believe in the name of his Son,
3:23 and to love one another as *he* **commanded** [*+1443*] us.
3:24 Those who obey his **commands** live in him, and he in them.
4:21 And he has given us this **command**: Whoever loves God must also
5: 2 children of God: by loving God and carrying out his **commands**.
5: 3 This is love for God: to obey his **commands**. And his commands
5: 3 to obey his commands. And his **commands** are not burdensome.
2Jn 1: 4 walking in the truth, just as the Father **commanded** [*+3284*] us.
1: 5 I am not writing you a new **command** but one we have had from
1: 6 And this is love: that we walk in obedience to his **commands**.
1: 6 heard from the beginning, his **command** is that you walk in love.
Rev 12:17 those who obey God's **commandments** and hold to the testimony
14:12 on the part of the saints who obey God's **commandments**

1954 ἐντόπιος, *entopios* [1] [√ *1877 + 5536*]

people there [1]

Ac 21:12 and the **people there** pleaded with Paul not to go up to Jerusalem.

1955 ἐντός, *entos* [2] [√ *1877*]

inside [1], within [1]

Mt 23:26 First clean the **inside** of the cup and dish, and then the outside also
Lk 17:21 or 'There it is,' because the kingdom of God is **within** you."

1956 ἐντρέπω, *entrepō* [9] [√ *1877 + 5572*]

respect [3], ashamed [1], care about [1], cared about [1], feel ashamed [1], respected [1], shame [1]

Mt 21:37 he sent his son to them. '*They will* **respect** my son,' he said.
Mk 12: 6 He sent him last of all, saying, '*They will* **respect** my son.'

Lk 18: 2 there was a judge who neither feared God nor **cared about** men.
   18: 4 said to himself, 'Even though I don't fear God or **care about** men,
   20:13 I will send my son, whom I love; perhaps *they will* **respect** him.'
1Co 4:14 I am not writing this *to* **shame** you, but to warn you, as my dear
2Th 3:14 Do not associate with him, in order that *he may* **feel ashamed**.
Tit 2: 8 so that those who oppose you *may be* **ashamed** because they have
Heb 12: 9 human fathers who disciplined us and *we* **respected** them for it.

1957 ἐντρέφω, *entrephō* [1] [√ 1877 + 5555]

brought up [1]

1Ti 4: 6 **brought up** in the truths of the faith and of the good teaching that

1958 ἔντρομος, *entromos* [3] [√ 1877 + 5554]

trembled with fear [+1181] [1], trembling [+1181] [1], trembling [1]

Ac 7:32 Moses **trembled** [+1181] **with fear** and did not dare to look.
   16:29 rushed in and fell **trembling** [+1181] before Paul and Silas.
Heb 12:21 sight was so terrifying that Moses said, "I am **trembling** with fear."

1959 ἐντροπή, *entropē* [2] [√ 1877 + 5572]

shame [2]

1Co 6: 5 I say this to **shame** you. Is it possible that there is nobody among
   15:34 there are some who are ignorant of God—I say this to your **shame**.

1960 ἐντρυφάω, *entryphaō* [1] [√ 1877 + 5588]

reveling [1]

2Pe 2:13 **reveling** in their pleasures while they feast with you.

1961 ἐντυγχάνω, *entynchanō* [5] [√ 1877 + 5593]

appealed [1], intercede [1], intercedes [1], interceding [1], petitioned [1]

Ac 25:24 The whole Jewish community *has* **petitioned** me about him in
Ro 8:27 because the Spirit **intercedes** for the saints in accordance with
   8:34 to life—is at the right hand of God and *is* also **interceding** for us.
   11: 2 the passage about Elijah—how *he* **appealed** to God against Israel:
Heb 7:25 God through him, because he always lives to **intercede** for them.

1962 ἐντυλίσσω, *entylissō* [3] [√ 1877]

wrapped [2], folded up [1]

Mt 27:59 Joseph took the body, **wrapped** it in a clean linen cloth,
Lk 23:53 Then *he* took it down, **wrapped** it in linen cloth and placed it in a
Jn 20: 7 The cloth *was* **folded up** by itself, separate from the linen.

1963 ἐντυπόω, *entypoō* [1] [√ 1877 + 5597]

engraved [1]

2Co 3: 7 *which was* **engraved** in letters on stone, came with glory,

1964 ἐνυβρίζω, *enybrizō* [1] [√ 1877 + 5615]

insulted [1]

Heb 10:29 that sanctified him, and who *has* **insulted** the Spirit of grace?

1965 ἐνυπνιάζομαι, *enypniazomai* [2] [√ 1877 + 5678]

dream [1], dreamers [1]

Ac 2:17 your young men will see visions, your old men *will* **dream** dreams.
Jude 1: 8 these **dreamers** pollute their own bodies, reject authority

1966 ἐνύπνιον, *enypnion* [1] [√ 1877 + 5678]

dreams [1]

Ac 2:17 your young men will see visions, your old men will dream **dreams**.

1967 ἐνώπιον, *enōpion* [94] [√ 1877 + 3972]

before [37], *untranslated* [10], in the presence [9], in the sight [5], in front [4], in the eyes [4], to [4], in sight [3], on behalf [3], against [2], in presence [2], publicly [+4246] [2], at [1], between [1], by [1], entice to sin [+965+4998] [1], in full view [1], in his sight [+899] [1], publicly [+3836+4436] [1], sight [1], with [1]

Lk 1:15 for he will be great **in the sight** of the Lord. He is never to take
   1:17 And he will go on **before** the Lord, in the spirit and power of
   1:19 I stand **in the presence** of God, and I have been sent to speak to
   1:75 in holiness and righteousness **before** him all our days.
   1:76 for you will go on **before** the Lord to prepare the way for him,
   4: 7 So if you worship [NIE] me, it will all be yours."
   5:18 and tried to take him into the house to lay him **before** Jesus.
   5:25 Immediately he stood up **in front** of them, took what he had been
   8:47 **In the presence** of all the people, she told why she had touched
   12: 6 sold for two pennies? Yet not one of them is forgotten **by** God.
   12: 9 But he who disowns me **before** men will be disowned before the
   12: 9 But he who disowns me before men will be disowned **before** the
   13:26 "Then you will say, 'We ate and drank **with** you, and you taught in
   14:10 Then you will be honored **in the presence** of all your fellow
   15:10 there is rejoicing **in the presence** of the angels of God over one
   15:18 say to him: Father, I have sinned against heaven and **against** you.
   15:21 said to him, 'Father, I have sinned against heaven and **against** you.
   16:15 "You are the ones who justify yourselves **in the eyes** of men,
   16:15 What is highly valued among men is detestable **in** God's **sight**.
   23:14 I have examined him **in** your **presence** and have found no basis for
   24:11 the women, because their words seemed **to** them like nonsense.
   24:43 and he took it and ate it **in** their **presence**.
Jn 20:30 Jesus did many other miraculous signs **in the presence** of his
Ac 2:25 David said about him: " 'I saw the Lord always **before** me.
   4:10 God raised from the dead, that this man stands **before** you healed.
   4:19 "Judge for yourselves whether it is right **in** God's **sight** to obey you
   6: 5 This proposal pleased the [NIE] whole group. They chose
   6: 6 They presented these men **to** the apostles, who prayed and laid
   7:46 who enjoyed [NIE] God's favor and asked that he might provide
   9:15 This man is my chosen instrument to carry my name **before** the
   10:30 the afternoon. Suddenly a man in shining clothes stood **before** me
   10:31 [NIE] God has heard your prayer and remembered your gifts to
   10:33 Now we are all here **in the presence** of God to listen to everything
   19: 9 refused to believe and **publicly** [+3836+4436] maligned the Way.
   19:19 brought their scrolls together and burned them **publicly** [+4246].
   27:35 he took some bread and gave thanks to God **in front** of them all.
Ro 3:20 Therefore no one will be declared righteous **in his sight** [+899] by
   12:17 for evil. Be careful to do what is right **in the eyes** of everybody.
   14:22 So whatever you believe about these things keep **between** yourself
1Co 1:29 so that no one may boast **before** him.
2Co 4: 2 ourselves to every man's conscience **in the sight** of God.
   7:12 but rather that **before** God you could see for yourselves how
   8:21 not only **in the eyes** of the Lord but also in the eyes of men.
   8:21 not only in the eyes of the Lord but also **in the eyes** of men.
Gal 1:20 I assure you **before** God that what I am writing you is no lie.
1Ti 2: 3 This is good, and pleases [NIE] God our Savior,
   5: 4 repaying their parents and grandparents, for this is pleasing **to** God.
   5:20 Those who sin are to be rebuked **publicly** [+4246], so that the
   5:21 **in the sight** of God and Christ Jesus and the elect angels,
   6:12 made your good confession **in the presence** of many witnesses.
   6:13 **In the sight** of God, who gives life to everything, and of Christ
2Ti 2:14 Warn them **before** God against quarreling about words; it is of no
   4: 1 **In the presence** of God and of Christ Jesus, who will judge the
Heb 4:13 Nothing in all creation is hidden from God's **sight** Everything is
   13:21 and may he work in us what is pleasing **to** him, through Jesus
Jas 4:10 Humble yourselves **before** the Lord, and he will lift you up.
1Pe 3: 4 of a gentle and quiet spirit, which is of great worth **in** God's **sight**.
1Jn 3:22 because we obey his commands and do what pleases [NIE] him.
3Jn 1: 6 They have told [NIE] the church about your love. You will do
Rev 1: 4 and who is to come, and from the seven spirits **before** his throne,
   2:14 who taught Balak to **entice** the Israelites **to sin** [+965+4998] and
   3: 2 for I have not found your deeds complete **in the sight** of my God.
   3: 5 but will acknowledge his name **before** my Father and his angels.
   3: 5 acknowledge his name before my Father and [RPG] his angels.
   3: 8 I have placed **before** you an open door that no one can shut.
   3: 9 I will make them come and fall down **at** your feet
   4: 5 and peals of thunder. **Before** the throne, seven lamps were blazing.
   4: 6 Also **before** the throne there was what looked like a sea of glass,

4:10   the twenty-four elders fall down **before** him who sits on the throne,
4:10   and ever. They lay their crowns **before** the throne and say:
5: 8   and the twenty-four elders fell down **before** the Lamb.
7: 9   and language, standing **before** the throne and in front of the Lamb.
7: 9   and language, standing before the throne and **in front** of the Lamb.
7:11   They fell down on their faces **before** the throne and worshiped
7:15   "they are **before** the throne of God and serve him day and night in
8: 2   And I saw the seven angels who stand **before** God, and to them
8: 3   the prayers of all the saints, on the golden altar **before** the throne.
8: 4   prayers of the saints, went up **before** God from the angel's hand.
9:13   voice coming from the horns of the golden altar that is **before** God.
11: 4   and the two lampstands that stand **before** the Lord of the earth.
11:16   who were seated on their thrones **before** God, fell on their faces
12: 4   The dragon stood **in front** of the woman who was about to give
12:10   who accuses them **before** our God day and night, has been hurled
13:12   He exercised all the authority of the first beast **on his behalf**,
13:13   even causing fire to come down from heaven to earth **in full view**
13:14   Because of the signs he was given power to do **on behalf** of the
14: 3   And they sang a new song **before** the throne and before the four
14: 3   the throne and **before** the four living creatures and the elders.
14:10   He will be tormented with burning sulfur **in the presence** of the
14:10   sulfur in the presence of the holy angels and **[RPG]** of the Lamb.
15: 4   All nations will come and worship **before** you, for your righteous
16:19   **[NIE]** God remembered Babylon the Great and gave her the cup
19:20   prophet who had performed the miraculous signs **on his behalf**.
20:12   And I saw the dead, great and small, standing **before** the throne,

1968 Ἐνώς, *Enōs* [1]

Enosh [1]

Lk   3:38   the son *of* **Enosh**, the son of Seth, the son of Adam, the son of

1969 ἐνωτίζομαι, *enōtizomai* [1] [√ *1877 + 4044*]

listen carefully [1]

Ac   2:14   let me explain this to you; **listen carefully** *to* what I say.

1970 Ἐνώχ, *Henōch* [3]

Enoch [3]

Lk   3:37   the son *of* **Enoch**, the son of Jared, the son of Mahalalel, the son of
Heb 11: 5   By faith **Enoch** was taken from this life, so that he did not
Jude 1:14   **Enoch**, the seventh from Adam, prophesied about these men:

1971 ἕξ, *hex* [13] [→ *1276, 1761, 1980, 2008*]

six [7], half [*+3604*] [2], 276 [*+1357+1573*] [1], 666
[*+1980+2008*] [1], a half [*+3604*] [1], forty-six [*+2779+5477*] [1]

Mt   17: 1   After **six** days Jesus took with him Peter, James and John the
Mk   9: 2   After **six** days Jesus took Peter, James and John with him and led
Lk   4:25   when the sky was shut for three and a **half** [*+3604*] years.
13:14   synagogue ruler said to the people, "There are **six** days for work.
Jn   2: 6   Nearby stood **six** stone water jars, the kind used by the Jews for
2:20   "It has taken **forty-six** [*+2779+5477*] years to build this temple,
12: 1   **Six** days before the Passover, Jesus arrived at Bethany,
Ac   11:12   These **six** brothers also went with me, and we entered the man's
18:11   So Paul stayed *for* a year and **a half** [*+3604*], teaching them the
27:37   Altogether there were **276** [*+1357+1573*] of us on board.
Jas   5:17   and it did not rain on the land *for* three and a **half** [*+3604*] years.
Rev   4: 8   Each of the four living creatures had **six** wings and was covered
13:18   for it is man's number. His number is **666** [*+1980+2008*].

1972 ἐξαγγέλλω, *exangellō* [2 / 1] [√ *1666 + 34*]

declare [1]

Mk   16: S   [UBS+ *commanded they **declared** briefly to those around Peter.*]
1Pe   2: 9   that *you* may **declare** the praises of him who called you out of

1973 ἐξαγοράζω, *exagorazō* [4] [√ *1666 + 60*]

make the most of opportunity [*+2789+3836*] [1], making the most
of [1], redeem [1], redeemed from [*RP1666*] [1]

Gal   3:13   Christ **redeemed** [*RP1666*] us **from** the curse of the law by
4: 5   to **redeem** those under law, that we might receive the full rights of
Eph   5:16   **making the most of** every opportunity, because the days are evil.
Col   4: 5   outsiders; **make the most of** *every* **opportunity** [*+2789+3836*].

1974 ἐξάγω, *exagō* [12] [√ *1666 + 72*]

led out [4], led out of [*RP1666*] [2], brought out [1], brought out of
[*RP1666*] [1], escort out [1], escorted from [1], lead out of
[*RP1666*] [1], leads out [1]

Mk   15:20   put his own clothes on him. Then *they* **led** him **out** to crucify him.
Lk   24:50   When *he had* **led** them **out** to the vicinity of Bethany, he lifted up
Jn   10: 3   to his voice. He calls his own sheep by name and **leads** them **out**.
Ac   5:19   of the Lord opened the doors of the jail and **brought** them **out**.
7:36   He **led** them **out** of Egypt and did wonders and miraculous signs in
7:40   As for this fellow Moses who **led** [*RP1666*] us **out of** Egypt—
12:17   and described how the Lord *had* **brought** [*RP1666*] him **out of**
13:17   with mighty power *he* **led** [*RP1666*] them **out of** that country,
16:37   or us quietly? No! *Let them* come themselves and **escort** us **out**."
16:39   They came to appease them and **escorted** them **from** the prison,
21:38   and **led** four thousand terrorists **out** into the desert some time ago?"
Heb   8: 9   I took them by the hand *to* **lead** [*RP1666*] them **out of** Egypt,

1975 ἐξαιρέω, *exaireō* [8] [√ *1666 + 145*]

rescued [3], gouge out [2], rescue [2], set free [1]

Mt   5:29   If your right eye causes you to sin, **gouge** it **out** and throw it away.
18: 9   And if your eye causes you to sin, **gouge** it **out** and throw it away.
Ac   7:10   and **rescued** him from all his troubles. He gave Joseph wisdom
7:34   I have heard their groaning and have come down *to* **set** them **free**.
12:11   that the Lord sent his angel and **rescued** me from Herod's clutches
23:27   about to kill him, but *I* came with my troops and **rescued** him,
26:17   *I will* **rescue** you from your own people and from the Gentiles.
Gal   1: 4   who gave himself *for* our sins to **rescue** us from the present evil

1976 ἐξαίρω, *exairō* [1] [√ *1666 + 149*]

expel [1]

1Co   5:13   will judge those outside. "**Expel** the wicked man from among you."

1977 ἐξαιτέω, *exaiteō* [1] [√ *1666 + 160*]

asked [1]

Lk   22:31   "Simon, Simon, Satan *has* **asked** to sift you as wheat.

1978 ἐξαίφνης, *exaiphnēs* [5] [√ *1666 + 167*]

suddenly [5]

Mk   13:36   If he comes **suddenly**, do not let him find you sleeping.
Lk   2:13   **Suddenly** a great company of the heavenly host appeared with the
9:39   A spirit seizes him and he **suddenly** screams; it throws him into
Ac   9: 3   on his journey, **suddenly** a light from heaven flashed around him.
22: 6   **suddenly** a bright light from heaven flashed around me.

1979 ἐξακολουθέω, *exakoloutheō* [3] [√ *1666 + 199*]
[1.3]

follow [3]

2Pe   1:16   *We did* not **follow** cleverly invented stories when we told you
2: 2   Many *will* **follow** their shameful ways and will bring the way of
2:15   and wandered off *to* **follow** the way of Balaam son of Beor,

1980 ἐξακόσιοι, *hexakosioi* [2] [√ *1971*]

1,600 [*+5943*] [1], 666 [*+1971+2008*] [1]

Rev   13:18   for it is man's number. His number is **666** [*+1971+2008*].
14:20   rising as high as the horses' bridles for a distance of **1,600** [*+5943*]

1981 ἐξαλείφω, *exaleiphō* [5] [√ *1666 + 230*]

blot out from [*RP1666*] [1], canceled [1], wipe away from [*RP1666*] [1], wipe from [*RP1666*] [1], wiped out [1]

Ac 3:19 then, and turn to God, so that your sins *may be* **wiped out**,
Col 2:14 *having* **canceled** the written code, with its regulations, that was
Rev 3: 5 *I will* never **blot** [*RP1666*] **out** his name **from** the book of life,
      7:17 And God *will* **wipe** [*RP1666*] **away** every tear **from** their eyes."
    21: 4 *He will* **wipe** [*RP1666*] every tear **from** their eyes. There will be

1982 ἐξάλλομαι, *exallomai* [1] [√ *1666 + 256*]

jumped [1]

Ac 3: 8 He **jumped** to his feet and began to walk. Then he went with them

1983 ἐξανάστασις, *exanastasis* [1]
[√ *1666 + 324 + 2705*]

resurrection [1]

Php 3:11 and so, somehow, to attain to the **resurrection** from the dead.

1984 ἐξανατέλλω, *exanatellō* [2] [√ *424; cf. 1666*]

sprang up [2]

Mt 13: 5 much soil. *It* **sprang up** quickly, because the soil was shallow.
Mk 4: 5 much soil. *It* **sprang up** quickly, because the soil was shallow.

1985 ἐξανίστημι, *exanistēmi* [3]
[√ *1666 + 324 + 2705*]

have children [+*5065*] [2], stood up [1]

Mk 12:19 must marry the widow and **have children** [+*5065*] for his brother.
Lk 20:28 must marry the widow and **have children** [+*5065*] for his brother.
Ac 15: 5 the believers who belonged to the party of the Pharisees **stood up**

1986 ἐξανοίγω, *exanoigō* Not used in UBS/NIV
[√ *487; cf. 1666*]

1987 ἐξαπατάω, *exapataō* [6] [√ *1666 + 573*]

deceive [3], deceived [3]

Ro 7:11 **deceived** me, and through the commandment put me to death.
   16:18 smooth talk and flattery *they* **deceive** the minds of naive people.
1Co 3:18 *Do* not **deceive** yourselves. If any one of you thinks he is wise by
2Co 11: 3 But I am afraid that just as Eve *was* **deceived** by the serpent's
2Th 2: 3 Don't *let* anyone **deceive** you in any way, for that day will not
1Ti 2:14 it was the woman *who was* **deceived** and became a sinner.

1988 ἐξάπινα, *exapina* [1] [√ *1666 + 167*]

suddenly [1]

Mk 9: 8 **Suddenly**, when they looked around, they no longer saw anyone

1989 ἐξαπορέω, *exaporeō* [2] [√ *1666 + 1.1 + 4513*]

despaired [1], in despair [1]

2Co 1: 8 far beyond our ability to endure, so that we **despaired** even of life.
    4: 8 on every side, but not crushed; perplexed, but not **in despair**;

1990 ἐξαποστέλλω, *exapostellō* [13 / 12]
[√ *1666 + 690*]

sent [7], sent away [3], send [1], sent off [1]

Mk 16: S [UBS+ *And after these things, Jesus himself sent out through them,*]
Lk 1:53 the hungry with good things but *has* **sent** the rich **away** empty.
  20:10 But the tenants beat him and **sent** him **away** empty-handed.
  20:11 they beat and treated shamefully and **sent away** empty-handed.
Ac 7:12 that there was grain in Egypt, *he* **sent** our fathers on their first visit.
  9:30 they took him down to Caesarea and **sent** him **off** to Tarsus.
  11:22 of the church at Jerusalem, and *they* **sent** Barnabas to Antioch.

  12:11 "Now I know without a doubt that the Lord **sent** his angel
  13:26 it is to us that this message of salvation *has been* **sent**.
  17:14 The brothers immediately **sent** Paul to the coast, but Silas
  22:21 Lord said to me, 'Go; I *will* **send** you far away to the Gentiles.' "
Gal 4: 4 fully come, God **sent** his Son, born of a woman, born under law,
    4: 6 you are sons, God **sent** the Spirit of his Son into our hearts,

1991 ἐξαρτάω, *exartaō* Not used in UBS/NIV

1992 ἐξαρτίζω, *exartizō* [2] [√ *1666 + 785*]

equipped [1], up [1]

Ac 21: 5 But when our time was **up**, we left and continued on our way.
2Ti 3:17 so that the man of God may be thoroughly **equipped** for every

1993 ἐξαστράπτω, *exastraptō* [1] [√ *1666 + 847*]

flash of lightning [1]

Lk 9:29 and his clothes became as bright as a **flash of lightning**.

1994 ἐξαυτῆς, *exautēs* [6] [√ *1666 + 899*]

at once [2], *untranslated* [1], immediately [1], right now [1], right then [1]

Mk 6:25 "I want you to give me **right now** the head of John the Baptist on a
Ac 10:33 So I sent for you **immediately**, and it was good of you to come.
  11:11 "**Right then** three men who had been sent to me from Cæsarea
  21:32 He **at once** took some officers and soldiers and ran down to the
  23:30 a plot to be carried out against the man, I sent him to you **at once**.
Php 2:23 to send him as soon as I see how things go with me. [**RPG**]

1995 ἐξεγείρω, *exegeirō* [2] [√ *1666 + 1586*]

raise [1], raised up [1]

Ro 9:17 "*I* **raised** you **up** for this very purpose, that I might display my
1Co 6:14 God raised the Lord from the dead, and *he will* **raise** us also.

1996 ἔξειμι¹, *exeimi*¹ [4] [√ *1666 + 1640*]

get [1], leave [1], leaving [*RP*] [1], left [1]

Ac 13:42 *As* Paul and Barnabas *were* **leaving** [*RP*] the synagogue,
  17:15 and then **left** with instructions for Silas and Timothy to join him as
  20: 7 spoke to the people and, because he intended to **leave** the next day,
  27:43 He ordered those who could swim *to* jump overboard first and **get**

1997 ἔξειμι², *exeimi*² Not used in UBS/NIV
[√ *1666 + 1639*]

1998 ἐξελέγχω, *exelenchō* Not used in UBS/NIV
[√ *1666 + 1794*]

1999 ἐξέλκω, *exelkō* [1] [√ *1666 + 1816*]

dragged away [1]

Jas 1:14 one is tempted *when*, by his own evil desire, *he is* **dragged away**

2000 ἐξέραμα, *exerama* [1] [√ *1666*]

vomit [1]

2Pe 2:22 "A dog returns to its **vomit**," and, "A sow that is washed goes back

2001 ἐξεραυνάω, *exeraunaō* [1] [√ *1666 + 2236*]

searched intently and with the greatest care [+*1699+2779*] [1]

1Pe 1:10 **searched** [+*1699+2779*] **intently and with the greatest care**,

2002 ἐξέρχομαι, *exerchomai* [218] [√ *1666 + 2262*]

went out [38], left [18], came out [14], go out [11], come out [9], came [8], leave [8], came out of [*RP1666*] [6], gone out [6], went [6], left [*RP1666*] [5], spread [5], come out of [*RP1666*] [4], come [4], go [4], gone [3], leaving [3], out of came [*RP1666*] [3], out of come [*RP1666*] [3], set out [3], comes out [2], coming [2], get out [2], go away [2], going out [2], got out of [*RP1666*] [2], landed [2], leave [*+2032*] [2], leave [*RP1666*] [2], went on [2], went out from [*RP1666*] [2], went out of [2], *untranslated* [1], at daybreak [*+1181+2465*] [1], bringing [1], came back [1], came from [*RP1666*] [1], came out of [1], comes from [*RP1666*] [1], came out [*RP1666*] [1], come out of [*+4047*] [1], comes [1], coming from [*RP1666*] [1], descended from [*+1666+3836+4019*] [1], driven out [1], escaped [*RP1666*] [1], flowed out of [*RP1666*] [1], followed out [*+199*] [1], gone out from [*RP1666*] [1], issued [1], known [1], leave [*RP1666+1666*] [1], led out of [*RP1666*] [1], on the journey [1], originate [1], out [1], rode out [1], set out from [1], slipping away from [*RP1666*] [1], started out [1], started [1], stepped [1], walked out [1], went out [*+2032*] [1], went through [1]

Mt 2: 6 for **out of** you *will* **come** [*RP1666*] a ruler who will be the
    5:26 the truth, *you will* not **get out** until you have paid the last penny.
    8:28 two demon-possessed men **coming** [*RP1666*] **from** the tombs met
    8:32 So they **came out** and went into the pigs, and the whole herd
    8:34 Then the whole town **went out** to meet Jesus. And when they saw
    9:26 News of this **spread** through all that region.
    9:31 But they **went out** and spread the news about him all over that
    9:32 *While* they *were* **going out**, a man who was demon-possessed
   10:11 some worthy person there and stay at his house until *you* **leave**.
   10:14 shake the dust off your feet *when you* **leave** [*+2032*] that home
   11: 7 "What *did you* **go out** into the desert to see? A reed swayed by the
   11: 8 If not, what *did you* **go out** to see? A man dressed in fine clothes?
   11: 9 Then what *did you* **go out** to see? A prophet? Yes, I tell you,
   12:14 But the Pharisees **went out** and plotted how they might kill Jesus.
   12:43 "When an evil spirit **comes out** of a man, it goes through arid
   12:44 Then it says, 'I will return to the house *I* **left**.' When it arrives,
   13: 1 That same day Jesus **went out of** the house and sat by the lake.
   13: 3 things in parables, saying: "A farmer **went out** to sow his seed.
   13:49 The angels *will* **come** and separate the wicked from the righteous
   14:14 *When* Jesus **landed** and saw a large crowd, he had compassion on
   15:18 But the things that come out of the mouth **come** [*RP1666*] **from**
   15:19 For **out of** the heart **come** [*RP1666*] evil thoughts, murder,
   15:21 **Leaving** that place, Jesus withdrew to the region of Tyre
   15:22 A Canaanite woman from that vicinity **came** to him, crying out,
   17:18 Jesus rebuked the demon, and it **came out** of the boy, and he was
   18:28 "But *when* that servant **went out**, he found one of his fellow
   20: 1 "For the kingdom of heaven is like a landowner who **went out** early
   20: 3 "About the third hour he **went out** and saw others standing in the
   20: 5 "*He* **went out** again about the sixth hour and the ninth hour
   20: 6 About the eleventh hour he **went out** and found still others
   21:17 And *he* left them and **went out of** the city to Bethany, where he
   22:10 So the servants **went out** into the streets and gathered all the
   24: 1 Jesus **left** the temple and was walking away when his disciples
   24:26 if anyone tells you, 'There he is, out in the desert,' *do* not **go out**;
   24:27 For as lightning that **comes** from the east is visible even in the
   25: 1 virgins who took their lamps and **went out** to meet the bridegroom.
   25: 6 the cry rang out: 'Here's the bridegroom! **Come out** to meet him!'
   26:30 they had sung a hymn, *they* **went out** to the Mount of Olives.
   26:55 that *you have* **come out** with swords and clubs to capture me?
   26:71 Then *he* **went out** to the gateway, where another girl saw him
   26:75 disown me three times." And *he* **went** outside and wept bitterly.
   27:32 *As they were* **going out**, they met a man from Cyrene,
   27:53 *They* **came** [*RP1666*] **out of** the tombs, and after Jesus'

Mk 1:25 "Be quiet!" said Jesus sternly. "**Come** [*RP1666*] **out of** him!"
    1:26 the man violently and **came** [*RP1666*] **out of** him with a shriek.
    1:28 News about him **spread** quickly over the whole region of Galilee.
    1:29 As soon as *they* **left** [*RP1666*] the synagogue, they went with
    1:35 Jesus got up, **left** the house and went off to a solitary place,
    1:38 so I can preach there also. That is why *I have* **come**."
    1:45 Instead he **went out** and began to talk freely, spreading the news.
    2:12 He got up, took his mat and **walked out** in full view of them all.
    2:13 Once again Jesus **went out** beside the lake. A large crowd came to
    3: 6 Then the Pharisees **went out** and began to plot with the Herodians
    3:21 *they* **went** to take charge of him, for they said, "He is out of his
    4: 3 "Listen! A farmer **went out** to sow his seed.

5: 2 *When* Jesus got [*RP1666*] **out of** the boat, a man with an evil
5: 8 had said to him, "**Come** [*RP1666*] **out of** this man, you evil spirit!"
5:13 and the evil spirits **came out** and went into the pigs.
5:30 At once Jesus realized that power *had* **gone** [*RP1666*] **out from**
6: 1 Jesus **left** there and went to his hometown, accompanied by his
6:10 Whenever you enter a house, stay there until *you* **leave** that town.
6:12 They **went out** and preached that people should repent.
6:24 She **went out** and said to her mother, "What shall I ask for?"
6:34 *When* Jesus **landed** and saw a large crowd, he had compassion on
6:54 As soon as they got [*RP1666*] **out of** the boat, people recognized
7:29 you may go; the demon *has* **left** [*RP1666*] your daughter."
7:30 and found her child lying on the bed, and the demon **gone**.
7:31 Then Jesus **left** [*RP1666*] the vicinity of Tyre and went through
8:11 The Pharisees **came** and began to question Jesus. To test him,
8:27 and his disciples **went on** to the villages *around* Caesarea Philippi.
9:25 **come** [*RP1666*] **out of** him and never enter him again."
9:26 The spirit shrieked, convulsed him violently and **came out**.
9:29 He replied, "This kind can **come out** only by prayer."
9:30 They **left** that place and passed through Galilee. Jesus did not want
11:11 since it was already late, *he* **went out** to Bethany with the Twelve.
11:12 The next day *as* they *were* **leaving** Bethany, Jesus was hungry.
14:16 The disciples **left**, went into the city and found things just as Jesus
14:26 they had sung a hymn, *they* **went out** to the Mount of Olives.
14:48 "that *you have* **come out** with swords and clubs to capture me?
14:68 talking about," he said, and **went** [*+2032*] **out** into the entryway.
16: 8 and bewildered, the women **went out** and fled from the tomb.
16:20 Then the disciples **went out** and preached everywhere,

Lk 1:22 *When he* **came out**, he could not speak to them. They realized he
    2: 1 In those days Caesar Augustus **issued** a decree that a census should
    4:14 and news about him **spread** through the whole countryside.
    4:35 "Be quiet!" Jesus said sternly. "**Come out** of him!" Then the demon
    4:35 the man down before them all and **came out** without injuring him.
    4:36 and power he gives orders to evil spirits and *they* **come out**!"
    4:41 Moreover, demons **came out** of many people, shouting, "You are
    4:42 **At daybreak** [*+1181+2465*] Jesus went out to a solitary place.
    5: 8 he fell at Jesus' knees and said, "**Go away** from me, Lord;
    5:27 Jesus **went out** and saw a tax collector by the name of Levi sitting
    6:12 One of those days Jesus **went out** to a mountainside to pray,
    6:19 because power *was* **coming** from him and healing them all.
    7:17 This news about Jesus **spread** throughout Judea and the
    7:24 "What *did you* **go out** into the desert to see? A reed swayed by the
    7:25 If not, what *did you* **go out** to see? A man dressed in fine clothes?
    7:26 But what *did you* **go out** to see? A prophet? Yes, I tell you,
    8: 2 (called Magdalene) from whom seven demons *had* **come out**;
    8: 5 "A farmer **went out** to sow his seed. As he was scattering the seed,
    8:27 *When* Jesus **stepped** ashore, he was met by a demon-possessed
    8:29 For Jesus had commanded the evil spirit *to* **come out** of the man.
    8:33 *When* the demons **came out** of the man, they went into the pigs,
    8:35 and the *people* **went out** to see what had happened. When they
    8:35 they found the man from whom the demons *had* **gone out**,
    8:38 The man from whom the demons *had* **gone out** begged to go with
    8:46 "Someone touched me; I know that power *has* **gone out** from me."
    9: 4 Whatever house you enter, stay there until *you* **leave** that town.
    9: 5 shake the dust off your feet *when you* **leave** their town, as a
    9: 6 So they **set out** and went from village to village,
   10:10 you enter a town and are not welcomed, **go** into its streets and say,
   11:14 *When* the demon **left**, the man who had been mute spoke,
   11:24 "When an evil spirit **comes out** of a man, it goes through arid
   11:24 and does not find it. Then it says, 'I will return to the house *I* **left**.'
   11:53 *When* Jesus **left** there, the Pharisees and the teachers of the law
   12:59 I tell you, *you will* not **get out** until you have paid the last penny."
   13:31 and said to him, "**Leave** this place and go somewhere else.
   14:18 The first said, 'I have just bought a field, and *I* must **go** and see it.
   14:21 '**Go out** quickly into the streets and alleys of the town and bring in
   14:23 '**Go out** to the roads and country lanes and make them come in,
   15:28 and refused to go in. So his father **went out** and pleaded with him.
   17:29 But the day Lot **left** Sodom, fire and sulfur rained down from
   21:37 and each evening he **went out** to spend the night on the hill called
   22:39 Jesus **went out** as usual to the Mount of Olives, and his disciples
   22:52 I leading a rebellion, that *you have* **come** with swords and clubs?
   22:62 And he **went** outside and wept bitterly.

Jn 1:43 The next day Jesus decided *to* **leave** for Galilee. Finding Philip,
    4:30 *They* **came** [*RP1666*] **out of** the town and made their way toward
    4:43 After the two days *he* **left** for Galilee.
    8: 9 At this, those who heard *began to* **go away** one at a time,
    8:42 would love me, for I **came** [*RP1666*] **from** God and now am here.

8: 59 hid himself, **slipping** [*RP1666*] **away from** the temple grounds.
10: 9 me will be saved. He will come in and **go out**, and find pasture.
10: 39 they tried to seize him, but *he* **escaped** [*RP1666*] their grasp.
11: 31 comforting her, noticed how quickly she got up and **went out**,
11: 44 The dead man **came out**, his hands and feet wrapped with strips of
12: 13 They took palm branches and **went out** to meet him, shouting,
13: 3 and that *he had* **come** from God and was returning to God;
13: 30 As soon as Judas had taken the bread, *he* **went out**. And it was
13: 31 When *he was* **gone**, Jesus said, "Now is the Son of Man glorified
16: 27 you have loved me and have believed that I **came** from God.
16: 28 *I* **came** from the Father and entered the world; now I am leaving
16: 30 ask you questions. This makes us believe that *you* **came** from God."
17: 8 They knew with certainty that *I* **came** from you, and they believed
18: 1 Jesus **left** with his disciples and crossed the Kidron Valley.
18: 4 to happen to him, **went out** and askcd thcm, "Who is it you want?"
18: 16 **came back**, spoke to the girl on duty there and brought Peter in.
18: 29 So Pilate **came out** to them and asked, "What charges are you
18: 38 With this *he* **went out** again to the Jews and said, "I find no basis
19: 4 Once more Pilate **came out** and said to the Jews, "Look, I am
19: 5 When Jesus **came out** wearing the crown of thorns and the purple
19: 17 *he* **went out** to the place of the Skull (which in Aramaic is called
19: 34 side with a spear, **bringing** a sudden flow of blood and water.
20: 3 So Peter and the other disciple **started** for the tomb.
21: 3 So *they* **went out** and got into the boat, but that night they caught
21: 23 the rumor **spread** among the brothers that this disciple would not
Ac 1: 21 with us the whole time the Lord Jesus went in and **out** among us,
7: 3 'Leave [*RP1666+1666*] your country and your people,' God said,
7: 4 "So he **left** [*RP1666*] the land of the Chaldeans and settled in
7: 7 'and afterward *they will* **come** [*+4047*] **out** of that country
8: 7 With shrieks, evil spirits **came out of** many, and many paralytics
10: 23 The next day Peter **started out** with them, and some of the
11: 25 Then Barnabas **went** to Tarsus to look for Saul,
12: 9 Peter **followed** him **out** [*+199*] of the prison, but he had no idea
12: 10 to the city. It opened for them by itself, and *they* **went through** it.
12: 17 about this," he said, and then [**RPG**] he left for another place.
14: 20 back into the city. The next day *he* and Barnabas **left** for Derbe.
15: 24 We have heard that some **went** [*RP1666*] **out from** us without our
15: 40 but Paul chose Silas and **left**, commended by the brothers to the
16: 3 Paul wanted to take him along **on the journey**, so he circumcised
16: 10 had seen the vision, we got ready at once *to* **leave** for Macedonia.
16: 13 On the Sabbath *we* **went** outside the city gate to the river,
16: 18 "In the name of Jesus Christ I command you *to* **come out** of her!"
16: 18 you to come out of her!" At that moment the spirit **left** her.
16: 19 the slave girl realized that their hope of making money *was* **gone**,
16: 36 that you and Silas be released. Now *you can* **leave**. Go in peace."
16: 40 *After* Paul and Silas **came out** of the prison, they went to Lydia's
16: 40 they met with the brothers and encouraged them. Then *they* **left**.
17: 33 At that, Paul **left** [*RP1666*] the Council.
18: 23 Paul **set out from** there and traveled from place to place
20: 1 after encouraging them, said good-by and **set out** for Macedonia.
20: 11 and broke bread and ate. After talking until daylight, *he* **left**.
21: 5 But when our time was up, we **left** and continued on our way.
21: 8 **Leaving** the next day, we reached Caesarea and stayed at the house
22: 18 'Leave [*RP1666*] Jerusalem immediately, because they will not
28: 3 as he put it on the fire, a viper, **driven out** by the heat,
Ro 10: 18 "Their voice *has* **gone out** into all the earth, their words to the ends
1Co 5: 10 In that case you would have to **leave** [*RP1666*] this world.
14: 36 *Did* the word of God **originate** with you? Or are you the only
2Co 2: 13 Titus there. So *I* said good-by to them and **went on** to Macedonia.
6: 17 "Therefore **come** [*RP1666*] **out** from them and be separate,
8: 17 but *hė is* **coming** to you with much enthusiasm and on his own
Php 4: 15 when *I* **set out** from Macedonia, not one church shared with me in
1Th 1: 8 and Achaia—your faith in God *has become* **known** everywhere.
Heb 3: 16 Were they not all those Moses **led** [*RP1666*] **out of** Egypt?
7: 5 their brothers *are* **descended** [*+1666+3836+4019*] **from** Abraham.
11: 8 when called *to* **go** to a place he would later receive as his
11: 8 obeyed and **went**, even though he did not know where he was
13: 13 *Let us*, then, **go** to him outside the camp, bearing the disgrace he
Jas 3: 10 **Out** of the same mouth **come** [*RP1666*] praise and cursing.
1Jn 2: 19 *They* **went** [*RP1666*] **out from** us, but they did not really belong
4: 1 because many false prophets *have* **gone out** into the world.
2Jn 1: 7 Jesus Christ as coming in the flesh, *have* **gone out** into the world.
3Jn 1: 7 It was for the sake of the Name that *they* **went out**, receiving no
Rev 3: 12 Never again *will he* **leave** [*+2032*] it. I will write on him the name
6: 2 given a crown, and *he* **rode out** as a conqueror bent on conquest.
6: 4 Then another horse **came out**, a fiery red one. Its rider was given

9: 3 And **out of** the smoke locusts **came** [*RP1666*] down upon the earth
14: 15 Then another angel **came** [*RP1666*] **out of** the temple and called in
14: 17 Another angel **came** [*RP1666*] **out of** the temple in heaven,
14: 18 **came** from the altar and called in a loud voice to him who had the
14: 20 outside the city, and blood **flowed** [*RP1666*] **out of** the press,
15: 6 **Out of** the temple came [*RP1666*] the seven angels with the seven
16: 17 and **out of** the temple came [*RP1666*] a loud voice from the
18: 4 "**Come** [*RP1666*] **out of** her, my people, so that you will not share
19: 5 Then a voice **came** from the throne, saying: "Praise our God,
19: 21 that **came** [*RP1666*] **out of** the mouth of the rider on the horse,
20: 8 and *will* **go out** to deceive the nations in the four corners of the

2003 ἔξεστι, *exesti* [31] [√ *1666 + 1639*]

lawful [10], permissible [4], unlawful [*+4024*] [4], right [3], can [1], have right [1], have the right [1], lawful for [*+4024*] [1], lawful for [1], legal [1], may [1], permitted [1], the law forbids [*+4024*] [1], the law [1]

Mt 12: 2 disciples are doing what *is* **unlawful** [*+4024*] on the Sabbath."
12: 4 ate the consecrated bread—which was not **lawful** for them to do,
12: 10 accuse Jesus, they asked him, "*Is it* **lawful** to heal on the Sabbath?"
12: 12 than a sheep! Therefore *it is* **lawful** to do good on the Sabbath."
14: 4 John had been saying to him: "*It is* not **lawful** for you to have her."
19: 3 "*Is it* **lawful** for a man to divorce his wife for any and every
20: 15 Don't I **have the right** to do what I want with my own money?
22: 17 what is your opinion? *Is it* **right** to pay taxes to Caesar or not?"
27: 6 and said, "*It is* against **the law** to put this into the treasury,
Mk 2: 24 why are they doing what *is* **unlawful** [*+4024*] on the Sabbath?"
2: 26 consecrated bread, which *is* **lawful** [*+4024*] only **for** priests to eat.
3: 4 Then Jesus asked them, "Which *is* **lawful** on the Sabbath: to do
6: 18 to Herod, "*It is* not **lawful** for you to have your brother's wife."
10: 2 tested him by asking, "*Is it* **lawful** for a man to divorce his wife?"
12: 14 accordance with the truth. *Is it* **right** to pay taxes to Caesar or not?
Lk 6: 2 "Why are you doing what *is* **unlawful** [*+4024*] on the Sabbath?"
6: 4 the consecrated bread, he ate what *is* **lawful** only **for** priests to eat.
6: 9 Jesus said to them, "I ask you, which *is* **lawful** on the Sabbath:
14: 3 and experts in the law, "*Is it* **lawful** to heal on the Sabbath or not?"
20: 22 *Is it* **right** for us to pay taxes to Caesar or not?"
Jn 5: 10 "It is the Sabbath; **the law** [*+4024*] **forbids** you to carry your mat."
18: 31 "But we **have** no **right** to execute anyone," the Jews objected.
Ac 2: 29 I **can** tell you confidently that the patriarch David died and was
16: 21 by advocating customs **unlawful** [*+4024*] for us Romans to accept
21: 37 he asked the commander, "**May** I say something to you?"
22: 25 "*Is it* **legal** for you to flog a Roman citizen who hasn't even been
1Co 6: 12 "Everything *is* **permissible** for me"—but not everything is
6: 12 "Everything *is* **permissible** for me"—but I will not be mastered by
10: 23 "Everything is **permissible**"—but not everything is beneficial.
10: 23 "Everything is **permissible**"—but not everything is constructive.
2Co 12: 4 heard inexpressible things, things that man *is* not **permitted** to tell.

2004 ἐξετάζω, *exetazō* [3] [√ *458; cf. 1666*]

ask [1], make a search [1], search for [1]

Mt 2: 8 and said, "Go and **make a** careful **search** for the child.
10: 11 **search for** some worthy person and stay at his house until
Jn 21: 12 None of the disciples dared **ask** him, "Who are you?"

2005 ἐξέφνης, *exephnēs* Not used in UBS/NIV
[√ *1666 + 167*]

2006 ἐξέχω, *exechō* Not used in UBS/NIV
[√ *1666 + 2400*]

2007 ἐξηγέομαι, *exēgeomai* [6] [√ *1666 + 72*]

told [2], described [1], made known [1], reported [1], telling about [1]

Lk 24: 35 Then the two **told** what had happened on the way, and how Jesus
Jn 1: 18 and Only, who is at the Father's side, *has* **made** him **known**.
Ac 10: 8 He **told** them everything that had happened and sent them to
15: 12 and Paul **telling about** the miraculous signs and wonders God had
15: 14 Simon *has* **described** to us how God at first showed his concern by

21:19 and **reported** in detail what God had done among the Gentiles

2008 ἐξήκοντα, *hexēkonta* [9] [√ *1971*]

sixty [4], 1 [+*1357*+*5943*] [2], 666 [+*1971*+*1980*] [1], seven miles [+*5084*] [1], sixty [+*2291*] [1]

Mt 13: 8 produced a crop—a hundred, **sixty** or thirty *times* what was sown.
13:23 a crop, yielding a hundred, **sixty** or thirty *times* what was sown."
Mk   4: 8 produced a crop, multiplying thirty, **sixty**, or even a hundred *times*."
4:20 a crop—thirty, **sixty** or even a hundred *times* what was sown."
Lk 24:13 called Emmaus, about **seven miles** [+*5084*] from Jerusalem.
1Ti 5: 9 may be put on the list of widows unless she is over **sixty** [+*2291*],
Rev 11: 3 and they will prophesy *for* **1** [+*1357*+*5943*],260 days, clothed in
12: 6 where she might be taken care of *for* **1** [+*1357*+*5943*],260 days.
13:18 for it is man's number. His number is **666** [+*1971*+*1980*].

2009 ἐξῆς, *hexēs* [5] [√ *2400*]

next [4], soon afterward [+*1877*+*3836*] [1]

Lk   7:11 **Soon afterward** [+*1877*+*3836*], Jesus went to a town called Nain,
9:37 The **next** day, when they came down from the mountain, a large
Ac 21: 1 The **next** *day* we went to Rhodes and from there to Patara.
25:17 but convened the court the **next** *day* and ordered the man to be
27:18 We took such a violent battering from the storm that the **next** *day*

2010 ἐξηχέω, *exēcheō* [1] [√ *1666* + *2491*]

rang out [1]

1Th 1: 8 The Lord's message **rang out** from you not only in Macedonia

2011 ἕξις, *hexis* [1] [√ *2400*]

constant use [1]

Heb 5:14 who by **constant use** have trained themselves to distinguish good

2012 ἐξιστάνω, *existanō* Not used in UBS/NIV
[√ *1666* + *2705*]

2013 ἐξιστάω, *existaō* Not used in UBS/NIV
[√ *1666* + *2705*]

2014 ἐξίστημι, *existēmi* [17] [√ *1666* + *2705*]

amazed [7], astonished [6], out of mind [2], astonished [+*1749*] [1], utterly amazed [+*2513*] [1]

Mt 12:23 All the people *were* **astonished** and said, "Could this be the Son of
Mk   2:12 This **amazed** everyone and they praised God, saying, "We have
3:21 went to take charge of him, for they said, "*He is* **out of** his **mind**."
5:42 years old). At this *they were* completely **astonished** [+*1749*].
6:51 and the wind died down. *They were* completely **amazed**,
Lk   2:47 Everyone who heard him *was* **amazed** at his understanding
8:56 Her parents *were* **astonished**,
24:22 In addition, some of our women **amazed** us. They went to the
Ac   2: 7 **Utterly amazed** [+*2513*], they asked: "Are not all these men who
2:12 **Amazed** and perplexed, they asked one another, "What does this
8: 9 practiced sorcery in the city and **amazed** all the people of Samaria.
8:11 because he *had* **amazed** them for a long time with his magic.
8:13 **astonished** by the great signs and miracles he saw.
9:21 All those who heard him *were* **astonished** and asked, "Isn't he the
10:45 *were* **astonished** that the gift of the Holy Spirit had been poured
12:16 when they opened the door and saw him, *they were* **astonished**.
2Co 5:13 If *we are* **out of** *our* **mind**, it is for the sake of God; if we are in

2015 ἐξισχύω, *exischyō* [1] [√ *1666* + *2709*]

power [1]

Eph 3:18 *may have* **power**, together with all the saints, to grasp how wide

2016 ἔξοδος, *exodos* [3] [√ *1666* + *3847*]

departure [2], exodus [1]

Lk   9:31 They spoke about his **departure**, which he was about to bring to
Heb 11:22 spoke about the **exodus** of the Israelites from Egypt and gave
2Pe 1:15 And I will make every effort to see that after my **departure** you

2017 ἐξολεθρεύω, *exolethreuō* [1] [√ *1666* + *3897*]

completely cut off from [RP*1666*] [1]

Ac   3:23 *will be* **completely cut** [RP*1666*] **off from** *among* his people.'

2018 ἐξομολογέω, *exomologeō* [10] [√ *1666* + *3933*]

confess [3], praise [3], confessing [2], consented [1], openly confessed [+*334*] [1]

Mt   3: 6 **Confessing** their sins, they were baptized by him in the Jordan
11:25 time Jesus said, "*I* **praise** you, Father, Lord of heaven and earth,
Mk   1: 5 **Confessing** their sins, they were baptized by him in the Jordan
Lk 10:21 Holy Spirit, said, "*I* **praise** you, Father, Lord of heaven and earth,
22: 6 *He* **consented**, and watched for an opportunity to hand Jesus over
Ac 19:18 believed now came and **openly confessed** [+*334*] their evil deeds.
Ro 14:11 knee will bow before me; every tongue *will* **confess** to God.' "
15: 9 "Therefore *I will* **praise** you among the Gentiles; I will sing hymns
Php 2:11 and every tongue **confess** that Jesus Christ is Lord, to the glory of
Jas   5:16 Therefore **confess** your sins to each other and pray for each other

2019 ἐξορκίζω, *exorkizō* [1] [√ *1666* + *3992*]

charge under oath [1]

Mt 26:63 priest said to him, "*I* **charge** you **under oath** by the living God:

2020 ἐξορκιστής, *exorkistēs* [1] [√ *1666* + *3992*]

driving out evil spirits [1]

Ac 19:13 Some Jews who went around **driving out evil spirits** tried to

2021 ἐξορύσσω, *exoryssō* [2] [√ *1666* + *4002*]

digging through [1], torn out [1]

Mk   2: 4 *after* **digging through** it, lowered the mat the paralyzed man was
Gal   4:15 you would have **torn out** your eyes and given them to me.

2022 ἐξουδενέω, *exoudeneō* [1]
[√ *1666* + *4024* + *1254* + *1651*]

rejected [1]

Mk   9:12 it written that the Son of Man must suffer much and *be* **rejected**?

2023 ἐξουδενόω, *exoudenoō* Not used in UBS/NIV
[√ *1666* + *4024* + *1254* + *1651*]

2024 ἐξουθενέω, *exoutheneō* [11]
[√ *1666* + *4024* + *1254* + *1651*]

look down on [2], treat with contempt [2], amounts to nothing [1], despised [1], looked down on [1], of little account [1], refuse to accept [1], rejected [1], ridiculed [1]

Lk 18: 9 of their own righteousness and **looked down on** everybody else,
23:11 Then Herod and his soldiers **ridiculed** and mocked him.
Ac   4:11 He is " 'the stone you builders **rejected**, which has become the
Ro 14: 3 The man who eats everything *must* not **look down on** him who
14:10 judge your brother? Or why *do* you **look down on** your brother?
1Co 1:28 He chose the lowly things of this world and the **despised** *things*—
6: 4 appoint as judges even men of **little account** in the church!
16:11 No one, then, *should* **refuse to accept** him. Send him on his way
2Co 10:10 person he is unimpressive and his speaking **amounts to nothing**."
Gal   4:14 was a trial to you, *you did* not **treat** me **with contempt** or scorn.
1Th 5:20 *do* not **treat** prophecies **with contempt**.

2025 ἐξουθενόω, exouthenoō Not used in UBS/NIV
[√ *1666 + 4024 + 1254 + 1651*]

2026 ἐξουσία, exousia [102] [→ *2027, 2028, 2980; cf. 1666 + 1639*]

ἐν ποίᾳ ἐξουσίᾳ (by what authority) [8] Mt 21:23,24,27; Mk 11:28,29,33; Lk 20:2,8

ἔχω ἐξουσία (to have authority) [31] Mt 7:29; 8:9; 9:6; Mk 1:22; 2:10; 3:15; Lk 5:24; 12:5; 19:17; Jn 10:18,18; 19:10,10,11; Ac 9:14; Ro 9:21; 1Co 7:37; 9:4,5,6; 11:10; 2Th 3:9; Heb 13:10; Rev 9:3; 11:6,6; 14:18; 16:9; 17:13; 18:1; 20:6

authority [54], power [11], right [9], authorities [8], *untranslated* [2], authority over [2], charge [2], control [2], ability [1], disposal [1], dominion [1], exercise of freedom [1], in charge [1], jurisdiction [1], kingdom [1], must [+2400] [1], on authority [+3284] [1], reigns [1], rights [1], sign of authority [1]

Mt 7:29 because he taught as one who had **authority**, and not as their
    8: 9 For I myself am a man under **authority**, with soldiers under me.
    9: 6 so that you may know that the Son of Man has **authority** on earth
    9: 8 and they praised God, who had given such **authority** to men.
   10: 1 and gave them **authority** to drive out evil spirits and to heal every
   21:23 "By what **authority** are you doing these things?" they asked.
   21:23 these things?" they asked. "And who gave you this **authority**?"
   21:24 I will tell you by what **authority** I am doing these things.
   21:27 "Neither will I tell you by what **authority** I am doing these things.
   28:18 "All **authority** in heaven and on earth has been given to me.
Mk 1:22 because he taught them as one who had **authority**, not as the
    1:27 each other, "What is this? A new teaching—and with **authority**!
    2:10 But that you may know that the Son of Man has **authority** on earth
    3:15 and to have **authority** to drive out demons.
    6: 7 them out two by two and gave them **authority over** evil spirits.
   11:28 "By what **authority** are you doing these things?" they asked.
   11:28 things?" they asked. "And who gave you **authority** to do this?"
   11:29 and I will tell you by what **authority** I am doing these things.
   11:33 "Neither will I tell you by what **authority** I am doing these things."
   11:34 He leaves his house and puts his servants **in charge**, each with his
Lk 4: 6 he said to him, "I will give you all their **authority** and splendor,
    4:32 were amazed at his teaching, because his message had **authority**.
    4:36 With **authority** and power he gives orders to evil spirits and they
    5:24 But that you may know that the Son of Man has **authority** on earth
    7: 8 For I myself am a man under **authority**, with soldiers under me.
    9: 1 he gave them power and **authority** to drive out all demons
   10:19 I have given you **authority** to trample on snakes and scorpions
   12: 5 after the killing of the body, has **power** to throw you into hell.
   12:11 "When you are brought before synagogues, rulers and **authorities**,
   19:17 been trustworthy in a very small matter, take **charge** of ten cities.'
   20: 2 "Tell us by what **authority** you are doing these things," they said.
   20: 2 are doing these things," they said. "Who gave you this **authority**?"
   20: 8 "Neither will I tell you by what **authority** I am doing these things."
   20:20 so that they might hand him over *to* the power and **authority** of the
   22:53 lay a hand on me. But this is your hour—when darkness **reigns**."
   23: 7 When he learned that Jesus was under Herod's **jurisdiction**,
Jn 1:12 in his name, he gave the **right** to become children of God—
    5:27 And he has given him **authority** to judge because he is the Son of
   10:18 I have **authority** to lay it down and authority to take it up again.
   10:18 I have authority to lay it down and **authority** to take it up again.
   17: 2 For you granted him **authority over** all people that he might give
   19:10 "Don't you realize I have **power** either to free you or to crucify
   19:10 realize I have power either to free you or to [RPG] to crucify you?"
   19:11 "You would have no **power** over me if it were not given to you
Ac 1: 7 to know the times or dates the Father has set by his own **authority**.
    5: 4 And after it was sold, wasn't the money at your **disposal**?
    8:19 "Give me also this **ability** so that everyone on whom I lay my hands
    9:14 And he has come here with **authority** from the chief priests to
   26:10 **On** the **authority** [+3284] of the chief priests I put many of the
   26:12 one of these journeys I was going to Damascus with the **authority**
   26:18 from darkness to light, and from the **power** of Satan to God,
Ro 9:21 Does not the potter have the **right** to make out of the same lump of
   13: 1 Everyone must submit himself *to* the governing **authorities**,
   13: 1 for there is no **authority** except that which God has established.
   13: 2 he who rebels against the **authority** is rebelling against what God
   13: 3 Do you want to be free from fear of the one in **authority**?
1Co 7:37 who is under no compulsion but has **control** over his own will,

    8: 9 that the **exercise of** your **freedom** does not become a stumbling
    9: 4 Don't we have the **right** to food and drink?
    9: 5 Don't we have the **right** to take a believing wife along with us,
    9: 6 Or is it only I and Barnabas *who* **must** [+2400] work for a living?
    9:12 If others have this **right** *of support* from you, shouldn't we have it
    9:12 But we did not use this **right**. On the contrary, we put up with
    9:18 it free of charge, and so not make use of my **rights** in preaching it.
   11:10 the woman ought to have a **sign of authority** on her head.
   15:24 Father after he has destroyed all dominion, **authority** and power.
2Co 10: 8 For even if I boast somewhat freely about the **authority** the Lord
   13:10 when I come I may not have to be harsh in my use of **authority**—
Eph 1:21 far above all rule and **authority**, power and dominion, and every
    2: 2 the ways of this world and of the ruler *of* the **kingdom** of the air,
    3:10 of God should be made known *to* the rulers and **authorities**
    6:12 and blood, but against the rulers, against the **authorities**,
Col 1:13 For he has rescued us from the **dominion** of darkness and brought
    1:16 and invisible, whether thrones or powers or rulers or **authorities**;
    2:10 fullness in Christ, who is the head over every power and **authority**.
    2:15 And having disarmed the powers and **authorities**, he made a
2Th 3: 9 We did this, not because we do not have the **right** to such help,
Tit 3: 1 Remind the people to be subject *to* rulers and **authorities**,
Heb 13:10 which those who minister at the tabernacle have no **right** to eat.
1Pe 3:22 *with* angels, **authorities** and powers in submission to him.
Jude 1:25 majesty, power and **authority**, through Jesus Christ our Lord,
Rev 2:26 does my will to the end, I will give **authority** over the nations—
    6: 8 They were given **power** over a fourth of the earth to kill by sword,
    9: 3 the earth and were given **power** like that of scorpions of the earth.
    9: 3 and were given power like that of scorpions of the earth. [RPG]
    9:10 and in their tails they had **power** to torment people for five months.
    9:19 The **power** of the horses was in their mouths and in their tails;
   11: 6 These men have **power** to shut up the sky so that it will not rain
   11: 6 and they have **power** to turn the waters into blood and to strike the
   12:10 and the kingdom of our God, and the **authority** of his Christ.
   13: 2 gave the beast his power and his throne and great **authority**.
   13: 4 worshiped the dragon because he had given **authority** to the beast,
   13: 5 blasphemies and to exercise his **authority** for forty-two months.
   13: 7 And he was given **authority** over every tribe, people, language
   13:12 He exercised all the **authority** of the first beast on his behalf,
   14:18 Still another angel, who had **charge** of the fire, came from the altar
   16: 9 who had **control** over these plagues, but they refused to repent
   17:12 but who for one hour will receive **authority** as kings along with
   17:13 one purpose and will give their power and **authority** to the beast.
   18: 1 He had great **authority**, and the earth was illuminated by his
   20: 6 The second death has no **power** over them, but they will be priests
   22:14 that they may have the **right** to the tree of life and may go through

2027 ἐξουσιάζω, exousiazō [4] [√ *2026*]

belong to [2], exercise authority over [1], mastered [1]

Lk 22:25 and those *who* **exercise authority over** them call themselves
1Co 6:12 is permissible for me"—but I *will* not be **mastered** by anything.
    7: 4 The wife's body *does* not **belong to** her alone but also to her
    7: 4 the husband's body *does* not **belong to** him alone but also to his

2028 ἐξουσιαστικός, exousiastikos Not used in UBS/NIV [√ *2026*]

2029 ἐξοχή, exochē [1] [√ *1666 + 2400*]

leading [1]

Ac 25:23 with the high ranking officers and the **leading** men of the city.

2030 ἐξυπνίζω, exypnizō [1] [√ *1666 + 5678*]

wake up [1]

Jn 11:11 Lazarus has fallen asleep; but I am going there to **wake** him **up**."

2031 ἔξυπνος, exypnos [1] [√ *1666 + 5678*]

woke up [+1181] [1]

Ac 16:27 The jailer **woke** [+1181] **up**, and when he saw the prison doors

2032 ἔξω, exō [63 / 62] [√ 1666]

outside [25], out [17], *untranslated* [6], away [3], from [2], leave
[+2002] [2], out of [2], outsiders [+3836] [2], foreign [1],
outwardly [+476+3836] [1], went out [+2002] [1]

Mt 5:13 good for anything, except to be thrown **out** and trampled by men.
  10:14 shake the dust off your feet *when you* **leave** [+2002] that home
  12:46 his mother and brothers stood **outside**, wanting to speak to him.
  12:47 Someone told him, "Your mother and brothers are standing **outside**,
  13:48 and collected the good fish in baskets, but threw the bad **away**.
  21:17 And he left them and went out of [RPG] the city to Bethany,
  21:39 and threw him out [RPG] of the vineyard and killed him.
  26:69 Now Peter was sitting **out** in the courtyard, and a servant girl came
  26:75 disown me three times." And he went **outside** and wept bitterly.
Mk 1:45 no longer enter a town openly but stayed **outside** in lonely places.
  3:31 Standing **outside**, they sent someone in to call him.
  3:32 told him, "Your mother and brothers are **outside** looking for you."
  4:11 But to those *on* the **outside** everything is said in parables
  5:10 he begged Jesus again and again not to send them **out** of the area.
  8:23 He took the blind man by the hand and led him **outside** the village.
  11: 4 They went and found a colt **outside** in the street, tied at a doorway.
  11:19 When evening came, they went **out** of the city.
  12: 8 they took him and killed him, and threw him **out** of the vineyard.
  14:68 talking about," he said, and **went out** [+2002] into the entryway.
Lk 1:10 incense came, all the assembled worshipers were praying **outside**.
  4:29 They got up, drove him out [RPG] of the town, and took him to
  8:20 Someone told him, "Your mother and brothers are standing **outside**,
  13:25 the door, you will stand **outside** knocking and pleading, 'Sir,
  13:28 prophets in the kingdom of God, but you yourselves thrown **out**.
  13:33 and the next day—for surely no prophet can die **outside** Jerusalem!
  14:35 It is fit neither for the soil nor for the manure pile; it is thrown **out**.
  20:15 So they threw him **out** of the vineyard and killed him. "What
  22:62 And he went **outside** and wept bitterly.
  24:50 he had led them out [UBS+ *outside*] to the vicinity of Bethany,
Jn 6:37 come to me, and whoever comes to me I will never drive **away**.
  9:34 in sin at birth; how dare you lecture us!" And they threw him **out**.
  9:35 Jesus heard that they had thrown him **out**, and when he found him,
  11:43 he had said this, Jesus called in a loud voice, "Lazarus, come **out**!"
  12:31 on this world; now the prince of this world will be driven **out**.
  15: 6 remain in me, he is like a branch that is thrown **away** and withers;
  18:16 but Peter had to wait **outside** at the door. The other disciple,
  18:29 So Pilate came out [RPG] to them and asked, "What charges are
  19: 4 Once more Pilate came out [RPG] and said to the Jews, "Look,
  19: 4 I am bringing him **out** to you to let you know that I find no basis
  19: 5 When Jesus came out [RPG] wearing the crown of thorns
  19:13 he brought Jesus **out** and sat down on the judge's seat at a place
  20:11 but Mary stood **outside** the tomb crying. As she wept, she bent
Ac 4:15 So they ordered them to withdraw **from** the Sanhedrin and
  5:34 and ordered that the men be put **outside** for a little while.
  7:58 dragged him **out** of the city and began to stone him. Meanwhile,
  9:40 Peter sent them all **out** of the room; then he got down on his knees
  14:19 They stoned Paul and dragged him **outside** the city, thinking he
  16:13 On the Sabbath we went **outside** the city gate to the river,
  16:30 He then brought them **out** and asked, "Sirs, what must I do to be
  21: 5 and their wives and children accompanied us **out** of the city,
  21:30 Seizing Paul, they dragged him **from** the temple, and immediately
  26:11 against them, I even went to **foreign** cities to persecute them.
1Co 5:12 What business is it of mine to judge those **outside** the church?
  5:13 God will judge those **outside**. "Expel the wicked man from among
2Co 4:16 Though **outwardly** [+476+3836] we are wasting away,
Col 4: 5 Be wise in the way you act toward **outsiders** [+3836];
1Th 4:12 so that your daily life may win the respect of **outsiders** [+3836]
Heb 13:11 Place as a sin offering, but the bodies are burned **outside** the camp.
  13:12 so Jesus also suffered **outside** the city gate to make the people holy
  13:13 Let us, then, go to him **outside** the camp, bearing the disgrace he
1Jn 4:18 But perfect love drives **out** fear, because fear has to do with
Rev 3:12 Never again *will he* **leave** [+2002] it. I will write on him the name
  22:15 **Outside** are the dogs, those who practice magic arts, the sexually

2033 ἔξωθεν, exōthen [13] [√ 1666]

outside [6], on the outside [2], *untranslated* [1], from outward [1],
from the outside [1], outer [1], outsiders [1]

Mt 23:25 You clean the **outside** of the cup and dish, but inside they are full
  23:27 which look beautiful **on the outside** but on the inside are full of
  23:28 **on the outside** you appear to people as righteous but on the inside
Mk 7:15 Nothing **outside** a man can make him 'unclean' by going into him.
  7:18 "Don't you see that nothing that enters a man **from the outside** can
Lk 11:39 "Now then, you Pharisees clean the **outside** of the cup and dish,
  11:40 Did not the one who made the **outside** make the inside also?
2Co 7: 5 were harassed at every turn—conflicts on the **outside**, fears within.
1Ti 3: 7 He must also have a good reputation with **outsiders**, so that he will
1Pe 3: 3 Your beauty should not come **from outward** adornment, such as
Rev 11: 2 But exclude [RPG] the outer court; do not measure it, because it
  11: 2 But exclude the **outer** court; do not measure it, because it has been
  14:20 They were trampled in the winepress **outside** the city, and blood

2034 ἐξωθέω, exōtheō [2] [√ 723; cf. 1666]

drove out [1], run aground [1]

Ac 7:45 they took the land from the nations God **drove out** before them.
  27:39 where they decided *to* **run** the ship **aground** if they could.

2035 ἐξώτερος, exōteros [3] [√ 1666]

outside [3]

Mt 8:12 But the subjects of the kingdom will be thrown **outside**,
  22:13 'Tie him hand and foot, and throw him **outside**, into the darkness,
  25:30 And throw that worthless servant **outside**, into the darkness,

2036 ἔοικα, eoika [2] [→ 1635, 2116, 2117]

like [2]

Jas 1: 6 because he who doubts *is* **like** a wave of the sea, blown and tossed
  1:23 but does not do what it says *is* **like** a man who looks at his face in

2037 ἑορτάζω, heortazō [1] [√ 2038]

keep the Festival [1]

1Co 5: 8 Therefore *let us* **keep the Festival**, not with the old yeast,

2038 ἑορτή, heortē [25] [→ 2037]

feast [22], Passover Feast [1], religious festival [1], there^s
[+1650+3836] [1]

Mt 26: 5 "But not during the **Feast**," they said, "or there may be a riot among
  27:15 Now it was the governor's custom at the **Feast** to release a prisoner
Mk 14: 2 "But not during the **Feast**," they said, "or the people may riot."
  15: 6 Now it was the custom at the **Feast** to release a prisoner whom he
Lk 2:41 Every year his parents went to Jerusalem *for* the **Feast** of the
  2:42 years old, they went up *to* the **Feast**, according to the custom.
  22: 1 Now the **Feast** of Unleavened Bread, called the Passover,
Jn 2:23 Now while he was in Jerusalem at the Passover **Feast**,
  4:45 had seen all that he had done in Jerusalem at the **Passover Feast**,
  4:45 at the Passover Feast, for they also had been **there**^s [+1650+3836].
  5: 1 Some time later, Jesus went up to Jerusalem for a **feast** of the Jews.
  6: 4 The Jewish Passover **Feast** was near.
  7: 2 But when the Jewish **Feast** of Tabernacles was near,
  7: 8 You go to the **Feast**. I am not yet going up to this Feast,
  7: 8 I am not yet going up to this **Feast**, because for me the right time
  7:10 However, after his brothers had left for the **Feast**, he went also,
  7:11 Now at the **Feast** the Jews were watching for him and asking,
  7:14 Not until halfway through the **Feast** did Jesus go up to the temple
  7:37 On the last and greatest day *of* the **Feast**, Jesus stood and said in a
  11:56 "What do you think? Isn't he coming to the **Feast** at all?"
  12:12 The next day the great crowd that had come for the **Feast** heard
  12:20 some Greeks among those who went up to worship at the **Feast**.
  13: 1 It was just before the Passover **Feast**. Jesus knew that the time had
  13:29 Jesus was telling him to buy what was needed for the **Feast**,
Col 2:16 you by what you eat or drink, or with regard to a **religious festival**,

2039 ἐπαγγελία, epangelia [52] [√ 2093 + 34]

promise [23], promised [9], promises [9], promised [+1181] [2],
what was promised [+3836] [2], consent [1], has promised [1],

promised [+2040] [1], was promised [1], what had been
promised [1], what has been promised [1], what was promised [1]

Lk 24:49 I am going to send you what my Father has **promised**; but stay in
Ac   1: 4 "Do not leave Jerusalem, but wait for the *gift* my Father **promised**,
     2:33 he has received from the Father the **promised** Holy Spirit
     2:39 The **promise** is for you and your children and for all who are far
     7:17 "As the time drew near for God to *fulfill* his **promise** to Abraham,
    13:23 God has brought to Israel the Savior Jesus, as he **promised**.
    13:32 tell you the good news: What God **promised** [+1181] our fathers
    23:21 They are ready now, waiting for your **consent** *to* their *request*."
    26: 6 because of my hope in what God *has* **promised** [+1181] our
Ro   4:13 and his offspring received the **promise** that he would be heir of the
     4:14 by law are heirs, faith has no value and the **promise** is worthless,
     4:16 Therefore, the **promise** comes by faith, so that it may be by grace
     4:20 Yet he did not waver through unbelief regarding the **promise** of
     9: 4 the receiving of the law, the temple worship and the **promises**.
     9: 8 but it is the children *of* the **promise** who are regarded as
     9: 9 For this was how the **promise** was stated: "At the appointed time I
    15: 8 of God's truth, to confirm the **promises** made to the patriarchs
2Co 1:20 For no matter how many **promises** God has made, they are "Yes" in
     7: 1 Since we have these **promises**, dear friends, let us purify ourselves
Gal 3:14 so that by faith we might receive the **promise** of the Spirit.
     3:16 The **promises** were spoken to Abraham and to his seed.
     3:17 established by God and thus do away with the **promise**.
     3:18 depends on the law, then it no longer depends on a **promise**;
     3:18 but God in his grace gave it to Abraham through a **promise**.
     3:21 Is the law, therefore, opposed to the **promises** of God? Absolutely
     3:22 so that what **was promised**, being given through faith in Jesus
     3:29 then you are Abraham's seed, and heirs according to the **promise**.
     4:23 but his son by the free woman was born as the result of a **promise**.
     4:28 Now you, brothers, like Isaac, are children *of* **promise**.
Eph 1:13 you were marked in him with a seal, the **promised** Holy Spirit,
     2:12 in Israel and foreigners to the covenants *of* the **promise**,
     3: 6 of one body, and sharers together in the **promise** in Christ Jesus.
     6: 2 and mother"—which is the first commandment with a **promise**—
1Ti 4: 8 holding **promise** for both the present life and the life to come.
2Ti 1: 1 will of God, according to the **promise** of life that is in Christ Jesus,
Heb 4: 1 Therefore, since the **promise** of entering his rest still stands,
     6:12 who through faith and patience inherit **what has been promised**.
     6:15 waiting patiently, Abraham received **what was promised** [+3836]
     6:17 his purpose very clear to the heirs *of* **what was promised** [+3836],
     7: 6 a tenth from Abraham and blessed him who had the **promises**.
     8: 6 is superior to the old one, and it is founded on better **promises**.
     9:15 that those who are called may receive the **promised** eternal
    10:36 have done the will of God, you will receive what he **has promised**.
    11: 9 By faith he made his home in the **promised** land like a stranger in
    11: 9 and Jacob, who were heirs with him *of* the same **promise**.
    11:13 They did not receive the things **promised**; they only saw them
    11:17 He who had received the **promises** was about to sacrifice his one
    11:33 administered justice, and gained **what was promised**;
    11:39 their faith, yet none of them received **what had been promised**.
2Pe 3: 4 They will say, "Where is this 'coming' he **promised**? Ever since
     3: 9 The Lord is not slow *in keeping* his **promise**, as some understand
1Jn 2:25 And this is what he **promised** [+2040] us—even eternal life.

2040 ἐπαγγέλλομαι, *epangellomai* [15]
[√ 2093 + 34]

promised [8], made promise [2], promise [2], profess [1],
professed [1], promised [+2039] [1]

Mk 14:11 They were delighted to hear this and **promised** to give him money.
Ac   7: 5 But God **promised** him that he and his descendants after him
Ro   4:21 fully persuaded that God had power to do what *he had* **promised**.
Gal 3:19 because of transgressions until the Seed to whom the **promise**
1Ti 2:10 good deeds, appropriate *for* women *who* **profess** to worship God.
     6:21 which some *have* **professed** and in so doing have wandered from
Tit 1: 2 who does not lie, **promised** before the beginning of time,
Heb 6:13 *When* God **made** his **promise** to Abraham, since there was no one
    10:23 to the hope we profess, for he *who* **promised** is faithful.
    11:11 because he considered him faithful *who had* **made** the **promise**.
    12:26 At that time his voice shook the earth, but now *he has* **promised**,
Jas 1:12 he will receive the crown of life that God *has* **promised** to those
     2: 5 and to inherit the kingdom *he* **promised** those who love him?
2Pe 2:19 *They* **promise** them freedom, while they themselves are slaves of

1Jn 2:25 And this is what he **promised** [+2039] us—even eternal life.

2041 ἐπάγγελμα, *epangelma* [2] [√ 2093 + 34]

promise [1], promises [1]

2Pe 1: 4 these he has given us his very great and precious **promises**,
     3:13 But in keeping with his **promise** we are looking forward to a new

2042 ἐπάγω, *epagō* [3] [√ 2093 + 72]

bringing on [1], brought on [1], make guilty of [+2093] [1]

Ac   5:28 and are determined *to* **make** [+2093] us **guilty of** this man's blood."
2Pe 2: 1 Lord who bought them—**bringing** swift destruction **on** themselves.
     2: 5 if he did not spare the ancient world *when he* **brought** the flood **on**

2043 ἐπαγωνίζομαι, *epagōnizomai* [1] [√ 2093 + 74]

contend [1]

Jude 1: 3 and urge you *to* **contend** for the faith that was once for all

2044 ἐπαθροίζω, *epathroizō* [1] [√ 2093 + 125]

increased [1]

Lk 11:29 *As* the crowds **increased**, Jesus said, "This is a wicked generation.

2045 Ἐπαίνετος, *Epainetos* [1] [√ 2093 + 142]

Epenetus [1]

Ro 16: 5 Greet my dear friend **Epenetus**, who was the first convert to Christ

2046 ἐπαινέω, *epaineō* [6] [√ 2093 + 142]

praise [2], *untranslated* [1], commended [1], have praise [1], sing
praises to [1]

Lk 16: 8 "The master **commended** the dishonest manager because he had
Ro 15:11 all you Gentiles, and **sing praises to** him, all *you* peoples."
1Co 11: 2 *I* **praise** you for remembering me in everything and for holding to
    11:17 In the following directives *I* **have** no **praise** for you, for your
    11:22 What shall I say to you? Shall *I* **praise** you for this? Certainly not!
    11:22 I say to you? Shall I **praise** you for this? Certainly not! **[RPG]**

2047 ἔπαινος, *epainos* [11] [√ 2093 + 142]

praise [7], commend [+2400] [1], commend [1], praised [1],
praiseworthy [1]

Ro   2:29 written code. Such a man's **praise** is not from men, but from God.
    13: 3 Then do what is right and he *will* **commend** [+2400] *you*.
1Co 4: 5 men's hearts. At that time each will receive his **praise** from God.
2Co 8:18 And we are sending along with him the brother who is **praised** by
Eph 1: 6 to the **praise** of his glorious grace, which he has freely given us in
     1:12 the first to hope in Christ, might be for the **praise** of his glory.
     1:14 of those who are God's possession—to the **praise** of his glory.
Php 1:11 that comes through Jesus Christ—to the glory and **praise** of God.
     4: 8 whatever is admirable—if anything is excellent or **praiseworthy**—
1Pe 1: 7 may be proved genuine and may result in **praise**, glory and honor
     2:14 punish those who do wrong and to **commend** those who do right.

2048 ἐπαίρω, *epairō* [19] [√ 2093 + 149]

looked up [+3836+4057] [3], lift up [2], lifted up [2], raised [2],
called out [+5889] [1], hoisted [1], look up [+3836+4057] [1],
looked [+3836+4057] [1], looking [+3836+4057] [1], open eyes
[+3836+4057] [1], pushes forward [1], sets up [1], shouted
[+3836+5889] [1], taken up [1]

Mt 17: 8 *When they* **looked up** [+3836+4057], they saw no one except
Lk   6:20 **Looking** [+3836+4057] at his disciples, he said: "Blessed are you
    11:27 was saying these things, a woman in the crowd **called out** [+5889],
    16:23 he **looked up** [+3836+4057] and saw Abraham far away,
    18:13 He would not even **look up** [+3836+4057] to heaven, but beat his
    21:28 these things begin to take place, stand up and **lift up** your heads,
    24:50 to the vicinity of Bethany, *he* **lifted up** his hands and blessed them.

Jn	4:35	I tell you, **open** your **eyes** [*+3836+4057*] and look at the fields!
	6: 5	When Jesus **looked up** [*+3836+4057*] and saw a great crowd
	13:18	'He who shares my bread *has* **lifted up** his heel against me.'
	17: 1	said this, *he* **looked** [*+3836+4057*] toward heaven and prayed:
Ac	1: 9	After he said this, *he was* **taken up** before their very eyes,
	2:14	up with the Eleven, **raised** his voice and addressed the crowd:
	14:11	had done, they **shouted** [*+3836+5889*] in the Lycaonian language,
	22:22	Then *they* **raised** their voices and shouted, "Rid the earth of him!
	27:40	Then they **hoisted** the foresail to the wind and made for the beach.
2Co	10: 5	and every pretension *that* **sets** *itself* **up** against the knowledge of
	11:20	of you or **pushes** *himself* **forward** or slaps you in the face.
1Ti	2: 8	I want men everywhere to **lift up** holy hands in prayer,

2049 ἐπαισχύνομαι, *epaischynomai* [11]
[√ *2093 + 156*]

ashamed of [7], ashamed [4]

Mk	8:38	If anyone *is* **ashamed of** me and my words in this adulterous
	8:38	the Son of Man *will be* **ashamed of** him when he comes in his
Lk	9:26	If anyone *is* **ashamed of** me and my words, the Son of Man will be
	9:26	the Son of Man *will be* **ashamed of** him when he comes in his
Ro	1:16	*I am* not **ashamed of** the gospel, because it is the power of God for
	6:21	you reap at that time from the things *you are* now **ashamed of**?
2Ti	1: 8	So *do* not *be* **ashamed** to testify about our Lord, or ashamed of me
	1:12	Yet *I am* not **ashamed**, because I know whom I have believed,
	1:16	because he often refreshed me and *was* not **ashamed of** my chains.
Heb	2:11	of the same family. So Jesus *is* not **ashamed** to call them brothers.
	11:16	Therefore God *is* not **ashamed** to be called their God, for he has

2050 ἐπαιτέω, *epaiteō* [2] [√ *2093 + 160*]

beg [1], begging [1]

Lk	16: 3	my job. I'm not strong enough to dig, and I'm ashamed *to* **beg**—
	18:35	a blind man was sitting by the roadside **begging**.

2051 ἐπακολουθέω, *epakoloutheō* [4]
[√ *2093 + 199 [1,3]*]

accompanied [1], devoting [1], follow [1], trail behind [1]

Mk	16:20	and confirmed his word by the signs that **accompanied** it.
1Ti	5:10	those in trouble and **devoting** *herself* to all kinds of good deeds.
	5:24	of judgment ahead of them; the sins of others **trail behind** them.
1Pe	2:21	leaving you an example, that *you should* **follow** in his steps.

2052 ἐπακούω, *epakouō* [1] [√ *2093 + 201*]

heard [1]

2Co	6: 2	For he says, "In the time of my favor *I* **heard** you, and in the day of

2053 ἐπακροάομαι, *epakroaomai* [1] [√ *2093 + 212*]

listening [1]

Ac	16:25	hymns to God, and the other prisoners *were* **listening** *to* them.

2054 ἐπάν, *epan* [3] [√ *2093 + 323*]

when [2], as soon as [1]

Mt	2: 8	**As soon as** you find him, report to me, so that I too may go
Lk	11:22	But **when** someone stronger attacks and overpowers him,
	11:34	But **when** they are bad, your body also is full of darkness.

2055 ἐπάναγκες, *epanankes* [1] [√ *2093 + 340*]

requirements [1]

Ac	15:28	to burden you with anything beyond the following **requirements**:

2056 ἐπανάγω, *epanagō* [3] [√ *2093 + 324 + 72*]

put out [2], on way back [1]

Mt	21:18	*as he was* **on** *his* **way back** to the city, he was hungry.
Lk	5: 3	belonging to Simon, and asked him *to* **put out** a little from shore.

	5: 4	had finished speaking, he said to Simon, "**Put out** into deep water,

2057 ἐπαναμιμνῄσκω, *epanamimnēskō* [1]
[√ *2093 + 324 + 3648*]

remind again [1]

Ro	15:15	as if *to* **remind** you of them **again**, because of the grace God gave

2058 ἐπαναπαύομαι, *epanapauomai* [2]
[√ *2093 + 324 + 4264*]

rely on [1], rest on [*RP2093*] [1]

Lk	10: 6	If a man of peace is there, your peace *will* **rest** [*RP2093*] **on** him;
Ro	2:17	if *you* **rely on** the law and brag about your relationship to God;

2059 ἐπανέρχομαι, *epanerchomai* [2]
[√ *2093 + 324 + 2262*]

return [1], returned home [1]

Lk	10:35	'Look after him,' he said, 'and when I **return**, I will reimburse you
	19:15	"He was made king, however, and **returned home**. Then he sent

2060 ἐπανίστημι, *epanistēmi* [2]
[√ *2093 + 324 + 2705*]

rebel against [*RP2093*] [2]

Mt	10:21	children *will* **rebel** [*RP2093*] **against** their parents and have them
Mk	13:12	Children *will* **rebel** [*RP2093*] **against** their parents and have them

2061 ἐπανόρθωσις, *epanorthōsis* [1]
[√ *2093 + 324 + 3981*]

correcting [1]

2Ti	3:16	for teaching, rebuking, **correcting** and training in righteousness,

2062 ἐπάνω, *epanō* [19] [√ *2093 + 539*]

on [7], over [4], above [3], more than [2], of [1], rider [*+2764*] [1], take charge of [*+1181*] [1]

Mt	2: 9	ahead of them until it stopped **over** the place where the child was.
	5:14	"You are the light of the world. A city **on** a hill cannot be hidden.
	21: 7	and the colt, placed their cloaks on them, and Jesus sat **on** them.
	23:18	but if anyone swears by the gift **on** it, he is bound by his oath.'
	23:20	he who swears by the altar swears by it and by everything **on** it.
	23:22	by heaven swears by God's throne and by the one who sits **on** it.
	27:37	**Above** his head they placed the written charge against him:
	28: 2	heaven and, going to the tomb, rolled back the stone and sat **on** it.
Mk	14: 5	It could have been sold for **more than** a year's wages
Lk	4:39	So he bent **over** her and rebuked the fever, and it left her. She got
	10:19	I have given you authority to trample **on** snakes and scorpions
	11:44	like unmarked graves, which men walk **over** without knowing it."
	19:17	been trustworthy in a very small matter, take charge of ten cities.'
	19:19	"His master answered, 'You **take charge** [*+1181*] **of** five cities.'
Jn	3:31	"The one who comes from above is **above** all; the one who is from
	3:31	one from the earth. The one who comes from heaven is **above** all.
1Co	15: 6	he appeared to **more than** five hundred of the brothers at the same
Rev	6: 8	Its **rider** [*+2764*] was named Death, and Hades was following
	20: 3	He threw him into the Abyss, and locked and sealed it **over** him,

2063 ἐπάρατος, *eparatos* [1] [√ *2093 + 725*]

curse on [1]

Jn	7:49	this mob that knows nothing of the law—there is a **curse on** them."

2064 ἐπαρκέω, *eparkeō* [3] [√ *2093 + 758*]

help [2], helping [1]

1Ti	5:10	**helping** those in trouble and devoting herself to all kinds of good
	5:16	*she should* **help** them and not let the church be burdened with
	5:16	so that the church *can* **help** those widows who are really in need.

2065 ἐπαρχεία, eparcheia [2] [√ 2093 + 806]

province [2]

Ac 23:34 The governor read the letter and asked what **province** he was from.
   25: 1 Three days after arriving in the **province**, Festus went up from

2066 ἐπάρχειος, eparcheios Not used in UBS/NIV
[√ 2093 + 806]

2067 ἐπαρχικός, eparchikos Not used in UBS/NIV
[√ 2093 + 806]

2068 ἔπαυλις, epaulis [1] [√ 2093 + 885]

place [1]

Ac 1:20 "it is written in the book of Psalms, " 'May his **place** be deserted;

2069 ἐπαύριον, epaurion [17] [√ 892; cf. 2093]

next day [15], following day [2]

Mt 27:62 The **next day**, the one after Preparation Day, the chief priests
Mk 11:12 The **next day** as they were leaving Bethany, Jesus was hungry.
Jn 1:29 The **next day** John saw Jesus coming toward him and said,
   1:35 The **next day** John was there again with two of his disciples.
   1:43 The **next day** Jesus decided to leave for Galilee. Finding Philip,
   6:22 The **next day** the crowd that had stayed on the opposite shore of
  12:12 The **next day** the great crowd that had come for the Feast heard
Ac 10: 9 About noon the **following day** as they were on their journey
  10:23 The **next day** Peter started out with them, and some of the brothers
  10:24 The **following day** he arrived in Caesarea. Cornelius was
  14:20 back into the city. The **next day** he and Barnabas left for Derbe.
  20: 7 spoke to the people and, because he intended to leave the **next day**,
  21: 8 Leaving the **next day**, we reached Caesarea and stayed at the
  22:30 The **next day**, since the commander wanted to find out exactly
  23:32 The **next day** they let the cavalry go on with him, while they
  25: 6 and the **next day** he convened the court and ordered that Paul be
  25:23 The **next day** Agrippa and Bernice came with great pomp

2070 ἐπαυτοφώρῳ, epautophōrō Not used in UBS/NIV [√ 2093 + 899]

2071 Ἐπαφρᾶς, Epaphras [3]

Epaphras [3]

Col 1: 7 You learned it from **Epaphras**, our dear fellow servant, who is a
  4:12 **Epaphras**, who is one of you and a servant of Christ Jesus,
Phm 1:23 **Epaphras**, my fellow prisoner in Christ Jesus, sends you greetings.

2072 ἐπαφρίζω, epaphrizō [1] [√ 2093 + 931]

foaming up [1]

Jude 1:13 They are wild waves of the sea, **foaming up** their shame;

2073 Ἐπαφρόδιτος, Epaphroditos [2]

Epaphroditus [2]

Php 2:25 But I think it is necessary to send back to you **Epaphroditus**,
  4:18 now that I have received from **Epaphroditus** the gifts-you sent.

2074 ἐπεγείρω, epegeirō [2] [√ 2093 + 1586]

stirred up against [RP2093] [1], stirred up [1]

Ac 13:50 *They* **stirred** [RP2093] **up** persecution **against** Paul and Barnabas,
  14: 2 But the Jews who refused to believe **stirred up** the Gentiles

2075 ἐπεί, epei [26] [√ 2093]

since [9], *untranslated* [4], because [4], if it could [1], if it were [1], if that were so [1], in that case [+726] [1], now if [1], otherwise [+726] [1], otherwise [1], so [1], then [1]

Mt 18:32 'I canceled all that debt of yours **because** you begged me to.
  21:46 afraid of the crowd **because** the people held that he was a prophet.
  27: 6 the law to put this into the treasury, **since** it is blood money."
Mk 15:42 (that is, the day before the Sabbath). **So** as evening approached,
Lk 1:34 "How will this be," Mary asked the angel, "**since** I am a virgin?"
Jn 13:29 **Since** Judas had charge of the money, some thought Jesus was
  19:31 Now [NIE] it was the day of Preparation, and the next day was to
Ro 3: 6 Certainly not! **If that were so**, how could God judge the world?
  11: 6 is no longer by works; **if it were**, grace would no longer be grace.
  11:22 you continue in his kindness. **Otherwise**, you also will be cut off.
1Co 5:10 **In** [+726] **that case** you would have to leave this world.
  7:14 **Otherwise** [+726] your children would be unclean, but as it is,
  14:12 **Since** you are eager to have spiritual gifts, try to excel in gifts that
  14:16 [NIE] If you are praising God with your spirit, how can one who
  15:29 **Now if** there is no resurrection, what will those do who are
2Co 11:18 **Since** many are boasting in the way the world does, I too will
  13: 3 **since** you are demanding proof that Christ is speaking through me.
Heb 2:14 **Since** the children have flesh and blood, he too shared in their
  4: 6 [NIE] It still remains that some will enter that rest, and those who
  5: 2 and are going astray, **since** he himself is subject to weakness.
  5:11 about this, but it is hard to explain **because** you are slow to learn.
  6:13 **since** there was no one greater for him to swear by, he swore by
  9:17 [NIE] it never takes effect while the one who made it is living.
  9:26 **Then** Christ would have had to suffer many times since the
  10: 2 **If it could**, would they not have stopped being offered? For the
  11:11 **because** he considered him faithful who had made the promise.

2076 ἐπειδή, epeidē [10] [√ 2093 + 1314]

since [4], *untranslated* [2], because [2], for [1], when [1]

Lk 7: 1 **When** Jesus had finished saying all this in the hearing of the
  11: 6 **because** a friend of mine on a journey has come to me, and I have
Ac 13:46 **Since** you reject it and do not consider yourselves worthy of
  14:12 and Paul they called Hermes **because** he was the chief speaker.
  15:24 [NIE] We have heard that some went out from us without our
1Co 1:21 **For since** in the wisdom of God the world through its wisdom did
  1:22 [NIE] Jews demand miraculous signs and Greeks look for
  14:16 to your thanksgiving, **since** he does not know what you are saying?
  15:21 **For since** death came through a man, the resurrection of the dead
Php 2:26 **For** he longs for all of you and is distressed because you heard he

2077 ἐπειδήπερ, epeidēper [1] [√ 2093 + 1314 + 4302]

untranslated [1]

Lk 1: 1 [NIE] Many have undertaken to draw up an account of the things

2078 ἐπεῖδον, epeidon [2] [√ 2093 + 1626]

consider [RP2093] [1], shown favor [1]

Lk 1:25 "In these days *he has* **shown** *his* **favor** and taken away my disgrace
Ac 4:29 **consider** [RP2093] their threats and enable your servants to speak

2079 ἔπειμι, epeimi [5] [√ 2093 + 1640]

next day [3], following [1], next [1]

Ac 7:26 The **next day** Moses came upon two Israelites who were fighting.
  16:11 sailed straight for Samothrace, and the **next day** on to Neapolis.
  20:15 The **next day** we set sail from there and arrived off Kios. The day
  21:18 The **next day** Paul and the rest of us went to see James, and all the
  23:11 The **following** night the Lord stood near Paul and said,

2080 ἐπείπερ, epeiper Not used in UBS/NIV
[√ 2093 + 4302]

2081 ἐπεισαγωγή, epeisagōgē [1]
[√ 2093 + 1650 + 72]

introduced [1]

Heb 7: 19 and a better hope is **introduced**, by which we draw near to God.

2082 ἐπεισέρχομαι, epeiserchomai [1]
[√ 2093 + 1650 + 2262]

come upon [RP2093] [1]

Lk 21: 35 For *it will* **come** [RP2093] **upon** all those who live on the face of

2083 ἔπειτα, epeita [16] [√ 2093 + 1663]

then [10], after that [2], later [2], also [1], and after [1]

Lk   16: 7 "**Then** he asked the second, 'And how much do you owe?'
Jn   11: 7 **Then** he said to his disciples, "Let us go back to Judea."
1Co 12: 28 second prophets, third teachers, **then** workers of miracles,
     12: 28 **also** those having gifts of healing, those able to help others,
     15: 6 **After that**, he appeared to more than five hundred of the brothers
     15: 7 **Then** he appeared to James, then to all the apostles,
     15: 23 the firstfruits; **then**, when he comes, those who belong to him.
     15: 46 did not come first, but the natural, **and after** that the spiritual.
Gal   1: 18 **Then** after three years, I went up to Jerusalem to get acquainted
      1: 21 **Later** I went to Syria and Cilicia.
      2: 1 Fourteen years **later** I went up again to Jerusalem, this time with
1Th   4: 17 **After that**, we who are still alive and are left will be caught up
Heb   7: 2 righteousness"; **then** also, "king of Salem" means "king of peace."
      7: 27 after day, first for his own sins, and **then** for the sins of the people.
Jas   3: 17 **then** peace-loving, considerate, submissive, full of mercy
      4: 14 You are a mist that appears for a little while and **then** vanishes.

2084 ἐπέκεινα, epekeina [1] [√ 2093 + 1695]

beyond [1]

Ac   7: 43 to worship. Therefore I will send you into exile' **beyond** Babylon.

2085 ἐπεκτείνομαι, epekteinomai [1] [√ 1753; cf. 2093]

straining toward [1]

Php   3: 13 Forgetting what is behind and **straining toward** what is ahead,

2086 ἐπενδύομαι, ependyomai [2]
[√ 2093 + 1877 + 1544]

clothed with [2]

2Co   5: 2 we groan, longing *to be* **clothed with** our heavenly dwelling,
      5: 4 to be unclothed but *to be* **clothed with** our heavenly dwelling,

2087 ἐπενδύτης, ependytēs [1] [√ 2093 + 1877 + 1544]

outer garment [1]

Jn   21: 7 he wrapped his **outer garment** around him (for he had taken it off)

2088 ἐπέρχομαι, eperchomai [9] [√ 2093 + 2262]

attacks [1], came [1], come upon [RP2093] [1], comes on [RP2093] [1], coming on [1], coming upon [1], coming [1], happen to [RP2093] [1], happen to [1]

Lk   1: 35 angel answered, "The Holy Spirit *will* **come** [RP2093] **upon** you,
     11: 22 But when someone stronger **attacks** and overpowers him,
     21: 26 faint from terror, apprehensive *of* what *is* **coming on** the world,
Ac   1: 8 will receive power *when* the Holy Spirit **comes** [RP2093] **on** you;
     8: 24 so that nothing you have said *may* **happen** [RP2093] **to** me.
     13: 40 Take care that what the prophets have said *does* not **happen to**
     14: 19 Then some Jews **came** from Antioch and Iconium and won the
Eph   2: 7 in order that in the **coming** ages he might show the incomparable
Jas   5: 1 weep and wail because of the misery that *is* **coming upon** you.

2089 ἐπερωτάω, eperōtaō [56] [√ 2093 + 2263]

asked [35], ask [5], question [4], ask questions [2], asking [2], questioned [2], ask about [1], ask for [1], asked about [1], asking questions [1], demanded [1], plied [1]

Mt   12: 10 accuse Jesus, *they* **asked** him, "Is it lawful to heal on the Sabbath?"
     16: 1 and tested him *by* **asking** him to show them a sign from heaven.
     17: 10 The disciples **asked** him, "Why then do the teachers of the law say
     22: 23 who say there is no resurrection, came to him with a **question**.
     22: 35 One of them, an expert in the law, tested him *with* this **question**:
     22: 41 While the Pharisees were gathered together, Jesus **asked** them,
     22: 46 and from that day on no one dared *to* **ask** him any more **questions**.
     27: 11 and the governor **asked** him, "Are you the king of the Jews?"
Mk   5: 9 Jesus **asked** him, "My name is Legion,"
     7: 5 So the Pharisees and teachers of the law **asked** Jesus, "Why don't
     7: 17 and entered the house, his disciples **asked** him **about** this parable.
     8: 23 and put his hands on him, Jesus **asked**, "Do you see anything?"
     8: 27 On the way *he* **asked** them, "Who do people say I am?"
     8: 29 "But what about you?" he **asked**. "Who do you say I am?" Peter
     9: 11 And *they* **asked** him, "Why do the teachers of the law say that
     9: 16 "What are you arguing with them about?" *he* **asked**.
     9: 21 Jesus **asked** the boy's father, "How long has he been like this?"
     9: 28 After Jesus had gone indoors, his disciples **asked** him privately,
     9: 32 not understand what he meant and were afraid *to* **ask** him **about** it.
     9: 33 When he was in the house, *he* **asked** them, "What were you arguing
     10: 2 Some Pharisees came and tested him *by* **asking**, "Is it lawful for a
     10: 10 they were in the house again, the disciples **asked** Jesus about this.
     10: 17 "Good teacher," *he* **asked**, "what must I do to inherit eternal life?"
     11: 29 Jesus replied, "*I will* **ask** you one question. Answer me, and I will
     12: 18 who say there is no resurrection, came to him with a **question**.
     12: 28 *he* **asked** him, "Of all the commandments, which is the most
     12: 34 And from then on no one dared **ask** him any more **questions**.
     13: 3 the temple, Peter, James, John and Andrew **asked** him privately,
     14: 60 Then the high priest stood up before them and **asked** Jesus,
     14: 61 Again the high priest **asked** him, "Are you the Christ, the Son of
     15: 2 of the Jews?" **asked** Pilate. "Yes, it is as you say," Jesus replied.
     15: 4 So again Pilate **asked** him, "Aren't you going to answer? See how
     15: 44 Summoning the centurion, *he* **asked** him if Jesus had already died.
Lk   2: 46 among the teachers, listening to them and **asking** them **questions**.
     3: 10 "What should we do then?" the crowd **asked**.
     3: 14 Then some soldiers **asked** him, "And what should we do?" He
     6: 9 Then Jesus said to them, "*I* **ask** you, which is lawful on the
     8: 9 His disciples **asked** him what this parable meant.
     8: 30 Jesus **asked** him, "What is your name?" "Legion," he replied,
     9: 18 were with him, *he* **asked** them, "Who do the crowds say I am?"
     17: 20 *having been* **asked** by the Pharisees when the kingdom of God
     18: 18 A certain ruler **asked** him, "Good teacher, what must I do to inherit
     18: 40 man to be brought to him. When he came near, Jesus **asked** him,
     20: 21 So the spies **questioned** him: "Teacher, we know that you speak
     20: 27 who say there is no resurrection, came to Jesus with a **question**.
     20: 40 And no one dared *to* **ask** him any more questions.
     21: 7 "Teacher," *they* **asked**, "when will these things happen? And what
     22: 64 *They* blindfolded him and **demanded**, "Prophesy! Who hit you?"
     23: 6 On hearing this, Pilate **asked** if the man was a Galilean.
     23: 9 He **plied** him with many questions, but Jesus gave him no answer.
Jn   9: 23 That was why his parents said, "He is of age; **ask** him."
     18: 7 Again he **asked** them, "Who is it you want?" And they said,
Ac   5: 27 they made him appear before the Sanhedrin *to be* **questioned** *by*
     23: 34 The governor read the letter and **asked** what province he was from.
Ro 10: 20 not seek me; I revealed myself *to* those *who did* not **ask for** me."
1Co 14: 35 about something, *they should* **ask** their own husbands at home;

2090 ἐπερώτημα, eperōtēma [1] [√ 2093 + 2263]

pledge [1]

1Pe   3: 21 from the body but the **pledge** of a good conscience toward God.

2091 ἐπέχω, epechō [5] [√ 2093 + 2400]

attention [1], hold out [1], noticed [1], stayed a little longer [+5989] [1], watch closely [1]

Lk   14: 7 *When he* **noticed** how the guests picked the places of honor at the
Ac   3: 5 So the man *gave* them *his* **attention**, expecting to get something
     19: 22 *while* he **stayed** [+5989] in the province of Asia a **little longer**.

Php 2: 16 *as* you **hold out** the word of life—in order that I may boast on the
1Ti 4: 16 **Watch** your life and doctrine **closely**. Persevere in them, because if

2092 ἐπηρεάζω, *epēreazō* [2]

mistreat [1], speak maliciously against [1]

Lk 6: 28 bless those who curse you, pray for those *who* **mistreat** you.
1Pe 3: 16 so that those *who* **speak maliciously against** your good behavior

2093 ἐπί, *epi* [890 / 888]

[→ 258, 454, 455, 2039, 2040, 2041, 2042, 2043, 2044, 2045, 2046,
2047, 2048, 2049, 2050, 2051, 2052, 2053, 2054, 2055, 2056, 2057,
2058, 2059, 2060, 2061, 2062, 2063, 2064, 2065, 2066, 2067, 2068,
2069, 2070, 2072, 2074, 2075, 2076, 2077, 2078, 2079, 2080, 2081,
2082, 2083, 2084, 2085, 2086, 2087, 2088, 2089, 2090, 2091, 2094,
2095, 2096, 2097, 2098, 2099, 2100, 2101, 2102, 2103, 2104, 2105,
2106, 2107, 2108, 2109, 2110, 2111, 2112, 2113, 2114, 2115, 2116,
2117, 2118, 2119, 2120, 2121, 2122, 2123, 2124, 2125, 2126, 2127,
2128, 2129, 2130, 2131, 2132, 2133, 2134, 2135, 2136, 2137, 2138,
2139, 2141, 2142, 2143, 2144, 2145, 2146, 2147, 2148, 2149,
2150, 2151, 2152, 2153, 2154, 2155, 2156, 2157, 2158, 2159, 2164,
2165, 2166, 2167, 2168, 2169, 2170, 2171, 2172, 2173, 2174, 2175,
2176, 2177, 2178, 2179, 2180, 2181, 2183, 2184, 2185, 2186, 2187,
2188, 2189, 2190, 2191, 2192, 2194, 2195, 2196, 2197, 2198, 2199,
2200, 2201, 2202, 2203, 2204, 2205, 2206, 2207, 2208, 2209, 2210,
2211, 2212, 2213, 2214, 2215, 2216, 2217, 2218, 2219, 2220, 2221,
2222, 2223, 2224, 2225, 2226, 2227, 2228, 2230, 2383, 2384, 2388,
2389, 2390, 2391, 2392, 2393, 2987, 3575, 4215, 4600, 5296, 5297,
5298, 5308; cf. 2160]

on [258], in [73], to [73], *untranslated* [52], at [39], over [38], for
[33], against [32], of [21], before [15], upon [14], by [12], about
[8], with [8], rider [+2764] [6], because of [5], put on [RP2202]
[5], together [+899+3836] [4], around [3], from [3], turn to
[RP2188] [3], above [2], after [2], against [+3836+5111] [2],
among [2], as long as [+4012+5989] [2], because [+4005] [2],
because [2], came on [RP2158] [2], during [2], earthly
[+1178+3836] [2], generously [+2330] [2], in accordance with
[2], in the account [2], into [2], laid on [RP2095] [2], landed
[+1178+2262+3836] [2], placed on [RP2202] [2], put on
[RP2097] [2], reached [+1181] [2], reached [+2262] [2], rebel
against [RP2060] [2], riders [+2764] [2], right at [2], seized
[+1181] [2], seized [+2095+3836+5931] [2], sews on [RP2095]
[2], toward [2], turned to [RP2188] [2], whatever [+4012] [2],
when [2], with face to the ground [+4725] [2], write on [RP2108]
[2], a long time [+4498] [1], a matter of [1], across [1], add to
[RP2202] [1], adds to [RP2202] [1], along [1], any further [+4498]
[1], arrest [+2095+3836+5931] [1], arrested [+2095+3836+5931]
[1], as long as [+4012] [1], ashore [+1178] [1], assure
[+237+3306] [1], at the time [1], bear [RP20932126] [1], bear
[RP2126+2093] [1], bedridden [+2879+3187] [1], belong
[RP2126] [1], beside [1], between [1], bring back to [RP2188] [1],
builds on [RP2224] [1], built on [RP2224] [1], call [RP2126] [1],
cast on [RP2166] [1], caught in the act [+900+2898] [1], certainly
[+237] [1], come together [+899+3836+5302] [1], come upon
[RP16392158] [1], come upon [RP2082] [1], come upon [RP2088]
[1], comes on [RP2088] [1], comes together [+899+3836+5302]
[1], consider [RP2078] [1], convened the court
[+1037+2767+3836] [1], court [+1037] [1], covers [+3023] [1],
decided [+326+2840+3836] [1], died [+3738] [1], drive out [1],
embraced [+2158+3836+5549] [1], facedown to the ground
[+4725] [1], fall down [+4406+4725] [1], fallen on [RP2158] [1],
fell into trance [+1181+1749] [1], found to be [1], from bad to
worse [+3836+5937] [1], gathered to [RP2191] [1], get very far
[+4498+4621] [1], given [1], go down [RP2115] [1], gripped with
[RP2158] [1], happen to [RP2088] [1], holding in [1], how true
[+237] [1], in addition [+1254] [1], in charge of [+1639] [1], in
connection with [1], in front of [1], in one place [+899+3836] [1],
in the days of [1], in the time of [1], inasmuch as
[+3525+4012+4036] [1], indeed [+237+1142] [1], jumped on
[RP2383] [1], just then [+4047] [1], laid across [RP2130] [1], lay
on [RP2095] [1], look at [RP2098] [1], make guilty of [+2042] [1],

mindful of [RP2098] [1], more and more [+4498] [1], near [+1581]
[1], near [1], on and on [+4498] [1], on the basis of [1], only as
long as [+4012+5989] [1], opposes [+482] [1], place on
[RP2202] [1], placing on [RP2202] [1], put on [RP2222] [1], puts
on [RP2202] [1], puts to [RP2095] [1], putting on [RP2202] [1],
reached [1], reaching [+1181] [1], rest on [RP2058] [1], rest on
[RP2172] [1], resting on [1], returned to [RP2188] [1], returns to
[RP2188] [1], right [+237] [1], seized with [RP2158] [1], set on
[RP2202] [1], show special attention to [RP2098] [1], spend time
[+3531+5989] [1], stirred up against [RP2074] [1], stone [+965]
[1], stopped at [RP2392] [1], struck [+2262] [1], struck [RP2158]
[1], that is why [+4047] [1], them [+1178+2997+3836+3836] [1],
threw arms around [+2158+3836+5549] [1], threw himself
[+4406+4725] [1], throughout [+4246] [1], to face [1], to
overcome [1], to see [1], to their number [+899+3836] [1], to
where [1], travel by ship [+4434+5536] [1], trusted personal
servant [+3131+3836] [1], turning back to [RP2188] [1], turning to
[RP2188] [1], under [1], wearing nothing [+1218+4314] [1], what
[+4005] [1], where [+4005] [1], while [+4012] [1]

Mt 1: 11 of Jeconiah and his brothers **at the time** of the exile to Babylon.
3: 7 of the Pharisees and Sadducees coming **to where** he was baptizing,
3: 13 Then Jesus came from Galilee **to** the Jordan to be baptized by
3: 16 saw the Spirit of God descending like a dove and lighting **on** him.
4: 4 'Man does not live **on** bread alone, but on every word that comes
4: 4 but **on** every word that comes from the mouth of God.' "
4: 5 the holy city and had him stand **on** the highest point of the temple.
4: 6 his angels concerning you, and they will lift you up **in** their hands,
5: 15 Instead they put it **on** its stand, and it gives light to everyone in the
5: 23 if you are offering your gift **at** the altar and there remember that
5: 45 He causes his sun to rise **on** the evil and the good, and sends rain
5: 45 and the good, and sends rain **on** the righteous and the unrighteous.
6: 10 your kingdom come, your will be done **on** earth as it is in heaven.
6: 19 "Do not store up for yourselves treasures **on** earth, where moth
6: 27 Who of you by worrying can add a single hour **to** his life?
7: 24 into practice is like a wise man who built his house **on** the rock.
7: 25 yet it did not fall, because it had its foundation **on** the rock.
7: 26 into practice is like a foolish man who built his house **on** sand.
7: 28 saying these things, the crowds were amazed **at** his teaching,
9: 2 Some men brought to him a paralytic, lying **on** a mat. When Jesus
9: 6 so that you may know that the Son of Man has authority **on** earth
9: 9 he saw a man named Matthew sitting **at** the tax collector's booth.
9: 15 "How can the guests of the bridegroom mourn **while** [+4012] he is
9: 16 "No one **sews** a patch of unshrunk cloth **on** [RP2095] an old
9: 18 But come and **put** your hand **on** [RP2202] her, and she will live."
10: 13 If the home is deserving, let your peace rest **on** it; if it is not,
10: 18 On my account you will be brought **before** governors and kings as
10: 21 children *will* **rebel against** [RP2060] their parents and have them
10: 27 what is whispered in your ear, proclaim **from** the roofs.
10: 29 Yet not one of them will fall **to** the ground apart from the will of
10: 34 "Do not suppose that I have come to bring peace **to** the earth.
11: 29 Take my yoke **upon** you and learn from me, for I am gentle
12: 18 I will put my Spirit **on** him, and he will proclaim justice to the
12: 26 If Satan drives out Satan, he is divided **against** himself. How
12: 28 by the Spirit of God, then the kingdom of God has come **upon** you.
12: 49 Pointing **to** his disciples, he said, "Here are my mother and my
13: 2 got into a boat and sat in it, while all the people stood **on** the shore.
13: 5 Some fell **on** rocky places, where it did not have much soil.
13: 7 Other seed fell **among** thorns, which grew up and choked the
13: 8 Still other seed fell **on** good soil, where it produced a crop—
13: 20 The one who received the seed that fell **on** rocky places is the man
13: 23 But the one who received the seed that fell **on** good soil is the man
13: 48 When it was full, the fishermen pulled it up **on** the shore.
14: 8 she said, "Give me here **on** a platter the head of John the Baptist."
14: 11 His head was brought in **on** a platter and given to the girl,
14: 14 a large crowd, he had compassion **on** them and healed their sick.
14: 19 And he directed the people to sit down **on** the grass.
14: 25 watch of the night Jesus went out to them, walking **on** the lake.
14: 26 When the disciples saw him walking **on** the lake, they were
14: 28 if it's you," Peter replied, "tell me to come to you **on** the water."
14: 29 down out of the boat, walked **on** the water and came toward Jesus.
14: 34 had crossed over, *they* **landed** [+1178+2262+3836] at Gennesaret.
15: 32 his disciples to him and said, "I have compassion **for** these people;
15: 35 He told the crowd to sit down **on** the ground.
16: 18 tell you that you are Peter, and **on** this rock I will build my church,

16: 19 whatever you bind **on** earth will be bound in heaven, and whatever
16: 19 and whatever you loose **on** earth will be loosed in heaven."
17: 6 heard this, they fell **facedown to the ground** [+4725], terrified.
18: 5 "And whoever welcomes a little child like this **in** my name
18: 12 will he not leave the ninety-nine **on** the hills and go to look for the
18: 13 he is happier **about** that one sheep than about the ninety-nine that
18: 13 he is happier about that one sheep than **about** the ninety-nine that
18: 16 so that 'every matter may be established **by** the testimony of two
18: 18 you the truth, whatever you bind **on** earth will be bound in heaven,
18: 18 and whatever you loose **on** earth will be loosed in heaven.
18: 19 I tell you that if two of you **on** earth agree about anything you ask
18: 26 'Be patient **with** me,' he begged, 'and I will pay back everything.'
18: 29 servant fell to his knees and begged him, 'Be patient **with** me,
19: 9 anyone who divorces his wife, except **for** marital unfaithfulness,
19: 28 of all things, when the Son of Man sits **on** his glorious throne,
19: 28 you who have followed me will also sit **on** twelve thrones,
21: 5 gentle and riding **on** a donkey, on a colt, the foal of a donkey.' "
21: 5 gentle and riding on a donkey, **on** a colt, the foal of a donkey.' "
21: 7 the donkey and the colt, **placed** their cloaks on [RP2202] them,
21: 19 Seeing a fig tree **by** the road, he went up to it but found nothing on
21: 19 by the road, he went up **to** it but found nothing on it except leaves.
21: 44 He who falls **on** this stone will be broken to pieces, but he on
21: 44 will be broken to pieces, but he **on** whom it falls will be crushed."
22: 5 no attention and went off—one to his field, another **to** his business.
22: 9 Go **to** the street corners and invite to the banquet anyone you find.'
22: 33 When the crowds heard this, they were astonished **at** his teaching.
22: 34 had silenced the Sadducees, the Pharisees got together. [RPG]
23: 2 "The teachers of the law and the Pharisees sit **in** Moses' seat.
23: 4 *They* tie up heavy loads and **put** them on [RP2202] men's
23: 9 And do not call anyone **on** earth 'father,' for you have one Father,
23: 35 so **upon** you will come all the righteous blood that has been shed
23: 35 upon you will come all the righteous blood that has been shed **on**
23: 36 I tell you the truth, all this will come **upon** this generation.
24: 2 "I tell you the truth, not one stone here will be left **on** another;
24: 3 As Jesus was sitting **on** the Mount of Olives, the disciples came to
24: 5 For many will come **in** my name, claiming, 'I am the Christ,'
24: 7 Nation will rise **against** nation, and kingdom against kingdom.
24: 7 Nation will rise against nation, and kingdom **against** kingdom.
24: 17 Let no one **on** the roof of his house go down to take anything out
24: 30 They will see the Son of Man coming **on** the clouds of the sky,
24: 33 you see all these things, you know that it is near, **right** at the door.
24: 45 whom the master has put in charge **of** the servants in his household
24: 47 I tell you the truth, he will put him in charge **of** all his possessions.
25: 21 You have been faithful **with** a few things; I will put you in charge
25: 21 faithful with a few things; I will put you in charge **of** many things.
25: 23 You have been faithful **with** a few things; I will put you in charge
25: 23 faithful with a few things; I will put you in charge **of** many things.
25: 31 all the angels with him, he will sit **on** his throne in heavenly glory.
25: 40 'I tell you the truth, **whatever** [+4012] you did for one of the least
25: 45 'I tell you the truth, **whatever** [+4012] you did not do for one of
26: 7 which she poured **on** his head as he was reclining at the table.
26: 12 When she poured this perfume **on** my body, she did it to prepare
26: 39 he fell with his **face to the ground** [+4725] and prayed, "My
26: 50 Jesus replied, "Friend, do **what** [+4005] you came for."
26: 50 Then the men stepped forward, **seized** [+2095+3836+5931] Jesus
26: 55 [NIE] "Am I leading a rebellion, that you have come out with
26: 64 right hand of the Mighty One and coming **on** the clouds of heaven."
27: 19 While Pilate was sitting **on** the judge's seat, his wife sent him this
27: 25 the people answered, "Let his blood be **on** us and on our children!"
27: 25 the people answered, "Let his blood be on us and **on** our children!"
27: 27 and gathered the whole company of soldiers **around** him.
27: 29 twisted together a crown of thorns and **set** it on [RP2202] his head.
27: 42 him come down now from the cross, and we will believe **in** him.
27: 43 He trusts **in** God. Let God rescue him now if he wants him,
27: 45 From the sixth hour until the ninth hour darkness came **over** all the
28: 14 If this report gets **to** the governor, we will satisfy him and keep you
28: 18 "All authority in heaven and **on** earth has been given to me.

Mk 1: 22 The people were amazed **at** his teaching, because he taught them
1: 45 no longer enter a town openly but stayed outside **in** lonely places.
2: 10 But that you may know that the Son of Man has authority **on** earth
2: 14 he saw Levi son of Alphaeus sitting **at** the tax collector's booth.
2: 21 "No one sews a patch of unshrunk cloth on an old garment.
2: 26 **In the days of** Abiathar the high priest, he entered the house of
3: 5 deeply distressed **at** their stubborn hearts, said to the man,
3: 24 If a kingdom is divided **against** itself, that kingdom cannot stand.
3: 25 If a house is divided **against** itself, that house cannot stand.

3: 26 And if Satan **opposes** [+482] himself and is divided, he cannot
4: 1 while all the people were **along** the shore at the water's edge.
4: 5 Some fell **on** rocky places, where it did not have much soil.
4: 16 Others, like seed sown **on** rocky places, hear the word and at once
4: 20 Others, like seed sown **on** good soil, hear the word, accept it,
4: 21 put it under a bowl or a bed? Instead, don't you put it **on** its stand?
4: 26 the kingdom of God is like. A man scatters seed **on** the ground.
4: 31 which is the smallest seed [RPG] you plant in the ground.
4: 31 a mustard seed, which is the smallest seed you plant **in** the ground.
4: 38 Jesus was in the stern, sleeping **on** a cushion. The disciples woke
5: 21 a large crowd gathered **around** him while he was by the lake.
6: 25 "I want you to give me right now the head of John the Baptist **on** a
6: 28 and brought back his head **on** a platter. He presented it to the girl,
6: 34 Jesus landed and saw a large crowd, he had compassion **on** them,
6: 39 them to have all the people sit down in groups **on** the green grass.
6: 47 the boat was in the middle of the lake, and he was alone **on** land.
6: 48 fourth watch of the night he went out to them, walking **on** the lake.
6: 49 but when they saw him walking **on** the lake, they thought he was a
6: 52 for they had not understood **about** the loaves; their hearts were
6: 53 When they had crossed over, *they* **landed** [+1178+2262+3836] at
      Gennesaret and anchored there.
6: 55 and carried the sick **on** mats to wherever they heard he was.
7: 30 She went home and found her child lying **on** the bed,
8: 2 "I have compassion **for** these people; they have already been with
8: 4 "But where **in** this remote place can anyone get enough bread to
8: 6 He told the crowd to sit down **on** the ground. When he had taken
8: 25 Once more Jesus **put** his hands on [RP2202] the man's eyes.
9: 3 dazzling white, whiter than anyone **in** the world could bleach them.
9: 12 then is it written that [NIE] the Son of Man must suffer much
9: 13 to him everything they wished, just as it is written **about** him."
9: 20 He fell **to** the ground and rolled around, foaming at the mouth.
9: 22 to kill him. But if you can do anything, take pity **on** us and help us."
9: 37 "Whoever welcomes one of these little children **in** my name
9: 39 "No one who does a miracle **in** my name can in the next moment
10: 11 and marries another woman commits adultery **against** her.
10: 16 the children in his arms, put his hands **on** them and blessed them.
10: 22 **At** this the man's face fell. He went away sad, because he had great
10: 24 The disciples were amazed **at** his words. But Jesus said again,
11: 2 will find a colt tied there, [NIE] which no one has ever ridden.
11: 4 They went and found a colt outside **in** the street, tied at a doorway.
11: 7 brought the colt to Jesus and threw their cloaks over it, he sat **on** it.
11: 13 *When he* **reached** [+2262] it, he found nothing but leaves,
11: 18 feared him, because the whole crowd was amazed **at** his teaching.
12: 14 but you teach the way of God **in accordance with** the truth.
12: 17 and to God what is God's." And they were amazed **at** him.
12: 26 **in the account** of the bush, how God said to him, 'I am the God of
12: 32 "You are **right** [+237] in saying that God is one and there is no
13: 2 "Not one stone here will be left **on** another; every one will be
13: 6 Many will come **in** my name, claiming, 'I am he,' and will deceive
13: 8 Nation will rise **against** nation, and kingdom against kingdom.
13: 8 Nation will rise against nation, and kingdom **against** kingdom.
13: 9 On account of me you will stand **before** governors and kings as
13: 12 Children *will* **rebel against** [RP2060] their parents and have them
13: 15 Let no one **on** the roof of his house go down or enter the house to
13: 29 these things happening, you know that it is near, **right at** the door.
14: 35 he fell **to** the ground and prayed that if possible the hour might
14: 48 [NIE] "Am I leading a rebellion," said Jesus, "that you have come
14: 51 young man, **wearing nothing** [+1218+4314] but a linen garment,
15: 22 They brought Jesus **to** the place called Golgotha (which means The
15: 24 up his clothes, they cast lots [NIE] to see what each would get.
15: 33 At the sixth hour darkness came **over** the whole land until the ninth
15: 46 of rock. Then he rolled a stone **against** the entrance of the tomb.
16: 2 of the week, just after sunrise, they were on their way **to** the tomb
16: 18 *they will* **place** their hands on [RP2202] sick people, and they will

Lk 1: 12 saw him, he was startled and *was* **gripped with** [RP2158] fear.
1: 14 and delight to you, and many will rejoice **because of** his birth,
1: 16 Many of the people of Israel *will he* **bring back to** [RP2188] the
1: 17 *to* **turn** the hearts of the fathers **to** [RP2188] their children
1: 29 Mary was greatly troubled **at** his words and wondered what kind of
1: 33 and he will reign **over** the house of Jacob forever, his kingdom will
1: 35 angel answered, "The Holy Spirit *will* **come upon** [RP2088] you,
1: 47 and my spirit rejoices **in** God my Savior,
1: 48 for *he has been* **mindful of** [RP2098] the humble state of his
1: 59 and they were going to name him **after** his father Zechariah,
1: 65 The neighbors were [NIE] all filled with awe, and throughout the
2: 8 out in the fields nearby, keeping watch **over** their flocks at night.

2: 14 in the highest, and **on** earth peace to men on whom his favor rests."
2: 20 and praising God **for** all the things they had heard and seen,
2: 25 for the consolation of Israel, and the Holy Spirit was **upon** him.
2: 33 child's father and mother marveled **at** what was said about him.
2: 40 he was filled with wisdom, and the grace of God was **upon** him.
2: 47 Everyone who heard him was amazed **at** his understanding
3: 2 **during** the high priesthood of Annas and Caiaphas, the word of
3: 2 the word of God came **to** John son of Zechariah in the desert.
3: 20 Herod added this **to** them all: He locked John up in prison.
3: 22 and the Holy Spirit descended **on** him in bodily form like a dove.
4: 4 Jesus answered, "It is written: 'Man does not live **on** bread alone.' "
4: 9 to Jerusalem and had him stand **on** the highest point of the temple.
4: 11 they will lift you up **in** their hands, so that you will not strike your
4: 18 "The Spirit of the Lord is **on** me,
4: 22 and were amazed **at** the gracious words that came from his lips.
4: 25 *I assure* [+237+3306] you that there were many widows in Israel
4: 25 when the sky was shut **for** three and a half years and there was a
4: 25 and there was a severe famine **throughout** [+4246] the land.
4: 27 And there were many in Israel with leprosy **in the time of** Elisha
4: 29 and took him to the brow of the hill **on** which the town was built,
4: 32 They were amazed **at** his teaching, because his message had
4: 36 **[NIE]** All the people were amazed and said to each other,
4: 43 to the other towns also, because **that is why** [+4047] I was sent."
5: 5 caught anything. But **because** you say so, I will let down the nets."
5: 9 and all his companions were astonished **at** the catch of fish they
5: 11 So they pulled their boats up **on** shore, left everything
5: 12 he fell **with** his **face to the ground** [+4725] and begged him,
5: 18 Some men came carrying a paralytic **on** a mat and tried to take him
5: 19 they went up **on** the roof and lowered him on his mat through the
5: 24 But that you may know that the Son of Man has authority **on** earth
5: 25 took what he had been lying **on** and went home praising God.
5: 27 and saw a tax collector by the name of Levi sitting **at** his tax booth.
5: 36 a patch from a new garment and **sews** it **on** [RP2095] an old one.
6: 17 He went down with them and stood **on** a level place. A large crowd
6: 29 If someone strikes you **on** one cheek, turn to him the other also.
6: 35 of the Most High, because he is kind **to** the ungrateful and wicked.
6: 48 a house, who dug down deep and laid the foundation **on** rock.
6: 49 like a man who built a house **on** the ground without a foundation.
7: 13 the Lord saw her, his heart went out **to** her and he said, "Don't cry."
7: 44 You did not give me any water **for** my feet, but she wet my feet
8: 6 Some fell **on** rock, and when it came up, the plants withered
8: 13 Those **on** the rock are the ones who receive the word with joy
8: 16 Instead, he puts it **on** a stand, so that those who come in can see the
8: 27 When Jesus stepped **ashore** [+1178], he was met by a
9: 1 he gave them power and authority *to* **drive out** all demons
9: 5 your feet when you leave their town, as a testimony **against** them."
9: 38 "Teacher, I beg you *to* **look at** [RP2098] my son, for he is my only
9: 43 And they were all amazed **at** the greatness of God. While everyone
9: 43 While everyone was marveling **at** all that Jesus did, he said to his
9: 48 "Whoever welcomes this little child **in** my name welcomes me;
9: 62 "No one *who* **puts** his hand **to** [RP2095] the plow and looks back is
10: 6 If a man of peace is there, your peace *will* **rest on** [RP2058] him;
10: 6 is there, your peace will rest on him; if not, it will return **to** you.
10: 9 and tell them, 'The kingdom of God *is* **near** [+1581] you.'
10: 19 and scorpions and **to overcome** all the power of the enemy;
10: 34 Then *he* **put** the man **on** [RP2097] his own donkey, took him to an
10: 35 **[NIE]** The next day he took out two silver coins and gave them to
11: 17 "Any kingdom divided **against** itself will be ruined, and a house
11: 17 itself will be ruined, and a house divided **against** itself will fall.
11: 18 If Satan is divided **against** himself, how can his kingdom stand?
11: 20 by the finger of God, then the kingdom of God has come **to** you.
11: 22 he takes away the armor **in** which the man trusted and divides up
11: 33 Instead he puts it **on** its stand, so that those who come in may see
12: 3 in the ear in the inner rooms will be proclaimed **from** the roofs.
12: 11 "When you are brought **before** synagogues, rulers and authorities,
12: 14 "Man, who appointed me a judge or an arbiter **between** you?"
12: 25 Who of you by worrying can add a single hour **to** his life?
12: 42 whom the master puts in charge **of** his servants to give them their
12: 44 I tell you the truth, he will put him in charge **of** all his possessions.
12: 49 "I have come to bring fire **on** the earth, and how I wish it were
12: 52 against each other, three **against** two and two against three.
12: 52 against each other, three against two and two **against** three.
12: 53 They will be divided, father **against** son and son against father,
12: 53 They will be divided, father against son and son **against** father,
12: 53 mother **against** daughter and daughter against mother,
12: 53 mother against daughter and daughter **against** mother,

12: 53 mother-in-law **against** daughter-in-law and daughter-in-law
12: 53 daughter-in-law and daughter-in-law **against** mother-in-law."
12: 54 "When you see a cloud rising **in** the west, immediately you say,
12: 58 As you are going with your adversary **to** the magistrate, try hard to
13: 4 Or those eighteen who died when the tower in Siloam fell **on**
13: 17 but the people were delighted **with** all the wonderful things he was
14: 31 men to oppose the one coming **against** him with twenty thousand?
15: 4 in the open country and go **after** the lost sheep until he finds it?
15: 5 when he finds it, *he* joyfully **puts** it **on** [RP2202] his shoulders
15: 7 **over** one sinner who repents than over ninety-nine righteous
15: 7 than **over** ninety-nine righteous persons who do not need to repent.
15: 10 there is rejoicing in the presence of the angels of God **over** one
15: 20 **threw** his **arms around** [+2158+3836+5549] him and kissed him.
17: 16 He **threw** himself [+4406+4725] at Jesus' feet and thanked him—
17: 31 On that day no one who is **on** the roof of his house, with his goods
17: 34 I tell you, on that night two people will be **in** one bed; one will be
17: 35 Two women will be grinding grain **together** [+899+3836];
18: 4 "**For** some time he refused. But finally he said to himself,
18: 7 out to him day and night? Will he keep putting **[NIE]** them off?
18: 8 when the Son of Man comes, will he find faith **on** the earth?"
18: 9 To some who were confident **of** their own righteousness
19: 4 he ran ahead and climbed **[NIE]** a sycamore-fig tree to see him,
19: 5 When Jesus **reached** [+2262] the spot, he looked up and said to
19: 14 after him to say, 'We don't want this man to be **[NIE]** our king.'
19: 23 Why then didn't you put my money **on** deposit,
19: 27 But those enemies of mine who did not want me to be king **over**
19: 30 will find a colt tied there, **[NIE]** which no one has ever ridden.
19: 35 threw their cloaks on the colt and put Jesus **on** [RP2097] it.
19: 41 As he approached Jerusalem and saw the city, he wept **over** it
19: 43 The days will come **upon** you when your enemies will build an
19: 44 within your walls. They will not leave one stone **on** another,
20: 18 Everyone who falls **on** that stone will be broken to pieces,
20: 18 will be broken to pieces, but he **on** whom it falls will be crushed."
20: 19 looked for a way *to* **arrest** [+2095+3836+5931] him immediately,
20: 21 partiality but teach the way of God **in accordance with** the truth.
20: 26 there in public. And astonished **by** his answer, they became silent.
20: 37 But **in the account** of the bush, even Moses showed that the dead
21: 6 the time will come when not one stone will be left **on** another;
21: 8 For many will come **in** my name, claiming, 'I am he,' and,
21: 10 "Nation will rise **against** nation, and kingdom against kingdom.
21: 10 "Nation will rise against nation, and kingdom **against** kingdom.
21: 12 all this, *they will* **lay** hands **on** [RP2095] you and persecute you.
21: 12 and prisons, and you will be brought **before** kings and governors,
21: 23 There will be great distress **in** the land and wrath against this
21: 25 **On** the earth, nations will be in anguish and perplexity at the
21: 34 of life, and that day will close **on** you unexpectedly like a trap.
21: 35 For *it will* **come upon** [RP2082] all those who live on the face of
21: 35 For it will come upon all those who live **on** the face of the whole
22: 21 But the hand of him who is going to betray me is with mine **on** the
22: 30 may eat and drink **at** my table in my kingdom and sit on thrones,
22: 30 may eat and drink at my table in my kingdom and sit **on** thrones,
22: 40 *On* **reaching** [+1181] the place, he said to them, "Pray that you will
22: 44 and his sweat was like drops of blood falling **to** the ground.
22: 52 and the elders, who had come **for** him, "Am I leading a rebellion,
22: 52 who had come for him, **[NIE]** "Am I leading a rebellion,
22: 53 with you in the temple courts, and you did not lay a hand **on** me.
22: 59 About an hour later another asserted, "**Certainly** [+237] this
23: 1 Then the whole assembly rose and led him off **to** Pilate.
23: 28 and said to them, "Daughters of Jerusalem, do not weep **for** me;
23: 28 do not weep for me; weep **for** yourselves and for your children.
23: 28 do not weep for me; weep for yourselves and **for** your children.
23: 30 " 'they will say to the mountains, "Fall **on** us!" and to the hills,
23: 33 When they came to the place called the Skull, there they crucified
23: 38 There was a written notice **above** him, which read: THIS IS THE
23: 44 and darkness came **over** the whole land until the ninth hour,
23: 48 When all the people who had gathered **to** *witness* this sight saw
24: 1 the women took the spices they had prepared and went **to** the tomb.
24: 12 Peter, however, got up and ran **to** the tomb. Bending over,
24: 22 our women amazed us. They went **to** the tomb early this morning
24: 24 Then some of our companions went **to** the tomb and found it just
24: 25 and how slow of heart to believe **[NIE]** all that the prophets have
24: 47 and forgiveness of sins will be preached **in** his name to all nations,
24: 49 I am going to send **[NIE]** you what my Father has promised;

Jn 1: 32 The Spirit come down from heaven as a dove and remain **on** him.
     1: 33 'The man **on** whom you see the Spirit come down and remain is he
     1: 33 and remain **[RPG]** is he who will baptize with the Holy Spirit.'

1:51 the angels of God ascending and descending **on** the Son of Man."
3:36 rejects the Son will not see life, for God's wrath remains **on** him."
4: 6 and Jesus, tired as he was from the journey, sat down **by** the well.
4:27 **Just then** [+4047] his disciples returned and were surprised to
5: 2 Now there is in Jerusalem **near** the Sheep Gate a pool, which in
6: 2 because they saw the miraculous signs he had performed **on** the
6:16 When evening came, his disciples went down **to** the lake,
6:19 they saw Jesus approaching the boat, walking **on** the water;
6:21 and immediately the boat **reached** [+1181] the shore where they
7:30 they tried to seize him, but no one **laid** a hand **on** [RP2095] him,
7:44 wanted to seize him, but no one **laid** a hand **on** [RP2095] him.
8: 3 and the Pharisees brought in a woman caught **in** adultery.
8: 4 this woman *was* **caught in the act** [+900+2898] of adultery.
8: 7 of you is without sin, let him be the first to throw a stone **at** her."
8:59 At this, they picked up stones to **stone** [+965] him, but Jesus hid
9: 6 some mud with the saliva, and **put** it **on** [RP2222] the man's eyes.
9:15 "*He* **put** mud **on** [RP2202] my eyes," the man replied, "and I
11:38 It was a cave with a stone **laid across** [RP2130] the entrance.
12:14 Jesus found a young donkey and sat **upon** it, as it is written,
12:15 of Zion; see, your king is coming, seated **on** a donkey's colt."
12:16 did they realize that these things had been written **about** him
13:18 'He who shares my bread has lifted up his heel **against** me.'
13:25 Leaning back **against** [+3836+5111] Jesus, he asked him,
17: 4 I have brought you glory **on** earth by completing the work you
18: 4 Jesus, knowing all that was going to happen **to** him, went out
19:13 and sat down **on** the judge's seat at a place known as the Stone
19:19 Pilate had a notice prepared and fastened **to** the cross. It read:
19:24 divided my garments among them and cast lots **for** my clothing."
19:31 Because the Jews did not want the bodies left **on** the crosses during
19:33 But when they came **to** Jesus and found that he was already dead,
20: 7 as well as the burial cloth that had been **around** Jesus' head.
21: 1 Jesus appeared again to his disciples, **by** the Sea of Tiberias.
21:20 (This was the one who had leaned back **against** [+3836+5111]

Ac 1: 8 will receive power *when* the Holy Spirit **comes on** [RP2088] you;
1:15 In those days Peter stood up among the believers (a group **[NIE]**
1:21 with us the whole time the Lord Jesus went in and out **among** us,
1:26 Then they cast lots, and the lot fell **to** Matthias; so he was added to
2: 1 Pentecost came, they were all together **in** [+899+3836] **one place.**
2: 3 be tongues of fire that separated and came to rest **on** each of them.
2:17 " 'In the last days, God says, I will pour out my Spirit **on** all people.
2:18 Even **on** my servants, both men and women, I will pour out my
2:18 Even on my servants, **[RPG]** both men and women, I will pour
2:19 show wonders in the heaven above and signs **on** the earth below,
2:26 is glad and my tongue rejoices; my body also will live **in** hope,
2:30 on oath that he would place one of his descendants **on** his throne.
2:38 **in** the name of Jesus Christ for the forgiveness of your sins.
2:44 All the believers were **together** [+899+3836] and had everything
2:47 And the Lord added **to** [+899+3836] **their number** daily those
3: 1 and John were going up to the temple **at** the time of prayer
3:10 they recognized him as the same man who used to sit begging **at**
3:10 filled with wonder and amazement **at** what had happened to him.
3:11 and came running to them **in** the place called Solomon's
3:12 he said to them: "Men of Israel, why does **[NIE]** this surprise you?
3:16 **By** faith in the name of Jesus, this man whom you see and know
4: 5 **[NIE]** The next day the rulers, elders and teachers of the law met
4: 9 If we are being called to account today **for** an act of kindness
4:17 But to stop this thing from spreading **any further** [+4498] among
4:17 we must warn these men to speak no longer to anyone **in** this
4:18 commanded them not to speak or teach at all **in** the name of Jesus.
4:21 because all the people were praising God **for** what had happened.
4:22 For the man **[NIE]** who was miraculously healed was over forty
4:26 and the rulers gather **together** [+899+3836] against the Lord
4:27 **Indeed** [+237+1142] Herod and Pontius Pilate met together with
4:27 the people of Israel in this city **to conspire against** your holy
4:29 **consider** [RP2078] their threats and enable your servants to speak
4:33 resurrection of the Lord Jesus, and much grace was **upon** them all.
5: 5 And great fear **seized** [+1181] all who heard what had happened.
5: 9 The feet of the men who buried your husband are **at** the door,
5:11 Great fear **seized** [+1181] the whole church and all who heard
5:11 the whole church and **[RPG]** all who heard about these events.
5:15 brought the sick into the streets and laid them **on** beds and mats
5:18 *They* **arrested** [+2095+3836+5931] the apostles and put them in
5:23 the jail securely locked, with the guards standing **at** the doors;
5:28 "We gave you strict orders not to teach **in** this name," he said.
5:28 are determined *to* **make** us **guilty of** [+2042] this man's blood."
5:30 from the dead—whom you had killed by hanging him **on** a tree.

5:35 of Israel, consider carefully what you intend to do **to** these men.
5:40 Then they ordered them not to speak **in** the name of Jesus,
6: 3 and wisdom. We will turn **[NIE]** this responsibility over to them
7:10 king of Egypt; so he made him ruler **over** Egypt and all his palace.
7:10 so he made him ruler over Egypt and [UBS+ *over*] all his palace.
7:11 "Then a famine **struck** [+2262] all Egypt and Canaan,
7:18 who knew nothing about Joseph, became ruler **of** Egypt.
7:23 he **decided** [+326+2840+3836] to visit his fellow Israelites.
7:27 Moses aside and said, 'Who made you ruler and judge **over** us?
7:33 the place **where** [4005] you are standing is holy ground.
7:54 they heard this, they were furious and gnashed their teeth **at** him.
7:57 ears and, yelling at the top of their voices, they all rushed **at** him,
8: 1 On that day a great persecution broke out **against** the church at
8: 2 Godly men buried Stephen and mourned deeply **for** him.
8:16 because the Holy Spirit *had* not yet **come upon** [RP1639+2158]
8:17 Then Peter and John **placed** their hands **on** [RP2202] them,
8:24 so that nothing you have said *may* **happen to** [RP2088] me."
8:26 Now an angel of the Lord said to Philip, "Go south to the road—
8:27 an important official **in charge** [+1639] **of** all the treasury of
8:28 and on his way home was sitting **in** his chariot reading the book of
8:32 "He was led like a sheep **to** the slaughter, and as a lamb before he
8:36 they came to some water and the eunuch said, "Look, here is water.
9: 4 He fell **to** the ground and heard a voice say to him, "Saul, Saul,
9:11 "Go to the house of Judas **on** Straight Street and ask for a man from
9:17 **Placing** his hands **on** [RP2202] Saul, he said, "Brother Saul,
9:21 And hasn't he come here to take them as prisoners **to** the chief
9:33 a paralytic *who had been* **bedridden** [+2879+3187] for eight years.
9:35 in Lydda and Sharon saw him and **turned to** [RP2188] the Lord.
9:42 known all over Joppa, and many people believed **in** the Lord.
10: 9 and approaching the city, Peter went up **on** the roof to pray.
10:10 the meal was being prepared, he **fell into** a **trance** [+1181+1749].
10:11 and something like a large sheet being let down **to** earth by its four
10:16 This happened **[NIE]** three times, and immediately the sheet was
10:17 out where Simon's house was and **stopped at** [RP2392] the gate.
10:25 the house, Cornelius met him and fell **at** his feet in reverence.
10:34 "I now realize **how true** [+237] it is that God does not show
10:39 and in Jerusalem. They killed him by hanging him **on** a tree,
10:44 the Holy Spirit **came on** [RP2158] all who heard the message.
10:45 gift of the Holy Spirit had been poured out even **on** the Gentiles.
11:10 This happened **[NIE]** three times, and then it was all pulled up to
11:11 then three men who had been sent to me from Caesarea stopped at
11:15 the Holy Spirit **came on** [RP2158] them as he had come on us at
11:15 the Holy Spirit came on them as he had come **on** us at the
11:17 who believed **in** the Lord Jesus Christ, who was I to think that I
11:19 **in connection with** Stephen traveled as far as Phoenicia,
11:21 great number of people believed and **turned to** [RP2188] the Lord.
11:28 that a severe famine would spread **over** the entire Roman world.
11:28 Roman world. (This happened **during** *the reign of* Claudius.)
12:10 and second guards and came **to** the iron gate leading to the city.
12:12 he went **to** the house of Mary the mother of John, also called Mark,
12:20 a **trusted personal servant** [+3131+3836] of the king, they asked
12:21 sat **on** his throne and delivered a public address to the people.
13:11 Now the hand of the Lord is **against** you. You are going to be
13:11 Immediately mist and darkness came **over** him, and he groped
13:12 he believed, for he was amazed **at** the teaching about the Lord.
13:31 and for many days he was seen by those who had traveled with
13:50 *They* **stirred up** persecution **against** [RP2074] Paul and Barnabas,
13:51 So they shook the dust from their feet in protest **against** them
14: 3 spent considerable time there, speaking boldly **for** the Lord,
14: 3 who confirmed **[NIE]** the message of his grace by enabling them
14:10 and called out, "Stand up **on** your feet!" At that, the man jumped up
14:13 brought bulls and wreaths **to** the city gates because he
14:15 telling you *to* **turn** from these worthless things **to** [RP2188] the
15:10 why do you try to test God *by* **putting on** [RP2202] the necks of
15:17 and all the Gentiles who **bear** [RP2126+2093] my name, says the
15:17 and all the Gentiles who **bear** [RP2093+2126] my name, says the
15:19 it difficult for the Gentiles who *are* **turning to** [RP2188] God.
15:31 The people read it and were glad **for** its encouraging message.
16:18 She kept this up **for** many days. Finally Paul became so troubled
16:19 and dragged them into the marketplace **to face** the authorities.
16:31 They replied, "Believe **in** the Lord Jesus, and you will be saved—
17: 2 and on three Sabbath days he reasoned with them from the
17: 6 dragged Jason and some other brothers **before** the city officials,
17:14 The brothers immediately sent Paul **to** the coast, but Silas
17:19 they took him and brought him **to** a meeting of the Areopagus,
17:26 nation of men, that they should inhabit **[NIE]** the whole earth;

18: 6 in protest and said to them, "Your blood be **on** your own heads!
18:12 the Jews made a united attack on Paul and brought him **into** court.
18:20 When they asked him *to* **spend** more **time** [*+3531+5989*] with
19: 6 the Holy Spirit came **on** them, and they spoke in tongues
19: 8 entered the synagogue and spoke boldly there **for** three months,
19:10 This went on **for** two years, so that all the Jews and Greeks who
19:12 and aprons that had touched him were taken **to** the sick,
19:13 the name of the Lord Jesus **over** those who were demon-possessed.
19:16 Then the man who had the evil spirit **jumped on** [*RP2383*] them
19:17 living in Ephesus, they *were* all **seized with** [*RP2158*] fear,
19:34 he was a Jew, they all shouted in unison **for** about two hours:
20: 9 Seated **in** a window was a young man named Eutychus, who was
20: 9 was sinking into a deep sleep as Paul talked **on and on** [*+4498*]
20:11 broke bread and ate. After talking **[NIE]** until daylight, he left.
20:13 We went on ahead **to** the ship and sailed for Assos, where we were
20:13 We went on ahead **to** the ship and sailed **for** Assos, where we were
20:37 They all wept as *they* **embraced** [*+2158+3836+5549*] him and
20:38 What grieved them most was **[NIE]** his statement that they would
21: 5 us out of the city, and there **on** the beach we knelt to pray.
21:23 There are four men with us who have made a vow. **[NIE]**
21:24 join in their purification rites and pay **[NIE]** their expenses,
21:27 stirred up the whole crowd and **seized** [*+2095+3836+5931*] him,
21:32 at once took some officers and soldiers and ran down **to** the crowd.
21:35 When Paul **reached** [*+1181*] the steps, the violence of the mob was
21:40 Paul stood **on** the steps and motioned to the crowd.
22:19 to another to imprison and beat those who believe **in** you.
23:30 I also ordered his accusers to present **to** you their case against him.
24: 4 But in order not to weary you **[NIE]** further, I would request that
24:19 who ought to be here **before** you and bring charges if they have
24:20 what crime they found in me when I stood **before** the Sanhedrin—
24:21 the resurrection of the dead that I am on trial **before** you today.' "
25: 6 and the next day he **convened the court** [*+1037+2767+3836*] and
25: 9 up to Jerusalem and stand trial **before** me there on these charges?"
25:10 "I am now standing **before** Caesar's court, where I ought to be tried.
25:12 he declared: "You have appealed to Caesar. **To** Caesar you will go!"
25:17 but convened the **court** [*+1037*] the next day and ordered the man
25:26 Therefore I have brought him before **[NIE]** all of you,
25:26 him before all of you, and especially **before** you, King Agrippa,
26: 2 I consider myself fortunate to *stand* **before** you today as I make
26: 6 **because of** my hope in what God has promised our fathers that I
26:16 'Now get up and stand **on** your feet. I have appeared to you to
26:18 them from darkness to light, and from the power of Satan **to** God,
26:20 I preached that they should repent and **turn to** [*RP2188*] God
27:20 When neither sun nor stars appeared **for** many days and the storm
27:43 those who could swim to jump overboard first and get **to** land.
27:44 The rest were to get there **on** planks or on pieces of the ship.
27:44 The rest were to get there **on** planks or **on** pieces of the ship.
27:44 on pieces of the ship. In this way everyone **reached** land in safety.
28: 3 *as he* **put** it **on** [*RP2202*] the fire, a viper, driven out by the heat,
28: 6 but after waiting **a long time** [*+4498*] and seeing nothing unusual

Ro   1:10 **in** my prayers at all times; and I pray that now at last by God's will
1:18 The wrath of God is being revealed from heaven **against** all the
2: 2 Now we know that God's judgment **against** those who do such
2: 9 will be trouble and distress **for** every human being who does evil:
4: 5 who does not work but trusts **[NIE]** God who justifies the wicked,
4: 9 Is this blessedness *only* **for** the circumcised, or also for the
4: 9 only for the circumcised, or also **for** the uncircumcised?
4:18 Abraham **in** hope believed and so became the father of many
4:24 for us who believe **in** him who raised Jesus our Lord from the
5: 2 we now stand. And we rejoice **in** the hope of the glory of God.
5:12 in this way death came to all men, **because** [*+4005*] all sinned—
5:14 even **over** those who did not sin by breaking a command, as did
5:14 even over those who did not sin **by** breaking a command, as did
6:21 What benefit did you reap at that time **from** the things you are now
7: 1 has authority over a man **only as long as** [*+4012+5989*] he lives?
8:20 its own choice, but by the will of the one who subjected it, **in** hope
9: 5 the human ancestry of Christ, who is God **over** all, forever praised!
9:23 What if he did this to make the riches of his glory known **to** the
9:28 For the Lord will carry out his sentence **on** earth with speed
9:33 and the one who trusts **in** him will never be put to shame."
10:11 "Anyone who trusts **in** him will never be put to shame."
10:19 "I will make you envious **by** those who are not a nation;
10:19 I will make you angry **by** a nation that has no understanding."
11:13 **Inasmuch as** [*+3525+4012+4036*] I am the apostle to the Gentiles,
11:22 sternness **to** those who fell, but kindness to you, provided that you
11:22 sternness to those who fell, but kindness **to** you, provided that you

12:20 to drink. In doing this, you will heap burning coals **on** his head."
15: 3 "The insults of those who insult you *have* **fallen on** [*RP2158*] me."
15:12 will arise to rule over the nations; the Gentiles will hope **in** him."
15:20 so that I would not be building **on** someone else's foundation.
16:19 has heard about your obedience, so I am full of joy **over** you;

1Co 1: 4 thank God for you **because of** his grace given you in Christ Jesus.
2: 9 no **[NIE]** mind has conceived what God has prepared for those
3:12 If any man **builds on** [*RP2224*] this foundation using gold,
6: 1 dare he take it **before** the ungodly for judgment instead of before
6: 1 dare he take it before the ungodly for judgment instead of **before**
6: 6 goes to law against another—and this **in front of** unbelievers!
7: 5 Then come **together** [*+899+3836*] again so that Satan will not
7:36 If anyone thinks he is acting improperly **toward** the virgin he is
7:39 A woman is bound to her husband **as long as** [*+4012+5989*] he
8: 5 or **on** earth (as indeed there are many "gods" and many "lords"),
9:10 they ought to do so **in** the hope of sharing in the harvest.
9:10 they ought to do so in the hope **[RPG]** of sharing in the harvest.
11:10 the woman ought to have a sign of authority **on** her head.
11:20 *When* you **come together** [*+899+3836+5302*], it is not the Lord's
13: 6 Love does not delight **in** evil but rejoices with the truth.
14:16 those who do not understand say "Amen" **to** your thanksgiving,
14:23 So if the whole church **comes together** [*+899+3836+5302*] and
14:25 So he will **fall down** [*+4406+4725*] and worship God, exclaiming,
16:17 I was glad **when** Stephanas, Fortunatus and Achaicus arrived,

2Co 1: 4 who comforts us **in** all our troubles,
1: 9 But this happened that we might not rely **on** ourselves but on God,
1: 9 But this happened that we might not rely on ourselves but **on** God,
1:23 I **call** [*RP2126*] God as my witness that it was in order to spare
2: 3 I had confidence **in** all of you, that you would all share my joy.
3:13 who would put a veil **over** his face to keep the Israelites from
3:14 for to this day the same veil remains **when** the old covenant is
3:15 to this day when Moses is read, a veil **covers** [*+3023*] their hearts.
5: 4 **because** [*+4005*] we do not wish to be unclothed but to be clothed
7: 4 greatly encouraged; **in** all our troubles my joy knows no bounds.
7: 7 by his coming but also by the comfort **[NIE]** you had given him.
7:13 **In addition** [*+1254*] to our own encouragement, we were
7:13 we were especially delighted **to see** how happy Titus was,
7:14 so our boasting about you **to** Titus has proved to be true as well.
9: 6 and whoever sows **generously** [*+2330*] will also reap generously.
9: 6 and whoever sows generously will also reap **generously** [*+2330*].
9:13 men will praise God **for** the obedience that accompanies your
9:14 go out to you, because of the surpassing grace God has **given** you.
9:15 Thanks be to God **for** his indescribable gift!
10: 2 **toward** some people who think that we live by the standards of
10: 7 he should consider again **[NIE]** that we belong to Christ just as
12: 9 my weaknesses, so that Christ's power *may* **rest on** [*RP2172*] me.
12:21 who have sinned earlier and have not repented **of** the impurity,
13: 1 "Every matter must be established **by** the testimony of two

Gal 3:13 for it is written: "Cursed is everyone who is hung **on** a tree."
3:16 meaning **[NIE]** many people, but "and to your seed," meaning one
3:16 but "and to your seed," meaning **[NIE]** one person, who is Christ.
4: 1 What I am saying is that **as long as** [*+4012+5989*] the heir is a
4: 9 how is it that *you are* **turning back to** [*RP2188*] those weak
5:13 You, my brothers, were called **to** be free. But do not use your
6:16 Peace **[NIE]** and mercy to all who follow this rule, even to the
6:16 and mercy to all who follow this rule, even **to** the Israel of God.

Eph 1:10 to bring all things **in** heaven and on earth together under one head,
1:10 to bring all things in heaven and **on** earth together under one head,
1:16 stopped giving thanks for you, remembering you **in** my prayers.
2: 7 riches of his grace, expressed in his kindness **to** us in Christ Jesus.
2:10 are God's workmanship, created in Christ Jesus **to** do good works,
2:20 **built on** [*RP2224*] the foundation of the apostles and prophets,
3:15 whom his whole family in heaven and **on** earth derives its name.
4: 6 and Father of all, who is **over** all and through all and in all.
4:26 *Do* not *let* the sun **go down** [*RP2115*] while you are still angry,
5: 6 because of such things God's wrath comes **on** those who are
6: 3 go well with you and that you may enjoy long life **on** the earth."

Php 1: 3 I thank my God **[NIE]** every time I remember you.
1: 5 **because** of your partnership in the gospel from the first day until
2:17 But even if I am being poured out like a drink offering **on** the
2:27 not on him only but also on me, to spare me sorrow **upon** sorrow.
3: 9 in Christ—the righteousness that comes from God and is **by** faith.
3:12 but I press on to take hold **of** that for which Christ Jesus took hold
4:10 **[NIE]** Indeed, you have been concerned, but you had no

Col 1:16 things in heaven and **on** earth, visible and invisible,
1:20 whether things **on** earth or things in heaven, by making peace

3: 2 your minds on things above, not on **earthly** [+*1178+3836*] things.
3: 5 therefore, whatever belongs to your **earthly** [+*1178+3836*] nature:
3: 6 the wrath of God is coming [UBS+ *on those who are disobedient.*]
3: 14 And **over** all these virtues put on love, which binds them all

1Th 1: 2 always thank God for all of you, mentioning you **in** our prayers.
2: 16 sins to the limit. The wrath of God has come **upon** them at last.
3: 7 **in** all our distress and persecution we were encouraged about you
3: 7 in all our distress and persecution we were encouraged **about** you
3: 9 How can we thank God enough for you in return **for** all the joy we
4: 7 For God did not call us **to** be impure, but to live a holy life.

2Th 1: 10 This includes you, because you believed our testimony **to** you.
2: 1 of our Lord Jesus Christ and our *being* **gathered to** [*RP2191*] him,
2: 4 and will exalt himself **over** everything that is called God
3: 4 are doing and will continue to do the things we command. [**NIE**]

1Ti 1: 16 patience as an example for those who would believe **on** him
1: 18 instruction in keeping with the prophecies once made **about** you,
4: 10 we labor and strive), that we have put our hope **in** the living God,
5: 5 and left all alone puts her hope **in** God and continues night
5: 19 entertain an accusation against an elder unless it is *brought* **by** two
6: 13 who while testifying **before** Pontius Pilate made the good
6: 17 present world not to be arrogant nor to put their hope **in** wealth,
6: 17 which is so uncertain, but to put their hope **in** God, who richly

2Ti 2: 14 about words; it is **of** no value, and only ruins those who listen.
2: 14 it is of no value, and only [**NIE**] ruins those who listen.
2: 16 those who indulge in it will become **more and more** [+*4498*]
3: 9 But *they will* not **get very far** [+*4498+4621*] because, as in the
3: 13 and impostors will go **from bad to worse** [+*3836+5937*],
4: 4 will turn their ears away from the truth and turn aside **to** myths.

Tit 1: 2 a faith and knowledge **resting** on the hope of eternal life,
3: 6 whom he poured out **on** us generously through Jesus Christ our

Phm 1: 4 I always thank my God as I remember you **in** my prayers,
1: 7 [**NIE**] Your love has given me great joy and encouragement,

Heb 1: 2 but **in** these last days he has spoken to us by his Son, whom he
2: 13 And again, "I will put my trust **in** him." And again he says, "Here
3: 6 But Christ is faithful as a son **over** God's house. And we are his
6: 1 leave the elementary teachings about Christ and go on **to** maturity,
6: 1 of repentance from acts that lead to death, and of faith **in** God,
6: 7 Land that drinks in the rain often falling **on** it and that produces a
7: 11 priesthood (for **on the basis of** it the law was given to the people),
7: 13 He **of** whom these things are said belonged to a different tribe,
8: 1 The point **of** what we are saying is this: We do have such a high
8: 4 If he were **on** earth, he would not be a priest, for there are already
8: 6 is superior to the old one, and it is founded **on** better promises.
8: 8 when I will make a new covenant **with** the house of Israel
8: 8 new covenant with the house of Israel and **with** the house of Judah.
8: 10 my laws in their minds and **write** them **on** [*RP2108*] their hearts.
9: 10 They are only **a matter of** food and drink and various ceremonial
9: 15 to set them free from the sins *committed* **under** the first covenant.
9: 17 because a will is in force only when somebody has **died** [+*3738*];
9: 26 But now he has appeared once for all **at** the end of the ages to do
10: 16 I will put my laws **in** their hearts, and I will write them on their
10: 16 in their hearts, and *I will* **write** them **on** [*RP2108*] their minds."
10: 21 and since we have a great priest **over** the house of God,
10: 28 Anyone who rejected the law of Moses died without mercy **on** the
11: 4 as a righteous man, when God spoke well **of** his offerings.
11: 13 And they admitted that they were aliens and strangers **on** earth.
11: 21 Joseph's sons, and worshiped as he *leaned* **on** the top of his staff.
11: 30 after the people had marched around them **for** seven days.
11: 38 They wandered **in** deserts and mountains, and in caves and holes in
12: 10 but God disciplines us **for** our good, that we may share in his
12: 25 If they did not escape when they refused him who warned them **on**

Jas 2: 3 *If you* **show special attention to** [*RP2098*] the man wearing fine
2: 7 slandering the noble name of him to whom you **belong** [*RP2126*]?
2: 21 for what he did when he offered his son Isaac **on** the altar?
5: 1 weep and wail **because of** the misery that is coming upon you.
5: 5 You have lived **on** earth in luxury and self-indulgence. You have
5: 7 and how patient [**NIE**] he is for the autumn and spring rains.
5: 14 He should call the elders of the church to pray **over** him and anoint
5: 17 not rain, and it did not rain **on** the land for three and a half years.

1Pe 1: 13 set your hope fully **on** the grace to be given you when Jesus Christ
1: 20 of the world, but was revealed **in** these last times for your sake.
2: 6 and the one who trusts **in** him will never be put to shame."
2: 24 He himself bore our sins in his body **on** the tree, so that we might
2: 25 but now *you have* **returned to** [*RP2188*] the Shepherd
3: 12 For the eyes of the Lord are **on** the righteous and his ears are
3: 12 their prayer, but the face of the Lord is **against** those who do evil."

4: 14 you are blessed, for the Spirit of glory and of God rests **on** you.
5: 7 **Cast** all your anxiety **on** [*RP2166*] him because he cares for you.

2Pe 1: 13 I think it is right to refresh your memory **as long as** [+*4012*] I live
2: 22 "A dog **returns to** [*RP2188*] its vomit," and, "A sow that is washed
3: 3 you must understand that **in** the last days scoffers will come,

1Jn 3: 3 Everyone who has this hope **in** him purifies himself, just as he is

3Jn 1: 10 Not satisfied **with** that, he refuses to welcome the brothers.

Jude 1: 18 "**In** the last times there will be scoffers who will follow their own

Rev 1: 7 and all the peoples of the earth will mourn **because of** him.
1: 17 Then he placed his right hand **on** me and said: "Do not be afraid.
1: 20 The mystery of the seven stars that you saw **in** my right hand
2: 17 I will also give him a white stone with a new name written **on** it,
2: 24 so-called deep secrets (I will not impose any other burden **on** you):
2: 26 and does my will to the end, I will give authority **over** the nations—
3: 3 like a thief, and you will not know at what time I will come **to** you.
3: 10 to come **upon** the whole world to test those who live on the earth.
3: 10 to come upon the whole world to test those who live **on** the earth.
3: 12 I will write **on** him the name of my God and the name of the city of
3: 20 Here I am! I stand **at** the door and knock. If anyone hears my voice
4: 2 there before me was a throne in heaven with someone sitting **on**
4: 4 other thrones, and seated **on** them were twenty-four elders.
4: 4 They were dressed in white and had crowns of gold **on** their heads.
4: 9 honor and thanks to him who sits **on** the throne and who lives for
4: 10 the twenty-four elders fall down before him who sits **on** the throne,
5: 1 Then I saw **in** the right hand of him who sat on the throne a scroll
5: 1 Then I saw in the right hand of him who sat **on** the throne a scroll
5: 3 But no one in heaven or **on** earth or under the earth could open the
5: 7 and took the scroll from the right hand of him who sat **on** the
5: 10 and priests to serve our God, and they will reign **on** the earth."
5: 13 creature in heaven and **on** earth and under the earth and on the sea,
5: 13 creature in heaven and on earth and under the earth and **on** the sea,
5: 13 "To him who sits **on** the throne and to the Lamb be praise and
6: 2 Its **rider** [+*2764*] held a bow, and he was given a crown, and he
6: 4 Its **rider** [+*2764*] was given power to take peace from the earth
6: 5 Its **rider** [+*2764*] was holding a pair of scales in his hand.
6: 8 They were given power **over** a fourth of the earth to kill by sword,
6: 10 until you judge the inhabitants **of** the earth and avenge our blood?"
6: 16 "Fall **on** us and hide us from the face of him who sits on the throne
6: 16 "Fall on us and hide us from the face of him who sits **on** the throne
7: 1 After this I saw four angels standing **at** the four corners of the
7: 1 winds of the earth to prevent any wind from blowing **on** the land
7: 1 any wind from blowing on the land or **on** the sea or on any tree.
7: 1 any wind from blowing on the land or on the sea or **on** any tree.
7: 3 or the trees until we put a seal **on** the foreheads of the servants of
7: 10 belongs to our God, who sits **on** the throne, and to the Lamb."
7: 11 They fell down **on** their faces before the throne and worshiped
7: 15 and he who sits **on** the throne will spread his tent over them.
7: 15 and he who sits on the throne will spread his tent **over** them.
7: 16 The sun will not beat **upon** them, nor any scorching heat.
7: 17 will be their shepherd; he will lead them **to** springs of living water.
8: 3 who had a golden censer, came and stood **at** the altar.
8: 3 the prayers of all the saints, **on** the golden altar before the throne.
8: 10 fell from the sky **on** a third of the rivers and on the springs of
8: 10 from the sky on a third of the rivers and **on** the springs of water—
8: 13 Woe to the inhabitants **of** the earth, because of the trumpet blasts
9: 4 but only those people who did not have the seal of God **on** their
9: 7 **On** their heads they *wore* something like crowns of gold, and their
9: 11 They had as king **over** them the angel of the Abyss, whose name in
9: 14 the four angels who are bound **at** the great river Euphrates."
9: 17 The horses and **riders** [+*2764*] I saw in my vision looked like this:
10: 1 He was robed in a cloud, with a rainbow **above** his head; his face
10: 2 He planted his right foot **on** the sea and his left foot on the land,
10: 2 He planted his right foot on the sea and his left foot **on** the land,
10: 5 Then the angel I had seen standing **on** the sea and on the land
10: 5 standing on the sea and **on** the land raised his right hand to heaven.
10: 8 that lies open in the hand of the angel who is standing **on** the sea
10: 8 the hand of the angel who is standing on the sea and **on** the land."
10: 11 "You must prophesy again **about** many peoples, nations, languages
11: 6 and they have power to turn [**NIE**] the waters into blood
11: 8 Their bodies will *lie* **in** the street of the great city, which is
11: 10 The inhabitants **of** the earth will gloat over them and will celebrate
11: 10 The inhabitants of the earth will gloat **over** them and will celebrate
11: 10 because these two prophets had tormented those who live **on** the
11: 11 and they stood **on** their feet, and terror struck those who saw them.
11: 11 on their feet, and terror **struck** [*RP2158*] those who saw them.
11: 16 who were seated **on** their thrones before God, fell on their faces

11: 16 on their thrones before God, fell **on** their faces and worshiped God,
12: 1 the moon under her feet and a crown of twelve stars **on** her head.
12: 3 with seven heads and ten horns and seven crowns **on** his heads.
12: 17 Then the dragon was enraged **at** the woman and went off to make
13: 1 And the dragon stood **on** the shore of the sea. And I saw a beast
13: 1 He had ten horns and seven heads, with ten crowns **on** his horns,
13: 1 ten crowns **on** his horns, and **on** each head a blasphemous name.
13: 7 And he was given authority **over** every tribe, people, language
13: 8 All inhabitants **of** the earth will worship the beast—all whose
13: 14 on behalf of the first beast, he deceived the inhabitants **of** the earth.
13: 14 He ordered them^s [+1178+2997+3836+3836] to set up an image
13: 16 and slave, to receive a mark **on** his right hand or **on** his forehead,
13: 16 and slave, to receive a mark **on** his right hand or **on** his forehead,
14: 1 and there before me was the Lamb, standing **on** Mount Zion,
14: 1 had his name and his Father's name written **on** their foreheads.
14: 6 and he had the eternal gospel to proclaim **to** those who live on the
14: 6 and he had the eternal gospel to proclaim to those who live **on** the
14: 6 who live on the earth—**to** every nation, tribe, language and people.
14: 9 and his image and receives his mark **on** the forehead or on the
14: 9 his image and receives his mark on the forehead or **on** the hand,
14: 14 and seated **on** the cloud was one "like a son of man" with a crown
14: 14 cloud was one "like a son of man" with a crown of gold **on** his head
14: 15 and called in a loud voice to him who was sitting **on** the cloud,
14: 16 So he who was seated **on** the cloud swung his sickle over the earth,
14: 16 So he who was seated on the cloud swung his sickle **over** the earth,
14: 18 Still another angel, who had charge **of** the fire, came from the altar
15: 2 standing **beside** the sea, those who had been victorious over the
16: 2 and painful sores broke out **on** the people who had the mark of the
16: 8 The fourth angel poured out his bowl **on** the sun, and the sun was
16: 9 who had control **over** these plagues, but they refused to repent
16: 10 The fifth angel poured out his bowl **on** the throne of the beast,
16: 12 The sixth angel poured out his bowl **on** the great river Euphrates,
16: 14 miraculous signs, and they go out **to** the kings of the whole world,
16: 17 The seventh angel poured out his bowl **into** the air, and out of the
16: 18 No earthquake like it has ever occurred since man has been **on**
16: 21 huge hailstones of about a hundred pounds each fell **upon** men.
17: 1 the punishment of the great prostitute, who sits **on** many waters.
17: 3 There I saw a woman sitting **on** a scarlet beast that was covered
17: 5 This title was written **on** her forehead: MYSTERY BABYLON
17: 8 The inhabitants **of** the earth whose names have not been written in
17: 8 The inhabitants of the earth whose names have not been written **in**
17: 9 The seven heads are seven hills **on** which the woman sits.
17: 18 The woman you saw is the great city that rules **over** the kings of
18: 9 see the smoke of her burning, they will weep and mourn **over** her.
18: 11 "The merchants of the earth will weep and mourn **over** her
18: 17 sea captain, and all who **travel by ship** [+4434+5536], the sailors,
18: 19 They will throw dust **on** their heads, and with weeping
18: 20 Rejoice **over** her, O heaven! Rejoice, saints and apostles
18: 24 and of the saints, and of all who have been killed **on** the earth."
19: 4 fell down and worshiped God, who was seated **on** the throne.
19: 11 a white horse, whose **rider** [+2764] is called Faithful and True.
19: 12 His eyes are like blazing fire, and **on** his head are many crowns.
19: 14 *riding* **on** white horses and dressed in fine linen, white and clean.
19: 16 **On** his robe and on his thigh he has this name written: KING OF
19: 16 On his robe and **on** his thigh he has this name written: KING OF
19: 18 generals, and mighty men, of horses and their **riders** [+2764],
19: 19 together to make war against the **rider** [+2764] on the horse
19: 21 that came out of the mouth *of* the **rider** [+2764] on the horse,
20: 1 having the key to the Abyss and **holding in** his hand a great chain.
20: 4 I saw thrones **on** which were seated those who had been given
20: 4 or his image and had not received his mark **on** their foreheads
20: 4 not received his mark on their foreheads or **[RPG]** their hands.
20: 6 The second death has no power **over** them, but they will be priests
20: 9 They marched **across** the breadth of the earth and surrounded the
20: 11 Then I saw a great white throne and him who was seated **on** it.
21: 5 He who was seated **on** the throne said, "I am making everything
21: 10 And he carried me away in the Spirit **to** a mountain great and high,
21: 12 high wall with twelve gates, and with twelve angels **at** the gates.
21: 14 and **on** them were the names of the twelve apostles of the Lamb.
21: 16 the city with the rod and **found** it **to** be 12,000 stadia in length,
22: 4 They will see his face, and his name will be **on** their foreheads.
22: 5 the light of the sun, for the Lord God will give **[NIE]** them light.
22: 14 that they may have the right **to** the tree of life and may go through
22: 16 have sent my angel to give you this testimony **for** the churches.
22: 18 If anyone **adds** *anything* **to** [RP2202] them, God will add to him
22: 18 God *will* **add to** [RP2202] him the plagues described in this book.

2094 ἐπιβαίνω, *epibainō* [6] [√ *2093 + 326*]

arriving in [1], boarded [1], came [1], go on [1], riding [1], went on board [1]

Mt 21: 5 gentle and **riding** on a donkey, on a colt, the foal of a donkey.' "
Ac 20: 18 I was with you, from the first day *I* **came** into the province of Asia.
21: 2 a ship crossing over to Phoenicia, **went on board** and set sail.
21: 4 Through the Spirit they urged Paul not *to* **go on** to Jerusalem.
25: 1 Three days after **arriving in** the province, Festus went up from
27: 2 *We* **boarded** a ship from Adramyttium about to sail for ports along

2095 ἐπιβάλλω, *epiballō* [18] [√ *2093 + 965*]

laid on [RP2093] [2], seized [+2093+3836+5931] [2], seized [+3836+5931] [2], sews on [RP2093] [2], arrest [+2093+3836+5931] [1], arrested [+2093+3836+5931] [1], arrested [+3836+5931] [1], broke down [1], broke [1], lay on [RP2093] [1], puts to [RP2093] [1], restrict [+1105] [1], share [+3538] [1], threw over [1]

Mt 9: 16 "No one **sews** [RP2093] a patch of unshrunk cloth **on** an old
26: 50 the men stepped forward, **seized** [+2093+3836+5931] Jesus and
Mk 4: 37 A furious squall came up, and the waves **broke** over the boat,
11: 7 When they brought the colt to Jesus and **threw** their cloaks **over** it,
14: 46 The men **seized** [+3836+5931] Jesus and arrested him.
14: 72 you will disown me three times." And he **broke down** and wept.
Lk 5: 36 a patch from a new garment and **sews** [RP2093] it **on** an old one.
9: 62 "No one *who* **puts** [RP2093] his hand to the plow and looks back is
15: 12 said to his father, 'Father, give me my **share** [+3538] of the estate.'
20: 19 looked for a way *to* **arrest** [+2093+3836+5931] him immediately,
21: 12 all this, *they will* **lay** [RP2093] hands **on** you and persecute you.
Jn 7: 30 they tried to seize him, but no one **laid** [RP2093] a hand **on** him,
7: 44 wanted to seize him, but no one **laid** [RP2093] a hand **on** him.
Ac 4: 3 *They* **seized** [+3836+5931] Peter and John, and because it was
5: 18 *They* **arrested** [+2093+3836+5931] the apostles and put them in
12: 1 It was about this time that King Herod **arrested** [+3836+5931]
21: 27 stirred up the whole crowd and **seized** [+2093+3836+5931] him,
1Co 7: 35 I am saying this for your own good, not to **restrict** [+1105] you,

2096 ἐπιβαρέω, *epibareō* [3] [√ *2093 + 983*]

burden to [2], put it too severely [1]

2Co 2: 5 has grieved all of you, to some extent—not to **put it too severely**.
1Th 2: 9 and day in order not to *be a* **burden to** anyone while we preached
2Th 3: 8 and toiling so that *we would* not *be a* **burden to** any of you.

2097 ἐπιβιβάζω, *epibibazō* [3] [√ *2093 + 326*]

put on [RP2093] [2], taken [1]

Lk 10: 34 Then *he* **put** [RP2093] the man **on** his own donkey, took him to an
19: 35 threw their cloaks on the colt and **put** [RP2093] Jesus **on** it.
Ac 23: 24 mounts for Paul so that he may be **taken** safely to Governor Felix."

2098 ἐπιβλέπω, *epiblepō* [3] [√ *2093 + 1063*]

look at [RP2093] [1], mindful of [RP2093] [1], show special attention to [RP2093] [1]

Lk 1: 48 for *he has been* **mindful** [RP2093] **of** the humble state of his
9: 38 "Teacher, I beg you *to* **look** [RP2093] **at** my son, for he is my only
Jas 2: 3 *If you* **show special attention** [RP2093] **to** the man wearing fine

2099 ἐπίβλημα, *epiblēma* [4] [√ *2093 + 965*]

patch [4]

Mt 9: 16 "No one sews a **patch** of unshrunk cloth on an old garment,
Mk 2: 21 "No one sews a **patch** of unshrunk cloth on an old garment,
Lk 5: 36 "No one tears a **patch** from a new garment and sews it on an old
5: 36 new garment, and the **patch** from the new will not match the old.

2100 ἐπιβοάω, *epiboaō* Not used in UBS/NIV

[√ *2093 + 1068*]

2101 ἐπιβουλή, *epiboulē* [4] [√ 2093 + 1089]

plot [2], plan [1], plots [1]

Ac   9:24 but Saul learned of their **plan**. Day and night they kept close watch
     20: 3 Because the Jews made a **plot** against him just as he was about to
     20:19 with tears, although I was severely tested by the **plots** of the Jews.
     23:30 When I was informed *of* a **plot** to be carried out against the man,

2102 ἐπιγαμβρεύω, *epigambreuō* [1] [√ 2093 + 1141]

marry [1]

Mt 22:24 his brother *must* **marry** the widow and have children for him.

2103 ἐπίγειος, *epigeios* [7] [√ 2093 + 1178]

earthly [4], earthly things [2], on earth [1]

Jn   3:12 I have spoken to you of **earthly things** and you do not believe;
1Co 15:40 There are also heavenly bodies and there are **earthly** bodies;
     15:40 is one kind, and the splendor *of* the **earthly** bodies is another.
2Co 5: 1 Now we know that if the **earthly** tent we live in is destroyed,
Php 2:10 knee should bow, in heaven and **on earth** and under the earth,
      3:19 and their glory is in their shame. Their mind is on **earthly things**.
Jas   3:15 Such "wisdom" does not come down from heaven but is **earthly**,

2104 ἐπιγίνομαι, *epiginomai* [1] [√ 2093 + 1181]

came up [1]

Ac 28:13 The next day the south wind **came up**, and on the following day

2105 ἐπιγινώσκω, *epiginōskō* [44] [√ 2093 + 1182]

recognized [6], know [5], recognize [4], known [3], learned [3], realized [3], knew [2], knows [2], understood [2], acknowledge [1], come to understand [1], find out [1], found out [1], fully known [1], know fully [1], learn the truth [1], realize [1], realized that [1], recognition [1], recognizing [1], took note [1], understand [1], verify [1]

Mt   7:16 By their fruit *you will* **recognize** them. Do people pick grapes
      7:20 Thus, by their fruit *you will* **recognize** them.
    11:27 No one **knows** the Son except the Father, and no one knows the
    11:27 and no one **knows** the Father except the Son and those to whom
    14:35 And *when* the men of that place **recognized** Jesus, they sent word
    17:12 Elijah has already come, and *they did* not **recognize** him,
Mk   2: 8 Immediately Jesus **knew** in his spirit that this was what they were
     5:30 At once Jesus **realized** that power had gone out from him.
     6:33 But many who saw them leaving **recognized** them and ran on foot
     6:54 As soon as they got out of the boat, *people* **recognized** Jesus.
Lk   1: 4 so that *you may* **know** the certainty of the things you have been
     1:22 *They* **realized** he had seen a vision in the temple, for he kept
     5:22 Jesus **knew** what they were thinking and asked, "Why are you
     7:37 When a woman who had lived a sinful life in that town **learned**
    23: 7 *When he* **learned** that Jesus was under Herod's jurisdiction,
    24:16 but they were kept from **recognizing** him.
    24:31 Then their eyes were opened and *they* **recognized** him, and he
Ac   3:10 *they* **recognized** him as the same man who used to sit begging at
     4:13 and *they* **took note** that these men had been with Jesus.
     9:30 *When* the brothers **learned** of this, they took him down to
    12:14 *When she* **recognized** Peter's voice, she was so overjoyed she ran
    19:34 But *when they* **realized** he was a Jew, they all shouted in unison
    22:24 and questioned in order to **find out** why the people were shouting
    22:29 The commander himself was alarmed *when he* **realized** that he
    23:28 I wanted *to* **know** why they were accusing him, so I brought him to
    24: 8 By examining him yourself you will be able *to* **learn the truth**
    24:11 You can *easily* **verify** that no more than twelve days ago I went up
    25:10 not done any wrong to the Jews, as *you* yourself **know** very well.
    27:39 When daylight came, *they did* not **recognize** the land, but they
    28: 1 safely on shore, *we* **found out** that the island was called Malta.
Ro   1:32 *Although* they **know** God's righteous decree that those who do
1Co 13:12 I know in part; then *I shall* **know fully**, even as I am fully known.
    13:12 I know in part; then I shall **know fully**, even as *I am* **fully known**.
    14:37 let him **acknowledge** that what I am writing to you is the Lord's
    16:18 refreshed my spirit and yours also. Such men *deserve* **recognition**.
2Co   1:13 For we do not write you anything you cannot read or **understand**.

1:14 as *you have* **understood** us in part, you will come to understand
1:14 *you will* **come to understand** fully that you can boast of us just as
6: 9 **known**, yet regarded as unknown; dying, and yet we live on;
13: 5 *Do you* not **realize** that Christ Jesus is in you—unless, of course,
Col 1: 6 the day you heard it and **understood** God's grace in all its truth.
1Ti 4: 3 received with thanksgiving *by* those who believe and who **know**
2Pe 2:21 It would have been better for them not *to have* **known** the way of
    2:21 than *to have* **known** it and then to turn their backs on the sacred

2106 ἐπίγνωσις, *epignōsis* [20] [√ 2093 + 1182]

knowledge [14], acknowledge [+*2262*] [1], conscious [1], full understanding [1], know better [1], know [1], knowing [1]

Ro   1:28 since they did not think it worthwhile to retain the **knowledge** of
    3:20 the law; rather, through the law we become **conscious** of sin.
   10: 2 they are zealous for God, but their zeal is not based on **knowledge**.
Eph 1:17 Spirit of wisdom and revelation, so that you may **know** him **better**.
    4:13 and *in* the **knowledge** of the Son of God and become mature,
Php 1: 9 may abound more and more in **knowledge** and depth of insight,
Col 1: 9 and asking God to fill you with the **knowledge** of his will through
    1:10 fruit in every good work, growing *in* the **knowledge** of God,
    2: 2 in order that they may **know** the mystery of God, namely,
    3:10 which is being renewed in **knowledge** in the image of its Creator.
1Ti 2: 4 wants all men to be saved and to come to a **knowledge** of the truth.
2Ti 2:25 grant them repentance leading them to a **knowledge** of the truth,
    3: 7 always learning but never able *to* **acknowledge** [+*2262*] the truth.
Tit   1: 1 God's elect and the **knowledge** of the truth that leads to godliness
Phm 1: 6 so that you will have a **full understanding** of every good thing we
Heb 10:26 keep on sinning after we have received the **knowledge** of the truth,
2Pe 1: 2 and peace be yours in abundance through the **knowledge** of God
    1: 3 and godliness through our **knowledge** of him who called us by his
    1: 8 and unproductive in your **knowledge** of our Lord Jesus Christ.
    2:20 If they have escaped the corruption of the world by **knowing** our

2107 ἐπιγραφή, *epigraphē* [5] [√ 2093 + 1211]

inscription [3], written notice [2]

Mt 22:20 he asked them, "Whose portrait is this? And whose **inscription**?"
Mk 12:16 portrait is this? And whose **inscription**?" "Caesar's," they replied.
    15:26 The **written notice** of the charge against him read: THE KING OF
Lk 20:24 "Show me a denarius. Whose portrait and **inscription** are on it?"
    23:38 There was a **written notice** above him, which read: THIS IS THE

2108 ἐπιγράφω, *epigraphō* [5] [√ 2093 + 1211]

write on [*RP2093*] [2], read [+*1639*] [1], this inscription [*+4005*] [1], written [1]

Mk 15:26 The written notice of the charge against him **read** [+*1639*]:
Ac 17:23 of worship, I even found an altar with **this inscription** [+*4005*]:
Heb 8:10 my laws in their minds and **write** [*RP2093*] them **on** their hearts.
    10:16 in their hearts, and *I will* **write** [*RP2093*] them **on** their minds."
Rev 21:12 On the gates *were* **written** the names of the twelve tribes of Israel.

2109 ἐπιδείκνυμι, *epideiknymi* [7] [√ 2093 + 1259]

show [3], call attention to [1], make clear [1], proving [1], showing [1]

Mt 16: 1 and tested him by asking him *to* **show** them a sign from heaven.
   22:19 **Show** me the coin used for paying the tax." They brought him a
   24: 1 his disciples came up to him *to* **call** his **attention to** its buildings.
Lk 17:14 When he saw them, he said, "Go, **show** yourselves to the priests."
Ac   9:39 crying and **showing** him the robes and other clothing that Dorcas
  18:28 **proving** from the Scriptures that Jesus was the Christ.
Heb 6:17 *to* **make** the unchanging nature of his purpose very **clear** to the

2110 ἐπιδέχομαι, *epidechomai* [2] [√ 2093 + 1312]

have to do with [1], welcome [1]

3Jn 1: 9 who loves to be first, *will* **have** nothing **to do with** us.
   1:10 Not satisfied with that, he refuses to **welcome** the brothers.

2111 ἐπιδημέω, *epidēmeō* [2] [√ 2093 + 1322]

lived there [1], visitors [1]

Ac   2:10 Egypt and the parts of Libya near Cyrene; **visitors** from Rome
     17:21 and the foreigners *who* **lived there** spent their time doing nothing

2112 ἐπιδιατάσσομαι, *epidiatassomai* [1]
[√ 2093 + 1328 + 5435]

add to [1]

Gal   3:15 or **add to** a human covenant that has been duly established,

2113 ἐπιδίδωμι, *epididōmi* [9] [√ 2093 + 1443]

give [5], delivered [1], gave way [1], gave [1], handed [1]

Mt   7: 9 "Which of you, if his son asks for bread, *will* **give** him a stone?
     7:10 Or if he asks for a fish, *will* **give** him a snake?
Lk   4:17 The scroll of the prophet Isaiah *was* **handed** to him. Unrolling it,
    11:11 if your son asks for a fish, *will* **give** him a snake instead?
    11:12 Or if he asks for an egg, *will* **give** him a scorpion?
    24:30 *he* took bread, gave thanks, broke it and *began to* **give** it to them.
    24:42 They **gave** him a piece of broiled fish,
Ac 15:30 where they gathered the church together and **delivered** the letter.
    27:15 head into the wind; so we **gave way** to it and were driven along.

2114 ἐπιδιορθόω, *epidiorthoō* [1]
[√ 2093 + 1328 + 3981]

straighten out [1]

Tit   1: 5 The reason I left you in Crete was that *you might* **straighten out**

2115 ἐπιδύω, *epidyō* [1] [√ 2093 + 1544]

go down [RP2093] [1]

Eph   4:26 *Do* not *let* the sun **go** [RP2093] **down** while you are still angry,

2116 ἐπιείκεια, *epieikeia* [2] [√ 2093 + 2036]

gentleness [1], kind [1]

Ac   24: 4 I would request that you be **kind** *enough* to hear us briefly.
2Co 10: 1 By the meekness and **gentleness** of Christ, I appeal to you—

2117 ἐπιεικής, *epieikēs* [5] [√ 2093 + 2036]

considerate [3], gentle [1], gentleness [1]

Php   4: 5 Let your **gentleness** be evident to all. The Lord is near.
1Ti   3: 3 not violent but **gentle**, not quarrelsome, not a lover of money.
Tit   3: 2 to slander no one, to be peaceable and **considerate**, and to show
Jas   3:17 **considerate**, submissive, full of mercy and good fruit, impartial
1Pe   2:18 not only *to* those who are good and **considerate**, but also to those

2118 ἐπιζητέω, *epizēteō* [13] [√ 2093 + 2426]

looking for [5], a thorough search made for [1], asks for [1], looks for [1], run after [1], runs after [1], sought so earnestly [1], want to bring up [1], wanted [1]

Mt   6:32 For the pagans **run after** all these things, and your heavenly Father
    12:39 "A wicked and adulterous generation **asks for** a miraculous sign!
    16: 4 A wicked and adulterous generation **looks for** a miraculous sign,
Lk   4:42 The people *were* **looking for** him and when they came to where he
    12:30 For the pagan world **runs after** all such things, and your Father
Ac 12:19 *After* Herod *had* **a thorough search made for** him and did not
    13: 7 and Saul *because* he **wanted** to hear the word of God.
    19:39 If there is anything further *you* **want to bring up**, it must be
Ro 11: 7 What then? What Israel **sought so earnestly** it did not obtain,
Php   4:17 Not that *I am* **looking for** a gift, but I am looking for what may be
    4:17 but *I am* **looking for** what may be credited to your account.
Heb 11:14 People who say such things show that *they are* **looking for** a
    13:14 an enduring city, but *we are* **looking for** the city that is to come.

2119 ἐπιθανάτιος, *epithanatios* [1] [√ 2093 + 2569]

condemned to die [1]

1Co   4: 9 the end of the procession, like *men* **condemned to die** in the arena.

2120 ἐπίθεσις, *epithesis* [4] [√ 2093 + 5502]

laying on [3], laid on [1]

Ac   8:18 When Simon saw that the Spirit was given at the **laying on** of the
1Ti   4:14 message when the body of elders **laid** their hands **on** you.
2Ti   1: 6 the gift of God, which is in you through the **laying on** of my hands.
Heb   6: 2 instruction about baptisms, the **laying on** of hands, the resurrection

2121 ἐπιθυμέω, *epithymeō* [16] [√ 2093 + 2596]

long [3], covet [2], desires [2], longed [2], want [2], coveted [1], did^s [1], eagerly desired [+2123] [1], longing [1], lustfully [+3836+4639] [1]

Mt   5:28 **lustfully** [+3836+4639] has already committed adultery with her in
    13:17 many prophets and righteous men **longed** to see what you see
Lk 15:16 *He* **longed** to fill his stomach with the pods that the pigs were
    16:21 and **longing** to eat what fell from the rich man's table. Even the
    17:22 "The time is coming when *you will* **long** to see one of the days of
    22:15 "*I have* **eagerly desired** [+2123] to eat this Passover with you
Ac 20:33 *I have* not **coveted** anyone's silver or gold or clothing.
Ro   7: 7 what coveting really was if the law had not said, "*Do* not **covet**."
    13: 9 commit adultery," "*Do* not murder," "*Do* not steal," "*Do* not **covet**,"
1Co 10: 6 to keep us from setting our hearts on evil things as they **did**^{s}.
Gal   5:17 For the sinful nature **desires** what is contrary to the Spirit,
1Ti   3: 1 anyone sets his heart on being an overseer, *he* **desires** a noble task.
Heb   6:11 *We* **want** each of you to show this same diligence to the very end,
Jas   4: 2 *You* **want** *something* but don't get it. You kill and covet,
1Pe   1:12 Spirit sent from heaven. Even angels **long** to look into these things.
Rev   9: 6 but will not find it; *they will* **long** to die, but death will elude them.

2122 ἐπιθυμητής, *epithymētēs* [1] [√ 2093 + 2596]

setting hearts on [1]

1Co 10: 6 to keep us from **setting** our **hearts on** evil things as they did.

2123 ἐπιθυμία, *epithymia* [38] [√ 2093 + 2596]

desires [11], evil desires [8], desire [3], cravings [2], lust [2], passions [2], coveting [1], covetous desire [1], desire [+2400] [1], eagerly desired [+2121] [1], evil desire [1], longed for [+3836+6034] [1], longing [1], lustful desires [+816] [1], passionate [1], sinful desires [1]

Mk   4:19 and the **desires** for other things come in and choke the word,
Lk 22:15 "*I have* **eagerly desired** [+2121] to eat this Passover with you
Jn   8:44 the devil, and you want to carry out your father's **desire**.
Ro   1:24 Therefore God gave them over in the **sinful desires** of their hearts
    6:12 let sin reign in your mortal body so that you obey its **evil desires**.
    7: 7 For I would not have known what **coveting** really was if the law
    7: 8 the commandment, produced in me every kind of **covetous desire**.
    13:14 and do not think about how to gratify the **desires** of the sinful
Gal   5:16 the Spirit, and you will not gratify the **desires** of the sinful nature.
    5:24 Jesus have crucified the sinful nature with its passions and **desires**.
Eph   2: 3 gratifying the **cravings** of our sinful nature and following its
    4:22 off your old self, which is being corrupted by its deceitful **desires**;
Php   1:23 I **desire** [+2400] to depart and be with Christ, which is better by
Col   3: 5 impurity, lust, evil **desires** and greed, which is idolatry.
1Th   2:17 out of our intense **longing** we made every effort to see you.
    4: 5 not in **passionate** lust like the heathen, who do not know God;
1Ti   6: 9 and harmful **desires** that plunge men into ruin and destruction.
2Ti   2:22 Flee the **evil desires** of youth, and pursue righteousness, faith,
    3: 6 loaded down with sins and are swayed by all kinds of **evil desires**,
    4: 3 Instead, to suit their own **desires**, they will gather around them a
Tit   2:12 It teaches us to say "No" to ungodliness and worldly **passions**,
    3: 3 deceived and enslaved by all kinds of **passions** and pleasures.
Jas   1:14 by his own **evil desire**, he is dragged away and enticed.
    1:15 Then, after **desire** has conceived, it gives birth to sin; and sin,
1Pe   1:14 do not conform *to* the **evil desires** you had when you lived in
    2:11 as aliens and strangers in the world, to abstain from sinful **desires**,

4: 2 he does not live the rest of his earthly life *for* **evil** human **desires**,
4: 3 **lust**, drunkenness, orgies, carousing and detestable idolatry.
2Pe 1: 4 and escape the corruption in the world caused by **evil desires**.
2: 10 This is especially true of those who follow the corrupt **desire** of the
2: 18 to the **lustful desires** [*+816*] of sinful human nature, they entice
3: 3 scoffers will come, scoffing and following their own **evil desires**.
1Jn 2: 16 the **cravings** of sinful man, the lust of his eyes and the boasting of
2: 16 the **lust** of his eyes and the boasting of what he has and does—
2: 17 The world and its **desires** pass away, but the man who does the
Jude 1: 16 are grumblers and faultfinders; they follow their own **evil desires**;
1: 18 there will be scoffers who will follow their own ungodly **desires**."
Rev 18: 14 'The fruit you **longed** [*+3836+6034*] **for** is gone from you.

2124 ἐπιθύω, *epithyō* Not used in UBS/NIV
[√ *2093 + 2604*]

2125 ἐπικαθίζω, *epikathizō* [1] [√ *2093 + 2767*]

sat [1]

Mt 21: 7 and the colt, placed their cloaks on them, and Jesus **sat** on them.

2126 ἐπικαλέω, *epikaleō* [30] [√ *2093 + 2813*]

called [8], call on [7], appeal to [2], calls on [2], known as [2],
appealed to [1], appealed [1], bear [*RP20932093*] [1], belong
[*RP2093*] [1], call [*RP2093*] [1], calling on [1], made appeal to [1],
made appeal [1], prayed [1]

Mt 10: 25 If the head of the house has been **called** Beelzebub, how much
Ac 1: 23 Joseph called Barsabbas (also **known as** Justus) and Matthias.
2: 21 And everyone who **calls on** the name of the Lord will be saved.'
4: 36 whom the apostles **called** Barnabas (which means Son of
7: 59 were stoning him, Stephen **prayed**, "Lord Jesus, receive my spirit."
9: 14 from the chief priests to arrest all who **call on** your name."
9: 21 raised havoc in Jerusalem among those *who* **call on** this name?
10: 5 to Joppa to bring back a man named Simon who *is* **called** Peter.
10: 18 asking if Simon who *was* **known as** Peter was staying there.
10: 32 Send to Joppa for Simon who *is* **called** Peter. He is a guest in the
11: 13 in his house and say, 'Send to Joppa for Simon who *is* **called** Peter.
12: 12 also **called** Mark, where many people had gathered and were
12: 25 returned from Jerusalem, taking with them John, also **called** Mark.
15: 17 and all the Gentiles who **bear** [*RP20932093*] my name, says the
22: 16 be baptized and wash your sins away, **calling on** his name.'
25: 11 no one has the right to hand me over to them. *I* **appeal to** Caesar!"
25: 12 with his council, he declared: "You *have* **appealed** to Caesar.
25: 21 *When* Paul **made** his **appeal** to be held over for the Emperor's
25: 25 *because* he **made** his **appeal to** the Emperor I decided to send him
26: 32 "This man could have been set free if *he had* not **appealed to** Caesar."
28: 19 when the Jews objected, I was compelled *to* **appeal to** Caesar—
Ro 10: 12 the same Lord is Lord of all and richly blesses all who **call on** him,
10: 13 "Everyone who **calls on** the name of the Lord will be saved."
10: 14 How, then, *can they* **call on** the one they have not believed in?
1Co 1: 2 together with all those everywhere *who* **call on** the name of our
2Co 1: 23 I **call** [*RP2093*] God as my witness that it was in order to spare
2Ti 2: 22 along with those *who* **call on** the Lord out of a pure heart.
Heb 11: 16 Therefore God is not ashamed *to be* **called** their God, for he has
Jas 2: 7 slandering the noble name of him to whom you **belong** [*RP2093*]?
1Pe 1: 17 Since *you* **call on** a Father who judges each man's work

2127 ἐπικάλυμμα, *epikalymma* [1] [√ *2093 + 2821*]

cover-up [1]

1Pe 2: 16 as free men, but do not use your freedom as a **cover-up** for evil;

2128 ἐπικαλύπτω, *epikalyptō* [1] [√ *2093 + 2821*]

covered [1]

Ro 4: 7 they whose transgressions are forgiven, whose sins *are* **covered**.

2129 ἐπικατάρατος, *epikataratos* [2]
[√ *2093 + 2848 + 725*]

cursed [2]

Gal 3: 10 "**Cursed** is everyone who does not continue to do everything
3: 13 for it is written: "**Cursed** is everyone who is hung on a tree."

2130 ἐπίκειμαι, *epikeimai* [7] [√ *2093 + 3023*]

applying [1], compelled [*+340*] [1], continued raging
[*+3900+4024*] [1], crowding around [1], insistently [1], laid across
[*RP2093*] [1], on [1]

Lk 5: 1 with the people **crowding around** him and listening to the word of
23: 23 But with loud shouts they **insistently** demanded that he be
Jn 11: 38 It was a cave with a stone **laid** [*RP2093*] **across** the entrance.
21: 9 they saw a fire of burning coals there with fish **on** it, and some
Ac 27: 20 for many days and the storm **continued raging** [*+3900+4024*],
1Co 9: 16 the gospel, I cannot boast, for I *am* **compelled** [*+340*] to preach.
Heb 9: 10 external regulations **applying** until the time of the new order.

2131 ἐπικέλλω, *epikellō* [1] [√ *2093 + 3027*]

ran aground [1]

Ac 27: 41 But the ship struck a sandbar and **ran aground**. The bow stuck fast

2132 ἐπικερδαίνω, *epikerdainō* Not used in
UBS/NIV [√ *2093 + 3046*]

2133 ἐπικεφάλαιον, *epikephalaion* Not used in
UBS/NIV [√ *2093 + 3051*]

2134 Ἐπικούρειος, *Epikoureios* [1] [√ *2093 + 3025*]

Epicurean [1]

Ac 17: 18 A group *of* **Epicurean** and Stoic philosophers began to dispute

2135 ἐπικουρία, *epikouria* [1] [√ *2093 + 3025*]

help [1]

Ac 26: 22 But I have had God's **help** to this very day,

2136 ἐπικράζω, *epikrazō* Not used in UBS/NIV
[√ *2093 + 3189*]

2137 ἐπικρίνω, *epikrinō* [1] [√ *2093 + 3212*]

decided [1]

Lk 23: 24 So Pilate **decided** to grant their demand.

2138 ἐπιλαμβάνομαι, *epilambanomai* [19]
[√ *2093 + 3284*]

took [6], seized [2], take hold [2], *untranslated* [1], arrested [1],
catch [1], caught [1], helps [1], seizing [1], taking hold of [1], trap
in [1], turned on [1]

Mt 14: 31 Immediately Jesus reached out his hand and **caught** him. "You of
Mk 8: 23 *He* **took** the blind man by the hand and led him outside the village.
Lk 9: 47 their thoughts, **took** a little child and had him stand beside him.
14: 4 So **taking hold of** the man, he healed him and sent him away.
20: 20 They hoped *to* **catch** Jesus in something he said so that they might
20: 26 They were unable *to* **trap** him **in** what he had said there in public.
23: 26 As they led him away, *they* **seized** Simon from Cyrene, who was
Ac 9: 27 But Barnabas **took** him and brought him to the apostles. He told
16: 19 they **seized** Paul and Silas and dragged them into the marketplace
17: 19 Then they **took** him and brought him to a meeting of the
18: 17 Then *they* all **turned on** Sosthenes the synagogue ruler and beat
21: 30 **Seizing** Paul, they dragged him from the temple, and immediately
21: 33 The commander came up and **arrested** him and ordered him to be
23: 19 The commander **took** the young man by the hand, drew him aside
1Ti 6: 12 **Take hold** of the eternal life to which you were called when you

6: 19 coming age, so that *they may* **take hold** of the life that is truly life.
Heb 2: 16 For surely it is not angels he **helps**, but Abraham's descendants.
      2: 16 it is not angels he helps, but Abraham's descendants. **[RPG]**
      8: 9 when I **took** them by the hand to lead them out of Egypt,

2139 ἐπιλάμπω, *epilampō*   Not used in UBS/NIV
[√ *2093 + 3290*]

2140 ἐπιλανθάνομαι, *epilanthanomai* [8]
[√ *2093 + 3291*]

forget [3], forgotten [2], forgets [1], forgetting [1], forgot [1]

Mt 16: 5 When they went across the lake, the disciples **forgot** to take bread.
Mk 8: 14 The disciples *had* **forgotten** to bring bread, except for one loaf
Lk 12: 6 sold for two pennies? Yet not one of them is **forgotten** by God.
Php 3: 13 **Forgetting** what is behind and straining toward what is ahead,
Heb 6: 10 he *will* not **forget** your work and the love you have shown him as
     13: 2 *Do* not **forget** to entertain strangers, for by so doing some people
     13: 16 And *do* not **forget** to do good and to share with others, for with
Jas 1: 24 at himself, goes away and immediately **forgets** what he looks like.

2141 ἐπιλέγω, *epilegō* [2] [√ *2093 + 3306*]

called [1], chose [1]

Jn 5: 2 which in Aramaic *is* **called** Bethesda and which is surrounded by
Ac 15: 40 but Paul **chose** Silas and left, commended by the brothers to the

2142 ἐπιλείπω, *epileipō* [1] [√ *2093 + 3309*]

not have [1]

Heb 11: 32 I *do* **not have** time to tell about Gideon, Barak, Samson, Jephthah,

2143 ἐπιλείχω, *epileichō* [1] [√ *2093 + 3314*]

licked [1]

Lk 16: 21 the rich man's table. Even the dogs came and **licked** his sores.

2144 ἐπιλησμονή, *epilēsmonē* [1] [√ *2093 + 3291*]

forgetting [1]

Jas 1: 25 to do this, not **forgetting** what he has heard, but doing it—

2145 ἐπίλοιπος, *epiloipos* [1] [√ *2093 + 3309*]

rest [1]

1Pe 4: 2 he does not live the **rest** of his earthly life for evil human desires,

2146 ἐπίλυσις, *epilysis* [1] [√ *2093 + 3395*]

interpretation [1]

2Pe 1: 20 of Scripture came about *by* the prophet's own **interpretation**.

2147 ἐπιλύω, *epilyō* [2] [√ *2093 + 3395*]

explained [1], settled [1]

Mk 4: 34 he was alone with his own disciples, *he* **explained** everything.
Ac 19: 39 you want to bring up, *it must be* **settled** in a legal assembly.

2148 ἐπιμαρτυρέω, *epimartyreō* [1] [√ *2093 + 3459*]

testifying that [1]

1Pe 5: 12 encouraging you and **testifying that** this is the true grace of God.

2149 ἐπιμέλεια, *epimeleia* [1] [√ *2093 + 3508*]

for needs [1]

Ac 27: 3 him to go to his friends so they might provide **for** his **needs**.

2150 ἐπιμελέομαι, *epimeleomai* [3] [√ *2093 + 3508*]

look after [1], take care of [1], took care of [1]

Lk 10: 34 man on his own donkey, took him to an inn and **took care of** him.
     10: 35 '**Look after** him,' he said, 'and when I return, I will reimburse you
1Ti 3: 5 manage his own family, how *can he* **take care of** God's church?)

2151 ἐπιμελῶς, *epimelōs* [1] [√ *2093 + 3508*]

carefully [1]

Lk 15: 8 a lamp, sweep the house and search **carefully** until she finds it?

2152 ἐπιμένω, *epimenō* [16] [√ *2093 + 3531*]

stayed [3], continue in [2], kept on [2], been there [1], go on [1],
persevere in [1], persist in [1], remain [1], spend time [+*5989*] [1],
spend [1], stay on [1], stay [1]

Jn 8: 7 When *they* **kept on** questioning him, he straightened up and said
Ac 10: 48 Then they asked Peter *to* **stay** *with* them for a few days.
     12: 16 But Peter **kept on** knocking, and when they opened the door
     21: 4 Finding the disciples there, *we* **stayed** *with* them seven days.
     21: 10 *After we had* **been there** a number of days, a prophet named
     28: 12 *We* put in at Syracuse and **stayed** there three days.
     28: 14 There we found some brothers who invited us *to* **spend** a week
Ro 6: 1 then? *Shall we* **go on** sinning so that grace may increase?
     11: 22 but kindness to you, provided that *you* **continue in** his kindness.
     11: 23 And if they *do not* **persist in** unbelief, they will be grafted in,
1Co 16: 7 I hope *to* **spend** some **time** [+*5989*] with you, if the Lord permits.
     16: 8 But *I will* **stay on** at Ephesus until Pentecost,
Gal 1: 18 to get acquainted with Peter and **stayed** with him fifteen days.
Php 1: 24 but it is more necessary for you that I **remain** in the body.
Col 1: 23 if *you* **continue in** your faith, established and firm, not moved
1Ti 4: 16 **Persevere in** them, because if you do, you will save both yourself

2153 ἐπινεύω, *epineuō* [1] [√ *2093 + 3748*]

declined [+*4024*] [1]

Ac 18: 20 asked him to spend more time with them, *he* **declined** [+*4024*].

2154 ἐπίνοια, *epinoia* [1] [√ *2093 + 3808*]

thought [1]

Ac 8: 22 Perhaps he will forgive you for having such a **thought** in your

2155 ἐπιορκέω, *epiorkeō* [1] [√ *2093 + 3992*]

break oath [1]

Mt 5: 33 '*Do* not **break** *your* **oath**, but keep the oaths you have made to the

2156 ἐπίορκος, *epiorkos* [1] [√ *2093 + 3992*]

perjurers [1]

1Ti 1: 10 and perverts, *for* slave traders and liars and **perjurers**—

2157 ἐπιούσιος, *epiousios* [2] [√ *2093 + 1639*]

daily [2]

Mt 6: 11 Give us today our **daily** bread.
Lk 11: 3 Give us each day our **daily** bread.

2158 ἐπιπίπτω, *epipiptō* [11] [√ *2093 + 4406*]

came on [*RP2093*] [2], come upon [*RP1639+2093*] [1], embraced
[+*2093+3836+5549*] [1], fallen on [*RP2093*] [1], gripped with
[*RP2093*] [1], pushing forward [1], seized with [*RP2093*] [1],
struck [*RP2093*] [1], threw arms around [+*2093+3836+5549*] [1],
threw himself on [1]

Mk 3: 10 so that those with diseases *were* **pushing forward** to touch him.
Lk 1: 12 saw him, he was startled and *was* **gripped** [*RP2093*] **with** fear.
     15: 20 **threw** [+*2093+3836+5549*] his **arms around** him and kissed him.
Ac 8: 16 because the Holy Spirit *had* not yet **come** [*RP1639+2093*] **upon**

10:44　the Holy Spirit **came** [*RP2093*] **on** all who heard the message.
11:15　the Holy Spirit [*RP2093*] **on** them as he had come on us at
19:17　living in Ephesus, they *were* all **seized** [*RP2093*] **with** fear,
20:10　**threw himself on** the young man and put his arms around him.
20:37　wept as *they* **embraced** [*+2093+3836+5549*] him and kissed him.
Ro　15: 3　"The insults of those who insult you *have* **fallen** [*RP2093*] **on** me."
Rev　11:11　on their feet, and terror **struck** [*RP2093*] those who saw them.

2159 ἐπιπλήσσω, *epiplēssō* [1] [√ *2093 + 4448*]

rebuke harshly [1]

1Ti　5: 1　*Do* not **rebuke** an older man **harshly**, but exhort him as if he were

2160 ἐπιποθέω, *epipotheō* [9] [→ *2161, 2162, 2163; cf. 2093*]

long [3], crave [1], hearts go out to [1], intensely [*+4639*] [1], long for [1], longing [1], longs for [*+1639*] [1]

Ro　1:11　*I* **long** to see you so that I may impart to you some spiritual gift to
2Co　5: 2　we groan, **longing** to be clothed with our heavenly dwelling,
　　9:14　And in their prayers for you their **hearts** *will* **go out to** you,
Php　1: 8　God can testify how *I* **long for** all of you with the affection of
　　2:26　For *he* **longs** [*+1639*] **for** all of you and is distressed because you
1Th　3: 6　always have pleasant memories of us and that *you* **long** to see us,
2Ti　1: 4　Recalling your tears, *I* **long** to see you, so that I may be filled with
Jas　4: 5　that the spirit he caused to live in us envies **intensely** [*+4639*]?
1Pe　2: 2　Like newborn babies, **crave** pure spiritual milk, so that by it you

2161 ἐπιπόθησις, *epipothēsis* [2] [√ *2160*]

longing for [1], longing [1]

2Co　7: 7　He told us about your **longing for** me, your deep sorrow, your
　　7:11　what indignation, what alarm, what **longing**, what concern,

2162 ἐπιπόθητος, *epipothētos* [1] [√ *2160*]

long for [1]

Php　4: 1　my brothers, you whom I love and **long for**, my joy and crown,

2163 ἐπιποθία, *epipothia* [1] [√ *2160*]

longing [*+2400*] [1]

Ro　15:23　and *since I have been* **longing** [*+2400*] for many years to see you,

2164 ἐπιπορεύομαι, *epiporeuomai* [1] [√ *2093 + 4513*]

coming [1]

Lk　8: 4　and people *were* **coming** to Jesus from town after town,

2165 ἐπιράπτω, *epiraptō* [1] [√ *2093 + 4827*]

sews [1]

Mk　2:21　"No one **sews** a patch of unshrunk cloth on an old garment.

2166 ἐπιρίπτω, *epiriptō* [2] [√ *2093 + 4849*]

cast on [*RP2093*] [1], threw on [1]

Lk　19:35　it to Jesus, **threw** their cloaks **on** the colt and put Jesus on it.
1Pe　5: 7　**Cast** [*RP2093*] all your anxiety **on** him because he cares for you.

2167 ἐπισείω, *episeiō* Not used in UBS/NIV [√ *2093 + 4940*]

2168 ἐπίσημος, *episēmos* [2] [√ *2093 + 4956*]

notorious [1], outstanding [1]

Mt　27:16　At that time they had a **notorious** prisoner, called Barabbas.
Ro　16: 7　They are **outstanding** among the apostles, and they were in Christ

2169 ἐπισιτισμός, *episitismos* [1] [√ *2093 + 4992*]

food [1]

Lk　9:12　surrounding villages and countryside and find **food** and lodging,

2170 ἐπισκέπτομαι, *episkeptomai* [11] [√ *2093 + 5023*]

look after [2], visit [2], care for [1], choose [1], come to help [1], come to [1], come [1], looked after [1], showed concern [1]

Mt　25:36　I was sick and *you* **looked after** me, I was in prison and you came
　　25:43　clothe me, I was sick and in prison and *you did* not **look after** me.'
Lk　1:68　God of Israel, because *he has* **come** and has redeemed his people.
　　1:78　of our God, by which the rising sun *will* **come to** us from heaven
　　7:16　appeared among us," they said. "God *has* **come to help** his people."
Ac　6: 3　**choose** seven men from among you who are known to be full of
　　7:23　Moses was forty years old, he decided *to* **visit** his fellow Israelites.
　　15:14　Simon has described to us how God at first **showed** *his* **concern** by
　　15:36　"*Let us* go back and **visit** the brothers in all the towns where we
Heb　2: 6　that you are mindful of him, the son of man that *you* **care for** him?
Jas　1:27　*to* **look after** orphans and widows in their distress and to keep

2171 ἐπισκευάζομαι, *episkeuazomai* [1] [√ *2093 + 5007*]

got ready [1]

Ac　21:15　After this, we **got ready** and went up to Jerusalem.

2172 ἐπισκηνόω, *episkēnoō* [1] [√ *2093 + 5008*]

rest on [*RP2093*] [1]

2Co　12: 9　my weaknesses, so that Christ's power *may* **rest** [*RP2093*] **on** me.

2173 ἐπισκιάζω, *episkiazō* [5] [√ *2093 + 5014*]

enveloped [3], fall on [1], overshadow [1]

Mt　17: 5　While he was still speaking, a bright cloud **enveloped** them,
Mk　9: 7　Then a cloud appeared and **enveloped** them, and a voice came
Lk　1:35　upon you, and the power of the Most High *will* **overshadow** you.
　　9:34　While he was speaking, a cloud appeared and **enveloped** them,
Ac　5:15　so that at least Peter's shadow *might* **fall on** some of them as he

2174 ἐπισκοπέω, *episkopeō* [2] [√ *2093 + 5023*]

see to it [1], serving as overseers [1]

Heb　12:15　**See to it** that no one misses the grace of God and that no bitter root
1Pe　5: 2　of God's flock that is under your care, **serving as overseers**—

2175 ἐπισκοπή, *episkopē* [4] [√ *2093 + 5023*]

coming [1], overseer [1], place of leadership [1], visits [1]

Lk　19:44　because you did not recognize the time *of* God's **coming** to you."
Ac　1:20　to dwell in it,' and, " 'May another take his **place of leadership**.'
1Ti　3: 1　If anyone sets his heart on being an **overseer**, he desires a noble
1Pe　2:12　may see your good deeds and glorify God on the day *he* **visits** us.

2176 ἐπίσκοπος, *episkopos* [5] [√ *2093 + 5023*]

overseer [3], overseers [2]

Ac　20:28　and all the flock of which the Holy Spirit has made you **overseers**.
Php　1: 1　Christ Jesus at Philippi, together with the **overseers** and deacons:
1Ti　3: 2　Now the **overseer** must be above reproach, the husband of
Tit　1: 7　Since an **overseer** is entrusted with God's work, he must be
1Pe　2:25　you have returned to the Shepherd and **Overseer** of your souls.

2177 ἐπισπάομαι, *epispaomai* [1] [√ *2093 + 5060*]

become uncircumcised [1]

1Co　7:18　*He should* not **become uncircumcised**. Was a man uncircumcised

2178 ἐπισπείρω, *epispeirō* [1] [√ *2093 + 5062*]

sowed [1]

Mt 13:25 his enemy came and **sowed** weeds among the wheat, and went

2179 ἐπίσταμαι, *epistamai* [14] [√ *2093 + 2705*]

know [6], understand [2], familiar [1], knew [1], know about [1], know that [1], understands [1], well aware [1]

Mk 14:68 "I don't know or **understand** what you're talking about," he said,
Ac 10:28 "You *are* **well aware** that it is against our law for a Jew to associate
    15: 7 you **know** that some time ago God made a choice among you that
    18:25 about Jesus accurately, *though he* **knew** only the baptism of John.
    19:15 "Jesus I know, and *I* **know about** Paul, but who are you?"
    19:25 "Men, *you* **know** we receive a good income from this business.
    20:18 "You **know** how I lived the whole time I was with you,
    22:19 'these men **know** that I went from one synagogue to another to
    24:10 "*I* **know that** for a number of years you have been a judge over
    26:26 The king *is* **familiar** with these things, and I can speak freely to
1Ti 6: 4 he is conceited and **understands** nothing. He has an unhealthy
Heb 11: 8 and went, *even though he did* not **know** where he was going.
Jas 4:14 Why, you *do* not even **know** what will happen tomorrow.
Jude 1:10 and what things *they do* **understand** by instinct, like unreasoning

2180 ἐπίστασις, *epistasis* [2] [√ *2093 + 2705*]

pressure [1], stirring up [*+4472*] [1]

Ac 24:12 or **stirring** [*+4472*] **up** a crowd in the synagogues or anywhere else
2Co 11:28 I face daily the **pressure** of my concern for all the churches.

2181 ἐπιστάτης, *epistatēs* [7] [√ *2093 + 2705*]

Master [7]

Lk 5: 5 Simon answered, "**Master**, we've worked hard all night
    8:24 The disciples went and woke him, saying, "**Master**, Master,
    8:24 The disciples went and woke him, saying, "Master, **Master**,
    8:45 When they all denied it, Peter said, "**Master**, the people are
    9:33 Peter said to him, "**Master**, it is good for us to be here.
    9:49 "**Master**," said John, "we saw a man driving out demons in your
    17:13 and called out in a loud voice, "Jesus, **Master**, have pity on us!"

2182 ἐπιστέλλω, *epistellō* [3] [√ *2186*]

write [1], written a letter [1], written [1]

Ac 15:20 Instead *we should* **write** to them, telling them to abstain from food
    21:25 we *have* **written** to them our decision that they should abstain
Heb 13:22 my word of exhortation, for *I have* **written** you only a short **letter**.

2183 ἐπιστήμη, *epistēmē* Not used in UBS/NIV
[√ *2093 + 2705*]

2184 ἐπιστήμων, *epistēmōn* [1] [√ *2093 + 2705*]

understanding [1]

Jas 3:13 Who is wise and **understanding** among you? Let him show it by

2185 ἐπιστηρίζω, *epistērizō* [4] [√ *2093 + 5114*]

strengthening [3], strengthen [1]

Ac 14:22 **strengthening** the disciples and encouraging them to remain true
    15:32 said much to encourage and **strengthen** the brothers.
    15:41 He went through Syria and Cilicia, **strengthening** the churches.
    18:23 the region of Galatia and Phrygia, **strengthening** all the disciples.

2186 ἐπιστολή, *epistolē* [24] [→ *2182; cf. 2093 + 5097*]

letter [15], letters [9]

Ac 9: 2 and asked him for **letters** to the synagogues in Damascus,
    15:30 where they gathered the church together and delivered the **letter**.
    22: 5 I even obtained **letters** from them to their brothers in Damascus,
    23:25 He wrote a **letter** as follows:

    23:33 they delivered the **letter** to the governor and handed Paul over to
Ro 16:22 I, Tertius, who wrote down this **letter**, greet you in the Lord.
1Co 5: 9 I have written you in my **letter** not to associate with sexually
    16: 3 I will give **letters** *of introduction* to the men you approve
2Co 3: 1 like some people, **letters** of recommendation to you or from you?
    3: 2 You yourselves are our **letter**, written on our hearts, known
    3: 3 You show that you are a **letter** from Christ, the result of our
    7: 8 Even if I caused you sorrow by my **letter**, I do not regret it.
    7: 8 regret it—I see that my **letter** hurt you, but only for a little while—
    10: 9 I do not want to seem to be trying to frighten you with my **letters**.
    10:10 For some say, "His **letters** are weighty and forceful, but in person
    10:11 Such people should realize that what we are in our **letters** when we
Col 4:16 After this **letter** has been read to you, see that it is also read in the
1Th 5:27 I charge you before the Lord to have this **letter** read to all the
2Th 2: 2 by some prophecy, report or **letter** supposed to have come from us,
    2:15 we passed on to you, whether by word of mouth or by **letter**.
    3:14 If anyone does not obey our instruction in this **letter**, take special
    3:17 in my own hand, which is the distinguishing mark in all my **letters**.
2Pe 3: 1 Dear friends, this is now my second **letter** to you. I have written
    3:16 He writes the same way in all his **letters**, speaking in them of these

2187 ἐπιστομίζω, *epistomizō* [1] [√ *2093 + 5125*]

silenced [1]

Tit 1:11 They must *be* **silenced**, because they are ruining whole households

2188 ἐπιστρέφω, *epistrephō* [36] [√ *2093 + 5138*]

turn [4], turned [4], go [3], turn to [*RP2093*] [3], turned around [3], return [2], returned [2], turned to [*RP2093*] [2], turns [2], bring back to [*RP2093*] [1], bring back [1], comes back [1], go back [1], returned to [*RP2093*] [1], returns to [*RP2093*] [1], turn to [1], turned back [1], turning back to [*RP2093*] [1], turning to [*RP2093*] [1], turning [1]

Mt 10:13 let your peace rest on it; if it is not, *let* your peace **return** to you.
    12:44 Then it says, '*I will* **return** to the house I left.' When it arrives,
    13:15 hear with their ears, understand with their hearts and **turn**,
    24:18 *Let* no one in the field **go** back to get his cloak.
Mk 4:12 never understanding; otherwise they *might* **turn** and be forgiven!' "
    5:30 He **turned around** in the crowd and asked, "Who touched my
    8:33 But *when* Jesus **turned** and looked at his disciples, he rebuked
    13:16 *Let* no one in the field **go** back to get his cloak.
Lk 1:16 Many of the people of Israel *will he* **bring** [*RP2093*] **back to** the
    1:17 *to* **turn** [*RP2093*] the hearts of the fathers **to** their children
    2:39 the Lord, *they* **returned** to Galilee to their own town of Nazareth.
    8:55 Her spirit **returned**, and at once she stood up. Then Jesus told
    17: 4 and seven times **comes back** to you and says, 'I repent,'
    17:31 Likewise, no one in the field *should* **go** back *for anything*.
    22:32 And when you *have* **turned back**, strengthen your brothers."
Jn 21:20 Peter **turned** and saw that the disciple whom Jesus loved was
Ac 3:19 Repent, then, and **turn to** God, so that your sins may be wiped out,
    9:35 in Lydda and Sharon saw him and **turned** [*RP2093*] **to** the Lord.
    9:40 **Turning** toward the dead woman, he said, "Tabitha, get up."
    11:21 great number of people believed and **turned** [*RP2093*] **to** the Lord.
    14:15 telling you *to* **turn** [*RP2093*] from these worthless things **to** the
    15:19 it difficult for the Gentiles who *are* **turning** [*RP2093*] **to** God.
    15:36 "Let us **go back** and visit the brothers in all the towns where we
    16:18 Finally Paul became so troubled that he **turned around** and said to
    26:18 to open their eyes and **turn** them from darkness to light, and from
    26:20 I preached that they should repent and **turn** [*RP2093*] **to** God
    28:27 hear with their ears, understand with their hearts and **turn**,
2Co 3:16 But whenever *anyone* **turns** to the Lord, the veil is taken away.
Gal 4: 9 how is it that *you are* **turning** [*RP2093*] **back to** those weak
1Th 1: 9 They tell how *you* **turned** to God from idols to serve the living
Jas 5:19 wander from the truth and someone *should* **bring** him **back**,
    5:20 Whoever **turns** a sinner from the error of his way will save him
1Pe 2:25 but now *you have* **returned** [*RP2093*] **to** the Shepherd
2Pe 2:22 "A dog **returns** [*RP2093*] **to** its vomit," and, "A sow that is washed
Rev 1:12 *I* **turned around** to see the voice that was speaking to me.
    1:12 to me. And *when I* **turned** I saw seven golden lampstands,

2189 ἐπιστροφή, *epistrophē* [1] [√ *2093 + 5138*]

converted [1]

Ac 15: 3 and Samaria, they told how the Gentiles had been **converted**.

2190 ἐπισυνάγω, *episynagō* [8] [√ 2093 + 5250 + 72]

gather [3], gather together [2], gathered [+*1639*] [1], gathered [1], gathers [1]

Mt 23:37 how often I have longed *to* **gather** your children **together**,
     23:37 as a hen **gathers** her chicks under her wings, but you were not
     24:31 and *they will* **gather** his elect from the four winds, from one end
Mk 1:33 The whole town **gathered** [+*1639*] at the door,
     13:27 he will send his angels and **gather** his elect from the four winds,
Lk 12: 1 Meanwhile, *when* a crowd of many thousands *had* **gathered**,
     13:34 how often I have longed *to* **gather** your children **together**,
     17:37 "Where there is a dead body, there the vultures *will* **gather**."

2191 ἐπισυναγωγή, *episynagōgē* [2] [√ 2093 + 5252]

gathered to [*RP2093*] [1], meeting together [1]

2Th 2: 1 of our Lord Jesus Christ and our *being* **gathered** [*RP2093*] **to** him,
Heb 10:25 Let us not give up **meeting together**, as some are in the habit of

2192 ἐπισυντρέχω, *episyntrechō* [1]
[√ 2093 + 5250 + 5556]

running [1]

Mk 9:25 When Jesus saw that a crowd *was* **running** to the scene,

2193 ἐπισυρράπτω, *episyrraptō* Not used in UBS/NIV

2194 ἐπισύστασις, *episystasis* Not used in UBS/NIV
[√ 2093 + 5250 + 2705]

2195 ἐπισφαλής, *episphalēs* [1] [√ 2093 + 5378]

dangerous [1]

Ac 27: 9 and sailing had already become **dangerous** because by now it was

2196 ἐπισχύω, *epischyō* [1] [√ 2093 + 2709]

insisted [1]

Lk 23: 5 But they **insisted**, "He stirs up the people all over Judea by his

2197 ἐπισωρεύω, *episōreuō* [1] [√ 2093 + 5397]

gather a great number [1]

2Ti 4: 3 *they will* **gather** around them **a great number** of teachers to say

2198 ἐπιταγή, *epitagē* [7] [√ 2093 + 5435]

command [5], authority [1], commanding [+*2848*+*3306*] [1]

Ro 16:26 and made known through the prophetic writings by the **command**
1Co 7: 6 I say this as a concession, not as a **command**.
     7:25 I have no **command** from the Lord, but I give a judgment as one
2Co 8: 8 *I am* not **commanding** [+*2848*+*3306*] you, but I want to test the
1Ti 1: 1 an apostle of Christ Jesus by the **command** of God our Savior,
Tit 1: 3 the preaching entrusted to me by the **command** of God our Savior,
     2:15 Encourage and rebuke with all **authority**. Do not let anyone

2199 ἐπιτάσσω, *epitassō* [10] [√ 2093 + 5435]

gives orders [2], order [2], ordered [2], command [1], commands [1], directed [1], orders [1]

Mk 1:27 *He* even **gives orders** to evil spirits and they obey him."
     6:27 So he immediately sent an executioner with **orders** to bring John's
     6:39 Then Jesus **directed** them to have all the people sit down in groups
     9:25 "You deaf and mute spirit," he said, "I **command** you, come out of
Lk 4:36 With authority and power *he* **gives orders** to evil spirits and they
     8:25 *He* **commands** even the winds and the water, and they obey him."
     8:31 And they begged him repeatedly not to **order** them to go into the
     14:22 " 'Sir,' the servant said, 'what *you* **ordered** has been done, but there
Ac 23: 2 At this the high priest Ananias **ordered** those standing near Paul to

Phm 1: 8 Christ I could be bold and **order** you to do what you ought to do,

2200 ἐπιτελέω, *epiteleō* [10] [√ 2093 + 5465]

attain goal [1], bring to completion [1], build [1], carry it on to completion [1], carry on [1], completed [1], completion [1], finish [1], perfecting [1], undergoing [1]

Ro 15:28 So *after I have* **completed** this task and have made sure that they
2Co 7: 1 and spirit, **perfecting** holiness out of reverence for God.
     8: 6 to **bring** also **to completion** this act of grace on your part.
     8:11 Now **finish** the work, so that your eager willingness to do it may
     8:11 willingness to do it may be matched by your **completion** of it,
Gal 3: 3 *are you* now *trying to* **attain** *your* **goal** by human effort?
Php 1: 6 in you *will* **carry it on to completion** until the day of Christ Jesus.
Heb 8: 5 This is why Moses was warned when he was about to **build** the
     9: 6 the priests entered regularly into the outer room *to* **carry on** their
1Pe 5: 9 throughout the world *are* **undergoing** the same kind of sufferings.

2201 ἐπιτήδειος, *epitēdeios* [1] [√ 2093 + 3836]

needs [1]

Jas 2:16 and well fed," but does nothing about his physical **needs**,

2202 ἐπιτίθημι, *epitithēmi* [39] [√ 2093 + 5502]

put on [*RP2093*] [5], put on [5], placed on [4], place on [3], gave [2], laying on [2], placed on [*RP2093*] [2], add to [*RP2093*] [1], adds to [*RP2093*] [1], attack [1], beat [+*4435*] [1], flogged [+*4435*] [1], furnished with [1], laid on [1], lay on [1], on lay [1], place on [*RP2093*] [1], placed [1], placing on [*RP2093*] [1], puts on [*RP2093*] [1], putting on [*RP2093*] [1], set on [*RP2093*] [1], to burden [+*983*] [1]

Mt 9:18 But come and **put** [*RP2093*] your hand **on** her, and she will live."
     19:13 children were brought to Jesus for *him to* **place** his hands **on** them
     19:15 *When he had* **placed** his hands **on** them, he went on from there.
     21: 7 the donkey and the colt, **placed** [*RP2093*] their cloaks **on** them,
     23: 4 *They* tie up heavy loads and **put** [*RP2093*] them **on** men's
     27:29 twisted together a crown of thorns and **set** [*RP2093*] it **on** his head.
     27:37 Above his head *they* **placed** the written charge against him:
Mk 3:16 the twelve he appointed: Simon (to whom *he* **gave** the name Peter);
     3:17 and his brother John (to them *he* **gave** the name Boanerges,
     5:23 Please come and **put** your hands **on** her so that she will be healed
     6: 5 except **lay** his hands **on** a few sick people and heal them.
     7:32 hardly talk, and they begged him to **place** his hand **on** the man.
     8:23 *When he had* spit on the man's eyes and **put** his hands **on** him,
     8:25 Once more Jesus **put** [*RP2093*] his hands **on** the man's eyes.
     16:18 *they will* **place** [*RP2093*] their hands **on** sick people, and they will
Lk 4:40 of sickness, and **laying** his hands **on** each one, he healed them.
     10:30 They stripped him of his clothes, **beat** [+*4435*] him and went away,
     13:13 Then *he* **put** his hands **on** her, and immediately she straightened up
     15: 5 when he finds it, *he* joyfully **puts** [*RP2093*] it **on** his shoulders
     23:26 and **put** the cross **on** him and made him carry it behind Jesus.
Jn 9:15 "*He* **put** [*RP2093*] mud **on** my eyes," the man replied, "and I
     19: 2 soldiers twisted together a crown of thorns and **put** it **on** his head.
Ac 6: 6 men to the apostles, who prayed and **laid** their hands **on** them.
     8:17 Then Peter and John **placed** [*RP2093*] their hands **on** them,
     8:19 so that everyone **on** whom *I* **lay** my hands may receive the Holy
     9:12 Ananias come and **place** his hands **on** him to restore his sight."
     9:17 **Placing** [*RP2093*] his hands **on** Saul, he said, "Brother Saul,
     13: 3 and prayed, *they* **placed** their hands **on** them and sent them off.
     15:10 why do you try to test God *by* **putting** [*RP2093*] **on** the necks of
     15:28 and to us not **to burden** you **with** [+*983*] anything beyond the
     16:23 *After they had been* severely **flogged** [+*4435*], they were thrown
     18:10 For I am with you, and no one *is going to* **attack** and harm you,
     19: 6 *When* Paul **placed** his hands **on** them, the Holy Spirit came on
     28: 3 *as he* **put** [*RP2093*] it **on** the fire, a viper, driven out by the heat,
     28: 8 see him and, after prayer, **placed** his hands **on** him and healed him.
     28:10 were ready to sail, *they* **furnished** us **with** the supplies we needed.
1Ti 5:22 *Do* not be hasty in the **laying on** of hands, and do not share in the
Rev 22:18 If anyone **adds** [*RP2093*] *anything* **to** them, God will add to him
     22:18 God *will* **add** [*RP2093*] **to** him the plagues described in this book.

2203 ἐπιτιμάω, *epitimaō* [29 / 30] [√ *2093 + 5507*]

rebuked [17], rebuke [6], sternly [2], warned [2], gave orders [1], strictly warned [+4133] [1], warning [1]

Mt 8:26 Then *he* got up and **rebuked** the winds and the waves, and it was
     12:16 **warning** them not to tell who he was.
     16:20 Then *he* **warned** [UBS *1403*] his disciples not to tell anyone that
     16:22 Peter took him aside and began *to* **rebuke** him. "Never, Lord!"
     17:18 Jesus **rebuked** the demon, and it came out of the boy, and he was
     19:13 pray for them. But the disciples **rebuked** those who brought them.
     20:31 The crowd **rebuked** them and told them to be quiet,
Mk 1:25 "Be quiet!" said Jesus **sternly**. "Come out of him!"
     3:12 But *he* **gave** them strict **orders** not to tell who he was.
     4:39 *He* got up, **rebuked** the wind and said to the waves, "Quiet!
     8:30 Jesus **warned** them not to tell anyone about him.
     8:32 about this, and Peter took him aside and began *to* **rebuke** him.
     8:33 when Jesus turned and looked at his disciples, *he* **rebuked** Peter.
     9:25 that a crowd was running to the scene, *he* **rebuked** the evil spirit.
    10:13 to Jesus to have him touch them, but the disciples **rebuked** them.
    10:48 Many **rebuked** him and told him to be quiet,
Lk 4:35 "Be quiet!" Jesus said **sternly**. "Come out of him!" Then the demon
     4:39 So *he* bent over her and **rebuked** the fever, and it left her.
     4:41 But *he* **rebuked** them and would not allow them to speak,
     8:24 He got up and **rebuked** the wind and the raging waters; the storm
     9:21 Jesus **strictly warned** [+4133] them not to tell this to anyone.
     9:42 But Jesus **rebuked** the evil spirit, healed the boy and gave him
     9:55 But Jesus turned and **rebuked** them,
    17: 3 "If your brother sins, **rebuke** him, and if he repents, forgive him.
    18:15 him touch them. When the disciples saw this, *they* **rebuked** them.
    18:39 Those who led the way **rebuked** him and told him to be quiet,
    19:39 in the crowd said to Jesus, "Teacher, **rebuke** your disciples!"
    23:40 But the other criminal **rebuked** him. "Don't you fear God,"
2Ti 4: 2 in season and out of season; correct, **rebuke** and encourage—
Jude 1: 9 accusation against him, but said, "The Lord **rebuke** you!"

2204 ἐπιτιμία, *epitimia* [1] [√ *2093 + 5507*]

punishment [1]

2Co 2: 6 The **punishment** inflicted on him by the majority is sufficient for

2205 ἐπιτρέπω, *epitrepō* [18] [√ *2093 + 5572*]

let [5], allowed [3], gave permission [2], permission [2], permitted [2], permit [1], permits [1], permitting [1], received permission [1]

Mt 8:21 disciple said to him, "Lord, first **let** me go and bury my father."
    19: 8 "Moses **permitted** you to divorce your wives because your hearts
Mk 5:13 *He* **gave** them **permission**, and the evil spirits came out and went
    10: 4 "Moses **permitted** a man to write a certificate of divorce and send
Lk 8:32 The demons begged Jesus to **let** them go into them, and he gave
     8:32 Jesus to let them go into them, and *he* **gave** them **permission**.
     9:59 But the man replied, "Lord, first **let** me go and bury my father."
     9:61 Lord; but first **let** me go back and say good-by to my family."
Jn 19:38 With Pilate's **permission**, he came and took the body away.
Ac 21:39 a citizen of no ordinary city. Please **let** me speak to the people."
    21:40 *Having* **received** the commander's **permission**, Paul stood on the
    26: 1 Agrippa said to Paul, "You *have* **permission** to speak for yourself."
    27: 3 **allowed** him to go to his friends so they might provide for his
    28:16 When we got to Rome, Paul *was* **allowed** to live by himself,
1Co 14:34 They *are* not **allowed** to speak, but must be in submission,
    16: 7 I hope to spend some time with you, if the Lord **permits**.
1Ti 2:12 *I do* not **permit** a woman to teach or to have authority over a man;
Heb 6: 3 And God **permitting**, we will do so.

2206 ἐπιτροπεύω, *epitropeuō*   Not used in UBS/NIV
[√ *2093 + 5572*]

2207 ἐπιτροπή, *epitropē* [1] [√ *2093 + 5572*]

commission [1]

Ac 26:12 Damascus with the authority and **commission** of the chief priests.

2208 ἐπίτροπος, *epitropos* [3] [√ *2093 + 5572*]

foreman [1], guardians [1], manager of household [1]

Mt 20: 8 the owner of the vineyard said *to* his **foreman**, 'Call the workers
Lk   8: 3 Joanna the wife of Cuza, the **manager of** Herod's **household**;
Gal 4: 2 He is subject to **guardians** and trustees until the time set by his

2209 ἐπιτυγχάνω, *epitynchanō* [5] [√ *2093 + 5593*]

did^s [1], gained [1], have [1], obtain [1], received [1]

Ro 11: 7 What then? What Israel sought so earnestly *it did* not **obtain**,
    11: 7 Israel sought so earnestly it did not obtain, but the elect **did**^{s}.
Heb 6:15 so after waiting patiently, Abraham **received** what was promised.
    11:33 administered justice, and **gained** what was promised;
Jas 4: 2 You kill and covet, but you cannot **have** what you want.

2210 ἐπιφαίνω, *epiphainō* [4] [√ *2093 + 5743*]

appeared [3], shine on [1]

Lk   1:79 *to* **shine on** those living in darkness and in the shadow of death,
Ac 27:20 *When* neither sun nor stars **appeared** for many days and the storm
Tit 2:11 For the grace of God that brings salvation *has* **appeared** to all
     3: 4 But when the kindness and love of God our Savior **appeared**,

2211 ἐπιφάνεια, *epiphaneia* [6] [√ *2093 + 5743*]

appearing [5], splendor [1]

2Th 2: 8 the breath of his mouth and destroy *by* the **splendor** of his coming.
1Ti 6:14 or blame until the **appearing** of our Lord Jesus Christ,
2Ti 1:10 but it has now been revealed through the **appearing** of our Savior,
     4: 1 and the dead, and in view of his **appearing** and his kingdom,
     4: 8 not only to me, but also to all who have longed for his **appearing**.
Tit 2:13 the glorious **appearing** of our great God and Savior, Jesus Christ,

2212 ἐπιφανής, *epiphanēs* [1] [√ *2093 + 5743*]

glorious [1]

Ac 2:20 blood before the coming of the great and **glorious** day of the Lord.

2213 ἐπιφαύσκω, *epiphauskō* [1] [√ *2093 + 5743*]

shine on [1]

Eph 5:14 O sleeper, rise from the dead, and Christ *will* **shine on** you."

2214 ἐπιφέρω, *epipherō* [2] [√ *2093 + 5770*]

bring against [1], bringing [1]

Ro 3: 5 what shall we say? That God is unjust in **bringing** his wrath on us?
Jude 1: 9 did not dare *to* **bring** a slanderous accusation **against** him,

2215 ἐπιφωνέω, *epiphōneō* [4] [√ *2093 + 5889*]

shouted [2], shouting at [1], shouting [1]

Lk 23:21 But they *kept* **shouting**, "Crucify him! Crucify him!"
Ac 12:22 They **shouted**, "This is the voice of a god, not of a man."
    21:34 Some in the crowd **shouted** one thing and some another, and since
    22:24 in order to find out why the *people were* **shouting at** him like this.

2216 ἐπιφώσκω, *epiphōskō* [2] [√ *2093 + 5743*]

about to begin [1], dawn [1]

Mt 28: 1 *at* **dawn** on the first day of the week, Mary Magdalene
Lk 23:54 It was Preparation Day, and the Sabbath *was* **about to begin**.

2217 ἐπιχειρέω, *epicheireō* [3] [√ *2093 + 5931*]

tried [2], undertaken [1]

Lk 1: 1 Many *have* **undertaken** to draw up an account of the things that
Ac 9:29 and debated with the Grecian Jews, but they **tried** to kill him.
    19:13 Some Jews who went around driving out evil spirits **tried** to

2218 ἐπιχείρησις, **epicheirēsis**   Not used in UBS/NIV   [√ *2093 + 5931*]

2219 ἐπιχέω, **epicheō**   [1]   [√ *1772; cf. 2093*]

pouring on [1]

Lk   10:34   went to him and bandaged his wounds, **pouring on** oil and wine.

2220 ἐπιχορηγέω, **epichorēgeō**   [5]
[√ *2093 + 5962 + 72*]

add [1], give [1], receive [1], supplies [1], supported [1]

2Co   9:10   Now he *who* **supplies** seed to the sower and bread for food will
Gal   3: 5   *Does* God **give** you his Spirit and work miracles among you
Col   2:19   **supported** and held together by its ligaments and sinews,
2Pe   1: 5   this very reason, make every effort *to* **add** to your faith goodness;
     1:11   and you *will* **receive** a rich welcome into the eternal kingdom of

2221 ἐπιχορηγία, **epichorēgia**   [2]
[√ *2093 + 5962 + 72*]

help given [1], supporting [1]

Eph   4:16   joined and held together by every **supporting** ligament, grows
Php   1:19   your prayers and the **help given** by the Spirit of Jesus Christ,

2222 ἐπιχρίω, **epichriō**   [2]   [√ *2093 + 5987*]

put on [RP2093] [1], put on [1]

Jn   9: 6   some mud with the saliva, and **put** [RP2093] it **on** the man's eyes.
     9:11   "The man they call Jesus made some mud and **put** it **on** my eyes.

2223 ἐπιψαύω, **epipsauō**   Not used in UBS/NIV
[√ *2093 + 6041*]

2224 ἐποικοδομέω, **epoikodomeō**   [7]
[√ *2093 + 3875 + 1560*]

build up [1], building on [1], builds on [RP2093] [1], builds [1],
built on [RP2093] [1], built up [1], built [1]

1Co   3:10   as an expert builder, and someone else *is* **building on** it.
     3:10   is building on it. But each one should be careful how *he* **builds**.
     3:12   If any man **builds** [RP2093] **on** this foundation using gold,
     3:14   If what *he has* **built** survives, he will receive his reward.
Eph   2:20   **built** [RP2093] **on** the foundation of the apostles and prophets,
Col   2: 7   rooted and **built up** in him, strengthened in the faith as you were
Jude   1:20   **build** yourselves **up** in your most holy faith and pray in the Holy

2225 ἐποκέλλω, **epokellō**   Not used in UBS/NIV
[√ *2093 + 3027*]

2226 ἐπονομάζω, **eponomazō**   [1]   [√ *2093 + 3950*]

call [1]

Ro   2:17   Now you, if *you* **call** *yourself* a Jew; if you rely on the law

2227 ἐποπτεύω, **epopteuō**   [2]   [√ *2093 + 3972*]

see [2]

1Pe   2:12   they may **see** your good deeds and glorify God on the day he visits
     3: 2   *when they* **see** the purity and reverence of your lives.

2228 ἐπόπτης, **epoptēs**   [1]   [√ *2093 + 3972*]

eyewitnesses [1]

2Pe   1:16   of our Lord Jesus Christ, but we were **eyewitnesses** of his majesty.

2229 ἔπος, **epos**   [1]

one might even say [+3306+6055] [1]

Heb   7: 9   **One might even say** [+3306+6055] that Levi, who collects the

2230 ἐπουράνιος, **epouranios**   [19]   [√ *2093 + 4041*]

heavenly [7], heavenly realms [5], heaven [3], heavenly things [2],
in heaven [2]

Jn   3:12   how then will you believe if I speak of **heavenly things**?
1Co   15:40   There are also **heavenly** bodies and there are earthly bodies;
     15:40   but the splendor *of* the **heavenly** bodies is one kind,
     15:48   and as is the *man from* **heaven**, so also are those who are of
     15:48   as is the man from heaven, so also are those who are *of* **heaven**.
     15:49   so shall we bear the likeness *of the man from* **heaven**.
Eph   1: 3   who has blessed us in the **heavenly realms** with every spiritual
     1:20   the dead and seated him at his right hand in the **heavenly realms**,
     2: 6   and seated us with him in the **heavenly realms** in Christ Jesus,
     3:10   made known to the rulers and authorities in the **heavenly realms**,
     6:12   and against the spiritual forces of evil in the **heavenly realms**.
Php   2:10   knee should bow, **in heaven** and on earth and under the earth,
2Ti   4:18   evil attack and will bring me safely to his **heavenly** kingdom.
Heb   3: 1   Therefore, holy brothers, who share in the **heavenly** calling,
     6: 4   who have tasted the **heavenly** gift, who have shared in the Holy
     8: 5   at a sanctuary that is a copy and shadow *of* what is **in heaven**.
     9:23   but the **heavenly things** themselves with better sacrifices than
     11:16   Instead, they were longing for a better country—a **heavenly** *one*.
     12:22   Mount Zion, to the **heavenly** Jerusalem, the city of the living God.

2231 ἐπτά, **hepta**   [88]   [→ *1573, 1574, 1575, 2232, 2233, 2234*]

seven [85], seventh [1], seventy-seven times [+*1574*] [1], week
[+*2465*] [1]

Mt   12:45   and takes with it **seven** other spirits more wicked than itself,
     15:34   have?" Jesus asked. "**Seven**," they replied, "and a few small fish."
     15:36   Then he took the **seven** loaves and the fish, and when he had given
     15:37   Afterward the disciples picked up **seven** basketfuls of broken
     16:10   Or the **seven** loaves for the four thousand, and how many
     18:22   "I tell you, not seven times, but **seventy-seven times** [+*1574*].
     22:25   Now there were **seven** brothers among us. The first one married
     22:26   to the second and third brother, right on down to the **seventh**.
     22:28   Now then, at the resurrection, whose wife will be *of* the **seven**,
Mk   8: 5   many loaves do you have?" Jesus asked. "**Seven**," they replied.
     8: 6   When he had taken the **seven** loaves and given thanks, he broke
     8: 8   Afterward the disciples picked up **seven** basketfuls of broken
     8:20   "And when I broke the **seven** loaves for the four thousand,
     8:20   basketfuls of pieces did you pick up?" They answered, "**Seven**."
     12:20   Now there were **seven** brothers. The first one married and died
     12:22   In fact, none of the **seven** left any children. Last of all, the woman
     12:23   whose wife will she be, since the **seven** were married to her?"
     16: 9   to Mary Magdalene, out of whom he had driven **seven** demons.
Lk   2:36   she had lived with her husband **seven** years after her marriage,
     8: 2   Mary (called Magdalene) from whom **seven** demons had come out;
     11:26   Then it goes and takes **seven** other spirits more wicked than itself,
     20:29   Now there were **seven** brothers. The first one married a woman
     20:31   and in the same way the **seven** died, leaving no children.
     20:33   whose wife will she be, since the **seven** were married to her?"
Ac   6: 3   choose **seven** men from among you who are known to be full of
     13:19   he overthrew **seven** nations in Canaan and gave their land to his
     19:14   **Seven** sons of Sceva, a Jewish chief priest, were doing this.
     20: 6   days later joined the others at Troas, where we stayed **seven** days.
     21: 4   Finding the disciples there, we stayed with them **seven** days.
     21: 8   and stayed at the house of Philip the evangelist, one of the **Seven**.
     21:27   When the **seven** days were nearly over, some Jews from the
     28:14   some brothers who invited us to spend a **week** [+*2465*] with them.
Heb   11:30   after the people had marched around them for **seven** days.
Rev   1: 4   John, *To* the **seven** churches in the province of Asia: Grace
     1: 4   and who is to come, and from the **seven** spirits before his throne,
     1:11   "Write on a scroll what you see and send it *to* the **seven** churches:
     1:12   speaking to me. And when I turned I saw **seven** golden lampstands,
     1:16   In his right hand he held **seven** stars, and out of his mouth came a
     1:20   The mystery *of* the **seven** stars that you saw in my right hand
     1:20   saw in my right hand and of the **seven** golden lampstands is this:

1: 20 The **seven** stars are the angels of the seven churches, and the seven
1: 20 The **seven** stars are the angels *of* the seven churches, and the seven
1: 20 seven churches, and the **seven** lampstands are the seven churches.
1: 20 seven churches, and the seven lampstands are the **seven** churches.
2: 1 These are the words of him who holds the **seven** stars in his right
2: 1 in his right hand and walks among the **seven** golden lampstands.
3: 1 These are the words of him who holds the **seven** spirits of God
3: 1 of him who holds the seven spirits of God and the **seven** stars.
4: 5 and peals of thunder. Before the throne, **seven** lamps were blazing.
4: 5 seven lamps were blazing. These are the **seven** spirits of God.
5: 1 a scroll with writing on both sides and sealed *with* **seven** seals.
5: 5 has triumphed. He is able to open the scroll and its **seven** seals."
5: 6 He had **seven** horns and seven eyes, which are the seven spirits of
5: 6 He had seven horns and **seven** eyes, which are the seven spirits of
5: 6 which are the **seven** spirits of God sent out into all the earth.
6: 1 I watched as the Lamb opened the first of the **seven** seals.
8: 2 And I saw the **seven** angels who stand before God, and to them
8: 2 who stand before God, and to them were given **seven** trumpets.
8: 6 Then the **seven** angels who had the seven trumpets prepared to
8: 6 Then the seven angels who had the **seven** trumpets prepared to
10: 3 When he shouted, the voices of the **seven** thunders spoke.
10: 4 And when the **seven** thunders spoke, I was about to write;
10: 4 "Seal up what the **seven** thunders have said and do not write it
11: 13 **Seven** thousand people were killed in the earthquake,
12: 3 an enormous red dragon with **seven** heads and ten horns and seven
12: 3 with seven heads and ten horns and **seven** crowns on his heads.
13: 1 He had ten horns and **seven** heads, with ten crowns on his horns,
15: 1 **seven** angels with the seven last plagues—last, because with them
15: 1 seven angels with the **seven** last plagues—last, because with them
15: 6 Out of the temple came the **seven** angels with the seven plagues.
15: 6 Out of the temple came the seven angels with the **seven** plagues.
15: 7 Then one of the four living creatures gave *to* the **seven** angels
15: 7 one of the four living creatures gave to the seven angels **seven**
15: 8 and no one could enter the temple until the **seven** plagues of the
15: 8 temple until the seven plagues *of* the **seven** angels were completed.
16: 1 Then I heard a loud voice from the temple saying *to* the **seven**
16: 1 "Go, pour out the **seven** bowls of God's wrath on the earth."
17: 1 One of the **seven** angels who had the seven bowls came and said to
17: 1 One of the seven angels who had the **seven** bowls came and said to
17: 3 with blasphemous names and had **seven** heads and ten horns.
17: 7 of the beast she rides, which has the **seven** heads and ten horns.
17: 9 The **seven** heads are seven hills on which the woman sits.
17: 9 The seven heads are **seven** hills on which the woman sits.
17: 10 They are also **seven** kings. Five have fallen, one is, the other has
17: 11 He belongs to the **seven** and is going to his destruction.
21: 9 One of the **seven** angels who had the seven bowls full of the seven
21: 9 One of the seven angels who had the **seven** bowls full of the seven
21: 9 One of the seven angels who had the seven bowls full *of* the **seven**

2232 ἐπτάκις, *heptakis* [4] [√ 2231]

seven times [4]

Mt 18: 21 I forgive my brother when he sins against me? Up to **seven times**?"
18: 22 Jesus answered, "I tell you, not **seven times**, but seventy-seven
Lk 17: 4 If he sins against you **seven times** in a day, and seven times comes
17: 4 and **seven times** comes back to you and says, 'I repent,'

2233 ἐπτακισχίλιοι, *heptakischilioi* [1]

[√ 2231 + 5943]

seven thousand [1]

Ro 11: 4 "I have reserved for myself **seven thousand** who have not bowed

2234 ἐπταπλασίων, *heptaplasiōn* Not used in
UBS/NIV [√ 2231]

2235 Ἔραστος, *Erastos* [3]

Erastus [3]

Ac 19: 22 He sent two of his helpers, Timothy and **Erastus**, to Macedonia,
Ro 16: 23 **Erastus**, who is the city's director of public works, and our brother
2Ti 4: 20 **Erastus** stayed in Corinth, and I left Trophimus sick in Miletus.

2236 ἐραυνάω, *eraunaō* [6] [→ 451, 2001; cf. 2263]

searches [3], diligently study [1], look into [1], trying to find out [1]

Jn 5: 39 You **diligently study** the Scriptures because you think that by
7: 52 **Look into** it, and you will find that a prophet does not come out of
Ro 8: 27 And he *who* **searches** our hearts knows the mind of the Spirit,
1Co 2: 10 The Spirit **searches** all things, even the deep things of God.
1Pe 1: 11 **trying to find out** the time and circumstances to which the Spirit
Rev 2: 23 Then all the churches will know that I am he *who* **searches** hearts

2237 ἐργάζομαι, *ergazomai* [41] [√ 2240]

work [7], do [6], worked [3], does [2], doing [2], done [2],
administered [1], at work [1], bring about [1], brings [1], busy [1],
carrying on [1], done [+1639] [1], earn living [1], earn [1],
evildoers [+490+3836] [1], for work [+1256+1877+4005] [1], put
to work [1], sin [+281] [1], work for a living [1], work for [1], work
hard [+3159] [1], worked for [1], working [1], works [1]

Mt 7: 23 'I never knew you. Away from me, *you* **evildoers** [+490+3836]!'
21: 28 to the first and said, 'Son, go and **work** today in the vineyard.'
25: 16 went at once and **put** his money **to work** and gained five more.
26: 10 you bothering this woman? *She has* **done** a beautiful thing to me.
Mk 14: 6 "Why are you bothering her? *She has* **done** a beautiful thing to me.
Lk 13: 14 to the people, "There are six days **for work** [+1256+1877+4005].
Jn 3: 21 plainly that what he has done *has been* **done** [+1639] through God."
5: 17 said to them, "My Father *is always* **at his work** to this very day,
5: 17 is always at his work to this very day, and I, too, *am* **working**."
6: 27 *Do* not **work for** food that spoils, but for food that endures to
6: 28 they asked him, "What must we do to **do** the works God requires?"
6: 30 you give that we may see it and believe you? What *will you* **do**?
9: 4 As long as it is day, we must **do** the work of him who sent me.
9: 4 of him who sent me. Night is coming, when no one can **work**.
Ac 10: 35 accepts men from every nation who fear him and **do** what is right.
13: 41 for I *am going to* **do** something in your days that you would never
18: 3 he was a tentmaker as they were, he stayed and **worked** with them.
Ro 2: 10 but glory, honor and peace *for* everyone who **does** good: first for
4: 4 Now *when* a man **works**, his wages are not credited to him as a
4: 5 *to* the man *who does not* **work** but trusts God who justifies the
13: 10 Love **does** no harm to its neighbor. Therefore love is the
1Co 4: 12 *We* **work hard** [+3159] with our own hands. When we are cursed,
9: 6 Or is it only I and Barnabas who must **work for a living**?
9: 13 Don't you know that those *who* **work** in the temple get their food
16: 10 with you, for *he is* **carrying on** the work of the Lord, just as I am.
2Co 7: 10 Godly sorrow **brings** repentance that leads to salvation and leaves
Gal 6: 10 Therefore, as we have opportunity, *let us* **do** good to all people,
Eph 4: 28 but must work, **doing** something useful with his own hands,
Col 3: 23 Whatever you do, **work** at it with all your heart, as working for the
1Th 2: 9 we **worked** night and day in order not to be a burden to anyone
4: 11 to mind your own business and *to* **work** with your hands, just as
2Th 3: 8 we **worked** night and day, laboring and toiling so that we would
3: 10 we gave you this rule: "If a man will not **work**, he shall not eat."
3: 11 some among you are idle. *They are* not **busy**; they are busybodies.
3: 12 in the Lord Jesus Christ to settle down and **earn** the bread they eat.
Heb 11: 33 **administered** justice, and gained what was promised;
Jas 1: 20 for man's anger *does* not **bring about** the righteous life that God
2: 9 *you* **sin** [+281] and are convicted by the law as lawbreakers.
2Jn 1: 8 Watch out that you do not lose what *you have* **worked for**,
3Jn 1: 5 you are faithful in what *you are* **doing** for the brothers,
Rev 18: 17 the sailors, and all *who* **earn** *their* **living** from the sea, will stand

2238 ἐργασία, *ergasia* [6] [√ 2240]

business [2], indulge [1], making money [1], money [1], try hard
[+1443] [1]

Lk 12: 58 **try hard** [+1443] to be reconciled to him on the way, or he may
Ac 16: 16 She earned a great deal of **money** for her owners by
16: 19 the slave girl realized that their hope *of* **making money** was gone,
19: 24 shrines of Artemis, brought in no little **business** for the craftsmen.
19: 25 "Men, you know we receive a good income from this **business**.
Eph 4: 19 over to sensuality so as to **indulge** in every kind of impurity,

2239 ἐργάτης, ergatēs [16] [√ 2240]

workers [5], worker [3], workmen [3], do [1], evildoers [+94] [1], men to work [1], them^s [+3836] [1], workman [1]

Mt   9:37   to his disciples, "The harvest is plentiful but the **workers** are few.
     9:38   of the harvest, therefore, to send out **workers** into his harvest field."
    10:10   extra tunic, or sandals or a staff; for the **worker** is worth his keep.
    20: 1   went out early in the morning to hire **men to work** in his vineyard.
    20: 2   He agreed to pay **them**^s [+3836] a denarius for the day and sent
    20: 8   'Call the **workers** and pay them their wages, beginning with the
Lk   10: 2   He told them, "The harvest is plentiful, but the **workers** are few.
    10: 2   of the harvest, therefore, to send out **workers** into his harvest field.
    10: 7   whatever they give you, for the **worker** deserves his wages.
    13:27   or where you come from. Away from me, all you **evildoers** [+94]!'
Ac   19:25   them together, along with the **workmen** in related trades, and said:
2Co   11:13   For such men are false apostles, deceitful **workmen**,
Php   3: 2   Watch out for those dogs, those men who **do** evil, those mutilators
1Ti   5:18   it is treading out the grain," and "The **worker** deserves his wages."
2Ti   2:15   a **workman** who does not need to be ashamed and who correctly
Jas   5: 4   The wages you failed to pay the **workmen** who mowed your fields

2240 ἔργον, ergon [169]

[→ 14, 15, 307, 733, 734, 1175, 1176, 1177, 1321, 1918, 1919, 1920, 1921, 2237, 2238, 2239, 2307, 2308, 2309, 2646, 2806, 2934, 2981, 3310, 3311, 3312, 3313, 4111, 4112, 4318, 4319, 4664, 5300, 5301, 5348; cf. 4816]

ἀγαθός ἔργον (good deed) [14] Ac 9:36; Ro 2:7; 13:3; 2Co 9:8; Eph 2:10; Php 1:6; Col 1:10; 2Th 2:17; 1Ti 2:10; 5:10; 2Ti 2:21; 3:17; Tit 1:16; 3:1

καλός ἔργον (good deed) [15] Mt 5:16; 26:10; Mk 14:6; Jn 10:32,33; 1Ti 3:1; 5:10,25; 6:18; Tit 2:7,14; 3:8,14; Heb 10:24; 1Pe 2:12

λόγος ... ἔργον (word ... deed) [6] Lk 24:19; Ac 7:22; Ro 15:18; Col 3:17; 2Th 2:17; 1Jn 3:18

πίστις ... ἔργον (faith ... work) [22] Ro 3:27,28; 9:32; Gal 2:16,16; 3:2,5; 1Th 1:3; 2Th 1:11; Heb 6:1; Jas 2:14,14,17,18,18,18,20,22,22,24,26; Rev 2:19

πονηρός ἔργον (evil deed) [6] Jn 3:19; 7:7; Col 1:21; 2Ti 4:18; 1Jn 3:12; 2Jn 1:11

τὸ ἔργον τοῦ θεοῦ (the work of God) [4] Jn 6:28,29; 9:3; Ro 14:20

τὸ ἔργον τοῦ νόμου (the work of the law) [9] Ro 2:15; 3:20,28; Gal 2:16,16,16; 3:2,5,10

work [35], deeds [29], done [10], works [9], doing [8], observing [8], actions [7], do [6], miracles [6], things [5], acts [4], *untranslated* [3], deed [3], action [2], did [2], does [2], thing [2], what he did [2], what^s [+3836] [2], act [1], actions deserve [+2848] [1], activity [1], assigned task [1], attack [1], behavior [1], everything^s [+3836] [1], it^s [+3836+5516] [1], it^s [1], labor [1], made [1], miracle [1], observe [1], practices [1], requirements [1], something [1], task [1], these^s [+2819] [1], this^s [+3836+4047] [1], ways [1], what he does [1], what she did [1], what^s [+3836+5516] [1], will [1]

Mt   5:16   that they may see your good **deeds** and praise your Father in
    11: 2   When John heard in prison what Christ was **doing**, he sent his
    11:19   and "sinners." ' But wisdom is proved right by her **actions**."
    23: 3   But do not do what they **do**, for they do not practice what they
    23: 5   "Everything they **do** is done for men to see: They make their
    26:10   you bothering this woman? She has done a beautiful **thing** to me.
Mk   13:34   and puts his servants in charge, each with his **assigned task**,
    14: 6   "Why are you bothering her? She has done a beautiful **thing** to me.
Lk   11:48   So you testify that you approve of what your forefathers **did**;
    24:19   powerful in word and **deed** before God and all the people.
Jn   3:19   men loved darkness instead of light because their **deeds** were evil.
    3:20   and will not come into the light for fear that his **deeds** will be
    3:21   so that it may be seen plainly that what he has **done** has been done
    4:34   "is to do the will of him who sent me and to finish his **work**.
    5:20   to your amazement he will show him even greater **things** than
    5:36   of John. For the very **work** that the Father has given me to finish,
    5:36   [RPG] and which I am doing, testifies that the Father has sent me.

    6:28   they asked him, "What must we do to do the **works** God requires?'
    6:29   Jesus answered, "The **work** of God is this: to believe in the one he
    7: 3   go to Judea, so that your disciples may see the **miracles** you do.
    7: 7   hate you, but it hates me because I testify that what it **does** is evil.
    7:21   Jesus said to them, "I did one **miracle**, and you are all astonished.
    8:39   said Jesus, "then you would do the **things** Abraham did.
    8:41   You are doing the **things** your own father does." "We are not
    9: 3   so that the **work** of God might be displayed in his life.
    9: 4   As long as it is day, we must do the **work** of him who sent me.
    10:25   not believe. The **miracles** I do in my Father's name speak for me,
    10:32   to them, "I have shown you many great **miracles** from the Father.
    10:32   from the Father. For which of these [RPG] do you stone me?"
    10:33   "We are not stoning you for *any of* these^s [+2819],"
    10:37   Do not believe me unless I do what my Father **does**.
    10:38   believe the **miracles**, that you may know and understand that the
    14:10   Rather, it is the Father, living in me, who is doing his **work**.
    14:11   or at least believe on the evidence of the **miracles** themselves.
    14:12   anyone who has faith in me will do **what**^s [+3836] I have been
    15:24   But now they have seen these **miracles**, and yet they have hated
    17: 4   I have brought you glory on earth by completing the **work** you
Ac   5:38   For if their purpose or **activity** is of human origin, it will fail.
    7:22   wisdom of the Egyptians and was powerful in speech and **action**.
    7:41   and held a celebration in honor of what their hands had **made**.
    9:36   is Dorcas), who was always **doing** good and helping the poor.
    13: 2   me Barnabas and Saul for the **work** to which I have called them."
    13:41   for I am going to do **something** in your days that you would never
    13:41   for I am going to do something in your days [RPG] that you
    14:26   where they had been committed to the grace of God for the **work**
    15:38   them in Pamphylia and had not continued with them in the **work**.
    26:20   and turn to God and prove their repentance by their **deeds**.
Ro   2: 6   God "will give to each person according to what he has **done**."
    2: 7   To those who by persistence in **doing** good seek glory, honor
    2:15   since they show that the **requirements** of the law are written on
    3:20   one will be declared righteous in his sight by **observing** the law;
    3:27   On that *of* **observing** the law? No, but on that of faith.
    3:28   that a man is justified by faith apart from **observing** the law.
    4: 2   If, in fact, Abraham was justified by **works**, he had something to
    4: 6   of the man to whom God credits righteousness apart from **works**:
    9:12   not by **works** but by him who calls   she was told, "The older will
    9:32   Because they pursued it not by faith but as if it were by **works**.
    11: 6   And if by grace, then it is no longer by **works**; if it were, grace
    13: 3   For rulers hold no terror *for* those *who* **do** right, but for those who
    13:12   So let us put aside the **deeds** of darkness and put on the armor of
    14:20   Do not destroy the **work** of God for the sake of food. All food is
    15:18   in leading the Gentiles to obey God *by* what I have said and **done**—
1Co   3:13   his **work** will be shown for what it is, because the Day will bring it
    3:13   with fire, and the fire will test the quality of each man's **work**.
    3:14   If **what**^s [+3836+5516] he has built survives, he will receive his
    3:15   If **it**^s [+3836+5516] is burned up, he will suffer loss; he himself
    5: 2   put out of your fellowship the man who did **this**^s [+3836+4047]?
    9: 1   Jesus our Lord? Are you not the *result of* my **work** in the Lord?
    15:58   Always give yourselves fully to the **work** of the Lord, because you
    16:10   with you, for he is carrying on the **work** of the Lord, just as I am.
2Co   9: 8   having all that you need, you will abound in every good **work**.
    10:11   we are absent, we will be *in* our **actions** when we are present.
    11:15   Their end will be *what* their **actions** [+2848] **deserve**.
Gal   2:16   know that a man is not justified by **observing** the law,
    2:16   may be justified by faith in Christ and not by **observing** the law,
    2:16   the law, because by **observing** the law no one will be justified.
    3: 2   Did you receive the Spirit by **observing** the law, or by believing
    3: 5   and work miracles among you because you **observe** the law,
    3:10   All who rely on **observing** the law are under a curse, for it is
    5:19   The **acts** of the sinful nature are obvious: sexual immorality,
    6: 4   Each one should test his own **actions**. Then he can take pride in
Eph   2: 9   not by **works**, so that no one can boast.
    2:10   are God's workmanship, created in Christ Jesus to do good **works**,
    4:12   to prepare God's people for **works** of service, so that the body of
    5:11   Have nothing to do with the fruitless **deeds** of darkness, but rather
Php   1: 6   that he who began a good **work** in you will carry it on to
    1:22   am to go on living in the body, this will mean fruitful **labor** for me.
    2:30   because he almost died for the **work** of Christ, risking his life to
Col   1:10   bearing fruit in every good **work**, growing in the knowledge of
    1:21   and were enemies in your minds because of your evil **behavior**.
    3:17   And whatever you do, whether in word or **deed**, do it all in the
1Th   1: 3   remember before our God and Father your **work** produced by faith,
    5:13   Hold them in the highest regard in love because of their **work**.

2Th 1:11 every good purpose of yours and every **act** prompted by your faith.
2:17 your hearts and strengthen you in every good **deed** and word.
1Ti 2:10 but with good **deeds**, appropriate for women who profess to
3: 1 anyone sets his heart on being an overseer, he desires a noble **task**.
5:10 and is well known for her good **deeds**, such as bringing up
5:10 those in trouble and devoting herself *to* all kinds of good **deeds**.
5:25 In the same way, good **deeds** are obvious, and even those that are
6:18 to be rich in good **deeds**, and to be generous and willing to share.
2Ti 1: 9 not because of anything we have **done** but because of his own
2:21 useful to the Master and prepared to do any good **work**.
3:17 the man of God may be thoroughly equipped for every good **work**.
4: 5 in all situations, endure hardship, do the **work** of an evangelist,
4:14 great deal of harm. The Lord will repay him for what he has **done**.
4:18 The Lord will rescue me from every evil **attack** and will bring me
Tit 1:16 They claim to know God, but *by* their **actions** they deny him.
1:16 They are detestable, disobedient and unfit for **doing** anything good.
2: 7 In everything set them an example *by* **doing** what is good.
2:14 himself a people that are his very own, eager to **do** what is good.
3: 1 and authorities, to be obedient, to be ready to **do** whatever is good,
3: 5 not because of righteous **things** we had done, but because of his
3: 8 in God may be careful to devote themselves *to* **doing** what is good,
3:14 Our people must learn to devote themselves to **doing** what is good,
Heb 1:10 of the earth, and the heavens are the **work** of your hands.
3: 9 your fathers tested and tried me and for forty years saw what I **did**.
4: 3 'They shall never enter my rest.' " And yet his **work** has been
4: 4 words: "And on the seventh day God rested from all his **work**."
4:10 for anyone who enters God's rest also rests from his own **work**,
6: 1 not laying again the foundation of repentance from **acts** that lead to
6:10 he will not forget your **work** and the love you have shown him as
9:14 to God, cleanse our consciences from **acts** that lead to death,
10:24 how we may spur one another on *toward* love and good **deeds**.
Jas 1: 4 Perseverance must finish its **work** so that you may be mature
1:25 to do this, not forgetting what he has heard, but doing it**s**—
2:14 my brothers, if a man claims to have faith but has no **deeds**?
2:17 faith by itself, if it is not accompanied by **action**, is dead.
2:18 But someone will say, "You have faith; I have **deeds**." Show me
2:18 "You have faith; I have deeds." Show me your faith without **deeds**,
2:18 faith without deeds, and I will show you my faith by what I **do**.
2:20 do you want evidence that faith without **deeds** is useless?
2:21 for **what he did** when he offered his son Isaac on the altar?
2:22 You see that his faith and his **actions** were working together,
2:22 and his faith was made complete by **what he did**.
2:24 You see that a person is justified by **what he does** and not by faith
2:25 righteous for **what she did** when she gave lodging to the spies
2:26 the body without the spirit is dead, so faith without **deeds** is dead.
3:13 good life, by **deeds** done in the humility that comes from wisdom.
1Pe 1:17 Since you call on a Father who judges each man's **work**
2:12 they may see your good **deeds** and glorify God on the day he visits
2Pe 2: 8 was tormented in his righteous soul *by* the lawless **deeds** he saw
3:10 and the earth and everything**s** [+*3836*] in it will be laid bare.
1Jn 3: 8 reason the Son of God appeared was to destroy the devil's **work**.
3:12 Because his own **actions** were evil and his brother's were
3:18 let us not love with words or tongue but with **actions** and in truth.
2Jn 1:11 Anyone who welcomes him shares *in* his wicked **work**.
3Jn 1:10 So if I come, I will call attention to **what**s [+*3836*] he is doing,
Jude 1:15 and to convict all the ungodly of all the ungodly **acts** they have
Rev 2: 2 I know your **deeds**, your hard work and your perseverance.
2: 5 Repent and do the **things** you did at first. If you do not repent,
2: 6 You hate the **practices** of the Nicolaitans, which I also hate.
2:19 I know your **deeds**, your love and faith, your service
2:19 and that you are now **doing** more than you did at first.
2:22 adultery with her suffer intensely, unless they repent of her **ways**.
2:23 and minds, and I will repay each of you according to your **deeds**.
2:26 To him who overcomes and does my **will** to the end, I will give
3: 1 I know your **deeds**; you have a reputation of being alive, but you
3: 2 for I have not found your **deeds** complete in the sight of my God.
3: 8 I know your **deeds**. See, I have placed before you an open door
3:15 I know your **deeds**, that you are neither cold nor hot. I wish you
9:20 by these plagues still did not repent of the **work** of their hands;
14:13 "they will rest from their labor, for their **deeds** will follow them."
15: 3 "Great and marvelous are your **deeds**, Lord God Almighty.
16:11 and their sores, but they refused to repent of what they had **done**.
18: 6 to her as she has given; pay her back double for what she has **done**.
20:12 The dead were judged according to what they had **done** as
20:13 and each person was judged according to what he had **done**.
22:12 and I will give to everyone according to what he has **done**.

2241 ἐρεθίζω, erethizō [2]

embitter [1], stirred to action [1]

2Co 9: 2 to give; and your enthusiasm *has* **stirred** most of them **to action**.
Col 3:21 Fathers, *do* not **embitter** your children, or they will become

2242 ἐρείδω, ereidō [1]

stuck fast [1]

Ac 27:41 and ran aground. The bow **stuck fast** and would not move,

2243 ἐρεύγομαι, ereugomai [1]

utter [1]

Mt 13:35 *I will* **utter** things hidden since the creation of the world."

2244 ἐρημία, erēmia [4] [√ *2245*]

remote place [2], country [1], deserts [1]

Mt 15:33 "Where could we get enough bread in this **remote place** to feed
Mk 8: 4 "But where in this **remote place** can anyone get enough bread to
2Co 11:26 in danger in the city, in danger in the **country**, in danger at sea;
Heb 11:38 They wandered in **deserts** and mountains, and in caves and holes

2245 ἔρημος, erēmos [48 / 49] [→ *2244, 2246, 2247*]

desert [32], solitary [4], desolate [3], remote [3], desert region [1],
deserted [1], lonely places [1], lonely [1], open country [1], quiet
[1], solitary places [1]

Mt 3: 1 days John the Baptist came, preaching in the **Desert** of Judea
3: 3 "A voice of one calling in the **desert**, 'Prepare the way for the Lord,
4: 1 Then Jesus was led by the Spirit into the **desert** to be tempted by
11: 7 "What did you go out into the **desert** to see? A reed swayed by the
14:13 had happened, he withdrew by boat privately to a **solitary** place.
14:15 the disciples came to him and said, "This is a **remote** place,
23:38 Look, your house is left to you **desolate**.
24:26 if anyone tells you, 'There he is, out in the **desert**,' do not go out;
Mk 1: 3 "a voice of one calling in the **desert**, 'Prepare the way for the Lord,
1: 4 baptizing in the **desert region** and preaching a baptism of
1:12 At once the Spirit sent him out into the **desert**,
1:13 and he was in the **desert** forty days, being tempted by Satan.
1:35 Jesus got up, left the house and went off to a **solitary** place,
1:45 no longer enter a town openly but stayed outside in **lonely** places.
6:31 "Come with me by yourselves to a **quiet** place and get some rest."
6:32 So they went away by themselves in a boat to a **solitary** place.
6:35 "This is a **remote** place," they said, "and it's already very late.
Lk 1:80 and he lived in the **desert** until he appeared publicly to Israel.
3: 2 the word of God came to John son of Zechariah in the **desert**.
3: 4 "A voice of one calling in the **desert**, 'Prepare the way for the Lord,
4: 1 returned from the Jordan and was led by the Spirit in the **desert**,
4:42 At daybreak Jesus went out to a **solitary** place. The people were
5:16 But Jesus often withdrew to **lonely places** and prayed.
7:24 "What did you go out into the **desert** to see? A reed swayed by the
8:29 his chains and had been driven by the demon into **solitary places**.
9:12 and find food and lodging, because we are in a **remote** place here."
13:35 Look, your house is left to you **desolate**. [UBS-] I tell you,
15: 4 Does he not leave the ninety-nine in the **open country** and go after
Jn 1:23 "I am the voice of one calling in the **desert**, 'Make straight the way
3:14 Just as Moses lifted up the snake in the **desert**, so the Son of Man
6:31 Our forefathers ate the manna in the **desert**; as it is written:
6:49 Your forefathers ate the manna in the **desert**, yet they died.
11:54 Instead he withdrew to a region near the **desert**, to a village called
Ac 1:20 "it is written in the book of Psalms, " 'May his place be **deserted**;
7:30 in the flames of a burning bush in the **desert** near Mount Sinai.
7:36 signs in Egypt, at the Red Sea and for forty years in the **desert**.
7:38 He was in the assembly in the **desert**, with the angel who spoke to
7:42 you bring me sacrifices and offerings forty years in the **desert**,
7:44 had the tabernacle of the Testimony with them in the **desert**.
8:26 of the Lord said to Philip, "Go south to the **desert** road—the **desert** road—
13:18 he endured their conduct for about forty years in the **desert**,
21:38 and led four thousand terrorists out into the **desert** some time ago?"
1Co 10: 5 with most of them; their bodies were scattered over the **desert**.
Gal 4:27 because more are the children *of* the **desolate** *woman* than of her

Heb 3: 8 as you did in the rebellion, during the time of testing in the **desert**,
      3: 17 Was it not with those who sinned, whose bodies fell in the **desert**?
Rev 12: 6 The woman fled into the **desert** to a place prepared for her by God,
     12: 14 so that she might fly to the place prepared for her in the **desert**,
     17: 3 Then the angel carried me away in the Spirit into a **desert**.

2246 ἐρημόω, *erēmoō* [5] [√ *2245*]

brought to ruin [2], ruined [2], ruin [1]

Mt 12: 25 "Every kingdom divided against itself *will be* **ruined**, and every
Lk 11: 17 "Any kingdom divided against itself *will be* **ruined**, and a house
Rev 17: 16 They will bring her *to* **ruin** and leave her naked; they will eat her
     18: 17 In one hour such great wealth *has been* **brought to ruin**!'
     18: 19 through her wealth! In one hour *she has been* **brought to ruin**!

2247 ἐρήμωσις, *erēmōsis* [3] [√ *2245*]

desolation [3]

Mt 24: 15 in the holy place 'the abomination that *causes* **desolation**,'
Mk 13: 14 "When you see 'the abomination that *causes* **desolation**' standing
Lk 21: 20 surrounded by armies, you will know that its **desolation** is near.

2248 ἐρίζω, *erizō* [1] [√ *2251*]

quarrel [1]

Mt 12: 19 *He will* not **quarrel** or cry out; no one will hear his voice in the

2249 ἐριθεία, *eritheia* [7] [√ *2251*]

selfish ambition [5], factions [1], self-seeking [1]

Ro   2: 8 But for those who are **self-seeking** and who reject the truth
2Co 12: 20 of anger, **factions**, slander, gossip, arrogance and disorder.
Gal 5: 20 hatred, discord, jealousy, fits of rage, **selfish ambition**,
Php 1: 17 The former preach Christ out of **selfish ambition**, not sincerely,
      2: 3 Do nothing out of **selfish ambition** or vain conceit, but in humility
Jas 3: 14 But if you harbor bitter envy and **selfish ambition** in your hearts,
      3: 16 For where you have envy and **selfish ambition**, there you find

2250 ἔριον, *erion* [2]

wool [2]

Heb 9: 19 together with water, scarlet **wool** and branches of hyssop,
Rev 1: 14 His head and hair were white like **wool**, as white as snow,

2251 ἔρις, *eris* [9] [→ *2248, 2249*]

quarreling [2], strife [2], arguments [1], discord [1], dissension
[1], quarrels [1], rivalry [1]

Ro   1: 29 They are full *of* envy, murder, **strife**, deceit and malice.
     13: 13 sexual immorality and debauchery, not *in* **dissension** and jealousy.
1Co 1: 11 household have informed me that there are **quarrels** among you.
      3: 3 For since there is jealousy and **quarreling** among you, are you not
2Co 12: 20 I fear that there may be **quarreling**, jealousy, outbursts of anger,
Gal 5: 20 hatred, **discord**, jealousy, fits of rage, selfish ambition,
Php 1: 15 It is true that some preach Christ out of envy and **rivalry**,
1Ti 6: 4 words that result in envy, **strife**, malicious talk, evil suspicions
Tit 3: 9 and genealogies and **arguments** and quarrels about the law,

2252 ἐρίφιον, *eriphion* [1] [√ *2253*]

goats [1]

Mt 25: 33 He will put the sheep on his right and the **goats** on his left.

2253 ἔριφος, *eriphos* [2] [→ *2252*]

goats [1], young goat [1]

Mt 25: 32 one from another as a shepherd separates the sheep from the **goats**.
Lk 15: 29 Yet you never gave me even a **young goat** so I could celebrate

2254 Ἑρμᾶς, *Hermas* [1]

Hermas [1]

Ro 16: 14 Phlegon, Hermes, Patrobas, **Hermas** and the brothers with them.

2255 ἑρμηνεία, *hermēneia* [2] [√ *2257*]

interpretation [2]

1Co 12: 10 kinds of tongues, and to still another the **interpretation** of tongues.
     14: 26 a word of instruction, a revelation, a tongue or an **interpretation**.

2256 ἑρμηνευτής, *hermēneutēs* Not used in UBS/NIV [√ *2257*]

2257 ἑρμηνεύω, *hermēneuō* [3] [→ *1448, 1449, 1450, 1549, 2255, 2256, 3493*]

means [2], translated [1]

Jn   1: 42 You will be called Cephas" (which, *when* **translated**, is Peter).
      9: 7 he told him, "wash in the Pool of Siloam" (this word **means** Sent).
Heb 7: 2 tenth of everything. First, his *name* **means** "king of righteousness";

2258 Ἑρμῆς, *Hermēs* [2]

Hermes [2]

Ac 14: 12 and Paul they called **Hermes** because he was the chief speaker.
Ro 16: 14 Phlegon, **Hermes**, Patrobas, Hermas and the brothers with them.

2259 Ἑρμογένης, *Hermogenēs* [1]

Hermogenes [1]

2Ti 1: 15 of Asia has deserted me, including Phygelus and **Hermogenes**.

2260 ἑρπετόν, *herpeton* [4]

reptiles [4]

Ac 10: 12 as well as **reptiles** of the earth and birds of the air.
     11: 6 animals of the earth, wild beasts, **reptiles**, and birds of the air.
Ro   1: 23 made to look like mortal man and birds and animals and **reptiles**.
Jas 3: 7 All kinds *of* animals, birds, **reptiles** and creatures of the sea are

2261 ἐρυθρός, *erythros* [2]

Red [2]

Ac   7: 36 signs in Egypt, at the **Red** Sea and for forty years in the desert.
Heb 11: 29 By faith the people passed through the **Red** Sea as on dry land;

2262 ἔρχομαι, *erchomai* [632] [→ *456, 524, 599, 1446, 1451, 1656, 1803, 2002, 2059, 2082, 2088, 2982, 4209, 4216, 4320, 4601, 4665, 4670, 5291, 5302*]

come [194], came [128], comes [58], coming [58], went [45],
arrived [13], go [10], *untranslated* [9], returned [6], entered
[+*1650*] [5], return [5], reached [+*1650*] [4], arrives [3], came
back [3], come back [3], going [3], gone [3], went back [3], went
out [3], brought out [2], joined [+*4639*] [2], landed
[+*1178+2093+3836*] [2], reached [+*2093*] [2], reached [2],
returns [2], rose [2], traveled [2], visit [+*4639*] [2], went up [2],
accompanied by [+*2779*] [1], acknowledge [+*2106*] [1],
approaching [+*4639*] [1], arrival [1], arrived [+*1650*] [1], been [1],
bound to come [+*450+3590*] [1], bring in [1], came home [1],
came up [1], come [+*1639*] [1], comes home [1], coming back
[1], coming of [1], condemned [+*1650+3213*] [1], fall [1], falling
[1], follow [+*3958*] [1], followed [1], gathered [1], get here [1], get
in [1], goes [1], going to happen [1], going to rain [+*3915*] [1],
grew [+*1650+3836*] [1], has served [1], here [1], hurried off
[+*5067*] [1], join [+*4639*] [1], landed [1], lighting [1], lose good
name [+*591+1650*] [1], made their way [1], make visit [1], next
[1], occurs [1], on his way [1], on their way [1], on way in [1], on
way [1], passed by [1], reaching [+*1650*] [1], rest [1], result [1],

return [+1650+3836+4099] [1], returning [1], see [+4639] [1], set off [1], struck [+2093] [1], to come [+3516] [1], traveled on [+3847] [1], visit [1], visited [+1650] [1], visited [+4639] [1], went on [1]

Mt 2: 2 We saw his star in the east and *have* **come** to worship him."
2: 8 you find him, report to me, so that I too may **go** and worship him."
2: 9 them until [**RPG**] it stopped over the place where the child was.
2:11 *On* **coming** to the house, they saw the child with his mother Mary,
2:23 and he **went** and lived in a town called Nazareth. So was fulfilled
3: 7 of the Pharisees and Sadducees **coming** to where he was baptizing,
3:11 But after me *will* **come** one who is more powerful than I,
3:14 saying, "I need to be baptized by you, and *do* you **come** to me?"
3:16 saw the Spirit of God descending like a dove and **lighting** on him.
4:13 Leaving Nazareth, he **went** and lived in Capernaum, which was by
5:17 "Do not think that *I have* **come** to abolish the Law or the Prophets;
5:17 the Prophets; *I have* not **come** to abolish them but to fulfill them.
5:24 and be reconciled to your brother; then **come** and offer your gift.
6:10 your kingdom **come**, your will be done on earth as it is in heaven.
7:15 They **come** to you in sheep's clothing, but inwardly they are
7:25 the streams **rose**, and the winds blew and beat against that house;
7:27 the streams **rose**, and the winds blew and beat against that house,
8: 7 Jesus said to him, "I will **go** and heal him."
8: 9 this one, 'Go,' and he goes; and that one, 'Come,' and he comes.
8: 9 this one, 'Go,' and he goes; and that one, 'Come,' and *he* **comes**.
8:14 *When* Jesus **came** into Peter's house, he saw Peter's
8:28 *When* he **arrived** at the other side in the region of the Gadarenes,
8:29 "*Have you* **come** here to torture us before the appointed time?"
9: 1 Jesus stepped into a boat, crossed over and **came** to his own town.
9:10 collectors and "sinners" **came** and ate with him and his disciples.
9:13 For *I have* not **come** to call the righteous, but sinners."
9:15 The time *will* **come** when the bridegroom will be taken from them;
9:18 he was saying this, a ruler **came** and knelt before him and said,
9:18 just died. But **come** and put your hand on her, and she will live."
9:23 *When* Jesus **entered** [+1650] the ruler's house and saw the flute
9:28 *When* he had **gone** indoors, the blind men came to him, and he
10:13 If the home is deserving, *let* your peace **rest** on it; if it is not,
10:23 going through the cities of Israel before the Son of Man **comes**.
10:34 "Do not suppose that *I have* **come** to bring peace to the earth.
10:34 peace to the earth. *I did* not **come** to bring peace, but a sword.
10:35 For *I have* **come** to turn " 'a man against his father, a daughter
11: 3 to ask him, "Are you the one *who was* to **come**, or should we expect
11:14 are willing to accept it, he is the Elijah who *was* to **come** [+3516].
11:18 For John **came** neither eating nor drinking, and they say, 'He has a
11:19 The Son of Man **came** eating and drinking, and they say, 'Here is a
12: 9 Going on from that place, *he* **went** into their synagogue,
12:42 for *she* **came** from the ends of the earth to listen to Solomon's
12:44 *When* it **arrives**, it finds the house unoccupied, swept clean
13: 4 some fell along the path, and the birds **came** and ate it up.
13:19 the evil one **comes** and snatches away what was sown in his heart.
13:25 his enemy **came** and sowed weeds among the wheat, and went
13:32 so that the birds of the air **come** and perch in its branches."
13:36 Then *he* left the crowd and **went** into the house. His disciples came
13:54 **Coming** to his hometown, he began teaching the people in their
14:12 and took his body and buried it. Then they **went** and told Jesus.
14:25 watch of the night Jesus went out [UBS **went**; NIV 599] to them,
14:28 if it's you," Peter replied, "tell me *to* **come** to you on the water."
14:29 "**Come**," he said. Then Peter got down out of the boat, and
14:29 down out of the boat, walked on the water and **came** toward Jesus.
14:34 had crossed over, *they* **landed** [+1178+2093+3836] at Gennesaret.
15:25 The woman **came** and knelt before him. "Lord, help me!" she said.
15:29 Jesus left there and **went** along the Sea of Galilee. Then he went up
15:39 he got into the boat and **went** to the vicinity of Magadan.
16: 5 *When they* **went** across the lake, the disciples forgot to take bread.
16:13 *When* Jesus **came** to the region of Caesarea Philippi, he asked his
16:24 "If anyone would **come** after me, he must deny himself and take up
16:27 For the Son of Man is going to **come** in his Father's glory with his
16:28 taste death before they see the Son of Man **coming** in his kingdom."
17:10 then do the teachers of the law say that Elijah must **come** first?"
17:11 Jesus replied, "To be sure, Elijah **comes** and will restore all things.
17:12 But I tell you, Elijah *has* already **come**, and they did not recognize
17:14 *When they* **came** to the crowd, a man approached Jesus and knelt
17:24 *After* Jesus and his disciples **arrived** in Capernaum, the collectors
17:25 *When* Peter **came** into the house, Jesus was the first to speak.
18: 7 Such things must **come**, but woe to the man through whom they
18: 7 things must come, but woe to the man through whom they **come**!

18:31 they were greatly distressed and **went** and told their master
19: 1 and **went** into the region of Judea to the other side of the Jordan.
19:14 Jesus said, "Let the little children **come** to me, and do not hinder
20: 9 "The workers who were hired about the eleventh hour **came**
20:10 So *when* those **came** who were hired first, they expected to receive
20:28 just as the Son of Man *did* not **come** to be served, but to serve,
21: 1 and **came** to Bethphage on the Mount of Olives,
21: 5 'See, your king **comes** to you, gentle and riding on a donkey,
21: 9 "Blessed is he who **comes** in the name of the Lord!" "Hosanna in
21:19 by the road, *he* **went** up to it but found nothing on it except leaves.
21:23 Jesus **entered** [+1650] the temple courts, and, while he was
21:32 For John **came** to you to show you the way of righteousness,
21:40 "Therefore, when the owner of the vineyard **comes**, what will he do
22: 3 to the banquet to tell them to come, but they refused *to* **come**.
23:35 so upon you *will* **come** all the righteous blood that has been shed
23:39 until you say, 'Blessed is he *who* **comes** in the name of the Lord.' "
24: 5 For many *will* **come** in my name, claiming, 'I am the Christ,'
24:30 They will see the Son of Man **coming** on the clouds of the sky,
24:39 they knew nothing about what would happen until the flood **came**
24:42 because you do not know on what day your Lord *will* **come**.
24:43 the house had known at what time of night the thief *was* **coming**,
24:44 because the Son of Man *will* **come** at an hour when you do not
24:46 for that servant whose master finds him doing so *when he* **returns**.
25:10 they were on their way to buy the oil, the bridegroom **arrived**.
25:11 "Later the others also **came**. 'Sir! Sir!' they said. 'Open the door for
25:19 "After a long time the master of those servants **returned** and settled
25:27 so that *when I* **returned** I would have received it back with
25:31 "When the Son of Man **comes** in his glory, and all the angels with
25:36 you looked after me, I was in prison and *you* **came** to visit me.'
25:39 When did we see you sick or in prison and **go** to visit you?'
26:36 Then Jesus **went** with his disciples to a place called Gethsemane,
26:40 Then *he* **returned** to his disciples and found them sleeping.
26:43 *When he* **came back**, he again found them sleeping, because their
26:45 Then *he* **returned** to the disciples and said to them, "Are you still
26:47 While he was still speaking, Judas, one of the Twelve, **arrived**.
26:64 right hand of the Mighty One and **coming** on the clouds of heaven."
27:33 *They* **came** to a place called Golgotha (which means The Place of
27:49 "Now leave him alone. Let's see if Elijah **comes** to save him."
27:57 *there* **came** a rich man from Arimathea, named Joseph,
27:64 his disciples *may* **come** and steal the body and tell the people that
28: 1 Mary Magdalene and the other Mary **went** to look at the tomb.
28:11 some of the guards **went** into the city and reported to the chief
28:13 'His disciples **came** during the night and stole him away while we

Mk 1: 7 "After me *will* **come** one more powerful than I, the thongs of whose
1: 9 At that time Jesus **came** from Nazareth in Galilee and was baptized
1:14 After John was put in prison, Jesus **went** into Galilee,
1:24 want with us, Jesus of Nazareth? *Have you* **come** to destroy us?
1:29 *they* **went** with James and John to the home of Simon and Andrew,
1:39 So *he* **traveled** throughout Galilee, preaching in their synagogues
1:40 A man with leprosy **came** to him and begged him on his knees,
1:45 lonely places. Yet the *people still* **came** to him from everywhere.
2: 3 *Some men* **came**, bringing to him a paralytic, carried by four of
2:13 the lake. A large crowd **came** to him, and he began to teach them.
2:17 but the sick. *I have* not **come** to call the righteous, but sinners."
2:18 *Some people* **came** and asked Jesus, "How is it that John's disciples
2:20 But the time *will* **come** when the bridegroom will be taken from
3: 8 many people **came** to him from Judea, Jerusalem, Idumea,
3:20 Then Jesus **entered** [+1650] a house, and again a crowd gathered,
3:31 Then Jesus' mother and brothers **arrived**. Standing outside,
4: 4 some fell along the path, and the birds **came** and ate it up.
4:15 Satan **comes** and takes away the word that was sown in them.
4:21 to them, "*Do* you **bring in** a lamp to put it under a bowl or a bed?
4:22 and whatever is concealed is meant to *be* **brought out** into the
5: 1 *They* **went** across the lake to the region of the Gerasenes.
5:14 and the *people* **went out** to see what had happened.
5:15 When *they* **came** to Jesus, they saw the man who had been
5:22 Then one of the synagogue rulers, named Jairus, **came** there.
5:23 Please **come** and put your hands on her so that she will be healed
5:26 yet instead of getting better *she* grew [+1650+3836] worse.
5:27 *she* **came up** behind him in the crowd and touched his cloak,
5:33 **came** and fell at his feet and, trembling with fear, told him the
5:35 *some men* **came** from the house of Jairus, the synagogue ruler.
5:38 When *they* **came** to the home of the synagogue ruler, Jesus saw a
6: 1 Jesus left there and **went** to his hometown, accompanied by his
6:29 John's disciples **came** and took his body and laid it in a tomb.
6:31 because so many people were **coming** and going that they did not

6: 48 About the fourth watch of the night *he* **went out** to them,
6: 53 had crossed over, *they* **landed** [+*1178+2093+3836*] at Gennesaret
7: 1 and some of the teachers of the law *who had* **come** from Jerusalem
7: 4 When *they* **come** [UBS-] from the marketplace they do not eat
7: 25 woman whose little daughter was possessed by an evil spirit **came**
7: 31 Then Jesus left the vicinity of Tyre and **went** through Sidon,
8: 10 the boat with his disciples and **went** to the region of Dalmanutha.
8: 22 *They* **came** to Bethsaida, and some people brought a blind man
8: 38 the Son of Man will be ashamed of him when *he* **comes** in his
9: 1 taste death before they see the kingdom of God **come** with power."
9: 11 "Why do the teachers of the law say that Elijah must **come** first?"
9: 12 Jesus replied, "To be sure, Elijah *does* **come** first, and restores all
9: 13 But I tell you, Elijah *has* **come**, and they have done to him
9: 14 *When they* **came** to the other disciples, they saw a large crowd
9: 33 *They* **came** to Capernaum. When he was in the house, he asked
10: 1 Jesus then left that place and **went** into the region of Judea
10: 14 He said to them, "Let the little children **come** to me, and do not
10: 30 and with them, persecutions) and in the age *to* **come**, eternal life.
10: 45 For even the Son of Man *did* not **come** to be served, but to serve,
10: 46 Then *they* **came** to Jericho. As Jesus and his disciples,
10: 50 Throwing his cloak aside, he jumped to his feet and **came** to Jesus.
11: 9 "Hosanna!" "Blessed is he *who* **comes** in the name of the Lord!"
11: 10 "Blessed is the **coming** kingdom of our father David!" "Hosanna in
11: 13 the distance a fig tree in leaf, *he* **went** to find out if it had any fruit.
11: 13 *When he* **reached** [+*2093*] it, he found nothing but leaves,
11: 15 On **reaching** [+*1650*] Jerusalem, Jesus entered the temple area
11: 27 *They* **arrived** [+*1650*] again in Jerusalem, and while Jesus was
11: 27 chief priests, the teachers of the law and the elders **came** to him.
12: 9 *He will* **come** and kill those tenants and give the vineyard to
12: 14 They **came** to him and said, "Teacher, we know you are a man of
12: 18 who say there is no resurrection, **came** to him with a question.
12: 42 But a poor widow **came** and put in two very small copper coins,
13: 6 Many *will* **come** in my name, claiming, 'I am he,' and will deceive
13: 26 "At that time men will see the Son of Man **coming** in clouds with
13: 35 you do not know when the owner of the house *will* **come back**—
13: 36 *If he* **comes** suddenly, do not let him find you sleeping.
14: 3 a woman **came** with an alabaster jar of very expensive perfume,
14: 16 **went** into the city and found things just as Jesus had told them.
14: 17 When evening came, Jesus **arrived** with the Twelve.
14: 32 *They* **went** to a place called Gethsemane, and Jesus said to his
14: 37 Then *he* **returned** to his disciples and found them sleeping.
14: 38 Watch and pray so that *you* will not **fall** into temptation. The spirit
14: 40 *When he* **came back**, he again found them sleeping, because their
14: 41 **Returning** the third time, he said to them, "Are you still sleeping
14: 41 The hour *has* **come**. Look, the Son of Man is betrayed into the
14: 45 **Going** at once to Jesus, Judas said, "Rabbi!" and kissed him.
14: 62 right hand of the Mighty One and **coming** on the clouds of heaven."
14: 66 the courtyard, one of the servant girls of the high priest **came** *by*.
15: 21 and Rufus, was passing by **on** his **way** in from the country,
15: 36 him alone. Let's see if Elijah **comes** to take him down," he said.
15: 43 [**RPG**] who was himself waiting for the kingdom of God,
16: 1 Salome bought spices so that they might **go** to anoint Jesus' body.
16: 2 the week, just after sunrise, *they were* **on their way** to the tomb
Lk 1: 43 so favored, that the mother of my Lord *should* **come** to me?
1: 59 On the eighth day *they* **came** to circumcise the child, and they
2: 16 So *they* **hurried off** [+*5067*] and found Mary and Joseph,
2: 27 Moved by the Spirit, *he* **went** into the temple courts. When the
2: 44 he was in their company, *they* **traveled** [+*3847*] **on** for a day.
2: 51 Then he went down [**RPG**] to Nazareth with them and was
3: 3 *He* **went** into all the country around the Jordan, preaching a
3: 12 Tax collectors also **came** to be baptized. "Teacher," they asked,
3: 16 But one more powerful than I *will* **come**, the thongs of whose
4: 16 *He* **went** to Nazareth, where he had been brought up, and on the
4: 34 want with us, Jesus of Nazareth? *Have you* **come** to destroy us?
4: 42 people were looking for him and when *they* **came** to where he was,
5: 7 So they signaled their partners in the other boat to **come** and help
5: 7 and *they* **came** and filled both boats so full that they began to sink.
5: 17 who *had* **come** [+*1639*] from every village of Galilee and from
5: 32 *I have* not **come** to call the righteous, but sinners to repentance."
5: 35 But the time *will* **come** when the bridegroom will be taken from
6: 18 who *had* **come** to hear him and to be healed of their diseases.
6: 47 I will show you what he is like who **comes** to me and hears my
7: 3 elders of the Jews to him, asking him to **come** and heal his servant.
7: 7 That is why I did not even consider myself worthy *to* **come** to you.
7: 8 this one, 'Go,' and he goes; and that one, '**Come**,' and he comes.
7: 8 this one, 'Go,' and he goes; and that one, 'Come,' and *he* **comes**.

7: 19 he sent them to the Lord to ask, "Are you the one *who was to* **come**,
7: 20 'Are you the one *who was to* **come**, or should we expect someone
7: 33 For John the Baptist **came** neither eating bread nor drinking wine,
7: 34 The Son of Man **came** eating and drinking, and you say, 'Here is a
8: 12 and then the devil **comes** and takes away the word from their
8: 17 concealed that will not be known or **brought out** into the open.
8: 35 When *they* **came** to Jesus, they found the man from whom the
8: 41 named Jairus, a ruler of the synagogue, **came** and fell at Jesus' feet,
8: 47 she could not go unnoticed, **came** trembling and fell at his feet.
8: 49 someone **came** from the house of Jairus, the synagogue ruler.
8: 51 *When he* **arrived** at the house of Jairus, he did not let anyone go
9: 23 "If anyone would **come** after me, he must deny himself and take up
9: 26 the Son of Man will be ashamed of him when *he* **comes** in his
10: 1 ahead of him to every town and place where he was about to **go**.
10: 32 a Levite, when he came to the place and [**RPG**] saw him,
10: 33 But a Samaritan, as he traveled, **came** where the man was;
11: 2 say: " 'Father, hallowed be your name, your kingdom **come**.
11: 25 *When it* **arrives**, it finds the house swept clean and put in order.
11: 31 for *she* **came** from the ends of the earth to listen to Solomon's
12: 36 so that *when he* **comes** and knocks they can immediately open the
12: 37 those servants whose master finds them watching *when he* **comes**.
12: 38 even if *he* **comes** in the second or third watch of the night.
12: 39 owner of the house had known at what hour the thief *was* **coming**,
12: 40 because the Son of Man *will* **come** at an hour when you do not
12: 43 for that servant whom the master finds doing so *when he* **returns**.
12: 45 'My master is taking a long time *in* **coming**,' and he then begins to
12: 49 "*I have* **come** to bring fire on the earth, and how I wish it were
12: 54 in the west, immediately you say, '*It's* **going to rain** [+*3915*],'
13: 6 and *he* **went** to look for fruit on it, but did not find any.
13: 7 'For three years now *I've been* **coming** to look for fruit on this fig
13: 14 So **come** and be healed on those days, not on the Sabbath."
13: 35 until you say, 'Blessed is he *who* **comes** in the name of the Lord.' "
14: 1 when Jesus **went** to eat in the house of a prominent Pharisee,
14: 9 the host who invited both of you will **come** and say to you,
14: 10 so that when your host **comes**, he will say to you, 'Friend,
14: 17 those who had been invited, '**Come**, for everything is now ready.'
14: 20 "Still another said, 'I just got married, so I can't **come**.'
14: 26 "If anyone **comes** to me and does not hate his father and mother,
14: 27 not carry his cross and **follow** [+*3958*] me cannot be my disciple.
14: 31 men to oppose the one **coming** against him with twenty thousand'?
15: 6 and **goes** home. Then he calls his friends and neighbors together
15: 17 "*When he* **came** to his senses, he said, 'How many of my father's
15: 20 So *he* got up and **went** to his father. "But while he was still a long
15: 25 When he **came** near the house, he heard music and dancing.
15: 30 who has squandered your property with prostitutes **comes home**,
16: 21 the rich man's table. Even the dogs **came** and licked his sores.
16: 28 so that they *will* not also **come** to this place of torment.'
17: 1 "Things that cause people to sin are **bound to come** [+*450+3590*],
17: 1 bound to come, but woe to that person through whom *they* **come**.
17: 20 asked by the Pharisees when the kingdom of God *would* **come**,
17: 20 "The kingdom of God *does* not **come** with your careful observation,
17: 22 "The time *is* **coming** when you will long to see one of the days of
17: 27 Noah entered the ark. Then the flood **came** and destroyed them all.
18: 3 And there was a widow in that town *who kept* **coming** to him with
18: 5 so that she won't eventually wear me out *with her* **coming**!' "
18: 8 However, *when* the Son of Man **comes**, will he find faith on the
18: 16 the children to him and said, "Let the little children **come** to me,
18: 30 times as much in this age and, in the age *to* **come**, eternal life."
19: 5 When Jesus **reached** [+*2093*] the spot, he looked up and said to
19: 10 For the Son of Man **came** to seek and to save what was lost."
19: 13 ten minas. 'Put this money to work,' he said, 'until *I* **come back**.'
19: 18 "The second **came** and said, 'Sir, your mina has earned five more.'
19: 20 "Then another servant **came** and said, 'Sir, here is your mina;
19: 23 so that *when* I **came back**, I could have collected it with interest?'
19: 38 "Blessed is the king who **comes** in the name of the Lord!" "Peace in
20: 16 *He will* **come** and kill those tenants and give the vineyard to
21: 6 the time *will* **come** when not one stone will be left on another;
21: 8 For many *will* **come** in my name, claiming, 'I am he,' and,
21: 27 At that time they will see the Son of Man **coming** in a cloud with
22: 7 Then **came** the day of Unleavened Bread on which the Passover
22: 18 again of the fruit of the vine until the kingdom of God **comes**."
22: 45 When he rose from prayer and **went back** to the disciples,
23: 26 *who was* **on** his **way in** from the country, and put the cross on him
23: 29 For the time *will* **come** when you will say, 'Blessed are the barren
23: 33 When *they* **came** to the place called the Skull, there they crucified
23: 42 he said, "Jesus, remember me when *you* **come** into your kingdom."

24: 1 women took the spices they had prepared and **went** to the tomb.
24:23 *They* **came** and told us that they had seen a vision of angels,

Jn 1: 7 He **came** as a witness to testify concerning that light, so that
1: 9 The true light that gives light to every man was **coming** into the
1:11 *He* **came** to that which was his own, but his own did not receive
1:15 'He *who* **comes** after me has surpassed me because he was before
1:27 He is the one *who* **comes** after me, the thongs of whose sandals I
1:29 The next day John saw Jesus **coming** toward him and said,
1:30 'A man who **comes** after me has surpassed me because he was
1:31 but the reason I **came** baptizing with water was that he might be
1:39 "**Come**," he replied, "and you will see." So they went and saw
1:39 So *they* **went** and saw where he was staying, and spent that day
1:46 come from there?" Nathanael asked. "**Come** and see," said Philip.
1:47 *When* Jesus saw Nathanael **approaching** [+4639], he said of him,
3: 2 He **came** to Jesus at night and said, "Rabbi, we know you are a
3: 2 "Rabbi, we know you are a teacher *who has* **come** from God.
3: 8 but you cannot tell where *it* **comes** from or where it is going.
3:19 Light *has* **come** into the world, but men loved darkness instead of
3:20 and *will* not **come** into the light for fear that his deeds will be
3:21 But whoever lives by the truth **comes** into the light, so that it may
3:22 Jesus and his disciples **went out** into the Judean countryside,
3:26 *They* **came** to John and said to him, "Rabbi, that man who was with
3:26 well, he is baptizing, and everyone *is* **going** to him."
3:31 "The one *who* **comes** from above is above all; the one who is from
3:31 one from the earth. The one *who* **comes** from heaven is above all.
4: 5 So *he* **came** to a town in Samaria called Sychar, near the plot of
4: 7 *When* a Samaritan woman **came** to draw water, Jesus said to her,
4:16 He told her, "Go, call your husband and **come** back."
4:21 a time *is* **coming** when you will worship the Father neither on this
4:23 Yet a time *is* **coming** and has now come when the true worshipers
4:25 The woman said, "I know that Messiah" (called Christ) "*is* **coming**.
4:25 "is coming. When *he* **comes**, he will explain everything to us."
4:27 Just then his disciples **returned** and were surprised to find him
4:30 They came out of the town and **made their way** toward him.
4:35 [NIE] I tell you, open your eyes and look at the fields!
4:40 So when the Samaritans **came** to him, they urged him to stay with
4:45 When *he* **arrived** in Galilee, the Galileans welcomed him.
4:45 in Jerusalem at the Passover Feast, for they also *had* **been** there.
4:46 Once more *he* **visited** [+1650] Cana in Galilee, where he had
4:54 sign that Jesus performed, *having* **come** from Judea to Galilee.
5: 7 While I *am trying to* **get in**, someone else goes down ahead of me."
5:24 sent me has eternal life and *will* not *be* **condemned** [+1650+3213];
5:25 a time *is* **coming** and has now come when the dead will hear the
5:28 for a time *is* **coming** when all who are in their graves will hear his
5:40 yet you refuse *to* **come** to me to have life.
5:43 I *have* **come** in my Father's name, and you do not accept me;
5:43 but if someone else **comes** in his own name, you will accept him.
6: 5 When Jesus looked up and saw a great crowd **coming** toward him,
6:14 to say, "Surely this is the Prophet who *is to* **come** into the world."
6:15 knowing that they intended to **come** and make him king by force,
6:17 they got into a boat and **set off** across the lake for Capernaum.
6:17 By now it was dark, and Jesus *had* not yet **joined** [+4639] them.
6:23 Then some boats from Tiberias **landed** near the place where the
6:24 they got into the boats and **went** to Capernaum in search of Jesus.
6:35 He *who* **comes** to me will never go hungry, and he who believes in
6:37 come to me, and whoever **comes** to me I will never drive away.
6:44 "No one can **come** to me unless the Father who sent me draws him,
6:45 who listens to the Father and learns from him **comes** to me.
6:65 "This is why I told you that no one can **come** to me unless the
7:27 when the Christ **comes**, no one will know where he is from."
7:28 *I am* not **here** on my own, but he who sent me is true. You do not
7:30 but no one laid a hand on him, because his time *had* not yet **come**.
7:31 They said, "When the Christ **comes**, will he do more miraculous
7:34 but you will not find me; and where I am, you cannot **come**."
7:36 but you will not find me,' and 'Where I am, you cannot **come**'?"
7:37 in a loud voice, "If anyone is thirsty, *let him* **come** to me and drink.
7:41 Still others asked, "How *can* the Christ **come** from Galilee?
7:42 Does not the Scripture say that the Christ *will* **come** from David's
7:45 Finally the temple guards **went back** to the chief priests
7:50 who *had* **gone** to Jesus earlier and who was one of their own
8: 2 where all the people **gathered** around him, and he sat down to
8:14 is valid, for I know where *I* **came** from and where I am going.
8:14 But you have no idea where *I* **came** from or where I am going.
8:20 Yet no one seized him, because his time *had* not yet **come**.
8:21 and you will die in your sin. Where I go, you cannot **come**."
8:22 kill himself? Is that why he says, 'Where I go, you cannot **come**'?"

8:42 and now am here. *I have* not **come** on my own; but he sent me.
9: 4 of him who sent me. Night *is* **coming**, when no one can work.
9: 7 So the man went and washed, and **came home** seeing.
9:39 Jesus said, "For judgment I *have* **come** into this world, so that the
10: 8 All who ever came before me were thieves and robbers,
10:10 The thief **comes** only to steal and kill and destroy; I have come that
10:10 I *have* **come** that they may have life, and have it to the full.
10:12 So when he sees the wolf **coming**, he abandons the sheep and runs
10:41 and many people **came** to him. They said, "Though John never
11:17 *On his* **arrival**, Jesus found that Lazarus had already been in the
11:19 and many Jews *had* **come** to Martha and Mary to comfort them in
11:20 When Martha heard that Jesus *was* **coming**, she went out to meet
11:27 are the Christ, the Son of God, who *was to* **come** into the world."
11:29 When Mary heard this, she got up quickly and **went** to him.
11:30 Now Jesus *had* not yet **entered** [+1650] the village, but was still at
11:32 When Mary reached the place where Jesus was and saw him,
11:34 have you laid him?" he asked. "**Come** and see, Lord," they replied.
11:38 Jesus, once more deeply moved, **came** to the tomb. It was a cave
11:45 Therefore many of the Jews who *had* **come** to visit Mary,
11:48 and then the Romans will **come** and take away both our place
11:56 "What do you think? Isn't *he* **coming** to the Feast at all?"
12: 1 the Passover, Jesus **arrived** at Bethany, where Lazarus lived,
12: 9 a large crowd of Jews found out that Jesus was there and **came**,
12:12 The next day the great crowd that *had* **come** for the Feast heard
12:12 come for the Feast heard that Jesus *was* **on his way** to Jerusalem.
12:13 "Hosanna!" "Blessed is he *who* **comes** in the name of the Lord!"
12:15 of Zion; see, your king *is* **coming**, seated on a donkey's colt."
12:22 Philip **went** to tell Andrew; Andrew and Philip in turn told Jesus.
12:22 went to tell Andrew; Andrew and Philip in turn [RPG] told Jesus.
12:23 "The hour *has* **come** for the Son of Man to be glorified.
12:27 from this hour'? No, it was for this very reason *I* **came** to this hour.
12:28 Then a voice **came** from heaven, "I have glorified it, and will
12:46 I *have* **come** into the world as a light, so that no one who believes
12:47 judge him. For *I did* not **come** to judge the world, but to save it.
13: 1 Jesus knew that the time *had* **come** for him to leave this world
13: 6 *He* **came** to Simon Peter, who said to him, "Lord, are you going to
13:33 the Jews, so I tell you now: Where I am going, you cannot **come**.
14: 3 *I will* **come** back and take you to be with me that you also may be
14: 6 and the life. No one **comes** to the Father except through me.
14:18 I will not leave you as orphans; *I will* **come** to you.
14:23 love him, and *we will* **come** to him and make our home with him.
14:28 heard me say, 'I am going away and *I am* **coming back** to you.'
14:30 with you much longer, for the prince of this world *is* **coming**.
15:22 If *I had* not **come** and spoken to them, they would not be guilty of
15:26 "When the Counselor **comes**, whom I will send to you from the
16: 2 a time *is* **coming** when anyone who kills you will think he is
16: 4 so that when the time **comes** you will remember that I warned you.
16: 7 Unless I go away, the Counselor *will* not **come** to you; but if I go,
16: 8 *When* he **comes**, he will convict the world of guilt in regard to sin
16:13 But when he, the Spirit of truth, **comes**, he will guide you into all
16:13 speak only what he hears, and he will tell you what *is yet to* **come**.
16:21 woman giving birth to a child has pain because her time *has* **come**;
16:25 a time *is* **coming** when I will no longer use this kind of language
16:28 I came from the Father and **entered** [+1650] the world; now I am
16:32 "But a time *is* **coming**, and has come, when you will be scattered,
16:32 "But a time is coming, and *has* **come**, when you will be scattered,
17: 1 he looked toward heaven and prayed: "Father, the time *has* **come**.
17:11 no longer, but they are still in the world, and I *am* **coming** to you.
17:13 "*I am* **coming** to you now, but I say these things while I am still in
18: 3 So Judas **came** to the grove, guiding a detachment of soldiers
18: 4 Jesus, knowing all that *was* **going to happen** to him, went out
18:37 was born, and for this I **came** into the world, to testify to the truth.
19: 3 and **went up** to him *again and again*, saying, "Hail, king of the
19:32 The soldiers therefore **came** and broke the legs of the first man
19:33 But *when they* **came** to Jesus and found that he was already dead,
19:38 With Pilate's permission, *he* **came** and took the body away.
19:39 *He was* **accompanied** [+2779] *by* Nicodemus, the man who earlier
19:39 the man *who* earlier *had* **visited** [+4639] Jesus at night.
20: 1 Mary Magdalene **went** to the tomb and saw that the stone had been
20: 2 So *she* **came** running to Simon Peter and the other disciple,
20: 3 So Peter and the other disciple started [RPG] for the tomb.
20: 4 the other disciple outran Peter and **reached** [+1650] the tomb first.
20: 6 who was behind him, **arrived** and went into the tomb.
20: 8 other disciple, who *had* **reached** the tomb first, also went inside.
20:18 Mary Magdalene **went** to the disciples with the news: "I have seen
20:19 Jesus **came** and stood among them and said, "Peace be with you!"

20:24   one of the Twelve, was not with the disciples when Jesus **came**.
20:26   Jesus **came** and stood among them and said, "Peace be with you!"
21: 3   to fish," Simon Peter told them, and they said, "We'll **go** with you."
21: 8   The other disciples **followed** in the boat, towing the net full of fish,
21:13   Jesus **came**, took the bread and gave it to them, and did the same
21:22   Jesus answered, "If I want him to remain alive until *I* **return**,
21:23   he only said, "If I want him to remain alive until *I* **return**, what is

Ac   1:11   *will* **come back** in the same way you have seen him go into
    2:20   and the moon to blood before the **coming of** the great and glorious
    3:19   be wiped out, that times of refreshing *may* **come** from the Lord,
    4:23   Peter and John **went back** to their own people and reported all that
    5:15   least Peter's shadow might fall on some of them *as he* **passed by**.
    7:11   "Then a famine **struck** [+2093] all Egypt and Canaan,
    8:27   of the Ethiopians. This man *had* **gone** to Jerusalem to worship,
    8:36   they **came** to some water and the eunuch said, "Look, here is water.
    8:40   preaching the gospel in all the towns until he **reached** [+1650]
    9:17   who appeared to you on the road *as you were* **coming** here—
    9:21   And *hasn't he* **come** here to take them as prisoners to the chief
  10:29   So when I was sent for, *I* **came** without raising any objection.
  11: 5   from heaven by its four corners, and *it* **came** down to where I was.
  11:12   These six brothers also **went** with me, and we entered the man's
  11:20   and Cyrene, **went** to Antioch and began to speak to Greeks also,
  12:10   and second guards and **came** to the iron gate leading to the city.
  12:12   he **went** to the house of Mary the mother of John, also called
  13:13   and his companions sailed [RPG] to Perga in Pamphylia,
  13:25   No, but *he is* **coming** after me, whose sandals I am not worthy to
  13:44   On the **next** Sabbath almost the whole city gathered to hear the
  13:51   dust from their feet in protest against them and **went** to Iconium.
  14:24   After going through Pisidia, *they* **came** into Pamphylia,
  16: 7   *When they* **came** to the border of Mysia, they tried to enter
  16:37   rid of us quietly? No! Let them **come** themselves and escort us out."
  16:39   *They* **came** to appease them and escorted them from the prison,
  17: 1   through Amphipolis and Apollonia, *they* **came** to Thessalonica,
  17:13   they **went** there too, agitating the crowds and stirring them up.
  17:15   for Silas and Timothy to **join** [+4639] him as soon as possible.
  18: 1   After this, Paul left Athens and **went** to Corinth.
  18: 2   *who had* recently **come** from Italy with his wife Priscilla,
  19: 4   He told the people to believe in the one **coming** after him,
  19: 6   the Holy Spirit **came** on them, and they spoke in tongues
  19:18   Many of those who believed *now* **came** and openly confessed their
  19:27   not only that our trade *will* **lose** [+591+1650] its **good name**,
  20: 2   of encouragement to the people, and *finally* **arrived** in Greece,
  20: 6   and five days later **joined** [+4639] the others at Troas, where we
  20:14   he met us at Assos, *we* took him aboard and **went on** to Mitylene.
  20:15   over to Samos, and on the following day **arrived** at Miletus.
  21: 1   The next day *we* **went** to Rhodes and from there to Patara.
  21: 8   *we* **reached** [+1650] Caesarea and stayed at the house of Philip the
  21:11   **Coming** over to us, he took Paul's belt, tied his own hands
  21:22   What shall we do? They will certainly hear that *you have* **come**,
  22:11   My companions led me by the hand [RPG] into Damascus,
  22:12   "A man named Ananias **came** to see me. He was a devout observer
  25:23   The next day Agrippa and Bernice **came** with great pomp
  27: 8   the coast with difficulty and **came** to a place called Fair Havens,
  28:13   came up, and on the following day *we* **reached** [+1650] Puteoli.
  28:14   invited us to spend a week with them. And so *we* **came** to Rome.
  28:15   and *they* **traveled** as far as the Forum of Appius and the Three
  28:23   and **came** in even larger numbers to the place where he was

Ro   1:10   last by God's will the way may be opened for me *to* **come** to you.
    1:13   that I planned many times *to* **come** to you (but have been
    3: 8   as some claim that we say—"Let us do evil that good *may* **result**"?
    7: 9   but *when* the commandment came, sin sprang to life and I died
    9: 9   "At the appointed time *I will* **return**, and Sarah will have a son."
  15:22   This is why I have often been hindered from **coming** to you.
  15:23   and since I have been longing for many years *to* **see** [+4639] you,
  15:29   I know that *when I* **come** to you, I will come in the full measure of
  15:29   to you, *I will* **come** in the full measure of the blessing of Christ.
  15:32   so that by God's will *I may* **come** to you with joy and together

1Co   2: 1   When I **came** to you, brothers, I did not come with eloquence
    2: 1   I *did not* **come** with eloquence or superior wisdom as I proclaimed
    4: 5   judge nothing before the appointed time; wait till the Lord **comes**.
    4:18   of you have become arrogant, as if *I* *were* not **coming** to you.
    4:19   But *I will* **come** to you very soon, if the Lord is willing, and
    4:21   Shall *I* **come** to you with a whip, or in love and with a gentle
  11:26   and drink this cup, you proclaim the Lord's death until *he* **comes**.
  11:34   result in judgment. And when *I* **come** I will give further directions.
  13:10   but when perfection **comes**, the imperfect disappears.

  14: 6   Now, brothers, if *I* **come** to you and speak in tongues, what good
  15:35   are the dead raised? With what kind of body *will they* **come**?"
  16: 2   it up, so that when *I* **come** no collections will have to be made.
  16: 5   After I go through Macedonia, *I will* **come** to you—for I will be
  16:10   If Timothy **comes**, see to it that he has nothing to fear while he is
  16:11   Send him on his way in peace so that *he may* **return** to me.
  16:12   I strongly urged him to **go** to you with the brothers.
  16:12   He was quite unwilling to **go** now, but he will go when he has the
  16:12   unwilling to go now, but *he will* **go** when he has the opportunity.

2Co   1:15   I planned *to* **visit** [+4639] you first so that you might benefit twice.
    1:16   my way to Macedonia and *to* **come** back to you from Macedonia,
    1:23   that it was in order to spare you that *I did* not **return** to Corinth.
    2: 1   So I made up my mind that I *would* not **make** another painful **visit**
    2: 3   so that *when I* **came** I should not be distressed by those who ought
    2:12   Now *when I* **came** to Troas to preach the gospel of Christ
    7: 5   For *when* we **came** into Macedonia, this body of ours had no rest,
    9: 4   For if any Macedonians **come** with me and find you unprepared,
  11: 4   For if someone **comes** to you and preaches a Jesus other than the
  11: 9   for the brothers who **came** from Macedonia supplied what I
  12: 1   to be gained, *I will* **go** on to visions and revelations from the Lord.
  12:14   Now I am ready *to* **visit** [+4639] you for the third time, and I will
  12:20   For I am afraid that *when I* **come** I may not find you as I want you
  12:21   I am afraid that *when I* **come** again my God will humble me before
  13: 1   This will be my third **visit** to you. "Every matter must be
  13: 2   On *my* **return** [+1650+3836+4099] I will not spare those who

Gal   1:21   Later *I* **went** to Syria and Cilicia.
    2:11   When Peter **came** to Antioch, I opposed him to his face,
    2:12   Before certain men **came** from James, he used to eat with the
    2:12   But when *they* **arrived**, he began to draw back and separate
    3:19   until the Seed to whom the promise referred *had* **come**.
    3:23   Before this faith **came**, we were held prisoners by the law,
    3:25   Now that faith *has* **come**, we are no longer under the supervision
    4: 4   But when the time *had* fully **come**, God sent his Son, born of a

Eph   2:17   He **came** and preached peace to you who were far away and peace
    5: 6   because of such things God's wrath **comes** on those who are

Php   1:12   that what has happened to me **has** really **served** to advance the
    1:27   whether *I* **come** and see you or only hear about you in my absence,
    2:24   And I am confident in the Lord that I myself *will* **come** soon.

Col   3: 6   Because of these, the wrath of God *is* **coming**.
    4:10   instructions about him; if *he* **comes** to you, welcome him.)

1Th   1:10   from the dead—Jesus, who rescues us from the **coming** wrath.
    2:18   For we wanted *to* **come** to you—certainly I, Paul, did, again
    3: 6   But Timothy *has* just now **come** to us from you and has brought
    5: 2   for you know very well that the day of the Lord *will* **come** like a

2Th   1:10   on the day *he* **comes** to be glorified in his holy people and to be
    2: 3   for ιhat day will not come, until the rebellion **occurs** and the man

1Ti   1:15   Christ Jesus **came** into the world to save sinners—of whom I am
    2: 4   wants all men to be saved and *to* **come** to a knowledge of the truth.
    3:14   Although I hope *to* **come** to you soon, I am writing you these
    4:13   Until *I* **come**, devote yourself to the public reading of Scripture,

2Ti   3: 7   always learning but never able *to* **acknowledge** [+2106] the truth.
    4: 9   Do your best *to* **come** to me quickly,
    4:13   *When* you **come**, bring the cloak that I left with Carpus at Troas,
    4:21   Do your best *to* **get here** before winter. Eubulus greets you,

Tit   3:12   or Tychicus to you, do your best *to* **come** to me at Nicopolis,

Heb   6: 7   Land that drinks in the rain often **falling** on it and that produces a
    8: 8   "The time *is* **coming**, declares the Lord, when I will make a new
  10:37   a very little while, "He *who is* **coming** will come and will not delay.
  11: 8   and went, even though he did not know where *he was* **going**.
  13:23   been released. If *he* **arrives** soon, I will come with him to see you.

2Pe   3: 3   you must understand that in the last days scoffers *will* **come**,

1Jn   2:18   and as you have heard that the antichrist *is* **coming**, even now
    4: 2   Every spirit that acknowledges that Jesus Christ *has* **come** in the
    4: 3   which you have heard *is* **coming** and even now is already in the
    5: 6   This is the *one who* **came** by water and blood—Jesus Christ.

2Jn   1: 7   who do not acknowledge Jesus Christ as **coming** in the flesh,
    1:10   If anyone **comes** to you and does not bring this teaching, do not

3Jn   1: 3   It gave me great joy to have some brothers **come** and tell about
    1:10   So if *I* **come**, I will call attention to what he is doing,

Jude   1:14   the Lord *is* **coming** with thousands upon thousands of his holy

Rev   1: 4   peace to you from him who is, and who was, and who *is to* **come**,
    1: 7   Look, *he is* **coming** with the clouds, and every eye will see him,
    1: 8   "who is, and who was, and who *is to* **come**, the Almighty."
    2: 5   *I will* **come** to you and remove your lampstand from its place.
    2:16   *I will* soon **come** to you and will fight against them with the sword
    3:10   I will also keep you from the hour of trial that is going to **come**

3:11 *I am* **coming** soon. Hold on to what you have, so that no one will
4: 8 holy is the Lord God Almighty, who was, and is, and *is to* **come**.”
5: 7 *He* **came** and took the scroll from the right hand of him who sat on
6: 1 one of the four living creatures say in a voice like thunder, “**Come!**”
6: 3 the second seal, I heard the second living creature say, “**Come!**”
6: 5 opened the third seal, I heard the third living creature say, “**Come!**”
6: 7 I heard the voice of the fourth living creature say, “**Come!**”
6:17 For the great day of their wrath *has* **come**, and who can stand?”
7:13 in white robes—who are they, and where *did they* **come** from?”
7:14 “These are they *who have* **come** out of the great tribulation;
8: 3 who had a golden censer, **came** and stood at the altar.
9:12 The first woe is past; two other woes are yet *to* **come**.
11:14 The second woe has passed; the third woe *is* **coming** soon.
11:18 The nations were angry; and your wrath *has* **come**. The time has
14: 7 and give him glory, because the hour of his judgment *has* **come**.
14:15 “Take your sickle and reap, because the time to reap *has* **come**,
16:15 “Behold, *I* **come** like a thief! Blessed is he who stays awake
17: 1 One of the seven angels who had the seven bowls **came** and said to
17:10 Five have fallen, one is, the other *has* not yet **come**; but when he
17:10 but when *he does* **come**, he must remain for a little while.
18:10 O Babylon, city of power! In one hour your doom *has* **come**!’
19: 7 For the wedding of the Lamb *has* **come**, and his bride has made
21: 9 angels who had the seven bowls full of the seven last plagues **came**
22: 7 “Behold, *I am* **coming** soon! Blessed is he who keeps the words of
22:12 “Behold, *I am* **coming** soon! My reward is with me, and I will give
22:17 The Spirit and the bride say, “**Come!**” And let him who hears say,
22:17 and the bride say, “**Come!**” And let him who hears say,
22:17 Whoever is thirsty, *let him* **come**; and whoever wishes, let him
22:20 He who testifies to these things says, “Yes, *I am* **coming** soon.”
22:20 things says, “Yes, I am coming soon.” Amen. **Come**, Lord Jesus.

2263 ἐρωτάω, erōtaō [63] [→ *1452, 2089, 2090; cf. 2236*]

asked [19], ask [18], urged [3], asks [2], begged [2], invited [2], please [+*5148*] [2], pray [2], prayer is [2], questioned [2], ask questions [1], asked for [1], asking [1], beg [1], praying [1], question [1], questioning [1], request [1], requesting [1]

Mt 15:23 So his disciples came to him and **urged** him, “Send her away,
    16:13 he **asked** his disciples, “Who do people say the Son of Man is?”
    19:17 “Why *do you* **ask** me about what is good?” Jesus replied. “There is
    21:24 Jesus replied, “I *will* also **ask** you one question. If you answer me,
Mk 4:10 and the others around him **asked** him *about* the parables.
    7:26 She **begged** Jesus to drive the demon out of her daughter.
    8: 5 many loaves do you have?” Jesus **asked**. “Seven,” they replied.
Lk 4:38 was suffering from a high fever, and *they* **asked** Jesus to help her.
    5: 3 belonging to Simon, and **asked** him to put out a little from shore.
    7: 3 elders of the Jews to him, **asking** him to come and heal his servant.
    7:36 Now one of the Pharisees **invited** Jesus to have dinner with him,
    8:37 Then all the people of the region of the Gerasenes **asked** Jesus to
    9:45 that they did not grasp it, and they were afraid *to* **ask** him about it.
    11:37 had finished speaking, a Pharisee **invited** him to eat with him;
    14:18 a field, and I must go and see it. **Please** [+*5148*] excuse me.’
    14:19 and I’m on my way to try them out. **Please** [+*5148*] excuse me.’
    14:32 the other is still a long way off and will **ask** for terms of peace.
    16:27 “He answered, ‘Then *I* **beg** you, father, send Lazarus to my father’s
    19:31 If anyone **asks** you, ‘Why are you untying it?’ tell him, ‘The Lord
    20: 3 He replied, “I *will* also **ask** you a question. Tell me,
    22:68 and if *I* **asked** you, you would not answer.
    23: 3 So Pilate **asked** Jesus, “Are you the king of the Jews?” “Yes,
Jn 1:19 Jews of Jerusalem sent priests and Levites to **ask** him who he was.
    1:21 *They* **asked** him, “Then who are you? Are you Elijah?” He said,
    1:25 **questioned** him, “Why then do you baptize if you are not the Christ
    4:31 Meanwhile his disciples **urged** him, “Rabbi, eat something.”
    4:40 *they* **urged** him to stay with them, and he stayed two days.
    4:47 he went to him and **begged** him to come and heal his son,
    5:12 So *they* **asked** him, “Who is this fellow who told you to pick it up
    8: 7 When they kept on **questioning** him, he straightened up and said to
    9: 2 His disciples **asked** him, “Rabbi, who sinned, this man or his
    9:15 Therefore the Pharisees also **asked** him how he had received his
    9:19 “Is this your son?” *they* **asked**. “Is this the one you say was born
    9:21 we don’t know. **Ask** him. He is of age; he will speak for himself.”
    12:21 came to Philip, who was from Bethsaida in Galilee, with a **request**.
    14:16 And I *will* **ask** the Father, and he will give you another Counselor
    16: 5 who sent me, yet none of you **asks** me, ‘Where are you going?’
    16:19 Jesus saw that they wanted to **ask** him *about* this, so he said to

    16:23 In that day *you will* no longer **ask** me anything. I tell you the truth,
    16:26 my name. I am not saying that I *will* **ask** the Father on your behalf.
    16:30 and that you do not even need to *have* anyone **ask** you **questions**.
    17: 9 I **pray** for them. I am not praying for the world, but for those you
    17: 9 *I am* not **praying** for the world, but for those you have given me,
    17:15 *My* **prayer is** not that you take them out of the world but that you
    17:20 “*My* **prayer is** not for them alone. I pray also for those who will
    18:19 the high priest **questioned** Jesus about his disciples and his
    18:21 Why **question** me? Ask those who heard me. Surely they know
    18:21 Why question me? **Ask** those who heard me. Surely they know
    19:31 *they* **asked** Pilate to have the legs broken and the bodies taken
    19:38 Later, Joseph of Arimathea **asked** Pilate for the body of Jesus.
Ac 1: 6 So when they met together, *they* **asked** him, “Lord, are you at this
    3: 3 he saw Peter and John about to enter, he **asked** them *for* money.
    10:48 Then *they* **asked** Peter to stay with them for a few days.
    16:39 escorted them from the prison, **requesting** them to leave the city.
    18:20 *When* they **asked** him to spend more time with them, he declined.
    23:18 sent for me and **asked** me to bring this young man to you
    23:20 “The Jews have agreed *to* **ask** you to bring Paul before the
Php 4: 3 Yes, and *I* **ask** you, loyal yokefellow, help these women who have
1Th 4: 1 *Now we* **ask** you and urge you in the Lord Jesus to do this more
    5:12 Now *we* **ask** you, brothers, to respect those who work hard among
2Th 2: 1 Jesus Christ and our being gathered to him, *we* **ask** you, brothers,
1Jn 5:16 that leads to death. I am not saying that *he should* **pray** about that.
2Jn 1: 5 we have had from the beginning. *I* **ask** that we love one another.

2264 ἐσθής, esthēs [8] [√ *2667*]

clothes [5], dressed [1], robe [1], robes [1]

Lk 23:11 Dressing him in an elegant **robe**, they sent him back to Pilate.
    24: 4 suddenly two men in **clothes** that gleamed like lightning stood
Ac 1:10 when suddenly two men **dressed** in white stood beside them.
    10:30 the afternoon. Suddenly a man in shining **clothes** stood before me
    12:21 wearing his royal **robes**, sat on his throne and delivered a public
Jas 2: 2 man comes into your meeting wearing a gold ring and fine **clothes**,
    2: 2 and fine clothes, and a poor man in shabby **clothes** also comes in.
    2: 3 If you show special attention to the man wearing fine **clothes**

2265 ἔσθησις, esthēsis   Not used in UBS/NIV [√ *2667*]

2266 ἐσθίω, esthiō [158] [→ *2267, 2983, 2984, 5303; cf. 3763, 5741*]

ἐσθίω … πίνω (eat … drink) [33] Mt 6:25,31; 11:18,19; 24:49; Lk 5:30,33; 7:33,34; 10:7; 12:19,29,45; 13:26; 17:8,8,27,28; 22:30; Ac 9:9; 23:12,21; Ro 14:21; 1Co 9:4; 10:7,31; 11:22,26,27,28,29,29; 15:32

ἐσθίω τὸ πάσχα (eat the Passover) [7] Mt 26:17; Mk 14:12,14; Lk 22:8,11,15; Jn 18:28

eat [92], ate [19], eating [19], eats [10], eaten [4], do[s] [2], does[s] [2], food [2], abstains [+*3590*] [1], consume [1], does[s] so [+*4024*] [1], drink [1], eating of [1], get food [1], have a feast [1], have dinner [1]

Mt 6:25 I tell you, do not worry about your life, what *you will* **eat** or drink;
    6:31 So do not worry, saying, ‘What *shall we* **eat**?’ or ‘What shall we
    9:11 “Why *does* your teacher **eat** with tax collectors and ‘sinners’?”
    11:18 For John came neither **eating** nor drinking, and they say, ‘He has a
    11:19 The Son of Man came **eating** and drinking, and they say, ‘Here is a
    12: 1 were hungry and began *to* pick some heads of grain and **eat** them.
    12: 4 of God, and he and his companions **ate** the consecrated bread—
    12: 4 ate the consecrated bread—which was not lawful for them *to* **do**[s],
    14:16 “They do not need to go away. You give them something *to* **eat**.”
    14:20 *They* all **ate** and were satisfied, and the disciples picked up twelve
    14:21 The number of those *who* **ate** was about five thousand men,
    15: 2 of the elders? They don’t wash their hands before *they* **eat**!”
    15:20 but **eating** with unwashed hands does not make him ‘unclean.’ ”
    15:27 even the dogs **eat** the crumbs that fall from their masters’ table.”
    15:32 they have already been with me three days and have nothing to **eat**.
    15:37 *They* all **ate** and were satisfied. Afterward the disciples picked up
    15:38 The number of those *who* **ate** was four thousand, besides women
    24:49 to beat his fellow servants and *to* **eat** and drink with drunkards.
    25:35 For I was hungry and you gave me something *to* **eat**, I was thirsty
    25:42 For I was hungry and you gave me nothing *to* **eat**, I was thirsty

26:17 "Where do you want us to make preparations for you *to* **eat** the
26:21 And *while* they *were* **eating**, he said, "I tell you the truth, one of
26:26 *While* they *were* **eating**, Jesus took bread, gave thanks and broke
26:26 and broke it, and gave it to his disciples, saying, "Take and **eat**;
Mk   1: 6 a leather belt around his waist, and *he* **ate** locusts and wild honey.
2:16 When the teachers of the law who were Pharisees saw *him* **eating**
2:16 his disciples: "Why *does he* **eat** with tax collectors and 'sinners'?"
2:26 he entered the house of God and **ate** the consecrated bread,
2:26 **ate** the consecrated bread, which is lawful only for priests *to* **eat**.
3:20 so that he and his disciples were not even able *to* **eat**.
5:43 know about this, and told them to give her something *to* **eat**.
6:31 and going that they did not even have a chance *to* **eat**,
6:36 and villages and buy themselves something *to* **eat**."
6:37 But he answered, "You give them something *to* **eat**." They said to
6:37 we to go and spend that much on bread and give it to them *to* **eat**?"
6:42 *They* all **ate** and were satisfied,
6:44 The number of the men who *had* **eaten** was five thousand.
7: 2 saw some of his disciples **eating** food with hands that were
7: 3 and all the Jews *do* not **eat** unless they give their hands a
7: 4 When they come from the marketplace *they do* not **eat** unless they
7: 5 of the elders instead of **eating** their food with 'unclean' hands?"
7:28 "but even the dogs under the table **eat** the children's crumbs."
8: 1 Since they had nothing *to* **eat**, Jesus called his disciples to him
8: 2 they have already been with me three days and have nothing *to* **eat**.
8: 8 The *people* **ate** and were satisfied. Afterward the disciples picked
11:14 he said to the tree, "*May* no one ever **eat** fruit from you again."
14:12 want us to go and make preparations for *you to* **eat** the Passover?"
14:14 my guest room, where *I may* **eat** the Passover with my disciples?'
14:18 *While* they were reclining at the table **eating**, he said, "I tell you the
14:18 the truth, one of you will betray me—one who *is* **eating** with me."
14:22 *While* they *were* **eating**, Jesus took bread, gave thanks and broke
Lk   4: 2 *He* **ate** nothing during those days, and at the end of them he was
5:30 "Why *do you* **eat** and drink with tax collectors and 'sinners'?"
5:33 the disciples of the Pharisees, but yours *go on* **eating** and drinking."
6: 1 some heads of grain, rub them in their hands and **eat** the kernels.
6: 4 the consecrated bread, *he* **ate** what is lawful only for priests to eat.
6: 4 the consecrated bread, he **ate** what is lawful only for priests *to* eat.
7:33 For John the Baptist came neither **eating** bread nor drinking wine,
7:34 The Son of Man came **eating** and drinking, and you say, 'Here is a
7:36 Now one of the Pharisees invited Jesus to **have dinner** with him,
8:55 she stood up. Then Jesus told them to give her something *to* **eat**.
9:13 He replied, "You give them something *to* **eat**." They answered,
9:17 *They* all **ate** and were satisfied, and the disciples picked up twelve
10: 7 Stay in that house, **eating** and drinking whatever they give you,
10: 8 you enter a town and are welcomed, **eat** what is set before you.
12:19 laid up for many years. Take life easy; **eat**, drink and be merry." '
12:22 I tell you, do not worry about your life, what *you will* **eat**;
12:29 And do not set your heart on what *you will* **eat** or drink; do not
12:45 and maidservants and *to* **eat** and drink and get drunk.
13:26 "Then you will say, '*We* **ate** and drank with you, and you taught in
14: 1 when Jesus went *to* **eat** in the house of a prominent Pharisee,
14:15 is the man who *will* **eat** at the feast in the kingdom of God."
15:16 longed to fill his stomach with the pods that the pigs *were* **eating**,
15:23 Bring the fattened calf and kill it. Let's **have a feast** and celebrate.
17: 8 get yourself ready and wait on me while *I* **eat** and drink;
17: 8 on me while I **eat** and drink; after that you *may* **eat** and drink'?
17:27 *People were* **eating**, drinking, marrying and being given in
17:28 *People were* **eating** and drinking, buying and selling, planting
22: 8 saying, "Go and make preparations for us to **eat** the Passover."
22:11 the guest room, where *I may* **eat** the Passover with my disciples?'
22:15 "I have eagerly desired *to* **eat** this Passover with you before I suffer.
22:16 *I will* not **eat** it *again* until it finds fulfillment in the kingdom of
22:30 so that *you may* **eat** and drink at my table in my kingdom
24:43 and *he* took it and **ate** it in their presence.
Jn   4:31 Meanwhile his disciples urged him, "Rabbi, **eat** *something*."
4:32 he said to them, "I have food *to* **eat** that you know nothing about."
4:33 said to each other, "Could someone have brought him **food**?"
6: 5 said to Philip, "Where shall we buy bread for these people *to* **eat**?"
6:23 the people *had* **eaten** the bread after the Lord had given thanks.
6:26 miraculous signs but because *you* **ate** the loaves and had your fill.
6:31 Our forefathers **ate** the manna in the desert; as it is written:
6:31 as it is written: 'He gave them bread from heaven *to* **eat**.' "
6:49 Your forefathers **ate** the manna in the desert, yet they died.
6:50 that comes down from heaven, which a man *may* **eat** and not die.
6:51 If anyone **eats** of this bread, he will live forever. This bread is my
6:52 among themselves, "How can this man give us his flesh *to* **eat**?"

6:53 unless *you* **eat** the flesh of the Son of Man and drink his blood,
6:58 Your forefathers **ate** manna and died, but he who feeds on this
18:28 not enter the palace; *they wanted to be able to* **eat** the Passover.
Ac   9: 9 For three days he was blind, and *did* not **eat** or drink anything.
10:13 Then a voice told him, "Get up, Peter. Kill and **eat**."
10:14 Peter replied. "*I* have never **eaten** anything impure or unclean."
11: 7 Then I heard a voice telling me, 'Get up, Peter. Kill and **eat**.'
23:12 and bound themselves with an oath not *to* **eat** or drink until they
23:21 They have taken an oath not *to* **eat** or drink until they have killed
27:35 to God in front of them all. Then he broke it and began *to* **eat**.
Ro 14: 2 One man's faith allows him *to* **eat** everything, but another man,
14: 2 but another man, whose faith is weak, **eats** only vegetables.
14: 3 The man *who* **eats** everything must not look down on him who
14: 3 who **eats** everything must not look down on him *who* **does**[s] not,
14: 3 and the man *who* **does** not **eat** everything must not condemn the
14: 3 does not eat everything must not condemn the man *who* **does**[s],
14: 6 He *who* **eats** meat, eats to the Lord, for he gives thanks to God;
14: 6 He who **eats** meat, **eats** to the Lord, for he gives thanks to God;
14: 6 and he *who* **abstains** [+3590], does so to the Lord and gives
14: 6 **does**[s] [+4024] **so** to the Lord and gives thanks to God.
14:20 but it is wrong for a man *to* **eat** anything that causes someone else
14:21 It is better not *to* **eat** meat or drink wine or to do anything else that
14:23 But the man who has doubts is condemned if *he* **eats**, because his
1Co 8: 7 so accustomed to idols that *when they* **eat** such food they think of
8: 8 to God; we are no worse if *we do* not **eat**, and no better if we do.
8: 8 we are no worse if we do not eat, and no better if *we* **do**[s].
8:10 won't be emboldened *to* **eat** what has been sacrificed to idols?
8:13 I **eat** causes my brother to fall into sin, *I will* never **eat** meat again,
9: 4 Don't we have the right *to* **food** and drink?
9: 7 Who plants a vineyard and *does* not **eat** of its grapes? Who tends a
9: 7 of its grapes? Who tends a flock and *does* not **drink** of the milk?
9:13 Don't you know that those who work in the temple **get** *their* **food**
10: 3 *They* all **ate** the same spiritual food
10: 7 "The people sat down *to* **eat** and drink and got up to indulge in
10:18 Do not those *who* **eat** the sacrifices participate in the altar?
10:25 **Eat** anything sold in the meat market without raising questions of
10:27 **eat** whatever is put before you without raising questions of
10:28 says to you, "This has been offered in sacrifice," then *do* not **eat** it,
10:31 So whether *you* **eat** or drink or whatever you do, do it all for the
11:20 When you come together, it is not the Lord's Supper *you* **eat**,
11:21 for as *you* **eat**, each of you goes ahead without waiting for
11:22 Don't you have homes to **eat** and drink in? Or do you despise the
11:26 For whenever *you* **eat** this bread and drink this cup, you proclaim
11:27 whoever **eats** the bread or drinks the cup of the Lord in an
11:28 A man ought to examine himself before *he* **eats** of the bread
11:29 For anyone *who* **eats** and drinks without recognizing the body of
11:29 who eats and drinks without recognizing the body of the Lord **eats**
11:33 So then, my brothers, when you come together to **eat**, wait for each
11:34 If anyone is hungry, *he should* **eat** at home, so that when you meet
15:32 dead are not raised, "*Let us* **eat** and drink, for tomorrow we die."
2Th 3: 8 nor *did we* **eat** anyone's food without paying for it. On the
3:10 we gave you this rule: "If a man will not work, *he shall* not **eat**."
3:12 in the Lord Jesus Christ to settle down and earn the bread they **eat**.
Heb 10:27 and of raging fire *that* will **consume** the enemies of God.
13:10 which those who minister at the tabernacle have no right *to* **eat**.
Jas   5: 3 Their corrosion will testify against you and **eat** your flesh like fire.
Rev   2: 7 who overcomes, I will give the right *to* **eat** from the tree of life,
2:14 who taught Balak to entice the Israelites to sin *by* **eating** food
2:20 into sexual immorality and the **eating of** food sacrificed to idols.
10:10 in my mouth, but when *I had* **eaten** it, my stomach turned sour.
17:16 and leave her naked; *they will* **eat** her flesh and burn her with fire.
19:18 so that *you may* **eat** the flesh of kings, generals, and mighty men,

2267 ἔσθω, *esthō* Not used in UBS/NIV [√ *2266*]

2268 Ἐσλί, *Hesli* [1]

Esli [1]

Lk   3:25 son of Amos, the son of Nahum, the son *of* **Esli**, the son of Naggai,

2269 ἔσοπτρον, *esoptron* [2] [√ *1650 + 3972*]

mirror [2]

1Co 13:12 Now we see but a poor reflection as in a **mirror**;

Jas   1:23 not do what it says is like a man who looks at his face in a **mirror**

2270 ἑσπέρα, *hespera* [3] [→ *2271*]

evening [3]

Lk   24:29 But they urged him strongly, "Stay with us, for it is nearly **evening**;
Ac   4: 3 They seized Peter and John, and because it was **evening**, they put
     28:23 From morning till **evening** he explained and declared to them the

2271 ἑσπερινός, *hesperinos* Not used in UBS/NIV
[√ *2270*]

2272 Ἑσρώμ, *Hesrōm* [3]

Hezron [3]

Mt   1: 3 was Tamar, Perez the father of **Hezron**, Hezron the father of Ram,
      1: 3 was Tamar, Perez the father of Hezron, **Hezron** the father of Ram,
Lk   3:33 the son of Ram, the son *of* **Hezron**, the son of Perez, the son of

2273 ἑσσόομαι, *hessoomai* [1] [√ *2482*]

inferior [1]

2Co 12:13 How were *you* **inferior** to the other churches, except that I was

2274 ἔσχατος, *eschatos* [52] [√ *1666*]

last [42], end [2], ends [2], final [2], last of all [1], least important
[1], lowest [1], now [1]

Mt   5:26 the truth, you will not get out until you have paid the **last** penny.
     12:45 And the **final** *condition* of that man is worse than the first.
     19:30 But many who are first will be **last**, and many who are last will be
     19:30 many who are first will be last, and many who are **last** will be first.
     20: 8 beginning with the **last** *ones* hired and going on to the first.'
     20:12 'These men who were hired **last** worked only one hour,' they said,
     20:14 I want to give the man who was hired **last** the same as I gave you.
     20:16 "So the **last** will be first, and the first will be last."
     20:16 "So the last will be first, and the **last** will be last."
     27:64 from the dead. This **last** deception will be worse than the first."
Mk   9:35 wants to be first, he must be the very **last**, and the servant of all."
     10:31 But many who are first will be **last**, and the last first."
     10:31 But many who are first will be last, and the **last** first."
     12: 6 He sent him **last of all**, saying, 'They will respect my son.'
     12:22 of the seven left any children. **Last** of all, the woman died too.
Lk   11:26 And the **final** *condition* of that man is worse than the first."
     12:59 I tell you, you will not get out until you have paid the **last** penny."
     13:30 Indeed there are *those who are* **last** who will be first, and first who
     13:30 are those who are last who will be first, and first who will be **last**."
     14: 9 humiliated, you will have to take the **least important** place.
     14:10 But when you are invited, take the **lowest** place, so that when your
Jn   6:39 none of all that he has given me, but raise them up at the **last** day.
      6:40 him shall have eternal life, and I will raise him up at the **last** day."
      6:44 who sent me draws him, and I will raise him up at the **last** day.
      6:54 my blood has eternal life, and I will raise him up *at* the **last** day.
      7:37 On the **last** and greatest day of the Feast, Jesus stood and said in a
     11:24 "I know he will rise again in the resurrection at the **last** day."
     12:48 that very word which I spoke will condemn him at the **last** day.
Ac   1: 8 and in all Judea and Samaria, and to the **ends** of the earth."
      2:17 " 'In the **last** days, God says, I will pour out my Spirit on all people.
     13:47 that you may bring salvation to the **ends** of the earth.' "
1Co   4: 9 God has put us apostles on display at the **end** *of the procession*,
     15: 8 and **last** of all he appeared to me also, as to one abnormally born.
     15:26 The **last** enemy to be destroyed is death.
     15:45 Adam became a living being"; the **last** Adam, a life-giving spirit.
     15:52 in a flash, in the twinkling of an eye, at the **last** trumpet.
2Ti   3: 1 But mark this: There will be terrible times in the **last** days.
Heb   1: 2 but in these **last** days he has spoken to us by his Son, whom he
Jas   5: 3 eat your flesh like fire. You have hoarded wealth in the **last** days.
1Pe   1: 5 coming of the salvation that is ready to be revealed in the **last** time.
      1:20 of the world, but was revealed in these **last** times for your sake.
2Pe   2:20 they are worse off at the **end** than they were at the beginning.
      3: 3 you must understand that in the **last** days scoffers will come,
1Jn   2:18 Dear children, this is the **last** hour; and as you have heard that the
      2:18 antichrists have come. This is how we know it is the **last** hour.

Jude 1:18 "In the **last** times there will be scoffers who will follow their own
Rev   1:17 hand on me and said: "Do not be afraid. I am the First and the **Last**.
      2: 8 These are the words of him who is the First and the **Last**, who died
      2:19 and that you are **now** doing more than you did at first.
     15: 1 seven angels with the seven **last** plagues—last, because with them
     21: 9 angels who had the seven bowls full *of* the seven **last** plagues came
     22:13 and the Omega, the First and the **Last**, the Beginning and the End.

2275 ἐσχάτως, *eschatōs* [1] [√ *1666*]

dying [1]

Mk   5:23 and pleaded earnestly with him, "My little daughter is **dying**."

2276 ἔσω, *esō* [9] [√ *1650*]

inner [2], inside [2], *untranslated* [1], in [1], into [1], inwardly
[+*3836*] [1], right into [+*1650+2401*] [1]

Mt   26:58 sat down with the guards to see the outcome.
Mk   14:54 Peter followed him at a distance, **right into** [+*1650+2401*] the
     15:16 The soldiers led Jesus away **into** the palace (that is,
Jn   20:26 A week later his disciples were **in** the *house* again, and Thomas
Ac   5:23 at the doors; but when we opened them, we found no one **inside**."
1Co   5:12 judge those outside the church? Are you not to judge those **inside**?
2Co   4:16 yet **inwardly** [+*3836*] we are being renewed day by day.
Eph   3:16 strengthen you with power through his Spirit in your **inner** being,

2277 ἔσωθεν, *esōthen* [12] [√ *1650*]

inside [4], on the inside [2], from inside [1], from within [1],
inwardly [1], on both sides [+*2779+3957*] [1], under [1], within [1]

Mt   7:15 to you in sheep's clothing, but **inwardly** they are ferocious wolves.
     23:25 and dish, but **inside** they are full of greed and self-indulgence.
     23:27 but **on the inside** are full of dead men's bones and everything
     23:28 but **on the inside** you are full of hypocrisy and wickedness.
Mk   7:21 For **from within**, out of men's hearts, come evil thoughts,
      7:23 All these evils come **from inside** and make a man 'unclean.' "
Lk   11: 7 "Then the one **inside** answers, 'Don't bother me. The door is
     11:39 and dish, but **inside** you are full of greed and wickedness.
     11:40 Did not the one who made the outside make the **inside** also?
2Co   7: 5 were harassed at every turn—conflicts on the outside, fears **within**.
Rev   4: 8 and was covered with eyes all around, even **under** his wings.
      5: 1 on the throne a scroll with writing **on** [+*2779+3957*] **both sides**

2278 ἐσώτερος, *esōteros* [2] [√ *1650*]

inner [2]

Ac   16:24 he put them in the **inner** cell and fastened their feet in the stocks.
Heb   6:19 and secure. It enters the **inner** *sanctuary* behind the curtain,

2279 ἑταῖρος, *hetairos* [3]

friend [3]

Mt   20:13 he answered one of them, '**Friend**, I am not being unfair to you.
     22:12 '**Friend**,' he asked, 'how did you get in here without wedding
     26:50 Jesus replied, "**Friend**, do what you came for." Then the men

2280 ἑτερόγλωσσος, *heteroglōssos* [1]
[√ *2283* + *1185*]

strange tongues [1]

1Co 14:21 "Through *men of* **strange tongues** and through the lips of

2281 ἑτεροδιδασκαλέω, *heterodidaskaleō* [2]
[√ *2283* + *1438*]

teach false doctrines [1], teaches false doctrines [1]

1Ti   1: 3 command certain men not *to* **teach false doctrines** any longer
      6: 3 If anyone **teaches false doctrines** and does not agree to the sound

2282 ἑτεροζυγέω, *heterozygeō* [1] [√ 2283 + 2413]

yoked together [1]

2Co 6:14 Do not be **yoked together** with unbelievers. For what do

2283 ἕτερος, *heteros* [98] [→ 2280, 2281, 2282, 2284, 4538]

ἄλλος ... ἕτερος (other ... another) [6] Mt 16:14; Ac 4:12; 1Co 10:29; 12:9,10; 2Co 11:4

εἷς ... ὁ ἕτερος (one ... the other) [10] Mt 6:24,24; Lk 7:41; 16:13,13; 17:34,35; 18:10; Ac 23:6; 1Co 4:6

another [29], other [29], others [14], different [4], else [3], some [3], different from [2], someone else [2], *untranslated* [1], another [+3836] [1], changed [+1181] [1], day after [1], elsewhere [+1877] [1], foreigners [1], his fellowman^s [+3836] [1], next [1], one kind [1], perversion [+599+3958+4922] [1], somebody else [1], the second^s [1]

Mt   6:24 Either he will hate the one and love the **other**, or he will be
     6:24 the other, or he will be devoted to the one and despise the **other**.
     8:21 **Another** disciple said to him, "Lord, first let me go and bury my
  10:23 When you are persecuted in one place, flee to **another**. I tell you
  11: 3 you the one who was to come, or should we expect **someone else**?"
  11:16 like children sitting in the marketplaces and calling out to **others**:
  12:45 and takes with it seven **other** spirits more wicked than itself,
  15:30 the lame, the blind, the crippled, the mute and many **others**,
  16:14 others say Elijah; and *still* **others**, Jeremiah or one of the prophets."
  21:30 "Then the father went to the **other** son and said the same thing.
Mk 16:12 Afterward Jesus appeared in a **different** form to two of them while
Lk   3:18 And with many **other** *words* John exhorted the people
    4:43 "I must preach the good news of the kingdom of God *to* the **other**
    5: 7 So they signaled their partners in the **other** boat to come and help
    6: 6 On **another** Sabbath he went into the synagogue and was teaching,
    7:41 One owed him five hundred denarii, and the **other** fifty.
    8: 3 the manager of Herod's household; Susanna; and many **others**.
    8: 6 **Some** fell on rock, and when it came up, the plants withered
    8: 7 **Other** seed fell among thorns, which grew up with it and choked
    8: 8 Still **other** seed fell on good soil. It came up and yielded a crop,
    9:29 As he was praying, the appearance of his face **changed** [+1181],
    9:56 and they went to **another** village.
    9:59 He said to **another** *man*, "Follow me." But the man replied,
    9:61 Still **another** said, "I will follow you, Lord; but first let me go back
  10: 1 After this the Lord appointed seventy-two **others** and sent them
  11:16 **Others** tested him by asking for a sign from heaven.
  11:26 Then it goes and takes seven **other** spirits more wicked than itself,
  14:19 "**Another** said, 'I have just bought five yoke of oxen, and I'm on
  14:20 "Still **another** said, 'I just got married,
  14:31 "Or suppose a king is about to go to war *against* **another** king.
  16: 7 "Then he asked the **second**^s, 'And how much do you owe?'
  16:13 Either he will hate the one and love the **other**, or he will be
  16:13 the other, or he will be devoted to the one and despise the **other**.
  16:18 divorces his wife and marries **another** *woman* commits adultery,
  17:34 two people will be in one bed; one will be taken and the **other** left.
  17:35 be grinding grain together; one will be taken and the **other** left."
  18:10 to the temple to pray, one a Pharisee and the **other** a tax collector.
  19:20 "Then **another** *servant* came and said, 'Sir, here is your mina;
  20:11 He sent **another** servant,
  22:58 A little later **someone else** saw him and said, "You also are one of
  22:65 And they said many **other** insulting *things* to him.
  23:32 Two **other** *men*, both criminals, were also led out with him to be
  23:40 But the **other** criminal rebuked him. "Don't you fear God," he said,
Jn 19:37 and, as **another** scripture says, "They will look on the one they
Ac   1:20 to dwell in it,' and, " 'May **another** take his place of leadership.'
    2: 4 and began to speak *in* **other** tongues as the Spirit enabled them.
    2:13 **Some**, however, made fun of them and said, "They have had too
    2:40 *With* many **other** words he warned them; and he pleaded with
    4:12 for there is no **other** name under heaven given to men by which we
    7:18 Then **another** king, who knew nothing about Joseph, became ruler
    8:34 who is the prophet talking about, himself or **someone else**?"
  12:17 the brothers about this," he said, and then he left for **another** place.
  13:35 it is stated **elsewhere** [+1877]: " 'You will not let your Holy One
  15:35 where they and many **others** taught and preached the word of the
  17: 7 saying that there is **another** king, one called Jesus."
  17:21 foreigners who lived there spent their time doing nothing **[NIE]**

17:34 also a woman named Damaris, and a *number of* **others**.
20:15 The **day after** that we crossed over to Samos, and on the following
23: 6 that some of them were Sadducees and the **others** Pharisees,
27: 1 and some **other** prisoners were handed over to a centurion named
27: 3 The **next** *day* we landed at Sidon; and Julius, in kindness to Paul,
Ro   2: 1 for at whatever point you judge the **other**, you are condemning
   2:21 you, then, who teach **others**, do you not teach yourself? You who
   7: 3 if she marries **another** man while her husband is still alive,
   7: 3 and is not an adulteress, even though she marries **another** man.
   7: 4 that you might belong *to* **another**, to him who was raised from the
   7:23 but I see **another** law at work in the members of my body,
   8:39 neither height nor depth, nor anything **else** in all creation, will be
  13: 8 for he who loves his **fellowman**^s [+3836] has fulfilled the law.
  13: 9 "Do not covet," and whatever **other** commandment there may be,
1Co 3: 4 when one says, "I follow Paul," and **another**, "I follow Apollos,"
   4: 6 you will not take pride in one man over against **another** [+3836].
   6: 1 If any of you has a dispute with **another**, dare he take it before the
  10:24 Nobody should seek his own good, but the good *of* **others**.
  10:29 the **other** *man's* conscience, I mean, not yours. For why should
  12: 9 *to* **another** faith by the same Spirit, to another gifts of healing by
  12:10 between spirits, *to* **another** speaking in different kinds of tongues,
  14:17 be giving thanks well enough, but the **other** *man* is not edified.
  14:21 and through the lips *of* **foreigners** I will speak to this people,
  15:40 but the splendor of the heavenly bodies is **one kind**,
  15:40 is one kind, and the splendor of the earthly bodies is **another**.
2Co 8: 8 of your love by comparing it with the earnestness *of* **others**.
  11: 4 or if you receive a **different** spirit *from* the one you received,
  11: 4 or a **different** gospel *from* the one you accepted, you put up with it
Gal 1: 6 you by the grace of Christ and are turning to a **different** gospel—
   1:19 I saw none of the **other** apostles—only James, the Lord's brother.
   6: 4 pride in himself, without comparing himself to **somebody else**,
Eph 3: 5 which was not made known to men *in* **other** generations as it has
Php 2: 4 not only to your own interests, but also to the interests *of* **others**.
1Ti 1:10 and for whatever **else** is contrary to the sound doctrine
2Ti 2: 2 entrust to reliable men who will also be qualified to teach **others**.
Heb 5: 6 And he says in **another** *place*, "You are a priest forever,
   7:11 the people), why was there still need for **another** priest to come—
   7:13 He of whom these things are said belonged to a **different** tribe,
   7:15 And what we have said is even more clear if **another** priest like
  11:36 **Some** faced jeers and flogging, while still others were chained
Jas 2:25 lodging to the spies and sent them off *in* a **different** direction?
Jude 1: 7 Sodom and Gomorrah and the surrounding towns gave themselves
        up to sexual immorality and **perversion** [+599+3958+4922].

2284 ἑτέρως, *heterōs* [1] [√ 2283]

differently [1]

Php 3:15 And if on some point you think **differently**, that too God will make

2285 ἔτι, *eti* [93] [→ 3600, 4033]

still [31], again [9], more [9], *untranslated* [8], longer [7], continue [5], any more [4], even [3], any longer [2], anymore [1], as long as still [1], as [1], before long [+3625] [1], besides [1], left [1], longer [+5989] [1], now [1], on [1], only [1], other [1], still [+3814] [1], very while [+4012+4012] [1], while still [1], yes [+5445] [1]

Mt   5:13 It is no **longer** good for anything, except to be thrown out
  12:46 While Jesus was **still** talking to the crowd, his mother and brothers
  17: 5 While he was **still** speaking, a bright cloud enveloped them,
  18:16 But if he will not listen, take one **[NIE]** or two others along,
  19:20 "All these I have kept," the young man said. "What do I **still** lack?"
  26:47 While he was **still** speaking, Judas, one of the Twelve, arrived.
  26:65 Why do we need **any more** witnesses? Look, now you have heard
  27:63 "we remember that **while** he was **still** alive that deceiver said,
Mk 5:35 While Jesus was **still** speaking, some men came from the house of
   5:35 daughter is dead," they said. "Why bother the teacher **any more**?"
  12: 6 "He had one **left** to send, a son, whom he loved. He sent him last of
  14:43 Just as **[NIE]** he was speaking, Judas, one of the Twelve,
  14:63 tore his clothes. "Why do we need **any more** witnesses?" he asked.
Lk   1:15 and he will be filled with the Holy Spirit **even** from birth.
   8:49 While Jesus was **still** speaking, someone came from the house of
   9:42 **Even** while the boy was coming, the demon threw him to the
  14:22 'what you ordered has been done, but there is **still** room.'

14:26 his wife and children, his brothers and sisters—**yes** [+5445],
14:32 he will send a delegation while the other is **still** a long way off
15:20 "But while he was **still** a long way off, his father saw him and was
16: 2 of your management, because you cannot be manager **any longer**.'
18:22 When Jesus heard this, he said to him, "You **still** lack one thing.
20:36 and they can no **longer** die; for they are like the angels. They are
22:47 While he was **still** speaking a crowd came up, and the man who
22:60 you're talking about!" Just **as** he was speaking, the rooster crowed.
22:71 Then they said, "Why do we need **any more** testimony? We have
24: 6 Remember how he told you, while he was **still** *with* you in Galilee:
24:41 And while they **still** did not believe it because of joy
24:44 He said to them, "This is what I told you while I was **still** with you:
Jn   4:35 Do you not say, 'Four months **more** and then the harvest'?
7:33 "I am with you for **only** a short time, and then I go to the one who
11:30 the village, but was **still** at the place where Martha had met him.
12:35 told them, "You are going to have the light just a little while **longer**.
13:33 "My children, I will be with you only a little **longer**. You will look
14:19 **Before long** [+3625], the world will not see me anymore,
16:12 "I have much **more** to say to you, more than you can now bear.
20: 1 Early on the first day of the week, while it was **still** dark,
Ac   2:26 and my tongue rejoices; [NIE] my body also will live in hope,
9: 1 Saul was **still** breathing out murderous threats against the Lord's
10:44 While Peter was **still** speaking these words, the Holy Spirit came
18:18 Paul stayed **on** in Corinth for some time. Then he left the brothers
21:28 And **besides**, he has brought Greeks into the temple area
Ro   3: 7 so increases his glory, why am I **still** condemned as a sinner?"
5: 6 at just the right time, [RPG] when we were still powerless,
5: 6 You see, at just the right time, when we were **still** powerless,
5: 8 love for us in this: While we were **still** sinners, Christ died for us.
6: 2 By no means! We died to sin; how can we live in it **any longer**?
9:19 "Then why does God **still** blame us? For who resists his will?"
1Co 3: 2 were not yet ready for it. Indeed, you are **still** [+3814] not ready.
3: 3 You are **still** worldly. For since there is jealousy and quarreling
12:31 the greater gifts. And **now** I will show you the most excellent way.
15:17 has not been raised, your faith is futile; you are **still** in your sins.
2Co 1:10 On him we have set our hope that he will **continue** to deliver us,
Gal 1:10 If I were **still** trying to please men, I would not be a servant of
5:11 Brothers, if I am **still** preaching circumcision, why am I still being
5:11 I am still preaching circumcision, why am I **still** being persecuted?
Php 1: 9 abound more and [NIE] more in knowledge and depth of insight,
2Th 2: 5 Don't you remember that when I was [NIE] with you I used to
Heb 7:10 met Abraham, Levi was **still** in the body of his ancestor.
7:11 to the people), why was there **still** need for another priest to come—
7:15 And what we have said is **even** more clear if another priest like
8:12 forgive their wickedness and will remember their sins no **more**."
9: 8 yet been disclosed **as long as** the first tabernacle was **still** standing.
10: 2 once for all, and would no **longer** have felt guilty for their sins.
10:17 he adds: "Their sins and lawless acts I will remember no **more**."
10:37 For in just a **very** little while [+4012+4012], "He who is coming
11: 4 his offerings. And by faith he **still** speaks, even though he is dead.
11:32 And what **more** shall I say? I do not have time to tell about
11:36 and flogging, while **still** others were chained and put in prison.
12:26 "Once **more** I will shake not only the earth but also the heavens."
12:27 The words "once **more**" indicate the removing of what can be
Rev 3:12 Never **again** will he leave it. I will write on him the name of my
6:11 and they were told to wait a little **longer** [+5989], until the number
7:16 Never **again** will they hunger; never again will they thirst.
7:16 Never again will they hunger; never **again** will they thirst.
9:12 The first woe is past; two **other** woes are yet to come.
12: 8 was not strong enough, and they lost their place [NIE] in heaven.
18:21 city of Babylon will be thrown down, never to be found **again**.
18:22 flute players and trumpeters, will never be heard in you **again**.
18:22 No workman of any trade will ever be found in you **again**.
18:22 The sound of a millstone will never be heard in you **again**.
18:23 The light of a lamp will never shine in you **again**. The voice of
18:23 voice of bridegroom and bride will never be heard in you **again**.
20: 3 to keep him from deceiving the nations **anymore** until the
21: 1 the first earth had passed away, and there was no **longer** any sea.
21: 4 There will be no **more** death or mourning or crying or pain,
21: 4 or pain, [RPG] for the old order of things has passed away."
22: 3 No **longer** will there be any curse. The throne of God and of the
22: 5 There will be no **more** night. They will not need the light of a lamp
22:11 Let him who does wrong **continue** to do wrong; let him who is vile
22:11 let him who is vile **continue** to be vile; let him who does right
22:11 continue to be vile; let him who does right **continue** to do right;
22:11 continue to do right; and let him who is holy **continue** to be holy."

2286 ἑτοιμάζω, *hetoimazō* [40] [√ 2289]

prepared [19], prepare [10], make preparations [5], get ready [3],
kept ready [1], made ready [1], make ready [1]

Mt   3: 3 '**Prepare** the way for the Lord, make straight paths for him.' "
20:23 These places belong to those for whom *they have been* **prepared**
22: 4 'Tell those who have been invited that *I have* **prepared** my dinner:
25:34 the kingdom **prepared** for you since the creation of the world.
25:41 into the eternal fire **prepared** for the devil and his angels.
26:17 "Where do you want *us to* **make preparations** for you to eat the
26:19 did as Jesus had directed them and **prepared** the Passover.
Mk   1: 3 '**Prepare** the way for the Lord, make straight paths for him.' "
10:40 These places belong to those for whom *they have been* **prepared**."
14:12 "Where do you want *us* to go and **make preparations** for you to eat
14:15 upper room, furnished and ready. **Make preparations** for us there."
14:16 things just as Jesus had told them. So they **prepared** the Passover.
Lk   1:17 of the righteous—*to* **make ready** a people prepared for the Lord."
1:76 for you will go on before the Lord *to* **prepare** the way for him,
2:31 which *you have* **prepared** in the sight of all people,
3: 4 '**Prepare** the way for the Lord, make straight paths for him.
9:52 who went into a Samaritan village to **get things ready** for him;
12:20 Then who will get what *you have* **prepared** for yourself?'
12:47 "That servant who knows his master's will and *does* not **get ready**
17: 8 '**Prepare** my supper, get yourself ready and wait on me while I eat
22: 8 saying, "Go and **make preparations** for us to eat the Passover.
22: 9 "Where do you want *us to* **prepare** for it?" they asked.
22:12 you a large upper room, all furnished. **Make preparations** there."
22:13 things just as Jesus had told them. So *they* **prepared** the Passover.
23:56 Then *they* went home and **prepared** spices and perfumes.
24: 1 the women took the spices *they had* **prepared** and went to the
Jn 14: 2 would have told you. I am going there *to* **prepare** a place for you.
14: 3 And if I go and **prepare** a place for you, I will come back
Ac 23:23 "**Get ready** a detachment of two hundred soldiers, seventy
1Co 2: 9 no mind has conceived what God *has* **prepared** for those who love
2Ti 2:21 useful to the Master and **prepared** to do any good work.
Phm 1:22 **Prepare** a guest room for me, because I hope to be restored to you
Heb 11:16 to be called their God, for *he has* **prepared** a city for them.
Rev 8: 6 Then the seven angels who had the seven trumpets **prepared** to
9: 7 The locusts looked like horses **prepared** for battle. On their heads
9:15 And the four angels who *had been* **kept ready** for this very hour
12: 6 The woman fled into the desert to a place **prepared** for her by
16:12 and its water was dried up to **prepare** the way for the kings from
19: 7 of the Lamb has come, and his bride *has* **made** herself **ready**.
21: 2 **prepared** as a bride beautifully dressed for her husband.

2287 Ἕτοιμας, *Hetoimas*   Not used in UBS/NIV
[√ *cf. 1829*]

2288 ἑτοιμασία, *hetoimasia* [1] [√ 2289]

readiness [1]

Eph 6:15 and with your feet fitted with the **readiness** that comes from the

2289 ἕτοιμος, *hetoimos* [17] [→ 2286, 2288, 2290, 4602]

ready [14], prepared [1], right [1], work already done [1]

Mt 22: 4 and fattened cattle have been butchered, and everything is **ready**.
22: 8 "Then he said to his servants, 'The wedding banquet is **ready**,
24:44 So you also must be **ready**, because the Son of Man will come at
25:10 The virgins who were **ready** went in with him to the wedding
Mk 14:15 He will show you a large upper room, furnished and **ready**.
Lk 12:40 You also must be **ready**, because the Son of Man will come at an
14:17 those who had been invited, 'Come, for everything is now **ready**.'
22:33 replied, "Lord, I am **ready** to go with you to prison and to death."
Jn   7: 6 "The right time for me has not yet come; for you any time is **right**."
Ac 23:15 about his case. We are **ready** to kill him before he gets here."
23:21 They are **ready** now, waiting for your consent to their request."
2Co 9: 5 Then it will be **ready** as a generous gift, not as one grudgingly
10: 6 And we will be **ready** to punish every act of disobedience.
10:16 For we do not want to boast about **work already done** in another
Tit 3: 1 and authorities, to be obedient, to be **ready** to do whatever is good,
1Pe 1: 5 of the salvation that is **ready** to be revealed in the last time.
3:15 Always be **prepared** to give an answer to everyone who asks you

2290 ἑτοίμως, *hetoimōs* [3] [√ *2289*]

ready [3]

Ac 21:13 I am **ready** not only to be bound, but also to die in Jerusalem for
2Co 12:14 Now I am **ready** to visit you for the third time, and I will not be a
1Pe 4: 5 But they will have to give account to him who is **ready** to judge

2291 ἔτος, *etos* [49] [→ *1453, 1454, 1670, 5474, 5478, 5562*]

years [40], year [3], years old [3], eighty-four [*+3837+5475*] [1], sixty [*+2008*] [1], twelve [*+1557*] [1]

Mt   9:20 then a woman who had been subject to bleeding *for* twelve **years**
Mk   5:25 was there who had been subject to bleeding *for* twelve **years**.
      5:42 the girl stood up and walked around (she was twelve **years** *old*).
Lk   2:36 she had lived with her husband seven **years** after her marriage,
      2:37 and then was a widow until she was **eighty-four** [*+3837+5475*].
      2:41 Every **year** his parents went to Jerusalem for the Feast of the
      2:42 When he was twelve **years old**, they went up to the Feast,
      3: 1 In the fifteenth **year** of the reign of Tiberius Caesar—when Pontius
      3:23 Now Jesus himself was about thirty **years old** when he began his
      4:25 when the sky was shut for three and a half **years** and there was a
      8:42 his only daughter, a girl *of* about **twelve** [*+1557*], was dying.
      8:43 was there who had been subject to bleeding for twelve **years**,
     12:19 to myself, "You have plenty of good things laid up for many **years**.
     13: 7 '*For* three **years** now I've been coming to look for fruit on this fig
     13: 8 " 'Sir,' the man replied, 'leave it alone *for* one more **year**,
     13:11 was there who had been crippled by a spirit *for* eighteen **years**.
     13:16 of Abraham, whom Satan has kept bound *for* eighteen *long* **years**,
     15:29 *All* these **years** I've been slaving for you and never disobeyed your
Jn   2:20 The Jews replied, "It has taken forty-six **years** to build this temple,
      5: 5 One who was there had been an invalid *for* thirty-eight **years**.
      8:57 "You are not yet fifty **years old**," the Jews said to him, "and you
Ac   4:22 the man who was miraculously healed was over forty **years** *old*.
      7: 6 and they will be enslaved and mistreated four hundred **years**.
      7:30 "After forty **years** had passed, an angel appeared to Moses in the
      7:36 signs in Egypt, at the Red Sea and *for* forty **years** in the desert.
      7:42 you bring me sacrifices and offerings forty **years** in the desert,
      9:33 a paralytic who had been bedridden for eight **years**.
     13:20 All this took about 450 **years**. "After this, God gave them judges
     13:21 Saul son of Kish, of the tribe of Benjamin, who ruled forty **years**.
     19:10 This went on for two **years**, so that all the Jews and Greeks who
     24:10 "I know that for a number *of* **years** you have been a judge over this
     24:17 "After an absence *of* several **years**, I came to Jerusalem to bring my
Ro 15:23 and since I have been longing for many **years** to see you,
2Co 12: 2 I know a man in Christ who fourteen **years** ago was caught up to
Gal 1:18 Then after three **years**, I went up to Jerusalem to get acquainted
      2: 1 Fourteen **years** later I went up again to Jerusalem, this time with
      3:17 The law, introduced 430 **years** later, does not set aside the
1Ti 5: 9 may be put on the list of widows unless she is over **sixty** [*+2008*],
Heb 1:12 But you remain the same, and your **years** will never end."
      3: 9 fathers tested and tried me and *for* forty **years** saw what I did.
      3:17 And with whom was he angry *for* forty **years**? Was it not with
2Pe 3: 8 With the Lord a day is like a thousand **years**, and a thousand years
      3: 8 a day is like a thousand years, and a thousand **years** are like a day.
Rev 20: 2 who is the devil, or Satan, and bound him *for* a thousand **years**.
     20: 3 the nations anymore until the thousand **years** were ended.
     20: 4 They came to life and reigned with Christ a thousand **years**.
     20: 5 (The rest of the dead did not come to life until the thousand **years**
     20: 6 and of Christ and will reign with him *for* a thousand **years**.
     20: 7 When the thousand **years** are over, Satan will be released from his

2292 εὖ, *eu* [5]

[→ *460, 1922, 2294, 2295, 2296, 2297, 2298, 2299, 2300, 2301, 2302, 2303, 2304, 2305, 2306, 2307, 2308, 2309, 2310, 2313, 2314, 2315, 2320, 2321, 2322, 2323, 2324, 2325, 2326, 2327, 2328, 2329, 2330, 2331, 2332, 2333, 2334, 2337, 2338, 2339, 2340, 2341, 2342, 2343, 2344, 2345, 2346, 2347, 2348, 2349, 2354, 2355, 2356, 2357, 2358, 2359, 2360, 2361, 2362, 2363, 2364, 2365, 2366, 2367, 2368, 2369, 2370, 2373, 2374, 2375, 2378, 2379, 2380, 2381, 2382, 2986, 4492, 4603, 5306, 5307*]

well done [2], well [2], help [*+4472*] [1]

Mt 25:21 "His master replied, '**Well done**, good and faithful servant!

25:23 "His master replied, '**Well done**, good and faithful servant!
Mk 14: 7 have with you, and you can **help** [*+4472*] them any time you want.
Ac 15:29 You will do **well** to avoid these things. Farewell.
Eph 6: 3 "that it may go **well** with you and that you may enjoy long life on

2293 Εὕα, *Heua* [2]

Eve [2]

2Co 11: 3 But I am afraid that just as **Eve** was deceived by the serpent's
1Ti 2:13 For Adam was formed first, then **Eve**.

2294 εὐαγγελίζω, *euangelizō* [54] [√ *2292 + 34*]

preach the gospel [7], preached [7], preaching the gospel [5], preached the good news [3], preach the good news [2], preach [2], preached the gospel [2], proclaiming the good news [2], the good news preached [2], the gospel preached [2], announced [1], bring good news [1], bring news [1], bringing good news [1], brought good news about [1], gospel preached [*+2295*] [1], gospel proclaim [*+2295*] [1], had the gospel preached [1], preach a gospel [1], preach good news [1], preaching a gospel [1], preaching the good news [1], preaching the gospel [*+2295*] [1], preaching [1], tell good news [1], tell the good news [1], telling the good news about [1], telling the good news [1], the good news is preached [1], told the good news about [1]

Mt 11: 5 the dead are raised, and **the good news is preached** *to* the poor.
Lk   1:19 I have been sent to speak to you and *to* **tell** you this **good news**.
      2:10 *I* **bring** you **good news** of great joy that will be for all the people.
      3:18 John exhorted the people and **preached the good news** to them.
      4:18 because he has anointed me *to* **preach the good news** to the poor.
      4:43 "I must **preach the good news** of the kingdom of God to the other
      7:22 the dead are raised, and **the good news** *is* **preached** *to* the poor.
      8: 1 to another, **proclaiming the good news** of the kingdom of God.
      9: 6 to village, **preaching the gospel** and healing people everywhere.
     16:16 **the good news** of the kingdom of God *is being* **preached**,
     20: 1 teaching the people in the temple courts and **preaching the gospel**,
Ac   5:42 and **proclaiming the good news** that Jesus is the Christ.
      8: 4 Those who had been scattered **preached** the word wherever they
      8:12 But when they believed Philip *as he* **preached the good news** of
      8:25 to Jerusalem, **preaching the gospel** in many Samaritan villages.
      8:35 passage of Scripture and **told** him **the good news about** Jesus.
      8:40 **preaching the gospel** in all the towns until he reached Caesarea.
     10:36 **telling the good news** of peace through Jesus Christ, who is Lord
     11:20 to Greeks also, **telling** them **the good news about** the Lord Jesus.
     13:32 "We **tell** you **the good news**: What God promised our fathers
     14: 7 where they continued *to* **preach the good news**.
     14:15 We are **bringing** you **good news**, telling you to turn from these
     14:21 *They* **preached the good news** in that city and won a large
     15:35 where *they* and many others taught and **preached** the word of the
     16:10 concluding that God had called us *to* **preach the gospel** to them.
     17:18 said this because Paul *was* **preaching the good news** about Jesus
Ro   1:15 so eager *to* **preach the gospel** also to you who are at Rome.
     10:15 "How beautiful are the feet *of* those *who* **bring** good news!"
     15:20 It has always been my ambition *to* **preach the gospel** where Christ
1Co 1:17 For Christ did not send me to baptize, but *to* **preach the gospel**—
      9:16 Yet when *I* **preach the gospel**, I cannot boast, for I am compelled
      9:16 am compelled to preach. Woe to me *if I do* not **preach the gospel**!
      9:18 that *in* **preaching the gospel** I may offer it free of charge,
     15: 1 brothers, I want to remind you of the gospel *I* **preached** to you,
     15: 2 you are saved, if you hold firmly to the word *I* **preached** to you.
2Co 10:16 *so that* we can **preach the gospel** in the regions beyond you.
     11: 7 by **preaching the gospel** [*+2295*] of God to you free of charge?
Gal 1: 8 or an angel from heaven *should* **preach a gospel** other than the
      1: 8 should preach a gospel other than the one *we* **preached** to you,
      1: 9 If anybody *is* **preaching** to you a gospel other than what you
      1:11 that the gospel I **preached** [*+2295*] is not something that man
      1:16 his Son in me so that *I might* **preach** him among the Gentiles,
      1:23 "The man who formerly persecuted us *is now* **preaching** the faith
      4:13 because of an illness that *I* first **preached the gospel** to you.
Eph 2:17 *He* came and **preached** peace to you who were far away and peace
      3: 8 *to* **preach** to the Gentiles the unsearchable riches of Christ,
1Th 3: 6 from you and **has brought good news about** your faith and love.
Heb 4: 2 For we also have had **the gospel preached** *to* us, just as they did;
      4: 6 and those who formerly **had the gospel preached** *to them* did not

1Pe 1:12 *who have* **preached the gospel** to you by the Holy Spirit sent from
1:25 stands forever." And this is the word that *was* **preached** to you.
4: 6 For this is the reason **the gospel** *was* **preached** even to those who
Rev 10: 7 just as *he* **announced** to his servants the prophets."
14: 6 and he had the eternal **gospel** *to* **proclaim** [+2295] to those who

2295 εὐαγγέλιον, *euangelion* [76] [√ 2292 + 34]

ἡ ἀλήθεια τοῦ εὐαγγελίου (the truth of the Gospel) [3] Gal 2:5,14; Col 1:5

εὐαγγέλιον μου, ἡμῶν (my/our Gospel) [6] Ro 2:16; 16:25; 2Co 4:3; 1Th 1:5; 2Th 2:14; 2Ti 2:8

εὐαγγέλιον τῆς βασιλείας (Gospel of the kingdom) [3] Mt 4:23; 9:35; 24:14

εὐαγγέλιον τοῦ θεοῦ (Gospel of God) [10] Mk 1:14; Ac 20:24; Ro 1:1; 15:16; 2Co 11:7; 1Th 2:2,8,9; 1Ti 1:11; 1Pe 4:17

εὐαγγέλιον τοῦ κυρίου (Gospel of the Lord) [1] 2Th 1:8

εὐαγγέλιον τοῦ Χρίστου (Gospel of Christ) [10] Mk 1:1; Ro 15:19; 1Co 9:12; 2Co 2:12; 4:4; 9:13; 10:14; Gal 1:7; Php 1:27; 1Th 3:2

κηρύσσω εὐαγγέλιον (preach the Gospel) [11] Mt 4:23; 9:35; 24:14; 26:13; Mk 1:14; 13:10; 14:9; 16:15; Gal 2:2; Col 1:23; 1Th 2:9

gospel [60], good news [6], preaching gospel [2], gospel preached [+2294] [1], gospel proclaim [+2294] [1], its [+3836] [1], preach gospel [1], preaching the gospel [+2294] [1], preaching [1], proclaiming gospel [1], spreading gospel [1]

Mt 4:23 preaching the **good news** of the kingdom, and healing every
9:35 preaching the **good news** of the kingdom and healing every disease
24:14 And this **gospel** of the kingdom will be preached in the whole
26:13 the truth, wherever this **gospel** is preached throughout the world,
Mk 1: 1 The beginning *of* the **gospel** about Jesus Christ, the Son of God.
1:14 Jesus went into Galilee, proclaiming the **good news** of God.
1:15 "The kingdom of God is near. Repent and believe the **good news**!"
8:35 but whoever loses his life for me and for the **gospel** will save it.
10:29 or mother or father or children or fields for me and the **gospel**
13:10 And the **gospel** must first be preached to all nations.
14: 9 the truth, wherever the **gospel** is preached throughout the world,
16:15 "Go into all the world and preach the **good news** to all creation.
Ac 15: 7 the Gentiles might hear from my lips the message *of* the **gospel**
20:24 has given me—the task of testifying to the **gospel** of God's grace.
Ro 1: 1 called to be an apostle and set apart for the **gospel** of God—
1: 9 whom I serve with my whole heart in **preaching** the **gospel** of his
1:16 I am not ashamed of the **gospel**, because it is the power of God for
2:16 judge men's secrets through Jesus Christ, as my **gospel** declares.
10:16 But not all the Israelites accepted the **good news**. For Isaiah says,
11:28 As far as the **gospel** is concerned, they are enemies on your
15:16 Gentiles with the priestly duty of **proclaiming** the **gospel** of God,
15:19 around to Illyricum, I have fully proclaimed the **gospel** of Christ.
16:25 Now to him who is able to establish you by my **gospel**
1Co 4:15 for in Christ Jesus I became your father through the **gospel**.
9:12 we put up with anything rather than hinder the **gospel** of Christ.
9:14 the Lord has commanded that those who preach the **gospel** should
9:14 who preach the gospel should receive their living from the **gospel**.
9:18 that in preaching the gospel I may offer **it**s [+3836] free of charge,
9:18 it free of charge, and so not make use of my rights in **preaching** it.
9:23 I do all this for the sake of the **gospel**, that I may share in its
15: 1 brothers, I want to remind you of the **gospel** I preached to you,
2Co 2:12 Now when I went to Troas to **preach** the **gospel** of Christ
4: 3 And even if our **gospel** is veiled, it is veiled to those who are
4: 4 so that they cannot see the light *of* the **gospel** of the glory of Christ,
8:18 who is praised by all the churches for his *service to* the **gospel**.
9:13 that accompanies your confession of the **gospel** of Christ,
10:14 come to you, for we did get as far as you with the **gospel** of Christ.
11: 4 or a different **gospel** from the one you accepted, you put up with it
11: 7 by **preaching the gospel** [+2294] of God to you free of charge?
Gal 1: 6 you by the grace of Christ and are turning to a different **gospel**—
1: 7 you into confusion and are trying to pervert the **gospel** of Christ.
1:11 that the **gospel** [+2294] I **preached** is not something that man
2: 2 and set before them the **gospel** that I preach among the Gentiles.
2: 5 a moment, so that the truth *of* the **gospel** might remain with you.
2: 7 entrusted with the task *of* **preaching** the **gospel** to the Gentiles,

2:14 I saw that they were not acting in line with the truth *of* the **gospel**,
Eph 1:13 when you heard the word of truth, the **gospel** of your salvation.
3: 6 This mystery is that through the **gospel** the Gentiles are heirs
6:15 feet fitted with the readiness that *comes from* the **gospel** of peace.
6:19 so that I will fearlessly make known the mystery *of* the **gospel**,
Php 1: 5 because of your partnership in the **gospel** from the first day until
1: 7 for whether I am in chains or defending and confirming the **gospel**,
1:12 what has happened to me has really served to advance the **gospel**.
1:16 in love, knowing that I am put here for the defense *of* the **gospel**.
1:27 conduct yourselves in a manner worthy *of* the **gospel** of Christ.
1:27 in one spirit, contending as one man for the faith *of* the **gospel**
2:22 with his father he has served with me in the *work of* the **gospel**.
4: 3 women who have contended at my side in the cause of the **gospel**,
4:15 in the early days *of* your *acquaintance with* the **gospel**,
Col 1: 5 that you have already heard about in the word *of* truth, the **gospel**
1:23 and firm, not moved from the hope *held out in* the **gospel**.
1Th 1: 5 because our **gospel** came to you not simply with words, but also
2: 2 but with the help of our God we dared to tell you his **gospel** in
2: 4 we speak as men approved by God to be entrusted with the **gospel**.
2: 8 we were delighted to share with you not only the **gospel** of God
2: 9 a burden to anyone while we preached the **gospel** of God to you.
3: 2 and God's fellow worker in **spreading** the **gospel** of Christ,
2Th 1: 8 do not know God and do not obey the **gospel** of our Lord Jesus.
2:14 He called you to this through our **gospel**, that you might share in
1Ti 1:11 that conforms to the glorious **gospel** of the blessed God, which he
2Ti 1: 8 But join with me in suffering *for* the **gospel**, by the power of God,
1:10 and has brought life and immortality to light through the **gospel**.
2: 8 raised from the dead, descended from David. This is my **gospel**,
Phm 1:13 take your place in helping me while I am in chains *for* the **gospel**.
1Pe 4:17 what will the outcome be for those who do not obey the **gospel** of
Rev 14: 6 and he had the eternal **gospel** [+2294] *to* **proclaim** to those who

2296 εὐαγγελιστής, *euangelistēs* [3] [√ 2292 + 34]

evangelist [2], evangelists [1]

Ac 21: 8 reached Caesarea and stayed at the house *of* Philip the **evangelist**,
Eph 4:11 some to be prophets, some to be **evangelists**, and some to be
2Ti 4: 5 in all situations, endure hardship, do the work *of* an **evangelist**,

2297 εὐαρεστέω, *euaresteō* [3] [√ 2292 + 743]

pleased [2], please [1]

Heb 11: 5 before he was taken, he was commended as one *who* **pleased** God.
11: 6 And without faith it is impossible *to* **please** God, because anyone
13:16 and to share with others, for with such sacrifices God *is* **pleased**.

2298 εὐάρεστος, *euarestos* [9] [√ 2292 + 743]

pleasing [5], pleases [+1639] [2], please [+1639] [1], please [1]

Ro 12: 1 to offer your bodies as living sacrifices, holy and **pleasing** to God—
12: 2 approve what God's will is—his good, **pleasing** and perfect will.
14:18 because anyone who serves Christ in this way is **pleasing** to God
2Co 5: 9 So we make it our goal *to* **please** [+1639] him, whether we are at
Eph 5:10 and find out what **pleases** [+1639] the Lord.
Php 4:18 are a fragrant offering, an acceptable sacrifice, **pleasing** to God.
Col 3:20 obey your parents in everything, for this **pleases** [+1639] the Lord.
Tit 2: 9 in everything, to try to **please** them, not to talk back to them,
Heb 13:21 and may he work in us what is **pleasing** to him, through Jesus

2299 εὐαρέστως, *euarestōs* [1] [√ 2292 + 743]

acceptably [1]

Heb 12:28 and so worship God **acceptably** with reverence and awe,

2300 Εὔβουλος, *Euboulos* [1] [√ 2292 + 1089]

Eubulus [1]

2Ti 4:21 **Eubulus** greets you, and so do Pudens, Linus, Claudia and all the

2301 εὖγε, *euge* [1] [√ 2292 + 1145]

well done [1]

Lk 19:17 " 'Well done, my good servant!' his master replied. 'Because you

2302 εὐγενής, *eugenēs* [3] [√ 2292 + 1181]

noble birth [1], of more noble character [1], of noble birth [1]

Lk 19:12 "A man *of* noble birth went to a distant country to have himself
Ac 17:11 Now the Bereans were of more noble character *than* the
1Co 1:26 not many were influential; not many were of noble birth.

2303 εὐγλωττία, *euglōttia*   Not used in UBS/NIV
[√ 2292 + 1185]

2304 εὐδία, *eudia* [1] [√ 2292 + 2416]

fair weather [1]

Mt 16: 2 you say, 'It will be fair weather, for the sky is red,'

2305 εὐδοκέω, *eudokeō* [21] [√ 2292 + 1506]

pleased [8], well pleased [5], delight [2], delighted [2], pleased with [1], prefer [+3437] [1], thought it best [1], with pleased [1]

Mt 3:17 "This is my Son, whom I love; with him *I am* well pleased."
12:18 my servant whom I have chosen, the one I love, in whom I delight;
17: 5 "This is my Son, whom I love; with him *I am* well pleased.
Mk 1:11 "You are my Son, whom I love; with you *I am* well pleased."
Lk 3:22 "You are my Son, whom I love; with you *I am* well pleased."
12:32 for your Father *has been* pleased to give you the kingdom.
Ro 15:26 and Achaia *were* pleased to make a contribution for the poor
15:27 *They were* pleased to do it, and indeed they owe it to them.
1Co 1:21 God *was* pleased through the foolishness of what was preached to
10: 5 Nevertheless, God *was* not pleased with most of them; their bodies
2Co 5: 8 and *would* prefer [+3437] to be away from the body and at home
12:10 *I* delight in weaknesses, in insults, in hardships, in persecutions,
Gal 1:15 set me apart from birth and called me by his grace, *was* pleased
Col 1:19 For God *was* pleased to have all his fullness dwell in him,
1Th 2: 8 so much that *we were* delighted to share with you not only the
3: 1 it no longer, *we* thought it best to be left by ourselves in Athens.
2Th 2:12 who have not believed the truth but *have* delighted in wickedness.
Heb 10: 6 with burnt offerings and sin offerings *you were* not pleased.
10: 8 nor *were you* pleased with them" (although the law required them
10:38 by faith. And if he shrinks back, I *will* not *be* pleased with him."
2Pe 1:17 "This is my Son, whom I love; with him *I am* well pleased."

2306 εὐδοκία, *eudokia* [9] [√ 2292 + 1506]

good pleasure [3], desire [1], good purpose [1], goodwill [1], on whom favor rests [1], pleasure [1], purpose [1]

Mt 11:26 Yes, Father, for this was your good pleasure.
Lk 2:14 the highest, and on earth peace to men on whom his favor rests."
10:21 to little children. Yes, Father, for this was your good pleasure.
Ro 10: 1 my heart's desire and prayer to God for the Israelites is that they
Eph 1: 5 through Jesus Christ, in accordance with his pleasure and will—
1: 9 to us the mystery of his will according to his good pleasure,
Php 1:15 preach Christ out of envy and rivalry, but others out of goodwill.
2:13 works in you to will and to act according to his good purpose.
2Th 1:11 and that by his power he may fulfill every good purpose of yours

2307 εὐεργεσία, *euergesia* [2] [√ 2292 + 2240]

act of kindness shown to [1], service [1]

Ac 4: 9 called to account today for an act of kindness shown to a cripple
1Ti 6: 2 because those who benefit *from* their service are believers,

2308 εὐεργετέω, *euergeteō* [1] [√ 2292 + 2240]

doing good [1]

Ac 10:38 and how he went around doing good and healing all who were

2309 εὐεργέτης, *euergetēs* [1] [√ 2292 + 2240]

Benefactors [1]

Lk 22:25 who exercise authority over them call themselves Benefactors.

2310 εὔθετος, *euthetos* [3] [√ 2292 + 5502]

fit for service [1], fit [1], useful [1]

Lk 9:62 the plow and looks back is fit for service in the kingdom of God."
14:35 It is fit neither for the soil nor for the manure pile; it is thrown out.
Heb 6: 7 and that produces a crop useful to those for whom it is farmed

2311 εὐθέως, *eutheōs* [36] [√ 2317]

immediately [19], at once [8], *untranslated* [1], as soon as [1], at that moment [1], at this [1], now [1], quickly [1], right away [1], soon [1], suddenly [1]

Mt 4:20 At once they left their nets and followed him.
4:22 and immediately they left the boat and their father and followed
8: 3 he said. "Be clean!" Immediately he was cured of his leprosy.
13: 5 have much soil. It sprang up quickly, because the soil was shallow.
14:22 Immediately Jesus made the disciples get into the boat and go on
14:31 Immediately Jesus reached out his hand and caught him. "You of
20:34 Immediately they received their sight and followed him.
21: 2 and at once you will find a donkey tied there, with her colt by her.
24:29 "Immediately after the distress of those days " 'the sun will be
25:16 The man who had received the five talents went at once and put
26:49 Going at once to Jesus, Judas said, "Greetings, Rabbi!" and kissed
26:74 to them, "I don't know the man!" Immediately a rooster crowed.
27:48 Immediately one of them ran and got a sponge. He filled it with
Mk 7:35 At this, the man's ears were opened, his tongue was loosened
Lk 5:13 he said. "Be clean!" And immediately the leprosy left him.
12:36 he comes and knocks they can immediately open the door for him.
12:54 cloud rising in the west, immediately you say, 'It's going to rain,'
14: 5 a well on the Sabbath day, will you not immediately pull him out?"
17: 7 he comes in from the field, 'Come along now and sit down to eat'?
21: 9 things must happen first, but the end will not come right away."
Jn 5: 9 At once the man was cured; he picked up his mat and walked.
6:21 and immediately the boat reached the shore where they were
18:27 Peter denied it, and at that moment a rooster began to crow.
Ac 9:18 Immediately, something like scales fell from Saul's eyes,
9:20 At once he began to preach in the synagogues that Jesus is the Son
9:34 Get up and take care of your mat." Immediately Aeneas got up.
12:10 had walked the length of one street, suddenly the angel left him.
16:10 had seen the vision, we got ready at once to leave for Macedonia,
17:10 As soon as it was night, the brothers sent Paul and Silas away to
17:14 The brothers immediately sent Paul to the coast, but Silas
21:30 him from the temple, and immediately the gates were shut.
22:29 Those who were about to question him withdrew immediately.
Gal 1:16 preach him among the Gentiles, [NIE] I did not consult any man,
Jas 1:24 at himself, goes away and immediately forgets what he looks like.
3Jn 1:14 I hope to see you soon, and we will talk face to face. Peace to you.
Rev 4: 2 At once I was in the Spirit, and there before me was a throne in

2312 εὐθυδρομέω, *euthydromeō* [2] [√ 2317 + 5556]

sailed straight [2]

Ac 16:11 From Troas *we* put out to sea and sailed straight for Samothrace,
21: 1 away from them, we put out to sea and sailed straight to Cos.

2313 εὐθυμέω, *euthymeō* [3] [√ 2292 + 2596]

keep up courage [2], happy [1]

Ac 27:22 But now I urge you *to* keep up your courage, because not one of
27:25 So keep up *your* courage, men, for I have faith in God that it will
Jas 5:13 Is any one of you in trouble? He should pray. *Is* anyone happy?

2314 εὔθυμος, *euthymos* [1] [√ 2292 + 2596]

encouraged [1]

Ac 27:36 They were all encouraged and ate some food themselves.

2315 εὐθύμως, euthymōs [1] [√ 2292 + 2596]

gladly [1]

Ac 24:10 have been a judge over this nation; so I **gladly** make my defense.

2316 εὐθύνω, euthynō [2] [√ 2317]

go [1], make straight [1]

Jn 1:23 of one calling in the desert, '**Make straight** the way for the Lord.' "
Jas 3: 4 are steered by a very small rudder wherever the pilot wants *to* **go**.

2317 εὐθύς¹, euthys¹ [51] [→ 2311, 2312, 2316, 2318, 2319, 2985]

immediately [13], at once [8], as soon as [6], *untranslated* [4], quickly [4], as soon as [+4020] [2], just as [2], as [1], at once [+4020] [1], at this [1], just then [1], right away [1], shortly [1], sudden [1], the moment [1], then [1], very early in the morning [+4745] [1], when [1], without delay [1]

Mt 3:16 **As soon as** Jesus was baptized, he went up out of the water.
    13:20 the man who hears the word and **at once** receives it with joy.
    13:21 or persecution comes because of the word, he **quickly** falls away.
    14:27 But Jesus **immediately** said to them: "Take courage! It is I.
    21: 3 him that the Lord needs them, and he will send them **right away**."
Mk 1:10 **As** Jesus was coming up out of the water, he saw heaven being torn
    1:12 **At once** the Spirit sent him out into the desert,
    1:18 **At once** they left their nets and followed him.
    1:20 **Without delay** he called them, and they left their father Zebedee in
    1:21 They went to Capernaum, and **when** the Sabbath *came*, Jesus went
    1:23 **Just then** a man in their synagogue who was possessed by an evil
    1:28 News about him spread **quickly** over the whole region of Galilee.
    1:29 **As soon as** they left the synagogue, they went with James
    1:30 was in bed with a fever, and [NIE] they told Jesus about her.
    1:42 **Immediately** the leprosy left him and he was cured.
    1:43 Jesus sent him away **at once** with a strong warning:
    2: 8 **Immediately** Jesus knew in his spirit that this was what they were
    2:12 [NIE] took his mat and walked out in full view of them all.
    3: 6 **Then** the Pharisees went out and began to plot with the Herodians
    4: 5 have much soil. It sprang up **quickly**, because the soil was shallow.
    4:15 **As soon** [+4020] **as** they hear it, Satan comes and takes away the
    4:16 hear the word and **at once** [+4020] receive it with joy.
    4:17 or persecution comes because of the word, they **quickly** fall away.
    4:29 **As soon** [+4020] **as** the grain is ripe, he puts the sickle to it,
    5: 2 [NIE] a man with an evil spirit came from the tombs to meet him.
    5:29 **Immediately** her bleeding stopped and she felt in her body that she
    5:30 **At once** Jesus realized that power had gone out from him.
    5:42 **Immediately** the girl stood up and walked around (she was twelve
    5:42 was twelve years old). **At this** they were completely astonished.
    6:25 **At once** the girl hurried in to the king with the request: "I want you
    6:27 So he **immediately** sent an executioner with orders to bring John's
    6:45 **Immediately** Jesus made his disciples get into the boat and go on
    6:50 **Immediately** he spoke to them and said, "Take courage! It is I.
    6:54 **As soon as** they got out of the boat, people recognized Jesus.
    7:25 In fact, **as soon as** she heard about him, a woman whose little
    8:10 [NIE] he got into the boat with his disciples and went to the
    9:15 **As soon as** all the people saw Jesus, they were overwhelmed with
    9:20 spirit saw Jesus, it **immediately** threw the boy into a convulsion.
    9:24 **Immediately** the boy's father exclaimed, "I do believe; help me
    10:52 **Immediately** he received his sight and followed Jesus along the
    11: 2 and **just as** you enter it, you will find a colt tied there, which no
    11: 3 tell him, 'The Lord needs it and will send it back here **shortly**.' "
    14:43 **Just as** he was speaking, Judas, one of the Twelve, appeared.
    14:45 Going **at once** to Jesus, Judas said, "Rabbi!" and kissed him.
    14:72 **Immediately** the rooster crowed the second time. Then Peter
    15: 1 **Very early in the morning** [+4745], the chief priests,
Lk 6:49 **The moment** the torrent struck that house, it collapsed and its
Jn 13:30 **As soon as** Judas had taken the bread, he went out. And it was
    13:32 God will glorify the Son in himself, and will glorify him **at once**.
    19:34 side with a spear, bringing a **sudden** flow of blood and water.
Ac 10:16 three times, and **immediately** the sheet was taken back to heaven.

2318 εὐθύς², euthys² [8] [√ 2317]

straight [6], right [2]

Mt 3: 3 'Prepare the way for the Lord, make **straight** paths for him.' "

Mk 1: 3 'Prepare the way for the Lord, make **straight** paths for him.' "
Lk 3: 4 'Prepare the way for the Lord, make **straight** paths for him.
    3: 5 The crooked roads shall become **straight**, the rough ways smooth.
Ac 8:21 share in this ministry, because your heart is not **right** before God.
    9:11 "Go to the house of Judas on **Straight** Street and ask for a man
    13:10 Will you never stop perverting the **right** ways of the Lord?
2Pe 2:15 They have left the **straight** way and wandered off to follow the

2319 εὐθύτης, euthytēs [1] [√ 2317]

righteousness [1]

Heb 1: 8 and ever, and **righteousness** will be the scepter of your kingdom.

2320 εὐκαιρέω, eukaireō [3] [√ 2292 + 2789]

has the opportunity [1], have a chance [1], spent time [1]

Mk 6:31 and going that *they did* not even **have a chance** to eat,
Ac 17:21 and the foreigners who lived there **spent** *their* **time** doing nothing
1Co 16:12 unwilling to go now, but he will go when *he* **has the opportunity**.

2321 εὐκαιρία, eukairia [2] [√ 2292 + 2789]

opportunity [2]

Mt 26:16 then on Judas watched for an **opportunity** to hand him over.
Lk 22: 6 and watched for an **opportunity** to hand Jesus over to them when

2322 εὔκαιρος, eukairos [2] [√ 2292 + 2789]

opportune [1], time of need [1]

Mk 6:21 Finally the **opportune** time came. On his birthday Herod gave a
Heb 4:16 may receive mercy and find grace to help us in our **time of need**.

2323 εὐκαίρως, eukairōs [2] [√ 2292 + 2789]

in season [1], opportunity [1]

Mk 14:11 him money. So he watched for an **opportunity** to hand him over.
2Ti 4: 2 be prepared **in season** and out of season; correct, rebuke

2324 εὔκοπος, eukopos [7] [√ 2292 + 3164]

easier [7]

Mt 9: 5 Which is **easier**: to say, 'Your sins are forgiven,' or to say,
    19:24 it is **easier** *for* a camel to go through the eye of a needle than for a
Mk 2: 9 Which is **easier**: to say to the paralytic, 'Your sins are forgiven,'
    10:25 It is **easier** *for* a camel to go through the eye of a needle than for a
Lk 5:23 Which is **easier**: to say, 'Your sins are forgiven,'
    16:17 It is **easier** *for* heaven and earth to disappear than for the least
    18:25 it is **easier** *for* a camel to go through the eye of a needle than for a

2325 εὐλάβεια, eulabeia [2] [√ 2292 + 3284]

reverence [1], reverent submission [1]

Heb 5: 7 from death, and he was heard because of his **reverent submission**.
    12:28 and so worship God acceptably with **reverence** and awe,

2326 εὐλαβέομαι, eulabeomai [1] [√ 2292 + 3284]

holy fear [1]

Heb 11: 7 things not yet seen, *in* **holy fear** built an ark to save his family.

2327 εὐλαβής, eulabēs [4] [√ 2292 + 3284]

devout [2], God-fearing [1], Godly [1]

Lk 2:25 a man in Jerusalem called Simeon, who was righteous and **devout**.
Ac 2: 5 Now there were staying in Jerusalem **God-fearing** Jews from
    8: 2 **Godly** men buried Stephen and mourned deeply for him.
    22:12 He was a **devout** observer of the law and highly respected by all

2328 εὐλογέω, eulogeō [41] [√ 2292 + 3306]

blessed [19], gave thanks [6], bless [5], praising [3], bless [+2328] [2], blessing [2], gave thanks for [1], give thanks [1], praise [1], praised [1]

Mt 14:19 and looking up to heaven, *he* **gave thanks** and broke the loaves.
    21: 9 "**Blessed** *is* he who comes in the name of the Lord!" "Hosanna in
    23:39 until you say, '**Blessed** *is* he who comes in the name of the Lord.' "
    25:34 to those on his right, 'Come, *you* who *are* **blessed** by my Father;
    26:26 they were eating, Jesus took bread, **gave thanks** and broke it,
Mk 6:41 and looking up to heaven, *he* **gave thanks** and broke the loaves.
    8: 7 *he* **gave thanks for** them also and told the disciples to distribute
  11: 9 "Hosanna!" "**Blessed** *is* he who comes in the name of the Lord!"
  11:10 "**Blessed** *is* the coming kingdom of our father David!" "Hosanna in
  14:22 they were eating, Jesus took bread, **gave thanks** and broke it,
Lk 1:42 "**Blessed** *are* you among women, and blessed is the child you will
    1:42 are you among women, and **blessed** *is* the child you will bear!
    1:64 and his tongue was loosed, and he began to speak, **praising** God.
    2:28 Simeon took him in his arms and **praised** God, saying:
    2:34 Then Simeon **blessed** them and said to Mary, his mother: "This
    6:28 **bless** those who curse you, pray for those who mistreat you.
    9:16 and looking up to heaven, *he* **gave thanks** and broke them.
  13:35 until you say, '**Blessed** *is* he who comes in the name of the Lord.' "
  19:38 "**Blessed** *is* the king who comes in the name of the Lord!" "Peace in
  24:30 *he* took bread, **gave thanks**, broke it and began to give it to them.
  24:50 to the vicinity of Bethany, he lifted up his hands and **blessed** them.
  24:51 While he *was* **blessing** them, he left them and was taken up into
  24:53 And they stayed continually at the temple, **praising** God.
Jn 12:13 "Hosanna!" "**Blessed** *is* he who comes in the name of the Lord!"
Ac 3:26 he sent him first to you *to* **bless** you by turning each of you from
Ro 12:14 **Bless** those who persecute you; bless and do not curse.
  12:14 Bless those who persecute you; **bless** and do not curse.
1Co 4:12 When we are cursed, *we* **bless**; when we are persecuted, we endure
  10:16 Is not the cup of thanksgiving for which *we* **give thanks** a
  14:16 If *you are* **praising** God with your spirit, how can one who finds
Gal 3: 9 So those who have faith *are* **blessed** along with Abraham,
Eph 1: 3 who *has* **blessed** us in the heavenly realms with every spiritual
Heb 6:14 "*I will* surely **bless** [+2328] you and give you many descendants."
    6:14 "*I will* surely **bless** [+2328] you and give you many descendants."
    7: 1 Abraham returning from the defeat of the kings and **blessed** him,
    7: 6 a tenth from Abraham and **blessed** him who had the promises.
    7: 7 And without doubt the lesser person *is* **blessed** by the greater.
  11:20 By faith Isaac **blessed** Jacob and Esau in regard to their future.
  11:21 By faith Jacob, when he was dying, **blessed** each of Joseph's sons,
Jas 3: 9 With the tongue we **praise** our Lord and Father, and with it we
1Pe 3: 9 Do not repay evil with evil or insult with insult, but with **blessing**,

2329 εὐλογητός, eulogētos [8] [√ 2292 + 3306]

praise [4], praised [3], blessed [1]

Mk 14:61 priest asked him, "Are you the Christ, the Son *of* the **Blessed** *One*?"
Lk 1:68 "**Praise** be to the Lord, the God of Israel, because he has come
Ro 1:25 created things rather than the Creator—who is forever **praised**.
    9: 5 human ancestry of Christ, who is God over all, forever **praised**!
2Co 1: 3 **Praise** be to the God and Father of our Lord Jesus Christ,
  11:31 who is to be **praised** forever, knows that I am not lying.
Eph 1: 3 **Praise** be to the God and Father of our Lord Jesus Christ,
1Pe 1: 3 **Praise** be to the God and Father of our Lord Jesus Christ!

2330 εὐλογία, eulogia [16] [√ 2292 + 3306]

blessing [6], praise [4], generous gift [2], generously [+2093] [2], flattery [1], thanksgiving [1]

Ro 15:29 to you, I will come in the full measure *of* the **blessing** of Christ.
  16:18 smooth talk and **flattery** they deceive the minds of naive people.
1Co 10:16 Is not the cup *of* **thanksgiving** for which we give thanks a
2Co 9: 5 and finish the arrangements for the **generous gift** you had
    9: 5 Then it will be ready as a **generous gift**, not as one grudgingly
    9: 6 and whoever sows **generously** [+2093] will also reap generously.
    9: 6 and whoever sows generously will also reap **generously** [+2093].
Gal 3:14 He redeemed us in order that the **blessing** given to Abraham might
Eph 1: 3 us in the heavenly realms with every spiritual **blessing** in Christ.
Heb 6: 7 useful to those for whom it is farmed receives the **blessing** of God.
  12:17 Afterward, as you know, when he wanted to inherit this **blessing**,

Jas 3:10 Out of the same mouth come **praise** and cursing. My brothers,
1Pe 3: 9 because to this you were called so that you may inherit a **blessing**.
Rev 5:12 and wisdom and strength and honor and glory and **praise**!"
    5:13 and to the Lamb be **praise** and honor and glory and power,
    7:12 **Praise** and glory and wisdom and thanks and honor and power

2331 εὐμετάδοτος, eumetadotos [1] [√ 2292 + 3552 + 1443]

generous [1]

1Ti 6:18 to be rich in good deeds, and to be **generous** and willing to share.

2332 Εὐνίκη, Eunikē [1] [√ 2292 + 3772]

Eunice [1]

2Ti 1: 5 lived in your grandmother Lois and in your mother **Eunice** and,

2333 εὐνοέω, eunoeō [1] [√ 2292 + 3808]

settle matters [+1639] [1]

Mt 5:25 "**Settle** [+1639] **matters** quickly with your adversary who is

2334 εὔνοια, eunoia [1] [√ 2292 + 3808]

wholeheartedly [+3552] [1]

Eph 6: 7 Serve **wholeheartedly** [+3552], as if you were serving the Lord,

2335 εὐνουχίζω, eunouchizō [2] [–→ 2336; cf. 2400]

made^s that way [+2336] [1], renounced marriage [+1571+2336] [1]

Mt 19:12 were born that way; others *were* **made^s** [+2336] **that way** by men;
  19:12 and others *have* **renounced marriage** [+1571+2336] because of

2336 εὐνοῦχος, eunouchos [8] [√ 2335]

eunuch [5], eunuchs [1], made that way [+2335] [1], renounced marriage [+1571+2335] [1]

Mt 19:12 For some are **eunuchs** because they were born that way; others
  19:12 were born that way; others *were* **made^s that way** [+2335] by men;
  19:12 and others *have* **renounced marriage** [+1571+2335] because of
Ac 8:27 So he started out, and on his way he met an Ethiopian **eunuch**,
    8:34 The **eunuch** asked Philip, "Tell me, please, who is the prophet
    8:36 they came to some water and the **eunuch** said, "Look, here is water.
    8:38 Then both Philip and the **eunuch** went down into the water
    8:39 and the **eunuch** did not see him again, but went on his way

2337 Εὐοδία, Euodia [1] [√ 2292 + 3847]

Euodia [1]

Php 4: 2 I plead with **Euodia** and I plead with Syntyche to agree with each

2338 εὐοδόω, euodoō [4] [√ 2292 + 3847]

go well [1], in keeping with income [+1569+4005+5516] [1], is getting along well [1], way opened for [1]

Ro 1:10 last by God's will the **way** *may be* **opened for** *me* to come to you.
1Co 16: 2 sum of money **in keeping with** *his* **income** [+1569+4005+5516],
3Jn 1: 2 that you may enjoy good health and that all *may* **go well** with you,
    1: 2 all may go well with you, even as your soul **is getting along well**.

2339 εὐπάρεδρος, euparedros [1] [√ 2292 + 4123 + 1612]

devotion [1]

1Co 7:35 but that you may live in a right way in undivided **devotion** to the

2340 εὐπειθής, eupeithēs [1] [√ 2292 + 4275]

submissive [1]

Jas 3:17 considerate, **submissive**, full of mercy and good fruit, impartial

2341 εὐπερίσπαστος, euperispastos Not used in UBS/NIV [√ 2292 + 4309 + 5060]

2342 εὐπερίστατος, euperistatos [1]
[√ 2292 + 4309 + 2705]

easily entangles [1]

Heb 12: 1 off everything that hinders and the sin that so **easily entangles**,

2343 εὐποιΐα, eupoiia [1] [√ 2292 + 4472]

do good [1]

Heb 13:16 And do not forget to **do good** and to share with others, for with

2344 εὐπορέω, euporeō [1] [√ 2292 + 4513]

ability [1]

Ac 11:29 The disciples, each according to his **ability**, decided to provide

2345 εὐπορία, euporia [1] [√ 2292 + 4513]

good income [1]

Ac 19:25 "Men, you know we receive a **good income** from this business.

2346 εὐπρέπεια, euprepeia [1] [√ 2292 + 4560]

beauty [1]

Jas 1:11 and withers the plant; its blossom falls and its **beauty** is destroyed.

2347 εὐπρόσδεκτος, euprosdektos [5]
[√ 2292 + 4639 + 1312]

acceptable [4], favor [1]

Ro 15:16 so that the Gentiles might become an offering **acceptable** to God,
     15:31 and that my service in Jerusalem may be **acceptable** to the saints
2Co 6: 2 I tell you, now is the time of God's **favor**, now is the day of
      8:12 is there, the gift is **acceptable** according to what one has,
1Pe 2: 5 offering spiritual sacrifices **acceptable** to God through Jesus

2348 εὐπρόσεδρος, euprosedros Not used in UBS/NIV [√ 2292 + 4639 + 1612]

2349 εὐπροσωπέω, euprosōpeō [1] [√ 2292 + 4725]

make a good impression [1]

Gal 6:12 Those who want to **make a good impression** outwardly are trying

2350 εὐρακύλων, eurakylōn [1]

the northeaster [1]

Ac 27:14 very long, a wind of hurricane force, called the "**northeaster**,"

2351 εὑρίσκω, heuriskō [176] [→ 461, 2388]

found [84], find [53], finds [13], met [3], finding [2], and lost [+4028] [1], appeared [1], bring about [1], came to [1], considered [1], decide [1], discovered [1], enjoyed [1], evident [1], find [+1639] [1], find out [1], finds [+1181] [1], found that [1], laid bare [1], obtained [1], prove [1], provide [1], recovered [1], result [1], was [1], were looking for [1]

Mt 1:18 she was **found** to be with child through the Holy Spirit.
     2: 8 As soon as you **find** him, report to me, so that I too may go
     7: 7 seek and you will **find**; knock and the door will be opened to you.
     7: 8 he who seeks **finds**; and to him who knocks, the door will be

     7:14 narrow the road that leads to life, and only a few **find** [+1639] it.
     8:10 the truth, I have not **found** anyone in Israel with such great faith.
    10:39 Whoever **finds** his life will lose it, and whoever loses his life for
    10:39 life will lose it, and whoever loses his life for my sake will **find** it.
    11:29 and humble in heart, and you will **find** rest for your souls.
    12:43 it goes through arid places seeking rest and does not **find** it.
    12:44 it **finds** the house unoccupied, swept clean and put in order.
    13:44 When a man **found** it, he hid it again, and then in his joy went
    13:46 When he **found** one of great value, he went away and sold
    16:25 his life will lose it, but whoever loses his life for me will **find** it.
    17:27 you catch; open its mouth and you will **find** a four-drachma coin.
    18:13 And if he **finds** [+1181] it, I tell you the truth, he is happier about
    18:28 he **found** one of his fellow servants who owed him a hundred
    20: 6 About the eleventh hour he went out and **found** still others
    21: 2 and at once you will **find** a donkey tied there, with her colt by her.
    21:19 by the road, he went up to it but **found** nothing on it except leaves.
    22: 9 Go to the street corners and invite to the banquet anyone you **find**.'
    22:10 out into the streets and gathered all the people they could **find**,
    24:46 It will be good for that servant whose master **finds** him doing
    26:40 Then he returned to his disciples and **found** them sleeping.
    26:43 When he came back, he again **found** them sleeping, because their
    26:60 But they did not **find** any, though many false witnesses came
    27:32 they were going out, they **met** a man from Cyrene, named Simon,
Mk 1:37 and when they **found** him, they exclaimed: "Everyone is looking
     7:30 She went home and **found** her child lying on the bed,
    11: 2 and just as you enter it, you will **find** a colt tied there, which no
    11: 4 They went and **found** a colt outside in the street, tied at a doorway.
    11:13 the distance a fig tree in leaf, he went to **find out** if it had any fruit.
    11:13 When he reached it, he **found** nothing but leaves, because it was
    13:36 If he comes suddenly, do not let him **find** you sleeping.
    14:16 went into the city and **found** things just as Jesus had told them.
    14:37 Then he returned to his disciples and **found** them sleeping.
    14:40 When he came back, he again **found** them sleeping, because their
    14:55 so that they could put him to death, but they did not **find** any.
Lk 1:30 to her, "Do not be afraid, Mary, you have **found** favor with God.
     2:12 You will **find** a baby wrapped in cloths and lying in a manger."
     2:45 When they did not **find** him, they went back to Jerusalem to look
     2:46 After three days they **found** him in the temple courts,
     4:17 handed to him. Unrolling it, he **found** the place where it is written:
     5:19 When they could not **find** a way to do this because of the crowd,
     6: 7 and the teachers of the law were **looking for** a reason to accuse
     7: 9 "I tell you, I have not **found** such great faith even in Israel."
     7:10 had been sent returned to the house and **found** the servant well.
     8:35 they **found** the man from whom the demons had gone out,
     9:12 surrounding villages and countryside and **find** food and lodging,
     9:36 When the voice had spoken, they **found** that Jesus was alone.
    11: 9 seek and you will **find**; knock and the door will be opened to you.
    11:10 he who seeks **finds**; and to him who knocks, the door will be
    11:24 it goes through arid places seeking rest and does not **find** it.
    11:25 When it arrives, it **finds** the house swept clean and put in order.
    12:37 It will be good for those servants whose master **finds** them
    12:38 It will be good for those servants whose master **finds** them ready,
    12:43 It will be good for that servant whom the master **finds** doing
    13: 6 and he went to look for fruit on it, but did not **find** any.
    13: 7 coming to look for fruit on this fig tree and haven't **found** any.
    15: 4 in the open country and go after the lost sheep until he **finds** it?
    15: 5 And when he **finds** it, he joyfully puts it on his shoulders
    15: 6 and says, 'Rejoice with me; I have **found** my lost sheep.'
    15: 8 a lamp, sweep the house and search carefully until she **finds** it?
    15: 9 And when she **finds** it, she calls her friends and neighbors together
    15: 9 and says, 'Rejoice with me; I have **found** my lost coin.'
    15:24 son of mine was dead and is alive again; he was lost and is **found**.'
    15:32 of yours was dead and is alive again; he was lost and is **found**.'"
    17:18 Was no one **found** to return and give praise to God except this
    18: 8 when the Son of Man comes, will he **find** faith on the earth?"
    19:30 and as you enter it, you will **find** a colt tied there, which no one
    19:32 who were sent ahead went and **found** it just as he had told them.
    19:48 Yet they could not **find** any way to do it, because all the people
    22:13 They left and **found** things just as Jesus had told them. So they
    22:45 to the disciples, he **found** them asleep, exhausted from sorrow.
    23: 2 saying, "We have **found** this man subverting our nation.
    23: 4 and the crowd, "I **find** no basis for a charge against this man."
    23:14 and have **found** no basis for your charges against him.
    23:22 I have **found** in him no grounds for the death penalty. Therefore I
    24: 2 They **found** the stone rolled away from the tomb,
    24: 3 when they entered, they did not **find** the body of the Lord Jesus.

	24:23	but didn't **find** his body. They came and told us that they had seen
	24:24	went to the tomb and **found** it just as the women had said,
	24:33	There *they* **found** the Eleven and those with them,
Jn	1:41	The first thing Andrew did was *to* **find** his brother Simon
	1:41	and tell him, "*We have* **found** the Messiah" (that is, the Christ).
	1:43	to leave for Galilee. **Finding** Philip, he said to him, "Follow me."
	1:45	Philip **found** Nathanael and told him, "We have found the one
	1:45	told him, "*We have* **found** the one Moses wrote about in the Law,
	2:14	In the temple courts he **found** men selling cattle, sheep and doves,
	5:14	Later Jesus **found** him at the temple and said to him, "See,
	6:25	*When they* **found** him on the other side of the lake, they asked
	7:34	You will look for me, but *you will* not **find** me; and where I am,
	7:35	"Where does this man intend to go that we cannot **find** him?
	7:36	but *you will* not **find** me,' and 'Where I am, you cannot come'?"
	9:35	and *when he* **found** him, he said, "Do you believe in the Son of
	10:9	me will be saved. He will come in and go out, and **find** pasture.
	11:17	Jesus **found that** Lazarus had already been in the tomb for four
	12:14	Jesus **found** a young donkey and sat upon it, as it is written,
	18:38	again to the Jews and said, "I **find** no basis for a charge against him.
	19:4	I am bringing him out to you to let you know that *I* **find** no basis
	19:6	crucify him. As for me, *I* **find** no basis for a charge against him."
	21:6	your net on the right side of the boat and *you will* **find** some."
Ac	4:21	*They could* not **decide** how to punish them, because all the people
	5:10	**finding** her dead, carried her out and buried her beside her
	5:22	But on arriving at the jail, the officers *did* not **find** them there.
	5:23	"*We* **found** the jail securely locked, with the guards standing at the
	5:23	at the doors; but when we opened them, *we* **found** no one inside."
	5:39	these men; *you will* only **find** *yourselves* fighting against God."
	7:11	bringing great suffering, and our fathers *could* not **find** food.
	7:46	who **enjoyed** God's favor and asked that he might provide a
	7:46	and asked that *he might* **provide** a dwelling place for the God of
	8:40	Philip, however, **appeared** at Azotus and traveled about,
	9:2	so that if *he* **found** any there who belonged to the Way,
	9:33	There *he* **found** a man named Aeneas, *a paralytic* who had been
	10:27	with him, Peter went inside and **found** a large gathering of people.
	11:26	and *when he* **found** him, he brought him to Antioch. So for a
	12:19	*After* Herod had a thorough search made for him and *did* not **find**
	13:6	There *they* **met** a Jewish sorcerer and false prophet named
	13:22	'*I have* **found** David son of Jesse a man after my own heart';
	13:28	*Though they* **found** no proper ground for a death sentence,
	17:6	But *when they did* not **find** them, they dragged Jason and some
	17:23	your objects of worship, *I* even **found** an altar with this inscription:
	17:27	men would seek him and perhaps reach out for him and **find** him,
	18:2	There *he* **met** a Jew named Aquila, a native of Pontus, who had
	19:1	interior and arrived at Ephesus. There *he* **found** some disciples
	19:19	the value of the scrolls, the total **came to** fifty thousand drachmas.
	21:2	*We* **found** a ship crossing over to Phoenicia, went on board
	23:9	"*We* **find** nothing wrong with this man," they said. "What if a spirit
	23:29	*I* **found** that the accusation had to do with questions about their
	24:5	"*We have* **found** this man to be a troublemaker, stirring up riots
	24:12	My accusers *did* not **find** me arguing with anyone at the temple,
	24:18	I was ceremonially clean when *they* **found** me in the temple courts
	24:20	Or these who are here should state what crime *they* **found** in me
	27:6	There the centurion **found** an Alexandrian ship sailing for Italy
	27:28	*They* took soundings and **found** that the water was a hundred
	27:28	A short time later *they* took soundings again and **found** it was
	28:14	There *we* **found** some brothers who invited us to spend a week
Ro	4:1	we say that Abraham, our forefather, **discovered** in this matter?
	7:10	I **found** that the very commandment that was intended to bring life
	7:21	So *I* **find** this law at work: When I want to do good, evil is right
	10:20	Isaiah boldly says, "*I was* **found** by those who did not seek me;
1Co	4:2	that those who have been given a trust *must* **prove** faithful.
	15:15	than that, *we are* then **found** to be false witnesses about God,
2Co	2:13	no peace of mind, *because* I *did* not **find** my brother Titus there.
	5:3	because when we are clothed, *we will* not *be* **found** naked.
	9:4	For if any Macedonians come with me and **find** you unprepared,
	11:12	to *be* **considered** equal with us in the things they boast about.
	12:20	For I am afraid that when I come *I may* not **find** you as I want you
	12:20	I want you to be, and you *may* not **find** me as you want me to be.
Gal	2:17	in Christ, *it becomes* **evident** that we ourselves are sinners,
Php	2:8	And *being* **found** in appearance as a man, he humbled himself
	3:9	and *be* **found** in him, not having a righteousness of my own that
2Ti	1:17	when he was in Rome, he searched hard for me until *he* **found** me.
	1:18	May the Lord grant that he *will* **find** mercy from the Lord on that
Heb	4:16	may receive mercy and **find** grace to help us in our time of need.
	9:12	for all by his own blood, *having* **obtained** eternal redemption.

	11:5	he *could* not *be* **found**, because God had taken him away.
	12:17	*He could* **bring about** no change of mind, though he sought the
1Pe	1:7	*may be* proved genuine and *may* **result** in praise, glory and honor
	2:22	"He committed no sin, and no deceit *was* **found** in his mouth."
2Pe	3:10	by fire, and the earth and everything in it *will be* **laid bare**.
	3:14	make every effort *to be* **found** spotless, blameless and at peace
2Jn	1:4	It has given me great joy to **find** some of your children walking in
Rev	2:2	who claim to be apostles but are not, and *have* **found** them false.
	3:2	for *I have* not **found** your deeds complete in the sight of my God.
	5:4	because no one *was* **found** who was worthy to open the scroll
	9:6	During those days men will seek death, but *will* not **find** it;
	12:8	not strong enough, **and** they lost [*+4028*] their place in heaven.
	14:5	No lie *was* **found** in their mouths; they are blameless.
	16:20	Every island fled away and the mountains *could* not *be* **found**.
	18:14	your riches and splendor have vanished, never *to be* **recovered**.'
	18:21	city of Babylon will be thrown down, never *to be* **found** again.
	18:22	No workman of any trade *will* ever *be* **found** in you again.
	18:24	In her *was* **found** the blood of prophets and of the saints, and of all
	20:11	and sky fled from his presence, and *there* **was** no place for them.
	20:15	If anyone's name *was* not **found** written in the book of life,

2352 εὐροκλύδων, *euroklydōn*   Not used in UBS/NIV
[√ *3114*]

2353 εὐρύχωρος, *eurychōros* [1] [√ *6003*]

broad [1]

Mt   7:13   For wide is the gate and **broad** is the road that leads to destruction,

2354 εὐσέβεια, *eusebeia* [15] [√ *2292 + 4936*]

godliness [12], godly [2], godly [*+2848*] [1]

Ac	3:12	Why do you stare at us as if *by* our own power or **godliness** we
1Ti	2:2	we may live peaceful and quiet lives in all **godliness** and holiness.
	3:16	Beyond all question, the mystery *of* **godliness** is great:
	4:7	and old wives' tales; rather, train yourself to be **godly**.
	4:8	training is of some value, but **godliness** has value for all things,
	6:3	instruction of our Lord Jesus Christ and to **godly** [*+2848*] teaching,
	6:5	and who think that **godliness** is a means to financial gain.
	6:6	But **godliness** with contentment is great gain.
	6:11	**godliness**, faith, love, endurance and gentleness.
2Ti	3:5	having a form *of* **godliness** but denying its power. Have nothing to
Tit	1:1	God's elect and the knowledge of the truth that leads to **godliness**—
2Pe	1:3	and **godliness** through our knowledge of him who called us by his
	1:6	and to self-control, perseverance; and to perseverance, **godliness**;
	1:7	and to **godliness**, brotherly kindness; and to brotherly kindness,
	3:11	of people ought you to be? You ought to live holy and **godly** *lives*

2355 εὐσεβέω, *eusebeō* [2] [√ *2292 + 4936*]

put religion into practice by caring for [1], worship [1]

Ac   17:23   Now what *you* **worship** as something unknown I am going to
1Ti   5:4   *to* **put** *their* **religion into practice by caring for** their own family

2356 εὐσεβής, *eusebēs* [3] [√ *2292 + 4936*]

devout [2], godly [1]

Ac   10:2   He and all his family were **devout** and God-fearing; he gave
       10:7   of his servants and a **devout** soldier who was one of his attendants.
2Pe   2:9   then the Lord knows how to rescue **godly** *men* from trials

2357 εὐσεβῶς, *eusebōs* [2] [√ *2292 + 4936*]

godly [2]

2Ti   3:12   everyone who wants to live a **godly** *life* in Christ Jesus will be
Tit   2:12   to live self-controlled, upright and **godly** *lives* in this present age,

2358 εὔσημος, *eusēmos* [1] [√ *2292 + 4956*]

intelligible [1]

1Co   14:9   Unless you speak **intelligible** words with your tongue, how will

2359 εὔσπλαγχνος, *eusplanchnos* [2]
[√ 2292 + 5073]

compassionate [2]

Eph 4:32 Be kind and **compassionate** to one another, forgiving each other,
1Pe 3: 8 be sympathetic, love as brothers, be **compassionate** and humble.

2360 εὐσχημονέω, *euschēmoneō* Not used in
UBS/NIV [√ 2292 + 5386]

2361 εὐσχημόνως, *euschēmonōs* [3] [√ 2292 + 5386]

decently [1], fitting [1], win the respect [1]

Ro 13:13 Let us behave **decently**, as in the daytime, not in orgies
1Co 14:40 But everything should be done in a **fitting** and orderly way.
1Th 4:12 so that your daily life may **win the respect** of outsiders and

2362 εὐσχημοσύνη, *euschēmosynē* [1]
[√ 2292 + 5386]

modesty [1]

1Co 12:23 the parts that are unpresentable are treated with special **modesty**,

2363 εὐσχήμων, *euschēmōn* [5] [√ 2292 + 5386]

prominent [2], high standing [1], presentable [1], right [1]

Mk 15:43 Joseph of Arimathea, a **prominent** member of the Council,
Ac 13:50 But the Jews incited the God-fearing women of **high standing**
    17:12 as did also a *number of* **prominent** Greek women and many
1Co 7:35 but that you may live in a **right** *way* in undivided devotion to the
    12:24 while our **presentable** parts need no special treatment. But God

2364 εὐτόνως, *eutonōs* [2] [√ 1753; cf. 2292]

vehemently [1], vigorously [1]

Lk 23:10 teachers of the law were standing there, **vehemently** accusing him.
Ac 18:28 For he **vigorously** refuted the Jews in public debate, proving from

2365 εὐτραπελία, *eutrapelia* [1] [√ 2292 + 5572]

coarse joking [1]

Eph 5: 4 foolish talk or **coarse joking**, which are out of place, but rather

2366 Εὔτυχος, *Eutychos* [1] [√ 2292 + 5593]

Eutychus [1]

Ac 20: 9 Seated in a window was a young man named **Eutychus**, who was

2367 εὐφημία, *euphēmia* [1] [√ 2292 + 5774]

good report [1]

2Co 6: 8 through glory and dishonor, bad report and **good report**; genuine,

2368 εὔφημος, *euphēmos* [1] [√ 2292 + 5774]

admirable [1]

Php 4: 8 whatever is pure, whatever is lovely, whatever is **admirable**—

2369 εὐφορέω, *euphoreō* [1] [√ 2292 + 5770]

produced a good crop [1]

Lk 12:16 "The ground of a certain rich man **produced a good crop**.

2370 εὐφραίνω, *euphrainō* [14] [→ 2371, 2372; cf. 2292 + 5856]

celebrate [5], rejoice [3], glad [2], held a celebration [1], lived [1], make glad [1], merry [1]

Lk 12:19 laid up for many years. Take life easy; eat, drink and *be* **merry**." '

15:23 Bring the fattened calf and kill it. *Let's* have a feast and **celebrate**.
15:24 alive again; he was lost and is found.' So they began *to* **celebrate**.
15:29 gave me even a young goat so *I could* **celebrate** with my friends.
15:32 But we had to **celebrate** and be glad, because this brother of yours
16:19 was dressed in purple and fine linen and **lived** in luxury every day.
Ac   2:26 Therefore my heart *is* **glad** and my tongue rejoices; my body also
     7:41 and **held a celebration** in honor of what their hands had made.
Ro 15:10 Again, it says, "**Rejoice**, O Gentiles, with his people."
2Co 2: 2 who is left to **make** me **glad** but you whom I have grieved?
Gal 4:27 "*Be* **glad**, O barren woman, who bears no children; break forth
Rev 11:10 will gloat over them and *will* **celebrate** by sending each other gifts,
    12:12 Therefore **rejoice**, *you* heavens and you who dwell in them!
    18:20 **Rejoice** over her, O heaven! Rejoice, saints and apostles

2371 Εὐφράτης, *Euphratēs* [2] [√ 2370]

Euphrates [2]

Rev 9:14 the four angels who are bound at the great river **Euphrates**."
    16:12 The sixth angel poured out his bowl on the great river **Euphrates**,

2372 εὐφροσύνη, *euphrosynē* [2] [√ 2370]

fills with joy [1], joy [1]

Ac   2:28 to me the paths of life; you will fill me with **joy** in your presence.'
    14:17 he provides you with plenty of food and **fills** your hearts **with joy**."

2373 εὐχαριστέω, *eucharisteō* [38] [√ 2292 + 5897]

thank [12], gave thanks [7], giving thanks [5], given thanks [4], give thanks [2], gives thanks [2], thanked [2], give thanks for [1], grateful [1], thank for [1], thankful [1]

Mt 15:36 took the seven loaves and the fish, and *when he had* **given thanks**,
    26:27 **gave thanks** and offered it to them, saying, "Drink from it,
Mk   8: 6 When he had taken the seven loaves and **given thanks**, he broke
    14:23 Then he took the cup, **gave thanks** and offered it to them,
Lk 17:16 He threw himself at Jesus' feet and **thanked** him—and he was a
    18:11 'God, *I* **thank** you that I am not like other men—robbers,
    22:17 *he* **gave thanks** and said, "Take this and divide it among you.
    22:19 And he took bread, **gave thanks** and broke it, and gave it to them,
Jn   6:11 Jesus then took the loaves, **gave thanks**, and distributed to those
     6:23 the people had eaten the bread *after* the Lord *had* **given thanks**.
    11:41 looked up and said, "Father, *I* **thank** you that you have heard me.
Ac 27:35 *he* took some bread and **gave thanks** to God in front of them all.
    28:15 At the sight of these men Paul **thanked** God and was encouraged.
Ro   1: 8 First, *I* **thank** my God through Jesus Christ for all of you,
     1:21 they neither glorified him as God nor **gave thanks** to him,
    14: 6 He who eats meat, eats to the Lord, for *he* **gives thanks** to God;
    14: 6 and he who abstains, does so to the Lord and **gives thanks** to God.
    16: 4 only I but all the churches of the Gentiles *are* **grateful** to them.
1Co 1: 4 *I* always **thank** God for you because of his grace given you in
     1:14 *I am* **thankful** that I did not baptize any of you except Crispus
    10:30 why am I denounced because of something I **thank** God **for**?
    11:24 and *when he had* **given thanks**, he broke it and said, "This is my
    14:17 You *may be* **giving thanks** well enough, but the other man is not
    14:18 *I* **thank** God that I speak in tongues more than all of you.
2Co 1:11 Then many *will* **give thanks** on our behalf **for** the gracious favor
Eph 1:16 I have not stopped **giving thanks** for you, remembering you in my
     5:20 always **giving thanks** to God the Father for everything,
Php 1: 3 *I* **thank** my God every time I remember you.
Col 1: 3 *We* always **thank** God, the Father of our Lord Jesus Christ,
     1:12 **giving thanks** to the Father, who has qualified you to share in the
     3:17 of the Lord Jesus, **giving thanks** to God the Father through him.
1Th 1: 2 *We* always **thank** God for all of you, mentioning you in our
     2:13 And we also **thank** God continually because, when you received
     5:18 **give thanks** in all circumstances, for this is God's will for you in
2Th 1: 3 *We* ought always *to* **thank** God for you, brothers, and rightly so,
     2:13 But we ought always *to* **thank** God for you, brothers loved by the
Phm 1: 4 *I* always **thank** my God as I remember you in my prayers,
Rev 11:17 "*We* **give thanks** to you, Lord God Almighty, the One who is

2374 εὐχαριστία, *eucharistia* [15] [√ 2292 + 5897]

thanksgiving [8], thanks [2], expressions of thanks [1], gratitude [1], thank [1], thankful [1], thankfulness [1]

Ac 24: 3 excellent Felix, we acknowledge this with profound **gratitude**.

1Co 14:16 those who do not understand say "Amen" to your **thanksgiving**,
2Co 4:15 and more people may cause **thanksgiving** to overflow to the glory
     9:11 and through us your generosity will result in **thanksgiving** to God.
     9:12 but is also overflowing in many **expressions of thanks** to God.
Eph 5: 4 or coarse joking, which are out of place, but rather **thanksgiving**.
Php 4: 6 but in everything, by prayer and petition, with **thanksgiving**,
Col 2: 7 the faith as you were taught, and overflowing with **thankfulness**.
     4: 2 Devote yourselves to prayer, being watchful and **thankful**.
1Th 3: 9 How can we **thank** God enough for you in return for all the joy we
1Ti 2: 1 prayers, intercession and **thanksgiving** be made for everyone—
     4: 3 which God created to be received with **thanksgiving** by those who
     4: 4 and nothing is to be rejected if it is received with **thanksgiving**,
Rev 4: 9 honor and **thanks** to him who sits on the throne and who lives for
     7:12 Praise and glory and wisdom and **thanks** and honor and power

2375 εὐχάριστος, *eucharistos* [1] [√ *2292 + 5897*]

thankful [1]

Col 3:15 members of one body you were called to peace. And be **thankful**.

2376 εὐχή, *euchē* [3] [√ *2377*]

vow [2], prayer [1]

Ac 18:18 he had his hair cut off at Cenchrea because of a **vow** he had taken.
     21:23 we tell you. There are four men with us who have made a **vow**.
Jas 5:15 And the **prayer** offered in faith will make the sick person well;

2377 εὔχομαι, *euchomai* [7] [→ *2376, 4666, 4667*]

pray [3], pray [+323] [1], prayed for [1], prayer for [1], wish [1]

Ac 26:29 *I* **pray** [+323] God that not only you but all who are listening to
     27:29 *they* dropped four anchors from the stern and **prayed for** daylight.
Ro 9: 3 For *I could* **wish** that I myself were cursed and cut off from Christ
2Co 13: 7 Now *we* **pray** to God that you will not do anything wrong.
     13: 9 but you are strong; and *our* **prayer** *is* **for** your perfection.
Jas 5:16 to each other and **pray** for each other so that you may be healed.
3Jn 1: 2 *I* **pray** that you may enjoy good health and that all may go well

2378 εὔχρηστος, *euchrēstos* [3] [√ *2292 + 5968*]

useful [2], helpful [1]

2Ti 2:21 made holy, **useful** to the Master and prepared to do any good work.
     4:11 bring him with you, because he is **helpful** to me in my ministry.
Phm 1:11 to you, but now he has become **useful** both to you and to me.

2379 εὐψυχέω, *eupsycheō* [1] [√ *2292 + 6038*]

cheered [1]

Php 2:19 that I also *may be* **cheered** when I receive news about you.

2380 εὐωδία, *euōdia* [3] [√ *2292 + 3853*]

fragrant [+4011] [2], aroma [1]

2Co 2:15 For we are to God the **aroma** of Christ among those who are being
Eph 5: 2 and gave himself up for us as a **fragrant** [+4011] offering
Php 4:18 They are a **fragrant** [+4011] offering, an acceptable sacrifice,

2381 εὐώνυμος, *euōnymos* [9] [√ *2292 + 3950*]

left [8], south of [1]

Mt 20:21 may sit at your right and the other at your **left** in your kingdom."
     20:23 from my cup, but to sit at my right or **left** is not for me to grant.
     25:33 He will put the sheep on his right and the goats on his **left**.
     25:41 "Then he will say to those on his **left**, 'Depart from me, you who
     27:38 were crucified with him, one on his right and one on his **left**.
Mk 10:40 but to sit at my right or **left** is not for me to grant. These places
     15:27 two robbers with him, one on his right and one on his **left**.
Ac 21: 3 After sighting Cyprus and passing to the **south of** it, we sailed on
Rev 10: 2 He planted his right foot on the sea and his **left** foot on the land,

2382 εὐωχία, *euōchia* Not used in UBS/NIV
[√ *2292 + 2400*]

2383 ἐφάλλομαι, *ephallomai* [1] [√ *2093 + 256*]

jumped on [*RP2093*] [1]

Ac 19:16 Then the man who had the evil spirit **jumped** [*RP2093*] **on** them

2384 ἐφάπαξ, *ephapax* [5] [√ *2093 + 562*]

once for all [4], at the same time [1]

Ro 6:10 The death he died, he died to sin **once for all**; but the life he lives,
1Co 15: 6 to more than five hundred of the brothers **at the same time**,
Heb 7:27 He sacrificed for their sins **once for all** when he offered himself.
     9:12 but he entered the Most Holy Place **once for all** by his own blood,
     10:10 holy through the sacrifice of the body of Jesus Christ **once for all**.

2385 Ἐφέσινος, *Ephesinos* Not used in UBS/NIV
[√ *2387*]

2386 Ἐφέσιος, *Ephesios* [5] [√ *2387*]

Ephesians [2], of Ephesus [2], Ephesian [1]

Ac 19:28 and began shouting: "Great is Artemis *of* the **Ephesians**!"
     19:34 in unison for about two hours: "Great is Artemis *of* the **Ephesians**!"
     19:35 "Men **of Ephesus**, doesn't all the world know that the city of
     19:35 doesn't all the world know that the city **of Ephesus** is the guardian
     21:29 (They had previously seen Trophimus the **Ephesian** in the city

2387 Ἔφεσος, *Ephesos* [16] [→ *2385, 2386*]

Ephesus [16]

Ac 18:19 They arrived at **Ephesus**, where Paul left Priscilla and Aquila.
     18:21 will come back if it is God's will." Then he set sail from **Ephesus**.
     18:24 a Jew named Apollos, a native of Alexandria, came to **Ephesus**.
     19: 1 Paul took the road through the interior and arrived at **Ephesus**.
     19:17 this became known to the Jews and Greeks living in **Ephesus**,
     19:26 and led astray large numbers of people here *in* **Ephesus**
     20:16 Paul had decided to sail past **Ephesus** to avoid spending time in
     20:17 From Miletus, Paul sent to **Ephesus** for the elders of the church.
1Co 15:32 If I fought wild beasts in **Ephesus** for merely human reasons,
     16: 8 But I will stay on at **Ephesus** until Pentecost,
Eph 1: 1 will of God, To the saints in **Ephesus**, the faithful in Christ Jesus:
1Ti 1: 3 stay there in **Ephesus** so that you may command certain men not
2Ti 1:18 You know very well in how many ways he helped me in **Ephesus**.
     4:12 I sent Tychicus to **Ephesus**.
Rev 1:11 to **Ephesus**, Smyrna, Pergamum, Thyatira, Sardis, Philadelphia
     2: 1 "To the angel of the church in **Ephesus** write: These are the words

2388 ἐφευρετής, *epheuretēs* [1] [√ *2093 + 2351*]

invent [1]

Ro 1:30 insolent, arrogant and boastful; they **invent** ways of doing evil;

2389 ἐφημερία, *ephēmeria* [2] [√ *2093 + 2465*]

division [1], priestly division [1]

Lk 1: 5 named Zechariah, who belonged to the **priestly division** of Abijah;
     1: 8 Once when Zechariah's **division** was on duty and he was serving

2390 ἐφήμερος, *ephēmeros* [1] [√ *2093 + 2465*]

daily [1]

Jas 2:15 Suppose a brother or sister is without clothes and **daily** food.

2391 ἐφικνέομαι, *ephikneomai* [2] [√ *2093 + 2653*]

come [1], reaches [1]

2Co 10:13 the field God has assigned to us, a field that **reaches** even to you.
     10:14 in our boasting, as would be the case *if we had* not **come** to you,

2392 ἐφίστημι, **ephistēmi** [21] [√ 2093 + 2705]

appeared [2], came up [2], came [2], stood beside [2], *untranslated* [1], bent [1], close [1], come on [1], come [1], coming up [1], prepared [1], rushed to [1], stood near [1], stood there [+1639] [1], stopped at [RP2093] [1], stopped [1], was [1]

Lk   2: 9 An angel of the Lord **appeared** to them, and the glory of the Lord
      2:38 **Coming up** to them at that very moment, she gave thanks to God
      4:39 So he **bent** over her and rebuked the fever, and it left her.
   10:40 She **came** to him and asked, "Lord, don't you care that my sister has
   20: 1 the teachers of the law, together with the elders, **came up** to him.
   21:34 of life, and that day *will* **close** on you unexpectedly like a trap.
   24: 4 two men in clothes that gleamed like lightning **stood beside** them.
Ac   4: 1 captain of the temple guard and the Sadducees **came up** to Peter
   6:12 **[NIE]** They seized Stephen and brought him before the
   10:17 out where Simon's house was and **stopped** [RP2093] at the gate.
   11:11 then three men who had been sent to me from Caesarea **stopped** at
   12: 7 Suddenly an angel of the Lord **appeared** and a light shone in the
   17: 5 *They* **rushed to** Jason's house in search of Paul and Silas in order
   22:13 He **stood beside** me and said, 'Brother Saul, receive your sight!'
   22:20 I **stood** [+1639] **there** giving my approval and guarding the clothes
   23:11 The following night the Lord **stood near** Paul and said,
   23:27 were about to kill him, but I **came** with my troops and rescued him,
   28: 2 built a fire and welcomed us all because *it* **was** raining and cold.
1Th 5: 3 "Peace and safety," destruction *will* **come** on them suddenly,
2Ti 4: 2 *be* **prepared** in season and out of season; correct, rebuke
   4: 6 out like a drink offering, and the time *has* **come** for my departure.

2393 ἐφοράω, **ephoraō** Not used in UBS/NIV
[√ 2093 + 3972]

2394 Ἐφραίμ, **Ephraim** [1]

Ephraim [1]

Jn 11:54 to a village called **Ephraim**, where he stayed with his disciples.

2395 ἐφφαθά, **ephphatha** [1]

ephphatha [1]

Mk   7:34 up to heaven and with a deep sigh said to him, "***Ephphatha!***"

2396 ἐχθές, **echthes** [3] [√ 5940]

yesterday [3]

Jn   4:52 said to him, "The fever left him **yesterday** at the seventh hour."
Ac   7:28 Do you want to kill me as you killed the Egyptian **yesterday**?'
Heb 13: 8 Jesus Christ is the same **yesterday** and today and forever.

2397 ἔχθρα, **echthra** [6] [√ 2398]

hatred [2], hostility [2], enemies [+1877] [1], hostile [1]

Lk 23:12 Pilate became friends—before this they had been **enemies** [+1877].
Ro   8: 7 the sinful mind is **hostile** to God. It does not submit to God's law,
Gal 5:20 **hatred**, discord, jealousy, fits of rage, selfish ambition,
Eph 2:14 and has destroyed the barrier, the dividing wall *of* **hostility**,
   2:16 to God through the cross, by which he put to death their **hostility**.
Jas 4: 4 don't you know that friendship with the world is **hatred** toward

2398 ἐχθρός, **echthros** [32] [→ 2397]

enemies [21], enemy [10], enemy [+476] [1]

Mt   5:43 heard that it was said, 'Love your neighbor and hate your **enemy**.'
   5:44 Love your **enemies** and pray for those who persecute you,
  10:36 a man's **enemies** will be the members of his own household.'
  13:25 his **enemy** came and sowed weeds among the wheat, and went
  13:28 " 'An **enemy** [+476] did this,' he replied. "The servants asked him,
  13:39 and the **enemy** who sows them is the devil. The harvest is the end
  22:44 "Sit at my right hand until I put your **enemies** under your feet." '
Mk 12:36 "Sit at my right hand until I put your **enemies** under your feet." '
Lk   1:71 salvation from our **enemies** and from the hand of all who hate us—
   1:74 to rescue us from the hand *of* our **enemies**, and to enable us to
   6:27 who hear me: Love your **enemies**, do good to those who hate you,

   6:35 But love your **enemies**, do good to them, and lend to them without
  10:19 and scorpions and to overcome all the power *of* the **enemy**;
  19:27 But those **enemies** of mine who did not want me to be king over
  19:43 The days will come upon you when your **enemies** will build an
  20:43 until I make your **enemies** a footstool for your feet." '
Ac   2:35 until I make your **enemies** a footstool for your feet." '
  13:10 are a child of the devil and an **enemy** of everything that is right!
Ro   5:10 For if, when we were God's **enemies**, we were reconciled to him
  11:28 far as the gospel is concerned, they are **enemies** on your account;
  12:20 "If your **enemy** is hungry, feed him; if he is thirsty, give him
1Co 15:25 For he must reign until he has put all his **enemies** under his feet.
  15:26 The last **enemy** to be destroyed is death.
Gal 4:16 Have I now become your **enemy** by telling you the truth?
Php 3:18 again even with tears, many live as **enemies** of the cross of Christ.
Col 1:21 and were **enemies** in your minds because of your evil behavior.
2Th 3:15 Yet do not regard him as an **enemy**, but warn him as a brother.
Heb 1:13 "Sit at my right hand until I make your **enemies** a footstool for your
  10:13 Since that time he waits for his **enemies** to be made his footstool.
Jas 4: 4 who chooses to be a friend of the world becomes an **enemy**
Rev 11: 5 fire comes from their mouths and devours their **enemies**.
  11:12 they went up to heaven in a cloud, while their **enemies** looked on.

2399 ἔχιδνα, **echidna** [5]

vipers [4], viper [1]

Mt   3: 7 to where he was baptizing, he said to them: "You brood *of* **vipers**!
  12:34 You brood *of* **vipers**, how can you who are evil say anything
  23:33 "You snakes! You brood *of* **vipers**! How will you escape being
Lk   3: 7 crowds coming out to be baptized by him, "You brood *of* **vipers**!
Ac 28: 3 as he put it on the fire, a **viper**, driven out by the heat,

2400 ἔχω, **echō** [708]

[→ 191, 445, 452, 462, 496, 504, 600, 1923, 1944, 2006, 2009, 2011, 2029, 2091, 2382, 2759, 2807, 2959, 2988, 3576, 3580, 3581, 3807, 4060, 4065, 4218, 4321, 4343, 4430, 4431, 4432, 4604, 4617, 4652, 4668, 4812, 5156, 5212, 5226, 5307, 5309, 5330, 5385, 5660, 5667, 5674; cf. 2335, 5386]

ἐλπίς ἔχειν (to have hope) [7] Ac 24:15; Ro 15:4; 2Co 3:12; 10:15; Eph 2:12; 1Th 4:13; 1Jn 3:3

ἔχειν ἁμαρτίαν (to have sin) [6] Jn 9:41; 15:22,22,24; 19:11; 1Jn 1:8

ἔχειν γυναῖκα (to have a wife) [8] Mk 6:18; 12:23; Lk 20:28,33; 1Co 5:1; 7:2,12,29

ἔχειν δαιμόνιον (to have [be possessed by] a demon) [9] Mt 11:18; Lk 4:33; 7:33; 8:27; Jn 7:20; 8:48,49,52; 10:20

ἔχειν ἐν γαστρί (to have in the womb) [7] Mt 1:18,23; 24:19; Mk 13:17; Lk 21:23; 1Th 5:3; Rev 12:2

ἔχειν ἐξουσία (to have authority) [31] Mt 7:29; 8:9; 9:6; Mk 1:22; 2:10; 3:15; Lk 5:24; 12:5; 19:17; Jn 10:18,18; 19:10,10,11; Ac 9:14; Ro 9:21; 1Co 7:37; 9:4,5,6; 11:10; 2Th 3:9; Heb 13:10; Rev 9:3; 11:6,6; 14:18; 16:9; 17:13; 18:1; 20:6

ἔχειν ζωήν (to have life) [19] Mt 19:16; Jn 3:15,16,36; 5:24,26, 26,39,40; 6:40,47,53,54; 10:10; 20:31; 1Jn 3:15; 5:12,12,13

ἔχειν πίστις (to have faith) [13] Mt 17:20; 21:21; Mk 4:40; 11:22; Lk 17:6; Ac 14:9; Ro 14:22; 1Co 13:2; 1Ti 1:19; Phm 1:5; Jas 2:1,14,18

ἔχειν πνεῦμα (to have a spirit/the Spirit) [9] Mk 3:30; 7:25; 9:17; Ac 8:7; 16:16; Ro 8:9; 1Co 7:40; Jude 1:19; Rev 3:1

ἔχειν χάριν (to have grace) [6] Lk 17:9; Ac 2:47; 2Co 1:15; 1Ti 1:12; 2Ti 1:3; Heb 12:28

have [207], has [89], had [74], need [+5970] [27], with [24], *untranslated* [17], is [13], having [11], was [10], are [8], sick [+2809] [8], held [6], demon-possessed [+1228] [5], get [5], needs [+5970] [5], possessed by [5], without [+3590] [5], hold [4], take [4], am [3], be [3], belongs to [3], felt [3], guilty of sin [+281] [3], hold to [3], holding [3], holds [3], keep [3], pregnant women [+1143+1877] [3], thank [+5921] [3], were [3], able [2], come [2], excuse [+4148] [2], had [+1639] [2], love [+27] [2], made [2], married to [2], needed [+5970] [2], possess [2], reap

[2], rich [*+3836+5975*] [2], with child [*+1143+1877*] [2], accompanied by [1], accusers [*+2991+3836*] [1], answer [*+4639*] [1], approach [*+4643*] [1], as follows [*+3836+4047+5596*] [1], been [1], believe about [*+4411*] [1], believers [*+3836+4411*] [1], benefit [*+5921*] [1], bold [*+4244+4498*] [1], bring [1], bringing [*+1571+3552*] [1], cans [1], cannots [*+4024*] [1], collect a tenth from [*+620*] [1], commend [*+2047*] [1], confident [*+4244*] [1], consider [1], considered [*+6055*] [1], contained [*+1877*] [1], could [1], covered [*+2848*] [1], crippled [*+819*] [1], demon-possessed [*+3836+3836+4460+4505*] [1], dependent on [*+5970*] [1], desire [*+2123*] [1], distressed [*+3383*] [1], doing [1], dwell [*+3531*] [1], encouraged [*+4155*] [1], end [*+5465*] [1], enjoy [1], enjoyed [1], enjoying [1], enough for now [*+3814+3836*] [1], face [1], filled with [1], finish [*+5455*] [1], following [1], forgiven [*+912*] [1], gained [1], gave [*+4639*] [1], gave [1], give [1], given [*+608*] [1], given [1], glory in [*+3018*] [1], glory over [*+3018*] [1], got [1], guilty [1], had [*+323*] [1], had charge of [1], harbor [1], hardened [*+4800*] [1], has enough [*+1650*] [1], has hold [1], has to do with [1], have [*+3836*] [1], haven't [*+3590*] [1], holding on to [1], honor [*+1952*] [1], in leaf [*+5877*] [1], in this condition [1], invalid [*+819+1877+3836*] [1], is ours [1], is under [1], keep hold of [1], keeper [1], keeping [1], kept [1], leaves [1], live [1], lived [*+2998+3836*] [1], living [*+3836+6034*] [1], longing [*+2163*] [1], made up of [1], maintained [1], means [1], must [*+2026*] [1], must [*+340*] [1], nearby [1], need [*+1181+5970*] [1], need [*+340*] [1], next day [1], next [1], obey [*+5717*] [1], persevered [*+5705*] [1], preached [*+3062*] [1], pregnant [*+1143+1877*] [1], pregnant woman [*+1143+1877*] [1], reaching [1], received [1], remember [*+3644*] [1], retain [*+993*] [1], rules [1], Sabbath day's walk from [*+1584+3847+4879*] [1], sealed with [*+3836+5382*] [1], shone with [1], sick [*1819*] [1], since going through [1], spare [*+3590*] [1], spread [*+3786*] [1], stop [*+398*] [1], suffer persecution [*+2568*] [1], surrounded by [1], take [*+1639*] [1], taken [1], thankful [*+5921*] [1], that accompany [1], trained [*+1214*] [1], treated with [1], trembling [*+5571*] [1], uncircumcised [*+213*] [1], use [1], want [1], whose [*+4005*] [1], whose [*+5515*] [1], whose [*+899*] [1], whoses [1], wounded [*+3836+4435*] [1]

Mt 1: 18 she was found *to be* **with child** [*+1143+1877*] through the Holy
1: 23 "The virgin *will be* **with child** [*+1143+1877*] and will give birth to
3: 4 John's clothes *were* **made** of camel's hair, and he had a leather
3: 9 think you can say to yourselves, 'We **have** Abraham as our father.'
3: 14 saying, "I **need** [*+5970*] to be baptized by you, and do you come to
4: 24 and people brought to him all who *were* **ill** [*+2809*] with various
5: 23 and there remember that your brother **has** something against you,
5: 46 If you love those who love you, what reward *will you* **get**?
6: 1 If you do, *you will* **have** no reward from your Father in heaven.
6: 8 for your Father knows what *you* **need** [*+5970*] before you ask him.
7: 29 because he taught as *one who* **had** authority, and not as their
8: 9 For I myself am a man under authority, **with** soldiers under me.
8: 16 drove out the spirits with a word and healed all the **sick** [*+2809*].
8: 20 Jesus replied, "Foxes **have** holes and birds of the air have nests,
8: 20 the air have nests, but the Son of Man **has** no place to lay his head."
9: 6 so that you may know that the Son of Man **has** authority on earth
9: 12 Jesus said, "It is not the healthy who **need** [*+5970*] a doctor, but the
9: 12 "It is not the healthy who need a doctor, but the **sick** [*+2809*].
9: 36 and helpless, like sheep **without** [*+3590*] a shepherd.
11: 15 He *who* **has** ears, let him hear.
11: 18 came neither eating nor drinking, and they say, '*He* **has** a demon.'
12: 10 and a man **with** a shriveled hand was there. Looking for a reason to
12: 11 "If any of you **has** a sheep and it falls into a pit on the Sabbath,
13: 5 Some fell on rocky places, where *it did* not **have** much soil.
13: 5 have much soil. It sprang up quickly, because the soil **was** shallow.
13: 6 plants were scorched, and they withered because they **had** no root.
13: 9 He *who* **has** ears, let him hear."
13: 12 Whoever **has** will be given more,
13: 12 Whoever *does* not **have**, even what he has will be taken from him.
13: 12 Whoever does not have, even what *he* **has** will be taken from him.
13: 21 But *since he* **has** no root, he lasts only a short time. When trouble
13: 27 good seed in your field? Where then *did* the weeds **come** from?'
13: 43 sun in the kingdom of their Father. He *who* **has** ears, let him hear.
13: 44 and then in his joy went and sold all *he* **had** and bought that field.
13: 46 he went away and sold everything *he* **had** and bought it.
14: 4 John had been saying to him: "It is not lawful for you *to* **have** her."

14: 5 of the people, because *they* **considered** [*+6055*] him a prophet.
14: 16 Jesus replied, "They do not **need** [*+5970*] to go away. You give
14: 17 "We **have** here only five loaves of bread and two fish," they
14: 35 surrounding country. People brought all their **sick** [*+2809*] to him
15: 30 **bringing** [*+1571+3552*] the lame, the blind, the crippled, the mute
15: 32 *they* have already been with me three days and **have** nothing to
15: 34 "How many loaves *do you* **have**?" Jesus asked. "Seven," they
16: 8 why are you talking among yourselves about **having** no bread?
17: 20 I tell you the truth, if *you* **have** faith as small as a mustard seed,
18: 8 or crippled than *to* **have** two hands or two feet and be thrown into
18: 9 It is better for you to enter life with one eye than *to* **have** two eyes
18: 25 *Since he was* not **able** to pay, the master ordered that he and his
18: 25 and his children and all that *he* **had** be sold to repay the debt.
19: 16 and asked, "Teacher, what good thing must I do to **get** eternal life?"
19: 21 and give to the poor, and *you will* **have** treasure in heaven.
19: 22 he went away sad, because *he* **had** [*+1639*] great wealth.
21: 3 says anything to you, tell him that the Lord **needs** [*+5970*] them,
21: 21 "I tell you the truth, if *you* **have** faith and do not doubt,
21: 26 are afraid of the people, for *they* all **hold** that John was a prophet."
21: 28 There was a man *who* **had** two sons. He went to the first and said,
21: 38 'This is the heir. Come, let's kill him and **take** his inheritance.'
21: 46 afraid of the crowd because the *people* **held** that he was a prophet.
22: 12 'how did you get in here **without** [*+3590*] wedding clothes?'
22: 24 said, "Moses told us that if a man dies without **having** children,
22: 25 The first one married and died, and *since he* **had** no children,
22: 28 will she be of the seven, since all of them *were* **married to** her?"
24: 19 it will be in those days *for* **pregnant women** [*+1143+1877*]
25: 25 hid your talent in the ground. See, here is what **belongs to** you.'
25: 28 the talent from him and give it *to* the one *who* **has** the ten talents.
25: 29 For everyone who **has** will be given more, and he will have an
25: 29 Whoever *does* not **have**, even what he has will be taken from him.
25: 29 Whoever does not have, even what *he* **has** will be taken from him.
26: 7 a woman came to him **with** an alabaster jar of very expensive
26: 11 The poor *you will* always **have** with you, but you will not always
26: 11 you will always have with you, but *you will* not always **have** me.
26: 65 Why *do we* **need** [*+5970*] any more witnesses? Look, now you
27: 16 At that time *they* **had** a notorious prisoner, called Barabbas.
27: 65 "**Take** a guard," Pilate answered. "Go, make the tomb as secure as

Mk 1: 22 because he taught them as *one who* **had** authority, not as the
1: 32 after sunset the people brought to Jesus all the **sick** [*+2809*]
1: 34 and Jesus healed many *who* **had** various diseases. He also drove
1: 38 to the **nearby** villages—so I can preach there also.
2: 10 But that you may know that the Son of Man **has** authority on earth
2: 17 "It is not the healthy *who* **need** [*+5970*] a doctor, but the sick.
2: 17 "It is not the healthy who need a doctor, but the **sick** [*+2809*].
2: 19 is with them? They cannot, so long as *they* **have** him with them.
2: 25 when he and his companions were hungry and *in* **need** [*+5970*]?
3: 1 into the synagogue, and a man **with** a shriveled hand was there.
3: 3 Jesus said to the man **with** the shriveled hand, "Stand up in front of
3: 10 so that those **with** diseases were pushing forward to touch him.
3: 15 and *to* **have** authority to drive out demons.
3: 22 came down from Jerusalem said, "*He is* **possessed by** Beelzebub!
3: 26 opposes himself and is divided, he cannot stand; *his* end *has* **come**.
3: 29 blasphemes against the Holy Spirit *will* never *be* **forgiven** [*+912*];
3: 30 He said this because they were saying, "*He* **has** an evil spirit."
4: 5 Some fell on rocky places, where *it did* not **have** much soil.
4: 5 have much soil. It sprang up quickly, because the soil **was** shallow.
4: 6 plants were scorched, and they withered because they **had** no root.
4: 9 Then Jesus said, "He *who* **has** ears to hear, let him hear."
4: 17 But *since they* **have** no root, they last only a short time.
4: 23 If anyone **has** ears to hear, let him hear."
4: 25 Whoever **has** will be given more; whoever does not have,
4: 25 whoever *does* not **have**, even what he has will be taken from him."
4: 25 whoever does not have, even what *he* **has** will be taken from him."
4: 40 his disciples, "Why are you so afraid? *Do you* still **have** no faith?"
5: 3 This man **lived** [*+2998+3836*] in the tombs, and no one could bind
5: 15 of demons, **[RPG]** sitting there, dressed and in his right mind;
5: 23 and pleaded earnestly with him, "My little daughter *is* dying.
6: 18 to Herod, "It is not lawful for you *to* **have** your brother's wife."
6: 34 because they were like sheep **without** [*+3590*] a shepherd.
6: 38 "How many loaves *do you* **have**?" he asked. "Go and see."
6: 55 and carried the **sick** [*+2809*] on mats to wherever they heard he
7: 25 a woman whose little daughter *was* **possessed by** an evil spirit
8: 1 *Since they* **had** nothing to eat, Jesus called his disciples to him
8: 2 they have already been with me three days and **have** nothing to eat.
8: 5 "How many loaves *do you* **have**?" Jesus asked. "Seven," they

8: 7 *They* had a few small fish as well; he gave thanks for them also
8: 14 to bring bread, except for one loaf *they* had with them in the boat.
8: 16 this with one another and said, "It is because *we* have no bread."
8: 17 Jesus asked them: "Why are you talking about having no bread?
8: 17 still not see or understand? *Are* your hearts hardened [+4800]?
8: 18 Do you have eyes but fail to see, and ears but fail to hear?
8: 18 Do you have eyes but fail to see, and [RPG] ears but fail to hear?
9: 17 who *is* possessed by a spirit that has robbed him of speech.
9: 43 It is better for you to enter life maimed than with two hands to go
9: 45 It is better for you to enter life crippled than *to* have two feet
9: 47 to enter the kingdom of God with one eye than *to* have two eyes
9: 50 Have salt in yourselves, and be at peace with each other."
10: 21 "Go, sell everything *you* have and give to the poor, and you will
10: 21 and give to the poor, and *you will* have treasure in heaven.
10: 22 face fell. He went away sad, because *he* had [+1639] great wealth.
10: 23 "How hard it is *for* the rich [+3836+5975] to enter the kingdom of
11: 3 'The Lord needs [+5970] it and will send it back here shortly.' "
11: 13 Seeing in the distance a fig tree in leaf [+5877], he went to find out
11: 22 "Have faith in God," Jesus answered.
11: 25 stand praying, if *you* hold anything against anyone, forgive him,
11: 32 the people, for everyone held [that John really was a prophet.)
12: 6 "*He* had one left to send, a son, whom he loved. He sent him last
12: 23 whose wife will she be, since the seven *were* married to her?"
12: 44 out of her poverty, put in everything—all she had to live on."
13: 17 it will be in those days *for* pregnant women [+1143+1877]
14: 3 a woman came with an alabaster jar of very expensive perfume,
14: 7 The poor *you will* always have with you, and you can help them
14: 7 help them any time you want. But *you will* not always have me.
14: 8 She did what *she* could. She poured perfume on my body
14: 63 "Why *do we* need [+5970] any more witnesses?" he asked.
16: 8 Trembling [+5557] and bewildered, the women went out
16: 18 they will place their hands on sick people, and *they will* get well."

Lk 3: 8 not begin to say to yourselves, '*We* have Abraham as our father.'
3: 11 "The man with two tunics should share with him who has none,
3: 11 "The man with two tunics should share with him *who* has none,
3: 11 him who has none, and the one *who* has food should do the same."
4: 33 In the synagogue there was a man possessed by a demon,
4: 40 the people brought to Jesus all who had various kinds of sickness,
5: 24 But that you may know that the Son of Man has authority on earth
5: 31 "It is not the healthy *who* need [+5970] a doctor, but the sick.
5: 31 "It is not the healthy who need a doctor, but the sick [+2809].
6: 8 they were thinking and said to the man with the shriveled hand,
7: 2 whom his master valued highly, *was* sick [+2809] and about to die.
7: 8 For I myself am a man under authority, with soldiers under me.
7: 33 eating bread nor drinking wine, and you say, '*He* has a demon.'
7: 40 Jesus answered him, "Simon, *I* have something to tell you."
7: 42 Neither of them had the money to pay him back, so he canceled
8: 6 it came up, the plants withered because they had no moisture.
8: 8 he said this, he called out, "He *who* has ears to hear, let him hear."
8: 13 receive the word with joy when they hear it, but they have no root.
8: 18 Whoever has will be given more; whoever does not have,
8: 18 whoever *does* not have, even what he thinks he has will be taken
8: 18 does not have, even what he thinks he has will be taken from him."
8: 27 he was met by a demon-possessed [+1228] man from the town.
9: 3 no staff, no bag, no bread, no money, [RPG] no extra tunic.
9: 11 kingdom of God, and healed those *who* needed [+5970] healing.
9: 58 Jesus replied, "Foxes have holes and birds of the air have nests,
9: 58 the air have nests, but the Son of Man has no place to lay his head."
11: 5 Then he said to them, "Suppose one of you has a friend, and he
11: 6 a journey has come to me, and *I* have nothing to set before him.'
11: 36 and no part of it [NIE] dark, it will be completely lighted,
12: 4 afraid of those who kill the body and after that can^s do no more.
12: 5 after the killing of the body, has power to throw you into hell.
12: 17 to himself, 'What shall I do? *I* have no place to store my crops.'
12: 19 to myself, "You have plenty of good things laid up for many years.
12: 50 But *I* have a baptism to undergo,
13: 6 "A man had a fig tree, planted in his vineyard, and he went to look
13: 11 and a woman was there *who had been* crippled by [+819] a spirit
13: 33 I must keep going today and tomorrow and the next day—
14: 14 Although *they* cannot^s [+4024] repay you, you will be repaid at
14: 18 'I have just bought a field, and I must [+340] go and see it.
14: 18 a field, and I must go and see it. Please excuse [+4148] me.'
14: 19 and I'm on my way to try them out. Please excuse [+4148] me.'
14: 28 and estimate the cost to see if *he* has [+1650] enough money to
14: 35 it is thrown out. "He *who* has ears to hear, let him hear."
15: 4 "Suppose one of you has a hundred sheep and loses one of them.

15: 7 ninety-nine righteous persons who *do* not need [+5970] to repent.
15: 8 "Or suppose a woman has ten silver coins and loses one. Does she
15: 11 Jesus continued: "There was a man *who* had two sons.
16: 1 "There was a rich man whose [+4005] manager was accused of
16: 28 for *I* have five brothers. Let him warn them, so that they will not
16: 29 "Abraham replied, '*They* have Moses and the Prophets; let them
17: 6 He replied, "If *you* have faith as small as a mustard seed, you can
17: 7 "Suppose one of you had a servant plowing or looking after the
17: 9 *Would he* thank [+5921] the servant because he did what he was
18: 22 Sell everything *you* have and give to the poor, and you will have
18: 22 and give to the poor, and *you will* have treasure in heaven.
18: 24 "How hard it is *for* the rich [+3836+5975] to enter the kingdom of
19: 17 you have been trustworthy in a very small matter, take [+1639]
19: 20 here is your mina; *I* have kept it laid away in a piece of cloth.
19: 24 his mina away from him and give it *to* the one *who* has ten minas.'
19: 25 " 'Sir,' they said, '*he already* has ten!'
19: 26 "He replied, 'I tell you that to everyone who has, more will be
19: 26 who has, more will be given, but as for the one *who* has nothing,
19: 26 for the one who has nothing, even what *he* has will be taken away.
19: 31 'Why are you untying it?' tell him, 'The Lord needs [+5970] it.' "
19: 34 They replied, "The Lord needs [+5970] it."
20: 24 me a denarius. Whose [+5515] portrait and inscription are on it?"
20: 28 us that if a man's brother dies and leaves a wife but no children,
20: 33 whose wife will she be, since the seven *were* married to her?"
21: 4 but she out of her poverty put in *all she* had to live on."
21: 23 it will be in those days *for* pregnant women [+1143+1877]
22: 36 "But now *if you* have [+3836] a purse, take it, and also a bag;
22: 36 and *if* you don't have a sword, sell your cloak and buy one.
22: 37 in me. Yes, what is written about me *is* reaching its fulfillment."
22: 71 Then they said, "Why *do we* need [+5970] any more testimony?"
24: 39 and see; a ghost *does* not have flesh and bones, as you see I have."
24: 39 and see; a ghost does not have flesh and bones, as you see I have.
24: 41 he asked them, "*Do you* have anything here to eat?"

Jn 2: 3 was gone, Jesus' mother said to him, "*They* have no more wine."
2: 25 *He did* not need [+5970] man's testimony about man, for he knew
3: 15 that everyone who believes in him *may* have eternal life.
3: 16 that whoever believes in him shall not perish but have eternal life.
3: 29 The bride belongs to the bridegroom. The friend who attends the
3: 36 Whoever believes in the Son has eternal life, but whoever rejects
4: 11 woman said, "*you* have nothing to draw with and the well is deep.
4: 11 and the well is deep. Where *can you* get this living water?
4: 17 "*I* have no husband," she replied. Jesus said to her, "You are right
4: 17 said to her, "You are right when you say *you* have no husband.
4: 18 The fact is, *you have* had five husbands, and the man you now
4: 18 had five husbands, and the man *you* now have is not your husband.
4: 32 he said to them, "I have food to eat that you know nothing about."
4: 44 (Now Jesus himself had pointed out that a prophet has no honor in
4: 52 When he inquired as to the time when his son got better, they said
5: 2 and which *is* surrounded by five covered colonnades.
5: 5 *had been an* invalid [+819+1877+3836] for thirty-eight years.
5: 6 and learned that *he* had been in this condition for a long time,
5: 7 "*I* have no one to help me into the pool when the water is stirred.
5: 24 hears my word and believes him who sent me has eternal life
5: 26 For as the Father has life in himself, so he has granted the Son to
5: 26 life in himself, so he has granted the Son *to* have life in himself.
5: 36 "I have testimony weightier than that of John. For the very work
5: 38 nor *does* his word dwell [+3531] in you, for you do not believe the
5: 39 because you think that by them you possess eternal life.
5: 40 yet you refuse to come to me to have life.
5: 42 I know that *you do* not have the love of God in your hearts.
6: 9 "Here is a boy with five small barley loaves and two small fish,
6: 40 who looks to the Son and believes in him *shall* have eternal life,
6: 47 I tell you the truth, he who believes has everlasting life.
6: 53 of the Son of Man and drink his blood, *you* have no life in you.
6: 54 Whoever eats my flesh and drinks my blood has eternal life,
6: 68 to whom shall we go? You have the words of eternal life.
7: 20 "*You are* demon-possessed [+1228]," the crowd answered.
8: 6 this question as a trap, in order to have *a basis* for accusing him.
8: 12 me will never walk in darkness, but *will* have the light of life."
8: 26 "*I* have much to say in judgment of you. But he who sent me is
8: 41 they protested. "The only Father *we* have is God himself."
8: 48 in saying that you are a Samaritan and demon-possessed [+1228]?"
8: 49 "*I am* not possessed by a demon," said Jesus, "but I honor my
8: 52 "Now we know that *you are* demon-possessed [+1228]!
8: 57 "*You are* not yet fifty years old," the Jews said to him, "and you
9: 21 we don't know. Ask him. *He is* of age; he will speak for himself."

9: 23　That was why his parents said, "*He* **is** of age; ask him."
9: 41　"If you were blind, *you* would not *be* **guilty of sin** [*+281*];
10: 10　I have come that *they may* **have** life, and have it to the full.
10: 10　I have come that they may have life, and **have** it to the full.
10: 16　*I* **have** other sheep that are not of this sheep pen. I must bring them
10: 18　*I* **have** authority to lay it down and authority to take it up again.
10: 18　authority to lay it down and authority **[RPG]** to take it up again.
10: 20　of them said, "*He is* **demon-possessed** [*+1228*] and raving mad.
11: 17　Jesus found that Lazarus *had* already **been** in the tomb for four
12: 6　as **keeper** of the money bag, he used to help himself to what was
12: 8　*You will* always **have** the poor among you, but you will not always
12: 8　have the poor among you, but *you will* not always **have** me."
12: 35　Walk while *you* **have** the light, before darkness overtakes you.
12: 36　Put your trust in the light while *you* **have** it, so that you may
12: 48　*There* **is** a judge for the one who rejects me and does not accept
13: 8　Jesus answered, "Unless I wash you, *you* **have** no part with me."
13: 10　"A person who has had a bath **needs** [*+5970*] only to wash his feet;
13: 29　Since Judas **had charge of** the money, some thought Jesus was
13: 29　was telling him to buy what *was* **needed** [*+5970*] for the Feast,
13: 35　will know that you are my disciples, if *you* **love** [*+27*] one another."
14: 21　Whoever **has** my commands and obeys them, he is the one who
14: 30　for the prince of this world is coming. *He* **has** no **hold** on me,
15: 13　Greater love **has** no one than this, that he lay down his life for his
15: 22　and spoken to them, *they would* not *be* **guilty of sin** [*+281*].
15: 22　be guilty of sin. Now, however, *they* **have** no excuse for their sin.
15: 24　them what no one else did, *they would* not *be* **guilty of sin** [*+281*].
16: 12　"*I* **have** much more to say to you, more than you can now bear.
16: 15　All that **belongs to** the Father is mine. That is why I said the Spirit
16: 21　A woman giving birth to a child **has** pain because her time has
16: 22　Now **is** *your* time of grief, but I will see you again and you will
16: 30　and that *you do* not even **need** [*+5970*] to have anyone ask you
16: 33　"I have told you these things, so that in me *you may* **have** peace.
16: 33　In this world *you will* **have** trouble. But take heart! I have
17: 5　glorify me in your presence with the glory *I* **had** with you before
17: 13　so that *they may* **have** the full measure of my joy within them.
18: 10　who **had** a sword, drew it and struck the high priest's servant,
19: 7　The Jews insisted, "*We* **have** a law, and according to that law he
19: 10　"Don't you realize *I* **have** power either to free you or to crucify
19: 10　realize I have power either to free you or **[RPG]** to crucify you?"
19: 11　"*You would* **have** no power over me if it were not given to you
19: 11　Therefore the one who handed me over to you *is* **guilty** of a greater
19: 15　"*We* **have** no king but Caesar," the chief priests answered.
20: 31　Son of God, and that by believing *you may* **have** life in his name.
21: 5　He called out to them, "Friends, **haven't** [*+3590*] you any fish?"

Ac　1: 12　Olives, a **Sabbath day's walk from** [*+1584+3847+4879*] the city.
2: 44　All the believers were together and **had** everything in common.
2: 45　their possessions and goods, they gave to anyone as he **had** need.
2: 47　praising God and **enjoying** the favor of all the people.
3: 6　Peter said, "Silver or gold I do not have, but what *I* **have** I give you.
4: 14　healed standing there with them, *there* **was** nothing they could say.
4: 35　and it was distributed to anyone as he **had** [*+323*] need.
7: 1　Then the high priest asked him, "**Are** these charges true?"
8: 7　With shrieks, **[NIE]** evil spirits came out of many, and many
9: 14　And he has come here **with** authority from the chief priests to
9: 31　throughout Judea, Galilee and Samaria **enjoyed** a time of peace.
11: 3　"You went into the house of **uncircumcised** [*+213*] men and ate
12: 15　When she kept insisting that *it* **was** so, they said, "It must be his
13: 5　in the Jewish synagogues. John *was* **with** *them* as their helper.
14: 9　Paul looked directly at him, saw that *he* **had** faith to be healed
15: 21　For Moses *has been* **preached** [*+3062*] in every city from the
15: 36　we preached the word of the Lord and see how *they are* **doing**."
16: 16　we were met by a slave girl *who* **had** a spirit by which she
17: 11　and examined the Scriptures every day to see if what Paul said **was**
18: 18　he had his hair cut off at Cenchrea because of a vow *he had* **taken**.
19: 13　those *who were* **demon-possessed** [*+3836+3836+4460+4505*].
19: 38　and his fellow craftsmen **have** a grievance against anybody,
20: 15　over to Samos, and *on* the **following** day arrived at Miletus.
21: 13　I **am** ready not only to be bound, but also to die in Jerusalem for
21: 23　we tell you. There are four men with us *who have* **made** a vow.
21: 26　The **next** day Paul took the men and purified himself along with
23: 17　this young man to the commander; *he* **has** something to tell him."
23: 18　bring this young man to you *because he* **has** something to tell you."
23: 19　drew him aside and asked, "What is it *you* **want** to tell me?"
23: 25　He wrote a letter **as follows** [*+3836+4047+5596*]:
23: 29　but *there* **was** no charge against him that deserved death
24: 9　Jews joined in the accusation, asserting that these things **were** true.

24: 15　and *I* **have** the same hope in God as these men, that there will be a
24: 16　So I strive always *to* **keep** my conscience clear before God
24: 19　before you and bring charges if *they* **have** anything against me.
24: 23　but *to* **give** him some freedom and permit his friends to take care of
24: 25　Felix was afraid and said, "That's **enough for now** [*+3814+3836*]!
25: 16　hand over any man before he has faced his **accusers** [*+2991+3836*]
25: 19　*they* **had** some points of dispute with him about their own religion
25: 26　But *I* **have** nothing definite to write to His Majesty about him.
25: 26　so that as a result of this investigation *I may* **have** something to
27: 39　did not recognize the land, but they saw a bay **with** a sandy beach,
28: 9　the rest of the **sick** [*+819*] on the island came and were cured.
28: 19　not that I **had** any charge to bring against my own people.

Ro　1: 13　in order that *I might* **have** a harvest among you, just as I have had
1: 28　since they did not think it worthwhile to **retain** the knowledge of
2: 14　(Indeed, when Gentiles, who *do* not **have** the law, do by nature
2: 14　are a law for themselves, *even though they do* not **have** the law,
2: 20　*because you* **have** in the law the embodiment of knowledge
4: 2　was justified by works, *he* **had** something to boast about—
5: 1　we **have** peace with God through our Lord Jesus Christ,
5: 2　through whom *we have* **gained** access by faith into this grace in
6: 21　What benefit *did you* **reap** at that time from the things you are
6: 22　the benefit *you reap* leads to holiness, and the result is eternal life.
8: 9　And if anyone *does* not **have** the Spirit of Christ, he does not
8: 23　only so, but we ourselves, *who* **have** the firstfruits of the Spirit,
9: 10　Not only that, but Rebekah's children **had** one and the same father,
9: 21　*Does* not the potter **have** the right to make out of the same lump of
10: 2　For I can testify about them that *they* **are** zealous for God,
12: 4　Just as each of *us* **has** one body with many members, and these
12: 4　and these members *do* not all **have** the same function,
12: 6　*We* **have** different gifts, according to the grace given us. If a man's
13: 3　Then do what is right and he *will* **commend you** [*+2047*].
14: 22　So whatever you **believe about** [*+4411*] these things keep between
14: 22　So whatever you believe about these things **keep** between yourself
15: 4　and the encouragement of the Scriptures *we might* **have** hope.
15: 17　Therefore *I* **glory** in Christ Jesus **in** [*+3018*] my service to God.
15: 23　But now *that there* **is** no more place for me to work in these
15: 23　and *since I have been* **longing** [*+2163*] for many years to see you,

1Co　2: 16　that he may instruct him?" But we **have** the mind of Christ.
4: 7　What *do you* **have** that you did not receive? And if you did receive
4: 15　Even though *you* **have** ten thousand guardians in Christ, you do
5: 1　does not occur even among pagans: A man **has** his father's wife.
6: 1　*If* any of *you* **has** a dispute with another, dare he take it before the
6: 4　Therefore, if *you* **have** disputes about such matters, appoint as
6: 7　The very fact that *you* **have** lawsuits among you means you have
6: 19　Holy Spirit, who is in you, whom *you have* **received** from God?
7: 2　so much immorality, each man *should* **have** his own wife,
7: 2　have his own wife, and each woman **[RPG]** her own husband.
7: 7　But each man **has** his own gift from God; one has this gift,
7: 12　If any brother **has** a wife who is not a believer and she is willing to
7: 13　And if a woman **has** a husband who is not a believer and he is
7: 25　*I* **have** no command from the Lord, but I give a judgment as one
7: 28　But those who marry will **face** many troubles in this life, and I
7: 29　From now on those *who* **have** wives should live as if they had
7: 29　From now on those who have wives should live as if *they* **had**
7: 37　*who* **is under** no compulsion but has control over his own will,
7: 37　who is under no compulsion but **has** control over his own will,
7: 40　if she stays as she is—and I think that I too **have** the Spirit of God.
8: 1　We know that *we* all **possess** knowledge. Knowledge puffs up,
8: 10　For if anyone with a weak conscience sees you who **have** this
9: 4　Don't *we* **have** the right to food and drink?
9: 5　Don't *we* **have** the right to take a believing wife along with us,
9: 6　Or is it only I and Barnabas *who* **must** [*+2026*] work for a living?
9: 17　If I preach voluntarily, *I* **have** a reward; if not voluntarily,
11: 4　or prophesies *with* his head **covered** [*+2848*] dishonors his head.
11: 10　the woman ought *to* **have** a sign of authority on her head.
11: 16　wants to be contentious about this, we **have** no other practice—
11: 22　Don't *you* **have** homes to eat and drink in? Or do you despise the
11: 22　despise the church of God and humiliate those *who* **have** nothing?
12: 12　The body is a unit, though *it is* **made up of** many parts; and though
12: 21　The eye cannot say to the hand, "*I don't* **need** [*+5970*] you!"
12: 21　And the head cannot say to the feet, "*I don't* **need** [*+5970*] you!"
12: 23　And the parts that are unpresentable *are* **treated** with special
12: 24　while our presentable parts **need** [*+5970*] no special treatment.
12: 30　Do all **have** gifts of healing? Do all speak in tongues? Do all
13: 1　If I speak in the tongues of men and of angels, but **have** not love,
13: 2　If *I* **have** the gift of prophecy and can fathom all mysteries

13: 2 and if *I* **have** a faith that can move mountains, but have not love,
13: 2 a faith that can move mountains, but **have** not love, I am nothing.
13: 3 surrender my body to the flames, but **have** not love, I gain nothing.
14:26 everyone **has** a hymn, or a word of instruction, a revelation,
14:26 or **[RPG]** a word of instruction, a revelation, a tongue or an
14:26 of instruction, **[RPG]** a revelation, a tongue or an interpretation.
14:26 of instruction, a revelation, **[RPG]** a tongue or an interpretation.
14:26 of instruction, a revelation, a tongue or **[RPG]** an interpretation.
15:31 just as surely as *I* **glory over** [+3018] you in Christ Jesus our Lord.
15:34 and stop sinning; for there are some *who* **are** ignorant of God—

2Co 1: 9 Indeed, in our hearts we **felt** the sentence of death. But this
1:15 planned to visit you first so that *you might* **benefit** [+5921] twice.
2: 3 so that when I came *I should* not *be* **distressed** [+3383] by those
2: 4 but to let you know the depth of my love **[NIE]** for you.
2:13 *I still* **had** no peace of mind,
3: 4 Such confidence as this **is ours** through Christ before God.
3:12 Therefore, *since we* **have** such a hope, we are very bold.
4: 1 Therefore, since through God's mercy we **have** this ministry,
4: 7 But *we* **have** this treasure in jars of clay to show that this
4:13 **With** that same spirit of faith we also believe and therefore speak,
5: 1 we **have** a building from God, an eternal house in heaven,
5:12 so that *you can* **answer** [+4639] those who take pride in what is
6:10 making many rich; **having** nothing, and yet possessing everything.
7: 1 *Since we* **have** these promises, dear friends, let us purify ourselves
7: 5 For when we came into Macedonia, this body of ours **had** no rest,
8:11 be matched by your completion of it, according to your **means**.
8:12 is there, the gift is acceptable according to what *one* **has**,
8:12 to what one has, not according to what *he does* not **have**.
9: 8 so that in all things at all times, **having** all that you need, you will
10: 6 And *we will* **be** ready to punish every act of disobedience,
10:15 Our hope **is** that, as your faith continues to grow, our area of
12:14 Now *I* **am** ready to visit you for the third time, and I will not be a

Gal 2: 4 infiltrated our ranks to spy on the freedom *we* **have** in Christ Jesus
4:22 For it is written that Abraham **had** two sons, one by the slave
4:27 The children of the desolate woman than *of her who* **has** a husband."
6: 4 Then *he can* **take** pride in himself, without comparing himself to
6:10 Therefore, as *we* **have** opportunity, let us do good to all people,

Eph 1: 7 In him *we* **have** redemption through his blood, the forgiveness of
2:12 and foreigners to the covenants of the promise, **without** [+3590]
2:18 For through him *we both* **have** access to the Father by one Spirit.
3:12 and through faith in him *we may* **approach** [+4643] God with
4:28 that *he may* **have** *something* to share with those in need.
4:28 that he may have something to share with those in **need** [+5970].
5: 5 **has** any inheritance in the kingdom of Christ and of God.
5:27 and to present her to himself as a radiant church, **without** [+3590]

Php 1: 7 me to feel this way about all of you, since *I* **have** you in my heart;
1:23 *I* **desire** [+2123] to depart and be with Christ, which is better for
1:30 **since** you *are going through* the same struggle you saw I had,
2: 2 **having** the same love, being one in spirit and purpose.
2:20 *I* **have** no one else like him, who takes a genuine interest in your
2:27 but also on me, to **spare** [+3590] me sorrow upon sorrow.
2:29 him in the Lord with great joy, and **honor** [+1952] men like him,
3: 4 though I myself **have** *reasons* for such confidence. If anyone else
3: 9 not **having** a righteousness of my own that comes from the law,
3:17 take note of those who live according to the pattern we **gave** *you*.

Col 1: 4 faith in Christ Jesus and of the love *you* **have** for all the saints—
1:14 in whom *we* **have** redemption, the forgiveness of sins.
2: 1 I want you to know how much *I* **am** struggling for you and for
2:23 Such regulations indeed **have** an appearance of wisdom, with their
3:13 and forgive whatever grievances *you may* **have** against one
4: 1 because you know that you also **have** a Master in heaven.
4:13 I vouch for him that *he* **is** working hard for you and for those at

1Th 1: 8 Therefore we *do* not **need** [+5970] to say anything about it,
1: 9 they themselves report what kind of reception you **gave** [+4639]
3: 6 He has told us that *you* always **have** pleasant memories of us
4: 9 Now about brotherly love *we do* not **need** [+5970] to write to you,
4:12 and so that *you will* not *be* **dependent on** [+5970] anybody.
4:13 fall asleep, or to grieve like the rest of men, who **have** no hope.
5: 1 about times and dates *we do* not **need** [+5970] to write to you,
5: 3 as labor pains *on* a **pregnant woman** [+1143+1877], and they will

2Th 3: 9 We did this, not because *we do* not **have** the right to such help,

1Ti 1:12 *I* **thank** [+5921] Christ Jesus our Lord, who has given me strength,
1:19 **holding on to** faith and a good conscience. Some have rejected
3: 4 and see that his children **obey** [+5717] him with proper respect.
3: 7 He must also **have** a good reputation with outsiders, so that he will
3: 9 They *must* **keep hold of** the deep truths of the faith with a clear

4: 8 **holding** promise for both the present life and the life to come.
5: 4 But if a widow **has** children or grandchildren, these should learn
5:12 Thus they **bring** judgment on themselves, because they have
5:16 If any woman who is a believer **has** widows *in* her *family*,
5:20 are to be rebuked publicly, so that the others *may* **take** warning.
5:25 deeds are obvious, and even those that **are** not cannot be hidden.
6: 2 Those *who* **have** believing masters are not to show less respect for
6: 8 But *if we* **have** food and clothing, we will be content with that.
6:16 who alone **is** immortal and who lives in unapproachable light,

2Ti 1: 3 *I* **thank** [+5921] God, whom I serve, as my forefathers did,
1: 3 and day *I* constantly **remember** [+3644] you in my prayers.
1:13 **keep** as the pattern of sound teaching, with faith and love in Christ
2:17 Their teaching *will* **spread** [+3786] like gangrene. Among them
2:19 God's solid foundation stands firm, **sealed with** [+3836+5382] this
3: 5 **having** a form of godliness but denying its power. Have nothing to

Tit 1: 6 a *man whose*[s] children believe and are not open to the charge of
2: 8 may be ashamed *because they* **have** nothing bad to say about us.

Phm 1: 5 because I hear about your faith **[NIE]** in the Lord Jesus and your
1: 7 Your love *has* **given** me great joy and encouragement,
1: 8 *although* in Christ I *could be* **bold** [+4244+4498] and order you to
1:17 So if *you* **consider** me a partner, welcome him as you would

Heb 2:14 so that by his death he might destroy him *who* **holds** the power of
3: 3 just as the builder of a house **has** greater honor than the house
4:14 *since we* **have** a great high priest who has gone through the
4:15 For *we do* not **have** a high priest who is unable to sympathize with
5:12 *you* **need** [+5970] someone to teach you the elementary truths of
5:12 word all over again. *You* **need** [+1181+5970] milk, not solid food!
5:14 who by constant use *have* **trained** [+1214] themselves to
6: 9 of better things in your case—things *that* **accompany** salvation.
6:13 since *there* **was** no one greater for him to swear by, he swore by
6:18 of the hope offered to us *may be* greatly **encouraged** [+4155].
6:19 *We* **have** this hope as an anchor for the soul, firm and secure.
7: 3 without beginning of days or **end** [+5465] of life,
7: 5 who become priests *to* **collect a tenth from** [+620] the people—
7: 6 a tenth from Abraham and blessed him *who* **had** the promises.
7:24 because Jesus lives forever, *he* **has** a permanent priesthood.
7:27 he *does* not **need** [+340] to offer sacrifices day after day, first for
7:28 For the law appoints as high priests men *who* **are** weak; but the
8: 1 *We do* **have** such a high priest, who sat down at the right hand of
8: 3 so it was necessary for this one also *to* **have** something to offer.
9: 1 Now the first covenant **had** regulations for worship and also an
9: 4 *which* **had** the golden altar of incense and the gold-covered ark of
9: 4 This ark **contained** [+1877] the gold jar of manna, Aaron's staff
9: 8 yet been disclosed as long as the first tabernacle **was** still standing.
10: 1 The law **is** only a shadow of the good things that are coming—
10: 2 once for all, and *would* no longer **have** **felt** guilty for their sins.
10:19 *since we* **have** confidence to enter the Most Holy Place by the
10:34 because you knew that you yourselves **had** better and lasting
10:35 So do not throw away your confidence; it *will* **be** richly rewarded.
10:36 *You* **need** [+5970] to persevere so that when you have done the
11:10 For he was looking forward to the city **with** foundations,
11:15 country they had left, *they* would have **had** opportunity to return.
11:25 of God rather than *to* **enjoy** the pleasures of sin for a short time.
12: 1 *since* we **are** surrounded by such a great cloud of witnesses,
12: 9 *we have all* **had** human fathers who disciplined us and we
12:28 a kingdom that cannot be shaken, *let us be* **thankful** [+5921],
13:10 *We* **have** an altar from which those who minister at the tabernacle
13:10 which those who minister at the tabernacle **have** no right to eat.
13:14 For here *we do* not **have** an enduring city, but we are looking for
13:18 We are sure that *we* **have** a clear conscience and desire to live

Jas 1: 4 Perseverance *must* **finish** [+5455] its work so that you may be
2: 1 as **believers** [+3836+4411] in our glorious Lord Jesus Christ,
2:14 my brothers, if a man claims *to* **have** faith but has no deeds?
2:14 my brothers, if a man claims to have faith but **has** no deeds?
2:17 faith by itself, if *it* is not **accompanied by** action, is dead.
2:18 But someone will say, "You **have** faith; I have deeds."
2:18 But someone will say, "You have faith; I **have** deeds." Show me
3:14 But if *you* **harbor** bitter envy and selfish ambition in your hearts,
4: 2 You want something but don't **get** it. You kill and covet, but you
4: 2 and fight. *You do* not **have**, because you do not ask God.

1Pe 2:12 **Live** such good lives among the pagans that, though they accuse
2:16 as free men, but *do* not **use** your freedom as a cover-up for evil;
3:16 **keeping** a clear conscience, so that those who speak maliciously
4: 5 But they will have to give account to him *who* **is** ready to judge the
4: 8 Above all, **love** [+27] each other deeply, because love covers over

2Pe 1:15 my departure you *will* always *be* **able** to remember these things.

1:19 And *we* **have** the word of the prophets made more certain,
2:14 **With** eyes full of adultery, they never stop sinning; they seduce the
2:14 seduce the unstable; *they* **are** experts in greed—an accursed brood!
2:16 But he **was** rebuked for his wrongdoing by a donkey—a beast

1Jn 1: 3 and heard, so that you also *may* **have** fellowship with us.
1: 6 If we claim *to* **have** fellowship with him yet walk in the darkness,
1: 7 as he is in the light, *we* **have** fellowship with one another,
1: 8 If we claim *to* **be** without sin, we deceive ourselves and the truth is
2: 1 does sin, *we* **have** one who speaks to the Father in our defense—
2: 7 but an old one, which *you have* **had** since the beginning.
2:20 But you **have** an anointing from the Holy One, and all of you know
2:23 No one who denies the Son **has** the Father; whoever acknowledges
2:23 has the Father; whoever acknowledges the Son **has** the Father also.
2:27 remains in you, and *you do* not **need** [+*5970*] anyone to teach you.
2:28 so that when he appears *we may be* **confident** [+*4244*]
3: 3 Everyone who **has** this hope in him purifies himself, just as he is
3:15 a murderer, and you know that no murderer **has** eternal life in him.
3:17 If anyone **has** material possessions and sees his brother in need
3:17 and sees his brother *in* **need** [+*5970*] but has no pity on him,
3:21 if our hearts do not condemn us, *we* **have** confidence before God
4:16 And so we know and rely on the love God **has** for us. God is love.
4:17 among us so that *we will* **have** confidence on the day of judgment,
4:18 love drives out fear, because fear **has to do with** punishment.
4:21 And he *has* **given** [+*608*] *us* this command: Whoever loves God
5:10 Anyone who believes in the Son of God **has** this testimony in his
5:12 He *who* **has** the Son has life; he who does not have the Son of God
5:12 He who has the Son **has** life; he who does not have the Son of God
5:12 has life; he *who* **does** not have the Son of God does not have
5:12 has life; he who does not have the Son of God *does* not **have** life.
5:13 of the Son of God so that you may know that *you* **have** eternal life.
5:14 This is the confidence *we* **have** in approaching God: that if we ask
5:15 whatever we ask—we know that *we* **have** what we asked of him.

2Jn 1: 5 you a new command but one *we have* **had** from the beginning.
1: 9 and does not continue in the teaching of Christ *does* not **have** God;
1: 9 whoever continues in the teaching **has** both the Father and the Son.
1:12 I **have** much to write to you, but I do not want to use paper

3Jn 1: 4 *I* **have** no greater joy than to hear that my children are walking in
1:13 I **have** much to write you, but I do not want to do so with pen

Jude 1: 3 *I* **felt** I had to write and urge you to contend for the faith that was
1:19 who follow mere natural instincts and *do* not **have** the Spirit.

Rev 1:16 In his right hand *he* **held** seven stars, and out of his mouth came a
1:18 alive for ever and ever! And *I* **hold** the keys of death and Hades.
2: 3 *You have* **persevered** [+*5705*] and have endured hardships for my
2: 4 Yet *I* **hold** this against you: You have forsaken your first love.
2: 6 But *you* **have** this *in your favor*. You hate the practices of the
2: 7 He *who* **has** an ear, let him hear what the Spirit says to the
2:10 to test you, and *you will* **suffer persecution** [+*2568*] for ten days.
2:11 He *who* **has** an ear, let him hear what the Spirit says to the
2:12 These are the words of him *who* **has** the sharp, double-edged
2:14 Nevertheless, *I* **have** a few things against you: You have people
2:14 You **have** people there who hold to the teaching of Balaam,
2:15 Likewise you also **have** those who hold to the teaching of the
2:17 He *who* **has** an ear, let him hear what the Spirit says to the
2:18 **whose** [+*899*] eyes are like blazing fire and whose feet are like
2:20 Nevertheless, *I* **have** this against you: You tolerate that woman
2:24 to you who *do* not **hold** to her teaching and have not learned
2:25 Only hold on to what *you* **have** until I come.
2:29 He *who* **has** an ear, let him hear what the Spirit says to the
3: 1 These are the words of him *who* **holds** the seven spirits of God
3: 1 your deeds; *you* **have** a reputation of being alive, but you are dead.
3: 4 Yet *you* **have** a few people in Sardis who have not soiled their
3: 6 He *who* **has** an ear, let him hear what the Spirit says to the
3: 7 words of him who is holy and true, who **holds** the key of David.
3: 8 I know that *you* **have** little strength, yet you have kept my word
3:11 Hold on to what *you* **have**, so that no one will take your crown.
3:13 He *who* **has** an ear, let him hear what the Spirit says to the
3:17 am rich; I **have** acquired wealth and *do* not **need** [+*5970*] a thing.'
3:22 He *who* **has** an ear, let him hear what the Spirit says to the
4: 7 the second was like an ox, the third **had** a face like a man,
4: 8 Each of the four living creatures **had** six wings and was covered
4: 8 Day and night *they* never **stop** [+*398*] saying: "Holy, holy,
5: 6 *He* **had** seven horns and seven eyes, which are the seven spirits of
5: 8 Each one **had** a harp and they were holding golden bowls full of
6: 2 Its rider **held** a bow, and he was given a crown, and he rode out as
6: 5 a black horse! Its rider *was* **holding** a pair of scales in his hand.
6: 9 of the word of God and the testimony *they had* **maintained**.

7: 2 angel coming up from the east, **having** the seal of the living God.
8: 3 *who* **had** a golden censer, came and stood at the altar.
8: 6 Then the seven angels who **had** the seven trumpets prepared to
8: 9 a third of the **living** [+*3836+6034*] creatures in the sea died,
9: 3 and were given power like that of scorpions of the earth. **[NIE]**
9: 4 but only those people who *did* not **have** the seal of God on their
9: 8 Their hair **was** like women's hair, and their teeth were like lions'
9: 9 *They* **had** breastplates like breastplates of iron, and the sound of
9:10 *They* **had** tails and stings like scorpions, and in their tails they had
9:11 *They* **had** as king over them the angel of the Abyss, whose name
9:11 name in Hebrew is Abaddon, and in Greek, **[RPG]** Apollyon.
9:14 It said to the sixth angel who **had** the trumpet, "Release the four
9:17 Their breastplates **were** fiery red, dark blue, and yellow as sulfur.
9:19 tails were like snakes, **having** heads with which they inflict injury.
10: 2 *He was* **holding** a little scroll, which lay open in his hand.
11: 6 These men **have** power to shut up the sky so that it will not rain
11: 6 and *they* **have** power to turn the waters into blood and to strike the
12: 2 *She was* **pregnant** [+*1143+1877*] and cried out in pain as she was
12: 3 an enormous red dragon **with** seven heads and ten horns and seven
12: 6 The woman fled into the desert to **[NIE]** a place prepared for her
12:12 *He is* **filled with** fury, because he knows that his time is short."
12:12 He is filled with fury, because he knows that *his* time **is** short."
12:17 obey God's commandments and **hold to** the testimony of Jesus.
13: 1 *He* **had** ten horns and seven heads, with ten crowns on his horns,
13: 9 He *who* **has** an ear, let him hear.
13:11 *He* **had** two horns like a lamb, but he spoke like a dragon.
13:14 honor of the beast who *was* **wounded** [+*3836+4435*] by the sword
13:17 so that no one could buy or sell unless he **had** the mark, which is
13:18 *If* anyone **has** insight, let him calculate the number of the beast,
14: 1 and with him 144,000 who **had** his name and his Father's name
14: 6 and *he* **had** the eternal gospel to proclaim to those who live on the
14:11 *There* is no rest day or night for those who worship the beast
14:14 and seated on the cloud was one "like a son of man" **with** a crown
14:17 came out of the temple in heaven, and he too **had** a sharp sickle.
14:18 Still another angel, who **had** charge of the fire, came from the altar
14:18 and called in a loud voice *to* him *who* **had** the sharp sickle,
15: 1 seven angels **with** the seven last plagues—last, because with them
15: 2 over the number of his name. *They* **held** harps given them by God
15: 6 Out of the temple came the seven angels **with** the seven plagues.
16: 2 and painful sores broke out on the people who **had** the mark of the
16: 9 who **had** control over these plagues, but they refused to repent
17: 1 One of the seven angels who **had** the seven bowls came and said to
17: 3 with blasphemous names and **had** seven heads and ten horns.
17: 4 *She* **held** a golden cup in her hand, filled with abominable things
17: 7 of the beast she rides, which **has** the seven heads and ten horns.
17: 9 "This calls for a mind **with** wisdom. The seven heads are seven
17:13 They **have** one purpose and will give their power and authority to
17:18 The woman you saw is the great city that **rules** [+*993*] over the
18: 1 *He* **had** great authority, and the earth was illuminated by his
18:19 where all who **had** ships on the sea became rich through her
19:10 and with your brothers who **hold to** the testimony of Jesus.
19:12 *He* **has** a name written on him that no one knows but he himself.
19:16 On his robe and on his thigh *he* **has** this name written: KING OF
20: 1 **having** the key to the Abyss and holding in his hand a great chain.
20: 6 and holy are those *who* **have** part in the first resurrection.
20: 6 The second death **has** no power over them, but they will be priests
21: 9 One of the seven angels who **had** the seven bowls full of the seven
21:11 *It* **shone with** the glory of God, and its brilliance was like that of a
21:12 *It* **had** a great, high wall with twelve gates, and with twelve angels
21:12 It had a great, high wall **with** twelve gates, and with twelve angels
21:14 The wall of the city **had** twelve foundations, and on them were the
21:15 The angel who talked with me **had** a measuring rod of gold to
21:23 The city *does* not **need** [+*5970*] the sun or the moon to shine on it,
22: 5 *They will* not **need** [+*5970*] the light of a lamp or the light of the

2401 ἕως, *heōs* [146]

to [31], until [29], until [+*323*] [14], until [+*4005*] [13], how long
[+*4536*] [7], *untranslated* [6], before [+*323*] [4], still [+*785*] [3], till
[3], until [+*4015*] [3], up to [3], while [3], even [2], for [2], till
[+*323*] [2], to the point [2], while [+*4005*] [2], all the way [1], and
[+*4015*] [1], and [1], as far as [1], as long as [1], before [+*4005*]
[1], before [1], fully [+*5465*] [1], going on to [1], no more [+*1572*]
[1], right into [+*1650+2276*] [1], right on down to [1], right up to

[1], to where [1], until [+2465] [1], when [+4005] [1], while still [+4015] [1]

Mt 1:17 Thus there were fourteen generations in all from Abraham **to**
1:17 fourteen from David **to** the exile to Babylon, and fourteen from the
1:17 to the exile to Babylon, and fourteen from the exile **to** the Christ.
1:25 But he had no union with her **until** [+4005] she gave birth to a son.
2: 9 and the star they had seen in the east went ahead of them **until** it
2:13 Stay there **until** [+323] I tell you, for Herod is going to search for
2:15 where he stayed **until** the death of Herod. And so was fulfilled
5:18 I tell you the truth, **until** [+323] heaven and earth disappear,
5:18 will by any means disappear from the Law **until** [+323] everything
5:25 Do it **while** [+4015] you are **still** with him on the way, or he may
5:26 you will not get out **until** [+323] you have paid the last penny.
10:11 worthy person there and stay at his house **until** [+323] you leave.
10:23 you will not finish going through the cities of Israel **before** [+323]
11:12 From the days of John the Baptist **until** now, the kingdom of
11:13 For all the Prophets and the Law prophesied **until** John.
11:23 And you, Capernaum, will you be lifted up **to** the skies? No,
11:23 you be lifted up to the skies? No, you will go down **to** the depths.
12:20 wick he will not snuff out, **till** [+323] he leads justice to victory.
13:30 Let both grow together **until** the harvest. At that time I will tell the
13:33 and mixed into a large amount of flour **until** [+4005] it worked all
14:22 of him to the other side, **while** [+4005] he dismissed the crowd.
16:28 some who are standing here will not taste death **before** [+323] they
17: 9 **until** [+4005] the Son of Man has been raised from the dead."
17:17 Jesus replied, "**how long** [+4536] shall I stay with you?
17:17 "how long shall I stay with you? **How long** [+4536] shall I put up
18:21 I forgive my brother when he sins against me? **Up to** seven times?"
18:22 Jesus answered, "I tell you, not [RPG] seven times,
18:22 "I tell you, not seven times, but [RPG] seventy-seven times.
18:30 and had the man thrown into prison **until** he could pay the debt.
18:34 to be tortured, **until** [+4005] he should pay back all he owed.
20: 8 beginning with the last ones hired and **going on to** the first.'
22:26 to the second and third brother, **right on down to** the seventh.
22:44 "Sit at my right hand **until** [+323] I put your enemies under your
23:35 from the blood of righteous Abel **to** the blood of Zechariah son of
23:39 For I tell you, you will not see me again **until** [+323] you say,
24:21 unequaled from the beginning of the world **until** now—
24:27 For as lightning that comes from the east is visible **even** in the
24:31 from the four winds, from one end of the heavens **to** the other.
24:34 this generation will certainly not pass away **until** [+323] all these
24:39 and they knew nothing about what would happen **until** the flood
26:29 I will not drink of this fruit of the vine from now on **until** that day
26:36 he said to them, "Sit here **while** [+4005] I go over there and pray."
26:38 "My soul is overwhelmed with sorrow **to the point** of death.
26:58 him at a distance, **right up to** the courtyard of the high priest.
27: 8 That is why it has been called the Field of Blood **to** this day.
27:45 From the sixth hour **until** the ninth hour darkness came over all the
27:51 the curtain of the temple was torn in two from top **to** bottom.
27:64 So give the order for the tomb to be made secure **until** the third
28:20 And surely I am with you always, **to** the very end of the age."
Mk 6:10 you enter a house, stay there **until** [+323] you leave that town.
6:23 "Whatever you ask I will give you, **up to** half my kingdom."
6:45 go on ahead of him to Bethsaida, **while** he dismissed the crowd.
9: 1 some who are standing here will not taste death **before** [+323] they
9:19 Jesus replied, "**how long** [+4536] shall I stay with you?
9:19 **How long** [+4536] shall I put up with you? Bring the boy to me."
12:36 "Sit at my right hand **until** [+323] I put your enemies under your
13:19 from the beginning, when God created the world, **until** now—
13:27 four winds, from the ends of the earth **to** the ends of the heavens.
14:25 I will not drink again of the fruit of the vine **until** that day when I
14:32 and Jesus said to his disciples, "Sit here **while** I pray."
14:34 "My soul is overwhelmed with sorrow **to the point** of death,"
14:54 Peter followed him at a distance, **right into** [+1650+2276] the
15:33 At the sixth hour darkness came over the whole land **until** the
15:38 The curtain of the temple was torn in two from top **to** bottom.
Lk 1:80 and he lived in the desert **until** [+2465] he appeared publicly to
2:15 "Let's go **to** Bethlehem and see this thing that has happened,
2:37 and then was a widow **until** she was eighty-four. She never left the
4:29 and took him **to** the brow of the hill on which the town was built,
4:42 people were looking for him and when they came **to where** he was,
9:27 some who are standing here will not taste death **before** [+323] they
9:41 Jesus replied, "**how long** [+4536] shall I stay with you and put up
10:15 And you, Capernaum, will you be lifted up **to** the skies? No,
10:15 you be lifted up to the skies? No, you will go down **to** the depths.

11:51 from the blood of Abel **to** the blood of Zechariah, who was killed
12:50 to undergo, and how distressed I am **until** [+4015] it is completed!
12:59 I tell you, you will not get out **until** you have paid the last penny."
13: 8 for one more year, **and** [+4015] I'll dig around it and fertilize it.
13:21 and mixed into a large amount of flour **until** [+4005] it worked all
13:35 I tell you, you will not see me again **until** you say, 'Blessed is he
15: 4 in the open country and go after the lost sheep **until** he finds it?
15: 8 sweep the house and search carefully **until** [+4005] she finds it?
17: 8 get yourself ready and wait on me **while** I eat and drink;
20:43 **until** [+323] I make your enemies a footstool for your feet." '
21:32 this generation will certainly not pass away **until** [+323] all these
22:16 I will not eat it again **until** [+4015] it finds fulfillment in the
22:18 of the fruit of the vine **until** [+4005] the kingdom of God comes."
22:34 Jesus answered, "I tell you, Peter, **before** the rooster crows today,
22:51 But Jesus answered, "**No more** [+1572] of this!" And he touched
23: 5 his teaching. He started in Galilee and has come **all the way** here."
23:44 and darkness came over the whole land **until** the ninth hour,
24:49 but stay in the city **until** [+4005] you have been clothed with
24:50 When he had led them out **to** the vicinity of Bethany, he lifted up
Jn 2: 7 "Fill the jars with water"; so they filled them **to** the brim.
2:10 have had too much to drink; but you have saved the best **till** now."
5:17 said to them, "My Father is always at his work **to** this very day,
9: 4 **As long as** it is day, we must do the work of him who sent me.
9:18 and had received his sight **until** [+4015] they sent for the man's
10:24 saying, "**How long** [+4536] will you keep us in suspense?
13:38 I tell you the truth, **before** [+4005] the rooster crows, you will
16:24 **Until** now you have not asked for anything in my name. Ask
21:22 Jesus answered, "If I want him to remain alive **until** I return,
21:23 he only said, "If I want him to remain alive **until** I return, what is
Ac 1: 8 and in all Judea and Samaria, and **to** the ends of the earth."
1:22 beginning from John's baptism **to** the time when Jesus was taken
2:35 **until** [+323] I make your enemies a footstool for your feet." '
7:45 out before them. It *remained* in the land **until** the time of David,
8:10 and all the people, both high **and** low, gave them their attention
8:40 preaching the gospel in all the towns **until** he reached Caesarea.
9:38 sent two men to him and urged him, "Please come [NIE] at once!"
11:19 in connection with Stephen traveled **as far as** Phoenicia,
11:22 ears of the church at Jerusalem, and they sent Barnabas **to** Antioch.
13:20 God gave them judges **until** the *time of* Samuel the prophet.
13:47 Gentiles, that you may bring salvation **to** the ends of the earth.' "
17:14 The brothers immediately sent Paul [NIE] to the coast, but Silas
17:15 The men who escorted Paul brought him **to** Athens and then left
21: 5 their wives and children accompanied us [NIE] out of the city,
21:26 he went to the temple to give notice of the *date* **when** [+4005]
23:12 with an oath not to eat or drink **until** [+4005] they had killed Paul.
23:14 "We have taken a solemn oath not to eat anything **until** [+4005] we
23:21 an oath not to eat or drink **until** [+4005] they have killed him.
23:23 and two hundred spearmen to go to Caesarea at nine tonight.
25:21 I ordered him held **until** [+4005] I could send him to Caesar."
26:11 I even went [NIE] to foreign cities to persecute them.
28:23 From morning **till** evening he explained and declared to them the
Ro 3:12 become worthless; there is no one who does good, not **even** one."
11: 8 could not see and ears so that they could not hear, **to** this very day."
1Co 1: 8 He will keep you strong **to** the end, so that you will be blameless
4: 5 nothing before the appointed time; wait **till** [+323] the Lord comes.
4:13 **Up to** this moment we have become the scum of the earth,
8: 7 Some people are still [+785] so accustomed to idols that when they
15: 6 most of whom are **still** [+785] living, though some have fallen
16: 8 But I will stay on at Ephesus **until** Pentecost,
2Co 1:14 you will come to understand **fully** [+5465] that you can boast of us
3:15 Even **to** this day when Moses is read, a veil covers their hearts.
12: 2 I know a man in Christ who fourteen years ago was caught up **to**
2Th 2: 7 but the one who now holds it back will *continue* to do so **till** he is
1Ti 4:13 **Until** I come, devote yourself to the public reading of Scripture,
Heb 1:13 "Sit at my right hand **until** [+323] I make your enemies a footstool
8:11 they will all know me, from the least of them **to** the greatest.
10:13 Since that time he waits **for** his enemies to be made his footstool,
Jas 5: 7 Be patient, then, brothers, **until** the Lord's coming. See how the
5: 7 and how patient he is **for** the autumn and spring rains.
2Pe 1:19 **until** [+4005] the day dawns and the morning star rises in your
1Jn 2: 9 be in the light but hates his brother is **still** [+785] in the darkness.
Rev 6:10 They called out in a loud voice, "**How long** [+4536], Sovereign
6:11 **until** the number of their fellow servants and brothers who were to

2402 ς, [*stigma*] Not used in UBS/NIV

Z, ζ

2403 ζ, z Not used in UBS/NIV

2404 Ζαβουλών, *Zaboulōn* [3]

Zebulun [3]

Mt 4:13 which was by the lake in the area *of* **Zebulun** and Naphtali—
      4:15 "Land *of* **Zebulun** and land of Naphtali, the way to the sea,
Rev 7:8 from the tribe *of* **Zebulun** 12,000, from the tribe of Joseph 12,000,

2405 Ζακχαῖος, *Zakchaios* [3]

Zacchaeus [3]

Lk 19:2 A man was there by the name *of* **Zacchaeus**; he was a chief tax
     19:5 he looked up and said to him, "**Zacchaeus**, come down
     19:8 But **Zacchaeus** stood up and said to the Lord, "Look, Lord!

2406 Ζάρα, *Zara* [1]

Zerah [1]

Mt 1:3 Judah the father of Perez and **Zerah**, whose mother was Tamar,

2407 ζαφθάνι, *zaphthani* Not used in UBS/NIV
[√ *cf. 4876*]

2408 Ζαχαρίας, *Zacharias* [11]

Zechariah [10], Zechariah's [1]

Mt 23:35 from the blood of righteous Abel to the blood *of* **Zechariah** son of
Lk   1:5 time of Herod king of Judea there was a priest named **Zechariah**,
     1:12 When **Zechariah** saw him, he was startled and was gripped with
     1:13 "Do not be afraid, **Zechariah**; your prayer has been heard
     1:18 **Zechariah** asked the angel, "How can I be sure of this? I am an old
     1:21 the people were waiting for **Zechariah** and wondering why he
     1:40 where she entered **Zechariah's** home and greeted Elizabeth.
     1:59 and they were going to name him after his father **Zechariah**,
     1:67 His father **Zechariah** was filled with the Holy Spirit
     3:2 the word of God came to John son *of* **Zechariah** in the desert.
   11:51 from the blood of Abel to the blood *of* **Zechariah**, who was killed

2409 ζάω, *zaō* [140 / 139] [→ *348, 351, 2436, 2437, 2441, 2442, 2443, 5182, 5188*]

ζῶν θεός (Living God) [15] Mt 16:16; 26:63; Ac 14:15; Ro 9:26; 2Co 3:3; 6:16; 1Th 1:9; 1Ti 3:15; 4:10; Heb 3:12; 9:14; 10:31; 12:22; Rev 7:2; 15:7

ζῶν ὕδωρ (living water) [3] Jn 4:10,11; 7:38

live [50], living [42], alive [18], lives [15], lived [4], came to life [2], as surely as I live [*+1609*] [1], belonged [1], brought to life [1], come to life [1], life [1], live on [1], receive living [1], returned to life [1]

Mt 4:4 'Man *does* not **live** on bread alone, but on every word that comes
     9:18 just died. But come and put your hand on her, and *she will* **live**."
   16:16 Peter answered, "You are the Christ, the Son *of* the **living** God."
   22:32 the God of Jacob'? He is not the God of the dead but *of* the **living**."
   26:63 high priest said to him, "I charge you under oath by the **living** God
   27:63 "we remember that while *he was* still **alive** that deceiver said,
Mk 5:23 and put your hands on her so that she will be healed and **live**."
  12:27 He is not the God of the dead, but *of* the **living**. You are badly
  16:11 When they heard that Jesus *was* **alive** and that she had seen him,
Lk 2:36 she had **lived** with her husband seven years after her marriage,
   4:4 Jesus answered, "It is written: 'Man *does* not **live** on bread alone.' "
 10:28 have answered correctly," Jesus replied. "Do this and *you will* **live**."
 15:13 a distant country and there squandered his wealth *in* wild **living**.
 15:32 this brother of yours was dead and *is* **alive** [UBS; NIV *348*] **again**;
 20:38 not the God of the dead, but *of* the **living**, for to him all are alive."
 20:38 not the God of the dead, but of the living, for to him all *are* **alive**."

   24:5 said to them, "Why do you look for the **living** among the dead?
  24:23 us that they had seen a vision of angels, who said he *was* **alive**.
Jn 4:10 would have asked him and he would have given you **living** water."
   4:11 and the well is deep. Where can you get this **living** water?
   4:50 Jesus replied, "You may go. Your son *will* **live**." The man took
   4:51 his servants met him with the news that his boy *was* **living**.
   4:53 the exact time at which Jesus had said to him, "Your son *will* **live**."
   5:25 will hear the voice of the Son of God and those who hear *will* **live**.
   6:51 I am the **living** bread that came down from heaven. If anyone eats
   6:51 If anyone eats of this bread, *he will* **live** forever. This bread is my
   6:57 Just as the **living** Father sent me and I live because of the Father,
   6:57 Just as the living Father sent me and I **live** because of the Father,
   6:57 of the Father, so the one who feeds on me *will* **live** because of me.
   6:58 and died, but he who feeds on this bread *will* **live** forever."
   7:38 has said, streams *of* **living** water will flow from within him."
 11:25 and the life. He who believes in me *will* **live**, even though he dies;
 11:26 and whoever **lives** and believes in me will never die. Do you
 14:19 but you will see me. Because I **live**, you also will live.
 14:19 but you will see me. Because I live, you also *will* **live**.
Ac 1:3 to these men and gave many convincing proofs that *he was* **alive**.
   7:38 and with our fathers; and he received **living** words to pass on to us.
   9:41 the believers and the widows and presented her to them **alive**.
 10:42 that he is the one whom God appointed as judge *of* the **living**
 14:15 telling you to turn from these worthless things to the **living** God,
 17:28 'For in him we **live** and move and have our being.' As some of
 20:12 The people took the young man home **alive** and were greatly
 22:22 voices and shouted, "Rid the earth of him! He's not fit *to* **live**!"
 25:19 and about a dead man named Jesus who Paul claimed *was* **alive**.
 25:24 and here in Caesarea, shouting that he ought not *to* **live** any longer.
 26:5 according to the strictest sect of our religion, *I* **lived** as a Pharisee.
 28:4 he escaped from the sea, Justice has not allowed him *to* **live**."
Ro 1:17 first to last, just as it is written: "The righteous *will* **live** by faith."
   6:2 By no means! We died to sin; how *can we* **live** in it any longer?
   6:10 he died to sin once for all; but the life *he* **lives**, he lives to God.
   6:10 he died to sin once for all; but the life he lives, *he* **lives** to God.
   6:11 count yourselves dead to sin but **alive** to God in Christ Jesus.
   6:13 to God, as *those who have been* **brought** from death to life;
   7:1 that the law has authority over a man only as long as *he* **lives**?
   7:2 a married woman is bound to her husband *as long as he is* **alive**,
   7:3 if she marries another man *while* her husband *is still* **alive**,
   7:9 Once I *was* **alive** apart from law; but when the commandment
   8:12 but it is not to the sinful nature, *to* **live** according to it.
   8:13 For if *you* **live** according to the sinful nature, you will die;
   8:13 the Spirit you put to death the misdeeds of the body, *you will* **live**,
   9:26 are not my people,' they will be called 'sons of the **living** God.' "
 10:5 is by the law: "The man who does these things *will* **live** by them."
 12:1 to offer your bodies as **living** sacrifices, holy and pleasing to God—
 14:7 For none of us **lives** to himself alone and none of us dies to himself
 14:8 If *we* **live**, we live to the Lord; and if we die, we die to the Lord.
 14:8 If we live, *we* **live** to the Lord; and if we die, we die to the Lord.
 14:8 die to the Lord. So, whether *we* **live** or die, we belong to the Lord.
 14:9 Christ died and **returned to life** so that he might be the Lord of
 14:9 so that he might be the Lord *of* both the dead and the **living**.
 14:11 " 'As surely [*+1609*] as I live,' says the Lord, 'every knee will
1Co 7:39 A woman is bound to her husband as long as *he* **lives**. But if her
   9:14 who preach the gospel *should* **receive** *their* **living** from the gospel.
 15:45 "The first man Adam became a **living** being"; the last Adam,
2Co 1:8 far beyond our ability to endure, so that we despaired even *of* **life**.
   3:3 written not with ink but with the Spirit of the **living** God, not on
   4:11 For we who *are* **alive** are always being given over to death for
   5:15 that those *who* **live** should no longer live for themselves but for
   5:15 that those who live *should* no longer **live** for themselves but for
   6:9 as unknown; dying, and yet *we* **live on**; beaten, and yet not killed;
   6:16 temple of God and idols? For we are the temple of the **living** God.
 13:4 he was crucified in weakness, yet *he* **lives** by God's power.
 13:4 in him, yet by God's power *we will* **live** with him to serve you.
Gal 2:14 "You are a Jew, yet *you* **live** like a Gentile and not like a Jew.
   2:19 For through the law I died to the law so that *I might* **live** for God.
   2:20 I have been crucified with Christ and I no longer **live**, but Christ
   2:20 crucified with Christ and I no longer live, but Christ **lives** in me.
   2:20 The life *I* **live** in the body, I live by faith in the Son of God,
   2:20 *I* **live** by faith in the Son of God, who loved me and gave himself
   3:11 before God by the law, because, "The righteous *will* **live** by faith."
   3:12 on the contrary, "The man who does these things *will* **live** by them."
   5:25 Since *we* **live** by the Spirit, let us keep in step with the Spirit.
Php 1:21 For to me, *to* **live** is Christ and to die is gain.

Col 1:22 If I am *to go on* living in the body, this will mean fruitful labor for
Col 2:20 why, as though *you still* belonged to it, do you submit to its rules:
     3: 7 You used to walk in these ways, in the life *you* once lived.
1Th 1: 9 They tell how you turned to God from idols to serve the living
     3: 8 For now *we really* live, since you are standing firm in the Lord.
     4:15 to the Lord's own word, we tell you that we who *are still* alive,
     4:17 we who *are still* alive and are left will be caught up together with
     5:10 whether we are awake or asleep, *we may* live together with him.
1Ti 3:15 which is the church *of* the living God, the pillar and foundation of
     4:10 we labor and strive), that we have put our hope in the living God,
     5: 6 But the widow who lives for pleasure is dead *even while she* lives.
2Ti 3:12 everyone who wants *to* live a godly life in Christ Jesus will be
     4: 1 and of Christ Jesus, who will judge the living and the dead,
Tit 2:12 and *to* live self-controlled, upright and godly lives in this present
Heb 2:15 and free those who all their lives were held in slavery by their fear
     3:12 has a sinful, unbelieving heart that turns away from the living God.
     4:12 For the word of God *is* living and active. Sharper than any
     7: 8 but in the other case, by him who is declared to be living.
     7:25 to God through him, *because he* always lives to intercede for them.
     9:14 from acts that lead to death, so that we may serve the living God!
     9:17 has died; it never takes effect while the one who made it *is* living.
  10:20 *by* a new and living way opened for us through the curtain,
  10:31 It is a dreadful thing to fall into the hands *of* the living God.
  10:38 But my righteous one *will* live by faith. And if he shrinks back,
  12: 9 much more should *we* submit to the Father of our spirits and live!
  12:22 Mount Zion, to the heavenly Jerusalem, the city *of* the living God.
Jas 4:15 to say, "If it is the Lord's will, *we will* live and do this or that."
1Pe 1: 3 In his great mercy he has given us new birth into a living hope
     1:23 but of imperishable, through the living and enduring word of God.
     2: 4 As you come to him, the living Stone—rejected by men but chosen
     2: 5 you also, like living stones, are being built into a spiritual house to
     2:24 on the tree, so that *we might* die to sins and live for righteousness;
     4: 5 will have to give account to him who is ready to judge the living
     4: 6 regard to the body, but live according to God in regard to the spirit.
1Jn 4: 9 and only Son into the world that *we might* live through him.
Rev 1:18 I am the Living *One*; I was dead, and behold I am alive for ever
     1:18 Living One; I was dead, and behold I am alive for ever and ever!
     2: 8 him who is the First and the Last, who died and came to life *again*.
     3: 1 your deeds; you have a reputation of *being* alive, but you are dead.
     4: 9 and thanks *to* him who sits on the throne and who lives for ever
     4:10 sits on the throne, and worship him *who* lives for ever and ever.
     7: 2 angel coming up from the east, having the seal *of* the living God.
  10: 6 And he swore by him *who* lives for ever and ever, who created the
  13:14 honor of the beast who was wounded by the sword and yet lived.
  15: 7 bowls filled with the wrath of God, who lives for ever and ever.
  19:20 The two of them were thrown alive into the fiery lake of burning
  20: 4 *They* came to life and reigned with Christ a thousand years.
  20: 5 (The rest of the dead *did* not come to life until the thousand years

2410 ζβέννυμι, zbennymi   Not used in UBS/NIV
[√ 4931]

2411 Ζεβεδαῖος, Zebedaios [12]

Zebedee [10], Zebedee's [2]

Mt 4:21 two other brothers, James son *of* Zebedee and his brother John.
     4:21 They were in a boat with their father Zebedee, preparing their nets.
  10: 2 his brother Andrew; James son *of* Zebedee, and his brother John;
  20:20 Then the mother *of* Zebedee's sons came to Jesus with her sons
  26:37 He took Peter and the two sons *of* Zebedee along with him,
  27:56 the mother of James and Joses, and the mother *of* Zebedee's sons.
Mk 1:19 he saw James son *of* Zebedee and his brother John in a boat,
     1:20 and they left their father Zebedee in the boat with the hired men
     3:17 James son *of* Zebedee and his brother John (to them he gave the
  10:35 Then James and John, the sons *of* Zebedee, came to him.
Lk 5:10 and so were James and John, the sons *of* Zebedee, Simon's
Jn 21: 2 Nathanael from Cana in Galilee, the sons *of* Zebedee,

2412 ζεστός, zestos [3] [√ 2417]

hot [2], the other^s [1]

Rev 3:15 I know your deeds, that you are neither cold nor hot. I wish you
     3:15 are neither cold nor hot. I wish you were either one or the other^s!
     3:16 So, because you are lukewarm—neither hot nor cold—I am about

2413 ζεύγνυμι, zeugnymi   Not used in UBS/NIV
[→ 2282, 2414, 2415, 2433, 5183, 5187, 5689]

2414 ζεῦγος, zeugos [2] [√ 2413]

pair [1], yoke [1]

Lk 2:24 in the Law of the Lord: "a pair of doves or two young pigeons."
  14:19 "Another said, 'I have just bought five yoke of oxen, and I'm on my

2415 ζευκτηρία, zeuktēria [1] [√ 2413]

ropes [1]

Ac 27:40 and at the same time untied the ropes that held the rudders.

2416 Ζεύς, Zeus [2] [→ 1479, 1483, 1485, 2304, 2424, 2425]

Zeus [2]

Ac 14:12 Barnabas they called Zeus, and Paul they called Hermes
  14:13 The priest *of* Zeus, whose temple was just outside the city,

2417 ζέω, zeō [2] [→ 2412; cf. 2419, 2434]

fervor [1], with great fervor [+3836+4460] [1]

Ac 18:25 and he spoke with great fervor [+3836+4460] and taught about
Ro 12:11 be lacking in zeal, but *keep* your spiritual fervor, serving the Lord.

2418 ζηλεύω, zēleuō [1] [√ 2419]

earnest [1]

Rev 3:19 whom I love I rebuke and discipline. So *be* earnest, and repent.

2419 ζῆλος, zēlos [16] [→ 2418, 2420, 2421, 4143; cf. 2417]

jealousy [7], envy [2], zeal [2], ardent concern [1], concern [1], enthusiasm [1], raging [1], zealous [1]

Jn 2:17 that it is written: "Zeal for your house will consume me."
Ac 5:17 members of the party of the Sadducees, were filled *with* jealousy.
  13:45 they were filled *with* jealousy and talked abusively against what
Ro 10: 2 For I can testify about them that they are zealous for God,
  13:13 sexual immorality and debauchery, not in dissension and jealousy.
1Co 3: 3 For since there is jealousy and quarreling among you, are you not
2Co 7: 7 your deep sorrow, your ardent concern for me, so that my joy was
     7:11 what indignation, what alarm, what longing, what concern,
     9: 2 to give; and your enthusiasm has stirred most of them to action.
    11: 2 I am jealous for you *with* a godly jealousy. I promised you to one
  12:20 jealousy, outbursts of anger, factions, slander, gossip, arrogance
Gal 5:20 hatred, discord, jealousy, fits of rage, selfish ambition, dissensions,
Php 3: 6 as for zeal, persecuting the church; as for legalistic righteousness,
Heb 10:27 and *of* raging fire that will consume the enemies of God.
Jas 3:14 But if you harbor bitter envy and selfish ambition in your hearts,
     3:16 For where you have envy and selfish ambition, there you find

2420 ζηλόω, zēloō [11] [√ 2419]

eagerly desire [2], zealous [2], covet [1], eager [1], envy [1], jealous for [1], jealous of [1], jealous [1], zealous for [1]

Ac 7: 9 "*Because* the patriarchs *were* jealous of Joseph, they sold him as a
  17: 5 But the Jews *were* jealous; so they rounded up some bad
1Co 12:31 But eagerly desire the greater gifts. And now I will show you the
  13: 4 love is kind. *It does* not envy, it does not boast, it is not proud.
  14: 1 Follow the way of love and eagerly desire spiritual gifts,
  14:39 Therefore, my brothers, *be* eager to prophesy, and do not forbid
2Co 11: 2 *I am* jealous for you with a godly jealousy. I promised you to one
Gal 4:17 *Those people are* zealous *to win* you over, but for no good.
     4:17 is to alienate you ᴌfrom usᴊ, so that *you may be* zealous for them.
     4:18 It is fine *to be* zealous, provided the purpose is good, and to be
Jas 4: 2 You kill and covet, but you cannot have what you want.

2421 ζηλωτής, zēlōtēs [8] [√ 2419]

eager [3], Zealot [2], zealous [2], zealous for [1]

Lk 6:15 James son of Alphaeus, Simon who was called the **Zealot**,
Ac 1:13 James son of Alphaeus and Simon the **Zealot**, and Judas son of
21:20 of Jews have believed, and all of them are **zealous** for the law.
22:3 and was just as **zealous** for God as any of you are today.
1Co 14:12 Since you are **eager** to have spiritual gifts, try to excel in gifts that
Gal 1:14 and was extremely **zealous for** the traditions of my fathers.
Tit 2:14 himself a people that are his very own, **eager** to do what is good.
1Pe 3:13 Who is going to harm you if you are **eager** to do good?

2422 ζημία, zēmia [4] [→ 2423]

loss [4]

Ac 27:10 is going to be disastrous and bring great **loss** to ship and cargo,
27:21 then you would have spared yourselves this damage and **loss**.
Php 3:7 But whatever was to my profit I now consider **loss** for the sake of
3:8 I consider everything a **loss** compared to the surpassing greatness

2423 ζημιόω, zēmioō [6] [√ 2422]

forfeit [2], forfeits [1], harmed [1], lost [1], suffer loss [1]

Mt 16:26 it be for a man if he gains the whole world, yet **forfeits** his soul?
Mk 8:36 good is it for a man to gain the whole world, yet **forfeit** his soul?
Lk 9:25 a man to gain the whole world, and yet lose or **forfeit** his very self?
1Co 3:15 If it is burned up, he will **suffer loss**; he himself will be saved,
2Co 7:9 as God intended and so were not **harmed** in any way by us.
Php 3:8 Christ Jesus my Lord, for whose sake I have **lost** all things.

2424 Ζηνᾶς, Zēnas [1] [√ 2416]

Zenas [1]

Tit 3:13 Do everything you can to help **Zenas** the lawyer and Apollos on

2425 Ζήνων, Zēnōn Not used in UBS/NIV [√ 2416]

2426 ζητέω, zēteō [117] [→ 349, 1699, 1700, 2118, 2427, 2428, 5184, 5185, 5186]

looking for [18], seek [14], look for [10], tried [9], trying [6], seeking [5], want [5], seeks [4], looked for a way [3], watched for [3], ask for [2], in search of [2], searching for [2], try [2], wanting [2], asked for [1], asking for [1], asking [1], asks for [1], attempt [1], demanded [1], demanding [1], determined [1], gain [1], got ready [1], looks out for [1], make effort to obtain [1], ready [1], required [1], search for [1], search [1], searched for [1], self-seeking [+1571+3836] [1], set heart on [1], set hearts on [1], sought for [1], sought [1], tries [1], trying to kill [+3836+6034] [1], trying to take [1], waiting [1], wanted [1], wants [1], watching for [1], works for [1]

Mt 2:13 I tell you, for Herod is going to **search for** the child to kill him."
2:20 for those who were **trying to take** the child's life are dead."
6:33 But **seek** first his kingdom and his righteousness, and all these
7:7 **seek** and you will find; knock and the door will be opened to you.
7:8 he who **seeks** finds; and to him who knocks, the door will be
12:43 it goes through arid places **seeking** rest and does not find it.
12:46 his mother and brothers stood outside, **wanting** to speak to him.
12:47 and brothers are standing outside, **wanting** to speak to you."
13:45 the kingdom of heaven is like a merchant **looking for** fine pearls.
18:12 on the hills and go to **look for** the one that wandered off?
21:46 They **looked for a way** to arrest him, but they were afraid of the
26:16 then on Judas **watched for** an opportunity to hand him over.
26:59 and the whole Sanhedrin were **looking for** false evidence against
28:5 "Do not be afraid, for I know that you are **looking for** Jesus,
Mk 1:37 they found him, they exclaimed: "Everyone is **looking for** you!"
3:32 told him, "Your mother and brothers are outside **looking for** you."
8:11 To test him, they **asked** him **for** a sign from heaven.
8:12 and said, "Why does this generation **ask for** a miraculous sign?
11:18 of the law heard this and began **looking for** a way to kill him,
12:12 Then they **looked for a way** to arrest him because they knew he
14:1 and the teachers of the law were **looking for** some sly way to

14:11 him money. So he **watched for** an opportunity to hand him over.
14:55 and the whole Sanhedrin were **looking for** evidence against Jesus
16:6 "You are **looking for** Jesus the Nazarene, who was crucified.
Lk 2:48 Your father and I have been anxiously **searching for** you."
2:49 "Why were you **searching for** me?" he asked. "Didn't you know I
5:18 and **tried** to take him into the house to lay him before Jesus.
6:19 and the people all **tried** to touch him, because power was coming
9:9 then, is this I hear such things about?" And he **tried** to see him.
11:9 **seek** and you will find; knock and the door will be opened to you.
11:10 he who **seeks** finds; and to him who knocks, the door will be
11:16 Others tested him by **asking for** a sign from heaven.
11:24 it goes through arid places **seeking** rest and does not find it.
11:29 It **asks for** a miraculous sign, but none will be given it except the
12:29 And do not set your **heart on** what you will eat or drink; do not
12:31 But **seek** his kingdom, and these things will be given to you as
12:48 everyone who has been given much, much will be **demanded**;
13:6 and he went to **look for** fruit on it, but did not find any.
13:7 'For three years now I've been coming to **look for** fruit on this fig
13:24 because many, I tell you, will **try** to enter and will not be able to.
15:8 a lamp, sweep the house and **search** carefully until she finds it?
17:33 Whoever **tries** to keep his life will lose it, and whoever loses his
19:3 He **wanted** to see who Jesus was, but being a short man he could
19:10 For the Son of Man came to **seek** and to save what was lost."
19:47 and the leaders among the people were **trying** to kill him.
20:19 and the chief priests **looked for a way** to arrest him immediately,
22:2 and the teachers of the law were **looking for** some way to get rid
22:6 and **watched for** an opportunity to hand Jesus over to them when
24:5 said to them, "Why do you **look for** the living among the dead?
Jn 1:38 Jesus saw them following and asked, "What do you **want**?"
4:23 and truth, for they are the kind of worshipers the Father **seeks**.
4:27 But no one asked, "What do you **want**?" or "Why are you talking
5:18 For this reason the Jews **tried** all the harder to kill him; not only
5:30 is just, for I **seek** not to please myself but him who sent me.
5:44 yet **make** no **effort to obtain** the praise that comes from the only
6:24 they got into the boats and went to Capernaum **in search of** Jesus.
6:26 you are **looking for** me, not because you saw miraculous signs
7:1 from Judea because the Jews there were **waiting** to take his life.
7:4 No one who **wants** to become a public figure acts in secret.
7:11 Now at the Feast the Jews were **watching for** him and asking,
7:18 He who speaks on his own does so to **gain** honor for himself,
7:18 but he who **works for** the honor of the one who sent him is a man
7:19 Yet not one of you keeps the law. Why are you **trying** to kill me?"
7:20 the crowd answered. "Who is **trying** to kill you?"
7:25 Jerusalem began to ask, "Isn't this the man they are **trying** to kill?
7:30 At this they **tried** to seize him, but no one laid a hand on him,
7:34 You will **look for** me, but you will not find me; and where I am,
7:36 'You will **look for** me, but you will not find me,' and 'Where I am,
8:21 "I am going away, and you will **look for** me, and you will die in
8:37 Yet you are **ready** to kill me, because you have no room for my
8:40 As it is, you are **determined** to kill me, a man who has told you
8:50 I am not **seeking** glory for myself; but there is one who seeks it,
8:50 glory for myself; but there is one who **seeks** it, and he is the judge.
10:39 Again they **tried** to seize him, but he escaped their grasp.
11:8 "But Rabbi," they said, "a short while ago the Jews **tried** to stone
11:56 They kept **looking for** Jesus, and as they stood in the temple area
13:33 You will **look for** me, and just as I told the Jews, so I tell you now:
16:19 to them, "Are you **asking** one another what I meant when I said,
18:4 to happen to him, went out and asked them, "Who is it you **want**?"
18:7 Again he asked them, "Who is it you **want**?" And they said,
18:8 Jesus answered. "If you are **looking for** me, then let these men go."
19:12 From then on, Pilate **tried** to set Jesus free, but the Jews kept
20:15 he said, "why are you crying? Who is it you are **looking for**?"
Ac 9:11 on Straight Street and ask for a man from Tarsus named Saul,
10:19 the Spirit said to him, "Simon, three men are **looking for** you,
10:21 went down and said to the men, "I'm the one you're **looking for**.
13:8 opposed them and **tried** to turn the proconsul from the faith.
13:11 and he groped about, **seeking** someone to lead him by the hand.
16:10 had seen the vision, we **got ready** at once to leave for Macedonia,
17:5 They rushed to Jason's house **in search of** Paul and Silas in order
17:27 God did this so that men would **seek** him and perhaps reach out
21:31 While they were **trying** to kill him, news reached the commander
27:30 In an **attempt** to escape from the ship, the sailors let the lifeboat
Ro 2:7 To those who by persistence in doing good **seek** glory, honor
10:3 that comes from God and **sought** to establish their own,
10:20 And Isaiah boldly says, "I was found by those who did not **seek** me;
11:3 the only one left, and they are **trying** [+3836+6034] **to kill** me"?

1Co 1:22   Jews demand miraculous signs and Greeks **look for** wisdom,
     4: 2   Now *it is* required that those who have been given a trust must
     7:27   Are you married? *Do* not **seek** a divorce. Are you unmarried?
     7:27   Do not seek a divorce. Are you unmarried? *Do* not **look for** a wife.
     10:24   Nobody *should* **seek** his own good, but the good of others.
     10:33   For *I am* not **seeking** my own good but the good of many,
     13: 5   It is not rude, *it is* not **self-seeking** [+1571+3836], it is not easily
     14:12   to have spiritual gifts, **try** to excel in gifts that build up the church.
2Co 12:14   to you, because what I **want** is not your possessions but you.
     13: 3   since *you are* **demanding** proof that Christ is speaking through
Gal 1:10   the approval of men, or of God? Or *am I* **trying** to please men?
     2:17   "If, *while we* **seek** to be justified in Christ, it becomes evident that
Php 2:21   For everyone **looks out for** his own interests, not those of Jesus
Col 3: 1   you have been raised with Christ, **set** *your* **hearts on** things above,
1Th 2: 6   *We were* not **looking for** praise from men, not from you or anyone
2Ti 1:17   when he was in Rome, *he* **searched** hard **for** me until he found me.
Heb 8: 7   that first covenant, no place would have *been* **sought for** another.
1Pe 3:11   turn from evil and do good; *he must* **seek** peace and pursue it.
     5: 8   Your enemy the devil prowls around like a roaring lion **looking for**
Rev 9: 6   During those days men *will* **seek** death, but will not find it;

2427 ζήτημα, zētēma [5] [√ 2426]

questions [2], controversies [1], points of dispute [1], question [1]

Ac 15: 2   up to Jerusalem to see the apostles and elders about this **question**.
     18:15   But since it involves **questions** about words and names and your
     23:29   I found that the accusation had to do with **questions** about their
     25:19   they had some **points of dispute** with him about their own religion
     26: 3   well acquainted with all the Jewish customs and **controversies**.

2428 ζήτησις, zētēsis [7] [√ 2426]

controversies [2], argument [1], arguments [1], debate [1], discussion [1], investigate [1]

Jn 3:25   An **argument** developed between some of John's disciples
Ac 15: 2   and Barnabas into sharp dispute and **debate** with them.
     15: 7   After much **discussion**, Peter got up and addressed them: "Brothers,
     25:20   I was at a loss how to **investigate** such matters; so I asked if he
1Ti 6: 4   He has an unhealthy interest in **controversies** and quarrels about
2Ti 2:23   Don't have anything to do with foolish and stupid **arguments**,
Tit 3: 9   But avoid foolish **controversies** and genealogies and arguments

2429 ζιζάνιον, zizanion [8]

weeds [8]

Mt 13:25   his enemy came and sowed **weeds** among the wheat, and went
     13:26   wheat sprouted and formed heads, then the **weeds** also appeared.
     13:27   good seed in your field? Where then did the **weeds** come from?'
     13:29   " 'No,' he answered, 'because while you are pulling the **weeds**,
     13:30   First collect the **weeds** and tie them in bundles to be burned;
     13:36   and said, "Explain to us the parable *of* the **weeds** in the field."
     13:38   the sons of the kingdom. The **weeds** are the sons of the evil one,
     13:40   "As the **weeds** are pulled up and burned in the fire, so it will be at

2430 Ζμύρνα, Zmyrna Not used in UBS/NIV [√ 5043]

2431 Ζοροβαβέλ, Zorobabel [3]

Zerubbabel [3]

Mt 1:12   was the father of Shealtiel, Shealtiel the father of **Zerubbabel**,
     1:13   **Zerubbabel** the father of Abiud, Abiud the father of Eliakim,
Lk 3:27   the son of Joanan, the son of Rhesa, the son *of* **Zerubbabel**,

2432 ζόφος, zophos [5]

blackest [2], darkness [1], gloom [1], gloomy [1]

Heb 12:18   and that is burning with fire; to darkness, **gloom** and storm;
2Pe 2: 4   putting them into **gloomy** dungeons to be held for judgment;
     2:17   mists driven by a storm. **Blackest** darkness is reserved for them.
Jude 1: 6   these he has kept in **darkness**, bound with everlasting chains for
     1:13   for whom **blackest** darkness has been reserved forever.

2433 ζυγός, zygos [6] [√ 2413]

yoke [5], pair of scales [1]

Mt 11:29   Take my **yoke** upon you and learn from me, for I am gentle
     11:30   For my **yoke** is easy and my burden is light."
Ac 15:10   a **yoke** that neither we nor our fathers have been able to bear?
Gal 5: 1   and do not let yourselves be burdened again *by* a **yoke** of slavery.
1Ti 6: 1   All who are under the **yoke** of slavery should consider their
Rev 6: 5   a black horse! Its rider was holding a **pair of scales** in his hand.

2434 ζύμη, zymē [13] [→ 109, 2435; cf. 2417]

yeast [12], that^s [+3836] [1]

Mt 13:33   "The kingdom of heaven is like **yeast** that a woman took and mixed
     16: 6   "Be on your guard against the **yeast** of the Pharisees and
     16:11   But be on your guard against the **yeast** of the Pharisees
     16:12   he was not telling them to guard against the **yeast** used in bread,
Mk 8:15   "Watch out for the **yeast** of the Pharisees and that of Herod."
     8:15   out for the yeast of the Pharisees and **that**^s [+3836] of Herod."
Lk 12: 1   "Be on your guard against the **yeast** of the Pharisees, which is
     13:21   It is like **yeast** that a woman took and mixed into a large amount of
1Co 5: 6   Don't you know that a little **yeast** works through the whole batch
     5: 7   Get rid of the old **yeast** that you may be a new batch without
     5: 8   not with the old **yeast**, the yeast of malice and wickedness,
     5: 8   not with the old yeast, the **yeast** of malice and wickedness,
Gal 5: 9   "A little **yeast** works through the whole batch of dough."

2435 ζυμόω, zymoō [4] [√ 2434]

worked through the dough [2], works through [2]

Mt 13:33   a large amount of flour until *it* **worked** all **through the dough**."
Lk 13:21   a large amount of flour until it **worked** all **through the dough**."
1Co 5: 6   Don't you know that a little yeast **works through** the whole batch
Gal 5: 9   "A little yeast **works through** the whole batch of dough."

2436 ζωγρέω, zōgreō [2] [√ 2409 + 62]

catch [+1639] [1], taken captive [1]

Lk 5:10   "Don't be afraid; from now on *you will* **catch** [+1639] men."
2Ti 2:26   the trap of the devil, *who has* **taken** them **captive** to do his will.

2437 ζωή, zōē [135] [√ 2409]

ὁ ἄρτος τῆς ζωῆς (bread of life) [2] Jn 6:35,48
βιβλίον τῆς ζωῆς (book of life) [4] Rev 13:8; 17:8; 20:12; 21:27
βίβλος [τῆς] ζωῆς (book of life) [3] Php 4:3; Rev 3:5; 20:15
ἔχειν ζωήν (to have life) [19] Mt 19:16; Jn 3:15,16,36; 5:24,26, 26,39,40; 6:40,47,53,54; 10:10; 20:31; 1Jn 3:15; 5:12,12,13
ζωή αἰώνιος (eternal life) [43] Mt 19:16,29; 25:46; Mk 10:17,30; Lk 10:25; 18:18,30; Jn 3:15,16,36; 4:14,36; 5:24,39; 6:27,40,47, 54,68; 10:28; 12:25,50; 17:2,3; Ac 13:46,48; Ro 2:7; 5:21; 6:22,23; Gal 6:8; 1Ti 1:16; 6:12; Tit 1:2; 3:7; 1Jn 1:2; 2:25; 3:15; 5:11,13,20; Jude 1:21
ζωή ... θάνατος (life ... death) [20] Jn 5:24; Ro 5:10,17,21; 6:4,23; 7:10; 8:2,6,38; 1Co 3:22; 2Co 2:16,16; 4:11,12; Php 1:20; 2Ti 1:10; 1Jn 3:14; 5:16; Rev 2:10
ὕδωρ ζωῆς (water of life) [4] Rev 7:17; 21:6; 22:1,17

life [128], living [2], *untranslated* [1], alive [1], brings life [1], lifetime [1], live [1]

Mt 7:14   But small is the gate and narrow the road that leads to **life**,
     18: 8   It is better for you to enter **life** maimed or crippled than to have
     18: 9   It is better for you to enter **life** with one eye than to have two eyes
     19:16   and asked, "Teacher, what good thing must I do to get eternal **life**?"
     19:17   who is good. If you want to enter **life**, obey the commandments."
     19:29   will receive a hundred times as much and will inherit eternal **life**.
     25:46   go away to eternal punishment, but the righteous to eternal **life**."
Mk 9:43   It is better for you to enter **life** maimed than with two hands to go
     9:45   It is better for you to enter **life** crippled than to have two feet
     10:17   "Good teacher," he asked, "what must I do to inherit eternal **life**?"
     10:30   and with them, persecutions) and in the age to come, eternal **life**.

Lk 10:25 "Teacher," he asked, "what must I do to inherit eternal **life**?"
12:15 a man's **life** does not consist in the abundance of his possessions."
16:25 remember that in your **lifetime** you received your good things,
18:18 asked him, "Good teacher, what must I do to inherit eternal **life**?"
18:30 times as much in this age and, in the age to come, eternal **life**."
Jn 1:4 In him was **life**, and that life was the light of men.
1:4 In him was life, and that **life** was the light of men.
3:15 that everyone who believes in him may have eternal **life**.
3:16 that whoever believes in him shall not perish but have eternal **life**.
3:36 Whoever believes in the Son has eternal **life**, but whoever rejects
3:36 but whoever rejects the Son will not see **life**, for God's wrath
4:14 will become in him a spring of water welling up to eternal **life**."
4:36 even now he harvests the crop for eternal **life**, so that the sower
5:24 hears my word and believes him who sent me has eternal **life**
5:24 and will not be condemned; he has crossed over from death to **life**.
5:26 For as the Father has **life** in himself, so he has granted the Son to
5:26 life in himself, so he has granted the Son to have **life** in himself.
5:29 those who have done good will rise to **live**, and those who have
5:39 because you think that by them you possess eternal **life**.
5:40 yet you refuse to come to me to have **life**.
6:27 work for food that spoils, but for food that endures to eternal **life**,
6:33 is he who comes down from heaven and gives **life** to the world."
6:35 Then Jesus declared, "I am the bread of **life**. He who comes to me
6:40 who looks to the Son and believes in him shall have eternal **life**,
6:47 I tell you the truth, he who believes has everlasting **life**.
6:48 I am the bread of **life**.
6:51 This bread is my flesh, which I will give for the **life** of the world."
6:53 of the Son of Man and drink his blood, you have no **life** in you.
6:54 Whoever eats my flesh and drinks my blood has eternal **life**,
6:63 The words I have spoken to you are spirit and they are **life**.
6:68 "Lord, to whom shall we go? You have the words of eternal **life**.
8:12 me will never walk in darkness, but will have the light of **life**."
10:10 I have come that they may have **life**, and have it to the full.
10:28 I give them eternal **life**, and they shall never perish; no one can
11:25 Jesus said to her, "I am the resurrection and the **life**. He who
12:25 the man who hates his life in this world will keep it for eternal **life**.
12:50 I know that his command leads to eternal **life**. So whatever I say is
14:6 Jesus answered, "I am the way and the truth and the **life**. No one
17:2 that he might give eternal **life** to all those you have given him.
17:3 Now this is eternal **life**: that they may know you, the only true
20:31 Son of God, and that by believing you may have **life** in his name.
Ac 2:28 You have made known to me the paths of **life**; you will fill me with
3:15 You killed the author of **life**, but God raised him from the dead.
5:20 he said, "and tell the people the full message of this new **life**."
8:33 speak of his descendants? For his **life** was taken from the earth."
11:18 "So then, God has granted even the Gentiles repentance unto **life**."
13:46 you reject it and do not consider yourselves worthy of eternal **life**,
13:48 of the Lord; and all who were appointed for eternal **life** believed.
17:25 because he himself gives all men **life** and breath and everything
Ro 2:7 good seek glory, honor and immortality, he will give eternal **life**.
5:10 having been reconciled, shall we be saved through his **life**!
5:17 and of the gift of righteousness reign in **life** through the one man,
5:18 act of righteousness was justification *that* brings **life** for all men.
5:21 also grace might reign through righteousness to bring eternal **life**
6:4 dead through the glory of the Father, we too may live a new **life**.
6:22 the benefit you reap leads to holiness, and the result is eternal **life**.
6:23 but the gift of God is eternal **life** in Christ Jesus our Lord.
7:10 I found that the very commandment that was intended to bring **life**
8:2 because through Christ Jesus the law of the Spirit of **life** set me
8:6 is death, but the mind controlled by the Spirit is **life** and peace;
8:10 because of sin, your spirit is **alive** because of righteousness.
8:38 For I am convinced that neither death nor **life**, neither angels nor
11:15 of the world, what will their acceptance be but **life** from the dead?
1Co 3:22 whether Paul or Apollos or Cephas or the world or **life** or death
15:19 If only for this **life** we have hope in Christ, we are to be pitied
2Co 2:16 the one we are the smell of death; to the other, the fragrance of **life**.
2:16 the fragrance of life. **[RPG]** And who is equal to such a task?
4:10 of Jesus, so that the **life** of Jesus may also be revealed in our body.
4:11 for Jesus' sake, so that his **life** may be revealed in our mortal body.
4:12 So then, death is at work in us, but **life** is at work in you.
5:4 so that what is mortal may be swallowed up by **life**.
Gal 6:8 who sows to please the Spirit, from the Spirit will reap eternal **life**.
Eph 4:18 darkened in their understanding and separated *from* the **life** of God
Php 1:20 Christ will be exalted in my body, whether by **life** or by death.
2:16 as you hold out the word of **life**—in order that I may boast on the
4:3 the rest of my fellow workers, whose names are in the book of **life**.

Col 3:3 For you died, and your **life** is now hidden with Christ in God.
3:4 When Christ, who is your **life**, appears, then you also will appear
1Ti 1:16 for those who would believe on him and receive eternal **life**.
4:8 holding promise for both the present **life** and the life to come.
6:12 Take hold of the eternal **life** to which you were called when you
6:19 coming age, so that they may take hold of the **life** that is truly life.
2Ti 1:1 will of God, according to the promise of **life** that is in Christ Jesus,
1:10 who has destroyed death and has brought **life** and immortality to
Tit 1:2 a faith and knowledge resting on the hope of eternal **life**,
3:7 his grace, we might become heirs having the hope of eternal **life**.
Heb 7:3 without genealogy, without beginning of days or end of **life**,
7:16 his ancestry but on the basis of the power of an indestructible **life**.
Jas 1:12 he will receive the crown of **life** that God has promised to those
4:14 What is your life? You are a mist that appears for a little while
1Pe 3:7 the weaker partner and as heirs with you of the gracious gift of **life**,
3:10 "Whoever would love **life** and see good days must keep his tongue
2Pe 1:3 His divine power has given us everything we need for **life**
1Jn 1:1 have touched—this we proclaim concerning the Word of **life**.
1:2 The **life** appeared; we have seen it and testify to it, and we
1:2 seen it and testify to it, and we proclaim to you the eternal **life**,
2:25 And this is what he promised us—even eternal **life**.
3:14 We know that we have passed from death to **life**, because we love
3:15 a murderer, and you know that no murderer has eternal **life** in him.
5:11 God has given us eternal **life**, and this life is in his Son.
5:11 God has given us eternal life, and this **life** is in his Son.
5:12 He who has the Son has **life**; he who does not have the Son of God
5:12 has life; he who does not have the Son of God does not have **life**.
5:13 of the Son of God so that you may know that you have eternal **life**.
5:16 does not lead to death, he should pray and God will give him **life**.
5:20 even in his Son Jesus Christ. He is the true God and eternal **life**.
Jude 1:21 for the mercy of our Lord Jesus Christ to bring you to eternal **life**.
Rev 2:7 who overcomes, I will give the right to eat from the tree of **life**,
2:10 even to the point of death, and I will give you the crown of **life**.
3:5 I will never blot out his name from the book of **life**, but will
7:17 will be their shepherd; he will lead them to springs of **living** water.
11:11 the three and a half days a breath of **life** from God entered them,
13:8 all whose names have not been written in the book of **life**
16:3 like that of a dead man, and every **living** thing in the sea died.
17:8 *of* **life** from the creation of the world will be astonished when they
20:12 were opened. Another book was opened, which is the book of **life**.
20:15 If anyone's name was not found written in the book of **life**,
21:6 I will give to drink without cost from the spring of the water of **life**.
21:27 but only those whose names are written in the Lamb's book of **life**.
22:1 Then the angel showed me the river of the water of **life**, as clear as
22:2 On each side of the river stood the tree of **life**, bearing twelve crops
22:2 that they may have the right to the tree of **life** and may go through
22:17 and whoever wishes, let him take the free gift of the water of **life**.
22:19 God will take away from him his share in the tree of **life** and in the

2438 ζώνη, zōnē [8] [√ 2439]

belt [4], belts [2], sash [1], sashes [1]

Mt 3:4 made of camel's hair, and he had a leather **belt** around his waist.
10:9 Do not take along any gold or silver or copper in your **belts**;
Mk 1:6 with a leather **belt** around his waist, and he ate locusts and wild
6:8 journey except a staff—no bread, no bag, no money in your **belts**.
Ac 21:11 he took Paul's **belt**, tied his own hands and feet with it and said,
21:11 'In this way the Jews of Jerusalem will bind the owner of this **belt**
Rev 1:13 reaching down to his feet and with a golden **sash** around his chest.
15:6 shining linen and wore golden **sashes** around their chests.

2439 ζώννυμι, zōnnymi [3] [→ 350, 1346, 2438, 2440, 4322, 4323, 5690]

dress [1], dressed [1], put on clothes [1]

Jn 21:18 when you were younger *you* **dressed** yourself and went where you
21:18 and someone else *will* **dress** you and lead you where you do not
Ac 12:8 Then the angel said to him, "**Put on** your **clothes** and sandals."

2440 ζωννύω, zōnnyō Not used in UBS/NIV [√ 2439]

2441 ζῳογονέω, zōogoneō [3] [√ 2409 + 1181]

die [+3590] [1], gives life to [1], preserve [1]

Lk 17:33 keep his life will lose it, and whoever loses his life *will* **preserve** it.
Ac 7:19 to throw out their newborn babies so that they *would* **die** [+3590].
1Ti 6:13 In the sight *of* God, who **gives life to** everything, and of Christ

2442 ζῷον, zōon [23] [√ 2409]

living creatures [13], living creature [4], *untranslated* [3], animals [2], beasts [1]

Heb 13:11 The high priest carries the blood *of* **animals** into the Most Holy
2Pe 2:12 They are like brute **beasts**, creatures of instinct, born only to be
Jude 1:10 things they do understand by instinct, like unreasoning **animals**—
Rev 4: 6 In the center, around the throne, were four **living creatures**,
    4: 7 The first **living creature** was like a lion, the second was like an ox,
    4: 7 the second **[RPG]** was like an ox, the third had a face like a man,
    4: 7 the second was like an ox, the third **[RPG]** had a face like a man,
    4: 7 had a face like a man, the fourth **[RPG]** was like a flying eagle.
    4: 8 Each of the four **living creatures** had six wings and was covered
    4: 9 Whenever the **living creatures** give glory, honor and thanks to him
    5: 6 of the throne, encircled by the four **living creatures** and the elders.
    5: 8 the four **living creatures** and the twenty-four elders fell down
    5:11 They encircled the throne and the **living creatures** and the elders.
    5:14 The four **living creatures** said, "Amen," and the elders fell down
    6: 1 Then I heard one of the four **living creatures** say in a voice like
    6: 3 the second seal, I heard the second **living creature** say, "Come!"
    6: 5 opened the third seal, I heard the third **living creature** say, "Come!"
    6: 6 I heard what sounded like a voice among the four **living creatures**,
    6: 7 I heard the voice *of* the fourth **living creature** say, "Come!"
    7:11 the throne and around the elders and the four **living creatures**.
    14: 3 the throne and before the four **living creatures** and the elders.
    15: 7 Then one of the four **living creatures** gave to the seven angels
    19: 4 and the four **living creatures** fell down and worshiped God,

2443 ζῳοποιέω, zōopoieō [11] [√ 2409 + 4472]

gives life [4], made alive [2], come to life [1], give life [1], gives life [+1639] [1], impart life [1], life-giving [1]

Jn 5:21 For just as the Father raises the dead and **gives** them **life**, even
    5:21 even so the Son **gives life** to whom he is pleased to give it.
    6:63 The Spirit **gives life** [+1639]; the flesh counts for nothing.
Ro 4:17 the God *who* **gives life** to the dead and calls things that are not as
    8:11 he who raised Christ from the dead *will* also **give life** to your
1Co 15:22 For as in Adam all die, so in Christ all *will be* **made alive**.
    15:36 How foolish! What you sow *does* not **come to life** unless it dies.
    15:45 Adam became a living being"; the last Adam, a **life-giving** spirit.
2Co 3: 6 but of the Spirit; for the letter kills, but the Spirit **gives life**.
Gal 3:21 For if a law had been given that could **impart life**,
1Pe 3:18 He was put to death in the body but **made alive** by the Spirit,

H, H

2444 η, ē Not used in UBS/NIV

2445 ἤ, ē [343 / 341] See Index of Articles, Etc.

[→ 2472, 2486]

or [241], *untranslated* [34], than [30], and [9], before [+4570] [4], either [2], instead of [+3437] [2], than [+3437] [2], before [+323+4570] [1], but [+247] [1], but [1], cannot [+247] [1], more than [1], nor [1], now [1], only [+4024+4498] [1], or again [1], or else [1], or even [1], some [1], three or three and a half miles [+1633+4297+5084+5558] [1], tune played [+884+3068] [1], twenty to thirty gallons [+1545+3583+5552] [1], unless [1], whether [1]

2446 ἤ, ē Not used in UBS/NIV [→ 2447]

2447 ἦ μήν, ē mēn Not used in UBS/NIV [√ 2446 + 3605]

2448 ἡγεμονεύω, hēgemoneuō [2] [√ 72]

governor [2]

Lk 2: 2 census that took place *while* Quirinius *was* **governor** of Syria.)
    3: 1 *when* Pontius Pilate *was* **governor** of Judea, Herod tetrarch of

2449 ἡγεμονία, hēgemonia [1] [√ 72]

reign [1]

Lk 3: 1 In the fifteenth year *of* the **reign** of Tiberius Caesar—when Pontius

2450 ἡγεμών, hēgemōn [20] [√ 72]

governor [13], governors [4], governor's [2], rulers [1]

Mt 2: 6 land of Judah, are by no means least among the **rulers** of Judah;
    10:18 On my account you will be brought before **governors** and kings as
    27: 2 led him away and handed him over to Pilate, the **governor**.
    27:11 Meanwhile Jesus stood before the **governor**, and the governor
    27:11 and the **governor** asked him, "Are you the king of the Jews?"
    27:14 even to a single charge—to the great amazement of the **governor**.
    27:15 Now it was the **governor's** custom at the Feast to release a
    27:21 to release to you?" asked the **governor**. "Barabbas," they answered.
    27:27 Then the **governor's** soldiers took Jesus into the Prætorium
    28:14 If this report gets to the **governor**, we will satisfy him and keep
Mk 13: 9 On account of me you will stand before **governors** and kings as
Lk 20:20 might hand him over to the power and authority *of* the **governor**.
    21:12 and prisons, and you will be brought before kings and **governors**,
Ac 23:24 mounts for Paul so that he may be taken safely to **Governor** Felix."
    23:26 Claudius Lysias, *To* His Excellency, **Governor** Felix: Greetings.
    23:33 they delivered the letter *to* the **governor** and handed Paul over to
    24: 1 and they brought their charges against Paul *before* the **governor**.
    24:10 When the **governor** motioned for him to speak, Paul replied:
    26:30 and with him the **governor** and Bernice and those sitting with
1Pe 2:14 or *to* **governors**, who are sent by him to punish those who do

2451 ἡγέομαι, hēgeomai [28] [√ 72]

consider [8], leaders [4], considered [2], ruler [2], think [2], bear in mind [1], chief [1], hold [1], idea [1], regard [1], regarded [1], rules [1], thought [1], treated [1], understand [1]

Mt 2: 6 for out of you will come a **ruler** who will be the shepherd of my
Lk 22:26 like the youngest, and the one *who* **rules** like the one who serves.
Ac 7:10 king of Egypt; so he made him **ruler** over Egypt and all his palace.
    14:12 and Paul they called Hermes because he was the **chief** speaker.
    15:22 and Silas, two men *who were* **leaders** among the brothers.
    26: 2 *I* **consider** myself fortunate to stand before you today as I make
2Co 9: 5 So *I* **thought** it necessary to urge the brothers to visit you in
Php 2: 3 but in humility **consider** others better than yourselves.
    2: 6 *did* not **consider** equality with God something to be grasped,
    2:25 But *I* **think** it is necessary to send back to you Epaphroditus,
    3: 7 But whatever was to my profit *I* now **consider** loss for the sake of
    3: 8 *I* **consider** everything a loss compared to the surpassing greatness
    3: 8 lost all things. *I* **consider** them rubbish, that I may gain Christ
1Th 5:13 **Hold** them in the highest regard in love because of their work.
2Th 3:15 Yet *do* not **regard** him as an enemy, but warn him as a brother.
1Ti 1:12 who has given me strength, that *he* **considered** me faithful,
    6: 1 All who are under the yoke of slavery *should* **consider** their
Heb 10:29 *who has* **treated** as an unholy thing the blood of the covenant that
    11:11 because *he* **considered** him faithful who had made the promise.
    11:26 *He* **regarded** disgrace for the sake of Christ as of greater value
    13:7 Remember your **leaders**, who spoke the word of God to you.
    13:17 Obey your **leaders** and submit to their authority. They keep watch
    13:24 Greet all your **leaders** and all God's people. Those from Italy send
Jas 1: 2 **Consider** it pure joy, my brothers, whenever you face trials of
2Pe 1:13 *I* **think** it is right to refresh your memory as long as I live in the
    2:13 *Their* **idea** of pleasure *is* to carouse in broad daylight. They are
    3: 9 is not slow in keeping his promise, as some **understand** slowness.
    3:15 **Bear in mind** that our Lord's patience means salvation, just as our

2452 ἡδέως, *hēdeōs* [5] [√ *2454*]

gladly [2], liked [1], very gladly [1], with delight [1]

Mk 6:20 heard John, he was greatly puzzled; yet he **liked** to listen to him.
     12:37 can he be his son?" The large crowd listened to him **with delight**.
2Co 11:19 You **gladly** put up with fools since you are so wise!
     12: 9 Therefore I will boast all the more **gladly** about my weaknesses,
     12:15 So I will **very gladly** spend for you everything I have and expend

2453 ἤδη, *ēdē* [61]

already [33], *untranslated* [6], now [5], by now [2], by this time [2], almost [1], as good as dead [+3739] [1], as soon as [+4020] [1], as [1], at last [+4537] [1], even now [1], had been [1], has come [1], nearly [1], not until [+1254] [1], now at last [+4537] [1], still [1], when [+4020] [1]

Mt   3:10 The ax is **already** at the root of the trees, and every tree that does
      5:28 lustfully has **already** committed adultery with her in his heart.
     14:15 and said, "This is a remote place, and it's **already** getting late.
     14:24 but the boat was **already** a considerable distance from land,
     15:32 they have **already** been with me three days and have nothing to
     17:12 But I tell you, Elijah has **already** come, and they did not recognize
     24:32 As soon as its twigs get tender and [NIE] its leaves come out,
Mk   4:37 and the waves broke over the boat, so that it was **nearly** swamped.
      6:35 **By this time** it was late in the day, so his disciples came to him.
      6:35 "This is a remote place," they said, "and it's **already** very late.
      8: 2 they have **already** been with me three days and have nothing to
     11:11 He looked around at everything, but since it was **already** late,
     13:28 **As soon as** [+4020] its twigs get tender and its leaves come out,
     15:42 (that is, the day before the Sabbath). So **as** evening approached,
     15:44 Pilate was surprised to hear that he was **already** dead. Summoning
Lk   3: 9 The ax is **already** at the root of the trees, and every tree that does
      7: 6 [NIE] He was not far from the house when the centurion sent
     11: 7 The door is **already** locked, and my children are with me in bed.
     12:49 to bring fire on the earth, and how I wish it were **already** kindled!
     14:17 those who had been invited, 'Come, for everything is **now** ready.'
     19:37 When he came near [NIE] the place where the road goes down
     21:30 **When** [+4020] they sprout leaves, you can see for yourselves
     21:30 you can see for yourselves and know that summer is [NIE] near.
     23:44 It was **now** about the sixth hour, and darkness came over the whole
     24:29 "Stay with us, for it is nearly evening; the day is **almost** over."
Jn   3:18 but whoever does not believe stands condemned **already**
      4:36 **Even** now the reaper draws his wages, even now he harvests the
      4:51 While he was **still** on the way, his servants met him with the news
      5: 6 and learned that he **had been** in this condition for a long time,
      6:17 **By now** it was dark, and Jesus had not yet joined them.
      7:14 **Not until** [+1254] halfway through the Feast did Jesus go up to the
      9:22 for **already** the Jews had decided that anyone who acknowledged
      9:27 He answered, "I have told you **already** and you did not listen.
     11:17 Jesus found that Lazarus had **already** been in the tomb for four
     11:39 the sister of the dead man, "**by this time** there is a bad odor,
     13: 2 and the devil had **already** prompted Judas Iscariot, son of Simon,
     15: 3 You are **already** clean because of the word I have spoken to you.
     19:28 knowing that all was **now** completed, and so that the Scripture
     19:33 But when they came to Jesus and found that he was **already** dead,
     21: 4 Early in the morning, [NIE] Jesus stood on the shore,
     21:14 This was **now** the third time Jesus appeared to his disciples after he
Ac   4: 3 it was evening, [NIE] they put them in jail until the next day.
     27: 9 and sailing had **already** become dangerous because by now it was
     27: 9 already become dangerous because **by now** it was after the Fast.
Ro   1:10 and I pray that **now** [+4537] **at last** by God's will the way may be
      4:19 he faced the fact that his body was **as good as dead** [+3739]—
     13:11 The hour **has come** for you to wake up from your slumber,
1Co 4: 8 **Already** you have all you want! Already you have become rich!
      4: 8 **Already** you have become rich! You have become kings—
      5: 3 And I have **already** passed judgment on the one who did this,
      6: 7 among you means you have been completely defeated **already**.
Php 3:12 Not that I have **already** obtained all this, or have already been
      3:12 have already obtained all this, or have **already** been made perfect,
      4:10 I rejoice greatly in the Lord that **at last** [+4537] you have renewed
2Th 2: 7 For the secret power of lawlessness is **already** at work; but the one
1Ti 5:15 Some have in fact **already** turned away to follow Satan.
2Ti 2:18 the truth. They say that the resurrection has **already** taken place,
      4: 6 For I am **already** being poured out like a drink offering,
2Pe 3: 1 Dear friends, this is **now** my second letter to you. I have written

1Jn 2: 8 the darkness is passing and the true light is **already** shining.
      4: 3 you have heard is coming and even now is **already** in the world.

2454 ἡδονή, *hēdonē* [5] [→ *112, 830, 881, 2452, 2455, 5310, 5798*]

pleasures [3], desires [1], pleasure [1]

Lk   8:14 by life's worries, riches and **pleasures**, and they do not mature.
Tit 3: 3 deceived and enslaved by all kinds of passions and **pleasures**.
Jas 4: 1 Don't they come from your **desires** that battle within you?
      4: 3 that you may spend what you get on your **pleasures**.
2Pe 2:13 Their idea of **pleasure** is to carouse in broad daylight. They are

2455 ἡδύοσμον, *hēdyosmon* [2] [√ *2454 + 3853*]

mint [1], spices mint [1]

Mt 23:23 You give a tenth of your **spices**—mint, dill and cummin.
Lk 11:42 because you give God a tenth of your **mint**, rue and all other kinds

2456 ἦθος, *ēthos* [1] [√ *1621*]

character [1]

1Co 15:33 Do not be misled: "Bad company corrupts good **character**."

2457 ἥκω, *hēkō* [26 / 25] [→ *465, 2763*]

come [18], has come [2], have come [2], arrived [1], here [1], overtake [1]

Mt   8:11 I say to you that many *will* **come** from the east and the west,
     23:36 I tell you the truth, all this *will* **come** upon this generation.
     24:14 world as a testimony to all nations, and then the end *will* **come**.
     24:50 The master of that servant *will* **come** on a day when he does not
Mk   8: 3 on the way, because some of them *have* **come** a long distance."
Lk 12:46 The master of that servant *will* **come** on a day when he does not
     13:29 *People will* **come** from east and west and north and south,
     13:35 will not see me again until [UBS+ *the time comes when*] you say,
     15:27 'Your brother **has come**,' he replied,
     19:43 The days *will* **come** upon you when your enemies will build an
Jn   2: 4 do you involve me?" Jesus replied. "My time *has* not yet **come**."
      4:47 When this man heard that Jesus had **arrived** in Galilee from
      6:37 All that the Father gives me *will* **come** to me, and whoever comes
      8:42 you would love me, for I came from God and *now am* **here**.
Ro 11:26 "The deliverer *will* **come** from Zion; he will turn godlessness away
Heb 10: 7 about me in the scroll—*I have* **come** to do your will, O God.' "
     10: 9 Then he said, "Here I am, *I have* **come** to do your will." He sets
     10:37 a very little while, "He who is coming *will* **come** and will not delay.
2Pe 3:10 But the day of the Lord *will* **come** like a thief. The heavens will
1Jn 5:20 We know also that the Son of God **has come** and has given us
Rev 2:25 Only hold on to what you have until *I* **come**.
      3: 3 But if you do not wake up, *I will* **come** like a thief, and you will
      3: 3 like a thief, and you will not know at what time *I will* **come** to you.
      3: 9 I will make them **come** and fall down at your feet
     15: 4 All nations *will* **come** and worship before you, for your righteous
     18: 8 Therefore in one day her plagues *will* **overtake** her: death,

2458 ἠλί¹, *ēli*¹ [2 / 0] [√ cf. *1830*]

Mt 27:46 voice, "*Eloi*, [UBS *Eli*; NIV *1830*] *Eloi, lama sabachthani?*"—
     27:46 voice, "*Eloi, Eloi*, [UBS *Eli*; NIV *1830*] *lama sabachthani?*"—

2459 Ἠλί², *Ēli*² [1]

Heli [1]

Lk   3:23 He was the son, so it was thought, of Joseph, the son *of* **Heli**,

2460 Ἠλίας, *Ēlias* [29]

Elijah [28], Elijah's [1]

Mt 11:14 if you are willing to accept it, he is the **Elijah** who was to come.
     16:14 others say **Elijah**; and still others, Jeremiah or one of the prophets."
     17: 3 Just then there appeared before them Moses and **Elijah**,
     17: 4 up three shelters—one for you, one for Moses and one *for* **Elijah**."

17:10   then do the teachers of the law say that **Elijah** must come first?"
17:11   Jesus replied, "To be sure, **Elijah** comes and will restore all things.
17:12   But I tell you, **Elijah** has already come, and they did not recognize
27:47   of those standing there heard this, they said, "He's calling **Elijah**."
27:49   "Now leave him alone. Let's see if **Elijah** comes to save him."
Mk   6:15   Others said, "He is **Elijah**." And still others claimed, "He is a
     8:28   the Baptist; others say **Elijah**; and still others, one of the prophets."
     9: 4   And there appeared before them **Elijah** and Moses, who were
     9: 5   up three shelters—one for you, one for Moses and one *for* **Elijah**."
     9:11   "Why do the teachers of the law say that **Elijah** must come first?"
     9:12   Jesus replied, "To be sure, **Elijah** does come first, and restores all
     9:13   But I tell you, **Elijah** has come, and they have done to him
     15:35   standing near heard this, they said, "Listen, he's calling **Elijah**."
     15:36   him alone. Let's see if **Elijah** comes to take him down," he said.
Lk   1:17   he will go on before the Lord, in the spirit and power *of* **Elijah**,
     4:25   I assure you that there were many widows in Israel in **Elijah's**
     4:26   Yet **Elijah** was not sent to any of them, but to a widow in
     9: 8   others that **Elijah** had appeared, and still others that one of the
     9:19   others say **Elijah**; and still others, that one of the prophets of long
     9:30   Two men, Moses and **Elijah**,
     9:33   up three shelters—one for you, one for Moses and one *for* **Elijah**."
Jn   1:21   him, "Then who are you? Are you **Elijah**?" He said, "I am not."
     1:25   you baptize if you are not the Christ, nor **Elijah**, nor the Prophet?"
Ro   11: 2   you know what the Scripture says in *the passage about* **Elijah**—
Jas   5:17   **Elijah** was a man just like us. He prayed earnestly that it would not

2461 ἡλικία, hēlikia [8] [√ 2462]

life [2], of age [2], age [+2789] [1], short [+3625+3836] [1], stature [1], whole measure [+3586] [1]

Mt   6:27   Who of you by worrying can add a single hour to his **life**?
Lk   2:52   And Jesus grew in wisdom and **stature**, and in favor with God
     12:25   Who of you by worrying can add a single hour to his **life**?
     19: 3   but being a **short man** [+3625+3836] he could not, because of the
Jn   9:21   we don't know. Ask him. He is **of age**; he will speak for himself."
     9:23   That was why his parents said, "He is **of age**; ask him."
Eph   4:13   attaining to the **whole measure** [+3586] of the fullness of Christ.
Heb 11:11   By faith Abraham, even though he was past **age** [+2789]—

2462 ἡλίκος, hēlikos [3] [→ 2461, 4383, 5312, 5496]

how much [1], small [1], what a great [1]

Col   2: 1   I want you to know **how much** I am struggling for you and for
Jas   3: 5   Consider **what a great** forest is set on fire by a small spark.
     3: 5   Consider what a great forest is set on fire by a **small** spark.

2463 ἥλιος, hēlios [32] [√ cf. 1637]

sun [27], east [+424] [2], just after sunrise [+422+3836] [1], light of the sun [1], sunset [+1544] [1]

Mt   5:45   He causes his **sun** to rise on the evil and the good, and sends rain
     13: 6   But when the **sun** came up, the plants were scorched, and they
     13:43   Then the righteous will shine like the **sun** in the kingdom of their
     17: 2   His face shone like the **sun**, and his clothes became as white as the
     24:29   "Immediately after the distress of those days " 'the **sun** will be
Mk   1:32   That evening after **sunset** [+1544] the people brought to Jesus all
     4: 6   But when the **sun** came up, the plants were scorched, and they
     13:24   in those days, following that distress, " 'the **sun** will be darkened,
     16: 2   **just after sunrise** [+422+3836], they were on their way to the
Lk   4:40   When the **sun** was setting, the people brought to Jesus all who had
     21:25   "There will be signs in the **sun**, moon and stars. On the earth,
     23:45   *for* the **sun** stopped shining. And the curtain of the temple was torn
Ac   2:20   The **sun** will be turned to darkness and the moon to blood before
     13:11   and for a time you will be unable to see the **light of the sun**."
     26:13   brighter than the **sun**, blazing around me and my companions.
     27:20   When neither **sun** nor stars appeared for many days and the storm
1Co 15:41   The **sun** has one kind of splendor, the moon another and the stars
Eph   4:26   do not sin": Do not let the **sun** go down while you are still angry,
Jas   1:11   For the **sun** rises with scorching heat and withers the plant;
Rev   1:16   His face was like the **sun** shining in all its brilliance.
     6:12   The **sun** turned black like sackcloth made of goat hair, the whole
     7: 2   Then I saw another angel coming up from the **east** [+424],
     7:16   The **sun** will not beat upon them, nor any scorching heat.
     8:12   and a third *of* the **sun** was struck, a third of the moon, and a third

     9: 2   The **sun** and sky were darkened by the smoke from the Abyss.
     10: 1   his face was like the **sun**, and his legs were like fiery pillars.
     12: 1   a woman clothed with the **sun**, with the moon under her feet
     16: 8   The fourth angel poured out his bowl on the **sun**, and the sun was
     16:12   dried up to prepare the way for the kings from the **East** [+424].
     19:17   And I saw an angel standing in the **sun**, who cried in a loud voice
     21:23   The city does not need the **sun** or the moon to shine on it,
     22: 5   They will not need the light of a lamp or the light *of* the **sun**,

2464 ἧλος, hēlos [2] [→ 4669]

nail [1], nails [1]

Jn   20:25   "Unless I see the **nail** marks in his hands and put my finger where
     20:25   the **nail** marks in his hands and put my finger where the **nails** were,

2465 ἡμέρα, hēmera [389] [→ 2389, 2390, 2765, 2766, 3540, 3819, 3892, 4958]

ἐκείνη ἡμέρα (that day) [49] Mt 3:1; 7:22; 13:1; 22:23,46; 24:19,22,29,36; 26:29; Mk 1:9; 2:20; 4:35; 8:1; 13:17,19,24,32; 14:25; Lk 2:1; 4:2; 5:35; 6:23; 9:36; 10:12; 17:31; 21:23,34; Jn 1:39; 5:9; 11:53; 14:20; 16:23,26; 19:31; 20:19; Ac 2:18,41; 7:41; 8:1; 9:37; 2Th 1:10; 2Ti 1:12,18; 4:8; Heb 8:10; 10:16; Rev 9:6

ἐν ἡμέραις (in the days [of]) [48] Mt 2:1; 3:1; 23:30; 24:19,38; 27:40; Mk 1:9; 8:1; 13:17,24; 15:29; Lk 1:5,7,18,25,39; 2:1,36; 4:2,25; 5:35; 6:12; 9:36; 17:26,26,28; 21:23; 23:7; 24:18; Jn 2:19,20; Ac 1:15; 2:17,18; 5:37; 6:1; 7:41; 9:37; 11:27; 13:41; 27:7; 2Ti 3:1; Heb 5:7; Jas 5:3; 1Pe 3:20; Rev 2:13; 9:6; 10:7

ἐσχάτη ἡμέρα (last day) [12] Jn 6:39,40,44,54; 7:37; 11:24; 12:48; Ac 2:17; 2Ti 3:1; Heb 1:2; Jas 5:3; 2Pe 3:3

ἡμέρα θεοῦ (day of God) [3] 2Pe 3:12; Rev 12:10; 16:14

ἡμέρα κρίσεως (day of judgment) [7] Mt 10:15; 11:22,24; 12:36; 2Pe 2:9; 3:7; 1Jn 4:17

ἡμέρα κυρίου (day of the Lord) [7] Ac 2:20; 1Co 1:8; 5:5; 2Co 1:14; 1Th 5:2; 2Th 2:2; 2Pe 3:10

ἡμέρα ... νύξ (day ... night) [23] Mt 4:2; 12:40,40; Mk 4:27; 5:5; Lk 2:37; 18:7; 21:37; Ac 9:24; 20:31; 26:7; Ro 13:12; 1Th 2:9; 3:10; 5:5; 2Th 3:8; 1Ti 5:5; 2Ti 1:3; Rev 4:8; 7:15; 12:10; 14:11; 20:10

ἡμέρα Χριστοῦ (day of Christ) [4] 1Co 1:8; Php 1:6,10; 2:16

μέγας ἡμέρα (great day) [5] Jn 7:37; Ac 2:20; Jude 1:6; Rev 6:17; 16:14

day [181], days [114], time [32], daily [+2848] [5], untranslated [4], daylight [4], day after day [+2848] [2], every day [+2848] [2], some time ago [+3836+4047+4574] [2], this^s [+3836] [2], very day [+4958] [2], years [2], a few days later [+1328] [1], a week later [+3552+3893] [1], about noon [+3545] [1], always [+3836+4246] [1], another^s [1], at daybreak [+1181+2002] [1], broad daylight [1], court [1], daily [+1667+2848] [1], dawn [+1181+3516] [1], day [+4958] [1], day after day [+4246] [1], day by day [+2848+4246] [1], daybreak [+1181] [1], daytime [1], during [1], each day [+3836] [1], Feast of Unleavened Bread [+109] [1], Feast [1], forever [+172+1650] [1], in the morning [+1181] [1], late in afternoon [+806+3111] [1], long [+4498] [1], morning [1], nine in the morning [+3836+5569+6052] [1], old [+1877+4581] [1], some time ago [+608+792] [1], that was the time [+1697+1877+3836] [1], the next day [+1651+3552] [1], the next morning [+1181] [1], them^s [+3836] [1], three in the afternoon [+1888+3836+6052] [1], today [+3836+4958] [1], until [+2401] [1], week [+2231] [1], when [+1877] [1], while [1]

Mt   2: 1   during the **time** of King Herod, Magi from the east came to
     3: 1   In those **days** John the Baptist came, preaching in the Desert of
     4: 2   After fasting forty **days** and forty nights, he was hungry.
     6:34   will worry about itself. Each **day** has enough trouble of its own.
     7:22   Many will say to me on that **day**, 'Lord, Lord, did we not prophesy
     9:15   The **time** will come when the bridegroom will be taken from them;
     10:15   and Gomorrah on the **day** of judgment than for that town.
     11:12   From the **days** of John the Baptist until now, the kingdom of
     11:22   bearable for Tyre and Sidon on the **day** of judgment than for you.
     11:24   But I tell you that it will be more bearable for Sodom on the **day** of

12:36 But I tell you that men will have to give account on the **day** of
12:40 For as Jonah was three **days** and three nights in the belly of a huge
12:40 so the Son of Man will be three **days** and three nights in the heart
13: 1 That same **day** Jesus went out of the house and sat by the lake.
15:32 they have already been with me three **days** and have nothing to eat.
16:21 and that he must be killed and *on* the third **day** be raised to life.
17: 1 After six **days** Jesus took with him Peter, James and John the
17:23 They will kill him, and *on* the third **day** he will be raised to life."
20: 2 He agreed to pay them a denarius *for* the **day** and sent them into
20: 6 'Why have you been standing here all **day** *long* doing nothing?'
20:12 us who have borne the burden of the work and the heat *of* the **day**.'
20:19 and crucified. *On* the third **day** he will be raised to life!"
22:23 That same **day** the Sadducees, who say there is no resurrection,
22:46 and from that **day** on no one dared to ask him any more questions.
23:30 And you say, 'If we had lived in the **days** of our forefathers,
24:19 How dreadful it will be in those **days** for pregnant women
24:22 If those **days** had not been cut short, no one would survive.
24:22 but for the sake of the elect those **days** will be shortened.
24:29 "Immediately after the distress *of* those **days** " 'the sun will be
24:36 "No one knows about that **day** or hour, not even the angels in
24:37 As it was in the **days** of Noah, so it will be at the coming of the
24:38 For in the **days** before the flood, people were eating and drinking,
24:38 and giving in marriage, up to the **day** Noah entered the ark;
24:42 because you do not know *on* what **day** your Lord will come.
24:50 The master of that servant will come on a **day** when he does not
25:13 keep watch, because you do not know the **day** or the hour.
26: 2 "As you know, the Passover is two **days** away—and the Son of
26:29 I will not drink of this fruit of the vine from now on until that **day**
26:55 and clubs to capture me? **Every day** [*+2848*] I sat in the temple
26:61 am able to destroy the temple of God and rebuild it in three **days**.' "
27:40 who are going to destroy the temple and build it in three **days**,
27:63 still alive that deceiver said, 'After three **days** I will rise again.'
27:64 give the order for the tomb to be made secure until the third **day**.
28:15 been widely circulated among the Jews to this **very day** [*+4958*].
28:20 And surely I am with you **always** [*+3836+4246*], to the very end of

Mk 1: 9 At that **time** Jesus came from Nazareth in Galilee and was baptized
    1:13 and he was in the desert forty **days**, being tempted by Satan.
    2: 1 **A few days** [*+1328*] later, when Jesus again entered Capernaum,
    2:20 But the **time** will come when the bridegroom will be taken from
    2:20 bridegroom will be taken from them, and on that **day** they will fast.
    4:27 Night and **day**, whether he sleeps or gets up, the seed sprouts
    4:35 That **day** when evening came, he said to his disciples, "Let us go
    5: 5 Night and **day** among the tombs and in the hills he would cry out
    6:21 Finally the opportune **time** came. On his birthday Herod gave a
    8: 1 During those **days** another large crowd gathered. Since they had
    8: 2 they have already been with me three **days** and have nothing to eat.
    8:31 the law, and that he must be killed and after three **days** rise again.
    9: 2 After six **days** Jesus took Peter, James and John with him
    9:31 hands of men. They will kill him, and after three **days** he will rise."
   10:34 spit on him, flog him and kill him. Three **days** later he will rise."
   13:17 How dreadful it will be in those **days** for pregnant women
   13:19 because those will be **days** of distress unequaled from the
   13:20 If the Lord had not cut short those **days**, no one would survive.
   13:20 the elect, whom he has chosen, he has shortened them^s [*+3836*].
   13:24 "But in those **days**, following that distress, " 'the sun will be
   13:32 "No one knows about that **day** or hour, not even the angels in
   14: 1 and the Feast of Unleavened Bread were only two **days** away,
   14:12 *On* the first **day** of the Feast of Unleavened Bread, when it was
   14:25 I will not drink again of the fruit of the vine until that **day** when I
   14:49 **Every day** [*+2848*] I was with you, teaching in the temple courts,
   14:58 destroy this man-made temple and in three **days** will build another,
   15:29 You who are going to destroy the temple and build it in three **days**,

Lk 1: 5 In the **time** of Herod king of Judea there was a priest named
    1: 7 Elizabeth was barren; and they were both well along in **years**.
    1:18 sure of this? I am an old man and my wife is well along in **years**."
    1:20 you will be silent and not able to speak until the **day** this happens,
    1:23 When his **time** of service was completed, he returned home.
    1:24 After this^s [*+3836*] his wife Elizabeth became pregnant and for
    1:25 "In *these* **days** he has shown his favor and taken away my disgrace
    1:39 At that **time** Mary got ready and hurried to a town in the hill
    1:59 On the eighth **day** they came to circumcise the child, and they were
    1:75 in holiness and righteousness before him all our **days**.
    1:80 and he lived in the desert **until** [*+2401*] he appeared publicly to
    2: 1 In those **days** Caesar Augustus issued a decree that a census should
    2: 6 While they were there, the **time** came for the baby to be born,
    2:21 On the eighth **day**, when it was time to circumcise him, he was

2:22 When the **time** of their purification according to the Law of Moses
2:36 She *was* very old [*+1877+4581*]; she had lived with her husband
2:37 She never left the temple but worshiped night and **day**, fasting
2:43 After the **Feast** was over, while his parents were returning home,
2:44 Thinking he was in their company, they traveled on *for* a **day**.
2:46 After three **days** they found him in the temple courts,
4: 2 where *for* forty **days** he was tempted by the devil. He ate nothing
4: 2 He ate nothing during those **days**, and at the end of them he was
4:16 and on the Sabbath **day** he went into the synagogue, as was his
4:25 assure you that there were many widows in Israel in Elijah's **time**,
4:42 **At daybreak** [*+1181+2002*] Jesus went out to a solitary place.
5:17 One **day** as he was teaching, Pharisees and teachers of the law,
5:35 But the **time** will come when the bridegroom will be taken from
5:35 bridegroom will be taken from them; in those **days** they will fast."
6:12 One of those **days** Jesus went out to a mountainside to pray,
6:13 When **morning** came, he called his disciples to him and chose
6:23 "Rejoice in that **day** and leap for joy,
8:22 One **day** Jesus said to his disciples, "Let's go over to the other side
9:12 **Late in** the **afternoon** [*+806+3111*] the Twelve came to him
9:22 and he must be killed and *on* the third **day** be raised to life.
9:23 deny himself and take up his cross **daily** [*+2848*] and follow me.
9:28 About eight **days** after Jesus said this, he took Peter, John
9:36 this to themselves, and told no one at that **time** what they had seen.
9:37 The next **day**, when they came down from the mountain, a large
9:51 As the **time** approached for him to be taken up to heaven,
10:12 it will be more bearable on that **day** for Sodom than for that town.
11: 3 Give us each **day** our daily bread.
12:46 The master of that servant will come on a **day** when he does not
13:14 synagogue ruler said to the people, "There are six **days** for work.
13:14 So come and be healed on those days, not [**RPG**] on the Sabbath."
13:16 long years, be set free *on* the Sabbath **day** from what bound her?"
14: 5 of you has a son or an ox that falls into a well on the Sabbath **day**,
15:13 "Not **long** [*+4498*] after that, the younger son got together all he
16:19 was dressed in purple and fine linen and lived in luxury every **day**.
17: 4 If he sins against you seven times *in* a **day**, and seven times comes
17:22 "The **time** is coming when you will long to see one of the days of
17:22 "The **time** is coming when you will long to see one *of* the **days** of
17:24 For the Son of Man in his **day** will be like the lightning,
17:26 "Just as it was in the **days** of Noah, so also will it be in the days of
17:26 the **days** of Noah, so also will it be in the **days** of the Son of Man.
17:27 and being given in marriage up to the **day** Noah entered the ark.
17:28 "It was the same in the **days** of Lot. People were eating
17:29 But the **day** Lot left Sodom, fire and sulfur rained down from
17:30 "It will be just like this *on* the **day** the Son of Man is revealed.
17:31 On that **day** no one who is on the roof of his house, with his goods
18: 7 justice for his chosen ones, who cry out to him **day** and night?
18:33 *On* the third **day** he will rise again."
19:42 had only known on this **day** what would bring you peace—
19:43 The **days** will come upon you when your enemies will build an
19:47 Every **day** he was teaching at the temple. But the chief priests,
20: 1 One **day** as he was teaching the people in the temple courts
21: 6 the **time** will come when not one stone will be left on another;
21:22 For this is the **time** of punishment in fulfillment of all that has been
21:23 How dreadful it will be in those **days** for pregnant women
21:34 of life, and that **day** will close on you unexpectedly like a trap.
21:37 **Each day** [*+3836*] Jesus was teaching at the temple, and each
22: 7 Then came the **day** of Unleavened Bread on which the Passover
22:53 Every **day** I was with you in the temple courts, and you did not lay
22:66 At **daybreak** [*+1181*] the council of the elders of the people,
23: 7 he sent him to Herod, who was also in Jerusalem at that **time**.
23:12 That **day** Herod and Pilate became friends—before this they had
23:29 For the **time** will come when you will say, 'Blessed are the barren
23:54 It was Preparation **Day**, and the Sabbath was about to begin.
24: 7 of sinful men, be crucified and *on* the third **day** be raised again.' "
24:13 Now that same **day** two of them were going to a village called
24:18 do not know the things that have happened there in these **days**?"
24:21 And what is more, it is the third **day** since all this took place.
24:29 "Stay with us, for it is nearly evening; the **day** is almost over."
24:46 The Christ will suffer and rise from the dead *on* the third **day**,

Jn 1:39 and saw where he was staying, and spent that **day** with him.
    2: 1 *On* the third **day** a wedding took place at Cana in Galilee.
    2:12 and brothers and his disciples. There they stayed *for* a few **days**.
    2:19 "Destroy this temple, and I will raise it again in three **days**."
    2:20 to build this temple, and you are going to raise it in three **days**?"
    4:40 they urged him to stay with them, and he stayed two **days**.
    4:43 After the two **days** he left for Galilee.

5: 9 and walked. The **day** on which this took place was a Sabbath,
6: 39 none of all that he has given me, but raise them up at the last **day**.
6: 40 him shall have eternal life, and I will raise him up at the last **day**."
6: 44 who sent me draws him, and I will raise him up at the last **day**.
6: 54 my blood has eternal life, and I will raise him up *at* the last **day**.
7: 37 On the last and greatest **day** of the Feast, Jesus stood and said in a
8: 56 Your father Abraham rejoiced at the thought of seeing my **day**;
9: 4 As long as it is **day**, we must do the work of him who sent me.
9: 14 Now the **day** on which Jesus had made the mud and opened the
11: 6 that Lazarus was sick, he stayed where he was two more **days**.
11: 9 Jesus answered, "Are there not twelve hours *of* **daylight**? A man
11: 9 A man who walks by **day** will not stumble, for he sees by this
11: 17 found that Lazarus had already been in the tomb *for* four **days**.
11: 24 "I know he will rise again in the resurrection at the last **day**."
11: 53 So from that **day** on they plotted to take his life.
12: 1 Six **days** before the Passover, Jesus arrived at Bethany,
12: 7 "˻It was intended˼ that she should save this perfume for the **day** of
12: 48 that very word which I spoke will condemn him at the last **day**.
14: 20 On that **day** you will realize that I am in my Father, and you are in
16: 23 In that **day** you will no longer ask me anything. I tell you the truth,
16: 26 In that **day** you will ask in my name. I am not saying that I will ask
19: 31 day of Preparation, and the next **day** was to be a special Sabbath.
20: 19 On the evening *of* that first **day** of the week, when the disciples
20: 26 **A week later** [+*3552*+*3893*] his disciples were in the house again,
Ac 1: 2 until the **day** he was taken up to heaven, after giving instructions
1: 3 He appeared to them over a period *of* forty **days** and spoke about
1: 5 but in a few **days** you will be baptized with the Holy Spirit."
1: 15 In those **days** Peter stood up among the believers (a group
1: 22 beginning from John's baptism to the **time** when Jesus was taken
2: 1 When the **day** of Pentecost came, they were all together in one
2: 15 It's *only* **nine in the morning** [+*3836*+*5569*+*6052*]!
2: 17 " 'In the last **days**, God says, I will pour out my Spirit on all people.
2: 18 both men and women, I will pour out my Spirit in those **days**,
2: 20 blood before the coming of the great and glorious **day** of the Lord.
2: 29 David died and was buried, and his tomb is here to this **day**.
2: 41 and about three thousand were added to their number that **day**.
2: 46 Every **day** they continued to meet together in the temple courts.
2: 47 And the Lord added to their number **daily** [+*2848*] those who were
3: 2 where he was put every **day** to beg from those going into the
3: 24 Samuel on, as many as have spoken, have foretold these **days**.
5: 36 **Some time ago** [+*3836*+*4047*+*4574*] Theudas appeared, claiming
5: 37 Judas the Galilean appeared in the **days** of the census and led a
5: 42 **Day** [+*4246*] **after day**, in the temple courts and from house to
6: 1 In those **days** when the number of disciples was increasing,
7: 8 the father of Isaac and circumcised him eight **days** after his birth.
7: 26 The next **day** Moses came upon two Israelites who were fighting.
7: 41 **That was the time** [+*1697*+*1877*+*3836*] they made an idol in the
form of a calf. They brought sacrifices to it and held a celebration in
7: 45 out before them. It remained in the land until the **time** of David,
8: 1 On that **day** a great persecution broke out against the church at
9: 9 *For* three **days** he was blind, and did not eat or drink anything.
9: 19 Saul spent several **days** with the disciples in Damascus.
9: 23 After many **days** had gone by, the Jews conspired to kill him,
9: 24 **Day** and night they kept close watch on the city gates in order to
9: 37 About that **time** she became sick and died, and her body was
9: 43 Peter stayed in Joppa *for* some **time** with a tanner named Simon.
10: 3 One day at about **three in the afternoon** [+*1888*+*3836*+*6052*] he
10: 30 "Four **days** ago I was in my house praying at this hour, at three in
10: 40 but God raised him from the dead on the third **day** and caused him
10: 48 Then they asked Peter to stay with them *for* a few **days**.
11: 27 During this **time** some prophets came down from Jerusalem to
12: 3 Peter also. This happened **during** the Feast of Unleavened Bread.
12: 18 **In the morning** [+*1181*], there was no small commotion among
12: 21 *On* the appointed **day** Herod, wearing his royal robes, sat on his
13: 14 On **[RPG]** the Sabbath they entered the synagogue and sat down.
13: 31 and for many **days** he was seen by those who had traveled with
13: 41 for I am going to do something in your **days** that you would never
15: 7 you know that **some time** [+*608*+*792*] **ago** God made a choice
15: 36 Some **time** later Paul said to Barnabas, "Let us go back and visit the
16: 5 were strengthened in the faith and grew **daily** [+*2848*] in numbers.
16: 12 of that district of Macedonia. And we stayed there several **days**.
16: 13 On **[RPG]** the Sabbath we went outside the city gate to the river,
16: 18 She kept this up for many **days**. Finally Paul became so troubled
16: 35 When it was **daylight**, the magistrates sent their officers to the
17: 11 and examined the Scriptures every **day** to see if what Paul said was
17: 17 as well as in the marketplace **day** [+*2848*+*4246*] **by day** with those
17: 31 For he has set a **day** when he will judge the world with justice by
18: 18 Paul stayed on in Corinth *for* some **time**. Then he left the brothers
19: 9 and had discussions **daily** [+*2848*] in the lecture hall of Tyrannus.
20: 6 sailed from Philippi after the **Feast of Unleavened Bread** [+*109*],
20: 6 and five **days** later joined the others at Troas, where we stayed
20: 6 days later joined the others at Troas, where we stayed seven **days**.
20: 16 in a hurry to reach Jerusalem, if possible, *by* the **day** of Pentecost.
20: 18 I was with you, from the first **day** I came into the province of Asia.
20: 26 I declare to you **today** [+*3836*+*4958*] that I am innocent of the
20: 31 I never stopped warning each of you night and **day** with tears.
21: 4 Finding the disciples there, we stayed with them seven **days**.
21: 5 But when our **time** was up, we left and continued on our way.
21: 7 where we greeted the brothers and stayed with them *for* a **day**.
21: 10 After we had been there a number of **days**, a prophet named
21: 15 After **this**[s] [+*3836*], we got ready and went up to Jerusalem.
21: 26 The next **day** Paul took the men and purified himself along with
21: 26 he went to the temple to give notice of the date when the **days**
21: 27 When the seven **days** were nearly over, some Jews from the
21: 38 terrorists out into the desert **some time ago** [+*3836*+*4047*+*4574*]?"
23: 1 I have fulfilled my duty to God in all good conscience to this **day**."
23: 12 **The next morning** [+*1181*] the Jews formed a conspiracy
24: 1 Five **days** later the high priest Ananias went down to Caesarea
24: 11 You can easily verify that no more than twelve **days** ago I went up
24: 24 Several **days** later Felix came with his wife Drusilla, who was a
25: 1 Three **days** after arriving in the province, Festus went up from
25: 6 After spending eight or ten **days** with them, he went down to
25: 13 A few **days** later King Agrippa and Bernice arrived at Caesarea to
25: 14 Since they were spending many **days** there, Festus discussed
26: 7 tribes are hoping to see fulfilled as they earnestly serve God **day**
26: 13 **About noon** [+*3545*], O king, as I was on the road, I saw a light
26: 22 But I have had God's help to this very **day**,
27: 7 We made slow headway for many **days** and had difficulty arriving
27: 20 When neither sun nor stars appeared for many **days** and the storm
27: 29 they dropped four anchors from the stern and prayed for **daylight**.
27: 33 Just before **dawn** [+*1181*+*3516*] Paul urged them all to eat.
27: 33 "For the last fourteen days," **[RPG]** he said, "you have been in
27: 39 When **daylight** came, they did not recognize the land, but they saw
28: 7 us to his home and *for* three **days** entertained us hospitably.
28: 12 We put in at Syracuse and stayed there three **days**.
28: 13 **The next day** [+*1651*+*3552*] the south wind came up, and on the
28: 14 some brothers who invited us to spend a **week** [+*2231*] with them.
28: 17 Three **days** later he called together the leaders of the Jews.
28: 23 They arranged to meet Paul on a *certain* **day**, and came in even
Ro 2: 5 you are storing up wrath against yourself for the **day** of God's
2: 16 This will take place on the **day** when God will judge men's secrets
8: 36 "For your sake we face death all **day** *long*; we are considered as
10: 21 "All **day** long I have held out my hands to a disobedient
11: 8 and ears so that they could not hear, to this **very day** [+*4958*]."
13: 12 The night is nearly over; the **day** is almost here. So let us put aside
13: 13 behave decently, as in the **daytime**, not in orgies and drunkenness,
14: 5 One man considers *one* **day** more sacred than another;
14: 5 One man considers one day more sacred than **another**[s];
14: 5 more sacred than another; another man considers every **day** alike.
14: 6 He who regards one **day** as special, does so to the Lord. He who
1Co 1: 8 so that you will be blameless on the **day** of our Lord Jesus Christ.
3: 13 will be shown for what it is, because the **Day** will bring it to light.
4: 3 I care very little if I am judged by you or by any human **court**;
5: 5 may be destroyed and his spirit saved on the **day** of the Lord.
10: 8 of them did—and *in* one **day** twenty-three thousand of them died.
15: 4 that he was raised *on* the third **day** according to the Scriptures,
15: 31 I die every **day**—I mean that, brothers—just as surely as I glory
2Co 1: 14 of us just as we will boast of you in the **day** of the Lord Jesus.
3: 14 for to this **day** [+*4958*] the same veil remains when the old
4: 16 are wasting away, yet inwardly we are being renewed **day** by day.
4: 16 are wasting away, yet inwardly we are being renewed day *by* **day**.
6: 2 of my favor I heard you, and in the **day** of salvation I helped you."
6: 2 now is the time of God's favor, now is the **day** of salvation.
11: 28 I face **daily** [+*2848*] the pressure of my concern for all the
Gal 1: 18 to get acquainted with Peter and stayed with him fifteen **days**.
4: 10 You are observing *special* **days** and months and seasons and years!
Eph 4: 30 of God, with whom you were sealed for the **day** of redemption.
5: 16 making the most of every opportunity, because the **days** are evil.
6: 13 so that when the **day** of evil comes, you may be able to stand your
Php 1: 5 because of your partnership in the gospel from the first **day** until
1: 6 in you will carry it on to completion until the **day** of Christ Jesus.
1: 10 what is best and may be pure and blameless until the **day** of Christ,

	2:16	in order that I may boast on the **day** of Christ that I did not run
Col	1: 6	just as it has been doing among you since the **day** you heard it
	1: 9	For this reason, since the **day** we heard about you, we have not
1Th	2: 9	and **day** in order not to be a burden to anyone while we preached
	3:10	and **day** we pray most earnestly that we may see you again
	5: 2	for you know very well that the **day** of the Lord will come like a
	5: 4	are not in darkness so that this **day** should surprise you like a thief.
	5: 5	You are all sons of the light and sons *of* the **day**. We do not belong
	5: 8	But since we belong to the **day**, let us be self-controlled, putting on
2Th	1:10	on the **day** he comes to be glorified in his holy people and to be
	2: 2	come from us, saying that the **day** of the Lord has already come.
	3: 8	we worked night and **day**, laboring and toiling so that we would
1Ti	5: 5	and continues night and **day** to pray and to ask God for help.
2Ti	1: 3	as night and **day** I constantly remember you in my prayers.
	1:12	that he is able to guard what I have entrusted to him for that **day**.
	1:18	the Lord grant that he will find mercy from the Lord on that **day**!
	3: 1	But mark this: There will be terrible times in the last **days**.
	4: 8	the Lord, the righteous Judge, will award to me on that **day**—
Heb	1: 2	but in these last **days** he has spoken to us by his Son, whom he
	3: 8	as you did in the rebellion, during the **time** of testing in the desert.
	3:13	But encourage one another **daily** [+*1667*+*2848*], as long as it is
	4: 4	words: "And on the seventh **day** God rested from all his work."
	4: 7	Therefore God again set a certain **day**, calling it Today, when a
	4: 8	them rest, God would not have spoken later about another **day**.
	5: 7	During the **days** of Jesus' life on earth, he offered up prayers
	7: 3	without genealogy, without beginning *of* **days** or end of life,
	7:27	he does not need to offer sacrifices **day** [+*2848*] **after day**,
	8: 8	"The **time** is coming, declares the Lord, when I will make a new
	8: 9	**when** [+*1877*] I took them by the hand to lead them out of Egypt,
	8:10	is the covenant I will make with the house of Israel after that **time**,
	10:11	**Day** [+*2848*] **after day** every priest stands and performs his
	10:16	"This is the covenant I will make with them after that **time**,
	10:25	one another—and all the more as you see the **Day** approaching.
	10:32	Remember those earlier **days** after you had received the light,
	11:30	after the people had marched around them for seven **days**.
	12:10	Our fathers disciplined us for a little **while** as they thought best;
Jas	5: 3	eat your flesh like fire. You have hoarded wealth in the last **days**.
	5: 5	You have fattened yourselves in the **day** of slaughter.
1Pe	2:12	may see your good deeds and glorify God on the **day** he visits us.
	3:10	would love life and see good **days** must keep his tongue from evil
	3:20	who disobeyed long ago when God waited patiently in the **days** of
2Pe	1:19	until the **day** dawns and the morning star rises in your hearts.
	2: 8	(for that righteous man, living among them **day** after day,
	2: 8	(for that righteous man, living among them day after **day**,
	2: 9	from trials and to hold the unrighteous for the **day** of judgment,
	2:13	Their idea of pleasure is to carouse in **broad daylight**. They are
	3: 3	you must understand that in the last **days** scoffers will come,
	3: 7	being kept for the **day** of judgment and destruction of ungodly
	3: 8	With the Lord a **day** is like a thousand years, and a thousand years
	3: 8	a day is like a thousand years, and a thousand years are like a **day**.
	3:10	But the **day** of the Lord will come like a thief. The heavens will
	3:12	as you look forward to the **day** of God and speed its coming.
	3:18	To him be glory both now and **forever** [+*172*+*1650*]! Amen.
1Jn	4:17	among us so that we will have confidence on the **day** of judgment,
Jude	1: 6	bound with everlasting chains for judgment on the great **Day**.
Rev	1:10	On the Lord's **Day** I was in the Spirit, and I heard behind me a
	2:10	in prison to test you, and you will suffer persecution *for* ten **days**.
	2:13	even in the **days** of Antipas, my faithful witness, who was put to
	4: 8	**Day** and night they never stop saying: "Holy, holy, holy is the Lord
	6:17	For the great **day** of their wrath has come, and who can stand?"
	7:15	the throne of God and serve him **day** and night in his temple;
	8:12	A third of the **day** was without light, and also a third of the night.
	9: 6	During those **days** men will seek death, but will not find it;
	9:15	and **day** and month and year were released to kill a third of
	10: 7	But in the **days** when the seventh angel is about to sound his
	11: 3	and they will prophesy *for* 1,260 **days**, clothed in sackcloth."
	11: 6	so that it will not rain *during* the **time** they are prophesying;
	11: 9	*For* three and a half **days** men from every people, tribe, language
	11:11	the three and a half **days** a breath of life from God entered them,
	12: 6	for her by God, where she might be taken care of *for* 1,260 **days**.
	12:10	who accuses them before our God **day** and night, has been hurled
	14:11	There is no rest **day** or night for those who worship the beast
	16:14	to gather them for the battle *on* the great **day** of God Almighty.
	18: 8	Therefore in one **day** her plagues will overtake her: death,
	20:10	They will be tormented **day** and night for ever and ever.
	21:25	On no **day** will its gates ever be shut, for there will be no night

2466 ἡμέτερος, *hēmeteros* [7] [√ *1609*]

our [4], our own [1], ours [1], us [1]

Ac	2:11	we hear them declaring the wonders of God *in* **our own** tongues!"
	26: 5	they are willing, that according to the strictest sect *of* **our** religion,
Ro	15: 4	For everything that was written in the past was written to teach **us**,
2Ti	4:15	your guard against him, because he strongly opposed **our** message.
Tit	3:14	**Our** people must learn to devote themselves to doing what is
1Jn	1: 3	And **our** fellowship is with the Father and with his Son,
	2: 2	and not only for **ours** but also for the sins of the whole world.

2467 ἡμιθανής, *hēmithanēs* [1] [√ *2468* + *2569*]

half dead [1]

Lk	10:30	of his clothes, beat him and went away, leaving him **half dead**.

2468 ἥμισυς, *hēmisys* [5] [→ *2467*, *2469*, *2470*]

half [5]

Mk	6:23	"Whatever you ask I will give you, up to **half** my kingdom."
Lk	19: 8	Here and now I give **half** of my possessions to the poor, and if I
Rev	11: 9	*For* three and a **half** days men from every people, tribe, language
	11:11	the three and a **half** days a breath of life from God entered them,
	12:14	care of for a time, times and **half** a time, out of the serpent's reach.

2469 ἡμιώριον, *hēmiōrion* [1] [√ *2468* + *6052*]

half an hour [1]

Rev	8: 1	seventh seal, there was silence in heaven for about **half an hour**.

2470 ἡμίωρον, *hēmiōron* Not used in UBS/NIV
[√ *2468* + *6052*]

2471 ἡνίκα, *hēnika* [2]

when [+*323*] [1], whenever [+*1569*] [1]

2Co	3:15	Even to this day **when** [+*323*] Moses is read, a veil covers their
	3:16	But **whenever** [+*1569*] anyone turns to the Lord, the veil is taken

2472 ἤπερ, *ēper* [1] [√ *2445* + *4302*]

than [1]

Jn	12:43	for they loved praise from men more **than** praise from God.

2473 ἤπιος, *ēpios* [1 / 2]

gentle [1], kind [1]

1Th	2: 7	but we were **gentle** [UBS *3758*] among you, like a mother caring
2Ti	2:24	instead, he must be **kind** to everyone, able to teach, not resentful.

2474 Ἤρ, *Ēr* [1]

Er [1]

Lk	3:28	son of Addi, the son of Cosam, the son of Elmadam, the son *of* **Er**,

2475 ἤρεμος, *ēremos* [1]

peaceful [1]

1Ti	2: 2	that we may live **peaceful** and quiet lives in all godliness

2476 Ἡρῴδης, *Hērōdēs* [43] [→ *2477*, *2478*, *2479*]

the "Great" [11] Mt 2:1,3,7,12,13,15,16,19,22; Lk 1:5; Ac 23:35

the Tetrarch [27] Mt 14:1,3,6,6; Mk 6:14,16,17,18,20,21,22; 8:15; Lk 3:1,19,19; 8:3; 9:7,9; 13:31; 23:7,7,8,11,12,15; Ac 4:27; 13:1

Agrippa I [5] Ac 12:1,6,11,19,21

Herod [37], Herod's [5], he^s [1]

Mt	2: 1	during the time *of* King **Herod**, Magi from the east came to
	2: 3	When King **Herod** heard this he was disturbed, and all Jerusalem

2: 7 Then **Herod** called the Magi secretly and found out from them the
2: 12 And having been warned in a dream not to go back to **Herod**,
2: 13 I tell you, for **Herod** is going to search for the child to kill him."
2: 15 where he stayed until the death of **Herod**. And so was fulfilled
2: 16 When **Herod** realized that he had been outwitted by the Magi,
2: 19 After **Herod** died, an angel of the Lord appeared in a dream to
2: 22 that Archelaus was reigning in Judea in place of his father **Herod**,
14: 1 At that time **Herod** the tetrarch heard the reports about Jesus,
14: 3 Now **Herod** had arrested John and bound him and put him in
14: 6 On **Herod's** birthday the daughter of Herodias danced for them
14: 6 daughter of Herodias danced for them and pleased **Herod** so much

Mk 6: 14 King **Herod** heard about this, for Jesus' name had become well
6: 16 But when **Herod** heard this, he said, "John, the man I beheaded,
6: 17 For **Herod** himself had given orders to have John arrested,
6: 18 For John had been saying to **Herod**, "It is not lawful for you to have
6: 20 because **Herod** feared John and protected him, knowing him to be
6: 21 On his birthday **Herod** gave a banquet for his high officials
6: 22 came in and danced, she pleased **Herod** and his dinner guests.
8: 15 "Watch out for the yeast of the Pharisees and that of **Herod**."

Lk 1: 5 In the time of **Herod** king of Judea there was a priest named
3: 1 **Herod** tetrarch of Galilee, his brother Philip tetrarch of Iturea
3: 19 But when John rebuked **Herod** the tetrarch because of Herodias,
3: 19 his brother's wife, and all the other evil things he[s] had done,
8: 3 Joanna the wife of Cuza, the manager of **Herod's** household;
9: 7 Now **Herod** the tetrarch heard about all that was going on.
9: 9 But **Herod** said, "I beheaded John. Who, then, is this I hear such
13: 31 "Leave this place and go somewhere else. **Herod** wants to kill you."
23: 7 When he learned that Jesus was under **Herod's** jurisdiction,
23: 7 he sent him to **Herod**, who was also in Jerusalem at that time.
23: 8 When **Herod** saw Jesus, he was greatly pleased, because for a long
23: 11 Then **Herod** and his soldiers ridiculed and mocked him.
23: 12 That day **Herod** and Pilate became friends—before this they had
23: 15 Neither has **Herod**, for he sent him back to us; as you can see,

Ac 4: 27 Indeed **Herod** and Pontius Pilate met together with the Gentiles
12: 1 It was about this time that King **Herod** arrested some who
12: 6 The night before **Herod** was to bring him to trial, Peter was
12: 11 that the Lord sent his angel and rescued me from **Herod's** clutches
12: 19 After **Herod** had a thorough search made for him and did not find
12: 21 On the appointed day **Herod**, wearing his royal robes, sat on his
13: 1 Manaen (who had been brought up with **Herod** the tetrarch)
23: 35 Then he ordered that Paul be kept under guard in **Herod's** palace.

2477 Ἡρῳδιανοί, *Hērōdianoi* [3] [√ 2476]

Herodians [3]

Mt 22: 16 They sent their disciples to him along with the **Herodians**.
Mk 3: 6 and began to plot with the **Herodians** how they might kill Jesus.
12: 13 Later they sent some of the Pharisees and **Herodians** to Jesus to

2478 Ἡρῳδιάς, *Hērōdias* [6] [√ 2476]

Herodias [6]

Mt 14: 3 and bound him and put him in prison because of **Herodias**,
14: 6 On Herod's birthday the daughter of **Herodias** danced for them
Mk 6: 17 He did this because of **Herodias**, his brother Philip's wife,
6: 19 So **Herodias** nursed a grudge against John and wanted to kill him.
6: 22 When the daughter of **Herodias** came in and danced, she pleased
Lk 3: 19 But when John rebuked Herod the tetrarch because of **Herodias**,

2479 Ἡρῳδίων, *Hērōdiōn* [1] [√ 2476]

Herodion [1]

Ro 16: 11 Greet **Herodion**, my relative. Greet those in the household of

2480 Ἡσαΐας, *Ēsaias* [22]

Isaiah [21], book of Isaiah [1]

Mt 3: 3 This is he who was spoken of through the prophet **Isaiah**:
4: 14 to fulfill what was said through the prophet **Isaiah**:
8: 17 This was to fulfill what was spoken through the prophet **Isaiah**:
12: 17 This was to fulfill what was spoken through the prophet **Isaiah**:
13: 14 In them is fulfilled the prophecy of **Isaiah**: " 'You will be ever
15: 7 You hypocrites! **Isaiah** was right when he prophesied about you:

Mk 1: 2 It is written in **Isaiah** the prophet: "I will send my messenger ahead
7: 6 "**Isaiah** was right when he prophesied about you hypocrites;
Lk 3: 4 As is written in the book of the words of **Isaiah** the prophet:
4: 17 The scroll of the prophet **Isaiah** was handed to him. Unrolling it,
Jn 1: 23 John replied in the words of **Isaiah** the prophet, "I am the voice of
12: 38 This was to fulfill the word of **Isaiah** the prophet: "Lord, who has
12: 39 reason they could not believe, because, as **Isaiah** says elsewhere:
12: 41 **Isaiah** said this because he saw Jesus' glory and spoke about him.
Ac 8: 28 was sitting in his chariot reading the **book of Isaiah** the prophet.
8: 30 ran up to the chariot and heard the man reading **Isaiah** the prophet.
28: 25 truth to your forefathers when he said through **Isaiah** the prophet:
Ro 9: 27 **Isaiah** cries out concerning Israel: "Though the number of the
9: 29 It is just as **Isaiah** said previously: "Unless the Lord Almighty had
10: 16 For **Isaiah** says, "Lord, who has believed our message?"
10: 20 **Isaiah** boldly says, "I was found by those who did not seek me;
15: 12 And again, **Isaiah** says, "The Root of Jesse will spring up, one who

2481 Ἠσαῦ, *Ēsau* [3]

Esau [3]

Ro 9: 13 Just as it is written: "Jacob I loved, but **Esau** I hated."
Heb 11: 20 By faith Isaac blessed Jacob and **Esau** in regard to their future.
12: 16 See that no one is sexually immoral, or is godless like **Esau**,

2482 ἥσσων, *hēssōn* [2] [→ 2273, 2487, 2488, 2489]

harm [1], less [1]

1Co 11: 17 no praise for you, for your meetings do more **harm** than good.
2Co 12: 15 expend myself as well. If I love you more, will you love me **less**?

2483 ἡσυχάζω, *hēsychazō* [5] [→ 2484, 2485]

gave up [1], had no objections [1], lead a quiet life [1], rested [1], silent [1]

Lk 14: 4 But they *remained* **silent**. So taking hold of the man, he healed
23: 56 But *they* **rested** on the Sabbath in obedience to the commandment.
Ac 11: 18 *they* **had no** *further* **objections** and praised God, saying,
21: 14 not be dissuaded, *we* **gave up** and said, "The Lord's will be done."
1Th 4: 11 Make it your ambition *to* **lead a quiet life**, to mind your own

2484 ἡσυχία, *hēsychia* [4] [√ 2483]

quiet [1], quietness [1], settle down [+3552] [1], silent [1]

Ac 22: 2 they heard him speak to them in Aramaic, they became very **quiet**.
2Th 3: 12 and urge in the Lord Jesus Christ to **settle** [+3552] **down**.
1Ti 2: 11 A woman should learn in **quietness** and full submission.
2: 12 to teach or to have authority over a man; she must be **silent**.

2485 ἡσύχιος, *hēsychios* [2] [√ 2483]

quiet [2]

1Ti 2: 2 we may live peaceful and **quiet** lives in all godliness and holiness.
1Pe 3: 4 of your inner self, the unfading beauty of a gentle and **quiet** spirit,

2486 ἤτοι, *ētoi* [1] [√ 2445 + 5520]

whether [1]

Ro 6: 16 **whether** you are slaves to sin, which leads to death, or to

2487 ἡττάομαι, *hēttaomai* [2] [√ 2482]

mastered [1], overcome [1]

2Pe 2: 19 of depravity—for a man is a slave to whatever *has* **mastered** him.
2: 20 Savior Jesus Christ and are again entangled in it and **overcome**,

2488 ἥττημα, *hēttēma* [2] [√ 2482]

defeated [1], loss [1]

Ro 11: 12 and their **loss** means riches for the Gentiles, how much greater
1Co 6: 7 among you means you have been completely **defeated** already.

2489 ἥττων, *hēttōn* Not used in UBS/NIV [√ *2482*]

2490 ἠχέω, *ēcheō* [1] [√ *2491*]

resounding [1]

1Co 13: 1 have not love, I am only a **resounding** gong or a clanging cymbal.

2491 ἦχος¹, *ēchos¹* [3] [→ *2010, 2490, 2492, 2493, 2994, 4654*]

blast [1], news [1], sound [1]

Lk 4:37 And the **news** about him spread throughout the surrounding area.
Ac 2: 2 Suddenly a **sound** like the blowing of a violent wind came from
Heb 12:19 *to* a trumpet **blast** or to such a voice speaking words that those

2492 ἦχος², *ēchos²* [1] [√ *2491*]

roaring [1]

Lk 21:25 be in anguish and perplexity at the **roaring** and tossing of the sea.

2493 ἠχώ, *ēchō* Not used in UBS/NIV [√ *2491*]

Θ, *Th*

2494 θ, *th* Not used in UBS/NIV

2495 θά, *tha* Not used in UBS/NIV [√ *cf. 3448*]

2496 θάβιτα, *thabita* Not used in UBS/NIV [√ *cf. 5412*]

2497 Θαδδαῖος, *Thaddaios* [2] [√ *cf. 3304*]

Thaddaeus [2]

Mt 10: 3 the tax collector; James son of Alphaeus, and **Thaddaeus**;
Mk 3:18 Thomas, James son of Alphaeus, **Thaddaeus**, Simon the Zealot

2498 θάλασσα, *thalassa* [91] [→ *1458, 4144; cf. 229*]

ἐρυθρός θάλασσα (Red Sea) [2] Ac 7:36; Heb 11:29

θάλασσα Τιβεριάς (Sea of Tiberias) [2] Jn 6:1; 21:1

θάλασσα τῆς Γαλιλαίας (Sea of Galilee) [5] Mt 4:18; 15:29; Mk 1:16; 7:31; Jn 6:1

sea [56], lake [23], waves [4], water [2], *untranslated* [1], coast [1], seashore [+*3836+5927*] [1], seashore [1], water's edge [1], waters [1]

Mt 4:15 and land of Naphtali, the way *to* the **sea**, along the Jordan,
 4:18 As Jesus was walking beside the **Sea** of Galilee, he saw two
 4:18 They were casting a net into the **lake**, for they were fishermen.
 8:24 Without warning, a furious storm came up on the **lake**, so that the
 8:26 Then he got up and rebuked the winds and the **waves**, and it was
 8:27 "What kind of man is this? Even the winds and the **waves** obey
 8:32 and the whole herd rushed down the steep bank into the **lake**
 13: 1 That same day Jesus went out of the house and sat by the **lake**.
 13:47 the kingdom of heaven is like a net that was let down into the **lake**
 14:25 watch of the night Jesus went out to them, walking on the **lake**.
 14:26 When the disciples saw him walking on the **lake**, they were
 15:29 Jesus left there and went along the **Sea** of Galilee. Then he went up
 17:27 we may not offend them, go to the **lake** and throw out your line.
 18: 6 hung around his neck and to be drowned in the depths *of* the **sea**.
 21:21 'Go, throw yourself into the **sea**,' and it will be done.
 23:15 You travel over land and **sea** to win a single convert, and when he
Mk 1:16 As Jesus walked beside the **Sea** of Galilee, he saw Simon and his
 1:16 he saw Simon and his brother Andrew casting a net into the **lake**,
 2:13 Once again Jesus went out beside the **lake**. A large crowd came to
 3: 7 Jesus withdrew with his disciples to the **lake**, and a large crowd
 4: 1 Again Jesus began to teach by the **lake**. The crowd that gathered
 4: 1 so large that he got into a boat and sat in it *out* on the **lake**,

 4: 1 while all the people were along the shore at the **water's edge**.
 4:39 He got up, rebuked the wind and said *to* the **waves**, "Quiet!
 4:41 each other, "Who is this? Even the wind and the **waves** obey him!"
 5: 1 They went across the **lake** to the region of the Gerasenes.
 5:13 rushed down the steep bank into the **lake** and were drowned.
 5:13 down the steep bank into the lake and were drowned. [RPG]
 5:21 a large crowd gathered around him while he was by the **lake**.
 6:47 When evening came, the boat was in the middle *of* the **lake**,
 6:48 fourth watch of the night he went out to them, walking on the **lake**.
 6:49 but when they saw him walking on the **lake**, they thought he was a
 7:31 down to the **Sea** of Galilee and into the region of the Decapolis.
 9:42 it would be better for him to be thrown into the **sea** with a large
 11:23 'Go, throw yourself into the **sea**,' and does not doubt in his heart
Lk 17: 2 It would be better for him to be thrown into the **sea** with a
 17: 6 'Be uprooted and planted in the **sea**,' and it will obey you.
 21:25 be in anguish and perplexity at the roaring and tossing of the **sea**.
Jn 6: 1 Jesus crossed to the far shore *of* the **Sea** of Galilee (that is,
 6:16 When evening came, his disciples went down to the **lake**,
 6:17 they got into a boat and set off across the **lake** for Capernaum.
 6:18 A strong wind was blowing and the **waters** grew rough.
 6:19 they saw Jesus approaching the boat, walking on the **water**;
 6:22 shore *of* the **lake** realized that only one boat had been there,
 6:25 When they found him on the other side of the **lake**, they asked him,
 21: 1 Jesus appeared again to his disciples, by the **Sea** of Tiberias.
 21: 7 around him (for he had taken it off) and jumped into the **water**.
Ac 4:24 they said, "you made the heaven and the earth and the **sea**,
 7:36 signs in Egypt, at the Red **Sea** and for forty years in the desert.
 10: 6 He is staying with Simon the tanner, whose house is by the **sea**."
 10:32 is a guest in the home of Simon the tanner, who lives by the **sea**.'
 14:15 who made heaven and earth and **sea** and everything in them.
 17:14 The brothers immediately sent Paul to the **coast**, but Silas
 27:30 escape from the ship, the sailors let the lifeboat down into the **sea**,
 27:38 they lightened the ship by throwing the grain into the **sea**.
 27:40 they left them in the **sea** and at the same time untied the ropes that
 28: 4 for though he escaped from the **sea**, Justice has not allowed him to
Ro 9:27 "Though the number of the Israelites be like the sand *by* the **sea**,
1Co 10: 1 were all under the cloud and that they all passed through the **sea**.
 10: 2 They were all baptized into Moses in the cloud and in the **sea**.
2Co 11:26 in danger in the city, in danger in the country, in danger at **sea**;
Heb 11:12 and as countless as the sand on the **seashore** [+*3836+5927*].
 11:29 By faith the people passed through the Red **Sea** as on dry land;
Jas 1: 6 because he who doubts is like a wave *of* the **sea**, blown and tossed
Jude 1:13 They are wild waves of the **sea**, foaming up their shame;
Rev 4: 6 Also before the throne there was what looked like a **sea** of glass,
 5:13 creature in heaven and on earth and under the earth and on the **sea**,
 7: 1 any wind from blowing on the land or on the **sea** or on any tree.
 7: 2 angels who had been given power to harm the land and the **sea**:
 7: 3 "Do not harm the land or the **sea** or the trees until we put a seal on
 8: 8 like a huge mountain, all ablaze, was thrown into the **sea**.
 8: 8 was thrown into the **sea**. A third *of* the **sea** turned into blood,
 8: 9 a third of the living creatures in the **sea** died, and a third of the
 10: 2 He planted his right foot on the **sea** and his left foot on the land,
 10: 5 Then the angel I had seen standing on the **sea** and on the land
 10: 6 and all that is in it, and the **sea** and all that is in it, and said,
 10: 8 that lies open in the hand of the angel who is standing on the **sea**
 12:12 But woe to the earth and the **sea**, because the devil has gone down
 13: 1 And the dragon stood on the shore *of* the **sea**. And I saw a beast
 13: 1 And I saw a beast coming out of the **sea**. He had ten horns
 14: 7 who made the heavens, the earth, the **sea** and the springs of water."
 15: 2 And I saw what looked like a **sea** of glass mixed with fire and,
 15: 2 standing beside the **sea**, those who had been victorious over the
 16: 3 The second angel poured out his bowl on the **sea**, and it turned into
 16: 3 like that of a dead man, and every living thing in the **sea** died.
 18:17 the sailors, and all who earn their living from the **sea**, will stand far
 18:19 where all who had ships on the **sea** became rich through her
 18:21 up a boulder the size of a large millstone and threw it into the **sea**,
 20: 8 them for battle. In number they are like the sand *on* the **seashore**.
 20:13 The **sea** gave up the dead that were in it, and death and Hades gave
 21: 1 the first earth had passed away, and there was no longer any **sea**.

2499 θάλπω, *thalpō* [2]

cares for [1], caring for [1]

Eph 5:29 but *he* feeds and **cares for** it, just as Christ does the church—
1Th 2: 7 were gentle among you, like a mother **caring for** her little children.

2500 Θαμάρ, *Thamar* [1]

Tamar [1]

Mt 1: 3 Judah the father of Perez and Zerah, whose mother was **Tamar**,

2501 θαμβέω, *thambeō* [3] [√ *2502*]

amazed [2], astonished [1]

Mk 1:27 The *people were* all so **amazed** that they asked each other,
    10:24 The disciples *were* **amazed** at his words. But Jesus said again,
    10:32 with Jesus leading the way, and the disciples *were* **astonished**,

2502 θάμβος, *thambos* [3] [→ *1701, 1702, 2501*]

amazed [1], astonished [+*4321*] [1], wonder [1]

Lk 4:36 All the people were **amazed** and said to each other, "What is this
    5: 9 and all his companions *were* **astonished** [+*4321*] at the catch of
Ac 3:10 and they were filled *with* **wonder** and amazement at what had

2503 θανάσιμος, *thanasimos* [1] [√ *2569*]

deadly poison [+*5516*] [1]

Mk 16:18 and when they drink **deadly** [+*5516*] **poison**, it will not hurt them

2504 θανατηφόρος, *thanatēphoros* [1]
[√ *2569 + 5770*]

deadly [1]

Jas 3: 8 man can tame the tongue. It is a restless evil, full *of* **deadly** poison.

2505 θάνατος, *thanatos* [120] [√ *2569*]

γεύομαι θανάτου (taste death) [5] Mt 16:28; Mk 9:1; Lk 9:27; Jn 8:52; Heb 2:9

ζωή ... θάνατος (life ... death) [20] Jn 5:24; Ro 5:10,17,21; 6:4,23; 7:10; 8:2,6,38; 1Co 3:22; 2Co 2:16,16; 4:11,12; Php 1:20; 2Ti 1:10; 1Jn 3:14; 5:16; Rev 2:10

θάνατος δεύτερος (second death) [4] Rev 2:11; 20:6,14; 21:8

death [104], fatal [3], died [2], put to death [+*5462*] [2], *untranslated* [1], deadly peril [1], death sentence [1], die [+*3972*] [1], died [+*1181*] [1], exposed to death [1], grounds for the death penalty [+*165*] [1], plague [1], strike dead [+*650+1877*] [1]

Mt 4:16 on those living in the land of the shadow *of* **death** a light has
    10:21 "Brother will betray brother to **death**, and a father his child;
    15: 4 who curses his father or mother *must be* **put to death** [+*5462*].'
    16:28 some who are standing here will not taste **death** before they see the
    20:18 and the teachers of the law. They will condemn him *to* **death**
    26:38 "My soul is overwhelmed with sorrow to the point *of* **death**.
    26:66 What do you think?" "He is worthy *of* **death**," they answered.
Mk 7:10 who curses his father or mother *must be* **put to death** [+*5462*].'
    9: 1 some who are standing here will not taste **death** before they see
    10:33 They will condemn him *to* **death** and will hand him over to the
    13:12 "Brother will betray brother to **death**, and a father his child.
    14:34 "My soul is overwhelmed with sorrow to the point *of* **death**,"
    14:64 What do you think?" They all condemned him as worthy *of* **death**.
Lk 1:79 to shine on those living in darkness and in the shadow *of* **death**,
    2:26 he *would* not **die** [+*3972*] before he had seen the Lord's Christ.
    9:27 some who are standing here will not taste **death** before they see the
    22:33 replied, "Lord, I am ready to go with you to prison and *to* **death**."
    23:15 back to us; as you can see, he has done nothing to deserve **death**.
    23:22 I have found in him no **grounds for the death penalty** [+*165*].
    24:20 and our rulers handed him over to be sentenced to **death**,
Jn 5:24 and will not be condemned; he has crossed over from **death** to life.
    8:51 you the truth, if anyone keeps my word, he will never see **death**."
    8:52 you say that if anyone keeps your word, he will never taste **death**.
    11: 4 he heard this, Jesus said, "This sickness will not end in **death**.
    11:13 Jesus had been speaking of his **death**, but his disciples thought he
    12:33 He said this to show the kind of **death** he was going to die.
    18:32 so that the words Jesus had spoken indicating the kind of **death** he
    21:19 Jesus said this to indicate the kind of **death** by which Peter would
Ac 2:24 raised him from the dead, freeing him from the agony *of* **death**,

13:28 Though they found no proper ground *for* a **death sentence**,
22: 4 I persecuted the followers of this Way to their **death**,
23:29 but there was no charge against him that deserved **death**
25:11 If, however, I am guilty of doing anything deserving **death**,
25:25 I found he had done nothing deserving *of* **death**, but because he
26:31 "This man is not doing anything that deserves **death**
28:18 because I was not guilty of any crime *deserving* **death**.
Ro 1:32 righteous decree that those who do such things deserve **death**,
    5:10 we were reconciled to him through the **death** of his Son,
    5:12 and **death** through sin, and in this way death came to all men,
    5:12 and death through sin, and in this way **death** came to all men,
    5:14 **death** reigned from the time of Adam to the time of Moses,
    5:17 the trespass of the one man, **death** reigned through that one man,
    5:21 so that, just as sin reigned in **death**, so also grace might reign
    6: 3 who were baptized into Christ Jesus were baptized into his **death**?
    6: 4 therefore buried with him through baptism into **death** in order that,
    6: 5 If we have been united with him like this *in* his **death**, we will
    6: 9 he cannot die again; **death** no longer has mastery over him.
    6:16 you are slaves to sin, which leads to **death**, or to obedience,
    6:21 the things you are now ashamed of? Those things result *in* **death**!
    6:23 For the wages of sin is **death**, but the gift of God is eternal life in
    7: 5 law were at work in our bodies, so that we bore fruit *for* **death**.
    7:10 that was intended to bring life actually brought **death**.
    7:13 Did that which is good, then, become **death** to me? By no means!
    7:13 recognized as sin, it produced **death** in me through what was good,
    7:24 wretched man I am! Who will rescue me from this body *of* **death**?
    8: 2 law of the Spirit of life set me free from the law *of* sin and **death**.
    8: 6 The mind of sinful man is **death**, but the mind controlled by the
    8:38 For I am convinced that neither **death** nor life, neither angels nor
1Co 3:22 whether Paul or Apollos or Cephas or the world or life or **death**
    11:26 and drink this cup, you proclaim the Lord's **death** until he comes.
    15:21 For since **death** came through a man, the resurrection of the dead
    15:26 The last enemy to be destroyed is **death**.
    15:54 written will come true: "**Death** has been swallowed up in victory."
    15:55 "Where, O **death**, is your victory? Where, O death, is your sting?"
    15:55 "Where, O death, is your victory? Where, O **death**, is your sting?"
    15:56 The sting of **death** is sin,
2Co 1: 9 Indeed, in our hearts we felt the sentence *of* **death**. But this
    1:10 He has delivered us from such a **deadly peril**, and he will deliver
    2:16 To the one we are the smell of **death**, the other, the fragrance of
    2:16 are the smell of death; [RPG] to the other, the fragrance of life.
    3: 7 Now if the ministry that *brought* **death**, which was engraved in
    4:11 For we who are alive are always being given over to **death** for
    4:12 So then, **death** is at work in us, but life is at work in you.
    7:10 to salvation and leaves no regret, but worldly sorrow brings **death**.
    11:23 more severely, and been **exposed to death** again and again.
Php 1:20 Christ will be exalted in my body, whether by life or by **death**.
    2: 8 as a man, he humbled himself and became obedient to **death**—
    2: 8 and became obedient to death—even **death** on a cross!
    2:27 Indeed he was ill, and almost **died**. But God had mercy on him,
    2:30 because he almost **died** for the work of Christ, risking his life to
    3:10 of sharing in his sufferings, becoming like him *in* his **death**,
Col 1:22 physical body through **death** to present you holy in his sight,
2Ti 1:10 who has destroyed **death** and has brought life and immortality to
Heb 2: 9 now crowned with glory and honor because he suffered **death**,
    2: 9 so that by the grace of God he might taste **death** for everyone.
    2:14 so that by his **death** he might destroy him who holds the power of
    2:14 by his death he might destroy him who holds the power *of* **death**—
    2:15 those who all their lives were held in slavery by their fear *of* **death**.
    5: 7 loud cries and tears to the one who could save him from **death**,
    7:23 since **death** prevented them from continuing in office;
    9:15 *now that he has* **died** [+*1181*] as a ransom to set them free from
    9:16 of a will, it is necessary to prove the **death** of the one who made it,
    11: 5 was taken from this life, so that *he did* not experience **death**;
Jas 1:15 birth to sin; and sin, when it is full-grown, gives birth to **death**
    5:20 turns a sinner from the error of his way will save him from **death**
1Jn 3:14 We know that we have passed from **death** to life, because we love
    3:14 we love our brothers. Anyone who does not love remains in **death**.
    5:16 If anyone sees his brother commit a sin that does not lead to **death**,
    5:16 will give him life. I refer to those whose sin does not lead to **death**.
    5:16 There is a sin that leads to **death**. I am not saying that he should
    5:17 All wrongdoing is sin, and there is sin that does not lead to **death**.
Rev 1:18 alive for ever and ever! And I hold the keys *of* **death** and Hades.
    2:10 Be faithful, even to the point of **death**, and I will give you the
    2:11 He who overcomes will not be hurt at all by the second **death**.
    2:23 *I will* **strike** her children **dead** [+*650+1877*]. Then all the churches

6: 8 Its rider was named **Death**, and Hades was following close behind
6: 8 by sword, famine and **plague**, and by the wild beasts of the earth.
9: 6 During those days men will seek **death**, but will not find it;
9: 6 but will not find it; they will long to die, but **death** will elude them.
12:11 they did not love their lives so much as to *shrink from* **death**.
13: 3 One of the heads of the beast seemed to have had a **fatal** wound,
13: 3 to have had a fatal wound, but the **fatal** wound had been healed.
13:12 worship the first beast, whose **fatal** wound had been healed.
18: 8 **death**, mourning and famine. She will be consumed by fire,
20: 6 The second **death** has no power over them, but they will be priests
20:13 and **death** and Hades gave up the dead that were in them,
20:14 Then **death** and Hades were thrown into the lake of fire. The lake
20:14 thrown into the lake of fire. The lake of fire is the second **death**.
21: 4 There will be no more **death** or mourning or crying or pain,
21: 8 in the fiery lake of burning sulfur. This is the second **death**."

2506 θανατόω, *thanatoō* [11] [√ 2569]

put to death [8], died [1], face death [1], killed [1]

Mt 10:21 will rebel against their parents and *have* them **put to death**.
  26:59 false evidence against Jesus so that *they could* **put** him **to death**.
  27: 1 the elders of the people came to the decision *to* **put** Jesus **to death**.
Mk 13:12 will rebel against their parents and *have* them **put to death**.
  14:55 for evidence against Jesus so that *they could* **put** him **to death**,
Lk 21:16 relatives and friends, and *they will* **put** some of you **to death**.
Ro 7: 4 my brothers, you also **died** to the law through the body of Christ,
  8:13 but if by the Spirit *you* **put to death** the misdeeds of the body,
  8:36 "For your sake *we* **face death** all day long; we are considered as
2Co 6: 9 as unknown; dying, and yet we live on; beaten, and yet not **killed**;
1Pe 3:18 *He was* **put to death** in the body but made alive by the Spirit,

2507 θάπτω, *thaptō* [11] [→ 5313; cf. 5439]

buried [7], bury [4]

Mt 8:21 disciple said to him, "Lord, first let me go and **bury** my father."
  8:22 Jesus told him, "Follow me, and let the dead **bury** their own dead."
  14:12 John's disciples came and took his body and **buried** it. Then they
Lk 9:59 But the man replied, "Lord, first let me go and **bury** my father."
  9:60 "Let the dead **bury** their own dead, but you go and proclaim the
  16:22 him to Abraham's side. The rich man also died and *was* **buried**.
Ac 2:29 tell you confidently that the patriarch David died and *was* **buried**,
  5: 6 wrapped up his body, and carried him out and **buried** him.
  5: 9 The feet of the men *who* **buried** your husband are at the door,
  5:10 her dead, carried her out and **buried** her beside her husband.
1Co 15: 4 that *he was* **buried**, that he was raised on the third day according

2508 Θάρα, *Thara* [1]

Terah [1]

Lk 3:34 of Isaac, the son of Abraham, the son *of* **Terah**, the son of Nahor,

2509 θαρρέω, *tharreō* [6] [√ 2511]

bold [2], confident [2], have confidence [1], with confidence [1]

2Co 5: 6 Therefore *we are* always **confident** and know that as long as we
  5: 8 *We are* **confident**, I say, and would prefer to be away from the
  7:16 I am glad *I can* **have** complete **confidence** in you.
  10: 1 "timid" when face to face with you, but "**bold**" when away!
  10: 2 I beg you that when I come *I may* not **have to be** as **bold** as I
Heb 13: 6 So we say **with confidence**, "The Lord is my helper; I will not be

2510 θαρσέω, *tharseō* [7] [√ 2511]

take courage [3], take heart [3], cheer up [1]

Mt 9: 2 Jesus saw their faith, he said to the paralytic, "**Take heart**, son;
  9:22 "**Take heart**, daughter," he said, "your faith has healed you."
  14:27 immediately said to them: "**Take courage**! It is I. Don't be afraid."
Mk 6:50 Immediately he spoke to them and said, "**Take courage**! It is I.
  10:49 and said, "Call him." So they called to the blind man, "**Cheer up**!
Jn 16:33 you will have trouble. But **take heart**! I have overcome the world."
Ac 23:11 following night the Lord stood near Paul and said, "**Take courage**!

2511 θάρσος, *tharsos* [1] [→ 2509, 2510]

encouraged [+3284] [1]

Ac 28:15 of these men Paul thanked God and *was* **encouraged** [+3284].

2512 θαῦμα, *thauma* [2] [√ 2513]

astonished [+2513] [1], wonder [1]

2Co 11:14 And no **wonder**, for Satan himself masquerades as an angel of
Rev 17: 6 to Jesus. When I saw her, *I was* greatly **astonished** [+2513].

2513 θαυμάζω, *thaumazō* [43] [→ 1703, 2512, 2514, 2515; cf. 2517]

amazed [12], astonished [8], surprised [5], amazement [4], amazed at [3], astonished [+2512] [1], astonishment [1], flatter [+4725] [1], marveled [+1639] [1], marveled at [1], marveling [1], surprise [1], utterly amazed [+2014] [1], wonder [1], wondering why [1], wondering [1]

Mt 8:10 he was **astonished** and said to those following him, "I tell you the
  8:27 The men *were* **amazed** and asked, "What kind of man is this?
  9:33 The crowd *was* **amazed** and said, "Nothing like this has ever been
  15:31 The people *were* **amazed** when they saw the mute speaking,
  21:20 When the disciples saw this, *they were* **amazed**. "How did the fig
  22:22 When they heard this, *they were* **amazed**. So they left him
  27:14 even to a single charge—to the great **amazement** of the governor.
Mk 5:20 much Jesus had done for him. And all the people *were* **amazed**.
  6: 6 And *he was* **amazed** at their lack of faith. Then Jesus went around
  15: 5 But Jesus still made no reply, and Pilate *was* **amazed**.
  15:44 Pilate *was* **surprised** to hear that he was already dead. Summoning
Lk 1:21 for Zechariah and **wondering why** he stayed so long in the temple.
  1:63 and to everyone's **astonishment** he wrote, "His name is John."
  2:18 and all who heard it *were* **amazed** at what the shepherds said to
  2:33 and mother **marveled** [+1639] at what was said about him.
  4:22 and *were* **amazed** at the gracious words that came from his lips.
  7: 9 When Jesus heard this, *he was* **amazed** at him, and turning to the
  8:25 In fear and **amazement** they asked one another, "Who is this?
  9:43 *While* everyone *was* **marveling** at all that Jesus did, he said to his
  11:14 the man who had been mute spoke, and the crowd *was* **amazed**.
  11:38 that Jesus did not first wash before the meal, *was* **surprised**.
  20:26 there in public. And **astonished** by his answer, they became silent.
  24:12 and he went away, **wondering** to himself what had happened.
  24:41 while they still did not believe it because of joy and **amazement**,
Jn 3: 7 *You should not be* **surprised** at my saying, 'You must be born
  4:27 and *were* **surprised** to find him talking with a woman.
  5:20 to your **amazement** he will show him even greater things than
  5:28 "*Do* not *be* **amazed at** this, for a time is coming when all who are
  7:15 The Jews *were* **amazed** and asked, "How did this man get such
  7:21 Jesus said to them, "I did one miracle, and *you are* all **astonished**.
Ac 2: 7 **Utterly amazed** [+2014], they asked: "Are not all these men who
  3:12 he said to them: "Men of Israel, why *does* this **surprise** *you*?
  4:13 *they were* **astonished** and they took note that these men had been
  7:31 When he saw this, he *was* **amazed at** the sight. As he went over to
  13:41 "'Look, you scoffers, **wonder** and perish, for I am going to do
Gal 1: 6 *I am* **astonished** that you are so quickly deserting the one who
2Th 1:10 and *to be* **marveled at** among all those who have believed.
1Jn 3:13 *Do* not *be* **surprised**, my brothers, if the world hates you.
Jude 1:16 and **flatter** [+4725] others for their own advantage.
Rev 13: 3 The whole world *was* **astonished** and followed the beast.
  17: 6 to Jesus. When I saw her, *I was* greatly **astonished** [+2512].
  17: 7 Then the angel said to me: "Why *are you* **astonished**? I will explain
  17: 8 creation of the world *will be* **astonished** when they see the beast,

2514 θαυμάσιος, *thaumasios* [1] [√ 2513]

wonderful [1]

Mt 21:15 and the teachers of the law saw the **wonderful** *things* he did

2515 θαυμαστός, *thaumastos* [6] [√ 2513]

marvelous [4], remarkable [1], wonderful [1]

Mt 21:42 the Lord has done this, and it is **marvelous** in our eyes'?
Mk 12:11 the Lord has done this, and it is **marvelous** in our eyes'?"

Jn   9:30 The man answered, "Now that is **remarkable**! You don't know
1Pe 2: 9 of him who called you out of darkness into his **wonderful** light.
Rev 15: 1 I saw in heaven another great and **marvelous** sign: seven angels
     15: 3 "Great and **marvelous** are your deeds, Lord God Almighty.

2516 θεά, thea [1] [√ 2536]

goddess [1]

Ac 19:27 but also that the temple *of* the great **goddess** Artemis will be

2517 θεάομαι, theaomai [22] [√ cf. 2513, 2519, 2555]

seen [8], saw [7], see [4], look at [1], looked at [1], visit [1]

Mt   6: 1 to do your 'acts of righteousness' before men, to *be* **seen** by them.
   11: 7 "What did you go out into the desert *to* **see**? A reed swayed by the
   22:11 "But when the king came in *to* **see** the guests, he noticed a man
   23: 5 "Everything they do is done for men *to* **see**: They make their
Mk 16:11 When they heard that Jesus was alive and that she *had* **seen** *him*,
   16:14 and their stubborn refusal to believe those *who had* **seen** him after
Lk   5:27 and **saw** a tax collector by the name of Levi sitting at his tax booth.
    7:24 "What did you go out into the desert *to* **see**? A reed swayed by the
  23:55 followed Joseph and **saw** the tomb and how his body was laid in it.
Jn   1:14 *We have* **seen** his glory, the glory of the One and Only, who came
    1:32 "*I* **saw** the Spirit come down from heaven as a dove and remain on
    1:38 Turning around, Jesus **saw** them following and asked, "What do
    4:35 then the harvest'? I tell you, open your eyes and **look at** the fields!
    6: 5 When Jesus looked up and **saw** a great crowd coming toward him,
  11:45 to visit Mary, and *had* **seen** what Jesus did, put their faith in him.
Ac   1:11 will come back in the same way *you have* **seen** him go into
   21:27 some Jews from the province of Asia **saw** Paul at the temple.
   22: 9 My companions **saw** the light, but they did not understand the
Ro 15:24 I hope *to* **visit** you while passing through and to have you assist me
1Jn 1: 1 our eyes, which *we have* **looked at** and our hands have touched—
    4:12 No one *has* ever **seen** God; but if we love one another, God lives in
    4:14 And we *have* **seen** and testify that the Father has sent his Son to be

2518 θεατρίζω, theatrizō [1] [√ 2519]

publicly exposed [1]

Heb 10:33 Sometimes *you were* **publicly exposed** to insult and persecution;

2519 θέατρον, theatron [3] [→ 2518; cf. 2517]

theater [2], spectacle [1]

Ac 19:29 from Macedonia, and rushed as one man into the **theater**.
   19:31 sent him a message begging him not to venture into the **theater**.
1Co 4: 9 We have been made a **spectacle** to the whole universe, to angels as

2520 θεῖον, theion [7] [→ 2523; cf. 2536 (or) 2604]

sulfur [7]

Lk 17:29 fire and **sulfur** rained down from heaven and destroyed them all.
Rev 9:17 of lions, and out of their mouths came fire, smoke and **sulfur**.
    9:18 plagues of fire, smoke and **sulfur** that came out of their mouths.
  14:10 He will be tormented with burning **sulfur** in the presence of the
  19:20 of them were thrown alive into the fiery lake of burning **sulfur**.
  20:10 was thrown into the lake of burning **sulfur**, where the beast
  21: 8 and all liars—their place will be in the fiery lake *of* burning **sulfur**.

2521 θεῖος, theios [3] [√ 2536]

divine [2], divine being [1]

Ac 17:29 we should not think that the **divine being** is like gold or silver
2Pe 1: 3 His **divine** power has given us everything we need for life
    1: 4 so that through them you may participate in the **divine** nature

2522 θειότης, theiotēs [1] [√ 2536]

divine nature [1]

Ro   1:20 his eternal power and **divine nature**—have been clearly seen,

2523 θειώδης, theiōdēs [1] [√ 2520]

yellow as sulfur [1]

Rev 9:17 Their breastplates were fiery red, dark blue, and **yellow as sulfur**.

2524 Θέκλα, Thekla   Not used in UBS/NIV

2525 θέλημα, thelēma [62] [√ 2527]

θέλημα [τοῦ] θεοῦ, αὐτοῦ, σου (will of God; his/your will)
[32] Mk 3:35; Jn 7:17; 9:31; Ac 22:14; Ro 1:10; 12:2; 15:32; 1Co
1:1; 2Co 1:1; 8:5; Gal 1:4; Eph 1:1,5,9,11; 6:6; Col 1:1,9; 4:12;
1Th 4:3; 5:18; 2Ti 1:1; Heb 10:7,36; 13:21; 1Pe 2:15; 3:17; 4:2,19;
1Jn 2:17; 5:14; Rev 4:11

θέλημα τοῦ κυρίου (will of the Lord) [3] Lk 12:47; 21:14; Eph
5:17

θέλημα τοῦ πατρός (will of the Father) [5] Mt 7:21; 12:50;
21:31; Jn 6:40; Gal 1:4

θέλημα [τῆς] σαρκός (will of the flesh) [2] Jn 1:13; Eph 2:3

will [52], *untranslated* [1], decision [1], desires [1], please [1],
unwilling [+4024] [1], want [1], wanted [1], wants [1], will [+2527]
[1], willing [1]

Mt   6:10 your kingdom come, your **will** be done on earth as it is in heaven.
    7:21 but only he who does the **will** of my Father who is in heaven.
  12:50 For whoever does the **will** of my Father in heaven is my brother
  18:14 In the same way your Father in heaven is not **willing** that any of
  21:31 "Which of the two did what his father **wanted**?" "The first,"
  26:42 this cup to be taken away unless I drink it, may your **will** be done."
Mk 3:35 Whoever does God's **will** is my brother and sister and mother."
Lk 12:47 "That servant who knows his master's **will** and does not get ready
  12:47 or does not do what his master **wants** will be beaten with many
  22:42 take this cup from me; yet not my **will**, but yours be done."
  23:25 the one they asked for, and surrendered Jesus *to* their **will**.
Jn   1:13 nor of human **decision** or a husband's will, but born of God.
    1:13 nor of human decision or a husband's **will**, but born of God.
    4:34 "is to do the **will** of him who sent me and to finish his work.
    5:30 is just, for I seek not to **please** myself but him who sent me.
    5:30 for I seek not to please myself but **[RPG]** him who sent me.
    6:38 For I have come down from heaven not to do my **will** but to do the
    6:38 heaven not to do my will but to do the **will** of him who sent me.
    6:39 And this is the **will** of him who sent me, that I shall lose none of all
    6:40 For my Father's **will** is that everyone who looks to the Son
    7:17 If anyone chooses to do God's **will**, he will find out whether my
    9:31 not listen to sinners. He listens to the godly man who does his **will**.
Ac 13:22 a man after my own heart; he will do everything I **want** him to do.'
  21:14 not be dissuaded, we gave up and said, "The Lord's **will** be done."
  22:14 'The God of our fathers has chosen you to know his **will** and to see
Ro   1:10 and I pray that now at last by God's **will** the way may be opened
    2:18 if you know his will and approve of what is superior because you
  12: 2 Then you will be able to test and approve what God's **will** is—
  15:32 so that by God's **will** I may come to you with joy and together with
1Co 1: 1 Paul, called to be an apostle of Christ Jesus by the **will** of God,
    7:37 who is under no compulsion but has control over his own **will**,
  16:12 He was quite **unwilling** [+4024] to go now, but he will go when he
2Co 1: 1 Paul, an apostle of Christ Jesus by the **will** of God, and Timothy
    8: 5 first to the Lord and then to us in keeping with God's **will**.
Gal 1: 4 the present evil age, according to the **will** of our God and Father,
Eph 1: 1 Paul, an apostle of Christ Jesus by the **will** of God, To the saints in
    1: 5 through Jesus Christ, in accordance with his pleasure and **will**—
    1: 9 And he made known to us the mystery *of* his **will** according to his
    1:11 works out everything in conformity with the purpose *of* his **will**,
    2: 3 of our sinful nature and following its **desires** and thoughts.
    5:17 Therefore do not be foolish, but understand what the Lord's **will** is.
    6: 6 but like slaves of Christ, doing the **will** of God from your heart.
Col 1: 1 Paul, an apostle of Christ Jesus by the **will** of God, and Timothy
    1: 9 and asking God to fill you with the knowledge *of* his **will** through
    4:12 that you may stand firm in all the **will** of God, mature and fully
1Th 4: 3 It is God's **will** that you should be sanctified: that you should avoid
    5:18 in all circumstances, for this is God's **will** for you in Christ Jesus.
2Ti 1: 1 Paul, an apostle of Christ Jesus by the **will** of God, according to the
    2:26 the trap of the devil, who has taken them captive to do his **will**.
Heb 10: 7 about me in the scroll—I have come to do your **will**, O God.' "
   10: 9 Then he said, "Here I am, I have come to do your **will**." He sets

10:10 And by that **will**, we have been made holy through the sacrifice of
10:36 You need to persevere so that when you have done the **will** of God,
13:21 equip you with everything good for doing his **will**, and may he
1Pe 2:15 For it is God's **will** that by doing good you should silence the
3:17 It is better, if *it is* God's **will** [+*2527*], to suffer for doing good than
4: 2 earthly life for evil human desires, but rather *for* the **will** of God.
4:19 those who suffer according to God's **will** should commit
2Pe 1:21 For prophecy never had its origin *in* the **will** of man, but men
1Jn 2:17 pass away, but the man who does the **will** of God lives forever.
5:14 that if we ask anything according to his **will**, he hears us.
Rev 4:11 all things, and by your **will** they were created and have their being."

2526 θέλησις, *thelēsis* [1] [√ *2527*]

will [1]

Heb 2: 4 and gifts of the Holy Spirit distributed according to his **will**.

2527 θέλω, *thelō* [208 / 207] [→ *1615, 2525, 2526*]

want [74], wants [19], wanted [17], willing [15], desire [8], like [7],
will [7], would [7], refused [+*4024*] [6], wish [6], wanting [3],
chosen [2], longed [2], mean [+*1639*] [2], trying [2], wished [2],
wishes [2], choose [1], chooses [1], choosing [1], chose [1],
decided [1], deliberately [1], delights [1], determined [1], in order
to [1], pleased [1], pleases [1], prefer [1], purposely [1], refuse
[+*4024*] [1], refusing [+*4024*] [1], request [1], tries [1], unwilling
[+*4024*] [1], want to [1], wants to [1], was [1], will [+*2525*] [1],
willingness [1], wish that [1], wishing [1], would rather [1]

Mt 1:19 a righteous man and *did* not **want** to expose her to public disgrace,
2:18 weeping for her children and **refusing** [+*4024*] to be comforted,
5:40 And if someone **wants** to sue you and take your tunic, let him have
5:42 and do not turn away from the one *who* **wants** to borrow from you.
7:12 in everything, do to others what *you* **would** have them do to you,
8: 2 and knelt before him and said, "Lord, if *you* are **willing**,
8: 3 his hand and touched the man. "*I am* **willing**," he said. "Be clean!"
9:13 and learn what this means: '*I* **desire** mercy, not sacrifice.'
11:14 And if *you* are **willing** to accept it, he is the Elijah who was to
12: 7 had known what these words mean, '*I* **desire** mercy, not sacrifice,'
12:38 said to him, "Teacher, *we* **want** to see a miraculous sign from you."
13:28 "The servants asked him, '*Do you* **want** us to go and pull them up?'
14: 5 Herod **wanted** to kill John, but he was afraid of the people,
15:28 "Woman, you have great faith! Your **request** is granted."
15:32 *I do* not **want** to send them away hungry, or they may collapse on
16:24 "If anyone **would** come after me, he must deny himself and take up
16:25 For whoever **wants** to save his life will lose it, but whoever loses
17: 4 If *you* **wish**, I will put up three shelters—one for you, one for
17:12 not recognize him, but have done to him everything *they* **wished**.
18:23 the kingdom of heaven is like a king who **wanted** to settle
18:30 "But he **refused** [+*4024*]. Instead, he went off and had the man
19:17 who is good. If *you* **want** to enter life, obey the commandments."
19:21 Jesus answered, "If *you* **want** to be perfect, go, sell your
20:14 *I* **want** to give the man who was hired last the same as I gave you.
20:15 Don't I have the right to do what *I* **want** with my own money?
20:21 "What is it *you* **want**?" he asked. She said, "Grant that one of these
20:26 whoever **wants** to become great among you must be your servant,
20:27 and whoever **wants** to be first must be your slave—
20:32 and called them. "What *do you* **want** me to do for you?" he asked.
21:29 " '*I* **will** not,' he answered,
22: 3 banquet to tell them to come, but *they* **refused** [+*4024*] to come.
23: 4 but they themselves *are* not **willing** to lift a finger to move them.
23:37 how often *I* have **longed** to gather your children together,
23:37 hen gathers her chicks under her wings, but *you* were not **willing**.
26:15 "What *are you* **willing** to give me if I hand him over to you?"
26:17 "Where *do you* **want** us to make preparations for you to eat the
26:39 may this cup be taken from me. Yet not as *I* **will**, but as you will."
27:15 custom at the Feast to release a prisoner **chosen** by the crowd.
27:17 Pilate asked them, "Which one *do you* **want** me to release to you:
27:21 "Which of the two *do you* **want** me to release to you?" asked the
27:34 mixed with gall; but after tasting it, *he* **refused** [+*4024*] to drink it.
27:43 Let God rescue him now if *he* **wants** him, for he said, 'I am the
Mk 1:40 him on his knees, "If *you* are **willing**, you can make me clean."
1:41 his hand and touched the man. "*I am* **willing**," he said. "Be clean!"
3:13 went up on a mountainside and called to him those he **wanted**,
6:19 So Herodias nursed a grudge against John and **wanted** to kill him.

6:22 to the girl, "Ask me for anything *you* **want**, and I'll give it to you."
6:25 "*I* **want** you to give me right now the head of John the Baptist on a
6:26 of his oaths and his dinner guests, *he did* not **want** to refuse her.
6:48 out to them, walking on the lake. *He* was about to pass by them,
7:24 *He* entered a house and *did* not **want** anyone to know it; yet he
8:34 "If anyone **would** come after me, he must deny himself and take up
8:35 For whoever **wants** to save his life will lose it, but whoever loses
9:13 has come, and they have done to him everything *they* **wished**,
9:30 Jesus *did* not **want** anyone to know where they were,
9:35 Jesus called the Twelve and said, "If anyone **wants** to be first,
10:35 "Teacher," they said, "*we* **want** you to do for us whatever we ask."
10:36 "What *do you* **want** me to do for you?" he asked.
10:43 whoever **wants** to become great among you must be your servant,
10:44 and whoever **wants** to be first must be slave of all.
10:51 "What *do you* **want** me to do for you?" Jesus asked him. The blind
12:38 *They* **like** to walk around in flowing robes and be greeted in the
14: 7 always have with you, and you can help them any time *you* **want**.
14:12 "Where *do you* **want** us to go and make preparations for you to eat
14:36 Take this cup from me. Yet not what *I* **will**, but what you will."
15: 9 "*Do you* **want** me to release to you the king of the Jews?"
15:12 "What [UBS+ *do you* **want** *that*] shall I do, then, with the one you
Lk 1:62 to his father, to find out what *he* would **like** to name the child.
4: 6 for it has been given to me, and I can give it to anyone *I* **want to**.
5:12 his face to the ground and begged him, "Lord, if *you* are **willing**,
5:13 his hand and touched the man. "*I am* **willing**," he said. "Be clean!"
5:39 And no one after drinking old wine **wants** the new, for he says,
6:31 Do to others as *you* **would** have them do to you.
8:20 and brothers are standing outside, **wanting** to see you."
9:23 "If anyone **would** come after me, he must deny himself and take up
9:24 For whoever **wants** to save his life will lose it, but whoever loses
9:54 *do you* **want** us to call fire down from heaven to destroy them?"
10:24 and kings **wanted** to see what you see but did not see it,
10:29 But he **wanted** to justify himself, so he asked Jesus, "And who is
12:49 to bring fire on the earth, and how *I* **wish** it were already kindled!"
13:31 "Leave this place and go somewhere else. Herod **wants** to kill you."
13:34 how often *I* have **longed** to gather your children together,
13:34 hen gathers her chicks under her wings, but *you* were not **willing**!
14:28 "Suppose one of you **wants** to build a tower. Will he not first sit
15:28 "The older brother became angry and **refused** [+*4024*] to go in.
16:26 been fixed, so that those *who* **want** to go from here to you cannot,
18: 4 "For some time *he* **refused** [+*4024*]. But finally he said to himself,
18:13 *He* **would** not even look up to heaven, but beat his breast and said,
18:41 "What *do you* **want** me to do for you?" "Lord, I want to see,"
19:14 after him to say, '*We* don't **want** this man to be our king.'
19:27 But those enemies of mine who *did* not **want** me to be king over
20:46 They **like** to walk around in flowing robes and love to be greeted in
22: 9 "Where *do you* **want** us to prepare for it?" they asked.
23: 8 because for a long time he had been **wanting** to see him.
23:20 **Wanting** to release Jesus, Pilate appealed to them again.
Jn 1:43 The next day Jesus **decided** to leave for Galilee. Finding Philip,
3: 8 The wind blows wherever *it* **pleases**. You hear its sound, but you
5: 6 for a long time, he asked him, "*Do you* **want** to get well?"
5:21 even so the Son gives life to whom *he is* **pleased** to give it.
5:35 and gave light, and you **chose** for a time to enjoy his light.
5:40 yet *you* **refuse** [+*4024*] to come to me to have life.
6:11 and distributed to those who were seated as much as *they* **wanted**.
6:21 Then *they* were **willing** to take him into the boat, and immediately
6:67 "You *do* not **want** to leave too, do you?" Jesus asked the Twelve.
7: 1 **purposely** staying away from Judea because the Jews there were
7:17 If anyone **chooses** to do God's will, he will find out whether my
7:44 Some **wanted** to seize him, but no one laid a hand on him.
8:44 the devil, and *you* **want** to carry out your father's desire.
9:27 and you did not listen. Why *do you* **want** to hear it again?
9:27 want to hear it again? *Do you* **want** to become his disciples, too?"
12:21 with a request. "Sir," they said, "*we would* **like** to see Jesus."
15: 7 remain in you, ask whatever *you* **wish**, and it will be given you.
16:19 Jesus saw that *they* **wanted** to ask him about this, so he said to
17:24 *I* **want** those you have given me to be with me where I am,
21:18 were younger you dressed yourself and went where *you* **wanted**;
21:18 else will dress you and lead you where *you do* not **want** to go."
21:22 Jesus answered, "If *I* **want** him to remain alive until I return,
21:23 he only said, "If *I* **want** him to remain alive until I return, what is
Ac 2:12 they asked one another, "What *does* this **mean** [+*1639*]?"
7:28 *Do* you **want** to kill me as you killed the Egyptian yesterday?'
7:39 "But our fathers **refused** [+*4024*] to obey him. Instead, they
10:10 He became hungry and **wanted** something to eat, and while the

14:13 *because he* and the crowd **wanted** to offer sacrifices to them.
16: 3 Paul **wanted** *to* take him along on the journey, so he circumcised
17:18 Some of them asked, "What *is* this babbler **trying** to say?" Others
17:20 ideas to our ears, and we want to know what they **mean** [+*1639*]."
18:21 But as he left, he promised, "I will come back *if it is* God's **will**."
19:33 He motioned for silence **in order to** make a defense before the
24:27 but *because* Felix **wanted** to grant a favor to the Jews, he left Paul
25: 9 Festus, **wishing** to do the Jews a favor, said to Paul, "Are you
25: 9 "*Are you* **willing** to go up to Jerusalem and stand trial before me
26: 5 have known me for a long time and can testify, if *they are* **willing**,
Ro   1:13 *I do not* **want** you to be unaware, brothers, that I planned many
    7:15 I do not understand what I do. For what *I* **want** to do I do not do,
    7:16 And if I do what *I do* not **want** to do, I agree that the law is good.
    7:18 For I have the **desire** to do what is good, but I cannot carry it out.
    7:19 For what I do is not the good *I* **want** to do; no, the evil I do not
    7:19 I want to do; no, the evil *I do* not **want** to do—this I keep on doing.
    7:20 Now if I do what *I do* not **want** to do, it is no longer I who do it,
    7:21 law at work: *When* I **want** to do good, evil is right there with me.
    9:16 It does not, therefore, *depend on* man's **desire** or effort, but on
    9:18 Therefore God has mercy on whom *he* **wants** to have mercy,
    9:18 he wants to have mercy, and he hardens whom *he* **wants to** harden.
    9:22 if God, **choosing** to show his wrath and make his power known,
   11:25 *I do* not **want** you to be ignorant of this mystery, brothers,
   13: 3 *Do you* **want** to be free from fear of the one in authority?
   16:19 but *I* **want** you to be wise about what is good, and innocent about
1Co 4:19 if the Lord *is* **willing**, and then I will find out not only how these
    4:21 What *do you* **prefer**? Shall I come to you with a whip, or in love
    7: 7 *I* **wish** that all men were as I am. But each man has his own gift
    7:32 *I would* **like** you to be free from concern. An unmarried man is
    7:36 and he feels he ought to marry, he should do as *he* **wants**.
    7:39 But if her husband dies, she is free to marry anyone she **wishes**,
   10: 1 For *I do* not **want** you to be ignorant of the fact, brothers,
   10:20 not to God, and *I do* not **want** you to be participants with demons.
   10:27 If some unbeliever invites you to a meal and *you* **want** to go,
   11: 3 Now *I* **want** you to realize that the head of every man is Christ,
   12: 1 about spiritual gifts, brothers, *I do* not **want** you to be ignorant.
   12:18 parts in the body, every one of them, just as *he* **wanted** them to be.
   14: 5 *I would* **like** every one of you to speak in tongues, but I would
   14:19 But in the church I **would rather** speak five intelligible words to
   14:35 If *they* **want** to inquire about something, they should ask their own
   15:38 But God gives it a body as *he has* **determined**, and to each kind of
   16: 7 *I do* not **want** to see you now and make only a passing visit;
2Co 1: 8 *We do* not **want** you to be uninformed, brothers,
    5: 4 because *we do* not **wish** to be unclothed but to be clothed with our
    8:10 were the first not only to give but also *to have* the **desire** to do so.
    8:11 so that your eager **willingness** to do it may be matched by your
   11:12 who **want** an opportunity to be considered equal with us in the
   12: 6 Even if *I should* **choose** to boast, I would not be a fool, because I
   12:20 For I am afraid that when I come I may not find you as *I* **want** you
   12:20 I want you to be, and you may not find me as *you* **want** me to be.
Gal   1: 7 you into confusion and *are* **trying** to pervert the gospel of Christ.
    3: 2 *I would* **like** to learn just one thing from you: Did you receive the
    4: 9 *Do you* **wish** to be enslaved by them all over again?
    4:17 What *they* **want** is to alienate you ⌞from us⌟, so that you may be
    4:20 how *I* **wish** I could be with you now and change my tone,
    4:21 Tell me, you *who* **want** to be under the law, are you not aware of
    5:17 in conflict with each other, so that you do not do what *you* **want**.
    6:12 Those *who* **want** to make a good impression outwardly are trying
    6:13 yet *they* **want** you to be circumcised that they may boast about
Php 2:13 for it is God who works in you *to* **will** and to act according to his
Col   1:27 To them God has **chosen** to make known among the Gentiles the
    2: 1 *I* **want** you to know how much I am struggling for you and for
    2:18 Do not let anyone *who* **delights** in false humility and the worship
1Th 2:18 For *we* **wanted** to come to you—certainly I, Paul, did, again
    4:13 *we do* not **want** you to be ignorant about those who fall asleep,
2Th 3:10 we gave you this rule: "If a man **will** not work, he shall not eat."
1Ti   1: 7 *They* **want** to be teachers of the law, but they do not know what
    2: 4 who **wants** all men to be saved and to come to a knowledge of the
    5:11 desires overcome their dedication to Christ, *they* **want** to marry.
2Ti   3:12 everyone who **wants** to live a godly life in Christ Jesus will be
Phm 1:14 But *I did* not **want** to do anything without your consent, so that
Heb 10: 5 "Sacrifice and offering *you did* not **desire**, but a body you prepared
   10: 8 and offerings, burnt offerings and sin offerings *you did* not **desire**,
   12:17 Afterward, as you know, *when* he **wanted** to inherit this blessing,
   13:18 have a clear conscience and **desire** to live honorably in every way.
Jas   2:20 *do you* **want** evidence that faith without deeds is useless?

    4:15 to say, "If it is the Lord's **will**, we will live and do this or that."
1Pe 3:10 "Whoever **would** love life and see good days must keep his tongue
    3:17 It is better, if *it is* God's **will** [+*2525*], to suffer for doing good than
2Pe 3: 5 But they **deliberately** forget that long ago by God's word the
3Jn   1:13 much to write you, but *I do* not **want** to do so with pen and ink.
Rev 2:21 her time to repent of her immorality, but *she is* **unwilling** [+*4024*].
   11: 5 If anyone **tries** to harm them, fire comes from their mouths
   11: 5 This is how anyone who **wants** to harm them must die.
   11: 6 to strike the earth with every kind of plague as often as *they* **want**.
   22:17 and whoever **wishes**, let him take the free gift of the water of life.

2528 θεμέλιον, *themelion* [1] [√ *2529*]

foundations [1]

Ac 16:26 Suddenly there was such a violent earthquake that the **foundations**

2529 θεμέλιος, *themelios* [15] [→ *2528, 2530; cf. 5502*]

foundation [12], foundations [3]

Lk   6:48 a house, who dug down deep and laid the **foundation** on rock.
    6:49 like a man who built a house on the ground without a **foundation**.
   14:29 For if he lays the **foundation** and is not able to finish it,
Ro 15:20 so that I would not be building on someone else's **foundation**.
1Co 3:10 grace God has given me, I laid a **foundation** as an expert builder,
    3:11 For no one can lay any **foundation** other than the one already laid,
    3:12 If any man builds on this **foundation** using gold, silver,
Eph 2:20 built on the **foundation** of the apostles and prophets, with Christ
1Ti   6:19 treasure for themselves as a firm **foundation** for the coming age,
2Ti   2:19 Nevertheless, God's solid **foundation** stands firm, sealed with this
Heb 6: 1 not laying again the **foundation** of repentance from acts that lead
   11:10 For he was looking forward to the city with **foundations**,
Rev 21:14 The wall of the city had twelve **foundations**, and on them were the
   21:19 The **foundations** of the city walls were decorated with every kind
   21:19 The first **foundation** was jasper, the second sapphire, the third

2530 θεμελιόω, *themelioō* [5] [√ *2529*]

established [2], foundation [1], laid the foundations of [1], make steadfast [1]

Mt   7:25 yet it did not fall, because *it had its* **foundation** on the rock.
Eph 3:17 And I pray that you, *being* rooted and **established** in love,
Col   1:23 if you continue in your faith, **established** and firm, not moved
Heb 1:10 "In the beginning, O Lord, you **laid the foundations of** the earth,
1Pe 5:10 *will* himself restore you and **make** you strong, firm and **steadfast**.

2531 θεοδίδακτος, *theodidaktos* [1] [√ *2536 + 1438*]

taught by God [1]

1Th 4: 9 for you yourselves have been **taught by God** to love each other.

2532 θεολόγος, *theologos* Not used in UBS/NIV [√ *2536 + 3306*]

2533 θεομαχέω, *theomacheō* Not used in UBS/NIV [√ *2536 + 3480*]

2534 θεομάχος, *theomachos* [1] [√ *2536 + 3480*]

fighting against God [1]

Ac   5:39 these men; you will only find yourselves **fighting against God**."

2535 θεόπνευστος, *theopneustos* [1] [√ *2536 + 4463*]

God-breathed [1]

2Ti   3:16 All Scripture is **God-breathed** and is useful for teaching, rebuking,

2536 θεός, *theos* [1317 / 1316] [→ *117, 2516, 2521, 2522, 2531, 2532, 2533, 2534, 2535, 2537, 2538, 2539, 2540, 2541, 2554, 5510, 5806; cf. 2520*]

θεοί (plural: gods) [8] Jn 10:34,35; Ac 7:40; 14:11; 19:26; 1Co 8:5,5; Gal 4:8

ἀγάπη τοῦ θεοῦ (love of God) [11] Lk 11:42; Jn 5:42; Ro 5:5; 8:39; 2Co 13:14; 2Th 3:5; 1Jn 2:5; 3:17; 4:9; 5:3; Jude 1:21

ἄγγελος θεοῦ (angel of God) [8] Lk 12:8,9; 15:10; Jn 1:51; Ac 10:3; 27:23; Gal 4:14; Heb 1:6

βασιλεία τοῦ θεοῦ (kingdom of God) [64] Mt 6:33; 12:28; 19:24; 21:31,43; Mk 1:15; 4:11,26,30; 9:1,47; 10:14,15,23,24,25; 12:34; 14:25; 15:43; Lk 4:43; 6:20; 7:28; 8:1,10; 9:2,11,27,60,62; 10:9,11; 11:20; 13:18,20,28,29; 14:15; 16:16; 17:20,20,21; 18:16,17,24,25,29; 19:11; 21:31; 22:16,18; 23:51; Jn 3:3,5; Ac 1:3; 8:12; 14:22; 19:8; 28:23,31; Ro 14:17; 1Co 4:20; Col 4:11; 2Th 1:5; Rev 12:10

βουλή τοῦ θεοῦ (will of God) [4] Lk 7:30; Ac 2:23; 13:36; 20:27

δικαιοσύνη θεοῦ (righteousness of God) [10] Ro 1:17; 3:5,21,22; 10:3,3; 2Co 5:21; Php 3:9; Jas 1:20; 2Pe 1:1

δόξα [τοῦ] θεοῦ (glory of God) [22] Jn 11:4,40; 12:43; Ac 7:55; Ro 1:23; 3:7,23; 5:2; 15:7; 1Co 10:31; 11:7; 2Co 4:6,15; Php 1:11; 2:11; 1Ti 1:11; Tit 2:13; 1Pe 4:14; Rev 15:8; 19:1; 21:11,23

δόξα τῷ θεῷ (glory to God) [6] Lk 2:14; 17:18; Jn 9:24; Ac 12:23; Ro 4:20; Rev 11:13

δοῦλος θεοῦ (slave of God) [6] Ac 16:17; Tit 1:1; Jas 1:1; 1Pe 2:16; Rev 7:3; 15:3

δύναμις [τοῦ] θεοῦ (power of God) [18] Mt 22:29; Mk 12:24; Lk 22:69; Ac 8:10; Ro 1:16; 15:19; 1Co 1:18,24; 2:5; 2Co 4:7; 6:7; 13:4,4; Eph 3:7; 2Ti 1:8; 1Pe 1:5; Rev 12:10; 19:1

εἰρήνη ἀπὸ θεοῦ (peace from God) [12] Ro 1:7; 1Co 1:3; 2Co 1:2; Gal 1:3; Eph 1:2; Php 1:2; Col 1:2; 2Th 1:2; 1Ti 1:2; 2Ti 1:2; Tit 1:4; Phm 1:3

ἐκκλησία θεοῦ (church of God) [12] Ac 20:28; 1Co 1:2; 10:32; 11:16,22; 15:9; 2Co 1:1; Gal 1:13; 1Th 2:14; 2Th 1:4; 1Ti 3:5,15

ἐκλεκτοὶ θεοῦ (churches of God) [3] Ro 8:33; Col 3:12; Tit 1:1

ἐντολή [τοῦ] θεοῦ (command of God) [6] Mt 15:3; Mk 7:8,9; 1Co 7:19; Rev 12:17; 14:12

ἐνώπιον [του] θεοῦ (before God) [25] Lk 1:19; 12:6; 16:15; Ac 4:19; 7:46; 10:31,33; Ro 14:22; 1Co 1:29; 2Co 4:2; 7:12; Gal 1:20; 1Ti 2:3; 5:4; 6:13; 1Pe 3:4; Rev 3:2; 8:2,4; 9:13; 11:16; 12:10; 14:10,10; 16:19

τὸ ἔργον τοῦ θεοῦ (the work of God) [4] Jn 6:28,29; 9:3; Ro 14:20

εὐαγγέλιον τοῦ θεοῦ (the Gospel of God) [10] Mk 1:14; Ac 20:24; Ro 1:1; 15:16; 2Co 11:7; 1Th 2:2,8,9; 1Ti 1:11; 1Pe 4:17

ζῶν θεός (Living God) [15] Mt 16:16; 26:63; Ac 14:15; Ro 9:26; 2Co 3:3; 6:16; 1Th 1:9; 1Ti 3:15; 4:10; Heb 3:12; 9:14; 10:31; 12:22; Rev 7:2; 15:7

ἡμέρα θεοῦ (day of God) [3] 2Pe 3:12; Rev 12:10; 16:14

θέλημα [τοῦ] θεοῦ (will of God) [23] Mk 3:35; Ro 1:10; 12:2; 15:32; 1Co 1:1; 2Co 1:1; 8:5; Gal 1:4; Eph 1:1; 6:6; Col 1:1,9; 4:12; 1Th 4:3; 5:18; 2Ti 1:1; Heb 10:7,36; 1Pe 2:15; 3:17; 4:2,19; 1Jn 2:17

θεὸς τῆς εἰρήνης (God of peace) [7] Ro 15:33; 16:20; 1Co 14:33; 2Co 13:11; Php 4:9; 1Th 5:23; Heb 13:20

θεός [καὶ] πατήρ (God [and] Father) [42] Jn 6:27; 8:42; Ro 1:7; 15:6; 1Co 1:3; 8:6; 15:24; 2Co 1:2,3; 11:31; Gal 1:1,3,4; Eph 1:2,3; 4:6; 5:20; 6:23; Php 1:2; 2:11; 4:20; Col 1:2,3; 3:17; 1Th 1:1,3; 3:11,13; 2Th 1:1,2; 2:16; 1Ti 1:2; 2Ti 1:2; Tit 1:4; Phm 1:3; Jas 1:27; 1Pe 1:2,3; 2Pe 1:17; 2Jn 1:3; Jude 1:1; Rev 1:6

θεός σωτήρ [ἡμῶν, μοῦ] (God [my, our] Saviour) [10] Lk 1:47; 1Ti 1:1; 2:3; 4:10; Tit 1:3; 2:10,13; 3:4; 2Pe 1:1; Jude 1:25

θρόνος τοῦ θεοῦ (throne of God) [7] Mt 5:34; 23:22; Heb 1:8; 12:2; Rev 7:15; 22:1,3

κύριος θεός (Lord God) [25] Mt 4:7,10; 22:37; Mk 12:29,30; Lk 1:16,32,68; 4:8,12; 10:27; 20:37; Ac 2:39; 3:22; Rev 1:8; 4:8,11; 11:17; 15:3; 16:7; 18:8; 19:6; 21:22; 22:5,6

λαός θεοῦ (people of God) [6] Ro 9:26; 2Co 6:16; Heb 4:9; 11:25; 1Pe 2:10; Rev 21:3

λόγος θεοῦ (word of God) [42] Mt 15:6; Mk 7:13; Lk 5:1; 8:11,21; 11:28; Jn 10:35; Ac 4:31; 6:2,7; 8:14; 11:1; 12:24; 13:5,7,46; 17:13; 18:11; Ro 9:6; 1Co 14:36; 2Co 2:17; 4:2; Php 1:14; Col 1:25; 1Th 2:13,13; 1Ti 4:5; 2Ti 2:9; Tit 2:5; Heb 4:12; 5:12; 13:7; 1Pe 1:23; 2Pe 3:5; 1Jn 2:14; Rev 1:2,9; 6:9; 17:17; 19:9,13; 20:4

μόνος θεός (only God) [5] Jn 5:44; 17:3; Ro 16:27; 1Ti 1:17; Jude 1:25

μυστήριον τοῦ θεοῦ (mystery of God) [4] 1Co 2:1; 4:1; Col 2:2; Rev 10:7

ναός θεοῦ (holy place [temple] of God) [10] Mt 26:61; 1Co 3:16,17,17; 2Co 6:16,16; 2Th 2:4; Rev 3:12; 11:1,19

οἶκος θεοῦ (house of God) [6] Mt 12:4; Mk 2:26; Lk 6:4; 1Ti 3:15; Heb 10:21; 1Pe 4:17

ὀργή θεοῦ (wrath of God) [9] Jn 3:36; Ro 1:18; 2:5; Eph 5:6; Col 3:6; 1Th 2:16; Rev 14:10; 16:19; 19:15

πνεῦμα θεοῦ (Spirit of God) [19] Mt 3:16; 12:28; Ro 8:9,14; 15:19; 1Co 2:11,14; 3:16; 6:11; 7:40; 12:3; 2Co 3:3; Eph 4:30; Php 3:3; 1Pe 4:14; 1Jn 4:2; Rev 3:1; 4:5; 5:6

ῥῆμα θεοῦ (word of God) [6] Lk 3:2; Jn 3:34; 8:47; Eph 6:17; Heb 6:5; 11:3

σοφία θεοῦ (wisdom of God) [7] Lk 11:49; Ro 11:33; 1Co 1:21,24,30; 2:7; Eph 3:10

τέκνον θεοῦ (child of God) [10] Jn 1:12; 11:52; Ro 8:16,21; 9:8; Php 2:15; 1Jn 3:1,2,10; 5:2

υἱοὶ θεοῦ (sons of God) [7] Mt 5:9; Lk 20:36; Ro 8:14,19; 9:26; Gal 3:26; 4:6

υἱός θεοῦ (Son of God) [45] Mt 4:3,6; 8:29; 14:33; 16:16; 26:63; 27:40,43,54; Mk 1:1; 3:11; 5:7; 15:39; Lk 1:35, 4:3,9,41; 8:28; 22:70; Jn 1:34,49; 3:18; 5:25; 10:36; 11:4,27; 19:7; 20:31; Ac 9:20; Ro 1:4; 2Co 1:19; Gal 2:20; Eph 4:13; Heb 4:14; 6:6; 7:3; 10:29; 1Jn 3:8; 4:15; 5:5,10,12,13,20; Rev 2:18

χάρις θεοῦ (grace of God) [16] Lk 2:40; Ac 11:23; 13:43; 14:26; 1Co 3:10; 15:10,10; 2Co 8:1; 9:14; Gal 2:21; 2Th 1:12; Tit 2:11; Heb 2:9; 12:15; 1Pe 5:12; Jude 1:4

χάρις τῷ θεῷ (grace to God) [9] Lk 1:30; Ro 6:17; 7:25; 1Co 15:57; 2Co 2:14; 8:16; 9:15; Col 3:16; 2Ti 1:3

God [1154], God's [125], gods [8], him[s] [+3836] [7], he[s] [+3836] [5], his[s] [+3836] [4], *untranslated* [2], divine [2], God-fearing [+3836+5828] [2], godly [+2848] [2], God-fearing Gentiles [+3836+5828] [1], goddess [1], godly [1], no ordinary [+842+3836] [1], of God [1]

Mt

1:23 and they will call him Immanuel"—which means, "**God** with us."
3: 9 I tell you that out of these stones **God** can raise up children for
3:16 and he saw the Spirit *of* **God** descending like a dove and lighting
4: 3 The tempter came to him and said, "If you are the Son *of* **God**,
4: 4 but on every word that comes from the mouth *of* **God**.' "
4: 6 "If you are the Son *of* **God**," he said, "throw yourself down. For it
4: 7 "It is also written: 'Do not put the Lord your **God** to the test.' "
4:10 it is written: 'Worship the Lord your **God**, and serve him only.' "
5: 8 Blessed are the pure in heart, for they will see **God**.
5: 9 Blessed are the peacemakers, for they will be called sons *of* **God**.
5:34 Do not swear at all: either by heaven, for it is **God's** throne;
6:24 and despise the other. You cannot serve both **God** and Money.
6:30 If that is how **God** clothes the grass of the field, which is here
6:33 But seek first his[s] [+3836] kingdom and his righteousness,
8:29 "What do you want with us, Son *of* **God**?" they shouted. "Have you
9: 8 and they praised **God**, who had given such authority to men.
12: 4 He entered the house *of* **God**, and he and his companions ate the
12:28 But if I drive out demons by the Spirit *of* **God**, then the kingdom of
12:28 by the Spirit of God, then the kingdom *of* **God** has come upon you.
14:33 in the boat worshiped him, saying, "Truly you are the Son *of* **God**."
15: 3 "And why do you break the command *of* **God** for the sake of your
15: 4 For **God** said, 'Honor your father and mother' and 'Anyone who

15: 6 Thus you nullify the word *of* God for the sake of your tradition.
15:31 and the blind seeing. And they praised the **God** of Israel.
16:16 Peter answered, "You are the Christ, the Son *of* the living **God.**"
16:23 you do not have in mind the things *of* **God,** but the things of men."
19: 6 Therefore what **God** has joined together, let man not separate."
19:24 eye of a needle than for a rich man to enter the kingdom *of* **God.**"
19:26 "With man this is impossible, but with **God** all things are possible."
21:31 and the prostitutes are entering the kingdom *of* **God** ahead of you.
21:43 "Therefore I tell you that the kingdom *of* **God** will be taken away
22:16 and that you teach the way *of* **God** in accordance with the truth.
22:21 "Give to Caesar what is Caesar's, and *to* **God** what is God's."
22:21 "Give to Caesar what is Caesar's, and to God what is **God's.**"
22:29 because you do not know the Scriptures or the power *of* **God.**
22:31 resurrection of the dead—have you not read what **God** said to you,
22:32 'I am the **God** of Abraham, the God of Isaac, and the God of
22:32 am the God of Abraham, the **God** of Isaac, and the God of Jacob'?
22:32 am the God of Abraham, the God of Isaac, and the **God** of Jacob'?
22:32 the God of Jacob'? He is not the **God** of the dead but of the living."
22:37 " 'Love the Lord your **God** with all your heart and with all your
23:22 And he who swears by heaven swears by **God's** throne and by the
26:61 'I am able to destroy the temple *of* **God** and rebuild it in three
26:63 high priest said to him, "I charge you under oath by the living **God:**
26:63 by the living God: Tell us if you are the Christ, the Son *of* **God.**"
27:40 Come down from the cross, if you are the Son *of* **God!**"
27:43 He trusts in **God.** Let God rescue him now if he wants him,
27:43 him now if he wants him, for he said, 'I am the Son *of* **God.**' "
27:46 which means, "My **God,** my God, why have you forsaken me?"
27:46 which means, "My God, my **God,** why have you forsaken me?"
27:54 they were terrified, and exclaimed, "Surely he was the Son *of* **God!**"
Mk 1: 1 The beginning of the gospel about Jesus Christ, the Son *of* **God.**
1:14 Jesus went into Galilee, proclaiming the good news *of* **God.**
1:15 "The kingdom *of* **God** is near. Repent and believe the good news!"
1:24 come to destroy us? I know who you are—the Holy One *of* **God!**"
2: 7 like that? He's blaspheming! Who can forgive sins but **God** alone?"
2:12 This amazed everyone and they praised **God,** saying, "We have
2:26 he entered the house *of* **God** and ate the consecrated bread,
3:11 they fell down before him and cried out, "You are the Son *of* **God.**"
3:35 Whoever does **God's** will is my brother and sister and mother."
4:11 "The secret of the kingdom *of* **God** has been given to you.
4:26 He also said, "This is what the kingdom *of* **God** is like. A man
4:30 Again he said, "What shall we say the kingdom *of* **God** is like,
5: 7 "What do you want with me, Jesus, Son *of* the Most High **God?**
5: 7 of the Most High God? Swear *to* **God** that you won't torture me!"
7: 8 You have let go of the commands *of* **God** and are holding on to the
7: 9 "You have a fine way of setting aside the commands *of* **God** in
7:13 Thus you nullify the word *of* **God** by your tradition that you have
8:33 do not have in mind the things *of* **God,** but the things of men."
9: 1 taste death before they see the kingdom *of* **God** come with power."
9:47 It is better for you to enter the kingdom *of* **God** with one eye than
10: 9 Therefore what **God** has joined together, let man not separate."
10:14 not hinder them, for the kingdom *of* **God** belongs to such as these.
10:15 anyone who will not receive the kingdom *of* **God** like a little child
10:18 me good?" Jesus answered. "No one is good—except **God** alone.
10:23 "How hard it is for the rich to enter the kingdom *of* **God!**"
10:24 said again, "Children, how hard it is to enter the kingdom *of* **God!**
10:25 eye of a needle than for a rich man to enter the kingdom *of* **God.**"
10:27 at them and said, "With man this is impossible, but not with **God;**
10:27 is impossible, but not with God; all things are possible with **God.**"
11:22 "Have faith *in* **God,**" Jesus answered.
12:14 but you teach the way *of* **God** in accordance with the truth.
12:17 "Give to Caesar what is Caesar's and *to* **God** what is God's."
12:17 "Give to Caesar what is Caesar's and to God what is **God's.**"
12:24 because you do not know the Scriptures or the power *of* **God?**
12:26 in the account of the bush, how **God** said to him, 'I am the God of
12:26 how God said to him, 'I am the **God** of Abraham, the God of Isaac,
12:26 am the God of Abraham, the **God** of Isaac, and the God of Jacob'?
12:26 am the God of Abraham, the God of Isaac, and the **God** of Jacob'?
12:27 He is not the **God** of the dead, but of the living. You are badly
12:29 "is this: 'Hear, O Israel, the Lord our **God,** the Lord is one.
12:30 Love the Lord your **God** with all your heart and with all your soul
12:34 he said to him, "You are not far from the kingdom *of* **God.**"
13:19 from the beginning, when **God** created the world, until now—
14:25 the vine until that day when I drink it anew in the kingdom *of* **God.**"
15:34 which means, "My **God,** my God, why have you forsaken me?"
15:34 which means, "My God, my **God,** why have you forsaken me?"
15:39 saw how he died, he said, "Surely this man was the Son *of* **God!**"

15:43 who was himself waiting for the kingdom *of* **God,** went boldly to
16:19 he was taken up into heaven and he sat at the right hand *of* **God.**
Lk 1: 6 Both of them were upright in the sight *of* **God,** observing all the
1: 8 division was on duty and he was serving as priest before **God,**
1:16 of the people of Israel will he bring back to the Lord their **God.**
1:19 I stand in the presence *of* **God,** and I have been sent to speak to
1:26 **God** sent the angel Gabriel to Nazareth, a town in Galilee,
1:30 to her, "Do not be afraid, Mary, you have found favor with **God.**
1:32 The Lord **God** will give him the throne of his father David,
1:35 So the holy one to be born will be called the Son *of* **God.**
1:37 For nothing is impossible with **God.**"
1:47 and my spirit rejoices in **God** my Savior,
1:64 and his tongue was loosed, and he began to speak, praising **God.**
1:68 the **God** of Israel, because he has come and has redeemed his
1:78 because of the tender mercy *of* our **God,** by which the rising sun
2:13 heavenly host appeared with the angel, praising **God** and saying,
2:14 "Glory *to* **God** in the highest, and on earth peace to men on whom
2:20 and praising **God** for all the things they had heard and seen,
2:28 Simeon took him in his arms and praised **God,** saying:
2:38 she gave thanks *to* **God** and spoke about the child to all who were
2:40 he was filled with wisdom, and the grace *of* **God** was upon him.
2:52 Jesus grew in wisdom and stature, and in favor with **God** and men.
3: 2 the word *of* **God** came to John son of Zechariah in the desert.
3: 6 And all mankind will see **God's** salvation.' "
3: 8 For I tell you that out of these stones **God** can raise up children for
3:38 son of Enosh, the son of Seth, the son of Adam, the son *of* **God.**
4: 3 The devil said to him, "If you are the Son *of* **God,** tell this stone to
4: 8 "It is written: 'Worship the Lord your **God** and serve him only.' "
4: 9 "If you are the Son *of* **God,**" he said, "throw yourself down from
4:12 "It says: 'Do not put the Lord your **God** to the test.' "
4:34 come to destroy us? I know who you are—the Holy One *of* **God!**"
4:41 came out of many people, shouting, "You are the Son *of* **God.**"
4:43 "I must preach the good news of the kingdom *of* **God** to the other
5: 1 the people crowding around him and listening to the word *of* **God,**
5:21 who speaks blasphemy? Who can forgive sins but **God** alone?"
5:25 took what he had been lying on and went home praising **God.**
5:26 Everyone was amazed and gave praise to **God.** They were filled
6: 4 He entered the house *of* **God,** and taking the consecrated bread,
6:12 out to a mountainside to pray, and spent the night praying *to* **God.**
6:20 "Blessed are you who are poor, for yours is the kingdom *of* **God.**
7:16 They were all filled with awe and praised **God.** "A great prophet
7:16 appeared among us," they said. "**God** has come to help his people."
7:28 yet the one who is least in the kingdom *of* **God** is greater than he."
7:29 they heard Jesus' words, acknowledged that **God's** way was right,
7:30 and experts in the law rejected **God's** purpose for themselves,
8: 1 to another, proclaiming the good news of the kingdom *of* **God.**
8:10 "The knowledge of the secrets of the kingdom *of* **God** has been
8:11 "This is the meaning of the parable: The seed is the word *of* **God.**
8:21 "My mother and brothers are those who hear **God's** word and put it
8:28 "What do you want with me, Jesus, Son *of* the Most High **God?**
8:39 "Return home and tell how much **God** has done for you."
9: 2 and he sent them out to preach the kingdom *of* **God** and to heal the
9:11 He welcomed them and spoke to them about the kingdom *of* **God,**
9:20 "Who do you say I am?" Peter answered, "The Christ *of* **God.**"
9:27 here will not taste death before they see the kingdom *of* **God.**"
9:43 And they were all amazed at the greatness *of* **God.** While everyone
9:60 bury their own dead, but you go and proclaim the kingdom *of* **God.**"
9:62 the plow and looks back is fit for service in the kingdom *of* **God.**"
10: 9 who are there and tell them, 'The kingdom *of* **God** is near you.'
10:11 off against you. Yet be sure of this: The kingdom *of* **God** is near.'
10:27 " 'Love the Lord your **God** with all your heart and with all your
11:20 But if I drive out demons by the finger *of* **God,** then the kingdom
11:20 by the finger of God, then the kingdom *of* **God** has come to you.
11:28 "Blessed rather are those who hear the word *of* **God** and obey it."
11:42 kinds of garden herbs, but you neglect justice and the love *of* **God.**
11:49 Because of this, **God** in his wisdom said, 'I will send them
12: 6 sold for two pennies? Yet not one of them is forgotten by **God.**
12: 8 Son of Man will also acknowledge him before the angels *of* **God.**
12: 9 me before men will be disowned before the angels *of* **God.**
12:20 "But God said to him, 'You fool! This very night your life will be
12:21 who stores up things for himself but is not rich toward **God.**"
12:24 or reap, they have no storeroom or barn; yet **God** feeds them.
12:28 If that is how **God** clothes the grass of the field, which is here
13:13 on her, and immediately she straightened up and praised **God.**
13:18 Then Jesus asked, "What is the kingdom *of* **God** like? What shall I
13:20 Again he asked, "What shall I compare the kingdom *of* **God** to?

13:28 Isaac and Jacob and all the prophets in the kingdom *of* **God**,
13:29 and will take their places at the feast in the kingdom *of* **God**.
14:15 is the man who will eat at the feast in the kingdom *of* **God**."
15:10 there is rejoicing in the presence of the angels *of* **God** over one
16:13 and despise the other. You cannot serve both **God** and Money."
16:15 justify yourselves in the eyes of men, but **God** knows your hearts.
16:15 What is highly valued among men is detestable in **God's** sight.
16:16 that time, the good news of the kingdom *of* **God** is being preached,
17:15 he saw he was healed, came back, praising **God** in a loud voice.
17:18 one found to return and give praise *to* **God** except this foreigner?"
17:20 having been asked by the Pharisees when the kingdom *of* **God**
17:20 "The kingdom *of* **God** does not come with your careful observation,
17:21 or 'There it is,' because the kingdom *of* **God** is within you."
18: 2 "In a certain town there was a judge who neither feared **God** nor
18: 4 said to himself, 'Even though I don't fear **God** or care about men,
18: 7 And will not **God** bring about justice for his chosen ones,
18:11 '**God**, I thank you that I am not like other men—robbers, evildoers,
18:13 but beat his breast and said, '**God**, have mercy on me, a sinner.'
18:16 not hinder them, for the kingdom *of* **God** belongs to such as these.
18:17 anyone who will not receive the kingdom *of* **God** like a little child
18:19 me good?" Jesus answered. "No one is good—except **God** alone.
18:24 and said, "How hard it is for the rich to enter the kingdom *of* **God**!
18:25 eye of a needle than for a rich man to enter the kingdom *of* **God**."
18:27 Jesus replied, "What is impossible with men is possible with **God**."
18:29 or parents or children for the sake of the kingdom *of* **God**
18:43 he received his sight and followed Jesus, praising **God**.
18:43 praising God. When all the people saw it, they also praised **God**.
19:11 and the people thought that the kingdom *of* **God** was going to
19:37 the whole crowd of disciples began joyfully to praise **God** in loud
20:21 partiality but teach the way *of* **God** in accordance with the truth.
20:25 "Then give to Caesar what is Caesar's, and *to* **God** what is God's."
20:25 "Then give to Caesar what is Caesar's, and to God what is **God's**."
20:36 They are **God's** children, since they are children of the
20:37 for he calls the Lord 'the **God** of Abraham, and the God of Isaac,
20:37 God of Abraham, and the **God** of Isaac, and the God of Jacob.'
20:37 God of Abraham, and the God of Isaac, and the **God** of Jacob.'
20:38 He is not the **God** of the dead, but of the living, for to him all are
21:31 these things happening, you know that the kingdom *of* **God** is near.
22:16 not eat it again until it finds fulfillment in the kingdom *of* **God**."
22:18 again of the fruit of the vine until the kingdom *of* **God** comes."
22:69 the Son of Man will be seated at the right hand *of* the mighty **God**."
22:70 They all asked, "Are you then the Son *of* **God**?" He replied,
23:35 let him save himself if he is the Christ *of* **God**, the Chosen One."
23:40 "Don't you fear **God**," he said, "since you are under the same
23:47 The centurion, seeing what had happened, praised **God** and said,
23:51 town of Arimathea and he was waiting for the kingdom *of* **God**.
24:19 powerful in word and deed before **God** and all the people.
24:53 And they stayed continually at the temple, praising **God**.
Jn   1: 1 the Word, and the Word was with **God**, and the Word was God.
1: 1 the Word, and the Word was with God, and the Word was **God**.
1: 2 He was with **God** in the beginning.
1: 6 There came a man who was sent from **God**; his name was John.
1:12 in his name, he gave the right to become children *of* **God**—
1:13 nor of human decision or a husband's will, but born of **God**.
1:18 No one has ever seen **God**, but God the One and Only, who is at
1:18 No one has ever seen God, but **God** the One and Only, who is at
1:29 saw Jesus coming toward him and said, "Look, the Lamb *of* **God**,
1:34 I have seen and I testify that this is the Son *of* **God**."
1:36 When he saw Jesus passing by, he said, "Look, the Lamb *of* **God**!"
1:49 Then Nathanael declared, "Rabbi, you are the Son *of* **God**;
1:51 and the angels *of* **God** ascending and descending on the Son of
3: 2 "Rabbi, we know you are a teacher who has come from **God**.
3: 2 the miraculous signs you are doing if **God** were not with him."
3: 3 no one can see the kingdom *of* **God** unless he is born again."
3: 5 no one can enter the kingdom *of* **God** unless he is born of water
3:16 "For **God** so loved the world that he gave his one and only Son,
3:17 For **God** did not send his Son into the world to condemn the world,
3:18 because he has not believed in the name of **God's** one and only
3:21 be seen plainly that what he has done has been done through **God**."
3:33 The man who has accepted it has certified that **God** is truthful.
3:34 For the one whom **God** has sent speaks the words of God,
3:34 For the one whom God has sent speaks the words of **God**,
3:36 rejects the Son will not see life, for **God's** wrath remains on him."
4:10 "If you knew the gift *of* **God** and who it is that asks you for a drink,
4:24 **God** is spirit, and his worshipers must worship in spirit and in
5:18 but he was even calling **God** his own Father, making himself equal

5:18 even calling God his own Father, making himself equal *with* **God**.
5:25 has now come when the dead will hear the voice of the Son *of* **God**
5:42 I know that you do not have the love *of* **God** in your hearts.
5:44 make no effort to obtain the praise that comes from the only **God**?
6:27 give you. On him **God** the Father has placed his seal of approval."
6:28 they asked him, "What must we do to do the works **God** *requires*?"
6:29 Jesus answered, "The work *of* **God** is this: to believe in the one he
6:33 For the bread *of* **God** is he who comes down from heaven
6:45 It is written in the Prophets: 'They will all be taught *by* **God**.'
6:46 No one has seen the Father except the one who is from **God**;
6:69 We believe and know that you are the Holy One *of* **God**."
7:17 he will find out whether my teaching comes from **God** or whether I
8:40 to kill me, a man who has told you the truth that I heard from **God**.
8:41 they protested. "The only Father we have is **God** himself."
8:42 Jesus said to them, "If **God** were your Father, you would love me,
8:42 you would love me, for I came from **God** and now am here.
8:47 He who belongs to **God** hears what God says. The reason you do
8:47 He who belongs to God hears what **God** says. The reason you do
8:47 The reason you do not hear is that you do not belong to **God**."
8:54 My Father, whom you claim as your God, is the one who glorifies
9: 3 so that the work *of* **God** might be displayed in his life.
9:16 Some of the Pharisees said, "This man is not from **God**, for he does
9:24 "Give glory *to* **God**," they said. "We know this man is a sinner."
9:29 We know that **God** spoke to Moses, but as for this fellow,
9:31 We know that **God** does not listen to sinners. He listens to the
9:33 If this man were not from **God**, he could do nothing."
10:33 "but for blasphemy, because you, a mere man, claim to be **God**."
10:34 "Is it not written in your Law, 'I have said you are **gods**'?
10:35 If he called them '**gods**,' to whom the word of God came—
10:35 If he called them 'gods,' to whom the word *of* **God** came—
10:36 do you accuse me of blasphemy because I said, 'I am **God's** Son'?
11: 4 it is for **God's** glory so that God's Son may be glorified through it."
11: 4 it is for God's glory so that **God's** Son may be glorified through it."
11:22 But I know that even now **God** will give you whatever you ask."
11:22 know that even now God will give you whatever you ask." [RPG]
11:27 she told him, "I believe that you are the Christ, the Son *of* **God**,
11:40 I not tell you that if you believed, you would see the glory *of* **God**?"
11:52 not only for that nation but also for the scattered children *of* **God**,
12:43 for they loved praise from men more than praise *from* **God**
13: 3 and that he had come from **God** and was returning to God;
13: 3 and that he had come from God and was returning to **God**;
13:31 "Now is the Son of Man glorified and **God** is glorified in him.
13:32 If **God** is glorified in him, God will glorify the Son in himself,
13:32 If God is glorified in him, **God** will glorify the Son in himself,
14: 1 "Do not let your hearts be troubled. Trust in **God**; trust also in me.
16: 2 anyone who kills you will think he is offering a service *to* **God**.
16:27 you have loved me and have believed that I came from **God**.
16:30 ask you questions. This makes us believe that you came from **God**."
17: 3 the only true **God**, and Jesus Christ, whom you have sent.
19: 7 to that law he must die, because he claimed to be the Son *of* **God**."
20:17 to my Father and your Father, to my **God** and your God.' "
20:17 to my Father and your Father, to my God and your **God**.' "
20:28 Thomas said to him, "My Lord and my **God**!"
20:31 the Son *of* **God**, and that by believing you may have life in his
21:19 to indicate the kind of death by which Peter would glorify **God**.
Ac   1: 3 over a period of forty days and spoke about the kingdom *of* **God**.
2:11 we hear them declaring the wonders *of* **God** in our own tongues!"
2:17 " 'In the last days, **God** says, I will pour out my Spirit on all people.
2:22 Jesus of Nazareth was a man accredited by **God** to you by
2:22 wonders and signs, which **God** did among you through him,
2:23 This man was handed over to you by **God's** set purpose
2:24 But **God** raised him from the dead, freeing him from the agony of
2:30 and knew that God had promised him on oath that he would place
2:32 **God** has raised this Jesus to life, and we are all witnesses of it.
2:33 Exalted to the right hand *of* **God**, he has received from the Father
2:36 **God** has made this Jesus, whom you crucified, both Lord
2:39 for all who are far off—for all whom the Lord our **God** will call."
2:47 praising **God** and enjoying the favor of all the people.
3: 8 into the temple courts, walking and jumping, and praising **God**.
3: 9 When all the people saw him walking and praising **God**,
3:13 The **God** of Abraham, Isaac and Jacob, the God of our fathers,
3:13 The God of Abraham, [UBS+ *the God of*] Isaac and Jacob,
3:13 The God of Abraham, Isaac and [UBS+ *the God of*] Jacob,
3:13 The God of Abraham, Isaac and Jacob, the **God** of our fathers,
3:15 You killed the author of life, but **God** raised him from the dead.
3:18 But this is how **God** fulfilled what he had foretold through all the

3:21 He must remain in heaven until the time comes for **God** to restore
3:22 'The Lord your **God** will raise up for you a prophet like me from
3:25 of the prophets and of the covenant **God** made with your fathers.
3:26 When **God** raised up his servant, he sent him first to you to bless
4:10 whom you crucified but whom **God** raised from the dead,
4:19 "Judge for yourselves whether it is right in **God's** sight to obey you
4:19 whether it is right in God's sight to obey you rather than **God**.
4:21 because all the people were praising **God** for what had happened.
4:24 they heard this, they raised their voices together in prayer to **God**.
4:31 all filled with the Holy Spirit and spoke the word *of* **God** boldly.
5: 4 think of doing such a thing? You have not lied to men but *to* **God**."
5:29 and the other apostles replied: "We must obey **God** rather than men!
5:30 The **God** of our fathers raised Jesus from the dead—whom you had
5:31 **God** exalted him to his own right hand as Prince and Savior that he
5:32 so is the Holy Spirit, whom **God** has given to those who obey him."
5:39 But if it is from **God**, you will not be able to stop these men;
6: 2 neglect the ministry of the word *of* **God** in order to wait on tables.
6: 7 So the word *of* **God** spread. The number of disciples in Jerusalem
6:11 speak words of blasphemy against Moses and against **God**."
7: 2 The **God** of glory appeared to our father Abraham while he was
7: 6 **God** spoke to him in this way: 'Your descendants will be strangers
7: 7 But I will punish the nation they serve as slaves,' **God** said,
7: 9 they sold him as a slave into Egypt. But **God** was with him
7:17 "As the time drew near for **God** to fulfill his promise to Abraham,
7:20 time Moses was born, and he was **no ordinary child** [*+842+3836*].
7:25 Moses thought that his own people would realize that **God** was
7:32 'I am the **God** of your fathers, the God of Abraham, Isaac
7:32 am the God of your fathers, the **God** of Abraham, Isaac and Jacob.'
7:35 He was sent to be their ruler and deliverer *by* **God** himself,
7:37 '**God** will send you a prophet like me from your own people.'
7:40 They told Aaron, 'Make us **gods** who will go before us. As for this
7:42 But **God** turned away and gave them over to the worship of the
7:43 lifted up the shrine of Molech and the star *of* your **god** Rephan,
7:45 they took the land from the nations **God** drove out before them.
7:46 who enjoyed **God's** favor and asked that he might provide a
7:46 might provide a dwelling place *for* the **God** [UBS *3875*] of Jacob.
7:55 of the Holy Spirit, looked up to heaven and saw the glory *of* **God**,
7:55 saw the glory of God, and Jesus standing at the right hand *of* **God**.
7:56 heaven open and the Son of Man standing at the right hand *of* **God**."
8:10 "This man is the **divine** power known as the Great Power."
8:12 Philip as he preached the good news of the kingdom *of* **God**
8:14 in Jerusalem heard that Samaria had accepted the word *of* **God**,
8:20 because you thought you could buy the gift *of* **God** with money!
8:21 share in this ministry, because your heart is not right before **God**.
9:20 he began to preach in the synagogues that Jesus is the Son *of* **God**.
10: 2 and all his family were devout and **God-fearing** [*+3836+5828*];
10: 2 he gave generously to those in need and prayed to **God** regularly.
10: 3 He distinctly saw an angel *of* **God**, who came to him and said,
10: 4 gifts to the poor have come up as a memorial offering before **God**.
10:15 time, "Do not call anything impure that **God** has made clean."
10:22 He is a righteous and **God-fearing** [*+3836+5828*] man, who is
10:28 But **God** has shown me that I should not call any man impure
10:31 **God** has heard your prayer and remembered your gifts to the poor.
10:33 Now we are all here in the presence *of* **God** to listen to everything
10:34 "I now realize how true it is that **God** does not show favoritism
10:38 how **God** anointed Jesus of Nazareth with the Holy Spirit
10:38 were under the power of the devil, because **God** was with him.
10:40 but **God** raised him from the dead on the third day and caused him
10:41 all the people, but by witnesses whom **God** had already chosen—
10:42 and to testify that he is the one whom **God** appointed as judge of
10:46 For they heard them speaking in tongues and praising **God**.
11: 1 Judea heard that the Gentiles also had received the word *of* **God**.
11: 9 'Do not call anything impure that **God** has made clean.'
11:17 So if **God** gave them the same gift as he gave us, who believed in
11:17 the Lord Jesus Christ, who was I to think that I could oppose **God**?"
11:18 they had no further objections and praised **God**, saying, "So then,
11:18 "So then, **God** has granted even the Gentiles repentance unto life."
11:23 When he arrived and saw the evidence of the grace *of* **God**,
12: 5 in prison, but the church was earnestly praying to **God** for him.
12:22 They shouted, "This is the voice of a **god**, not of a man."
12:23 Immediately, because Herod did not give praise *to* **God**, an angel
12:24 But the word *of* **God** continued to increase and spread.
13: 5 they proclaimed the word *of* **God** in the Jewish synagogues.
13: 7 for Barnabas and Saul because he wanted to hear the word *of* **God**.
13:16 "Men of Israel and you Gentiles who worship **God**, listen to me!
13:17 The **God** of the people of Israel chose our fathers; he made the

13:21 and he^s [*+3836*] gave them Saul son of Kish, of the tribe of
13:23 "From this man's descendants **God** has brought to Israel the Savior
13:26 of Abraham, and you **God-fearing Gentiles** [*+3836+5828*],
13:30 But **God** raised him from the dead,
13:33 he^s [*+3836*] has fulfilled for us, their children, by raising up Jesus.
13:36 "For when David had served **God's** purpose in his own generation,
13:37 But the one whom **God** raised from the dead did not see decay.
13:43 talked with them and urged them to continue in the grace *of* **God**.
13:46 "We had to speak the word *of* **God** to you first. Since you reject it
14:11 "The **gods** have come down to us in human form!"
14:15 telling you to turn from these worthless things to the living **God**,
14:22 must go through many hardships to enter the kingdom *of* **God**,"
14:26 where they had been committed to the grace *of* **God** for the work
14:27 church together and reported all that **God** had done through them
15: 4 to whom they reported everything **God** had done through them.
15: 7 you know that some time ago **God** made a choice among you that
15: 8 **God**, who knows the heart, showed that he accepted them by
15:10 why do you try to test **God** by putting on the necks of the disciples
15:12 and wonders **God** had done among the Gentiles through them.
15:14 Simon has described to us how **God** at first showed his concern by
15:19 not make it difficult for the Gentiles who are turning to **God**.
16:10 concluding that **God** had called us to preach the gospel to them.
16:14 cloth from the city of Thyatira, who was a worshiper *of* **God**.
16:17 rest of us, shouting, "These men are servants of the Most High **God**,
16:25 midnight Paul and Silas were praying and singing hymns to **God**,
16:34 he was filled with joy because he had come to believe *in* **God**—
17:13 learned that Paul was preaching the word *of* **God** at Berea,
17:23 found an altar with this inscription: TO AN UNKNOWN **GOD**.
17:24 "The **God** who made the world and everything in it is the Lord of
17:27 God did this so that men would seek him^s [*+3836*] and perhaps
17:29 "Therefore since we are **God's** offspring, we should not think that
17:30 In the past **God** overlooked such ignorance, but now he commands
18: 7 went next door to the house of Titius Justus, a worshiper *of* **God**.
18:11 Paul stayed for a year and a half, teaching them the word *of* **God**.
18:13 "is persuading the people to worship **God** in ways contrary to the
18:21 But as he left, he promised, "I will come back if it is **God's** will."
18:26 their home and explained to him the way *of* **God** more adequately.
19: 8 for three months, arguing persuasively about the kingdom *of* **God**.
19:11 **God** did extraordinary miracles through Paul,
19:26 province of Asia. He says that man-made gods are no **gods** at all.
19:37 they have neither robbed temples nor blasphemed our **goddess**.
20:21 to both Jews and Greeks that they must turn to **God** in repentance
20:24 has given me—the task of testifying to the gospel *of* **God's** grace.
20:27 For I have not hesitated to proclaim to you the whole will *of* **God**.
20:28 Be shepherds of the church *of* **God**, which he bought with his own
20:32 "Now I commit you *to* **God** and to the word of his grace, which can
21:19 and reported in detail what **God** had done among the Gentiles
21:20 When they heard this, they praised **God**. Then they said to Paul:
22: 3 and was just as zealous *for* **God** as any of you are today.
22:14 'The **God** of our fathers has chosen you to know his will and to see
23: 1 I have fulfilled my duty *to* **God** in all good conscience to this day."
23: 3 Then Paul said to him, "**God** will strike you, you whitewashed
23: 4 standing near Paul said, "You dare to insult **God's** high priest?"
24:14 I admit that I worship the **God** of our fathers as a follower of the
24:15 and I have the same hope in **God** as these men, that there will be a
24:16 So I strive always to keep my conscience clear before **God**
26: 6 because of my hope in what **God** has promised our fathers that I
26: 8 Why should any of you consider it incredible that **God** raises the
26:18 them from darkness to light, and from the power of Satan to **God**,
26:20 I preached that they should repent and turn to **God** and prove their
26:22 But I have had **God's** help to this very day,
26:29 I pray **God** that not only you but all who are listening to me today
27:23 Last night an angel *of the* **God** whose I am and whom I serve
27:24 and **God** has graciously given you the lives of all who sail with
27:25 for I have faith *in* **God** that it will happen just as he told me.
27:35 he took some bread and gave thanks *to* **God** in front of them all.
28: 6 happen to him, they changed their minds and said he was a **god**.
28:15 At the sight of these men Paul thanked **God** and was encouraged.
28:23 till evening he explained and declared to them the kingdom *of* **God**
28:28 "Therefore I want you to know that **God's** salvation has been sent
28:31 Boldly and without hindrance he preached the kingdom *of* **God**
Ro 1: 1 called to be an apostle and set apart for the gospel *of* **God**—
1: 4 with power to be the Son *of* **God** by his resurrection from the dead:
1: 7 To all in Rome who are loved *by* **God** and called to be saints:
1: 7 Grace and peace to you from **God** our Father and from the Lord
1: 8 First, I thank my **God** through Jesus Christ for all of you,

1: 9 **God**, whom I serve with my whole heart in preaching the gospel of
1: 10 and I pray that now at last by **God's** will the way may be opened
1: 16 because it is the power *of* **God** for the salvation of everyone who
1: 17 For in the gospel a righteousness *from* **God** is revealed,
1: 18 The wrath *of* **God** is being revealed from heaven against all the
1: 19 since what may be known *about* **God** is plain to them,
1: 19 about God is plain to them, because **God** has made it plain to them.
1: 21 For although they knew **God**, they neither glorified him as God nor
1: 21 they neither glorified him as **God** nor gave thanks to him,
1: 23 and exchanged the glory *of* the immortal **God** for images made to
1: 24 Therefore **God** gave them over in the sinful desires of their hearts
1: 25 They exchanged the truth *of* **God** for a lie, and worshiped
1: 26 Because of this, **God** gave them over to shameful lusts. Even their
1: 28 they did not think it worthwhile to retain the knowledge of **God**,
1: 28 think it worthwhile to retain the knowledge of God, **he**[S] [+*3836*]
1: 32 Although they know **God's** righteous decree that those who do
2: 2 Now we know that **God's** judgment against those who do such
2: 3 do the same things, do you think you will escape **God's** judgment?
2: 4 not realizing that **God's** kindness leads you toward repentance?
2: 5 you are storing up wrath against yourself for the day of **God's**
2: 11 For **God** does not show favoritism.
2: 13 For it is not those who hear the law who are righteous in **God's**
2: 16 This will take place on the day when **God** will judge men's secrets
2: 17 if you rely on the law and brag about your relationship to **God**;
2: 23 brag about the law, do you dishonor **God** by breaking the law?
2: 24 "**God's** name is blasphemed among the Gentiles because of you."
2: 29 written code. Such a man's praise is not from men, but from **God**.
3: 2 First of all, they have been entrusted with the very words *of* **God**.
3: 3 not have faith? Will their lack of faith nullify **God's** faithfulness?
3: 4 Not at all! Let **God** be true, and every man a liar. As it is written:
3: 5 But if our unrighteousness brings out **God's** righteousness more
3: 5 what shall we say? That **God** is unjust in bringing his wrath on us?
3: 6 Certainly not! If that were so, how could **God** judge the world?
3: 7 "If my falsehood enhances **God's** truthfulness and so increases his
3: 11 there is no one who understands, no one who seeks **God**.
3: 18 "There is no fear *of* **God** before their eyes."
3: 19 may be silenced and the whole world held accountable *to* **God**.
3: 21 But now a righteousness *from* **God**, apart from law, has been made
3: 22 This righteousness *from* **God** comes through faith in Jesus Christ
3: 23 for all have sinned and fall short of the glory *of* **God**,
3: 25 **God** presented him as a sacrifice of atonement, through faith in his
3: 25 because in **his**[S] [+*3836*] forbearance he had left the sins committed
3: 29 Is God the **God** of Jews only? Is he not the God of Gentiles too?
3: 30 since there is only one **God**, who will justify the circumcised by
4: 2 by works, he had something to boast about—but not before **God**.
4: 3 "Abraham believed **God**, and it was credited to him as
4: 6 of the man to whom **God** credits righteousness apart from works:
4: 17 the **God** who gives life to the dead and calls things that are not as
4: 20 he did not waver through unbelief regarding the promise *of* **God**,
4: 20 of God, but was strengthened in his faith and gave glory *to* **God**,
5: 1 we have peace with **God** through our Lord Jesus Christ,
5: 2 we now stand. And we rejoice in the hope of the glory *of* **God**.
5: 5 because **God** has poured out his love into our hearts by the Holy
5: 8 But **God** demonstrates his own love for us in this: While we were
5: 10 we were reconciled *to* **him**[S] [+*3836*] through the death of his Son,
5: 11 but we also rejoice in **God** through our Lord Jesus Christ,
5: 15 how much more did **God's** grace and the gift that came by the
6: 10 he died to sin once for all; but the life he lives, he lives *to* **God**.
6: 11 count yourselves dead to sin but alive *to* **God** in Christ Jesus.
6: 13 as instruments of wickedness, but rather offer yourselves *to* **God**,
6: 13 and offer the parts of your body *to* **him**[S] [+*3836*] as instruments of
6: 17 But thanks be *to* **God** that, though you used to be slaves to sin,
6: 22 you have been set free from sin and have become slaves *to* **God**,
6: 23 but the gift *of* **God** is eternal life in Christ Jesus our Lord.
7: 4 was raised from the dead, in order that we might bear fruit *to* **God**.
7: 22 For in my inner being I delight in **God's** law;
7: 25 Thanks be *to* **God**—through Jesus Christ our Lord! So then,
7: 25 So then, I myself in my mind am a slave *to* **God's** law, but in the
8: 3 **God** did by sending his own Son in the likeness of sinful man to be
8: 7 the sinful mind is hostile to **God**. It does not submit to God's law,
8: 7 is hostile to God. It does not submit *to* **God's** law, nor can it do so.
8: 8 Those controlled by the sinful nature cannot please **God**.
8: 9 the sinful nature but by the Spirit, if the Spirit *of* **God** lives in you.
8: 14 because those who are led by the Spirit *of* **God** are sons of God.
8: 14 because those who are led by the Spirit of God are sons *of* **God**.
8: 16 The Spirit himself testifies with our spirit that we are **God's**
8: 17 heirs *of* **God** and co-heirs with Christ, if indeed we share in his
8: 19 The creation waits in eager expectation for the sons *of* **God** to be
8: 21 and brought into the glorious freedom of the children *of* **God**.
8: 27 the Spirit intercedes for the saints in accordance with **God's** will.
8: 28 things God works for the good of those who love **him**[S] [+*3836*],
8: 31 we say in response to this? If **God** is for us, who can be against us?
8: 33 Who will bring any charge against those whom **God** has chosen?
8: 33 against those whom God has chosen? It is **God** who justifies.
8: 34 to life—is at the right hand *of* **God** and is also interceding for us.
8: 39 will be able to separate us from the love *of* **God** that is in Christ
9: 5 the human ancestry of Christ, who is **God** over all, forever praised!
9: 6 It is not as though **God's** word had failed. For not all who are
9: 8 other words, it is not the natural children who are **God's** children,
9: 11 or bad—in order that **God's** purpose in election might stand:
9: 14 What then shall we say? Is **God** unjust? Not at all!
9: 16 therefore, depend on man's desire or effort, but *on* **God's** mercy.
9: 20 But who are you, O man, to talk back *to* **God**? "Shall what is
9: 22 What if **God**, choosing to show his wrath and make his power
9: 26 are not my people,' they will be called 'sons *of* the living **God**.' "
10: 1 and prayer to **God** for the Israelites is that they may be saved.
10: 2 For I can testify about them that they are zealous *for* **God**,
10: 3 Since they did not know the righteousness that *comes from* **God**
10: 3 to establish their own, they did not submit to **God's** righteousness.
10: 9 and believe in your heart that **God** raised him from the dead,
11: 1 I ask then: Did **God** reject his people? By no means! I am an
11: 2 **God** did not reject his people, whom he foreknew. Don't you know
11: 2 the passage about Elijah—how he appealed *to* **God** against Israel:
11: 8 "**God** gave them a spirit of stupor, eyes so that they could not see
11: 21 For if **God** did not spare the natural branches, he will not spare you
11: 22 Consider therefore the kindness and sternness *of* **God**: sternness to
11: 22 sternness to those who fell, but kindness **[RPG]** to you,
11: 23 they will be grafted in, for **God** is able to graft them in again.
11: 29 for **God's** gifts and his call are irrevocable.
11: 30 Just as you who were at one time disobedient *to* **God** have now
11: 32 For **God** has bound all men over to disobedience so that he may
11: 33 the depth of the riches of the wisdom and knowledge *of* **God**!
12: 1 Therefore, I urge you, brothers, in view of **God's** mercy, to offer
12: 1 to offer your bodies as living sacrifices, holy and pleasing *to* **God**—
12: 2 Then you will be able to test and approve what **God's** will is—
12: 3 in accordance with the measure of faith **God** has given you.
13: 1 for there is no authority except that which **God** has established.
13: 1 The authorities that exist have been established by **God**.
13: 2 he who rebels against the authority is rebelling against what **God**
13: 4 For he is **God's** servant to do you good. But if you do wrong,
13: 4 He is **God's** servant, an agent of wrath to bring punishment on the
13: 6 is also why you pay taxes, for the authorities are **God's** servants,
14: 3 must not condemn the man who does, for **God** has accepted him.
14: 6 He who eats meat, eats to the Lord, for he gives thanks *to* **God**;
14: 6 and he who abstains, does so to the Lord and gives thanks *to* **God**.
14: 10 on your brother? For we will all stand before **God's** judgment seat.
14: 11 knee will bow before me; every tongue will confess *to* **God**.' "
14: 12 So then, each of us will give an account of himself *to* **God**.
14: 17 For the kingdom *of* **God** is not a matter of eating and drinking,
14: 18 because anyone who serves Christ in this way is pleasing *to* **God**
14: 20 Do not destroy the work *of* **God** for the sake of food. All food is
14: 22 you believe about these things keep between yourself and **God**.
15: 5 May the **God** who gives endurance and encouragement give you a
15: 6 so that with one heart and mouth you may glorify the **God**
15: 7 just as Christ accepted you, in order to bring praise *to* **God**.
15: 8 Christ has become a servant of the Jews on behalf of **God's** truth,
15: 9 so that the Gentiles may glorify **God** for his mercy, as it is written:
15: 13 May the **God** of hope fill you with all joy and peace as you trust in
15: 15 if to remind you of them again, because of the grace **God** gave me
15: 16 Gentiles with the priestly duty of proclaiming the gospel *of* **God**,
15: 17 Therefore I glory in Christ Jesus in my service to **God**.
15: 19 signs and miracles, through the power of the Spirit [UBS+ *of God*,]
15: 30 of the Spirit, to join me in my struggle by praying to **God** for me.
15: 32 so that by **God's** will I may come to you with joy and together
15: 33 The **God** of peace be with you all. Amen.
16: 20 The **God** of peace will soon crush Satan under your feet. The grace
16: 26 through the prophetic writings by the command *of* the eternal **God**,
16: 27 *to* the only wise **God** be glory forever through Jesus Christ!
1Co 1: 1 Paul, called to be an apostle of Christ Jesus by the will *of* **God**,
1: 2 To the church *of* **God** in Corinth, to those sanctified in Christ Jesus
1: 3 Grace and peace to you from **God** our Father and the Lord Jesus
1: 4 I always thank **God** for you because of his grace given you in

1: 4 for you because of his[s] [+3836] grace given you in Christ Jesus.
1: 9 **God**, who has called you into fellowship with his Son Jesus Christ
1:14 I am thankful [UBS+ *to God*] that I did not baptize any of you
1:18 are perishing, but to us who are being saved it is the power *of God.*
1:20 of this age? Has not **God** made foolish the wisdom of the world?
1:21 For since in the wisdom *of* **God** the world through its wisdom did
1:21 of God the world through its wisdom did not know **him**[s] [+3836],
1:21 **God** was pleased through the foolishness of what was preached to
1:24 and Greeks, Christ the power *of* **God** and the wisdom of God.
1:24 and Greeks, Christ the power of God and the wisdom of **God**,
1:25 For the foolishness *of* **God** is wiser than man's wisdom,
1:25 and the weakness *of* **God** is stronger than man's strength.
1:27 But **God** chose the foolish things of the world to shame the wise;
1:27 **God** chose the weak things of the world to shame the strong.
1:28 **He**[s] [+3836] chose the lowly things of this world and the despised
1:29 so that no one may boast before **him**[s] [+3836].
1:30 are in Christ Jesus, who has become for us wisdom from **God**—
2: 1 superior wisdom as I proclaimed to you the testimony *about* **God.**
2: 5 your faith might not rest on men's wisdom, but on **God's** power.
2: 7 No, we speak *of* **God's** secret wisdom, a wisdom that has been
2: 7 and that **God** destined for our glory before time began.
2: 9 no mind has conceived what **God** has prepared for those who love
2:10 but **God** has revealed it to us by his Spirit. The Spirit searches all
2:10 The Spirit searches all things, even the deep things *of* **God.**
2:11 In the same way no one knows the thoughts *of* **God** except the
2:11 way no one knows the thoughts of God except the Spirit *of* **God.**
2:12 not received the spirit of the world but the Spirit who is from **God,**
2:12 from God, that we may understand what **God** has freely given us.
2:14 Spirit does not accept the things that come from the Spirit *of* **God,**
3: 6 I planted the seed, Apollos watered it, but **God** made it grow.
3: 7 he who waters is anything, but only **God,** who makes things grow.
3: 9 For we are **God's** fellow workers; you are God's field,
3: 9 we are God's fellow workers; you are **God's** field, God's building.
3: 9 we are God's fellow workers; you are God's field, **God's** building.
3:10 By the grace **God** has given me, I laid a foundation as an expert
3:16 Don't you know that you yourselves are **God's** temple and that
3:16 yourselves are God's temple and that **God's** Spirit lives in you?
3:17 If anyone destroys **God's** temple, God will destroy him; for God's
3:17 If anyone destroys God's temple, **God** will destroy him; for God's
3:17 destroy him; for **God's** temple is sacred, and you are that temple.
3:19 For the wisdom of this world is foolishness in **God's** sight.
3:23 and you are of Christ, and Christ is *of* **God.**
4: 1 of Christ and as those entrusted with the secret things *of* **God.**
4: 5 men's hearts. At that time each will receive his praise from **God.**
4: 9 For it seems to me that **God** has put us apostles on display at the
4:20 For the kingdom *of* **God** is not a matter of talk but of power.
5:13 **God** will judge those outside. "Expel the wicked man from among
6: 9 you not know that the wicked will not inherit the kingdom *of* **God?**
6:10 nor slanderers nor swindlers will inherit the kingdom *of* **God.**
6:11 in the name of the Lord Jesus Christ and by the Spirit *of* our **God.**
6:13 and the stomach for food"—but **God** will destroy them both.
6:14 By his power **God** raised the Lord from the dead, and he will raise
6:19 Holy Spirit, who is in you, whom you have received from **God?**
6:20 you were bought at a price. Therefore honor **God** with your body.
7: 7 But each man has his own gift from **God;** one has this gift,
7:15 bound in such circumstances; **God** has called us to live in peace.
7:17 that the Lord assigned to him and to which **God** has called him.
7:19 is nothing. Keeping **God's** commands is what counts.
7:24 Brothers, each man, as responsible to **God,** should remain in the
7:40 if she stays as she is—and I think that I too have the Spirit *of* **God.**
8: 3 But the man who loves **God** is known by God.
8: 4 idol is nothing at all in the world and that there is no **God** but one.
8: 5 For even if there are so-called **gods,** whether in heaven or on earth
8: 5 or on earth (as indeed there are many "**gods**" and many "lords"),
8: 6 yet for us there is but one **God,** the Father, from whom all things
8: 8 But food does not bring us near *to* **God;** we are no worse if we do
9: 9 it is about oxen that **God** is concerned? Is it about oxen that God is
9:21 like one not having the law (though I am not free from **God's** law
10: 5 Nevertheless, **God** was not pleased with most of them; their bodies
10:13 And **God** is faithful; he will not let you be tempted beyond what
10:20 but the sacrifices of pagans are offered to demons, not *to* **God,**
10:31 or drink or whatever you do, do it all for the glory *of* **God.**
10:32 anyone to stumble, whether Jews, Greeks or the church *of* **God**—
11: 3 and the head of the woman is man, and the head of Christ is **God.**
11: 7 not to cover his head, since he is the image and glory *of* **God;**
11:12 so also man is born of woman. But everything comes from **God.**

11:13 Is it proper for a woman to pray *to* **God** with her head uncovered?
11:16 about this, we have no other practice—nor do the churches *of* **God.**
11:22 Or do you despise the church *of* **God** and humiliate those who
12: 3 I tell you that no one who is speaking by the Spirit *of* **God** says,
12: 6 kinds of working, but the same **God** works all of them in all men.
12:18 But in fact **God** has arranged the parts in the body, every one of
12:24 But **God** has combined the members of the body and has given
12:28 And in the church **God** has appointed first of all apostles,
14: 2 anyone who speaks in a tongue does not speak to men but *to* **God.**
14:18 I thank **God** that I speak in tongues more than all of you.
14:25 So he will fall down and worship **God,** exclaiming, "God is really
14:25 and worship God, exclaiming, "**God** is really among you!"
14:28 should keep quiet in the church and speak *to* himself and **God.**
14:33 For **God** is not a God of disorder but of peace. As in all the
14:36 Did the word *of* **God** originate with you? Or are you the only
15: 9 to be called an apostle, because I persecuted the church *of* **God.**
15:10 But by the grace *of* **God** I am what I am, and his grace to me was
15:10 than all of them—yet not I, but the grace *of* **God** that was with me.
15:15 than that, we are then found to be false witnesses *about* **God,**
15:15 for we have testified about **God** that he raised Christ from the
15:24 when he hands over the kingdom *to* **God** the Father after he has
15:28 him who put everything under him, so that **God** may be all in all.
15:34 and stop sinning; for there are some who are ignorant *of* **God**—
15:38 But **God** gives it a body as he has determined, and to each kind of
15:50 brothers, that flesh and blood cannot inherit the kingdom *of* **God,**
15:57 But thanks be *to* **God!** He gives us the victory through our Lord
2Co 1: 1 Paul, an apostle of Christ Jesus by the will *of* **God,** and Timothy
1: 1 and Timothy our brother, To the church *of* **God** in Corinth,
1: 2 Grace and peace to you from **God** our Father and the Lord Jesus
1: 3 Praise be to the **God** and Father of our Lord Jesus Christ,
1: 3 Jesus Christ, the Father of compassion and the **God** of all comfort,
1: 4 trouble with the comfort we ourselves have received from **God.**
1: 9 But this happened that we might not rely on ourselves but on **God,**
1:12 relations with you, in the holiness and sincerity that are *from* **God.**
1:12 so not according to worldly wisdom but according to **God's** grace.
1:18 But as surely as **God** is faithful, our message to you is not "Yes"
1:19 For the Son of **God,** Jesus Christ, who was preached among you by
1:20 For no matter how many promises **God** has made, they are "Yes" in
1:20 so through him the "Amen" is spoken by us to the glory *of* **God.**
1:21 Now it is **God** who makes both us and you stand firm in Christ.
1:23 I call God as my witness that it was in order to spare you that I did
2:14 But thanks be *to* **God,** who always leads us in triumphal
2:15 For we are *to* **God** the aroma of Christ among those who are being
2:17 Unlike so many, we do not peddle the word *of* **God** for profit.
2:17 On the contrary, in Christ we speak before **God** with sincerity,
2:17 we speak before God with sincerity, like men sent from **God.**
3: 3 written not with ink but with the Spirit *of* the living **God,** not on
3: 4 Such confidence as this is ours through Christ before **God.**
3: 5 anything for ourselves, but our competence comes from **God.**
4: 2 we do not use deception, nor do we distort the word *of* **God.**
4: 2 commend ourselves to every man's conscience in the sight *of* **God.**
4: 4 The **god** of this age has blinded the minds of unbelievers,
4: 4 light of the gospel of the glory of Christ, who is the image *of* **God.**
4: 6 For **God,** who said, "Let light shine out of darkness," made his light
4: 6 the light of the knowledge of the glory *of* **God** in the face of Christ.
4: 7 in jars of clay to show that this all-surpassing power is *from* **God**
4:15 people may cause thanksgiving to overflow to the glory *of* **God.**
5: 1 we have a building from **God,** an eternal house in heaven,
5: 5 Now it is **God** who has made us for this very purpose and has
5:11 What we are is plain *to* **God,** and I hope it is also plain to your
5:13 If we are out of our mind, it is *for the sake of* **God;** if we are in
5:18 All this is from **God,** who reconciled us to himself through Christ
5:19 that **God** was reconciling the world to himself in Christ,
5:20 as though **God** were making his appeal through us.
5:20 We implore you on Christ's behalf: Be reconciled *to* **God.**
5:21 so that in him we might become the righteousness *of* **God.**
6: 1 As **God's** fellow workers we urge you not to receive **God's** grace
6: 4 Rather, as servants *of* **God** we commend ourselves in every way:
6: 7 in truthful speech and in the power *of* **God;** with weapons of
6:16 What agreement is there between the temple *of* **God** and idols?
6:16 temple of God and idols? For we are the temple *of* the living **God.**
6:16 As **God** has said: "I will live with them and walk among them,
6:16 will live with them and walk among them, and I will be their **God,**
7: 1 and spirit, perfecting holiness out of reverence *for* **God.**
7: 6 But **God,** who comforts the downcast, comforted us by the coming
7: 9 For you became sorrowful as **God** intended and so were not

7:10 **Godly** [+2848] sorrow brings repentance that leads to salvation
7:11 See what this **godly** [+2848] sorrow has produced in you:
7:12 but rather that before **God** you could see for yourselves how
8: 1 we want you to know about the grace that **God** has given the
8: 5 first to the Lord and then to us in keeping with **God's** will.
8:16 I thank **God**, who put into the heart of Titus the same concern I
9: 7 or under compulsion, for **God** loves a cheerful giver.
9: 8 And **God** is able to make all grace abound to you, so that in all
9:11 and through us your generosity will result in thanksgiving to **God**.
9:12 but is also overflowing in many expressions of thanks to **God**.
9:13 men will praise **God** for the obedience that accompanies your
9:14 go out to you, because of the surpassing grace **God** has given you.
9:15 Thanks be to **God** for his indescribable gift!
10: 4 On the contrary, they have **divine** power to demolish strongholds.
10: 5 every pretension that sets itself up against the knowledge of **God**,
10:13 but will confine our boasting to the field **God** has assigned to us,
11: 2 I am jealous for you with a **godly** jealousy. I promised you to one
11: 7 elevate you by preaching the gospel of **God** to you free of charge?
11:11 Why? Because I do not love you? **God** knows I do!
11:31 The **God** and Father of the Lord Jesus, who is to be praised
12: 2 it was in the body or out of the body I do not know—**God** knows.
12: 3 in the body or apart from the body I do not know, but **God** knows
12:19 We have been speaking in the sight of **God** as those in Christ;
12:21 I am afraid that when I come again my **God** will humble me before
13: 4 he was crucified in weakness, yet he lives by **God's** power.
13: 4 in him, yet by **God's** power we will live with him to serve you.
13: 7 Now we pray to **God** that you will not do anything wrong.
13:11 live in peace. And the **God** of love and peace will be with you.
13:14 May the grace of the Lord Jesus Christ, and the love of **God**,
Gal 1: 1 not from men nor by man, but by Jesus Christ and **God** the Father,
1: 3 Grace and peace to you from **God** our Father and the Lord Jesus
1: 4 the present evil age, according to the will of our **God** and Father,
1:10 Am I now trying to win the approval of men, or of **God**? Or am I
1:13 how intensely I persecuted the church of **God** and tried to destroy
1:15 But when **God**, who set me apart from birth and called me by his
1:20 I assure you before **God** that what I am writing you is no lie.
1:24 And they praised **God** because of me.
2: 6 **God** does not judge by external appearance—those men added
2:19 For through the law I died to the law so that I might live for **God**.
2:20 I live by faith in the Son of **God**, who loved me and gave himself
2:21 I do not set aside the grace of **God**, for if righteousness could be
3: 6 "He believed **God**, and it was credited to him as righteousness."
3: 8 The Scripture foresaw that **God** would justify the Gentiles by faith,
3:11 Clearly no one is justified before **God** by the law, because,
3:17 does not set aside the covenant previously established by **God**
3:18 but **God** in his grace gave it to Abraham through a promise.
3:20 however, does not represent just one party; but **God** is one.
3:21 Is the law, therefore, opposed to the promises of **God**? Absolutely
3:26 You are all sons of **God** through faith in Christ Jesus,
4: 4 fully come, **God** sent his Son, born of a woman, born under law,
4: 6 you are sons, **God** sent the Spirit of his Son into our hearts,
4: 7 but a son; and since you are a son, **God** has made you also an heir.
4: 8 Formerly, when you did not know **God**, you were slaves to those
4: 8 know God, you were slaves to those who by nature are not **gods**.
4: 9 But now that you know **God**—or rather are known by God—
4: 9 But now that you know God—or rather are known by **God**—
4:14 Instead, you welcomed me as if I were an angel of **God**, as if I
5:21 that those who live like this will not inherit the kingdom of **God**.
6: 7 Do not be deceived: **God** cannot be mocked. A man reaps what he
6:16 and mercy to all who follow this rule, even to the Israel of **God**.
Eph 1: 1 Paul, an apostle of Christ Jesus by the will of **God**, To the saints in
1: 2 Grace and peace to you from **God** our Father and the Lord Jesus
1: 3 Praise be to the **God** and Father of our Lord Jesus Christ, who has
1:17 I keep asking that the **God** of our Lord Jesus Christ, the glorious
2: 4 because of his great love for us, **God**, who is rich in mercy,
2: 8 through faith—and this not from yourselves, it is the gift of **God**—
2:10 to do good works, which **God** prepared in advance for us to do.
2:16 and in this one body to reconcile both of them to **God** through the
2:19 citizens with God's people and members of **God's** household,
2:22 together to become a dwelling in which **God** lives by his Spirit.
3: 2 Surely you have heard about the administration of **God's** grace that
3: 7 I became a servant of this gospel by the gift of **God's** grace given
3: 9 which for ages past was kept hidden in **God**, who created all
3:10 the manifold wisdom of **God** should be made known to the rulers
3:19 that you may be filled to the measure of all the fullness of **God**.
4: 6 one **God** and Father of all, who is over all and through all

4:13 and in the knowledge of the Son of **God** and become mature,
4:18 darkened in their understanding and separated from the life of **God**
4:24 new self, created to be like **God** in true righteousness and holiness.
4:30 And do not grieve the Holy Spirit of **God**, with whom you were
4:32 forgiving each other, just as in Christ **God** forgave you.
5: 1 Be imitators of **God**, therefore, as dearly loved children
5: 2 gave himself up for us as a fragrant offering and sacrifice to **God**.
5: 5 has any inheritance in the kingdom of Christ and of **God**.
5: 6 because of such things **God's** wrath comes on those who are
5:20 always giving thanks to **God** the Father for everything, in the name
6: 6 but like slaves of Christ, doing the will of **God** from your heart.
6:11 Put on the full armor of **God** so that you can take your stand
6:13 Therefore put on the full armor of **God**, so that when the day of
6:17 of salvation and the sword of the Spirit, which is the word of **God**.
6:23 and love with faith from **God** the Father and the Lord Jesus Christ.
Php 1: 2 Grace and peace to you from **God** our Father and the Lord Jesus
1: 3 I thank my **God** every time I remember you.
1: 8 **God** can testify how I long for all of you with the affection of
1:11 that comes through Jesus Christ—to the glory and praise of **God**.
1:14 encouraged to speak the word of **God** [UBS-] more courageously
1:28 will be destroyed, but that you will be saved—and that by **God**.
2: 6 Who, being in very nature **God**, did not consider equality with God
2: 6 did not consider equality with **God** something to be grasped,
2: 9 Therefore **God** exalted him to the highest place and gave him the
2:11 confess that Jesus Christ is Lord, to the glory of **God** the Father.
2:13 for it is **God** who works in you to will and to act according to his
2:15 children of **God** without fault in a crooked and depraved
2:27 But **God** had mercy on him, and not on him only but also on me,
3: 3 we who worship by the Spirit of **God**, who glory in Christ Jesus,
3: 9 in Christ—the righteousness that comes from **God** and is by faith.
3:14 I press on toward the goal to win the prize for which **God** has
3:15 point you think differently, that too **God** will make clear to you.
3:19 Their destiny is destruction, their **god** is their stomach, and their
4: 6 and petition, with thanksgiving, present your requests to **God**.
4: 7 And the peace of **God**, which transcends all understanding,
4: 9 put it into practice. And the **God** of peace will be with you.
4:18 are a fragrant offering, an acceptable sacrifice, pleasing to **God**.
4:19 And my **God** will meet all your needs according to his glorious
4:20 *To* our **God** and Father be glory for ever and ever. Amen.
Col 1: 1 Paul, an apostle of Christ Jesus by the will of **God**, and Timothy
1: 2 in Christ at Colosse: Grace and peace to you from **God** our Father.
1: 3 We always thank **God**, the Father of our Lord Jesus Christ,
1: 6 the day you heard it and understood **God's** grace in all its truth.
1:10 fruit in every good work, growing in the knowledge of **God**,
1:15 He is the image of the invisible **God**, the firstborn over all creation.
1:25 I have become its servant by the commission **God** gave me to
1:25 God gave me to present to you the word of **God** in its fullness—
1:27 To them **God** has chosen to make known among the Gentiles the
2: 2 in order that they may know the mystery of **God**, namely,
2:12 and raised with him through your faith in the power of **God**,
2:19 by its ligaments and sinews, grows as **God** causes it to grow.
3: 1 on things above, where Christ is seated at the right hand of **God**.
3: 3 For you died, and your life is now hidden with Christ in **God**.
3: 6 Because of these, the wrath of **God** is coming.
3:12 Therefore, as **God's** chosen people, holy and dearly loved,
3:16 hymns and spiritual songs with gratitude in your hearts to **God**.
3:17 of the Lord Jesus, giving thanks to **God** the Father through him.
4: 3 And pray for us, too, that **God** may open a door for our message,
4:11 the only Jews among my fellow workers for the kingdom of **God**,
4:12 that you may stand firm in all the will of **God**, mature and fully
1Th 1: 1 To the church of the Thessalonians in **God** the Father and the Lord
1: 2 We always thank **God** for all of you, mentioning you in our
1: 3 We continually remember before our **God** and Father your work
1: 4 For we know, brothers loved by **God**, that he has chosen you,
1: 8 and Achaia—your faith in **God** has become known everywhere.
1: 9 They tell how you turned to **God** from idols to serve the living
1: 9 how you turned to God from idols to serve the living and true **God**,
2: 2 but with the help of our **God** we dared to tell you his gospel in
2: 2 but with the help of our God we dared to tell you **his**[s] [+3836]
2: 4 we speak as men approved by **God** to be entrusted with the gospel.
2: 4 We were not trying to please men but **God**, who tests our hearts.
2: 5 nor did we put on a mask to cover up greed—**God** is our witness.
2: 8 we were delighted to share with you not only the gospel of **God**
2: 9 a burden to anyone while we preached the gospel of **God** to you.
2:10 and so is **God**, of how holy, righteous and blameless we were
2:12 and urging you to live lives worthy of **God**,

2: 13 And we also thank **God** continually because, when you received
2: 13 when you received the word *of* **God**, which you heard from us,
2: 13 but as it actually is, the word *of* **God**, which is at work in you who
2: 14 For you, brothers, became imitators *of* **God's** churches in Judea,
2: 15 also drove us out. They displease **God** and are hostile to all men
2: 16 the limit. The wrath *of* **God** [UBS-] has come upon them at last.
3: 2 and **God's** fellow worker in spreading the gospel of Christ,
3: 9 How can we thank **God** enough for you in return for all the joy we
3: 9 for you in return for all the joy we have in the presence *of* **God**
3: 11 Now may our **God** and Father himself and our Lord Jesus clear the
3: 13 so that you will be blameless and holy in the presence *of* our **God**
4: 1 brothers, we instructed you how to live in order to please **God**,
4: 3 It is **God's** will that you should be sanctified: that you should
4: 5 not in passionate lust like the heathen, who do not know **God**;
4: 7 For **God** did not call us to be impure, but to live a holy life.
4: 8 he who rejects this instruction does not reject man but **God**,
4: 14 so we believe that **God** will bring with Jesus those who have fallen
4: 16 with the voice of the archangel and with the trumpet call *of* **God**,
5: 9 For **God** did not appoint us to suffer wrath but to receive salvation
5: 18 in all circumstances, for this is **God's** will for you in Christ Jesus.
5: 23 May God himself, the **God** of peace, sanctify you through

2Th 1: 1 To the church of the Thessalonians in **God** our Father and the Lord
1: 2 Grace and peace to you from **God** the Father and the Lord Jesus
1: 3 We ought always to thank **God** for you, brothers, and rightly so,
1: 4 among **God's** churches we boast about your perseverance
1: 5 All this is evidence that **God's** judgment is right, and as a result
1: 5 and as a result you will be counted worthy of the kingdom *of* **God**,
1: 6 **God** is just: He will pay back trouble to those who trouble you
1: 8 He will punish those who do not know **God** and do not obey the
1: 11 pray for you, that our **God** may count you worthy of his calling,
1: 12 according to the grace *of* our **God** and the Lord Jesus Christ.
2: 4 and will exalt himself over everything that is called **God**
2: 4 or is worshiped, so that he sets himself up in **God's** temple,
2: 4 he sets himself up in God's temple, proclaiming himself to be **God**.
2: 11 For this reason **God** sends them a powerful delusion so that they
2: 13 But we ought always to thank **God** for you, brothers loved by the
2: 13 because from the beginning **God** chose you to be saved through the
2: 16 May our Lord Jesus Christ himself and **God** our Father, who loved
3: 5 May the Lord direct your hearts into **God's** love and Christ's

1Ti 1: 1 an apostle of Christ Jesus by the command *of* **God** our Savior
1: 2 mercy and peace from **God** the Father and Christ Jesus our Lord.
1: 4 These promote controversies rather than **God's** work—which is by
1: 11 that conforms to the glorious gospel *of* the blessed **God**, which he
1: 17 invisible, the only **God**, be honor and glory for ever and ever.
2: 3 This is good, and pleases **God** our Savior,
2: 5 For there is one **God** and one mediator between God and men,
2: 5 For there is one God and one mediator between **God** and men,
3: 5 to manage his own family, how can he take care of **God's** church?)
3: 15 you will know how people ought to conduct themselves in **God's**
3: 15 which is the church *of* the living **God**, the pillar and foundation of
4: 3 which **God** created to be received with thanksgiving by those who
4: 4 For everything **God** created is good, and nothing is to be rejected if
4: 5 because it is consecrated by the word *of* **God** and prayer.
4: 10 we labor and strive), that we have put our hope in the living **God**,
5: 4 their parents and grandparents, for this is pleasing to **God**.
5: 5 and left all alone puts her hope in **God** and continues night
5: 21 in the sight *of* **God** and Christ Jesus and the elect angels,
6: 1 so that **God's** name and our teaching may not be slandered.
6: 11 But you, man *of* **God**, flee from all this, and pursue righteousness,
6: 13 In the sight *of* **God**, who gives life to everything, and of Christ
6: 17 which is so uncertain, but to put their hope in **God**, who richly

2Ti 1: 1 Paul, an apostle of Christ Jesus by the will *of* **God**, according to
1: 2 mercy and peace from **God** the Father and Christ Jesus our Lord.
1: 3 I thank **God**, whom I serve, as my forefathers did, with a clear
1: 6 For this reason I remind you to fan into flame the gift *of* **God**,
1: 7 For **God** did not give us a spirit of timidity, but a spirit of power,
1: 8 But join with me in suffering for the gospel, by the power *of* **God**,
2: 9 of being chained like a criminal. But **God's** word is not chained.
2: 14 Warn them before **God** against quarreling about words; it is of no
2: 15 Do your best to present yourself *to* **God** as one approved,
2: 19 Nevertheless, **God's** solid foundation stands firm, sealed with this
2: 25 in the hope that **God** will grant them repentance leading them to a
3: 17 so that the man *of* **God** may be thoroughly equipped for every
4: 1 In the presence *of* **God** and of Christ Jesus, who will judge the

Tit 1: 1 a servant *of* **God** and an apostle of Jesus Christ for the faith of
1: 1 of God and an apostle of Jesus Christ for the faith *of* **God's** elect

1: 2 which **God**, who does not lie, promised before the beginning of
1: 3 the preaching entrusted to me by the command *of* **God** our Savior.
1: 4 Grace and peace from **God** the Father and Christ Jesus our Savior.
1: 7 Since an overseer is entrusted with **God's** work, he must be
1: 16 They claim to know **God**, but by their actions they deny him.
2: 5 to their husbands, so that no one will malign the word *of* **God**.
2: 10 so that in every way they will make the teaching *about* **God** our
2: 11 For the grace *of* **God** that brings salvation has appeared to all men.
2: 13 the glorious appearing *of* our great **God** and Savior, Jesus Christ,
3: 4 But when the kindness and love *of* **God** our Savior appeared,
3: 8 so that those who have trusted *in* **God** may be careful to devote

Phm 1: 3 Grace to you and peace from **God** our Father and the Lord Jesus
1: 4 I always thank my **God** as I remember you in my prayers,

Heb 1: 1 In the past **God** spoke to our forefathers through the prophets at
1: 6 into the world, he says, "Let all **God's** angels worship him."
1: 8 the Son he says, "Your throne, O **God**, will last for ever and ever,
1: 9 therefore **God**, your God, has set you above your companions by
1: 9 therefore God, your **God**, has set you above your companions by
2: 4 **God** also testified to it by signs, wonders and various miracles,
2: 9 so that by the grace *of* **God** he might taste death for everyone.
2: 13 again he says, "Here am I, and the children **God** has given me."
2: 17 might become a merciful and faithful high priest in service to **God**,
3: 4 house is built by someone, but **God** is the builder of everything.
3: 12 has a sinful, unbelieving heart that turns away from the living **God**.
4: 4 words: "And on the seventh day **God** rested from all his work."
4: 9 There remains, then, a Sabbath-rest for the people *of* **God**;
4: 10 God's rest also rests from his own work, just as **God** did from his.
4: 12 For the word *of* **God** is living and active. Sharper than any
4: 14 Jesus the Son *of* **God**, let us hold firmly to the faith we profess.
5: 1 and is appointed to represent them in matters related to **God**,
5: 4 honor upon himself; he must be called by **God**, just as Aaron was.
5: 10 and was designated by **God** to be high priest in the order of
5: 12 you need someone to teach you the elementary truths of **God's**
6: 1 of repentance from acts that lead to death, and of faith in **God**,
6: 3 And **God** permitting, we will do so.
6: 5 who have tasted the goodness of the word *of* **God** and the powers
6: 6 because to their loss they are crucifying the Son *of* **God** all over
6: 7 useful to those for whom it is farmed receives the blessing of **God**.
6: 10 **God** is not unjust; he will not forget your work and the love you
6: 13 When **God** made his promise to Abraham, since there was no one
6: 17 Because **God** wanted to make the unchanging nature of his
6: 18 by two unchangeable things in which it is impossible *for* **God** to
7: 1 This Melchizedek was king of Salem and priest *of* **God** Most High.
7: 3 or end of life, like the Son *of* **God** he remains a priest forever.
7: 19 and a better hope is introduced, by which we draw near *to* **God**.
7: 25 Therefore he is able to save completely those who come to **God**
8: 10 on their hearts. I will be their **God**, and they will be my people.
9: 14 through the eternal Spirit offered himself unblemished *to* **God**,
9: 14 from acts that lead to death, so that we may serve the living **God**!
9: 20 blood of the covenant, which **God** has commanded you to keep."
9: 24 he entered heaven itself, now to appear for us in **God's** presence.
10: 7 about me in the scroll—I have come to do your will, O **God**.' "
10: 12 time one sacrifice for sins, he sat down at the right hand *of* **God**,
10: 21 and since we have a great priest over the house *of* **God**,
10: 29 to be punished who has trampled the Son *of* **God** under foot,
10: 31 It is a dreadful thing to fall into the hands *of* the living **God**.
10: 36 need to persevere so that when you have done the will *of* **God**,
11: 3 By faith we understand that the universe was formed at **God's**
11: 4 By faith Abel offered a better sacrifice than Cain did.
11: 4 as a righteous man, when **God** spoke well of his offerings.
11: 5 he could not be found, because **God** had taken him away.
11: 5 before he was taken, he was commended as one who pleased **God**.
11: 6 because anyone who comes *to* him[s] [+3836] must believe that he
11: 10 to the city with foundations, whose architect and builder is **God**.
11: 16 Therefore **God** is not ashamed to be called their God, for he has
11: 16 Therefore God is not ashamed to be called their **God**, for he has
11: 19 Abraham reasoned that **God** could raise the dead, and figuratively
11: 25 He chose to be mistreated along with the people *of* **God** rather than
11: 40 **God** had planned something better for us so that only together with
12: 2 its shame, and sat down at the right hand of the throne *of* **God**.
12: 7 Endure hardship as discipline; **God** is treating you as sons.
12: 15 See to it that no one misses the grace *of* **God** and that no bitter root
12: 22 Mount Zion, to the heavenly Jerusalem, the city *of* the living **God**.
12: 23 You have come to **God**, the judge of all men, to the spirits of
12: 28 and so worship **God** acceptably with reverence and awe,
12: 29 for our "**God** is a consuming fire."

13: 4   for **God** will judge the adulterer and all the sexually immoral.
13: 7   Remember your leaders, who spoke the word *of* **God** to you.
13:15   therefore, let us continually offer *to* **God** a sacrifice of praise—
13:16   and to share with others, for with such sacrifices **God** is pleased.
13:20   May the **God** of peace, who through the blood of the eternal
Jas 1: 1   James, a servant *of* **God** and of the Lord Jesus Christ,
1: 5   If any of you lacks wisdom, he should ask **God**, who gives
1:13   When tempted, no one should say, "**God** is tempting me." For God
1:13   For **God** cannot be tempted by evil, nor does he tempt anyone;
1:20   anger does not bring about the righteous life that **God** *desires*.
1:27   Religion that **God** our Father accepts as pure and faultless is this:
2: 5   Has not **God** chosen those who are poor in the eyes of the world to
2:19   You believe that there is one **God**. Good! Even the demons believe
2:23   And the scripture was fulfilled that says, "Abraham believed **God**,
2:23   credited to him as righteousness," and he was called **God's** friend.
3: 9   and with it we curse men, who have been made in **God's** likeness.
4: 4   you know that friendship with the world is hatred *toward* **God**?
4: 4   chooses to be a friend of the world becomes an enemy *of* **God**.
4: 6   "**God** opposes the proud but gives grace to the humble."
4: 7   Submit yourselves, then, *to* **God**. Resist the devil, and he will flee
4: 8   Come near *to* **God** and he will come near to you. Wash your
1Pe 1: 2   who have been chosen according to the foreknowledge *of* **God** the
1: 3   Praise be to the **God** and Father of our Lord Jesus Christ! In his
1: 5   who through faith are shielded by **God's** power until the coming of
1:21   Through him you believe in **God**, who raised him from the dead
1:21   the dead and glorified him, and so your faith and hope are in **God**.
1:23   but of imperishable, through the living and enduring word *of* **God**.
2: 4   rejected by men but chosen by **God** and precious to him—
2: 5   offering spiritual sacrifices acceptable *to* **God** through Jesus
2:10   Once you were not a people, but now you are the people *of* **God**;
2:12   may see your good deeds and glorify **God** on the day he visits us.
2:15   For it is **God's** will that by doing good you should silence the
2:16   use your freedom as a cover-up for evil; live as servants *of* **God**.
2:17   Love the brotherhood of believers, fear **God**, honor the king.
2:19   under the pain of unjust suffering because he is conscious *of* **God**.
2:20   for doing good and you endure it, this is commendable before **God**.
3: 4   of a gentle and quiet spirit, which is of great worth in **God's** sight.
3. 5   past who put their hope in **God** used to make themselves beautiful.
3:17   It is better, if it is **God's** will, to suffer for doing good than for
3:18   once for all, the righteous for the unrighteous, to bring you *to* **God**.
3:20   who disobeyed long ago when **God** waited patiently in the days of
3:21   from the body but the pledge of a good conscience toward **God**.
3:22   who has gone into heaven and is at **God's** right hand—with angels,
4: 2   earthly life for evil human desires, but rather for the will *of* **God**.
4: 6   regard to the body, but live according to **God** in regard to the spirit.
4:10   faithfully administering **God's** grace in its various forms.
4:11   he should do it as one speaking the very words *of* **God**.
4:11   If anyone serves, he should do it with the strength **God** provides,
4:11   so that in all things **God** may be praised through Jesus Christ.
4:14   you are blessed, for the Spirit of glory and *of* **God** rests on you.
4:16   do not be ashamed, but praise **God** that you bear that name.
4:17   For it is time for judgment to begin with the family *of* **God**;
4:17   will the outcome be for those who do not obey the gospel *of* **God**?
4:19   those who suffer according to **God's** will should commit
5: 2   Be shepherds of **God's** flock that is under your care, serving as
5: 2   you must, but because you are willing, as **God** wants you to be;
5: 5   because, "**God** opposes the proud but gives grace to the humble."
5: 6   Humble yourselves, therefore, under **God's** mighty hand, that he
5:10   And the **God** of all grace, who called you to his eternal glory in
5:12   encouraging you and testifying that this is the true grace *of* **God**.
2Pe 1: 1   To those who through the righteousness *of* our **God** and Savior
1: 2   and peace be yours in abundance through the knowledge *of* **God**
1:17   and glory from **God** the Father when the voice came to him from
1:21   but men spoke from **God** as they were carried along by the Holy
2: 4   For if **God** did not spare angels when they sinned, but sent them to
3: 5   But they deliberately forget that long ago by **God's** word the
3:12   as you look forward to the day *of* **God** and speed its coming.
1Jn 1: 5   and declare to you: **God** is light; in him there is no darkness at all.
2: 5   anyone obeys his word, **God's** love is truly made complete in him.
2:14   because you are strong, and the word *of* **God** lives in you,
2:17   pass away, but the man who does the will *of* **God** lives forever.
3: 1   has lavished on us, that we should be called children *of* **God**!
3: 2   Dear friends, now we are children *of* **God**, and what we will be has
3: 8   The reason the Son *of* **God** appeared was to destroy the devil's
3: 9   No one who is born of **God** will continue to sin, because God's
3: 9   he cannot go on sinning, because he has been born of **God**.

3:10   This is how we know who the children *of* **God** are and who the
3:10   Anyone who does not do what is right is not a child of **God**;
3:17   but has no pity on him, how can the love *of* **God** be in him?
3:20   For **God** is greater than our hearts, and he knows everything.
3:21   if our hearts do not condemn us, we have confidence before **God**
4: 1   every spirit, but test the spirits to see whether they are from **God**,
4: 2   This is how you can recognize the Spirit *of* **God**: Every spirit that
4: 2   acknowledges that Jesus Christ has come in the flesh is from **God**,
4: 3   but every spirit that does not acknowledge Jesus is not from **God**.
4: 4   You, dear children, are from **God** and have overcome them,
4: 6   We are from **God**, and whoever knows God listens to us;
4: 6   We are from God, and whoever knows **God** listens to us;
4: 6   listens to us; but whoever is not from **God** does not listen to us.
4: 7   Dear friends, let us love one another, for love comes from **God**.
4: 7   Everyone who loves has been born of **God** and knows God.
4: 7   Everyone who loves has been born of God and knows **God**.
4: 8   Whoever does not love does not know **God**, because God is love.
4: 8   Whoever does not love does not know God, because **God** is love.
4: 9   This is how **God** showed his love among us: He sent his one
4: 9   This is how God showed his love among us: He^s [*+3836*] sent his
4:10   not that we loved **God**, but that he loved us and sent his Son as an
4:11   Dear friends, since **God** so loved us, we also ought to love one
4:12   No one has ever seen **God**; but if we love one another, God lives in
4:12   one another, **God** lives in us and his love is made complete in us.
4:15   If anyone acknowledges that Jesus is the Son *of* **God**, God lives in
4:15   that Jesus is the Son of God, **God** lives in him and he in God.
4:15   that Jesus is the Son of God, God lives in him and he in **God**.
4:16   And so we know and rely on the love **God** has for us. God is love.
4:16   **God** is love. Whoever lives in love lives in God, and God in him.
4:16   God is love. Whoever lives in love lives in **God**, and God in him.
4:16   God is love. Whoever lives in love lives in God, and **God** in him.
4:20   If anyone says, "I love **God**," yet hates his brother, he is a liar.
4:20   whom he has seen, cannot love **God**, whom he has not seen.
4:21   us this command: Whoever loves **God** must also love his brother.
5: 1   Everyone who believes that Jesus is the Christ is born of **God**,
5: 2   This is how we know that we love the children *of* **God**: by loving
5: 2   children of God: by loving **God** and carrying out his commands.
5: 3   This is love *for* **God**: to obey his commands. And his commands
5: 4   for everyone born of **God** overcomes the world. This is the victory
5: 5   the world? Only he who believes that Jesus is the Son *of* **God**.
5: 9   but **God's** testimony is greater because it is the testimony of God,
5: 9   but God's testimony is greater because it is the testimony *of* **God**,
5:10   Anyone who believes in the Son *of* **God** has this testimony in his
5:10   Anyone who does not believe **God** has made him out to be a liar,
5:10   because he has not believed the testimony **God** has given about his
5:11   **God** has given us eternal life, and this life is in his Son.
5:12   has life; he who does not have the Son *of* **God** does not have life.
5:13   these things to you who believe in the name of the Son *of* **God**
5:18   We know that anyone born of **God** does not continue to sin;
5:18   the one who was born of **God** keeps him safe, and the evil one
5:19   We know that we are children of **God**, and that the whole world is
5:20   We know also that the Son *of* **God** has come and has given us
5:20   even in his Son Jesus Christ. He is the true **God** and eternal life.
2Jn 1: 3   mercy and peace from **God** the Father and from Jesus Christ,
1: 9   and does not continue in the teaching of Christ does not have **God**;
3Jn 1: 6   will do well to send them on their way in a manner worthy **of** **God**.
1:11   but what is good. Anyone who does what is good is from **God**.
1:11   is from God. Anyone who does what is evil has not seen **God**.
Jude 1: 1   who are loved by **God** the Father and kept by Jesus Christ:
1: 4   who change the grace *of* our **God** into a license for immorality
1:21   Keep yourselves in **God's** love as you wait for the mercy of our
1:25   *to* the only **God** our Savior be glory, majesty, power and authority,
Rev 1: 1   which **God** gave him to show his servants what must soon take
1: 2   that is, the word *of* **God** and the testimony of Jesus Christ.
1: 6   made us to be a kingdom and priests *to serve* his **God** and Father—
1: 8   and the Omega," says the Lord **God**, "who is, and who was,
1: 9   of Patmos because of the word *of* **God** and the testimony of Jesus.
2: 7   right to eat from the tree of life, which is in the paradise *of* **God**.
2:18   These are the words of the Son *of* **God**, whose eyes are like
3: 1   These are the words of him who holds the seven spirits *of* **God**
3: 2   for I have not found your deeds complete in the sight *of* my **God**.
3:12   Him who overcomes I will make a pillar in the temple *of* my **God**.
3:12   I will write on him the name *of* my **God** and the name of the city
3:12   on him the name of my God and the name of the city *of* my **God**,
3:12   which is coming down out of heaven from my **God**;
3:14   the faithful and true witness, the ruler *of* **God's** creation.

4: 5 seven lamps were blazing. These are the seven spirits *of* **God**.
4: 8 "Holy, holy, holy is the Lord **God** Almighty, who was, and is,
4: 11 our Lord and **God**, to receive glory and honor and power,
5: 6 which are the seven spirits *of* **God** sent out into all the earth.
5: 9 and with your blood you purchased men *for* **God** from every tribe
5: 10 have made them to be a kingdom and priests *to serve* our **God**,
6: 9 because of the word *of* **God** and the testimony they had
7: 2 angel coming up from the east, having the seal *of* the living **God**.
7: 3 until we have put a seal on the foreheads of the servants *of* our **God**."
7: 10 "Salvation *belongs to* our **God**, who sits on the throne, and to the
7: 11 fell down on their faces before the throne and worshiped **God**,
7: 12 and honor and power and strength be *to* our **God** for ever and ever.
7: 15 "they are before the throne *of* **God** and serve him day and night in
7: 17 living water. And **God** will wipe away every tear from their eyes."
8: 2 And I saw the seven angels who stand before **God**, and to them
8: 4 prayers of the saints, went up before **God** from the angel's hand.
9: 4 but only those people who did not have the seal *of* **God** on their
9: 13 voice coming from the horns of the golden altar that is before **God**.
10: 7 the mystery *of* **God** will be accomplished, just as he announced to
11: 1 and was told, "Go and measure the temple *of* **God** and the altar,
11: 11 the three and a half days a breath of life from **God** entered them,
11: 13 the survivors were terrified and gave glory *to* the **God** of heaven.
11: 16 who were seated on their thrones before **God**, fell on their faces
11: 16 on their thrones before **God**, fell on their faces and worshiped **God**,
11: 17 thanks to you, Lord **God** Almighty, the One who is and who was,
11: 19 Then **God's** temple in heaven was opened, and within his temple
12: 5 And her child was snatched up to **God** and to his throne.
12: 6 The woman fled into the desert to a place prepared for her by **God**,
12: 10 come the salvation and the power and the kingdom *of* our **God**,
12: 10 who accuses them before our **God** day and night, has been hurled
12: 17 those who obey **God's** commandments and hold to the testimony
13: 6 He opened his mouth to blaspheme **God**, and to slander his name
14: 4 from among men and offered as firstfruits *to* **God** and the Lamb.
14: 7 He said in a loud voice, "Fear **God** and give him glory,
14: 10 he, too, will drink of the wine *of* **God's** fury, which has been
14: 12 on the part of the saints who obey **God's** commandments
14: 19 its grapes and threw them into the great winepress of **God's** wrath.
15: 1 last plagues—last, because with them **God's** wrath is completed.
15: 2 over the number of his name. They held harps *given* them *by* **God**
15: 3 and sang the song of Moses the servant *of* **God** and the song of the
15: 3 "Great and marvelous are your deeds, Lord **God** Almighty.
15: 7 the seven angels seven golden bowls filled with the wrath *of* **God**,
15: 8 And the temple was filled with smoke from the glory *of* **God**
16: 1 "Go, pour out the seven bowls *of* **God's** wrath on the earth."
16: 7 "Yes, Lord **God** Almighty, true and just are your judgments."
16: 9 were seared by the intense heat and they cursed the name *of* **God**,
16: 11 and cursed the **God** of heaven because of their pains and their
16: 14 to gather them for the battle on the great day *of* **God** Almighty.
16: 19 **God** remembered Babylon the Great and gave her the cup filled
16: 21 And they cursed **God** on account of the plague of hail,
17: 17 For **God** has put it into their hearts to accomplish his purpose by
17: 17 give the beast their power to rule, until **God's** words are fulfilled.
18: 5 sins are piled up to heaven, and **God** has remembered her crimes.
18: 8 be consumed by fire, for mighty is the Lord **God** who judges her.
18: 20 and prophets! **God** has judged her for the way she treated you.' "
19: 1 "Hallelujah! Salvation and glory and power *belong to* our **God**,
19: 4 and the four living creatures fell down and worshiped **God**,
19: 5 "Praise our **God**, all you his servants, you who fear him, both small
19: 6 shouting: "Hallelujah! For our Lord **God** Almighty reigns.
19: 9 of the Lamb!' " And he added, "These are the true words *of* **God**."
19: 10 Worship **God**! For the testimony of Jesus is the spirit of prophecy."
19: 13 in a robe dipped in blood, and his name is the Word *of* **God**.
19: 15 He treads the winepress of the fury of the wrath *of* **God** Almighty.
19: 17 in midair, "Come, gather together for the great supper *of* **God**,
20: 4 of their testimony for Jesus and because of the word *of* **God**.
20: 6 but they will be priests *of* **God** and of Christ and will reign with
21: 2 the new Jerusalem, coming down out of heaven from **God**,
21: 3 "Now the dwelling *of* **God** is with men, and he will live with them.
21: 3 be his people, and **God** himself will be with them and be their God.
21: 3 be his people, and **God** himself will be with them and be their **God**.
21: 7 will inherit all this, and I will be his **God** and he will be my son.
21: 10 the Holy City, Jerusalem, coming down out of heaven from **God**.
21: 11 It shone with the glory *of* **God**, and its brilliance was like that of a
21: 22 because the Lord **God** Almighty and the Lamb are its temple.
21: 23 for the glory *of* **God** gives it light, and the Lamb is its lamp.
22: 1 clear as crystal, flowing from the throne *of* **God** and of the Lamb

22: 3 The throne *of* **God** and of the Lamb will be in the city, and his
22: 5 or the light of the sun, for the Lord **God** will give them light.
22: 6 The Lord, the **God** of the spirits of the prophets, sent his angel to
22: 9 and of all who keep the words of this book. Worship **God**!"
22: 18 to them, **God** will add to him the plagues described in this book.
22: 19 **God** will take away from him his share in the tree of life and in the

2537 θεοσέβεια, *theosebeia* [1] [√ 2536 + 4936]

worship God [1]

1Ti 2: 10 good deeds, appropriate for women who profess to **worship God**.

2538 θεοσεβής, *theosebēs* [1] [√ 2536 + 4936]

godly man [1]

Jn 9: 31 not listen to sinners. He listens to the **godly man** who does his will.

2539 θεοστυγής, *theostygēs* [1] [√ 2536 + 5144]

God-haters [1]

Ro 1: 30 slanderers, **God-haters**, insolent, arrogant and boastful;

2540 θεότης, *theotēs* [1] [√ 2536]

Deity [1]

Col 2: 9 For in Christ all the fullness *of* the **Deity** lives in bodily form,

2541 Θεόφιλος, *Theophilos* [2] [√ 2536 + 5813]

Theophilus [2]

Lk 1: 3 me to write an orderly account for you, most excellent **Theophilus**,
Ac 1: 1 In my former book, **Theophilus**, I wrote about all that Jesus began

2542 θεραπεία, *therapeia* [3] [√ 2544]

healing [2], servants [1]

Lk 9: 11 about the kingdom of God, and healed those who needed **healing**.
12: 42 whom the master puts in charge of his **servants** to give them their
Rev 22: 2 And the leaves of the tree are for the **healing** of the nations.

2543 θεραπεύω, *therapeuō* [43] [√ 2544]

healed [22], heal [12], cured [3], healing [3], cure [1], cured [+1639] [1], served [1]

Mt 4: 23 and **healing** every disease and sickness among the people.
4: 24 those having seizures, and the paralyzed, and *he* **healed** them.
8: 7 Jesus said to him, "I *will* go and **heal** him."
8: 16 and he drove out the spirits with a word and **healed** all the sick.
9: 35 good news of the kingdom and **healing** every disease and sickness.
10: 1 to drive out evil spirits and *to* **heal** every disease and sickness.
10: 8 **Heal** the sick, raise the dead, cleanse those who have leprosy,
12: 10 accuse Jesus, they asked him, "Is it lawful *to* **heal** on the Sabbath?"
12: 15 from that place. Many followed him, and *he* **healed** all their *sick*,
12: 22 man who was blind and mute, and Jesus **healed** him,
14: 14 a large crowd, he had compassion on them and **healed** their sick.
15: 30 and many others, and laid them at his feet; and *he* **healed** them.
17: 16 I brought him to your disciples, but they could not **heal** him."
17: 18 and it came out of the boy, and he *was* **healed** from that moment.
19: 2 Large crowds followed him, and *he* **healed** them there.
21: 14 and the lame came to him at the temple, and he **healed** them.
Mk 1: 34 and Jesus **healed** many who had various diseases. He also drove
3: 2 so they watched him closely to see if *he would* **heal** him on the
3: 10 For *he had* **healed** many, so that those with diseases were pushing
6: 5 except lay his hands on a few sick people and **heal** them.
6: 13 and anointed many sick people with oil and **healed** them.
Lk 4: 23 you will quote this proverb to me: 'Physician, **heal** yourself!
4: 40 of sickness, and laying his hands on each one, he **healed** them.
5: 15 of people came to hear him and *to be* **healed** of their sicknesses.
6: 7 so they watched him closely to see if *he would* **heal** on the
6: 18 **healed** of their diseases. Those troubled by evil spirits *were* **cured**.
7: 21 At that very time Jesus **cured** many who had diseases, sicknesses
8: 2 and also some women who *had been* **cured** [+1639] of evil spirits

8: 43 subject to bleeding for twelve years, but no one could **heal** her.
9: 1 and authority to drive out all demons and *to* **cure** diseases,
9: 6 to village, preaching the gospel and **healing** people everywhere.
10: 9 **Heal** the sick who are there and tell them, 'The kingdom of God is
13: 14 Indignant because Jesus *had* **healed** on the Sabbath, the synagogue
13: 14 So come and *be* **healed** on those days, not on the Sabbath."
14: 3 and experts in the law, "Is it lawful *to* **heal** on the Sabbath or not?"
Jn   5: 10 and so the Jews said *to* the man *who had been* **healed**, "It is the
Ac   4: 14 But since they could see the man who *had been* **healed** standing
5: 16 and those tormented by evil spirits, and all of them *were* **healed**.
8: 7 came out of many, and many paralytics and cripples *were* **healed**.
17: 25 And *he is* not **served** by human hands, as if he needed anything,
28: 9 the rest of the sick on the island came and *were* **cured**.
Rev 13: 3 to have had a fatal wound, but the fatal wound *had been* **healed**.
13: 12 worship the first beast, whose fatal wound *had been* **healed**.

2544 θεράπων, *therapōn* [1] [→ *2542, 2543*]

servant [1]

Heb 3: 5 Moses was faithful as a **servant** in all God's house, testifying to

2545 θερίζω, *therizō* [21] [√ *2549*]

reap [10], reaper [2], reaps [2], harvest [1], harvested [1],
harvesters [1], harvesting [1], reap a harvest [1], reap harvest [1],
reaping [1]

Mt   6: 26 they do not sow or **reap** or store away in barns, and yet your
25: 24 **harvesting** where you have not sown and gathering where you
25: 26 So you knew that *I* **harvest** where I have not sown and gather
Lk 12: 24 They do not sow or **reap**, they have no storeroom or barn;
19: 21 take out what you did not put in and **reap** what you did not sow.'
19: 22 taking out what I did not put in, and **reaping** what I did not sow?
Jn   4: 36 Even now the **reaper** draws his wages, even now he harvests the
4: 36 eternal life, so that the sower and the **reaper** may be glad together.
4: 37 Thus the saying 'One sows and another **reaps**' is true.
4: 38 I sent you *to* **reap** what you have not worked for. Others have done
1Co 9: 11 among you, is it too much if we **reap** a material **harvest** from you?
2Co 9: 6 Whoever sows sparingly *will* also **reap** sparingly, and whoever
9: 6 and whoever sows generously *will* also **reap** generously.
Gal   6: 7 be deceived: God cannot be mocked. A man **reaps** what he sows.
6: 8 to please his sinful nature, from that nature *will* **reap** destruction;
6: 8 who sows to please the Spirit, from the Spirit *will* **reap** eternal life.
6: 9 for at the proper time we will **reap a harvest** if we do not give up.
Jas   5: 4 The cries *of* the **harvesters** have reached the ears of the Lord
Rev 14: 15 "Take your sickle and **reap**, because the time to reap has come,
14: 15 "Take your sickle and reap, because the time *to* **reap** has come,
14: 16 cloud swung his sickle over the earth, and the earth *was* **harvested**.

2546 θερισμός, *therismos* [13] [√ *2549*]

harvest [10], harvest field [2], that^s [*+3836*] [1]

Mt   9: 37 to his disciples, "The **harvest** is plentiful but the workers are few.
9: 38 Ask the Lord *of* the **harvest**, therefore, to send out workers into his
9: 38 the harvest, therefore, to send out workers into his **harvest field**."
13: 30 Let both grow together until the **harvest**. At that time I will tell the
13: 30 At that^s [*+3836*] time I will tell the harvesters: First collect the
13: 39 The **harvest** is the end of the age, and the harvesters are angels.
Mk   4: 29 grain is ripe, he puts the sickle to it, because the **harvest** has come."
Lk 10: 2 He told them, "The **harvest** is plentiful, but the workers are few.
10: 2 Ask the Lord *of* the **harvest**, therefore, to send out workers into his
10: 2 of the harvest, therefore, to send out workers into his **harvest field**.
Jn   4: 35 Do you not say, 'Four months more and then the **harvest**'?
4: 35 open your eyes and look at the fields! They are ripe for **harvest**.
Rev 14: 15 the time to reap has come, for the **harvest** of the earth is ripe."

2547 θεριστής, *theristēs* [2] [√ *2549*]

harvesters [2]

Mt 13: 30 At that time I will tell the **harvesters**: First collect the weeds
13: 39 The harvest is the end of the age, and the **harvesters** are angels.

2548 θερμαίνω, *thermainō* [6] [√ *2549*]

warming [3], keep warm [1], warm [1], warmed [1]

Mk 14: 54 There he sat with the guards and **warmed** *himself* at the fire.
14: 67 When she saw Peter **warming** *himself*, she looked closely at him.
Jn 18: 18 and officials stood around a fire they had made *to* **keep warm**.
18: 18 keep warm. Peter also was standing with them, **warming** *himself*.
18: 25 As Simon Peter stood **warming** *himself*, he was asked, "You are
Jas   2: 16 *keep* **warm** and well fed," but does nothing about his physical

2549 θέρμη, *thermē* [1] [→ *2545, 2546, 2547, 2548, 2550*]

heat [1]

Ac 28: 3 as he put it on the fire, a viper, driven out by the **heat**,

2550 θέρος, *theros* [3] [√ *2549*]

summer [3]

Mt 24: 32 get tender and its leaves come out, you know that **summer** is near.
Mk 13: 28 get tender and its leaves come out, you know that **summer** is near.
Lk 21: 30 you can see for yourselves and know that **summer** is near.

2551 Θεσσαλία, *Thessalia*   Not used in UBS/NIV
[→ *2552, 2553*]

2552 Θεσσαλονικεύς, *Thessalonikeus* [4]
[√ *2551 + 3772*]

from Thessalonica [2], Thessalonians [2]

Ac 20: 4 Aristarchus and Secundus **from Thessalonica**, Gaius from Derbe,
27: 2 Aristarchus, a Macedonian **from Thessalonica**, was with us.
1Th 1: 1 To the church *of* the **Thessalonians** in God the Father and the Lord
2Th 1: 1 To the church *of* the **Thessalonians** in God our Father

2553 Θεσσαλονίκη, *Thessalonikē* [5] [√ *2551 + 3772*]

Thessalonica [4], Thessalonians [*+1877*] [1]

Ac 17: 1 through Amphipolis and Apollonia, they came to **Thessalonica**,
17: 11 of more noble character than the **Thessalonians** [*+1877*],
17: 13 When the Jews in **Thessalonica** learned that Paul was preaching
Php   4: 16 for even when I was in **Thessalonica**, you sent me aid again
2Ti   4: 10 loved this world, has deserted me and has gone to **Thessalonica**.

2554 Θευδᾶς, *Theudas* [1] [√ *2536 + 1565*]

Theudas [1]

Ac   5: 36 Some time ago **Theudas** appeared, claiming to be somebody,

2555 θεωρέω, *theōreō* [58] [→ *355, 2556, 4145; cf. 2517*]

see [23], saw [18], sees [5], watching [3], look at [1], looked on
[1], looks at [1], looks [1], see here [*+4047*] [1], seeing [1], seen
[1], think [1], watched [1]

Mt 27: 55 Many women were there, **watching** from a distance. They had
28: 1 Mary Magdalene and the other Mary went *to* **look at** the tomb.
Mk   3: 11 Whenever the evil spirits **saw** him, they fell down before him
5: 15 *they* **saw** the man who had been possessed by the legion of
5: 38 Jesus **saw** a commotion, with people crying and wailing loudly.
12: 41 and **watched** the crowd putting their money into the temple
15: 40 Some women were **watching** from a distance. Among them were
15: 47 and Mary the mother of Joses **saw** where he was laid.
16: 4 *they* **saw** that the stone, which was very large, had been rolled
Lk 10: 18 He replied, "*I* **saw** Satan fall like lightning from heaven.
14: 29 and is not able to finish it, everyone who **sees** it will ridicule him,
21: 6 "As for what *you* **see** [*+4047*] here, the time will come when not
23: 35 The people stood **watching**, and the rulers even sneered at him.
23: 48 When all the people who had gathered to witness this sight **saw**
24: 37 They were startled and frightened, thinking *they* **saw** a ghost.
24: 39 and see; a ghost does not have flesh and bones, as *you* **see** I have."
Jn   2: 23 many people **saw** the miraculous signs he was doing and believed
4: 19 "Sir," the woman said, "*I can* **see** that you are a prophet.

6: 2 because *they* **saw** the miraculous signs he had performed on the
6: 19 or three and a half miles, *they* **saw** Jesus approaching the boat,
6: 40 For my Father's will is that everyone who **looks** to the Son
6: 62 What if *you* **see** the Son of Man ascend to where he was before!
7: 3 go to Judea, so that your disciples *may* **see** the miracles you do.
8: 51 you the truth, if anyone keeps my word, *he* **will** never **see** death."
9: 8 and those *who had* formerly **seen** him begging asked,
10: 12 So *when he* **sees** the wolf coming, he abandons the sheep
12: 19 the Pharisees said to one another, "**See**, this is getting us nowhere.
12: 45 When he **looks at** me, he sees the one who sent me.
12: 45 When he looks at me, *he* **sees** the one who sent me.
14: 17 cannot accept him, because *it* neither **sees** him nor knows him.
14: 19 Before long, the world *will* not **see** me anymore, but you will see
14: 19 the world will not **see** me anymore, but you *will* **see** me.
16: 10 because I am going to the Father, where *you can* **see** me no longer;
16: 16 "In a little while *you will* **see** me no more, and then after a little
16: 17 'In a little while *you will* **see** me no more, and then after a little
16: 19 'In a little while *you will* **see** me no more, and then after a little
17: 24 and to **see** my glory, the glory you have given me because you
20: 6 and went into the tomb. *He* **saw** the strips of linen lying there,
20: 12 and **saw** two angels in white, seated where Jesus' body had been,
20: 14 At this, she turned around and **saw** Jesus standing there, but she
Ac 3: 16 name of Jesus, this man whom *you* **see** and know was made strong.
4: 13 *When they* **saw** the courage of Peter and John and realized that
7: 56 "*I* **see** heaven open and the Son of Man standing at the right hand
8: 13 astonished by the great signs and miracles *he* **saw**.
9: 7 there speechless; they heard the sound but *did* not **see** anyone.
10: 11 *He* **saw** heaven opened and something like a large sheet being let
17: 16 he was greatly distressed *to* **see** that the city was full of idols.
17: 22 "Men of Athens! *I* **see** that in every way you are very religious.
19: 26 And *you* **see** and hear how this fellow Paul has convinced
20: 38 most was his statement that they would never **see** his face again.
21: 20 "*You* **see**, brother, how many thousands of Jews have believed,
25: 24 "King Agrippa, and all who are present with us, you **see** this man!
27: 10 *I can* **see** that our voyage is going to be disastrous and bring great
28: 6 waiting a long time and **seeing** nothing unusual happen to him,
Heb 7: 4 Just **think** how great he was: Even the patriarch Abraham gave
1Jn 3: 17 and **sees** his brother in need but has no pity on him,
Rev 11: 11 and they stood on their feet, and terror struck those *who* **saw** them.
11: 12 they went up to heaven in a cloud, while their enemies **looked on**.

2556   θεωρία, *theōria*   [1]   [√ 2555]

sight [1]

Lk 23: 48 When all the people who had gathered to witness this **sight** saw

2557   θήκη, *thēkē*   [1]   [√ 5502]

away [+1650+3836] [1]

Jn 18: 11 Jesus commanded Peter, "Put your sword **away**[s] [+1650+3836]!

2558   θηλάζω, *thēlazō*   [5]   [→ 352, 2559]

nursing mothers [3], infants [1], nursed [1]

Mt 21: 16 " 'From the lips of children and **infants** you have ordained praise'?"
24: 19 it will be in those days for pregnant women and **nursing mothers**!
Mk 13: 17 it will be in those days for pregnant women and **nursing mothers**!
Lk 11: 27 "Blessed is the mother who gave you birth and **nursed** you."
21: 23 it will be in those days for pregnant women and **nursing mothers**!

2559   θῆλυς, *thēlys*   [5]   [√ 2558]

female [3], women [2]

Mt 19: 4 "that at the beginning the Creator 'made them male and **female**,'
Mk 10: 6 at the beginning of creation God 'made them male and **female**.'
Ro 1: 26 Even their **women** exchanged natural relations for unnatural ones.
1: 27 same way the men also abandoned natural relations *with* **women**
Gal 3: 28 There is neither Jew nor Greek, slave nor free, male nor **female**,

2560   θήρα, *thēra*   [1]   [√ 2563]

trap [1]

Ro 11: 9 "May their table become a snare and a **trap**, a stumbling block

2561   θηρεύω, *thēreuō*   [1]   [√ 2563]

catch [1]

Lk 11: 54 waiting *to* **catch** him in something he might say.

2562   θηριομαχέω, *thēriomacheō*   [1]   [√ 2563 + 3480]

fought wild beasts [1]

1Co 15: 32 If *I* **fought wild beasts** in Ephesus for merely human reasons,

2563   θηρίον, *thērion*   [46 / 45]   [→ 2560, 2561, 2562]

beast [35], snake [2], wild beasts [2], *untranslated* [1], animal [1],
animals [1], brutes [1], it [+1635+3836+3836] [1], wild animals [1]

Mk 1: 13 by Satan. He was with the **wild animals**, and angels attended him.
Ac 11: 6 animals of the earth, **wild beasts**, reptiles, and birds of the air.
28: 4 When the islanders saw the **snake** hanging from his hand,
28: 5 But Paul shook the **snake** off into the fire and suffered no ill
Tit 1: 12 has said, "Cretans are always liars, evil **brutes**, lazy gluttons."
Heb 12: 20 "If even an **animal** touches the mountain, it must be stoned."
Jas 3: 7 All kinds *of* **animals**, birds, reptiles and creatures of the sea are
Rev 6: 8 by sword, famine and plague, and by the **wild beasts** of the earth.
11: 7 the **beast** that comes up from the Abyss will attack them,
13: 1 And I saw a **beast** coming out of the sea. He had ten horns
13: 2 The **beast** I saw resembled a leopard, but had feet like those of a
13: 3 The whole world was astonished and followed the **beast**.
13: 4 worshiped the dragon because he had given authority *to* the **beast**,
13: 4 and they also worshiped the **beast** and asked, "Who is like the
13: 4 they also worshiped the beast and asked, "Who is like the **beast**?
13: 11 Then I saw another **beast**, coming out of the earth. He had two
13: 12 He exercised all the authority *of* the first **beast** on his behalf,
13: 12 and made the earth and its inhabitants worship the first **beast**,
13: 14 of the signs he was given power to do on behalf *of* the first **beast**,
13: 14 He ordered them to set up an image *in honor of* the **beast** who was
13: 15 He was given power to give breath to the image *of* the first **beast**,
13: 15 so that **it**[s] [+1635+3836+3836] could speak and cause all who
13: 15 and cause all who refused to worship the image **[RPG]** to be
13: 17 which is the name *of* the **beast** or the number of his name.
13: 18 If anyone has insight, let him calculate the number *of* the **beast**,
14: 9 "If anyone worships the **beast** and his image and receives his mark
14: 11 no rest day or night for those who worship the **beast** and his image,
15: 2 those who had been victorious over the **beast** and his image
16: 2 sores broke out on the people who had the mark *of* the **beast**
16: 10 The fifth angel poured out his bowl on the throne *of* the **beast**,
16: 13 out of the mouth *of* the **beast** and out of the mouth of the false
17: 3 There I saw a woman sitting on a scarlet **beast** that was covered
17: 7 to you the mystery of the woman and *of* the **beast** she rides,
17: 8 The **beast**, which you saw, once was, now is not, and will come up
17: 8 creation of the world will be astonished when they see the **beast**,
17: 11 The **beast** who once was, and now is not, is an eighth king.
17: 12 for one hour will receive authority as kings along with the **beast**.
17: 13 one purpose and will give their power and authority *to* the **beast**.
17: 16 The **beast** and the ten horns you saw will hate the prostitute.
17: 17 his purpose by agreeing to give the **beast** their power to rule,
18: 2 bird, [UBS+ *a haunt for every unclean and detestable **beast**.*]
19: 19 Then I saw the **beast** and the kings of the earth and their armies
19: 20 But the **beast** was captured, and with him the false prophet who
19: 20 signs he had deluded those who had received the mark *of* the **beast**
20: 4 They had not worshiped the **beast** or his image and had not
20: 10 where the **beast** and the false prophet had been thrown.

2564   θησαυρίζω, *thēsaurizō*   [8]   [√ 2565]

store up [2], hoarded wealth [1], reserved [1], save up [1], stores
up [1], storing up [1], sum of money [1]

Mt 6: 19 "*Do* not **store up** for yourselves treasures on earth, where moth
6: 20 But **store up** for yourselves treasures in heaven, where moth
Lk 12: 21 "This is how it will be with anyone *who* **stores up** things for
Ro 2: 5 *you are* **storing up** wrath against yourself for the day of God's
1Co 16: 2 each one of you should set aside a **sum of money** in keeping with
2Co 12: 14 After all, children should not have *to* **save up** for their parents,
Jas 5: 3 eat your flesh like fire. *You have* **hoarded wealth** in the last days.
2Pe 3: 7 the same word the present heavens and earth are **reserved** for fire,

2565 θησαυρός, thēsauros [17 / 18] [→ 630, 631, 2564; cf. 5502]

treasure [8], treasures [5], stored up [4], storeroom [1]

Mt 2:11 Then they opened their **treasures** and presented him with gifts of
  6:19 "Do not store up for yourselves **treasures** on earth, where moth
  6:20 But store up for yourselves **treasures** in heaven, where moth
  6:21 For where your **treasure** is, there your heart will be also.
  12:35 The good man brings good things out of the good **stored up** in
  12:35 and the evil man brings evil things out of the evil **stored up** in him.
  13:44 "The kingdom of heaven is like **treasure** hidden in a field.
  13:52 who brings out of his **storeroom** new treasures as well as old."
  19:21 and give to the poor, and you will have **treasure** in heaven.
Mk 10:21 and give to the poor, and you will have **treasure** in heaven.
Lk 6:45 The good man brings good things out of the good **stored up** in his
  6:45 brings evil things out of the evil **stored** [UBS-] **up** in his heart.
  12:33 a **treasure** in heaven that will not be exhausted, where no thief
  12:34 For where your **treasure** is, there your heart will be also.
  18:22 and give to the poor, and you will have **treasure** in heaven.
2Co 4:7 But we have this **treasure** in jars of clay to show that this
Col 2:3 in whom are hidden all the **treasures** of wisdom and knowledge.
Heb 11:26 the sake of Christ as of greater value than the **treasures** of Egypt,

2566 θιγγάνω, thinganō [3]

touch [2], touches [1]

Col 2:21 "Do not handle! Do not taste! *Do* not **touch**!"?
Heb 11:28 so that the destroyer of the firstborn *would* not **touch** the firstborn
  12:20 "If even an animal **touches** the mountain, it must be stoned."

2567 θλίβω, thlibō [10] [→ 632, 2568, 5315]

persecuted [2], crowding [1], distressed [1], harassed [1], hard pressed [1], narrow [1], those in trouble [1], trouble [1], troubled [1]

Mt 7:14 But small is the gate and **narrow** the road that leads to life,
Mk 3:9 a small boat ready for him, to keep the *people* from **crowding** him.
2Co 1:6 If *we are* **distressed**, it is for your comfort and salvation; if we are
  4:8 We *are* **hard pressed** on every side, but not crushed; perplexed,
  7:5 this body of ours had no rest, but *we were* **harassed** at every turn—
1Th 3:4 were with you, we kept telling you that we would *be* **persecuted**,
2Th 1:6 God is just: He will pay back trouble *to* those *who* **trouble** you
  1:7 and give relief *to* you who *are* **troubled**, and to us as well.
1Ti 5:10 helping **those in trouble** and devoting herself to all kinds of good
Heb 11:37 in sheepskins and goatskins, destitute, **persecuted** and mistreated—

2568 θλῖψις, thlipsis [45] [√ 2567]

trouble [8], distress [6], troubles [6], suffering [4], hardships [3], persecution [3], afflictions [2], sufferings [2], trials [2], affliction [1], anguish [1], hard pressed [1], many troubles [1], persecuted [1], severe trial [+1509] [1], suffer persecution [+2400] [1], suffer [1], tribulation [1]

Mt 13:21 When **trouble** or persecution comes because of the word,
  24:9 "Then you will be handed over to be **persecuted** and put to death,
  24:21 For then there will be great **distress**, unequaled from the beginning
  24:29 "Immediately after the **distress** of those days " 'the sun will be
Mk 4:17 When **trouble** or persecution comes because of the word,
  13:19 because those will be days of **distress** unequaled from the
  13:24 "But in those days, following that **distress**, " 'the sun will be
Jn 16:21 but when her baby is born she forgets the **anguish** because of her
  16:33 In this world you will have **trouble**. But take heart! I have
Ac 7:10 and rescued him from all his **troubles**. He gave Joseph wisdom
  7:11 a famine struck all Egypt and Canaan, bringing great **suffering**,
  11:19 Now those who had been scattered by the **persecution** in
  14:22 must go through many **hardships** to enter the kingdom of God,"
  20:23 the Holy Spirit warns me that prison and **hardships** are facing me.
Ro 2:9 There will be **trouble** and distress for every human being who does
  5:3 Not only so, but we also rejoice in our **sufferings**, because we
  5:3 because we know that **suffering** produces perseverance,
  8:35 Shall **trouble** or hardship or persecution or famine or nakedness
  12:12 Be joyful in hope, patient *in* **affliction**, faithful in prayer.
1Co 7:28 But those who marry *will* face **many troubles** in this life,
2Co 1:4 who comforts us in all our **troubles**, so that we can comfort

  1:4 so that we can comfort those in any **trouble** with the comfort we
  1:8 brothers, about the **hardships** we suffered in the province of Asia.
  2:4 For I wrote you out of great **distress** and anguish of heart and with
  4:17 and momentary **troubles** are achieving for us an eternal glory that
  6:4 in great endurance; in **troubles**, hardships and distresses;
  7:4 greatly encouraged; in all our **troubles** my joy knows no bounds.
  8:2 Out of the most **severe trial** [+1509], their overflowing joy
  8:13 is not that others might be relieved while you are **hard pressed**,
Eph 3:13 therefore, not to be discouraged because of my **sufferings** for you,
Php 1:17 supposing that they can stir up **trouble** for me while I am in
  4:14 Yet it was good of you to share *in* my **troubles**.
Col 1:24 in my flesh what is still lacking *in regard to* Christ's **afflictions**,
1Th 1:6 in spite of severe **suffering**, you welcomed the message with the
  3:3 so that no one would be unsettled by these **trials**. You know quite
  3:7 in all our distress and **persecution** we were encouraged about you
2Th 1:4 and faith in all the persecutions and **trials** you are enduring.
  1:6 God is just: He will pay back **trouble** to those who trouble you
Heb 10:33 Sometimes you were publicly exposed to insult and **persecution**;
Jas 1:27 to look after orphans and widows in their **distress** and to keep
Rev 1:9 your brother and companion in the **suffering** and kingdom
  2:9 I know your **afflictions** and your poverty—yet you are rich!
  2:10 to test you, and *you will* **suffer persecution** [+2400] for ten days.
  2:22 and I will make those who commit adultery with her **suffer**
  7:14 "These are they who have come out of the great **tribulation**;

2569 θνήσκω, thnēskō [9] [→ 114, 115, 633, 2119, 2467, 2503, 2504, 2505, 2506, 2570, 5271]

dead [9]

Mt 2:20 for those who were trying to take the child's life *are* **dead**."
Mk 15:44 Pilate was surprised to hear that *he* was already **dead**. Summoning
Lk 7:12 approached the town gate, a **dead** *person* was being carried out—
  8:49 of Jairus, the synagogue ruler. "Your daughter *is* **dead**," he said.
Jn 11:44 The **dead** *man* came out, his hands and feet wrapped with strips of
  19:33 But when they came to Jesus and found that he *was* already **dead**,
Ac 14:19 and dragged him outside the city, thinking he *was* **dead**.
  25:19 and about a **dead** *man* named Jesus who Paul claimed was alive.
1Ti 5:6 But the widow who lives for pleasure *is* **dead** even while she lives.

2570 θνητός, thnētos [6] [√ 2569]

mortal [6]

Ro 6:12 Therefore do not let sin reign in your **mortal** body so that you
  8:11 dead will also give life *to* your **mortal** bodies through his Spirit,
1Co 15:53 itself with the imperishable, and the **mortal** with immortality,
  15:54 and the **mortal** with immortality, then the saying that is written
2Co 4:11 for Jesus' sake, so that his life may be revealed in our **mortal** body.
  5:4 so that what is **mortal** may be swallowed up by life.

2571 θορυβάζω, thorybazō [1] [√ 2573]

upset [1]

Lk 10:41 the Lord answered, "you are worried and **upset** about many things,

2572 θορυβέω, thorybeō [4] [√ 2573]

alarmed [1], commotion [1], noisy [1], riot [1]

Mt 9:23 the ruler's house and saw the flute players and the **noisy** crowd,
Mk 5:39 went in and said to them, "Why all this **commotion** and wailing?
Ac 17:5 from the marketplace, formed a mob and *started* a **riot** in the city.
  20:10 his arms around him. "Don't *be* **alarmed**," he said. "He's alive!"

2573 θόρυβος, thorybos [7] [→ 2571, 2572]

uproar [3], commotion [1], disturbance [1], riot [+1639] [1], riot [1]

Mt 26:5 the Feast," they said, "or there may be a **riot** among the people."
  27:24 but that instead an **uproar** was starting, he took water and washed
Mk 5:38 Jesus saw a **commotion**, with people crying and wailing loudly,
  14:2 not during the Feast," they said, "or the people *may* **riot** [+1639]."
Ac 20:1 When the **uproar** had ended, Paul sent for the disciples and,
  21:34 the commander could not get at the truth because of the **uproar**,
  24:18 was no crowd with me, nor was I involved in any **disturbance**.

2574 θραυματίζω, **thraumatizō**　Not used in UBS/NIV [√ *2575*]

2575 θραύω, **thrauō** [1] [→ *2574*]

oppressed [1]

Lk　4: 18　and recovery of sight for the blind, to release the **oppressed**,

2576 θρέμμα, **thremma** [1] [√ *5555*]

flocks and herds [1]

Jn　4: 12　from it himself, as did also his sons and his **flocks and herds**?"

2577 θρηνέω, **thrēneō** [4] [→ *2578, 2583; cf. 125*]

sang a dirge [2], mourn [1], wailed for [1]

Mt　11: 17　and you did not dance; *we* **sang a dirge**, and you did not mourn.'
Lk　7: 32　and you did not dance; *we* **sang a dirge**, and you did not cry.'
　　23: 27　followed him, including women who mourned and **wailed for** him.
Jn　16: 20　you the truth, you will weep and **mourn** while the world rejoices.

2578 θρῆνος, **thrēnos**　Not used in UBS/NIV [√ *2577*]

2579 θρησκεία, **thrēskeia** [4] [√ *2580*]

religion [3], worship [1]

Ac　26: 5　they are willing, that according to the strictest sect *of* our **religion**,
Col　2: 18　and the **worship** of angels disqualify you for the prize.
Jas　1: 26　on his tongue, he deceives himself and his **religion** is worthless.
　　1: 27　**Religion** that God our Father accepts as pure and faultless is this:

2580 θρῆσκος, **thrēskos** [1] [→ *1615, 2579*]

religious [1]

Jas　1: 26　If anyone considers himself **religious** and yet does not keep a tight

2581 θριαμβεύω, **thriambeuō** [2]

leads in triumphal procession [1], triumphing over [1]

2Co　2: 14　who always **leads** us **in triumphal procession** in Christ
Col　2: 15　a public spectacle of them, **triumphing over** them by the cross.

2582 θρίξ, **thrix** [15] [→ *5570*]

hair [13], hairs [2]

Mt　3: 4　John's clothes were made of camel's **hair**, and he had a leather belt
　　5: 36　by your head, for you cannot make even one **hair** white or black.
　　10: 30　And even the very **hairs** of your head are all numbered.
Mk　1: 6　John wore clothing *made of* camel's **hair**, with a leather belt
Lk　7: 38　Then she wiped them *with* her **hair**, kissed them and poured
　　7: 44　but she wet my feet with her tears and wiped them *with* her **hair**.
　　12: 7　Indeed, the very **hairs** of your head are all numbered. Don't be
　　21: 18　But not a **hair** of your head will perish.
Jn　11: 2　who poured perfume on the Lord and wiped his feet *with* her **hair**,
　　12: 3　she poured it on Jesus' feet and wiped his feet *with* her **hair**.
Ac　27: 34　it to survive. Not one of you will lose a *single* **hair** from his head."
1Pe　3: 3　such as braided **hair** and the wearing of gold jewelry and fine
Rev　1: 14　His head and **hair** were white like wool, as white as snow,
　　9: 8　Their **hair** was like women's hair, and their teeth were like lions'
　　9: 8　Their hair was like women's **hair**, and their teeth were like lions'

2583 θροέω, **throeō** [3] [√ *2577*]

alarmed [3]

Mt　24: 6　and rumors of wars, but see to it that *you are* not **alarmed**.
Mk　13: 7　When you hear of wars and rumors of wars, *do* not *be* **alarmed**.
2Th　2: 2　not to become easily unsettled or **alarmed** by some prophecy,

2584 θρόμβος, **thrombos** [1]

drops [1]

Lk　22: 44　and his sweat was like **drops** of blood falling to the ground.

2585 θρόνος, **thronos** [62]

ἐνώπιον τοῦ θρόνου (before the throne) [11] Rev 1:4; 4:5,6,10; 7:9,9,11,15; 8:3; 14:3; 20:12

θρόνος τοῦ θεοῦ (throne of God) [7] Mt 5:34; 23:22; Heb 1:8; 12:2; Rev 7:15; 22:1,3

throne [52], thrones [7], *untranslated* [1], it[s] [+3836] [1], them[s] [+3836] [1]

Mt　5: 34　Do not swear at all: either by heaven, for it is God's **throne**;
　　19: 28　of all things, when the Son of Man sits on his glorious **throne**,
　　19: 28　you who have followed me will also sit on twelve **thrones**,
　　23: 22　And he who swears by heaven swears by God's **throne** and by the
　　25: 31　all the angels with him, he will sit on his **throne** in heavenly glory.
Lk　1: 32　The Lord God will give him the **throne** of his father David,
　　1: 52　He has brought down rulers from their **thrones** but has lifted up
　　22: 30　may eat and drink at my table in my kingdom and sit on **thrones**,
Ac　2: 30　on oath that he would place one of his descendants on his **throne**.
　　7: 49　' 'Heaven is my **throne**, and the earth is my footstool. What kind of
Col　1: 16　and invisible, whether **thrones** or powers or rulers or authorities;
Heb　1: 8　the Son he says, "Your **throne**, O God, will last for ever and ever,
　　4: 16　Let us then approach the **throne** of grace with confidence,
　　8: 1　who sat down at the right hand *of* the **throne** of the Majesty in
　　12: 2　its shame, and sat down at the right hand *of* the **throne** of God.
Rev　1: 4　and who is to come, and from the seven spirits before his **throne**,
　　2: 13　I know where you live—where Satan has his **throne**. Yet you
　　3: 21　I will give the right to sit with me on my **throne**, just as I
　　3: 21　just as I overcame and sat down with my Father on his **throne**.
　　4: 2　and there before me was a **throne** in heaven with someone sitting
　　4: 2　me was a throne in heaven with someone sitting on it[s] [+3836]
　　4: 3　A rainbow, resembling an emerald, encircled the **throne**.
　　4: 4　Surrounding the **throne** were twenty-four other thrones, and seated
　　4: 4　Surrounding the throne were twenty-four *other* **thrones**,
　　4: 4　and seated on them[s] [+3836] were twenty-four elders.
　　4: 5　From the **throne** came flashes of lightning, rumblings and peals of
　　4: 5　and peals of thunder. Before the **throne**, seven lamps were blazing.
　　4: 6　Also before the **throne** there was what looked like a sea of glass,
　　4: 6　In the center, **[RPG]** around the throne, were four living
　　4: 6　In the center, around the **throne**, were four living creatures,
　　4: 9　honor and thanks to him who sits on the **throne** and who lives for
　　4: 10　twenty-four elders fall down before him who sits on the **throne**,
　　4: 10　and ever. They lay their crowns before the **throne** and say:
　　5: 1　Then I saw in the right hand of him who sat on the **throne** a scroll
　　5: 6　looking as if it had been slain, standing in the center *of* the **throne**,
　　5: 7　took the scroll from the right hand of him who sat on the **throne**.
　　5: 11　They encircled the **throne** and the living creatures and the elders.
　　5: 13　"To him who sits on the **throne** and to the Lamb be praise
　　6: 16　"Fall on us and hide us from the face of him who sits on the **throne**
　　7: 9　and language, standing before the **throne** and in front of the Lamb.
　　7: 10　belongs to our God, who sits on the **throne**, and to the Lamb."
　　7: 11　All the angels were standing around the **throne** and around the
　　7: 11　They fell down on their faces before the **throne** and worshiped
　　7: 15　"they are before the **throne** of God and serve him day and night in
　　7: 15　and he who sits on the **throne** will spread his tent over them.
　　7: 17　For the Lamb at the center *of* the **throne** will be their shepherd;
　　8: 3　the prayers of all the saints, on the golden altar before the **throne**.
　　11: 16　who were seated on their **thrones** before God, fell on their faces
　　12: 5　And her child was snatched up to God and to his **throne**.
　　13: 2　gave the beast his power and his **throne** and great authority.
　　14: 3　And they sang a new song before the **throne** and before the four
　　16: 10　The fifth angel poured out his bowl on the **throne** of the beast,
　　16: 17　and out of the temple came a loud voice from the **throne**,
　　19: 4　fell down and worshiped God, who was seated on the **throne**.
　　19: 5　Then a voice came from the **throne**, saying: "Praise our God,
　　20: 4　I saw **thrones** on which were seated those who had been given
　　20: 11　Then I saw a great white **throne** and him who was seated on it.
　　20: 12　And I saw the dead, great and small, standing before the **throne**,
　　21: 3　And I heard a loud voice from the **throne** saying,
　　21: 5　He who was seated on the **throne** said, "I am making everything
　　22: 1　clear as crystal, flowing from the **throne** of God and of the Lamb

22: 3 The **throne** of God and of the Lamb will be in the city, and his

2586 θρύπτω, *thryptō* Not used in UBS/NIV [→ *5316;* cf. *5588*]

2587 Θυάτειρα, *Thyateira* [4]

Thyatira [4]

Ac   16:14 a dealer in purple cloth from the city *of* **Thyatira**, who was a
Rev   1:11 to Ephesus, Smyrna, Pergamum, **Thyatira**, Sardis, Philadelphia
      2:18 "To the angel of the church in **Thyatira** write: These are the words
      2:24 Now I say to the rest of you in **Thyatira**, to you who do not hold

2588 θυγάτηρ, *thygatēr* [28] [→ *2589*]

daughter [23], daughters [4], descendant [+*1666+3836*] [1]

Mt   9:18 and knelt before him and said, "My **daughter** has just died.
     9:22 "Take heart, **daughter**," he said, "your faith has healed you."
     10:35 a **daughter** against her mother, a daughter-in-law against her
     10:37 who loves his son or **daughter** more than me is not worthy of me;
     14: 6 On Herod's birthday the **daughter** of Herodias danced for them
     15:22 My **daughter** is suffering terribly from demon-possession."
     15:28 is granted." And her **daughter** was healed from that very hour.
     21: 5 "Say *to* the **Daughter** of Zion, 'See, your king comes to you,
Mk   5:34 He said to her, "**Daughter**, your faith has healed you. Go in peace
     5:35 of Jairus, the synagogue ruler. "Your **daughter** is dead," they said.
     6:22 When the **daughter** of Herodias came in and danced, she pleased
     7:26 She begged Jesus to drive the demon out *of* her **daughter**.
     7:29 "For such a reply, you may go; the demon has left your **daughter**."
Lk   1: 5 his wife Elizabeth was also a **descendant** [+*1666+3836*] of Aaron.
     2:36 a prophetess, Anna, the **daughter** of Phanuel, of the tribe of Asher.
     8:42 because his only **daughter**, a girl of about twelve, was dying.
     8:48 Then he said to her, "**Daughter**, your faith has healed you.
     8:49 of Jairus, the synagogue ruler. "Your **daughter** is dead," he said.
     12:53 mother against **daughter** and daughter against mother,
     12:53 mother against daughter and **daughter** against mother,
     13:16 Then should not this woman, a **daughter** of Abraham, whom Satan
     23:28 Jesus turned and said to them, "**Daughters** of Jerusalem, do not
Jn   12:15 "Do not be afraid, O **Daughter** of Zion; see, your king is coming,
Ac   2:17 Your sons and **daughters** will prophesy, your young men will see
     7:21 Pharaoh's **daughter** took him and brought him up as her own son.
     21: 9 He had four unmarried **daughters** who prophesied.
2Co   6:18 and you will be my sons and **daughters**, says the Lord Almighty."
Heb 11:24 grown up, refused to be known as the son *of* Pharaoh's **daughter**.

2589 θυγάτριον, *thygatrion* [2] [√ *2588*]

little daughter [2]

Mk   5:23 and pleaded earnestly with him, "My **little daughter** is dying.
     7:25 a woman whose **little daughter** was possessed by an evil spirit

2590 θύελλα, *thyella* [1] [√ *2596*]

storm [1]

Heb 12:18 and that is burning with fire; to darkness, gloom and **storm**;

2591 θύϊνος, *thyinos* [1] [√ *2604*]

citron [1]

Rev 18:12 every sort *of* **citron** wood, and articles of every kind made of

2592 θυμίαμα, *thymiama* [6] [√ *2604*]

incense [5], burning of incense [1]

Lk   1:10 And when the time *for* the **burning of incense** came,
     1:11 appeared to him, standing at the right side of the altar *of* **incense**.
Rev 5: 8 one had a harp and they were holding golden bowls full *of* **incense**,
     8: 3 He was given much **incense** to offer, with the prayers of all the
     8: 4 The smoke *of* the **incense**, together with the prayers of the saints,
     18:13 of **incense**, myrrh and frankincense, of wine and olive oil,

2593 θυμιατήριον, *thymiatērion* [1] [√ *2604*]

altar of incense [1]

Heb 9: 4 which had the golden **altar of incense** and the gold-covered ark of

2594 θυμιάω, *thymiaō* [1] [√ *2604*]

burn incense [1]

Lk   1: 9 the priesthood, to go into the temple of the Lord and **burn incense**.

2595 θυμομαχέω, *thymomacheō* [1] [√ *2596 + 3480*]

quarreling [1]

Ac   12:20 He had been **quarreling** with the people of Tyre and Sidon;

2596 θυμός, *thymos* [18] [→ *126, 1445, 1926, 1927, 2121, 2122, 2123, 2313, 2314, 2315, 2590, 2595, 2597, 3428, 3429, 3430, 3924, 4608, 4609, 4610*]

wrath [4], fury [3], anger [2], maddening [2], rage [2], fits of rage [1], furious [+*4398*] [1], furious [+*4441*] [1], fury [+*3489*] [1], outbursts of anger [1]

Lk   4:28 All the people in the synagogue *were* **furious** [+*4398*] when they
Ac   19:28 heard this, they were **furious** [+*4441*] and began shouting:
Ro   2: 8 who reject the truth and follow evil, there will be wrath and **anger**.
2Co 12:20 jealousy, **outbursts of anger**, factions, slander, gossip, arrogance
Gal   5:20 hatred, discord, jealousy, **fits of rage**, selfish ambition,
Eph   4:31 Get rid of all bitterness, **rage** and anger, brawling and slander,
Col   3: 8 anger, **rage**, malice, slander, and filthy language from your lips.
Heb 11:27 By faith he left Egypt, not fearing the king's **anger**; he persevered
Rev 12:12 He is filled with **fury** [+*3489*], because he knows that his time is
     14: 8 which made all the nations drink the **maddening** wine of her
     14:10 he, too, will drink of the wine *of* God's **fury**, which has been
     14:19 its grapes and threw them into the great winepress *of* God's **wrath**.
     15: 1 last plagues—last, because with them God's **wrath** is completed.
     15: 7 the seven angels seven golden bowls filled *with* the **wrath** of God,
     16: 1 "Go, pour out the seven bowls *of* God's **wrath** on the earth."
     16:19 and gave her the cup filled with the wine *of* the **fury** of his wrath.
     18: 3 For all the nations have drunk the **maddening** wine of her
     19:15 He treads the winepress *of* the **fury** of the wrath of God Almighty.

2597 θυμόω, *thymoō* [1] [√ *2596*]

furious [+*3336*] [1]

Mt   2:16 that he had been outwitted by the Magi, *he was* **furious** [+*3336*],

2598 θύρα, *thyra* [39] [→ *2599, 2600, 2601*]

door [21], doors [6], gate [5], entrance [4], doorway [1], gates [1], outer entrance [+*4784*] [1]

Mt   6: 6 your room, close the **door** and pray to your Father, who is unseen.
     24:33 you see all these things, you know that it is near, right at the **door**.
     25:10 went in with him to the wedding banquet. And the **door** was shut.
     27:60 He rolled a big stone in front of the **entrance** to the tomb and went
Mk   1:33 The whole town gathered at the **door**,
     2: 2 not even outside the **door**, and he preached the word to them.
     11: 4 They went and found a colt outside in the street, tied at a **doorway**.
     13:29 these things happening, you know that it is near, right at the **door**.
     15:46 of rock. Then he rolled a stone against the **entrance** of the tomb.
     16: 3 "Who will roll the stone away from the **entrance** of the tomb?"
Lk   11: 7 The **door** is already locked, and my children are with me in bed.
     13:24 "Make every effort to enter through the narrow **door**,
     13:25 Once the owner of the house gets up and closes the **door**, you will
     13:25 stand outside knocking and pleading, 'Sir, open the **door** for us.'
Jn   10: 1 the truth, the man who does not enter the sheep pen by the **gate**,
     10: 2 The man who enters by the **gate** is the shepherd of his sheep.
     10: 7 Jesus said again, "I tell you the truth, I am the **gate** for the sheep.
     10: 9 I am the **gate**; whoever enters through me will be saved. He will
     18:16 but Peter had to wait outside at the **door**. The other disciple,
     20:19 with the **doors** locked for fear of the Jews, Jesus came and stood
     20:26 Though the **doors** were locked, Jesus came and stood among them
Ac   3: 2 a man crippled from birth was being carried to the temple **gate**

5: 9 The feet of the men who buried your husband are at the **door**,
5: 19 But during the night an angel of the Lord opened the **doors** of the
5: 23 the jail securely locked, with the guards standing at the **doors**;
12: 6 bound with two chains, and sentries stood guard at the **entrance**.
12: 13 Peter knocked at the **outer entrance** [+*4784*], and a servant girl
14: 27 and how he had opened the **door** of faith to the Gentiles.
16: 26 At once all the prison **doors** flew open, and everybody's chains
16: 27 and when he saw the prison **doors** open, he drew his sword
21: 30 him from the temple, and immediately the **gates** were shut.
1Co 16: 9 because a great **door** for effective work has opened to me,
2Co 2: 12 gospel of Christ and found that the Lord had opened a **door** for me,
Col 4: 3 And pray for us, too, that God may open a **door** for our message,
Jas 5: 9 brothers, or you will be judged. The Judge is standing at the **door**!
Rev 3: 8 I have placed before you an open **door** that no one can shut.
3: 20 Here I am! I stand at the **door** and knock. If anyone hears my voice
3: 20 If anyone hears my voice and opens the **door**, I will come in
4: 1 I looked, and there before me was a **door** standing open in heaven.

2599 θυρεός, *thyreos* [1] [√ *2598*]

shield [1]

Eph 6: 16 In addition to all this, take up the **shield** of faith, with which you

2600 θυρίς, *thyris* [2] [√ *2598*]

window [2]

Ac 20: 9 Seated in a **window** was a young man named Eutychus, who was
2Co 11: 33 But I was lowered in a basket from a **window** in the wall

2601 θυρωρός, *thyrōros* [4] [√ *2598*]

door [1], girl on duty [1], one at the door [1], watchman [1]

Mk 13: 34 with his assigned task, and tells the **one at the door** to keep watch.
Jn 10: 3 The **watchman** opens the gate for him, and the sheep listen to his
18: 16 came back, spoke to the **girl on duty** there and brought Peter in.
18: 17 not one of his disciples, are you?" the girl *at* the **door** asked Peter.

2602 θυσία, *thysia* [28] [√ *2604*]

sacrifices [16], sacrifice [11], offering [1]

Mt 9: 13 and learn what this means: 'I desire mercy, not **sacrifice**.'
12: 7 had known what these words mean, 'I desire mercy, not **sacrifice**,'
Mk 12: 33 yourself is more important than all burnt offerings and **sacrifices**."
Lk 2: 24 and to offer a **sacrifice** in keeping with what is said in the Law of
13: 1 the Galileans whose blood Pilate had mixed with their **sacrifices**.
Ac 7: 41 They brought **sacrifices** to it and held a celebration in honor of
7: 42 " 'Did you bring me **sacrifices** and offerings forty years in the
Ro 12: 1 to offer your bodies as living **sacrifices**, holy and pleasing to God—
1Co 10: 18 Do not those who eat the **sacrifices** participate in the altar?
Eph 5: 2 gave himself up for us as a fragrant offering and **sacrifice** to God.
Php 2: 17 even if I am being poured out like a drink offering on the **sacrifice**
4: 18 They are a fragrant **offering**, an acceptable sacrifice, pleasing to
Heb 5: 1 in matters related to God, to offer gifts and **sacrifices** for sins.
7: 27 he does not need to offer **sacrifices** day after day, first for his own
8: 3 Every high priest is appointed to offer both gifts and **sacrifices**,
9: 9 and **sacrifices** being offered were not able to clear the conscience
9: 23 but the heavenly things themselves *with* better **sacrifices** than
9: 26 the end of the ages to do away with sin by the **sacrifice** of himself.
10: 1 *by* the same **sacrifices** repeated endlessly year after year,
10: 5 "**Sacrifice** and offering you did not desire, but a body you
10: 8 First he said, "**Sacrifices** and offerings, burnt offerings and sin
10: 11 again and again he offers the same **sacrifices**, which can never take
10: 12 But when this priest had offered for all time one **sacrifice** for sins,
10: 26 received the knowledge of the truth, no **sacrifice** for sins is left,
11: 4 By faith Abel offered God a better **sacrifice** than Cain did.
13: 15 therefore, let us continually offer to God a **sacrifice** of praise—
13: 16 and to share with others, for *with* such **sacrifices** God is pleased.
1Pe 2: 5 offering spiritual **sacrifices** acceptable to God through Jesus

2603 θυσιαστήριον, *thysiastērion* [23] [√ *2604*]

altar [22], altars [1]

Mt 5: 23 if you are offering your gift at the **altar** and there remember that

5: 24 leave your gift there in front of the **altar**. First go and be
23: 18 You also say, 'If anyone swears by the **altar**, it means nothing;
23: 19 Which is greater: the gift, or the **altar** that makes the gift sacred?
23: 20 he who swears by the **altar** swears by it and by everything on it.
23: 35 whom you murdered between the temple and the **altar**.
Lk 1: 11 appeared to him, standing at the right side *of* the **altar** of incense.
11: 51 of Zechariah, who was killed between the **altar** and the sanctuary.
Ro 11: 3 they have killed your prophets and torn down your **altars**;
1Co 9: 13 and those who serve at the **altar** share in what is offered on the
9: 13 those who serve at the altar share *in* what is offered on the **altar**?
10: 18 Do not those who eat the sacrifices participate in the **altar**?
Heb 7: 13 and no one from that tribe has ever served at the **altar**.
13: 10 We have an **altar** from which those who minister at the tabernacle
Jas 2: 21 for what he did when he offered his son Isaac on the **altar**?
Rev 6: 9 I saw under the **altar** the souls of those who had been slain
8: 3 who had a golden censer, came and stood at the **altar**.
8: 3 the prayers of all the saints, on the golden **altar** before the throne.
8: 5 filled it with fire *from* the **altar**, and hurled it on the earth;
9: 13 and I heard a voice coming from the horns *of* the golden **altar** that
11: 1 and was told, "Go and measure the temple of God and the **altar**,
14: 18 came from the **altar** and called in a loud voice to him who had the
16: 7 And I heard the **altar** respond: "Yes, Lord God Almighty, true

2604 θύω, *thyō* [14] [→ *1628, 2124, 2591, 2592, 2593, 2594, 2602, 2603, 2638; cf. 2520*]

kill [5], sacrificed [2], *untranslated* [1], butchered [1], killed [1], offer sacrifices [1], offered [1], sacrifice [1], sacrificing [1]

Mt 22: 4 My oxen and fattened cattle *have been* **butchered**, and everything
Mk 14: 12 when *it was customary to* **sacrifice** the Passover lamb,
Lk 15: 23 Bring the fattened calf and **kill** it. Let's have a feast and celebrate.
15: 27 'and your father *has* **killed** the fattened calf because he has him
15: 30 with prostitutes comes home, *you* **kill** the fattened calf for him!'
22: 7 Bread on which the Passover lamb had to *be* **sacrificed**.
Jn 10: 10 The thief comes only to steal and **kill** and destroy; I have come that
Ac 10: 13 Then a voice told him, "Get up, Peter. **Kill** and eat."
11: 7 Then I heard a voice telling me, 'Get up, Peter. **Kill** and eat.'
14: 13 because he and the crowd wanted *to* **offer sacrifices** to them.
14: 18 they had difficulty keeping the crowd from **sacrificing** to them.
1Co 5: 7 you really are. For Christ, our Passover lamb, *has been* **sacrificed**.
10: 20 No, but the sacrifices of pagans *are* **offered** to demons, not to God,
10: 20 the sacrifices of pagans are offered to demons, not [**RPG**] to God,

2605 Θωμᾶς, *Thōmas* [11]

Thomas [11]

Mt 10: 3 and Bartholomew; **Thomas** and Matthew the tax collector;
Mk 3: 18 Andrew, Philip, Bartholomew, Matthew, **Thomas**, James son of
Lk 6: 15 Matthew, **Thomas**, James son of Alphaeus, Simon who was called
Jn 11: 16 Then **Thomas** (called Didymus) said to the rest of the disciples,
14: 5 **Thomas** said to him, "Lord, we don't know where you are going,
20: 24 Now **Thomas** (called Didymus), one of the Twelve, was not with
20: 26 his disciples were in the house again, and **Thomas** was with them.
20: 27 Then he said *to* **Thomas**, "Put your finger here; see my hands.
20: 28 **Thomas** said to him, "My Lord and my God!"
21: 2 Simon Peter, **Thomas** (called Didymus), Nathanael from Cana in
Ac 1: 13 and Andrew; Philip and **Thomas**, Bartholomew and Matthew;

2606 θώραξ, *thōrax* [5]

breastplates [3], breastplate [2]

Eph 6: 14 around your waist, with the **breastplate** of righteousness in place,
1Th 5: 8 let us be self-controlled, putting on faith and love as a **breastplate**,
Rev 9: 9 They had **breastplates** like breastplates of iron, and the sound of
9: 9 They had breastplates like **breastplates** of iron, and the sound of
9: 17 Their **breastplates** were fiery red, dark blue, and yellow as sulfur.

I, *I*

2607 ι, *i*   Not used in UBS/NIV [→ *2740*]

2608 Ἰάϊρος, Iairos [2]

Jairus [2]

Mk 5:22 Then one of the synagogue rulers, named **Jairus**, came there.
Lk   8:41 Then a man named **Jairus**, a ruler of the synagogue, came

2609 Ἰακώβ, Iakōb [27] [→ 2610]

Jacob [26], Jacob's [1]

Mt   1: 2 Isaac the father of **Jacob**, Jacob the father of Judah and his
     1: 2 the father of Jacob, **Jacob** the father of Judah and his brothers,
     1:15 Eleazar the father of Matthan, Matthan the father of **Jacob**,
     1:16 and **Jacob** the father of Joseph, the husband of Mary, of whom was
     8:11 feast with Abraham, Isaac and **Jacob** in the kingdom of heaven.
    22:32 am the God of Abraham, the God of Isaac, and the God of **Jacob**'?
Mk 12:26 am the God of Abraham, the God of Isaac, and the God of **Jacob**'?
Lk   1:33 and he will reign over the house of **Jacob** forever; his kingdom
     3:34 the son of **Jacob**, the son of Isaac, the son of Abraham, the son of
    13:28 Isaac and **Jacob** and all the prophets in the kingdom of God,
    20:37 God of Abraham, and the God of Isaac, and the God of **Jacob**.'
Jn   4: 5 near the plot of ground **Jacob** had given to his son Joseph.
     4: 6 **Jacob's** well was there, and Jesus, tired as he was from the
     4:12 Are you greater than our father **Jacob**, who gave us the well
Ac   3:13 The God of Abraham, Isaac and **Jacob**, the God of our fathers,
     7: 8 Later Isaac became the father of **Jacob**, and Jacob became the
     7: 8 of Jacob, and **Jacob** became the father of the twelve patriarchs.
     7:12 When **Jacob** heard that there was grain in Egypt, he sent our
     7:14 After this, Joseph sent for his father **Jacob** and his whole family,
     7:15 Then **Jacob** went down to Egypt, where he and our fathers died.
     7:32 the God of your fathers, the God of Abraham, Isaac and **Jacob**.'
     7:46 asked that he might provide a dwelling place for the God of **Jacob**.
Ro   9:13 Just as it is written: "**Jacob** I loved, but Esau I hated."
    11:26 will come from Zion; he will turn godlessness away from **Jacob**.
Heb 11: 9 he lived in tents, as did Isaac and **Jacob**, who were heirs with him
    11:20 By faith Isaac blessed **Jacob** and Esau in regard to their future.
    11:21 By faith **Jacob**, when he was dying, blessed each of Joseph's sons,

2610 Ἰάκωβος, Iakōbos [42] [√ 2609]

Πέτρος ... Ἰωάννης ... Ἰάκωβος (Peter ... John ... James)
[10] Mt 10:2; 17:1; Mk 5:37; 9:2; 13:3; 14:33; Lk 6:14; 8:51; 9:28;
Ac 1:13

James [41], his^s [+3836] [1]

Mt   4:21 two other brothers, **James** son of Zebedee and his brother John.
    10: 2 his brother Andrew; **James** son of Zebedee, and his brother John;
    10: 3 Matthew the tax collector; **James** son of Alphaeus, and Thaddaeus;
    13:55 and aren't his brothers **James**, Joseph, Simon and Judas?
    17: 1 Jesus took with him Peter, **James** and John the brother of James,
    27:56 Mary the mother of **James** and Joses, and the mother of Zebedee's
Mk   1:19 he saw **James** son of Zebedee and his brother John in a boat,
     1:29 they went with **James** and John to the home of Simon and Andrew.
     3:17 **James** son of Zebedee and his brother John (to them he gave the
     3:17 and his^s [+3836] brother John (to them he gave the name
     3:18 Thomas, **James** son of Alphaeus, Thaddaeus,
     5:37 follow him except Peter, **James** and John the brother of James.
     5:37 follow him except Peter, James and John the brother of **James**.
     6: 3 Isn't this Mary's son and the brother of **James**, Joseph, Judas
     9: 2 **James** and John with him and led them up a high mountain,
    10:35 Then **James** and John, the sons of Zebedee, came to him.
    10:41 ten heard about this, they became indignant with **James** and John.
    13: 3 the temple, Peter, **James**, John and Andrew asked him privately,
    14:33 He took Peter, **James** and John along with him, and he began to be
    15:40 Mary the mother of **James** the younger and of Joses, and Salome.
    16: 1 Mary Magdalene, Mary the mother of **James**, and Salome bought
Lk   5:10 and so were **James** and John, the sons of Zebedee, Simon's
     6:14 his brother Andrew, **James**, John, Philip, Bartholomew,
     6:15 Matthew, Thomas, **James** son of Alphaeus, Simon who was called
     6:16 Judas son of **James**, and Judas Iscariot, who became a traitor.
     8:51 except Peter, John and **James**, and the child's father and mother.
     9:28 John and **James** with him and went up onto a mountain to pray.
     9:54 When the disciples **James** and John saw this, they asked, "Lord,
    24:10 It was Mary Magdalene, Joanna, Mary the mother of **James**,
Ac   1:13 Those present were Peter, John, **James** and Andrew; Philip
     1:13 **James** son of Alphaeus and Simon the Zealot, and Judas son of

     1:13 son of Alphaeus and Simon the Zealot, and Judas son of **James**.
    12: 2 He had **James**, the brother of John, put to death with the sword.
    12:17 "Tell **James** and the brothers about this," he said, and then he left
    15:13 When they finished, **James** spoke up: "Brothers, listen to me.
    21:18 The next day Paul and the rest of us went to see **James**, and all the
1Co 15: 7 Then he appeared to **James**, then to all the apostles,
Gal 1:19 I saw none of the other apostles—only **James**, the Lord's brother.
     2: 9 **James**, Peter and John, those reputed to be pillars, gave me
     2:12 Before certain men came from **James**, he used to eat with the
Jas 1: 1 **James**, a servant of God and of the Lord Jesus Christ,
Jude 1: 1 Jude, a servant of Jesus Christ and a brother of **James**, To those

2611 ἴαμα, iama [3] [√ 2615]

healing [3]

1Co 12: 9 by the same Spirit, to another gifts of **healing** by that one Spirit,
    12:28 also those having gifts of **healing**, those able to help others,
    12:30 Do all have gifts of **healing**? Do all speak in tongues? Do all

2612 Ἰαμβρῆς, Iambrēs [1]

Jambres [1]

2Ti 3: 8 Just as Jannes and **Jambres** opposed Moses, so also these men

2613 Ἰανναί, Iannai [1]

Jannai [1]

Lk   3:24 the son of Levi, the son of Melki, the son of **Jannai**, the son of

2614 Ἰάννης, Iannēs [1]

Jannes [1]

2Ti 3: 8 Just as **Jannes** and Jambres opposed Moses, so also these men

2615 ἰάομαι, iaomai [26] [→ 2611, 2617, 2620]

healed [16], heal [6], healing [2], freed [1], heals [1]

Mt   8: 8 my roof. But just say the word, and my servant will be **healed**.
     8:13 believed it would." And his servant was **healed** at that very hour.
    13:15 understand with their hearts and turn, and I would **heal** them.'
    15:28 is granted." And her daughter was **healed** from that very hour.
Mk   5:29 and she felt in her body that she was **freed** from her suffering.
Lk   5:17 And the power of the Lord was present for him to **heal** the sick.
     6:18 who had come to hear him and to be **healed** of their diseases.
     6:19 because power was coming from him and **healing** them all.
     7: 7 to come to you. But say the word, and my servant will be **healed**.
     8:47 why she had touched him and how she had been instantly **healed**.
     9: 2 sent them out to preach the kingdom of God and to **heal** the sick.
     9:11 about the kingdom of God, and **healed** those who needed healing.
     9:42 the evil spirit, **healed** the boy and gave him back to his father.
    14: 4 So taking hold of the man, he **healed** him and sent him away.
    17:15 One of them, when he saw he was **healed**, came back,
    22:51 "No more of this!" And he touched the man's ear and **healed** him.
Jn   4:47 he went to him and begged him to come and **heal** his son,
     5:13 The man who was **healed** had no idea who it was, for Jesus had
    12:40 nor understand with their hearts, nor turn—and I would **heal** them."
Ac   9:34 "Aeneas," Peter said to him, "Jesus Christ **heals** you. Get up and
    10:38 doing good and **healing** all who were under the power of the devil,
    28: 8 see him and, after prayer, placed his hands on him and **healed** him.
    28:27 understand with their hearts and turn, and I would **heal** them.'
Heb 12:13 your feet," so that the lame may not be disabled, but rather **healed**.
Jas 5:16 to each other and pray for each other so that you may be **healed**.
1Pe 2:24 and live for righteousness; by his wounds you have been **healed**.

2616 Ἰάρετ, Iaret [1]

Jared [1]

Lk   3:37 the son of Enoch, the son of **Jared**, the son of Mahalalel, the son of

2617 ἴασις, iasis [3] [√ 2615]

heal people [+699] [1], heal [1], healed [1]

Lk 13:32 drive out demons and **heal** [+699] **people** today and tomorrow,
Ac   4:22 For the man who was miraculously **healed** was over forty years
     4:30 Stretch out your hand to **heal** and perform miraculous signs

2618 ἴασπις, iaspis [4]

jasper [3], jasper [+3345] [1]

Rev 4: 3 And the one who sat there had the appearance of **jasper**
     21:11 of a very precious jewel, like a **jasper** [+3345], clear as crystal.
     21:18 The wall was made of **jasper**, and the city of pure gold, as pure as
     21:19 The first foundation was **jasper**, the second sapphire, the third

2619 Ἰάσων, Iasōn [5]

Jason [4], Jason's [1]

Ac 17: 5 They rushed to **Jason's** house in search of Paul and Silas in order
    17: 6 they dragged **Jason** and some other brothers before the city
    17: 7 **Jason** has welcomed them into his house. They are all defying
    17: 9 Then they made **Jason** and the others post bond and let them go.
Ro 16:21 greetings to you, as do Lucius, **Jason** and Sosipater, my relatives.

2620 ἰατρός, iatros [7 / 6] [√ 2615]

doctor [4], doctors [1], physician [1]

Mt   9:12 Jesus said, "It is not the healthy who need a **doctor**, but the sick.
Mk   2:17 said to them, "It is not the healthy who need a **doctor**, but the sick.
     5:26 She had suffered a great deal under the care of many **doctors**
Lk   4:23 you will quote this proverb to me: '**Physician**, heal yourself!
     5:31 "It is not the healthy who need a **doctor**, but the sick.
     8:43 [UBS+ *and she had spent all she had on doctors,*] but no one could
Col 4:14 Our dear friend Luke, the **doctor**, and Demas send greetings.

2621 Ἰαχίν, Iachin Not used in UBS/NIV

2622 ιβ, ib Not used in UBS/NIV

2623 ἴδε, ide [34] [√ 1626]

see also 3972 ὁράω

see [10], look [9], here [6], *untranslated* [2], consider [1], find [1], listen [1], look how [1], mark my words [1], surely [1], well [1]

Mt 25:20 'you entrusted me with five talents. **See**, I have gained five more.'
    25:22 'you entrusted me with two talents; **see**, I have gained two more.'
    25:25 hid your talent in the ground. **See**, here is what belongs to you.'
    26:65 any more witnesses? **Look**, now you have heard the blasphemy.
Mk   2:24 The Pharisees said to him, "**Look**, why are they doing what is
     3:34 around him and said, "**Here** *are* my mother and my brothers!
    11:21 Peter remembered and said to Jesus, "Rabbi, **look**! The fig tree you
    13: 1 the temple, one of his disciples said to him, "**Look**, Teacher!
    13:21 At that time if anyone says to you, '**Look**, here is the Christ!'
    13:21 here is the Christ!' or, '**Look**, there he is!' do not believe it.
    15: 4 going to answer? **See** how many things they are accusing you of."
    15:35 standing near heard this, they said, "**Listen**, he's calling Elijah."
    16: 6 He has risen! He is not here. **See** the place where they laid him.
Jn   1:29 The next day John saw Jesus coming toward him and said, "**Look**,
     1:36 When he saw Jesus passing by, he said, "**Look**, the Lamb of God!"
     1:46 come from there?" Nathanael asked. "Come and **see**," said Philip.
     1:47 he said of him, "**Here** *is* a true Israelite, in whom there is nothing
     3:26 **well**, he is baptizing, and everyone is going to him."
     5:14 Later Jesus found him at the temple and said to him, "**See**,
     7:26 **Here** *he is*, speaking publicly, and they are not saying a word to
     7:52 and *you will* **find** that a prophet does not come out of Galilee."
    11: 3 sisters sent word to Jesus, "Lord, [NIE] the one you love is sick."
    11:34 have you laid him?" he asked. "Come and **see**, Lord," they replied.
    11:36 Then the Jews said, "**See** how he loved him!"
    12:19 us nowhere. **Look how** the whole world has gone after him!"
    16:29 [NIE] "Now you are speaking clearly and without figures of
    18:21 Ask those who heard me. **Surely** they know what I said."
    19: 4 Once more Pilate came out and said to the Jews, "**Look**, I am

    19:14 about the sixth hour. "**Here** *is* your king," Pilate said to the Jews.
    19:26 he said to his mother, "Dear woman, **here** *is* your son,"
    19:27 and to the disciple, "**Here** *is* your mother." From that time on,
    20:27 Then he said to Thomas, "Put your finger here; **see** my hands.
Ro 11:22 **Consider** therefore the kindness and sternness of God: sternness to
Gal 5: 2 **Mark my words**! I, Paul, tell you that if you let yourselves be

2624 ἰδέα, idea Not used in UBS/NIV [√ 1626]

2625 ἴδιος, idios [114 / 112] [→ 2626]

his own [37], their own [11], his [10], privately [+2848] [6], aside ⌊+2848] [3], its own [3], own [3], their [3], themselves [3], your [3], *untranslated* [2], himself [2], its [2], our own [2], your own [2], all [+2848] [1], all had [+3836] [1], alone [+2848] [1], belongs [1], friends [1], her alone [1], her own [1], him alone [1], his home [+3836] [1], his native language [+1666+3836] [1], his own home [+3836] [1], his relatives [1], home [+3836] [1], owns [+1639] [1], private [1], proper [1], whose [1], you [1], your own [+3836] [1], yourselves [1]

Mt   9: 1 Jesus stepped into a boat, crossed over and came to **his own** town.
    14:13 he withdrew by boat **privately** [+2848] to a solitary place.
    14:23 dismissed them, he went up on a mountainside by **himself** to pray.
    17: 1 brother of James, and led them up a high mountain by **themselves**.
    17:19 Then the disciples came to Jesus in **private** and asked, "Why
    20:17 he took the twelve disciples **aside** [+2848] and said to them,
    22: 5 no attention and went off—one to **his** field, another to his business.
    24: 3 the Mount of Olives, the disciples came to him **privately** [+2848].
    25:14 who called **his** servants and entrusted his property to them.
    25:15 two talents, and to another one talent, each according to **his** ability.
Mk   4:34 But when he was **alone** [+2848] with his own disciples,
     4:34 But when he was alone *with* **his own** disciples, he explained
     6:31 "Come with me by **yourselves** to a quiet place and get some rest."
     6:32 So they went away by **themselves** in a boat to a solitary place.
     7:33 After he took him **aside** [+2848], away from the crowd, Jesus put
     9: 2 led them up a high mountain, where they were **all** [+2848] alone.
     9:28 Jesus had gone indoors, his disciples asked him **privately** [+2848],
    13: 3 Peter, James, John and Andrew asked him **privately** [+2848].
Lk   6:41 brother's eye and pay no attention to the plank in **your own** eye?
     6:44 Each tree is recognized by **its own** fruit. People do not pick figs
     9:10 and they withdrew by **themselves** to a town called Bethsaida,
    10:23 Then he turned to his disciples and said **privately** [+2848],
    10:34 Then he put the man on **his own** donkey, took him to an inn
    18:28 Peter said to him, "We have left **all** *we* **had** [+3836] to follow you!"
Jn   1:11 He came to that which was **his own**, but his own did not receive
     1:11 came to that which was his own, but *his* **own** did not receive him.
     1:41 The first thing Andrew did was to find **his** brother Simon and tell
     4:44 had pointed out that a prophet has no honor in **his own** country.)
     5:18 but he was even calling God **his own** Father, making himself equal
     5:43 but if someone else comes in **his own** name, you will accept him.
     7:18 He who speaks on his own does so to gain honor for **himself**,
     8:44 When he lies, he speaks **his** [+1666+3836] **native language**,
    10: 3 to his voice. He calls **his own** sheep by name and leads them out.
    10: 4 When he has brought out all **his own**, he goes on ahead of them,
    10:12 The hired hand is not the shepherd who **owns** [+1639] the sheep.
    13: 1 Having loved **his own** who were in the world, he now showed
    15:19 If you belonged to the world, it would love you as **its own**.
    16:32 when you will be scattered, each to **his own** [+3836] home, leaving
    19:27 From that time on, this disciple took her into **his** [+3836] **home**.
Ac   1: 7 to know the times or dates the Father has set by **his own** authority.
     1:19 so they called that field in their [UBS+ *own*] language Akeldama,
     1:25 this apostolic ministry, from which Judas left to go where **he belongs**."
     2: 6 because each one heard them speaking in **his own** language.
     2: 8 Then how is it that each of us hears them *in* **his own** native
     3:12 Why do you stare at us as if by **our own** power or godliness we
     4:23 Peter and John went back to **their own** *people* and reported all that
     4:32 No one claimed that any of his possessions was **his own**, but they
    13:36 "For when David had served God's purpose *in* **his own** generation,
    20:28 of the church of God, which he bought with **his own** blood.
    21: 6 we went aboard the ship, and they returned **home** [+3836].
    23:19 drew him **aside** [+2848] and asked, "What is it you want to tell
    24:23 him some freedom and permit his **friends** to take care of his needs.
    24:24 Several days later Felix came with **his** wife Drusilla, who was a
    25:19 they had some points of dispute with him about **their own** religion

	28:30	For two whole years Paul stayed there in **his own** rented house
Ro	8:32	He who did not spare **his own** Son, but gave him up for us all—
	10: 3	that comes from God and sought to establish **their own**,
	11:24	the natural branches, be grafted into *their* **own** olive tree!
	14: 4	*To* **his own** master he stands or falls. And he will stand,
	14: 5	day alike. Each one should be fully convinced in **his own** mind.
1Co	3: 8	and each **[RPG]** will be rewarded according to his own labor.
	3: 8	and each will be rewarded according to **his own** labor.
	4:12	We work hard *with* **our own** hands. When we are cursed,
	6:18	his body, but he who sins sexually sins against **his own** body.
	7: 2	man should have his own wife, and each woman **her own** husband.
	7: 4	The wife's body does not belong to **her alone** but also to her
	7: 4	the husband's body does not belong to **him alone** but also to his
	7: 7	But each man has **his own** gift from God; one has this gift,
	7:37	who is under no compulsion but has control over **his own** will,
	7:37	own will, and who has made up **his** mind not to marry the virgin—
	9: 7	Who serves as a soldier *at* **his own** expense? Who plants a
	11:21	each of **you** goes ahead without waiting for anybody else.
	12:11	and the same Spirit, and he gives them **[RPG]** to each one,
	14:35	about something, they should ask **their own** husbands at home;
	15:23	But each in **his own** turn: Christ, the firstfruits; then, when he
	15:38	he has determined, and to each kind of seed he gives **its own** body.
Gal	2: 2	But I did this **privately** [+2848] to those who seemed to be leaders,
	6: 5	for each one should carry **his own** load.
	6: 9	for *at* the **proper** time we will reap a harvest if we do not give up.
Eph	4:28	but must work, doing something useful *with* **his own** hands,
	5:22	Wives, submit *to* **your** husbands as to the Lord.
1Th	2:14	You suffered from **your own** countrymen the same things those
	4:11	to mind **your own** [+3836] business and to work with your hands,
	4:11	mind your own business and to work with your [UBS+ *own*] hands,
1Ti	2: 6	as a ransom for all men—the testimony given *in* **its** proper time.
	3: 4	He must manage **his own** family well and see that his children
	3: 5	(If anyone does not know how to manage **his own** family,
	3:12	but one wife and must manage his children and **his** household well.
	4: 2	**whose** consciences have been seared as with a hot iron.
	5: 4	all to put their religion into practice by caring for **their own** family
	5: 8	If anyone does not provide for **his relatives**, and especially for his
	6: 1	All who are under the yoke of slavery should consider **their**
	6:15	which God will bring about *in* **his own** time—God, the blessed
2Ti	1: 9	anything we have done but because of **his own** purpose and grace.
	4: 3	Instead, to suit **their own** desires, they will gather around them a
Tit	1: 3	and *at* **his** appointed season he brought his word to light through
	1:12	Even one of **their own** prophets has said, "Cretans are always liars,
	2: 5	to be busy at home, to be kind, and to be subject *to* **their** husbands,
	2: 9	Teach slaves to be subject *to* **their** masters in everything, to try to
Heb	4:10	God's rest also rests from his own work, just as God did from **his**.
	7:27	after day, first for **his own** sins, and then for the sins of the people.
	9:12	but he entered the Most Holy Place once for all by **his own** blood,
	13:12	the city gate to make the people holy through **his own** blood.
Jas	1:14	by **his own** evil desire, he is dragged away and enticed.
1Pe	3: 1	Wives, in the same way be submissive *to* **your** husbands so that,
	3: 5	They were submissive *to* **their own** husbands,
2Pe	1: 3	through our knowledge of him who called us *by* **his own** glory
	1:20	of Scripture came about by the prophet's **own** interpretation.
	2:16	But he was rebuked *for* **his** wrongdoing by a donkey—a beast
	2:22	"A dog returns to **its** vomit," and, "A sow that is washed goes back
	3: 3	scoffers will come, scoffing and following **their own** evil desires.
	3:16	as they do the other Scriptures, to **their own** destruction.
	3:17	by the error of lawless men and fall from **your** secure position.
Jude	1: 6	keep their positions of authority but abandoned **their own** home—

2626 ἰδιώτης, *idiōtēs* [5] [√ 2625]

not understand [3], not trained [1], ordinary [1]

Ac	4:13	**ordinary** men, they were astonished and they took note that these
1Co	14:16	those who do **not understand** say "Amen" to your thanksgiving,
	14:23	and *some who* do **not understand** or some unbelievers come in,
	14:24	or *someone who* does **not understand** comes in while everybody
2Co	11: 6	I may **not** be a **trained** speaker, but I do have knowledge.

2627 ἰδού, *idou* [200] [√ 1626]

untranslated [75], look [14], here [12], see [10], and [+2779] [9], now [9], there before [9], behold [4], now [+2779] [4], suddenly [+2779] [4], no [3], now [+3814] [3], at that moment [+2779] [2],

here [+6045] [2], just then [+2779] [2], now [+2779+3814] [2], then [+2779] [2], there [2], as can see [+2779] [1], as know [1], at this [+2779] [1], but [1], came along [+2779] [1], came up [1], consider [1], even [+2779] [1], here is [1], here's [1], I assure you [1], I tell you [1], indeed [+2779] [1], listen [+201] [1], listen [1], met [+2779] [1], on one occasion [+2779] [1], or take as an example [+2779] [1], see how [1], so [1], suddenly [1], surely [1], that [1], there [+2779] [1], there is [1], when [+2779] [1], where [+2779] [1], with that [+2779] [1], without warning [+2779] [1], yes [+1609] [1], yet [+2779] [1], yet [1]

Mt	1:20	**[NIE]** an angel of the Lord appeared to him in a dream and said,
	1:23	**[NIE]** "The virgin will be with child and will give birth to a son,
	2: 1	time of King Herod, **[NIE]** Magi from the east came to Jerusalem
	2: 9	**and** [+2779] the star they had seen in the east went ahead of them
	2:13	**[NIE]** an angel of the Lord appeared to Joseph in a dream.
	2:19	**[NIE]** an angel of the Lord appeared in a dream to Joseph in
	3:16	he went up out of the water. **At that moment** [+2779] heaven was
	3:17	**And** [+2779] a voice from heaven said, "This is my Son, whom I
	4:11	the devil left him, **and** [+2779] angels came and attended him.
	7: 4	of your eye,' when all the time **there is** a plank in your own eye?
	8: 2	**[NIE]** A man with leprosy came and knelt before him and said,
	8:24	**Without warning** [+2779], a furious storm came up on the lake,
	8:29	**[NIE]** "What do you want with us, Son of God?" they shouted.
	8:32	**and** [+2779] the whole herd rushed down the steep bank into the
	8:34	**Then** [+2779] the whole town went out to meet Jesus. And when
	9: 2	**[NIE]** Some men brought to him a paralytic, lying on a mat.
	9: 3	**At this** [+2779], some of the teachers of the law said to
	9:10	**[NIE]** many tax collectors and "sinners" came and ate with him
	9:18	saying this, **[NIE]** a ruler came and knelt before him and said,
	9:20	**Just then** [+2779] a woman who had been subject to bleeding for
	9:32	**[NIE]** a man who was demon-possessed and could not talk was
	10:16	**[NIE]** I am sending you out like sheep among wolves.
	11: 8	fine clothes? **No**, those who wear fine clothes are in kings' palaces.
	11:10	**[NIE]** " 'I will send my messenger ahead of you, who will prepare
	11:19	and drinking, and they say, '**Here** is a glutton and a drunkard,
	12: 2	When the Pharisees saw this, they said to him, "**Look**!
	12:10	and a man with a shriveled hand was **there**. Looking for a reason
	12:18	"**Here** is my servant whom I have chosen, the one I love, in whom
	12:41	at the preaching of Jonah, and **now** one greater than Jonah is here.
	12:42	to Solomon's wisdom, and **now** one greater than Solomon is here.
	12:46	**[NIE]** his mother and brothers stood outside, wanting to speak to
	12:47	told him, **[NIE]** "Your mother and brothers are standing outside,
	12:49	to his disciples, he said, "**Here** are my mother and my brothers.
	13: 3	in parables, saying: **[NIE]** "A farmer went out to sow his seed.
	15:22	**[NIE]** A Canaanite woman from that vicinity came to him,
	17: 3	**Just then** [+2779] there appeared before them Moses and Elijah,
	17: 5	he was still speaking, **[NIE]** a bright cloud enveloped them,
	17: 5	**and** [+2779] a voice from the cloud said, "This is my Son,
	19:16	**Now** [+2779] a man came up to Jesus and asked, "Teacher,
	19:27	answered him, **[NIE]** "We have left everything to follow you!
	20:18	**[NIE]** "We are going up to Jerusalem, and the Son of Man will be
	20:30	**[NIE]** Two blind men were sitting by the roadside, and when they
	21: 5	'**See**, your king comes to you, gentle and riding on a donkey,
	22: 4	'Tell those who have been invited that I have prepared my dinner:
	23:34	Therefore **[NIE]** I am sending you prophets and wise men
	23:38	**Look**, your house is left to you desolate.
	24:23	At that time if anyone says to you, '**Look**, here is the Christ!'
	24:25	**See**, I have told you ahead of time.
	24:26	if anyone tells you, '**There** he is, out in the desert,' do not go out;
	24:26	not go out; or, '**Here** he is, in the inner rooms,' do not believe it.
	25: 6	the cry rang out: '**Here's** the bridegroom! Come out to meet him!'
	26:45	**Look**, the hour is near, and the Son of Man is betrayed into the
	26:46	Rise, let us go! **Here** comes my betrayer!"
	26:47	he was still speaking, **[NIE]** Judas, one of the Twelve, arrived.
	26:51	**With that** [+2779], one of Jesus' companions reached for his
	27:51	**At that moment** [+2779] the curtain of the temple was torn in two
	28: 2	**[NIE]** There was a violent earthquake, for an angel of the Lord
	28: 7	from the dead **and** [+2779] is going ahead of you into Galilee.
	28: 7	of you into Galilee. There you will see him.' **Now** I have told you."
	28: 9	**Suddenly** [+2779] Jesus met them. "Greetings," he said.
	28:11	**[NIE]** some of the guards went into the city and reported to the
	28:20	And **surely** I am with you always, to the very end of the age."
Mk	1: 2	**[NIE]** "I will send my messenger ahead of you, who will prepare
	3:32	**[NIE]** "Your mother and brothers are outside looking for you."
	4: 3	"**Listen** [+201]! A farmer went out to sow his seed.

10: 28　Peter said to him, **[NIE]** "We have left everything to follow you!"
10: 33　**[NIE]** "We are going up to Jerusalem," he said, "and the Son of
14: 41　**Look**, the Son of Man is betrayed into the hands of sinners.
14: 42　Rise! Let us go! **Here** comes my betrayer!"

Lk　1: 20　And **now** you will be silent and not able to speak until the day this
1: 31　**[NIE]** You will be with child and give birth to a son, and you are
1: 36　**Even** [+2779] Elizabeth your relative is going to have a child in
1: 38　**[NIE]** "I am the Lord's servant," Mary answered. "May it be to me
1: 44　**[NIE]** As soon as the sound of your greeting reached my ears,
1: 48　**[NIE]** From now on all generations will call me blessed,
2: 10　**[NIE]** I bring you good news of great joy that will be for all the
2: 25　**Now** [+2779] there was a man in Jerusalem called Simeon,
2: 34　**[NIE]** "This child is destined to cause the falling and rising of
2: 48　**[NIE]** Your father and I have been anxiously searching for you."
5: 12　a man **came along** [+2779] who was covered with leprosy.
5: 18　**[NIE]** Some men came carrying a paralytic on a mat and tried to
6: 23　and leap for joy, **[NIE]** because great is your reward in heaven.
7: 12　the town gate, **[NIE]** a dead person was being carried out—
7: 25　**No**, those who wear expensive clothes and indulge in luxury are in
7: 27　**[NIE]** " 'I will send my messenger ahead of you, who will prepare
7: 34　and drinking, and you say, '**Here** *is* a glutton and a drunkard,
7: 37　**When** [+2779] a woman who had lived a sinful life in that town
8: 41　**Then** [+2779] a man named Jairus, a ruler of the synagogue,
9: 30　**[NIE]** Two men, Moses and Elijah,
9: 38　**[NIE]** A man in the crowd called out, "Teacher, I beg you to look
9: 39　**[NIE]** A spirit seizes him and he suddenly screams; it throws him
10: 3　Go! **[NIE]** I am sending you out like lambs among wolves.
10: 19　**[NIE]** I have given you authority to trample on snakes
10: 25　**On one occasion** [+2779] an expert in the law stood up to test
11: 31　to Solomon's wisdom, and **now** one greater than Solomon is here.
11: 32　at the preaching of Jonah, and **now** one greater than Jonah is here.
11: 41　dish, to the poor, and [+2779] everything will be clean for you.
13: 7　**[NIE]** 'For three years now I've been coming to look for fruit on
13: 11　**and** [+2779] a woman was there who had been crippled by a spirit
13: 16　whom Satan has kept bound for **[NIE]** eighteen long years,
13: 30　**Indeed** [+2779] there are those who are last who will be first,
13: 32　**[NIE]** 'I will drive out demons and heal people today
13: 35　**Look**, your house is left to you desolate. I tell you, you will not see
14: 2　**There** [+2779] in front of him was a man suffering from dropsy.
15: 29　But he answered his father, '**Look**! All these years I've been
17: 21　nor will people say, '**Here** [+6045] it is,' or 'There it is,'
17: 21　or 'There it is,' **[NIE]** because the kingdom of God is within you."
17: 23　Men will tell you, **[NIE]** 'There he is!' or 'Here he is!' Do not go
17: 23　Men will tell you, 'There he is!' or '**Here** [+6045] he is!' Do not
18: 28　Peter said to him, **[NIE]** "We have left all we had to follow you!"
18: 31　Twelve aside and told them, **[NIE]** "We are going up to Jerusalem,
19: 2　**[NIE]** A man was there by the name of Zacchaeus; he was a chief
19: 8　But Zacchaeus stood up and said to the Lord, "**Look**, Lord!
19: 20　"Then another servant came and said, 'Sir, **here** is your mina;
22: 10　He replied, **[NIE]** "As you enter the city, a man carrying a jar of
22: 21　But **[NIE]** the hand of him who is going to betray me is with mine
22: 31　"Simon, Simon, **[NIE]** Satan has asked to sift you as wheat.
22: 38　The disciples said, "**See**, Lord, here are two swords." "That is
22: 47　While he was still speaking a crowd **came up**, and the man who
23: 14　**[NIE]** I have examined him in your presence and have found no
23: 15　has Herod, for he sent him back to us; **as** *you* **can see** [+2779],
23: 29　For **[NIE]** the time will come when you will say, 'Blessed are the
23: 50　**Now** [+2779] there was a man named Joseph, a member of the
24: 4　While they were wondering about this, **suddenly** [+2779] two men
24: 13　**Now** [+2779] that same day two of them were going to a village
24: 49　**[NIE]** I am going to send you what my Father has promised."

Jn　4: 35　**[NIE]** I tell you, open your eyes and look at the fields!
12: 15　of Zion; **see**, your king is coming, seated on a donkey's colt."
16: 32　"**But** a time is coming, and has come, when you will be scattered,
19: 5　and the purple robe, Pilate said to them, "**Here is** the man!"

Ac　1: 10　when **suddenly** two men dressed in white stood beside them.
2: 7　**[NIE]** "Are not all these men who are speaking Galileans?
5: 9　"How could you agree to test the Spirit of the Lord? **Look**!
5: 25　Then someone came and said, "**Look**! The men you put in jail are
5: 28　he said. "**Yet** [+2779] you have filled Jerusalem with your
7: 56　"**Look**," he said, "I see heaven open and the Son of Man standing at
8: 27　started out, and on his way he **met** [+2779] an Ethiopian eunuch,
8: 36　came to some water and the eunuch said, "**Look**, here is water.
9: 10　to him in a vision, "Ananias!" "**Yes** [+1609], Lord," he answered.
9: 11　ask for a man from Tarsus named Saul, **[NIE]** for he is praying.
10: 17　**[NIE]** the men sent by Cornelius found out where Simon's house

10: 19　the Spirit said to him, **[NIE]** "Simon, three men are looking for
10: 21　and said to the men, **[NIE]** "I'm the one you're looking for.
10: 30　at three in the afternoon. **Suddenly** [+2779] a man in shining
11: 11　**[NIE]** "Right then three men who had been sent to me from
12: 7　**Suddenly** [+2779] an angel of the Lord appeared and a light shone
13: 11　**Now** [+2779+3814] the hand of the Lord is against you. You are
13: 25　**No**, but he is coming after me, whose sandals I am not worthy to
13: 46　yourselves worthy of eternal life, we **now** turn to the Gentiles.
16: 1　then to Lystra, **where** [+2779] a disciple named Timothy lived,
20: 22　"And **now** [+3814], compelled by the Spirit, I am going to
20: 25　"**Now** [+2779+3814] I know that none of you among whom I have
27: 24　**and** [+2779] God has graciously given you the lives of all who sail

Ro　9: 33　"**See**, I lay in Zion a stone that causes men to stumble and a rock
1Co 15: 51　**Listen**, I tell you a mystery: We will not all sleep, but we will all
2Co　5: 17　he is a new creation; the old has gone, **[NIE]** the new has come!
6: 2　I tell you, **now** [+3814] is the time of God's favor, now is the day
6: 2　is the time of God's favor, **now** [+3814] is the day of salvation.
6: 9　as unknown; dying, and **yet** we live on; beaten, and yet not killed;
7: 11　**See** what this godly sorrow has produced in you: what earnestness,
12: 14　**Now** I am ready to visit you for the third time, and I will not be a

Gal　1: 20　**I assure you** before God that what I am writing you is no lie.
Heb　2: 13　And again he says, "**Here** am I, and the children God has given
8: 8　**[NIE]** "The time is coming, declares the Lord, when I will make a
10: 7　Then I said, '**Here** I am—it is written about me in the scroll—
10: 9　Then he said, "**Here** I am, I have come to do your will." He sets
Jas　3: 4　**Or take ships as an example** [+2779]. Although they are
3: 5　**Consider** what a great forest is set on fire by a small spark.
5: 4　**Look**! The wages you failed to pay the workmen who mowed your
5: 7　**See how** the farmer waits for the land to yield its valuable crop
5: 9　or you will be judged. **[NIE]** The Judge is standing at the door!
5: 11　**As** *you* **know**, we consider blessed those who have persevered.
1Pe　2: 6　"**See**, I lay a stone in Zion, a chosen and precious cornerstone,
Jude　1: 14　"**See**, the Lord is coming with thousands upon thousands of his
Rev　1: 7　**Look**, he is coming with the clouds, and every eye will see him,
1: 18　Living One; I was dead, and **behold** I am alive for ever and ever!
2: 10　**I tell you**, the devil will put some of you in prison to test you,
2: 22　**So** I will cast her on a bed of suffering, and I will make those who
3: 8　**See**, I have placed before you an open door that no one can shut.
3: 9　**[NIE]** I will make those who are of the synagogue of Satan,
3: 9　**[NIE]** I will make them come and fall down at your feet
3: 20　**Here** I am! I stand at the door and knock. If anyone hears my voice
4: 1　and **there before** me was a door standing open in heaven.
4: 2　and **there before** me was a throne in heaven with someone sitting
5: 5　**See**, the Lion of the tribe of Judah, the Root of David,
6: 2　I looked, and **there before** me was a white horse! Its rider held a
6: 5　"**Come**!" I looked, and **there before** me was a black horse!
6: 8　I looked, and **there before** me was a pale horse! Its rider was
7: 9　and **there before** me was a great multitude that no one could
9: 12　The first woe is past; **[NIE]** two other woes are yet to come.
11: 14　The second woe has passed; **[NIE]** the third woe is coming soon.
12: 3　**[NIE]** an enormous red dragon with seven heads and ten horns
14: 1　Then I looked, and **there before** me was the Lamb, standing on
14: 14　I looked, and **there before** me was a white cloud, and seated on the
16: 15　"**Behold**, I come like a thief! Blessed is he who stays awake
19: 11　saw heaven standing open and **there before** me was a white horse,
21: 3　"**Now** the dwelling of God is with men, and he will live with them.
21: 5　seated on the throne said, **[NIE]** "I am making everything new!"
22: 7　"**Behold**, I am coming soon! Blessed is he who keeps the words of
22: 12　"**Behold**, I am coming soon! My reward is with me, and I will give

2628　Ἰδουμαία, *Idoumaia* [1]

Idumea [1]

Mk　3: 8　Jerusalem, **Idumea**, and the regions across the Jordan and around

2629　ἱδρώς, *hidrōs* [1]

sweat [1]

Lk　22: 44　and his **sweat** was like drops of blood falling to the ground.

2630　Ἰεζάβελ, *Iezabel* [1]

Jezabel [1]

Rev　2: 20　You tolerate that woman **Jezebel**, who calls herself a prophetess.

2631 Ἱεράπολις, *Hierapolis* [1] [√ 2641 + 4484]

Hierapolis [1]

Col 4:13 is working hard for you and for those at Laodicea and **Hierapolis**.

2632 ἱερατεία, *hierateia* [2] [√ 2641]

priesthood [1], priests [1]

Lk   1: 9 he was chosen by lot, according to the custom *of* the **priesthood**,
Heb 7: 5 Now the law requires the descendants of Levi who become **priests**

2633 ἱεράτευμα, *hierateuma* [2] [√ 2641]

priesthood [2]

1Pe 2: 5 are being built into a spiritual house to be a holy **priesthood**,
      2: 9 a royal **priesthood**, a holy nation, a people belonging to God,

2634 ἱερατεύω, *hierateuō* [1] [√ 2641]

serving as priest [1]

Lk   1: 8 division was on duty and he *was* **serving as priest** before God,

2635 Ἱερεμίας, *Ieremias* [3]

Jeremiah [3]

Mt   2:17 Then what was said through the prophet **Jeremiah** was fulfilled:
   16:14 others say Elijah; and still others, **Jeremiah** or one of the prophets.'
   27: 9 Then what was spoken by **Jeremiah** the prophet was fulfilled:

2636 ἱερεύς, *hiereus* [31] [√ 2641]

priest [16], priests [15]

Mt   8: 4 show yourself *to* the **priest** and offer the gift Moses commanded,
   12: 4 which was not lawful for them to do, but only *for* the **priests**.
   12: 5 Or haven't you read in the Law that on the Sabbath the **priests** in
Mk   1:44 show yourself *to* the **priest** and offer the sacrifices that Moses
    2:26 ate the consecrated bread, which is lawful only for **priests** to eat.
Lk   1: 5 In the time of Herod king of Judea there was a **priest** named
    5:14 show yourself *to* the **priest** and offer the sacrifices that Moses
    6: 4 the consecrated bread, he ate what is lawful only for **priests** to eat.
   10:31 A **priest** happened to be going down the same road, and when he
   17:14 When he saw them, he said, "Go, show yourselves *to* the **priests**."
Jn   1:19 this was John's testimony when the Jews of Jerusalem sent **priests**
Ac   4: 1 The **priests** and the captain of the temple guard and the Sadducees
    6: 7 and a large number *of* **priests** became obedient to the faith.
   14:13 The **priest** of Zeus, whose temple was just outside the city,
Heb 5: 6 "You are a **priest** forever, in the order of Melchizedek."
    7: 1 Melchizedek was king of Salem and **priest** of God Most High.
    7: 3 or end of life, like the Son of God he remains a **priest** forever.
    7:11 the people), why was there still need for another **priest** to come—
    7:14 and in regard to that tribe Moses said nothing about **priests**.
    7:15 And what we have said is even more clear if another **priest** like
    7:17 is declared: "You are a **priest** forever, in the order of Melchizedek."
    7:20 was not without an oath! Others became **priests** without any oath,
    7:21 and will not change his mind: 'You are a **priest** forever.' "
    7:23 Now there have been many of those **priests**, since death prevented
    8: 4 If he were on earth, he would not be a **priest**, for there are already
    9: 6 the **priests** entered regularly into the outer room to carry on their
   10:11 Day after day every **priest** stands and performs his religious duties;
   10:21 and since we have a great **priest** over the house of God,
Rev 1: 6 made us to be a kingdom and **priests** to serve his God and Father—
    5:10 have made them to be a kingdom and **priests** to serve our God,
   20: 6 but they will be **priests** of God and of Christ and will reign with

2637 Ἱεριχώ, *Ierichō* [7]

Jericho [6], the city[s] [1]

Mt 20:29 As Jesus and his disciples were leaving **Jericho**, a large crowd
Mk 10:46 Then they came to **Jericho**. As Jesus and his disciples,
   10:46 were leaving **the city**[s], a blind man, Bartimaeus (that is, the Son of
Lk   10:30 "A man was going down from Jerusalem to **Jericho**, when he fell
   18:35 As Jesus approached **Jericho**, a blind man was sitting by the

   19: 1 Jesus entered **Jericho** and was passing through.
Heb 11:30 By faith the walls *of* **Jericho** fell, after the people had marched

2638 ἱερόθυτος, *hierothytos* [1] [√ 2641 + 2604]

offered in sacrifice [1]

1Co 10:28 says to you, "This has been **offered in sacrifice**," then do not eat it,

2639 ἱερόν, *hieron* [71] [√ 2641]

temple [31], temple courts [23], temple area [10], temple guard
[2], there[s] [+1877+3836] [2], *untranslated* [1], its[s] [+3836] [1],
temple grounds [1]

Mt   4: 5 the holy city and had him stand on the highest point *of* the **temple**.
   12: 5 Law that on the Sabbath the priests in the **temple** desecrate the day
   12: 6 I tell you that one greater than the **temple** is here.
   21:12 Jesus entered the **temple area** and drove out all who were buying
   21:12 drove out all who were buying and selling **there**[s] [+1877+3836].
   21:14 The blind and the lame came to him at the **temple**, and he healed
   21:15 things he did and the children shouting in the **temple area**,
   21:23 Jesus entered the **temple courts**, and, while he was teaching,
   24: 1 Jesus left the **temple** and was walking away when his disciples
   24: 1 came up to him to call his attention to **its**[s] [+3836] buildings.
   26:55 Every day I sat in the **temple courts** teaching, and you did not
Mk 11:11 Jesus entered Jerusalem and went to the **temple**. He looked around
   11:15 Jesus entered the **temple area** and began driving out those who
   11:15 out those who were buying and selling **there**[s] [+1877+3836].
   11:16 not allow anyone to carry merchandise through the **temple courts**.
   11:27 and while Jesus was walking in the **temple courts**, the chief
   12:35 While Jesus was teaching in the **temple courts**, he asked,
   13: 1 As he was leaving the **temple**, one of his disciples said to him,
   13: 3 As Jesus was sitting on the Mount of Olives opposite the **temple**,
   14:49 with you, teaching in the **temple courts**, and you did not arrest me.
Lk   2:27 Moved by the Spirit, he went into the **temple courts**. When the
    2:37 She never left the **temple** but worshiped night and day, fasting
    2:46 After three days they found him in the **temple courts**,
    4: 9 to Jerusalem and had him stand on the highest point *of* the **temple**.
   18:10 "Two men went up to the **temple** to pray, one a Pharisee
   19:45 Then he entered the **temple area** and began driving out those who
   19:47 Every day he was teaching at the **temple**. But the chief priests,
   20: 1 One day as he was teaching the people in the **temple courts**
   21: 5 Some of his disciples were remarking about how the **temple** was
   21:37 Each day Jesus was teaching at the **temple**, and each evening he
   21:38 all the people came early in the morning to hear him at the **temple**.
   22:52 the officers of the **temple** guard, and the elders, who had come for
   22:53 Every day I was with you in the **temple courts**, and you did not lay
   24:53 And they stayed continually at the **temple**, praising God.
Jn   2:14 In the **temple courts** he found men selling cattle, sheep and doves,
    2:15 and drove all from the **temple area**, both sheep and cattle;
    5:14 Later Jesus found him at the **temple** and said to him, "See,
    7:14 halfway through the Feast did Jesus go up to the **temple courts**
    7:28 Then Jesus, still teaching in the **temple courts**, cried out, "Yes,
    8: 2 At dawn he appeared again in the **temple courts**, where all the
    8:20 He spoke these words while teaching in the **temple area** near the
    8:59 but Jesus hid himself, slipping away from the **temple grounds**.
   10:23 and Jesus was in the **temple area** walking in Solomon's
   11:56 and as they stood in the **temple area** they asked one another,
   18:20 "I always taught in synagogues or at the **temple**, where all the Jews
Ac   2:46 Every day they continued to meet together in the **temple courts**.
    3: 1 and John were going up to the **temple** at the time of prayer—
    3: 2 Now a man crippled from birth was being carried to the **temple**
    3: 2 was put every day to beg from those going into the **temple courts**.
    3: 3 and John about to enter, [RPG] he asked them for money.
    3: 8 Then he went with them into the **temple courts**, walking
   3:10 man who used to sit begging at the **temple** gate called Beautiful,
    4: 1 The priests and the captain *of* the **temple guard** and the Sadducees
    5:20 "Go, stand in the **temple courts**," he said, "and tell the people the
    5:21 At daybreak they entered the **temple courts**, as they had been told,
    5:24 the captain of the **temple guard** and the chief priests were puzzled;
    5:25 The men you put in jail are standing in the **temple courts** teaching
    5:42 Day after day, in the **temple courts** and from house to house,
   19:27 but also that the **temple** of the great goddess Artemis will be
   21:26 Then he went to the **temple** to give notice of the date when the
   21:27 some Jews from the province of Asia saw Paul at the **temple**.

21:28 he has brought Greeks into the **temple area** and defiled this holy
21:29 and assumed that Paul had brought him into the **temple area**.)
21:30 Seizing Paul, they dragged him from the **temple**, and immediately
22:17 "When I returned to Jerusalem and was praying at the **temple**,
24: 6 and even tried to desecrate the **temple**; so we seized him.
24:12 My accusers did not find me arguing with anyone at the **temple**,
24:18 I was ceremonially clean when they found me in the **temple courts**
25: 8 against the law of the Jews or against the **temple** or against Caesar."
26:21 That is why the Jews seized me in the **temple courts** and tried to
1Co 9:13 that those who work in the temple get their food from the **temple**,

2640 ἱεροπρεπής, *hieroprepēs* [1] [√ 2641 + 4560]

reverent [1]

Tit 2: 3 teach the older women to be **reverent** in the way they live,

2641 ἱερός, *hieros* [3 / 2] [→ 796, 797, 2631, 2632, 2633, 2634, 2636, 2638, 2639, 2640, 2644, 2645, 2646, 2648]

holy [1], temple [1]

Mk 16: S [UBS+ *holy and imperishable proclamation of eternal salvation.*]
1Co 9:13 Don't you know that those who work in the **temple** get their food
2Ti 3:15 and how from infancy you have known the **holy** Scriptures,

2642 Ἱεροσόλυμα, *Hierosolyma* Not used in UBS/NIV [√ 2647]

2643 Ἱεροσολυμίτης, *Hierosolymitēs* [2] [√ 2647]

people of Jerusalem [2]

Mk 1: 5 and all the **people of Jerusalem** went out to him.
Jn 7:25 At that point some of the **people of Jerusalem** began to ask,

2644 ἱεροσυλέω, *hierosyleō* [1] [√ 2641 + 5195]

rob temples [1]

Ro 2:22 you commit adultery? You who abhor idols, *do you* **rob temples**?

2645 ἱερόσυλος, *hierosylos* [1] [√ 2641 + 5195]

robbed temples [1]

Ac 19:37 *though they have* neither **robbed temples** nor blasphemed our

2646 ἱερουργέω, *hierourgeō* [1] [√ 2641 + 2240]

priestly duty [1]

Ro 15:16 Gentiles *with* the **priestly duty** of proclaiming the gospel of God,

2647 Ἱερουσαλήμ, *Ierousalēm* [139] [→ 2642, 2643]

Jerusalem [136], city of Jerusalem [2], the city[s] [1]

Mt 2: 1 the time of King Herod, Magi from the east came to **Jerusalem**
2: 3 Herod heard this he was disturbed, and all **Jerusalem** with him.
3: 5 People went out to him from **Jerusalem** and all Judea
4:25 **Jerusalem**, Judea and the region across the Jordan followed him.
5:35 his footstool; or by **Jerusalem**, for it is the city of the Great King.
15: 1 and teachers of the law came to Jesus from **Jerusalem** and asked,
16:21 began to explain to his disciples that he must go to **Jerusalem**
20:17 Now as Jesus was going up to **Jerusalem**, he took the twelve
20:18 "We are going up to **Jerusalem**, and the Son of Man will be
21: 1 As they approached **Jerusalem** and came to Bethphage on the
21:10 When Jesus entered **Jerusalem**, the whole city was stirred
23:37 "O **Jerusalem**, Jerusalem, you who kill the prophets and stone
23:37 "O Jerusalem, **Jerusalem**, you who kill the prophets and stone
Mk 3: 8 **Jerusalem**, Idumea, and the regions across the Jordan and around
3:22 And the teachers of the law who came down from **Jerusalem** said,
7: 1 of the law who had come from **Jerusalem** gathered around Jesus
10:32 They were on their way up to **Jerusalem**, with Jesus leading the
10:33 "We are going up to **Jerusalem**," he said, "and the Son of Man will
11: 1 As they approached **Jerusalem** and came to Bethphage
11:11 Jesus entered **Jerusalem** and went to the temple. He looked around

11:15 On reaching **Jerusalem**, Jesus entered the temple area and began
11:27 They arrived again in **Jerusalem**, and while Jesus was walking in
15:41 Many other women who had come up with him to **Jerusalem** were
Lk 2:22 and Mary took him to **Jerusalem** to present him to the Lord
2:25 Now there was a man in **Jerusalem** called Simeon, who was
2:38 to all who were looking forward to the redemption *of* **Jerusalem**.
2:41 Every year his parents went to **Jerusalem** for the Feast of the
2:43 the boy Jesus stayed behind in **Jerusalem**, but they were unaware
2:45 did not find him, they went back to **Jerusalem** to look for him.
4: 9 The devil led him to **Jerusalem** and had him stand on the highest
5:17 come from every village of Galilee and from Judea and **Jerusalem**.
6:17 from **Jerusalem**, and from the coast of Tyre and Sidon,
9:31 which he was about to bring to fulfillment at **Jerusalem**.
9:51 to be taken up to heaven, Jesus resolutely set out for **Jerusalem**.
9:53 did not welcome him, because he was heading for **Jerusalem**.
10:30 "A man was going down from **Jerusalem** to Jericho, when he fell
13: 4 they were more guilty than all the others living in **Jerusalem**?
13:22 the towns and villages, teaching as he made his way to **Jerusalem**.
13:33 the next day—for surely no prophet can die outside **Jerusalem**!
13:34 "O **Jerusalem**, Jerusalem, you who kill the prophets and stone
13:34 "O Jerusalem, **Jerusalem**, you who kill the prophets and stone
17:11 Now on his way to **Jerusalem**, Jesus traveled along the border
18:31 the Twelve aside and told them, "We are going up to **Jerusalem**,
19:11 because he was near **Jerusalem** and the people thought that the
19:28 Jesus had said this, he went on ahead, going up to **Jerusalem**.
21:20 "When you see **Jerusalem** being surrounded by armies, you will
21:24 **Jerusalem** will be trampled on by the Gentiles until the times of
23: 7 he sent him to Herod, who was also in **Jerusalem** at that time.
23:28 Jesus turned and said to them, "Daughters *of* **Jerusalem**, do not
24:13 to a village called Emmaus, about seven miles from **Jerusalem**.
24:18 "Are you only a visitor to **Jerusalem** and do not know the things
24:33 They got up and returned at once to **Jerusalem**. There they found
24:47 be preached in his name to all nations, beginning at **Jerusalem**.
24:52 they worshiped him and returned to **Jerusalem** with great joy.
Jn 1:19 Now this was John's testimony when the Jews of **Jerusalem** sent
2:13 almost time for the Jewish Passover, Jesus went up to **Jerusalem**.
2:23 Now while he was in **Jerusalem** at the Passover Feast,
4:20 Jews claim that the place where we must worship is in **Jerusalem**."
4:21 will worship the Father neither on this mountain nor in **Jerusalem**.
4:45 They had seen all that he had done in **Jerusalem** at the Passover
5: 1 time later, Jesus went up to **Jerusalem** for a feast of the Jews.
5: 2 Now there is in **Jerusalem** near the Sheep Gate a pool, which in
10:22 Then came the Feast of Dedication at **Jerusalem**. It was winter,
11:18 Bethany was less than two miles from **Jerusalem**,
11:55 many went up from the country to **Jerusalem** for their ceremonial
12:12 come for the Feast heard that Jesus was on his way to **Jerusalem**.
Ac 1: 4 "Do not leave **Jerusalem**, but wait for the gift my Father promised,
1: 8 and you will be my witnesses in **Jerusalem**, and in all Judea
1:12 Then they returned to **Jerusalem** from the hill called the Mount of
1:12 called the Mount of Olives, a Sabbath day's walk from **the city**[s]
1:19 Everyone in **Jerusalem** heard about this, so they called that field in
2: 5 Now there were staying in **Jerusalem** God-fearing Jews from
2:14 "Fellow Jews and all of you who live in **Jerusalem**, let me explain
4: 5 day the rulers, elders and teachers of the law met in **Jerusalem**.
4:16 "Everybody living *in* **Jerusalem** knows they have done an
5:16 Crowds gathered also from the towns around **Jerusalem**,
5:28 "Yet you have filled **Jerusalem** with your teaching and are
6: 7 The number of disciples in **Jerusalem** increased rapidly, and a
8: 1 day a great persecution broke out against the church at **Jerusalem**,
8:14 When the apostles in **Jerusalem** heard that Samaria had accepted
8:25 the word of the Lord, Peter and John returned to **Jerusalem**,
8:26 the desert road—that goes down from **Jerusalem** to Gaza."
8:27 of the Ethiopians. This man had gone to **Jerusalem** to worship,
9: 2 or women, he might take them as prisoners to **Jerusalem**.
9:13 and all the harm he has done to your saints in **Jerusalem**.
9:21 "Isn't he the man who raised havoc in **Jerusalem** among those who
9:26 When he came to **Jerusalem**, he tried to join the disciples,
9:28 So Saul stayed with them and moved about freely in **Jerusalem**,
10:39 of everything he did in the country of the Jews and in **Jerusalem**.
11: 2 So when Peter went up to **Jerusalem**, the circumcised believers
11:22 News of this reached the ears of the church at **Jerusalem**,
11:27 During this time some prophets came down from **Jerusalem** to
12:25 they returned from **Jerusalem**, taking with them John, also called
13:13 Perga in Pamphylia, where John left them to return to **Jerusalem**.
13:27 The people of **Jerusalem** and their rulers did not recognize Jesus,
13:31 by those who had traveled with him from Galilee to **Jerusalem**.

15: 2   to go up to **Jerusalem** to see the apostles and elders about this
15: 4   When they came to **Jerusalem**, they were welcomed by the church
16: 4   by the apostles and elders in **Jerusalem** for the people to obey.
19:21   Paul decided to go to **Jerusalem**, passing through Macedonia
20:16   for he was in a hurry to reach **Jerusalem**, if possible, by the day of
20:22   "And now, compelled by the Spirit, I am going to **Jerusalem**,
21: 4   Through the Spirit they urged Paul not to go on to **Jerusalem**.
21:11   'In this way the Jews of **Jerusalem** will bind the owner of this belt
21:12   and the people there pleaded with Paul not to go up to **Jerusalem**.
21:13   but also to die in **Jerusalem** for the name of the Lord Jesus."
21:15   After this, we got ready and went up to **Jerusalem**.
21:17   When we arrived at **Jerusalem**, the brothers received us warmly.
21:31   Roman troops that the whole **city of Jerusalem** was in an uproar.
22: 5   and went there to bring these people as prisoners to **Jerusalem** to
22:17   "When I returned to **Jerusalem** and was praying at the temple,
22:18   'Leave **Jerusalem** immediately, because they will not accept your
23:11   As you have testified about me in **Jerusalem**, so you must also
24:11   no more than twelve days ago I went up to **Jerusalem** to worship.
25: 1   in the province, Festus went up from Caesarea to **Jerusalem**,
25: 3   as a favor to them, to have Paul transferred to **Jerusalem**,
25: 7   the Jews who had come down from **Jerusalem** stood around him,
25: 9   "Are you willing to go up to **Jerusalem** and stand trial before me
25:15   When I went to **Jerusalem**, the chief priests and elders of the Jews
25:20   so I asked if he would be willing to go to **Jerusalem** and stand
25:24   Jewish community has petitioned me about him in **Jerusalem**
26: 4   beginning of my life in my own country, and also in **Jerusalem**.
26:10   And that is just what I did in **Jerusalem**. On the authority of the
26:20   then to those *in* **Jerusalem** and in all Judea, and to the Gentiles
28:17   I was arrested in **Jerusalem** and handed over to the Romans.
Ro 15:19   So from **Jerusalem** all the way around to Illyricum, I have fully
15:25   I am on my way to **Jerusalem** in the service of the saints there.
15:26   to make a contribution for the poor among the saints in **Jerusalem**.
15:31   and that my service in **Jerusalem** may be acceptable to the saints
1Co 16: 3   the men you approve and send them with your gift to **Jerusalem**.
Gal 1:17   nor did I go up to **Jerusalem** to see those who were apostles before
1:18   I went up to **Jerusalem** to get acquainted with Peter and stayed
2: 1   Fourteen years later I went up again to **Jerusalem**, this time with
4:25   Sinai in Arabia and corresponds *to* the present **city of Jerusalem**,
4:26   But the **Jerusalem** that is above is free, and she is our mother.
Heb 12:22   Mount Zion, to the heavenly **Jerusalem**, the city of the living God.
Rev 3:12   my God and the name of the city of my God, the new **Jerusalem**,
21: 2   I saw the Holy City, the new **Jerusalem**, coming down out of
21:10   and high, and showed me the Holy City, **Jerusalem**,

2648 ἱερωσύνη, *hierōsynē* [3] [√ *2641*]

priesthood [3]

Heb 7:11   **priesthood** (for on the basis of it the law was given to the people),
7:12   For when there is a change *of* the **priesthood**, there must also be a
7:24   because Jesus lives forever, he has a permanent **priesthood**.

2649 Ἰεσσαί, *Iessai* [5]

Jesse [5]

Mt 1: 5   father of Obed, whose mother was Ruth, Obed the father of **Jesse**,
1: 6   and **Jesse** the father of King David. David was the father of
Lk 3:32   the son *of* **Jesse**, the son of Obed, the son of Boaz, the son of
Ac 13:22   'I have found David son *of* **Jesse** a man after my own heart;
Ro 15:12   And again, Isaiah says, "The Root *of* **Jesse** will spring up, one who

2650 Ἰεφθάε, *Iephthae* [1]

Jephthah [1]

Heb 11:32   Barak, Samson, **Jephthah**, David, Samuel and the prophets,

2651 Ἰεχονίας, *Iechonias* [2]

Jeconiah [2]

Mt 1:11   and Josiah the father of **Jeconiah** and his brothers at the time of the
1:12   **Jeconiah** was the father of Shealtiel, Shealtiel the father of

2652 Ἰησοῦς, *Iēsous* [917 / 916]

ἀδελφοὶ Ἰησοῦ (brothers of Jesus) [21] Mt 12:46,47,48,49; 13:55; 28:10; Mk 3:31,32,33,34,35; Lk 8:19,20,21; Jn 2:12; 7:3,5,10; 20:17; Ac 1:14; 1Co 9:5

Ἰησοῦς Χριστός (Jesus Christ) [136 / 135] Mt 1:1,18; Mk 1:1; Jn 1:17; 17:3; Ac 2:38; 3:6; 4:10; 8:12; 9:34; 10:36,48; 11:17; 15:26; 16:18; 28:31; Ro 1:4,6,7,8; 2:16[NIV]; 3:22; 5:1,11,15,17,21; 7:25; 13:14; 15:6,30; 16:25,27; 1Co 1:2,3,7,8,9,10; 2:2; 3:11; 6:11; 8:6; 15:57; 2Co 1:2,3,19; 4:5,6[UBS]; 8:9; 13:5[UBS],14; Gal 1:1,3,12; 2:16; 3:1,22; 6:14,18; Eph 1:2,3,5,17; 5:20; 6:23,24; Php 1:2,11, 19; 2:11,21; 3:20; 4:23; Col 1:3; 1Th 1:1,3; 5:9,23,28; 2Th 1:1,2, 12; 2:1,14,16; 3:6,12,18; 1Ti 6:3,14; 2Ti 2:8; Tit 1:1; 2:13; 3:6; Phm 1:3,25; Heb 10:10; 13:8,21; Jas 1:1; 2:1; 1Pe 1:1,2,3,3,7,13; 2:5; 3:21; 4:11; 2Pe 1:1,1,8,11,14,16; 2:20; 3:18; 1Jn 1:3; 2:1; 3:23; 4:2; 5:6,20; 2Jn 1:3,7; Jude 1:1,1,4,17,21,25; Rev 1:1,2,5

κύριος Ἰησοῦς (Lord Jesus) [101] Mk 16:19; Lk 24:3; Ac 1:21; 4:33; 7:59; 8:16; 11:17,20; 15:11,26; 16:31; 19:5,13,17; 20:21,24,35; 21:13; 28:31; Ro 1:7; 5:1,11; 13:14; 14:14; 15:6,30; 16:20; 1Co 1:2,3,7,8,10; 5:4,4; 6:11; 8:6; 11:23; 15:57; 16:23; 2Co 1:2,3; 4:14; 8:9; 11:31; 13:14; Gal 1:3; 6:14,18; Eph 1:2,3,15,17; 5:20; 6:23,24; Php 1:2; 2:19; 3:20; 4:23; Col 1:3; 3:17; 1Th 1:1,3; 2:15,19; 3:11,13; 4:1,2; 5:9,23,28; 2Th 1:1,2,7,8,12,12; 2:1,8,14,16; 3:6,12,18; 1Ti 6:3,14; Phm 1:3,5,25; Heb 13:20; Jas 1:1; 2:1; 1Pe 1:3; 2Pe 1:8,14,16; Jude 1:17,21; Rev 22:20,21

λόγος Ἰησοῦ (word of Jesus) [2] Jn 18:32; Ac 20:35

μαρτυρία Ἰησοῦ (testimony of Jesus) [7] Mk 14:55; Rev 1:2,9; 12:17; 19:10,10; 20:4

ὄνομα Ἰησοῦ (name of Jesus) [12] Ac 2:38; 3:6; 4:10,18; 5:40; 8:12; 9:27; 10:48; 16:18; 26:9; Php 2:10; Col 3:17

πίστις εἰς Ἰησοῦν (faith in Jesus) [?] Ac 20:21; 24:24

πίστις ἐν Ἰησοῦς (faith in Jesus) [7] Gal 3:26; Eph 1:15; Col 1:4; 1Ti 1:14; 3:13; 2Ti 1:13; 3:15

πίστις Ἰησοῦ (faith in Jesus) [5] Ro 3:22,26; Gal 2:16; 3:22; Rev 14:12

πνεῦμα Ἰησοῦ (Spirit of Jesus) [2] Ac 16:7; Php 1:19

σῶμα Ἰησοῦ (body of Jesus) [13] Mt 26:26; 27:58; Mk 14:22; 15:43; Lk 23:52; 24:3; Jn 19:38,38,40; 20:12; Ro 8:11; 2Co 4:10; Heb 10:10

σωτήρ Ἰησοῦς (Savior Jesus) [9] Ac 13:23; Php 3:20; 2Ti 1:10; Tit 1:4; 2:13; 2Pe 1:1,11; 2:20; 3:18

Χριστός Ἰησοῦς (Christ Jesus) [91 / 90] Ac 24:24; Ro 1:1; 2:16[UBS]; 3:24; 6:3,11,23; 8:1,2,34,39; 15:5,16,17; 16:3; 1Co 1:1,2,4,30; 4:15,17; 15:31; 16:24; 2Co 1:1; 13:5[NIV]; Gal 2:4,16; 3:14,26,28; 4:14; 5:6,24; Eph 1:1,1; 2:6,7,10,13,20; 3:1,6,11,21; Php 1:1,1,6,8,26; 2:5; 3:3,8,12,14; 4:7,19,21; Col 1:1,4; 2:6; 4:12; 1Th 2:14; 5:18; 1Ti 1:1,1,2,14,15,16; 2:5; 3:13; 4:6; 5:21; 6:13; 2Ti 1:1,1,2,9,10,13; 2:1,3,10; 3:12,15; 4:1; Tit 1:4; Phm 1:1,9,23; 1Pe 5:10[UBS]

Joshua [3] Lk 3:29; Ac 7:45; Heb 4:8

Jesus [897], heˢ [+*3836*] [7], himˢ [+*3836*] [6], Joshua [3], *untranslated* [1], heˢ [1], hisˢ [+*3836*] [1]

Mt 1: 1   A record of the genealogy *of* **Jesus** Christ the son of David,
1:16   husband of Mary, of whom was born **Jesus**, who is called Christ.
1:18   This is how the birth *of* **Jesus** Christ came about: His mother Mary
1:21   will give birth to a son, and you are to give him the name **Jesus**,
1:25   her until she gave birth to a son. And he gave him the name **Jesus**.
2: 1   After **Jesus** was born in Bethlehem in Judea, during the time of
3:13   Then **Jesus** came from Galilee to the Jordan to be baptized by
3:15   **Jesus** replied, "Let it be so now; it is proper for us to do this to
3:16   As soon as **Jesus** was baptized, he went up out of the water.
4: 1   Then **Jesus** was led by the Spirit into the desert to be tempted by
4: 7   **Jesus** answered him, "It is also written: 'Do not put the Lord your
4:10   **Jesus** said to him, "Away from me, Satan! For it is written:
4:17   From that time on **Jesus** began to preach, "Repent, for the kingdom
7:28   When **Jesus** had finished saying these things, the crowds were
8: 4   Then **Jesus** said to him, "See that you don't tell anyone. But go,
8:10   When **Jesus** heard this, he was astonished and said to those
8:13   Then **Jesus** said to the centurion, "Go! It will be done just as you
8:14   When **Jesus** came into Peter's house, he saw Peter's mother-in-law

8:18 When **Jesus** saw the crowd around him, he gave orders to cross to
8:20 **Jesus** replied, "Foxes have holes and birds of the air have nests,
8:22 But **Jesus** told him, "Follow me, and let the dead bury their own
8:34 Then the whole town went out to meet **Jesus**. And when they saw
9: 1 **Jesus** [UBS-] stepped into a boat, crossed over and came to his
9: 2 When **Jesus** saw their faith, he said to the paralytic, "Take heart,
9: 4 Knowing their thoughts, **Jesus** said, "Why do you entertain evil
9: 9 As **Jesus** went on from there, he saw a man named Matthew sitting
9:10 and "sinners" came and ate with **him**[s] [+3836] and his disciples.
9:15 **Jesus** answered, "How can the guests of the bridegroom mourn
9:19 **Jesus** got up and went with him, and so did his disciples.
9:22 **Jesus** turned and saw her. "Take heart, daughter," he said, "your
9:23 When **Jesus** entered the ruler's house and saw the flute players
9:27 As **Jesus** went on from there, two blind men followed him,
9:28 the blind men came to him, and **he**[s] [+3836] asked them,
9:30 **Jesus** warned them sternly, "See that no one knows about this."
9:35 **Jesus** went through all the towns and villages, teaching in their
10: 5 These twelve **Jesus** sent out with the following instructions:
11: 1 After **Jesus** had finished instructing his twelve disciples, he went
11: 4 **Jesus** replied, "Go back and report to John what you hear and see:
11: 7 were leaving, **Jesus** began to speak to the crowd about John:
11:20 Then **Jesus** [UBS-] began to denounce the cities in which most of
11:25 At that time **Jesus** said, "I praise you, Father, Lord of heaven
12: 1 At that time **Jesus** went through the grainfields on the Sabbath.
12:15 Aware of this, **Jesus** withdrew from that place. Many followed
13: 1 That same day **Jesus** went out of the house and sat by the lake.
13:34 **Jesus** spoke all these things to the crowd in parables; he did not
13:51 all these things?" **Jesus** [UBS-] asked. "Yes," they replied.
13:53 When **Jesus** had finished these parables, he moved on from there.
13:57 But **Jesus** said to them, "Only in his hometown and in his own
14: 1 At that time Herod the tetrarch heard the reports *about* **Jesus**,
14:12 and took his body and buried it. Then they went and told **Jesus**.
14:13 When **Jesus** heard what had happened, he withdrew by boat
14:16 **Jesus** replied, "They do not need to go away. You give them
14:27 But **Jesus** immediately said to them: "Take courage! It is I.
14:29 down out of the boat, walked on the water and came toward **Jesus**.
14:31 Immediately **Jesus** reached out his hand and caught him. "You of
15: 1 and teachers of the law came to **Jesus** from Jerusalem and asked,
15:21 that place, **Jesus** withdrew to the region of Tyre and Sidon.
15:28 Then **Jesus** answered, "Woman, you have great faith! Your request
15:29 **Jesus** left there and went along the Sea of Galilee. Then he went
15:32 **Jesus** called his disciples to him and said, "I have compassion for
15:34 "How many loaves do you have?" **Jesus** asked. "Seven," they
16: 6 "Be careful," **Jesus** said to them. "Be on your guard against the
16: 8 Aware of their discussion, **Jesus** asked, "You of little faith,
16:13 When **Jesus** came to the region of Caesarea Philippi, he asked his
16:17 **Jesus** replied, "Blessed are you, Simon son of Jonah, for this was
16:21 From that time on **Jesus** began to explain to his disciples that he
16:24 Then **Jesus** said to his disciples, "If anyone would come after me,
17: 1 After six days **Jesus** took with him Peter, James and John the
17: 4 Peter said *to* **Jesus**, "Lord, it is good for us to be here. If you wish,
17: 7 But **Jesus** came and touched them. "Get up," he said. "Don't be
17: 8 When they looked up, they saw no one except **Jesus**.
17: 9 **Jesus** instructed them, "Don't tell anyone what you have seen,
17:17 "O unbelieving and perverse generation," **Jesus** replied, "how long
17:18 **Jesus** rebuked the demon, and it came out of the boy, and he was
17:19 Then the disciples came to **Jesus** in private and asked, "Why
17:22 When they came together in Galilee, **he**[s] [+3836] said to them,
17:25 When Peter came into the house, **Jesus** was the first to speak.
17:26 Peter answered. "Then the sons are exempt," **Jesus** said to him.
18: 1 At that time the disciples came to **Jesus** and asked, "Who is the
18:22 **Jesus** answered, "I tell you, not seven times, but seventy-seven
19: 1 When **Jesus** had finished saying these things, he left Galilee
19:14 **Jesus** said, "Let the little children come to me, and do not hinder
19:18 **Jesus** replied, " 'Do not murder, do not commit adultery, do not
19:21 **Jesus** answered, "If you want to be perfect, go, sell your
19:23 Then **Jesus** said to his disciples, "I tell you the truth, it is hard for a
19:26 **Jesus** looked at them and said, "With man this is impossible,
19:28 **Jesus** said to them, "I tell you the truth, at the renewal of all things,
20:17 Now as **Jesus** was going up to Jerusalem, he took the twelve
20:22 "You don't know what you are asking," **Jesus** said to them.
20:25 **Jesus** called them together and said, "You know that the rulers of
20:30 and when they heard that **Jesus** was going by, they shouted,
20:32 **Jesus** stopped and called them. "What do you want me to do for
20:34 **Jesus** had compassion on them and touched their eyes.
21: 1 to Bethphage on the Mount of Olives, **Jesus** sent two disciples,

21: 6 The disciples went and did as **Jesus** had instructed them.
21:11 The crowds answered, "This is **Jesus**, the prophet from Nazareth in
21:12 **Jesus** entered the temple area and drove out all who were buying
21:16 "Yes," replied **Jesus**, "have you never read, " 'From the lips of
21:21 **Jesus** replied, "I tell you the truth, if you have faith and do not
21:24 **Jesus** replied, "I will also ask you one question. If you answer me,
21:27 So they answered **Jesus**, "We don't know." Then he said, "Neither
21:31 **Jesus** said to them, "I tell you the truth, the tax collectors
21:42 **Jesus** said to them, "Have you never read in the Scriptures:
22: 1 **Jesus** spoke to them again in parables, saying:
22:18 But **Jesus**, knowing their evil intent, said, "You hypocrites,
22:29 **Jesus** replied, "You are in error because you do not know the
22:41 While the Pharisees were gathered together, **Jesus** asked them,
23: 1 Then **Jesus** said to the crowds and to his disciples:
24: 1 **Jesus** left the temple and was walking away when his disciples
24: 4 **Jesus** answered: "Watch out that no one deceives you.
26: 1 When **Jesus** had finished saying all these things, he said to his
26: 4 and they plotted to arrest **Jesus** in some sly way and kill him.
26: 6 While **Jesus** was in Bethany in the home of a man known as Simon
26:10 Aware of this, **Jesus** said to them, "Why are you bothering this
26:17 Feast of Unleavened Bread, the disciples came to **Jesus** and asked,
26:19 So the disciples did as **Jesus** had directed them and prepared the
26:26 they were eating, **Jesus** took bread, gave thanks and broke it,
26:31 Then **Jesus** told them, "This very night you will all fall away on
26:34 "I tell you the truth," **Jesus** answered, "this very night,
26:36 Then **Jesus** went with his disciples to a place called Gethsemane,
26:49 Going at once to **Jesus**, Judas said, "Greetings, Rabbi!" and kissed
26:50 **Jesus** replied, "Friend, do what you came for." Then the men
26:50 Then the men stepped forward, seized **Jesus** and arrested him.
26:51 With that, one of **Jesus**' companions reached for his sword,
26:52 "Put your sword back in its place," **Jesus** said to him, "for all who
26:55 At that time **Jesus** said to the crowd, "Am I leading a rebellion,
26:57 Those who had arrested **Jesus** took him to Caiaphas, the high
26:59 the whole Sanhedrin were looking for false evidence against **Jesus**
26:63 But **Jesus** remained silent. The high priest said to him, "I charge
26:64 "Yes, it is as you say," **Jesus** replied. "But I say to all of you:
26:69 girl came to him. "You also were with **Jesus** of Galilee," she said.
26:71 said to the people there, "This fellow was with **Jesus** of Nazareth."
26:75 Then Peter remembered the word **Jesus** had spoken: "Before the
27: 1 and the elders of the people came to the decision to put **Jesus** to
27:11 Meanwhile **Jesus** stood before the governor, and the governor
27:11 you the king of the Jews?" "Yes, it is as you say," **Jesus** replied.
27:16 they had a notorious prisoner, called [UBS+ *Jesus*] Barabbas.
27:17 to you: [UBS+ *Jesus*] Barabbas, or Jesus who is called Christ?"
27:17 to release to you: Barabbas, or **Jesus** who is called Christ?"
27:20 the crowd to ask for Barabbas and to have **Jesus** executed.
27:22 "What shall I do, then, with **Jesus** who is called Christ?" Pilate
27:26 But he had **Jesus** flogged, and handed him over to be crucified.
27:27 Then the governor's soldiers took **Jesus** into the Praetorium
27:37 against him: THIS IS JESUS, THE KING OF THE JEWS.
27:46 About the ninth hour **Jesus** cried out in a loud voice, "*Eloi*,
27:50 And when **Jesus** had cried out again in a loud voice, he gave up his
27:54 and those with him who were guarding **Jesus** saw the earthquake
27:55 They had followed **Jesus** from Galilee to care for his needs.
27:57 named Joseph, who had himself become a disciple *of* **Jesus**.
27:58 Going to Pilate, he asked for **Jesus**' body, and Pilate ordered that it
28: 5 "Do not be afraid, for I know that you are looking for **Jesus**,
28: 9 Suddenly **Jesus** met them. "Greetings," he said. They came to him,
28:10 Then **Jesus** said to them, "Do not be afraid. Go and tell my brothers
28:16 went to Galilee, to the mountain where **Jesus** had told them to go.
28:18 Then **Jesus** came to them and said, "All authority in heaven
Mk 1: 1 The beginning of the gospel *about* **Jesus** Christ, the Son of God.
1: 9 At that time **Jesus** came from Nazareth in Galilee and was baptized
1:14 After John was put in prison, **Jesus** went into Galilee,
1:17 follow me," **Jesus** said, "and I will make you fishers of men."
1:24 "What do you want with us, **Jesus** of Nazareth? Have you come to
1:25 "Be quiet!" said **Jesus** sternly. "Come out of him!"
2: 5 When **Jesus** saw their faith, he said to the paralytic, "Son, your sins
2: 8 Immediately **Jesus** knew in his spirit that this was what they were
2:15 and "sinners" were eating with **him**[s] [+3836] and his disciples,
2:17 On hearing this, **Jesus** said to them, "It is not the healthy who need
2:19 **Jesus** answered, "How can the guests of the bridegroom fast while
3: 7 **Jesus** withdrew with his disciples to the lake, and a large crowd
5: 6 When he saw **Jesus** from a distance, he ran and fell on his knees in
5: 7 "What do you want with me, **Jesus**, Son of the Most High God?
5:15 When they came to **Jesus**, they saw the man who had been

5:20 and began to tell in the Decapolis how much **Jesus** had done for
5:21 When **Jesus** had again crossed over by boat to the other side of the
5:27 When she heard about **Jesus**, she came up behind him in the crowd
5:30 At once **Jesus** realized that power had gone out from him.
5:36 what they said, **Jesus** told the synagogue ruler, "Don't be afraid;
6:4 **Jesus** said to them, "Only in his hometown, among his relatives
6:30 The apostles gathered around **Jesus** and reported to him all they
8:17 Aware of their discussion, **Jesus** [UBS-] asked them: "Why are
8:27 **Jesus** and his disciples went on to the villages around Caesarea
9:2 After six days **Jesus** took Peter, James and John with him
9:4 before them Elijah and Moses, who were talking with **Jesus**.
9:5 Peter said to **Jesus**, "Rabbi, it is good for us to be here. Let us put
9:8 looked around, they no longer saw anyone with them except **Jesus**
9:23 " 'If you can'?" said **Jesus**. "Everything is possible for him who
9:25 When **Jesus** saw that a crowd was running to the scene, he rebuked
9:27 But **Jesus** took him by the hand and lifted him to his feet,
9:39 "Do not stop him," **Jesus** said. "No one who does a miracle in my
10:5 hearts were hard that Moses wrote you this law," **Jesus** replied.
10:14 When **Jesus** saw this, he was indignant. He said to them,
10:18 me good?" **Jesus** answered. "No one is good—except God alone.
10:21 **Jesus** looked at him and loved him. "One thing you lack," he said.
10:23 **Jesus** looked around and said to his disciples, "How hard it is for
10:24 But **Jesus** said again, "Children, how hard it is to enter the kingdom
10:27 **Jesus** looked at them and said, "With man this is impossible,
10:29 "I tell you the truth," **Jesus** replied, "no one who has left home
10:32 with **Jesus** leading the way, and the disciples were astonished,
10:38 "You don't know what you are asking," **Jesus** said. "Can you drink
10:39 **Jesus** said to them, "You will drink the cup I drink and be baptized
10:42 **Jesus** called them together and said, "You know that those who are
10:47 When he heard that it was **Jesus** of Nazareth, he began to shout,
10:47 he began to shout, "**Jesus**, Son of David, have mercy on me!"
10:49 **Jesus** stopped and said, "Call him." So they called to the blind man,
10:50 Throwing his cloak aside, he jumped to his feet and came to **Jesus**.
10:51 **Jesus** asked him. The blind man said, "Rabbi, I want to see."
10:52 "Go," said **Jesus**, "your faith has healed you." Immediately he
11:6 They answered as **Jesus** had told them to, and the people let them
11:7 When they brought the colt to **Jesus** and threw their cloaks over it,
11:22 "Have faith in God," **Jesus** answered.
11:29 **Jesus** replied, "I will ask you one question. Answer me, and I will
11:33 So they answered **Jesus**, "We don't know." Jesus said, "Neither
11:33 **Jesus** said, "Neither will I tell you by what authority I am doing
12:17 Then **Jesus** said to them, "Give to Caesar what is Caesar's and to
12:24 **Jesus** replied, "Are you not in error because you do not know the
12:29 "The most important one," answered **Jesus**, "is this: 'Hear, O Israel,
12:34 When **Jesus** saw that he had answered wisely, he said to him,
12:35 While **Jesus** was teaching in the temple courts, he asked, "How is it
13:2 "Do you see all these great buildings?" replied **Jesus**. "Not one
13:5 **Jesus** said to them: "Watch out that no one deceives you.
14:6 "Leave her alone," said **Jesus**. "Why are you bothering her?
14:18 While they were reclining at the table eating, he[s] [+3836] said,
14:22 were eating, **Jesus** [UBS-] took bread, gave thanks and broke it,
14:27 "You will all fall away," **Jesus** told them, "for it is written: " 'I will
14:30 "I tell you the truth," **Jesus** answered, "today—yes, tonight—
14:48 "Am I leading a rebellion," said **Jesus**, "that you have come out
14:53 They took **Jesus** to the high priest, and all the chief priests,
14:55 and the whole Sanhedrin were looking for evidence against **Jesus**
14:60 Then the high priest stood up before them and asked **Jesus**,
14:62 "I am," said **Jesus**. "And you will see the Son of Man sitting at the
14:67 closely at him. "You also were with that Nazarene, **Jesus**," she said.
14:72 Then Peter remembered the word **Jesus** had spoken to him:
15:1 They bound **Jesus**, led him away and handed him over to Pilate.
15:5 But **Jesus** still made no reply,
15:15 He had **Jesus** flogged, and handed him over to be crucified.
15:34 And at the ninth hour **Jesus** cried out in a loud voice, "*Eloi*,
15:37 With a loud cry, **Jesus** breathed his last.
15:43 kingdom of God, went boldly to Pilate and asked for **Jesus**' body.
16:6 "You are looking for **Jesus** the Nazarene, who was crucified.
16:19 After the Lord **Jesus** had spoken to them, he was taken up into
16:S [UBS+ *And after these things Jesus himself sent out through them*,]
Lk 1:31 and give birth to a son, and you are to give him the name **Jesus**.
2:21 when it was time to circumcise him, he was named **Jesus**,
2:27 When the parents brought in the child **Jesus** to do for him what the
2:43 the boy **Jesus** stayed behind in Jerusalem, but they were unaware
2:52 And **Jesus** grew in wisdom and stature, and in favor with God
3:21 When all the people were being baptized, **Jesus** was baptized too.
3:23 Now **Jesus** himself was about thirty years old when he began his

3:29 the son *of* Joshua, the son of Eliezer, the son of Jorim, the son of
4:1 **Jesus**, full of the Holy Spirit, returned from the Jordan and was led
4:4 **Jesus** answered, "It is written: 'Man does not live on bread alone.' "
4:8 **Jesus** answered, "It is written: 'Worship the Lord your God
4:12 **Jesus** answered, "It says: 'Do not put the Lord your God to the test.'
4:14 **Jesus** returned to Galilee in the power of the Spirit, and news about
4:34 What do you want with us, **Jesus** of Nazareth? Have you come
4:35 "Be quiet!" **Jesus** said sternly. "Come out of him!" Then the demon
5:8 saw this, he fell at **Jesus**' knees and said, "Go away from me, Lord;
5:10 Then **Jesus** said to Simon, "Don't be afraid; from now on you will
5:12 When he saw **Jesus**, he fell with his face to the ground and begged
5:19 the tiles into the middle of the crowd, right in front of **Jesus**.
5:22 **Jesus** knew what they were thinking and asked, "Why are you
5:31 **Jesus** answered them, "It is not the healthy who need a doctor,
5:34 **Jesus** answered, "Can you make the guests of the bridegroom fast
6:3 **Jesus** answered them, "Have you never read what David did when
6:9 Then **Jesus** said to them, "I ask you, which is lawful on the
6:11 began to discuss with one another what they might do *to* **Jesus**.
7:3 The centurion heard of **Jesus** and sent some elders of the Jews to
7:4 When they came to **Jesus**, they pleaded earnestly with him,
7:6 So **Jesus** went with them. He was not far from the house when the
7:9 When **Jesus** heard this, he was amazed at him, and turning to the
7:40 **Jesus** answered him, "Simon, I have something to tell you."
8:28 When he saw **Jesus**, he cried out and fell at his feet, shouting at the
8:28 "What do you want with me, **Jesus**, Son of the Most High God?
8:30 **Jesus** asked him, "What is your name?" "Legion," he replied,
8:35 When they came to **Jesus**, they found the man from whom the
8:35 had gone out, sitting at **Jesus**' feet, dressed and in his right mind;
8:39 and told all over town how much **Jesus** had done for him.
8:40 Now when **Jesus** returned, a crowd welcomed him, for they were
8:41 named Jairus, a ruler of the synagogue, came and fell at **Jesus**' feet,
8:45 "Who touched me?" **Jesus** asked. When they all denied it, Peter
8:46 But **Jesus** said, "Someone touched me; I know that power has gone
8:50 Hearing this, **Jesus** said to Jairus, "Don't be afraid; just believe,
9:33 As the men were leaving **Jesus**, Peter said to him, "Master,
9:36 When the voice had spoken, they found that **Jesus** was alone.
9:41 "O unbelieving and perverse generation," **Jesus** replied, "how long
9:42 But **Jesus** rebuked the evil spirit, healed the boy and gave him
9:47 **Jesus**, knowing their thoughts, took a little child and had him stand
9:50 "Do not stop him," **Jesus** said, "for whoever is not against you is
9:58 **Jesus** replied, "Foxes have holes and birds of the air have nests,
9:62 **Jesus** replied, "No one who puts his hand to the plow and looks
10:29 to justify himself, so he asked **Jesus**, "And who is my neighbor?"
10:30 In reply **Jesus** said: "A man was going down from Jerusalem to
10:37 one who had mercy on him." **Jesus** told him, "Go and do likewise."
13:12 When **Jesus** saw her, he called her forward and said to her,
13:14 Indignant because **Jesus** had healed on the Sabbath, the synagogue
14:3 **Jesus** asked the Pharisees and experts in the law, "Is it lawful to
17:13 and called out in a loud voice, "**Jesus**, Master, have pity on us!"
17:17 **Jesus** asked, "Were not all ten cleansed? Where are the other nine?
18:16 But **Jesus** called the children to him and said, "Let the little
18:19 me good?" **Jesus** answered. "No one is good—except God alone.
18:22 When **Jesus** heard this, he said to him, "You still lack one thing.
18:24 **Jesus** looked at him and said, "How hard it is for the rich to enter
18:37 They told him, "**Jesus** of Nazareth is passing by."
18:38 He called out, "**Jesus**, Son of David, have mercy on me!"
18:40 **Jesus** stopped and ordered the man to be brought to him. When he
18:42 **Jesus** said to him, "Receive your sight; your faith has healed you."
19:3 He wanted to see who **Jesus** was, but being a short man he could
19:5 When **Jesus** reached the spot, he looked up and said to him,
19:9 **Jesus** said to him, "Today salvation has come to this house,
19:35 They brought it to **Jesus**, threw their cloaks on the colt and put
19:35 it to Jesus, threw their cloaks on the colt and put **Jesus** on it.
20:8 **Jesus** said, "Neither will I tell you by what authority I am doing
20:34 **Jesus** replied, "The people of this age marry and are given in
22:47 of the Twelve, was leading them. He approached **Jesus** to kiss him,
22:48 but **Jesus** asked him, "Judas, are you betraying the Son of Man with
22:51 But **Jesus** answered, "No more of this!" And he touched the man's
22:52 Then **Jesus** said to the chief priests, the officers of the temple
23:8 When Herod saw **Jesus**, he was greatly pleased, because for a long
23:20 Wanting to release **Jesus**, Pilate appealed to them again.
23:25 the one they asked for, and surrendered **Jesus** to their will.
23:26 and put the cross on him and made him carry it behind **Jesus**.
23:28 **Jesus** turned and said to them, "Daughters of Jerusalem, do not
23:34 **Jesus** said, "Father, forgive them, for they do not know what they
23:42 Then he said, "**Jesus**, remember me when you come into your

23:46 **Jesus** called out with a loud voice, "Father, into your hands I
23:52 Going to Pilate, he asked for **Jesus'** body.
24: 3 when they entered, they did not find the body *of* the Lord **Jesus**.
24:15 each other, **Jesus** himself came up and walked along with them;
24:19 "What things?" he asked. "About **Jesus** of Nazareth," they replied.

Jn 1:17 given through Moses; grace and truth came through **Jesus** Christ.
1:29 The next day John saw **Jesus** coming toward him and said,
1:36 When he saw **Jesus** passing by, he said, "Look, the Lamb of God!"
1:37 When the two disciples heard him say this, they followed **Jesus**.
1:38 Turning around, **Jesus** saw them following and asked, "What do
1:42 And he brought him to **Jesus**. Jesus looked at him and said,
1:42 looked at him and said, "You are Simon son of John.
1:43 for Galilee. Finding Philip, he^s [*+3836*] said to him, "Follow me."
1:45 the prophets also wrote—**Jesus** of Nazareth, the son of Joseph."
1:47 When **Jesus** saw Nathanael approaching, he said of him, "Here is a
1:48 **Jesus** answered, "I saw you while you were still under the fig tree
1:50 **Jesus** said, "You believe because I told you I saw you under the fig
2: 1 a wedding took place at Cana in Galilee. **Jesus'** mother was there,
2: 2 and **Jesus** and his disciples had also been invited to the wedding.
2: 3 was gone, **Jesus'** mother said to him, "They have no more wine."
2: 4 "Dear woman, why do you involve me?" **Jesus** replied. "My time
2: 7 **Jesus** said to the servants, "Fill the jars with water"; so they filled
2:11 first of his miraculous signs, **Jesus** performed at Cana in Galilee.
2:13 almost time for the Jewish Passover, **Jesus** went up to Jerusalem.
2:19 **Jesus** answered them, "Destroy this temple, and I will raise it again
2:22 they believed the Scripture and the words that **Jesus** had spoken.
2:24 But **Jesus** would not entrust himself to them, for he knew all men.
3: 3 In reply **Jesus** declared, "I tell you the truth, no one can see the
3: 5 **Jesus** answered, "I tell you the truth, no one can enter the kingdom
3:10 "You are Israel's teacher," said **Jesus**, "and do you not understand
3:22 **Jesus** and his disciples went out into the Judean countryside,
4: 1 The Pharisees heard that **Jesus** was gaining and baptizing more
4: 2 although in fact it was not **Jesus** who baptized, but his disciples.
4: 3 When the Lord [UBS **Jesus**; NIV *3261*] learned of this, he left
4: 6 Jacob's well was there, and **Jesus**, tired as he was from the
4: 7 came to draw water, **Jesus** said to her, "Will you give me a drink?"
4:10 **Jesus** answered her, "If you knew the gift of God and who it is that
4:13 **Jesus** answered, "Everyone who drinks this water will be thirsty
4:17 **Jesus** said to her, "You are right when you say you have no
4:21 **Jesus** declared, "Believe me, woman, a time is coming when you
4:26 Then **Jesus** declared, "I who speak to you am he."
4:34 "My food," said **Jesus**, "is to do the will of him who sent me
4:44 (Now **Jesus** himself had pointed out that a prophet has no honor in
4:47 When this man heard that **Jesus** had arrived in Galilee from Judea,
4:48 you people see miraculous signs and wonders," **Jesus** told him,
4:50 **Jesus** replied, "You may go. Your son will live." The man took
4:50 Your son will live." The man took **Jesus** at his word and departed.
4:53 Then the father realized that this was the exact time at which **Jesus**
4:54 This was the second miraculous sign that **Jesus** performed,
5: 1 time later, **Jesus** went up to Jerusalem for a feast of the Jews.
5: 6 When **Jesus** saw him lying there and learned that he had been in
5: 8 Then **Jesus** said to him, "Get up! Pick up your mat and walk."
5:13 it was, for **Jesus** had slipped away into the crowd that was there.
5:14 Later **Jesus** found him at the temple and said to him, "See,
5:15 and told the Jews that it was **Jesus** who had made him well.
5:16 So, because **Jesus** was doing these things on the Sabbath,
5:17 **Jesus** said to them, "My Father is always at his work to this very
5:19 **Jesus** gave them this answer: "I tell you the truth, the Son can do
6: 1 **Jesus** crossed to the far shore of the Sea of Galilee (that is,
6: 3 Then **Jesus** went up on a mountainside and sat down with his
6: 5 When **Jesus** looked up and saw a great crowd coming toward him,
6:10 **Jesus** said, "Have the people sit down." There was plenty of grass
6:11 **Jesus** then took the loaves, gave thanks, and distributed to those
6:15 **Jesus**, knowing that they intended to come and make him king by
6:17 By now it was dark, and **Jesus** had not yet joined them.
6:19 or three and a half miles, they saw **Jesus** approaching the boat,
6:22 and that **Jesus** had not entered it with his disciples, but that they
6:24 Once the crowd realized that neither **Jesus** nor his disciples were
6:24 they got into the boats and went to Capernaum in search of **Jesus**.
6:26 **Jesus** answered, "I tell you the truth, you are looking for me,
6:29 **Jesus** answered, "The work of God is this: to believe in the one he
6:32 **Jesus** said to them, "I tell you the truth, it is not Moses who has
6:35 Then **Jesus** declared, "I am the bread of life. He who comes to me
6:42 They said, "Is this not **Jesus**, the son of Joseph, whose father
6:43 "Stop grumbling among yourselves," **Jesus** answered.
6:53 **Jesus** said to them, "I tell you the truth, unless you eat the flesh of

6:61 grumbling about this, **Jesus** said to them, "Does this offend you?
6:64 For **Jesus** had known from the beginning which of them did not
6:67 "You do not want to leave too, do you?" **Jesus** asked the Twelve.
6:70 Then **Jesus** replied, "Have I not chosen you, the Twelve? Yet one
7: 1 After this, **Jesus** went around in Galilee, purposely staying away
7: 6 Therefore **Jesus** told them, "The right time for me has not yet come;
7:14 Not until halfway through the Feast did **Jesus** go up to the temple
7:16 **Jesus** answered, "My teaching is not my own. It comes from him
7:21 **Jesus** said to them, "I did one miracle, and you are all astonished.
7:28 Then **Jesus**, still teaching in the temple courts, cried out, "Yes,
7:33 **Jesus** said, "I am with you for only a short time, and then I go to the
7:37 **Jesus** stood and said in a loud voice, "If anyone is thirsty, let him
7:39 Spirit had not been given, since **Jesus** had not yet been glorified.
8: 1 But **Jesus** went to the Mount of Olives.
8: 6 But **Jesus** bent down and started to write on the ground with his
8:10 **Jesus** straightened up and asked her, "Woman, where are they?
8:11 "Then neither do I condemn you," **Jesus** declared. "Go now and
8:12 When **Jesus** spoke again to the people, he said, "I am the light of
8:14 **Jesus** answered, "Even if I testify on my own behalf, my testimony
8:19 "You do not know me or my Father," **Jesus** replied. "If you knew
8:25 "Just what I have been claiming all along," **Jesus** replied.
8:28 So **Jesus** said, "When you have lifted up the Son of Man, then you
8:31 **Jesus** said, "If you hold to my teaching, you are really my disciples.
8:34 **Jesus** replied, "I tell you the truth, everyone who sins is a slave to
8:39 "If you were Abraham's children," said **Jesus**, "then you would do
8:42 **Jesus** said to them, "If God were your Father, you would love me,
8:49 a demon," said **Jesus**, "but I honor my Father and you dishonor me.
8:54 **Jesus** replied, "If I glorify myself, my glory means nothing.
8:58 "I tell you the truth," **Jesus** answered, "before Abraham was born,
8:59 they picked up stones to stone him, but **Jesus** hid himself,
9: 3 said **Jesus**, "but this happened so that the work of God might be
9:11 "The man they call **Jesus** made some mud and put it on my eyes.
9:14 Now the day on which **Jesus** had made the mud and opened the
9:35 **Jesus** heard that they had thrown him out, and when he found him,
9:37 **Jesus** said, "You have now seen him; in fact, he is the one speaking
9:39 **Jesus** said, "For judgment I have come into this world, so that the
9:41 **Jesus** said, "If you were blind, you would not be guilty of sin;
10: 6 **Jesus** used this figure of speech,
10: 7 Therefore **Jesus** said again, "I tell you the truth, I am the gate for
10:23 and **Jesus** was in the temple area walking in Solomon's
10:25 **Jesus** answered, "I did tell you, but you do not believe.
10:32 but **Jesus** said to them, "I have shown you many great miracles
10:34 **Jesus** answered them, "Is it not written in your Law, 'I have said
11: 4 he heard this, **Jesus** said, "This sickness will not end in death.
11: 5 **Jesus** loved Martha and her sister and Lazarus.
11: 9 **Jesus** answered, "Are there not twelve hours of daylight? A man
11:13 **Jesus** had been speaking of his death, but his disciples thought he
11:14 So then he^s [*+3836*] told them plainly, "Lazarus is dead,
11:17 **Jesus** found that Lazarus had already been in the tomb for four
11:20 When Martha heard that **Jesus** was coming, she went out to meet
11:21 "Lord," Martha said to **Jesus**, "if you had been here, my brother
11:23 **Jesus** said to her, "Your brother will rise again."
11:25 **Jesus** said to her, "I am the resurrection and the life. He who
11:30 Now **Jesus** had not yet entered the village, but was still at the place
11:32 When Mary reached the place where **Jesus** was and saw him,
11:33 When **Jesus** saw her weeping, and the Jews who had come along
11:35 **Jesus** wept.
11:38 **Jesus**, once more deeply moved, came to the tomb. It was a cave
11:39 "Take away the stone," he^s [*+3836*] said. "But, Lord," said Martha,
11:40 Then **Jesus** said, "Did I not tell you that if you believed, you would
11:41 Then **Jesus** looked up and said, "Father, I thank you that you have
11:44 **Jesus** said to them, "Take off the grave clothes and let him go."
11:46 of them went to the Pharisees and told them what **Jesus** had done.
11:51 but as high priest that year he prophesied that **Jesus** would die for
11:54 Therefore **Jesus** no longer moved about publicly among the Jews.
11:56 They kept looking for **Jesus**, and as they stood in the temple area
12: 1 the Passover, **Jesus** arrived at Bethany, where Lazarus lived,
12: 1 where Lazarus lived, whom **Jesus** had raised from the dead.
12: 3 she poured it on **Jesus'** feet and wiped his feet with her hair.
12: 7 "Leave her alone," **Jesus** replied. "It was intended, that she should
12: 9 not only because of him^s [*+3836*] but also to see Lazarus,
12:11 for on account of him many of the Jews were going over to **Jesus**
12:12 come for the Feast heard that **Jesus** was on his way to Jerusalem.
12:14 **Jesus** found a young donkey and sat upon it, as it is written,
12:16 Only after **Jesus** was glorified did they realize that these things had
12:21 with a request. "Sir," they said, "we would like to see **Jesus**."

12:22　Philip went to tell Andrew; Andrew and Philip in turn told **Jesus**.
12:23　**Jesus** replied, "The hour has come for the Son of Man to be
12:30　**Jesus** said, "This voice was for your benefit, not mine.
12:35　Then **Jesus** told them, "You are going to have the light just a little
12:36　he had finished speaking, **Jesus** left and hid himself from them.
12:44　Then **Jesus** cried out, "When a man believes in me, he does not
13: 1　**Jesus** knew that the time had come for him to leave this world
13: 7　**Jesus** replied, "You do not realize now what I am doing, but later
13: 8　**Jesus** answered, "Unless I wash you, you have no part with me."
13:10　**Jesus** answered, "A person who has had a bath needs only to wash
13:21　**Jesus** was troubled in spirit and testified, "I tell you the truth,
13:23　One of them, the disciple whom **Jesus** loved, was reclining next to
13:23　disciple whom Jesus loved, was reclining next to **him**ˢ [+3836].
13:25　Leaning back against **Jesus**, he asked him, "Lord, who is it?"
13:26　**Jesus** answered, "It is the one to whom I will give this piece of
13:27　into him. "What you are about to do, do quickly," **Jesus** told him,
13:29　some thought **Jesus** was telling him to buy what was needed for
13:31　When he was gone, **Jesus** said, "Now is the Son of Man glorified
13:36　**Jesus** replied, "Where I am going, you cannot follow now,
13:38　Then **Jesus** answered, "Will you really lay down your life for me?
14: 6　**Jesus** answered, "I am the way and the truth and the life. No one
14: 9　**Jesus** answered: "Don't you know me, Philip, even after I have
14:23　**Jesus** replied, "If anyone loves me, he will obey my teaching.
16:19　**Jesus** saw that they wanted to ask him about this, so he said to
16:31　"You believe at last!" **Jesus** answered.
17: 1　After **Jesus** said this, he looked toward heaven and prayed:
17: 3　the only true God, and **Jesus** Christ, whom you have sent.
18: 1　**Jesus** left with his disciples and crossed the Kidron Valley.
18: 2　the place, because **Jesus** had often met there with his disciples.
18: 4　**Jesus**, knowing all that was going to happen to him, went out
18: 5　"**Jesus** of Nazareth," they replied. "I am he," Jesus said. (And Judas
18: 7　"Who is it you want?" And they said, "**Jesus** of Nazareth."
18: 8　"I told you that I am he," **Jesus** answered. "If you are looking for
18:11　**Jesus** commanded Peter, "Put your sword away! Shall I not drink
18:12　with its commander and the Jewish officials arrested **Jesus**.
18:15　Simon Peter and another disciple were following **Jesus**.
18:15　the high priest, he went with **Jesus** into the high priest's courtyard,
18:19　the high priest questioned **Jesus** about his disciples and his
18:20　"I have spoken openly to the world," **Jesus** replied. "I always
18:22　one of the officials nearby struck **him**ˢ [+3836] in the face.
18:23　"If I said something wrong," **Jesus** replied, "testify as to what is
18:28　Then the Jews led **Jesus** from Caiaphas to the palace of the Roman
18:32　so that the words **Jesus** had spoken indicating the kind of death he
18:33　summoned **Jesus** and asked him, "Are you the king of the Jews?"
18:34　"Is that your own idea," **Jesus** asked, "or did others talk to you
18:36　**Jesus** said, "My kingdom is not of this world. If it were, my
18:37　**Jesus** answered, "You are right in saying I am a king. In fact,
19: 1　Then Pilate took **Jesus** and had him flogged.
19: 5　When **Jesus** came out wearing the crown of thorns and the purple
19: 9　do you come from?" he asked **Jesus**, but Jesus gave him no answer.
19: 9　do you come from?" he asked Jesus, but **Jesus** gave him no answer.
19:11　**Jesus** answered, "You would have no power over me if it were not
19:13　he brought **Jesus** out and sat down on the judge's seat at a place
19:16　over to them to be crucified. So the soldiers took charge of **Jesus**.
19:18　with him two others—one on each side and **Jesus** in the middle.
19:19　It read: **JESUS** OF NAZARETH, THE KING OF THE JEWS.
19:20　for the place where **Jesus** was crucified was near the city,
19:23　When the soldiers crucified **Jesus**, they took his clothes, dividing
19:25　Near the cross of **Jesus** stood his mother, his mother's sister,
19:26　When **Jesus** saw his mother there, and the disciple whom he loved
19:28　so that the Scripture would be fulfilled, **Jesus** said, "I am thirsty."
19:30　When he had received the drink, **Jesus** said, "It is finished."
19:33　But when they came to **Jesus** and found that he was already dead,
19:38　Later, Joseph of Arimathea asked Pilate for the body of **Jesus**.
19:38　Now Joseph was a disciple of **Jesus**, but secretly because he feared
19:40　Taking **Jesus**' body, the two of them wrapped it, with the spices,
19:42　and since the tomb was nearby, they laid **Jesus** there.
20: 2　Simon Peter and the other disciple, the one **Jesus** loved, and said,
20:12　seated where **Jesus**' body had been, one at the head and the other at
20:14　At this, she turned around and saw **Jesus** standing there, but she
20:14　saw Jesus standing there, but she did not realize that it was **Jesus**.
20:15　"Woman," **he**ˢ said, "why are you crying? Who is it you are
20:16　**Jesus** said to her, "Mary." She turned toward him and cried out in
20:17　**Jesus** said, "Do not hold on to me, for I have not yet returned to the
20:19　**Jesus** came and stood among them and said, "Peace be with you!"
20:21　Again **Jesus** said, "Peace be with you! As the Father has sent me,

20:24　one of the Twelve, was not with the disciples when **Jesus** came.
20:26　**Jesus** came and stood among them and said, "Peace be with you!"
20:29　Then **Jesus** told him, "Because you have seen me, you have
20:30　**Jesus** did many other miraculous signs in the presence of his
20:31　But these are written that you may believe that **Jesus** is the Christ,
21: 1　Afterward **Jesus** appeared again to his disciples, by the Sea of
21: 4　Early in the morning, **Jesus** stood on the shore, but the disciples
21: 4　on the shore, but the disciples did not realize that it was **Jesus**.
21: 5　**He**ˢ [+3836] called out to them, "Friends, haven't you any fish?"
21: 7　Then the disciple whom **Jesus** loved said to Peter, "It is the Lord!"
21:10　**Jesus** said to them, "Bring some of the fish you have just caught."
21:12　**Jesus** said to them, "Come and have breakfast." None of the
21:13　**Jesus** came, took the bread and gave it to them, and did the same
21:14　This was now the third time **Jesus** appeared to his disciples after
21:15　had finished eating, **Jesus** said to Simon Peter, "Simon son of John,
21:17　all things; you know that I love you." **Jesus** said, "Feed my sheep.
21:20　and saw that the disciple whom **Jesus** loved was following them.
21:21　When Peter saw him, he asked, **[RPG]** "Lord, what about him?"
21:22　**Jesus** answered, "If I want him to remain alive until I return,
21:23　But **Jesus** did not say that he would not die; he only said, "If I want
21:25　**Jesus** did many other things as well. If every one of them were

Ac　1: 1　Theophilus, I wrote about all that **Jesus** began to do and to teach
1:11　This same **Jesus**, who has been taken from you into heaven,
1:14　along with the women and Mary the mother of **Jesus**, and with his
1:16　who served as guide for those who arrested **Jesus**—
1:21　men who have been with us the whole time the Lord **Jesus** went in
2:22　**Jesus** of Nazareth was a man accredited by God to you by
2:32　God has raised this **Jesus** to life, and we are all witnesses of the
2:36　God has made this **Jesus**, whom you crucified, both Lord
2:38　in the name of **Jesus** Christ for the forgiveness of your sins.
3: 6　I have I give you. In the name of **Jesus** Christ of Nazareth, walk."
3:13　and Jacob, the God of our fathers, has glorified his servant **Jesus**.
3:20　may send the Christ, who has been appointed for you—even **Jesus**.
4: 2　the people and proclaiming in **Jesus** the resurrection of the dead.
4:10　It is by the name of **Jesus** Christ of Nazareth, whom you crucified
4:13　and they took note that these men had been with **Jesus**.
4:18　commanded them not to speak or teach at all in the name of **Jesus**.
4:27　of Israel in this city to conspire against your holy servant **Jesus**,
4:30　and wonders through the name of your holy servant **Jesus**."
4:33　apostles continued to testify to the resurrection of the Lord **Jesus**,
5:30　The God of our fathers raised **Jesus** from the dead—whom you had
5:40　Then they ordered them not to speak in the name of **Jesus**,
5:42　and proclaiming the good news that **Jesus** is the Christ.
6:14　For we have heard him say that this **Jesus** of Nazareth will destroy
7:45　our fathers under **Joshua** brought it with them when they took the
7:55　saw the glory of God, and **Jesus** standing at the right hand of God.
7:59　were stoning him, Stephen prayed, "Lord **Jesus**, receive my spirit."
8:12　good news of the kingdom of God and the name of **Jesus** Christ,
8:16　they had simply been baptized into the name of the Lord **Jesus**.
8:35　very passage of Scripture and told him the good news about **Jesus**.
9: 5　Saul asked. "I am **Jesus**, whom you are persecuting," he replied.
9:17　**Jesus**, who appeared to you on the road as you were coming here—
9:20　At once he began to preach in the synagogues that **Jesus** is the Son
9:27　how in Damascus he had preached fearlessly in the name of **Jesus**.
9:34　"Aeneas," Peter said to him, "**Jesus** Christ heals you. Get up
10:36　telling the good news of peace through **Jesus** Christ, who is Lord
10:38　how God anointed **Jesus** of Nazareth with the Holy Spirit
10:48　So he ordered that they be baptized in the name of **Jesus** Christ.
11:17　who believed in the Lord **Jesus** Christ, who was I to think that I
11:20　to Greeks also, telling them the good news about the Lord **Jesus**.
13:23　this man's descendants God has brought to Israel the Savior **Jesus**,
13:33　he has fulfilled for us, their children, by raising up **Jesus**. As it is
15:11　We believe it is through the grace of our Lord **Jesus** that we are
15:26　men who have risked their lives for the name of our Lord **Jesus**
16: 7　to enter Bithynia, but the Spirit of **Jesus** would not allow them to.
16:18　"In the name of **Jesus** Christ I command you to come out of her!"
16:31　They replied, "Believe in the Lord **Jesus**, and you will be saved—
17: 3　"This **Jesus** I am proclaiming to you is the Christ," he said.
17: 7　saying that there is another king, one called **Jesus**."
17:18　said this because Paul was preaching the good news *about* **Jesus**
18: 5　to preaching, testifying to the Jews that **Jesus** was the Christ.
18:25　and he spoke with great fervor and taught about **Jesus** accurately,
18:28　proving from the Scriptures that **Jesus** was the Christ.
19: 4　the people to believe in the one coming after him, that is, in **Jesus**."
19: 5　hearing this, they were baptized into the name of the Lord **Jesus**.
19:13　the name of the Lord **Jesus** over those who were demon-possessed.

19:13 They would say, "In the name of **Jesus**, whom Paul preaches,
19:15 "**Jesus** I know, and I know about Paul, but who are you?"
19:17 with fear, and the name *of* the Lord **Jesus** was held in high honor.
20:21 must turn to God in repentance and have faith in our Lord **Jesus**.
20:24 finish the race and complete the task the Lord **Jesus** has given me—
20:35 the weak, remembering the words the Lord **Jesus** himself said:
21:13 but also to die in Jerusalem for the name *of* the Lord **Jesus**."
22: 8 " 'I am **Jesus** of Nazareth, whom you are persecuting,' he replied.
24:24 and listened to him as he spoke about faith in Christ **Jesus**.
25:19 and about a dead man named **Jesus** who Paul claimed was alive.
26: 9 do all that was possible to oppose the name *of* **Jesus** of Nazareth.
26:15 " 'I am **Jesus**, whom you are persecuting,' the Lord replied.
28:23 and tried to convince them about **Jesus** from the Law of Moses
28:31 the kingdom of God and taught about the Lord **Jesus** Christ.
Ro 1: 1 Paul, a servant *of* Christ **Jesus**, called to be an apostle and set apart
1: 4 of God by his resurrection from the dead: **Jesus** Christ our Lord.
1: 6 And you also are among those who are called to *belong to* **Jesus**
1: 7 peace to you from God our Father and from the Lord **Jesus** Christ.
1: 8 First, I thank my God through **Jesus** Christ for all of you,
2:16 the day when God will judge men's secrets through **Jesus** Christ,
3:22 This righteousness from God comes through faith *in* **Jesus** Christ
3:24 by his grace through the redemption that came by Christ **Jesus**.
3:26 to be just and the one who justifies those who have faith *in* **Jesus**.
4:24 for us who believe in him who raised **Jesus** our Lord from the
5: 1 we have peace with God through our Lord **Jesus** Christ,
5:11 but we also rejoice in God through our Lord **Jesus** Christ,
5:15 and the gift that came by the grace *of* the one man, **Jesus** Christ,
5:17 of righteousness reign in life through the one man, **Jesus** Christ.
5:21 righteousness to bring eternal life through **Jesus** Christ our Lord.
6: 3 who were baptized into Christ **Jesus** were baptized into his death?
6:11 count yourselves dead to sin but alive to God in Christ **Jesus**.
6:23 but the gift of God is eternal life in Christ **Jesus** our Lord.
7:25 Thanks be to God—through **Jesus** Christ our Lord! So then,
8: 1 there is now no condemnation for those who are in Christ **Jesus**,
8: 2 because through Christ **Jesus** the law of the Spirit of life set me
8:11 And if the Spirit of him who raised **Jesus** from the dead is living in
8:34 Christ **Jesus**, who died—more than that, who was raised to life—
8:39 separate us from the love of God that is in Christ **Jesus** our Lord.
10: 9 That if you confess with your mouth, "**Jesus** is Lord," and believe
13:14 Rather, clothe yourselves with the Lord **Jesus** Christ, and do not
14:14 As one who is in the Lord **Jesus**, I am fully convinced that no food
15: 5 you a spirit of unity among yourselves as you follow Christ **Jesus**,
15: 6 you may glorify the God and Father *of* our Lord **Jesus** Christ.
15:16 to be a minister *of* Christ **Jesus** to the Gentiles with the priestly
15:17 Therefore I glory in Christ **Jesus** in my service to God.
15:30 brothers, by our Lord **Jesus** Christ and by the love of the Spirit,
16: 3 Greet Priscilla and Aquila, my fellow workers in Christ **Jesus**.
16:20 Satan under your feet. The grace *of* our Lord **Jesus** be with you.
16:25 establish you by my gospel and the proclamation *of* **Jesus** Christ,
16:27 to the only wise God be glory forever through **Jesus** Christ!
1Co 1: 1 called to be an apostle *of* Christ **Jesus** by the will of God,
1: 2 in Corinth, to those sanctified in Christ **Jesus** and called to be holy,
1: 2 those everywhere who call on the name *of* our Lord **Jesus** Christ—
1: 3 and peace to you from God our Father and the Lord **Jesus** Christ.
1: 4 thank God for you because of his grace given you in Christ **Jesus**.
1: 7 gift as you eagerly wait for our Lord **Jesus** Christ to be revealed.
1: 8 so that you will be blameless on the day *of* our Lord **Jesus** Christ.
1: 9 who has called you into fellowship with his Son **Jesus** Christ our
1:10 I appeal to you, brothers, in the name *of* our Lord **Jesus** Christ,
1:30 It is because of him that you are in Christ **Jesus**, who has become
2: 2 For I resolved to know nothing while I was with you except **Jesus**
3:11 foundation other than the one already laid, which is **Jesus** Christ.
4:15 for in Christ **Jesus** I became your father through the gospel.
4:17 He will remind you of my way of life in Christ **Jesus**, which agrees
5: 4 When you are assembled in the name *of* our Lord **Jesus** and I am
5: 4 I am with you in spirit, and the power *of* our Lord **Jesus** is present,
6:11 you were justified in the name *of* the Lord **Jesus** Christ and by the
8: 6 and there is but one Lord, **Jesus** Christ, through whom all things
9: 1 I not free? Am I not an apostle? Have I not seen **Jesus** our Lord?
11:23 The Lord **Jesus**, on the night he was betrayed, took bread,
12: 3 "**Jesus** be cursed," and no one can say, "Jesus is Lord," except by
12: 3 "Jesus be cursed," and no one can say, "**Jesus** is Lord," except by
15:31 just as surely as I glory over you in Christ **Jesus** our Lord.
15:57 be to God! He gives us the victory through our Lord **Jesus** Christ.
16:23 The grace *of* the Lord **Jesus** be with you.
16:24 My love to all of you in Christ **Jesus**. Amen.

2Co 1: 1 Paul, an apostle *of* Christ **Jesus** by the will of God, and Timothy
1: 2 and peace to you from God our Father and the Lord **Jesus** Christ.
1: 3 Praise be to the God and Father *of* our Lord **Jesus** Christ,
1:14 of us just as we will boast of you in the day of the Lord **Jesus**.
1:19 For the Son of God, **Jesus** Christ, who was preached among you
4: 5 For we do not preach ourselves, but **Jesus** Christ as Lord,
4: 5 Jesus Christ as Lord, and ourselves as your servants for **Jesus**' sake.
4: 6 knowledge of the glory of God in the face of [UBS+ *Jesus*] Christ.
4:10 We always carry around in our body the death *of* **Jesus**, so that the
4:10 so that the life *of* **Jesus** may also be revealed in our body.
4:11 who are alive are always being given over to death for **Jesus**' sake,
4:11 so that his[s] [+3836] life may be revealed in our mortal body.
4:14 because we know that the one who raised the Lord **Jesus** from the
4:14 raised the Lord Jesus from the dead will also raise us with **Jesus**
8: 9 For you know the grace *of* our Lord **Jesus** Christ, that though he
11: 4 to you and preaches a **Jesus** other than the Jesus we preached,
11:31 The God and Father *of* the Lord **Jesus**, who is to be praised
13: 5 Do you not realize that Christ **Jesus** is in you—unless, of course,
13:14 May the grace *of* the Lord **Jesus** Christ, and the love of God,
Gal 1: 1 not from men nor by man, but by **Jesus** Christ and God the Father,
1: 3 and peace to you from God our Father and the Lord **Jesus** Christ.
1:12 I taught it; rather, I received it by revelation *from* **Jesus** Christ.
2: 4 infiltrated our ranks to spy on the freedom we have in Christ **Jesus**
2:16 is not justified by observing the law, but by faith *in* **Jesus** Christ.
2:16 have put our faith in Christ **Jesus** that we may be justified by faith
3: 1 Before your very eyes **Jesus** Christ was clearly portrayed as
3:14 to Abraham might come to the Gentiles through Christ **Jesus**,
3:22 that what was promised, being given through faith *in* **Jesus** Christ,
3:26 You are all sons of God through faith in Christ **Jesus**,
3:28 slave nor free, male nor female, for you are all one in Christ **Jesus**.
4:14 me as if I were an angel of God, as if I were Christ **Jesus** himself.
5: 6 For in Christ **Jesus** neither circumcision nor uncircumcision has
5:24 Those who *belong to* Christ **Jesus** have crucified the sinful nature
6:14 May I never boast except in the cross *of* our Lord **Jesus** Christ,
6:17 no one cause me trouble, for I bear on my body the marks *of* **Jesus**.
6:18 The grace *of* our Lord **Jesus** Christ be with your spirit, brothers.
Eph 1: 1 Paul, an apostle *of* Christ **Jesus** by the will of God, To the saints in
1: 1 will of God, To the saints in Ephesus, the faithful in Christ **Jesus**:
1: 2 and peace to you from God our Father and the Lord **Jesus** Christ.
1: 3 Praise be to the God and Father *of* our Lord **Jesus** Christ, who has
1: 5 he predestined us to be adopted as his sons through **Jesus** Christ,
1:15 ever since I heard about your faith in the Lord **Jesus** and your love
1:17 I keep asking that the God *of* our Lord **Jesus** Christ, the glorious
2: 6 and seated us with him in the heavenly realms in Christ **Jesus**,
2: 7 riches of his grace, expressed in his kindness to us in Christ **Jesus**.
2:10 are God's workmanship, created in Christ **Jesus** to do good works,
2:13 But now in Christ **Jesus** you who once were far away have been
2:20 and prophets, with Christ **Jesus** himself as the chief cornerstone.
3: 1 the prisoner *of* Christ **Jesus** for the sake of you Gentiles—
3: 6 of one body, and sharers together in the promise in Christ **Jesus**.
3:11 eternal purpose which he accomplished in Christ **Jesus** our Lord.
3:21 glory in the church and *of* Christ **Jesus** throughout all generations,
4:21 were taught in him in accordance with the truth that is in **Jesus**.
5:20 the Father for everything, in the name *of* our Lord **Jesus** Christ.
6:23 and love with faith from God the Father and the Lord **Jesus** Christ.
6:24 Grace to all who love our Lord **Jesus** Christ with an undying love.
Php 1: 1 Paul and Timothy, servants *of* Christ **Jesus**, To all the saints in
1: 1 of Christ Jesus, To all the saints in Christ **Jesus** at Philippi,
1: 2 and peace to you from God our Father and the Lord **Jesus** Christ.
1: 6 in you will carry it on to completion until the day *of* Christ **Jesus**.
1: 8 testify how I long for all of you with the affection *of* Christ **Jesus**.
1:11 filled with the fruit of righteousness that comes through **Jesus**
1:19 your prayers and the help given by the Spirit *of* **Jesus** Christ,
1:26 so that through my being with you again your joy in Christ **Jesus**
2: 5 Your attitude should be the same as that of Christ **Jesus**:
2:10 that at the name *of* **Jesus** every knee should bow, in heaven
2:11 and every tongue confess that **Jesus** Christ is Lord, to the glory of
2:19 I hope in the Lord **Jesus** to send Timothy to you soon, that I also
2:21 everyone looks out for his own interests, not those *of* **Jesus** Christ.
3: 3 we who worship by the Spirit of God, who glory in Christ **Jesus**,
3: 8 to the surpassing greatness of knowing Christ **Jesus** my Lord,
3:12 but I press on to take hold of that for which Christ **Jesus** took hold
3:14 the prize for which God has called me heavenward in Christ **Jesus**.
3:20 And we eagerly await a Savior from there, the Lord **Jesus** Christ,
4: 7 will guard your hearts and your minds in Christ **Jesus**.
4:19 all your needs according to his glorious riches in Christ **Jesus**.

4:21 Greet all the saints in Christ **Jesus**. The brothers who are with me
4:23 The grace of the Lord **Jesus** Christ be with your spirit. Amen.
Col 1: 1 Paul, an apostle of Christ **Jesus** by the will of God, and Timothy
1: 3 the Father of our Lord **Jesus** Christ, when we pray for you,
1: 4 because we have heard of your faith in Christ **Jesus** and of the love
2: 6 So then, just as you received Christ **Jesus** as Lord, continue to live
3:17 whether in word or deed, do it all in the name of the Lord **Jesus**,
4:11 **Jesus**, who is called Justus, also sends greetings. These are the
4:12 Epaphras, who is one of you and a servant of Christ **Jesus**,
1Th 1: 1 of the Thessalonians in God the Father and the Lord **Jesus** Christ:
1: 3 and your endurance inspired by hope *in* our Lord **Jesus** Christ.
1:10 from the dead—**Jesus**, who rescues us from the coming wrath.
2:14 imitators of God's churches in Judea, which are in Christ **Jesus**:
2:15 who killed the Lord **Jesus** and the prophets and also drove us out.
2:19 we will glory in the presence of our Lord **Jesus** when he comes?
3:11 and our Lord **Jesus** clear the way for us to come to you.
3:13 and Father when our Lord **Jesus** comes with all his holy ones.
4: 1 ask you and urge you in the Lord **Jesus** to do this more and more.
4: 2 what instructions we gave you by the authority of the Lord **Jesus**.
4:14 We believe that **Jesus** died and rose again and so we believe that
4:14 bring with **Jesus** those who have fallen asleep in him[s] [+3836].
5: 9 suffer wrath but to receive salvation through our Lord **Jesus** Christ.
5:18 in all circumstances, for this is God's will for you in Christ **Jesus**.
5:23 and body be kept blameless at the coming of our Lord **Jesus**
5:28 The grace of our Lord **Jesus** Christ be with you.
2Th 1: 1 of the Thessalonians in God our Father and the Lord **Jesus** Christ:
1: 2 and peace to you from God the Father and the Lord **Jesus** Christ.
1: 7 This will happen when the Lord **Jesus** is revealed from heaven in
1: 8 do not know God and do not obey the gospel of our Lord **Jesus**.
1:12 so that the name of our Lord **Jesus** may be glorified in you,
1:12 according to the grace of our God and the Lord **Jesus** Christ.
2: 1 Concerning the coming of our Lord **Jesus** Christ and our being
2: 8 whom the Lord **Jesus** will overthrow with the breath of his mouth
2:14 that you might share in the glory of our Lord **Jesus** Christ.
2:16 May our Lord **Jesus** Christ himself and God our Father, who loved
3: 6 In the name of the Lord **Jesus** Christ, we command you, brothers,
3:12 we command and urge in the Lord **Jesus** Christ to settle down
3:18 The grace of our Lord **Jesus** Christ be with you all.
1Ti 1: 1 an apostle of Christ **Jesus** by the command of God our Savior
1: 1 by the command of God our Savior and of Christ **Jesus** our hope,
1: 2 and peace from God the Father and Christ **Jesus** our Lord.
1:12 I thank Christ **Jesus** our Lord, who has given me strength,
1:14 along with the faith and love that are in Christ **Jesus**.
1:15 Christ **Jesus** came into the world to save sinners—of whom I am
1:16 Christ **Jesus** might display his unlimited patience as an example
2: 5 and one mediator between God and men, the man Christ **Jesus**,
3:13 standing and great assurance in their faith in Christ **Jesus**.
4: 6 you will be a good minister of Christ **Jesus**, brought up in the
5:21 in the sight of God and Christ **Jesus** and the elect angels,
6: 3 and does not agree to the sound instruction of our Lord **Jesus**
6:13 the sight of God, who gives life to everything, and of Christ **Jesus**,
6:14 without spot or blame until the appearing of our Lord **Jesus** Christ,
2Ti 1: 1 Paul, an apostle of Christ **Jesus** by the will of God, according to
1: 1 will of God, according to the promise of life that is in Christ **Jesus**,
1: 2 and peace from God the Father and Christ **Jesus** our Lord.
1: 9 This grace was given us in Christ **Jesus** before the beginning of
1:10 been revealed through the appearing of our Savior, Christ **Jesus**,
1:13 the pattern of sound teaching, with faith and love in Christ **Jesus**.
2: 1 You then, my son, be strong in the grace that is in Christ **Jesus**.
2: 3 Endure hardship with us like a good soldier of Christ **Jesus**.
2: 8 Remember **Jesus** Christ, raised from the dead, descended from
2:10 that they too may obtain the salvation that is in Christ **Jesus**,
2:12 everyone who wants to live a godly life in Christ **Jesus** will be
3:15 able to make you wise for salvation through faith in Christ **Jesus**.
4: 1 In the presence of God and of Christ **Jesus**, who will judge the
Tit 1: 1 of God and an apostle of **Jesus** Christ for the faith of God's elect
1: 4 and peace from God the Father and Christ **Jesus** our Savior.
2:13 the glorious appearing of our great God and Savior, **Jesus** Christ,
3: 6 whom he poured out on us generously through **Jesus** Christ our
Phm 1: 1 Paul, a prisoner of Christ **Jesus**, and Timothy our brother,
1: 3 and peace from God our Father and the Lord **Jesus** Christ.
1: 5 because I hear about your faith in the Lord **Jesus** and your love for
1: 9 as Paul—an old man and now also a prisoner of Christ **Jesus**—
1:23 Epaphras, my fellow prisoner in Christ **Jesus**, sends you greetings.
1:25 The grace of the Lord **Jesus** Christ be with your spirit.
Heb 2: 9 But we see **Jesus**, who was made a little lower than the angels,

3: 1 fix your thoughts on **Jesus**, the apostle and high priest whom we
4: 8 For if **Joshua** had given them rest, God would not have spoken
4:14 **Jesus** the Son of God, let us hold firmly to the faith we profess.
6:20 where **Jesus**, who went before us, has entered on our behalf.
7:22 of this oath, **Jesus** has become the guarantee of a better covenant.
10:10 we have been made holy through the sacrifice of the body of **Jesus**
10:19 confidence to enter the Most Holy Place by the blood of **Jesus**,
12: 2 Let us fix our eyes on **Jesus**, the author and perfecter of our faith,
12:24 *to* **Jesus** the mediator of a new covenant, and to the sprinkled
13: 8 **Jesus** Christ is the same yesterday and today and forever.
13:12 so **Jesus** also suffered outside the city gate to make the people holy
13:20 of the eternal covenant brought back from the dead our Lord **Jesus**,
13:21 through **Jesus** Christ, to whom be glory for ever and ever.
Jas 1: 1 James, a servant of God and of the Lord **Jesus** Christ,
2: 1 My brothers, as believers *in* our glorious Lord **Jesus** Christ,
1Pe 1: 1 Peter, an apostle of **Jesus** Christ, To God's elect, strangers in the
1: 2 for obedience *to* **Jesus** Christ and sprinkling by his blood:
1: 3 Praise be to the God and Father of our Lord **Jesus** Christ!
1: 3 living hope through the resurrection of **Jesus** Christ from the dead,
1: 7 result in praise, glory and honor when **Jesus** Christ is revealed.
1:13 set your hope fully on the grace to be given you when **Jesus** Christ
2: 5 offering spiritual sacrifices acceptable to God through **Jesus**
3:21 toward God. It saves you by the resurrection of **Jesus** Christ,
4:11 so that in all things God may be praised through **Jesus** Christ.
5:10 who called you to his eternal glory in Christ [UBS+ *Jesus*,]
2Pe 1: 1 Simon Peter, a servant and apostle of **Jesus** Christ, To those who
1: 1 and Savior **Jesus** Christ have received a faith as precious as ours:
1: 2 abundance through the knowledge of God and of **Jesus** our Lord.
1: 8 and unproductive in your knowledge of our Lord **Jesus** Christ.
1:11 into the eternal kingdom of our Lord and Savior **Jesus** Christ.
1:14 soon put it aside, as our Lord **Jesus** Christ has made clear to me.
1:16 we told you about the power and coming of our Lord **Jesus** Christ,
2:20 and Savior **Jesus** Christ and are again entangled in it
3:18 in the grace and knowledge of our Lord and Savior **Jesus** Christ.
1Jn 1: 3 our fellowship is with the Father and with his Son, **Jesus** Christ.
1: 7 and the blood of **Jesus**, his Son, purifies us from all sin.
2: 1 to the Father in our defense—**Jesus** Christ, the Righteous One.
2:22 Who is the liar? It is the man who denies that **Jesus** is the Christ.
3:23 to believe in the name of his Son, **Jesus** Christ, and to love one
4: 2 Every spirit that acknowledges that **Jesus** Christ has come in the
4: 3 but every spirit that does not acknowledge **Jesus** is not from God.
4:15 If anyone acknowledges that **Jesus** is the Son of God, God lives in
5: 1 Everyone who believes that **Jesus** is the Christ is born of God,
5: 5 the world? Only he who believes that **Jesus** is the Son of God.
5: 6 This is the one who came by water and blood—**Jesus** Christ.
5:20 And we are in him who is true—even in his Son **Jesus** Christ.
2Jn 1: 3 mercy and peace from God the Father and from **Jesus** Christ,
1: 7 who do not acknowledge **Jesus** Christ as coming in the flesh,
Jude 1: 1 Jude, a servant of **Jesus** Christ and a brother of James, To those
1: 1 who are loved by God the Father and kept *by* **Jesus** Christ:
1: 4 for immorality and deny **Jesus** Christ our only Sovereign and Lord.
1:17 remember what the apostles of our Lord **Jesus** Christ foretold.
1:21 for the mercy of our Lord **Jesus** Christ to bring you to eternal life.
1:25 majesty, power and authority, through **Jesus** Christ our Lord,
Rev 1: 1 The revelation of **Jesus** Christ, which God gave him to show his
1: 2 that is, the word of God and the testimony of **Jesus** Christ.
1: 5 and from **Jesus** Christ, who is the faithful witness, the firstborn
1: 9 and kingdom and patient endurance that are ours in **Jesus**,
1: 9 of Patmos because of the word of God and the testimony of **Jesus**.
12:17 obey God's commandments and hold to the testimony of **Jesus**.
14:12 who obey God's commandments and remain faithful *to* **Jesus**.
17: 6 of the saints, the blood of those who bore testimony *to* **Jesus**.
19:10 and with your brothers who hold to the testimony of **Jesus**.
19:10 Worship God! For the testimony of **Jesus** is the spirit of prophecy."
20: 4 because of their testimony *for* **Jesus** and because of the word of
22:16 "I, **Jesus**, have sent my angel to give you this testimony for the
22:20 things says, "Yes, I am coming soon." Amen. Come, Lord **Jesus**.
22:21 The grace of the Lord **Jesus** be with God's people. Amen.

2653 ἱκανός, *hikanos* [39] [→ *919, 922, 1459, 2391, 2654, 2655, 2656*]

many [5], large [4], long [4], deserve [+*1639*] [2], great [2], number [2], some [2], worthy [2], *untranslated* [1], bright [1], competent [1], considerable [1], deserve [1], enough [1], equal

[1], fit [1], large number [1], large sum [1], much [1], post bond [1], qualified [1], satisfy [+4472] [1], sufficient [1], wept [+1181+3088] [1]

Mt	3:11 who is more powerful than I, whose sandals I am not **fit** to carry.
	8: 8 *I do* not **deserve** [+1639] to have you come under my roof.
	28:12 and devised a plan, they gave the soldiers a **large sum** of money,
Mk	1: 7 the thongs of whose sandals I am not **worthy** to stoop down
	10:46 As Jesus and his disciples, together with a **large** crowd,
	15:15 Wanting *to* **satisfy** [+4472] the crowd, Pilate released Barabbas to
Lk	3:16 I will come, the thongs of whose sandals I am not **worthy** to untie.
	7: 6 for *I do* not **deserve** [+1639] to have you come under my roof.
	7:12 she was a widow. And a **large** crowd from the town was with her.
	8:27 *For* a **long** time this man had not worn clothes or lived in a house,
	8:32 A **large** herd of pigs was feeding there on the hillside. The demons
	20: 9 rented it to some farmers and went away *for* a **long** time.
	22:38 "See, Lord, here are two swords." "That is **enough**," he replied.
	23: 8 because for a **long** time he had been wanting to see him.
	23: 9 He plied him with **many** questions, but Jesus gave him no answer.
Ac	8:11 because he had amazed them *for* a **long** time with his magic.
	9:23 After **many** days had gone by, the Jews conspired to kill him,
	9:43 Peter stayed in Joppa *for* **some** time with a tanner named Simon.
	11:24 and faith, and a **great** many of people were brought to the Lord.
	11:26 and Saul met with the church and taught **great** numbers of people.
	12:12 called Mark, where **many** *people* had gathered and were praying.
	14: 3 So Paul and Barnabas spent **considerable** time there,
	14:21 the good news in that city and won a **large number** *of* disciples.
	17: 9 Then they made Jason and the others **post bond** and let them go.
	18:18 Paul stayed on in Corinth *for* **some** time. Then he left the brothers
	19:19 A **number** who had practiced sorcery brought their scrolls together
	19:26 and led astray **large** numbers of people here in Ephesus
	20: 8 There were **many** lamps in the upstairs room where we were
	20:11 broke bread and ate. After talking [NIE] until daylight, he left.
	20:37 *They* all **wept** [+1181+3088] as they embraced him and kissed
	22: 6 suddenly a **bright** light from heaven flashed around me.
	27: 7 We made slow headway for **many** days and had difficulty arriving
	27: 9 **Much** time had been lost, and sailing had already become
1Co	11:30 you are weak and sick, and a **number** *of* you have fallen asleep.
	15: 9 of the apostles and do not even **deserve** to be called an apostle,
2Co	2: 6 The punishment inflicted on him by the majority is **sufficient** for
	2:16 to the other, the fragrance of life. And who is **equal** to such a task?
	3: 5 Not that we are **competent** in ourselves to claim anything for
2Ti	2: 2 entrust to reliable men who will also be **qualified** to teach others.

2654 ἱκανότης, *hikanotēs* [1] [√ 2653]

competence [1]

2Co   3: 5 anything for ourselves, but our **competence** comes from God.

2655 ἱκανόω, *hikanoō* [2] [√ 2653]

made competent [1], qualified [1]

2Co   3: 6 He *has* **made** us **competent** as ministers of a new covenant—
Col   1:12 giving thanks *to* the Father, who *has* **qualified** you to share in the

2656 ἱκετηρία, *hiketēria* [1] [√ 2653]

petitions [1]

Heb   5: 7 he offered up prayers and **petitions** with loud cries and tears to the

2657 ἱκμάς, *ikmas* [1]

moisture [1]

Lk   8: 6 it came up, the plants withered because they had no **moisture**.

2658 Ἰκόνιον, *Ikonion* [6]

Iconium [6]

Ac	13:51 dust from their feet in protest against them and went to **Iconium**.
	14: 1 At **Iconium** Paul and Barnabas went as usual into the Jewish
	14:19 Jews came from Antioch and **Iconium** and won the crowd over.
	14:21 of disciples. Then they returned to Lystra, **Iconium** and Antioch,
	16: 2 The brothers at Lystra and **Iconium** spoke well of him.

2Ti   3:11 to me in Antioch, **Iconium** and Lystra, the persecutions I endured.

2659 ἱλαρός, *hilaros* [1] [√ 2661]

cheerful [1]

2Co   9: 7 or under compulsion, for God loves a **cheerful** giver.

2660 ἱλαρότης, *hilarotēs* [1] [√ 2661]

cheerfully [+1877] [1]

Ro   12: 8 if it is showing mercy, let him do it **cheerfully** [+1877].

2661 ἱλάσκομαι, *hilaskomai* [2] [→ 480, 2659, 2660, 2662, 2663, 2664]

make atonement for [1], mercy on [1]

Lk   18:13 but beat his breast and said, 'God, *have* **mercy on** me, a sinner.'
Heb   2:17 and that he *might* **make atonement for** the sins of the people.

2662 ἱλασμός, *hilasmos* [2] [√ 2661]

atoning sacrifice [2]

1Jn   2: 2 He is the **atoning sacrifice** for our sins, and not only for ours
   4:10 he loved us and sent his Son as an **atoning sacrifice** for our sins.

2663 ἱλαστήριον, *hilastērion* [2] [√ 2661]

atonement cover [1], sacrifice of atonement [1]

Ro   3:25 God presented him as a **sacrifice of atonement**, through faith in
Heb   9: 5 the cherubim of the Glory, overshadowing the **atonement cover**.

2664 ἵλεως, *hileōs* [2] [√ 2661]

forgive [+1639] [1], never [1]

Mt   16:22 took him aside and began to rebuke him. "**Never**, Lord!" he said.
Heb   8:12 For *I will* **forgive** [+1639] their wickedness and will remember

2665 Ἰλλυρικόν, *Illyrikon* [1]

Illyricum [1]

Ro   15:19 So from Jerusalem all the way around to **Illyricum**, I have fully

2666 ἱμάς, *himas* [4]

thongs [3], flog [1]

Mk	1: 7 the **thongs** of whose sandals I am not worthy to stoop down
Lk	3:16 I will come, the **thongs** of whose sandals I am not worthy to untie.
Jn	1:27 after me, the **thongs** of whose sandals I am not worthy to untie."
Ac	22:25 As they stretched him out *to* **flog** him, Paul said to the centurion

2667 ἱματίζω, *himatizō* [2] [→ 2264, 2265, 2668, 2669; cf. 313]

dressed [2]

Mk   5:15 the legion of demons, sitting there, **dressed** and in his right mind;
Lk   8:35 had gone out, sitting at Jesus' feet, **dressed** and in his right mind;

2668 ἱμάτιον, *himation* [60 / 61] [√ 2667]

clothes [22], cloak [13], cloaks [7], garment [6], robe [4], dressed [+4314] [2], garments [2], clothing [1], fine clothes [+1906] [1], ones [1], outer clothing [1], stripped [+3836+4351] [1]

Mt	5:40 to sue you and take your tunic, let him have your **cloak** as well.
	9:16 "No one sews a patch of unshrunk cloth on an old **garment**,
	9:16 for the patch will pull away from the **garment**, making the tear
	9:20 years came up behind him and touched the edge *of* his **cloak**.
	9:21 She said to herself, "If I only touch his **cloak**, I will be healed."
	14:36 and begged him to let the sick just touch the edge *of* his **cloak**,
	17: 2 shone like the sun, and his **clothes** became as white as the light.
	21: 7 They brought the donkey and the colt, placed their **cloaks** on them,

21: 8 A very large crowd spread their **cloaks** on the road, while others
23: 5 phylacteries wide and the tassels *on* their **garments** [UBS-] long;
24: 18 Let no one in the field go back to get his **cloak**.
26: 65 Then the high priest tore his **clothes** and said, "He has spoken
27: 31 they took off the robe and put his own **clothes** on him.
27: 35 they had crucified him, they divided up his **clothes** by casting lots.
Mk 2: 21 "No one sews a patch of unshrunk cloth on an old **garment**.
5: 27 she came up behind him in the crowd and touched his **cloak**,
5: 28 because she thought, "If I just touch his **clothes**, I will be healed."
5: 30 turned around in the crowd and asked, "Who touched my **clothes**?"
6: 56 They begged him to let them touch even the edge *of* his **cloak**,
9: 3 His **clothes** became dazzling white, whiter than anyone in the
10: 50 Throwing his **cloak** aside, he jumped to his feet and came to Jesus.
11: 7 When they brought the colt to Jesus and threw their **cloaks** over it,
11: 8 Many people spread their **cloaks** on the road, while others spread
13: 16 Let no one in the field go back to get his **cloak**.
15: 20 they took off the purple robe and put his own **clothes** on him.
15: 24 Dividing up his **clothes**, they cast lots to see what each would get.
Lk 5: 36 "No one tears a patch from a new **garment** and sews it on an old
5: 36 one tears a patch from a new garment and sews it on an old **one**[S].
6: 29 If someone takes your **cloak**, do not stop him from taking your
7: 25 A man dressed in fine **clothes**? No, those who wear expensive
8: 27 For a long time this man had not worn **clothes** or lived in a house,
8: 44 She came up behind him and touched the edge *of* his **cloak**,
19: 35 it to Jesus, threw their **cloaks** on the colt and put Jesus on it.
19: 36 As he went along, people spread their **cloaks** on the road.
22: 36 and if you don't have a sword, sell your **cloak** and buy one.
23: 34 they are doing." And they divided up his **clothes** by casting lots.
Jn 13: 4 so he got up from the meal, took off his **outer clothing**,
13: 12 washing their feet, he put on his **clothes** and returned to his place.
19: 2 and put it on his head. They clothed him in a purple **robe**
19: 5 Jesus came out wearing the crown of thorns and the purple **robe**,
19: 23 they took his **clothes**, dividing them into four shares, one for each
19: 24 "They divided my **garments** among them and cast lots for my
Ac 7: 58 the witnesses laid their **clothes** at the feet of a young man named
9: 39 and *other* **clothing** that Dorcas had made while she was still with
12: 8 "Wrap your **cloak** around you and follow me," the angel told him.
14: 14 they tore their **clothes** and rushed out into the crowd, shouting:
16: 22 and the magistrates ordered them *to be* **stripped** [*+3836+4351*]
18: 6 he shook out his **clothes** in protest and said to them,
22: 20 and guarding the **clothes** of those who were killing him.'
22: 23 As they were shouting and throwing off their **cloaks** and flinging
Heb 1: 11 will perish, but you remain; they will all wear out like a **garment**.
1: 12 will roll them up like a robe; like a **garment** they will be changed.
Jas 5: 2 Your wealth has rotted, and moths have eaten your **clothes**.
1Pe 3: 3 and the wearing of gold jewelry and **fine clothes** [*+1906*].
Rev 3: 4 you have a few people in Sardis who have not soiled their **clothes**.
3: 5 He who overcomes *will*, like them, *be* **dressed** [*+4314*] in white.
3: 18 and white **clothes** to wear, so you can cover your shameful
4: 4 *They were* **dressed** [*+4314*] in white and had crowns of gold on
16: 15 Blessed is he who stays awake and keeps his **clothes** with him,
19: 13 He is dressed in a **robe** dipped in blood, and his name is the Word
19: 16 On his **robe** and on his thigh he has this name written: KING OF

2669 ἱματισμός, himatismos [5] [√ *2667*]

clothes [3], clothing [2]

Lk 7: 25 those who wear expensive **clothes** and indulge in luxury are in
9: 29 and his **clothes** became as bright as a flash of lightning.
Jn 19: 24 divided my garments among them and cast lots for my **clothing**."
Ac 20: 33 I have not coveted anyone's silver or gold or **clothing**.
1Ti 2: 9 not with braided hair or gold or pearls or expensive **clothes**,

2670 ἱμείρομαι, himeiromai Not used in UBS/NIV

2671 ἵνα, hina [663] [→ *2672*]

so that [197], to [179], that [116], *untranslated* [42], in order that [16], for [12], so [12], in order to [10], or [*+3590*] [8], then [6], to let [6], and [5], want [5], have [3], reason [3], so as to [3], let [2], meant to [2], therefore [2], when [2], aim is to [1], allow [1], and then [1], as to [1], as [1], at [1], because [1], before [*+3590*] [1], bent on [1], by [1], expecting to [1], for fear [*+3590*] [1], for fear that [*+3590*] [1], from [*+3590*] [1], hoped [1], if [1], in the hope that [1], instead [1], intent that [1], lest [*+3590*] [1], must [1], only [1], please [1], purpose that [1], purpose [1], rather than [*+3590*] [1], see that [1], to keep from [*+3590*] [1], to make [1], to show that [1], wants [1], which [1]

Mt 1: 22 All this took place **to** fulfill what the Lord had said through the
2: 15 **so** was fulfilled what the Lord had said through the prophet:
4: 3 you are the Son of God, tell **[NIE]** these stones to become bread."
4: 14 **to** fulfill what was said through the prophet Isaiah:
5: 29 It is better for you **to** lose one part of your body than for your
5: 30 It is better for you **to** lose one part of your body than for your
7: 1 "Do not judge, **or** [*+3590*] you too will be judged.
7: 12 in everything, do to others what you would **have** them do to you,
8: 8 "Lord, I do not deserve **to** have you come under my roof.
9: 6 **so that** you may know that the Son of Man has authority on earth
10: 25 It is enough for the student **to** be like his teacher, and the servant
12: 10 Looking for a **reason** to accuse Jesus, they asked him, "Is it lawful
12: 16 warning them not **to** tell who he was.
12: 17 This was **to** fulfill what was spoken through the prophet Isaiah:
14: 15 **so** they can go to the villages and buy themselves some food."
14: 36 and begged him **to let** the sick just touch the edge of his cloak,
16: 20 Then he warned his disciples **[NIE]** not to tell anyone that he was
17: 27 "But **so that** we may not offend them, go to the lake and throw out
18: 6 it would be better for him **to** have a large millstone hung around
18: 14 In the same way your Father in heaven is not willing **that** any of
18: 16 **so that** 'every matter may be established by the testimony of two
19: 13 Then little children were brought to Jesus **for** him to place his
19: 16 and asked, "Teacher, what good thing must I do **to** get eternal life?"
20: 21 "Grant **that** one of these two sons of mine may sit at your right
20: 31 The crowd rebuked them and told them **to** be quiet,
20: 33 "Lord," they answered, "we **want** our sight."
21: 4 This took place **to** fulfill what was spoken through the prophet:
23: 26 inside of the cup and dish, **and then** the outside also will be clean.
24: 20 Pray **that** your flight will not take place in winter or on the
26: 4 and they plotted **to** arrest Jesus in some sly way and kill him.
26: 5 they said, "**or** [*+3590*] there may be a riot among the people."
26: 16 then on Judas watched for an opportunity **to** hand him over.
26: 41 "Watch and pray **so that** you will not fall into temptation. The spirit
26: 56 But this has all taken place **that** the writings of the prophets might
26: 63 living God: **[NIE]** Tell us if you are the Christ, the Son of God."
27: 20 and the elders persuaded the crowd **to** ask for Barabbas
27: 26 But he had Jesus flogged, and handed him over **to** be crucified.
27: 32 named Simon, and they forced him **to** carry the cross.
28: 10 Go and tell my brothers **to** go to Galilee; there they will see me."
Mk 1: 38 to the nearby villages—**so** I can preach there also.
2: 10 But **that** you may know that the Son of Man has authority on earth
3: 2 Some of them were looking for a **reason** to accuse Jesus, so they
3: 9 Because of the crowd he told his disciples **to** have a small boat
3: 9 ready for him, **to** [*+3590*] **keep** the people **from** crowding him.
3: 10 so that those with diseases were pushing forward **to** touch him.
3: 12 But he gave them strict orders not **to** tell who he was.
3: 14 **that** they might be with him and that he might send them out to
3: 14 they might be with him and **that** he might send them out to preach
4: 12 **so that**, " 'they may be ever seeing but never perceiving, and ever
4: 21 to them, "Do you bring in a lamp **to** put it under a bowl or a bed?
4: 21 put it under a bowl or a bed? **Instead**, don't you put it on its stand?
4: 22 For whatever is hidden is **meant to** be disclosed, and whatever is
4: 22 and whatever is concealed is **meant to** be brought out into the
5: 10 he begged Jesus again and again not **to** send them out of the area.
5: 12 begged Jesus, "Send us among the pigs; **allow** us to go into them."
5: 18 the man who had been demon-possessed begged **to** go with him.
5: 23 **Please** come and put your hands on her so that she will be healed
5: 23 and put your hands on her **so that** she will be healed and live."
5: 43 He gave strict orders not **to let** anyone know about this, and told
6: 8 **[NIE]** "Take nothing for the journey except a staff—no bread,
6: 12 They went out and preached **that** people should repent.
6: 25 "I want **[NIE]** you to give me right now the head of John the
6: 36 **so** they can go to the surrounding countryside and villages
6: 41 Then he gave them to his disciples **to** set before the people.
6: 56 They begged him **to let** them touch even the edge of his cloak,
7: 9 the commands of God **in order to** observe your own traditions!
7: 26 She begged Jesus **to** drive the demon out of her daughter.
7: 32 hardly talk, and they begged him **to** place his hand on the man.
7: 36 Jesus commanded them not **to** tell anyone. But the more he did so,
8: 6 broke them and gave them to his disciples **to** set before the people,
8: 22 some people brought a blind man and begged Jesus **to** touch him.

8:30 Jesus warned them not **to** tell anyone about him.
9: 9 Jesus gave them orders not **to** tell anyone what they had seen until
9:12 Why then is it written **that** the Son of Man must suffer much
9:18 I asked your disciples **to** drive out the spirit, but they could not."
9:22 "It has often thrown him into fire or water **to** kill him. But if you
9:30 Jesus did not want anyone **to** know where they were,
10:13 People were bringing little children to Jesus **to** have him touch
10:17 "Good teacher," he asked, "what must I do **to** inherit eternal life?"
10:35 they said, "we want [NIE] you to do for us whatever we ask."
10:37 "Let one of us [NIE] sit at your right and the other at your left in
10:48 Many rebuked him and told him **to** be quiet,
10:51 Jesus asked him. The blind man said, "Rabbi, I **want** to see."
11:16 and would not allow [NIE] anyone to carry merchandise through
11:25 **so that** your Father in heaven may forgive your sins."
11:28 things?" they asked. "And who gave you authority **to** do this?"
12: 2 At harvest time he sent a servant to the tenants **to** collect from
12:13 of the Pharisees and Herodians to Jesus **to** catch him in his words.
12:15 to trap me?" he asked. "Bring me a denarius and **let** me look at it."
12:19 [NIE] The man must marry the widow and have children for his
13:18 Pray **that** this will not take place in winter,
13:34 with his assigned task, and tells the one at the door **to** keep watch.
14:10 one of the Twelve, went to the chief priests **to** betray Jesus to them.
14:12 want us to go and make preparations **for** you to eat the Passover?"
14:35 and prayed **that** if possible the hour might pass from him.
14:38 Watch and pray **so that** you will not fall into temptation. The spirit
14:49 you did not arrest me. But [NIE] the Scriptures must be fulfilled."
15:11 But the chief priests stirred up the crowd **to** have Pilate release
15:15 He had Jesus flogged, and handed him over **to** be crucified.
15:20 put his own clothes on him. Then they led him out **to** crucify him.
15:21 his way in from the country, and they forced him **to** carry the cross.
15:32 come down now from the cross, **that** we may see and believe."
16: 1 Salome bought spices **so that** they might go to anoint Jesus' body.

Lk 1: 4 **so that** you may know the certainty of the things you have been
1:43 so favored, **that** the mother of my Lord should come to me?
4: 3 "If you are the Son of God, tell this stone **to** become bread."
5:24 But **that** you may know that the Son of Man has authority on earth
6: 7 and the teachers of the law were looking for a **reason** to accuse
6:31 Do to others as you would **have** them do to you.
6:34 Even 'sinners' lend to 'sinners,' **expecting to** be repaid in full.
7: 6 for I do not deserve **to** have you come under my roof.
7:36 Now one of the Pharisees invited Jesus **to** have dinner with him,
8:10 I speak in parables, **so that,** " 'though seeing, they may not see;
8:12 word from their hearts, **so that** they may not believe and be saved.
8:16 he puts it on a stand, **so that** those who come in can see the light.
8:31 And they begged him repeatedly not **to** order them to go into the
8:32 The demons begged Jesus **to** let them go into them, and he gave
9:12 **so** they can go to the surrounding villages and countryside
9:40 I begged your disciples **to** drive it out, but they could not."
9:45 It was hidden from them, **so that** they did not grasp it, and they
10:40 sister has left me to do the work by myself! Tell her **to** help me!"
11:33 he puts it on its stand, **so that** those who come in may see the light.
11:50 **Therefore** this generation will be held responsible for the blood of
12:36 **so that** when he comes and knocks they can immediately open the
14:10 **so that** when your host comes, he will say to you, 'Friend,
14:23 and make them come in, **so that** my house will be full.
14:29 **For** if he lays the foundation and is not able to finish it,
15:29 gave me even a young goat **so** I could celebrate with my friends.
16: 4 I know what I'll do **so that,** when I lose my job here, people will
16: 9 **so that** when it is gone, you will be welcomed into eternal
16:24 pity on me and send Lazarus **to** dip the tip of his finger in water
16:27 'Then I beg you, father, [NIE] send Lazarus to my father's house,
16:28 **so that** they will not also come to this place of torment.'
17: 2 his neck than **for** him to cause one of these little ones to sin.
18: 5 **so that** she won't eventually wear me out with her coming!' "
18:15 People were also bringing babies to Jesus **to** have him touch them.
18:39 Those who led the way rebuked him and told him **to** be quiet,
18:41 do you want me to do for you?" "Lord, I **want** to see," he replied.
19: 4 So he ran ahead and climbed a sycamore-fig tree **to** see him,
19:15 given the money, **in order to** find out what they had gained with it.
20:10 **so** they would give him some of the fruit of the vineyard.
20:14 they said. 'Let's kill him, **and** the inheritance will be ours.'
20:20 They **hoped** to catch Jesus in something he said so that they might
20:28 [NIE] The man must marry the widow and have children for his
21:36 and pray **that** you may be able to escape all that is about to happen,
22: 8 saying, "Go and make preparations for us **to** eat the Passover."
22:30 **so that** you may eat and drink at my table in my kingdom

22:32 But I have prayed for you, Simon, **that** your faith may not fail.
22:46 "Get up and pray **so that** you will not fall into temptation."

Jn 1: 7 He came as a witness **to** testify concerning that light, so that
1: 7 concerning that light, **so that** through him all men might believe.
1: 8 himself was not the light; he came only **as** a witness to the light.
1:19 Jews of Jerusalem sent priests and Levites **to** ask him who he was.
1:22 "Who are you? Give us an answer **to** take back to those who sent
1:27 after me, the thongs of whose sandals I am not worthy **to** untie."
1:31 but the reason I came baptizing with water was **that** he might be
2:25 He did not need [NIE] man's testimony about man, for he knew
3:15 **that** everyone who believes in him may have eternal life.
3:16 **that** whoever believes in him shall not perish but have eternal life.
3:17 For God did not send his Son into the world **to** condemn the world,
3:17 world to condemn the world, but **to** save the world through him.
3:20 and will not come into the light **for fear that** [+3590] his deeds
3:21 **so that** it may be seen plainly that what he has done has been done
4: 8 (His disciples had gone into the town **to** buy food.)
4:15 give me this water **so that** I won't get thirsty and have to keep
4:34 "is **to** do the will of him who sent me and to finish his work.
4:36 eternal life, **so that** the sower and the reaper may be glad together.
4:47 he went to him and begged him **to** come and heal his son,
5: 7 "I have no one to help me into the pool [NIE] when the water is
5:14 Stop sinning or [+3590] something worse may happen to you."
5:20 **to** your amazement he will show him even greater things than
5:23 **that** all may honor the Son just as they honor the Father. He who
5:34 I accept human testimony; but I mention it **that** you may be saved.
5:36 of John. For the very work that the Father has given me **to** finish,
5:40 yet you refuse to come to me **to** have life.
6: 5 said to Philip, "Where shall we buy bread **for** these people to eat?"
6: 7 "Eight months' wages would not buy enough bread **for** each one to
6:12 "Gather the pieces that are left over. **Let** nothing be wasted."
6:15 that they intended to come and **make** him king by force,
6:28 they asked him, "What must we do **to** do the works God requires?"
6:29 "The work of God is this: **to** believe in the one he has sent."
6:30 then will you give **that** we may see it and believe you?
6:38 For I have come down from heaven not to do my will but **to** do the
6:39 **that** I shall lose none of all that he has given me, but raise them up
6:40 For my Father's will is **that** everyone who looks to the Son
6:50 that comes down from heaven, **which** a man may eat and not die.
7: 3 go to Judea, **so that** your disciples may see the miracles you do.
7:23 on the Sabbath **so that** the law of Moses may not be broken,
7:32 the chief priests and the Pharisees sent temple guards **to** arrest him.
8: 6 this question as a trap, **in order to** have a basis for accusing him.
8:56 Your father Abraham rejoiced **at** the thought of seeing my day;
8:59 At this, they picked up stones **to** stone him, but Jesus hid himself,
9: 2 who sinned, this man or his parents, **that** he was born blind?"
9: 3 **so that** the work of God might be displayed in his life.
9:22 for already the Jews had decided **that** anyone who acknowledged
9:36 is he, sir?" the man asked. "Tell me **so that** I may believe in him."
9:39 **so that** the blind will see and those who see will become blind."
10:10 The thief comes only **to** steal and kill and destroy; I have come that
10:10 I have come **that** they may have life, and have it to the full.
10:17 loves me is that I lay down my life—**only** to take it up again.
10:31 Again the Jews picked up stones **to** stone him,
10:38 **that** you may know and understand that the Father is in me,
11: 4 it is for God's glory **so that** God's Son may be glorified through it."
11:11 Lazarus has fallen asleep; but I am going there **to** wake him up."
11:15 for your sake I am glad I was not there, **so that** you may believe.
11:16 the rest of the disciples, "Let us also go, **that** we may die with him."
11:19 to Martha and Mary **to** comfort them in the loss of their brother.
11:31 followed her, supposing she was going to the tomb **to** mourn there.
11:37 the eyes of the blind man have kept this man **from** [+3590] dying?"
11:42 the people standing here, **that** they may believe that you sent me."
11:50 You do not realize that it is better for you **that** one man die for the
11:52 children of God, **to** bring them together and make them one.
11:53 So from that day on they plotted **to** take his life.
11:55 many went up from the country to Jerusalem **for** their ceremonial
11:57 and Pharisees had given orders **that** if anyone found out where
12: 7 "It was intended, **that** she should save this perfume for the day of
12: 9 and came, not only because of him but also **to** see Lazarus,
12:10 So the chief priests made plans **to** kill Lazarus as well,
12:20 Now there were some Greeks among those who went up **to**
12:23 "The hour has come **for** the Son of Man to be glorified.
12:35 while you have the light, **before** [+3590] darkness overtakes you.
12:36 the light while you have it, **so that** you may become sons of light.
12:38 This was **to** fulfill the word of Isaiah the prophet: "Lord, who has

12:40 and deadened their hearts, **so** they can neither see with their eyes,
12:42 faith **for** [+*3590*] **fear** they would be put out of the synagogue;
12:46 **so that** no one who believes in me should stay in darkness.
12:47 not judge him. For I did not come **to** judge the world, but to save it.
12:47 not judge him. For I did not come to judge the world, but **to** save it.
13: 1 Jesus knew that the time had come **for** him to leave this world
13: 2 had already prompted Judas Iscariot, son of Simon, **to** betray Jesus.
13:15 I have set you an example **that** you should do as I have done for
13:18 I know those I have chosen. But this is **to** fulfill the scripture:
13:19 **so that** when it does happen you will believe that I am He.
13:29 what was needed for the Feast, or **to** give something to the poor.
13:34 I give you: [NIE] Love one another. As I have loved you,
13:34 As I have loved you, [NIE] **so** you must love one another.
14: 3 and take you to be with me **that** you also may be where I am.
14:13 you ask in my name, **so that** the Son may bring glory to the Father.
14:16 and he will give you another Counselor **to** be with you forever—
14:29 before it happens, **so that** when it does happen you will believe.
14:31 but [NIE] the world must learn that I love the Father and that I do
15: 2 that does bear fruit he prunes **so that** it will be even more fruitful.
15: 8 This is to my Father's glory, **that** you bear much fruit, showing
15:11 I have told you this **so that** my joy may be in you and that your joy
15:12 My command is this: [NIE] Love each other as I have loved you,
15:13 love has no one than this, **that** he lay down his life for his friends.
15:16 but I chose you and appointed you **to** go and bear fruit—
15:16 **Then** the Father will give you whatever you ask in my name.
15:17 This is my command: [NIE] Love each other.
15:25 But this is **to** fulfill what is written in their Law: 'They hated me
16: 1 "All this I have told you **so that** you will not go astray.
16: 2 a time is coming **when** anyone who kills you will think he is
16: 4 **so that** when the time comes you will remember that I warned you.
16: 7 It is for your good **that** I am going away. Unless I go away,
16:24 Ask and you will receive, **and** your joy will be complete.
16:30 and that you do not even need **to** have anyone ask you questions.
16:32 "But a time is coming, and has come, **when** you will be scattered,
16:33 "I have told you these things, **so that** in me you may have peace.
17: 1 time has come. Glorify your Son, **that** your Son may glorify you.
17: 2 For you granted him authority over all people **that** he might give
17: 3 **that** they may know you, the only true God, and Jesus Christ,
17: 4 you glory on earth by completing the work you gave me **to** do.
17:11 the name you gave me—**so that** they may be one as we are one.
17:12 the one doomed to destruction **so that** Scripture would be fulfilled.
17:13 **so that** they may have the full measure of my joy within them.
17:15 My prayer is not **that** you take them out of the world but that you
17:15 them out of the world but **that** you protect them from the evil one.
17:19 For them I sanctify myself, **that** they too may be truly sanctified.
17:21 **that** all of them may be one, Father, just as you are in me
17:21 [NIE] May they also be in us so that the world may believe that
17:21 also be in us **so that** the world may believe that you have sent me.
17:22 the glory that you gave me, **that** they may be one as we are one:
17:23 [NIE] May they be brought to complete unity to let the world
17:23 May they be brought to complete unity **to let** the world know that
17:24 I want those you have given me **to** be with me where I am,
17:24 and **to** see my glory, the glory you have given me because you
17:26 and will continue to make you known **in order that** the love you
18: 9 This happened **so that** the words he had spoken would be fulfilled:
18:28 and to avoid ceremonial uncleanness the Jews did not enter the
18:32 **so that** the words Jesus had spoken indicating the kind of death he
18:36 my servants would fight **to** prevent my arrest by the Jews.
18:37 was born, and for this I came into the world, **to** testify to the truth.
18:39 But it is your custom **for** me to release to you one prisoner at the
19: 4 I am bringing him out to you **to let** you know that I find no basis
19:16 Finally Pilate handed him over to them **to** be crucified.
19:24 This happened **that** the scripture might be fulfilled which said,
19:28 and **so that** the Scripture would be fulfilled, Jesus said, "I am
19:31 **Because** the Jews did not want the bodies left on the crosses during
19:31 they asked Pilate **to** have the legs broken and the bodies taken
19:35 that he tells the truth, and he testifies **so that** you also may believe.
19:36 These things happened **so that** the scripture would be fulfilled:
19:38 Later, Joseph of Arimathea asked Pilate **for** the body of Jesus.
20:31 But these are written **that** you may believe that Jesus is the Christ,
20:31 Son of God, and that by believing you may have life in his name.
Ac 2:25 Because he is at my right hand, [NIE] I will not be shaken.
4:17 But **to** stop this thing from spreading any further among the
5:15 **so that** at least Peter's shadow might fall on some of them as he
8:19 **so that** everyone on whom I lay my hands may receive the Holy
9:21 And hasn't he come here **to** take them as prisoners to the chief

16:30 brought them out and asked, "Sirs, what must I do **to** be saved?"
16:36 "The magistrates have ordered **that** you and Silas be released.
17:15 instructions for Silas and Timothy **to** join him as soon as possible.
19: 4 He told the people **to** believe in the one coming after him,
21:24 and pay their expenses, **so that** they can have their heads shaved.
22: 5 and went there to bring these people as prisoners to Jerusalem **to**
22:24 and questioned **in order to** find out why the people were shouting
23:24 mounts for Paul **so that** he may be taken safely to Governor Felix."
24: 4 But **in order** not **to** weary you further, I would request that you be
27:42 The soldiers planned **to** kill the prisoners to prevent any of them
Ro 1:11 **so that** I may impart to you some spiritual gift to make you
1:13 **in order that** I might have a harvest among you, just as I have had
3: 8 as some claim that we say—"Let us do evil **that** good may result"?
3:19 **so that** every mouth may be silenced and the whole world held
4:16 **so that** it may be by grace and may be guaranteed to all Abraham's
5:20 The law was added **so that** the trespass might increase. But where
5:21 **so that**, just as sin reigned in death, so also grace might reign
6: 1 then? Shall we go on sinning **so that** grace may increase?
6: 4 buried with him through baptism into death **in order that**,
6: 6 with him **so that** the body of sin might be done away with,
7: 4 raised from the dead, **in order that** we might bear fruit to God.
7:13 But **in order that** sin might be recognized as sin, it produced death
7:13 **so that** through the commandment sin might become utterly sinful.
8: 4 **in order that** the righteous requirements of the law might be fully
8:17 if indeed we share in his sufferings **in order that** we may also
9:11 or bad—**in order that** God's purpose in election might stand:
9:23 What if he did this **to** make the riches of his glory known to the
11:11 Did they stumble **so as to** fall beyond recovery? Not at all!
11:19 say then, "Branches were broken off **so that** I could be grafted in."
11:25 of this mystery, brothers, **so that** you may not be conceited:
11:31 so they too have now become disobedient **in order that** they too
11:32 men over to disobedience **so that** he may have mercy on them all.
14: 9 **so that** he might be the Lord of both the dead and the living.
15: 4 **so that** through endurance and the encouragement of the Scriptures
15: 6 **so that** with one heart and mouth you may glorify the God
15:16 **so that** the Gentiles might become an offering acceptable to God,
15:20 **so that** I would not be building on someone else's foundation.
15:31 Pray **that** I may be rescued from the unbelievers in Judea and that
15:32 **so that** by God's will I may come to you with joy and together
16: 2 I ask you to receive her in the Lord in a way worthy of the saints
1Co 1:10 **that** all of you agree with one another so that there may be no
1:15 **so** no one can say that you were baptized into my name.
1:17 **lest** [+*3590*] the cross of Christ be emptied of its power.
1:27 But God chose the foolish things of the world **to** shame the wise;
1:27 God chose the weak things of the world **to** shame the strong.
1:28 and the things that are not—**to** nullify the things that are,
1:31 **Therefore**, as it is written: "Let him who boasts boast in the Lord."
2: 5 **so that** your faith might not rest on men's wisdom, but on God's
2:12 from God, **that** we may understand what God has freely given us.
3:18 of this age, he should become a "fool" **so that** he may become wise.
4: 2 Now it is required **that** those who have been given a trust must
4: 3 I care very little **if** I am judged by you or by any human court;
4: 6 **so that** you may learn from us the meaning of the saying,
4: 6 **Then** you will not take pride in one man over against another.
4: 8 you really had become kings **so that** we might be kings with you!
5: 2 and [NIE] have put out of your fellowship the man who did this?
5: 5 may be destroyed **and** his spirit saved on the day of the Lord.
5: 7 Get rid of the old yeast **that** you may be a new batch without
7: 5 and for a time, **so that** you may devote yourselves to prayer.
7: 5 Then come together again **so that** Satan will not tempt you
7:29 From now on [NIE] those who have wives should live as if they
7:34 Her **aim is to** be devoted to the Lord in both body and spirit.
7:35 I am saying this for your own good, not **to** restrict you, but that you
8:13 I will never eat meat again, **so that** I will not cause him to fall.
9:12 we put up with anything **rather than** [+*3590*] hinder the gospel of
9:15 And I am not writing this **in the hope that** you will do such things
9:18 **that** in preaching the gospel I may offer it free of charge, and
9:19 I make myself a slave to everyone, **to** win as many as possible.
9:20 To the Jews I became like a Jew, **to** win the Jews. To those under
9:20 I myself am not under the law), **so as to** win those under the law.
9:21 but am under Christ's law), **so as to** win those not having the law.
9:22 To the weak I became weak, **to** win the weak. I have become all
9:22 things to all men **so that** by all possible means I might save some.
9:23 all this for the sake of the gospel, **that** I may share in its blessings.
9:24 but only one gets the prize? Run in such a way **as to** get the prize.
9:25 They do it **to** get a crown that will not last; but we do it to get a

10:33 my own good but the good of many, **so that** they may be saved.
11:19 No doubt there have to be differences among you **to** show which of
11:32 **so that** we will not be condemned with the world.
11:34 **so that** when you meet together it may not result in judgment.
12:25 **so that** there should be no division in the body, but that its parts
13: 3 I possess to the poor and surrender my body **[NIE]** to the flames,
14: 1 desire spiritual gifts, especially **[NIE]** the gift of prophecy.
14: 5 of you to speak in tongues, but I would rather **have** you prophesy.
14: 5 in tongues, unless he interprets, **so that** the church may be edified.
14:12 to have spiritual gifts, try **to** excel in gifts that build up the church.
14:13 For this reason anyone who speaks in a tongue should pray **that** he
14:19 But in the church I would rather speak five intelligible words **to**
14:31 in turn **so that** everyone may be instructed and encouraged.
15:28 him who put everything under him, **so that** God may be all in all.
16: 2 it up, **so that** when I come no collections will have to be made.
16: 6 the winter, **so that** you can help me on my journey, wherever I go.
16:10 see to it **that** he has nothing to fear while he is with you,
16:11 Send him on his way in peace **so that** he may return to me.
16:12 I strongly urged him **to** go to you with the brothers.
16:12 He was quite unwilling **to** go now, but he will go when he has the
16:16 **to** submit to such as these and to everyone who joins in the work,
2Co 1: 9 But this happened **that** we might not rely on ourselves but on God,
1:11 **Then** many will give thanks on our behalf for the gracious favor
1:15 I planned to visit you first **so that** you might benefit twice.
1:17 my plans in a worldly manner **so that** in the same breath I say,
2: 3 **so that** when I came I should not be distressed by those who ought
2: 4 not **to** grieve you but to let you know the depth of my love for you.
2: 4 not to grieve you but **to let** you know the depth of my love for you.
2: 5 has grieved all of you, to some extent—not **to** put it too severely.
2: 9 The reason I wrote you was **to** see if you would stand the test
2:11 **in order that** Satan might not outwit us. For we are not unaware of
4: 7 But we have this treasure in jars of clay **to show that** this
4:10 **so that** the life of Jesus may also be revealed in our body.
4:11 for Jesus' sake, **so that** his life may be revealed in our mortal body.
4:15 **so that** the grace that is reaching more and more people may cause
5: 4 **so that** what is mortal may be swallowed up by life.
5:10 **that** each one may receive what is due him for the things done
5:12 **so that** you can answer those who take pride in what is seen rather
5:15 **so that** those who live should no longer live for themselves but for
5:21 **so that** in him we might become the righteousness of God.
6: 3 block in anyone's path, **so that** our ministry will not be discredited.
7: 9 as God intended and **so** were not harmed in any way by us.
8: 6 So we urged Titus, **[NIE]** since he had earlier made a beginning,
8: 7 in your love for us—**see that** you also excel in this grace of giving.
8: 9 became poor, **so that** you through his poverty might become rich.
8:13 Our desire is not **that** others might be relieved while you are hard
8:14 they need, **so that** in turn their plenty will supply what you need.
9: 3 But I am sending the brothers **in order that** our boasting about you
9: 3 prove hollow, but **that** you may be ready, as I said you would be.
9: 4 and find you unprepared, we—not **to** say anything about you—
9: 5 So I thought it necessary to urge the brothers **to** visit you in
9: 8 **so that** in all things at all times, having all that you need, you will
10: 9 I do not **want** to seem to be trying to frighten you with my letters.
11: 7 Was it a sin for me to lower myself **in order to** elevate you by
11:12 And I will keep on doing what I am doing **in order to** cut the
11:12 **to** be considered equal with us in the things they boast about.
11:16 me just as you would a fool, **so that** I may do a little boasting.
12: 7 **To** keep me from becoming conceited because of these
12: 7 given me a thorn in my flesh, a messenger of Satan, **to** torment me.
12: 7 a thorn in my flesh, a messenger of Satan, to torment me. **[RPG]**
12: 8 Three times I pleaded with the Lord **to** take it away from me.
12: 9 about my weaknesses, **so that** Christ's power may rest on me.
13: 7 Not that people will see **that** we have stood the test but that you
13: 7 but **that** you will do what is right even though we may seem to
13:10 **that** when I come I may not have to be harsh in my use of
Gal 1:16 his Son in me **so that** I might preach him among the Gentiles,
2: 4 spy on the freedom we have in Christ Jesus and **to** make us slaves.
2: 5 a moment, **so that** the truth of the gospel might remain with you.
2: 9 They agreed **that** we should go to the Gentiles, and they to the
2:10 All they asked was **that** we should continue to remember the poor,
2:16 have put our faith in Christ Jesus **that** we may be justified by faith
2:19 For through the law I died to the law **so that** I might live for God.
3:14 He redeemed us **in order that** the blessing given to Abraham
3:14 **so that** by faith we might receive the promise of the Spirit.
3:22 **so that** what was promised, being given through faith in Jesus
3:24 So the law was put in charge to lead us to Christ **that** we might be

4: 5 **to** redeem those under law, that we might receive the full rights of
4: 5 those under law, **that** we might receive the full rights of sons.
4:17 is to alienate you ⌊from us⌋, **so that** you may be zealous for them.
5:17 in conflict with each other, **so that** you do not do what you want.
6:12 The only reason they do this is **to** avoid being persecuted for the
6:13 yet they want you to be circumcised **that** they may boast about
Eph 1:17 I keep asking **that** the God of our Lord Jesus Christ, the glorious
2: 7 **in order that** in the coming ages he might show the incomparable
2: 9 not by works, **so that** no one can boast.
2:10 to do good works, which God prepared in advance **for** us to do.
2:15 His **purpose** was to create in himself one new man out of the two,
3:10 His **intent** was **that** now, through the church, the manifold wisdom
3:16 I pray **that** out of his glorious riches he may strengthen you with
3:18 **[RPG]** may have power, together with all the saints, to grasp how
3:19 **that** you may be filled to the measure of all the fullness of God.
4:10 higher than all the heavens, **in order to** fill the whole universe.)
4:14 **Then** we will no longer be infants, tossed back and forth by the
4:28 **that** he may have something to share with those in need.
4:29 up according to their needs, **that** it may benefit those who listen.
5:26 **to** make her holy, cleansing her by the washing with water through
5:27 and **to** present her to himself as a radiant church, without stain
5:27 or wrinkle or any other blemish, but **[RPG]** holy and blameless.
5:33 wife as he loves himself, and the wife **must** respect her husband.
6: 3 "**that** it may go well with you and that you may enjoy long life on
6:13 **so that** when the day of evil comes, you may be able to stand your
6:19 Pray also for me, **that** whenever I open my mouth, words may be
6:20 in chains. Pray **that** I may declare it fearlessly, as I should.
6:21 **so that** you also may know how I am and what I am doing.
6:22 **that** you may know how we are, and that he may encourage you.
Php 1: 9 **that** your love may abound more and more in knowledge
1:10 what is best **and** may be pure and blameless until the day of Christ,
1:26 **so that** through my being with you again your joy in Christ Jesus
1:27 **Then**, whether I come and see you or only hear about you in my
2: 2 then make my joy complete **by** being like-minded, having the same
2:10 **that** at the name of Jesus every knee should bow, in heaven
2:15 **so that** you may become blameless and pure, children of God
2:19 **that** I also may be cheered when I receive news about you.
2:27 not on him only but also on me, **to** spare me sorrow upon sorrow.
2:28 **so that** when you see him again you may be glad and I may have
2:30 risking his life to make up for the help you could not give me.
3: 8 lost all things. I consider them rubbish, **that** I may gain Christ
Col 1: 9 and asking God **to** fill you with the knowledge of his will through
1:18 the dead, **so that** in everything he might have the supremacy.
1:28 all wisdom, **so that** we may present everyone perfect in Christ.
2: 2 My **purpose** is **that** they may be encouraged in heart and united in
2: 4 **so that** no one may deceive you by fine-sounding arguments.
3:21 embitter your children, or **[+3590]** they will become discouraged.
4: 3 And pray for us, too, **that** God may open a door for our message,
4: 4 Pray **that** I may proclaim it clearly, as I should.
4: 8 I am sending him to you for the express purpose **that** you may
4:12 **that** you may stand firm in all the will of God, mature and fully
4:16 see **that** it is also read in the church of the Laodiceans and that you
4:16 the Laodiceans and **that** you in turn read the letter from Laodicea.
4:17 "See to it **that** you complete the work you have received in the
1Th 2:16 keep us from speaking to the Gentiles **so that** they may be saved.
4: 1 brothers, we instructed you how to live **in order to** please God,
4: 1 ask you and urge you in the Lord Jesus **to** do this more and more.
4:12 **so that** your daily life may win the respect of outsiders and
4:13 or **[+3590]** to grieve like the rest of men, who have no hope.
5: 4 are not in darkness **so that** this day should surprise you like a thief.
5:10 He died for us **so that**, whether we are awake or asleep, we may
2Th 1:11 pray for you, **that** our God may count you worthy of his calling,
2:12 **so that** all will be condemned who have not believed the truth
3: 1 pray for us **that** the message of the Lord may spread rapidly
3: 2 And pray **that** we may be delivered from wicked and evil men,
3: 9 but **in order to** make ourselves a model for you to follow.
3:12 we command and urge you in the Lord Jesus Christ **to** settle down
3:14 Do not associate with him, **in order that** he may feel ashamed.
1Ti 1: 3 **so that** you may command certain men not to teach false doctrines
1:16 But for that very reason I was shown mercy **so that** in me,
1:18 about you, **so that** by following them you may fight the good fight,
1:20 whom I have handed over to Satan **to** be taught not to blaspheme.
2: 2 **that** we may live peaceful and quiet lives in all godliness
3: 6 or **[+3590]** he may become conceited and fall under the same
3: 7 **so that** he will not fall into disgrace and into the devil's trap.
3:14 to come to you soon, I am writing you these instructions **so that,**

4:15 yourself wholly to them, **so that** everyone may see your progress.
5: 7 these instructions, too, **so that** no one may be open to blame.
5:16 **so that** the church can help those widows who are really in need.
5:20 are to be rebuked publicly, **so that** the others may take warning.
5:21 and the elect angels, **to** keep these instructions without partiality,
6: 1 **so that** God's name and our teaching may not be slandered.
6:19 coming age, **so that** they may take hold of the life that is truly life.

2Ti 1: 4 your tears, I long to see you, **so that** I may be filled with joy.
2: 4 in civilian affairs—he **wants** to please his commanding officer.
2:10 **that** they too may obtain the salvation that is in Christ Jesus,
3:17 **so that** the man of God may be thoroughly equipped for every
4:17 **so that** through me the message might be fully proclaimed

Tit 1: 5 The reason I left you in Crete was **that** you might straighten out
1: 9 **so that** he can encourage others by sound doctrine and refute those
1:13 rebuke them sharply, **so that** they will be sound in the faith
2: 4 **Then** they can train the younger women to love their husbands
2: 5 to their husbands, **so that** no one will malign the word of God.
2: 8 **so that** those who oppose you may be ashamed because they have
2:10 **so that** in every way they will make the teaching about God our
2:12 It teaches us **to** say "No" to ungodliness and worldly passions,
2:14 who gave himself for us **to** redeem us from all wickedness
3: 7 **so that**, having been justified by his grace, we might become heirs
3: 8 **so that** those who have trusted in God may be careful to devote
3:13 Apollos on their way and see **that** they have everything they need.
3:14 **in order that** they may provide for daily necessities and not live

Phm 1:13 **so that** he could take your place in helping me while I am in chains
1:14 **so that** any favor you do will be spontaneous and not forced.
1:15 you for a little while was **that** you might have him back for good—
1:19 I will pay it back—not **to** mention that you owe me your very self.

Heb 2:14 **so that** by his death he might destroy him who holds the power of
2:17 **in order that** he might become a merciful and faithful high priest
3:13 **so that** none of you may be hardened by sin's deceitfulness.
4:11 **so that** no one will fall by following their example of
4:16 **so that** we may receive mercy and find grace to help us in our time
5: 1 them in matters related to God, **to** offer gifts and sacrifices for sins.
6:12 We do not **want** you to become lazy, but to imitate those who
6:18 God did this **so that**, by two unchangeable things in which it is
9:25 Nor did he enter heaven **to** offer himself again and again, the way
10: 9 to do your will." He sets aside the first **to** establish the second.
10:36 need to persevere **so that** when you have done the will of God,
11:28 *so that* the destroyer of the firstborn would not touch the firstborn
11:35 to be released, **so that** they might gain a better resurrection.
11:40 **so that** only together with us would they be made perfect.
12: 3 from sinful men, **so that** you will not grow weary and lose heart.
12:13 your feet," **so that** the lame may not be disabled, but rather healed.
12:27 created things—**so that** what cannot be shaken may remain.
13:12 so Jesus also suffered outside the city gate **to** make the people holy
13:17 Obey them **so that** their work will be a joy, not a burden, for that
13:19 urge you to pray **so that** I may be restored to you soon.

Jas 1: 4 must finish its work **so that** you may be mature and complete.
4: 3 **that** you may spend what you get on your pleasures.
5: 9 against each other, brothers, **or** [+*3590*] you will be judged.
5:12 be yes, and your "No," no, **or** [+*3590*] you will be condemned.

1Pe 1: 7 These have come **so that** your faith—of greater worth than gold,
2: 2 spiritual milk, **so that** by it you may grow up in your salvation,
2:12 Live such good lives among the pagans **that**, though they accuse
2:21 leaving you an example, **that** you should follow in his steps.
2:24 on the tree, **so that** we might die to sins and live for righteousness;
3: 1 Wives, in the same way be submissive to your husbands **so that**,
3: 9 because to this you were called **so that** you may inherit a blessing.
3:16 **so that** those who speak maliciously against your good behavior in
3:18 once for all, the righteous for the unrighteous, **to** bring you to God.
4: 6 **so that** they might be judged according to men in regard to the
4:11 **so that** in all things God may be praised through Jesus Christ.
4:13 **so that** you may be overjoyed when his glory is revealed.
5: 6 under God's mighty hand, **that** he may lift you up in due time.

2Pe 1: 4 **so that** through them you may participate in the divine nature
3:17 **so that** you may not be carried away by the error of lawless men

1Jn 1: 3 and heard, **so that** you also may have fellowship with us.
1: 4 We write this **to** make our joy complete.
1: 9 he is faithful and just **and** will forgive us our sins and purify us
2: 1 My dear children, I write this to you **so that** you will not sin.
2:19 but their going [NIE] showed that none of them belonged to us.
2:27 remains in you, and you do not need [NIE] anyone to teach you.
2:28 **so that** when he appears we may be confident and unashamed
3: 1 has lavished on us, **that** we should be called children of God!

3: 5 you know that he appeared **so that** he might take away our sins.
3: 8 The reason the Son of God appeared was **to** destroy the devil's
3:11 you heard from the beginning: [NIE] We should love one another.
3:23 **to** believe in the name of his Son, Jesus Christ, and to love one
4: 9 and only Son into the world **that** we might live through him.
4:17 among us **so that** we will have confidence on the day of judgment,
4:21 [NIE] Whoever loves God must also love his brother.
5: 3 This is love for God: **to** obey his commands. And his commands
5:13 of the Son of God **so that** you may know that you have eternal life.
5:16 that leads to death. I am not saying **that** he should pray about that.
5:20 has given us understanding, **so that** we may know him who is true.

2Jn 1: 5 we have had from the beginning. I ask **that** we love one another.
1: 6 And this is love: **that** we walk in obedience to his commands.
1: 6 heard from the beginning, his command is **that** you walk in love.
1: 8 Watch out **that** you do not lose what you have worked for,
1:12 and talk with you face to face, **so that** our joy may be complete.

3Jn 1: 4 I have no greater joy than to hear **that** my children are walking in
1: 8 hospitality to such men **so that** we may work together for the truth.

Rev 2:10 I tell you, the devil will put some of you in prison **to** test you,
2:21 I have given her time **to** repent of her immorality, but she is
3: 9 I will make them [NIE] come and fall down at your feet
3:11 Hold on to what you have, **so that** no one will take your crown.
3:18 to buy from me gold refined in the fire, **so** you can become rich;
3:18 and white clothes **to** wear, **so** you can cover your shameful
3:18 shameful nakedness; and salve to put on your eyes, **so** you can see.
6: 2 given a crown, and he rode out as a conqueror bent **on** conquest.
6: 4 to take peace from the earth and **to make** men slay each other.
6:11 and they were told **to** wait a little longer, until the number of their
7: 1 holding back the four winds of the earth **to** prevent any wind from
8: 3 He was given much incense **to** offer, with the prayers of all the
8: 6 Then the seven angels who had the seven trumpets prepared **to**
8:12 and a third of the stars, **so that** a third of them turned dark.
9: 4 They were told not **to** harm the grass of the earth or any plant
9: 5 They were not given power **to** kill them, but only to torture them
9: 5 given power to kill them, but only **to** torture them for five months.
9:15 and month and year were released **to** kill a third of mankind.
9:20 [NIE] they did not stop worshiping demons, and idols of gold,
11: 6 **so that** it will not rain during the time they are prophesying;
12: 4 **so that** he might devour her child the moment it was born.
12: 6 by God, where [NIE] she might be taken care of for 1,260 days.
12:14 **so that** she might fly to the place prepared for her in the desert,
12:15 **to** overtake the woman and sweep her away with the torrent.
13:12 made the earth and its inhabitants [NIE] worship the first beast,
13:13 [NIE] even causing fire to come down from heaven to earth in
13:15 **so that** it could speak and cause all who refused to worship the
13:15 and cause [NIE] all who refused to worship the image to be
13:16 and slave, **to** receive a mark on his right hand or on his forehead,
13:17 **so that** no one could buy or sell unless he had the mark, which is
14:13 "Yes," says the Spirit, [NIE] "they will rest from their labor,
16:12 and its water was dried up **to** prepare the way for the kings from
16:15 him, **so that** he may not go naked and be shamefully exposed."
18: 4 "Come out of her, my people, **so that** you will not share in her sins,
18: 4 share in her sins, **so that** you will not receive any of her plagues;
19: 8 Fine linen, bright and clean, was given her **to** wear." (Fine linen
19:15 Out of his mouth comes a sharp sword with which **to** strike down
19:18 **so that** you may eat the flesh of kings, generals, and mighty men,
20: 3 **to** keep him from deceiving the nations anymore until the thousand
21:15 The angel who talked with me had a measuring rod of gold **to**
21:23 The city does not need the sun or the moon **to** shine on it,
22:14 **that** they may have the right to the tree of life and may go through

2672 ἱνατί, *hinati* [6] [√ *2671* + *5515*]

why [6]

Mt 9: 4 Jesus said, "**Why** do you entertain evil thoughts in your hearts?
27:46 which means, "My God, my God, **why** have you forsaken me?"
Lk 13: 7 haven't found any. Cut it down! **Why** should it use up the soil?'
Ac 4:25 " '**Why** do the nations rage and the peoples plot in vain?
7:26 'Men, you are brothers; **why** do you want to hurt each other?'
1Co 10:29 For **why** should my freedom be judged by another's conscience?

2673 Ἰόππη, *Ioppē* [10]

Joppa [10]

Ac 9:36 In **Joppa** there was a disciple named Tabitha (which,

9:38 Lydda was near **Joppa**; so when the disciples heard that Peter was
9:42 This became known all over **Joppa**, and many people believed in
9:43 Peter stayed in **Joppa** for some time with a tanner named Simon.
10: 5 Now send men to **Joppa** to bring back a man named Simon who is
10: 8 told them everything that had happened and sent them to **Joppa**.
10:23 out with them, and some of the brothers from **Joppa** went along.
10:32 Send to **Joppa** for Simon who is called Peter. He is a guest in the
11: 5 "I was in the city *of* **Joppa** praying, and in a trance I saw a vision.
11:13 his house and say, 'Send to **Joppa** for Simon who is called Peter.

2674 Ἰορδάνης, *Iordanēs* [15]

Jordan [15]

Mt 3: 5 from Jerusalem and all Judea and the whole region *of* the **Jordan**.
3: 6 their sins, they were baptized by him in the **Jordan** River.
3:13 Then Jesus came from Galilee to the **Jordan** to be baptized by
4:15 and land of Naphtali, the way to the sea, along the **Jordan**,
4:25 Jerusalem, Judea and the region across the **Jordan** followed him.
19: 1 and went into the region of Judea to the other side *of* the **Jordan**.
Mk 1: 5 their sins, they were baptized by him in the **Jordan** River.
1: 9 from Nazareth in Galilee and was baptized by John in the **Jordan**.
3: 8 and the regions across the **Jordan** and around Tyre and Sidon.
10: 1 that place and went into the region of Judea and across the **Jordan**.
Lk 3: 3 He went into all the country around the **Jordan**, preaching a
4: 1 returned from the **Jordan** and was led by the Spirit in the desert,
Jn 1:28 This all happened at Bethany on the other side *of* the **Jordan**,
3:26 that man who was with you on the other side *of* the **Jordan**—
10:40 Then Jesus went back across the **Jordan** to the place where John

2675 ἰός, *ios* [3] [→ 2995]

poison [2], corrosion [1]

Ro 3:13 tongues practice deceit." "The **poison** of vipers is on their lips."
Jas 3: 8 man can tame the tongue. It is a restless evil, full *of* deadly **poison**.
5: 3 Their **corrosion** will testify against you and eat your flesh like fire.

2676 Ἰουδά, *Iouda*   Not used in UBS/NIV [√ 2683]

2677 Ἰουδαία, *Ioudaia* [43] [√ 2683]

Judea [41], Judea [+6001] [2]

Mt 2: 1 After Jesus was born in Bethlehem *in* **Judea**, during the time of
2: 5 "In Bethlehem *in* **Judea**," they replied, "for this is what the prophet
2:22 But when he heard that Archelaus was reigning *in* **Judea** in place
3: 1 days John the Baptist came, preaching in the Desert of **Judea**
3: 5 from Jerusalem and all **Judea** and the whole region of the Jordan.
4:25 Jerusalem, **Judea** and the region across the Jordan followed him.
19: 1 and went into the region *of* **Judea** to the other side of the Jordan.
24:16 then let those who are in **Judea** flee to the mountains.
Mk 3: 8 many people came to him from **Judea**, Jerusalem, Idumea,
10: 1 Jesus then left that place and went into the region *of* **Judea**
13:14 then let those who are in **Judea** flee to the mountains.
Lk 1: 5 In the time of Herod king *of* **Judea** there was a priest named
1:65 and throughout the hill country *of* **Judea** people were talking about
2: 4 also went up from the town of Nazareth in Galilee to **Judea**,
3: 1 when Pontius Pilate was governor *of* **Judea**, Herod tetrarch of
4:44 And he kept on preaching in the synagogues of **Judea**.
5:17 come from every village of Galilee and from **Judea** and Jerusalem,
6:17 was there and a great number of people from all over **Judea**,
7:17 This news about Jesus spread throughout **Judea** and the
21:21 Then let those who are in **Judea** flee to the mountains, let those in
23: 5 they insisted, "He stirs up the people all over **Judea** by his teaching.
Jn 4: 3 learned of this, he left **Judea** and went back once more to Galilee.
4:47 When this man heard that Jesus had arrived in Galilee from **Judea**,
4:54 sign that Jesus performed, having come from **Judea** to Galilee.
7: 1 purposely staying away from **Judea** because the Jews there were
7: 3 brothers said to him, "You ought to leave here and go to **Judea**,
11: 7 Then he said to his disciples, "Let us go back to **Judea**."
Ac 1: 8 and in all **Judea** and Samaria, and to the ends of the earth."
2: 9 of Mesopotamia, **Judea** and Cappadocia, Pontus and Asia,
8: 1 all except the apostles were scattered throughout **Judea** [+6001]
9:31 Then the church throughout **Judea**, Galilee and Samaria enjoyed a
10:37 You know what has happened throughout **Judea**, beginning in

11: 1 and the brothers throughout **Judea** heard that the Gentiles also had
11:29 his ability, decided to provide help for the brothers living in **Judea**.
12:19 Then Herod went from **Judea** to Caesarea and stayed there a
15: 1 Some men came down from **Judea** to Antioch and were teaching
21:10 number of days, a prophet named Agabus came down from **Judea**.
26:20 then to those in Jerusalem and in all **Judea** [+6001], and to the
28:21 "We have not received any letters from **Judea** concerning you,
Ro 15:31 Pray that I may be rescued from the unbelievers in **Judea**
2Co 1:16 and then to have you send me on my way to **Judea**.
Gal 1:22 I was personally unknown to the churches *of* **Judea** that are in
1Th 2:14 For you, brothers, became imitators of God's churches in **Judea**,

2678 ἰουδαΐζω, *ioudaizō* [1] [√ 2683]

follow Jewish customs [1]

Gal 2:14 How is it, then, that you force Gentiles *to* **follow Jewish customs**?

2679 Ἰουδαϊκός, *Ioudaikos* [1] [√ 2683]

Jewish [1]

Tit 1:14 and will pay no attention *to* **Jewish** myths or to the commands of

2680 Ἰουδαϊκῶς, *Ioudaikōs* [1] [√ 2683]

like a Jew [1]

Gal 2:14 "You are a Jew, yet you live like a Gentile and not **like a Jew**."

2681 Ἰουδαῖος, *Ioudaios* [195] [√ 2683]

βασιλεύς τῶν Ἰουδαίων (king of the Jews) [18] Mt 2:2;
27:11,29,37; Mk 15:2,9,12,18,26; Lk 23:3,37,38; Jn 18:33,39;
19:3,19,21,21

Jews [149], Jew [18], Jewish [18], Judean [3], Jew [+467] [2],
Jewess [2], Jew [+476] [1], Jewish community [+4436] [1], Jews
[+467] [1]

Mt 2: 2 and asked, "Where is the one who has been born king *of* the **Jews**?
27:11 and the governor asked him, "Are you the king *of* the **Jews**?"
27:29 in front of him and mocked him. "Hail, king *of* the **Jews**!" they said.
27:37 against him: THIS IS JESUS, THE KING *OF* THE **JEWS**.
28:15 And this story has been widely circulated among the **Jews** to this
Mk 1: 5 The whole **Judean** countryside and all the people of Jerusalem
7: 3 and all the **Jews** do not eat unless they give their hands a
15: 2 "Are you the king *of* the **Jews**?" asked Pilate. "Yes, it is as you
15: 9 "Do you want me to release to you the king *of* the **Jews**?"
15:12 "What shall I do, then, with the one you call the king *of* the **Jews**?"
15:18 And they began to call out to him, "Hail, king *of* the **Jews**!"
15:26 of the charge against him read: THE KING *OF* THE **JEWS**.
Lk 7: 3 centurion heard of Jesus and sent some elders *of* the **Jews** to him,
23: 3 So Pilate asked Jesus, "Are you the king *of* the **Jews**?" "Yes,
23:37 and said, "If you are the king *of* the **Jews**, save yourself."
23:38 above him, which read: THIS IS THE KING *OF* THE **JEWS**.
23:51 He came from the **Judean** town of Arimathea and he was waiting
Jn 1:19 Now this was John's testimony when the **Jews** of Jerusalem sent
2: 6 water jars, the kind *used by* the **Jews** for ceremonial washing,
2:13 When it was almost time for the **Jewish** Passover, Jesus went up to
2:18 Then the **Jews** demanded of him, "What miraculous sign can you
2:20 The **Jews** replied, "It has taken forty-six years to build this temple,
3: 1 named Nicodemus, a member of the **Jewish** ruling council.
3:22 Jesus and his disciples went out into the **Judean** countryside,
3:25 and a certain **Jew** over the matter of ceremonial washing.
4: 9 woman said to him, "You are a **Jew** and I am a Samaritan woman.
4: 9 ask me for a drink?" (For **Jews** do not associate with Samaritans.)
4:22 we worship what we do know, for salvation is from the **Jews**.
5: 1 Some time later, Jesus went up to Jerusalem for a feast *of* the **Jews**.
5:10 and so the **Jews** said to the man who had been healed, "It is the
5:15 and told the **Jews** that it was Jesus who had made him well.
5:16 was doing these things on the Sabbath, the **Jews** persecuted him.
5:18 For this reason the **Jews** tried all the harder to kill him; not only
6: 4 The **Jewish** Passover Feast was near.
6:41 At this the **Jews** began to grumble about him because he said,
6:52 Then the **Jews** began to argue sharply among themselves,
7: 1 from Judea because the **Jews** there were waiting to take his life.
7: 2 But when the **Jewish** Feast of Tabernacles was near,

7: 11 Now at the Feast the **Jews** were watching for him and asking,
7: 13 no one would say anything publicly about him for fear *of* the **Jews**.
7: 15 The **Jews** were amazed and asked, "How did this man get such
7: 35 The **Jews** said to one another, "Where does this man intend to go
8: 22 This made the **Jews** ask, "Will he kill himself? Is that why he says,
8: 31 To the **Jews** who had believed him, Jesus said, "If you hold to my
8: 48 The **Jews** answered him, "Aren't we right in saying that you are a
8: 52 At this the **Jews** exclaimed, "Now we know that you are
8: 57 years old," the **Jews** said to him, "and you have seen Abraham!"
9: 18 The **Jews** still did not believe that he had been blind and had
9: 22 His parents said this because they were afraid of the **Jews**,
9: 22 for already the **Jews** had decided that anyone who acknowledged
10: 19 At these words the **Jews** were again divided.
10: 24 The **Jews** gathered around him, saying, "How long will you keep us
10: 31 Again the **Jews** picked up stones to stone him,
10: 33 stoning you for any of these," replied the **Jews**, "but for blasphemy,
11: 8 "But Rabbi," they said, "a short while ago the **Jews** tried to stone
11: 19 and many **Jews** had come to Martha and Mary to comfort them in
11: 31 When the **Jews** who had been with Mary in the house, comforting
11: 33 and the **Jews** who had come along with her also weeping,
11: 36 Then the **Jews** said, "See how he loved him!"
11: 45 Therefore many of the **Jews** who had come to visit Mary,
11: 54 Therefore Jesus no longer moved about publicly among the **Jews**.
11: 55 When it was almost time for the **Jewish** Passover, many went up
12: 9 Meanwhile a large crowd of **Jews** found out that Jesus was there
12: 11 for on account of him many of the **Jews** were going over to Jesus
13: 33 You will look for me, and just as I told the **Jews**, so I tell you now:
18: 12 with its commander and the **Jewish** officials arrested Jesus.
18: 14 Caiaphas was the one who had advised the **Jews** that it would be
18: 20 in synagogues or at the temple, where all the **Jews** come together.
18: 31 "But we have no right to execute anyone," the **Jews** objected.
18: 33 summoned Jesus and asked him, "Are you the king *of the* **Jews**?"
18: 35 "Am I a **Jew**?" Pilate replied. "It was your people and your chief
18: 36 my servants would fight to prevent my arrest *by* the **Jews**.
18: 38 With this he went out again to the **Jews** and said, "I find no basis
18: 39 of the Passover. Do you want me to release 'the king *of the* **Jews**'?"
19: 3 went up to him again and again, saying, "Hail, king *of the* **Jews**!"
19: 7 The **Jews** insisted, "We have a law, and according to that law he
19: 12 but the **Jews** kept shouting, "If you let this man go, you are no
19: 14 about the sixth hour. "Here is your king," Pilate said *to* the **Jews**.
19: 19 JESUS OF NAZARETH, THE KING *OF* THE JEWS.
19: 20 Many *of the* **Jews** read this sign, for the place where Jesus was
19: 21 The chief priests *of the* **Jews** protested to Pilate, "Do not write 'The
19: 21 the Jews protested to Pilate, "Do not write 'The King *of the* **Jews**,'
19: 21 of the Jews,' but that this man claimed to be king *of the* **Jews**."
19: 31 Because the **Jews** did not want the bodies left on the crosses during
19: 38 was a disciple of Jesus, but secretly because he feared the **Jews**.
19: 40 strips of linen. This was in accordance with **Jewish** burial customs.
19: 42 Because it was the **Jewish** day of Preparation and since the tomb
20: 19 with the doors locked for fear *of* the **Jews**, Jesus came and stood
Ac 2: 5 Now there were staying in Jerusalem God-fearing **Jews** from every
2: 11 (both **Jews** and converts to Judaism); Cretans and Arabs—
2: 14 raised his voice and addressed the crowd: "*Fellow* **Jews** [+467]
9: 22 and baffled the **Jews** living in Damascus by proving that Jesus is
9: 23 After many days had gone by, the **Jews** conspired to kill him,
10: 22 and God-fearing man, who is respected by all the **Jewish** people.
10: 28 "You are well aware that it is against our law *for* a **Jew** [+467] to
10: 39 "We are witnesses of everything he did in the country of the **Jews**
11: 19 Cyprus and Antioch, telling the message only *to* **Jews**.
12: 3 When he saw that this pleased the **Jews**, he proceeded to seize
12: 11 and from everything the **Jewish** people were anticipating."
13: 5 they proclaimed the word of God in the **Jewish** synagogues.
13: 6 There they met a **Jewish** sorcerer and false prophet named
13: 43 many *of the* **Jews** and devout converts to Judaism followed Paul
13: 45 When the **Jews** saw the crowds, they were filled with jealousy
13: 50 But the **Jews** incited the God-fearing women of high standing
14: 1 and Barnabas went as usual into the **Jewish** synagogue.
14: 1 There they spoke so effectively that a great number *of* **Jews**
14: 2 But the **Jews** who refused to believe stirred up the Gentiles
14: 4 were divided; some sided with the **Jews**, others with the apostles.
14: 5 There was a plot afoot *among* the Gentiles and **Jews**, together with
14: 19 Then *some* **Jews** came from Antioch and Iconium and won the
16: 1 whose mother was a **Jewess** and a believer, but whose father was a
16: 3 so he circumcised him because of the **Jews** who lived in that area,
16: 20 brought them before the magistrates and said, "These men are **Jews**,
17: 1 they came to Thessalonica, where there was a **Jewish** synagogue.

17: 5 But the **Jews** were jealous; so they rounded up some bad characters
17: 10 to Berea. On arriving there, they went to the **Jewish** synagogue.
17: 13 When the **Jews** in Thessalonica learned that Paul was preaching
17: 17 So he reasoned in the synagogue *with* the **Jews**
18: 2 There he met a **Jew** named Aquila, a native of Pontus, who had
18: 2 because Claudius had ordered all the **Jews** to leave Rome.
18: 4 he reasoned in the synagogue, trying to persuade **Jews** and Greeks.
18: 5 to preaching, testifying *to* the **Jews** that Jesus was the Christ.
18: 12 the **Jews** made a united attack on Paul and brought him into court.
18: 14 Just as Paul was about to speak, Gallio said to the **Jews**, "If you
18: 14 "If you **Jews** were making a complaint about some misdemeanor
18: 19 He himself went into the synagogue and reasoned *with* the **Jews**.
18: 24 Meanwhile a **Jew** named Apollos, a native of Alexandria,
18: 28 For he vigorously refuted the **Jews** in public debate, proving from
19: 10 so that all the **Jews** and Greeks who lived in the province of Asia
19: 13 Some **Jews** who went around driving out evil spirits tried to invoke
19: 14 Seven sons of Sceva, a **Jewish** chief priest, were doing this.
19: 17 When this became known *to* the **Jews** and Greeks living in
19: 33 The **Jews** pushed Alexander to the front, and some of the crowd
19: 34 But when they realized he was a **Jew**, they all shouted in unison
20: 3 Because the **Jews** made a plot against him just as he was about to
20: 19 with tears, although I was severely tested by the plots *of* the **Jews**.
20: 21 I have declared *to* both **Jews** and Greeks that they must turn to
21: 11 'In this way the **Jews** of Jerusalem will bind the owner of this belt
21: 20 "You see, brother, how many thousands of **Jews** have believed,
21: 21 They have been informed that you teach all the **Jews** who live
21: 27 some **Jews** from the province of Asia saw Paul at the temple.
21: 39 Paul answered, "I am a **Jew** [+476], from Tarsus in Cilicia,
22: 3 "I am a **Jew** [+467], born in Tarsus of Cilicia, but brought up in
22: 12 of the law and highly respected by all the **Jews** living there.
22: 30 to find out exactly why Paul was being accused by the **Jews**,
23: 12 The next morning the **Jews** formed a conspiracy and bound
23: 20 "The **Jews** have agreed to ask you to bring Paul before the
23: 27 This man was seized by the **Jews** and they were about to kill him,
24: 5 stirring up riots *among* the **Jews** all over the world.
24: 9 The **Jews** joined in the accusation, asserting that these things were
24: 19 But there are some **Jews** from the province of Asia, who ought to
24: 24 days later Felix came with his wife Drusilla, who was a **Jewess**.
24: 27 but because Felix wanted to grant a favor *to* the **Jews**, he left Paul
25: 2 where the chief priests and **Jewish** leaders appeared before him
25: 7 the **Jews** who had come down from Jerusalem stood around him,
25: 8 "I have done nothing wrong against the law of the **Jews** or against
25: 9 Festus, wishing to do the **Jews** a favor, said to Paul, "Are you
25: 10 I have not done any wrong *to* the **Jews**, as you yourself know very
25: 15 chief priests and elders of the **Jews** brought charges against him
25: 24 The whole **Jewish** [+4436] **community** has petitioned me about
26: 2 today as I make my defense against all the accusations of the **Jews**,
26: 3 because you are well acquainted with all the **Jewish** customs
26: 4 "The **Jews** all know the way I have lived ever since I was a child,
26: 7 O king, it is because of this hope that the **Jews** are accusing me.
26: 21 That is why the **Jews** seized me in the temple courts and tried to
28: 17 Three days later he called together the leaders *of* the **Jews**.
28: 19 But when the **Jews** objected, I was compelled to appeal to Caesar—
Ro 1: 16 of everyone who believes: first *for* the **Jew**, then for the Gentile.
2: 9 human being who does evil: first for the **Jew**, then for the Gentile;
2: 10 for everyone who does good: first for the **Jew**, then for the Gentile.
2: 17 Now you, if you call yourself a **Jew**; if you rely on the law
2: 28 A man is not a **Jew** if he is only one outwardly, nor is circumcision
2: 29 No, a man is a **Jew** if he is one inwardly; and circumcision is
3: 1 What advantage, then, is there *in* being a **Jew**, or what value is
3: 9 We have already made the charge that **Jews** and Gentiles alike are
3: 29 Is God the God *of* **Jews** only? Is he not the God of Gentiles too?
9: 24 he also called, not only from the **Jews** but also from the Gentiles?
10: 12 For there is no difference between **Jew** and Gentile—the same
1Co 1: 22 **Jews** demand miraculous signs and Greeks look for wisdom,
1: 23 a stumbling block *to* **Jews** and foolishness to Gentiles,
1: 24 both **Jews** and Greeks, Christ the power of God and the wisdom of
9: 20 *To* the **Jews** I became like a **Jew**, to win the Jews. To those under
9: 20 To the Jews I became like a Jew, to win the **Jews**. To those under
9: 20 To the Jews I became like a Jew, to win the Jews. To those under
10: 32 anyone to stumble, whether **Jews**, Greeks or the church of God—
12: 13 whether **Jews** or Greeks, slave or free—and we were all given the
2Co 11: 24 Five times I received from the **Jews** the forty lashes minus one.
Gal 2: 13 The other **Jews** joined him in his hypocrisy, so that by their
2: 14 "You are a **Jew**, yet you live like a Gentile and not like a Jew.
2: 15 "We who are **Jews** by birth and not 'Gentile sinners'

3:28 There is neither **Jew** nor Greek, slave nor free, male nor female,
Col 3:11 Here there is no Greek or **Jew**, circumcised or uncircumcised,
1Th 2:14 the same things those churches suffered from the **Jews**,
Rev 2: 9 I know the slander of those who say they are **Jews** and are not,
3: 9 of Satan, who claim to be **Jews** though they are not, but are liars—

2682 Ἰουδαϊσμός, *Ioudaismos* [2] [√ 2683]

Judaism [2]

Gal 1:13 For you have heard of my previous way of life in **Judaism**,
1:14 I was advancing in **Judaism** beyond many Jews of my own age

2683 Ἰούδας, *Ioudas* [44] [→ 2676, 2677, 2678, 2679, 2680, 2681, 2682]

Judas [32], Judah [10], Jude [1], Judea [1]

Mt   1: 2 the father of Jacob, Jacob the father of **Judah** and his brothers,
1: 3 **Judah** the father of Perez and Zerah, whose mother was Tamar,
2: 6 " 'But you, Bethlehem, in the land *of* **Judah**, are by no means least
2: 6 land of Judah, are by no means least among the rulers *of* **Judah**;
10: 4 Simon the Zealot and **Judas** Iscariot, who betrayed him.
13:55 and aren't his brothers James, Joseph, Simon and **Judas**?
26:14 the one called **Judas** Iscariot—went to the chief priests
26:25 Then **Judas**, the one who would betray him, said, "Surely not I,
26:47 While he was still speaking, **Judas**, one of the Twelve, arrived.
27: 3 When **Judas**, who had betrayed him, saw that Jesus was
Mk   3:19 and **Judas** Iscariot, who betrayed him.
6: 3 Mary's son and the brother *of* James, Joseph, **Judas** and Simon?
14:10 Then **Judas** Iscariot, one of the Twelve, went to the chief priests to
14:43 Just as he was speaking, **Judas**, one of the Twelve, appeared.
Lk   1:39 Mary got ready and hurried to a town in the hill country *of* **Judea**,
3:30 of Simeon, the son *of* **Judah**, the son of Joseph, the son of Jonam,
3:33 son of Ram, the son of Hezron, the son of Perez, the son of **Judah**,
6:16 **Judas** son of James, and Judas Iscariot, who became a traitor.
6:16 Judas son of James, and **Judas** Iscariot, who became a traitor.
22: 3 Then Satan entered **Judas**, called Iscariot, one of the Twelve.
22:47 and the man who was called **Judas**, one of the Twelve,
22:48 but Jesus asked him, "**Judas**, are you betraying the Son of Man
Jn   6:71 (He meant **Judas**, the son of Simon Iscariot, who, though one of
12: 4 But one of his disciples, **Judas** Iscariot, who was later to betray
13: 2 and the devil had already prompted **Judas** Iscariot, son of Simon,
13:26 the piece of bread, he gave it *to* **Judas** Iscariot, son of Simon.
13:29 Since **Judas** had charge of the money, some thought Jesus was
14:22 Then **Judas** (not Judas Iscariot) said, "But, Lord, why do you intend
18: 2 Now **Judas**, who betrayed him, knew the place, because Jesus had
18: 3 So **Judas** came to the grove, guiding a detachment of soldiers
18: 5 Jesus said. (And **Judas** the traitor was standing there with them.)
Ac   1:13 son of Alphaeus and Simon the Zealot, and **Judas** son of James.
1:16 spoke long ago through the mouth of David concerning **Judas**,
1:25 this apostolic ministry, which **Judas** left to go where he belongs."
5:37 **Judas** the Galilean appeared in the days of the census and led a
9:11 "Go to the house *of* **Judas** on Straight Street and ask for a man from
15:22 They chose **Judas** (called Barsabbas) and Silas, two men who were
15:27 Therefore we are sending **Judas** and Silas to confirm by word of
15:32 **Judas** and Silas, who themselves were prophets, said much to
Heb 7:14 For it is clear that our Lord descended from **Judah**, and in regard
8: 8 covenant with the house of Israel and with the house *of* **Judah**.
Jude 1: 1 **Jude**, a servant of Jesus Christ and a brother of James, To those
Rev 5: 5 See, the Lion of the tribe *of* **Judah**, the Root of David,
7: 5 From the tribe *of* **Judah** 12,000 were sealed, from the tribe of

2684 Ἰουλία, *Ioulia* [1] [√ 2685]

Julia [1]

Ro 16:15 **Julia**, Nereus and his sister, and Olympas and all the saints with

2685 Ἰούλιος, *Ioulios* [2] [→ 549, 2684]

Julius [2]

Ac 27: 1 other prisoners were handed over *to* a centurion named **Julius**,
27: 3 and **Julius**, in kindness to Paul, allowed him to go to his friends

2686 Ἰουνία, *Iounia* Not used in UBS/NIV [→ 2687]

2687 Ἰουνιᾶς, *Iounias* [1] [√ 2686]

Junias [1]

Ro 16: 7 Greet Andronicus and **Junias**, my relatives who have been in

2688 Ἰοῦστος, *Ioustos* [3]

Justus [3]

Ac   1:23 Joseph called Barsabbas (also known as **Justus**) and Matthias.
18: 7 the synagogue and went next door to the house *of* Titius **Justus**,
Col 4:11 Jesus, who is called **Justus**, also sends greetings. These are the

2689 ἱππεύς, *hippeus* [2] [√ 2691]

cavalry [1], horsemen [1]

Ac 23:23 seventy **horsemen** and two hundred spearmen to go to Caesarea at
23:32 The next day they let the **cavalry** go on with him, while they

2690 ἱππικός, *hippikos* [1] [√ 2691]

mounted [1]

Rev 9:16 The number of the **mounted** troops was two hundred million.

2691 ἵππος, *hippos* [17] [→ 68, 800, 2689, 2690, 5803, 5804, 5805]

horses [10], horse [7]

Jas   3: 3 When we put bits into the mouths *of* **horses** to make them obey us,
Rev   6: 2 I looked, and there before me was a white **horse**! Its rider held a
6: 4 Then another **horse** came out, a fiery red one. Its rider was given
6: 5 "Come!" I looked, and there before me was a black **horse**!
6: 8 I looked, and there before me was a pale **horse**! Its rider was
9: 7 The locusts looked like **horses** prepared for battle. On their heads
9: 9 the sound of their wings was like the thundering *of* many **horses**
9:17 The **horses** and riders I saw in my vision looked like this:
9:17 The heads *of* the **horses** resembled the heads of lions, and out of
9:19 The power *of* the **horses** was in their mouths and in their tails;
14:20 rising as high as the **horses**' bridles for a distance of 1,600 stadia.
18:13 cattle and sheep; **horses** and carriages; and bodies and souls of
19:11 saw heaven standing open and there before me was a white **horse**,
19:14 riding on white **horses** and dressed in fine linen, white and clean.
19:18 of kings, generals, and mighty men, *of* **horses** and their riders,
19:19 gathered together to make war against the rider *on* the **horse**
19:21 the sword that came out of the mouth of the rider *on* the **horse**,

2692 ἶρις, *iris* [2]

rainbow [2]

Rev   4: 3 A **rainbow**, resembling an emerald, encircled the throne.
10: 1 He was robed in a cloud, with a **rainbow** above his head; his face

2693 Ἰσαάκ, *Isaak* [20]

Isaac [20]

Mt   1: 2 Abraham was the father of **Isaac**, Isaac the father of Jacob,
1: 2 **Isaac** the father of Jacob, Jacob the father of Judah and his
8:11 the feast with Abraham, **Isaac** and Jacob in the kingdom of heaven.
22:32 am the God of Abraham, the God *of* **Isaac**, and the God of Jacob'?
Mk 12:26 am the God of Abraham, the God *of* **Isaac**, and the God of Jacob'?
Lk   3:34 the son of Jacob, the son *of* **Isaac**, the son of Abraham, the son of
13:28 **Isaac** and Jacob and all the prophets in the kingdom of God,
20:37 God of Abraham, and the God *of* **Isaac**, and the God of Jacob.'
Ac   3:13 The God of Abraham, **Isaac** and Jacob, the God of our fathers,
7: 8 And Abraham became the father of **Isaac** and circumcised him
7: 8 Later **Isaac** became the father of Jacob, and Jacob became the
7:32 the God of your fathers, the God *of* Abraham, **Isaac** and Jacob.'
Ro   9: 7 "It is through **Isaac** that your offspring will be reckoned."
9:10 Rebekah's children had one and the same father, our father **Isaac**.
Gal   4:28 Now you, brothers, like **Isaac**, are children of promise.
Heb 11: 9 he lived in tents, as did **Isaac** and Jacob, who were heirs with him

11:17 faith Abraham, when God tested him, offered **Isaac** as a sacrifice.
11:18 to him, "It is through **Isaac** that your offspring will be reckoned."
11:20 By faith **Isaac** blessed Jacob and Esau in regard to their future.
Jas 2:21 for what he did when he offered his son **Isaac** on the altar?

2694 ἰσάγγελος, *isangelos* [1] [√ 2698 + 34]

like angels [1]

Lk 20:36 and they can no longer die; for they are **like** the **angels**. They are

2695 Ἰσαχάρ, *Isachar* Not used in UBS/NIV [√ cf. 2704]

2696 Ἰσκαριώθ, *Iskariōth* Not used in UBS/NIV [→ 2697, 5000, 5001]

2697 Ἰσκαριώτης, *Iskariōtēs* [11] [√ 2696]

Iscariot [11]

Mt 10:4 Simon the Zealot and Judas **Iscariot**, who betrayed him.
26:14 the one called Judas **Iscariot**—went to the chief priests
Mk 3:19 and Judas **Iscariot**, who betrayed him.
14:10 Then Judas **Iscariot**, one of the Twelve, went to the chief priests to
Lk 6:16 Judas son of James, and Judas **Iscariot**, who became a traitor.
22:3 Then Satan entered Judas, called **Iscariot**, one of the Twelve.
Jn 6:71 (He meant Judas, the son of Simon **Iscariot**, who, though one of
12:4 But one of his disciples, Judas **Iscariot**, who was later to betray
13:2 and the devil had already prompted Judas **Iscariot**, son of Simon,
13:26 the piece of bread, he gave it to Judas **Iscariot**, son of Simon.
14:22 Then Judas (not Judas **Iscariot**) said, "But, Lord, why do you

2698 ἴσος, *isos* [8] [→ 2694, 2699, 2700, 2701, 2711]

agree [2], equal [2], as [1], equality [+1639+3836] [1], in full [+3836] [1], same [1]

Mt 20:12 'and you have made them **equal** to us who have borne the burden
Mk 14:56 testified falsely against him, but their statements did not **agree**.
14:59 Yet even then their testimony did not **agree**.
Lk 6:34 'sinners' lend to 'sinners,' expecting to be repaid **in full** [+3836].
Jn 5:18 even calling God his own Father, making himself **equal** with God.
Ac 11:17 So if God gave them the **same** gift as he gave us, who believed in
Php 2:6 did not consider **equality** [+1639+3836] with God something to be
Rev 21:16 it to be 12,000 stadia in length, and as wide and high **as** it is long.

2699 ἰσότης, *isotēs* [3] [√ 2698]

equality [2], fair [1]

2Co 8:13 while you are hard pressed, but that there might be **equality**.
8:14 plenty will supply what you need. Then there will be **equality**,
Col 4:1 Masters, provide your slaves with what is right and **fair**,

2700 ἰσότιμος, *isotimos* [1] [√ 2698 + 5507]

as precious as [1]

2Pe 1:1 and Savior Jesus Christ have received a faith **as precious as** ours:

2701 ἰσόψυχος, *isopsychos* [1] [√ 2698 + 6038]

like [1]

Php 2:20 I have no one else **like** *him*, who takes a genuine interest in your

2702 Ἰσραήλ, *Israēl* [68] [→ 2703]

βασιλεύς Ἰσραήλ (king of Israel) [4] Mt 27:42; Mk 15:32; Jn 1:49; 12:13

θεός Ἰσραήλ (God of Israel) [2] Mt 15:31; Lk 1:68

υἱοί Ἰσραήλ (sons of Israel) [14] Mt 27:9; Lk 1:16; Ac 5:21; 7:23,37; 9:15; 10:36; Ro 9:27; 2Co 3:7,13; Heb 11:22; Rev 2:14; 7:4; 21:12

Israel [53], Israelites [+5626] [7], Israel [+3875] [3], Israel [+5626] [3], Israel's [1], people of Israel [+2848+4922] [1]

Mt 2:6 will come a ruler who will be the shepherd of my people **Israel**.' "
2:20 take the child and his mother and go to the land *of* **Israel**.
2:21 took the child and his mother and went to the land *of* **Israel**.
8:10 the truth, I have not found anyone in **Israel** with such great faith.
9:33 and said, "Nothing like this has ever been seen in **Israel**."
10:6 Go rather to the lost sheep *of* **Israel** [+3875].
10:23 you will not finish going through the cities *of* **Israel** before the Son
15:24 He answered, "I was sent only to the lost sheep *of* **Israel** [+3875]."
15:31 and the blind seeing. And they praised the God *of* **Israel**.
19:28 will also sit on twelve thrones, judging the twelve tribes *of* **Israel**.
27:9 the thirty silver coins, the price set on him by the people *of* **Israel**,
27:42 they said, "but he can't save himself! He's the King *of* **Israel**!
Mk 12:29 "is this: 'Hear, O **Israel**, the Lord our God, the Lord is one.
15:32 Let this Christ, this King *of* **Israel**, come down now from the cross,
Lk 1:16 Many of the people *of* **Israel** will he bring back to the Lord their
1:54 He has helped his servant **Israel**, remembering to be merciful
1:68 the God *of* **Israel**, because he has come and has redeemed his
1:80 and he lived in the desert until he appeared publicly to **Israel**.
2:25 He was waiting for the consolation *of* **Israel**, and the Holy Spirit
2:32 for revelation to the Gentiles and for glory to your people **Israel**."
2:34 child is destined to cause the falling and rising of many in **Israel**
4:25 I assure you that there were many widows in **Israel** in Elijah's
4:27 And there were many in **Israel** with leprosy in the time of Elisha
7:9 "I tell you, I have not found such great faith even in **Israel**."
22:30 my kingdom and sit on thrones, judging the twelve tribes *of* **Israel**.
24:21 we had hoped that he was the one who was going to redeem **Israel**.
Jn 1:31 came baptizing with water was that he might be revealed *to* **Israel**."
1:49 "Rabbi, you are the Son of God; you are the King *of* **Israel**."
3:10 "You are **Israel's** teacher," said Jesus, "and do you not understand
12:13 comes in the name of the Lord!" "Blessed is the King *of* **Israel**!"
Ac 1:6 are you at this time going to restore the kingdom *to* **Israel**?"
2:36 "Therefore let all **Israel** [+3875] be assured of this: God has made
4:10 then know this, you and all the people *of* **Israel**: It is by the name
4:27 and the people *of* **Israel** in this city to conspire against your holy
5:21 the full assembly of the elders *of* **Israel** [+5626]—and sent to the
5:31 that he might give repentance and forgiveness of sins *to* **Israel**.
7:23 forty years old, he decided to visit his fellow **Israelites** [+5626].
7:37 "This is that Moses who told the **Israelites** [+5626], 'God will send
7:42 and offerings forty years in the desert, O house *of* **Israel**?
9:15 before the Gentiles and their kings and before the people *of* **Israel**.
10:36 You know the message God sent to the people *of* **Israel**,
13:17 The God of the people *of* **Israel** chose our fathers; he made the
13:23 "From this man's descendants God has brought *to* **Israel** the Savior
13:24 John preached repentance and baptism to all the people *of* **Israel**.
28:20 because of the hope *of* **Israel** that I am bound with this chain."
Ro 9:6 had failed. For not all who are descended from **Israel** are Israel.
9:6 had failed. For not all who are descended from Israel are **Israel**.
9:27 Isaiah cries out concerning **Israel**: "Though the number of the
9:27 "Though the number of the **Israelites** [+5626] be like the sand by
9:31 but **Israel**, who pursued a law of righteousness, has not attained it.
10:19 Did **Israel** not understand? First, Moses says, "I will make you
10:21 But concerning **Israel** he says, "All day long I have held out my
11:2 the passage about Elijah—how he appealed to God against **Israel**:
11:7 What then? What **Israel** sought so earnestly it did not obtain,
11:25 **Israel** has experienced a hardening in part until the full number of
11:26 And so all **Israel** will be saved, as it is written: "The deliverer will
1Co 10:18 Consider the **people of Israel** [+2848+4922]: Do not those who eat
2Co 3:7 so that the **Israelites** [+5626] could not look steadily at the face of
3:13 who would put a veil over his face to keep the **Israelites** [+5626]
Gal 6:16 and mercy to all who follow this rule, even to the **Israel** of God.
Eph 2:12 excluded from citizenship *in* **Israel** and foreigners to the covenants
Php 3:5 of the people *of* **Israel**, of the tribe of Benjamin, a Hebrew of
Heb 8:8 when I will make a new covenant with the house *of* **Israel**
8:10 This is the covenant I will make with the house *of* **Israel** after that
11:22 spoke about the exodus *of* the **Israelites** [+5626] from Egypt
Rev 2:14 who taught Balak to entice the **Israelites** [+5626] to sin by eating
7:4 who were sealed: 144,000 from all the tribes *of* **Israel** [+5626].
21:12 were written the names of the twelve tribes *of* **Israel** [+5626].

2703 Ἰσραηλίτης, *Israēlitēs* [9] [√ 2702]

of Israel [6], Israelite [2], Israelites [1]

Jn 1:47 he said of him, "Here is a true **Israelite**, in whom there is nothing

Ac   2:22 "Men **of Israel**, listen to this: Jesus of Nazareth was a man
     3:12 he said to them: "Men **of Israel**, why does this surprise you?
     5:35 "Men **of Israel**, consider carefully what you intend to do to these
    13:16 "Men **of Israel** and you Gentiles who worship God, listen to me!
    21:28 shouting, "Men **of Israel**, help us! This is the man who teaches all
Ro   9: 4 the people **of Israel**. Theirs is the adoption as sons; theirs the
    11: 1 I am an **Israelite** myself, a descendant of Abraham, from the tribe
2Co 11:22 Are they Hebrews? So am I. Are they **Israelites**? So am I.

2704 Ἰσσαχάρ, **Issachar** [1] [√ cf. 2695]

Issachar [1]

Rev 7: 7 from the tribe of Levi 12,000, from the tribe *of* **Issachar** 12,000,

2705 ἵστημι, **histēmi** [155 / 154]

[→ *189, 190, 414, 415, 468, 482, 510, 634, 635, 640, 686, 687, 688, 841, 923, 1404, 1460, 1496, 1749, 1931, 1983, 1985, 2012, 2013, 2014, 2060, 2179, 2180, 2181, 2183, 2184, 2194, 2342, 2392, 2706, 2769, 2770, 2949, 2987, 3495, 3496, 4188, 4224, 4225, 4325, 4613, 4706, 4756, 5084, 5085, 5086, 5087, 5088, 5112, 5308, 5318, 5319, 5363, 5364, 5712; cf. 5089, 5119*]

standing [34], stand [30], stood [26], standing there [5], stood up [5], stopped [5], stand firm [3], establish [2], established [2], got up [2], stand here [2], stands [2], stood still [2], there [2], appear [1], brought [1], counted out [1], feet [1], hold [1], holding [1], is [1], made appear [1], made stand [1], make stand [1], on trial [+3212] [1], present [1], presented [1], produced [1], proposed [1], put [1], set [1], settled the matter [+1612] [1], stand fast [1], standing [+1639] [1], standing firm [1], stands firm [1], stayed [1], stood [+1639] [1], stood there [1], stop [1], take stand [1], taken stand [1], uphold [1], wait [1], waits [1], was there [1]

Mt   2: 9 ahead of them until *it* **stopped** over the place where the child was.
     4: 5 the holy city and *had* him **stand** on the highest point of the temple.
     6: 5 for they love to pray **standing** in the synagogues and on the street
    12:25 and every city or household divided against itself *will* not **stand**.
    12:26 he is divided against himself. How *can* his kingdom **stand**?
    12:46 his mother and brothers **stood** outside, wanting to speak to him.
    12:47 told him, "Your mother and brothers *are* **standing** outside,
    13: 2 got into a boat and sat in it, while all the people **stood** on the shore.
    16:28 some who are **standing** here will not taste death before they see
    18: 2 *He* called a little child and *had* him **stand** among them.
    18:16 so that 'every matter *may be* **established** by the testimony of two
    20: 3 and saw others **standing** in the marketplace doing nothing.
    20: 6 eleventh hour he went out and found still others **standing** *around*.
    20: 6 'Why *have you been* **standing** here all day long doing nothing?'
    20:32 Jesus **stopped** and called them. "What do you want me to do for
    24:15 "So when you see **standing** in the holy place 'the abomination that
    25:33 *He will* **put** the sheep on his right and the goats on his left.
    26:15 him over to you?" So they **counted out** for him thirty silver coins.
    26:73 After a little while, those **standing** there went up to Peter and said,
    27:11 Meanwhile Jesus **stood** before the governor, and the governor
    27:47 When some *of* those **standing** there heard this, they said, "He's
Mk   3:24 If a kingdom is divided against itself, that kingdom cannot **stand**.
     3:25 If a house is divided against itself, that house cannot **stand**.
     3:26 And if Satan opposes himself and is divided, he cannot **stand**;
     7: 9 in order to observe [UBS *set up*; NIV *5498*] your own traditions!
     9: 1 some who are **standing** here will not taste death before they see
     9:36 *He* took a little child and *had* him **stand** among them. Taking him
    10:49 Jesus **stopped** and said, "Call him." So they called to the blind man,
    11: 5 some people **standing** there asked, "What are you doing,
    13: 9 On account of me *you will* **stand** before governors and kings as
    13:14 "When you see 'the abomination that causes desolation' **standing**
Lk   1:11 appeared to him, **standing** at the right side of the altar of incense.
     4: 9 to Jerusalem and *had* him **stand** on the highest point of the temple.
     5: 1 One day as Jesus was **standing** by the Lake of Gennesaret,
     5: 2 left **there** by the fishermen, who were washing their nets.
     6: 8 with the shriveled hand, "Get up and **stand** in front of everyone."
     6: 8 and stand in front of everyone." So *he* **got up** and stood there.
     6:17 *He* went down with them and **stood** on a level place. A large
     7:14 he went up and touched the coffin, and those carrying it **stood still**.
     7:38 and *as* she **stood** behind him at his feet weeping, she began to wet
     8:20 told him, "Your mother and brothers *are* **standing** outside,

     8:44 the edge of his cloak, and immediately her bleeding **stopped**.
     9:27 some who are **standing** here will not taste death before they see
     9:47 their thoughts, took a little child and *had* him **stand** beside him.
    11:18 If Satan is divided against himself, how *can* his kingdom **stand**?
    13:25 the door, you will **stand** outside knocking and pleading, 'Sir,
    17:12 ten men who had leprosy met him. They **stood** at a distance
    18:11 The Pharisee **stood up** and prayed about himself: 'God, I thank
    18:13 "But the tax collector **stood** at a distance. He would not even look
    18:40 Jesus **stopped** and ordered the man to be brought to him. When he
    19: 8 But Zacchaeus **stood up** and said to the Lord, "Look, Lord!
    21:36 and that you *may be able to* **stand** before the Son of Man."
    23:10 The chief priests and the teachers of the law *were* **standing there**,
    23:35 The people **stood** watching, and the rulers even sneered at him.
    23:49 him from Galilee, **stood** at a distance, watching these things.
    24:17 together as you walk along?" *They* **stood still**, their faces downcast.
    24:36 Jesus himself **stood** among them and said to them, "Peace be with
Jn   1:26 John replied, "but among you **stands** one you do not know.
     1:35 The next day John **was there** again with two of his disciples.
     3:29 The friend who attends the bridegroom **waits** and listens for him,
     6:22 The next day the crowd that *had* **stayed** on the opposite shore of
     7:37 Jesus **stood** and said in a loud voice, "If anyone is thirsty, let him
     8: 3 woman caught in adultery. They **made** her **stand** before the group
     8:44 the beginning, not **holding** to the truth, for there is no truth in him.
    11:56 and *as they* **stood** in the temple area they asked one another,
    12:29 The crowd that *was* **there** and heard it said it had thundered;
    18: 5 Jesus said. (And Judas the traitor *was* **standing there** with them.)
    18:16 but Peter *had to* **wait** outside at the door. The other disciple,
    18:18 and officials **stood** *around* a fire they had made to keep warm.
    18:18 keep warm. Peter also was **standing** with them, warming himself.
    18:25 As Simon Peter **stood** [+*1639*] warming himself, he was asked,
    19:25 Near the cross of Jesus **stood** his mother, his mother's sister,
    20:11 but Mary **stood** outside the tomb crying. As she wept, she bent
    20:14 At this, she turned around and saw Jesus **standing there**,
    20:19 Jesus came and **stood** among them and said, "Peace be with you!"
    20:26 Jesus came and **stood** among them and said, "Peace be with you!"
    21: 4 Early in the morning, Jesus **stood** on the shore, but the disciples
Ac   1:11 Galilee," they said, "why *do you* **stand here** looking into the sky?
     1:23 So *they* **proposed** two men: Joseph called Barsabbas (also known
     2:14 Then Peter **stood up** with the Eleven, raised his voice
     3: 8 *He* jumped *to his* **feet** and began to walk. Then he went with them
     4: 7 *They had* Peter and John **brought** before them and began to
     4:14 could see the man who had been healed **standing there** with them,
     5:20 "Go, **stand** in the temple courts," he said, "and tell the people the
     5:23 the jail securely locked, with the guards **standing** at the doors;
     5:25 The men you put in jail are **standing** in the temple courts teaching
     5:27 *they* **made** them **appear** before the Sanhedrin to be questioned by
     6: 6 *They* **presented** these men to the apostles, who prayed and laid
     6:13 *They* **produced** false witnesses, who testified, "This fellow never
     7:33 off your sandals, the place where *you are* **standing** is holy ground.
     7:55 saw the glory of God, and Jesus **standing** at the right hand of God.
     7:56 and the Son of Man **standing** at the right hand of God."
     7:60 his knees and cried out, "Lord, *do* not **hold** this sin against them."
     8:38 And he gave orders *to* **stop** the chariot. Then both Philip
     9: 7 The men traveling with Saul **stood there** speechless; they heard
    10:30 the afternoon. Suddenly a man in shining clothes **stood** before me
    11:13 He told us how he had seen an angel **appear** in his house and say,
    12:14 ran back without opening it and exclaimed, "Peter **is** at the door!"
    16: 9 night Paul had a vision of a man of Macedonia **standing** [+*1639*]
    17:22 Paul then **stood up** in the meeting of the Areopagus and said:
    17:31 For *he has* **set** a day when he will judge the world with justice by
    21:40 Paul **stood** on the steps and motioned to the crowd.
    22:25 him out to flog him, Paul said to the centurion **standing there**,
    22:30 Then *he* brought Paul and *had* him **stand** before them.
    24:20 what crime they found in me *when* I **stood** before the Sanhedrin—
    24:21 unless it was this one thing I shouted *as I* **stood** in their presence:
    25:10 "I am *now* **standing** before Caesar's court, where I ought to be
    25:18 *When* his accusers **got up** to speak, they did not charge him with
    26: 6 God has promised our fathers that *I am* **on trial** [+*3212*] today.
    26:16 'Now get up and **stand** on your feet. I have appeared to you to
    26:22 very day, and so *I* **stand here** and testify to small and great alike.
    27:21 a long time without food, Paul **stood up** before them and said:
Ro   3:31 nullify the law by this faith? Not at all! Rather, *we* **uphold** the law.
     5: 2 have gained access by faith into this grace in which *we now* **stand**.
    10: 3 that comes from God and sought *to* **establish** their own,
    11:20 they were broken off because of unbelief, and you **stand** by faith.
    14: 4 And *he will* **stand**, for the Lord is able to make him stand.

14: 4 And he will stand, for the Lord is able *to* **make** him **stand.**
1Co 7:37 But the man *who has* **settled the matter** [+*1612*] in his own mind,
   10:12 So, if you think you *are* **standing firm,** be careful that you don't
   15: 1 which you received and on which *you have* **taken** your **stand.**
2Co 1:24 work with you for your joy, because it is by faith *you* **stand firm.**
   13: 1 "Every matter *must be* **established** by the testimony of two
Eph 6:11 so that you can **take** your **stand** against the devil's schemes.
   6:13 stand your ground, and after you have done everything, *to* **stand.**
   6:14 **Stand firm** then, with the belt of truth buckled around your waist,
Col 4:12 that *you may* **stand firm** in all the will of God, mature and fully
2Ti 2:19 Nevertheless, God's solid foundation **stands firm,** sealed with this
Heb 10: 9 to do your will." He sets aside the first to **establish** the second.
   10:11 Day after day every priest **stands** and performs his religious duties;
Jas 2: 3 to the poor man, "You **stand** there" or "Sit on the floor by my feet,"
   5: 9 brothers, or you will be judged. The Judge *is* **standing** at the door!
1Pe 5:12 and testifying that this is the true grace of God. **Stand fast** in it.
Jude 1:24 and *to* **present** you before his glorious presence without fault
Rev 3:20 Here I am! *I* **stand** at the door and knock. If anyone hears my
   5: 6 looking as if it had been slain, **standing** in the center of the throne,
   6:17 For the great day of their wrath has come, and who can **stand?**"
   7: 1 After this I saw four angels **standing** at the four corners of the
   7: 9 and language, **standing** before the throne and in front of the Lamb.
   7:11 All the angels *were* **standing** around the throne and around the
   8: 2 And I saw the seven angels who **stand** before God, and to them
   8: 3 who had a golden censer, came and **stood** at the altar.
   10: 5 Then the angel I had seen **standing** on the sea and on the land
   10: 8 that lies open in the hand of the angel who *is* **standing** on the sea
   11: 4 and the two lampstands that **stand** before the Lord of the earth.
   11:11 and *they* **stood** on their feet, and terror struck those who saw them.
   12: 4 The dragon **stood** in front of the woman who was about to give
   13: 1 And the dragon **stood** on the shore of the sea. And I saw a beast
   14: 1 and there before me was the Lamb, **standing** on Mount Zion,
   15: 2 **standing** beside the sea, those who had been victorious over the
   18:10 Terrified at her torment, *they will* **stand** far off and cry: " 'Woe!
   18:15 these things and gained their wealth from her *will* **stand** far off,
   18:17 and all who earn their living from the sea, *will* **stand** far off.
   19:17 And I saw an angel **standing** in the sun, who cried in a loud voice
   20:12 And I saw the dead, great and small, **standing** before the throne,

2706 ἰστίον, **histion**   Not used in UBS/NIV [√ *2705*]

2707 ἰστορέω, **historeō**   [1] [→ *1461*]

get acquainted with [1]

Gal 1:18 I went up to Jerusalem *to* **get acquainted with** Peter and stayed

2708 ἰσχυρός, **ischyros**   [29 / 28] [√ *2709*]

strong [8], mighty [7], more powerful [3], stronger [3], loud [2], forceful [1], greatly [1], power [1], powerful [1], severe [1]

Mt 3:11 But after me will come one who is **more powerful** *than* I,
   12:29 how can anyone enter a **strong** *man's* house and carry off his
   12:29 carry off his possessions unless he first ties up the **strong** *man?*
   14:30 But when he saw the [UBS+ **strong**] wind, he was afraid and,
Mk 1: 7 "After me will come one **more powerful** *than* I, the thongs of
   3:27 no one can enter a **strong** *man's* house and carry off his
   3:27 and carry off his possessions unless he first ties up the **strong** man.
Lk 3:16 But one **more powerful** *than* I will come, the thongs of whose
   11:21 "When a **strong** *man,* fully armed, guards his own house, his
   11:22 But when *someone* **stronger** attacks and overpowers him,
   15:14 there was a **severe** famine in that whole country, and he began to
1Co 1:25 and the weakness of God is **stronger** *than* man's strength.
   1:27 God chose the weak things of the world to shame the **strong.**
   4:10 We are weak, but you are **strong!** You are honored, we are
   10:22 we trying to arouse the Lord's jealousy? Are we **stronger** *than* he?
2Co 10:10 For some say, "His letters are weighty and **forceful,** but in person
Heb 5: 7 he offered up prayers and petitions with **loud** cries and tears to the
   6:18 to take hold of the hope offered to us may be **greatly** encouraged.
   11:34 and who became **powerful** in battle and routed foreign armies.
1Jn 2:14 I write to you, young men, because you are **strong,** and the word
Rev 5: 2 And I saw a **mighty** angel proclaiming in a loud voice, "Who is
   6:15 the princes, the generals, the rich, the **mighty,** and every slave
   10: 1 Then I saw another **mighty** angel coming down from heaven.
   18: 2 With a **mighty** voice he shouted: "Fallen! Fallen is Babylon the

18: 8 be consumed by fire, for **mighty** is the Lord God who judges her.
18:10 and cry: " 'Woe! Woe, O great city, O Babylon, city of **power!**
18:21 Then a **mighty** angel picked up a boulder the size of a large
19: 6 like the roar of rushing waters and like **loud** peals of thunder,
19:18 of kings, generals, and **mighty** men, of horses and their riders,

2709 ἰσχύς, **ischys**   [10] [→ *1462, 1932, 2015, 2196, 2708, 2710, 2996*]

strength [6], mighty [2], power [1], stronger [1]

Mk 12:30 all your soul and with all your mind and with all your **strength.'**
   12:33 your heart, with all your understanding and with all your **strength,**
Lk 10:27 and with all your soul and with all your **strength** and with all your
Eph 1:19 That power is like the working *of* his **mighty** strength,
   6:10 Finally, be strong in the Lord and in his **mighty** power.
2Th 1: 9 from the presence of the Lord and from the majesty *of* his **power**
1Pe 4:11 If anyone serves, he should do it with the **strength** God provides,
2Pe 2:11 yet even angels, although they are **stronger** and more powerful,
Rev 5:12 and wisdom and **strength** and honor and glory and praise!"
   7:12 and power and **strength** be to our God for ever and ever.

2710 ἰσχύω, **ischyō**   [28] [√ *2709*]

could [8], able [5], strong [3], healthy [2], can do [1], gave beating [1], good [1], grew [1], had [1], powerful [+*4498*] [1], takes effect [1], unable [+*4024*] [1], unable [+*4033*] [1], value [1]

Mt 5:13 *It is* no longer **good** for anything, except to be thrown out
   8:28 met him. They were so violent that no one **could** pass that way.
   9:12 Jesus said, "It is not the **healthy** who need a doctor, but the sick.
   26:40 "**Could** *you* men not keep watch with me for one hour?" he asked
Mk 2:17 said to them, "*It is* not the **healthy** who need a doctor, but the sick.
   5: 4 the irons on his feet. No one *was* **strong** *enough* to subdue him.
   9:18 I asked your disciples to drive out the spirit, but *they* **could** not."
   14:37 to Peter, "are you asleep? **Could** *you* not keep watch for one hour?
Lk 6:48 a flood came, the torrent struck that house but **could** not shake it,
   8:43 subject to bleeding for twelve years, but no one **could** heal her.
   13:24 because many, I tell you, will try to enter and *will* not *be* **able** to.
   14: 6 And *they* **had** nothing to say.
   14:29 For if he lays the foundation and *is* not **able** to finish it,
   14:30 saying, 'This fellow began to build and *was* not **able** to finish.'
   16: 3 my job. *I'm* not **strong** *enough* to dig, and I'm ashamed to beg—
   20:26 *They were* **unable** [+*4024*] to trap him in what he had said there in
Jn 21: 6 *they were* **unable** [+*4033*] to haul the net in because of the large
Ac 6:10 but *they* **could** not stand up against his wisdom or the Spirit by
   15:10 a yoke that neither we nor our fathers *have been* **able** to bear?
   19:16 *He* **gave** them such a **beating** that they ran out of the house naked
   19:20 In this way the word of the Lord spread widely and **grew** in power.
   25: 7 many serious charges against him, which *they* **could** not prove.
   27:16 called Cauda, *we were* hardly **able** to make the lifeboat secure.
Gal 5: 6 Jesus neither circumcision nor uncircumcision *has* any **value.**
Php 4:13 *I* **can do** everything through him who gives me strength.
Heb 9:17 has died; it never **takes effect** while the one who made it is living.
Jas 5:16 The prayer of a righteous man *is* **powerful** [+*4498*] and effective.
Rev 12: 8 But *he was* not **strong** enough, and they lost their place in heaven.

2711 ἴσως, **isōs**   [1] [√ *2698*]

perhaps [1]

Lk 20:13 I will send my son, whom I love; **perhaps** they will respect him.'

2712 Ἰταλία, **Italia**   [4] [→ *2713*]

Italy [4]

Ac 18: 2 who had recently come from **Italy** with his wife Priscilla,
   27: 1 When it was decided that we would sail for **Italy,** Paul and some
   27: 6 There the centurion found an Alexandrian ship sailing for **Italy**
Heb 13:24 and all God's people. Those from **Italy** send you their greetings.

2713 Ἰταλικός, **Italikos**   [1] [√ *2712*]

Italian [1]

Ac 10: 1 a centurion in what was known as the **Italian** Regiment.

2714 Ἰτουραῖος, *Itouraios* [1]

Iturea [1]

Lk   3: 1 of Galilee, his brother Philip tetrarch *of* **Iturea** and Traconitis,

2715 ἰχθύδιον, *ichthydion* [2] [√ *2716*]

small fish [2]

Mt 15:34 have?" Jesus asked. "Seven," they replied, "and a few **small fish**."
Mk   8: 7 They had a few **small fish** as well; he gave thanks for them also

2716 ἰχθύς, *ichthys* [20] [→ *2715*]

fish [19], *untranslated* [1]

Mt   7:10 Or if he asks for a **fish**, will give him a snake?
     14:17 "We have here only five loaves of bread and two **fish**," they
     14:19 Taking the five loaves and the two **fish** and looking up to heaven,
     15:36 Then he took the seven loaves and the **fish**, and when he had given
     17:27 Take the first **fish** you catch; open its mouth and you will find a
Mk   6:38 and see." When they found out, they said, "Five—and two **fish**."
      6:41 Taking the five loaves and the two **fish** and looking up to heaven,
      6:41 set before the people. He also divided the two **fish** among them all.
      6:43 picked up twelve basketfuls of broken pieces of bread and **fish**.
Lk   5: 6 they caught such a large number *of* **fish** that their nets began to
      5: 9 and all his companions were astonished at the catch *of* **fish** they
      9:13 They answered, "We have only five loaves of bread and two **fish**—
      9:16 Taking the five loaves and the two **fish** and looking up to heaven,
     11:11 "Which of you fathers, if your son asks for a **fish**, will give him a
     11:11 if your son asks for a fish, will give him a snake instead? **[RPG]**
     24:42 They gave him a piece *of* broiled **fish**,
Jn   21: 6 were unable to haul the net in because of the large number *of* **fish**.
     21: 8 towing the net *full of* **fish**, for they were not far from shore,
     21:11 and dragged the net ashore. It was full of large **fish**, 153,
1Co 15:39 of flesh, animals have another, birds another and **fish** another.

2717 ἴχνος, *ichnos* [3] [→ *453*]

course [1], footsteps [1], steps [1]

Ro   4:12 but who also walk *in* the **footsteps** of the faith that our father
2Co 12:18 Did we not act in the same spirit and follow the same **course**?
1Pe   2:21 leaving you an example, that you should follow *in* his **steps**.

2718 Ἰωαθάμ, *Iōatham* [2]

Jotham [2]

Mt   1: 9 Uzziah the father of **Jotham**, Jotham the father of Ahaz, Ahaz the
      1: 9 Uzziah the father of Jotham, **Jotham** the father of Ahaz, Ahaz the

2719 Ἰωακίμ, *Iōakim*   Not used in UBS/NIV

2720 Ἰωανάν, *Iōanan* [1] [√ *cf. 2722*]

Joanan [1]

Lk   3:27 the son *of* **Joanan**, the son of Rhesa, the son of Zerubbabel,

2721 Ἰωάννα, *Iōanna* [2] [√ *cf. 2722*]

Joanna [2]

Lk   8: 3 **Joanna** the wife of Cuza, the manager of Herod's household;
     24:10 It was Mary Magdalene, **Joanna**, Mary the mother of James,

2722 Ἰωάννης, *Iōannēs* [135] [√ *cf. 2720, 2721, 2728*]

Baptist [92] Mt 3:1,4,13,14; 4:12; 9:14; 11:2,4,7,11,12,13,18;
     14:2,3,4,8,10; 16:14; 17:13; 21:25,26,32; Mk 1:4,6,9,14; 2:18,18;
     6:14,16,17,18,20,24,25; 8:28; 11:30,32; Lk 1:13,60,63; 3:2,15,16,
     20; 5:33; 7:18,18,20,22,24,24,28,29,33; 9:7,9,19; 11:1; 16:16;
     20:4,6; Jn 1:6,15,19,26,28,32,35,40; 3:23,24,25,26,27; 4:1;
     5:33,36; 10:40,41,41; Ac 1:5,22; 10:37; 11:16; 12:2; 13:24,25;
     18:25; 19:3,4

son of Zebedee [30] Mt 4:21; 10:2; 17:1; Mk 1:19,29; 3:17; 5:37;
     9:2,38; 10:35,41; 13:3; 14:33; Lk 5:10; 6:14; 8:51; 9:28,49,54;
     22:8; Ac 1:13; 3:1,3,4,11; 4:13,19; 8:14; 12:2; Gal 2:9

of the Apocalypse [son of Zebedee?] [4] Rev 1:1,4,9; 22:8

father of Peter [4] Jn 1:42; 21:15,16,17

John Mark [5] Ac 12:12,25; 13:5,13; 15:37

μαθηταὶ Ἰωάννου (disciples of John) [7] Mt 9:14; Mk 2:18,18;
     Lk 5:33; 7:18,18; Jn 3:25; cf. Mt 14:12; Mk 6:29

Πέτρος ... Ἰωάννης ... Ἰάκωβος (Peter ... John ... James)
     [10] Mt 10:2; 17:1; Mk 5:37; 9:2; 13:3; 14:33; Lk 6:14; 8:51; 9:28;
     Ac 1:13

John [119], John's [14], *untranslated* [1], John's [+*899*] [1]

Mt   3: 1 In those days **John** the Baptist came, preaching in the Desert of
      3: 4 **John's** [+*899*] clothes were made of camel's hair, and he had a
      3:13 Jesus came from Galilee to the Jordan to be baptized by **John**.
      3:14 But **John** tried to deter him, saying, "I need to be baptized by you,
      4:12 When Jesus heard that **John** had been put in prison, he returned to
      4:21 two other brothers, James son of Zebedee and his brother **John**.
      9:14 Then **John's** disciples came and asked him, "How is it that we
     10: 2 his brother Andrew; James son of Zebedee, and his brother **John**;
     11: 2 When **John** heard in prison what Christ was doing, he sent his
     11: 4 Jesus replied, "Go back and report *to* **John** what you hear and see:
     11: 7 were leaving, Jesus began to speak to the crowd about **John**:
     11:11 of women there has not risen anyone greater than **John** the Baptist;
     11:12 From the days *of* **John** the Baptist until now, the kingdom of
     11:13 For all the Prophets and the Law prophesied until **John**.
     11:18 For **John** came neither eating nor drinking, and they say, 'He has a
     14: 2 and he said to his attendants, "This is **John** the Baptist; he has risen
     14: 3 Now Herod had arrested **John** and bound him and put him in
     14: 4 for **John** had been saying to him: "It is not lawful for you to have
     14: 8 she said, "Give me here on a platter the head *of* **John** the Baptist."
     14:10 and had **John** beheaded in the prison.
     16:14 They replied, "Some say **John** the Baptist; others say Elijah;
     17: 1 Jesus took with him Peter, James and **John** the brother of James,
     17:13 understood that he was talking to them about **John** the Baptist.
     21:25 **John's** baptism—where did it come from? Was it from heaven,
     21:26 are afraid of the people, for they all hold that **John** was a prophet."
     21:32 For **John** came to you to show you the way of righteousness,
Mk   1: 4 And so **John** came, baptizing in the desert region and preaching a
      1: 6 **John** wore clothing made of camel's hair, with a leather belt
      1: 9 from Nazareth in Galilee and was baptized by **John** in the Jordan.
      1:14 After **John** was put in prison, Jesus went into Galilee,
      1:19 he saw James son of Zebedee and his brother **John** in a boat,
      1:29 they went with James and **John** to the home of Simon and Andrew.
      2:18 Now **John's** disciples and the Pharisees were fasting. Some people
      2:18 "How is it that **John's** disciples and the disciples of the Pharisees
      3:17 and his brother **John** (to them he gave the name Boanerges,
      5:37 follow him except Peter, James and **John** the brother of James.
      6:14 were saying, "**John** the Baptist has been raised from the dead,
      6:16 But when Herod heard this, he said, "**John**, the man I beheaded,
      6:17 For Herod himself had given orders to have **John** arrested,
      6:18 For **John** had been saying to Herod, "It is not lawful for you to have
      6:20 because Herod feared **John** and protected him, knowing him to be
      6:24 shall I ask for?" "The head *of* **John** the Baptist," she answered.
      6:25 "I want you to give me right now the head *of* **John** the Baptist on a
      8:28 They replied, "Some say **John** the Baptist; others say Elijah;
      9: 2 James and **John** with him and led them up a high mountain,
      9:38 "Teacher," said **John**, "we saw a man driving out demons in your
     10:35 Then James and **John**, the sons of Zebedee, came to him.
     10:41 ten heard about this, they became indignant with James and **John**.
     11:30 **John's** baptism—was it from heaven, or from men? Tell me!"
     11:32 The people, for everyone held that **John** really was a prophet.)
     13: 3 the temple, Peter, James, **John** and Andrew asked him privately,
     14:33 He took Peter, James and **John** along with him, and he began to be
Lk   1:13 will bear you a son, and you are to give him the name **John**.
      1:60 but his mother spoke up and said, "No! He is to be called **John**."
      1:63 and to everyone's astonishment he wrote, "His name is **John**."
      3: 2 the word of God came to **John** son of Zechariah in the desert.
      3:15 and were all wondering in their hearts if **John** might possibly be
      3:16 **John** answered them all, "I baptize you with water. But one more
      3:20 Herod added this to them all: He locked **John** up in prison.

	5: 10	and so were James and **John**, the sons of Zebedee, Simon's
	5: 33	"**John's** disciples often fast and pray, and so do the disciples of the
	6: 14	his brother Andrew, James, **John**, Philip, Bartholomew,
	7: 18	**John's** disciples told him about all these things. Calling two of
	7: 18	told him about all these things. Calling two of them, **[RPG]**
	7: 20	came to Jesus, they said, "**John** the Baptist sent us to you to ask,
	7: 22	"Go back and report *to* **John** what you have seen and heard:
	7: 24	After **John's** messengers left, Jesus began to speak to the crowd
	7: 24	messengers left, Jesus began to speak to the crowd about **John**:
	7: 28	among those born of women there is no one greater than **John**.
	7: 29	God's way was right, because they had been baptized *by* **John**.
	7: 33	For **John** the Baptist came neither eating bread nor drinking wine,
	8: 51	except Peter, **John** and James, and the child's father and mother.
	9: 7	because some were saying that **John** had been raised from the
	9: 9	But Herod said, "I beheaded **John**. Who, then, is this I hear such
	9: 19	They replied, "Some say **John** the Baptist; others say Elijah;
	9: 28	**John** and James with him and went up onto a mountain to pray.
	9: 49	"Master," said **John**, "we saw a man driving out demons in your
	9: 54	When the disciples James and **John** saw this, they asked, "Lord,
	11: 1	to him, "Lord, teach us to pray, just as **John** taught his disciples."
	16: 16	"The Law and the Prophets were proclaimed until **John**. Since that
	20: 4	**John's** baptism—was it from heaven, or from men?"
	20: 6	will stone us, because they are persuaded that **John** was a prophet."
	22: 8	Jesus sent Peter and **John**, saying, "Go and make preparations for
Jn	1: 6	There came a man who was sent from God; his name was **John**.
	1: 15	**John** testifies concerning him. He cries out, saying, "This was he of
	1: 19	Now this was **John's** testimony when the Jews of Jerusalem sent
	1: 26	"I baptize with water," **John** replied, "but among you stands one
	1: 28	Bethany on the other side of the Jordan, where **John** was baptizing.
	1: 32	Then **John** gave this testimony: "I saw the Spirit come down from
	1: 35	The next day **John** was there again with two of his disciples.
	1: 40	was one of the two who heard what **John** had said and who had
	1: 42	Jesus looked at him and said, "You are Simon son *of* **John**.
	3: 23	Now **John** also was baptizing at Aenon near Salim, because there
	3: 24	(This was before **John** was put in prison.)
	3: 25	An argument developed between some of **John's** disciples
	3: 26	They came to **John** and said to him, "Rabbi, that man who was
	3: 27	To this **John** replied, "A man can receive only what is given him
	4: 1	that Jesus was gaining and baptizing more disciples than **John**,
	5: 33	"You have sent to **John** and he has testified to the truth.
	5: 36	"I have testimony weightier than that *of* **John**. For the very work
	10: 40	Then Jesus went back across the Jordan to the place where **John**
	10: 41	They said, "Though **John** never performed a miraculous sign,
	10: 41	a miraculous sign, all that **John** said about this man was true."
	21: 15	had finished eating, Jesus said to Simon Peter, "Simon *son of* **John**,
	21: 16	Again Jesus said, "Simon *son of* **John**, do you truly love me?"
	21: 17	third time he said to him, "Simon *son of* **John**, do you love me?"
Ac	1: 5	For **John** baptized with water, but in a few days you will be
	1: 13	Those present were Peter, **John**, James and Andrew; Philip
	1: 22	beginning from **John's** baptism to the time when Jesus was taken
	3: 1	and **John** were going up to the temple at the time of prayer—
	3: 3	When he saw Peter and **John** about to enter, he asked them for
	3: 4	Peter looked straight at him, as did **John**. Then Peter said,
	3: 11	While the beggar held on to Peter and **John**, all the people were
	4: 6	**John**, Alexander and the other men of the high priest's family.
	4: 13	When they saw the courage of Peter and **John** and realized that
	4: 19	But Peter and **John** replied, "Judge for yourselves whether it is
	8: 14	had accepted the word of God, they sent Peter and **John** to them.
	10: 37	beginning in Galilee after the baptism that **John** preached—
	11: 16	'**John** baptized with water, but you will be baptized with the Holy
	12: 2	He had James, the brother *of* **John**, put to death with the sword.
	12: 12	he went to the house of Mary the mother *of* **John**, also called
	12: 25	returned from Jerusalem, taking with them **John**, also called Mark.
	13: 5	God in the Jewish synagogues. **John** was with them as their helper.
	13: 13	Perga in Pamphylia, where **John** left them to return to Jerusalem.
	13: 24	**John** preached repentance and baptism to all the people of Israel.
	13: 25	As **John** was completing his work, he said: 'Who do you think I
	15: 37	Barnabas wanted to take **John**, also called Mark, with them,
	18: 25	about Jesus accurately, though he knew only the baptism *of* **John**.
	19: 3	what baptism did you receive?" "**John's** baptism," they replied.
	19: 4	Paul said, "**John's** baptism was a baptism of repentance. He told
Gal	2: 9	James, Peter and **John**, those reputed to be pillars, gave me
Rev	1: 1	He made it known by sending his angel to his servant **John**,
	1: 4	**John**, To the seven churches in the province of Asia: Grace
	1: 9	I, **John**, your brother and companion in the suffering and kingdom
	22: 8	I, **John**, am the one who heard and saw these things. And when I

2723 Ἰωάς, Iōas   Not used in UBS/NIV

2724 Ἰώβ, Iōb   [1]

Job's [1]

Jas   5: 11   You have heard of **Job's** perseverance and have seen what the

2725 Ἰωβήδ, Iōbēd   [3]   [→ 6044]

Obed [3]

Mt   1: 5   Boaz the father of **Obed**, whose mother was Ruth, Obed the father
     1: 5   father of Obed, whose mother was Ruth, **Obed** the father of Jesse,
Lk   3: 32   the son of Jesse, the son *of* **Obed**, the son of Boaz, the son of

2726 Ἰωδά, Iōda   [1]

Joda [1]

Lk   3: 26   the son of Semein, the son of Josech, the son *of* **Joda**,

2727 Ἰωήλ, Iōēl   [1]

Joel [1]

Ac   2: 16   No, this is what was spoken by the prophet **Joel**:

2728 Ἰωνάθας, Iōnathas   Not used in UBS/NIV
[√ cf. 2722]

2729 Ἰωνάμ, Iōnam   [1]

Jonam [1]

Lk   3: 30   of Simeon, the son of Judah, the son of Joseph, the son *of* **Jonam**,

2730 Ἰωνάν, Iōnan   Not used in UBS/NIV

2731 Ἰωνᾶς, Iōnas   [9]

Jonah [9]

Mt   12: 39   But none will be given it except the sign *of* the prophet **Jonah**.
     12: 40   For as **Jonah** was three days and three nights in the belly of a huge
     12: 41   for they repented at the preaching *of* **Jonah**, and now one greater
     12: 41   at the preaching of Jonah, and now one greater than **Jonah** is here.
     16: 4   but none will be given it except the sign *of* **Jonah**."
Lk   11: 29   but none will be given it except the sign *of* **Jonah**.
     11: 30   For as **Jonah** was a sign to the Ninevites, so also will the Son of
     11: 32   for they repented at the preaching *of* **Jonah**, and now one greater
     11: 32   at the preaching of Jonah, and now one greater than **Jonah** is here.

2732 Ἰωράμ, Iōram   [2]

Jehoram [2]

Mt   1: 8   Jehoshaphat the father of **Jehoram**, Jehoram the father of Uzziah,
     1: 8   Jehoshaphat the father of Jehoram, **Jehoram** the father of Uzziah,

2733 Ἰωρίμ, Iōrim   [1]

Jorim [1]

Lk   3: 29   the son of Joshua, the son of Eliezer, the son *of* **Jorim**, the son of

2734 Ἰωσαφάτ, Iōsaphat   [2]

Jehoshaphat [2]

Mt   1: 8   Asa the father of **Jehoshaphat**, Jehoshaphat the father of Jehoram,
     1: 8   **Jehoshaphat** the father of Jehoram, Jehoram the father of Uzziah,

2735 Ἰωσή, Iōsē   Not used in UBS/NIV   [√ cf. 2736]

2736 Ἰωσῆς, *Iōsēs* [3 / 4] [√ cf. 2735]

Joses [3], Joseph [1]

Mt 27:56 Mary the mother *of* James and **Joses**, [UBS 2737] and the mother
Mk   6: 3 Isn't this Mary's son and the brother *of* James, **Joseph**, Judas
    15:40 Mary the mother *of* James the younger and *of* **Joses**, and Salome.
    15:47 and Mary the mother *of* **Joses** saw where he was laid.

2737 Ἰωσήφ, *Iōsēph* [35 / 34]

Joseph [31], Joseph's [3]

Mt   1:16 and Jacob the father of **Joseph**, the husband of Mary, of whom was
     1:18 His mother Mary was pledged to be married *to* **Joseph**, but before
     1:19 Because **Joseph** her husband was a righteous man and did not want
     1:20 Lord appeared to him in a dream and said, "**Joseph** son of David,
     1:24 When **Joseph** woke up, he did what the angel of the Lord had
     2:13 had gone, an angel of the Lord appeared *to* **Joseph** in a dream.
     2:19 an angel of the Lord appeared in a dream *to* **Joseph** in Egypt
    13:55 and aren't his brothers James, **Joseph**, Simon and Judas?
    27:56 Mary the mother *of* James and **Joses**, [UBS *Joseph*; NIV 2736]
    27:57 there came a rich man from Arimathea, named **Joseph**,
    27:59 **Joseph** took the body, wrapped it in a clean linen cloth,
Mk 15:43 **Joseph** of Arimathea, a prominent member of the Council,
    15:45 from the centurion that it was so, he gave the body *to* **Joseph**.
Lk   1:27 to a virgin pledged to be married to a man named **Joseph**,
     2: 4 So **Joseph** also went up from the town of Nazareth in Galilee to
     2:16 So they hurried off and found Mary and **Joseph**, and the baby,
     3:23 He was the son, so it was thought, *of* **Joseph**, the son of Heli,
     3:24 son of Levi, the son of Melki, the son of Jannai, the son *of* **Joseph**,
     3:30 of Simeon, the son of Judah, the son *of* **Joseph**, the son of Jonam,
     4:22 that came from his lips. "Isn't this **Joseph's** son?" they asked.
    23:50 Now there was a man named **Joseph**, a member of the Council,
Jn   1:45 the prophets also wrote—Jesus of Nazareth, the son *of* **Joseph**."
     4: 5 near the plot of ground Jacob had given to his son **Joseph**.
     6:42 not Jesus, the son *of* **Joseph**, whose father and mother we know?
    19:38 Later, **Joseph** of Arimathea asked Pilate for the body of Jesus.
Ac   1:23 **Joseph** called Barsabbas (also known as Justus) and Matthias.
     4:36 **Joseph**, a Levite from Cyprus, whom the apostles called Barnabas
     7: 9 "Because the patriarchs were jealous of **Joseph**, they sold him as a
     7:13 On their second visit, **Joseph** told his brothers who he was,
     7:13 brothers who he was, and Pharaoh learned about **Joseph's** family.
     7:14 After this, **Joseph** sent for his father Jacob and his whole family,
     7:18 Then another king, who knew nothing about **Joseph**, became ruler
Heb 11:21 By faith Jacob, when he was dying, blessed each *of* **Joseph's** sons,
    11:22 By faith **Joseph**, when his end was near, spoke about the exodus of
Rev 7: 8 from the tribe of Zebulun 12,000, from the tribe *of* **Joseph** 12,000,

2738 Ἰωσήχ, *Iōsēch* [1]

Josech [1]

Lk   3:26 the son of Semein, the son *of* **Josech**, the son of Joda,

2739 Ἰωσίας, *Iōsias* [2]

Josiah [2]

Mt   1:10 Manasseh the father of Amon, Amon the father of **Josiah**,
     1:11 and **Josiah** the father of Jeconiah and his brothers at the time of the

2740 ἰῶτα, *iōta* [1] [√ cf. 2607]

smallest letter [1]

Mt   5:18 the truth, until heaven and earth disappear, not the **smallest letter**,

Κ, κ

2741 κ, *k* Not used in UBS/NIV

2742 κάβος, *kabos* Not used in UBS/NIV

2743 κἀγώ, *kagō* [84] See Index of Articles, Etc.

[√ 2779 + 1609]

I [28], and I [24], I also [8], so I [5], I too [3], me also [3], me [3],
and I too [2], also me [1], and I myself [1], and me [1], but I [1],
but me [1], I myself [1], if I [1], so that I [1]

2744 κάδος, *kados* Not used in UBS/NIV

2745 καθά, *katha* [1] [√ 2848 + 4005]

as [1]

Mt 27:10 used them to buy the potter's field, **as** the Lord commanded me."

2746 καθαίρεσις, *kathairesis* [3] [√ 2848 + 145]

demolish [1], pulling down [1], tearing down [1]

2Co 10: 4 On the contrary, they have divine power to **demolish** strongholds.
    10: 8 Lord gave us for building you up rather than **pulling** you **down**,
    13:10 the Lord gave me for building you up, not for **tearing** you **down**.

2747 καθαιρέω, *kathaireō* [9] [√ 2848 + 145]

took down [3], brought down [1], demolish [1], overthrew [1],
robbed [1], take down [1], tear down [1]

Mk 15:36 him alone. Let's see if Elijah comes *to* **take** him **down**," he said.
    15:46 some linen cloth, **took down** the body, wrapped it in the linen,
Lk   1:52 He has **brought down** rulers from their thrones but has lifted up
    12:18 I will **tear down** my barns and build bigger ones, and there I will
    23:53 Then he **took** it **down**, wrapped it in linen cloth and placed it in a
Ac 13:19 he **overthrew** seven nations in Canaan and gave their land to his
    13:29 they **took** him **down** from the tree and laid him in a tomb.
    19:27 of Asia and the world, will *be* **robbed** of her divine majesty."
2Co 10: 5 We **demolish** arguments and every pretension that sets itself up

2748 καθαίρω, *kathairō* [1] [√ 2754]

prunes [1]

Jn 15: 2 while every branch that does bear fruit he **prunes** so that it will be

2749 καθάπερ, *kathaper* [13] [√ 2848 + 4005 + 4302]

just as [5], *untranslated* [2], like [2], as [1], for [1], the same thing
[1], which [1]

Ro   4: 6 David says **the same thing** when he speaks of the blessedness of
    12: 4 **Just as** each of us has one body with many members, and these
1Co 10:10 And do not grumble, **as** some of them did—and were killed by the
    12:12 [NIE] The body is a unit, though it is made up of many parts;
2Co 1:14 you will come to understand fully that you can boast of us **just as**
     3:13 We are not **like** Moses, who would put a veil over his face to keep
     3:18 **which** comes from the Lord, who is the Spirit.
     8:11 so that [RPG] your eager willingness to do it may be matched by
1Th 2:11 **For** you know that we dealt with each of you as a father deals with
     3: 6 and that you long to see us, **just as** we also long to see you.
     3:12 for each other and for everyone else, **just as** ours does for you.
     4: 5 not in passionate lust **like** the heathen, who do not know God;
Heb 4: 2 For we also have had the gospel preached to us, **just as** they did;

2750 καθάπτω, *kathaptō* [1] [√ 2848 + 721]

fastened [1]

Ac 28: 3 a viper, driven out by the heat, **fastened** *itself* on his hand.

2751 καθαρίζω, *katharizō* [31] [√ 2754]

clean [7], cleansed [5], cured [4], make clean [3], purify [3],
cleanse [2], made clean [2], purified [2], cleansing [1], purifies
[1], wash [1]

Mt   8: 2 and said, "Lord, if you are willing, you can **make** me **clean**."
     8: 3 his hand and touched the man. "I am willing," he said. "*Be* **clean**!"
     8: 3 he said. "Be clean!" Immediately *he was* **cured** of his leprosy.

10: 8 Heal the sick, raise the dead, **cleanse** those who have leprosy,
11: 5 the lame walk, those who have leprosy *are* **cured**, the deaf hear,
23: 25 *You* **clean** the outside of the cup and dish, but inside they are full
23: 26 First **clean** the inside of the cup and dish, and then the outside also
Mk 1: 40 him on his knees, "If you are willing, you can **make** me **clean**."
1: 41 his hand and touched the man. "I am willing," he said. "*Be* **clean**!"
1: 42 Immediately the leprosy left him and *he was* **cured**.
7: 19 out of his body." (In saying this, Jesus declared all foods "**clean**.")
Lk 4: 27 time of Elisha the prophet, yet not one of them *was* **cleansed**—
5: 12 begged him, "Lord, if you are willing, you can **make** me **clean**."
5: 13 his hand and touched the man. "I am willing," he said. "*Be* **clean**!"
7: 22 the lame walk, those who have leprosy *are* **cured**, the deaf hear,
11: 39 "Now then, you Pharisees **clean** the outside of the cup and dish,
17: 14 yourselves to the priests." And as they went, *they were* **cleansed**.
17: 17 Jesus asked, "*Were* not all ten **cleansed**? Where are the other
Ac 10: 15 "Do not call anything impure that God *has* **made clean**."
11: 9 'Do not call anything impure that God *has* **made clean**.'
15: 9 between us and them, for *he* **purified** their hearts by faith.
2Co 7: 1 *let us* **purify** ourselves from everything that contaminates body
Eph 5: 26 **cleansing** her by the washing with water through the word,
Tit 2: 14 and *to* **purify** for himself a people that are his very own,
Heb 9: 14 to God, **cleanse** our consciences from acts that lead to death,
9: 22 the law requires that nearly everything *be* **cleansed** with blood,
9: 23 for the copies of the heavenly things *to be* **purified** with these
10: 2 For the worshipers *would have been* **cleansed** once for all,
Jas 4: 8 **Wash** your hands, you sinners, and purify your hearts,
1Jn 1: 7 and the blood of Jesus, his Son, **purifies** us from all sin.
1: 9 will forgive us our sins and **purify** us from all unrighteousness.

2752 καθαρισμός, *katharismos* [7] [√ *2754*]

ceremonial washing [2], cleansing [2], purification [2], cleansed [1]

Mk 1: 44 and offer the sacrifices that Moses commanded for your **cleansing**,
Lk 2: 22 When the time *of* their **purification** according to the Law of Moses
5: 14 and offer the sacrifices that Moses commanded for your **cleansing**,
Jn 2: 6 water jars, the kind used by the Jews for **ceremonial washing**,
3: 25 and a certain Jew over the matter of **ceremonial washing**.
Heb 1: 3 After he had provided **purification** for sins, he sat down at the
2Pe 1: 9 and has forgotten that he has been **cleansed** from his past sins.

2753 κάθαρμα, *katharma* Not used in UBS/NIV
[√ *2754*]

2754 καθαρός, *katharos* [27 / 26] [→ *174, 175, 176, 1350, 1351, 1705, 2748, 2751, 2752, 2753, 2755, 2760, 4326*]

clean [11], pure [11], clear [2], clear of responsibility [1], innocent [1]

Mt 5: 8 Blessed are the **pure** in heart, for they will see God.
23: 26 inside of the cup and dish, and then the outside also will be **clean**.
27: 59 Joseph took the body, wrapped it in a **clean** linen cloth,
Lk 11: 41 inside the dish; to the poor, and everything will be **clean** for you.
Jn 13: 10 has had a bath needs only to wash his feet; his whole body is **clean**.
13: 10 body is clean. And you are **clean**, though not every one of you."
13: 11 to betray him, and that was why he said not every one was **clean**.
15: 3 You are already **clean** because of the word I have spoken to you.
Ac 18: 6 blood be on your own heads! I am **clear of** my **responsibility**.
20: 26 I declare to you today that I am **innocent** of the blood of all men.
Ro 14: 20 All food is **clean**, but it is wrong for a man to eat anything that
1Ti 1: 5 which comes from a **pure** heart and a good conscience and a
3: 9 They must keep hold of the deep truths of the faith with a **clear**
2Ti 1: 3 with a **clear** conscience, as night and day I constantly remember
2: 22 along with those who call on the Lord out of a **pure** heart.
Tit 1: 15 *To* the **pure**, all things are pure, but to those who are corrupted
1: 15 To the pure, all things are **pure**, but to those who are corrupted
1: 15 but to those who are corrupted and do not believe, nothing is **pure**.
Heb 10: 22 guilty conscience and having our bodies washed *with* **pure** water.
Jas 1: 27 Religion that God our Father accepts as **pure** and faultless is this:
1Pe 1: 22 brothers, love one another deeply, from [UBS+ *a pure*] the heart.
Rev 15: 6 They were dressed in **clean**, shining linen and wore golden sashes
19: 8 Fine linen, bright and **clean**, was given her to wear." (Fine linen
19: 14 riding on white horses and dressed in fine linen, white and **clean**.
21: 18 was made of jasper, and the city of **pure** gold, as pure as glass.

21: 18 was made of jasper, and the city of pure gold, as **pure** as glass.
21: 21 The great street of the city was of **pure** gold, like transparent glass.

2755 καθαρότης, *katharotēs* [1] [√ *2754*]

clean [1]

Heb 9: 13 unclean sanctify them so that they are outwardly **clean**.

2756 καθέδρα, *kathedra* [3] [√ *2757*]

benches [2], seat [1]

Mt 21: 12 of the money changers and the **benches** of those selling doves,
23: 2 "The teachers of the law and the Pharisees sit in Moses' **seat**.
Mk 11: 15 of the money changers and the **benches** of those selling doves,

2757 καθέζομαι, *kathezomai* [7] [→ *2756, 2764, 4149, 4751, 5153; cf. 2848 + 1612*]

seated [2], sitting [2], sat down [1], sat [1], stayed [1]

Mt 26: 55 Every day *I* **sat** in the temple courts teaching, and you did not
Lk 2: 46 **sitting** among the teachers, listening to them and asking them
Jn 4: 6 and Jesus, tired as he was from the journey, **sat down** by the well.
11: 20 was coming, she went out to meet him, but Mary **stayed** at home.
20: 12 **seated** where Jesus' body had been, one at the head and the other at
Ac 6: 15 All who *were* **sitting** in the Sanhedrin looked intently at Stephen,
20: 9 **Seated** in a window was a young man named Eutychus, who was

2758 καθεῖς, *katheis* Not used in UBS/NIV
[√ *2848 + 1651*]

2759 καθεξῆς, *kathexēs* [5] [√ *2848 + 2400*]

after this [+*1877+3836*] [1], from place to place [1], on [+*2779+3836*] [1], orderly [1], precisely as it had happened [1]

Lk 1: 3 it seemed good also to me to write an **orderly** account for you,
8: 1 **After** [+*1877+3836*] **this**, Jesus traveled about from one town
Ac 3: 24 "Indeed, all the prophets from Samuel **on** [+*2779+3836*], as many
11: 4 and explained everything to them **precisely as it had happened**:
18: 23 and traveled **from place to place** throughout the region of Galatia

2760 καθερίζω, *katherizō* Not used in UBS/NIV
[√ *2754*]

2761 καθεύδω, *katheudō* [22] [√ *2848*]

sleeping [11], asleep [6], sleep [2], fell asleep [1], sleeper [1], sleeps [1]

Mt 8: 24 so that the waves swept over the boat. But Jesus *was* **sleeping**.
9: 24 he said, "Go away. The girl is not dead but **asleep**." But they
13: 25 But while everyone *was* **sleeping**, his enemy came and sowed
25: 5 a long time in coming, and they all became drowsy and **fell asleep**.
26: 40 Then he returned to his disciples and found them **sleeping**.
26: 43 When he came back, he again found them **sleeping**, because their
26: 45 the disciples and said to them, "*Are you* still **sleeping** and resting?
Mk 4: 27 Night and day, whether *he* **sleeps** or gets up, the seed sprouts
4: 38 Jesus was in the stern, **sleeping** on a cushion. The disciples woke
5: 39 all this commotion and wailing? The child is not dead but **asleep**."
13: 36 If he comes suddenly, do not let him find you **sleeping**.
14: 37 Then he returned to his disciples and found them **sleeping**.
14: 37 found them sleeping. "Simon," he said to Peter, "*are you* **asleep**?
14: 40 When he came back, he again found them **sleeping**, because their
14: 41 the third time, he said to them, "*Are you* still **sleeping** and resting?
Lk 8: 52 for her. "Stop wailing," Jesus said. "She is not dead but **asleep**."
22: 46 "Why *are you* **sleeping**?" he asked them. "Get up and pray so that
Eph 5: 14 "Wake up, O **sleeper**, rise from the dead, and Christ will shine on
1Th 5: 6 So then, *let us* not *be* like others, *who are* **asleep**, but let us be
5: 7 For those *who* **sleep**, sleep at night, and those who get drunk,
5: 7 For those who sleep, **sleep** at night, and those who get drunk,
5: 10 He died for us so that, whether we are awake or **asleep**, we may

2762 καθηγητής, *kathēgētēs* [2] [√ 2848 + 72]

teacher [2]

Mt 23:10 Nor are you to be called 'teacher,' for you have one Teacher,
   23:10 you to be called 'teacher,' for you have one Teacher, the Christ.

2763 καθήκω, *kathēkō* [2] [√ 2848 + 2457]

fit [1], ought to be done [1]

Ac 22:22 their voices and shouted, "Rid the earth of him! He's not fit to live!"
Ro 1:28 them over to a depraved mind, to do what ought not to be done.

2764 κάθημαι, *kathēmai* [91] [√ 2757]

sitting [28], seated [12], sit [12], sits [10], sat [8], rider [+2093]
[6], sat down [4], living [3], live [2], riders [+2093] [2], sitting
down [2], rider [+2062] [1], seat [1]

Mt 4:16 the people living in darkness have seen a great light; on those
    4:16 on those living in the land of the shadow of death a light has
    9: 9 he saw a man named Matthew sitting at the tax collector's booth.
   11:16 They are like children sitting in the marketplaces and calling out
   13: 1 That same day Jesus went out of the house and sat by the lake.
   13: 2 crowds gathered around him that he got into a boat and sat in it,
   15:29 Sea of Galilee. Then he went up on a mountainside and sat down.
   19:28 you who have followed me will also sit on twelve thrones,
   20:30 Two blind men were sitting by the roadside, and when they heard
   22:44 "Sit at my right hand until I put your enemies under your feet." '
   23:22 by heaven swears by God's throne and by the one who sits on it.
   24: 3 As Jesus was sitting on the Mount of Olives, the disciples came to
   26:58 He entered and sat down with the guards to see the outcome.
   26:64 In the future you will see the Son of Man sitting at the right hand
   26:69 Now Peter was sitting out in the courtyard, and a servant girl came
   27:19 While Pilate was sitting on the judge's seat, his wife sent him this
   27:36 And sitting down, they kept watch over him there.
   27:61 and the other Mary were sitting there opposite the tomb.
   28: 2 heaven and, going to the tomb, rolled back the stone and sat on it.
Mk 2: 6 Now some teachers of the law were sitting there, thinking to
    2:14 he saw Levi son of Alphaeus sitting at the tax collector's booth.
    3:32 A crowd was sitting around him, and they told him, "Your mother
    3:34 Then he looked at those seated in a circle around him and said,
    4: 1 so large that he got into a boat and sat in it out on the lake,
    5:15 the legion of demons, sitting there, dressed and in his right mind;
   10:46 the Son of Timaeus), was sitting by the roadside begging.
   12:36 "Sit at my right hand until I put your enemies under your feet." '
   13: 3 As Jesus was sitting on the Mount of Olives opposite the temple,
   14:62 "And you will see the Son of Man sitting at the right hand of the
   16: 5 they saw a young man dressed in a white robe sitting on the right
Lk 1:79 to shine on those living in darkness and in the shadow of death,
    5:17 of Galilee and from Judea and Jerusalem, were sitting there.
    5:27 and saw a tax collector by the name of Levi sitting at his tax booth.
    7:32 They are like children sitting in the marketplace and calling out to
    8:35 had gone out, sitting at Jesus' feet, dressed and in his right mind;
   10:13 they would have repented long ago, sitting in sackcloth and ashes.
   18:35 a blind man was sitting by the roadside begging.
   20:42 Book of Psalms: " 'The Lord said to my Lord: "Sit at my right hand
   21:35 For it will come upon all those who live on the face of the whole
   22:30 may eat and drink at my table in my kingdom and sit on thrones,
   22:55 and had sat down together, Peter sat down with them.
   22:56 A servant girl saw him seated there in the firelight. She looked
   22:69 the Son of Man will be seated at the right hand of the mighty God."
Jn 2:14 and doves, and others sitting at tables exchanging money.
    6: 3 Jesus went up on a mountainside and sat down with his disciples.
    9: 8 begging asked, "Isn't this the same man who used to sit and beg?"
   12:15 of Zion; see, your king is coming, seated on a donkey's colt."
Ac 2: 2 from heaven and filled the whole house where they were sitting.
    2:34 and yet he said, " 'The Lord said to my Lord: "Sit at my right hand
    3:10 they recognized him as the same man who used to sit begging at
    8:28 and on his way home was sitting in his chariot reading the book of
   14: 8 In Lystra there sat a man crippled in his feet, who was lame from
   23: 3 You sit there to judge me according to the law, yet you yourself
1Co 14:30 And if a revelation comes to someone who is sitting down,
Col 3: 1 on things above, where Christ is seated at the right hand of God.
Heb 1:13 "Sit at my right hand until I make your enemies a footstool for
Jas 2: 3 the man wearing fine clothes and say, "Here's a good seat for you,"

    2: 3 to the poor man, "You stand there" or "Sit on the floor by my feet,"
Rev 4: 2 and there before me was a throne in heaven with someone sitting
    4: 3 And the one who sat there had the appearance of jasper
    4: 4 other thrones, and seated on them were twenty-four elders.
    4: 9 honor and thanks to him who sits on the throne and who lives for
    4:10 the twenty-four elders fall down before him who sits on the throne,
    5: 1 Then I saw in the right hand of him who sat on the throne a scroll
    5: 7 and took the scroll from the right hand of him who sat on the
    5:13 "To him who sits on the throne and to the Lamb be praise
    6: 2 Its rider [+2093] held a bow, and he was given a crown, and he
    6: 4 Its rider [+2093] was given power to take peace from the earth
    6: 5 Its rider [+2093] was holding a pair of scales in his hand.
    6: 8 Its rider [+2062] was named Death, and Hades was following
    6:16 "Fall on us and hide us from the face of him who sits on the throne
    7:10 belongs to our God, who sits on the throne, and to the Lamb."
    7:15 and he who sits on the throne will spread his tent over them.
    9:17 The horses and riders [+2093] I saw in my vision looked like this:
   11:16 who were seated on their thrones before God, fell on their faces
   14: 6 and he had the eternal gospel to proclaim to those who live on the
   14:14 and seated on the cloud was one "like a son of man" with a crown
   14:15 and called in a loud voice to him who was sitting on the cloud,
   14:16 So he who was seated on the cloud swung his sickle over the
   17: 1 the punishment of the great prostitute, who sits on many waters.
   17: 3 There I saw a woman sitting on a scarlet beast that was covered
   17: 9 The seven heads are seven hills on which the woman sits.
   17:15 where the prostitute sits, are peoples, multitudes, nations
   18: 7 In her heart she boasts, 'I sit as queen; I am not a widow, and I will
   19: 4 fell down and worshiped God, who was seated on the throne.
   19:11 a white horse, whose rider [+2093] is called Faithful and True.
   19:18 generals, and mighty men, of horses and their riders [+2093],
   19:19 together to make war against the rider [+2093] on the horse
   19:21 that came out of the mouth of the rider [+2093] on the horse,
   20:11 Then I saw a great white throne and him who was seated on it.
   21: 5 He who was seated on the throne said, "I am making everything

2765 καθημέραν, *kathēmeran* Not used in UBS/NIV
[√ 2848 + 2465]

2766 καθημερινός, *kathēmerinos* [1] [√ 2848 + 2465]

daily [1]

Ac 6: 1 because their widows were being overlooked in the daily

2767 καθίζω, *kathizō* [46] [→ 361, 2125, 4150, 4327, 5154]

sat down [15], sit [10], sat [4], sit down [3], ridden [2], seated [2],
appoint as judges [1], came to rest [1], convened the court
[+1037+2093+3836] [1], convened [1], place [1], sets up [1], sits
[1], sitting down [1], stay [1], stayed [1]

Mt 5: 1 he saw the crowds, he went up on a mountainside and sat down.
   13:48 Then they sat down and collected the good fish in baskets,
   19:28 of all things, when the Son of Man sits on his glorious throne,
   20:21 "Grant that one of these two sons of mine may sit at your right
   20:23 from my cup, but to sit at my right or left is not for me to grant.
   23: 2 "The teachers of the law and the Pharisees sit in Moses' seat.
   25:31 all the angels with him, he will sit on his throne in heavenly glory.
   26:36 and he said to them, "Sit here while I go over there and pray."
Mk 9:35 Sitting down, Jesus called the Twelve and said, "If anyone wants to
   10:37 "Let one of us sit at your right and the other at your left in your
   10:40 but to sit at my right or left is not for me to grant. These places
   11: 2 you will find a colt tied there, which no one has ever ridden.
   11: 7 brought the colt to Jesus and threw their cloaks over it, he sat on it.
   12:41 Jesus sat down opposite the place where the offerings were put
   14:32 and Jesus said to his disciples, "Sit here while I pray."
   16:19 he was taken up into heaven and he sat at the right hand of God.
Lk 4:20 he rolled up the scroll, gave it back to the attendant and sat down.
    5: 3 from shore. Then he sat down and taught the people from the boat.
   14:28 Will he not first sit down and estimate the cost to see if he has
   14:31 Will he not first sit down and consider whether he is able with ten
   16: 6 "The manager told him, 'Take your bill, sit down quickly,
   19:30 you will find a colt tied there, which no one has ever ridden.
   24:49 but stay in the city until you have been clothed with power from on
Jn 8: 2 the people gathered around him, and he sat down to teach them.

    12:14 Jesus found a young donkey and **sat** upon it, as it is written,
    19:13 and **sat down** on the judge's seat at a place known as the Stone
Ac 2: 3 be tongues of fire that separated and **came to rest** on each of them.
    2:30 and knew that God had promised him on oath that he *would* **place**
    8:31 it to me?" So he invited Philip to come up and **sit** with him.
    12:21 **sat** on his throne and delivered a public address to the people.
    13:14 On the Sabbath *they* entered the synagogue and **sat down**.
    16:13 We **sat down** and began to speak to the women who had gathered
    18:11 So Paul **stayed** for a year and a half, teaching them the word of
    25: 6 and the next day he **convened the court** [*+1037+2093+3836*] and
    25:17 but **convened** the court the next day and ordered the man to be
1Co 6: 4 **appoint as judges** even men of little account in the church!
    10: 7 "The people **sat down** to eat and drink and got up to indulge in
Eph 1:20 the dead and **seated** him at his right hand in the heavenly realms,
2Th 2: 4 or is worshiped, so that he **sets** himself **up** in God's temple,
Heb 1: 3 for sins, *he* **sat down** at the right hand of the Majesty in heaven.
    8: 1 who **sat down** at the right hand of the throne of the Majesty in
    10:12 time one sacrifice for sins, *he* **sat down** at the right hand of God.
    12: 2 its shame, and **sat down** at the right hand of the throne of God.
Rev 3:21 I will give the right *to* **sit** with me on my throne, just as I overcame
    3:21 just as I overcame and **sat down** with my Father on his throne.
    20: 4 I saw thrones on which *were* **seated** those who had been given

2768 καθίημι, *kathiēmi* [4] [√ *2848 + 1640*]

  untranslated [1], let down [1], lowered [*+5899*] [1], lowered [1]

Lk 5:19 and **lowered** him on his mat through the tiles into the middle of the
Ac 9:25 and **lowered** [*+5899*] him in a basket through an opening in the
    10:11 and something like a large sheet being let down **[RPG]** to earth
    11: 5 I saw something like a large sheet *being* **let down** from heaven by

2769 καθιστάνω, *kathistanō*   Not used in UBS/NIV
  [√ *2848 + 2705*]

2770 καθίστημι, *kathistēmi* [21] [√ *2848 + 2705*]

  made [5], put in charge [5], appointed [3], *untranslated* [1],
  appoint [1], appoints [1], becomes [1], escorted [1], keep [1],
  puts in charge [1], turn over to [1]

Mt 24:45 whom the master *has* **put in charge** of the servants in his
    24:47 tell you the truth, *he will* **put** him **in charge** of all his possessions.
    25:21 faithful with a few things; *I will* **put** you **in charge** of many things.
    25:23 faithful with a few things; *I will* **put** you **in charge** of many things.
Lk 12:14 "Man, who **appointed** me a judge or an arbiter between you?"
    12:42 whom the master **puts in charge** of his servants to give them their
    12:44 tell you the truth, *he will* **put** him **in charge** of all his possessions.
Ac 6: 3 and wisdom. *We will* **turn** this responsibility **over to** them
    7:10 king of Egypt; so *he* **made** him ruler over Egypt and all his palace.
    7:27 Moses aside and said, 'Who **made** you ruler and judge over us?
    7:35 had rejected with the words, 'Who **made** you ruler and judge?'
 —17:15 The men *who* **escorted** Paul brought him to Athens and then left
Ro 5:19 the disobedience of the one man the many *were* **made** sinners,
    5:19 the obedience of the one man the many *will be* **made** righteous.
Tit 1: 5 out what was left unfinished and **appoint** elders in every town,
Heb 5: 1 and *is* **appointed** to represent them in matters related to God,
    7:28 For the law **appoints** as high priests men who are weak; but the
    8: 3 Every high priest *is* **appointed** to offer both gifts and sacrifices,
Jas 3: 6 also is a fire, a world of evil **[NIE]** among the parts of the body.
    4: 4 Anyone who chooses to be a friend of the world **becomes** an
2Pe 1: 8 *they will* **keep** you from being ineffective and unproductive in

2771 καθό, *katho* [4] [√ *2848 + 4005*]

  untranslated [1], according to what [*+1569+2848+4005*] [1],
  according to what [1], that [*+2848+4005*] [1]

Ro 8:26 We do not know what we **[NIE] [NIE]** ought to pray for,
2Co 8:12 is there, the gift is acceptable **according to what** one has,
    8:12 to what one has, not **according to what** he does not have.
1Pe 4:13 But rejoice **that** you participate in the sufferings of Christ,

2772 καθολικός, *katholikos*   Not used in UBS/NIV
  [√ *2848 + 3910*]

2773 καθόλου, *katholou* [1] [√ *2848 + 3910*]

  at all [1]

Ac 4:18 commanded them not to speak or teach **at all** in the name of Jesus.

2774 καθοπλίζω, *kathoplizō* [1] [√ *2848 + 3960*]

  fully armed [1]

Lk 11:21 "When a strong man, **fully armed**, guards his own house, his

2775 καθοράω, *kathoraō* [1] [√ *2848 + 3972*]

  clearly seen [1]

Ro 1:20 *have been* **clearly seen**, being understood from what has been

2776 καθότι, *kathoti* [6] [√ *2848 + 4005 + 5515*]

  because [3], as [*+323*] [1], as [1], for [1]

Lk 1: 7 But they had no children, **because** Elizabeth was barren; and they
   19: 9 come to this house, **because** this man, too, is a son of Abraham.
Ac 2:24 **because** it was impossible for death to keep its hold on him.
    2:45 and goods, they gave to anyone **as** [*+323*] he had need.
    4:35 the apostles' feet, and it was distributed to anyone **as** he had need.
    17:31 **For** he has set a day when he will judge the world with justice by

2777 καθώς, *kathōs* [182] [√ *2848 + 6055*]

  καθώς γέγραπται, γεγραμμένος (as it is written) [28] Mt
    26:24; Mk 1:2; 9:13; 14:21; Lk 2:23; Jn 6:31; 12:14; Ac 7:42;
    15:15; Ro 1:17; 2:24; 3:4,10; 4:17; 8:36; 9:13,33; 10:15; 11:8,26;
    15:3,9,21; 1Co 1:31; 2:9; 10:7; 2Co 8:15; 9:9; cf. 2Pe 3:15

  as [80], just as [50], *untranslated* [9], even as [6], like [3], since
  [3], and [2], because [2], for [2], how [2], in accordance with [2],
  what [2], according to [1], any more than [*+4024*] [1], as much as
  [1], as well as [1], but [*+4024*] [1], consider§ [1], equal with
  [*+2779*] [1], in the words§ of [1], just what [1], just [1], suffered§
  [1], that way [1], that [1], the same [*+3931*] [1], this agrees with
  [1], this is why [1], what usually did [1], whatever [1], which
  agrees with [1]

Mt 21: 6 The disciples went and did **as** Jesus had instructed them.
    26:24 The Son of Man will go **just as** it is written about him. But woe to
    28: 6 He is not here; he has risen, **just as** he said. Come and see the
Mk 1: 2 **[NIE]** It is written in Isaiah the prophet: "I will send my messenger
    4:33 Jesus spoke the word to them, **as much as** they could understand.
    9:13 to him everything they wished, **just as** it is written about him."
    11: 6 They answered **as** Jesus had told them to, and the people let them
    14:16 went into the city and found things **just as** Jesus had told them.
    14:21 The Son of Man will go **just as** it is written about him. But woe to
    15: 8 came up and asked Pilate to do for them **what** he **usually did**.
    16: 7 of you into Galilee. There you will see him, **just as** he told you.' "
Lk 1: 2 **just as** they were handed down to us by those who from the first
    1:55 and his descendants forever, **even as** he said to our fathers."
    1:70 (**as** he said through his holy prophets of long ago),
    2:20 they had heard and seen, which were **just as** they had been told.
    2:23 (**as** it is written in the Law of the Lord, "Every firstborn male is to
    5:14 and offer the sacrifices **that** Moses commanded for your cleansing,
    6:31 Do to others **as** you would have them do to you.
    6:36 Be merciful, **just as** your Father is merciful.
    11: 1 to him, "Lord, teach us to pray, **just as** John taught his disciples."
    11:30 For **as** Jonah was a sign to the Ninevites, so also will the Son of
    17:26 "**Just as** it was in the days of Noah, so also will it be in the days of
    17:28 "It was **the same** [*+3931*] in the days of Lot. People were eating
    19:32 who were sent ahead went and found it **just as** he had told them.
    22:13 They left and found things **just as** Jesus had told them. So they
    22:29 I confer on you a kingdom, **just as** my Father conferred one on me,
    24:24 went to the tomb and found it **just as** the women had said,
    24:39 and see; a ghost does not have flesh and bones, **as** you see I have."
Jn 1:23 John replied **in the words§ of** Isaiah the prophet, "I am the voice of
    3:14 **Just as** Moses lifted up the snake in the desert, so the Son of Man

5: 23 that all may honor the Son **just as** they honor the Father. He who
5: 30 I judge *only* **as** I hear, and my judgment is just, for I seek not to
6: 31 Our forefathers ate the manna in the desert; **as** it is written:
6: 57 **Just as** the living Father sent me and I live because of the Father,
6: 58 and died, **but** [*+4024*] he who feeds on this bread will live forever."
7: 38 Whoever believes in me, **as** the Scripture has said, streams of
8: 28 nothing on my own but speak **just** what the Father has taught me.
10: 15 **just as** the Father knows me and I know the Father—and I lay
12: 14 Jesus found a young donkey and sat upon it, **as** it is written,
12: 50 So whatever I say is **just what** the Father has told me to say."
13: 15 I have set you an example that you should do **as** I have done for
13: 33 You will look for me, and **just as** I told the Jews, so I tell you now:
13: 34 new command I give you: Love one another. **As** I have loved you,
14: 27 my peace I give you. I do not give to you **as** the world gives.
14: 31 and that I do exactly **what** my Father has commanded me.
15: 4 **[NIE]** No branch can bear fruit by itself; it must remain in the
15: 9 "**As** the Father has loved me, so have I loved you. Now remain in
15: 10 **just as** I have obeyed my Father's commands and remain in his
15: 12 My command is this: Love each other **as** I have loved you.
17: 2 **For** you granted him authority over all people that he might give
17: 11 the name you gave me—so that they may be one **as** we are one.
17: 14 for they are not of the world **any more** [*+4024*] **than** I am of the
17: 16 They are not of the world, **even as** I am not of it.
17: 18 **As** you sent me into the world, I have sent them into the world.
17: 21 of them may be one, Father, **just as** you are in me and I am in you.
17: 22 the glory that you gave me, that they may be one **as** we are one:
17: 23 that you sent me and have loved them **even as** you have loved me.
19: 40 of linen. This was **in accordance with** Jewish burial customs.
20: 21 "Peace be with you! **As** the Father has sent me, I am sending you."
Ac   2: 4 and began to speak in other tongues **as** the Spirit enabled them.
2: 22 which God did among you through him, **as** you yourselves know.
7: 17 "**As** the time drew near for God to fulfill his promise to Abraham,
7: 42 **This agrees with** what is written in the book of the prophets:
7: 44 It had been made **as** God directed Moses, according to the pattern
7: 48 High does not live in houses made by men. **As** the prophet says:
11: 29 The disciples, each **according to** his ability, decided to provide
15: 8 them by giving the Holy Spirit to them, **just as** he did to us.
15: 14 Simon has described to us **how** God at first showed his concern by
15: 15 words of the prophets are in agreement with this, **as** it is written:
22: 3 and was just as zealous for God **as** any of you are today.
Ro   1: 13 a harvest among you, **just as** I have had among the other Gentiles.
1: 17 righteousness that is by faith from first to last, **just as** it is written:
1: 28 **since** they did not think it worthwhile to retain the knowledge of
2: 24 **As** it is written: "God's name is blasphemed among the Gentiles
3: 4 Not at all! Let God be true, and every man a liar. **As** it is written:
3: 8 **as** we are being slanderously reported as saying and as some claim
3: 8 slanderously reported as saying and **as** some claim that we say—
3: 10 **As** it is written: "There is no one righteous, not even one;
4: 17 **As** it is written: "I have made you a father of many nations."
8: 36 **As** it is written: "For your sake we face death all day long; we are
9: 13 **Just as** it is written: "Jacob I loved, but Esau I hated."
9: 29 It is **just as** Isaiah said previously: "Unless the Lord Almighty had
9: 33 **As** it is written: "See, I lay in Zion a stone that causes men to
10: 15 **As** it is written, "How beautiful are the feet of those who bring good
11: 8 **as** it is written: "God gave them a spirit of stupor, eyes so that they
11: 26 And so all Israel will be saved, **as** it is written: "The deliverer will
15: 3 For even Christ did not please himself but, **as** it is written:
15: 7 Accept one another, then, **just as** Christ accepted you, in order to
15: 9 so that the Gentiles may glorify God for his mercy, **as** it is written:
15: 21 Rather, **as** it is written: "Those who were not told about him will
1Co 1: 6 **because** our testimony about Christ was confirmed in you.
1: 31 Therefore, **as** it is written: "Let him who boasts boast in the Lord."
2: 9 However, **as** it is written: "No eye has seen, no ear has heard,
4: 17 **which agrees with** what I teach everywhere in every church.
5: 7 that you may be a new batch without yeast—**as** you really are.
8: 2 The man who thinks he knows something does not yet know **as** he
10: 6 to keep us from setting our hearts on evil things **as** they did.
10: 7 Do not be idolaters, **as** some of them were; as it is written:
10: 8 We should not commit sexual immorality, **as** some of them did—
10: 9 We should not test the Lord, **as** some of them did—and were killed
10: 33 **even as** I try to please everybody in every way. For I am not
11: 1 Follow my example, **as** I follow the example of Christ.
11: 2 and for holding to the teachings, **just as** I passed them on to you.
12: 11 same Spirit, and he gives them to each one, **just as** he determines.
12: 18 parts in the body, every one of them, **just as** he wanted them to be.
13: 12 I know in part; then I shall know fully, **even as** I am fully known.

14: 34 not allowed to speak, but must be in submission, **as** the Law says.
15: 38 But God gives it a body **as** he has determined, and to each kind of
15: 49 And **just as** we have borne the likeness of the earthly man,
2Co 1: 5 For **just as** the sufferings of Christ flow over into our lives,
1: 14 **as** you have understood us in part, you will come to understand
4: 1 Therefore, **since** through God's mercy we have this ministry,
6: 16 **As** God has said: "I will live with them and walk among them,
8: 5 And they did not do **as** we expected, but they gave themselves first
8: 6 So we urged Titus, **since** he had earlier made a beginning,
8: 15 **as** it is written: "He who gathered much did not have too much,
9: 3 prove hollow, but that you may be ready, **as** I said you would be.
9: 7 Each *man* should give **what** he has decided in his heart to give,
9: 9 **As** it is written: "He has scattered abroad his gifts to the poor;
10: 7 he should consider again that we belong to Christ **just as** much as
11: 12 considered **equal** [*+2779*] **with** us in the things they boast about.
Gal 2: 7 the gospel to the Gentiles, **just as** Peter had been to the Jews.
3: 6 **Consider**[s] Abraham: "He believed God, and it was credited to him
5: 21 I warn you, **as** I did before, that those who live like this will not
Eph 1: 4 **For** he chose us in him before the creation of the world to be holy
3: 3 made known to me by revelation, **as** I have already written briefly.
4: 4 **just as** you were called to one hope when you were called—
4: 17 on it in the Lord, that you must no longer live **as** the Gentiles do,
4: 21 and were taught in him **in accordance with** the truth that is in
4: 32 forgiving each other, **just as** in Christ God forgave you.
5: 2 **just as** Christ loved us and gave himself up for us as a fragrant
5: 3 or of greed, **because** these are improper for God's holy people.
5: 25 **just as** Christ loved the church and gave himself up for her
5: 29 but he feeds and cares for it, **just as** Christ does the church—
Php 1: 7 **[NIE]** It is right for me to feel this way about all of you, since I
2: 12 Therefore, my dear friends, **as** you have always obeyed—not only
3: 17 and take note of those who live according to the pattern we **[NIE]**
Col 1: 6 All over the world **[RPG]** this gospel is bearing fruit
1: 6 **just as** it has been doing among you since the day you heard it
1: 7 **[NIE]** You learned it from Epaphras, our dear fellow servant,
2: 7 and built up in him, strengthened in the faith **as** you were taught,
3: 13 may have against one another. Forgive **as** the Lord forgave you.
1Th 1: 5 **[NIE]** You know how we lived among you for your sake.
2: 2 had previously suffered and been insulted in Philippi, **as** you know,
2: 4 we speak **as** men approved by God to be entrusted with the gospel.
2: 5 **[NIE]** You know now we never used flattery, nor did we put on a
2: 13 but as it actually is, the word of God, which is at work in you who
2: 14 the same things those churches **suffered**[s] from the Jews,
3: 4 be persecuted. And it turned out **that way**, as you well know.
4: 1 we **[NIE]** instructed you how to live in order to please God,
4: 1 you how to live in order to please God, **as** in fact you are living.
4: 6 men for all such sins, **as** we have already told you and warned you.
4: 11 own business and to work with your hands, **just as** we told you,
4: 13 fall asleep, or to grieve **like** the rest of men, who have no hope.
5: 11 one another and build each other up, **just as** in fact you are doing.
2Th 1: 3 We ought always to thank God for you, brothers, **and** rightly so,
3: 1 Lord may spread rapidly and be honored, **just as** it was with you.
1Ti 1: 3 **As** I urged you when I went into Macedonia, stay there in Ephesus
Heb 3: 7 So, **as** the Holy Spirit says: "Today, if you hear his voice,
4: 3 that rest, **just as** God has said, "So I declared on oath in my anger,
4: 7 when a long time later he spoke through David, **as** was said before:
5: 3 sacrifices for his own sins, **as well as** for the sins of the people.
5: 6 **And** he says in another place, "You are a priest forever, in the order
8: 5 **This is why** Moses was warned when he was about to build the
10: 25 **as** some are in the habit of doing, but let us encourage one
11: 12 came descendants as numerous **as** the stars in the sky and as
1Pe 4: 10 Each one should use **whatever** gift he has received to serve others,
2Pe 1: 14 soon put it aside, **as** our Lord Jesus Christ has made clear to me.
3: 15 **just as** our dear brother Paul also wrote you with the wisdom that
1Jn 2: 6 Whoever claims to live in him must walk **as** Jesus did.
2: 18 and **as** you have heard that the antichrist is coming, even now
2: 27 is real, not counterfeit—**just as** it has taught you, remain in him.
3: 2 he appears, we shall be like him, for we shall see him **as** he is.
3: 3 who has this hope in him purifies himself, **just as** he is pure.
3: 7 He who does what is right is righteous, **just as** he is righteous.
3: 12 Do not be **like** Cain, who belonged to the evil one and murdered
3: 23 Jesus Christ, and to love one another **as** he commanded us.
4: 17 on the day of judgment, because in this world we are **like** him.
2Jn 1: 4 children walking in the truth, **just as** the Father commanded us.
1: 6 **As** you have heard from the beginning, his command is that you
3Jn 1: 2 all may go well with you, **even as** your soul is getting along well.
1: 3 faithfulness to the truth and **how** you continue to walk in the truth.

2778 καθώσπερ, *kathōsper* [1] [√ *2848 + 6055 + 4302*]

just as [1]

Heb 5: 4 honor upon himself; he must be called by God, **just as** Aaron was.

2779 καί, *kai* [9161 / 9140] See Index of Articles, Etc.

[→ *2743, 2781, 2788, 2792, 2793, 2795, 2796, 2797, 2817, 2829, 4298, 5476*]

and [4829], *untranslated* [2904], also [239], then [228], but [174], even [97], so [94], or [57], yet [35], too [34], with [34], and then [25], when [22], and also [14], both [14], as [12], and so [11], and yet [11], now [11], and [+2627] [9], as well [9], so that [9], if [8], in fact [8], while [8], still [7], and even [6], as well as [6], where [6], nor [5], what do want with [+5515] [5], now [+2627] [4], suddenly [+2627] [4], that [4], though [+1623] [4], though [4], whether [4], again [3], along with [3], and too [3], as for [3], but [+247] [3], even though [3], in turn [3], including [3], nor [+4024] [3], until [3], afterward [2], and as well [2], and when [2], at that moment [+2627] [2], because [2], but also [2], but even [2], he [2], in the same way [+4048] [2], indeed [2], just then [+2627] [2], later [2], man [+135+4922] [2], meanwhile [2], now [+2627+3814] [2], or even [2], rather than [+4024] [2], than for [+3590] [2], then [+2627] [2], therefore [2], thus [2], yet even [2], 42 [+1545+5477] [1], 430 [+5484+5558] [1], 450 [+4299+5484] [1], accompanied by [+2262] [1], although [+247] [1], and [+1181] [1], and [+247+1145] [1], and also [+247] [1], and as good as [+4047] [1], and both [1], and even more [+4707+5148] [1], and indeed [1], and now [1], and others [1], and still [1], and though [1], and up [1], as can see [+2627] [1], as it is [1], at least [+1569] [1], at that [1], at this [+2627] [1], at this [1], because [+1145+1623] [1], before [+4048] [1], both [+4047] [1], both of you [+899+5148] [1], but only [+1623] [1], but still [1], by [1], came along [+2627] [1], eighteen [+1274+3893] [1], equal with [+2777] [1], even [+1145] [1], even [+1569] [1], even [+247] [1], even [+2627] [1], even when [1], finally [1], for [1], forty-six [+1971+5477] [1], forty-two [+1545+5477] [1], fully convinced [+3857+4275] [1], furthermore [1], greatly increased [+889+4437] [1], if so [1], in addition [+247] [1], in fact [+1142] [1], in this same way [+4048] [1], including [+899] [1], indeed [+247] [1], indeed [+2627] [1], instead of [+4049] [1], it is the same [+4048] [1], it is true [1], just [+1569] [1], just as though [+899+1651+3836] [1], likewise [+4048] [1], matched [+4048] [1], met [+2627] [1], more than that [1], moved about freely [+1660+1744] [1], neither [+4024] [1], nor [+3590] [1], now [+1181] [1], on [+2759+3836] [1], on both sides [+2277+3957] [1], on each side [+1696+1949] [1], on one occasion [+2627] [1], on one occasion [1], on [1], once [+1181] [1], once [1], one day [+1181] [1], one on each side [+1949+1949] [1], or [+4024] [1], or take as an example [+2627] [1], rather than [+3590] [1], same as [+4005] [1], searched intently and with the greatest care [+1699+2001] [1], since [1], so too [1], some [1], soon [1], than that [+3590] [1], the same as [+6055] [1], the same way [+6055] [1], the two of you [+899+5148] [1], their [1], then [+1696] [1], there [+2627] [1], they [+899+899+3412+3836] [1], thirty-eight [+3893+5558] [1], though [+1145] [1], though [+247+1623] [1], to this [1], together with [1], too [+899+3836] [1], what if [1], what is more [+247+1254+3667+4024] [1], what is more [+247+3529] [1], when [+2627] [1], where [+2627] [1], why do involve [+5515] [1], with that [+2627] [1], with that [1], without [+3590] [1], without [+4024] [1], without warning [+2627] [1], yet [+2627] [1]

2780 Καϊάφας, *Kaiaphas* [9]

Caiaphas [9]

Mt 26: 3 in the palace of the high priest, whose name was **Caiaphas,**
26:57 Those who had arrested Jesus took him to **Caiaphas,** the high
Lk 3: 2 during the high priesthood of Annas and **Caiaphas,** the word of
Jn 11:49 Then one of them, named **Caiaphas,** who was high priest that year,
18:13 who was the father-in-law *of* **Caiaphas,** the high priest that year.
18:14 **Caiaphas** was the one who had advised the Jews that it would be
18:24 Then Annas sent him, still bound, to **Caiaphas** the high priest.

18:28 Then the Jews led Jesus from **Caiaphas** to the palace of the Roman
Ac 4: 6 and so were **Caiaphas,** John, Alexander and the other men of the

2781 καίγε, *kaige* Not used in UBS/NIV [√ *2779 + 1145*]

2782 Κάϊν, *Kain* [3]

Cain [3]

Heb 11: 4 By faith Abel offered God a better sacrifice than **Cain** did.
1Jn 3:12 Do not be like **Cain,** who belonged to the evil one and murdered
Jude 1:11 They have taken the way *of* **Cain;** they have rushed for profit into

2783 Καϊνάμ, *Kainam* [2] [→ *2784*]

Cainan [1], Kenan [1]

Lk 3:36 the son *of* **Cainan,** the son of Arphaxad, the son of Shem,
3:37 of Enoch, the son of Jared, the son of Mahalalel, the son *of* **Kenan,**

2784 Καϊνάν, *Kainan* Not used in UBS/NIV [√ *2783*]

2785 καινός, *kainos* [42] [→ *362, 363, 364, 1589, 1590, 2786, 2787*]

καινός γῆ (new earth) [2] 2Pe 3:13; Rev 21:1

καινός διαθήκη (new covenant) [5] Lk 22:20; 1Co 11:25; 2Co 3:6; Heb 8:8; 9:15

καινός ἐντολή (new commandment) [4] Jn 13:34; 1Jn 2:7,8; 2Jn 1:5

καινός Ἰερουσαλήμ (new Jerusalem) [2] Rev 3:12; 21:2

καινός οὐρανός (new heaven) [2] 2Pe 3:13; Rev 21:1

new [39], anew [2], latest [1]

Mt 9:17 No, they pour new wine into **new** wineskins, and both are
13:52 who brings out of his storeroom **new** *treasures* as well as old."
26:29 that day when I drink it **anew** with you in my Father's kingdom."
27:60 and placed it in his own **new** tomb that he had cut out of the rock.
Mk 1:27 each other, "What is this? A **new** teaching—and with authority!
2:21 If he does, the **new** piece will pull away from the old, making the
2:22 will be ruined. No, he pours new wine into **new** wineskins."
14:25 vine until that day when I drink it **anew** in the kingdom of God."
16:17 name they will drive out demons; they will speak *in* **new** tongues;
Lk 5:36 "No one tears a patch from a **new** garment and sews it on an old
5:36 If he does, he will have torn the **new** garment, and the patch from
5:36 new garment, and the patch from the **new** will not match the old.
5:38 No, new wine must be poured into **new** wineskins.
22:20 saying, "This cup is the **new** covenant in my blood, which is poured
Jn 13:34 "A **new** command I give you: Love one another. As I have loved
19:41 there was a garden, and in the garden a **new** tomb, in which no one
Ac 17:19 "May we know what this **new** teaching is that you are presenting?
17:21 doing nothing but talking about and listening to the **latest** ideas.)
1Co 11:25 he took the cup, saying, "This cup is the **new** covenant in my blood;
2Co 3: 6 He has made us competent as ministers *of* a **new** covenant—
5:17 Therefore, if anyone is in Christ, he is a **new** creation; the old has
5:17 he is a new creation; the old has gone, the **new** has come!
Gal 6:15 nor uncircumcision means anything; what counts is a **new** creation.
Eph 2:15 His purpose was to create in himself one **new** man out of the two,
4:24 and to put on the **new** self, created to be like God in true
Heb 8: 8 when I will make a **new** covenant with the house of Israel
8:13 By calling this covenant "**new,**" he has made the first one obsolete;
9:15 For this reason Christ is the mediator *of* a **new** covenant, that those
2Pc 3:13 But in keeping with his promise we are looking forward to a **new**
3:13 promise we are looking forward to a new heaven and a **new** earth,
1Jn 2: 7 Dear friends, I am not writing you a **new** command but an old one,
2: 8 Yet I am writing you a **new** command; its truth is seen in him
2Jn 1: 5 I am not writing you a **new** command but one we have had from
Rev 2:17 I will also give him a white stone with a **new** name written on it,
3:12 of my God and the name of the city of my God, the **new** Jerusalem,
3:12 heaven from my God; and I will also write on him my **new** name.
5: 9 And they sang a **new** song: "You are worthy to take the scroll
14: 3 And they sang a **new** song before the throne and before the four
21: 1 Then I saw a **new** heaven and a new earth, for the first heaven
21: 1 Then I saw a new heaven and a **new** earth, for the first heaven

21: 2 I saw the Holy City, the **new** Jerusalem, coming down out of
21: 5 who was seated on the throne said, "I am making everything **new**!"

2786 καινότης, *kainotēs* [2] [√ *2785*]

new way [1], new [1]

Ro 6: 4 dead through the glory of the Father, we too may live a **new** life.
7: 6 released from the law so that we serve in the **new way** of the Spirit,

2787 καινοφωνία, *kainophōnia* Not used in UBS/NIV [√ *2785 + 5889*]

2788 καίπερ, *kaiper* [5] [√ *2779 + 4302*]

even though [2], though [2], although [1]

Php 3: 4 **though** I myself have reasons for such confidence. If anyone else
Heb 5: 8 **Although** he was a son, he learned obedience from what he
7: 5 **even though** their brothers are descended from Abraham.
12:17 about no change of mind, **though** he sought the blessing with tears.
2Pe 1:12 **even though** you know them and are firmly established in the truth

2789 καιρός, *kairos* [85] [→ *177, 178, 2320, 2321, 2322, 2323, 4672*]

time [42], times [8], proper time [4], appointed time [3], harvest time [3], opportunity [3], right time [3], age [2], dates [2], present time [2], seasons [2], a while [1], age [*+2461*] [1], always [*+1877+4246*] [1], appointed season [1], due time [1], find convenient [*+3561*] [1], make the most of opportunity [*+1973+3836*] [1], occasions [1], opportune time [1], present [*+3814+3836*] [1], season [1]

Mt 8:29 "Have you come here to torture us before the **appointed time**?"
11:25 At that **time** Jesus said, "I praise you, Father, Lord of heaven
12: 1 At that **time** Jesus went through the grainfields on the Sabbath.
13:30 At that **time** I will tell the harvesters: First collect the weeds
14: 1 At that **time** Herod the tetrarch heard the reports about Jesus,
16: 3 of the sky, but you cannot interpret the signs *of* the **times**.
21:34 When the harvest **time** approached, he sent his servants to the
21:41 who will give him his share of the crop at **harvest time**."
24:45 in his household to give them their food at the **proper time**?
26:18 and tell him, 'The Teacher says: My **appointed time** is near.
Mk 1:15 "The **time** has come," he said. "The kingdom of God is near.
10:30 will fail to receive a hundred **times** as much in this present **age**
11:13 he found nothing but leaves, because it was not the **season** for figs.
12: 2 At **harvest time** he sent a servant to the tenants to collect from
13:33 Be on guard! Be alert! You do not know when that **time** will come.
Lk 1:20 not believe my words, which will come true at their **proper time**."
4:13 had finished all this tempting, he left him until an **opportune time**.
8:13 They believe for **a while**, but in the time of testing they fall away.
8:13 They believe for a while, but in the **time** of testing they fall away.
12:42 his servants to give them their food allowance at the **proper time**?
12:56 How is it that you don't know how to interpret this **present time**?
13: 1 Now there were some present at that **time** who told Jesus about the
18:30 will fail to receive many times as much in this **age** and, in the age
19:44 because you did not recognize the **time** of God's coming to you."
20:10 At **harvest time** he sent a servant to the tenants so they would give
21: 8 come in my name, claiming, 'I am he,' and, 'The **time** is near.'
21:24 Jerusalem will be trampled on by the Gentiles until the **times** of the
21:36 Be **always** [*+1877+4246*] on the watch, and pray that you may be
Jn 7: 6 Jesus told them, "The **right time** for me has not yet come;
7: 6 "The right time for me has not yet come; for you any **time** is right.
7: 8 up to this Feast, because for me the **right time** has not yet come."
Ac 1: 7 to know the times or **dates** the Father has set by his own authority.
3:19 be wiped out, that **times** of refreshing may come from the Lord,
7:20 "At that **time** Moses was born, and he was no ordinary child.
12: 1 It was about this **time** that King Herod arrested some who
13:11 and for a **time** you will be unable to see the light of the sun."
14:17 by giving you rain from heaven and crops in their **seasons**,
17:26 and he determined the **times** set for them and the exact places
19:23 About that **time** there arose a great disturbance about the Way.
24:25 may leave. When *I* **find** it **convenient** [*+3561*], I will send for you."
Ro 3:26 he did it to demonstrate his justice at the present **time**, so as to be
5: 6 You see, at just the **right time**, when we were still powerless,

8:18 I consider that our **present** [*+3814+3836*] sufferings are not worth
9: 9 "At the appointed **time** I will return, and Sarah will have a son."
11: 5 So too, at the present **time** there is a remnant chosen by grace.
13:11 And do this, understanding the **present time**. The hour has come
1Co 4: 5 Therefore judge nothing before the **appointed time**; wait till the
7: 5 Do not deprive each other except by mutual consent and for a **time**,
7:29 What I mean, brothers, is that the **time** is short. From now on those
2Co 6: 2 For he says, "In the **time** of my favor I heard you, and in the day
6: 2 I tell you, now is the **time** of God's favor, now is the day of
8:14 At the present **time** your plenty will supply what they need,
Gal 4:10 You are observing *special* days and months and **seasons** and years!
6: 9 for at the proper **time** we will reap a harvest if we do not give up.
6:10 Therefore, as we have **opportunity**, let us do good to all people,
Eph 1:10 to be put into effect when the **times** will have reached their
2:12 remember that *at* that **time** you were separate from Christ,
5:16 making the most of every **opportunity**, because the days are evil.
6:18 And pray in the Spirit on all **occasions** with all kinds of prayers
Col 4: 5 outsiders; **make the most of** *every* **opportunity** [*+1973+3836*].
1Th 2:17 when we were torn away from you for a short **time** (in person,
5: 1 brothers, about times and **dates** we do not need to write to you,
2Th 2: 6 is holding him back, so that he may be revealed at the proper **time**.
1Ti 2: 6 as a ransom for all men—the testimony given *in* its **proper time**.
4: 1 The Spirit clearly says that in later **times** some will abandon the
6:15 which God will bring about *in* his own **time**—God, the blessed
2Ti 3: 1 But mark this: There will be terrible **times** in the last days.
4: 3 For the **time** will come when men will not put up with sound
4: 6 out like a drink offering, and the **time** has come for my departure.
Tit 1: 3 and at his **appointed season** he brought his word to light through
Heb 9: 9 This is an illustration for the present **time**, indicating that the gifts
9:10 external regulations applying until the **time** of the new order.
11:11 By faith Abraham, even though he was past **age** [*+2461*]—
11:15 country they had left, they would have had **opportunity** to return.
1Pe 1: 5 coming of the salvation that is ready to be revealed in the last **time**.
1:11 trying to find out the **time** and circumstances to which the Spirit of
4:17 For it is **time** for judgment to begin with the family of God;
5: 6 under God's mighty hand, that he may lift you up in **due time**.
Rev 1: 3 and take to heart what is written in it, because the **time** is near.
11:18 The **time** has come for judging the dead, and for rewarding your
12:12 He is filled with fury, because he knows that his **time** is short."
12:14 where she would be taken care of *for* a **time**, times and half a time,
12:14 where she would be taken care of *for* a time, **times** and half a time,
12:14 care of for a time, times and half a **time**, out of the serpent's reach.
22:10 the words of the prophecy of this book, because the **time** is near.

2790 Καῖσαρ, *Kaisar* [29] [→ *2791*]

Caesar [20], Caesar's [9]

Mt 22:17 what is your opinion? Is it right to pay taxes *to* **Caesar** or not?"
22:21 "**Caesar's**," they replied. Then he said to them, "Give to Caesar
22:21 Then he said to them, "Give *to* **Caesar** what is Caesar's, and to God
22:21 Then he said to them, "Give to Caesar what is **Caesar's**, and to God
Mk 12:14 accordance with the truth. Is it right to pay taxes *to* **Caesar** or not?
12:16 portrait is this? And whose inscription?" "**Caesar's**," they replied.
12:17 "Give *to* **Caesar** what is Caesar's and to God what is God's."
12:17 "Give to Caesar what is **Caesar's** and to God what is God's."
Lk 2: 1 In those days **Caesar** Augustus issued a decree that a census
3: 1 In the fifteenth year of the reign *of* Tiberius **Caesar**—when Pontius
20:22 Is it right for us to pay taxes *to* **Caesar** or not?"
20:25 "**Caesar's**," they replied. He said to them, "Then give to Caesar
20:25 He said to them, "Then give *to* **Caesar** what is Caesar's, and to God
20:25 said to them, "Then give to Cæsar what is **Caesar's**, and to God
23: 2 He opposes payment of taxes *to* **Caesar** and claims to be Christ,
Jn 19:12 kept shouting, "If you let this man go, you are no friend *of* **Caesar**.
19:12 friend of Caesar. Anyone who claims to be a king opposes **Caesar**."
19:15 "We have no king but **Caesar**," the chief priests answered.
Ac 17: 7 They are all defying **Caesar's** decrees, saying that there is another
25: 8 the law of the Jews or against the temple or against **Caesar**."
25:10 "I am now standing before **Caesar's** court, where I ought to be
25:11 no one has the right to hand me over to them. I appeal to **Caesar**!"
25:12 with his council, he declared: "You have appealed *to* **Caesar**.
25:12 declared: "You have appealed to Caesar. To **Caesar** you will go!"
25:21 I ordered him held until I could send him to **Caesar**."
26:32 man could have been set free if he had not appealed to **Caesar**."
27:24 You must stand trial before **Caesar**; and God has graciously given
28:19 when the Jews objected, I was compelled to appeal to **Caesar**—

Php 4:22 you greetings, especially those who belong to **Caesar's** household.

2791 Καισάρεια, *Kaisareia* [17] [√ *2790*]

Caesarea [17]

Mt 16:13 When Jesus came to the region *of* **Caesarea** Philippi, he asked his
Mk   8:27 and his disciples went on to the villages around **Caesarea** Philippi.
Ac   8:40 preaching the gospel in all the towns until he reached **Caesarea**.
     9:30 they took him down to **Caesarea** and sent him off to Tarsus.
    10: 1 At **Caesarea** there was a man named Cornelius, a centurion in
    10:24 The following day he arrived in **Caesarea**. Cornelius had
    11:11 then three men who had been sent to me from **Caesarea** stopped at
    12:19 Then Herod went from Judea to **Caesarea** and stayed there a
    18:22 When he landed at **Caesarea**, he went up and greeted the church
    21: 8 we reached **Caesarea** and stayed at the house of Philip the
    21:16 Some of the disciples from **Caesarea** accompanied us and brought
    23:23 and two hundred spearmen to go to **Caesarea** at nine tonight.
    23:33 When the cavalry arrived in **Caesarea**, they delivered the letter to
    25: 1 in the province, Festus went up from **Caesarea** to Jerusalem,
    25: 4 Festus answered, "Paul is being held at **Caesarea**, and I myself am
    25: 6 spending eight or ten days with them, he went down to **Caesarea**,
    25:13 and Bernice arrived at **Caesarea** to pay their respects to Festus.

2792 καίτοι, *kaitoi* [2] [√ *2779 + 5520*]

and yet [1], yet [1]

Ac 14:17 **Yet** he has not left himself without testimony: He has shown
Heb 4: 3 'They shall never enter my rest.' " **And yet** his work has been

2793 καίτοιγε, *kaitoige* [1] [√ *2779 + 5520 + 1145*]

although in fact [1]

Jn   4: 2 **although in fact** it was not Jesus who baptized, but his disciples.

2794 καίω, *kaiō* [11 / 12] [→ *1706, 2825, 2876, 3008, 3009, 3010, 3011, 3012, 3013, 3014, 3015, 3906*]

burning [5], burned [2], all ablaze [+*4786*] [1], blazing [+*4786*] [1], blazing [1], flames [1], light [1]

Mt   5:15 Neither *do people* **light** a lamp and put it under a bowl.
Lk 12:35 "Be dressed ready for service and keep your lamps **burning**,
    24:32 "Were not our hearts **burning** within us while he talked with us on
Jn   5:35 John was a lamp that **burned** and gave light, and you chose for a
    15: 6 such branches are picked up, thrown into the fire and **burned**.
1Co 13: 3 to the poor and surrender my body to the **flames**, [UBS *3016*]
Heb 12:18 to a mountain that can be touched and that *is* **burning** with fire;
Rev 4: 5 of thunder. Before the throne, seven lamps *were* **blazing** [+*4786*].
     8: 8 and something like a huge mountain, **all ablaze** [+*4786*],
     8:10 angel sounded his trumpet, and a great star, **blazing** like a torch,
    19:20 The two of them were thrown alive into the fiery lake *of* **burning**
    21: 8 and all liars—their place will be in the fiery lake *of* **burning** sulfur.

2795 κἀκεῖ, *kakei* [10] [√ *2779 + 1695*]

there [3], where [3], and there [2], and at his house [1], there too [1]

Mt   5:23 if you are offering your gift at the altar **and there** remember that
    10:11 search for some worthy person there **and stay at his house** until
    28:10 and tell my brothers to go to Galilee; [NIE] **there** they will see
Mk   1:35 and went off to a solitary place, [NIE] **where** he prayed.
Jn 11:54 to a village called Ephraim, [NIE] **where** he stayed with his
Ac 14: 7 [NIE] **where** they continued to preach the good news.
    17:13 they went **there too**, agitating the crowds and stirring them up.
    22:10 'and go into Damascus. [NIE] **There** you will be told all that you
    25:20 if he would be willing to go to Jerusalem **and** stand trial **there**
    27: 6 [NIE] **There** the centurion found an Alexandrian ship sailing for

2796 κἀκεῖθεν, *kakeithen* [10] [√ *2779 + 1695*]

from there [3], there [2], *untranslated* [1], and from there [1], from [1], that place [1], then [+*1696+2779*] [1]

Mk   9:30 They left [NIE] **that place** and passed through Galilee. Jesus did

Lk 11:53 When Jesus left [NIE] **there**, the Pharisees and the teachers of the
Ac   7: 4 and settled in Haran. [NIE] [RPG] After the death of his father,
    13:21 **Then** the people asked for a king, and he gave them Saul son of
    14:26 [NIE] **From** Attalia they sailed back to Antioch, where they had
    16:12 [NIE] **From there** we traveled to Philippi, a Roman colony
    20:15 The next day we set sail [NIE] **from there** and arrived off Kios.
    21: 1 The next day we went to Rhodes **and from there** to Patara.
    27: 4 [NIE] **From there** we put out to sea again and passed to the lee
    28:15 The brothers [NIE] **there** had heard that we were coming,

2797 κἀκεῖνος, *kakeinos* [22] [√ *2779 + 1695*]

they [5], *untranslated* [2], the former[s] [2], and he [1], and that [1], and these [1], but that also [1], he also [1], he too [1], he [1], Priscilla and Aquila[s] [1], them also [1], then the one [1], these [1], this [1], those [1]

Mt 15:18 things that come out of the mouth come from the heart, **and these**
    23:23 have practiced the latter, without neglecting [NIE] **the former**[s].
Mk 12: 4 they struck [NIE] **this** *man* on the head and treated him
    12: 5 He sent still another, **and that** *one* they killed. He sent many
    16:11 When [NIE] **they** heard that Jesus was alive and that she had seen
    16:13 [NIE] **These** returned and reported it to the rest; but they did not
Lk 11: 7 "**Then the one** inside answers, 'Don't bother me. The door is
    11:42 practiced the latter without leaving **the** [NIE] **former**[s] undone.
    20:11 He sent another servant, **but that** *one* **also** they beat and treated
    22:12 [NIE] **He** will show you a large upper room, all furnished.
Jn   6:57 so the one who feeds on me [NIE] [RPG] will live because of
     7:29 but I know him because I am from him **and he** sent me."
    10:16 I must bring **them also**. They too will listen to my voice, and there
    14:12 anyone who has faith in me [NIE] [RPG] will do what I have
    17:24 I want [NIE] **those** you have given me to be with me where I am,
Ac   5:37 of the census and led a band of people in revolt. **He too** was killed,
    15:11 grace of our Lord Jesus that we are saved, just as [NIE] **they** are."
    18:19 arrived at Ephesus, where Paul left [NIE] **Priscilla and Aquila**[s].
Ro 11:23 And if [NIE] **they** do not persist in unbelief, they will be grafted
1Co 10: 6 keep us from setting our hearts on evil things as [NIE] **they** did.
2Ti 2:12 will also reign with him. If we disown him, **he** will **also** disown us;
Heb 4: 2 also have had the gospel preached to us, just as [NIE] **they** did;

2798 κακία, *kakia* [11] [√ *2805*]

malice [5], evil [3], depravity [1], trouble [1], wickedness [1]

Mt   6:34 will worry about itself. Each day has enough **trouble** of its own.
Ac   8:22 Repent of this **wickedness** and pray to the Lord. Perhaps he will
Ro   1:29 filled with every kind of wickedness, evil, greed and **depravity**.
1Co 5: 8 not with the old yeast, the yeast *of* **malice** and wickedness,
    14:20 *In regard to* **evil** be infants, but in your thinking be adults.
Eph 4:31 and anger, brawling and slander, along with every form of **malice**.
Col 3: 8 anger, rage, **malice**, slander, and filthy language from your lips.
Tit 3: 3 We lived in **malice** and envy, being hated and hating one another.
Jas 1:21 get rid of all moral filth and the **evil** that is so prevalent
1Pe 2: 1 Therefore, rid yourselves of all **malice** and all deceit, hypocrisy,
     2:16 as free men, but do not use your freedom as a cover-up *for* **evil**;

2799 κακοήθεια, *kakoētheia* [1] [√ *2805 + 1621*]

malice [1]

Ro   1:29 They are full *of* envy, murder, strife, deceit and **malice**.

2800 κακολογέω, *kakologeō* [4] [√ *2805 + 3306*]

curses [2], maligned [1], say bad about [1]

Mt 15: 4 your father and mother' and 'Anyone *who* **curses** his father
Mk   7:10 'Anyone *who* **curses** his father or mother must be put to death.'
     9:39 in my name can in the next moment **say** *anything* **bad about** me,
Ac 19: 9 they refused to believe and publicly **maligned** the Way.

2801 κακοπάθεια, *kakopatheia* [1] [√ *2805 + 4248*]

suffering [1]

Jas 5:10 Brothers, as an example of patience *in the face of* **suffering**,

2802 κακοπαθέω, *kakopatheō* [3] [√ 2805 + 4248]

endure hardship [1], suffering [1], trouble [1]

2Ti	2: 9	for which I *am* **suffering** even to the point of being chained like a
	4: 5	in all situations, **endure hardship**, do the work of an evangelist,
Jas	5:13	*Is* any one of you *in* **trouble**? He should pray. Is anyone happy?

2803 κακοποιέω, *kakopoieō* [4] [√ 2805 + 4472]

do evil [2], does what is evil [1], doing evil [1]

Mk	3: 4	to do good or *to* **do evil**, to save life or to kill?" But they remained
Lk	6: 9	the Sabbath: to do good or *to* **do evil**, to save life or to destroy it?"
1Pe	3:17	if it is God's will, to suffer for doing good than *for* **doing evil**.
3Jn	1:11	is from God. Anyone *who* **does what is evil** has not seen God.

2804 κακοποιός, *kakopoios* [3] [√ 2805 + 4472]

criminal [1], do wrong [1], doing wrong [1]

1Pe	2:12	though they accuse you of **doing wrong**, they may see your good
	2:14	who are sent by him to punish *those who* **do wrong** and to
	4:15	not be as a murderer or thief or *any other kind of* **criminal**,

2805 κακός, *kakos* [50] [→ 179, 452, 1591, 1707, 2798, 2799, 2800, 2801, 2802, 2803, 2804, 2806, 2807, 2808, 2809, 2810, 5155, 5156]

evil [25], wrong [8], crime [3], harm [3], bad [2], wicked [2], criminal [+4472] [1], harm [+4556] [1], ill effects [1], ugly [1], wretches [1], wrongdoer [+4556] [1], wrongs [1]

Mt	21:41	"He will bring those **wretches** to a wretched end," they replied,
	24:48	But suppose that servant is **wicked** and says to himself,
	27:23	"Why? What **crime** has he committed?" asked Pilate. But they
Mk	7:21	come **evil** thoughts, sexual immorality, theft, murder, adultery,
	15:14	"Why? What **crime** has he committed?" asked Pilate. But they
Lk	16:25	while Lazarus received **bad** *things*, but now he is comforted here
	23:22	he spoke to them: "Why? What **crime** has this man committed?"
Jn	18:23	I said something wrong," Jesus replied, "testify as to what is **wrong**
	18:30	"If he were not a **criminal** [+4472]," they replied, "we would not
Ac	9:13	this man and all the **harm** he has done to your saints in Jerusalem.
	16:28	But Paul shouted, "Don't **harm** [+4556] yourself! We are all here!"
	23: 9	"We find nothing **wrong** with this man," they said. "What if a spirit
	28: 5	Paul shook the snake off into the fire and suffered no **ill effects**.
Ro	1:30	insolent, arrogant and boastful; they invent *ways of doing* **evil**;
	2: 9	will be trouble and distress for every human being who does **evil**;
	3: 8	as some claim that we say—"Let us do **evil** that good may result"?
	7:19	I want to do; no, the **evil** I do not want to do—this I keep on doing.
	7:21	law at work: When I want to do good, **evil** is right there with me.
	12:17	Do not repay anyone **evil** for evil. Be careful to do what is right in
	12:17	Do not repay anyone evil for **evil**. Be careful to do what is right in
	12:21	Do not be overcome by **evil**, but overcome evil with good.
	12:21	Do not be overcome by evil, but overcome **evil** with good.
	13: 3	hold no terror for those who do right, but *for* those who do **wrong**.
	13: 4	But if you do **wrong**, be afraid, for he does not bear the sword for
	13: 4	an agent of wrath to bring punishment *on* the **wrongdoer** [+4556].
	13:10	Love does no **harm** to its neighbor. Therefore love is the
	14:20	but it is **wrong** for a man to eat anything that causes someone else
	16:19	you to be wise about what is good, and innocent about what is **evil**.
1Co	10: 6	to keep us from setting our hearts on **evil** *things* as they did.
	13: 5	it is not easily angered, it keeps no record of **wrongs**.
	15:33	Do not be misled: "**Bad** company corrupts good character."
2Co	13: 7	Now we pray to God that you will not do anything **wrong**.
Php	3: 2	Watch out for those dogs, those men who do **evil**, those mutilators
Col	3: 5	impurity, lust, **evil** desires and greed, which is idolatry.
1Th	5:15	Make sure that nobody pays back **wrong** for wrong, but always try
	5:15	Make sure that nobody pays back wrong for **wrong**, but always try
1Ti	6:10	For the love of money is a root of all kinds *of* **evil**. Some people,
2Ti	4:14	Alexander the metalworker did me a great deal of **harm**. The Lord
Tit	1:12	has said, "Cretans are always liars, **evil** brutes, lazy gluttons."
Heb	5:14	constant use have trained themselves to distinguish good from **evil**.
Jas	1:13	For God cannot be tempted *by* **evil**, nor does he tempt anyone;
	3: 8	man can tame the tongue. It is a restless **evil**, full of deadly poison.
1Pe	3: 9	Do not repay **evil** with evil or insult with insult,
	3: 9	Do not repay evil with **evil** or insult with insult,
	3:10	would love life and see good days must keep his tongue from **evil**

	3:11	He must turn from **evil** and do good; he must seek peace
	3:12	their prayer, but the face of the Lord is against those who do **evil**."
3Jn	1:11	Dear friend, do not imitate what is **evil** but what is good.
Rev	2: 2	I know that you cannot tolerate **wicked** *men*, that you have tested
	16: 2	and **ugly** and painful sores broke out on the people who had the

2806 κακοῦργος, *kakourgos* [4] [√ 2805 + 2240]

criminals [3], criminal [1]

Lk	23:32	Two other men, *both* **criminals**, were also led out with him to be
	23:33	the Skull, there they crucified him, along with the **criminals**—
	23:39	One *of* the **criminals** who hung there hurled insults at him:
2Ti	2: 9	I am suffering even to the point of being chained like a **criminal**.

2807 κακουχέω, *kakoucheō* [2] [√ 2805 + 2400]

mistreated [2]

Heb	11:37	in sheepskins and goatskins, destitute, persecuted and **mistreated**—
	13: 3	and those *who are* **mistreated** as if you yourselves were suffering.

2808 κακόω, *kakoō* [6] [√ 2805]

harm [2], mistreated [1], oppressed [1], persecute [1], poisoned [1]

Ac	7: 6	and they will be enslaved and **mistreated** four hundred years.
	7:19	and **oppressed** our forefathers by forcing them to throw out their
	12: 1	some who belonged to the church, *intending to* **persecute** them.
	14: 2	up the Gentiles and **poisoned** their minds against the brothers.
	18:10	For I am with you, and no one is going to attack and **harm** you,
1Pe	3:13	Who *is going to* **harm** you if you are eager to do good?

2809 κακῶς, *kakōs* [16] [√ 2805]

sick [+2400] [8], diseases [+3798] [1], evil [1], greatly [1], ill [+2400] [1], terribly [1], with wrong motives [1], wretched [1], wrong [1]

Mt	4:24	and people brought to him all who *were* **ill** [+2400] with various
	8:16	drove out the spirits with a word and healed all the **sick** [+2400].
	9:12	"It is not the healthy who need a doctor, but the **sick** [+2400]
	14:35	surrounding country. People brought all their **sick** [+2400] to him
	15:22	My daughter is suffering **terribly** from demon-possession."
	17:15	on my son," he said. "He has seizures and is suffering **greatly**.
	21:41	"He will bring those wretches to a **wretched** end," they replied,
Mk	1:32	after sunset the people brought to Jesus all the **sick** [+2400]
	1:34	and Jesus healed many who had various **diseases** [+3798].
	2:17	"It is not the healthy who need a doctor, but the **sick** [+2400].
	6:55	and carried the **sick** [+2400] on mats to wherever they heard he
Lk	5:31	"It is not the healthy who need a doctor, but the **sick** [+2400]
	7: 2	whom his master valued highly, *was* **sick** [+2400] and about to die.
Jn	18:23	"If I said *something* **wrong**," Jesus replied, "testify as to what is
Ac	23: 5	for it is written: 'Do not speak **evil** about the ruler of your people.' "
Jas	4: 3	you do not receive, because you ask **with wrong motives**,

2810 κάκωσις, *kakōsis* [1] [√ 2805]

oppression [1]

Ac	7:34	I have indeed seen the **oppression** of my people in Egypt.

2811 καλάμη, *kalamē* [1] [√ 2812]

straw [1]

1Co	3:12	foundation *using* gold, silver, costly stones, wood, hay or **straw**,

2812 κάλαμος, *kalamos* [12] [→ 2811]

reed [4], staff [3], rod [2], stick [2], pen [1]

Mt	11: 7	did you go out into the desert to see? A **reed** swayed by the wind?
	12:20	A bruised **reed** he will not break, and a smoldering wick he will
	27:29	They put a **staff** in his right hand and knelt in front of him
	27:30	and took the **staff** and struck him on the head again and again.
	27:48	He filled it with wine vinegar, put it on a **stick**, and offered it to
Mk	15:19	Again and again they struck him on the head *with* a **staff** and spit

15:36 with wine vinegar, put it on a **stick**, and offered it to Jesus to drink.
Lk   7:24 did you go out into the desert to see? A **reed** swayed by the wind?
3Jn   1:13 much to write you, but I do not want to do so with **pen** and ink.
Rev 11: 1 I was given a **reed** like a measuring rod and was told, "Go
      21:15 The angel who talked with me had a measuring **rod** of gold to
      21:16 He measured the city *with* the **rod** and found it to be 12,000 stadia

2813 καλέω, *kaleō* [148 / 147] [→ *440, 441, 511, 1269, 1592, 1598, 1657, 1711, 2126, 3104, 3105, 3559, 4151, 4155, 4156, 4614, 4673, 4678, 5157, 5220*]

καλέω ... ὄνομα (to call ... name)   [10] Mt 1:21,23,25; Lk 1:13,31,59,61; 2:21; 19:2; Rev 19:13

called [84], call [12], invited [11], calls [8], give [3], *untranslated* [2], host [2], invite [2], invites [2], known as [2], reckoned [2], call [*+3836+3950*] [1], called in [1], calling received [*+3104*] [1], consecrated [*+41*] [1], gave [1], given [1], guests [1], has^s [1], host invited [1], is^s [1], name [*+3836+3950*] [1], name [1], named [*+3836+3950*] [1], named [1], of^s [1], said to be [1], tell [1]

Mt   1:21 will give birth to a son, and *you are to* **give** him the name Jesus,
     1:23 birth to a son, and *they will* **call** [*+3836+3950*] him Immanuel"—
     1:25 her until she gave birth to a son. And he **gave** him the name Jesus.
     2: 7 Then Herod **called** the Magi secretly and found out from them the
     2:15 Lord had said through the prophet: "Out of Egypt *I* **called** my son."
     2:23 was said through the prophets: "He will be **called** a Nazarene."
     4:21 with their father Zebedee, preparing their nets. Jesus **called** them,
     5: 9 Blessed are the peacemakers, for they *will be* **called** sons of God.
     5:19 and teaches others to do the same *will be* **called** least in the
     5:19 and teaches these commands *will be* **called** great in the kingdom of
     9:13 For I have not come *to* **call** the righteous, but sinners."
     20: 8 '**Call** the workers and pay them their wages, beginning with the
     21:13 he said to them, " 'My house *will be* **called** a house of prayer,'
     22: 3 He sent his servants to those *who had been* **invited** to the banquet
     22: 3 to those who had been invited to the banquet *to* **tell** them to come,
     22: 4 'Tell those *who have been* **invited** that I have prepared my dinner:
     22: 8 banquet is ready, but those I **invited** did not deserve to come.
     22: 9 Go to the street corners and **invite** to the banquet anyone you find.'
     22:43 "How is it then that David, speaking by the Spirit, **calls** him 'Lord'?
     22:45 If then David **calls** him 'Lord,' how can he be his son?"
     23: 7 be greeted in the marketplaces and to have men **call** them 'Rabbi.'
     23: 8 "But you *are* not *to be* **called** 'Rabbi,' for you have only one
     23: 9 And *do* not **call** anyone on earth 'father,' for you have one Father,
     23:10 Nor *are you to be* **called** 'teacher,' for you have one Teacher,
     25:14 who **called** his servants and entrusted his property to them.
     27: 8 That is why it *has been* **called** the Field of Blood to this day.
Mk   1:20 Without delay he **called** them, and they left their father Zebedee in
     2:17 but the sick. I have not come *to* **call** the righteous, but sinners."
     3:31 Standing outside, they sent someone in *to* **call** him.
     11:17 " 'My house *will be* **called** a house of prayer for all nations'?
Lk   1:13 will bear you a son, and *you are to* **give** him the name John.
     1:31 and give birth to a son, and *you are to* **give** him the name Jesus.
     1:32 He will be great and *will be* **called** the Son of the Most High.
     1:35 So the holy one to be born *will be* **called** the Son of God.
     1:36 old age, and she who *was* **said to be** barren is in her sixth month.
     1:59 and *they were going to* **name** [*+3836+3950*] him after his father
     1:60 but his mother spoke up and said, "No! *He is to be* **called** John."
     1:61 "There is no one among your relatives who has^s that name."
     1:62 to his father, to find out what he would like *to* **name** the child.
     1:76 And you, my child, *will be* **called** a prophet of the Most High;
     2: 4 [NIE] because he belonged to the house and line of David.
     2:21 it was time to circumcise him, he *was* **named** [*+3836+3950*] Jesus,
     2:21 the name the angel *had* **given** him before he had been conceived.
     2:23 "Every firstborn male *is to be* **consecrated** [*+41*] to the Lord"),
     5:32 I have not come *to* **call** the righteous, but sinners to repentance."
     6:15 James son of Alphaeus, Simon who *was* **called** the Zealot,
     6:46 "Why *do you* **call** me, 'Lord, Lord,' and do not do what I say?
     7:11 Soon afterward, Jesus went to a town **called** Nain, and his disciples
     7:39 When the Pharisee who *had* **invited** him saw this, he said to
     8: 2 Mary (**called** Magdalene) from whom seven demons had come out;
     9:10 and they withdrew by themselves to a town **called** Bethsaida.
     10:39 She had a sister **called** Mary, who sat at the Lord's feet listening to
     14: 7 When he noticed how the **guests** picked the places of honor at the
     14: 8 "When someone **invites** you to a wedding feast, do not take the
     14: 8 for a person more distinguished than you may have been **invited**.

     14: 9 the **host** *who* **invited** both of you will come and say to you,
     14:10 But when *you are* **invited**, take the lowest place, so that when your
     14:10 so that when your **host** comes, he will say to you, 'Friend,
     14:12 Then Jesus said *to* his **host**, "When you give a luncheon or dinner,
     14:13 give a banquet, **invite** the poor, the crippled, the lame, the blind,
     14:16 man was preparing a great banquet and **invited** many guests.
     14:17 the banquet he sent his servant to tell those *who had been* **invited**,
     14:24 not one of those men who *were* **invited** will get a taste of my
     15:19 I am no longer worthy *to be* **called** your son; make me like one of
     15:21 and against you. I am no longer worthy *to be* **called** your son.'
     19: 2 A man was there [UBS+ *called*] by the name of Zacchaeus;
     19:13 So he **called** ten of his servants and gave them ten minas. 'Put this
     19:29 and Bethany at the hill **called** the Mount of Olives,
     20:44 David **calls** him 'Lord.' How then can he be his son?"
     21:37 and each evening he went out to spend the night on the hill **called**
     22: 3 Then Satan entered Judas, **called** Iscariot, one of the Twelve.
     22:25 and those who exercise authority over them **call** *themselves*
     23:33 When they came to the place **called** the Skull, there they crucified
Jn   1:42 You *will be* **called** Cephas" (which, when translated, is Peter).
     2: 2 and Jesus and his disciples *had also been* **invited** to the wedding.
Ac   1:12 Then they returned to Jerusalem from the hill **called** the Mount of
     1:19 so they **called** that field in their language Akeldama, that is,
     1:23 Joseph **called** Barsabbas (also known as Justus) and Matthias.
     3:11 and came running to them in the place **called** Solomon's
     4:18 Then *they* **called** them *in* again and commanded them not to speak
     7:58 the witnesses laid their clothes at the feet *of* a young man **named**
     8:10 "This man is the divine power **known as** the Great Power."
     9:11 "Go to the house of Judas on [NIE] Straight Street and ask for a
     10: 1 a centurion *in* what *was* **known as** the Italian Regiment.
     13: 1 Barnabas, Simeon **called** Niger, Lucius of Cyrene, Manaen (who
     14:12 Barnabas *they* **called** Zeus, and Paul they called Hermes
     15:22 They chose Judas (**called** Barsabbas) and Silas, two men who were
     15:37 Barnabas wanted to take John, also **called** Mark, with them,
     24: 2 *When* Paul *was* **called** in, Tertullus presented his case before
     27: 8 the coast with difficulty and came to a place **called** Fair Havens,
     27:14 very long, a wind of hurricane force, **called** the "northeaster,"
     27:16 As we passed to the lee of a small island **called** Cauda, we were
     28: 1 safely on shore, we found out that the island *was* **called** Malta.
Ro   4:17 life to the dead and **calls** things that *are* not as though they were.
     8:30 And those he predestined, he also **called**; those he called, he also
     8:30 he predestined, he also called; those *he* **called**, he also justified;
     9: 7 "It is through Isaac that your offspring *will be* **reckoned**."
     9:12 not by works but by him *who* **calls**—she was told, "The older will
     9:24 even us, whom *he also* **called**, not only from the Jews but also
     9:25 "*I will* **call** them 'my people' who are not my people; and I will
     9:26 are not my people,' *they will be* **called** 'sons of the living God.' "
1Co 1: 9 who has **called** you into fellowship with his Son Jesus Christ our
     7:15 bound in such circumstances; God has **called** us to live in peace.
     7:17 that the Lord assigned to him and to which God has **called** him.
     7:18 Was a man already circumcised *when he was* **called**? He should
     7:18 Was a man uncircumcised *when he was* **called**? He should not be
     7:20 remain in the situation which *he was* in *when* God **called** him.
     7:21 Were you a slave *when you were* **called**? Don't let it trouble you—
     7:22 For he who was a slave *when he was* **called** by the Lord is the
     7:22 he who was a free man *when he was* **called** is Christ's slave.
     7:24 to God, should remain in the situation God **called** *him* to.
     10:27 If some unbeliever **invites** you *to a meal* and you want to go,
     15: 9 of the apostles and do not even deserve *to be* **called** an apostle,
Gal 1: 6 so quickly deserting the one *who* **called** you by the grace of Christ
     1:15 who set me apart from birth and **called** me by his grace,
     5: 8 That kind of persuasion does not come from the one *who* **calls** you.
     5:13 You, my brothers, *were* **called** to be free. But do not use your
Eph 4: 1 you to live a life worthy *of* the **calling** you have **received** [*+3104*].
     4: 4 just as *you were* **called** to one hope when you were called—
Col 3:15 since as members of one body *you were* **called** to peace.
1Th 2:12 lives worthy of God, who **calls** you into his kingdom and glory.
     4: 7 For God *did* not **call** us to be impure, but to live a holy life.
     5:24 The one *who* **calls** you is faithful and he will do it.
2Th 2:14 He **called** you to this through our gospel, that you might share in
1Ti 6:12 Take hold of the eternal life to which *you were* **called** when you
2Ti 1: 9 who has saved us and **called** us to a holy life—not because of
Heb 2:11 of the same family. So Jesus is not ashamed *to* **call** them brothers.
     3:13 But encourage one another daily, as long as *it is* **called** Today,
     5: 4 honor upon himself; *he must be* **called** by God, just as Aaron was.
     9:15 that those *who are* **called** may receive the promised eternal
     11: 8 *when* **called** to go to a place he would later receive as his

	11:18	to him, "It is through Isaac that your offspring *will be* **reckoned**."
Jas	2:23	credited to him as righteousness," and *he was* **called** God's friend.
1Pe	1:15	But just as he *who* **called** you is holy, so be holy in all you do;
	2:9	that you may declare the praises *of* him *who* **called** you out of
	2:21	To this *you were* **called**, because Christ suffered for you,
	3:6	like Sarah, who obeyed Abraham and **called** him her master.
	3:9	because to this *you were* **called** so that you may inherit a blessing.
	5:10	the God of all grace, who **called** you to his eternal glory in Christ,
2Pe	1:3	and godliness through our knowledge *of* him who **called** us by his
1Jn	3:1	has lavished on us, that *we should be* **called** children of God!
Rev	1:9	was on the island of[s] Patmos because of the word of God
	11:8	which *is* figuratively **called** Sodom and Egypt, where also their
	12:9	that ancient serpent **called** the devil, or Satan, who leads the whole
	16:16	kings together to the place that in Hebrew *is* **called** Armageddon.
	19:9	'Blessed are those *who are* **invited** to the wedding supper of the
	19:11	me was a white horse, whose rider *is* **called** Faithful and True.
	19:13	in a robe dipped in blood, and his name **is**[s] the Word of God.

2814 καλλιέλαιος, *kallielaios* [1] [√ 2819 + 1777]

cultivated olive tree [1]

Ro   11:24   and contrary to nature were grafted into a **cultivated olive tree**,

2815 καλοδιδάσκαλος, *kalodidaskalos* [1] [√ 2819 + 1438]

teach what is good [1]

Tit   2:3   be slanderers or addicted to much wine, but to **teach what is good**.

2816 Καλοὶ λιμένες, *Kaloi limenes* [1] [√ 2819 + 3348]

Fair Havens [1]

Ac   27:8   the coast with difficulty and came to a place called **Fair Havens**,

2817 καλοκαγαθία, *kalokagathia*   Not used in UBS/NIV [√ 2819 + 2779 + 19]

2818 καλοποιέω, *kalopoieō* [1] [√ 2819 + 4472]

doing what is right [1]

2Th   3:13   And as for you, brothers, never tire of **doing what is right**.

2819 καλός, *kalos* [100] [→ 2814, 2815, 2816, 2817, 2818, 2822]

καλός ἔργον (good work) [15] Mt 5:16; 26:10; Mk 14:6; Jn 10:32,33; 1Ti 3:1; 5:10,25; 6:18; Tit 2:7,14; 3:8,14; Heb 10:24; 1Pe 2:12

καλός καρπός (good fruit) [7] Mt 3:10; 7:17,18,19; 12:33; Lk 3:9; 6:43

καλός ποιεῖν (to do good) [12] Mt 3:10; 7:17,18,19; 12:33,33; Lk 3:9; 6:43; Ro 7:21; 2Co 13:7; Gal 6:9; Jas 4:17

good [61], better [9], right [4], what is good [4], beautiful [3], noble [3], *untranslated* [2], excellent [2], fine [2], best [1], choice [1], clear [1], faithfully [+6055] [1], firm [1], goodness [1], great [1], it[s] [+3836] [1], these [+2240] [1], what is right [1]

Mt	3:10	and every tree that does not produce **good** fruit will be cut down
	5:16	that they may see your **good** deeds and praise your Father in
	7:17	Likewise every good tree bears **good** fruit, but a bad tree bears bad
	7:18	tree cannot bear bad fruit, and a bad tree cannot bear **good** fruit.
	7:19	Every tree that does not bear **good** fruit is cut down and thrown
	12:33	"Make a tree **good** and its fruit will be good, or make a tree bad
	12:33	"Make a tree good and its fruit will be **good**, or make a tree bad
	13:8	Still other seed fell on **good** soil, where it produced a crop—
	13:23	But the one who received the seed that fell on **good** soil is the man
	13:24	"The kingdom of heaven is like a man who sowed **good** seed in his
	13:27	came to him and said, 'Sir, didn't you sow **good** seed in your field?
	13:37	"The one who sowed the **good** seed is the Son of Man.
	13:38	is the world, and the **good** seed stands for the sons of the kingdom.

	13:45	the kingdom of heaven is like a merchant looking for **fine** pearls.
	13:48	Then they sat down and collected the **good** fish in baskets,
	15:26	"It is not **right** to take the children's bread and toss it to their dogs."
	17:4	Peter said to Jesus, "Lord, it is **good** for us to be here. If you wish,
	18:8	It is **better** for you to enter life maimed or crippled than to have
	18:9	It is **better** for you to enter life with one eye than to have two eyes
	26:10	you bothering this woman? She has done a **beautiful** thing to me.
	26:24	Son of Man! It would be **better** for him if he had not been born."
Mk	4:8	Still other seed fell on **good** soil. It came up, grew and produced a
	4:20	Others, like seed sown on **good** soil, hear the word, accept it,
	7:27	"for it is not **right** to take the children's bread and toss it to their
	9:5	Peter said to Jesus, "Rabbi, it is **good** for us to be here. Let us put up
	9:42	it would be **better** for him to be thrown into the sea with a large
	9:43	It is **better** for you to enter life maimed than with two hands to go
	9:45	It is **better** for you to enter life crippled than to have two feet
	9:47	It is **better** for you to enter the kingdom of God with one eye than
	9:50	"Salt is **good**, but if it loses its saltiness, how can you make it salty
	14:6	"Why are you bothering her? She has done a **beautiful** thing to me.
	14:21	Son of Man! It would be **better** for him if he had not been born."
Lk	3:9	and every tree that does not produce **good** fruit will be cut down
	6:38	A **good** measure, pressed down, shaken together and running over,
	6:43	"No **good** tree bears bad fruit, nor does a bad tree bear good fruit.
	6:43	"No good tree bears bad fruit, nor does a bad tree bear **good** fruit.
	8:15	But the seed on **good** soil stands for those with a noble and good
	8:15	But the seed on good soil stands for those with a **noble** and good
	9:33	Peter said to him, "Master, it is **good** for us to be here.
	14:34	"Salt is **good**, but if it loses its saltiness, how can it be made salty
	21:5	about how the temple was adorned *with* **beautiful** stones
Jn	2:10	"Everyone brings out the **choice** wine first and then the cheaper
	2:10	have had too much to drink; but you have saved the **best** till now."
	10:11	"I am the **good** shepherd. The good shepherd lays down his life for
	10:11	The **good** shepherd lays down his life for the sheep.
	10:14	"I am the **good** shepherd; I know my sheep and my sheep know
	10:32	to them, "I have shown you many **great** miracles from the Father.
	10:33	"We are not stoning you for *any of* these[s] [+2240],"
Ro	7:16	And if I do what I do not want to do, I agree that the law is **good**.
	7:18	the desire to do good, but I cannot carry it[s] [+3836] out.
	7:21	law at work: When I want to do **good**, evil is right there with me.
	12:17	for evil. Be careful to do what is **right** in the eyes of everybody.
	14:21	It is **better** not to eat meat or drink wine or to do anything else that
1Co	5:6	Your boasting is not **good**. Don't you know that a little yeast works
	7:1	for the matters you wrote about: It is **good** for a man not to marry.
	7:8	the widows I say: It is **good** for them to stay unmarried, as I am.
	7:26	I think **[RPG]** that it is good for you to remain as you are.
	7:26	present crisis, I think that it is **good** for you to remain as you are.
	9:15	**[RPG]** I would rather die than have anyone deprive me of this
2Co	8:21	For we are taking pains to do **what is right**, not only in the eyes of
	13:7	but that you will do what is **right** even though we may seem to
Gal	4:18	It is **fine** to be zealous, provided the purpose is good, and to be
	4:18	provided the purpose is **good**, and to be so always and not just
	6:9	Let us not become weary in doing **good**, for at the proper time we
1Th	5:21	Test everything. Hold on to the **good**.
1Ti	1:8	We know that the law is **good** if one uses it properly.
	1:18	about you, so that by following them you may fight the **good** fight,
	2:3	This is **good**, and pleases God our Savior,
	3:1	anyone sets his heart on being an overseer, he desires a **noble** task.
	3:7	He must also have a **good** reputation with outsiders, so that he will
	3:13	Those who have served well gain an **excellent** standing and great
	4:4	For everything God created is **good**, and nothing is to be rejected if
	4:6	you will be a good minister of Christ Jesus, brought up in the
	4:6	truths of the faith and *of* the **good** teaching that you have followed.
	5:10	and is well known for her **good** deeds, such as bringing up
	5:25	In the same way, **good** deeds are obvious, and even those that are
	6:12	Fight the **good** fight of the faith. Take hold of the eternal life to
	6:12	you made your **good** confession in the presence of many witnesses.
	6:13	who while testifying before Pontius Pilate made the **good**
	6:18	to be rich in **good** deeds, and to be generous and willing to share.
	6:19	In this way they will lay up treasure for themselves as a **firm**
2Ti	1:14	Guard the **good** deposit that was entrusted to you—guard it with
	2:3	Endure hardship with us like a **good** soldier of Christ Jesus.
	4:7	I have fought the **good** fight, I have finished the race, I have kept
Tit	2:7	In everything set them an example by doing **what is good**.
	2:14	himself a people that are his very own, eager to do **what is good**.
	3:8	in God may be careful to devote themselves to doing **what is good**.
	3:8	is good. These things are **excellent** and profitable for everyone.
	3:14	Our people must learn to devote themselves to doing **what is good**,

Heb 5:14 who by constant use have trained themselves to distinguish **good**
     6: 5 who have tasted the **goodness** of the word of God and the powers
   10:24 consider how we may spur one another on *toward* love and **good**
   13: 9 It is **good** for our hearts to be strengthened by grace, not by
   13:18 We are sure that we have a **clear** conscience and desire to live
Jas   2: 7 Are they not the ones who are slandering the **noble** name of him to
   3:13 Let him show it by his **good** life, by deeds done in the humility that
   4:17 who knows the **good** he ought to do and doesn't do it, sins.
1Pe 2:12 Live *such* **good** lives among the pagans that, though they accuse
   2:12 they may see your **good** deeds and glorify God on the day he visits
   4:10 whatever gift he has received to serve others, **faithfully** [*+6055*]

2820 κάλυμμα, *kalymma* [4] [√ *2821*]

veil [4]

2Co 3:13 who would put a **veil** over his face to keep the Israelites from
   3:14 for to this day the same **veil** remains when the old covenant is read.
   3:15 Even to this day when Moses is read, a **veil** covers their hearts.
   3:16 But whenever anyone turns to the Lord, the **veil** is taken away.

2821 καλύπτω, *kalyptō* [8] [→ *184, 365, 636, 637, 2127, 2128, 2820, 2877, 4152, 4328, 5158*]

veiled [2], concealed [1], cover over [1], cover [1], covers over [1], hides [1], swept over [1]

Mt   8:24 storm came up on the lake, so that the waves **swept over** the boat.
  10:26 There is nothing **concealed** that will not be disclosed, or hidden
Lk   8:16 "No one lights a lamp and **hides** it in a jar or puts it under a bed.
  23:30 say to the mountains, "Fall on us!" and to the hills, "**Cover** us!" '
2Co 4: 3 And even if our gospel is **veiled**, it is veiled to those who are
   4: 3 even if our gospel is veiled, it is **veiled** to those who are perishing.
Jas 5:20 way will save him from death and **cover over** a multitude of sins.
1Pe 4: 8 each other deeply, because love **covers over** a multitude of sins.

2822 καλῶς, *kalos* [37] [√ *2819*]

well [12], good [8], right [6], the truth [2], easily [1], fine way [1], good [*+4472*] [1], granted [1], honorably [1], rightly so [1], the right thing [1], very well [1], well said [1]

Mt 12:12 than a sheep! Therefore it is lawful to do **good** on the Sabbath."
  15: 7 You hypocrites! Isaiah was **right** when he prophesied about you:
Mk   7: 6 "Isaiah was **right** when he prophesied about you hypocrites;
   7: 9 "You have a **fine way** of setting aside the commands of God in
   7:37 "He has done everything **well**," they said. "He even makes the deaf
  12:28 Noticing that Jesus had given them a **good** answer, he asked him,
  12:32 "**Well** said, teacher," the man replied. "You are right in saying that
  16:18 they will place their hands on sick people, and they will get **well**."
Lk   6:26 Woe to you when all men speak **well** of you, for that is how their
   6:27 who hear me: Love your enemies, do **good** to those who hate you,
   6:48 struck that house but could not shake it, because it was **well** built.
  20:39 Some of the teachers of the law responded, "**Well** said, teacher!"
Jn   4:17 said to her, "You are **right** when you say you have no husband.
   8:48 "Aren't we **right** in saying that you are a Samaritan
  13:13 "You call me 'Teacher' and 'Lord,' and **rightly so**, for that is what
  18:23 to what is wrong. But if I spoke **the truth**, why did you strike me?"
Ac 10:33 So I sent for you immediately, and it was **good** of you to come.
  25:10 not done any wrong to the Jews, as you yourself know **very well**.
  28:25 "The Holy Spirit spoke **the truth** to your forefathers when he said
Ro 11:20 **Granted**. But they were broken off because of unbelief, and you
1Co 7:37 mind not to marry the virgin—this man also does **the right thing**.
   7:38 So then, he who marries the virgin does **right**, but he who does not
  14:17 You may be giving thanks **well** *enough*, but the other man is not
2Co 11: 4 from the one you accepted, you put up with it **easily** *enough*.
Gal 4:17 Those people are zealous to win you over, but for no **good**.
   5: 7 You were running a **good** race. Who cut in on you and kept you
Php 4:14 Yet it was **good** of you to share in my troubles.
1Ti   3: 4 He must manage his own family **well** and see that his children
   3:12 but one wife and must manage his children and his household **well**.
   3:13 Those who have served **well** gain an excellent standing and great
   5:17 The elders who direct the affairs of the church **well** are worthy of
Heb 13:18 have a clear conscience and desire to live **honorably** in every way.
Jas   2: 3 the man wearing fine clothes and say, "Here's a **good** seat for you,"
   2: 8 in Scripture, "Love your neighbor as yourself," you are doing **right**.
   2:19 **Good** [*+4472*]! Even the demons believe that—and shudder.

2Pe 1:19 and *you* will do **well** to pay attention to it, as to a light shining in a
3Jn 1: 6 You will do **well** to send them on their way in a manner worthy of

2823 κάμηλος, *kamēlos* [6]

camel [4], camel's [2]

Mt   3: 4 John's clothes were made of **camel's** hair, and he had a leather belt
  19:24 it is easier for a **camel** to go through the eye of a needle than for a
  23:24 You blind guides! You strain out a gnat but swallow a **camel**.
Mk   1: 6 John wore clothing made *of* **camel's** hair, with a leather belt
  10:25 It is easier for a **camel** to go through the eye of a needle than for a
Lk 18:25 it is easier for a **camel** to go through the eye of a needle than for a

2824 κάμιλος, *kamilos*   Not used in UBS/NIV

2825 κάμινος, *kaminos* [4] [√ *2794*]

furnace [4]

Mt 13:42 They will throw them into the fiery **furnace**, where there will be
  13:50 and throw them into the fiery **furnace**, where there will be
Rev   1:15 His feet were like bronze glowing in a **furnace**, and his voice was
   9: 2 smoke rose from it like the smoke *from* a gigantic **furnace**.

2826 κάμμύω, *kammyō* [2]

closed [2]

Mt 13:15 they hardly hear with their ears, and *they have* **closed** their eyes.
Ac 28:27 they hardly hear with their ears, and *they have* **closed** their eyes.

2827 κάμνω, *kamnō* [2]

sick [1], weary [1]

Heb 12: 3 from sinful men, so that *you will* not grow **weary** and lose heart.
Jas   5:15 And the prayer offered in faith will make the **sick** *person* well;

2828 κάμπτω, *kamptō* [4] [→ *366, 5159*]

bow [2], bowed [1], kneel [*+1205+3836*] [1]

Ro 11: 4 "I have reserved for myself seven thousand who *have* not **bowed**
  14:11 surely as I live,' says the Lord, 'every knee *will* **bow** before me;
Eph   3:14 For this reason *I* **kneel** [*+1205+3836*] before the Father,
Php   2:10 that at the name of Jesus every knee *should* **bow**, in heaven

2829 κἄν, *kan* [17] [√ *2779 + 1623 + 323*]

if [4], even if [3], even though [2], also [1], and when [1], at least [*+1569+2779*] [1], even [*+1569+2779*] [1], if even [1], just [*+1569+2779*] [1], or [1], would [1]

Mt 21:21 but **also** [NIE] you can say to this mountain, 'Go, throw yourself
  26:35 But Peter declared, "**Even if** I have to die with you, I will never
Mk   5:28 because she thought, "If I **just** touch his clothes, I will be healed."
   6:56 They begged him to let them touch **even** the edge of his cloak,
  16:18 they will pick up snakes with their hands; **and when** they drink
Lk 12:38 be good for those servants whose master finds them ready, **even if**
  12:38 even if he comes in the second **or** [RPG] third watch of the
  13: 9 [NIE] **If** it bears fruit next year, fine! If not, then cut it down.' '
Jn   8:14 Jesus answered, "**Even if** I testify on my own behalf, my testimony
   8:55 I know him. [NIE] **If** I said I did not, I would be a liar like you,
  10:38 But if I do it, **even though** you do not believe me,
  11:25 and the life. He who believes in me will live, **even though** he dies;
Ac   5:15 so that **at least** Peter's shadow might fall on some of them as he
1Co 13: 3 [NIE] **If** I give all I possess to the poor and surrender my body to
2Co 11:16 But if you do, then receive me just as you [NIE] **would** a fool,
Heb 12:20 because they could not bear what was commanded: "**If even** an
Jas   5:15 the Lord will raise him up. [NIE] **If** he has sinned, he will be

2830 Κανά, *Kana* [4] [→ *2832*]

Cana [4]

Jn   2: 1 On the third day a wedding took place at **Cana** in Galilee.
   2:11 first of his miraculous signs, Jesus performed at **Cana** in Galilee.

4:46 Once more he visited **Cana** in Galilee, where he had turned the
21: 2 Nathanael from **Cana** in Galilee, the sons of Zebedee,

2831 Καναναῖος, *Kananaios* [2]

Zealot [2]

Mt 10: 4 Simon the **Zealot** and Judas Iscariot, who betrayed him.
Mk 3:18 Thomas, James son of Alphaeus, Thaddaeus, Simon the **Zealot**

2832 Κανανίτης, *Kananitēs* Not used in UBS/NIV
[√ 2830]

2833 Κανδάκη, *Kandakē* [1]

Candace [1]

Ac 8:27 an important official in charge of all the treasury *of* **Candace**,

2834 κανών, *kanōn* [4]

area of activity [1], field [+3586+3836] [1], rule [1], territory [1]

2Co 10:13 but will confine our boasting to the **field** [+3586+3836] God has
10:15 to grow, our **area of activity** among you will greatly expand,
10:16 want to boast about work already done in another man's **territory**.
Gal 6:16 Peace and mercy to all who follow this **rule**, even to the Israel of

2835 Καπερναούμ, *Kapernaoum* Not used in UBS/NIV [√ cf. 3019]

2836 καπηλεύω, *kapēleuō* [1]

peddle for profit [1]

2Co 2:17 Unlike so many, we do not **peddle** the word of God **for profit**.

2837 καπνός, *kapnos* [13]

smoke [13]

Ac 2:19 and signs on the earth below, blood and fire and billows *of* **smoke**.
Rev 8: 4 The **smoke** of the incense, together with the prayers of the saints,
9: 2 **smoke** rose from it like the smoke from a gigantic furnace.
9: 2 smoke rose from it like the **smoke** from a gigantic furnace.
9: 2 The sun and sky were darkened by the **smoke** from the Abyss.
9: 3 And out of the **smoke** locusts came down upon the earth and were
9:17 of lions, and out of their mouths came fire, **smoke** and sulfur.
9:18 plagues of fire, **smoke** and sulfur that came out of their mouths.
14:11 And the **smoke** of their torment rises for ever and ever. There is no
15: 8 And the temple was filled *with* **smoke** from the glory of God
18: 9 with her and shared her luxury see the **smoke** of her burning,
18:18 When they see the **smoke** of her burning, they will exclaim,
19: 3 "Hallelujah! The **smoke** from her goes up for ever and ever."

2838 Καππαδοκία, *Kappadokia* [2]

Cappadocia [2]

Ac 2: 9 of Mesopotamia, Judea and **Cappadocia**, Pontus and Asia,
1Pe 1: 1 throughout Pontus, Galatia, **Cappadocia**, Asia and Bithynia,

2839 καραδοκία, *karadokia* Not used in UBS/NIV [√ 3191 + 1312]

2840 καρδία, *kardia* [156 / 157] [→ 2841, 5016]

hearts [69], heart [60], mind [3], you [+3836+5148] [3], himself
[+899+3836] [2], minds [2], untranslated [1], decided
[+326+2093+3836] [1], experts [+1214] [1], furious
[+1391+3836] [1], heart's [1], himself [+899] [1], inmost [1], made
think [+1877+3836+5502] [1], make up mind
[+1877+3836+5502] [1], prompted [+965+1650+3836] [1], self
[+476+3836] [1], stand firm [+3836+5114] [1], themselves
[+899+3836] [1], thought [1], thoughts [+1369+3836] [1],

wholeheartedly [+1666] [1], wondered about
[+1877+3836+5502] [1], yourselves [+3836+5148] [1]

Mt 5: 8 Blessed are the pure *in* **heart**, for they will see God.
5:28 lustfully has already committed adultery with her in his **heart**.
6:21 For where your treasure is, there your **heart** will be also.
9: 4 Jesus said, "Why do you entertain evil thoughts in your **hearts**?
11:29 upon you and learn from me, for I am gentle and humble *in* **heart**,
12:34 For out of the overflow *of* the **heart** the mouth speaks.
12:40 of Man will be three days and three nights in the **heart** of the earth.
13:15 For this people's **heart** has become calloused; they hardly hear
13:15 hear with their ears, understand *with* their **hearts** and turn,
13:19 the evil one comes and snatches away what was sown in his **heart**.
15: 8 people honor me with their lips, but their **hearts** are far from me.
15:18 But the things that come out of the mouth come from the **heart**,
15:19 For out of the **heart** come evil thoughts, murder, adultery,
18:35 treat each of you unless you forgive your brother from your **heart**."
22:37 " 'Love the Lord your God with all your **heart** and with all your
24:48 suppose that servant is wicked and says to **himself** [+899+3836],
Mk 2: 6 of the law were sitting there, thinking to **themselves** [+899+3836],
2: 8 and he said to them, "Why are you thinking these things? [RPG]
3: 5 deeply distressed at their stubborn **hearts**, said to the man,
6:52 had not understood about the loaves; their **hearts** were hardened.
7: 6 people honor me with their lips, but their **hearts** are far from me.
7:19 For it doesn't go into his **heart** but into his stomach, and then out
7:21 For from within, out of men's **hearts**, come evil thoughts,
8:17 Do you still not see or understand? Are your **hearts** hardened?
11:23 and does not doubt in his **heart** but believes that what he says will
12:30 Love the Lord your God with all your **heart** and with all your soul
12:33 To love him with all your **heart**, with all your understanding
Lk 1:17 to turn the **hearts** of the fathers to their children
1:51 he has scattered those who are proud in their **inmost** thoughts.
1:66 Everyone who heard this **wondered about** [+1877+3836+5502] it,
2:19 Mary treasured up all these things and pondered them in her **heart**.
2:35 so that the thoughts of many **hearts** will be revealed. And a sword
2:51 to them. But his mother treasured all these things in her **heart**.
3:15 and were all wondering in their **hearts** if John might possibly be
5:22 and asked, "Why are you thinking these things in your **hearts**?
6:45 man brings good things out of the good stored up *in* his **heart**,
6:45 brings evil things out of the evil stored up *in* his **heart**. [UBS-]
6:45 in his heart. For out of the overflow *of* his **heart** his mouth speaks.
8:12 then the devil comes and takes away the word from their **hearts**,
8:15 the seed on good soil stands for those with a noble and good **heart**,
9:47 Jesus, knowing their **thoughts** [+1369+3836], took a little child
10:27 " 'Love the Lord your God with all your **heart** and with all your
12:34 For where your treasure is, there your **heart** will be also.
12:45 But suppose the servant says to **himself** [+899+3836], 'My master
16:15 justify yourselves in the eyes of men, but God knows your **hearts**.
21:14 But **make up** your **mind** [+1877+3836+5502] not to worry
21:34 "Be careful, or your **hearts** will be weighed down with dissipation,
24:25 and how slow *of* **heart** to believe all that the prophets have
24:32 "Were not our **hearts** burning within us while he talked with us on
24:38 "Why are you troubled, and why do doubts rise in your **minds**?
Jn 12:40 "He has blinded their eyes and deadened their **hearts**, so they can
12:40 see with their eyes, nor understand *with* their **hearts**, nor turn—
13: 2 devil *had* already **prompted** [+965+1650+3836] Judas Iscariot,
14: 1 "Do not let your **hearts** be troubled. Trust in God; trust also in me.
14:27 Do not let your **hearts** be troubled and do not be afraid.
16: 6 I have said these things, you [+3836+5148] are filled with grief.
16:22 but I will see you again and **you** [+3836+5148] will rejoice,
Ac 2:26 Therefore my **heart** is glad and my tongue rejoices; my body also
2:37 they were cut to the **heart** and said to Peter and the other apostles,
2:46 bread in their homes and ate together with glad and sincere **hearts**,
4:32 All the believers were one *in* **heart** and mind. No one claimed that
5: 3 Satan has so filled your **heart** that you have lied to the Holy Spirit
5: 4 What **made** you **think** [+1877+3836+5502] of doing such a thing?
7:23 he **decided** [+326+2093+3836] to visit his fellow Israelites.
7:39 they rejected him and in their **hearts** turned back to Egypt.
7:51 "You stiff-necked people, with uncircumcised **hearts** and ears!
7:54 they *were* **furious** [+1391+3836] and gnashed their teeth at him.
8:21 share in this ministry, because your **heart** is not right before God.
8:22 he will forgive you for having such a thought *in* your **heart**.
11:23 them all to remain true to the Lord *with all* their **hearts**.
13:22 'I have found David son of Jesse a man after my own **heart**;
14:17 he provides you with plenty of food and fills your **hearts** with joy."
15: 9 between us and them, for he purified their **hearts** by faith.

16:14 The Lord opened her **heart** to respond to Paul's message.
21:13 Paul answered, "Why are you weeping and breaking my **heart**?
28:27 For this people's **heart** has become calloused; they hardly hear
28:27 hear with their ears, understand *with* their **hearts** and turn,

Ro 1:21 thinking became futile and their foolish **hearts** were darkened.
1:24 Therefore God gave them over in the sinful desires *of* their **hearts**
2: 5 because of your stubbornness and your unrepentant **heart**,
2:15 show that the requirements of the law are written on their **hearts**,
2:29 and circumcision is circumcision *of* the **heart**, by the Spirit,
5: 5 because God has poured out his love into our **hearts** by the Holy
6:17 you **wholeheartedly** [+1666] obeyed the form of teaching to
8:27 And he who searches our **hearts** knows the mind of the Spirit,
9: 2 I have great sorrow and unceasing anguish *in* my **heart**.
10: 1 my **heart's** desire and prayer to God for the Israelites is that they
10: 6 "Do not say in your **heart**, 'Who will ascend into heaven?'" (that
10: 8 it is in your mouth and in your **heart**," that is, the word of faith we
10: 9 and believe in your **heart** that God raised him from the dead,
10:10 For it is *with* your **heart** that you believe and are justified,
16:18 smooth talk and flattery they deceive the **minds** of naive people.

1Co 2: 9 no **mind** has conceived what God has prepared for those who love
4: 5 is hidden in darkness and will expose the motives *of* men's **hearts**.
7:37 But the man who has settled the matter in his own **mind**, who is
7:37 own will, and who has made up his **mind** not to marry the virgin—
14:25 and the secrets *of* his **heart** will be laid bare. So he will fall down

2Co 1:22 and put his Spirit in our **hearts** as a deposit, guaranteeing what is
2: 4 you out of great distress and anguish *of* **heart** and with many tears,
3: 2 our letter, written on our **hearts**, known and read by everybody.
3: 3 living God, not on tablets of stone but on tablets of human **hearts**.
3:15 Even to this day when Moses is read, a veil covers their **hearts**.
4: 6 made his light shine in our **hearts** to give us the light of the
5:12 who take pride in what is seen rather than in what is in the **heart**.
6:11 freely to you, Corinthians, and opened wide our **hearts** to you.
7: 3 I have said before that you have such a place in our **hearts** that we
8:16 who put into the **heart** of Titus the same concern I have for you.
9: 7 Each man should give what he has decided *in* his **heart** to give,

Gal 4: 6 you are sons, God sent the Spirit of his Son into our **hearts**,

Eph 1:18 I pray also that the eyes *of* your **heart** may be enlightened in order
3:17 so that Christ may dwell in your **hearts** through faith. And I pray
4:18 the ignorance that is in them due to the hardening *of* their **hearts**.
5:19 spiritual songs. Sing and make music *in* your **heart** to the Lord,
6: 5 earthly masters with respect and fear, and with sincerity *of* **heart**,
6:22 know how we are, and that he may encourage **you** [+3836+5148].

Php 1: 7 me to feel this way about all of you, since I have you in my **heart**;
4: 7 will guard your **hearts** and your minds in Christ Jesus.

Col 2: 2 My purpose is that they may be encouraged in **heart** and united in
3:15 Let the peace of Christ rule in your **hearts**, since as members of
3:16 hymns and spiritual songs with gratitude in your **hearts** to God.
3:22 their favor, but with sincerity *of* **heart** and reverence for the Lord.
4: 8 about our circumstances and that he may encourage your **hearts**.

1Th 2: 4 We are not trying to please men but God, who tests our **hearts**.
2:17 not *in* **thought**), out of our intense longing we made every effort to
3:13 May he strengthen your **hearts** so that you will be blameless

2Th 2:17 encourage your **hearts** and strengthen you in every good deed
3: 5 May the Lord direct your **hearts** into God's love and Christ's

1Ti 1: 5 which comes from a pure **heart** and a good conscience and a

2Ti 2:22 along with those who call on the Lord out of a pure **heart**.

Heb 3: 8 do not harden your **hearts** as you did in the rebellion,
3:10 and I said, 'Their **hearts** are always going astray, and they have
3:12 a sinful, unbelieving **heart** that turns away from the living God.
3:15 his voice, do not harden your **hearts** as you did in the rebellion."
4: 7 "Today, if you hear his voice, do not harden your **hearts**."
4:12 and marrow; it judges the thoughts and attitudes *of* the **heart**.
8:10 I will put my laws in their minds and write them on their **hearts**.
10:16 I will put my laws in their **hearts**, and I will write them on their
10:22 let us draw near to God with a sincere **heart** in full assurance of
10:22 having our **hearts** sprinkled to cleanse us from a guilty conscience
13: 9 It is good for our **hearts** to be strengthened by grace, not by

Jas 1:26 he deceives **himself** [+899] and his religion is worthless.
3:14 But if you harbor bitter envy and selfish ambition in your **hearts**,
4: 8 Wash your hands, you sinners, and purify your **hearts**,
5: 5 have fattened **yourselves** [+3836+5148] in the day of slaughter.
5: 8 You too, be patient and **stand firm** [+3836+5114],

1Pe 1:22 love for your brothers, love one another deeply, from the **heart**.
3: 4 Instead, it should be that of your inner **self** [+476+3836].
3:15 But in your **hearts** set apart Christ as Lord. Always be prepared to

2Pe 1:19 until the day dawns and the morning star rises in your **hearts**.

2:14 they are **experts** [+1214] in greed—an accursed brood!

1Jn 3:19 to the truth, and how we set our **hearts** at rest in his presence
3:20 whenever our **hearts** condemn us. For God is greater than our
3:20 For God is greater than our **hearts**, and he knows everything.
3:21 Dear friends, if our **hearts** do not condemn us, we have

Rev 2:23 Then all the churches will know that I am he who searches **hearts**
17:17 For God has put it into their **hearts** to accomplish his purpose by
18: 7 In her **heart** she boasts, 'I sit as queen; I am not a widow,

2841 καρδιογνώστης, *kardiognōstēs* [2]
[√ 2840 + 1182]

know heart [1], knows heart [1]

Ac 1:24 Then they prayed, "Lord, you **know** everyone's **heart**. Show us
15: 8 God, who **knows** the **heart**, showed that he accepted them by

2842 Κάρπος, *Karpos* [1] [√ 2843]

Carpus [1]

2Ti 4:13 bring the cloak that I left with **Carpus** at Troas, and my scrolls,

2843 καρπός, *karpos* [66] [→ 182, 2842, 2844, 2845]

fruit [41], crop [6], harvest [4], crops [3], benefit [2], grain [2],
child bear [+3120+3836] [1], descendants [+3836+4019] [1],
fruitful [+5770] [1], fruitful [1], grapes [1], heads [1], seeds [1],
what**s** [+3836] [1]

Mt 3: 8 Produce **fruit** in keeping with repentance.
3:10 and every tree that does not produce good **fruit** will be cut down
7:16 By their **fruit** you will recognize them. Do people pick grapes
7:17 Likewise every good tree bears good **fruit**, but a bad tree bears bad
7:17 every good tree bears good fruit, but a bad tree bears bad **fruit**.
7:18 A good tree cannot bear bad **fruit**, and a bad tree cannot bear good
7:18 tree cannot bear bad fruit, and a bad tree cannot bear good **fruit**.
7:19 Every tree that does not bear good **fruit** is cut down and thrown
7:20 Thus, by their **fruit** you will recognize them.
12:33 "Make a tree good and its **fruit** will be good, or make a tree bad
12:33 its fruit will be good, or make a tree bad and its **fruit** will be bad,
12:33 and its fruit will be bad, for a tree is recognized by its **fruit**.
13: 8 Still other seed fell on good soil, where it produced a **crop**—
13:26 When the wheat sprouted and formed **heads**, then the weeds also
21:19 Then he said to it, "May you never bear **fruit** again!" Immediately
21:34 When the **harvest** time approached, he sent his servants to the
21:34 he sent his servants to the tenants to collect his **fruit**.
21:41 who will give him his share of the **crop** at harvest time."
21:43 away from you and given to a people who will produce its **fruit**.

Mk 4: 7 grew up and choked the plants, so that they did not bear **grain**.
4: 8 It came up, grew and produced a **crop**, multiplying thirty,
4:29 As soon as the **grain** is ripe, he puts the sickle to it,
11:14 he said to the tree, "May no one ever eat **fruit** from you again."
12: 2 the tenants to collect from them some *of* the **fruit** of the vineyard.

Lk 1:42 and blessed is the **child** [+3120+3836] you will **bear**!
3: 8 Produce **fruit** in keeping with repentance. And do not begin to say
3: 9 and every tree that does not produce good **fruit** will be cut down
6:43 "No good tree bears bad **fruit**, nor does a bad tree bear good fruit.
6:43 "No good trees bears bad fruit, nor does a bad tree bear good **fruit**.
6:44 Each tree is recognized by its own **fruit**. People do not pick figs
8: 8 It came up and yielded a **crop**, a hundred times more than was
12:17 to himself, 'What shall I do? I have no place to store my **crops**.'
13: 6 and he went to look for **fruit** on it, but did not find any.
13: 7 'For three years now I've been coming to look for **fruit** on this fig
13: 9 If it bears **fruit** next year, fine! If not, then cut it down.'"
20:10 so they would give him some *of* the **fruit** of the vineyard.

Jn 4:36 even now he harvests the **crop** for eternal life, so that the sower
12:24 it remains only a single seed. But if it dies, it produces many **seeds**.
15: 2 He cuts off every branch in me that bears no **fruit**, while every
15: 2 while every branch that does bear **fruit** he prunes so that it will be
15: 2 bear fruit he prunes so that *it will be even* more **fruitful** [+5770].
15: 4 No branch can bear **fruit** by itself; it must remain in the vine.
15: 5 If a man remains in me and I in him, he will bear much **fruit**;
15: 8 This is to my Father's glory, that you bear much **fruit**, showing
15:16 but I chose you and appointed you to go and bear **fruit**—
15:16 and appointed you to go and bear fruit—**fruit** that will last.

Ac 2:30 would place one of his **descendants** [+3836+4019] on his throne.

Ro   1:13 in order that I might have a **harvest** among you, just as I have had
    6:21 What **benefit** did you reap at that time from the things you are now
    6:22 the **benefit** you reap leads to holiness, and the result is eternal life.
   15:28 this task and have made sure that they have received this **fruit**,
1Co 9: 7 Who plants a vineyard and does not eat of its **grapes**? Who tends a
Gal 5:22 But the **fruit** of the Spirit is love, joy, peace, patience, kindness,
Eph 5: 9 (for the **fruit** of the light consists in all goodness, righteousness
Php 1:11 filled with the **fruit** of righteousness that comes through Jesus
    1:22 to go on living in the body, this will mean **fruitful** labor for me.
    4:17 but I am looking for **what**ˢ [+3836] may be credited to your
2Ti 2: 6 farmer should be the first to receive a share *of* the **crops**.
Heb 12:11 it produces a **harvest** of righteousness and peace for those who
   13:15 to God a sacrifice of praise—the **fruit** of lips that confess his name.
Jas 3:17 submissive, full of mercy and good **fruit**, impartial and sincere.
    3:18 Peacemakers who sow in peace raise a **harvest** of righteousness.
    5: 7 See how the farmer waits for the land to yield its valuable **crop**
    5:18 and the heavens gave rain, and the earth produced its **crops**.
Rev 22: 2 bearing twelve crops of **fruit**, yielding its fruit every month.
   22: 2 bearing twelve crops of fruit, yielding its **fruit** every month.

2844 καρποφορέω, *karpophoreō* [8] [√ 2843 + 5770]

bearing fruit [2], produce a crop [2], bear fruit [1], bore fruit [1], produces a crop [1], produces grain [1]

Mt 13:23 He **produces a crop**, yielding a hundred, sixty or thirty times
Mk   4:20 sown on good soil, hear the word, accept it, and **produce a crop**—
    4:28 All by itself the soil **produces grain**—first the stalk, then the head,
Lk   8:15 who hear the word, retain it, and by persevering **produce a crop**.
Ro   7: 4 raised from the dead, in order that *we might* **bear fruit** to God.
    7: 5 law were at work in our bodies, so that we **bore fruit** for death.
Col 1: 6 All over the world this gospel is **bearing fruit** and growing,
    1:10 **bearing fruit** in every good work, growing in the knowledge of

2845 καρποφόρος, *karpophoros* [1] [√ 2843 + 5770]

crops [1]

Ac 14:17 by giving you rain from heaven and **crops** in their seasons;

2846 καρτερέω, *kartereō* [1] [→ 4674, 4675; cf. 3197]

persevered [1]

Heb 11:27 king's anger; *he* **persevered** because he saw him who is invisible.

2847 κάρφος, *karphos* [6]

speck [4], speck of sawdust [2]

Mt   7: 3 "Why do you look at the **speck of sawdust** in your brother's eye
    7: 4 you say to your brother, 'Let me take the **speck** out of your eye,'
    7: 5 then you will see clearly to remove the **speck** from your brother's
Lk   6:41 "Why do you look at the **speck of sawdust** in your brother's eye
    6:42 to your brother, 'Brother, let me take the **speck** out of your eye,'
    6:42 then you will see clearly to remove the **speck** from your brother's

2848 κατά, *kata* [477]

[→ 183, 184, 185, 186, 187, 188, 189, 190, 191, 510, 634, 635, 639, 640, 896, 1352, 1588, 1593, 1594, 2129, 2745, 2746, 2747, 2749, 2750, 2757, 2758, 2759, 2761, 2762, 2763, 2765, 2766, 2768, 2769, 2770, 2771, 2772, 2773, 2774, 2775, 2776, 2777, 2778, 2849, 2850, 2851, 2852, 2853, 2854, 2855, 2856, 2857, 2858, 2859, 2860, 2861, 2863, 2864, 2865, 2866, 2867, 2868, 2869, 2870, 2871, 2872, 2874, 2875, 2876, 2877, 2878, 2879, 2880, 2881, 2882, 2883, 2884, 2885, 2886, 2887, 2888, 2889, 2890, 2891, 2892, 2893, 2894, 2895, 2896, 2897, 2898, 2899, 2900, 2901, 2902, 2903, 2904, 2905, 2906, 2907, 2908, 2909, 2910, 2911, 2912, 2913, 2914, 2915, 2916, 2917, 2918, 2919, 2920, 2921, 2922, 2923, 2924, 2925, 2926, 2927, 2928, 2929, 2930, 2931, 2932, 2933, 2934, 2935, 2936, 2937, 2938, 2939, 2940, 2941, 2942, 2943, 2944, 2945, 2946, 2947, 2948, 2949, 2950, 2951, 2952, 2953, 2954, 2955, 2956, 2957, 2958, 2959, 2960, 2961, 2962, 2963, 2964, 2965, 2966, 2967, 2968, 2969, 2971, 2972, 2973, 2974, 2975, 2976, 2977, 2978, 2979, 2980, 2981, 2982, 2983, 2984, 2985, 2986, 2987, 2988, 2989, 2993, 2994, 2995, 2996, 2997, 2998, 2999,
3000, 3001, 3002, 3003, 3004, 3005, 3006, 4153, 4615, 4616, 4617, 5160, 5161, 5162, 5163, 5164, 5691; cf. 2862]

against [47], according to [46], in [42], by [34], *untranslated* [29], as [16], every [11], to [7], about [6], at [6], in accordance with [6], privately [+2625] [6], because of [5], daily [+2465] [5], for [5], like [5], on [4], over [4], with [4], along [3], aside [+2625] [3], based on [3], down [3], in every [3], in keeping with [3], in various [3], of [3], through [3], as for [2], case [+3836] [2], contrary to [2], day after day [+2465] [2], earthly [+4922] [2], every [+4246] [2], every day [+2465] [2], follow [+4513] [2], from house to house [+3875] [2], from one to another [2], godly [+2536] [2], in obedience to [2], in the ordinary way [+4922] [2], Is concerned [2], just as [+4012] [2], just as [2], natural [+5882] [2], off [2], on the basis of [2], out of [2], required [2], that is how [+899+3836] [2], throughout [+3910] [2], throughout [2], your own [+5148] [2], a follower of [1], actions deserve [+2240] [1], after [1], agrees with [1], all [+2625] [1], all over [+3910] [1], alone [+2625] [1], alone [+3668] [1], among [1], annual [+1929] [1], anywhere else in [1], as does [1], as intended [1], as much as were able [+1539] [1], as to [1], as usual [+1621+3836] [1], as usual [+899+3836] [1], as was [1], before [+4725] [1], before [1], both [1], by means of [1], by standards [1], by the standards of [1], carrying out [1], commanding [+2198+3306] [1], conforms to [1], considerate [+1194] [1], covered [+2400] [1], daily [+1667+2465] [1], day by day [+2465+4246] [1], deny [+6017] [1], depends on [1], down from [1], during [1], each [+1651+1651] [1], each [1], everyone [+4246] [1], extreme [+958] [1], face to face [+4725] [1], faced [+4725] [1], follow [1], followed [1], following [+4513] [1], for reasons [1], forced [+340] [1], forefather [+4635+4922] [1], found in [1], from after town [1], from everyday life [+476] [1], from house to house [+3836+3875] [1], from human point of view [+476] [1], from one synagogue to another [+3836+4246+5252] [1], from village to village [+3267+3836] [1], from [1], godly [+2354] [1], great [+5651] [1], happened [+5175] [1], having [1], how [+3836] [1], how [+5515] [1], human [+476] [1], human ancestry [+4922] [1], in any way [+3594+5573] [1], in conformity with [1], in each [1], in homes [+3875] [1], in regard to [1], in response to [1], in the way [1], in this way [+4922] [1], in turn [+1651] [1], in whole [1], indicating that [+4005] [1], intensely [+5651] [1], just as [+3928] [1], just as [+4005+4048+5573] [1], just as [+4005+5573] [1], just like this [+899+3836] [1], leads to [1], member [+3517+3836] [1], most excellent [+5651] [1], near [1], observerˢ [1], one at a time [+1651+1651] [1], opposed to [1], opposite [1], orderly way [+5423] [1], out of favoritism [+4680] [1], over against [1], people of Israel [+2702+4922] [1], prescribed by [1], race [+4922+5150] [1], reasonable [+3364] [1], required by [1], requires [1], something man made up [+476] [1], spontaneous [+1730] [1], surface of things [+4725] [1], that [+4005] [1], that far outweighs them all [+983+1650+5651+5651] [1], this is [+3836] [1], thoroughly [+205] [1], to suit [1], toward [1], utterly [+5651] [1], what has happened to [+3836] [1], when [1], where [1], with regard to [1], year after year [+1929] [1], your [+5148] [1]

Mt   1:20 an angel of the Lord appeared to him **in** a dream and said,
    2:12 And having been warned **in** a dream not to go back to Herod,
    2:13 they had gone, an angel of the Lord appeared to Joseph **in** a dream.
    2:16 **in accordance with** the time he had learned from the Magi.
    2:19 an angel of the Lord appeared **in** a dream to Joseph in Egypt
    2:22 Having been warned **in** a dream, he withdrew to the district of
    5:11 persecute you and falsely say all kinds of evil **against** you
    5:23 and there remember that your brother has something **against** you,
    8:32 and the whole herd rushed **down** the steep bank into the lake
    9:29 and said, "**According to** your faith will it be done to you";
   10:35 For I have come to turn " 'a man **against** his father, a daughter
   10:35 a daughter **against** her mother, a daughter-in-law against her
   10:35 against her mother, a daughter-in-law **against** her mother-in-law—
   12:14 Pharisees went out and plotted [NIE] how they might kill Jesus.
   12:25 "Every kingdom divided **against** itself will be ruined, and every
   12:25 and every city or household divided **against** itself will not stand.
   12:30 "He who is not with me is **against** me, and he who does not gather
   12:32 Anyone who speaks a word **against** the Son of Man will be
   12:32 but anyone who speaks **against** the Holy Spirit will not be

14:13 he withdrew by boat **privately** [+*2625*] to a solitary place.
14:23 dismissed them, he went up on a mountainside **by** himself to pray.
16:27 then he will reward each person **according to** what he has done.
17: 1 brother of James, and led them up a high mountain **by** themselves.
17:19 Then the disciples came to Jesus **in** private and asked, "Why
19: 3 lawful for a man to divorce his wife **for** any and every reason?"
20:11 they received it, they began to grumble **against** the landowner.
20:17 he took the twelve disciples **aside** [+*2625*] and said to them,
23: 3 But do not do what [NIE] they do, for they do not practice what
24: 3 the Mount of Olives, the disciples came to him **privately** [+*2625*].
24: 7 There will be famines and earthquakes **in various** places.
25:15 and to another one talent, each **according to** his ability.
26:55 and clubs to capture me? **Every day** [+*2465*] I sat in the temple
26:59 and the whole Sanhedrin were looking for false evidence **against**
26:63 high priest said to him, "I charge you under oath **by** the living God:
27: 1 and the elders of the people came to the decision to put [NIE]
27:15 Now it was the governor's custom **at** the Feast to release a prisoner
27:19 for I have suffered a great deal today **in** a dream because of him."

Mk 1:27 each other, "What is this? A new teaching—and **with** authority!
3: 6 and began to plot [NIE] **with** the Herodians how they might kill
4:10 When he was **alone** [+*3668*], the Twelve and the others around
4:34 But when he was **alone** [+*2625*] with his own disciples,
5:13 rushed **down** the steep bank into the lake and were drowned.
6:31 "Come with me **by** yourselves to a quiet place and get some rest."
6:32 So they went away **by** themselves in a boat to a solitary place.
6:40 So they sat down in groups **of** hundreds and fifties.
6:40 So they sat down in groups of hundreds and [RPG] fifties.
7: 5 "Why don't your disciples live **according to** the tradition of the
7:33 After he took him **aside** [+*2625*], away from the crowd, Jesus put
9: 2 led them up a high mountain, where they were **all** [+*2625*] alone.
9:28 Jesus had gone indoors, his disciples asked him **privately** [+*2625*],
9:40 for whoever is not **against** us is for us.
11:25 stand praying, if you hold anything **against** anyone, forgive him,
13: 3 Peter, James, John and Andrew asked him **privately** [+*2625*],
13: 8 There will be earthquakes **in various** places, and famines.
14:19 were saddened, and one **by** one they said to him, "Surely not I?"
14:49 **Every day** [+*2465*] I was with you, teaching in the temple courts,
14:55 and the whole Sanhedrin were looking for evidence **against** Jesus
14:56 Many testified falsely **against** him, but their statements did not
14:57 Then some stood up and gave this false testimony **against** him:
15: 6 Now it was the custom **at** the Feast to release a prisoner whom the

Lk 1: 9 he was chosen by lot, **according to** the custom of the priesthood,
1:18 Zechariah asked the angel, "**How** [+*5515*] can I be sure of this?
1:38 servant," Mary answered. "May it be to me **as** you have said."
2:22 When the time of their purification **according to** the Law of Moses
2:24 and to offer a sacrifice **in keeping with** what is said in the Law of
2:27 the child Jesus to do for him what the custom of the Law **required**,
2:29 "Sovereign Lord, **as** you have promised, you now dismiss your
2:31 which you have prepared **in** the sight of all people,
2:39 and Mary had done everything **required by** the Law of the Lord,
2:41 **Every** year his parents went to Jerusalem for the Feast of the
2:42 years old, they went up to the Feast, **according to** the custom.
4:14 and news about him spread **through** the whole countryside.
4:16 on the Sabbath day he went into the synagogue, **as was** his custom.
6:23 For **that is how** [+*899*+*3836*] their fathers treated the prophets.
6:26 for **that is how** [+*899*+*3836*] their fathers treated the false
8: 1 Jesus traveled about **from one** town and village **to another,**
8: 4 and people were coming to Jesus **from** town **after town,**
8:33 and the herd rushed **down** the steep bank into the lake and was
8:39 and told **all over** [+*3910*] town how much Jesus had done for him.
9: 6 So they set out and went **from village to village** [+*3267*+*3836*],
9:10 and they withdrew **by** themselves to a town called Bethsaida.
9:18 Once when Jesus was praying **in** private and his disciples were
9:23 deny himself and take up his cross **daily** [+*2465*] and follow me.
9:50 stop him," Jesus said, "for whoever is not **against** you is for you."
10: 4 take a purse or bag or sandals; and do not greet anyone **on** the road.
10:23 Then he turned to his disciples and said **privately** [+*2625*],
10:31 A priest **happened** [+*5175*] to be going down the same road,
10:32 So too, a Levite, when he came **to** the place and saw him,
10:33 But a Samaritan, as he traveled, came **where** the man was;
11: 3 Give us **each** day our daily bread.
11:23 "He who is not with me is **against** me, and he who does not gather
13:22 Then Jesus went through [NIE] the towns and villages,
15:14 there was a severe famine **in** that **whole** country, and he began to
16:19 was dressed in purple and fine linen and lived in luxury **every** day.
17:30 "It will be **just like this** [+*899*+*3836*] on the day the Son of Man is

19:47 **Every** day he was teaching at the temple. But the chief priests,
21:11 famines and pestilences **in various** places, and fearful events
22:22 The Son of Man will go **as** it has been decreed, but woe to that
22:39 Jesus went out **as usual** [+*1621*+*3836*] to the Mount of Olives,
22:53 **Every** day I was with you in the temple courts, and you did not lay
23: 5 they insisted, "He stirs up the people all **over** Judea by his teaching.
23:14 and have found no basis for your charges **against** him.
23:56 But they rested on the Sabbath **in obedience to** the commandment.

Jn 2: 6 water jars, the kind used by the Jews **for** ceremonial washing,
7:24 Stop judging **by** mere appearances, and make a right judgment."
8: 9 those who heard began to go away **one at a time** [+*1651*+*1651*],
8:15 You judge **by** human standards; I pass judgment on no one.
10: 3 to his voice. He calls his own sheep **by** name and leads them out.
18:29 and asked, "What charges are you bringing **against** this man?"
18:31 Pilate said, "Take him yourselves and judge him **by** your own law."
19: 7 "We have a law, and **according to** that law he must die,
19:11 "You would have no power **over** me if it were not given to you
21:25 If **every** one of them were written down, I suppose that even the

Ac 2:10 and Pamphylia, Egypt and the parts of Libya **near** Cyrene;
2:46 **Every** day they continued to meet together in the temple courts.
2:46 They broke bread **in** their **homes** [+*3875*] and ate together with
2:47 And the Lord added to their number **daily** [+*2465*] those who were
3: 2 where he was put **every** day to beg from those going into the
3:13 over to be killed, and you disowned him **before** [+*4725*] Pilate,
3:17 "Now, brothers, I know that you acted **in** ignorance, as did your
3:22 your own people; you must listen **to** everything he tells you.
4:26 and the rulers gather together **against** the Lord and against his
4:26 gather together **against** the Lord and **against** his Anointed One.'
5:42 after day, in the temple courts and **from house to house** [+*3875*],
6:13 "This fellow never stops speaking **against** this holy place
7:44 made as God directed Moses, **according to** the pattern he had seen.
8: 1 and all except the apostles were scattered **throughout** Judea
8: 3 Going **from house to house** [+*3836*+*3875*], he dragged off men
8:26 an angel of the Lord said to Philip, "Go [NIE] south to the road—
8:36 As they traveled **along** the road, they came to some water
9:31 Then the church **throughout** [+*3910*] Judea, Galilee and Samaria
9:42 This became known all **over** [+*3910*] Joppa, and many people believed in
10:37 You know what has happened **throughout** [+*3910*] Judea,
11: 1 and the brothers **throughout** Judea heard that the Gentiles also had
12: 1 It was about this time that King Herod arrested some who
13: 1 **In** the church at Antioch there were prophets and teachers:
13:22 'I have found David son of Jesse a man **after** my own heart;
13:23 God has brought to Israel the Savior Jesus, **as** he promised.
13:27 the words of the prophets that are read **every** [+*4246*] Sabbath.
14: 1 and Barnabas went **as usual** [+*899*+*3836*] into the Jewish
14: 2 up the Gentiles and poisoned their minds **against** the brothers.
14:23 and Barnabas appointed elders for them **in each** church and,
15:11 our Lord Jesus that we are saved, **just as** [+*4005*+*5573*] they are."
15:21 For Moses has been preached **in every** city from the earliest times
15:21 the earliest times and is read in the synagogues **on** every Sabbath."
15:23 To the Gentile believers **in** Antioch, Syria and Cilicia:
15:36 and visit the brothers **in** all the towns where we preached the word
16: 5 were strengthened in the faith and grew **daily** [+*2465*] in numbers.
16: 7 When they came **to** *the border* of Mysia, they tried to enter
16:22 The crowd joined in the attack **against** Paul and Silas,
16:25 **About** midnight Paul and Silas were praying and singing hymns to
17: 2 **As** his custom was, Paul went into the synagogue, and on three
17:11 and examined the Scriptures **every** day to see if what Paul said was
17:17 as well as in the marketplace **day by day** [+*2465*+*4246*] with those
17:22 "Men of Athens! I see that **in** every way you are very religious.
17:28 As some of **your own** [+*5148*] poets have said, 'We are his
18: 4 **Every** [+*4246*] Sabbath he reasoned in the synagogue, trying to
18:14 it would be **reasonable** [+*3364*] for me to listen to you.
18:15 questions about words and names and **your own** [+*5148*] law—
19: 9 and had discussions **daily** [+*2465*] in the lecture hall of Tyrannus.
19:16 He gave [NIE] them such a beating that they ran out of the house
19:20 In this way the word of the Lord spread widely and grew **in** power.
19:23 **About** that time there arose a great disturbance about the Way.
20:20 but have taught you publicly and **from house to house** [+*3875*].
20:23 I only know that in **every** city the Holy Spirit warns me that prison
21:19 and reported **in** detail what God had done among the Gentiles
21:21 the Jews who *live* **among** the Gentiles to turn away from Moses,
21:28 This is the man who teaches all men everywhere **against** our
22: 3 Under Gamaliel I was **thoroughly** [+*205*] trained in the law of our
22:12 He was a devout **observer**[s] of the law and highly respected by all
22:19 'these men know that I went **from one** synagogue **to another** to

23: 3 You sit there to judge me **according to** the law, yet you yourself
23:19 drew him **aside** [*+2625*] and asked, "What is it you want to tell
23:31 So the soldiers, **carrying out** their orders, took Paul with them
24: 1 and they brought their charges **against** Paul before the governor.
24: 5 a troublemaker, stirring up riots among the Jews all **over** the world.
24:12 stirring up a crowd in the synagogues or **anywhere else in** the city.
24:14 I admit that I worship the God of our fathers as **a follower of** the
24:14 I believe everything that **agrees with** the Law and that is written in
24:22 the commander comes," he said, "I will decide your **case** [*+3836*]."
25: 2 appeared before him and presented the charges **against** Paul.
25: 3 They urgently requested Festus, as a favor **to** them, to have Paul
25: 3 for they were preparing an ambush to kill him **along** the way.
25:14 days there, Festus discussed Paul's **case** [*+3836*] with the king.
25:15 chief priests and elders of the Jews brought charges **against** him
25:16 to hand over any man before he has **faced** [*+4725*] his accusers
25:23 the high ranking officers and the **[NIE]** leading men of the city.
25:27 to send on a prisoner without specifying the charges **against** him."
26: 3 because you are well acquainted with all the **[NIE]** Jewish
26: 5 they are willing, that **according to** the strictest sect of our religion,
26:11 I went **from** one synagogue to another [*+3836+4246+5252*] to
26:13 About noon, O king, *as* I was **on** the road, I saw a light from
27: 2 about to sail for ports **along** the *coast* of the province of Asia,
27: 5 When we had sailed across the open sea **off** the *coast* of Cilicia
27: 7 headway for many days and had difficulty arriving **off** Cnidus.
27: 7 to hold our course, we sailed to the lee of Crete, **opposite** Salmone.
27:12 This was a harbor in Crete, facing **both** southwest and northwest.
27:12 a harbor in Crete, facing both southwest and **[RPG]** northwest.
27:14 called the "northeaster," swept **down from** the island.
27:25 in God that it will happen **just as** [*+4005+4048+5573*] he told me.
27:27 when **about** midnight the sailors sensed they were approaching
27:29 Fearing that we would be dashed **against** the rocks, they dropped
28:16 When we got to Rome, Paul was allowed to live **by** himself,
Ro 1: 3 his Son, who **as to** his human nature was a descendant of David,
    1: 4 and who **through** the Spirit of holiness was declared with power to
    1:15 That is why **[NIE]** I am so eager to preach the gospel also to you
    2: 2 judgment against those who do such things is **based on** truth.
    2: 5 But **because of** your stubbornness and your unrepentant heart,
    2: 6 God "will give to each person **according to** what he has done."
    2: 7 To those who **by** persistence in doing good seek glory, honor
    2:16 judge men's secrets through Jesus Christ, **as** my gospel *declares*,
    3: 2 Much **in** every way! First of all, they have been entrusted with the
    3: 5 bringing his wrath on us? (I am using a **human** [*+476*] argument.)
    4: 1 that Abraham, our **forefather** [*+4635+4922*], discovered in this
    4: 4 his wages are not credited to him **as** a gift, but as an obligation.
    4: 4 his wages are not credited to him as a gift, but **as** an obligation.
    4:16 so that it may be **by** grace and may be guaranteed to all Abraham's
    4:18 **just as** it had been said to him, "So shall your offspring be."
    5: 6 You see, **at** just the right time, when we were still powerless,
    7:13 the commandment sin might become **utterly** [*+5651*] sinful.
    7:22 For **in** my inner being I delight in God's law;
    8: 4 who do not live **according to** the sinful nature but according to the
    8: 4 not live according to the sinful nature but **according to** the Spirit.
    8: 5 Those who live **according to** the sinful nature have their minds set
    8: 5 but those who live **in accordance with** the Spirit have their minds
    8:12 but it is not to the sinful nature, to live **according to** it.
    8:13 For if you live **according to** the sinful nature, you will die;
    8:26 We do not know what we **[NIE]** ought to pray for, but the Spirit
    8:27 because the Spirit intercedes for the saints **in accordance with**
    8:28 who love him, who have been called **according to** his purpose.
    8:31 we say in response to this? If God is for us, who can be **against** us?
    8:33 Who will bring any charge **against** those whom God has chosen?
    9: 3 for the sake of my brothers, those *of* my own **race** [*+4922+5150*],
    9: 5 and from them is traced the **human ancestry** [*+4922*] of Christ,
    9: 9 "**At** the appointed time I will return, and Sarah will have a son."
    9:11 or bad—in order that God's purpose **in** election might stand:
   10: 2 they are zealous for God, but their zeal is not **based on** knowledge.
   11: 2 the passage about Elijah—how he appealed to God **against** Israel:
   11: 5 So too, at the present time there is a remnant chosen **by** grace.
   11:21 For if God did not spare the **natural** [*+5882*] branches, he will not
   11:24 After all, if you were cut out of an olive tree that is wild **by** nature,
   11:24 how much more readily will these, the **natural** [*+5882*] branches,
   11:28 As far as the gospel **is concerned**, they are enemies on your
   11:28 but as far as election **is concerned**, they are loved on account of
   12: 5 and each **member** [*+3517+3836*] belongs to all the others.
   12: 6 We have different gifts, **according to** the grace given us. If a
   12: 6 a man's gift is prophesying, let him use it **in** proportion to his faith.

14:15 because of what you eat, you are no longer acting **in** love.
14:22 So whatever you believe about these things keep between **[NIE]**
15: 5 you a spirit of unity among yourselves as you **follow** Christ Jesus,
16: 5 Greet also the church that *meets* **at** their house. Greet my dear
16:25 Now to him who is able to establish you **by** my gospel
16:25 **according to** the revelation of the mystery hidden for long ages
16:26 and made known through the prophetic writings **by** the command
1Co 1:26 Not many of you were wise **by** human **standards**; not many were
    2: 1 I did not come **with** eloquence or superior wisdom as I proclaimed
    3: 3 are you not worldly? Are you not acting **like** mere men?
    3: 8 and each will be rewarded **according to** his own labor.
    3:10 **By** the grace God has given me, I laid a foundation as an expert
    4: 6 Then you will not take pride in one man **over against** another.
    7: 6 I say this **as** a concession, not as a command.
    7: 6 I say this as a concession, not **as** a command.
    7:40 **In** my judgment, she is happier if she stays as she is—and I think
    9: 8 Do I say this merely **from** a **human point of view** [*+476*]?
   10:18 Consider the **people of Israel** [*+2702+4922*]: Do not those who eat
   11: 4 or prophesies *with* his head **covered** [*+2400*] dishonors his head.
   12: 8 to another the message of knowledge **by means of** the same Spirit,
   12:31 And now I will show you the **most excellent** [*+5651*] way.
   14:27 If anyone speaks in a tongue, **[NIE]** two—or at the most three—
   14:31 For you can all prophesy in [*+1651*] **turn** so that everyone may be
   14:40 everything should be done in a fitting and **orderly way** [*+5423*].
   15: 3 that Christ died for our sins **according to** the Scriptures,
   15: 4 that he was raised on the third day **according to** the Scriptures,
   15:15 for we have testified **about** God that he raised Christ from the
   15:31 I die **every** day—I mean that, brothers—just as surely as I glory
   15:32 If I fought wild beasts in Ephesus for merely human **reasons**,
   16: 2 On the first day of **every** week, each one of you should set aside a
   16:19 in the Lord, and so does the church that *meets* **at** their house.
2Co 1: 8 We were under **great** [*+5651*] pressure, far beyond our ability to
    1:17 Or do I make my plans in a worldly manner so that in the same
    4:13 It **[NIE]** is written: "I believed; therefore I have spoken." With that
    4:17 glory **that far outweighs them all** [*+983+1650+5651+5651*].
    5:16 So from now on we regard no one **from** a worldly point of view.
    5:16 Though we once regarded Christ **in this way**ˢ [*+4922*], we do
    7: 9 For you became sorrowful **as** God **intended** and so were not
    7:10 **Godly** [*+2536*] sorrow brings repentance that leads to salvation
    7:11 See what this **godly** [*+2536*] sorrow has produced in you:
    8: 2 and their **extreme** [*+958*] poverty welled up in rich generosity.
    8: 3 For I testify that they gave **as much as** they **were able** [*+1539*],
    8: 8 *I am* not **commanding** [*+2198+3306*] you, but I want to test the
    8:12 is there, the gift is acceptable **according to** what one has,
    8:12 to what one has, not **according to** what he does not have.
   10: 1 I, Paul, who am "timid" when **face to face** [*+4725*] with you,
   10: 2 people who think that we live **by the standards of** this world.
   10: 3 we live in the world, we do not wage war **as** the world **does**.
   10: 5 and every pretension that sets itself up **against** the knowledge of
   10: 7 You are looking only on the **surface of things** [*+4725*]. If anyone
   10:13 but will *confine* our boasting to the field God has assigned to us,
   10:15 **[NIE]** our area of activity among you will greatly expand,
   11:15 Their end will be *what* their **actions deserve** [*+2240*].
   11:17 In this self-confident boasting I am not talking **as** the Lord would,
   11:18 Since many are boasting **in the way** the world does, I too will
   11:21 **To** my shame I admit that we were too weak for that! What anyone
   11:28 I face **daily** [*+2465*] the pressure of my concern for all the
   13: 8 For we cannot do anything **against** the truth, but only for the truth.
   13:10 that when I come I may not have to be harsh in my use **of**
Gal 1: 4 the present evil age, **according to** the will of our God and Father,
    1:11 the gospel I preached is not **something** that **man made up** [*+476*].
    1:13 how **intensely** [*+5651*] I persecuted the church of God and tried to
    2: 1 I went **in response to** a revelation and set before them the gospel
    2: 2 But I did this **privately** [*+2625*] to those who seemed to be leaders,
    2:11 When Peter came to Antioch, I opposed him **to** his face,
    3: 1 **Before** your very eyes Jesus Christ was clearly portrayed as
    3:15 Brothers, let me take an example **from everyday life** [*+476*].
    3:21 Is the law, therefore, **opposed to** the promises of God? Absolutely
    3:29 then you are Abraham's seed, and heirs **according to** the promise.
    4:23 son by the slave woman was born **in the ordinary way** [*+4922*];
    4:28 Now you, brothers, **like** Isaac, are children of promise.
    4:29 At that time the son born **in the ordinary way** [*+4922*] persecuted
    4:29 ordinary way persecuted the son born **by** *the power* of the Spirit.
    5:17 For the sinful nature desires what is **contrary to** the Spirit,
    5:17 to the Spirit, and the Spirit what is **contrary to** the sinful nature.
    5:23 gentleness and self-control. **Against** such things there is no law.

Eph 1: 5 through Jesus Christ, **in accordance with** his pleasure and will—
1: 7 forgiveness of sins, **in accordance with** the riches of God's grace
1: 9 And he made known to us the mystery of his will **according to** his
1:11 having been predestined **according to** the plan of him who works
1:11 works out everything **in conformity with** the purpose of his will,
1:15 ever since I heard about **your** [+5148] faith in the Lord Jesus
1:19 who believe. That power is **like** the working of his mighty strength,
2: 2 in which you used to live when you **followed** the ways of this
2: 2 of this world and **[RPG]** of the ruler of the kingdom of the air,
3: 3 that is, the mystery made known to me **by** revelation, as I have
3: 7 I became a servant of this gospel **by** the gift of God's grace given
3: 7 gift of God's grace given me **through** the working of his power.
3:11 **according to** his eternal purpose which he accomplished in Christ
3:16 I pray that **out of** his glorious riches he may strengthen you with
3:20 or imagine, **according to** his power that is at work within us,
4: 7 But to each one of us grace has been given **as** Christ apportioned it.
4:16 grows and builds itself up in love, **as** each part does its work.
4:22 You were taught, **with regard to** your former way of life,
4:22 off your old self, which is being corrupted **by** its deceitful desires;
4:24 new self, created to be **like** God in true righteousness and holiness.
5:33 **[NIE]** each one of you also must love his wife as he loves
6: 5 Slaves, obey your **earthly** [+4922] masters with respect and fear,
6: 6 Obey them not only to win their favor **when** their eye is on you,
6:21 so that you also may know **how** [+3836] I am and what I am doing.

Php 1:12 that **what has happened** [+3836] to me has really served to
1:20 **[NIE]** I eagerly expect and hope that I will in no way be ashamed,
2: 3 Do nothing **out of** selfish ambition or vain conceit, but in humility
2: 3 Do nothing out of selfish ambition or **[RPG]** vain conceit,
3: 5 a Hebrew of Hebrews; **in regard to** the law, a Pharisee;
3: 6 **as for** zeal, persecuting the church; as for legalistic righteousness,
3: 6 persecuting the church; **as for** legalistic righteousness, faultless.
3:14 I press on **toward** the goal to win the prize for which God has
3:21 **by** the power that enables him to bring everything under his
4:11 I am not saying this because I am **in** need, for I have learned to be
4:19 And my God will meet all your needs **according to** his glorious

Col 1:11 being strengthened with all power **according to** his glorious might
1:25 I have become its servant **by** the commission God gave me to
1:29 struggling **with** all his energy, which so powerfully works in me.
2: 8 which **depends on** human tradition and the basic principles of this
2: 8 and **[RPG]** the basic principles of this world rather than on Christ.
2: 8 and the basic principles of this world rather than **on** Christ.
2:14 its regulations, that was **against** us and that stood opposed to us;
2:22 because they are **based on** human commands and teachings.
3:10 which is being renewed in knowledge **in** the image of its Creator.
3:20 Children, obey your parents **in** everything, for this pleases the
3:22 Slaves, obey your **earthly** [+4922] masters in everything;
3:22 Slaves, obey your earthly masters **in** everything; and do it,
4: 7 Tychicus will tell you all the news **about** me. He is a dear brother,
4:15 brothers at Laodicea, and to Nympha and the church **in** her house.

2Th 1:12 **according to** the grace of our God and the Lord Jesus Christ.
2: 3 Don't let anyone deceive you **in any way** [+3594+5573], for that
2: 9 The coming of the lawless one will be **in accordance with**
3: 6 and does not live **according to** the teaching you received from us.

1Ti 1: 1 an apostle of Christ Jesus **by** the command of God our Savior
1:11 that **conforms to** the glorious gospel of the blessed God, which he
1:18 I give you this instruction **in keeping with** the prophecies once
5:19 Do not entertain an accusation **against** an elder unless it is brought
5:21 without partiality, and to do nothing **out of favoritism** [+4680].
6: 3 instruction of our Lord Jesus Christ and to **godly** [+2354] teaching,

2Ti 1: 1 will of God, **according to** the promise of life that is in Christ Jesus,
1: 8 But join with me in suffering for the gospel, **by** the power of God,
1: 9 not **because of** anything we have done but because of his own
1: 9 anything we have done but **because of** his own purpose and grace.
2: 8 from the dead, descended from David. **This is** [+3836] my gospel,
4: 3 Instead, **to suit** their own desires, they will gather around them a
4:14 great deal of harm. The Lord will repay him **for** what he has done.

Tit 1: 1 of God and an apostle of Jesus Christ **for** the faith of God's elect
1: 1 God's elect and the knowledge of the truth that **leads to** godliness
1: 3 the preaching entrusted to me **by** the command of God our Savior,
1: 4 To Titus, my true son **in** our common faith: Grace and peace from
1: 5 out what was left unfinished and appoint elders in **every** town,
1: 9 He must hold firmly to the trustworthy message **as** it has been
3: 5 of righteous things we had done, but **because of** his mercy.
3: 7 his grace, we might become heirs **having** the hope of eternal life.

Phm 1: 2 our fellow soldier and to the church that *meets* **in** your home:
1:14 so that any favor you do will be **spontaneous** [+1730] and not

1:14 that any favor you do will be spontaneous and not **forced** [+340].

Heb 1:10 He also says, "**In** the beginning, O Lord, you laid the foundations
2: 4 and gifts of the Holy Spirit distributed **according to** his will.
2:17 For this reason he had to be made like his brothers **in** every way,
3: 3 been found worthy of greater honor than Moses, **just as** [+4012]
3: 8 as you did in the rebellion, **during** the time of testing in the desert,
3:13 But encourage one another **daily** [+1667+2465], as long as it is
4:15 but we have one who has been tempted **in** every way, just as we
4:15 one who has been tempted in every way, **just as** [+3928] we are—
5: 6 "You are a priest forever, **in** the order of Melchizedek."
5:10 and was designated by God to be high priest **in** the order of
6:13 since there was **[NIE]** no one greater for him to swear by,
6:13 there was no one greater for him to swear by, he swore **by** himself,
6:16 Men swear **by** someone greater than themselves, and the oath
6:20 He has become a high priest forever, **in** the order of Melchizedek.
7: 5 Now **[NIE]** the law requires the descendants of Levi who become
7:11 one **in** the order of Melchizedek, not in the order of Aaron?
7:11 one in the order of Melchizedek, not **in** the order of Aaron?
7:15 And what we have said is even more **[NIE]** clear if another priest
7:16 one who has become a priest not **on the basis of** a regulation as to
7:16 his ancestry but **on the basis of** the power of an indestructible life.
7:17 is declared: "You are a priest forever, **in** the order of Melchizedek."
7:20 And **[NIE]** it was not without an oath! Others became priests
7:22 **Because of** this oath, Jesus has become the guarantee of a better
7:27 he does not need to offer sacrifices **day after day** [+2465],
8: 4 for there are already men who offer the gifts **prescribed by** the
8: 5 "See to it that you make everything **according to** the pattern shown
8: 9 It will not be **like** the covenant I made with their forefathers when I
9: 5 atonement cover. But we cannot discuss these things **in** detail now.
9: 9 This is an illustration for the present time, **indicating that** [+4005]
9: 9 and sacrifices being offered were not able to clear **[NIE]** the
9:19 When Moses had proclaimed every commandment **of** the law to all
9:22 the law **requires** that nearly everything be cleansed with blood,
9:25 the way the high priest enters the Most Holy Place **every** year with
9:27 **Just as** [+4012] man is destined to die once, and after that to face
10: 1 by the same sacrifices repeated endlessly **year after year** [+1929],
10: 3 But those sacrifices are an **annual** [+1929] reminder of sins,
10: 8 nor were you pleased with them" (although the law **required** them
10:11 **Day after day** [+2465] every priest stands and performs his
11: 7 and became heir of the righteousness that *comes* **by** faith.
11:13 All these people were still *living* **by** faith when they died.
12:10 Our fathers disciplined us for a little while **as** they thought best;

Jas 2: 8 If you really keep the royal law **found in** Scripture, "Love your
2:17 In the same way, faith **by** itself, if it is not accompanied by action,
3: 9 and with it we curse men, who have been made **in** God's likeness.
3:14 in your hearts, do not boast about it or **deny** [+6017] the truth.
5: 9 Don't grumble **against** each other, brothers, or you will be judged.

1Pe 1: 2 who have been chosen **according to** the foreknowledge of God the
1: 3 **In** his great mercy he has given us new birth into a living hope
1:15 But **just as** he who called you is holy, so be holy in all you do;
1:17 Since you call on a Father who judges **[NIE]** each man's work
2:11 to abstain from sinful desires, which war **against** your soul.
3: 7 in the same way *be* **considerate** [+1194] as you live with your
4: 6 so that they might be judged **according to** men in regard to the
4: 6 to the body, but live **according to** God in regard to the spirit.
4:13 But rejoice **that** [+4005] you participate in the sufferings of Christ,
4:19 those who suffer **according to** God's will should commit
5: 2 you must, but because you are willing, **as** God wants you to be;

2Pe 2:11 do not bring slanderous accusations **against** such beings in the
3: 3 will come, scoffing and **following** [+4513] their own evil desires.
3:13 But **in keeping with** his promise we are looking forward to a new
3:15 just as our dear brother Paul also wrote you **with** the wisdom that

1Jn 5:14 that if we ask anything **according to** his will, he hears us.

2Jn 1: 6 And this is love: that we walk **in obedience to** his commands.

3Jn 1:14 friends here send their greetings. Greet the friends there **by** name.

Jude 1:15 to judge **everyone** [+4246], and to convict all the ungodly of all the
1:15 and of all the harsh words ungodly sinners have spoken **against**
1:16 and faultfinders; *they* **follow** [+4513] their own evil desires;
1:18 "In the last times there will be scoffers *who will* **follow** [+4513]

Rev 2: 4 Yet I hold this **against** you: You have forsaken your first love.
2:14 Nevertheless, I have a few things **against** you: You have people
2:20 Nevertheless, I have this **against** you: You tolerate that woman
2:23 and minds, and I will repay each of you **according to** your deeds.
4: 8 **Each** [+1651+1651] of the four living creatures had six wings
18: 6 to her as she has given; pay her back double **for** what she has done.
20:12 The dead were judged **according to** what they had done as

20:13 and each person was judged **according to** what he had done.
22: 2 bearing twelve crops of fruit, yielding its fruit **[NIE]** every month.

2849 καταβαίνω, *katabainō* [81] [√ 2848 + 326]

come down [14], went down [13], came down [12], coming down [9], go down [6], descended [3], descending [3], comes down [2], down [2], goes down [2], going down [2], arrived [1], came [1], come [1], comes [1], descend [1], falling [1], fell [1], go downstairs [1], gone down [1], got down [1], let down [1], on the way [1], went [1]

Mt   3:16 and he saw the Spirit of God **descending** like a dove and lighting
    7:25 The rain **came down**, the streams rose, and the winds blew
    7:27 The rain **came down**, the streams rose, and the winds blew
    8: 1 *When* he **came down** from the mountainside, large crowds
   11:23 you be lifted up to the skies? No, *you will* **go down** to the depths.
   14:29 Then Peter **got down** out of the boat, walked on the water
   17: 9 *As they were* **coming down** the mountain, Jesus instructed them,
   24:17 *Let* no one on the roof of his house **go down** to take anything out
   27:40 **Come down** from the cross, if you are the Son of God!"
   27:42 *Let him* **come down** now from the cross, and we will believe in
   28: 2 for an angel of the Lord **came down** from heaven and, going to the
Mk   1:10 being torn open and the Spirit **descending** on him like a dove.
    3:22 And the teachers of the law who **came down** from Jerusalem said,
    9: 9 *As they were* **coming down** the mountain, Jesus gave them orders
   13:15 *Let* no one on the roof of his house **go down** or enter the house to
   15:30 **come down** from the cross and save yourself!"
   15:32 *Let* this Christ, this King of Israel, **come down** now from the
Lk   2:51 Then *he* **went down** to Nazareth with them and was obedient to
    3:22 and the Holy Spirit **descended** on him in bodily form like a dove.
    6:17 He **went down** with them and stood on a level place. A large
    8:23 A squall **came down** on the lake, so that the boat was being
    9:54 do you want us to call fire **down** from heaven to destroy them?"
   10:15 you be lifted up to the skies? No, *you will* **go down** to the depths.
   10:30 "A man *was* **going down** from Jerusalem to Jericho, when he fell
   10:31 A priest happened *to be* **going down** the same road, and when he
   17:31 of his house, with his goods inside, *should* **go down** to get them.
   18:14 this man, rather than the other, **went** home justified before God.
   19: 5 looked up and said to him, "Zacchaeus, **come down** immediately.
   19: 6 So *he* **came down** at once and welcomed him gladly.
   22:44 and his sweat was like drops of blood **falling** to the ground.
Jn   1:32 "I saw the Spirit **come down** from heaven as a dove and remain on
    1:33 'The man on whom you see the Spirit **come down** and remain is he
    1:51 the angels of God ascending and **descending** on the Son of Man."
    2:12 After this *he* **went down** to Capernaum with his mother
    3:13 No one has ever gone into heaven except the one *who* **came** from
    4:47 he went to him and begged him to **come** and heal his son,
    4:49 The royal official said, "Sir, **come down** before my child dies."
    4:51 *While* he *was* still **on the way**, his servants met him with the news
    5: 7 While I am trying to get in, someone else **goes down** ahead of me."
    6:16 When evening came, his disciples **went down** to the lake,
    6:33 For the bread of God is he *who* **comes down** from heaven
    6:38 For *I have* **come down** from heaven not to do my will but to do the
    6:41 because he said, "I am the bread that **came down** from heaven."
    6:42 we know? How can he now say, '*I* **came down** from heaven'?"
    6:50 But here is the bread that **comes down** from heaven, which a man
    6:51 I am the living bread that **came down** from heaven. If anyone eats
    6:58 This is the bread that **came down** from heaven. Your forefathers
Ac   7:15 Then Jacob **went down** to Egypt, where he and our fathers died.
    7:34 I have heard their groaning and *have* **come down** to set them free.
    8:15 *When they* **arrived**, they prayed for them that they might receive
    8:26 the desert road—that **goes down** from Jerusalem to Gaza."
    8:38 Then both Philip and the eunuch **went down** into the water
   10:11 and something like a large sheet *being* **let down** to earth by its four
   10:20 So get up and **go downstairs**. Do not hesitate to go with them,
   10:21 Peter **went down** and said to the men, "I'm the one you're looking
   11: 5 from heaven by its four corners, and it came **down** to where I was.
   14:11 "The gods *have* **come down** to us in human form!"
   14:25 they had preached the word in Perga, *they* **went down** to Attalia.
   16: 8 So they passed by Mysia and **went down** to Troas.
   18:22 he went up and greeted the church and then **went down** to Antioch.
   20:10 Paul **went down**, threw himself on the young man and put his arms
   23:10 He ordered the troops to **go down** and take him away from them by
   24: 1 Five days later the high priest Ananias **went down** to Caesarea
   24:22 "When Lysias the commander **comes**," he said, "I will decide your

   25: 6 spending eight or ten days with them, *he* **went down** to Caesarea,
   25: 7 the Jews *who had* **come down** from Jerusalem stood around him,
Ro 10: 7 "or 'Who *will* **descend** into the deep?' " (that is, to bring Christ up
Eph   4: 9 (What does "he ascended" mean except that *he* also **descended** to
    4:10 He *who* **descended** is the very one who ascended higher than all
1Th   4:16 For the Lord himself *will* **come down** from heaven, with a loud
Jas   1:17 from above, **coming down** from the Father of the heavenly lights,
Rev   3:12 which *is* **coming down** out of heaven from my God;
   10: 1 Then I saw another mighty angel **coming down** from heaven.
   12:12 to the earth and the sea, because the devil *has* **gone down** to you!
   13:13 even causing fire *to* **come down** from heaven to earth in full view
   16:21 From the sky huge hailstones of about a hundred pounds *each* **fell**
   18: 1 After this I saw another angel **coming down** from heaven.
   20: 1 And I saw an angel **coming down** out of heaven, having the key to
   20: 9 he loves. But fire **came down** from heaven and devoured them.
   21: 2 the new Jerusalem, **coming down** out of heaven from God,
   21:10 the Holy City, Jerusalem, **coming down** out of heaven from God.

2850 καταβάλλω, *kataballō* [2] [√ 2848 + 965]

laying [1], struck down [1]

2Co   4: 9 persecuted, but not abandoned; **struck down**, but not destroyed.
Heb   6: 1 not **laying** again the foundation of repentance from acts that lead to

2851 καταβαρέω, *katabareō* [1] [√ 2848 + 983]

burden to [1]

2Co 12:16 Be that as it may, I *have* not *been* a **burden to** you. Yet,

2852 καταβαρύνω, *katabarynō* [1] [√ 2848 + 983]

heavy [1]

Mk 14:40 he again found them sleeping, because their eyes were **heavy**.

2853 κατάβασις, *katabasis* [1] [√ 2848 + 326]

place where the road goes down [1]

Lk 19:37 When he came near the **place where the road goes down** the

2854 καταβιβάζω, *katabibazo* Not used in UBS/NIV [√ 2848 + 326]

2855 καταβοάω, *kataboaō* Not used in UBS/NIV [√ 2848 + 1068]

2856 καταβολή, *katabolē* [11] [√ 2848 + 965]

creation [9], become a father [+3284+5065] [1], beginning [1]

Mt 13:35 I will utter things hidden since the **creation** of the world."
   25:34 the kingdom prepared for you since the **creation** of the world.
Lk 11:50 the prophets that has been shed since the **beginning** of the world,
Jn 17:24 given me because you loved me before the **creation** of the world.
Eph   1: 4 For he chose us in him before the **creation** of the world to be holy
Heb   4: 3 And yet his work has been finished since the **creation** of the world.
    9:26 have had to suffer many times since the **creation** of the world.
   11:11 was enabled to **become a father** [+3284+5065] because he
1Pe   1:20 He was chosen before the **creation** of the world, but was revealed
Rev 13: 8 to the Lamb that was slain from the **creation** of the world.
   17: 8 **creation** of the world will be astonished when they see the beast,

2857 καταβραβεύω, *katabrabeuō* [1] [√ 2848 + 1093]

disqualify for the prize [1]

Col   2:18 *Do* not *let* anyone who delights in false humility and the worship of angels **disqualify** you **for the prize**.

2858 καταγγελεύς, *katangeleus* [1] [√ 2848 + 34]

advocating [1]

Ac 17:18 Others remarked, "He seems to be **advocating** foreign gods."

2859 καταγγέλλω, **katangellō** [18] [√ 2848 + 34]

proclaim [4], proclaimed [3], preach [2], preached [2], proclaiming [2], advocating [1], foretold [1], preaching [1], reported [1], telling [1]

Ac   3:24   Samuel on, as many as have spoken, *have* **foretold** these days.
       4: 2   the people and **proclaiming** in Jesus the resurrection of the dead.
      13: 5   *they* **proclaimed** the word of God in the Jewish synagogues.
      13:38   that through Jesus the forgiveness of sins *is* **proclaimed** to you.
      15:36   and visit the brothers in all the towns where *we* **preached** the word
      16:17   of the Most High God, who *are* **telling** you the way to be saved."
      16:21   *by* **advocating** customs unlawful for us Romans to accept
      17: 3   "This Jesus I *am* **proclaiming** to you is the Christ," he said.
      17:13   When the Jews in Thessalonica learned that Paul *was* **preaching**
      17:23   worship as something unknown I *am going to* **proclaim** to you.
      26:23   would **proclaim** light to his own people and to the Gentiles."
Ro   1: 8   all of you, because your faith *is being* **reported** all over the world.
1Co   2: 1   or superior wisdom *as I* **proclaimed** to you the testimony about
       9:14   the Lord has commanded that those *who* **preach** the gospel should
      11:26   and drink this cup, *you* **proclaim** the Lord's death until he comes.
Php   1:17   The former **preach** Christ out of selfish ambition, not sincerely,
       1:18   every way, whether from false motives or true, Christ *is* **preached**.
Col   1:28   We **proclaim** him, admonishing and teaching everyone with all

2860 καταγελάω, **katagelaō** [3] [√ 2848 + 1151]

laughed at [3]

Mt   9:24   The girl is not dead but asleep." But *they* **laughed at** him.
Mk   5:40   But *they* **laughed at** him. After he put them all out, he took the
Lk   8:53   *They* **laughed at** him, knowing that she was dead.

2861 καταγινώσκω, **kataginōskō** [3] [√ 2848 + 1182]

condemn [2], clearly in the wrong [1]

Gal   2:11   I opposed him to his face, because he was **clearly in the wrong**.
1Jn   3:20   whenever our hearts **condemn** us. For God is greater than our
       3:21   Dear friends, if our hearts *do* not **condemn** us, we have

2862 κατάγνυμι, **katagnymi** [4] [→ 544, 3728; cf. 2848]

break [2], broke [1], broken [1]

Mt   12:20   A bruised reed he will not **break**, and a smoldering wick he will
Jn   19:31   they asked Pilate to *have* the legs **broken** and the bodies taken
     19:32   and **broke** the legs of the first man who had been crucified with
     19:33   and found that he was already dead, *they did* not **break** his legs.

2863 καταγράφω, **katagraphō** [1] [√ 2848 + 1211]

write [1]

Jn   8: 6   bent down and *started to* **write** on the ground with his finger.

2864 κατάγω, **katagō** [9] [√ 2848 + 72]

bring [2], brought [2], bring down [1], landed [1], pulled up [1], put in [1], took down [1]

Lk   5:11   So *they* **pulled** their boats **up** on shore, left everything
Ac   9:30   *they* **took** him **down** to Caesarea and sent him off to Tarsus.
      22:30   to assemble. Then he **brought** Paul and had him stand before them.
      23:15   and the Sanhedrin petition the commander to **bring** him before you
      23:20   "The Jews have agreed to ask you to **bring** Paul before the
      23:28   why they were accusing him, so *I* **brought** him to their Sanhedrin.
      27: 3   The next day *we* **landed** at Sidon; and Julius, in kindness to Paul,
      28:12   We **put in** at Syracuse and stayed there three days.
Ro   10: 6   'Who will ascend into heaven?' " (that is, *to* **bring** Christ **down**)

2865 καταγωνίζομαι, **katagōnizomai** [1]
       [√ 2848 + 74]

conquered [1]

Heb 11:33   who through faith **conquered** kingdoms, administered justice,

2866 καταδέω, **katadeō** [1] [√ 2848 + 1313]

bandaged [1]

Lk   10:34   He went to him and **bandaged** his wounds, pouring on oil

2867 κατάδηλος, **katadēlos** [1] [√ 2848 + 1316]

clear [1]

Heb   7:15   And what we have said is even more **clear** if another priest like

2868 καταδικάζω, **katadikazō** [5] [√ 2848 + 1472]

condemned [4], condemn [1]

Mt   12: 7   not sacrifice,' *you* would not have **condemned** the innocent.
      12:37   you will be acquitted, and by your words *you will be* **condemned**."
Lk   6:37   *Do* not **condemn**, and you will not be condemned. Forgive,
       6:37   Do not condemn, and *you will* not *be* **condemned**. Forgive,
Jas   5: 6   *You have* **condemned** and murdered innocent men, who were not

2869 καταδίκη, **katadikē** [1] [√ 2848 + 1472]

condemned [1]

Ac   25:15   brought charges against him and asked that he be **condemned**.

2870 καταδιώκω, **katadiōkō** [1] [√ 2848 + 1503]

to look for [1]

Mk   1:36   Simon and his companions *went* **to look for** him,

2871 καταδουλόω, **katadouloō** [2] [√ 2848 + 1528]

enslaves [1], make slaves [1]

2Co 11:20   you even put up with anyone *who* **enslaves** you or exploits you
Gal   2: 4   spy on the freedom we have in Christ Jesus and to **make** us **slaves**.

2872 καταδυναστεύω, **katadynasteuō** [2]
       [√ 2848 + 1538]

exploiting [1], under the power [1]

Ac   10:38   and healing all who *were* **under the power** of the devil,
Jas   2: 6   have insulted the poor. Is it not the rich *who are* **exploiting** you?

2873 κατάθεμα, **katathema** [1] [√ 2874]

curse [1]

Rev 22: 3   No longer will there be any **curse**. The throne of God and of the

2874 καταθεματίζω, **katathematizō** [1] [→ 2873; cf. 2848 + 5502]

call down curses [1]

Mt   26:74   Then he began *to* **call down curses** *on* himself and he swore to

2875 καταισχύνω, **kataischynō** [13] [√ 2848 + 156]

put to shame [3], ashamed of [2], dishonors [2], shame [2], disappoint [1], embarrassed [1], humiliate [1], humiliated [1]

Lk   13:17   When he said this, all his opponents *were* **humiliated**, but the
Ro   5: 5   And hope *does* not **disappoint** us, because God has poured out his
       9:33   and the one who trusts in him *will* never *be* **put to shame**."
      10:11   "Anyone who trusts in him *will* never *be* **put to shame**.
1Co   1:27   But God chose the foolish things of the world to **shame** the wise;
       1:27   God chose the weak things of the world to **shame** the strong.
      11: 4   who prays or prophesies with his head covered **dishonors** his head.
      11: 5   or prophesies with her head uncovered **dishonors** her head—
      11:22   despise the church of God and **humiliate** those who have nothing?
2Co   7:14   had boasted to him about you, and you *have* not **embarrassed** me.
       9: 4   about you—*would be* **ashamed of** having been so confident.
1Pe   2: 6   and the one who trusts in him *will* never *be* **put to shame**."
       3:16   your good behavior in Christ *may be* **ashamed of** their slander.

2876 κατακαίω, *katakaiō* [12] [√ 2848 + 2794]

burned up [4], burned [4], burn up [1], burn [1], burning up [1],
consumed [2]

Mt   3:12 into the barn and **burning up** the chaff with unquenchable fire."
     13:30 First collect the weeds and tie them in bundles to *be* **burned**;
     13:40 "As the weeds are pulled up and **burned** in the fire, so it will be at
Lk   3:17 his barn, but *he will* **burn up** the chaff with unquenchable fire."
Ac 19:19 sorcery brought their scrolls together and **burned** them publicly.
1Co 3:15 If it *is* **burned up**, he will suffer loss; he himself will be saved,
Heb 13:11 as a sin offering, but the bodies *are* **burned** outside the camp.
Rev 8: 7 A third of the earth *was* **burned up**, a third of the trees were
      8: 7 of the earth was burned up, a third of the trees *were* **burned up**,
      8: 7 the trees were burned up, and all the green grass *was* **burned up**.
    17:16 and leave her naked; they will eat her flesh and **burn** her with fire.
    18: 8 *She will be* **consumed** by fire, for mighty is the Lord God who

2877 κατακαλύπτω, *katakalyptō* [3] [√ 2848 + 2821]

cover [3]

1Co 11: 6 If a woman *does* not **cover** her head, she should have her hair cut
    11: 6 to have her hair cut or shaved off, *she should* **cover** her head.
    11: 7 A man ought not *to* **cover** his head, since he is the image and glory

2878 κατακαυχάομαι, *katakauchaomai* [4]
[√ 2848 + 3016]

boast over [1], boast [1], do^s [1], triumphs over [1]

Ro 11:18 *do* not **boast over** those branches. If you do, consider this:
    11:18 If you do^s, consider this: You do not support the root, but the root
Jas   2:13 who has not been merciful. Mercy **triumphs over** judgment!
     3:14 ambition in your hearts, *do* not **boast** *about* it or deny the truth.

2879 κατάκειμαι, *katakeimai* [12] [√ 2848 + 3023]

eating [3], lying [2], bedridden [+2093+3187] [1], dinner [1], in
bed [1], lie [1], lying on [1], reclining at the table [1], sick in bed
[1]

Mk 1:30 Simon's mother-in-law *was* **in bed** with a fever, and they told
     2: 4 through it, lowered the mat the paralyzed man *was* **lying on**.
     2:15 While Jesus *was having* **dinner** at Levi's house, many tax
    14: 3 **reclining at the table** in the home of a man known as Simon the
Lk   5:25 took what *he had been* **lying** on and went home praising God.
     5:29 a large crowd of tax collectors and others were **eating** with them.
     7:37 in that town learned that Jesus *was* **eating** at the Pharisee's house,
Jn   5: 3 Here a great number of disabled people *used to* **lie**—the blind,
     5: 6 When Jesus saw him **lying** there and learned that he had been in
Ac   9:33 a paralytic *who had been* **bedridden** [+2093+3187] for eight years.
    28: 8 His father *was* **sick in bed**, suffering from fever and dysentery.
1Co 8:10 sees you who have this knowledge **eating** in an idol's temple,

2880 κατακλάω, *kataklaō* [2] [√ 2848 + 3089]

broke [2]

Mk 6:41 and looking up to heaven, he gave thanks and **broke** the loaves.
Lk 9:16 and looking up to heaven, he gave thanks and **broke** them.

2881 κατακλείω, *katakleiō* [2] [√ 2848 + 3091]

locked up [1], put [1]

Lk 3:20 Herod added this to them all: *He* **locked** John **up** in prison.
Ac 26:10 On the authority of the chief priests I **put** many of the saints in

2882 κατακληροδοτέω, *kataklērodoteō* Not used in
UBS/NIV [√ 2848 + 3102 + 1443]

2883 κατακληρονομέω, *kataklēronomeō* [1]
[√ 2848 + 3102 + 3795]

gave to as inheritance [1]

Ac 13:19 in Canaan and **gave** their land **to** his people **as** their **inheritance**.

2884 κατακλίνω, *kataklinō* [5] [√ 2848 + 3111]

at the table [1], reclined at the table [1], sat down [1], sit down
[1], take [+1650] [1]

Lk 7:36 so he went to the Pharisee's house and **reclined at the table**.
     9:14 his disciples, "Have them **sit down** in groups of about fifty each."
     9:15 The disciples did so, and everybody **sat down**.
    14: 8 you to a wedding feast, *do* not **take** [+1650] the place of honor,
    24:30 When he *was* **at the table** with them, he took bread, gave thanks,

2885 κατακλύζω, *kataklyzō* [1] [√ 2848 + 3114]

deluged [+5623] [1]

2Pe 3: 6 By these waters also the world of that time *was* **deluged** [+5623]

2886 κατακλυσμός, *kataklysmos* [4] [√ 2848 + 3114]

flood [4]

Mt 24:38 For in the days before the **flood**, people were eating and drinking,
    24:39 and they knew nothing about what would happen until the **flood**
Lk 17:27 Noah entered the ark. Then the **flood** came and destroyed them all.
2Pe 2: 5 if he did not spare the ancient world when he brought the **flood** on

2887 κατακολουθέω, *katakoloutheō* [2]
[√ 2848 + 199 [1.3]]

followed [2]

Lk 23:55 The women who had come with Jesus from Galilee **followed**
Ac 16:17 This girl **followed** Paul and the rest of us, shouting, "These men are

2888 κατακόπτω, *katakoptō* [1] [√ 2848 + 3164]

cut [1]

Mk 5: 5 and in the hills he would cry out and **cut** himself with stones.

2889 κατακρημνίζω, *katakrēmnizō* [1]
[√ 2848 + 3203]

throw down the cliff [1]

Lk 4:29 on which the town was built, in order to **throw** him **down the cliff**.

2890 κατάκριμα, *katakrima* [3] [√ 2848 + 3212]

condemnation [3]

Ro 5:16 The judgment followed one sin and brought **condemnation**,
    5:18 just as the result of one trespass was **condemnation** for all men,
    8: 1 there is now no **condemnation** for those who are in Christ Jesus,

2891 κατακρίνω, *katakrinō* [18] [√ 2848 + 3212]

condemned [9], condemn [7], condemning [1], condemns [1]

Mt 12:41 will stand up at the judgment with this generation and **condemn** it;
    12:42 will rise at the judgment with this generation and **condemn** it;
    20:18 and the teachers of the law. They will **condemn** him to death
    27: 3 who had betrayed him, saw that Jesus *was* **condemned**,
Mk 10:33 *They will* **condemn** him to death and will hand him over to the
    14:64 What do you think?" They all **condemned** him as worthy of death.
    16:16 will be saved, but whoever does not believe *will be* **condemned**.
Lk 11:31 the judgment with the men of this generation and **condemn** them;
    11:32 will stand up at the judgment with this generation and **condemn**
Jn   8:10 asked her, "Woman, where are they? *Has* no one **condemned** you?"
     8:11 "Then neither *do* I **condemn** you," Jesus declared. "Go now and
Ro 2: 1 whatever point you judge the other, *you are* **condemning** yourself,
     8: 3 man to be a sin offering. And so *he* **condemned** sin in sinful man,
     8:34 Who is he that **condemns**? Christ Jesus, who died—more than that,
    14:23 But the man who has doubts *is* **condemned** if he eats, because his
1Co 11:32 so that *we will* not *be* **condemned** with the world.
Heb 11: 7 By his faith *he* **condemned** the world and became heir of the
2Pe 2: 6 if *he* **condemned** the cities of Sodom and Gomorrah by burning

2892 κατάκρισις, *katakrisis* [2] [√ 2848 + 3212]

condemn [1], condemns [1]

2Co 3: 9 If the ministry that **condemns** men is glorious, how much more
7: 3 I do not say this to **condemn** you; I have said before that you have

2893 κατακύπτω, *katakyptō* [1] [√ 2848 + 3252]

stooped down [1]

Jn 8: 8 Again *he* **stooped down** and wrote on the ground.

2894 κατακυριεύω, *katakyrieuō* [4] [√ 2848 + 3261]

lord it over [2], lording it over [1], overpowered [1]

Mt 20: 25 "You know that the rulers of the Gentiles **lord it over** them,
Mk 10: 42 those who are regarded as rulers of the Gentiles **lord it over** them,
Ac 19: 16 who had the evil spirit jumped on them and **overpowered** them all.
1Pe 5: 3 not **lording it over** those entrusted to you, but being examples to

2895 καταλαλέω, *katalaleō* [5] [√ 2848 + 3281]

slander [2], speaks against [2], accuse [1]

Jas 4: 11 Brothers, *do* not **slander** one another. Anyone who speaks against
4: 11 Anyone *who* **speaks against** his brother or judges him speaks
4: 11 his brother or judges him **speaks against** the law and judges it.
1Pe 2: 12 *though they* **accuse** you of doing wrong, they may see your good
3: 16 your good behavior in Christ may be ashamed of their **slander.**

2896 καταλαλιά, *katalalia* [2] [√ 2848 + 3281]

slander [2]

2Co 12: 20 of anger, factions, **slander**, gossip, arrogance and disorder.
1Pe 2: 1 and all deceit, hypocrisy, envy, and **slander** of every kind.

2897 κατάλαλος, *katalalos* [1] [√ 2848 + 3281]

slanderers [1]

Ro 1: 30 **slanderers**, God-haters, insolent, arrogant and boastful;

2898 καταλαμβάνω, *katalambanō* [15]
[√ 2848 + 3284]

caught in the act [+900+2093] [1], caught [1], found [1], get the prize [1], grasp [1], obtained [1], overtakes [1], realize [1], realized [1], seizes [1], surprise [1], take hold [1], taken hold of [1], took hold of [1], understood [1]

Mk 9: 18 Whenever *it* **seizes** him, it throws him to the ground. He foams at
Jn 1: 5 shines in the darkness, but the darkness *has* not **understood** it.
8: 3 and the Pharisees brought in a woman **caught** in adultery.
8: 4 this woman *was* **caught** [+900+2093] **in the act** of adultery.
12: 35 Walk while you have the light, before darkness **overtakes** you.
Ac 4: 13 courage of Peter and John and **realized** that they were unschooled,
10: 34 "*I now* **realize** how true it is that God does not show favoritism.
25: 25 I **found** he had done nothing deserving of death, but because he
Ro 9: 30 *have* **obtained** it, a righteousness that is by faith;
1Co 9: 24 but only one gets the prize? Run in such a way as to **get the prize.**
Eph 3: 18 *to* **grasp** how wide and long and high and deep is the love of
Php 3: 12 but I press on to **take hold** of that for which Christ Jesus took hold
3: 12 on to take hold of that for which Christ Jesus **took hold of** *me.*
3: 13 Brothers, I do not consider myself yet *to have* **taken hold of** it.
1Th 5: 4 not in darkness so that this day *should* **surprise** you like a thief.

2899 καταλέγω, *katalegō* [1] [√ 2848 + 3306]

put on the list [1]

1Ti 5: 9 No widow *may be* **put on the list** of widows unless she is over

2900 κατάλειμμα, *kataleimma* Not used in UBS/NIV
[√ 2848 + 3309]

2901 καταλείπω, *kataleipō* [24] [√ 2848 + 3309]

left [11], leave [4], leaving [3], leaves [1], leaving behind [1], neglect [1], passing [1], reserved [1], stands [1]

Mt 4: 13 **Leaving** Nazareth, he went and lived in Capernaum, which was by
16: 4 it except the sign of Jonah." Jesus then **left** them and went away.
19: 5 'For this reason a man *will* **leave** his father and mother and be
21: 17 And he **left** them and went out of the city to Bethany, where he
Mk 10: 7 'For this reason a man *will* **leave** his father and mother and be
12: 19 us that if a man's brother dies and **leaves** a wife but no children,
12: 21 second one married the widow, but he also died, **leaving** no child.
14: 52 he fled naked, **leaving** his garment **behind.**
Lk 5: 28 and Levi got up, **left** everything and followed him.
10: 40 don't you care that my sister *has* **left** me to do the work by myself?
15: 4 *Does he* not **leave** the ninety-nine in the open country and go after
20: 31 and in the same way the seven died, **leaving** no children.
Jn 8: 9 the older ones first, until only Jesus *was* **left**, with the woman still
Ac 6: 2 "It would not be right for us *to* **neglect** the ministry of the word of
18: 19 They arrived at Ephesus, where Paul **left** Priscilla and Aquila.
21: 3 After sighting Cyprus and **passing** to the south of it, we sailed on
24: 27 Felix wanted to grant a favor to the Jews, *he* **left** Paul in prison.
25: 14 He said: "There is a man here whom Felix **left** as a prisoner.
Ro 11: 4 "*I have* **reserved** for myself seven thousand who have not bowed
Eph 5: 31 "For this reason a man *will* **leave** his father and mother and be
1Th 3: 1 it no longer, we thought it best *to be* **left** by ourselves in Athens.
Heb 4: 1 Therefore, *since* the promise of entering his rest *still* **stands,**
11: 27 By faith *he* **left** Egypt, not fearing the king's anger; he persevered
2Pe 2: 15 They have **left** the straight way and wandered off to follow the

2902 καταλιθάζω, *katalithazō* [1] [√ 2848 + 3345]

stone [1]

Lk 20: 6 But if we say, 'From men,' all the people *will* **stone** us,

2903 καταλλαγή, *katallagē* [4] [√ 2848 + 248]

reconciliation [4]

Ro 5: 11 Jesus Christ, through whom we have now received **reconciliation.**
11: 15 For if their rejection is the **reconciliation** of the world, what will
2Co 5: 18 himself through Christ and gave us the ministry *of* **reconciliation:**
5: 19 And he has committed to us the message *of* **reconciliation.**

2904 καταλλάσσω, *katallassō* [6] [√ 2848 + 248]

reconciled [5], reconciling [1]

Ro 5: 10 *we were* **reconciled** to him through the death of his Son,
5: 10 how much more, *having been* **reconciled**, shall we be saved
1Co 7: 11 she must remain unmarried or else *be* **reconciled** to her husband.
2Co 5: 18 who **reconciled** us to himself through Christ and gave us the
5: 19 that God was **reconciling** the world to himself in Christ,
5: 20 We implore *you* on Christ's behalf: *Be* **reconciled** to God.

2905 κατάλοιπος, *kataloipos* [1] [√ 2848 + 3309]

remnant [1]

Ac 15: 17 that the **remnant** of men may seek the Lord, and all the Gentiles

2906 κατάλυμα, *katalyma* [3] [√ 2848 + 3395]

guest room [2], inn [1]

Mk 14: 14 Where is my **guest room**, where I may eat the Passover with my
Lk 2: 7 him in a manger, because there was no room for them in the **inn.**
22: 11 Where is the **guest room**, where I may eat the Passover with my

2907 καταλύω, *katalyō* [17] [√ 2848 + 3395]

destroy [6], thrown down [3], abolish [2], destroyed [2], fail [1], guest [1], lodging [1], stop [1]

Mt 5: 17 "Do not think that I have come *to* **abolish** the Law or the Prophets;
5: 17 the Prophets; I have not come *to* **abolish** them but to fulfill them.
24: 2 stone here will be left on another; every one *will be* **thrown down.**"
26: 61 'I am able *to* **destroy** the temple of God and rebuild it in three

27:40 "You *who are going to* **destroy** the temple and build it in three
Mk 13: 2 stone here will be left on another; every one *will be* **thrown down**."
14:58 'I *will* **destroy** this man-made temple and in three days will build
15:29 You who *are going to* **destroy** the temple and build it in three
Lk 9:12 surrounding villages and countryside and find food and **lodging**,
19: 7 and began to mutter, "He has gone *to be* the **guest** of a 'sinner.' "
21: 6 will be left on another; every one of them *will be* **thrown down**."
Ac 5:38 For if their purpose or activity is of human origin, *it will* **fail**.
5:39 But if it is from God, you will not be able *to* **stop** these men;
6:14 For we have heard him say that this Jesus of Nazareth *will* **destroy**
Ro 14:20 *Do* not **destroy** the work of God for the sake of food. All food is
2Co 5: 1 Now we know that if the earthly tent we live in *is* **destroyed**,
Gal 2:18 If I rebuild what *I* **destroyed**, I prove that I am a lawbreaker.

2908 καταμανθάνω, *katamanthanō* [1]
[√ 2848 + 3443]

see [1]

Mt 6:28 **See** how the lilies of the field grow. They do not labor or spin.

2909 καταμαρτυρέω, *katamartyreō* [3]
[√ 2848 + 3459]

testimony bringing against [3]

Mt 26:62 What *is this* **testimony** that these men *are* **bringing against** you?"
27:13 "Don't you hear the **testimony** they *are* **bringing against** you?"
Mk 14:60 What *is this* **testimony** that these men are **bringing against** you?"

2910 καταμένω, *katamenō* [1] [√ 2848 + 3531]

staying [1]

Ac 1:13 they went upstairs to the room where *they* were **staying**.

2911 καταμόνας, *katamonas*   Not used in UBS/NIV
[√ 2848 + 3668]

2912 κατανάθεμα, *katanathema*   Not used in UBS/NIV [√ 2848 + 353]

2913 καταναθεματίζω, *katanathematizō*   Not used in UBS/NIV [√ 2848 + 353]

2914 καταναλίσκω, *katanaliskō* [1]
[√ 2848 + 324 + 274]

consuming [1]

Heb 12:29 for our "God is a **consuming** fire."

2915 καταναρκάω, *katanarkaō* [3] [√ 2848]

burden [2], burden to [1]

2Co 11: 9 with you and needed something, *I was* not a **burden to** anyone,
12:13 to the other churches, except that I *was* never a **burden** to you?
12:14 and I will not *be* a **burden** to you, because what I want is not your

2916 κατανεύω, *kataneuō* [1] [√ 2848 + 3748]

signaled [1]

Lk 5: 7 So *they* **signaled** their partners in the other boat to come and help

2917 κατανοέω, *katanoeō* [14] [√ 2848 + 3808]

consider [3], pay attention to [2], faced the fact [1], fix thoughts on [1], look more closely [1], look [1], looked [+867] [1], looking at [1], looks at [1], saw through [1], saw [1]

Mt 7: 3 brother's eye and **pay** no **attention to** the plank in your own eye?
Lk 6:41 brother's eye and **pay** no **attention to** the plank in your own eye?
12:24 **Consider** the ravens: They do not sow or reap, they have no
12:27 "**Consider** how the lilies grow. They do not labor or spin.

20:23 He **saw through** their duplicity and said to them,
Ac 7:31 As he went over *to* **look more closely**, he heard the Lord's voice:
7:32 and Jacob.' Moses trembled with fear and did not dare *to* **look**.
11: 6 *I* **looked** [+867] into it and saw four-footed animals of the earth,
27:39 did not recognize the land, but *they* **saw** a bay with a sandy beach,
Ro 4:19 in his faith, *he* **faced the fact** that his body was as good as dead—
Heb 3: 1 **fix** *your* **thoughts on** Jesus, the apostle and high priest whom we
10:24 And *let us* **consider** how we may spur one another on toward love
Jas 1:23 but does not do what it says is like a man *who* **looks at** his face in
1:24 and, *after* **looking at** himself, goes away and immediately forgets

2918 καταντάω, *katantaō* [13] [√ 2848 + 505]

arrived [4], came [2], reach [2], attain [1], come [1], landed [1], reached [1], see fulfilled [1]

Ac 16: 1 *He* **came** to Derbe and then to Lystra, where a disciple named
18:19 *They* **arrived** at Ephesus, where Paul left Priscilla and Aquila.
18:24 a Jew named Apollos, a native of Alexandria, **came** to Ephesus.
20:15 The next day *we* set sail from there and **arrived** off Kios.
21: 7 We continued our voyage from Tyre and **landed** at Ptolemais,
25:13 and Bernice **arrived** at Caesarea to pay their respects to Festus.
26: 7 This is the promise our twelve tribes are hoping *to* **see fulfilled** as
27:12 that we should sail on, hoping *to* **reach** Phoenix and winter there.
28:13 From there *we* set sail and **arrived** at Rhegium. The next day the
1Co 10:11 as warnings for us, on whom the fulfillment of the ages *has* **come**.
14:36 originate with you? Or are you the only people *it has* **reached**?
Eph 4:13 until *we* all **reach** unity in the faith and in the knowledge of the
Php 3:11 and so, somehow, to **attain** to the resurrection from the dead.

2919 κατάνυξις, *katanyxis* [1] [√ 2848 + 3817]

stupor [1]

Ro 11: 8 "God gave them a spirit *of* **stupor**, eyes so that they could not see

2920 κατανύσσομαι, *katanyssomai* [1]
[√ 2848 + 3817]

cut to [1]

Ac 2:37 *they were* **cut to** the heart and said to Peter and the other apostles,

2921 καταξιόω, *kataxioō* [3] [√ 2848 + 545]

counted worthy [2], considered worthy of [1]

Lk 20:35 But those *who are* **considered worthy of** taking part in that age
Ac 5:41 because *they had been* **counted worthy** of suffering disgrace for
2Th 1: 5 and as a result you *will be* **counted worthy** of the kingdom of

2922 καταπατέω, *katapateō* [5] [√ 2848 + 4251]

trample [1], trampled on [1], trampled under foot [1], trampled [1], trampling on [1]

Mt 5:13 good for anything, except to be thrown out and **trampled** by men.
7: 6 *they may* **trample** them under their feet, and then turn and tear
Lk 8: 5 the path; *it was* **trampled on**, and the birds of the air ate it up.
12: 1 so that *they were* **trampling on** one another, Jesus began to speak
Heb 10:29 to be punished who *has* **trampled** the Son of God **under foot**,

2923 κατάπαυσις, *katapausis* [9] [√ 2848 + 4264]

rest [8], resting [1]

Ac 7:49 build for me? says the Lord. Or where will my **resting** place be?
Heb 3:11 I declared on oath in my anger, 'They shall never enter my **rest**.' "
3:18 And to whom did God swear that they would never enter his **rest** if
4: 1 Therefore, since the promise of entering his **rest** still stands,
4: 3 Now we who have believed enter that **rest**, just as God has said,
4: 3 'They shall never enter my **rest**.' " And yet his work has been
4: 5 in the passage above he says, "They shall never enter my **rest**."
4:10 for anyone who enters God's **rest** also rests from his own work,
4:11 Let us, therefore, make every effort to enter that **rest**, so that no

2924 καταπαύω, *katapauō* [4] [√ 2848 + 4264]

given rest [1], keeping [1], rested [1], rests [1]

Ac 14:18 *they* had difficulty **keeping** the crowd from sacrificing to them.
Heb 4: 4 words: "And on the seventh day God **rested** from all his work."
      4: 8 For if Joshua *had* **given** them **rest**, God would not have spoken
      4:10 for anyone who enters God's rest also **rests** from his own work,

2925 καταπέτασμα, *katapetasma* [6] [√ 2848 + 4375]

curtain [6]

Mt 27:51 At that moment the **curtain** of the temple was torn in two from top
Mk 15:38 The **curtain** of the temple was torn in two from top to bottom.
Lk 23:45 stopped shining. And the **curtain** of the temple was torn in two.
Heb 6:19 and secure. It enters the inner sanctuary *behind* the **curtain**,
      9: 3 Behind the second **curtain** was a room called the Most Holy Place,
     10:20 by a new and living way opened for us through the **curtain**,

2926 καταπίμπρημι, *katapimprēmi* Not used in
UBS/NIV [√ 2848 + 4399]

2927 καταπίνω, *katapinō* [7] [√ 2848 + 4403]

swallowed up [2], devour [1], drowned [1], overwhelmed [1],
swallow [1], swallowing [1]

Mt 23:24 You blind guides! You strain out a gnat but **swallow** a camel.
1Co 15:54 written will come true: "Death *has been* **swallowed up** in victory."
2Co 2: 7 so that he *will* not *be* **overwhelmed** by excessive sorrow.
      5: 4 so that what is mortal *may be* **swallowed up** by life.
Heb 11:29 but when the Egyptians tried to do so, *they were* **drowned**.
1Pe 5: 8 prowls around like a roaring lion looking for someone *to* **devour**.
Rev 12:16 and **swallowing** the river that the dragon had spewed out of his

2928 καταπίπτω, *katapiptō* [3] [√ 2848 + 4406]

fell [2], fall [1]

Lk   8: 6 Some **fell** on rock, and when it came up, the plants withered
Ac 26:14 We all **fell** to the ground, and I heard a voice saying to me in
     28: 6 The people expected him to swell up or suddenly **fall** dead,

2929 καταπλέω, *katapleō* [1] [√ 2848 + 4434]

sailed [1]

Lk   8:26 *They* **sailed** to the region of the Gerasenes, which is across the

2930 καταπονέω, *kataponeō* [2] [√ 2848 + 4506]

distressed [1], him^s [+3836] [1]

Ac   7:24 to his defense and avenged **him**^{s} [+3836] by killing the Egyptian.
2Pe 2: 7 *who was* **distressed** by the filthy lives of lawless men

2931 καταποντίζω, *katapontizō* [2] [√ 2848 + 4509]

drowned [1], sink [1]

Mt 14:30 he was afraid and, beginning *to* **sink**, cried out, "Lord, save me!"
     18: 6 hung around his neck and *to be* **drowned** in the depths of the sea.

2932 κατάρα, *katara* [6] [√ 2848 + 725]

curse [3], accursed [1], being cursed [1], cursing [1]

Gal 3:10 All who rely on observing the law are under a **curse**, for it is
      3:13 Christ redeemed us from the **curse** of the law by becoming a curse
      3:13 Christ redeemed us from the curse of the law by becoming a **curse**
Heb 6: 8 and thistles is worthless and is in danger of **being cursed**.
Jas 3:10 Out of the same mouth come praise and **cursing**. My brothers,
2Pe 2:14 seduce the unstable; they are experts in greed—an **accursed** brood!

2933 καταράομαι, *kataraomai* [5] [√ 2848 + 725]

curse [3], cursed [2]

Mt 25:41 will say to those on his left, 'Depart from me, you *who are* **cursed**,
Mk 11:21 said to Jesus, "Rabbi, look! The fig tree *you* **cursed** has withered!"
Lk   6:28 bless those *who* **curse** you, pray for those who mistreat you.
Ro 12:14 Bless those who persecute you; bless and *do* not **curse**.
Jas 3: 9 tongue we praise our Lord and Father, and with it *we* **curse** men,

2934 καταργέω, *katargeō* [27] [√ 2848 + 1.1 + 2240]

destroy [3], destroyed [3], nullify [3], fading away [2], released
[2], abolished [1], abolishing [1], alienated [1], cease [1], coming
to nothing [1], disappears [1], do away with [1], done away with
[1], fading [1], pass away [1], put behind [1], taken away [1], use
up [1], worthless [1]

Lk 13: 7 haven't found any. Cut it down! Why *should it* **use up** the soil?'
Ro   3: 3 not have faith? *Will* their lack of faith **nullify** God's faithfulness?
      3:31 *Do we*, then, **nullify** the law by this faith? Not at all! Rather,
      4:14 by law are heirs, faith has no value and the promise *is* **worthless**,
      6: 6 with him so that the body of sin *might be* **done away with**,
      7: 2 but if her husband dies, *she is* **released** from the law of marriage.
      7: 6 *we have been* **released** from the law so that we serve in the new
1Co 1:28 and the things that are not—to **nullify** the things that are,
      2: 6 of this age or of the rulers of this age, who *are* **coming to nothing**.
      6:13 and the stomach for food"—but God *will* **destroy** them both.
     13: 8 But where there are prophecies, *they will* **cease**; where there are
     13: 8 they will be stilled; where there is knowledge, *it will* **pass away**.
     13:10 but when perfection comes, the imperfect **disappears**.
     13:11 a child. When I became a man, *I* **put** childish ways **behind** *me*.
     15:24 kingdom to God the Father after *he has* **destroyed** all dominion,
     15:26 The last enemy *to be* **destroyed** is death.
2Co 3: 7 at the face of Moses because of its glory, **fading** *though it was*,
      3:11 And if what *was* **fading away** came with glory, how much greater
      3:13 Israelites from gazing at it *while* the radiance *was* **fading away**.
      3:14 It has not been removed, because only in Christ *is it* **taken away**.
Gal 3:17 established by God and thus **do away with** the promise.
      5: 4 You who are trying to be justified by law *have been* **alienated**
      5:11 In that case the offense of the cross *has been* **abolished**.
Eph 2:15 *by* **abolishing** in his flesh the law with its commandments
2Th 2: 8 the breath of his mouth and **destroy** by the splendor of his coming.
2Ti 1:10 who has **destroyed** death and has brought life and immortality to
Heb 2:14 so that by his death *he might* **destroy** him who holds the power of

2935 καταριθμέω, *katarithmeō* [1] [√ 2848 + 750]

number [1]

Ac   1:17 he was *one* of our **number** and shared in this ministry."

2936 καταρτίζω, *katartizō* [13] [√ 2848 + 785]

prepared [2], preparing [2], restore [2], aim for perfection [1],
equip [1], formed [1], fully trained [1], ordained [1], perfectly
united [+899+3836] [1], supply [1]

Mt   4:21 were in a boat with their father Zebedee, **preparing** their nets.
     21:16 'From the lips of children and infants *you have* **ordained** praise'?"
Mk   1:19 of Zebedee and his brother John in a boat, **preparing** their nets.
Lk   6:40 but everyone *who is* **fully trained** will be like his teacher.
Ro   9:22 great patience the objects of his wrath—**prepared** for destruction?
1Co 1:10 and that you may be **perfectly** [+899+3836] **united** in mind
2Co 13:11 **Aim for perfection**, listen to my appeal, be of one mind, live in
Gal 6: 1 is caught in a sin, you who are spiritual *should* **restore** him gently.
1Th 3:10 we may see you again and **supply** what is lacking in your faith.
Heb 10: 5 and offering you did not desire, but a body *you* **prepared** for me;
     11: 3 By faith we understand that the universe *was* **formed** at God's
     13:21 **equip** you with everything good for doing his will, and may he
1Pe 5:10 *will* himself **restore** you and make you strong, firm and steadfast.

2937 κατάρτισις, *katartisis* [1] [√ 2848 + 785]

perfection [1]

2Co 13: 9 are weak but you are strong; and our prayer is for your **perfection**.

2938 καταρτισμός, *katartismos* [1] [√ 2848 + 785]

prepare [1]

Eph   4: 12 to **prepare** God's people for works of service, so that the body of

2939 κατασείω, *kataseiō* [4] [√ 2848 + 4940]

motioned [+3836+5931] [2], motioned [2]

Ac   12: 17 Peter **motioned** with his hand for them to be quiet and described
      13: 16 Standing up, Paul **motioned** with his hand and said: "Men of Israel
      19: 33 He **motioned** [+3836+5931] *for silence* in order to make a defense
      21: 40 Paul stood on the steps and **motioned** [+3836+5931] to the crowd.

2940 κατασκάπτω, *kataskaptō* [2] [√ 2848 + 4999]

ruins [1], torn down [1]

Ac   15: 16 David's fallen tent. Its **ruins** I will rebuild, and I will restore it,
Ro   11: 3 they have killed your prophets and **torn down** your altars;

2941 κατασκευάζω, *kataskeuazō* [11] [√ 2848 + 5007]

built [3], prepare [3], builder [2], arranged [1], prepared [1], set up [1]

Mt   11: 10 messenger ahead of you, who *will* **prepare** your way before you.'
Mk   1: 2 send my messenger ahead of you, who *will* **prepare** your way"—
Lk   1: 17 of the righteous—to make ready a people **prepared** for the Lord."
      7: 27 messenger ahead of you, who *will* **prepare** your way before you.'
Heb 3: 3 just as the **builder** of a house has greater honor than the house
      3: 4 For every house *is* **built** by someone, but God is the builder of
      3: 4 house is built by someone, but God *is* the **builder** of everything.
      9: 2 A tabernacle *was* **set up**. In its first room were the lampstand,
      9: 6 *When* everything *had been* **arranged** like this, the priests entered
      11: 7 things not yet seen, in holy fear **built** an ark to save his family.
1Pe 3: 20 waited patiently in the days of Noah *while* the ark *was being* **built**.

2942 κατασκηνόω, *kataskēnoō* [4] [√ 2848 + 5008]

perch [2], live [1], perched [1]

Mt   13: 32 so that the birds of the air come and **perch** in its branches."
Mk   4: 32 with such big branches that the birds of the air can **perch** in its
Lk   13: 19 and became a tree, and the birds of the air **perched** in its branches."
Ac   2: 26 is glad and my tongue rejoices; my body also *will* **live** in hope,

2943 κατασκήνωσις, *kataskēnōsis* [2] [√ 2848 + 5008]

nests [2]

Mt   8: 20 Jesus replied, "Foxes have holes and birds of the air have **nests**,
Lk   9: 58 Jesus replied, "Foxes have holes and birds of the air have **nests**,

2944 κατασκιάζω, *kataskiazō* [1] [√ 2848 + 5014]

overshadowing [1]

Heb 9: 5 the cherubim of the Glory, **overshadowing** the atonement cover.

2945 κατασκοπέω, *kataskopeō* [1] [√ 2848 + 5023]

spy on [1]

Gal 2: 4 because some false brothers had infiltrated our ranks *to* **spy on** the

2946 κατάσκοπος, *kataskopos* [1] [√ 2848 + 5023]

spies [1]

Heb 11: 31 By faith the prostitute Rahab, because she welcomed the **spies**,

2947 κατασοφίζομαι, *katasophizomai* [1] [√ 2848 + 5055]

dealt treacherously with [1]

Ac   7: 19 He **dealt treacherously with** our people and oppressed our

2948 καταστέλλω, *katastellō* [2] [√ 2848 + 5097]

quiet [1], quieted [1]

Ac   19: 35 The city clerk **quieted** the crowd and said: "Men of Ephesus,
      19: 36 are undeniable, you ought to be **quiet** and not do anything rash.

2949 κατάστημα, *katastēma* [1] [√ 2848 + 2705]

way live [1]

Tit   2: 3 teach the older women to be reverent in the **way** they **live**,

2950 καταστολή, *katastolē* [1] [√ 2848 + 5097]

modestly [+1877+3177] [1]

1Ti 2: 9 I also want women to dress **modestly** [+1877+3177], with decency

2951 καταστρέφω, *katastrephō* [2] [√ 2848 + 5138]

overturned [2]

Mt   21: 12 He **overturned** the tables of the money changers and the benches
Mk   11: 15 He **overturned** the tables of the money changers and the benches

2952 καταστρηνιάω, *katastrēniaō* [1] [√ 2848 + 5140]

sensual desires overcome their dedication to [1]

1Ti 5: 11 For when *their* **sensual desires overcome their dedication to**

2953 καταστροφή, *katastrophē* [2 / 1] [√ 2848 + 5138]

ruins [1]

2Ti 2: 14 about words; it is of no value, and only **ruins** those who listen.
2Pe 2: 6 if he condemned [UBS+ *to* **ruin**] the cities of Sodom and Gomorrah

2954 καταστρώννυμι, *katastrōnnymi* [1] [√ 2848 + 5143]

scattered [1]

1Co 10: 5 with most of them; *their bodies were* **scattered** over the desert.

2955 κατασύρω, *katasyrō* [1] [√ 2848 + 5359]

drag off [1]

Lk   12: 58 or *he may* **drag** you **off** to the judge, and the judge turn you over

2956 κατασφάζω, *katasphazō* [1] [√ 2848 + 5377]

kill [1]

Lk   19: 27 be king over them—bring them here and **kill** them in front of me.' "

2957 κατασφάττω, *katasphattō* Not used in UBS/NIV [√ 2848 + 5377]

2958 κατασφραγίζω, *katasphragizō* [1] [√ 2848 + 5382]

sealed [1]

Rev 5: 1 a scroll with writing on both sides and **sealed** with seven seals.

2959 κατάσχεσις, *kataschesis* [2] [√ *2848 + 2400*]

possess [+*1650*] [1], took [1]

Ac 7: 5 and his descendants after him *would* **possess** [+*1650*] the land,
    7:45 our fathers under Joshua brought it with them when they **took** the

2960 κατατίθημι, *katatithēmi* [2] [√ *2848 + 5502*]

do [1], grant [1]

Ac 24:27 but because Felix wanted *to* **grant** a favor to the Jews, he left Paul
   25: 9 Festus, wishing *to* **do** the Jews a favor, said to Paul, "Are you

2961 κατατομή, *katatomē* [1] [√ *2848 + 5533*]

mutilators of the flesh [1]

Php 3: 2 those dogs, those men who do evil, those **mutilators of the flesh**.

2962 κατατοξεύω, *katatoxeuō* Not used in UBS/NIV
[√ *2848 + 5534*]

2963 κατατρέχω, *katatrechō* [1] [√ *2848 + 5556*]

ran down [1]

Ac 21:32 once took some officers and soldiers and **ran down** to the crowd.

2964 καταυγάζω, *kataugazō* Not used in UBS/NIV
[√ *2848 + 879*]

2965 καταφέρω, *katapherō* [4] [√ *2848 + 5770*]

bringing against [1], cast against [1], sinking [1], sound asleep
[+*608+3836+5678*] [1]

Ac 20: 9 *who was* **sinking** into a deep sleep as Paul talked on and on.
   20: 9 *When he was* **sound asleep** [+*608+3836+5678*], he fell to the
   25: 7 **bringing** many serious charges **against** him, which they could not
   26:10 and when they were put to death, *I* **cast** my vote **against** them.

2966 καταφεύγω, *katapheugō* [2] [√ *2848 + 5771*]

fled [2]

Ac 14: 6 out about it and **fled** to the Lycaonian cities of Lystra and Derbe
Heb 6:18 we *who have* **fled** to take hold of the hope offered to us may be

2967 καταφθείρω, *kataphtheirō* [1] [√ *2848 + 5780*]

depraved [1]

2Ti 3: 8 men of **depraved** minds, who, as far as the faith is concerned,

2968 καταφιλέω, *kataphileō* [6] [√ *2848 + 5813*]

kissed [5], kissing [1]

Mt 26:49 at once to Jesus, Judas said, "Greetings, Rabbi!" and **kissed** him.
Mk 14:45 Going at once to Jesus, Judas said, "Rabbi!" and **kissed** him.
Lk 7:38 them with her hair, **kissed** them and poured perfume on them.
    7:45 from the time I entered, has not stopped **kissing** my feet.
   15:20 he ran to his son, threw his arms around him and **kissed** him.
Ac 20:37 They all wept as they embraced him and **kissed** him.

2969 καταφρονέω, *kataphroneō* [9] [→ *2970; cf. 2848
+ 5856*]

despise [4], look down on [2], scorning [1], show contempt for
[1], show less respect [1]

Mt 6:24 the other, or he will be devoted to the one and **despise** the other.
   18:10 "See that *you do* not **look down on** one of these little ones.
Lk 16:13 the other, or he will be devoted to the one and **despise** the other.
Ro 2: 4 Or *do you* **show contempt for** the riches of his kindness, tolerance
1Co 11:22 Or *do you* **despise** the church of God and humiliate those who
1Ti 4:12 Don't *let* anyone **look down on** you because you are young,
    6: 2 Those who have believing masters *are* not *to* **show less respect** for

Heb 12: 2 for the joy set before him endured the cross, **scorning** its shame,
2Pe 2:10 follow the corrupt desire of the sinful nature and **despise** authority.

2970 καταφρονητής, *kataphronētēs* [1] [√ *2969*]

scoffers [1]

Ac 13:41 " 'Look, *you* **scoffers**, wonder and perish, for I am going to do

2971 καταφωνέω, *kataphōneō* Not used in UBS/NIV
[√ *2848 + 5889*]

2972 καταχέω, *katacheō* [2] [√ *1772; cf. 2848*]

poured on [1], poured [1]

Mt 26: 7 which *she* **poured** on his head as he was reclining at the table.
Mk 14: 3 pure nard. *She* broke the jar and **poured** the perfume **on** his head.

2973 καταχθόνιος, *katachthonios* [1] [√ *2848*]

under the earth [1]

Php 2:10 knee should bow, in heaven and on earth and **under the earth**,

2974 καταχράομαι, *katachraomai* [2]
[√ *2848 + 5968*]

engrossed in [1], make use of [1]

1Co 7:31 those who use the things of the world, as if not **engrossed in** them.
    9:18 it free of charge, and so not **make use of** my rights in preaching it.

2975 καταψηφίζομαι, *katapsēphizomai* Not used
in UBS/NIV [√ *2848 + 6029*]

2976 καταψύχω, *katapsychō* [1] [√ *2848 + 6038*]

cool [1]

Lk 16:24 Lazarus to dip the tip of his finger in water and **cool** my tongue,

2977 κατείδωλος, *kateidōlos* [1] [√ *2848 + 1631*]

full of idols [1]

Ac 17:16 he was greatly distressed to see that the city was **full of idols**.

2978 κατέναντι, *katenanti* [8] [√ *2848 + 1882*]

ahead [3], in the sight [2], opposite [2], before [1]

Mt 21: 2 saying to them, "Go to the village **ahead** of you, and at once you
Mk 11: 2 saying to them, "Go to the village **ahead** of you, and just as you
   12:41 Jesus sat down **opposite** the place where the offerings were put
   13: 3 As Jesus was sitting on the Mount of Olives **opposite** the temple,
Lk 19:30 "Go to the village **ahead** of you, and as you enter it, you will find a
Ro 4:17 He is our father **in the sight** of God, in whom he believed—
2Co 2:17 On the contrary, in Christ we speak **before** God with sincerity,
   12:19 We have been speaking **in the sight** of God as those in Christ;

2979 κατενώπιον, *katenōpion* [3]
[√ *2848 + 1877 + 3972*]

in sight [2], before [1]

Eph 1: 4 the creation of the world to be holy and blameless **in his sight**.
Col 1:22 physical body through death to present you holy **in his sight**,
Jude 1:24 and to present you **before** his glorious presence without fault

2980 κατεξουσιάζω, *katexousiazo* [2] [√ *2026;
cf. 2848*]

exercise authority over [2]

Mt 20:25 it over them, and their high officials **exercise authority over** them.
Mk 10:42 it over them, and their high officials **exercise authority over** them.

2981 κατεργάζομαι, *katergazomai* [22]
[√ 2848 + 2240]

do [3], produced [3], brings [2], done [2], accomplished [1], achieving [1], carry out [1], committed [1], develops [1], did [1], does [1], doing [1], made [1], produces [1], result in [1], work out [1]

Ro 1:27 Men **committed** indecent acts with other men, and received in
      2: 9 will be trouble and distress for every human being who **does** evil:
      4:15 because law **brings** wrath. And where there is no law there is no
      5: 3 because we know that suffering **produces** perseverance;
      7: 8 the commandment, **produced** in me every kind of covetous desire.
      7:13 as sin, it **produced** death in me through what was good,
      7:15 I do not understand what *I do.* For what I want to do I do not do,
      7:17 As it is, it is no longer I myself *who* **do** it, but it is sin living in me.
      7:18 For I have the desire to do what is good, but I cannot **carry** it **out.**
      7:20 it is no longer I *who* **do** it, but it is sin living in me that does it.
   15:18 *has* **accomplished** through me in leading the Gentiles to obey God
1Co 5: 3 And I have already passed judgment on the one *who* **did** this,
2Co 4:17 and momentary troubles *are* **achieving** for us an eternal glory that
      5: 5 Now it is God who *has* **made** us for this very purpose and has
      7:10 to salvation and leaves no regret, but worldly sorrow **brings** death.
      7:11 See what this godly sorrow *has* **produced** in you:
      9:11 and through us your generosity *will* **result in** thanksgiving to God.
   12:12 and miracles—*were* **done** among you with great perseverance.
Eph 6:13 stand your ground, and *after you have* **done** everything, to stand.
Php 2:12 *continue to* **work out** your salvation with fear and trembling,
Jas 1: 3 because you know that the testing of your faith **develops**
1Pe 4: 3 For you have spent enough time in the past **doing** what pagans

2982 κατέρχομαι, *katerchomai* [16] [√ 2848 + 2262]

came down [4], went down [4], landed [3], went [2], arrived [1], came [1], come down [1]

Lk 4:31 Then *he* **went down** to Capernaum, a town in Galilee, and on the
      9:37 The next day, *when* they **came down** from the mountain, a large
Ac 8: 5 Philip **went down** to a city in Samaria and proclaimed the Christ
      9:32 traveled about the country, he **went** to visit the saints in Lydda.
   11:27 During this time some prophets **came down** from Jerusalem to
   12:19 Then Herod **went** from Judea to Caesarea and stayed there a while.
   13: 4 **went down** to Seleucia and sailed from there to Cyprus.
   15: 1 Some men **came down** from Judea to Antioch and were teaching
   15:30 The men were sent off and **went down** to Antioch, where they
   18: 5 When Silas and Timothy **came** from Macedonia, Paul devoted
   18:22 *When he* **landed** at Caesarea, he went up and greeted the church
   19: 1 Paul took the road through the interior and **arrived** at Ephesus.
   21: 3 *We* **landed** at Tyre, where our ship was to unload its cargo.
   21:10 number of days, a prophet named Agabus **came down** from Judea.
   27: 5 the coast of Cilicia and Pamphylia, *we* **landed** at Myra in Lycia.
Jas 3:15 Such "wisdom" *does* not **come down** from heaven but is earthly,

2983 κατεσθίω, *katesthiō* [14] [√ 2848 + 2266]

ate up [3], devour [3], ate [1], consume [1], devoured [1], devouring [1], devours [1], eat [1], exploits [1], squandered [1]

Mt 13: 4 some fell along the path, and the birds came and **ate** it **up.**
Mk 4: 4 some fell along the path, and the birds came and **ate** it **up.**
   12:40 *They* **devour** widows' houses and for a show make lengthy prayers.
Lk 8: 5 the path; it was trampled on, and the birds of the air **ate** it **up.**
   15:30 But when this son of yours who *has* **squandered** your property
   20:47 They **devour** widows' houses and for a show make lengthy prayers.
Jn 2:17 that it is written: "Zeal for your house *will* **consume** me."
2Co 11:20 or **exploits** you or takes advantage of you or pushes himself
Gal 5:15 If *you* **keep on** biting and **devouring** each other, watch out
Rev 10: 9 He said to me, "Take it and **eat** it. It will turn your stomach sour,
   10:10 I took the little scroll from the angel's hand and **ate** it. It tasted as
   11: 5 fire comes from their mouths and **devours** their enemies.
   12: 4 so that *he might* **devour** her child the moment it was born.
   20: 9 he loves. But fire came down from heaven and **devoured** them.

2984 κατέσθω, *katesthō* Not used in UBS/NIV
[√ 2848 + 2266]

2985 κατευθύνω, *kateuthynō* [3] [√ 2848 + 2317]

clear [1], direct [1], guide [1]

Lk 1:79 in the shadow of death, *to* **guide** our feet into the path of peace."
1Th 3:11 Now *may* our God and Father himself and our Lord Jesus **clear** the
2Th 3: 5 *May* the Lord **direct** your hearts into God's love and Christ's

2986 κατευλογέω, *kateulogeō* [1]
[√ 2848 + 2292 + 3306]

blessed [1]

Mk 10:16 the children in his arms, put his hands on them and **blessed** them.

2987 κατεφίσταμαι, *katephistamai* [1]
[√ 2848 + 2093 + 2705]

made a attack on [1]

Ac 18:12 the Jews **made a** united **attack on** Paul and brought him into court.

2988 κατέχω, *katechō* [17] [√ 2848 + 2400]

hold on to [2], keep [2], bound [1], hold firmly [1], hold to [1], hold [1], holding back [1], holding to [1], holds back [1], made [1], possessing [1], retain [1], suppress [1], take [1], theirs to keep [1]

Lk 4:42 came to where he was, *they tried to* **keep** him from leaving them.
    8:15 for those with a noble and good heart, who hear the word, **retain** it,
   14: 9 humiliated, you will *have to* **take** the least important place.
Ac 27:40 Then *they* hoisted the foresail to the wind and **made** for the beach.
Ro 1:18 and wickedness of men who **suppress** the truth by their
    7: 6 But now, by dying to what *once* **bound** us, we have been released
1Co 7:30 those who buy something, as if *it were* not **theirs to keep**;
   11: 2 remembering me in everything and for **holding to** the teachings,
   15: 2 you are saved, if *you* **hold firmly** to the word I preached to you.
2Co 6:10 making many rich; having nothing, and yet **possessing** everything.
1Th 5:21 Test everything. **Hold on to** the good.
2Th 2: 6 And now you know what *is* **holding** him **back,**
    2: 7 but the one *who* now **holds** it **back** will continue to do so till he is
Phm 1:13 I would have liked *to* **keep** him with me so that he could take your
Heb 3: 6 if *we* **hold on to** our courage and the hope of which we boast.
    3:14 We have come to share in Christ if *we* **hold** firmly till the end the
  10:23 *Let us* **hold** unswervingly **to** the hope we profess, for he who

2989 κατηγορέω, *katēgoreō* [23] [→ 2990, 2991, 2992; cf. 2848 + 72]

accuse [5], accusing [3], accused [2], accused of [1], accuser [1], accuses [1], accusing of [1], bring charges [1], charge to bring against [1], charges bringing against [1], charges brought against [1], charges making against [1], charges [1], he^s [+3836] [1], presented case [+806] [1], press charges against [1]

Mt 12:10 *Looking* for a reason *to* **accuse** Jesus, they asked him, "Is it lawful
   27:12 When he *was* **accused** by the chief priests and the elders, he gave
Mk 3: 2 *Some* of them *were looking* for a reason *to* **accuse** Jesus,
   15: 3 The chief priests **accused** him **of** many things.
   15: 4 going to answer? See how many things *they are* **accusing** you **of.**"
Lk 6: 7 and the teachers of the law were looking for a reason *to* **accuse**
   23: 2 And they began *to* **accuse** him, saying, "We have found this man
   23:10 teachers of the law were standing there, vehemently **accusing** him.
   23:14 and have found no basis for *your* **charges** against him.
Jn 5:45 "But do not think I *will* **accuse** you before the Father. Your accuser
    5:45 the Father. Your **accuser** is Moses, on whom your hopes are set.
    8: 6 this question as a trap, in order to have a basis *for* **accusing** him.
Ac 22:30 to find out exactly why Paul *was being* **accused** by the Jews,
   24: 2 was called in, Tertullus **presented** [+806] his **case** before Felix:
   24: 8 the truth about all these **charges** we *are* **bringing against** him."
   24:13 prove to you the **charges** *they are* now **making against** me.
   24:19 before you and **bring charges** if they have anything against me.
   25: 5 *Let* some of your leaders come with me and **press charges against**
   25:11 But if the **charges brought against** me by these Jews are not true,
   25:16 to hand over any man before he^s [+3836] has faced his accusers
   28:19 not that I had any **charge to bring against** my own people.
Ro 2:15 and their thoughts now **accusing,** now even defending them.)
Rev 12:10 who **accuses** them before our God day and night, has been hurled

2990 κατηγορία, *katēgoria* [3] [√ 2989]

accusation [1], charge [1], charges [1]

Jn   18:29 and asked, "What **charges** are you bringing against this man?"
1Ti   5:19 Do not entertain an **accusation** against an elder unless it is brought
Tit   1: 6 and are not open to the **charge** of being wild and disobedient.

2991 κατήγορος, *katēgoros* [4] [√ 2989]

accusers [3], accusers [+2400+3836] [1]

Ac   23:30 I also ordered his **accusers** to present to you their case against him.
      23:35 he said, "I will hear your case when your **accusers** get here."
      25:16 hand over any man before he has faced his **accusers** [+2400+3836]
      25:18 When his **accusers** got up to speak, they did not charge him with

2992 κατήγωρ, *katēgōr* [1] [√ 2989]

accuser [1]

Rev 12:10 For the **accuser** of our brothers, who accuses them before our God

2993 κατήφεια, *katēpheia* [1] [√ 2848 + 5743]

gloom [1]

Jas   4: 9 Change your laughter to mourning and your joy to **gloom**.

2994 κατηχέω, *katēcheō* [8] [√ 2848 + 2491]

informed [1], instruct [1], instructed in [1], instructed [1], instructor [1], receives instruction in [1], reports [1], taught [1]

Lk   1: 4 you may know the certainty of the things *you have been* **taught**.
Ac 18:25 He had been **instructed in** the way of the Lord, and he spoke with
      21:21 *They have been* **informed** that you teach all the Jews who live
      21:24 Then everybody will know there is no truth in these **reports** about
Ro   2.18 of what is superior *because you are* **instructed** by the law;
1Co 14:19 words to **instruct** others than ten thousand words in a tongue.
Gal 6: 6 Anyone *who* **receives instruction in** the word must share all good
     6: 6 in the word must share all good things *with* his **instructor**.

2995 κατιόω, *katioō* [1] [√ 2848 + 2675]

corroded [1]

Jas   5: 3 Your gold and silver *are* **corroded**. Their corrosion will testify

2996 κατισχύω, *katischyō* [3] [√ 2848 + 2709]

able [1], overcome [1], prevailed [1]

Mt 16:18 will build my church, and the gates of Hades *will* not **overcome** it.
Lk 21:36 and pray that *you may be* **able** to escape all that is about to
      23:23 demanded that he be crucified, and their shouts **prevailed**.

2997 κατοικέω, *katoikeō* [44] [√ 2848 + 3875]

inhabitants [7], live [7], living [5], lived [4], dwell [3], in [2], lived in [2], lives [2], living in [2], dwells in [1], home [1], inhabit [1], inhabitants of [1], live in [1], people [1], residents of [1], settled [1], staying [1], thems [+1178+2093+3836+3836] [1]

Mt   2:23 and *he* went and **lived** in a town called Nazareth. So was fulfilled
     4:13 Leaving Nazareth, *he* went and **lived** in Capernaum, which was by
   12:45 other spirits more wicked than itself, and they go in and **live** there.
   23:21 swears by the temple swears by it and by the one who **dwells in** it.
Lk 11:26 other spirits more wicked than itself, and *they* go in and **live** there.
    13: 4 do you think they were more guilty than all the others **living in**
Ac   1:19 Everyone in Jerusalem heard about this, so they called that field in
    1:20 there be no one *to* **dwell** in it,' and, " 'May another take his place
    2: 5 Now there were **staying** in Jerusalem God-fearing Jews from every
    2: 9 **residents of** Mesopotamia, Judea and Cappadocia, Pontus
    2:14 "Fellow Jews and all of you who **live** in Jerusalem, let me explain
    4:16 "Everybody **living** in Jerusalem knows they have done an
    7: 2 while he was still in Mesopotamia, before he **lived** in Haran.
    7: 4 "So he left the land of the Chaldeans and **settled** in Haran. After the
    7: 4 of his father, God sent him to this land where you *are* now **living**.

    7:48 "However, the Most High *does* not **live** in houses made by men.
    9:22 and baffled the Jews **living** in Damascus by proving that Jesus is
    9:32 traveled about the country, he went to visit the saints **in** Lydda.
    9:35 All those *who* **lived in** Lydda and Sharon saw him and turned to
  11:29 his ability, decided to provide help *for* the brothers **living** in Judea.
  13:27 The **people** of Jerusalem and their rulers did not recognize Jesus,
  17:24 of heaven and earth and *does* not **live** in temples built by hands.
  17:26 every nation of men, that *they should* **inhabit** the whole earth;
  19:10 and Greeks who **lived in** the province of Asia heard the word of
  19:17 this became known to the Jews and Greeks **living in** Ephesus,
  22:12 of the law and highly respected by all the Jews **living** there.
Eph 3:17 so that Christ *may* **dwell** in your hearts through faith. And I pray
Col 1:19 For God was pleased *to have* all his fullness **dwell** in him,
    2: 9 For in Christ all the fullness of the Deity **lives** in bodily form,
Heb 11: 9 *he* **lived** in tents, as did Isaac and Jacob, who were heirs with him
2Pe 3:13 to a new heaven and a new earth, the **home** of righteousness.
Rev 2:13 I know where *you* **live**—where Satan has his throne. Yet you
    2:13 who was put to death in your city—where Satan **lives**.
    3:10 to come upon the whole world to test those *who* **live** on the earth.
    6:10 until you judge the **inhabitants** of the earth and avenge our blood?"
    8:13 Woe *to* the **inhabitants** of the earth, because of the trumpet blasts
  11:10 The **inhabitants** of the earth will gloat over them and will
  11:10 because these two prophets had tormented those *who* **live** on the
  13: 8 All **inhabitants** of the earth will worship the beast—all whose
  13:12 and made the earth and its **inhabitants** worship the first beast,
  13:14 behalf of the first beast, he deceived the **inhabitants** of the earth.
  13:14 He ordered them^s [+1178+2093+3836+3836] to set up an image
  17: 2 and the **inhabitants of** the earth were intoxicated with the wine of
  17: 8 The **inhabitants** of the earth whose names have not been written in

2998 κατοίκησις, *katoikēsis* [1] [√ 2848 + 3875]

lived [+2400+3836] [1]

Mk   5: 3 This man **lived** [+2400+3836] in the tombs, and no one could bind

2999 κατοικητήριον, *katoikētērion* [2]
[√ 2848 + 3875]

dwelling [1], home [1]

Eph 2:22 And in him you too are being built together to become a **dwelling**
Rev 18: 2 She has become a **home** for demons and a haunt for every evil

3000 κατοικία, *katoikia* [1] [√ 2848 + 3875]

live [1]

Ac 17:26 the times set for them and the exact places where they should **live**.

3001 κατοικίζω, *katoikizō* [1] [√ 2848 + 3875]

caused to live [1]

Jas   4: 5 reason that the spirit he **caused to live** in us envies intensely?

3002 κατοπτρίζω, *katoptrizō* [1] [√ 2848 + 3972]

reflect [1]

2Co 3:18 And we, who with unveiled faces all **reflect** the Lord's glory,

3003 κατόρθωμα, *katorthōma* Not used in UBS/NIV
[√ 2848 + 3981]

3004 κάτω, *katō* [9] [√ 2848]

below [3], down [3], bottom [2], to the ground [1]

Mt   4: 6 "If you are the Son of God," he said, "throw yourself **down**. For it
  27:51 the curtain of the temple was torn in two from top to **bottom**.
Mk 14:66 While Peter was **below** in the courtyard, one of the servant girls of
  15:38 The curtain of the temple was torn in two from top to **bottom**.
Lk   4: 9 "If you are the Son of God," he said, "throw yourself **down** from
Jn   8: 6 But Jesus bent **down** and started to write on the ground with his
    8:23 But he continued, "You are from **below**; I am from above. You are
Ac   2:19 show wonders in the heaven above and signs on the earth **below**,

20: 9 he fell **to the ground** from the third story and was picked up dead.

3005 κατώτερος, *katōteros* [1] [√ *2848*]

lower [1]

Eph 4: 9 "he ascended" mean except that he also descended to the **lower**,

3006 κατωτέρω, *katōterō* [1] [√ *2848*]

under [1]

Mt 2:16 in Bethlehem and its vicinity who were two years old and **under**,

3007 Καῦδα, *Kauda* [1] [√ *cf. 1144, 3084, 3085*]

Cauda [1]

Ac 27:16 As we passed to the lee of a small island called **Cauda**, we were

3008 καῦμα, *kauma* [2] [√ *2794*]

heat [1], scorching heat [1]

Rev 7:16 The sun will not beat upon them, nor any **scorching heat**.
16: 9 They were seared by the intense **heat** and they cursed the name of

3009 καυματίζω, *kaumatizō* [4] [√ *2794*]

scorched [2], scorch [1], seared [1]

Mt 13: 6 the *plants were* **scorched**, and they withered because they had no
Mk 4: 6 the *plants were* **scorched**, and they withered because they had no
Rev 16: 8 the sun, and the sun was given power *to* **scorch** people with fire.
16: 9 They *were* **seared** *by* the intense heat and they cursed the name of

3010 καυματόω, *kaumatoō* Not used in UBS/NIV [√ *2794*]

3011 καῦσις, *kausis* [1] [√ *2794*]

burned [1]

Heb 6: 8 and is in danger of being cursed. In the end it will be **burned**.

3012 καυσόω, *kausoō* [2] [√ *2794*]

fire [1], heat [1]

2Pe 3:10 the elements will be destroyed *by* **fire**, and the earth
3:12 of the heavens by fire, and the elements will melt *in* the **heat**.

3013 καυστηριάζω, *kaustēriazō* [1] [√ *2794*]

seared as with a hot iron [1]

1Ti 4: 2 whose consciences *have been* **seared as with a hot iron**.

3014 καύσων, *kausōn* [3] [√ *2794*]

heat [1], hot [1], scorching heat [1]

Mt 20:12 us who have borne the burden of the work and the **heat** of the day.'
Lk 12:55 the south wind blows, you say, 'It's going to be **hot**,' and it is.
Jas 1:11 For the sun rises with **scorching heat** and withers the plant;

3015 καυτηριάζω, *kautēriazō* Not used in UBS/NIV [√ *2794*]

3016 καυχάομαι, *kauchaomai* [37 / 36] [→ *1595, 2878, 3017, 3018*]

boast [17], boasting [5], rejoice [3], boasts [2], take pride [2], boast about [1], boast of [1], boasted [1], boasting of [1], brag about [1], brag [1], glory [1]

Ro 2:17 if you rely on the law and **brag about** your relationship to God;
2:23 You who **brag** about the law, do you dishonor God by breaking the

5: 2 we now stand. And *we* **rejoice** in the hope of the glory of God.
5: 3 Not only so, but *we* also **rejoice** in our sufferings, because we
5:11 but *we* also **rejoice** in God through our Lord Jesus Christ,
1Co 1:29 so that no one *may* **boast** before him.
1:31 Therefore, as it is written: "Let him *who* **boasts** boast in the Lord."
1:31 Therefore, as it is written: "*Let* him who boasts **boast** in the Lord."
3:21 So then, no more **boasting** about men! All things are yours,
4: 7 And if you did receive it, why *do* you **boast** as though you did not?
13: 3 and surrender my body to the flames, [UBS *body that I may* **boast**; NIV *2794*] but have not love, I gain nothing.
2Co 5:12 so that you can answer those *who* **take pride** in what is seen rather
7:14 *I had* **boasted** to him about you, and you have not embarrassed
9: 2 to help, and *I have been* **boasting** about it to the Macedonians,
10: 8 For even if *I* **boast** somewhat freely about the authority the Lord
10:13 We, however, *will* not **boast** beyond proper limits, but will confine
10:15 Neither do we go beyond our limits *by* **boasting of** work done by
10:16 For we *do* not *want to* **boast** about work already done in another
10:17 But, "*Let* him *who* **boasts** boast in the Lord."
10:17 But, "Let him who boasts **boast** in the Lord."
11:12 to be considered equal with us in the things *they* **boast about**.
11:16 me just as you would a fool, so that I *may do* a little **boasting**.
11:18 Since many *are* **boasting** in the way the world does, I too will
11:18 many are boasting in the way the world does, I too *will* **boast**.
11:30 If I must **boast**, I will boast of the things that show my weakness.
11:30 If I must boast, *I will* **boast of** the things that show my weakness.
12: 1 I must *go on* **boasting**. Although there is nothing to be gained,
12: 5 *I will* **boast** about a man like that, but I will not boast about
12: 5 but *I will* not **boast** about myself, except about my weaknesses.
12: 6 Even if I should choose *to* **boast**, I would not be a fool, because I
12: 9 Therefore *I will* **boast** all the more gladly about my weaknesses,
Gal 6:13 yet they want you to be circumcised that *they may* **boast** about
6:14 May I never **boast** except in the cross of our Lord Jesus Christ,
Eph 2: 9 not by works, so that no one *can* **boast**.
Php 3: 3 we who worship by the Spirit of God, who **glory** in Christ Jesus,
Jas 1: 9 The brother in humble circumstances *ought to* **take pride** in his
4:16 As it is, you **boast** and brag. All such boasting is evil.

3017 καύχημα, *kauchēma* [11] [√ *3016*]

boast [4], boasting [2], pride [2], boast [+*1639*] [1], joy [1], something to boast about [1]

Ro 4: 2 was justified by works, he had **something to boast about**—
1Co 5: 6 Your **boasting** is not good. Don't you know that a little yeast
9:15 I would rather die than have anyone deprive me of this **boast**.
9:16 I preach the gospel, I cannot **boast**, for I am compelled to preach.
2Co 1:14 just as *we will* **boast** [+*1639*] of you in the day of the Lord Jesus.
5:12 to you again, but are giving you an opportunity to take **pride** in us,
9: 3 But I am sending the brothers in order that our **boasting** about you
Gal 6: 4 Then he can take **pride** in himself, without comparing himself to
Php 1:26 so that through my being with you again your **joy** in Christ Jesus
2:16 in order that I may **boast** on the day of Christ that I did not run
Heb 3: 6 if we hold on to our courage and the hope of which we **boast**.

3018 καύχησις, *kauchēsis* [11] [√ *3016*]

boasting [4], pride [2], boast [1], boasting about [1], glory in [+*2400*] [1], glory over [+*2400*] [1], glory [1]

Ro 3:27 Where, then, is **boasting**? It is excluded. On what principle?
15:17 Therefore *I* **glory** [+*2400*] in Christ Jesus *in* my service to God.
1Co 15:31 just as surely as *I* **glory** [+*2400*] *over* you in Christ Jesus our Lord.
2Co 1:12 Now this is our **boast**: Our conscience testifies that we have
7: 4 I have great confidence in you; I take great **pride** in you. I am
7:14 so our **boasting about** you to Titus has proved to be true as well.
8:24 men the proof of your love and the reason for our **pride** in you,
11:10 nobody in the regions of Achaia will stop this **boasting** of mine.
11:17 In this self-confident **boasting** I am not talking as the Lord would,
1Th 2:19 or the crown in which we will **glory** in the presence of our Lord
Jas 4:16 As it is, you boast and brag. All such **boasting** is evil.

3019 Καφαρναούμ, *Kapharnaoum* [16] [√ *cf. 2835*]

Capernaum [16]

Mt 4:13 Leaving Nazareth, he went and lived in **Capernaum**, which was
8: 5 When Jesus had entered **Capernaum**, a centurion came to him,

	11:23	And you, **Capernaum**, will you be lifted up to the skies? No,
	17:24	After Jesus and his disciples arrived in **Capernaum**, the collectors
Mk	1:21	They went to **Capernaum**, and when the Sabbath came,
	2: 1	A few days later, when Jesus again entered **Capernaum**,
	9:33	They came to **Capernaum**. When he was in the house, he asked
Lk	4:23	your hometown what we have heard that you did in **Capernaum**.' "
	4:31	Then he went down to **Capernaum**, a town in Galilee, and on the
	7: 1	saying all this in the hearing of the people, he entered **Capernaum**.
	10:15	And you, **Capernaum**, will you be lifted up to the skies? No,
Jn	2:12	After this he went down to **Capernaum** with his mother
	4:46	was a certain royal official whose son lay sick at **Capernaum**.
	6:17	they got into a boat and set off across the lake for **Capernaum**.
	6:24	they got into the boats and went to **Capernaum** in search of Jesus.
	6:59	He said this while teaching in the synagogue in **Capernaum**.

3020 Κεγχρεαί, *Kenchreai* [2]

Cenchrea [2]

Ac	18:18	he had his hair cut off at **Cenchrea** because of a vow he had taken.
Ro	16: 1	to you our sister Phoebe, a servant of the church in **Cenchrea**.

3021 κέδρος, *kedros* Not used in UBS/NIV

3022 Κεδρών, *Kedrōn* [1]

Kidron [1]

Jn	18: 1	Jesus left with his disciples and crossed the **Kidron** Valley.

3023 κεῖμαι, *keimai* [24] [→ 367, 512, 641, 780, 2130, 2879, 3121, 3122, 3130, 3131, 4154, 4329, 4618, 5165, 5263, 5692]

lying [4], destined [2], is [2], laid [2], there [2], *untranslated* [1], been [1], by itself [+1650+1651+5536+6006] [1], covers [+2093] [1], laid out [1], laid up [1], lay [1], made [1], put here [1], stood [+1639] [1], under the control [1], was [1]

Mt	3:10	The ax **is** already at the root of the trees, and every tree that does
	5:14	are the light of the world. A city [NIE] on a hill cannot be hidden.
	28: 6	he has risen, just as he said. Come and see the place where *he* **lay**.
Lk	2:12	You will find a baby wrapped in cloths and **lying** in a manger."
	2:16	and Joseph, and the baby, *who was* **lying** in the manger.
	2:34	"This child *is* **destined** to cause the falling and rising of many in
	3: 9	The ax **is** already at the root of the trees, and every tree that does
	12:19	to myself, "You have plenty of good things **laid up** for many years.
	23:53	it in a tomb cut in the rock, one in which no one had yet been **laid**.
Jn	2: 6	Nearby **stood** [+1639] six stone water jars, the kind used by the
	19:29	A jar of wine vinegar *was* **there**,
	20: 5	He bent over and looked in at the strips of linen **lying** there
	20: 6	and went into the tomb. He saw the strips of linen **lying** there,
	20: 7	The cloth was folded up **by itself** [+1650+1651+5536+6006],
	20:12	seated where Jesus' body *had* **been**, one at the head and the other at
	21: 9	they saw a fire of burning coals **there** with fish on it, and some
1Co	3:11	For no one can lay any foundation other than the one *already* **laid**,
2Co	3:15	to this day when Moses is read, a veil **covers** [+2093] their hearts.
Php	1:16	knowing that *I am* **put here** for the defense of the gospel.
1Th	3: 3	these trials. You know quite well that *we were* **destined** for them.
1Ti	1: 9	We also know that law *is* **made** not for the righteous but for
1Jn	5:19	and that the whole world *is* **under the control** of the evil one.
Rev	4: 2	and there before me **was** a throne in heaven with someone sitting
	21:16	The city *was* **laid out** like a square, as long as it was wide.

3024 κειρία, *keiria* [1] [√ 3025]

strips of linen [1]

Jn	11:44	man came out, his hands and feet wrapped *with* **strips of linen**,

3025 κείρω, *keirō* [4] [→ 1483, 2134, 2135, 3024, 3047, 3048, 3166]

cut off [2], hair cut [1], shearer [1]

Ac	8:32	and as a lamb before the **shearer** is silent, so he did not open his
	18:18	*he had* his hair **cut off** at Cenchrea because of a vow he had taken.

1Co	11: 6	woman does not cover her head, *she should have* her hair **cut off**;
	11: 6	and if it is a disgrace for a woman *to have her* **hair cut** or shaved

3026 κέλευσμα, *keleusma* [1] [√ 3027]

loud command [1]

1Th	4:16	with a **loud command**, with the voice of the archangel and with

3027 κελεύω, *keleuō* [25] [→ 1353, 2131, 2225, 3026]

ordered [18], gave orders [2], command [1], commanding [1], directed [1], give order [1], tell [1]

Mt	8:18	around him, *he* **gave orders** to cross to the other side of the lake.
	14: 9	and his dinner guests, *he* **ordered** that her request be granted
	14:19	And *he* **directed** the people to sit down on the grass.
	14:28	if it's you," Peter replied, "**tell** me to come to you on the water."
	18:25	the master **ordered** that he and his wife and his children and all
	27:58	he asked for Jesus' body, and Pilate **ordered** that it be given to him.
	27:64	So **give** the **order** for the tomb to be made secure until the third
Lk	18:40	Jesus stopped and **ordered** the man to be brought to him. When he
Ac	4:15	So *they* **ordered** them to withdraw from the Sanhedrin and
	5:34	and **ordered** that the men be put outside for a little while.
	8:38	And *he* **gave orders** to stop the chariot. Then both Philip
	12:19	he cross-examined the guards and **ordered** that they be executed.
	16:22	and the magistrates **ordered** them to be stripped and beaten.
	21:33	and arrested him and **ordered** him to be bound with two chains.
	21:34	of the uproar, *he* **ordered** that Paul be taken into the barracks.
	22:24	the commander **ordered** Paul to be taken into the barracks.
	22:30	he released him and **ordered** the chief priests and all the Sanhedrin
	23: 3	yet *you yourself* violate the law *by* **commanding** that I be struck!"
	23:10	*He* **ordered** the troops to go down and take him away from them
	23:35	Then *he* **ordered** that Paul be kept under guard in Herod's palace.
	25: 6	and the next day *he* convened the court and **ordered** that Paul be
	25:17	the court the next day and **ordered** the man to be brought in.
	25:21	*I* **ordered** him held until I could send him to Caesar."
	25:23	men of the city. *At the* **command** of Festus, Paul was brought in.
	27:43	*He* **ordered** those who could swim to jump overboard first

3028 κενεμβατεύω, *kenembateuō* Not used in UBS/NIV [√ 3031 + 1877 + 326]

3029 κενοδοξία, *kenodoxia* [1] [√ 3031 + 1518]

vain conceit [1]

Php	2: 3	Do nothing out of selfish ambition or **vain conceit**, but in humility

3030 κενόδοξος, *kenodoxos* [1] [√ 3031 + 1518]

conceited [1]

Gal	5:26	Let us not become **conceited**, provoking and envying each other.

3031 κενός, *kenos* [18] [→ 3028, 3029, 3030, 3032, 3033, 3036]

empty-handed [3], empty [2], in vain [2], useless [2], vain [2], *untranslated* [1], failure [1], foolish [1], hollow [1], nothing [1], so[s] [1], without effect [1]

Mk	12: 3	But they seized him, beat him and sent him away **empty-handed**.
Lk	1:53	the hungry with good things but has sent the rich away **empty**.
	20:10	But the tenants beat him and sent him away **empty-handed**.
	20:11	they beat and treated shamefully and sent away **empty-handed**.
Ac	4:25	" 'Why do the nations rage and the peoples plot **in vain**?
1Co	15:10	God I am what I am, and his grace to me was not **without effect**.
	15:14	has not been raised, our preaching is **useless** and so is your faith.
	15:14	has not been raised, our preaching is useless and so[s] is your faith.
	15:58	because you know that your labor in the Lord is not **in vain**.
2Co	6: 1	fellow workers we urge you not to receive God's grace **in vain**.
Gal	2: 2	be leaders, for fear that I was running or had run my race **in vain**.
Eph	5: 6	Let no one deceive you *with* **empty** words, for because of such
Php	2:16	boast on the day of Christ that I did not run or labor for **nothing**.
	2:16	on the day of Christ that I did not run or labor for nothing. [RPG]
Col	2: 8	See to it that no one takes you captive through **hollow**

1Th 2: 1 You know, brothers, that our visit to you was not a **failure.**
      3: 5 might have tempted you and our efforts might have been **useless.**
Jas 2:20 You **foolish** man, do you want evidence that faith without deeds is

3032 κενοφωνία, kenophōnia [2] [√ 3031 + 5889]

chatter [2]

1Ti 6:20 Turn away from godless **chatter** and the opposing ideas of what is
2Ti 2:16 Avoid godless **chatter,** because those who indulge in it will

3033 κενόω, kenoō [5] [√ 3031]

deprive [1], emptied [1], made nothing [1], no value [1], prove hollow [1]

Ro   4:14 by law are heirs, faith *has* **no value** and the promise is worthless,
1Co 1:17 of human wisdom, lest the cross of Christ *be* **emptied** of its power.
      9:15 I would rather die than have anyone **deprive** me of this boast.
2Co 9: 3 our boasting about you in this matter *should* not **prove hollow,**
Php 2: 7 but **made** himself **nothing,** taking the very nature of a servant,

3034 κέντρον, kentron [4] [→ 1596, 1708]

sting [2], goads [1], stings [1]

Ac 26:14 do you persecute me? It is hard for you to kick against the **goads.'**
1Co 15:55 "Where, O death, is your victory? Where, O death, is your **sting?"**
     15:56 The **sting** of death is sin,
Rev 9:10 They had tails and **stings** like scorpions, and in their tails they had

3035 κεντυρίων, kentyriōn [3]

centurion [3]

Mk 15:39 And when the **centurion,** who stood there in front of Jesus,
     15:44 Summoning the **centurion,** he asked him if Jesus had already died.
     15:45 When he learned from the **centurion** that it was so, he gave the

3036 κενῶς, kenōs [1] [√ 3031]

without reason [1]

Jas 4: 5 Or do you think Scripture says **without reason** that the spirit he

3037 κεραία, keraia [2] [√ 3043]

least stroke of a pen [2]

Mt   5:18 not the smallest letter, not the **least stroke of a pen,**
Lk 16:17 and earth to disappear than *for* the **least stroke of a pen** to drop

3038 κεραμεύς, kerameus [3] [√ 3041]

potter's [2], potter [1]

Mt 27: 7 So they decided to use the money to buy the **potter's** field as a
     27:10 and they used them to buy the **potter's** field, as the Lord
Ro   9:21 Does not the **potter** have the right to make out of the same lump of

3039 κεραμικός, keramikos [1] [√ 3041]

pottery [+5007] [1]

Rev 2:27 an iron scepter; he will dash them to pieces like **pottery'** [+5007]—

3040 κεράμιον, keramion [2] [√ 3041]

jar [2]

Mk 14:13 "Go into the city, and a man carrying a **jar** of water will meet you.
Lk 22:10 "As you enter the city, a man carrying a **jar** of water will meet you.

3041 κέραμος, keramos [1] [→ 3038, 3039, 3040]

tiles [1]

Lk   5:19 and lowered him on his mat through the **tiles** into the middle of the

3042 κεράννυμι, kerannymi [3] [→ 193, 204, 5166]

untranslated [1], mix [1], poured [1]

Rev 14:10 which *has been* **poured** full strength into the cup of his wrath.
     18: 6 for what she has done. **Mix** her a double portion from her own cup.
     18: 6 she has done. Mix her a double portion from her own cup. **[RPG]**

3043 κέρας, keras [11] [→ 3037, 3044]

horns [10], horn [1]

Lk   1:69 He has raised up a **horn** of salvation for us in the house of his
Rev 5: 6 He had seven **horns** and seven eyes, which are the seven spirits of
      9:13 and I heard a voice coming from the **horns** of the golden altar that
     12: 3 with seven heads and ten **horns** and seven crowns on his heads.
     13: 1 He had ten **horns** and seven heads, with ten crowns on his horns,
     13: 1 He had ten horns and seven heads, with ten crowns on his **horns,**
     13:11 He had two **horns** like a lamb, but he spoke like a dragon.
     17: 3 with blasphemous names and had seven heads and ten **horns.**
     17: 7 of the beast she rides, which has the seven heads and ten **horns.**
     17:12 "The ten **horns** you saw are ten kings who have not yet received a
     17:16 The beast and the ten **horns** you saw will hate the prostitute.

3044 κεράτιον, keration [1] [√ 3043]

pods [1]

Lk 15:16 He longed to fill his stomach with the **pods** that the pigs were

3045 κερδαίνω, kerdainō [17] [√ 3046]

win [5], gained [4], gain [3], won over [2], gains [1], make money [1], spared [1]

Mt 16:26 What good will it be for a man if *he* **gains** the whole world,
     18:15 two of you. If he listens to you, *you have* **won** your brother **over.**
     25:16 went at once and put his money to work and **gained** five more.
     25:17 So also, the one with the two talents **gained** two more.
     25:20 'you entrusted me with five talents. See, I have **gained** five more.'
     25:22 'you entrusted me with two talents; see, I have **gained** two more.'
Mk   8:36 What good is it for a man *to* **gain** the whole world, yet forfeit his
Lk   9:25 What good is it for a man *to* **gain** the whole world, and yet lose
Ac 27:21 then you *would have* **spared** yourselves this damage and loss.
1Co 9:19 I make myself a slave to everyone, to **win** as many as possible.
      9:20 To the Jews I became like a Jew, to **win** the Jews. To those under
      9:20 I myself am not under the law), so as to **win** those under the law.
      9:21 but am under Christ's law), so as to **win** those not having the law.
      9:22 To the weak I became weak, to **win** the weak. I have become all
Php 3: 8 lost all things. I consider them rubbish, that *I may* **gain** Christ
Jas 4:13 that city, spend a year there, carry on business and **make money."**
1Pe 3: 1 *they may be* **won over** without words by the behavior of their

3046 κέρδος, kerdos [3] [→ 153, 154, 2132, 3045]

gain [2], profit [1]

Php 1:21 For to me, to live is Christ and to die is **gain.**
      3: 7 But whatever was to my **profit** I now consider loss for the sake of
Tit 1:11 they ought not to teach—and that for the sake of dishonest **gain.**

3047 κέρμα, kerma [1] [√ 3025]

coins [1]

Jn   2:15 he scattered the **coins** of the money changers and overturned their

3048 κερματιστής, kermatistēs [1] [√ 3025]

exchanging money [1]

Jn   2:14 and doves, and others sitting at tables **exchanging money.**

3049 κεφάλαιον, kephalaion [2] [√ 3051]

price [1], the point is this [1]

Ac 22:28 the commander said, "I had to pay a big **price** for my citizenship."
Heb 8: 1 **The point** of what we are saying **is this:** We do have such a high

3050 κεφαλαιόω, *kephalaioō* Not used in UBS/NIV
[√ *3051*]

3051 κεφαλή, *kephalē* [75] [→ *368, 642, 2133, 3049, 3050, 3052, 3053, 4330, 4676*]

head [50], heads [18], capstone [+*1224*] [5], *untranslated* [1], hair [1]

Mt	5:36 And do not swear by your **head**, for you cannot make even one
	6:17 But when you fast, put oil on your **head** and wash your face,
	8:20 the air have nests, but the Son of Man has no place to lay his **head**."
	10:30 And even the very hairs *of* your **head** are all numbered.
	14: 8 she said, "Give me here on a platter the **head** of John the Baptist."
	14:11 His **head** was brought in on a platter and given to the girl,
	21:42 'The stone the builders rejected has become the **capstone** [+*1224*];
	26: 7 which she poured on his **head** as he was reclining at the table.
	27:29 then twisted together a crown of thorns and set it on his **head**.
	27:30 and took the staff and struck him on the **head** again and again.
	27:37 Above his **head** they placed the written charge against him:
	27:39 Those who passed by hurled insults at him, shaking their **heads**
Mk	6:24 shall I ask for?" "The **head** of John the Baptist," she answered.
	6:25 "I want you to give me right now the **head** of John the Baptist on a
	6:27 immediately sent an executioner with orders to bring John's **head**.
	6:28 and brought back his **head** on a platter. He presented it to the girl,
	12:10 'The stone the builders rejected has become the **capstone** [+*1224*];
	14: 3 pure nard. She broke the jar and poured the perfume on his **head**.
	15:19 Again and again they struck him *on* the **head** with a staff and spit
	15:29 by hurled insults at him, shaking their **heads** and saying, "So!
Lk	7:38 with her hair, [NIE] kissed them and poured perfume on them.
	7:46 You did not put oil on my **head**, but she has poured perfume on my
	9:58 the air have nests, but the Son of Man has no place to lay his **head**."
	12: 7 Indeed, the very hairs *of* your **head** are all numbered. Don't be
	20:17 stone the builders rejected has become the **capstone**' [+*1224*]?
	21:18 But not a hair of your **head** will perish.
	21:28 these things begin to take place, stand up and lift up your **heads**,
Jn	13: 9 Peter replied, "not just my feet but my hands and my **head** as well!"
	19: 2 soldiers twisted together a crown of thorns and put it on his **head**.
	19:30 "It is finished." With that, he bowed his **head** and gave up his spirit.
	20: 7 as well as the burial cloth that had been around Jesus' **head**.
	20:12 Jesus' body had been, one at the **head** and the other at the foot.
Ac	4:11 you builders rejected, which has become the **capstone** [+*1224*].'
	18: 6 in protest and said to them, "Your blood be on your own **heads**!
	18:18 he had his **hair** cut off at Cenchrea because of a vow he had taken.
	21:24 and pay their expenses, so that they can have their **heads** shaved.
	27:34 it to survive. Not one of you will lose a single hair from his **head**."
Ro	12:20 to drink. In doing this, you will heap burning coals on his **head**."
1Co	11: 3 Now I want you to realize that the **head** of every man is Christ,
	11: 3 and the **head** of the woman is man, and the head of Christ is God.
	11: 3 and the head of the woman is man, and the **head** of Christ is God.
	11: 4 who prays or prophesies with his **head** covered dishonors his head.
	11: 4 who prays or prophesies with his head covered dishonors his **head**.
	11: 5 or prophesies *with* her **head** uncovered dishonors her head—
	11: 5 or prophesies with her head uncovered dishonors her **head**—
	11: 7 A man ought not to cover his **head**, since he is the image and glory
	11:10 the woman ought to have a sign of authority on her **head**.
	12:21 need you!" And the **head** cannot say to the feet, "I don't need you!"
Eph	1:22 and appointed him to be **head** over everything for the church,
	4:15 we will in all things grow up into him who is the **Head**, that is,
	5:23 For the husband is the **head** of the wife as Christ is the head of the
	5:23 For the husband is the head of the wife as Christ is the **head** of the
Col	1:18 And he is the **head** of the body, the church; he is the beginning
	2:10 fullness in Christ, who is the **head** over every power and authority.
	2:19 He has lost connection with the **Head**, from whom the whole body,
1Pe	2: 7 stone the builders rejected has become the **capstone** [+*1224*],"
Rev	1:14 His **head** and hair were white like wool, as white as snow,
	4: 4 They were dressed in white and had crowns of gold on their **heads**.
	9: 7 On their **heads** they wore something like crowns of gold, and their
	9:17 The **heads** of the horses resembled the heads of lions, and out of
	9:17 The heads of the horses resembled the **heads** of lions, and out of
	9:19 tails were like snakes, having **heads** with which they inflict injury.
	10: 1 He was robed in a cloud, with a rainbow above his **head**; his face
	12: 1 the moon under her feet and a crown of twelve stars on her **head**.
	12: 3 an enormous red dragon with seven **heads** and ten horns and seven
	12: 3 with seven heads and ten horns and seven crowns on his **heads**.
	13: 1 He had ten horns and seven **heads**, with ten crowns on his horns,
	13: 1 ten crowns on his horns, and on each **head** a blasphemous name.
	13: 3 One of the **heads** of the beast seemed to have had a fatal wound,
	14:14 was one "like a son of man" with a crown of gold on his **head**
	17: 3 with blasphemous names and had seven **heads** and ten horns.
	17: 7 of the beast she rides, which has the seven **heads** and ten horns.
	17: 9 The seven **heads** are seven hills on which the woman sits.
	18:19 They will throw dust on their **heads**, and with weeping
	19:12 His eyes are like blazing fire, and on his **head** are many crowns.

3052 κεφαλιόω, *kephalioō* [1] [√ *3051*]

struck on the head [1]

Mk 12: 4 *they* **struck** this man **on the head** and treated him shamefully.

3053 κεφαλίς, *kephalis* [1] [√ *3051*]

scroll [+*1046*] [1]

Heb 10: 7 I said, 'Here I am—it is written about me in the **scroll** [+*1046*]—

3054 κηδεύω, *kēdeuō* Not used in UBS/NIV

3055 κημόω, *kēmoō* [1]

muzzle [1]

1Co 9: 9 of Moses: "*Do* not **muzzle** an ox while it is treading out the grain."

3056 κῆνσος, *kēnsos* [4]

taxes [3], tax [1]

Mt	17:25 "From whom do the kings of the earth collect duty and **taxes**—
	22:17 what is your opinion? Is it right to pay **taxes** to Caesar or not?"
	22:19 Show me the coin *used for paying* the **tax**." They brought him a
Mk	12:14 accordance with the truth. Is it right to pay **taxes** to Caesar or not?

3057 κῆπος, *kēpos* [5] [→ *3058*]

garden [3], olive grove [2]

Lk	13:19 like a mustard seed, which a man took and planted in his **garden**.
Jn	18: 1 On the other side there was an **olive grove**, and he and his disciples
	18:26 challenged him, "Didn't I see you with him in the **olive grove**?"
	19:41 there was a **garden**, and in the garden a new tomb, in which no one
	19:41 there was a garden, and in the **garden** a new tomb, in which no one

3058 κηπουρός, *kēpouros* [1] [√ *3057*]

gardener [1]

Jn 20:15 Thinking he was the **gardener**, she said, "Sir, if you have carried

3059 κηρίον, *kērion* Not used in UBS/NIV

3060 κήρυγμα, *kērygma* [9 / 8] [√ *3061*]

preaching [5], message [1], proclamation [1], what was preached [1]

Mt	12:41 for they repented at the **preaching** of Jonah, and now one greater
Mk	16: S [UBS+ *holy and imperishable* **proclamation** *of eternal salvation*.]
Lk	11:32 for they repented at the **preaching** of Jonah, and now one greater
Ro	16:25 establish you by my gospel and the **proclamation** of Jesus Christ,
1Co	1:21 God was pleased through the foolishness of **what was preached** to
	2: 4 My message and my **preaching** were not with wise and persuasive
	15:14 has not been raised, our **preaching** is useless and so is your faith.
2Ti	4:17 so that through me the **message** might be fully proclaimed
Tit	1: 3 the **preaching** entrusted to me by the command of God our Savior,

3061 κῆρυξ, *kēryx* [3] [→ *3060, 3062, 4619*]

herald [2], preacher [1]

1Ti	2: 7 And for this purpose I was appointed a **herald** and an apostle—
2Ti	1:11 And of this gospel I was appointed a **herald** and an apostle
2Pe	2: 5 but protected Noah, a **preacher** of righteousness, and seven others;

3062 κηρύσσω, kēryssō [61] [√ 3061]

preach [17], preached [16], preaching [10], proclaim [3], proclaimed [3], proclaiming [3], preaches [2], *untranslated* [1], message [1], preached [+2400] [1], talk [1], talking about [1], tell [1], told [1]

Mt 3: 1 days John the Baptist came, **preaching** in the Desert of Judea
     4: 17 From that time on Jesus began to **preach**, "Repent, for the kingdom
     4: 23 **preaching** the good news of the kingdom, and healing every
     9: 35 **preaching** the good news of the kingdom and healing every
     10: 7 As *you go*, **preach** this message: 'The kingdom of heaven is near.'
     10: 27 what is whispered in your ear, **proclaim** from the roofs.
     11: 1 he went on from there to teach and **preach** in the towns of Galilee.
     24: 14 And this gospel of the kingdom *will be* **preached** in the whole
     26: 13 the truth, wherever this gospel *is* **preached** throughout the world,
Mk 1: 4 and **preaching** a baptism of repentance for the forgiveness of sins.
     1: 7 And this *was his* **message**: "After me will come one more powerful
     1: 14 Jesus went into Galilee, **proclaiming** the good news of God.
     1: 38 to the nearby villages—so *I can* **preach** there also.
     1: 39 **preaching** in their synagogues and driving out demons.
     1: 45 Instead he went out and began to **talk** freely, spreading the news.
     3: 14 they might be with him and that he might send them out *to* **preach**
     5: 20 and began *to* **tell** in the Decapolis how much Jesus had done for
     6: 12 *They* went out and **preached** that people should repent.
     7: 36 But the more he did so, the more they *kept* **talking about** it.
     13: 10 And the gospel must first *be* **preached** to all nations.
     14: 9 the truth, wherever the gospel *is* **preached** throughout the world,
     16: 15 "Go into all the world and **preach** the good news to all creation.
     16: 20 Then the disciples went out and **preached** everywhere,
Lk 3: 3 **preaching** a baptism of repentance for the forgiveness of sins.
     4: 18 He has sent me *to* **proclaim** freedom for the prisoners
     4: 19 *to* **proclaim** the year of the Lord's favor."
     4: 44 And he kept on **preaching** in the synagogues of Judea.
     8: 1 [RPG] **proclaiming** the good news of the kingdom of God.
     8: 39 and **told** all over town how much Jesus had done for him.
     9: 2 and he sent them out *to* **preach** the kingdom of God and to heal the
     12: 3 in the ear in the inner rooms *will be* **proclaimed** from the roofs.
     24: 47 and forgiveness of sins *will be* **preached** in his name to all nations,
Ac 8: 5 went down to a city in Samaria and **proclaimed** the Christ there.
     9: 20 At once *he began to* **preach** in the synagogues that Jesus is the
     10: 37 beginning in Galilee after the baptism that John **preached**—
     10: 42 He commanded us *to* **preach** to the people and to testify that he is
     15: 21 For Moses *has been* **preached** [+2400] in every city from the
     19: 13 They would say, "In the name of Jesus, whom Paul **preaches**,
     20: 25 I have gone about **preaching** the kingdom will ever see me again.
     28: 31 Boldly and without hindrance *he* **preached** the kingdom of God
Ro 2: 21 not teach yourself? You *who* **preach** against stealing, do you steal?
     10: 8 and in your heart," that is, the word of faith *we are* **proclaiming**:
     10: 14 And how can they hear without *someone* **preaching** to them?
     10: 15 And how *can they* **preach** unless they are sent? As it is written,
1Co 1: 23 but we **preach** Christ crucified: a stumbling block to Jews
     9: 27 and make it my slave so that *after I have* **preached** to others,
     15: 11 Whether, then, it was I or they, this is what *we* **preach**, and this is
     15: 12 But if *it is* **preached** that Christ has been raised from the dead,
2Co 1: 19 who *was* **preached** among you by me and Silas and Timothy,
     4: 5 For *we do* not **preach** ourselves, but Jesus Christ as Lord,
     11: 4 to you and **preaches** a Jesus other than the Jesus we preached,
     11: 4 to you and preaches a Jesus other than the Jesus *we* **preached**,
Gal 2: 2 and set before them the gospel that *I* **preach** among the Gentiles.
     5: 11 Brothers, if I *am* still **preaching** circumcision, why am I still being
Php 1: 15 It is true that some **preach** Christ out of envy and rivalry,
Col 1: 23 and that *has been* **proclaimed** to every creature under heaven,
1Th 2: 9 and day in order not to be a burden to anyone *while we* **preached**
1Ti 3: 16 the Spirit, *was* seen by angels, *was* **preached** among the nations,
2Ti 4: 2 **Preach** the Word; be prepared in season and out of season;
1Pe 3: 19 through whom also *he* went and **preached** to the spirits in prison
Rev 5: 2 And I saw a mighty angel **proclaiming** in a loud voice, "Who is

3063 κῆτος, kētos [1]

huge fish [1]

Mt 12: 40 Jonah was three days and three nights in the belly *of* a **huge fish**,

3064 Κηφᾶς, Kēphas [9]

Peter [5], Cephas [4]

Jn 1: 42 You will be called **Cephas**" (which, when translated, is Peter).
1Co 1: 12 another, "I follow **Cephas**"; still another, "I follow Christ."
     3: 22 whether Paul or Apollos or **Cephas** or the world or life or death
     9: 5 as do the other apostles and the Lord's brothers and **Cephas**?
     15: 5 and that he appeared *to* **Peter**, and then to the Twelve.
Gal 1: 18 I went up to Jerusalem to get acquainted with **Peter** and stayed
     2: 9 James, **Peter** and John, those reputed to be pillars, gave me
     2: 11 When **Peter** came to Antioch, I opposed him to his face,
     2: 14 I said *to* **Peter** in front of them all, "You are a Jew, yet you live like

3065 κιβώριον, kibōrion Not used in UBS/NIV

3066 κιβωτός, kibōtos [6]

ark [6]

Mt 24: 38 and giving in marriage, up to the day Noah entered the **ark**;
Lk 17: 27 and being given in marriage up to the day Noah entered the **ark**.
Heb 9: 4 golden altar of incense and the gold-covered **ark** of the covenant.
     11: 7 things not yet seen, in holy fear built an **ark** to save his family.
1Pe 3: 20 waited patiently in the days of Noah while the **ark** was being built.
Rev 11: 19 and within his temple was seen the **ark** of his covenant.

3067 κιθάρα, kithara [4] [→ 3068, 3069]

harp [2], harps [2]

1Co 14: 7 case of lifeless things that make sounds, such as the flute or **harp**,
Rev 5: 8 Each one had a **harp** and they were holding golden bowls full of
     14: 2 The sound I heard was like that of harpists playing their **harps**.
     15: 2 over the number of his name. They held **harps** given them by God

3068 κιθαρίζω, kitharizō [2] [√ 3067]

playing [1], tune played [+884+2445] [1]

1Co 14: 7 how will anyone know what **tune** *is being* **played** [+884+2445]
Rev 14: 2 The sound I heard was like that of harpists **playing** their harps.

3069 κιθαρῳδός, kitharōdos [2] [√ 3067 + 6046]

harpists [2]

Rev 14: 2 The sound I heard was like that *of* **harpists** playing their harps.
     18: 22 The music *of* **harpists** and musicians, flute players and trumpeters,

3070 Κιλικία, Kilikia [8] [√ 3071]

Cilicia [7], provinces of Cilicia [1]

Ac 6: 9 and Alexandria as well as the **provinces of Cilicia** and Asia.
     15: 23 To the Gentile believers in Antioch, Syria and **Cilicia**:
     15: 41 He went through Syria and **Cilicia**, strengthening the churches.
     21: 39 Paul answered, "I am a Jew, from Tarsus *in* **Cilicia**, a citizen of no
     22: 3 "I am a Jew, born in Tarsus *of* **Cilicia**, but brought up in this city.
     23: 34 what province he was from. Learning that he was from **Cilicia**,
     27: 5 When we had sailed across the open sea off the coast of **Cilicia**
Gal 1: 21 Later I went to Syria and **Cilicia**.

3071 Κίλιξ, Kilix Not used in UBS/NIV [→ 3070]

3072 κινάμωμον, kinamōmon Not used in UBS/NIV
[√ 3077]

3073 κινδυνεύω, kindyneuō [4] [√ 3074]

danger that [1], endanger [1], in danger of [1], in great danger [1]

Lk 8: 23 that the boat was being swamped, and *they were* **in great danger**.
Ac 19: 27 *There is* **danger** not only *that* our trade will lose its good name,
     19: 40 *we are* **in danger of** being charged with rioting because of today's
1Co 15: 30 And as for us, why *do we* **endanger** ourselves every hour?

3074 κίνδυνος, kindynos [9] [→ 3073]

danger [9]

Ro   8:35   or persecution or famine or nakedness or **danger** or sword?
2Co 11:26   I have been in **danger** from rivers, in danger from bandits,
     11:26   I have been in danger from rivers, *in* **danger** from bandits,
     11:26   in danger from bandits, *in* **danger** from my own countrymen,
     11:26   in danger from my own countrymen, *in* **danger** from Gentiles;
     11:26   *in* **danger** in the city, in danger in the country, in danger at sea;
     11:26   in danger in the city, *in* **danger** in the country, in danger at sea;
     11:26   in danger in the city, in danger in the country, *in* **danger** at sea;
     11:26   in the country, in danger at sea; and *in* **danger** from false brothers.

3075 κινέω, kineō [8] [→ 293, 3076, 3560, 5167]

move [2], shaking [2], aroused [1], remove [1], removed [1], stirring up [1]

Mt   23: 4   but they themselves are not willing to lift a finger *to* **move** them.
     27:39   Those who passed by hurled insults at him, **shaking** their heads
Mk 15:29   by hurled insults at him, **shaking** their heads and saying, "So!
Ac   17:28   'For in him *we* live and **move** and have our being.' As some of
     21:30   The whole city *was* **aroused**, and the people came running from all
     24: 5   **stirring up** riots among the Jews all over the world.
Rev   2: 5   I will come to you and **remove** your lampstand from its place.
     6:14   and every mountain and island *was* **removed** from its place.

3076 κίνησις, kinēsis   Not used in UBS/NIV [√ 3075]

3077 κιννάμωμον, kinnamōmon [1] [→ 3072]

cinnamon [1]

Rev 18:13   cargoes of **cinnamon** and spice, of incense, myrrh

3078 Κίς, Kis [1]

Kish [1]

Ac 13:21   and he gave them Saul son *of* **Kish**, of the tribe of Benjamin,

3079 κίχρημι, kichrēmi [1] [√ cf. 5968, 5969]

lend [1]

Lk 11: 5   him at midnight and says, 'Friend, **lend** me three loaves of bread,

3080 κλάδος, klados [11] [√ 3089]

branches [9], twigs [2]

Mt   13:32   so that the birds of the air come and perch in its **branches**."
     21: 8   while others cut **branches** from the trees and spread them on the
     24:32   As soon as its **twigs** get tender and its leaves come out, you know
Mk   4:32   with such big **branches** that the birds of the air can perch in its
     13:28   As soon as its **twigs** get tender and its leaves come out, you know
Lk   13:19   and became a tree, and the birds of the air perched in its **branches**."
Ro   11:16   the whole batch is holy; if the root is holy, so are the **branches**.
     11:17   If some *of the* **branches** have been broken off, and you, though a
     11:18   do not boast over those **branches**. If you do, consider this:
     11:19   say then, "**Branches** were broken off so that I could be grafted in."
     11:21   For if God did not spare the natural **branches**, he will not spare

3081 κλαίω, klaiō [40] [→ 3088]

weep [10], crying [5], weeping [5], wept [5], mourn [4], wailing [3], cry [2], did⁵ [1], wail [1], weeping [+4472] [1], weeping for [1], wept and wept [+4498] [1], with tears [1]

Mt   2:18   Rachel **weeping for** her children and refusing to be comforted,
     26:75   disown me three times." And he went outside and **wept** bitterly.
Mk   5:38   Jesus saw a commotion, with *people* **crying** and wailing loudly.
     5:39   went in and said to them, "Why all this commotion and **wailing**?
     14:72   you will disown me three times." And *he* broke down and **wept**.
     16:10   who had been with him and who were mourning and **weeping**.
Lk   6:21   be satisfied. Blessed are you who **weep** now, for you will laugh.
     6:25   Woe to you who laugh now, for *you will* mourn and **weep**.
     7:13   the Lord saw her, his heart went out to her and he said, "Don't **cry**."

     7:32   and you did not dance; we sang a dirge, and *you did* not **cry**.'
     7:38   and as she stood behind him at his feet **weeping**, she began to wet
     8:52   Meanwhile, all the people *were* **wailing** and mourning for her.
     8:52   for her. "Stop **wailing**," Jesus said. "She is not dead but asleep."
     19:41   As he approached Jerusalem and saw the city, he **wept** over it
     22:62   And *he* went outside and **wept** bitterly.
     23:28   and said to them, "Daughters of Jerusalem, *do* not **weep** for me;
     23:28   do not weep for me; **weep** for yourselves and for your children.
Jn   11:31   followed her, supposing she was going to the tomb to **mourn** there.
     11:33   When Jesus saw her **weeping**, and the Jews who had come along
     11:33   and the Jews who had come along with her also **weeping**,
     16:20   you the truth, you *will* **weep** and mourn while the world rejoices.
     20:11   but Mary stood outside the tomb **crying**. As she wept, she bent over
     20:11   the tomb crying. As *she* **wept**, she bent over to look into the tomb
     20:13   They asked her, "Woman, why *are you* **crying**?" "They have taken
     20:15   "Woman," he said, "why *are you* **crying**? Who is it you are looking
Ac   9:39   **crying** and showing him the robes and other clothing that Dorcas
     21:13   "Why *are you* **weeping** [+4472] and breaking my heart?
Ro   12:15   Rejoice with those who rejoice; **mourn** with those who mourn.
     12:15   Rejoice with those who rejoice; mourn with *those who* **mourn**.
1Co   7:30   those *who* **mourn**, as if they did not; those who are happy,
     7:30   those who mourn, as if they did⁵ not; those who are happy,
Php   3:18   as I have often told you before and now say again even **with tears**,
Jas   4: 9   Grieve, mourn and **wail**. Change your laughter to mourning
     5: 1   **weep** and wail because of the misery that is coming upon you.
Rev   5: 4   *I* **wept** [+4498] **and wept** because no one was found who was
     5: 5   Then one of the elders said to me, "*Do* not **weep**! See, the Lion of
     18: 9   see the smoke of her burning, *they will* **weep** and mourn over her.
     18:11   "The merchants of the earth *will* **weep** and mourn over her
     18:15   stand far off, terrified at her torment. *They will* **weep** and mourn
     18:19   dust on their heads, and *with* **weeping** and mourning cry out:

3082 κλάσις, klasis [2] [√ 3089]

breaking [1], broke [1]

Lk   24:35   and how Jesus was recognized by them when he **broke** the bread.
Ac   2:42   and to the fellowship, to the **breaking** of bread and to prayer.

3083 κλάσμα, klasma [9] [√ 3089]

broken pieces [5], pieces [4]

Mt   14:20   and the disciples picked up twelve basketfuls *of* **broken pieces** that
     15:37   picked up seven basketfuls *of* **broken pieces** that were left over.
Mk   6:43   and the disciples picked up twelve basketfuls *of* **broken pieces** of
     8: 8   picked up seven basketfuls *of* **broken pieces** that were left over.
     8:19   the five thousand, how many basketfuls *of* **pieces** did you pick up?"
     8:20   the four thousand, how many basketfuls *of* **pieces** did you pick up?"
Lk   9:17   and the disciples picked up twelve basketfuls *of* **broken pieces** that
Jn   6:12   he said to his disciples, "Gather the **pieces** that are left over.
     6:13   and filled twelve baskets *with* the **pieces** of the five barley loaves

3084 Κλαῦδα, Klauda   Not used in UBS/NIV [√ cf. 3007]

3085 Κλαύδη, Klaudē   Not used in UBS/NIV [√ cf. 3007]

3086 Κλαυδία, Klaudia [1] [→ 3087]

Claudia [1]

2Ti   4:21   greets you, and so do Pudens, Linus, **Claudia** and all the brothers.

3087 Κλαύδιος, Klaudios [3] [√ 3086]

Claudius [3]

Ac   11:28   Roman world. (This happened during the reign of **Claudius**.)
     18: 2   because **Claudius** had ordered all the Jews to leave Rome.
     23:26   **Claudius** Lysias, To His Excellency, Governor Felix: Greetings.

3088 κλαυθμός, klauthmos [9] [√ 3081]

weeping [7], weeping [+3836] [1], wept [+1181+2653] [1]

Mt   2:18   "A voice is heard in Ramah, **weeping** and great mourning,
     8:12   the darkness, where there will be **weeping** and gnashing of teeth."

13:42 fiery furnace, where there will be **weeping** and gnashing of teeth.
13:50 fiery furnace, where there will be **weeping** and gnashing of teeth.
22:13 the darkness, where there will be **weeping** and gnashing of teeth.'
24:51 the hypocrites, where there will be **weeping** and gnashing of teeth.
25:30 the darkness, where there will be **weeping** and gnashing of teeth.'
Lk 13:28 "There will be **weeping** [*+3836*] there, and gnashing of teeth,
Ac 20:37 *They* all **wept** [*+1181+2653*] as they embraced him and kissed

3089 κλάω, *klaō* [14] [→ *1709, 2880, 3080, 3082, 3083, 3097*]

broke [12], break [2]

Mt 14:19 and looking up to heaven, he gave thanks and **broke** the loaves.
15:36 *he* **broke** them and gave them to the disciples, and they in turn to
26:26 they were eating, Jesus took bread, gave thanks and **broke** it,
Mk 8: 6 *he* **broke** them and gave them to his disciples to set before the
8:19 When *I* **broke** the five loaves for the five thousand, how many
14:22 they were eating, Jesus took bread, gave thanks and **broke** it,
Lk 22:19 And *he* took bread, gave thanks and **broke** it, and gave it to them,
24:30 he took bread, gave thanks, **broke** it and began to give it to them.
Ac 2:46 They **broke** bread in their homes and ate together with glad
20: 7 On the first day of the week we came together *to* **break** bread.
20:11 Then *he* went upstairs again and **broke** bread and ate. After talking
27:35 to God in front of them all. Then he **broke** it and began to eat.
1Co 10:16 And is not the bread that *we* **break** a participation in the body of
11:24 he **broke** it and said, "This is my body, which is for you;

3090 κλείς, *kleis* [6] [√ *3091*]

key [4], keys [2]

Mt 16:19 I will give you the **keys** of the kingdom of heaven; whatever you
Lk 11:52 in the law, because you have taken away the **key** to knowledge.
Rev 1:18 alive for ever and ever! And I hold the **keys** of death and Hades.
3: 7 words of him who is holy and true, who holds the **key** of David.
9: 1 to the earth. The star was given the **key** to the shaft of the Abyss.
20: 1 having the **key** to the Abyss and holding in his hand a great chain.

3091 κλείω, *kleiō* [16] [→ *643, 1597, 1710, 2881, 3090, 5168*]

shut [8], locked [5], close [1], has no pity [*+3836+5073*] [1], shuts [1]

Mt 6: 6 your room, **close** the door and pray to your Father, who is unseen.
23:13 you hypocrites! *You* **shut** the kingdom of heaven in men's faces.
25:10 went in with him to the wedding banquet. And the door *was* **shut**.
Lk 4:25 when the sky *was* **shut** for three and a half years and there was a
11: 7 The door *is* already **locked**, and my children are with me in bed.
Jn 20:19 with the doors **locked** for fear of the Jews, Jesus came and stood
20:26 *Though* the doors *were* **locked**, Jesus came and stood among them
Ac 5:23 "We found the jail securely **locked**, with the guards standing at the
21:30 him from the temple, and immediately the gates *were* **shut**.
1Jn 3:17 and sees his brother in need but **has no pity** [*+3836+5073*] on him,
Rev 3: 7 What he opens no one *can* **shut**, and what he shuts no one can
3: 7 he opens no one can shut, and what he **shuts** no one can open.
3: 8 I have placed before you an open door that no one can **shut**.
11: 6 These men have power *to* **shut** up the sky so that it will not rain
20: 3 He threw him into the Abyss, and **locked** and sealed it over him,
21:25 On no day *will* its gates ever *be* **shut**, for there will be no night

3092 κλέμμα, *klemma* [1] [√ *3096*]

thefts [1]

Rev 9:21 their magic arts, their sexual immorality or their **thefts**.

3093 Κλεοπᾶς, *Kleopas* [1] [√ *3094 + 4252*]

Cleopas [1]

Lk 24:18 One of them, named **Cleopas**, asked him, "Are you only a visitor to

3094 κλέος, *kleos* [1] [→ *3093*]

credit [1]

1Pe 2:20 But how is it to your **credit** if you receive a beating for doing

3095 κλέπτης, *kleptēs* [16] [√ *3096*]

thief [12], thieves [4]

Mt 6:19 where moth and rust destroy, and where **thieves** break in and steal.
6:20 rust do not destroy, and where **thieves** do not break in and steal.
24:43 If the owner of the house had known at what time of night the **thief**
Lk 12:33 not be exhausted, where no **thief** comes near and no moth destroys.
12:39 If the owner of the house had known at what hour the **thief** was
Jn 10: 1 the gate, but climbs in by some other way, is a **thief** and a robber.
10: 8 All who ever came before me were **thieves** and robbers,
10:10 The **thief** comes only to steal and kill and destroy; I have come that
12: 6 because he cared about the poor but because he was a **thief**;
1Co 6:10 nor **thieves** nor the greedy nor drunkards nor slanderers nor
1Th 5: 2 well that the day of the Lord will come like a **thief** in the night.
5: 4 are not in darkness so that this day should surprise you like a **thief**.
1Pe 4:15 should not be as a murderer or **thief** or any other kind of criminal,
2Pe 3:10 But the day of the Lord will come like a **thief**. The heavens will
Rev 3: 3 But if you do not wake up, I will come like a **thief**, and you will
16:15 "Behold, I come like a **thief**! Blessed is he who stays awake

3096 κλέπτω, *kleptō* [13] [→ *3092, 3095, 3113*]

steal [10], stealing [2], stole [1]

Mt 6:19 where moth and rust destroy, and where thieves break in and **steal**.
6:20 rust do not destroy, and where thieves do not break in and **steal**.
19:18 " 'Do not murder, do not commit adultery, *do* not **steal**,
27:64 his disciples may come and **steal** the body and tell the people that
28:13 came during the night and **stole** him *away* while we were asleep.'
Mk 10:19 'Do not murder, do not commit adultery, *do* not **steal**, do not give
Lk 18:20 'Do not commit adultery, do not murder, *do* not **steal**, do not give
Jn 10:10 The thief comes only to **steal** and kill and destroy; I have come that
Ro 2:21 not teach yourself? You who preach against **stealing**, do you steal?
2:21 not teach yourself? You who preach against stealing, *do you* **steal**?
13: 9 "Do not murder," "*Do* not **steal**," "Do not covet,"
Eph 4:28 He *who has been* **stealing** must steal no longer, but must work,
4:28 He who has been stealing *must* **steal** no longer, but must work,

3097 κλῆμα, *klēma* [4] [√ *3089*]

branch [3], branches [1]

Jn 15: 2 He cuts off every **branch** in me that bears no fruit, while every
15: 4 No **branch** can bear fruit by itself; it must remain in the vine.
15: 5 "I am the vine; you are the **branches**. If a man remains in me
15: 6 remain in me, he is like a **branch** that is thrown away and withers;

3098 Κλήμης, *Klēmēs* [1]

Clement [1]

Php 4: 3 along with **Clement** and the rest of my fellow workers,

3099 κληρονομέω, *klēronomeō* [18] [√ *3102 + 3795*]

inherit [15], inherited [1], share in the inheritance [1], take inheritance [1]

Mt 5: 5 Blessed are the meek, for they *will* **inherit** the earth.
19:29 will receive a hundred times as much and *will* **inherit** eternal life.
25:34 **take** *your* **inheritance**, the kingdom prepared for you since the
Mk 10:17 "Good teacher," he asked, "what must I do to **inherit** eternal life?"
Lk 10:25 "Teacher," he asked, "what must I do *to* **inherit** eternal life?"
18:18 asked him, "Good teacher, what must I do *to* **inherit** eternal life?"
1Co 6: 9 Do you not know that the wicked *will* not **inherit** the kingdom of
6:10 nor slanderers nor swindlers *will* **inherit** the kingdom of God.
15:50 brothers, that flesh and blood cannot **inherit** the kingdom of God.
15:50 kingdom of God, nor *does* the perishable **inherit** the imperishable.
Gal 4:30 for the slave woman's son *will* never **share in the inheritance**
5:21 that those who live like this *will* not **inherit** the kingdom of God.
Heb 1: 4 to the angels as the name *he has* **inherited** is superior to theirs.
1:14 ministering spirits sent to serve those *who* will **inherit** salvation?

6:12 but to imitate those *who* through faith and patience **inherit** what
12:17 Afterward, as you know, when he wanted *to* **inherit** this blessing,
1Pe 3: 9 because to this you were called so that *you may* **inherit** a blessing.
Rev 21: 7 He who overcomes *will* **inherit** all this, and I will be his God

3100 κληρονομία, *klēronomia* [14] [√ *3102 + 3795*]

inheritance [14]

Mt 21:38 'This is the heir. Come, let's kill him and take his **inheritance**.'
Mk 12: 7 is the heir. Come, let's kill him, and the **inheritance** will be ours.'
Lk 12:13 "Teacher, tell my brother to divide the **inheritance** with me.'
20:14 they said. 'Let's kill him, and the **inheritance** will be ours.'
Ac 7: 5 He gave him no **inheritance** here, not even a foot of ground.
20:32 and give you an **inheritance** among all those who are sanctified.
Gal 3:18 For if the **inheritance** depends on the law, then it no longer
Eph 1:14 who is a deposit guaranteeing our **inheritance** until the redemption
1:18 has called you, the riches *of* his glorious **inheritance** in the saints,
5: 5 has any **inheritance** in the kingdom of Christ and of God.
Col 3:24 since you know that you will receive an **inheritance** from the Lord
Heb 9:15 who are called may receive the promised eternal **inheritance**—
11: 8 called to go to a place he would later receive as his **inheritance**,
1Pe 1: 4 and into an **inheritance** that can never perish, spoil or fade—

3101 κληρονόμος, *klēronomos* [15] [√ *3102 + 3795*]

heir [8], heirs [6], inherit [1]

Mt 21:38 the tenants saw the son, they said to each other, 'This is the **heir**.
Mk 12: 7 "But the tenants said to one another, 'This is the **heir**. Come,
Lk 20:14 'This is the **heir**,' they said. 'Let's kill him, and the inheritance
Ro 4:13 and his offspring received the promise that he would be **heir** of the
4:14 For if those who live by law are **heirs**, faith has no value
8:17 Now if we are children, then we are **heirs**—heirs of God
8:17 **heirs** of God and co-heirs with Christ, if indeed we share in his
Gal 3:29 then you are Abraham's seed, and **heirs** according to the promise.
4: 1 What I am saying is that as long as the **heir** is a child, he is no
4: 7 but a son; and since you are a son, God has made you also an **heir**.
Tit 3: 7 his grace, we might become **heirs** having the hope of eternal life.
Heb 1: 2 whom he appointed **heir** of all things, and through whom he made
6:17 nature of his purpose very clear *to* the **heirs** of what was promised,
11: 7 and became **heir** of the righteousness that comes by faith.
Jas 2: 5 and to **inherit** the kingdom he promised those who love him?

3102 κλῆρος, *klēros* [11] [→ *2882, 2883, 3099, 3100,*
3101, 3103, 3729, 3907, 3908, 4677, 5169]

lots [5], entrusted to [1], inheritance [1], lot [1], place [1], share
[1], shared [+*3275+3836*] [1]

Mt 27:35 they had crucified him, they divided up his clothes by casting **lots**.
Mk 15:24 Dividing up his clothes, they cast **lots** to see what each would get.
Lk 23:34 they are doing." And they divided up his clothes by casting **lots**.
Jn 19:24 divided my garments among them and cast **lots** for my clothing."
Ac 1:17 one of our number and **shared** [+*3275+3836*] in this ministry."
1:26 Then they cast **lots**, and the lot fell to Matthias; so he was added to
1:26 Then they cast lots, and the **lot** fell to Matthias; so he was added to
8:21 You have no part or **share** in this ministry, because your heart is
26:18 and a **place** among those who are sanctified by faith in me.'
Col 1:12 who has qualified you to share *in* the **inheritance** of the saints in
1Pe 5: 3 not lording it over those **entrusted to** you, but being examples to

3103 κληρόω, *klēroō* [1] [√ *3102*]

chosen [1]

Eph 1:11 In him *we were* also **chosen**, having been predestined according to

3104 κλῆσις, *klēsis* [11] [√ *2813*]

called [4], calling [3], call [1], calling received [+*2813*] [1], life [1],
situation [1]

Ro 11:29 for God's gifts and his **call** are irrevocable.
1Co 1:26 Brothers, think of what you were when you were **called**. Not many
7:20 Each one should remain in the **situation** which he was in when
Eph 1:18 in order that you may know the hope to which he has **called** you,
4: 1 you to live a life worthy *of* the **calling** [+*2813*] *you have* **received**.

4: 4 just as you were called to one hope when you were **called**—
Php 3:14 the prize for which God has **called** me heavenward in Christ Jesus.
2Th 1:11 pray for you, that our God may count you worthy *of* his **calling**,
2Ti 1: 9 who has saved us and called us *to* a holy **life**—not because of
Heb 3: 1 Therefore, holy brothers, who share in the heavenly **calling**,
2Pe 1:10 be all the more eager to make your **calling** and election sure.

3105 κλητός, *klētos* [10] [√ *2813*]

called [9], invited [1]

Mt 22:14 "For many are **invited**, but few are chosen."
Ro 1: 1 **called** to be an apostle and set apart for the gospel of God—
1: 6 And you also are among those who are **called** to belong to Jesus
1: 7 To all in Rome who are loved by God and **called** to be saints:
8:28 who love him, who have been **called** according to his purpose.
1Co 1: 1 Paul, **called** to be an apostle of Christ Jesus by the will of God,
1: 2 in Corinth, to those sanctified in Christ Jesus and **called** to be holy,
1:24 but to those whom God has **called**, both Jews and Greeks,
Jude 1: 1 and a brother of James, To those who have been **called**,
Rev 17:14 and with him will be his **called**, chosen and faithful followers."

3106 κλίβανος, *klibanos* [2]

fire [2]

Mt 6:30 which is here today and tomorrow is thrown into the **fire**, will he
Lk 12:28 which is here today, and tomorrow is thrown into the **fire**,

3107 κλίμα, *klima* [3] [√ *3111*]

regions [2], *untranslated* [1]

Ro 15:23 now that there is no more place for me to work in these **regions**,
2Co 11:10 nobody in the **regions** of Achaia will stop this boasting of mine.
Gal 1:21 Later I went to Syria **[NIE]** and Cilicia.

3108 κλινάριον, *klinarion* [1] [√ *3111*]

beds [1]

Ac 5:15 brought the sick into the streets and laid them on **beds** and mats

3109 κλίνη, *klinē* [9 / 8] [√ *3111*]

bed [4], mat [3], bed of suffering [1]

Mt 9: 2 Some men brought to him a paralytic, lying on a **mat**. When Jesus
9: 6 Then he said to the paralytic, "Get up, take your **mat** and go home."
Mk 4:21 to them, "Do you bring in a lamp to put it under a bowl or a **bed**?
7: 4 washing of cups, pitchers and kettles.) [UBS+ *and dining couches*.]
7:30 She went home and found her child lying on the **bed**,
Lk 5:18 Some men came carrying a paralytic on a **mat** and tried to take him
8:16 "No one lights a lamp and hides it in a jar or puts it under a **bed**.
17:34 I tell you, on that night two people will be in one **bed**; one will be
Rev 2:22 So I will cast her on a **bed of suffering**, and I will make those who

3110 κλινίδιον, *klinidion* [2] [√ *3111*]

mat [2]

Lk 5:19 and lowered him on his **mat** through the tiles into the middle of the
5:24 the paralyzed man, "I tell you, get up, take your **mat** and go home."

3111 κλίνω, *klinō* [7] [→ *195, 369, 804, 1712, 2884, 3107,*
3108, 3109, 3110, 3112, 4679, 4680, 4752]

lay [2], bowed down [1], bowed [1], late in afternoon
[+*806+2465*] [1], over [1], routed [1]

Mt 8:20 the air have nests, but the Son of Man has no place to **lay** his head."
Lk 9:12 **Late in the afternoon** [+*806+2465*] the Twelve came to him
9:58 the air have nests, but the Son of Man has no place *to* **lay** his head."
24: 5 In their fright the *women* **bowed down** with their faces to the
24:29 "Stay with us, for it is nearly evening; the day *is* almost **over**."
Jn 19:30 "It is finished." With that, he **bowed** his head and gave up his spirit.
Heb 11:34 and who became powerful in battle and **routed** foreign armies.

3112 κλισία, *klisia* [1] [√ 3111]

groups [1]

Lk   9:14 his disciples, "Have them sit down in **groups** of about fifty each."

3113 κλοπή, *klopē* [2] [√ 3096]

theft [2]

Mt   15:19 adultery, sexual immorality, **theft**, false testimony, slander.
Mk   7:21 come evil thoughts, sexual immorality, **theft**, murder, adultery,

3114 κλύδων, *klydōn* [2] [→ 2352, 2885, 2886, 3115]

raging [1], wave [1]

Lk   8:24 He got up and rebuked the wind and the **raging** waters; the storm
Jas   1: 6 because he who doubts is like a **wave** of the sea, blown and tossed

3115 κλυδωνίζομαι, *klydōnizomai* [1] [√ 3114]

tossed back and forth by the waves [1]

Eph   4:14 **tossed back and forth by the waves**, and blown here and there by

3116 Κλωπᾶς, *Klōpas* [1]

Clopas [1]

Jn   19:25 his mother's sister, Mary the wife *of* **Clopas**, and Mary

3117 κνήθω, *knēthō* [1] [√ cf. 1187]

itching [1]

2Ti   4: 3 number of teachers to say what their **itching** ears want to hear.

3118 Κνίδος, *Knidos* [1]

Cnidus [1]

Ac   27: 7 headway for many days and had difficulty arriving off **Cnidus**.

3119 κοδράντης, *kodrantēs* [2]

a fraction of a penny [1], penny [1]

Mt   5:26 the truth, you will not get out until you have paid the last **penny**.
Mk   12:42 in two very small copper coins, worth only **a fraction of a penny**.

3120 κοιλία, *koilia* [22 / 23]

stomach [8], birth [+3613] [4], womb [3], *untranslated* [1],
appetites [1], belly [1], child bear [+2843+3836] [1], conceived
[+1877+3836+5197] [1], mother [1], within [1], wombs [1]

Mt   12:40 as Jonah was three days and three nights in the **belly** of a huge fish,
     15:17 you see that whatever enters the mouth goes into the **stomach**
     19:12 For some are eunuchs **[NIE]** because they were born that way;
Mk   7:19 For it doesn't go into his heart but into his **stomach**, and then out
Lk   1:15 and he will be filled with the Holy Spirit even from **birth** [+3613].
      1:41 Elizabeth heard Mary's greeting, the baby leaped in her **womb**,
      1:42 and blessed is the **child** you will **bear** [+2843+3836]!
      1:44 greeting reached my ears, the baby in my **womb** leaped for joy.
      2:21 had given him before he *had been* **conceived** [+1877+3836+5197].
     11:27 "Blessed is the **mother** who gave you birth and nursed you."
     15:16 He longed to fill his **stomach** [UBS-] with the pods that the pigs
     23:29 the **wombs** that never bore and the breasts that never nursed!'
Jn   3: 4 "Surely he cannot enter a second time into his mother's **womb** to be
      7:38 has said, streams of living water will flow from **within** him."
Ac   3: 2 Now a man crippled from **birth** [+3613] was being carried to the
     14: 8 who was lame from **birth** [+3613] and had never walked.
Ro   16:18 people are not serving our Lord Christ, but their own **appetites**.
1Co   6:13 "Food *for* the **stomach** and the stomach for food"—but God will
      6:13 "Food for the stomach and the **stomach** for food"—but God will
Gal   1:15 who set me apart from **birth** [+3613] and called me by his grace,
Php   3:19 Their destiny is destruction, their god is their **stomach**, and their
Rev 10: 9 It will turn your **stomach** sour, but in your mouth it will be as
     10:10 in my mouth, but when I had eaten it, my **stomach** turned sour.

3121 κοιμάω, *koimaō* [18] [√ 3023]

fallen asleep [7], asleep [2], died [2], fell asleep [2], dies [1], fall
asleep [1], sleep [1], sleeping [1], sleeps [1]

Mt   27:52 and the bodies of many holy people who *had* **died** were raised to
     28:13 came during the night and stole him away *while* we *were* **asleep**.'
Lk   22:45 to the disciples, he found them **asleep**, exhausted from sorrow.
Jn   11:11 he went on to tell them, "Our friend Lazarus *has* **fallen asleep**;
     11:12 His disciples replied, "Lord, *if he* **sleeps**, he will get better."
Ac   7:60 hold this sin against them." When he had said this, *he* **fell asleep**.
     12: 6 Peter was **sleeping** between two soldiers, bound with two chains,
     13:36 had served God's purpose in his own generation, *he* **fell asleep**;
1Co   7:39 But if her husband **dies**, she is free to marry anyone she wishes,
     11:30 you are weak and sick, and a number of you *have* **fallen asleep**.
     15: 6 most of whom are still living, though some *have* **fallen asleep**.
     15:18 Then those also *who have* **fallen asleep** in Christ are lost.
     15:20 from the dead, the firstfruits *of* those *who have* **fallen asleep**.
     15:51 you a mystery: *We will* not all **sleep**, but we will all be changed—
1Th   4:13 we do not want you to be ignorant about those *who* **fall asleep**,
      4:14 God will bring with Jesus those *who have* **fallen asleep** in him.
      4:15 the Lord, will certainly not precede those *who have* **fallen asleep**.
2Pe   3: 4 Ever since our fathers **died**, everything goes on as it has since the

3122 κοίμησις, *koimēsis* [1] [√ 3023]

natural sleep [+3836+3836+5678] [1]

Jn   11:13 Jesus had been speaking of his death, but his disciples thought he
            meant **natural sleep** [+3836+3836+5678].

3123 κοινός, *koinos* [14] [→ 3124, 3125, 3126, 3127, 3128, 3129, 5170, 5171]

unclean [5], impure [4], common [1], in common [1], share [1],
shared [1], unholy [1]

Mk   7: 2 some of his disciples eating food *with* hands that were "**unclean**,"
      7: 5 of the elders instead of eating their food *with* 'unclean' hands?"
Ac   2:44 All the believers were together and had everything **in common**.
      4:32 his possessions was his own, but they **shared** everything they had.
     10:14 Peter replied. "I have never eaten anything **impure** or unclean."
     10:28 But God has shown me that I should not call any man **impure**
     11: 8 Lord! Nothing **impure** or unclean has ever entered my mouth.'
Ro   14:14 Lord Jesus, I am fully convinced that no food is **unclean** in itself.
     14:14 But if anyone regards something as **unclean**, then for him it is
     14:14 if anyone regards something as unclean, then for him it is **unclean**.
Tit   1: 4 To Titus, my true son in our **common** faith: Grace and peace from
Heb 10:29 who has treated as an **unholy** *thing* the blood of the covenant that
Jude 1: 3 I was very eager to write to you about the salvation we **share**,
Rev 21:27 Nothing **impure** will ever enter it, nor will anyone who does what

3124 κοινόω, *koinoō* [14] [√ 3123]

make unclean [7], call impure [2], makes unclean [2],
ceremonially unclean [1], defiled [1], what makes unclean [1]

Mt   15:11 What goes into a man's mouth *does* not **make** him 'unclean,'
     15:11 what comes out of his mouth, that *is* **what makes** him 'unclean.' "
     15:18 the mouth come from the heart, and these **make** a man 'unclean.'
     15:20 These are what **make** a man 'unclean'; but eating with unwashed
     15:20 but eating with unwashed hands *does* not **make** him 'unclean.' "
Mk   7:15 Nothing outside a man can **make** him 'unclean' by going into him.
      7:15 it is what comes out of a man that **makes** him 'unclean.' "
      7:18 that enters a man from the outside can **make** him 'unclean'?
      7:20 went on: "What comes out of a man is what **makes** him 'unclean.'
      7:23 All these evils come from inside and **make** a man 'unclean.' "
Ac   10:15 "*Do* not **call** anything **impure** that God has made clean."
     11: 9 '*Do* not **call** anything **impure** that God has made clean.'
     21:28 brought Greeks into the temple area and **defiled** this holy place."
Heb   9:13 sprinkled on those *who are* **ceremonially unclean** sanctify them

3125 κοινωνέω, *koinōneō* [8] [√ 3123]

share [2], shared [2], have [1], participate [1], share with [1],
shares [1]

Ro   12:13 **Share with** God's people who are in need. Practice hospitality.

15:27 For if the Gentiles *have* **shared** in the Jews' spiritual blessings,
Gal   6: 6 Anyone who receives instruction in the word *must* **share** all good
Php   4:15 not one church **shared** with me in the matter of giving
1Ti   5:22 in the laying on of hands, and *do* not **share** in the sins of others.
Heb   2:14 Since the children **have** flesh and blood, he too shared in their
1Pe   4:13 But rejoice that *you* **participate** in the sufferings of Christ,
2Jn   1:11 Anyone who welcomes him **shares** in his wicked work.

3126 κοινωνία, *koinōnia* [19] [√ *3123*]

fellowship [10], sharing [3], participation [2], contribution [1],
fellowship of sharing [1], partnership [1], share [1]

Ac   2:42 devoted themselves to the apostles' teaching and to the **fellowship**,
Ro   15:26 and Achaia were pleased to make a **contribution** for the poor
1Co   1: 9 who has called you into **fellowship** with his Son Jesus Christ our
     10:16 for which we give thanks a **participation** in the blood of Christ?
     10:16 And is not the bread that we break a **participation** in the body of
2Co   6:14 in common? Or what **fellowship** can light have with darkness?
      8: 4 they urgently pleaded with us for the privilege of **sharing** in this
      9:13 and for your generosity *in* **sharing** with them and with everyone
     13:14 love of God, and the **fellowship** of the Holy Spirit be with you all.
Gal   2: 9 and Barnabas the right hand *of* **fellowship** when they recognized
Php   1: 5 because of your **partnership** in the gospel from the first day until
      2: 1 if any **fellowship** with the Spirit, if any tenderness
      3:10 of his resurrection and the **fellowship of sharing** in his sufferings,
Phm   1: 6 I pray that you may be active in **sharing** your faith, so that you will
Heb 13:16 And do not forget to do good and to **share** *with* others, for with
1Jn   1: 3 have seen and heard, so that you also may have **fellowship** with us.
      1: 3 And our **fellowship** is with the Father and with his Son,
      1: 6 If we claim to have **fellowship** with him yet walk in the darkness,
      1: 7 as he is in the light, we have **fellowship** with one another,

3127 κοινωνικός, *koinōnikos* [1] [√ *3123*]

willing to share [1]

1Ti   6:18 to be rich in good deeds, and to be generous and **willing to share**.

3128 κοινωνός, *koinōnos* [10] [√ *3123*]

partner [2], participants [1], participate [+*1639*] [1], participate in
[+*1181*] [1], partners [1], share [+*1639*] [1], share [1], side by
side [1], taken part [+*1639*] [1]

Mt   23:30 *we* would not have **taken part** [+*1639*] with them in shedding the
Lk   5:10 so were James and John, the sons of Zebedee, Simon's **partners**.
1Co 10:18 *Do* not those who eat the sacrifices **participate** [+*1639*] in the
     10:20 not to God, and I do not want you to be **participants** with demons.
2Co   1: 7 because we know that just as *you* **share** [+*1639*] in our sufferings,
      8:23 As for Titus, he is my **partner** and fellow worker among you;
Phm   1:17 So if you consider me a **partner**, welcome him as you would
Heb 10:33 at other times you stood **side by side** with those who were
1Pe   5: 1 and one who also will **share** in the glory to be revealed:
2Pe   1: 4 so that through them *you may* **participate** [+*1181*] **in** the divine

3129 κοινῶς, *koinōs* Not used in UBS/NIV [√ *3123*]

3130 κοίτη, *koitē* [4] [√ *3023*]

bed [1], father^s [+*1666*] [1], marriage bed [1], sexual immorality
[1]

Lk   11: 7 The door is already locked, and my children are with me in **bed**.
Ro   9:10 but Rebekah's children had one and the same **father**^s [+*1666*],
     13:13 not *in* **sexual immorality** and debauchery, not in dissension
Heb 13: 4 and the **marriage bed** kept pure, for God will judge the adulterer

3131 κοιτών, *koitōn* [1] [√ *3023*]

trusted personal servant [+*2093*+*3836*] [1]

Ac   12:20 a **trusted** [+*2093*+*3836*] **personal servant** of the king, they asked

3132 κόκκινος, *kokkinos* [6] [√ *3133*]

scarlet [5], scarlet cloth [1]

Mt   27:28 They stripped him and put a **scarlet** robe on him,
Heb   9:19 together with water, **scarlet** wool and branches of hyssop,
Rev 17: 3 There I saw a woman sitting on a **scarlet** beast that was covered
     17: 4 The woman was dressed in purple and **scarlet**, and was glittering
     18:12 precious stones and pearls; fine linen, purple, silk and **scarlet cloth**;
     18:16 Woe, O great city, dressed in fine linen, purple and **scarlet**,

3133 κόκκος, *kokkos* [7] [→ *3132*]

seed [6], kernel [1]

Mt   13:31 "The kingdom of heaven is like a mustard **seed**, which a man took
     17:20 I tell you the truth, if you have faith as small as a mustard **seed**,
Mk   4:31 It is like a mustard **seed**, which is the smallest seed you plant in the
Lk   13:19 It is like a mustard **seed**, which a man took and planted in his
     17: 6 He replied, "If you have faith as small as a mustard **seed**, you can
Jn   12:24 you the truth, unless a **kernel** of wheat falls to the ground and dies,
1Co 15:37 that will be, but just a **seed**, perhaps of wheat or of something else.

3134 κολάζω, *kolazō* [2] [√ *3266*]

punish [1], punishment [1]

Ac   4:21 They could not decide how *to* **punish** them, because all the people
2Pe   2: 9 for the day of judgment, *while continuing* their **punishment**.

3135 κολακεία, *kolakeia* [1]

flattery [+*3364*] [1]

1Th   2: 5 You know we never used **flattery** [+*3364*], nor did we put on a

3136 κόλασις, *kolasis* [2] [√ *3266*]

punishment [2]

Mt   25:46 "Then they will go away to eternal **punishment**, but the righteous
1Jn   4:18 love drives out fear, because fear has to do with **punishment**.

3137 Κολασσαεύς, *Kolassaeus* Not used in UBS/NIV [√ *3145*]

3138 Κολασσαί, *Kolassai* Not used in UBS/NIV [√ *3145*]

3139 κολαφίζω, *kolaphizō* [5]

struck with fists [2], brutally treated [1], receive a beating [1],
torment [1]

Mt   26:67 Then they spit in his face and **struck** him **with** *their* **fists**.
Mk   14:65 blindfolded him, **struck** him **with** their **fists**, and said, "Prophesy!"
1Co   4:11 we go hungry and thirsty, we are in rags, *we are* **brutally treated**,
2Co 12: 7 me a thorn in my flesh, a messenger of Satan, to **torment** me.
1Pe   2:20 But how is it to your credit if you **receive a beating** for doing

3140 κολλάω, *kollaō* [12] [→ *4681*]

join [2], unites [2], associate with [1], cling [1], followers of [1],
hired out to [1], piled up [1], stay near [1], sticks [1], united to [1]

Mt   19: 5 a man will leave his father and mother and *be* **united to** his wife,
Lk   10:11 'Even the dust of your town that **sticks** to our feet we wipe off
     15:15 So *he* went and **hired** *himself* **out** to a citizen of that country,
Ac   5:13 No one else dared **join** them, even though they were highly
      8:29 The Spirit told Philip, "Go to that chariot and **stay near** it."
      9:26 When he came to Jerusalem, he tried *to* **join** the disciples,
     10:28 that it is against our law for a Jew *to* **associate with** a Gentile
     17:34 A few men *became* **followers of** Paul and believed. Among them
Ro   12: 9 Love must be sincere. Hate what is evil; **cling** to what is good.
1Co   6:16 Do you not know that he *who* **unites** *himself* with a prostitute is
      6:17 But he *who* **unites** *himself* with the Lord is one with him in spirit.
Rev 18: 5 for her sins *are* **piled up** to heaven, and God has remembered her

3141 κολλούριον, *kollourion* [1]

salve [1]

Rev   3:18 shameful nakedness; and **salve** to put on your eyes, so you can see.

3142 κολλυβιστής, *kollybistēs* [3]

money changers [3]

Mt   21:12 He overturned the tables *of* the **money changers** and the benches
Mk   11:15 He overturned the tables *of* the **money changers** and the benches
Jn   2:15 he scattered the coins *of* the **money changers** and overturned their

3143 κολοβόω, *koloboō* [4] [√ *3266*]

cut short [2], shortened [2]

Mt   24:22 If those days *had* not *been* **cut short**, no one would survive,
     24:22 but for the sake of the elect those days *will be* **shortened**.
Mk   13:20 If the Lord *had* not **cut short** those days, no one would survive.
     13:20 the sake of the elect, whom he has chosen, *he has* **shortened** them.

3144 Κολοσσαεύς, *Kolossaeus*   Not used in UBS/NIV
[√ *3145*]

3145 Κολοσσαί, *Kolossai* [1] [→ *3137, 3138, 3144*]

Colosse [1]

Col   1: 2 To the holy and faithful brothers in Christ at **Colosse**: Grace

3146 κόλπος, *kolpos* [6]

side [3], bay [1], lap [1], next to [+*1877+3836*] [1]

Lk   6:38 shaken together and running over, will be poured into your **lap**.
     16:22 the beggar died and the angels carried him to Abraham's **side**.
     16:23 he looked up and saw Abraham far away, with Lazarus by his **side**.
Jn   1:18 but God the One and Only, who is at the Father's **side**, has made
     13:23 whom Jesus loved, was reclining **next to** [+*1877+3836*] him.
Ac   27:39 did not recognize the land, but they saw a **bay** with a sandy beach,

3147 κολυμβάω, *kolymbaō* [1] [→ *1713, 3148*]

swim [1]

Ac   27:43 He ordered those who could **swim** to jump overboard first

3148 κολυμβήθρα, *kolymbēthra* [3] [√ *3147*]

pool [3]

Jn   5: 2 Now there is in Jerusalem near the Sheep Gate a **pool**, which in
     5: 7 "I have no one to help me into the **pool** when the water is stirred.
     9: 7 he told him, "wash in the **Pool** of Siloam" (this word means Sent).

3149 κολωνία, *kolōnia* [1]

Roman colony [1]

Ac   16:12 a **Roman colony** and the leading city of that district of Macedonia.

3150 κομάω, *komaō* [2] [√ *3151*]

has long hair [2]

1Co 11:14 not the very nature of things teach you that if a man **has long hair**,
     11:15 but that if a woman **has long hair**, it is her glory? For long hair is

3151 κόμη, *komē* [1] [→ *3150*]

long hair [1]

1Co 11:15 it is her glory? For **long hair** is given to her as a covering.

3152 κομίζω, *komizō* [10] [√ *3180*]

receive [2], brought [1], receive back [1], receive what is due [1], received back [1], received [1], receiving [1], repaid [1], reward [1]

Mt   25:27 so that when I returned I would have **received** it **back** with
Lk   7:37 at the Pharisee's house, *she* **brought** an alabaster jar of perfume,
2Co   5:10 that each one *may* **receive what is due** him for the things done
Eph   6: 8 because you know that the Lord *will* **reward** everyone for
Col   3:25 Anyone who does wrong *will be* **repaid** for his wrong, and there is
Heb 10:36 have done the will of God, *you* will **receive** what he has promised.
     11:19 and figuratively speaking, *he* did **receive** Isaac **back** from death.
     11:39 for their faith, yet none of them **received** what had been promised.
1Pe   1: 9 for *you are* **receiving** the goal of your faith, the salvation of your
     5: 4 *you will* **receive** the crown of glory that will never fade away.

3153 κομψότερον, *kompsoteron* [1] [√ *3180*]

better [1]

Jn   4:52 When he inquired as to the time when his son got **better**, they said

3154 κονιάω, *koniaō* [2] [→ *3155*]

whitewashed [2]

Mt   23:27 You are like **whitewashed** tombs, which look beautiful on the
Ac   23: 3 Paul said to him, "God will strike you, *you* **whitewashed** wall!

3155 κονιορτός, *koniortos* [5] [√ *3154 + 3995*]

dust [5]

Mt   10:14 shake the **dust** off your feet when you leave that home or town.
Lk   9: 5 shake the **dust** off your feet when you leave their town, as a
     10:11 'Even the **dust** of your town that sticks to our feet we wipe off
Ac   13:51 So they shook the **dust** from their feet in protest against them
     22:23 and throwing off their cloaks and flinging **dust** into the air,

3156 κοπάζω, *kopazō* [3] [√ *3164*]

died down [3]

Mt   14:32 And when they climbed into the boat, the wind **died down**.
Mk   4:39 Be still!" Then the wind **died down** and it was completely calm.
     6:51 Then he climbed into the boat with them, and the wind **died down**.

3157 κοπετός, *kopetos* [1] [√ *3164*]

mourned deeply [+*3489+4472*] [1]

Ac   8: 2 men buried Stephen and **mourned** [+*3489+4472*] **deeply** for him.

3158 κοπή, *kopē* [1] [√ *3164*]

defeat [1]

Heb   7: 1 He met Abraham returning from the **defeat** of the kings

3159 κοπιάω, *kopiaō* [23] [√ *3164*]

labor [5], worked hard [3], weary [2], work hard [2], work [2], done hard work [1], efforts [1], hard work [1], hardworking [1], labors [1], tired [1], work hard [+*2237*] [1], worked for [1], worked [1]

Mt   6:28 See how the lilies of the field grow. *They do* not **labor** or spin.
     11:28 "Come to me, all you who *are* **weary** and burdened,
Lk   5: 5 we've **worked hard** all night and haven't caught anything.
     12:27 *They do* not **labor** or spin. Yet I tell you, not even Solomon in all
Jn   4: 6 and Jesus, **tired** as he was from the journey, sat down by the well.
     4:38 I sent you to reap what you *have* not **worked for**. Others have
     4:38 Others *have* **done** the **hard work**, and you have reaped the
Ac   20:35 I showed you that by this kind of **hard work** we must help the
Ro   16: 6 Greet Mary, who **worked** very **hard** for you.
     16:12 and Tryphosa, those women *who* **work hard** in the Lord.
     16:12 another woman *who has* **worked** very **hard** in the Lord.
1Co   4:12 *We* **work** [+*2237*] **hard** with our own hands. When we are cursed,

	15:10	No, *I* **worked** harder than all of them—yet not I, but the grace of
	16:16	as these and *to* everyone who joins in the work, and **labors** at it.
Gal	4:11	I fear for you, that somehow *I have* wasted *my* **efforts** on you.
Eph	4:28	but *must* **work**, doing something useful with his own hands,
Php	2:16	boast on the day of Christ that I did not run or **labor** for nothing.
Col	1:29	To this end *I* **labor**, struggling with all his energy, which
1Th	5:12	we ask you, brothers, to respect those *who* **work hard** among you,
1Ti	4:10	(and for this *we* **labor** and strive), that we have put our hope in the
	5:17	especially those whose **work** is preaching and teaching.
2Ti	2:6	The **hardworking** farmer should be the first to receive a share of
Rev	2:3	have endured hardships for my name, and *have* not *grown* **weary**.

3160 κόπος, *kopos* [18] [√ 3164]

labor [5], bothering [+4218] [3], hard work [2], bother [+4218] [1], efforts [1], labored [1], laboring [1], toil [1], trouble [1], work [1], worked [1]

Mt	26:10	Jesus said to them, "Why *are you* **bothering** [+4218] this woman?
Mk	14:6	her alone," said Jesus. "Why *are you* **bothering** [+4218] her?
Lk	11:7	"Then the one inside answers, 'Don't **bother** [+4218] me. The door
	18:5	yet because this widow *keeps* **bothering** [+4218] me, I will see
Jn	4:38	the hard work, and you have reaped the benefits of their **labor**."
1Co	3:8	and each will be rewarded according to his own **labor**.
	15:58	because you know that your **labor** in the Lord is not in vain.
2Co	6:5	and riots; in **hard work**, sleepless nights and hunger;
	10:15	Neither do we go beyond our limits by boasting of **work** done by
	11:23	I have **worked** much harder, been in prison more frequently,
	11:27	I have **labored** and toiled and have often gone without sleep;
Gal	6:17	Finally, let no one cause me **trouble**, for I bear on my body the
1Th	1:3	Father your work produced by faith, your **labor** prompted by love,
	2:9	Surely you remember, brothers, our **toil** and hardship; we worked
	3:5	might have tempted you and our **efforts** might have been useless.
2Th	3:8	**laboring** and toiling so that we would not be a burden to any of
Rev	2:2	I know your deeds, your **hard work** and your perseverance.
	14:13	"Yes," says the Spirit, "they will rest from their **labor**, for their

3161 κοπρία, *kopria* [1] [→ 3162, 3163]

manure pile [1]

Lk	14:35	It is fit neither for the soil nor for the **manure pile**; it is thrown out.

3162 κόπριον, *koprion* [1] [√ 3161]

fertilize [+965] [1]

Lk	13:8	for one more year, and I'll dig around it and **fertilize** [+965] it.

3163 κόπρος, *kopros* Not used in UBS/NIV [√ 3161]

3164 κόπτω, *koptō* [8] [→ 370, 644, 718, 737, 1600, 1601, 1715, 1716, 2324, 2888, 3156, 3157, 3158, 3159, 3160, 3273, 4620, 4621, 4682, 4683, 4684]

mourn [4], cut [2], mourned [1], mourning [1]

Mt	11:17	and you did not dance; we sang a dirge, and *you did* not **mourn**.'
	21:8	while others **cut** branches from the trees and spread them on the
	24:30	will appear in the sky, and all the nations of the earth *will* **mourn**.
Mk	11:8	the road, while others spread branches *they had* **cut** in the fields.
Lk	8:52	Meanwhile, all the people *were* wailing and **mourning** for her.
	23:27	followed him, including women who **mourned** and wailed for him.
Rev	1:7	and all the peoples of the earth *will* **mourn** because of him.
	18:9	see the smoke of her burning, *they will* weep and **mourn** over her.

3165 κόραξ, *korax* [1]

ravens [1]

Lk	12:24	Consider the **ravens**: They do not sow or reap, they have no

3166 κοράσιον, *korasion* [8] [√ 3025]

girl [6], little girl [1], she^s [+3836] [1]

Mt	9:24	said, "Go away. The **girl** is not dead but asleep." But they laughed

	9:25	had been put outside, he went in and took the **girl** by the hand,
	14:11	His head was brought in on a platter and given *to* the **girl**,
Mk	5:41	(which means, "**Little girl**, I say to you, get up!").
	5:42	Immediately the **girl** stood up and walked around (she was twelve
	6:22	The king said *to* the **girl**, "Ask me for anything you want, and I'll
	6:28	a platter. He presented it *to* the **girl**, and she gave it to her mother.
	6:28	He presented it to the girl, and she^s [+3836] gave it to her mother.

3167 κορβᾶν, *korban* [1] [→ 3168]

Corban [1]

Mk	7:11	you might otherwise have received from me is **Corban**' (that is,

3168 κορβανᾶς, *korbanas* [1] [√ 3167]

treasury [1]

Mt	27:6	and said, "It is against the law to put this into the **treasury**,

3169 Κόρε, *Kore* [1]

Korah's [1]

Jude	1:11	Balaam's error; they have been destroyed in **Korah's** rebellion.

3170 κορέννυμι, *korennymi* [2]

eaten as much as wanted [+5575] [1], have all you want [+1639] [1]

Ac	27:38	*When they had* **eaten** [+5575] **as much as** *they* **wanted**,
1Co	4:8	Already *you* **have** [+1639] **all you want**! Already you have

3171 Κορίνθιος, *Korinthios* [2] [√ 3172]

Corinthians [2]

Ac	18:8	and many *of* the **Corinthians** who heard him believed and were
2Co	6:11	We have spoken freely to you, **Corinthians**, and opened wide our

3172 Κόρινθος, *Korinthos* [6] [→ 3171]

Corinth [6]

Ac	18:1	After this, Paul left Athens and went to **Corinth**.
	19:1	While Apollos was at **Corinth**, Paul took the road through the
1Co	1:2	To the church of God in **Corinth**, to those sanctified in Christ
2Co	1:1	and Timothy our brother, To the church of God in **Corinth**,
	1:23	that it was in order to spare you that I did not return to **Corinth**.
2Ti	4:20	Erastus stayed in **Corinth**, and I left Trophimus sick in Miletus.

3173 Κορνήλιος, *Kornēlios* [8]

Cornelius [8]

Ac	10:1	At Caesarea there was a man named **Cornelius**, a centurion in
	10:3	saw an angel of God, who came to him and said, "**Cornelius**!"
	10:17	the men sent by **Cornelius** found out where Simon's house was
	10:22	The men replied, "We have come from **Cornelius** the centurion.
	10:24	**Cornelius** was expecting them and had called together his relatives
	10:25	the house, **Cornelius** met him and fell at his feet in reverence.
	10:30	**Cornelius** answered: "Four days ago I was in my house praying at
	10:31	and said, '**Cornelius**, God has heard your prayer and remembered

3174 κόρος, *koros* [1]

thousand bushels [+1669] [1]

Lk	16:7	'And how much do you owe?' " 'A **thousand bushels** [+1669] of

3175 κοσμέω, *kosmeō* [10] [√ 3180]

put in order [2], adorned [1], beautifully dressed [1], decorate [1], decorated [1], dress [1], make attractive [1], make beautiful [1], trimmed [1]

Mt	12:44	it finds the house unoccupied, swept clean and **put in order**.
	23:29	tombs for the prophets and **decorate** the graves of the righteous.

25: 7 "Then all the virgins woke up and **trimmed** their lamps.
Lk 11:25 When it arrives, it finds the house swept clean and **put in order**.
   21: 5 about how the temple *was* **adorned** with beautiful stones
1Ti 2: 9 I also want women *to* **dress** modestly, with decency and propriety,
Tit 2:10 way *they will* **make** the teaching about God our Savior **attractive**.
1Pe 3: 5 who put their hope in God *used to* **make** themselves **beautiful**.
Rev 21: 2 prepared as a bride **beautifully dressed** for her husband.
   21:19 The foundations of the city walls *were* **decorated** with every kind

3176 κοσμικός, *kosmikos* [2] [√ *3180*]

earthly [1], worldly [1]

Tit 2:12 It teaches us to say "No" to ungodliness and **worldly** passions,
Heb 9: 1 had regulations for worship and also an **earthly** sanctuary.

3177 κόσμιος, *kosmios* [2] [√ *3180*]

modestly [*+1877+2950*] [1], respectable [1]

1Ti 2: 9 I also want women to dress **modestly** [*+1877+2950*], with decency
   3: 2 temperate, self-controlled, **respectable**, hospitable, able to teach,

3178 κοσμίως, *kosmiōs* Not used in UBS/NIV [√ *3180*]

3179 κοσμοκράτωρ, *kosmokratōr* [1] [√ *3180 + 3197*]

powers of world [1]

Eph 6:12 against the **powers of** this dark **world** and against the spiritual

3180 κόσμος, *kosmos* [186] [→ *1186, 1714, 3152, 3153, 3175, 3176, 3177, 3178, 3179, 5172*]

καταβολῆς κόσμου (foundation of the world) [10] Mt 13:35; 25:34; Lk 11:50; Jn 17:24; Eph 1:4; Heb 4:3; 9:26; 1Pe 1:20; Rev 13:8; 17:8

κρίνω τὸν κόσμον (judge the world) [6] Jn 3:17; 12:47,48; Ro 3:6; 1Co 6:2,2

ὅλος κόσμος (whole world) [8] Mt 16:26; 26:13; Mk 8:36; 14:9; Lk 9:25; Jn 12:19[NIV]; Ro 1:8; 1Jn 2:2; 5:19

οὗτος κόσμος (this world) [16] Jn 8:23,23; 9:39; 11:9; 12:25,31, 31; 13:1; 16:11; 18:36,36; 1Co 3:19; 5:10; 7:31; Eph 2:2; 1Jn 4:17

φῶς τοῦ κόσμου (light of the world) [5] Mt 5:14; Jn 8:12; 9:5; 11:9; 12:46

world [173], it^s [*+3836*] [3], *untranslated* [1], adornment [1], earth [1], it^s [1], material [1], people [1], universe [1], whole universe [1], world's [1], worldly [*+3836*] [1]

Mt 4: 8 and showed him all the kingdoms *of* the **world** and their splendor.
   5:14 "You are the light of the **world**. A city on a hill cannot be hidden.
  13:35 I will utter things hidden since the creation *of* the **world**."
  13:38 The field is the **world**, and the good seed stands for the sons of the
  16:26 What good will it be for a man if he gains the whole **world**,
  18: 7 "Woe *to* the **world** because of the things that cause people to sin!
  24:21 unequaled from the beginning *of* the **world** until now—
  25:34 the kingdom prepared for you since the creation *of* the **world**.
  26:13 the truth, wherever this gospel is preached throughout the **world**,
Mk 8:36 What good is it for a man to gain the whole **world**, yet forfeit his
  14: 9 the truth, wherever the gospel is preached throughout the **world**,
  16:15 "Go into all the **world** and preach the good news to all creation.
Lk 9:25 What good is it for a man to gain the whole **world**, and yet lose
  11:50 the prophets that has been shed since the beginning *of* the **world**,
  12:30 For the pagan **world** runs after all such things, and your Father
Jn 1: 9 true light that gives light to every man was coming into the **world**.
  1:10 He was in the **world**, and though the world was made through him,
  1:10 He was in the world, and though the **world** was made through him,
  1:10 the world was made through him, the **world** did not recognize him.
  1:29 "Look, the Lamb of God, who takes away the sin *of* the **world**!
  3:16 "For God so loved the **world** that he gave his one and only Son,
  3:17 For God did not send his Son into the **world** to condemn the world,
  3:17 For God did not send his Son into the world to condemn the **world**,
  3:17 world to condemn the world, but to save the **world** through him.
  3:19 Light has come into the **world**, but men loved darkness instead of
  4:42 and we know that this man really is the Savior *of* the **world**."

  6:14 to say, "Surely this is the Prophet who is to come into the **world**."
  6:33 is he who comes down from heaven and gives life *to* the **world**."
  6:51 This bread is my flesh, which I will give for the life *of* the **world**."
  7: 4 Since you are doing these things, show yourself *to* the **world**."
  7: 7 The **world** cannot hate you, but it hates me because I testify that
  8:12 spoke again to the people, he said, "I am the light *of* the **world**.
  8:23 I am from above. You are of this **world**; I am not of this world.
  8:23 I am from above. You are of this world; I am not of this **world**.
  8:26 me is reliable, and what I have heard from him I tell the **world**."
  9: 5 While I am in the **world**, I am the light of the world."
  9: 5 While I am in the world, I am the light *of* the **world**."
  9:39 Jesus said, "For judgment I have come into this **world**, so that the
  10:36 whom the Father set apart as his very own and sent into the **world**?
  11: 9 walks by day will not stumble, for he sees by this **world's** light.
  11:27 are the Christ, the Son of God, who was to come into the **world**."
  12:19 us nowhere. Look how the whole **world** has gone after him!"
  12:25 while the man who hates his life in this **world** will keep it for
  12:31 Now is the time for judgment *on* this **world**; now the prince of this
  12:31 on this world; now the prince *of* this **world** will be driven out.
  12:46 I have come into the **world** as a light, so that no one who believes
  12:47 judge him. For I did not come to judge the **world**, but to save it.
  12:47 For I did not come to judge the world, but to save it^s [*+3836*]
  13: 1 Jesus knew that the time had come for him to leave this **world**
  13: 1 Having loved his own who were in the **world**, he now showed
  14:17 The **world** cannot accept him, because it neither sees him nor
  14:19 Before long, the **world** will not see me anymore, but you will see
  14:22 why do you intend to show yourself to us and not *to* the **world**?"
  14:27 my peace I give you. I do not give to you as the **world** gives.
  14:30 with you much longer, for the prince *of* this **world** is coming.
  14:31 but the **world** must learn that I love the Father and that I do exactly
  15:18 "If the **world** hates you, keep in mind that it hated me first.
  15:19 If you belonged to the **world**, it would love you as its own.
  15:19 If you belonged to the world, it^s [*+3836*] would love you as its
  15:19 As it is, you do not belong to the **world**, but I have chosen you out
  15:19 do not belong to the world, but I have chosen you out of the **world**.
  15:19 chosen you out of the world. That is why the **world** hates you.
  16: 8 he will convict the **world** of guilt in regard to sin and righteousness
  16:11 because the prince *of* this **world** now stands condemned.
  16:20 you the truth, you will weep and mourn while the **world** rejoices.
  16:21 the anguish because of her joy that a child is born into the **world**.
  16:28 I came from the Father and entered the **world**; now I am leaving
  16:28 now I am leaving the **world** and going back to the Father."
  16:33 In this **world** you will have trouble. But take heart! I have
  16:33 you will have trouble. But take heart! I have overcome the **world**."
  17: 5 presence with the glory I had with you before the **world** began.
  17: 6 "I have revealed you to those whom you gave me out of the **world**.
  17: 9 I am not praying for the **world**, but for those you have given me,
  17:11 I will remain in the **world** no longer, but they are still in the world,
  17:11 I will remain in the world no longer, but they are still in the **world**,
  17:13 to you now, but I say these things while I am still in the **world**,
  17:14 I have given them your word and the **world** has hated them,
  17:14 for they are not of the **world** any more than I am of the world.
  17:14 for they are not of the world any more than I am of the **world**.
  17:15 My prayer is not that you take them out of the **world** but that you
  17:16 They are not of the **world**, even as I am not of it.
  17:16 They are not of the world, even as I am not of it^s [*+3836*].
  17:18 As you sent me into the **world**, I have sent them into the world.
  17:18 As you sent me into the world, I have sent them into the **world**.
  17:21 also be in us so that the **world** may believe that you have sent me.
  17:23 May they be brought to complete unity to let the **world** know that
  17:24 given me because you loved me before the creation *of* the **world**.
  17:25 though the **world** does not know you, I know you,
  18:20 "I have spoken openly *to* the **world**," Jesus replied. "I always taught
  18:36 Jesus said, "My kingdom is not of this **world**. If it were, my
  18:36 **[RPG]** my servants would fight to prevent my arrest by the Jews.
  18:37 was born, and for this I came into the **world**, to testify to the truth.
  21:25 I suppose that even the whole **world** would not have room for the
Ac 17:24 "The God who made the **world** and everything in it is the Lord of
Ro 1: 8 all of you, because your faith is being reported all over the **world**.
  1:20 For since the creation *of* the **world** God's invisible qualities—
  3: 6 Certainly not! If that were so, how could God judge the **world**?
  3:19 may be silenced and the whole **world** held accountable to God.
  4:13 offspring received the promise that he would be heir *of* the **world**,
  5:12 Therefore, just as sin entered the **world** through one man,
  5:13 for before the law was given, sin was in the **world**. But sin is not
  11:12 But if their transgression means riches *for* the **world**, and their loss

11:15 For if their rejection is the reconciliation *of* the **world**, what will
1Co 1:20 of this age? Has not God made foolish the wisdom *of* the **world**?
1:21 For since in the wisdom of God the **world** through its wisdom did
1:27 But God chose the foolish things *of* the **world** to shame the wise;
1:27 God chose the weak things *of* the **world** to shame the strong.
1:28 He chose the lowly things *of* this **world** and the despised things—
2:12 We have not received the spirit of the **world** but the Spirit who is
3:19 For the wisdom *of* this **world** is foolishness in God's sight.
3:22 whether Paul or Apollos or Cephas or the **world** or life or death
4: 9 We have been made a spectacle *to* the **whole universe**, to angels as
4:13 Up to this moment we have become the scum *of* the **earth**,
5:10 not at all meaning the people *of* this **world** who are immoral,
5:10 or idolaters. In that case you would have to leave this **world**.
6: 2 Do you not know that the saints will judge the **world**? And if you
6: 2 And if you are to judge the **world**, are you not competent to judge
7:31 those who use the things *of* the **world**, as if not engrossed in them.
7:31 in them. For this **world** in its present form is passing away.
7:33 But a married man is concerned about the affairs *of* this **world**—
7:34 But a married woman is concerned about the affairs *of* this **world**—
8: 4 We know that an idol is nothing at all in the **world** and that there is
11:32 so that we will not be condemned with the **world**.
14:10 Undoubtedly there are all sorts of languages in the **world**,
2Co 1:12 conscience testifies that we have conducted ourselves in the **world**,
5:19 that God was reconciling the **world** to himself in Christ,
7:10 and leaves no regret, but **worldly** [+*3836*] sorrow brings death.
Gal 4: 3 we were in slavery under the basic principles *of* the **world**.
6:14 Jesus Christ, through which the **world** has been crucified to me,
6:14 which the world has been crucified to me, and I *to* the **world**.
Eph 1: 4 For he chose us in him before the creation *of* the **world** to be holy
2: 2 which you used to live when you followed the ways of this **world**
2:12 of the promise, without hope and without God in the **world**.
Php 2:15 depraved generation, in which you shine like stars in the **universe**
Col 1: 6 All over the **world** this gospel is bearing fruit and growing,
2: 8 and the basic principles *of* this **world** rather than on Christ.
2:20 Since you died with Christ to the basic principles *of* the **world**,
2:20 why, as though you still belonged to it[s], do you submit to its rules:
1Ti 1:15 Christ Jesus came into the **world** to save sinners—of whom I am
3:16 the nations, was believed on in the **world**, was taken up in glory.
6: 7 For we brought nothing into the **world**,
Heb 4: 3 And yet his work has been finished since the creation *of* the **world**.
9:26 have had to suffer many times since the creation of the **world**.
10: 5 Therefore, when Christ came into the **world**, he said: "Sacrifice
11: 7 By his faith he condemned the **world** and became heir of the
11:38 the **world** was not worthy of them. They wandered in deserts
Jas 1:27 their distress and to keep oneself from being polluted by the **world**.
2: 5 Has not God chosen those who are poor *in* the eyes of the **world** to
3: 6 tongue also is a fire, a **world** of evil among the parts of the body.
4: 4 don't you know that friendship *with* the **world** is hatred toward
4: 4 Anyone who chooses to be a friend *of* the **world** becomes an
1Pe 1:20 He was chosen before the creation *of* the **world**, but was revealed
3: 3 Your beauty should not come from outward **adornment**, such as
5: 9 because you know that your brothers throughout the **world** are
2Pe 1: 4 and escape the corruption in the **world** caused by evil desires.
2: 5 if he did not spare the ancient **world** when he brought the flood on
2: 5 the ancient world when he brought the flood on its ungodly **people**,
2:20 If they have escaped the corruption of the **world** by knowing our
3: 6 By these waters also the **world** of that time was deluged
1Jn 2: 2 and not only for ours but also for the sins *of* the whole **world**.
2:15 Do not love the **world** or anything in the world. If anyone loves the
2:15 Do not love the world or anything in the **world**. If anyone loves the
2:15 If anyone loves the **world**, the love of the Father is not in him.
2:16 For everything in the **world**—the cravings of sinful man, the lust of
2:16 and does—comes not from the Father but from the **world**.
2:17 The **world** and its desires pass away, but the man who does the
3: 1 The reason the **world** does not know us is that it did not know him.
3:13 Do not be surprised, my brothers, if the **world** hates you.
3:17 If anyone has **material** possessions and sees his brother in need
4: 1 because many false prophets have gone out into the **world**.
4: 3 you have heard is coming and even now is already in the **world**.
4: 4 the one who is in you is greater than the one who is in the **world**.
4: 5 They are from the **world** and therefore speak from the viewpoint
4: 5 the world and therefore speak from the viewpoint *of* the **world**,
4: 5 from the viewpoint of the world, and the **world** listens to them.
4: 9 and only Son into the **world** that we might live through him.
4:14 that the Father has sent his Son to be the Savior *of* the **world**.
4:17 on the day of judgment, because in this **world** we are like him.

5: 4 for everyone born of God overcomes the **world**. This is the victory
5: 4 This is the victory that has overcome the **world**, even our faith.
5: 5 Who is it that overcomes the **world**? Only he who believes that
5:19 and that the whole **world** is under the control of the evil one.
2Jn 1: 7 Jesus Christ as coming in the flesh, have gone out into the **world**.
Rev 11:15 "The kingdom of the **world** has become the kingdom of our Lord
13: 8 to the Lamb that was slain from the creation *of* the **world**.
17: 8 creation *of* the **world** will be astonished when they see the beast,

3181 Κούαρτος, *Kouartos* [1]

Quartus [1]

Ro 16:23 of public works, and our brother **Quartus** send you their greetings.

3182 κοῦμ, *koum* [1] [→ *3183*]

koum [1]

Mk 5:41 He took her by the hand and said to her, *"Talitha koum!"*

3183 κούμι, *koumi* Not used in UBS/NIV [√ *3182*]

3184 κουστωδία, *koustōdia* [3]

guard [2], guards [1]

Mt 27:65 "Take a **guard**," Pilate answered. "Go, make the tomb as secure as
27:66 tomb secure by putting a seal on the stone and posting the **guard**.
28:11 some *of* the **guards** went into the city and reported to the chief

3185 κουφίζω, *kouphizō* [1]

lightened [1]

Ac 27:38 *they* **lightened** the ship by throwing the grain into the sea.

3186 κόφινος, *kophinos* [6]

basketfuls [+*4441*] [2], basketfuls [2], basketfuls [+*4445*] [1],
baskets [1]

Mt 14:20 and the disciples picked up twelve **basketfuls** [+*4441*] of broken
16: 9 for the five thousand, and how many **basketfuls** you gathered?
Mk 6:43 and the disciples picked up twelve **basketfuls** [+*4445*] of broken
8:19 how many **basketfuls** [+*4441*] of pieces did you pick up?"
Lk 9:17 and the disciples picked up twelve **basketfuls** of broken pieces that
Jn 6:13 and filled twelve **baskets** with the pieces of the five barley loaves

3187 κράβαττος, *krabattos* [11] [→ *3188*]

mat [8], mats [2], bedridden [+*2093*+*2879*] [1]

Mk 2: 4 through it, lowered the **mat** the paralyzed man was lying on.
2: 9 sins are forgiven,' or to say, 'Get up, take your **mat** and walk'?
2:11 "I tell you, get up, take your **mat** and go home."
2:12 He got up, took his **mat** and walked out in full view of them all.
6:55 and carried the sick on **mats** to wherever they heard he was.
Jn 5: 8 Then Jesus said to him, "Get up! Pick up your **mat** and walk."
5: 9 At once the man was cured; he picked up his **mat** and walked.
5:10 "It is the Sabbath; the law forbids you to carry your **mat**."
5:11 man who made me well said to me, 'Pick up your **mat** and walk.' "
Ac 5:15 brought the sick into the streets and laid them on beds and **mats**
9:33 paralytic *who had been* **bedridden** [+*2093*+*2879*] for eight years.

3188 κράββατος, *krabbatos* Not used in UBS/NIV
[√ *3187*]

3189 κράζω, *krazō* [55 / 56] [→ *371, 372, 2136, 3198,*
3199]

shouted [15], cried out [8], shouting [7], called out [3], cry out [3],
crying out [3], cries out [2], cry [2], a loud voice [1], called [1],
calling out [1], calls out [1], cried out [+*3489*+*5889*] [1], cried [1],

exclaim [1], exclaimed [1], gave a shout [+*5889*] [1], screams [1], shout [1], shrieked [1], yelling [1]

Mt   8:29   "What do you want with us, Son of God?" *they* **shouted**. "Have you
    9:27   men followed him, **calling out**, "Have mercy on us, Son of David!"
    14:26   they were terrified. "It's a ghost," they said, and **cried out** in fear.
    14:30   he was afraid and, beginning to sink, **cried out**, "Lord, save me!"
    15:22   came to him, **crying out**, "Lord, Son of David, have mercy on me!
    15:23   and urged him, "Send her away, for *she* keeps **crying out** after us.
    20:30   going by, *they* **shouted**, "Lord, Son of David, have mercy on us!"
    20:31   but they **shouted** all the louder, "Lord, Son of David, have mercy
    21: 9   crowds that went ahead of him and those that followed **shouted**,
    21:15   things he did and the children **shouting** in the temple area,
    27:23   asked Pilate. But they **shouted** all the louder, "Crucify him!"
    27:50   And *when Jesus had* **cried out** again in a loud voice, he gave up
Mk   3:11   they fell down before him and **cried out**, "You are the Son of God."
    5: 5   and day among the tombs and in the hills he would **cry out**
    5: 7   *He* **shouted** at the top of his voice, "What do you want with me,
    9:24   Immediately the boy's father **exclaimed**, "I do believe; help me
    9:26   The spirit **shrieked**, convulsed him violently and came out.
    10:47   he began *to* **shout**, "Jesus, Son of David, have mercy on me!"
    10:48   but he **shouted** all the more, "Son of David, have mercy on me!"
    11: 9   who went ahead and those who followed **shouted**, "Hosanna!"
    15:13   "Crucify him!" they **shouted**.
    15:14   asked Pilate. But they **shouted** all the louder, "Crucify him!"
    15:39   front of Jesus, heard his **cry** [UBS-] and saw how he died, he said,
Lk   9:39   A spirit seizes him and he suddenly **screams**; it throws him into
    18:39   but he **shouted** all the more, "Son of David, have mercy on me!"
    19:40   "I tell you," he replied, "if they keep quiet, the stones *will* **cry out**."
Jn   1:15   *He* **cries out**, saying, "This was he of whom I said, 'He who comes
    7:28   **cried out**, "Yes, you know me, and you know where I am from.
    7:37   Jesus stood and said in **a loud voice**, "If anyone is thirsty, let him
    12:44   Then Jesus **cried out**, "When a man believes in me, he does not
Ac   7:57   ears and, **yelling** at the top of their voices, they all rushed at him,
    7:60   Then *he* fell on his knees and **cried** [+*3489*+*5889*] **out**, "Lord,
    14:14   they tore their clothes and rushed out into the crowd, **shouting**:
    16:17   This girl followed Paul and the rest of us, **shouting**, "These men are
    19:28   When they heard this, they were furious and *began* **shouting**:
    19:32   was in confusion: Some *were* **shouting** one thing, some another.
    19:34   he was a Jew, *they* all **shouted** in unison for about two hours:
    21:28   **shouting**, "Men of Israel, help us! This is the man who teaches all
    21:36   The crowd that followed *kept* **shouting**, "Away with him!"
    23: 6   **called out** in the Sanhedrin, "My brothers, I am a Pharisee,
    24:21   unless it was this one thing *I* **shouted** as I stood in their presence:
Ro   8:15   received the Spirit of sonship. And by him *we* **cry**, "Abba, Father."
    9:27   Isaiah **cries out** concerning Israel: "Though the number of the
Gal   4: 6   of his Son into our hearts, the Spirit *who* **calls out**, "Abba, Father."
Jas   5: 4   the workmen who mowed your fields *are* **crying out** against you.
Rev   6:10   *They* **called out** in a loud voice, "How long, Sovereign Lord,
    7: 2   *He* **called out** in a loud voice to the four angels who had been
    7:10   And *they* **cried out** in a loud voice: "Salvation belongs to our God,
    10: 3   and he **gave a** loud **shout** [+*5889*] like the roar of a lion. When he
    10: 3   When *he* **shouted**, the voices of the seven thunders spoke.
    12: 2   was pregnant and **cried out** in pain as she was about to give birth.
    14:15   and **called** in a loud voice to him who was sitting on the cloud,
    18: 2   With a mighty voice *he* **shouted**: "Fallen! Fallen is Babylon the
    18:18   When they see the smoke of her burning, *they will* **exclaim**,
    18:19   dust on their heads, and with weeping and mourning **cry out**:
    19:17   *who* **cried** in a loud voice to all the birds flying in midair,

3190 κραιπάλη, *kraipalē* [1]

dissipation [1]

Lk   21:34   "Be careful, or your hearts will be weighed down with **dissipation**,

3191 κρανίον, *kranion* [4] [→ *638, 2839*]

Skull [4]

Mt   27:33   to a place called Golgotha (which means The Place *of* the **Skull**).
Mk   15:22   to the place called Golgotha (which means The Place *of* the **Skull**).
Lk   23:33   When they came to the place called the **Skull**, there they crucified
Jn   19:17   he went out to the place *of* the **Skull** (which in Aramaic is called

3192 κράσπεδον, *kraspedon* [5]

edge [4], tassels [1]

Mt   9:20   years came up behind him and touched the **edge** of his cloak.
    14:36   and begged him to let the sick just touch the **edge** of his cloak,
    23: 5   their phylacteries wide and the **tassels** on their garments long;
Mk   6:56   They begged him to let them touch even the **edge** of his cloak,
Lk   8:44   She came up behind him and touched the **edge** of his cloak,

3193 κραταιός, *krataios* [1] [√ *3197*]

mighty [1]

1Pe   5: 6   Humble yourselves, therefore, under God's **mighty** hand,

3194 κραταιόω, *krataioō* [4] [√ *3197*]

strong [3], strengthen [+*1443*] [1]

Lk   1:80   And the child grew and *became* **strong** in spirit; and he lived in
    2:40   And the child grew and *became* **strong**; he was filled with
1Co   16:13   your guard; stand firm in the faith; be men of courage; *be* **strong**.
Eph   3:16   I pray that out of his glorious riches *he may* **strengthen** [+*1443*]

3195 κρατέω, *krateō* [47] [√ *3197*]

arrest [8], arrested [5], took [5], seized [4], hold to [3], hold on to [2], clasped [1], grabbed [1], held on to [1], hold firmly to [1], hold on [1], holding back [1], holding on to [1], holding to [1], holds [1], kept from [+*3590*] [1], kept [1], lost connection with [+*4024*] [1], not forgive [1], not forgiven [1], observe [1], obtained [1], remain true to [1], take charge of [1], take hold of [1], take hold [1]

Mt   9:25   had been put outside, *he* went in and **took** the girl by the hand,
    12:11   a pit on the Sabbath, *will you* not **take hold of** it and lift it out?
    14: 3   Now Herod *had* **arrested** John and bound him and put him in
    18:28   *He* **grabbed** him and began to choke him. 'Pay back what you owe
    21:46   They looked for a way to **arrest** him, but they were afraid of the
    22: 6   The rest **seized** his servants, mistreated them and killed them.
    26: 4   and they plotted to **arrest** Jesus in some sly way and kill him.
    26:48   a signal with them: "The one I kiss is the man; **arrest** him."
    26:50   Then the men stepped forward, seized Jesus and **arrested** him.
    26:55   day I sat in the temple courts teaching, and *you did* not **arrest** me.
    26:57   Those *who had* **arrested** Jesus took him to Caiaphas, the high
    28: 9   he said. They came to him, **clasped** his feet and worshiped him.
Mk   1:31   So he went to her, **took** her hand and helped her up. The fever left
    3:21   they went *to* **take charge of** him, for they said, "He is out of his
    5:41   He **took** her by the hand and said to her, *"Talitha koum!"*
    6:17   For Herod himself had given orders to *have* John **arrested**,
    7: 3   hands a ceremonial washing, **holding to** the tradition of the elders.
    7: 4   And *they* **observe** many other traditions, such as the washing of
    7: 8   the commands of God and *are* **holding on to** the traditions of men."
    9:10   *They* **kept** the matter to themselves, discussing what "rising from
    9:27   But Jesus **took** him by the hand and lifted him to his feet, and he
    12:12   Then they looked for a way *to* **arrest** him because they knew he
    14: 1   teachers of the law were looking for some sly way *to* **arrest** Jesus
    14:44   one I kiss is the man; **arrest** him and lead him away under guard."
    14:46   The men seized Jesus and **arrested** him.
    14:49   teaching in the temple courts, and *you did* not **arrest** me.
    14:51   but a linen garment, was following Jesus. When *they* **seized** him,
Lk   8:54   But he **took** her by the hand and said, "My child, get up!"
    24:16   but they *were* **kept** [+*3590*] **from** recognizing him.
Jn   20:23   are forgiven; *if you do* **not forgive** them, they are not forgiven."
    20:23   are forgiven; if you do not forgive them, *they are* **not forgiven**."
Ac   2:24   because it was impossible for death *to* **keep** its **hold on** him.
    3:11   *While* the beggar **held on to** Peter and John, all the people were
    24: 6   and even tried to desecrate the temple; so *we* **seized** him.
    27:13   began to blow, they thought *they had* **obtained** what they wanted;
Col   2:19   He *has* **lost connection** [+*4024*] with the Head, from whom the
2Th   2:15   stand firm and **hold to** the teachings we passed on to you,
Heb   4:14   Jesus the Son of God, *let us* **hold firmly to** the faith we profess.
    6:18   we who have fled *to* **take hold** of the hope offered to us may be
Rev   2: 1   These are the words of him *who* **holds** the seven stars in his right
    2:13   where Satan has his throne. Yet *you* **remain true to** my name.
    2:14   You have *people* there *who* **hold to** the teaching of Balaam,
    2:15   Likewise you also have *those who* **hold to** the teaching of the

2:25 Only **hold on to** what you have until I come.
3:11 **Hold on to** what you have, so that no one will take your crown.
7: 1 **holding back** the four winds of the earth to prevent any wind from
20: 2 *He* **seized** the dragon, that ancient serpent, who is the devil,

3196 κράτιστος, *kratistos* [4] [√ *3197*]

most excellent [3], excellency [1]

Lk   1: 3 me to write an orderly account for you, **most excellent** Theophilus,
Ac 23:26 Claudius Lysias, *To* His **Excellency**, Governor Felix: Greetings.
    24: 3 Everywhere and in every way, **most excellent** Felix,
    26:25 "I am not insane, **most excellent** Festus," Paul replied. "What I am

3197 κράτος, *kratos* [12] [→ 202, 203, 1602, 1603, 1604, 3179, 3193, 3194, 3195, 3196, 3201, 3202, 4120, 4331; cf. 2846]

power [8], might [2], mighty deeds [1], strength [1]

Lk   1:51 He has performed **mighty deeds** with his arm; he has scattered
Ac 19:20 In this way the word of the Lord spread widely and grew in **power**.
Eph 1:19 That power is like the working *of* his mighty **strength**,
     6:10 Finally, be strong in the Lord and in his mighty **power**.
Col 1:11 being strengthened with all power according to his glorious **might**
1Ti 6:16 has seen or can see. To him be honor and **might** forever. Amen.
Heb 2:14 so that by his death he might destroy him who holds the **power** of
1Pe 4:11 To him be the glory and the **power** for ever and ever. Amen.
     5:11 To him be the **power** for ever and ever. Amen.
Jude 1:25 majesty, **power** and authority, through Jesus Christ our Lord,
Rev 1: 6 and Father—to him be glory and **power** for ever and ever!
     5:13 and to the Lamb be praise and honor and glory and **power**,

3198 κραυγάζω, *kraugazō* [9] [√ *3189*]

shouting [4], shouted [3], called [1], cry out [1]

Mt 12:19 He will not quarrel or **cry out**; no one will hear his voice in the
Lk   4:41 came out of many people, **shouting**, "You are the Son of God!"
Jn 11:43 he had said this, Jesus **called** in a loud voice, "Lazarus, come out!"
    12:13 palm branches and went out to meet him, **shouting**, "Hosanna!"
    18:40 *They* **shouted** back, "No, not him! Give us Barabbas!"
    19: 6 chief priests and their officials saw him, *they* **shouted**, "Crucify!
    19:12 but the Jews *kept* **shouting**, "If you let this man go, you are no
    19:15 But they **shouted**, "Take him away! Take him away! Crucify him!"
Ac 22:23 *As* they *were* **shouting** and throwing off their cloaks and flinging

3199 κραυγή, *kraugē* [6] [√ *3189*]

brawling [1], cries [1], cry [1], crying [1], uproar [1], voice [1]

Mt 25: 6 "At midnight the **cry** rang out: 'Here's the bridegroom! Come out
Lk   1:42 *In* a loud **voice** she exclaimed: "Blessed are you among women,
Ac 23: 9 There was a great **uproar**, and some of the teachers of the law who
Eph 4:31 Get rid of all bitterness, rage and anger, **brawling** and slander,
Heb 5: 7 he offered up prayers and petitions with loud **cries** and tears to the
Rev 21: 4 There will be no more death or mourning or **crying** or pain,

3200 κρέας, *kreas* [2]

meat [2]

Ro 14:21 It is better not to eat **meat** or drink wine or to do anything else that
1Co 8:13 I eat causes my brother to fall into sin, I will never eat **meat** again,

3201 κρείσσων, *kreissōn* Not used in UBS/NIV [√ *3197*]

3202 κρείττων, *kreittōn* [19] [√ *3197*]

better [14], superior to [2], better [+*3437*] [1], good [1], greater [1]

1Co 7: 9 should marry, for it is **better** to marry than to burn with passion.
     7:38 virgin does right, but he who does not marry her does *even* **better**.
    11:17 have no praise for you, for your meetings do more harm than **good**.
Php 1:23 desire to depart and be with Christ, which is **better** [+*3437*] by far;
Heb 1: 4 So he became as much **superior to** the angels as the name he has

6: 9 dear friends, we are confident of **better** *things* in your case—
7: 7 And without doubt the lesser person is blessed by the **greater**.
7:19 and a **better** hope is introduced, by which we draw near to God.
7:22 of this oath, Jesus has become the guarantee *of* a **better** covenant.
8: 6 as the covenant of which he is mediator is **superior to** the old one,
8: 6 is superior to the old one, and it is founded on **better** promises.
9:23 but the heavenly things themselves *with* **better** sacrifices than
10:34 because you knew that you yourselves had **better** and lasting
11:16 Instead, they were longing for a **better** *country*—a heavenly one.
11:35 to be released, so that they might gain a **better** resurrection.
11:40 God had planned something **better** for us so that only together
12:24 and to the sprinkled blood that speaks a **better** *word* than the
1Pe 3:17 It is **better**, if it is God's will, to suffer for doing good than for
2Pe 2:21 It would have been **better** for them not to have known the way of

3203 κρεμάννυμι, *kremannymi* [7] [→ *1717, 2889, 3204*]

hanging [3], hung [3], hang [1]

Mt 18: 6 it would be better for him to *have* a large millstone **hung** around
    22:40 All the Law and the Prophets **hang** on these two commandments."
Lk 23:39 One of the criminals *who* **hung** there hurled insults at him:
Ac   5:30 from the dead—whom you had killed *by* **hanging** him on a tree.
    10:39 and in Jerusalem. They killed him *by* **hanging** him on a tree,
    28: 4 When the islanders saw the snake **hanging** from his hand,
Gal 3:13 for it is written: "Cursed is everyone who *is* **hung** on a tree."

3204 κρημνός, *krēmnos* [3] [√ *3203*]

steep bank [3]

Mt   8:32 and the whole herd rushed down the **steep bank** into the lake
Mk   5:13 rushed down the **steep bank** into the lake and were drowned.
Lk   8:33 and the herd rushed down the **steep bank** into the lake and was

3205 Κρής, *Krēs* [2] [→ *3207*]

Cretans [2]

Ac   2:11 (both Jews and converts to Judaism); **Cretans** and Arabs—
Tit 1:12 has said, "**Cretans** are always liars, evil brutes, lazy gluttons."

3206 Κρήσκης, *Krēskēs* [1]

Crescens [1]

2Ti 4:10 **Crescens** has gone to Galatia, and Titus to Dalmatia.

3207 Κρήτη, *Krētē* [5] [√ *3205*]

Crete [5]

Ac 27: 7 to hold our course, we sailed to the lee of **Crete**, opposite Salmone.
    27:12 This was a harbor *in* **Crete**, facing both southwest and northwest.
    27:13 so they weighed anchor and sailed along the shore of **Crete**.
    27:21 "Men, you should have taken my advice not to sail from **Crete**;
Tit 1: 5 The reason I left you in **Crete** was that you might straighten out

3208 κριθή, *krithē* [1] [→ *3209*]

barley [1]

Rev 6: 6 and three quarts *of* **barley** for a day's wages, and do not damage

3209 κρίθινος, *krithinos* [2] [√ *3208*]

barley [1], small barley [1]

Jn   6: 9 "Here is a boy with five **small barley** loaves and two small fish,
     6:13 and filled twelve baskets with the pieces of the five **barley** loaves

3210 κρίμα, *krima* [27] [√ *3212*]

judgment [12], condemnation [3], punished [+*3284*] [2], judge [1], judged [+*3284*] [1], judgments [1], lawsuits [1], penalty [1], punishment [1], sentence [1], sentenced [1], the same way^s [1], way treated^s [1]

Mt	7: 2	For in **the same way**^{s} you judge others, you will be judged,
Mk	12:40	Such men *will be* **punished** [*+3284*] most severely."
Lk	20:47	Such men *will be* **punished** [*+3284*] most severely."
	23:40	you fear God," he said, "since you are under the same **sentence**?
	24:20	and our rulers handed him over to be **sentenced** to death,
Jn	9:39	Jesus said, "For **judgment** I have come into this world, so that the
Ac	24:25	self-control and the **judgment** to come, Felix was afraid and said,
Ro	2: 2	Now we know that God's **judgment** against those who do such
	2: 3	do the same things, do you think you will escape God's **judgment**?
	3: 8	us do evil that good may result"? Their **condemnation** is deserved.
	5:16	The **judgment** followed one sin and brought condemnation,
	11:33	How unsearchable his **judgments**, and his paths beyond tracing
	13: 2	and those who do so will bring **judgment** on themselves.
1Co	6: 7	The very fact that you have **lawsuits** among you means you have
	11:29	the body of the Lord eats and drinks **judgment** on himself.
	11:34	so that when you meet together it may not result in **judgment**.
Gal	5:10	The one who is throwing you into confusion will pay the **penalty**,
1Ti	3: 6	become conceited and fall under the same **judgment** as the devil.
	5:12	Thus they bring **judgment** on themselves, because they have
Heb	6: 2	of hands, the resurrection of the dead, and eternal **judgment**.
Jas	3: 1	because you know that *we* who teach *will be* **judged** [*+3284*] more
1Pe	4:17	For it is time *for* **judgment** to begin with the family of God;
2Pe	2: 3	Their **condemnation** has long been hanging over them, and their
Jude	1: 4	For certain men whose **condemnation** was written about long ago
Rev	17: 1	"Come, I will show you the **punishment** of the great prostitute,
	18:20	and prophets! God has judged her *for* the **way** she **treated**^{s} you.' "
	20: 4	which were seated those who had been given authority *to* **judge**.

3211 κρίνον, **krinon** [2]

lilies [2]

Mt	6:28	See how the **lilies** of the field grow. They do not labor or spin.
Lk	12:27	"Consider how the **lilies** grow. They do not labor or spin. Yet I tell

3212 κρίνω, **krinō** [114] [→ *88, 95, 185, 373, 374, 503, 537, 645, 646, 647, 850, 896, 1359, 1360, 1464, 1605, 1637, 2137, 2890, 2891, 2892, 3210, 3213, 3215, 3216, 3217, 4622, 5173, 5347, 5693, 5694, 5695; cf. 1637*]

κρίνω τὸν κόσμον (to judge the world) [6] Jn 3:17; 12:47,48; Ro 3:6; 1Co 6:2,2

judge [38], judged [14], judges [7], condemn [6], condemned [6], decided [4], judging [4], consider [3], pass judgment on [3], considers [2], stand trial [2], come under judgment [1], condemning [1], convinced [1], decided that [1], decision that [1], goes to law [1], judgment that [1], judgment [1], made up mind [1], made up [1], make judgment [*+3213*] [1], make up mind [1], on trial [*+2705*] [1], on trial [1], pass judgment [1], passed judgment on [1], passing judgment on [1], punish [1], reached [1], resolved [1], stand on trial [1], sue [1], take judgment [1], tried [1], until judge [*+4024*] [1]

Mt	5:40	And if someone wants *to* **sue** you and take your tunic, let him have
	7: 1	"*Do* not **judge**, or you too will be judged.
	7: 1	"Do not judge, or *you* too *will be* **judged**.
	7: 2	For in the same way *you* **judge** others, you will be judged,
	7: 2	*you will be* **judged**, and with the measure you use, it will be
	19:28	will also sit on twelve thrones, **judging** the twelve tribes of Israel.
Lk	6:37	"*Do* not **judge**, and you will not be judged. Do not condemn,
	6:37	"Do not judge, and *you will not be* **judged**. Do not condemn,
	7:43	the bigger debt canceled." "*You have* **judged** correctly," Jesus said.
	12:57	"Why don't *you* **judge** for yourselves what is right?
	19:22	"His master replied, '*I will* **judge** you by your own words,
	22:30	my kingdom and sit on thrones, **judging** the twelve tribes of Israel.
Jn	3:17	For God did not send his Son into the world to **condemn** the
	3:18	Whoever believes in him *is* not **condemned**, but whoever does not
	3:18	but whoever does not believe *stands* **condemned** already
	5:22	Moreover, the Father **judges** no one, but has entrusted all judgment
	5:30	*I* **judge** only as I hear, and my judgment is just, for I seek not to
	7:24	Stop **judging** by mere appearances, and make a right judgment."
	7:24	by mere appearances, and **make** a right **judgment** [*+3213*]."
	7:51	"*Does* our law **condemn** anyone without first hearing him to find

	8:15	You **judge** by human standards; I pass judgment on no one.
	8:15	You judge by human standards; I **pass judgment on** no one.
	8:16	But if I *do* **judge**, my decisions are right, because I am not alone.
	8:26	"I have much to say in **judgment** of you. But he who sent me is
	8:50	glory for myself; but there is one who seeks it, and *he is* the **judge**.
	12:47	who hears my words but does not keep them, I *do* not **judge** him.
	12:47	judge him. For I did not come to **judge** the world, but to save it.
	12:48	There is a **judge** for the one who rejects me and does not accept
	12:48	that very word which I spoke *will* **condemn** him at the last day.
	16:11	because the prince of this world *now stands* **condemned**.
	18:31	Pilate said, "Take him yourselves and **judge** him by your own law."
Ac	3:13	disowned him before Pilate, *though he had* **decided** to let him go.
	4:19	"**Judge** *for yourselves* whether it is right in God's sight to obey
	7: 7	But I *will* **punish** the nation they serve as slaves,' God said,
	13:27	yet *in* **condemning** him they fulfilled the words of the prophets
	13:46	you reject it and *do* not **consider** yourselves worthy of eternal life,
	15:19	"*It is* my **judgment**, therefore, *that* we should not make it difficult
	16: 4	they delivered the decisions **reached** by the apostles and elders in
	16:15	"*If you* **consider** me a believer in the Lord," she said, "come
	17:31	For he has set a day when he will **judge** the world with justice by
	20:16	Paul *had* **decided** to sail past Ephesus to avoid spending time in
	21:25	we have written to them *our* **decision** that they should abstain
	23: 3	You sit there *to* **judge** me according to the law, yet you yourself
	23: 6	I **stand on trial** because of my hope in the resurrection of the dead."
	24:21	'It is concerning the resurrection of the dead that I *am* **on trial**
	25: 9	"Are you willing *to* go up to Jerusalem and **stand trial** before me
	25:10	am now standing before Caesar's court, where I ought *to be* **tried**."
	25:20	willing to go to Jerusalem and **stand trial** there on these charges.
	25:25	because he made his appeal to the Emperor *I* **decided** to send him
	26: 6	God has promised our fathers that *I am* **on trial** [*+2705*] today.
	26: 8	Why *should* any of you **consider** it incredible that God raises the
	27: 1	When *it was* **decided** that we would sail for Italy, Paul and some
Ro	2: 1	have no excuse, you *who* **pass judgment on** someone else,
	2: 1	for at whatever point *you* **judge** the other, you are condemning
	2: 1	because you *who* **pass judgment** do the same things.
	2: 3	So *when* you, a mere man, **pass judgment on** them and yet do the
	2:12	the law, and all who sin under the law *will be* **judged** by the law.
	2:16	This will take place on the day when God *will* **judge** men's secrets
	2:27	and yet obeys the law *will* **condemn** you who,
	3: 4	may be proved right when you speak and prevail when you **judge**."
	3: 6	Certainly not! If that were so, how *could* God **judge** the world?
	3: 7	so increases his glory, why *am* I still **condemned** as a sinner?"
	14: 3	and the man who does not eat everything *must* not **condemn** the
	14: 4	Who are you *to* **judge** someone else's servant? To his own master
	14: 5	One man **considers** one day more sacred than another;
	14: 5	more sacred than another; another man **considers** every day alike.
	14:10	You, then, why *do you* **judge** your brother? Or why do you look
	14:13	Therefore *let us* stop **passing judgment** on one another. Instead,
	14:13	**make up** *your* **mind** not to put any stumbling block or obstacle in
	14:22	Blessed is the man *who does* not **condemn** himself by what he
1Co	2: 2	For *I* **resolved** to know nothing while I was with you except Jesus
	4: 5	Therefore **judge** nothing before the appointed time; wait till the
	5: 3	And *I have* already **passed judgment on** the one who did this,
	5:12	What business is it of mine *to* **judge** those outside the church?
	5:12	judge those outside the church? *Are* you not *to* **judge** those inside?
	5:13	God *will* **judge** those outside. "Expel the wicked man from among
	6: 1	dare he **take** it before the ungodly *for* **judgment** instead of before
	6: 2	Do you not know that the saints *will* **judge** the world? And if you
	6: 2	And if you *are to* **judge** the world, are you not competent to judge
	6: 3	Do you not know that *we will* **judge** angels? How much more the
	6: 6	But instead, one brother **goes to law** against another—and this in
	7:37	own will, and *who has* **made up** his mind not to marry the virgin—
	10:15	I speak to sensible people; **judge** for yourselves what I say.
	10:29	For why *should* my freedom *be* **judged** by another's conscience?
	11:13	**Judge** for yourselves: Is it proper for a woman to pray to God with
	11:31	But if we judged ourselves, *we* would not **come under judgment**.
	11:32	*When we are* **judged** by the Lord, we are being disciplined
2Co	5:14	So *I* **made up** my **mind** that I would not make another painful visit
	5:14	*because we are* **convinced** that one died for all, and therefore all
Col	2:16	Therefore *do* not *let* anyone **judge** you by what you eat or drink,
2Th	2:12	so that all will *be* **condemned** who have not believed the truth
2Ti	4: 1	and of Christ Jesus, who will **judge** the living and the dead,
Tit	3:12	come to me at Nicopolis, because *I have* **decided** to winter there.
Heb	10:30	avenge; I will repay," and again, "The Lord *will* **judge** his people."
	13: 4	for God *will* **judge** the adulterer and all the sexually immoral.
Jas	2:12	and act as those who are going to *be* **judged** by the law that gives

4: 11 his brother or **judges** him speaks against the law and judges it.
4: 11 his brother or judges him speaks against the law and **judges** it.
4: 11 When *you* **judge** the law, you are not keeping it, but sitting in
4: 12 and destroy. But you—who are you to **judge** your neighbor?
5: 9 Don't grumble against each other, brothers, or *you will be* **judged**.
1Pe 1: 17 Since you call on a Father who **judges** each man's work
2: 23 no threats. Instead, he entrusted himself to him *who* **judges** justly.
4: 5 But they will have to give account to him who is ready *to* **judge**
4: 6 so that *they might be* **judged** according to men in regard to the
Rev 6: 10 and true, **until** *you* judge [+4024] the inhabitants of the earth
11: 18 The time has come *for* **judging** the dead, and for rewarding your
16: 5 and who were, the Holy One, because *you have* so **judged**;
18: 8 be consumed by fire, for mighty is the Lord God who **judges** her.
18: 20 and prophets! God *has* **judged** her for the way she treated you.' "
19: 2 He has **condemned** the great prostitute who corrupted the earth by
19: 11 is called Faithful and True. With justice *he* **judges** and makes war.
20: 12 The dead *were* **judged** according to what they had done as
20: 13 and each person *was* **judged** according to what he had done.

3213 κρίσις, *krisis* [47] [√ *3212*]

ἡμέρα κρίσεως (day of judgment) [7] Mt 10:15; 11:22,24;
    12:36; 2Pe 2:9; 3:7; 1Jn 4:17

judgment [28], justice [5], condemned [2], judge [+4472] [2],
judgments [2], accusation [1], accusations [1], condemned
[+1650+2262] [1], condemned [+4406+5679] [1], decisions [1],
doom [1], make judgment [+3212] [1], verdict [1]

Mt 5: 21 and anyone who murders will be subject *to* **judgment**.'
5: 22 anyone who is angry with his brother will be subject *to* **judgment**.
10: 15 and Gomorrah on the day *of* **judgment** than for that town.
11: 22 bearable for Tyre and Sidon on the day *of* **judgment** than for you.
11: 24 be more bearable for Sodom on the day *of* **judgment** than for you."
12: 18 put my Spirit on him, and he will proclaim **justice** to the nations.
12: 20 wick he will not snuff out, till he leads **justice** to victory.
12: 36 on the day *of* **judgment** for every careless word they have spoken.
12: 41 The men of Nineveh will stand up at the **judgment** with this
12: 42 The Queen of the South will rise at the **judgment** with this
23: 23 important matters of the law—**justice**, mercy and faithfulness.
23: 33 brood of vipers! How will you escape being **condemned** to hell?
Lk 10: 14 be more bearable for Tyre and Sidon at the **judgment** than for you.
11: 31 The Queen of the South will rise at the **judgment** with the men of
11: 32 The men of Nineveh will stand up at the **judgment** with this
11: 42 kinds of garden herbs, but you neglect **justice** and the love of God.
Jn 3: 19 This is the **verdict**: Light has come into the world, but men loved
5: 22 Father judges no one, but has entrusted all **judgment** to the Son,
5: 24 sent me has eternal life and *will not be* **condemned** [+1650+2262];
5: 27 And he has given him authority *to* **judge** [+4472] because he is the
5: 29 to live, and those who have done evil will rise to be **condemned**.
5: 30 I judge only as I hear, and my **judgment** is just, for I seek not to
7: 24 by mere appearances, but **make** a right **judgment** [+3212]."
8: 16 But if I do judge, my **decisions** are right, because I am not alone.
12: 31 Now is the time for **judgment** on this world; now the prince of this
16: 8 the world of guilt in regard to sin and righteousness and **judgment**:
16: 11 and in regard to **judgment**, because the prince of this world now
Ac 8: 33 In his humiliation he was deprived of **justice**. Who can speak of
2Th 1: 5 All this is evidence that God's **judgment** is right, and as a result
1Ti 5: 24 men are obvious, reaching the place of **judgment** ahead of them;
Heb 9: 27 as man is destined to die once, and after that to *face* **judgment**,
10: 27 but only a fearful expectation *of* **judgment** and of raging fire that
Jas 2: 13 because **judgment** without mercy will be shown to anyone who
2: 13 who has not been merciful. Mercy triumphs over **judgment**!
5: 12 yes, and your "No," no, or *you will be* **condemned** [+4406+5679].
2Pe 2: 4 putting them into gloomy dungeons to be held for **judgment**;
2: 9 from trials and to hold the unrighteous for the day *of* **judgment**,
2: 11 do not bring slanderous **accusations** against such beings in the
3: 7 being kept for the day *of* **judgment** and destruction of ungodly
1Jn 4: 17 among us so that we will have confidence on the day *of* **judgment**,
Jude 1: 6 bound with everlasting chains for **judgment** on the great Day.
1: 9 did not dare to bring a slanderous **accusation** against him,
1: 15 *to* **judge** [+4472] everyone, and to convict all the ungodly of all
Rev 14: 7 and give him glory, because the hour *of* his **judgment** has come.
16: 7 "Yes, Lord God Almighty, true and just are your **judgments**."
18: 10 O Babylon, city of power! In one hour your **doom** has come!'
19: 2 for true and just are his **judgments**. He has condemned the great

3214 Κρίσπος, *Krispos* [2]

Crispus [2]

Ac 18: 8 **Crispus**, the synagogue ruler, and his entire household believed in
1Co 1: 14 I am thankful that I did not baptize any of you except **Crispus**

3215 κριτήριον, *kritērion* [3] [√ *3212*]

court [1], disputes [1], judge cases [1]

1Co 6: 2 to judge the world, are you not competent *to* **judge** trivial **cases**?
6: 4 Therefore, if you have **disputes** about such matters, appoint as
Jas 2: 6 Are they not the ones who are dragging you into **court**?

3216 κριτής, *kritēs* [19] [√ *3212*]

judge [14], judges [4], sitting in judgment [1]

Mt 5: 25 still with him on the way, or he may hand you over *to* the **judge**,
5: 25 and the **judge** may hand you over to the officer, and you may be
12: 27 do your people drive them out? So then, they will be your **judges**.
Lk 11: 19 your followers drive them out? So then, they will be your **judges**.
12: 14 "Man, who appointed me a **judge** or an arbiter between you?"
12: 58 or he may drag you off to the **judge**, and the judge turn you over to
12: 58 you off to the judge, and the **judge** turn you over to the officer,
18: 2 "In a certain town there was a **judge** who neither feared God nor
18: 6 And the Lord said, "Listen to what the unjust **judge** says.
Ac 10: 42 and to testify that he is the one whom God appointed as **judge** of
13: 20 God gave them **judges** until the time of Samuel the prophet.
18: 15 settle the matter yourselves. I will not be a **judge** of such things."
24: 10 "I know that for a number of years you have been a **judge** over this
2Ti 4: 8 which the Lord, the righteous **Judge**, will award to me on that
Heb 12: 23 You have come to God, the **judge** of all men, to the spirits of
Jas 2: 4 among yourselves and become **judges** with evil thoughts?
4: 11 the law, you are not keeping it, but **sitting in judgment** on it.
4: 12 There is only one Lawgiver and **Judge**, the one who is able to save
5: 9 brothers, or you will be judged. The **Judge** is standing at the door!

3217 κριτικός, *kritikos* [1] [√ *3212*]

judges [1]

Heb 4: 12 and marrow; it **judges** the thoughts and attitudes of the heart.

3218 κρούω, *krouō* [9]

knock [3], knocks [3], knocking [2], knocked at [1]

Mt 7: 7 and you will find; **knock** and the door will be opened to you.
7: 8 who seeks finds; and *to* him *who* **knocks**, the door will be opened.
Lk 11: 9 who seeks finds; and **knock** and the door will be opened to you.
11: 10 who seeks finds; and *to* him *who* **knocks**, the door will be opened.
12: 36 he comes and **knocks** they can immediately open the door for him.
13: 25 the door, you will stand outside **knocking** and pleading, 'Sir,
Ac 12: 13 Peter **knocked at** the outer entrance, and a servant girl named
12: 16 But Peter kept on **knocking**, and when they opened the door
Rev 3: 20 Here I am! I stand at the door and **knock**. If anyone hears my voice

3219 κρύπτη, *kryptē* [1] [√ *3221*]

place hidden [1]

Lk 11: 33 one lights a lamp and puts it in a **place** where it will be **hidden**,

3220 κρυπτός, *kryptos* [17] [√ *3221*]

secret [7], hidden [5], secrets [2], inner [1], inwardly
[+1877+3836] [1], unseen [+1877+3836] [1]

Mt 6: 4 so that your giving may be in **secret**. Then your Father, who sees
6: 4 your Father, who sees what is done in **secret**, will reward you.
6: 6 the door and pray to your Father, who is **unseen** [+1877+3836].
6: 6 your Father, who sees what is done in **secret**, will reward you.
10: 26 that will not be disclosed, or **hidden** that will not be made known.
Mk 4: 22 For whatever is **hidden** is meant to be disclosed, and whatever is
Lk 8: 17 For there is nothing **hidden** that will not be disclosed, and nothing
12: 2 that will not be disclosed, or **hidden** that will not be made known.
Jn 7: 4 No one who wants to become a public figure acts in **secret**.

	7: 10	had left for the Feast, he went also, not publicly, but in **secret**.
	18: 20	where all the Jews come together. I said nothing in **secret**.
Ro	2: 16	This will take place on the day when God will judge men's **secrets**
	2: 29	No, a man is a Jew if he is one **inwardly** [+1877+3836]; and
1Co	4: 5	He will bring to light what is **hidden** in darkness and will expose
	14: 25	and the **secrets** of his heart will be laid bare. So he will fall down
2Co	4: 2	Rather, we have renounced **secret** and shameful *ways*; we do not
1Pe	3: 4	Instead, it should be that of your **inner** self, the unfading beauty of

3221 κρύπτω, kryptō [18] [→ 648, 649, 1606, 3219, 3220, 3224, 3225, 3226, 4332]

hidden [9], hid [7], hide [1], secretly [1]

Mt	5: 14	"You are the light of the world. A city on a hill cannot *be* **hidden**.
	11: 25	because *you have* **hidden** these things from the wise and learned,
	13: 35	I will utter *things* **hidden** since the creation of the world."
	13: 44	"The kingdom of heaven is like treasure **hidden** in a field. When a
	13: 44	he **hid** it again, and then in his joy went and sold all he had
	25: 18	went off, dug a hole in the ground and **hid** his master's money.
	25: 25	So I was afraid and went out and **hid** your talent in the ground.
Lk	18: 34	Its meaning was **hidden** from them, and they did not know what he
	19: 42	what would bring you peace—but now *it is* **hidden** from your eyes.
Jn	8: 59	they picked up stones to stone him, but Jesus **hid** *himself*,
	12: 36	he had finished speaking, Jesus left and **hid** *himself* from them.
	19: 38	was a disciple of Jesus, but **secretly** because he feared the Jews.
Col	3: 3	For you died, and your life *is now* **hidden** with Christ in God.
1Ti	5: 25	deeds are obvious, and even those that are not cannot *be* **hidden**.
Heb	11: 23	By faith Moses' parents **hid** *him* for three months after he was
Rev	2: 17	To him who overcomes, I will give some of the **hidden** manna.
	6: 15	and every slave and every free man **hid** in caves and among the
	6: 16	"Fall on us and **hide** us from the face of him who sits on the throne

3222 κρυσταλλίζω, krystallizō [1] [√ 3223]

clear as crystal [1]

Rev	21: 11	like that of a very precious jewel, like a jasper, **clear as crystal**.

3223 κρύσταλλος, krystallos [2] [→ 3222]

crystal [2]

Rev	4: 6	throne there was what looked like a sea of glass, clear as **crystal**.
	22: 1	as clear as **crystal**, flowing from the throne of God and of the

3224 κρυφαῖος, kryphaios [2] [√ 3221]

secret [1], unseen [+1877+3836] [1]

Mt	6: 18	are fasting, but only to your Father, who is **unseen** [+1877+3836];
	6: 18	and your Father, who sees what is done in **secret**, will reward you.

3225 κρυφῇ, kryphē [1] [√ 3221]

secret [1]

Eph	5: 12	it is shameful even to mention what the disobedient do *in* **secret**.

3226 κρύφιος, kryphios Not used in UBS/NIV [√ 3221]

3227 κτάομαι, ktaomai [7] [→ 3228, 3229, 3230]

bought [1], buy [1], control [1], gain [1], get [1], pay for [1], take along [1]

Mt	10: 9	*Do* not **take along** any gold or silver or copper in your belts;
Lk	18: 12	I fast twice a week and give a tenth of all *I* **get**.'
	21: 19	By standing firm *you will* **gain** life.
Ac	1: 18	(With the reward he got for his wickedness, Judas **bought** a field;
	8: 20	because you thought you *could* **buy** the gift of God with money!
	22: 28	the commander said, "I had to **pay** a big price **for** my citizenship."
1Th	4: 4	that each of you should learn *to* **control** his own body in a way that

3228 κτῆμα, ktēma [4] [√ 3227]

wealth [2], piece of property [1], possessions [1]

Mt	19: 22	man heard this, he went away sad, because he had great **wealth**.
Mk	10: 22	man's face fell. He went away sad, because he had great **wealth**.
Ac	2: 45	Selling their **possessions** and goods, they gave to anyone as he had
	5: 1	together with his wife Sapphira, also sold a **piece of property**.

3229 κτῆνος, ktēnos [4] [√ 3227]

animals [1], cattle [1], donkey [1], mounts [1]

Lk	10: 34	Then he put the man on his own **donkey**, took him to an inn
Ac	23: 24	Provide **mounts** for Paul that he may be taken safely to
1Co	15: 39	of flesh, **animals** have another, birds another and fish another.
Rev	18: 13	**cattle** and sheep; horses and carriages; and bodies and souls of

3230 κτήτωρ, ktētōr [1] [√ 3227]

owned [+5639] [1]

Ac	4: 34	For from time to time those *who* **owned** [+5639] lands or houses

3231 κτίζω, ktizō [15] [→ 3232, 3233, 3234]

created [11], Creator [3], create [1]

Mt	19: 4	"that at the beginning the **Creator** 'made them male and female,'
Mk	13: 19	from the beginning, *when* God **created** the world, until now—
Ro	1: 25	and worshiped and served **created** things rather than the **Creator**—
1Co	11: 9	neither *was* man **created** for woman, but woman for man.
Eph	2: 10	are God's workmanship, **created** in Christ Jesus to do good works,
	2: 15	His purpose *was to* **create** in himself one new man out of the two,
	3: 9	for ages past was kept hidden in God, who **created** all things.
	4: 24	**created** to be like God in true righteousness and holiness.
Col	1: 16	For by him all things *were* **created**: things in heaven and on earth,
	1: 16	or authorities; all things *were* **created** by him and for him.
	3: 10	which is being renewed in knowledge in the image *of* its **Creator**.
1Ti	4: 3	which God **created** to be received with thanksgiving by those who
Rev	4: 11	to receive glory and honor and power, for you **created** all things,
	4: 11	and by your will *they were* **created** and have their being."
	10: 6	who **created** the heavens and all that is in them, the earth and all

3232 κτίσις, ktisis [19] [√ 3231]

creation [15], authority [1], created things [1], creature [1], world [1]

Mk	10: 6	"But at the beginning *of* **creation** God 'made them male
	13: 19	from the beginning, when God created the **world**, until now—
	16: 15	"Go into all the world and preach the good news *to* all **creation**.
Ro	1: 20	For since the **creation** of the world God's invisible qualities—
	1: 25	and worshiped and served **created things** rather than the Creator—
	8: 19	The **creation** waits in eager expectation for the sons of God to be
	8: 20	For the **creation** was subjected to frustration, not by its own
	8: 21	that the **creation** itself will be liberated from its bondage to decay
	8: 22	We know that the whole **creation** has been groaning as in the pains
	8: 39	neither height nor depth, nor anything else in *all* **creation**,
2Co	5: 17	Therefore, if anyone is in Christ, he is a new **creation**; the old has
Gal	6: 15	uncircumcision means anything; what counts is a new **creation**.
Col	1: 15	is the image of the invisible God, the firstborn *over* all **creation**.
	1: 23	and that has been proclaimed to every **creature** under heaven,
Heb	4: 13	Nothing in all **creation** is hidden from God's sight Everything is
	9: 11	that is not man-made, that is to say, not *a part of* this **creation**.
1Pe	2: 13	Submit yourselves for the Lord's sake to every **authority** instituted
2Pe	3: 4	everything goes on as it has since the beginning *of* **creation**."
Rev	3: 14	the faithful and true witness, the ruler *of* God's **creation**.

3233 κτίσμα, ktisma [4] [√ 3231]

created [2], creature [1], creatures [1]

1Ti	4: 4	For everything God **created** is good, and nothing is to be rejected
Jas	1: 18	of truth, that we might be a kind of firstfruits *of all* he **created**.
Rev	5: 13	Then I heard every **creature** in heaven and on earth and under the
	8: 9	a third *of* the living **creatures** in the sea died, and a third of the

3234 κτίστης, *ktistēs* [1] [√ *3231*]

Creator [1]

1Pe 4: 19 to God's will should commit themselves *to* their faithful **Creator**

3235 κυβεία, *kybeia* [1]

cunning [1]

Eph 4: 14 and there by every wind of teaching and by the **cunning**

3236 κυβέρνησις, *kybernēsis* [1] [→ *3237*]

those with gifts of administration [1]

1Co 12: 28 those able to help others, **those with gifts of administration,**

3237 κυβερνήτης, *kybernētēs* [2] [√ *3236*]

pilot [1], sea captain [1]

Ac 27: 11 followed the advice of the **pilot** and of the owner of the ship.
Rev 18: 17 "Every **sea captain**, and all who travel by ship, the sailors,

3238 κυκλεύω, *kykleuō* [1] [√ *3241*]

surrounded [1]

Rev 20: 9 breadth of the earth and **surrounded** the camp of God's people,

3239 κυκλόθεν, *kyklothen* [3] [√ *3241*]

all around [1], encircled [1], surrounding [1]

Rev 4: 3 A rainbow, resembling an emerald, **encircled** the throne.
      4: 4 **Surrounding** the throne were twenty-four other thrones,
      4: 8 creatures had six wings and was covered with eyes **all around,**

3240 κυκλόω, *kykloō* [4] [√ *3241*]

gathered around [2], marched around [1], surrounded [1]

Lk 21: 20 "When you see Jerusalem *being* **surrounded** by armies, you will
Jn 10: 24 The Jews **gathered around** him, saying, "How long will you keep
Ac 14: 20 But *after* the disciples *had* **gathered around** him, he got up
Heb 11: 30 *after* the people had **marched around** them for seven days.

3241 κύκλῳ, *kyklō* [8] [→ *3238, 3239, 3240, 4333*]

around [3], surrounding [2], encircled [1], from village to village [+*3267*] [1], in a circle [1]

Mk   3: 34 Then he looked at those seated **in a circle** around him and said,
      6: 6 Then Jesus went around teaching **from village to village** [+*3267*].
      6: 36 so they can go to the **surrounding** countryside and villages
Lk   9: 12 so they can go to the **surrounding** villages and countryside
Ro 15: 19 So from Jerusalem all the way **around** to Illyricum, I have fully
Rev 4: 6 In the center, **around** the throne, were four living creatures,
      5: 11 They **encircled** the throne and the living creatures and the elders.
      7: 11 All the angels were standing **around** the throne and around the

3242 κύλισμα, *kylisma* Not used in UBS/NIV [√ *3244*]

3243 κυλισμός, *kylismos* [1] [√ *3244*]

wallowing [1]

2Pe 2: 22 "A sow that is washed goes back to her **wallowing** in the mud."

3244 κυλίω, *kyliō* [1] [→ *375, 653, 3242, 3243, 4685*]

rolled around [1]

Mk   9: 20 *He* fell to the ground and **rolled around**, foaming at the mouth.

3245 κυλλός, *kyllos* [4]

crippled [2], maimed [2]

Mt 15: 30 the lame, the blind, the **crippled**, the mute and many others,
    15: 31 the **crippled** made well, the lame walking and the blind seeing.
    18: 8 It is better for you to enter life **maimed** or crippled than to have
Mk   9: 43 It is better for you to enter life **maimed** than with two hands to go

3246 κῦμα, *kyma* [5] [→ *652, 1607*]

waves [4], surf [1]

Mt   8: 24 storm came up on the lake, so that the **waves** swept over the boat.
    14: 24 from land, buffeted by the **waves** because the wind was against it.
Mk   4: 37 A furious squall came up, and the **waves** broke over the boat,
Ac 27: 41 and the stern was broken to pieces by the pounding *of* the **surf**.
Jude 1: 13 They are wild **waves** of the sea, foaming up their shame;

3247 κύμβαλον, *kymbalon* [1]

cymbal [1]

1Co 13: 1 have not love, I am only a resounding gong or a clanging **cymbal**.

3248 κύμινον, *kyminon* [1]

cummin [1]

Mt 23: 23 You give a tenth of your spices—mint, dill and **cummin**.

3249 κυνάριον, *kynarion* [4] [√ *3264*]

dogs [4]

Mt 15: 26 "It is not right to take the children's bread and toss it *to* their **dogs**."
    15: 27 even the **dogs** eat the crumbs that fall from their masters' table."
Mk   7: 27 it is not right to take the children's bread and toss it *to* their **dogs**."
      7: 28 "but even the **dogs** under the table eat the children's crumbs."

3250 Κύπριος, *Kyprios* [3] [√ *3251*]

from Cyprus [3]

Ac   4: 36 Joseph, a Levite **from Cyprus**, whom the apostles called Barnabas
    11: 20 Some of them, however, men **from Cyprus** and Cyrene, went to
    21: 16 He was a man **from Cyprus** and one of the early disciples.

3251 Κύπρος, *Kypros* [5] [→ *3250*]

Cyprus [5]

Ac 11: 19 **Cyprus** and Antioch, telling the message only to Jews.
    13: 4 went down to Seleucia and sailed from there to **Cyprus**.
    15: 39 they parted company. Barnabas took Mark and sailed for **Cyprus**,
    21: 3 After sighting **Cyprus** and passing to the south of it, we sailed on
    27: 4 there we put out to sea again and passed to the lee of **Cyprus**

3252 κύπτω, *kyptō* [2] [→ *376, 2893, 4160, 5174*]

bent [1], stoop down [1]

Mk   1: 7 the thongs of whose sandals I am not worthy to **stoop down**
Jn   8: 6 But Jesus **bent** down and started to write on the ground with his

3253 Κυρεῖνος, *Kyreinos* Not used in UBS/NIV
[√ *3256*]

3254 Κυρηναῖος, *Kyrēnaios* [6] [√ *3255*]

from Cyrene [4], of Cyrene [2]

Mt 27: 32 they were going out, they met a man **from Cyrene**, named Simon,
Mk 15: 21 A certain man **from Cyrene**, Simon, the father of Alexander
Lk 23: 26 As they led him away, they seized Simon **from Cyrene**, who was
Ac   6: 9 Jews **of Cyrene** and Alexandria as well as the provinces of Cilicia
    11: 20 Some of them, however, men from Cyprus and **Cyrene**, went to
    13: 1 Barnabas, Simeon called Niger, Lucius **of Cyrene**, Manaen (who

3255 Κυρήνη, *Kyrēnē* [1] [→ *3254*]

Cyrene [1]

Ac 2: 10 and Pamphylia, Egypt and the parts of Libya near **Cyrene**;

3256 Κυρήνιος, *Kyrēnios* [1] [→ *3253, 3260*]

Quirinius [1]

Lk 2: 2 (This was the first census that took place while **Quirinius** was

3257 κυρία, *kyria* [2] [√ *3261*]

dear lady [1], lady [1]

2Jn 1: 1 The elder, *To* the chosen **lady** and her children, whom I love in the
1: 5 And now, **dear lady**, I am not writing you a new command

3258 κυριακός, *kyriakos* [2] [√ *3261*]

Lord's [2]

1Co 11:20 When you come together, it is not the **Lord's** Supper you eat,
Rev 1: 10 On the **Lord's** Day I was in the Spirit, and I heard behind me a

3259 κυριεύω, *kyrieuō* [7] [√ *3261*]

lord it over [2], has authority over [1], has mastery over [1], Lord [1], lords [1], master [1]

Lk 22:25 Jesus said to them, "The kings of the Gentiles **lord it over** them;
Ro 6: 9 he cannot die again; death no longer **has mastery over** him.
6:14 For sin *shall* not *be* your **master**, because you are not under law,
7: 1 that the law **has authority over** a man only as long as he lives?
14: 9 so that *he* might *be* the **Lord** of both the dead and the living.
2Co 1:24 Not that *we* **lord it over** your faith, but we work with you for your
1Ti 6:15 the blessed and only Ruler, the King of kings and Lord *of* **lords**,

3260 Κυρίνιος, *Kyrinios* Not used in UBS/NIV [√ *3256*]

3261 κύριος, *kyrios* [717 / 720] [→ *2894, 3257, 3258, 3259, 3262;* cf. *3263*]

ἄγγελος κυρίου (angel of the Lord) [11] Mt 1:20,24; 2:13,19; 28:2; Lk 1:11; 2:9; Ac 5:19; 8:26; 12:7,23; cf. Ac 12:11

βασιλεία τοῦ κυρίου (kingdom of the Lord) [2] 2Pe 1:11; Rev 11:15

δόξα [τοῦ] κυρίου (glory of the Lord) [5] Lk 2:9; 2Co 3:18; 8:19; 2Th 2:14; Jas 2:1

δύναμις [τοῦ] κυρίου (power of the Lord) [3] Lk 5:17; 1Co 5:4; 2Pe 1:16

ἐντολή [τοῦ] κυρίου (command of the Lord) [3] Lk 1:6; 1Co 14:37; 2Pe 3:2

ἡμέρα κυρίου (day of the Lord) [7] Ac 2:20; 1Co 1:8; 5:5; 2Co 1:14; 1Th 5:2; 2Th 2:2; 2Pe 3:10

κύριε κύριε (Lord, Lord) [4] Mt 7:21,22; 25:11; Lk 6:46

κύριοι (lords) [14] Mt 6:24; 15:27; Lk 16:13; 19:33; Ac 16:16,19, 30; 1Co 8:5; Eph 6:5,9; Col 3:22; 4:1; Rev 17:14; 19:16

κύριος Ἰησοῦς (Lord Jesus) [100] Mk 16:19; Lk 24:3; Ac 1:21; 4:33; 8:16; 11:17,20; 15:11,26; 16:31; 19:5,13,17; 20:21,24,35; 21:13; 28:31; Ro 1:7; 5:1,11; 13:14; 14:14; 15:6,30; 16:20; 1Co 1:2,3,7,8,10; 5:4,4; 6:11; 8:6; 11:23; 15:57; 16:23; 2Co 1:2,3; 4:14; 8:9; 11:31; 13:14; Gal 1:3; 6:14,18; Eph 1:2,3,15,17; 5:20; 6:23, 24; Php 1:2; 2:19; 3:20; 4:23; Col 1:3; 3:17; 1Th 1:1,3; 2:15,19; 3:11,13; 4:1,2; 5:9,23,28; 2Th 1:1,2,7,8,12,12; 2:1,8,14,16; 3:6,12, 18; 1Ti 6:3,14; Phm 1:3,5,25; Heb 13:20; Jas 1:1; 2:1; 1Pe 1:3; 2Pe 1:8,14,16; Jude 1:17,21; Rev 22:20,21

κύριος ὁ θεός (Lord God) [14] Mk 12:29; Lk 1:32,68; Ac 3:22; Rev 1:8; 4:8; 11:17; 15:3; 16:7; 18:8; 19:6; 21:22; 22:5,6

κύριος τὸν θεὸν [σου] (the Lord [your] God) [9] Mt 4:7,10; 22:37; Mk 12:30; Lk 1:16; 4:8,12, 10:27; 20:37

κύριος κυρίων (Lord of lords) [2] Rev 17:14; 19:16

κύριος Χριστός (Lord Christ) [4] Lk 2:11; Ro 16:18; Col 3:24; 1Pe 3:15

λόγος κυρίου (word of the Lord) [13] Ac 8:25; 13:44,48,49; 15:35,36; 16:32; 19:10,20; 20:35; 1Th 1:8; 4:15; 2Th 3:1

νόμος κυρίου (law of the Lord) [3] Lk 2:23,24,39

ὁδός κυρίου (way of the Lord) [7] Mt 3:3; Mk 1:3; Lk 1:76; 3:4; Jn 1:23; Ac 13:10; 18:25

ὄνομα κυρίου (name of the Lord) [21] Mt 21:9; 23:39; Mk 11:9; Lk 13:35; 19:38; Jn 12:13; Ac 2:21; 8:16; 9:28; 19:5,13,17; 21:13; Ro 10:13; 1Co 6:11; Col 3:17; 2Th 1:12; 3:6; 2Ti 2:19; Jas 5:10,14

πνεῦμα κυρίου (Spirit of the Lord) [5] Lk 4:18; Ac 5:9; 8:39; 2Co 3:17,18

ῥῆμα κυρίου (word of the Lord) [3] Lk 22:61; Ac 11:16; 1Pe 1:25

χάρις κυρίου (grace of the Lord) [15] Ac 15:11,40; Ro 16:20; 1Co 16:23; 2Co 8:9; 13:14; Gal 6:18; Php 4:23; 1Th 5:28; 2Th 1:12; 3:18; 1Ti 1:14; Phm 1:25; 2Pe 3:18; Rev 22:21

Lord/lord [601], master [35], Lord's [32], sir [23], masters [7], master's [6], owner [6], lords [3], owners [3], he[s] [+*3836*] [1], His Majesty [1], owns [+*1639*] [1], sirs [1]

Mt 1: 20 an angel *of* the **Lord** appeared to him in a dream and said,
1: 22 All this took place to fulfill what the **Lord** had said through the
1: 24 he did what the angel *of* the **Lord** had commanded him and took
2: 13 they had gone, an angel *of* the **Lord** appeared to Joseph in a dream.
2: 15 so was fulfilled what the **Lord** had said through the prophet:
2: 19 an angel *of* the **Lord** appeared in a dream to Joseph in Egypt
3: 3 'Prepare the way *for* the **Lord**, make straight paths for him.' "
4: 7 "It is also written: 'Do not put the **Lord** your God to the test.' "
4: 10 it is written: 'Worship the **Lord** your God, and serve him only.' "
5: 33 break your oath, but keep the oaths you have made *to* the **Lord**.'
6: 24 "No one can serve two **masters**. Either he will hate the one
7: 21 "Not everyone who says to me, '**Lord**, Lord,' will enter the
7: 21 "Not everyone who says to me, 'Lord, **Lord**,' will enter the
7: 22 Many will say to me on that day, '**Lord**, Lord, did we not prophesy
7: 22 Many will say to me on that day, 'Lord, **Lord**, did we not prophesy
8: 2 A man with leprosy came and knelt before him and said, "**Lord**,
8: 6 "**Lord**," he said, "my servant lies at home paralyzed and in terrible
8: 8 The centurion replied, "**Lord**, I do not deserve to have you come
8: 21 disciple said to him, "**Lord**, first let me go and bury my father."
8: 25 The disciples went and woke him, saying, "**Lord**, save us!
9: 28 you believe that I am able to do this?" "Yes, **Lord**," they replied.
9: 38 Ask the **Lord** of the harvest, therefore, to send out workers into his
10: 24 "A student is not above his teacher, nor a servant above his **master**.
10: 25 the student to be like his teacher, and the servant like his **master**.
11: 25 time Jesus said, "I praise you, Father, **Lord** of heaven and earth,
12: 8 For the Son of Man is **Lord** of the Sabbath."
13: 27 "The owner's servants came to him and said, '**Sir**, didn't you sow
14: 28 "**Lord**, if it's you," Peter replied, "tell me to come to you on the
14: 30 he was afraid and, beginning to sink, cried out, "**Lord**, save me!"
15: 22 came to him, crying out, "**Lord**, Son of David, have mercy on me!
15: 25 The woman came and knelt before him. "**Lord**, help me!" she said.
15: 27 "Yes, **Lord**," she said, "but even the dogs eat the crumbs that fall
15: 27 even the dogs eat the crumbs that fall from their **masters'** table."
16: 22 took him aside and began to rebuke him. "Never, **Lord**!" he said.
17: 4 Peter said to Jesus, "**Lord**, it is good for us to be here. If you wish,
17: 15 "**Lord**, have mercy on my son," he said. "He has seizures and is
18: 21 Then Peter came to Jesus and asked, "**Lord**, how many times shall
18: 25 the **master** ordered that he and his wife and his children and all
18: 27 The servant's **master** took pity on him, canceled the debt
18: 31 and went and told their **master** everything that had happened.
18: 32 "Then the **master** called the servant in. 'You wicked servant,'
18: 34 In anger his **master** turned him over to the jailers to be tortured,
20: 8 the **owner** of the vineyard said to his foreman, 'Call the workers
20: 30 going by, they shouted, "**Lord**, Son of David, have mercy on us!"
20: 31 shouted all the louder, "**Lord**, Son of David, have mercy on us!"
20: 33 "**Lord**," they answered, "we want our sight."
21: 3 If anyone says anything to you, tell him that the **Lord** needs them,
21: 9 "Blessed is he who comes in the name *of* the **Lord**!" "Hosanna in
21: 30 to the other son and said the same thing. He answered, 'I will, **sir**,'
21: 40 "Therefore, when the **owner** of the vineyard comes, what will he do
21: 42 the **Lord** has done this, and it is marvelous in our eyes'?
22: 37 " 'Love the **Lord** your God with all your heart and with all your

22:43 then that David, speaking by the Spirit, calls him '**Lord**'?
22:44 " 'The **Lord** said to my Lord: "Sit at my right hand until I put your
22:44 " 'The Lord said *to* my **Lord**: "Sit at my right hand until I put your
22:45 If then David calls him '**Lord**,' how can he be his son?"
23:39 until you say, 'Blessed is he who comes in the name *of* the **Lord**.' "
24:42 because you do not know on what day your **Lord** will come.
24:45 whom the **master** has put in charge of the servants in his
24:46 It will be good for that servant whose **master** finds him doing
24:48 and says to himself, 'My **master** is staying away a long time,'
24:50 The **master** of that servant will come on a day when he does not
25:11 the others also came. '**Sir**! Sir!' they said. 'Open the door for us!'
25:11 the others also came. 'Sir! **Sir**!' they said. 'Open the door for us!'
25:18 went off, dug a hole in the ground and hid his **master's** money.
25:19 "After a long time the **master** of those servants returned and settled
25:20 '**Master**,' he said, 'you entrusted me with five talents. See,
25:21 "His **master** replied, 'Well done, good and faithful servant!
25:21 charge of many things. Come and share your **master's** happiness!'
25:22 '**Master**,' he said, 'you entrusted me with two talents; see,
25:23 "His **master** replied, 'Well done, good and faithful servant!
25:23 charge of many things. Come and share your **master's** happiness!'
25:24 '**Master**,' he said, 'I knew that you are a hard man,
25:26 "His **master** replied, 'You wicked, lazy servant! So you knew that I
25:37 '**Lord**, when did we see you hungry and feed you, or thirsty
25:44 "They also will answer, '**Lord**, when did we see you hungry
26:22 and began to say to him one after the other, "Surely not I, **Lord**?"
27:10 used them to buy the potter's field, as the **Lord** commanded me."
27:63 "**Sir**," they said, "we remember that while he was still alive that
28: 2 for an angel *of* the **Lord** came down from heaven and, going to the

Mk 1: 3 'Prepare the way *for* the **Lord**, make straight paths for him.' "
2:28 So the Son of Man is **Lord** even of the Sabbath."
5:19 to your family and tell them how much the **Lord** has done for you,
7:28 "Yes, **Lord**," she replied, "but even the dogs under the table eat the
11: 3 tell him, 'The **Lord** needs it and will send it back here shortly.' "
11: 9 "Hosanna!" "Blessed is he who comes in the name *of* the **Lord**!"
12: 9 "What then will the **owner** of the vineyard do? He will come
12:11 the **Lord** has done this, and it is marvelous in our eyes'?"
12:29 "is this: 'Hear, O Israel, the **Lord** our God, the Lord is one.
12:29 "is this: 'Hear, O Israel, the Lord our God, the **Lord** is one.
12:30 Love the **Lord** your God with all your heart and with all your soul
12:36 speaking by the Holy Spirit, declared: " 'The **Lord** said to my Lord:
12:36 speaking by the Holy Spirit, declared: " 'The Lord said *to* my **Lord**:
12:37 David himself calls him '**Lord**.' How then can he be his son?"
13:20 If the **Lord** had not cut short those days, no one would survive.
13:35 because you do not know when the **owner** of the house will come
16:19 After the **Lord** Jesus had spoken to them, he was taken up into
16:20 and the **Lord** worked with them and confirmed his word by the

Lk 1: 6 observing all the **Lord's** commandments and regulations
1: 9 the priesthood, to go into the temple *of* the **Lord** and burn incense.
1:11 Then an angel *of* the **Lord** appeared to him, standing at the right
1:15 for he will be great in the sight *of* the **Lord**. He is never to take
1:16 Many of the people of Israel will he bring back to the **Lord** their
1:17 of the righteous—to make ready a people prepared *for* the **Lord**."
1:25 "The **Lord** has done this for me," she said. "In these days he has
1:28 "Greetings, you who are highly favored! The **Lord** is with you."
1:32 The **Lord** God will give him the throne of his father David,
1:38 "I am the **Lord's** servant," Mary answered. "May it be to me as you
1:43 so favored, that the mother *of* my **Lord** should come to me?
1:45 Blessed is she who has believed that what the **Lord** has said to her
1:46 And Mary said: "My soul glorifies the **Lord**
1:58 and relatives heard that the **Lord** had shown her great mercy,
1:66 then is this child going to be?" For the **Lord's** hand was with him.
1:68 "Praise be to the **Lord**, the God of Israel, because he has come
1:76 for you will go on before the **Lord** to prepare the way for him,
2: 9 An angel *of* the **Lord** appeared to them, and the glory of the Lord
2: 9 and the glory *of* the **Lord** shone around them, and they were
2:11 of David a Savior has been born to you; he is Christ the **Lord**.
2:15 see this thing that has happened, which the **Lord** has told us about."
2:22 and Mary took him to Jerusalem to present him *to* the **Lord**
2:23 (as it is written in the Law *of* the **Lord**, "Every firstborn male is to
2:23 the Lord, "Every firstborn male is to be consecrated *to* the **Lord**"),
2:24 a sacrifice in keeping with what is said in the Law *of* the **Lord's** Christ.
2:26 Spirit that he would not die before he had seen the **Lord's** Christ.
2:39 and Mary had done everything required by the Law *of* the **Lord**,
3: 4 'Prepare the way *for* the **Lord**, make straight paths for him.' "
4: 8 "It is written: 'Worship the **Lord** your God and serve him only.' "
4:12 "It says: 'Do not put the **Lord** your God to the test.' "

4:18 "The Spirit *of* the **Lord** is on me,
4:19 to proclaim the year *of* the **Lord's** favor."
5: 8 saw this, he fell at Jesus' knees and said, "Go away from me, **Lord**;
5:12 he fell with his face to the ground and begged him, "**Lord**,
5:17 And the power *of* the **Lord** was present for him to heal the sick.
6: 5 Then Jesus said to them, "The Son of Man is **Lord** of the Sabbath."
6:46 "Why do you call me, '**Lord**, Lord,' and do not do what I say?
6:46 "Why do you call me, 'Lord, **Lord**,' and do not do what I say?
7: 6 "**Lord**, don't trouble yourself, for I do not deserve to have you
7:13 When the **Lord** saw her, his heart went out to her and he said,
7:19 sent them to the **Lord** to ask, "Are you the one who was to come,
9:54 When the disciples James and John saw this, they asked, "**Lord**,
9:59 But the man replied, "**Lord**, first let me go and bury my father."
9:61 Still another said, "I will follow you, **Lord**; but first let me go back
10: 1 After this the **Lord** appointed seventy-two others and sent them
10: 2 Ask the **Lord** of the harvest, therefore, to send out workers into his
10:17 The seventy-two returned with joy and said, "**Lord**,
10:21 Holy Spirit, said, "I praise you, Father, **Lord** of heaven and earth,
10:27 " 'Love the **Lord** your God with all your heart and with all your
10:39 called Mary, who sat at the **Lord's** feet listening to what he said.
10:40 She came to him and asked, "**Lord**, don't you care that my sister
10:41 "Martha, Martha," the **Lord** answered, "you are worried and upset
11: 1 one of his disciples said to him, "**Lord**, teach us to pray,
11:39 Then the **Lord** said to him, "Now then, you Pharisees clean the
12:36 like men waiting for their **master** to return from a wedding
12:37 It will be good for those servants whose **master** finds them
12:41 Peter asked, "**Lord**, are you telling this parable to us, or to
12:42 The **Lord** answered, "Who then is the faithful and wise manager,
12:42 whom the **master** puts in charge of his servants to give them their
12:43 It will be good for that servant whom the **master** finds doing
12:45 'My **master** is taking a long time in coming,' and he then begins to
12:46 The **master** of that servant will come on a day when he does not
12:47 "That servant who knows his **master's** will and does not get ready
13: 8 " '**Sir**,' the man replied, 'leave it alone for one more year,
13:15 The **Lord** answered him, "You hypocrites! Doesn't each of you on
13:23 Someone asked him, "**Lord**, are only a few people going to be
13:25 closes the door, you will stand outside knocking and pleading, '**Sir**,
13:35 until you say, 'Blessed is he who comes in the name *of* the **Lord**.' "
14:21 "The servant came back and reported this *to* his **master**.
14:22 " '**Sir**,' the servant said, 'what you ordered has been done,
14:23 "Then the **master** told his servant, 'Go out to the roads and country
16: 3 'What shall I do now? My **master** is taking away my job.
16: 5 "So he called in each one of his **master's** debtors. He asked the
16: 5 He asked the first, 'How much do you owe my **master**?'
16: 8 "The **master** commended the dishonest manager because he had
16:13 "No servant can serve two **masters**. Either he will hate the one
17: 5 The apostles said *to* the **Lord**, "Increase our faith!"
17: 6 He[s] [+*3836*] replied, "If you have faith as small as a mustard seed,
17:37 "Where, **Lord**?" they asked. He replied, "Where there is a dead
18: 6 And the **Lord** said, "Listen to what the unjust judge says.
18:41 do you want me to do for you?" "**Lord**, I want to see," he replied.
19: 8 But Zacchaeus stood up and said to the **Lord**, "Look, Lord!
19: 8 But Zacchaeus stood up and said to the Lord, "Look, **Lord**!
19:16 "The first one came and said, '**Sir**, your mina has earned ten more.'
19:18 "The second one came and said, '**Sir**, your mina has earned five more.'
19:20 "Then another servant came and said, '**Sir**, here is your mina;
19:25 " '**Sir**,' they said, 'he already has ten!'
19:31 asks you, 'Why are you untying it?' tell him, 'The **Lord** needs it.' "
19:33 As they were untying the colt, its **owners** asked them, "Why are
19:34 They replied, "The **Lord** needs it."
19:38 "Blessed is the king who comes in the name *of* the **Lord**!" "Peace
20:13 "Then the **owner** of the vineyard said, 'What shall I do? I will send
20:15 killed him. "What then will the **owner** of the vineyard do to them?
20:37 for he calls the **Lord** 'the God of Abraham, and the God of Isaac,
20:42 of Psalms: " 'The **Lord** said to my Lord: "Sit at my right hand
20:42 of Psalms: " 'The Lord said *to* my **Lord**: "Sit at my right hand
20:44 David calls him '**Lord**.' How then can he be his son?"
22:33 But he replied, "**Lord**, I am ready to go with you to prison
22:38 The disciples said, "See, **Lord**, here are two swords." "That is
22:49 to happen, they said, "**Lord**, should we strike with our swords?"
22:61 The **Lord** turned and looked straight at Peter. Then Peter
22:61 Then Peter remembered the word the **Lord** had spoken to him:
24: 3 when they entered, they did not find the body *of* the **Lord** Jesus.
24:34 "It is true! The **Lord** has risen and has appeared to Simon."

Jn 1:23 of one calling in the desert, 'Make straight the way *for* the **Lord**.' "
4: 3 When the **Lord** [UBS *2652*] learned of this, he left Judea

4:11 "**Sir**," the woman said, "you have nothing to draw with and the well
4:15 "**Sir**, give me this water so that I won't get thirsty and have to keep
4:19 "**Sir**," the woman said, "I can see that you are a prophet.
4:49 The royal official said, "**Sir**, come down before my child dies."
5: 7 "**Sir**," the invalid replied, "I have no one to help me into the pool
6:23 the people had eaten the bread after the **Lord** had given thanks.
6:34 "**Sir**," they said, "from now on give us this bread."
6:68 Simon Peter answered him, "**Lord**, to whom shall we go?
8:11 "No one, **sir**," she said. "Then neither do I condemn you," Jesus
9:36 "Who is he, **sir**?" the man asked. "Tell me so that I may believe in
9:38 Then the man said, "**Lord**, I believe," and he worshiped him.
11: 2 was the same one who poured perfume on the **Lord** and wiped his
11: 3 So the sisters sent word to Jesus, "**Lord**, the one you love is sick."
11:12 His disciples replied, "**Lord**, if he sleeps, he will get better."
11:21 "**Lord**," Martha said to Jesus, "if you had been here, my brother
11:27 "Yes, **Lord**," she told him, "I believe that you are the Christ,
11:32 where Jesus was and saw him, she fell at his feet and said, "**Lord**,
11:34 have you laid him?" he asked. "Come and see, **Lord**," they replied.
11:39 "But, **Lord**," said Martha, the sister of the dead man, "by this time
12:13 "Hosanna!" "Blessed is he who comes in the name of the **Lord**!"
12:21 with a request. "**Sir**," they said, "we would like to see Jesus.
12:38 "**Lord**, who has believed our message and to whom has the arm of
12:38 our message and to whom has the arm of the **Lord** been revealed?"
13: 6 He came to Simon Peter, who said to him, "**Lord**, are you going to
13: 9 "Then, **Lord**," Simon Peter replied, "not just my feet but my hands
13:13 "You call me 'Teacher' and '**Lord**,' and rightly so, for that is what I
13:14 Now that I, your **Lord** and Teacher, have washed your feet,
13:16 I tell you the truth, no servant is greater than his **master**, nor is a
13:25 Leaning back against Jesus, he asked him, "**Lord**, who is it?"
13:36 Simon Peter asked him, "**Lord**, where are you going?"
13:37 Peter asked, "**Lord**, why can't I follow you now? I will lay down
14: 5 Thomas said to him, "**Lord**, we don't know where you are going,
14: 8 Philip said, "**Lord**, show us the Father and that will be enough for
14:22 said, "But, **Lord**, why do you intend to show yourself to us
15:15 because a servant does not know his **master's** business.
15:20 'No servant is greater than his **master**.' If they persecuted me,
20: 2 Jesus loved, and said, "They have taken the **Lord** out of the tomb,
20:13 "They have taken my **Lord** away," she said, "and I don't know
20:15 he was the gardener, she said, "**Sir**, if you have carried him away,
20:18 went to the disciples with the news: "I have seen the **Lord**!"
20:20 and side. The disciples were overjoyed when they saw the **Lord**.
20:25 So the other disciples told him, "We have seen the **Lord**!" But he
20:28 Thomas said to him, "My **Lord** and my God!"
21: 7 Then the disciple whom Jesus loved said to Peter, "It is the **Lord**!"
21: 7 As soon as Simon Peter heard him say, "It is the **Lord**," he wrapped
21:12 dared ask him, "Who are you?" They knew it was the **Lord**.
21:15 "Yes, **Lord**," he said, "you know that I love you." Jesus said,
21:16 He answered, "Yes, **Lord**, you know that I love you." Jesus said,
21:17 He said, "**Lord**, you know all things; you know that I love you."
21:20 had leaned back against Jesus at the supper and had said, "**Lord**,
21:21 When Peter saw him, he asked, "**Lord**, what about him?"
Ac 1: 6 So when they met together, they asked him, "**Lord**, are you at this
1:21 men who have been with us the whole time the **Lord** Jesus went in
1:24 Then they prayed, "**Lord**, you know everyone's heart. Show us
2:20 blood before the coming of the great and glorious day of the **Lord**.
2:21 And everyone who calls on the name of the **Lord** will be saved.'
2:25 David said about him: " 'I saw the **Lord** always before me.
2:34 not ascend to heaven, and yet he said, " 'The **Lord** said to my Lord:
2:34 not ascend to heaven, and yet he said, " 'The Lord said to my **Lord**:
2:36 has made this Jesus, whom you crucified, both **Lord** and Christ."
2:39 for all who are far off—for all whom the **Lord** our God will call."
2:47 And the **Lord** added to their number daily those who were being
3:19 be wiped out, that times of refreshing may come from the **Lord**,
3:22 'The **Lord** your God will raise up for you a prophet like me from
4:26 and the rulers gather together against the **Lord** and against his
4:29 Now, **Lord**, consider their threats and enable your servants to
4:33 apostles continued to testify to the resurrection of the **Lord** Jesus,
5: 9 said to her, "How could you agree to test the Spirit of the **Lord**?
5:14 more and more men and women believed in the **Lord** and were
5:19 But during the night an angel of the **Lord** opened the doors of the
7:31 As he went over to look more closely, he heard the **Lord's** voice:
7:33 "Then the **Lord** said to him, 'Take off your sandals; the place where
7:49 build for me? says the **Lord**. Or where will my resting place be?
7:59 were stoning him, Stephen prayed, "**Lord** Jesus, receive my spirit."
7:60 Then he fell on his knees and cried out, "**Lord**, do not hold this sin
8:16 they had simply been baptized into the name of the **Lord** Jesus.

8:22 Repent of this wickedness and pray to the **Lord**. Perhaps he will
8:24 "Pray to the **Lord** for me so that nothing you have said may happen
8:25 When they had testified and proclaimed the word of the **Lord**,
8:26 Now an angel of the **Lord** said to Philip, "Go south to the road—
8:39 out of the water, the Spirit of the **Lord** suddenly took Philip away,
9: 1 Saul was still breathing out murderous threats against the **Lord's**
9: 5 "Who are you, **Lord**?" Saul asked. "I am Jesus, whom you are
9:10 The **Lord** called to him in a vision, "Ananias!" "Yes, Lord," he
9:10 called to him in a vision, "Ananias!" "Yes, **Lord**," he answered.
9:11 The **Lord** told him, "Go to the house of Judas on Straight Street
9:13 "**Lord**," Ananias answered, "I have heard many reports about this
9:15 But the **Lord** said to Ananias, "Go! This man is my chosen
9:17 Placing his hands on Saul, he said, "Brother Saul, the **Lord**—
9:27 He told them how Saul on his journey had seen the **Lord** and that
9:28 freely in Jerusalem, speaking boldly in the name of the **Lord**.
9:31 the Holy Spirit, it grew in numbers, living in the fear of the **Lord**.
9:35 who lived in Lydda and Sharon saw him and turned to the **Lord**.
9:42 known all over Joppa, and many people believed in the **Lord**.
10: 4 "What is it, **Lord**?" he asked. The angel answered, "Your prayers
10:14 "Surely not, **Lord**!" Peter replied. "I have never eaten anything
10:33 to listen to everything the **Lord** has commanded you to tell us."
10:36 the good news of peace through Jesus Christ, who is **Lord** of all.
11: 8 "I replied, 'Surely not, **Lord**! Nothing impure or unclean has ever
11:16 Then I remembered what the **Lord** had said: 'John baptized with
11:17 who believed in the **Lord** Jesus Christ, who was I to think that I
11:20 to Greeks also, telling them the good news about the **Lord** Jesus.
11:21 The **Lord's** hand was with them, and a great number of people
11:21 and a great number of people believed and turned to the **Lord**.
11:23 and encouraged them all to remain true to the **Lord** with all their
11:24 and faith, and a great number of people were brought to the **Lord**.
12: 7 Suddenly an angel of the **Lord** appeared and a light shone in the
12:11 "Now I know without a doubt that the **Lord** sent his angel
12:17 and described how the **Lord** had brought him out of prison.
12:23 an angel of the **Lord** struck him down, and he was eaten by worms
13: 2 While they were worshiping the **Lord** and fasting, the Holy Spirit
13:10 Will you never stop perverting the right ways of the **Lord**?
13:11 Now the hand of the **Lord** is against you. You are going to be
13:12 he believed, for he was amazed at the teaching about the **Lord**.
13:44 almost the whole city gathered to hear the word of the **Lord**.
13:47 For this is what the **Lord** has commanded us: " 'I have made you a
13:48 heard this, they were glad and honored the word of the **Lord**;
13:49 The word of the **Lord** spread through the whole region.
14: 3 spent considerable time there, speaking boldly for the **Lord**,
14:23 with prayer and fasting, committed them to the **Lord**, in whom
15:11 We believe it is through the grace of our **Lord** Jesus that we are
15:17 that the remnant of men may seek the **Lord**, and all the Gentiles
15:17 who bear my name, says the **Lord**, who does these things'
15:26 men who have risked their lives for the name of our **Lord** Jesus
15:35 and many others taught and preached the word of the **Lord**.
15:36 brothers in all the towns where we preached the word of the **Lord**
15:40 and left, commended by the brothers to the grace of the **Lord**.
16:14 The **Lord** opened her heart to respond to Paul's message.
16:15 "If you consider me a believer in the **Lord**," she said, "come
16:16 She earned a great deal of money for her **owners** by
16:19 When the **owners** of the slave girl realized that their hope of
16:30 He then brought them out and asked, "**Sirs**, what must I do to be
16:31 They replied, "Believe in the **Lord** Jesus, and you will be saved—
16:32 Then they spoke the word of the **Lord** to him and to all the others
17:24 the world and everything in it is the **Lord** of heaven and earth
18: 8 the synagogue ruler, and his entire household believed in the **Lord**;
18: 9 One night the **Lord** spoke to Paul in a vision: "Do not be afraid;
18:25 He had been instructed in the way of the **Lord**, and he spoke with
19: 5 hearing this, they were baptized into the name of the **Lord** Jesus.
19:10 who lived in the province of Asia heard the word of the **Lord**.
19:13 the name of the **Lord** Jesus over those who were demon-possessed.
19:17 with fear, and the name of the **Lord** Jesus was held in high honor.
19:20 In this way the word of the **Lord** spread widely and grew in power.
20:19 I served the **Lord** with great humility and with tears, although I
20:21 must turn to God in repentance and have faith in our **Lord** Jesus.
20:24 the race and complete the task the **Lord** Jesus has given me—
20:35 the weak, remembering the words the **Lord** Jesus himself said:
21:13 but also to die in Jerusalem for the name of the **Lord** Jesus."
21:14 not be dissuaded, we gave up and said, "The **Lord's** will be done."
22: 8 " 'Who are you, **Lord**?' I asked. " 'I am Jesus of Nazareth,
22:10 " 'What shall I do, **Lord**?' I asked. " 'Get up,' the Lord said,
22:10 " 'What shall I do, Lord?' I asked. " 'Get up,' the **Lord** said,

22: 19   " 'Lord,' I replied, 'these men know that I went from one
23: 11   The following night the Lord stood near Paul and said,
25: 26   But I have nothing definite to write *to* His Majesty about him.
26: 15   "Then I asked, 'Who are you, Lord?' " 'I am Jesus, whom you are
26: 15   " 'I am Jesus, whom you are persecuting,' the Lord replied.
28: 31   the kingdom of God and taught about the Lord Jesus Christ.
Ro 1: 4   of God by his resurrection from the dead: Jesus Christ our Lord.
1: 7   peace to you from God our Father and from the Lord Jesus Christ.
4: 8   Blessed is the man whose sin the Lord will never count against
4: 24   for us who believe in him who raised Jesus our Lord from the
5: 1   we have peace with God through our Lord Jesus Christ,
5: 11   but we also rejoice in God through our Lord Jesus Christ,
5: 21   righteousness to bring eternal life through Jesus Christ our Lord.
6: 23   but the gift of God is eternal life in Christ Jesus our Lord.
7: 25   Thanks be to God—through Jesus Christ our Lord! So then,
8: 39   separate us from the love of God that is in Christ Jesus our Lord.
9: 28   For the Lord will carry out his sentence on earth with speed
9: 29   "Unless the Lord Almighty had left us descendants, we would have
10: 9   That if you confess with your mouth, "Jesus is Lord," and believe
10: 12   the same Lord is Lord of all and richly blesses all who call on him,
10: 13   "Everyone who calls on the name *of* the Lord will be saved."
10: 16   For Isaiah says, "Lord, who has believed our message?"
11: 3   "Lord, they have killed your prophets and torn down your altars;
11: 34   "Who has known the mind *of* the Lord? Or who has been his
12: 11   be lacking in zeal, but keep your spiritual fervor, serving the Lord.
12: 19   for it is written: "It is mine to avenge; I will repay," says the Lord.
13: 14   Rather, clothe yourselves with the Lord Jesus Christ, and do not
14: 4   *To* his own master he stands or falls. And he will stand,
14: 4   And he will stand, for the Lord is able to make him stand.
14: 6   He who regards one day as special, does so *to* the Lord. He who
14: 6   He who eats meat, eats *to* the Lord, for he gives thanks to God;
14: 6   and he who abstains, does so *to* the Lord and gives thanks to God.
14: 8   If we live, wc live *to* the Lord; and if we die, we die to the Lord.
14: 8   If we live, we live to the Lord; and if we die, we die *to* the Lord.
14: 8   die to the Lord. So, whether we live or die, we belong to the Lord.
14: 11   " 'As surely as I live,' says the Lord, 'every knee will bow before
14: 14   As one who is in the Lord Jesus, I am fully convinced that no food
15: 6   you may glorify the God and Father *of* our Lord Jesus Christ.
15: 11   And again, "Praise the Lord, all you Gentiles, and sing praises to
15: 30   brothers, by our Lord Jesus Christ and by the love of the Spirit,
16: 2   I ask you to receive her in the Lord in a way worthy of the saints
16: 8   Greet Ampliatus, whom I love in the Lord.
16: 11   Greet those in the household of Narcissus who are in the Lord.
16: 12   and Tryphosa, those women who work hard in the Lord.
16: 12   another woman who has worked very hard in the Lord.
16: 13   Greet Rufus, chosen in the Lord, and his mother, who has been a
16: 18   For such people are not serving our Lord Christ, but their own
16: 20   Satan under your feet. The grace *of* our Lord Jesus be with you.
16: 22   Tertius, who wrote down this letter, greet you in the Lord.
1Co 1: 2   those everywhere who call on the name *of* our Lord Jesus Christ—
1: 3   and peace to you from God our Father and the Lord Jesus Christ.
1: 7   gift as you eagerly wait for our Lord Jesus Christ to be revealed.
1: 8   so that you will be blameless on the day *of* our Lord Jesus Christ.
1: 9   has called you into fellowship with his Son Jesus Christ our Lord,
1: 10   I appeal to you, brothers, in the name *of* our Lord Jesus Christ,
1: 31   Therefore, as it is written: "Let him who boasts boast in the Lord."
2: 8   for if they had, they would not have crucified the Lord of glory.
2: 16   "For who has known the mind *of* the Lord that he may instruct
3: 5   you came to believe—as the Lord has assigned to each his task.
3: 20   again, "The Lord knows that the thoughts of the wise are futile."
4: 4   but that does not make me innocent. It is the Lord who judges me.
4: 5   judge nothing before the appointed time; wait till the Lord comes.
4: 17   to you Timothy, my son whom I love, who is faithful in the Lord.
4: 19   if the Lord is willing, and then I will find out not only how these
5: 4   When you are assembled in the name *of* our Lord Jesus and I am
5: 4   I am with you in spirit, and the power *of* our Lord Jesus is present,
5: 5   may be destroyed and his spirit saved on the day *of* the Lord.
6: 11   you were justified in the name *of* the Lord Jesus Christ and by the
6: 13   for sexual immorality, but *for* the Lord, and the Lord for the body.
6: 13   for sexual immorality, but for the Lord, and the Lord for the body.
6: 14   By his power God raised the Lord from the dead, and he will raise
6: 17   But he who unites himself *with* the Lord is one with him in spirit.
7: 10   To the married I give this command (not I, but the Lord):
7: 12   To the rest I say this (I, not the Lord): If any brother has a wife
7: 17   each one should retain the place in life that the Lord assigned to
7: 22   For he who was a slave when he was called by the Lord is the

7: 22   a slave when he was called by the Lord is the Lord's freedman;
7: 25   I have no command *from* the Lord, but I give a judgment as one
7: 25   but I give a judgment as one who by the Lord's mercy is
7: 32   An unmarried man is concerned about the Lord's affairs—
7: 32   concerned about the Lord's affairs—how he can please the Lord.
7: 34   unmarried woman or virgin is concemed about the Lord's affairs:
7: 35   that you may live in a right way in undivided devotion *to* the Lord.
7: 39   free to marry anyone she wishes, but he must belong to the Lord.
8: 5   or on earth (as indeed there are many "gods" and many "lords"),
8: 6   and there is but one Lord, Jesus Christ, through whom all things
9: 1   I not free? Am I not an apostle? Have I not seen Jesus our Lord?
9: 1   Jesus our Lord? Are you not the result of my work in the Lord?
9: 2   I am to you! For you are the seal of my apostleship in the Lord.
9: 5   as do the other apostles and the Lord's brothers and Cephas?
9: 14   the Lord has commanded that those who preach the gospel should
10: 9   We should not test the Lord, [UBS *5986*] as some of them did—
10: 21   You cannot drink the cup *of* the Lord and the cup of demons too;
10: 21   you cannot have a part in both the Lord's table and the table of
10: 22   Are we trying to arouse the Lord's jealousy? Are we stronger than
10: 26   for, "The earth is the Lord's, and everything in it."
11: 11   In the Lord, however, woman is not independent of man,
11: 23   For I received from the Lord what I also passed on to you:
11: 23   The Lord Jesus, on the night he was betrayed, took bread,
11: 26   and drink this cup, you proclaim the Lord's death until he comes.
11: 27   or drinks the cup *of* the Lord in an unworthy manner will be guilty
11: 27   will be guilty of sinning against the body and blood *of* the Lord.
11: 29   and drinks without recognizing the body *of* the Lord [UBS-] eats
11: 32   When we are judged by the Lord, we are being disciplined
12: 3   "Jesus be cursed," and no one can say, "Jesus is Lord," except by
12: 5   There are different kinds of service, but the same Lord.
14: 21   this people, but even then they will not listen to me," says the Lord.
14: 37   let him acknowledge that what I am writing to you is the Lord's
15: 31   just as surely as I glory over you in Christ Jesus our Lord.
15: 57   be to God! He gives us the victory through our Lord Jesus Christ.
15: 58   Always give yourselves fully to the work *of* the Lord, because you
15: 58   because you know that your labor in the Lord is not in vain.
16: 7   I hope to spend some time with you, if the Lord permits.
16: 10   with you, for he is carrying on the work *of* the Lord, just as I am.
16: 19   Aquila and Priscilla greet you warmly in the Lord, and so does the
16: 22   If anyone does not love the Lord—a curse be on him. Come,
16: 23   The grace *of* the Lord Jesus be with you.
2Co 1: 2   and peace to you from God our Father and the Lord Jesus Christ.
1: 3   Praise be to the God and Father *of* our Lord Jesus Christ,
1: 14   of us just as we will boast of you in the day *of* the Lord Jesus.
2: 12   of Christ and found that the Lord had opened a door for me,
3: 16   But whenever anyone turns to the Lord, the veil is taken away.
3: 17   Now the Lord is the Spirit, and where the Spirit of the Lord is,
3: 17   is the Spirit, and where the Spirit *of* the Lord is, there is freedom.
3: 18   And we, who with unveiled faces all reflect the Lord's glory,
3: 18   which comes from the Lord, who is the Spirit.
4: 5   For we do not preach ourselves, but Jesus Christ as Lord,
4: 14   because we know that the one who raised the Lord Jesus from the
5: 6   as long as we are at home in the body we are away from the Lord.
5: 8   would prefer to be away from the body and at home with the Lord.
5: 11   Since, then, we know what it is to fear the Lord, we try to
6: 17   "Therefore come out from them and be separate, says the Lord.
6: 18   and you will be my sons and daughters, says the Lord Almighty."
8: 5   but they gave themselves first *to* the Lord and then to us in
8: 9   For you know the grace *of* our Lord Jesus Christ, that though he
8: 19   which we administer in order to honor the Lord himself and to
8: 21   not only in the eyes *of* the Lord but also in the eyes of men.
10: 8   For even if I boast somewhat freely about the authority the Lord
10: 17   But, "Let him who boasts boast in the Lord."
10: 18   himself who is approved, but the one whom the Lord commends.
11: 17   In this self-confident boasting I am not talking as the Lord would,
11: 31   The God and Father *of* the Lord Jesus, who is to be praised
12: 1   to be gained, I will go on to visions and revelations *from* the Lord.
12: 8   Three times I pleaded with the Lord to take it away from me.
13: 10   the authority the Lord gave me for building you up, not for tearing
13: 14   May the grace *of* the Lord Jesus Christ, and the love of God,
Gal 1: 3   and peace to you from God our Father and the Lord Jesus Christ,
1: 19   I saw none of the other apostles—only James, the Lord's brother.
4: 1   different from a slave, *although he owns* [*+1639*] the whole estate.
5: 10   I am confident in the Lord that you will take no other view.
6: 14   May I never boast except in the cross *of* our Lord Jesus Christ,
6: 18   The grace *of* our Lord Jesus Christ be with your spirit, brothers.

Eph 1: 2 and peace to you from God our Father and the **Lord** Jesus Christ.
1: 3 Praise be to the God and Father *of* our **Lord** Jesus Christ,
1: 15 ever since I heard about your faith in the **Lord** Jesus and your love
1: 17 I keep asking that the God *of* our **Lord** Jesus Christ, the glorious
2: 21 is joined together and rises to become a holy temple in the **Lord**
3: 11 eternal purpose which he accomplished in Christ Jesus our **Lord**.
4: 1 As a prisoner for the **Lord**, then, I urge you to live a life worthy of
4: 5 one **Lord**, one faith, one baptism;
4: 17 So I tell you this, and insist on it in the **Lord**, that you must no
5: 8 For you were once darkness, but now you are light in the **Lord**.
5: 10 and find out what pleases the **Lord**.
5: 17 do not be foolish, but understand what the **Lord's** will is.
5: 19 spiritual songs. Sing and make music in your heart *to* the **Lord**,
5: 20 the Father for everything, in the name *of* our **Lord** Jesus Christ.
5: 22 Wives, submit to your husbands as *to* the **Lord**.
6: 1 Children, obey your parents in the **Lord**, for this is right.
6: 4 instead, bring them up in the training and instruction *of* the **Lord**.
6: 5 Slaves, obey your earthly **masters** with respect and fear, and with
6: 7 Serve wholeheartedly, as if you were serving the **Lord**, not men,
6: 8 because you know that the **Lord** will reward everyone for
6: 9 And **masters**, treat your slaves in the same way. Do not threaten
6: 9 since you know that he who is both their **Master** and yours is in
6: 10 Finally, be strong in the **Lord** and in his mighty power.
6: 21 Tychicus, the dear brother and faithful servant in the **Lord**,
6: 23 and love with faith from God the Father and the **Lord** Jesus Christ.
6: 24 Grace to all who love our **Lord** Jesus Christ with an undying love.
Php 1: 2 and peace to you from God our Father and the **Lord** Jesus Christ.
1: 14 most of the brothers in the **Lord** have been encouraged to speak
2: 11 and every tongue confess that Jesus Christ is **Lord**, to the glory of
2: 19 I hope in the **Lord** Jesus to send Timothy to you soon, that I also
2: 24 And I am confident in the **Lord** that I myself will come soon.
2: 29 Welcome him in the **Lord** with great joy, and honor men like him,
3: 1 Finally, my brothers, rejoice in the **Lord**! It is no trouble for me to
3: 8 to the surpassing greatness of knowing Christ Jesus my **Lord**,
3: 20 And we eagerly await a Savior from there, the **Lord** Jesus Christ,
4: 1 and crown, that is how you should stand firm in the **Lord**,
4: 2 and I plead with Syntyche to agree with each other in the **Lord**.
4: 4 Rejoice in the **Lord** always. I will say it again: Rejoice!
4: 5 Let your gentleness be evident to all. The **Lord** is near.
4: 10 I rejoice greatly in the **Lord** that at last you have renewed your
4: 23 The grace *of* the **Lord** Jesus Christ be with your spirit. Amen.
Col 1: 3 the Father *of* our **Lord** Jesus Christ, when we pray for you,
1: 10 we pray this in order that you may live a life worthy of the **Lord**
2: 6 So then, just as you received Christ Jesus as **Lord**, continue to live
3: 13 may have against one another. Forgive as the **Lord** forgave you.
3: 17 whether in word or deed, do it all in the name *of* the **Lord** Jesus,
3: 18 Wives, submit to your husbands, as is fitting in the **Lord**.
3: 20 obey your parents in everything, for this pleases the **Lord**.
3: 22 Slaves, obey your earthly **masters** in everything; and do it,
3: 22 their favor, but with sincerity of heart and reverence for the **Lord**.
3: 23 at it with all your heart, as working *for* the **Lord**, not for men,
3: 24 since you know that you will receive an inheritance from the **Lord**
3: 24 from the Lord as a reward. It is the **Lord** Christ you are serving.
4: 1 **Masters**, provide your slaves with what is right and fair,
4: 1 because you know that you also have a **Master** in heaven.
4: 7 is a dear brother, a faithful minister and fellow servant in the **Lord**.
4: 17 to it that you complete the work you have received in the **Lord**."
1Th 1: 1 of the Thessalonians in God the Father and the **Lord** Jesus Christ:
1: 3 and your endurance inspired by hope *in* our **Lord** Jesus Christ.
1: 6 You became imitators of us and *of* the **Lord**; in spite of severe
1: 8 The **Lord's** message rang out from you not only in Macedonia
2: 15 who killed the **Lord** Jesus and the prophets and also drove us out.
2: 19 or the crown in which we will glory in the presence *of* our **Lord**
3: 8 For now we really live, since you are standing firm in the **Lord**.
3: 11 and our **Lord** Jesus clear the way for us to come to you.
3: 12 May the **Lord** make your love increase and overflow for each
3: 13 and Father when our **Lord** Jesus comes with all his holy ones.
4: 1 and urge you in the **Lord** Jesus to do this more and more.
4: 2 what instructions we gave you by the authority of the **Lord** Jesus.
4: 6 The **Lord** will punish men for all such sins, as we have already
4: 15 According to the **Lord's** *own* word, we tell you that we who are
4: 15 that we who are still alive, who are left till the coming *of* the **Lord**,
4: 16 For the **Lord** himself will come down from heaven, with a loud
4: 17 up together with them in the clouds to meet the **Lord** in the air.
4: 17 meet the Lord in the air. And so we will be with the **Lord** forever.
5: 2 for you know very well that the day *of* the **Lord** will come like a

5: 9 but to receive salvation through our **Lord** Jesus Christ.
5: 12 among you, who are over you in the **Lord** and who admonish you.
5: 23 and body be kept blameless at the coming *of* our **Lord** Jesus
5: 27 I charge you before the **Lord** to have this letter read to all the
5: 28 The grace *of* our **Lord** Jesus Christ be with you.
2Th 1: 1 of the Thessalonians in God our Father and the **Lord** Jesus Christ:
1: 2 and peace to you from God the Father and the **Lord** Jesus Christ.
1: 7 This will happen when the **Lord** Jesus is revealed from heaven in
1: 8 do not know God and do not obey the gospel *of* our **Lord** Jesus.
1: 9 and shut out from the presence *of* the **Lord** and from the majesty
1: 12 so that the name *of* our **Lord** Jesus may be glorified in you,
1: 12 according to the grace of our God and the **Lord** Jesus Christ.
2: 1 Concerning the coming *of* our **Lord** Jesus Christ and our being
2: 2 come from us, saying that the day *of* the **Lord** has already come.
2: 8 whom the **Lord** Jesus will overthrow with the breath of his mouth
2: 13 we ought always to thank God for you, brothers loved by the **Lord**,
2: 14 that you might share in the glory *of* our **Lord** Jesus Christ.
2: 16 May our **Lord** Jesus Christ himself and God our Father, who loved
3: 1 pray for us that the message *of* the **Lord** may spread rapidly
3: 3 But the **Lord** is faithful, and he will strengthen and protect you
3: 4 We have confidence in the **Lord** that you are doing and will
3: 5 May the **Lord** direct your hearts into God's love and Christ's
3: 6 In the name *of* the **Lord** Jesus Christ, we command you, brothers,
3: 12 we command and urge in the **Lord** Jesus Christ to settle down
3: 16 Now may the **Lord** of peace himself give you peace at all times
3: 16 peace at all times and in every way. The **Lord** be with all of you.
3: 18 The grace *of* our **Lord** Jesus Christ be with you all.
1Ti 1: 2 and peace from God the Father and Christ Jesus our **Lord**.
1: 12 I thank Christ Jesus our **Lord**, who has given me strength,
1: 14 The grace *of* our **Lord** was poured out on me abundantly,
6: 3 and does not agree to the sound instruction *of* our **Lord** Jesus
6: 14 without spot or blame until the appearing *of* our **Lord** Jesus Christ,
6: 15 the blessed and only Ruler, the King of kings and **Lord** of lords,
2Ti 1: 2 and peace from God the Father and Christ Jesus our **Lord**.
1: 8 So do not be ashamed to testify *about* our **Lord**, or ashamed of me
1: 16 May the **Lord** show mercy to the household of Onesiphorus,
1: 18 May the **Lord** grant that he will find mercy from the Lord on that
1: 18 May the Lord grant that he will find mercy from the **Lord** on that
2: 7 what I am saying, for the **Lord** will give you insight into all this.
2: 19 "The **Lord** knows those who are his," and, "Everyone who
2: 19 "Everyone who confesses the name *of* the **Lord** must turn away
2: 22 along with those who call on the **Lord** out of a pure heart.
2: 24 And the **Lord's** servant must not quarrel; instead, he must be kind
3: 11 persecutions I endured. Yet the **Lord** rescued me from all of them.
4: 8 which the **Lord**, the righteous Judge, will award to me on that
4: 14 great deal of harm. The **Lord** will repay him for what he has done.
4: 17 But the **Lord** stood at my side and gave me strength, so that
4: 18 The **Lord** will rescue me from every evil attack and will bring me
4: 22 The **Lord** be with your spirit. Grace be with you.
Phm 1: 3 and peace from God our Father and the **Lord** Jesus Christ.
1: 5 because I hear about your faith in the **Lord** Jesus and your love for
1: 16 but even dearer to you, both as a man and as a brother in the **Lord**.
1: 20 brother, that I may have some benefit from you in the **Lord**;
1: 25 The grace *of* the **Lord** Jesus Christ be with your spirit.
Heb 1: 10 He also says, "In the beginning, O **Lord**, you laid the foundations
2: 3 This salvation, which was first announced by the **Lord**,
7: 14 For it is clear that our **Lord** descended from Judah, and in regard
7: 21 "The **Lord** has sworn and will not change his mind: 'You are a
8: 2 the sanctuary, the true tabernacle set up by the **Lord**, not by man.
8: 8 "The time is coming, declares the **Lord**, when I will make a new
8: 9 to my covenant, and I turned away from them, declares the **Lord**.
8: 10 make with the house of Israel after that time, declares the **Lord**.
8: 11 or a man his brother, saying, 'Know the **Lord**,' because they will
10: 16 the covenant I will make with them after that time, says the **Lord**.
10: 30 avenge; I will repay," and again, "The **Lord** will judge his people."
12: 5 "My son, do not make light of the **Lord's** discipline, and do not
12: 6 because the **Lord** disciplines those he loves, and he punishes
12: 14 and to be holy; without holiness no one will see the **Lord**.
13: 6 So we say with confidence, "The **Lord** is my helper; I will not be
13: 20 the eternal covenant brought back from the dead our **Lord** Jesus,
Jas 1: 1 James, a servant of God and *of* the **Lord** Jesus Christ,
1: 7 That man should not think he will receive anything from the **Lord**;
2: 1 My brothers, as believers *in* our glorious **Lord** Jesus Christ,
3: 9 With the tongue we praise our **Lord** and Father, and with it we
4: 10 Humble yourselves before the **Lord**, and he will lift you up.
4: 15 to say, "If it is the **Lord's** will, we will live and do this or that."

5: 4 The cries of the harvesters have reached the ears *of* the **Lord**
5: 7 Be patient, then, brothers, until the **Lord's** coming. See how the
5: 8 be patient and stand firm, because the **Lord's** coming is near.
5: 10 of suffering, take the prophets who spoke in the name *of* the **Lord**.
5: 11 and have seen what the **Lord** finally brought about.
5: 11 finally brought about. The **Lord** is full of compassion and mercy.
5: 14 to pray over him and anoint him with oil in the name *of* the **Lord**
5: 15 in faith will make the sick person well; the **Lord** will raise him up.
1Pe 1: 3 Praise be to the God and Father *of* our **Lord** Jesus Christ!
1: 25 but the word *of* the **Lord** stands forever." And this is the word that
2: 3 now that you have tasted that the **Lord** is good.
2: 13 Submit yourselves for the **Lord's** sake to every authority instituted
3: 6 like Sarah, who obeyed Abraham and called him her **master**.
3: 12 For the eyes *of* the **Lord** are on the righteous and his ears are
3: 12 their prayer, but the face *of* the **Lord** is against those who do evil."
3: 15 But in your hearts set apart Christ *as* **Lord**. Always be prepared to
2Pe 1: 2 abundance through the knowledge of God and *of* Jesus our **Lord**.
1: 8 and unproductive in your knowledge *of* our **Lord** Jesus Christ.
1: 11 will receive a rich welcome into the eternal kingdom of our **Lord**
1: 14 soon put it aside, as our **Lord** Jesus Christ has made clear to me.
1: 16 we told you about the power and coming *of* our **Lord** Jesus Christ,
2: 9 then the **Lord** knows how to rescue godly men from trials
2: 11 accusations against such beings in the presence *of* the **Lord**.
2: 20 have escaped the corruption of the world by knowing our **Lord**
3: 2 and the command *given by* our **Lord** and Savior through your
3: 8 With the **Lord** a day is like a thousand years, and a thousand years
3: 9 The **Lord** is not slow in keeping his promise, as some understand
3: 10 But the day *of* the **Lord** will come like a thief. The heavens will
3: 15 Bear in mind that our **Lord's** patience means salvation, just as our
3: 18 But grow in the grace and knowledge *of* our **Lord** and Savior Jesus
Jude 1: 4 and deny Jesus Christ our only Sovereign and **Lord**.
1: 5 I want to remind you that the **Lord** delivered his people out of
1: 9 accusation against him, but said, "The **Lord** rebuke you!"
1: 14 the **Lord** is coming with thousands upon thousands of his holy
1: 17 remember what the apostles *of* our **Lord** Jesus Christ foretold.
1: 21 for the mercy *of* our **Lord** Jesus Christ to bring you to eternal life.
1: 25 majesty, power and authority, through Jesus Christ our **Lord**,
Rev 1: 8 and the Omega," says the **Lord** God, "who is, and who was,
4: 8 "Holy, holy, holy is the **Lord** God Almighty, who was, and is,
4: 11 our **Lord** and God, to receive glory and honor and power,
7: 14 I answered, "**Sir**, you know." And he said, "These are they who
11: 4 and the two lampstands that stand before the **Lord** of the earth.
11: 8 called Sodom and Egypt, where also their **Lord** was crucified.
11: 15 "The kingdom of the world has become the kingdom of our **Lord**
11: 17 thanks to you, **Lord** God Almighty, the One who is and who was,
14: 13 Blessed are the dead who die in the **Lord** from now on." "Yes,"
15: 3 "Great and marvelous are your deeds, **Lord** God Almighty.
15: 4 Who will not fear *you*, O **Lord**, and bring glory to your name?
16: 7 "Yes, **Lord** God Almighty, true and just are your judgments."
17: 14 overcome them because he is **Lord** of lords and King of kings—
17: 14 overcome them because he is Lord *of* **lords** and King of kings—
18: 8 be consumed by fire, for mighty is the **Lord** God who judges her.
19: 6 shouting: "Hallelujah! For our **Lord** God Almighty reigns.
19: 16 this name written: KING OF KINGS AND **LORD** OF LORDS.
19: 16 this name written: KING OF KINGS AND LORD *OF* **LORDS**.
21: 22 because the **Lord** God Almighty and the Lamb are its temple.
22: 5 or the light of the sun, for the **Lord** God will give them light.
22: 6 The **Lord**, the God of the spirits of the prophets, sent his angel to
22: 20 things says, "Yes, I am coming soon." Amen. Come, **Lord** Jesus.
22: 21 The grace *of* the **Lord** Jesus be with God's people. Amen.

3262 κυριότης, *kyriotēs* [4] [√ *3261*]

authority [2], dominion [1], powers [1]

Eph 1: 21 far above all rule and authority, power and **dominion**, and every
Col 1: 16 and invisible, whether thrones or **powers** or rulers or authorities;
2Pe 2: 10 the corrupt desire of the sinful nature and despise **authority**.
Jude 1: 8 their own bodies, reject **authority** and slander celestial beings.

3263 κυρόω, *kyroō* [2] [→ *218, 4623; cf. 3261*]

duly established [1], reaffirm [1]

2Co 2: 8 I urge you, therefore, *to* **reaffirm** your love for him.
Gal 3: 15 or add to a human covenant *that has been* **duly established**,

3264 κύων, *kyōn* [5] [→ *3249*]

dogs [4], dog [1]

Mt 7: 6 "Do not give **dogs** what is sacred; do not throw your pearls to pigs.
Lk 16: 21 the rich man's table. Even the **dogs** came and licked his sores.
Php 3: 2 Watch out for those **dogs**, those men who do evil, those mutilators
2Pe 2: 22 "A **dog** returns to its vomit," and, "A sow that is washed goes back
Rev 22: 15 Outside are the **dogs**, those who practice magic arts, the sexually

3265 κῶλον, *kōlon* [1]

bodies [1]

Heb 3: 17 Was it not with those who sinned, whose **bodies** fell in the desert?

3266 κωλύω, *kōlyō* [23] [→ *219, 1361, 3134, 3136, 3143; cf. 1551*]

hinder [3], stop [3], forbid [2], keep from [2], kept from [2],
prevented from [2], hindered [1], oppose [1], opposes [1], permit
[+*3594*] [1], restrained [1], shouldn't [1], stop from taking [1],
stops [1], told to stop [1]

Mt 19: 14 "Let the little children come to me, and *do* not **hinder** them,
Mk 9: 38 a man driving out demons in your name and *we* told him **to stop**,
9: 39 "*Do* not **stop** him," Jesus said. "No one who does a miracle in my
10: 14 "Let the little children come to me, and *do* not **hinder** them,
Lk 6: 29 takes your cloak, *do* not **stop** him **from taking** your tunic.
9: 49 a man driving out demons in your name and *we tried to* **stop** him,
9: 50 "*Do* not **stop** him," Jesus said, "for whoever is not against you is
11: 52 have not entered, and *you have* **hindered** those who were entering."
18: 16 "Let the little children come to me, and *do* not **hinder** them,
23: 2 *He* **opposes** payment of taxes to Caesar and claims to be Christ,
Ac 8: 36 eunuch said, "Look, here is water. Why **shouldn't** I be baptized?"
10: 47 "Can anyone **keep** these people **from** being baptized with water?
11: 17 the Lord Jesus Christ, who was I to think that I could **oppose** God?"
16: 6 *having been* **kept** by the Holy Spirit **from** preaching the word in
24: 23 and **permit** [+*3594*] his friends to take care of his needs.
27: 43 to spare Paul's life and **kept** them **from** *carrying out* their plan.
Ro 1: 13 come to you (but *have been* **prevented from** doing so until now)
1Co 14: 39 be eager to prophesy, and *do* not **forbid** speaking in tongues.
1Th 2: 16 *in their* effort to **keep** us **from** speaking to the Gentiles so that
1Ti 4: 3 *They* **forbid** people to marry and order them to abstain from
Heb 7: 23 since death **prevented** them **from** continuing in office;
2Pe 2: 16 spoke with a man's voice and **restrained** the prophet's madness.
3Jn 1: 10 *He* also **stops** those who want to do so and puts them out of the

3267 κώμη, *kōmē* [27] [→ *3268, 3269*]

village [16], villages [8], from village to village [+*2848*+*3836*] [1],
from village to village [+*3241*] [1], town [1]

Mt 9: 35 Jesus went through all the towns and **villages**, teaching in their
10: 11 "Whatever town or **village** you enter, search for some worthy
14: 15 so they can go to the **villages** and buy themselves some food."
21: 2 saying to them, "Go to the **village** ahead of you, and at once you
Mk 6: 6 Then Jesus went around teaching **from village** [+*3241*] **to village**.
6: 36 and **villages** and buy themselves something to eat."
6: 56 And wherever he went—into **villages**, towns or countryside—
8: 23 He took the blind man by the hand and led him outside the **village**.
8: 26 Jesus sent him home, saying, "Don't go into the **village**."
8: 27 and his disciples went to the **villages** around Caesarea Philippi.
11: 2 saying to them, "Go to the **village** ahead of you, and just as you
Lk 5: 17 who had come from every **village** of Galilee and from Judea
8: 1 Jesus traveled about from one town and **village** to another,
9: 6 So they set out and went **from village** [+*2848*+*3836*] **to village**,
9: 12 so they can go to the surrounding **villages** and countryside
9: 52 who went into a Samaritan **village** to get things ready for him;
9: 56 and they went to another **village**.
10: 38 he came to a **village** where a woman named Martha opened her
13: 22 Then Jesus went through the towns and **villages**, teaching as he
17: 12 As he was going into a **village**, ten men who had leprosy met him.
19: 30 "Go to the **village** ahead of you, and as you enter it, you will find a
24: 13 Now that same day two of them were going to a **village** called
24: 28 As they approached the **village** to which they were going,
Jn 7: 42 David's family and from Bethlehem, the **town** where David lived?"
11: 1 He was from Bethany, the **village** of Mary and her sister Martha.

11:30 Now Jesus had not yet entered the **village**, but was still at the place
Ac   8:25 to Jerusalem, preaching the gospel *in* many Samaritan **villages**.

3268 κωμόπολις, kōmopolis [1] [√ 3267 + 4484]

villages [1]

Mk   1:38 to the nearby **villages**—so I can preach there also.

3269 κῶμος, kōmos [3] [√ 3267]

orgies [3]

Ro   13:13 behave decently, as in the daytime, not *in* **orgies** and drunkenness,
Gal   5:21 and envy; drunkenness, **orgies**, and the like. I warn you, as I did
1Pe   4: 3 lust, drunkenness, **orgies**, carousing and detestable idolatry.

3270 κώνωψ, kōnōps [1]

gnat [1]

Mt   23:24 You blind guides! You strain out a **gnat** but swallow a camel.

3271 Κῶς, Kōs [1]

Cos [1]

Ac   21: 1 away from them, we put out to sea and sailed straight to **Cos**.

3272 Κωσάμ, Kōsam [1]

Cosam [1]

Lk   3:28 the son of Melki, the son of Addi, the son *of* **Cosam**, the son of

3273 κωφός, kōphos [14] [√ 3164]

deaf [4], mute [4], man who had been mute [2], could not talk [1],
he^s [+3836] [1], man who was deaf [1], unable to speak [1]

Mt   9:32 was demon-possessed and **could not talk** was brought to Jesus.
    9:33 the demon was driven out, the **man who had been mute** spoke.
    11: 5 who have leprosy are cured, the **deaf** hear, the dead are raised,
    12:22 brought him a demon-possessed man who was blind and **mute**,
    12:22 and Jesus healed him, so that **he**^s [+3836] could both talk and see.
    15:30 the lame, the blind, the crippled, the **mute** and many others,
    15:31 The people were amazed when they saw the **mute** speaking,
Mk   7:32 There some people brought to him a **man who was deaf** and could
    7:37 they said. "He even makes the **deaf** hear and the mute speak."
    9:25 "*You* **deaf** and mute spirit," he said, "I command you, come out of
Lk   1:22 for he kept making signs to them but remained **unable to speak**.
    7:22 who have leprosy are cured, the **deaf** hear, the dead are raised,
    11:14 Jesus was driving out a demon that was **mute**. When the demon
    11:14 When the demon left, the **man who had been mute** spoke,

Λ, L

3274 λ, l   Not used in UBS/NIV

3275 λαγχάνω, lanchanō [4]

chosen by lot [1], decide by lot [1], received [1], shared
[+3102+3836] [1]

Lk   1: 9 he was **chosen by lot**, according to the custom of the priesthood,
Jn   19:24 they said to one another. "*Let's* **decide by lot** who will get it."
Ac   1:17 was one of our number and **shared** [+3102+3836] in this ministry."
2Pe   1: 1 and Savior Jesus Christ *have* **received** a faith as precious as ours:

3276 Λάζαρος, Lazaros [15]

Lazarus [15]

Lk   16:20 At his gate was laid a beggar named **Lazarus**, covered with sores
    16:23 looked up and saw Abraham far away, with **Lazarus** by his side.
    16:24 pity on me and send **Lazarus** to dip the tip of his finger in water

    16:25 while **Lazarus** received bad things, but now he is comforted here
Jn   11: 1 Now a man named **Lazarus** was sick. He was from Bethany,
    11: 2 This Mary, whose brother **Lazarus** now lay sick, was the same one
    11: 5 Jesus loved Martha and her sister and **Lazarus**.
    11:11 he went on to tell them, "Our friend **Lazarus** has fallen asleep;
    11:14 So then he told them plainly, "**Lazarus** is dead,
    11:43 he had said this, Jesus called in a loud voice, "**Lazarus**, come out!"
    12: 1 the Passover, Jesus arrived at Bethany, where **Lazarus** lived,
    12: 2 while **Lazarus** was among those reclining at the table with him.
    12: 9 and came, not only because of him but also to see **Lazarus**,
    12:10 So the chief priests made plans to kill **Lazarus** as well,
    12:17 Now the crowd that was with him when he called **Lazarus** from

3277 λάθρᾳ, lathra [4] [√ 3291]

quietly [2], aside [1], secretly [1]

Mt   1:19 her to public disgrace, he had in mind to divorce her **quietly**.
    2: 7 Then Herod called the Magi **secretly** and found out from them the
Jn   11:28 she had said this, she went back and called her sister Mary **aside**.
Ac   16:37 us into prison. And now do they want to get rid of us **quietly**? No!

3278 λαῖλαψ, lailaps [3]

squall [+449] [2], storm [1]

Mk   4:37 A furious **squall** [+449] came up, and the waves broke over the
Lk   8:23 A **squall** [+449] came down on the lake, so that the boat was being
2Pe   2:17 These men are springs without water and mists driven by a **storm**.

3279 λακάω, lakaō [1] [√ cf. 3299]

burst [1]

Ac   1:18 fell headlong, his body **burst** open and all his intestines spilled out.

3280 λακτίζω, laktizō [1]

kick [1]

Ac   26:14 do you persecute me? It is hard for you *to* **kick** against the goads.'

3281 λαλέω, laleō [296] [→ 227, 228, 443, 654, 1362,
1718, 2895, 2896, 2897, 3282, 3651, 3652, 4493, 4688, 5196]

λαλεῖν γλῶσσαι (to speak in tongues) [17] Mk 16:17; Ac
2:4,11; 10:46; 19:6; 1Co 12:30; 13:1; 14:2,4,5,6,13,18,23,27,39

speak [62], speaking [38], spoke [33], said [26], speaks [18],
spoken [17], say [16], told [16], saying [6], talk [6], tell [5],
untranslated [4], talked [4], talking [4], telling [3], preached [2],
proclaimed [2], says [2], teach [2], address [1], announced
[+3284] [1], boast about [+5665] [1], bring a message [+4839]
[1], bring [1], claiming [1], declare [1], declaring [1], distort the
truth [+1406] [1], God^s [+3836] [1], he^s [+3836] [1], help
speaking about [+3590] [1], insisted [1], lies [+3836+6022] [1],
message [1], preaching [1], presenting [1], proclaim [1],
promised [1], say about [1], speak about [1], speaker [1], speech
[1], spoke about [1], talking about [1], tells [1], use language [1],
utter [1], utters [1], whispered [1]

Mt   9:18 *While* he *was* **saying** this, a ruler came and knelt before him
    9:33 the demon was driven out, the man who had been mute **spoke**.
    10:19 they arrest you, do not worry about what *to* **say** or how to say it.
    10:19 or how to say it. At that time you will be given what *to* **say**,
    10:20 for it will not be you **speaking**, but the Spirit of your Father
    10:20 you speaking, but the Spirit of your Father **speaking** through you.
    12:22 and mute, and Jesus healed him, so that he *could* both **talk** and see.
    12:34 You brood of vipers, how can you who are evil **say** anything good?
    12:34 For out of the overflow of the heart the mouth **speaks**.
    12:36 on the day of judgment for every careless word *they have* **spoken**.
    12:46 *While* Jesus *was* still **talking** to the crowd, his mother and brothers
    12:46 his mother and brothers stood outside, wanting *to* **speak** to him.
    12:47 and brothers are standing outside, wanting *to* **speak** to you."
    13: 3 Then *he* **told** them many things in parables, saying: "A farmer went
    13:10 to him and asked, "Why *do you* **speak** to the people in parables?"
    13:13 This is why *I* **speak** to them in parables: "Though seeing, they do
    13:33 *He* **told** them still another parable: "The kingdom of heaven is like

13:34 Jesus **spoke** all these things to the crowd in parables; he did not say
13:34 he did not **say** anything to them without using a parable.
14:27 But Jesus immediately **said** to them: "Take courage! It is I.
15:31 The people were amazed when they saw the mute **speaking**,
17: 5 *While* he *was* still **speaking**, a bright cloud enveloped them,
23: 1 Then Jesus **said** to the crowds and to his disciples:
26:13 the world, what she has done *will* also *be* **told**, in memory of her."
26:47 *While* he *was* still **speaking**, Judas, one of the Twelve, arrived.
28:18 Then Jesus came to them and **said**, "All authority in heaven

Mk 1:34 but he would not let the demons **speak** because they knew who he
2: 2 not even outside the door, and *he* **preached** the word to them.
2: 7 "Why *does* this fellow **talk** like that? He's blaspheming! Who can
4:33 With many similar parables Jesus **spoke** the word to them,
4:34 He did not **say** *anything* to them without using a parable.
5:35 *While* Jesus *was* still **speaking**, some men came from the house of
5:36 Ignoring what they **said**, Jesus told the synagogue ruler, "Don't be
6:50 Immediately he **spoke** to them and said, "Take courage! It is I.
7:35 his tongue was loosened and *he began to* **speak** plainly.
7:37 they said. "He even makes the deaf hear and the mute **speak**."
8:32 *He* **spoke** plainly **about** this, and Peter took him aside and began
11:23 not doubt in his heart but believes that what *he* **says** will happen,
12: 1 He then began to **speak** to them in parables: "A man planted a
13:11 and brought to trial, do not worry beforehand about what *to* **say**.
13:11 Just **say** whatever is given you at the time, for it is not you
13:11 you at the time, for it is not you **speaking**, but the Holy Spirit.
14: 9 the world, what she has done *will* also *be* **told**, in memory of her."
14:31 But Peter **insisted** emphatically, "Even if I have to die with you,
14:43 Just as he *was* **speaking**, Judas, one of the Twelve, appeared.
16:17 name they will drive out demons; *they* will **speak** in new tongues;
16:19 After the Lord Jesus *had* **spoken** to them, he was taken up into

Lk 1:19 and I have been sent *to* **speak** to you and to tell you this good
1:20 you will be silent and not able *to* **speak** until the day this happens,
1:22 When he came out, he could not **speak** to them. They realized he
1:45 Blessed is she who has believed that what the Lord *has* **said** to her
1:55 and his descendants forever, even as *he* **said** to our fathers."
1:64 and his tongue was loosed, and *he began to* **speak**, praising God.
1:70 (as *he* **said** through his holy prophets of long ago),
2:15 left them and gone into heaven, the shepherds **said** to one another,
2:17 they spread the word *concerning* what *had been* **told** them about
2:18 and all who heard it were amazed at what the shepherds **said** to
2:20 they had heard and seen, which were just as they *had been* **told**.
2:33 child's father and mother marveled at what *was* **said** about him.
2:38 and **spoke** about the child to all who were looking forward to the
2:50 But they did not understand what *he was* **saying** to them.
4:41 But he rebuked them and would not allow them *to* **speak**,
5: 4 When he had finished **speaking**, he said to Simon, "Put out into
5:21 to themselves, "Who is this fellow who **speaks** blasphemy?
6:45 in his heart. For out of the overflow of his heart his mouth **speaks**.
7:15 The dead man sat up and began *to* **talk**, and Jesus gave him back to
8:49 *While* Jesus *was* still **speaking**, someone came from the house of
9:11 *He* welcomed them and **spoke** to them about the kingdom of God,
11:14 When the demon left, the man who had been mute **spoke**,
11:37 When Jesus had finished **speaking**, a Pharisee invited him to eat
12: 3 and what *you have* **whispered** in the ear in the inner rooms will be
22:47 *While* he *was* still **speaking** a crowd came up, and the man who
22:60 you're talking about!" Just as he *was* **speaking**, the rooster crowed.
24: 6 Remember how *he* **told** you, while he was still with you in Galilee:
24:25 how slow of heart to believe all that the prophets *have* **spoken**!
24:32 "Were not our hearts burning within us while *he* **talked** with us on
24:36 *While* they *were still* **talking** about this, Jesus himself stood
24:44 He said to them, "This is what *I* **told** you while I was still with you:

Jn 1:37 When the two disciples heard him **say** this, they followed Jesus.
3:11 I tell you the truth, *we* **speak** of what we know, and we testify to
3:31 the earth belongs to the earth, and **speaks** as one from the earth.
3:34 For the one whom God has sent **speaks** the words of God,
4:26 Then Jesus declared, "I who **speak** to you am he."
4:27 and were surprised to find *him* **talking** with a woman.
4:27 asked, "What do you want?" or "Why *are you* **talking** with her?"
6:63 The words I *have* **spoken** to you are spirit and they are life.
7:13 But no one *would* **say** *anything* publicly about him for fear of the
7:17 my teaching comes from God or whether I **speak** on my own.
7:18 He who **speaks** on his own does so to gain honor for himself,
7:26 Here he is, **speaking** publicly, and they are not saying a word to
7:46 "No one ever **spoke** the way this man does," the guards declared.
8:12 When Jesus **spoke** again to the people, he said, "I am the light of
8:20 *He* **spoke** these words while teaching in the temple area near the

8:25 "Just what *I have been* **claiming** all along," Jesus replied.
8:26 "I have much *to* **say** in judgment of you. But he who sent me is
8:26 me is reliable, and what I have heard from him *I* **tell** the world."
8:28 nothing on my own but **speak** just what the Father has taught me.
8:30 *Even as* he **spoke**, many put their faith in him.
8:38 *I am* **telling** you what I have seen in the Father's presence,
8:40 to kill me, a man who *has* **told** you the truth that I heard from God.
8:44 When *he* **lies** [+*3836*+*6022*], he speaks his native language,
8:44 When he lies, *he* **speaks** his native language, for he is a liar
9:21 we don't know. Ask him. He is of age; he *will* **speak** for himself."
9:29 We know that God **spoke** to Moses, but as for this fellow,
9:37 "You have now seen him; in fact, he is the one **speaking** with you."
10: 6 of speech, but they did not understand what he was **telling** them.
12:29 it said it had thundered; others said an angel *had* **spoken** to him.
12:36 *When he had finished* **speaking**, Jesus left and hid himself from
12:41 Isaiah said this because he saw Jesus' glory and **spoke** about him.
12:48 that very word which *I* **spoke** will condemn him at the last day.
12:49 For I *did* not **speak** of my own accord, but the Father who sent me
12:49 Father who sent me commanded me what to say and how *to* **say** it.
12:50 So whatever I **say** is just what the Father has told me to say."
12:50 So whatever I say is just what the Father has told me *to* **say**."
14:10 The words I say to you [**RPG**] are not just my own. Rather,
14:25 "All this *I have* **spoken** while still with you.
14:30 *I will* not **speak** with you much longer, for the prince of this world
15: 3 You are already clean because of the word *I have* **spoken** to you.
15:11 *I have* **told** you this so that my joy may be in you and that your joy
15:22 If I had not come and **spoken** to them, they would not be guilty of
16: 1 "All this *I have* **told** you so that you will not go astray.
16: 4 *I have* **told** you this, so that when the time comes you will
16: 6 Because *I have* **said** these things, you are filled with grief.
16:13 *He will* not **speak** on his own; he will speak only what he hears,
16:13 *he will* **speak** only what he hears, and he will tell you what is yet
16:18 mean by 'a little while'? We don't understand what *he is* **saying**."
16:25 "Though *I have been* **speaking** figuratively, a time is coming when
16:25 a time is coming when *I will* no longer **use** this kind of **language**
16:29 "Now *you are* **speaking** clearly and without figures of speech.
16:33 "*I have* **told** you these things, so that in me you may have peace.
17: 1 *After* Jesus **said** this, he looked toward heaven and prayed:
17:13 to you now, but *I* **say** these things while I am still in the world,
18:20 "*I have* **spoken** openly to the world," Jesus replied. "I always
18:20 where all the Jews come together. *I* **said** nothing in secret.
18:21 Ask those who heard me. [**RPG**] Surely they know what I said."
18:23 "If *I* **said** something wrong," Jesus replied, "testify as to what is
19:10 "*Do you* refuse *to* **speak** to me?" Pilate said. "Don't you realize I

Ac 2: 4 and began *to* **speak** in other tongues as the Spirit enabled them.
2: 6 because each one heard them **speaking** in his own language.
2: 7 they asked: "Are not all these men who *are* **speaking** Galileans?
2:11 we hear them **declaring** the wonders of God in our own tongues!"
2:31 Seeing what was ahead, *he* **spoke** of the resurrection of the Christ,
3:21 as *he* **promised** long ago through his holy prophets.
3:22 your own people; you must listen to everything *he* **tells** you.
3:24 Samuel on, as many as *have* **spoken**, have foretold these days.
4: 1 came up to Peter and John *while* they *were* **speaking** to the people.
4:17 we must warn these men *to* **speak** no longer to anyone in this
4:20 For we cannot **help speaking** [+*3590*] **about** what we have seen
4:29 and enable your servants *to* **speak** your word with great boldness.
4:31 all filled with the Holy Spirit and **spoke** the word of God boldly.
5:20 he said, "and **tell** the people the full message of this new life."
5:40 Then they ordered them not *to* **speak** in the name of Jesus,
6:10 not stand up against his wisdom or the Spirit by whom *he* **spoke**.
6:11 "We have heard Stephen **speak** words of blasphemy against Moses
6:13 "This fellow never stops **speaking** against this holy place
7: 6 God **spoke** to him in this way: 'Your descendants will be strangers
7:38 with the angel who **spoke** to him on Mount Sinai, and with our
7:44 It had been made as God's [+*3836*] directed Moses, according to
8:25 When *they had* testified and **proclaimed** the word of the Lord,
8:26 Now an angel of the Lord **said** to Philip, "Go south to the road—
9: 6 and go into the city, and you *will be* **told** what you must do."
9:27 journey had seen the Lord and that the Lord *had* **spoken** to him,
9:29 He **talked** and debated with the Grecian Jews,
10: 7 When the angel who **spoke** to him had gone, Cornelius called two
10:44 *While* Peter *was* still **speaking** these words, the Holy Spirit came
10:46 For they heard them **speaking** in tongues and praising God.
11:14 He *will* **bring** you **a message** [+*4839*] through which you
11:15 "As I began *to* **speak**, the Holy Spirit came on them as he had come
11:19 Cyprus and Antioch, **telling** the message only to Jews.

11:20 and Cyrene, went to Antioch and *began to* **speak** to Greeks also,
13:42 the people invited them *to* **speak** *further* **about** these things on the
13:45 with jealousy and talked abusively against what Paul *was* **saying**.
13:46 "We had to **speak** the word of God to you first. Since you reject it
14: 1 There they **spoke** so effectively that a great number of Jews
14: 9 He listened to Paul *as he was* **speaking**. Paul looked directly at
14:25 and *when they had* **preached** the word in Perga, they went down
16: 6 having been kept by the Holy Spirit from **preaching** the word in
16:13 *We* sat down and *began to* **speak** to the women who had gathered
16:14 of God. The Lord opened her heart to respond to Paul's **message**.
16:32 Then *they* **spoke** the word of the Lord to him and to all the others
17:19 "May we know what this new teaching is that you *are* **presenting**?
18: 9 in a vision: "Do not be afraid; *keep on* **speaking**, do not be silent.
18:25 and he **spoke** with great fervor and taught about Jesus accurately,
19: 6 Spirit came on them, and *they* **spoke** in tongues and prophesied.
20:30 and **distort the truth** [+*1406*] in order to draw away disciples after
21:39 a citizen of no ordinary city. Please let me **speak** to the people."
22: 9 but they did not understand the voice *of* him *who was* **speaking** to
22:10 There you *will be* **told** all that you have been assigned to do.'
23: 9 they said. "What if a spirit or an angel *has* **spoken** to him?"
23:18 bring this young man to you because he has something *to* **tell** you."
26:22 nothing beyond what the prophets and Moses **said** would happen—
26:26 king is familiar with these things, and *I can* **speak** freely to him.
26:31 They left the room, and while talking with one another, *they* **said**,
27:25 for I have faith in God that it will happen just as *he* **told** me.
28:21 have come from there has reported or **said** anything bad about you.
28:25 "The Holy Spirit **spoke** the truth to your forefathers when he said
Ro 3:19 *it* **says** to those who are under the law, so that every mouth may be
    7: 1 brothers—for *I am* **speaking** to men who know the law—
   15:18 I will not venture *to* **speak** of anything except what Christ has
1Co 2: 6 *We do,* however, **speak** a message of wisdom among the mature,
    2: 7 No, *we* **speak** of God's secret wisdom, a wisdom that has been
    2:13 This is what *we* **speak**, not in words taught us by human wisdom
    3: 1 Brothers, I could not **address** you as spiritual but as worldly—
    9: 8 *Do I* **say** this merely from a human point of view? Doesn't the Law
   12: 3 Therefore I tell you that no one *who is* **speaking** by the Spirit of
   12:30 all have gifts of healing? Do all **speak** in tongues? Do all interpret?
   13: 1 If *I* **speak** in the tongues of men and of angels, but have not love,
   13:11 When I was a child, *I* **talked** like a child, I thought like a child,
   14: 2 For anyone *who* **speaks** in a tongue does not speak to men
   14: 2 For anyone who speaks in a tongue *does* not **speak** to men
   14: 2 no one understands him; *he* **utters** mysteries with his spirit.
   14: 3 But everyone who prophesies **speaks** to men for their
   14: 4 He *who* **speaks** in a tongue edifies himself, but he who prophesies
   14: 5 I would like every one of you *to* **speak** in tongues, but I would
   14: 5 He who prophesies is greater than one *who* **speaks** in tongues,
   14: 6 Now, brothers, if I come to you and **speak** in tongues, what good
   14: 6 unless *I* **bring** you some revelation or knowledge or prophecy
   14: 9 with your tongue, how will anyone know what *you are* **saying**?
   14: 9 know what you are saying? You will just be **speaking** into the air.
   14:11 I am a foreigner *to* the **speaker**, and he is a foreigner to me.
   14:11 a foreigner to the speaker, and he^s [+*3836*] is a foreigner to me.
   14:13 For this reason anyone *who* **speaks** in a tongue should pray that he
   14:18 I thank God that *I* **speak** in tongues more than all of you.
   14:19 But in the church I would rather **speak** five intelligible words to
   14:21 and through the lips of foreigners *I will* **speak** to this people,
   14:23 the whole church comes together and everyone **speaks** in tongues,
   14:27 If anyone **speaks** in a tongue, two—or at the most three—
   14:28 the speaker *should* keep quiet in the church and **speak** to himself
   14:29 Two or three prophets *should* **speak**, and the others should weigh
   14:34 They are not allowed *to* **speak**, but must be in submission,
   14:35 at home; for it is disgraceful for a woman *to* **speak** in the church.
   14:39 be eager to prophesy, and do not forbid **speaking** in tongues.
   15:34 there are some who are ignorant of God—*I* **say** this to your shame.
2Co 2:17 On the contrary, in Christ *we* **speak** before God with sincerity,
    4:13 It is written: "I believed; therefore *I have* **spoken**." With that same
    4:13 With that same spirit of faith we also believe and therefore **speak**,
    7:14 But just as everything *we* **said** to you was true, so our boasting
   11:17 In this self-confident boasting **[RPG]** I am not talking as the Lord
   11:17 In this self-confident boasting *I am* not **talking** as the Lord would,
   11:23 of Christ? (*I am* out of my mind *to* **talk** like this.) I am more.
   12: 4 heard inexpressible things, things that man is not permitted *to* **tell**.
   12:19 *We have been* **speaking** in the sight of God as those in Christ;
   13: 3 since you are demanding proof that Christ *is* **speaking** through me.
Eph 4:25 of you must put off falsehood and **speak** truthfully to his neighbor,
    5:19 **Speak** to one another with psalms, hymns and spiritual songs.

6:20 in chains. Pray that I *may* **declare** it fearlessly, as I should.
Php 1:14 most of the brothers in the Lord have been encouraged *to* **speak**
Col 4: 3 *so that* we *may* **proclaim** the mystery of Christ, for which I am in
    4: 4 Pray that I may proclaim it clearly, as I should. **[RPG]**
1Th 1: 8 Therefore we do not need *to* **say** anything **about** it,
    2: 2 but with the help of our God we dared *to* **tell** you his gospel in
    2: 4 *we* **speak** as men approved by God to be entrusted with the gospel.
    2:16 in their effort to keep us from **speaking** to the Gentiles so that they
1Ti 5:13 but also gossips and busybodies, **saying** things they ought not to.
Tit 2: 1 You *must* **teach** what is in accord with sound doctrine.
    2:15 These, then, are the things *you should* **teach**. Encourage
Heb 1: 1 In the past God **spoke** to our forefathers through the prophets at
    1: 2 but in these last days *he has* **spoken** to us by his Son, whom he
    2: 2 For if the message **spoken** by angels was binding, and every
    2: 3 This salvation, which *was* first **announced** [+*3284*] by the Lord,
    2: 5 he has subjected the world to come, about which *we are* **speaking**.
    3: 5 in all God's house, testifying *to* what *would be* **said** in the *future*.
    4: 8 them rest, God would not have **spoken** later about another day.
    5: 5 But God **said** to him, "You are my Son; today I have become your
    6: 9 Even though *we* **speak** like this, dear friends, we are confident of
    7:14 and in regard to that tribe Moses **said** nothing about priests.
    9:19 *When* Moses *had* **proclaimed** every commandment of the law to
   11: 4 his offerings. And by faith *he* still **speaks**, even though he is dead.
   11:18 even though God *had* **said** to him, "It is through Isaac that your
   12:24 and to the sprinkled blood that **speaks** a better word than the blood
   12:25 See to it that you do not refuse him *who* **speaks**. If they did not
   13: 7 Remember your leaders, who **spoke** the word of God to you.
Jas 1:19 should be quick to listen, slow *to* **speak** and slow to become angry,
    2:12 **Speak** and act as those who are going to be judged by the law that
    5:10 of suffering, take the prophets who **spoke** in the name of the Lord.
1Pe 3:10 must keep his tongue from evil and his lips from deceitful **speech**.
    4:11 If anyone **speaks**, he should do it as one speaking the very words
2Pe 1:21 but men **spoke** from God as they were carried along by the Holy
    3:16 the same way in all his letters, **speaking** in them of these matters.
1Jn 4: 5 the world and therefore **speak** from the viewpoint of the world,
2Jn 1:12 Instead, I hope to visit you and **talk** *with* you face to face,
3Jn 1:14 I hope to see you soon, and *we will* **talk** face to face. Peace to you.
Jude 1:15 and of all the harsh words ungodly sinners *have* **spoken** against
    1:16 they **boast about** [+*5665*] themselves and flatter others for their
Rev 1:12 I turned around to see the voice that *was* **speaking** to me.
    4: 1 And the voice I had first heard **speaking** to me like a trumpet said,
   10: 3 When he shouted, the voices of the seven thunders **spoke**.
   10: 4 And when the seven thunders **spoke**, I was about to write;
   10: 4 "Seal up what the seven thunders *have* **said** and do not write it
   10: 8 Then the voice that I had heard from heaven **spoke** to me once
   13: 5 The beast was given a mouth *to* **utter** proud words
   13:11 He had two horns like a lamb, but *he* **spoke** like a dragon.
   13:15 so that it *could* **speak** and cause all who refused to worship the
   17: 1 of the seven angels who had the seven bowls came and **said** to me,
   21: 9 the seven bowls full of the seven last plagues came and **said** to me,
   21:15 The angel *who* **talked** with me had a measuring rod of gold to

3282 λαλιά, *lalia* [3] [√ *3281*]

accent [1], language [1], said [1]

Mt 26:73 "Surely you are one of them, for your **accent** gives you away."
Jn 4:42 to the woman, "We no longer believe just because of what you **said**;
    8:43 Why is my **language** not clear to you? Because you are unable to

3283 λαμά, *lama* Not used in UBS/NIV [→ *3316*]

3284 λαμβάνω, *lambanō* [258 / 257] [→ *377, 378, 455,*
514, 516, 655, 719, 1287, 2138, 2325, 2326, 2327, 2898, 3331,
3335, 3561, 3562, 4161, 4624, 4647, 4689, 4691, 4692, 4719,
4720, 4721, 4722, 4723, 4724, 5197, 5221, 5227, 5269, 5696]

λαμβάνω ἄρτος (take bread) [20] Mt 14:19; 15:26,36; 16:5,7;
26:26; Mk 6:41; 7:27; 8:6,14,16; 14:22; Lk 6:4; 9:16; 22:19; 24:30;
Jn 6:11; 21:13; Ac 27:35; 1Co 11:23

λαμβάνω γυναῖκα (take a wife) [5] Mk 12:19,20,21; Lk
20:28,29,31

receive [38], took [38], received [37], take [24], accept [9], taking
[9], receives [7], accepts [5], taken [4], bring [3], collect [3],

married [3], receiving [3], seized [3], *untranslated* [2], accepted [2], caught [2], gathered [2], get [2], marry [2], punished [*+3210*] [2], seizing [2], take up [2], amazed [*+1749*] [1], announced [*+3281*] [1], appointed [1], become a father [*+2856+5065*] [1], become [1], circumcised [*+4362*] [1], circumcised [*+4364*] [1], collected [1], collectors of tax [1], collects [1], commanded [*+1953*] [1], decided to [*+5206*] [1], devised a plan [*+5206*] [1], dids [1], draw [1], draws [1], edified [*+3869*] [1], encouraged [*+2511*] [1], faced [*+4278*] [1], filled with awe [*+5832*] [1], forgotten that [*+3330*] [1], gets [1], given [1], got [1], guiding [1], had [1], have [1], judge by external appearance [*+476+4725*] [1], judged [*+3210*] [1], laid plans [*+5206*] [1], made king [*+993+3836*] [1], made [1], married [*+1222*] [1], obtained [1], on authority [*+2026*] [1], picked up [1], plotted [*+5206*] [1], put on [1], reminded [*+5704*] [1], repayment [1], rewarded [*+3635*] [1], seizes [1], selected [1], show partiality [*+4725*] [1], succeeded [*+1345*] [1], take over [*+3836+5536*] [1], takes advantage of [1], takes [1], to the decision [*+5206*] [1], took up [1], tried to do [*+4278*] [1], with instructions [*+1953*] [1], wrapped around waist [*+1346*] [1]

Mt 5: 40 And if someone wants to sue you and **take** your tunic, let him have
     7: 8 For everyone who asks **receives**; he who seeks finds; and to him
     8: 17 Isaiah: "He **took up** our infirmities and carried our diseases."
    10: 8 drive out demons. Freely you have **received**, freely give.
    10: 38 and anyone *who does* not **take** his cross and follow me is not
    10: 41 a prophet because he is a prophet *will* **receive** a prophet's reward,
    10: 41 because he is a righteous man *will* **receive** a righteous man's
    12: 14 Pharisees went out and **plotted** [*+5206*] how they might kill Jesus.
    13: 20 is the man who hears the word and at once **receives** it with joy.
    13: 31 is like a mustard seed, which a man **took** and planted in his field.
    13: 33 "The kingdom of heaven is like yeast that a woman **took** and mixed
    14: 19 **Taking** the five loaves and the two fish and looking up to heaven,
    15: 26 "It is not right *to* **take** the children's bread and toss it to their dogs."
    15: 36 Then *he* **took** the seven loaves and the fish, and when he had given
    16: 5 When they went across the lake, the disciples forgot *to* **take** bread.
    16: 7 and said, "It is because *we* didn't **bring** any bread."
    16: 9 for the five thousand, and how many basketfuls *you* **gathered**?
    16: 10 for the four thousand, and how many basketfuls *you* **gathered**?
    17: 24 the **collectors of** the two-drachma **tax** came to Peter and asked,
    17: 25 "From whom *do* the kings of the earth **collect** duty and taxes—
    17: 27 **Take** it and give it to them for my tax and yours."
    19: 29 or fields for my sake *will* **receive** a hundred times as much
    20: 9 hired about the eleventh hour came and each **received** a denarius.
    20: 10 those came who were hired first, they expected *to* **receive** more.
    20: 10 to receive more. But each one of them also **received** a denarius.
    20: 11 *When they* **received** it, they began to grumble against the
    21: 22 If you believe, *you will* **receive** whatever you ask for in prayer."
    21: 34 he sent his servants to the tenants *to* **collect** his fruit.
    21: 35 "The tenants **seized** his servants; they beat one, killed another,
    21: 39 So they **took** him and threw him out of the vineyard and killed
    22: 15 went out and **laid plans** [*+5206*] to trap him in his words.
    25: 1 kingdom of heaven will be like ten virgins who **took** their lamps
    25: 3 The foolish ones **took** their lamps but did not take any oil with
    25: 3 foolish ones took their lamps but *did* not **take** any oil with them.
    25: 4 The wise, however, **took** oil in jars along with their lamps.
    25: 16 The man *who had* **received** the five talents went at once and put
    25: 18 But the man *who had* **received** the one talent went off, dug a hole
    25: 20 The man *who had* **received** the five talents brought the other five.
    25: 24 "Then the man *who had* **received** the one talent came. 'Master,'
    26: 26 they were eating, Jesus **took** bread, gave thanks and broke it,
    26: 26 and broke it, and gave it to his disciples, saying, "**Take** and eat;
    26: 27 Then he **took** the cup, gave thanks and offered it to them, saying,
    26: 52 said to him, "for all who **draw** the sword will die by the sword."
    27: 1 and the elders of the people came **to the decision** [*+5206*] to put
    27: 6 The chief priests **picked up** the coins and said, "It is against the law
    27: 7 So *they* **decided to** [*+5206*] use the money to buy the potter's field
    27: 9 *They* **took** the thirty silver coins, the price set on him by the
    27: 24 he **took** water and washed his hands in front of the crowd.
    27: 30 and **took** the staff and struck him on the head again and again.
    27: 48 Immediately one of them ran and **got** a sponge. He filled it with
    27: 59 Joseph **took** the body, wrapped it in a clean linen cloth,
    28: 12 chief priests had met with the elders and **devised a plan** [*+5206*],
    28: 15 So the soldiers **took** the money and did as they were instructed.
Mk   4: 16 on rocky places, hear the word and at once **receive** it with joy.

    6: 41 **Taking** the five loaves and the two fish and looking up to heaven,
    7: 27 "for it is not right *to* **take** the children's bread and toss it to their
    8: 6 *When he had* **taken** the seven loaves and given thanks, he broke
    8: 14 The disciples had forgotten *to* **bring** bread, except for one loaf
    9: 36 He **took** a little child and had him stand among them. Taking him
   10: 30 *will* fail *to* **receive** a hundred times as much in this present age
   11: 24 in prayer, believe that *you have* **received** it, and it will be yours.
   12: 2 At harvest time he sent a servant to the tenants to **collect** from
   12: 3 But they **seized** him, beat him and sent him away empty-handed.
   12: 8 So they **took** him and killed him, and threw him out of the
   12: 19 the man *must* **marry** the widow and have children for his brother.
   12: 20 The first one **married** [*+1222*] and died without leaving any
   12: 21 The second one **married** the widow, but he also died, leaving no
   12: 40 Such men *will be* **punished** [*+3210*] most severely."
   14: 22 they were eating, Jesus **took** bread, gave thanks and broke it,
   14: 22 and broke it, and gave it to his disciples, saying, "**Take** it;
   14: 23 Then he **took** the cup, gave thanks and offered it to them, and they
   14: 65 and said, "Prophesy!" And the guards **took** him and beat him.
   15: 23 they offered him wine mixed with myrrh, but he *did* not **take** it.
Lk   5: 5 *we've* worked hard all night and haven't **caught** anything.
     5: 26 Everyone *was* **amazed** [*+1749*] and gave praise to God. They
     6: 4 He entered the house of God, and **taking** the consecrated bread,
     6: 34 And if you lend to those from whom you expect **repayment**,
     7: 16 They *were* all **filled with awe** [*+5832*] and praised God. "A great
     9: 16 **Taking** the five loaves and the two fish and looking up to heaven,
     9: 39 A spirit **seizes** him and he suddenly screams; it throws him into
    11: 10 For everyone who asks **receives**; he who seeks finds; and to him
    13: 19 is like a mustard seed, which a man **took** and planted in his garden.
    13: 21 It is like yeast that a woman **took** and mixed into a large amount of
    19: 12 birth went to a distant country *to have* himself **appointed** king
    19: 15 "He *was* **made king** [*+993+3836*], however, and returned home.
    20: 21 and that *you do* not **show partiality** [*+4725*] but teach the way of
    20: 28 the man *must* **marry** the widow and have children *for him.* Now
    20: 29 seven brothers. The first one **married** a woman and died childless.
    20: 31 and then the third **married** her, and in the same way the seven
    20: 47 Such men *will be* **punished** [*+3210*] most severely."
    22: 17 he gave thanks and said, "**Take** this and divide it among you.
    22: 19 And he **took** bread, gave thanks and broke it, and gave it to them,
    24: 30 he **took** bread, gave thanks, broke it and began to give it to them,
    24: 43 and he **took** it and ate it in their presence.
Jn   1: 12 Yet to all who **received** him, to those who believed in his name,
     1: 16 From the fullness of his grace we *have* all **received** one blessing
     3: 11 we have seen, but still *you people do* not **accept** our testimony.
     3: 27 "A man can **receive** only what is given him from heaven.
     3: 32 to what he has seen and heard, but no one **accepts** his testimony.
     3: 33 The man *who has* **accepted** it has certified that God is truthful.
     4: 36 Even now the reaper **draws** his wages, even now he harvests the
     5: 34 Not that I **accept** human testimony; but I mention it that you may
     5: 41 "*I do* not **accept** praise from men,
     5: 43 I have come in my Father's name, and *you do* not **accept** me;
     5: 43 but if someone else comes in his own name, *you will* **accept** him.
     5: 44 How can you believe *if you* **accept** praise from one another,
     6: 7 wages would not buy enough bread for each one *to* **have** a bite!"
     6: 11 Jesus then **took** the loaves, gave thanks, and distributed to those
     6: 21 Then they were willing *to* **take** him into the boat, and immediately
     7: 23 Now if a child *can* **circumcised** [*+4364*] on the Sabbath
     7: 39 the Spirit, whom those who believed in him *were* later *to* **receive**.
    10: 17 loves me is that I lay down my life—only *to* **take** it **up** again.
    10: 18 I have authority to lay it down and authority *to* **take** it **up** again.
    10: 18 to take it up again. This command I **received** from my Father."
    12: 3 Then Mary **took** about a pint of pure nard, an expensive perfume;
    12: 13 *They* **took** palm branches and went out to meet him, shouting,
    12: 48 a judge for the one who rejects me and *does* not **accept** my words;
    13: 4 outer clothing, and **wrapped** a towel **around** his **waist** [*+1346*];
    13: 12 washing their feet, *he* **put on** his clothes and returned to his place.
    13: 20 I tell you the truth, whoever **accepts** anyone I send accepts me;
    13: 20 I tell you the truth, whoever accepts anyone I send **accepts** me;
    13: 20 accepts me; and whoever **accepts** me accepts the one who sent me."
    13: 20 accepts me; and whoever accepts me **accepts** the one who sent me."
    13: 26 [UBS+ *he* **took** *it and*] he gave it to Judas Iscariot, son of Simon.
    13: 30 As soon as Judas *had* **taken** the bread, he went out. And it was
    14: 17 The world cannot **accept** him, because it neither sees him nor
    16: 14 He will bring glory to me by **taking** from what is mine and making
    16: 15 That is why I said the Spirit *will* **take** from what is mine and make
    16: 24 Ask and *you will* **receive**, and your joy will be complete.
    17: 8 For I gave them the words you gave me and they **accepted** them.

18: 3 **guiding** a detachment of soldiers and some officials from the chief
18: 31 Pilate said, "**Take** him yourselves and judge him by your own law."
19: 1 Then Pilate **took** Jesus and had him flogged.
19: 6 Crucify!" But Pilate answered, "You **take** him and crucify him.
19: 23 *they* **took** his clothes, dividing them into four shares, one for each
19: 27 From that time on, this disciple **took** her into his home.
19: 30 When *he had* **received** the drink, Jesus said, "It is finished."
19: 40 **Taking** Jesus' body, the two of them wrapped it, with the spices,
20: 22 with that he breathed on them and said, "**Receive** the Holy Spirit.
21: 13 Jesus came, **took** the bread and gave it to them, and did the same

Ac   1: 8 But *you will* **receive** power when the Holy Spirit comes on you;
1: 20 to dwell in it,' and, " '*May* another **take** his place of leadership.'
1: 25 *to* **take** [+3836+5536] **over** this apostolic ministry, which Judas
2: 33 he has **received** from the Father the promised Holy Spirit
2: 38 of your sins. And *you will* **receive** the gift of the Holy Spirit.
3: 3 and John about to enter, he asked them for **[RPG]** money.
3: 5 gave them his attention, expecting *to* **get** something from them.
7: 53 *you* who *have* **received** the law that was put into effect through
8: 15 they prayed for them that *they might* **receive** the Holy Spirit,
8: 17 placed their hands on them, and *they* **received** the Holy Spirit.
8: 19 so that everyone on whom I lay my hands *may* **receive** the Holy
9: 19 and *after* **taking** some food, he regained his strength. Saul spent
9: 25 But his followers **took** him by night and lowered him in a basket
10: 43 who believes in him **receives** forgiveness of sins through his name."
10: 47 with water? They *have* **received** the Holy Spirit just as we have."
15: 14 his concern *by* **taking** from the Gentiles a people for himself.
16: 3 so he **circumcised** [+4362] him because of the Jews who lived in
16: 24 *Upon* **receiving** such orders, he put them in the inner cell
17: 9 Then *they* **made** Jason and the others post bond and let them go.
17: 15 and then left **with instructions** [+1953] for Silas and Timothy to
19: 2 asked them, "*Did you* **receive** the Holy Spirit when you believed?"
20: 24 finish the race and complete the task the Lord Jesus *has* **given** me—
20: 35 Jesus himself said: 'It is more blessed to give than *to* **receive**.' "
24: 27 Felix *was* **succeeded by** [+1345] Porcius Festus, but because Felix
25: 16 and *has* **had** an opportunity to defend himself against their
26: 10 **On the authority** [+2026] of the chief priests I put many of the
26: 18 so that they *may* **receive** forgiveness of sins and a place among
27: 35 he **took** some bread and gave thanks to God in front of them all.
28: 15 of these men Paul thanked God and *was* **encouraged** [+2511].

Ro   1: 5 *we* **received** grace and apostleship to call people from among all
4: 11 And *he* **received** the sign of circumcision, a seal of the
5: 11 Jesus Christ, through whom *we have* now **received** reconciliation.
5: 17 how much more will those *who* **receive** God's abundant provision
7: 8 But sin, **seizing** the opportunity afforded by the commandment,
7: 11 For sin, **seizing** the opportunity afforded by the commandment,
8: 15 For *you did* not **receive** a spirit that makes you a slave again to
8: 15 you a slave again to fear, but *you* **received** the Spirit of sonship.
13: 2 and those who do so *will* **bring** judgment on themselves.

1Co 2: 12 We *have* not **received** the spirit of the world but the Spirit who is
3: 8 and each *will be* **rewarded** [+3635] according to his own labor.
3: 14 If what he has built survives, *he will* **receive** his reward.
4: 7 What do you have that *you did* not **receive**? And if you did receive
4: 7 And if *you did* **receive** it, why do you boast as though you did not?
4: 7 if you did receive it, why do you boast as though you **did**[s] not?
9: 24 know that in a race all the runners run, but only one **gets** the prize?
9: 25 They do it to **get** a crown that will not last; but we do it to get a
10: 13 No temptation *has* **seized** you except what is common to man.
11: 23 The Lord Jesus, on the night he was betrayed, **took** bread,
14: 5 unless he interprets, so that the church *may be* **edified** [+3869].

2Co 11: 4 or if *you* **receive** a different spirit from the one you received,
11: 4 or if you receive a different spirit from the one *you* **received**,
11: 8 I robbed other churches *by* **receiving** support *from* them so as to
11: 20 or exploits you or **takes advantage of** you or pushes himself
11: 24 Five times *I* **received** from the Jews the forty lashes minus one.
12: 16 to you. Yet, crafty fellow that I am, *I* **caught** you by trickery!

Gal 2: 6 God *does* not **judge by external appearance** [+476+4725]—those
3: 2 *Did you* **receive** the Spirit by observing the law, or by believing
3: 14 so that by faith *we might* **receive** the promise of the Spirit.

Php 2: 7 but made himself nothing, **taking** the very nature of a servant,
3: 12 Not that *I have* already **obtained** all this, or have already been

Col 4: 10 (*You have* **received** instructions about him; if he comes to you,
1Ti 4: 4 and nothing is to be rejected *if it is* **received** with thanksgiving,
2Ti 1: 5 *I have been* **reminded** [+5704] of your sincere faith, which first
Heb 2: 2 and every violation and disobedience **received** its just punishment,
2: 3 This salvation, which *was* first **announced** [+3281] by the Lord,
4: 16 so that *we may* **receive** mercy and find grace to help us in our time

5: 1 Every high priest *is* **selected** from among men and is appointed to
5: 4 No one **takes** this honor upon himself; he must be called by God,
7: 5 Now the law requires the descendants of Levi who **become** priests
7: 8 In the one case, the tenth *is* **collected** *by* men who die; but in the
7: 9 One might even say that Levi, who **collects** the tenth,
9: 15 that those who are called *may* **receive** the promised eternal
9: 19 he **took** the blood of calves, together with water, scarlet wool
10: 26 If we deliberately keep on sinning after *we have* **received** the
11: 8 when called to go to a place he would later **receive** as his
11: 11 was enabled to **become** [+2856+5065] **a father** because he
11: 13 *They did* not **receive** the things promised; they only saw them
11: 29 but *when* the Egyptians **tried to do** [+4278] so, they were
11: 35 Women **received** back their dead, raised to life again. Others were
11: 36 Some **faced** [+4278] jeers and flogging, while still others were

Jas 1: 7 That man should not think *he will* **receive** anything from the Lord;
1: 12 *he will* **receive** the crown of life that God has promised to those
3: 1 because you know that *we* who teach *will be* **judged** [+3210] more
4: 3 When you ask, *you do* not **receive**, because you ask with wrong
5: 7 and how patient he is for **[NIE]** the autumn and spring rains.
5: 10 of suffering, **take** the prophets who spoke in the name of the Lord.

1Pe 4: 10 Each one should use whatever gift *he has* **received** to serve others,
2Pe 1: 9 and *has* **forgotten that** [+3330] he has been cleansed from his past
1: 17 For *he* **received** honor and glory from God the Father when the
1Jn 2: 27 As for you, the anointing *you* **received** from him remains in you,
3: 22 and **receive** from him anything we ask, because we obey his
5: 9 *We* **accept** man's testimony, but God's testimony is greater
2Jn 1: 4 walking in the truth, just as the Father **commanded** [+1953] us.
1: 10 this teaching, *do* not **take** him into your house or welcome him.
3Jn 1: 7 of the Name that they went out, **receiving** no help from the pagans.
Rev 2: 17 with a new name written on it, known only to him *who* **receives** it.
2: 27 like pottery'—just as I *have* **received** authority from my Father.
3: 3 Remember, therefore, what *you have* **received** and heard;
3: 11 Hold on to what you have, so that no one *will* **take** your crown.
4: 11 our Lord and God, *to* **receive** glory and honor and power,
5: 7 and **took** the scroll from the right hand of him who sat on the
5: 8 And when *he had* **taken** it, the four living creatures
5: 9 "You are worthy *to* **take** the scroll and to open its seals,
5: 12 *to* **receive** power and wealth and wisdom and strength and honor
6: 4 Its rider was given power *to* **take** peace from the earth and to make
8: 5 Then the angel **took** the censer, filled it with fire from the altar,
10: 8 **take** the scroll that lies open in the hand of the angel who is
10: 9 He said to me, "**Take** it and eat it. It will turn your stomach sour,
10: 10 *I* **took** the little scroll from the angel's hand and ate it. It tasted as
11: 17 because *you have* **taken** your great power and have begun to
14: 9 and his image and **receives** his mark on the forehead or on the
14: 11 and his image, or for anyone *who* **receives** the mark of his name."
17: 12 "The ten horns you saw are ten kings who *have* not yet **received** a
17: 12 but who for one hour *will* **receive** authority as kings along with the
18: 4 share in her sins, so that *you will* not **receive** any of her plagues;
19: 20 With these signs he had deluded those *who had* **received** the mark
20: 4 or his image and *had* not **received** his mark on their foreheads
22: 17 and whoever wishes, *let him* **take** the free gift of the water of life.

3285 Λάμεχ, *Lamech* [1]

Lamech [1]

Lk   3: 36 the son of Shem, the son of Noah, the son *of* **Lamech**,

3286 λαμπάς, *lampas* [9] [√ 3290]

lamps [7], lanterns [1], torch [1]

Mt 25: 1 kingdom of heaven will be like ten virgins who took their **lamps**
25: 3 The foolish ones took their **lamps** but did not take any oil with
25: 4 The wise, however, took oil in jars along with their **lamps**.
25: 7 "Then all the virgins woke up and trimmed their **lamps**.
25: 8 to the wise, 'Give us some of your oil; our **lamps** are going out.'
Jn 18: 3 and Pharisees. They were carrying torches, **lanterns** and weapons.
Ac 20: 8 There were many **lamps** in the upstairs room where we were
Rev 4: 5 and peals of thunder. Before the throne, seven **lamps** were blazing.
8: 10 angel sounded his trumpet, and a great star, blazing like a **torch**,

3287 λαμπρός, lampros [9] [√ 3290]

bright [2], fine [2], shining [2], clear [1], elegant [1], splendor [1]

Lk 23:11 Dressing him in an **elegant** robe, they sent him back to Pilate.
Ac 10:30 the afternoon. Suddenly a man in **shining** clothes stood before me
Jas 2: 2 man comes into your meeting wearing a gold ring and **fine** clothes,
    2: 3 If you show special attention to the man wearing **fine** clothes
Rev 15: 6 **shining** linen and wore golden sashes around their chests.
    18:14 All your riches and **splendor** have vanished, never to be
    19: 8 Fine linen, **bright** and clean, was given her to wear." (Fine linen
    22: 1 as **clear** as crystal, flowing from the throne of God and of the
    22:16 and the Offspring of David, and the **bright** Morning Star."

3288 λαμπρότης, lamprotēs [1] [√ 3290]

brighter [+5642] [1]

Ac 26:13 I saw a light from heaven, **brighter** [+5642] *than* the sun,

3289 λαμπρῶς, lamprōs [1] [√ 3290]

in luxury [1]

Lk 16:19 was dressed in purple and fine linen and lived **in luxury** every day.

3290 λάμπω, lampō [7] [→ 1719, 2139, 3286, 3287, 3288, 3289, 4334, 5697]

shine [2], shone [2], gives light [1], lights up [1], made shine [1]

Mt 5:15 they put it on its stand, and *it* **gives light** to everyone in the house.
    5:16 In the same way, *let* your light **shine** before men, that they may see
    17: 2 His face **shone** like the sun, and his clothes became as white as the
Lk 17:24 which flashes and **lights up** the sky from one end to the other.
Ac 12: 7 an angel of the Lord appeared and a light **shone** in the cell.
2Co 4: 6 For God, who said, "*Let* light **shine** out of darkness," made his light
    4: 6 **made** his light **shine** in our hearts to give us the light of the

3291 λανθάνω, lanthanō [6] [→ 237, 238, 239, 240, 242, 1720, 2140, 2144, 3277, 3330]

forget [2], escaped notice [1], go unnoticed [1], keep secret [1], without knowing [1]

Mk 7:24 want anyone to know it; yet he could not **keep** his presence **secret**.
Lk 8:47 seeing that *she could* not **go unnoticed**, came trembling and fell at
Ac 26:26 I am convinced that none of this *has* **escaped** his **notice**, because it
Heb 13: 2 so doing some people have entertained angels **without knowing** it.
2Pe 3: 5 But they deliberately **forget** that long ago by God's word the
    3: 8 But *do* not **forget** this one thing, dear friends: With the Lord a day

3292 λαξευτός, laxeutos [1]

cut in the rock [1]

Lk 23:53 wrapped it in linen cloth and placed it in a tomb **cut in the rock**,

3293 Λαοδίκεια, Laodikeia [6] [√ 3295 + 1472]

Laodicea [6]

Col 2: 1 know how much I am struggling for you and for those at **Laodicea**,
    4:13 is working hard for you and for those at **Laodicea** and Hierapolis.
    4:15 Give my greetings to the brothers at **Laodicea**, and to Nympha
    4:16 the Laodiceans and that you in turn read the letter from **Laodicea**.
Rev 1:11 Smyrna, Pergamum, Thyatira, Sardis, Philadelphia and **Laodicea**."
    3:14 "To the angel of the church in **Laodicea** write: These are the words

3294 Λαοδικεύς, Laodikeus [1] [√ 3295 + 1472]

Laodiceans [1]

Col 4:16 see that it is also read in the church *of* the **Laodiceans** and that you

3295 λαός, laos [142] [→ 793, 3293, 3294, 3310, 3311, 3312, 3313, 3774, 3775]

λαὸς θεοῦ (people of God) [5] Ro 9:26; 2Co 6:16; Heb 4:9; 11:25; 1Pe 2:10

λαὸς Ἰσραήλ (people of Israel) [6] Mt 2:6; Lk 2:32; Ac 4:10,27; 13:17,24

people [126], peoples [4], people's [3], crowd [2], assembled worshipers [+3836+4436] [1], band of people [1], crowd [+3836+4436] [1], in public [+1883+3836] [1], public [1], thems [+3836] [1], thoses [+3836] [1]

Mt 1:21 the name Jesus, because he will save his **people** from their sins."
    2: 4 When he had called together all the **people's** chief priests
    2: 6 will come a ruler who will be the shepherd of my **people** Israel.' "
    4:16 the **people** living in darkness have seen a great light; on those
    4:23 and healing every disease and sickness among the **people**.
    13:15 For this **people's** heart has become calloused; they hardly hear
    15: 8 " 'These **people** honor me with their lips, but their hearts are far
    21:23 the chief priests and the elders *of* the **people** came to him.
    26: 3 and the elders *of* the **people** assembled in the palace of the high
    26: 5 the Feast," they said, "or there may be a riot among the **people**."
    26:47 and clubs, sent from the chief priests and the elders *of* the **people**.
    27: 1 and the elders *of* the **people** came to the decision to put Jesus to
    27:25 All the **people** answered, "Let his blood be on us and on our
    27:64 the body and tell the **people** that he has been raised from the dead.
Mk 7: 6 " 'These **people** honor me with their lips, but their hearts are far
    14:2 "But not during the Feast," they said, "or the **people** may riot."
Lk 1:10 all the **assembled worshipers** [+3836+4436] were praying outside.
    1:17 of the righteous—to make ready a **people** prepared for the Lord."
    1:21 the **people** were waiting for Zechariah and wondering why he
    1:68 God of Israel, because he has come and has redeemed his **people**.
    1:77 to give his **people** the knowledge of salvation through the
    2:10 I bring you good news of great joy that will be *for* all the **people**.
    2:31 which you have prepared in the sight *of* all **people**,
    2:32 for revelation to the Gentiles and for glory *to* your **people** Israel."
    3:15 The **people** were waiting expectantly and were all wondering in
    3:18 And with many other words John exhorted the **people**
    3:21 When all the **people** were being baptized, Jesus was baptized too.
    6:17 was there and a great number of **people** from all over Judea,
    7: 1 Jesus had finished saying all this in the hearing *of* the **people**,
    7:16 appeared among us," they said. "God has come to help his **people**."
    7:29 (All the **people**, even the tax collectors, when they heard Jesus'
    8:47 In the presence *of* all the **people**, she told why she had touched him
    9:13 and two fish—unless we go and buy food for all this **crowd**."
    18:43 praising God. When all the **people** saw it, they also praised God.
    19:47 and the leaders *among* the **people** were trying to kill him.
    19:48 find any way to do it, because all the **people** hung on his words.
    20: 1 One day as he was teaching the **people** in the temple courts
    20: 6 But if we say, 'From men,' all the **people** will stone us,
    20: 9 He went on to tell the **people** this parable: "A man planted a
    20:19 this parable against them. But they were afraid of the **people**.
    20:26 to trap him in what he had said there **in public** [+1883+3836].
    20:45 While all the **people** were listening, Jesus said to his disciples,
    21:23 will be great distress in the land and wrath *against* this **people**.
    21:38 and all the **people** came early in the morning to hear him at the
    22: 2 for some way to get rid of Jesus, for they were afraid of the **people**.
    22:66 At daybreak the council of the elders *of* the **people**, both the chief
    23: 5 they insisted, "He stirs up the **people** all over Judea by his teaching.
    23:13 Pilate called together the chief priests, the rulers and the **people**,
    23:14 "You brought me this man as one who was inciting the **people** to
    23:27 A large number of **people** followed him, including women who
    23:35 The **people** stood watching, and the rulers even sneered at him.
    24:19 powerful in word and deed before God and all the **people**.
Jn 8: 2 where all the **people** gathered around him, and he sat down to
    11:50 that one man die for the **people** than that the whole nation perish."
    18:14 the Jews that it would be good if one man died for the **people**.
Ac 2:47 praising God and enjoying the favor of all the **people**.
    3: 9 When all the **people** saw him walking and praising God,
    3:11 all the **people** were astonished and came running to them in the
    3:12 When Peter saw this, he said to them **s** [+3836]: "Men of Israel,
    3:23 listen to him will be completely cut off from among his **people**.'
    4: 1 came up to Peter and John while they were speaking to the **people**.
    4: 2 greatly disturbed because the apostles were teaching the **people**
    4: 8 with the Holy Spirit, said to them: "Rulers and elders *of* the **people**!

4:10 then know this, you and all the **people** of Israel: It is by the name
4:17 to stop this thing from spreading any further among the **people**,
4:21 because all the **people** were praising God for what had happened.
4:25 " 'Why do the nations rage and the **peoples** plot in vain?'
4:27 and the **people** of Israel in this city to conspire against your holy
5:12 performed many miraculous signs and wonders among the **people**.
5:13 join them, even though they were highly regarded by the **people**.
5:20 he said, "and tell the **people** the full message of this new life."
5:25 put in jail are standing in the temple courts teaching the **people**."
5:26 use force, because they feared that the **people** would stone them.
5:34 a teacher of the law, who was honored *by* all the **people**, stood up
5:37 in the days of the census and led a **band of people** in revolt.
6:8 did great wonders and miraculous signs among the **people**.
6:12 So they stirred up the **people** and the elders and the teachers of the
7:17 to Abraham, the number of our **people** in Egypt greatly increased.
7:34 I have indeed seen the oppression *of* my **people** in Egypt.
10:2 he gave generously to those[s] [*+3836*] in need and prayed to God
10:41 He was not seen *by* all the **people**, but by witnesses whom God
10:42 He commanded us to preach *to* the **people** and to testify that he is
12:4 Herod intended to bring him out for **public** trial after the Passover.
12:11 and from everything the Jewish **people** were anticipating."
13:15 "Brothers, if you have a message of encouragement for the **people**,
13:17 The God *of* the **people** of Israel chose our fathers; he made the
13:17 he made the **people** prosper during their stay in Egypt, with mighty
13:24 John preached repentance and baptism *to* all the **people** of Israel.
13:31 Galilee to Jerusalem. They are now his witnesses to our **people**.
15:14 his concern by taking from the Gentiles a **people** for himself.
18:10 to attack and harm you, because I have many **people** in this city."
19:4 He told the **people** to believe in the one coming after him,
21:28 is the man who teaches all men everywhere against our **people**
21:30 city was aroused, and the **people** came running from all directions.
21:36 The **crowd** [*+3836+4436*] that followed kept shouting, "Away with
21:39 a citizen of no ordinary city. Please let me speak to the **people**."
21:40 Paul stood on the steps and motioned *to* the **crowd**.
23:5 for it is written: 'Do not speak evil about the ruler *of* your **people**.' "
26:17 I will rescue you from your own **people** and from the Gentiles.
26:23 would proclaim light *to* his own **people** and to the Gentiles."
28:17 although I have done nothing against our **people** or against the
28:26 " 'Go to this **people** and say, "You will be ever hearing but never
28:27 For this **people's** heart has become calloused; they hardly hear
Ro 9:25 "I will call them 'my **people**' who are not my people; and I will call
9:25 "I will call them 'my **people**' who are not my **people**; and I will call
9:26 'You are not my **people**,' they will be called 'sons of the living
10:21 I have held out my hands to a disobedient and obstinate **people**."
11:1 I ask then: Did God reject his **people**? By no means! I am an
11:2 God did not reject his **people**, whom he foreknew. Don't you know
15:10 Again, it says, "Rejoice, O Gentiles, with his **people**."
15:11 the Lord, all you Gentiles, and sing praises to him, all you **peoples**."
1Co 10:7 "The **people** sat down to eat and drink and got up to indulge in
14:21 and through the lips of foreigners I will speak *to* this **people**,
2Co 6:16 among them, and I will be their God, and they will be my **people**."
Tit 2:14 and to purify for himself a **people** that are his very own,
Heb 2:17 and that he might make atonement for the sins *of* the **people**.
4:9 There remains, then, a Sabbath-rest *for* the **people** of God;
5:3 sacrifices for his own sins, as well as for the sins *of* the **people**.
7:5 of Levi who become priests to collect a tenth from the **people**—
7:11 priesthood (for on the basis of it the law was given to the **people**),
7:27 after that, first for his own sins, and then for the sins *of* the **people**.
8:10 on their hearts. I will be their God, and they will be my **people**.
9:7 for himself and for the sins the **people** had committed in ignorance.
9:19 had proclaimed every commandment of the law *to* all the **people**,
9:19 and branches of hyssop, and sprinkled the scroll and all the **people**.
10:30 avenge; I will repay," and again, "The Lord will judge his **people**."
11:25 He chose to be mistreated along with the **people** of God rather than
13:12 so Jesus also suffered outside the city gate to make the **people** holy
1Pe 2:9 a royal priesthood, a holy nation, a **people** belonging to God,
2:10 Once you were not a **people**, but now you are the people of God;
2:10 Once you were not a people, but now you are the **people** of God;
2Pe 2:1 But there were also false prophets among the **people**, just as there
Jude 1:5 I want to remind you that the Lord delivered his **people** out of
Rev 5:9 men for God from every tribe and language and **people** and nation.
7:9 from every nation, tribe, **people** and language, standing before the
10:11 "You must prophesy again about many **peoples**, nations, languages
11:9 For three and a half days men from *every* **people**, tribe, language
13:7 was given authority over every tribe, **people**, language and nation.
14:6 who live on the earth—to every nation, tribe, language and **people**.

17:15 the prostitute sits, are **peoples**, multitudes, nations and languages.
18:4 "Come out of her, my **people**, so that you will not share in her sins,
21:3 They will be his **people**, and God himself will be with them

3296 λάρυγξ, *larynx* [1]

throats [1]

Ro 3:13 "Their **throats** are open graves; their tongues practice deceit."

3297 Λασαία, *Lasaia* [1] [→ *3298*]

Lasea [1]

Ac 27:8 and came to a place called Fair Havens, near the town of **Lasea**.

3298 Λασέα, *Lasea* Not used in UBS/NIV [√ *3297*]

3299 λάσκω, *laskō* Not used in UBS/NIV [√ *cf. 3279*]

3300 λατομέω, *latomeō* [2]

cut [*+1639*] [1], cut out [1]

Mt 27:60 and placed it in his own new tomb that *he had* **cut out** of the rock.
Mk 15:46 it in the linen, and placed it in a tomb **cut** [*+1639*] out of rock.

3301 λατρεία, *latreia* [5] [→ *1629, 1630, 3302*]

act of worship [1], ministry [1], service [1], temple worship [1], worship [1]

Jn 16:2 anyone who kills you will think he is offering a **service** to God.
Ro 9:4 the receiving of the law, the **temple worship** and the promises.
12:1 and pleasing to God—this is your spiritual **act of worship**.
Heb 9:1 Now the first covenant had regulations *for* **worship** and also an
9:6 entered regularly into the outer room to carry on their **ministry**.

3302 λατρεύω, *latreuō* [21] [√ *3301*]

serve [10], worship [5], minister [1], serve at a sanctuary [1], served [1], worshiped [1], worshiper [1], worshipers [1]

Mt 4:10 it is written: 'Worship the Lord your God, and **serve** him only.' "
Lk 1:74 hand of our enemies, and to enable us *to* **serve** him without fear
2:37 She never left the temple but **worshiped** night and day, fasting
4:8 "It is written: 'Worship the Lord your God and **serve** him only.' "
Ac 7:7 they will come out of that country and **worship** me in this place.'
7:42 and gave them over *to* the **worship** of the heavenly bodies.
24:14 I admit that *I* **worship** the God of our fathers as a follower of the
26:7 tribes are hoping to see fulfilled as they earnestly **serve** God day
27:23 angel of the God whose I am and whom *I* **serve** stood beside me
Ro 1:9 whom *I* **serve** with my whole heart in preaching the gospel of his
1:25 and worshiped and **served** created things rather than the Creator—
Php 3:3 we who **worship** by the Spirit of God, who glory in Christ Jesus,
2Ti 1:3 I thank God, whom *I* **serve**, as my forefathers did, with a clear
Heb 8:5 They **serve at a sanctuary** that is a copy and shadow of what is in
9:9 offered were not able to clear the conscience of the **worshiper**.
9:14 from acts that lead to death, so that we *may* **serve** the living God!
10:2 For the **worshipers** would have been cleansed once for all,
12:28 and so **worship** God acceptably with reverence and awe,
13:10 We have an altar from which those *who* **minister** at the tabernacle
Rev 7:15 the throne of God and **serve** him day and night in his temple;
22:3 of the Lamb will be in the city, and his servants *will* **serve** him.

3303 λάχανον, *lachanon* [4]

garden plants [2], garden herbs [1], vegetables [1]

Mt 13:32 it grows, it is the largest *of* **garden plants** and becomes a tree,
Mk 4:32 it grows and becomes the largest of all **garden plants**,
Lk 11:42 rue and all other kinds of **garden herbs**, but you neglect justice
Ro 14:2 but another man, whose faith is weak, eats *only* **vegetables**.

3304 Λεββαῖος, *Lebbaios* Not used in UBS/NIV [√ *cf. 2497*]

3305 λεγιών, legion [4]

legion [3], legions [1]

Mt	26:53	and he will at once put at my disposal more than twelve **legions** of
Mk	5: 9	your name?" "My name is **Legion**," he replied, "for we are many."
	5:15	they saw the man who had been possessed by the **legion** of
Lk	8:30	"**Legion**," he replied, because many demons had gone into him.

3306 λέγω, lego [2353 / 2356]

[→ 37, 155, 224, 381, 382, 406, 515, 517, 584, 664, 665, 1006, 1156, 1157, 1363, 1365, 1368, 1369, 1474, 1721, 1723, 1724, 1823, 1824, 1922, 2141, 2328, 2329, 2330, 2532, 2800, 2899, 2986, 3315, 3356, 3357, 3358, 3359, 3360, 3361, 3362, 3363, 3364, 3467, 3468, 3703, 3933, 4162, 4165, 4391, 4494, 4597, 4625, 4690, 5066, 5133, 5198, 5199, 5274, 5293, 5807, 5981, 6016; cf. 3933]

ἀπεκρίθη καὶ εἶπεν (answered and said) [25] Mk 12:34; Lk 13:15; 17:20; Jn 1:48,50; 2:19; 3:3,9,10,27; 4:10,13,17; 6:26,29,43; 7:16,21; 8:14; 9:30,36; 12:30; 13:7; 14:23; 20:28

ἀποκριθεὶς εἶπεν (answering, said) [69] Mt 3:15; 4:4; 11:4,25; 12:39,48; 13:11, 37; 15:3,13,24,26,28; 16:2,16; 17:4,11,17; 19:4, 27; 20:13,22; 21:21,24,29,30; 22:1,29; 24:2,4; 25:12,26; 26:23,25, 33; 27:21,25; 28:5; Mk 6:37; 10:3,51; 11:14; 14:48; Lk 1:19,35; 4:8,12; 5:5,22,31; 6:3; 7:22,40,43; 8:21; 9:20,41; 10:27,41; 13:2; 14:3; 15:29; 17:17; 19:40; 20:3; 22:51; 24:18; Ac 8:24; 25:9

said [784], *untranslated* [290], tell [216], say [183], asked [153], replied [92], told [91], says [83], saying [79], answered [52], called [31], spoken [17], ask [15], speak [12], telling [10], call [9], spoke [9], declared [8], words [8], claim [7], talking about [7], talking [7], speaking [6], claimed [4], continued [4], declares [4], exclaimed [4], said [+806] [4], yes it is as you say [ı5148] [4], asking [3], asks [3], calls [3], claiming [3], claims [3], demanded [3], is [3], mean [3], mention [3], ordered [3], speaks [3], spoken of [3], tells [3], added [2], answer [2], calling [2], challenged [2], claim [+1571] [2], known as [2], means [2], meant [+4309] [2], meant [2], name [2], objected [2], protested [2], shouted [2], shouting [2], speak of [2], spoke up [2], stated [2], told [+4192] [2], accuse [1], addressed [+4639] [1], addressed [1], adds [1], admit [1], advise [1], agree with one another [+899+3836] [1], announced [1], asks for [1], assure [+237+2093] [1], at this [+4047] [1], began to speak [+487+3836+5125] [1], begged [1], boasted [1], boasts [1], bys [+4005] [1], call out [1], called out [+3489+5889] [1], called out [1], charged [1], claiming [+1571] [1], claims [+1571] [1], commanded [1], commanding [+2198+2848] [1], cried out [1], cried [1], cry out [1], cry [1], directed [1], discuss [1], explain [1], grant [1], inquired [1], insisted [1], made [1], means [+1639] [1], means [+3493] [1], named [1], one might even say [+2229+6055] [1], order [1], pleading [1], prayed [1], praying [1], preach [1], present [1], promised [1], put [1], question [1], quote [1], referring [1], remarking [1], repeat [+4099] [1], reply [1], respond [1], sang [1], say about [1], sent for [+5888] [1], shouting at the top of voice [+3489+5889] [1], singing [1], so-called [+6055] [1], so-called [1], speak about [1], speaks of [1], spoke about [1], state [1], take an example [1], talk [1], telling about [1], testified [1], this message [1], thought [1], told [+806] [1], turned [1], urged [1], used [1], using argument [1], warned [1], welcome [+5897] [1], welcomes [+5897] [1], went on [1], whats [+3836] [1], with that [+4047] [1], with the news [1], with the plea [1], with the words [1], with this [+4047] [1], word [1], yes [+5148] [1]

Mt	1:16	husband of Mary, of whom was born Jesus, who *is* **called** Christ.
	1:20	an angel of the Lord appeared to him in a dream and **said**,
	1:22	All this took place to fulfill what the Lord *had* **said** through
	1:22	to fulfill what the Lord had said through the prophet: **[RPG]**
	2: 2	and **asked**, "Where is the one who has been born king of the Jews?
	2: 5	"In Bethlehem in Judea," they **replied**, "for this is what the prophet
	2: 8	*He* sent them to Bethlehem and **said**, "Go and make a careful
	2:13	"Get up," *he* **said**, "take the child and his mother and escape to
	2:13	Stay there until *I* **tell** you, for Herod is going to search for the child
	2:15	so was fulfilled what the Lord *had* **said** through the prophet:
	2:15	said through the prophet: **[RPG]** "Out of Egypt I called my son."
	2:17	Then what *was* **said** through the prophet Jeremiah was fulfilled:

	2:17	what was said through the prophet Jeremiah was fulfilled: **[RPG]**
	2:20	and **said**, "Get up, take the child and his mother and go to the land
	2:23	and he went and lived in a town **called** Nazareth. So was fulfilled
	2:23	So was fulfilled what *was* **said** through the prophets: "He will be
	3: 2	and **saying**, "Repent, for the kingdom of heaven is near."
	3: 3	This is he *who was* **spoken of** through the prophet Isaiah:
	3: 3	**[RPG]** "A voice of one calling in the desert, 'Prepare the way for
	3: 7	and Sadducees coming to where he was baptizing, *he* **said** to them:
	3: 9	And do not think you *can* **say** to yourselves, 'We have Abraham as
	3: 9	*I* **tell** you that out of these stones God can raise up children for
	3:14	But John tried to deter him, **saying**, "I need to be baptized by you,
	3:15	Jesus replied, **[RPG]** "Let it be so now; it is proper for us to do this
	3:17	And a voice from heaven **said**, "This is my Son, whom I love;
	4: 3	The tempter came to him and **said**, "If you are the Son of God,
	4: 3	"If you are the Son of God, **tell** these stones to become bread."
	4: 4	Jesus answered, **[RPG]** "It is written: 'Man does not live on bread
	4: 6	"If you are the Son of God," *he* **said**, "throw yourself down. For it
	4: 9	I will give you," *he* **said**, "if you will bow down and worship me."
	4:10	Jesus **said** to him, "Away from me, Satan! For it is written:
	4:14	to fulfill what *was* **said** through the prophet Isaiah:
	4:14	to fulfill what was said through the prophet Isaiah: **[RPG]**
	4:17	to preach, **[RPG]** "Repent, for the kingdom of heaven is near."
	4:18	he saw two brothers, Simon **called** Peter and his brother Andrew.
	4:19	follow me," Jesus **said**, "and I will make you fishers of men."
	5: 2	and he began to teach them, **saying**:
	5:11	persecute you and falsely **say** all kinds of evil against you
	5:18	*I* **tell** you the truth, until heaven and earth disappear,
	5:20	For *I* **tell** you that unless your righteousness surpasses that of the
	5:21	"You have heard that *it was* **said** to the people long ago, 'Do not
	5:22	But I **tell** you that anyone who is angry with his brother will be
	5:22	Again, anyone *who* **says** to his brother, 'Raca,' is answerable to
	5:22	is answerable to the Sanhedrin. But anyone *who* **says**, 'You fool!'
	5:26	*I* **tell** you the truth, you will not get out until you have paid the last
	5:27	"You have heard that *it was* **said**, 'Do not commit adultery.'
	5:28	But I **tell** you that anyone who looks at a woman lustfully has
	5:31	"*It has been* **said**, 'Anyone who divorces his wife must give her a
	5:32	But I **tell** you that anyone who divorces his wife, except for marital
	5:33	"Again, you have heard that *it was* **said** to the people long ago,
	5:34	But I **tell** you, Do not swear at all: either by heaven, for it is God's
	5:38	"You have heard that *it was* **said**, 'Eye for eye, and tooth for tooth.'
	5:39	But I **tell** you, Do not resist an evil person. If someone strikes you
	5:43	"You have heard that *it was* **said**, 'Love your neighbor and hate
	5:44	But I **tell** you: Love your enemies and pray for those who
	6: 2	*I* **tell** you the truth, they have received their reward in full.
	6: 5	*I* **tell** you the truth, they have received their reward in full.
	6:16	*I* **tell** you the truth, they have received their reward in full.
	6:25	"Therefore *I* **tell** you, do not worry about your life, what you will
	6:29	Yet *I* **tell** you that not even Solomon in all his splendor was
	6:31	So do not worry, **saying**, 'What shall we eat?' or 'What shall we
	7: 4	How *can you* **say** to your brother, 'Let me take the speck out of
	7:21	"Not everyone who **says** to me, 'Lord, Lord,' will enter the
	7:22	Many *will* **say** to me on that day, 'Lord, Lord, did we not prophesy
	8: 2	A man with leprosy came and knelt before him and **said**, "Lord,
	8: 3	his hand and touched the man. "I am willing," *he* **said**. "Be clean!"
	8: 4	Then Jesus **said** to him, "See that you don't tell anyone. But go,
	8: 4	Then Jesus said to him, "See that *you* don't **tell** anyone. But go,
	8: 6	"Lord," *he* **said**, "my servant lies at home paralyzed and in terrible
	8: 7	Jesus **said** to him, "I will go and heal him."
	8: 8	my roof. But just **say** the word, and my servant will be healed.
	8: 9	*I* **tell** this one, 'Go,' and he goes; and that one, 'Come,' and he
	8:10	he was astonished and **said** to those following him, "I tell you the
	8:10	and said to those following him, "*I* **tell** you the truth,
	8:11	*I* **say** to you that many will come from the east and the west,
	8:13	Then Jesus **said** to the centurion, "Go! It will be done just as you
	8:17	This was to fulfill what *was* **spoken** through the prophet Isaiah:
	8:17	**[RPG]** "He took up our infirmities and carried our diseases."
	8:19	Then a teacher of the law came to him and **said**, "Teacher, I will
	8:20	Jesus **replied**, "Foxes have holes and birds of the air have nests,
	8:21	Another disciple **said** to him, "Lord, first let me go and bury my
	8:22	But Jesus **told** him, "Follow me, and let the dead bury their own
	8:25	The disciples went and woke him, **saying**, "Lord, save us!
	8:26	*He* **replied**, "You of little faith, why are you so afraid?" Then he
	8:27	The men were amazed and **asked**, "What kind of man is this?
	8:29	**[RPG]** "Have you come here to torture us before the appointed
	8:31	The demons begged Jesus, **[RPG]** "If you drive us out, send us
	8:32	*He* **said** to them, "Go!" So they came out and went into the pigs,

9: 2   Jesus saw their faith, *he* **said** to the paralytic, "Take heart, son;
9: 3   At this, some of the teachers of the law **said** to themselves,
9: 4   Knowing their thoughts, Jesus **said**, "Why do you entertain evil
9: 5   *to* **say**, 'Your sins are forgiven,' or to say, 'Get up and walk'?
9: 5   to say, 'Your sins are forgiven,' or *to* **say**, 'Get up and walk'?
9: 6   Then *he* **said** to the paralytic, "Get up, take your mat and go home."
9: 9   he saw a man **named** Matthew sitting at the tax collector's booth.
9: 9   "Follow me," *he* **told** him, and Matthew got up and followed him.
9: 11   When the Pharisees saw this, *they* **asked** his disciples, "Why does
9: 12   On hearing this, Jesus **said**, "It is not the healthy who need a doctor,
9: 14   Then John's disciples came and **asked** him, "How is it that we
9: 15   Jesus **answered**, "How can the guests of the bridegroom mourn
9: 18   he was saying this, a ruler came and knelt before him and **said**,
9: 21   *She* **said** to herself, "If I only touch his cloak, I will be healed."
9: 22   "Take heart, daughter," *he* **said**, "your faith has healed you."
9: 24   *he* **said**, "Go away. The girl is not dead but asleep." But they
9: 27   calling out, **[RPG]** "Have mercy on us, Son of David!"
9: 28   had gone indoors, the blind men came to him, and he **asked** them,
9: 28   you believe that I am able to do this?" "Yes, Lord," *they* **replied**.
9: 29   Then he touched their eyes and **said**, "According to your faith will it
9: 30   warned them sternly, **[RPG]** "See that no one knows about this."
9: 33   The crowd was amazed and **said**, "Nothing like this has ever been
9: 34   But the Pharisees **said**, "It is by the prince of demons that he drives
9: 37   Then *he* **said** to his disciples, "The harvest is plentiful
10: 2   first, Simon (who *is* **called** Peter) and his brother Andrew;
10: 5   **[RPG]** "Do not go among the Gentiles or enter any town of the
10: 7   As you go, preach **this** message: 'The kingdom of heaven is near.'
10: 15   *I* **tell** you the truth, it will be more bearable for Sodom
10: 23   *I* **tell** you the truth, you will not finish going through the cities of
10: 27   What *I* **tell** you in the dark, speak in the daylight; what is
10: 27   What I tell you in the dark, **speak** in the daylight; what is
10: 42   of these little ones because he is my disciple, *I* **tell** you the truth,
11: 3   to **ask** him, "Are you the one who was to come, or should we expect
11: 4   **[RPG]** "Go back and report to John what you hear and see:
11: 7   were leaving, Jesus began to **speak** to the crowd about John:
11: 9   go out to see? A prophet? Yes, *I* **tell** you, and more than a prophet.
11: 11   *I* **tell** you the truth: Among those born of women there has not
11: 17   **[RPG]** " 'We played the flute for you, and you did not dance;
11: 18   came neither eating nor drinking, and *they* **say**, 'He has a demon.'
11: 19   The Son of Man came eating and drinking, and *they* **say**, 'Here is a
11: 22   But *I* **tell** you, it will be more bearable for Tyre and Sidon on the
11: 24   But *I* **tell** you that it will be more bearable for Sodom on the day of
11: 25   At that time Jesus **said**, "I praise you, Father, Lord of heaven
12: 2   When the Pharisees saw this, *they* **said** to him, "Look!
12: 3   He **answered**, "Haven't you read what David did when he and his
12: 6   *I* **tell** you that one greater than the temple is here.
12: 10   they asked him, **[RPG]** "Is it lawful to heal on the Sabbath?"
12: 11   He **said** to them, "If any of you has a sheep and it falls into a pit on
12: 13   Then *he* **said** to the man, "Stretch out your hand." So he stretched it
12: 17   This was to fulfill what *was* **spoken** through the prophet Isaiah:
12: 17   was to fulfill what was spoken through the prophet Isaiah: **[RPG]**
12: 23   All the people were astonished and **said**, "Could this be the Son of
12: 24   *they* **said**, "It is only by Beelzebub, the prince of demons,
12: 25   Jesus knew their thoughts and **said** to them, "Every kingdom
12: 31   And so *I* **tell** you, every sin and blasphemy will be forgiven men,
12: 32   Anyone *who* **speaks** a word against the Son of Man will be
12: 32   but anyone *who* **speaks** against the Holy Spirit will not be
12: 36   But *I* **tell** you that men will have to give account on the day of
12: 38   Then some of the Pharisees and teachers of the law **said** to him,
12: 39   **[RPG]** "A wicked and adulterous generation asks for a miraculous
12: 44   Then *it* **says**, 'I will return to the house I left.' When it arrives,
12: 47   Someone **told** him, "Your mother and brothers are standing outside,
12: 48   He replied **[RPG]** to him, "Who is my mother, and who are my
12: 48   He replied **[RPG]** to him, "Who is my mother, and who are my
12: 49   to his disciples, *he* **said**, "Here are my mother and my brothers.
13: 3   Then he told them many things in parables, **saying**: "A farmer went
13: 10   The disciples came to him and **asked**, "Why do you speak to the
13: 11   **[RPG]** "The knowledge of the secrets of the kingdom of heaven
13: 14   **[RPG]** " 'You will be ever hearing but never understanding;
13: 17   For *I* **tell** you the truth, many prophets and righteous men longed to
13: 24   Jesus **told** [+4192] them another parable: "The kingdom of heaven
13: 27   "The owner's servants came to him and **said**, 'Sir, didn't you sow
13: 28   "The servants **asked** him, 'Do you want us to go and pull them up?'
13: 30   At that time *I* **will tell** the harvesters: First collect the weeds
13: 31   *He* **told** [+4192] them another parable: "The kingdom of heaven is
13: 35   So was fulfilled what *was* **spoken** through the prophet: "I will open

13: 35   **[RPG]** "I will open my mouth in parables, I will utter things
13: 36   His disciples came to him and **said**, "Explain to us the parable of
13: 37   **[RPG]** "The one who sowed the good seed is the Son of Man.
13: 51   all these things?" Jesus **asked**. [UBS-] "Yes," they replied.
13: 51   you understood all these things?" Jesus asked. "Yes," *they* **replied**.
13: 52   He **said** to them, "Therefore every teacher of the law who has been
13: 54   man get this wisdom and these miraculous powers?" they **asked**.
13: 55   Isn't his mother's **name** Mary, and aren't his brothers James,
13: 57   But Jesus **said** to them, "Only in his hometown and in his own
14: 2   and *he* **said** to his attendants, "This is John the Baptist; he has risen
14: 4   for John *had been* **saying** to him: "It is not lawful for you to have
14: 15   the disciples came to him and **said**, "This is a remote place.
14: 16   Jesus **replied**, "They do not need to go away. You give them
14: 17   have here only five loaves of bread and two fish," they **answered**.
14: 18   "Bring them here to me," he **said**.
14: 26   walking on the lake, they were terrified. "It's a ghost," *they* **said**,
14: 27   said to them: **[RPG]** "Take courage! It is I. Don't be afraid."
14: 28   "Lord, if it's you," **[RPG]** Peter replied, "tell me to come to you on
14: 29   "Come," he **said**. Then Peter got down out of the boat, walked on
14: 30   afraid and, beginning to sink, cried out, **[RPG]** "Lord, save me!"
14: 31   and caught him. "You of little faith," *he* **said**, "why did you doubt?"
14: 33   in the boat worshiped him, **saying**, "Truly you are the Son of God."
15: 1   and teachers of the law came to Jesus from Jerusalem and **asked**,
15: 3   **[RPG]** "And why do you break the command of God for the sake
15: 4   For God **said**, 'Honor your father and mother' and 'Anyone who
15: 5   But you **say** that if a man says to his father or mother,
15: 5   But you say that if a man **says** to his father or mother,
15: 7   Isaiah was right when he prophesied about you: **[RPG]**
15: 10   Jesus called the crowd to him and **said**, "Listen and understand.
15: 12   Then the disciples came to him and **asked**, "Do you know that the
15: 13   **[RPG]** "Every plant that my heavenly Father has not planted will
15: 15   Peter **said**, "Explain the parable to us."
15: 16   "Are you still so dull?" Jesus **asked** them.
15: 22   crying out, **[RPG]** "Lord, Son of David, have mercy on me!
15: 23   his disciples came to him and urged him, **[RPG]** "Send her away,
15: 24   He answered, **[RPG]** "I was sent only to the lost sheep of Israel."
15: 25   The woman came and knelt before him. "Lord, help me!" she **said**.
15: 26   **[RPG]** "It is not right to take the children's bread and toss it to
15: 27   "Yes, Lord," she **said**, "but even the dogs eat the crumbs that fall
15: 28   Then Jesus answered, **[RPG]** "Woman, you have great faith!
15: 32   Jesus called his disciples to him and **said**, "I have compassion for
15: 33   His disciples **answered**, "Where could we get enough bread in this
15: 34   "How many loaves do you have?" Jesus **asked**. "Seven," they
15: 34   have?" Jesus asked. "Seven," *they* **replied**, "and a few small fish."
16: 2   He replied, **[RPG]** "When evening comes, you say, 'It will be fair
16: 2   He replied, "When evening comes, *you* **say**, 'It will be fair weather,
16: 6   "Be careful," Jesus **said** to them. "Be on your guard against the
16: 7   They discussed this among themselves and **said**, "It is because we
16: 8   Aware of their discussion, Jesus **asked**, "You of little faith,
16: 11   How is it you don't understand that *I* **was** not **talking** to you about
16: 12   Then they understood that *he was* not **telling** them to guard against
16: 13   asked his disciples, **[RPG]** "Who do people say the Son of Man is?"
16: 13   he asked his disciples, "Who *do* people **say** the Son of Man is?"
16: 14   They **replied**, "Some say John the Baptist; others say Elijah;
16: 15   "But what about you?" *he* **asked**. "Who do you say I am?"
16: 15   "But what about you?" he asked. "Who *do you* **say** I am?"
16: 16   Simon Peter answered, **[RPG]** "You are the Christ, the Son of the
16: 17   Jesus replied, "Blessed are you, **[RPG]** Simon son of Jonah,
16: 18   And *I* **tell** you that you are Peter, and on this rock I will build my
16: 20   Then he warned his disciples not *to* **tell** anyone that he was the
16: 22   took him aside and began to rebuke him. "Never, Lord!" *he* **said**.
16: 23   Jesus turned and **said** to Peter, "Get behind me, Satan! You are a
16: 24   Then Jesus **said** to his disciples, "If anyone would come after me,
16: 28   *I* **tell** you the truth, some who are standing here will not taste death
17: 4   Peter **said** to Jesus, "Lord, it is good for us to be here. If you wish,
17: 5   and a voice from the cloud **said**, "This is my Son, whom I love;
17: 7   Jesus came and touched them. "Get up," *he* **said**. "Don't be afraid."
17: 9   instructed them, **[RPG]** "Don't tell anyone what you have seen,
17: 9   Jesus instructed them, "Don't **tell** anyone what you have seen,
17: 10   **[RPG]** "Why then do the teachers of the law say that Elijah must
17: 10   then *do* the teachers of the law **say** that Elijah must come first?"
17: 11   **[RPG]** "To be sure, Elijah comes and will restore all things.
17: 12   But *I* **tell** you, Elijah has already come, and they did not recognize
17: 13   Then the disciples understood that *he was* **talking** to them about
17: 15   "Lord, have mercy on my son," *he* **said**. "He has seizures and is
17: 17   Jesus replied, **[RPG]** "how long shall I stay with you?

17:19 Then the disciples came to Jesus in private and **asked**, "Why
17:20 He **replied**, "Because you have so little faith. I tell you the truth,
17:20 *I* **tell** you the truth, if you have faith as small as a mustard seed,
17:20 *you can* **say** to this mountain, 'Move from here to there' and it will
17:22 When they came together in Galilee, he **said** to them, "The Son of
17:24 the collectors of the two-drachma tax came to Peter and **asked**,
17:25 "Yes, he does," *he* **replied**. When Peter came into the house,
17:25 When Peter came into the house, Jesus was the first *to* **speak**.
17:26 "From others," Peter **answered**. "Then the sons are exempt," Jesus
18: 1 At that time the disciples came to Jesus and **asked**, "Who is the
18: 3 And *he* **said**: "I tell you the truth, unless you change and become
18: 3 "*I* **tell** you the truth, unless you change and become like little
18:10 For *I* **tell** you that their angels in heaven always see the face of my
18:13 And if he finds it, *I* **tell** you the truth, he is happier about that one
18:17 If he refuses to listen to them, **tell** it to the church; and if he refuses
18:18 "*I* **tell** you the truth, whatever you bind on earth will be bound in
18:19 *I* **tell** you that if two of you on earth agree about anything you ask
18:21 Then Peter came to Jesus and **asked**, "Lord, how many times shall I
18:22 Jesus **answered**, "I tell you, not seven times, but seventy-seven
18:22 Jesus answered, "*I* **tell** you, not seven times, but seventy-seven
18:26 'Be patient with me,' *he* **begged**, 'and I will pay back everything.'
18:28 began to choke him. 'Pay back what you owe me!' *he* **demanded**.
18:29 fell to his knees and begged him, **[RPG]** 'Be patient with me,
18:32 'You wicked servant,' *he* **said**, 'I canceled all that debt of yours
19: 3 *They* **asked**, "Is it lawful for a man to divorce his wife for any
19: 4 **[RPG]** "that at the beginning the Creator 'made them male
19: 5 and **said**, 'For this reason a man will leave his father and mother
19: 7 "Why then," *they* **asked**, "did Moses command that a man give his
19: 8 Jesus **replied**, "Moses permitted you to divorce your wives
19: 9 *I* **tell** you that anyone who divorces his wife, except for marital
19:10 The disciples **said** to him, "If this is the situation between a
19:11 Jesus **replied**, "Not everyone can accept this word, but only those
19:14 Jesus **said**, "Let the little children come to me, and do not hinder
19:16 Now a man came up to Jesus and **asked**, "Teacher, what good thing
19:17 Jesus **replied**. "There is only One who is good. If you want to enter
19:18 "Which ones?" the man **inquired**. Jesus replied, " 'Do not murder,
19:18 Jesus **replied**, " 'Do not murder, do not commit adultery, do not
19:20 "All these I have kept," the young man **said**. "What do I still lack?"
19:23 Then Jesus **said** to his disciples, "I tell you the truth, it is hard for a
19:23 Then Jesus said to his disciples, "*I* **tell** you the truth, it is hard for a
19:24 Again *I* **tell** you, it is easier for a camel to go through the eye of a
19:25 they were greatly astonished and **asked**, "Who then can be saved?"
19:26 Jesus looked at them and **said**, "With man this is impossible,
19:27 answered him, **[RPG]** "We have left everything to follow you!
19:28 Jesus **said** to them, "I tell you the truth, at the renewal of all things,
19:28 Jesus said to them, "*I* **tell** you the truth, at the renewal of all things,
20: 4 *He* **told** them, 'You also go and work in my vineyard, and I will
20: 6 *He* **asked** them, 'Why have you been standing here all day long
20: 7 " 'Because no one has hired us,' *they* **answered**. "He said to them,
20: 7 "*He* **said** to them, 'You also go and work in my vineyard.'
20: 8 the owner of the vineyard **said** to his foreman, 'Call the workers
20:12 'These men who were hired last worked only one hour,' *they* **said**,
20:13 one of them, **[RPG]** 'Friend, I am not being unfair to you.
20:17 to Jerusalem, he took the twelve disciples aside and **said** to them,
20:21 he **asked**. She said, "Grant that one of these two sons of mine may
20:21 *She* **said**, "Grant that one of these two sons of mine may sit at your
20:21 "**Grant** that one of these two sons of mine may sit at your right
20:22 "You don't know what you are asking," Jesus **said** to them. "Can
20:22 you drink the cup I am going to drink?" "We can," *they* **answered**.
20:23 Jesus **said** to them, "You will indeed drink from my cup, but to sit
20:25 Jesus called them together and **said**, "You know that the rulers of
20:30 they shouted, **[RPG]** "Lord, Son of David, have mercy on us!"
20:31 but they shouted **[RPG]** all the louder, "Lord, Son of David,
20:32 and called them. "What do you want me to do for you?" *he* **asked**.
20:33 "Lord," *they* **answered**, "we want our sight."
21: 2 **saying** to them, "Go to the village ahead of you, and at once you
21: 3 If anyone **says** anything to you, tell him that the Lord needs them,
21: 3 If anyone says anything to you, **tell** him that the Lord needs them,
21: 4 This took place to fulfill what *was* **spoken** through the prophet:
21: 4 took place to fulfill what was spoken through the prophet: **[RPG]**
21: 5 "**Say** to the Daughter of Zion, 'See, your king comes to you,
21: 9 that followed shouted, **[RPG]** "Hosanna to the Son of David!"
21:10 the whole city was stirred and **asked**, "Who is this?"
21:11 The crowds **answered**, "This is Jesus, the prophet from Nazareth in
21:13 "It is written," *he* **said** to them, " 'My house will be called a house
21:15 **[RPG]** "Hosanna to the Son of David," they were indignant.

21:16 "Do you hear what these children *are* **saying**?" they asked him.
21:16 "Do you hear what these children are saying?" *they* **asked** him.
21:16 "Yes," **replied** Jesus, "have you never read, " 'From the lips of
21:19 Then *he* **said** to it, "May you never bear fruit again!" Immediately
21:20 were amazed. "How did the fig tree wither so quickly?" *they* **asked**.
21:21 Jesus replied, **[RPG]** "I tell you the truth, if you have faith
21:21 Jesus replied, "*I* **tell** you the truth, if you have faith and do not
21:21 but also *you can* **say** to this mountain, 'Go, throw yourself into the
21:23 these things?" *they* **asked**. "And who gave you this authority?"
21:24 Jesus replied, **[RPG]** "I will also ask you one question. If you
21:24 If *you* **answer** me, I will tell you by what authority I am doing
21:24 I *will* **tell** you by what authority I am doing these things.
21:25 They discussed it among themselves and **said**, "If we say,
21:25 They discussed it among themselves and said, "If *we* **say**,
21:25 among themselves and said, "If we say, 'From heaven,' *he will* **ask**,
21:26 But if *we* **say**, 'From men'—we are afraid of the people, for they
21:27 So they answered Jesus, **[RPG]** "We don't know." Then he said,
21:27 "Neither *will I* **tell** you by what authority I am doing these things.
21:28 He went to the first and **said**, 'Son, go and work today in the
21:29 he answered, **[RPG]** but later he changed his mind and went.
21:30 "Then the father went to the other son and **said** the same thing.
21:30 same thing. He answered, 'I will, sir,' **[RPG]** but he did not go.
21:31 "The first," *they* **answered**. Jesus said to them, "I tell you the truth,
21:31 Jesus **said** to them, "I tell you the truth, the tax collectors
21:31 "*I* **tell** you the truth, the tax collectors and the prostitutes are
21:37 he sent his son to them. 'They will respect my son,' *he* **said**.
21:38 the tenants saw the son, *they* **said** to each other, 'This is the heir.
21:41 *they* **replied**, "and he will rent the vineyard to other tenants,
21:42 Jesus **said** to them, "Have you never read in the Scriptures:
21:43 "Therefore *I* **tell** you that the kingdom of God will be taken away
21:45 heard Jesus' parables, they knew *he was* **talking** about them.
22: 1 Jesus **spoke** to them again in parables, saying:
22: 1 Jesus spoke to them again in parables, **saying**:
22: 4 "Then he sent some more servants and **said**, 'Tell those who have
22: 4 '**Tell** those who have been invited that I have prepared my dinner:
22: 8 "Then *he* **said** to his servants, 'The wedding banquet is ready,
22:12 'Friend,' *he* **asked**, 'how did you get in here without wedding
22:13 "Then the king **told** the attendants, 'Tie him hand and foot,
22:16 "Teacher," *they* **said**, "we know you are a man of integrity and that
22:17 **Tell** us then, what is your opinion? Is it right to pay taxes to Caesar
22:18 But Jesus, knowing their evil intent, **said**, "You hypocrites,
22:20 *he* **asked** them, "Whose portrait is this? And whose inscription?"
22:21 "Caesar's," *they* **replied**. Then he said to them, "Give to Caesar
22:21 Then *he* **said** to them, "Give to Caesar what is Caesar's, and to God
22:23 who **say** there is no resurrection, came to him with a question.
22:24 "Teacher," *they* **said**, "Moses told us that if a man dies without
22:24 said, "Moses **told** us that if a man dies without having children,
22:29 **[RPG]** "You are in error because you do not know the Scriptures
22:31 of the dead—have you not read what⁵ [+3836] God said to you,
22:31 resurrection of the dead—have you not read what God **said** to you,
22:42 **[RPG]** "What do you think about the Christ? Whose son is he?"
22:42 the Christ? Whose son is he?" "The son of David," *they* **replied**.
22:43 *He* **said** to them, "How is it then that David, speaking by the Spirit,
22:43 He said to them, "How is it then that David, **speaking** by the Spirit,
22:44 " 'The Lord **said** to my Lord: "Sit at my right hand until I put your
23: 2 **[RPG]** "The teachers of the law and the Pharisees sit in Moses'
23: 3 So you must obey them and do everything *they* **tell** you. But do
23: 3 do not do what they do, for they do not practice what *they* **preach**.
23:16 You **say**, 'If anyone swears by the temple, it means nothing;
23:30 And *you* **say**, 'If we had lived in the days of our forefathers,
23:36 *I* **tell** you the truth, all this will come upon this generation.
23:39 For *I* **tell** you, you will not see me again until you say, 'Blessed is
23:39 For I tell you, you will not see me again until *you* **say**, 'Blessed is
24: 2 he **asked**. "I tell you the truth, not one stone here will be left on
24: 2 "*I* **tell** you the truth, not one stone here will be left on another;
24: 3 "**Tell** us," they said, "when will this happen, and what will be the
24: 3 "Tell us," they said, "when will this happen, and what will be the
24: 4 Jesus answered: **[RPG]** "Watch out that no one deceives you.
24: 5 in my name, **claiming**, 'I am the Christ,' and will deceive many.
24:15 that causes desolation,' **spoken of** through the prophet Daniel—
24:23 At that time if anyone **says** to you, 'Look, here is the Christ!'
24:26 "So if *anyone* **tells** you, 'There he is, out in the desert,' do not go
24:34 *I* **tell** you the truth, this generation will certainly not pass away
24:47 *I* **tell** you the truth, he will put him in charge of all his possessions.
24:48 But suppose that servant is wicked and **says** to himself, 'My master
25: 8 The foolish ones **said** to the wise, 'Give us some of your oil;

25: 9 'there may not be enough [RPG] for both us and you.
25: 11 the others also came. 'Sir! Sir!' they said. 'Open the door for us!'
25: 12 "But he replied, [RPG] 'I tell you the truth, I don't know you.'
25: 12 "But he replied, '*I tell* you the truth, I don't know you.'
25: 20 'Master,' *he* said, 'you entrusted me with five talents. See,
25: 22 'Master,' *he* said, 'you entrusted me with two talents; see,
25: 24 'Master,' *he* said, 'I knew that you are a hard man,
25: 26 "His master replied, [RPG] 'You wicked, lazy servant! So you
25: 34 "Then the King *will* say to those on his right, 'Come, you who are
25: 37 [RPG] 'Lord, when did we see you hungry and feed you,
25: 40 "The King will reply, [RPG] 'I tell you the truth, whatever you did
25: 40 "The King will reply, '*I tell* you the truth, whatever you did for one
25: 41 "Then *he will* say to those on his left, 'Depart from me, you who
25: 44 "They also will answer, [RPG] 'Lord, when did we see you hungry
25: 45 "He will reply, [RPG] 'I tell you the truth, whatever you did not do
25: 45 "He will reply, '*I tell* you the truth, whatever you did not do for one
26: 1 Jesus had finished saying all these things, *he* said to his disciples.
26: 3 in the palace of the high priest, whose **name** *was* Caiaphas,
26: 5 "But not during the Feast," *they* said, "or there may be a riot among
26: 8 saw this, they were indignant. "Why this waste?" *they* asked.
26: 10 Aware of this, Jesus said to them, "Why are you bothering this
26: 13 *I* tell you the truth, wherever this gospel is preached throughout the
26: 14 the one **called** Judas Iscariot—went to the chief priests
26: 15 and asked, "What are you willing to give me if I hand him over to
26: 17 Feast of Unleavened Bread, the disciples came to Jesus and asked,
26: 18 He replied, "Go into the city to a certain man and tell him,
26: 18 He replied, "Go into the city to a certain man and tell him,
26: 18 "Go into the city to a certain man and tell him, 'The Teacher **says**:
26: 21 eating, *he* said, "I tell you the truth, one of you will betray me."
26: 21 he said, "*I tell* you the truth, one of you will betray me."
26: 22 They were very sad and began *to* say to him one after the other,
26: 23 [RPG] "The one who has dipped his hand into the bowl with me
26: 25 the one who would betray him, said, "Surely not I, Rabbi?"
26: 25 said, "Surely not I, Rabbi?" Jesus answered, "Yes, it is you."
26: 25 "Surely not I, Rabbi?" Jesus answered, "**Yes** [+*5148*], it is you.
26: 26 and broke it, and gave it to his disciples, **saying**, "Take and eat;
26: 27 and offered it to them, **saying**, "Drink from it, all of you.
26: 29 *I* tell you, I will not drink of this fruit of the vine from now on until
26: 31 Then Jesus **told** them, "This very night you will all fall away on
26: 33 [RPG] "Even if all fall away on account of you, I never will."
26: 34 "*I* tell you the truth," Jesus answered, "this very night,
26: 35 But Peter **declared**, "Even if I have to die with you, I will never
26: 35 I will never disown you." And all the other disciples **said** the same.
26: 36 Then Jesus went with his disciples to a place **called** Gethsemane,
26: 36 and *he* said to them, "Sit here while I go over there and pray."
26: 38 Then *he* said to them, "My soul is overwhelmed with sorrow to the
26: 39 he fell with his face to the ground and prayed, [RPG] "My Father,
26: 40 you men not keep watch with me for one hour?" *he* asked Peter.
26: 42 He went away a second time and prayed, [RPG] "My Father,
26: 44 away once more and prayed the third time, **saying** the same thing.
26: 45 He returned to the disciples and said to them, "Are you still
26: 48 a signal with them: [RPG] "The one I kiss is the man; arrest him."
26: 49 Going at once to Jesus, Judas said, "Greetings, Rabbi!" and kissed
26: 50 Jesus replied, "Friend, do what you came for." Then the men
26: 52 "Put your sword back in its place," Jesus said to him, "for all who
26: 55 At that time Jesus said to the crowd, "Am I leading a rebellion,
26: 61 and **declared**, "This fellow said, 'I am able to destroy the temple of
26: 62 then the high priest stood up and said to Jesus, "Are you not going
26: 63 The high priest said to him, "I charge you under oath by the living
26: 63 by the living God: **Tell** us if you are the Christ, the Son of God."
26: 64 "**Yes, it is as you say** [+*5148*]," Jesus replied. "But I say to all of
26: 64 "Yes, it is as you say," Jesus **replied**. "But I say to all of you:
26: 64 "Yes, it is as you say," Jesus replied. "But *I* say to all of you:
26: 65 Then the high priest tore his clothes and said, "He has spoken
26: 66 do you think?" "He is worthy of death," they answered. [RPG]
26: 68 and said, "Prophesy to us, Christ. Who hit you?"
26: 69 girl came to him. "You also were with Jesus of Galilee," *she* said.
26: 70 before them all. "I don't know what *you're* **talking about**," he said.
26: 70 before them all. "I don't know what you're talking about," *he* **said**.
26: 71 where another girl saw him and **said** to the people there,
26: 73 After a little while, those standing there went up to Peter and said,
26: 75 Then Peter remembered the word Jesus *had* **spoken**: "Before the
27: 4 "I have sinned," *he* said, "for I have betrayed innocent blood."
27: 4 "What is that to us?" *they* **replied**. "That's your responsibility."
27: 6 The chief priests picked up the coins and said, "It is against the law
27: 9 Then what *was* **spoken** by Jeremiah the prophet was fulfilled:

27: 9 [RPG] "They took the thirty silver coins, the price set on him by
27: 11 the governor asked him, [RPG] "Are you the king of the Jews?"
27: 11 king of the Jews?" "**Yes, it is as you say** [+*5148*]," Jesus replied.
27: 13 Then Pilate **asked** him, "Don't you hear the testimony they are
27: 16 At that time they had a notorious prisoner, **called** Barabbas.
27: 17 So when the crowd had gathered, Pilate **asked** them, "Which one do
27: 17 want me to release to you: Barabbas, or Jesus who *is* **called** Christ?"
27: 19 [RPG] "Don't have anything to do with that innocent man,
27: 21 to you?" [RPG] asked the governor. "Barabbas," they answered.
27: 21 to release to you?" asked the governor. "Barabbas," they **answered**.
27: 22 "What shall I do, then, with Jesus who *is* **called** Christ?" Pilate
27: 22 is called Christ?" Pilate **asked**. They all answered, "Crucify him!"
27: 22 is called Christ?" Pilate asked. *They* all **answered**, "Crucify him!"
27: 23 asked Pilate. But they shouted all the louder, [RPG] "Crucify him!"
27: 24 "I am innocent of this man's blood," *he* said. "It is your
27: 25 [RPG] "Let his blood be on us and on our children!"
27: 29 in front of him and mocked him. "Hail, king of the Jews!" *they* said.
27: 33 They came to a place **called** Golgotha (which means The Place of
27: 33 They came to a place called Golgotha (which **means** [+*1639*] The
27: 40 and **saying**, "You who are going to destroy the temple and build it
27: 42 "He saved others," *they* said, "but he can't save himself! He's the
27: 43 him now if he wants him, for *he* said, 'I am the Son of God.' "
27: 46 in a loud voice, [RPG] "*Eloi, Eloi, lama sabachthani?*"—
27: 47 of those standing there heard this, *they* said, "He's calling Elijah."
27: 49 The rest said, "Now leave him alone. Let's see if Elijah comes to
27: 54 and all that had happened, they were terrified, and **exclaimed**,
27: 63 "Sir," *they* said, "we remember that while he was still alive that
27: 63 "we remember that while he was still alive that deceiver **said**,
27: 64 the body and **tell** the people that he has been raised from the dead.
28: 5 The angel **said** to the women, "Do not be afraid, for I know that you
28: 6 He is not here; he has risen, just as *he* **said**. Come and see the place
28: 7 Then go quickly and **tell** his disciples: 'He has risen from the dead
28: 7 of you into Galilee. There you will see him.' Now *I have* **told** you."
28: 9 "Greetings," *he* said. They came to him, clasped his feet
28: 10 Then Jesus **said** to them, "Do not be afraid. Go and tell my brothers
28: 13 **telling** them, "You are to say, 'His disciples came during the night
28: 13 telling them, "*You are to* say, 'His disciples came during the night
28: 18 [RPG] "All authority in heaven and on earth has been given to me.
Mk 1: 7 [RPG] "After me will come one more powerful than I, the thongs
1: 15 "The time has come," *he* said. "The kingdom of God is near.
1: 17 follow me," Jesus said, "and I will make you fishers of men."
1: 24 [RPG] "What do you want with us, Jesus of Nazareth? Have you
1: 25 "Be quiet!" said Jesus sternly. "Come out of him!"
1: 27 so amazed that they asked each other, [RPG] "What is this?
1: 30 was in bed with a fever, and *they* **told** Jesus about her.
1: 37 and when they found him, *they* **exclaimed**: "Everyone is looking
1: 38 Jesus **replied**, "Let us go somewhere else—to the nearby villages—
1: 40 on his knees, [RPG] "If you are willing, you can make me clean."
1: 41 his hand and touched the man. "I am willing," *he* said. "Be clean!"
1: 44 [RPG] "See that you don't tell this to anyone. But go,
1: 44 "See that *you* don't **tell** this to anyone. But go, show yourself to the
2: 5 their faith, *he* said to the paralytic, "Son, your sins are forgiven."
2: 8 and *he* said to them, "Why are you thinking these things?
2: 9 *to* say to the paralytic, 'Your sins are forgiven,' or to say,
2: 9 sins are forgiven,' or *to* **say**, 'Get up, take your mat and walk'?
2: 10 has authority on earth to forgive sins...." *He* said to the paralytic,
2: 11 "*I tell* you, get up, take your mat and go home."
2: 12 This amazed everyone and they praised God, **saying**, "We have
2: 14 "Follow me," Jesus **told** him, and Levi got up and followed him.
2: 16 with the "sinners" and tax collectors, *they* **asked** his disciples:
2: 17 On hearing this, Jesus said to them, "It is not the healthy who need
2: 18 Some people came and **asked** Jesus, "How is it that John's disciples
2: 19 Jesus **answered**, "How can the guests of the bridegroom fast while
2: 24 The Pharisees said to him, "Look, why are they doing what is
2: 25 *He* **answered**, "Have you never read what David did when he
2: 27 Then *he* said to them, "The Sabbath was made for man, not man for
3: 3 Jesus said to the man with the shriveled hand, "Stand up in front of
3: 4 Then Jesus **asked** them, "Which is lawful on the Sabbath: to do
3: 5 at their stubborn hearts, said to the man, "Stretch out your hand."
3: 9 Because of the crowd *he* **told** his disciples to have a small boat
3: 11 down before him and cried out, [RPG] "You are the Son of God."
3: 21 went to take charge of him, for *they* said, "He is out of his mind."
3: 22 And the teachers of the law who came down from Jerusalem said,
3: 23 So Jesus called them and **spoke** to them in parables: "How can
3: 28 *I* tell you the truth, all the sins and blasphemies of men will be
3: 30 He said this because *they* were **saying**, "He has an evil spirit."

3:32 and *they* **told** him, "Your mother and brothers are outside looking
3:33 "Who are my mother and my brothers?" **[RPG]** he asked.
3:34 Then he looked at those seated in a circle around him and **said**,
4: 2 He taught them many things by parables, and in his teaching **said**:
4: 9 Then Jesus **said**, "He who has ears to hear, let him hear."
4:11 *He* **told** them, "The secret of the kingdom of God has been given to
4:13 Then Jesus **said** to them, "Don't you understand this parable?
4:21 *He* **said** to them, "Do you bring in a lamp to put it under a bowl
4:24 "Consider carefully what you hear," *he* **continued**. "With the
4:26 *He* also **said**, "This is what the kingdom of God is like. A man
4:30 Again *he* **said**, "What shall we say the kingdom of God is like,
4:35 That day when evening came, *he* **said** to his disciples, "Let us go
4:38 The disciples woke him and **said** to him, "Teacher, don't you care
4:39 *He* got up, rebuked the wind and **said** to the waves, "Quiet!
4:40 *He* **said** to his disciples, "Why are you so afraid? Do you still have
4:41 They were terrified and **asked** each other, "Who is this? Even the
5: 7 **[RPG]** He shouted at the top of his voice, "What do you want with
5: 8 For Jesus *had* **said** to him, "Come out of this man, you evil spirit!"
5: 9 your name?" "My name is Legion," *he* **replied**, "for we are many."
5:12 The demons begged Jesus, **[RPG]** "Send us among the pigs;
5:19 Jesus did not let him, but **said**, "Go home to your family and tell
5:23 pleaded earnestly with him, **[RPG]** "My little daughter is dying.
5:28 because *she* **thought**, "If I just touch his clothes, I will be healed."
5:30 *He* turned around in the crowd and **asked**, "Who touched me?
5:31 his disciples **answered**, "and yet you can ask, 'Who touched me?' "
5:31 his disciples answered, "and yet *you* can **ask**, 'Who touched me?' "
5:33 fell at his feet and, trembling with fear, **told** him the whole truth.
5:34 He **said** to her, "Daughter, your faith has healed you. Go in peace
5:35 of Jairus, the synagogue ruler. "Your daughter is dead," *they* **said**.
5:36 what they said, Jesus **told** the synagogue ruler, "Don't be afraid;
5:39 *He* went in and **said** to them, "Why all this commotion and
5:41 *He* took her by the hand and **said** to her, *"Talitha koum!"*
5:41 *"Talitha koum!"* (which means, "Little girl, *I* **say** to you, get up!").
5:43 know about this, and **told** them to give her something to eat.
6: 2 were amazed. "Where did this man get these things?" *they* **asked**.
6: 4 Jesus **said** to them, "Only in his hometown, among his relatives
6:10 **[RPG]** Whenever you enter a house, stay there until you leave
6:14 *Some were* **saying**, "John the Baptist has been raised from the dead,
6:15 Others **said**, "He is Elijah." And still others claimed, "He is a
6:15 And still others **claimed**, "He is a prophet, like one of the prophets
6:16 But when Herod heard this, *he* **said**, "John, the man I beheaded,
6:18 For John *had been* **saying** to Herod, "It is not lawful for you to
6:22 The king **said** to the girl, "Ask me for anything you want, and I'll
6:24 *She* went out and **said** to her mother, "What shall I ask for?"
6:24 shall I ask for?" "The head of John the Baptist," she **answered**.
6:25 **[RPG]** "I want you to give me right now the head of John the
6:31 *he* **said** to them, "Come with me by yourselves to a quiet place
6:35 "This is a remote place," *they* **said**, "and it's already very late.
6:37 But he answered, **[RPG]** "You give them something to eat."
6:37 *They* **said** to him, "That would take eight months of a man's wages!
6:38 he **asked**. "Go and see." When they found out, they said, "Five—
6:38 and see." When they found out, *they* **said**, "Five—and two fish."
6:50 Immediately he spoke to them and **said**, "Take courage! It is I.
7: 6 He **replied**, "Isaiah was right when he prophesied about you
7: 9 And *he* **said** to them: "You have a fine way of setting aside the
7:10 For Moses **said**, 'Honor your father and your mother,' and,
7:11 But you **say** that if a man says to his father or mother:
7:11 But you say that if a man **says** to his father or mother:
7:14 Again Jesus called the crowd to him and **said**, "Listen to me,
7:18 "Are you so dull?" *he* **asked**. "Don't you see that nothing that
7:20 *He* **went on**: "What comes out of a man is what makes him
7:27 "First let the children eat all they want," *he* **told** her, "for it is not
7:28 **[RPG]** "but even the dogs under the table eat the children's
7:29 Then *he* **told** her, "For such a reply, you may go; the demon has left
7:34 He looked up to heaven and with a deep sigh **said** to him,
7:36 Jesus commanded them not to **tell** anyone. But the more he did so,
7:37 "He has done everything well," *they* **said**. "He even makes the deaf
8: 1 they had nothing to eat, Jesus called his disciples to him and **said**,
8: 5 many loaves do you have?" Jesus asked. "Seven," they **replied**.
8: 7 he gave thanks for them also and **told** the disciples to distribute
8:12 He sighed deeply and **said**, "Why does this generation ask for a
8:12 a miraculous sign? *I* **tell** you the truth, no sign will be given to it."
8:15 "Be careful," Jesus warned **[RPG]** them. "Watch out for the yeast
8:16 They discussed this with one another and said, [UBS-] "It is
8:17 Aware of their discussion, Jesus **asked** them: "Why are you talking
8:19 basketfuls of pieces did you pick up?" "Twelve," *they* **replied**.

8:20 basketfuls of pieces did you pick up?" *They* **answered**, "Seven."
8:21 *He* **said** to them, "Do you still not understand?"
8:24 *He* looked up and **said**, "I see people; they look like trees walking
8:26 Jesus sent him home, **saying**, "Don't go into the village."
8:27 On the way he asked them, **[RPG]** "Who do people say I am?"
8:27 On the way he asked them, "Who *do* people **say** I am?"
8:28 They **replied**, "Some say John the Baptist; others say Elijah;
8:28 They replied, **[RPG]** "Some say John the Baptist; others say
8:29 he asked. "Who *do* you **say** I am?" Peter answered, "You are the
8:29 do you say I am?" Peter answered, **[RPG]** "You are the Christ."
8:30 Jesus warned them not to **tell** anyone about him.
8:33 at his disciples, he rebuked Peter. "Get behind me, Satan!" *he* **said**.
8:34 Then he called the crowd to him along with his disciples and **said**:
9: 1 And *he* **said** to them, "I tell you the truth, some who are standing
9: 1 And he said to them, "*I* **tell** you the truth, some who are standing
9: 5 Peter **said** to Jesus, "Rabbi, it is good for us to be here. Let us put
9:11 **[RPG]** "Why do the teachers of the law say that Elijah must come
9:11 "Why *do* the teachers of the law **say** that Elijah must come first?"
9:13 But *I* **tell** you, Elijah has come, and they have done to him
9:18 *I* **asked** your disciples to drive out the spirit, but they could not."
9:19 Jesus replied, **[RPG]** "how long shall I stay with you?
9:21 "How long has he been like this?" "From childhood," he **answered**.
9:23 " 'If you can'?" **said** Jesus. "Everything is possible for him who
9:24 Immediately the boy's father exclaimed, **[RPG]** "I do believe;
9:25 "You deaf and mute spirit," *he* **said**, "I command you, come out of
9:26 The boy looked so much like a corpse that many **said**, "He's dead."
9:29 *He* **replied**, "This kind can come out only by prayer."
9:31 *He* **said** to them, "The Son of Man is going to be betrayed into the
9:35 Sitting down, Jesus called the Twelve and **said**, "If anyone wants to
9:36 him stand among them. Taking him in his arms, *he* **said** to them,
9:39 "Do not stop him," Jesus **said**. "No one who does a miracle in my
9:41 *I* **tell** you the truth, anyone who gives you a cup of water in my
10: 3 "What did Moses command you?" he replied. **[RPG]**
10: 4 They **said**, "Moses permitted a man to write a certificate of divorce
10: 5 hearts were hard that Moses wrote you this law," Jesus **replied**.
10:11 *He* **answered**, "Anyone who divorces his wife and marries another
10:14 *He* **said** to them, "Let the little children come to me, and do not
10:15 *I* **tell** you the truth, anyone who will not receive the kingdom of
10:18 "Why *do you* **call** me good?" Jesus answered. "No one is good—
10:18 me good?" Jesus **answered**. "No one is good—except God alone.
10:21 "One thing you lack," *he* **said**. "Go, sell everything you have
10:23 Jesus looked around and **said** to his disciples, "How hard it is for
10:24 But Jesus **said** again, "Children, how hard it is to enter the kingdom
10:26 more amazed, and **said** to each other, "Who then can be saved?"
10:27 Jesus looked at them and **said**, "With man this is impossible,
10:28 Peter **said** [+*806*] to him, "We have left everything to follow you!"
10:29 "*I* **tell** you the truth," Jesus replied, "no one has left home
10:32 Again *he* took the Twelve aside and **told** [+*806*] them what was
10:35 "Teacher," *they* **said**, "we want you to do for us whatever we ask."
10:36 "What do you want me to do for you?" he **asked**.
10:37 They **replied**, "Let one of us sit at your right and the other at your
10:38 "You don't know what you are asking," Jesus **said**. "Can you drink
10:39 "We can," they **answered**. Jesus said to them, "You will drink the
10:39 Jesus **said** to them, "You will drink the cup I drink and be baptized
10:42 Jesus called them together and **said**, "You know that those who are
10:47 he began to shout, **[RPG]** "Jesus, Son of David, have mercy on
10:49 Jesus stopped and **said**, "Call him." So they called to the blind man,
10:49 "Call him." So they called to the blind man, **[RPG]** "Cheer up!
10:51 Jesus asked **[RPG]** him. The blind man said, "Rabbi, I want to see."
10:51 Jesus asked him. The blind man **said**, "Rabbi, I want to see.
10:52 "Go," **said** Jesus, "your faith has healed you." Immediately he
11: 2 **saying** to them, "Go to the village ahead of you, and just as you
11: 3 If anyone **asks** you, 'Why are you doing this?' tell him, 'The Lord
11: 3 **tell** him, 'The Lord needs it and will send it back here shortly.' "
11: 5 some people standing there **asked**, "What are you doing,
11: 6 They **answered** as Jesus had told them to, and the people let them
11: 6 They answered as Jesus *had* **told** them to, and the people let them
11:14 *he* **said** to the tree, "May no one ever eat fruit from you again."
11:17 And as he taught them, *he* **said**, "Is it not written: " 'My house will
11:21 Peter remembered and **said** to Jesus, "Rabbi, look! The fig tree you
11:22 "Have faith in God," Jesus **answered**. **[RPG]**
11:23 "*I* **tell** you the truth, if anyone says to this mountain, 'Go,
11:23 "I tell you the truth, if anyone **says** to this mountain, 'Go, throw
11:24 Therefore *I* **tell** you, whatever you ask for in prayer, believe that
11:28 things?" *they* **asked**. "And who gave you authority to do this?"
11:29 Jesus **replied**, "I will ask you one question. Answer me, and I will

11:29 and *I will* **tell** you by what authority I am doing these things.
11:31 They discussed it among themselves and **said**, "If we say,
11:31 They discussed it among themselves and said, "If *we* **say**,
11:31 among themselves and said, "If we say, 'From heaven,' *he will* **ask**,
11:32 But if *we* **say**, 'From men'…." (They feared the people, for
11:33 So they answered **[RPG]** Jesus, "We don't know." Jesus said,
11:33 Jesus **said**, "Neither will I tell you by what authority I am doing
11:33 "Neither *will* I **tell** you by what authority I am doing these things."
12: 6 He sent him last of all, **saying**, 'They will respect my son.'
12: 7 "But the tenants **said** to one another, 'This is the heir. Come,
12:12 because they knew *he had* **spoken** the parable against them.
12:14 *They* came to him and **said**, "Teacher, we know you are a man of
12:15 to trap me?" *he* **asked**. "Bring me a denarius and let me look at it."
12:16 They brought the coin, and *he* **asked** them, "Whose portrait is this?
12:16 portrait is this? And whose inscription?" "Caesar's," they **replied**.
12:17 Then Jesus **said** to them, "Give to Caesar what is Caesar's and to
12:18 Then the Sadducees, who **say** there is no resurrection, came to him
12:19 "Teacher," *they* **said**, "Moses wrote for us that if a man's brother
12:26 in the account of the bush, how God **said** to him, 'I am the God of
12:26 said to him, **[RPG]** 'I am the God of Abraham, the God of Isaac,
12:32 "Well said, teacher," the man **replied**. "You are right in saying that
12:32 "You are right in **saying** that God is one and there is no other
12:34 *he* **said** to him, "You are not far from the kingdom of God."
12:35 While Jesus was teaching in the temple courts, *he* **asked**, "How is it
12:35 "How is it that the teachers of the law **say** that the Christ is the son
12:36 David himself, speaking by the Holy Spirit, **declared**: " 'The Lord
12:36 speaking by the Holy Spirit, declared: " 'The Lord **said** to my Lord:
12:37 David himself **calls** him 'Lord.' How then can he be his son?"
12:38 As he taught, Jesus **said**, "Watch out for the teachers of the law.
12:43 Calling his disciples to him, Jesus **said**, "I tell you the truth,
12:43 Calling his disciples to him, Jesus said, "*I* **tell** you the truth,
13: 1 the temple, one of his disciples **said** to him, "Look, Teacher!
13: 2 "Do you see all these great buildings?" **replied** Jesus. "Not one
13: 4 "**Tell** us, when will these things happen? And what will be the sign
13: 5 Jesus **said** [+*806*] to them: "Watch out that no one deceives you.
13: 6 come in my name, **claiming**, 'I am he,' and will deceive many.
13:21 At that time if anyone **says** to you, 'Look, here is the Christ!'
13:30 *I* **tell** you the truth, this generation will certainly not pass away
13:37 What *I* **say** to you, I say to everyone: 'Watch!' "
13:37 What I say to you, *I* **say** to everyone: 'Watch!' "
14: 2 "But not during the Feast, *they* **said**, "or the people may riot."
14: 6 "Leave her alone," **said** Jesus. "Why are you bothering her? She has
14: 9 *I* **tell** you the truth, wherever the gospel is preached throughout the
14:12 Jesus' disciples **asked** him, "Where do you want us to go and make
14:13 So he sent two of his disciples, **telling** them, "Go into the city,
14:14 **Say** to the owner of the house he enters, 'The Teacher asks:
14:14 Say to the owner of the house he enters, 'The Teacher **asks**:
14:16 went into the city and found things just as Jesus *had* **told** them.
14:18 he **said**, "I tell you the truth, one of you will betray me—
14:18 he said, "*I* **tell** you the truth, one of you will betray me—
14:19 were saddened, and one by one they **said** to him, "Surely not I?"
14:20 "It is one of the Twelve," he **replied**, "one who dips bread into the
14:22 and broke it, and gave it to his disciples, **saying**, "Take it;
14:24 of the covenant, which is poured out for many," *he* **said** to them.
14:25 "*I* **tell** you the truth, I will not drink again of the fruit of the vine
14:27 "You will all fall away," Jesus **told** them, "for it is written: " 'I will
14:30 "*I* **tell** you the truth," Jesus answered, "today—yes, tonight—
14:30 "I tell you the truth," Jesus **answered**, "today—yes, tonight—
14:31 I will never disown you." And all the others **said** the same.
14:32 and Jesus **said** to his disciples, "Sit here while I pray."
14:34 is overwhelmed with sorrow to the point of death," *he* **said** to them.
14:36 "*Abba*, Father," *he* **said**, "everything is possible for you. Take this
14:37 found them sleeping. "Simon," *he* **said** to Peter, "are you asleep?
14:39 Once more he went away and prayed the same thing. **[RPG]**
14:41 the third time, *he* **said** to them, "Are you still sleeping and resting?
14:44 **[RPG]** "The one I kiss is the man; arrest him and lead him away
14:45 Going at once to Jesus, Judas **said**, "Rabbi!" and kissed him.
14:48 "Am I leading a rebellion," **said** Jesus, "that you have come out
14:57 some stood up and gave this false testimony against him: **[RPG]**
14:58 "We heard him **say**, 'I will destroy this man-made temple and in
14:60 them and asked Jesus, **[RPG]** "Are you not going to answer?
14:61 **[RPG]** "Are you the Christ, the Son of the Blessed One?"
14:62 "I am," **said** Jesus. "And you will see the Son of Man sitting at the
14:63 tore his clothes. "Why do we need any more witnesses?" *he* **asked**.
14:65 blindfolded him, struck him with their fists, and **said**, "Prophesy!"
14:67 closely at him. "You also were with that Nazarene, Jesus," *she* **said**.

14:68 **[RPG]** "I don't know or understand what you're talking about,"
14:68 "I don't know or understand what you're **talking about**," he said,
14:69 she **said** [+*806*] again to those standing around, "This fellow is one
14:70 After a little while, those standing near **said** to Peter, "Surely you
14:71 he swore to them, "I don't know this man *you're* **talking about**."
14:72 Then Peter remembered the word Jesus *had* **spoken** to him:
15: 2 asked Pilate. "**Yes, it is as you say** [+*5148*]," Jesus replied.
15: 2 Jews?" asked Pilate. "Yes, it is as you say," Jesus replied. **[RPG]**
15: 4 So again Pilate asked him, **[RPG]** "Aren't you going to answer?
15: 7 A man **called** Barabbas was in prison with the insurrectionists who
15: 9 me to release to you the king of the Jews?" asked Pilate, **[RPG]**
15:12 "What shall I do, then, with the one *you* **call** the king of the Jews?"
15:12 the one you call the king of the Jews?" Pilate asked **[RPG]** them.
15:14 "Why? What crime has he committed?" **asked** Pilate. But they
15:29 by hurled insults at him, shaking their heads and **saying**, "So!
15:31 "He saved others," *they* **said**, "but he can't save himself!
15:35 standing near heard this, *they* **said**, "Listen, he's calling Elijah."
15:36 him alone. Let's see if Elijah comes to take him down," *he* **said**.
15:39 there in front of Jesus, heard his cry and saw how he died, *he* **said**,
16: 3 and *they* **asked** each other, "Who will roll the stone away from the
16: 6 "Don't be alarmed," he **said**. "You are looking for Jesus the
16: 7 But go, **tell** his disciples and Peter, 'He is going ahead of you into
16: 7 of you into Galilee. There you will see him, just as *he* **told** you.' "
16: 8 the tomb. *They* **said** nothing to anyone, because they were afraid.
16:15 *He* **said** to them, "Go into all the world and preach the good news to

Lk   1:13 But the angel **said** to him: "Do not be afraid, Zechariah; your prayer
1:18 Zechariah **asked** the angel, "How can I be sure of this? I am an old
1:19 The angel answered, **[RPG]** "I am Gabriel. I stand in the presence
1:25 "The Lord has done this for me," *she* **said**. "In these days he has
1:28 The angel went to her and **said**, "Greetings, you who are highly
1:30 But the angel **said** to her, "Do not be afraid, Mary, you have found
1:34 "How will this be," Mary **asked** the angel, "since I am a virgin?"
1:35 The angel answered, **[RPG]** "The Holy Spirit will come upon you,
1:38 "I am the Lord's servant," Mary **answered**. "May it be to me as you
1:42 **[RPG]** "Blessed are you among women, and blessed is the child
1:46 And Mary **said**: "My soul glorifies the Lord
1:60 but his mother spoke up and **said**, "No! He is to be called John."
1:61 *They* **said** to her, "There is no one among your relatives who has
1:63 to everyone's astonishment he wrote, **[RPG]** "His name is John."
1:66 wondered about it, **asking**, "What then is this child going to be?"
1:67 Zechariah was filled with the Holy Spirit and prophesied: **[RPG]**
2:10 But the angel **said** to them, "Do not be afraid. I bring you good
2:13 heavenly host appeared with the angel, praising God and **saying**,
2:24 and to offer a sacrifice in keeping with what *is* **said** in the Law of
2:28 Simeon took him in his arms and praised God, **saying**:
2:34 Then Simeon blessed them and **said** to Mary, his mother: "This
2:48 His mother **said** to him, "Son, why have you treated us like this?
2:49 "Why were you searching for me?" *he* **asked**. "Didn't you know I
3: 7 John **said** to the crowds coming out to be baptized by him,
3: 8 And do not begin *to* **say** to yourselves, 'We have Abraham as our
3: 8 For *I* **tell** you that out of these stones God can raise up children for
3:10 "What should we do then?" the crowd asked. **[RPG]**
3:11 **[RPG]** "The man with two tunics should share with him who has
3:12 came to be baptized. "Teacher," *they* **asked**, "what should we do?"
3:13 "Don't collect any more than you are required to," he **told** them.
3:14 Then some soldiers asked him, **[RPG]** "And what should we do?"
3:14 *He* **replied**, "Don't extort money and don't accuse people falsely—
3:16 John answered **[RPG]** them all, "I baptize you with water.
4: 3 The devil **said** to him, "If you are the Son of God, tell this stone to
4: 3 "If you are the Son of God, **tell** this stone to become bread."
4: 6 And he **said** to him, "I will give you all their authority
4: 8 Jesus answered, **[RPG]** "It is written: 'Worship the Lord your God
4: 9 "If you are the Son of God," *he* **said**, "throw yourself down from
4:12 Jesus answered, **[RPG]** "It says: 'Do not put the Lord your God to
4:12 Jesus answered, "*It* **says**: 'Do not put the Lord your God to the
4:21 and he began *by* **saying** to them, "Today this scripture is fulfilled in
4:22 words that came from his lips. "Isn't this Joseph's son?" *they* **asked**.
4:23 Jesus **said** to them, "Surely you will quote this proverb to me:
4:23 Jesus said to them, "Surely *you will* **quote** this proverb to me:
4:24 "*I* **tell** you the truth," he continued, "no prophet is accepted in his
4:24 "I tell you the truth," he **continued**, "no prophet is accepted in his
4:25 *I* **assure** [+*237*+*2093*] you that there were many widows in Israel
4:35 "Be quiet!" Jesus **said** sternly. "Come out of him!" Then the demon
4:36 and said to each other, **[RPG]** "What is this teaching?
4:41 out of many people, shouting, **[RPG]** "You are the Son of God!"
4:43 But he **said**, "I must preach the good news of the kingdom of God

5: 4	had finished speaking, he **said** to Simon, "Put out into deep water,
5: 5	Simon answered, **[RPG]** "Master, we've worked hard all night
5: 8	saw this, he fell at Jesus' knees and **said**, "Go away from me, Lord;
5:10	Then Jesus **said** to Simon, "Don't be afraid; from now on you will
5:12	he fell with his face to the ground and begged him, **[RPG]** "Lord,
5:13	his hand and touched the man. "I am willing," he **said**. "Be clean!"
5:14	Then Jesus ordered him, "Don't **tell** anyone, but go, show yourself
5:20	Jesus saw their faith, he **said**, "Friend, your sins are forgiven."
5:21	to themselves, **[RPG]** "Who is this fellow who speaks blasphemy?
5:22	**[RPG]** "Why are you thinking these things in your hearts?
5:23	Which is easier: to **say**, 'Your sins are forgiven,'
5:23	to say, 'Your sins are forgiven,' or to **say**, 'Get up and walk'?
5:24	He **said** to the paralyzed man, "I tell you, get up, take your mat
5:24	the paralyzed man, "I **tell** you, get up, take your mat and go home."
5:26	They were filled with awe and **said**, "We have seen remarkable
5:27	of Levi sitting at his tax booth. "Follow me," Jesus **said** to him,
5:30	**[RPG]** "Why do you eat and drink with tax collectors
5:31	Jesus answered **[RPG]** them, "It is not the healthy who need a
5:33	They **said** to him, "John's disciples often fast and pray, and
5:34	Jesus **answered**, "Can you make the guests of the bridegroom fast
5:36	He **told** them this parable: "No one tears a patch from a new
5:39	drinking old wine wants the new, for he **says**, 'The old is better.' "
6: 2	Some of the Pharisees **asked**, "Why are you doing what is unlawful
6: 3	**[RPG]** "Have you never read what David did when he and his
6: 5	Then Jesus **said** to them, "The Son of Man is Lord of the Sabbath."
6: 8	they were thinking and **said** to the man with the shriveled hand,
6: 9	Jesus **said** to them, "I ask you, which is lawful on the Sabbath:
6:10	He looked around at them all, and then **said** to the man, "Stretch out
6:20	Looking at his disciples, he **said**: "Blessed are you who are poor,
6:26	Woe to you when all men **speak** well of you, for that is how their
6:27	"But I **tell** you who hear me: Love your enemies, do good to those
6:39	He also **told** them this parable: "Can a blind man lead a blind man?
6:42	How can you **say** to your brother, 'Brother, let me take the speck
6:46	"Why do you call me, 'Lord, Lord,' and do not do what I **say**?
7: 4	earnestly with him, **[RPG]** "This man deserves to have you do this,
7: 6	far from the house when the centurion sent friends to **say** to him:
7: 7	to come to you. But **say** the word, and my servant will be healed.
7: 8	I **tell** this one, 'Go,' and he goes; and that one, 'Come,' and he
7: 9	and turning to the crowd following him, he **said**, "I tell you,
7: 9	and turning to the crowd following him, he said, "I **tell** you,
7:13	the Lord saw her, his heart went out to her and he **said**, "Don't cry."
7:14	carrying it stood still. He **said**, "Young man, I say to you, get up!"
7:14	carrying it stood still. He said, "Young man, I **say** to you, get up!"
7:16	praised God. "A great prophet has appeared among us," they **said**.
7:19	sent them to the Lord to **ask**, "Are you the one who was to come,
7:20	When the men came to Jesus, they **said**, "John the Baptist sent us to
7:20	came to Jesus, they said, "John the Baptist sent us to you to **ask**,
7:22	**[RPG]** "Go back and report to John what you have seen and heard:
7:24	messengers left, Jesus began to **speak** to the crowd about John:
7:26	go out to see? A prophet? Yes, I **tell** you, and more than a prophet.
7:28	I **tell** you, among those born of women there is no one greater than
7:32	**[RPG]** " 'We played the flute for you, and you did not dance;
7:33	eating bread nor drinking wine, and you **say**, 'He has a demon.'
7:34	The Son of Man came eating and drinking, and you **say**, 'Here is a
7:39	he **said** to himself, "If this man were a prophet, he would know
7:39	he said to himself, **[RPG]** "If this man were a prophet, he would
7:40	Jesus answered **[RPG]** him, "Simon, I have something to tell you."
7:40	answered him, "Simon, I have something to **tell** you."
7:40	"Simon, I have something to tell you." "**Tell** me, teacher," he said.
7:43	**[RPG]** "I suppose the one who had the bigger debt canceled."
7:43	the bigger debt canceled." "You have judged correctly," Jesus **said**.
7:47	Therefore, I **tell** you, her many sins have been forgiven—for she
7:48	Then Jesus **said** to her, "Your sins are forgiven."
7:49	The other guests began to **say** among themselves, "Who is this who
7:50	Jesus **said** to the woman, "Your faith has saved you; go in peace."
8: 4	were coming to Jesus from town after town, he **told** this parable:
8: 8	When he **said** this, he called out, "He who has ears to hear,
8:10	He **said**, "The knowledge of the secrets of the kingdom of God has
8:21	**[RPG]** "My mother and brothers are those who hear God's word
8:22	One day Jesus **said** to his disciples, "Let's go over to the other side
8:24	The disciples went and woke him, **saying**, "Master, Master,
8:25	he **asked** his disciples. In fear and amazement they asked one
8:25	In fear and amazement they **asked** one another, "Who is this?
8:28	and fell at his feet, **shouting** [+3489+5889] at the top of his voice,
8:30	"Legion," he **replied**, because many demons had gone into him.
8:38	gone out begged to go with him, but Jesus sent him away, **saying**,

8:45	"Who touched me?" Jesus **asked**. When they all denied it, Peter
8:45	When they all denied it, Peter **said**, "Master, the people are
8:46	But Jesus **said**, "Someone touched me; I know that power has gone
8:48	Then he **said** to her, "Daughter, your faith has healed you. Go in
8:49	of Jairus, the synagogue ruler. "Your daughter is dead," he **said**.
8:52	for her. "Stop wailing," Jesus **said**. "She is not dead but asleep."
8:54	But he took her by the hand and said, **[RPG]** "My child, get up!"
8:56	but he ordered them not to **tell** anyone what had happened.
9: 3	He **told** them: "Take nothing for the journey—no staff, no bag,
9: 7	because some were **saying** that John had been raised from the
9: 9	But Herod **said**, "I beheaded John. Who, then, is this I hear such
9:12	Late in the afternoon the Twelve came to him and **said**,
9:13	He **replied**, "You give them something to eat." They answered,
9:13	They **answered**, "We have only five loaves of bread and two fish—
9:14	But he **said** to his disciples, "Have them sit down in groups of
9:18	with him, he asked them, **[RPG]** "Who do the crowds say I am?"
9:18	were with him, he asked them, "Who do the crowds **say** I am?"
9:19	They replied, **[RPG]** "Some say John the Baptist; others say
9:20	"But what about you?" he **asked**. "Who do you say I am?" Peter
9:20	he asked. "Who do you **say** I am?" Peter answered, "The Christ of
9:20	do you say I am?" Peter answered, **[RPG]** "The Christ of God."
9:21	Jesus strictly warned them not to **tell** this to anyone.
9:22	And he **said**, "The Son of Man must suffer many things and be
9:23	Then he **said** to them all: "If anyone would come after me,
9:27	I **tell** you the truth, some who are standing here will not taste death
9:31	They **spoke about** his departure, which he was about to bring to
9:33	Peter **said** to him, "Master, it is good for us to be here.
9:33	and one for Elijah." (He did not know what he was **saying**.)
9:34	While he was **speaking**, a cloud appeared and enveloped them,
9:35	from the cloud, **saying**, "This is my Son, whom I have chosen;
9:38	**[RPG]** "Teacher, I beg you to look at my son, for he is my only
9:41	**[RPG]** "how long shall I stay with you and put up with you?
9:43	was marveling at all that Jesus did, he **said** to his disciples,
9:48	Then he **said** to them, "Whoever welcomes this little child in my
9:49	"Master," **said** John, "we saw a man driving out demons in your
9:50	"Do not stop him," Jesus **said**, "for whoever is not against you is
9:54	When the disciples James and John saw this, they **asked**, "Lord,
9:54	do you want us to **call** fire down from heaven to destroy them?"
9:57	the road, a man **said** to him, "I will follow you wherever you go."
9:58	Jesus **replied**, "Foxes have holes and birds of the air have nests,
9:59	He **said** to another man, "Follow me." But the man replied, "Lord,
9:59	But the man **replied**, "Lord, first let me go and bury my father."
9:60	Jesus **said** to him, "Let the dead bury their own dead, but you go
9:61	Still another **said**, "I will follow you, Lord; but first let me go back
9:62	Jesus **replied**, "No one who puts his hand to the plow and looks
10: 2	He **told** them, "The harvest is plentiful, but the workers are few.
10: 5	"When you enter a house, first **say**, 'Peace to this house.'
10: 9	Heal the sick who are there and **tell** them, 'The kingdom of God is
10:10	you enter a town and are not welcomed, go into its streets and **say**,
10:12	I **tell** you, it will be more bearable on that day for Sodom than for
10:17	The seventy-two returned with joy and **said**, "Lord,
10:18	He **replied**, "I saw Satan fall like lightning from heaven.
10:21	Holy Spirit, **said**, "I praise you, Father, Lord of heaven and earth,
10:23	Then he turned to his disciples and **said** privately, "Blessed are the
10:24	For I **tell** you that many prophets and kings wanted to see what you
10:25	"Teacher," he **asked**, "what must I do to inherit eternal life?"
10:26	"What is written in the Law?" he **replied**. "How do you read it?"
10:27	**[RPG]** " 'Love the Lord your God with all your heart and with all
10:28	"You have **answered** correctly," Jesus replied. "Do this and you
10:29	to justify himself, so he **asked** Jesus, "And who is my neighbor?"
10:30	In reply Jesus **said**: "A man was going down from Jerusalem to
10:35	'Look after him,' he **said**, 'and when I return, I will reimburse you
10:37	The expert in the law **replied**, "The one who had mercy on him."
10:37	one who had mercy on him." Jesus **told** him, "Go and do likewise."
10:40	She came to him and **asked**, "Lord, don't you care that my sister
10:40	sister has left me to do the work by myself? **Tell** her to help me!"
10:41	**[RPG]** "you are worried and upset about many things,
11: 1	finished, one of his disciples **said** to him, "Lord, teach us to pray,
11: 2	He **said** to them, "When you pray, say: " 'Father, hallowed be your
11: 2	He said to them, "When you pray, **say**: " 'Father, hallowed be your
11: 5	Then he **said** to them, "Suppose one of you has a friend, and he
11: 5	and he goes to him at midnight and **says**, 'Friend, lend me three
11: 7	"Then the one inside answers, **[RPG]** 'Don't bother me. The door
11: 8	I **tell** you, though he will not get up and give him the bread
11: 9	"So I **say** to you: Ask and it will be given to you; seek and you will
11:15	But some of them **said**, "By Beelzebub, the prince of demons,

11:17 Jesus knew their thoughts and **said** to them: "Any kingdom divided
11:18 because *you* **claim** that I drive out demons by Beelzebub.
11:24 and does not find it. Then *it* says, 'I will return to the house I left.'
11:27 As Jesus was **saying** these things, a woman in the crowd called
11:27 **[RPG]** "Blessed is the mother who gave you birth and nursed you."
11:28 He **replied**, "Blessed rather are those who hear the word of God
11:29 As the crowds increased, Jesus **said** [*+806*], "This is a wicked
11:39 Then the Lord **said** to him, "Now then, you Pharisees clean the
11:45 One of the experts in the law answered **[RPG]** him, "Teacher,
11:45 "Teacher, *when you* **say** these things, you insult us also."
11:46 Jesus **replied**, "And you experts in the law, woe to you, because
11:49 Because of this, God in his wisdom **said**, 'I will send them
11:51 Yes, *I* **tell** you, this generation will be held responsible for it all.
12: 1 on one another, Jesus began *to* **speak** first to his disciples, saying:
12: 3 What *you have* **said** in the dark will be heard in the daylight,
12: 4 "*I* **tell** you, my friends, do not be afraid of those who kill the body
12: 5 has power to throw you into hell. Yes, *I* **tell** you, fear him.
12: 8 "*I* **tell** you, whoever acknowledges me before men, the Son of
12:10 And everyone who **speaks** a word against the Son of Man will be
12:11 worry about how you will defend yourselves or what *you will* **say**,
12:12 for the Holy Spirit will teach you at that time what *you* should **say**."
12:13 Someone in the crowd **said** to him, "Teacher, tell my brother to
12:13 "Teacher, **tell** my brother to divide the inheritance with me."
12:14 Jesus **replied**, "Man, who appointed me a judge or an arbiter
12:15 Then *he* **said** to them, "Watch out! Be on your guard against all
12:16 And *he* **told** them this parable: "The ground of a certain rich man
12:16 **[RPG]** "The ground of a certain rich man produced a good crop.
12:17 He thought to himself, **[RPG]** 'What shall I do? I have no place to
12:18 "Then *he* **said**, 'This is what I'll do. I will tear down my barns
12:19 And *I'll* **say** to myself, "You have plenty of good things laid up for
12:20 "But God **said** to him, 'You fool! This very night your life will be
12:22 Then Jesus **said** to his disciples: "Therefore I tell you, do not worry
12:22 "Therefore *I* **tell** you, do not worry about your life, what you will
12:27 Yet *I* **tell** you, not even Solomon in all his splendor was dressed
12:37 *I* **tell** you the truth, he will dress himself to serve, will have them
12:41 Peter **asked**, "Lord, are you telling this parable to us, or to
12:41 Peter asked, "Lord, *are you* **telling** this parable to us, or to
12:42 The Lord **answered**, "Who then is the faithful and wise manager,
12:44 *I* **tell** you the truth, he will put him in charge of all his possessions.
12:45 But suppose the servant **says** to himself, 'My master is taking a
12:51 think I came to bring peace on earth? No, *I* **tell** you, but division.
12:54 *He* **said** to the crowd: "When you see a cloud rising in the west,
12:54 cloud rising in the west, immediately *you* **say**, 'It's going to rain,'
12:55 the south wind blows, *you* **say**, 'It's going to be hot,' and it is.
12:59 *I* **tell** you, you will not get out until you have paid the last penny."
13: 2 **[RPG]** "Do you think that these Galileans were worse sinners than
13: 3 *I* **tell** you, no! But unless you repent, you too will all perish.
13: 5 *I* **tell** you, no! But unless you repent, you too will all perish."
13: 6 Then *he* **told** this parable: "A man had a fig tree, planted in his
13: 7 So *he* **said** to the man who took care of the vineyard, 'For three
13: 8 the man replied, **[RPG]** 'leave it alone for one more year,
13:12 Jesus saw her, he called her forward and **said** to her, "Woman,
13:14 the synagogue ruler **said** to the people, "There are six days for
13:15 The Lord answered him, **[RPG]** "You hypocrites! Doesn't each of
13:17 *When* he **said** this, all his opponents were humiliated, but the
13:18 Then Jesus **asked**, "What is the kingdom of God like? What shall I
13:20 Again *he* **asked**, "What shall I compare the kingdom of God to?
13:23 Someone **asked** him, "Lord, are only a few people going to be
13:23 are only a few people going to be saved?" He **said** to them,
13:24 because many, *I* **tell** you, will try to enter and will not be able to.
13:25 the door, you will stand outside knocking and **pleading**, 'Sir,
13:25 will answer, **[RPG]** 'I don't know you or where you come from.'
13:26 "Then you will **say**, 'We ate and drank with you, and you taught in
13:27 "But *he will* **reply**, 'I don't know you or where you come from.
13:27 he will reply, **[RPG]** 'I don't know you or where you come from.
13:31 At that time some Pharisees came to Jesus and **said** to him,
13:32 *He* **replied**, "Go tell that fox, 'I will drive out demons and heal
13:32 He replied, "Go **tell** that fox, 'I will drive out demons and heal
13:35 *I* **tell** you, you will not see me again until you say, 'Blessed is he
13:35 I tell you, you will not see me again until *you* **say**, 'Blessed is he
14: 3 Jesus **[RPG]** asked the Pharisees and experts in the law, "Is it
14: 3 in the law, **[RPG]** "Is it lawful to heal on the Sabbath or not?"
14: 5 Then *he* **asked** them, "If one of you has a son or an ox that falls into
14: 7 picked the places of honor at the table, *he* **told** them this parable:
14: 7 the places of honor at the table, he told them this parable: **[RPG]**
14: 9 the host who invited both of you *will* come and **say** to you,

14:10 host comes, *he will* **say** to you, 'Friend, move up to a better place.'
14:12 Then Jesus **said** to his host, "When you give a luncheon or dinner,
14:15 one of those at the table with him heard this, *he* **said** to Jesus,
14:16 Jesus **replied**: "A certain man was preparing a great banquet
14:17 At the time of the banquet he sent his servant *to* **tell** those who had
14:18 The first **said**, 'I have just bought a field, and I must go and see it.
14:19 "Another **said**, 'I have just bought five yoke of oxen, and I'm on
14:20 "Still another **said**, 'I just got married,
14:21 the owner of the house became angry and **ordered** his servant,
14:22 " 'Sir,' the servant **said**, 'what you ordered has been done, but there
14:23 "Then the master **told** his servant, 'Go out to the roads and country
14:24 *I* **tell** you, not one of those men who were invited will get a taste
14:25 crowds were traveling with Jesus, and turning to them *he* **said**:
14:30 **saying**, 'This fellow began to build and was not able to finish.'
15: 2 **[RPG]** "This man welcomes sinners and eats with them."
15: 3 Then Jesus **told** them this parable:
15: 3 Then Jesus told **[RPG]** them this parable:
15: 6 Then he calls his friends and neighbors together and **says**,
15: 7 *I* **tell** you that in the same way there will be more rejoicing in
15: 9 she calls her friends and neighbors together and **says**, 'Rejoice with
15:10 In the same way, *I* **tell** you, there is rejoicing in the presence of the
15:11 Jesus **continued**: "There was a man who had two sons.
15:12 The younger one **said** to his father, 'Father, give me my share of
15:18 *I will* set out and go back to my father and **say** to him: Father,
15:21 "The son **said** to him, 'Father, I have sinned against heaven
15:22 "But the father **said** to his servants, 'Quick! Bring the best robe
15:27 'Your brother has come,' he **replied**,
15:29 But he answered **[RPG]** his father, 'Look! All these years I've
15:31 " 'My son,' the father **said**, 'you are always with me, and
16: 1 Jesus **told** his disciples: "There was a rich man whose manager was
16: 2 So *he* called him in and **asked** him, 'What is this I hear about you?
16: 3 "The manager **said** to himself, 'What shall I do now? My master is
16: 5 *He* **asked** the first, 'How much do you owe my master?'
16: 6 " 'Eight hundred gallons of olive oil,' he **replied**. "The manager
16: 6 "The manager **told** him, 'Take your bill, sit down quickly, and
16: 7 "Then *he* **asked** the second, 'And how much do you owe?'
16: 7 " 'A thousand bushels of wheat,' he **replied**. "He told him,
16: 7 "*He* **told** him, 'Take your bill and make it eight hundred.'
16: 9 I tell you, use worldly wealth to gain friends for yourselves,
16:15 *He* **said** to them, "You are the ones who justify yourselves in the
16:24 So he called **[RPG]** to him, 'Father Abraham, have pity on me
16:25 "But Abraham **replied**, 'Son, remember that in your lifetime you
16:27 "*He* **answered**, 'Then I beg you, father, send Lazarus to my
16:29 "Abraham **replied**, 'They have Moses and the Prophets; let them
16:30 " 'No, father Abraham,' he **said**, 'but if someone from the dead
16:31 "He **said** to him, 'If they do not listen to Moses and the Prophets,
17: 1 Jesus **said** to his disciples: "Things that cause people to sin are
17: 4 and seven times comes back to you and **says**, 'I repent,'
17: 5 The apostles **said** to the Lord, "Increase our faith!"
17: 6 He **replied**, "If you have faith as small as a mustard seed, you can
17: 6 *you can* **say** to this mulberry tree, 'Be uprooted and planted in the
17: 7 *Would he* **say** to the servant when he comes in from the field,
17: 8 *Would he* not rather **say**, 'Prepare my supper, get yourself ready
17:10 you were told to do, *should* **say**, 'We are unworthy servants;
17:13 and **[RPG]** called out in a loud voice, "Jesus, Master, have pity on
17:14 When he saw them, *he* **said**, "Go, show yourselves to the priests."
17:17 Jesus asked, **[RPG]** "Were not all ten cleansed? Where are the
17:19 Then *he* **said** to him, "Rise and go; your faith has made you well."
17:20 **[RPG]** "The kingdom of God does not come with your careful
17:21 nor *will people* **say**, 'Here it is,' or 'There it is,'
17:22 Then *he* **said** to his disciples, "The time is coming when you will
17:23 *Men will* **tell** you, 'There he is!' or 'Here he is!' Do not go running
17:34 *I* **tell** you, on that night two people will be in one bed; one will be
17:37 **[RPG]** He replied, "Where there is a dead body, there the vultures
17:37 He **replied**, "Where there is a dead body, there the vultures will
18: 1 Then Jesus **told** his disciples a parable to show them that they
18: 2 *He* **said**: "In a certain town there was a judge who neither feared
18: 3 was a widow in that town who kept coming to him **with the plea**,
18: 4 But finally *he* **said** to himself, 'Even though I don't fear God
18: 6 And the Lord **said**, "Listen to what the unjust judge says.
18: 6 And the Lord said, "Listen to what the unjust judge **says**.
18: 8 *I* **tell** you, he will see that they get justice, and quickly. However,
18: 9 and looked down on everybody else, Jesus **told** this parable:
18:13 but beat his breast and **said**, 'God, have mercy on me, a sinner.'
18:14 "*I* **tell** you that this man, rather than the other, went home justified
18:16 But Jesus called the children to him and **said**, "Let the little children

18: 17   *I* **tell** you the truth, anyone who will not receive the kingdom of
18: 18   A certain ruler asked him, **[RPG]** "Good teacher, what must I do to
18: 19   "Why *do you* **call** me good?" Jesus answered. "No one is good—
18: 19   me good?" Jesus **answered**. "No one is good—except God alone.
18: 21   "All these I have kept since I was a boy," he **said**.
18: 22   When Jesus heard this, *he* **said** to him, "You still lack one thing.
18: 24   Jesus looked at him and **said**, "How hard it is for the rich to enter
18: 26   Those who heard this **asked**, "Who then can be saved?"
18: 27   Jesus **replied**, "What is impossible with men is possible with God."
18: 28   Peter **said** to him, "We have left all we had to follow you!"
18: 29   "*I* **tell** you the truth," Jesus said to them, "no one who has left home
18: 29   "I **tell** you the truth," Jesus **said** to them, "no one who has left home
18: 31   Jesus took the Twelve aside and **told** them, "We are going up to
18: 34   from them, and they did not know what *he was* **talking about**.
18: 38   He called out, **[RPG]** "Jesus, Son of David, have mercy on me!"
18: 41   do you want me to do for you?" "Lord, I want to see," he **replied**.
18: 42   Jesus **said** to him, "Receive your sight; your faith has healed you."
19: 5   looked up and **said** to him, "Zacchaeus, come down immediately.
19: 7   to mutter, **[RPG]** "He has gone to be the guest of a 'sinner.' "
19: 8   But Zacchaeus stood up and **said** to the Lord, "Look, Lord!
19: 9   Jesus **said** to him, "Today salvation has come to this house,
19: 11   While they were listening to this, *he* went on *to* **tell** them a parable,
19: 12   *He* **said**: "A man of noble birth went to a distant country to have
19: 13   ten minas. 'Put this money to work,' *he* **said**, 'until I come back.'
19: 14   "But his subjects hated him and sent a delegation after him *to* **say**,
19: 15   Then *he* **sent for** [+*5888*] the servants to whom he had given the
19: 16   "The first one came and **said**, 'Sir, your mina has earned ten more.'
19: 17   " 'Well done, my good servant!' his master **replied**. 'Because you
19: 18   "The second came and **said**, 'Sir, your mina has earned five more.'
19: 19   "His master **answered**, 'You take charge of five cities.'
19: 20   "Then another servant came and **said**, 'Sir, here is your mina;
19: 22   "His master **replied**, 'I will judge you by your own words,
19: 24   "Then *he* **said** to those standing by, 'Take his mina away from him
19: 25   " 'Sir,' *they* **said**, 'he already has ten!'
19: 26   "He **replied**, '*I* **tell** you that to everyone who has, more will be
19: 28   *After* Jesus had **said** this, he went on ahead, going up to
19: 29   the Mount of Olives, he sent two of his disciples, **saying** to them,
19: 31   asks you, 'Why are you untying it?' **tell** him, 'The Lord needs it.' "
19: 32   who were sent ahead went and found it just as *he had* **told** them.
19: 33   As they were untying the colt, its owners **asked** them, "Why are
19: 34   They **replied**, "The Lord needs it."
19: 38   **[RPG]** "Blessed is the king who comes in the name of the Lord!"
19: 39   Some of the Pharisees in the crowd **said** to Jesus, "Teacher,
19: 40   "*I* **tell** you," he replied, "if they keep quiet, the stones will cry out."
19: 40   "I tell you," **[RPG]** he replied, "if they keep quiet, the stones will
19: 42   and **said**, "If you, even you, had only known on this day what
19: 46   "It is written," *he* **said** to them, " 'My house will be a house of
20: 2   "**Tell** us by what authority you are doing these things," they said.
20: 2   "Tell us by what authority you are doing these things," *they* **said**.
20: 2   these things," they said. **[RPG]** "Who gave you this authority?"
20: 3   He replied, **[RPG]** "I will also ask you a question. Tell me,
20: 3   He replied, "I will also ask you a question. **Tell** me,
20: 5   They discussed it among themselves and **said**, "If we say,
20: 5   They discussed it among themselves and said, "If *we* **say**,
20: 5   among themselves and said, "If we say, 'From heaven,' *he will* **ask**,
20: 6   But if *we* **say**, 'From men,' all the people will stone us,
20: 8   Jesus **said**, "Neither will I tell you by what authority I am doing
20: 8   "Neither will I **tell** you by what authority I am doing these things."
20: 9   He went on *to* **tell** the people this parable: "A man planted a
20: 13   "Then the owner of the vineyard **said**, 'What shall I do? I will send
20: 14   'This is the heir,' *they* **said**. 'Let's kill him, and the inheritance
20: 16   When the people heard this, *they* **said**, "May this never be!"
20: 17   Jesus looked directly at them and **asked**, "Then what is the meaning
20: 19   because they knew *he had* **spoken** this parable against them.
20: 21   **[RPG]** "Teacher, we know that you speak and teach what is right,
20: 21   "Teacher, we know that *you* **speak** and teach what is right,
20: 23   *He* saw through their duplicity and **said** to them,
20: 25   "Caesar's," they **replied**. He said to them, "Then give to Caesar
20: 25   He **said** to them, "Then give to Caesar what is Caesar's, and to God
20: 28   "Teacher," *they* **said**, "Moses wrote for us that if a man's brother
20: 34   Jesus **replied**, "The people of this age marry and are given in
20: 37   for *he* **calls** the Lord 'the God of Abraham, and the God of Isaac,
20: 39   of the teachers of the law responded, **[RPG]** "Well said, teacher!"
20: 39   Some of the teachers of the law responded, "Well **said**, teacher!"
20: 41   Then Jesus **said** to them, "How is it that they say the Christ is the
20: 41   to them, "How is it that *they* **say** the Christ is the Son of David?

20: 42   David himself **declares** in the Book of Psalms: " 'The Lord said to
20: 42   Book of Psalms: " 'The Lord **said** to my Lord: "Sit at my right hand
20: 45   While all the people were listening, Jesus **said** to his disciples,
21: 3   "*I* **tell** you the truth," he said, "this poor widow has put in more
21: 3   "I tell you the truth," *he* **said**, "this poor widow has put in more
21: 5   Some of his disciples *were* **remarking** about how the temple was
21: 5   beautiful stones and with gifts dedicated to God. But Jesus **said**,
21: 7   "Teacher," they said, **[RPG]** "when will these things happen?"
21: 8   He **replied**: "Watch out that you are not deceived. For many will
21: 8   come in my name, **claiming**, 'I am he,' and, 'The time is near.'
21: 10   Then *he* **said** to them: "Nation will rise against nation, and kingdom
21: 29   *He* **told** them this parable: "Look at the fig tree and all the trees.
21: 32   "*I* **tell** you the truth, this generation will certainly not pass away
22: 1   Feast of Unleavened Bread, **called** the Passover, was approaching,
22: 8   **saying**, "Go and make preparations for us to eat the Passover."
22: 9   "Where do you want us to prepare for it?" they **asked**.
22: 10   He **replied**, "As you enter the city, a man carrying a jar of water
22: 11   and **say** to the owner of the house, 'The Teacher asks: Where is the
22: 11   and say to the owner of the house, 'The Teacher **asks**: Where is the
22: 13   They left and found things just as Jesus *had* **told** them. So they
22: 15   And *he* **said** to them, "I have eagerly desired to eat this Passover
22: 16   For *I* **tell** you, I will not eat it again until it finds fulfillment in the
22: 17   he gave thanks and **said**, "Take this and divide it among you.
22: 18   For *I* **tell** you I will not drink again of the fruit of the vine until the
22: 19   took bread, gave thanks and broke it, and gave it to them, **saying**,
22: 20   In the same way, after the supper he took the cup, **saying**,
22: 25   Jesus **said** to them, "The kings of the Gentiles lord it over them;
22: 33   But he **replied**, "Lord, I am ready to go with you to prison and to
22: 34   Jesus **answered**, "I tell you, Peter, before the rooster crows today,
22: 34   Jesus answered, "*I* **tell** you, Peter, before the rooster crows today,
22: 35   Then Jesus **asked** them, "When I sent you without purse, bag
22: 35   or sandals, did you lack anything?" "Nothing," they **answered**.
22: 36   *He* **said** to them, "But now if you have a purse, take it, and also a
22: 37   the transgressors'; and *I* **tell** you that this must be fulfilled in me.
22: 38   The disciples **said**, "See, Lord, here are two swords." "That is
22: 38   "See, Lord, here are two swords." "That is enough," he **replied**.
22: 40   On reaching the place, *he* **said** to them, "Pray that you will not fall
22: 42   **[RPG]** "Father, if you are willing, take this cup from me; yet not
22: 46   *he* **asked** them. "Get up and pray so that you will not fall into
22: 47   and the man *who was* **called** Judas, one of the Twelve, was leading
22: 48   but Jesus **asked** him, "Judas, are you betraying the Son of Man with
22: 49   to happen, *they* **said**, "Lord, should we strike with our swords?"
22: 51   But Jesus answered, **[RPG]** "No more of this!" And he touched the
22: 52   Then Jesus **said** to the chief priests, the officers of the temple
22: 56   *She* looked closely at him and **said**, "This man was with him."
22: 57   But he denied it. "Woman, I don't know him," he **said**.
22: 59   **[RPG]** "Certainly this fellow was with him, for he is a Galilean."
22: 60   Peter **replied**, "Man, I don't know what you're talking about!"
22: 60   Peter replied, "Man, I don't know what *you're* **talking about**!"
22: 61   Then Peter remembered the word the Lord *had* **spoken** to him:
22: 64   They blindfolded him and demanded, **[RPG]** "Prophesy! Who hit
22: 65   And *they* **said** many other insulting things to him.
22: 67   "If you are the Christ," *they* **said**, "tell us." Jesus answered, "If I tell
22: 67   "If you are the Christ," they said, "**tell** us." Jesus answered, "If I tell
22: 67   "tell us." Jesus **answered**, "If I tell you, you will not believe me,
22: 67   "tell us." Jesus answered, "If *I* **tell** you, you will not believe me,
22: 70   *They* all **asked**, "Are you then the Son of God?" He replied,
22: 70   then the Son of God?" He replied, "You *are right in* **saying** I am."
22: 71   Then they **said**, "Why do we need any more testimony? We have
23: 2   And they began to accuse him, **saying**, "We have found this man
23: 2   payment of taxes to Caesar and **claims** [+*1571*] to be Christ,
23: 3   the king of the Jews?" **[RPG]** "Yes, it is as you say," Jesus replied.
23: 3   king of the Jews?" **Yes, it is as you say** [+*5148*]," Jesus replied.
23: 4   Then Pilate **announced** to the chief priests and the crowd,
23: 5   **[RPG]** "He stirs up the people all over Judea by his teaching.
23: 14   and **said** to them, "You brought me this man as one who was
23: 18   With one voice they cried out, **[RPG]** "Away with this man!
23: 21   But they kept shouting, **[RPG]** "Crucify him! Crucify him!"
23: 22   For the third time he **spoke** to them: "Why? What crime has this
23: 28   Jesus turned and **said** to them, "Daughters of Jerusalem, do not
23: 29   For the time will come when *you will* **say**, 'Blessed are the barren
23: 30   " 'they will **say** to the mountains, "Fall on us!" and to the hills,
23: 34   Jesus said, "Father, forgive them, for they do not know what they
23: 35   *They* **said**, "He saved others; let him save himself if he is the Christ
23: 37   and **said**, "If you are the king of the Jews, save yourself."
23: 39   at him: **[RPG]** "Aren't you the Christ? Save yourself and us!"

23:42 Then *he* **said**, "Jesus, remember me when you come into your
23:43 Jesus **answered** him, "I tell you the truth, today you will be with me ,
23:43 Jesus answered him, "*I* **tell** you the truth, today you will be with
23:46 Jesus called out with a loud voice, **[RPG]** "Father, into your hands
23:46 I commit my spirit." *When he had* **said** this, he breathed his last.
23:47 The centurion, seeing what had happened, praised God and **said**,
24: 5 but the *men* **said** to them, "Why do you look for the living among
24: 7 **[RPG]** 'The Son of Man must be delivered into the hands of
24:10 of James, and the others with them *who* **told** this to the apostles.
24:17 *He* **asked** them, "What are you discussing together as you walk
24:18 One of them, named Cleopas, asked **[RPG]** him, "Are you only a
24:19 "What things?" *he* **asked**. "About Jesus of Nazareth," they **said**,
24:19 "What things?" he asked. "About Jesus of Nazareth," they **replied**.
24:23 They came and **told** us that they had seen a vision of angels,
24:23 us that they had seen a vision of angels, who **said** he was alive.
24:24 went to the tomb and found it just as the women *had* **said**,
24:25 He **said** to them, "How foolish you are, and how slow of heart to
24:29 urged him strongly, **[RPG]** "Stay with us, for it is nearly evening;
24:32 *They* **asked** each other, "Were not our hearts burning within us
24:34 and **saying**, "It is true! The Lord has risen and has appeared to
24:36 Jesus himself stood among them and **said** to them, "Peace be with
24:38 *He* **said** to them, "Why are you troubled, and why do doubts rise in
24:40 *When he had* **said** this, he showed them his hands and feet.
24:41 did not believe it because of joy and amazement, *he* **asked** them,
24:44 *He* **said** to them, "This is what I told you while I was still with you:
24:46 *He* **told** them, "This is what is written: The Christ will suffer
Jn   1:15 He cries out, **saying**, "This was he of whom I said, 'He who comes
1:15 He cries out, saying, "This was he *of* whom *I* said, 'He who comes
1:21 him, "Then who are you? Are you Elijah?" *He* **said**, "I am not."
1:22 Finally *they* **said**, "Who are you? Give us an answer to take back to
1:22 take back to those who sent us. What *do you* **say** about yourself?"
1:23 **[RPG]** "I am the voice of one calling in the desert, 'Make straight
1:25 **[RPG]** "Why then do you baptize if you are not the Christ,
1:26 John replied, **[RPG]** "but among you stands one you do not know.
1:29 The next day John saw Jesus coming toward him and **said**,
1:30 This is the one I meant *when* I **said**, 'A man who comes after me
1:32 **[RPG]** "I saw the Spirit come down from heaven as a dove
1:33 except that the one who sent me to baptize with water **told** me,
1:36 When he saw Jesus passing by, *he* **said**, "Look, the Lamb of God!"
1:38 Turning around, Jesus saw them following and **asked**, "What do
1:38 They **said**, "Rabbi" (which means Teacher), "where are you
1:38 They said, "Rabbi" (which **means** [+3493] Teacher), "where are
1:39 "Come," *he* **replied**, "and you will see." So they went and saw
1:41 first thing Andrew did was to find his brother Simon and **tell** him,
1:42 Jesus looked at him and **said**, "You are Simon son of John.
1:43 to leave for Galilee. Finding Philip, he **said** to him, "Follow me."
1:45 Philip found Nathanael and **told** him, "We have found the one
1:46 come from there?" Nathanael **asked**. "Come and see," said Philip.
1:46 come from there?" Nathanael asked. "Come and see," **said** Philip.
1:47 *he* **said** of him, "Here is a true Israelite, in whom there is nothing
1:48 Nathanael **asked**. Jesus answered, "I saw you while you were still
1:48 **[RPG]** "I saw you while you were still under the fig tree before
1:50 Jesus **said**, "You believe because I told you I saw you under the fig
1:50 "You believe because *I* **told** you I saw you under the fig tree.
1:51 *He* then **added**, "I tell you the truth, you shall see heaven open,
1:51 He then added, "*I* **tell** you the truth, you shall see heaven open,
2: 3 was gone, Jesus' mother **said** to him, "They have no more wine."
2: 4 "Dear woman, why do you involve me?" Jesus **replied**. "My time
2: 5 His mother **said** to the servants, "Do whatever he tells you."
2: 5 His mother said to the servants, "Do whatever *he* **tells** you."
2: 7 Jesus **said** to the servants, "Fill the jars with water"; so they filled
2: 8 Then *he* **told** them, "Now draw some out and take it to the master of
2:10 and **said**, "Everyone brings out the choice wine first and
2:16 To those who sold doves *he* **said**, "Get these out of here! How dare
2:18 Then the Jews demanded **[RPG]** of him, "What miraculous sign
2:19 Jesus answered **[RPG]** them, "Destroy this temple, and I will raise
2:20 The Jews **replied**, "It has taken forty-six years to build this temple,
2:21 But the temple he *had* **spoken** of was his body.
2:22 was raised from the dead, his disciples recalled what *he had* **said**.
2:22 they believed the Scripture and the words that Jesus *had* **spoken**.
3: 2 He came to Jesus at night and **said**, "Rabbi, we know you are a
3: 3 In reply Jesus **declared**, "I tell you the truth, no one can see the
3: 3 In reply Jesus declared, "*I* **tell** you the truth, no one can see the
3: 4 "How can a man be born when he is old?" Nicodemus **asked**.
3: 5 Jesus answered, "*I* **tell** you the truth, no one can enter the kingdom
3: 7 You should not be surprised at *my* **saying**, 'You must be born

3: 9 "How can this be?" Nicodemus asked. **[RPG]**
3:10 "You are Israel's teacher," **said** Jesus, "and do you not understand
3:11 *I* **tell** you the truth, we speak of what we know, and we testify to
3:12 *I have* **spoken** to you *of* earthly things and you do not believe;
3:12 how then will you believe if *I* **speak of** heavenly things?
3:26 They came to John and **said** to him, "Rabbi, that man who was with
3:27 **[RPG]** "A man can receive only what is given him from heaven.
3:28 You yourselves can testify that *I* **said**, 'I am not the Christ
4: 5 So he came to a town in Samaria **called** Sychar, near the plot of
4: 7 came to draw water, Jesus **said** to her, "Will you give me a drink?"
4: 9 The Samaritan woman **said** to him, "You are a Jew and I am a
4:10 Jesus answered **[RPG]** her, "If you knew the gift of God and who
4:10 "If you knew the gift of God and who it is that **asks** you **for** a drink,
4:11 "Sir," the woman **said**, "you have nothing to draw with and the
4:13 **[RPG]** "Everyone who drinks this water will be thirsty again,
4:15 The woman **said**, "Sir, give me this water so that I won't get
4:16 *He* **told** her, "Go, call your husband and come back."
4:17 **[RPG]** Jesus said to her, "You are right when you say you have no
4:17 Jesus **said** to her, "You are right when you say you have no
4:17 said to her, "You are right *when you* **say** you have no husband.
4:18 have is not your husband. What *you have just* **said** is quite true."
4:19 "Sir," the woman **said**, "I can see that you are a prophet.
4:20 but you Jews **claim** that the place where we must worship is in
4:21 Jesus **declared**, "Believe me, woman, a time is coming when you
4:25 The woman **said**, "I know that Messiah" (called Christ) "is coming.
4:25 The woman said, "I know that Messiah" (**called** Christ) "is coming.
4:26 Then Jesus **declared**, "I who speak to you am he."
4:27 But no one **asked**, "What do you want?" or "Why are you talking
4:28 water jar, the woman went back to the town and **said** to the people,
4:29 "Come, see a man who **told** me everything I ever did. Could this be
4:31 Meanwhile his disciples urged him, **[RPG]** "Rabbi, eat something."
4:32 But he **said** to them, "I have food to eat that you know nothing
4:33 Then his disciples **said** to each other, "Could someone have brought
4:34 "My food," **said** Jesus, "is to do the will of him who sent me and to
4:35 *Do you not* **say**, 'Four months more and then the harvest'?
4:35 then the harvest'? *I* **tell** you, open your eyes and look at the fields!
4:39 of the woman's testimony, "*He* **told** me everything I ever did."
4:42 *They* **said** to the woman, "We no longer believe just because of
4:48 you people see miraculous signs and wonders," Jesus **told** him,
4:49 The royal official **said**, "Sir, come down before my child dies."
4:50 Jesus **replied**, "You may go. Your son will live." The man took
4:50 will live." The man took Jesus at his word **[RPG]** and departed.
4:51 his servants met him **with the news** that his boy was living.
4:52 *they* **said** to him, "The fever left him yesterday at the seventh hour."
4:53 that this was the exact time at which Jesus *had* **said** to him,
5: 6 condition for a long time, *he* **asked** him, "Do you want to get well?"
5: 8 Then Jesus **said** to him, "Get up! Pick up your mat and walk."
5:10 and so the Jews **said** to the man who had been healed, "It is the
5:11 But he replied, "The man who made me well **said** to me, 'Pick up
5:12 him, "Who is this fellow who **told** you to pick it up and walk?"
5:14 Later Jesus found him at the temple and **said** to him, "See, you are
5:18 but *he was* even **calling** God his own Father, making himself equal
5:19 **[RPG]** "I tell you the truth, the Son can do nothing by himself;
5:19 "*I* **tell** you the truth, the Son can do nothing by himself; he can do
5:24 "*I* **tell** you the truth, whoever hears my word and believes him who
5:25 *I* **tell** you the truth, a time is coming and has now come when the
5:34 I accept human testimony; but *I* **mention** it that you may be saved.
6: 5 and saw a great crowd coming toward him, *he* **said** to Philip,
6: 6 *He* **asked** this only to test him, for he already had in mind what he
6: 8 of his disciples, Andrew, Simon Peter's brother, **spoke up**,
6:10 Jesus **said**, "Have the people sit down." There was plenty of grass
6:12 *he* **said** to his disciples, "Gather the pieces that are left over.
6:14 people saw the miraculous sign that Jesus did, *they began to* **say**,
6:20 But he **said** to them, "It is I; don't be afraid."
6:25 side of the lake, *they* **asked** him, "Rabbi, when did you get here?"
6:26 Jesus answered, **[RPG]** "I tell you the truth, you are looking for
6:26 Jesus answered, "*I* **tell** you the truth, you are looking for me,
6:28 Then *they* **asked** him, "What must we do to do the works God
6:29 Jesus answered, **[RPG]** "The work of God is this: to believe in the
6:30 So *they* **asked** him, "What miraculous sign then will you give that
6:32 Jesus **said** to them, "I tell you the truth, it is not Moses who has
6:32 Jesus said to them, "*I* **tell** you the truth, it is not Moses who has
6:34 "Sir," *they* **said**, "from now on give us this bread."
6:35 Then Jesus **declared**, "I am the bread of life. He who comes to me
6:36 But as *I* **told** you, you have seen me and still you do not believe.
6:41 At this the Jews began to grumble about him because *he* **said**,

6:42 *They* **said**, "Is this not Jesus, the son of Joseph, whose father
6:42 we know? How *can* he now **say**, 'I came down from heaven'?"
6:43 "Stop grumbling among yourselves," Jesus answered. **[RPG]**
6:47 *I* **tell** you the truth, he who believes has everlasting life.
6:52 **[RPG]** "How can this man give us his flesh to eat?"
6:53 Jesus **said** to them, "I tell you the truth, unless you eat the flesh of
6:53 Jesus said to them, "*I* **tell** you the truth, unless you eat the flesh of
6:59 He **said** this while teaching in the synagogue in Capernaum.
6:60 On hearing it, many of his disciples **said**, "This is a hard teaching.
6:61 grumbling about this, Jesus **said** to them, "Does this offend you?
6:65 *He* went on to **say**, "This is why I told you that no one can come to
6:65 "This is why *I* **told** you that no one can come to me unless the
6:67 "You do not want to leave too, do you?" Jesus **asked** the Twelve.
6:71 (*He* **meant** Judas, the son of Simon Iscariot, who, though one of
7: 3 Jesus' brothers **said** to him, "You ought to leave here and go to
7: 6 Therefore Jesus **told** them, "The right time for me has not yet come;
7: 9 *Having* **said** this, he stayed in Galilee.
7:11 Now at the Feast the Jews were watching for him and **asking**,
7:12 Some **said**, "He is a good man." Others replied, "No, he deceives
7:12 "He is a good man." Others **replied**, "No, he deceives the people."
7:15 The Jews were amazed and **asked**, "How did this man get such
7:16 Jesus answered, **[RPG]** "My teaching is not my own. It comes
7:21 Jesus **said** to them, "I did one miracle, and you are all astonished.
7:25 At that point some of the people of Jerusalem *began to* **ask**,
7:26 speaking publicly, and *they are* not **saying** a word to him.
7:28 cried out, **[RPG]** "Yes, you know me, and you know where I am
7:31 *They* **said**, "When the Christ comes, will he do more miraculous
7:33 Jesus **said**, "I am with you for only a short time, and then I go to the
7:35 The Jews **said** to one another, "Where does this man intend to go
7:36 What did he mean *when* he **said**, 'You will look for me, but you
7:37 Jesus stood and **said** in a loud voice, "If anyone is thirsty, let him
7:38 Whoever believes in me, as the Scripture *has* **said**, streams of
7:39 By this *he* **meant** [+4309] the Spirit, whom those who believed in
7:40 On hearing his words, some of the people **said**, "Surely this man is
7:41 Others **said**, "He is the Christ." Still others asked, "How can the
7:41 Still others **asked**, "How can the Christ come from Galilee?
7:42 *Does* not the Scripture **say** that the Christ will come from David's
7:45 went back to the chief priests and Pharisees, who **asked** them,
7:50 gone to Jesus earlier and who was one of their own number, **asked**,
7:52 They replied, **[RPG]** "Are you from Galilee, too? Look into it,
8: 4 and **said** to Jesus, "Teacher, this woman was caught in the act of
8: 5 commanded us to stone such women. Now what *do* you **say**?"
8: 6 *They were* using this **question** as a trap, in order to have a basis
8: 7 he straightened up and **said** to them, "If any one of you is without
8:10 Jesus straightened up and **asked** her, "Woman, where are they?
8:11 "No one, sir," she **said**. "Then neither do I condemn you," Jesus
8:11 "Then neither do I condemn you," Jesus **declared**. "Go now and
8:12 spoke again to the people, *he* **said**, "I am the light of the world.
8:13 The Pharisees **challenged** him, "Here you are, appearing as your
8:14 Jesus answered, **[RPG]** "Even if I testify on my own behalf,
8:19 Then *they* **asked** him, "Where is your father?" "You do not know
8:21 Once more Jesus **said** to them, "I am going away, and you will look
8:22 This made the Jews **ask**, "Will he kill himself? Is that why he says,
8:22 kill himself? Is that why *he* **says**, 'Where I go, you cannot come'?"
8:23 But *he* **continued**, "You are from below; I am from above.
8:24 *I* **told** you that you would die in your sins; if you do not believe
8:25 "Who are you?" *they* **asked**. "Just what I have been claiming all
8:25 "Just what I have been claiming all along," Jesus **replied**.
8:27 They did not understand that *he was* **telling** them **about** his Father.
8:28 So Jesus **said**, "When you have lifted up the Son of Man, then you
8:31 Jesus **said**, "If you hold to my teaching, you are really my disciples.
8:33 been slaves of anyone. How *can* you **say** that we shall be set free?"
8:34 Jesus replied, "*I* **tell** you the truth, everyone who sins is a slave to
8:39 **[RPG]** "If you were Abraham's children," said Jesus, "then you
8:39 "If you were Abraham's children," **said** Jesus, "then you would do
8:41 "We are not illegitimate children," *they* **protested**. "The only Father
8:42 Jesus **said** to them, "If God were your Father, you would love me,
8:45 Yet because I **tell** the truth, you do not believe me!
8:46 guilty of sin? If *I am* **telling** the truth, why don't you believe me?
8:48 The Jews answered **[RPG]** him, "Aren't we right in saying that
8:48 "Aren't we right in **saying** that you are a Samaritan
8:51 *I* **tell** you the truth, if anyone keeps my word, he will never see
8:52 At this the Jews **exclaimed**, "Now we know that you are
8:52 so did the prophets, yet you **say** that if anyone keeps your word,
8:54 My Father, whom you **claim** as your God, is the one who glorifies
8:55 If *I* **said** I did not, I would be a liar like you, but I do know him

8:57 years old," the Jews **said** to him, "and you have seen Abraham!"
8:58 "*I* **tell** you the truth," Jesus answered, "before Abraham was born,
8:58 "I tell you the truth," Jesus **answered**, "before Abraham was born,
9: 2 **[RPG]** "Rabbi, who sinned, this man or his parents, that he was
9: 6 *Having* **said** this, he spit on the ground, made some mud with the
9: 7 "Go," *he* **told** him, "wash in the Pool of Siloam" (this word means
9: 8 and those who had formerly seen him begging **asked**,
9: 9 Some **claimed** that he was. Others said, "No, he only looks like
9: 9 Others **said**, "No, he only looks like him." But he himself insisted,
9: 9 he only looks like him." But he himself **insisted**, "I am the man."
9:10 "How then were your eyes opened?" *they* **demanded**.
9:11 "The man they **call** Jesus made some mud and put it on my eyes.
9:11 *He* **told** me to go to Siloam and wash. So I went and washed,
9:12 "Where is this man?" *they* **asked** him. "I don't know," he said.
9:12 "Where is this man?" they asked him. "I don't know," *he* **said**.
9:15 mud on my eyes," the man **replied**, "and I washed, and now I see."
9:16 Some of the Pharisees **said**, "This man is not from God, for he does
9:16 But others **asked**, "How can a sinner do such miraculous signs?"
9:17 Finally *they* **turned** again to the blind man, "What have you to say
9:17 turned again to the blind man, "What *have* you *to* **say** about him?
9:17 It was your eyes he opened." The man **replied**, "He is a prophet."
9:19 they asked. **[RPG]** "Is this the one you say was born blind?
9:19 this your son?" they asked. "Is this the one you **say** was born blind?
9:20 the parents answered, **[RPG]** "and we know he was born blind.
9:22 His parents **said** this because they were afraid of the Jews,
9:23 That was why his parents **said**, "He is of age; ask him."
9:24 "Give glory to God," *they* **said**. "We know this man is a sinner."
9:26 Then *they* **asked** him, "What did he do to you? How did he open
9:27 He answered, "*I have* **told** you already and you did not listen.
9:28 Then they hurled insults at him and **said**, "You are this fellow's
9:30 The man answered, **[RPG]** "Now that is remarkable! You don't
9:34 To this they replied, **[RPG]** "You were steeped in sin at birth;
9:35 and when he found him, *he* **said**, "Do you believe in the Son of
9:36 the man asked. **[RPG]** "Tell me so that I may believe in him."
9:37 Jesus **said**, "You have now seen him; in fact, he is the one speaking
9:39 Jesus **said**, "For judgment I have come into this world, so that the
9:40 Some Pharisees who were with him heard him say this and **asked**,
9:41 Jesus **said**, "If you were blind, you would not be guilty of sin;
9:41 of sin; but now that *you* **claim** you can see, your guilt remains.
10: 1 "*I* **tell** you the truth, the man who does not enter the sheep pen by
10: 6 Jesus **used** this figure of speech,
10: 7 Therefore Jesus **said** again, "I tell you the truth, I am the gate for
10: 7 Therefore Jesus said again, "*I* **tell** you the truth, I am the gate for
10:20 Many of them **said**, "He is demon-possessed and raving mad.
10:21 But others **said**, "These are not the sayings of a man possessed by a
10:24 The Jews gathered around him, **saying**, "How long will you keep us
10:24 will you keep us in suspense? If you are the Christ, **tell** us plainly."
10:25 Jesus answered, "*I did* **tell** you, but you do not believe.
10:34 "Is it not written in your Law, 'I *have* **said** you are gods'?
10:35 If *he* **called** them 'gods,' to whom the word of God came—
10:36 Why then *do* you **accuse** me of blasphemy because I said,
10:36 Why then do you accuse me of blasphemy because *I* **said**,
10:41 *They* **said**, "Though John never performed a miraculous sign,
10:41 a miraculous sign, all that John **said** about this man was true."
11: 3 So the sisters sent **word** to Jesus, "Lord, the one you love is sick."
11: 4 he heard this, Jesus **said**, "This sickness will not end in death.
11: 7 Then *he* **said** to his disciples, "Let us go back to Judea."
11: 8 "But Rabbi," they **said**, "a short while ago the Jews tried to stone
11:11 After *he* had **said** this, he went on to tell them, "Our friend Lazarus
11:11 After he had said this, *he* went on to **tell** them, "Our friend Lazarus
11:12 His disciples **replied**, "Lord, if he sleeps, he will get better."
11:13 Jesus *had been* **speaking** of his death, but his disciples thought he
11:13 but his disciples thought *he* **meant** [+4309] natural sleep.
11:14 So then he **told** them plainly, "Lazarus is dead,
11:16 Then Thomas (**called** Didymus) said to the rest of the disciples,
11:16 **said** to the rest of the disciples, "Let us also go, that we may die
11:21 "Lord," Martha said to Jesus, "if you had been here, my brother
11:23 Jesus **said** to her, "Your brother will rise again."
11:24 Martha **answered**, "I know he will rise again in the resurrection at
11:25 Jesus **said** to her, "I am the resurrection and the life. He who
11:27 "Yes, Lord," *she* **told** him, "I believe that you are the Christ, the
11:28 And *after she had* **said** this, she went back and called her sister
11:28 "The Teacher is here," *she* **said**, "and is asking for you."
11:32 where Jesus was and saw him, she fell at his feet and **said**, "Lord,
11:34 have you laid him?" *he* **asked**. "Come and see, Lord," they replied.
11:34 have you laid him?" he asked. "Come and see, Lord," *they* **replied**.

11:36   Then the Jews **said**, "See how he loved him!"
11:37   But some of them **said**, "Could not he who opened the eyes of the
11:39   "Take away the stone," he **said**. "But, Lord," said Martha, the sister
11:39   "But, Lord," **said** Martha, the sister of the dead man, "by this time
11:40   Then Jesus **said**, "Did I not tell you that if you believed, you would
11:40   Then Jesus **said**, "*Did I* not **tell** you that if you believed,
11:41   Then Jesus looked up and **said**, "Father, I thank you that you have
11:42   hear me, but *I* **said** this for the benefit of the people standing here,
11:43   *When he had* **said** this, Jesus called in a loud voice, "Lazarus,
11:44   Jesus **said** to them, "Take off the grave clothes and let him go."
11:46   of them went to the Pharisees and **told** them what Jesus had done.
11:47   of the Sanhedrin. "What are we accomplishing?" *they* **asked**.
11:49   who was high priest that year, **spoke up**, "You know nothing at all!
11:51   *He did* not **say** this on his own, but as high priest that year he
11:54   to a village **called** Ephraim, where he stayed with his disciples.
11:56   and as they stood in the temple area *they* **asked** one another,
12: 4   his disciples, Judas Iscariot, who was later to betray him, **objected**,
12: 6   *He did* not **say** this because he cared about the poor but because he
12: 7   "Leave her alone," Jesus **replied**. "*It was intended* that she should
12:19   So the Pharisees **said** to one another, "See, this is getting us
12:21   with a request. "Sir," *they* **said**, "we would like to see Jesus."
12:22   Philip went *to* **tell** Andrew; Andrew and Philip in turn told Jesus.
12:22   Philip went to tell Andrew; Andrew and Philip in turn **told** Jesus.
12:23   **[RPG]** "The hour has come for the Son of Man to be glorified.
12:24   *I* **tell** you the truth, unless a kernel of wheat falls to the ground
12:27   "Now my heart is troubled, and what *shall I* **say**? 'Father, save me
12:29   The crowd that was there and heard it **said** it had thundered;
12:29   it said it had thundered; others **said** an angel had spoken to him.
12:30   Jesus **said**, "This voice was for your benefit, not mine.
12:33   *He* **said** this to show the kind of death he was going to die.
12:34   so how *can* you **say**, 'The Son of Man must be lifted up'?
12:35   Then Jesus **told** them, "You are going to have the light just a little
12:38   **[RPG]** "Lord, who has believed our message and to whom has the
12:39   reason they could not believe, because, as Isaiah **says** elsewhere:
12:41   Isaiah **said** this because he saw Jesus' glory and spoke about him.
12:44   Then Jesus cried out, **[RPG]** "When a man believes in me,
12:49   but the Father who sent me commanded me what *to* **say** and how
12:50   So whatever I say is just what the Father *has* **told** me to say."
13: 6   He came to Simon Peter, *who* **said** to him, "Lord, are you going to
13: 7   Jesus replied, **[RPG]** "You do not realize now what I am doing,
13: 8   "No," **said** Peter, "you shall never wash my feet." Jesus answered,
13: 9   "Then, Lord," Simon Peter **replied**, "not just my feet but my hands
13:10   Jesus **answered**, "A person who has had a bath needs only to wash
13:11   to betray him, and that was why he **said** not every one was clean.
13:12   "Do you understand what *I* have done for you?" *he* **asked** them.
13:13   and 'Lord,' and rightly so, **[RPG]** for that is what I am.
13:16   *I* **tell** you the truth, no servant is greater than his master, nor is a
13:18   "*I am* not **referring** to all of you; I know those I have chosen.
13:19   "*I am* **telling** you now before it happens, so that when it does
13:20   *I* **tell** you the truth, whoever accepts anyone I send accepts me;
13:21   *After he had* **said** this, Jesus was troubled in spirit and testified,
13:21   was troubled in spirit and testified, "I **[RPG]** tell you the truth,
13:21   Jesus was troubled in spirit and testified, "*I* **tell** you the truth,
13:22   stared at one another, at a loss to know which of them *he* **meant**.
13:24   motioned to this disciple and said, "Ask him which one *he* **means**."
13:25   Leaning back against Jesus, he **asked** him, "Lord, who is it?"
13:27   into him. "What you are about to do, do quickly," Jesus **told** him,
13:28   but no one at the meal understood why Jesus **said** this to him.
13:29   some thought Jesus *was* **telling** him to buy what was needed for
13:31   When he was gone, Jesus said, "Now is the Son of Man glorified
13:33   You will look for me, and just as *I* **told** the Jews, so I tell you now:
13:33   You will look for me, and just as I told the Jews, so *I* **tell** you now:
13:36   Simon Peter **asked** him, "Lord, where are you going?" Jesus
13:37   Peter **asked**, "Lord, why can't I follow you now? I will lay down
13:38   *I* **tell** you the truth, before the rooster crows, you will disown me
14: 2   house are many rooms; if it were not so, *I* would have **told** you.
14: 5   Thomas **said** to him, "Lord, we don't know where you are going,
14: 6   Jesus **answered**, "I am the way and the truth and the life. No one
14: 8   Philip **said**, "Lord, show us the Father and that will be enough for
14: 9   Jesus **answered**: "Don't you know me, Philip, even after I have
14: 9   me has seen the Father. How *can* you **say**, 'Show us the Father'?
14:10   The words I **say** to you are not just my own. Rather, it is the
14:12   *I* **tell** you the truth, anyone who has faith in me will do what I have
14:22   **said**, "But, Lord, why do you intend to show yourself to us
14:23   Jesus replied, **[RPG]** "If anyone loves me, he will obey my
14:26   all things and will remind you of everything I *have* **said** to you.

14:28   "You heard me **say**, 'I am going away and I am coming back to
14:29   *I have* **told** you now before it happens, so that when it does happen
15:15   *I* no longer **call** you servants, because a servant does not know his
15:15   Instead, *I have* **called** you friends, for everything that I learned
15:20   Remember the words I **spoke** to you: 'No servant is greater than
16: 4   so that when the time comes you will remember that I **warned** you.
16: 4   I warned you. *I did* not **tell** you this at first because I was with you.
16: 7   But I **tell** you the truth: It is for your good that I am going away.
16:12   "I have much more *to* **say** to you, more than you can now bear.
16:15   That is why *I* **said** the Spirit will take from what is mine and make
16:17   Some of his disciples **said** to one another, "What does he mean by
16:17   of his disciples said to one another, "What does he mean *by* **saying**,
16:18   *They kept* **asking**, "What does he mean by 'a little while'?
16:18   They kept asking, "What does he mean by[s] [+4005] 'a little while'?
16:19   saw that they wanted to ask him about this, so *he* **said** to them,
16:19   to them, "Are you asking one another what I meant when *I* **said**,
16:20   *I* **tell** you the truth, you will weep and mourn while the world
16:23   *I* **tell** you the truth, my Father will give you whatever you ask in
16:26   my name. *I am* not **saying** that I will ask the Father on your behalf.
16:29   Then Jesus' disciples **said**, "Now you are speaking clearly
16:29   you are speaking clearly and **[RPG]** without figures of speech.
17: 1   After Jesus said this, he looked toward heaven and **prayed**:
18: 1   *When he had finished* **praying**, Jesus left with his disciples
18: 4   to happen to him, went out and **asked** them, "Who is it you want?"
18: 5   "Jesus of Nazareth," they replied. "I am he," Jesus **said**.
18: 6   When Jesus **said**, "I am he," they drew back and fell to the ground.
18: 7   them, "Who is it you want?" And they **said**, "Jesus of Nazareth."
18: 8   "*I* **told** you that I am he," Jesus answered. "If you are looking for
18: 9   This happened so that the words *he had* **spoken** would be fulfilled:
18:11   Jesus **commanded** Peter, "Put your sword away! Shall I not drink
18:16   came back, **spoke** to the girl on duty there and brought Peter in.
18:17   not one of his disciples, are you?" the girl at the door **asked** Peter.
18:17   are you?" the girl at the door asked Peter. He **replied**, "I am not."
18:21   Ask those who heard me. Surely they know what I **said**."
18:22   *When* Jesus **said** this, one of the officials nearby struck him in the
18:22   "Is this the way you answer the high priest?" *he* **demanded**.
18:25   he *was* **asked**, "You are not one of his disciples, are you?"
18:25   not one of his disciples, are you?" He denied it, **saying**, "I am not."
18:26   **challenged** him, "Didn't I see you with him in the olive grove?"
18:30   they replied, **[RPG]** "we would not have handed him over to you."
18:31   Pilate said, "Take him yourselves and judge him by your own law."
18:31   "But we have no right to execute anyone," the Jews **objected**.
18:32   so that the words Jesus *had* **spoken** indicating the kind of death he
18:33   summoned Jesus and **asked** him, "Are you the king of the Jews?"
18:34   "Is that your own idea," Jesus asked, "or did others talk to you
18:34   your own idea," Jesus asked, "or *did* others **talk** to you about me?"
18:37   "You are a king, then!" **said** Pilate. Jesus answered, "You are right
18:37   Jesus answered, "You *are right in* **saying** I am a king. In fact,
18:38   "What is truth?" Pilate **asked**. With this he went out again to the
18:38   **With this** [+4047] he went out again to the Jews and said,
18:38   With this he went out again to the Jews and **said**, "I find no basis
18:40   They shouted back, **[RPG]** "No, not him! Give us Barabbas!"
19: 3   and went up to him again and again, **saying**, "Hail, king of the
19: 4   Once more Pilate came out and **said** to the Jews, "Look, I am
19: 5   thorns and the purple robe, Pilate **said** to them, "Here is the man!"
19: 6   and their officials saw him, they shouted, **[RPG]** "Crucify!
19: 6   Crucify!" But Pilate **answered**, "You take him and crucify him.
19: 9   do you come from?" *he* **asked** Jesus, but Jesus gave him no answer.
19:10   "Do you refuse to speak to me?" Pilate **said**. "Don't you realize I
19:12   but the Jews kept shouting, **[RPG]** "If you let this man go,
19:13   and sat down on the judge's seat at a place **known as** the Stone
19:14   about the sixth hour. "Here is your king," Pilate **said** to the Jews.
19:15   Pilate **asked**. "We have no king but Caesar," the chief priests
19:17   he went out to the place of **[RPG]** the Skull (which in Aramaic is
19:17   he went out to the place of the Skull (which in Aramaic *is* **called**
19:21   The chief priests of the Jews **protested** to Pilate, "Do not write 'The
19:21   of the Jews,' but that this man **claimed** to be king of the Jews."
19:24   "Let's not tear it," *they* **said** to one another. "Let's decide by lot
19:24   This happened that the scripture might be fulfilled which **said**,
19:26   *he* **said** to his mother, "Dear woman, here is your son,"
19:27   and to the disciple, **[RPG]** "Here is your mother." From that time
19:28   so that the Scripture would be fulfilled, Jesus **said**, "I am thirsty."
19:30   When he had received the drink, Jesus **said**, "It is finished."
19:35   He knows that *he* **tells** the truth, and he testifies so that you also
19:37   and, *as* another scripture **says**, "They will look on the one they have
20: 2   Simon Peter and the other disciple, the one Jesus loved, and **said**,

20: 13 They **asked** her, "Woman, why are you crying?" "They have taken
20: 13 "They have taken my Lord away," *she* **said**, "and I don't know
20: 14 **At this** [+4047], she turned around and saw Jesus standing there,
20: 15 "Woman," he **said**, "why are you crying? Who is it you are looking
20: 15 he was the gardener, she **said**, "Sir, if you have carried him away,
20: 15 if you have carried him away, **tell** me where you have put him,
20: 16 Jesus **said** to her, "Mary." She turned toward him and cried out in
20: 16 She turned toward him and **cried out** in Aramaic, "Rabboni!"
20: 16 and cried out in Aramaic, "Rabboni!" (which **means** Teacher).
20: 17 Jesus **said**, "Do not hold on to me, for I have not yet returned to the
20: 17 Go instead to my brothers and **tell** them, 'I am returning to my
20: 18 the Lord!" And she told them that *he had* **said** these things to her.
20: 19 Jesus came and stood among them and **said**, "Peace be with you!"
20: 20 *After he* **said** this, he showed them his hands and side. The
20: 21 Again Jesus **said**, "Peace be with you! As the Father has sent me,
20: 22 And **with that** [+4047] he breathed on them and said,
20: 22 And with that he breathed on them and **said**, "Receive the Holy
20: 24 Now Thomas (**called** Didymus), one of the Twelve, was not with
20: 25 So the other disciples **told** him, "We have seen the Lord!" But he
20: 25 But he **said** to them, "Unless I see the nail marks in his hands
20: 26 Jesus came and stood among them and **said**, "Peace be with you!"
20: 27 Then *he* **said** to Thomas, "Put your finger here; see my hands.
20: 28 Thomas **said** to him, "My Lord and my God!"
20: 29 Then Jesus **told** him, "Because you have seen me, you have
21: 2 Simon Peter, Thomas, (**called** Didymus), Nathanael from Cana in
21: 3 to fish," Simon Peter **told** them, and they said, "We'll go with you."
21: 3 Simon Peter told them, and *they* **said**, "We'll go with you."
21: 5 He **called out** to them, "Friends, haven't you any fish?" "No,"
21: 6 He **said**, "Throw your net on the right side of the boat and you will
21: 7 Then the disciple whom Jesus loved **said** to Peter, "It is the Lord!"
21: 10 Jesus **said** to them, "Bring some of the fish you have just caught."
21: 12 Jesus **said** to them, "Come and have breakfast." None of the
21: 15 had finished eating, Jesus **said** to Simon Peter, "Simon son of John,
21: 15 "Yes, Lord," he **said**, "you know that I love you." Jesus said,
21: 15 he said, "you know that I love you." Jesus **said**, "Feed my lambs."
21: 16 Again Jesus **said**, "Simon son of John, do you truly love me?"
21: 16 *He* **answered**, "Yes, Lord, you know that I love you." Jesus said,
21: 16 you know that I love you." Jesus **said**, "Take care of my sheep."
21: 17 third time *he* **said** to him, "Simon son of John, do you love me?"
21: 17 Peter was hurt because Jesus **asked** him the third time, "Do you
21: 17 *He* **said**, "Lord, you know all things; you know that I love you."
21: 17 all things; you know that I love you." Jesus **said**, "Feed my sheep.
21: 18 *I* **tell** you the truth, when you were younger you dressed yourself
21: 19 Jesus **said** this to indicate the kind of death by which Peter would
21: 19 Peter would glorify God. **[RPG]** Then he said to him, "Follow me!"
21: 19 which Peter would glorify God. Then *he* **said** to him, "Follow me!"
21: 20 one who had leaned back against Jesus at the supper and *had* **said**,
21: 21 When Peter saw him, he **asked**, "Lord, what about him?"
21: 22 Jesus **answered**, "If I want him to remain alive until I return,
21: 23 But Jesus *did* not **say** that he would not die; he only said, "If I want

Ac   1: 3 over a period of forty days and **spoke** about the kingdom of God.
1: 6 So when they met together, they asked him, **[RPG]** "Lord,
1: 7 *He* **said** to them: "It is not for you to know the times or dates the
1: 9 *After he* **said** this, he was taken up before their very eyes,
1: 11 "Men of Galilee," they **said**, "why do you stand here looking into
1: 16 and **said**, "Brothers, the Scripture had to be fulfilled which the Holy
1: 24 Then they **[RPG]** prayed, "Lord, you know everyone's heart.
2: 7 Utterly amazed, *they* **asked**: "Are not all these men who are
2: 12 Amazed and perplexed, *they* **asked** one another, "What does this
2: 13 Some, however, made fun of them and **said**, "They have had too
2: 16 No, this is what *was* **spoken** by the prophet Joel:
2: 17 " 'In the last days, God **says**, I will pour out my Spirit on all people.
2: 25 David **said** about him: " 'I saw the Lord always before me.
2: 29 *I* can **tell** you confidently that the patriarch David died and was
2: 34 not ascend to heaven, and yet he **said**, " 'The Lord said to my Lord:
2: 34 not ascend to heaven, and yet he said, " 'The Lord **said** to my Lord:
2: 37 they were cut to the heart and **said** to Peter and the other apostles,
2: 40 with them, **[RPG]** "Save yourselves from this corrupt generation."
3: 2 from birth was being carried to the temple gate **called** Beautiful,
3: 4 looked straight at him, as did John. Then Peter **said**, "Look at us!"
3: 6 Then Peter **said**, "Silver or gold I do not have, but what I have I
3: 22 For Moses **said**, 'The Lord your God will raise up for you a
3: 25 *He* **said** to Abraham, 'Through your offspring all peoples on earth
4: 8 Then Peter, filled with the Holy Spirit, **said** to them: "Rulers
4: 16 "What are we going to do with these men?" *they* **asked**.
4: 19 **[RPG]** "Judge for yourselves whether it is right in God's sight to

4: 23 and reported all that the chief priests and elders *had* **said** to them.
4: 24 "Sovereign Lord," *they* **said**, "you made the heaven and the earth
4: 25 You **spoke** by the Holy Spirit through the mouth of your servant,
4: 32 No one **claimed** that any of his possessions was his own, but they
5: 3 Then Peter **said**, "Ananias, how is it that Satan has so filled your
5: 8 Peter asked her, "**Tell** me, is this the price you and Ananias got for
5: 8 and Ananias got for the land?" "Yes," she **said**, "that is the price."
5: 20 "Go, stand in the temple courts," *he* **said**, "and tell the people the
5: 23 **[RPG]** "We found the jail securely locked, with the guards
5: 28 "We gave you strict orders not to teach in this name," *he* **said**.
5: 29 apostles replied: **[RPG]** "We must obey God rather than men!
5: 35 Then *he* **addressed** them: "Men of Israel, consider carefully what
5: 36 time ago Theudas appeared, **claiming** [+1571] to be somebody,
5: 38 Therefore, in the present case *I* **advise** you: Leave these men
6: 2 So the Twelve gathered all the disciples together and **said**,
6: 9 members of the Synagogue of the Freedmen (as *it was* **called**)—
6: 11 Then they secretly persuaded some men *to* **say**, "We have heard
6: 13 They produced false witnesses, *who* **testified**, "This fellow never
6: 14 For we have heard him **say** that this Jesus of Nazareth will destroy
7: 1 Then the high priest **asked** him, "Are these charges true?"
7: 3 'Leave your country and your people,' God **said**,
7: 7 But I will punish the nation they serve as slaves,' God **said**,
7: 26 He tried to reconcile them *by* **saying**, 'Men, you are brothers;
7: 27 man who was mistreating the other pushed Moses aside and **said**,
7: 33 "Then the Lord **said** to him, 'Take off your sandals; the place where
7: 35 "This is the same Moses whom they had rejected **with the words**,
7: 37 "This is that Moses who **told** the Israelites, 'God will send you a
7: 40 *They* **told** Aaron, 'Make us gods who will go before us. As for this
7: 48 High does not live in houses made by men. As the prophet **says**:
7: 49 build for me? **says** the Lord. Or where will my resting place be?
7: 56 "Look," he **said**, "I see heaven open and the Son of Man standing at
7: 59 Stephen prayed, **[RPG]** "Lord Jesus, receive my spirit."
7: 60 hold this sin against them." *When he had* **said** this, he fell asleep.
8: 6 signs he did, they all paid close attention *to what* he **said**.
8: 9 all the people of Samaria. *He* **boasted** that he was someone great,
8: 10 both high and low, gave him their attention and **exclaimed**,
8: 19 and **said**, "Give me also this ability so that everyone on whom I lay
8: 20 Peter **answered**: "May your money perish with you, because you
8: 24 **[RPG]** "Pray to the Lord for me so that nothing you have said may
8: 24 the Lord for me so that nothing *you have* **said** may happen to me."
8: 26 an angel of the Lord said to Philip, **[RPG]** "Go south to the road—
8: 29 The Spirit **told** Philip, "Go to that chariot and stay near it."
8: 30 "Do you understand what you are reading?" Philip **asked**.
8: 31 "How can I," he **said**, "unless someone explains it to me?" So he
8: 34 The eunuch asked Philip, **[RPG]** "Tell me, please, who is the
8: 34 please, who *is* the prophet **talking** about, himself or someone else?"
9: 4 He fell to the ground and heard a voice **say** to him, "Saul, Saul,
9: 5 "Who are you, Lord?" Saul **asked**. "I am Jesus, whom you are
9: 10 The Lord **called** to him in a vision, "Ananias!" "Yes, Lord," he
9: 10 called to him in a vision, "Ananias!" "Yes, Lord," he **answered**.
9: 15 But the Lord said to Ananias, "Go! This man is my chosen
9: 17 Placing his hands on Saul, he **said**, "Brother Saul, the Lord—
9: 21 All those who heard him were astonished and **asked**, "Isn't he the
9: 34 "Aeneas," Peter **said** to him, "Jesus Christ heals you. Get up and
9: 36 when translated, **is** Dorcas), who was always doing good
9: 40 Turning toward the dead woman, he **said**, "Tabitha, get up."
10: 3 saw an angel of God, who came to him and **said**, "Cornelius!"
10: 4 "What is it, Lord?" he **asked**. The angel answered, "Your prayers
10: 4 The angel **answered**, "Your prayers and gifts to the poor have
10: 14 "Surely not, Lord!" Peter **replied**. "I have never eaten anything
10: 19 the Spirit **said** to him, "Simon, three men are looking for you.
10: 21 Peter went down and **said** to the men, "I'm the one you're looking
10: 22 The men **replied**, "We have come from Cornelius the centurion.
10: 26 made him get up. "Stand up," *he* **said**, "I am only a man myself."
10: 28 But God has shown me that I *should* not **call** any man impure
10: 34 Then Peter **began to speak** [+487+3836+5125]: "I now realize
11: 3 and **said**, "You went into the house of uncircumcised men and ate
11: 4 everything to them precisely as it had happened: **[RPG]**
11: 7 Then I heard a voice **telling** me, 'Get up, Peter. Kill and eat.'
11: 8 "*I* **replied**, 'Surely not, Lord! Nothing impure or unclean has ever
11: 12 The Spirit **told** me to have no hesitation about going with them.
11: 13 He told us how he had seen an angel appear in his house and **say**,
11: 16 Then I remembered what the Lord *had* **said**: 'John baptized with
11: 18 they had no further objections and praised God, **saying**, "So then,
12: 7 "Quick, get up!" *he* **said**, and the chains fell off Peter's wrists.
12: 8 Then the angel **said** to him, "Put on your clothes and sandals."

12: 8 "Wrap your cloak around you and follow me," the angel **told** him.
12:11 Then Peter came to himself and **said**, "Now I know without a doubt
12:15 "You're out of your mind," they **told** her. When she kept insisting
12:15 she kept insisting that it was so, they **said**, "It must be his angel."
12:17 the brothers about this," *he* **said**, and then he left for another place.
13: 2 they were worshiping the Lord and fasting, the Holy Spirit **said**,
13: 9 filled with the Holy Spirit, looked straight at Elymas and **said**,
13:15 the synagogue rulers sent word to them, **saying**, "Brothers,
13:15 have a message of encouragement for the people, *please* **speak**."
13:16 Standing up, Paul motioned with his hand and **said**: "Men of Israel
13:22 he made David their king. He **[RPG]** testified concerning him:
13:25 As John was completing his work, *he* **said**: 'Who do you think I
13:34 raised him from the dead, never to decay, *is* **stated** in these words:
13:35 So *it is* **stated** elsewhere: " 'You will not let your Holy One see
13:40 Take care that what the prophets *have* **said** does not happen to
13:46 Then Paul and Barnabas **answered** them boldly: "We had to speak
14:10 and **called** [+3489+5889] out, "Stand up on your feet!" At that,
14:11 **[RPG]** "The gods have come down to us in human form!"
14:15 **[RPG]** "Men, why are you doing this? We too are only men,
14:18 Even *with* these **words**, they had difficulty keeping the crowd
15: 5 who belonged to the party of the Pharisees stood up and **said**,
15: 7 After much discussion, Peter got up and **addressed** [+4639] them:
15:13 they finished, James spoke up: **[RPG]** "Brothers, listen to me.
15:17 who bear my name, **says** the Lord, who does these things'
15:36 Some time later Paul **said** to Barnabas, "Let us go back and visit the
16: 9 and begging him, **[RPG]** "Come over to Macedonia and help us."
16:15 me a believer in the Lord," *she* **said**, "come and stay at my house."
16:17 shouting, **[RPG]** "These men are servants of the Most High God,
16:18 so troubled that *he* turned around and **said** to the spirit,
16:20 *They* brought them before the magistrates and **said**, "These men are
16:28 But Paul shouted, **[RPG]** "Don't harm yourself! We are all here!"
16:31 They **replied**, "Believe in the Lord Jesus, and you will be saved—
16:35 the magistrates sent their officers to the jailer with the **order**:
17: 7 **saying** that there is another king, one called Jesus."
17:18 Some of them **asked**, "What is this babbler trying to say?" Others
17:18 Some of them asked, "What is this babbler trying *to* **say**?" Others
17:19 him to a meeting of the Areopagus, where *they* **said** to him,
17:21 doing nothing but **talking about** and listening to the latest ideas.)
17:28 As some of your own poets *have* **said**, 'We are his offspring.'
17:32 some of them sneered, but others **said**, "We want to hear you again
18: 6 he shook out his clothes in protest and **said** to them,
18: 9 One night the Lord **spoke** to Paul in a vision: "Do not be afraid;
18:13 "This man," *they* **charged**, "is persuading the people to worship
18:14 Just as Paul was about to speak, Gallio **said** to the Jews, "If you
18:21 But as he left, *he* **promised**, "I will come back if it is God's will."
19: 2 and **asked** them, "Did you receive the Holy Spirit when you
19: 3 So Paul **asked**, "Then what baptism did you receive?" "John's
19: 3 what baptism did you receive?" "John's baptism," they **replied**.
19: 4 Paul **said**, "John's baptism was a baptism of repentance. He told the
19: 4 *He* **told** the people to believe in the one coming after him,
19:13 *They would* **say**, "In the name of Jesus, whom Paul preaches,
19:15 ₍One day₎ the evil spirit answered **[RPG]** them, "Jesus I know,
19:21 "After I have been there," *he* **said**, "I must visit Rome also."
19:25 them together, along with the workmen in related trades, and **said**:
19:26 province of Asia. *He* **says** that man-made gods are no gods at all.
19:28 and began shouting: **[RPG]** "Great is Artemis of the Ephesians!"
19:41 *After he had* **said** this, he dismissed the assembly.
20:10 put his arms around him. "Don't be alarmed," *he* **said**. "He's alive!
20:18 When they arrived, *he* **said** to them: "You know how I lived the
20:23 I only know that in every city the Holy Spirit warns me **[RPG]**
20:35 the weak, remembering the words the Lord Jesus himself **said**:
20:36 *When he had* **said** this, he knelt down with all of them and prayed.
20:38 What grieved them most was his statement **[RPG]** that they
21: 4 Through the Spirit they **urged** Paul not to go on to Jerusalem.
21:11 he took Paul's belt, tied his own hands and feet with it and **said**,
21:11 tied his own hands and feet with it and said, "The Holy Spirit **says**,
21:14 not be dissuaded, we gave up and **said**, "The Lord's will be done."
21:20 Then *they* **said** to Paul: "You see, brother, how many thousands of
21:21 **telling** them not to circumcise their children or live according to
21:23 so do what *we* **tell** you. There are four men with us who have made
21:37 *he* **asked** the commander, "May I say something to you?"
21:37 he asked the commander, "May I **say** something to you?"
21:39 Paul **answered**, "I am a Jew, from Tarsus in Cilicia, a citizen of no
21:40 When they were all silent, he said **[RPG]** to them in Aramaic:
22: 7 I fell to the ground and heard a voice **say** to me, 'Saul! Saul!
22: 8 " 'I am Jesus of Nazareth, whom you are persecuting,' *he* **replied**.

22:10 " 'What shall I do, Lord?' *I* **asked**. " 'Get up,' the Lord said,
22:10 " 'What shall I do, Lord?' I asked. " 'Get up,' the Lord **said**,
22:13 *He* stood beside me and **said**, 'Brother Saul, receive your sight!'
22:14 "Then he **said**: 'The God of our fathers has chosen you to know his
22:18 and saw the Lord **speaking**. 'Quick!' he said to me. 'Leave
22:19 " 'Lord,' I **replied**, 'these men know that I went from one
22:21 "Then the Lord **said** to me, 'Go; I will send you far away to the
22:22 Then they raised their voices and **shouted**, "Rid the earth of him!
22:24 *He* **directed** that he be flogged and questioned in order to find out
22:25 him out to flog him, Paul **said** to the centurion standing there,
22:26 and reported it. "What are you going to do?" *he* **asked**.
22:27 The commander went to Paul and **asked**, "Tell me, are you a
22:27 The commander went to Paul and asked, "**Tell** me, are you a
23: 1 Paul looked straight at the Sanhedrin and **said**, "My brothers,
23: 3 Then Paul **said** to him, "God will strike you, you whitewashed wall!
23: 4 Those who were standing near Paul **said**, "You dare to insult God's
23: 5 it is written: '*Do* not **speak** evil **about** the ruler of your people.' "
23: 7 *When* he **said** this, a dispute broke out between the Pharisees
23: 8 (The Sadducees **say** that there is no resurrection, and that there are
23: 9 "We find nothing wrong with this man," *they* **said**. "What if a spirit
23:11 The following night the Lord stood near Paul and **said**,
23:12 and bound themselves with an oath **[RPG]** not to eat or drink
23:14 They went to the chief priests and elders and **said**, "We have taken
23:20 *He* **said**: "The Jews have agreed to ask you to bring Paul before the
23:23 then *he* called two of his centurions and **ordered** them, "Get ready
23:30 I also ordered his accusers to **present** to you their case against him.
24: 2 was called in, Tertullus presented his case **[RPG]** before Felix:
24:10 When the governor motioned for him *to* **speak**, Paul replied:
24:14 God of our fathers as a follower of the Way, which *they* **call** a sect.
24:20 Or these who are here *should* **state** what crime they found in me
24:22 Lysias the commander comes," *he* **said**, "I will decide your case."
25: 9 Festus, wishing to do the Jews a favor, **said** to Paul, "Are you
25:10 Paul **answered**: "I am now standing before Caesar's court,
25:14 days there, Festus discussed Paul's case with the king. *He* **said**:
25:20 so *I* **asked** if he would be willing to go to Jerusalem and stand trial
26: 1 Agrippa said to Paul, "You have permission *to* **speak** for yourself."
26:14 and I heard a voice **saying** to me in Aramaic, 'Saul, Saul,
26:15 "Then *I* **asked**, 'Who are you, Lord?' " 'I am Jesus, whom you are
26:15 " 'I am Jesus, whom you are persecuting,' the Lord **replied**.
26:22 *I am* **saying** nothing beyond what the prophets and Moses said
26:31 They left the room, and *while* **talking** with one another, they said,
27:10 **[RPG]** "Men, I can see that our voyage is going to be disastrous
27:11 But the centurion, instead of listening to what Paul **said**,
27:21 gone a long time without food, Paul stood up before them and **said**:
27:24 and **said**, 'Do not be afraid, Paul. You must stand trial before
27:31 Then Paul **said** to the centurion and the soldiers, "Unless these men
27:33 "For the last fourteen days," *he* **said**, "you have been in constant
27:35 *After he had* **said** this, he took some bread and gave thanks to God in
28: 4 his hand, *they* **said** to each other, "This man must be a murderer;
28: 6 happen to him, *they* changed their minds and **said** he was a god.
28:17 When they had assembled, Paul **said** to them: "My brothers,
28:21 They **replied**, "We have not received any letters from Judea
28:24 Some were convinced by what he **said**, but others would not
28:25 and began to leave after Paul *had* **made** this final statement:
28:25 "The Holy Spirit spoke the truth to your forefathers *when he* **said**
28:26 " 'Go to this people and **say**, "You will be ever hearing but never

Ro   2:12 You *who* **say** that people should not commit adultery, do you
3: 5 brings out God's righteousness more clearly, what *shall we* **say**?
3: 5 in bringing his wrath on us? (*I am* **using** a human **argument**.)
3: 8 slanderously reported as saying and as some claim that we **say**—
3:19 Now we know that whatever the law **says**, it says to those who are
4: 1 What then *shall we* **say** that Abraham, our forefather, discovered
4: 3 What *does* the Scripture **say**? "Abraham believed God, and it was
4: 6 David says the same thing *when he* **speaks** of the blessedness of
4: 9 *We have been* **saying** that Abraham's faith was credited to him as
4:18 just as it *had been* **said** to him, "So shall your offspring be."
6: 1 What *shall we* **say**, then? Shall we go on sinning so that grace may
6:19 *I* **put** this in human terms because you are weak in your natural
7: 7 What *shall we* **say**, then? Is the law sin? Certainly not! Indeed I
7: 7 not have known what coveting really was if the law *had* not **said**,
8:31 What, then, *shall we* **say** in response to this? If God is for us,
9: 1 *I* **speak** the truth in Christ—I am not lying, my conscience
9:12 him who calls—she *was* **told**, "The older will serve the younger."
9:14 What then *shall we* **say**? Is God unjust? Not at all!
9:15 For *he* **says** to Moses, "I will have mercy on whom I have mercy,
9:17 For the Scripture **says** to Pharaoh: "I raised you up for this very

9: 19   One of *you will* **say** to me: "Then why does God still blame us?
9: 20   "*Shall* what is formed **say** to him who formed it, 'Why did you
9: 25   as *he* **says** in Hosea: "I will call them 'my people' who are not my
9: 26   "It will happen that in the very place where *it was* **said** to them,
9: 30   What then *shall we* **say**? That the Gentiles, who did not pursue
10: 6   But the righteousness that is by faith **says**: "Do not say in your
10: 6   "*Do* not **say** in your heart, 'Who will ascend into heaven?'
10: 8   But what *does it* **say**? "The word is near you; it is in your mouth
10: 11   As the Scripture **says**, "Anyone who trusts in him will never be put
10: 16   good news. For Isaiah **says**, "Lord, who has believed our message?"
10: 18   But *I* **ask**: Did they not hear? Of course they did: "Their voice has
10: 19   Again *I* **ask**: Did Israel not understand? First, Moses says,
10: 19   First, Moses **says**, "I will make you envious by those who are not a
10: 20   And Isaiah boldly **says**, "I was found by those who did not seek me;
10: 21   But concerning Israel he **says**, "All day long I have held out my
11: 1   *I* **ask** then: Did God reject his people? By no means! I am an
11: 2   Don't you know what the Scripture **says** in the passage about
11: 4   And what *was* God's **answer** to him? "I have reserved for myself
11: 9   And David **says**: "May their table become a snare and a trap,
11: 11   Again *I* **ask**: Did they stumble so as to fall beyond recovery?
11: 13   *I am* **talking** to you Gentiles. Inasmuch as I am the apostle to the
11: 19   *You will* **say** then, "Branches were broken off so that I could be
12: 3   For by the grace given me *I* **say** to every one of you: Do not think
12: 19   for it is written: "It is mine to avenge; I will repay," **says** the Lord.
14: 11   " 'As surely as I live,' **says** the Lord, 'every knee will bow before
15: 8   For *I* **tell** you that Christ has become a servant of the Jews on
15: 10   Again, *it* **says**, "Rejoice, O Gentiles, with his people."
15: 12   And again, Isaiah **says**, "The Root of Jesse will spring up, one who
1Co 1: 10   that all of *you* **agree** [+899+3836] **with one another** so that there
1: 12   What *I* **mean** is this: One of you says, "I follow Paul"; another,
1: 12   One of you says, "I follow Paul"; another, "I follow Apollos";
1: 15   so no one *can* **say** that you were baptized into my name.
3: 4   when one **says**, "I follow Paul," and another, "I follow Apollos,"
6: 5   *I* **say** this to shame you. Is it possible that there is nobody among
7: 6   *I* **say** this as a concession, not as a command.
7: 8   Now to the unmarried and the widows *I* **say**: It is good for them to
7: 12   To the rest *I* **say** this (I, not the Lord): If any brother has a wife
7: 35   *I am* **saying** this for your own good, not to restrict you, but that
8: 5   For even if there are **so-called** gods, whether in heaven or on earth
9: 8   from a human point of view? Doesn't the Law **say** the same thing?
9: 10   Surely *he* **says** this for us, doesn't he? Yes, this was written for us,
10: 15   I **speak** to sensible people; judge for yourselves what I say.
10: 28   But if anyone **says** to you, "This has been offered in sacrifice,"
10: 29   the other man's conscience, *I* **mean**, not yours. For why should my
11: 22   What *shall I* **say** to you? Shall I praise you for this? Certainly not!
11: 24   he broke it and **said**, "This is my body, which is for you;
11: 25   In the same way, after supper he took the cup, **saying**, "This cup is
12: 3   I tell you that no one who is speaking by the Spirit of God **says**,
12: 3   "Jesus be cursed," and no one can say, "Jesus is Lord," except by
12: 15   If the foot *should* **say**, "Because I am not a hand, I do not belong to
12: 16   And if the ear *should* **say**, "Because I am not an eye, I do not
12: 21   The eye cannot **say** to the hand, "I don't need you!" And the head
14: 16   *can* one who finds himself among those who do not understand **say**
14: 16   your thanksgiving, since he does not know what *you are* **saying**?
14: 21   this people, but even then they will not listen to me," **says** the Lord.
14: 23   come in, *will they* not **say** that you are out of your mind?
14: 34   not allowed to speak, but must be in submission, as the Law **says**.
15: 12   how *can* some of you **say** that there is no resurrection of the dead?
15: 27   Now when *it* **says** that "everything" has been put under him,
15: 35   But someone *may* **ask**, "How are the dead raised? With what kind
15: 51   Listen, *I* **tell** you a mystery: We will not all sleep, but we will all
2Co 4: 6   For God, who **said**, "Let light shine out of darkness," made his light
6: 2   For *he* **says**, "In the time of my favor I heard you, and in the day of
6: 13   As a fair exchange—*I* **speak** as to my children—open wide your
6: 16   As God *has* **said**: "I will live with them and walk among them,
6: 17   "Therefore come out from them and be separate, **says** the Lord.
6: 18   and you will be my sons and daughters, **says** the Lord Almighty."
7: 3   *I do* not **say** this to condemn you; I have said before that you have
8: 8   *I am* not **commanding** [+2198+2848] you, but I want to test the
9: 3   prove hollow, but that you may be ready, as *I* **said** you would be.
9: 4   and find you unprepared, we—not to **say** *anything* **about** you—
11: 16   *I* **repeat** [+4099]: Let no one take me for a fool. But if you do,
11: 21   To my shame *I* **admit** that we were too weak for that! What
11: 21   boast about—*I am* **speaking** as a fool—I also dare to boast about.
12: 6   I would not be a fool, because *I would be* **speaking** the truth.
12: 9   But *he* **said** to me, "My grace is sufficient for you, for my power is

Gal 1: 9   As we have already said, so now *I* **say** again: If anybody is
2: 14   *I* **said** to Peter in front of them all, "You are a Jew, yet you live like
3: 15   Brothers, *let me* **take an example** from everyday life. Just as no
3: 16   The promises *were* **spoken** to Abraham and to his seed.
3: 16   The *Scripture does* not **say** "and to seeds," meaning many people,
3: 17   What *I* **mean** is this: The law, introduced 430 years later, does not
4: 1   What *I am* **saying** is that as long as the heir is a child, he is no
4: 21   **Tell** me, you who want to be under the law, are you not aware of
4: 30   But what *does* the Scripture **say**? "Get rid of the slave woman
5: 2   I, Paul, **tell** you that if you let yourselves be circumcised,
5: 16   So *I* **say**, live by the Spirit, and you will not gratify the desires of
Eph 2: 11   and **called** "uncircumcised" by those who call themselves "the
2: 11   and called "uncircumcised" by those *who* **call** *themselves* "the
4: 8   This is why *it* **says**: "When he ascended on high, he led captives in
4: 17   So *I* **tell** you this, and insist on it in the Lord, that you must no
5: 12   For it is shameful even *to* **mention** what the disobedient do in
5: 14   This is why *it is* **said**: "Wake up, O sleeper, rise from the dead,
5: 32   a profound mystery—but I *am* **talking** about or what Christ and the church.
Php 3: 18   as *I have* often **told** you before and now say again even with tears,
3: 18   as I have often told you before and now **say** again even with tears,
4: 4   Rejoice in the Lord always. *I will* **say** it again: Rejoice!
4: 11   *I am* not **saying** this because I am in need, for I have learned to be
Col 2: 4   *I* **tell** you this so that no one may deceive you by fine-sounding
4: 11   Jesus, who *is* **called** Justus, also sends greetings. These are the
4: 17   **Tell** Archippus: "See to it that you complete the work you have
1Th 4: 15   to the Lord's own word, *we* **tell** you that we who are still alive,
5: 3   While *people are* **saying**, "Peace and safety," destruction will come
2Th 2: 4   and will exalt himself over everything *that is* **called** God
2: 5   Don't you remember that when I was with you *I used to* **tell** you
1Ti 1: 7   but they do not know what *they are* **talking about** or what they
2: 7   a herald and an apostle—*I am* **telling** the truth, I am not lying—
4: 1   The Spirit clearly **says** that in later times some will abandon the
5: 18   For the Scripture **says**, "Do not muzzle the ox while it is treading
2Ti 2: 7   Reflect on what *I am* **saying**, for the Lord will give you insight
2: 18   the truth. *They* **say** that the resurrection has already taken place,
Tit 1: 12   Even one of their own prophets *has* **said**, "Cretans are always liars,
2: 8   may be ashamed because they have nothing bad *to* **say** about us.
Phm 1: 19   I will pay it back—not to **mention** that you owe me your very self.
1: 21   I write to you, knowing that you will do even more than *I* **ask**.
Heb 1: 5   For to which of the angels *did* God ever **say**, "You are my Son;
1: 6   into the world, *he* **says**, "Let all God's angels worship him."
1: 7   In speaking of the angels *he* **says**, "He makes his angels winds,
1: 13   To which of the angels *did* God ever **say**, "Sit at my right hand until
2: 6   **[RPG]** "What is man that you are mindful of him, the son of man
2: 12   *He* **says**, "I will declare your name to my brothers; in the presence
3: 7   So, as the Holy Spirit **says**: "Today, if you hear my voice,
3: 10   and *I* **said**, 'Their hearts are always going astray, and they have not
3: 15   As *has just been* **said**: "Today, if you hear his voice, do not harden
4: 3   that rest, just as God *has* **said**, "So I declared on oath in my anger,
4: 4   For somewhere *he has* **spoken** about the seventh day in these
4: 7   calling it Today, when a long time later *he* **spoke** through David,
5: 6   And *he* **says** in another place, "You are a priest forever, in the order
5: 11   We have much *to* **say** about this,
6: 14   **saying**, "I will surely bless you and give you many descendants."
7: 9   **One might even say** [+2229+6055] that Levi, who collects the
7: 11   in the order of Melchizedek, not in the order of Aaron? **[RPG]**
7: 13   He of whom these things *are* **said** belonged to a different tribe,
7: 21   but he became a priest with an oath when God **said** to him:
8: 1   The point of what *we are* **saying** is this: We do have such a high
8: 8   But God found fault with the people and **said**: "The time is coming,
8: 8   "The time is coming, **declares** the Lord, when I will make a new
8: 9   to my covenant, and I turned away from them, **declares** the Lord.
8: 10   make with the house of Israel after that time, **declares** the Lord.
8: 11   or a man his brother, **saying**, 'Know the Lord,' because they will
8: 13   By **calling** this covenant "new," he has made the first one obsolete;
9: 2   and the consecrated bread; this *was* **called** the Holy Place.
9: 3   Behind the second curtain was a room **called** the Most Holy Place,
9: 5   atonement cover. But we cannot **discuss** these things in detail now.
9: 20   *He* **said**, "This is the blood of the covenant, which God has
10: 5   Therefore, when Christ came into the world, *he* **said**: "Sacrifice
10: 7   Then *I* **said**, 'Here I am—it is written about me in the scroll—
10: 8   First *he* **said**, "Sacrifices and offerings, burnt offerings and sin
10: 9   Then *he* **said**, "Here I am, I have come to do your will." He sets
10: 15   The Holy Spirit also testifies to us about this. First he **says**:
10: 16   the covenant I will make with them after that time, **says** the Lord.
10: 17   Then *he* **adds**: [UBS-] "Their sins and lawless acts I will

10:30	For we know him *who* said, "It is mine to avenge; I will repay,"
11:14	People *who* say such things show that they are looking for a
11:24	grown up, refused *to be* **known** as the son of Pharaoh's daughter.
11:32	And what more *shall I* say? I do not have time to tell about
12:21	The sight was so terrifying that Moses said, "I am trembling with
12:26	**[RPG]** "Once more I will shake not only the earth but also the
13: 5	with what you have, because God *has* said, "Never will I leave you;
13: 6	So we say with confidence, "The Lord is my helper; I will not be

Jas
1:13	When tempted, no one *should* say, "God is tempting me." For God
2: 3	show special attention to the man wearing fine clothes and say,
2: 3	but say to the poor man, "You stand there" or "Sit on the floor by
2:11	For he *who* said, "Do not commit adultery," also said, "Do not
2:11	he who said, "Do not commit adultery," also **said**, "Do not murder."
2:14	my brothers, if a man **claims** to have faith but has no deeds?
2:16	*If* one of you says to him, "Go, I wish you well; keep warm
2:18	But someone *will* say, "You have faith; I have deeds." Show me
2:23	And the scripture was fulfilled that says, "Abraham believed God,
4: 5	Or do you think Scripture says without reason that the spirit he
4: 6	That is why *Scripture* says: "God opposes the proud but gives
4:13	*you* who say, "Today or tomorrow we will go to this or that city,
4:15	Instead, you *ought to* say, "If it is the Lord's will, we will live

2Pe
| 3: 4 | *They will* say, "Where is this 'coming' he promised? Ever since our |

1Jn
1: 6	If *we* **claim** to have fellowship with him yet walk in the darkness,
1: 8	If *we* **claim** to be without sin, we deceive ourselves and the truth is
1:10	If *we* **claim** we have not sinned, we make him out to be a liar
2: 4	The *man who* says, "I know him," but does not do what he
2: 6	Whoever **claims** to live in him must walk as Jesus did.
2: 9	Anyone *who* **claims** to be in the light but hates his brother is still
4:20	If anyone says, "I love God," yet hates his brother, he is a liar.
5:16	that leads to death. *I am* not **saying** he should pray about that.

2Jn
| 1:10 | do not take him into your house or **welcome** [+*5897*] him. |
| 1:11 | Anyone *who* **welcomes** [+*5897*] him shares in his wicked work. |

Jude
1: 9	accusation against him, but said, "The Lord rebuke you!"
1:14	**[RPG]** "See, the Lord is coming with thousands upon thousands
1:18	*They* said to you, "In the last times there will be scoffers who will

Rev
1: 8	and the Omega," says the Lord God, "who is, and who was,
1:11	*which* said: "Write on a scroll what you see and send it to the seven
1:17	Then he placed his right hand on me and said: "Do not be afraid.
2: 1	These *are* the **words** *of* him who holds the seven stars in his right
2: 2	that you have tested those *who* **claim** [+*1571*] to be apostles
2: 7	who has an ear, let him hear what the Spirit says to the churches.
2: 8	These are the **words** *of* him who is the First and the Last,
2: 9	I know the slander of those *who* say they are Jews and are not,
2:11	who has an ear, let him hear what the Spirit says to the churches.
2:12	These *are* the **words** *of* him who has the sharp, double-edged
2:17	who has an ear, let him hear what the Spirit says to the churches.
2:18	These *are* the **words** *of* the Son of God, whose eyes are like
2:20	You tolerate that woman Jezebel, who **calls** herself a prophetess.
2:24	Now *I* say to the rest of you in Thyatira, to you who do not hold to
2:24	and have not learned Satan's **so-called** [+*6055*] deep secrets (I will
2:29	who has an ear, let him hear what the Spirit says to the churches.
3: 1	These *are* the **words** *of* him who holds the seven spirits of God
3: 6	who has an ear, let him hear what the Spirit says to the churches.
3: 7	These *are* the **words** *of* him who is holy and true, who holds the
3: 9	who **claim** [+*1571*] to be Jews though they are not, but are liars—
3:13	who has an ear, let him hear what the Spirit says to the churches.
3:14	These *are* the **words** *of* the Amen, the faithful and true witness,
3:17	*You* say, 'I am rich; I have acquired wealth and do not need a
3:22	who has an ear, let him hear what the Spirit says to the churches."
4: 1	And the voice I had first heard speaking to me like a trumpet said,
4: 8	Day and night they never stop **saying**: "Holy, holy, holy is the Lord
4:10	and ever. They lay their crowns before the throne and say:
5: 5	Then one of the elders said to me, "Do not weep! See, the Lion of
5: 9	**[RPG]** "You are worthy to take the scroll and to open its seals,
5:12	In a loud voice *they* **sang**: "Worthy is the Lamb, who was slain,
5:13	and under the earth and on the sea, and all that is in them, **singing**:
5:14	The four living creatures said, "Amen," and the elders fell down
6: 1	Then I heard one of the four living creatures say in a voice like
6: 3	the second seal, I heard the second living creature say, "Come!"
6: 5	opened the third seal, I heard the third living creature say, "Come!"
6: 6	**saying**, "A quart of wheat for a day's wages, and three quarts of
6: 7	I heard the voice of the fourth living creature say, "Come!"
6:10	in a loud voice, **[RPG]** "How long, Sovereign Lord, holy and true,
6:11	and they *were* **told** to wait a little longer, until the number of their
6:16	*They* **called** to the mountains and the rocks, "Fall on us and hide us
7: 3	**[RPG]** "Do not harm the land or the sea or the trees until we put a

7:10	**[RPG]** "Salvation belongs to our God, who sits on the throne,
7:12	**saying**: "Amen! Praise and glory and wisdom and thanks and honor
7:13	Then one of the elders asked me, **[RPG]** "These in white robes—
7:14	*I* **answered**, "Sir, you know." And he said, "These are they who
7:14	And *he* said, "These are they who have come out of the great
8:11	the name of the star **is** Wormwood. A third of the waters turned
8:13	I heard an eagle that was flying in midair **call out** in a loud voice:
9: 4	They *were* **told** not to harm the grass of the earth or any plant
9:14	It said to the sixth angel who had the trumpet, "Release the four
10: 4	but I heard a voice from heaven say, "Seal up what the seven
10: 8	**[RPG]** "Go, take the scroll that lies open in the hand of the angel
10: 9	So I went to the angel and **asked** him to give me the little scroll.
10: 9	*He* said to me, "Take it and eat it. It will turn your stomach sour,
10:11	Then I *was* **told**, "You must prophesy again about many peoples,
11: 1	I was given a reed like a measuring rod and *was* **told**, "Go
11:12	Then they heard a loud voice from heaven **saying** to them,
11:15	his trumpet, and there were loud voices in heaven, *which* said:
11:17	**saying**: "We give thanks to you, Lord God Almighty, the One who
12:10	Then I heard a loud voice in heaven say: "Now have come the
13: 4	and they also worshiped the beast and **asked**, "Who is like the
13:14	*He* **ordered** them to set up an image in honor of the beast who was
14: 7	*He* **said** in a loud voice, "Fear God and give him glory,
14: 8	A second angel followed and **said**, "Fallen! Fallen is Babylon the
14: 9	A third angel followed them and said in a loud voice: "If anyone
14:13	Then I heard a voice from heaven say, "Write: Blessed are the dead
14:13	"Yes," says the Spirit, "they will rest from their labor, for their
14:18	**[RPG]** "Take your sharp sickle and gather the clusters of grapes
15: 3	**[RPG]** "Great and marvelous are your deeds, Lord God Almighty.
16: 1	Then I heard a loud voice from the temple **saying** to the seven
16: 5	Then I heard the angel in charge of the waters say: "You are just in
16: 7	And I heard the altar **respond**: "Yes, Lord God Almighty, true
16:17	the temple came a loud voice from the throne, **saying**, "It is done!"
17: 1	who had the seven bowls came and said to me, **[RPG]** "Come,
17: 7	Then the angel said to me: "Why are you astonished? I will explain
17: 7	I *will* **explain** to you the mystery of the woman and of the beast
17:15	Then the angel said to me, "The waters you saw,
18: 2	voice he shouted: **[RPG]** "Fallen! Fallen is Babylon the Great!
18: 4	Then I heard another voice from heaven say: "Come out of her,
18: 7	In her heart *she* **boasts**, 'I sit as queen; I am not a widow,
18:10	Terrified at her torment, they will stand far off and **cry**: " 'Woe!
18:16	and **cry out**: " 'Woe! Woe, O great city, dressed in fine linen,
18:18	will exclaim, **[RPG]** 'Was there ever a city like this great city?'
18:19	**[RPG]** " 'Woe! Woe, O great city, where all who had ships on the
18:21	the size of a large millstone and threw it into the sea, and **said**:
19: 1	what sounded like the roar of a great multitude in heaven **shouting**:
19: 3	And again *they* **shouted**: "Hallelujah! The smoke from her goes up
19: 4	who was seated on the throne. And *they* **cried**: "Amen, Hallelujah!"
19: 5	Then a voice came from the throne, **saying**: "Praise our God,
19: 6	the roar of rushing waters and like loud peals of thunder, **shouting**:
19: 9	Then the angel said to me, "Write: 'Blessed are those who are
19: 9	are invited to the wedding supper of the Lamb!' " And *he* **added**,
19:10	But *he* said to me, "Do not do it! I am a fellow servant with you
19:17	who cried in a loud voice **[RPG]** to all the birds flying in midair,
21: 3	I heard a loud voice from the throne **saying**, "Now the dwelling
21: 5	He who was seated on the throne said, "I am making everything
21: 5	Then *he* said, "Write this down, for these words are trustworthy
21: 6	*He* **said** to me: "It is done. I am the Alpha and the Omega,
21: 9	full of the seven last plagues came and said to me, **[RPG]** "Come,
22: 6	The angel said to me, "These words are trustworthy and true.
22: 9	But *he* said to me, "Do not do it! I am a fellow servant with you
22:10	Then he **told** me, "Do not seal up the words of the prophecy of this
22:17	The Spirit and the bride say, "Come!" And let him who hears say,
22:17	and the bride say, "Come!" And *let* him who hears say, "Come!"
22:20	He who testifies to these things **says**, "Yes, I am coming soon."

3307 λεῖμμα, *leimma* [1] [√ *3309*]

remnant [1]

Ro   11: 5   So too, at the present time there is a **remnant** chosen by grace.

3308 λεῖος, *leios* [1]

smooth [1]

Lk   3: 5   The crooked roads shall become straight, the rough ways **smooth**.

3309 λείπω, *leipō* [6] [→ *89, 90, 444, 657, 659, 1364, 1366, 1593, 1722, 2142, 2145, 2900, 2901, 2905, 3307, 3370, 4335, 5698, 5699, 5701*]

untranslated [1], have everything need [*+3594*] [1], lack [1], lacking [1], lacks [1], left [1]

Lk 18:22 When Jesus heard this, he said to him, "You still **lack** one thing.
Tit 1: 5 Crete was that you might straighten out what *was* **left** *unfinished*
      3:13 their way and see that they **have** [*+3594*] **everything** they **need**.
Jas 1: 4 so that you may be mature and complete, not **lacking** anything.
      1: 5 If any of you **lacks** wisdom, he should ask God, who gives
      2:15 a brother or sister is without clothes and **[RPG]** daily food.

3310 λειτουργέω, *leitourgeō* [3] [√ *3295 + 2240*]

performs religious duties [1], share [1], worshiping [1]

Ac 13: 2 *While* they *were* **worshiping** the Lord and fasting, the Holy Spirit
Ro 15:27 they owe it to the Jews *to* **share** with them their material blessings.
Heb 10:11 after day every priest stands and **performs** his **religious duties**;

3311 λειτουργία, *leitourgia* [6] [√ *3295 + 2240*]

service [2], ceremonies [1], help [1], ministry [1], service that perform [*+1355+3836+4047*] [1]

Lk 1:23 When his time *of* **service** was completed, he returned home.
2Co 9:12 This **service that** *you* **perform** [*+1355+3836+4047*] is not only
Php 2:17 drink offering on the sacrifice and **service** coming from your faith,
      2:30 risking his life to make up for the **help** you could not give me.
Heb 8: 6 But the **ministry** Jesus has received is as superior to theirs as the
      9:21 blood both the tabernacle and everything *used in* its **ceremonies**.

3312 λειτουργικός, *leitourgikos* [1] [√ *3295 + 2240*]

ministering [1]

Heb 1:14 Are not all angels **ministering** spirits sent to serve those who will

3313 λειτουργός, *leitourgos* [5] [√ *3295 + 2240*]

servants [2], minister [1], serves [1], take care [1]

Ro 13: 6 is also why you pay taxes, for the authorities are God's **servants**,
      15:16 to be a **minister** of Christ Jesus to the Gentiles with the priestly
Php 2:25 is also your messenger, whom you sent to **take care** of my needs.
Heb 1: 7 he says, "He makes his angels winds, his **servants** flames of fire."
      8: 2 and who **serves** in the sanctuary, the true tabernacle set up by the

3314 λείχω, *leichō* Not used in UBS/NIV [→ *658, 2143, 4336*]

3315 Λέκτρα, *Lektra* Not used in UBS/NIV [√ *3306*]

3316 λεμά, *lema* [2] [√ *3283*]

lama [2]

Mt 27:46 cried out in a loud voice, "*Eloi, Eloi,* **lama** *sabachthani?*"—
Mk 15:34 cried out in a loud voice, "*Eloi, Eloi,* **lama** *sabachthani?*"—

3317 λέντιον, *lention* [2]

towel [2]

Jn 13: 4 took off his outer clothing, and wrapped a **towel** around his waist.
      13: 5 drying them *with* the **towel** that was wrapped around him.

3318 λεπίς, *lepis* [1] [→ *3319, 3320, 3321*]

scales [1]

Ac 9:18 Immediately, something like **scales** fell from Saul's eyes, and he

3319 λέπρα, *lepra* [4] [√ *3318*]

leprosy [4]

Mt 8: 3 he said. "Be clean!" Immediately he was cured of his **leprosy**.
Mk 1:42 Immediately the **leprosy** left him and he was cured.
Lk 5:12 of the towns, a man came along who was covered *with* **leprosy**.
      5:13 he said. "Be clean!" And immediately the **leprosy** left him.

3320 λεπρός, *lepros* [9] [√ *3318*]

have leprosy [3], leper [2], man with leprosy [2], had leprosy [1], with leprosy [1]

Mt 8: 2 A **man with leprosy** came and knelt before him and said,
      10: 8 Heal the sick, raise the dead, cleanse *those who* **have leprosy**,
      11: 5 the lame walk, *those who* **have leprosy** are cured, the deaf hear,
      26: 6 was in Bethany in the home of a man known as Simon the **Leper**,
Mk 1:40 A **man with leprosy** came to him and begged him on his knees,
      14: 3 at the table in the home of a man known as Simon the **Leper**,
Lk 4:27 And there were many in Israel **with leprosy** in the time of Elisha
      7:22 the lame walk, *those who* **have leprosy** are cured, the deaf hear,
      17:12 As he was going into a village, ten men *who* **had leprosy** met him.

3321 λεπτός, *leptos* [3] [√ *3318*]

very small copper coins [2], penny [1]

Mk 12:42 But a poor widow came and put in two **very small copper coins**,
Lk 12:59 I tell you, you will not get out until you have paid the last **penny**."
      21: 2 He also saw a poor widow put in two **very small copper coins**.

3322 Λευί, *Leui* [8] [→ *3323, 3324, 3325*]

Levi [8]

Mk 2:14 he saw **Levi** son of Alphaeus sitting at the tax collector's booth.
Lk 3:24 the son *of* **Levi**, the son of Melki, the son of Jannai, the son of
      3:29 of Eliezer, the son of Jorim, the son of Matthat, the son *of* **Levi**,
      5:27 and saw a tax collector by the name *of* **Levi** sitting at his tax booth.
      5:29 Then **Levi** held a great banquet for Jesus at his house, and a large
Heb 7: 5 Now the law requires the descendants of **Levi** who become priests
      7: 9 One might even say that **Levi**, who collects the tenth,
Rev 7: 7 from the tribe of Simeon 12,000, from the tribe *of* **Levi** 12,000,

3323 Λευίς, *Leuis* Not used in UBS/NIV [√ *3322*]

3324 Λευίτης, *Leuitēs* [3] [√ *3322*]

Levite [2], Levites [1]

Lk 10:32 So too, a **Levite**, when he came to the place and saw him,
Jn 1:19 Jews of Jerusalem sent priests and **Levites** to ask him who he was.
Ac 4:36 Joseph, a **Levite** from Cyprus, whom the apostles called Barnabas

3325 Λευιτικός, *Leuitikos* [1] [√ *3322*]

Levitical [1]

Heb 7:11 If perfection could have been attained through the **Levitical**

3326 λευκαίνω, *leukainō* [2] [√ *3328*]

bleach [1], made white [1]

Mk 9: 3 whiter than anyone in the world could **bleach** them.
Rev 7:14 washed their robes and **made** them **white** in the blood of the Lamb.

3327 λευκοβύσσινος, *leukobyssinos* Not used in UBS/NIV [√ *3328 + 1116*]

3328 λευκός, *leukos* [25] [→ *3326, 3327*]

white [23], bright [1], ripe [1]

Mt 5:36 by your head, for you cannot make even one hair **white** or black.
      17: 2 shone like the sun, and his clothes became as **white** as the light.
      28: 3 appearance was like lightning, and his clothes were **white** as snow.

Mk   9: 3 His clothes became dazzling **white**, whiter than anyone in the
     16: 5 they saw a young man dressed in a **white** robe sitting on the right
Lk   9: 29 and his clothes became **bright** as a flash of lightning.
Jn   4: 35 open your eyes and look at the fields! They are **ripe** for harvest.
     20: 12 and saw two angels in **white**, seated where Jesus' body had been,
Ac   1: 10 when suddenly two men dressed in **white** stood beside them.
Rev 1: 14 His head and hair were **white** like wool, as white as snow,
     1: 14 His head and hair were white like wool, as **white** as snow,
     2: 17 I will also give him a **white** stone with a new name written on it,
     3: 4 They will walk with me, dressed in **white**, for they are worthy.
     3: 5 He who overcomes will, like them, be dressed in **white**. I will
     3: 18 and **white** clothes to wear, so you can cover your shameful
     4: 4 They were dressed in **white** and had crowns of gold on their heads.
     6: 2 I looked, and there before me was a **white** horse! Its rider had a
     6: 11 Then each of them was given a **white** robe, and they were told to
     7: 9 They were wearing **white** robes and were holding palm branches in
     7: 13 Then one of the elders asked me, "These in **white** robes—who are
     14: 14 I looked, and there before me was a **white** cloud, and seated on the
     19: 11 I saw heaven standing open and there before me was a **white** horse,
     19: 14 riding on **white** horses and dressed in fine linen, white and clean.
     19: 14 riding on white horses and dressed in fine linen, **white** and clean.
     20: 11 Then I saw a great **white** throne and him who was seated on it.

3329 λέων, leōn [9]

lion [5], lions [3], lion's [1]

2Ti   4: 17 Gentiles might hear it. And I was delivered from the **lion's** mouth.
Heb 11: 33 and gained what was promised; who shut the mouths of **lions**,
1Pe   5: 8 Your enemy the devil prowls around like a roaring **lion** looking for
Rev   4: 7 The first living creature was like a **lion**, the second was like an ox,
     5: 5 See, the **Lion** of the tribe of Judah, the Root of David,
     9: 8 hair was like women's hair, and their teeth were like **lions**' teeth.
     9: 17 The heads of the horses resembled the heads of **lions**, and out of
     10: 3 and he gave a loud shout like the roar of a **lion**. When he shouted,
     13: 2 but had feet like those of a bear and a mouth like that of a **lion**.

3330 λήθη, lēthē [1] [√ 3291]

forgotten that [+3284] [1]

2Pe   1: 9 and **has forgotten** [+3284] **that** he has been cleansed from his past

3331 λῆμψις, lēmpsis [1] [√ 3284]

receiving [1]

Php   4: 15 one church shared with me in the matter of giving and **receiving**,

3332 ληνός, lēnos [5] [→ 5700]

winepress [3], press [1], winepress [+3836+3885] [1]

Mt   21: 33 put a wall around it, dug a **winepress** in it and built a watchtower.
Rev 14: 19 its grapes and threw them into the great **winepress** of God's wrath.
     14: 20 They were trampled in the **winepress** outside the city, and blood
     14: 20 the winepress outside the city, and blood flowed out of the **press**,
     19: 15 He treads the **winepress** [+3836+3885] of the fury of the wrath of

3333 λῆρος, lēros [1]

nonsense [1]

Lk   24: 11 the women, because their words seemed to them like **nonsense**.

3334 λῃστής, lēstēs [15] [→ 798]

robbers [9], leading a rebellion [3], bandits [1], had taken part in
a rebellion [+1639] [1], robber [1]

Mt   21: 13 a house of prayer,' but you are making it a 'den of **robbers**.' "
     26: 55 "Am I **leading a rebellion**, that you have come out with swords
     27: 38 Two **robbers** were crucified with him, one on his right and one on
     27: 44 In the same way the **robbers** who were crucified with him also
Mk   11: 17 prayer for all nations'? But you have made it 'a den of **robbers**.' "
     14: 48 "Am I **leading a rebellion**," said Jesus, "that you have come out
     15: 27 They crucified two **robbers** with him, one on his right and one on
Lk   10: 30 from Jerusalem to Jericho, when he fell into the hands of **robbers**.

     10: 36 was a neighbor to the man who fell into the hands of **robbers**?"
     19: 46 be a house of prayer'; but you have made it 'a den of **robbers**.' "
     22: 52 and the elders, who had come for him, "Am I **leading a rebellion**,
Jn   10: 1 the gate, but climbs in by some other way, is a thief and a **robber**.
     10: 8 All who ever came before me were thieves and **robbers**,
     18: 40 Now Barabbas **had taken part in a rebellion** [+1639].
2Co 11: 26 I have been in danger from rivers, in danger from **bandits**,

3335 λῆψις, lēpsis   Not used in UBS/NIV [√ 3284]

3336 λίαν, lian [12] [→ 5663]

great [3], very [3], completely [+1666+4356] [1], dazzling
[+5118] [1], furious [+2597] [1], greatly [1], so violent [+5901] [1],
strongly [1]

Mt   2: 16 that he had been outwitted by the Magi, he was **furious** [+2597],
     4: 8 the devil took him to a **very** high mountain and showed him all the
     8: 28 They were **so violent** [+5901] that no one could pass that way.
     27: 14 even to a single charge—to the **great** amazement of the governor.
Mk   1: 35 **Very** early in the morning, while it was still dark, Jesus got up,
     6: 51 the wind died down. They were **completely** [+1666+4356] amazed,
     9: 3 His clothes became **dazzling** [+5118] white, whiter than anyone in
     16: 2 **Very** early on the first day of the week, just after sunrise,
Lk   23: 8 When Herod saw Jesus, he was **greatly** pleased, because for a long
2Ti   4: 15 your guard against him, because he **strongly** opposed our message.
2Jn   1: 4 It has given me **great** joy to find some of your children walking in
3Jn   1: 3 It gave me **great** joy to have some brothers come and tell about

3337 λίβανος, libanos [2] [→ 3338]

frankincense [1], incense [1]

Mt   2: 11 and presented him with gifts of gold and of **incense** and of myrrh.
Rev 18: 13 of incense, myrrh and **frankincense**, of wine and olive oil,

3338 λιβανωτός, libanōtos [2] [√ 3337]

censer [2]

Rev   8: 3 who had a golden **censer**, came and stood at the altar.
     8: 5 Then the angel took the **censer**, filled it with fire from the altar,

3339 Λιβερτῖνος, Libertinos [1]

Freedmen [1]

Ac   6: 9 from members of the Synagogue of the **Freedmen** (as it was

3340 Λιβύη, Libyē [1] [√ cf. 3341]

Libya [1]

Ac   2: 10 and Pamphylia, Egypt and the parts of **Libya** near Cyrene;

3341 Λιβυστῖνος, Libystinos   Not used in UBS/NIV
[√ cf. 3340]

3342 λιθάζω, lithazō [9] [√ 3345]

stone [5], stoned [3], stoning [1]

Jn   8: 5 In the Law Moses commanded us to **stone** such women. Now what
     10: 31 Again the Jews picked up stones to **stone** him,
     10: 32 miracles from the Father. For which of these do you **stone** me?"
     10: 33 "We are not **stoning** you for any of these," replied the Jews,
     11: 8 Rabbi," they said, "a short while ago the Jews tried to **stone** you,
Ac   5: 26 use force, because they feared that the people would **stone** them.
     14: 19 They **stoned** Paul and dragged him outside the city, thinking he
2Co 11: 25 once I was **stoned**, three times I was shipwrecked, I spent a night
Heb 11: 37 They were **stoned**; they were sawed in two; they were put to death

3343 λίθινος, lithinos [3] [√ 3345]

of stone [2], stone [1]

Jn   2: 6 Nearby stood six **stone** water jars, the kind used by the Jews for

2Co 3: 3   living God, not on tablets **of stone** but on tablets of human hearts.
Rev 9:20   and idols **of** gold, silver, bronze, **stone** and wood—

3344 λιθοβολέω, *lithoboleō* [7] [√ *3345* + *965*]

stone [4], stoned [2], stoning [1]

Mt 21:35   his servants; they beat one, killed another, and **stoned** a third.
    23:37   Jerusalem, you who kill the prophets and **stone** those sent to you,
Lk 13:34   Jerusalem, you who kill the prophets and **stone** those sent to you,
Ac 7:58   dragged him out of the city and *began to* **stone** him. Meanwhile,
    7:59   *While they were* **stoning** him, Stephen prayed, "Lord Jesus,
    14: 5   together with their leaders, to mistreat them and **stone** them.
Heb 12:20   "If even an animal touches the mountain, *it must be* **stoned**."

3345 λίθος, *lithos* [59] [→ *2902, 3342, 3343, 3344, 3346, 5994*]

stone [35], stones [14], another[s] [4], *untranslated* [1], boulder [1], jasper [+*2618*] [1], jewel [1], millstone [+*3683*] [1], stone's [1]

Mt 3: 9   I tell you that out of these **stones** God can raise up children for
    4: 3   "If you are the Son of God, tell these **stones** to become bread."
    4: 6   their hands, so that you will not strike your foot against a **stone**.' "
    7: 9   "Which of you, if his son asks for bread, will give him a **stone**?
    21:42   " 'The **stone** the builders rejected has become the capstone;
    21:44   He who falls on this **stone** will be broken to pieces, but he on
    24: 2   "I tell you the truth, not *one* **stone** here will be left on another;
    24: 2   "I tell you the truth, not *one* stone here will be left on **another**[s];
    27:60   He rolled a big **stone** in front of the entrance to the tomb and went
    27:66   they went and made the tomb secure by putting a seal on the **stone**
    28: 2   heaven and, going to the tomb, rolled back the **stone** and sat on it.
Mk 5: 5   and in the hills he would cry out and cut himself *with* **stones**.
    12:10   " 'The **stone** the builders rejected has become the capstone;
    13: 1   of his disciples said to him, "Look, Teacher! What massive **stones**!
    13: 2   "Not one **stone** here will be left on another; every one will be
    13: 2   "Not one stone here will be left on **another**[s]; every one will be
    15:46   of rock. Then he rolled a **stone** against the entrance of the tomb.
    16: 3   "Who will roll the **stone** away from the entrance of the tomb?"
    16: 4   they saw that the **stone**, which was very large, had been rolled
Lk 3: 8   For I tell you that out of these **stones** God can raise up children for
    4: 3   "If you are the Son of God, tell this **stone** to become bread."
    17: 2   **millstone** [+*3683*] tied around his neck than for him to cause one
    19:40   "I tell you," he replied, "if they keep quiet, the **stones** will cry out."
    19:44   within your walls. They will not leave one **stone** on another,
    19:44   within your walls. They will not leave one stone on **another**[s],
    20:17   " 'The **stone** the builders rejected has become the capstone'?
    20:18   Everyone who falls on that **stone** will be broken to pieces,
    21: 5   about how the temple was adorned *with* beautiful **stones**
    21: 6   the time will come when not one **stone** will be left on another;
    21: 6   the time will come when not one stone will be left on **another**[s];
    22:41   He withdrew about a **stone's** throw beyond them, knelt down
    24: 2   They found the **stone** rolled away from the tomb,
Jn 8: 7   of you is without sin, let him be the first to throw a **stone** at her."
    8:59   At this, they picked up **stones** to stone him, but Jesus hid himself,
    10:31   Again the Jews picked up **stones** to stone him,
    11:38   to the tomb. It was a cave with a **stone** laid across the entrance.
    11:39   "Take away the **stone**," he said. "But, Lord," said Martha, the
    11:41   So they took away the **stone**. Then Jesus looked up and said,
    20: 1   and saw that the **stone** had been removed from the entrance.
Ac 4:11   He is " 'the **stone** you builders rejected, which has become the
    17:29   not think that the divine being is like gold or silver or **stone**—
Ro 9:32   as if it were by works. They stumbled over the "stumbling **stone**."
    9:33   I lay in Zion a **stone** that causes men to stumble and a rock that
1Co 3:12   any man builds on this foundation *using* gold, silver, costly **stones**,
2Co 3: 7   which was engraved in letters *on* **stone**, came with glory,
1Pe 2: 4   As you come to him, the living **Stone**—rejected by men but chosen
    2: 5   you also, like living **stones**, are being built into a spiritual house to
    2: 6   "See, I lay a **stone** in Zion, a chosen and precious cornerstone,
    2: 7   "The **stone** the builders rejected has become the capstone,"
    2: 8   "A **stone** that causes men to stumble and a rock that makes them
Rev 4: 3   And the one who sat there had the appearance of jasper **[NIE]**
    17: 4   and was glittering *with* gold, precious **stones** and pearls.
    18:12   cargoes *of* gold, silver, precious **stones** and pearls; fine linen,
    18:16   and scarlet, and glittering with gold, precious **stones** and pearls!

    18:21   Then a mighty angel picked up a **boulder** the size of a large
    21:11   and its brilliance was like that of a very precious **jewel**, like a
    21:11   of a very precious jewel, like a **jasper** [+*2618*], clear as crystal.
    21:19   of the city walls were decorated *with* every kind of precious **stone**.

3346 λιθόστρωτος, *lithostrōtos* [1] [√ *3345* + *5143*]

Stone Pavement [1]

Jn 19:13   known as the **Stone Pavement** (which in Aramaic is Gabbatha).

3347 λικμάω, *likmaō* [2]

crushed [2]

Mt 21:44   will be broken to pieces, but *he* on whom it falls *will be* **crushed**."
Lk 20:18   will be broken to pieces, but he on whom it falls *will be* **crushed**."

3348 λιμήν, *limēn* [2] [→ *2816, 3349*]

harbor [2]

Ac 27:12   Since the **harbor** was unsuitable to winter in, the majority decided
    27:12   This was a **harbor** in Crete, facing both southwest and northwest.

3349 λίμνη, *limnē* [11] [√ *3348*]

lake [10], water's [1]

Lk 5: 1   One day as Jesus was standing by the **Lake** of Gennesaret,
    5: 2   he saw at the **water's** edge two boats, left there by the fishermen,
    8:22   said to his disciples, "Let's go over to the other side *of* the **lake**."
    8:23   A squall came down on the **lake**, so that the boat was being
    8:33   and the herd rushed down the steep bank into the **lake** and was
Rev 19:20   The two of them were thrown alive into the fiery **lake** of burning
    20:10   was thrown into the **lake** of burning sulfur, where the beast
    20:14   Then death and Hades were thrown into the **lake** of fire. The lake
    20:14   thrown into the lake of fire. The **lake** of fire is the second death.
    20:15   written in the book of life, he was thrown into the **lake** of fire.
    21: 8   and all liars—their place will be in the fiery **lake** of burning sulfur.

3350 λιμός, *limos* [12]

famine [7], famines [3], hunger [1], starving to death [+*660*] [1]

Mt 24: 7   There will be **famines** and earthquakes in various places.
Mk 13: 8   There will be earthquakes in various places, and **famines**.
Lk 4:25   a half years and there was a severe **famine** throughout the land.
    15:14   there was a severe **famine** in that whole country, and he began to
    15:17   men have food to spare, and here I *am* **starving to death** [+*660*]!
    21:11   **famines** and pestilences in various places, and fearful events
Ac 7:11   "Then a **famine** struck all Egypt and Canaan, bringing great
    11:28   and through the Spirit predicted that a severe **famine** would spread
Ro 8:35   or persecution or **famine** or nakedness or danger or sword?
2Co 11:27   I have known **hunger** and thirst and have often gone without food;
Rev 6: 8   by sword, **famine** and plague, and by the wild beasts of the earth.
    18: 8   death, mourning and **famine**. She will be consumed by fire,

3351 λίνον, *linon* [2]

linen [1], wick [1]

Mt 12:20   and a smoldering **wick** he will not snuff out, till he leads justice to
Rev 15: 6   shining **linen** and wore golden sashes around their chests.

3352 Λίνος, *Linos* [1]

Linus [1]

2Ti 4:21   greets you, and so do Pudens, **Linus**, Claudia and all the brothers.

3353 λιπαρός, *liparos* [1]

riches [1]

Rev 18:14   All your **riches** and splendor have vanished, never to be

3354 λίτρα, *litra* [2]

about a pint [1], seventy-five pounds [+1669] [1]

Jn   12: 3 Then Mary took **about a pint** of pure nard, an expensive perfume;
     19:39 a mixture of myrrh and aloes, about **seventy-five pounds** [+1669]

3355 λίψ, *lips* [1]

southwest [1]

Ac 27:12 This was a harbor in Crete, facing both **southwest** and northwest.

3356 λογεία, *logeia* [2] [√ 3306]

collection [1], collections [1]

1Co 16: 1 Now about the **collection** for God's people: Do what I told the
    16: 2 it up, so that when I come no **collections** will have to be made.

3357 λογίζομαι, *logizomai* [40] [√ 3306]

credited [10], consider [3], think [3], count [2], realize [2],
reasoned [2], regard [2], regarded [2], claim [1], considered [1],
counting [1], credit [1], credits [1], discredited [+1650+4029] [1],
expect [1], held [1], maintain [1], numbered [1], record of [1],
regards [1], think about [1], think that [1]

Lk 22:37 'And he was **numbered** with the transgressors'; and I tell you that
Jn 11:50 You do not **realize** that it is better for you that one man die for the
Ac 19:27 of the great goddess Artemis *will be* **discredited** [+1650+4029],
Ro   2: 3 do the same things, *do you* **think** you will escape God's judgment?
     2:26 *will* they not *be* **regarded** as though they were circumcised?
     3:28 For *we* **maintain** that a man is justified by faith apart from
     4: 3 believed God, and *it was* **credited** to him as righteousness."
     4: 4 his wages *are* not **credited** to him as a gift, but as an obligation.
     4: 5 who justifies the wicked, his faith *is* **credited** as righteousness.
     4: 6 of the man to whom God **credits** righteousness apart from works:
     4: 8 Blessed *is* the man whose sin the Lord *will* never **count** *against*
     4: 9 We have been saying that Abraham's faith *was* **credited** *to* him as
     4:10 Under what circumstances *was it* **credited**? Was it after he was
     4:11 in order that righteousness *might be* **credited** to them.
     4:22 This is why "*it was* **credited** to him as righteousness."
     4:23 The words "*it was* **credited** to him" were written not for him alone,
     4:24 but also for us, to whom God will **credit** righteousness—for us
     6:11 **count** yourselves dead to sin but alive to God in Christ Jesus.
     8:18 *I* **consider** that our present sufferings are not worth comparing
     8:36 death all day long; *we are* **considered** as sheep to be slaughtered."
     9: 8 but it is the children of the promise *who are* **regarded** as
    14:14 But if anyone **regards** something as unclean, then for him it is
1Co 4: 1 men *ought to* **regard** us as servants of Christ and as those
    13: 5 it is not easily angered, *it keeps* no **record of** wrongs.
    13:11 I talked like a child, I thought like a child, *I* **reasoned** like a child.
2Co 3: 5 Not that we are competent in ourselves *to* **claim** anything for
     5:19 world to himself in Christ, not **counting** men's sins against them.
    10: 2 beg you that when I come I may not have to be as bold as *I* **expect**
    10: 2 some people who **think that** we live by the standards of this world.
    10: 7 he should **consider** again that we belong to Christ just as much as
    10:11 Such people *should* **realize** that what we are in our letters when
    11: 5 *I do* not **think** I am in the least inferior to those "super-apostles."
    12: 6 so no one *will* **think** more of me than is warranted by what I do
Gal 3: 6 "He believed God, and *it was* **credited** to him as righteousness."
Php 3:13 Brothers, I *do* not **consider** myself yet to have taken hold of it.
     4: 8 if anything is excellent or praiseworthy—**think about** such things.
2Ti 4:16 but everyone deserted me. *May it* not *be* **held** against them.
Heb 11:19 Abraham **reasoned** that God could raise the dead, and figuratively
Jas 2:23 believed God, and *it was* **credited** to him as righteousness,"
1Pe 5:12 With the help of Silas, whom *I* **regard** as a faithful brother,

3358 λογικός, *logikos* [2] [√ 3306]

spiritual [2]

Ro 12: 1 and pleasing to God—this is your **spiritual** act of worship.
1Pe 2: 2 Like newborn babies, crave pure **spiritual** milk, so that by it you

3359 λόγιον, *logion* [4] [√ 3306]

words [3], word [1]

Ac   7:38 and with our fathers; and he received living **words** to pass on to us.
Ro   3: 2 First of all, they have been entrusted with the very **words** of God.
Heb 5:12 to teach you the elementary truths *of* God's **word** all over again.
1Pe 4:11 he should do it as one speaking the very **words** of God.

3360 λόγιος, *logios* [1] [√ 3306]

learned [1]

Ac 18:24 He was a **learned** man, with a thorough knowledge of the

3361 λογισμός, *logismos* [2] [√ 3306]

arguments [1], thoughts [1]

Ro   2:15 and their **thoughts** now accusing, now even defending them.)
2Co 10: 5 We demolish **arguments** and every pretension that sets itself up

3362 λογομαχέω, *logomacheō* [1] [√ 3306 + 3480]

quarreling about words [1]

2Ti 2:14 Warn them before God against **quarreling about words**; it is of no

3363 λογομαχία, *logomachia* [1] [√ 3306 + 3480]

quarrels about words [1]

1Ti 6: 4 in controversies and **quarrels about words** that result in envy,

3364 λόγος, *logos* [330] [√ 3306]

Λόγος (the Word) [7] Jn 1:1,1,1,14; 1Jn 1:1; Rev 19:13; 2Ti 4:2
λόγος ἀληθείας (word of truth) [5] 2Co 6:7; Eph 1:13; Col 1:5;
    2Ti 2:15; Jas 1:18
λόγος ... ἔργον (word ... deed) [6] Lk 24:19; Ac 7:22; Ro 15:18;
    Col 3:17; 2Th 2:17; 1Jn 3:18
λόγος θεοῦ (word of God) [42] Mt 15:6; Mk 7:13; Lk 5:1;
    8:11,21; 11:28; Jn 10:35; Ac 4:31; 6:2,7; 8:14; 11:1; 12:24;
    13:5,7,46; 17:13; 18:11; Ro 9:6; 1Co 14:36; 2Co 2:17; 4:2; Php
    1:14; Col 1:25; 1Th 2:13,13; 1Ti 4:5; 2Ti 2:9; Tit 2:5; Heb 4:12;
    5:12; 13:7; 1Pe 1:23; 2Pe 3:5; 1Jn 2:14; Rev 1:2,9; 6:9; 17:17;
    19:9,13; 20:4
λόγος Ἰησοῦ (word of Jesus) [2] Jn 18:32; Ac 20:35
λόγος κυρίου (word of the Lord) [13] Ac 8:25; 13:44,48,49;
    15:35,36; 16:32; 19:10,20; 20:35; 1Th 1:8; 4:15; 2Th 3:1
λόγος Χριστοῦ (word of Christ) [2] Col 3:16; Heb 6:1
τηρέω λόγον (keep the word) [12] Jn 8:51,52,55; 14:23,24;
    15:20; 17:6; 1Jn 2:5; Rev 3:8,10; 22:7,9

word [125], words [53], message [29], saying [10], teaching [9],
this^s [+3836] [9], untranslated [7], account [6], said [5], speech
[5], news [4], question [4], command [2], instruction [2], matter
[2], report [2], speaker [2], speaking [2], talk [2], talking [2], thing
[2], word of mouth [2], account [+625] [1], accounts [1],
appearance [1], book [1], conversation [1], eloquence [1], except
for [+4211] [1], flattery [+3135] [1], further word spoken [+4707]
[1], give account for [+625] [1], grievance [1], heard [1], its
[+3836] [1], maliciously [+4505] [1], ministry [1], nothing [+4029]
[1], preaching [+1877] [1], preaching [+3836] [1], proposal [1],
questions [1], reason [1], reasonable [+2848] [1], reply [1], rule
[1], rumor [1], say [1], sentence [1], settled accounts [+5256] [1],
something said [1], speak [1], stated [1], statement [1], stories
[1], story [1], teachings [1], testimony [+3455] [1], things [1], this^s
[+3836+4047] [1], truths [1], what am about to tell [+3836+4047]
[1], what said [1], what says [1], what^s [+3836] [1], why [+5515]
[1]

Mt   5:32 **except for** [+4211] marital unfaithfulness, causes her to become an
     5:37 Simply let [NIE] your 'Yes' be 'Yes,' and your 'No,' 'No';
     7:24 "Therefore everyone who hears these **words** of mine and puts them
     7:26 But everyone who hears these **words** of mine and does not put

7:28 When Jesus had finished **saying** these things, the crowds were
8: 8 my roof. But just say the **word**, and my servant will be healed.
8:16 and he drove out the spirits *with* a **word** and healed all the sick.
10:14 If anyone will not welcome you or listen to your **words**,
12:32 Anyone who speaks a **word** against the Son of Man will be
12:36 *will have to* **give account** on the day of judgment **for** [+625] every
12:37 For by your **words** you will be acquitted, and by your words you
12:37 you will be acquitted, and by your **words** you will be condemned."
13:19 When anyone hears the **message** about the kingdom and does not
13:20 the seed that fell on rocky places is the man who hears the **word**
13:21 When trouble or persecution comes because of the **word**,
13:22 the seed that fell among the thorns is the man who hears the **word**,
13:22 of this life and the deceitfulness of wealth choke it^s [+3836],
13:23 the seed that fell on good soil is the man who hears the **word**
15: 6 Thus you nullify the **word** of God for the sake of your tradition.
15:12 that the Pharisees were offended when they heard this^s [+3836]?"
15:23 Jesus did not answer a **word**. So his disciples came to him
18:23 kingdom of heaven is like a king who wanted to settle **accounts**
19: 1 When Jesus had finished **saying** these things, he left Galilee
19:11 Jesus replied, "Not everyone can accept this **word**, but only those to
19:22 When the young man heard this^s [+3836], he went away sad,
21:24 Jesus replied, "I will also ask you one **question**. If you answer me,
22:15 the Pharisees went out and laid plans to trap him in his **words**.
22:46 No one could say a **word** in reply,
24:35 and earth will pass away, but my **words** will never pass away.
25:19 of those servants returned and **settled accounts** [+5256] with them.
26: 1 When Jesus had finished **saying** all these things, he said to his
26:44 away once more and prayed the third time, saying the same **thing**.
28:15 And this **story** has been widely circulated among the Jews to this

Mk 1:45 Instead he went out and began to talk freely, spreading the **news**.
2: 2 not even outside the door, and he preached the **word** to them.
4:14 The farmer sows the **word**.
4:15 Some people are like seed along the path, where the **word** is sown.
4:15 Satan comes and takes away the **word** that was sown in them.
4:16 on rocky places, hear the **word** and at once receive it with joy.
4:17 When trouble or persecution comes because of the **word**,
4:18 Still others, like seed sown among thorns, hear the **word**;
4:19 and the desires for other things come in and choke the **word**,
4:20 sown on good soil, hear the **word**, accept it, and produce a crop—
4:33 With many similar parables Jesus spoke the **word** to them,
5:36 Ignoring **what**^s [+3836] they said, Jesus told the synagogue ruler,
7:13 Thus you nullify the **word** of God by your tradition that you have
7:29 Then he told her, "For such a **reply**, you may go, the demon has left
8:32 He spoke plainly about this^s [+3836], and Peter took him aside
8:38 of me and my **words** in this adulterous and sinful generation,
9:10 They kept the **matter** to themselves, discussing what "rising from
10:22 At this^s [+3836] the man's face fell. He went away sad,
10:24 The disciples were amazed at his **words**. But Jesus said again,
11:29 Jesus replied, "I will ask you one **question**. Answer me, and I will
12:13 of the Pharisees and Herodians to Jesus to catch him *in* his **words**.
13:31 and earth will pass away, but my **words** will never pass away.
14:39 Once more he went away and prayed the same **thing**.
16:20 and confirmed his **word** by the signs that accompanied it.

Lk 1: 2 who from the first were eyewitnesses and servants *of* the **word**.
1: 4 so that you may know the certainty of the **things** you have been
1:20 because you did not believe my **words**, which will come true at
1:29 Mary was greatly troubled at his **words** and wondered what kind of
3: 4 As is written in the book *of* the **words** of Isaiah the prophet:
4:22 and were amazed at the gracious **words** that came from his lips.
4:32 were amazed at his teaching, because his **message** had authority.
4:36 people were amazed and said to each other, "What is this **teaching**?
5: 1 the people crowding around him and listening to the **word** of God,
5:15 Yet the **news** about him spread all the more, so that crowds of
6:47 who comes to me and hears my **words** and puts them into practice.
7: 7 to come to you. But say the **word**, and my servant will be healed.
7:17 This **news** about Jesus spread throughout Judea and the
8:11 "This is the meaning of the parable: The seed is the **word** of God.
8:12 then the devil comes and takes away the **word** from their hearts,
8:13 Those on the rock are the ones who receive the **word** with joy
8:15 for those with a noble and good heart, who hear the **word**, retain it,
8:21 "My mother and brothers are those who hear God's **word** and put it
9:26 If anyone is ashamed of me and my **words**, the Son of Man will be
9:28 About eight days after Jesus **said** this, he took Peter, John
9:44 "Listen carefully to **what I am about to tell** [+3836+4047] *you*:
10:39 called Mary, who sat at the Lord's feet listening to what he **said**.
11:28 "Blessed rather are those who hear the **word** of God and obey it."

12:10 And everyone who speaks a **word** against the Son of Man will be
16: 2 Give an **account** of your management, because you cannot be
20: 3 He replied, "I will also ask you a **question**. Tell me,
20:20 They hoped to catch Jesus in **something** he **said** so that they might
21:33 and earth will pass away, but my **words** will never pass away.
23: 9 *He* plied him with many **questions**, but Jesus gave him no answer.
24:17 "What [NIE] are you discussing together as you walk along?"
24:19 powerful in **word** and deed before God and all the people.
24:44 He said to them, "This^s [+3836] is what I told you while I was

Jn 1: 1 In the beginning was the **Word**, and the Word was with God,
1: 1 the Word, and the **Word** was with God, and the Word was God.
1: 1 the Word, and the Word was with God, and the **Word** was God.
1:14 The **Word** became flesh and made his dwelling among us.
2:22 they believed the Scripture and the **words** that Jesus had spoken.
4:37 Thus the **saying** 'One sows and another reaps' is true.
4:39 town believed in him because of the woman's **testimony** [+3455],
4:41 And because of his **words** many more became believers.
4:50 Your son will live." The man took Jesus at his **word** and departed.
5:24 whoever hears my **word** and believes him who sent me has eternal
5:38 nor does his **word** dwell in you, for you do not believe the one he
6:60 On hearing it, many of his disciples said, "This is a hard **teaching**.
7:36 What did he mean [RPG] when he said, 'You will look for me,
7:40 On hearing his **words**, some of the people said, "Surely this man is
8:31 Jesus said, "If you hold to my **teaching**, you are really my disciples.
8:37 you are ready to kill me, because you have no room for my **word**.
8:43 not clear to you? Because you are unable to hear what I **say**.
8:51 I tell you the truth, if anyone keeps my **word**, he will never see
8:52 so did the prophets, yet you say that if anyone keeps your **word**,
8:55 I would be a liar like you, but I do know him and keep his **word**.
10:19 At these **words** the Jews were again divided.
10:35 If he called them 'gods,' to whom the **word** of God came—
12:38 This was to fulfill the **word** of Isaiah the prophet: "Lord, who has
12:48 that very **word** which I spoke will condemn him at the last day.
14:23 Jesus replied, "If anyone loves me, he will obey my **teaching**.
14:24 He who does not love me will not obey my **teaching**. These words
14:24 These **words** you hear are not my own; they belong to the Father
15: 3 You are already clean because of the **word** I have spoken to you.
15:20 Remember the **words** I spoke to you: 'No servant is greater than
15:20 you also. If they obeyed my **teaching**, they will obey yours also.
15:25 But this^s [+3836] is to fulfill what is written in their Law:
17: 6 you gave them to me and they have obeyed your **word**.
17:14 I have given them your **word** and the world has hated them,
17:17 Sanctify them by the truth; your **word** is truth.
17:20 I pray also for those who will believe in me through their **message**,
18: 9 This happened so that the **words** he had spoken would be fulfilled:
18:32 so that the **words** Jesus had spoken indicating the kind of death he
19: 8 When Pilate heard this^s [+3836], he was even more afraid,
19:13 When Pilate heard this^s [+3836], he brought Jesus out and sat
21:23 the **rumor** spread among the brothers that this disciple would not

Ac 1: 1 In my former **book**, Theophilus, I wrote about all that Jesus began
2:22 "Men of Israel, listen to this^s [+3836]: Jesus of Nazareth was a man
2:40 *With* many other **words** he warned them; and he pleaded with
2:41 Those who accepted his **message** were baptized, and about three
4: 4 But many who heard the **message** believed, and the number of men
4:29 and enable your servants to speak your **word** with great boldness.
4:31 all filled with the Holy Spirit and spoke the **word** of God boldly.
5: 5 When Ananias heard this^s [+3836+4047], he fell down and died.
5:24 On hearing this **report**, the captain of the temple guard
6: 2 "It would not be right for us to neglect the ministry of the **word** of
6: 4 and will give our attention to prayer and the ministry *of* the **word**."
6: 5 This **proposal** pleased the whole group. They chose Stephen,
6: 7 So the **word** of God spread. The number of disciples in Jerusalem
7:22 wisdom of the Egyptians and was powerful in **speech** and action.
7:29 When Moses **heard** this, he fled to Midian, where he settled as a
8: 4 Those who had been scattered preached the **word** wherever they
8:14 in Jerusalem heard that Samaria had accepted the **word** of God,
8:21 You have no part or share in this **ministry**, because your heart is
8:25 When they had testified and proclaimed the **word** of the Lord,
10:29 raising any objection. May I ask **why** [+5515] you sent for me?"
10:36 You know the **message** God sent to the people of Israel,
10:44 these words, the Holy Spirit came on all who heard the **message**.
11: 1 Judea heard that the Gentiles also had received the **word** of God.
11:19 Cyprus and Antioch, telling the **message** only to Jews.
11:22 **News** of this reached the ears of the church at Jerusalem, and they
12:24 But the **word** of God continued to increase and spread.
13: 5 they proclaimed the **word** of God in the Jewish synagogues.

13: 7 for Barnabas and Saul because he wanted to hear the **word** of God.
13:15 "Brothers, if you have a **message** of encouragement for the people,
13:26 it is to us that this **message** of salvation has been sent.
13:44 almost the whole city gathered to hear the **word** of the Lord.
13:46 "We had to speak the **word** of God to you first. Since you reject it
13:48 heard this, they were glad and honored the **word** of the Lord;
13:49 The **word** of the Lord spread through the whole region.
14: 3 who confirmed the **message** of his grace by enabling them to do
14:12 and Paul they called Hermes because he was the chief **speaker**.
14:25 and when they had preached the **word** in Perga, they went down to
15: 6 The apostles and elders met to consider this **question**.
15: 7 the Gentiles might hear from my lips the **message** of the gospel
15:15 The **words** of the prophets are in agreement with this, as it is
15:24 and disturbed you, troubling your minds *by what they said*.
15:27 and Silas to confirm by **word of mouth** what we are writing.
15:32 **said** much to encourage and strengthen the brothers.
15:35 and many others taught and preached the **word** of the Lord.
15:36 and visit the brothers in all the towns where we preached the **word**
16: 6 having been kept by the Holy Spirit from preaching the **word** in
16:32 Then they spoke the **word** of the Lord to him and to all the others
16:36 The jailer told **[NIE]** Paul, "The magistrates have ordered that you
17:11 for they received the **message** with great eagerness and examined
17:13 learned that Paul was preaching the **word** of God at Berea,
18: 5 Paul devoted himself exclusively *to* **preaching** [+3836],
18:11 Paul stayed for a year and a half, teaching them the **word** of God.
18:14 it would be **reasonable** [+2848] for me to listen to you.
18:15 But since it involves questions about **words** and names and your
19:10 and Greeks who lived in the province of Asia heard the **word** of
19:20 In this way the **word** of the Lord spread widely and grew in power.
19:38 and his fellow craftsmen have a **grievance** against anybody,
19:40 In that case we would not be able *to* **account** [+625] for this
20: 2 speaking many **words** of encouragement to the people, and finally
20: 7 he intended to leave the next day, kept on **talking** until midnight.
20:24 However, I consider my life worth **nothing** [+4029] to me,
20:32 "Now I commit you to God and *to* the **word** of his grace, which can
20:35 the weak, remembering the **words** the Lord Jesus himself said:
20:38 What grieved them most was his **statement** that they would never
22:22 The crowd listened to Paul until he **said** this. Then they raised their
Ro   3: 4 "So that you may be proved right when you **speak** and prevail when
9: 6 It is not as though God's **word** had failed. For not all who are
9: 9 For this was how the promise was **stated**: "At the appointed time I
9:28 For the Lord will carry out his **sentence** on earth with speed
13: 9 other commandment there may be, are summed up in this one **rule**:
14:12 So then, each of us will give an **account** of himself to God.
15:18 me in leading the Gentiles to obey God *by* what I have **said**.
1Co   1: 5 in every way—in all your **speaking** and in all your knowledge—
1:17 not with **words** of human wisdom, lest the cross of Christ be
1:18 For the **message** of the cross is foolishness to those who are
2: 1 I did not come with **eloquence** or superior wisdom as I proclaimed
2: 4 My **message** and my preaching were not with wise and persuasive
2: 4 and my preaching were not with wise and persuasive **words**,
2:13 not in **words** taught us by human wisdom but in words taught by
4:19 then I will find out not only how these arrogant people are **talking**,
4:20 For the kingdom of God is not a matter of **talk** but of power.
12: 8 To one there is given through the Spirit the **message** of wisdom,
12: 8 to another the **message** of knowledge by means of the same Spirit,
14: 9 Unless you speak intelligible **words** with your tongue, how will
14:19 But in the church I would rather speak five intelligible **words** to
14:19 words to instruct others than ten thousand **words** in a tongue.
14:36 Did the **word** of God originate with you? Or are you the only
15: 2 you are saved, if you hold firmly *to* the **word** I preached to you.
15:54 with immortality, then the **saying** that is written will come true:
2Co   1:18 as God is faithful, our **message** to you is not "Yes" and "No."
2:17 Unlike so many, we do not peddle the **word** of God for profit.
4: 2 we do not use deception, nor do we distort the **word** of God.
5:19 And he has committed to us the **message** of reconciliation.
6: 7 in truthful **speech** and in the power of God; with weapons of
8: 7 in faith, *in* **speech**, in knowledge, in complete earnestness
10:10 in person he is unimpressive and his **speaking** amounts to nothing."
10:11 Such people should realize that what we are **[NIE]** in our letters
11: 6 I may not be a trained **speaker**, but I do have knowledge. We have
Gal   5:14 The entire law is summed up in a single **command**: "Love your
6: 6 Anyone who receives instruction in the **word** must share all good
Eph   1:13 And you also were included in Christ when you heard the **word** of
4:29 Do not let any unwholesome **talk** come out of your mouths,
5: 6 Let no one deceive you *with* empty **words**, for because of such

6:19 **words** may be given me so that I will fearlessly make known the
Php   1:14 been encouraged to speak the **word** of God more courageously
2:16 as you hold out the **word** of life—in order that I may boast on the
4:15 not one church shared with me in the **matter** of giving
4:17 but I am looking for what may be credited to your **account**.
Col   1: 5 and that you have already heard about in the **word** of truth,
1:25 God gave me to present to you the **word** of God in its fullness—
2:23 Such regulations indeed have an **appearance** of wisdom, with their
3:16 Let the **word** of Christ dwell in you richly as you teach
3:17 And whatever you do, whether in **word** or deed, do it all in the
4: 3 And pray for us, too, that God may open a door for our **message**,
4: 6 Let your **conversation** be always full of grace, seasoned with salt,
1Th   1: 5 because our gospel came to you not simply with **words**, but also
1: 6 you welcomed the **message** with the joy given by the Holy Spirit.
1: 8 The Lord's **message** rang out from you not only in Macedonia
2: 5 You know we never used **flattery** [+3135], nor did we put on a
2:13 when you received the **word** of God, which you heard from us,
2:13 you accepted it not as the **word** of men, but as it actually is,
2:13 but as it actually is, the **word** of God, which is at work in you who
4:15 According to the Lord's own **word**, we tell you that we who are
4:18 Therefore encourage each other with these **words**.
2Th   2: 2 some prophecy, **report** or letter supposed to have come from us,
2:15 we passed on to you, whether by **word of mouth** or by letter.
2:17 your hearts and strengthen you in every good deed and **word**.
3: 1 I pray for us that the **message** of the Lord may spread rapidly
3:14 If anyone does not obey our **instruction** in this letter, take special
1Ti   1:15 Here is a trustworthy **saying** that deserves full acceptance:
3: 1 Here is a trustworthy **saying**: If anyone sets his heart on being an
4: 5 because it is consecrated by the **word** of God and prayer.
4: 6 brought up *in* the **truths** of the faith and of the good teaching that
4: 9 This is a trustworthy **saying** that deserves full acceptance
4:12 but set an example for the believers in **speech**, in life, in love,
5:17 especially those whose work is **preaching** [+1877] and teaching.
6: 3 and does not agree to the sound **instruction** of our Lord Jesus
2Ti   1:13 keep as the pattern *of* sound **teaching**, with faith and love in Christ
2: 9 of being chained like a criminal. But God's **word** is not chained.
2:11 Here is a trustworthy **saying**: If we died with him, we will also live
2:15 need to be ashamed and who correctly handles the **word** of truth.
2:17 Their **teaching** will spread like gangrene. Among them are
4: 2 Preach the **Word**; be prepared in season and out of season;
4:15 your guard against him, because he strongly opposed our **message**.
Tit   1: 3 and at his appointed season he brought his **word** to light through
1: 9 He must hold firmly to the trustworthy **message** as it has been
2: 5 to their husbands, so that no one will malign the **word** of God.
2: 8 and soundness of **speech** that cannot be condemned, so that those
3: 8 This is a trustworthy **saying**. And I want you to stress these things,
Heb   2: 2 For if the **message** spoken by angels was binding, and every
4: 2 but the **message** they heard was of no value to them, because those
4:12 For the **word** of God is living and active. Sharper than any
4:13 laid bare before the eyes of him to whom we must give **account**.
5:11 **[RPG]** but it is hard to explain because you are slow to learn.
5:13 an infant, is not acquainted with the **teaching** about righteousness.
6: 1 Therefore let us leave the elementary **teachings** about Christ
7:28 but **[RPG]** the oath, which came after the law, appointed the Son,
12:19 heard it begged that no **further word** [+4707] *be* **spoken** to them,
13: 7 Remember your leaders, who spoke the **word** of God to you.
13:17 They keep watch over you as men who must give an **account**.
13:22 Brothers, I urge you to bear with my **word** of exhortation,
Jas   1:18 He chose to give us birth *through* the **word** of truth, that we might
1:21 that is so prevalent and humbly accept the **word** planted in you,
1:22 Do not merely listen to the **word**, and so deceive yourselves.
1:23 Anyone who listens to the **word** but does not do what it says is
3: 2 If anyone is never at fault in what he **says**, he is a perfect man,
1Pe   1:23 but of imperishable, through the living and enduring **word** of God.
2: 8 They stumble because they disobey the **message**—which is also
3: 1 to your husbands so that, if any of them do not believe the **word**,
3: 1 they may be won over without **words** by the behavior of their
3:15 who asks you to give the **reason** for the hope that you have.
4: 5 But they will have to give **account** to him who is ready to judge
2Pe   1:19 And we have the **word** of the prophets made more certain,
2: 3 In their greed these teachers will exploit you *with* **stories** they
3: 5 But they deliberately forget that long ago *by* God's **word**
3: 7 *By* the same **word** the present heavens and earth are reserved for
1Jn   1: 1 have touched—this we proclaim concerning the **Word** of life.
1:10 make him out to be a liar and his **word** has no place in our lives.
2: 5 But if anyone obeys his **word**, God's love is truly made complete

2: 7 the beginning. This old command is the **message** you have heard.
2:14 because you are strong, and the **word** of God lives in you,
3:18 let us not love *with* **words** or tongue but with actions and in truth.
3Jn 1:10 to what he is doing, gossiping **maliciously** [+*4505*] about us.
Rev 1: 2 that is, the **word** of God and the testimony of Jesus Christ.
1: 3 Blessed is the one who reads the **words** of this prophecy,
1: 9 of Patmos because of the **word** of God and the testimony of Jesus.
3: 8 yet you have kept my **word** and have not denied my name.
3:10 Since you have kept my **command** to endure patiently, I will also
6: 9 because of the **word** of God and the testimony they had
12:11 him by the blood of the Lamb and by the **word** of their testimony;
17:17 give the beast their power to rule, until God's **words** are fulfilled.
19: 9 of the Lamb!' " And he added, "These are the true **words** of God."
19:13 in a robe dipped in blood, and his name is the **Word** of God.
20: 4 of their testimony for Jesus and because of the **word** of God.
21: 5 "Write this down, for these **words** are trustworthy and true."
22: 6 The angel said to me, "These **words** are trustworthy and true.
22: 7 Blessed is he who keeps the **words** of the prophecy in this book."
22: 9 brothers the prophets and of all who keep the **words** of this book.
22:10 he told me, "Do not seal up the **words** of the prophecy of this book,
22:18 I warn everyone who hears the **words** of the prophecy of this book:
22:19 And if anyone takes **words** away from this book of prophecy,

3365 λόγχη, *lonchē* [1]

spear [1]

Jn 19:34 Instead, one of the soldiers pierced Jesus' side *with* a **spear**,

3366 λοιδορέω, *loidoreō* [4] [√ *3368*]

hurled insults at [2], cursed [1], insult [1]

Jn 9:28 Then *they* **hurled insults at** him and said, "You are this fellow's
Ac 23: 4 standing near Paul said, "*You dare to* **insult** God's high priest?"
1Co 4:12 *When we are* **cursed**, we bless; when we are persecuted,
1Pe 2:23 *When they* **hurled** *their* **insults at** him, he did not retaliate;

3367 λοιδορία, *loidoria* [3] [√ *3368*]

insult [2], slander [1]

1Ti 5:14 their homes and to give the enemy no opportunity for **slander**.
1Pe 3: 9 Do not repay evil with evil or **insult** with insult,
3: 9 Do not repay evil with evil or insult with **insult**,

3368 λοίδορος, *loidoros* [2] [→ *518, 3366, 3367*]

slanderer [1], slanderers [1]

1Co 5:11 but is sexually immoral or greedy, an idolater or a **slanderer**,
6:10 nor thieves nor the greedy nor drunkards nor **slanderers** nor

3369 λοιμός, *loimos* [2]

pestilences [1], troublemaker [1]

Lk 21:11 famines and **pestilences** in various places, and fearful events
Ac 24: 5 "We have found this man to be a **troublemaker**, stirring up riots

3370 λοιπός, *loipos* [55] [√ *3309*]

rest [15], other [9], others [9], finally [+*3836*] [5], else [3], finally
[3], still [+*3836*] [2], beyond that [1], everybody else [1], from now
on [+*3836*] [1], further [1], now [+*6045*] [1], now [1], remains [1],
since that time [+*3836*] [1], survivors [1]

Mt 22: 6 The **rest** seized his servants, mistreated them and killed them.
25:11 "Later the **others** also came. 'Sir! Sir!' they said. 'Open the door
26:45 and said to them, "Are you **still** [+*3836*] sleeping and resting?
27:49 The **rest** said, "Now leave him alone. Let's see if Elijah comes to
Mk 4:19 and the desires for **other** *things* come in and choke the word,
14:41 he said to them, "Are you **still** [+*3836*] sleeping and resting?
16:13 These returned and reported it *to* the **rest**; but they did not believe
Lk 8:10 but *to* **others** I speak in parables, so that, " 'though seeing, they
12:26 cannot do this very little thing, why do you worry about the **rest**?
18: 9 of their own righteousness and looked down on **everybody else**,
18:11 'God, I thank you that I am not like **other** men—robbers, evildoers,

24: 9 they told all these things to the Eleven and *to* all the **others**.
24:10 of James, and the **others** with them who told this to the apostles.
Ac 2:37 they were cut to the heart and said to Peter and the **other** apostles,
5:13 No one **else** dared join them, even though they were highly
17: 9 Then they made Jason and the **others** post bond and let them go.
27:20 continued raging, we **finally** gave up all hope of being saved.
27:44 The **rest** were to get there on planks or on pieces of the ship.
28: 9 the **rest** of the sick on the island came and were cured.
Ro 1:13 a harvest among you, just as I have had among the **other** Gentiles.
11: 7 it did not obtain, but the elect did. The **others** were hardened,
1Co 1:16 **beyond that**, I don't remember if I baptized anyone else.)
4: 2 **Now** [+*6045*] it is required that those who have been given a trust
7:12 *To* the **rest** I say this (I, not the Lord): If any brother has a wife
7:29 **From now** [+*3836*] **on** those who have wives should live as if they
9: 5 as do the **other** apostles and the Lord's brothers and Cephas?
11:34 in judgment. And when I come I will give **further** directions.
15:37 that will be, but just a seed, perhaps of wheat or *of* something **else**.
2Co 12:13 How were you inferior to the **other** churches, except that I was
13: 2 I will not spare those who sinned earlier or any *of* the **others**,
13:11 **Finally**, brothers, good-by. Aim for perfection, listen to my appeal,
Gal 2:13 The **other** Jews joined him in his hypocrisy, so that by their
6:17 **Finally** [+*3836*], let no one cause me trouble, for I bear on my
Eph 2: 3 and thoughts. Like the **rest**, we were by nature objects of wrath.
6:10 **Finally** [+*3836*], be strong in the Lord and in his mighty power.
Php 1:13 palace guard and *to* everyone **else** that I am in chains for Christ.
3: 1 **Finally** [+*3836*], my brothers, rejoice in the Lord! It is no trouble
4: 3 along with Clement and the **rest** of my fellow workers,
4: 8 **Finally** [+*3836*], brothers, whatever is true, whatever is noble,
1Th 4: 1 **Finally**, brothers, we instructed you how to live in order to please
4:13 fall asleep, or to grieve like the **rest** *of men*, who have no hope.
5: 6 So then, let us not be like **others**, who are asleep, but let us be alert
2Th 3: 1 **Finally** [+*3836*], brothers, pray for us that the message of the Lord
1Ti 5:20 are to be rebuked publicly, so that the **others** may take warning.
2Ti 4: 8 **Now** there is in store for me the crown of righteousness,
Heb 10:13 **Since** [+*3836*] **that time** he waits for his enemies to be made his
2Pe 3:16 as they do the **other** Scriptures, to their own destruction.
Rev 2:24 Now I say *to* the **rest** *of* you in Thyatira, to you who do not hold
3: 2 Strengthen what **remains** and is about to die, for I have not found
8:13 because of the trumpet blasts about to be sounded by the **other**
9:20 The **rest** of mankind that were not killed by these plagues still did
11:13 and the **survivors** were terrified and gave glory to the God of
12:17 and went off to make war against the **rest** of her offspring—
19:21 The **rest** of them were killed with the sword that came out of the
20: 5 (The **rest** of the dead did not come to life until the thousand years

3371 Λουκᾶς, *Loukas* [3] [√ *3372*]

Luke [3]

Col 4:14 Our dear friend **Luke**, the doctor, and Demas send greetings.
2Ti 4:11 Only **Luke** is with me. Get Mark and bring him with you,
Phm 1:24 And so do Mark, Aristarchus, Demas and **Luke**, my fellow

3372 Λούκιος, *Loukios* [2] [→ *3371*]

Lucius [2]

Ac 13: 1 Barnabas, Simeon called Niger, **Lucius** of Cyrene, Manaen (who
Ro 16:21 greetings to you, as do **Lucius**, Jason and Sosipater, my relatives.

3373 λουτρόν, *loutron* [2] [√ *3374*]

washing [2]

Eph 5:26 cleansing her *by* the **washing** with water through the word,
Tit 3: 5 He saved us through the **washing** of rebirth and renewal by the

3374 λούω, *louō* [5] [→ *666, 3373*]

washed [4], had a bath [1]

Jn 13:10 "A person *who has* **had a bath** needs only to wash his feet;
Ac 9:37 and her body was **washed** and placed in an upstairs room.
16:33 hour of the night the jailer took them and **washed** their wounds;
Heb 10:22 guilty conscience and *having* our bodies **washed** with pure water.
2Pe 2:22 "A sow *that is* **washed** goes back to her wallowing in the mud."

3375　Λύδδα, *Lydda* [3]

Lydda [3]

Ac　9:32　traveled about the country, he went to visit the saints in **Lydda**.
　　9:35　All those who lived in **Lydda** and Sharon saw him and turned to
　　9:38　**Lydda** was near Joppa; so when the disciples heard that Peter was

3376　Λυδία, *Lydia* [2]

Lydia [1], Lydia's [1]

Ac　16:14　One of those listening was a woman named **Lydia**, a dealer in
　　16:40　and Silas came out of the prison, they went to **Lydia's** house,

3377　Λυκαονία, *Lykaonia* [1] [→ *3378*]

Lycaonian [1]

Ac　14:6　out about it and fled to the **Lycaonian** cities of Lystra and Derbe

3378　Λυκαονιστί, *Lykaonisti* [1] [√ *3377*]

in Lycaonian language [1]

Ac　14:11　saw what Paul had done, they shouted **in** the **Lycaonian language**,

3379　Λυκία, *Lykia* [1]

Lycia [1]

Ac　27:5　the coast of Cilicia and Pamphylia, we landed at Myra *in* **Lycia**.

3380　λύκος, *lykos* [6]

wolves [4], wolf [2]

Mt　7:15　to you in sheep's clothing, but inwardly they are ferocious **wolves**.
　　10:16　I am sending you out like sheep among **wolves**. Therefore be as
Lk　10:3　Go! I am sending you out like lambs among **wolves**.
Jn　10:12　So when he sees the **wolf** coming, he abandons the sheep and runs
　　10:12　and runs away. Then the **wolf** attacks the flock and scatters it.
Ac　20:29　savage **wolves** will come in among you and will not spare the

3381　λυμαίνω, *lymainō* [1]

began destroy [1]

Ac　8:3　But Saul **began** *to* **destroy** the church. Going from house to house,

3382　λυπέω, *lypeō* [26] [√ *3383*]

grieve [5], distressed [3], sad [3], sorrowful [3], grieved [2], hurt [2], sorrow [2], caused grief [1], caused sorrow [1], filled with grief [+*5379*] [1], made sorry [1], saddened [+*806*] [1], suffer grief [1]

Mt　14:9　The king *was* **distressed**, but because of his oaths and his dinner
　　17:23　be raised to life." And the disciples *were* **filled with grief** [+*5379*].
　　18:31　*they were* greatly **distressed** and went and told their master
　　19:22　man heard this, he went away **sad**, because he had great wealth.
　　26:22　They *were* very **sad** and began to say to him one after the other,
　　26:37　along with him, and he began *to be* **sorrowful** and troubled.
Mk　10:22　man's face fell. He went away **sad**, because he had great wealth.
　　14:19　*They were* **saddened** [+*806*], and one by one they said to him,
Jn　16:20　the world rejoices. You *will* **grieve**, but your grief will turn to joy.
　　21:17　Peter *was* **hurt** because Jesus asked him the third time, "Do you
Ro　14:15　If your brother *is* **distressed** because of what you eat, you are no
2Co　2:2　For if I **grieve** you, who is left to make me glad but you whom I
　　2:2　who is left to make me glad but you whom I *have* **grieved**?
　　2:4　not to **grieve** *you* but to let you know the depth of my love for you.
　　2:5　If anyone *has* **caused grief**, he has not so much grieved me as he
　　2:5　*he* has not so much **grieved** me as he has grieved all of you,
　　6:10　**sorrowful**, yet always rejoicing; poor, yet making many rich;
　　7:8　Even if *I* **caused** you **sorrow** by my letter, I do not regret it.
　　7:8　I regret it—I see that my letter **hurt** you, but only for a little while—
　　7:9　not because *you were* **made sorry**, but because your sorrow led
　　7:9　were made sorry, but because *your* **sorrow** led you to repentance.
　　7:9　For *you became* **sorrowful** as God intended and so were not
　　7:11　See what this godly **sorrow** has produced in you: what earnestness,

Eph　4:30　And *do* not **grieve** the Holy Spirit of God, with whom you were
1Th　4:13　fall asleep, or *to* **grieve** like the rest of men, who have no hope.
1Pe　1:6　though now for a little while you may have had to **suffer grief** in

3383　λύπη, *lypē* [16] [→ *267, 3382, 4337, 5200*]

sorrow [7], grief [3], pain [2], distressed [+*2400*] [1], painful [+*1877*] [1], painful [1], reluctantly [+*1666*] [1]

Lk　22:45　to the disciples, he found them asleep, exhausted from **sorrow**.
Jn　16:6　Because I have said these things, you are filled with **grief**.
　　16:20　the world rejoices. You will grieve, but your **grief** will turn to joy.
　　16:21　A woman giving birth to a child has **pain** because her time has
　　16:22　Now is your *time of* **grief**, but I will see you again and you will
Ro　9:2　I have great **sorrow** and unceasing anguish in my heart.
2Co　2:1　mind that I would not make another **painful** [+*1877*] visit to you.
　　2:3　so that when I came I *should* not *be* **distressed** [+*2400*] by those
　　2:7　so that he will not be overwhelmed *by* excessive **sorrow**.
　　7:10　Godly **sorrow** brings repentance that leads to salvation and leaves
　　7:10　to salvation and leaves no regret, but worldly **sorrow** brings death.
　　9:7　not **reluctantly** [+*1666*] or under compulsion, for God loves a
Php　2:27　not on him only but also on me, to spare me **sorrow** upon sorrow.
　　2:27　not on him only but also on me, to spare me sorrow upon **sorrow**.
Heb　12:11　No discipline seems pleasant at the time, but **painful**. Later on,
1Pe　2:19　For it is commendable if a man bears up under the **pain** of unjust

3384　Λυσανίας, *Lysanias* [1]

Lysanias [1]

Lk　3:1　of Iturea and Traconitis, and **Lysanias** tetrarch of Abilene—

3385　Λυσίας, *Lysias* [2]

Lysias [2]

Ac　23:26　Claudius **Lysias**, To His Excellency, Governor Felix: Greetings.
　　24:22　"When **Lysias** the commander comes," he said, "I will decide your

3386　λύσις, *lysis* [1] [√ *3395*]

divorce [1]

1Co　7:27　Are you married? Do not seek a **divorce**. Are you unmarried?

3387　λυσιτελέω, *lysiteleō* [1] [√ *3395 + 5465*]

better [1]

Lk　17:2　*It would be* **better** for him to be thrown into the sea with a

3388　Λύστρα, *Lystra* [6]

Lystra [6]

Ac　14:6　out about it and fled to the Lycaonian cities of **Lystra** and Derbe
　　14:8　In **Lystra** there sat a man crippled in his feet, who was lame from
　　14:21　of disciples. Then they returned to **Lystra**, Iconium and Antioch,
　　16:1　He came to Derbe and then to **Lystra**, where a disciple named
　　16:2　The brothers at **Lystra** and Iconium spoke well of him.
2Ti　3:11　to me in Antioch, Iconium and **Lystra**, the persecutions I endured.

3389　λύτρον, *lytron* [2] [√ *3395*]

ransom [2]

Mt　20:28　be served, but to serve, and to give his life as a **ransom** for many."
Mk　10:45　be served, but to serve, and to give his life as a **ransom** for many."

3390　λυτρόω, *lytroō* [3] [√ *3395*]

redeem [2], redeemed [1]

Lk　24:21　but we had hoped that he was the one who was going to **redeem**
Tit　2:14　who gave himself for us to **redeem** us from all wickedness
1Pe　1:18　or gold that *you were* **redeemed** from the empty way of life

3391 λύτρωσις, *lytrōsis* [3] [√ *3395*]

redemption [2], redeemed [+*4472*] [1]

Lk   1:68 because he has come and *has* **redeemed** [+*4472*] his people.
       2:38 to all who were looking forward to the **redemption** of Jerusalem.
Heb 9:12 for all by his own blood, having obtained eternal **redemption**.

3392 λυτρωτής, *lytrōtēs* [1] [√ *3395*]

deliverer [1]

Ac   7:35 He was sent to be their ruler and **deliverer** by God himself,

3393 λυχνία, *lychnia* [12] [√ *3394*]

lampstands [6], stand [4], lampstand [2]

Mt   5:15 Instead they put it on its **stand**, and it gives light to everyone in the
Mk   4:21 put it under a bowl or a bed? Instead, don't you put it on its **stand**?
Lk   8:16 Instead, he puts it on a **stand**, so that those who come in can see
    11:33 Instead he puts it on a **stand**, so that those who come in may see
Heb 9: 2 In its first room were the **lampstand**, the table and the consecrated
Rev 1:12 to me. And when I turned I saw seven golden **lampstands**,
     1:13 and among the **lampstands** was someone "like a son of man,"
     1:20 saw in my right hand and of the seven golden **lampstands** is this:
     1:20 seven churches, and the seven **lampstands** are the seven churches.
     2: 1 in his right hand and walks among the seven golden **lampstands**:
     2: 5 I will come to you and remove your **lampstand** from its place.
   11: 4 and the two **lampstands** that stand before the Lord of the earth.

3394 λύχνος, *lychnos* [14] [→ *3393*]

lamp [12], lamps [1], light [1]

Mt   5:15 Neither do people light a **lamp** and put it under a bowl.
     6:22 "The eye is the **lamp** of the body. If your eyes are good, your whole
Mk   4:21 to them, "Do you bring in a **lamp** to put it under a bowl or a bed?
Lk   8:16 "No one lights a **lamp** and hides it in a jar or puts it under a bed.
    11:33 "No one lights a **lamp** and puts it in a place where it will be hidden,
    11:34 Your eye is the **lamp** of your body. When your eyes are good,
    11:36 be completely lighted, as when the light of a **lamp** shines on you."
    12:35 "Be dressed ready for service and keep your **lamps** burning,
    15: 8 Does she not light a **lamp**, sweep the house and search carefully
Jn   5:35 John was a **lamp** that burned and gave light, and you chose for a
2Pe 1:19 as *to* a **light** shining in a dark place, until the day dawns
Rev 18:23 The light *of* a **lamp** will never shine in you again. The voice of
    21:23 for the glory of God gives it light, and the Lamb is its **lamp**.
    22: 5 They will not need the light *of* a **lamp** or the light of the sun,

3395 λύω, *lyō* [42] [→ *186, 269, 385, 386, 519, 667, 668, 1370, 1725, 2146, 2147, 2906, 2907, 3386, 3387, 3389, 3390, 3391, 3392, 4166, 4167, 4168*]

untie [8], untying [4], destroyed [3], released [3], broken [2], destroy [2], loose [2], loosed [2], set free [2], take off [2], break [1], breaking [1], breaks [1], broken to pieces [1], destruction [1], dismissed [1], freed [1], freeing [1], loosened [1], release [1], unmarried [+*608*+*1222*] [1], untied [1]

Mt   5:19 Anyone *who* **breaks** one of the least of these commandments
   16:19 and whatever *you* **loose** on earth will be loosed in heaven."
   16:19 and whatever you loose on earth will be **loosed** in heaven."
   18:18 and whatever *you* **loose** on earth will be loosed in heaven.
   18:18 and whatever you loose on earth will be **loosed** in heaven.
   21: 2 tied there, with her colt by her. **Untie** them and bring them to me.
Mk   1: 7 thongs of whose sandals I am not worthy *to* stoop down and **untie**
    7:35 his tongue *was* **loosened** and he began to speak plainly.
   11: 2 tied there, which no one has ever ridden. **Untie** it and bring it here.
   11: 4 a colt outside in the street, tied at a doorway. As *they* **untied** it,
   11: 5 standing there asked, "What are you doing, **untying** that colt?"
Lk   3:16 I will come, the thongs of whose sandals I am not worthy *to* **untie**.
   13:15 Doesn't each of you on the Sabbath **untie** his ox or donkey from
   13:16 long years, *be* **set free** on the Sabbath day from what bound her?"
   19:30 tied there, which no one has ever ridden. **Untie** it and bring it here.
   19:31 If anyone asks you, 'Why *are you* **untying** it?' tell him, 'The Lord
   19:33 *As* they *were* **untying** the colt, its owners asked them, "Why are
   19:33 the colt, its owners asked them, "Why *are you* **untying** the colt?"

Jn   1:27 after me, the thongs of whose sandals I am not worthy to **untie**."
    2:19 Jesus answered them, "**Destroy** this temple, and I will raise it
    5:18 not only *was he* **breaking** the Sabbath, but he was even calling
    7:23 on the Sabbath so that the law of Moses *may* not *be* **broken**,
  10:35 the word of God came—and the Scripture cannot *be* **broken**—
  11:44 Jesus said to them, "**Take off** the grave clothes and let him go."
Ac   2:24 raised him from the dead, **freeing** him from the agony of death,
    7:33 "Then the Lord said to him, '**Take off** your sandals; the place
   13:25 he is coming after me, whose sandals I am not worthy *to* **untie**.'
   13:43 When the congregation *was* **dismissed**, many of the Jews
   22:30 *he* **released** him and ordered the chief priests and all the Sanhedrin
   27:41 and the stern *was* **broken to pieces** by the pounding of the surf.
1Co 7:27 *Are* you **unmarried** [+*608*+*1222*]? Do not look for a wife.
Eph 2:14 who has made the two one and *has* **destroyed** the barrier,
2Pe 3:10 the elements *will be* **destroyed** by fire, and the earth
    3:11 *Since* everything *will be* **destroyed** in this way, what kind of
    3:12 That day *will* bring about the **destruction** of the heavens by fire,
1Jn 3: 8 The reason the Son of God appeared was to **destroy** the devil's
Rev 1: 5 *To* him who loves us and *has* **freed** us from our sins by his blood,
    5: 2 loud voice, "Who is worthy *to* **break** the seals and open the scroll?"
    9:14 "**Release** the four angels who are bound at the great river
    9:15 and month and year *were* **released** to kill a third of mankind.
   20: 3 years were ended. After that, he must *be* **set free** for a short time.
   20: 7 thousand years are over, Satan *will be* **released** from his prison

3396 Λωΐς, *Lōis* [1]

Lois [1]

2Ti 1: 5 which first lived in your grandmother **Lois** and in your mother

3397 Λώτ, *Lōt* [4]

Lot [3], Lot's [1]

Lk 17:28 "It was the same in the days *of* **Lot**. People were eating
   17:29 But the day **Lot** left Sodom, fire and sulfur rained down from
   17:32 Remember **Lot's** wife!
2Pe 2: 7 and if he rescued **Lot**, a righteous man, who was distressed by the

---

M, Μ

3398 μ, *m* Not used in UBS/NIV

3399 Μάαθ, *Maath* [1]

Maath [1]

Lk   3:26 the son *of* **Maath**, the son of Mattathias, the son of Semein,

3400 Μαγαδάν, *Magadan* [1]

Magadan [1]

Mt 15:39 he got into the boat and went to the vicinity *of* **Magadan**.

3401 Μαγδαλά, *Magdala* Not used in UBS/NIV [√ *cf. 3402*]

3402 Μαγδαληνή, *Magdalēnē* [12] [√ *cf. 3401*]

Magdalene [12]

Mt 27:56 Among them were Mary **Magdalene**, Mary the mother of James
   27:61 Mary **Magdalene** and the other Mary were sitting there opposite
   28: 1 Mary **Magdalene** and the other Mary went to look at the tomb.
Mk 15:40 Among them were Mary **Magdalene**, Mary the mother of James
   15:47 Mary **Magdalene** and Mary the mother of Joses saw where he was
   16: 1 Mary **Magdalene**, Mary the mother of James, and Salome bought
   16: 9 he appeared first to Mary **Magdalene**, out of whom he had driven
Lk   8: 2 Mary (called **Magdalene**) from whom seven demons had come
   24:10 It was Mary **Magdalene**, Joanna, Mary the mother of James,
Jn 19:25 mother's sister, Mary the wife of Clopas, and Mary **Magdalene**.
   20: 1 Mary **Magdalene** went to the tomb and saw that the stone had

20:18 Mary **Magdalene** went to the disciples with the news: "I have seen

3403 Μαγεδών, *Magedōn* Not used in UBS/NIV
[√ *cf. 762*]

3404 μαγεία, *mageia* [1] [√ *3405*]

magic [1]

Ac 8:11 because he had amazed them for a long time *with* his **magic**.

3405 μαγεύω, *mageuō* [1] [→ *3404, 3406, 3407*]

practiced sorcery [1]

Ac 8:9 Now for some time a man named Simon *had* **practiced sorcery** in

3406 μαγία, *magia* Not used in UBS/NIV [√ *3405*]

3407 μάγος, *magos* [6] [√ *3405*]

Magi [4], sorcerer [2]

Mt 2:1 the time of King Herod, **Magi** from the east came to Jerusalem
   2:7 Then Herod called the **Magi** secretly and found out from them the
   2:16 When Herod realized that he had been outwitted by the **Magi**,
   2:16 in accordance with the time he had learned from the **Magi**.
Ac 13:6 There they met a Jewish **sorcerer** and false prophet named
  13:8 But Elymas the **sorcerer** (for that is what his name means)

3408 Μαγώγ, *Magōg* [1]

Magog [1]

Rev 20:8 corners of the earth—Gog and **Magog**—to gather them for battle.

3409 Μαδιάμ, *Madiam* [1]

Midian [+*1178*] [1]

Ac 7:29 When Moses heard this, he fled to **Midian** [+*1178*], where he

3410 μαζός, *mazos* Not used in UBS/NIV [√ *3466*]

3411 μαθητεύω, *mathēteuō* [4] [√ *3443*]

become a disciple [1], instructed [1], make disciples [1], won disciples [1]

Mt 13:52 "Therefore every teacher of the law *who has been* **instructed** about
  27:57 named Joseph, who *had* himself **become a disciple** of Jesus.
  28:19 Therefore go and **make disciples** of all nations, baptizing them in
Ac 14:21 the good news in that city and **won** a large number of **disciples**.

3412 μαθητής, *mathētēs* [261] [√ *3443*]

δύο μαθηταί (two disciples) [8] Mt 21:1; Mk 11:1; 14:13; Lk 7:18; 19:29; Jn 1:35,37; 21:2

δώδεκα μαθηταί (twelve disciples) [3] Mt 10:1; 11:1; 20:17

ἕνδεκα μαθηταί (eleven disciples) [1] Mt 28:16

μαθηταὶ Ἰωάννου (disciples of John) [7] Mt 9:14; Mk 2:18,18; Lk 5:33; 7:18,18; Jn 3:25; cf. Mt 14:12; Mk 6:29

disciples [222], disciple [24], student [3], them[s] [+*899+3836*] [3], they[s] [+*3836*] [2], *untranslated* [1], all disciples [+*3836+4436*] [1], disciples [+*6034*] [1], followers [1], them[s] [+*3836*] [1], they[s] [+*899+3836*] [1], they[s] [+*899+899+2779+3836*] [1]

Mt 5:1 up on a mountainside and sat down. His **disciples** came to him,
  8:21 Another **disciple** said to him, "Lord, first let me go and bury my
  8:23 Then he got into the boat and his **disciples** followed him.
  9:10 collectors and "sinners" came and ate with him and his **disciples**.
  9:11 When the Pharisees saw this, they asked his **disciples**, "Why does
  9:14 Then John's **disciples** came and asked him, "How is it that we
  9:14 is it that we and the Pharisees fast, but your **disciples** do not fast?"
  9:19 Jesus got up and went with him, and so did his **disciples**.

9:37 Then he said *to* his **disciples**, "The harvest is plentiful
10:1 He called his twelve **disciples** to him and gave them authority to
10:24 "A **student** is not above his teacher, nor a servant above his master.
10:25 It is enough *for* the **student** to be like his teacher, and the servant
10:42 of cold water to one of these little ones because he is my **disciple**,
11:1 After Jesus had finished instructing his twelve **disciples**, he went
11:2 John heard in prison what Christ was doing, he sent his **disciples**
12:1 His **disciples** were hungry and began to pick some heads of grain
12:2 Your **disciples** are doing what is unlawful on the Sabbath."
12:49 Pointing to his **disciples**, he said, "Here are my mother and my
13:10 The **disciples** came to him and asked, "Why do you speak to the
13:36 His **disciples** came to him and said, "Explain to us the parable of
14:12 John's **disciples** came and took his body and buried it. Then they
14:15 the **disciples** came to him and said, "This is a remote place,
14:19 Then he gave them *to* the **disciples**, and the disciples gave them to
14:19 them to the disciples, and the **disciples** gave them to the people.
14:22 Immediately Jesus made the **disciples** get into the boat and go on
14:26 When the **disciples** saw him walking on the lake, they were
15:2 "Why do your **disciples** break the tradition of the elders? They
15:12 Then the **disciples** came to him and asked, "Do you know that the
15:23 So his **disciples** came to him and urged him, "Send her away,
15:32 Jesus called his **disciples** to him and said, "I have compassion for
15:33 His **disciples** answered, "Where could we get enough bread in this
15:36 he broke them and gave them *to* the **disciples**, and they in turn to
15:36 gave them to the disciples, and they[s] [+*3836*] in turn to the people.
16:5 When they went across the lake, the **disciples** forgot to take bread.
16:13 he asked his **disciples**, "Who do people say the Son of Man is?"
16:20 Then he warned his **disciples** not to tell anyone that he was the
16:21 From that time on Jesus began to explain *to* his **disciples** that he
16:24 Then Jesus said *to* his **disciples**, "If anyone would come after me,
17:6 When the **disciples** heard this, they fell facedown to the ground,
17:10 The **disciples** asked him, "Why then do the teachers of the law say
17:13 Then the **disciples** understood that he was talking to them about
17:16 I brought him *to* your **disciples**, but they could not heal him."
17:19 Then the **disciples** came to Jesus in private and asked, "Why
18:1 At that time the **disciples** came to Jesus and asked, "Who is the
19:10 The **disciples** said to him, "If this is the situation between a husband
19:13 pray for them. But the **disciples** rebuked those who brought them.
19:23 Then Jesus said *to* his **disciples**, "I tell you the truth, it is hard for a
19:25 When the **disciples** heard this, they were greatly astonished
20:17 to Jerusalem, he took the twelve **disciples** aside and said to them,
21:1 to Bethphage on the Mount of Olives, Jesus sent two **disciples**,
21:6 The **disciples** went and did as Jesus had instructed them.
21:20 When the **disciples** saw this, they were amazed. "How did the fig
22:16 They sent their **disciples** to him along with the Herodians.
23:1 Then Jesus said to the crowds and *to* his **disciples**:
24:1 and was walking away when his **disciples** came up to him to call
24:3 sitting on the Mount of Olives, the **disciples** came to him privately.
26:1 Jesus had finished saying all these things, he said *to* his **disciples**,
26:8 the **disciples** saw this, they were indignant. "Why this waste?"
26:17 Feast of Unleavened Bread, the **disciples** came to Jesus and asked,
26:18 I am going to celebrate the Passover with my **disciples** at your
26:19 So the **disciples** did as Jesus had directed them and prepared the
26:26 and broke it, and gave it *to* his **disciples**, saying, "Take and eat;
26:35 I will never disown you." And all the other **disciples** said the same.
26:36 and he said *to* them[s] [+*3836*], "Sit here while I go over there
26:40 Then he returned to his **disciples** and found them sleeping.
26:45 Then he returned to the **disciples** and said to them, "Are you still
26:56 might be fulfilled." Then all the **disciples** deserted him and fled.
27:64 his **disciples** may come and steal the body and tell the people that
28:7 Then go quickly and tell his **disciples**: 'He has risen from the dead
28:8 the tomb, afraid yet filled with joy, and ran to tell his **disciples**.
28:13 'His **disciples** came during the night and stole him away while we
28:16 Then the eleven **disciples** went to Galilee, to the mountain where
Mk 2:15 tax collectors and "sinners" were eating with him and his **disciples**,
  2:16 with the "sinners" and tax collectors, they asked his **disciples**:
  2:18 Now John's **disciples** and the Pharisees were fasting. Some people
  2:18 "How is it that John's **disciples** and the disciples of the Pharisees
  2:18 that John's disciples and the **disciples** of the Pharisees are fasting,
  2:18 disciples of the Pharisees are fasting, but yours [RPG] are not?"
  2:23 and as his **disciples** walked along, they began to pick some heads
  3:7 Jesus withdrew with his **disciples** to the lake, and a large crowd
  3:9 Because of the crowd he told his **disciples** to have a small boat
  4:34 But when he was alone *with* his own **disciples**, he explained
  5:31 his **disciples** answered, "and yet you can ask, 'Who touched me?' "
  6:1 and went to his hometown, accompanied by his **disciples**.

6:29   John's **disciples** came and took his body and laid it in a tomb.
6:35   By this time it was late in the day, so his **disciples** came to him.
6:41   Then he gave them *to* his **disciples** to set before the people.
6:45   Immediately Jesus made his **disciples** get into the boat and go on
7: 2   saw some *of* his **disciples** eating food with hands that were
7: 5   "Why don't your **disciples** live according to the tradition of the
7:17   and entered the house, his **disciples** asked him about this parable.
8: 1   they had nothing to eat, Jesus called his **disciples** to him and said,
8: 4   His **disciples** answered, "But where in this remote place can anyone
8: 6   broke them and gave them *to* his **disciples** to set before the people,
8:10   he got into the boat with his **disciples** and went to the region of
8:27   and his **disciples** went on to the villages around Caesarea Philippi.
8:27   On the way he asked **them**ˢ [+899+3836], "Who do people say I
8:33   But when Jesus turned and looked at his **disciples**, he rebuked
8:34   Then he called the crowd to him along with his **disciples** and said:
9:14   When they came to the other **disciples**, they saw a large crowd
9:18   I asked your **disciples** to drive out the spirit, but they could not."
9:28   After Jesus had gone indoors, his **disciples** asked him privately,
9:31   because he was teaching his **disciples**. He said to them, "The Son of
10:10   they were in the house again, the **disciples** asked Jesus about this.
10:13   to Jesus to have him touch them, but the **disciples** rebuked them.
10:23   Jesus looked around and said *to* his **disciples**, "How hard it is for
10:24   The **disciples** were amazed at his words. But Jesus said again,
10:46   As Jesus and his **disciples**, together with a large crowd,
11: 1   Bethany at the Mount of Olives, Jesus sent two *of* his **disciples**,
11:14   ever eat fruit from you again." And his **disciples** heard him say it.
12:43   Calling his **disciples** to him, Jesus said, "I tell you the truth,
13: 1   the temple, one *of* his **disciples** said to him, "Look, Teacher!
14:12   Jesus' **disciples** asked him, "Where do you want us to go and make
14:13   So he sent two *of* his **disciples**, telling them, "Go into the city,
14:14   my guest room, where I may eat the Passover with my **disciples**?'
14:16   The **disciples** left, went into the city and found things just as Jesus
14:32   and Jesus said *to* his **disciples**, "Sit here while I pray."
16: 7   But go, tell his **disciples** and Peter, 'He is going ahead of you into

Lk 5:30   of the law who belonged to their sect complained to his **disciples**,
5:33   "John's **disciples** often fast and pray, and so do the disciples of the
6: 1   his **disciples** began to pick some heads of grain, rub them in
6:13   he called his **disciples** to him and chose twelve of them,
6:17   A large crowd *of* his **disciples** was there and a great number of
6:20   Looking at his **disciples**, he said: "Blessed are you who are poor,
6:40   A **student** is not above his teacher, but everyone who is fully
7:11   and his **disciples** and a large crowd went along with him.
7:18   John's **disciples** told him about all these things. Calling two of
7:18   him about all these things. Calling two *of* **them**ˢ [+899+3836],
8: 9   His **disciples** asked him what this parable meant.
8:22   So **they**ˢ [+899+899+2779+3836] got into a boat and set out.
9:14   But he said to his **disciples**, "Have them sit down in groups of
9:16   Then he gave them *to* the **disciples** to set before the people.
9:18   when Jesus was praying in private and his **disciples** were with him,
9:40   I begged your **disciples** to drive it out, but they could not."
9:43   was marveling at all that Jesus did, he said to his **disciples**,
9:54   When the **disciples** James and John saw this, they asked, "Lord,
10:23   Then he turned to his **disciples** and said privately, "Blessed are the
11: 1   he finished, one *of* his **disciples** said to him, "Lord, teach us to pray,
11: 1   to him, "Lord, teach us to pray, just as John taught his **disciples**."
12: 1   on one another, Jesus began to speak first to his **disciples**, saying:
12:22   Then Jesus said to his **disciples**: "Therefore I tell you, do not worry
14:26   and sisters—yes, even his own life—he cannot be my **disciple**.
14:27   who does not carry his cross and follow me cannot be my **disciple**.
14:33   you who does not give up everything he has cannot be my **disciple**.
16: 1   Jesus told his **disciples**: "There was a rich man whose manager was
17: 1   Jesus said to his **disciples**: "Things that cause people to sin are
17:22   Then he said to his **disciples**, "The time is coming when you will
18:15   him touch them. When the **disciples** saw this, they rebuked them.
19:29   the Mount of Olives, he sent two *of* his **disciples**, saying to them,
19:37   the whole crowd *of* **disciples** began joyfully to praise God in loud
19:39   in the crowd said to Jesus, "Teacher, rebuke your **disciples**!"
20:45   While all the people were listening, Jesus said *to* his **disciples**,
22:11   the guest room, where I may eat the Passover with my **disciples**?'
22:39   as usual to the Mount of Olives, and his **disciples** followed him.
22:45   When he rose from prayer and went back to the **disciples**,

Jn 1:35   The next day John was there again with two of his **disciples**.
1:37   When the two **disciples** heard him say this, they followed Jesus.
2: 2   and Jesus and his **disciples** had also been invited to the wedding.
2:11   He thus revealed his glory, and his **disciples** put their faith in him.
2:12   to Capernaum with his mother and brothers and his **disciples**.

2:17   His **disciples** remembered that it is written: "Zeal for your house
2:22   was raised from the dead, his **disciples** recalled what he had said.
3:22   Jesus and his **disciples** went out into the Judean countryside,
3:25   An argument developed between some of John's **disciples**
4: 1   that Jesus was gaining and baptizing more **disciples** than John,
4: 2   although in fact it was not Jesus who baptized, but his **disciples**.
4: 8   (His **disciples** had gone into the town to buy food.)
4:27   Just then his **disciples** returned and were surprised to find him
4:31   Meanwhile his **disciples** urged him, "Rabbi, eat something."
4:33   Then his **disciples** said to each other, "Could someone have brought
6: 3   Jesus went up on a mountainside and sat down with his **disciples**.
6: 8   Another of his **disciples**, Andrew, Simon Peter's brother, spoke up,
6:12   he said *to* his **disciples**, "Gather the pieces that are left over.
6:16   When evening came, his **disciples** went down to the lake,
6:22   and that Jesus had not entered it *with* his **disciples**, but that they
6:22   his disciples, but that **they**ˢ [+899+3836] had gone away alone.
6:24   Once the crowd realized that neither Jesus nor his **disciples** were
6:60   On hearing it, many of his **disciples** said, "This is a hard teaching.
6:61   Aware that his **disciples** were grumbling about this, Jesus said to
6:66   From this time many of his **disciples** turned back and no longer
7: 3   go to Judea, so that your **disciples** may see the miracles you do.
8:31   Jesus said, "If you hold to my teaching, you are really my **disciples**.
9: 2   His **disciples** asked him, "Rabbi, who sinned, this man or his
9:27   want to hear it again? Do you want to become his **disciples**, too?"
9:28   they hurled insults at him and said, "You are this fellow's **disciple**!
9:28   "You are this fellow's disciple! We are **disciples** of Moses!
11: 7   Then he said *to* his **disciples**, "Let us go back to Judea."
11: 8   "But Rabbi," **they**ˢ [+3836] said, "a short while ago the Jews tried
11:12   His **disciples** replied, "Lord, if he sleeps, he will get better."
11:54   to a village called Ephraim, where he stayed with his **disciples**.
12: 4   But one of his **disciples**, Judas Iscariot, who was later to betray
12:16   At first his **disciples** did not understand all this. Only after Jesus
13: 5   he poured water into a basin and began to wash his **disciples**' feet,
13:22   His **disciples** stared at one another, at a loss to know which of
13:23   One of **them**ˢ [+899+3836], the disciple whom Jesus loved,
13:35   By this all men will know that you are my **disciples**, if you love
15: 8   that you bear much fruit, showing yourselves to be my **disciples**.
16:17   Some of his **disciples** said to one another, "What does he mean by
16:29   Then Jesus' **disciples** said, "Now you are speaking clearly
18: 1   Jesus left with his **disciples** and crossed the Kidron Valley.
18: 1   side there was an olive grove, and he and his **disciples** went into it.
18: 2   the place, because Jesus had often met there with his **disciples**.
18:15   Simon Peter and another **disciple** were following Jesus.
18:15   Because this **disciple** was known to the high priest, he went with
18:16   The other **disciple**, who was known to the high priest, came back,
18:17   "You are not one of his **disciples**, are you?" the girl at the door
18:19   the high priest questioned Jesus about his **disciples** and his
18:25   he was asked, "You are not one of his **disciples**, are you?"
19:26   and the **disciple** whom he loved standing nearby, he said to his
19:27   and *to* the **disciple**, "Here is your mother." From that time on,
19:27   From that time on, this **disciple** took her into his home.
19:38   Now Joseph was a **disciple** of Jesus, but secretly because he feared
20: 2   So she came running to Simon Peter and the other **disciple**,
20: 3   So Peter and the other **disciple** started for the tomb.
20: 4   but the other **disciple** outran Peter and reached the tomb first.
20: 8   Finally the other **disciple**, who had reached the tomb first,
20:10   Then the **disciples** went back to their homes,
20:18   Mary Magdalene went *to* the **disciples** with the news: "I have seen
20:19   when the **disciples** were together, with the doors locked for fear of
20:20   and side. The **disciples** were overjoyed when they saw the Lord.
20:25   So the other **disciples** told him, "We have seen the Lord!" But he
20:26   A week later his **disciples** were in the house again, and Thomas
20:30   did many other miraculous signs in the presence *of* his **disciples**,
21: 1   Afterward Jesus appeared again *to* his **disciples**, by the Sea of
21: 2   the sons of Zebedee, and two other **disciples** were together.
21: 4   on the shore, but the **disciples** did not realize that it was Jesus.
21: 7   Then the **disciple** whom Jesus loved said to Peter, "It is the Lord!"
21: 8   The other **disciples** followed in the boat, towing the net full of fish,
21:12   breakfast." None *of* the **disciples** dared ask him, "Who are you?"
21:14   This was now the third time Jesus appeared *to* his **disciples** after
21:20   and saw that the **disciple** whom Jesus loved was following them.
21:23   the rumor spread among the brothers that this **disciple** would not
21:24   This is the **disciple** who testifies to these things and who wrote

Ac 6: 1   In those days when the number of **disciples** was increasing,
6: 2   So the Twelve gathered **all** the **disciples** [+3836+4436] together
6: 7   The number *of* **disciples** in Jerusalem increased rapidly, and a

9: 1   still breathing out murderous threats against the Lord's **disciples**.
9: 10   In Damascus there was a **disciple** named Ananias. The Lord called
9: 19   Saul spent several days with the **disciples** in Damascus.
9: 25   But his **followers** took him by night and lowered him in a basket
9: 26   When he came to Jerusalem, he tried to join the **disciples**,
9: 26   were all afraid of him, not believing that he really was a **disciple**.
9: 38   so when the **disciples** heard that Peter was in Lydda, they sent two
11: 26   of people. The **disciples** were called Christians first at Antioch.
11: 29   The **disciples**, each according to his ability, decided to provide
13: 52   And the **disciples** were filled with joy and with the Holy Spirit.
14: 20   But after the **disciples** had gathered around him, he got up
14: 22   strengthening the **disciples** [+6034] and encouraging them to
14: 28   And they stayed there a long time with the **disciples**.
15: 10   why do you try to test God by putting on the necks of the **disciples**
16: 1   and then to Lystra, where a **disciple** named Timothy lived,
18: 23   the region of Galatia and Phrygia, strengthening all the **disciples**.
18: 27   encouraged him and wrote to the **disciples** there to welcome him.
19: 1   interior and arrived at Ephesus. There he found some **disciples**
19: 9   He took the **disciples** with him and had discussions daily in the
19: 30   to appear before the crowd, but the **disciples** would not let him.
20: 1   Paul sent for the **disciples** and, after encouraging them,
20: 30   and distort the truth in order to draw away **disciples** after them.
21: 4   Finding the **disciples** there, we stayed with them seven days.
21: 16   Some of the **disciples** from Caesarea accompanied us and brought
21: 16   He was a man from Cyprus and one of the early **disciples**.

3413 μαθήτρια, **mathētria** [1] [√ 3443]

disciple [1]

Ac   9: 36   In Joppa there was a **disciple** named Tabitha (which,

3414 Μαθθαῖος, **Maththaios** [5] [→ 3473]

Matthew [5]

Mt   9: 9   he saw a man named **Matthew** sitting at the tax collector's booth.
     10: 3   and Bartholomew; Thomas and **Matthew** the tax collector;
Mk   3: 18   Andrew, Philip, Bartholomew, **Matthew**, Thomas, James son of
Lk   6: 15   **Matthew**, Thomas, James son of Alphaeus, Simon who was called
Ac   1: 13   and Andrew; Philip and Thomas, Bartholomew and **Matthew**;

3415 Μαθθάτ, **Maththat** [2] [→ 3475]

Matthat [2]

Lk   3: 24   the son of **Matthat**, the son of Levi, the son of Melki, the son of
     3: 29   of Eliezer, the son of Jorim, the son of **Matthat**, the son of Levi,

3416 Μαθθίας, **Maththias** [2] [→ 3476]

Matthias [2]

Ac   1: 23   Joseph called Barsabbas (also known as Justus) and **Matthias**.
     1: 26   Then they cast lots, and the lot fell to **Matthias**; so he was added

3417 Μαθουσαλά, **Mathousala** [1]

Methuselah [1]

Lk   3: 37   the son of **Methuselah**, the son of Enoch, the son of Jared,

3418 Μαϊνάν, **Mainan**   Not used in UBS/NIV
[√ cf. 3527]

3419 μαίνομαι, **mainomai** [5] [→ 1841, 3444, 3446]

out of mind [3], insane [1], raving mad [1]

Jn   10: 20   Many of them said, "He is demon-possessed and **raving mad**.
Ac   12: 15   "You're **out of** your **mind**," they told her. When she kept insisting
     26: 24   "You are **out of** your **mind**, Paul!" he shouted. "Your great learning
     26: 25   "I am not **insane**, most excellent Festus," Paul replied. "What I am
1Co 14: 23   come in, will they not say that you are **out of** your **mind**?

3420 μακαρίζω, **makarizō** [2] [→ 3421, 3422]

call blessed [1], consider blessed [1]

Lk   1: 48   of his servant. From now on all generations will **call** me blessed,
Jas 5: 11   As you know, we **consider blessed** those who have persevered.

3421 μακάριος, **makarios** [50] [√ 3420]

blessed [44], good [4], fortunate [1], happier [1]

Mt   5: 3   "**Blessed** are the poor in spirit, for theirs is the kingdom of heaven.
     5: 4   **Blessed** are those who mourn, for they will be comforted.
     5: 5   **Blessed** are the meek, for they will inherit the earth.
     5: 6   **Blessed** are those who hunger and thirst for righteousness,
     5: 7   **Blessed** are the merciful, for they will be shown mercy.
     5: 8   **Blessed** are the pure in heart, for they will see God.
     5: 9   **Blessed** are the peacemakers, for they will be called sons of God.
     5: 10   **Blessed** are those who are persecuted because of righteousness,
     5: 11   "**Blessed** are you when people insult you, persecute you
     11: 6   **Blessed** is the man who does not fall away on account of me."
     13: 16   But **blessed** are your eyes because they see, and your ears
     16: 17   Jesus replied, "**Blessed** are you, Simon son of Jonah, for this was
     24: 46   It will be **good** for that servant whose master finds him doing
Lk   1: 45   **Blessed** is she who has believed that what the Lord has said to her
     6: 20   "**Blessed** are you who are poor, for yours is the kingdom of God.
     6: 21   **Blessed** are you who hunger now, for you will be satisfied.
     6: 21   be satisfied. **Blessed** are you who weep now, for you will laugh.
     6: 22   **Blessed** are you when men hate you, when they exclude you
     7: 23   **Blessed** is the man who does not fall away on account of me."
     10: 23   and said privately, "**Blessed** are the eyes that see what you see.
     11: 27   "**Blessed** is the mother who gave you birth and nursed you."
     11: 28   "**Blessed** rather are those who hear the word of God and obey it."
     12: 37   It will be **good** for those servants whose master finds them
     12: 38   It will be **good** for those servants whose master finds them ready,
     12: 43   It will be **good** for that servant whom the master finds doing
     14: 14   and you will be **blessed**. Although they cannot repay you,
     14: 15   "**Blessed** is the man who will eat at the feast in the kingdom of
     23: 29   'Blessed are the barren women, the wombs that never bore
Jn   13: 17   that you know these things, you will be **blessed** if you do them.
     20: 29   **blessed** are those who have not seen and yet have believed."
Ac   20: 35   Jesus himself said: 'It is more **blessed** to give than to receive.' "
     26: 2   I consider myself **fortunate** to stand before you today as I make
Ro   4: 7   "**Blessed** are they whose transgressions are forgiven, whose sins
     4: 8   **Blessed** is the man whose sin the Lord will never count against
     14: 22   **Blessed** is the man who does not condemn himself by what he
1Co 7: 40   In my judgment, she is **happier** if she stays as she is—and I think
1Ti 1: 11   that conforms to the glorious gospel of the **blessed** God, which he
     6: 15   God, the **blessed** and only Ruler, the King of kings and Lord of
Tit 2: 13   while we wait for the **blessed** hope—the glorious appearing of our
Jas 1: 12   **Blessed** is the man who perseveres under trial, because when he
     1: 25   he has heard, but doing it—he will be **blessed** in what he does.
1Pe 3: 14   But even if you should suffer for what is right, you are **blessed**.
     4: 14   you are **blessed**, for the Spirit of glory and of God rests on you.
Rev 1: 3   **Blessed** is the one who reads the words of this prophecy.
     14: 13   **Blessed** are the dead who die in the Lord from now on." "Yes,"
     16: 15   **Blessed** is he who stays awake and keeps his clothes with him,
     19: 9   'Blessed are those who are invited to the wedding supper of the
     20: 6   **Blessed** and holy are those who have part in the first resurrection.
     22: 7   **Blessed** is he who keeps the words of the prophecy in this book."
     22: 14   "**Blessed** are those who wash their robes, that they may have the

3422 μακαρισμός, **makarismos** [3] [√ 3420]

blessedness [2], joy [1]

Ro   4: 6   David says the same thing when he speaks of the **blessedness** of
     4: 9   Is this **blessedness** only for the circumcised, or also for the
Gal 4: 15   What has happened to all your **joy**? I can testify that, if you could

3423 Μακεδονία, **Makedonia** [22] [√ 3424]

Macedonia [21], Macedonian [1]

Ac   16: 9   and begging him, "Come over to **Macedonia** and help us."
     16: 10   had seen the vision, we got ready at once to leave for **Macedonia**,
     16: 12   a Roman colony and the leading city of that district of **Macedonia**.
     18: 5   When Silas and Timothy came from **Macedonia**, Paul devoted

19:21 to go to Jerusalem, passing through **Macedonia** and Achaia.	18:29 servant fell to his knees and begged him, '*Be* **patient** with me,

19:21 to go to Jerusalem, passing through **Macedonia** and Achaia.
19:22 He sent two of his helpers, Timothy and Erastus, to **Macedonia**,
20: 1 after encouraging them, said good-by and set out for **Macedonia**
20: 3 about to sail for Syria, he decided to go back through **Macedonia**.
Ro 15:26 For **Macedonia** and Achaia were pleased to make a contribution
1Co 16: 5 After I go through **Macedonia**, I will come to you—for I will be
16: 5 I will come to you—for I will be going through **Macedonia**.
2Co 1:16 I planned to visit you on my way to **Macedonia** and to come back
1:16 my way to Macedonia and to come back to you from **Macedonia**,
2:13 Titus there. So I said good-by to them and went on to **Macedonia**.
7: 5 For when we came into **Macedonia**, this body of ours had no rest,
8: 1 about the grace that God has given the **Macedonian** churches.
11: 9 for the brothers who came from **Macedonia** supplied what I
Php 4:15 when I set out from **Macedonia**, not one church shared with me in
1Th 1: 7 so you became a model to all the believers in **Macedonia**
1: 8 The Lord's message rang out from you not only in **Macedonia**
4:10 And in fact, you do love all the brothers throughout **Macedonia**.
1Ti 1: 3 As I urged you when I went into **Macedonia**, stay there in Ephesus

3424 Μακεδών, *Makedōn* [5] [→ *3423*]

Macedonians [2], from Macedonia [1], Macedonian [1], of Macedonia [1]

Ac 16: 9 During the night Paul had a vision of a man **of Macedonia**
19:29 and Aristarchus, Paul's traveling companions **from Macedonia**,
27: 2 Aristarchus, a **Macedonian** from Thessalonica, was with us.
2Co 9: 2 to help, and I have been boasting about it *to* the **Macedonians**,
9: 4 For if any **Macedonians** come with me and find you unprepared,

3425 μάκελλον, *makellon* [1]

meat market [1]

1Co 10:25 Eat anything sold in the **meat market** without raising questions of

3426 μακράν, *makran* [10] [√ *3601*]

far [4], far away [3], far off [+*1650*] [1], long way off [1], some distance [1]

Mt 8:30 **Some distance** from them a large herd of pigs was feeding.
Mk 12:34 he said to him, "You are not **far** from the kingdom of God."
Lk 7: 6 He was not **far** from the house when the centurion sent friends to
15:20 "But while he was still a **long way off**, his father saw him and was
Jn 21: 8 of fish, for they were not **far** from shore, about a hundred yards.
Ac 2:39 is for you and your children and for all who are **far** [+*1650*] **off**—
17:27 out for him and find him, though he is not **far** from each one of us.
22:21 Lord said to me, 'Go; I will send you **far away** to the Gentiles.' "
Eph 2:13 But now in Christ Jesus you who once were **far away** have been
2:17 He came and preached peace to you who were **far away** and peace

3427 μακρόθεν, *makrothen* [14] [√ *3601*]

distance [7], far off [+*608*] [3], at a distance [2], far away [+*608*] [1], long distance [1]

Mt 26:58 But Peter followed him at a **distance**, right up to the courtyard of
27:55 Many women were there, watching from a **distance**. They had
Mk 5: 6 When he saw Jesus from a **distance**, he ran and fell on his knees in
8: 3 on the way, because some of them have come a **long distance**."
11:13 Seeing in the **distance** a fig tree in leaf, he went to find out if it had
14:54 Peter followed him at a **distance**, right into the courtyard of the
15:40 Some women were watching from a **distance**. Among them were
Lk 16:23 he looked up and saw Abraham **far** [+*608*] **away**, with Lazarus by
18:13 "But the tax collector stood **at a distance**. He would not even look
22:54 him into the house of the high priest. Peter followed **at a distance**.
23:49 him from Galilee, stood at a **distance**, watching these things.
Rev 18:10 Terrified at her torment, they will stand **far** [+*608*] **off** and cry:
18:15 and gained their wealth from her will stand **far** [+*608*] **off**,
18:17 all who earn their living from the sea, will stand **far** [+*608*] **off**.

3428 μακροθυμέω, *makrothymeō* [10]
[√ *3601* + *2596*]

patient [8], putting off [1], waiting patiently [1]

Mt 18:26 '*Be* **patient** with me,' he begged, 'and I will pay back everything.'

Lk 18: 7 who cry out to him day and night? *Will he keep* **putting** them **off**?
1Co 13: 4 Love *is* **patient**, love is kind. It does not envy, it does not boast,
1Th 5:14 encourage the timid, help the weak, *be* **patient** with everyone.
Heb 6:15 And so *after* **waiting patiently**, Abraham received what was
Jas 5: 7 *Be* **patient**, then, brothers, until the Lord's coming. See how the
5: 7 and how **patient** he is for the autumn and spring rains.
5: 8 You too, *be* **patient** and stand firm,
2Pe 3: 9 *He is* **patient** with you, not wanting anyone to perish, but everyone

3429 μακροθυμία, *makrothymia* [14] [√ *3601* + *2596*]

patience [11], great patience [+*4246*] [1], patient [1], patiently [1]

Ro 2: 4 contempt for the riches *of* his kindness, tolerance and **patience**,
9:22 power known, bore with great **patience** the objects of his wrath—
2Co 6: 6 in purity, understanding, **patience** and kindness; in the Holy Spirit
Gal 5:22 is love, joy, peace, **patience**, kindness, goodness, faithfulness,
Eph 4: 2 and gentle; be **patient**, bearing with one another in love.
Col 1:11 glorious might so that you may have great endurance and **patience**,
3:12 with compassion, kindness, humility, gentleness and **patience**.
1Ti 1:16 Christ Jesus might display his unlimited **patience** as an example
2Ti 3:10 my way of life, my purpose, faith, **patience**, love, endurance,
4: 2 with **great patience** [+*4246*] and careful instruction.
Heb 6:12 who through faith and **patience** inherit what has been promised.
Jas 5:10 Brothers, as an example *of* **patience** in the face of suffering,
1Pe 3:20 who disobeyed long ago when God waited **patiently** in the days of
2Pe 3:15 Bear in mind that our Lord's **patience** means salvation, just as our

3430 μακροθύμως, *makrothymōs* [1] [√ *3601* + *2596*]

patiently [1]

Ac 26: 3 and controversies. Therefore, I beg you to listen to me **patiently**.

3431 μακρός, *makros* [4] [√ *3601*]

distant [2], lengthy [2]

Mk 12:40 They devour widows' houses and for a show make **lengthy** prayers.
Lk 15:13 set off for a **distant** country and there squandered his wealth in
19:12 "A man of noble birth went to a **distant** country to have himself
20:47 They devour widows' houses and for a show make **lengthy** prayers.

3432 μακροχρόνιος, *makrochronios* [1]
[√ *3601* + *5989*]

long life [1]

Eph 6: 3 go well with you and that you may enjoy **long life** on the earth."

3433 μαλακία, *malakia* [3] [√ *3434*]

sickness [3]

Mt 4:23 and healing every disease and **sickness** among the people.
9:35 good news of the kingdom and healing every disease and **sickness**.
10: 1 to drive out evil spirits and to heal every disease and **sickness**.

3434 μαλακός, *malakos* [4] [→ *3433*]

fine clothes [2], fine [1], male prostitutes [1]

Mt 11: 8 A man dressed in **fine clothes**? No, those who wear fine clothes
11: 8 fine clothes? No, those who wear **fine clothes** are in kings' palaces.
Lk 7:25 A man dressed in **fine** clothes? No, those who wear expensive
1Co 6: 9 nor adulterers nor **male prostitutes** nor homosexual offenders

3435 Μαλελεήλ, *Maleleēl* [1]

Mahalalel [1]

Lk 3:37 the son of Enoch, the son of Jared, the son *of* **Mahalalel**, the son of

3436 μάλιστα, *malista* [12] [√ *3437*]

especially [9], especially so [1], most [1], very [1]

Ac 20:38 What grieved them **most** was his statement that they would never

25:26 him before all of you, and **especially** before you, King Agrippa,
26: 3 and **especially so** because you are well acquainted with all the
Gal 6:10 **especially** to those who belong to the family of believers.
Php 4:22 you greetings, **especially** those who belong to Caesar's household.
1Ti 4:10 who is the Savior of all men, and **especially** of those who believe.
5: 8 and **especially** for his immediate family, he has denied the faith
5:17 **especially** those whose work is preaching and teaching.
2Ti 4:13 with Carpus at Troas, and my scrolls, **especially** the parchments.
Tit 1:10 and deceivers, **especially** those of the circumcision group.
Phm 1:16 He is **very** dear to me but even dearer to you, both as a man
2Pe 2:10 This is **especially** true of those who follow the corrupt desire of the

3437 μᾶλλον, *mallon* [81] [→ 3436]

more [21], rather [14], all the more [4], instead [3], *untranslated* [2], all the more [+4498] [2], greater [2], instead of [+2445] [2], more than [2], rather [+1254] [2], than [+2445] [2], all the harder [1], all the more [+5537] [1], better [+3202] [1], but [+1254] [1], do so [+5968] [1], do so more and more [+4355] [1], do this more and more [+4355] [1], especially [+1254] [1], especially [+4359] [1], even [+4531] [1], greater than ever [1], instead [+1883+3836] [1], instead [+247] [1], less [1], more [+4358] [1], more and more [1], more and [1], more than that [+1254] [1], much [1], on the contrary [+247+4498] [1], prefer [+2305] [1], really [1], then [1], very [1], yet [+247] [1]

Mt 6:26 Father feeds them. Are you not **much** more valuable than they?
6:30 the fire, will he not much **more** clothe you, O you of little faith?
7:11 how much **more** will your Father in heaven give good gifts to
10: 6 Go **rather** [+1254] to the lost sheep of Israel.
10:25 called Beelzebub, how much **more** the members of his household!
10:28 **Rather** [+1254], be afraid of the One who can destroy both soul
18:13 he is happier about that one sheep **than** [+2445] about the
25: 9 **Instead**, go to those who sell oil and buy some for yourselves.'
27:24 but that **instead** an uproar was starting, he took water and washed
Mk 5:26 all she had, **yet** [+247] instead of getting better she grew worse.
7:36 the more he did so, the **more** [+4358] they kept talking about it.
9:42 it would be better **[NIE]** for him to be thrown into the sea with a
10:48 but he shouted **all the more** [+4498], "Son of David, have mercy
15:11 stirred up the crowd to have Pilate release Barabbas **instead**.
Lk 5:15 Yet the news about him spread **all the more**, so that crowds of
11:13 how much **more** will your Father in heaven give the Holy Spirit to
12:24 feeds them. And how much **more** valuable you are **than** birds!
12:28 the fire, how much **more** will he clothe you, O you of little faith!
18:39 but he shouted **all the more** [+4498], "Son of David, have mercy
Jn 3:19 but men loved darkness **instead** [+2445] **of** light because their
5:18 For this reason the Jews tried **all the harder** to kill him; not only
12:43 for they loved praise from men **more** than praise from God.
19: 8 When Pilate heard this, he was *even* **more** afraid,
Ac 4:19 whether it is right in God's sight to obey you **rather** than God.
5:14 **more and more** men and women believed in the Lord and were
5:29 the other apostles replied: "We must obey God **rather** than men!
9:22 Yet Saul grew **more and** more powerful and baffled the Jews
20:35 Jesus himself said: 'It is **more** blessed to give than to receive.' "
22: 2 they heard him speak to them in Aramaic, they became **very** quiet.
27:11 But the centurion, **instead** [+2445] **of** listening to what Paul said,
Ro 5: 9 how much **more** shall we be saved from God's wrath through him!
5:10 how much **more**, having been reconciled, shall we be saved
5:15 how much **more** did God's grace and the gift that came by the
5:17 how much **more** will those who receive God's abundant provision
8:34 Christ Jesus, who died—**more** [+1254] **than that**, who was raised
11:12 for the Gentiles, how much **greater** riches will their fullness bring!
11:24 how much **more** *readily* will these, the natural branches,
14:13 make up your mind **[NIE]** not to put any stumbling block
1Co 5: 2 Shouldn't you **rather** have been filled with grief and have put out
6: 7 Why not **rather** be wronged? Why not rather be cheated?
6: 7 Why not rather be wronged? Why not **rather** be cheated?
7:21 although if you can gain your freedom, **do so** [+5968].
9:12 this right of support from you, shouldn't we have it **all the more**?
9:15 I would **rather** die than have anyone deprive me of this boast.
12:22 **On the contrary** [+247+4498], those parts of the body that seem
14: 1 desire spiritual gifts, **especially** [+1254] the gift of prophecy.
14: 5 of you to speak in tongues, but I would **rather** have you prophesy.
14:18 I thank God that I speak in tongues **more than** all of you.
2Co 2: 7 Now **instead** [+1883+3836], you ought to forgive and comfort
3: 8 will not the ministry of the Spirit be even **more** glorious?

3: 9 how much **more** glorious is the ministry that brings righteousness!
3:11 with glory, how much **greater** is the glory of that which lasts!
5: 8 and *would* **prefer** [+2305] to be away from the body and at home
7: 7 your ardent concern for me, so that my joy was **greater than ever**.
7:13 we were **especially** [+4359] delighted to see how happy Titus was,
12: 9 Therefore I will boast **all the more** gladly about my weaknesses,
Gal 4: 9 But now that you know God—or **rather** are known by God—
4:27 because more are the children of the desolate woman **than** [+2445]
Eph 4:28 **but** [+1254] must work, doing something useful with his own
5: 4 or coarse joking, which are out of place, but **rather** thanksgiving.
5:11 to do with the fruitless deeds of darkness, but **rather** expose them.
Php 1: 9 that your love may abound **more** and more in knowledge and depth
1: 9 may abound more and **more** in knowledge and depth of insight,
1:12 that what has happened to me has **really** served to advance the
1:23 desire to depart and be with Christ, which is **better** [+3202] by far;
2:12 not only in my presence, but now much **more** in my absence—
3: 4 thinks he has reasons to put confidence in the flesh, I have **more**:
1Th 4: 1 and urge you in the Lord Jesus to **do this more and more** [+4355].
4:10 Yet we urge you, brothers, *to* **do so more and more** [+4355].
1Ti 1: 4 These promote controversies **rather** than God's work—which is by
6: 2 **Instead** [+247], they are to serve them even better, because those
2Ti 3: 4 rash, conceited, lovers of pleasure **rather** than lovers of God—
Phm 1: 9 I **then**, as Paul—an old man and now also a prisoner of Christ
1:16 He is very dear to me but **even** [+4531] dearer to you, both as a
Heb 9:14 How much **more**, then, will the blood of Christ, who through the
10:25 and **all the more** [+5537] as you see the Day approaching.
11:25 He chose to be mistreated along with the people of God **rather**
12: 9 How much **more** should we submit to the Father of our spirits
12:13 your feet," so that the lame may not be disabled, but **rather** healed.
12:25 how much **less** will we, if we turn away from him who warns us
2Pe 1:10 be **all the more** eager to make your calling and election sure.

3438 Μάλχος, *Malchos* [1]

Malchus [1]

Jn 18:10 cutting off his right ear. (The servant's name was **Malchus**.)

3439 μάμμη, *mammē* [1]

grandmother [1]

2Ti 1: 5 which first lived in your **grandmother** Lois and in your mother

3440 μαμωνᾶς, *mamōnas* [4]

Money [2], wealth [2]

Mt 6:24 and despise the other. You cannot serve both God and **Money**.
Lk 16: 9 I tell you, use worldly **wealth** to gain friends for yourselves,
16:11 So if you have not been trustworthy in handling worldly **wealth**,
16:13 and despise the other. You cannot serve both God and **Money**."

3441 Μαναήν, *Manaēn* [1]

Manaen [1]

Ac 13: 1 **Manaen** (who had been brought up with Herod the tetrarch)

3442 Μανασσῆς, *Manassēs* [3]

Manasseh [3]

Mt 1:10 Hezekiah the father of **Manasseh**, Manasseh the father of Amon,
1:10 **Manasseh** the father of Amon, Amon the father of Josiah,
Rev 7: 6 the tribe of Naphtali 12,000, from the tribe *of* **Manasseh** 12,000,

3443 μανθάνω, *manthanō* [25] [→ 276, 2908, 3411, 3412, 3413, 5209]

learn [10], learned [8], get into the habit of being [1], inquire about [1], instructed [1], know [1], learning [1], learns [1], studied [1]

Mt 9:13 But go and **learn** what this means: 'I desire mercy, not sacrifice.'
11:29 Take my yoke upon me and **learn** from me, for I am gentle
24:32 "Now **learn** this lesson from the fig tree: As soon as its twigs get
Mk 13:28 "Now **learn** this lesson from the fig tree: As soon as its twigs get

Jn   6:45 who listens to the Father and **learns** from him comes to me.
      7:15 "How did this man get such learning without *having* **studied**?"
Ac   23:27 and rescued him, *for I had* **learned** that he is a Roman citizen.
Ro   16:17 in your way that are contrary to the teaching you *have* **learned**.
1Co   4: 6 so that *you may* **learn** from us the meaning of the saying,
     14:31 in turn so that everyone *may be* **instructed** and encouraged.
     14:35 If they want *to* **inquire about** something, they should ask their
Gal   3: 2 I would like *to* **learn** just one thing from you: Did you receive the
Eph   4:20 You, however, *did* not *come to* **know** Christ that way.
Php   4: 9 Whatever *you have* **learned** or received or heard from me,
      4:11 for I *have* **learned** to be content whatever the circumstances.
Col   1: 7 *You* **learned** it from Epaphras, our dear fellow servant, who is a
1Ti   2:11 A woman *should* **learn** in quietness and full submission.
      5: 4 *these should* **learn** first of all to put their religion into practice by
      5:13 *they* **get into the habit of being** idle and going about from house
2Ti   3: 7 always **learning** but never able to acknowledge the truth.
      3:14 continue in what *you have* **learned** and have become convinced
      3:14 convinced of, because you know those from whom *you* **learned** it,
Tit   3:14 Our people *must* **learn** to devote themselves to doing what is
Heb   5: 8 he was a son, *he* **learned** obedience from what he suffered
Rev 14: 3 No one could **learn** the song except the 144,000 who had been

3444 μανία, *mania* [1] [√ 3419]

insane [1]

Ac   26:24 Paul!" he shouted. "Your great learning is driving you **insane**."

3445 μάννα, *manna* [4 / 5]

manna [5]

Jn   6:31 Our forefathers ate the **manna** in the desert; as it is written:
      6:49 Your forefathers ate the **manna** in the desert, yet they died.
      6:58 Your forefathers ate **manna** [UBS-] and died, but he who feeds
Heb   9: 4 This ark contained the gold jar of **manna**, Aaron's staff that had
Rev   2:17 To him who overcomes, I will give some of the hidden **manna**.

3446 μαντεύομαι, *manteuomai* [1] [√ 3419]

fortune-telling [1]

Ac   16:16 earned a great deal of money for her owners *by* **fortune-telling**.

3447 μαραίνω, *marainō* [1] [→ 277, 278]

fade away [1]

Jas   1:11 the rich man *will* **fade away** even while he goes about his business.

3448 μαράνα θά, *marana tha* [1] [√ cf. 2495]

Come Lord [1]

1Co 16:22 does not love the Lord—a curse be on him. **Come**, O **Lord**!

3449 μαργαρίτης, *margaritēs* [9]

pearls [7], *untranslated* [1], pearl [1]

Mt   7: 6 "Do not give dogs what is sacred; do not throw your **pearls** to pigs.
     13:45 the kingdom of heaven is like a merchant looking for fine **pearls**.
     13:46 When he found [RPG] one of great value, he went away
1Ti   2: 9 not with braided hair or gold or **pearls** or expensive clothes,
Rev 17: 4 and was glittering *with* gold, precious stones and **pearls**.
     18:12 cargoes *of* gold, silver, precious stones and **pearls**; fine linen,
     18:16 and scarlet, and glittering with gold, precious stones and **pearls**!
     21:21 The twelve gates were twelve **pearls**, each gate made of a single
     21:21 twelve gates were twelve pearls, each gate made of a single **pearl**.

3450 Μάρθα, *Martha* [13]

Martha [13]

Lk   10:38 he came to a village where a woman named **Martha** opened her
     10:40 But **Martha** was distracted by all the preparations that had to be
     10:41 "**Martha**, Martha," the Lord answered, "you are worried and upset
     10:41 "Martha, **Martha**," the Lord answered, "you are worried and upset
Jn   11: 1 He was from Bethany, the village of Mary and her sister **Martha**.
     11: 5 Jesus loved **Martha** and her sister and Lazarus.
     11:19 and many Jews had come to **Martha** and Mary to comfort them in
     11:20 When **Martha** heard that Jesus was coming, she went out to meet
     11:21 "Lord," **Martha** said to Jesus, "if you had been here, my brother
     11:24 **Martha** answered, "I know he will rise again in the resurrection at
     11:30 the village, but was still at the place where **Martha** had met him.
     11:39 "But, Lord," said **Martha**, the sister of the dead man, "by this time
     12: 2 **Martha** served, while Lazarus was among those reclining at the

3451 Μαρία, *Maria* [54] [→ 3452]

ἄλλη Μαρία (the other Mary) [2] Mt 27:61; 28:1

Ἰάκωβος (mother of James) [4] Mt 27:56; Mk 15:40; 16:1; Lk
24:10

Ἰησοῦς (mother of Jesus) [19] Mt 1:16,18,20; 2:11; 13:55; Mk
6:3; Lk 1:27,30,34,38,39,41,46,56; 2:5,16,19,34; Ac 1:14

Ἰωάννης ... Μᾶρκος (mother of John Mark) [1] Ac 12:12

Ἰωσῆς (mother of Joses) [1] Mk 15:47

Κλωπᾶς (wife of Clopas) [1] Jn 19:25

Λάζαρος ... Μάρθα (sister of Lazarus and Martha) [11] Lk
10:39,42; Jn 11:1,2,19,20,28,31,32,45; 12:3

of Rome [1] Ro 16:6

ἡ Μαγδαληνή (Magdalene) [14] Mt 27:56,61; 28:1; Mk
15:40,47; 16:1,9; Lk 8:2; 24:10; Jn 19:25; 20:1,11,16,18

Mary [51], Mary's [2], she[s] [+3836] [1]

Mt   1:16 the husband *of* **Mary**, of whom was born Jesus, who is called
      1:18 His mother **Mary** was pledged to be married to Joseph, but before
      1:20 son of David, do not be afraid to take **Mary** home as your wife,
      2:11 they saw the child with his mother **Mary**, and they bowed down
     13:55 Isn't his mother's name **Mary**, and aren't his brothers James,
     27:56 Among them were **Mary** Magdalene, Mary the mother of James
     27:56 **Mary** the mother of James and Joses, and the mother of Zebedee's
     27:61 **Mary** Magdalene and the other Mary were sitting there opposite
     27:61 and the other **Mary** were sitting there opposite the tomb.
     28: 1 **Mary** Magdalene and the other Mary went to look at the tomb.
     28: 1 Mary Magdalene and the other **Mary** went to look at the tomb.
Mk   6: 3 Isn't this **Mary's** son and the brother of James, Joseph, Judas
     15:40 Among them were **Mary** Magdalene, Mary the mother of James
     15:40 **Mary** the mother of James the younger and of Joses, and Salome.
     15:47 **Mary** Magdalene and Mary the mother of Joses saw where he was
     15:47 and **Mary** the mother of Joses saw where he was laid.
     16: 1 **Mary** Magdalene, Mary the mother of James, and Salome bought
     16: 1 Mary Magdalene, **Mary** the mother of James, and Salome bought
     16: 9 he appeared first *to* **Mary** Magdalene, out of whom he had driven
Lk   1:27 a descendant of David. The virgin's name was **Mary**.
      1:30 But the angel said to her, "Do not be afraid, **Mary**, you have found
      1:34 "How will this be," **Mary** asked the angel, "since I am a virgin?"
      1:38 "I am the Lord's servant," **Mary** answered. "May it be to me as you
      1:39 At that time **Mary** got ready and hurried to a town in the hill
      1:41 When Elizabeth heard **Mary's** greeting, the baby leaped in her
      1:46 And **Mary** said: "My soul glorifies the Lord
      1:56 **Mary** stayed with Elizabeth for about three months and
      2: 5 He went there to register with **Mary**, who was pledged to be
      2:16 So they hurried off and found **Mary** and Joseph, and the baby,
      2:19 But **Mary** treasured up all these things and pondered them in her
      2:34 Then Simeon blessed them and said to **Mary**, his mother:
      8: 2 **Mary** (called Magdalene) from whom seven demons had come
     10:39 She had a sister called **Mary**, who sat at the Lord's feet listening to
     10:42 **Mary** has chosen what is better, and it will not be taken away from
     24:10 It was **Mary** Magdalene, Joanna, Mary the mother of James,
     24:10 It was Mary Magdalene, Joanna, **Mary** the mother of James,
Jn   11: 1 He was from Bethany, the village *of* **Mary** and her sister Martha.
     11: 2 This **Mary**, whose brother Lazarus now lay sick, was the same one
     11:19 to Martha and **Mary** to comfort them in the loss of their brother.
     11:20 was coming, she went out to meet him, but **Mary** stayed at home.
     11:28 she had said this, she went back and called her sister **Mary** aside.
     11:31 noticed how quickly **she**[s] [+3836] got up and went out,
     11:32 When **Mary** reached the place where Jesus was and saw him,
     11:45 Therefore many of the Jews who had come to visit **Mary**,
     12: 3 Then **Mary** took about a pint of pure nard, an expensive perfume;
     19:25 his mother's sister, **Mary** the wife of Clopas, and Mary
     19:25 mother's sister, Mary the wife of Clopas, and **Mary** Magdalene.

20: 1 **Mary** Magdalene went to the tomb and saw that the stone had been
20: 11 but **Mary** stood outside the tomb crying. As she wept, she bent
20: 16 Jesus said to her, "**Mary**." She turned toward him and cried out in
20: 18 **Mary** Magdalene went to the disciples with the news: "I have seen
Ac 1: 14 along with the women and **Mary** the mother of Jesus, and with his
12: 12 he went to the house *of* **Mary** the mother of John, also called
Ro 16: 6 Greet **Mary**, who worked very hard for you.

3452 Μαριάμ, *Mariam* Not used in UBS/NIV [√ *3451*]

3453 Μᾶρκος, *Markos* [8]

Mark [8]

Ac 12: 12 also called **Mark**, where many people had gathered and were
12: 25 returned from Jerusalem, taking with them John, also called **Mark**.
15: 37 Barnabas wanted to take John, also called **Mark**, with them,
15: 39 they parted company. Barnabas took **Mark** and sailed for Cyprus,
Col 4: 10 sends you his greetings, as does **Mark**, the cousin of Barnabas.
2Ti 4: 11 Get **Mark** and bring him with you, because he is helpful to me in
Phm 1: 24 And so do **Mark**, Aristarchus, Demas and Luke, my fellow
1Pe 5: 13 with you, sends you her greetings, and so does my son **Mark**.

3454 μάρμαρος, *marmaros* [1]

marble [1]

Rev 18: 12 every kind made of ivory, costly wood, bronze, iron and **marble**;

3455 μαρτυρέω, *martyreō* [76] [√ *3459*]

testify [22], testifies [6], testified [5], commended [4], testifies to [3], witness [3], declared [2], given^s [2], spoke well of [2], testify to [2], confirmed [1], gave testimony [1], give testimony [1], given testimony [1], highly respected [1], known [1], pointed out [1], respected [1], showed that accepted [1], speak well of [1], speak [1], spoke well [1], spread the word [1], tell about [1], testified about [1], testifies about [1], testifying [1], testimony [*+3364*] [1], testimony [*+3456+4005*] [1], testimony [1], told about [1], vouch [1], warn [1], well known [1], well spoken of [1]

Mt 23: 31 So *you* **testify** against yourselves that you are the descendants of
Lk 4: 22 All **spoke well of** him and were amazed at the gracious words that
Jn 1: 7 He came as a witness to **testify** concerning that light, so that
1: 8 himself was not the light; he came only as a **witness** to the light.
1: 15 John **testifies** concerning him. He cries out, saying, "This was he of
1: 32 Then John **gave** this **testimony**: "I saw the Spirit come down from
1: 34 I have seen and *I* **testify** that this is the Son of God."
2: 25 He did not need man's **testimony** about man, for he knew what
3: 11 we speak of what we know, and *we* **testify to** what we have seen,
3: 26 the one you **testified about**—well, he is baptizing, and everyone is
3: 28 You yourselves *can* **testify** that I said, 'I am not the Christ
3: 32 He **testifies to** what he has seen and heard, but no one accepts his
4: 39 town believed in him because of the woman's **testimony** [*+3364*],
4: 44 (Now Jesus himself *had* **pointed out** that a prophet has no honor
5: 31 "If I **testify** about myself, my testimony is not valid.
5: 32 There is another *who* **testifies** in my favor, and I know that his
5: 32 and I know that *his* **testimony** [*+3456+4005*] about me is valid.
5: 33 "You have sent to John and *he has* **testified** to the truth.
5: 36 and which I am doing, **testifies** that the Father has sent me.
5: 37 And the Father who sent me *has* himself **testified** concerning me.
5: 39 possess eternal life. These are the Scriptures that **testify** about me,
7: 7 hate you, but it hates me because I **testify** that what it does is evil.
8: 13 challenged him, "Here you are, *appearing* as your own **witness**;
8: 14 Jesus answered, "Even if I **testify** on my own behalf, my testimony
8: 18 I am one *who* **testifies** for myself; my other witness is the Father,
8: 18 testifies for myself; my *other* **witness** is the Father, who sent me."
10: 25 not believe. The miracles I do in my Father's name **speak** for me,
12: 17 and raised him from the dead *continued to* **spread the word**.
13: 21 Jesus was troubled in spirit and **testified**, "I tell you the truth,
15: 26 of truth who goes out from the Father, he *will* **testify** about me.
15: 27 And you also *must* **testify**, for you have been with me from the
18: 23 I said something wrong," Jesus replied, "**testify** as to what is wrong.
18: 37 was born, and for this I came into the world, to **testify** to the truth.
19: 35 The man who saw it *has* **given testimony**, and his testimony is
21: 24 This is the disciple who **testifies** to these things and who wrote
Ac 6: 3 choose seven men from among you *who are* **known** to be full of
10: 22 and God-fearing man, *who is* **respected** by all the Jewish people.
10: 43 All the prophets **testify** about him that everyone who believes in
13: 22 he made David their king. *He* **testified** concerning him:
14: 3 who **confirmed** the message of his grace by enabling them to do
15: 8 **showed that** he **accepted** them by giving the Holy Spirit to them,
16: 2 The brothers at Lystra and Iconium **spoke well of** him.
22: 5 as also the high priest and all the Council *can* **testify**. I even
22: 12 of the law and **highly respected** by all the Jews living there.
23: 11 testified about me in Jerusalem, so you must also **testify** in Rome."
26: 5 They have known me for a long time and *can* **testify**, if they are
Ro 3: 21 has been made known, to which the Law and the Prophets **testify**.
10: 2 For *I can* **testify** about them that they are zealous for God,
1Co 15: 15 for *we have* **testified** about God that he raised Christ from the
2Co 8: 3 For *I* **testify** that they gave as much as they were able, and even
Gal 4: 15 *I can* **testify** that, if you could have done so, you would have torn
Col 4: 13 *I* **vouch** for him that he is working hard for you and for those at
1Ti 5: 10 and *is* **well known** for her good deeds, such as bringing up
6: 13 and *of* Christ Jesus, who *while* **testifying** before Pontius Pilate
Heb 7: 8 but in the other case, *by him who is* **declared** to be living.
7: 17 For *it is* **declared**: "You are a priest forever, in the order of
10: 15 The Holy Spirit also **testifies** to us **about** this. First he says:
11: 2 This is what the ancients *were* **commended** for.
11: 4 By faith *he was* **commended** as a righteous man, when God spoke
11: 4 as a righteous man, *when* God **spoke well** of his offerings.
11: 5 before he was taken, *he was* **commended** as one who pleased God.
11: 39 These *were* all **commended** for their faith, yet none of them
1Jn 1: 2 we have seen it and **testify to** it, and we proclaim to you the eternal
4: 14 and **testify** that the Father has sent his Son to be the Savior of the
5: 6 And it is the Spirit who **testifies**, because the Spirit is the truth.
5: 7 For there are three that **testify**:
5: 9 it is the testimony of God, which *he has* **given**^s about his Son.
5: 10 because he has not believed the testimony God *has* **given**^s about
3Jn 1: 3 and **tell about** your faithfulness to the truth and how you continue
1: 6 They *have* **told** the church **about** your love. You will do well to
1: 12 Demetrius *is* **well spoken of** by everyone—and even by the truth
1: 12 We also **speak well of** him, and you know that our testimony is
Rev 1: 2 who **testifies to** everything he saw—that is, the word of God
22: 16 have sent my angel *to* **give** you this **testimony** for the churches.
22: 18 I **warn** everyone who hears the words of the prophecy of this
22: 20 He *who* **testifies to** these things says, "Yes, I am coming soon."

3456 μαρτυρία, *martyria* [37] [√ *3459*]

testimony [31], certified [*+3836+5381*] [1], evidence [1], reputation [1], statements [1], testimony [*+3455+4005*] [1], witness [1]

Mk 14: 55 and the whole Sanhedrin were looking for **evidence** against Jesus
14: 56 testified falsely against him, but their **statements** did not agree.
14: 59 Yet even then their **testimony** did not agree.
Lk 22: 71 Then they said, "Why do we need any more **testimony**? We have
Jn 1: 7 He came as a **witness** to testify concerning that light, so that
1: 19 Now this was John's **testimony** when the Jews of Jerusalem sent
3: 11 we have seen, but still you people do not accept our **testimony**.
3: 32 to what he has seen and heard, but no one accepts his **testimony**.
3: 33 The man who has accepted it *has* **certified** [*+3836+5381*] that God
5: 31 "If I testify about myself, my **testimony** is not valid.
5: 32 and I know that *his* **testimony** [*+3455+4005*] about me is valid.
5: 34 Not that I accept human **testimony**; but I mention it that you may
5: 36 "I have **testimony** weightier than that of John. For the very work
8: 13 appearing as your own witness; your **testimony** is not valid."
8: 14 my **testimony** is valid, for I know where I came from and where I
8: 17 In your own Law it is written that the **testimony** of two men is
19: 35 man who saw it has given testimony, and his **testimony** is true.
21: 24 and who wrote them down. We know that his **testimony** is true.
Ac 22: 18 because they will not accept your **testimony** about me.'
1Ti 3: 7 He must also have a good **reputation** with outsiders, so that he
Tit 1: 13 This **testimony** is true. Therefore, rebuke them sharply, so that
1Jn 5: 9 We accept man's **testimony**, but God's testimony is greater
5: 9 but God's **testimony** is greater because it is the testimony of God,
5: 9 but God's testimony is greater because it is the **testimony** of God,
5: 10 Anyone who believes in the Son of God has this **testimony** in his
5: 10 because he has not believed the **testimony** God has given about his
5: 11 And this is the **testimony**: God has given us eternal life, and this
3Jn 1: 12 also speak well of him, and you know that our **testimony** is true.

Rev 1: 2 that is, the word of God and the **testimony** of Jesus Christ.
      1: 9 of Patmos because of the word of God and the **testimony** of Jesus.
      6: 9 of the word of God and the **testimony** they had maintained.
    11: 7 Now when they have finished their **testimony**, the beast that comes
    12:11 him by the blood of the Lamb and by the word *of* their **testimony**;
    12:17 obey God's commandments and hold to the **testimony** of Jesus.
    19:10 and with your brothers who hold to the **testimony** of Jesus.
    19:10 Worship God! For the **testimony** of Jesus is the spirit of prophecy."
    20: 4 because of their **testimony** for Jesus and because of the word of

3457 μαρτύριον, *martyrion* [19 / 20] [√ *3459*]

testimony [12], witnesses [3], testifies [1], testify [+*1639*] [1], testify to [+*625*] [1], testify [1], testifying [1]

Mt   8: 4 and offer the gift Moses commanded, as a **testimony** to them."
    10:18 and kings as **witnesses** to them and to the Gentiles.
    24:14 will be preached in the whole world as a **testimony** to all nations,
Mk   1:44 Moses commanded for your cleansing, as a **testimony** to them."
    6:11 dust off your feet when you leave, as a **testimony** against them."
    13: 9 you will stand before governors and kings as **witnesses** to them.
Lk   5:14 Moses commanded for your cleansing, as a **testimony** to them."
    9: 5 your feet when you leave their town, as a **testimony** against them."
    21:13 This will result in your being **witnesses** to them.
Ac   4:33 With great power the apostles *continued* to **testify** [+*625*] **to** the
    7:44 "Our forefathers had the tabernacle *of* the **Testimony** with them in
1Co 1: 6 because our **testimony** about Christ was confirmed in you.
    2: 1 as I proclaimed to you the **testimony** [UBS *3696*] about God.
2Co 1:12 Our conscience **testifies** that we have conducted ourselves in the
2Th 1:10 This includes you, because you believed our **testimony** to you.
1Ti 2: 6 as a ransom for all men—the **testimony** given in its proper time.
2Ti 1: 8 So do not be ashamed to **testify** about our Lord, or ashamed of me
Heb 3: 5 in all God's house, **testifying** to what would be said in the future.
Jas 5: 3 Their corrosion *will* **testify** [+*1639*] against you and eat your flesh
Rev 15: 5 the temple, that is, the tabernacle *of* the **Testimony**, was opened.

3458 μαρτύρομαι, *martyromai* [5] [√ *3459*]

declare [2], insist on it [1], testify [1], urging [1]

Ac 20:26 *I* **declare** to you today that I am innocent of the blood of all men.
    26:22 very day, and so I stand here and **testify** to small and great alike.
Gal 5: 3 Again *I* **declare** to every man who lets himself be circumcised that
Eph 4:17 So I tell you this, and **insist on it** in the Lord, that you must no
1Th 2:12 and **urging** you to live lives worthy of God,

3459 μάρτυς, *martys* [35] [→ *282, 1371, 2148, 2909, 3455, 3456, 3457, 3458, 4626, 4753, 5210, 5296, 6018, 6019, 6020*]

witnesses [20], witness [10], bore testimony [1], martyr [1], testify [+*1639*] [1], testify [1], testimony [1]

Mt 18:16 may be established by the testimony *of* two or three **witnesses**.'
    26:65 Why do we need any more **witnesses**? Look, now you have heard
Mk 14:63 tore his clothes. "Why do we need any more **witnesses**?" he asked.
Lk 11:48 So *you* **testify** [+*1639*] that you approve of what your forefathers
    24:48 You are **witnesses** of these things.
Ac   1: 8 and you will be my **witnesses** in Jerusalem, and in all Judea
    1:22 one of these must become a **witness** with us of his resurrection."
    2:32 has raised this Jesus to life, and we are all **witnesses** of the fact.
    3:15 but God raised him from the dead. We are **witnesses** of this.
    5:32 We are **witnesses** of these things, and so is the Holy Spirit,
    6:13 They produced false **witnesses**, who testified, "This fellow never
    7:58 the **witnesses** laid their clothes at the feet of a young man named
    10:39 "We are **witnesses** of everything he did in the country of the Jews
    10:41 all the people, but *by* **witnesses** whom God had already chosen—
    13:31 Galilee to Jerusalem. They are now his **witnesses** to our people.
    22:15 You will be his **witness** to all men of what you have seen
    22:20 And when the blood *of* your **martyr** Stephen was shed, I stood
    26:16 and as a **witness** of what you have seen of me and what I will show
Ro   1: 9 gospel of his Son, is my **witness** how constantly I remember you
2Co 1:23 I call God as my **witness** that it was in order to spare you that I did
    13: 1 must be established by the testimony of two or three **witnesses**."
Php 1: 8 God can **testify** how I long for all of you with the affection of
1Th 2: 5 nor did we put on a mask to cover up greed—God is our **witness**.
    2:10 You are **witnesses**, and so is God, of how holy, righteous

1Ti 5:19 against an elder unless it is brought by two or three **witnesses**.
    6:12 you made your good confession in the presence *of* many **witnesses**.
2Ti 2: 2 **witnesses** entrust to reliable men who will also be qualified to
Heb 10:28 the law of Moses died without mercy on the **testimony** of two
    12: 1 since we are surrounded by such a great cloud *of* **witnesses**,
1Pe 5: 1 a **witness** of Christ's sufferings and one who also will share in the
Rev 1: 5 and from Jesus Christ, who is the faithful **witness**, the firstborn
    2:13 even in the days of Antipas, my faithful **witness**, who was put to
    3:14 the faithful and true **witness**, the ruler of God's creation.
    11: 3 And I will give power *to* my two **witnesses**, and they will prophesy
    17: 6 of the saints, the blood *of* those *who* **bore testimony** to Jesus.

3460 μασάομαι, *masaomai* [1] [√ *3463*]

gnawed [1]

Rev 16:10 was plunged into darkness. *Men* **gnawed** their tongues in agony

3461 μασθός, *masthos* Not used in UBS/NIV [√ *3466*]

3462 μασσάομαι, *massaomai* Not used in UBS/NIV [√ *3463*]

3463 μαστιγόω, *mastigoō* [7] [→ *669, 1726, 3460, 3462, 3464, 3465*]

flog [4], flogged [2], punishes [1]

Mt 10:17 you over to the local councils and **flog** you in their synagogues.
    20:19 and will turn him over to the Gentiles to *be* mocked and **flogged**
    23:34 others *you will* **flog** in your synagogues and pursue from town to
Mk 10:34 who will mock him and spit on him, **flog** him and kill him.
Lk 18:32 They will mock him, insult him, spit on him, **flog** him and kill him.
Jn 19: 1 Then Pilate took Jesus and *had* him **flogged**.
Heb 12: 6 those he loves, and *he* **punishes** everyone he accepts as a son."

3464 μαστίζω, *mastizō* [1] [√ *3463*]

flog [1]

Ac 22:25 "Is it legal for you *to* **flog** a Roman citizen who hasn't even been

3465 μάστιξ, *mastix* [6] [√ *3463*]

suffering [2], diseases [1], flogged [1], flogging [1], sicknesses [1]

Mk 3:10 so that those with **diseases** were pushing forward to touch him.
    5:29 and she felt in her body that she was freed from her **suffering**.
    5:34 has healed you. Go in peace and be freed from your **suffering**."
Lk 7:21 **sicknesses** and evil spirits, and gave sight to many who were blind.
Ac 22:24 He directed that he be **flogged** and questioned in order to find out
Heb 11:36 Some faced jeers and **flogging**, while still others were chained

3466 μαστός, *mastos* [3] [→ *3410, 3461*]

untranslated [1], breasts [1], chest [1]

Lk 11:27 "Blessed is the mother who gave you birth and nursed **[NIE]** you."
    23:29 the wombs that never bore and the **breasts** that never nursed!'
Rev 1:13 reaching down to his feet and with a golden sash around his **chest**.

3467 ματαιολογία, *mataiologia* [1] [√ *3469* + *3306*]

meaningless talk [1]

1Ti 1: 6 have wandered away from these and turned to **meaningless talk**.

3468 ματαιολόγος, *mataiologos* [1] [√ *3469* + *3306*]

mere talkers [1]

Tit 1:10 For there are many rebellious people, **mere talkers** and deceivers,

3469 μάταιος, *mataios* [6] [→ 3467, 3468, 3470, 3471, 3472]

futile [2], worthless [2], empty [1], useless [1]

Ac 14:15 telling you to turn from these **worthless** *things* to the living God,
1Co 3:20 again, "The Lord knows that the thoughts of the wise are **futile**."
   15:17 And if Christ has not been raised, your faith is **futile**; you are still
Tit 3: 9 quarrels about the law, because these are unprofitable and **useless**.
Jas · 1:26 on his tongue, he deceives himself and his religion is **worthless**.
1Pe 1:18 or gold that you were redeemed from the **empty** way of life handed

3470 ματαιότης, *mataiotēs* [3] [√ 3469]

empty [1], frustration [1], futility [1]

Ro 8:20 For the creation was subjected *to* **frustration**, not by its own
Eph 4:17 no longer live as the Gentiles do, in the **futility** of their thinking.
2Pe 2:18 For they mouth **empty**, boastful words and, by appealing to the

3471 ματαιόω, *mataioō* [1] [√ 3469]

futile [1]

Ro 1:21 but their thinking *became* **futile** and their foolish hearts were

3472 μάτην, *matēn* [2] [√ 3469]

in vain [2]

Mt 15: 9 They worship me **in vain**; their teachings are but rules taught by
Mk 7: 7 They worship me **in vain**; their teachings are but rules taught by

3473 Ματθαῖος, *Matthaios*   Not used in UBS/NIV [√ 3414]

3474 Ματθάν, *Matthan* [2]

Matthan [2]

Mt 1:15 Eliud the father of Eleazar, Eleazar the father of **Matthan**,
   1:15 Eleazar the father of Matthan, **Matthan** the father of Jacob,

3475 Ματθάτ, *Matthat*   Not used in UBS/NIV [√ 3415]

3476 Ματθίας, *Matthias*   Not used in UBS/NIV [√ 3416]

3477 Ματταθά, *Mattatha* [1]

Mattatha [1]

Lk 3:31 the son of Melea, the son of Menna, the son *of* **Mattatha**,

3478 Ματταθίας, *Mattathias* [2]

Mattathias [1], of Mattathias [1]

Lk 3:25 the son **of Mattathias**, the son of Amos, the son of Nahum,
   3:26 the son of Maath, the son *of* **Mattathias**, the son of Semein,

3479 μάχαιρα, *machaira* [29] [√ 3480]

sword [21], swords [7], sword [+5125] [1]

Mt 10:34 peace to the earth. I did not come to bring peace, but a **sword**.
   26:47 With him was a large crowd armed with **swords** and clubs,
   26:51 With that, one of Jesus' companions reached for his **sword**,
   26:52 "Put your **sword** back in its place," Jesus said to him, "for all who
   26:52 said to him, "for all who draw the **sword** will die by the sword.
   26:52 said to him, "for all who draw the sword will die by the **sword**.
   26:55 that you have come out with **swords** and clubs to capture me?
Mk 14:43 With him was a crowd armed with **swords** and clubs, sent from the
   14:47 Then one of those standing near drew his **sword** and struck the
   14:48 "that you have come out with **swords** and clubs to capture me?
Lk 21:24 They will fall *by* the **sword** [+5125] and will be taken as prisoners
   22:36 and if you don't have a **sword**, sell your cloak and buy one.
   22:38 The disciples said, "See, Lord, here are two **swords**." "That is

22:49 to happen, they said, "Lord, should we strike with our **swords**?"
22:52 I leading a rebellion, that you have come with **swords** and clubs?
Jn 18:10 who had a **sword**, drew it and struck the high priest's servant,
   18:11 Jesus commanded Peter, "Put your **sword** away! Shall I not drink
Ac 12: 2 He had James, the brother of John, put to death *with* the **sword**.
   16:27 he drew his **sword** and was about to kill himself because he
Ro 8:35 or persecution or famine or nakedness or danger or **sword**?
   13: 4 do wrong, be afraid, for he does not bear the **sword** for nothing.
Eph 6:17 Take the helmet of salvation and the **sword** of the Spirit, which is
Heb 4:12 Sharper than any double-edged **sword**, it penetrates even to
   11:34 the fury of the flames, and escaped the edge *of* the **sword**;
   11:37 they were sawed in two; they were put to death *by* the **sword**.
Rev 6: 4 and to make men slay each other. To him was given a large **sword**.
   13:10 If anyone is to be killed with the **sword**, with the sword he will be
   13:10 is to be killed with the sword, with the **sword** he will be killed.
   13:14 up an image in honor of the beast who was wounded *by* the **sword**

3480 μάχη, *machē* [4] [→ 285, 1372, 2533, 2534, 2562, 2595, 3362, 3363, 3479, 3481]

quarrels [3], conflicts [1]

2Co 7: 5 were harassed at every turn—**conflicts** on the outside, fears within.
2Ti 2:23 and stupid arguments, because you know they produce **quarrels**.
Tit 3: 9 and genealogies and arguments and **quarrels** about the law,
Jas 4: 1 What causes fights and **quarrels** among you? Don't they come

3481 μάχομαι, *machomai* [4] [√ 3480]

quarrel [2], argue sharply [1], fighting [1]

Jn 6:52 Then the Jews *began to* **argue sharply** among themselves,
Ac 7:26 The next day Moses came upon two Israelites *who were* **fighting**,
2Ti 2:24 And the Lord's servant must not **quarrel**; instead, he must be kind
Jas 4: 2 *You* **quarrel** and fight. You do not have, because you do not ask

3482 μεγαλαυχέω, *megalaucheō*   Not used in UBS/NIV [√ 3489 + 902]

3483 μεγαλεῖος, *megaleios* [1] [√ 3489]

wonders [1]

Ac 2:11 we hear them declaring the **wonders** of God in our own tongues!"

3484 μεγαλειότης, *megaleiotēs* [3] [√ 3489]

divine majesty [1], greatness [1], majesty [1]

Lk 9:43 And they were all amazed at the **greatness** of God. While
Ac 19:27 of Asia and the world, will be robbed *of* her **divine majesty**."
2Pe 1:16 of our Lord Jesus Christ, but we were eyewitnesses *of* his **majesty**.

3485 μεγαλοπρεπής, *megaloprepēs* [1] [√ 3489 + 4560]

Majestic [1]

2Pe 1:17 the Father when the voice came to him from the **Majestic** Glory,

3486 μεγαλύνω, *megalynō* [8] [√ 3489]

exalted [1], expand [1], glorifies [1], held in high honor [1], highly regarded [1], long [1], praising [1], shown great [1]

Mt 23: 5 make their phylacteries wide and the tassels on their garments **long**;
Lk 1:46 And Mary said: "My soul **glorifies** the Lord
   1:58 and relatives heard that the Lord *had* **shown** her **great** mercy,
Ac 5:13 join them, even though they *were* **highly regarded** *by* the people.
   10:46 For they heard them speaking in tongues and **praising** God.
   19:17 with fear, and the name of the Lord Jesus *was* **held in high honor**.
2Co 10:15 to grow, our area of activity among you *will* greatly **expand**,
Php 1:20 so that now as always Christ *will* be **exalted** in my body,

3487 μεγάλως, *megalōs* [1] [√ 3489]

greatly [1]

Php   4:10   I rejoice **greatly** in the Lord that at last you have renewed your

3488 μεγαλωσύνη, *megalōsynē* [3] [√ 3489]

majesty [3]

Heb   1: 3   for sins, he sat down at the right hand *of* the **Majesty** in heaven.
     8: 1   who sat down at the right hand of the throne *of* the **Majesty** in
Jude   1:25   **majesty**, power and authority, through Jesus Christ our Lord,

3489 μέγας, *megas* [194] [→ 3482, 3483, 3484, 3485, 3486, 3487, 3488, 3490, 3491, 3492, 3504, 3505]

μέγας ἐντολή (great commandment)   [2]   Mt 22:36,38

μέγας ἡμέρα (great day)   [5]   Jn 7:37; Ac 2:20; Jude 1:6; Rev 6:17; 16:14

μέγας θλῖψις (great tribulation)   [4]   Mt 24:21; Ac 7:11; Rev 2:22; 7:14

μέγας ... μικρός (great ... small)   [10]   Lk 9:48; Ac 8:10; 26:22; Heb 8:11; Jas 3:5; Rev 11:18; 13:16; 19:5,18; 20:12

μέγας φόβος (great fear)   [6]   Mk 4:41; Lk 2:9; 8:37; Ac 5:5,11; Rev 11:11

μέγας φωνή (great voice)   [40]   Mt 27:46,50; Mk 1:26; 5:7; 15:34,37; Lk 4:33; 8:28; 17:15; 19:37; 23:23,46; Jn 11:43; Ac 7:57,60; 8:7; 14:10; 16:28; 26:24; Rev 1:10; 5:2,12; 6:10; 7:2,10; 8:13; 10:3; 11:12,15; 12:10; 14:2,7,9,15,18; 16:1,17; 19:1,17; 21:3

μέγας χαρά (great joy)   [5]   Mt 2:10; 28:8; Lk 2:10; 24:52; Ac 15:3

great [90], loud [31], large [10], greatest [5], severe [4], completely [3], big [2], furious [2], high officials [2], high [2], huge [2], much [2], strong [2], terrified [+5828+5832] [2], violent [2], at the top of voice [+5889] [1], at the top of voices [+5889] [1], at the top of [1], called out [+3306+5889] [1], complete [1], cried out [+3189+5889] [1], enormous [1], fear [+5832] [1], filled with joy [+5915] [1], fury [+2596] [1], gigantic [1], greatly [1], grown up [+1181] [1], intense [1], intensely [1], long [1], mourned deeply [+3157+4472] [1], overjoyed [+5379+5897+5915] [1], profound [1], proud [1], richly [1], roar [+5889] [1], shouted [+3836+5774+5889] [1], shouted [+5888+5889] [1], shouting at the top of voice [+3306+5889] [1], shriek [+5888+5889] [1], shrieks [+1066+5889] [1], special [1], surprising [1], terrible [1], terror [+5832] [1], tremendous [+5496] [1], very [1]

Mt   2:10   they saw the star, *they were* **overjoyed** [+5379+5897+5915].
     4:16   the people living in darkness have seen a **great** light; on those
     5:19   and teaches these commands will be called **great** in the kingdom of
     5:35   his footstool; or by Jerusalem, for it is the city *of* the **Great** King.
     7:27   and beat against that house, and it fell with a **great** crash."
     8:24   Without warning, a **furious** storm came up on the lake, so that the
     8:26   and rebuked the winds and the waves, and it was **completely** calm.
   15:28   Then Jesus answered, "Woman, you have **great** faith! Your request
   20:25   it over them, and their **high officials** exercise authority over them.
   20:26   whoever wants to become **great** among you must be your servant,
   22:36   "Teacher, which is the **greatest** commandment in the Law?"
   22:38   This is the first and **greatest** commandment.
   24:21   For then there will be **great** distress, unequaled from the beginning
   24:24   and false prophets will appear and perform **great** signs
   24:31   And he will send his angels with a **loud** trumpet call, and they will
   27:46   About the ninth hour Jesus cried out *in* a **loud** voice, "*Eloi,*
   27:50   And when Jesus had cried out again *in* a **loud** voice, he gave up his
   27:60   He rolled a **big** stone in front of the entrance to the tomb and went
   28: 2   There was a **violent** earthquake, for an angel of the Lord came
   28: 8   hurried away from the tomb, afraid yet **filled with joy** [+5915],
Mk   1:26   man violently and came out of him *with* a **shriek** [+5888+5889].
     4:32   with such **big** branches that the birds of the air can perch in its
     4:37   A **furious** squall came up, and the waves broke over the boat,
     4:39   Be still!" Then the wind died down and it was **completely** calm.
     4:41   *They were* **terrified** [+5828+5832] and asked each other,
     5: 7   He shouted **at the top of** his voice, "What do you want with me,
     5:11   A **large** herd of pigs was feeding on the nearby hillside.
     5:42   was twelve years old). At this they were **completely** astonished.

   10:42   it over them, and their **high officials** exercise authority over them.
   10:43   whoever wants to become **great** among you must be your servant,
   13: 2   "Do you see all these **great** buildings?" replied Jesus. "Not one
   14:15   He will show you a **large** upper room, furnished and ready.
   15:34   And at the ninth hour Jesus cried out *in* a **loud** voice, "*Eloi,*
   15:37   With a **loud** cry, Jesus breathed his last.
   16: 4   saw that the stone, which was very **large**, had been rolled away.
Lk   1:15   for he will be **great** in the sight of the Lord. He is never to take
     1:32   He will be **great** and will be called the Son of the Most High.
     1:42   *In* a **loud** voice she exclaimed: "Blessed are you among women,
     1:49   for the Mighty One has done **great** *things* for me—holy is his
     2: 9   Lord shone around them, and *they were* **terrified** [+5828+5832].
     2:10   I bring you good news of **great** joy that will be for all the people.
     4:25   a half years and there was a **severe** famine throughout the land.
     4:33   an evil spirit. He cried out **at the top of** his voice [+5889].
     4:38   Now Simon's mother-in-law was suffering *from* a **high** fever,
     5:29   Then Levi held a **great** banquet for Jesus at his house, and a large
     6:49   struck that house, it collapsed and its destruction was **complete**."
     7:16   praised God. "A **great** prophet has appeared among us," they said.
     8:28   and fell at his feet, **shouting at the top of** *his* voice [+3306+5889],
     8:37   to leave them, because they were overcome *with* **fear** [+5832]."
     9:48   sent me. For he who is least among you all—he is the **greatest**."
   14:16   "A certain man was preparing a **great** banquet and invited many
   16:26   besides all this, between us and you a **great** chasm has been fixed,
   17:15   he saw he was healed, came back, praising God in a **loud** voice.
   19:37   the whole crowd of disciples began joyfully to praise God *in* **loud**
   21:11   There will be **great** earthquakes, famines and pestilences in
   21:11   in various places, and fearful events and **great** signs from heaven.
   21:23   There will be **great** distress in the land and wrath against this
   22:12   He will show you a **large** upper room, all furnished.
   23:23   But *with* **loud** shouts they insistently demanded that he be
   23:46   Jesus called out *with* a **loud** voice, "Father, into your hands I
   24:52   they worshiped him and returned to Jerusalem with **great** joy.
Jn   6:18   A **strong** wind was blowing and the waters grew rough.
     7:37   On the last and **greatest** day of the Feast, Jesus stood and said in a
   11:43   he had said this, Jesus called *in* a **loud** voice, "Lazarus, come out!"
   19:31   day of Preparation, and the next day was to be a **special** Sabbath.
   21:11   and dragged the net ashore. It was full *of* **large** fish, 153,
Ac   2:20   and the moon to blood before the coming of the **great** and glorious
     4:33   *With* **great** power the apostles continued to testify to the
     4:33   resurrection of the Lord Jesus, and **much** grace was upon them all.
     5: 5   and died. And **great** fear seized all who heard what had happened.
     5:11   **Great** fear seized the whole church and all who heard about these
     6: 8   did **great** wonders and miraculous signs among the people.
     7:11   a famine struck all Egypt and Canaan, bringing **great** suffering,
     7:57   yelling **at the top of** their voices [+5889], they all rushed at him,
     7:60   Then *he* fell on his knees and **cried out** [+3189+5889], "Lord,
     8: 1   On that day a **great** persecution broke out against the church at
     8: 2   men buried Stephen and **mourned deeply** [+3157+4472] for him.
     8: 7   *With* **shrieks** [+1066+5889], evil spirits came out of many,
     8: 9   all the people of Samaria. He boasted that he was someone **great**,
     8:10   and all the people, both **high** and low, gave him their attention
     8:10   "This man is the divine power known as the **Great** Power."
     8:13   astonished *by* the **great** signs and miracles he saw.
   10:11   and something like a **large** sheet being let down to earth by its four
   11: 5   I saw something like a **large** sheet being let down from heaven by
   11:28   and through the Spirit predicted that a **severe** famine would spread
   14:10   and **called out** [+3306+5889], "Stand up on your feet!" At that,
   15: 3   had been converted. This news made all the brothers **very** glad.
   16:26   Suddenly there was such a **violent** earthquake that the foundations
   16:28   But Paul **shouted** [+5888+5889], "Don't harm yourself! We are all
   19:27   but also that the temple *of* the **great** goddess Artemis will be
   19:28   and began shouting: "**Great** is Artemis of the Ephesians!"
   19:34   in unison for about two hours: "**Great** is Artemis of the Ephesians!"
   19:35   city of Ephesus is the guardian of the temple *of* the **great** Artemis
   23: 9   There was a **great** uproar, and some of the teachers of the law who
   26:22   very day, and so I stand here and testify *to* small and **great** alike.
   26:24   are out of your mind, Paul!" *he* **shouted** [+3836+5774+5889].
   26:29   Paul replied, "Short time or **long**—I pray God that not only you
Ro   9: 2   I have **great** sorrow and unceasing anguish in my heart.
1Co   9:11   among you, is it *too* **much** if we reap a material harvest from you?
   16: 9   because a **great** door for effective work has opened to me,
2Co   11:15   It is not **surprising**, then, if his servants masquerade as servants of
Eph   5:32   This is a **profound** mystery—but I am talking about Christ
1Ti   3:16   Beyond all question, the mystery of godliness is **great**:
     6: 6   But godliness with contentment is **great** gain.

2Ti 2:20 In a **large** house there are articles not only of gold and silver,
Tit 2:13 the glorious appearing *of* our **great** God and Savior, Jesus Christ,
Heb 4:14 since we have a **great** high priest who has gone through the
     8:11 they will all know me, from the least of them to the **greatest**.
     10:21 and since we have a **great** priest over the house of God,
     10:35 So do not throw away your confidence; it will be **richly** rewarded.
     11:24 By faith Moses, *when he had* **grown** [+*1181*] **up**, refused to be
     13:20 from the dead our Lord Jesus, that **great** Shepherd of the sheep,
Jas 3:5 the tongue is a small part of the body, but it makes **great** boasts.
Jude 1:6 bound with everlasting chains for judgment on the **great** Day.
Rev 1:10 in the Spirit, and I heard behind me a **loud** voice like a trumpet,
     2:22 I will make those who commit adultery with her suffer **intensely**,
     5:2 And I saw a mighty angel proclaiming in a **loud** voice, "Who is
     5:12 *In* a **loud** voice they sang: "Worthy is the Lamb, who was slain,
     6:4 and to make men slay each other. To him was given a **large** sword.
     6:10 They called out in a **loud** voice, "How long, Sovereign Lord,
     6:12 watched as he opened the sixth seal. There was a **great** earthquake.
     6:13 as late figs drop from a fig tree when shaken by a **strong** wind.
     6:17 For the **great** day of their wrath has come, and who can stand?"
     7:2 He called out *in* a **loud** voice to the four angels who had been
     7:10 And they cried out *in* a **loud** voice: "Salvation belongs to our God,
     7:14 "These are they who have come out of the **great** tribulation;
     8:8 and something like a **huge** mountain, all ablaze, was thrown into
     8:10 angel sounded his trumpet, and a **great** star, blazing like a torch,
     8:13 I heard an eagle that was flying in midair call out in a **loud** voice:
     9:2 smoke rose from it like the smoke *from* a **gigantic** furnace.
     9:14 "Release the four angels who are bound at the **great** river
     10:3 and he gave a **loud** shout like the roar of a lion. When he shouted,
     11:8 Their bodies will lie in the street *of* the **great** city, which is
     11:11 stood on their feet, and **terror** [+*5832*] struck those who saw them.
     11:12 Then they heard a **loud** voice from heaven saying to them,
     11:13 At that very hour there was a **severe** earthquake and a tenth of the
     11:15 his trumpet, and there were **loud** voices in heaven, which said:
     11:17 because you have taken your **great** power and have begun to reign.
     11:18 and those who reverence your name, both small and **great**—
     11:19 rumblings, peals of thunder, an earthquake and a **great** hailstorm.
     12:1 A **great** and wondrous sign appeared in heaven: a woman clothed
     12:3 an **enormous** red dragon with seven heads and ten horns and seven
     12:9 The **great** dragon was hurled down—that ancient serpent called the
     12:10 Then I heard a **loud** voice in heaven say: "Now have come the
     12:12 He is filled with **fury** [+*2596*], because he knows that his time is
     12:14 The woman was given the two wings *of* a **great** eagle, so that she
     13:2 gave the beast his power and his throne and **great** authority.
     13:5 The beast was given a mouth to utter **proud** *words*
     13:13 And he performed **great** and miraculous signs, even causing fire to
     13:16 forced everyone, small and **great**, rich and poor, free and slave,
     14:2 like the roar of rushing waters and like a **loud** peal of thunder.
     14:7 He said in a **loud** voice, "Fear God and give him glory,
     14:8 Fallen is Babylon the **Great**, which made all the nations drink the
     14:9 A third angel followed them and said in a **loud** voice: "If anyone
     14:15 and called in a **loud** voice to him who was sitting on the cloud,
     14:18 and called *in* a **loud** voice to him who had the sharp sickle,
     14:19 its grapes and threw them into the **great** winepress of God's wrath.
     15:1 I saw in heaven another **great** and marvelous sign: seven angels
     15:3 "**Great** and marvelous are your deeds, Lord God Almighty.
     16:1 Then I heard a **loud** voice from the temple saying to the seven
     16:9 They were seared by the **intense** heat and they cursed the name of
     16:12 The sixth angel poured out his bowl on the **great** river Euphrates,
     16:14 to gather them for the battle *on* the **great** day of God Almighty.
     16:17 and out of the temple came a **loud** voice from the throne, saying,
     16:18 of lightning, rumblings, peals of thunder and a **severe** earthquake.
     16:18 man has been on earth, so **tremendous** [+*5496*] was the quake.
     16:19 The **great** city split into three parts, and the cities of the nations
     16:19 God remembered Babylon the **Great** and gave her the cup filled
     16:21 From the sky **huge** hailstones of about a hundred pounds each fell
     16:21 account of the plague of hail, because the plague was so **terrible**.
     17:1 "Come, I will show you the punishment *of* the **great** prostitute,
     17:5 MYSTERY BABYLON THE **GREAT** THE MOTHER OF
     17:6 bore testimony to Jesus. When I saw her, I was **greatly** astonished.
     17:18 The woman you saw is the **great** city that rules over the kings of
     18:1 He had **great** authority, and the earth was illuminated by his
     18:2 a mighty voice he shouted: "Fallen! Fallen is Babylon the **Great**!
     18:10 and cry: " 'Woe! Woe, O **great** city, O Babylon, city of power!
     18:16 Woe, O **great** city, dressed in fine linen, purple and scarlet,
     18:18 they will exclaim, 'Was there ever a city like this **great** city?'
     18:19 Woe, O **great** city, where all who had ships on the sea became rich

     18:21 Then a mighty angel picked up a boulder the size of a **large**
     18:21 "With such violence the **great** city of Babylon will be thrown down,
     19:1 After this I heard what sounded like the **roar** [+*5889*] of a great
     19:2 He has condemned the **great** prostitute who corrupted the earth by
     19:5 all you his servants, you who fear him, both small and **great**!"
     19:17 who cried in a **loud** voice to all the birds flying in midair,
     19:17 in midair, "Come, gather together for the **great** supper of God,
     19:18 and the flesh *of* all people, free and slave, small and **great**."
     20:1 having the key to the Abyss and holding in his hand a **great** chain.
     20:11 Then I saw a **great** white throne and him who was seated on it.
     20:12 And I saw the dead, **great** and small, standing before the throne,
     21:3 I heard a **loud** voice from the throne saying, "Now the dwelling
     21:10 And he carried me away in the Spirit to a mountain **great** and high,
     21:12 It had a **great**, high wall with twelve gates, and with twelve angels

3490 μέγεθος, *megethos* [1] [√ *3489*]

great [1]

Eph 1:19 and his incomparably **great** power for us who believe. That power

3491 μεγιστάν, *megistan* [3] [√ *3489*]

great [1], high officials [1], princes [1]

Mk 6:21 On his birthday Herod gave a banquet *for* his **high officials**
Rev 6:15 the **princes**, the generals, the rich, the mighty, and every slave
     18:23 heard in you again. Your merchants were the world's **great** *men*.

3492 μέγιστος, *megistos* [1] [√ *3489*]

very great [1]

2Pe 1:4 Through these he has given us his **very great** and precious

3493 μεθερμηνεύω, *methermēneuō* [8]
[√ *3552* + *2257*]

means [+*1639*] [5], is [+*1639*] [1], means [+*3306*] [1], means [1]

Mt 1:23 will call him Immanuel"—which **means** [+*1639*], "God with us."
Mk 5:41 (which **means** [+*1639*], "Little girl, I say to you, get up!").
     15:22 called Golgotha (which **means** [+*1639*] The Place of the Skull).
     15:34 which **means** [+*1639*], "My God, my God, why have you forsaken
Jn 1:38 They said, "Rabbi" (which **means** [+*3306*] Teacher), "where are
     1:41 tell him, "We have found the Messiah" (that **is** [+*1639*], the Christ).
Ac 4:36 whom the apostles called Barnabas (which **means** [+*1639*] Son of
     13:8 But Elymas the sorcerer (for that *is what* his name **means**)

3494 μέθη, *methē* [3] [√ *3501*]

drunkenness [3]

Lk 21:34 down with dissipation, **drunkenness** and the anxieties of life,
Ro 13:13 behave decently, as in the daytime, not in orgies and **drunkenness**,
Gal 5:21 and envy; **drunkenness**, orgies, and the like. I warn you, as I did

3495 μεθιστάνω, *methistanō* Not used in UBS/NIV
[√ *3552* + *2705*]

3496 μεθίστημι, *methistēmi* [5] [√ *3552* + *2705*]

brought [1], led astray [1], lose [+*1666*] [1], move [1], removing [1]

Lk 16:4 I know what I'll do so that, when *I* **lose** [+*1666*] my job here,
Ac 13:22 *After* **removing** Saul, he made David their king. He testified
     19:26 **led astray** large numbers of people here in Ephesus
1Co 13:2 and if I have a faith that *can* **move** mountains, but have not love,
Col 1:13 of darkness and **brought** us into the kingdom of the Son he loves,

3497 μεθοδεία, *methodeia* [2] [√ *3552* + *3847*]

schemes [1], scheming [1]

Eph 4:14 by the cunning and craftiness of men in their deceitful **scheming**.
     6:11 so that you can take your stand against the devil's **schemes**.

3498 μεθόριον, **methorion**   Not used in UBS/NIV
[√ *3552 + 4000*]

3499 μεθύσκω, **methyskō**   [5]   [√ *3501*]

get drunk [3], had too much to drink [1], intoxicated [1]

Lk 12:45 and maidservants and *to* eat and drink and **get drunk**.
Jn   2:10 the cheaper wine after the *guests have* **had too much to drink**;
Eph 5:18 *Do* not **get drunk** on wine, which leads to debauchery. Instead,
1Th 5: 7 sleep at night, and those *who* **get drunk**, get drunk at night.
Rev 17: 2 and the inhabitants of the earth *were* **intoxicated** with the wine of

3500 μέθυσος, **methysos**   [2]   [√ *3501*]

drunkard [1], drunkards [1]

1Co 5:11 or greedy, an idolater or a slanderer, a **drunkard** or a swindler.
     6:10 nor thieves nor the greedy nor **drunkards** nor slanderers nor

3501 μεθύω, **methyō**   [5]   [→ *287, 3494, 3499, 3500*]

drunk [2], drunkards [1], get drunk [1], gets drunk [1]

Mt 24:49 to beat his fellow servants and to eat and drink with **drunkards**.
Ac   2:15 These men *are* not **drunk**, as you suppose. It's only nine in the
1Co 11:21 for anybody else. One remains hungry, another **gets drunk**.
1Th 5: 7 sleep at night, and those who get drunk, **get drunk** at night.
Rev 17: 6 I saw that the woman *was* **drunk** with the blood of the saints,

3502 μείγνυμι, **meignymi**   [4]   [→ *3503, 3623, 3624, 5042, 5264*]

mixed [4]

Mt 27:34 There they offered Jesus wine to drink, **mixed** with gall; but after
Lk 13: 1 the Galileans whose blood Pilate *had* **mixed** with their sacrifices.
Rev 8: 7 his trumpet, and there came hail and fire **mixed** with blood,
    15: 2 And I saw what looked like a sea of glass **mixed** with fire and,

3503 μειγνύω, **meignyō**   Not used in UBS/NIV [√ *3502*]

3504 μειζότερος, **meizoteros**   Not used in UBS/NIV
[√ *3489*]

3505 μείζων, **meizōn**   [48]   [√ *3489*]

greater than [20], greater [10], greatest [8], more [3], largest [2],
all the louder [1], bigger [1], older [1], one greater than [1],
weightier than [1]

Mt 11:11 women there has not risen anyone **greater than** John the Baptist;
    11:11 yet he who is least in the kingdom of heaven is **greater than** he.
    12: 6 I tell you that **one greater than** the temple is here.
    13:32 it grows, it is the **largest** of garden plants and becomes a tree,
    18: 1 and asked, "Who is the **greatest** in the kingdom of heaven?"
    18: 4 whoever humbles himself like this child is the **greatest** in the
    20:31 but they shouted **all the louder**, "Lord, Son of David, have mercy
    23:11 The **greatest** among you will be your servant.
    23:17 Which is **greater**: the gold, or the temple that makes the gold
    23:19 Which is **greater**: the gift, or the altar that makes the gift sacred?
Mk   4:32 it grows and becomes the **largest** of all garden plants,
     9:34 because on the way they had argued about who was the **greatest**.
    12:31 as yourself.' There is no commandment **greater than** these."
Lk   7:28 among those born of women there is no one **greater than** John;
     7:28 yet the one who is least in the kingdom of God is **greater than** he."
     9:46 among the disciples as to which of them would be the **greatest**.
    12:18 I will tear down my barns and build **bigger** *ones*, and there I will
    22:24 among them as to which of them was considered to be **greatest**.
    22:26 Instead, the **greatest** among you should be like the youngest,
    22:27 For who is **greater**, the one who is at the table or the one who
Jn   1:50 saw you under the fig tree. You shall see **greater** *things* **than** that."
     4:12 Are you **greater than** our father Jacob, who gave us the well
     5:20 to your amazement he will show him even **greater** things **than**
     5:36 "I have testimony **weightier than** that of John. For the very work
     8:53 Are you **greater than** our father Abraham? He died, and so did the

    10:29 My Father, who has given them to me, is **greater than** all;
    13:16 I tell you the truth, no servant is **greater than** his master, nor is a
    13:16 his master, nor is a messenger **greater than** the one who sent him.
    14:12 He will do even **greater** things **than** these, because I am going to
    14:28 glad that I am going to the Father, for the Father is **greater than** I.
    15:13 **Greater** love has no one **than** this, that he lay down his life for his
    15:20 'No servant is **greater than** his master.' If they persecuted me,
    19:11 the one who handed me over to you is guilty *of* a **greater** sin."
Ro   9:12 him who calls—she was told, "The **older** will serve the younger."
1Co 12:31 But eagerly desire the **greater** gifts. And now I will show you the
    13:13 faith, hope and love. But the **greatest** of these is love.
    14: 5 He who prophesies is **greater** than one who speaks in tongues,
Heb 6:13 since there was no one **greater** for him to swear by, he swore by
     6:16 Men swear by someone **greater than** themselves, and the oath
     9:11 he went through the **greater** and more perfect tabernacle that is not
    11:26 the sake of Christ as *of* **greater** value **than** the treasures of Egypt,
Jas 1: 1 because you know that we who teach will be judged **more** *strictly*.
     4: 6 But he gives us **more** grace. That is why Scripture says: "God
2Pe 2:11 yet even angels, although they are stronger and **more** powerful,
1Jn 3:20 For God is **greater than** our hearts, and he knows everything.
     4: 4 because the one who is in you is **greater** than the one who is in the
     5: 9 but God's testimony is **greater** because it is the testimony of God,
3Jn 1: 4 I have no **greater** joy **than** to hear that my children are walking in

3506 μέλας, **melas**   [6]

black [3], ink [3]

Mt   5:36 by your head, for you cannot make even one hair white or **black**.
2Co 3: 3 written not *with* **ink** but with the Spirit of the living God,
2Jn 1:12 have much to write to you, but I do not want to use paper and **ink**.
3Jn 1:13 much to write you, but I do not want to do so with pen and **ink**.
Rev 6: 5 "Come!" I looked, and there before me was a **black** horse!
     6:12 The sun turned **black** like sackcloth made of goat hair, the whole

3507 Μελεά, **Melea**   [1]

Melea [1]

Lk   3:31 the son *of* **Melea**, the son of Menna, the son of Mattatha, the son of

3508 μέλει, **melei**   [10]   [→ *288, 294, 2149, 2150, 2151, 3509, 3520, 3564, 4627*]

care [2], cares [2], swayed [2], cared [1], concerned [1], showed
concern [1], trouble [1]

Mt 22:16 You aren't **swayed** by men, because you pay no attention to who
Mk   4:38 woke him and said to him, "Teacher, don't you **care** if we drown?"
    12:14 You aren't **swayed** by men, because you pay no attention to who
Lk 10:40 don't you **care** that my sister has left me to do the work by myself?
Jn 10:13 because he is a hired hand and **cares** nothing for the sheep.
    12: 6 He did not say this because he **cared** about the poor but because he
Ac 18:17 him in front of the court. But Gallio **showed** no **concern** whatever.
1Co 7:21 Don't *let it* **trouble** you—although if you can gain your freedom,
     9: 9 it is treading out the grain." Is it about oxen that God *is* **concerned**?
1Pe 5: 7 Cast all your anxiety on him because he **cares** for you.

3509 μελετάω, **meletaō**   [2]   [√ *3508*]

give yourself wholly to [1], plot [1]

Ac   4:25 " 'Why do the nations rage and the peoples **plot** in vain?
1Ti 4:15 **give yourself wholly to** them, so that everyone may see your

3510 μέλι, **meli**   [4]   [→ *3511, 3512, 3513*]

honey [4]

Mt   3: 4 leather belt around his waist. His food was locusts and wild **honey**.
Mk   1: 6 a leather belt around his waist, and he ate locusts and wild **honey**.
Rev 10: 9 your stomach sour, but in your mouth it will be as sweet as **honey**."
    10:10 It tasted as sweet as **honey** in my mouth, but when I had eaten it,

3511 μελισσεῖον, **melisseion**   Not used in UBS/NIV
[√ *3510*]

3512 μελισσίον, **melission**   Not used in UBS/NIV
[√ *3510*]

3513 μελίσσιος, **melissios**   Not used in UBS/NIV
[√ *3510*]

3514 Μελίτη, **Melitē**   [1]   [→ *3515*]

Malta [1]

Ac 28: 1 safely on shore, we found out that the island was called **Malta**.

3515 Μελιτήνη, **Melitēnē**   Not used in UBS/NIV
[√ *3514*]

3516 μέλλω, **mellō**   [109]

about to [22], going to [18], will [17], to come [8], would [8],
coming [4], later [4], intend to [2], intended to [2], the future [2], to
be [2], wanting [2], *untranslated* [1], am [1], as [1], close to [1],
dawn [*+1181+2465*] [1], future [1], going to happen to [1], intend
[1], nearly [1], never [*+3600*] [1], next [*+1650+3836*] [1], should
[1], that are coming [1], to come [*+2262*] [1], to [1], waiting for
[1], was to [1], was [1]

Mt 2:13 I tell you, for Herod *is* **going to** search for the child to kill him."
     3: 7 brood of vipers! Who warned you to flee from the **coming** wrath?
    11:14 are willing to accept it, he is the Elijah who *was* **to come** [*+2262*].
    12:32 Spirit will not be forgiven, either in this age or in the age **to come**.
    16:27 For the Son of Man *is* **going to** come in his Father's glory with his
    17:12 In the same way the Son of Man *is* **going to** suffer at their hands."
    17:22 "The Son of Man *is* **going to** be betrayed into the hands of men.
    20:22 "Can you drink the cup I *am* **going to** drink?" "We can,"
    24: 6 *You* **will** hear of wars and rumors of wars, but see to it that you are
Mk 10:32 the Twelve aside and told them what *was* **going to** happen to him.
    13: 4 And what will be the sign that they *are* all **about to** be fulfilled?"
Lk 3: 7 brood of vipers! Who warned you to flee from the **coming** wrath?
     7: 2 whom his master valued highly, was sick and **about to** die.
     9:31 which he *was* **about to** bring to fulfillment at Jerusalem.
     9:44 The Son of Man *is* **going to** be betrayed into the hands of men."
    10: 1 ahead of him to every town and place where he *was* **about to** go.
    13: 9 If it bears fruit next [*+1650+3836*] year, fine! If not, then cut it
    19: 4 a sycamore-fig tree to see him, since Jesus **was** coming that way.
    19:11 and the people thought that the kingdom of God *was* **going to**
    21: 7 And what will be the sign that they *are* **about to** take place?"
    21:36 and pray that you may be able to escape all that *is* **about to**
    22:23 among themselves which of them it might be who **would** do this.
    24:21 but we had hoped that he was the one *who was* **going to** redeem
Jn 4:47 and begged him to come and heal his son, *who was* **close to** death.
     6: 6 to test him, for he already had in mind what *he was* **going to** do.
     6:15 knowing that *they* **intended to** come and make him king by force,
     6:71 who, though one of the Twelve, *was* **later** to betray him.)
     7:35 "Where *does* this man **intend to** go that we cannot find him?
     7:35 **Will** he go where our people live scattered among the Greeks,
     7:39 the Spirit, whom those who believed in him were **later** to receive.
    11:51 but as high priest that year he prophesied that Jesus **would** die for
    12: 4 his disciples, Judas Iscariot, who *was* **later** to betray him, objected,
    12:33 He said this to show the kind of death *he was* **going to** die.
    14:22 why *do you* **intend to** show yourself to us and not to the world?"
    18:32 indicating the kind of death *he was* **going to** die would be fulfilled.
Ac 3: 3 When he saw Peter and John **about to** enter, he asked them for
     5:35 of Israel, consider carefully what *you* **intend** to do to these men.
    11:28 and through the Spirit predicted that a severe famine **would** spread
    12: 6 The night before Herod **was to** bring him to trial, Peter was
    13:34 from the dead, **never** [*+3600*] to decay, is stated in these words:
    16:27 he drew his sword and *was* **about to** kill himself because he
    17:31 For he has set a day when *he* **will** judge the world with justice by
    18:14 Just as Paul *was* **about to** speak, Gallio said to the Jews, "If you
    19:27 of Asia and the world, **will** be robbed of her divine majesty."
    20: 3 Because the Jews made a plot against him just *as he was* **about to**
    20: 7 to the people and, *because* he **intended to** leave the next day,
    20:13 and sailed for Assos, where *we were* **going to** take Paul aboard.
    20:13 made this arrangement *because* he was **[NIE]** going there on foot.
    20:38 What grieved them most was his statement that *they* **would** never
    21:27 When the seven days were **nearly** over, some Jews from the

21:37 *As* the soldiers *were* **about to** take Paul into the barracks,
22:16 And now what *are you* **waiting for**? Get up, be baptized and wash
22:26 and reported it. "What *are you* **going to** do?" he asked.
22:29 Those *who were* **about to** question him withdrew immediately.
23: 3 Then Paul said to him, "God **will** strike you, you whitewashed wall!
23:15 the pretext of **wanting** more accurate information about his case.
23:20 on the pretext of **wanting** more accurate information about him.
23:27 This man was seized by the Jews and they *were* **about to** kill him,
24:15 that there **will** be a resurrection of both the righteous
24:25 self-control and the judgment **to come**, Felix was afraid and said,
25: 4 "Paul is being held at Caesarea, and I myself *am* **going** there soon.
26: 2 I consider myself fortunate to stand before you today **as** I make my
26:22 nothing beyond what the prophets and Moses said **would** happen—
26:23 **would** proclaim light to his own people and to the Gentiles."
27: 2 We boarded a ship from Adramyttium **about to** sail for ports along
27:10 I can see that our voyage *is* **going to** be disastrous and bring great
27:30 pretending *they were* **going to** lower some anchors from the bow.
27:33 Just before **dawn** [*+1181+2465*] Paul urged them all to eat.
28: 6 The people expected him **to** swell up or suddenly fall dead,
Ro 4:24 but also for us, to whom God **will** credit righteousness—for us who
     5:14 a command, as did Adam, who was a pattern *of* the one **to come**.
     8:13 For if you live according to the sinful nature, *you* **will** die;
     8:18 are not worth comparing with the glory that **will** be revealed in us.
     8:38 nor demons, neither the present nor **the future**, nor any powers,
1Co 3:22 or the world or life or death or the present or **the future**—
Gal 3:23 held prisoners by the law, locked up until faith **should** be revealed.
Eph 1:21 be given, not only in the present age but also in the one **to come**.
Col 2:17 These are a shadow of the *things that were* **to come**; the reality,
1Th 3: 4 were with you, we kept telling you that *we* **would** be persecuted.
1Ti 1:16 patience as an example *for* those *who* **would** believe on him
     4: 8 holding promise for both the present life and the life **to come**.
     6:19 treasure for themselves as a firm foundation for the **coming** age,
2Ti 4: 1 and of Christ Jesus, who **will** judge the living and the dead,
Heb 1:14 Are not all angels ministering spirits sent to serve those who **will**
     2: 5 It is not to angels that he has subjected the world **to come**,
     6: 5 goodness of the word of God and the powers *of* the **coming** age,
     8: 5 This is why Moses was warned *when he was* **about to** build the
    10: 1 The law is only a shadow *of* the good things **that are coming**—
    10:27 and of raging fire that **will** consume the enemies of God.
    11: 8 when called to go to a place he *would* **later** receive as his
    11:20 By faith Isaac blessed Jacob and Esau in regard to their **future**.
    13:14 an enduring city, but we are looking for the city that *is* **to come**.
Jas 2:12 and act as *those who are* **going to** be judged by the law that gives
1Pe 5: 1 and one who also will share in the glory **to be** revealed:
2Pe 1:12 So *I* **will** always remind you of these things, even though you
     2: 6 and made them an example *of what is* **going to happen to** the
Rev 1:19 what you have seen, what is now and what **will** take place later.
     2:10 Do not be afraid of what you *are* **about to** suffer. I tell you,
     2:10 I tell you, the devil **will** put some of you in prison to test you,
     3: 2 Strengthen what remains and *is* **about to** die, for I have not found
     3:10 I will also keep you from the hour of trial that *is* **going to** come
     3:16 neither hot nor cold—*I am* **about to** spit you out of my mouth.
     6:11 and brothers who *were* **to be** killed as they had been was
     8:13 because of the trumpet blasts **about to** be sounded by the other
    10: 4 And when the seven thunders spoke, *I was* **about to** write;
    10: 7 But in the days when the seventh angel *is* **about to** sound his
    12: 4 The dragon stood in front of the woman who *was* **about to** give
    12: 5 a male child, who **will** rule all the nations with an iron scepter.
    17: 8 and **will** come up out of the Abyss and go to his destruction.

3517 μέλος, **melos**   [34]

members [7], part [6], parts [6], parts of body [3], part of body
[2], bodies [1], each one$ [1], member [*+2848+3836*] [1],
members of body [1], nature [1], part of the body [1], parts of the
body [1], them$ [*+3836+5148*] [1], unite [*+4472*] [1], within
[*+1877+3836*] [1]

Mt 5:29 It is better for you to lose one **part of** your **body** than for your
     5:30 It is better for you to lose one **part of** your **body** than for your
Ro 6:13 Do not offer the **parts of** your **body** to sin, as instruments of
     6:13 and offer the **parts of** your **body** to him as instruments of
     6:19 Just as you used to offer the **parts of** your **body** in slavery to
     6:19 so now offer **them**$ [*+3836+5148*] in slavery to righteousness
     7: 5 the sinful passions aroused by the law were at work in our **bodies**,
     7:23 but I see another law at work in the **members of** my **body**,

7:23   me a prisoner of the law of sin at work within my **members**.
12: 4   Just as each of us has one body with many **members**, and these
12: 4   and these **members** do not all have the same function,
12: 5   and each **member** [+2848+3836] belongs to all the others.
1Co   6:15   Do you not know that your bodies are **members** of Christ himself?
6:15   Shall I then take the **members** of Christ and unite them with a
6:15   *Shall I* then take the members of Christ and **unite** [+4472] them
12:12   The body is a unit, though it is made up of many **parts**; and though
12:12   many parts; and though all its **parts** are many, they form one body.
12:14   Now the body is not made up of one **part** but of many.
12:18   But in fact God has arranged the **parts** in the body, every one of
12:19   If they were all one **part**, where would the body be?
12:20   As it is, there are many **parts**, but one body.
12:22   those **parts** of the body that seem to be weaker are indispensable,
12:25   but that its **parts** should have equal concern for each other.
12:26   If one **part** suffers, every part suffers with it; if one part is
12:26   If one part suffers, every **part** suffers with it; if one part is
12:26   suffers with it; if one **part** is honored, every part rejoices with it.
12:26   suffers with it; if one part is honored, every **part** rejoices with it.
12:27   you are the body of Christ, and **each one**s of you is a part of it.
Eph   4:25   truthfully to his neighbor, for we are all **members** of one body.
5:30   for we are **members** of his body.
Col   3: 5   Put to death, therefore, whatever *belongs to* your earthly **nature**:
Jas   3: 5   Likewise the tongue is a small **part of the body**, but it makes great
3: 6   tongue also is a fire, a world of evil among the **parts of the body**.
4: 1   they come from your desires that battle **within** [+1877+3836] you?

3518 Μελχί, *Melchi* [2]

Melki [2]

Lk   3:24   the son of Levi, the son of **Melki**, the son of Jannai, the son of
3:28   the son of **Melki**, the son of Addi, the son of Cosam, the son of

3519 Μελχισέδεκ, *Melchisedek* [8]

Melchizedek [8]

Heb   5: 6   "You are a priest forever, in the order of **Melchizedek**."
5:10   designated by God to be high priest in the order of **Melchizedek**.
6:20   He has become a high priest forever, in the order of **Melchizedek**.
7: 1   This **Melchizedek** was king of Salem and priest of God Most
7:10   because when **Melchizedek** met Abraham, Levi was still in the
7:11   one in the order of **Melchizedek**, not in the order of Aaron?
7:15   said is even more clear if another priest like **Melchizedek** appears,
7:17   is declared: "You are a priest forever, in the order of **Melchizedek**."

3520 μέλω, *melō*   Not used in UBS/NIV [√ 3508]

3521 μεμβράνα, *membrana* [1]

parchments [1]

2Ti   4:13   with Carpus at Troas, and my scrolls, especially the **parchments**.

3522 μέμφομαι, *memphomai* [2] [→ 289, 290, 318, 320, 3523, 3524, 3664, 3699, 3700]

blame [1], found fault with [1]

Ro   9:19   "Then why *does* God still **blame** us? For who resists his will?"
Heb   8: 8   But God **found fault with** the people and said: "The time is

3523 μεμψίμοιρος, *mempsimoiros* [1] [√ 3522]

faultfinders [1]

Jude   1:16   These men are grumblers and **faultfinders**; they follow their own

3524 μέμψις, *mempsis*   Not used in UBS/NIV [√ 3522]

3525 μέν, *men* [179 / 178] [→ 3528, 3529, 3530; cf. 3605]

untranslated [115], one [+4005] [8], if [+1623] [7], some [+4005]
[6], some [+3836] [5], some [3], indeed [2], though [2], to be sure
[2], as far as [1], certainly [1], even though [+1142] [1], fine [1],

for [+1142] [1], he [+3836] [1], in the one case [+6045] [1],
inasmuch as [+2093+4012+4036] [1], latter [1], moreover
[+1663] [1], now [1], one [+3836] [1], one kind [+257] [1], others
[+3836] [1], our fathers [+3836] [1], Paul [+3836] [1], Peter and
John [+3836] [1], some [+5516] [1], sometimes [+4047] [1], son
[+3836] [1], the apostles [+3836] [1], the men [+3836] [1], the
one [+4005] [1], then [1], they [+3836] [1], those [+4005] [1],
whatever [+4012] [1], who [+4005] [1]

Mt   3:11   [NIE] "I baptize you with water for repentance. But after me will
9:37   [NIE] "The harvest is plentiful but the workers are few.
10:13   [NIE] If the home is deserving, let your peace rest on it; if it is
13: 4   **some** [+4005] fell along the path, and the birds came and ate it up.
13: 8   a crop—[RPG] a hundred, sixty or thirty times what was sown.
13:23   yielding [RPG] a hundred, sixty or thirty times what was sown."
13:32   **Though** it is the smallest of all your seeds, yet when it grows,
16: 3   [NIE] You know how to interpret the appearance of the sky,
16:14   They replied, "**Some** [+3836] say John the Baptist; others say
17:11   "**To be sure**, Elijah comes and will restore all things.
20:23   Jesus said to them, "You will **indeed** drink from my cup, but to sit
21:35   tenants seized his servants; they beat **one** [+4005], killed another,
22: 5   and went off—**one** [+4005] to his field, another to his business.
22: 8   he said to his servants, 'The [NIE] wedding banquet is ready,
23:27   which [NIE] look beautiful on the outside but on the inside are
23:28   [NIE] on the outside you appear to people as righteous but on the
25:15   *To* one [+4005] he gave five talents of money, to another two
25:33   He will put [NIE] the sheep on his right and the goats on his left.
26:24   [NIE] The Son of Man will go just as it is written about him.
26:41   into temptation. [NIE] The spirit is willing, but the body is weak."
Mk   4: 4   **some** [+4005] fell along the path, and the birds came and ate it up.
9:12   Jesus replied, "**To be sure**, Elijah does come first, and restores all
12: 5   many others; **some** [+4005] of them they beat, others they killed.
14:21   The [NIE] Son of Man will go just as it is written about him.
14:38   into temptation. [NIE] The spirit is willing, but the body is weak."
16:19   [NIE] After the Lord Jesus had spoken to them, he was taken up
Lk   3:16   John answered them all, [NIE] "I baptize you with water.
3:18   [NIE] And with many other words John exhorted the people
8: 5   As he was scattering the seed, **some** [+4005] fell along the path;
10: 2   He told them, [NIE] "The harvest is plentiful, but the workers are
11:48   [NIE] they killed the prophets, and you build their tombs.
13: 9   If it bears fruit next year, **fine**! If not, then cut it down.' "
22:22   [NIE] The Son of Man will go as it has been decreed, but woe to
23:33   with the criminals—**one** [+4005] on his right, the other on his left.
23:41   [NIE] We are punished justly, for we are getting what our deeds
23:56   But [NIE] they rested on the Sabbath in obedience to the
Jn   7:12   **Some** [+3836] said, "He is a good man." Others replied, "No,
10:41   They said, "**Though** John never performed a miraculous sign,
11: 6   Lazarus was sick, [NIE] he stayed where he was two more days.
16: 9   [NIE] in regard to sin, because men do not believe in me;
16:22   [NIE] Now is your time of grief, but I will see you again
19:24   cast lots for my clothing." [NIE] So this is what the soldiers did.
19:32   and broke [NIE] the legs of the first man who had been crucified
20:30   [NIE] Jesus did many other miraculous signs in the presence of
Ac   1: 1   [NIE] In my former book, Theophilus, I wrote about all that Jesus
1: 5   For [NIE] John baptized with water, but in a few days you will be
1: 6   [NIE] So when they met together, they asked him, "Lord,
1:18   [NIE] (With the reward he got for his wickedness, Judas bought a
2:41   [NIE] Those who accepted his message were baptized, and about
3:13   [UBS+ (*NIE*)] You handed him over to be killed, and you
3:21   He must [NIE] remain in heaven until the time comes for God to
3:22   [NIE] For Moses said, 'The Lord your God will raise up for you a
4:16   "Everybody living in Jerusalem knows they have done an
5:41   The apostles [+3836] left the Sanhedrin, rejoicing because they
8: 4   [NIE] Those who had been scattered preached the word wherever
8:25   word of the Lord, Peters and John [+3836] returned to Jerusalem,
9: 7   [NIE] they heard the sound but did not see anyone.
9:31   [NIE] Then the church throughout Judea, Galilee and Samaria
11:16   [NIE] 'John baptized with water, but you will be baptized with
11:19   [NIE] Now those who had been scattered by the persecution in
12: 5   So [NIE] Peter was kept in prison, but the church was earnestly
13: 4   [NIE] The two of them, sent on their way by the Holy Spirit,
13:36   "For [+1142] when David had served God's purpose in his own
14: 3   [NIE] So Paul and Barnabas spent considerable time there,
14: 4   **some** [+3836] sided with the Jews, others with the apostles.
15: 3   and as **they** [+3836] traveled through Phoenicia and Samaria,
15:30   The men s [+3836] were sent off and went down to Antioch,

16: 5 [NIE] So the churches were strengthened in the faith and grew
17:12 [NIE] Many of the Jews believed, as did also a number of
17:17 [NIE] So he reasoned in the synagogue with the Jews
17:30 [NIE] In the past God overlooked such ignorance, but now he
17:32 **some** [+3836] of them sneered, but others said, "We want to hear
18:14 "**If** [+1623] you Jews were making a complaint about some
19:15 [NIE] "Jesus I know, and I know about Paul, but who are you?"
19:32 was in confusion: **Some** were shouting one thing, some another.
19:38 **If** [+1623], then, Demetrius and his fellow craftsmen have a
21:39 Paul answered, "I [NIE] am a Jew, from Tarsus in Cilicia,
22: 9 My companions [NIE] saw the light, but they did not understand
23: 8 [NIE] (The Sadducees say that there is no resurrection, and that
23:18 So **he** [+3836] took him to the commander. The centurion said,
23:22 [NIE] The commander dismissed the young man and cautioned
23:31 [NIE] So the soldiers, carrying out their orders, took Paul with
25: 4 [NIE] Festus answered, "Paul is being held at Caesarea, and I
25:11 **If** [+1623], however, I am guilty of doing anything deserving
26: 4 [NIE] "The Jews all know the way I have lived ever since I was a
26: 9 [NIE] "I too was convinced that I ought to do all that was possible
27:21 [NIE] "Men, you should have taken my advice not to sail from
27:41 and ran aground. [NIE] The bow stuck fast and would not move,
27:44 The rest [NIE] were to get there on planks or on pieces of the
28: 5 But **Paul**ˢ [+3836] shook the snake off into the fire and suffered
28:22 for we know that people everywhere are talking against [NIE]
28:24 **Some** [+3836] were convinced by what he said, but others would
Ro 1: 8 [NIE] I thank my God through Jesus Christ for all of you,
2: 7 [NIE] To those who by persistence in doing good seek glory,
2:25 [NIE] Circumcision has value if you observe the law, but if you
3: 2 [NIE] First of all, they have been entrusted with the very words of
5:16 [NIE] The judgment followed one sin and brought condemnation,
6:11 count yourselves [NIE] dead to sin but alive to God in Christ
7:12 So **then**, the law is holy, and the commandment is holy, righteous
7:25 So then, I myself [NIE] in my mind am a slave to God's law,
8:10 [NIE] your body is dead because of sin, yet your spirit is alive
8:17 [NIE] heirs of God and co-heirs with Christ, if indeed we share in
9:21 of the same lump of clay **some** [+4005] pottery for noble purposes
10: 1 [NIE] my heart's desire and prayer to God for the Israelites is that
11:13 **Inasmuch as** [+2093+4012+4036] I am the apostle to the Gentiles,
11:22 [NIE] sternness to those who fell, but kindness to you,
11:28 **As far as** the gospel is concerned, they are enemies on your
14: 2 **One man's** [+4005] faith allows him to eat everything, but another
14: 5 **One man** [+4005] considers one day more sacred than another;
14:20 [NIE] All food is clean, but it is wrong for a man to eat anything
1Co 1:12 of you says, [NIE] "I follow Paul"; another, "I follow Apollos";
1:18 For the message of the cross [NIE] is foolishness to those who are
1:23 [NIE] a stumbling block to Jews and foolishness to Gentiles,
3: 4 one says, [NIE] "I follow Paul," and another, "I follow Apollos,"
5: 3 **Even though** [+1142] I am not physically present, I am with you
6: 4 [NIE] Therefore, if you have disputes about such matters,
6: 7 [NIE] The very fact that you have lawsuits among you means you
7: 7 his own gift from God; **one** [+3836] has this gift, another has that.
9:24 Do you not know that in a race [NIE] all the runners run,
9:25 [NIE] They do it to get a crown that will not last; but we do it to
11: 7 [NIE] A man ought not to cover his head, since he is the image
11:14 Does not the very nature of things teach you that [NIE] if a man
11:18 [NIE] In the first place, I hear that when you come together as a
11:21 anybody else. **One** [+4005] remains hungry, another gets drunk.
12: 8 *To* **one** [+4005] there is given through the Spirit the message of
12:20 As it is, [NIE] there are many parts, but one body.
12:28 And [NIE] in the church God has appointed first of all apostles,
14:17 [NIE] You may be giving thanks well enough, but the other man
15:39 Men have **one kind** [+257] of flesh, animals have another,
15:40 but [NIE] the splendor of the heavenly bodies is one kind,
2Co 2:16 *To* **the one** [+4005] we are the smell of death; to the other,
8:17 For [NIE] Titus not only welcomed our appeal, but he is coming
9: 1 [NIE] There is no need for me to write to you about this service
10: 1 I, Paul, **who** [+4005] am "timid" when face to face with you,
10:10 For **some** say, "His letters are weighty and forceful, but in person he
11: 4 For **if** [+1623] someone comes to you and preaches a Jesus other
12: 1 [NIE] Although there is nothing to be gained, I will go on to
12:12 [NIE] The things that mark an apostle—signs, wonders
Gal 4: 8 [NIE] Formerly, when you did not know God, you were slaves to
4:23 His **son**ˢ [+3836] by the slave woman was born in the ordinary
4:24 [NIE] One covenant is from Mount Sinai and bears children who
Eph 4:11 It was he who gave **some** to be apostles, some to be prophets,
Php 1:15 It is true that **some** [+5516] preach Christ out of envy and rivalry,

1:16 The **latter** do so in love, knowing that I am put here for the defense
2:23 [NIE] I hope, therefore, to send him as soon as I see how things
3: 1 It is no trouble for me to write [NIE] the same things to you
3:13 Forgetting what is [NIE] behind and straining toward what is
Col 2:23 Such regulations **indeed** have an appearance of wisdom, with their
1Th 2:18 **certainly** I, Paul, did, again and again—but Satan stopped us.
2Ti 1:10 who has destroyed [NIE] death and has brought life
2:20 but also of wood and clay; **some** [+4005] are for noble purposes
4: 4 They will turn their ears away from [NIE] the truth and turn aside
Heb 1: 7 In speaking [NIE] of the angels he says, "He makes his angels
3: 5 [NIE] Moses was faithful as a servant in all God's house,
7: 2 of everything. [NIE] First, his name means "king of righteousness";
7: 5 [NIE] Now the law requires the descendants of Levi who become
7: 8 **In the one case** [+6045], the tenth is collected by men who die;
7:11 **If** [+1623] perfection could have been attained through the
7:18 [NIE] The former regulation is set aside because it was weak
7:20 without an oath! **Others** [+3836] became priests without any oath,
7:23 **Now** there have been many of those priests, since death prevented
8: 4 **If** [+1623] he were on earth, he would not be a priest, for there are
9: 1 [NIE] Now the first covenant had regulations for worship
9: 6 the priests entered regularly into [NIE] the outer room to carry on
9:23 [NIE] for the copies of the heavenly things to be purified with
10:11 Day after day [NIE] every priest stands and performs his religious
10:33 **Sometimes** [+4047] you were publicly exposed to insult
11:15 **If** [+1623] they had been thinking of the country they had left,
12: 9 **Moreover** [+1663], we have all had human fathers who disciplined
12:10 **Our fathers**ˢ [+3836] disciplined us for a little while as they
12:11 No discipline seems pleasant [NIE] at the time, but painful.
Jas 3:17 But the wisdom that comes from heaven is [NIE] first of all pure;
1Pe 1:20 [NIE] He was chosen before the creation of the world, but was
2: 4 [NIE] rejected by men but chosen by God and precious to him—
3:18 [NIE] He was put to death in the body but made alive by the
4: 6 so that [NIE] they might be judged according to men in regard to
Jude 1: 8 these dreamers [NIE] pollute their own bodies, reject authority
1:10 Yet these men speak abusively against **whatever** [+4012] they do
1:22 Be merciful to **those** [+4005] who doubt;

3526 Μενάμ, *Menam*   Not used in UBS/NIV

3527 Μεννά, *Menna*   [1]   [√ *cf. 3418*]

Menna [1]

Lk 3:31 the son of Melea, the son *of* **Menna**, the son of Mattatha, the son

3528 μενοῦν, *menoun*   [1]   [√ 3525 + 4036]

rather [1]

Lk 11:28 "Blessed **rather** are those who hear the word of God and obey it."

3529 μενοῦνγε, *menounge*   [3]   [√ 3525 + 4036 + 1145]

but [1], of course [1], what is more [+247+2779] [1]

Ro 9:20 **But** who are you, O man, to talk back to God? "Shall what is
10:18 But I ask: Did they not hear? **Of course** they did: "Their voice has
Php 3: 8 **What is more** [+247+2779], I consider everything a loss compared

3530 μέντοι, *mentoi*   [8]   [√ 3525 + 5520]

but [4], nevertheless [1], really [1], very [1], yet [1]

Jn 4:27 **But** no one asked, "What do you want?" or "Why are you talking
7:13 **But** no one would say anything publicly about him for fear of the
12:42 **Yet** at the same time many even among the leaders believed in
20: 5 and looked in at the strips of linen lying there **but** did not go in.
21: 4 on the shore, **but** the disciples did not realize that it was Jesus.
2Ti 2:19 **Nevertheless**, God's solid foundation stands firm, sealed with this
Jas 2: 8 If you **really** keep the royal law found in Scripture, "Love your
Jude 1: 8 In the **very** same way, these dreamers pollute their own bodies,

3531 μένω, menō [118] [→ *388, 670, 1373, 1844, 2152, 2910, 3665, 4169, 4338, 4693, 5222, 5702, 5705*]

remain [24], stay [14], lives [12], remains [11], stayed [11], continue [4], live [4], *untranslated* [3], endures [2], enduring [2], living [2], remained [2], staying [2], be [1], belong [1], belongs [1], continues [1], does^s [*+1877+5148*] [1], dwell [*+2400*] [1], facing [1], hold [1], keep on [1], last [1], lasting [1], lasts [1], left [1], lived [1], not move [*+810*] [1], permanent place [1], spend time [*+2093+5989*] [1], spent [1], stand [1], stands [1], stayed [*+1695*] [1], stays [1], still [1], survives [1], waited for [1]

Mt 10:11   some worthy person there and **stay** at his house until you leave.
     11:23   been performed in Sodom, *it* would have **remained** to this day.
     26:38   sorrow to the point of death. **Stay** here and keep watch with me."
Mk   6:10   Whenever you enter a house, **stay** there until you leave that town.
     14:34   to the point of death," he said to them. "**Stay** here and keep watch."
Lk   1:56   Mary **stayed** with Elizabeth for about three months and
     8:27   For a long time this man had not worn clothes or **lived** in a house,
     9: 4   Whatever house you enter, **stay** there until you leave that town.
     10: 7   **Stay** in that house, eating and drinking whatever they give you,
     19: 5   come down immediately. I must **stay** at your house today."
     24:29   they urged him strongly, "**Stay** with us, for it is nearly evening;
     24:29   the day is almost over." So he went in to **stay** with them.
Jn   1:32   the Spirit come down from heaven as a dove and **remain** on him.
     1:33   and **remain** is he who will baptize with the Holy Spirit.'
     1:38   said, "Rabbi" (which means Teacher), "where *are you* **staying**?"
     1:39   So they went and saw where *he was* **staying**, and spent that day
     1:39   and saw where he was staying, and **spent** that day with him.
     2:12   and brothers and his disciples. There *they* **stayed** for a few days.
     3:36   rejects the Son will not see life, for God's wrath **remains** on him."
     4:40   they urged him *to* **stay** with them, and he stayed two days.
     4:40   they urged him to stay with them, and he **stayed** [*+1695*] two days.
     5:38   nor *does* his word **dwell** [*+2400*] in you, for you do not believe the
     6:27   work for food that spoils, but for food that **endures** to eternal life,
     6:56   Whoever eats my flesh and drinks my blood **remains** in me,
     7: 9   Having said this, he **stayed** in Galilee.
     8:31   Jesus said, "If you **hold** to my teaching, you are really my disciples.
     8:35   Now a slave *has* no **permanent place** in the family,
     8:35   no permanent place in the family, but a son **belongs** to it forever.
     9:41   of sin; but now that you claim you can see, your guilt **remains**.
     10:40   where John had been baptizing in the early days. Here *he* **stayed**
     11: 6   that Lazarus was sick, *he* **stayed** where he was two more days.
     11:54   to a village called Ephraim, where *he* **stayed** with his disciples.
     12:24   of wheat falls to the ground and dies, *it* **remains** only a single seed.
     12:34   "We have heard from the Law that the Christ *will* **remain** forever,
     12:46   so that no one who believes in me *should* **stay** in darkness.
     14:10   Rather, it is the Father, **living** in me, who is doing his work.
     14:17   But you know him, for *he* **lives** with you and will be in you.
     14:25   "All this I have spoken *while* **still** with you.
     15: 4   **Remain** in me, and I will remain in you. No branch can bear fruit
     15: 4   No branch can bear fruit by itself; *it must* **remain** in the vine.
     15: 4   in the vine. Neither can you bear fruit unless *you* **remain** in me.
     15: 5   *If* a man **remains** in me and I in him, he will bear much fruit;
     15: 6   If anyone *does* not **remain** in me, he is like a branch that is thrown
     15: 7   If *you* **remain** in me and my words remain in you, ask whatever
     15: 7   If you remain in me and my words **remain** in you, ask whatever
     15: 9   Father has loved me, so have I loved you. *Now* **remain** in my love.
     15:10   If you obey my commands, *you* **will remain** in my love, just as I
     15:10   as I have obeyed my Father's commands and **remain** in his love.
     15:16   and appointed you to go and bear fruit—fruit that *will* **last**.
     19:31   Because the Jews did not want the bodies **left** on the crosses during
     21:22   Jesus answered, "If I want him *to* **remain** *alive* until I return,
     21:23   he only said, "If I want him *to* **remain** *alive* until I return, what is
Ac   5: 4   Didn't *it* **belong** to you before it was sold? And after it was sold,
     5: 4   Didn't it belong to you **[RPG]** before it was sold? And after it
     9:43   Peter **stayed** in Joppa for some time with a tanner named Simon.
     16:15   me a believer in the Lord," she said, "come and **stay** at my house."
     18: 3   he was a tentmaker as they were, *he* **stayed** and worked with them.
     18:20   When they asked him *to* **spend** more *time* [*+2093+5989*] with
     20: 5   These men went on ahead and **waited for** us at Troas.
     20:23   the Holy Spirit warns me that prison and hardships *are* **facing** me.
     21: 7   where we greeted the brothers and **stayed** with them for a day.
     21: 8   reached Caesarea and **stayed** at the house of Philip the evangelist,
     27:31   centurion and the soldiers, "Unless these men **stay** with the ship,
     27:41   and ran aground. The bow stuck fast and *would* **not move** [*+810*],

     28:16   When we got to Rome, Paul was allowed *to* **live** by himself,
Ro   9:11   or bad—in order that God's purpose in election *might* **stand**:
1Co 3:14   If what he has built **survives**, he will receive his reward.
     7: 8   the widows I say: It is good for them *to* **stay** unmarried, as I am.
     7:11   *she must* **remain** unmarried or else be reconciled to her husband.
     7:20   Each one *should* **remain** in the situation which he was in when
     7:24   to God, *should* **remain** in the situation God called him to.
     7:40   In my judgment, she is happier if *she* **stays** as she is—and I think
     13:13   And now these three **remain**: faith, hope and love. But the greatest
     15: 6   most of whom *are* still **living**, though some have fallen asleep.
2Co 3:11   came with glory, how much greater is the glory of that which **lasts**!
     3:14   for to this day the same veil **remains** when the old covenant is
     9: 9   abroad his gifts to the poor; his righteousness **endures** forever."
Php 1:25   Convinced of this, I know that *I will* **remain**, and I will continue
1Ti 2:15   if *they* **continue** in faith, love and holiness with propriety.
2Ti 2:13   if we are faithless, he *will* **remain** faithful, for he cannot disown
     3:14   **continue** in what you have learned and have become convinced of,
     4:20   Erastus **stayed** in Corinth, and I left Trophimus sick in Miletus.
Heb 7: 3   or end of life, like the Son of God *he* **remains** a priest forever.
     7:24   but because Jesus **lives** forever, he has a permanent priesthood.
     10:34   you knew that you yourselves had better and **lasting** possessions.
     12:27   created things—so that what cannot be shaken *may* **remain**.
     13: 1   **Keep on** loving each other as brothers.
     13:14   For here we do not have an **enduring** city, but we are looking for
1Pe 1:23   but of imperishable, through the living and **enduring** word of God.
     1:25   but the word of the Lord **stands** forever." And this is the word that
1Jn 2: 6   Whoever claims *to* **live** in him must walk as Jesus did.
     2:10   Whoever loves his brother **lives** in the light, and there is nothing in
     2:14   because you are strong, and the word of God **lives** in you,
     2:17   pass away, but the man who does the will of God **lives** forever.
     2:19   For if they had belonged to us, *they* would have **remained** with us;
     2:24   *See that* what you have heard from the beginning **remains** in you.
     2:24   If it **does**^{s} [*+1877+5148*], you also will remain in the Son
     2:24   If it does, you also *will* **remain** in the Son and in the Father.
     2:27   As for you, the anointing you received from him **remains** in you,
     2:27   is real, not counterfeit—just as it has taught you, **remain** in him.
     2:28   And now, dear children, **continue** in him, so that when he appears
     3: 6   No one who **lives** in him keeps on sinning. No one who continues
     3: 9   of God will continue to sin, because God's seed **remains** in him;
     3:14   we love our brothers. Anyone who does not love **remains** in death.
     3:15   and you know that no murderer has eternal life **[RPG]** in him.
     3:17   but has no pity on him, how *can* the love of God **be** in him?
     3:24   Those who obey his commands **live** in him, and he in them.
     3:24   and he in them. And this is how we know that *he* **lives** in us:
     4:12   one another, God **lives** in us and his love is made complete in us.
     4:13   We know that *we* **live** in him and he in us, because he has given us
     4:15   that Jesus is the Son of God, God **lives** in him and he in God.
     4:16   God is love. Whoever **lives** in love lives in God, and God in him.
     4:16   God is love. Whoever lives in love **lives** in God, and God in him.
     4:16   Whoever lives in love lives in God, and God in him. **[RPG]**
2Jn 1: 2   because of the truth, which **lives** in us and will be with us forever:
     1: 9   and *does* not **continue** in the teaching of Christ does not have God;
     1: 9   whoever **continues** in the teaching has both the Father and the Son.
Rev 17:10   but when he does come, he must **remain** for a little while.

3532 μερίζω, merizō [14] [√ *3538*]

divided [9], assigned [2], divide [1], gave [1], given [1]

Mt 12:25   "Every kingdom **divided** against itself will be ruined, and every
     12:25   and every city or household **divided** against itself will not stand.
     12:26   If Satan drives out Satan, *he is* **divided** against himself. How
Mk 3:24   If a kingdom *is* **divided** against itself, that kingdom cannot stand.
     3:25   If a house *is* **divided** against itself, that house cannot stand.
     3:26   And if Satan opposes himself and *is* **divided**, he cannot stand;
     6:41   set before the people. *He* also **divided** the two fish among them all.
Lk 12:13   "Teacher, tell my brother *to* **divide** the inheritance with me."
Ro 12: 3   in accordance with the measure of faith God *has* **given** you.
1Co 1:13   *Is* Christ **divided**? Was Paul crucified for you? Were you baptized
     7:17   each one should retain the place in life that the Lord **assigned** to
     7:34   and his *interests are* **divided**. An unmarried woman or virgin is
2Co 10:13   but will confine our boasting to the field God *has* **assigned** to us,
Heb 7: 2   and Abraham **gave** him a tenth of everything. First, his name

3533 μέριμνα, merimna [6] [→ 291, 3534, 4628; cf. 3538]

worries [3], anxieties [1], anxiety [1], concern [1]

Mt 13:22 but the **worries** of this life and the deceitfulness of wealth choke it,
Mk   4:19 but the **worries** of this life, the deceitfulness of wealth
Lk   8:14 but as they go on their way they are choked by life's **worries**,
    21:34 down with dissipation, drunkenness and the **anxieties** of life,
2Co 11:28 I face daily the pressure of my **concern** for all the churches.
1Pe   5: 7 Cast all your **anxiety** on him because he cares for you.

3534 μεριμνάω, merimnaō [19] [√ 3533]

worry about [5], concerned about [4], worry [4], worrying [2], anxious about [1], have concern [1], takes interest [1], worried [1]

Mt   6:25 tell you, *do* not **worry about** your life, what you will eat or drink;
    6:27 Who of you *by* **worrying** can add a single hour to his life?
    6:28 "And why *do you* **worry** about clothes? See how the lilies of the
    6:31 So *do* not **worry**, saying, 'What shall we eat?' or 'What shall we
    6:34 Therefore *do* not **worry** about tomorrow, for tomorrow will worry
    6:34 not worry about tomorrow, for tomorrow *will* **worry about** itself.
  10:19 they arrest you, *do* not **worry about** what to say or how to say it.
Lk 10:41 Lord answered, "*you are* **worried** and upset about many things,
  12:11 *do* not **worry about** how you will defend yourselves or what you
  12:22 I tell you, *do* not **worry about** your life, what you will eat;
  12:25 Who of you *by* **worrying** can add a single hour to his life?
  12:26 cannot do this very little thing, why *do you* **worry** about the rest?
1Co 7:32 An unmarried man *is* **concerned about** the Lord's affairs—
    7:33 But a married man *is* **concerned about** the affairs of this world—
    7:34 unmarried woman or virgin *is* **concerned about** the Lord's affairs:
    7:34 But a married woman *is* **concerned about** the affairs of this
  12:25 but that its parts *should* **have** equal **concern** for each other.
Php 2:20 no one else like him, who **takes** a genuine **interest** *in* your welfare.
    4: 6 *Do* not *be* **anxious about** anything, but in everything, by prayer

3535 μερίς, meris [5] [√ 3538]

district [1], in common [1], part [1], share [1], what[s] [1]

Lk 10:42 Mary has chosen **what**[s] is better, and it will not be taken away
Ac   8:21 You have no **part** or share in this ministry, because your heart is
  16:12 a Roman colony and the leading city *of* that **district** of Macedonia.
2Co 6:15 What does a believer have **in common** with an unbeliever?
Col   1:12 who has qualified you to **share** in the inheritance of the saints in

3536 μερισμός, merismos [2] [√ 3538]

dividing [1], gifts distributed [1]

Heb 2: 4 and **gifts** of the Holy Spirit **distributed** according to his will.
    4:12 it penetrates even to **dividing** soul and spirit, joints and marrow;

3537 μεριστής, meristēs [1] [√ 3538]

arbiter [1]

Lk 12:14 "Man, who appointed me a judge or an **arbiter** between you?"

3538 μέρος, meros [42] [→ 1374, 1375, 3532, 3535, 3536, 3537, 4495, 5211; cf. 3533]

part [8], place [3], region [3], in part [+608] [2], parts [2], *untranslated* [1], area [1], detail [1], district [1], dividing into shares [+4472] [1], extent [1], imperfect [+1666] [1], in comparison with [+1641+1877+3836+4047] [1], interior [+541] [1], matter [1], one at a time [+324] [1], one[s] [1], piece [1], points [1], regions [1], share [+2095] [1], share [1], side [1], some [+1651+3836] [1], the rest [+5516] [1], to some extent [+247+608] [1], trade [1], while [1], with regard to [+1877] [1]

Mt   2:22 been warned in a dream, he withdrew to the **district** of Galilee,
  15:21 that place, Jesus withdrew to the **region** of Tyre and Sidon.
  16:13 When Jesus came to the **region** of Caesarea Philippi, he asked his
  24:51 will cut him to pieces and assign him a **place** with the hypocrites,
Mk   8:10 the boat with his disciples and went to the **region** of Dalmanutha
Lk 11:36 is full of light, and no **part** of it dark, it will be completely lighted,

  12:46 will cut him to pieces and assign him a **place** with the unbelievers.
  15:12 said to his father, 'Father, give me my **share** [+2095] of the estate.'
  24:42 They gave him a **piece** of broiled fish,
Jn 13: 8 Jesus answered, "Unless I wash you, you have no **part** with me."
  19:23 they took his clothes, **dividing** them **into** four **shares** [+4472],
  19:23 his clothes, dividing them into four shares, one[s] for each of them,
  21: 6 "Throw your net on the right **side** of the boat and you will find
Ac   2:10 and Pamphylia, Egypt and the **parts** of Libya near Cyrene;
    5: 2 but brought the **rest** [+5516] and put it at the apostles' feet.
  19: 1 Paul took the road through the **interior** [+541] and arrived at
  19:27 There is danger not only that our **trade** will lose its good name,
  20: 2 He traveled through that **area**, speaking many words of
  23: 6 knowing that **some** [+1651+3836] of them were Sadducees
  23: 9 and some of the teachers of the law **[NIE]** who were Pharisees
Ro 11:25 Israel has experienced a hardening **in part** [+608] until the full
  15:15 I have written you quite boldly *on* some **points**, as if to remind you
  15:24 my journey there, after I have enjoyed your company for a **while**.
1Co 11:18 there are divisions among you, and to some **extent** I believe it.
  12:27 you are the body of Christ, and each one of you is a **part** of it.
  13: 9 For we know in **part** and we prophesy in part,
  13: 9 For we know in part and we prophesy in **part**,
  13:10 but when perfection comes, the **imperfect** [+1666] disappears.
  13:12 Now I know in **part**; then I shall know fully, even as I am fully
  14:27 should speak, **one** [+324] **at a time**, and someone must interpret.
2Co 1:14 as you have understood us **in part** [+608], you will come to
    2: 5 me as he has grieved all of you, **to some** [+247+608] **extent**—
    3:10 has no glory now **in comparison** [+1641+1877+3836+4047] **with**
    9: 3 our boasting about you in this **matter** should not prove hollow,
Eph 4: 9 mean except that he also descended to the lower, earthly **regions**?
    4:16 grows and builds itself up in love, as each **part** does its work.
Col   2:16 you eat or drink, or **with regard** [+1877] **to** a religious festival,
Heb 9: 5 atonement cover. But we cannot discuss these things in **detail** now.
Rev 16:19 The great city split into three **parts**, and the cities of the nations
  20: 6 and holy are those who have **part** in the first resurrection.
  21: 8 and all liars—their **place** will be in the fiery lake of burning sulfur.
  22:19 God will take away from him his **share** in the tree of life and in the

3539 μεσάζω, mesazō Not used in UBS/NIV [√ 3545]

3540 μεσημβρία, mesēmbria [2] [√ 3545 + 2465]

noon [1], south [1]

Ac   8:26 Now an angel of the Lord said to Philip, "Go **south** to the road—
  22: 6 "About **noon** as I came near Damascus, suddenly a bright light from

3541 μεσιτεύω, mesiteuō [1] [√ 3545]

confirmed [1]

Heb 6:17 to the heirs of what was promised, *he* **confirmed** it with an oath.

3542 μεσίτης, mesitēs [6] [√ 3545]

mediator [5], mediator between [1]

Gal 3:19 The law was put into effect through angels by a **mediator**.
    3:20 A **mediator**, however, does not represent just one party; but God is
1Ti   2: 5 For there is one God and one **mediator between** God and men,
Heb 8: 6 as the covenant *of* which he is **mediator** is superior to the old one,
    9:15 For this reason Christ is the **mediator** of a new covenant,
  12:24 to Jesus the **mediator** of a new covenant, and to the sprinkled

3543 μεσονύκτιον, mesonyktion [4] [√ 3545 + 3816]

midnight [3], at midnight [1]

Mk 13:35 whether in the evening, or **at midnight**, or when the rooster crows,
Lk 11: 5 and he goes to him *at* **midnight** and says, 'Friend, lend me three
Ac 16:25 About **midnight** Paul and Silas were praying and singing hymns to
  20: 7 he intended to leave the next day, kept on talking until **midnight**.

3544 Μεσοποταμία, *Mesopotamia* [2]

[√ 3545 + 4532]

Mesopotamia [2]

Ac   2: 9 residents of **Mesopotamia**, Judea and Cappadocia, Pontus
       7: 2 to our father Abraham while he was still in **Mesopotamia**,

3545 μέσος, *mesos* [58] [→ 1845, 3539, 3540, 3541, 3542, 3543, 3544, 3546, 3547, 3548]

among [+1877] [14], middle [5], center [3], among [+1650+3836] [2], front of everyone [+3836] [2], in [+1877] [2], untranslated [1], about noon [+2465] [1], among [+324] [1], among [1], at midnight [+3816] [1], away [+1666+3836] [1], away from [+1666] [1], before [+1650+3836] [1], before [+1877+3836] [1], before [+1877] [1], before the group [+1877] [1], before them [+1650] [1], between [+324] [1], between [1], encircleds by [+1877] [1], fellowship [1], for [+1877+3836] [1], from [+1666] [1], from [1], in two [1], in [1], into [+324] [1], midnight [+3816+3836] [1], open [1], presence [1], there [+1877] [1], walked right through [+1328+1451] [1], way [1], with [+1877] [1], with [1]

Mt 10:16 I am sending you out like sheep **among** [+1877] wolves.
      13:25 his enemy came and sowed weeds **among** [+324] the wheat,
      13:49 will come and separate the wicked **from** [+1666] the righteous
      14: 6 birthday the daughter of Herodias danced **for** [+1877+3836] them
      18: 2 He called a little child and had him stand **among** [+1877] them.
      18:20 or three come together in my name, there am I **with** [+1877] them."
      25: 6 "At **midnight** [+3816] the cry rang out: 'Here's the bridegroom!
Mk   3: 3 with the shriveled hand, "Stand up in **front** [+3836] **of everyone**."
       6:47 When evening came, the boat was in the **middle** of the lake,
       7:31 to the Sea of Galilee and **into** [+324] the region of the Decapolis.
       9:36 He took a little child and had him stand **among** [+1877] them.
      14:60 Then the high priest stood up **before them** [+1650] and asked
Lk   2:46 sitting **among** [+1877] the teachers, listening to them and asking
       4:30 But he **walked right through** [+1328+1451] the crowd and went
       4:35 Then the demon threw the man down **before** [+1650+3836] them and
       5:19 and lowered him on his mat through the tiles into the **middle** of the
       6: 8 shriveled hand, "Get up and stand in **front** [+3836] **of everyone**."
       8: 7 Other seed fell **among** [+1877] thorns, which grew up with it
      10: 3 Go! I am sending you out like lambs **among** [+1877] wolves.
      17:11 Jesus traveled along the *border* **between** Samaria and Galilee.
      21:21 let those **in** [+1877] the city get out, and let those in the country not
      22:27 is at the table? But I am **among** [+1877] you as one who serves.
      22:55 But when they had kindled a fire in the **middle** of the courtyard
      22:55 and had sat down together, Peter sat down **with** them.
      23:45 sun stopped shining. And the curtain of the temple was torn **in two**.
      24:36 Jesus himself stood **among** [+1877] them and said to them,
Jn   1:26 John replied, "but **among** you stands one you do not know.
       8: 3 in adultery. They made her stand **before** [+1877] **the group**
       8: 9 only Jesus was left, with the woman still standing **there** [+1877].
      19:18 with him two others—one on each side and Jesus in the **middle**.
      20:19 Jesus came and stood **among** [+1650+3836] them and said,
      20:26 Jesus came and stood **among** [+1650+3836] them and said,
Ac   1:15 In those days Peter stood up **among** [+1877] the believers (a group
       1:18 fell headlong, his body burst **open** and all his intestines spilled out.
       2:22 and signs, which God did **among** [+1877] you through him,
       4: 7 They had Peter and John brought **before** [+1877+3836] them
      17:22 Paul then stood up **in** [+1877] the meeting of the Areopagus
      17:33 At that, Paul left the **[NIE]** Council.
      23:10 and take him **away from** [+1666] them by force and bring him into
      26:13 **About noon** [+2465], O king, as I was on the road, I saw a light
      27:21 time without food, Paul stood up **before** [+1877] them and said:
      27:27 when about **midnight** [+3816+3836] the sailors sensed they were
1Co 5: 2 and have put out of your **fellowship** the man who did this?
       6: 5 you wise enough to judge a dispute **between** [+324] believers?
2Co 6:17 "Therefore come out **from** them and be separate, says the Lord.
Php 2:15 children of God without fault **in** a crooked and depraved
Col 2:14 to us; he took it **away** [+1666+3836], nailing it to the cross.
1Th 2: 7 but we were gentle **among** [+1877] you, like a mother caring for
2Th 2: 7 holds it back will continue to do so till he is taken out of the **way**.
Heb 2:12 in the **presence** of the congregation I will sing your praises."
Rev 1:13 and **among** [+1877] the lampstands was someone "like a son of
       2: 1 right hand and walks **among** [+1877] the seven golden lampstands:
       4: 6 In the **center**, around the throne, were four living creatures,

       5: 6 looking as if it had been slain, standing in the **center** of the throne,
       5: 6 standing in the center of the throne, **encircled**s [+1877] **by** the
       6: 6 Then I heard what sounded like a voice **among** [+1877] the four
       7:17 For the Lamb at the **center** of the throne will be their shepherd;
      22: 2 down the **middle** of the great street of the city. On each side of the

3546 μεσότοιχον, *mesotoichon* [1] [√ 3545 + 5446]

dividing wall [1]

Eph 2:14 and has destroyed the barrier, the **dividing wall** of hostility,

3547 μεσουράνημα, *mesouranēma* [3]

[√ 3545 + 4041]

midair [3]

Rev 8:13 I heard an eagle that was flying in **midair** call out in a loud voice:
      14: 6 Then I saw another angel flying in **midair**, and he had the eternal
      19:17 who cried in a loud voice to all the birds flying in **midair**,

3548 μεσόω, *mesoō* [1] [√ 3545]

halfway through [1]

Jn   7:14 Not until **halfway through** the Feast did Jesus go up to the temple

3549 Μεσσίας, *Messias* [2]

Messiah [2]

Jn   1:41 and tell him, "We have found the **Messiah**" (that is, the Christ)
       4:25 The woman said, "I know that **Messiah**" (called Christ) "is coming.

3550 μεστός, *mestos* [9] [→ 3551]

full [7], untranslated [1], soaked [1]

Mt 23:28 but on the inside you are **full** of hypocrisy and wickedness.
Jn   19:29 of wine vinegar was there, **[RPG]** so they soaked a sponge in it,
      19:29 A jar of wine vinegar was there, so they **soaked** a sponge in it,
      21:11 and dragged the net ashore. It was **full** of large fish, 153,
Ro   1:29 They are **full** of envy, murder, strife, deceit and malice.
      15:14 my brothers, that you yourselves are **full** of goodness, complete in
Jas   3: 8 man can tame the tongue. It is a restless evil, **full** of deadly poison.
       3:17 submissive, **full** of mercy and good fruit, impartial and sincere.
2Pe 2:14 With eyes **full** of adultery, they never stop sinning; they seduce the

3551 μεστόω, *mestoō* [1] [√ 3550]

had too much [+1639] [1]

Ac   2:13 fun of them and said, "*They have* **had too much** [+1639] wine."

3552 μετά, *meta* [469 / 468] [→ 292, 293, 294, 295, 2331, 3493, 3495, 3496, 3497, 3498, 3553, 3554, 3555, 3556, 3557, 3558, 3559, 3560, 3561, 3562, 3563, 3564, 3565, 3566, 3567, 3568, 3569, 3570, 3571, 3572, 3573, 3574, 3575, 3576, 3578, 3579, 3580, 3581, 3587, 5212]

with [263], after [59], untranslated [19], to [11], after [+3836] [9], along with [9], against [8], later [7], among [6], later [+4047] [6], companions [+3836] [5], between [3], in [3], afterward [+4047] [2], away [2], by [2], companions [+1639+3836] [2], joyfully [+5915] [2], on [2], through [2], when [+3836] [2], a week later [+2465+3893] [1], afraid [+5832] [1], afterward [1], along [1], and as well [1], and [1], as dids [1], before very long [+4024+4498] [1], behind [1], boldly [+4244+4246] [1], boldly [+4244] [1], bringing [+1571+2400] [1], carrying [1], close [1], companions [1], confidently [+4244] [1], disastrous [+5615] [1], finally [+4047] [1], first [+3836] [1], followed [+4244] [1], following [1], humiliated [+158] [1], hurried [+4513+5082] [1], hurried [+5082] [1], in presence [+3836+4725] [1], involved in [1], is one of us [+199+1609] [1], posting [1], received with [RP3562] [1], separate from [+4024] [1], settle down [+2484] [1], some time after [1], some time later [+4047] [1], that would follow [+4047] [1], the next day [+1651+2465] [1], together with [1], under [1],

urgently [*+4155+4498*] [1], use force [*+1040*] [1], welcomed
[*+1312+1645*] [1], when later [1], when [1], wholeheartedly
[*+2334*] [1], yet [*+4047*] [1]

Mt 1:12 **After** the exile to Babylon: Jeconiah was the father of Shealtiel,
    1:23 and they will call him Immanuel"—which means, "God **with** us."
    2: 3 Herod heard this he was disturbed, and all Jerusalem **with** him.
    2:11 they saw the child **with** his mother Mary, and they bowed down
    4:21 They were in a boat **with** their father Zebedee, preparing their nets.
    5:25 Do it while you are still **with** him on the way, or he may hand you
    5:41 If someone forces you to go one mile, go **with** him two miles.
    8:11 and will take their places at the feast **with** Abraham, Isaac
    9:11 "Why does your teacher eat **with** tax collectors and 'sinners'?"
    9:15 "How can the guests of the bridegroom mourn while he is **with**
   12: 3 David did when he and his **companions** [*+3836*] were hungry?
   12: 4 and he and his **companions** [*+3836*] ate the consecrated bread—
   12:30 "He who is not **with** me is against me, and he who does not gather
   12:30 me is against me, and he who does not gather **with** me scatters.
   12:41 The men of Nineveh will stand up at the judgment **with** this
   12:42 The Queen of the South will rise at the judgment **with** this
   12:45 and takes **with** it seven other spirits more wicked than itself,
   13:20 is the man who hears the word and at once receives it **with** joy.
   14: 7 that he promised **with** an oath to give her whatever she asked.
   15:30 **bringing** [*+1571+2400*] the lame, the blind, the crippled, the mute
   16:27 For the Son of Man is going to come in his Father's glory **with** his
   17: 1 **After** six days Jesus took with him Peter, James and John the
   17: 3 appeared before them Moses and Elijah, talking with [**NIE**] Jesus.
   17:17 generation," Jesus replied, "how long shall I stay **with** you?
   18:16 But if he will not listen, take one or two others **along**,
   18:23 is like a king who wanted to settle accounts **with** his servants.
   19:10 "If this is the situation **between** a husband and wife, it is better not
   20: 2 He agreed [**NIE**] to pay them a denarius for the day and sent them
   20:20 Then the mother of Zebedee's sons came to Jesus **with** her sons
   21: 2 and at once you will find a donkey tied there, with her colt **by** her.
   22:16 They sent their disciples to him **along with** the Herodians.
   24:29 "Immediately **after** the distress of those days " 'the sun will be
   24:30 Man coming on the clouds of the sky, **with** power and great glory.
   24:31 And he will send his angels **with** a loud trumpet call, and they will
   24:49 to beat his fellow servants and to eat and drink **with** drunkards.
   24:51 will cut him to pieces and assign him a place **with** the hypocrites,
   25: 3 foolish ones took their lamps but did not take any oil **with** them.
   25: 4 The wise, however, took oil in jars **along with** their lamps.
   25:10 The virgins who were ready went in **with** him to the wedding
   25:19 "**After** a long time the master of those servants returned
   25:19 master of those servants returned and settled accounts **with** them.
   25:31 the Son of Man comes in his glory, and all the angels **with** him,
   26: 2 "As you know, the Passover is two days **away**—and the Son of
   26:11 The poor you will always have **with** you, but you will not always
   26:18 I am going to celebrate the Passover **with** my disciples at your
   26:20 evening came, Jesus was reclining at the table **with** the Twelve.
   26:23 "The one who has dipped his hand into the bowl **with** me will
   26:29 that day when I drink it anew **with** you in my Father's kingdom."
   26:32 But **after** [*+3836*] I have risen, I will go ahead of you into Galilee."
   26:36 Then Jesus went **with** his disciples to a place called Gethsemane,
   26:38 sorrow to the point of death. Stay here and keep watch **with** me."
   26:40 "Could you men not keep watch **with** me for one hour?" he asked
   26:47 **With** him was a large crowd armed with swords and clubs,
   26:47 With him was a large crowd *armed* **with** swords and clubs,
   26:51 one of Jesus' **companions** [*+3836*] reached for his sword,
   26:55 that you have come out **with** swords and clubs to capture me?
   26:58 He entered and sat down **with** the guards to see the outcome.
   26:69 girl came to him. "You also were **with** Jesus of Galilee," she said.
   26:71 said to the people there, "This fellow was **with** Jesus of Nazareth."
   26:72 He denied it again, **with** an oath: "I don't know the man!"
   26:73 **After** a little while, those standing there went up to Peter and said,
   27:34 There they offered Jesus wine to drink, mixed **with** gall; but after
   27:41 [**NIE**] the teachers of the law and the elders mocked him.
   27:53 and **after** Jesus' resurrection they went into the holy city
   27:54 and those **with** him who were guarding Jesus saw the earthquake
   27:62 The next day, the one **after** Preparation Day, the chief priests
   27:63 still alive that deceiver said, '**After** three days I will rise again.'
   27:66 tomb secure by putting a seal on the stone and **posting** the guard.
   28: 8 So the women hurried away from the tomb, **afraid** [*+5832*] yet
   28:12 When the chief priests had met **with** the elders and devised a plan,
   28:20 And surely I am **with** you always, to the very end of the age."

Mk 1:13 by Satan. He was **with** the wild animals, and angels attended him.

    1:14 **After** [*+3836*] John was put in prison, Jesus went into Galilee,
    1:20 and they left their father Zebedee in the boat **with** the hired men
    1:29 they went **with** James and John to the home of Simon and Andrew.
    1:36 Simon and his **companions** [*+3836*] went to look for him,
    2:16 of the law who were Pharisees saw him eating **with** the "sinners"
    2:16 his disciples: "Why does he eat **with** tax collectors and 'sinners'?"
    2:19 "How can the guests of the bridegroom fast while he is **with** them?
    2:19 is with them? They cannot, so long as they have him **with** them.
    2:25 when he and his **companions** [*+3836*] were hungry and in need?
    3: 5 He looked around at them in anger and, deeply distressed at their
    3: 6 and began to plot **with** the Herodians how they might kill Jesus.
    3: 7 Jesus withdrew **with** his disciples to the lake, and a large crowd
    3:14 that they might be **with** him and that he might send them out to
    4:16 on rocky places, hear the word and at once receive it **with** joy.
    4:36 just as he was, in the boat. There were also other boats **with** him.
    5:18 the man who had been demon-possessed begged to go **with** him.
    5:24 So Jesus went **with** him. A large crowd followed and pressed
    5:37 He did not let anyone follow [**NIE**] him except Peter, James
    5:40 the child's father and mother and the disciples who were **with** him,
    6:25 At once the girl **hurried** [*+5082*] in to the king with the request:
    6:50 Immediately he spoke **to** them and said, "Take courage! It is I.
    8:10 he got into the boat **with** his disciples and went to the region of
    8:14 to bring bread, except for one loaf they had **with** them in the boat.
    8:31 and that he must be killed and **after** three days rise again.
    8:38 of him when he comes in his Father's glory **with** the holy angels."
    9: 2 **After** six days Jesus took Peter, James and John with him
    9: 8 looked around, they no longer saw anyone **with** them except Jesus.
    9:31 hands of men. They will kill him, and **after** three days he will rise."
   10:30 mothers, children and fields—and **with** them, persecutions)
   10:34 spit on him, flog him and kill him. Three days **later** he will rise."
   11:11 since it was already late, he went out to Bethany **with** the Twelve.
   13:24 "But in those days, **following** that distress, " 'the sun will be
   13:26 "At that time men will see the Son of Man coming in clouds **with**
   14: 1 and the Feast of Unleavened Bread were only two days **away**,
   14: 7 The poor you will always have **with** you, and you can help them
   14:14 my guest room, where I may eat the Passover **with** my disciples?'
   14:17 When evening came, Jesus arrived **with** the Twelve.
   14:18 the truth, one of you will betray me—one who is eating **with** me."
   14:20 Twelve," he replied, "one who dips bread into the bowl **with** me.
   14:28 But **after** [*+3836*] I have risen, I will go ahead of you into Galilee."
   14:33 He took Peter, James and John **along with** him, and he began to be
   14:43 **With** him was a crowd armed with swords and clubs, sent from the
   14:43 With him was a crowd *armed* **with** swords and clubs, sent from
   14:48 "that you have come out **with** swords and clubs to capture me?
   14:54 There he sat **with** the guards and warmed himself at the fire.
   14:62 right hand of the Mighty One and coming **on** the clouds of heaven."
   14:67 closely at him. "You also were **with** that Nazarene, Jesus," she said.
   14:70 **After** a little while, those standing near said to Peter, "Surely you
   15: 1 the chief priests, **with** the elders, the teachers of the law
   15: 7 A man called Barabbas was in prison **with** the insurrectionists who
   15:31 **and** the teachers of the law mocked him among themselves.
   16:10 She went and told those who had been **with** him and who were
   16:12 **Afterward** [*+4047*] Jesus appeared in a different form to two of
   16:19 **After** [*+3836*] the Lord Jesus had spoken to them, he was taken up
   16: S [UBS+ *And after these things Jesus himself sent out* through them]

Lk 1:24 **After** this his wife Elizabeth became pregnant and for five months
    1:28 "Greetings, you who are highly favored! The Lord is **with** you."
    1:39 and **hurried** [*+4513+5082*] to a town in the hill country of Judea,
    1:58 and relatives heard that the Lord had shown [**NIE**] her great
    1:66 then is this child going to be?" For the Lord's hand was **with** him.
    1:72 to show mercy **to** our fathers and to remember his holy covenant,
    2:36 she had lived **with** her husband seven years after her marriage,
    2:46 **After** three days they found him in the temple courts,
    2:51 Then he went down to Nazareth **with** them and was obedient to
    5:27 **After** this, Jesus went out and saw a tax collector by the name of
    5:29 a large crowd of tax collectors and others were eating **with** them.
    5:30 "Why do you eat and drink **with** tax collectors and 'sinners'?"
    5:34 "Can you make the guests of the bridegroom fast while he is **with**
    6: 3 did when he and his **companions** [*+1639+3836*] were hungry?
    6: 4 only for priests to eat. And he also gave some *to* his **companions**."
    6:17 He went down **with** them and stood on a level place. A large
    7:36 Now one of the Pharisees invited Jesus to have dinner **with** him,
    8:13 Those on the rock are the ones who receive the word **with** joy
    9:28 About eight days **after** Jesus said this, he took Peter, John
    9:39 throws him into convulsions so that he [**NIE**] foams at the mouth.
    9:49 we tried to stop him, because he is not **one of us** [*+199+1609*]."

10: 1　**After** this the Lord appointed seventy-two others and sent them
10:17　The seventy-two returned **with** joy and said, "Lord,
10:37　The expert in the law replied, "The one who had mercy **on** him."
11: 7　The door is already locked, and my children are **with** me in bed.
11:23　"He who is not **with** me is against me, and he who does not gather
11:23　me is against me, and he who does not gather **with** me, scatters.
11:31　The Queen of the South will rise at the judgment **with** the men of
11:32　The men of Nineveh will stand up at the judgment **with** this
12: 4　be afraid of those who kill the body and **after** that can do no more.
12: 5　Fear him who, **after** the killing of the body, has power to throw
12:13　"Teacher, tell my brother to divide the inheritance **with** me."
12:46　will cut him to pieces and assign him a place **with** the unbelievers.
12:58　As you are going **with** your adversary to the magistrate, try hard to
13: 1　the Galileans whose blood Pilate had mixed **with** their sacrifices.
14: 9　Then, **humiliated** [+*158*], you will have to take the least important
14:31　men to oppose the one coming against him **with** twenty thousand?
15:13　"Not long **after** that, the younger son got together all he had,
15:29　gave me even a young goat so I could celebrate **with** my friends.
15:30　But when this son of yours who has squandered your property **with**
15:31　" 'My son,' the father said, 'you are always **with** me, and
17: 8　on me while I eat and drink; **after** that you may eat and drink'?
17:15　he saw he was healed, came back, praising God **in** a loud voice.
17:20　"The kingdom of God does not come **with** your careful observation,
18: 4　But **finally** [+*4047*] he said to himself, 'Even though I don't fear
21:27　At that time they will see the Son of Man coming in a cloud **with**
22:11　the guest room, where I may eat the Passover **with** my disciples?'
22:15　"I have eagerly desired to eat this Passover **with** you before I suffer.
22:20　In the same way, **after** the supper he took the cup, saying,
22:21　But the hand of him who is going to betray me is **with** mine on the
22:28　You are those who have stood **by** me in my trials.
22:33　replied, "Lord, I am ready to go **with** you to prison and to death."
22:37　'And he was numbered **with** the transgressors'; and I tell you that
22:52　I leading a rebellion, that you have come **with** swords and clubs?
22:53　Every day I was **with** you in the temple courts, and you did not lay
22:58　A little **later** someone else saw him and said, "You also are one of
22:59　"Certainly this fellow was **with** him, for he is a Galilean."
23:12　Pilate became friends—**[NIE]** before this they had been enemies.
23:43　"I tell you the truth, today you will be **with** me in paradise."
24: 5　said to them, "Why do you look for the living **among** the dead?
24:29　But they urged him strongly, "Stay **with** us, for it is nearly evening;
24:30　When he was at the table **with** them, he took bread, gave thanks,
24:52　Then they worshiped him and returned to Jerusalem **with** great joy.

Jn　2:12　**After** this he went down to Capernaum with his mother
3: 2　the miraculous signs you are doing if God were not **with** him."
3:22　**After** this, Jesus and his disciples went out into the Judean
3:22　where he spent some time **with** them, and baptized.
3:25　An argument developed **between** some of John's disciples
3:26　that man who was **with** you on the other side of the Jordan—
4:27　and were surprised to find him talking **with** a woman.
4:27　asked, "What do you want?" or "Why are you talking **with** her?"
4:43　**After** the two days he left for Galilee.
5: 1　**Some time later** [+*4047*], Jesus went up to Jerusalem for a feast of
5:14　**Later** [+*4047*] Jesus found him at the temple and said to him,
6: 1　**Some time after** this, Jesus crossed to the far shore of the Sea of
6: 3　Jesus went up on a mountainside and sat down **with** his disciples.
6:43　"Stop grumbling **among** yourselves," Jesus answered.
6:66　of his disciples turned back and no longer **followed** [+*4344*] him.
7: 1　**After** this, Jesus went around in Galilee, purposely staying away
7:33　"I am **with** you for only a short time, and then I go to the one who
8:29　The one who sent me is **with** me; he has not left me alone,
9:37　"You have now seen him; in fact, he is the one speaking **with** you."
9:40　Some Pharisees who were **with** him heard him say this and asked,
11: 7　Then **[NIE]** he said to his disciples, "Let us go back to Judea."
11:11　**After** he had said this, he went on to tell them, "Our friend Lazarus
11:16　the rest of the disciples, "Let us also go, that we may die **with** him."
11:31　When the Jews who had been **with** Mary in the house, comforting
11:54　to a village called Ephraim, where he stayed **with** his disciples.
11:56　and as they stood in the temple area they asked **[NIE]** one
12: 8　You will always have the poor **among** you, but you will not always
12:17　Now the crowd that was **with** him when he called Lazarus from the
13: 7　now what I am doing, but **later** [+*4047*] you will understand."
13: 8　Jesus answered, "Unless I wash you, you have no part **with** me."
13:27　**[NIE]** As soon as Judas took the bread, Satan entered into him.
13:33　"My children, I will be **with** you only a little longer. You will look
14: 9　Philip, even after I have been **among** you such a long time?
14:16　and he will give you another Counselor to be **with** you forever—

14:30　I will not speak **with** you much longer, for the prince of this world
15:27　also must testify, for you have been **with** me from the beginning.
16: 4　I warned you. I did not tell you this at first because I was **with** you.
16:19　"Are you asking **[NIE]** one another what I meant when I said,
16:32　leave me all alone. Yet I am not alone, for my Father is **with** me.
17:12　While I was **with** them, I protected them and kept them safe by
17:24　I want those you have given me to be **with** me where I am,
18: 2　the place, because Jesus had often met there **with** his disciples.
18: 3　and Pharisees. They were **carrying** torches, lanterns and weapons.
18: 5　Jesus said. (And Judas the traitor was standing there **with** them.)
18:18　keep warm. Peter also was standing **with** them, warming himself.
18:26　challenged him, "Didn't I see you **with** him in the olive grove?"
19:18　Here they crucified him, and **with** him two others—one on each
19:28　**Later** [+*4047*], knowing that all was now completed, and
19:38　**Later** [+*4047*], Joseph of Arimathea asked Pilate for the body of
19:40　the two of them wrapped it, **with** the spices, in strips of linen.
20: 7　The cloth was folded up by itself, **separate** [+*4024*] **from** the
20:24　one of the Twelve, was not **with** the disciples when Jesus came.
20:26　**A week later** [+*2465*+*3893*] his disciples were in the house again,
20:26　his disciples were in the house again, and Thomas was **with** them.
21: 1　**Afterward** [+*4047*] Jesus appeared again to his disciples,
Ac　1: 3　**After** [+*3836*] his suffering, he showed himself to these men
1: 5　but **in** a few days you will be baptized with the Holy Spirit."
1:26　and the lot fell to Matthias; so he was added **to** the eleven apostles.
2:28　of life; you will fill me with joy in your **presence** [+*3836*+*4725*].'
2:29　I can tell you **confidently** [+*4244*] that the patriarch David died
4:29　and enable your servants to speak your word **with** great boldness.
4:31　with the Holy Spirit and spoke the word of God **boldly** [+*4244*].
5:26　They did not **use force** [+*1040*], because they feared that the
5:37　**After** him, Judas the Galilean appeared in the days of the census
7: 4　**After** the death of his father, God sent him to this land where you
7: 5　him that he and his descendants **after** him would possess the land,
7: 7　'and **afterward** they will come out of that country and worship me
7: 9　they sold him as a slave into Egypt. But God was **with** him
7:38　**with** the angel who spoke to him on Mount Sinai, and with our
7:45　our fathers **under** Joshua brought it with them when they took the
9:19　Saul spent several days **with** the disciples in Damascus.
9:28　So Saul stayed **with** them and moved about freely in Jerusalem,
9:39　and other clothing that Dorcas had made while she was still **with**
10:37　beginning in Galilee **after** the baptism that John preached—
10:38　were under the power of the devil, because God was **with** him.
10:41　who ate and drank with him **after** [+*3836*] he rose from the dead.
11:21　The Lord's hand was **with** them, and a great number of people
12: 4　Herod intended to bring him out for public trial **after** the Passover.
13:15　**After** the reading from the Law and the Prophets, the synagogue
13:17　stay in Egypt, **with** mighty power he led them out of that country,
13:20　"**After** this, God gave them judges until the time of Samuel the
13:25　No, but he is coming **after** me, whose sandals I am not worthy to
14:23　**with** prayer and fasting, committed them to the Lord, in whom
14:27　church together and reported all that God had done **through** them
15: 4　to whom they reported everything God had done **through** them.
15:13　**When** [+*3836*] they finished, James spoke up: "Brothers, listen to
15:16　" '**After** this I will return and rebuild David's fallen tent.
15:33　they were sent off by the brothers **with** the blessing of peace to
15:35　where they **[NIE]** and many others taught and preached the word
15:36　Some time **later** Paul said to Barnabas, "Let us go back and visit
17:11　for they received the message **with** great eagerness and examined
18: 1　**After** this, Paul left Athens and went to Corinth.
18:10　For I am **with** you, and no one is going to attack and harm you,
19: 4　He told the people to believe in the one coming **after** him,
19:21　"**After** [+*3836*] I have been there," he said, "I must visit Rome
20: 1　**When** [+*3836*] the uproar had ended, Paul sent for the disciples
20: 6　But we sailed from Philippi **after** the Feast of Unleavened Bread,
20:18　"You know how I lived the whole time I was **with** you,
20:19　I served the Lord **with** great humility and with tears, although I
20:29　I know that **after** I leave, savage wolves will come in among you
20:31　I never stopped warning each of you night and day **with** tears.
20:34　my own needs and the needs of my **companions** [+*1639*+*3836*].
21:15　**After** this, we got ready and went up to Jerusalem.
24: 1　Five days **later** the high priest Ananias went down to Caesarea
24: 1　high priest Ananias went down to Caesarea **with** some of the elders
24: 3　excellent Felix, we acknowledge this **with** profound gratitude.
24:18　There was no crowd **with** me, nor was I involved in any
24:18　was no crowd with me, nor was I **involved in** any disturbance.
24:24　Several days **later** Felix came with his wife Drusilla, who was a
25: 1　Three days **after** arriving in the province, Festus went up from

25:12 After Festus had conferred with [NIE] his council, he declared:
25:23 The next day Agrippa and Bernice came **with** great pomp
26:12 "On one of these journeys I was going to Damascus **with** the
27:10 I can see that our voyage is going to be **disastrous** [+5615]
27:14 **Before very long** [+4024+4498], a wind of hurricane force,
27:24 and God has graciously given you the lives of all who sail **with**
28:11 **After** three months we put out to sea in a ship that had wintered in
28:13 **The next day** [+1651+2465] the south wind came up, and on the
28:17 Three days **later** he called together the leaders of the Jews.
28:31 **Boldly** [+4244+4246] and without hindrance he preached the

Ro 12:15 Rejoice **with** those who rejoice; mourn with those who mourn.
12:15 Rejoice with those who rejoice; mourn **with** those who mourn.
12:18 as far as it depends on you, live at peace **with** everyone.
15:10 Again, it says, "Rejoice, O Gentiles, **with** his people."
15:33 The God of peace be **with** you all. Amen.
16:20 Satan under your feet. The grace of our Lord Jesus be **with** you.

1Co 6: 6 But instead, one brother goes to law **against** another—and this in
6: 7 The very fact that you have lawsuits **among** you means you have
7:12 has a wife who is not a believer and she is willing to live **with** him,
7:13 a husband who is not a believer and he is willing to live **with** her,
11:25 In the same way, **after** [+3836] supper he took the cup, saying,
16:11 he may return to me. I am expecting him **along with** the brothers.
16:12 I strongly urged him to go to you **with** the brothers.
16:23 The grace of the Lord Jesus be **with** you.
16:24 My love to all of you in Christ Jesus. Amen.

2Co 6:15 What does a believer have in common **with** an unbeliever?
6:16 What agreement is there **between** the temple of God and idols?
7:15 that you were all obedient, receiving him **with** fear and trembling.
8: 4 they **urgently** [+4155+4498] pleaded with us for the privilege of
8:18 And we are sending **along with** him the brother who is praised by
13:11 live in peace. And the God of love and peace will be **with** you.
13:14 love of God, and the fellowship of the Holy Spirit be **with** you all.

Gal 1:18 Then **after** three years, I went up to Jerusalem to get acquainted
2: 1 years later I went up again to Jerusalem, this time with Barnabas.
2:12 certain men came from James, he used to eat **with** the Gentiles.
3:17 The law, introduced 430 years **later**, does not set aside the
4:25 city of Jerusalem, because she is in slavery **with** her children.
4:30 for the slave woman's son will never share in the inheritance **with**
6:18 The grace of our Lord Jesus Christ be **with** your spirit, brothers.

Eph 4: 2 [NIE] Be completely humble and gentle; be patient, bearing with
4: 2 and gentle; [RPG] be patient, bearing with one another in love.
4:25 of you must put off falsehood and speak truthfully **to** his neighbor,
6: 5 Slaves, obey your earthly masters **with** respect and fear, and with
6: 7 Serve **wholeheartedly** [+2334], as if you were serving the Lord,
6:23 and love **with** faith from God the Father and the Lord Jesus Christ.
6:24 Grace **to** all who love our Lord Jesus Christ with an undying love.

Php 1: 4 In all my prayers for all of you, I always pray **with** joy
2:12 continue to work out your salvation **with** fear and trembling,
2:29 Welcome him in the Lord **with** great joy, and honor men like him,
4: 3 **along with** Clement and the rest of my fellow workers,
4: 6 but in everything, by prayer and petition, **with** thanksgiving,
4: 9 put it into practice. And the God of peace will be **with** you.
4:23 The grace of the Lord Jesus Christ be **with** your spirit. Amen.

Col 1:11 you may have great endurance and patience, and **joyfully** [+5915]
4:18 in my own hand. Remember my chains. Grace be **with** you.

1Th 1: 6 you welcomed the message **with** the joy given by the Holy Spirit.
3:13 and Father when our Lord Jesus comes **with** all his holy ones.
5:28 The grace of our Lord Jesus Christ be **with** you.

2Th 1: 7 and give relief to you who are troubled, **and** to us **as well**.
1: 7 is revealed from heaven in blazing fire **with** his powerful angels.
3:12 and urge in the Lord Jesus Christ to **settle down** [+2484]
3:16 peace at all times and in every way. The Lord be **with** all of you.
3:18 The grace of our Lord Jesus Christ be **with** you all.

1Ti 1:14 **along with** the faith and love that are in Christ Jesus.
2: 9 **with** decency and propriety, not with braided hair or gold
2:15 if they continue in faith, love and holiness **with** propriety.
3: 4 family well and see that his children obey him **with** proper respect.
4: 3 which God created to be **received with** [RP3562] thanksgiving by
4: 4 and nothing is to be rejected if it is received **with** thanksgiving,
4:14 which was given you through a prophetic message **when** the body
6: 6 But godliness **with** contentment is great gain.
6:21 so doing have wandered from the faith. Grace be **with** you.

2Ti 2:10 may obtain the salvation that is in Christ Jesus, **with** eternal glory.
2:22 **along with** those who call on the Lord out of a pure heart.
4:11 Only Luke is **with** me. Get Mark and bring him with you,
4:11 Get Mark and bring him **with** you, because he is helpful to me in

4:22 The Lord be **with** your spirit. Grace be with you.
4:22 The Lord be with your spirit. Grace be **with** you.

Tit 2:15 Encourage and rebuke with all authority. Do not let anyone despise
3:10 warn him a second time. **After** that, have nothing to do with him.
3:15 Everyone **with** me sends you greetings. Greet those who love us in
3:15 Greet those who love us in the faith. Grace be **with** you all.

Phm 1:25 The grace of the Lord Jesus Christ be **with** your spirit.

Heb 4: 7 calling it Today, **when** a long time **later** he spoke through David,
4: 8 God would not have spoken **later** [+4047] about another day.
4:16 Let us then approach the throne of grace **with** confidence,
5: 7 he offered up prayers and petitions **with** loud cries and tears to the
7:21 but he became a priest **with** an oath when God said to him:
7:28 but the oath, which *came* **after** the law, appointed the Son,
8:10 This is the covenant I will make with the house of Israel **after** that
9: 3 **Behind** the second curtain was a room called the Most Holy Place,
9:19 **together with** water, scarlet wool and branches of hyssop,
9:27 Just as man is destined to die once, and **after** that to face judgment,
10:15 Holy Spirit also testifies to us about this. **First** [+3836] he says:
10:16 "This is the covenant I will make with them **after** that time,
10:22 let us draw near to God **with** a sincere heart in full assurance of
10:26 If we deliberately keep on sinning **after** [+3836] we have received
10:34 and **joyfully** [+5915] accepted the confiscation of your property,
11: 9 he lived in tents, **as did**[s] Isaac and Jacob, who were heirs with him
11:31 prostitute Rahab, *because she* **welcomed** [+1312+1645] the spies,
12:14 Make every effort to live in peace **with** all men and to be holy;
12:17 about no change of mind, though he sought the blessing **with** tears.
12:28 and so worship God acceptably **with** reverence and awe,
13:17 Obey them so that their work will be [NIE] a joy, not a burden,
13:23 been released. If he arrives soon, I will *come* **with** him to see you.
13:25 Grace be **with** you all.

1Pe 1:11 the sufferings of Christ and the glories **that would follow** [+4047].
3:15 for the hope that you have. But do this **with** gentleness and respect,

2Pe 1:15 And I will make every effort to see that **after** my departure you

1Jn 1: 3 have seen and heard, so that you also may have fellowship **with** us.
1: 3 And our fellowship is **with** the Father and with his Son,
1: 3 And our fellowship is with the Father and **with** his Son,
1: 6 If we claim to have fellowship with him yet walk in the darkness,
1: 7 as he is in the light, we have fellowship **with** one another,
2:19 For if they had belonged to us, they would have remained **with** us;
4:17 love is made complete **among** us so that we will have confidence

2Jn 1: 2 because of the truth, which lives in us and will be **with** us forever:
1: 3 Jesus Christ, the Father's Son, will be **with** us in truth and love.

Rev 1: 7 Look, he is coming **with** the clouds, and every eye will see him,
1:12 I turned around to see the voice that was speaking **to** me.
1:19 you have seen, what is now and what will take place **later** [+4047].
2:16 to you and will fight **against** them with the sword of my mouth.
2:22 and I will make those who commit adultery **with** her suffer
3: 4 They will walk **with** me, dressed in white, for they are worthy.
3:20 opens the door, I will come in and eat **with** him, and he with me.
3:20 opens the door, I will come in and eat with him, and he **with** me.
3:21 I will give the right to sit **with** me on my throne, just as I overcame
3:21 just as I overcame and sat down **with** my Father on his throne.
4: 1 **After** this I looked, and there before me was a door standing open
4: 1 And the voice I had first heard speaking **to** me like a trumpet said,
4: 1 up here, and I will show you what must take place **after** this."
6: 8 was named Death, and Hades was following **close** behind him.
7: 1 **After** this I saw four angels standing at the four corners of the
7: 9 **After** this I looked and there before me was a great multitude that
9:12 The first woe is past; two other woes are **yet** [+4047] to come.
10: 8 Then the voice that I had heard from heaven spoke **to** me once
11: 7 the beast that comes up from the Abyss will attack [NIE] them,
11:11 But **after** the three and a half days a breath of life from God
12: 7 Michael and his angels fought **against** the dragon, and the dragon
12: 9 world astray. He was hurled to the earth, and his angels **with** him.
12:17 and went off to make war **against** the rest of her offspring—
13: 4 asked, "Who is like the beast? Who can make war **against** him?"
13: 7 He was given power to make war **against** the saints and to conquer
14: 1 and with him 144,000 who had his name and his Father's name
14: 4 These are those who did not defile themselves **with** women,
14:13 will rest from their labor, for their deeds will follow [NIE] them."
15: 5 **After** this I looked and in heaven the temple, that is, the tabernacle
17: 1 of the seven angels who had the seven bowls came and said **to** me,
17: 2 **With** her the kings of the earth committed adultery
17:12 but who for one hour will receive authority as kings **along with** the
17:14 They will make war **against** the Lamb, but the Lamb will
17:14 and **with** him will be his called, chosen and faithful followers."

18: 1 **After** this I saw another angel coming down from heaven.
18: 3 The kings of the earth committed adultery **with** her,
18: 9 "When the kings of the earth who committed adultery **with** her
19: 1 **After** this I heard what sounded like the roar of a great multitude in
19:19 and their armies gathered together to make war **against** the rider on
19:19 to make war against the rider on the horse and **[RPG]** his army.
19:20 and **with** him the false prophet who had performed the miraculous
20: 3 years were ended. **After** that, he must be set free for a short time.
20: 4 They came to life and reigned **with** Christ a thousand years.
20: 6 and of Christ and will reign **with** him for a thousand years.
21: 3 "Now the dwelling of God is **with** men, and he will live with them.
21: 3 "Now the dwelling of God is with men, and he will live **with** them.
21: 3 be his people, and God himself will be **with** them and be their God.
21: 9 the seven bowls full of the seven last plagues came and said **to** me,
21:15 The angel who talked **with** me had a measuring rod of gold to
22:12 My reward is **with** me, and I will give to everyone according to
22:21 The grace of the Lord Jesus be **with** God's people. Amen.

3553 μεταβαίνω, *metabainō* [12] [√ 3552 + 326]

leave [3], left [2], move [2], crossed over [1], going on [1], move around [1], passed [1], went on [1]

Mt 8:34 when they saw him, they pleaded with him to **leave** their region.
    11: 1 he **went on** from there to teach and preach in the towns of Galilee.
    12: 9 **Going on** from that place, he went into their synagogue,
    15:29 Jesus **left** there and went along the Sea of Galilee. Then he went up
    17:20 say to this mountain, 'Move from here to there' and it will move.
    17:20 say to this mountain, 'Move from here to there' and it will **move**.
Lk 10: 7 deserves his wages. Do not **move around** from house to house.
Jn 5:24 will not be condemned; he has **crossed over** from death to life.
    7: 3 brothers said to him, "You ought to **leave** here and go to Judea,
    13: 1 Jesus knew that the time had come for him to **leave** this world
Ac 18: 7 Then Paul **left** the synagogue and went next door to the house of
1Jn 3:14 We know that we have **passed** from death to life, because we love

3554 μεταβάλλω, *metaballō* [1] [√ 3552 + 965]

changed minds [1]

Ac 28: 6 happen to him, they **changed** *their* **minds** and said he was a god.

3555 μετάγω, *metagō* [2] [√ 3552 + 72]

steered [1], turn [1]

Jas 3: 3 of horses to make them obey us, *we can* **turn** the whole animal.
    3: 4 they are **steered** by a very small rudder wherever the pilot wants

3556 μεταδίδωμι, *metadidōmi* [5] [√ 3552 + 1443]

share with [2], contributing to the needs of others [1], impart [1], share [1]

Lk 3:11 "The man with two tunics *should* **share with** him who has none,
Ro 1:11 so that *I may* **impart** to you some spiritual gift to make you
    12: 8 if it is **contributing to the needs of others**, let him give
Eph 4:28 that he may have something *to* **share** with those in need.
1Th 2: 8 so much that we were delighted *to* **share with** you not only the

3557 μετάθεσις, *metathesis* [3] [√ 3552 + 5502]

change [1], removing [1], taken [1]

Heb 7:12 a change of the priesthood, there must also be a **change** of the law.
    11: 5 For before he was **taken**, he was commended as one who pleased
    12:27 The words "once more" indicate the **removing** of what can be

3558 μεταίρω, *metairō* [2] [√ 3552 + 149]

left [1], moved on [1]

Mt 13:53 When Jesus had finished these parables, *he* **moved on** from there.
    19: 1 he **left** Galilee and went into the region of Judea to the other side

3559 μετακαλέω, *metakaleō* [4] [√ 3552 + 2813]

untranslated [1], for [1], send for [1], sent for [+690] [1]

Ac 7:14 Joseph **sent** [+690] **for** his father Jacob and his whole family,
    10:32 Send to Joppa for Simon **[RPG]** who is called Peter. He is a guest
    20:17 From Miletus, Paul sent to Ephesus **for** the elders of the church.
    24:25 You may leave. When I find it convenient, *I will* **send for** you."

3560 μετακινέω, *metakineō* [1] [√ 3552 + 3075]

moved [1]

Col 1:23 and firm, not **moved** from the hope held out in the gospel.

3561 μεταλαμβάνω, *metalambanō* [7] [√ 3552 + 3284]

eat [+5575] [1], find convenient [+2789] [1], receive a share [1], receives [1], share in [1], take [1], together [1]

Ac 2:46 bread in their homes and ate **together** with glad and sincere hearts,
    24:25 may leave. *When I* **find** [+2789] it **convenient**, I will send for you."
    27:33 Just before dawn Paul urged them all *to* **eat** [+5575]. "For the last
    27:34 Now I urge you to **take** some food. You need it to survive.
2Ti 2: 6 The hardworking farmer should be the first *to* **receive a share** of
Heb 6: 7 useful to those for whom it is farmed **receives** the blessing of God.
    12:10 God disciplines us for our good, that we *may* **share in** his holiness.

3562 μετάλημψις, *metalēmpsis* [1] [√ 3552 + 3284]

received with [RP3552] [1]

1Ti 4: 3 which God created to be **received** [RP3552] **with** thanksgiving by

3563 μεταλλάσσω, *metallassō* [2] [√ 3552 + 248]

exchanged [2]

Ro 1:25 They **exchanged** the truth of God for a lie, and worshiped
    1:26 Even their women **exchanged** natural relations for unnatural ones.

3564 μεταμέλομαι, *metamelomai* [6] [√ 3552 + 3508]

regret [2], change mind [1], changed mind [1], repent [1], seized with remorse [1]

Mt 21:29 " 'I will not,' he answered, but later *he* **changed** *his* **mind** and
    21:32 And even after you saw this, *you did* not **repent** and believe him.
    27: 3 he *was* **seized with remorse** and returned the thirty silver coins to
2Co 7: 8 Even if I caused you sorrow by my letter, *I do* not **regret** it.
    7: 8 Though *I did* **regret** it—I see that my letter hurt you, but only for a
Heb 7:21 "The Lord has sworn and *will* not **change** *his* **mind**: 'You are a

3565 μεταμορφόω, *metamorphoō* [4] [√ 3552 + 3671]

transfigured [2], transformed into [1], transformed [1]

Mt 17: 2 There he was **transfigured** before them. His face shone like the
Mk 9: 2 they were all alone. There he was **transfigured** before them.
Ro 12: 2 of this world, but be **transformed** by the renewing of your mind.
2Co 3:18 are being **transformed into** his likeness with ever-increasing

3566 μετανοέω, *metanoeō* [34] [√ 3552 + 3808]

repent [23], repented [5], repents [3], refused to repent [+4024] [2], untranslated [1]

Mt 3: 2 and saying, "**Repent**, for the kingdom of heaven is near."
    4:17 began to preach, "**Repent**, for the kingdom of heaven is near."
    11:20 of his miracles had been performed, because *they did* not **repent**.
    11:21 *they* would have **repented** long ago in sackcloth and ashes.
    12:41 for *they* **repented** at the preaching of Jonah, and now one greater
Mk 1:15 "The kingdom of God is near. **Repent** and believe the good news!"
    6:12 They went out and preached that *people should* **repent**.
Lk 10:13 performed in Tyre and Sidon, *they* would have **repented** long ago,
    11:32 for *they* **repented** at the preaching of Jonah, and now one greater
    13: 3 I tell you, no! But unless *you* **repent**, you too will all perish.

13: 5 I tell you, no! But unless *you* repent, you too will all perish."
15: 7 *who* repents than over ninety-nine righteous persons who do not
15: 10 in the presence of the angels of God over one sinner *who* repents."
16: 30 'but if someone from the dead goes to them, *they will* repent.'
17: 3 "If your brother sins, rebuke him, and if *he* repents, forgive him.
17: 4 and seven times comes back to you and says, '*I* repent,'
Ac 2: 38 Peter replied, "Repent and be baptized, every one of you,
3: 19 Repent, then, and turn to God, so that your sins may be wiped out,
8: 22 Repent of this wickedness and pray to the Lord. Perhaps he will
17: 30 but now he commands all people everywhere *to* repent.
26: 20 I preached that they *should* repent and turn to God and prove their
2Co 12: 21 who have sinned earlier and *have* not repented of the impurity,
Rev 2: 5 Repent and do the things you did at first. If you do not repent,
2: 5 If *you do* not repent, I will come to you and remove your
2: 16 Repent therefore! Otherwise, I will soon come to you and will
2: 21 I have given her time to repent of her immorality, but she is
2: 21 her time to repent of her immorality, but she is unwilling. [RPG]
2: 22 adultery with her suffer intensely, unless *they* repent of her ways.
3: 3 therefore, what *you have* received and heard; obey it, and repent.
3: 19 whom I love I rebuke and discipline. So be earnest, and repent.
9: 20 by these plagues *still did* not repent of the work of their hands;
9: 21 Nor *did they* repent of their murders, their magic arts, their sexual
16: 9 these plagues, but *they* refused to repent [+4024] and glorify him.
16: 11 but *they* refused to repent [+4024] of what they had done.

3567 μετάνοια, *metanoia* [22] [√ 3552 + 3808]

repentance [19], change of mind [1], repent [1], turn in
repentance [1]

Mt 3: 8 Produce fruit in keeping with repentance.
3: 11 "I baptize you with water for repentance. But after me will come
Mk 1: 4 and preaching a baptism *of* repentance for the forgiveness of sins.
Lk 3: 3 preaching a baptism *of* repentance for the forgiveness of sins.
3: 8 Produce fruit in keeping with repentance. And do not begin to say
5: 32 I have not come to call the righteous, but sinners to repentance."
15: 7 over ninety-nine righteous persons who do not need *to* repent.
24: 47 and repentance and forgiveness of sins will be preached in his
Ac 5: 31 and Savior that he might give repentance and forgiveness of sins
11: 18 "So then, God has granted even the Gentiles repentance unto life."
13: 24 John preached repentance and baptism to all the people of Israel.
19: 4 Paul said, "John's baptism was a baptism *of* repentance. He told
20: 21 to both Jews and Greeks that they must turn to God in repentance
26: 20 and turn to God and prove their repentance by their deeds.
Ro 2: 4 not realizing that God's kindness leads you toward repentance?
2Co 7: 9 were made sorry, but because your sorrow led you to repentance.
7: 10 Godly sorrow brings repentance that leads to salvation and leaves
2Ti 2: 25 in the hope that God will grant them repentance leading them to a
Heb 6: 1 not laying again the foundation *of* repentance from acts that lead
6: 6 if they fall away, to be brought back to repentance, because to
12: 17 He could bring about no change of mind, though he sought the
2Pe 3: 9 not wanting anyone to perish, but everyone to come to repentance.

3568 μεταξύ, *metaxy* [9] [√ 3552 + 5250]

between [6], *untranslated* [1], meanwhile [+1877+3836] [1], next
[1]

Mt 18: 15 go and show him his fault, just between the two of you.
23: 35 whom you murdered between the temple and the altar.
Lk 11: 51 of Zechariah, who was killed between the altar and the sanctuary.
16: 26 besides all this, between us and you a great chasm has been fixed,
Jn 4: 31 Meanwhile [+1877+3836] his disciples urged him, "Rabbi, eat
Ac 12: 6 Peter was sleeping between two soldiers, bound with two chains,
13: 42 them to speak further about these things on the next Sabbath.
15: 9 He made no distinction between us and them, for he purified their
Ro 2: 15 their thoughts now accusing, now even defending [NIE] them.)

3569 μεταπέμπω, *metapempō* [9] [√ 3552 + 4287]

sent for [5], bring back [1], come [1], for [1], have transferred [1]

Ac 10: 5 Now send men to Joppa *to* bring back a man named Simon who is
10: 22 A holy angel told him *to have* you come to his house so that he
10: 29 So *when I was* sent for, I came without raising any objection.
10: 29 without raising any objection. May I ask why *you* sent for me?"
11: 13 in his house and say, 'Send to Joppa for Simon who is called Peter.

20: 1 Paul sent for the disciples and, after encouraging them,
24: 24 He sent for Paul and listened to him as he spoke about faith in
24: 26 him a bribe, so he sent for him frequently and talked with him.
25: 3 as a favor to them, to have Paul transferred to Jerusalem,

3570 μεταστρέφω, *metastrephō* [2] [√ 3552 + 5138]

pervert [1], turned [1]

Ac 2: 20 The sun *will be* turned to darkness and the moon to blood before
Gal 1: 7 you into confusion and are trying *to* pervert the gospel of Christ.

3571 μετασχηματίζω, *metaschēmatizō* [5]
[√ 3552 + 5386]

applied [1], masquerade [1], masquerades [1], masquerading
[1], transform [1]

1Co 4: 6 *I have* applied these things to myself and Apollos for your benefit,
2Co 11: 13 deceitful workmen, masquerading as apostles of Christ.
11: 14 no wonder, for Satan himself masquerades as an angel of light.
11: 15 then, if his servants masquerade as servants of righteousness.
Php 3: 21 *will* transform our lowly bodies so that they will be like his

3572 μετατίθημι, *metatithēmi* [6] [√ 3552 + 5502]

change [2], brought back [1], deserting [+608] [1], taken away
[1], taken from [1]

Ac 7: 16 Their *bodies* were brought back to Shechem and placed in the
Gal 1: 6 I am astonished that *you are* so quickly deserting [+608] the one
Heb 7: 12 For *when there is* a change of the priesthood, there must also be a
11: 5 By faith Enoch *was* taken from *this life*, so that he did not
11: 5 he could not be found, because God *had* taken him away.
Jude 1: 4 *who* change the grace of our God into a license for immorality

3573 μετατρέπω, *metatrepō* [1] [√ 3552 + 5572]

change [1]

Jas 4: 9 Change your laughter to mourning and your joy to gloom.

3574 μεταφυτεύω, *metaphyteuō* Not used in
UBS/NIV [√ 3552 + 5886]

3575 μετέπειτα, *metepeita* [1] [√ 3552 + 2093 + 1663]

afterward [1]

Heb 12: 17 Afterward, as you know, when he wanted to inherit this blessing,

3576 μετέχω, *metechō* [8] [√ 3552 + 2400]

belonged to [1], have a part [1], have [1], lives on [1], partake [1],
shared in [1], sharing in [1], take part [1]

1Co 9: 10 they ought to do so in the hope *of* sharing in the *harvest*.
9: 12 If others have this right of support from you, shouldn't we have it
10: 17 who are many, are one body, for *we* all partake of the one loaf.
10: 21 you cannot have a part in both the Lord's table and the table of
10: 30 If I take part *in the meal* with thankfulness, why am I denounced
Heb 2: 14 he too shared in their humanity so that by his death he might
5: 13 Anyone who lives on milk, being still an infant, is not acquainted
7: 13 He of whom these things are said belonged to a different tribe,

3577 μετεωρίζομαι, *meteōrizomai* [1]

worry about [1]

Lk 12: 29 set your heart on what you will eat or drink; *do* not worry about it.

3578 μετοικεσία, *metoikesia* [4] [√ 3552 + 3875]

exile [4]

Mt 1: 11 of Jeconiah and his brothers at the time *of* the exile to Babylon.
1: 12 After the exile to Babylon: Jeconiah was the father of Shealtiel,
1: 17 fourteen from David to the exile to Babylon, and fourteen from the

1: 17 to the exile to Babylon, and fourteen from the **exile** to the Christ.

3579 μετοικίζω, *metoikizō* [2] [√ *3552 + 3875*]

send into exile [1], sent [1]

Ac   7: 4 of his father, God **sent** him to this land where you are now living.
     7: 43 to worship. Therefore *I will* **send** you **into exile**' beyond Babylon.

3580 μετοχή, *metochē* [1] [√ *3552 + 2400*]

in common [1]

2Co   6: 14 For what do righteousness and wickedness have **in common**?

3581 μέτοχος, *metochos* [6] [√ *3552 + 2400*]

share in [2], companions [1], partners [1], shared in [+*1181*] [1],
undergoes [+*1181*] [1]

Lk   5: 7 So they signaled their **partners** in the other boat to come and help
Heb   1: 9 has set you above your **companions** by anointing you with the oil
     3: 1 Therefore, holy brothers, *who* **share in** the heavenly calling,
     3: 14 We have come to **share in** Christ if we hold firmly till the end the
     6: 4 the heavenly gift, who *have* **shared** [+*1181*] **in** the Holy Spirit,
    12: 8 are not disciplined (and everyone **undergoes** [+*1181*] discipline),

3582 μετρέω, *metreō* [11] [√ *3586*]

measure [4], measured [4], use[s] [3]

Mt   7: 2 you will be judged, and with the measure *you* **use**[s], it will be
     7: 2 and with the measure you use, *it will be* **measured** to you.
Mk   4: 24 "With the measure *you* **use**[s], it will be measured to you—
     4: 24 "With the measure you use, *it will be* **measured** to you—
Lk   6: 38 For with the measure *you* **use**[s], it will be measured to you."
2Co 10: 12 *When* they **measure** themselves by themselves and compare
Rev 11: 1 and was told, "Go and **measure** the temple of God and the altar,
    11: 2 *do* not **measure** it, because it has been given to the Gentiles.
    21: 15 talked with me had a measuring rod of gold to **measure** the city,
    21: 16 *He* **measured** the city with the rod and found it to be 12,000 stadia
    21: 17 *He* **measured** its wall and it was 144 cubits thick, by man's

3583 μετρητής, *metrētēs* [1] [√ *3586*]

twenty to thirty gallons [+*1545+2445+5552*] [1]

Jn   2: 6 each holding from **twenty to thirty gallons** [+*1545+2445+5552*].

3584 μετριοπαθέω, *metriopatheō* [1] [√ *3586 + 4248*]

deal gently [1]

Heb   5: 2 He is able *to* **deal gently** with those who are ignorant and are

3585 μετρίως, *metriōs* [1] [√ *3586*]

greatly [+*4024*] [1]

Ac   20: 12 the young man home alive and were **greatly** [+*4024*] comforted.

3586 μέτρον, *metron* [14] [→ *296, 520, 3582, 3583,* *3584, 3585, 4991*]

measure [6], *untranslated* [1], apportioned [1], field
[+*2834+3836*] [1], field [1], limit [1], measurement [1], measuring
[1], whole measure [+*2461*] [1]

Mt   7: 2 you will be judged, and with the **measure** you use, it will be
    23: 32 Fill up, then, the **measure** of the sin of your forefathers!
Mk   4: 24 "With the **measure** you use, it will be measured to you—
Lk   6: 38 A good **measure**, pressed down, shaken together and running over,
     6: 38 For *with* the **measure** you use, it will be measured to you."
Jn   3: 34 speaks the words of God, for God gives the Spirit without **limit**.
Ro   12: 3 in accordance with the **measure** of faith God has given you.
2Co 10: 13 but will confine our boasting to the **field** [+*2834+3836*] God has
    10: 13 to the **field** God has assigned to us, a **field** that reaches even to you.
Eph   4: 7 But to each one of us grace has been given as Christ **apportioned**
     4: 13 attaining to the **whole measure** [+*2461*] of the fullness of Christ.

     4: 16 and builds itself up in love, as each part [**NIE**] does its work.
Rev 21: 15 The angel who talked with me had a **measuring** rod of gold to
    21: 17 cubits thick, by man's **measurement**, which the angel was using.

3587 μέτωπον, *metōpon* [8] [√ *3552 + 3972*]

foreheads [5], forehead [3]

Rev   7: 3 or the trees until we put a seal on the **foreheads** of the servants of
     9: 4 those people who did not have the seal of God on their **foreheads**.
    13: 16 and slave, to receive a mark on his right hand or on his **forehead**,
    14: 1 had his name and his Father's name written on their **foreheads**.
    14: 9 and his image and receives his mark on the **forehead** or on the
    17: 5 This title was written on her **forehead**: MYSTERY BABYLON
    20: 4 or his image and had not received his mark on their **foreheads**
    22: 4 They will see his face, and his name will be on their **foreheads**.

3588 μέχρι, *mechri* [17] [→ *3589*]

until [5], to [4], until [+*4005*] [2], *untranslated* [1], all the way to
[1], at [1], even to the point of [1], till [1], to the point of [1]

Mt   11: 23 had been performed in Sodom, it would have remained **to** this day.
    28: 15 And this story has been widely circulated among the Jews **to** this
Mk   13: 30 this generation will certainly not pass away **until** [+*4005*] all these
Lk   16: 16 "The Law and the Prophets were proclaimed **until** John. Since that
Ac   10: 30 "Four days ago I was in my house praying **at** this hour, at three in
    20: 7 he intended to leave the next day, kept on talking **until** midnight.
Ro   5: 14 death reigned from the time of Adam **to** the time of Moses,
    15: 19 So from Jerusalem **all the way** around to Illyricum, I have fully
Gal   4: 19 for whom I am again in the pains of childbirth **until** [+*4005*] Christ
Eph   4: 13 **until** we all reach unity in the faith and in the knowledge of the
Php   2: 8 as a man, he humbled himself and became obedient **to** death—
     2: 30 because he almost [**RPG**] died for the work of Christ, risking his
1Ti   6: 14 without spot or blame **until** the appearing of our Lord Jesus Christ,
2Ti   2: 9 for which I am suffering **even to the point of** being chained like a
Heb   3: 14 We have come to share in Christ if we hold firmly **till** the end the
     9: 10 external regulations applying **until** the time of the new order.
    12: 4 you have not yet resisted **to the point of** shedding your blood.

3589 μέχρις, *mechris* Not used in UBS/NIV [√ *3588*]

3590 μή, *mē* [1041 / 1040] See Index of Articles, Etc.

[→ *3591, 3592, 3593, 3594, 3595, 3596, 3598, 3599, 3600, 3607,* *3608, 3609, 3610, 3612, 3614, 3615*]

not [525], no [58], *untranslated* [53], except [+*1623*] [36], never
[+*4024*] [33], unless [+*1569*] [31], not [+*4024*] [30], don't [24],
but [+*1623*] [11], only [+*1623*] [8], or [+*2671*] [8], without [8],
certainly not [+*4024*] [7], nothing [6], stop [6], never
[+*172+1650+3836+4024*] [5], never [5], only [+*1623+4024*] [5],
without [+*2400*] [5], by no means [+*1181*] [4], from [4], neither
[4], not at all [+*1181*] [4], or [4], avoid [3], but only [+*1623*] [3],
cannot [+*1538*] [3], cannot [3], do[s] [+*1145*] [3], don't [+*4024*] [3],
none [3], not only [3], that [+*4803*] [3], that [3], won't [3],
absolutely not [+*1181*] [2], against [2], blind [+*1063*] [2], certainly
not [+*1181*] [2], does[s] [+*1145*] [2], doesn't [2], how [2], if he does
[+*1254+1623*] [2], keep from [2], never again [+*4024*] [2], no
[+*4024*] [2], not at all [+*4024*] [2], nothing [+*5516*] [2], prevent
[2], shallow [+*958*] [2], than for [+*2779*] [2], unless [+*1623+1760*]
[2], unless [+*1623*] [2], unseen [+*1063*] [2], abstains [+*2266*] [1],
afraid[s] that [1], at once [+*3890*] [1], before [+*2671*] [1], bound to
come [+*450+2262*] [1], but [+*1569*] [1], but if [+*1623*] [1], could
[1], cover [+*5746*] [1], didn't [1], die [+*2441*] [1], displease
[+*743*] [1], ever [1], evidently [+*1623*] [1], except for [+*1623*] [1],
except [1], fail [+*1569*] [1], fail [+*4049*] [1], fearing that [+*5828*]
[1], for [+*4803*] [1], for fear [+*2671*] [1], for fear that [+*2671*] [1],
for fear that [+*4803*] [1], free from fear of [+*5828*] [1], from
[+*2671*] [1], haven't [+*2400*] [1], help speaking about [+*3281*] [1],
how [+*1142*] [1], how dare you [1], isn't at all [+*4024*] [1], kept
from [+*3195*] [1], kept from [1], lest [+*2671*] [1], may never
[+*1181*] [1], may this never [1], never [+*1181*] [1], never
[+*4024+4033*] [1], never [+*4024+4537*] [1], never [+*4024+4799*]
[1], never again [+*172+1650+3836+4024*] [1], nevertheless

[+1623] [1], no ever [+4024] [1], no longer [+4024] [1], nobody [+5516] [1], none [+5516] [1], nor [+2779] [1], not [+4029] [1], not again [+4024] [1], not anything [+3594] [1], not are you [1], not by any means [+4024] [1], not one [+4024] [1], nothing [+4024+4029] [1], nothing [+5515] [1], nothing ever [1], only [+1569] [1], only [+1623+3667] [1], only [+1623+3668] [1], only to [+1623+4029] [1], or at least [+1254+1623] [1], otherwise [+1254+1623] [1], otherwise [+1623+1760] [1], rather than [+2671] [1], rather than [+2779] [1], refused to worship [+4686] [1], shouldn't [+1474] [1], sincere [+1474] [1], spare [+2400] [1], stop for [+1142] [1], than that [+2779] [1], that [+4543] [1], to keep from [+2671] [1], to keep from [+3836+4639] [1], to prevent [1], together with [+6006] [1], unable [+1538] [1], unable [1], unashamed [+159] [1], until [+1569+4754] [1], until [+1623+4020] [1], without [+1569] [1], without [+1650] [1], without [+2779] [1], without light [+5743] [1], you mean [1]

3591 μήγε, mēge   Not used in UBS/NIV [√ 3590 + 1145]

3592 μηδαμῶς, mēdamōs [2] [√ 3590 + 1254 + 1609]

surely not [2]

Ac 10:14 "**Surely not**, Lord!" Peter replied. "I have never eaten anything
   11: 8 "I replied, '**Surely not**, Lord! Nothing impure or unclean has ever

3593 μηδέ, mēde [57] [√ 3590 + 1254]

or [26], not [11], and not [5], nor [5], not even [4], *untranslated* [3], and don't [1], and [1], don't [1]

Mt 6:25 you will eat or drink; **or** about your body, what you will wear.
   7: 6 "Do not give dogs what is sacred; do **not** throw your pearls to pigs.
   10: 9 Do not take along any gold **or** silver or copper in your belts;
   10: 9 Do not take along any gold **or** silver or copper in your belts;
   10:10 take no bag for the journey, **or** extra tunic, or sandals or a staff;
   10:10 take no bag for the journey, or extra tunic, **or** sandals or a staff;
   10:10 take no bag for the journey, or extra tunic, or sandals **or** a staff;
   10:14 If anyone will not welcome you **or** listen to your words,
   22:29 because you do not know the Scriptures **or** the power of God.
   23:10 **Nor** are you to be called 'teacher,' for you have one Teacher,
   24:20 that your flight will not take place in winter **or** on the Sabbath.
Mk 2: 2 **not even** outside the door, and he preached the word to them.
   3:20 so that he and his disciples were **not even** able to eat.
   6:11 And if any place will not welcome you **or** listen to you,
   8:26 Jesus sent him home, saying, "**Don't** go into the village."
   12:24 because you do not know the Scriptures **or** the power of God?
   13:15 roof of his house go down **or** enter the house to take anything out.
Lk 3:14 He replied, "Don't extort money **and don't** accuse people falsely—
   12:22 what you will eat; **or** about your body, what you will wear.
   14:12 do not invite your friends, **[RPG]** your brothers or relatives,
   14:12 or dinner, do not invite your friends, your brothers **or** relatives,
   14:12 your friends, your brothers or relatives, **or** your rich neighbors;
   16:26 here to you cannot, **nor** can anyone cross over from there to us.'
   17:23 or 'Here he is!' Do not go running off after **[RPG]** them.
Jn 4:15 I won't get thirsty **and** have to keep coming here to draw water."
   14:27 Do not let your hearts be troubled **and** do **not** be afraid.
Ac 4:18 commanded them not to speak **or** teach at all in the name of Jesus.
   21:21 not to circumcise their children **or** live according to our customs.
Ro 6:13 Do **not** offer the parts of your body to sin, as instruments of
   9:11 before the twins were born **or** had done anything good or bad—
   14:21 It is better not to eat meat **or** drink wine or to do anything else that
   14:21 **or** to do anything else that will cause your brother to fall.
1Co 5: 8 not with the old yeast, **[RPG]** the yeast of malice and wickedness,
   5:11 a drunkard or a swindler. With such a man do **not even** eat.
   10: 7 Do **not** be idolaters, as some of them were; as it is written:
   10: 8 We should **not** commit sexual immorality, as some of them did—
   10: 9 We should **not** test the Lord, as some of them did—and were killed
   10:10 **And** do **not** grumble, as some of them did—and were killed by the
2Co 4: 2 we do not use deception, **nor** do we distort the word of God.
Eph 4:27 **and** do **not** give the devil a foothold.
   5: 3 But among you there must **not** be **even** a hint of sexual immorality,
Php 2: 3 Do nothing out of selfish ambition **or** vain conceit, but in humility
Col 2:21 "Do not handle! Do **not** taste! Do not touch!"?
   2:21 "Do not handle! Do not taste! Do **not** touch!"?

2Th 2: 2 not to become easily unsettled **or** alarmed by some prophecy,
   3:10 we gave you this rule: "If a man will not work, he shall **not** eat."
1Ti 1: 4 **nor** to devote themselves to myths and endless genealogies.
   5:22 in the laying on of hands, **and** do **not** share in the sins of others.
   6:17 present world not to be arrogant **nor** to put their hope in wealth,
2Ti 1: 8 ashamed to testify about our Lord, **or** ashamed of me his prisoner.
Tit 2: 3 not to be slanderers **or** addicted to much wine, but to teach what is
Heb 12: 5 the Lord's discipline, **and** do **not** lose heart when he rebukes you,
1Pe 3:14 you are blessed. "Do not fear what they fear; do **not** be frightened."
   5: 2 as God wants you to be; **not** greedy for money, but eager to serve;
   5: 3 **not** lording it over those entrusted to you, but being examples to
1Jn 2:15 Do not love the world **or** anything in the world. If anyone loves the
   3:18 let us not love with words **or** tongue but with actions and in truth.

3594 μηδείς, mēdeis [90] [√ 3590 + 1254 + 1651]

not anyone [13], nothing [11], no one [9], no [9], not [8], don't anyone [5], not anything [5], *untranslated* [3], without [3], don't [2], not any [2], any way [1], any [1], anyone [+476] [1], anyone [1], anyone's [1], don't any [1], don't anything [1], don't this [1], have everything need [+3309] [1], haven't anything [1], in any way [+2848+5573] [1], instead of [1], no more [1], nobody [1], not any way [1], not anybody [1], not anything [+3590] [1], not in the least [1], permit [+3266] [1], without anything [1]

Mt 8: 4 Then Jesus said to him, "See that you **don't** tell **anyone**. But go,
   9:30 Jesus warned them sternly, "See that **no one** knows about this."
   16:20 Then he warned his disciples **not** to tell **anyone** that he was the
   17: 9 Jesus instructed them, "**Don't** tell **anyone** what you have seen,
   27:19 "**Don't** have **anything** to do with that innocent man, for I have
Mk 1:44 "See that you **don't** tell **this** to anyone. But go, show yourself to the
   1:44 "See that you don't tell this *to* anyone. But go, show yourself to the
   5:26 had spent all she had, yet *instead of* getting better she grew worse.
   5:43 He gave strict orders **not** to let **anyone** know about this, and told
   6: 8 "Take **nothing** for the journey except a staff—no bread, no bag,
   7:36 Jesus commanded them **not** to tell **anyone**. But the more he did so,
   8:30 Jesus warned them **not** to tell **anyone** about him.
   9: 9 Jesus gave them orders **not** to tell **anyone** what they had seen until
   11:14 he said to the tree, "May **no one** ever eat fruit from you again."
Lk 3:13 "**Don't** collect **any** more than you are required to," he told them.
   3:14 He replied, "**Don't** extort money and don't accuse people falsely—
   4:35 the man down before them all and came out **without** injuring him.
   5:14 Then Jesus ordered him, "**Don't** tell **anyone**, but go, show yourself
   6:35 and lend to them **without** expecting to get **anything** back.
   8:56 but he ordered them **not** to tell **anyone** what had happened.
   9: 3 "Take **nothing** for the journey—no staff, no bag, no bread,
   9:21 Jesus strictly warned them **not** to tell this *to* **anyone**.
   10: 4 a purse or bag or sandals; and do **not** greet **anyone** on the road.
Ac 4:17 we must warn these men to speak **no** longer *to* **anyone** [+476] in
   4:21 They could **not** decide how to punish them, because all the people
   8:24 the Lord for me so that **nothing** you have said may happen to me."
   9: 7 there speechless; they heard the sound but did **not** see **anyone**.
   10:20 Do **not** hesitate to go with them, for I have sent them."
   10:28 But God has shown me that I should **not** call **any** man impure
   11:12 The Spirit told me to have **no** hesitation about going with them.
   11:19 Cyprus and Antioch, telling **[RPG]** the message only to Jews.
   13:28 Though they found **no** proper ground for a death sentence,
   15:28 and to us **not** to burden you with **anything** beyond the following
   16:28 But Paul shouted, "**Don't** harm yourself! We are all here!"
   19:36 are undeniable, you ought to be quiet and **not** do **anything** rash.
   19:40 able to account for this commotion, since there is **no** reason for it."
   23:14 "We have taken a solemn oath **not** to eat **anything** until we have
   23:22 "**Don't** tell **anyone** that you have reported this to me."
   23:29 but there was **no** charge against him that deserved death
   24:23 and **permit** [+3266] his friends to take care of his needs.
   25:17 When they came here with me, I did **not** delay the case,
   25:25 I found he had done **nothing** deserving of death, but because he
   27:33 and have gone without food—you **haven't** eaten **anything**.
   28: 6 waiting a long time and seeing **nothing** unusual happen to him,
   28:18 release me, because I was **not** guilty of **any** crime deserving death.
Ro 12:17 Do **not** repay **anyone** evil for evil. Be careful to do what is right in
   13: 8 Let **no** debt remain outstanding, except the continuing debt to love
   13: 8 **[RPG]** except the continuing debt to love one another,
1Co 1: 7 Therefore you do not lack **any** spiritual gift as you eagerly wait for
   3:18 Do **not** deceive yourselves. If any one of you thinks he is wise by
   3:21 So then, **no more** boasting about men! All things are yours,

10: 24 **Nobody** should seek his own good, but the good of others.
10: 25 Eat anything sold in the meat market **without** raising questions of
10: 27 eat whatever is put before you **without** raising questions of
2Co 6: 3 We put **no** stumbling block in anyone's path, so that our ministry
6: 3 We put no stumbling block in **anyone's** path, so that our ministry
6: 10 making many rich; having **nothing**, and yet possessing everything.
7: 9 as God intended and so were **not** harmed in **any way** by us.
11: 5 I do **not** think I am **in the least** inferior to those "super-apostles."
13: 7 Now we pray to God that you will **not** do **anything** [+*3590*]
Gal 6: 3 If anyone thinks he is something when he is **nothing**, he deceives
6: 17 Finally, let **no one** cause me trouble, for I bear on my body the
Eph 5: 6 Let **no one** deceive you with empty words, for because of such
Php 1: 28 without being frightened in **any way** by those who oppose you.
2: 3 Do **nothing** out of selfish ambition or vain conceit, but in humility
4: 6 Do **not** be anxious about **anything**, but in everything, by prayer
Col 2: 4 so that **no one** may deceive you by fine-sounding arguments.
2: 18 Do **not** let **anyone** who delights in false humility and the worship
1Th 3: 3 so that **no one** would be unsettled when he is tried. You know quite
4: 12 of outsiders and so that you will **not** be dependent on **anybody**.
2Th 2: 3 Don't let anyone deceive you **in any way** [+*2848*+*5573*], for ιthat
3: 11 some among you are idle. They are **not** busy; they are busybodies.
1Ti 4: 12 **Don't** let **anyone** look down on you because you are young,
5: 14 their homes and to give the enemy **no** opportunity for slander.
5: 21 instructions without partiality, and to do **nothing** out of favoritism.
5: 22 Do **not** be hasty in the laying on of hands, and do not share in the
6: 4 he is conceited and understands **nothing**. He has an unhealthy
Tit 2: 8 may be ashamed because they have **nothing** bad to say about us.
2: 15 and rebuke with all authority. Do **not** let **anyone** despise you.
3: 2 to slander **no one**, to be peaceable and considerate, and to show
3: 13 their way and see that they **have everything** they need [+*3309*].
Heb 10: 2 once for all, and would **no** longer have felt guilty for their sins.
Jas 1: 4 so that you may be mature and complete, **not** lacking **anything**.
1: 6 But when he asks, he must believe and **not** doubt, because he who
1: 13 When tempted, **no one** should say, "God is tempting me." For God
1Pe 3: 6 if you do what is right and do not give way to fear. **[NIE]**
1Jn 3: 7 Dear children, do **not** let **anyone** lead you astray. He who does
3Jn 1: 7 of the Name that they went out, receiving **no** *help* from the pagans.
Rcv 2: 10 Do **not** be afraid of what you are about to suffer. I tell you,
3: 11 Hold on to what you have, so that **no one** will take your crown.

3595 μηδέποτε, *mēdepote* [1] [√ *3590* + *1254* + *4544*]

never [1]

2Ti 3: 7 always learning but **never** able to acknowledge the truth.

3596 μηδέπω, *mēdepō* [1] [√ *3590* + *1254*]

not yet [1]

Heb 11: 7 By faith Noah, when warned about things **not yet** seen, in holy fear

3597 Μῆδος, *Mēdos* [1]

Medes [1]

Ac 2: 9 Parthians, **Medes** and Elamites; residents of Mesopotamia,

3598 μηθαμῶς, *mēthamōs* Not used in UBS/NIV
[√ *3590* + *1254* + *1609*]

3599 μηθείς, *mētheis* Not used in UBS/NIV
[√ *3590* + *1254* + *1651*]

3600 μηκέτι, *mēketi* [22] [√ *3590* + *2285*]

no longer [9], stop [3], again [1], any longer [1], don't any more
[1], leave your life of sin [+*279*] [1], never [+*3516*] [1], never
again [1], never [1], no more [1], no [1], not [1]

Mt 21: 19 Then he said to it, "May you **never** bear fruit again!" Immediately
Mk 1: 45 Jesus could **no longer** enter a town openly but stayed outside in
2: 2 So many gathered that there was **no** room *left*, not even outside the
9: 25 "I command you, come out of him and **never** enter him **again**."
11: 14 he said to the tree, "May no one ever eat fruit from you **again**."
Lk 8: 49 daughter is dead," he said. "**Don't** bother the teacher **any more**."

Jn 5: 14 well again. **Stop** sinning or something worse may happen to you."
8: 11 Jesus declared. "Go now and **leave your life of sin** [+*279*]."
Ac 4: 17 we must warn these men to speak **no longer** to anyone in this
13: 34 from the dead, **never** [+*3516*] to decay, is stated in these words:
25: 24 here in Caesarea, shouting that he ought not to live **any longer**.
Ro 6: 6 be done away with, that we should **no longer** be slaves to sin—
14: 13 Therefore let us **stop** passing judgment on one another. Instead,
15: 23 But now that there is **no more** place for me to work in these
2Co 5: 15 that those who live should **no longer** live for themselves but for
Eph 4: 14 Then we will **no longer** be infants, tossed back and forth by the
4: 17 on it in the Lord, that you must **no longer** live as the Gentiles do,
4: 28 He who has been stealing must steal **no longer**, but must work,
1Th 3: 1 So when we could stand it **no longer**, we thought it best to be left
3: 5 For this reason, when I could stand it **no longer**, I sent to find out
1Ti 5: 23 **Stop** drinking only water, and use a little wine because of your
1Pe 4: 2 he does **not** live the rest of his earthly life for evil human desires,

3601 μῆκος, *mēkos* [3] [→ *3426*, *3427*, *3428*, *3429*, *3430*, *3431*, *3432*, *3602*]

long [3]

Eph 3: 18 to grasp how wide and **long** and high and deep is the love of
Rev 21: 16 The city was laid out like a square, as **long** as it was wide.
21: 16 it to be 12,000 stadia in length, and as wide and high as it is **long**.

3602 μηκύνω, *mēkynō* [1] [√ *3601*]

grows [1]

Mk 4: 27 and day, whether he sleeps or gets up, the seed sprouts and **grows**,

3603 μηλωτή, *mēlōtē* [1]

sheepskins [1]

Heb 11: 37 They went about in **sheepskins** and goatskins, destitute, persecuted

3604 μήν¹, *mēn¹* [18] [→ *3741*, *3806*, *5485*, *5564*]

months [11], month [4], half [+*1971*] [2], a half [+*1971*] [1]

Lk 1: 24 became pregnant and *for* five **months** remained in seclusion.
1: 26 In the sixth **month**, God sent the angel Gabriel to Nazareth,
1: 36 old age, and she who was said to be barren is in her sixth **month**.
1: 56 Mary stayed with Elizabeth *for* about three **months** and
4: 25 when the sky was shut for three and a **half** [+*1971*] years
Ac 7: 20 *For* three **months** he was cared for in his father's house.
18: 11 So Paul stayed *for* a year and **a half** [+*1971*], teaching them the
19: 8 entered the synagogue and spoke boldly there for three **months**,
20: 3 where he stayed three **months**. Because the Jews had made a plot
28: 11 After three **months** we put out to sea in a ship that had wintered in
Gal 4: 10 You are observing *special* days and **months** and seasons
Jas 5: 17 and it did not rain on the land *for* three and a **half** [+*1971*] years.
Rev 9: 5 given power to kill them, but only to torture them *for* five **months**.
9: 10 in their tails they had power to torment people *for* five **months**.
9: 15 and day and **month** and year were released to kill a third of
11: 2 to the Gentiles. They will trample on the holy city *for* 42 **months**.
13: 5 blasphemies and to exercise his authority for forty-two **months**.
22: 2 bearing twelve crops of fruit, yielding its fruit every **month**.

3605 μήν², *mēn²* [1] [→ *1638*, *2447*; *cf. 3525*]

surely [+*1623*] [1]

Heb 6: 14 "I will **surely** [+*1623*] bless you and give you many descendants."

3606 μηνύω, *mēnyō* [4]

informed [1], report [1], showed [1], told [1]

Lk 20: 37 in the account of the bush, even Moses **showed** that the dead rise,
Jn 11: 57 where Jesus was, *he should* **report** it so that they might arrest him.
Ac 23: 30 *When I was* **informed** of a plot to be carried out against the man,
1Co 10: 28 both for the sake of the man who **told** you and for conscience'

3607 μήποτε, *mēpote* [25] [√ *3590 + 4544*]

or [5], otherwise [4], so that not [3], if you do [2], if [2], that none [+*5516*] [2], *untranslated* [1], because [1], for [1], in the hope that [1], never [1], no [1], only [1]

Mt 4: 6 their hands, **so that** you will **not** strike your foot against a stone.' "
5: 25 still with him on the way, **or** he may hand you over to the judge,
7: 6 **If you do**, they may trample them under their feet, and then turn
13: 15 **Otherwise** they might see with their eyes, hear with their ears,
13: 29 " 'No,' he answered, '**because** while you are pulling the weeds,
15: 32 want to send them away hungry, **or** they may collapse on the way."
25: 9 " 'No,' they replied, 'there may not be enough for both us
27: 64 **Otherwise**, his disciples may come and steal the body and tell the
Mk 4: 12 never understanding; **otherwise** they might turn and be forgiven!' "
14: 2 "But not during the Feast," they said, "**or** the people may riot."
Lk 3: 15 and were all wondering in their hearts **if** John might possibly be the
4: 11 their hands, **so that** you will **not** strike your foot against a stone.' "
12: 58 **or** he may drag you off to the judge, and the judge turn you over to
14: 8 **for** a person more distinguished than you may have been invited.
14: 12 **if you do**, they may invite you back and so you will be repaid.
14: 29 For **if** he lays the foundation and is not able to finish it,
21: 34 "Be careful, **or** your hearts will be weighed down with dissipation,
Jn 7: 26 **[NIE]** Have the authorities really concluded that he is the Christ?
Ac 5: 39 these men; you will **only** find yourselves fighting against God."
28: 27 **Otherwise** they might see with their eyes, hear with their ears,
2Ti 2: 25 **in the hope that** God will grant them repentance leading them to a
Heb 2: 1 therefore, to what we have heard, **so that** we do **not** drift away.
3: 12 See to it, brothers, **that** [+*5516*] **none** of you has a sinful,
4: 1 let us be careful **that** [+*5516*] **none** of you be found to have fallen
9: 17 has died; it **never** takes effect while the one who made it is living.

3608 μήπου, *mēpou* Not used in UBS/NIV
[√ *3590 + 4544*]

3609 μήπω, *mēpō* [2] [√ *3590*]

not yet [1], yet before [1]

Ro 9: 11 **Yet, before** the twins were born or had done anything good
Heb 9: 8 **not yet** been disclosed as long as the first tabernacle was still

3610 μήπως, *mēpōs* Not used in UBS/NIV
[√ *3590 + 4544*]

3611 μηρός, *mēros* [1]

thigh [1]

Rev 19: 16 On his robe and on his **thigh** he has this name written: KING OF

3612 μήτε, *mēte* [34] [√ *3590 + 5445*]

or [13], no [5], nor [4], *untranslated* [3], neither [3], not [3], and not [1], either [1], without [1]

Mt 5: 34 Do not swear at all: **either** by heaven, for it is God's throne;
5: 35 **or** by the earth, for it is his footstool;
5: 35 his footstool; **or** by Jerusalem, for it is the city of the Great King.
5: 36 **And** do **not** swear by your head, for you cannot make even one
11: 18 For John came **neither** eating nor drinking, and they say, 'He has a
11: 18 For John came neither eating **nor** drinking, and they say, 'He has a
Lk 7: 33 For John the Baptist came neither eating bread **nor** drinking wine,
9: 3 the journey—**no** staff, no bag, no bread, no money, no extra tunic.
9: 3 the journey—no staff, **no** bag, no bread, no money, no extra tunic.
9: 3 the journey—no staff, no bag, **no** bread, no money, no extra tunic.
9: 3 the journey—no staff, no bag, no bread, **no** money, no extra tunic.
9: 3 the journey—no staff, no bag, no bread, no money, **no** extra tunic.
Ac 23: 8 and that there are **neither** angels nor spirits, but the Pharisees
23: 8 and that there are neither angels **nor** spirits, but the Pharisees
23: 12 bound themselves with an oath **not** to eat or drink until they
23: 12 with an oath not to eat **or** drink until they had killed Paul.
23: 21 They have taken an oath **not** to eat or drink until they have killed
23: 21 have taken an oath not to eat **or** drink until they have killed him.
27: 20 When **neither** sun nor stars appeared for many days and the storm
27: 20 When neither sun **nor** stars appeared for many days and the storm

---

2Th 2: 2 to become easily unsettled or alarmed **[RPG]** by some prophecy,
2: 2 **[RPG]** report or letter supposed to have come from us,
2: 2 by some prophecy, report **or** letter supposed to have come from us,
1Ti 1: 7 but they do not know **[RPG]** what they are talking about
1: 7 what they are talking about **or** what they so confidently affirm.
Heb 7: 3 without genealogy, **without** beginning of days or end of life,
7: 3 without genealogy, without beginning of days **or** end of life,
Jas 5: 12 do not swear—**not** by heaven or by earth or by anything else.
5: 12 do not swear—not by heaven **or** by earth or by anything else.
5: 12 do not swear—not by heaven or by earth **or** by anything else.
Rev 7: 1 any wind from blowing on the land **or** on the sea or on any tree.
7: 1 any wind from blowing on the land or on the sea **or** on any tree.
7: 3 "Do not harm the land **or** the sea or the trees until we put a seal on
7: 3 **or** the trees until we put a seal on the foreheads of the servants of

3613 μήτηρ, *mētēr* [83] [→ *298, 3616, 3617, 3618, 3619*]

mother [73], birth [+*3120*] [4], mother's [3], mothers [2], *untranslated* [1]

Mt 1: 18 His **mother** Mary was pledged to be married to Joseph, but before
2: 11 they saw the child with his **mother** Mary, and they bowed down
2: 13 he said, "take the child and his **mother** and escape to Egypt.
2: 14 took the child and his **mother** during the night and left for Egypt,
2: 20 take the child and his **mother** and go to the land of Israel,
2: 21 took the child and his **mother** and went to the land of Israel.
10: 35 a daughter against her **mother**, a daughter-in-law against her
10: 37 who loves his father or **mother** more than me is not worthy of me;
12: 46 his **mother** and brothers stood outside, wanting to speak to him.
12: 47 Someone told him, "Your **mother** and brothers are standing outside,
12: 48 He replied to him, "Who is my **mother**, and who are my brothers?"
12: 49 to his disciples, he said, "Here are my **mother** and my brothers.
12: 50 will of my Father in heaven is my brother and sister and **mother**."
13: 55 Isn't his **mother's** name Mary, and aren't his brothers James,
14: 8 Prompted by her **mother**, she said, "Give me here on a platter the
14: 11 in on a platter and given to the girl, who carried it *to* her **mother**.
15: 4 'Honor your father and **mother**' and 'Anyone who curses his
15: 4 'Anyone who curses his father or **mother** must be put to death.'
15: 5 But you say that if a man says *to* his father or **mother**,
19: 5 a man will leave his father and **mother** and be united to his wife,
19: 12 For some are eunuchs **[NIE]** because they were born that way;
19: 19 honor your father and **mother**,' and 'love your neighbor as
19: 29 left houses or brothers or sisters or father or **mother** or children
20: 20 Then the **mother** of Zebedee's sons came to Jesus with her sons
27: 56 Mary the **mother** of James and Joses, and the mother of Zebedee's
27: 56 the mother of James and Joses, and the **mother** of Zebedee's sons.
Mk 3: 31 Then Jesus' **mother** and brothers arrived. Standing outside,
3: 32 told him, "Your **mother** and brothers are outside looking for you."
3: 33 "Who are my **mother** and my brothers?" he asked.
3: 34 circle around him and said, "Here are my **mother** and my brothers!
3: 35 Whoever does God's will is my brother and sister and **mother**."
5: 40 he took the child's father and **mother** and the disciples who were
6: 24 She went out and said *to* her **mother**, "What shall I ask for?"
6: 28 a platter. He presented it to the girl, and she gave it *to* her **mother**.
7: 10 For Moses said, 'Honor your father and your **mother**,' and,
7: 10 'Anyone who curses his father or **mother** must be put to death.'
7: 11 But you say that if a man says to his father or **mother**:
7: 12 then you no longer let him do anything *for* his father or **mother**.
10: 7 a man will leave his father and **mother** and be united to his wife,
10: 19 false testimony, do not defraud, honor your father and **mother**.' "
10: 29 or brothers or sisters or **mother** or father or children or fields for
10: 30 age (homes, brothers, sisters, **mothers**, children and fields—
15: 40 Mary the **mother** of James the younger and of Joses, and Salome.
Lk 1: 15 and he will be filled with the Holy Spirit even from **birth** [+*3120*].
1: 43 so favored, that the **mother** of my Lord should come to me?
1: 60 but his **mother** spoke up and said, "No! He is to be called John."
2: 33 child's father and **mother** marveled at what was said about him.
2: 34 Then Simeon blessed them and said to Mary, his **mother**:
2: 48 His **mother** said to him, "Son, why have you treated us like this?
2: 51 to them. But his **mother** treasured all these things in her heart.
7: 12 carried out—the only son *of* his **mother**, and she was a widow.
7: 15 and began to talk, and Jesus gave him back to his **mother**.
8: 19 Now Jesus' **mother** and brothers came to see him, but they were
8: 20 Someone told him, "Your **mother** and brothers are standing outside,
8: 21 "My **mother** and brothers are those who hear God's word and put it
8: 51 except Peter, John and James, and the child's father and **mother**.

12:53 **mother** against daughter and daughter against mother,
12:53 mother against daughter and daughter against **mother**,
14:26 "If anyone comes to me and does not hate his father and **mother**,
18:20 do not give false testimony, honor your father and **mother**.' "
Jn   2: 1 a wedding took place at Cana in Galilee. Jesus' **mother** was there,
     2: 3 was gone, Jesus' **mother** said to him, "They have no more wine."
     2: 5 His **mother** said to the servants, "Do whatever he tells you."
     2:12 After this he went down to Capernaum with his **mother**
     3: 4 "Surely he cannot enter a second time into his **mother's** womb to
     6:42 not Jesus, the son of Joseph, whose father and **mother** we know?
   19:25 Near the cross of Jesus stood his **mother**, his mother's sister,
   19:25 his **mother's** sister, Mary the wife of Clopas, and Mary
   19:26 When Jesus saw his **mother** there, and the disciple whom he loved
   19:26 he said *to* his **mother**, "Dear woman, here is your son,"
   19:27 and to the disciple, "Here is your **mother**." From that time on,
Ac   1:14 along with the women and Mary the **mother** of Jesus, and with his
     3: 2 Now a man crippled from **birth** [+*3120*] was being carried to the
   12:12 he went to the house of Mary the **mother** of John, also called
   14: 8 who was lame from **birth** [+*3120*] and had never walked.
Ro 16:13 Greet Rufus, chosen in the Lord, and his **mother**, who has been a
Gal   1:15 who set me apart from **birth** [+*3120*] and called me by his grace,
     4:26 But the Jerusalem that is above is free, and she is our **mother**.
Eph 5:31 a man will leave his father and **mother** and be united to his wife,
     6: 2 "Honor your father and **mother**"—which is the first commandment
1Ti   5: 2 older women as **mothers**, and younger women as sisters,
2Ti   1: 5 lived in your grandmother Lois and in your **mother** Eunice and,
Rev 17: 5 MYSTERY BABYLON THE GREAT THE **MOTHER** OF

3614 μήτι, *mēti* [17] [√ 3590 + 5516]

untranslated [7], surely not [3], could [2], unless [+*1623*] [2], can [1], except [+*323+1623*] [1], not [1]

Mt   7:16 [NIE] Do people pick grapes from thornbushes, or figs from
   12:23 people were astonished and said, "**Could** this be the Son of David?"
   26:22 and began to say to him one after the other, "**Surely not** I, Lord?"
   26:25 the one who would betray him, said, "**Surely not** I, Rabbi?"
Mk   4:21 [NIE] "Do you bring in a lamp to put it under a bowl or a bed?
   14:19 were saddened, and one by one they said to him, "**Surely not** I?"
Lk   6:39 told them this parable: [RPG] "Can a blind man lead a blind man?
     9:13 two fish—**unless** [+*1623*] we go and buy food for all this crowd."
Jn   4:29 man who told me everything I ever did. **Could** this be the Christ?"
     8:22 This made the Jews ask, [NIE] "Will he kill himself? Is that why
   18:35 "Am [NIE] I a Jew?" Pilate replied. "It was your people and your
Ac 10:47 [NIE] "Can anyone keep these people from being baptized with
1Co   7: 5 Do not deprive each other **except** [+*323+1623*] by mutual consent
2Co   1:17 When I planned this, [NIE] did I do it lightly? Or do I make my
   12:18 and I sent our brother with him. Titus did **not** exploit you, did he?
   13: 5 Christ Jesus is in you—**unless** [+*1623*], of course, you fail the test?
Jas   3:11 **Can** both fresh water and salt water flow from the same spring?

3615 μήτιγε, *mētige* [1] [√ 3590 + 5516 + 1145]

how much more [1]

1Co   6: 3 that we will judge angels? **How much more** the things of this life!

3616 μήτρα, *mētra* [2] [√ 3613]

firstborn [+*1380*] [1], womb [1]

Lk   2:23 "Every **firstborn** [+*1380*] male is to be consecrated to the Lord"),
Ro   4:19 about a hundred years old—and that Sarah's **womb** was also dead.

3617 μητραλῴας, *mētralōas* Not used in UBS/NIV
[√ 3613 + 262]

3618 μητρολῴας, *mētrolōas* [1] [√ 3613 + 262]

kill their mothers [1]

1Ti   1: 9 *for those who* **kill their** fathers or **mothers**, for murderers,

3619 μητρόπολις, *mētropolis* Not used in UBS/NIV
[√ 3613 + 4484]

3620 μιαίνω, *miainō* [5] [→ 299, 3621, 3622]

corrupted [2], ceremonial uncleanness [1], defile [1], pollute [1]

Jn 18:28 and to avoid **ceremonial uncleanness** the Jews did not enter the
Tit   1:15 but *to* those *who are* **corrupted** and do not believe, nothing is
     1:15 is pure. In fact, both their minds and consciences *are* **corrupted**.
Heb 12:15 and that no bitter root grows up to cause trouble and **defile** many.
Jude 1: 8 these dreamers **pollute** their own bodies, reject authority

3621 μίασμα, *miasma* [1] [√ 3620]

corruption [1]

2Pe   2:20 If they have escaped the **corruption** of the world by knowing our

3622 μιασμός, *miasmos* [1] [√ 3620]

corrupt [1]

2Pe   2:10 This is especially true of those who follow the **corrupt** desire of

3623 μίγμα, *migma* [1] [√ 3502]

mixture [1]

Jn 19:39 Nicodemus brought a **mixture** of myrrh and aloes,

3624 μίγνυμι, *mignymi* Not used in UBS/NIV [√ 3502]

3625 μικρός, *mikros* [46]

little [20], a little while [7], small [7], least [4], short [2], smallest [2], before long [+*2285*] [1], low [1], short [+*2461+3836*] [1], younger [1]

Mt 10:42 if anyone gives even a cup of cold water to one *of* these **little** *ones*
   11:11 yet he who is **least** in the kingdom of heaven is greater than he.
   13:32 Though it is the **smallest** of all your seeds, yet when it grows,
   18: 6 But if anyone causes one *of* these **little** *ones* who believe in me to
   18:10 "See that you do not look down on one *of* these **little** *ones*.
   18:14 in heaven is not willing that any *of* these **little** *ones* should be lost.
   26:39 Going a **little** farther, he fell with his face to the ground
   26:73 After a **little** *while*, those standing there went up to Peter and said,
Mk   4:31 a mustard seed, which is the **smallest** seed you plant in the ground.
     9:42 "And if anyone causes one *of* these **little** *ones* who believe in me to
   14:35 Going a **little** farther, he fell to the ground and prayed that if
   14:70 After a **little** *while*, those standing near said to Peter, "Surely you
   15:40 Mary the mother of James the **younger** and of Joses, and Salome.
Lk   7:28 yet the one who is **least** in the kingdom of God is greater than he."
     9:48 sent me. For he who is **least** among you all—he is the greatest."
   12:32 "Do not be afraid, **little** flock, for your Father has been pleased to
   17: 2 his neck than for him to cause one *of* these **little** *ones* to sin.
Jn   7:33 "I am with you for only a **short** time, and then I go to the one who
   12:35 told them, "You are going to have the light just a **little** while longer.
   13:33 "My children, I will be with you only a **little** longer. You will look
   14:19 **Before long** [+*2285*], the world will not see me anymore,
   16:16 "*In* **a little while** you will see me no more, and then after a little
   16:16 will see me no more, and then after **a little while** you will see me."
   16:17 '*In* **a little while** you will see me no more, and then after a little
   16:17 and then after **a little while** you will see me,' and 'Because I am
   16:18 They kept asking, "What does he mean by '**a little while**'?
   16:19 '*In* **a little while** you will see me no more, and then after a little
   16:19 will see me no more, and then after **a little while** you will see me'?
Ac   8:10 and all the people, both high and **low**, gave him their attention
   26:22 very day, and so I stand here and testify *to* **small** and great alike.
1Co   5: 6 Don't you know that a **little** yeast works through the whole batch
2Co 11: 1 I hope you will put up with a **little** of my foolishness; but you are
   11:16 me just as you would a fool, so that I may do a **little** boasting.
Gal   5: 9 "A **little** yeast works through the whole batch of dough."
Heb 8:11 they will all know me, from the **least** of them to the greatest.
   10:37 For in just a very **little** while, "He who is coming will come
Jas   3: 5 Likewise the tongue is a **small** part of the body, but it makes great
Rev   3: 8 I know that you have **little** strength, yet you have kept my word
     6:11 and they were told to wait a **little** longer, until the number of their
   11:18 and those who reverence your name, both **small** and great—
   13:16 forced everyone, **small** and great, rich and poor, free and slave,

19: 5 all you his servants, you who fear him, both **small** and great!"
19:18 and the flesh *of* all people, free and slave, **small** and great."
20: 3 years were ended. After that, he must be set free *for* a **short** time.
20:12 And I saw the dead, great and **small**, standing before the throne,

3626 Μίλητος, *Milētos* [3]

Miletus [3]

Ac 20:15 over to Samos, and on the following day arrived at **Miletus**.
   20:17 From **Miletus**, Paul sent to Ephesus for the elders of the church.
2Ti 4:20 Erastus stayed in Corinth, and I left Trophimus sick in **Miletus**.

3627 μίλιον, *milion* [1]

mile [1]

Mt 5:41 If someone forces you to go one **mile**, go with him two miles.

3628 μιμέομαι, *mimeomai* [4] [→ *3629, 5213*]

imitate [2], follow example [1], follow [1]

2Th 3: 7 For you yourselves know how you ought *to* **follow** our **example**.
     3: 9 but in order to make ourselves a model for you to **follow**.
Heb 13: 7 Consider the outcome of their way of life and **imitate** their faith.
3Jn 1:11 Dear friend, *do* not **imitate** what is evil but what is good.

3629 μιμητής, *mimētēs* [6] [√ *3628*]

imitators [3], follow example [*+1181*] [1], imitate [*+1181*] [1], imitate [1]

1Co 4:16 Therefore I urge you to **imitate** [*+1181*] me.
     11: 1 **Follow** my **example** [*+1181*], as I follow the example of Christ.
Eph 5: 1 Be **imitators** of God, therefore, as dearly loved children
1Th 1: 6 You became **imitators** of us and of the Lord; in spite of severe
     2:14 For you, brothers, became **imitators** of God's churches in Judea,
Heb 6:12 but to **imitate** those who through faith and patience inherit what

3630 μιμνήσκομαι, *mimnēskomai* [23] [√ *3648*]

remember [10], remembered [6], remembering [2], are mindful [1], realize [1], recall [1], recalled [1], recalling [1]

Mt 5:23 and there **remember** that your brother has something against you,
   26:75 Then Peter **remembered** the word Jesus had spoken: "Before the
   27:63 *"we* **remember** that while he was still alive that deceiver said,
Lk 1:54 He has helped his servant Israel, **remembering** to be merciful
     1:72 to show mercy to our fathers and *to* **remember** his holy covenant,
  16:25 **remember** that in your lifetime you received your good things,
  23:42 "Jesus, **remember** me when you come into your kingdom."
  24: 6 **Remember** how he told you, while he was still with you in
  24: 8 Then *they* **remembered** his words.
Jn 2:17 His disciples **remembered** that it is written: "Zeal for your house
     2:22 was raised from the dead, his disciples **recalled** what he had said.
  12:16 Only after Jesus was glorified *did they* **realize** that these things
Ac 10:31 God has heard your prayer and **remembered** your gifts to the poor.
  11:16 Then *I* **remembered** what the Lord had said: 'John baptized with
1Co 11: 2 I praise you for **remembering** me in everything and for holding to
2Ti 1: 4 **Recalling** your tears, I long to see you, so that I may be filled with
Heb 2: 6 "What is man that *you* **are mindful** of him, the son of man that you
    8:12 forgive their wickedness and *will* **remember** their sins no more."
  10:17 he adds: "Their sins and lawless acts *I will* **remember** no more."
  13: 3 **Remember** those in prison as if you were their fellow prisoners,
2Pe 3: 2 I *want you to* **recall** the words spoken in the past by the holy
Jude 1:17 **remember** what the apostles of our Lord Jesus Christ foretold.
Rev 16:19 God **remembered** Babylon the Great and gave her the cup filled

3631 μισέω, *miseō* [40]

hate [13], hates [12], hated [9], hate [*+1639*] [3], hating [2], detestable [1]

Mt 5:43 heard that it was said, 'Love your neighbor and **hate** your enemy.'
   6:24 Either *he will* **hate** the one and love the other, or he will be
  10:22 All men *will* **hate** [*+1639*] you because of me, but he who stands
  24: 9 put to death, and you will be **hated** by all nations because of me.

  24:10 will turn away from the faith and will betray and **hate** each other,
Mk 13:13 All men *will* **hate** [*+1639*] you because of me, but he who stands
Lk 1:71 salvation from our enemies and from the hand of all who **hate** us—
   6:22 Blessed are you when men **hate** you, when they exclude you
   6:27 who hear me: Love your enemies, do good *to* those *who* **hate** you,
  14:26 "If anyone comes to me and *does* not **hate** his father and mother,
  16:13 Either *he will* **hate** the one and love the other, or he will be
  19:14 "But his subjects **hated** him and sent a delegation after him to say,
  21:17 All men *will* **hate** [*+1639*] you because of me.
Jn 3:20 Everyone who does evil **hates** the light, and will not come into the
   7: 7 The world cannot **hate** you, but it hates me because I testify that
   7: 7 hate you, but *it* **hates** me because I testify that what it does is evil.
  12:25 while the man *who* **hates** his life in this world will keep it for
  15:18 "If the world **hates** you, keep in mind that it hated me first.
  15:18 "If the world hates you, keep in mind that *it* **hated** me first.
  15:19 chosen you out of the world. That is why the world **hates** you.
  15:23 He *who* **hates** me hates my Father as well.
  15:23 He who hates me **hates** my Father as well.
  15:24 these miracles, and yet *they* have **hated** both me and my Father.
  15:25 what is written in their Law: *'They* **hated** me without reason.'
  17:14 I have given them your word and the world *has* **hated** them,
Ro 7:15 what I do. For what I want to do I do not do, but what *I* **hate** I do.
   9:13 Just as it is written: "Jacob I loved, but Esau *I* **hated**."
Eph 5:29 After all, no one ever **hated** his own body, but he feeds and cares
Tit 3: 3 We lived in malice and envy, being hated and **hating** one another.
Heb 1: 9 You have loved righteousness and **hated** wickedness;
1Jn 2: 9 to be in the light but **hates** his brother is still in the darkness.
   2:11 But whoever **hates** his brother is in the darkness and walks around
   3:13 Do not be surprised, my brothers, if the world **hates** you.
   3:15 Anyone who **hates** his brother is a murderer, and you know that no
   4:20 If anyone says, "I love God," yet **hates** his brother, he is a liar.
Jude 1:23 with fear—**hating** even the clothing stained by corrupted flesh.
Rev 2: 6 *You* **hate** the practices of the Nicolaitans, which I also hate.
   2: 6 You hate the practices of the Nicolaitans, which I also **hate**.
  17:16 The beast and the ten horns you saw *will* **hate** the prostitute.
  18: 2 for every evil spirit, a haunt *for* every unclean and **detestable** bird.

3632 μισθαποδοσία, *misthapodosia* [3] [√ *3635 + 608 + 1443*]

punishment [1], reward [1], rewarded [1]

Heb 2: 2 and every violation and disobedience received its just **punishment**,
  10:35 So do not throw away your confidence; it will be richly **rewarded**.
  11:26 treasures of Egypt, because he was looking ahead to his **reward**.

3633 μισθαποδότης, *misthapodotēs* [1] [√ *3635 + 608 + 1443*]

rewards [*+1181*] [1]

Heb 11: 6 and that *he* **rewards** [*+1181*] those who earnestly seek him.

3634 μίσθιος, *misthios* [2] [√ *3635*]

hired men [2]

Lk 15:17 'How many of my father's **hired men** have food to spare,
  15:19 to be called your son; make me like one *of* your **hired men**.'

3635 μισθός, *misthos* [29] [→ *521, 3632, 3633, 3634, 3636, 3637, 3638*]

reward [17], wages [7], paid back [1], profit [1], rewarded [*+3284*] [1], rewarded [*+655*] [1], rewarding [*+1443+3836*] [1]

Mt 5:12 Rejoice and be glad, because great is your **reward** in heaven,
   5:46 If you love those who love you, what **reward** will you get?
   6: 1 If you do, you will have no **reward** from your Father in heaven.
   6: 2 I tell you the truth, they have received their **reward** in full.
   6: 5 I tell you the truth, they have received their **reward** in full.
   6:16 I tell you the truth, they have received their **reward** in full.
  10:41 a prophet because he is a prophet will receive a prophet's **reward**,
  10:41 he is a righteous man will receive a righteous man's **reward**.
  10:42 I tell you the truth, he will certainly not lose his **reward**."
  20: 8 'Call the workers and pay them their **wages**, beginning with the
Mk 9:41 because you belong to Christ will certainly not lose his **reward**.

Lk   6:23 and leap for joy, because great is your **reward** in heaven.
      6:35 Then your **reward** will be great, and you will be sons of the Most
     10: 7 whatever they give you, for the worker deserves his **wages**.
Jn   4:36 Even now the reaper draws his **wages**, even now he harvests the
Ac   1:18 (With the **reward** he got for his wickedness, Judas bought a field;
Ro   4: 4 his **wages** are not credited to him as a gift, but as an obligation.
1Co   3: 8 and each *will be* **rewarded** [+3284] according to his own labor.
      3:14 If what he has built survives, he will receive his **reward**.
      9:17 If I preach voluntarily, I have a **reward**; if not voluntarily,
      9:18 What then is my **reward**? Just this: that in preaching the gospel I
1Ti   5:18 it is treading out the grain," and "The worker deserves his **wages**."
Jas   5: 4 The **wages** you failed to pay the workmen who mowed your fields
2Pe   2:13 They will be **paid back** with harm for the harm they have done.
      2:15 way of Balaam son of Beor, who loved the **wages** of wickedness.
2Jn   1: 8 you have worked for, but that *you may be* **rewarded** [+655] fully.
Jude 1:11 the way of Cain; they have rushed *for* **profit** into Balaam's error;
Rev 11:18 and *for* **rewarding** [+1443+3836] your servants the prophets and
     22:12 My **reward** is with me, and I will give to everyone according to

3636 μισθόω, *misthoō* [2] [√ *3635*]

hire [1], hired [1]

Mt   20: 1 went out early in the morning *to* **hire** men to work in his vineyard.
     20: 7 " 'Because no one *has* **hired** us,' they answered. "He said to them,

3637 μίσθωμα, *misthōma* [1] [√ *3635*]

rented house [1]

Ac   28:30 For two whole years Paul stayed there in his own **rented house**

3638 μισθωτός, *misthōtos* [3] [√ *3635*]

hired hand [2], hired men [1]

Mk   1:20 and they left their father Zebedee in the boat with the **hired men**
Jn   10:12 The **hired hand** is not the shepherd who owns the sheep. So when
     10:13 The man runs away because he is a **hired hand** and cares nothing

3639 Μιτυλήνη, *Mitylēnē* [1]

Mitylene [1]

Ac   20:14 he met us at Assos, we took him aboard and went on to **Mitylene**.

3640 Μιχαήλ, *Michaēl* [2]

Michael [2]

Jude 1: 9 But even the archangel **Michael**, when he was disputing with the
Rev 12: 7 **Michael** and his angels fought against the dragon, and the dragon

3641 μνᾶ, *mna* [9]

mina [4], *untranslated* [2], minas [2], more[s] [1]

Lk   19:13 So he called ten of his servants and gave them ten **minas**.
     19:16 "The first one came and said, 'Sir, your **mina** has earned ten more.'
     19:16 one came and said, 'Sir, your **mina** has earned ten **[RPG]** more.'
     19:18 "The second came and said, 'Sir, your **mina** has earned five more.'
     19:18 "The second came and said, 'Sir, your **mina** has earned five **more**[s].'
     19:20 "Then another servant came and said, 'Sir, here is your **mina**;
     19:24 'Take his **mina** away from him and give it to the one who has ten
     19:24 his mina away from him and give it to the one who has ten **minas**.'
     19:25 " 'Sir,' they said, 'he already has ten!' **[RPG]**

3642 μνάομαι, *mnaomai*   Not used in UBS/NIV
[→ *3650*]

3643 Μνάσων, *Mnasōn* [1]

Mnason [1]

Ac   21:16 Caesarea accompanied us and brought us to the home of **Mnason**,

3644 μνεία, *mneia* [7] [√ *3648*]

remember [+4472] [2], memories [1], mentioning [+4472] [1],
remember [+2400] [1], remember [1], remembering [+4472] [1]

Ro   1: 9 his Son, is my witness how constantly *I* **remember** [+4472] you
Eph   1:16 I have not stopped giving thanks for you, **remembering** [+4472]
Php   1: 3 I thank my God every time I **remember** you.
1Th   1: 2 We always thank God for all of you, **mentioning** [+4472] you in
      3: 6 He has told us that you always have pleasant **memories** of us
2Ti   1: 3 and day *I* constantly **remember** [+2400] you in my prayers.
Phm   1: 4 I always thank my God *as* I **remember** [+4472] you in my prayers,

3645 μνῆμα, *mnēma* [8] [√ *3648*]

tomb [4], tombs [3], burial [+1650+5502] [1]

Mk   5: 3 This man lived in the **tombs**, and no one could bind him any more,
      5: 5 Night and day among the **tombs** and in the hills he would cry out
Lk   8:27 not worn clothes or lived in a house, but had lived in the **tombs**.
     23:53 wrapped it in linen cloth and placed it in a **tomb** cut in the rock,
     24: 1 women took the spices they had prepared and went to the **tomb**.
Ac   2:29 David died and was buried, and his **tomb** is here to this day.
      7:16 and placed in the **tomb** that Abraham had bought from the sons of
Rev 11: 9 will gaze on their bodies and refuse them **burial** [+1650+5502].

3646 μνημεῖον, *mnēmeion* [40] [√ *3648*]

tomb [31], tombs [5], graves [3], entrance[s] [1]

Mt   8:28 two demon-possessed men coming from the **tombs** met him.
     23:29 tombs for the prophets and decorate the **graves** of the righteous.
     27:52 The **tombs** broke open and the bodies of many holy people who
     27:53 They came out of the **tombs**, and after Jesus' resurrection they went
     27:60 and placed it in his own new **tomb** that he had cut out of the rock.
     27:60 He rolled a big stone in front of the entrance *to* the **tomb** and went
     28: 8 So the women hurried away from the **tomb**, afraid yet filled with
Mk   5: 2 a man with an evil spirit came from the **tombs** to meet him.
      6:29 John's disciples came and took his body and laid it in a **tomb**.
     15:46 wrapped it in the linen, and placed it in a **tomb** cut out of rock.
     15:46 of rock. Then he rolled a stone against the entrance *of* the **tomb**.
     16: 2 of the week, just after sunrise, they were on their way to the **tomb**
     16: 3 "Who will roll the stone away from the entrance *of* the **tomb**?"
     16: 5 As they entered the **tomb**, they saw a young man dressed in a
     16: 8 and bewildered, the women went out and fled from the **tomb**.
Lk   11:44 "Woe to you, because you are like unmarked **graves**, which men
     11:47 "Woe to you, because you build **tombs** for the prophets, and it was
     23:55 followed Joseph and saw the **tomb** and how his body was laid in it.
     24: 2 They found the stone rolled away from the **tomb**,
     24: 9 When they came back from the **tomb**, they told all these things to
     24:12 Peter, however, got up and ran to the **tomb**. Bending over,
     24:22 our women amazed us. They went to the **tomb** early this morning
     24:24 Then some of our companions went to the **tomb** and found it just
Jn   5:28 for a time is coming when all who are in their **graves** will hear his
     11:17 Jesus found that Lazarus had already been in the **tomb** for four
     11:31 followed her, supposing she was going to the **tomb** to mourn there.
     11:38 Jesus, once more deeply moved, came to the **tomb**. It was a cave
     12:17 crowd that was with him when he called Lazarus from the **tomb**
     19:41 there was a garden, and in the garden a new **tomb**, in which no one
     19:42 was the Jewish day of Preparation and since the **tomb** was nearby,
     20: 1 Mary Magdalene went to the **tomb** and saw that the stone had been
     20: 1 and saw that the stone had been removed from the **entrance**[s].
     20: 2 Jesus loved, and said, "They have taken the Lord out of the **tomb**,
     20: 3 So Peter and the other disciple started for the **tomb**.
     20: 4 but the other disciple outran Peter and reached the **tomb** first.
     20: 6 Simon Peter, who was behind him, arrived and went into the **tomb**.
     20: 8 other disciple, who had reached the **tomb** first, also went inside.
     20:11 but Mary stood outside the **tomb** crying. As she wept, she bent
     20:11 the tomb crying. As she wept, she bent over to look into the **tomb**
Ac   13:29 they took him down from the tree and laid him in a **tomb**.

3647 μνήμη, *mnēmē* [1] [√ *3648*]

remember [+4472] [1]

2Pe   1:15 you will always be able *to* **remember** [+4472] these things.

3648 μνημονεύω, *mnēmoneuō* [21] [→ 389, 390, 2057, 3630, 3644, 3645, 3646, 3647, 3649, 5703, 5704]

remember [16], forgets [+4033] [1], remembered [1], remembering [1], spoke [1], thinking [1]

Mt 16: 9 Don't *you* **remember** the five loaves for the five thousand,
Mk 8:18 fail to see, and ears but fail to hear? And don't *you* **remember**?
Lk 17:32 **Remember** Lot's wife!
Jn 15:20 **Remember** the words I spoke to you: 'No servant is greater than
    16: 4 so that when the time comes *you will* **remember** that I warned
    16:21 but when her baby is born *she* **forgets** [+4033] the anguish
Ac 20:31 **Remember** that for three years I never stopped warning each of
    20:35 the weak, **remembering** the words the Lord Jesus himself said:
Gal 2:10 All they asked was that *we should continue to* **remember** the
Eph 2:11 **remember** that formerly you who are Gentiles by birth and called
Col 4:18 in my own hand. **Remember** my chains. Grace be with you.
1Th 1: 3 *We* continually **remember** before our God and Father your work
    2: 9 Surely *you* **remember**, brothers, our toil and hardship; we worked
2Th 2: 5 Don't *you* **remember** that when I was with you I used to tell you
2Ti 2: 8 **Remember** Jesus Christ, raised from the dead, descended from
Heb 11:15 If *they had been* **thinking** of the country they had left, they would
    11:22 **spoke** about the exodus of the Israelites from Egypt and gave
    13: 7 **Remember** your leaders, who spoke the word of God to you.
Rev 2: 5 **Remember** the height from which you have fallen! Repent
    3: 3 **Remember**, therefore, what you have received and heard;
    18: 5 sins are piled up to heaven, and God *has* **remembered** her crimes.

3649 μνημόσυνον, *mnēmosynon* [3] [√ 3648]

memory [2], memorial offering [1]

Mt 26:13 the world, what she has done will also be told, in **memory** of her."
Mk 14: 9 the world, what she has done will also be told, in **memory** of her."
Ac 10: 4 and gifts to the poor have come up as a **memorial offering** before

3650 μνηστεύω, *mnēsteuō* [3] [√ 3642]

pledged to be married [3]

Mt 1:18 His mother Mary *was* **pledged to be married** to Joseph, but before
Lk 1:27 to a virgin **pledged to be married** to a man named Joseph,
    2: 5 who *was* **pledged to be married** to him and was expecting a child.

3651 μογγιλάλος, *mongilalos*   Not used in UBS/NIV [√ 3281]

3652 μογιλάλος, *mogilalos* [1] [√ 3653 + 3281]

could hardly talk [1]

Mk 7:32 people brought to him a man who was deaf and **could hardly talk**,

3653 μόγις, *mogis* [1] [→ 3652, 3660, 3677]

scarcely ever [1]

Lk 9:39 at the mouth. It **scarcely ever** leaves him and is destroying him.

3654 μόδιος, *modios* [3]

bowl [3]

Mt 5:15 Neither do people light a lamp and put it under a **bowl**.
Mk 4:21 to them, "Do you bring in a lamp to put it under a **bowl** or a bed?
Lk 11:33 and puts it in a place where it will be hidden, or under a **bowl**.

3655 μοιχαλίς, *moichalis* [7] [√ 3659]

adulterous [4], adulteress [2], adultery [1]

Mt 12:39 "A wicked and **adulterous** generation asks for a miraculous sign!
    16: 4 A wicked and **adulterous** generation looks for a miraculous sign,
Mk 8:38 of me and my words in this **adulterous** and sinful generation,
Ro 7: 3 man while her husband is still alive, she is called an **adulteress**.
    7: 3 she is released from that law and is not an **adulteress**,
Jas 4: 4 *You* **adulterous** *people*, don't you know that friendship with the
2Pe 2:14 With eyes full *of* **adultery**, they never stop sinning; they seduce

3656 μοιχάω, *moichaō* [4] [√ 3659]

commits adultery [4]

Mt 5:32 and anyone who marries the divorced woman **commits adultery**.
    19: 9 and marries another woman **commits adultery**."
Mk 10:11 and marries another woman **commits adultery** against her.
    10:12 her husband and marries another man, *she* **commits adultery**."

3657 μοιχεία, *moicheia* [3] [√ 3659]

adultery [3]

Mt 15:19 murder, **adultery**, sexual immorality, theft, false testimony,
Mk 7:21 come evil thoughts, sexual immorality, theft, murder, **adultery**,
Jn 8: 3 and the Pharisees brought in a woman caught in **adultery**.

3658 μοιχεύω, *moicheuō* [15] [√ 3659]

commit adultery [10], commits adultery [2], adultery [1], become an adulteress [1], committed adultery with [1]

Mt 5:27 "You have heard that it was said, '*Do* not **commit adultery**.'
    5:28 lustfully *has* already **committed adultery with** her in his heart.
    5:32 for marital unfaithfulness, causes her *to* **become an adulteress**,
    19:18 " '*Do* not murder, *do* not **commit adultery**, do not steal,
Mk 10:19 '*Do* not murder, *do* not **commit adultery**, do not steal, do not give
Lk 16:18 divorces his wife and marries another woman **commits adultery**.
    16:18 and the man who marries a divorced woman **commits adultery**.
    18:20 '*Do* not **commit adultery**, do not murder, do not steal, do not give
Jn 8: 4 to Jesus, "Teacher, this woman was caught in the act *of* **adultery**.
Ro 2:22 You who say that people *should* not **commit adultery**, do you
    2:22 that people should not commit adultery, *do you* **commit adultery**?
    13: 9 "*Do* not **commit adultery**," "Do not murder," "Do not steal,"
Jas 2:11 who said, "*Do* not **commit adultery**," also said, "Do not murder."
    2:11 If *you do* not **commit adultery** but do commit murder, you have
Rev 2:22 and I will make those *who* **commit adultery** with her suffer

3659 μοιχός, *moichos* [3] [→ 3655, 3656, 3657, 3658]

adulterers [2], adulterer [1]

Lk 18:11 robbers, evildoers, **adulterers**—or even like this tax collector.
1Co 6: 9 Neither the sexually immoral nor idolaters nor **adulterers** nor
Heb 13: 4 for God will judge the **adulterer** and all the sexually immoral.

3660 μόλις, *molis* [6] [√ 3653]

difficulty [2], hard [1], hardly [1], very rarely [1], with difficulty [1]

Ac 14:18 they had **difficulty** keeping the crowd from sacrificing to them.
    27: 7 headway for many days and had **difficulty** arriving off Cnidus.
    27: 8 We moved along the coast **with difficulty** and came to a place
    27:16 called Cauda, we were **hardly** able to make the lifeboat secure.
Ro 5: 7 **Very rarely** will anyone die for a righteous man, though for a
1Pe 4:18 And, "If it is **hard** for the righteous to be saved, what will become

3661 Μολόχ, *Moloch* [1]

Molech [1]

Ac 7:43 You have lifted up the shrine *of* **Molech** and the star of your god

3662 μολύνω, *molynō* [3] [→ 3663]

defile [1], defiled [1], soiled [1]

1Co 8: 7 to an idol, and since their conscience is weak, *it is* **defiled**.
Rev 3: 4 Yet you have a few people in Sardis who *have* not **soiled** their
    14: 4 These are those who *did* not **defile** *themselves* with women,

3663 μολυσμός, *molysmos* [1] [√ 3662]

that contaminates [1]

2Co 7: 1 let us purify ourselves from everything **that contaminates** body

3664 μομφή, momphē [1] [√ 3522]

grievances [1]

Col 3:13 and forgive whatever **grievances** you may have against one

3665 μονή, monē [2] [√ 3531]

home [1], rooms [1]

Jn 14: 2 In my Father's house are many **rooms**; if it were not so, I would
      14:23 love him, and we will come to him and make our **home** with him.

3666 μονογενής, monogenēs [9] [√ 3668 + 1181]

one and only [5], only [2], one and only son [1], only child [1]

Lk 7:12 carried out—the **only** son of his mother, and she was a widow.
      8:42 because his **only** daughter, a girl of about twelve, was dying.
      9:38 "Teacher, I beg you to look at my son, for he is my **only child**.
Jn 1:14 We have seen his glory, the glory of the **One and Only**, who came
      1:18 No one has ever seen God, but God the **One and Only**, who is at
      3:16 "For God so loved the world that he gave his **one and only** Son,
      3:18 because he has not believed in the name of God's **one and only**
Heb 11:17 received the promises was about to sacrifice his **one and only son**,
1Jn 4: 9 He sent his **one and only** Son into the world that we might live

3667 μόνον, monon [66] [√ 3668]

only [41], just [6], *untranslated* [4], alone [3], but [3], simply [2], all they asked was [1], even [1], just one [+4047] [1], merely [1], only [+1623+3590] [1], what is more [+247+1254+2779+4024] [1], whatever happens [1]

Mt 5:47 And if you greet **only** your brothers, what are you doing more than
      8: 8 my roof. But **just** say the word, and my servant will be healed.
      9:21 She said to herself, "If I **only** touch his cloak, I will be healed."
    10:42 And if anyone gives **even** a cup of cold water to one of these little
    14:36 and begged him to let the sick **just** touch the edge of his cloak,
    21:19 **[RPG]** Then he said to it, "May you never bear fruit again!"
    21:21 do not doubt, not **only** can you do what was done to the fig tree,
Mk 5:36 Jesus told the synagogue ruler, "Don't be afraid; **just** believe."
      6: 8 except a staff—**[RPG]** no bread, no bag, no money in your belts.
Lk 8:50 to Jairus, "Don't be afraid; **just** believe, and she will be healed."
Jn 5:18 not **only** was he breaking the Sabbath, but he was even calling God
    11:52 and not **only** for that nation but also for the scattered children of
    12: 9 and came, not **only** because of him but also to see Lazarus,
    13: 9 Peter replied, "not **just** my feet but my hands and my head as well!"
    17:20 "My prayer is not for them **alone**. I pray also for those who will
Ac 8:16 they had **simply** been baptized into the name of the Lord Jesus.
    11:19 and Antioch, telling the message **only** [+1623+3590] to Jews.
    18:25 about Jesus accurately, though he knew **only** the baptism of John.
    19:26 and led astray large numbers of people here **[NIE]** in Ephesus
    19:27 There is danger not **only** that our trade will lose its good name,
    21:13 I am ready not **only** to be bound, but also to die in Jerusalem for
    26:29 I pray God that not **only** you but all who are listening to me today
    27:10 to be disastrous and bring great loss **[NIE]** to ship and cargo,
Ro 1:32 they not **only** continue to do these very things but also approve of
    3:29 Is God the God of Jews **only**? Is he not the God of Gentiles too?
    4:12 And he is also the father of the circumcised who not **only** are
    4:16 not **only** to those who are of the law but also to those who are of
    4:23 The words "it was credited to him" were written not for him **alone**,
    5: 3 Not **only** so, but we also rejoice in our sufferings, because we
    5:11 Not **only** is this so, but we also rejoice in God through our Lord
    8:23 Not **only** so, but we ourselves, who have the firstfruits of the Spirit,
    9:10 Not **only** that, but Rebekah's children had one and the same father,
    9:24 he also called, not **only** from the Jews but also from the Gentiles?
    13: 5 not **only** because of possible punishment but also because of
1Co 7:39 free to marry anyone she wishes, **but** he must belong to the Lord.
    15:19 If **only** for this life we have hope in Christ, we are to be pitied
2Co 7: 7 and not **only** by his coming but also by the comfort you had given
    8:10 Last year you were the first not **only** to give but also to have the
    8:19 **What is more** [+247+1254+2779+4024], he was chosen by the
          churches to accompany us as we carry the offering, which we
    8:21 not **only** in the eyes of the Lord but also in the eyes of men. ˙
    9:12 This service that you perform is not **only** supplying the needs of
Gal 1:23 They **only** heard the report: "The man who formerly persecuted us
    2:10 **All they asked was** that we should continue to remember the poor,

    3: 2 I would like to learn **just one** [+4047] *thing* from you: Did you
    4:18 is good, and to be so always and not **just** when I am with you.
    5:13 **But** do not use your freedom to indulge the sinful nature; rather,
    6:12 The **only** *reason* they do this is to avoid being persecuted for the
Eph 1:21 be given, not **only** in the present age but also in the one to come.
Php 1:27 **Whatever happens**, conduct yourselves in a manner worthy of the
    1:29 For it has been granted to you on behalf of Christ not **only** to
    2:12 not **only** in my presence, but now much more in my absence—
    2:27 But God had mercy on him, and not on him **only** but also on me,
1Th 1: 5 because our gospel came to you not **simply** with words, but also
    1: 8 The Lord's message rang out from you not **only** in Macedonia
    2: 8 so much that we were delighted to share with you not **only** the
2Th 2: 7 **but** the one who now holds it back will continue to do so till he is
1Ti 5:13 And not **only** do they become idlers, but also gossips
2Ti 2:20 In a large house there are articles not **only** of gold and silver,
    4: 8 and not **only** to me, but also to all who have longed for his
Heb 9:10 They are **only** a matter of food and drink and various ceremonial
  12:26 "Once more I will shake not **only** the earth but also the heavens."
Jas 1:22 Do not **merely** listen to the word, and so deceive yourselves.
    2:24 that a person is justified by what he does and not by faith **alone**.
1Pe 2:18 not **only** to those who are good and considerate, but also to those
1Jn 2: 2 and not **only** for ours but also for the sins of the whole world.
    5: 6 He did not come by water **only**, but by water and blood.

3668 μόνος, monos [48] [→ 2911, 3666, 3667, 3669, 3670]

μόνος θεός (the only God) [5] Jn 5:44; 17:3; Ro 16:27; 1Ti 1:17; Jude 1:25

only [22], alone [13], *untranslated* [3], all alone [1], alone [+2848] [1], by himself [+899] [1], by myself [1], by ourselves [1], by themselves [1], just [1], only [+1623+3590] [1], only a single [1], private [1]

Mt 4: 4 'Man does not live on bread **alone**, but on every word that comes
    4:10 it is written: 'Worship the Lord your God, and serve him **only**.' "
    12: 4 which was not lawful for them to do, but **only** for the priests.
    14:23 by himself to pray. When evening came, he was there **alone**,
    17. 8 When they looked up, they saw no one except Jesus. **[RPG]**
    18:15 go and show him his fault, **just** between the two of you.
    24:36 not even the angels in heaven, nor the Son, but **only** the Father.
Mk 4:10 When he was **alone** [+2848], the Twelve and the others around
    6:47 the boat was in the middle of the lake, and he was **alone** on land.
    9: 2 and led them up a high mountain, where they were all **alone**.
    9: 8 they no longer saw anyone with them except Jesus. **[RPG]**
Lk 4: 4 Jesus answered, "It is written: 'Man does not live on bread **alone**.' "
    4: 8 "It is written: 'Worship the Lord your God and serve him **only**.' "
    5:21 who speaks blasphemy? Who can forgive sins but God **alone**?"
    6: 4 he ate what is lawful **only** [+1623+3590] for priests to eat.
    9:18 Once when Jesus was praying in **private** and his disciples were
    9:36 When the voice had spoken, they found that Jesus was **alone**.
    10:40 don't you care that my sister has left me to do the work **by myself**?
    24:12 Bending over, he saw the strips of linen lying **by themselves**,
    24:18 "Are you **only** a visitor to Jerusalem and do not know the things
Jn 5:44 yet make no effort to obtain the praise that comes from the **only**
    6:15 king by force, withdrew again to a mountain **by himself** [+899].
    6:22 not entered it with his disciples, but that they had gone away **alone**.
    8: 9 the older ones first, until **only** Jesus was left, with the woman still
    8:16 But if I do judge, my decisions are right, because I am not **alone**.
    8:29 he has not left me **alone**, for I always do what pleases him."
    12:24 of wheat falls to the ground and dies, it remains **only a single** seed.
    16:32 You will leave me **all alone**. Yet I am not alone, for my Father is
    16:32 leave me all alone. Yet I am not **alone**, for my Father is with me.
    17: 3 the **only** true God, and Jesus Christ, whom you have sent.
Ro 11: 3 your altars; I am the **only** *one* left, and they are trying to kill me"?
    16: 4 Not **only** I but all the churches of the Gentiles are grateful to them.
    16:27 *to* the **only** wise God be glory forever through Jesus Christ!
1Co 9: 6 Or is it **only** I and Barnabas who must work for a living?
    14:36 originate with you? Or are you the **only** *people* it has reached?
Gal 6: 4 in himself, **[RPG]** without comparing himself to somebody else,
Php 4:15 with me in the matter of giving and receiving, except you **only**;
Col 4:11 These are the **only** Jews among my fellow workers for the
1Th 3: 1 it no longer, we thought it best to be left **by ourselves** in Athens.
1Ti 1:17 invisible, the **only** God, be honor and glory for ever and ever.
    6:15 God, the blessed and **only** Ruler, the King of kings and Lord of
    6:16 who **alone** is immortal and who lives in unapproachable light,

2Ti 4:11 **Only** Luke is with me. Get Mark and bring him with you,
Heb 9: 7 But **only** the high priest entered the inner room, and that only once
2Jn 1: 1 love in the truth—and not I **only**, but also all who know the truth—
Jude 1: 4 for immorality and deny Jesus Christ our **only** Sovereign and Lord.
  1:25 *to* the **only** God our Savior be glory, majesty, power and authority,
Rev 15: 4 For you **alone** are holy. All nations will come and worship before

3669 μονόφθαλμος, *monophthalmos* [2]
[√ *3668 + 4057*]

one eye [2]

Mt 18: 9 It is better for you to enter life with **one eye** than to have two eyes
Mk 9:47 It is better for you to enter the kingdom of God with **one eye** than

3670 μονόω, *monoō* [1] [√ *3668*]

left all alone [1]

1Ti 5: 5 and **left all alone** puts her hope in God and continues night

3671 μορφή, *morphē* [3] [→ *305, 3565, 3672, 3673, 5214, 5215, 5216*]

nature [2], form [1]

Mk 16:12 Afterward Jesus appeared in a different **form** to two of them while
Php 2: 6 Who, being in very **nature** God, did not consider equality with
  2: 7 but made himself nothing, taking the very **nature** of a servant,

3672 μορφόω, *morphoō* [1] [√ *3671*]

formed [1]

Gal 4:19 I am again in the pains of childbirth until Christ *is* **formed** in you,

3673 μόρφωσις, *morphōsis* [2] [√ *3671*]

embodiment [1], form [1]

Ro 2:20 because you have in the law the **embodiment** of knowledge
2Ti 3: 5 having a **form** of godliness but denying its power. Have nothing to

3674 μοσχοποιέω, *moschopoieō* [1] [√ *3675 + 4472*]

made an idol in the form of a calf [1]

Ac 7:41 That was the time *they* **made an idol in the form of a calf**.

3675 μόσχος, *moschos* [6] [→ *3674*]

calf [3], calves [2], ox [1]

Lk 15:23 Bring the fattened **calf** and kill it. Let's have a feast and celebrate.
  15:27 'and your father has killed the fattened **calf** because he has him
  15:30 with prostitutes comes home, you kill the fattened **calf** for him!'
Heb 9:12 He did not enter by means of the blood of goats and **calves**;
  9:19 he took the blood *of* **calves**, together with water, scarlet wool
Rev 4: 7 the second was like an **ox**, the third had a face like a man,

3676 μουσικός, *mousikos* [1]

musicians [1]

Rev 18:22 The music of harpists and **musicians**, flute players and trumpeters,

3677 μόχθος, *mochthos* [3] [√ *3653*]

hardship [1], toiled [1], toiling [1]

2Co 11:27 I have labored and **toiled** and have often gone without sleep;
1Th 2: 9 Surely you remember, brothers, our toil and **hardship**; we worked
2Th 3: 8 laboring and **toiling** so that we would not be a burden to any of

3678 μυελός, *myelos* [1]

marrow [1]

Heb 4:12 it penetrates even to dividing soul and spirit, joints and **marrow**;

3679 μυέω, *myeō* [1] [→ *3696*]

learned the secret [1]

Php 4:12 *I have* **learned the secret** of being content in any and every

3680 μῦθος, *mythos* [5] [→ *4170, 4171, 4172*]

myths [4], stories [1]

1Ti 1: 4 nor to devote themselves *to* **myths** and endless genealogies.
  4: 7 Have nothing to do with godless **myths** and old wives' tales;
2Ti 4: 4 will turn their ears away from the truth and turn aside to **myths**.
Tit 1:14 and will pay no attention *to* Jewish **myths** or to the commands of
2Pe 1:16 We did not follow cleverly invented **stories** when we told you

3681 μυκάομαι, *mykaomai* [1]

roar [1]

Rev 10: 3 and he gave a loud shout like the **roar** of a lion. When he shouted,

3682 μυκτηρίζω, *myktērizō* [1] [→ *1727*]

mocked [1]

Gal 6: 7 Do not be deceived: God cannot *be* **mocked**. A man reaps what he

3683 μυλικός, *mylikos* [1] [√ *3685*]

millstone [+*3345*] [1]

Lk 17: 2 **millstone** [+*3345*] tied around his neck than for him to cause one

3684 μύλινος, *mylinos* [1] [√ *3685*]

millstone [1]

Rev 18:21 a mighty angel picked up a boulder the size of a large **millstone**

3685 μύλος, *mylos* [4] [→ *3683, 3684, 3686, 3687*]

large millstone [+*3948*] [2], hand mill [1], millstone [1]

Mt 18: 6 it would be better for him to have a **large millstone** [+*3948*] hung
  24:41 Two women will be grinding with a **hand mill**; one will be taken
Mk 9:42 into the sea with a **large millstone** [+*3948*] tied around his neck.
Rev 18:22 The sound *of* a **millstone** will never be heard in you again.

3686 μυλών, *mylōn* Not used in UBS/NIV [√ *3685*]

3687 μυλωνικός, *mylōnikos* Not used in UBS/NIV [√ *3685*]

3688 Μύρα, *Myra* [1] [→ *3694*]

Myra [1]

Ac 27: 5 the coast of Cilicia and Pamphylia, we landed at **Myra** in Lycia.

3689 μυριάς, *myrias* [8] [√ *3692*]

ten thousand [2], thousands upon thousands [2], fifty thousand [+*4297*] [1], many thousands [1], thousands [1], two hundred million [+*1490*] [1]

Lk 12: 1 Meanwhile, when a crowd *of* **many thousands** had gathered,
Ac 19:19 of the scrolls, the total came to **fifty thousand** [+*4297*] drachmas.
  21:20 "You see, brother, how many **thousands** of Jews have believed,
Heb 12:22 You have come to **thousands upon thousands** of angels in joyful
Jude 1:14 the Lord is coming with **thousands upon thousands** of his holy
Rev 5:11 thousands upon thousands, and **ten thousand** times ten thousand.
  5:11 thousands upon thousands, and ten thousand times **ten thousand**.
  9:16 number of the mounted troops was **two hundred million** [+*1490*]

3690 μυρίζω, *myrizō* [1] [√ *3693*]

poured perfume on to prepare [1]

Mk 14: 8　She **poured perfume on** my body beforehand **to prepare** for my

3691 μύριοι, *myrioi* [1] [√ *3692*]

ten thousand [1]

Mt 18:24　a man who owed him **ten thousand** talents was brought to him.

3692 μυρίος, *myrios* [2] [→ *1490, 3689, 3691*]

ten thousand [2]

1Co 4:15　Even though you have **ten thousand** guardians in Christ, you do
　　14:19　words to instruct others than **ten thousand** words in a tongue.

3693 μύρον, *myron* [14 / 15] [→ *3690*]

perfume [12], its [+*3836*] [1], myrrh [1], perfumes [1]

Mt 26: 7　came to him with an alabaster jar *of* very expensive **perfume**,
　　26: 9　"This **perfume** [UBS-] could have been sold at a high price
　　26:12　When she poured this **perfume** on my body, she did it to prepare
Mk 14: 3　a woman came with an alabaster jar of very expensive **perfume**,
　　14: 4　saying indignantly to one another, "Why this waste *of* **perfume**?
　　14: 5　It's [+*3836*] could have been sold for more than a year's wages
Lk 7:37　at the Pharisee's house, she brought an alabaster jar *of* **perfume**,
　　7:38　them with her hair, kissed them and poured **perfume** on them.
　　7:46　not put oil on my head, but she has poured **perfume** on my feet.
　　23:56　Then they went home and prepared spices and **perfumes**.
Jn 11: 2　was the same one who poured **perfume** on the Lord and wiped his
　　12: 3　Then Mary took about a pint of pure nard, an expensive **perfume**;
　　12: 3　And the house was filled with the fragrance *of* the **perfume**.
　　12: 5　"Why wasn't this **perfume** sold and the money given to the poor?
Rev 18:13　of incense, **myrrh** and frankincense, of wine and olive oil,

3694 Μύρρα, *Myrra*　Not used in UBS/NIV [√ *3688*]

3695 Μυσία, *Mysia* [2]

　Mysia [2]

Ac 16: 7　When they came to the border of **Mysia**, they tried to enter
　　16: 8　So they passed by **Mysia** and went down to Troas.

3696 μυστήριον, *mystērion* [28 / 27] [√ *3679*]

　mystery [18], secret [3], mysteries [2], secrets [2], deep truths [1],
　secret [+*1877*] [1]

Mt 13:11　"The knowledge of the **secrets** of the kingdom of heaven has been
Mk 4:11　"The **secret** of the kingdom of God has been given to you.
Lk 8:10　"The knowledge of the **secrets** of the kingdom of God has been
Ro 11:25　I do not want you to be ignorant of this **mystery**, brothers,
　　16:25　according to the revelation *of* the **mystery** hidden for long ages
1Co 2: 1　to you the testimony [UBS *mystery*; NIV *3457*] about God.
　　2: 7　No, we speak of God's **secret** [+*1877*] wisdom, a wisdom that has
　　4: 1　of Christ and as those entrusted with the **secret** *things* of God.
　　13: 2　gift of prophecy and can fathom all **mysteries** and all knowledge,
　　14: 2　no one understands him; he utters **mysteries** with his spirit.
　　15:51　Listen, I tell you a **mystery**: We will not all sleep, but we will all
Eph 1: 9　And he made known to us the **mystery** of his will according to his
　　3: 3　that is, the **mystery** made known to me by revelation, as I have
　　3: 4　you will be able to understand my insight into the **mystery** of
　　3: 9　and to make plain to everyone the administration *of* this **mystery**
　　5:32　This is a profound **mystery**—but I am talking about Christ
　　6:19　so that I will fearlessly make known the **mystery** of the gospel,
Col 1:26　the **mystery** that has been kept hidden for ages and generations,
　　1:27　known among the Gentiles the glorious riches *of* this **mystery**,
　　2: 2　in order that they may know the **mystery** of God, namely,
　　4: 3　so that we may proclaim the **mystery** of Christ, for which I am in
2Th 2: 7　For the secret *power* of lawlessness is already at work; but the one
1Ti 3: 9　They must keep hold of the **deep truths** of the faith with a clear
　　3:16　Beyond all question, the **mystery** of godliness is great:
Rev 1:20　The **mystery** of the seven stars that you saw in my right hand

10: 7　the **mystery** of God will be accomplished, just as he announced to
17: 5　MYSTERY BABYLON THE GREAT THE MOTHER OF
17: 7　I will explain to you the **mystery** of the woman and of the beast

3697 μυωπάζω, *myōpazō* [1]

nearsighted [1]

2Pe 1: 9　But if anyone does not have them, he is **nearsighted** and blind,

3698 μώλωψ, *mōlōps* [1]

wounds [1]

1Pe 2:24　and live for righteousness; *by* his **wounds** you have been healed.

3699 μωμάομαι, *mōmaomai* [2] [√ *3522*]

criticism [1], discredited [1]

2Co 6: 3　in anyone's path, so that our ministry *will* not *be* **discredited**.
　　8:20　We want to avoid any **criticism** of the way we administer this

3700 μῶμος, *mōmos* [1] [√ *3522*]

blemishes [1]

2Pe 2:13　They are blots and **blemishes**, reveling in their pleasures while

3701 μωραίνω, *mōrainō* [4] [√ *3704*]

loses its saltiness [2], fools [1], made foolish [1]

Mt 5:13　But if the salt **loses its saltiness**, how can it be made salty again?
Lk 14:34　"Salt is good, but if it **loses its saltiness**, how can it be made salty
Ro 1:22　Although they claimed to be wise, *they became* **fools**
1Co 1:20　of this age? *Has* not God **made foolish** the wisdom of the world?

3702 μωρία, *mōria* [5] [√ *3704*]

foolishness [5]

1Co 1:18　For the message of the cross is **foolishness** to those who are
　　1:21　God was pleased through the **foolishness** of what was preached to
　　1:23　a stumbling block to Jews and **foolishness** to Gentiles,
　　2:14　for they are **foolishness** to him, and he cannot understand them,
　　3:19　For the wisdom of this world is **foolishness** in God's sight.

3703 μωρολογία, *mōrologia* [1] [√ *3704 + 3306*]

foolish talk [1]

Eph 5: 4　**foolish talk** or coarse joking, which are out of place, but rather

3704 μωρός, *mōros* [12] [→ *3701, 3702, 3703*]

foolish [7], fool [2], fools [2], foolishness [1]

Mt 5:22　is answerable to the Sanhedrin. But anyone who says, '*You* **fool!**'
　　7:26　and does not put them into practice is like a **foolish** man who built
　　23:17　*You* blind **fools**! Which is greater: the gold, or the temple that
　　25: 2　Five of them were **foolish** and five were wise.
　　25: 3　The **foolish** *ones* took their lamps but did not take any oil with
　　25: 8　The **foolish** *ones* said to the wise, 'Give us some of your oil;
1Co 1:25　For the **foolishness** of God is wiser than man's wisdom,
　　1:27　But God chose the **foolish** *things* of the world to shame the wise;
　　3:18　of this age, he should become a "**fool**" so that he may become wise.
　　4:10　We are **fools** for Christ, but you are so wise in Christ! We are
2Ti 2:23　Don't have anything to do with **foolish** and stupid arguments,
Tit 3: 9　But avoid **foolish** controversies and genealogies and arguments

3705 Μωσεύς, *Mōseus*　Not used in UBS/NIV [√ *3707*]

3706 Μωσῆς, *Mōsēs*　Not used in UBS/NIV [√ *3707*]

3707   Μωϋσῆς, Mōysēs   [80]   [→ 3705, 3706]

Μωϋσῆς ... ἔγραψεν (Moses ... wrote) [5] Mk 12:19; Lk 20:28; Jn 1:45; 5:46; Ro 10:5; cf. Mk 10:5

Μωϋσῆς ... νόμος (Moses ... law) [14] Lk 2:22; 24:44; Jn 1:17,45; 7:19,23; 8:5; Ac 13:38; 15:5; 28:23; Ro 10:5; 1Co 9:9; Heb 9:19; 10:28

Moses [79], he^s [+3836] [1]

Mt	8: 4	show yourself to the priest and offer the gift **Moses** commanded,
	17: 3	Just then there appeared before them **Moses** and Elijah,
	17: 4	up three shelters—one for you, one *for* **Moses** and one for Elijah."
	19: 7	"did **Moses** command that a man give his wife a certificate of
	19: 8	"**Moses** permitted you to divorce your wives because your hearts
	22:24	"**Moses** told us that if a man dies without having children,
	23: 2	"The teachers of the law and the Pharisees sit in **Moses**' seat.
Mk	1:44	and offer the sacrifices that **Moses** commanded for your cleansing,
	7:10	For **Moses** said, 'Honor your father and your mother,' and,
	9: 4	And there appeared before them Elijah and **Moses**, who were
	9: 5	up three shelters—one for you, one *for* **Moses** and one for Elijah."
	10: 3	"What did **Moses** command you?" he replied.
	10: 4	"**Moses** permitted a man to write a certificate of divorce and send
	12:19	"**Moses** wrote for us that if a man's brother dies and leaves a wife
	12:26	have you not read in the book *of* **Moses**, in the account of the bush,
Lk	2:22	according to the Law *of* **Moses**
	5:14	and offer the sacrifices that **Moses** commanded for your cleansing,
	9:30	Two men, **Moses** and Elijah,
	9:33	up three shelters—one for you, one *for* **Moses** and one for Elijah."
	16:29	"Abraham replied, 'They have **Moses** and the Prophets; let them
	16:31	"He said to him, 'If they do not listen to **Moses** and the Prophets,
	20:28	"**Moses** wrote for us that if a man's brother dies and leaves a wife
	20:37	in the account of the bush, even **Moses** showed that the dead rise,
	24:27	And beginning with **Moses** and all the Prophets, he explained to
	24:44	must be fulfilled that is written about me in the Law *of* **Moses**,
Jn	1:17	For the law was given through **Moses**; grace and truth came
	1:45	told him, "We have found the one **Moses** wrote about in the Law,
	3:14	Just as **Moses** lifted up the snake in the desert, so the Son of Man
	5:45	the Father. Your accuser is **Moses**, on whom your hopes are set.
	5:46	If you believed **Moses**, you would believe me, for he wrote about
	6:32	it is not **Moses** who has given you the bread from heaven,
	7:19	Has not **Moses** given you the law? Yet not one of you keeps the
	7:22	because **Moses** gave you circumcision (though actually it did not
	7:22	you circumcision (though actually it did not come from **Moses**,
	7:23	on the Sabbath so that the law *of* **Moses** may not be broken,
	8: 5	In the Law **Moses** commanded us to stone such women. Now what
	9:28	"You are this fellow's disciple! We are disciples *of* **Moses**!
	9:29	We know that God spoke *to* **Moses**, but as for this fellow,
Ac	3:22	For **Moses** said, 'The Lord your God will raise up for you a
	6:11	"We have heard Stephen speak words of blasphemy against **Moses**
	6:14	this place and change the customs **Moses** handed down to us."
	7:20	"At that time **Moses** was born, and he was no ordinary child.
	7:22	**Moses** was educated in all the wisdom of the Egyptians and was
	7:29	When **Moses** heard this, he fled to Midian, where he settled as a
	7:31	When he saw this, he^s [+3836] was amazed at the sight. As he
	7:32	and Jacob.' **Moses** trembled with fear and did not dare to look.
	7:35	"This is the same **Moses** whom they had rejected with the words,
	7:37	"This is that **Moses** who told the Israelites, 'God will send you a
	7:40	As for this fellow **Moses** who led us out of Egypt—we don't know
	7:44	It had been made as God directed **Moses**, according to the pattern
	13:39	everything you could not be justified from by the law *of* **Moses**.
	15: 1	*according to* the custom *taught by* **Moses**, you cannot be saved."
	15: 5	must be circumcised and required to obey the law *of* **Moses**."
	15:21	For **Moses** has been preached in every city from the earliest times
	21:21	all the Jews who live among the Gentiles to turn away from **Moses**,
	26:22	nothing beyond what the prophets and **Moses** said would happen—
	28:23	and tried to convince them about Jesus from the Law *of* **Moses**
Ro	5:14	death reigned from the time of Adam to the time *of* **Moses**,
	9:15	For he says *to* **Moses**, "I will have mercy on whom I have mercy,
	10: 5	**Moses** describes in this way the righteousness that is by the law:
	10:19	First, **Moses** says, "I will make you envious by those who are not a
1Co	9: 9	For it is written in the Law *of* **Moses**: "Do not muzzle an ox while it
	10: 2	They were all baptized into **Moses** in the cloud and in the sea.
2Co	3: 7	so that the Israelites could not look steadily at the face *of* **Moses**
	3:13	We are not like **Moses**, who would put a veil over his face to keep
	3:15	Even to this day when **Moses** is read, a veil covers their hearts.
2Ti	3: 8	Just as Jannes and Jambres opposed **Moses**, so also these men

Heb	3: 2	who appointed him, just as **Moses** was faithful in all God's house.
	3: 3	Jesus has been found worthy of greater honor than **Moses**,
	3: 5	**Moses** was faithful as a servant in all God's house, testifying to
	3:16	and rebelled? Were they not all those **Moses** led out of Egypt?
	7:14	and in regard to that tribe **Moses** said nothing about priests.
	8: 5	This is why **Moses** was warned when he was about to build the
	9:19	When **Moses** had proclaimed every commandment of the law to all
	10:28	Anyone who rejected the law *of* **Moses** died without mercy on the
	11:23	By faith **Moses**' parents hid him for three months after he was born,
	11:24	By faith **Moses**, when he had grown up, refused to be known as the
	12:21	The sight was so terrifying that **Moses** said, "I am trembling with
Jude	1: 9	when he was disputing with the devil about the body *of* **Moses**,
Rev	15: 3	and sang the song *of* **Moses** the servant of God and the song of the

---

N, N

3708   ν, n   Not used in UBS/NIV

3709   Ναασσών, Naassōn   [3]

Nahshon [3]

Mt	1: 4	Amminadab the father of **Nahshon**, Nahshon the father of Salmon,
	1: 4	Amminadab the father of Nahshon, **Nahshon** the father of Salmon,
Lk	3:32	of Obed, the son of Boaz, the son of Salmon, the son *of* **Nahshon**,

3710   Ναγγαί, Nangai   [1]

Naggai [1]

Lk	3:25	son of Amos, the son of Nahum, the son of Esli, the son *of* **Naggai**,

3711   Ναζαρά, Nazara   Not used in UBS/NIV   [→ 3712, 3713, 3714, 3715, 3716, 3717]

3712   Ναζαράθ, Nazarath   Not used in UBS/NIV   [√ 3711]

3713   Ναζαράτ, Nazarat   Not used in UBS/NIV   [√ 3711]

3714   Ναζαρέθ, Nazareth   [12]   [√ 3711]

Nazareth [12]

Mt	2:23	and he went and lived in a town called **Nazareth**. So was fulfilled
	4:13	Leaving **Nazareth**, he went and lived in Capernaum, which was by
	21:11	"This is Jesus, the prophet from **Nazareth** in Galilee."
Mk	1: 9	At that time Jesus came from **Nazareth** in Galilee and was
Lk	1:26	God sent the angel Gabriel to **Nazareth**, a town in Galilee,
	2: 4	So Joseph also went up from the town of **Nazareth** in Galilee to
	2:39	the Lord, they returned to Galilee to their own town *of* **Nazareth**.
	2:51	Then he went down to **Nazareth** with them and was obedient to
	4:16	He went to **Nazareth**, where he had been brought up, and on the
Jn	1:45	the prophets also wrote—Jesus of **Nazareth**, the son of Joseph."
	1:46	"**Nazareth**! Can anything good come from there?"
Ac	10:38	how God anointed Jesus of **Nazareth** with the Holy Spirit

3715   Ναζαρέτ, Nazaret   Not used in UBS/NIV   [√ 3711]

3716   Ναζαρηνός, Nazarēnos   [6]   [√ 3711]

of Nazareth [4], Nazarene [2]

Mk	1:24	"What do you want with us, Jesus **of Nazareth**? Have you come to
	10:47	When he heard that it was Jesus **of Nazareth**, he began to shout,
	14:67	closely at him. "You also were with that **Nazarene**, Jesus," she said.
	16: 6	"You are looking for Jesus the **Nazarene**, who was crucified.
Lk	4:34	"Ha! What do you want with us, Jesus **of Nazareth**? Have you
	24:19	"What things?" he asked. "About Jesus **of Nazareth**," they replied.

3717 Ναζωραῖος, *Nazōraios* [13] [√ *3711*]

of Nazareth [11], Nazarene [2]

Mt 2:23 was said through the prophets: "He will be called a **Nazarene**."
26:71 said to the people there, "This fellow was with Jesus **of Nazareth**."
Lk 18:37 They told him, "Jesus **of Nazareth** is passing by."
Jn 18: 5 "Jesus **of Nazareth**," they replied. "I am he," Jesus said.
18: 7 them, "Who is it you want?" And they said, "Jesus **of Nazareth**."
19:19 JESUS **OF NAZARETH**, THE KING OF THE JEWS.
Ac 2:22 Jesus **of Nazareth** was a man accredited by God to you by
3: 6 I have I give you. In the name of Jesus Christ **of Nazareth**, walk."
4:10 It is by the name of Jesus Christ **of Nazareth**, whom you crucified
6:14 For we have heard him say that this Jesus **of Nazareth** will destroy
22: 8 " 'I am Jesus **of Nazareth**, whom you are persecuting,' he replied.
24: 5 Jews all over the world. He is a ringleader of the **Nazarene** sect
26: 9 do all that was possible to oppose the name of Jesus **of Nazareth**.

3718 Ναθάμ, *Natham* [1] [→ *3719*]

Nathan [1]

Lk 3:31 the son of Mattatha, the son *of* **Nathan**, the son of David,

3719 Ναθάν, *Nathan* Not used in UBS/NIV [√ *3718*]

3720 Ναθαναήλ, *Nathanaēl* [6]

Nathanael [6]

Jn 1:45 Philip found **Nathanael** and told him, "We have found the one
1:46 come from there?" **Nathanael** asked. "Come and see," said Philip.
1:47 When Jesus saw **Nathanael** approaching, he said of him, "Here is a
1:48 **Nathanael** asked. Jesus answered, "I saw you while you were still
1:49 Then **Nathanael** declared, "Rabbi, you are the Son of God;
21: 2 **Nathanael** from Cana in Galilee, the sons of Zebedee,

3721 ναί, *nai* [33 / 34]

yes [32], so shall it be [1], wish [1]

Mt 5:37 Simply let your '**Yes**' be 'Yes,' and your 'No,' 'No'; anything
5:37 Simply let your 'Yes' be '**Yes**,' and your 'No,' 'No'; anything
9:28 you believe that I am able to do this?" "**Yes**, Lord," they replied.
11: 9 go out to see? A prophet? **Yes**, I tell you, and more than a prophet.
11:26 **Yes**, Father, for this was your good pleasure.
13:51 you understood all these things?" Jesus asked. "**Yes**," they replied.
15:27 "**Yes**, Lord," she said, "but even the dogs eat the crumbs that fall
17:25 "**Yes**, he does," he replied. When Peter came into the house,
21:16 "**Yes**," replied Jesus, "have you never read, " 'From the lips of
Mk 7:28 "**Yes**, [UBS-] Lord," she replied, "but even the dogs under the table
Lk 7:26 go out to see? A prophet? **Yes**, I tell you, and more than a prophet.
10:21 to little children. **Yes**, Father, for this was your good pleasure.
11:51 **Yes**, I tell you, this generation will be held responsible for it all.
12: 5 has power to throw you into hell. **Yes**, I tell you, fear him.
Jn 11:27 "**Yes**, Lord," she told him, "I believe that you are the Christ,
21:15 "**Yes**, Lord," he said, "you know that I love you." Jesus said,
21:16 He answered, "**Yes**, Lord, you know that I love you." Jesus said,
Ac 5: 8 and Ananias got for the land?" "**Yes**," she said, "that is the price."
22:27 "Tell me, are you a Roman citizen?" "**Yes**, I am," he answered.
Ro 3:29 Jews only? Is he not the God of Gentiles too? **Yes**, of Gentiles too,
2Co 1:17 so that in the same breath I say, "**Yes**, yes" and "No, no"?
1:17 so that in the same breath I say, "Yes, **yes**" and "No, no"?
1:18 surely as God is faithful, our message to you is not "**Yes**" and "No."
1:19 among you by me and Silas and Timothy, was not "**Yes**" and "No,"
1:19 was not "Yes" and "No," but in him it has always been "**Yes**."
1:20 matter how many promises God has made, they are "**Yes**" in Christ.
Php 4: 3 **Yes**, and I ask you, loyal yokefellow, help these women who have
Phm 1:20 I *do* **wish**, brother, that I may have some benefit from you in the
Jas 5:12 your "**Yes**" be yes, and your "No," no, or you will be condemned.
5:12 your "Yes" be **yes**, and your "No," no, or you will be condemned.
Rev 1: 7 of the earth will mourn because of him. **So shall it be**! Amen.
14:13 "**Yes**," says the Spirit, "they will rest from their labor, for their
16: 7 "**Yes**, Lord God Almighty, true and just are your judgments."
22:20 He who testifies to these things says, "**Yes**, I am coming soon."

3722 Ναιμάν, *Naiman* [1] [→ *3737*]

Naaman [1]

Lk 4:27 yet not one of them was cleansed—only **Naaman** the Syrian."

3723 Ναΐν, *Nain* [1]

Nain [1]

Lk 7:11 Soon afterward, Jesus went to a town called **Nain**, and his disciples

3724 ναός, *naos* [45] [→ *3753*]

temple [42], *untranslated* [1], shrines [1], temples [1]

Mt 23:16 You say, 'If anyone swears by the **temple**, it means nothing;
23:16 but if anyone swears by the gold *of* the **temple**, he is bound by his
23:17 is greater: the gold, or the **temple** that makes the gold sacred?
23:21 And he who swears by the **temple** swears by it and by the one who
23:35 whom you murdered between the **temple** and the altar.
26:61 'I am able to destroy the **temple** of God and rebuild it in three
27: 5 So Judas threw the money into the **temple** and left. Then he went
27:40 who are going to destroy the **temple** and build it in three days,
27:51 At that moment the curtain *of* the **temple** was torn in two from top
Mk 14:58 'I will destroy this man-made **temple** and in three days will build
15:29 You who are going to destroy the **temple** and build it in three days,
15:38 The curtain *of* the **temple** was torn in two from top to bottom.
Lk 1: 9 the priesthood, to go into the **temple** of the Lord and burn incense.
1:21 for Zechariah and wondering why he stayed so long in the **temple**.
1:22 They realized he had seen a vision in the **temple**, for he kept
23:45 stopped shining. And the curtain *of* the **temple** was torn in two.
Jn 2:19 Jesus answered them, "Destroy this **temple**, and I will raise it again
2:20 The Jews replied, "It has taken forty-six years to build this **temple**,
2:21 But the **temple** he had spoken of was his body.
Ac 17:24 of heaven and earth and does not live in **temples** built by hands.
19:24 silversmith named Demetrius, who made silver **shrines** of Artemis,
1Co 3:16 Don't you know that you yourselves are God's **temple** and that God's
3:17 If anyone destroys God's **temple**, God will destroy him; for God's
3:17 destroy him; for God's **temple** is sacred, and you are that temple.
6:19 Do you not know that your body is a **temple** of the Holy Spirit,
2Co 6:16 What agreement is there between the **temple** of God and idols?
6:16 temple of God and idols? For we are the **temple** of the living God.
Eph 2:21 is joined together and rises to become a holy **temple** in the Lord.
2Th 2: 4 or is worshiped, so that he sets himself up in God's **temple**,
Rev 3:12 Him who overcomes I will make a pillar in the **temple** of my God.
7:15 the throne of God and serve him day and night in his **temple**;
11: 1 and was told, "Go and measure the **temple** of God and the altar,
11: 2 **[RPG]** do not measure it, because it has been given to the
11:19 Then God's **temple** in heaven was opened, and within his temple
11:19 and within his **temple** was seen the ark of his covenant.
14:15 Then another angel came out of the **temple** and called in a loud
14:17 Another angel came out of the **temple** in heaven, and he too had a
15: 5 After this I looked and in heaven the **temple**, that is, the tabernacle
15: 6 Out of the **temple** came the seven angels with the seven plagues.
15: 8 And the **temple** was filled with smoke from the glory of God
15: 8 and no one could enter the **temple** until the seven plagues of the
16: 1 Then I heard a loud voice from the **temple** saying to the seven
16:17 and out of the **temple** came a loud voice from the throne, saying,
21:22 I did not see a **temple** in the city, because the Lord God Almighty
21:22 because the Lord God Almighty and the Lamb are its **temple**.

3725 Ναούμ, *Naoum* [1]

Nahum [1]

Lk 3:25 the son of Amos, the son *of* **Nahum**, the son of Esli, the son of

3726 νάρδος, *nardos* [2]

nard [2]

Mk 14: 3 an alabaster jar of very expensive perfume, *made of* pure **nard**.
Jn 12: 3 Then Mary took about a pint *of* pure **nard**, an expensive perfume;

3727 Νάρκισσος, *Narkissos* [1]

Narcissus [1]

Ro 16:11 Greet those in the *household of* **Narcissus** who are in the Lord.

3728 ναυαγέω, *nauageō* [2] [√ 3730 + 2862]

shipwrecked [2]

2Co 11:25 three times *I was* **shipwrecked**, I spent a night and a day in the
1Ti 1:19 Some have rejected these and so *have* **shipwrecked** their faith.

3729 ναύκληρος, *nauklēros* [1] [√ 3730 + 3102]

owner of the ship [1]

Ac 27:11 followed the advice of the pilot and of the **owner of the ship**.

3730 ναῦς, *naus* [1] [→ 3728, 3729, 3731]

ship [1]

Ac 27:41 But the **ship** struck a sandbar and ran aground. The bow stuck fast

3731 ναύτης, *nautēs* [3] [√ 3730]

sailors [3]

Ac 27:27 when about midnight the **sailors** sensed they were approaching
   27:30 escape from the ship, the **sailors** let the lifeboat down into the sea,
Rev 18:17 "Every sea captain, and all who travel by ship, the **sailors**, and all

3732 Ναχώρ, *Nachōr* [1]

Nahor [1]

Lk 3:34 of Isaac, the son of Abraham, the son of Terah, the son *of* **Nahor**,

3733 νεανίας, *neanias* [3] [√ 3742]

young man [3]

Ac 7:58 the witnesses laid their clothes at the feet *of* a **young man** named
   20: 9 Seated in a window was a **young man** named Eutychus, who was
   23:17 the centurions and said, "Take this **young man** to the commander;

3734 νεανίσκος, *neaniskos* [11] [√ 3742]

young man [7], young men [4]

Mt 19:20 "All these I have kept," the **young man** said. "What do I still lack?"
   19:22 When the **young man** heard this, he went away sad, because he
Mk 14:51 A **young man**, wearing nothing but a linen garment,
   16: 5 they saw a **young man** dressed in a white robe sitting on the right
Lk 7:14 carrying it stood still. He said, "**Young man**, I say to you, get up!"
Ac 2:17 and daughters will prophesy, your **young men** will see visions,
    5:10 Then the **young men** came in and, finding her dead, carried her out
   23:18 sent for me and asked me to bring this **young man** to you
   23:22 The commander dismissed the **young man** and cautioned him,
1Jn 2:13 I write to you, **young men**, because you have overcome the evil
    2:14 I write to you, **young men**, because you are strong, and the word

3735 Νέα πολις, *Nea polis* [1] [√ 3742 + 4484]

Neapolis [1]

Ac 16:11 sailed straight for Samothrace, and the next day on to **Neapolis**.

3736 Νεάπολις, *Neapolis* Not used in UBS/NIV
[√ 3742 + 4484]

3737 Νεεμάν, *Neeman* Not used in UBS/NIV [√ 3722]

3738 νεκρός, *nekros* [128 / 129] [→ 3739, 3740]

ἀνάστασις [ἐκ] νεκροῦ (resurrection of the dead) [15] Mt
   22:31; Lk 20:35; Ac 4:2; 17:32; 23:6; 24:21; 26:23; Ro 1:4; 1Co
   15:12,13,21,42; Heb 6:2; 11:35; 1Pe 1:3

ἀναστῆναι ἐκ νεκρῶν (to rise from the dead) [11] Mk 9:9,10;
   12:25; Lk 16:31; 24:46; Jn 20:9; Ac 10:41; 13:34; 17:3,31; Eph
   5:14

ἀπὸ νεκρῶν (from the dead) [6] Mt 14:2; 27:64; 28:7; Lk 16:30;
   Heb 6:1; 9:14

ἐγείρω ἀπὸ τῶν νεκρῶν (to raise from the dead) [3] Mt 14:2;
   27:64; 28:7

ἐγείρω ἐκ νεκρῶν (to raise from the dead) [26] Mt 17:9; Mk
   6:14,16; Lk 9:7; Jn 2:22; 12:1,9,17; 21:14; Ac 3:15; 4:10; 13:30;
   Ro 6:4,9; 7:4; 8:11; 10:9; 1Co 15:12,20; Gal 1:1; Eph 1:20; Col
   2:12; 1Th 1:10; 2Ti 2:8; Heb 11:19; 1Pe 1:21

ἐγείρω νεκρούς (to raise the dead) [4] Mt 10:8; Jn 5:21; Ac
   26:8; 2Co 1:9

ἐκ νεκρῶν (from the dead) [38] Mt 17:9; Mk 6:14,16; Lk 9:7;
   20:35; Jn 2:22; 12:1,9,17; 21:14; Ac 3:15; 4:2,10; 13:30; 26:23; Ro
   4:24; 6:4,9,13; 7:4; 8:11,11; 10:7,9; 11:15; 1Co 15:12,20; Gal 1:1;
   Eph 1:20; Php 3:11; Col 1:18; 2:12; 1Th 1:10; 2Ti 2:8; Heb 11:19;
   13:20; 1Pe 1:3,21

dead [123], death [3], corpse [1], died [+1181] [1], died [+2093]
   [1]

Mt 8:22 Jesus told him, "Follow me, and let the **dead** bury their own dead."
    8:22 Jesus told him, "Follow me, and let the dead bury their own **dead**."
   10: 8 Heal the sick, raise the **dead**, cleanse those who have leprosy,
   11: 5 who have leprosy are cured, the deaf hear, the **dead** are raised,
   14: 2 his attendants, "This is John the Baptist; he has risen from the **dead**!
   17: 9 have seen, until the Son of Man has been raised from the **dead**."
   22:31 But about the resurrection *of* the **dead**—have you not read what
   22:32 the God of Jacob'? He is not the God *of* the **dead** but of the living."
   23:27 but on the inside are full *of* **dead** *men's* bones and everything
   27:64 the body and tell the people that he has been raised from the **dead**.
   28: 4 so afraid of him that they shook and became like **dead** *men*.
   28: 7 'He has risen from the **dead** and is going ahead of you into Galilee.
Mk 6:14 Some were saying, "John the Baptist has been raised from the **dead**,
    6:16 the man I beheaded, has been raised from the **dead**!" [UBS-]
    9: 9 what they had seen until the Son of Man had risen from the **dead**.
    9:10 to themselves, discussing what "rising from the **dead**" meant.
    9:26 The boy looked so much like a **corpse** that many said, "He's dead."
   12:25 When the **dead** rise, they will neither marry nor be given in
   12:26 Now about the **dead** rising—have you not read in the book of
   12:27 He is not the God *of* the **dead**, but of the living. You are badly
Lk 7:15 The **dead** *man* sat up and began to talk, and Jesus gave him back
    7:22 who have leprosy are cured, the deaf hear, the **dead** are raised,
    9: 7 some were saying that John had been raised from the **dead**,
    9:60 "Let the **dead** bury their own dead, but you go and proclaim the
    9:60 "Let the dead bury their own **dead**, but you go and proclaim the
   15:24 For this son of mine was **dead** and is alive again; he was lost
   15:32 because this brother of yours was **dead** and is alive again;
   16:30 but if someone from the **dead** goes to them, they will
   16:31 they will not be convinced even if someone rises from the **dead**.' "
   20:35 and in the resurrection from the **dead** will neither marry nor be
   20:37 in the account of the bush, even Moses showed that the **dead** rise,
   20:38 He is not the God *of* the **dead**, but of the living, for to him all are
   24: 5 said to them, "Why do you look for the living among the **dead**?
   24:46 The Christ will suffer and rise from the **dead** on the third day,
Jn 2:22 After he was raised from the **dead**, his disciples recalled what he
    5:21 For just as the Father raises the **dead** and gives them life, even
    5:25 and has now come when the **dead** will hear the voice of the Son of
   12: 1 where Lazarus lived, whom Jesus had raised from the **dead**.
   12: 9 but also to see Lazarus, whom he had raised from the **dead**.
   12:17 and raised him from the **dead** continued to spread the word.
   20: 9 understand from Scripture that Jesus had to rise from the **dead**.)
   21:14 Jesus appeared to his disciples after he was raised from the **dead**.
Ac 3:15 You killed the author of life, but God raised him from the **dead**.
    4: 2 the people and proclaiming in Jesus the resurrection of the **dead**.
    4:10 whom you crucified but whom God raised from the **dead**,
    5:10 finding her **dead**, carried her out and buried her beside her
   10:41 by us who ate and drank with him after he rose from the **dead**.
   10:42 the one whom God appointed as judge *of* the living and the **dead**.
   13:30 But God raised him from the **dead**,
   13:34 The fact that God raised him from the **dead**, never to decay,
   17: 3 and proving that the Christ had to suffer and rise from the **dead**.
   17:31 He has given proof of this to all men by raising him from the **dead**."
   17:32 When they heard about the resurrection *of* the **dead**, some of them

	20: 9	he fell to the ground from the third story and was picked up **dead**.
	23: 6	I stand on trial because of my hope in the resurrection of the **dead**."
	24:21	'It is concerning the resurrection of the **dead** that I am on trial
	26: 8	should any of you consider it incredible that God raises the **dead**?
	26:23	that the Christ would suffer and, as the first to rise from the **dead**,
	28: 6	The people expected him to swell up or suddenly fall **dead**,
Ro	1: 4	power to be the Son of God by his resurrection from the **dead**:
	4:17	the God who gives life to the **dead** and calls things that are not as
	4:24	us who believe in him who raised Jesus our Lord from the **dead**.
	6: 4	just as Christ was raised from the **dead** through the glory of the
	6: 9	For we know that since Christ was raised from the **dead**, he cannot
	6:11	count yourselves **dead** to sin but alive to God in Christ Jesus.
	6:13	to God, as those who have been brought from **dead** to life;
	7: 4	might belong to another, to him who was raised from the **dead**,
	7: 8	me every kind of covetous desire. For apart from law, sin is **dead**.
	8:10	your body is **dead** because of sin, yet your spirit is alive because of
	8:11	And if the Spirit of him who raised Jesus from the **dead** is living in
	8:11	he who raised Christ from the **dead** will also give life to your
	10: 7	descend into the deep?' " (that is, to bring Christ up from the **dead**).
	10: 9	and believe in your heart that God raised him from the **dead**,
	11:15	of the world, what will their acceptance be but life from the **dead**?
	14: 9	so that he might be the Lord of both the **dead** and the living.
1Co	15:12	But if it is preached that Christ has been raised from the **dead**,
	15:12	how can some of you say that there is no resurrection of the **dead**?
	15:13	If there is no resurrection of the **dead**, then not even Christ has
	15:15	the dead. But he did not raise him if in fact the **dead** are not raised.
	15:16	For if the **dead** are not raised, then Christ has not been raised
	15:20	But Christ has indeed been raised from the **dead**, the firstfruits of
	15:21	a man, the resurrection of the **dead** comes also through a man.
	15:29	no resurrection, what will those do who are baptized for the **dead**?
	15:29	If the **dead** are not raised at all, why are people baptized for them?
	15:32	If the **dead** are not raised, "Let us eat and drink, for tomorrow we
	15:35	But someone may ask, "How are the **dead** raised? With what kind
	15:42	So will it be with the resurrection of the **dead**. The body that is
	15:52	the **dead** will be raised imperishable, and we will be changed.
2Co	1: 9	we might not rely on ourselves but on God, who raises the **dead**.
Gal	1: 1	Jesus Christ and God the Father, who raised him from the **dead**—
Eph	1:20	which he exerted in Christ when he raised him from the **dead**
	2: 1	As for you, you were **dead** in your transgressions and sins,
	2: 5	made us alive with Christ even when we were **dead** in
	5:14	"Wake up, O sleeper, rise from the **dead**, and Christ will shine on
Php	3:11	and so, somehow, to attain to the resurrection from the **dead**.
Col	1:18	he is the beginning and the firstborn from among the **dead**,
	2:12	your faith in the power of God, who raised him from the **dead**.
	2:13	When you were **dead** in your sins and in the uncircumcision of
1Th	1:10	to wait for his Son from heaven, whom he raised from the **dead**—
	4:16	with the trumpet call of God, and the **dead** in Christ will rise first.
2Ti	2: 8	Jesus Christ, raised from the **dead**, descended from David.
	4: 1	and of Christ Jesus, who will judge the living and the **dead**,
Heb	6: 1	again the foundation of repentance from acts that lead to **death**,
	6: 2	on of hands, the resurrection of the **dead**, and eternal judgment.
	9:14	to God, cleanse our consciences from acts that lead to **death**,
	9:17	because a will is in force only when somebody has **died** [+2093];
	11:19	Abraham reasoned that God could raise the **dead**, and figuratively
	11:35	Women received back their **dead**, raised to life again. Others were
	13:20	of the eternal covenant brought back from the **dead** our Lord Jesus,
Jas	2:17	faith by itself, if it is not accompanied by action, is **dead**.
	2:26	As the body without the spirit is **dead**, so faith without deeds is
	2:26	the body without the spirit is dead, so faith without deeds is **dead**.
1Pe	1: 3	living hope through the resurrection of Jesus Christ from the **dead**,
	1:21	who raised him from the **dead** and glorified him, and so your faith
	4: 5	give account to him who is ready to judge the living and the **dead**.
	4: 6	reason the gospel was preached even to those who are now **dead**,
Rev	1: 5	who is the faithful witness, the firstborn from the **dead**,
	1:17	When I saw him, I fell at his feet as though **dead**. Then he placed
	1:18	Living One; I was **dead**, and behold I am alive for ever and ever!
	2: 8	is the First and the Last, who **died** [+1181] and came to life again.
	3: 1	your deeds; you have a reputation of being alive, but you are **dead**.
	11:18	The time has come for judging the **dead**, and for rewarding your
	14:13	Blessed are the **dead** who die in the Lord from now on." "Yes,
	16: 3	and it turned into blood like that of a **dead** man, and every living
	20: 5	(The rest of the **dead** did not come to life until the thousand years
	20:12	And I saw the **dead**, great and small, standing before the throne,
	20:12	The **dead** were judged according to what they had done as
	20:13	The sea gave up the **dead** that were in it, and death and Hades gave
	20:13	in it, and death and Hades gave up the **dead** that were in them,

3739 νεκρόω, *nekroō* [3] [√ *3738*]

as good as dead [+2453] [1], dead [1], put to death [1]

Ro	4:19	he faced the fact that his body was **as good as dead** [+2453]—
Col	3: 5	**Put to death**, therefore, whatever belongs to your earthly nature:
Heb	11:12	And so from this one man, and he as good as **dead**,

3740 νέκρωσις, *nekrōsis* [2] [√ *3738*]

dead [1], death [1]

Ro	4:19	about a hundred years old—and that Sarah's womb was also **dead**.
2Co	4:10	We always carry around in our body the **death** of Jesus, so that the

3741 νεομηνία, *neomēnia* [1] [√ *3742 + 3604*]

New Moon celebration [1]

Col	2:16	to a religious festival, a **New Moon celebration** or a Sabbath day.

3742 νέος, *neos* [23] [→ *391, 3733, 3734, 3735, 3736, 3741, 3743, 3744, 3745, 3754, 3799, 3800, 3801, 3806*]

new [11], younger [8], young [3], youngest [1]

Mt	9:17	Neither do men pour **new** wine into old wineskins. If they do,
	9:17	No, they pour **new** wine into new wineskins, and both are
Mk	2:22	And no one pours **new** wine into old wineskins. If he does,
	2:22	will be ruined. No, he pours **new** wine into new wineskins."
Lk	5:37	And no one pours **new** wine into old wineskins. If he does,
	5:37	If he does, the **new** wine will burst the skins, the wine will run out
	5:38	No, **new** wine must be poured into new wineskins.
	5:39	And no one after drinking old wine wants the **new**, for he says,
	15:12	The **younger** one said to his father, 'Father, give me my share of
	15:13	"Not long after that, the **younger** son got together all he had,
	22:26	Instead, the greatest among you should be like the **youngest**,
Jn	21:18	when you were **younger** you dressed yourself and went where you
Ac	5: 6	Then the **young** men came forward, wrapped up his body,
1Co	5: 7	Get rid of the old yeast that you may be a **new** batch without
Col	3:10	and have put on the **new** self, which is being renewed in
1Ti	5: 1	him as if he were your father. Treat **younger** men as brothers,
	5: 2	as mothers, and **younger** women as sisters, with absolute purity.
	5:11	As for **younger** widows, do not put them on such a list. For when
	5:14	So I counsel **younger** widows to marry, to have children,
Tit	2: 4	then they can train the **younger** women to love their husbands
	2: 6	Similarly, encourage the **young** men to be self-controlled.
Heb	12:24	to Jesus the mediator of a **new** covenant, and to the sprinkled blood
1Pe	5: 5	**Young** men, in the same way be submissive to those who are

3743 νεοσσός, *neossos*   Not used in UBS/NIV [√ *3742*]

3744 νεότης, *neotēs* [4] [√ *3742*]

boy [2], child [1], young [1]

Mk	10:20	"Teacher," he declared, "all these I have kept since I was a **boy**."
Lk	18:21	"All these I have kept since I was a **boy**," he said.
Ac	26: 4	"The Jews all know the way I have lived ever since I was a **child**,
1Ti	4:12	Don't let anyone look down on you because you are **young**,

3745 νεόφυτος, *neophytos* [1] [√ *3742 + 5886*]

recent convert [1]

1Ti	3: 6	He must not be a **recent convert**, or he may become conceited

3746 Νέρων, *Nerōn*   Not used in UBS/NIV

3747 Νεύης, *Neuēs*   Not used in UBS/NIV

3748 νεύω, *neuō* [2] [→ *1377, 1728, 1935, 2153, 2916, 5162*]

motioned [2]

Jn	13:24	Simon Peter **motioned** to this disciple and said, "Ask him which

Ac   24:10 *When* the governor **motioned** for him to speak, Paul replied:

3749 νεφέλη, nephelē [25] [→ *3751*]

cloud [18], clouds [7]

Mt   17: 5 While he was still speaking, a bright **cloud** enveloped them,
     17: 5 and a voice from the **cloud** said, "This is my Son, whom I love;
     24:30 They will see the Son of Man coming on the **clouds** of the sky,
     26:64 right hand of the Mighty One and coming on the **clouds** of heaven."
Mk   9: 7 Then a **cloud** appeared and enveloped them, and a voice came
      9: 7 and enveloped them, and a voice came from the **cloud**:
     13:26 "At that time men will see the Son of Man coming in **clouds** with
     14:62 right hand of the Mighty One and coming on the **clouds** of heaven."
Lk   9:34 While he was speaking, a **cloud** appeared and enveloped them,
      9:34 enveloped them, and they were afraid as they entered the **cloud**.
      9:35 A voice came from the **cloud**, saying, "This is my Son, whom I
     12:54 "When you see a **cloud** rising in the west, immediately you say,
     21:27 At that time they will see the Son of Man coming in a **cloud** with
Ac   1: 9 up before their very eyes, and a **cloud** hid him from their sight.
1Co 10: 1 that our forefathers were all under the **cloud** and that they all
     10: 2 They were all baptized into Moses in the **cloud** and in the sea.
1Th   4:17 and are left will be caught up together with them in the **clouds** to
Jude 1:12 They are **clouds** without rain, blown along by the wind;
Rev   1: 7 Look, he is coming with the **clouds**, and every eye will see him,
     10: 1 He was robed in a **cloud**, with a rainbow above his head; his face
     11:12 And they went up to heaven in a **cloud**, while their enemies looked
     14:14 I looked, and there before me was a white **cloud**, and seated on the
     14:14 and seated on the **cloud** was one "like a son of man" with a crown
     14:15 and called in a loud voice to him who was sitting on the **cloud**,
     14:16 So he who was seated on the **cloud** swung his sickle over the earth,

3750 Νεφθαλίμ, Nephthalim [3]

Naphtali [3]

Mt   4:13 which was by the lake in the area of Zebulun and **Naphtali**—
      4:15 "Land of Zebulun and land *of* **Naphtali**, the way to the sea,
Rev   7: 6 from the tribe of Asher 12,000, from the tribe *of* **Naphtali** 12,000,

3751 νέφος, nephos [1] [√ *3749*]

cloud [1]

Heb 12: 1 since we are surrounded by such a great **cloud** of witnesses,

3752 νεφρός, nephros [1]

minds [1]

Rev   2:23 churches will know that I am he who searches hearts and **minds**,

3753 νεωκόρος, neōkoros [1] [√ *3724*]

guardian of the temple [1]

Ac   19:35 city of Ephesus is the **guardian of the temple** of the great Artemis

3754 νεωτερικός, neōterikos [1] [√ *3742*]

of youth [1]

2Ti   2:22 Flee the evil desires **of youth**, and pursue righteousness, faith,

3755 νή, nē [1]

I mean that just as surely as [1]

1Co 15:31 **I mean that**, brothers—**just as surely as** I glory over you in Christ

3756 νήθω, nēthō [2]

spin [2]

Mt   6:28 See how the lilies of the field grow. They do not labor or **spin**.
Lk   12:27 They do not labor or **spin**. Yet I tell you, not even Solomon in all

3757 νηπιάζω, nēpiazō [1] [√ *3758*]

infants [1]

1Co 14:20 In regard to evil be **infants**, but in your thinking be adults.

3758 νήπιος, nēpios [15 / 14] [→ *3757*]

child [5], infants [3], children [2], little children [2], childish [1],
infant [1]

Mt   11:25 from the wise and learned, and revealed them *to* **little children**.
     21:16 " 'From the lips *of* **children** and infants you have ordained praise'?"
Lk   10:21 from the wise and learned, and revealed them *to* **little children**.
Ro   2:20 an instructor of the foolish, a teacher *of* **infants**, because you have
1Co   3: 1 address you as spiritual but as worldly—*mere* **infants** in Christ.
     13:11 When I was a **child**, I talked like a child, I thought like a child,
     13:11 When I was a child, I talked like a **child**, I thought like a child,
     13:11 When I was a child, I talked like a child, I thought like a **child**,
     13:11 I talked like a child, I thought like a child, I reasoned like a **child**.
     13:11 like a child. When I became a man, I put **childish** ways behind me.
Gal   4: 1 What I am saying is that as long as the heir is a **child**, he is no
      4: 3 So also, when we were **children**, we were in slavery under the
Eph   4:14 Then we will no longer be **infants**, tossed back and forth by the
1Th   2: 7 but we were gentle [UBS *infants*; NIV *2473*] among you, like a
Heb   5:13 Anyone who lives on milk, being still an **infant**, is not acquainted

3759 Νηρεύς, Nēreus [1]

Nereus [1]

Ro   16:15 Julia, **Nereus** and his sister, and Olympas and all the saints with

3760 Νηρί, Nēri [1]

Neri [1]

Lk   3:27 the son of Zerubbabel, the son of Shealtiel, the son *of* **Neri**,

3761 νησίον, nēsion [1] [√ *3762*]

small island [1]

Ac   27:16 As we passed to the lee of a **small island** called Cauda, we were

3762 νῆσος, nēsos [9] [→ *3761*]

island [9]

Ac   13: 6 They traveled through the whole **island** until they came to Paphos.
     27:26 Nevertheless, we must run aground on some **island**."
     28: 1 safely on shore, we found out that the **island** was called Malta.
     28: 7 nearby that belonged to Publius, the chief official *of* the **island**.
     28: 9 the rest of the sick on the **island** came and were cured.
     28:11 months we put out to sea in a ship that had wintered in the **island**.
Rev   1: 9 was on the **island** of Patmos because of the word of God
      6:14 and every mountain and **island** was removed from its place.
     16:20 Every **island** fled away and the mountains could not be found.

3763 νηστεία, nēsteia [5] [→ *3764, 3765; cf. 2266*]

fasting [2], fast [1], gone without food [1], hunger [1]

Lk   2:37 left the temple but worshiped night and day, **fasting** and praying.
Ac   14:23 with prayer and **fasting**, committed them to the Lord, in whom
     27: 9 already become dangerous because by now it was after the **Fast**.
2Co   6: 5 and riots; in hard work, sleepless nights and **hunger**;
     11:27 I have known hunger and thirst and have often **gone without food**;

3764 νηστεύω, nēsteuō [20] [√ *3763*]

fast [11], fasting [6], *untranslated* [2], fasted [1]

Mt   4: 2 After **fasting** forty days and forty nights, he was hungry.
      6:16 "When *you* **fast**, do not look somber as the hypocrites do, for they
      6:16 they disfigure their faces to show men *they are* **fasting**.
      6:17 But *when* you **fast**, put oil on your head and wash your face,
      6:18 so that it will not be obvious to men that *you are* **fasting**, but only
      9:14 and asked him, "How is it that we and the Pharisees **fast**,
      9:14 is it that we and the Pharisees fast, but your disciples *do* not **fast**?"

9:15 when the bridegroom will be taken from them; then *they will* **fast**.
Mk 2:18 Now John's disciples and the Pharisees were **fasting**. Some people
2:18 that John's disciples and the disciples of the Pharisees *are* **fasting**,
2:18 disciples of the Pharisees are fasting, but yours are not?" **[RPG]**
2:19 "How can the guests of the bridegroom **fast** while he is with them?
2:19 They cannot, **[RPG]** so long as they have him with them.
2:20 will be taken from them, and on that day *they will* **fast**.
Lk 5:33 "John's disciples often **fast** and pray, and so do the disciples of the
5:34 "Can you make the guests of the bridegroom **fast** while he is with
5:35 bridegroom will be taken from them; in those days *they will* **fast**."
18:12 *I* **fast** twice a week and give a tenth of all I get.'
Ac 13: 2 *While* they *were* worshiping the Lord and **fasting**, the Holy Spirit
13: 3 So *after they had* **fasted** and prayed, they placed their hands on

3765 νῆστις, *nēstis* [2] [√ *3763*]

hungry [2]

Mt 15:32 I do not want to send them away **hungry**, or they may collapse on
Mk 8: 3 If I send them home **hungry**, they will collapse on the way,

3766 νηφαλέος, *nēphaleos* Not used in UBS/NIV [√ *3768*]

3767 νηφάλιος, *nēphalios* [3] [√ *3768*]

temperate [3]

1Ti 3: 2 the husband of but one wife, **temperate**, self-controlled,
3:11 not malicious talkers but **temperate** and trustworthy in everything.
Tit 2: 2 Teach the older men to be **temperate**, worthy of respect,

3768 νήφω, *nēphō* [6] [→ *392, 1729, 3766, 3767*]

self-controlled [5], keep head [1]

1Th 5: 6 like others, who are asleep, but *let us be* alert and **self-controlled**.
5: 8 *let us be* **self-controlled**, putting on faith and love as a breastplate,
2Ti 4: 5 But you, **keep** *your* **head** in all situations, endure hardship,
1Pe 1:13 Therefore, prepare your minds for action; *be* **self-controlled**;
4: 7 Therefore *be* clear minded and **self-controlled** so that you can
5: 8 *Be* **self-controlled** and alert. Your enemy the devil prowls around

3769 Νίγερ, *Niger* [1]

Niger [1]

Ac 13: 1 Barnabas, Simeon called **Niger**, Lucius of Cyrene, Manaen (who

3770 Νικάνωρ, *Nikanōr* [1] [√ *3772 + 467*]

Nicanor [1]

Ac 6: 5 also Philip, Procorus, **Nicanor**, Timon, Parmenas, and Nicolas

3771 νικάω, *nikaō* [28] [√ *3772*]

overcomes [10], overcome [8], overcame [2], conquer [1],
conqueror [1], conquest [1], overpower [1], overpowers [1],
prevail [1], triumphed [1], victorious [1]

Lk 11:22 But when someone stronger attacks and **overpowers** him,
Jn 16:33 you will have trouble. But take heart! I *have* **overcome** the world."
Ro 3: 4 may be proved right when you speak and **prevail** when you judge."
12:21 *Do* not *be* **overcome** by evil, but overcome evil with good.
12:21 Do not be overcome by evil, but **overcome** evil with good.
1Jn 2:13 to you, young men, because *you have* **overcome** the evil one.
2:14 the word of God lives in you, and *you have* **overcome** the evil one.
4: 4 You, dear children, are from God and *have* **overcome** them,
5: 4 for everyone born of God **overcomes** the world. This is the victory
5: 4 This is the victory that *has* **overcome** the world, even our faith.
5: 5 Who is it that **overcomes** the world? Only he who believes that
Rev 2: 7 *To* him who **overcomes**, I will give the right to eat from the tree of
2:11 He *who* **overcomes** will not be hurt at all by the second death.
2:17 *To* him who **overcomes**, I will give some of the hidden manna.
2:26 To him *who* **overcomes** and does my will to the end, I will give
3: 5 He *who* **overcomes** will, like them, be dressed in white. I will

3:12 Him who **overcomes** I will make a pillar in the temple of my God.
3:21 To him who **overcomes**, I will give the right to sit with me on my
3:21 just as I **overcame** and sat down with my Father on his throne.
5: 5 the Lion of the tribe of Judah, the Root of David, *has* **triumphed**.
6: 2 given a crown, and he rode out as a **conqueror** bent on conquest.
6: 2 given a crown, and he rode out as a conqueror bent on **conquest**.
11: 7 up from the Abyss will attack them, and **overpower** and kill them.
12:11 They **overcame** him by the blood of the Lamb and by the word of
13: 7 given power to make war against the saints and *to* **conquer** them.
15: 2 those *who had been* **victorious** over the beast and his image
17:14 but the Lamb *will* **overcome** them because he is Lord of lords
21: 7 He *who* **overcomes** will inherit all this, and I will be his God

3772 νίκη, *nikē* [1] [→ *438, 1022, 2332, 2552, 2553, 3770, 3771, 3773, 3774, 3775, 3776, 3777, 5664*]

victory [1]

1Jn 5: 4 This is the **victory** that has overcome the world, even our faith.

3773 Νικόδημος, *Nikodēmos* [5] [√ *3772 + 1322*]

Nicodemus [5]

Jn 3: 1 Now there was a man of the Pharisees named **Nicodemus**,
3: 4 "How can a man be born when he is old?" **Nicodemus** asked.
3: 9 "How can this be?" **Nicodemus** asked.
7:50 **Nicodemus**, who had gone to Jesus earlier and who was one of
19:39 He was accompanied by **Nicodemus**, the man who earlier had

3774 Νικολαΐτης, *Nikolaitēs* [2] [√ *3772 + 3295*]

Nicolaitans [2]

Rev 2: 6 You hate the practices *of* the **Nicolaitans**, which I also hate.
2:15 you also have those who hold to the teaching *of* the **Nicolaitans**.

3775 Νικόλαος, *Nikolaos* [1] [√ *3772 + 3295*]

Nicolas [1]

Ac 6: 5 Procorus, Nicanor, Timon, Parmenas, and **Nicolas** from Antioch,

3776 Νικόπολις, *Nikopolis* [1] [√ *3772 + 4484*]

Nicopolis [1]

Tit 3:12 or Tychicus to you, do your best to come to me at **Nicopolis**,

3777 νῖκος, *nikos* [4] [√ *3772*]

victory [4]

Mt 12:20 wick he will not snuff out, till he leads justice to **victory**.
1Co 15:54 written will come true: "Death has been swallowed up in **victory**."
15:55 "Where, O death, is your **victory**? Where, O death, is your sting?"
15:57 be to God! He gives us the **victory** through our Lord Jesus Christ.

3778 Νινευή, *Nineuē* Not used in UBS/NIV [→ *3779, 3780*]

3779 Νινευΐ, *Nineui* Not used in UBS/NIV [√ *3778*]

3780 Νινευΐτης, *Nineuitēs* [3] [√ *3778*]

of Nineveh [2], Ninevites [1]

Mt 12:41 The men **of Nineveh** will stand up at the judgment with this
Lk 11:30 For as Jonah was a sign *to* the **Ninevites**, so also will the Son of
11:32 The men **of Nineveh** will stand up at the judgment with this

3781 νιπτήρ, *niptēr* [1] [√ *3782*]

basin [1]

Jn 13: 5 he poured water into a **basin** and began to wash his disciples' feet,

3782 νίπτω, niptō [17] [→ 481, 672, 3781, 4469]

wash [10], washed [4], washing [3]

Mt   6: 17   But when you fast, put oil on your head and **wash** your face,
     15: 2   of the elders? *They* don't **wash** their hands before they eat!"
Mk   7: 3   Jews do not eat unless *they give* their hands a ceremonial **washing**,
Jn   9: 7   he told him, "**wash** in the Pool of Siloam" (this word means Sent).
     9: 7   So the man went and **washed**, and came home seeing.
     9: 11   He told me to go to Siloam and **wash**. So I went and washed,
     9: 11   to Siloam and wash. So *I* went and **washed**, and then I could see."
     9: 15   mud on my eyes," the man replied, "and *I* **washed**, and now I see."
     13: 5   he poured water into a basin and began *to* **wash** his disciples' feet,
     13: 6   who said to him, "Lord, *are* you *going to* **wash** my feet?"
     13: 8   "No," said Peter, "*you shall* never **wash** my feet." Jesus answered,
     13: 8   Jesus answered, "Unless *I* **wash** you, you have no part with me."
     13: 10   "A person who has had a bath needs only *to* **wash** his feet,
     13: 12   When *he had finished* **washing** their feet, he put on his clothes
     13: 14   Now that I, your Lord and Teacher, *have* **washed** your feet,
     13: 14   have washed your feet, you also should **wash** one another's feet.
1Ti   5: 10   showing hospitality, **washing** the feet of the saints, helping those

3783 νοέω, noeō [14] [√ 3808]

understand [7], see [3], imagine [1], know [1], reflect on [1],
understood [1]

Mt   15: 17   "Don't *you* **see** that whatever enters the mouth goes into the
     16: 9   *Do you* still not **understand**? Don't you remember the five loaves
     16: 11   How is it *you* don't **understand** that I was not talking to you about
     24: 15   spoken of through the prophet Daniel—*let* the reader **understand**—
Mk   7: 18   "Don't *you* **see** that nothing that enters a man from the outside can
     8: 17   *Do you* still not **see** or understand? Are your hearts hardened?
     13: 14   *let* the reader **understand**—then let those who are in Judea flee to
Jn   12: 40   see with their eyes, nor **understand** with their hearts, nor turn—
Ro   1: 20   been clearly seen, *being* **understood** from what has been made,
Eph   3: 4   you will be able *to* **understand** my insight into the mystery of
     3: 20   who is able to do immeasurably more than all *we* ask or **imagine**,
1Ti   1: 7   but *they do not* **know** what they are talking about or what they
2Ti   2: 7   **Reflect on** what I am saying, for the Lord will give you insight
Heb   11: 3   By faith *we* **understand** that the universe was formed at God's

3784 νόημα, noēma [6] [√ 3808]

minds [4], schemes [1], thought [1]

2Co   2: 11   Satan might not outwit us. For we are not unaware of his **schemes**.
     3: 14   But their **minds** were made dull, for to this day the same veil
     4: 4   The god of this age has blinded the **minds** of unbelievers,
     10: 5   and we take captive every **thought** to make it obedient to Christ.
     11: 3   your **minds** may somehow be led astray from your sincere
Php   4: 7   will guard your hearts and your **minds** in Christ Jesus.

3785 νόθος, nothos [1]

illegitimate children [1]

Heb   12: 8   then you are **illegitimate children** and not true sons.

3786 νομή, nomē [2] [√ 3795]

pasture [1], spread [+2400] [1]

Jn   10: 9   me will be saved. He will come in and go out, and find **pasture**.
2Ti   2: 17   Their teaching *will* **spread** [+2400] like gangrene. Among them

3787 νομίζω, nomizō [15] [√ 3795]

think [4], thought [4], expected [2], thinking [2], assumed [1],
suppose [1], thinks [1]

Mt   5: 17   "*Do* not **think** that I have come to abolish the Law or the Prophets;
     10: 34   *Do* not **suppose** that I have come to bring peace to the earth.
     20: 10   those came who were hired first, *they* **expected** to receive more.
Lk   2: 44   **Thinking** he was in their company, they traveled on for a day.
     3: 23   He was the son, so *it was* **thought**, of Joseph, the son of Heli,
Ac   7: 25   Moses **thought** that his own people would realize that God was
     8: 20   because *you* **thought** you could buy the gift of God with money!
     14: 19   and dragged him outside the city, **thinking** he was dead.

     16: 13   city gate to the river, where *we* **expected** to find a place of prayer.
     16: 27   to kill himself *because he* **thought** the prisoners had escaped.
     17: 29   we should not **think** that the divine being is like gold or silver
     21: 29   and **assumed** that Paul had brought him into the temple area.)
1Co   7: 26   present crisis, *I* **think** that it is good for you to remain as you are.
     7: 36   If anyone **thinks** he is acting improperly toward the virgin he is
1Ti   6: 5   and *who* **think** that godliness is a means to financial gain.

3788 νομικός, nomikos [9] [√ 3795]

experts in the law [5], expert in the law [2], about law [1], lawyer
[1]

Mt   22: 35   One of them, an **expert in the law**, tested him with this question:
Lk   7: 30   and **experts in the law** rejected God's purpose for themselves,
     10: 25   On one occasion an **expert in the law** stood up to test Jesus.
     11: 45   One *of* the **experts in the law** answered him, "Teacher, when you
     11: 46   Jesus replied, "And you **experts in the law**, woe to you,
     11: 52   "Woe to you **experts in the law**, because you have taken away the
     14: 3   Jesus asked the Pharisees and **experts in the law**, "Is it lawful to
Tit   3: 9   and genealogies and arguments and quarrels **about** the **law**,
     3: 13   Do everything you can to help Zenas the **lawyer** and Apollos on

3789 νομίμως, nomimōs [2] [√ 3795]

according to the rules [1], properly [1]

1Ti   1: 8   We know that the law is good if one uses it **properly**.
2Ti   2: 5   the victor's crown unless he competes **according to the rules**.

3790 νόμισμα, nomisma [1] [√ 3795]

coin [1]

Mt   22: 19   Show me the **coin** used for paying the tax." They brought him a

3791 νομοδιδάσκαλος, nomodidaskalos [3]
     [√ 3795 + 1438]

teachers of the law [2], teacher of the law [1]

Lk   5: 17   One day as he was teaching, Pharisees and **teachers of the law**,
Ac   5: 34   But a Pharisee named Gamaliel, a **teacher of the law**, who was
1Ti   1: 7   They want to be **teachers of the law**, but they do not know what

3792 νομοθεσία, nomothesia [1] [√ 3795 + 5502]

receiving of the law [1]

Ro   9: 4   the covenants, the **receiving of the law**, the temple worship

3793 νομοθετέω, nomotheteō [2] [√ 3795 + 5502]

founded [1], law was given [1]

Heb   7: 11   priesthood (for on the basis of it the **law was given** to the people),
     8: 6   is superior to the old one, and it *is* **founded** on better promises.

3794 νομοθέτης, nomothetēs [1] [√ 3795 + 5502]

Lawgiver [1]

Jas   4: 12   There is only one **Lawgiver** and Judge, the one who is able to save

3795 νόμος, nomos [194] [→ 490, 491, 492, 671, 1376,
     1937, 1938, 2883, 3099, 3100, 3101, 3786, 3787, 3788, 3789,
     3790, 3791, 3792, 3793, 3794, 3872, 3873, 3874, 4174, 4175,
     5169]

     τὸ ἔργον τοῦ νόμου (the work of the law) [9] Ro 2:15;
     3:20,28; Gal 2:16,16,16; 3:2,5,10

     κατὰ νόμον (according to law) [14] Lk 2:22,39; Jn 18:31; 19:7;
     Ac 22:12; 23:3; 24:14; Php 3:5; Heb 7:5,16; 8:4; 9:19,22; 10:8

     Μωϋσῆς ... νόμος (Moses ... law) [14] Lk 2:22; 24:44; Jn
     1:17,45; 7:19,23; 8:5; Ac 13:38; 15:5; 28:23; Ro 10:5; 1Co 9:9;
     Heb 9:19; 10:28

νόμος ... ἁμαρτία (law ... sin) [14] Ro 3:20,20; 5:13;
   7:5,7,7,8,9,23,25; 8:2,3; 1Co 15:56; Jas 2:9

νόμος ... δικαιοσύνη (law ... righteousness) [8] Ro 3:21; 9:31;
   10:4,5; Gal 2:21; 3:21; Php 3:6,9

νόμος θεοῦ (law of God) [3] Ro 7:22,25; 8:7

νόμος κυρίου (law of the Lord) [3] Lk 2:23,24,39

νόμος πνεύματος (law of the Spirit) [1] Ro 8:2

νόμος ... προφῆται (Law ... Prophets) [11] Mt 5:17; 7:12;
   11:13; 22:40; Lk 16:16; 24:44; Jn 1:45; Ac 13:15; 24:14; 28:23; Ro
   3:21

νόμος Χριστοῦ (law of Christ) [1] Gal 6:2

τηρέω νόμον (keep the law) [2] Ac 15:5; Jas 2:10

ὑπὸ νόμον [νόμου] (under law) [13] Ro 3:21; 6:14,15; 1Co
   9:20,20,20,20; Gal 3:23; 4:4,5,21; 5:18; Jas 2:9

law [182], its [2], lawbreaker [+4127] [2], laws [2], its [+1650] [1],
law's [1], legalistic [+1877] [1], principle [1], regulation [+1953]
[1], that [1]

Mt	5:17	"Do not think that I have come to abolish the **Law** or the Prophets;
	5:18	will by any means disappear from the **Law** until everything is
	7:12	have them do to you, for this sums up the **Law** and the Prophets.
	11:13	For all the Prophets and the **Law** prophesied until John.
	12: 5	Or haven't you read in the **Law** that on the Sabbath the priests in
	22:36	"Teacher, which is the greatest commandment in the **Law**?"
	22:40	All the **Law** and the Prophets hang on these two commandments."
	23:23	But you have neglected the more important matters *of* the **law**—
Lk	2:22	When the time of their purification according to the **Law** of Moses
	2:23	(as it is written in the **Law** of the Lord, "Every firstborn male is to
	2:24	and to offer a sacrifice in keeping with what is said in the **Law** of
	2:27	the child Jesus to do for him what the custom *of* the **Law** required,
	2:39	and Mary had done everything required by the **Law** of the Lord,
	10:26	"What is written in the **Law**?" he replied. "How do you read it?"
	16:16	"The **Law** and the Prophets were proclaimed until John. Since that
	16:17	disappear than for the least stroke of a pen to drop out *of* the **Law**.
	24:44	Everything must be fulfilled that is written about me in the **Law** of
Jn	1:17	For the **law** was given through Moses; grace and truth came
	1:45	told him, "We have found the one Moses wrote about in the **Law**,
	7:19	Has not Moses given you the **law**? Yet not one of you keeps the
	7:19	Yet not one of you keeps the **law**. Why are you trying to kill me?"
	7:23	on the Sabbath so that the **law** of Moses may not be broken,
	7:49	But this mob that knows nothing of the **law**—there is a curse on
	7:51	"Does our **law** condemn anyone without first hearing him to find
	8: 5	In the **Law** Moses commanded us to stone such women. Now what
	8:17	In your own **Law** it is written that the testimony of two men is
	10:34	Jesus answered them, "Is it not written in your **Law**, 'I have said
	12:34	"We have heard from the **Law** that the Christ will remain forever,
	15:25	But this is to fulfill what is written in their **Law**: 'They hated me
	18:31	Pilate said, "Take him yourselves and judge him by your own **law**."
	19: 7	The Jews insisted, "We have a **law**, and according to that law he
	19: 7	"We have a law, and according to that **law** he must die,
Ac	6:13	never stops speaking against this holy place and against the **law**.
	7:53	you who have received the **law** that was put into effect through
	13:15	After the reading *from* the **Law** and the Prophets, the synagogue
	13:39	everything you could not be justified from by the **law** of Moses.
	15: 5	must be circumcised and required to obey the **law** of Moses."
	18:13	persuading the people to worship God in ways contrary to the **law**."
	18:15	it involves questions about words and names and your own **law**—
	21:20	of Jews have believed, and all of them are zealous *for* the **law**.
	21:24	about you, but that you yourself are living in obedience to the **law**.
	21:28	all men everywhere against our people and our **law** and this place.
	22: 3	Under Gamaliel I was thoroughly trained *in* the **law** of our fathers
	22:12	He was a devout observer *of* the **law** and highly respected by all
	23: 3	You sit there to judge me according to the **law**, yet you yourself
	23:29	found that the accusation had to do with questions *about* their **law**,
	24:14	I believe everything that agrees with the **Law** and that is written in
	25: 8	"I have done nothing wrong against the **law** of the Jews or against
	28:23	and tried to convince them about Jesus from the **Law** of Moses
Ro	2:12	the law, and all who sin under the **law** will be judged by the law.
	2:12	the law, and all who sin under the law will be judged by the **law**.
	2:13	For it is not those who hear the **law** who are righteous in God's
	2:13	but it is those who obey the **law** who will be declared righteous.
	2:14	(Indeed, when Gentiles, who do not have the **law**, do by nature
	2:14	who do not have the law, do by nature things *required by* the **law**,

	2:14	they are a **law** for themselves, even though they do not have the
	2:14	are a law for themselves, even though they do not have the **law**,
	2:15	since they show that the requirements *of* the **law** are written on
	2:17	if you rely on the **law** and brag about your relationship to God;
	2:18	approve of what is superior because you are instructed by the **law**;
	2:20	because you have in the **law** the embodiment of knowledge
	2:23	You who brag about the **law**, do you dishonor God by breaking the
	2:23	who brag about the law, do you dishonor God by breaking the **law**?
	2:25	Circumcision has value if you observe the **law**, but if you break the
	2:25	has value if you observe the law, but if you break the **law**,
	2:26	If those who are not circumcised keep the **law's** requirements,
	2:27	and yet obeys the **law** will condemn you who,
	2:27	have the written code and circumcision, are a **lawbreaker** [+4127].
	3:19	Now we know that whatever the **law** says, it says to those who are
	3:19	it says *to* those who are under the **law**, so that every mouth may be
	3:20	no one will be declared righteous in his sight by observing the **law**;
	3:20	the law; rather, through the **law** we become conscious of sin.
	3:21	apart from **law**, has been made known, to which the Law
	3:21	has been made known, to which the **Law** and the Prophets testify.
	3:27	Where, then, is boasting? It is excluded. On what **principle**?
	3:27	On that of observing the law? No, but on **that** of faith.
	3:28	that a man is justified by faith apart from observing the **law**.
	3:31	Do we, then, nullify the **law** by this faith? Not at all! Rather,
	3:31	nullify the law by this faith? Not at all! Rather, we uphold the **law**.
	4:13	It was not through **law** that Abraham and his offspring received the
	4:14	For if those who live by **law** are heirs, faith has no value
	4:15	because **law** brings wrath. And where there is no law there is no
	4:15	brings wrath. And where there is no law there is no transgression.
	4:16	not only *to* those who are of the **law** but also to those who are of
	5:13	for before the **law** was given, sin was in the world. But sin is not
	5:13	the world. But sin is not taken into account when there is no **law**.
	5:20	The **law** was added so that the trespass might increase. But where
	6:14	be your master, because you are not under **law**, but under grace.
	6:15	Shall we sin because we are not under **law** but under grace?
	7: 1	not know, brothers—for I am speaking to men who know the **law**—
	7: 1	that the **law** has authority over a man only as long as he lives?
	7: 2	*by* **law** a married woman is bound to her husband as long as he is
	7: 2	but if her husband dies, she is released from the **law** of marriage.
	7: 3	husband dies, she is released from that **law** and is not an adulteress,
	7: 4	my brothers, you also died *to* the **law** through the body of Christ,
	7: 5	the sinful passions aroused by the **law** were at work in our bodies,
	7: 6	we have been released from the **law** so that we serve in the new
	7: 7	What shall we say, then? Is the **law** sin? Certainly not! Indeed I
	7: 7	I would not have known what sin was except through the **law**.
	7: 7	For I would not have known what coveting really was if the **law**
	7: 8	me every kind of covetous desire. For apart from **law**, sin is dead.
	7: 9	Once I was alive apart from law; but when the commandment
	7:12	So then, the **law** is holy, and the commandment is holy, righteous
	7:14	We know that the **law** is spiritual; but I am unspiritual, sold as a
	7:16	And if I do what I do not want to do, I agree that the **law** is good.
	7:21	So I find this **law** at work: When I want to do good, evil is right
	7:22	For in my inner being I delight *in* God's **law**;
	7:23	but I see another **law** at work in the members of my body,
	7:23	waging war against the **law** of my mind and making me a prisoner
	7:23	and making me a prisoner of the **law** of sin at work within my
	7:25	So then, I myself in my mind am a slave *to* God's **law**, but in the
	7:25	to God's law, but in the sinful nature a slave *to* the **law** of sin.
	8: 2	because through Christ Jesus the **law** of the Spirit of life set me
	8: 2	Jesus the law of the Spirit of life set me free from the **law** of sin
	8: 3	For what the **law** was powerless to do in that it was weakened by
	8: 4	in order that the righteous requirements *of* the **law** might be fully
	8: 7	is hostile to God. It does not submit *to* God's **law**, nor can it do so.
	9:31	but Israel, who pursued a **law** of righteousness, has not attained it.
	9:31	who pursued a law of righteousness, has not attained **it** [+1650].
	10: 4	Christ is the end *of* the **law** so that there may be righteousness for
	10: 5	Moses describes in this way the righteousness that is by the **law**:
	13: 8	one another, for he who loves his fellowman has fulfilled the **law**.
	13:10	harm to its neighbor. Therefore love is the fulfillment *of* the **law**.
1Co	9: 8	from a human point of view? Doesn't the **Law** say the same thing?
	9: 9	For it is written in the **Law** of Moses: "Do not muzzle an ox while
	9:20	To those under the **law** I became like one under the law (though I
	9:20	To those under the law I became like one under the **law** (though I
	9:20	like one under the law (though I myself am not under the **law**),
	9:20	I myself am not under the law), so as to win those under the **law**.
	14:21	In the **Law** it is written: "Through men of strange tongues
	14:34	not allowed to speak, but must be in submission, as the **Law** says.

15:56 The sting of death is sin, and the power of sin is the **law**.
Gal 2:16 know that a man is not justified by observing the **law**,
2:16 may be justified by faith in Christ and not by observing the **law**,
2:16 the law, because by observing the **law** no one will be justified.
2:19 For through the **law** I died to the law so that I might live for God.
2:19 For through the **law** I died *to* the law so that I might live for God.
2:21 for if righteousness could be gained through the **law**, Christ died
3:2 Did you receive the Spirit by observing the **law**, or by believing
3:5 and work miracles among you because you observe the **law**,
3:10 All who rely on observing the **law** are under a curse, for it is
3:10 does not continue to do everything written in the Book *of* the **Law**."
3:11 Clearly no one is justified before God by the **law**, because,
3:12 The **law** is not based on faith; on the contrary, "The man who does
3:13 Christ redeemed us from the curse *of* the **law** by becoming a curse
3:17 The **law**, introduced 430 years later, does not set aside the
3:18 For if the inheritance depends on the **law**, then it no longer depends
3:19 What, then, was the purpose of the **law**? It was added because of
3:21 Is the **law**, therefore, opposed to the promises of God? Absolutely
3:21 For if a **law** had been given that could impart life,
3:21 then righteousness would certainly have come by the **law**.
3:23 Before this faith came, we were held prisoners by the **law**,
3:24 So the **law** was put in charge to lead us to Christ that we might be
4:4 fully come, God sent his Son, born of a woman, born under the **law**,
4:5 to redeem those under **law**, that we might receive the full rights of
4:21 Tell me, you who want to be under the **law**, are you not aware of
4:21 want to be under the law, are you not aware of what the **law** says?
5:3 himself be circumcised that he is obligated to obey the whole **law**.
5:4 You who are trying to be justified by **law** have been alienated from
5:14 The entire **law** is summed up in a single command: "Love your
5:18 But if you are led by the Spirit, you are not under **law**.
5:23 gentleness and self-control. Against such things there is no **law**.
6:2 other's burdens, and in this way you will fulfill the **law** of Christ.
6:13 Not even those who are circumcised obey the **law**, yet they want
Eph 2:15 by abolishing in his flesh the **law** with its commandments
Php 3:5 a Hebrew of Hebrews; in regard to the **law**, a Pharisee,
3:6 the church; as for **legalistic** [+*1877*] righteousness, faultless.
3:9 not having a righteousness of my own that comes from the **law**,
1Ti 1:8 We know that the **law** is good if one uses it properly.
1:9 We also know that **law** is made not for the righteous but for
Heb 7:5 Now the **law** requires the descendants of Levi who become priests
7:12 a change of the priesthood, there must also be a change *of* the **law**.
7:16 a priest not on the basis of a **regulation** [+*1953*] as to his ancestry
7:19 (for the **law** made nothing perfect), and a better hope is introduced,
7:28 For the **law** appoints as high priests men who are weak; but the
7:28 but the oath, which came after the **law**, appointed the Son,
8:4 for there are already men who offer the gifts prescribed by the **law**.
8:10 I will put my **laws** in their minds and write them on their hearts.
9:19 When Moses had proclaimed every commandment of the **law** to all
9:22 the **law** requires that nearly everything be cleansed with blood,
10:1 The **law** is only a shadow of the good things that are coming—
10:8 nor were you pleased with them" (although the **law** required them to
10:16 I will put my **laws** in their hearts, and I will write them on their
10:28 Anyone who rejected the **law** of Moses died without mercy on the
Jas 1:25 But the man who looks intently into the perfect **law** that gives
2:8 If you really keep the royal **law** found in Scripture, "Love your
2:9 you sin and are convicted by the **law** as lawbreakers.
2:10 For whoever keeps the whole **law** and yet stumbles at just one
2:11 but do commit murder, you have become a **lawbreaker** [+*4127*].
2:12 and act as those who are going to be judged by the **law** that gives
4:11 his brother or judges him speaks against the **law** and judges it.
4:11 his brother or judges him speaks against the law and judges it[s].
4:11 When you judge the **law**, you are not keeping it, but sitting in
4:11 When you judge the law, you are not keeping it[s], but sitting in

3796 νοσέω, **noseō** [1] [√ *3798*]

unhealthy [1]

1Ti 6:4 *He has* an **unhealthy** interest in controversies and quarrels about

3797 νόσημα, **nosēma**   Not used in UBS/NIV [√ *3798*]

3798 νόσος, **nosos** [11] [→ *3796, 3797*]

diseases [5], disease [3], diseases [+*2809*] [1], illnesses [1], sickness [+*820*] [1]

Mt 4:23 and healing every **disease** and sickness among the people.
4:24 and people brought to him all who were ill *with* various **diseases**,
8:17 Isaiah: "He took up our infirmities and carried our **diseases**."
9:35 good news of the kingdom and healing every **disease** and sickness.
10:1 to drive out evil spirits and to heal every **disease** and sickness.
Mk 1:34 and Jesus healed many who had various **diseases** [+*2809*].
Lk 4:40 brought to Jesus all who had various kinds *of* **sickness** [+*820*],
6:18 who had come to hear him and to be healed of their **diseases**.
7:21 At that very time Jesus cured many who had **diseases**, sicknesses
9:1 and authority to drive out all demons and to cure **diseases**,
Ac 19:12 and their **illnesses** were cured and the evil spirits left them.

3799 νοσσιά, **nossia** [1] [√ *3742*]

chicks [1]

Lk 13:34 as a hen gathers her **chicks** under her wings, but you were not

3800 νοσσίον, **nossion** [1] [√ *3742*]

chicks [1]

Mt 23:37 as a hen gathers her **chicks** under her wings, but you were not

3801 νοσσός, **nossos** [1] [√ *3742*]

young [1]

Lk 2:24 said in the Law of the Lord: "a pair of doves or two **young** pigeons."

3802 νοσφίζω, **nosphizō** [3]

kept back [1], kept [1], steal [1]

Ac 5:2 wife's full knowledge *he* **kept back** part of the money *for himself*,
5:3 and *have* **kept** *for yourself* some of the money you received for
Tit 2:10 and not to **steal** from them, but to show that they can be fully

3803 νότος, **notos** [7]

south [4], south wind [3]

Mt 12:42 The Queen *of* the **South** will rise at the judgment with this
Lk 11:31 The Queen *of* the **South** will rise at the judgment with the men of
12:55 And when the **south wind** blows, you say, 'It's going to be hot,'
13:29 People will come from east and west and north and **south**,
Ac 27:13 When a gentle **south wind** began to blow, they thought they had
28:13 The next day the **south wind** came up, and on the following day
Rev 21:13 three on the north, three on the **south** and three on the west.

3804 νουθεσία, **nouthesia** [3] [√ *3808 + 5502*]

instruction [1], warn [1], warnings [1]

1Co 10:11 to them as examples and were written down as **warnings** for us,
Eph 6:4 bring them up in the training and **instruction** of the Lord.
Tit 3:10 **Warn** a divisive person once, and then warn him a second time.

3805 νουθετέω, **noutheteō** [8] [√ *3808 + 5502*]

warn [3], admonish [2], admonishing [1], instruct [1], warning [1]

Ac 20:31 Remember that for three years I never stopped **warning** each of
Ro 15:14 complete in knowledge and competent *to* **instruct** one another.
1Co 4:14 writing this to shame you, but *to* **warn** you, as my dear children.
Col 1:28 **admonishing** and teaching everyone with all wisdom,
3:16 the word of Christ dwell in you richly *as you* teach and **admonish**
1Th 5:12 among you, who are over you in the Lord and *who* **admonish** you.
5:14 And we urge you, brothers, **warn** those who are idle,
2Th 3:15 Yet do not regard him as an enemy, but **warn** him as a brother.

3806 νουμηνία, **noumēnia**   Not used in UBS/NIV [√ *3742 + 3604*]

3807 νουνεχῶς, *nounechōs* [1] [√ *3808 + 2400*]

wisely [1]

Mk 12:34 When Jesus saw that he had answered **wisely**, he said to him,

3808 νοῦς, *nous* [24] [→ *295, 485, 486, 1378, 1379, 1554, 1936, 2154, 2333, 2334, 2917, 3566, 3567, 3783, 3784, 3804, 3805, 3807, 4173, 4629, 4630, 5706, 5707*]

mind [15], minds [4], insight [1], intelligible [*+3836*] [1], thinking [1], understanding [1], unsettled [*+608+3836+4888*] [1]

Lk 24:45 Then he opened their **minds** so they could understand the
Ro 1:28 he gave them over to a depraved **mind**, to do what ought not to be
    7:23 waging war against the law *of* my **mind** and making me a prisoner
    7:25 So then, I myself *in* my **mind** am a slave to God's law, but in the
   11:34 "Who has known the **mind** of the Lord? Or who has been his
   12: 2 of this world, but be transformed by the renewing *of* your **mind**.
   14: 5 day alike. Each one should be fully convinced in his own **mind**.
1Co 1:10 and that you may be perfectly united in **mind** and thought.
    2:16 who has known the **mind** of the Lord that he may instruct him?"
    2:16 Lord that he may instruct him?" But we have the **mind** of Christ.
   14:14 if I pray in a tongue, my spirit prays, but my **mind** is unfruitful.
   14:15 I will pray with my spirit, but I will also pray *with* my **mind**;
   14:15 I will sing with my spirit, but I will also sing *with* my **mind**.
   14:19 But in the church I would rather speak five **intelligible** [*+3836*]
Eph 4:17 no longer live as the Gentiles do, in the futility *of* their **thinking**.
    4:23 to be made new in the attitude *of* your **minds**;
Php 4: 7 which transcends all **understanding**, will guard your hearts
Col 2:18 has seen, and his unspiritual **mind** puffs him up with idle notions.
2Th 2: 2 not *to become* easily **unsettled** [*+608+3836+4888*] or alarmed by
1Ti 6: 5 and constant friction between men of corrupt **mind**, who have been
2Ti 3: 8 men of depraved **minds**, who, as far as the faith is concerned,
Tit 1:15 is pure. In fact, both their **minds** and consciences are corrupted.
Rev 13:18 If anyone has **insight**, let him calculate the number of the beast,
   17: 9 "This calls for a **mind** with wisdom. The seven heads are seven

3809 Νύμφαν, *Nymphan* [1] [√ *3811*]

Nympha [1]

Col 4:15 brothers at Laodicea, and to **Nympha** and the church in her house.

3810 Νυμφᾶς, *Nymphas* Not used in UBS/NIV [√ *3811*]

3811 νύμφη, *nymphē* [8] [→ *3809, 3810, 3812, 3813*]

bride [5], daughter-in-law [3]

Mt 10:35 against her mother, a **daughter-in-law** against her mother-in-law—
Lk 12:53 mother-in-law against **daughter-in-law** and daughter-in-law
   12:53 daughter-in-law and **daughter-in-law** against mother-in-law."
Jn 3:29 The **bride** belongs to the bridegroom. The friend who attends
Rev 18:23 voice of bridegroom and **bride** will never be heard in you again.
   21: 2 from God, prepared as a **bride** beautifully dressed for her husband.
   21: 9 came and said to me, "Come, I will show you the **bride**,
   22:17 The Spirit and the **bride** say, "Come!" And let him who hears,

3812 νυμφίος, *nymphios* [16] [√ *3811*]

bridegroom [11], he^s [*+3836*] [3], bridegroom's [1], him^s [1]

Mt 9:15 "How can the guests of the bridegroom mourn while **he**^s [*+3836*] is
    9:15 The time will come when the **bridegroom** will be taken from
   25: 1 who took their lamps and went out to meet the **bridegroom**.
   25: 5 The **bridegroom** was a long time in coming, and they all became
   25: 6 the cry rang out: 'Here's the **bridegroom**! Come out to meet him!'
   25:10 they were on their way to buy the oil, the **bridegroom** arrived.
Mk 2:19 "How can the guests of the bridegroom fast while **he**^s [*+3836*] is
    2:19 is with them? They cannot, so long as they have **him**^s with them.
    2:20 But the time will come when the **bridegroom** will be taken from
Lk 5:34 "Can you make the guests of the bridegroom fast while **he**^s [*+3836*]
    5:35 But the time will come when the **bridegroom** will be taken from
Jn 2: 9 had drawn the water knew. Then he called the **bridegroom** aside
    3:29 The Bride belongs to the **bridegroom**. The friend who attends the

    3:29 The friend who *attends* the **bridegroom** waits and listens for him,
    3:29 for him, and is full of joy when he hears the **bridegroom's** voice.
Rev 18:23 The voice *of* **bridegroom** and bride will never be heard in you

3813 νυμφών, *nymphōn* [3] [√ *3811*]

bridegroom [3]

Mt 9:15 "How can the guests *of* the **bridegroom** mourn while he is with
Mk 2:19 "How can the guests *of* the **bridegroom** fast while he is with them?
Lk 5:34 "Can you make the guests *of* the **bridegroom** fast while he is with

3814 νῦν, *nyn* [147] [→ *3815, 5422, 5523*]

now [101], present [9], now [*+3836*] [7], now on [*+3836*] [6], as it is [*+1254*] [3], now [*+2627*] [3], untranslated [2], now [*+2627+2779*] [2], a short while ago [1], again [*+608+3836*] [1], as it is [1], at present [1], enough for now [*+2400+3836*] [1], in the present case [*+3836*] [1], instead [*+1254*] [1], just [1], now [*+608+3836*] [1], now then [1], present [*+2789+3836*] [1], present time [1], still [*+2285*] [1], this^s [*+3836*] [1]

Mt 24:21 unequaled from the beginning of the world until **now** [*+3836*]—
   26:65 any more witnesses? Look, **now** you have heard the blasphemy.
   27:42 Let him come down **now** from the cross, and we will believe in
   27:43 Let God rescue him **now** if he wants him, for he said, 'I am the
Mk 10:30 will fail to receive a hundred times as much in this **present** age
   13:19 the beginning, when God created the world, until **now** [*+3836*]—
   15:32 come down **now** from the cross, that we may see and believe."
Lk 1:48 From **now** [*+3836*] **on** all generations will call me blessed,
    2:29 as you have promised, you **now** dismiss your servant in peace.
    5:10 "Don't be afraid; from **now** [*+3836*] **on** you will catch men."
    6:21 Blessed are you who hunger **now**, for you will be satisfied.
    6:21 be satisfied. Blessed are you who weep **now**, for you will laugh.
    6:25 Woe to you who are well fed **now**, for you will go hungry.
    6:25 Woe to you who laugh **now**, for you will mourn and weep.
   11:39 Then the Lord said to him, "**Now then**, you Pharisees clean the
   12:52 From **now** [*+3836*] **on** there will be five in one family divided
   16:25 bad things, but **now** he is comforted here and you are in agony.
   19:42 what would bring you peace—but **now** it is hidden from your eyes.
   22:18 For I tell you I will not drink **again** [*+608+3836*] of the fruit of the
   22:36 said to them, "But **now** if you have a purse, take it, and also a bag;
   22:69 But from **now** [*+3836*] **on**, the Son of Man will be seated at the
Jn 2: 8 "**Now** draw some out and take it to the master of the banquet."
    4:18 had five husbands, and the man you **now** have is not your husband.
    4:23 and has **now** come when the true worshipers will worship the
    5:25 and has **now** come when the dead will hear the voice of the Son of
    6:42 we know? How can he **now** say, 'I came down from heaven'?"
    8:11 Jesus declared. "Go **now** [*+608+3836*] and leave your life of sin."
    8:40 As [*+1254*] **it** is, you are determined to kill me, a man who has told
    8:52 Jews exclaimed, "**Now** we know that you are demon-possessed!
    9:21 But how he can see **now**, or who opened his eyes, we don't know.
    9:41 of sin; but **now** that you claim you can see, your guilt remains.
   11: 8 they said, "**a short while ago** the Jews tried to stone you,
   11:22 But I know that even **now** God will give you whatever you ask."
   12:27 "**Now** my heart is troubled, and what shall I say? 'Father,
   12:31 **Now** is the time for judgment on this world; now the prince of this
   12:31 on this world; **now** the prince of this world will be driven out.
   13:31 "**Now** is the Son of Man glorified and God is glorified in him.
   13:36 Jesus replied, "Where I am going, you cannot follow **now**, but you
   14:29 I have told you **now** before it happens, so that when it does happen
   15:22 be guilty of sin. **Now**, however, they have no excuse for their sin."
   15:24 But **now** they have seen these miracles, and yet they have hated
   16: 5 "**Now** I am going to him who sent me, yet none of you asks me,
   16:22 **Now** is your time of grief, but I will see you again and you will
   16:29 "**Now** you are speaking clearly and without figures of speech.
   16:30 **Now** we can see that you know all things and that you do not even
   17: 5 And **now**, Father, glorify me in your presence with the glory I had
   17: 7 **Now** they know that everything you have given me comes from
   17:13 "I am coming to you **now**, but I say these things while I am still in
   18:36 arrest by the Jews. But **now** my kingdom is from another place."
   21:10 Jesus said to them, "Bring some of the fish you have **just** caught."
Ac 7: 4 "**Now**, brothers, I know that you acted in ignorance, as did your
    4:29 **Now** [*+3836*], Lord, consider their threats and enable your servants
    5:38 Therefore, **in the present** [*+3836*] **case** I advise you: Leave these
    7: 4 of his father, God sent him to this land where you are **now** living.

7:34 down to set them free. **Now** come, I will send you back to Egypt.'
7:52 Righteous One. And **now** you have betrayed and murdered him—
10: 5 **Now** send men to Joppa to bring back a man named Simon who is
10:33 **Now** we are all here in the presence of God to listen to everything
12:11 "**Now** I know without a doubt that the Lord sent his angel
13:11 **Now** [+2627+2779] the hand of the Lord is against you. You are
13:31 Galilee to Jerusalem. They are **now** his witnesses to our people.
15:10 **Now** then, why do you try to test God by putting on the necks of
16:36 that you and Silas be released. **Now** you can leave. Go in peace."
16:37 us into prison. And **now** do they want to get rid of us quietly? No!
17:30 but **now** [+3836] he commands all people everywhere to repent.
18: 6 my responsibility. From **now** [+3836] **on** I will go to the Gentiles."
20:22 "And **now** [+2627], compelled by the Spirit, I am going to
20:25 "**Now** [+2627+2779] I know that none of you among whom I have
20:32 "**Now** [+3836] I commit you to God and to the word of his grace,
22:16 And **now** what are you waiting for? Get up, be baptized and wash
23:15 **Now** then, you and the Sanhedrin petition the commander to bring
23:21 They are ready **now**, waiting for your consent to their request."
24:25 Felix was afraid and said, "That's **enough for now** [+2400+3836].
26: 6 And **now** it is because of my hope in what God has promised our
27:22 But **now** [+3836] I urge you to keep up your courage, because not
Ro 3:26 he did it to demonstrate his justice at the **present** time, so as to be
5: 9 Since we have **now** been justified by his blood, how much more
5:11 Jesus Christ, through whom we have **now** received reconciliation.
6:19 so **now** offer them in slavery to righteousness leading to holiness.
6:21 What benefit did you reap at that time from the things you are **now**
8: 1 there is **now** no condemnation for those who are in Christ Jesus,
8:18 I consider that our **present** [+2789+3836] sufferings are not worth
8:22 groaning as in the pains of childbirth right up to the **present time**.
11: 5 So too, at the **present** time there is a remnant chosen by grace.
11:30 Just as you who were at one time disobedient to God have **now**
11:31 so they too have **now** become disobedient in order that they too
11:31 they too may **now** receive mercy as a result of God's mercy to you.
13:11 because our salvation is nearer **now** than when we first believed.
16:26 but **now** revealed and made known through the prophetic writings
1Co 3: 2 were not yet ready for it. Indeed, you are **still** [+2285] not ready.
5:11 But **now** I am writing you that you must not associate with anyone
7:14 your children would be unclean, but **as it is**, they are holy.
12:20 **As it is** [+1254], there are many parts, but one body.
14: 6 **Now**, brothers, if I come to you and speak in tongues, what good
16:12 He was quite unwilling to go **now**, but he will go when he has the
2Co 5:16 So from **now** [+3836] **on** we regard no one from a worldly point of
5:16 we once regarded Christ in this way, **[NIE]** we do so no longer.
6: 2 I tell you, **now** [+2627] is the time of God's favor, now is the day
6: 2 is the time of God's favor, **now** [+2627] is the day of salvation.
7: 9 yet **now** I am happy, not because you were made sorry, but
8:14 At the **present** time your plenty will supply what they need,
13: 2 I **now** repeat it while absent: On my return I will not spare those
Gal 1:23 "The man who formerly persecuted us is **now** preaching the faith he
2:20 The life **[NIE]** I live in the body, I live by faith in the Son of God,
3: 3 the Spirit, are you **now** trying to attain your goal by human effort?
4: 9 But **now** that you know God—or rather are known by God—
4:25 Sinai in Arabia and corresponds *to* the **present** city of Jerusalem,
4:29 the son born by the power of the Spirit. It is the same **now**.
Eph 2: 2 the spirit who is **now** at work in those who are disobedient.
3: 5 as it has **now** been revealed by the Spirit to God's holy apostles
3:10 His intent was that **now**, through the church, the manifold wisdom
5: 8 For you were once darkness, but **now** you are light in the Lord.
Php 1: 5 your partnership in the gospel from the first day until **now** [+3836],
1:20 so that **now** as always Christ will be exalted in my body,
1:30 the same struggle you saw I had, and **now** hear that I still have.
2:12 not only in my presence, but **now** much more in my absence—
3:18 as I have often told you before and **now** say again even with tears,
Col 1:24 **Now** I rejoice in what was suffered for you, and I fill up in my
1:26 hidden for ages and generations, but is **now** disclosed to the saints.
1Th 3: 8 For **now** we really live, since you are standing firm in the Lord.
2Th 2: 6 And **now** you know what is holding him back,
1Ti 4: 8 holding promise *for* both the **present** life and the life to come.
6:17 Command those who are rich in this **present** world not to be
2Ti 1:10 but it has **now** been revealed through the appearing of our Savior,
4:10 for Demas, because he loved this[s] [+3836] world, has deserted me
Tit 2:12 to live self-controlled, upright and godly lives in this **present** age,
Heb 2: 8 to him. Yet **at present** we do not see everything subject to him.
9: 5 atonement cover. But we cannot discuss these things in detail **now**.
9:24 he entered heaven itself, **now** to appear for us in God's presence.
11:16 **Instead** [+1254], they were longing for a better country—a

12:26 At that time his voice shook the earth, but **now** he has promised,
Jas 4:13 **Now** listen, you who say, "Today or tomorrow we will go to this
4:16 **As it is** [+1254], you boast and brag. All such boasting is evil.
5: 1 **Now** listen, you rich people, weep and wail because of the misery
1Pe 1:12 when they spoke of the things that have **now** been told you by
2:10 Once you were not a people, but **now** you are the people of God;
2:10 you had not received mercy, but **now** you have received mercy.
2:25 but **now** you have returned to the Shepherd and Overseer of your
3:21 and this water symbolizes baptism that **now** saves you also—
2Pe 3: 7 By the same word the **present** heavens and earth are reserved for
3:18 Savior Jesus Christ. To him be glory both **now** and forever! Amen.
1Jn 2:18 the antichrist is coming, even **now** many antichrists have come.
2:28 And **now**, dear children, continue in him, so that when he appears
3: 2 Dear friends, **now** we are children of God, and what we will be has
4: 3 you have heard is coming and even **now** is already in the world.
2Jn 1: 5 And **now**, dear lady, I am not writing you a new command
Jude 1:25 Jesus Christ our Lord, before all ages, **now** and forevermore!

3815 νυνί, *nyni* [20] [√ 3814]

now [16], *untranslated* [1], as it is [+1254] [1], in fact [1], indeed [1]

Ac 22: 1 "Brothers and fathers, listen **now** to my defense."
24:13 And they cannot prove to you the charges they are **now** making
Ro 3:21 But **now** a righteousness from God, apart from law, has been made
6:22 But **now** that you have been set free from sin and have become
7: 6 But **now**, by dying to what once bound us, we have been released
7:17 **As it is** [+1254], it is no longer I myself who do it, but it is sin
15:23 But **now** that there is no more place for me to work in these
15:25 **Now**, however, I am on my way to Jerusalem in the service of the
1Co 12:18 But **in fact** God has arranged the parts in the body, every one of
13:13 And **now** these three remain: faith, hope and love. But the greatest
15:20 But Christ has **indeed** been raised from the dead, the firstfruits of
2Co 8:11 **Now** finish the work, so that your eager willingness to do it may be
8:22 and even more so because of his great confidence in you.
Eph 2:13 But **now** in Christ Jesus you who once were far away have been
Col 1:22 But **now** he has reconciled you by Christ's physical body through
3: 8 But **now** you must rid yourselves of all such things as these:
Phm 1: 9 as Paul—an old man and **now** also a prisoner of Christ Jesus—
1:11 to you, but **now** he has become useful both to you and to me.
Heb 8: 6 But **[NIE]** the ministry Jesus has received is as superior to theirs
9:26 But **now** he has appeared once for all at the end of the ages to do

3816 νύξ, *nyx* [61] [→ 1381, 1939, 3543, 3819]

διὰ νυκτός (by night) [6] Mk 5:5; Lk 5:5; Ac 5:19; 16:9; 17:10; 23:31

ἡμέρα ... νύξ (day ... night) [23] Mt 4:2; 12:40,40; Mk 4:27; 5:5; Lk 2:37; 18:7; 21:37; Ac 9:24; 20:31; 26:7; Ro 13:12; 1Th 2:9; 3:10; 5:5; 2Th 3:8; 1Ti 5:5; 2Ti 1:3; Rev 4:8; 7:15; 12:10; 14:11; 20:10

night [51], nights [3], at midnight [+3545] [1], evening [1], last night [+3836+4047] [1], midnight [+3545+3836] [1], night [+1328+4246] [1], tonight [+3836+4047] [1], tonight [1]

Mt 2:14 took the child and his mother *during* the **night** and left for Egypt,
4: 2 After fasting forty days and forty **nights**, he was hungry.
12:40 Jonah was three days and three **nights** in the belly of a huge fish,
12:40 of Man will be three days and three **nights** in the heart of the earth.
14:25 During the fourth watch *of* the **night** Jesus went out to them,
25: 6 "**At midnight** [+3545] the cry rang out: 'Here's the bridegroom!
26:31 "This very **night** you will all fall away on account of me, for it is
26:34 "I tell you the truth," Jesus answered, "this very **night**,
28:13 'His disciples came *during* the **night** and stole him away while we
Mk 4:27 **Night** and day, whether he sleeps or gets up, the seed sprouts
5: 5 **Night** [+1328+4246] and day among the tombs and in the hills he
6:48 About the fourth watch *of* the **night** he went out to them,
14:30 the truth," Jesus answered, "today—yes, **tonight** [+3836+4047]—
Lk 2: 8 out in the fields nearby, keeping watch over their flocks *at* **night**.
2:37 She never left the temple but worshiped **night** and day, fasting
5: 5 we've worked hard all **night** and haven't caught anything.
12:20 'You fool! This very **night** your life will be demanded from you.
17:34 I tell you, *on* that **night** two people will be in one bed; one will be
18: 7 justice for his chosen ones, who cry out to him day and **night**?
21:37 and each **evening** he went out to spend the night on the hill called

Jn   3: 2 He came to Jesus *at* **night** and said, "Rabbi, we know you are a
      9: 4 of him who sent me. **Night** is coming, when no one can work.
   11:10 It is when he walks by **night** that he stumbles, for he has no light."
   13:30 soon as Judas had taken the bread, he went out. And it was **night**.
   19:39 by Nicodemus, the man who earlier had visited Jesus *at* **night**.
   21: 3 went out and got into the boat, but that **night** they caught nothing.
Ac   5:19 But during the **night** an angel of the Lord opened the doors of the
    9:24 and **night** they kept close watch on the city gates in order to kill
    9:25 But his followers took him *by* **night** and lowered him in a basket
   12: 6 The **night** before Herod was to bring him to trial, Peter was
   16: 9 During the **night** Paul had a vision of a man of Macedonia
   16:33 At that hour *of* the **night** the jailer took them and washed their
   17:10 As soon as it was **night**, the brothers sent Paul and Silas away to
   18: 9 One **night** the Lord spoke to Paul in a vision: "Do not be afraid;
   20:31 that for three years I never stopped warning each of you **night**
   23:11 The following **night** the Lord stood near Paul and said,
   23:23 and two hundred spearmen to go to Caesarea at nine **tonight**.
   23:31 took Paul with them during the **night** and brought him as far as
   26: 7 hoping to see fulfilled as they earnestly serve God day and **night**.
   27:23 **Last night** [*+3836+4047*] an angel of the God whose I am
   27:27 On the fourteenth **night** we were still being driven across the
   27:27 when about **midnight** [*+3545+3836*] the sailors sensed they were
Ro 13:12 The **night** is nearly over; the day is almost here. So let us put aside
1Co 11:23 The Lord Jesus, on the **night** he was betrayed, took bread,
1Th 2: 9 we worked **night** and day in order not to be a burden to anyone
    3:10 **Night** and day we pray most earnestly that we may see you again
    5: 2 well that the day of the Lord will come like a thief in the **night**.
    5: 5 sons of the day. We do not belong to the **night** or to the darkness.
    5: 7 For those who sleep, sleep *at* **night**, and those who get drunk,
    5: 7 sleep at night, and those who get drunk, get drunk *at* **night**.
2Th 3: 8 we worked **night** and day, laboring and toiling so that we would
1Ti 5: 5 and continues **night** and day to pray and to ask God for help.
2Ti 1: 3 as **night** and day I constantly remember you in my prayers.
Rev 4: 8 Day and **night** they never stop saying: "Holy, holy, holy is the Lord
    7:15 the throne of God and serve him day and **night** in his temple;
    8:12 A third of the day was without light, and also a third of the **night**.
   12:10 who accuses them before our God day and **night**, has been hurled
   14:11 no rest day or **night** for those who worship the beast and his image,
   20:10 They will be tormented day and **night** for ever and ever.
   21:25 no day will its gates ever be shut, for there will be no **night** there.
   22: 5 There will be no more **night**. They will not need the light of a lamp

3817 νύσσω, *nyssō* [1] [→ *2919, 2920*]

pierced [1]

Jn 19:34 Instead, one of the soldiers **pierced** Jesus' side with a spear,

3818 νυστάζω, *nystazō* [2]

drowsy [1], sleeping [1]

Mt 25: 5 long time in coming, and *they* all *became* **drowsy** and fell asleep.
2Pe 2: 3 hanging over them, and their destruction *has* not *been* **sleeping**.

3819 νυχθήμερον, *nychthēmeron* [1] [√ *3816 + 2465*]

a night and a day [1]

2Co 11:25 I was shipwrecked, I spent **a night and a day** in the open sea,

3820 Νῶε, *Nōe* [8]

Noah [8]

Mt 24:37 As it was in the days *of* **Noah**, so it will be at the coming of the
   24:38 and giving in marriage, up to the day **Noah** entered the ark;
Lk   3:36 the son of Shem, the son *of* **Noah**, the son of Lamech,
   17:26 "Just as it was in the days of **Noah**, so also will it be in the days of
   17:27 and being given in marriage up to the day **Noah** entered the ark.
Heb 11: 7 By faith **Noah**, when warned about things not yet seen, in holy fear
1Pe 3:20 waited patiently in the days *of* **Noah** while the ark was being built.
2Pe 2: 5 but protected **Noah**, a preacher of righteousness, and seven others;

3821 νωθρός, *nōthros* [2]

lazy [1], slow [1]

Heb 5:11 about this, but it is hard to explain because you are **slow** to learn.
    6:12 We do not want you to become **lazy**, but to imitate those who

3822 νῶτος, *nōtos* [1]

backs [1]

Ro 11:10 be darkened so they cannot see, and their **backs** be bent forever."

Ξ, X

3823 ξ, x   Not used in UBS/NIV

3824 ξαίνω, xainō   Not used in UBS/NIV

3825 ξενία, *xenia* [2] [√ *3828*]

guest room [1], place where staying [1]

Ac 28:23 came in even larger numbers to the **place where** *he* was **staying**.
Phm 1:22 Prepare a **guest room** for me, because I hope to be restored to you

3826 ξενίζω, *xenizō* [10] [√ *3828*]

entertained [2], staying [2], guest [1], guests [1], stay [1], strange [1], surprised [1], think it strange [1]

Ac 10: 6 He *is* **staying** with Simon the tanner, whose house is by the sea."
   10:18 asking if Simon who was known as Peter *was* **staying** there.
   10:23 Then Peter invited the men into the house *to be* his **guests**.
   10:32 He *is* a **guest** in the home of Simon the tanner, who lives by the
   17:20 You are bringing some **strange** *ideas* to our ears, and we want to
   21:16 and brought us to the home of Mnason, where *we were to* **stay**.
   28: 7 us to his home and for three days **entertained** us hospitably.
Heb 13: 2 so doing some people *have* **entertained** angels without knowing it.
1Pe 4: 4 *They* **think it strange** that you do not plunge with them into the
    4:12 *do* not *be* **surprised** at the painful trial you are suffering,

3827 ξενοδοχέω, *xenodocheō* [1] [√ *3828 + 1312*]

showing hospitality [1]

1Ti 5:10 such as bringing up children, **showing hospitality**, washing the

3828 ξένος, *xenos* [14] [→ *3825, 3826, 3827, 5810, 5811*]

foreigners [4], stranger [4], strange [2], aliens [1], foreign [1], hospitality [1], strangers [1]

Mt 25:35 me something to drink, I was a **stranger** and you invited me in,
   25:38 When did we see you a **stranger** and invite you in, or needing
   25:43 I was a **stranger** and you did not invite me in, I needed clothes
   25:44 or thirsty or a **stranger** or needing clothes or sick or in prison,
   27: 7 the money to buy the potter's field as a burial place *for* **foreigners**.
Ac 17:18 Others remarked, "He seems to be advocating **foreign** gods."
   17:21 and the **foreigners** who lived there spent their time doing nothing
Ro 16:23 Gaius, whose **hospitality** I and the whole church here enjoy,
Eph 2:12 in Israel and **foreigners** to the covenants of the promise,
    2:19 Consequently, you are no longer **foreigners** and aliens, but fellow
Heb 11:13 And they admitted that they were **aliens** and strangers on earth.
   13: 9 Do not be carried away by all kinds of **strange** teachings.
1Pe 4:12 as though *something* **strange** were happening to you.
3Jn 1: 5 are doing for the brothers, even though they are **strangers** to you.

3829 ξέστης, *xestēs* [1]

pitchers [1]

Mk 7: 4 other traditions, such as the washing of cups, **pitchers** and kettles.)

3830 ξηραίνω, xērainō [15] [√ 3831]

withered [6], withers [3], becomes rigid [1], dried up [1], ripe [1], shriveled [1], stopped [1], wither [1]

Mt 13: 6 plants were scorched, and *they* **withered** because they had no root.
21:19 "May you never bear fruit again!" Immediately the tree **withered**.
21:20 were amazed. "How *did* the fig tree **wither** so quickly?" they asked.
Mk 3: 1 into the synagogue, and a man with a **shriveled** hand was there.
4: 6 plants were scorched, and *they* **withered** because they had no root.
5:29 Immediately her bleeding **stopped** and she felt in her body that she
9:18 He foams at the mouth, gnashes his teeth and **becomes rigid**.
11:20 as they went along, they saw the fig tree **withered** from the roots.
11:21 said to Jesus, "Rabbi, look! The fig tree you cursed *has* **withered**!"
Lk 8: 6 it came up, the *plants* **withered** because they had no moisture.
Jn 15: 6 remain in me, he is like a branch that is thrown away and **withers**;
Jas 1:11 For the sun rises with scorching heat and **withers** the plant;
1Pe 1:24 like the flowers of the field; the grass **withers** and the flowers fall,
Rev 14:15 the time to reap has come, for the harvest of the earth *is* **ripe**."
16:12 and its water *was* **dried up** to prepare the way for the kings from

3831 ξηρός, xēros [8] [→ 3830]

shriveled [4], dry [2], land [1], paralyzed [1]

Mt 12:10 and a man with a **shriveled** hand was there. Looking for a reason
23:15 You travel over **land** and sea to win a single convert, and when he
Mk 3: 3 Jesus said to the man with the **shriveled** hand, "Stand up in front of
Lk 6: 6 and a man was there whose right hand was **shriveled**.
6: 8 they were thinking and said to the man with the **shriveled** hand,
23:31 things when the tree is green, what will happen when it is **dry**?"
Jn 5: 3 of disabled people used to lie—the blind, the lame, the **paralyzed**.
Heb 11:29 By faith the people passed through the Red Sea as on **dry** land;

3832 ξύλινος, xylinos [2] [→ 3833, 3834]

of wood [2]

2Ti 2:20 are articles not only of gold and silver, but also **of wood** and clay;
Rev 9:20 and idols **of** gold, silver, bronze, stone and **wood**—

3833 ξύλον, xylon [20] [√ 3832]

tree [11], clubs [5], wood [3], stocks [1]

Mt 26:47 With him was a large crowd armed with swords and **clubs**,
26:55 that you have come out with swords and **clubs** to capture me?
Mk 14:43 With him was a crowd armed with swords and **clubs**, sent from the
14:48 "that you have come out with swords and **clubs** to capture me?
Lk 22:52 I leading a rebellion, that you have come with swords and **clubs**?
23:31 For if men do these things when the **tree** is green, what will
Ac 5:30 from the dead—whom you had killed by hanging him on a **tree**.
10:39 and in Jerusalem. They killed him by hanging him on a **tree**,
13:29 they took him down from the **tree** and laid him in a tomb.
16:24 he put them in the inner cell and fastened their feet in the **stocks**.
1Co 3:12 builds on this foundation *using* gold, silver, costly stones, **wood**,
Gal 3:13 for it is written: "Cursed is everyone who is hung on a **tree**."
1Pe 2:24 He himself bore our sins in his body on the **tree**, so that we might
Rev 2: 7 who overcomes, I will give the right to eat from the **tree** of life,
18:12 every sort of citron **wood**, and articles of every kind made of ivory,
18:12 of every kind made of ivory, costly **wood**, bronze, iron and marble;
22: 2 On each side of the river stood the **tree** of life, bearing twelve
22: 2 And the leaves *of* the **tree** are for the healing of the nations.
22:14 that they may have the right to the **tree** of life and may go through
22:19 God will take away from him his share in the **tree** of life and in the

3834 ξυράω, xyraō [3] [√ 3832]

shaved [2], shaved off [1]

Ac 21:24 and pay their expenses, so that *they can have* their heads **shaved**.
1Co 11: 5 dishonors her head—it is just as though her head *were* **shaved**.
11: 6 if it is a disgrace for a woman *to have her* hair cut or **shaved off**,

O, ο

3835 ο, o Not used in UBS/NIV

3836 ὁ, ho [19862 / 19863] See Index of Articles, Etc.

[→ 2201, 3840, 3888, 5422, 5437, 5524, 5525, 5539, 5540, 5541, 6045]

untranslated [8784], the [7565], who [385], those [344], his [203], what [183], a [169], that [150], he [144], their [96], your [80], him [77], this [76], the son [75], he [+1254] [70], our [55], they [+1254] [49], my [41], whoever [35], anyone [31], which [29], her [27], Jesus⁵ [+1254] [25], one [25], they [24], forever [+172+1650] [23], because [+1328] [21], its [21], to [+1650] [21], as [+1877] [17], you [17], all things [+4246] [16], an [15], so that [+1650] [15], when [+1877] [15], everything [+4246] [14], whom [13], these [10], things [10], after [+3552] [9], before [+4574] [9], son [9], this [+3364] [9], she [+1254] [8], he [+2652] [7], him [+2536] [7], now [+3814] [7], O [7], that [+1650] [7], God's⁵ [6], him [+2652] [6], now on [+3814] [6], so that [6], some [6], while [+1877] [6], companions [+3552] [5], finally [+3370] [5], God⁵ [5], he [+2536] [5], him [+476] [5], Jesus⁵ [5], never [+172+1650+3590+4024] [5], people [5], some [+3525] [5], someone [5], we [5], anything [4], back [+1650+3958] [4], his [+2536] [4], it [4], me [+1609+3950] [4], men [+476+3836+5626] [4], the man⁵ [+1254] [4], together [+899+2093] [4], what [+4839] [4], a man⁵ [3], all [+4246] [3], and so [+1650] [3], companions [+5250] [3], each [3], he [+3812] [3], in order that [+1650] [3], it [+3180] [3], looked up [+2048+4057] [3], mother [3], others [+1254] [3], others [3], that [+899] [3], that which [3], the man⁵ [3], them [+899+3412] [3], those [+1254] [3], whose [3], you [+2840+5148] [3], affairs [2], against [+2093+5111] [2], all this [+4246] [2], all [2], among [+1650+3545] [2], any [2], associates [+5250] [2], by [+1877] [2], case [+2848] [2], case⁵ [2], companions [+1639+3552] [2], companions [+1639+5250] [2], demon-possessed [+2400+3836+4460+4505] [2], earthly [+1178+2093] [2], for [+1328] [2], for [+1650] [2], forever [+1457+1650] [2], front of everyone [+3545] [2], God-fearing [+2536+5828] [2], he [+476] [2], him [+81+899] [2], himself [+899+2840] [2], his own [2], home [+1650+3875+5148] [2], home [+899+3875] [2], household [2], I have [+1847] [2], in person [+3836+4242+5393] [2], in [2], interests [2], it [+1046] [2], it [+1635+2563+3836] [2], it [+229] [2], it [+4450] [2], it [+993+1847+3836] [2], its [+899+4725] [2], knelt down [+1205+5502] [2], landed [+1178+2093+2262] [2], me [+1609+4725] [2], men⁵ [2], motioned [+2939+5931] [2], natural sleep [+3122+3836+5678] [2], never [+172+1650+4024] [2], on [+1877] [2], outsiders [+2032] [2], rich [+2400+5975] [2], seized [+2093+2095+5931] [2], seized [+2095+5931] [2], service⁵ [2], she [2], since [+1328] [2], sins [+281+4472] [2], some time ago [+2465+4047+4574] [2], still [+3370] [2], such [2], that is how [+899+2848] [2], the disciples [+1254] [2], the men⁵ [+1254] [2], the One [2], the son⁵ [2], them [+1178+2093+2997+3836] [2], them [+3836+4556+5525] [2], them [+476] [2], them [2], there [+1877+2639] [2], they [+3412] [2], they [+476] [2], this [+2465] [2], those that [2], those who are [+5626] [2], what [+2240] [2], what desires⁵ [2], what was promised [+2039] [2], when [+3552] [2], which [+180] [2], whoever [+4246] [2], you [+3950+5148] [2], you [+4725+5148] [2], you [+5148+6034] [2], Abraham's⁵ [1], according to [+1666] [1], accusers [+2400+2991] [1], across [+1650+4305] [1], across the lake [+1650+4305] [1], after this [+1877+2759] [1], again [+172+1650] [1], again [+608+3814] [1], agree with each other [+899+5858] [1], agree with one another [+899+3306] [1], all along [+794] [1], all disciples [+3412+4436] [1], all had [+2625] [1], altogether [+4246] [1], always [+2465+4246] [1], and [+1877] [1], and thus [+1650] [1], another [+1254] [1], another [+2283] [1], any way [+5515] [1], anyone [+476] [1], anyone⁵ [1], arrest [+2093+2095+5931] [1], arrested [+2093+2095+5931] [1], arrested [+2095+5931] [1], arrived [+4242] [1], as [+4301] [1], as a result [+1650] [1], as follows [+2400+4047+5596] [1], as to [1], as usual [+1621+2848] [1], as usual [+899+2848] [1], ashore [+1178+1650] [1], assembled worshipers [+3295+4436] [1], at [+1877] [1], at all [+1650+4117] [1], at once [+899+6052] [1], at the meal [+367] [1], away [+1650+2557] [1], away [+1666+3545] [1], before [+1650+3545] [1], before [+1877+3545] [1], began to speak [+487+3306+5125] [1], began to teach [+487+1438+5125] [1], begging [+1797+4639] [1], being like-minded [+899+5858] [1], believers [+2400+4411] [1], believers [+4411] [1], besides everything else [+4211+6006] [1], bleeding [+135+4380] [1], bleeding [+135+4868] [1], blemish [+5525] [1], blinded [+4057+5604] [1], blindfolded [+4328+4725] [1], both [+1545+3938] [1], brag [+224+1877] [1], but [+1254+1883] [1], call [+2813+3950] [1], called [+3950+4005] [1], certified [+3456+5381] [1], child bear [+2843+3120] [1], circumstances [1], come together [+899+2093+5302] [1], comes together [+899+2093+5302] [1], companions [+4309] [1], companions [+4513+5250] [1], completely [+1650+4117] [1], conceived [+1877+3120+5197] [1], convened the court [+1037+2093+2767] [1], Cornelius[s] [+1254] [1], crowd [+3295+4436] [1], decided [+1877+4460+5502] [1], decided [+326+2093+2840] [1], descendant [+1666+2588] [1], descendants [+2843+4019] [1], descended from [+1666+2002+4019] [1], does [+3847] [1], dressed ready for service [+4019+4322] [1], each day [+2465] [1], each one [+324] [1], each other [+1651+1651] [1], elementary truths [+794+5122] [1], embraced [+2093+2158+5549] [1], enabling [+1328+1443+5931] [1], endlessly [+1457+1650] [1], enough for now [+2400+3814] [1], envious [+1639+4057+4505] [1], equal [+899] [1], equality [+1639+2698] [1], ever [+172+1650] [1], ever [+172+1666] [1], ever-increasing wickedness [+490+490+1650] [1], every[s] [1], everyone [+4246] [1], everyone [1], everything [+2240] [1], everything [+4246+5007] [1], evildoers [+490+2237] [1], extraordinary [+4024+5593] [1], family [+3875] [1], family [+4123] [1], family [1], fellow [+5250] [1], field [+2834+3586] [1], finally [+5465] [1], first [+3552] [1], for [+1877+3545] [1], for [+4639] [1], for all time [+1457+1650] [1], forevermore [+172+1650+4246] [1], from bad to worse [+2093+5937] [1], from house to house [+2848+3875] [1], from house to house [+3864] [1], from now on [+3370] [1], from one synagogue to another [+2848+4246+5252] [1], from town to town [+4484] [1], from village to village [+2848+3267] [1], furious [+1391+2840] [1], give in [+1634+5717] [1], God [+3281] [1], God-fearing Gentiles [+2536+5828] [1], gods[s] [1], grasp the meaning [+1539+3857] [1], grew [+1650+2262] [1], had[s] [+4123] [1], handed over [+4140+5931] [1], has [+5639] [1], has no pity [+3091+5073] [1], have [+2400] [1], he [+1333] [1], he [+235] [1], he [+2989] [1], he [+3261] [1], he [+3273] [1], he [+3281] [1], he [+3525] [1], he [+3707] [1], he [+467] [1], he [+508] [1], he [+804] [1], he [+899+1328+5931] [1], he [+899+4725] [1], he [+899+899+1877+4460] [1], he [+995] [1], he that [1], he's [+899+1639+6034] [1], heavenly [+1877+4041] [1], heavenly things [+1877+4041] [1], her [+4086] [1], her own [1], highly valued [+5734] [1], him [+2930] [1], him [+4263] [1], him [+467] [1], him [+4737] [1], him [+5108] [1], him [+5986] [1], him [+81+1609] [1], him [+899+3950] [1], himself [+899+3950] [1], his [+2610] [1], his [+2652] [1], his [+4511] [1], his [+476+4047] [1], his [+899] [1], his fellowman [+2283] [1], his home [+2625] [1], his native language [+1666+2625] [1], his own home [+2625] [1], his son[s] [1], home [+2625] [1], home [+899+1650+3875] [1], house [1], how [+2848] [1], how [+4309] [1], I [+1609+6034] [1], illness [+819+4922] [1], immediately [+899+1877+6052] [1], in agreement [+1650+1651] [1], in comparison with [+1641+1877+3538+4047] [1], in full [+2698] [1], in one place [+899+2093] [1], in order to [+4639] [1], in presence [+3552+4725] [1], in public [+1883+3295] [1], in the present case [+3814] [1], in this way [+1650] [1], indoors [+1650+3864] [1], instead [+1883+3437] [1], intelligible [+3808] [1], invalid [+819+1877+2400] [1], inwardly [+1877+3220] [1], inwardly [+2276] [1], it [+1155+4047] [1], it [+1561] [1], it [+1631] [1], it [+1847] [1], it [+2240+5516] [1], it [+2295] [1], it [+2585] [1], it [+27] [1], it [+2819] [1], it [+3364] [1], it [+3693] [1], it [+3954] [1], it [+4047+4839] [1], it [+4384] [1], it [+4784] [1], it [+5013]

[1], it [+5853] [1], it [+5890] [1], it [+6029] [1], it [+6052] [1], it [+69] [1], it that [1], its [+1178] [1], its [+2639] [1], its [+4922] [1], its [+5393] [1], Jesus followers[s] [+1254] [1], Jews [+1169+1609+1877] [1], just after sunrise [+422+2463] [1], just as though [+899+1651+2779] [1], just like this [+899+2848] [1], keep in suspense [+149+6034] [1], kneel [+1205+2828] [1], knelt [+1205+5502] [1], landed [+609+1178+1650] [1], last night [+3816+4047] [1], lies [+3281+6022] [1], listen carefully [+1650+4044+5148+5148+5502] [1], live in harmony [+899+5858] [1], lived [+2400+2998] [1], living [+2400+6034] [1], longed for [+2123+6034] [1], look up [+2048+4057] [1], looked [+149+4057] [1], looked [+2048+4057] [1], looking [+2048+4057] [1], lustfully [+2121+4639] [1], made king [+993+3284] [1], made think [+1877+2840+5502] [1], make the most of opportunity [+1973+2789] [1], make up mind [+1877+2840+5502] [1], man's[s] [1], man[s] [1], Mary[s] [+1254] [1], matters [1], me [+1609+5889] [1], me [+1609+6034] [1], meanwhile [+1877+3568] [1], member [+2848+3517] [1], men's [1], midnight [+3545+3816] [1], money [1], most [+4498] [1], my [+1609+3950] [1], my [+1831+4309] [1], name [+2813+3950] [1], named [+2813+3950] [1], nearby [+4309+5536] [1], nearby [+899] [1], never again [+172+1650+3590+4024] [1], next [+1650+3516] [1], next to [+1877+3146] [1], nine in the morning [+2465+5569+6052] [1], no ordinary [+842+2536] [1], now [+608+3814] [1], on [+2759+2779] [1], on board [+1877+4450] [1], on duty [+1877+5423] [1], one [+1651] [1], one [+3525] [1], one [+899] [1], one Sabbath [+1877+4879] [1], open eyes [+2048+4057] [1], others [+3525] [1], our fathers[s] [+3525] [1], out of his body [+909+1650+1744] [1], outward [+1877+5745] [1], outwardly [+1877+5745] [1], outwardly [+476+2032] [1], own [1], parts [1], Paul[s] [+3525] [1], people live scattered among [+1402] [1], perfectly united [+899+2936] [1], performed [+1181+1328+5931] [1], person [1], Peter[s] and John [+3525] [1], Peter[s] [1], Pilate[s] [+1254] [1], Pointing [+1753+5931] [1], possessions [1], preaching [+3364] [1], prepare for action [+350+4019] [1], present [+2789+3814] [1], prompted [+965+1650+2840] [1], proud [+5731+5858] [1], publicly [+1967+4436] [1], reached for [+1753+5931] [1], reaching more and more [+1328+4429+4498] [1], realities [+1635+4547] [1], resolutely [+4725+5114] [1], result [+1650] [1], return [+1650+2262+4099] [1], rewarding [+1443+3635] [1], risked lives [+5549+5719] [1], say [+1666+5125] [1], sealed with [+2400+5382] [1], seashore [+2498+5927] [1], seeds[s] [1], self [+476+2840] [1], self-seeking [+1571+2426] [1], service that perform [+1355+3311+4047] [1], shared [+3102+3275] [1], she [+1222] [1], she [+3166] [1], she [+3451] [1], short [+2461+3625] [1], shouted [+2048+5889] [1], shouted [+3489+5774+5889] [1], sighed deeply [+417+4460] [1], sight [+487+4057] [1], since that time [+3370] [1], sinful [+5393] [1], so [+1650] [1], so as [+1650] [1], so, so he [+1254] [1], so that [+4639] [1], so then [+1650] [1], so they [+1254] [1], so [1], some [+1651+3538] [1], something [1], son[s] [+3525] [1], soon afterward [+1877+2009] [1], sound asleep [+608+2965+5678] [1], speak [+487+5125] [1], spirit of unity [+899+5858] [1], spoken freely [+487+5125] [1], stand firm [+2840+5114] [1], still others [+1254] [1], stripped [+2668+4351] [1], such a [1], such things [+4998] [1], take over [+3284+5536] [1], terms [1], terrorists [+467+4974] [1], that [+1877] [1], that [+2434] [1], that [+2546] [1], that [+4309] [1], that had touched [+608+5999] [1], that is [1], that same [1], that was the time [+1697+1877+2465] [1], the affairs [1], the affairs[s] [1], the apostles[s] [+3525] [1],
the expert in the law[s] [+1254] [1], the father[s] [+1254] [1], the interests [1], the man's[s] [+1254] [1], the manager[s] [+1254] [1], the men[s] [+3525] [1], the news[s] [1], the parts [+4047+5393] [1], the people[s] [+1254] [1], the rioters[s] [+1254] [1], the soldiers[s] [1], the very [1], the wife [1], them [+1177] [1], them [+1609+4252] [1], them [+2239] [1], them [+2465] [1], them [+2585] [1], them [+3295] [1], them [+3412] [1], them [+3517+5148] [1], them [+4063] [1], them [+899+4546] [1], them [+899+5284] [1], themselves [+899+2840] [1], themselves [+899+6034] [1], then will be able [+1650] [1], there [+1650+2038] [1], there [+1877+4047+4484] [1], there [+1877+5536] [1], they [+1322] [1], they [+213] [1], they [+3525] [1], they [+4998] [1], they

[+5861] [1], they [+899+1204] [1], they [+899+3412] [1], they [+899+4057] [1], they [+899+5125] [1], they [+899+6001] [1], they [+899+899+2779+3412] [1], thinking like [+1181+5856] [1], this [+2240+4047] [1], this [+3364+4047] [1], this [+3814] [1], this [+4047+4839] [1], this [+4246] [1], this is [+2848] [1], this mans [1], this or that [+3840] [1], this very [1], those [+3295] [1], those [+476] [1], those who marry [+5525] [1], those who [1], thoses present [1], thoughts [+1369+2840] [1], three in the afternoon [+1888+2465+6052] [1], threw arms around [+2093+2158+5549] [1], through [+1328+5931] [1], to keep from [+3590+4639] [1], to show that [+4639] [1], to their number [+899+2093] [1], today [+2465+4958] [1], tonight [+3816+4047] [1], too [+899+2779] [1], trusted personal servant [+2093+3131] [1], trying to kill [+2426+6034] [1], turned around [+1650+3958+5138] [1], turned back [+599+1650+3958] [1], under [+4123+4546] [1], unnatural ones [+4123+5882] [1], unseen [+1877+3220] [1], unseen [+1877+3224] [1], unsettled [+608+3808+4888] [1], us [1], wayss [1], weapons fight with [+3960+5127] [1], weeping [+3088] [1], welfare [+4309] [1], what [+2240+5516] [1], what [+2843] [1], what [+3306] [1], what [+3364] [1], what am about to tell [+3364+4047] [1], what had happened to [1], what has happened to [+2848] [1], what is [1], what we are writing [+899] [1], whatever [+4246] [1], whatever give [1], whatever [1], where [+1650+5536] [1], where [+1650+5596] [1], while [+1639+1877] [1], who [+476+4047] [1], whoever [+323] [1], whose temples [1], why [+162+1328+4005] [1], why [+162+5515] [1], wife [1], winepress [+3332+3885] [1], with [+1650] [1], with [+1877] [1], with great fervor [+2417+4460] [1], within [+1877+3517] [1], wondered about [+1877+2840+5502] [1], worldly [+3180] [1], wounded [+2400+4435] [1], you [+4364] [1], you have [+5050] [1], your family [+5050] [1], your own [+2625] [1], your own [1], yours [+5050] [1], yourselves [+2840+5148] [1]

3837 ὀγδοήκοντα, ogdoēkonta [2] [√ 3893]

eight hundred [1], eighty-four [+2291+5475] [1]

Lk   2:37 and then was a widow until she was **eighty-four** [+2291+5475]. She never left the temple but worshiped night and day, fasting
     16: 7 "He told him, 'Take your bill and make it **eight hundred**.'

3838 ὄγδοος, ogdoos [5] [√ 3893]

eighth [3], and sevens others [1], eight [1]

Lk   1:59 On the **eighth** day they came to circumcise the child, and they
Ac   7: 8 the father of Isaac and circumcised him **eight** days after his birth.
2Pe 2: 5 protected Noah, a preacher of righteousness, **and sevens others**;
Rev 17:11 The beast who once was, and now is not, is an **eighth** king.
     21:20 the **eighth** beryl, the ninth topaz, the tenth chrysoprase,

3839 ὄγκος, onkos [1] [→ 5665]

hinders [1]

Heb 12: 1 let us throw off everything that **hinders** and the sin that so easily

3840 ὅδε, hode [10] [√ 3836]

these [7], *untranslated* [1], she [1], this or that [+3836] [1]

Lk   10:39 **She** had a sister called Mary, who sat at the Lord's feet listening to
Ac   21:11 **[NIE]** 'In this way the Jews of Jerusalem will bind the owner of
Jas   4:13 "Today or tomorrow we will go to **this** [+3836] **or that** city,
Rev   2: 1 **These** are the words of him who holds the seven stars in his right
      2: 8 **These** are the words of him who is the First and the Last, who died
      2:12 **These** are the words of him who has the sharp, double-edged
      2:18 **These** are the words of the Son of God, whose eyes are like
      3: 1 **These** are the words of him who holds the seven spirits of God
      3: 7 **These** are the words of him who is holy and true, who holds the
      3:14 **These** are the words of the Amen, the faithful and true witness,

3841 ὁδεύω, hodeuō [1] [√ 3847]

traveled [1]

Lk   10:33 But a Samaritan, *as he* **traveled**, came where the man was;

3842 ὁδηγέω, hodēgeō [5] [√ 3847 + 72]

lead [2], explains to [1], guide [1], leads [1]

Mt   15:14 If a blind man **leads** a blind man, both will fall into a pit."
Lk   6:39 He also told them this parable: "Can a blind man **lead** a blind man?
Jn   16:13 the Spirit of truth, comes, *he will* **guide** you into all truth.
Ac   8:31 "How can I," he said, "unless someone **explains** it **to** me?" So he
Rev   7:17 will be their shepherd; *he will* **lead** them to springs of living water.

3843 ὁδηγός, hodēgos [5] [√ 3847 + 72]

guides [3], guide [2]

Mt   15:14 Leave them; they are blind **guides**. If a blind man leads a blind
     23:16 "Woe to you, blind **guides**! You say, 'If anyone swears by the
     23:24 *You* blind **guides**! You strain out a gnat but swallow a camel.
Ac   1:16 who served as **guide** for those who arrested Jesus—
Ro   2:19 if you are convinced that you are a **guide** for the blind, a light for

3844 ὁδοιπορέω, hodoiporeō [1] [√ 3847 + 4513]

on their journey [1]

Ac   10: 9 About noon the following day *as* they *were* **on their journey**

3845 ὁδοιπορία, hodoiporia [2] [√ 3847 + 4513]

journey [1], on the move [1]

Jn   4: 6 and Jesus, tired as he was from the **journey**, sat down by the well.
2Co 11:26 I have been constantly **on the move**. I have been in danger from

3846 ὁδοποιέω, hodopoieō   Not used in UBS/NIV
[√ 3847 + 4472]

3847 ὁδός, hodos [101 / 100] [→ 316, 1447, 1476, 1658, 2016, 2337, 2338, 3497, 3841, 3842, 3843, 3844, 3845, 3846, 4227, 5321, 5322]

ὁ Ὁδός (the Way) [6] Ac 9:2; 19:9,23; 22:4; 24:14,22

ὁδός τοῦ θεοῦ [αὐτοῦ] (God's [his] way) [5] Mt 22:16; Mk 12:14; Lk 20:21; Ac 18:26; Ro 11:33

ὁδός κυρίου (way of the Lord) [7] Mt 3:3; Mk 1:3; Lk 1:76; 3:4; Jn 1:23; Ac 13:10; 18:25

way [50], road [17], path [7], ways [5], journey [4], roadside [3], paths [2], among [+1650] [1], direction [1], doess [+3836] [1], on a journey [+1666] [1], roads [1], route [1], Sabbath day's walk from [+1584+2400+4879] [1], street [1], streets [1], traveled on [+2262] [1], walked along [+4472] [1], way of life [1]

Mt   2:12 go back to Herod, they returned to their country by another **route**.
      3: 3 'Prepare the **way** for the Lord, make straight paths for him.' "
      4:15 and land of Naphtali, the **way** to the sea, along the Jordan,
      5:25 Do it while you are still with him on the **way**, or he may hand you
      7:13 For wide is the gate and broad is the **road** that leads to destruction,
      7:14 But small is the gate and narrow the **road** that leads to life,
      8:28 met him. They were so violent that no one could pass that **way**.
     10: 5 "Do not go **among** [+1650] the Gentiles or enter any town of the
     10:10 take no bag for the **journey**, or extra tunic, or sandals or a staff;
     11:10 messenger ahead of you, who will prepare your **way** before you.'
     13: 4 some fell along the **path**, and the birds came and ate it up.
     13:19 what was sown in his heart. This is the seed sown along the **path**
     15:32 want to send them away hungry, or they may collapse on the **way**."
     20:17 twelve disciples aside and said to them, [UBS+ *on the* **way**]
     20:30 Two blind men were sitting by the **roadside**, and when they heard
     21: 8 A very large crowd spread their cloaks on the **road**, while others
     21: 8 others cut branches from the trees and spread them on the **road**.
     21:19 Seeing a fig tree by the **road**, he went up to it but found nothing on
     21:32 For John came to you to show you the **way** of righteousness,
     22: 9 Go to the **street** corners and invite to the banquet anyone you find.'

22: 10 So the servants went out into the **streets** and gathered all the
22: 16 and that you teach the **way** of God in accordance with the truth.

Mk   1: 2 send my messenger ahead of you, who will prepare your **way**"—
    1: 3 'Prepare the **way** for the Lord, make straight paths for him.' "
    2: 23 and as his disciples **walked along** [+4472], they began to pick
    4: 4 some fell along the **path**, and the birds came and ate it up.
    4: 15 Some people are like seed along the **path**, where the word is sown.
    6: 8 "Take nothing for the **journey** except a staff—no bread, no bag,
    8: 3 If I send them home hungry, they will collapse on the **way**,
    8: 27 On the **way** he asked them, "Who do people say I am?"
    9: 33 he asked them, "What were you arguing about on the **road**?"
    9: 34 because on the **way** they had argued about who was the greatest.
    10: 17 As Jesus started on his **way**, a man ran up to him and fell on his
    10: 32 They were on their **way** up to Jerusalem, with Jesus leading the
    10: 46 the Son of Timaeus), was sitting by the **roadside** begging.
    10: 52 he received his sight and followed Jesus along the **road**.
    11: 8 Many people spread their cloaks on the **road**, while others spread
    12: 14 but you teach the **way** of God in accordance with the truth.

Lk   1: 76 for you will go on before the Lord to prepare the **way** for him,
    1: 79 in the shadow of death, to guide our feet into the **path** of peace."
    2: 44 he was in their company, *they* **traveled on** [+2262] for a day.
    3: 4 'Prepare the **way** for the Lord, make straight paths for him.
    3: 5 The crooked roads shall become straight, the rough **ways** smooth.
    7: 27 messenger ahead of you, who will prepare your **way** before you.'
    8: 5 As he was scattering the seed, some fell along the **path**; it was
    8: 12 Those along the **path** are the ones who hear, and then the devil
    9: 3 "Take nothing for the **journey**—no staff, no bag, no bread,
    9: 57 As they were walking along the **road**, a man said to him, "I will
    10: 4 a purse or bag or sandals; and do not greet anyone on the **road**.
    10: 31 A priest happened to be going down the same **road**, and when he
    11: 6 because a friend of mine **on a journey** [+1666] has come to me,
    12: 58 try hard to be reconciled to him on the **way**, or he may drag you off
    14: 23 'Go out to the **roads** and country lanes and make them come in,
    18: 35 a blind man was sitting by the **roadside** begging.
    19: 36 As he went along, people spread their cloaks on the **road**.
    20: 21 partiality but teach the **way** of God in accordance with the truth.
    24: 32 our hearts burning within us while he talked with us on the **road**
    24: 35 Then the two told what had happened on the **way**, and how Jesus

Jn   1: 23 of one calling in the desert, 'Make straight the **way** for the Lord.' "
    14: 4 You know the **way** to the place where I am going."
    14: 5 don't know where you are going, so how can we know the **way**?"
    14: 6 Jesus answered, "I am the **way** and the truth and the life. No one

Ac   1: 12 Olives, a **Sabbath day's walk from** [+1584+2400+4879] the city.
    2: 28 You have made known to me the **paths** of life; you will fill me
    8: 26 Now an angel of the Lord said to Philip, "Go south to the **road**—
    8: 36 As they traveled along the **road**, they came to some water
    8: 39 the eunuch did not see him again, but went on his **way** rejoicing.
    9: 2 so that if he found any there who belonged to the **Way**,
    9: 17 who appeared to you on the **road** as you were coming here—
    9: 27 He told them how Saul on his **journey** had seen the Lord and that
    13: 10 Will you never stop perverting the right **ways** of the Lord?
    14: 16 In the past, he let all nations go their own **way**.
    16: 17 of the Most High God, who are telling you the **way** to be saved."
    18: 25 He had been instructed in the **way** of the Lord, and he spoke with
    18: 26 their home and explained to him the **way** of God more adequately.
    19: 9 they refused to believe and publicly maligned the **Way**.
    19: 23 About that time there arose a great disturbance about the **Way**.
    22: 4 I persecuted the *followers of* this **Way** to their death,
    24: 14 that I worship the God of our fathers as a follower of the **Way**,
    24: 22 Then Felix, who was well acquainted with the **Way**,
    25: 3 for they were preparing an ambush to kill him along the **way**.
    26: 13 About noon, O king, as I was on the **road**, I saw a light from

Ro   3: 16 ruin and misery mark their **ways**,
    3: 17 and the **way** of peace they do not know."
    11: 33 unsearchable his judgments, and his **paths** beyond tracing out!

1Co   4: 17 He will remind you of my **way of life** in Christ Jesus, which agrees
    12: 31 the greater gifts. And now I will show you the most excellent **way**.

1Th   3: 11 and our Lord Jesus clear the **way** for us to come to you.

Heb   3: 10 are always going astray, and they have not known my **ways**.'
    9: 8 The Holy Spirit was showing by this that the **way** into the Most
    10: 20 *by* a new and living **way** opened for us through the curtain,

Jas   1: 8 he is a double-minded man, unstable in all he **does**s [+3836].
    2: 25 lodging the spies and sent them off *in* a different **direction**?
    5: 20 Whoever turns a sinner from the error *of* his **way** will save him

2Pe   2: 2 their shameful ways and will bring the **way** of truth into disrepute.
    2: 15 They have left the straight **way** and wandered off to follow the way

---

    2: 15 and wandered off to follow the **way** of Balaam son of Beor,
    2: 21 It would have been better for them not to have known the **way** of

Jude   1: 11 They have taken the **way** of Cain; they have rushed for profit into

Rev   15: 3 Lord God Almighty. Just and true are your **ways**, King of the ages.
    16: 12 and its water was dried up to prepare the **way** for the kings from

3848 ὀδούς, *odous* [12]

teeth [10], tooth [2]

Mt   5: 38 "You have heard that it was said, 'Eye for eye, and **tooth** for tooth.'
    5: 38 "You have heard that it was said, 'Eye for eye, and tooth for **tooth**.'
    8: 12 the darkness, where there will be weeping and gnashing *of* **teeth**."
    13: 42 fiery furnace, where there will be weeping and gnashing *of* **teeth**.
    13: 50 fiery furnace, where there will be weeping and gnashing *of* **teeth**.
    22: 13 the darkness, where there will be weeping and gnashing *of* **teeth**.'
    24: 51 the hypocrites, where there will be weeping and gnashing *of* **teeth**.
    25: 30 the darkness, where there will be weeping and gnashing *of* **teeth**.'
Mk   9: 18 He foams at the mouth, gnashes his **teeth** and becomes rigid.
Lk   13: 28 and gnashing *of* **teeth**, when you see Abraham, Isaac and Jacob
Ac   7: 54 they heard this, they were furious and gnashed their **teeth** at him.
Rev   9: 8 hair was like women's hair, and their **teeth** were like lions' teeth.

3849 ὀδυνάω, *odynaō* [4] [√ *3850*]

in agony [2], anxiously [1], grieved [1]

Lk   2: 48 Your father and I have been **anxiously** searching for you."
    16: 24 in water and cool my tongue, because *I am* **in agony** in this fire.'
    16: 25 bad things, but now he is comforted here and you *are* **in agony**.
Ac   20: 38 What **grieved** them most was his statement that they would never

3850 ὀδύνη, *odynē* [2] [→ *3849*]

anguish [1], griefs [1]

Ro   9: 2 I have great sorrow and unceasing **anguish** in my heart.
1Ti   6: 10 wandered from the faith and pierced themselves *with* many **griefs**.

3851 ὀδυρμός, *odyrmos* [2]

deep sorrow [1], mourning [1]

Mt   2: 18 "A voice is heard in Ramah, weeping and great **mourning**,
2Co   7: 7 your **deep sorrow**, your ardent concern for me, so that my joy was

3852 'Οζίας, *Ozias* [2]

Uzziah [2]

Mt   1: 8 Jehoshaphat the father of Jehoram, Jehoram the father of **Uzziah**,
    1: 9 **Uzziah** the father of Jotham, Jotham the father of Ahaz, Ahaz the

3853 ὄζω, *ozō* [1] [→ *2380, 2455, 4011, 4018*]

bad odor [1]

Jn   11: 39 the sister of the dead man, "by this time *there is* a **bad odor**,

3854 ὅθεν, *hothen* [15] [√ *4005*]

where [3], *untranslated* [2], therefore [2], and so [1], for this
reason [1], from deaths [1], from there [1], then [1], that [1],
this is how [1], this is why [1]

Mt   12: 44 Then it says, 'I will return to the house **[RPG]** I left.' When it
    14: 7 **that** he promised with an oath to give her whatever she asked.
    25: 24 have not sown and gathering **where** you have not scattered seed.
    25: 26 where I have not sown and gather **where** I have not scattered seed?
Lk   11: 24 not find it. Then it says, 'I will return to the house **[RPG]** I left.'
Ac   14: 26 **where** they had been committed to the grace of God for the work
    26: 19 "So then, King Agrippa, I was not disobedient to the vision from
    28: 13 **From there** we set sail and arrived at Rhegium. The next day the
Heb   2: 17 **For this reason** he had to be made like his brothers in every way,
    3: 1 **Therefore**, holy brothers, who share in the heavenly calling,
    7: 25 **Therefore** he is able to save completely those who come to God
    8: 3 **and so** it was necessary for this one also to have something to
    9: 18 **This is why** even the first covenant was not put into effect without
    11: 19 and figuratively speaking, he did receive Isaac back **from death**s.

1Jn   2:18 antichrists have come. **This is how** we know it is the last hour.

3855 ὀθόνη, *othonē* [2] [→ *3856*]

sheet [2]

Ac   10:11 and something like a large **sheet** being let down to earth by its four
     11: 5 I saw something like a large **sheet** being let down from heaven by

3856 ὀθόνιον, *othonion* [5] [√ *3855*]

strips of linen [4], linen [1]

Lk   24:12 Bending over, he saw the **strips of linen** lying by themselves,
Jn   19:40 the two of them wrapped it, with the spices, *in* **strips of linen**.
     20: 5 He bent over and looked in *at* the **strips of linen** lying there
     20: 6 and went into the tomb. He saw the **strips of linen** lying there,
     20: 7 The cloth was folded up by itself, separate from the **linen**.

3857 οἶδα, *oida* [318 / 320] [→ *4631, 5287?, 5288?, 5323*]

know [219], knew [20], knows [14], knowing [12], realize [8], know how [7], known [7], understand [5], *untranslated* [2], idea [2], acquainted with [1], aware [1], did[s] [1], fathom [1], fully convinced [*+2779+4275*] [1], get learning [*+1207*] [1], grasp the meaning [*+1539+3836*] [1], had idea [1], in mind [1], knew about [1], know about [1], knows how [1], knows thoughts [1], learn [1], recognize [1], regard [1], remember [1], respect [1], see [1], sure [*+1182*] [1], sure [1], take note of [1], tell [1], understanding [1]

Mt   6: 8 for your Father **knows** what you need before you ask him.
     6:32 these things, and your heavenly Father **knows** that you need them.
     7:11 though *you* are evil, **know how** to give good gifts to your children,
     9: 4 **Knowing** [UBS *3972*] their thoughts, Jesus said, "Why do you
     9: 6 so that *you may* **know** that the Son of Man has authority on earth
     12:25 Jesus **knew** their thoughts and said to them, "Every kingdom
     15:12 *Do you* **know** that the Pharisees were offended when they heard
     20:22 *You* don't **know** what you are asking," Jesus said to them.
     20:25 *You* **know** that the rulers of the Gentiles lord it over them,
     21:27 So they answered Jesus, *"We* don't **know."** Then he said, "Neither
     22:16 *"we* **know** you are a man of integrity and that you teach the way of
     22:29 "You are in error *because you do* not **know** the Scriptures
     24:36 "No one **knows** about that day or hour, not even the angels in
     24:42 because *you do* not **know** on what day your Lord will come.
     24:43 If the owner of the house *had* **known** at what time of night the
     25:12 "But he replied, 'I tell you the truth, *I* don't **know** you.'
     25:13 keep watch, because *you do* not **know** the day or the hour.
     25:26 So *you* **knew** that I harvest where I have not sown and gather
     26: 2 "As *you* **know**, the Passover is two days away—and the Son of Man
     26:70 before them all. *"I* don't **know** what you're talking about," he said.
     26:72 He denied it again, with an oath: *"I* don't **know** the man!"
     26:74 curses on himself and he swore to them, *"I* don't **know** the man!"
     27:18 For *he* **knew** it was out of envy that they had handed Jesus over to
     27:65 Pilate answered. "Go, make the tomb as secure as *you* **know how."**
     28: 5 "Do not be afraid, for *I* **know** that you are looking for Jesus,
Mk   1:24 come to destroy us? *I* **know** who you are—the Holy One of God!"
     1:34 would not let the demons speak because *they* **knew** who he was.
     2:10 But that *you may* **know** that the Son of Man has authority on earth
     4:13 Then Jesus said to them, "Don't *you* **understand** this parable?
     4:27 the seed sprouts and grows, though he *does* not **know how.**
     5:33 **knowing** what had happened to her, came and fell at his feet and,
     6:20 and protected him, **knowing** him to be a righteous and holy man.
     9: 6 (*He did* not **know** what to say, they were so frightened.)
     10:19 *You* **know** the commandments: 'Do not murder, do not commit
     10:38 *"You* don't **know** what you are asking," Jesus said. "Can you drink
     10:42 *You* **know** that those who are regarded as rulers of the Gentiles
     11:33 So they answered Jesus, *"We* don't **know."** Jesus said, "Neither will
     12:14 to him and said, "Teacher, *we* **know** you are a man of integrity.
     12:15 Should we pay or shouldn't we?" But Jesus **knew** their hypocrisy.
     12:24 "Are you not in error because *you do* not **know** the Scriptures
     13:32 "No one **knows** about that day or hour, not even the angels in
     13:33 on guard! Be alert! *You do* not **know** when that time will come.
     13:35 because *you do* not **know** when the owner of the house will come
     14:40 their eyes were heavy. *They did* not **know** what to say to him.
     14:68 *"I* don't **know** or understand what you're talking about," he said,
     14:71 he swore to them, *"I* don't **know** this man you're talking about."
Lk   2:49 he asked. "Didn't *you* **know** I had to be in my Father's house?"

4:34 come to destroy us? *I* **know** who you are—the Holy One of God!"
4:41 not allow them to speak, because *they* **knew** he was the Christ.
5:24 But that *you may* **know** that the Son of Man has authority on earth
6: 8 But Jesus **knew** what they were thinking and said to the man with
8:53 They laughed at him, **knowing** that she was dead.
9:33 and one for Elijah." (*He did* not **know** what he was saying.)
9:47 Jesus, **knowing** their thoughts, took a little child and had him stand
11:13 though you are evil, **know how** to give good gifts to your children,
11:17 Jesus **knew** their thoughts and said to them: "Any kingdom divided
11:44 like unmarked graves, which men walk over without **knowing** it."
12:30 after all such things, and your Father **knows** that you need them.
12:39 If the owner of the house *had* **known** at what hour the thief was
12:56 *You* **know how** to interpret the appearance of the earth
12:56 How is it that *you* don't **know how** to interpret this present time?
13:25 "But he will answer, '*I* don't **know** you or where you come from.'
13:27 "But he will reply, '*I* don't **know** you or where you come from.
18:20 *You* **know** the commandments: 'Do not commit adultery,
19:22 *You* **knew**, did you, that I am a hard man, taking out what I did not
20: 7 So they answered, *"We* don't **know** where it was from."
20:21 "Teacher, *we* **know** that you speak and teach what is right,
22:34 rooster crows today, you will deny three times that *you* **know** me."
22:57 But he denied it. "Woman, *I* don't **know** him," he said.
22:60 Peter replied, "Man, *I* don't **know** what you're talking about!"
23:34 "Father, forgive them, for *they do* not **know** what they are doing."
Jn   1:26 John replied, "but among you stands one you *do* not **know.**
     1:31 I myself *did* not **know** him, but the reason I came baptizing with
     1:33 I *would* not *have* **known** him, except that the one who sent me to
     2: 9 *He did* not **realize** where it had come from, though the servants
     2: 9 come from, though the servants who had drawn the water **knew.**
     3: 2 "Rabbi, *we* **know** you are a teacher who has come from God.
     3: 8 but *you* cannot **tell** where it comes from or where it is going.
     3:11 I tell you the truth, we speak of what *we* **know**, and we testify to
     4:10 "If *you* **knew** the gift of God and who it is that asks you for a drink,
     4:22 You Samaritans worship what *you do* not **know**; we worship what
     4:22 we worship what *we do* **know**, for salvation is from the Jews.
     4:25 The woman said, *"I* **know** that Messiah" (called Christ) "is coming.
     4:32 he said to them, "I have food to eat that you **know** nothing **about.**"
     4:42 and *we* **know** that this man really is the Savior of the world."
     5:13 The man who was healed *had* no **idea** who it was, for Jesus had
     5:32 in my favor, and *I* **know** that his testimony about me is valid.
     6: 6 to test him, for he *already had* in **mind** what he was going to do.
     6:42 not Jesus, the son of Joseph, whose father and mother we **know**?
     6:61 **Aware** that his disciples were grumbling about this, Jesus said to
     6:64 For Jesus *had* **known** from the beginning which of them did not
     7:15 "How *did* this man **get** *such* **learning** [*+1207*] without having
     7:27 But *we* **know** where this man is from; when the Christ comes,
     7:28 cried out, "Yes, *you* **know** me, and you know where I am from.
     7:28 cried out, "Yes, you know me, and *you* **know** where I am from.
     7:28 on my own, but he who sent me is true. You *do* not **know** him,
     7:29 but I **know** him because I am from him and he sent me."
     8:14 is valid, for *I* **know** where I came from and where I am going.
     8:14 But you *have* no **idea** where I come from or where I am going.
     8:19 *"You do* not **know** me or my Father," Jesus replied. "If you knew
     8:19 Jesus replied. "If *you* **knew** me, you would know my Father also."
     8:19 Jesus replied. "If you knew me, *you* would **know** my Father also."
     8:37 *I* **know** you are Abraham's descendants. Yet you are ready to kill
     8:55 Though you do not know him, I **know** him. If I said I did not,
     8:55 If I said I did[s] not, I would be a liar like you, but I do know him
     8:55 I would be a liar like you, but *I do* **know** him and keep his word.
     9:12 "Where is this man?" they asked him. *"I* don't **know**," he said.
     9:20 *"We* **know** he is our son," the parents answered, "and we know he
     9:21 But how he can see now, or who opened his eyes, we don't **know.**
     9:21 **[RPG]** Ask him. He is of age; he will speak for himself."
     9:24 "Give glory to God," they said. "We **know** this man is a sinner."
     9:25 He replied, "Whether he is a sinner or not, *I* don't **know**. One thing
     9:25 I don't know. One thing *I do* **know**. I was blind but now I see!"
     9:29 We **know** that God spoke to Moses, but as for this fellow,
     9:29 but as for this fellow, we don't *even* **know** where he comes from."
     9:30 You don't **know** where he comes from, yet he opened my eyes.
     9:31 *We* **know** that God does not listen to sinners. He listens to the
     10: 4 of them, and his sheep follow him because *they* **know** his voice.
     10: 5 away from him because *they do* not **recognize** a stranger's voice."
     11:22 But *I* **know** that even now God will give you whatever you ask.
     11:24 *"I* **know** he will rise again in the resurrection at the last day."
     11:42 I **knew** that you always hear me, but I said this for the benefit of
     11:49 who was high priest that year, spoke up, "You **know** nothing at all!

12:35 The man who walks in the dark *does* not **know** where he is going.
12:50 *I* **know** that his command leads to eternal life. So whatever I say is
13: 1 Jesus **knew** that the time had come for him to leave this world
13: 3 Jesus **knew** that the Father had put all things under his power,
13: 7 Jesus replied, "You do not **realize** now what I am doing, but later
13:11 For *he* **knew** who was going to betray him, and that was why he
13:17 Now that *you* **know** these things, you will be blessed if you do
13:18 "I am not referring to all of you; I **know** those I have chosen.
14: 4 *You* **know** the way to the place where I am going."
14: 5 Thomas said to him, "Lord, *we* don't **know** where you are going,
14: 5 don't know where you are going, so how can *we* **know** the way?"
14: 7 really knew me, *you* would **know** [UBS *1182*] my Father as well.
15:15 because a servant *does* not **know** his master's business.
15:21 because of my name, for *they* do not **know** the One who sent me.
16:18 mean by 'a little while'? *We* don't **understand** what he is saying."
16:30 Now *we can* **see** that you know all things and that you do not even
16:30 Now we can see that *you* **know** all things and that you do not even
18: 2 Now Judas, who betrayed him, **knew** the place, because Jesus had
18: 4 Jesus, **knowing** all that was going to happen to him, went out
18:21 Ask those who heard me. Surely they **know** what I said."
19:10 "Don't *you* **realize** I have power either to free you or to crucify
19:28 **knowing** that all was now completed, and so that the Scripture
19:35 He **knows** that he tells the truth, and he testifies so that you also
20: 2 out of the tomb, and *we* don't **know** where they have put him!"
20: 9 (*They* still *did not* **understand** from Scripture that Jesus had to
20:13 Lord away," she said, "and *I don't* **know** where they have put him."
20:14 saw Jesus standing there, but *she did* not **realize** that it was Jesus.
21: 4 on the shore, but the disciples *did* not **realize** that it was Jesus.
21:12 dared ask him, "Who are you?" *They* **knew** it was the Lord.
21:15 "Yes, Lord," he said, "you **know** that I love you." Jesus said,
21:16 He answered, "Yes, Lord, you **know** that I love you." Jesus said,
21:17 He said, "Lord, you **know** all things; you know that I love you."
21:24 and who wrote them down. *We* **know** that his testimony is true.
Ac 2:22 which God did among you through him, as *you* yourselves **know**.
2:30 But *he* was a prophet and **knew** that God had promised him on
3:16 of Jesus, this man whom you see and **know** was made strong.
3:17 "Now, brothers, *I* **know** that you acted in ignorance, as did your
5: 7 hours later his wife came in, not **knowing** what had happened.
7:18 Then another king, who **knew** *nothing* **about** Joseph, became ruler
7:40 led us out of Egypt—*we* don't **know** what has happened to him!'
10:37 You **know** what has happened throughout Judea, beginning in
12: 9 but *he* had no **idea** that what the angel was doing was really
12:11 "Now *I* **know** without a doubt that the Lord sent his angel
16: 3 lived in that area, for *they* all **knew** that his father was a Greek.
19:32 Most of the people *did* not even **know** why they were there.
20:22 am going to Jerusalem, not **knowing** what will happen to me there.
20:25 "Now *I* **know** that none of you among whom I have gone about
20:29 I **know** that after I leave, savage wolves will come in among you
23: 5 Paul replied, "Brothers, *I did* not **realize** that he was the high priest;
24:22 Then Felix, *who was* well **acquainted with** the Way,
26: 4 "The Jews all **know** the way I have lived ever since I was a child,
26:27 King Agrippa, do you believe the prophets? *I* **know** you do."
Ro 2: 2 Now *we* **know** that God's judgment against those who do such
3:19 Now *we* **know** that whatever the law says, it says to those who are
5: 3 *because we* **know** that suffering produces perseverance;
6: 9 *For we* **know** that since Christ was raised from the dead, he cannot
6:16 Don't *you* **know** that when you offer yourselves to someone to
7: 7 For *I would* not *have* **known** what coveting really was if the law
7:14 *We* **know** that the law is spiritual; but I am unspiritual, sold as a
7:18 *I* **know** that nothing good lives in me, that is, in my sinful nature.
8:22 *We* **know** that the whole creation has been groaning as in the pains
8:26 *We do* not **know** what we ought to pray for, but the Spirit himself
8:27 And he who searches our hearts **knows** the mind of the Spirit,
8:28 And *we* **know** that in all things God works for the good of those
11: 2 Don't *you* **know** what the Scripture says in the passage about
13:11 And do this, **understanding** the present time. The hour has come
14:14 who is in the Lord Jesus, *I am* **fully convinced** [+*2779+4275*] that
15:29 *I* **know** that when I come to you, I will come in the full measure of
1Co 1:16 beyond that, *I don't* **remember** if I baptized anyone else.)
2: 2 For I resolved *to* **know** nothing while I was with you except Jesus
2:11 For who among men **knows** the **thoughts** of a man except the
2:12 from God, that *we may* **understand** what God has freely given us.
3:16 Don't *you* **know** that you yourselves are God's temple and that
5: 6 Don't *you* **know** that a little yeast works through the whole batch
6: 2 *Do you* not **know** that the saints will judge the world? And if you
6: 3 *Do you* not **know** that we will judge angels? How much more the

6: 9 *Do you* not **know** that the wicked will not inherit the kingdom of
6:15 *Do you* not **know** that your bodies are members of Christ himself?
6:16 *Do you* not **know** that he who unites himself with a prostitute is
6:19 *Do you* not **know** that your body is a temple of the Holy Spirit,
7:16 How *do you* **know**, wife, whether you will save your husband?
7:16 Or, how *do you* **know**, husband, whether you will save your wife?
8: 1 *We* **know** that we all possess knowledge. Knowledge puffs up,
8: 4 *We* **know** that an idol is nothing at all in the world and that there is
9:13 Don't *you* **know** that those who work in the temple get their food
9:24 *Do you* not **know** that in a race all the runners run, but only one
11: 3 Now I want you *to* **realize** that the head of every man is Christ,
12: 2 *You* **know** that when you were pagans, somehow or other you
13: 2 gift of prophecy and *can* **fathom** all mysteries and all knowledge,
14:11 then *I do* not **grasp the meaning** [+*1539+3836*] of what someone
14:16 your thanksgiving, since *he does* not **know** what you are saying?
15:58 *because you* **know** that your labor in the Lord is not in vain.
16:15 You **know** that the household of Stephanas were the first converts
2Co 1: 7 *because we* **know** that just as you share in our sufferings,
4:14 *because we* **know** that the one who raised the Lord Jesus from the
5: 1 Now *we* **know** that if the earthly tent we live in is destroyed,
5: 6 Therefore *we* are always confident and **know** that as long as we are
5:11 *Since*, then, *we* **know** what it is to fear the Lord, we try to persuade
5:16 So from now on we **regard** no one from a worldly point of view.
9: 2 For *I* **know** your eagerness to help,
11:11 Why? Because I *do* not love you? God **knows** I do!
11:31 who is to be praised forever, **knows** that I am not lying.
12: 2 *I* **know** a man in Christ who fourteen years ago was caught up to
12: 2 Whether it was in the body or out of the body *I do* not **know**—
12: 2 in the body or out of the body I do not know—**[RPG]** God knows.
12: 2 it was in the body or out of the body I do not know—God **knows**.
12: 3 And *I* **know** that this man—whether in the body or apart from the
12: 3 whether in the body or apart from the body *I do* not **know**,
12: 3 the body or apart from the body I do not know, but God **knows**—
Gal 2:16 **know** that a man is not justified by observing the law,
4: 8 Formerly, *when you did* not **know** God, you were slaves to those
4:13 As *you* **know**, it was because of an illness that I first preached the
Eph 1:18 in order that you *may* **know** the hope to which he has called you,
5: 5 For of this *you can be* **sure** [+*1182*]: No immoral, impure
6: 8 *because* you **know** that the Lord will reward everyone for
6: 9 *since* you **know** that he who is both their Master and yours is in
6:21 so that you also *may* **know** how I am and what I am doing.
Php 1:16 in love, **knowing** that I am put here for the defense of the gospel.
1:19 for *I* **know** that through your prayers and the help given by the
1:25 Convinced of this, *I* **know** that I will remain, and I will continue
4:12 *I* **know** what it is to be in need, and I know what it is to have
4:12 know what it is to be in need, and *I* **know** what it is to have plenty.
4:15 Moreover, as you Philippians **know**, in the early days of your
Col 2: 1 I want you *to* **know** how much I am struggling for you and for
3:24 *since you* **know** that you will receive an inheritance from the Lord
4: 1 *because you* **know** that you also have a Master in heaven.
4: 6 with salt, *so that you may* **know** how to answer everyone.
1Th 1: 4 *For we* **know**, brothers loved by God, that he has chosen you,
1: 5 *You* **know** how we lived among you for your sake.
2: 1 You **know**, brothers, that our visit to you was not a failure.
2: 2 previously suffered and been insulted in Philippi, as *you* **know**,
2: 5 *You* **know** we never used flattery, nor did we put on a mask to
2:11 For *you* **know** that we dealt with each of you as a father deals with
3: 3 these trials. You **know** *quite well* that we were destined for them.
3: 4 be persecuted. And it turned out that way, as *you well* **know**.
4: 2 For *you* **know** what instructions we gave you by the authority of
4: 4 that each of you *should* **learn** to control his own body in a way
4: 5 not in passionate lust like the heathen, who *do* not **know** God;
5: 2 for you **know** very well that the day of the Lord will come like a
5:12 we ask you, brothers, *to* **respect** those who work hard among you,
2Th 1: 8 He will punish those *who do* not **know** God and do not obey the
2: 6 And now *you* **know** what *is* holding him back,
3: 7 For *you* yourselves **know** how you ought to follow our example.
1Ti 1: 8 *We* **know** that the law is good if one uses it properly.
1: 9 We also **know** that law is made not for the righteous but for
3: 5 (If anyone *does* not **know** how to manage his own family,
3:15 *you will* **know** how people ought to conduct themselves in God's
2Ti 1:12 Yet I am not ashamed, because *I* **know** whom I have believed,
1:15 *You* **know** that everyone in the province of Asia has deserted me,
2:23 and stupid arguments, *because you* **know** they produce quarrels.
3:14 convinced of, *because you* **know** those from whom you learned it,
3:15 and how from infancy *you have* **known** the holy Scriptures,

Tit 1:16 They claim *to* **know** God, but by their actions they deny him.
     3:11 *You may be* **sure** that such a man is warped and sinful; he is
Phm 1:21 I write to you, **knowing** that you will do even more than I ask.
Heb 8:11 saying, 'Know the Lord,' because *they will* all **know** me,
    10:30 For *we* **know** him who said, "It is mine to avenge; I will repay,"
    12:17 Afterward, as *you* **know**, when he wanted to inherit this blessing,
Jas 1:19 My dear brothers, **take note of** this: Everyone should be quick to
     3:1 *because you* **know** that we who teach will be judged more strictly.
     4:4 don't *you* **know** that friendship with the world is hatred toward
     4:17 *Anyone*, then, *who* **knows** the good he ought to do and doesn't do
1Pe 1:18 *For you* **know** that it was not with perishable things such as silver
     5:9 *because you* **know** that your brothers throughout the world are
2Pe 1:12 even though *you* **know** them and are firmly established in the truth
     1:14 *because I* **know** that I will soon put it aside, as our Lord Jesus
     2:9 then the Lord **knows how** to rescue godly men from trials
1Jn 2:11 *he does* not **know** where he is going, because the darkness has
     2:20 an anointing from the Holy One, and all of *you* **know** the truth.
     2:21 I do not write to you because *you do* not **know** the truth, but
     2:21 but because *you do* **know** it and because no lie comes from the
     2:29 If *you* **know** that he is righteous, you know that everyone who
     3:2 But *we* **know** that when he appears, we shall be like him, for we
     3:5 But *you* **know** that he appeared so that he might take away our
     3:14 We **know** that we have passed from death to life, because we love
     3:15 a murderer, and *you* **know** that no murderer has eternal life in him.
     5:13 of the Son of God so that *you may* **know** that you have eternal life.
     5:15 And if *we* **know** that he hears us—whatever we ask—we know that
     5:15 whatever we ask—*we* **know** that we have what we asked of him.
     5:18 We **know** that anyone born of God does not continue to sin;
     5:19 We **know** that we are children of God, and that the whole world is
     5:20 We **know** also that the Son of God has come and has given us
3Jn 1:12 also speak well of him, and *you* **know** that our testimony is true.
Jude 1:5 *Though* you already **know** all this, I want to remind you that the
     1:10 men speak abusively against whatever *they do* not **understand**;
Rev 2:2 *I* **know** your deeds, your hard work and your perseverance.
     2:9 *I* **know** your afflictions and your poverty—yet you are rich!
     2:13 *I* **know** where you live—where Satan has his throne. Yet you
     2:17 with a new name written on it, **known** only to him who receives it.
     2:19 *I* **know** your deeds, your love and faith, your service
     3:1 *I* **know** your deeds; you have a reputation of being alive, but you
     3:8 *I* **know** your deeds. See, I have placed before you an open door
     3:15 *I* **know** your deeds, that you are neither cold nor hot. I wish you
     3:17 But *you do* not **realize** that you are wretched, pitiful, poor,
     7:14 I answered, "Sir, you **know**." And he said, "These are they who
    12:12 He is filled with fury, *because he* **knows** that his time is short."
    19:12 He has a name written on him that no one **knows** but he himself.

3858 οἰκεῖος, *oikeios* [3] [√ *3875*]

belong to family [1], immediate family [1], members of household
[1]

Gal 6:10 especially *to those who* **belong to** the **family** of believers.
Eph 2:19 citizens with God's people and **members of** God's **household**,
1Ti 5:8 and especially for his **immediate family**, he has denied the faith

3859 οἰκετεία, *oiketeia* [1] [√ *3875*]

servants in household [1]

Mt 24:45 **servants in** his **household** to give them their food at the proper

3860 οἰκέτης, *oiketēs* [4] [√ *3875*]

servant [2], servants [1], slaves [1]

Lk 16:13 "No **servant** can serve two masters. Either he will hate the one
Ac 10:7 Cornelius called two *of* his **servants** and a devout soldier who was
Ro 14:4 Who are you to judge someone else's **servant**? To his own master
1Pe 2:18 **Slaves**, submit yourselves to your masters with all respect,

3861 οἰκέω, *oikeō* [9] [√ *3875*]

lives [3], living [3], live [2], lives in [1]

Ro 7:17 it is no longer I myself who do it, but it is sin **living** in me.
     7:18 I know that nothing good **lives** in me, that is, in my sinful nature.
     7:20 it is no longer I who do it, but it is sin **living** in me that does it.

     8:9 the sinful nature but by the Spirit, if the Spirit of God **lives** in you.
     8:11 And if the Spirit of him who raised Jesus from the dead *is* **living** in
1Co 3:16 yourselves are God's temple and that God's Spirit **lives** in you?
     7:12 has a wife who is not a believer and she is willing *to* **live** with him,
     7:13 a husband who is not a believer and he is willing *to* **live** with her,
1Ti 6:16 who alone is immortal and *who* **lives in** unapproachable light,

3862 οἴκημα, *oikēma* [1] [√ *3875*]

cell [1]

Ac 12:7 an angel of the Lord appeared and a light shone in the **cell**.

3863 οἰκητήριον, *oikētērion* [2] [√ *3875*]

dwelling [1], home [1]

2Co 5:2 we groan, longing to be clothed with our heavenly **dwelling**,
Jude 1:6 keep their positions of authority but abandoned their own **home**—

3864 οἰκία, *oikia* [93] [√ *3875*]

house [66], home [11], household [4], houses [4], homes [3],
untranslated [1], family [1], from house to house [*+3836*] [1],
indoors [*+1650+3836*] [1], live in [1]

Mt 2:11 On coming to the **house**, they saw the child with his mother Mary,
     5:15 they put it on its stand, and it gives light to everyone in the **house**.
     7:24 and puts them into practice is like a wise man who built his **house**
     7:25 the streams rose, and the winds blew and beat against that **house**;
     7:26 into practice is like a foolish man who built his **house** on sand.
     7:27 the streams rose, and the winds blew and beat against that **house**,
     8:6 "my servant lies at **home** paralyzed and in terrible suffering."
     8:14 When Jesus came into Peter's **house**, he saw Peter's mother-in-law
     9:10 While Jesus was having dinner at Matthew's **house**, many tax
     9:23 When Jesus entered the ruler's **house** and saw the flute players
     9:28 When he had gone **indoors** [*+1650+3836*], the blind men came to
    10:12 As you enter the **house**, give it your greeting.
    10:13 If the **home** is deserving, let your peace rest on it; if it is not,
    10:14 shake the dust off your feet when you leave that **home** or town.
    12:25 and every city or **household** divided against itself will not stand.
    12:29 how can anyone enter a strong man's **house** and carry off his
    12:29 unless he first ties up the strong man? Then he can rob his **house**.
    13:1 That same day Jesus went out of the **house** and sat by the lake.
    13:36 Then he left the crowd and went into the **house**. His disciples came
    13:57 in his hometown and in his own **house** is a prophet without honor."
    17:25 When Peter came into the **house**, Jesus was the first to speak.
    19:29 And everyone who has left **houses** or brothers or sisters or father
    24:17 on the roof of his house go down to take anything out of the **house**.
    24:43 have kept watch and would not have let his **house** be broken into.
    26:6 While Jesus was in Bethany in the **home** of a man known as Simon
Mk 1:29 they went with James and John to the **home** of Simon and Andrew.
     2:15 While Jesus was having dinner at Levi's **house**, many tax
     3:25 If a **house** is divided against itself, that house cannot stand.
     3:25 If a house is divided against itself, that **house** cannot stand.
     3:27 no one can enter a strong man's **house** and carry off his
     3:27 unless he first ties up the strong man. Then he can rob his **house**.
     6:4 his relatives and in his own **house** is a prophet without honor."
     6:10 Whenever you enter a **house**, stay there until you leave that town.
     7:24 He entered a **house** and did not want anyone to know it; yet he
     9:33 When he was in the **house**, he asked them, "What were you arguing
    10:10 When they were in the **house** again, the disciples asked Jesus about
    10:29 "no one who has left **home** or brothers or sisters or mother
    10:30 fail to receive a hundred times as much in this present age (**homes**,
    12:40 They devour widows' **houses** and for a show make lengthy prayers.
    13:15 Let no one on the roof *of* his **house** go down or enter the house to
    13:34 He leaves his **house** and puts his servants in charge, each with his
    13:35 because you do not know when the owner *of* the **house** will come
    14:3 reclining at the table in the **home** of a man known as Simon the
Lk   4:38 Jesus left the synagogue and went to the **home** of Simon.
     5:29 Then Levi held a great banquet for Jesus at his **house**, and a large
     6:48 He is like a man building a **house**, who dug down deep and laid the
     6:48 a flood came, the torrent struck that **house** but could not shake it,
     6:49 and does not put them into practice is like a man who built a **house**
     6:49 The moment the torrent struck that **house**, it collapsed and its
     7:6 He was not far from the **house** when the centurion sent friends to
     7:37 in that town learned that Jesus was eating at the Pharisee's **house**,

   7:44   said to Simon, "Do you see this woman? I came into your **house**,
   8:27   For a long time this man had not worn clothes or lived in a **house**,
   8:51   When he arrived at the **house** of Jairus, he did not let anyone go in
   9: 4   Whatever **house** you enter, stay there until you leave that town.
  10: 5   "When you enter a **house**, first say, 'Peace to this house.'
  10: 7   Stay in that **house**, eating and drinking whatever they give you,
  10: 7   deserves his wages. Do not move around from **house** to house.
  10: 7   deserves his wages. Do not move around from house to **house**.
  15: 8   a lamp, sweep the **house** and search carefully until she finds it?
  15:25   When he came near the **house**, he heard music and dancing.
  17:31   On that day no one who is on the roof *of* his **house**, with his goods
  18:29   "no one who has left **home** or wife or brothers or parents
  20:47   They devour widows' **houses** and for a show make lengthy prayers.
  22:10   jar of water will meet you. Follow him to the **house** that he enters,
  22:11   and say to the owner *of* the **house**, 'The Teacher asks: Where is the
  22:54   they led him away and took him into the **house** of the high priest.
Jn   4:53   to him, "Your son will live." So he and all his **household** believed.
   8:35   Now a slave has no permanent place in the **family**,
  11:31   When the Jews who had been with Mary in the **house**, comforting
  12: 3   And the **house** was filled with the fragrance of the perfume.
  14: 2   In my Father's **house** are many rooms; if it were not so, I would
Ac   4:34   For from time to time those who owned lands or **houses** sold them,
   9:11   "Go to the **house** of Judas on Straight Street and ask for a man from
   9:17   Then Ananias went to the **house** and entered it. Placing his hands
  10: 6   He is staying with Simon the tanner, whose **house** is by the sea."
  10:17   the men sent by Cornelius found out where Simon's **house** was
  10:32   He is a guest in the **home** of Simon the tanner, who lives by the
  11:11   to me from Caesarea stopped at the **house** where I was staying.
  12:12   he went to the **house** of Mary the mother of John, also called Mark,
  16:32   the word of the Lord to him and to all the others in his **house**.
  17: 5   They rushed to Jason's **house** in search of Paul and Silas in order
  18: 7   the synagogue and went next door to the **house** of Titius Justus,
  18: 7   door to the house of Titius Justus, a worshiper of God. **[RPG]**
1Co 11:22   Don't you have **homes** to eat and drink in? Or do you despise the
  16:15   You know that the **household** of Stephanas were the first converts
2Co 5: 1   Now we know that if the earthly tent we **live in** is destroyed,
   5: 1   from God, an eternal **house** in heaven, not built by human hands.
Php 4:22   you greetings, especially those who belong to Caesar's **household**.
1Ti 5:13   habit of being idle and going about **from house** [+*3836*] **to house**.
2Ti 2:20   In a large **house** there are articles not only of gold and silver,
   3: 6   They are the kind who worm their way into **homes** and gain
2Jn 1:10   this teaching, do not take him into your **house** or welcome him.

3865   οἰκιακός, *oikiakos*   [2]   [√ *3875*]

   members of household [2]

Mt 10:25   called Beelzebub, how much more the **members of** his **household**!
  10:36   a man's enemies will be the **members of** his own **household**.'

3866   οἰκοδεσποτέω, *oikodespoteō*   [1]
   [√ *3875* + *1305*]

   manage homes [1]

1Ti 5:14   *to* **manage** *their* **homes** and to give the enemy no opportunity for

3867   οἰκοδεσπότης, *oikodespotēs*   [12]
   [√ *3875* + *1305*]

   owner of the house [5], landowner [+*476*] [2], head of the house
   [1], landowner [1], owner of a house [+*476*] [1], owner [1],
   owner's [1]

Mt 10:25   If the **head of the house** has been called Beelzebub, how much
  13:27   "The **owner's** servants came to him and said, 'Sir, didn't you sow
  13:52   **owner** [+*476*] **of a house** who brings out of his storeroom new
  20: 1   "For the kingdom of heaven is like a **landowner** [+*476*] who went
  20:11   they received it, they began to grumble against the **landowner**.
  21:33   There was a **landowner** [+*476*] who planted a vineyard. He put a
  24:43   If the **owner of the house** had known at what time of night the
Mk 14:14   Say *to* the **owner of the house** he enters, 'The Teacher asks:
Lk 12:39   If the **owner of the house** had known at what hour the thief was
  13:25   Once the **owner of the house** gets up and closes the door,
  14:21   Then the **owner of the house** became angry and ordered his
  22:11   and say *to* the **owner** of the house, 'The Teacher asks: Where is

3868   οἰκοδομέω, *oikodomeō*   [40]   [√ *3875* + *1560*]

   build [12], built [10], builders [4], building [3], build up [2], edifies
   [2], builds up [1], constructive [1], edified [1], emboldened [1],
   rebuild [+*4099*] [1], rebuild [1], strengthened [1]

Mt 7:24   and puts them into practice is like a wise man who **built** his house
   7:26   and does not put them into practice is like a foolish man who **built**
  16:18   tell you that you are Peter, and on this rock *I will* **build** my church,
  21:33   put a wall around it, dug a winepress in it and **built** a watchtower.
  21:42   " 'The stone the **builders** rejected has become the capstone;
  23:29   *You* **build** tombs for the prophets and decorate the graves of the
  26:61   able to destroy the temple of God and **rebuild** it in three days.' "
  27:40   who are going to destroy the temple and **build** it in three days,
Mk 12: 1   wall around it, dug a pit for the winepress and **built** a watchtower.
  12:10   " 'The stone the **builders** rejected has become the capstone;
  14:58   destroy this man-made temple and in three days *will* **build** another,
  15:29   You who are going to destroy the temple and **build** it in three days,
Lk 4:29   and took him to the brow of the hill on which the town *was* **built**
   6:48   He is like a man **building** a house, who dug down deep and laid
   6:48   struck that house but could not shake it, because it *was* well **built**.
   6:49   and does not put them into practice is like a man *who* **built** a house
   7: 5   because he loves our nation and *has* **built** our synagogue."
  11:47   "Woe to you, because *you* **build** tombs for the prophets, and it was
  11:48   forefathers did; they killed the prophets, and you **build** their tombs.
  12:18   *I will* tear down my barns and **build** bigger ones, and there I will
  14:28   "Suppose one of you wants *to* **build** a tower. Will he not first sit
  14:30   saying, 'This fellow began *to* **build** and was not able to finish.'
  17:28   and drinking, buying and selling, planting and **building**.
  20:17   " 'The stone the **builders** rejected has become the capstone'?
Jn 2:20   The Jews replied, "It has taken forty-six years *to* **build** this temple,
Ac 7:47   But it was Solomon *who* **built** the house for him.
   7:49   What kind of house *will you* **build** for me? says the Lord.
   9:31   *It was* **strengthened**; and encouraged by the Holy Spirit, it grew in
  20:32   which can **build** you **up** and give you an inheritance among all
Ro 15:20   so that *I would* not *be* **building** on someone else's foundation.
1Co 8: 1   all possess knowledge. Knowledge puffs up, but love **builds up**.
   8:10   won't *he be* **emboldened** to eat what has been sacrificed to idols?
  10:23   "Everything *is* permissible"—but not everything *is* **constructive**.
  14: 4   He who speaks in a tongue **edifies** himself, but he who prophesies
  14: 4   a tongue edifies himself, but he who prophesies **edifies** the church.
  14:17   be giving thanks well enough, but the other man *is* not **edified**.
Gal 2:18   If *I* **rebuild** [+*4099*] what I destroyed, I prove that I am a
1Th 5:11   Therefore encourage one another and **build** each other **up**,
1Pe 2: 5   *are being* **built** *into* a spiritual house to be a holy priesthood,
   2: 7   "The stone the **builders** rejected has become the capstone,"

3869   οἰκοδομή, *oikodomē*   [18]   [√ *3875* + *1560*]

   building up [3], building [3], buildings [3], strengthening [3], build
   up [2], builds up [1], built up [1], edification [1], edified [+*3284*]
   [1]

Mt 24: 1   his disciples came up to him to call his attention to its **buildings**.
Mk 13: 1   Teacher! What massive stones! What magnificent **buildings**!"
  13: 2   "Do you see all these great **buildings**?" replied Jesus. "Not one
Ro 14:19   every effort to do what leads to peace and to mutual **edification**.
  15: 2   of us should please his neighbor for his good, to **build** him **up**.
1Co 3: 9   we are God's fellow workers; you are God's field, God's **building**.
  14: 3   everyone who prophesies speaks to men *for* their **strengthening**,
  14: 5   unless he interprets, so that the church *may be* **edified** [+*3284*].
  14:12   to have spiritual gifts, try to excel in gifts that **build up** the church.
  14:26   All of these must be done for the **strengthening** of the church.
2Co 5: 1   we have a **building** from God, an eternal house in heaven,
  10: 8   Lord gave us for **building** you **up** rather than pulling you down,
  12:19   and everything we do, dear friends, is for your **strengthening**.
  13:10   the authority the Lord gave me for **building** you **up**, not for tearing
Eph 2:21   In him the whole **building** is joined together and rises to become a
   4:12   for works of service, so that the body of Christ may be **built up**
   4:16   grows and **builds** itself **up** in love, as each part does its work.
   4:29   but only what is helpful for **building** others **up** according to their

3870   οἰκοδομία, *oikodomia*   Not used in UBS/NIV
   [√ *3875* + *1560*]

3871 οἰκοδόμος, *oikodomos* [1] [√ 3875 + 1560]

builders [1]

Ac 4: 11 He is " 'the stone you **builders** rejected, which has become the

3872 οἰκονομέω, *oikonomeō* [1] [√ 3875 + 3795]

manager [1]

Lk 16: 2 of your management, because you cannot *be* **manager** any longer.'

3873 οἰκονομία, *oikonomia* [9] [√ 3875 + 3795]

administration [2], job [2], commission [1], management [1], put
into effect [1], trust [1], work [1]

Lk 16: 2 Give an account *of* your **management**, because you cannot be
　　 16: 3 'What shall I do now? My master is taking away my **job**.
　　 16: 4 I know what I'll do so that, when I lose my **job** here, people will
1Co 9: 17 I am simply discharging the **trust** committed to me.
Eph 1: 10 to be **put into effect** when the times will have reached their
　　 3: 2 Surely you have heard about the **administration** of God's grace
　　 3: 9 and to make plain to everyone the **administration** of this mystery,
Col 1: 25 I have become its servant by the **commission** God gave me to
1Ti 1: 4 These promote controversies rather than God's **work**—which is by

3874 οἰκονόμος, *oikonomos* [10] [√ 3875 + 3795]

manager [4], administering [1], director of public works [1],
entrusted with work [1], given a trust [+1877] [1], those entrusted
with [1], trustees [1]

Lk 12: 42 The Lord answered, "Who then is the faithful and wise **manager**,
　　 16: 1 "There was a rich man whose **manager** was accused of wasting his
　　 16: 3 "The **manager** said to himself, 'What shall I do now? My master is
　　 16: 8 "The master commended the dishonest **manager** because he had
Ro 16: 23 Erastus, who is the city's **director of public works**, and our
1Co 4: 1 of Christ and as **those entrusted** with the secret things of God.
　　 4: 2 Now it is required that those who have been **given a trust** [+1877]
Gal 4: 2 is subject to guardians and **trustees** until the time set by his father.
Tit 1: 7 Since an overseer is **entrusted with** God's **work**, he must be
1Pe 4: 10 faithfully **administering** God's grace in its various forms.

3875 οἶκος, *oikos* [114] [→ 488, 1594, 1940, 2224, 2997,

2998, 2999, 3000, 3001, 3578, 3579, 3858, 3859, 3860, 3861,
3862, 3863, 3864, 3865, 3866, 3867, 3868, 3869, 3870, 3871,
3872, 3873, 3874, 3876, 3877, 3878, 4109, 4228, 4229, 4230,
4340, 4341, 5324, 5325]

οἶκος Δαυίδ (house of David) [3] Lk 1:27,69; 2:4

οἶκος θεοῦ (house of God) [6] Mt 12:4; Mk 2:26; Lk 6:4; 1Ti
3:15; Heb 10:21; 1Pe 4:17

οἶκος Ἰακώβ (house of Jacob) [2] Lk 1:33; Ac 7:46

οἶκος Ἰούδας (house of Judah) [1] Heb 8:8

οἶκος Ἰσραήλ (house of Israel) [6] Mt 10:6; 15:24; Ac 2:36;
7:42; Heb 8:8,10

οἶκος πατρός (father's house) [3] Lk 16:27; Jn 2:16; Ac 7:20

οἶκος προσευχῆς (house of prayer) [3] Mt 21:13; Mk 11:17; Lk
19:46

house [59], home [9], household [8], family [7], home [+899] [5],
home [+5148] [3], Israel [+2702] [3], from house to house
[+2848] [2], home [+1650+3836+5148] [2], home [+899+3836]
[2], descendant [+1666] [1], family [+3836] [1], from house to
house [+2848+3836] [1], home [+899+1650+3836] [1],
households [1], houses [1], in homes [+2848] [1], indoors
[+1650] [1], itself[s] [1], market [+1866] [1], members of household
[1], palace [1], palaces [1], sanctuary [1]

Mt 9: 6 said to the paralytic, "Get up, take your mat and go **home** [+5148]."
　　 9: 7 and the man got up and went **home** [+899].
　　 10: 6 Go rather to the lost sheep *of* **Israel** [+2702].
　　 11: 8 fine clothes? No, those who wear fine clothes are in kings' **palaces**.
　　 12: 4 He entered the **house** of God, and he and his companions ate the
　　 12: 44 Then it says, 'I will return to the **house** I left.' When it arrives,

12: 44 it finds the **house** [UBS-] unoccupied, swept clean and put in
15: 24 He answered, "I was sent only to the lost sheep *of* **Israel** [+2702]."
21: 13 he said to them, " 'My **house** will be called a house of prayer,'
21: 13 he said to them, " 'My **house** will be called a **house** of prayer,'
23: 38 Look, your **house** is left to you desolate.
Mk 2: 1 entered Capernaum, the people heard that he had come **home**.
　　 2: 11 tell you, get up, take your mat and go **home** [+1650+3836+5148]."
　　 2: 26 he entered the **house** of God and ate the consecrated bread,
　　 3: 20 Then Jesus entered a **house**, and again a crowd gathered, so that he
　　 5: 19 "Go **home** [+5148] to your family and tell them how much the Lord
　　 5: 38 When they came to the **home** of the synagogue ruler, Jesus saw a
　　 7: 17 After he had left the crowd and entered the **house**, his disciples
　　 7: 30 She went **home** [+899+3836] and found her child lying on the
　　 8: 3 If I send them **home** [+899] hungry, they will collapse on the way,
　　 8: 26 Jesus sent him **home** [+899], saying, "Don't go into the village."
　　 9: 28 After Jesus had gone **indoors** [+1650], his disciples asked him
　　 11: 17 " 'My **house** will be called a house of prayer for all nations'?
　　 11: 17 " 'My house will be called a **house** of prayer for all nations'?
Lk 1: 23 his time of service was completed, he returned **home** [+899].
　　 1: 27 married to a man named Joseph, a **descendant** [+1666] of David.
　　 1: 33 and he will reign over the **house** of Jacob forever; his kingdom will
　　 1: 40 where she entered Zechariah's **home** and greeted Elizabeth.
　　 1: 56 Elizabeth for about three months and then returned **home** [+899].
　　 1: 69 He has raised up a horn of salvation for us in the **house** of his
　　 2: 4 of David, because he belonged to the **house** and line of David.
　　 5: 24 tell you, get up, take your mat and go **home** [+1650+3836+5148]."
　　 5: 25 been lying on and went **home** [+899+1650+3836] praising God.
　　 6: 4 He entered the **house** of God, and taking the consecrated bread,
　　 7: 10 Then the men who had been sent returned to the **house** and found
　　 7: 36 so he went to the Pharisee's **house** and reclined at the table.
　　 8: 39 "Return **home** [+5148] and tell how much God has done for you."
　　 8: 41 and fell at Jesus' feet, pleading with him to come to his **house**
　　 9: 61 Lord; but first let me go back and say good-by to my **family**."
　　 10: 5 "When you enter a house, first say, 'Peace *to* this **house**.'
　　 11: 17 itself will be ruined, and a **house** divided against itself will fall.
　　 11: 17 itself will be ruined, and a house divided against **itself**[s] will fall.
　　 11: 24 and does not find it. Then it says, 'I will return to the **house** I left.'
　　 11: 51 of Zechariah, who was killed between the altar and the **sanctuary**.
　　 12: 39 thief was coming, he would not have let his **house** be broken into.
　　 12: 52 From now on there will be five in one **family** divided against each
　　 13: 35 Look, your **house** is left to you desolate. I tell you, you will not see
　　 14: 1 when Jesus went to eat in the **house** of a prominent Pharisee,
　　 14: 23 and make them come in, so that my **house** will be full.
　　 15: 6 and goes **home**. Then he calls his friends and neighbors together
　　 16: 4 I lose my job here, people will welcome me into their **houses**.'
　　 16: 27 'Then I beg you, father, send Lazarus to my father's **house**,
　　 18: 14 than the other, went **home** [+899+3836] justified before God.
　　 19: 5 come down immediately. I must stay at your **house** today."
　　 19: 9 Jesus said to him, "Today salvation has come *to* this **house**,
　　 19: 46 is written," he said to them, " 'My **house** will be a house of prayer';
　　 19: 46 is written," he said to them, " 'My house will be a **house** of prayer';
Jn 2: 16 out of here! How dare you turn my Father's **house** into a market!"
　　 2: 16 How dare you turn my Father's house into a **market** [+1866]!"
　　 2: 17 that it is written: "Zeal *for* your **house** will consume me."
　　 7: 53 Then each went to his own **home**.
　　 11: 20 was coming, she went out to meet him, but Mary stayed at **home**.
Ac 2: 2 from heaven and filled the whole **house** where they were sitting.
　　 2: 36 "Therefore let all **Israel** [+2702] be assured of this: God has made
　　 2: 46 They broke bread in their **homes** [+2848] and ate together with
　　 5: 42 after day, in the temple courts and **from house** [+2848] **to house**,
　　 7: 10 king of Egypt; so he made him ruler over Egypt and all his **palace**.
　　 7: 20 For three months he was cared for in his father's **house**.
　　 7: 42 and offerings forty years in the desert, O **house** of Israel?
　　 7: 46 a dwelling place *for* the God [UBS **house**; NIV 2536] of Jacob.
　　 7: 47 But it was Solomon who built the **house** for him.
　　 7: 49 What kind of **house** will you build for me? says the Lord.
　　 8: 3 Going **from house** [+2848+3836] **to house**, he dragged off men
　　 10: 2 He and all his **family** were devout and God-fearing; he gave
　　 10: 22 A holy angel told him to have you come to his **house** so that he
　　 10: 30 "Four days ago I was in my **house** praying at this hour, at three in
　　 11: 12 six brothers also went with me, and we entered the man's **house**.
　　 11: 13 He told us how he had seen an angel appear in his **house** and say,
　　 11: 14 message through which you and all your **household** will be saved.'
　　 16: 15 When she and the **members of** her **household** were baptized,
　　 16: 15 me a believer in the Lord," she said, "come and stay at my **house**."
　　 16: 31 the Lord Jesus, and you will be saved—you and your **household**."

16:34 The jailer brought them into his **house** and set a meal before them;
18: 8 the synagogue ruler, and his entire **household** believed in the Lord;
19:16 He gave them such a beating that they ran out of the **house** naked
20:20 but have taught you publicly and **from house** [+2848] **to house.**
21: 8 reached Caesarea and stayed at the **house** of Philip the evangelist,
Ro 16: 5 Greet also the church that meets at their **house.** Greet my dear
1Co 1:16 (Yes, I also baptized the **household** of Stephanas; beyond that,
11:34 If anyone is hungry, he should eat at **home,** so that when you meet
14:35 about something, they should ask their own husbands at **home;**
16:19 in the Lord, and so does the church that meets at their **house.**
Col 4:15 brothers at Laodicea, and to Nympha and the church in her **house.**
1Ti 3: 4 He must manage his own **family** well and see that his children
3: 5 (If anyone does not know how to manage his own **family,**
3:12 one wife and must manage his children and his **household** well.
3:15 how people ought to conduct themselves in God's **household,**
5: 4 all to put their religion into practice by caring for their own **family**
2Ti 1:16 May the Lord show mercy *to* the **household** of Onesiphorus,
4:19 Greet Priscilla and Aquila and the **household** of Onesiphorus.
Tit 1:11 because they are ruining whole **households** by teaching things they
Phm 1: 2 our fellow soldier and to the church that meets in your **home:**
Heb 3: 2 who appointed him, just as Moses was faithful in all God's **house.**
3: 3 just as the builder of a house has greater honor than the **house**
3: 4 For every **house** is built by someone, but God is the builder of
3: 5 Moses was faithful as a servant in all God's **house,** testifying to
3: 6 But Christ is faithful as a son over God's **house.** And we are his
3: 6 And we are his **house,** if we hold on to our courage and the hope of
8: 8 when I will make a new covenant with the **house** of Israel
8: 8 new covenant with the **house** of Isræl and with the **house** of Judah.
8:10 This is the covenant I will make *with* the **house** of Israel after that
10:21 and since we have a great priest over the **house** of God,
11: 7 not yet seen, in holy fear built an ark to save his **family** [+3836].
1Pe 2: 5 are being built into a spiritual **house** to be a holy priesthood,
4:17 For it is time for judgment to begin with the **family** of God;

3876 οἰκουμένη, **oikoumenē** [15] [√ 3875]

world [13], Roman world [2]

Mt 24:14 will be preached in the whole **world** as a testimony to all nations,
Lk 2: 1 a decree that a census should be taken of the entire **Roman world.**
4: 5 and showed him in an instant all the kingdoms *of* the **world.**
21:26 faint from terror, apprehensive of what is coming on the **world,**
Ac 11:28 that a severe famine would spread over the entire **Roman world.**
17: 6 "These men who have caused trouble all *over* the **world** have now
17:31 For he has set a day when he will judge the **world** with justice by
19:27 who is worshiped throughout the province of Asia and the **world,**
24: 5 stirring up riots among the Jews all over the **world.**
Ro 10:18 gone out into all the earth, their words to the ends *of* the **world."**
Heb 1: 6 And again, when God brings his firstborn into the **world,** he says,
2: 5 It is not to angels that he has subjected the **world** to come,
Rev 3:10 to come upon the whole **world** to test those who live on the earth.
12: 9 called the devil, or Satan, who leads the whole **world** astray.
16:14 miraculous signs, and they go out to the kings *of* the whole **world,**

3877 οἰκουργός, **oikourgos** [1] [√ 3875]

busy at home [1]

Tit 2: 5 to be self-controlled and pure, to be **busy at home,** to be kind,

3878 οἰκουρός, **oikouros** Not used in UBS/NIV [√ 3875]

3879 οἰκτείρω, **oikteirō** Not used in UBS/NIV [√ 3882]

3880 οἰκτιρμός, **oiktirmos** [5] [√ 3882]

compassion [3], mercy [2]

Ro 12: 1 Therefore, I urge you, brothers, in view of God's **mercy,** to offer
2Co 1: 3 Jesus Christ, the Father *of* **compassion** and the God of all comfort,
Php 2: 1 any fellowship with the Spirit, if any tenderness and **compassion,**
Col 3:12 clothe yourselves with **compassion,** kindness, humility, gentleness
Heb 10:28 Anyone who rejected the law of Moses died without **mercy** on the

3881 οἰκτίρμων, **oiktirmōn** [3] [√ 3882]

merciful [2], mercy [1]

Lk 6:36 Be **merciful,** just as your Father is merciful.
6:36 Be **merciful,** just as your Father is merciful.
Jas 5:11 finally brought about. The Lord is full of compassion and **mercy.**

3882 οἰκτίρω, **oiktirō** [2] [→ 3879, 3880, 3881]

have compassion [2]

Ro 9:15 and *I will* **have compassion** on whom I have compassion."
9:15 and I will have compassion on whom *I* **have compassion.**"

3883 οἶμαι, **oimai** Not used in UBS/NIV [√ 3887]

3884 οἰνοπότης, **oinopotēs** [2] [√ 3885 + 4403]

drunkard [2]

Mt 11:19 and drinking, and they say, 'Here is a glutton and a **drunkard,**
Lk 7:34 and drinking, and you say, 'Here is a glutton and a **drunkard,**

3885 οἶνος, **oinos** [34] [→ 3884, 3886, 4232]

wine [32], *untranslated* [1], winepress [+3332+3836] [1]

Mt 9:17 Neither do men pour new **wine** into old wineskins. If they do,
9:17 will burst, the **wine** will run out and the wineskins will be ruined.
9:17 No, they pour new **wine** into new wineskins, and both are
27:34 There they offered Jesus **wine** to drink, mixed with gall; but after
Mk 2:22 And no one pours new **wine** into old wineskins. If he does,
2:22 If he does, the **wine** will burst the skins, and both the wine
2:22 burst the skins, and both the **wine** and the wineskins will be ruined.
2:22 will be ruined. No, he pours new **wine** into new wineskins."
15:23 Then they offered him **wine** mixed with myrrh, but he did not take
Lk 1:15 He is never to take **wine** or other fermented drink, and he will be
5:37 And no one pours new **wine** into old wineskins. If he does,
5:37 If he does, the new **wine** will burst the skins, the wine will run out
5:38 No, new **wine** must be poured into new wineskins.
7:33 For John the Baptist came neither eating bread nor drinking **wine,**
10:34 went to him and bandaged his wounds, pouring on oil and **wine.**
Jn 2: 3 When the **wine** was gone, Jesus' mother said to him, "They have no
2: 3 was gone, Jesus' mother said to him, "They have no more **wine."**
2: 9 of the banquet tasted the water that had been turned into **wine.**
2:10 "Everyone brings out the choice **wine** first and then the cheaper
2:10 too much to drink; but you have saved the best **[RPG]** till now."
4:46 visited Cana in Galilee, where he had turned the water into **wine.**
Ro 14:21 It is better not to eat meat or drink **wine** or to do anything else that
Eph 5:18 Do not get drunk *on* **wine,** which leads to debauchery. Instead,
1Ti 3: 8 to be men worthy of respect, sincere, not indulging *in* much **wine,**
5:23 and use a little **wine** because of your stomach and your frequent
Tit 2: 3 not to be slanderers or addicted *to* much **wine,** but to teach what is
Rev 6: 6 barley for a day's wages, and do not damage the oil and the **wine!"**
14: 8 which made all the nations drink the maddening **wine** of her
14:10 he, too, will drink of the **wine** of God's fury, which has been
16:19 and gave her the cup *filled with* the **wine** of the fury of his wrath.
17: 2 and the inhabitants of the earth were intoxicated with the **wine** of her
18: 3 For all the nations have drunk the maddening **wine** of her
18:13 and frankincense, of **wine** and olive oil, of fine flour and wheat;
19:15 He treads the **winepress** [+3332+3836] of the fury of the wrath of

3886 οἰνοφλυγία, **oinophlygia** [1] [√ 3885 + 5827]

drunkenness [1]

1Pe 4: 3 lust, **drunkenness,** orgies, carousing and detestable idolatry.

3887 οἴομαι, **oiomai** [3] [→ 3883]

suppose [1], supposing [1], think [1]

Jn 21:25 *I* **suppose** that even the whole world would not have room for the
Php 1:17 **supposing** that they can stir up trouble for me while I am in chains.
Jas 1: 7 That man *should* not **think** he will receive anything from the Lord;

3888 οἷος, hoios [14] [→ 3889, 4481; cf. 3836 + 4005]

as [5], *untranslated* [1], how [1], like [1], than [1], the [1], unequaled [+1181+4024+5525] [1], unequaled [+1181+4024] [1], what kinds of [1], what [1]

Mt	24:21	For then there will be great distress, **unequaled** [+1181+4024]
Mk	9: 3	whiter **than** anyone in the world could bleach them.
	13:19	those will be days of distress **unequaled** [+1181+4024+5525]
Ro	9: 6	It is not **as** though God's word had failed. For not all who are
1Co	15:48	**As** was the earthly man, so are those who are of the earth;
	15:48	and **as** is the man from heaven, so also are those who are of
2Co	10:11	Such people should realize that **what** we are in our letters when we
	12:20	For I am afraid that when I come I may not find you **as** I want you
	12:20	I want you to be, and you may not find me **as** you want me to be.
Php	1:30	since you are going through the same struggle **[RPG]** you saw I
1Th	1: 5	You know **how** we lived among you for your sake.
2Ti	3:11	**what kinds of** *things* happened to me in Antioch, Iconium
	3:11	to me in Antioch, Iconium and Lystra, **the** persecutions I endured.
Rev	16:18	No earthquake **like** *it* has ever occurred since man has been on

3889 οἱοσδηποτοῦν, hoiosdēpotoun Not used in UBS/NIV [√ 3888 + 1314 + 4544 + 4036]

3890 ὀκνέω, okneō [1] [→ 3891]

at once [+3590] [1]

Ac	9:38	two men to him and urged him, "*Please* come at once [+3590]!"

3891 ὀκνηρός, oknēros [3] [√ 3890]

lacking [1], lazy [1], trouble [1]

Mt	25:26	"His master replied, '*You* wicked, **lazy** servant! So you knew that I
Ro	12:11	Never be **lacking** in zeal, but keep your spiritual fervor,
Php	3: 1	It is no **trouble** for me to write the same things to you again,

3892 ὀκταήμερος, oktaēmeros [1] [√ 3893 + 2465]

eighth day [1]

Php	3: 5	circumcised on the **eighth day**, of the people of Israel, of the tribe

3893 ὀκτώ, oktō [8] [→ 1277, 3837, 3838, 3892]

eight [4], a week later [+2465+3552] [1], eighteen [+1274+2779] [1], eighth [1], thirty-eight [+2779+5558] [1]

Lk	2:21	On the **eighth** day, when it was time to circumcise him, he was
	9:28	About **eight** days after Jesus said this, he took Peter, John
	13:16	whom Satan has kept bound *for* **eighteen** [+1274+2779] long
Jn	5: 5	had been an invalid *for* **thirty-eight** [+2779+5558] years.
	20:26	A **week later** [+2465+3552] his disciples were in the house again,
Ac	9:33	named Aeneas, a paralytic who had been bedridden for **eight** years.
	25: 6	After spending **eight** or ten days with them, he went down to
1Pe	3:20	In it only a few people, **eight** in all, were saved through water,

3894 ὀλεθρευτής, olethreutēs Not used in UBS/NIV [√ 3897]

3895 ὀλεθρεύω, olethreuō Not used in UBS/NIV [√ 3897]

3896 ὀλέθριος, olethrios Not used in UBS/NIV [√ 3897]

3897 ὄλεθρος, olethros [4] [→ 660, 661, 724, 2017, 3894, 3895, 3896, 3904, 3905, 5272]

destruction [2], destroyed [1], ruin [1]

1Co	5: 5	so that the sinful nature may be **destroyed** and his spirit saved on
1Th	5: 3	"Peace and safety," **destruction** will come on them suddenly,
2Th	1: 9	They will be punished with everlasting **destruction** and shut out
1Ti	6: 9	and harmful desires that plunge men into **ruin** and destruction.

3898 ὀλιγοπιστία, oligopistia [1] [√ 3900 + 4412]

little faith [1]

Mt	17:20	He replied, "Because you have so **little faith**. I tell you the truth,

3899 ὀλιγόπιστος, oligopistos [5] [√ 3900 + 4412]

of little faith [5]

Mt	6:30	the fire, will he not much more clothe you, O you **of little faith**?
	8:26	He replied, "*You* **of little faith**, why are you so afraid?" Then he
	14:31	and caught him. "*You* **of little faith**," he said, "why did you doubt?"
	16: 8	Aware of their discussion, Jesus asked, "*You* **of little faith**,
Lk	12:28	the fire, how much more will he clothe you, O you **of little faith**!

3900 ὀλίγος, oligos [40] [→ 3898, 3899, 3901, 3902, 3903]

few [15], little [8], little while [4], some [2], a long time [+4024+5989] [1], a short time [1], briefly [+1328] [1], briefly [+1877] [1], continued raging [+2130+4024] [1], great disturbance [+4024+5431] [1], many [+4024] [1], sharp [+4024] [1], short time [1], short [1], small [1]

Mt	7:14	and narrow the road that leads to life, and *only a* **few** find it.
	9:37	to his disciples, "The harvest is plentiful but the workers are **few**.
	15:34	have?" Jesus asked. "Seven," they replied, "and a **few** small fish."
	22:14	"For many are invited, but **few** are chosen."
	25:21	You have been faithful with a **few** *things*; I will put you in charge
	25:23	You have been faithful with a **few** *things*; I will put you in charge
Mk	1:19	When he had gone a **little** farther, he saw James son of Zebedee
	6: 5	except lay his hands on a **few** sick people and heal them.
	6:31	"Come with me by yourselves to a quiet place and get **some** rest."
	8: 7	They had a **few** small fish as well; he gave thanks for them also
Lk	5: 3	belonging to Simon, and asked him to put out a **little** from shore.
	7:47	she loved much. But he who has been forgiven **little** loves little."
	7:47	she loved much. But he who has been forgiven little loves **little**."
	10: 2	He told them, "The harvest is plentiful, but the workers are **few**.
	12:48	and does things deserving punishment will be beaten with **few**
	13:23	asked him, "Lord, are only a **few** people going to be saved?"
Ac	12:18	there was no **small** commotion among the soldiers as to what had
	14:28	And they stayed there **a long time** [+4024+5989] with the
	15: 2	This brought Paul and Barnabas into **sharp** [+4024] dispute
	17: 4	number of God-fearing Greeks and not a **few** prominent women.
	17:12	of prominent Greek women and **many** [+4024] Greek men.
	19:23	there arose a **great disturbance** [+4024+5431] about the Way.
	19:24	shrines of Artemis, brought in no **little** business for the craftsmen.
	26:28	"Do you think that in such **a short time** you can persuade me to be
	26:29	Paul replied, "**Short time** or long—I pray God that not only you
	27:20	for many days and the storm **continued raging** [+2130+4024],
2Co	8:15	have too much, and he who gathered **little** did not have too little."
Eph	3: 3	to me by revelation, as I have already written **briefly** [+1877].
1Ti	4: 8	For physical training is of **some** value, but godliness has value for
	5:23	and use a **little** wine because of your stomach and your frequent
Heb	12:10	Our fathers disciplined us for a **little** while as they thought best;
Jas	4:14	You are a mist that appears for a **little while** and then vanishes.
1Pe	1: 6	though now *for* a **little while** you may have had to suffer grief in
	3:20	In it *only* a **few** people, eight in all, were saved through water,
	5:10	after you have suffered a **little while**, will himself restore you
	5:12	I have written to you **briefly** [+1328], encouraging you
Rev	2:14	Nevertheless, I have a **few** *things* against you: You have people
	3: 4	Yet you have a **few** people in Sardis who have not soiled their
	12:12	He is filled with fury, because he knows that his time is **short**."
	17:10	but when he does come, he must remain *for* a **little while**.

3901 ὀλιγόψυχος, oligopsychos [1] [√ 3900 + 6038]

timid [1]

1Th	5:14	warn those who are idle, encourage the **timid**, help the weak,

3902 ὀλιγωρέω, oligōreō [1] [√ 3900]

make light of [1]

Heb	12: 5	"My son, *do* not **make light of** the Lord's discipline, and do not

3903 ὀλίγως, *oligōs* [1] [√ *3900*]

just [1]

2Pe   2:18   they entice people who are **just** escaping from those who live in

3904 ὀλοθρευτής, *olothreutēs* [1] [√ *3897*]

destroying [1]

1Co 10:10   as some of them did—and were killed by the **destroying** angel.

3905 ὀλοθρεύω, *olothreuō* [1] [√ *3897*]

destroyer [1]

Heb 11:28   so that the **destroyer** *of* the firstborn would not touch the firstborn

3906 ὁλοκαύτωμα, *holokautōma* [3] [√ *3910 + 2794*]

burnt offerings [3]

Mk 12:33   neighbor as yourself is more important than all **burnt offerings**
Heb 10: 6   with **burnt offerings** and sin offerings you were not pleased.
     10: 8   and offerings, **burnt offerings** and sin offerings you did not desire,

3907 ὁλοκληρία, *holoklēria* [1] [√ *3910 + 3102*]

complete healing [1]

Ac   3:16   comes through him that has given this **complete healing** to him,

3908 ὁλόκληρος, *holoklēros* [2] [√ *3910 + 3102*]

complete [1], whole [1]

1Th   5:23   May your **whole** spirit, soul and body be kept blameless at the
Jas   1: 4   must finish its work so that you may be mature and **complete**,

3909 ὀλολύζω, *ololyzō* [1]

wail [1]

Jas   5: 1   weep and **wail** because of the misery that is coming upon you.

3910 ὅλος, *holos* [109] [→ *2772, 2773, 3906, 3907, 3908, 3911, 3914*]

ὅλος καρδία (whole heart) [4] Mt 22:37; Mk 12:30,33; Lk 10:27
ὅλος κόσμος (whole world) [9] Mt 16:26; 26:13; Mk 8:36; 14:9; Lk 9:25; Jn 12:19[NIV]; Ro 1:8; 1Jn 2:2; 5:19
ὅλος νόμος (whole law) [3] Mt 22:40; Gal 5:3; Jas 2:10
ὅλος σῶμα (whole body) [10] Mt 5:29,30; 6:22,23; Lk 11:34,36; 1Co 12:17; Jas 3:2,3,6

whole [53], all [34], throughout [+*1877*] [6], entire [2], throughout [+*1650*] [2], throughout [+*2848*] [2], all [+*4012*] [1], all long [1], all over [+*1650*] [1], all over [+*2848*] [1], all over [1], completely [1], steeped [1], throughout [1], to bottom [+*1328*] [1], whole [+*4116*] [1]

Mt   1:22   **All** this took place to fulfill what the Lord had said through the
     4:23   Jesus went **throughout** [+*1877*] Galilee, teaching in their
     4:24   News about him spread **all over** [+*1650*] Syria, and people brought
     5:29   is better for you to lose one part of your body than for your **whole**
     5:30   is better for you to lose one part of your body than for your **whole**
     6:22   If your eyes are good, your **whole** body will be full of light.
     6:23   But if your eyes are bad, your **whole** body will be full of darkness.
     9:26   News of this spread through **all** that region.
     9:31   they went out and spread the news about him **all over** that region.
     13:33   and mixed into a large amount of flour until it worked **all** through
     14:35   recognized Jesus, they sent word to **all** the surrounding country.
     16:26   What good will it be for a man if he gains the **whole** world,
     20: 6   'Why have you been standing here **all** day long doing nothing?'
     22:37   " 'Love the Lord your God with **all** your heart and with all your
     22:37   with all your heart and with **all** your soul and with all your mind.'
     22:37   with all your heart and with all your soul and with **all** your mind.'
     22:40   **All** the Law and the Prophets hang on these two commandments."
     24:14   And this gospel of the kingdom will be preached in the **whole**

     26:13   wherever this gospel is preached **throughout** [+*1877*] the world,
     26:56   But this has **all** taken place that the writings of the prophets might
     26:59   and the **whole** Sanhedrin were looking for false evidence against
     27:27   and gathered the **whole** company of soldiers around him.
Mk   1:28   News about him spread quickly over the **whole** [+*4116*] region of
     1:33   The **whole** town gathered at the door,
     1:39   So he traveled **throughout** [+*1650*] Galilee, preaching in their
     6:55   They ran throughout that **whole** region and carried the sick on mats
     8:36   What good is it for a man to gain the **whole** world, yet forfeit his
     12:30   Love the Lord your God with **all** your heart and with all your soul
     12:30   and with **all** your soul and with all your mind and with all your
     12:30   and with all your soul and with **all** your mind and with all your
     12:30   all your soul and with all your mind and with **all** your strength.'
     12:33   To love him with **all** your heart, with all your understanding
     12:33   your heart, with **all** your understanding and with all your strength,
     12:33   your heart, with all your understanding and with **all** your strength,
     12:44   of her poverty, put in everything—**all** [+*4012*] she had to live on."
     14: 9   wherever the gospel is preached **throughout** [+*1650*] the world,
     14:55   and the **whole** Sanhedrin were looking for evidence against Jesus
     15: 1   with the elders, the teachers of the law and the **whole** Sanhedrin,
     15:16   the Praetorium) and called together the **whole** company of soldiers.
     15:33   At the sixth hour darkness came over the **whole** land until the ninth
Lk   1:65   and **throughout** [+*1877*] the hill country of Judea people were
     4:14   and news about him spread through the **whole** countryside.
     5: 5   we've worked hard **all** night and haven't caught anything.
     7:17   This news about Jesus spread **throughout** [+*1877*] Judea and the
     8:39   and told **all** [+*2848*] over town how much Jesus had done for him.
     8:43   [UBS+ *and she had spent all she had on doctors*] but no one could
     9:25   What good is it for a man to gain the **whole** world, and yet lose
     10:27   " 'Love the Lord your God with **all** your heart and with all your
     10:27   and with **all** your soul and with all your strength and with all your
     10:27   and with all your soul and with **all** your strength and with all your
     10:27   all your soul and with all your strength and with **all** your mind';
     11:34   When your eyes are good, your **whole** body also is full of light.
     11:36   Therefore, if your **whole** body is full of light, and no part of it dark,
     11:36   is full of light, and no part of it dark, it will be **completely** lighted,
     13:21   and mixed into a large amount of flour until it worked **all** through
     23: 5   they insisted, "He stirs up the people **all** over Judea by his teaching.
     23:44   and darkness came over the **whole** land until the ninth hour,
Jn   4:53   to him, "Your son will live." So he and **all** his household believed.
     7:23   why are you angry with me for healing the **whole** man on the
     9:34   To this they replied, "You were **steeped** in sin at birth; how dare
     11:50   that one man die for the people than that the **whole** nation perish."
     12:19   Look how the **whole** [UBS+] world has gone after him!"
     13:10   had a bath needs only to wash his feet; his **whole** *body* is clean.
     19:23   was seamless, woven in one piece from top **to bottom** [+*1328*].
Ac   2: 2   from heaven and filled the **whole** house where they were sitting.
     2:47   praising God and enjoying the favor of **all** the people.
     5:11   Great fear seized the **whole** church and all who heard about these
     7:10   king of Egypt; so he made him ruler over Egypt and **all** his palace.
     7:11   "Then a famine struck **all** Egypt and Canaan, bringing great
     9:31   Then the church **throughout** [+*2848*] Judea, Galilee and Samaria
     9:42   This became known **all** over Joppa, and many people believed in
     10:22   and God-fearing man, who is respected by **all** the Jewish people.
     10:37   You know what has happened **throughout** [+*2848*] Judea,
     11:26   So *for* a **whole** year Barnabas and Saul met with the church
     11:28   that a severe famine would spread over the **entire** Roman world.
     13: 6   They traveled through the **whole** island until they came to Paphos.
     13:49   The word of the Lord spread through the **whole** region.
     15:22   Then the apostles and elders, with the **whole** church, decided to
     18: 8   the synagogue ruler, and his **entire** household believed in the Lord;
     19:27   who is worshiped **throughout** the province of Asia and the world,
     21:30   The **whole** city was aroused, and the people came running from all
     21:31   news reached the commander of the Roman troops that the **whole**
     28:30   For two **whole** years Paul stayed there in his own rented house
Ro   1: 8   all of you, because your faith is being reported **all** over the world.
     8:36   "For your sake we face death **all** day long; we are considered as
     10:21   "**All** day long I have held out my hands to a disobedient
     16:23   Gaius, whose hospitality I and the **whole** church here enjoy,
1Co   5: 6   Don't you know that a little yeast works through the **whole** batch
     12:17   If the **whole** body were an eye, where would the sense of hearing
     12:17   If the **whole** body were an ear, where would the sense of smell be?
     14:23   So if the **whole** church comes together and everyone speaks in
2Co   1: 1   together with all the saints **throughout** [+*1877*] Achaia:
Gal   5: 3   himself be circumcised that he is obligated to obey the **whole** law.
     5: 9   "A little yeast works through the **whole** batch of dough."

Php 1:13 it has become clear throughout the **whole** palace guard and to
1Th 4:10 you do love all the brothers **throughout** [+*1877*] Macedonia.
Tit 1:11 because they are ruining **whole** households by teaching things they
Heb 3: 2 who appointed him, just as Moses was faithful in **all** God's house.
     3: 5 Moses was faithful as a servant in **all** God's house, testifying to
Jas 2:10 For whoever keeps the **whole** law and yet stumbles at just one
     3: 2 he is a perfect man, able to keep his **whole** body in check.
     3: 3 of horses to make them obey us, we can turn the **whole** animal.
     3: 6 It corrupts the **whole** person, sets the whole course of his life on
1Jn 2: 2 and not only for ours but also for the sins *of* the **whole** world.
     5:19 and that the **whole** world is under the control of the evil one.
Rev 3:10 to come upon the **whole** world to test those who live on the earth.
     6:12 like sackcloth made of goat hair, the **whole** moon turned blood red,
    12: 9 called the devil, or Satan, who leads the **whole** world astray.
    13: 3 The **whole** world was astonished and followed the beast.
    16:14 miraculous signs, and they go out to the kings *of* the **whole** world,

3911 ὁλοτελής, **holotelēs** [1] [√ *3910 + 5465*]

through and through [1]

1Th 5:23 the God of peace, sanctify you **through and through**.

3912 Ὀλυμπᾶς, **Olympas** [1]

Olympas [1]

Ro 16:15 Nereus and his sister, and **Olympas** and all the saints with them.

3913 ὄλυνθος, **olynthos** [1]

late [1]

Rev 6:13 as **late** figs drop from a fig tree when shaken by a strong wind.

3914 ὅλως, **holōs** [4] [√ *3910*]

at all [2], actually [1], completely [1]

Mt   5:34 But I tell you, Do not swear **at all**: either by heaven, for it is God's
1Co 5: 1 It is **actually** reported that there is sexual immorality among you,
     6: 7 among you means you have been **completely** defeated already.
    15:29 If the dead are not raised **at all**, why are people baptized for them?

3915 ὄμβρος, **ombros** [1]

going to rain [+*2262*] [1]

Lk 12:54 in the west, immediately you say, '*It's* **going to rain** [+*2262*],'

3916 ὁμείρομαι, **homeiromai** [1]

loved [1]

1Th 2: 8 We **loved** you so much that we were delighted to share with you

3917 ὁμιλέω, **homileō** [4] [→ *3918, 3919, 5326; cf. 3927*]

talked [2], talking [2]

Lk 24:14 They *were* **talking** with each other about everything that had
    24:15 As they **talked** and discussed these things with each other,
Ac 20:11 and broke bread and ate. *After* **talking** until daylight, he left.
    24:26 him a bribe, so *he* sent for him frequently and **talked** with him.

3918 ὁμιλία, **homilia** [1] [√ *3917*]

company [1]

1Co 15:33 Do not be misled: "Bad **company** corrupts good character."

3919 ὅμιλος, **homilos** Not used in UBS/NIV [√ *3917*]

3920 ὁμίχλη, **homichlē** [1]

mists [1]

2Pe 2:17 These men are springs without water and **mists** driven by a storm.

3921 ὄμμα, **omma** [2] [√ *3972*]

eyes [2]

Mt 20:34 Jesus had compassion on them and touched their **eyes**.
Mk   8:23 When he had spit on the man's **eyes** and put his hands on him,

3922 ὄμνυμι, **omnymi** Not used in UBS/NIV [√ *3923*]

3923 ὀμνύω, **omnyō** [26] [→ *3922, 3993, 5350*]

swears [10], swore [5], swear [4], declared on oath [2], swear by
[2], promised with an oath [1], promised [1], sworn [1]

Mt   5:34 But I tell you, *Do* not **swear** at all: either by heaven, for it is God's
     5:36 And *do* not **swear** by your head, for you cannot make even one
    23:16 You say, 'If anyone **swears** by the temple, it means nothing;
    23:16 but if anyone **swears** by the gold of the temple, he is bound by his
    23:18 You also say, 'If anyone **swears** by the altar, it means nothing;
    23:18 but if anyone **swears** by the gift on it, he is bound by his oath.'
    23:20 he *who* **swears** by the altar swears by it and by everything on it.
    23:20 he who **swears** by the altar **swears** by it and by everything on it.
    23:21 And he *who* **swears** by the temple swears by it and by the one who
    23:21 And he who swears by the temple **swears** by it and by the one who
    23:22 And he *who* **swears** by heaven swears by God's throne and by the
    23:22 And he who swears by heaven **swears** by God's throne and by the
    26:74 he began to call down curses on himself and he **swore** to them,
Mk   6:23 And *he* **promised** her **with an oath**, "Whatever you ask I will give
    14:71 He began to call down curses on himself, and he **swore** to them,
Lk   1:73 the **swore** to our father Abraham:
Ac   2:30 and knew that God *had* **promised** him on oath that he would place
Heb 3:11 So *I* **declared on oath** in my anger, 'They shall never enter my
     3:18 And to whom *did* God **swear** that they would never enter his rest if
     4: 3 that rest, just as God has said, "So *I* **declared on oath** in my anger,
     6:13 since there was no one greater for him *to* **swear by**, he swore by
     6:13 there was no one greater for him to swear by, *he* **swore** by himself,
     6:16 Men **swear** by someone greater than themselves, and the oath
     7:21 "The Lord has **sworn** and will not change his mind: 'You are a
Jas 5:12 *do* not **swear**—not **by** heaven or by earth or by anything else.
Rev 10: 6 And *he* **swore** by him who lives for ever and ever, who created the

3924 ὁμοθυμαδόν, **homothymadon** [11]
[√ *3927 + 2596*]

together [4], all [2], agreed [+*1181*] [1], as one man [1], heart [1],
joined together [1], united [1]

Ac   1:14 They all joined **together** constantly in prayer, along with the
     2:46 Every day they continued to meet **together** in the temple courts.
     4:24 they heard this, they raised their voices **together** in prayer to God.
     5:12 And all the believers used to meet **together** in Solomon's
     7:57 ears and, yelling at the top of their voices, they **all** rushed at him,
     8: 6 signs he did, they **all** paid close attention to what he said.
    12:20 *they* now **joined together** and sought an audience with him.
    15:25 So we all **agreed** [+*1181*] to choose some men and send them to
    18:12 the Jews made a **united** attack on Paul and brought him into court.
    19:29 from Macedonia, and rushed **as one man** into the theater.
Ro 15: 6 so that with one **heart** and mouth you may glorify the God

3925 ὁμοιάζω, **homoiazō** Not used in UBS/NIV
[√ *3927*]

3926 ὁμοιοπαθής, **homoiopathēs** [2] [√ *3927 + 4248*]

just like [1], like [1]

Ac 14:15 why are you doing this? We too are only men, human **like** you.
Jas 5:17 Elijah was a man **just like** us. He prayed earnestly that it would not

3927 ὅμοιος, **homoios** [45] [→ *926, 3924, 3925, 3926,*
3928, 3929, 3930, 3931, 3932, 3933, 3936, 3937, 3938, 3939,
3940, 4234, 4235, 5327; cf. 3917, 3933]

like [37], as [2], like [+*4047*] [1], looked like [+*3930*] [1], of [1],
resembled [+*1639*] [1], resembling [+*3970*] [1], similar [1]

Mt 11:16 They are **like** children sitting in the marketplaces and calling out

	13:31	"The kingdom of heaven is **like** a mustard seed, which a man took
	13:33	"The kingdom of heaven is **like** yeast that a woman took and mixed
	13:44	"The kingdom of heaven is **like** treasure hidden in a field. When a
	13:45	the kingdom of heaven is **like** a merchant looking for fine pearls.
	13:47	the kingdom of heaven is **like** a net that was let down into the lake
	13:52	**like** the owner of a house who brings out of his storeroom new
	20: 1	"For the kingdom of heaven is **like** a landowner who went out early
	22:39	And the second is **like** it: 'Love your neighbor as yourself.'
Lk	6:47	I will show you what he is **like** who comes to me and hears my
	6:48	He is **like** a man building a house, who dug down deep and laid the
	6:49	and does not put them into practice is **like** a man who built a house
	7:31	can I compare the people of this generation? What are they **like**?
	7:32	They are **like** children sitting in the marketplace and calling out to
	12:36	**like** men waiting for their master to return from a wedding
	13:18	Then Jesus asked, "What is the kingdom of God **like**? What shall I
	13:19	It is **like** a mustard seed, which a man took and planted in his
	13:21	It is **like** yeast that a woman took and mixed into a large amount of
Jn	8:55	If I said I did not, I would be a liar **like** you, but I do know him
	9: 9	Others said, "No, he only looks **like** him." But he himself insisted,
Ac	17:29	we should not think that the divine being is **like** gold or silver
Gal	5:21	and envy; drunkenness, orgies, and the **like** [+*4047*]. I warn you,
1Jn	3: 2	he appears, we shall be **like** him, for we shall see him as he is.
Jude	1: 7	In a **similar** way, Sodom and Gomorrah and the surrounding towns
Rev	1:13	and among the lampstands as someone "**like** a son of man,"
	1:15	His feet were **like** bronze glowing in a furnace, and his voice was
	2:18	eyes are like blazing fire and whose feet are **like** burnished bronze.
	4: 3	And the one who sat there had the appearance **of** jasper
	4: 3	A rainbow, **resembling** [+*3970*] an emerald, encircled the throne.
	4: 6	throne there was what looked like a sea of glass, **clear as** crystal.
	4: 7	The first living creature was **like** a lion, the second was like an ox,
	4: 7	the second was **like** an ox, the third had a face like a man,
	4: 7	the third had a face like a man, the fourth was **like** a flying eagle.
	9: 7	The locusts **looked like** [+*3930*] horses prepared for battle.
	9: 7	On their heads they wore something **like** crowns of gold, and their
	9:10	They had tails and stings **like** scorpions, and in their tails they had
	9:19	for their tails were **like** snakes, having heads with which they
	11: 1	I was given a reed **like** a measuring rod and was told, "Go
	13: 2	The beast I saw **resembled** [+*1639*] a leopard, but had feet like
	13: 4	they also worshiped the beast and asked, "Who is **like** the beast?"
	13:11	He had two horns **like** a lamb, but he spoke like a dragon.
	14:14	and seated on the cloud was *one* "**like** a son of man" with a crown
	18:18	they will exclaim, 'Was there ever a city **like** this great city?'
	21:11	and its brilliance was **like** that of a very precious jewel, like a
	21:18	wall was made of jasper, and the city of pure gold, **as** pure as glass.

3928 ὁμοιότης, *homoiotēs* [2] [√ *3927*]

just as [+*2848*] [1], like [1]

Heb	4:15	one who has been tempted in every way, **just as** [+*2848*] we are—
	7:15	And what we have said is even more clear if another priest **like**

3929 ὁμοιόω, *homoioō* [15] [√ *3927*]

like [8], compare [4], form [1], made like [1], say is like [1]

Mt	6: 8	*Do* not **be like** them, for your Father knows what you need before
	7:24	and puts them into practice *is* **like** a wise man who built his house
	7:26	and does not put them into practice *is* **like** a foolish man who built
	11:16	"To what *can I* **compare** this generation? They are like children
	13:24	"The kingdom of heaven *is* **like** a man who sowed good seed in his
	18:23	the kingdom of heaven *is* **like** a king who wanted to settle accounts
	22: 2	"The kingdom of heaven *is* **like** a king who prepared a wedding
	25: 1	"At that time the kingdom of heaven *will be* **like** ten virgins who
Mk	4:30	Again he said, "What *shall* we **say** the kingdom of God **is like**,
Lk	7:31	"To what, then, *can I* **compare** the people of this generation?
	13:18	"What is the kingdom of God like? What *shall I* **compare** it to?
	13:20	Again he asked, "What *shall I* **compare** the kingdom of God to?
Ac	14:11	"The gods have come down to us in human **form**!"
Ro	9:29	have become like Sodom, *we* would have *been* **like** Gomorrah."
Heb	2:17	For this reason he had to *be* **made like** his brothers in every way,

3930 ὁμοίωμα, *homoiōma* [6] [√ *3927*]

likeness [2], as [1], like [1], look like [1], looked like [+*3927*] [1]

Ro	1:23	of the immortal God for images made to **look like** mortal man

---

	5:14	a command, **as** did Adam, who was a pattern of the one to come.
	6: 5	If we have been united with him **like** this in his death, we will
	8: 3	God did by sending his own Son in the **likeness** of sinful man to be
Php	2: 7	taking the very nature of a servant, being made in human **likeness**.
Rev	9: 7	The locusts **looked like** [+*3927*] horses prepared for battle.

3931 ὁμοίως, *homoiōs* [30 / 31] [√ *3927*]

in the same way [10], the same [4], *untranslated* [3], likewise [3], also [2], too [2], like [1], received[s] [1], similarly [1], so do [1], so [1], the same [+*2777*] [1], the same thing [1]

Mt	22:26	**The same thing** happened to the second and third brother,
	26:35	I will never disown you." And all the other disciples said **the same**.
	27:41	**In the same way** the chief priests, the teachers of the law
Mk	4:16	Others, **like** [UBS-] seed sown on rocky places, hear the word
	15:31	**In the same way** the chief priests and the teachers of the law
Lk	3:11	him who has none, and the one who has food should do **the same**."
	5:10	and **so** were James and John, the sons of Zebedee, Simon's
	5:33	often fast and pray, and **so do** the disciples of the Pharisees,
	6:31	Do to others as you would have them do to you. [RPG]
	10:32	So **too**, a Levite, when he came to the place and saw him,
	10:37	one who had mercy on him." Jesus told him, "Go and do **likewise**."
	13: 3	I tell you, no! But unless you repent, you **too** will all perish.
	16:25	while Lazarus **received**[s] bad things, but now he is comforted here
	17:28	"It was **the same** [+*2777*] in the days of Lot. People were eating
	17:31	**Likewise**, no one in the field should go back for anything.
	22:36	said to them, "But now if you have a purse, take it, and **also** a bag;
Jn	5:19	because whatever the Father does the Son **also** does. [RPG]
	6:11	seated as much as they wanted. He did **the same** with the fish.
	21:13	took the bread and gave it to them, and did **the same** with the fish.
Ro	1:27	**In the same way** the men also abandoned natural relations with
1Co	7: 3	his marital duty to his wife, and **likewise** the wife to her husband.
	7: 4	**In the same way**, the husband's body does not belong to him alone
	7:22	**similarly**, he who was a free man when he was called is Christ's
Heb	9:21	**In the same way**, he sprinkled with the blood both the tabernacle
Jas	2:25	**In the same way**, was not even Rahab the prostitute considered
1Pe	3: 1	Wives, **in the same way** be submissive to your husbands so that,
	3: 7	**in the same way** be considerate as you live with your wives,
	5: 5	**in the same way** be submissive to those who are older.
Jude	1: 8	**In the** very **same way**, these dreamers pollute their own bodies,
Rev	2:15	have those who hold to the teaching of the Nicolaitans. [RPG]
	8:12	A third of the day was without light, and **also** a third of the night.

3932 ὁμοίωσις, *homoiōsis* [1] [√ *3927*]

likeness [1]

Jas	3: 9	and with it we curse men, who have been made in God's **likeness**.

3933 ὁμολογέω, *homologeō* [26] [→ *469, 2018, 3934,* *3935; cf. 3927 + 3306*]

acknowledge [6], confess [5], acknowledges [4], *untranslated* [1], acknowledged that [1], acknowledges that [1], admit [1], admitted [1], claim [1], confess faith [1], confessed [1], made confession [+*3934*] [1], promised [1], tell plainly [1]

Mt	7:23	Then *I will* **tell** them **plainly**, 'I never knew you. Away from me,
	10:32	"Whoever **acknowledges** me before men, I will also acknowledge
	10:32	I *will* also **acknowledge** him before my Father in heaven.
	14: 7	that *he* **promised** with an oath to give her whatever she asked.
Lk	12: 8	"I tell you, whoever **acknowledges** me before men, the Son of Man
	12: 8	the Son of Man *will* also **acknowledge** him before the angels of
Jn	1:20	He did not fail *to* **confess**, but confessed freely, "I am not the
	1:20	did not fail to confess, but **confessed** *freely*, "I am not the Christ."
	9:22	who **acknowledged that** Jesus was the Christ would be put out of
	12:42	because of the Pharisees *they would* not **confess** their **faith** in
Ac	7:17	"As the time drew near for God to fulfill his promise [RPG] to
	23: 8	neither angels nor spirits, but the Pharisees **acknowledge** them all.)
	24:14	I **admit** that I worship the God of our fathers as a follower of the
Ro	10: 9	That *if you* **confess** with your mouth, "Jesus is Lord," and believe
	10:10	and it is with your mouth that *you* **confess** and are saved.
1Ti	6:12	*when you* **made** *your* good **confession** [+*3934*] in the presence of
Tit	1:16	*They* **claim** to know God, but by their actions they deny him.
Heb	11:13	And *they* **admitted** that they were aliens and strangers on earth.
	13:15	to God a sacrifice of praise—the fruit of lips that **confess** his name.

1Jn 1: 9 If *we* **confess** our sins, he is faithful and just and will forgive us
      2:23 has the Father; whoever **acknowledges** the Son has the Father also.
      4: 2 Every spirit that **acknowledges that** Jesus Christ has come in the
      4: 3 but every spirit that *does* not **acknowledge** Jesus is not from God.
      4:15 If anyone **acknowledges** that Jesus is the Son of God, God lives in
2Jn 1: 7 who *do* not **acknowledge** Jesus Christ as coming in the flesh,
Rev 3: 5 but *will* **acknowledge** his name before my Father and his angels.

3934 ὁμολογία, *homologia* [6] [√ 3933]

confess [1], confession [1], faith we profess [1], made confession [+3933] [1], made confession [1], profess [1]

2Co 9:13 that *accompanies* your **confession** of the gospel of Christ,
1Ti 6:12 *when you* **made** *your* good **confession** [+3933] in the presence of
      6:13 while testifying before Pontius Pilate **made** the good **confession**,
Heb 3: 1 thoughts on Jesus, the apostle and high priest whom we **confess**.
      4:14 Jesus the Son of God, let us hold firmly to the **faith we profess**.
   10:23 Let us hold unswervingly to the hope we **profess**, for he who

3935 ὁμολογουμένως, *homologoumenōs* [1] [√ 3933]

Beyond all question [1]

1Ti 3:16 **Beyond all question**, the mystery of godliness is great:

3936 ὁμόσε, *homose* Not used in UBS/NIV [√ 3927]

3937 ὁμότεχνος, *homotechnos* [1] [√ 3927 + 5492]

as [1]

Ac 18: 3 and because he was a tentmaker **as** they were, he stayed

3938 ὁμοῦ, *homou* [4] [√ 3927]

together [3], both [+1545+3836] [1]

Jn 4:36 eternal life, so that the sower and the reaper may be glad **together**.
  20: 4 **Both** [+1545+3836] were running, but the other disciple outran
  21: 2 the sons of Zebedee, and two other disciples were **together**.
Ac 2: 1 the day of Pentecost came, they were all **together** in one place.

3939 ὁμόφρων, *homophrōn* [1] [√ 3927 + 5856]

live in harmony with [1]

1Pe 3: 8 Finally, all of you, **live in harmony with** *one another*;

3940 ὅμως, *homōs* [3] [√ 3927]

at the same time [1], even in the case of [1], just as [1]

Jn 12:42 Yet **at the same time** many even among the leaders believed in
1Co 14: 7 **Even in the case of** lifeless things that make sounds, such as the
Gal 3:15 **Just as** no one can set aside or add to a human covenant that has

3941 ὄναρ, *onar* [6]

dream [6]

Mt 1:20 an angel of the Lord appeared to him in a **dream** and said,
    2:12 And having been warned in a **dream** not to go back to Herod,
    2:13 had gone, an angel of the Lord appeared to Joseph in a **dream**.
    2:19 an angel of the Lord appeared in a **dream** to Joseph in Egypt
    2:22 Having been warned in a **dream**, he withdrew to the district of
  27:19 for I have suffered a great deal today in a **dream** because of him."

3942 ὀνάριον, *onarion* [1] [√ 3952]

young donkey [1]

Jn 12:14 Jesus found a **young donkey** and sat upon it, as it is written,

3943 ὀνειδίζω, *oneidizō* [9] [√ 3945]

insult [3], heaped insults on [2], denounce [1], finding fault [1], insulted [1], rebuked [1]

Mt 5:11 "Blessed are you when *people* **insult** you, persecute you and falsely
  11:20 Then Jesus began *to* **denounce** the cities in which most of his
  27:44 robbers who were crucified with him also **heaped insults on** him.
Mk 15:32 and believe." Those crucified with him also **heaped insults on** him.
  16:14 he **rebuked** them for their lack of faith and their stubborn refusal
Lk 6:22 when they exclude you and **insult** you and reject your name as
Ro 15: 3 is written: "The insults *of those who* **insult** you have fallen on me."
Jas 1: 5 should ask God, who gives generously to all without **finding fault**,
1Pe 4:14 If *you are* **insulted** because of the name of Christ, you are blessed,

3944 ὀνειδισμός, *oneidismos* [5] [√ 3945]

disgrace [3], insult [1], insults [1]

Ro 15: 3 is written: "The **insults** of those who insult you have fallen on me."
1Ti 3: 7 so that he will not fall into **disgrace** and into the devil's trap.
Heb 10:33 Sometimes you were publicly exposed *to* **insult** and persecution;
  11:26 He regarded **disgrace** for the sake of Christ as of greater value than
  13:13 go to him outside the camp, bearing the **disgrace** he bore.

3945 ὄνειδος, *oneidos* [1] [→ 3943, 3944]

disgrace [1]

Lk 1:25 shown his favor and taken away my **disgrace** among the people."

3946 Ὀνήσιμος, *Onēsimos* [2] [√ 3949]

Onesimus [2]

Col 4: 9 He is coming with **Onesimus**, our faithful and dear brother,
Phm 1:10 I appeal to you for my son **Onesimus**, who became my son while I

3947 Ὀνησίφορος, *Onēsiphoros* [2] [√ 3949 + 5770]

Onesiphorus [2]

2Ti 1:16 May the Lord show mercy to the household *of* **Onesiphorus**,
    4:19 Greet Priscilla and Aquila and the household *of* **Onesiphorus**.

3948 ὀνικός, *onikos* [2] [√ 3952]

large millstone [+3685] [2]

Mt 18: 6 it would be better for him to have a **large millstone** [+3685] hung
Mk 9:42 into the sea with a **large millstone** [+3685] tied around his neck.

3949 ὀνίνημι, *oninēmi* [1] [→ 493, 3946, 3947]

benefit [1]

Phm 1:20 brother, *that I may have some* **benefit** from you in the Lord;

3950 ὄνομα, *onoma* [231] [→ 2226, 2381, 3951, 5540, 6024]

ἐπικαλεῖν τὸ ὄνομα (to call upon the name) [8] Ac 2:21; 9:14,21; 15:17; 22:16; Ro 10:13; 1Co 1:2; Jas 2:7
καλέω ... ὄνομα (call ... name) [9] Mt 1:21,23,25; Lk 1:13,31, 59,61; 2:21; 19:2; Rev 19:13
ὄνομα θεοῦ (name of God) [5] Jn 3:18; Ro 2:24; 1Ti 6:1; Rev 3:12; 16:9
ὄνομα Ἰησοῦ (name of Jesus) [12] Ac 2:38; 3:6; 4:10,18; 5:40; 8:12; 9:27; 10:48; 16:18; 26:9; Php 2:10; Col 3:17
ὄνομα κυρίου (name of the Lord) [21] Mt 21:9; 23:39; Mk 11:9; Lk 13:35; 19:38; Jn 12:13; Ac 2:21; 8:16; 9:28; 19:5,13,17; 21:13; Ro 10:13; 1Co 6:11; Col 3:17; 2Th 1:12; 3:6; 2Ti 2:19; Jas 5:10,14
ὄνομα Χριστοῦ (name of Christ) [7] Ac 2:38; 3:6; 4:10; 8:12; 10:48; 16:18; 1Pe 4:14

name [156], named [31], names [9], *untranslated* [7], me [+1609+3836] [4], because heˢ is [+1650] [3], named [+899] [2], you [+3836+5148] [2], call [+2813+3836] [1], called

[+3836+4005] [1], called [+4005] [1], called [1], group [+4063] [1], him [+899+3836] [1], himself^s [+899+3836] [1], invoke the name [+3951] [1], my [+1609+3836] [1], name [+2813+3836] [1], name's [1], named [+2813+3836] [1], people [+476] [1], people [1], reputation [1], title given [+3951] [1], title [1]

Mt   1:21 will give birth to a son, and you are to give him the **name** Jesus,
    1:23 birth to a son, and *they will* **call** [+2813+3836] him Immanuel"—
    1:25 her until she gave birth to a son. And he gave him the **name** Jesus.
    6: 9 you should pray: " 'Our Father in heaven, hallowed be your **name**,
    7:22 to me on that day, 'Lord, Lord, did we not prophesy *in* your **name**,
    7:22 and *in* your **name** drive out demons and perform many miracles?'
    7:22 and in your name drive out demons **[RPG]** and perform many
  10: 2 These are the **names** of the twelve apostles: first, Simon (who is
  10:22 All men will hate you because of **me** [+1609+3836], but he who
  10:41 Anyone who receives a prophet **because he**^s [+1650] **is** a prophet
  10:41 and anyone who receives a righteous man **because he**^s [+1650] **is**
  10:42 of cold water to one of these little ones **because he**^s [+1650] **is**
  12:21 *In* his **name** the nations will put their hope."
  18: 5 "And whoever welcomes a little child like this in my **name**
  18:20 For where two or three come together in my **name**, there am I with
  19:29 or fields for **my** [+1609+3836] sake will receive a hundred times
  21: 9 "Blessed is he who comes in the **name** of the Lord!" "Hosanna in
  23:39 until you say, 'Blessed is he who comes in the **name** of the Lord.' "
  24: 5 For many will come in my **name**, claiming, 'I am the Christ,'
  24: 9 and you will be hated by all nations because of **me** [+1609+3836].
  27:32 they were going out, they met a man from Cyrene, **named** Simon,
  27:57 there came a rich man from Arimathea, **named** Joseph,
  28:19 baptizing them in the **name** of the Father and of the Son and of the
Mk   3:16 twelve he appointed: Simon (to whom he gave the **name** Peter);
    3:17 and his brother John (to them he gave the **name** Boanerges,
    5: 9 Jesus asked him, "What is your **name**?" "My name is Legion,"
    5: 9 your name?" "My **name** is Legion," he replied, "for we are many."
    5:22 Then one of the synagogue rulers, **named** Jairus, came there.
    6:14 Herod heard about this, for Jesus' **name** had become well known.
    9:37 "Whoever welcomes one of these little children in my **name**
    9:38 "we saw a man driving out demons in your **name** and we told him
    9:39 "No one who does a miracle in my **name** can in the next moment
    9:41 anyone who gives you a cup of water in my **name** because you
  11: 9 "Hosanna!" "Blessed is he who comes in the **name** of the Lord!"
  13: 6 Many will come in my **name**, claiming, 'I am he,' and will deceive
  13:13 All men will hate you because of **me** [+1609+3836], but he who
  14:32 They went to a place **called** [+3836+4005] Gethsemane, and Jesus
  16:17 In my **name** they will drive out demons; they will speak in new
Lk   1: 5 In the time of Herod king of Judea there was a priest **named**
    1: 5 his wife **[RPG]** Elizabeth was also a descendant of Aaron.
    1:13 will bear you a son, and you are to give him the **name** John.
    1:26 God sent the angel Gabriel **[NIE]** to Nazareth, a town in Galilee,
    1:27 to a virgin pledged to be married to a man **named** Joseph,
    1:27 a descendant of David. The virgin's **name** was Mary.
    1:31 and give birth to a son, and you are to give him the **name** Jesus.
    1:49 the Mighty One has done great things for me—holy is his **name**.
    1:59 and *they were going to* **name** [+2813+3836] him after his father
    1:61 "There is no one among your relatives who has that **name**."
    1:63 and to everyone's astonishment he wrote, "His **name** is John."
    2:21 it was time to circumcise him, he *was* **named** [+2813+3836] Jesus,
    2:25 Now there was a man in Jerusalem **called** [+4005] Simeon,
    5:27 and saw a tax collector *by* the **name** of Levi sitting at his tax
    6:22 they exclude you and insult you and reject your **name** as evil,
    8:30 Jesus asked him, "What is your **name**?" "Legion," he replied,
    8:41 Then a man **named** Jairus, a ruler of the synagogue, came
    9:48 "Whoever welcomes this little child in my **name** welcomes me;
    9:49 "we saw a man driving out demons in your **name** and we tried to
  10:17 and said, "Lord, even the demons submit to us in your **name**."
  10:20 submit to you, but rejoice that your **names** are written in heaven."
  10:38 he came to a village where a woman **named** Martha opened her
  11: 2 say: "Father, hallowed be your **name**, your kingdom come.
  13:35 until you say, 'Blessed is he who comes in the **name** of the Lord.' "
  16:20 At his gate was laid a beggar **named** Lazarus, covered with sores
  19: 2 A man was there *by* the **name** of Zacchaeus; he was a chief tax
  19:38 "Blessed is the king who comes in the **name** of the Lord!" "Peace
  21: 8 For many will come in my **name**, claiming, 'I am he,' and,
  21:12 before kings and governors, and all on account of my **name**.
  21:17 All men will hate you because of **me** [+1609+3836].
  23:50 Now there was a man **named** Joseph, a member of the Council,
  24:13 Now that same day two of them were going to a village **called**

  24:18 One of them, **named** Cleopas, asked him, "Are you only a visitor to
  24:47 and forgiveness of sins will be preached in his **name** to all nations,
Jn   1: 6 There came a man who was sent from God; his **name** was John.
    1:12 Yet to all who received him, to those who believed in his **name**,
    2:23 saw the miraculous signs he was doing and believed in his **name**.
    3: 1 Now there was a man of the Pharisees **named** [+899] Nicodemus,
    3:18 because he has not believed in the **name** of God's one and only
    5:43 I have come in my Father's **name**, and you do not accept me;
    5:43 but if someone else comes in his own **name**, you will accept him.
  10: 3 to his voice. He calls his own sheep by **name** and leads them out.
  10:25 not believe. The miracles I do in my Father's **name** speak for me,
  12:13 "Hosanna!" "Blessed is he who comes in the **name** of the Lord!"
  12:28 Father, glorify your **name**!" Then a voice came from heaven,
  14:13 And I will do whatever you ask in my **name**, so that the Son may
  14:14 You may ask me for anything in my **name**, and I will do it.
  14:26 the Holy Spirit, whom the Father will send in my **name**,
  15:16 Then the Father will give you whatever you ask in my **name**.
  15:21 They will treat you this way because of my **name**, for they do not
  16:23 the truth, my Father will give you whatever you ask in my **name**.
  16:24 Until now you have not asked for anything in my **name**. Ask
  16:26 In that day you will ask in my **name**. I am not saying that I will ask
  17: 6 "I have revealed **you** [+3836+5148] to those whom you gave me
  17:11 Holy Father, protect them by the power of your **name**—the name
  17:12 I protected them and kept them safe by that **name** you gave me.
  17:26 I have made **you** [+3836+5148] known to them, and will continue
  18:10 cutting off his right ear. (The servant's **name** was Malchus.)
  20:31 Son of God, and that by believing you may have life in his **name**.
Ac   1:15 In those days Peter stood up among the believers (a **group** [+4063]
    2:21 And everyone who calls on the **name** of the Lord will be saved.'
    2:38 in the **name** of Jesus Christ for the forgiveness of your sins.
    3: 6 I have I give you. In the **name** of Jesus Christ of Nazareth, walk."
    3:16 By faith *in* the **name** of Jesus, this man whom you see and know
    3:16 It is Jesus' **name** and the faith that comes through him that has
    4: 7 to question them: "By what power or what **name** did you do this?"
    4:10 It is by the **name** of Jesus Christ of Nazareth, whom you crucified
    4:12 for there is no other **name** under heaven given to men by which we
    4:17 must warn these men to speak no longer to anyone in this **name**."
    4:18 commanded them not to speak or teach at all in the **name** of Jesus.
    4:30 and wonders through the **name** of your holy servant Jesus."
    5: 1 Now a man **named** Ananias, together with his wife Sapphira,
    5:28 "We gave you strict orders not to teach in this **name**," he said.
    5:34 But a Pharisee **named** Gamaliel, a teacher of the law, who was
    5:40 Then they ordered them not to speak in the **name** of Jesus,
    5:41 they had been counted worthy of suffering disgrace for the **Name**.
    8: 9 Now for some time a man **named** Simon had practiced sorcery in
    8:12 good news of the kingdom of God and the **name** of Jesus Christ,
    8:16 they had simply been baptized into the **name** of the Lord Jesus.
    9:10 In Damascus there was a disciple **named** Ananias. The Lord called
    9:11 on Straight Street and ask for a man from Tarsus **named** Saul,
    9:12 In a vision he has seen a man **named** Ananias come and place his
    9:14 from the chief priests to arrest all who call on your **name**."
    9:15 This man is my chosen instrument to carry my **name** before the
    9:16 I will show him how much he must suffer for my **name**."
    9:21 raised havoc in Jerusalem among those who call on this **name**?
    9:27 and how in Damascus he had preached fearlessly in the **name** of
    9:28 about freely in Jerusalem, speaking boldly in the **name** of the Lord.
    9:33 There he found a man **named** Aeneas, a paralytic who had been
    9:36 In Joppa there was a disciple **named** Tabitha, (which,
  10: 1 At Caesarea there was a man **named** Cornelius, a centurion who
  10:43 believes in him receives forgiveness of sins through his **name**."
  10:48 So he ordered that they be baptized in the **name** of Jesus Christ.
  11:28 **named** Agabus, stood up and through the Spirit predicted that a
  12:13 and a servant girl **named** Rhoda came to answer the door.
  13: 6 they met a Jewish sorcerer and false prophet **named** Bar-Jesus,
  13: 8 But Elymas the sorcerer (for that is what his **name** means)
  15:14 by taking from the Gentiles a people *for* **himself**^s [+899+3836].
  15:17 and all the Gentiles who bear my **name**, says the Lord, who does
  15:26 men who have risked their lives for the **name** of our Lord Jesus
  16: 1 and then to Lystra, where a disciple **named** Timothy lived,
  16:14 One of those listening was a woman **named** Lydia, a dealer in
  16:18 "In the **name** of Jesus Christ I command you to come out of her!"
  17:34 also a woman **named** Damaris, and a number of others.
  18: 2 There he met a Jew **named** Aquila, a native of Pontus, who had
  18: 7 and went next door to the house **[NIE]** of Titius Justus,
  18:15 it involves questions about words and **names** and your own law—
  18:24 Meanwhile a Jew **named** Apollos, a native of Alexandria,

19: 5 hearing this, they were baptized into the **name** of the Lord Jesus.
19:13 to **invoke the name** [+3951] of the Lord Jesus over those who
19:17 with fear, and the **name** of the Lord Jesus was held in high honor.
19:24 A silversmith **named** Demetrius, who made silver shrines of
20: 9 Seated in a window was a young man **named** Eutychus, who was
21:10 number of days, a prophet **named** Agabus came down from Judea.
21:13 but also to die in Jerusalem for the **name** of the Lord Jesus."
22:16 be baptized and wash your sins away, calling on his **name**.'
26: 9 do all that was possible to oppose the **name** of Jesus of Nazareth.
27: 1 and some other prisoners were handed over to a centurion **named**
28: 7 There was an estate nearby that belonged to [NIE] Publius,

Ro 1: 5 Through him and for his **name's** sake, we received grace
    2:24 "God's **name** is blasphemed among the Gentiles because of you."
    9:17 in you and that my **name** might be proclaimed in all the earth."
   10:13 "Everyone who calls on the **name** of the Lord will be saved."
   15: 9 praise you among the Gentiles; I will sing hymns to your **name**."

1Co 1: 2 together with all those everywhere who call on the **name** of our
    1:10 I appeal to you, brothers, in the **name** of our Lord Jesus Christ,
    1:13 Paul crucified for you? Were you baptized into the **name** of Paul?
    1:15 so no one can say that you were baptized into my **name**.
    5: 4 When you are assembled in the **name** of our Lord Jesus and I am
    6:11 you were justified in the **name** of the Lord Jesus Christ and by the

Eph 1:21 and dominion, and every **title** that can be given [+3951],
    5:20 for everything, in the **name** of our Lord Jesus Christ.

Php 2: 9 the highest place and gave him the **name** that is above every name,
    2: 9 the highest place and gave him the name that is above every **name**,
    2:10 that at the **name** of Jesus every knee should bow, in heaven
    4: 3 the rest of my fellow workers, whose **names** are in the book of life.

Col 3:17 whether in word or deed, do it all in the **name** of the Lord Jesus,
2Th 1:12 so that the **name** of our Lord Jesus may be glorified in you,
    3: 6 In the **name** of the Lord Jesus Christ, we command you, brothers,
1Ti 6: 1 so that God's **name** and our teaching may not be slandered.
2Ti 2:19 "Everyone who confesses the **name** of the Lord must turn away
Heb 1: 4 So he became as much superior to the angels as the **name** he has
    2:12 He says, "I will declare your **name** to my brothers; in the presence
    6:10 and the love you have shown **him** [+899+3836] as you have helped
   13:15 to God a sacrifice of praise—the fruit of lips that confess his **name**.
Jas 2: 7 Are they not the ones who are slandering the noble **name** of him to
    5:10 suffering, take the prophets who spoke in the **name** of the Lord.
    5:14 to pray over him and anoint him with oil in the **name** of the Lord.
1Pe 4:14 If you are insulted because of the **name** of Christ, you are blessed,
    4:16 do not be ashamed, but praise God that you bear that **name**.
1Jn 2:12 because your sins have been forgiven on account of his **name**.
    3:23 to believe in the **name** of his Son, Jesus Christ, and to love one
    5:13 I write these things to you who believe in the **name** of the Son of
3Jn 1: 7 It was for the sake of the **Name** that they went out, receiving no
    1:14 friends here send their greetings. Greet the friends there by **name**.
Rev 2: 3 You have persevered and have endured hardships for my **name**,
    2:13 where Satan has his throne. Yet you remain true to my **name**.
    2:17 I will also give him a white stone with a new **name** written on it,
    3: 1 you have a **reputation** of being alive, but you are dead.
    3: 4 Yet you have a few **people** in Sardis who have not soiled their
    3: 5 I will never blot out his **name** from the book of life, but will
    3: 5 but will acknowledge his **name** before my Father and his angels.
    3: 8 yet you have kept my word and have not denied my **name**.
    3:12 I will write on him the **name** of my God and the name of the city
    3:12 on him the name of my God and the **name** of the city of my God,
    3:12 heaven from my God; and I will also write on him my new **name**.
    6: 8 Its rider was **named** [+899] Death, and Hades was following close
    8:11 the **name** of the star is Wormwood. A third of the waters turned
    9:11 whose **name** in Hebrew is Abaddon, and in Greek, Apollyon.
    9:11 name in Hebrew is Abaddon, and in Greek, [RPG] Apollyon.
   11:13 Seven thousand **people** [+476] were killed in the earthquake,
   11:18 the prophets and your saints and those who reverence your **name**,
   13: 1 ten crowns on his horns, and on each head a blasphemous **name**.
   13: 6 and to slander his **name** and his dwelling place and those who live
   13: 8 all whose **names** have not been written in the book of life
   13:17 which is the **name** of the beast or the number of his name.
   13:17 which is the name of the beast or the number of his **name**.
   14: 1 and with him 144,000 who had his **name** and his Father's name
   14: 1 had his name and his Father's **name** written on their foreheads.
   14:11 and his image, or for anyone who receives the mark of his **name**."
   15: 2 over the beast and his image and over the number of his **name**.
   15: 4 Who will not fear you, O Lord, and bring glory to your **name**?
   16: 9 were seared by the intense heat and they cursed the **name** of God,
   17: 3 on a scarlet beast that was covered with blasphemous **names**

17: 5 This **title** was written on her forehead: MYSTERY BABYLON
17: 8 The inhabitants of the earth whose **names** have not been written in
19:12 He has a **name** written on him that no one knows but he himself.
19:13 in a robe dipped in blood, and his **name** is the Word of God.
19:16 On his robe and on his thigh he has this **name** written: KING OF
21:12 On the gates were written the **names** of the twelve tribes of Israel.
21:12 On the gates were written the names [RPG] of the twelve tribes
21:14 and on them were the **names** of the twelve apostles of the Lamb.
22: 4 They will see his face, and his **name** will be on their foreheads.

3951   ὀνομάζω, onomazō [10] [√ 3950]

a hint of [1], calls [1], confesses [1], derives name [1], designated [1], designating [1], invoke the name [+3950] [1], known [1], named [1], title given [+3950] [1]

Mk 3:14 He appointed twelve—**designating** them apostles—that they might
Lk 6:13 and chose twelve of them, whom he also **designated** apostles:
    6:14 Simon (whom he **named** Peter), his brother Andrew, James,
Ac 19:13 to **invoke the name** [+3950] of the Lord Jesus over those who
Ro 15:20 my ambition to preach the gospel where Christ was not **known**,
1Co 5:11 you must not associate with anyone who **calls** himself a brother
Eph 1:21 and dominion, and every **title** [+3950] that can be given,
    3:15 whom his whole family in heaven and on earth **derives** its **name**.
    5: 3 But among you there must not be even **a hint of** sexual
2Ti 2:19 "Everyone who **confesses** the name of the Lord must turn away

3952   ὄνος, onos [5] [→ 3942, 3948]

donkey [4], donkey's [1]

Mt 21: 2 and at once you will find a **donkey** tied there, with her colt by her.
   21: 5 gentle and riding on a **donkey**, on a colt, the foal of a donkey.' "
   21: 7 They brought the **donkey** and the colt, placed their cloaks on them,
Lk 13:15 his ox or **donkey** from the stall and lead it out to give it water?
Jn 12:15 of Zion; see, your king is coming, seated on a **donkey's** colt."

3953   ὄντως, ontōs [10] [√ 1639]

really in need [3], really [2], certainly [1], indeed [1], it is true [1], surely [1], truly [1]

Mk 11:32 the people, for everyone held that John **really** was a prophet.)
Lk 23:47 praised God and said, "**Surely** this was a righteous man."
   24:34 and saying, "**It is true**! The Lord has risen and has appeared to
Jn 8:36 So if the Son sets you free, you will be free **indeed**.
1Co 14:25 down and worship God, exclaiming, "God is **really** among you!"
Gal 3:21 then righteousness would **certainly** have come by the law.
1Ti 5: 3 Give proper recognition to those widows who are **really in need**.
    5: 5 The widow who is **really in need** and left all alone puts her hope
    5:16 so that the church can help those widows who are **really in need**.
    6:19 coming age, so that they may take hold of the life that is **truly** life.

3954   ὄξος, oxos [6] [√ 3955]

wine vinegar [4], drink [1], its [+3836] [1]

Mt 27:48 He filled it with **wine vinegar**, put it on a stick, and offered it to
Mk 15:36 One man ran, filled a sponge with **wine vinegar**, put it on a stick,
Lk 23:36 also came up and mocked him. They offered him **wine vinegar**
Jn 19:29 A jar of **wine vinegar** was there,
   19:29 of wine vinegar was there, so they soaked a sponge in **its** [+3836],
   19:30 When he had received the **drink**, Jesus said, "It is finished."

3955   ὄξύς, oxys [8] [→ 3954, 4236, 4237]

sharp [7], swift [1]

Ro 3:15 "Their feet are **swift** to shed blood;
Rev 1:16 and out of his mouth came a **sharp** double-edged sword.
    2:12 These are the words of him who has the **sharp**, double-edged
   14:14 with a crown of gold on his head and a **sharp** sickle in his hand.
   14:17 came out of the temple in heaven, and he too had a **sharp** sickle.
   14:18 and called in a loud voice to him who had the **sharp** sickle,
   14:18 "Take your **sharp** sickle and gather the clusters of grapes from the
   19:15 Out of his mouth comes a **sharp** sword with which to strike down

3956 ὀπή, opē [2]

holes [1], spring [1]

Heb 11:38   in deserts and mountains, and in caves and **holes** in the ground.
Jas   3:11   Can both fresh water and salt water flow from the same **spring**?

3957 ὄπισθεν, opisthen [7] [√ 3958]

behind [4], after [1], in back [1], on both sides [+2277+2779] [1]

Mt   9:20   had been subject to bleeding for twelve years came up **behind** him
    15:23   and urged him, "Send her away, for she keeps crying out **after** us."
Mk   5:27   she came up **behind** him in the crowd and touched his cloak,
Lk   8:44   She came up **behind** him and touched the edge of his cloak,
   23:26   and put the cross on him and made him carry it **behind** Jesus.
Rev   4:6   and they were covered with eyes, in front and **in back**.
    5:1   on the throne a scroll with writing **on both sides** [+2277+2779]

3958 ὀπίσω, opisō [35 / 36] [→ 3957, 5541]

after [11], behind [5], back [+1650+3836] [4], follow [3], follow [+4513] [2], back [1], follow [+199] [1], follow [+2262] [1], followed [+599] [1], followed [1], from [1], led in revolt [+923] [1], overtake [1], perversion [+599+2283+4922] [1], turned around [+1650+3836+5138] [1], turned back [+599+1650+3836] [1]

Mt   3:11   But **after** me will come one who is more powerful than I,
    4:10   Jesus said to him, "Away **from** [UBS−] me, Satan! For it is written:
    4:19   "Come, **follow** me," Jesus said, "and I will make you fishers of
   10:38   does not take his cross and **follow** [+199] me is not worthy of me.
   16:23   Jesus turned and said to Peter, "Get **behind** me, Satan! You are a
   16:24   "If anyone would come **after** me, he must deny himself and take up
   24:18   Let no one in the field go **back** to get his cloak.
Mk   1:7   "**After** me will come one more powerful than I, the thongs of
    1:17   "Come, **follow** me," Jesus said, "and I will make you fishers of
    1:20   Zebedee in the boat with the hired men and **followed** [+599] him.
    8:33   at his disciples, he rebuked Peter. "Get **behind** me, Satan!" he said.
    8:34   "If anyone would come **after** me, he must deny himself and take up
   13:16   Let no one in the field go **back** [+1650+3836] to get his cloak.
Lk   7:38   and as she stood **behind** him at his feet weeping, she began to wet
    9:23   "If anyone would come **after** me, he must deny himself and take up
    9:62   and looks **back** [+1650+3836] is fit for service in the kingdom of
   14:27   not carry his cross and **follow** [+2262] me cannot be my disciple.
   17:31   no one in the field should go **back** [+1650+3836] for anything.
   19:14   "But his subjects hated him and sent a delegation **after** him to say,
   21:8   'I am he,' and, 'The time is near.' Do not **follow** [+4513] them.
Jn   1:15   'He who comes **after** me has surpassed me because he was before
    1:27   He is the one who comes **after** me, the thongs of whose sandals I
    1:30   'A man who comes **after** me has surpassed me because he was
    6:66   many of his disciples **turned back** [+599+1650+3836] and no
   12:19   us nowhere. Look how the whole world has gone **after** him!"
   18:6   "I am he," they drew **back** [+1650+3836] and fell to the ground.
   20:14   At this, *she* **turned around** [+1650+3836+5138] and saw Jesus
Ac   5:37   in the days of the census and **led** a band of people **in revolt** [+923].
   20:30   and distort the truth in order to draw away disciples **after** them.
Php   3:13   Forgetting what is **behind** and straining toward what is ahead,
1Ti   5:15   Some have in fact already turned away to **follow** Satan.
2Pe   2:10   This is especially true of those *who* **follow** [+4513] the corrupt
Jude   1:7   Sodom and Gomorrah and the surrounding towns gave themselves up to sexual immorality and **perversion** [+599+2283+4922].
Rev   1:10   in the Spirit, and I heard **behind** me a loud voice like a trumpet,
   12:15   to **overtake** the woman and sweep her away with the torrent.
   13:3   The whole world was astonished and **followed** the beast.

3959 ὁπλίζω, hoplizō [1] [√ 3960]

arm [1]

1Pe   4:1   suffered in his body, **arm** yourselves also *with* the same attitude,

3960 ὅπλον, hoplon [6] [→ 2774, 3959, 4110]

instruments [2], weapons [2], armor [1], weapons fight with [+3836+5127] [1]

Jn   18:3   and Pharisees. They were carrying torches, lanterns and **weapons**.
Ro   6:13   as **instruments** of wickedness, but rather offer yourselves to God,
   6:13   and offer the parts of your body to him as **instruments** of
   13:12   us put aside the deeds of darkness and put on the **armor** of light.
2Co   6:7   with **weapons** of righteousness in the right hand and in the left;
   10:4   The **weapons** [+3836+5127] we **fight with** are not the weapons of

3961 ὁποῖος, hopoios [5] [√ 4544]

the quality [1], what [+5525] [1], what kind of [1], what [1], whatever [1]

Ac   26:29   but all who are listening to me today may become **what** [+5525] I
1Co   3:13   with fire, and the fire will test **the quality** of each man's work.
Gal   2:6   to be important—**whatever** they were makes no difference to me;
1Th   1:9   for they themselves report **what kind of** reception you gave us.
Jas   1:24   at himself, goes away and immediately forgets **what** he looks like.

3962 ὁπότε, hopote   Not used in UBS/NIV   [√ 4544]

3963 ὅπου, hopou [82] [√ 4544]

where [58], wherever [+1569] [5], *untranslated* [3], wherever [3], here [2], whenever [+1569] [2], wherever [+323] [2], above Jesus [1], in the case of [1], on[s] the other side [1], since [1], the place where [1], together [1], yet even [1]

Mt   6:19   **where** moth and rust destroy, and where thieves break in and steal.
    6:19   where moth and rust destroy, and **where** thieves break in and steal.
    6:20   **where** moth and rust do not destroy, and where thieves do not
    6:20   rust do not destroy, and **where** thieves do not break in and steal.
    6:21   For **where** your treasure is, there your heart will be also.
    8:19   and said, "Teacher, I will follow you **wherever** [+1569] you go."
   13:5   Some fell on rocky places, **where** it did not have much soil.
   24:28   **Wherever** [+1569] there is a carcass, there the vultures will gather.
   25:24   harvesting **where** you have not sown and gathering where you
   25:26   So you knew that I harvest **where** I have not sown and gather
   26:13   **wherever** [+1569] this gospel is preached throughout the world,
   26:57   where the teachers of the law and the elders had assembled.
   28:6   he has risen, just as he said. Come and see the place **where** he lay.
Mk   2:4   of the crowd, they made an opening in the roof **above Jesus** and,
    2:4   lowered the mat **[RPG]** the paralyzed man was lying on.
    4:5   Some fell on rocky places, **where** it did not have much soil.
    4:15   Some people are like seed along the path, **where** the word is sown.
    5:40   the disciples who were with him, and went in **where** the child was.
    6:10   **Whenever** [+1569] you enter a house, stay there until you leave
    6:55   and carried the sick on mats to **wherever** they heard he was.
    6:56   And **wherever** [+323] he went—into villages, towns
    9:18   **Whenever** [+1569] it seizes him, it throws him to the ground.
    9:48   **where** " 'their worm does not die, and the fire is not quenched.'
   13:14   that causes desolation' standing **where** it docs not belong—
   14:9   **wherever** [+1569] the gospel is preached throughout the world,
   14:14   Say to the owner of the house **[NIE]** he enters, 'The Teacher asks:
   14:14   my guest room, **where** I may eat the Passover with my disciples?'
   16:6   He has risen! He is not here. See the place **where** they laid him.
Lk   9:57   a man said to him, "I will follow you **wherever** [+1569] you go."
   12:33   not be exhausted, **where** no thief comes near and no moth destroys.
   12:34   For **where** your treasure is, there your heart will be also.
   17:37   He replied, "**Where** there is a dead body, there the vultures will
   22:11   the guest room, **where** I may eat the Passover with my disciples?'
Jn   1:28   Bethany on the other side of the Jordan, **where** John was baptizing.
    3:8   The wind blows **wherever** it pleases. You hear its sound, but you
    4:20   but we Jews claim that the place **where** we must worship is in
    4:46   visited Cana in Galilee, **where** he had turned the water into wine.
    6:23   Then some boats from Tiberias landed near the place **where** the
    6:62   What if you see the Son of Man ascend to **where** he was before!
    7:34   but you will not find me; and **where** I am, you cannot come."
    7:36   but you will not find me,' and 'Where I am, you cannot come'?"
    7:42   David's family and from Bethlehem, the town **where** David lived?'
    8:21   and you will die in your sin. **Where** I go, you cannot come."
    8:22   kill himself? Is that why he says, 'Where I go, you cannot come'?"
   10:40   Then Jesus went back across the Jordan to the place **where** John
   11:30   the village, but was still at the place **where** Martha had met him.
   11:32   When Mary reached **the place where** Jesus was and saw him,
   12:1   the Passover, Jesus arrived at Bethany, **where** Lazarus lived,
   12:26   me must follow me; and **where** I am, my servant also will be.
   13:33   the Jews, so I tell you now: **Where** I am going, you cannot come.
   13:36   Jesus replied, "**Where** I am going, you cannot follow now,

14: 3 and take you to be with me that you also may be **where** I am.
14: 4 You know the way *to the place* **where** I am going."
17:24 I want those you have given me to be with me **where** I am,
18: 1 On[s] **the other side** there was an olive grove, and he and his
18:20 in synagogues or at the temple, **where** all the Jews come together.
19:18 **Here** they crucified him, and with him two others—one on each
19:20 for the place **where** Jesus was crucified was near the city,
19:41 At the place **where** Jesus was crucified, there was a garden,
20:12 seated **where** Jesus' body had been, one at the head and the other at
20:19 when the disciples were **together**, with the doors locked for fear of
21:18 were younger you dressed yourself and went **where** you wanted;
21:18 else will dress you and lead you **where** you do not want to go."
Ac 17: 1 they came to Thessalonica, **where** there was a Jewish synagogue.
20: 6 days later joined the others at Troas, **where** we stayed seven days.
Ro 15:20 It has always been my ambition to preach the gospel **where** Christ
1Co 3: 3 For **since** there is jealousy and quarreling among you, are you not
Col 3:11 **Here** there is no Greek or Jew, circumcised or uncircumcised,
Heb 6:20 **where** Jesus, who went before us, has entered on our behalf.
9:16 **In the case of** a will, it is necessary to prove the death of the one
10:18 And **where** these have been forgiven, there is no longer any
Jas 3: 4 they are steered by a very small rudder **wherever** the pilot wants to
3:16 For **where** you have envy and selfish ambition, there you find
2Pe 2:11 **yet even** angels, although they are stronger and more powerful,
Rev 2:13 I know where you live—**where** Satan has his throne. Yet you
2:13 who was put to death in your city—**where** Satan lives.
11: 8 called Sodom and Egypt, **where** also their Lord was crucified.
12: 6 for her by God, **where** she might be taken care of for 1,260 days.
12:14 **where** she would be taken care of for a time, times and half a time,
14: 4 themselves pure. They follow the Lamb **wherever** [+323] he goes.
17: 9 The seven heads are seven hills [RPG] on which the woman sits.
20:10 **where** the beast and the false prophet had been thrown.

3964 ὀπτάνομαι, *optanomai* [1] [√ 3972]

appeared [1]

Ac 1: 3 *He* **appeared** to them over a period of forty days and spoke about

3965 ὀπτασία, *optasia* [4] [√ 3972]

vision [3], visions [1]

Lk 1:22 They realized he had seen a **vision** in the temple, for he kept
24:23 They came and told us that they had seen a **vision** of angels,
Ac 26:19 King Agrippa, I was not disobedient *to* the **vision** from heaven.
2Co 12: 1 to be gained, I will go on to **visions** and revelations from the Lord.

3966 ὀπτός, *optos* [1]

broiled [1]

Lk 24:42 They gave him a piece *of* **broiled** fish,

3967 ὀπώρα, *opōra* [1] [→ 5781]

fruit [1]

Rev 18:14 "They will say, 'The **fruit** you longed for is gone from you.

3968 ὅπως, *hopōs* [53] [√ 4544]

to [17], so that [15], that [8], so [3], how [2], so that [+323] [2],
that [+323] [2], *untranslated* [1], in order to [1], let [1], then [1]

Mt 2: 8 you find him, report to me, **so that** I too may go and worship him."
2:23 **So** was fulfilled what was said through the prophets: "He will be
5:16 **that** they may see your good deeds and praise your Father in
5:45 **that** you may be sons of your Father in heaven. He causes his sun
6: 2 do in the synagogues and on the streets, **to** be honored by men.
6: 4 **so that** your giving may be in secret. Then your Father, who sees
6: 5 in the synagogues and on the street corners **to** be seen by men.
6:16 for they disfigure their faces **to** show men they are fasting.
6:18 **so that** it will not be obvious to men that you are fasting, but only
8:17 This was **to** fulfill what was spoken through the prophet Isaiah:
8:34 when they saw him, they pleaded with him **to** leave their region.
9:38 of the harvest, therefore, **to** send out workers into his harvest field."

12:14 But the Pharisees went out and plotted **how** they might kill Jesus.
13:35 **So** was fulfilled what was spoken through the prophet: "I will open
22:15 the Pharisees went out and laid plans **to** trap him in his words.
23:35 **so** upon you will come all the righteous blood that has been shed
26:59 false evidence against Jesus **so that** they could put him to death.
Mk 3: 6 and began to plot with the Herodians **how** they might kill Jesus.
Lk 2:35 **so that** [+323] the thoughts of many hearts will be revealed.
7: 3 elders of the Jews to him, asking him **to** come and heal his servant.
10: 2 of the harvest, therefore, **to** send out workers into his harvest field.
11:37 had finished speaking, a Pharisee invited him **to** eat with him;
16:26 been fixed, **so that** those who want to go from here to you cannot,
16:28 **Let** him warn them, so that they will not also come to this place of
24:20 [NIE] The chief priests and our rulers handed him over to be
Jn 11:57 where Jesus was, he should report it **so that** they might arrest him.
Ac 3:19 **that** [+323] times of refreshing may come from the Lord,
8:15 they prayed for them **that** they might receive the Holy Spirit,
8:24 the Lord for me so that nothing you have said may happen to me."
9: 2 **so that** if he found any there who belonged to the Way,
9:12 Ananias come and place his hands on him **to** restore his sight."
9:17 has sent me **so that** you may see again and be filled with the Holy
9:24 and night they kept close watch on the city gates **in order to** kill
15:17 **that** [+323] the remnant of men may seek the Lord, and all the
20:16 Paul had decided to sail past Ephesus **to** avoid spending time in the
23:15 and the Sanhedrin petition the commander **to** bring him before you
23:20 "The Jews have agreed to ask you **to** bring Paul before the
23:23 and two hundred spearmen **to** go to Caesarea at nine tonight.
25: 3 as a favor to them, **to** have Paul transferred to Jerusalem,
25:26 **so that** as a result of this investigation I may have something to
Ro 3: 4 "So that [+323] you may be proved right when you speak
9:17 **that** I might display my power in you and that my name might be
9:17 in you and **that** my name might be proclaimed in all the earth."
1Co 1:29 **so that** no one may boast before him.
2Co 8:11 **so that** your eager willingness to do it may be matched by your
8:14 plenty will supply what you need. **Then** there will be equality,
Gal 1: 4 who gave himself for our sins **to** rescue us from the present evil
2Th 1:12 **so that** the name of our Lord Jesus may be glorified in you,
Phm 1: 6 I pray that you may be active in sharing your faith, so that you will
Heb 2: 9 **so that** by the grace of God he might taste death for everyone.
9:15 **that** those who are called may receive the promised eternal
Jas 5:16 to each other and pray for each other **so that** you may be healed.
1Pe 2: 9 **that** you may declare the praises of him who called you out of

3969 ὅραμα, *horama* [12] [√ 3972]

vision [8], had a vision [+3972] [1], seen [1], sight [1], vision
[+3972] [1]

Mt 17: 9 Jesus instructed them, "Don't tell anyone what you have **seen**,
Ac 7:31 When he saw this, he was amazed at the **sight**. As he went over to
9:10 The Lord called to him in a **vision**, "Ananias!" "Yes, Lord," he
9:12 In a **vision** he has seen a man named Ananias come and place his
10: 3 One day at about three in the afternoon he had a **vision**.
10:17 Peter was wondering about the meaning of the **vision** [+3972],
10:19 While Peter was still thinking about the **vision**, the Spirit said to
11: 5 "I was in the city of Joppa praying, and in a trance I saw a **vision**.
12: 9 doing was really happening; he thought he was seeing a **vision**.
16: 9 During the night Paul **had a vision** [+3972] of a man of Macedonia
16:10 After Paul had seen the **vision**, we got ready at once to leave for
18: 9 One night the Lord spoke to Paul in a **vision**: "Do not be afraid;

3970 ὅρασις, *horasis* [4] [√ 3972]

appearance [1], resembling [+3927] [1], vision [1], visions [1]

Ac 2:17 and daughters will prophesy, your young men will see **visions**,
Rev 4: 3 And the one who sat there had the **appearance** of jasper
4: 3 A rainbow, **resembling** [+3927] an emerald, encircled the throne.
9:17 The horses and riders I saw in my **vision** looked like this:

3971 ὁρατός, *horatos* [1] [√ 3972]

visible [1]

Col 1:16 things in heaven and on earth, **visible** and invisible,

3972 ὁράω, horaō [449 / 448] see also ἴδε

[→ 548, 898, 927, 1967, 2227, 2228, 2269, 2393, 2775, 2979, 3002, 3587, 3921, 3964, 3965, 3969, 3970, 3971, 4071, 4238, 4632, 4725, 5034, 5287?, 5288?, 5328, 5666, 5708, 5724, 5864; cf. 4057, 4725]

saw [182], see [112], seen [62], appeared [17], looked [9], seeing [7], look [4], realized [4], perceiving [3], see that [3], watched [3], careful [2], dos it [2], indeed seen [+3972] [2], look at [2], looked at [2], noticed [2], noticing [2], responsibility [2], see to it [2], sees [2], *untranslated* [1], appear [1], body decayed [+1426] [1], came upon [1], consider [+4309] [1], die [+2505] [1], experience [1], found [1], had a vision [+3969] [1], make sure that [1], met with [1], met [1], mourn [+4292] [1], saw that [1], seen of [1], settle the matter [1], show [1], the sight of [1], vision [+3969] [1], visit [1], watch out [1], watching [1]

Mt 2: 2 *We saw* his star in the east and have come to worship him."
    2: 9 and the star *they had* **seen** in the east went ahead of them until it
    2:10 *When they* **saw** the star, they were overjoyed.
    2:11 *they saw* the child with his mother Mary, and they bowed down
    2:16 When Herod **realized** that he had been outwitted by the Magi,
    3: 7 But *when he saw* many of the Pharisees and Sadducees coming to
    3:16 and *he saw* the Spirit of God descending like a dove and lighting
    4:16 the people living in darkness *have* **seen** a great light; on those
    4:18 *he saw* two brothers, Simon called Peter and his brother Andrew.
    4:21 Going on from there, *he saw* two other brothers, James son of
    5: 1 Now *when he saw* the crowds, he went up on a mountainside
    5: 8 Blessed are the pure in heart, for they *will* **see** God.
    5:16 that *they may* **see** your good deeds and praise your Father in
    8: 4 Then Jesus said to him, "**See that** you don't tell anyone. But go,
    8:14 *he saw* Peter's mother-in-law lying in bed with a fever.
    8:18 *When* Jesus **saw** the crowd around him, he gave orders to cross to
    8:34 And *when they saw* him, they pleaded with him to leave their
    9: 2 *When* Jesus **saw** their faith, he said to the paralytic, "Take heart,
    9: 4 Knowing [UBS *perceiving*; NIV 3857] their thoughts, Jesus said,
    9: 8 *When* the crowd **saw** this, they were filled with awe; and they
    9: 9 *he saw* a man named Matthew sitting at the tax collector's booth.
    9:11 *When* the Pharisees **saw** this, they asked his disciples, "Why does
    9.22 Jesus turned and **saw** her. "Take heart, daughter," he said, "your
    9:23 the ruler's house and **saw** the flute players and the noisy crowd,
    9:30 Jesus warned them sternly, "**See that** no one knows about this."
    9:36 *When he* **saw** the crowds, he had compassion on them,
   11: 8 If not, what did you go out *to* **see**? A man dressed in fine clothes?
   11: 9 Then what did you go out *to* **see**? A prophet? Yes, I tell you,
   12: 2 *When* the Pharisees **saw** this, they said to him, "Look!
   12:38 said to him, "Teacher, we want *to* **see** a miraculous sign from you."
   13:14 never understanding; you will be ever seeing but never **perceiving**.
   13:15 Otherwise *they might* **see** with their eyes, hear with their ears,
   13:17 many prophets and righteous men longed *to* **see** what you see
   13:17 and righteous men longed *to* **see** what you see but *did* not **see** it,
   14:14 When Jesus landed and **saw** a large crowd, he had compassion on
   14:26 *When* the disciples **saw** him walking on the lake, they were
   16: 6 "*Be* **careful**," Jesus said to them. "Be on your guard against the
   16:28 some who are standing here will not taste death before *they* **see** the
   17: 3 Just then *there* **appeared** before them Moses and Elijah,
   17: 8 When they looked up, *they* **saw** no one except Jesus.
   18:10 "**See that** you do not look down on one of these little ones.
   18:31 When the other servants **saw** what had happened, they were greatly
   20: 3 "About the third hour *he* went out and **saw** others standing in the
   21:15 But *when* the chief priests and the teachers of the law **saw** the
   21:19 **Seeing** a fig tree by the road, he went up to it but found nothing on
   21:20 *When* the disciples **saw** this, they were amazed. "How did the fig
   21:32 And even *after* you **saw** this, you did not repent and believe him.
   21:38 "But *when* the tenants **saw** the son, they said to each other,
   22:11 *he* **noticed** a man there who was not wearing wedding clothes.
   23:39 For I tell you, *you will* not **see** me again until you say, 'Blessed is
   24: 6 and rumors of wars, but **see to it** that you are not alarmed.
   24:15 "So when *you* **see** standing in the holy place 'the abomination that
   24:30 *They will* **see** the Son of Man coming on the clouds of the sky,
   24:33 Even so, when *you* **see** all these things, you know that it is near,
   25:37 'Lord, when *did we* **see** you hungry and feed you, or thirsty
   25:38 When *did we* **see** you a stranger and invite you in, or needing
   25:39 When *did we* **see** you sick or in prison and go to visit you?'
   25:44 when *did we* **see** you hungry or thirsty or a stranger or needing
   26: 8 *When* the disciples **saw** this, they were indignant. "Why this
   26:58 He entered and sat down with the guards *to* **see** the outcome.

   26:64 In the future *you will* **see** the Son of Man sitting at the right hand
   26:71 where another girl **saw** him and said to the people there,
   27: 3 who had betrayed him, **saw** that Jesus was condemned,
   27: 4 "What is that to us?" they replied. "*That's* your **responsibility**."
   27:24 *When* Pilate **saw** that he was getting nowhere,
   27:24 innocent of this man's blood," he said. "*It is* your **responsibility**!"
   27:49 "Now leave him alone. *Let's* **see** if Elijah comes to save him."
   27:54 the centurion and those with him who were guarding Jesus **saw**
   28: 6 he has risen, just as he said. Come and **see** the place where he lay.
   28: 7 of you into Galilee. There *you will* **see** him.' Now I have told you."
   28:10 and tell my brothers to go to Galilee; there *they will* **see** me."
   28:17 *When they* **saw** him, they worshiped him;
Mk 1:10 *saw* heaven being torn open and the Spirit descending on him
    1:16 *he* **saw** Simon and his brother Andrew casting a net into the lake,
    1:19 *he* **saw** James son of Zebedee and his brother John in a boat,
    1:44 "**See that** you don't tell this to anyone. But go, show yourself to
    2: 5 *When* Jesus **saw** their faith, he said to the paralytic, "Son, your sins
    2:12 they praised God, saying, "*We have* never **seen** anything like this!"
    2:14 *he* **saw** Levi son of Alphaeus sitting at the tax collector's booth.
    2:16 When the teachers of the law who were Pharisees **saw** him eating
    4:12 so that, " *they may be ever seeing but never* **perceiving**, and ever
    5: 6 *When he* **saw** Jesus from a distance, he ran and fell on his knees in
    5:14 and the people went out *to* **see** what had happened.
    5:16 Those *who had* **seen** it told the people what had happened to the
    5:22 named Jairus, came there. **Seeing** Jesus, he fell at his feet
    5:32 But Jesus kept looking around *to* **see** who had done it.
    6:33 But many *who* **saw** them leaving recognized them and ran on foot
    6:34 When Jesus landed and **saw** a large crowd, he had compassion on
    6:38 he asked. "Go and **see**." When they found out, they said, "Five—
    6:48 *He* **saw** the disciples straining at the oars, because the wind was
    6:49 but *when they* **saw** him walking on the lake, they thought he was a
    6:50 because they all **saw** him and were terrified. Immediately he spoke
    7: 2 **saw** some of his disciples eating food with hands that were
    8:15 "*Be* **careful**," Jesus warned them. "Watch out for the yeast of the
    8:24 and said, "I see people; they **look** like trees walking around."
    8:33 But *when* Jesus turned and **looked at** his disciples, he rebuked
    9: 1 some who are standing here will not taste death before *they* **see** the
    9: 4 And *there* **appeared** before them Elijah and Moses, who were
    9: 8 looked around, *they* no longer **saw** anyone with them except Jesus.
    9: 9 Jesus gave them orders not to tell anyone what *they had* **seen** until
    9:14 *they* **saw** a large crowd around them and the teachers of the law
    9:15 As soon as all the people **saw** Jesus, they were overwhelmed with
    9:20 *When* the spirit **saw** Jesus, it immediately threw the boy into a
    9:25 *When* Jesus **saw** that a crowd was running to the scene, he rebuked
    9:38 "*we* **saw** a man driving out demons in your name and we told him
   10:14 *When* Jesus **saw** this, he was indignant. He said to them,
   11:13 **Seeing** in the distance a fig tree in leaf, he went to find out if it had
   11:20 as they went along, *they* **saw** the fig tree withered from the roots.
   12:15 to trap me?" he asked. "Bring me a denarius and let *me* **look** *at* it."
   12:28 **Noticing** that Jesus had given them a good answer, he asked him,
   12:34 *When* Jesus **saw** that he had answered wisely, he said to him,
   13:14 "When *you* **see** 'the abomination that causes desolation' standing
   13:26 "At that time *men will* **see** the Son of Man coming in clouds with
   13:29 Even so, when you **see** these things happening, you know that it is
   14:62 "And *you will* **see** the Son of Man sitting at the right hand of the
   14:67 *When she* **saw** Peter warming himself, she looked closely at him.
   14:69 *When* the servant girl **saw** him there, she said again to those
   15:32 come down now from the cross, that *we may* **see** and believe."
   15:36 him alone. *Let's* **see** if Elijah comes to take him down," he said.
   15:39 there in front of Jesus, heard his cry and **saw** how he died, he said,
   16: 5 *they* **saw** a young man dressed in a white robe sitting on the right
   16: 7 of you into Galilee. There *you will* **see** him, just as he told you.' "
Lk 1:11 Then an angel of the Lord **appeared** to him, standing at the right
    1:12 *When* Zechariah **saw** him, he was startled and was gripped with
    1:22 They realized *he had* **seen** a vision in the temple, for he kept
    2:15 "Let's go to Bethlehem and **see** this thing that has happened,
    2:17 *When they had* **seen** him, they spread the word concerning what
    2:20 and praising God for all the things they had heard and **seen**,
    2:26 he *would* not **die** [+2505] before he had seen the Lord's Christ.
    2:26 Spirit that he would not die before *he had* **seen** the Lord's Christ.
    2:30 For my eyes *have* **seen** your salvation,
    2:48 *When* his parents **saw** him, they were astonished. His mother said
    3: 6 And all mankind *will* **see** God's salvation.' "
    5: 2 *he* **saw** at the water's edge two boats, left there by the fishermen,
    5: 8 *When* Simon Peter **saw** this, he fell at Jesus' knees and said,
    5:12 *When he* **saw** Jesus, he fell with his face to the ground and begged

5:20 *When* Jesus **saw** their faith, he said, "Friend, your sins are
5:26 filled with awe and said, "*We have* **seen** remarkable things today."
7:13 *When* the Lord **saw** her, his heart went out to her and he said,
7:22 "Go back and report to John what *you have* **seen** and heard:
7:25 If not, what did you go out *to* **see**? A man dressed in fine clothes?
7:26 But what did you go out *to* **see**? A prophet? Yes, I tell you,
7:39 *When* the Pharisee who had invited him **saw** this, he said to
8:20 mother and brothers are standing outside, wanting *to* **see** you."
8:28 *When* he **saw** Jesus, he cried out and fell at his feet, shouting at
8:34 *When* those tending the pigs **saw** what had happened, they ran off
8:35 and the people went out *to* **see** what had happened. When they
8:36 Those *who had* **seen** it told the people how the demon-possessed
8:47 **seeing** that she could not go unnoticed, came trembling and fell at
9: 9 then, is this I hear such things about?" And he tried *to* **see** him.
9:27 some who are standing here will not taste death before *they* **see** the
9:31 **appeared** in glorious splendor, talking with Jesus. They spoke
9:32 *they* **saw** his glory and the two men standing with him.
9:36 to themselves, and told no one at that time what *they had* **seen**.
9:49 "*we* **saw** a man driving out demons in your name and we tried to
9:54 *When* the disciples James and John **saw** this, they asked, "Lord,
10:24 and kings wanted *to* **see** what you see but did not see it,
10:24 and kings wanted to see what you see but *did* not **see** it,
10:31 and *when he* **saw** the man, he passed by on the other side.
10:32 So too, a Levite, when he came to the place and **saw** him,
10:33 where the man was; and *when he* **saw** him, he took pity on him.
11:38 **noticing** that Jesus did not first wash before the meal,
12:15 Then he said to them, "**Watch out!** Be on your guard against all
12:54 "When *you* **see** a cloud rising in the west, immediately you say,
13:12 *When* Jesus **saw** her, he called her forward and said to her,
13:28 when *you* **see** Abraham, Isaac and Jacob and all the prophets in the
13:35 I tell you, *you will* not **see** me again until you say, 'Blessed is he
14:18 The first said, 'I have just bought a field, and I must go and **see** it.
15:20 his father **saw** him and was filled with compassion for him;
16:23 he looked up and **saw** Abraham far away, with Lazarus by his side.
17:14 *When he* **saw** them, he said, "Go, show yourselves to the priests."
17:15 One of them, *when he* **saw** he was healed, came back,
17:22 "The time is coming when you will long *to* **see** one of the days of
17:22 to see one of the days of the Son of Man, but *you will* not **see** it.
18:15 him touch them. *When* the disciples **saw** this, they rebuked them.
18:24 Jesus **looked at** him and said, "How hard it is for the rich to enter
18:43 praising God. *When* all the people **saw** it, they also praised God.
19: 3 He wanted *to* **see** who Jesus was, but being a short man he could
19: 4 So he ran ahead and climbed a sycamore-fig tree to **see** him,
19: 7 All the people **saw** this and began to mutter, "He has gone to be the
19:37 to praise God in loud voices for all the miracles *they had* **seen**:
19:41 As he approached Jerusalem and **saw** the city, he wept over it
20:14 "But *when* the tenants **saw** him, they talked the matter over.
21: 1 Jesus **saw** the rich putting their gifts into the temple treasury.
21: 2 *He* also **saw** a poor widow put in two very small copper coins.
21:20 "When *you* **see** Jerusalem being surrounded by armies, you will
21:27 At that time *they will* **see** the Son of Man coming in a cloud with
21:29 He told them this parable: "**Look at** the fig tree and all the trees.
21:31 Even so, when *you* **see** these things happening, you know that the
22:43 An angel from heaven **appeared** to him and strengthened him.
22:49 *When* Jesus' followers **saw** what was going to happen, they said,
22:56 A servant girl **saw** him seated there in the firelight. She looked
22:58 A little later someone else **saw** him and said, "You also are one of
23: 8 *When* Herod **saw** Jesus, he was greatly pleased, because for a long
23: 8 because for a long time he had been wanting *to* **see** him.
23: 8 had heard about him, he hoped *to* **see** him perform some miracle.
23:47 The centurion, **seeing** what had happened, praised God and said,
23:49 him from Galilee, stood at a distance, **watching** these things.
24:23 They came and told us that they *had* **seen** a vision of angels,
24:24 and found it just as the women had said, but him *they did* not **see**."
24:34 "It is true! The Lord has risen and *has* **appeared** to Simon."
24:39 **Look at** my hands and my feet. It is I myself! Touch me and see;
24:39 Touch me and see; a ghost does not have flesh and bones,

Jn 1:18 No one *has* ever **seen** God, but God the One and Only, who is at
1:33 'The man on whom *you* **see** the Spirit come down and remain is he
1:34 I *have* **seen** and I testify that this is the Son of God."
1:39 "Come," he replied, "and *you will* **see**." So they went and saw
1:39 So they went and **saw** where he was staying, and spent that day
1:47 When Jesus **saw** Nathanael approaching, he said of him, "Here is a
1:48 "*I* **saw** you while you were still under the fig tree before Philip
1:50 "You believe because I told you *I* **saw** you under the fig tree.
1:50 I saw you under the fig tree. *You shall* **see** greater things than that."

1:51 then added, "I tell you the truth, *you shall* **see** heaven open,
3: 3 no one can **see** the kingdom of God unless he is born again."
3:11 we speak of what we know, and we testify to what *we have* **seen**,
3:32 He testifies to what *he has* **seen** and heard, but no one accepts his
3:36 but whoever rejects the Son *will* not **see** life, for God's wrath
4:29 "Come, **see** a man who told me everything I ever did. Could this be
4:45 *They had* **seen** all that he had done in Jerusalem at the Passover
4:48 "Unless *you people* **see** miraculous signs and wonders," Jesus told
5: 6 *When* Jesus **saw** him lying there and learned that he had been in
5:37 concerning it. You have never heard his voice nor **seen** his form,
6:14 *After* the people **saw** the miraculous sign that Jesus did,
6:22 shore of the lake **realized** that only one boat had been there,
6:24 Once the crowd **realized** that neither Jesus nor his disciples were
6:26 not because *you* **saw** miraculous signs but because you ate the
6:30 then will you give that *we may* **see** it and believe you?
6:36 But as I told you, *you have* **seen** me and still you do not believe.
6:46 No one *has* **seen** the Father except the one who is from God;
6:46 except the one who is from God; only he *has* **seen** the Father.
8:38 I am telling you what I *have* **seen** in the Father's presence,
8:56 Your father Abraham rejoiced at the thought of **seeing** my day;
8:56 rejoiced at the thought of seeing my day; *he* **saw** it and was glad."
8:57 years old," the Jews said to him, "and *you have* **seen** Abraham!"
9: 1 As he went along, *he* **saw** a man blind from birth.
9:37 Jesus said, "*You have* now **seen** him; in fact, he is the one
11:31 comforting her, **noticed** how quickly she got up and went out,
11:32 When Mary reached the place where Jesus was and **saw** him,
11:33 When Jesus **saw** her weeping, and the Jews who had come along
11:40 I not tell you that if you believed, *you would* **see** the glory of God?"
12: 9 and came, not only because of him but also to **see** Lazarus,
12:21 with a request. "Sir," they said, "we would like *to* **see** Jesus."
12:40 and deadened their hearts, so *they can* neither **see** with their eyes,
12:41 Isaiah said this because *he* **saw** Jesus' glory and spoke about him.
14: 7 as well. From now on, you do know him and *have* **seen** him."
14: 9 Anyone *who has* **seen** me has seen the Father. How can you say,
14: 9 Anyone who has seen me *has* **seen** the Father. How can you say,
15:24 But now *they have* **seen** these miracles, and yet they have hated
16:16 will see me no more, and then after a little while *you will* **see** me."
16:17 and then after a little while *you will* **see** me,' and 'Because I am
16:19 will see me no more, and then after a little while *you will* **see** me'?
16:22 is your time of grief, but *I will* **see** you again and you will rejoice,
18:26 challenged him, "Didn't *I* **see** you with him in the olive grove?"
19: 6 As soon as the chief priests and their officials **saw** him,
19:26 When Jesus **saw** his mother there, and the disciple whom he loved
19:33 But when they came to Jesus and **found** that he was already dead,
19:35 The man *who* **saw** it has given testimony, and his testimony is true.
19:37 scripture says, "They will **look** on the one they have pierced."
20: 8 had reached the tomb first, also went inside. *He* **saw** and believed.
20:18 went to the disciples with the news: "*I have* **seen** the Lord!"
20:20 and side. The disciples were overjoyed *when they* **saw** the Lord.
20:25 So the other disciples told him, "*We have* **seen** the Lord!"
20:25 "Unless *I* **see** the nail marks in his hands and put my finger where
20:29 Jesus told him, "Because *you have* **seen** me, you have believed;
20:29 blessed are those *who have* not **seen** and yet have believed."
21:21 When Peter **saw** him, he asked, "Lord, what about him?"

Ac 2: 3 They **saw** what seemed to be tongues of fire that separated
2:17 and daughters will prophesy, your young men *will* **see** visions,
2:27 me to the grave, nor will you let your Holy One **see** decay.
2:31 he was not abandoned to the grave, nor *did* his body **see** decay.
3: 3 *When he* **saw** Peter and John about to enter, he asked them for
3: 9 When all the people **saw** him walking and praising God,
3:12 *When* Peter **saw** this, he said to them: "Men of Israel, why does this
4:20 For we cannot help speaking about what *we have* **seen** and heard."
6:15 and *they* **saw** that his face was like the face of an angel.
7: 2 The God of glory **appeared** to our father Abraham while he was
7:24 *He* **saw** one of them being mistreated by an Egyptian, so he went
7:26 The next day Moses **came upon** two Israelites who were fighting.
7:30 an angel **appeared** to Moses in the flames of a burning bush in the
7:31 *When he* **saw** this, he was amazed at the sight. As he went over to
7:34 *I have* **indeed seen** [+*3972*] the oppression of my people in Egypt.
7:34 *I have* **indeed seen** [+*3972*] the oppression of my people in Egypt.
7:35 God himself, through the angel who **appeared** to him in the bush.
7:44 made as God directed Moses, according to the pattern *he had* **seen**.
7:55 of the Holy Spirit, looked up to heaven and **saw** the glory of God,
8:18 *When* Simon **saw** that the Spirit was given at the laying on of the
8:23 For *I* **see** that you are full of bitterness and captive to sin."
8:39 and the eunuch *did* not **see** him again, but went on his way

9: 12   In a vision he has **seen** a man named Ananias come and place his
9: 17   who **appeared** to you on the road as you were coming here—
9: 27   He told them how Saul on his journey *had* **seen** the Lord and that
9: 35   who lived in Lydda and Sharon **saw** him and turned to the Lord.
9: 40   "Tabitha, get up." She opened her eyes, and **seeing** Peter she sat up.
10: 3   *He* distinctly **saw** an angel of God, who came to him and said,
10: 17   Peter was wondering about the meaning of the **vision** [*+3969*],
11: 5   "I was in the city of Joppa praying, and in a trance *I* **saw** a vision.
11: 6   I looked into it and **saw** four-footed animals of the earth, wild
11: 13   He told us how *he had* **seen** an angel appear in his house and say,
11: 23   *When* he arrived and **saw** the evidence of the grace of God,
12: 3   *When he* **saw** that this pleased the Jews, he proceeded to seize
12: 16   and when *they* opened the door and **saw** him, they were
13: 12   When the proconsul **saw** what had happened, he believed,
13: 31   and for many days he *was* **seen** by those who had traveled with
13: 35   it is stated elsewhere: " 'You will not let your Holy One **see** decay.'
13: 36   he was buried with his fathers and *his* **body decayed** [*+1426*].
13: 37   But the one whom God raised from the dead *did* not **see** decay.
13: 41   " '**Look**, you scoffers, wonder and perish, for I am going to do
13: 45   *When* the Jews **saw** the crowds, they were filled with jealousy
14: 9   Paul looked directly at him, **saw** that he had faith to be healed
14: 11   When the crowd **saw** what Paul had done, they shouted in the
15: 6   The apostles and elders met *to* **consider** [*+4309*] this question.
16: 9   During the night Paul **had a vision** [*+3969*] of a man of Macedonia
16: 10   After Paul *had* **seen** the vision, we got ready at once to leave for
16: 19   When the owners of the slave girl **realized** that their hope of
16: 27   and *when he* **saw** the prison doors open, he drew his sword
16: 40   where *they* **met with** the brothers and encouraged them.
18: 15   and names and your own law—**settle the matter** yourselves.
19: 21   "After I have been there," he said, "I must **visit** Rome also."
20: 25   I have gone about preaching the kingdom *will* ever **see** me again.
21: 32   *When* the rioters **saw** the commander and his soldiers,
22: 14   and *to* **see** the Righteous One and to hear words from his mouth.
22: 15   You will be his witness to all men of what *you have* **seen**
22: 18   and **saw** the Lord speaking. 'Quick!' he said to me. 'Leave
26: 13   O king, as I was on the road, *I* **saw** a light from heaven,
26: 16   *I have* **appeared** to you to appoint you as a servant and as a
26: 16   as a witness of what *you have* **seen** of me and what I will
26: 16   a witness of what *you have seen of me* and what *I will* **show** you.
28: 4   When the islanders **saw** the snake hanging from his hand,
28: 15   *At* **the sight of** these men Paul thanked God and was encouraged.
28: 20   For this reason I have asked *to* **see** you and talk with you.
28: 26   never understanding; you will be ever seeing but never **perceiving**."
28: 27   Otherwise *they might* **see** with their eyes, hear with their ears,
Ro   1: 11   I long *to* **see** you so that I may impart to you some spiritual gift to
15: 21   "Those who were not told about him *will* **see**, and those who have
1Co   2: 9   "No eye *has* **seen**, no ear has heard, no mind has conceived what
8: 10   For if anyone with a weak conscience **sees** you who have this
9: 1   I not free? Am I not an apostle? *Have I* not **seen** Jesus our Lord?
15: 5   and that *he* **appeared** to Peter, and then to the Twelve.
15: 6   *he* **appeared** to more than five hundred of the brothers at the same
15: 7   Then *he* **appeared** to James, then to all the apostles,
15: 8   and last of all *he* **appeared** to me also, as to one abnormally born.
16: 7   I do not want *to* **see** you now and make only a passing visit;
Gal   1: 19   *I* **saw** none of the other apostles—only James, the Lord's brother.
2: 7   *they* **saw** that I had been entrusted with the task of preaching the
2: 14   When *I* **saw** that they were not acting in line with the truth of the
6: 11   **See** what large letters I use as I write to you with my own hand!
Php   1: 27   whether I come and **see** you or only hear about you in my absence,
1: 30   since you are going through the same struggle *you* **saw** I had,
2: 28   so that *when* you **see** him again you may be glad and I may have
4: 9   you have learned or received or heard from me, or **seen** in me—
Col   2: 1   for those at Laodicea, and for all *who have* not **met** me personally.
2: 18   Such a person goes into great detail about what *he has* **seen**,
1Th   2: 17   out of our intense longing we made every effort *to* **see** you.
3: 6   always have pleasant memories of us and that you long *to* **see** us,
3: 10   and day we pray most earnestly that we *may* **see** you again
5: 15   **Make sure that** nobody pays back wrong for wrong, but always
1Ti   3: 16   in a body, was vindicated by the Spirit, was **seen** by angels,
6: 16   lives in unapproachable light, whom no one *has* **seen** or can see.
6: 16   lives in unapproachable light, whom no one has seen or can **see**.
2Ti   1: 4   Recalling your tears, I long *to* **see** you, so that I may be filled with
Heb   2: 8   to him. Yet at present *we do* not **see** everything subject to him.
3: 9   your fathers tested and tried me and for forty years **saw** what I did.
8: 5   "**See to it** that you make everything according to the pattern shown
9: 28   and *he will* **appear** a second time, not to bear sin, but to bring

11: 5   was taken from this life, so that he did not **experience** death;
11: 13   *they* only **saw** them and welcomed them from a distance.
11: 23   because *they* **saw** he was no ordinary child, and they were not
11: 27   king's anger; he persevered because *he* **saw** him who is invisible.
12: 14   and to be holy; without holiness no one *will* **see** the Lord.
13: 23   been released. If he arrives soon, I will come with him *to* **see** you.
Jas   2: 24   *You* **see** that a person is justified by what he does and not by faith
5: 11   and *have* **seen** what the Lord finally brought about.
1Pe   1: 8   *Though* you *have* not **seen** him, you love him; and even though
1: 8   and *even though you do* not **see** him now, you believe in him
3: 10   would love life and **see** good days must keep his tongue from evil
1Jn   1: 1   which we have heard, which *we have* **seen** with our eyes,
1: 2   *we have* **seen** it and testify to it, and we proclaim to you the eternal
1: 3   We proclaim to you what *we have* **seen** and heard, so that you also
3: 1   [NIE] How great is the love the Father has lavished on us,
3: 2   he appears, we shall be like him, for *we shall* **see** him as he is.
3: 6   No one who continues to sin *has* either **seen** him or known him.
4: 20   whom *he has* **seen**, cannot love God, whom he has not seen.
4: 20   whom he has seen, cannot love God, whom *he has* not **seen**.
5: 16   If anyone **sees** his brother commit a sin that does not lead to death,
3Jn   1: 11   is from God. Anyone who does what is evil *has* not **seen** God.
1: 14   I hope *to* **see** you soon, and we will talk face to face. Peace to you.
Rev   1: 2   who testifies to everything *he* **saw**—that is, the word of God
1: 7   and every eye *will* **see** him, even those who pierced him;
1: 12   to me. And when I turned *I* **saw** seven golden lampstands,
1: 17   When *I* **saw** him, I fell at his feet as though dead. Then he placed
1: 19   "Write, therefore, what *you have* **seen**, what is now and what will
1: 20   The mystery of the seven stars that *you* **saw** in my right hand
4: 1   After this *I* **looked**, and there before me was a door standing open
5: 1   Then *I* **saw** in the right hand of him who sat on the throne a scroll
5: 2   And *I* **saw** a mighty angel proclaiming in a loud voice, "Who is
5: 6   Then *I* **saw** a Lamb, looking as if it had been slain, standing in the
5: 11   Then *I* **looked** and heard the voice of many angels, numbering
6: 1   *I* **watched** as the Lamb opened the first of the seven seals.
6: 2   *I* **looked**, and there before me was a white horse! Its rider held a
6: 5   "Come!" *I* **looked**, and there before me was a black horse!
6: 8   *I* **looked**, and there before me was a pale horse! Its rider was
6: 9   *I* **saw** under the altar the souls of those who had been slain
6: 12   *I* **watched** as he opened the sixth seal. There was a great
7: 1   After this *I* **saw** four angels standing at the four corners of the
7: 2   Then *I* **saw** another angel coming up from the east, having the seal
7: 9   After this *I* **looked** and there before me was a great multitude that
8: 2   And *I* **saw** the seven angels who stand before God, and to them
8: 13   As *I* **watched**, I heard an eagle that was flying in midair call out in
9: 1   and *I* **saw** a star that had fallen from the sky to the earth.
9: 17   The horses and riders *I* **saw** in my vision looked like this:
10: 1   Then *I* **saw** another mighty angel coming down from heaven.
10: 5   Then the angel *I had* **seen** standing on the sea and on the land
11: 19   and within his temple *was* **seen** the ark of his covenant.
12: 1   A great and wondrous sign **appeared** in heaven: a woman clothed
12: 3   Then another sign **appeared** in heaven: an enormous red dragon
12: 13   When the dragon **saw** that he had been hurled to the earth,
13: 1   And *I* **saw** a beast coming out of the sea. He had ten horns
13: 2   The beast *I* **saw** resembled a leopard, but had feet like those of a
13: 11   Then *I* **saw** another beast, coming out of the earth. He had two
14: 1   Then *I* **looked**, and there before me was the Lamb, standing on
14: 6   Then *I* **saw** another angel flying in midair, and he had the eternal
14: 14   *I* **looked**, and there before me was a white cloud, and seated on the
15: 1   *I* **saw** in heaven another great and marvelous sign: seven angels
15: 2   And *I* **saw** what looked like a sea of glass mixed with fire and,
15: 5   After this *I* **looked** and in heaven the temple, that is, the tabernacle
16: 13   Then *I* **saw** three evil spirits that looked like frogs; they came out
17: 3   There *I* **saw** a woman sitting on a scarlet beast that was covered
17: 6   *I* **saw that** the woman was drunk with the blood of the saints,
17: 6   bore testimony to Jesus. *When I* **saw** her, I was greatly astonished.
17: 8   The beast, which *you* **saw**, once was, now is not, and will come up
17: 12   "The ten horns *you* **saw** are ten kings who have not yet received a
17: 15   The waters *you* **saw**, where the prostitute sits, are peoples,
17: 16   The beast and the ten horns *you* **saw** will hate the prostitute.
17: 18   The woman *you* **saw** is the great city that rules over the kings of
18: 1   After this *I* **saw** another angel coming down from heaven.
18: 7   sit as queen; I am not a widow, and *I will* never **mourn** [*+4292*].'
19: 10   But he said to me, "*Do* not **do**ˢ it! I am a fellow servant with you
19: 11   *I* **saw** heaven standing open and there before me was a white horse,
19: 17   And *I* **saw** an angel standing in the sun, who cried in a loud voice
19: 19   Then *I* **saw** the beast and the kings of the earth and their armies

20: 1 And *I* saw an angel coming down out of heaven, having the key to
20: 4 *I* saw thrones on which were seated those who had been given
20:11 Then *I* saw a great white throne and him who was seated on it.
20:12 And *I* saw the dead, great and small, standing before the throne,
21: 1 Then *I* saw a new heaven and a new earth, for the first heaven
21: 2 *I* saw the Holy City, the new Jerusalem, coming down out of
21:22 *I* did not see a temple in the city, because the Lord God Almighty
22: 4 *They will* see his face, and his name will be on their foreheads.
22: 9 But he said to me, "*Do* not do^s it! I am a fellow servant with you

3973 ὀργή, *orgē* [36] [→ *3974, 3975, 4239, 4240; cf. 3977*]

wrath [27], anger [7], angry [1], punishment [1]

Mt   3: 7 brood of vipers! Who warned you to flee from the coming **wrath**?
Mk   3: 5 He looked around at them in **anger** and, deeply distressed at their
Lk   3: 7 brood of vipers! Who warned you to flee from the coming **wrath**?
    21:23 will be great distress in the land and **wrath** against this people.
Jn   3:36 rejects the Son will not see life, for God's **wrath** remains on him."
Ro   1:18 The **wrath** of God is being revealed from heaven against all the
     2: 5 you are storing up **wrath** against yourself for the day of God's
     2: 5 are storing up wrath against yourself for the day *of* God's **wrath**,
     2: 8 who reject the truth and follow evil, there will be **wrath** and anger.
     3: 5 what shall we say? That God is unjust in bringing his **wrath** on us?
     4:15 because law brings **wrath**. And where there is no law there is no
     5: 9 how much more shall we be saved from God's **wrath** through him!
     9:22 if God, choosing to show his **wrath** and make his power known,
     9:22 power known, bore with great patience the objects *of* his **wrath**—
    12:19 my friends, but leave room *for* God's **wrath**, for it is written:
    13: 4 an agent of **wrath** to bring punishment on the wrongdoer.
    13: 5 not only because of possible **punishment** but also because of
Eph 2: 3 and thoughts. Like the rest, we were by nature objects *of* **wrath**.
     4:31 Get rid of all bitterness, rage and **anger**, brawling and slander,
     5: 6 because of such things God's **wrath** comes on those who are
Col 3: 6 Because of these, the **wrath** of God is coming.
     3: 8 **anger**, rage, malice, slander, and filthy language from your lips.
1Th 1:10 from the dead—Jesus, who rescues us from the coming **wrath**.
     2:16 sins to the limit. The **wrath** of God has come upon them at last.
     5: 9 For God did not appoint us to suffer **wrath** but to receive salvation
1Ti 2: 8 to lift up holy hands in prayer, without **anger** or disputing.
Heb 3:11 So I declared on oath in my **anger**, 'They shall never enter my
     4: 3 that rest, just as God has said, "So I declared on oath in my **anger**,
Jas 1:19 should be quick to listen, slow to speak and slow to become **angry**,
     1:20 for man's **anger** does not bring about the righteous life that God
Rev 6:16 of him who sits on the throne and from the **wrath** of the Lamb!
     6:17 For the great day *of* their **wrath** has come, and who can stand?"
    11:18 The nations were angry; and your **wrath** has come. The time has
    14:10 which has been poured full strength into the cup *of* his **wrath**.
    16:19 and gave her the cup filled with the wine of the fury *of* his **wrath**.
    19:15 He treads the winepress of the fury *of* the **wrath** of God Almighty.

3974 ὀργίζω, *orgizō* [8] [√ *3973*]

angry [4], anger [2], enraged [2]

Mt   5:22 But I tell you that anyone who *is* **angry** with his brother will be
    18:34 *In* **anger** his master turned him over to the jailers to be tortured,
    22: 7 The king *was* **enraged**. He sent his army and destroyed those
Lk 14:21 Then the owner of the house *became* **angry** and ordered his
    15:28 "The older brother *became* **angry** and refused to go in. So his father
Eph 4:26 "*In your* **anger** do not sin": Do not let the sun go down while you
Rev 11:18 The nations *were* **angry**; and your wrath has come. The time has
    12:17 Then the dragon *was* **enraged** at the woman and went off to make

3975 ὀργίλος, *orgilos* [1] [√ *3973*]

quick-tempered [1]

Tit 1: 7 not overbearing, not **quick-tempered**, not given to drunkenness,

3976 ὀργυιά, *orgyia* [2] [√ *3977*]

a hundred and twenty feet deep [+*1633*] [1], ninety feet deep [+*1278*] [1]

Ac 27:28 that the *water* was **a hundred and twenty feet** [+*1633*] **deep**.
    27:28 took soundings again and found it was **ninety feet** [+*1278*] **deep**.

3977 ὀρέγω, *oregō* [3] [→ *3976, 3979; cf. 3973*]

eager for [1], longing for [1], sets heart on being [1]

1Ti 3: 1 If anyone **sets** his **heart on being** an overseer, he desires a noble
     6:10 Some people, **eager for** *money*, have wandered from the faith
Heb 11:16 Instead, *they were* **longing for** a better country—a heavenly one.

3978 ὀρεινός, *oreinos* [2] [√ *4001*]

hill country [2]

Lk   1:39 Mary got ready and hurried to a town in the **hill country** of Judea,
     1:65 and throughout the **hill country** of Judea people were talking about

3979 ὄρεξις, *orexis* [1] [√ *3977*]

lust [1]

Ro   1:27 relations with women and were inflamed with **lust** for one another.

3980 ὀρθοποδέω, *orthopodeō* [1] [√ *3981 + 4546*]

acting in line [1]

Gal 2:14 When I saw that *they were* not **acting in line** with the truth of the

3981 ὀρθός, *orthos* [2] [→ *494, 1480, 1481, 2061, 2114,*
            3003, 3980, 3982, 3987]

level [1], stand up [+*482*] [1]

Ac 14:10 and called out, "**Stand up** [+*482*] on your feet!" At that, the man
Heb 12:13 "Make **level** paths for your feet," so that the lame may not be

3982 ὀρθοτομέω, *orthotomeō* [1] [√ *3981 + 5533*]

correctly handles [1]

2Ti 2:15 need to be ashamed and *who* **correctly handles** the word of truth.

3983 ὀρθρίζω, *orthrizō* [1] [√ *3986*]

came early in the morning [1]

Lk 21:38 and all the people **came early in the morning** to hear him at the

3984 ὀρθρινός, *orthrinos* [1] [√ *3986*]

early morning [1]

Lk 24:22 our women amazed us. They went to the tomb **early** this **morning**

3985 ὄρθριος, *orthrios*   Not used in UBS/NIV [√ *3986*]

3986 ὄρθρος, *orthros* [3] [→ *3983, 3984, 3985*]

dawn [1], daybreak [1], very early in the morning [+*960*] [1]

Lk 24: 1 On the first day of the week, **very early** [+*960*] **in the morning**,
Jn   8: 2 *At* **dawn** he appeared again in the temple courts, where all the
Ac   5:21 At **daybreak** they entered the temple courts, as they had been told,

3987 ὀρθῶς, *orthōs* [4] [√ *3981*]

correctly [2], plainly [1], what is right [1]

Mk   7:35 his tongue was loosened and he began to speak **plainly**.
Lk   7:43 the bigger debt canceled." "You have judged **correctly**," Jesus said.
    10:28 "You have answered **correctly**," Jesus replied. "Do this and you
    20:21 "Teacher, we know that you speak and teach **what is right**,

3988 ὁρίζω, *horizō* [8] [√ *4000*]

appointed [2], set [2], decided [1], declared [1], decreed [1],
determined [1]

Lk 22:22 The Son of Man will go as *it has been* **decreed**, but woe to that
Ac   2:23 This man was handed over to you *by* God's **set** purpose
    10:42 and to testify that he is the one whom God **appointed** as judge of

11:29 his ability, **decided** to provide help for the brothers living in Judea.
17:26 and *he* **determined** the times set for them and the exact places
17:31 he will judge the world with justice by the man *he has* **appointed**.
Ro 1: 4 *was* **declared** with power *to be* the Son of God by his resurrection
Heb 4: 7 Therefore God again **set** a certain day, calling it Today, when a

3989 ὄρνιξ, *ornix* Not used in UBS/NIV [√ *3998*]

3990 ὅριον, *horion* [12] [√ *4000*]

region [6], vicinity [5], area [1]

Mt 2:16 in Bethlehem and its **vicinity** who were two years old and under,
     4:13 which was by the lake in the **area** of Zebulun and Naphtali—
     8:34 when they saw him, they pleaded with him to leave their **region**.
    15:22 A Canaanite woman from that **vicinity** came to him, crying out,
    15:39 he got into the boat and went to the **vicinity** of Magadan.
    19: 1 and went into the **region** of Judea to the other side of the Jordan.
Mk 5:17 Then the people began to plead with Jesus to leave their **region**.
     7:24 Jesus left that place and went to the **vicinity** of Tyre. He entered a
     7:31 Then Jesus left the **vicinity** of Tyre and went through Sidon,
     7:31 down to the Sea of Galilee and into the **region** of the Decapolis.
    10: 1 Jesus then left that place and went into the **region** of Judea
Ac 13:50 against Paul and Barnabas, and expelled them from their **region**.

3991 ὁρκίζω, *horkizō* [2] [√ *3992*]

command to come out [1], swear [1]

Mk 5: 7 of the Most High God? **Swear** to God that you won't torture me!"
Ac 19:13 of Jesus, whom Paul preaches, *I* **command** you **to come out**."

3992 ὅρκος, *horkos* [10] [→ *1941, 2019, 2020, 2155, 2156, 3991, 3993*]

oath [6], oaths [3], *untranslated* [1]

Mt 5:33 break your oath, but keep the **oaths** you have made to the Lord.'
    14: 7 that he promised with an **oath** to give her whatever she asked.
    14: 9 king was distressed, but because of his **oaths** and his dinner guests,
    26:72 He denied it again, with an **oath**: "I don't know the man!"
Mk 6:26 but because of his **oaths** and his dinner guests, he did not want to
Lk 1:73 the **oath** he swore to our father Abraham:
Ac 2:30 and knew that God had promised him *on* **oath** that he would place
Heb 6:16 and the **oath** confirms what is said and puts an end to all argument.
     6:17 to the heirs of what was promised, he confirmed it *with* an **oath**.
Jas 5:12 [RPG] Let your "Yes" be yes, and your "No," no, or you will be

3993 ὁρκωμοσία, *horkōmosia* [4] [√ *3992* + *3923*]

oath [4]

Heb 7:20 And it was not without an **oath**! Others became priests without any
     7:20 was not without an oath! Others became priests without any **oath**,
     7:21 but he became a priest with an **oath** when God said to him:
     7:28 but the **oath**, which came after the law, appointed the Son,

3994 ὁρμάω, *hormaō* [5] [√ *3995*]

rushed [5]

Mt 8:32 and the whole herd **rushed** down the steep bank into the lake
Mk 5:13 **rushed** down the steep bank into the lake and were drowned.
Lk 8:33 and the herd **rushed** down the steep bank into the lake and was
Ac 7:57 ears and, yelling at the top of their voices, *they* all **rushed** at him,
    19:29 from Macedonia, and **rushed** as one man into the theater.

3995 ὁρμή, *hormē* [2] [→ *929, 3155, 3994, 3996*]

pilot [1], plot afoot [1]

Ac 14: 5 There was a **plot afoot** among the Gentiles and Jews, together with
Jas 3: 4 they are steered by a very small rudder wherever the **pilot** wants to

3996 ὅρμημα, *hormēma* [1] [√ *3995*]

violence [1]

Rev 18:21 "With such **violence** the great city of Babylon will be thrown down,

3997 ὄρνεον, *orneon* [3] [√ *3998*]

birds [2], bird [1]

Rev 18: 2 for every evil spirit, a haunt *for* every unclean and detestable **bird**.
    19:17 who cried in a loud voice *to* all the **birds** flying in midair,
    19:21 on the horse, and all the **birds** gorged themselves on their flesh.

3998 ὄρνις, *ornis* [2] [→ *3989, 3997*]

hen [2]

Mt 23:37 as a **hen** gathers her chicks under her wings, but you were not
Lk 13:34 as a **hen** gathers her chicks under her wings, but you were not

3999 ὁροθεσία, *horothesia* [1] [√ *4000* + *5502*]

exact places [1]

Ac 17:26 the times set for them and the **exact places** where they should live.

4000 ὅρος, *horos* Not used in UBS/NIV [→ *626, 928, 3498, 3988, 3990, 3999, 4633, 5327, 5329*]

4001 ὄρος, *oros* [63 / 65] [→ *3978*]

ὄρος Ἐλαιῶν, Ἐλαιῶνος (Mount of Olives) [12] Mt 21:1; 24:3; 26:30; Mk 11:1; 13:3; 14:26; Lk 19:29,37; 21:37; 22:39; Jn 8:1; Ac 1:12
ὄρος Σινᾶ (Mount Sinai) [4] Ac 7:30,38; Gal 4:24,25
ὄρος Σιών (Mount Zion) [2] Heb 12:22; Rev 14:1
ὑψηλός ὄρος (high mountain) [5] Mt 4:8; 17:1; Mk 9:2; Lk 4:5; Rev 21:10

mountain [22], mount [15], mountains [9], mountainside [8], hill [5], hills [3], hillside [2], place [1]

Mt 4: 8 the devil took him to a very high **mountain** and showed him all the
     5: 1 he saw the crowds, he went up on a **mountainside** and sat down.
     5:14 "You are the light of the world. A city on a **hill** cannot be hidden.
     8: 1 When he came down from the **mountainside**, large crowds
    14:23 dismissed them, he went up on a **mountainside** by himself to pray.
    15:29 Sea of Galilee. Then he went up on a **mountainside** and sat down.
    17: 1 brother of James, and led them up a high **mountain** by themselves.
    17: 9 As they were coming down the **mountain**, Jesus instructed them,
    17:20 you can say *to* this **mountain**, 'Move from here to there' and it
    18:12 will he not leave the ninety-nine on the **hills** and go to look for the
    21: 1 and came to Bethphage on the **Mount** of Olives,
    21:21 but also you can say *to* this **mountain**, 'Go, throw yourself into the
    24: 3 As Jesus was sitting on the **Mount** of Olives, the disciples came to
    24:16 then let those who are in Judea flee to the **mountains**.
    26:30 they had sung a hymn, they went out to the **Mount** of Olives.
    28:16 went to Galilee, to the **mountain** where Jesus had told them to go.
Mk 3:13 Jesus went up on a **mountainside** and called to him those he
     5: 5 and day among the tombs and in the **hills** he would cry out
     5:11 A large herd of pigs was feeding on the nearby **hillside**.
     6:46 After leaving them, he went up on a **mountainside** to pray.
     9: 2 James and John with him and led them up a high **mountain**,
     9: 9 As they were coming down the **mountain**, Jesus gave them orders
    11: 1 and came to Bethphage and Bethany at the **Mount** of Olives,
    11:23 "I tell you the truth, if anyone says *to* this **mountain**, 'Go, throw
    13: 3 As Jesus was sitting on the **Mount** of Olives opposite the temple,
    13:14 then let those who are in Judea flee to the **mountains**.
    14:26 they had sung a hymn, they went out to the **Mount** of Olives.
Lk 3: 5 Every valley shall be filled in, every **mountain** and hill made low.
     4: 5 The devil led him up to a high **place** [UBS-] and showed him in
     4:29 and took him to the brow *of* the **hill** on which the town was built,
     6:12 One of those days Jesus went out to a **mountainside** to pray,
     8:32 A large herd of pigs was feeding there on the **hillside**. The demons
     9:28 and James with him and went up onto a **mountain** to pray.
     9:37 The next day, when they came down from the **mountain**, a large

	19:29	and Bethany at the **hill** called the Mount of Olives,
	19:37	he came near the place where the road goes down the **Mount**
	21:21	Then let those who are in Judea flee to the **mountains**, let those in
	21:37	and each evening he went out to spend the night on the **hill** called
	22:39	Jesus went out as usual to the **Mount** of Olives, and his disciples
	23:30	" 'they will say *to* the **mountains**, "Fall on us!" and to the hills,
Jn	4:20	Our fathers worshiped on this **mountain**, but you Jews claim that
	4:21	will worship the Father neither on this **mountain** nor in Jerusalem.
	6: 3	Then Jesus went up on a **mountainside** and sat down with his
	6:15	him king by force, withdrew again to a **mountain** by himself.
	8: 1	But Jesus went to the **Mount** of Olives.
Ac	1:12	Then they returned to Jerusalem from the **hill** called the Mount of
	7:30	in the flames of a burning bush in the desert *near* **Mount** Sinai.
	7:38	with the angel who spoke to him on **Mount** Sinai, and with our
1Co	13: 2	and if I have a faith that can move **mountains**, but have not love,
Gal	4:24	One covenant is from **Mount** Sinai and bears children who are to
	4:25	Now Hagar stands for **Mount** Sinai in Arabia and corresponds to
Heb	8: 5	everything according to the pattern shown you on the **mountain**."
	11:38	They wandered in deserts and **mountains**, and in caves and holes
	12:18	You have not come to a **mountain** [UBS-] that can be touched
	12:20	"If even an animal touches the **mountain**, it must be stoned."
	12:22	But you have come to **Mount** Zion, to the heavenly Jerusalem,
2Pe	1:18	from heaven when we were with him on the sacred **mountain**.
Rev	6:14	and every **mountain** and island was removed from its place.
	6:15	free man hid in caves and among the rocks *of* the **mountains**.
	6:16	They called *to* the **mountains** and the rocks, "Fall on us and hide us
	8: 8	and something like a huge **mountain**, all ablaze, was thrown into
	14: 1	and there before me was the Lamb, standing on **Mount** Zion,
	16:20	Every island fled away and the **mountains** could not be found.
	17: 9	The seven heads are seven **hills** on which the woman sits.
	21:10	And he carried me away in the Spirit to a **mountain** great

4002 ὀρύσσω, *oryssō* [3] [→ *1482, 2021*]

dug [2], dug a hole [1]

Mt	21:33	put a wall around it, **dug** a winepress in it and built a watchtower.
	25:18	went off, **dug a hole** in the ground and hid his master's money.
Mk	12: 1	wall around it, **dug** a pit for the winepress and built a watchtower.

4003 ὀρφανός, *orphanos* [2] [→ *682*]

orphans [2]

Jn	14:18	I will not leave you as **orphans**; I will come to you.
Jas	1:27	to look after **orphans** and widows in their distress and to keep

4004 ὀρχέομαι, *orcheomai* [4]

dance [2], danced [2]

Mt	11:17	" 'We played the flute for you, and *you did* not **dance**; we sang a
	14: 6	On Herod's birthday the daughter of Herodias **danced** for them
Mk	6:22	When the daughter of Herodias came in and **danced**, she pleased
Lk	7:32	" 'We played the flute for you, and *you did* not **dance**; we sang a

4005 ὅς, *hos* [1411] See Index of Articles, Etc.

[→ *1475, 1478, 1484, 1668, 1930, 2745, 2749, 2771, 2776, 3854, 3888, 4007, 4013, 4015, 4020, 4021, 4022, 4023, 4121, 4529, 5538*]

untranslated [266], what [130], whom [114], which [112], who [106], that [79], him [58], he [44], them [24], whose [23], the [19], whoever [+323] [19], anyone [18], the one [18], it [14], these [14], this [14], they [13], until [+2401] [13], whatever [+1569] [11], anyone [+323] [10], those [10], one [+3525] [8], their [7], whatever [7], when [+1877] [7], another [+1254] [6], his [6], some [+3525] [6], whoever [+1569] [6], anyone [+1569] [5], one [5], those who [5], until [+948] [5], whoever [5], whom [+323] [5], because [+505] [4], what [+1569] [4], where [+1877] [4], as [+5573] [3], her [3], others [+1254] [3], the lifeˢ [3], the manˢ [3], this gospelˢ [3], when [3], where [+1650] [3], while [+1877] [3], and some [+1254] [2], anything [+1569] [2], as [2], because [+2093] [2], ever since [+608] [2], its [2], or [+1254] [2], since [+608] [2], that which [2], the one [+323] [2], the other [+1254] [2], theirs [2], until [+3588] [2], whatever [+323+5516] [2], whatever [+323] [2], when [+323] [2], while [+2401] [2], who

[+1328] [2], who [+323] [2], why [+162+1328] [2], a manˢ [1], about [+4309] [1], Abrahamˢ [1], ago [+608] [1], all the world [+476+1639+5515] [1], also [1], any [+323+5516] [1], any [+323] [1], anything that [1], as long as [+948] [1], be [1], because [+1641] [1], because [+1877] [1], before [+2401] [1], both of them [+1877] [1], by [+3306] [1], called [+3836+3950] [1], called [+3950] [1], childrenˢ [1], Christˢ [1], disciplineˢ [1], duty [+4053+4472] [1], faithˢ [1], for work [+1256+1877+2237] [1], from the time [+608] [1], Godˢ [1], him [+4123] [1], his faithˢ [1], his lettersˢ [1], holinessˢ [1], I [1], if any [+323] [1], in keeping with income [+1569+2338+5516] [1], in that case [+4309] [1], in the same way [+5573] [1], in these [1], including [+1639] [1], indicating that [+2848] [1], itˢ [+201+608+794] [1], just as [+2848+4048+5573] [1], just as [+2848+5573] [1], just as [+5573] [1], just before [+948] [1], man [+1569] [1], matters [1], meanwhile [+1877] [1], native [+1164+1877] [1], nothing [+4024] [1], now [+608] [1], once [+323+608] [1], one of these journeysˢ [1], owner of [+467] [1], Paulˢ [1], peaceˢ [1], same as [+2779] [1], she [1], so [+1328] [1], so [+162+1328] [1], someone [1], something [1], such a man [1], such a man'sˢ [1], testimony [+3455+3456] [1], that [+2848] [1], that dayˢ [1], that is why [+162+1328] [1], that tribeˢ [1], the authorityˢ [1], the deathˢ [1], the factˢ [1], the gloryˢ [1], the gospelˢ [1], the Jesusˢ [1], the lawlessˢ one [1], the manˢ [+1569] [1], the matters [1], the menˢ [+1569] [1], the menˢ [1], the nameˢ [1], the one [+3525] [1], the peopleˢ [1], the promiseˢ [1], the sacrificesˢ [1], the situation [1], the Sonˢ [1], the tabernacleˢ [1], the whom [1], then [+948] [1], therefore [+162+1328] [1], therefore [+5920] [1], these menˢ [1], these watersˢ [1], things [1], thirdˢ [1], this arkˢ [1], this hopeˢ [1], this inscription [+2108] [1], this manˢ [1], those [+3525] [1], those whom [+1569] [1], to this end [+1650] [1], took at [+4409] [1], until [+1877] [1], until [+323+948] [1], what [+2093] [1], what [+323+1254+1877] [1], what [+5515] [1], what [+5516] [1], whatever [+1569+5516] [1], when [+2401] [1], where [+1877+5536] [1], where [+2093] [1], where [+4123] [1], who [+3525] [1], whom [+1569] [1], whose [+2400] [1], why [+162+1328+3836] [1], worth [+1639] [1], you [1], your [1]

4006 ὁσάκις, *hosakis* [3] [√ *4012*]

whenever [+1569] [2], as often as [+1569] [1]

1Co	11:25	do this, **whenever** [+1569] you drink it, in remembrance of me."
	11:26	For **whenever** [+1569] you eat this bread and drink this cup,
Rev	11: 6	the earth with every kind of plague **as often** [+1569] **as** they want.

4007 ὅσγε, *hosge* Not used in UBS/NIV [√ *4005 + 1145*]

4008 ὅσιος, *hosios* [8] [→ *495, 4009, 4010*]

holy [7], holy blessings promised [1]

Ac	2:27	me to the grave, nor will you let your **Holy** *One* see decay.
	13:34	" 'I will give you the **holy** and sure **blessings promised** to David.'
	13:35	it is stated elsewhere: " 'You will not let your **Holy** *One* see decay.'
1Ti	2: 8	I want men everywhere to lift up **holy** hands in prayer,
Tit	1: 8	what is good, who is self-controlled, upright, **holy** and disciplined.
Heb	7:26	one who is **holy**, blameless, pure, set apart from sinners, exalted
Rev	15: 4	For you alone are **holy**. All nations will come and worship before
	16: 5	you who are and who were, the **Holy** *One*, because you have

4009 ὁσιότης, *hosiotēs* [2] [√ *4008*]

holiness [2]

Lk	1:75	in **holiness** and righteousness before him all our days.
Eph	4:24	new self, created to be like God in true righteousness and **holiness**.

4010 ὁσίως, *hosiōs* [1] [√ *4008*]

holy [1]

1Th	2:10	of how **holy**, righteous and blameless we were among you who

4011 ὀσμή, *osmē* [6] [√ *3853*]

fragrance [3], fragrant [+*2380*] [2], smell [1]

Jn   12: 3   And the house was filled with the **fragrance** of the perfume.
2Co   2:14   and through us spreads everywhere the **fragrance** of the
     2:16   To the one we are the **smell** of death; to the other, the fragrance of
     2:16   one we are the smell of death; to the other, the **fragrance** of life.
Eph   5: 2   and gave himself up for us as a **fragrant** [+*2380*] offering
Php   4:18   They are a **fragrant** [+*2380*] offering, an acceptable sacrifice,

4012 ὅσος, *hosos* [110] [→ *4006, 4531*]

all [12], whatever [7], all [+*4246*] [6], what [6], as [5], everything [5], how much [5], *untranslated* [4], everything [+*4246*] [4], that [4], those [4], who [4], all that [2], all who [2], as long as [+*2093*+*5989*] [2], as much as [2], how many [2], just as [+*2848*] [2], very while [+*2285*+*4012*] [2], whatever [+*1569*] [2], whatever [+*2093*] [2], whatever [+*4246*] [2], all [+*323*] [1], all [+*3910*] [1], all of [1], all who [+*1569*] [1], all whom [+*323*] [1], anyone [+*1569*] [1], as long as [+*2093*] [1], as many as [1], ever [1], everything [+*1569*+*4246*] [1], everything [+*323*+*4246*] [1], everything that [1], inasmuch as [+*2093*+*3525*+*4036*] [1], more [1], only as long as [+*2093*+*5989*] [1], other [1], people [1], so long as [+*5989*] [1], those whom [+*1569*] [1], what [+*1569*] [1], whatever [+*323*] [1], whatever [+*3525*] [1], while [+*2093*] [1], who ever [1]

Mt   7:12   do to others **what** [+*1569*] you would have them do to you,
     9:15   "How can the guests of the bridegroom mourn **while** [+*2093*] he is
   13:44   and then in his joy went and sold **all** [+*4246*] he had and bought
   13:46   he went away and sold **everything** [+*4246*] he had and bought it.
   14:36   touch the edge of his cloak, and **all** who touched him were healed.
   17:12   not recognize him, but have done to him **everything** they wished.
   18:18   **whatever** [+*1569*] you bind on earth will be bound in heaven,
   18:18   and **whatever** [+*1569*] you loose on earth will be loosed in heaven.
   18:25   his children and **all** [+*4246*] that he had be sold to repay the debt.
   21:22   you will receive **whatever** [+*4246*] you ask for in prayer,
   22: 9   street corners and invite to the banquet **anyone** [+*1569*] you find.'
   23: 3   So you must obey them and do **everything** [+*1569*+*4246*] they tell
   25:40   'I tell you the truth, **whatever** [+*2093*] you did for one of the least
   25:45   'I tell you the truth, **whatever** [+*2093*] you did not do for one of
   28:20   and teaching them to obey **everything** [+*4246*] I have commanded
Mk   2:19   They cannot, **so** [+*5989*] **long as** they have him with them.
   3: 8   When they heard **all** he was doing, many people came to him from
   3:10   so that those with diseases were pushing forward to touch him.
   3:28   the sins and blasphemies of men will be forgiven them. [RPG]
   5:19   to your family and tell them **how much** the Lord has done for you,
   5:20   and began to tell in the Decapolis **how much** Jesus had done for
   6:30   and reported to him **all** [+*4246*] they had done and taught.
   6:30   and reported to him all they had done and [RPG] taught.
   6:56   the edge of his cloak, and **all** [+*323*] who touched him were healed.
   7:36   But the **more** he did so, the more they kept talking about it.
   9:13   has come, and they have done to him **everything** they wished,
   10:21   "Go, sell **everything** you have and give to the poor, and you will
   11:24   Therefore I tell you, **whatever** [+*4246*] you ask for in prayer,
   12:44   of her poverty, put in everything—**all** [+*3910*] she had to live on."
Lk   4:23   Do here in your hometown **what** we have heard that you did in
   4:40   the people brought to Jesus all **who** had various kinds of sickness,
   8:39   "Return home and tell **how much** God has done for you."
   8:39   and told all over town **how much** Jesus had done for him.
   9: 5   If **people** do not welcome you, shake the dust off your feet when
   9:10   the apostles returned, they reported to Jesus **what** they had done.
   11: 8   man's boldness he will get up and give him **as much as** he needs.
   12: 3   **What** you have said in the dark will be heard in the daylight,
   18:12   I fast twice a week and give a tenth of **all** [+*4246*] I get.'
   18:22   Sell **everything** [+*4246*] you have and give to the poor, and you
Jn   1:12   Yet to **all who** received him, to those who believed in his name,
   4:29   "Come, see a man who told me everything I **ever** did. Could this be
   4:45   They had seen all **that** he had done in Jerusalem at the Passover
   6:11   and distributed to those who were seated **as much as** they wanted.
   10: 8   All **who ever** came before me were thieves and robbers,
   10:41   a miraculous sign, all **that** John said about this man was true."
   11:22   But I know that even now God will give you **whatever** [+*323*] you
   16:13   he will speak only **what** he hears, and he will tell you what is yet
   16:15   All **that** belongs to the Father is mine. That is why I said the Spirit
   17: 7   Now they know that **everything** [+*4246*] you have given me

Ac   2:39   who are far off—for **all whom** [+*323*] the Lord our God will call."
   3:22   you must listen to **everything** [+*323*+*4246*] he tells you.
   3:24   Samuel on, **as many as** have spoken, have foretold these days.
   4: 6   John, Alexander and the **other** *men* of the high priest's family.
   4:23   and reported **all that** the chief priests and elders had said to them.
   4:28   They did **what** your power and will had decided beforehand should
   4:34   For from time to time **those** who owned lands or houses sold them,
   5:36   He was killed, **all** [+*4246*] his followers were dispersed, and it all
   5:37   He too was killed, and **all** [+*4246*] his followers were scattered.
   9:13   this man and **all** the harm he has done to your saints in Jerusalem.
   9:16   I will show him **how much** he must suffer for my name."
   9:39   and other clothing **that** Dorcas had made while she was still with
   10:45   The circumcised believers **who** had come with Peter were
   13:48   of the Lord; and **all** who were appointed for eternal life believed.
   14:27   church together and reported **all that** God had done through them
   15: 4   to whom they reported **everything** God had done through them.
   15:12   and Paul telling about [RPG] the miraculous signs and wonders
Ro   2:12   **All** who sin apart from the law will also perish apart from the law,
   2:12   the law, and **all** who sin under the law will be judged by the law.
   3:19   Now we know that **whatever** the law says, it says to those who are
   6: 3   Or don't you know that **all** of us who were baptized into Christ
   7: 1   has authority over a man **only as** [+*2093*+*5989*] **long as** he lives?
   8:14   because **those** who are led by the Spirit of God are sons of God.
   11:13   **Inasmuch** [+*2093*+*3525*+*4036*] **as** I am the apostle to the Gentiles,
   15: 4   For **everything that** was written in the past was written to teach
1Co   7:39   A woman is bound to her husband **as** [+*2093*+*5989*] **long as** he
2Co   1:20   For no matter **how many** promises God has made, they are "Yes"
Gal   3:10   **All** who rely on observing the law are under a curse, for it is
   3:27   for **all** *of you* who were baptized into Christ have clothed
   4: 1   What I am saying is that **as** [+*2093*+*5989*] **long as** the heir is a
   6:12   **Those** who want to make a good impression outwardly are trying
   6:16   Peace and mercy to **all** who follow this rule, even to the Israel of
Php   3:15   **All** of us who are mature should take such a view of things.
   4: 8   Finally, brothers, **whatever** is true, whatever is noble, whatever is
   4: 8   Finally, brothers, whatever is true, **whatever** is noble, whatever is
   4: 8   is true, whatever is noble, **whatever** is right, whatever is pure,
   4: 8   is true, whatever is noble, whatever is right, **whatever** is pure,
   4: 8   is noble, whatever is right, whatever is pure, **whatever** is lovely,
   4: 8   whatever is pure, whatever is lovely, **whatever** is admirable—
Col   2: 1   for those at Laodicea, and for **all** who have not met me personally.
1Ti   6: 1   **All** who are under the yoke of slavery should consider their
2Ti   1:18   You know very well in **how many** *ways* he helped me in Ephesus.
Heb   1: 4   So he became as much superior to the angels **as** the name he has
   2:15   and free those **who** all their lives were held in slavery by their fear
   3: 3   been found worthy of greater honor than Moses, **just as** [+*2848*]
   7:20   And [NIE] it was not without an oath! Others became priests
   8: 6   But the ministry Jesus has received is as superior to theirs **as** the
   9:27   **Just as** [+*2848*] man is destined to die once, and after that to face
   10:25   one another—and all the more **as** you see the Day approaching.
   10:37   For in just a **very** little **while** [+*2285*+*4012*], "He who is coming
   10:37   For in just a **very** little **while** [+*2285*+*4012*], "He who is coming
2Pe   1:13   I think it is right to refresh your memory **as** [+*2093*] **long as** I live
Jude   1:10   Yet these men speak abusively against **whatever** [+*3525*] they do
   1:10   and **what** *things* they do understand by instinct, like unreasoning
Rev   1: 2   who testifies to **everything** he saw—that is, the word of God
   2:24   to you **who** do not hold to her teaching and have not learned
   3:19   **Those** [+*1569*] **whom** I love I rebuke and discipline. So be earnest,
   13:15   and cause **all who** [+*1569*] refused to worship the image to be
   18: 7   Give her as much torture and grief **as** the glory and luxury she gave
   18:17   the sailors, and **all** who earn their living from the sea, will stand far
   21:16   The city was laid out like a square, as long **as** it was wide.

4013 ὅσπερ, *hosper*   Not used in UBS/NIV
[√ *4005* + *4302*]

4014 ὀστέον, *osteon* [4] [→ *4016*]

bones [4]

Mt   23:27   but on the inside are full *of* dead men's **bones** and everything
Lk   24:39   and see; a ghost does not have flesh and **bones**, as you see I have."
Jn   19:36   scripture would be fulfilled: "Not one of his **bones** will be broken,"
Heb   11:22   of the Israelites from Egypt and gave instructions about his **bones**.

4015 ὅστις, **hostis** [144] [√ *4005* + *5516*]

who [32], they [23], which [15], *untranslated* [11], whoever [6],
that [5], this [5], it [4], them [3], these [3], until [+*2401*] [3], you
[3], others [2], she [2], some [2], someone [2], those [2], whoever
[+*323*] [2], a [1], and [+*2401*] [1], another [1], anyone [1],
Barabbas^s [1], he [1], her [1], such regulations^s [1], that temple^s
[1], the cavalry^s [1], the one [1], the people^s [1], we [1], whatever
[1], while still [+*2401*] [1], who [+*1569*] [1], whoever [+*1569*] [1],
whoever [+*4246*] [1], your generosity^s [1]

Mt 2: 6 for out of you will come a ruler **who** will be the shepherd of my
    5:25 Do it **while** you are still [+*2401*] with him on the way, or he may
    5:39 If **someone** strikes you on the right cheek, turn to him the other
    5:41 If **someone** forces you to go one mile, go with him two miles.
    7:15 **They** come to you in sheep's clothing, but inwardly they are
    7:24 "Therefore everyone **who** hears these words of mine and puts them
    7:24 and puts them into practice is like a wise man **who** built his house
    7:26 and does not put them into practice is like a foolish man **who** built
   10:32 "**Whoever** [+*4246*] acknowledges me before men, I will also
   10:33 But **whoever** [+*323*] disowns me before men, I will disown him
   12:50 For **whoever** [+*323*] does the will of my Father in heaven is my
   13:12 **Whoever** has will be given more,
   13:12 **Whoever** does not have, even what he has will be taken from him.
   13:52 **who** brings out of his storeroom new treasures as well as old."
   16:28 some who are standing here **[RPG]** will not taste death before the
   18: 4 **whoever** humbles himself like this child is the greatest in the
   19:12 For **some** are eunuchs because they were born that way; others
   19:12 they were born that way; **others** were made that way by men;
   19:12 and **others** have renounced marriage because of the kingdom of
   19:29 And everyone **who** has left houses or brothers or sisters or father
   20: 1 "For the kingdom of heaven is like a landowner **who** went out early
   21:33 There was a landowner **who** planted a vineyard. He put a wall
   21:41 **who** will give him his share of the crop at harvest time."
   22: 2 "The kingdom of heaven is like a king **who** prepared a wedding
   23:12 For **whoever** exalts himself will be humbled, and whoever
   23:12 will be humbled, and **whoever** humbles himself will be exalted,
   23:27 **which** look beautiful on the outside but on the inside are full of
   25: 1 "At that time the kingdom of heaven will be like ten virgins **who**
   27:55 **They** had followed Jesus from Galilee to care for his needs.
   27:62 The next day, **the one** after Preparation Day, the chief priests
Mk 4:20 good soil, **[RPG]** hear the word, accept it, and produce a crop—
    9: 1 some **who** are standing here will not taste death before they see the
   12:18 Then the Sadducees, **who** say there is no resurrection, came to him
   15: 7 A man called Barabbas was in prison with the insurrectionists who
Lk 1:20 not believe my words, **which** will come true at their proper time."
    2: 4 **[RPG]** because he belonged to the house and line of David.
    2:10 I bring you good news of great joy **that** will be for all the people.
    7:37 When **a** woman who had lived a sinful life in that town learned that
    7:39 he would know who **[RPG]** is touching him and what kind of
    8: 3 **These** *women* were helping to support them out of their own
    8:15 But the seed on good soil stands for **those** with a noble and good
    8:26 the region of the Gerasenes, **which** is across the lake from Galilee.
    8:43 subject to bleeding for twelve years, but no one could heal **her**.
    9:30 Two men, **[RPG]** Moses and Elijah,
   10:42 has chosen what is better, and **it** will not be taken away from her."
   12: 1 your guard against the yeast of the Pharisees, **which** is hypocrisy.
   12:50 to undergo, and how distressed I am **until** [+*2401*] it is completed!
   13: 8 for one more year, **and** [+*2401*] I'll dig around it and fertilize it.
   14:15 "Blessed is the *man* **who** will eat at the feast in the kingdom of
   14:27 And **anyone** who does not carry his cross and follow me cannot be
   15: 7 than over ninety-nine righteous persons **who** do not need to repent.
   22:16 I will not eat it again **until** [+*2401*] it finds fulfillment in the
   23:19 (**Barabbas**^{s} had been thrown into prison for an insurrection in the
   23:55 The women **who** had come with Jesus from Galilee followed
Jn 8:53 **He** died, and so did the prophets. Who do you think you are?"
    9:18 and had received his sight **until** [+*2401*] they sent for the man's
   21:25 If every one of **them** were written down, I suppose that even the
Ac 3:23 Anyone **who** [+*1569*] does not listen to him will be completely cut
    5:16 and those tormented by evil spirits, and all of **them** were healed.
    7:53 you **who** have received the law that was put into effect through
    8:15 they prayed for them that they might receive the Holy Spirit,
    9:35 in Lydda and Sharon saw him and **[RPG]** turned to the Lord.
   10:41 by us **who** ate and drank with him after he rose from the dead.
   10:47 with water? **They** have received the Holy Spirit just as we have."
   11:20 **[RPG]** went to Antioch and began to speak to Greeks also,

   11:28 entire Roman world. (**This** happened during the reign of Claudius.)
   12:10 to the city. **It** opened for them by itself, and they went through it.
   13:31 Galilee to Jerusalem. **They** are now his witnesses to our people.
   13:43 **who** talked with them and urged them to continue in the grace of
   16:12 **[RPG]** a Roman colony and the leading city of that district of
   16:16 **She** earned a great deal of money for her owners by fortune-telling.
   16:17 of the Most High God, **who** are telling you the way to be saved."
   17:10 to Berea. On arriving there, **they** went to the Jewish synagogue.
   17:11 for **they** received the message with great eagerness and examined
   21: 4 Through the Spirit **they** urged Paul not to go on to Jerusalem.
   23:14 **They** went to the chief priests and elders and said, "We have taken
   23:21 **They** have taken an oath not to eat or drink until they have killed
   23:33 When **the cavalry**^{s} arrived in Caesarea, they delivered the letter to
   24: 1 and **they** brought their charges against Paul before the governor.
   28:18 **They** examined me and wanted to release me,
Ro 1:25 **They** exchanged the truth of God for a lie, and worshiped
    1:32 Although **they** know God's righteous decree that those who do
    2:15 since **they** show that the requirements of the law are written on
    6: 2 By no means! **We** died to sin; how can we live in it any longer?
    9: 4 **the people**^{s} of Israel. Theirs is the adoption as sons; theirs the
   11: 4 "I have reserved for myself seven thousand **who** have not bowed the
   16: 4 **They** risked their lives for me. Not only I but all the churches of
   16: 6 Greet Mary, **who** worked very hard for you.
   16: 7 **They** are outstanding among the apostles, and they were in Christ
   16:12 **another** *woman* who has worked very hard in the Lord.
1Co 3:17 destroy him; for God's temple is sacred, and you are **that temple**^{s}.
    5: 1 among you, and of a kind **that** does not occur even among pagans:
2Co 8:10 Last year **you** were the first not only to give but also to have the
    9:11 and through us **your generosity**^{s} will result in thanksgiving to
Gal 2: 4 because **some** false brothers had infiltrated our ranks to spy on the
    4:24 **These** *things* may be taken figuratively, for the women represent
    4:24 and bears children who are to be slaves: **This** is Hagar.
    4:26 But the Jerusalem that is above is free, and **she** is our mother.
    5: 4 **You** who are trying to be justified by law have been alienated from
    5:10 into confusion will pay the penalty, **whoever** [+*1569*] he may be.
    5:19 are obvious: **[RPG]** sexual immorality, impurity and debauchery;
Eph 1:23 **which** is his body, the fullness of him who fills everything in every
    3:13 because of my sufferings for you, **which** are your glory.
    4:19 **they** have given themselves over to sensuality so as to indulge in
    6: 2 and mother"—**which** is the first commandment with a promise—
Php 1:28 **This** is a sign to them that they will be destroyed, but that you will
    2:20 no one else like him, **who** takes a genuine interest in your welfare.
    3: 7 But **whatever** was to my profit I now consider loss for the sake of
    4: 3 help these women **who** have contended at my side in the cause of
Col 2:23 **Such regulations**^{s} indeed have an appearance of wisdom,
    3: 5 impurity, lust, evil desires and greed, **which** is idolatry.
    4:11 kingdom of God, and they have proved a comfort **[RPG]** to me.
2Th 1: 9 **They** will be punished with everlasting destruction and shut out
1Ti 1: 4 **These** promote controversies rather than God's work—which is by
    3:15 **which** is the church of the living God, the pillar and foundation of
    6: 9 and harmful desires **that** plunge men into ruin and destruction.
2Ti 1: 5 **which** first lived in your grandmother Lois and in your mother
    2: 2 entrust to reliable men **who** will also be qualified to teach others.
    2:18 **who** have wandered away from the truth. They say that the
Tit 1:11 because **they** are ruining whole households by teaching things they
Heb 2: 3 This salvation, **which** was first announced by the Lord,
    8: 5 **They** serve at a sanctuary that is a copy and shadow of what is in
    8: 6 is superior to the old one, and **it** is founded on better promises.
    9: 2 and the consecrated bread; **this** was called the Holy Place.
    9: 9 **This** is an illustration for the present time, indicating that the gifts
   10: 8 nor were you pleased with them" (although the law required **them**
   10:11 he offers the same sacrifices, **which** can never take away sins.
   10:35 So do not throw away your confidence; **it** will be richly rewarded.
   12: 5 And you have forgotten that word of encouragement **that**
   13: 7 Remember your leaders, **who** spoke the word of God to you.
Jas 2:10 For **whoever** keeps the whole law and yet stumbles at just one
    4:14 Why, **you** do not even know what will happen tomorrow. What is
1Pe 2:11 to abstain from sinful desires, **which** war against your soul.
2Pe 2: 1 **They** will secretly introduce destructive heresies, even denying the
1Jn 1: 2 the eternal life, **which** was with the Father and has appeared to us.
Rev 1: 7 and every eye will see him, even **those** who pierced him;
    1:12 I turned around to see the voice **that** was speaking to me.
    2:24 and **[RPG]** have not learned Satan's so-called deep secrets (I will
    9: 4 but only those people **who** did not have the seal of God on their
   11: 8 **which** is figuratively called Sodom and Egypt, where also their
   12:13 he pursued the woman **who** had given birth to the male child.

17: 12   "The ten horns you saw are ten kings **who** have not yet received a
19: 2   He has condemned the great prostitute **who** corrupted the earth by
20: 4   **They** had not worshiped the beast or his image and had not

4016 ὀστοῦν, **ostoun**   Not used in UBS/NIV [√ *4014*]

4017 ὀστράκινος, **ostrakinos** [2]

of clay [2]

2Co   4: 7   But we have this treasure in jars **of clay** to show that this
2Ti   2: 20   are articles not only **of** gold and silver, but also of wood and **clay**;

4018 ὄσφρησις, **osphrēsis** [1] [√ *3853*]

sense of smell [1]

1Co 12: 17   If the whole body were an ear, where would the **sense of smell** be?

4019 ὀσφῦς, **osphys** [8]

waist [2], belt [1], body [1], descendants [+2843+3836] [1], descended from [+1666+2002+3836] [1], dressed ready for service [+3836+4322] [1], prepare for action [+350+3836] [1]

Mt   3: 4   made of camel's hair, and he had a leather belt around his **waist**.
Mk   1: 6   with a leather belt around his **waist**, and he ate locusts and wild
Lk   12: 35   "Be **dressed ready for service** [+3836+4322] and keep your lamps
Ac   2: 30   was a prophet and knew that God had promised him on oath that he
         would place one of his **descendants** [+2843+3836] on his throne.
Eph   6: 14   Stand firm then, with the **belt** of truth buckled around your waist,
Heb   7: 5   a tenth from the people—that is, their brothers—even though their
         brothers *are* **descended from** [+1666+2002+3836] Abraham.
     7: 10   met Abraham, Levi was still in the **body** of his ancestor.
1Pe   1: 13   Therefore, **prepare** your minds **for action** [+350+3836];

4020 ὅταν, **hotan** [123] [√ *4005 + 5445 + 323*]

when [94], whenever [5], after [4], *untranslated* [3], as soon as [+2317] [2], as soon as [2], that [2], while [2], any time [1], as soon as [+2453] [1], at once [+2317] [1], before [1], by [1], once [1], the moment [1], until [+1623+3590] [1], when [+2453] [1]

Mt   5: 11   "Blessed are you **when** people insult you, persecute you and falsely
     6: 2   "So **when** you give to the needy, do not announce it with trumpets,
     6: 5   "And **when** you pray, do not be like the hypocrites, for they love to
     6: 6   But **when** you pray, go into your room, close the door and pray to
     6: 16   "**When** you fast, do not look somber as the hypocrites do,
     9: 15   The time will come **when** the bridegroom will be taken from them;
     10: 19   But **when** they arrest you, do not worry about what to say
     10: 23   **When** you are persecuted in one place, flee to another. I tell you
     12: 43   "**When** an evil spirit comes out of a man, it goes through arid
     13: 32   yet **when** it grows, it is the largest of garden plants and becomes a
     15: 2   of the elders? They don't wash their hands **before** they eat!"
     19: 28   of all things, **when** the Son of Man sits on his glorious throne,
     21: 40   "Therefore, **when** the owner of the vineyard comes, what will he do
     23: 15   and sea to win a single convert, and **when** he becomes one,
     24: 15   "So **when** you see standing in the holy place 'the abomination that
     24: 32   **As soon as** its twigs get tender and its leaves come out, you know
     24: 33   Even so, **when** you see all these things, you know that it is near,
     25: 31   "**When** the Son of Man comes in his glory, and all the angels with
     26: 29   that day **when** I drink it anew with you in my Father's kingdom."
Mk   2: 20   But the time will come **when** the bridegroom will be taken from
     3: 11   **Whenever** the evil spirits saw him, they fell down before him
     4: 15   **As soon as** [+2317] they hear it, Satan comes and takes away the
     4: 16   hear the word and **at once** [+2317] receive it with joy.
     4: 29   **As soon as** [+2317] the grain is ripe, he puts the sickle to it,
     4: 31   which is the smallest seed [NIE] you plant in the ground.
     4: 32   Yet **when** planted, it grows and becomes the largest of all garden
     7: 4   **When** [UBS-] they come from the marketplace they do not eat
     8: 38   the Son of Man will be ashamed of him **when** he comes in his
     9: 9   seen **until** [+1623+3590] the Son of Man had risen from the dead.
     11: 19   When evening came, they went out of the city.
     11: 25   And **when** you stand praying, if you hold anything against anyone,
     12: 23   At the resurrection [UBS+ *when men rise from the dead*] whose
     12: 25   **When** the dead rise, they will neither marry nor be given in
     13: 4   And what will be the sign **that** they are all about to be fulfilled?"
     13: 7   **When** you hear of wars and rumors of wars, do not be alarmed.
     13: 11   **Whenever** you are arrested and brought to trial, do not worry
     13: 14   "**When** you see 'the abomination that causes desolation' standing
     13: 28   **As soon** [+2453] **as** its twigs get tender and its leaves come out,
     13: 29   Even so, **when** you see these things happening, you know that it is
     14: 7   always have with you, and you can help them **any time** you want.
     14: 25   I will not drink again of the fruit of the vine until that day **when** I
Lk   5: 35   But the time will come **when** the bridegroom will be taken from
     6: 22   Blessed are you **when** men hate you, when they exclude you
     6: 22   **when** they exclude you and insult you and reject your name as evil,
     6: 26   Woe to you **when** all men speak well of you, for that is how their
     8: 13   rock are the ones who receive the word with joy **when** they hear it,
     9: 26   the Son of Man will be ashamed of him **when** he comes in his
     11: 2   He said to them, "**When** you pray, say: " 'Father, hallowed be your
     11: 21   "**When** a strong man, fully armed, guards his own house,
     11: 24   "**When** an evil spirit comes out of a man, it goes through arid
     11: 34   "**When** your eyes are good, your whole body also is full of light.
     11: 36   be completely lighted, as **when** the light of a lamp shines on you."
     12: 11   "**When** you are brought before synagogues, rulers and authorities,
     12: 54   "**When** you see a cloud rising in the west, immediately you say,
     12: 55   And **when** the south wind blows, you say, 'It's going to be hot,'
     13: 28   **when** you see Abraham, Isaac and Jacob and all the prophets in the
     14: 8   "**When** someone invites you to a wedding feast, do not take the
     14: 10   But **when** you are invited, take the lowest place, so that when your
     14: 10   so that **when** your host comes, he will say to you, 'Friend,
     14: 12   "**When** you give a luncheon or dinner, do not invite your friends,
     14: 13   But **when** you give a banquet, invite the poor, the crippled,
     16: 4   I know what I'll do so that, **when** I lose my job here, people will
     16: 9   so that **when** it is gone, you will be welcomed into eternal
     17: 10   **when** you have done everything you were told to do, should say,
     21: 7   And what will be the sign **that** they are about to take place?"
     21: 9   **When** you hear of wars and revolutions, do not be frightened.
     21: 20   "**When** you see Jerusalem being surrounded by armies, you will
     21: 30   **When** [+2453] they sprout leaves, you can see for yourselves
     21: 31   Even so, **when** you see these things happening, you know that the
     23: 42   he said, "Jesus, remember me **when** you come into your kingdom."
Jn   2: 10   then the cheaper wine **after** the guests have had too much to drink;
     4: 25   "is coming. When he comes, he will explain everything to us."
     5: 7   "I have no one to help me into the pool **when** the water is stirred.
     7: 27   **when** the Christ comes, no one will know where he is from."
     7: 31   They said, "**When** the Christ comes, will he do more miraculous
     8: 28   So Jesus said, "**When** you have lifted up the Son of Man,
     8: 44   **When** he lies, he speaks his native language, for he is a liar
     9: 5   **While** I am in the world, I am the light of the world."
     10: 4   **When** he has brought out all his own, he goes on ahead of them,
     13: 19   so that **when** it does happen you will believe that I am He.
     14: 29   before it happens, so that **when** it does happen you will believe.
     15: 26   "**When** the Counselor comes, whom I will send to you from the
     16: 4   so that **when** the time comes you will remember that I warned you.
     16: 13   But **when** he, the Spirit of truth, comes, he will guide you into all
     16: 21   A woman [NIE] giving birth to a child has pain because her time
     16: 21   but **when** her baby is born she forgets the anguish because of her
     21: 18   but **when** you are old you will stretch out your hands, and someone
Ac   23: 35   he said, "I will hear your case **when** your accusers get here."
     24: 22   "**When** Lysias the commander comes," he said, "I will decide your
Ro   2: 14   (Indeed, **when** Gentiles, who do not have the law, do by nature
     11: 27   And this is my covenant with them **when** I take away their sins."
1Co   3: 4   For **when** one says, "I follow Paul," and another, "I follow
     13: 10   but **when** perfection comes, the imperfect disappears.
     14: 26   **When** you come together, everyone has a hymn, or a word of
     15: 24   **when** he hands over the kingdom to God the Father after he has
     15: 24   when he hands over the kingdom to God the Father **after** he has
     15: 27   Now **when** it says that "everything" has been put under him,
     15: 28   **When** he has done this, then the Son himself will be made subject
     15: 54   **When** the perishable has been clothed with the imperishable,
     16: 2   it up, so that **when** I come no collections will have to be made.
     16: 3   Then, **when** I arrive, I will give letters of introduction to the men
     16: 5   **After** I go through Macedonia, I will come to you—for I will be
     16: 12   unwilling to go now, but he will go **when** he has the opportunity.
2Co   10: 6   punish every act of disobedience, **once** your obedience is complete.
     12: 10   in difficulties. For **when** I am weak, then I am strong.
     13: 9   We are glad **whenever** we are weak but you are strong; and our
Col   3: 4   **When** Christ, who is your life, appears, then you also will appear
     4: 16   **After** this letter has been read to you, see that it is also read in the
1Th   5: 3   **While** people are saying, "Peace and safety," destruction will come
2Th   1: 10   [NIE] on the day he comes to be glorified in his holy people

1Ti 5:11 For **when** their sensual desires overcome their dedication to Christ,
Tit 3:12 **As soon as** I send Artemas or Tychicus to you, do your best to
Heb 1: 6 And again, **when** God brings his firstborn into the world, he says,
Jas 1: 2 it pure joy, my brothers, **whenever** you face trials of many kinds,
1Jn 5: 2 children of God: **by** loving God and carrying out his commands.
Rev 4: 9 **Whenever** the living creatures give glory, honor and thanks to him
     8: 1 **When** he opened the seventh seal, there was silence in heaven for
     9: 5 was like that of the sting of a scorpion **when** it strikes a man.
    10: 7 But in the days **when** the seventh angel is about to sound his
    11: 7 Now **when** they have finished their testimony, the beast that comes
    12: 4 so that he might devour her child **the moment** it was born.
    17:10 but **when** he does come, he must remain for a little while.
    18: 9 "**When** the kings of the earth who committed adultery with her
    20: 7 **When** the thousand years are over, Satan will be released from his

4021 ὅτε, *hote* [103 / 102] [√ *4005 + 5445*]

when [83], after [7], as [4], *untranslated* [2], once [2], while [2], as soon as [1], before [1]

Mt   7:28 **When** Jesus had finished saying these things, the crowds were
     9:25 **After** the crowd had been put outside, he went in and took the girl
    11: 1 **After** Jesus had finished instructing his twelve disciples, he went
    12: 3 "Haven't you read what David did **when** he and his companions
    13:26 **When** the wheat sprouted and formed heads, then the weeds also
    13:48 **When** it was full, the fishermen pulled it up on the shore.
    13:53 **When** Jesus had finished these parables, he moved on from there.
    19: 1 **When** Jesus had finished saying these things, he left Galilee
    21: 1 **As** they approached Jerusalem and came to Bethphage on the
    21:34 **When** the harvest time approached, he sent his servants to the
    26: 1 **When** Jesus had finished saying all these things, he said to his
    27:31 **After** they had mocked him, they took off the robe and put his own
Mk   1:32 That evening **after** sunset the people brought to Jesus all the sick
     2:25 "Have you never read what David did **when** he and his companions
     4: 6 But **when** the sun came up, the plants were scorched, and they
     4:10 **When** he was alone, the Twelve and the others around him asked
     6:21 [NIE] On his birthday Herod gave a banquet for his high officials
     7:17 **After** he had left the crowd and entered the house, his disciples
     8:19 **When** I broke the five loaves for the five thousand, how many
     8:20 "And **when** I broke the seven loaves for the four thousand,
    11: 1 **As** they approached Jerusalem and came to Bethphage
    14:12 **when** it was customary to sacrifice the Passover lamb,
    15:20 And **when** they had mocked him, they took off the purple robe
    15:41 [NIE] In Galilee these women had followed him and cared for his
Lk   2:21 On the eighth day, **when** it was time to circumcise him, he was
     2:22 **When** the time of their purification according to the Law of Moses
     2:42 **When** he was twelve years old, they went up to the Feast,
     4:25 **when** the sky was shut for three and a half years and there was a
     6: 3 "Have you never read what David did **when** he and his companions
     6:13 **When** morning came, he called his disciples to him and chose
    13:35 will not see me again until [UBS+ *the time comes* **when**] you say,
    15:30 But **when** this son of yours who has squandered your property with
    17:22 "The time is coming **when** you will long to see one of the days of
    22:14 **When** the hour came, Jesus and his apostles reclined at the table.
    22:35 "**When** I sent you without purse, bag or sandals, did you lack
    23:33 **When** they came to the place called the Skull, there they crucified
Jn   1:19 Now this was John's testimony **when** the Jews of Jerusalem sent
     2:22 **After** he was raised from the dead, his disciples recalled what he
     4:21 a time is coming **when** you will worship the Father neither on this
     4:23 and has now come **when** the true worshipers will worship the
     4:45 **When** he arrived in Galilee, the Galileans welcomed him.
     5:25 and has now come **when** the dead will hear the voice of the Son of
     6:24 **Once** the crowd realized that neither Jesus nor his disciples were
     9: 4 of him who sent me. Night is coming, **when** no one can work.
    12:16 Only **after** Jesus was glorified did they realize that these things had
    12:17 Now the crowd that was with him **when** he called Lazarus from the
    13:12 **When** he had finished washing their feet, he put on his clothes
    13:31 **When** he was gone, Jesus said, "Now is the Son of Man glorified
    16:25 a time is coming **when** I will no longer use this kind of language
    17:12 **While** I was with them, I protected them and kept them safe by
    19: 6 **As soon as** the chief priests and their officials saw him,
    19: 8 **When** Pilate heard this, he was even more afraid,
    19:23 **When** the soldiers crucified Jesus, they took his clothes, dividing
    19:30 **When** he had received the drink, Jesus said, "It is finished."
    20:24 one of the Twelve, was not with the disciples **when** Jesus came.
    21:15 **When** they had finished eating, Jesus said to Simon Peter,

      21:18 **when** you were younger you dressed yourself and went where you
Ac   1:13 **When** they arrived, they went upstairs to the room where they
     8:12 But **when** they believed Philip as he preached the good news of the
     8:39 **When** they came up out of the water, the Spirit of the Lord
    11: 2 So **when** Peter went up to Jerusalem, the circumcised believers
    12: 6 The night **before** Herod was to bring him to trial, Peter was
    21: 5 But **when** our time was up, we left and continued on our way.
    21:35 **When** Paul reached the steps, the violence of the mob was
    22:20 And **when** the blood of your martyr Stephen was shed, I stood
    27:39 **When** daylight came, they did not recognize the land, but they saw
    28:16 **When** we got to Rome, Paul was allowed to live by himself,
Ro   2:16 This will take place on the day **when** God will judge men's secrets
     6:20 **When** you were slaves to sin, you were free from the control of
     7: 5 For **when** we were controlled by the sinful nature, the sinful
    13:11 because our salvation is nearer now than **when** we first believed.
1Co 12: 2 You know that **when** you were pagans, somehow or other you
    13:11 **When** I was a child, I talked like a child, I thought like a child,
    13:11 like a child. **When** I became a man, I put childish ways behind me.
Gal 1:15 But **when** God, who set me apart from birth and called me by his
     2:11 **When** Peter came to Antioch, I opposed him to his face,
     2:12 But **when** they arrived, he began to draw back and separate himself
     2:14 **When** I saw that they were not acting in line with the truth of the
     4: 3 So also, **when** we were children, we were in slavery under the
     4: 4 But **when** the time had fully come, God sent his Son, born of a
Php 4:15 **When** I set out from Macedonia, not one church shared with me in
Col 3: 7 You used to walk in these ways, in the life you **once** lived.
1Th 3: 4 In fact, **when** we were with you, we kept telling you that we would
2Th 3:10 For even **when** we were with you, we gave you this rule: "If a man
2Ti 4: 3 For the time will come **when** men will not put up with sound
Tit 3: 4 But **when** the kindness and love of God our Savior appeared,
Heb 7:10 because **when** Melchizedek met Abraham, Levi was still in the
     9:17 has died; it never takes effect **while** the one who made it is living.
1Pe 3:20 who disobeyed long ago **when** God waited patiently in the days of
Jude 1: 9 **when** he was disputing with the devil about the body of Moses,
Rev 1:17 **When** I saw him, I fell at his feet as though dead. Then he placed
     5: 8 And **when** he had taken it, the four living creatures
     6: 1 I watched **as** the Lamb opened the first of the seven seals.
     6: 3 **When** the Lamb opened the second seal, I heard the second living
     6: 5 **When** the Lamb opened the third seal, I heard the third living
     6: 7 **When** the Lamb opened the fourth seal, I heard the voice of the
     6: 9 **When** he opened the fifth seal, I saw under the altar the souls of
     6:12 I watched **as** he opened the sixth seal. There was a great
    10: 3 **When** he shouted, the voices of the seven thunders spoke.
    10: 4 And **when** the seven thunders spoke, I was about to write;
    10:10 in my mouth, but **when** I had eaten it, my stomach turned sour.
    12:13 **When** the dragon saw that he had been hurled to the earth,
    22: 8 And **when** I had heard and seen them, I fell down to worship at the

4022 ὅτι, *hoti* [1296 / 1298] See Index of Articles, Etc.

[√ *4005 + 5515*]

that [491], *untranslated* [419], because [205], for [145], how [6], since [5], this [3], as [2], by [2], of [2], about [1], although [1], as it is [+*1254*] [1], but [+*5515*] [1], here [1], if [1], in this [1], is that why [1], the fact that [1], the very fact that [1], though actually [1], though [1], to be [1], to find^s [1], what [1], when [1], which [1], why [1]

4023 οὗ, *hou* [25] [√ *4005*]

where [19], there [2], one in which [1], the place where [1], to which [1], wherever [+*1569*] [1]

Mt   2: 9 ahead of them until it stopped over **the place where** the child was.
    18:20 For **where** two or three come together in my name, there am I with
    28:16 went to Galilee, to the mountain **where** Jesus had told them to go.
Lk   4:16 He went to Nazareth, **where** he had been brought up, and on the
     4:17 handed to him. Unrolling it, he found the place **where** it is written:
    10: 1 ahead of him to every town and place **where** he was about to go.
    23:53 it in a tomb cut in the rock, **one in which** no one had yet been laid.
    24:28 As they approached the village **to which** they were going,
Ac   1:13 they went upstairs to the room **where** they were staying.
     2: 2 from heaven and filled the whole house **where** they were sitting.
     7:29 fled to Midian, **where** he settled as a foreigner and had two sons.
    12:12 called Mark, **where** many people had gathered and were praying.

16:13   city gate to the river, **where** we expected to find a place of prayer.
20: 8   There were many lamps in the upstairs room **where** we were
25:10   am now standing before Caesar's court, **where** I ought to be tried.
28:14   **There** we found some brothers who invited us to spend a week
Ro   4:15   brings wrath. And **where** there is no law there is no transgression.
5:20   But **where** sin increased, grace increased all the more,
9:26   "It will happen that in the very place **where** it was said to them,
1Co 16: 6   so that you can help me on my journey, **wherever** [+*1569*] I go.
2Co 3:17   is the Spirit, and **where** the Spirit of the Lord is, there is freedom.
Php 3:20   And we eagerly await a Savior from **there**, the Lord Jesus Christ,
Col   3: 1   on things above, **where** Christ is seated at the right hand of God.
Heb 3: 9   **where** your fathers tested and tried me and for forty years saw
Rev 17:15   **where** the prostitute sits, are peoples, multitudes, nations

4024   οὐ, *ou*   [1623 / 1619]   See Index of Articles, Etc.

[→ *2022, 2023, 2024, 2025, 4027, 4028, 4029, 4030, 4031, 4032, 4033, 4034, 4037, 4046, 4049*]

not [1026], no [146], don't [55], cannot [+*1538*] [40], *untranslated* [34], never [+*3590*] [33], not [+*3590*] [30], never [16], nothing [14], didn't [8], certainly not [+*3590*] [7], cannot [6], refused [+*2527*] [6], can't [+*1538*] [5], doesn't [5], isn't [+*1639*] [5], neither [5], never [+*172+1650+3590+3836*] [5], no [+*4246*] [5], nothing [+*4029*] [5], aren't [4], haven't [4], no more [4], not even [4], only [+*1623+3590*] [4], unlawful [+*2003*] [4], without [4], don't [+*3590*] [3], fail [3], no one [+*4029*] [3], none [+*4956*] [3], none [3], nor [+*2779*] [3], nor [3], aren't [+*1639*] [2], cannot [+*1639*] [2], cease to be [+*1639*] [2], couldn't [+*1538*] [2], few [+*4498*] [2], never [+*172+1650+3836*] [2], never again [+*3590*] [2], no [+*3590*] [2], not at all [+*3590*] [2], nothing [+*5515*] [2], nothing [+*5516*] [2], rather than [+*2779*] [2], refused to repent [+*3566*] [2], [+*3590*] [1], a long time [+*3900+5989*] [1], against [1], am a virgin [+*467+1182*] [1], any more than [+*2777*] [1], before very long [+*3552+4498*] [1], blinded [+*1838*] [1], but [+*2777*] [1], cannot [+*2400*] [1], cannot do [+*1538*] [1], continued raging [+*2130+3900*] [1], declined [+*2153*] [1], does so [+*2266*] [1], extraordinary [+*3836+5593*] [1], from [1], getting nowhere [+*4029+6067*] [1], great disturbance [+*3900+5431*] [1], greatly [+*3585*] [1], hanging over [+*733*] [1], haves [1], impossible [+*1543*] [1], is it possible that [1], isn't at all [+*3590*] [1], isn't [1], lack [1], lawful for [+*2003*] [1], lost connection with [+*3195*] [1], many [+*3900*] [1], more than [1], neither [+*2779*] [1], never [+*3590+4033*] [1], never [+*3590+4537*] [1], never [+*3590+4799*] [1], never [+*4537*] [1], never again [+*172+1650+3590+3836*] [1], no [+*4029*] [1], no ever [+*3590*] [1], no longer [+*3590*] [1], no place [+*4544*] [1], nobody [+*5516*] [1], nobody [1], none [+*4029*] [1], none [+*4246*] [1], none [+*570*] [1], not again [+*3590*] [1], not by any means [+*3590*] [1], not clear [+*1182*] [1], not even [+*4028*] [1], not one [+*3590*] [1], nothing [+*3590+4029*] [1], nothing [+*4005*] [1], nothing [+*4246+4839*] [1], nothing [+*4246*] [1], nothing at all [+*4029*] [1], nothing false [+*94*] [1], only [+*2445+4498*] [1], or [+*2779*] [1], out of place [+*465*] [1], refusal [1], refuse [+*2527*] [1], refuse [+*918*] [1], refuse [1], refused [+*1312*] [1], refused [+*4657*] [1], refusing [+*2527*] [1], separate from [+*3552*] [1], sharp [+*3900*] [1], shouldn't have [+*1256*] [1], shouldn't [1], staying away from [+*1877+4344*] [1], the law forbids [+*2003*] [1], unable [+*1538*] [1], unable [+*2710*] [1], unaware [+*1182*] [1], unequaled [+*1181+3888+5525*] [1], unequaled [+*1181+3888*] [1], unless [+*1623*] [1], unlike [+*6055*] [1], until judge [+*3212*] [1], unusual [+*5593*] [1], unwilling [+*2525*] [1], unwilling [+*2527*] [1], wasn't [1], what is more [+*247+1254+2779+3667*] [1], without [+*1666*] [1], without [+*2779*] [1], without sin [+*281*] [1], yet [+*4037*] [1]

4025   οὐά, *oua*   [1]

so [1]

Mk 15:29   by hurled insults at him, shaking their heads and saying, "**So**!

4026   οὐαί, *ouai*   [46]

woe [42], how dreadful [3], woes [1]

Mt 11:21   "**Woe** to you, Korazin! Woe to you, Bethsaida! If the miracles that

11:21   "**Woe** to you, Korazin! **Woe** to you, Bethsaida! If the miracles that
18: 7   "**Woe** to the world because of the things that cause people to sin!
18: 7   things must come, but **woe** to the man through whom they come!
23:13   "**Woe** to you, teachers of the law and Pharisees, you hypocrites!
23:15   "**Woe** to you, teachers of the law and Pharisees, you hypocrites!
23:16   "**Woe** to you, blind guides! You say, 'If anyone swears by the
23:23   "**Woe** to you, teachers of the law and Pharisees, you hypocrites!
23:25   "**Woe** to you, teachers of the law and Pharisees, you hypocrites!
23:27   "**Woe** to you, teachers of the law and Pharisees, you hypocrites!
23:29   "**Woe** to you, teachers of the law and Pharisees, you hypocrites!
24:19   **How dreadful** it will be in those days for pregnant women
26:24   But **woe** to that man who betrays the Son of Man! It would be
Mk 13:17   **How dreadful** it will be in those days for pregnant women
14:21   But **woe** to that man who betrays the Son of Man! It would be
Lk   6:24   "But **woe** to you who are rich, for you have already received your
6:25   **Woe** to you who are well fed now, for you will go hungry.
6:25   **Woe** to you who laugh now, for you will mourn and weep.
6:26   **Woe** to you when all men speak well of you, for that is how their
10:13   "**Woe** to you, Korazin! Woe to you, Bethsaida! For if the miracles
10:13   "Woe to you, Korazin! **Woe** to you, Bethsaida! For if the miracles
11:42   "**Woe** to you Pharisees, because you give God a tenth of your
11:43   "**Woe** to you Pharisees, because you love the most important seats
11:44   "**Woe** to you, because you are like unmarked graves, which men
11:46   Jesus replied, "And you experts in the law, **woe** to you, because you
11:47   "**Woe** to you, because you build tombs for the prophets, and it was
11:52   "**Woe** to you experts in the law, because you have taken away the
17: 1   bound to come, but **woe** to that person through whom they come.
21:23   **How dreadful** it will be in those days for pregnant women
22:22   go as it has been decreed, but **woe** to that man who betrays him."
1Co 9:16   I am compelled to preach. **Woe** to me if I do not preach the gospel!
Jude 1:11   **Woe** to them! They have taken the way of Cain; they have rushed
Rev 8:13   "**Woe**! Woe! Woe to the inhabitants of the earth, because of the
8:13   "Woe! **Woe**! Woe to the inhabitants of the earth, because of the
8:13   **Woe** to the inhabitants of the earth, because of the trumpet blasts
9:12   The first **woe** is past; two other woes are yet to come.
9:12   The first woe is past; two other **woes** are yet to come.
11:14   The second **woe** has passed; the third woe is coming soon.
11:14   The second woe has passed; the third **woe** is coming soon.
12:12   But **woe** to the earth and the sea, because the devil has gone down
18:10   and cry: " '**Woe**! Woe, O great city, O Babylon, city of power!
18:10   and cry: " 'Woe! **Woe**, O great city, O Babylon, city of power!
18:16   " '**Woe**! Woe, O great city, dressed in fine linen, purple
18:16   **Woe**, O great city, dressed in fine linen, purple and scarlet,
18:19   " '**Woe**! Woe, O great city, where all who had ships on the sea
18:19   **Woe**, O great city, where all who had ships on the sea became rich

4027   οὐδαμῶς, *oudamōs*   [1]   [√ *4024 + 1254*]

by no means [1]

Mt   2: 6   land of Judah, are **by no means** least among the rulers of Judah;

4028   οὐδέ, *oude*   [143]   [√ *4024 + 1254*]

or [35], nor [28], not even [17], not [16], neither [8], no [7], and [5], *untranslated* [4], and no [3], don't [2], even not [2], never [2], not either [2], and cannot [+*1538*] [1], and lost [+*2351*] [1], and not [1], and nothing [+*5516*] [1], and nothing [1], but not either [1], cannot do [+*1538*] [1], haven't [1], no [+*4246*] [1], not even [+*4024*] [1], nothing [+*1651*] [1], only [+*1651*] [1]

Mt   5:15   **Neither** do people light a lamp and put it under a bowl.
6:15   not forgive men their sins, your Father will **not** forgive your sins.
6:20   rust do not destroy, and where thieves do not break in **and** steal.
6:26   they do not sow **or** reap or store away in barns, and yet your
6:26   they do not sow or reap **or** store away in barns, and yet your
6:28   See how the lilies of the field grow. They do not labor **or** spin.
6:29   Yet I tell you that **not even** Solomon in all his splendor was
7:18   tree cannot bear bad fruit, **and** a bad tree cannot bear good fruit.
9:17   **Neither** do men pour new wine into old wineskins. If they do,
10:24   "A student is not above his teacher, **nor** a servant above his master.
11:27   **and no** one knows the Father except the Son and those to whom
12: 4   was not lawful for them to do, **[RPG]** but only for the priests.
12:19   He will not quarrel **or** cry out; no one will hear his voice in the
12:19   will not quarrel or cry out; **no** one will hear his voice in the streets.
13:13   they do not see; though hearing, they do not hear **or** understand.

16: 9 **Don't** you remember the five loaves for the five thousand,
16:10 **Or** the seven loaves for the four thousand, and how many
21:27 "**Neither** will I tell you by what authority I am doing these things.
21:32 And even after you saw this, you did **not** repent and believe him.
22:46 and from that day on **no** one dared to ask him any more questions.
23:13 do not enter, **nor** will you let those enter who are trying to.
24:21 beginning of the world until now—**and** never to be equaled again.
24:36 one knows about that day or hour, **not even** the angels in heaven,
24:36 not even the angels in heaven, **nor** the Son, but only the Father.
25:13 keep watch, because you do not know the day **or** the hour.
25:45 you did not do for one of the least of these, you did **not** do for me.'
27:14 But Jesus made no reply, **not even** to a single charge—to the great
Mk 4:22 **and** whatever is concealed is meant to be brought out into the
5: 3 and no one could bind him any more, **not even** with a chain.
6:31 were coming and going that they did **not** even have a chance to eat,
8:17 Do you still not see **or** understand? Are your hearts hardened?
11:33 "**Neither** will I tell you by what authority I am doing these things."
12:10 **Haven't** you read this scripture: " 'The stone the builders rejected
13:32 one knows about that day or hour, **not even** the angels in heaven,
13:32 not even the angels in heaven, **nor** the Son, but only the Father.
14:59 Yet even then their testimony did **not** agree.
16:13 and reported it to the rest; **but** they did **not** believe them **either.**
Lk 6: 3 "Have you **never** read what David did when he and his companions
6:43 "No good tree bears bad fruit, **nor** does a bad tree bear good fruit.
6:44 People do not pick figs from thornbushes, **or** grapes from briers.
7: 7 That is why I did **not even** consider myself worthy to come to you.
7: 9 "I tell you, I have **not** found such great faith **even** in Israel."
8:17 **and nothing** concealed that will not be known or brought out into
11:33 and puts it in a place where it will be hidden, **or** under a bowl.
12:24 They do not sow **or** reap, they have no storeroom or barn;
12:24 They do not sow or reap, they have no storeroom **or** barn;
12:26 Since **you cannot do** [+*1538*] this very little thing, why do you
12:27 They do not labor **or** spin. Yet I tell you, not even Solomon in all
12:27 **not even** Solomon in all his splendor was dressed like one of these.
12:33 be exhausted, where no thief comes near **and no** moth destroys.
16:31 they will **not** be convinced **even** if someone rises from the dead.' "
17:21 **nor** will people say, 'Here it is,' or 'There it is,'
18: 4 said to himself, 'Even though I don't fear God **or** care about men,
18:13 He would **not** [+*4024*] **even** look up to heaven, but beat his breast
20: 8 "**Neither** will I tell you by what authority I am doing these things."
20:36 and they can **no** longer die; for they are like the angels. They are
23:15 **Neither** has Herod, for he sent him back to us; as you can see,
23:40 "**Don't** you fear God," he said, "since you are under the same
Jn 1: 3 without him **nothing** [+*1651*] was made that has been made.
1:13 **nor** of human decision or a husband's will, but born of God.
1:13 nor of human decision **or** a husband's will, but born of God.
1:25 you baptize if you are not the Christ, **nor** Elijah, nor the Prophet?"
1:25 you baptize if you are not the Christ, nor Elijah, **nor** the Prophet?"
3:27 "A man can receive **only** [+*1651*] what is given him from heaven.
5:22 Moreover, [**RPG**] the Father judges no one, but has entrusted all
6:24 Once the crowd realized that neither Jesus **nor** his disciples were
7: 5 For **even** his own brothers did **not** believe in him.
8:11 "Then **neither** do I condemn you," Jesus declared. "Go now and
8:42 and now am here. I have **not** come on my own; but he sent me.
11:50 You do **not** realize that it is better for you that one man die for the
13:16 his master, **nor** is a messenger greater than the one who sent him.
14:17 cannot accept him, because it neither sees him **nor** knows him.
15: 4 in the vine. **Neither** can you bear fruit unless you remain in me.
16: 3 will do such things because they have not known the Father **or** me.
21:25 I suppose that **even** the whole world would **not** have room for the
Ac 2:27 me to the grave, **nor** will you let your Holy One see decay.
4:12 for there is **no** other name under heaven given to men by which we
4:32 **No** one claimed that any of his possessions was his own, but they
4:34 There were **no** needy persons among them. For from time to time
7: 5 He gave him no inheritance here, **not even** a foot of ground.
8:21 You have no part **or** share in this ministry, because your heart is
9: 9 For three days he was blind, and did not eat **or** drink *anything.*
16:21 advocating customs unlawful for us Romans to accept **or** practice."
17:25 **And** he is **not** served by human hands, as if he needed anything,
19: 2 "No, we have **not even** heard that there is a Holy Spirit."
24:13 **And** *they* **cannot** [+*1538*] prove to you the charges they are now
24:18 was no crowd with me, **nor** was I involved in any disturbance.
Ro 2:28 one outwardly, **nor** is circumcision merely outward and physical.
3:10 As it is written: "There is no one righteous, **not even** one;
4:15 brings wrath. And where there is no law there is **no** transgression.
8: 7 is hostile to God. It does not submit to God's law, **nor** can it do so.

9: 7 **Nor** because they are his descendants are they all Abraham's
9:16 It does not, therefore, depend on man's desire **or** effort, but on
11:21 did not spare the natural branches, he will **not** spare you **either.**
1Co 2: 6 but not the wisdom of this age **or** of the rulers of this age,
3: 2 for you were not yet ready for it. Indeed, you are still **not** ready.
4: 3 or by any human court; indeed, I do **not even** judge myself.
5: 1 among you, and of a kind that does **not** occur **even** among pagans:
11:14 Does **not** the very nature of things teach you that if a man has long
11:16 about this, we have no other practice—**nor** do the churches of God.
14:21 this people, but even then they will **not** listen to me," says the Lord.
15:13 is no resurrection of the dead, then **not even** Christ has been raised.
15:16 if the dead are not raised, then Christ has **not** been raised **either.**
15:50 kingdom of God, **nor** does the perishable inherit the imperishable.
2Co 7:12 on account of the one who did the wrong **or** of the injured party,
Gal 1: 1 sent not from men **nor** by man, but by Jesus Christ and God the
1:12 I did **not** receive it from any man, nor was I taught it; rather,
1:17 **nor** did I go up to Jerusalem to see those who were apostles before
2: 3 Yet **not even** Titus, who was with me, was compelled to be
2: 5 We did **not** give in to them for a moment, so that the truth of the
3:28 There is neither Jew **nor** Greek, slave nor free, male nor female,
3:28 There is neither Jew nor Greek, slave **nor** free, male nor female,
4:14 was a trial to you, you did not treat me with contempt **or** scorn.
6:13 **Not even** those who are circumcised obey the law, yet they want
Php 2:16 boast on the day of Christ that I did not run **or** labor for nothing.
1Th 2: 3 the appeal we make does not spring from error **or** impure motives,
2: 3 from error or impure motives, **nor** are we trying to trick you.
5: 5 sons of the day. We do not belong to the night **or** to the darkness.
2Th 3: 8 **nor** did we eat anyone's food without paying for it. On the
1Ti 2:12 I do not permit a woman to teach **or** to have authority over a man;
6: 7 nothing into the world, **and** we can take **nothing** [+*5516*] out of it.
6:16 lives in unapproachable light, whom no one has seen **or** can see.
Heb 8: 4 If he were on earth, he would **not** be a priest, for there are already
9:12 He did **not** enter by means of the blood of goats and calves;
9:18 This is why even the first covenant was **not** put into effect without
9:25 **Nor** did he enter heaven to offer himself again and again, the way
10: 8 **nor** were you pleased with them" (although the law required them
13: 5 has said, "Never will I leave you; [**NIE**] never will I forsake you."
1Pe 2:22 "He committed no sin, **and no** deceit was found in his mouth."
2Pe 1: 8 **and** unproductive in your knowledge of our Lord Jesus Christ.
1Jn 2:23 **No** [+*4246*] one who denies the Son has the Father;
3: 6 No one who continues to sin has either seen him **or** known him.
Rev 5: 3 But no one in heaven **or** on earth or under the earth could open the
5: 3 one in heaven or on earth **or** under the earth could open the scroll
7:16 Never again will they hunger; **never** again will they thirst.
7:16 The sun [**RPG**] will not beat upon them, nor any scorching heat.
7:16 The sun will not beat upon them, **nor** any scorching heat.
9: 4 were told not to harm the grass of the earth **or** any plant or tree,
9: 4 were told not to harm the grass of the earth or any plant **or** tree,
9:20 by these plagues still did **not** repent of the work of their hands;
12: 8 not strong enough, **and** they lost [+*2351*] their place in heaven.
20: 4 They had not worshiped the beast **or** his image and had not
21:23 The city does not need the sun **or** the moon to shine on it,

4029 οὐδείς, *oudeis* [234] [√ *4024 + 1254 + 1651*]

no one [89], nothing [37], no [23], *untranslated* [7], anyone [7], none [7], not any [6], not one [5], nothing [+*4024*] [5], any [3], anything [3], no one [+*4024*] [3], not anything [3], not anyone [2], not [2], at all [1], conscience is clear [+*5323*] [1], discredited [+*1650+3357*] [1], getting nowhere [+*4024+6067*] [1], haven't anything [1], men [1], men^s [1], never [1], no [+*4024*] [1], no anything [1], no at all [1], no one else [1], no truth [1], no way [1], no whatever [1], nobody [1], none [+*4024*] [1], nor anyone [+*1254*] [1], not [+*3590*] [1], not a thing [1], not a word [1], not anyone's [1], not in the least [1], not one [+*6034*] [1], nothing [+*3364*] [1], nothing [+*3590+4024*] [1], nothing at all [+*4024*] [1], one [1], only to [+*1623+3590*] [1], questions^s [1], was getting nowhere [+*6067*] [1], without [1]

Mt 5:13 It is **no** longer good for **anything,** except to be thrown out
6:24 "**No one** can serve two masters. Either he will hate the one
8:10 the truth, I have **not** found **anyone** in Israel with such great faith.
9:16 "**No one** sews a patch of unshrunk cloth on an old garment,
10:26 There is **nothing** concealed that will not be disclosed, or hidden
11:27 **No one** knows the Son except the Father, and no one knows the

13:34   he did **not** say **anything** to them without using a parable.
17: 8   When they looked up, they saw **no one** except Jesus.
17:20   to there' and it will move. **Nothing** will be impossible for you."
20: 7   " 'Because **no one** has hired us,' they answered. "He said to them,
21:19   by the road, he went up to it but found **nothing** on it except leaves.
22:16   You aren't swayed by **men**, because you pay no attention to who
22:46   **No one** could say a word in reply,
23:16   You say, 'If anyone swears by the temple, it means **nothing**;
23:18   You also say, 'If anyone swears by the altar, it means **nothing**;
24:36   "**No one** knows about that day or hour, not even the angels in
26:62   priest stood up and said to Jesus, "Are you **not** going to answer?
27:12   was accused by the chief priests and the elders, he gave **no** answer.
27:24   When Pilate saw that *he* **was getting nowhere** [+6067],

Mk   2:21   "**No one** sews a patch of unshrunk cloth on an old garment.
2:22   And **no one** pours new wine into old wineskins. If he does,
3:27   **no one** can enter a strong man's house and carry off his
5: 3   and **no one** could bind him any more, not even with a chain.
5: 4   the irons on his feet. **No one** was strong enough to subdue him.
5:37   He did not let **anyone** follow him except Peter, James and John the
6: 5   He could not do **any** miracles there, except lay his hands on a few
7:12   then you no longer let him do **anything** for his father or mother.
7:15   **Nothing** outside a man can make him 'unclean' by going into him.
7:24   He entered a house and did **not** want **anyone** to know it; yet he
9: 8   looked around, they no longer saw **anyone** with them except Jesus.
9:29   He replied, "This kind **[RPG]** can come out only by prayer."
9:39   "**No one** who does a miracle in my name can in the next moment
10:18   me good?" Jesus answered. "**No one** is good—except God alone.
10:29   "**no one** who has left home or brothers or sisters or mother
11: 2   you will find a colt tied there, which **no** one has ever ridden.
11:13   When he reached it, he found **nothing** but leaves, because it was
12:14   You aren't swayed by **men**s, because you pay no attention to who
12:34   And from then on **no one** dared ask him any more questions.
13:32   "**No one** knows about that day or hour, not even the angels in
14:60   **[RPG]** What is this testimony that these men are bringing against
14:61   **[RPG]** Again the high priest asked him, "Are you the Christ,
15: 4   to answer? **[RPG]** See how many things they are accusing you of."
15: 5   But Jesus still made no reply, **[RPG]** and Pilate was amazed.
16: 8   the tomb. They said **nothing** to anyone, because they were afraid.
16: 8   the tomb. They said nothing *to* **anyone**, because they were afraid.

Lk   1:61   to her, "There is **no one** among your relatives who has that name."
4: 2   He ate **nothing** during those days, and at the end of them he was
4:24   the truth," he continued, "**no** prophet is accepted in his hometown.
4:26   Yet Elijah was **not** sent to **any** of them, but to a widow in
4:27   the time of Elisha the prophet, yet **not one** of them was cleansed—
5: 5   we've worked hard all night and **haven't** caught **anything**.
5:36   "**No one** tears a patch from a new garment and sews it on an old
5:37   And **no one** pours new wine into old wineskins. If he does,
5:39   And **no one** after drinking old wine wants the new, for he says,
7:28   among those born of women there is **no one** greater than John;
8:16   "**No one** lights a lamp and hides it in a jar or puts it under a bed.
8:43   to bleeding for twelve years, but **no one** [+4024] could heal her.
9:36   this to themselves, and told **no one** at that time what they had seen.
9:36   and told no one at that time **[RPG]** what they had seen.
9:62   "**No one** who puts his hand to the plow and looks back is fit for
10:19   all the power of the enemy; **nothing** [+3590+4024] will harm you.
10:22   **No one** knows who the Son is except the Father, and no one knows
11:33   "**No one** lights a lamp and puts it in a place where it will be
12: 2   There is **nothing** concealed that will not be disclosed, or hidden
14:24   **not one** of those men who were invited will get a taste of my
15:16   the pods that the pigs were eating, but **no one** gave him anything.
16:13   "**No** servant can serve two masters. Either he will hate the one
18:19   me good?" Jesus answered. "**No one** is good—except God alone.
18:29   "**no one** who has left home or wife or brothers or parents
18:34   The disciples did **not** understand **any** of this. Its meaning was
19:30   you will find a colt tied there, which **no one** has ever ridden.
20:40   And no one dared to ask him any more **questions**s.
22:35   or sandals, did you lack anything?" "**Nothing**," they answered.
23: 4   and the crowd, "I find **no** basis for a charge against this man."
23: 9   He plied him with many questions, but Jesus gave him **no** answer.
23:14   and have found **no** basis for your charges against him.
23:15   back to us; as you can see, he has done **nothing** to deserve death.
23:22   I have found in him **no** grounds for the death penalty. Therefore I
23:41   what our deeds deserve. But this man has done **nothing** wrong."
23:53   it in a tomb cut in the rock, one in which **no one** had yet been laid.

Jn   1:18   **No one** has ever seen God, but God the One and Only, who is at
3: 2   For **no one** could perform the miraculous signs you are doing if

3:13   **No one** has ever gone into heaven except the one who came from
3:32   to what he has seen and heard, but **no one** accepts his testimony.
4:27   But **no one** asked, "What do you want?" or "Why are you talking
5:19   "I tell you the truth, the Son can do **nothing** [+4024] by himself;
5:22   Moreover, the Father judges **no one**, but has entrusted all judgment
5:30   By myself I can do **nothing** [+4024]; I judge only as I hear,
6:44   "**No one** can come to me unless the Father who sent me draws
6:63   The Spirit gives life; the flesh counts for **nothing** [+4024].
6:65   "This is why I told you that **no one** can come to me unless the
7: 4   **No one** who wants to become a public figure acts in secret.
7:13   But **no one** would say anything publicly about him for fear of the
7:19   Yet **not one** of you keeps the law. Why are you trying to kill me?"
7:26   speaking publicly, and they are **not** saying a **word** to him.
7:27   when the Christ comes, **no one** will know where he is from."
7:30   At this they tried to seize him, but **no one** laid a hand on him,
7:44   Some wanted to seize him, but **no one** laid a hand on him.
8:10   asked her, "Woman, where are they? Has **no one** condemned you?"
8:11   "**No one**, sir," she said. "Then neither do I condemn you," Jesus
8:15   judge by human standards; I pass judgment on **no one** [+4024].
8:20   Yet **no one** seized him, because his time had not yet come.
8:28   and that I do **nothing** on my own but speak just what the Father
8:33   are Abraham's descendants and have never been slaves *of* **anyone**.
8:54   Jesus replied, "If I glorify myself, my glory means **nothing**.
9: 4   of him who sent me. Night is coming, when **no one** can work.
9:33   If this man were not from God, he could do **nothing** [+4024]."
10:18   **No one** takes it from me, but I lay it down of my own accord.
10:29   greater than all; **no one** can snatch them out of my Father's hand.
10:41   They said, "Though John **never** performed a miraculous sign,
11:49   high priest that year, spoke up, "You know **nothing** [+4024] **at all**!
12:19   to one another, "See, *this is* **getting** us **nowhere** [+4024+6067].
13:28   but **no one** at the meal understood why Jesus said this to him.
14: 6   and the life. **No one** comes to the Father except through me.
14:30   the prince of this world is coming. He has **no** [+4024] hold on me,
15: 5   will bear much fruit; apart from me you can do **nothing** [+4024].
15:13   Greater love has **no one** than this, that he lay down his life for his
15:24   If I had not done among them what **no one** else did, they would not
16: 5   who sent me, yet **none** of you asks me, 'Where are you going?'
16:22   and you will rejoice, and **no one** will take away your joy.
16:23   In that day you will no longer ask me **anything**. I tell you the truth,
16:24   Until now you have not asked for **anything** in my name. Ask
16:29   "Now you are speaking clearly and **without** figures of speech.
17:12   **None** has been lost except the one doomed to destruction so that
18: 9   would be fulfilled: "I have not lost **one** of those you gave me."
18:20   where all the Jews come together. I said **nothing** in secret.
18:31   "But we have no right to execute **anyone**," the Jews objected.
18:38   again to the Jews and said, "I find **no** basis for a charge against him.
19: 4   I am bringing him out to you to let you know that I find **no** basis
19:11   "You would have no power over me **[RPG]** if it were not given to
19:41   and in the garden a new tomb, in which **no one** had ever been laid.
21: 3   went out and got into the boat, but that night they caught **nothing**.
21:12   **None** of the disciples dared ask him, "Who are you?"

Ac   4:12   Salvation is found in **no one** [+4024] else, for there is no other
4:14   healed standing there with them, there was **nothing** they could say.
5:13   **No one** else dared join them, even though they were highly
5:23   at the doors; but when we opened them, we found **no one** inside."
5:36   all his followers were dispersed, and it all came to **nothing**.
8:16   because the Holy Spirit had not yet come upon **any** of them;
9: 8   the ground, but when he opened his eyes he could see **nothing**.
15: 9   He made **no** distinction between us and them, for he purified their
17:21   and the foreigners who lived there spent their time doing **nothing**
18:10   For I am with you, and **no one** is going to attack and harm you,
18:17   him in front of the court. But Gallio showed **no** concern **whatever**.
19:27   only that our trade will lose its good name, but also that the temple
         of the great goddess Artemis *will be* **discredited** [+1650+3357],
20:20   You know that I have **not** [+3590] hesitated to preach anything that
20:24   However, I consider my life worth **nothing** [+3364] to me,
20:33   I have not coveted **anyone's** silver or gold or clothing.
21:24   Then everybody will know there is **no truth** in these reports about
23: 9   "We find **nothing** wrong with this man," they said. "What if a spirit
25:10   I have **not** done **any** wrong to the Jews, as you yourself know very
25:11   But if the charges brought against me by these Jews are **not** *true*,
25:11   Jews are not true, **no one** has the right to hand me over to them.
25:18   they did **not** charge him with **any** of the crimes I had expected.
26:22   I am saying **nothing** beyond what the prophets and Moses said
26:26   I am convinced that **none** [+4024] of this has escaped his notice,
26:31   "This man is **not** doing **anything** that deserves death

27:22 keep up your courage, because **not one** [+*6034*] of you will be lost;
27:34 it to survive. **Not one** of you will lose a single hair from his head."
28: 5 Paul shook the snake off into the fire and suffered **no** ill effects.
28:17 although I have done **nothing** against our people or against the
Ro   8: 1 there is now **no** condemnation for those who are in Christ Jesus,
14: 7 For **none** of us lives to himself alone and none of us dies to himself
14: 7 of us lives to himself alone and **none** of us dies to himself alone.
14:14 Lord Jesus, I am fully convinced that **no** *food* is unclean in itself.
1Co   1:14 I am thankful that I did **not** baptize **any** of you except Crispus
2: 8 **None** of the rulers of this age understood it, for if they had,
2:11 In the same way **no one** knows the thoughts of God except the
2:15 all things, but he himself is **not** subject to **any** *man's* judgment:
3:11 For **no one** can lay any foundation other than the one already laid,
4: 4 My **conscience is clear** [+*5323*], but that does not make me
6: 5 Is it possible that there is **nobody** among you wise enough to judge
7:19 Circumcision is **nothing** and uncircumcision is nothing.
7:19 Circumcision is nothing and uncircumcision is **nothing**.
8: 4 We know that an idol is **nothing** *at all* in the world and that there
8: 4 idol is nothing at all in the world and that there is **no** God but one.
9:15 But I have not used **any** of these rights. And I am not writing this
9:15 I would rather die than have **anyone** deprive me of this boast.
12: 3 Therefore I tell you that **no one** who is speaking by the Spirit of
12: 3 "Jesus be cursed," and **no one** can say, "Jesus is Lord," except by
13: 2 a faith that can move mountains, but have not love, I am **nothing**.
13: 3 surrender my body to the flames, but have not love, I gain **nothing**.
14: 2 Indeed, **no one** understands him; he utters mysteries with his spirit.
14:10 of languages in the world, yet **none** of them is without meaning.
2Co   5:16 So from now on we regard **no one** from a worldly point of view.
7: 2 We have wronged **no one**, we have corrupted no one, we have
7: 2 We have wronged no one, we have corrupted **no one**, we have
7: 2 no one, we have corrupted no one, we have exploited **no one**.
7: 5 For when we came into Macedonia, this body of ours had **no** rest,
11: 9 was with you and needed something, I was not a burden to **anyone**,
12:11 for I am **not in the least** inferior to the "super-apostles," even
12:11 the least inferior to the "super-apostles," even though I am **nothing**.
Gal   2: 6 to be important—whatever they were makes **no** difference to me;
2: 6 by external appearance—those men added **nothing** to my message.
3:11 Clearly **no one** is justified before God by the law, because,
3:15 Just as **no one** can set aside or add to a human covenant that has
4: 1 he is **no** different from a slave, although he owns the whole estate.
4:12 like me, for I became like you. You have done me **no** wrong.
5: 2 yourselves be circumcised, Christ will be of **no** value to you **at all**.
5:10 I am confident in the Lord that you will take **no** other view.
Eph   5:29 After all, **no one** ever hated his own body, but he feeds and cares
Php   1:20 I eagerly expect and hope that I will in **no way** be ashamed,
2:20 I have **no one else** like him, who takes a genuine interest in your
4:15 **not one** church shared with me in the matter of giving
1Ti   4: 4 and **nothing** is to be rejected if it is received with thanksgiving,
6: 7 For we brought **nothing** into the world,
6:16 lives in unapproachable light, whom **no** one has seen or can see.
2Ti   2: 4 **No one** serving as a soldier gets involved in civilian affairs—
2:14 about words; it is of **no** value, and only ruins those who listen.
4:16 At my first defense, **no one** came to my support, but everyone
Tit   1:15 but to those who are corrupted and do not believe, **nothing** is pure.
Phm   1:14 But I did **not** want to do **anything** without your consent, so that
Heb   4: 8 everything under him, God left **nothing** that is not subject to him.
6:13 since there was **no one** greater for him to swear by, he swore by
7:13 and **no one** from that tribe has ever served at the altar.
7:14 and in regard to that tribe Moses said **nothing** about priests.
7:19 (for the law made **nothing** perfect), and a better hope is introduced,
12:14 and to be holy; without holiness **no one** will see the Lord.
Jas   1:13 cannot be tempted by evil, **nor** does he tempt **anyone** [+*1254*];
3: 8 but no man can tame the tongue. It is a restless evil, full of deadly
1Jn   1: 5 and declare to you: God is light; in him there is **no** darkness **at all**.
4:12 **No one** has ever seen God; but if we love one another, God lives in
Rev   2:17 written on it, known **only** [+*1623+3590*] **to** him who receives it.
3: 7 What he opens **no one** can shut, and what he shuts no one can
3: 7 he opens no one can shut, and what he shuts **no one** can open.
3: 8 I have placed before you an open door that **no one** can shut.
3:17 'I am rich; I have acquired wealth and do **not** need **a thing**.'
5: 3 But **no one** in heaven or on earth or under the earth could open the
5: 4 because **no one** was found who was worthy to open the scroll
7: 9 and there before me was a great multitude that **no one** could count,
14: 3 **No one** could learn the song except the 144,000 who had been
15: 8 and **no one** could enter the temple until the seven plagues of the
18:11 and mourn over her because **no one** buys their cargoes any more—

19:12 He has a name written on him that **no one** knows but he himself.

4030 οὐδέποτε, *oudepote* [16]
[√ *4024* + *1254* + *4544* + *5445*]

never [13], nothing ever [2], no one ever [1]

Mt   7:23 Then I will tell them plainly, 'I **never** knew you. Away from me,
9:33 and said, "**Nothing** like this has **ever** been seen in Israel."
21:16 replied Jesus, "have you **never** read, " 'From the lips of children
21:42 Jesus said to them, "Have you **never** read in the Scriptures:
26:33 Peter replied, "Even if all fall away on account of you, I **never**
Mk   2:12 they praised God, saying, "We have **never** seen anything like this!"
2:25 "Have you **never** read what David did when he and his companions
Lk   15:29 years I've been slaving for you and **never** disobeyed your orders.
15:29 Yet you **never** gave me even a young goat so I could celebrate
Jn   7:46 "**No one** ever spoke the way this man does," the guards declared.
Ac   10:14 Peter replied. "I have **never** eaten anything impure or unclean."
11: 8 Lord! **Nothing** impure or unclean has **ever** entered my mouth.'
14: 8 in his feet, who was lame from birth and had **never** walked.
1Co   13: 8 Love **never** fails. But where there are prophecies, they will cease;
Heb   10: 1 For this reason it can **never**, by the same sacrifices repeated
10:11 he offers the same sacrifices, which can **never** take away sins.

4031 οὐδέπω, *oudepō* [4] [√ *4024* + *1254*]

not yet [2], ever [1], still not [1]

Jn   7:39 Spirit had not been given, since Jesus had **not yet** been glorified.
19:41 and in the garden a new tomb, in which no one had **ever** been laid.
20: 9 (They **still** did **not** understand from Scripture that Jesus had to rise
Ac   8:16 because the Holy Spirit had **not yet** come upon any of them;

4032 οὐθείς, *outheis*   Not used in UBS/NIV
[√ *4024* + *1254* + *1651*]

4033 οὐκέτι, *ouketi* [47] [√ *4024* + *2285*]

no longer [27], any more [3], again [2], no more [2], cannot again [1], ever again [1], forgets [+*3648*] [1], from then on [1], never [+*3590+4024*] [1], never again [1], no any more [1], no [1], not anymore [1], not longer [1], not [1], still no [1], unable [+*2710*] [1]

Mt   19: 6 So they are **no longer** two, but one. Therefore what God has joined
22:46 and from that day on no one dared to ask him **any more** questions.
Mk   5: 3 and no one could bind him **any more**, not even with a chain.
7:12 then you **no longer** let him do anything for his father or mother.
9: 8 looked around, they **no longer** saw anyone with them except Jesus.
10: 8 two will become one flesh.' So they are **no longer** two, but one.
12:34 And **from then on** no one dared ask him any more questions.
14:25 I will not drink **again** of the fruit of the vine until that day when I
15: 5 But Jesus **still** made **no** reply,
Lk   15:19 I am **no longer** worthy to be called your son; make me like one of
15:21 and against you. I am **no longer** worthy to be called your son.'
20:40 And **no** one dared to ask him **any more** questions.
Jn   4:42 the woman, "We **no longer** believe just because of what you said;
6:66 many of his disciples turned back and **no longer** followed him.
11:54 Therefore Jesus **no longer** moved about publicly among the Jews.
14:19 Before long, the world will **not** see me **anymore**, but you will see
14:30 I will **not** speak with you much longer, for the prince of this world
15:15 I **no longer** call you servants, because a servant does not know his
16:10 because I am going to the Father, where you can see me **no longer**;
16:16 "In a little while you will see me **no more**, and then after a little
16:21 but when her baby is born *she* **forgets** [+*3648*] the anguish
16:25 a time is coming when I will **no longer** use this kind of language
17:11 I will remain in the world **no longer**, but they are still in the world,
21: 6 *they were* **unable** [+*2710*] to haul the net in because of the large
Ac   8:39 and the eunuch did not see him **again**, but went on his way
20:25 I have gone about preaching the kingdom will **ever** see me **again**.
20:38 most was his statement that they would **never** see his face **again**.
Ro   6: 9 that since Christ was raised from the dead, he **cannot** die **again**;
6: 9 he cannot die again; death no longer has mastery over him.
7:17 As it is, it is **no longer** I myself who do it, but it is sin living in me.
7:20 it is **no longer** I who do it, but it is sin living in me that does it.
11: 6 And if by grace, then it is **no longer** by works; if it were, grace
11: 6 is no longer by works; if it were, grace would **no longer** be grace.

14:15 because of what you eat, you are **no longer** acting in love.
2Co 1:23 that it was in order to spare you that I did **not** return to Corinth.
     5:16 Though we have once regarded Christ in this way, we do so **no longer**.
Gal 2:20 I have been crucified with Christ and I **no longer** live, but Christ
     3:18 depends on the law, then it **no longer** depends on a promise;
     3:25 faith has come, we are **no longer** under the supervision of the law.
     4: 7 So you are **no longer** a slave, but a son; and since you are a son,
Eph 2:19 Consequently, you are **no longer** foreigners and aliens, but fellow
Phm 1:16 **no longer** as a slave, but better than a slave, as a dear brother.
Heb 10:18 these have been forgiven, there is **no longer** any sacrifice for sin.
    10:26 received the knowledge of the truth, **no** sacrifice for sins is left,
Rev 10: 6 and all that is in it, and said, "There will be **no more** delay!
    18:11 and mourn over her because no one buys their cargoes **any more**—
    18:14 and splendor have vanished, **never** [+3590+4024] to be recovered.'

4034 οὐκοῦν, *oukoun* [1] [√ 4024 + 4036]

then [1]

Jn 18:37 "You are a king, **then**!" said Pilate. Jesus answered, "You are right

4035 Οὐλαμμαούς, *Oulammaous* Not used in UBS/NIV [√ cf. 1843]

4036 οὖν, *oun* [499 / 497] [→ 1326, 3528, 3529, 3889, 4034, 5521]

untranslated [180], then [110], therefore [71], so [62], now [12], when [11], but [6], and [5], therefore [+726] [5], at this [4], finally [3], consequently [+726] [2], finally [+5538] [2], meanwhile [2], now then [2], so then [2], thus [2], after all [1], again [1], as [1], at that point [1], because of [1], conclude then [1], however [1], inasmuch as [+2093+3525+4012] [1], still [1], that [1], this made [1], too [1], well then [1], what has happened [+4544] [1], what shall we do [+1639+5515] [1], yet [1]

Mt   1:17 **Thus** there were fourteen generations in all from Abraham to
     3: 8 [NIE] Produce fruit in keeping with repentance.
     3:10 **and** every tree that does not produce good fruit will be cut down
     5:19 [NIE] Anyone who breaks one of the least of these
     5:23 "**Therefore**, if you are offering your gift at the altar and there
     5:48 Be perfect, **therefore**, as your heavenly Father is perfect.
     6: 2 "**So** when you give to the needy, do not announce it with trumpets,
     6: 8 [NIE] Do not be like them, for your Father knows what you need
     6: 9 "This, **then**, is how you should pray: " 'Our Father in heaven,
     6:22 [NIE] If your eyes are good, your whole body will be full of light.
     6:23 If **then** the light within you is darkness, how great is that darkness!
     6:31 **So** do not worry, saying, 'What shall we eat?' or 'What shall we
     6:34 **Therefore** do not worry about tomorrow, for tomorrow will worry
     7:11 If you, **then**, though you are evil, know how to give good gifts to
     7:12 **So** in everything, do to others what you would have them do to
     7:24 "**Therefore** everyone who hears these words of mine and puts
     9:38 Ask the Lord of the harvest, **therefore**, to send out workers into his
    10:16 **Therefore** be as shrewd as snakes and as innocent as doves.
    10:26 "**So** do not be afraid of them. There is nothing concealed that will
    10:31 **So** don't be afraid; you are worth more than many sparrows.
    10:32 [NIE] "Whoever acknowledges me before men, I will also
    12:12 [NIE] How much more valuable is a man than a sheep!
    12:26 he is divided against himself. How **then** can his kingdom stand?
    13:18 "Listen **then** to what the parable of the sower means:
    13:27 good seed in your field? Where **then** did the weeds come from?'
    13:28 asked him, 'Do you want [NIE] us to go and pull them up?'
    13:40 [NIE] "As the weeds are pulled up and burned in the fire,
    13:56 his sisters with us? Where **then** did this man get all these things?"
    17:10 **then** do the teachers of the law say that Elijah must come first?"
    18: 4 **Therefore**, whoever humbles himself like this child is the greatest
    18:26 [NIE] "The servant fell on his knees before him. 'Be patient with
    18:29 [NIE] "His fellow servant fell to his knees and begged him,
    18:31 **When** the other servants saw what had happened, they were
    19: 6 **Therefore** what God has joined together, let man not separate."
    19: 7 "Why **then**," they asked, "did Moses command that a man give his
    21:25 'From heaven,' he will ask, '**Then** why didn't you believe him?'
    21:40 "**Therefore**, when the owner of the vineyard comes, what will he

22: 9 [NIE] Go to the street corners and invite to the banquet anyone
    22:17 Tell us then, what is your opinion? Is it right to pay taxes to Caesar
    22:21 Then he said to them, [NIE] "Give to Caesar what is Caesar's,
    22:28 **Now then**, at the resurrection, whose wife will she be of the seven,
    22:43 He said to them, "How is it **then** that David, speaking by the Spirit,
    22:45 If **then** David calls him 'Lord,' how can he be his son?"
    23: 3 **So** you must obey them and do everything they tell you. But do not
    23:20 **Therefore**, he who swears by the altar swears by it and by
    24:15 "**So** when you see standing in the holy place 'the abomination that
    24:26 "**So** if anyone tells you, 'There he is, out in the desert,' do not go
    24:42 "**Therefore** keep watch, because you do not know on what day
    25:13 "**Therefore** keep watch, because you do not know the day
    25:27 **Well then**, you should have put my money on deposit with the
    25:28 [NIE] " 'Take the talent from him and give it to the one who has
    26:54 **then** would the Scriptures be fulfilled that say it must happen in
    27:17 **So** when the crowd had gathered, Pilate asked them, "Which one do
    27:22 "What shall I do, **then**, with Jesus who is called Christ?" Pilate
    27:64 **So** give the order for the tomb to be made secure until the third
    28:19 **Therefore** go and make disciples of all nations, baptizing them in
Mk 10: 9 **Therefore** what God has joined together, let man not separate."
    11:31 'From heaven,' he will ask, '**Then** why didn't you believe him?'
    12: 9 "What **then** will the owner of the vineyard do? He will come
    13:35 "**Therefore** keep watch because you do not know when the owner
    15:12 "What shall I do, **then**, with the one you call the king of the Jews?"
    16:19 [NIE] After the Lord Jesus had spoken to them, he was taken up
Lk   3: 7 [NIE] John said to the crowds coming out to be baptized by him,
     3: 8 [NIE] Produce fruit in keeping with repentance. And do not begin
     3: 9 **and** every tree that does not produce good fruit will be cut down
     3:10 "What should we do **then**?" the crowd asked.
     3:18 And [NIE] with many other words John exhorted the people
     4: 7 **So** if you worship me, it will all be yours."
     7:31 "To what, **then**, can I compare the people of this generation?
     7:42 the debts of both. **Now** which of them will love him more?"
     8:18 **Therefore** consider carefully how you listen. Whoever has will be
    10: 2 Ask the Lord of the harvest, **therefore**, to send out workers into his
    10:40 has left me to do the work by myself? [NIE] Tell her to help me!"
    11:13 If you **then**, though you are evil, know how to give good gifts to
    11:35 See to it, **then**, that the light within you is not darkness.
    11:36 **Therefore**, if your whole body is full of light, and no part of it
    12:26 [NIE] Since you cannot do this very little thing, why do you
    13: 7 on this fig tree and haven't found any. [UBS+ *So*] Cut it down!
    13:14 **So** come and be healed on those days, not on the Sabbath."
    13:18 **Then** Jesus asked, "What is the kingdom of God like? What shall I
    14:33 [NIE] In the same way, any of you who does not give up
    14:34 [NIE] "Salt is good, but if it loses its saltiness, how can it be made
    16:11 **So** if you have not been trustworthy in handling worldly wealth,
    16:27 "He answered, '**Then** I beg you, father, send Lazarus to my father's
    19:12 [NIE] He said: "A man of noble birth went to a distant country to
    20: 5 killed him. "What **then** will the owner of the vineyard do to them?
    20:17 and asked, "**Then** what is the meaning of that which is written:
    20:29 **Now** there were seven brothers. The first one married a woman
    20:33 **Now** then, at the resurrection whose wife will she be,
    20:44 [NIE] David calls him 'Lord.' How then can he be his son?"
    21: 7 "Teacher," they asked, [NIE] "when will these things happen?
    21:14 **But** make up your mind not to worry beforehand how you will
    22:70 They all asked, "Are you **then** the Son of God?" He replied,
    23:16 **Therefore**, I will punish him and then release him."
    23:22 **Therefore** I will have him punished and then release him."
Jn   1:21 They asked him, "**Then** who are you? Are you Elijah?" He said,
     1:22 **Finally** they said, "Who are you? Give us an answer to take back to
     1:25 "Why **then** do you baptize if you are not the Christ, nor Elijah,
     1:39 **So** they went and saw where he was staying, and spent that day
     2:18 **Then** the Jews demanded of him, "What miraculous sign can you
     2:20 [NIE] The Jews replied, "It has taken forty-six years to build this
     2:22 After [NIE] he was raised from the dead, his disciples recalled
     3:25 [NIE] An argument developed between some of John's disciples
     3:29 [NIE] That joy is mine, and it is now complete.
     4: 1 [NIE] The Pharisees heard that Jesus was gaining and baptizing
     4: 5 **So** he came to a town in Samaria called Sychar, near the plot of
     4: 6 Jacob's well was there, **and** Jesus, tired as he was from the
     4: 9 [NIE] The Samaritan woman said to him, "You are a Jew
     4:11 and the well is deep. [NIE] Where can you get this living water?
     4:28 **Then**, leaving her water jar, the woman went back to the town
     4:33 **Then** his disciples said to each other, "Could someone have
     4:40 **So** when the Samaritans came to him, they urged him to stay with
     4:45 [NIE] When he arrived in Galilee, the Galileans welcomed him.

4:46 **[NIE]** Once more he visited Cana in Galilee, where he had turned
4:48 **[NIE]** "Unless you people see miraculous signs and wonders,"
4:52 **[NIE]** When he inquired as to the time when his son got better,
4:52 **[NIE]** they said to him, "The fever left him yesterday at the
4:53 **Then** the father realized that this was the exact time at which Jesus
5:10 and **so** the Jews said to the man who had been healed, "It is the
5:18 For this reason **[NIE]** the Jews tried all the harder to kill him;
5:19 **[NIE]** Jesus gave them this answer: "I tell you the truth, the Son
6: 5 **When** Jesus looked up and saw a great crowd coming toward him,
6:10 in that place, **and** the men sat down, about five thousand of them.
6:11 Jesus **then** took the loaves, gave thanks, and distributed to those
6:13 **So** they gathered them and filled twelve baskets with the pieces of
6:14 **[NIE]** After the people saw the miraculous sign that Jesus did,
6:15 **[NIE]** knowing that they intended to come and make him king by
6:19 **[NIE]** When they had rowed three or three and a half miles,
6:21 **Then** they were willing to take him into the boat, and immediately
6:24 **[NIE]** Once the crowd realized that neither Jesus nor his disciples
6:28 **Then** they asked him, "What must we do to do the works God
6:30 **So** they asked him, "What miraculous sign then will you give that
6:30 **then** will you give that we may see it and believe you?
6:32 **[NIE]** Jesus said to them, "I tell you the truth, it is not Moses who
6:34 **[NIE]** "Sir," they said, "from now on give us this bread."
6:35 **Then** [UBS-] Jesus declared, "I am the bread of life. He who
6:41 **At this** the Jews began to grumble about him because he said,
6:52 **Then** the Jews began to argue sharply among themselves,
6:53 **[NIE]** Jesus said to them, "I tell you the truth, unless you eat the
6:60 **[NIE]** On hearing it, many of his disciples said, "This is a hard
6:62 **[NIE]** What if you see the Son of Man ascend to where he was
6:67 **[NIE]** "You do not want to leave too, do you?" Jesus asked the
7: 3 **[NIE]** Jesus' brothers said to him, "You ought to leave here
7: 6 **Therefore** Jesus told them, "The right time for me has not yet
7:11 **Now** at the Feast the Jews were watching for him and asking,
7:15 **[NIE]** The Jews were amazed and asked, "How did this man get
7:16 **[NIE]** Jesus answered, "My teaching is not my own. It comes from
7:25 **At that point** some of the people of Jerusalem began to ask,
7:28 **Then** Jesus, still teaching in the temple courts, cried out, "Yes,
7:30 **At this** they tried to seize him, but no one laid a hand on him,
7:33 **[NIE]** Jesus said, "I am with you for only a short time, and
7:35 **[NIE]** The Jews said to one another, "Where does this man intend
7:40 **[NIE]** On hearing his words, some of the people said, "Surely this
7:43 **Thus** the people were divided because of Jesus.
7:45 **Finally** the temple guards went back to the chief priests
7:47 **[NIE]** "You mean he has deceived you also?" the Pharisees
8: 5 commanded us to stone such women. **Now** what do you say?"
8:12 **When** Jesus spoke again to the people, he said, "I am the light of
8:13 **[NIE]** The Pharisees challenged him, "Here you are, appearing as
8:19 **Then** they asked him, "Where is your father?" "You do not know
8:21 **[NIE]** Once more Jesus said to them, "I am going away, and you
8:22 **This made** the Jews ask, "Will he kill himself? Is that why he says,
8:24 **[NIE]** I told you that you would die in your sins; if you do not
8:25 **[NIE]** "Who are you?" they asked. "Just what I have been claiming
8:28 **So** Jesus said, "When you have lifted up the Son of Man, then you
8:31 **[NIE]** To the Jews who had believed him, Jesus said, "If you hold
8:36 **So** if the Son sets you free, you will be free indeed.
8:38 and **[NIE]** you do what you have heard from your father."
8:41 "We are not illegitimate children," [UBS+ *so*] they protested.
8:52 **At this** the Jews exclaimed, "Now we know that you are
8:57 **[NIE]** "You are not yet fifty years old," the Jews said to him,
8:59 **At this**, they picked up stones to stone him, but Jesus hid himself,
9: 7 means Sent). **So** the man went and washed, and came home seeing.
9: 8 **[NIE]** His neighbors and those who had formerly seen him
9:10 **[NIE]** "How then were your eyes opened?" they demanded.
9:10 "How **then** were your eyes opened?" they demanded.
9:11 to Siloam and wash. **So** I went and washed, and then I could see."
9:15 **Therefore** the Pharisees also asked him how he had received his
9:16 **[NIE]** Some of the Pharisees said, "This man is not from God,
9:17 **Finally** they turned again to the blind man, "What have you to say
9:18 The Jews **still** did not believe that he had been blind and had
9:19 the one you say was born blind? How is it **that** now he can see?"
9:20 **[NIE]** "We know he is our son," the parents answered, "and we
9:24 **[NIE]** A second time they summoned the man who had been
9:25 **[NIE]** He replied, "Whether he is a sinner or not, I don't know.
9:26 **Then** they asked him, "What did he do to you? How did he open
10: 7 **Therefore** Jesus said again, "I tell you the truth, I am the gate for
10:24 **[NIE]** The Jews gathered around him, saying, "How long will you
10:39 **[NIE]** Again they tried to seize him, but he escaped their grasp.

11: 3 **So** the sisters sent word to Jesus, "Lord, the one you love is sick."
11: 6 **Yet** when he heard that Lazarus was sick, he stayed where he was
11:12 **[NIE]** His disciples replied, "Lord, if he sleeps, he will get better."
11:14 **So** then he told them plainly, "Lazarus is dead,
11:16 **Then** Thomas (called Didymus) said to the rest of the disciples,
11:17 **[NIE]** On his arrival, Jesus found that Lazarus had already been
11:20 **[NIE]** When Martha heard that Jesus was coming, she went out to
11:21 **[NIE]** "Lord," Martha said to Jesus, "if you had been here,
11:31 **When** the Jews who had been with Mary in the house, comforting
11:32 **[NIE]** When Mary reached the place where Jesus was and saw
11:33 **[NIE]** When Jesus saw her weeping, and the Jews who had come
11:36 **Then** the Jews said, "See how he loved him!"
11:38 **[NIE]** Jesus, once more deeply moved, came to the tomb.
11:41 **So** they took away the stone. Then Jesus looked up and said,
11:45 **Therefore** many of the Jews who had come to visit Mary,
11:47 **Then** the chief priests and the Pharisees called a meeting of the
11:53 **So** from that day on they plotted to take his life.
11:54 **Therefore** Jesus no longer moved about publicly among the Jews.
11:56 **[NIE]** They kept looking for Jesus, and as they stood in the
12: 1 **[NIE]** Six days before the Passover, Jesus arrived at Bethany,
12: 2 **[NIE]** Here a dinner was given in Jesus' honor. Martha served,
12: 3 **Then** Mary took about a pint of pure nard, an expensive perfume;
12: 7 **[NIE]** "Leave her alone," Jesus replied. ".It was intended, that she
12: 9 **Meanwhile** a large crowd of Jews found out that Jesus was there
12:17 **Now** the crowd that was with him when he called Lazarus from the
12:19 **So** the Pharisees said to one another, "See, this is getting us
12:21 **[NIE]** They came to Philip, who was from Bethsaida in Galilee,
12:28 **Then** a voice came from heaven, "I have glorified it, and will
12:29 **[NIE]** The crowd that was there and heard it said it had
12:34 **[NIE]** The crowd spoke up, "We have heard from the Law that the
12:35 **Then** Jesus told them, "You are going to have the light just a little
12:50 **So** whatever I say is just what the Father has told me to say."
13: 6 **[NIE]** He came to Simon Peter, who said to him, "Lord, are you
13:12 **[NIE]** When he had finished washing their feet, he put on his
13:14 **Now** that I, your Lord and Teacher, have washed your feet,
13:24 **[NIE]** Simon Peter motioned to this disciple and said, "Ask him
13:25 **[NIE]** Leaning back against Jesus, he asked him, "Lord, who is it?"
13:26 **Then**, dipping the piece of bread, he gave it to Judas Iscariot,
13:27 **[NIE]** "What you are about to do, do quickly," Jesus told him,
13:30 **[NIE]** As soon as Judas had taken the bread, he went out.
13:31 **[NIE]** When he was gone, Jesus said, "Now is the Son of Man
16:17 **[NIE]** Some of his disciples said to one another, "What does he
16:18 They kept asking, **[NIE]** "What does he mean by 'a little while'?
16:22 **So** with you: Now is your time of grief, but I will see you again
18: 3 **So** Judas came to the grove, guiding a detachment of soldiers
18: 4 **[NIE]** Jesus, knowing all that was going to happen to him,
18: 6 **[NIE]** When Jesus said, "I am he," they drew back and fell to the
18: 7 **[NIE]** Again he asked them, "Who is it you want?" And they said,
18: 8 Jesus answered. "If you are looking for me, **then** let these men go."
18:10 **Then** Simon Peter, who had a sword, drew it and struck the high
18:11 **[NIE]** Jesus commanded Peter, "Put your sword away! Shall I not
18:12 **Then** the detachment of soldiers with its commander
18:16 **[NIE]** The other disciple, who was known to the high priest,
18:17 **[NIE]** "You are not one of his disciples, are you?" the girl at the
18:19 **Meanwhile**, the high priest questioned Jesus about his disciples
18:24 **Then** Annas sent him, still bound, to Caiaphas the high priest.
18:25 **As** Simon Peter stood warming himself, he was asked, "You are not
18:27 **[NIE]** Again Peter denied it, and at that moment a rooster began
18:28 **Then** the Jews led Jesus from Caiaphas to the palace of the Roman
18:29 **So** Pilate came out to them and asked, "What charges are you
18:31 **[NIE]** Pilate said, "Take him yourselves and judge him by your
18:33 Pilate **then** went back inside the palace, summoned Jesus
18:37 **[NIE]** "You are a king, then!" said Pilate. Jesus answered, "You are
18:39 **[NIE]** Do you want me to release 'the king of the Jews'?"
18:40 **[NIE]** They shouted back, "No, not him! Give us Barabbas!"
19: 1 **[NIE]** Then Pilate took Jesus and had him flogged.
19: 5 **When** Jesus came out wearing the crown of thorns and the purple
19: 6 **[NIE]** As soon as the chief priests and their officials saw him,
19: 8 **[NIE]** When Pilate heard this, he was even more afraid,
19:10 **[NIE]** "Do you refuse to speak to me?" Pilate said. "Don't you
19:13 **When** Pilate heard this, he brought Jesus out and sat down on the
19:15 **But** they shouted, "Take him away! Take him away! Crucify him!"
19:16 **Finally** [+5538] Pilate handed him over to them to be crucified.
19:16 over to them to be crucified. **So** the soldiers took charge of Jesus.
19:20 **[NIE]** Many of the Jews read this sign, for the place where Jesus
19:21 **[NIE]** The chief priests of the Jews protested to Pilate, "Do not

19:23 [NIE] When the soldiers crucified Jesus, they took his clothes,
19:24 [NIE] "Let's not tear it," they said to one another. "Let's decide by
19:24 and cast lots for my clothing." **So** this is what the soldiers did.
19:26 **When** Jesus saw his mother there, and the disciple whom he loved
19:29 A jar of wine vinegar was there, **so** they soaked a sponge in it,
19:30 [NIE] When he had received the drink, Jesus said, "It is finished."
19:31 **Now** it was the day of Preparation, and the next day was to be a
19:32 The soldiers **therefore** came and broke the legs of the first man
19:38 With Pilate's permission, [NIE] he came and took the body away.
19:40 [NIE] Taking Jesus' body, the two of them wrapped it,
19:42 [NIE] Because it was the Jewish day of Preparation and since the
20: 2 **So** she came running to Simon Peter and the other disciple,
20: 3 **So** Peter and the other disciple started for the tomb.
20: 6 **Then** Simon Peter, who was behind him, arrived and went into the
20: 8 **Finally** [+*5538*] the other disciple, who had reached the tomb first,
20:10 **Then** the disciples went back to their homes,
20:11 [NIE] As she wept, she bent over to look into the tomb
20:19 [NIE] On the evening of that first day of the week,
20:20 [NIE] The disciples were overjoyed when they saw the Lord.
20:21 [NIE] Again Jesus said, "Peace be with you! As the Father has sent
20:25 **So** the other disciples told him, "We have seen the Lord!" But he
20:30 [NIE] Jesus did many other miraculous signs in the presence of
21: 5 [NIE] He called out to them, "Friends, haven't you any fish?"
21: 6 **When** they did, they were unable to haul the net in because of the
21: 7 **Then** the disciple whom Jesus loved said to Peter, "It is the Lord!"
21: 7 [NIE] As soon as Simon Peter heard him say, "It is the Lord,"
21: 9 [NIE] When they landed, they saw a fire of burning coals there
21:11 [NIE] Simon Peter climbed aboard and dragged the net ashore.
21:15 [NIE] When they had finished eating, Jesus said to Simon Peter,
21:21 **When** Peter saw him, he asked, "Lord, what about him?"
21:23 **Because of** this, the rumor spread among the brothers that this
Ac 1: 6 **So** when they met together, they asked him, "Lord, are you at this
1:18 [NIE] (With the reward he got for his wickedness, Judas bought a
1:21 **Therefore** it is necessary to choose one of the men who have been
2:30 **But** he was a prophet and knew that God had promised him on
2:33 [NIE] Exalted to the right hand of God, he has received from the
2:36 "**Therefore** let all Israel be assured of this: God has made this
2:41 [NIE] Those who accepted his message were baptized, and about
3:19 Repent, **then**, and turn to God, so that your sins may be wiped out,
5:41 [NIE] The apostles left the Sanhedrin, rejoicing because they had
8: 4 [NIE] Those who had been scattered preached the word wherever
8:22 [NIE] Repent of this wickedness and pray to the Lord.
8:25 **When** they had testified and proclaimed the word of the Lord,
9:31 **Then** the church throughout Judea, Galilee and Samaria enjoyed a
10:23 **Then** Peter invited the men into the house to be his guests.
10:29 raising any objection. [NIE] May I ask why you sent for me?"
10:32 [NIE] Send to Joppa for Simon who is called Peter. He is a guest
10:33 **So** I sent for you immediately, and it was good of you to come.
10:33 Now [NIE] we are all here in the presence of God to listen to
11:17 **So** if God gave them the same gift as he gave us, who believed in
11:19 **Now** those who had been scattered by the persecution in
12: 5 **So** Peter was kept in prison, but the church was earnestly praying
13: 4 [NIE] The two of them, sent on their way by the Holy Spirit,
13:38 "**Therefore**, my brothers, I want you to know that through Jesus
13:40 [NIE] Take care that what the prophets have said does not happen
14: 3 **So** Paul and Barnabas spent considerable time there,
15: 3 [NIE] The church sent them on their way, and as they traveled
15:10 Now **then**, why do you try to test God by putting on the necks of
15:27 **Therefore** we are sending Judas and Silas to confirm by word of
15:30 [NIE] The men were sent off and went down to Antioch,
16: 5 **So** the churches were strengthened in the faith and grew daily in
16:36 and Silas be released. Now [NIE] you can leave. Go in peace."
17:12 [NIE] Many of the Jews believed, as did also a number of
17:17 **So** he reasoned in the synagogue with the Jews
17:20 strange ideas to our ears, **and** we want to know what they mean."
17:23 **Now** what you worship as something unknown I am going to
17:29 "**Therefore** since we are God's offspring, we should not think that
17:30 [NIE] In the past God overlooked such ignorance, but now he
19: 3 So Paul asked, "**Then** what baptism did you receive?" "John's
19:32 in confusion: [NIE] Some were shouting one thing, some another.
19:36 **Therefore**, since these facts are undeniable, you ought to be quiet
19:38 If, **then**, Demetrius and his fellow craftsmen have a grievance
21:22 **What shall we do** [+*1639*+*5515*]? They will certainly hear that
21:23 **so** do what we tell you. There are four men with us who have made
22:29 [NIE] Those who were about to question him withdrew
23:15 Now **then**, you and the Sanhedrin petition the commander to bring

23:18 **So** he took him to the commander. The centurion said, "Paul,
23:21 [NIE] Don't give in to them, because more than forty of them are
23:22 [NIE] The commander dismissed the young man and cautioned
23:31 **So** the soldiers, carrying out their orders, took Paul with them
25: 1 [NIE] Three days after arriving in the province, Festus went up
25: 4 [NIE] Festus answered, "Paul is being held at Caesarea, and I
25: 5 [NIE] Let some of your leaders come with me and press charges
25:11 If, **however**, I am guilty of doing anything deserving death,
25:17 **When** they came here with me, I did not delay the case,
25:23 [NIE] The next day Agrippa and Bernice came with great pomp
26: 4 [NIE] "The Jews all know the way I have lived ever since I was a
26: 9 "**I too** was convinced that I ought to do all that was possible to
26:22 **But** I have had God's help to this very day,
28: 5 **But** Paul shook the snake off into the fire and suffered no ill
28:20 For this [NIE] reason I have asked to see you and talk with you.
28:28 "**Therefore** I want you to know that God's salvation has been sent
Ro 2:21 you, **then**, who teach others, do you not teach yourself? You who
2:26 If [NIE] those who are not circumcised keep the law's
3: 1 What advantage, **then**, is there in being a Jew, or what value is
3: 9 What shall we **conclude then**? Are we any better? Not at all!
3:27 Where, then, is boasting? It is excluded. On what principle?
3:31 Do we, **then**, nullify the law by this faith? Not at all! Rather,
4: 1 What **then** shall we say that Abraham, our forefather, discovered
4: 9 [NIE] Is this blessedness only for the circumcised, or also for the
4:10 [NIE] Under what circumstances was it credited? Was it after he
5: 1 **Therefore**, since we have been justified through faith, we have
5: 9 [NIE] Since we have now been justified by his blood, how much
5:18 **Consequently** [+*726*], just as the result of one trespass was
6: 1 What shall we say, **then**? Shall we go on sinning so that grace may
6: 4 **therefore** buried with him through baptism into death in order that,
6:12 **Therefore** do not let sin reign in your mortal body so that you
6:15 What **then**? Shall we sin because we are not under law but under
6:21 [NIE] What benefit did you reap at that time from the things you
7: 3 So **then**, if she marries another man while her husband is still
7: 7 What shall we say, **then**? Is the law sin? Certainly not! Indeed I
7:13 Did that which is good, **then**, become death to me? By no means!
7:25 So **then**, I myself in my mind am a slave to God's law, but in the
8:12 **Therefore** [+*726*], brothers, we have an obligation—but it is not to
8:31 What, **then**, shall we say in response to this? If God is for us,
9:14 What **then** shall we say? Is God unjust? Not at all!
9:16 It does not, **therefore** [+*726*], depend on man's desire or effort,
9:18 **Therefore** [+*726*] God has mercy on whom he wants to have
9:19 [NIE] One of you will say to me: "Then why does God still blame
9:19 "**Then** why does God still blame us? For who resists his will?"
9:30 What **then** shall we say? That the Gentiles, who did not pursue
10:14 How, **then**, can they call on the one they have not believed in?
11: 1 I ask **then**: Did God reject his people? By no means! I am an
11: 5 So [NIE] too, at the present time there is a remnant chosen by
11: 7 What **then**? What Israel sought so earnestly it did not obtain,
11:11 **Again** I ask: Did they stumble so as to fall beyond recovery?
11:13 **Inasmuch as** [+*2093*+*3525*+*4012*] I am the apostle to the Gentiles,
11:19 You will say **then**, "Branches were broken off so that I could be
11:22 Consider **therefore** the kindness and sternness of God: sternness to
12: 1 **Therefore**, I urge you, brothers, in view of God's mercy, to offer
13:10 harm to its neighbor. **Therefore** love is the fulfillment of the law.
13:12 **So** let us put aside the deeds of darkness and put on the armor of
14: 8 die to the Lord. **So**, whether we live or die, we belong to the Lord.
14:12 So **then**, each of us will give an account of himself to God.
14:13 **Therefore** let us stop passing judgment on one another. Instead,
14:16 [NIE] Do not allow what you consider good to be spoken of as
14:19 **therefore** [+*726*] make every effort to do what leads to peace
15:17 **Therefore** I glory in Christ Jesus in my service to God.
15:28 **So** after I have completed this task and have made sure that they
16:19 has heard about your obedience, **so** I am full of joy over you;
1Co 3: 5 What, **after all**, is Apollos? And what is Paul? Only servants,
4:16 **Therefore** I urge you to imitate me.
6: 4 **Therefore**, if you have disputes about such matters, appoint as
6: 7 The very fact [UBS+ *then*] that you have lawsuits among you
6:15 Shall I **then** take the members of Christ and unite them with a
7:26 [NIE] Because of the present crisis, I think that it is good for you
8: 4 So **then**, about eating food sacrificed to idols: We know that an
9:18 What **then** is my reward? Just this: that in preaching the gospel I
9:25 [NIE] They do it to get a crown that will not last; but we do it to
10:19 Do I mean **then** that a sacrifice offered to an idol is anything,
10:31 **So** whether you eat or drink or whatever you do, do it all for the
11:20 [NIE] When you come together, it is not the Lord's Supper you

14:11   **then** I do not grasp the meaning of what someone is saying,
14:15   **So** what shall I do? I will pray with my spirit, but I will also pray
14:23   **So** if the whole church comes together and everyone speaks in
14:26   What **then** shall we say, brothers? When you come together,
15:11   Whether, **then**, it was I or they, this is what we preach, and this is
16:11   No one, **then**, should refuse to accept him. Send him on his way in
16:18   my spirit and yours also. [NIE] Such men deserve recognition.
2Co   1:17   [NIE] When I planned this, did I do it lightly? Or do I make my
    3:12   **Therefore**, since we have such a hope, we are very bold.
    5: 6   **Therefore** we are always confident and know that as long as we
    5:11   Since, **then**, we know what it is to fear the Lord, we try to persuade
    5:20   We are **therefore** Christ's ambassadors, as though God were
    7: 1   [NIE] Since we have these promises, dear friends, let us purify
    8:24   **Therefore** show these men the proof of your love and the reason
    9: 5   **So** I thought it necessary to urge the brothers to visit you in
   11:15   It is not surprising, **then**, if his servants masquerade as servants of
   12: 9   **Therefore** I will boast all the more gladly about my weaknesses,
Gal   3: 5   Does God give [NIE] you his Spirit and work miracles among
    3:19   What, **then**, was the purpose of the law? It was added because of
    3:21   Is the law, **therefore**, opposed to the promises of God? Absolutely
    4:15   **What has happened to** [+4544] all your joy? I can testify that,
    5: 1   Stand firm, **then**, and do not let yourselves be burdened again by a
    6:10   **Therefore** [+726], as we have opportunity, let us do good to all
Eph   2:19   **Consequently** [+726], you are no longer foreigners and aliens,
    4: 1   As a prisoner for the Lord, **then**, I urge you to live a life worthy of
    4:17   **So** I tell you this, and insist on it in the Lord, that you must no
    5: 1   Be imitators of God, **therefore**, as dearly loved children
    5: 7   **Therefore** do not be partners with them.
    5:15   Be very careful, **then**, how you live—not as unwise but as wise,
    6:14   Stand firm **then**, with the belt of truth buckled around your waist,
Php   2: 1   [NIE] If you have any encouragement from being united with
    2:23   I hope, **therefore**, to send him as soon as I see how things go with
    2:28   **Therefore** I am all the more eager to send him, so that when you
    2:29   [NIE] Welcome him in the Lord with great joy, and honor men
    3:15   [NIE] All of us who are mature should take such a view of things.
Col   2: 6   **So then**, just as you received Christ Jesus as Lord, continue to live
    2:16   **Therefore** do not let anyone judge you by what you eat or drink,
    3: 1   Since, **then**, you have been raised with Christ, set your hearts on
    3: 5   Put to death, **therefore**, whatever belongs to your earthly nature:
    3:12   **Therefore**, as God's chosen people, holy and dearly loved,
1Th   4: 1   [NIE] Finally, brothers, we instructed you how to live in order to
    5: 6   So **then**, let us not be like others, who are asleep, but let us be alert
2Th   2:15   So **then**, brothers, stand firm and hold to the teachings we passed
1Ti   2: 1   I urge, **then**, first of all, that requests, prayers, intercession
    2: 8   [NIE] I want men everywhere to lift up holy hands in prayer,
    3: 2   **Now** the overseer must be above reproach, the husband of
    5:14   **So** I counsel younger widows to marry, to have children,
2Ti   1: 8   **So** do not be ashamed to testify about our Lord, or ashamed of me
    2: 1   You **then**, my son, be strong in the grace that is in Christ Jesus.
    2:21   [NIE] If a man cleanses himself from the latter, he will be an
Phm   1:17   **So** if you consider me a partner, welcome him as you would
Heb   2:14   Since [NIE] the children have flesh and blood, he too shared in
    4: 1   **Therefore**, since the promise of entering his rest still stands,
    4: 6   [NIE] It still remains that some will enter that rest, and those who
    4:11   Let us, **therefore**, make every effort to enter that rest, so that no
    4:14   **Therefore**, since we have a great high priest who has gone through
    4:16   Let us **then** approach the throne of grace with confidence,
    7:11   If perfection [NIE] could have been attained through the Levitical
    8: 4   If [NIE] he were on earth, he would not be a priest, for there are
    9: 1   **Now** the first covenant had regulations for worship and also an
    9:23   It was necessary, **then**, for the copies of the heavenly things to be
   10:19   **Therefore**, brothers, since we have confidence to enter the Most
   10:35   **So** do not throw away your confidence; it will be richly rewarded.
   13:15   Through Jesus, **therefore**, let us continually offer to God a
Jas   4: 4   [NIE] Anyone who chooses to be a friend of the world becomes
    4: 7   Submit yourselves, **then**, to God. Resist the devil, and he will flee
    4:17   Anyone, **then**, who knows the good he ought to do and doesn't do
    5: 7   Be patient, **then**, brothers, until the Lord's coming. See how the
    5:16   **Therefore** confess your sins to each other and pray for each other
1Pe   2: 1   **Therefore**, rid yourselves of all malice and all deceit, hypocrisy,
    2: 7   **Now** to you who believe, this stone is precious. But to those who
    4: 1   **Therefore**, since Christ suffered in his body, arm yourselves also
    4: 7   **Therefore** be clear minded and self-controlled so that you can
    5: 1   [NIE] To the elders among you, I appeal as a fellow elder,
    5: 6   Humble yourselves, **therefore**, under God's mighty hand,
2Pe   3:17   **Therefore**, dear friends, since you already know this, be on your

3Jn   1: 8   We ought **therefore** to show hospitality to such men so that we
Rev   1:19   "Write, **therefore**, what you have seen, what is now and what will
    2: 5   [NIE] Remember the height from which you have fallen!
    2:16   Repent **therefore**! Otherwise, I will soon come to you and will
    3: 3   Remember, **therefore**, what you have received and heard;
    3: 3   **But** if you do not wake up, I will come like a thief, and you will
    3:19   whom I love I rebuke and discipline. **So** be earnest, and repent.

4037   οὔπω, *oupō*   [26 / 28]   [√ 4024]

not yet [17], still not [3], still to come [2], before [1], ever [1], still no [1], up to that time not [1], yet [+4024] [1], yet not [1]

Mt   16: 9   Do you **still not** understand? Don't you remember the five loaves
   24: 6   not alarmed. Such things must happen, but the end is **still to come**.
Mk   4:40   his disciples, "Why are you so afraid? Do you **still** have **no** faith?"
    8:17   Do you **still not** see or understand? Are your hearts hardened?
    8:21   He said to them, "Do you **still not** understand?"
   11: 2   you will find a colt tied there, which no one has **ever** ridden.
   13: 7   be alarmed. Such things must happen, but the end is **still to come**.
Lk   23:53   cut in the rock, one in which no one had **yet** [+4024] been laid.
Jn   2: 4   do you involve me?" Jesus replied. "My time has **not yet** come."
    3:24   (This was **before** John was put in prison.)
    6:17   By now it was dark, and Jesus had **not** yet joined them.
    7: 6   Therefore Jesus told them, "The right time for me has **not yet** come;
    7: 8   I am **not yet** [UBS 4024] going up to this Feast, because for me
    7: 8   up to this Feast, because for me the right time has **not yet** come."
    7:30   but no one laid a hand on him, because his time had **not yet** come.
    7:39   **Up to that time** the Spirit had **not** been given, since Jesus had not
    8:20   Yet no one seized him, because his time had **not yet** come.
    8:57   "You are **not yet** fifty years old," the Jews said to him, "and you
   11:30   Now Jesus had **not** yet entered the village, but was still at the place
   20:17   "Do not hold on to me, for I have **not yet** returned to the Father."
1Co   3: 2   I gave you milk, not solid food, for you were **not yet** ready for it.
    8: 2   The man who thinks he knows something does **not yet** know as he
Php   3:13   I do **not** [UBS 4024] consider myself yet to have taken hold of it.
Heb   2: 8   to him. **Yet** at present we do **not** see everything subject to him.
   12: 4   you have **not yet** resisted to the point of shedding your blood.
1Jn   3: 2   of God, and what we will be has **not yet** been made known.
Rev   17:10   Five have fallen, one is, the other has **not yet** come; but when he
   17:12   "The ten horns you saw are ten kings who have **not yet** received a

4038   οὐρά, *oura*   [5]

tails [4], tail [1]

Rev   9:10   They had **tails** and stings like scorpions, and in their tails they had
    9:10   and in their **tails** they had power to torment people for five months.
    9:19   The power of the horses was in their mouths and in their **tails**;
    9:19   for their **tails** were like snakes, having heads with which they
   12: 4   His **tail** swept a third of the stars out of the sky and flung them to

4039   οὐράνιος, *ouranios*   [9]   [√ 4041]

heavenly [7], from heaven [1], in heaven [1]

Mt   5:48   Be perfect, therefore, as your **heavenly** Father is perfect.
    6:14   they sin against you, your **heavenly** Father will also forgive you.
    6:26   or store away in barns, and yet your **heavenly** Father feeds them.
    6:32   these things, and your **heavenly** Father knows that you need them.
   15:13   "Every plant that my **heavenly** Father has not planted will be pulled
   18:35   "This is how my **heavenly** Father will treat each of you unless you
   23: 9   on earth 'father,' for you have one Father, and he is **in heaven**.
Lk   2:13   Suddenly a great company *of* the **heavenly** host appeared with the
Ac   26:19   King Agrippa, I was not disobedient *to* the vision **from heaven**.

4040   οὐρανόθεν, *ouranothen*   [2]   [√ 4041]

from heaven [2]

Ac   14:17   He has shown kindness by giving you rain **from heaven** and crops
   26:13   O king, as I was on the road, I saw a light **from heaven**,

4041 οὐρανός, *ouranos* [273] [→ *2230, 3547, 4039, 4040*]

ἀπ' οὐρανοῦ (from heaven) [13] Mt 24:29,31; Mk 8:11; Lk 9:54; 17:29; 21:11; 22:43; Jn 6:38; Ro 1:18; 1Th 4:16; 2Th 1:7; Heb 12:25; 1Pe 1:12

ὁ ἄρτος ἐκ οὐρανοῦ (the bread from heaven) [7] Jn 6:31,32, 32,41,50,51,58

βασιλεία οὐρανῶν (kingdom of heaven) [32] Mt 3:2; 4:17; 5:3,10,19,19,20; 7:21; 8:11; 10:7; 11:11,12; 13:11,24,31,33,44, 45,47,52; 16:19; 18:1,3,4,23; 19:12,14,23; 20:1; 22:2; 23:13; 25:1

ἐκ οὐρανοῦ (out of heaven) [57] Mt 3:17; 16:1; 21:25,25; 28:2; Mk 1:11; 11:30,31; 13:25; Lk 3:22; 10:18; 11:13,16; 17:24; 20:4,5; Jn 1:32; 3:13,27,31; 6:31,32,32,33,41,42,50,51,58; 12:28; Ac 2:2; 9:3; 11:5,9; 22:6; 1Co 15:47; 2Co 5:2; Gal 1:8; 1Th 1:10; 2Pe 1:18; Rev 3:12; 8:10; 9:1; 10:1,4,8; 11:12; 13:13; 14:2,13; 16:21; 18:1,4; 20:1,9; 21:2,10

θεός τοῦ οὐρανοῦ (God of heaven) [2] Rev 11:13; 16:11

θησαυρός ἐν οὐρανῷ, οὐρανοῖς (treasure in heaven) [5] Mt 6:20; 19:21; Mk 10:21; Lk 12:33; 18:22

καινός οὐρανός (new heaven) [2] 2Pe 3:13; Rev 21:1

οὐρανὸς ... γῆ (heaven ... earth) [58] Mt 5:18; 6:10; 11:25; 16:19,19; 18:18,19; 24:30,35; 28:18; Mk 13:27,31; Lk 4:25; 10:21; 12:56; 16:17; 21:33; Jn 3:31; Ac 2:19; 4:24; 7:49; 10:11,12; 11:6; 14:15; 17:24; 1Co 8:5; 15:47; Eph 1:10; 3:15; Col 1:16,20; Heb 1:10; 12:25,26; Jas 5:12,18; 2Pe 3:5,7,10,13; Rev 5:3,13; 6:13; 9:1; 10:5,6,8; 11:6; 12:4,12; 13:13; 14:7; 18:1; 20:9,11; 21:1,1

heaven [219], sky [21], heavens [15], air [9], heavenly [3], skies [2], heavenly [+*1666*] [1], heavenly [+*1877+3836*] [1], heavenly things [+*1877+3836*] [1], others [1]

Mt   3: 2 and saying, "Repent, for the kingdom *of* **heaven** is near."
     3: 16 he went up out of the water. At that moment **heaven** was opened,
     3: 17 And a voice from **heaven** said, "This is my Son, whom I love;
     4: 17 Jesus began to preach, "Repent, for the kingdom *of* **heaven** is near."
     5: 3 "Blessed are the poor in spirit, for theirs is the kingdom *of* **heaven**.
     5: 10 because of righteousness, for theirs is the kingdom *of* **heaven**.
     5: 12 Rejoice and be glad, because great is your reward in **heaven**,
     5: 16 they may see your good deeds and praise your Father in **heaven**.
     5: 18 I tell you the truth, until **heaven** and earth disappear,
     5: 19 to do the same will be called least in the kingdom *of* **heaven**,
     5: 19 these commands will be called great in the kingdom *of* **heaven**.
     5: 20 of the law, you will certainly not enter the kingdom *of* **heaven**.
     5: 34 Do not swear at all: either by **heaven**, for it is God's throne;
     5: 45 that you may be sons of your Father in **heaven**. He causes his sun
     6: 1 If you do, you will have no reward from your Father in **heaven**.
     6: 9 you should pray: " 'Our Father in **heaven**, hallowed be your name,
     6: 10 your kingdom come, your will be done on earth as it is in **heaven**.
     6: 20 But store up for yourselves treasures in **heaven**, where moth
     6: 26 Look at the birds *of* the **air**; they do not sow or reap or store away
     7: 11 how much more will your Father in **heaven** give good gifts to
     7: 21 who says to me, 'Lord, Lord,' will enter the kingdom *of* **heaven**,
     7: 21 but only he who does the will of my Father who is in **heaven**.
     8: 11 the feast with Abraham, Isaac and Jacob in the kingdom *of* **heaven**.
     8: 20 Jesus replied, "Foxes have holes and birds *of* the **air** have nests,
     10: 7 As you go, preach this message: 'The kingdom *of* **heaven** is near.'
     10: 32 I will also acknowledge him before my Father in **heaven**.
     10: 33 me before men, I will disown him before my Father in **heaven**.
     11: 11 yet he who is least in the kingdom *of* **heaven** is greater than he.
     11: 12 the kingdom *of* **heaven** has been forcefully advancing, and forceful
     11: 23 And you, Capernaum, will you be lifted up to the **skies**? No,
     11: 25 time Jesus said, "I praise you, Father, Lord *of* **heaven** and earth,
     12: 50 For whoever does the will of my Father in **heaven** is my brother
     13: 11 "The knowledge of the secrets of the kingdom *of* **heaven** has been
     13: 24 "The kingdom *of* **heaven** is like a man who sowed good seed in his
     13: 31 "The kingdom *of* **heaven** is like a mustard seed, which a man took
     13: 32 so that the birds *of* the **air** come and perch in its branches."
     13: 33 "The kingdom *of* **heaven** is like yeast that a woman took and mixed
     13: 44 "The kingdom *of* **heaven** is like treasure hidden in a field. When a
     13: 45 the kingdom *of* **heaven** is like a merchant looking for fine pearls.
     13: 47 the kingdom *of* **heaven** is like a net that was let down into the lake
     13: 52 *of* **heaven** is like the owner of a house who brings out of his
     14: 19 Taking the five loaves and the two fish and looking up to **heaven**,
     16: 1 and tested him by asking him to show them a sign from **heaven**.

16: 2 evening comes, you say, 'It will be fair weather, for the **sky** is red,'
16: 3 'Today it will be stormy, for the **sky** is red and overcast.'
16: 3 You know how to interpret the appearance *of* the **sky**, but you
16: 17 this was not revealed to you by man, but by my Father in **heaven**.
16: 19 I will give you the keys of the kingdom *of* **heaven**; whatever you
16: 19 whatever you bind on earth will be bound in **heaven**, and whatever
16: 19 and whatever you loose on earth will be loosed in **heaven**."
18: 1 and asked, "Who is the greatest in the kingdom *of* **heaven**?"
18: 3 like little children, you will never enter the kingdom *of* **heaven**.
18: 4 himself like this child is the greatest in the kingdom *of* **heaven**.
18: 10 For I tell you that their angels in **heaven** always see the face of my
18: 10 their angels in heaven always see the face of my Father in **heaven**.
18: 14 In the same way your Father in **heaven** is not willing that any of
18: 18 you the truth, whatever you bind on earth will be bound in **heaven**,
18: 18 and whatever you loose on earth will be loosed in **heaven**.
18: 19 you ask for, it will be done for you by my Father in **heaven**.
18: 23 the kingdom *of* **heaven** is like a king who wanted to settle accounts
19: 12 have renounced marriage because of the kingdom *of* **heaven**.
19: 14 hinder them, for the kingdom *of* **heaven** belongs to such as these."
19: 21 and give to the poor, and you will have treasure in **heaven**.
19: 23 the truth, it is hard for a rich man to enter the kingdom *of* **heaven**.
20: 1 "For the kingdom *of* **heaven** is like a landowner who went out early
21: 25 where did it come from? Was it from **heaven**, or from men?"
21: 25 discussed it among themselves and said, "If we say, 'From **heaven**,'
22: 2 "The kingdom *of* **heaven** is like a king who prepared a wedding
22: 30 nor be given in marriage; they will be like the angels in **heaven**.
23: 13 you hypocrites! You shut the kingdom *of* **heaven** in men's faces.
23: 22 And he who swears by **heaven** swears by God's throne and by the
24: 29 the stars will fall from the **sky**, and the heavenly bodies will be
24: 29 will fall from the sky, and the **heavenly** bodies will be shaken.'
24: 30 "At that time the sign of the Son of Man will appear in the **sky**,
24: 30 They will see the Son of Man coming on the clouds *of* the **sky**,
24: 31 from the four winds, from one end *of* the **heaven** to the other.
24: 35 **Heaven** and earth will pass away, but my words will never pass
24: 36 one knows about that day or hour, not even the angels *in* **heaven**,
25: 1 "At that time the kingdom *of* **heaven** will be like ten virgins who
26: 64 right hand of the Mighty One and coming on the clouds *of* **heaven**."
28: 2 for an angel of the Lord came down from **heaven** and, going to the
28: 18 "All authority in **heaven** and on earth has been given to me.
Mk   1: 10 he saw **heaven** being torn open and the Spirit descending on him
     1: 11 And a voice came from **heaven**: "You are my Son, whom I love;
     4: 32 with such big branches that the birds *of* the **air** can perch in its
     6: 41 Taking the five loaves and the two fish and looking up to **heaven**,
     7: 34 He looked up to **heaven** and with a deep sigh said to him,
     8: 11 To test him, they asked him for a sign from **heaven**.
     10: 21 and give to the poor, and you will have treasure in **heaven**.
     11: 25 so that your Father in **heaven** may forgive you your sins."
     11: 30 John's baptism—was it from **heaven**, or from men? Tell me!"
     11: 31 discussed it among themselves and said, "If we say, 'From **heaven**,'
     12: 25 nor be given in marriage; they will be like the angels in **heaven**.
     13: 25 the stars will fall from the **sky**, and the heavenly bodies will be
     13: 25 the sky, and the **heavenly** [+*1877+3836*] bodies will be shaken.'
     13: 27 four winds, from the ends of the earth to the ends *of* the **heavens**.
     13: 31 **Heaven** and earth will pass away, but my words will never pass
     13: 32 one knows about that day or hour, not even the angels in **heaven**,
     14: 62 right hand of the Mighty One and coming on the clouds *of* **heaven**."
     16: 19 he was taken up into **heaven** and he sat at the right hand of God.
Lk   2: 15 When the angels had left them and gone into **heaven**,
     3: 21 was baptized too. And as he was praying, **heaven** was opened
     3: 22 And a voice came from **heaven**: "You are my Son, whom I love;
     4: 25 when the **sky** was shut for three and a half years and there was a
     6: 23 and leap for joy, because great is your reward in **heaven**.
     8: 5 along the path; it was trampled on, and the birds *of* the **air** ate it up.
     9: 16 Taking the five loaves and the two fish and looking up to **heaven**,
     9: 54 do you want us to call fire down from **heaven** to destroy them?"
     9: 58 Jesus replied, "Foxes have holes and birds *of* the **air** have nests,
     10: 15 And you, Capernaum, will you be lifted up to the **skies**? No,
     10: 18 He replied, "I saw Satan fall like lightning from **heaven**.
     10: 20 submit to you, but rejoice that your names are written in **heaven**."
     10: 21 Holy Spirit, said, "I praise you, Father, Lord *of* **heaven** and earth,
     11: 13 how much more will your Father in **heaven** give the Holy Spirit to
     11: 16 Others tested him by asking him for a sign from **heaven**.
     12: 33 a treasure in **heaven** that will not be exhausted, where no thief
     12: 56 You know how to interpret the appearance *of* the earth and the **sky**.
     13: 19 and became a tree, and the birds *of* the **air** perched in its branches."
     15: 7 **heaven** over one sinner who repents than over ninety-nine

15: 18 say to him: Father, I have sinned against **heaven** and against you.
15: 21 said to him, 'Father, I have sinned against **heaven** and against you.
16: 17 It is easier *for* **heaven** and earth to disappear than for the least
17: 24 which flashes and lights up the **sky** from one end to the other.
17: 24 which flashes and lights up the sky from one end to the **other**s.
17: 29 fire and sulfur rained down from **heaven** and destroyed them all.
18: 13 He would not even look up to **heaven**, but beat his breast and said,
18: 22 and give to the poor, and you will have treasure in **heaven**.
19: 38 the name of the Lord!" "Peace in **heaven** and glory in the highest!"
20: 4 John's baptism—was it from **heaven**, or from men?"
20: 5 discussed it among themselves and said, "If we say, 'From **heaven**,'
21: 11 in various places, and fearful events and great signs from **heaven**.
21: 26 is coming on the world, for the **heavenly** bodies will be shaken.
21: 33 **Heaven** and earth will pass away, but my words will never pass
22: 43 An angel from **heaven** appeared to him and strengthened him.
24: 51 he was blessing them, he left them and was taken up into **heaven**.

Jn 1: 32 "I saw the Spirit come down from **heaven** as a dove and remain on
1: 51 then added, "I tell you the truth, you shall see **heaven** open,
3: 13 No one has ever gone into **heaven** except the one who came from
3: 13 has ever gone into heaven except the one who came from **heaven**—
3: 27 "A man can receive only what is given him from **heaven**.
3: 31 one from the earth. The one who comes from **heaven** is above all.
6: 31 as it is written: 'He gave them bread from **heaven** to eat.' "
6: 32 it is not Moses who has given you the bread from **heaven**,
6: 32 but it is my Father who gives you the true bread from **heaven**.
6: 33 For the bread of God is he who comes down from **heaven**
6: 38 For I have come down from **heaven** not to do my will but to do the
6: 41 because he said, "I am the bread that came down from **heaven**."
6: 42 we know? How can he now say, 'I came down from **heaven**'?"
6: 50 But here is the bread that comes down from **heaven**, which a man
6: 51 I am the living bread that came down from **heaven**. If anyone eats
6: 58 This is the bread that came down from **heaven**. Your forefathers
12: 28 Then a voice came from **heaven**, "I have glorified it, and will
17: 1 After Jesus said this, he looked toward **heaven** and prayed:

Ac 1: 10 They were looking intently up into the **sky** as he was going,
1: 11 of Galilee," they said, "why do you stand here looking into the **sky**?
1: 11 This same Jesus, who has been taken from you into **heaven**,
1: 11 come back in the same way you have seen him go into **heaven**."
2: 2 a sound like the blowing of a violent wind came from **heaven**
2: 5 in Jerusalem God-fearing Jews from every nation under **heaven**.
2: 19 I will show wonders in the **heaven** above and signs on the earth
2: 34 For David did not ascend to **heaven**, and yet he said, " 'The Lord
3: 21 He must remain *in* **heaven** until the time comes for God to restore
4: 12 there is no other name under **heaven** given to men by which we
4: 24 they said, "you made the **heaven** and the earth and the sea,
7: 42 and gave them over to the worship *of* the **heavenly** bodies.
7: 49 " '**Heaven** is my throne, and the earth is my footstool. What kind
7: 55 of the Holy Spirit, looked up to **heaven** and saw the glory of God,
7: 56 "I see **heaven** open and the Son of Man standing at the right hand of
9: 3 on his journey, suddenly a light from **heaven** flashed around him.
10: 11 He saw **heaven** opened and something like a large sheet being let
10: 12 as well as reptiles of the earth and birds *of* the **air**.
10: 16 three times, and immediately the sheet was taken back to **heaven**.
11: 5 I saw something like a large sheet being let down from **heaven** by
11: 6 animals of the earth, wild beasts, reptiles, and birds *of* the **air**.
11: 9 "The voice spoke from **heaven** a second time, 'Do not call anything
11: 10 three times, and then it was all pulled up to **heaven** again.
14: 15 who made **heaven** and earth and sea and everything in them.
17: 24 the world and everything in it is the Lord *of* **heaven** and earth
22: 6 suddenly a bright light from **heaven** flashed around me.

Ro 1: 18 The wrath of God is being revealed from **heaven** against all the
10: 6 'Who will ascend into **heaven**?' " (that is, to bring Christ down)
1Co 8: 5 whether in **heaven** or on earth (as indeed there are many "gods"
15: 47 man was of the dust of the earth, the second man from **heaven**.
2Co 5: 1 from God, an eternal house in **heaven**, not built by human hands.
5: 2 longing to be clothed with our **heavenly** [+*1666*] dwelling,
12: 2 Christ who fourteen years ago was caught up to the third **heaven**.
Gal 1: 8 or an angel from **heaven** should preach a gospel other than the one
Eph 1: 10 to bring all things in **heaven** and on earth together under one head,
3: 15 from whom his whole family in **heaven** and on earth derives its
4: 10 is the very one who ascended higher than all the **heavens**,
6: 9 you know that he who is both their Master and yours is in **heaven**,
Php 3: 20 But our citizenship is in **heaven**. And we eagerly await a Savior
Col 1: 5 love that spring from the hope that is stored up for you in **heaven**
1: 16 things in **heaven** and on earth, visible and invisible,
1: 20 whether things on earth or things in **heaven**, by making peace

1: 23 and that has been proclaimed to every creature under **heaven**,
4: 1 because you know that you also have a Master in **heaven**.
1Th 1: 10 and to wait for his Son from **heaven**, whom he raised from the
4: 16 For the Lord himself will come down from **heaven**, with a loud
2Th 1: 7 This will happen when the Lord Jesus is revealed from **heaven** in
Heb 1: 10 of the earth, and the **heavens** are the work of your hands.
4: 14 we have a great high priest who has gone through the **heavens**,
7: 26 blameless, pure, set apart from sinners, exalted above the **heavens**.
8: 1 sat down at the right hand of the throne of the Majesty in **heaven**,
9: 23 for the copies of the **heavenly** [+*1877*+*3836*] **things** to be purified
9: 24 he entered **heaven** itself, now to appear for us in God's presence.
11: 12 came descendants as numerous as the stars *in* the **sky** and as
12: 23 to the church of the firstborn, whose names are written in **heaven**.
12: 25 which *we,* if we turn away from him who warns us from **heaven**?
12: 26 "Once more I will shake not only the earth but also the **heavens**."
Jas 5: 12 do not swear—not by **heaven** or by earth or by anything else.
5: 18 Again he prayed, and the **heavens** gave rain, and the earth
1Pe 1: 4 that can never perish, spoil or fade—kept in **heaven** for you,
1: 12 preached the gospel to you by the Holy Spirit sent from **heaven**.
3: 22 who has gone into **heaven** and is at God's right hand—with angels,
2Pe 1: 18 We ourselves heard this voice that came from **heaven** when we
3: 5 forget that long ago by God's word the **heavens** existed
3: 7 By the same word the present **heavens** and earth are reserved for
3: 10 The **heavens** will disappear with a roar; the elements will be
3: 12 That day will bring about the destruction of the **heavens** by fire,
3: 13 keeping with his promise we are looking forward to a new **heaven**
Rev 3: 12 which is coming down out of **heaven** from my God;
4: 1 I looked, and there before me was a door standing open in **heaven**.
4: 2 and there before me was a throne in **heaven** with someone sitting
5: 3 But no one in **heaven** or on earth or under the earth could open the
5: 13 Then I heard every creature in **heaven** and on earth and under the
6: 13 and the stars *in* the **sky** fell to earth, as late figs drop from a fig tree
6: 14 The **sky** receded like a scroll, rolling up, and every mountain
8: 1 seventh seal, there was silence in **heaven** for about half an hour.
8: 10 fell from the **sky** on a third of the rivers and on the springs of
9: 1 and I saw a star that had fallen from the **sky** to the earth.
10: 1 Then I saw another mighty angel coming down from **heaven**.
10: 4 but I heard a voice from **heaven** say, "Seal up what the seven
10: 5 standing on the sea and on the land raised his right hand to **heaven**.
10: 6 who created the **heavens** and all that is in them, the earth and all
10: 8 Then the voice that I had heard from **heaven** spoke to me once
11: 6 These men have power to shut up the **sky** so that it will not rain
11: 12 Then they heard a loud voice from **heaven** saying to them,
11: 12 And they went up to **heaven** in a cloud, while their enemies looked
11: 13 the survivors were terrified and gave glory to the God *of* **heaven**:
11: 15 his trumpet, and there were loud voices in **heaven**, which said:
11: 19 Then God's temple in **heaven** was opened, and within his temple
12: 1 A great and wondrous sign appeared in **heaven**: a woman clothed
12: 3 Then another sign appeared in **heaven**: an enormous red dragon
12: 4 His tail swept a third of the stars *out of* the **sky** and flung them to
12: 7 And there was war in **heaven**. Michael and his angels fought
12: 8 But he was not strong enough, and they lost their place in **heaven**.
12: 10 Then I heard a loud voice in **heaven** say: "Now have come the
12: 12 Therefore rejoice, you **heavens** and you who dwell in them!
13: 6 his name and his dwelling place and those who live in **heaven**.
13: 13 even causing fire to come down from **heaven** to earth in full view
14: 2 And I heard a sound from **heaven** like the roar of rushing waters
14: 7 Worship him who made the **heavens**, the earth, the sea
14: 13 Then I heard a voice from **heaven** say, "Write: Blessed are the dead
14: 17 Another angel came out of the temple in **heaven**, and he too had a
15: 1 I saw in **heaven** another great and marvelous sign: seven angels
15: 5 After this I looked and in **heaven** the temple, that is, the tabernacle
16: 11 and cursed the God *of* **heaven** because of their pains and their
16: 21 From the **sky** huge hailstones of about a hundred pounds each fell
18: 1 After this I saw another angel coming down from **heaven**.
18: 4 Then I heard another voice from **heaven** say: "Come out of her,
18: 5 for her sins are piled up to **heaven**, and God has remembered her
18: 20 Rejoice over her, O **heaven**! Rejoice, saints and apostles
19: 1 what sounded like the roar of a great multitude in **heaven** shouting:
19: 11 I saw **heaven** standing open and there before me was a white
19: 14 The armies of **heaven** were following him, riding on white horses
20: 1 And I saw an angel coming down out of **heaven**, having the key to
20: 9 he loves. But fire came down from **heaven** and devoured them.
20: 11 Earth and **sky** fled from his presence, and there was no place for
21: 1 Then I saw a new **heaven** and a new earth, for the first heaven
21: 1 new earth, for the first **heaven** and the first earth had passed away,

21: 2 the new Jerusalem, coming down out of **heaven** from God,
21:10 the Holy City, Jerusalem, coming down out of **heaven** from God.

4042 Οὐρβανός, *Ourbanos* [1]

Urbanus [1]

Ro 16: 9 Greet **Urbanus**, our fellow worker in Christ, and my dear friend

4043 Οὐρίας, *Ourias* [1]

Uriah's [1]

Mt 1: 6 was the father of Solomon, whose mother had been **Uriah's** wife,

4044 οὖς, *ous* [36] [→ *1969, 6064, 6065*]

ears [21], ear [13], hearing [1], listen carefully
[*+1650+3836+5148+5148+5502*] [1]

Mt 10:27 what is whispered in your **ear**, proclaim from the roofs.
11:15 He who has **ears**, let him hear.
13: 9 He who has **ears**, let him hear."
13:15 they hardly hear *with* their **ears**, and they have closed their eyes.
13:15 hear *with* their **ears**, understand with their hearts and turn,
13:16 are your eyes because they see, and your **ears** because they hear.
13:43 sun in the kingdom of their Father. He who has **ears**, let him hear.
Mk 4: 9 Then Jesus said, "He who has **ears** to hear, let him hear."
4:23 If anyone has **ears** to hear, let him hear."
7:33 away from the crowd, Jesus put his fingers into the man's **ears**.
8:18 Do you have eyes but fail to see, and **ears** but fail to hear?
Lk 1:44 As soon as the sound of your greeting reached my **ears**, the baby in
4:21 saying to them, "Today this scripture is fulfilled in your **hearing**."
8: 8 he said this, he called out, "He who has **ears** to hear, let him hear."
9:44 "**Listen** [*+1650+3836+5148+5148+5502*] **carefully** *to* what I am
12: 3 and what you have whispered in the **ear** in the inner rooms will be
14:35 it is thrown out. "He who has **ears** to hear, let him hear."
22:50 them struck the servant of the high priest, cutting off his right **ear**.
Ac 7:51 "You stiff-necked people, with uncircumcised hearts and **ears**!
7:57 At this they covered their **ears** and, yelling at the top of their
11:22 News of this reached the **ears** of the church at Jerusalem, and they
28:27 they hardly hear *with* their **ears**, and they have closed their eyes.
28:27 hear *with* their **ears**, understand with their hearts and turn,
Ro 11: 8 eyes so that they could not see and **ears** so that they could not hear,
1Co 2: 9 "No eye has seen, no **ear** has heard, no mind has conceived what
12:16 if the **ear** should say, "Because I am not an eye, I do not belong
Jas 5: 4 The cries of the harvesters have reached the **ears** of the Lord
1Pe 3:12 Lord are on the righteous and his **ears** are attentive to their prayer,
Rev 2: 7 He who has an **ear**, let him hear what the Spirit says to the
2:11 He who has an **ear**, let him hear what the Spirit says to the
2:17 He who has an **ear**, let him hear what the Spirit says to the
2:29 He who has an **ear**, let him hear what the Spirit says to the
3: 6 He who has an **ear**, let him hear what the Spirit says to the
3:13 He who has an **ear**, let him hear what the Spirit says to the
3:22 He who has an **ear**, let him hear what the Spirit says to the
13: 9 He who has an **ear**, let him hear.

4045 οὐσία, *ousia* [2] [√ *1639*]

estate [1], wealth [1]

Lk 15:12 one said to his father, 'Father, give me my share *of* the **estate**.'
15:13 a distant country and there squandered his **wealth** in wild living.

4046 οὔτε, *oute* [87] [√ *4024 + 5445*]

nor [30], neither [19], or [14], not [7], *untranslated* [3], and no [1],
and none [*+5516*] [1], and [1], cannot [*+1538*] [1], don't [1],
either [1], never [*+4537*] [1], never [*+4799*] [1], no [1], not any [1],
nothing [*+5516*] [1], nothing [1], or even [1], refuses to [1]

Mt 6:20 where moth **and** rust do not destroy, and where thieves do not
6:20 where moth and rust do **not** destroy, and where thieves do not
12:32 Spirit will not be forgiven, **either** in this age or in the age to come.
12:32 Spirit will not be forgiven, either in this age **or** in the age to come.
22:30 At the resurrection people will **neither** marry nor be given in
22:30 At the resurrection people will neither marry **nor** be given in
Mk 12:25 the dead rise, they will **neither** marry nor be given in marriage;

12:25 the dead rise, they will neither marry **nor** be given in marriage;
14:68 "I **don't** know or understand what you're talking about," he said,
14:68 "I don't know **or** understand what you're talking about," he said,
Lk 14:35 It is fit **neither** for the soil nor for the manure pile; it is thrown out.
14:35 It is fit neither for the soil **nor** for the manure pile; it is thrown out.
20:35 and in the resurrection from the dead will **neither** marry nor be
20:35 and in the resurrection from the dead will neither marry **nor** be
Jn 4:11 woman said, "you have **nothing** to draw with and the well is deep.
4:21 a time is coming when you will worship the Father **neither** on this
4:21 will worship the Father neither on this mountain **nor** in Jerusalem.
5:37 You have **never** [*+4799*] heard his voice nor seen his form,
5:37 concerning me. You have never heard his voice **nor** seen his form,
8:19 "You do **not** know me or my Father," Jesus replied. "If you knew
8:19 "You do not know me **or** my Father," Jesus replied. "If you knew
9: 3 "**Neither** this man nor his parents sinned," said Jesus, "but this
9: 3 "Neither this man **nor** his parents sinned," said Jesus, "but this
Ac 2:31 that he was **not** abandoned to the grave, nor did his body see
2:31 he was not abandoned to the grave, **nor** did his body see decay.
15:10 a yoke that **neither** we nor our fathers have been able to bear?
15:10 a yoke that neither we **nor** our fathers have been able to bear?
19:37 though they have **neither** robbed temples nor blasphemed our
19:37 though they have neither robbed temples **nor** blasphemed our
24:12 My accusers did **not** find me arguing with anyone at the temple,
24:12 or stirring up a crowd **[RPG]** in the synagogues or anywhere else
24:12 stirring up a crowd in the synagogues **or** anywhere else in the city.
25: 8 "I have done **nothing** [*+5516*] wrong against the law of the Jews
25: 8 against the law of the Jews **or** against the temple or against Caesar."
25: 8 against the law of the Jews or against the temple **or** against Caesar."
28:21 "We have **not** received **any** letters from Judea concerning you,
28:21 **and none** [*+5516*] of the brothers who have come from there has
Ro 8:38 For I am convinced that **neither** death nor life, neither angels nor
8:38 For I am convinced that neither death **nor** life, neither angels nor
8:38 **neither** angels nor demons, neither the present nor the future,
8:38 neither angels **nor** demons, neither the present nor the future,
8:38 nor demons, **neither** the present nor the future, nor any powers,
8:38 nor demons, neither the present **nor** the future, nor any powers,
8:38 nor demons, neither the present nor the future, **nor** any powers,
8:39 **neither** height nor depth, nor anything else in all creation,
8:39 neither height **nor** depth, nor anything else in all creation,
8:39 neither height nor depth, **nor** anything else in all creation,
1Co 3: 7 So **neither** he who plants nor he who waters is anything, but only
3: 7 So neither he who plants **nor** he who waters is anything, but only
6: 9 **Neither** the sexually immoral nor idolaters nor adulterers nor male
6: 9 Neither the sexually immoral **nor** idolaters nor adulterers nor male
6: 9 Neither the sexually immoral nor idolaters **nor** adulterers nor male
6: 9 Neither the sexually immoral nor idolaters nor adulterers **nor** male
6: 9 nor adulterers nor male prostitutes **nor** homosexual offenders
6:10 **nor** thieves nor the greedy nor drunkards nor slanderers nor
6:10 nor thieves **nor** the greedy nor drunkards nor slanderers nor
8: 8 to God; we are **no** worse if we do not eat, and no better if we do.
8: 8 to God; we are no worse if we do not eat, **and no** better if we do.
11:11 In the Lord, however, woman is **not** independent of man, nor is
11:11 is not independent of man, **nor** is man independent of woman.
Gal 1:12 I did not receive it from any man, **nor** was I taught it; rather,
5: 6 For in Christ Jesus **neither** circumcision nor uncircumcision has
5: 6 For in Christ Jesus neither circumcision **nor** uncircumcision has
6:15 **Neither** circumcision nor uncircumcision means anything;
6:15 Neither circumcision **nor** uncircumcision means anything;
1Th 2: 5 You know we **never** [*+4537*] used flattery, nor did we put on a
2: 5 never used flattery, **nor** did we put on a mask to cover up greed—
2: 6 We were **not** looking for praise from men, not from you or anyone
2: 6 not looking for praise from men, **not** from you or anyone else.
2: 6 not looking for praise from men, not from you **or** anyone else.
Jas 3:12 grapevine bear figs? **Neither** can a salt spring produce fresh water.
3Jn 1:10 Not satisfied with that, he **refuses to** welcome the brothers.
Rev 3:15 I know your deeds, that you are **neither** cold nor hot. I wish you
3:15 I know your deeds, that you are neither cold **nor** hot. I wish you
3:16 So, because you are lukewarm—**neither** hot nor cold—I am about
3:16 So, because you are lukewarm—neither hot **nor** cold—I am about
5: 3 or under the earth could open the scroll **or even** look inside it.
5: 4 one was found who was worthy to open the scroll **or** look inside.
9:20 and wood—idols that **cannot** [*+1538*] see or hear or walk.
9:20 bronze, stone and wood—idols that cannot see **or** hear or walk.
9:20 bronze, stone and wood—idols that cannot see or hear **or** walk.
9:21 **[NIE]** their magic arts, their sexual immorality or their thefts.
9:21 their magic arts, **[NIE]** their sexual immorality or their thefts.

9: 21   their magic arts, their sexual immorality **or** their thefts.
21: 4   There will be no more death **or** mourning or crying or pain,
21: 4   There will be no more death or mourning **or** crying or pain,
21: 4   There will be no more death or mourning or crying **or** pain,

4047 οὗτος, *houtos* [1387 / 1384] See Index of Articles, Etc.

[→ *4048, 5496, 5525, 5537, 5542*]

this [621], these [207], *untranslated* [158], he [42], that [38], him [25], therefore [*+1328*] [23], they [22], such [15], them [15], it [12], for this reason [*+1328*] [9], she [9], those [7], later [*+3552*] [6], this is how [*+1877*] [6], what [6], that is why [*+1328*] [5], the reason [*+1328*] [5], who [5], Jesus$ [4], so [*+1328*] [4], this is why [*+1328*] [4], this very [4], because [*+1328*] [3], so [3], the latter$ [3], afterward [*+3552*] [2], for that reason [*+4123*] [2], for this reason [*+5920*] [2], so then [*+1328*] [2], some time ago [*+2465+3836+4574*] [2], that was why [*+1328*] [2], the reason [*+1650*] [2], the [2], this one [2], above all [*+4754*] [1], and as good as [*+2779*] [1], Andrew$ [1], any such person [1], appointed [1], as follows [*+2400+3836+5596*] [1], as I did [*+899*] [1], as [1], at other times [*+1254*] [1], at this [*+3306*] [1], at this point [*+1254*] [1], both [*+2779*] [1], by all this [*+1328*] [1], come out of [*+2002*] [1], everything [1], finally [*+3552*] [1], first of all [*+4754*] [1], following [1], for that very reason [*+1328*] [1], for the express purpose [*+899+1650*] [1], for this reason [*+1650*] [1], for this reason [*+505*] [1], for this very reason [*+1328*] [1], for this very reason [*+899*] [1], from then on [*+1666*] [1], governing$ [*+899*] [1], happening$ [1], he's [1], here [*+1877*] [1], here [1], his [*+476+3836*] [1], his [1], how far will they go [*+1639+5515*] [1], in all [*+1639*] [1], in comparison with [*+1641+1877+3538+3836*] [1], in other words [*+1639*] [1], in the following [1], it [*+1155+3836*] [1], it [*+3836+4839*] [1], John's disciples$ [1], Judas$ [1], just one [*+3667*] [1], just then [*+2093*] [1], last night [*+3816+3836*] [1], like [*+3927*] [1], meanwhile [*+1877*] [1], men$ [1], one [1], one$ more [1], others [1], pray [*+4472*] [1], present [1], remember this [*+1254*] [1], sacrificed [*+4472*] [1], see here [*+2555*] [1], service that perform [*+1355+3311+3836*] [1], so doing$ [1], so favored$ [1], some time later [*+3552*] [1], some [1], sometimes [*+3525*] [1], such a man [1], such sins$ [1], that is why [*+1650*] [1], that is why [*+2093*] [1], that very [1], that would follow [*+3552*] [1], the Bereans$ [1], the parts$ [*+3836+5393*] [1], the passage above [1], the reason [*+5920*] [1], the same as [1], the same [1], the women$ [1], their work$ [1], their [1], there [*+1877+3836+4484*] [1], these very [1], thing [1], this [*+2240+3836*] [1], this [*+3364+3836*] [1], this [*+3836+4839*] [1], this is how [*+1666*] [1], this is the reason [*+1650*] [1], this makes [*+1877*] [1], this same [1], this very reason [*+1650*] [1], this way [*+4246*] [1], thus [*+1877*] [1], to [*+1650*] [1], tonight [*+3816+3836*] [1], what am about to tell [*+3364+3836*] [1], what going on [*+323+5515*] [1], what happened$ [1], what I meant [*+4309*] [1], what is more [*+4246+5250*] [1], what it says [1], what Paul said$ [1], which [1], who [*+476+3836*] [1], who are here [1], with that [*+3306*] [1], with this [*+3306*] [1], yet [*+3552*] [1]

4048 οὕτως, *houtōs* [208] [√ *4047*]

so [65], *untranslated* [31], in the same way [11], in this way [8], this is how [8], this [8], like this [7], this is what [6], that is how [5], like [3], then [3], true [3], in the same way [*+2779*] [2], in these words [2], like that [2], likewise [2], that way [2], that [2], this way [2], according to [1], and [1], as it has [1], as you are [1], as [1], as$ is [1], at that [1], bear$ fruit [1], before$ [*+2779*] [1], by this kind [1], does [*+1181*] [1], exactly [1], in such a way [1], in this same way [*+2779*] [1], in way [1], it is the same [*+2779*] [1], just as [*+2848+4005+5573*] [1], just as if [1], likewise [*+2779*] [1], looked like this [1], matched [*+2779*] [1], only [1], ready$ [1], so much [1], so then [1], such things [1], that is why [1], the same [1], the way [1], this is the way [1], this is the way [1], the way [1], to marry$ [*+1181*] [1], to [1], with such [1]

Mt   1: 18   **This is how** the birth of Jesus Christ came about: His mother Mary

2: 5   in Judea," they replied, "for **this is what** the prophet has written:
3: 15   Jesus replied, "Let it be **so** now; it is proper for us to do this to
5: 12   for **in the same way** they persecuted the prophets who were before
5: 16   **In the same way,** let your light shine before men, that they may
5: 19   and teaches others to do **the same** will be called least in the
6: 9   "**This,** then, **is how** you should pray: " 'Our Father in heaven,
6: 30   If **that is how** God clothes the grass of the field, which is here
7: 12   **[NIE]** do to others what you would have them do to you,
7: 17   **Likewise** every good tree bears good fruit, but a bad tree bears bad
9: 33   and said, "Nothing **like this** has ever been seen in Israel."
11: 26   Yes, Father, for **this** was your good pleasure.
12: 40   **so** the Son of Man will be three days and three nights in the heart
12: 45   than the first. **That is how** it will be with this wicked generation."
13: 40   pulled up and burned in the fire, **so** it will be at the end of the age.
13: 49   **This is how** it will be at the end of the age. The angels will come
17: 12   **In the same way** [*+2779*] the Son of Man is going to suffer at their
18: 14   **In the same way** your Father in heaven is not willing that any of
18: 35   "**This is how** my heavenly Father will treat each of you unless you
19: 8   your hearts were hard. But it was not **this way** from the beginning.
19: 10   "If **this** is the situation between a husband and wife, it is better not
19: 12   For some are eunuchs because they were born **that way**; others
20: 16   "**So** the last will be first, and the first will be last."
20: 26   Not **so** with you. Instead, whoever wants to become great among
23: 28   **In the same way,** on the outside you appear to people as righteous
24: 27   visible even in the west, **so** will be the coming of the Son of Man.
24: 33   Even **so,** when you see all these things, you know that it is near,
24: 37   in the days of Noah, **so** it will be at the coming of the Son of Man.
24: 39   all away. **That is how** it will be at the coming of the Son of Man.
24: 46   for that servant whose master finds him doing **so** when he returns.
26: 40   "Could you men not keep watch with me **[NIE]** for one hour?"
26: 54   the Scriptures be fulfilled that say it must happen **in this way**?"

Mk   2: 7   "Why does this fellow talk **like that**? He's blaspheming! Who can
2: 8   Immediately Jesus knew in his spirit that **this** was what they were
2: 12   they praised God, saying, "We have never seen anything **like this**!"
4: 26   He also said, "**This is what** the kingdom of God is like. A man
7: 18   "Are you so dull?" he asked. "Don't you see that nothing that
9: 3   whiter than anyone in the world could **[NIE]** bleach them.
10: 43   Not **so** with you. Instead, whoever wants to become great among
13: 29   Even **so,** when you see these things happening, you know that it is
14: 59   Yet even **then** their testimony did not agree.
15: 39   there in front of Jesus, heard his cry and saw **how** he died, he said,

Lk   1: 25   "The Lord has done **this** for me," she said. "In these days he has
2: 48   His mother said to him, "Son, why have you treated us **like this**?
9: 15   The disciples did **so,** and everybody sat down.
10: 21   to little children. Yes, Father, for **this** was your good pleasure.
11: 30   to the Ninevites. Yes, Father, for **this** was your good pleasure.
11: 30   to the Ninevites. **so** also will the Son of Man be to this generation.
12: 21   "**This is how** it will be with anyone who stores up things for
12: 28   If **that is how** God clothes the grass of the field, which is here
12: 38   It will be good for those servants whose master finds them **ready$,**
12: 43   for that servant whom the master finds doing **so** when he returns.
12: 54   immediately you say, 'It's going to rain,' and it **does$** [*+1181*].
14: 33   **In the same way,** any of you who does not give up everything he
15: 7   I tell you that **in the same way** there will be more rejoicing in
15: 10   **In the same way,** I tell you, there is rejoicing in the presence of
17: 10   **So** you also, when you have done everything you were told to do,
17: 24   and lights up the sky from one end to the other. **[NIE]**
17: 26   the days of Noah, **so** also will it be in the days of the Son of Man.
19: 31   'Why are you untying it?' tell him, **[NIE]** 'The Lord needs it.' "
21: 31   Even **so,** when you see these things happening, you know that the
22: 26   But you are not to be **like that**. Instead, the greatest among you
24: 24   went to the tomb and found it **[RPG]** just as the women had said,
24: 46   He told them, "**This is what** is written: The Christ will suffer

Jn   3: 8   or where it is going. **So** it is **with** everyone born of the Spirit."
3: 14   up the snake in the desert, **so** the Son of Man must be lifted up,
3: 16   "For God **so** loved the world that he gave his one and only Son,
4: 6   tired as he was from the journey, sat down **[NIE]** by the well.
5: 21   even **so** the Son gives life to whom he is pleased to give it.
5: 26   life in himself, **so** he has granted the Son to have life in himself.
7: 46   "No one ever spoke **the way** this man does," the guards declared.
11: 48   If we let him go on **like this,** everyone will believe in him,
12: 50   So whatever I say is just what the Father has told me **[NIE]** to
13: 25   Leaning back **[NIE]** against Jesus, he asked him, "Lord, who is it?"
14: 31   and that I do **exactly** what my Father has commanded me.
15: 4   in the vine. Neither *can* you bear$ fruit unless you remain in me.
18: 22   "Is **this the way** you answer the high priest?" he demanded.
21: 1   again to his disciples, by the Sea of Tiberias. It happened **this way:**

Ac   1:11   **[NIE]** will come back in the same way you have seen him go into
    3:18   But **this is how** God fulfilled what he had foretold through all the
    7: 1   Then the high priest asked them, "Are these charges **true?**"
    7: 6   God spoke to him **in this way**: 'Your descendants will be strangers
    7: 8   And **[NIE]** Abraham became the father of Isaac and circumcised
    8:32   as a lamb before the shearer is silent, **so** he did not open his mouth.
   12: 8   said to him, "Put on your clothes and sandals." And Peter did **so.**
   12:15   When she kept insisting that it was **so,** they said, "It must be his
   13: 8   But Elymas the sorcerer (for **that** is what his name means)
   13:34   raised him from the dead, never to decay, is stated **in these words**:
   13:47   For **this is what** the Lord has commanded us: " 'I have made you a
   14: 1   There they spoke **so** *effectively* that a great number of Jews
   17:11   the Scriptures every day to see if what Paul said was **true.**
   17:33   **At that,** Paul left the Council.
   19:20   **In this way** the word of the Lord spread widely and grew in
   20:11   broke bread and ate. After talking until daylight, **[NIE]** he left.
   20:13   He had made **this** arrangement because he was going there on foot.
   20:35   I showed you that **by this kind** of hard work we must help the
   21:11   'In this way' the Jews of Jerusalem will bind the owner of this belt
   22:24   in order to find out why the people were shouting at him **like** this.
   23:11   testified about me in Jerusalem, **so** you must also testify in Rome."
   24: 9   Jews joined in the accusation, asserting that these things were **true.**
   24:14   I admit that I worship the God of our fathers **as** a follower of the
   27:17   they lowered the sea anchor **and** let the ship be driven along.
   27:25   in God that it will happen **just as** [+2848+4005+5573] he told me.
   27:44   on pieces of the ship. **In this way** everyone reached land in safety.
   28:14   invited us to spend a week with them. And **so** we came to Rome.
Ro   1:15   **That is why** I am so eager to preach the gospel also to you who are
    4:18   just as it had been said to him, "So shall your offspring be."
    5:12   and death through sin, and **in this way** death came to all men,
    5:15   But the gift is not **like** the trespass. For if the many died by the
    5:18   **so** also the result of one act of righteousness was justification that
    5:19   **so** also through the obedience of the one man the many will be
    5:21   **so** also grace might reign through righteousness to bring eternal
    6: 4   through the glory of the Father, **[NIE]** we too may live a new life.
    6:11   **In the same way,** count yourselves dead to sin but alive to God in
    6:19   **so** now offer them in slavery to righteousness leading to holiness.
    9:20   say to him who formed it, 'Why did you make me **like this**?' "
   10: 6   **[NIE]** "Do not say in your heart, 'Who will ascend into heaven?' "
   11: 5   **So** too, at the present time there is a remnant chosen by grace.
   11:26   And **so** all Israel will be saved, as it is written: "The deliverer will
   11:31   **so** they too have now become disobedient in order that they too
   12: 5   **so** in Christ we who are many form one body, and each member
   15:20   **[NIE]** has always been my ambition to preach the gospel where
1Co 2:11   **In the same** [+2779] **way** no one knows the thoughts of God
    3:15   himself will be saved, but **only** as one escaping through the flames.
    4: 1   **So then,** men ought to regard us as servants of Christ and as those
    5: 3   passed judgment on the one who did this, **just as if** I were present.
    6: 5   I say **this** to shame you. Is it possible that there is nobody among
    7: 7   man has his own gift from God; one has **this** gift, another has that.
    7: 7   man has his own gift from God; one has this gift, another has **that.**
    7:17   each one should retain the place in life **[NIE]** that the Lord
    7:17   God has called him. **This is** the rule I lay down in all the churches.
    7:26   present crisis, I think that it is good for you to remain **as you are.**
    7:36   is getting along in years and he feels he ought to marryˢ [+1181],
    7:40   In my judgment, she is happier if she stays **as**ˢ she **is**—and I think
    8:12   When you sin against your brothers **in this way** and wound their
    9:14   **In the same way,** the Lord has commanded that those who preach
    9:15   And I am not writing this in the hope that you will do such **things**
    9:24   but only one gets the prize? Run in **such a way** as to get the prize.
    9:26   Therefore **[NIE]** I do not run like a man running aimlessly;
    9:26   running aimlessly; **[NIE]** I do not fight like a man beating the air.
   11:12   For as woman came from man, **so** also man is born of woman.
   11:28   A man ought to examine himself **before**ˢ [+2779] he eats of the
   12:12   all its parts are many, they form one body. **So** it is with Christ.
   14: 9   **So** it is with you. Unless you speak intelligible words with your
   14:12   **So** it is with you. Since you are eager to have spiritual gifts,
   14:21   this people, but even **then** they will not listen to me," says the Lord.
   14:25   **So** he will fall down and worship God, exclaiming, "God is really
   15:11   Whether, then, it was I or they, **this is what** we preach, and this is
   15:11   or they, this is what we preach, and **this is what** you believed.
   15:22   For as in Adam all die, **so** in Christ all will be made alive.
   15:42   **So** will it be with the resurrection of the dead. The body that is
   15:45   **So** it is written: "The first man Adam became a living being";
   16: 1   God's people: **[NIE]** Do what I told the Galatian churches to do.
2Co 1: 5   over into our lives, **so** also through Christ our comfort overflows.

    1: 7   as you share in our sufferings, **so** also you share in our comfort.
    7:14   **so** our boasting about you to Titus has proved to be true as well.
    8: 6   **to** bring also to completion this act of grace on your part.
    8:11   so that your eager willingness to do it may be **matched** [+2779] by
    9: 5   **Then** it will be ready as a generous gift, not as one grudgingly
   10: 7   he should consider again that **[NIE]** we belong to Christ just as
Gal 1: 6   **so** quickly deserting the one who called you by the grace of Christ
    3: 3   Are you **so** foolish? After beginning with the Spirit, are you now
    4: 3   **So** also, when we were children, we were in slavery under the
    4:29   son born by the power of the Spirit. **It is the same** [+2779] now.
    6: 2   other's burdens, and **in this way** you will fulfill the law of Christ.
Eph 4:20   You, however, did not come to know Christ **that way.**
    5:24   **so** also wives should submit to their husbands in everything.
    5:28   **In this same way** [+2779], husbands ought to love their wives as
    5:33   each one of you also must love his wife **[NIE]** as he loves
Php 3:17   and take note of those who live **according to** the pattern we gave
    4: 1   and crown, **that is how** you should stand firm in the Lord,
Col   3:13   have against one another. **[NIE]** Forgive as the Lord forgave you.
1Th 2: 4   **[NIE]** we speak as men approved by God to be entrusted with the
    2: 8   **so much** that we were delighted to share with you not only the
    4:14   **so** we believe that God will bring with Jesus those who have fallen
    4:17   meet the Lord in the air. And **so** we will be with the Lord forever.
    5: 2   for you know very well that the day of the Lord **[NIE]** will come
2Th 3:17   is the distinguishing mark in all my letters. **This is how** I write.
2Ti   3: 8   and Jambres opposed Moses, **so** also these men oppose the truth—
Heb 4: 4   somewhere he has spoken about the seventh day **in these words**:
    5: 3   for his own sins, as well as for the sins of the people. **[NIE]**
    5: 5   **So** Christ also did not take upon himself the glory of becoming a
    6: 9   Even though we speak **like this,** dear friends, we are confident of
    6:15   And **so** after waiting patiently, Abraham received what was
    9: 6   When everything had been arranged **like this,** the priests entered
    9:28   **so** Christ was sacrificed once to take away the sins of many people;
   10:33   other times you stood side by side with those who were **so** treated.
   12:21   The sight was **so** terrifying that Moses said, "I am trembling with
Jas   1:11   **In the same way,** the rich man will fade away even while he goes
    2:12   **[NIE]** Speak and act as those who are going to be judged by the
    2:12   and **[NIE]** act as those who are going to be judged by the law that
    2:17   **In the same way,** faith by itself, if it is not accompanied by action,
    2:26   the body without the spirit is dead, **so** faith without deeds is dead.
    3: 5   **Likewise** [+2779] the tongue is a small part of the body, but it
    3:10   come praise and cursing. My brothers, this should not **[NIE]** be.
1Pe 2:15   For **[NIE]** it is God's will that by doing good you should silence
    3: 5   For **this is the way** the holy women of the past who put their hope
2Pe 1:11   and **[NIE]** you will receive a rich welcome into the eternal
    3: 4   everything goes on **as it has** since the beginning of creation."
    3:11   Since everything will be destroyed **in** this **way,** what kind of
1Jn   2: 6   Whoever claims to live in him must **[RPG]** walk as Jesus did.
    4:11   Dear friends, since God **so** loved us, we also ought to love one
Rev 2:15   **Likewise** you also have those who hold to the teaching of the
    3: 5   He who overcomes will, **like** them, be dressed in white. I will
    3:16   **So,** because you are lukewarm—neither hot nor cold—I am about
    9:17   The horses and riders I saw in my vision **looked like this**:
   11: 5   **This is how** anyone who wants to harm them must die.
   16:18   since man has been on earth, **so** tremendous was the quake.
   18:21   "With **such** violence the great city of Babylon will be thrown

4049 οὐχί, *ouchi* [54] [√ 4024]

not [37], no [7], didn't [3], aren't [+1639] [2], fail [+3590] [1],
instead of [+2779] [1], isn't [+1639] [1], shouldn't [1], won't [1]

Mt   5:46   reward will you get? Are **not** even the tax collectors doing that?
    5:47   what are you doing more than others? Do **not** even pagans do that?
    6:25   Is **not** life more important than food, and the body more important
   10:29   Are **not** two sparrows sold for a penny? Yet not one of them will
   12:11   into a pit on the Sabbath, will you **not** take hold of it and lift it out?
   13:27   to him and said, 'Sir, **didn't** you sow good seed in your field?
   13:56   **Aren't** [+1639] all his sisters with us? Where then did this man get
   18:12   will he **not** leave the ninety-nine on the hills and go to look for the
   20:13   not being unfair to you. **Didn't** you agree to work for a denarius?
Lk   1:60   but his mother spoke up and said, "No! He is to be called John."
    4:22   came from his lips. "**Isn't** [+1639] this Joseph's son?" they asked.
    6:39   a blind man lead a blind man? Will they **not** both fall into a pit?
   12: 6   Are **not** five sparrows sold for two pennies? Yet not one of them is
   12:51   think I came to bring peace on earth? **No,** I tell you, but division.
   13: 3   I tell you, **no**! But unless you repent, you too will all perish.

13: 5 I tell you, no! But unless you repent, you too will all perish."
14:28 Will he **not** first sit down and estimate the cost to see if he has
14:31 Will he **not** first sit down and consider whether he is able with ten
15: 8 Does she **not** light a lamp, sweep the house and search carefully
16:30 " 'No, father Abraham,' he said, 'but if someone from the dead
17: 8 Would he **not** rather say, 'Prepare my supper, get yourself ready
17:17 Jesus asked, "Were **not** all ten cleansed? Where are the other nine?
18:30 will **fail** [+3590] to receive many times as much in this age and,
22:27 or the one who serves? Is it **not** the one who is at the table?
23:39 at him: "**Aren't** [+1639] you the Christ? Save yourself and us!"
24:26 Did **not** the Christ have to suffer these things and then enter his
24:32 "Were **not** our hearts burning within us while he talked with us on
Jn   9: 9 Others said, "**No**, he only looks like him." But he himself insisted,
11: 9 Jesus answered, "Are there **not** twelve hours of daylight? A man
13:10 body is clean. And you are clean, though **not** every one of you."
13:11 to betray him, and that was why he said **not** every one was clean.
14:22 why do you intend to show yourself to us and **not** to the world?"
Ac   5: 4 **Didn't** it belong to you before it was sold? And after it was sold,
7:50 Has **not** my hand made all these things?'
Ro   3:27 On that of observing the law? **No**, but on that of faith.
3:29 Jews only? Is he **not** the God of Gentiles too? Yes, of Gentiles too,
8:32 how will he **not** also, along with him, graciously give us all things?
1Co 1:20 of this age? Has **not** God made foolish the wisdom of the world?
3: 3 there is jealousy and quarreling among you, are you **not** worldly?
5: 2 **Shouldn't** you rather have been filled with grief and have put out
5:12 judge those outside the church? Are you **not** to judge those inside?
6: 1 dare he take it before the ungodly for judgment **instead** [+2779] **of**
6: 7 Why **not** rather be wronged? Why **not** rather be cheated?
6: 7 Why not rather be wronged? Why **not** rather be cheated?
8:10 **won't** he be emboldened to eat what has been sacrificed to idols?
9: 1 I not free? Am I not an apostle? Have I **not** seen Jesus our Lord?
10:16 Is **not** the cup of thanksgiving for which we give thanks a
10:16 And is **not** the bread that we break a participation in the body of
10:29 the other man's conscience, I mean, **not** yours. For why should my
2Co 3: 8 will **not** the ministry of the Spirit be even more glorious?
Gal   2:14 "You are a Jew, yet you live like a Gentile and **not** like a Jew.
1Th   2:19 in the presence of our Lord Jesus when he comes? Is it **not** you?
Heb   1:14 Are **not** all angels ministering spirits sent to serve those who will
3:17 Was it **not** with those who sinned, whose bodies fell in the desert?

4050 ὀφειλέτης, *opheiletēs* [7] [√ 4053]

obligated [2], debtors [1], guilty [1], obligation [1], owe [+1639]
[1], owed [1]

Mt   6:12 Forgive us our debts, as we also have forgiven our **debtors**.
18:24 a man *who* **owed** him ten thousand talents was brought to him.
Lk 13: 4 do you think they were more **guilty** than all the others living in
Ro   1:14 I am **obligated** both to Greeks and non-Greeks, both to the wise
8:12 Therefore, brothers, we have an **obligation**—but it is not to the
15:27 were pleased to do it, and indeed *they* **owe** [+1639] it to them.
Gal   5: 3 himself be circumcised that he is **obligated** to obey the whole law.

4051 ὀφειλή, *opheilē* [3] [√ 4053]

debt [1], duty [1], owe [1]

Mt 18:32 'I canceled all that **debt** of yours because you begged me to.
Ro 13: 7 Give everyone what *you* **owe** him: If you owe taxes, pay taxes;
1Co 7: 3 The husband should fulfill his *marital* **duty** to his wife,

4052 ὀφείλημα, *opheilēma* [2] [√ 4053]

debts [1], obligation [1]

Mt   6:12 Forgive us our **debts**, as we also have forgiven our debtors.
Ro   4: 4 his wages are not credited to him as a gift, but as an **obligation**.

4053 ὀφείλω, *opheilō* [35] [→ 4050, 4051, 4052, 4054, 4695, 5971, 5972]

ought [13], owe [4], owed [3], bound by his oath [2], must [2],
should [2], debt remain outstanding [1], debt [1], duty
[+4005+4472] [1], had to [1], has to [1], have to [1], owes [1],
should have [1], sins [1]

Mt 18:28 he found one of his fellow servants who **owed** him a hundred

18:28 began to choke him. 'Pay back what *you* **owe** me!' he demanded.
18:30 and had the man thrown into prison until he could pay the **debt**.
18:34 to the jailers to be tortured, until he should pay back all he **owed**.
23:16 anyone swears by the gold of the temple, *he is* **bound by his oath**.'
23:18 but if anyone swears by the gift on it, *he is* **bound by his oath**.'
Lk   7:41 One **owed** him five hundred denarii, and the other fifty.
11: 4 us our sins, for we also forgive everyone *who* **sins** against us.
16: 5 He asked the first, 'How much *do you* **owe** my master?'
16: 7 "Then he asked the second, 'And how much *do you* **owe**?'
17:10 unworthy servants; we have only done our **duty** [+4005+4472].' "
Jn 13:14 have washed your feet, you also **should** wash one another's feet.
19: 7 "We have a law, and according to that law he **must** die,
Ac 17:29 we **should** not think that the divine being is like gold or silver
Ro 13: 8 *Let* no **debt remain outstanding**, except the continuing debt to
15: 1 We who are strong **ought** to bear with the failings of the weak
15:27 *they* **owe** it to the Jews to share with them their material blessings.
1Co 5:10 or idolaters. In that case *you would* **have** to leave this world.
7:36 and if she is getting along in years and *he feels he* **ought** to marry,
9:10 *they* **ought** to do so in the hope of sharing in the harvest.
11: 7 A man **ought** not to cover his head, since he is the image and glory
11:10 the woman **ought** to have a sign of authority on her head.
2Co 12:11 I **ought** to have been commended by you, for I am not in the least
12:14 After all, children **should** not **have** to save up for their parents,
Eph   5:28 same way, husbands **ought** to love their wives as their own bodies.
2Th   1: 3 We **ought** always to thank God for you, brothers, and rightly so,
2:13 But we **ought** always to thank God for you, brothers loved by the
Phm   1:18 If he has done you any wrong or **owes** you *anything*, charge it to
Heb   2:17 For this reason *he* **had to** be made like his brothers in every way,
5: 3 This is why *he* **has to** offer sacrifices for his own sins, as well as
5:12 In fact, *though* by this time *you* **ought** to be teachers, you need
1Jn   2: 6 Whoever claims to live in him **must** walk as Jesus did.
3:16 life for us. And we **ought** to lay down our lives for our brothers.
4:11 since God so loved us, we also **ought** to love one another.
3Jn   1: 8 We **ought** therefore to show hospitality to such men so that we

4054 ὄφελον, *ophelon* [4] [√ 4053]

I wish [2], how I wish that [1], I hope [1]

1Co   4: 8 **How I wish that** you really had become kings so that we might be
2Co 11: 1 **I hope** you will put up with a little of my foolishness; but you are
Gal   5:12 **I wish** they would go the whole way and emasculate themselves!
Rev   3:15 are neither cold nor hot. **I wish** you were either one or the other!

4055 ὄφελος, *ophelos* [3] [√ 6067]

good [2], gained [1]

1Co 15:32 beasts in Ephesus for merely human reasons, what have I **gained**?
Jas   2:14 What **good** is it, my brothers, if a man claims to have faith
2:16 but does nothing about his physical needs, what **good** is it?

4056 ὀφθαλμοδουλία, *ophthalmodoulia* [2] [√ 4057 + 1528]

eye is on [2]

Eph   6: 6 Obey them not only to win their favor when their **eye is on** you,
Col   3:22 and do it, not only when their **eye is on** you and to win their favor,

4057 ὀφθαλμός, *ophthalmos* [100] [→ 535, 3669, 4056; cf. 3972]

ἀνοίγω οἱ ὀφθαλμοί (to open the eyes) [14] Mt 9:30; 20:33; Jn
9:10,14,17,21,26,30,32; 10:21; 11:37; Ac 9:8,40; 26:18

eyes [60], eye [25], looked up [+2048+3836] [3], sight [2],
blinded [+3836+5604] [1], envious [+1639+3836+4505] [1], envy
[+4505] [1], look up [+2048+3836] [1], looked [+149+3836] [1],
looked [+2048+3836] [1], looking [+2048+3836] [1], open eyes
[+2048+3836] [1], sight [+487+3836] [1], they [+899+3836] [1]

Mt   5:29 If your right **eye** causes you to sin, gouge it out and throw it away.
5:38 "You have heard that it was said, '**Eye** for eye, and tooth for tooth.'
5:38 "You have heard that it was said, 'Eye for **eye**, and tooth for tooth.'
6:22 The **eye** is the lamp of the body. If your eyes are good, your whole
6:22 If your **eyes** are good, your whole body will be full of light.
6:23 But if your **eyes** are bad, your whole body will be full of darkness.

7: 3 "Why do you look at the speck of sawdust in your brother's **eye**
7: 3 brother's eye and pay no attention to the plank in your own **eye**?
7: 4 you say to your brother, 'Let me take the speck out *of* your **eye**,'
7: 4 of your eye,' when all the time there is a plank in your own **eye**?
7: 5 first take the plank out *of* your own **eye**, and then you will see
7: 5 you will see clearly to remove the speck from your brother's **eye**.
9: 29 Then he touched their **eyes** and said, "According to your faith will it
9: 30 and their **sight** was restored. Jesus warned them sternly, "See that
13: 15 they hardly hear with their ears, and they have closed their **eyes**.
13: 15 Otherwise they might see *with* their **eyes**, hear with their ears,
13: 16 But blessed are your **eyes** because they see, and your ears
17: 8 *When they* **looked** [*+2048+3836*] **up**, they saw no one except
18: 9 And if your **eye** causes you to sin, gouge it out and throw it away.
18: 9 It is better for you to enter life with one eye than to have two **eyes**
20: 15 Or are you **envious** [*+1639+3836+4505*] because I am generous?'
20: 33 "Lord," they answered, "we want our **sight** [*+487+3836*]."
21: 42 the Lord has done this, and it is marvelous in our **eyes**'?
26: 43 he again found them sleeping, because their **eyes** were heavy.
Mk 7: 22 greed, malice, deceit, lewdness, **envy** [*+4505*], slander, arrogance
8: 18 Do you have **eyes** but fail to see, and ears but fail to hear?
8: 25 Once more Jesus put his hands on the man's **eyes**. Then his eyes
9: 47 And if your **eye** causes you to sin, pluck it out. It is better for you
9: 47 to enter the kingdom of God with one eye than to have two **eyes**
12: 11 the Lord has done this, and it is marvelous in our **eyes**'?"
14: 40 he again found them sleeping, because their **eyes** were heavy.
Lk 2: 30 For my **eyes** have seen your salvation,
4: 20 The **eyes** of everyone in the synagogue were fastened on him,
6: 20 **Looking** [*+2048+3836*] at his disciples, he said: "Blessed are you
6: 41 "Why do you look at the speck of sawdust in your brother's **eye**
6: 41 brother's eye and pay no attention to the plank in your own **eye**?
6: 42 to your brother, 'Brother, let me take the speck out of your **eye**,'
6: 42 your eye,' when you yourself fail to see the plank in your own **eye**?
6: 42 first take the plank out of your **eye**, and then you will see clearly to
6: 42 you will see clearly to remove the speck from your brother's **eye**.
10: 23 and said privately, "Blessed are the **eyes** that see what you see.
11: 34 Your **eye** is the lamp of your body. When your eyes are good,
11: 34 When your **eyes** are good, your whole body also is full of light.
16: 23 he **looked** [*+2048+3836*] **up** and saw Abraham far away,
18: 13 He would not even **look** [*+2048+3836*] **up** to heaven, but beat his
19: 42 what would bring you peace—but now it is hidden from your **eyes**.
24: 16 but **they** [*+899+3836*] were kept from recognizing him.
24: 31 Then their **eyes** were opened and they recognized him, and he
Jn 4: 35 I tell you, **open** your **eyes** [*+2048+3836*] and look at the fields!
6: 5 When Jesus **looked** [*+2048+3836*] **up** and saw a great crowd
9: 6 made some mud with the saliva, and put it on the man's **eyes**.
9: 10 "How then were your **eyes** opened?" they demanded.
9: 11 "The man they call Jesus made some mud and put it on my **eyes**.
9: 14 Jesus had made the mud and opened the man's **eyes** was a Sabbath.
9: 15 "He put mud on my **eyes**," the man replied, "and I washed, and
9: 17 It was your **eyes** he opened." The man replied, "He is a prophet."
9: 21 But how he can see now, or who opened his **eyes**, we don't know.
9: 26 asked him, "What did he do to you? How did he open your **eyes**?"
9: 30 You don't know where he comes from, yet he opened my **eyes**.
9: 32 Nobody has ever heard of opening the **eyes** of a man born blind.
10: 21 possessed by a demon. Can a demon open the **eyes** of the blind?"
11: 37 "Could not he who opened the **eyes** of the blind man have kept this
11: 41 Then Jesus **looked** [*+149+3836*] up and said, "Father, I thank you
12: 40 "He has blinded their **eyes** and deadened their hearts, so they can
12: 40 and deadened their hearts, so they can neither see *with* their **eyes**,
17: 1 said this, *he* **looked** [*+2048+3836*] toward heaven and prayed:
Ac 1: 9 up before their very eyes, and a cloud hid him from their **sight**.
9: 8 the ground, but when he opened his **eyes** he could see nothing.
9: 18 Immediately, something like scales fell from Saul's **eyes**, and he
9: 40 "Tabitha, get up." She opened her **eyes**, and seeing Peter she sat up.
26: 18 to open their **eyes** and turn them from darkness to light, and from
28: 27 they hardly hear with their ears, and they have closed their **eyes**.
28: 27 Otherwise they might see *with* their **eyes**, hear with their ears,
Ro 3: 18 "There is no fear of God before their **eyes**."
11: 8 **eyes** so that they could not see and ears so that they could not hear,
11: 10 May their **eyes** be darkened so they cannot see, and their backs be
1Co 2: 9 "No **eye** has seen, no ear has heard, no mind has conceived what
12: 16 And if the ear should say, "Because I am not an **eye**, I do not belong
12: 17 If the whole body were an **eye**, where would the sense of hearing
12: 21 The **eye** cannot say to the hand, "I don't need you!" And the head
15: 52 in a flash, in the twinkling *of* an **eye**, at the last trumpet.
Gal 3: 1 Before your very **eyes** Jesus Christ was clearly portrayed as
4: 15 you would have torn out your **eyes** and given them to me.
Eph 1: 18 I pray also that the **eyes** of your heart may be enlightened in order
Heb 4: 13 and laid bare *before* the **eyes** of him to whom we must give
1Pe 3: 12 For the **eyes** of the Lord are on the righteous and his ears are
2Pe 2: 14 With **eyes** full of adultery, they never stop sinning; they seduce the
1Jn 1: 1 which we have heard, which we have seen *with* our **eyes**,
2: 11 he is going, because the darkness *has* **blinded** [*+3836+5604*] him.
2: 16 the lust *of* his **eyes** and the boasting of what he has and does—
Rev 1: 7 and every **eye** will see him, even those who pierced him;
1: 14 like wool, as white as snow, and his **eyes** were like blazing fire.
2: 18 whose **eyes** are like blazing fire and whose feet are like burnished
3: 18 shameful nakedness; and salve to put on your **eyes**, so you can see.
4: 6 and they were covered with **eyes**, in front and in back.
4: 8 creatures had six wings and was covered with **eyes** all around,
5: 6 He had seven horns and seven **eyes**, which are the seven spirits of
7: 17 living water. And God will wipe away every tear from their **eyes**."
19: 12 His **eyes** are like blazing fire, and on his head are many crowns.
21: 4 He will wipe every tear from their **eyes**. There will be no more

4058 ὄφις, *ophis* [14]

snakes [6], serpent [3], snake [3], serpent's [*+899*] [1], serpent's [1]

Mt 7: 10 Or if he asks for a fish, will give him a **snake**?
10: 16 Therefore be as shrewd as **snakes** and as innocent as doves.
23: 33 "*You* **snakes**! You brood of vipers! How will you escape being
Mk 16: 18 they will pick up **snakes** with their hands;
Lk 10: 19 I have given you authority to trample on **snakes** and scorpions
11: 11 if your son asks for a fish, will give him a **snake** instead?
Jn 3: 14 Just as Moses lifted up the **snake** in the desert, so the Son of Man
1Co 10: 9 not test the Lord, as some of them did—and were killed by **snakes**.
2Co 11: 3 that just as Eve was deceived by the **serpent's** [*+899*] cunning,
Rev 9: 19 for their tails were like **snakes**, having heads with which they
12: 9 that ancient **serpent** called the devil, or Satan, who leads the whole
12: 14 care of for a time, times and half a time, out of the **serpent's** reach.
12: 15 Then from his mouth the **serpent** spewed water like a river,
20: 2 seized the dragon, that ancient **serpent**, who is the devil, or Satan,

4059 ὀφρῦς, *ophrys* [1]

brow [1]

Lk 4: 29 and took him to the **brow** of the hill on which the town was built,

4060 ὀχετός, *ochetos* Not used in UBS/NIV [√ *2400*]

4061 ὀχλέω, *ochleō* [1] [√ *4063*]

tormented [1]

Ac 5: 16 bringing their sick and *those* **tormented** by evil spirits, and all of

4062 ὀχλοποιέω, *ochlopoieō* [1] [√ *4063 + 4472*]

formed a mob [1]

Ac 17: 5 from the marketplace, **formed a mob** and started a riot in the city.

4063 ὄχλος, *ochlos* [175 / 174] [→ *1943, 4061, 4062, 4214*]

crowd [106], people [29], crowds [25], multitude [3], mob [2], numbers of people [2], crowd of people [1], group [*+3950*] [1], many people [1], multitudes [1], number of people [1], number [1], them[s] [*+3836*] [1]

Mt 4: 25 Large **crowds** from Galilee, the Decapolis, Jerusalem, Judea
5: 1 Now when he saw the **crowds**, he went up on a mountainside
7: 28 saying these things, the **crowds** were amazed at his teaching,
8: 1 he came down from the mountainside, large **crowds** followed him.
8: 18 When Jesus saw the **crowd** around him, he gave orders to cross to
9: 8 When the **crowd** saw this, they were filled with awe; and they
9: 23 the ruler's house and saw the flute players and the noisy **crowd**,
9: 25 After the **crowd** had been put outside, he went in and took the girl
9: 33 The **crowd** was amazed and said, "Nothing like this has ever been
9: 36 When he saw the **crowds**, he had compassion on them,

11: 7 were leaving, Jesus began to speak *to* the **crowd** about John:
12:15 Many [UBS+ *crowds*] followed him, and he healed all their sick,
12:23 All the **people** were astonished and said, "Could this be the Son of
12:46 While Jesus was still talking *to* the **crowd**, his mother and brothers
13: 2 Such large **crowds** gathered around him that he got into a boat
13: 2 got into a boat and sat in it, while all the **people** stood on the shore.
13:34 Jesus spoke all these things *to* the **crowd** in parables; he did not
13:36 Then he left the **crowd** and went into the house. His disciples came
14: 5 Herod wanted to kill John, but he was afraid of the **people**,
14:13 Hearing of this, the **crowds** followed him on foot from the towns.
14:14 When Jesus landed and saw a large **crowd**, he had compassion on
14:15 Send the **crowds** away, so they can go to the villages and buy
14:19 And he directed the **people** to sit down on the grass.
14:19 them to the disciples, and the disciples gave them *to* the **people**.
14:22 on ahead of him to the other side, while he dismissed the **crowd**.
14:23 After he had dismissed them[s] [+3836], he went up on a
15:10 Jesus called the **crowd** to him and said, "Listen and understand.
15:30 Great **crowds** came to him, bringing the lame, the blind,
15:31 The **people** were amazed when they saw the mute speaking,
15:32 his disciples to him and said, "I have compassion for these **people**;
15:33 we get enough bread in this remote place to feed such a **crowd**?"
15:35 He told the **crowd** to sit down on the ground.
15:36 and gave them to the disciples, and they in turn *to* the **people**.
15:39 After Jesus had sent the **crowd** away, he got into the boat
17:14 When they came to the **crowd**, a man approached Jesus and knelt
19: 2 Large **crowds** followed him, and he healed them there.
20:29 his disciples were leaving Jericho, a large **crowd** followed him.
20:31 The **crowd** rebuked them and told them to be quiet,
21: 8 A very large **crowd** spread their cloaks on the road, while others
21: 9 The **crowds** that went ahead of him and those that followed
21:11 The **crowds** answered, "This is Jesus, the prophet from Nazareth in
21:26 we are afraid of the **people**, for they all hold that John was a
21:46 but they were afraid of the **crowd** because the people held that he
22:33 *When* the **crowds** heard this, they were astonished at his teaching.
23: 1 Then Jesus said *to* the **crowds** and to his disciples:
26:47 With him was a large **crowd** armed with swords and clubs,
26:55 At that time Jesus said *to* the **crowd**, "Am I leading a rebellion,
27:15 custom at the Feast to release a prisoner chosen *by* the **crowd**.
27:20 and the elders persuaded the **crowd** to ask for Barabbas
27:24 he took water and washed his hands in front of the **crowd**.

Mk 2: 4 Since they could not get him to Jesus because of the **crowd**,
2:13 the lake. A large **crowd** came to him, and he began to teach them.
3: 9 Because of the **crowd** he told his disciples to have a small boat
3:20 and again a **crowd** gathered, so that he and his disciples were not
3:32 A **crowd** was sitting around him, and they told him, "Your mother
4: 1 The **crowd** that gathered around him was so large that he got into a
4: 1 while all the **people** were along the shore at the water's edge.
4:36 Leaving the **crowd** behind, they took him along, just as he was,
5:21 a large **crowd** gathered around him while he was by the lake.
5:24 went with him. A large **crowd** followed and pressed around him.
5:27 she came up behind him in the **crowd** and touched his cloak,
5:30 He turned around in the **crowd** and asked, "Who touched my
5:31 "You see the **people** crowding against you," his disciples answered,
6:34 When Jesus landed and saw a large **crowd**, he had compassion on
6:45 go on ahead of him to Bethsaida, while he dismissed the **crowd**.
7:14 Again Jesus called the **crowd** to him and said, "Listen to me,
7:17 After he had left the **crowd** and entered the house, his disciples
7:33 After he took him aside, away from the **crowd**, Jesus put his
8: 1 During those days another large **crowd** gathered. Since they had
8: 2 "I have compassion for these **people**; they have already been with
8: 6 He told the **crowd** to sit down on the ground. When he had taken
8: 6 broke them and gave them to his disciples to set before the **people**,
8:34 Then he called the **crowd** to him along with his disciples and said:
9:14 they saw a large **crowd** around them and the teachers of the law
9:15 As soon as all the **people** saw Jesus, they were overwhelmed with
9:17 A man in the **crowd** answered, "Teacher, I brought you my son,
9:25 When Jesus saw that a **crowd** was running to the scene, he rebuked
10: 1 Again **crowds** of people came to him, and as was his custom,
10:46 As Jesus and his disciples, together with a large **crowd**,
11:18 feared him, because the whole **crowd** was amazed at his teaching.
11:32 (They feared the **people**, for everyone held that John really was a
12:12 But they were afraid of the **crowd**; so they left him and went away.
12:37 can he be his son?" The large **crowd** listened to him with delight.
12:41 and watched the **crowd** putting their money into the temple
14:43 With him was a **crowd** armed with swords and clubs, sent from the
15: 8 The **crowd** came up and asked Pilate to do for them what he

15:11 But the chief priests stirred up the **crowd** to have Pilate release
15:15 Wanting to satisfy the **crowd**, Pilate released Barabbas to them.
Lk 3: 7 John said *to* the **crowds** coming out to be baptized by him,
3:10 "What should we do then?" the **crowd** asked.
4:42 The **people** were looking for him and when they came to where he
5: 1 with the **people** crowding around him and listening to the word of
5: 3 from shore. Then he sat down and taught the **people** from the boat.
5:15 so that crowds of **people** came to hear him and to be healed of their
5:19 When they could not find a way to do this because of the **crowd**,
5:29 and a large **crowd** of tax collectors and others were eating with
6:17 A large **crowd** of his disciples was there and a great number of
6:19 and the **people** all tried to touch him, because power was coming
7: 9 and turning to the **crowd** following him, he said, "I tell you,
7:11 and his disciples and a large **crowd** went along with him.
7:12 she was a widow. And a large **crowd** from the town was with her.
7:24 messengers left, Jesus began to speak to the **crowd** about John:
8: 4 While a large **crowd** was gathering and people were coming to
8:19 but they were not able to get near him because of the **crowd**.
8:40 Now when Jesus returned, a **crowd** welcomed him, for they were
8:42 As Jesus was on his way, the **crowds** almost crushed him.
8:45 "Master, the **people** are crowding and pressing against you."
9:11 but the **crowds** learned about it and followed him. He welcomed
9:12 "Send the **crowd** away so they can go to the surrounding villages
9:16 then he gave them to the disciples to set before the **people**.
9:18 were with him, he asked them, "Who do the **crowds** say I am?"
9:37 when they came down from the mountain, a large **crowd** met him.
9:38 A man in the **crowd** called out, "Teacher, I beg you to look at my
11:14 the man who had been mute spoke, and the **crowd** was amazed.
11:27 Jesus was saying these things, a woman in the **crowd** called out,
11:29 As the **crowds** increased, Jesus said, "This is a wicked generation,
12: 1 Meanwhile, when a **crowd** of many thousands had gathered,
12:13 Someone in the **crowd** said to him, "Teacher, tell my brother to
12:54 He said *to* the **crowd**: "When you see a cloud rising in the west,
13:14 the synagogue ruler said *to* the **people**, "There are six days for
13:17 but the **people** were delighted with all the wonderful things he was
14:25 Large **crowds** were traveling with Jesus, and turning to them he
18:36 When he heard the **crowd** going by, he asked what was happening.
19: 3 but being a short man he could not, because of the **crowd**.
19:39 Some of the Pharisees in the **crowd** said to Jesus, "Teacher,
22: 6 to hand Jesus over to them when no **crowd** was present.
22:47 While he was still speaking a **crowd** came up, and the man who
23: 4 Then Pilate announced to the chief priests and the **crowd**,
23:48 When all the **people** who had gathered to witness this sight saw
Jn 5:13 for Jesus had slipped away *into* the **crowd** that was there.
6: 2 and a great **crowd** of people followed him because they saw the
6: 5 When Jesus looked up and saw a great **crowd** coming toward him,
6:22 The next day the **crowd** that had stayed on the opposite shore of
6:24 Once the **crowd** realized that neither Jesus nor his disciples were
7:12 Among the **crowds** there was widespread whispering about him.
7:12 "He is a good man." Others replied, "No, he deceives the **people**."
7:20 "You are demon-possessed," the **crowd** answered. "Who is trying
7:31 Still, many in the **crowd** put their faith in him. They said,
7:32 The Pharisees heard the **crowd** whispering such things about him.
7:40 On hearing his words, some of the **people** said, "Surely this man is
7:43 Thus the **people** were divided because of Jesus.
7:49 But this **mob** that knows nothing of the law—there is a curse on
11:42 hear me, but I said this for the benefit of the **people** standing here,
12: 9 Meanwhile a large **crowd** of Jews found out that Jesus was there
12:12 The next day the great **crowd** that had come for the Feast heard
12:17 Now the **crowd** that was with him when he called Lazarus from
12:18 **Many people**, because they had heard that he had given this
12:29 The **crowd** that was there and heard it said it had thundered;
12:34 The **crowd** spoke up, "We have heard from the Law that the Christ
Ac 1:15 In those days Peter stood up among the believers (a **group** [+3950]
6: 7 and a large **number** of priests became obedient to the faith.
8: 6 When the **crowds** heard Philip and saw the miraculous signs he
11:24 and faith, and a great **number of people** were brought to the Lord.
11:26 and Saul met with the church and taught great **numbers of people**.
13:45 When the Jews saw the **crowds**, they were filled with jealousy
14:11 When the **crowd** saw what Paul had done, they shouted in the
14:13 because he and the **crowd** wanted to offer sacrifices to them.
14:14 they tore their clothes and rushed out into the **crowd**, shouting:
14:18 they had difficulty keeping the **crowd** from sacrificing to them.
14:19 Jews came from Antioch and Iconium and won the **crowd** over.
16:22 The **crowd** joined in the attack against Paul and Silas,
17: 8 the **crowd** and the city officials were thrown into turmoil.

17:13 they went there too, agitating the **crowds** and stirring them up.
19:26 and led astray large **numbers of people** here in Ephesus
19:33 to the front, and some of the **crowd** shouted instructions to him.
19:35 The city clerk quieted the **crowd** and said: "Men of Ephesus,
21:27 at the temple. They stirred up the whole **crowd** and seized him,
21:34 Some in the **crowd** shouted one thing and some another, and since
21:35 the violence of the **mob** was so great he had to be carried by the
24:12 or stirring up a **crowd** in the synagogues or anywhere else in the
24:18 There was no **crowd** with me, nor was I involved in any
Rev 7: 9 and there before me was a great **multitude** that no one could count,
    17:15 the prostitute sits, are peoples, **multitudes**, nations and languages.
    19: 1 After this I heard what sounded like the roar *of* a great **multitude**
    19: 6 Then I heard what sounded like a great **multitude**, like the roar of

4064 Ὀχοζίας, *Ochozias* Not used in UBS/NIV

4065 ὀχύρωμα, *ochyrōma* [1] [√ *2400*]

strongholds [1]

2Co 10: 4 On the contrary, they have divine power to demolish **strongholds**.

4066 ὀψάριον, *opsarion* [5] [→ *4072, 4243*]

fish [4], small fish [1]

Jn 6: 9 "Here is a boy with five small barley loaves and two **small fish**,
    6:11 were seated as much as they wanted. He did the same with the **fish**.
    21: 9 they saw a fire of burning coals there with **fish** on it, and some
    21:10 Jesus said to them, "Bring some *of* the **fish** you have just caught."
    21:13 took the bread and gave it to them, and did the same with the **fish**.

4067 ὀψέ, *opse* [3] [→ *4068, 4069, 4070*]

after the Sabbath [+*4879*] [1], evening [1], in the evening [1]

Mt 28: 1 **After the Sabbath** [+*4879*], at dawn on the first day of the week,
Mk 11:19 When **evening** came, they went out of the city.
    13:35 whether **in the evening**, or at midnight, or when the rooster crows,

4068 ὀψία, *opsia* [14] [√ *4067*]

evening [12], on the evening [+*1639*] [1], that evening [+*1181*] [1]

Mt 8:16 When **evening** came, many who were demon-possessed were
    14:15 As **evening** approached, the disciples came to him and said,
    14:23 by himself to pray. When **evening** came, he was there alone,
    16: 2 He replied, "When **evening** comes, you say, 'It will be fair weather,
    20: 8 "When **evening** came, the owner of the vineyard said to his
    26:20 When **evening** came, Jesus was reclining at the table with the
    27:57 As **evening** approached, there came a rich man from Arimathea,
Mk 1:32 **That evening** [+*1181*] after sunset the people brought to Jesus all
    4:35 That day when **evening** came, he said to his disciples, "Let us go
    6:47 When **evening** came, the boat was in the middle of the lake,
    14:17 When **evening** came, Jesus arrived with the Twelve.
    15:42 (that is, the day before the Sabbath). So as **evening** approached,
Jn 6:16 When **evening** came, his disciples went down to the lake,
    20:19 **On the evening** [+*1639*] of that first day of the week,

4069 ὄψιμος, *opsimos* [1] [√ *4067*]

spring rains [1]

Jas 5: 7 and how patient he is for the autumn and **spring rains**.

4070 ὄψιος, *opsios* [1] [√ *4067*]

late [1]

Mk 11:11 He looked around at everything, but since it was already **late**,

4071 ὄψις, *opsis* [3] [√ *3972*]

face [2], appearances [1]

Jn 7:24 Stop judging by *mere* **appearances**, and make a right judgment."
    11:44 and feet wrapped with strips of linen, and a cloth around his **face**.
Rev 1:16 His **face** was like the sun shining in all its brilliance.

4072 ὀψώνιον, *opsōnion* [4] [√ *4066 + 6050*]

expense [1], pay [1], support [1], wages [1]

Lk 3:14 and don't accuse people falsely—be content *with* your **pay**."
Ro 6:23 For the **wages** of sin is death, but the gift of God is eternal life in
1Co 9: 7 Who serves as a soldier *at* his own **expense**? Who plants a
2Co 11: 8 I robbed other churches by receiving **support** from them so as to

Π, Ρ

4073 π, *p* Not used in UBS/NIV

4074 παγιδεύω, *pagideuō* [1] [√ *4381*]

trap [1]

Mt 22:15 the Pharisees went out and laid plans to **trap** him in his words.

4075 παγίς, *pagis* [5] [√ *4381*]

trap [4], snare [1]

Lk 21:34 of life, and that day will close on you unexpectedly like a **trap**.
Ro 11: 9 "May their table become a **snare** and a trap, a stumbling block
1Ti 3: 7 so that he will not fall into disgrace and into the devil's **trap**.
    6: 9 and a **trap** and into many foolish and harmful desires that plunge
2Ti 2:26 will come to their senses and escape from the **trap** of the devil,

4076 πάγος, *pagos* Not used in UBS/NIV [→ *740, 741*]

4077 πάθημα, *pathēma* [16] [√ *4248*]

sufferings [10], passions [2], suffered [2], suffering [2]

Ro 7: 5 the sinful **passions** aroused by the law were at work in our bodies,
    8:18 I consider that our present **sufferings** are not worth comparing
2Co 1: 5 For just as the **sufferings** of Christ flow over into our lives,
    1: 6 which produces in you patient endurance *of* the same **sufferings**
    1: 7 because we know that just as you share *in* our **sufferings**,
Gal 5:24 to Christ Jesus have crucified the sinful nature with its **passions**
Php 3:10 of his resurrection and the fellowship of sharing *in* his **sufferings**,
Col 1:24 Now I rejoice in what was **suffered** for you, and I fill up in my
2Ti 3:11 persecutions, **sufferings**—what kinds of things happened to me in
Heb 2: 9 now crowned with glory and honor because he **suffered** death,
    2:10 make the author of their salvation perfect through **suffering**.
    10:32 you stood your ground in a great contest *in the face of* **suffering**.
1Pe 1:11 in them was pointing when he predicted the **sufferings** of Christ
    4:13 But rejoice that you participate *in* the **sufferings** of Christ,
    5: 1 a witness *of* Christ's **sufferings** and one who also will share in the
    5: 9 throughout the world are undergoing the same kind *of* **sufferings**.

4078 παθητός, *pathētos* [1] [√ *4248*]

suffer [1]

Ac 26:23 that the Christ would **suffer** and, as the first to rise from the dead,

4079 πάθος, *pathos* [3] [√ *4248*]

lust [2], lusts [1]

Ro 1:26 Because of this, God gave them over to shameful **lusts**. Even their
Col 3: 5 impurity, **lust**, evil desires and greed, which is idolatry.
1Th 4: 5 not in passionate **lust** like the heathen, who do not know God;

4080 παιδαγωγός, *paidagōgos* [3] [√ *4090 + 72*]

guardians [1], put in charge to lead [1], supervision [1]

1Co 4:15 Even though you have ten thousand **guardians** in Christ, you do
Gal 3:24 So the law was **put in charge to lead** us to Christ that we might be
    3:25 faith has come, we are no longer under the **supervision** of the law.

4081 παιδάριον, *paidarion* [1] [√ *4090*]

boy [1]

Jn   6: 9 "Here is a **boy** with five small barley loaves and two small fish,

4082 παιδεία, *paideia* [6] [√ *4090*]

discipline [3], training [2], disciplined [1]

Eph   6: 4 bring them up in the **training** and instruction of the Lord.
2Ti   3:16 for teaching, rebuking, correcting and **training** in righteousness,
Heb 12: 5 "My son, do not make light of the Lord's **discipline**, and do not lose
     12: 7 Endure hardship as **discipline**; God is treating you as sons.
     12: 8 If you are not **disciplined** (and everyone undergoes discipline),
     12:11 No **discipline** seems pleasant at the time, but painful. Later on,

4083 παιδευτής, *paideutēs* [2] [√ *4090*]

disciplined [1], instructor [1]

Ro   2:20 an **instructor** of the foolish, a teacher of infants, because you have
Heb 12: 9 we have all had human fathers who **disciplined** us and we

4084 παιδεύω, *paideuō* [13] [√ *4090*]

disciplined [3], beaten [1], discipline [1], disciplines [1], educated [1], instruct [1], punish [1], punished [1], taught [1], teaches [1], trained [1]

Lk   23:16 Therefore, I will **punish** him and then release him."
     23:22 Therefore *I will* have him **punished** and then release him."
Ac   7:22 Moses *was* **educated** in all the wisdom of the Egyptians and was
     22: 3 Under Gamaliel *I was* thoroughly **trained** in the law of our fathers
1Co 11:32 *we are being* **disciplined** so that we will not be condemned with
2Co   6: 9 as unknown; dying, and yet we live on; **beaten**, and yet not killed;
1Ti   1:20 whom I have handed over to Satan *to be* **taught** not to blaspheme.
2Ti   2:25 Those who oppose him *he must* gently **instruct**, in the hope that
Tit   2:12 *It* **teaches** us to say "No" to ungodliness and worldly passions,
Heb 12: 6 because the Lord **disciplines** those he loves, and he punishes
     12: 7 treating you as sons. For what son *is not* **disciplined** by his father?
     12:10 Our fathers **disciplined** us for a little while as they thought best;
Rev   3:19 Those whom I love I rebuke and **discipline**. So be earnest,

4085 παιδιόθεν, *paidiothen* [1] [√ *4090*]

childhood [1]

Mk   9:21 "How long has he been like this?" "From **childhood**," he answered.

4086 παιδίον, *paidion* [52] [√ *4090*]

child [21], children [8], little child [7], little children [7], child's [2], dear children [2], baby [1], boy's [1], children's [1], friends [1], her[s] [+*3836*] [1]

Mt   2: 8 to Bethlehem and said, "Go and make a careful search for the **child**.
      2: 9 ahead of them until it stopped over the place where the **child** was.
      2:11 they saw the **child** with his mother Mary, and they bowed down
      2:13 he said, "take the **child** and his mother and escape to Egypt.
      2:13 I tell you, for Herod is going to search for the **child** to kill him."
      2:14 took the **child** and his mother during the night and left for Egypt,
      2:20 "Get up, take the **child** and his mother and go to the land of Israel,
      2:20 for those who were trying to take the **child's** life are dead."
      2:21 took the **child** and his mother and went to the land of Israel.
     11:16 They are like **children** sitting in the marketplaces and calling out
     14:21 ate was about five thousand men, besides women and **children**.
     15:38 of those who ate was four thousand, besides women and **children**.
     18: 2 He called a **little child** and had him stand among them.
     18: 3 you the truth, unless you change and become like **little children**,
     18: 4 whoever humbles himself like this **child** is the greatest in the
     18: 5 "And whoever welcomes a **little child** like this in my name
     19:13 Then **little children** were brought to Jesus for him to place his
     19:14 Jesus said, "Let the **little children** come to me, and do not hinder
Mk   5:39 all this commotion and wailing? The **child** is not dead but asleep."
      5:40 he took the **child's** father and mother and the disciples who were
      5:40 the disciples who were with him, and went in where the **child** was.
      5:41 He took her[s] [+*3836*] by the hand and said to her,
      7:28 "but even the dogs under the table eat the **children's** crumbs."

7:30 She went home and found her **child** lying on the bed,
9:24 Immediately the **boy's** father exclaimed, "I do believe; help me
9:36 He took a **little child** and had him stand among them. Taking him
9:37 "Whoever welcomes one *of* these **little children** in my name
10:13 People were bringing **little children** to Jesus to have him touch
10:14 He said to them, "Let the **little children** come to me, and do not
10:15 anyone who will not receive the kingdom of God like a **little child**
Lk   1:59 On the eighth day they came to circumcise the **child**, and they were
      1:66 wondered about it, asking, "What then is this **child** going to be?"
      1:76 And you, my **child**, will be called a prophet of the Most High;
      1:80 And the **child** grew and became strong in spirit; and he lived in the
      2:17 the word concerning what had been told them about this **child**,
      2:27 When the parents brought in the **child** Jesus to do for him what the
      2:40 And the **child** grew and became strong; he was filled with wisdom,
      7:32 They are like **children** sitting in the marketplace and calling out to
      9:47 their thoughts, took a **little child** and had him stand beside him.
      9:48 "Whoever welcomes this **little child** in my name welcomes me;
     11: 7 The door is already locked, and my **children** are with me in bed.
     18:16 the children to him and said, "Let the **little children** come to me,
     18:17 anyone who will not receive the kingdom of God like a **little child**
Jn   4:49 The royal official said, "Sir, come down before my **child** dies."
     16:21 but when her **baby** is born she forgets the anguish because of her
     21: 5 He called out to them, "**Friends**, haven't you any fish?" "No,"
1Co 14:20 Brothers, stop thinking like **children**. In regard to evil be infants,
Heb   2:13 again he says, "Here am I, and the **children** God has given me."
      2:14 Since the **children** have flesh and blood, he too shared in their
     11:23 because they saw he was no ordinary **child**, and they were not
1Jn   2:13 I write to you, **dear children**, because you have known the Father.
      2:18 **Dear children**, this is the last hour; and as you have heard that the

4087 παιδίσκη, *paidiskē* [13] [√ *4090*]

servant girl [4], slave woman [4], girl [1], maidservants [1], servant girls [1], slave girl [1], slave woman's [1]

Mt   26:69 was sitting out in the courtyard, and a **servant girl** came to him.
Mk   14:66 the courtyard, one *of* the **servant girls** of the high priest came by.
     14:69 When the **servant girl** saw him there, she said again to those
Lk   12:45 and **maidservants**, and to eat and drink and get drunk.
     22:56 A **servant girl** saw him seated there in the firelight. She looked
Jn   18:17 not one of his disciples, are you?" the **girl** at the door asked Peter.
Ac   12:13 and a **servant girl** named Rhoda came to answer the door.
     16:16 we were met by a **slave girl** who had a spirit by which she
Gal   4:22 one by the **slave woman** and the other by the free woman.
      4:23 His son by the **slave woman** was born in the ordinary way;
      4:30 "Get rid of the **slave woman** and her son, for the slave woman's son
      4:30 for the **slave woman's** son will never share in the inheritance with
      4:31 Therefore, brothers, we are not children *of* the **slave woman**,

4088 παιδόθεν, *paidothen*   Not used in UBS/NIV
[√ *4090*]

4089 παίζω, *paizō* [1] [→ *1848, 1849, 1850, 1851; cf. 4090*]

indulge in pagan revelry [1]

1Co 10: 7 sat down to eat and drink and got up *to* **indulge in pagan revelry**."

4090 παῖς, *pais* [24] [→ *553, 4080, 4081, 4082, 4083, 4084, 4085, 4086, 4087, 4088; cf. 4089*]

servant [12], boy [4], attendants [1], boys [1], child [1], child's [1], children [1], menservants [1], servants [1], young man [1]

Mt   2:16 and he gave orders to kill all the **boys** in Bethlehem and its
      8: 6 "my **servant** lies at home paralyzed and in terrible suffering."
      8: 8 my roof. But just say the word, and my **servant** will be healed.
      8:13 believed it would." And his **servant** was healed at that very hour.
     12:18 "Here is my **servant** whom I have chosen, the one I love, in whom I
     14: 2 and he said *to* his **attendants**, "This is John the Baptist; he has risen
     17:18 Jesus rebuked the demon, and it came out of the **boy**, and he was
     21:15 things he did and the **children** shouting in the temple area,
Lk   1:54 He has helped his **servant** Israel, remembering to be merciful
      1:69 up a horn of salvation for us in the house *of* his **servant** David
      2:43 the **boy** Jesus stayed behind in Jerusalem, but they were unaware
      7: 7 to come to you. But say the word, and my **servant** will be healed.

8:51 except Peter, John and James, and the **child's** father and mother.
8:54 But he took her by the hand and said, "My **child**, get up!"
9:42 the evil spirit, healed the **boy** and gave him back to his father.
12:45 and he then begins to beat the **menservants** and maidservants
15:26 So he called one *of* the **servants** and asked him what was going on.
Jn   4:51 his servants met him with the news that his **boy** was living.
Ac   3:13 and Jacob, the God of our fathers, has glorified his **servant** Jesus.
3:26 When God raised up his **servant**, he sent him first to you to bless
4:25 You spoke by the Holy Spirit through the mouth *of* your **servant**,
4:27 of Israel in this city to conspire against your holy **servant** Jesus,
4:30 and wonders through the name *of* your holy **servant** Jesus."
20:12 The people took the **young man** home alive and were greatly

4091 παίω, *paiō* [5] [→ *4697*]

hit [+*1639*] [2], struck [2], strikes [1]

Mt   26:68 and said, "Prophesy to us, Christ. Who **hit** [+*1639*] you?"
Mk   14:47 near drew his sword and **struck** the servant of the high priest,
Lk   22:64 him and demanded, "Prophesy! Who **hit** [+*1639*] you?"
Jn   18:10 who had a sword, drew it and **struck** the high priest's servant,
Rev   9: 5 was like that of the sting of a scorpion when *it* **strikes** a man.

4092 Πακατιανός, *Pakatianos*   Not used in UBS/NIV

4093 πάλαι, *palai* [7] [→ *1732, 4094, 4095, 4096*]

long ago [3], all along [1], already [1], in the past [1], past [1]

Mt   11:21 they would have repented **long ago** in sackcloth and ashes.
Mk   15:44 Summoning the centurion, he asked him if Jesus had **already** died.
Lk   10:13 performed in Tyre and Sidon, they would have repented **long ago**,
2Co 12:19 Have you been thinking **all along** that we have been defending
Heb   1: 1 **In the past** God spoke to our forefathers through the prophets at
2Pe   1: 9 and has forgotten that he has been cleansed from his **past** sins.
Jude 1: 4 For certain men whose condemnation was written about **long ago**

4094 παλαιός, *palaios* [19] [√ *4093*]

old [19]

Mt   9:16 "No one sews a patch of unshrunk cloth on an **old** garment,
9:17 Neither do men pour new wine into **old** wineskins. If they do,
13:52 who brings out of his storeroom new treasures as well as **old**."
Mk   2:21 "No one sews a patch of unshrunk cloth on an **old** garment.
2:21 If he does, the new piece will pull away from the **old**, making the
2:22 And no one pours new wine into **old** wineskins. If he does,
Lk   5:36 one tears a patch from a new garment and sews it on an **old** one.
5:36 new garment, and the patch from the new will not match the **old**.
5:37 And no one pours new wine into **old** wineskins. If he does,
5:39 And no one after drinking **old** wine wants the new, for he says,
5:39 drinking old wine wants the new, for he says, 'The **old** is better.' "
Ro   6: 6 For we know that our **old** self was crucified with him so that the
1Co 5: 7 Get rid of the **old** yeast that you may be a new batch without
5: 8 not with the **old** yeast, the yeast of malice and wickedness,
2Co 3:14 for to this day the same veil remains when the **old** covenant is read.
Eph 4:22 with regard to your former way of life, to put off your **old** self,
Col 3: 9 since you have taken off your **old** self with its practices
1Jn 2: 7 Dear friends, I am not writing you a new command but an **old** one,
2: 7 the beginning. This **old** command is the message you have heard.

4095 παλαιότης, *palaiotēs* [1] [√ *4093*]

old way [1]

Ro   7: 6 new way of the Spirit, and not in the **old way** of the written code.

4096 παλαιόω, *palaioō* [4] [√ *4093*]

wear out [2], made obsolete [1], obsolete [1]

Lk   12:33 Provide purses for yourselves *that will* not **wear out**, a treasure in
Heb   1:11 will perish, but you remain; *they will* all **wear out** like a garment.
8:13 By calling this covenant "new," *he has* **made** the first one **obsolete**;
8:13 one obsolete; and what *is* **obsolete** and aging will soon disappear.

4097 πάλη, *palē* [1]

struggle [1]

Eph 6:12 For our **struggle** is not against flesh and blood, but against the

4098 παλιγγενεσία, *palingenesia* [2] [√ *4099 + 1181*]

rebirth [1], renewal [1]

Mt   19:28 Jesus said to them, "I tell you the truth, at the **renewal** *of all things*,
Tit   3: 5 He saved us through the washing *of* **rebirth** and renewal by the

4099 πάλιν, *palin* [141] [→ *4098, 4100*]

again [83], *untranslated* [21], once more [9], back [7], then after
[3], another [2], then [2], again [+*1309*] [1], all over again [+*540*]
[1], all over again [1], also [1], another time [1], elsewhere [1],
later [1], now [1], once again [1], rebuild [+*3868*] [1], repeat
[+*3306*] [1], return [+*1650+2262+3836*] [1], returned to place
[+*404*] [1], yet [1]

Mt   4: 7 Jesus answered him, "It is **also** written: 'Do not put the Lord your
4: 8 **Again**, the devil took him to a very high mountain and showed him
5:33 "**Again**, you have heard that it was said to the people long ago,
13:45 "**Again**, the kingdom of heaven is like a merchant looking for fine
13:47 "**Once again**, the kingdom of heaven is like a net that was let
18:19 "**Again**, I tell you that if two of you on earth agree about anything
19:24 **Again** I tell you, it is easier for a camel to go through the eye of a
20: 5 "He went out **again** about the sixth hour and the ninth hour
21:36 **Then** he sent other servants to them, more than the first time,
22: 1 Jesus spoke to them **again** in parables, saying:
22: 4 "**Then** he sent some more servants and said, 'Tell those who have
26:42 **[RPG]** He went away a second time and prayed, "My Father,
26:43 When he came back, he **again** found them sleeping, because their
26:44 So he left them and went away **once more** and prayed the third
26:44 and prayed the third time, saying the same thing. **[RPG]**
26:72 He denied it **again**, with an oath: "I don't know the man!"
27:50 And when Jesus had cried out **again** in a loud voice, he gave up his
Mk   2: 1 A few days later, when Jesus **again** entered Capernaum, the people
2:13 Once **again** Jesus went out beside the lake. A large crowd came to
3: 1 **Another time** he went into the synagogue, and a man with a
3:20 and **again** a crowd gathered, so that he and his disciples were not
4: 1 **Again** Jesus began to teach by the lake. The crowd that gathered
5:21 When Jesus had **again** crossed over by boat to the other side of the
7:14 **Again** Jesus called the crowd to him and said, "Listen to me,
7:31 Then **[NIE]** Jesus left the vicinity of Tyre and went through
8: 1 During those days **another** large crowd gathered. Since they had
8:13 he left them, got **back** into the boat and crossed to the other side.
8:25 **Once more** Jesus put his hands on the man's eyes. Then his eyes
10: 1 **Again** crowds of people came to him, and as was his custom,
10: 1 came to him, and as was his custom, **[RPG]** he taught them.
10:10 When they were in the house **again**, the disciples asked Jesus
10:24 But Jesus said **again**, "Children, how hard it is to enter the kingdom
10:32 **Again** he took the Twelve aside and told them what was going to
11: 3 'The Lord needs it and will send it back **[RPG]** here shortly.' "
11:27 They arrived **again** in Jerusalem, and while Jesus was walking in
12: 4 Then **[NIE]** he sent another servant to them; they struck this man
14:39 **Once more** he went away and prayed the same thing.
14:40 When he came back, he **again** found them sleeping, because their
14:61 **Again** the high priest asked him, "Are you the Christ, the Son of the
14:69 she said **again** to those standing around, "This fellow is one of
14:70 **Again** he denied it. After a little while, those standing near said to
14:70 After a little while, **[RPG]** those standing near said to Peter,
15: 4 So **again** Pilate asked him, "Aren't you going to answer? See how
15:12 the one you call the king of the Jews?" Pilate asked **[NIE]** them.
15:13 "Crucify him!" they shouted. **[NIE]**
Lk   6:43 tree bears bad fruit, nor **[NIE]** does a bad tree bear good fruit.
13:20 **Again** he asked, "What shall I compare the kingdom of God to?
23:20 Wanting to release Jesus, Pilate appealed to them **again**.
Jn   1:35 The next day John was there **again** with two of his disciples.
4: 3 learned of this, he left Judea and went back **once more** to Galilee.
4:13 "Everyone who drinks this water will be thirsty **again**,
4:46 **Once more** he visited Cana in Galilee, where he had turned the
4:54 **[RPG]** This was the second miraculous sign that Jesus performed,
6:15 make him king by force, withdrew **again** to a mountain by himself.
8: 2 At dawn he appeared **again** in the temple courts, where all the

8: 8 **Again** he stooped down and wrote on the ground.
8:12 When Jesus spoke **again** to the people, he said, "I am the light of
8:21 **Once more** Jesus said to them, "I am going away, and you will look
9:15 Therefore **[NIE]** the Pharisees also asked him how he had
9:17 Finally they turned **again** to the blind man, "What have you to say
9:27 and you did not listen. Why do you want to hear it **again**?
10: 7 Therefore Jesus said **again**, "I tell you the truth, I am the gate for
10:17 loves me is that I lay down my life—only to take it up **again**.
10:18 I have authority to lay it down and authority to take it up **again**.
10:19 At these words the Jews were **again** divided.
10:31 **Again** the Jews picked up stones to stone him,
10:39 **Again** they tried to seize him, but he escaped their grasp.
10:40 Then Jesus went back **[RPG]** across the Jordan to the place where
11: 7 Then he said to his disciples, "Let us go **back** to Judea."
11: 8 Jews tried to stone you, and yet **[RPG]** you are going back there?"
11:38 Jesus, **once more** deeply moved, came to the tomb. It was a cave
12:28 came from heaven, "I have glorified it, and will glorify it **again**."
12:39 reason they could not believe, because, as Isaiah says **elsewhere**:
13:12 their feet, he put on his clothes and **returned** to *his* place **[+404]**.
14: 3 I will come **back** and take you to be with me that you also may be
16:16 will see me no more, and **then after** a little while you will see me."
16:17 and **then after** a little while you will see me,' and 'Because I am
16:19 see me no more, and **then after** a little while you will see me'?
16:22 is your time of grief, but I will see you **again** and you will rejoice,
16:28 **now** I am leaving the world and going back to the Father."
18: 7 **Again** he asked them, "Who is it you want?" And they said,
18:27 **Again** Peter denied it, and at that moment a rooster began to crow.
18:33 Pilate then went **back** inside the palace, summoned Jesus
18:38 With this he went out **again** to the Jews and said, "I find no basis
18:40 They shouted **back**, "No, not him! Give us Barabbas!"
19: 4 **Once more** Pilate came out and said to the Jews, "Look, I am
19: 9 and he went **back** inside the palace. "Where do you come from?"
19:37 and, **[RPG]** as another scripture says, "They will look on the one
20:10 Then the disciples went back **[RPG]** to their homes,
20:21 **Again** Jesus said, "Peace be with you! As the Father has sent me,
20:26 A week later his disciples were in the house **again**, and Thomas
21: 1 Afterward Jesus appeared **again** to his disciples, by the Sea of
21:16 **Again** **[+1309]** Jesus said, "Simon son of John, do you truly love
Ac 10:15 The voice spoke to him **[RPG]** a second time, "Do not call
11:10 three times, and then it was all pulled up to heaven **again**.
17:32 but others said, "We want to hear you **again** on this subject."
18:21 he left, he promised, "I will come back **[RPG]** if it is God's will."
27:28 A short time later they took soundings **again** and found it was
Ro 8:15 For you did not receive a spirit that makes you a slave **again** to
11:23 they will be grafted in, for God is able to graft them in **again**.
15:10 **Again**, it says, "Rejoice, O Gentiles, with his people."
15:11 And **again**, "Praise the Lord, all you Gentiles, and sing praises to
15:12 And **again**, Isaiah says, "The Root of Jesse will spring up, one who
1Co 3:20 **again**, "The Lord knows that the thoughts of the wise are futile."
7: 5 Then come together **again** so that Satan will not tempt you
12:21 And **[RPG]** the head cannot say to the feet, "I don't need you!"
2Co 1:16 my way to Macedonia and to come **back** to you from Macedonia,
2: 1 So I made up my mind that I would not make **another** painful visit
3: 1 Are we beginning to commend ourselves **again**? Or do we need,
5:12 We are not trying to commend ourselves to you **again**, but are
10: 7 he should consider **again** that we belong to Christ just as much as
11:16 *I repeat* **[+3306]**: Let no one take me for a fool. But if you do,
12:21 I am afraid that when I come **again** my God will humble me before
13: 2 On *my* **return** **[+1650+2262+3836]** I will not spare those who
Gal 1: 9 As we have already said, so now I say **again**: If anybody is
1:17 I went immediately into Arabia and **later** returned to Damascus.
2: 1 Fourteen years later I went up **again** to Jerusalem, this time with
2:18 If *I* **rebuild** **[+3868]** what I destroyed, I prove that I am a
4: 9 how is it that you are turning back to **[RPG]** those weak
4: 9 Do you wish to be enslaved by them **all over again** **[+540]**?
4:19 for whom I am **again** in the pains of childbirth until Christ is
5: 1 and do not let yourselves be burdened **again** by a yoke of slavery.
5: 3 **Again** I declare to every man who lets himself be circumcised that
Php 1:26 so that through my being with you **again** your joy in Christ Jesus
2:28 so that when you see him **again** you may be glad and I may have
4: 4 Rejoice in the Lord always. I will say it **again**: Rejoice!
Heb 1: 5 Or **again**, "I will be his Father, and he will be my Son"?
1: 6 And **again**, when God brings his firstborn into the world, he says,
2:13 And **again**, "I will put my trust in him." And again he says, "Here
2:13 **again** he says, "Here am I, and the children God has given me."
4: 5 And **again** in the passage above he says, "They shall never enter my

4: 7 Therefore God **again** set a certain day, calling it Today, when a
5:12 to teach you the elementary truths of God's word **all over again**.
6: 1 not laying **again** the foundation of repentance from acts that lead to
6: 6 if they fall away, to be brought back **[RPG]** to repentance,
10:30 avenge," and **again**, "The Lord will judge his people."
Jas 5:18 **Again** he prayed, and the heavens gave rain, and the earth
2Pe 2:20 Savior Jesus Christ and are **again** entangled in it and overcome,
1Jn 2: 8 **Yet** I am writing you a new command; its truth is seen in him
Rev 10: 8 the voice that I had heard from heaven spoke to me **once more**:
10:11 "You must prophesy **again** about many peoples, nations, languages

4100 παλινγενεσία, *palingenesia* Not used in UBS/NIV [√ *4099 + 1181*]

4101 παμπληθεί, *pamplēthei* [1] [√ *4246 + 4398*]

with one voice [1]

Lk 23:18 **With one voice** they cried out, "Away with this man! Release

4102 πάμπολυς, *pampolys* Not used in UBS/NIV [√ *4246 + 4498*]

4103 Παμφυλία, *Pamphylia* [5] [√ *4246 + 5886*]

Pamphylia [5]

Ac 2:10 Phrygia and **Pamphylia**, Egypt and the parts of Libya near Cyrene;
13:13 Paul and his companions sailed from Perga *in* **Pamphylia**,
14:24 After going through Pisidia, they came into **Pamphylia**,
15:38 because he had deserted them in **Pamphylia** and had not
27: 5 sailed across the open sea off the coast of Cilicia and **Pamphylia**,

4104 πανδοκεῖον, *pandokeion* Not used in UBS/NIV [√ *4246 + 1312*]

4105 πανδοκεύς, *pandokeus* Not used in UBS/NIV [√ *4246 + 1312*]

4106 πανδοχεῖον, *pandocheion* [1] [√ *4246 + 1312*]

inn [1]

Lk 10:34 man on his own donkey, took him to an **inn** and took care of him.

4107 πανδοχεύς, *pandocheus* [1] [√ *4246 + 1312*]

innkeeper [1]

Lk 10:35 day he took out two silver coins and gave them *to* the **innkeeper**.

4108 πανήγυρις, *panēgyris* [1] [√ *4246 + 72*]

joyful assembly [1]

Heb 12:22 come to thousands upon thousands of angels *in* **joyful assembly**,

4109 πανοικεί, *panoikei* [1] [√ *4246 + 3875*]

whole family [1]

Ac 16:34 because he had come to believe in God—he and his **whole family**.

4110 πανοπλία, *panoplia* [3] [√ *4246 + 3960*]

full armor [2], armor [1]

Lk 11:22 he takes away the **armor** in which the man trusted and divides up
Eph 6:11 Put on the **full armor** of God so that you can take your stand
6:13 Therefore put on the **full armor** of God, so that when the day of

4111 πανουργία, *panourgia* [5] [√ *4246 + 2240*]

craftiness [2], cunning [1], deception [1], duplicity [1]

Lk 20:23 He saw through their **duplicity** and said to them,

1Co 3:19 As it is written: "He catches the wise in their **craftiness**";
2Co 4: 2 we do not use **deception**, nor do we distort the word of God.
     11: 3 I am afraid that just as Eve was deceived by the serpent's **cunning**,
Eph 4:14 by the cunning and **craftiness** of men in their deceitful scheming.

4112 πανοῦργος, *panourgos* [1] [√ 4246 + 2240]

crafty [1]

2Co 12:16 to you. Yet, **crafty** *fellow* that I am, I caught you by trickery!

4113 πανπληθεί, *panplēthei* Not used in UBS/NIV [√ 4246 + 4398]

4114 πανταχῆ, *pantachē* [1] [√ 4246]

everywhere [1]

Ac 21:28 This is the man who teaches all men **everywhere** against our

4115 πανταχόθεν, *pantachothen* Not used in UBS/NIV [√ 4246]

4116 πανταχοῦ, *pantachou* [7] [√ 4246]

everywhere [6], whole [+*3910*] [1]

Mk 1:28 News about him spread quickly over the **whole** [+*3910*] region of
    16:20 Then the disciples went out and preached **everywhere**,
Lk 9: 6 to village, preaching the gospel and healing people **everywhere**.
Ac 17:30 but now he commands all people **everywhere** to repent.
    24: 3 **Everywhere** and in every way, most excellent Felix,
    28:22 for we know that people **everywhere** are talking against this sect."
1Co 4:17 which agrees with what I teach **everywhere** in every church.

4117 παντελής, *pantelēs* [2] [√ 4246 + 5465]

at all [+*1650+3836*] [1], completely [+*1650+3836*] [1]

Lk 13:11 was bent over and could not straighten up **at all** [+*1650+3836*].
Heb 7:25 Therefore he is able to save **completely** [+*1650+3836*] those who

4118 πάντη, *pantē* [1] [√ 4246]

in every way [1]

Ac 24: 3 Everywhere and **in every way**, most excellent Felix,

4119 πάντοθεν, *pantothen* [3] [√ 4246]

from everywhere [1], gold-covered [+*4328+5992*] [1], on every side [1]

Mk 1:45 lonely places. Yet the people still came to him **from everywhere**.
Lk 19:43 against you and encircle you and hem you in **on every side**.
Heb 9: 4 incense and the **gold-covered** [+*4328+5992*] ark of the covenant.

4120 παντοκράτωρ, *pantokratōr* [10] [√ 4246 + 3197]

Almighty [10]

2Co 6:18 and you will be my sons and daughters, says the Lord **Almighty**."
Rev 1: 8 "who is, and who was, and who is to come, the **Almighty**."
    4: 8 "Holy, holy, holy is the Lord God **Almighty**, who was, and is,
    11:17 thanks to you, Lord God **Almighty**, the One who is and who was,
    15: 3 "Great and marvelous are your deeds, Lord God **Almighty**.
    16: 7 "Yes, Lord God **Almighty**, true and just are your judgments."
    16:14 to gather them for the battle on the great day *of* God **Almighty**.
    19: 6 shouting: "Hallelujah! For our Lord God **Almighty** reigns.
    19:15 He treads the winepress of the fury of the wrath of God **Almighty**.
    21:22 because the Lord God **Almighty** and the Lamb are its temple.

4121 πάντοτε, *pantote* [41] [√ 4246 + 4005 + 5445]

always [35], at all times [2], any [1], constantly [1], forever [1], from now on [1]

Mt 26:11 The poor you will **always** have with you, but you will not always

26:11 you will always have with you, but you will not **always** have me.
Mk 14: 7 The poor you will **always** have with you, and you can help them
    14: 7 help them any time you want. But you will not **always** have me.
Lk 15:31 " 'My son,' the father said, 'you are **always** with me, and
    18: 1 his disciples a parable to show them that they should **always** pray
Jn 6:34 "Sir," they said, "**from now on** give us this bread."
    7: 6 "The right time for me has not yet come; for you **any** time is right.
    8:29 he has not left me alone, for I **always** do what pleases him."
    11:42 I knew that you **always** hear me, but I said this for the benefit of
    12: 8 You will **always** have the poor among you, but you will not always
    12: 8 have the poor among you, but you will not **always** have me."
    18:20 "I **always** taught in synagogues or at the temple, where all the Jews
Ro 1:10 in my prayers **at all times**; and I pray that now at last by God's
1Co 1: 4 I **always** thank God for you because of his grace given you in
    15:58 **Always** give yourselves fully to the work of the Lord, because you
2Co 2:14 who **always** leads us in triumphal procession in Christ and through
    4:10 We **always** carry around in our body the death of Jesus, so that the
    5: 6 Therefore we are **always** confident and know that as long as we are
    9: 8 so that in all things **at all times**, having all that you need, you will
Gal 4:18 is good, and to be so **always** and not just when I am with you.
Eph 5:20 **always** giving thanks to God the Father for everything, in the name
Php 1: 4 In all my prayers for all of you, I **always** pray with joy
    1:20 so that now as **always** Christ will be exalted in my body,
    2:12 Therefore, my dear friends, as you have **always** obeyed—not only
    4: 4 Rejoice in the Lord **always**. I will say it again: Rejoice!
Col 1: 3 We **always** thank God, the Father of our Lord Jesus Christ,
    4: 6 Let your conversation be **always** full of grace, seasoned with salt,
    4:12 He is **always** wrestling in prayer for you, that you may stand firm
1Th 2: 2 We **always** thank God for all of you, mentioning you in our
    2:16 be saved. In this way they **always** heap up their sins to the limit.
    3: 6 He has told us that you **always** have pleasant memories of us
    4:17 meet the Lord in the air. And so we will be with the Lord **forever**.
    5:15 but **always** try to be kind to each other and to everyone else.
    5:16 Be joyful **always**;
2Th 1: 3 We ought **always** to thank God for you, brothers, and rightly so,
    1:11 With this in mind, we **constantly** pray for you, that our God may
    2:13 But we ought **always** to thank God for you, brothers loved by the
2Ti 3: 7 **always** learning but never able to acknowledge the truth.
Phm 1: 4 I **always** thank my God as I remember you in my prayers,
Heb 7:25 to God through him, because he **always** lives to intercede for them.

4122 πάντως, *pantōs* [8] [√ 4246]

at all [2], surely [2], by all possible means [1], certainly [1], must [1], quite [1]

Lk 4:23 Jesus said to them, "**Surely** you will quote this proverb to me:
Ac 21:22 What shall we do? They will **certainly** hear that you have come,
    28: 4 his hand, they said to each other, "This man **must** be a murderer,
Ro 3: 9 What shall we conclude then? Are we any better? Not **at all**!
1Co 5:10 not **at all** meaning the people of this world who are immoral,
    9:10 **Surely** he says this for us, doesn't he? Yes, this was written for us,
    9:22 things to all men so that **by all possible means** I might save some.
    16:12 He was **quite** unwilling to go now, but he will go when he has the

4123 παρά, *para* [194]

[→ *524, 563, 564, 1384, 2339, 4124, 4125, 4126, 4127, 4128, 4129, 4130, 4131, 4132, 4133, 4134, 4135, 4136, 4138, 4139, 4140, 4141, 4142, 4143, 4144, 4145, 4146, 4147, 4148, 4149, 4150, 4151, 4152, 4153, 4154, 4155, 4156, 4157, 4158, 4159, 4160, 4161, 4162, 4163, 4164, 4165, 4166, 4167, 4168, 4169, 4170, 4171, 4172, 4173, 4174, 4175, 4176, 4177, 4178, 4179, 4180, 4181, 4182, 4183, 4184, 4185, 4186, 4187, 4188, 4189, 4190, 4191, 4192, 4193, 4194, 4195, 4196, 4199, 4200, 4201, 4202, 4204, 4205, 4206, 4207, 4208, 4209, 4210, 4211, 4212, 4213, 4214, 4215, 4216, 4217, 4218, 4219, 4223, 4224, 4225, 4227, 4228, 4229, 4230, 4232, 4233, 4234, 4235, 4236, 4237, 4238, 4239, 4240, 4241, 4242, 4243, 4261, 5219, 5220, 5221, 5222, 5223*]

from [47], *untranslated* [27], with [26], by [11], at [9], than [9], along [7], to [4], beside [3], contrary to [3], among [2], before [2], conceited [+*1571+5861*] [2], for that reason [+*4047*] [2], in sight [2], more than [2], of [2], other than [2], rather than [2], above [1], accepts [1], against [1], any of [1], beyond [1], family [+*3836*] [1], had [+*3836*] [1], have [1], him [+*4005*] [1], in presence [1], in the presence [1], in [1], instructed [*RP4161*] [1], me say [*+1609*] [1], minus [1], more [*+4498*] [1], near [1], on [1], out [1], past [1], presence [1], received from [*RP4161*] [1], say [*+1639*] [1], sent[s] [1], set aside [*+1571+5502*] [1], they [*+899*] [1], under [*+3836+4546*] [1], unnatural ones [*+3836+5882*] [1], walked beside [*RP4135*] [1], where [*+4005*] [1]

Mt   2: 4   of the law, he asked [NIE] them where the Christ was to be born.
    2: 7   and found out **from** them the exact time the star had appeared.
    2:16   in accordance with the time he had learned **from** the Magi.
    4:18   As Jesus was walking **beside** the Sea of Galilee, he saw two
    6: 1   If you do, you will have no reward **from** your Father in heaven.
    8:10   the truth, I have not found anyone in Israel **with** such great faith.
   13: 1   That same day Jesus went out of the house and sat **by** the lake.
   13: 4   some fell **along** the path, and the birds came and ate it up.
   13:19   what was sown in his heart. This is the seed sown **along** the path.
   15:29   Jesus left there and went **along** the Sea of Galilee. Then he went up
   15:30   the crippled, the mute and many others, and laid them **at** his feet;
   18:19   you ask for, it will be done for you **by** my Father in heaven.
   19:26   Jesus looked at them and said, "**With** man this is impossible,
   19:26   "With man this is impossible, but **with** God all things are possible."
   20:30   Two blind men were sitting **by** the roadside, and when they heard
   21:42   the [NIE] Lord has done this, and it is marvelous in our eyes'?
   22:25   Now there were seven brothers **among** us. The first one married
   28:15   And this story has been widely circulated **among** the Jews to this

Mk   1:16   As Jesus **walked beside** [*RP4135*] the Sea of Galilee, he saw
    2:13   Once again Jesus went out **beside** the lake. A large crowd came to
    3:21   When his **family** [*+3836*] heard about this, they went to take
    4: 1   Again Jesus began to teach **by** the lake. The crowd that gathered
    4: 4   some fell **along** the path, and the birds came and ate it up.
    4:15   Some people are like seed **along** the path, where the word is sown.
    5:21   a large crowd gathered around him while he was **by** the lake.
    5:26   the care of many doctors and had spent all she had[s] [*+3836*],
    8:11   To test him, they asked [NIE] him for a sign from heaven.
   10:27   Jesus looked at them and said, "**With** man this is impossible,
   10:27   at them and said, "With man this is impossible, but not **with** God;
   10:27   is impossible, but not with God; all things are possible **with** God."
   10:46   the Son of Timaeus), was sitting **by** the roadside begging.
   12: 2   At harvest time he sent a servant to the tenants to collect **from**
   12:11   [NIE] the Lord has done this, and it is marvelous in our eyes'?"
   14:43   a crowd armed with swords and clubs, *sent* **from** the chief priests,
   16: 9   to Mary Magdalene, **out** of whom he had driven seven demons.

Lk   1:30   to her, "Do not be afraid, Mary, you have found favor **with** God.
    1:37   For nothing is impossible **with** God."
    1:45   Blessed is she who has believed that what the [NIE] Lord has said
    2: 1   In those days [NIE] Caesar Augustus issued a decree that a
    2:52   Jesus grew in wisdom and stature, and in favor **with** God and men.
    3:13   "Don't collect any **more than** [*+4498*] you are required to,"
    5: 1   One day as Jesus was standing **by** the Lake of Gennesaret,
    5: 2   he saw **at** the water's *edge* two boats, left there by the fishermen,
    6:19   because power was coming **from** him and healing them all.
    6:34   And if you lend to those **from** whom you expect repayment,
    7:38   and as she stood behind him **at** his feet weeping, she began to wet
    8: 5   As he was scattering the seed, some fell **along** the path; it was
    8:12   Those **along** the path are the ones who hear, and then the devil
    8:35   had gone out, sitting **at** Jesus' feet, dressed and in his right mind;
    8:41   named Jairus, a ruler of the synagogue, came and fell **at** Jesus' feet,
    8:49   someone came **from** the house of Jairus, the synagogue ruler.
    9:47   their thoughts, took a little child and had him stand **beside** him.
   10: 7   in that house, eating and drinking whatever they [*+899*] give you,
   11:16   Others tested [NIE] him by asking for a sign from heaven.
   11:37   had finished speaking, a Pharisee invited him to eat **with** him;
   12:48   [NIE] and from the one who has been entrusted with much,
   13: 2   "Do you think that these Galileans were *worse* sinners **than** all the
   13: 4   do you think they were *more* guilty **than** all the others living in
   17:16   He threw himself **at** Jesus' feet and thanked him—and he was a
   18:14   "I tell you that this man, **rather than** the other, went home justified
   18:27   Jesus replied, "What is impossible **with** men is possible with God."
   18:27   Jesus replied, "What is impossible with men is possible **with** God."
   18:35   a blind man was sitting **by** the roadside begging.
   19: 7   and began to mutter, "He has gone to be the guest **of** a 'sinner.' "

Jn   1: 6   There came a man who was sent **from** God; his name was John.
    1:14   the glory of the One and Only, who *came* **from** the Father,
    1:39   and saw where he was staying, and spent that day **with** him.
    1:40   was one of the two who heard what [NIE] John had said
    4: 9   I am a Samaritan woman. How can you ask [NIE] me for a drink?"

    4:40   they urged him to stay **with** them, and he stayed two days.
    4:52   When he inquired [NIE] as to the time when his son got better,
    5:34   Not that I accept [NIE] human testimony; but I mention it that
    5:41   "I do not accept praise **from** men,
    5:44   How can you believe if you accept praise **from** one another,
    5:44   yet make no effort to obtain the praise that *comes* **from** the only
    6:45   who listens to the Father and learns **from** him comes to me.
    6:46   No one has seen the Father except the one who is **from** God;
    7:29   but I know him because I am **from** him and he sent me."
    7:51   "Does our law condemn anyone without first hearing [NIE] him to
    8:26   me is reliable, and what I have heard **from** him I tell the world."
    8:38   I am telling you what I have seen in the Father's **presence**,
    8:38   and you do what you have heard **from** your father."
    8:40   to kill me, a man who has told you the truth that I heard **from** God.
    9:16   Some of the Pharisees said, "This man is not **from** God, for he does
    9:33   If this man were not **from** God, he could do nothing."
   10:18   to take it up again. This command I received **from** my Father."
   14:17   But you know him, for he lives **with** you and will be in you.
   14:23   love him, and we will come to him and make our home **with** him.
   14:25   "All this I have spoken while still **with** you.
   15:15   for everything that I learned **from** my Father I have made known
   15:26   the Counselor comes, whom I will send to you **from** the Father,
   15:26   the Spirit of truth who goes out **from** the Father, he will testify
   16:27   you have loved me and have believed that I came **from** God.
   16:28   I came **from** the Father and entered the world; now I am leaving
   17: 5   glorify me in your **presence** with the glory I had with you before
   17: 5   glorify me in your presence with the glory I had **with** you before
   17: 7   Now they know that everything you have given me comes **from**
   17: 8   They knew with certainty that I came **from** you, and they believed
   19:25   **Near** the cross of Jesus stood his mother, his mother's sister,

Ac   2:33   he has received **from** the Father the promised Holy Spirit and has
    3: 2   where he was put every day to beg **from** those going into the
    3: 5   gave them his attention, expecting to get something **from** them.
    4:35   and put it **at** the apostles' feet, and it was distributed to anyone as
    5: 2   for himself, but brought the rest and put it **at** the apostles' feet.
    7:16   and placed in the tomb that Abraham had bought **from** the sons of
    7:58   the witnesses laid their clothes **at** the feet of a young man named
    9: 2   and asked [NIE] him for letters to the synagogues in Damascus,
    9:14   And he has come here with authority **from** the chief priests to
    9:43   Peter stayed in Joppa for some time **with** a tanner named Simon.
   10: 6   He is staying **with** Simon the tanner, whose house is by the sea."
   10: 6   He is staying with Simon the tanner, whose house is **by** the sea."
   10:22   you come to his house so that he could hear what you **have** to say."
   10:32   is a guest in the home of Simon the tanner, who *lives* **by** the sea.'
   16:13   On the Sabbath we went outside the city gate **to** the river,
   17: 9   Then they made [NIE] Jason and the others post bond and let
   18: 3   he was a tentmaker as they were, he stayed and worked **with** them.
   18:13   "is persuading the people to worship God *in ways* **contrary to** the
   20:24   and complete the task [NIE] the Lord Jesus has given me—
   21: 7   where we greeted the brothers and stayed **with** them for a day.
   21: 8   and stayed [NIE] at the house of Philip the evangelist,
   21:16   and brought us to the home of Mnason, **where** [*+4005*] we were to
   22: 3   **Under** [*+3836+4546*] Gamaliel I was thoroughly trained in the law
   22: 5   I even obtained letters **from** them to their brothers in Damascus,
   24: 8   By examining **him** [*+4005*] yourself you will be able to learn the
   26: 8   Why should **any of** you consider it incredible that God raises the
   26:10   On the authority **of** the chief priests I put many of the saints in
   28:14   found some brothers who invited us to spend a week **with** them.
   28:22   But we want to hear [NIE] what your views are, for we know that

Ro   1:25   and worshiped and served created things **rather than** the Creator—
    1:26   exchanged natural relations for **unnatural ones** [*+3836+5882*].
    2:11   For [NIE] God does not show favoritism.
    2:13   it is not those who hear the law who are righteous in God's **sight**,
    4:18   **Against** all hope, Abraham in hope believed and so became the
    9:14   What then shall we say? Is [NIE] God unjust? Not at all!
   11:24   and **contrary to** nature were grafted into a cultivated olive tree,
   11:25   brothers, so that you may not be **conceited** [*+1571+5861*].
   11:27   And this is [NIE] my covenant with them when I take away their
   12: 3   one of you: Do not think of yourself **more** highly **than** you ought,
   12:16   with people of low position. Do not be **conceited** [*+1571+5861*].
   14: 5   One man considers one day **more** *sacred* **than** another;
   16:17   and put obstacles in your way that are **contrary to** the teaching

1Co   3:11   For no one can lay any foundation other **than** the one already laid,
    3:19   For the wisdom of this world is foolishness **in** God's **sight**.
    7:24   Brothers, each man, as *responsible* **to** God, should remain in the
   12:15   it would not **for** [*+4047*] **that reason** cease to be part of the body.

12: 16 it would not **for** [+*4047*] **that reason** cease to be part of the body.
16: 2 each one of you *should* **set aside** [+*1571*+*5502*] a sum of money in
2Co 1: 17 in a worldly manner so that *in the same breath* I **say** [+*1639*],
8: 3 gave as much as they were able, and even **beyond** their ability.
11: 24 Five times I received from the Jews the forty lashes **minus** one.
Gal 1: 8 or an angel from heaven should preach a gospel **other than** the one
1: 9 If anybody is preaching to you a gospel **other than** what you
1: 12 I did not receive it **from** any man, nor was I taught it; rather,
3: 11 Clearly no one is justified **before** God by the law, because,
Eph 6: 8 because you know that the **[NIE]** Lord will reward everyone for
6: 9 and yours is in heaven, and there is no favoritism **with** him.
Php 4: 18 now that I have received **from** Epaphroditus the gifts you sent.
4: 18 now that I have received from Epaphroditus the gifts you sent[s].
Col 4: 16 After this letter has been read **to** you, see that it is also read in the
1Th 2: 13 when you received the word of God, which you heard **from** us,
4: 1 we **instructed you** [*RP4161*] how to live in order to please God,
2Th 1: 6 **[NIE]** God is just: He will pay back trouble to those who trouble
3: 6 not live according to the teaching *you* **received from** [*RP4161*] us.
3: 8 nor did we eat **[NIE]** anyone's food without paying for it.
2Ti 1: 13 What you heard **from** me, keep as the pattern of sound teaching,
1: 18 May the Lord grant that he will find mercy **from** the Lord on that
2: 2 And the things you have heard **me say** [+*1609*] in the presence of
3: 14 convinced of, because you know those **from** whom you learned it,
4: 13 bring the cloak that I left **with** Carpus at Troas, and my scrolls,
Heb 1: 4 to the angels as the name he has inherited is superior **to** theirs.
1: 9 has *set* you **above** your companions by anointing you with the oil
2: 7 You made him a little lower **than** the angels; you crowned him
2: 9 But we see Jesus, who was made a little lower **than** the angels,
3: 3 Jesus has been found worthy of greater honor **than** Moses,
9: 23 but the heavenly things themselves with better sacrifices **than**
11: 4 By faith Abel offered God a better sacrifice **than** Cain did.
11: 11 By faith Abraham, even though he was **past** age—and Sarah
11: 12 as the stars in the sky and as countless as the sand **on** the seashore.
12: 24 and to the sprinkled blood that speaks a better word **than** the blood
Jas 1: 5 If any of you lacks wisdom, he should ask **[NIE]** God, who gives
1: 7 That man should not think he will receive anything **from** the Lord;
1: 17 **[NIE]** who does not change like shifting shadows.
1: 27 Religion that God our Father **accepts** as pure and faultless is this:
1Pe 2: 4 rejected by men but chosen **by** God and precious to him—
2: 20 doing good and you endure it, this is commendable **before** God.
2Pe 1: 17 and glory **from** God the Father when the voice came to him from
2: 11 accusations against such beings **in the presence** of the Lord.
3: 8 **With** the Lord a day is like a thousand years, and a thousand years
2Jn 1: 3 mercy and peace **from** God the Father and from Jesus Christ,
1: 3 mercy and peace **from** God the Father and **from** Jesus Christ,
1: 4 walking in the truth, just as **[NIE]** the Father commanded us.
Rev 2: 13 my faithful witness, who was put to death **in** your *city*—
2: 27 like pottery'—just as I have received authority **from** my Father.
3: 18 I counsel you to buy **from** me gold refined in the fire, so you can

4124 παραβαίνω, *parabainō* [3] [√ *4123 + 326*]

break [2], left [1]

Mt 15: 2 "Why *do* your disciples **break** the tradition of the elders? They
15: 3 "And why *do* you **break** the command of God for the sake of your
Ac 1: 25 this apostolic ministry, which Judas **left** to go where he belongs."

4125 παραβάλλω, *paraballō* [1] [√ *4123 + 965*]

crossed over [1]

Ac 20: 15 The day after that *we* **crossed over** to Samos, and on the following

4126 παράβασις, *parabasis* [7] [√ *4123 + 326*]

breaking a command [1], breaking [1], sinner [1], sins [1],
transgression [1], transgressions [1], violation [1]

Ro 2: 23 brag about the law, do you dishonor God by **breaking** the law?
4: 15 brings wrath. And where there is no law there is no **transgression**.
5: 14 even over those who did not sin by **breaking a command**,
Gal 3: 19 because of **transgressions** until the Seed to whom the promise
1Ti 2: 14 it was the woman who was deceived and became a **sinner**.
Heb 2: 2 and every **violation** and disobedience received its just punishment,
9: 15 now that he has died as a ransom to set them free *from* the **sins**

4127 παραβάτης, *parabatēs* [5] [√ *4123 + 326*]

lawbreaker [+*3795*] [2], break [+*1639*] [1], lawbreaker [1],
lawbreakers [1]

Ro 2: 25 has value if you observe the law, but if *you* **break** [+*1639*] the law,
2: 27 have the written code and circumcision, are a **lawbreaker** [+*3795*].
Gal 2: 18 If I rebuild what I destroyed, I prove that I am a **lawbreaker**.
Jas 2: 9 you sin and are convicted by the law as **lawbreakers**.
2: 11 but do commit murder, you have become a **lawbreaker** [+*3795*].

4128 παραβιάζομαι, *parabiazomai* [2] [√ *4123 + 1040*]

persuaded [1], urged strongly [1]

Lk 24: 29 But *they* **urged** him **strongly**, "Stay with us, for it is nearly
Ac 16: 15 she said, "come and stay at my house." And *she* **persuaded** us.

4129 παραβολεύομαι, *paraboleuomai* [1] [√ *4123 + 965*]

risking [1]

Php 2: 30 **risking** his life to make up for the help you could not give me.

4130 παραβολή, *parabolē* [50] [√ *4123 + 965*]

parable [30], parables [15], lesson [2], figuratively speaking
[+*1877*] [1], illustration [1], proverb [1]

Mt 13: 3 Then he told them many things in **parables**, saying: "A farmer
13: 10 to him and asked, "Why do you speak to the people in **parables**?"
13: 13 This is why I speak to them in **parables**: "Though seeing, they do
13: 18 "Listen then to what the **parable** of the sower means:
13: 24 Jesus told them another **parable**: "The kingdom of heaven is like a
13: 31 He told them another **parable**: "The kingdom of heaven is like a
13: 33 He told them still another **parable**: "The kingdom of heaven is like
13: 34 Jesus spoke all these things to the crowd in **parables**; he did not
13: 34 he did not say anything to them without using a **parable**.
13: 35 "I will open my mouth in **parables**, I will utter things hidden since
13: 36 and said, "Explain to us the **parable** of the weeds in the field."
13: 53 When Jesus had finished these **parables**, he moved on from there.
15: 15 Peter said, "Explain the **parable** to us."
21: 33 "Listen to another **parable**: There was a landowner who planted a
21: 45 When the chief priests and the Pharisees heard Jesus' **parables**,
22: 1 Jesus spoke to them again in **parables**, saying:
24: 32 "Now learn this **lesson** from the fig tree: As soon as its twigs get
Mk 3: 23 So Jesus called them and spoke to them in **parables**: "How can
4: 2 He taught them many things by **parables**, and in his teaching said:
4: 10 and the others around him asked him about the **parables**.
4: 11 But to those on the outside everything is said in **parables**
4: 13 Then Jesus said to them, "Don't you understand this **parable**?
4: 13 this parable? How then will you understand any **parable**?
4: 30 of God is like, or what **parable** shall we use to describe it?
4: 33 *With* many similar **parables** Jesus spoke the word to them,
4: 34 He did not say anything to them without using a **parable**.
7: 17 and entered the house, his disciples asked him about this **parable**.
12: 1 He then began to speak to them in **parables**: "A man planted a
12: 12 because they knew he had spoken the **parable** against them.
13: 28 "Now learn this **lesson** from the fig tree: As soon as its twigs get
Lk 4: 23 Jesus said to them, "Surely you will quote this **proverb** to me:
5: 36 He told them this **parable**: "No one tears a patch from a new
6: 39 He also told them this **parable**: "Can a blind man lead a blind man?
8: 4 were coming to Jesus from town after town, he told this **parable**:
8: 9 His disciples asked him what this **parable** meant.
8: 10 but to others I speak in **parables**, so that, " 'though seeing, they
8: 11 "This is the meaning of the **parable**: The seed is the word of God.
12: 16 And he told them this **parable**: "The ground of a certain rich man
12: 41 Peter asked, "Lord, are you telling this **parable** to us, or to
13: 6 Then he told this **parable**: "A man had a fig tree, planted in his
14: 7 picked the places of honor at the table, he told this **parable**:
15: 3 Then Jesus told them this **parable**:
18: 1 Then Jesus told his disciples a **parable** to show them that they
18: 9 and looked down on everybody else, Jesus told this **parable**:
19: 11 they were listening to this, he went on to tell them a **parable**,
20: 9 He went on to tell the people this **parable**: "A man planted a
20: 19 because they knew he had spoken this **parable** against them.

21:29 He told them this **parable**: "Look at the fig tree and all the trees.
Heb 9: 9 This is an **illustration** for the present time, indicating that the gifts
11:19 and **figuratively** [+1877] **speaking**, he did receive Isaac back from

4131 παραβουλεύομαι, parabouleuomai Not used
in UBS/NIV [√ 4123 + 1089]

4132 παραγγελία, parangelia [5] [√ 4123 + 34]

command [1], gave strict orders [+4133] [1], instruction [1],
instructions [1], orders [1]

Ac 5:28 "We gave you **strict orders** [+4133] not to teach in this name,"
16:24 Upon receiving such **orders**, he put them in the inner cell
1Th 4: 2 For you know what **instructions** we gave you by the authority of
1Ti 1: 5 The goal of this **command** is love, which comes from a pure heart
1:18 I give you this **instruction** in keeping with the prophecies once

4133 παραγγέλλω, parangellō [32 / 31] [√ 4123 + 34]

command [7], commanded [4], ordered [4], told [3], instructions
[2], cautioned [1], charge [1], commands [1], directives [1], gave
command [1], gave rule [1], gave strict orders [+4132] [1], give
instructions [1], give this command [1], required [1], strictly
warned [+2203] [1]

Mt 10: 5 These twelve Jesus sent out with the following **instructions**:
15:35 He **told** the crowd to sit down on the ground.
Mk 6: 8 These were his **instructions**: "Take nothing for the journey except
8: 6 He **told** the crowd to sit down on the ground. When he had taken
16: S [UBS+ And all that had been **commanded** them they told briefly]
Lk 5:14 Then Jesus **ordered** him, "Don't tell anyone, but go, show yourself
8:29 For Jesus had **commanded** the evil spirit to come out of the man.
8:56 but he **ordered** them not to tell anyone what had happened.
9:21 Jesus **strictly warned** [+2203] them not to tell this to anyone.
Ac 1: 4 while he was eating with them, he **gave** them this **command**:
4:18 Then they called them in again and **commanded** them not to speak
5:28 "We **gave** you strict orders [+4132] not to teach in this name,"
5:40 Then they **ordered** them not to speak in the name of Jesus,
10:42 He **commanded** us to preach to the people and to testify that he is
15: 5 must be circumcised and **required** to obey the law of Moses."
16:18 "In the name of Jesus Christ I **command** you to come out of her!"
16:23 and the jailer was **commanded** to guard them carefully.
17:30 but now he **commands** all people everywhere to repent.
23:22 The commander dismissed the young man and **cautioned** him,
23:30 I also **ordered** his accusers to present to you their case against
1Co 7:10 To the married I **give this command** (not I, but the Lord):
11:17 In the following **directives** I have no praise for you, for your
1Th 4:11 own business and to work with your hands, just as we **told** you,
2Th 3: 4 that you are doing and will continue to do the things we **command**.
3: 6 In the name of the Lord Jesus Christ, we **command** you, brothers,
3:10 For even when we were with you, we **gave** you this **rule**: "If a man
3:12 Such people we **command** and urge in the Lord Jesus Christ to
1Ti 1: 3 so that you may **command** certain men not to teach false
4:11 **Command** and teach these things.
5: 7 Give the people these **instructions**, too, so that no one may be
6:13 before Pontius Pilate made the good confession, I **charge** you
6:17 **Command** those who are rich in this present world not to be

4134 παραγίνομαι, paraginomai [37] [√ 4123 + 1181]

came [14], arrived [4], arriving [4], appeared [3], come [3],
untranslated [1], arrive [1], came back [1], came to support [1],
come from [1], coming [1], get here [1], present [1], went on
[+1451] [1]

Mt 2: 1 the time of King Herod, Magi from the east **came** to Jerusalem
3: 1 In those days John the Baptist **came**, preaching in the Desert of
3:13 Then Jesus **came** from Galilee to the Jordan to be baptized by
Mk 14:43 Just as he was speaking, Judas, one of the Twelve, **appeared**.
Lk 7: 4 When they **came** to Jesus, they pleaded earnestly with him,
7:20 When the men **came** to Jesus, they said, "John the Baptist sent us to
8:19 Now Jesus' mother and brothers **came** to see him, but they were not
11: 6 because a friend of mine on a journey has **come** to me, and I have
12:51 Do you think I **came** to bring peace on earth? No, I tell you,
14:21 "The servant **came back** and reported this to his master.

19:16 "The first one **came** and said, 'Sir, your mina has earned ten more.'
22:52 and the elders, who had **come** for him, "Am I leading a rebellion,
Jn 3:23 of water, and people were constantly **coming** to be baptized.
8: 2 At dawn he **appeared** again in the temple courts, where all the
Ac 5:21 When the high priest and his associates **arrived**, they called
5:22 But on **arriving** at the jail, the officers did not find them there.
5:25 Then someone **came** and said, "Look! The men you put in jail are
9:26 When he **came** to Jerusalem, he tried to join the disciples,
9:39 with them, and when he **arrived** he was taken upstairs to the room.
10:33 So I sent for you immediately, and it was good of you to **come**.
11:23 When he **arrived** and saw the evidence of the grace of God,
13:14 From Perga they **went on** [+1451] to Pisidian Antioch. On the
14:27 On **arriving** there, they gathered the church together and reported
15: 4 When they **came** to Jerusalem, they were welcomed by the church
17:10 to Berea. On **arriving** there, they went to the Jewish synagogue.
18:27 On **arriving**, he was a great help to those who by grace had
20:18 When they **arrived**, he said to them: "You know how I lived the
21:18 the rest of us went to see James, and all the elders were **present**.
23:16 heard of this plot, he [RPG] went into the barracks and told Paul.
23:35 he said, "I will hear your case when your accusers **get here**."
24:17 I **came** to Jerusalem to bring my people gifts for the poor
24:24 Several days later Felix **came** with his wife Drusilla, who was a
25: 7 When Paul **appeared**, the Jews who had come down from
28:21 and none of the brothers who have **come from** there has reported
1Co 16: 3 Then, when I **arrive**, I will give letters of introduction to the men
2Ti 4:16 At my first defense, no one **came to** my **support**, but everyone
Heb 9:11 When Christ **came** as high priest of the good things that are

4135 παράγω, paragō [10] [√ 4123 + 72]

went on [2], going by [1], pass away [1], passing away [1],
passing by [1], passing [1], walked along [1], walked beside
[RP4123] [1], went along [1]

Mt 9: 9 As Jesus **went on** from there, he saw a man named Matthew sitting
9:27 As Jesus **went on** from there, two blind men followed him,
20:30 and when they heard that Jesus was **going by**, they shouted,
Mk 1:16 As Jesus **walked** [RP4123] **beside** the Sea of Galilee, he saw
2:14 As he **walked along**, he saw Levi son of Alphaeus sitting at the tax
15:21 and Rufus, was **passing by** on his way in from the country,
Jn 9: 1 As he **went along**, he saw a man blind from birth.
1Co 7:31 in them. For this world in its present form is **passing away**.
1Jn 2: 8 because the darkness is **passing** and the true light is already
2:17 The world and its desires **pass away**, but the man who does the

4136 παραδειγματίζω, paradeigmatizō [1]
[√ 4123 + 1257]

subjecting to public disgrace [1]

Heb 6: 6 Son of God all over again and **subjecting** him **to public disgrace**.

4137 παράδεισος, paradeisos [3]

paradise [3]

Lk 23:43 "I tell you the truth, today you will be with me in **paradise**."
2Co 12: 4 was caught up to **paradise**. He heard inexpressible things,
Rev 2: 7 right to eat from the tree of life, which is in the **paradise** of God.

4138 παραδέχομαι, paradechomai [6]
[√ 4123 + 1312]

accept [3], accepts [1], entertain [1], welcomed [1]

Mk 4:20 sown on good soil, hear the word, **accept** it, and produce a crop—
Ac 15: 4 they were **welcomed** by the church and the apostles and elders,
16:21 by advocating customs unlawful for us Romans to **accept**
22:18 because they will not **accept** your testimony about me.'
1Ti 5:19 Do not **entertain** an accusation against an elder unless it is brought
Heb 12: 6 those he loves, and he punishes everyone he **accepts** as a son."

4139 παραδιατριβή, paradiatribē Not used in
UBS/NIV [√ 4123 + 1328 + 5561]

4140 παραδίδωμι, *paradidōmi* [119] [√ 4123 + 1443]

handed over [18], betray [16], betrayed [14], hand over [9], entrusted [6], betrayer [4], gave over [4], passed on [4], betrays [3], committed [3], gave up [3], handed down [3], arrest [2], delivered [2], gave [2], given over [2], put in prison [2], turn over [2], arrested [1], betray [+*1639*] [1], betraying [1], commended [1], deliver [1], delivered over [1], given [1], hand over to [+*1650+5931*] [1], handed over [+*3836+5931*] [1], handing over [1], hands over [1], put [1], putting into [1], ripe [1], risked [1], surrender [1], surrendered [1], throwing [1], traitor [1], turned over [1]

Mt	4:12	When Jesus heard that John *had been* **put in prison**, he returned to
	5:25	still with him on the way, or he *may* **hand** you **over** to the judge,
	10:4	Simon the Zealot and Judas Iscariot, who **betrayed** him.
	10:17	*they will* **hand** you **over** to the local councils and flog you in their
	10:19	But when *they* **arrest** you, do not worry about what to say
	10:21	"Brother *will* **betray** brother to death, and a father his child;
	11:27	"All things *have been* **committed** to me by my Father. No one
	17:22	"The Son of Man is going to *be* **betrayed** into the hands of men.
	18:34	In anger his master **turned** him **over** to the jailers to be tortured,
	20:18	and the Son of Man *will be* **betrayed** to the chief priests
	20:19	and *will* **turn** him **over** to the Gentiles to be mocked and flogged
	24:9	"Then you *will be* **handed over** to be persecuted and put to death,
	24:10	will turn away from the faith and *will* **betray** and hate each other,
	25:14	who called his servants and **entrusted** his property to them.
	25:20	'Master,' he said, '*you* **entrusted** me *with* five talents. See,
	25:22	'Master,' he said, '*you* **entrusted** me *with* two talents; see,
	26:2	and the Son of Man *will be* **handed over** to be crucified."
	26:15	"What are you willing to give me if I **hand** him **over** to you?"
	26:16	then on Judas watched for an opportunity to **hand** him **over**.
	26:21	eating, he said, "I tell you the truth, one of you *will* **betray** me."
	26:23	who has dipped his hand into the bowl with me *will* **betray** me.
	26:24	But woe to that man who **betrays** the Son of Man! That man
	26:25	Then Judas, the one *who would* **betray** him, said, "Surely not I,
	26:45	and the Son of Man *is* **betrayed** into the hands of sinners.
	26:46	Rise, let us go! Here comes my **betrayer**!"
	26:48	Now the **betrayer** had arranged a signal with them: "The one I kiss
	27:2	*They* bound him, led him away and **handed** him **over** to Pilate,
	27:3	When Judas, who *had* **betrayed** him, saw that Jesus was
	27:4	"I have sinned," he said, "*for I have* **betrayed** innocent blood."
	27:18	For he knew it was out of envy that *they had* **handed** Jesus **over**
	27:26	But he had Jesus flogged, and **handed** him **over** to be crucified.
Mk	1:14	After John *was* **put in prison**, Jesus went into Galilee,
	3:19	and Judas Iscariot, who **betrayed** him.
	4:29	As soon as the grain *is* **ripe**, he puts the sickle to it,
	7:13	the word of God by your tradition that *you have* **handed down**.
	9:31	"The Son of Man *is going to be* **betrayed** into the hands of men.
	10:33	"and the Son of Man *will be* **betrayed** to the chief priests
	10:33	will condemn him to death and *will* **hand** him **over** to the Gentiles.
	13:9	You *will be* **handed over** to the local councils and flogged in the
	13:11	Whenever you *are* **arrested** and brought to trial, do not worry
	13:12	"Brother *will* **betray** brother to death, and a father his child.
	14:10	of the Twelve, went to the chief priests to **betray** Jesus to them.
	14:11	him money. So he watched for an opportunity *to* **hand** him **over**.
	14:18	he said, "I tell you the truth, one of you *will* **betray** me—
	14:21	But woe to that man who **betrays** the Son of Man! It would be
	14:41	Look, the Son of Man *is* **betrayed** into the hands of sinners.
	14:42	Rise! Let us go! Here comes my **betrayer**!"
	14:44	Now the **betrayer** had arranged a signal with them: "The one I kiss
	15:1	They bound Jesus, led him away and **handed** him **over** to Pilate.
	15:10	out of envy that the chief priests *had* **handed** Jesus **over** to him.
	15:15	*He* had Jesus flogged, and **handed** him **over** to be crucified.
Lk	1:2	just as *they were* **handed down** to us *by* those who from the first
	4:6	you all their authority and splendor, for *it has been* **given** to me,
	9:44	The Son of Man is going to *be* **betrayed** into the hands of men."
	10:22	"All things *have been* **committed** to me by my Father. No one
	12:58	you off to the judge, and the judge **turn** you **over** to the officer,
	18:32	*He will be* **handed over** to the Gentiles. They will mock him,
	20:20	so that they *might* **hand** him **over** to the power and authority of
	21:12	*They will* **deliver** you to synagogues and prisons, and you will be
	21:16	*You will be* **betrayed** even by parents, brothers, relatives
	22:4	temple guard and discussed with them how *he might* **betray** Jesus.
	22:6	and watched for an opportunity *to* **hand** Jesus **over** to them when
	22:21	But the hand *of* him *who is going to* **betray** me is with mine on the

	22:22	go as it has been decreed, but woe to that man who **betrays** *him*."
	22:48	asked him, "Judas, *are you* **betraying** the Son of Man with a kiss?"
	23:25	the one they asked for, and **surrendered** Jesus to their will.
	24:7	'The Son of Man must *be* **delivered** into the hands of sinful men,
	24:20	and our rulers **handed** him **over** to be sentenced to death,
Jn	6:64	of them did not believe and who *would* **betray** [+*1639*] him.
	6:71	who, though one of the Twelve, was later *to* **betray** him.)
	12:4	his disciples, Judas Iscariot, who was later *to* **betray** him, objected,
	13:2	already prompted Judas Iscariot, son of Simon, to **betray** Jesus.
	13:11	For he knew who *was going to* **betray** him, and that was why he
	13:21	testified, "I tell you the truth, one of you *is going to* **betray** me."
	18:2	Now Judas, who **betrayed** him, knew the place, because Jesus had
	18:5	Jesus said. (And Judas the **traitor** was standing there with them.)
	18:30	they replied, "*we* would not have **handed** him **over** to you."
	18:35	your people and your chief priests *who* **handed** you **over** to me.
	18:36	my servants would fight to prevent *my* **arrest** by the Jews.
	19:11	Therefore the one *who* **handed** me **over** to you is guilty of a
	19:16	Finally Pilate **handed** him **over** to them to be crucified.
	19:30	"It is finished." With that, *he* bowed his head and **gave up** his spirit.
	21:20	at the supper and had said, "Lord, who is *going to* **betray** you?")
Ac	3:13	You **handed** him **over** *to be killed*, and you disowned him before
	6:14	this place and change the customs Moses **handed down** to us."
	7:42	and **gave** them **over** to the worship of the heavenly bodies.
	8:3	to house, he dragged off men and women and **put** them in prison.
	12:4	**handing** him **over** to be guarded by four squads of four soldiers
	14:26	where they had been **committed** to the grace of God for the work
	15:26	men *who have* **risked** their lives for the name of our Lord Jesus
	15:40	and left, **commended** by the brothers to the grace of the Lord.
	16:4	*they* **delivered** the decisions reached by the apostles and elders in
	21:11	this belt and *will* **hand** [+*1650+5931*] him **over** to the Gentiles.' "
	22:4	arresting both men and women and **throwing** them into prison,
	27:1	and some other prisoners *were* **handed over** to a centurion named
	28:17	*I was* arrested in Jerusalem and **handed** [+*3836+5931*] **over** to the
Ro	1:24	Therefore God **gave** them **over** in the sinful desires of their hearts
	1:26	Because of this, God **gave** them **over** to shameful lusts. Even their
	1:28	he **gave** them **over** to a depraved mind, to do what ought not to be
	4:25	He *was* **delivered over** *to death* for our sins and was raised to life
	6:17	obeyed the form of teaching to which *you were* **entrusted**.
	8:32	He who did not spare his own Son, but **gave** him **up** for us all—
1Co	5:5	**hand** this man **over** to Satan, so that the sinful nature may be
	11:2	and for holding to the teachings, just as *I* **passed** them **on** to you.
	11:23	For I received from the Lord what *I* also **passed on** to you:
	11:23	The Lord Jesus, on the night he *was* **betrayed**, took bread,
	13:3	If *I* give all I possess to the poor and **surrender** my body to the
	15:3	For what I received *I* **passed on** to you as of first importance:
	15:24	when *he* **hands over** the kingdom to God the Father after he has
2Co	4:11	For we who are alive *are* always *being* **given over** to death for
Gal	2:20	by faith in the Son of God, who loved me and **gave** himself for me.
Eph	4:19	they *have* **given** themselves **over** to sensuality so as to indulge in
	5:2	and **gave** himself up for us as a fragrant offering and sacrifice to
	5:25	just as Christ loved the church and **gave** himself **up** for her
1Ti	1:20	whom *I have* **handed over** to Satan to be taught not to blaspheme.
1Pe	2:23	no threats. Instead, *he* **entrusted** *himself* to him who judges justly.
2Pe	2:4	**putting** them **into** gloomy dungeons to be held for judgment;
	2:21	their backs on the sacred command *that was* **passed on** to them.
Jude	1:3	contend for the faith that was once for all **entrusted** to the saints.

4141 παράδοξος, *paradoxos* [1] [√ 4123 + 1518]

remarkable [1]

Lk	5:26	filled with awe and said, "We have seen **remarkable** *things* today."

4142 παράδοσις, *paradosis* [13] [√ 4123 + 1443]

tradition [7], traditions [3], teachings [2], teaching [1]

Mt	15:2	"Why do your disciples break the **tradition** of the elders? They
	15:3	do you break the command of God for the sake of your **tradition**?
	15:6	Thus you nullify the word of God for the sake of your **tradition**.
Mk	7:3	hands a ceremonial washing, holding to the **tradition** of the elders.
	7:5	"Why don't your disciples live according to the **tradition** of the
	7:8	the commands of God and are holding on to the **traditions** of men."
	7:9	the commands of God in order to observe your own **traditions**!
	7:13	Thus you nullify the word of God *by* your **tradition** that you have
1Co	11:2	remembering me in everything and for holding to the **teachings**,

Gal 1:14 and was extremely zealous for the **traditions** of my fathers.
Col 2: 8 which depends on human **tradition** and the basic principles of this
2Th 2:15 stand firm and hold to the **teachings** we passed on to you,
     3: 6 and does not live according to the **teaching** you received from us.

4143 παραζηλόω, *parazēloō* [4] [√ 4123 + 2419]

make envious [2], arouse jealousy [1], arouse to envy [1]

Ro 10:19 "I *will* **make** you **envious** by those who are not a nation;
    11:11 salvation has come to the Gentiles to **make** Israel **envious**.
    11:14 in the hope that *I may* somehow **arouse** my own people **to envy**
1Co 10:22 *Are we trying to* **arouse** the Lord's **jealousy**? Are we stronger

4144 παραθαλάσσιος, *parathalassios* [1]
[√ 4123 + 2498]

by the lake [1]

Mt 4:13 which was **by the lake** in the area of Zebulun and Naphtali—

4145 παραθεωρέω, *paratheōreō* [1] [√ 4123 + 2555]

overlooked [1]

Ac 6: 1 because their widows *were being* **overlooked** in the daily

4146 παραθήκη, *parathēkē* [3] [√ 4123 + 5502]

deposit entrusted to [1], entrusted to care [1], entrusted to [1]

1Ti 6:20 Timothy, guard what has been **entrusted to** your **care**. Turn away
2Ti 1:12 and am convinced that he is able to guard what I have **entrusted to**
     1:14 Guard the good **deposit** that was **entrusted to** you—guard it with

4147 παραινέω, *paraineō* [2] [√ 4123 + 142]

urge [1], warned [1]

Ac 27: 9 because by now it was after the Fast. So Paul **warned** them,
    27:22 But now *I* **urge** you to keep up your courage, because not one of

4148 παραιτέομαι, *paraiteomai* [12] [√ 4123 + 160]

excuse [+2400] [2], have nothing to do with [2], refuse [2],
begged [1], don't have anything to do with [1], make excuses [1],
not put on such a list [1], refused [1], requested [1]

Mk 15: 6 at the Feast to release a prisoner whom the *people* **requested**.
Lk 14:18 "But they all alike began *to* **make excuses**. The first said, 'I have
    14:18 a field, and I must go and see it. Please **excuse** [+2400] me.'
    14:19 and I'm on my way to try them out. Please **excuse** [+2400] me.'
Ac 25:11 guilty of doing anything deserving death, *I do* not **refuse** to die.
1Ti 4: 7 **Have nothing to do with** godless myths and old wives' tales,
     5:11 As for younger widows, *do* **not put** them **on such a list**. For when
2Ti 2:23 **Don't have anything to do with** foolish and stupid arguments,
Tit 3:10 warn him a second time. After that, **have nothing to do with** him.
Heb 12:19 or to such a voice speaking words that those who heard it **begged**
    12:25 See to it that *you do* not **refuse** him who speaks. If they did not
    12:25 If they did not escape *when they* **refused** him who warned them

4149 παρακαθέζομαι, *parakathezomai* [1]
[√ 4123 + 2757]

sat [1]

Lk 10:39 called Mary, who **sat** at the Lord's feet listening to what he said.

4150 παρακαθίζω, *parakathizō* Not used in
UBS/NIV [√ 4123 + 2767]

4151 παρακαλέω, *parakaleō* [109] [√ 4123 + 2813]

urge [20], begged [13], encourage [13], pleaded with [7],
comforted [6], encouraged [6], urged [6], encouraging [5],
appeal to [4], invited [4], plead with [3], begging [2], comfort [2],
comforts [2], answer kindly [1], appeal [1], appease [1], asked

[1], asking for help [1], call on [1], exhort [1], exhorted [1], given
[1], listen to appeal [1], making appeal [1], pleading with [1],
received [1], request that [1], speaking encouragement to [1],
urgently requested [+160] [1]

Mt   2:18 Rachel weeping for her children and refusing *to be* **comforted**,
     5: 4 Blessed are those who mourn, for they *will be* **comforted**.
     8: 5 had entered Capernaum, a centurion came to him, **asking for help**.
     8:31 The demons **begged** Jesus, "If you drive us out, send us into the
     8:34 when they saw him, *they* **pleaded with** him to leave their region.
    14:36 and **begged** him to let the sick just touch the edge of his cloak,
    18:29 "His fellow servant fell to his knees and **begged** him, 'Be patient
    18:32 'I canceled all that debt of yours because *you* **begged** me to.
    26:53 Do you think I cannot **call on** my Father, and he will at once put at
Mk   1:40 A man with leprosy came to him and **begged** him on his knees,
     5:10 And *he* **begged** Jesus again and again not to send them out of the
     5:12 The demons **begged** Jesus, "Send us among the pigs; allow us to go
     5:17 Then the people began *to* **plead with** Jesus to leave their region.
     5:18 the man who had been demon-possessed **begged** to go with him.
     5:23 and **pleaded** earnestly **with** him, "My little daughter is dying.
     6:56 *They* **begged** him to let them touch even the edge of his cloak,
     7:32 hardly talk, and *they* **begged** him to place his hand on the man.
     8:22 some people brought a blind man and **begged** Jesus to touch him.
Lk   3:18 And with many other words John **exhorted** the people
     7: 4 When they came to Jesus, *they* **pleaded** earnestly **with** him,
     8:31 And *they* **begged** him *repeatedly* not to order them to go into the
     8:32 The demons **begged** Jesus to let them go into them, and he gave
     8:41 and fell at Jesus' feet, **pleading with** him to come to his house
    15:28 and refused to go in. So his father went out and **pleaded with** him.
    16:25 bad things, but now *he is* **comforted** here and you are in agony.
Ac   2:40 and *he* **pleaded with** them, "Save yourselves from this corrupt
     8:31 it to me?" So *he* **invited** Philip to come up and sit with him.
     9:38 they sent two men to him and **urged** him, "Please come at once!"
    11:23 and **encouraged** them all to remain true to the Lord with all their
    13:42 the *people* **invited** them to speak further about these things on the
    14:22 the disciples and **encouraging** them to remain true to the faith.
    15:32 said much *to* **encourage** and strengthen the brothers.
    16: 9 had a vision of a man of Macedonia standing and **begging** him,
    16:15 of her household were baptized, *she* **invited** us to her home.
    16:39 They came *to* **appease** them and escorted them from the prison,
    16:40 where they met with the brothers and **encouraged** them.
    19:31 sent him a message **begging** him not to venture into the theater.
    20: 1 *after* **encouraging** them, said good-by and set out for Macedonia.
    20: 2 **speaking** many words of **encouragement** to the people,
    20:12 took the young man home alive and *were* greatly **comforted**.
    21:12 and the people there **pleaded with** Paul not to go up to Jerusalem.
    24: 4 *I would* **request that** you be kind enough to hear us briefly.
    25: 3 *They* **urgently requested** [+160] Festus, as a favor to them,
    27:33 Just before dawn Paul **urged** them all to eat. "For the last fourteen
    27:34 Now *I* **urge** you to take some food. You need it to survive.
    28:14 There we found some brothers *who* **invited** *us* to spend a week
    28:20 For this reason *I have* **asked** to see you and talk with you.
Ro 12: 1 Therefore, *I* **urge** you, brothers, in view of God's mercy, to offer
    12: 8 if it is **encouraging**, let him encourage; if it is contributing to the
    15:30 *I* **urge** you, brothers, by our Lord Jesus Christ and by the love of
    16:17 *I* **urge** you, brothers, to watch out for those who cause divisions
1Co 1:10 *I* **appeal to** you, brothers, in the name of our Lord Jesus Christ,
     4:13 when we are slandered, *we* **answer kindly**. Up to this moment we
     4:16 Therefore *I* **urge** you to imitate me.
    14:31 in turn so that everyone *may be* instructed and **encouraged**.
    16:12 *I* strongly **urged** him to go to you with the brothers.
    16:15 themselves to the service of the saints. *I* **urge** you, brothers,
2Co 1: 4 who **comforts** us in all our troubles,
     1: 4 so that we can **comfort** those in any trouble with the comfort we
     1: 4 trouble with the comfort *we* ourselves *have* **received** from God.
     1: 6 if *we are* **comforted**, it is for your comfort, which produces in you
     2: 7 Now instead, *you* *ought to* forgive and **comfort** him, so that he
     2: 8 *I* **urge** you, therefore, to reaffirm your love for him.
     5:20 as though God *were* **making** *his* **appeal** through us.
     6: 1 As God's fellow workers *we* **urge** you not to receive God's grace
     7: 6 But God, who **comforts** the downcast, comforted us by the coming
     7: 6 who comforts the downcast, **comforted** us by the coming of Titus,
     7: 7 only by his coming but also by the comfort you *had* **given** *him*.
     7:13 By all this *we are* **encouraged**. In addition to our own
     8: 6 So we **urged** Titus, since he had earlier made a beginning,
     9: 5 So I thought it necessary *to* **urge** the brothers to visit you in

10:	1	By the meekness and gentleness of Christ, I **appeal to** you—
12:	8	Three times *I* **pleaded with** the Lord to take it away from me.
12:	18	*I* **urged** Titus to go to you and I sent our brother with him.
13:	11	for perfection, **listen to** my **appeal**, be of one mind, live in peace.

Eph 4: 1 I **urge** you to live a life worthy of the calling you have received.
    6: 22 that you may know how we are, and that *he may* **encourage** you.
Php 4: 2 *I* **plead with** Euodia and I plead with Syntyche to agree with each
    4: 2 and *I* **plead with** Syntyche to agree with each other in the Lord.
Col 2: 2 My purpose is that they *may be* **encouraged** in heart and united in
    4: 8 about our circumstances and that *he may* **encourage** your hearts.
1Th 2: 12 **encouraging**, comforting and urging you to live lives worthy of
    3: 2 gospel of Christ, to strengthen and **encourage** you in your faith,
    3: 7 in all our distress and persecution *we were* **encouraged** about you
    4: 1 *Now we* ask you and **urge** you in the Lord Jesus to do this more
    4: 10 Yet *we* **urge** you, brothers, to do so more and more.
    4: 18 Therefore **encourage** each other with these words.
    5: 11 Therefore **encourage** one another and build each other up,
    5: 14 And *we* **urge** you, brothers, warn those who are idle,
2Th 2: 17 **encourage** your hearts and strengthen you in every good deed
    3: 12 we command and **urge** in the Lord Jesus Christ to settle down
1Ti 1: 3 As *I* **urged** you when I went into Macedonia, stay there in Ephesus
    2: 1 *I* **urge**, then, first of all, that requests, prayers, intercession
    5: 1 an older man harshly, but **exhort** him as if he were your father.
    6: 2 to them. These are the things *you are to* teach and **urge** on them.
2Ti 4: 2 in season and out of season; correct, rebuke and **encourage**—
Tit 1: 9 so that he can **encourage** others by sound doctrine and refute those
    2: 6 Similarly, **encourage** the young men to be self-controlled.
    2: 15 **Encourage** and rebuke with all authority. Do not let anyone
Phm 1: 9 yet *I* **appeal to** you on the basis of love. I then, as Paul—an old
    1: 10 *I* **appeal to** you for my son Onesimus, who became my son while I
Heb 3: 13 But **encourage** one another daily, as long as it is called Today,
    10: 25 some are in the habit of doing, but let us **encourage** one another—
    13: 19 *I* particularly **urge** you to pray so that I may be restored to you
    13: 22 Brothers, *I* **urge** you to bear with my word of exhortation,
1Pe 2: 11 Dear friends, *I* **urge** you, as aliens and strangers in the world,
    5: 1 To the elders among you, *I* **appeal** as a fellow elder, a witness of
    5: 12 **encouraging** you and testifying that this is the true grace of God.
Jude 1: 3 and **urge** you to contend for the faith that was once for all

4152 παρακαλύπτω, *parakalyptō* [1] [√ *4123 + 2821*]

hidden [1]

Lk 9: 45 It was **hidden** from them, so that they did not grasp it, and they

4153 παρακαταθήκη, *parakatathēkē* Not used in UBS/NIV [√ *4123 + 2848 + 5502*]

4154 παράκειμαι, *parakeimai* [2] [√ *4123 + 3023*]

have [1], right there [1]

Ro 7: 18 For I **have** the desire to do what is good, but I cannot carry it out.
    7: 21 law at work: When I want to do good, evil *is* **right there** with me.

4155 παράκλησις, *paraklēsis* [29] [√ *4123 + 2813*]

encouragement [10], comfort [8], appeal [2], consolation [1], encourage [1], encouraged [+*2400*] [1], encouraged [1], encouraging message [1], exhortation [1], greatly encouraged [+*4444*] [1], preaching [1], urgently [+*3552+4498*] [1]

Lk 2: 25 He was waiting for the **consolation** of Israel, and the Holy Spirit
    6: 24 to you who are rich, for you have already received your **comfort**.
Ac 4: 36 apostles called Barnabas (which means Son of **Encouragement**),
    9: 31 and **encouraged** by the Holy Spirit, it grew in numbers, living in
    13: 15 "Brothers, if you have a message of **encouragement** for the people,
    15: 31 The people read it and were glad for its **encouraging message**.
Ro 12: 8 if it is encouraging, let him **encourage**; if it is contributing to the
    15: 4 and the **encouragement** of the Scriptures we might have hope.
    15: 5 May the God who *gives* endurance and **encouragement** give you a
1Co 14: 3 to men for their strengthening, **encouragement** and comfort.
2Co 1: 3 Jesus Christ, the Father of compassion and the God *of* all **comfort**,
    1: 4 so that we can comfort those in any trouble with the **comfort** we
    1: 5 over into our lives, so also through Christ our **comfort** overflows.
    1: 6 If we are distressed, it is for your **comfort** and salvation; if we are

    1: 6 if we are comforted, it is for your **comfort**, which produces in you
    1: 7 as you share in our sufferings, so also you share *in* our **comfort**.
    7: 4 *I am* **greatly encouraged** [+*4444*]; in all our troubles my joy
    7: 7 not only by his coming but also by the **comfort** you had given him.
    7: 13 In addition *to* our own **encouragement**, we were especially
    8: 4 they **urgently** [+*3552+4498*] pleaded with us for the privilege of
    8: 17 For Titus not only welcomed our **appeal**, but he is coming to you
Php 2: 1 If you have any **encouragement** from being united with Christ,
1Th 2: 3 For the **appeal** we make does not spring from error or impure
2Th 2: 16 who loved us and by his grace gave us eternal **encouragement**
1Ti 4: 13 to the public reading of Scripture, *to* **preaching** and to teaching.
Phm 1: 7 Your love has given me great joy and **encouragement**,
Heb 6: 18 of the hope offered to us *may be* greatly **encouraged** [+*2400*].
    12: 5 And you have forgotten that *word of* **encouragement** that
    13: 22 Brothers, I urge you to bear with my word *of* **exhortation**,

4156 παράκλητος, *paraklētos* [5] [√ *4123 + 2813*]

Counselor [4], speaks in defense [1]

Jn 14: 16 and he will give you another **Counselor** to be with you forever—
    14: 26 But the **Counselor**, the Holy Spirit, whom the Father will send in
    15: 26 "When the **Counselor** comes, whom I will send to you from the
    16: 7 Unless I go away, the **Counselor** will not come to you; but if I go,
1Jn 2: 1 does sin, we have *one who* **speaks** to the Father **in** *our* **defense**—

4157 παρακοή, *parakoē* [3] [√ *4123 + 201*]

disobedience [2], act of disobedience [1]

Ro 5: 19 For just as through the **disobedience** of the one man the many
2Co 10: 6 And we will be ready to punish every **act of disobedience**,
Heb 2: 2 and every violation and **disobedience** received its just punishment,

4158 παρακολουθέω, *parakoloutheō* [4] [√ *4123 + 199 [1.3]*]

accompany [1], followed [1], investigated [1], know all about [1]

Mk 16: 17 And these signs *will* **accompany** those who believe: In my name
Lk 1: 3 *since I* myself *have* carefully **investigated** everything from the
1Ti 4: 6 truths of the faith and of the good teaching that *you have* **followed**.
2Ti 3: 10 You, however, **know all about** my teaching, my way of life,

4159 παρακούω, *parakouō* [3] [√ *4123 + 201*]

refuses to listen [2], ignoring [1]

Mt 18: 17 If *he* **refuses to listen** *to* them, tell it to the church; and if he
    18: 17 and if *he* **refuses to listen** even *to* the church, treat him as you
Mk 5: 36 **Ignoring** what they said, Jesus told the synagogue ruler, "Don't be

4160 παρακύπτω, *parakyptō* [5] [√ *4123 + 3252*]

bending over [1], bent over to look [1], bent over [1], look [1], looks intently [1]

Lk 24: 12 **Bending over**, he saw the strips of linen lying by themselves,
Jn 20: 5 He **bent over** and looked in at the strips of linen lying there
    20: 11 the tomb crying. As she wept, *she* **bent over to look** into the tomb
Jas 1: 25 But the man *who* **looks intently** into the perfect law that gives
1Pe 1: 12 Spirit sent from heaven. Even angels long *to* **look** into these things.

4161 παραλαμβάνω, *paralambanō* [49] [√ *4123 + 3284*]

took [12], received [7], take [5], taken [4], took with [4], receive [2], takes [2], took along [2], took aside [2], accepted [1], instructed [*RP4123*] [1], received from [*RP4123*] [1], receiving [1], take home [1], took [+*72*] [1], took charge of [1], took home [1], traditions [1]

Mt 1: 20 son of David, do not be afraid *to* **take** Mary **home** as your wife,
    1: 24 of the Lord had commanded him and **took** Mary **home** as his wife.
    2: 13 he said, "**take** the child and his mother and escape to Egypt,
    2: 14 **took** the child and his mother during the night and left for Egypt,
    2: 20 "Get up, **take** the child and his mother and go to the land of Israel,
    2: 21 **took** the child and his mother and went to the land of Israel.

4: 5   Then the devil **took** him to the holy city and had him stand on the
4: 8   the devil **took** him to a very high mountain and showed him all the
12:45   and **takes** with it seven other spirits more wicked than itself,
17: 1   After six days Jesus **took** with him Peter, James and John the
18:16   But if he will not listen, **take** one or two others along,
20:17   to Jerusalem, *he* **took** the twelve disciples aside and said to them,
24:40   Two men will be in the field; one *will be* **taken** and the other left.
24:41   be grinding with a hand mill; one *will be* **taken** and the other left.
26:37   *He* **took** Peter and the two sons of Zebedee **along** with him,
27:27   Then the governor's soldiers **took** Jesus into the Prætorium
Mk   4:36   the crowd behind, *they* **took** him **along**, just as he was, in the boat.
5:40   he **took** the child's father and mother and the disciples who were
7: 4   And they observe many other **traditions**, such as the washing of
9: 2   After six days Jesus **took** Peter, James and John **with** him
10:32   Again he **took** the Twelve **aside** and told them what was going to
14:33   *He* **took** Peter, James and John along with him, and he began to be
Lk   9:10   Then *he* **took** them **with** him and they withdrew by themselves to a
9:28   he **took** Peter, John and James **with** him and went up onto a
11:26   Then it goes and **takes** seven other spirits more wicked than itself,
17:34   two people will be in one bed; one *will be* **taken** and the other left.
17:35   be grinding grain together; one *will be* **taken** and the other left."
18:31   Jesus **took** the Twelve **aside** and told them, "We are going up to
Jn   1:11   came to that which was his own, but his own *did* not **receive** him.
14: 3   and **take** you to be with me that you also may be where I am.
19:16   over to them to be crucified. So the *soldiers* **took charge of** Jesus.
Ac   15:39   they parted company. Barnabas **took** Mark and sailed for Cyprus,
16:33   At that hour of the night the jailer **took** them and washed their
21:24   **Take** these men, join in their purification rites and pay their
21:26   The next day Paul **took** the men and purified himself along with
21:32   He at once **took** some officers and soldiers and ran down to the
23:18   So he **took** [+72] him to the commander. The centurion said,
1Co 11:23   For I **received** from the Lord what I also passed on to you:
15: 1   which *you* **received** and on which you have taken your stand.
15: 3   For what *I* **received** I passed on to you as of first importance:
Gal   1: 9   is preaching to you a gospel other than what *you* **accepted**,
1:12   I *did* not **receive** it from any man, nor was I taught it; rather,
Php   4: 9   Whatever you have learned or **received** or heard from me,
Col   2: 6   So then, just as *you* **received** Christ Jesus as Lord, continue to live
4:17   "See to it that you complete the work *you have* **received** in the
1Th   2:13   *when you* **received** the word of God, which you heard from us,
4: 1   we **instructed** [RP4123] *you* how to live in order to please God,
2Th   3: 6   not live according to the teaching *you* **received** [RP4123] *from* us.
Heb 12:28   *since we are* **receiving** a kingdom that cannot be shaken,

4162 παραλέγομαι, *paralegomai* [2] [√ 4123 + 3306]

moved along [1], sailed [1]

Ac 27: 8   *We* **moved along** the coast with difficulty and came to a place
27:13   so *they* weighed anchor and **sailed** along the shore of Crete.

4163 παράλιος, *paralios* [1] [√ 4123 + 229]

coast [1]

Lk   6:17   over Judea, from Jerusalem, and from the **coast** of Tyre and Sidon,

4164 παραλλαγή, *parallagē* [1] [√ 4123 + 248]

change [1]

Jas   1:17   of the heavenly lights, who does not **change** like shifting shadows.

4165 παραλογίζομαι, *paralogizomai* [2] [√ 4123 + 3306]

deceive [2]

Col   2: 4   so that no one *may* **deceive** you by fine-sounding arguments.
Jas   1:22   Do not merely listen to the word, and so **deceive** yourselves.

4166 παραλυτικός, *paralytikos* [10] [√ 4123 + 3395]

paralytic [7], paralyzed [3]

Mt   4:24   those having seizures, and the **paralyzed**, and he healed them.
8: 6   "my servant lies at home **paralyzed** and in terrible suffering."
9: 2   Some men brought to him a **paralytic**, lying on a mat. When Jesus

9: 2   Jesus saw their faith, he said *to* the **paralytic**, "Take heart, son;
9: 6   he said *to* the **paralytic**, "Get up, take your mat and go home."
Mk   2: 3   Some men came, bringing to him a **paralytic**, carried by four of
2: 4   through it, lowered the mat the **paralyzed** *man* was lying on.
2: 5   their faith, he said *to* the **paralytic**, "Son, your sins are forgiven."
2: 9   to say *to* the **paralytic**, 'Your sins are forgiven,' or to say,
2:10   has authority on earth to forgive sins...." He said *to* the **paralytic**,

4167 παράλυτος, *paralytos*   Not used in UBS/NIV
[√ 4123 + 3395]

4168 παραλύω, *paralyō* [5] [√ 4123 + 3395]

paralytic [+1639] [1], paralytic [+476] [1], paralytics [1],
paralyzed [1], weak [1]

Lk   5:18   Some men came carrying a **paralytic** [+476] on a mat and tried to
5:24   He said *to* the **paralyzed** *man*, "I tell you, get up, take your mat
Ac   8: 7   came out of many, and many **paralytics** and cripples were healed.
9:33   There he found a man named Aeneas, a **paralytic** [+1639] who
Heb 12:12   Therefore, strengthen your feeble arms and **weak** knees.

4169 παραμένω, *paramenō* [4] [√ 4123 + 3531]

continue with [1], continues [1], continuing [1], stay awhile [1]

1Co 16: 6   Perhaps *I will* **stay** with you **awhile**, or even spend the winter,
Php   1:25   and *I will* **continue with** all of you for your progress and joy in the
Heb   7:23   since death prevented them from **continuing** *in office*;
Jas   1:25   and **continues** to do this, not forgetting what he has heard,

4170 παραμυθέομαι, *paramytheomai* [4]
[√ 4123 + 3680]

comforting [2], comfort [1], encourage [1]

Jn   11:19   to Martha and Mary to **comfort** them in the loss of their brother.
11:31   **comforting** her, noticed how quickly she got up and went out,
1Th   2:12   **comforting** and urging you to live lives worthy of God,
5:14   warn those who are idle, **encourage** the timid, help the weak,

4171 παραμυθία, *paramythia* [1] [√ 4123 + 3680]

comfort [1]

1Co 14: 3   to men for their strengthening, encouragement and **comfort**.

4172 παραμύθιον, *paramythion* [1] [√ 4123 + 3680]

comfort [1]

Php   2: 1   if any **comfort** from his love, if any fellowship with the Spirit,

4173 παράνοια, *paranoia*   Not used in UBS/NIV
[√ 4123 + 3808]

4174 παρανομέω, *paranomeō* [1] [√ 4123 + 3795]

violate the law [1]

Ac 23: 3   yet you yourself **violate the law** by commanding that I be struck!"

4175 παρανομία, *paranomia* [1] [√ 4123 + 3795]

wrongdoing [1]

2Pe   2:16   But he was rebuked *for* his **wrongdoing** by a donkey—a beast

4176 παραπικραίνω, *parapikrainō* [1]
[√ 4123 + 4395]

rebelled [1]

Heb   3:16   Who were they who heard and **rebelled**? Were they not all those

4177 παραπικρασμός, *parapikrasmos* [2]
[√ *4123 + 4395*]

rebellion [2]

Heb   3: 8   do not harden your hearts as you did in the **rebellion**,
        3: 15   his voice, do not harden your hearts as you did in the **rebellion**."

4178 παραπίπτω, *parapiptō* [1] [√ *4123 + 4406*]

fall away [1]

Heb   6: 6   *if they* **fall away**, to be brought back to repentance, because to

4179 παραπλέω, *parapleō* [1] [√ *4123 + 4434*]

sail past [1]

Ac   20: 16   Paul had decided *to* **sail past** Ephesus to avoid spending time in

4180 παραπλήσιος, *paraplēsios* [1] [√ *4123 + 4446*]

almost [1]

Php   2: 27   Indeed he was ill, and **almost** died. But God had mercy on him,

4181 παραπλησίως, *paraplēsiōs* [1] [√ *4123 + 4446*]

too [1]

Heb   2: 14   he **too** shared in their humanity so that by his death he might

4182 παραπορεύομαι, *paraporeuomai* [5]
[√ *4123 + 4513*]

passed by [2], going [1], passed [1], went along [1]

Mt   27: 39   Those *who* **passed by** hurled insults at him, shaking their heads
Mk   2: 23   One Sabbath Jesus *was* **going** through the grainfields, and as his
         9: 30   *They* left that place and **passed** through Galilee. Jesus did not want
        11: 20   In the morning, *as they* **went along**, they saw the fig tree withered
        15: 29   Those *who* **passed by** hurled insults at him, shaking their heads

4183 παράπτωμα, *paraptōma* [19 / 20]
[√ *4123 + 4406*]

sins [7], trespass [5], transgression [2], transgressions [2], sin
against [1], sin [1], sins against [1], trespasses [1]

Mt   6: 14   For if you forgive men *when* they **sin against** you, your heavenly
        6: 15   But if you do not forgive men their **sins**, [UBS-] your Father will
        6: 15   not forgive men their sins, your Father will not forgive your **sins**.
Mk   11: 25   so that your Father in heaven may forgive you your **sins**."
Ro   4: 25   He was delivered over to death for our **sins** and was raised to life
        5: 15   But the gift is not like the **trespass**. For if the many died by the
        5: 15   For if the many died *by* the **trespass** of the one man, how much
        5: 16   but the gift followed many **trespasses** and brought justification.
        5: 17   For if, *by* the **trespass** of the one man, death reigned through that
        5: 18   just as the result of one **trespass** was condemnation for all men,
        5: 20   The law was added so that the **trespass** might increase. But where
       11: 11   Rather, *because of* their **transgression**, salvation has come to the
       11: 12   But if their **transgression** means riches for the world, and their
2Co   5: 19   world to himself in Christ, not counting men's **sins against** them.
Gal   6: 1   Brothers, if someone is caught in a **sin**, you who are spiritual
Eph   1: 7   the forgiveness *of* **sins**, in accordance with the riches of God's
        2: 1   As for you, you were dead in your **transgressions** and sins,
        2: 5   us alive with Christ even when we were dead *in* **transgressions**—
Col   2: 13   When you were dead in your **sins** and in the uncircumcision of
        2: 13   God made you alive with Christ. He forgave us all our **sins**,

4184 παραρρέω, *pararreō* [1] [√ *4123 + 4835*]

drift away [1]

Heb   2: 1   therefore, to what we have heard, so that *we do* not **drift away**.

4185 παράσημος, *parasēmos* [1] [√ *4123 + 4956*]

figurehead [1]

Ac   28: 11   It was an Alexandrian ship *with* the **figurehead** of the twin gods

4186 παρασκευάζω, *paraskeuazō* [4] [√ *4123 + 5007*]

ready [2], get ready [1], prepared [1]

Ac   10: 10   and *while* the meal *was being* **prepared**, he fell into a trance.
1Co 14: 8   trumpet does not sound a clear call, who *will* **get ready** for battle?
2Co   9: 2   telling them that since last year *you* in Achaia *were* **ready** to give;
         9: 3   prove hollow, but that you may be **ready**, as I said you would be.

4187 παρασκευή, *paraskeuē* [6] [√ *4123 + 5007*]

day of Preparation [3], Preparation Day [2], Preparation [1]

Mt   27: 62   The next day, the one after **Preparation Day**, the chief priests
Mk   15: 42   It was **Preparation Day** (that is, the day before the Sabbath).
Lk   23: 54   It was **Preparation** Day, and the Sabbath was about to begin.
Jn   19: 14   It was the **day of Preparation** of Passover Week, about the sixth
       19: 31   Now it was the **day of Preparation**, and the next day was to be a
       19: 42   Because it was the Jewish **day of Preparation** and since the tomb

4188 παραστάτις, *parastatis*   Not used in UBS/NIV
[√ *4123 + 2705*]

4189 παρατείνω, *parateinō* [1] [√ *1753; cf. 4123*]

kept on [1]

Ac   20: 7   because *he* intended to leave the next day, **kept on** talking until

4190 παρατηρέω, *paratēreō* [6] [√ *4123 + 5498*]

watched closely [2], carefully watched [1], keeping a close watch
[1], kept close watch on [1], observing [1]

Mk   3: 2   so *they* **watched** him **closely** to see if he would heal him on the
Lk   6: 7   so *they* **watched** him **closely** to see if he would heal on the
       14: 1   house of a prominent Pharisee, he was *being* **carefully watched**.
       20: 20   **Keeping a close watch** on him, they sent spies, who pretended to
Ac   9: 24   and night *they* **kept close watch on** the city gates in order to kill
Gal   4: 10   *You are* **observing** special days and months and seasons

4191 παρατήρησις, *paratērēsis* [1] [√ *4123 + 5498*]

careful observation [1]

Lk   17: 20   kingdom of God does not come with your **careful observation**,

4192 παρατίθημι, *paratithēmi* [19] [√ *4123 + 5502*]

set before [5], commit [3], told [+*3306*] [2], committed [1], did[s] so
[1], distribute [1], entrust [1], entrusted with [1], give [1], proving
[1], put before [1], set a meal before [+*5544*] [1]

Mt   13: 24   Jesus **told** [+*3306*] them another parable: "The kingdom of heaven
       13: 31   He **told** [+*3306*] them another parable: "The kingdom of heaven is
Mk   6: 41   Then he gave them to his disciples to **set before** the people.
        8: 6   broke them and gave them to his disciples to **set before** the people,
        8: 6   them to his disciples to set before the people, and *they* **did[s] so**.
        8: 7   gave thanks for them also and told the disciples *to* **distribute** them.
Lk   9: 16   Then he gave them to the disciples *to* **set before** the people.
       10: 8   you enter a town and are welcomed, eat what *is* **set before** you.
       11: 6   a journey has come to me, and I have nothing *to* **set before** him.'
       12: 48   and from the one *who has been* **entrusted with** much, much more
       23: 46   out with a loud voice, "Father, into your hands *I* **commit** my spirit."
Ac   14: 23   with prayer and fasting, **committed** them to the Lord, in whom
       16: 34   brought them into his house and **set** [+*5544*] **a meal before** them;
       17: 3   explaining and **proving** that the Christ had to suffer and rise from
       20: 32   "Now *I* **commit** you to God and to the word of his grace, which can
1Co 10: 27   eat whatever *is* **put before** you without raising questions of
1Ti   1: 18   *I* **give** you this instruction in keeping with the prophecies once
2Ti   2: 2   **entrust** to reliable men who will also be qualified to teach others.
1Pe   4: 19   those who suffer according to God's will *should* **commit**

4193 παρατυγχάνω, *paratynchanō* [1]
[√ *4123 + 5593*]

happened to be there [1]

Ac 17:17 the marketplace day by day with those *who* **happened to be there.**

4194 παραυτίκα, *parautika* [1] [√ *4123 + 899*]

momentary [1]

2Co 4:17 and **momentary** troubles are achieving for us an eternal glory that

4195 παραφέρω, *parapherō* [4] [√ *4123 + 5770*]

take [2], blown along [1], carried away [1]

Mk 14:36 **Take** this cup from me. Yet not what I will, but what you will."
Lk 22:42 "Father, if you are willing, **take** this cup from me; yet not my will,
Heb 13: 9 *Do not be* **carried away** by all kinds of strange teachings.
Jude 1:12 They are clouds without rain, **blown along** by the wind;

4196 παραφρονέω, *paraphroneō* [1] [→ *4197, 4198;*
cf. 4123 + 5856]

out of mind [1]

2Co 11:23 of Christ? (I am **out of** *my* **mind** to talk like this.) I am more.

4197 παραφρονία, *paraphronia* [1] [√ *4196*]

madness [1]

2Pe 2:16 spoke with a man's voice and restrained the prophet's **madness.**

4198 παραφροσύνη, *paraphrosynē* Not used in
UBS/NIV [√ *4196*]

4199 παραχειμάζω, *paracheimazō* [4]
[√ *4123 + 5946*]

winter [2], spend the winter [1], wintered [1]

Ac 27:12 that we should sail on, hoping to reach Phoenix and **winter** there.
    28:11 After three months we put out to sea in a ship *that had* **wintered**
1Co 16: 6 Perhaps I will stay with you awhile, or even **spend the winter,**
Tit 3:12 come to me at Nicopolis, because I have decided *to* **winter** there.

4200 παραχειμασία, *paracheimasia* [1]
[√ *4123 + 5946*]

winter in [1]

Ac 27:12 Since the harbor was unsuitable to **winter in**, the majority decided

4201 παραχράομαι, *parachraomai* Not used in
UBS/NIV [√ *4123 + 5968*]

4202 παραχρῆμα, *parachrēma* [18] [√ *4123 + 5968*]

immediately [9], at once [4], instantly [2], at that moment [1], just
[1], so quickly [1]

Mt 21:19 "May you never bear fruit again!" **Immediately** the tree withered.
    21:20 were amazed. "How did the fig tree wither **so quickly**?" they asked.
Lk 1:64 **Immediately** his mouth was opened and his tongue was loosed,
    4:39 and it left her. She got up **at once** and began to wait on them.
    5:25 **Immediately** he stood up in front of them, took what he had been
    8:44 the edge of his cloak, and **immediately** her bleeding stopped.
    8:47 why she had touched him and how she had been **instantly** healed.
    8:55 Her spirit returned, and **at once** she stood up. Then Jesus told them
    13:13 on her, and **immediately** she straightened up and praised God.
    18:43 **Immediately** he received his sight and followed Jesus,
    19:11 thought that the kingdom of God was going to appear **at once**.
    22:60 you're talking about!" **Just** as he was speaking, the rooster crowed.
Ac 3: 7 him up, and **instantly** the man's feet and ankles became strong.
    5:10 **At that moment** she fell down at his feet and died. Then the young
    12:23 **Immediately**, because Herod did not give praise to God, an angel

13:11 **Immediately** mist and darkness came over him, and he groped
16:26 **At once** all the prison doors flew open, and everybody's chains
16:33 then **immediately** he and all his family were baptized.

4203 πάρδαλις, *pardalis* [1]

leopard [1]

Rev 13: 2 The beast I saw resembled a **leopard**, but had feet like those of a

4204 παρεδρεύω, *paredreuō* [1] [√ *4123 + 1612*]

serve at [1]

1Co 9:13 and those *who* **serve at** the altar share in what is offered on the

4205 πάρειμι, *pareimi* [24] [√ *4123 + 1639*]

come [7], have [2], am with [1], am [1], are here [1], are present
[1], be [1], came for [1], here [1], is here [1], now have [1],
present [1], sought an audience [1], time [1], was with [1], was
[1], were present [1]

Mt 26:50 Jesus replied, "Friend, *do* what *you* **came for**." Then the men
Lk 13: 1 Now *there were* some **present** at that time who told Jesus about
Jn 7: 6 Therefore Jesus told them, "The right time for me *has* not yet **come**;
    11:28 "The Teacher **is here**," she said, "and is asking for you."
Ac 10:21 to the men, "I'm the one you're looking for. Why *have* you **come**?"
    10:33 Now we **are** all **here** in the presence of God to listen to everything
    12:20 they now joined together and **sought an audience** with him.
    17: 6 who have caused trouble all over the world *have* now **come** here,
    24:19 who ought *to be* **here** before you and bring charges if they have
1Co 5: 3 Even though I am not physically present, I **am with** you in spirit.
    5: 3 passed judgment on the one who did this, just as if *I* **were present**.
2Co 10: 2 I beg you that *when I* **come** I may not have to be as bold as I
    10:11 we are absent, we will be in our actions *when we* **are present**.
    11: 9 And *when I* **was** with you and needed something, I was not a
    13: 2 I already gave you a warning when *I* **was with** you the second
    13:10 that *when I* **come** I may not have to be harsh in my use of
Gal 4:18 is good, and to be so always and not just when I **am** with you.
    4:20 how I wish *I could* **be** with you now and change my tone,
Col 1: 6 that *has* **come** to you. All over the world this gospel is bearing fruit
Heb 12:11 No discipline seems pleasant at the **time**, but painful. Later on,
    13: 5 free from the love of money and be content *with* what *you* **have**,
2Pe 1: 9 But *if* anyone *does* not **have** them, he is nearsighted and blind,
    1:12 know them and are firmly established in the truth *you* **now have**.
Rev 17: 8 see the beast, because he once was, now is not, and yet *will* **come**.

4206 παρεισάγω, *pareisagō* [1] [√ *4123 + 1650 + 72*]

secretly introduce [1]

2Pe 2: 1 They *will* **secretly introduce** destructive heresies, even denying

4207 παρείσακτος, *pareisaktos* [1]
[√ *4123 + 1650 + 72*]

infiltrated ranks [+4209] [1]

Gal 2: 4 because some false brothers *had* **infiltrated** [+4209] *our* **ranks** to

4208 παρεισδύω, *pareisdyō* [1] [√ *4123 + 1650 + 1544*]

secretly slipped in [1]

Jude 1: 4 was written about long ago *have* **secretly slipped in** among you.

4209 παρεισέρχομαι, *pareiserchomai* [2]
[√ *4123 + 1650 + 2262*]

added [1], infiltrated ranks [+4207] [1]

Ro 5:20 The law *was* **added** so that the trespass might increase. But where
Gal 2: 4 because some false brothers *had* **infiltrated** *our* **ranks** [+4207] to

4210 παρεισφέρω, *pareispherō* [1]
[√ *4123 + 1650 + 5770*]

make [1]

2Pe 1: 5 this very reason, **make** every effort to add to your faith goodness;

4211 παρεκτός, *parektos* [3] [√ *4123 + 1666*]

besides everything else [*+3836+6006*] [1], except for [*+3364*] [1], except for [1]

Mt 5:32 **except** [*+3364*] **for** marital unfaithfulness, causes her to become an
Ac 26:29 to me today may become what I am, **except for** these chains."
2Co 11:28 **Besides everything else** [*+3836+6006*], I face daily the pressure of

4212 παρεμβάλλω, *paremballō* [1]
[√ *4123 + 1877 + 965*]

build [1]

Lk 19:43 The days will come upon you when your enemies *will* **build** an

4213 παρεμβολή, *parembolē* [10]
[√ *4123 + 1877 + 965*]

barracks [6], camp [3], armies [1]

Ac 21:34 of the uproar, he ordered that Paul be taken into the **barracks**.
21:37 As the soldiers were about to take Paul into the **barracks**,
22:24 the commander ordered Paul to be taken into the **barracks**.
23:10 him away from them by force and bring him into the **barracks**.
23:16 sister heard of this plot, he went into the **barracks** and told Paul.
23:32 the cavalry go on with him, while they returned to the **barracks**.
Heb 11:34 and who became powerful in battle and routed foreign **armies**.
13:11 Place as a sin offering, but the bodies are burned outside the **camp**.
13:13 Let us, then, go to him outside the **camp**, bearing the disgrace he
Rev 20: 9 the breadth of the earth and surrounded the **camp** of God's people,

4214 παρενοχλέω, *parenochleō* [1]
[√ *4123 + 1877 + 4063*]

make it difficult for [1]

Ac 15:19 that *we should* not **make it difficult for** the Gentiles who are

4215 παρεπίδημος, *parepidēmos* [3]
[√ *4123 + 2093 + 1322*]

strangers [3]

Heb 11:13 And they admitted that they were aliens and **strangers** on earth.
1Pe 1: 1 an apostle of Jesus Christ, *To* God's elect, **strangers** *in the world*,
2:11 Dear friends, I urge you, as aliens and **strangers** *in the world*,

4216 παρέρχομαι, *parerchomai* [29] [√ *4123 + 2262*]

pass away [10], disappear [4], pass [2], after [1], come along [1], come [1], disobeyed [1], getting [1], gone [1], neglect [1], pass by [1], passed by [1], passing by [1], past [1], taken away [1], taken [1]

Mt 5:18 I tell you the truth, until heaven and earth **disappear**,
5:18 *will* by any means **disappear** from the Law until everything is
8:28 met him. They were so violent that no one could **pass** that way.
14:15 and said, "This is a remote place, and *it's* already **getting** late.
24:34 this generation *will* certainly not **pass away** until all these things
24:35 Heaven and earth *will* **pass away**, but my words will never pass
24:35 and earth will pass away, but my words *will* never **pass away**.
26:39 "My Father, if it is possible, *may* this cup *be* **taken** from me.
26:42 if it is not possible for this cup *to be* **taken away** unless I drink it,
Mk 6:48 out to them, walking on the lake. He was *about to* **pass by** them,
13:30 this generation *will* certainly not **pass away** until all these things
13:31 Heaven and earth *will* **pass away**, but my words will never pass
13:31 and earth will pass away, but my words *will* never **pass away**.
14:35 and prayed that if possible the hour *might* **pass** from him.
Lk 11:42 kinds of garden herbs, but *you* **neglect** justice and the love of God.
12:37 will have them recline at the table and will **come** and wait on them.

15:29 years I've been slaving for you and never **disobeyed** your orders.
16:17 and earth *to* **disappear** than for the least stroke of a pen to drop out
17: 7 he comes in from the field, 'Come along now and sit down to eat'?
18:37 They told him, "Jesus of Nazareth *is* **passing by**."
21:32 this generation *will* certainly not **pass away** until all these things
21:33 Heaven and earth *will* **pass away**, but my words will never pass
21:33 and earth will pass away, but my words *will* never **pass away**.
Ac 16: 8 So *they* **passed by** Mysia and went down to Troas.
27: 9 already become dangerous because by now it *was* **after** the Fast.
2Co 5:17 he is a new creation; the old *has* **gone**, the new has come!
Jas 1:10 in his low position, because *he will* **pass away** like a wild flower.
1Pe 4: 3 For you *have spent* enough time *in the* **past** doing what pagans
2Pe 3:10 The heavens *will* **disappear** with a roar; the elements will be

4217 πάρεσις, *paresis* [1] [√ *918; cf. 4123*]

left unpunished [1]

Ro 3:25 he had **left** the sins committed beforehand **unpunished**—

4218 παρέχω, *parechō* [16] [√ *4123 + 2400*]

bothering [*+3160*] [3], became [1], bother [*+3160*] [1], brought in [1], cause [1], do [1], earned [1], given proof [*+4411*] [1], promote [1], provide with [1], provides with [1], set [1], showed [1], turn [1]

Mt 26:10 Jesus said to them, "Why *are you* **bothering** [*+3160*] this woman?
Mk 14: 6 her alone," said Jesus. "Why *are you* **bothering** [*+3160*] her?
Lk 6:29 If someone strikes you on one cheek, **turn** to him the other also.
7: 4 earnestly with him, "This man deserves *to have you* **do** this,
11: 7 "Then the one inside answers, 'Don't **bother** [*+3160*] me. The door
18: 5 yet because this widow *keeps* **bothering** [*+3160*] me, I will see
Ac 16:16 She **earned** a great deal of money for her owners by
17:31 *He has* **given** [*+4411*] **proof** of this to all men by raising him from
19:24 shrines of Artemis, **brought in** no little business for the craftsmen.
22: 2 they heard him speak to them in Aramaic, *they* **became** very quiet.
28: 2 The islanders **showed** us unusual kindness. They built a fire
Gal 6:17 Finally, *let* no one **cause** me trouble, for I bear on my body the
Col 4: 1 Masters, **provide** your slaves **with** what is right and fair,
1Ti 4: 1 These **promote** controversies rather than God's work—which is by
6:17 who richly **provides** us **with** everything for our enjoyment.
Tit 2: 7 In everything **set** them an example by doing what is good.

4219 παρηγορία, *parēgoria* [1] [√ *4123 + 72*]

comfort [1]

Col 4:11 for the kingdom of God, and they have proved a **comfort** to me.

4220 παρθενία, *parthenia* [1] [√ *4221*]

after marriage [*+608*] [1]

Lk 2:36 had lived with her husband seven years **after** her **marriage** [*+608*],

4221 παρθένος, *parthenos* [15] [→ *4220*]

virgin [8], virgins [3], *untranslated* [1], pure [1], unmarried [1], virgin's [1]

Mt 1:23 "The **virgin** will be with child and will give birth to a son, and they
25: 1 "At that time the kingdom of heaven will be like ten **virgins** who
25: 7 "Then all the **virgins** woke up and trimmed their lamps.
25:11 "Later the others **[RPG]** also came. 'Sir! Sir!' they said.
Lk 1:27 to a **virgin** pledged to be married to a man named Joseph,
1:27 a descendant of David. The **virgin's** name was Mary.
Ac 21: 9 He had four **unmarried** daughters who prophesied.
1Co 7:25 Now about **virgins**: I have no command from the Lord, but I give a
7:28 you have not sinned; and if a **virgin** marries, she has not sinned.
7:34 unmarried woman or **virgin** is concerned about the Lord's affairs:
7:36 If anyone thinks he is acting improperly toward the **virgin** he is
7:37 own will, and who has made up his mind not to marry the **virgin**—
7:38 So then, he who marries the **virgin** does right, but he who does not
2Co 11: 2 to Christ, so that I might present you as a pure **virgin** to him.
Rev 14: 4 not defile themselves with women, for they kept themselves **pure**.

4222 Πάρθοι, *Parthoi* [1]

Parthians [1]

Ac   2: 9 **Parthians**, Medes and Elamites; residents of Mesopotamia,

4223 παρίημι, *pariēmi* [2] [√ *918; cf. 4123*]

feeble [1], leaving undone [1]

Lk   11:42 have practiced the latter without **leaving** the former **undone**.
Heb 12:12 Therefore, strengthen your **feeble** arms and weak knees.

4224 παριστάνω, *paristanō*   Not used in UBS/NIV
[√ *4123 + 2705*]

4225 παρίστημι, *paristēmi* [41] [√ *4123 + 2705*]

present [7], offer [6], standing near [5], stood beside [2], bring near [1], come [1], give [1], handed over [1], nearby [1], presented [1], prove [1], provide [1], put at disposal [1], showed [1], stand before [1], stand trial before [1], stand [1], standing around [1], standing by [1], standing nearby [1], stands [1], stood around [1], stood at side [1], stood there [1], take stand [1]

Mt   26:53 and *he will* at once **put at** my **disposal** more than twelve legions of
Mk   4:29 grain is ripe, he puts the sickle to it, because the harvest *has* **come.**"
     14:47 Then one *of* those **standing near** drew his sword and struck the
     14:69 she said again to those **standing around**, "This fellow is one of
     14:70 After a little while, those **standing near** said to Peter, "Surely you
     15:35 When some *of* those **standing near** heard this, they said, "Listen,
     15:39 And *when* the centurion, who **stood there** in front of Jesus,
Lk   1: 19 I **stand** in the presence of God, and I have been sent to speak to
      2:22 and Mary took him to Jerusalem to **present** him to the Lord
     19:24 "Then he said to those **standing by**, 'Take his mina away from him
Jn   18:22 Jesus said this, one of the officials **nearby** struck him in the face.
     19:26 and the disciple whom he loved **standing nearby**, he said to his
Ac   1: 3 he **showed** himself to these men and gave many convincing proofs
      1: 10 when suddenly two men dressed in white **stood beside** them.
      4: 10 God raised from the dead, that this man **stands** before you healed.
      4:26 The kings of the earth **take** *their* **stand** and the rulers gather
      9:39 All the widows **stood around** him, crying and showing him the
      9:41 Then *he* called the believers and the widows and **presented** her to
     23: 2 At this the high priest Ananias ordered those **standing near** Paul to
     23: 4 Those *who were* **standing near** Paul said, "You dare to insult
     23:24 **Provide** mounts for Paul so that he may be taken safely to
     23:33 *they* delivered the letter to the governor and **handed** Paul **over** to
     24: 13 And they cannot **prove** to you the charges they are now making
     27:23 angel of the God whose I am and whom I serve **stood beside** me
     27:24 You must **stand trial before** Caesar; and God has graciously given
Ro   6: 13 *Do* not **offer** the parts of your body to sin, as instruments of
      6: 13 as instruments of wickedness, but rather **offer** yourselves to God,
      6: 16 Don't you know that *when* you **offer** yourselves to someone to
      6: 19 Just as *you used to* **offer** the parts of your body in slavery to
      6: 19 so now **offer** them in slavery to righteousness leading to holiness.
     12: 1 *to* **offer** your bodies as living sacrifices, holy and pleasing to God—
     14: 10 your brother? For *we will* all **stand before** God's judgment seat.
     16: 2 of the saints and *to* **give** her any help she may need from you,
1Co   8: 8 But food *does* not **bring** us **near** to God; we are no worse if we do
2Co   4: 14 also raise us with Jesus and **present** us with you in his presence.
     11: 2 to Christ, *so that* I *might* **present** you as a pure virgin to him.
Eph   5:27 and to **present** her to himself as a radiant church, without stain
Col   1:22 physical body through death *to* **present** you holy in his sight,
      1:28 all wisdom, so that *we may* **present** everyone perfect in Christ.
2Ti   2: 15 Do your best *to* **present** yourself to God as one approved,
      4: 17 But the Lord **stood at** my **side** and gave me strength, so that

4226 Παρμενᾶς, *Parmenas* [1]

Parmenas [1]

Ac   6: 5 also Philip, Procorus, Nicanor, Timon, **Parmenas**, and Nicolas

4227 πάροδος, *parodos* [1] [√ *4123 + 3847*]

passing visit [1]

1Co 16: 7 I do not want to see you now and make *only* a **passing visit**;

4228 παροικέω, *paroikeō* [2] [√ *4123 + 3875*]

made home [1], visitor to [1]

Lk   24:18 "*Are* you only a **visitor to** Jerusalem and do not know the things
Heb 11: 9 By faith *he* **made** *his* **home** in the promised land like a stranger in

4229 παροικία, *paroikia* [2] [√ *4123 + 3875*]

stay [1], strangers [1]

Ac   13:17 he made the people prosper during their **stay** in Egypt, with mighty
1Pe   1: 17 work impartially, live your lives as **strangers** here in reverent fear.

4230 πάροικος, *paroikos* [4] [√ *4123 + 3875*]

aliens [2], foreigner [1], strangers [1]

Ac   7: 6 'Your descendants will be **strangers** in a country not their own,
      7:29 fled to Midian, where he settled *as* a **foreigner** and had two sons.
Eph   2: 19 Consequently, you are no longer foreigners and **aliens**, but fellow
1Pe   2: 11 Dear friends, I urge you, as **aliens** and strangers in the world,

4231 παροιμία, *paroimia* [5]

figuratively [*+1877*] [1], figure of speech [1], figures of speech [1], proverbs [1], this[s] kind of [*+1877*] [1]

Jn   10: 6 Jesus used this **figure of speech**,
     16:25 "Though I have been speaking **figuratively** [*+1877*], a time is
     16:25 a time is coming when I will no longer use **this**[s] [*+1877*] **kind of**
     16:29 "Now you are speaking clearly and without **figures of speech**.
2Pe   2:22 Of them the **proverbs** are true: "A dog returns to its vomit,"

4232 πάροινος, *paroinos* [2] [√ *4123 + 3885*]

given to drunkenness [2]

1Ti   3: 3 not **given to drunkenness**, not violent but gentle, not quarrelsome,
Tit   1: 7 not quick-tempered, not **given to drunkenness**, not violent,

4233 παροίχομαι, *paroichomai* [1] [√ *4123*]

past [*+1155*] [1]

Ac   14:16 In the **past** [*+1155*], he let all nations go their own way.

4234 παρομοιάζω, *paromoiazō* [1] [√ *4123 + 3927*]

like [1]

Mt   23:27 *You are* **like** whitewashed tombs, which look beautiful on the

4235 παρόμοιος, *paromoios* [1] [√ *4123 + 3927*]

like [1]

Mk   7: 13 that you have handed down. And you do many things **like** that."

4236 παροξύνω, *paroxynō* [2] [√ *4123 + 3955*]

easily angered [1], greatly distressed [1]

Ac   17:16 he *was* **greatly distressed** to see that the city was full of idols.
1Co 13: 5 It is not rude, it is not self-seeking, *it is* not **easily angered**,

4237 παροξυσμός, *paroxysmos* [2] [√ *4123 + 3955*]

sharp disagreement [1], spur on [*+1650*] [1]

Ac   15:39 They had *such* a **sharp disagreement** that they parted company.
Heb 10:24 And let us consider how we may **spur** [*+1650*] one another **on**

4238 παροράω, *paroraō* Not used in UBS/NIV
[√ 4123 + 3972]

4239 παροργίζω, *parorgizō* [2] [√ 4123 + 3973]
exasperate [1], make angry [1]

Ro 10:19 *I will* **make** you **angry** by a nation that has no understanding."
Eph 6: 4 Fathers, *do* not **exasperate** your children; instead, bring them up in

4240 παροργισμός, *parorgismos* [1] [√ 4123 + 3973]
angry [1]

Eph 4:26 do not sin": Do not let the sun go down while you are still **angry**,

4241 παροτρύνω, *parotrynō* [1] [√ 4123]
incited [1]

Ac 13:50 But the Jews **incited** the God-fearing women of high standing

4242 παρουσία, *parousia* [24] [√ 4123 + 1639]
coming [17], comes [3], arrived [+3836] [1], being [1], in person [+3836+3836+5393] [1], presence [1]

Mt 24: 3 and what will be the sign *of* your **coming** and of the end of the
  24:27 visible even in the west, so will be the **coming** of the Son of Man.
  24:37 in the days of Noah, so it will be at the **coming** of the Son of Man.
  24:39 all away. That is how it will be at the **coming** of the Son of Man.
1Co 15:23 the firstfruits; then, when he **comes**, those who belong to him.
  16:17 glad when Stephanas, Fortunatus and Achaicus **arrived** [+3836],
2Co 7: 6 who comforts the downcast, comforted us by the **coming** of Titus,
  7: 7 and not only by his **coming** but also by the comfort you had given
  10:10 but **in person** [+3836+3836+5393] he is unimpressive and his
Php 1:26 so that through my **being** with you again your joy in Christ Jesus
  2:12 not only in my **presence**, but now much more in my absence—
1Th 2:19 we will glory in the presence of our Lord Jesus when he **comes**?
  3:13 and Father when our Lord Jesus **comes** with all his holy ones.
  4:15 that we who are still alive, who are left till the **coming** of the Lord,
  5:23 and body be kept blameless at the **coming** of our Lord Jesus Christ.
2Th 2: 1 Concerning the **coming** of our Lord Jesus Christ and our being
  2: 8 the breath of his mouth and destroy by the splendor *of* his **coming**.
  2: 9 The **coming** of the lawless one will be in accordance with the work
Jas 5: 7 Be patient, then, brothers, until the Lord's **coming**. See how the
  5: 8 be patient and stand firm, because the Lord's **coming** is near.
2Pe 1:16 we told you about the power and **coming** of our Lord Jesus Christ,
  3: 4 They will say, "Where is this '**coming**' he promised? Ever since
  3:12 as you look forward to the day of God and speed its **coming**.
1Jn 2:28 we may be confident and unashamed before him at his **coming**.

4243 παροψίς, *paropsis* [1 / 2] [√ 4123 + 4066]
dish [2]

Mt 23:25 You clean the outside of the cup and **dish**, but inside they are full
  23:26 First clean the inside of the cup and **dish**, [UBS-] and

4244 παρρησία, *parrēsia* [31] [√ 4246 + 4839]
confidence [7], plainly [4], courage [3], publicly [3], a public figure [+1877] [1], assurance [1], bold [+2400+4498] [1], bold [+5968] [1], boldly [+3552+4246] [1], boldly [+3552] [1], boldness [1], clearly [+1877] [1], confident [+2400] [1], confidently [+3552] [1], fearlessly [+1877] [1], freedom [1], openly [1], public [1]

Mk 8:32 He spoke **plainly** about this, and Peter took him aside and began to
Jn 7: 4 No one who wants to become a **public** [+1877] **figure** acts in
  7:13 But no one would say anything **publicly** about him for fear of the
  7:26 Here he is, speaking **publicly**, and they are not saying a word to
  10:24 will you keep us in suspense? If you are the Christ, tell us **plainly**."
  11:14 So then he told them **plainly**, "Lazarus is dead,
  11:54 Therefore Jesus no longer moved about **publicly** among the Jews.
  16:25 this kind of language but will tell you **plainly** about my Father.
  16:29 "Now you are speaking **clearly** [+1877] and without figures of
  18:20 "I have spoken **openly** to the world," Jesus replied. "I always

Ac 2:29 I can tell you **confidently** [+3552] that the patriarch David died
  4:13 When they saw the **courage** of Peter and John and realized that
  4:29 and enable your servants to speak your word with great **boldness**.
  4:31 with the Holy Spirit and spoke the word of God **boldly** [+3552].
  28:31 **Boldly** [+3552+4246] and without hindrance he preached the
2Co 3:12 Therefore, since we have such a hope, *we are* very **bold** [+5968].
  7: 4 I have great **confidence** in you; I take great pride in you. I am
Eph 3:12 and through faith in him we may approach God with **freedom**
  6:19 so that I will **fearlessly** [+1877] make known the mystery of the
Php 1:20 but will have sufficient **courage** so that now as always Christ will
Col 2:15 the powers and authorities, he made a **public** spectacle of them,
1Ti 3:13 standing and great **assurance** in their faith in Christ Jesus.
Phm 1: 8 *although* in Christ I *could be* **bold** [+2400+4498] and order you to
Heb 3: 6 if we hold on to our **courage** and the hope of which we boast.
  4:16 Let us then approach the throne of grace with **confidence**,
  10:19 since we have **confidence** to enter the Most Holy Place by the
  10:35 So do not throw away your **confidence**; it will be richly rewarded.
1Jn 2:28 so that when he appears *we may be* **confident** [+2400]
  3:21 if our hearts do not condemn us, we have **confidence** before God
  4:17 among us so that we will have **confidence** on the day of judgment,
  5:14 This is the **confidence** we have in approaching God: that if we ask

4245 παρρησιάζομαι, *parrēsiazomai* [9]
[√ 4246 + 4839]
speaking boldly [2], boldly [1], dared [1], fearlessly [1], freely [1], preached fearlessly [1], speak boldly [1], spoke boldly [1]

Ac 9:27 and how in Damascus *he had* **preached fearlessly** in the name of
  9:28 freely in Jerusalem, **speaking boldly** in the name of the Lord.
  13:46 Then Paul and Barnabas answered them **boldly**: "We had to speak
  14: 3 spent considerable time there, **speaking boldly** for the Lord,
  18:26 He began *to* **speak boldly** in the synagogue. When Priscilla
  19: 8 entered the synagogue and **spoke boldly** there for three months,
  26:26 king is familiar with these things, and I can speak **freely** to him.
Eph 6:20 in chains. Pray that I may declare it **fearlessly**, as I should.
1Th 2: 2 but with the help of our God *we* **dared** to tell you his gospel in

4246 πᾶς, *pas* [1243 / 1240]
[→ 570, 1383, 4101, 4102, 4103, 4104, 4105, 4106, 4107, 4108, 4109, 4110, 4111, 4112, 4113, 4114, 4115, 4116, 4117, 4118, 4119, 4120, 4121, 4122, 4244, 4245]

τὰ πάντα (all things) [41] Mk 4:11; Ac 17:25; Ro 8:32; 11:36; 1Co 2:15; 8:6,6; 11:12; 12:6,19; 15:27,28,28,28; 2Co 4:15; 5:18; 12:19; Gal 3:22; Eph 1:10,11,23; 3:9; 4:10,15; 5:13; Php 3:8,21; Col 1:16,16,17,20; 3:8,11; 4:7; 1Ti 6:13; Heb 1:3; 2:8,8,10,10; Rev 4:11

all [651], every [127], everything [101], everyone [93], *untranslated* [26], whole [23], any [17], all things [+3836] [16], anyone [15], everything [+3836] [14], full [8], all [+4012] [6], everyone [+476] [6], great [6], always [5], no [+4024] [5], one [+4922] [5], anything [4], everybody [4], everything [+4012] [4], one [4], all [+3836] [3], always [+1328] [3], everywhere [+1877+5536] [3], all over [2], all this [+3836] [2], continually [+1328] [2], entire [2], every [+2848] [2], everybody [+476] [2], everyone [+6034] [2], everyone's [2], publicly [+1967] [2], regularly [+1328] [2], very [2], whatever [+4012] [2], whatever [2], whoever [+3836] [2], absolute [1], all [+476] [1], altogether [+3836] [1], always [+1877+2789] [1], always [+2465+3836] [1], any and every [1], anyone [+6034] [1], anything [+4547] [1], boldly [+3552+4244] [1], complete [+1877] [1], complete [+4444] [1], complete [1], completely [1], day after day [+2465] [1], day by day [+2465+2848] [1], depth [1], everybody's [1], everyone [+1667] [1], everyone [+2848] [1], everyone [+3836] [1], everything [+1569+4012] [1], everything [+323+4012] [1], everything [+3836+5007] [1], everywhere [+5536] [1], finally [+5731] [1], forever [+1328] [1], forevermore [+172+1650+3836] [1], free and belong to no man [+1666+1801] [1], from one synagogue to another [+2848+3836+5252] [1], fully [+19] [1], great patience [+3429] [1], in all [1], in everything [1], large [1], night [+1328+3816] [1], no [+4028] [1], none [+4024] [1], none [1], nothing [+4024+4839] [1], nothing [+4024] [1], perfectly [+1877] [1], profound [1], proper [1], pure [1], securely

[*+854+1877*] [1], strict [1], sufficient [1], the country[s] [1], the whole [1], the world[s] [1], this way [*+4047*] [1], this[s] [*+3836*] [1], throughout [*+1650*] [1], throughout [*+2093*] [1], true [1], what is more [*+4047+5250*] [1], whatever [*+3836*] [1], whoever [*+4015*] [1], whole [*+4725*] [1], whole universe [1], whole world [1], without [*+6006*] [1], you [1]

Mt 1:17 Thus there were fourteen generations *in* **all** from Abraham to
2: 3 Herod heard this he was disturbed, and **all** Jerusalem with him.
2: 4 When he had called together **all** the people's chief priests
2:16 and he gave orders to kill **all** the boys in Bethlehem and its
2:16 and **[RPG]** its vicinity who were two years old and under,
3: 5 from Jerusalem and **all** Judea and the whole region of the Jordan.
3: 5 from Jerusalem and all Judea and the **whole** region of the Jordan.
3:10 and **every** tree that does not produce good fruit will be cut down
3:15 so now; it is proper for us to do this to fulfill **all** righteousness."
4: 4 but on **every** word that comes from the mouth of God.' "
4: 8 and showed him **all** the kingdoms of the world and their splendor.
4: 9 "**All** this I will give you," he said, "if you will bow down
4:23 and healing **every** disease and sickness among the people.
4:23 and healing every disease and **[RPG]** sickness among the people.
4:24 and people brought to him **all** who were ill with various diseases,
5:11 persecute you and falsely say **all** *kinds* of evil against you
5:15 they put it on its stand, and it gives light *to* **everyone** in the house.
5:18 will by any means disappear from the Law until **everything** is
5:22 But I tell you that **anyone** who is angry with his brother will be
5:28 But I tell you that **anyone** who looks at a woman lustfully has
5:32 But I tell you that **anyone** who divorces his wife, except for marital
6:29 Yet I tell you that not even Solomon in **all** his splendor was
6:32 For the pagans run after **all** these things, and your heavenly Father
6:33 his righteousness, and **all** these things will be given to you as well.
7: 8 For **everyone** who asks receives; he who seeks finds; and to him
7:12 So in **everything**, do to others what you would have them do to
7:17 Likewise **every** good tree bears good fruit, but a bad tree bears bad
7:19 **Every** tree that does not bear good fruit is cut down and thrown
7:21 "Not **everyone** who says to me, 'Lord, Lord,' will enter the
7:24 "Therefore **everyone** who hears these words of mine and puts them
7:26 But **everyone** who hears these words of mine and does not put
8:16 and he drove out the spirits with a word and healed **all** the sick.
8:32 and the **whole** herd rushed down the steep bank into the lake
8:33 tending the pigs ran off, went into the town and reported **all** *this*,
8:34 Then the **whole** town went out to meet Jesus. And when they saw
9:35 Jesus went through **all** the towns and villages, teaching in their
9:35 good news of the kingdom and healing **every** disease and sickness.
9:35 of the kingdom and healing every disease and **[RPG]** sickness.
10: 1 to drive out evil spirits and to heal **every** disease and sickness.
10: 1 out evil spirits and to heal every disease and **[RPG]** sickness.
10:22 **All** *men* will hate you because of me, but he who stands firm to the
10:30 And even the very hairs of your head are **all** numbered.
10:32 "**Whoever** [*+4015*] acknowledges me before men, I will also
11:13 For **all** the Prophets and the Law prophesied until John.
11:27 "**All** *things* have been committed to me by my Father. No one
11:28 "Come to me, **all** you who are weary and burdened,
12:15 from that place. Many followed him, and he healed **all** their sick,
12:23 **All** the people were astonished and said, "Could this be the Son of
12:25 "**Every** kingdom divided against itself will be ruined, and every
12:25 and **every** city or household divided against itself will not stand.
12:31 so I tell you, **every** sin and blasphemy will be forgiven men,
12:36 on the day of judgment for **every** careless word they have spoken.
13: 2 got into a boat and sat in it, while **all** the people stood on the shore.
13:19 When **anyone** hears the message about the kingdom and does not
13:32 Though it is the smallest *of* **all** your seeds, yet when it grows,
13:34 Jesus spoke **all** these things to the crowd in parables; he did not say
13:41 and they will weed out of his kingdom **everything** that causes sin
13:44 and then in his joy went and sold **all** [*+4012*] he had and bought
13:46 he went away and sold **everything** [*+4012*] he had and bought it.
13:47 a net that was let down into the lake and caught **all** kinds of fish.
13:51 "Have you understood **all** these things?" Jesus asked. "Yes,"
13:52 "Therefore **every** teacher of the law who has been instructed about
13:56 Aren't **all** his sisters with us? Where then did this man get all these
13:56 his sisters with us? Where then did this man get **all** these things?"
14:20 They **all** ate and were satisfied, and the disciples picked up twelve
14:35 to all the surrounding country. People brought **all** their sick to him
15:13 "**Every** plant that my heavenly Father has not planted will be
15:17 "Don't you see that **whatever** [*+3836*] enters the mouth goes into
15:37 They **all** ate and were satisfied. Afterward the disciples picked up
17:11 Jesus replied, "To be sure, Elijah comes and will restore **all** *things*.
18:10 For I tell you that their angels in heaven **always** [*+1328*] see the
18:16 so that '**every** matter may be established by the testimony of two
18:19 I tell you that if two of you on earth agree about **anything** [*+4547*]
18:25 his children and **all** [*+4012*] that he had be sold to repay the debt.
18:26 'Be patient with me,' he begged, 'and I will pay back **everything**.'
18:31 and went and told their master **everything** that had happened.
18:32 'I canceled **all** that debt of yours because you begged me to.
18:34 to the jailers to be tortured, until he should pay back **all** he owed.
19: 3 "Is it lawful for a man to divorce his wife for **any and every**
19:11 Jesus replied, "Not **everyone** can accept this word, but only those to
19:20 "**All** these I have kept," the young man said. "What do I still lack?"
19:26 "With man this is impossible, but with God **all** *things* are possible."
19:27 Peter answered him, "We have left **everything** to follow you!
19:29 And **everyone** who has left houses or brothers or sisters or father
21:10 the **whole** city was stirred and asked, "Who is this?"
21:12 temple area and drove out **all** who were buying and selling there.
21:22 you will receive **whatever** [*+4012*] you ask for in prayer."
21:26 are afraid of the people, for they **all** hold that John was a prophet."
22: 4 and fattened cattle have been butchered, and **everything** is ready.
22:10 out into the streets and gathered **all** the people they could find,
22:27 **Finally** [*+5731*], the woman died.
22:28 will she be of the seven, since **all** *of them* were married to her?"
23: 3 So you must obey them and do **everything** [*+1569+4012*] they tell
23: 5 "**Everything** they do is done for men to see: They make their
23: 8 for you have only one Master and you are **all** brothers.
23:20 he who swears by the altar swears by it and by **everything** on it.
23:27 on the inside are full of dead men's bones and **everything** unclean.
23:35 so upon you will come **all** the righteous blood that has been shed
23:36 I tell you the truth, **all** this will come upon this generation.
24: 2 "Do you see **all** these things?" he asked. "I tell you the truth, not
24: 8 **All** these are the beginning of birth pains.
24: 9 put to death, and you will be hated by **all** nations because of me.
24:14 will be preached in the whole world as a testimony *to* **all** nations,
24:22 those days had not been cut short, no **one** [*+4922*] would survive,
24:30 will appear in the sky, and **all** the nations of the earth will mourn.
24:33 Even so, when you see **all** these things, you know that it is near,
24:34 this generation will certainly not pass away until **all** these things
24:47 I tell you the truth, he will put him in charge of **all** his possessions.
25: 5 a long time in coming, and they **all** became drowsy and fell asleep.
25: 7 "Then **all** the virgins woke up and trimmed their lamps.
25:29 For **everyone** who has will be given more, and he will have an
25:31 the Son of Man comes in his glory, and **all** the angels with him,
25:32 **All** the nations will be gathered before him, and he will separate
26: 1 When Jesus had finished saying **all** these things, he said to his
26:27 and offered it to them, saying, "Drink from it, **all** of you.
26:31 "This very night you will **all** fall away on account of me, for it is
26:33 Peter replied, "Even if **all** fall away on account of you, I never will."
26:35 I will never disown you." And **all** the other disciples said the same.
26:52 said to him, "for **all** who draw the sword will die by the sword.
26:56 might be fulfilled." Then **all** the disciples deserted him and fled.
26:70 But he denied it before *them* **all**. "I don't know what you're talking
27: 1 **all** the chief priests and the elders of the people came to the
27:22 is called Christ?" Pilate asked. They **all** answered, "Crucify him!"
27:25 **All** the people answered, "Let his blood be on us and on our
27:45 From the sixth hour until the ninth hour darkness came over **all** the
28:18 "**All** authority in heaven and on earth has been given to me.
28:19 Therefore go and make disciples of **all** nations, baptizing them in
28:20 and teaching them to obey **everything** [*+4012*] I have commanded
28:20 And surely I am with you **always** [*+2465+3836*], to the very end of

Mk 1: 5 The **whole** Judean countryside and all the people of Jerusalem
1: 5 and **all** the people of Jerusalem went out to him.
1:32 That evening after sunset the people brought to Jesus **all** the sick
1:37 they found him, they exclaimed: "**Everyone** is looking for you!"
2:12 He got up, took his mat and walked out in full view of *them* **all**.
2:12 This amazed **everyone** and they praised God, saying, "We have
2:13 the lake. A **large** crowd came to him, and he began to teach them.
3:28 **all** the sins and blasphemies of men will be forgiven them.
4: 1 while **all** the people were along the shore at the water's edge.
4:11 But to those on the outside **everything** [*+3836*] is said in parables
4:13 this parable? How then will you understand **any** parable?
4:31 which is the smallest seed **[NIE]** you plant in the ground.
4:32 it grows and becomes the largest *of* **all** garden plants,
4:34 he was alone with his own disciples, he explained **everything**.
5: 5 **Night** [*+1328+3816*] and day among the tombs and in the hills he
5:20 much Jesus had done for him. And **all** the *people* were amazed.

5: 26   deal under the care of many doctors and had spent **all** she had,
5: 33   fell at his feet and, trembling with fear, told him the **whole** truth.
5: 40   After he put *them* **all** out, he took the child's father and mother
6: 30   and reported to him **all** [+*4012*] they had done and taught.
6: 33   and ran on foot from **all** the towns and got there ahead of them.
6: 39   Then Jesus directed them to have **all** the *people* sit down in groups
6: 41   set before the people. He also divided the two fish among them **all**.
6: 42   They **all** ate and were satisfied,
6: 50   because they **all** saw him and were terrified. Immediately he spoke
7: 3   and **all** the Jews do not eat unless they give their hands a
7: 14   Jesus called the crowd to him and said, "Listen to me, **everyone**,
7: 18   "Don't you see that **nothing** [+*4024*] that enters a man from the
7: 19   out of his body." (In saying this, Jesus declared **all** foods "clean.")
7: 23   **All** these evils come from inside and make a man 'unclean.' "
7: 37   "He has done **everything** well," they said. "He even makes the deaf
9: 12   "To be sure, Elijah does come first, and restores **all** *things*.
9: 15   As soon as **all** the people saw Jesus, they were overwhelmed with
9: 23   said Jesus. "**Everything** is possible for him who believes."
9: 35   wants to be first, he must be the **very** last, and the servant of all."
9: 35   wants to be first, he must be the very last, and the servant *of* **all**."
9: 49   **Everyone** will be salted with fire.
10: 20   "Teacher," he declared, "**all** these I have kept since I was a boy."
10: 27   is impossible, but not with God; **all** *things* are possible with God."
10: 28   Peter said to him, "We have left **everything** to follow you!"
10: 44   and whoever wants to be first must be slave *of* **all**.
11: 11   He looked around at **everything**, but since it was already late,
11: 17   " 'My house will be called a house of prayer *for* **all** nations'?
11: 18   feared him, because the **whole** crowd was amazed at his teaching.
11: 24   Therefore I tell you, **whatever** [+*4012*] you ask for in prayer,
12: 22   of the seven left any children. Last *of* **all**, the woman died too.
12: 28   he asked him, "*Of* **all** the commandments, which is the most
12: 33   and to love your neighbor as yourself is more important than **all**
12: 43   this poor widow has put more into the treasury than **all** the others.
12: 44   They **all** gave out of their wealth; but she, out of her poverty,
12: 44   but she, out of her poverty, put in **everything**—all she had to live
13: 4   And what will be the sign that they are **all** about to be fulfilled?"
13: 10   And the gospel must first be preached to **all** nations.
13: 13   **All** *men* will hate you because of me, but he who stands firm to the
13: 20   Lord had not cut short those days, no **one** [+*4922*] would survive.
13: 23   So be on your guard; I have told you **everything** ahead of time.
13: 30   this generation will certainly not pass away until **all** these things
13: 37   What I say to you, I say *to* **everyone**: 'Watch!' "
14: 23   gave thanks and offered it to them, and they **all** drank from it.
14: 27   "You will **all** fall away," Jesus told them, "for it is written: " 'I will
14: 29   Peter declared, "Even if **all** fall away, I will not."
14: 31   I will never disown you." And **all** the *others* said the same.
14: 36   "*Abba*, Father," he said, "**everything** is possible for you. Take this
14: 50   Then **everyone** deserted him and fled.
14: 53   and **all** the chief priests, elders and teachers of the law came
14: 64   What do you think?" They **all** condemned him as worthy of death.
16: 15   "Go into all the world and preach the good news to **all** creation.
16: S   [UBS+ *And* **all** *that had been commanded them they told briefly*]

Lk   1: 3   since I myself have carefully investigated **everything** from the
1: 6   observing **all** the Lord's commandments and regulations
1: 10   incense came, **all** the assembled worshipers were praying outside.
1: 37   For **nothing** [+*4024*+*4839*] is impossible with God."
1: 48   of his servant. From now on **all** generations will call me blessed,
1: 63   and to **everyone's** astonishment he wrote, "His name is John."
1: 65   The neighbors were **all** filled with awe, and throughout the hill
1: 65   the hill country of Judea people were talking about **all** these things.
1: 66   **Everyone** who heard this wondered about it, asking, "What
1: 71   salvation from our enemies and from the hand *of* **all** who hate us—
1: 75   in holiness and righteousness before him **all** our days.
2: 1   a decree that a census should be taken of the **entire** Roman world.
2: 3   And **everyone** [+*1667*] went to his own town to register.
2: 10   I bring you good news of great joy that will be *for* **all** the people.
2: 18   and **all** who heard it were amazed at what the shepherds said to
2: 19   But Mary treasured up **all** these things and pondered them in her
2: 20   and praising God for **all** the things they had heard and seen,
2: 23   the Lord, "**Every** firstborn male is to be consecrated to the Lord"),
2: 31   which you have prepared in the sight *of* **all** people,
2: 38   and spoke about the child *to* **all** who were looking forward to the
2: 39   and Mary had done **everything** required by the Law of the Lord,
2: 47   **Everyone** who heard him was amazed at his understanding
2: 51   to them. But his mother treasured **all** these things in her heart.
3: 3   He went into **all** the country around the Jordan, preaching a

3: 5   **Every** valley shall be filled in, every mountain and hill made low.
3: 5   Every valley shall be filled in, **every** mountain and hill made low.
3: 6   And **all** mankind will see God's salvation.' "
3: 9   and **every** tree that does not produce good fruit will be cut down
3: 15   and were **all** wondering in their hearts if John might possibly be
3: 16   John answered *them* **all**, "I baptize you with water. But one more
3: 19   his brother's wife, and **all** the *other* evil things he had done,
3: 20   Herod added this to *them* **all**: He locked John up in prison.
4: 5   and showed him in an instant **all** the kingdoms of the world.
4: 7   So if you worship me, it will **all** be yours."
4: 13   When the devil had finished **all** *this* tempting, he left him until an
4: 15   He taught in their synagogues, and **everyone** praised him.
4: 20   The eyes *of* **everyone** in the synagogue were fastened on him,
4: 22   **All** spoke well of him and were amazed at the gracious words that
4: 25   and there was a severe famine **throughout** [+*2093*] the land.
4: 28   **All** the *people* in the synagogue were furious when they heard this.
4: 36   **All** the *people* were amazed and said to each other, "What is this
4: 37   And the news about him spread **throughout** [+*1650*] the
5: 9   and **all** his companions were astonished at the catch of fish they
5: 11   pulled their boats up on shore, left **everything** and followed him.
5: 17   who had come from **every** village of Galilee and from Judea
5: 28   and Levi got up, left **everything** and followed him.
6: 10   He looked around at them **all**, and then said to the man, "Stretch out
6: 17   was there and a great number of people from **all over** Judea,
6: 19   and the people **all** tried to touch him, because power was coming
6: 19   because power was coming from him and healing *them* **all**.
6: 26   Woe to you when **all** men speak well of you, for that is how their
6: 30   Give *to* **everyone** who asks you, and if anyone takes what belongs
6: 40   but **everyone** who is fully trained will be like his teacher.
6: 47   I will show you what he is like **[RPG]** who comes to me
7: 1   When Jesus had finished saying **all** *this* in the hearing of the
7: 16   They were **all** filled with awe and praised God. "A great prophet
7: 17   spread throughout Judea and **[RPG]** the surrounding country.
7: 18   John's disciples told him about **all** these things. Calling two of
7: 29   (**All** the people, even the tax collectors, when they heard Jesus'
7: 35   But wisdom is proved right by **all** her children."
8: 40   a crowd welcomed him, for they were **all** expecting him.
8: 45   When they **all** denied it, Peter said, "Master, the people are
8: 47   In the presence *of* **all** the people, she told why she had touched him
8: 52   Meanwhile, **all** the *people* were wailing and mourning for her.
9: 1   he gave them power and authority to drive out **all** demons
9: 7   Now Herod the tetrarch heard about **all** that was going on.
9: 13   and two fish—unless we go and buy food for **all** this crowd."
9: 17   They **all** ate and were satisfied, and the disciples picked up twelve
9: 23   Then he said to *them* **all**: "If anyone would come after me,
9: 43   And they were **all** amazed at the greatness of God. While everyone
9: 43   While **everyone** was marveling at all that Jesus did, he said to his
9: 43   While everyone was marveling at **all** that Jesus did, he said to his
9: 48   sent me. For he who is least among you **all**—he is the greatest."
10: 1   and sent them two by two ahead of him to **every** town and place
10: 19   and scorpions and to overcome **all** the power of the enemy.
10: 22   "**All** *things* have been committed to me by my Father. No one
11: 4   us our sins, for we also forgive **everyone** who sins against us.
11: 10   For **everyone** who asks receives; he who seeks finds; and to him
11: 17   "**Any** kingdom divided against itself will be ruined, and a house
11: 41   inside the dish, to the poor, and **everything** will be clean for you.
11: 42   rue and **all** *other kinds* of garden herbs, but you neglect justice
11: 50   *of* **all** the prophets that has been shed since the beginning of the
12: 7   Indeed, the very hairs of your head are **all** numbered. Don't be
12: 8   "I tell you, **[RPG]** whoever acknowledges me before men,
12: 10   And **everyone** who speaks a word against the Son of Man will be
12: 15   Be on your guard against **all** *kinds* of greed; a man's life does not
12: 18   build bigger ones, and there I will store **all** my grain and my goods.
12: 27   not even Solomon in **all** his splendor was dressed like one of these.
12: 30   For the pagan world runs after **all** such things, and your Father
12: 41   "Lord, are you telling this parable to us, or to **everyone**?"
12: 44   I tell you the truth, he will put him in charge of **all** his possessions.
12: 48   *From* **everyone** who has been given much, much will be
13: 2   "Do you think that these Galileans were worse sinners than **all** the
13: 3   I tell you, no! But unless you repent, you too will **all** perish.
13: 4   do you think they were more guilty than **all** the others living in
13: 5   I tell you, no! But unless you repent, you too will **all** perish."
13: 17   When he said this, **all** his opponents were humiliated, but the
13: 17   but **[RPG]** the people were delighted with all the wonderful
13: 17   but the people were delighted with **all** the wonderful things he was
13: 27   or where you come from. Away from me, **all** you evildoers!'

13:28 Isaac and Jacob and **all** the prophets in the kingdom of God,
14:10 Then you will be honored in the presence *of* **all** your fellow guests.
14:11 For **everyone** who exalts himself will be humbled, and he who
14:18 "But they **all** alike began to make excuses. The first said, 'I have
14:29 and is not able to finish it, **everyone** who sees it will ridicule him,
14:33 **any** of you who does not give up everything he has cannot be my
14:33 any of you who does not give up **everything** he has cannot be my
15: 1 tax collectors and "sinners" were **all** gathering around to hear him.
15:13 "Not long after that, the younger son got together **all** he had,
15:14 After he had spent **everything**, there was a severe famine in that
15:31 'you are always with me, and **everything** I have is yours.
16:14 who loved money, heard **all** this and were sneering at Jesus.
16:16 of God is being preached, and **everyone** is forcing his way into it.
16:18 "**Anyone** who divorces his wife and marries another woman
16:26 And besides **all** this, between us and you a great chasm has been
17:10 when you have done **everything** you were told to do, should say,
17:27 Noah entered the ark. Then the flood came and destroyed *them* **all**.
17:29 and sulfur rained down from heaven and destroyed *them* **all**.
18:12 I fast twice a week and give a tenth of **all** [+4012] I get.'
18:14 For **everyone** who exalts himself will be humbled, and he who
18:21 "**All** these I have kept since I was a boy," he said.
18:22 Sell **everything** [+4012] you have and give to the poor, and you
18:31 and **everything** that is written by the prophets about the Son of
18:43 praising God. When **all** the people saw it, thcy also praised God.
19: 7 **All** the *people* saw this and began to mutter, "He has gone to be the
19:26 "He replied, 'I tell you that *to* **everyone** who has, more will be
19:37 to praise God in loud voices for **all** the miracles they had seen:
20:18 **Everyone** who falls on that stone will be broken to pieces,
20:38 is not the God of the dead, but of the living, for to him **all** are alive."
20:45 While **all** the people were listening, Jesus said to his disciples,
21: 3 he said, "this poor widow has put in more than **all** the *others*.
21: 4 **All** these people gave their gifts out of their wealth; but she out of
21: 4 wealth; but she out of her poverty put in **all** she had to live on."
21:12 "But before **all** this, they will lay hands on you and persecute you.
21:17 **All** *men* will hate you because of me.
21:22 For this is the time of punishment in fulfillment of **all** that has been
21:24 fall by the sword and will be taken as prisoners to **all** the nations.
21:29 He told them this parable: "Look at the fig tree and **all** the trees.
21:32 this generation will certainly not pass away until **all** these *things*
21:35 For it will come upon **all** those who live on the face of the whole
21:35 For it will come upon all those who live on the face *of* the **whole**
21:36 Be **always** [+1877+2789] on the watch, and pray that you may be
21:36 and pray that you may be able to escape **all** that is about to happen,
21:38 and **all** the people came early in the morning to hear him at the
22:70 They **all** asked, "Are you then the Son of God?" He replied,
23:48 When **all** the people who had gathered to witness this sight saw
23:49 But **all** those who knew him, including the women who had
24: 9 they told **all** these things to the Eleven and to all the others.
24: 9 they told all these things to the Eleven and *to* **all** the others.
24:14 They were talking with each other about **everything** that had
24:19 powerful in word and deed before God and **all** the people.
24:21 And **what is more** [+4047+5250], it is the third day since all this
24:25 and how slow of heart to believe **all** that the prophets have spoken!
24:27 And beginning with Moses and **all** the Prophets, he explained to
24:27 he explained to them what was said in **all** the Scriptures concerning
24:44 **Everything** must be fulfilled that is written about me in the Law of
24:47 and forgiveness of sins will be preached in his name to **all** nations,
24:53 And they stayed **continually** [+1328] at the temple, praising God.
Jn 1: 3 Through him **all** *things* were made; without him nothing was made
1: 7 concerning that light, so that through him **all** *men* might believe.
1: 9 The true light that gives light to **every** man was coming into the
1:16 From the fullness of his grace we have **all** received one blessing
2:10 "**Everyone** [+476] brings out the choice wine first and
2:15 and drove **all** from the temple area, both sheep and cattle;
2:24 But Jesus would not entrust himself to them, for he knew **all** *men*.
3: 8 it is going. So it is with **everyone** [+3836] born of the Spirit."
3:15 that **everyone** who believes in him may have eternal life.
3:16 that **whoever** [+3836] believes in him shall not perish but have
3:20 **Everyone** who does evil hates the light, and will not come into the
3:26 well, he is baptizing, and **everyone** is going to him."
3:31 "The one who comes from above is above **all**; the one who is from
3:31 one from the earth. The one who comes from heaven is above **all**.
3:35 The Father loves the Son and has placed **everything** in his hands.
4:13 "**Everyone** who drinks this water will be thirsty again,
4:29 "Come, see a man who told me **everything** I ever did. Could this be
4:39 of the woman's testimony, "He told me **everything** I ever did."

4:45 They had seen **all** that he had done in Jerusalem at the Passover
5:20 For the Father loves the Son and shows him **all** he does. Yes,
5:22 the Father judges no one, but has entrusted **all** judgment to the Son,
5:23 that **all** may honor the Son just as they honor the Father. He who
5:28 for a time is coming when **all** who are in their graves will hear his
6:37 **All** that the Father gives me will come to me, and whoever comes
6:39 that I shall lose none of **all** that he has given me, but raise them up
6:40 For my Father's will is that **everyone** who looks to the Son
6:45 It is written in the Prophets: 'They will **all** be taught by God.'
6:45 **Everyone** who listens to the Father and learns from him comes to
7:21 Jesus said to them, "I did one miracle, and you are **all** astonished.
8: 2 where **all** the people gathered around him, and he sat down to teach
8:34 "I tell you the truth, **everyone** who sins is a slave to sin.
10: 4 When he has brought out **all** his own, he goes on ahead of thcm,
10: 8 **All** who ever came before me were thieves and robbers,
10:29 My Father, who has given them to me, is greater than **all**; no one
10:41 a miraculous sign, **all** that John said about this man was true."
11:26 and **whoever** [+3836] lives and believes in me will never die.
11:48 **everyone** will believe in him, and then the Romans will come
12:32 when I am lifted up from the earth, will draw **all** *men* to myself."
12:46 so that no **one** who believes in me should stay in darkness.
13: 3 Jesus knew that the Father had put **all** *things* under his power,
13:10 body is clean. And you are clean, though not **every** *one* of you."
13:11 to betray him, and that was why he said not **every** *one* was clean.
13:18 "I am not referring to **all** of you; I know those I have chosen.
13:35 By this **all** *men* will know that you are my disciples, if you love
14:26 will teach you **all** *things* and will remind you of everything I have
14:26 all things and will remind you of **everything** I have said to you.
15: 2 He cuts off **every** branch in me that bears no fruit, while every
15: 2 while **every** branch that does bear fruit he prunes so that it will be
15:15 for **everything** that I learned from my Father I have made known
15:21 They will treat you **this way** [+4047] because of my name,
16: 2 a time is coming when **anyone** who kills you will think he is
16:13 when he, the Spirit of truth, comes, he will guide you into **all** truth.
16:15 **All** that belongs to the Father is mine. That is why I said the Spirit
16:30 Now we can see that you know **all** *things* and that you do not even
17: 2 For you granted him authority over **all** people that he might give
17: 2 that he might give eternal life to **all** those you have given him.
17: 7 Now they know that **everything** [+4012] you have given me
17:10 **All** I have is yours, and all you have is mine. And glory has come
17:21 that **all** *of them* may be one, Father, just as you are in me
18: 4 Jesus, knowing **all** that was going to happen to him, went out
18:20 in synagogues or at the temple, where **all** the Jews come together.
18:37 to testify to the truth. **Everyone** on the side of truth listens to me."
19:12 friend of Caesar. **Anyone** who claims to be a king opposes Caesar."
19:28 knowing that **all** was now completed, and so that the Scripture
21:17 He said, "Lord, you know **all** *things*; you know that I love you."
Ac 1: 1 Theophilus, I wrote about **all** that Jesus began to do and to teach
1: 8 and in **all** Judea and Samaria, and to the ends of the earth."
1:14 They **all** joined together constantly in prayer, along with the
1:18 fell headlong, his body burst open and **all** his intestines spilled out.
1:19 **Everyone** in Jerusalem heard about this, so they called that field in
1:21 men who have been with us the **whole** time the Lord Jesus went in
1:24 Then they prayed, "Lord, you know **everyone's** heart. Show us
2: 1 the day of Pentecost came, they were **all** together in one place.
2: 4 **All** *of them* were filled with the Holy Spirit and began to speak in
2: 5 Now there were staying in Jerusalem God-fearing Jews from **every**
2:12 Amazed **[RPG]** and perplexed, they asked one another, "What
2:14 "Fellow Jews and **all** *of you* who live in Jerusalem, let me explain
2:17 " 'In the last days, God says, I will pour out my Spirit on **all** people.
2:21 And **everyone** who calls on the name of the Lord will be saved.'
2:25 David said about him: " 'I saw the Lord **always** [+1328] before me.
2:32 has raised this Jesus to life, and we are **all** witnesses of the fact.
2:36 "Therefore let **all** Israel be assured of this: God has made this Jesus,
2:39 promise is for you and your children and *for* **all** who are far off—
2:43 **Everyone** [+6034] was filled with awe, and many wonders
2:44 **All** the believers were together and had everything in common.
2:45 their possessions and goods, they gave *to* **anyone** as he had need.
3: 9 When **all** the people saw him walking and praising God,
3:11 **all** the people were astonished and came running to them in the
3:16 him that has given this complete healing to him, as you can all see.
3:18 But this is how God fulfilled what he had foretold through **all** the
3:21 in heaven until the time comes for God to restore **everything**,
3:22 you must listen to **everything** [+323+4012] he tells you.
3:23 **Anyone** [+6034] who does not listen to him will be completely cut
3:24 "Indeed, **all** the prophets from Samuel on, as many as have spoken,

3:25	'Through your offspring all peoples on earth will be blessed.'
4:10	then know this, [RPG] you and all the people of Israel: It is by the
4:10	then know this, you and all the people of Israel: It is by the name
4:16	"Everybody living in Jerusalem knows they have done an
4:21	because all the people were praising God for what had happened.
4:24	the heaven and the earth and the sea, and everything in them.
4:29	and enable your servants to speak your word with great boldness.
4:33	resurrection of the Lord Jesus, and much grace was upon them all.
5: 5	and died. And great fear seized all who heard what had happened.
5:11	fear seized the whole church and all who heard about these events.
5:17	Then the high priest and all his associates, who were members of
5:20	he said, "and tell the people the full message of this new life."
5:21	the full assembly of the elders of Israel—and sent to the jail for the
5:23	"We found the jail securely [+854+1877] locked, with the guards
5:34	a teacher of the law, who was honored by all the people, stood up
5:36	He was killed, all [+4012] his followers were dispersed, and it all
5:37	He too was killed, and all [+4012] his followers were scattered.
5:42	Day after day [+2465], in the temple courts and from house to
6: 5	This proposal pleased the whole group. They chose Stephen,
6:15	All who were sitting in the Sanhedrin looked intently at Stephen,
7:10	and rescued him from all his troubles. He gave Joseph wisdom
7:14	After this, Joseph sent for his father Jacob and his whole family,
7:22	Moses was educated in all the wisdom of the Egyptians and was
7:50	Has not my hand made all these things?'
8: 1	and all except the apostles were scattered throughout Judea
8:10	and all the people, both high and low, gave him their attention
8:27	an important official in charge of all the treasury of Candace.
8:40	preaching the gospel in all the towns until he reached Caesarea.
9:14	authority from the chief priests to arrest all who call on your name."
9:21	All those who heard him were astonished and asked, "Isn't he the
9:26	he tried to join the disciples, but they were all afraid of him,
9:32	As Peter traveled about the countrys, he went to visit the saints in
9:35	All those who lived in Lydda and Sharon saw him and turned to
9:39	All the widows stood around him, crying and showing him the
9:40	Peter sent them all out of the room; then he got down on his knees
10: 2	He and all his family were devout and God-fearing; he gave
10: 2	generously to those in need and prayed to God regularly [+1328].
10:12	It contained all kinds of four-footed animals, as well as reptiles of
10:14	Peter replied. "I have never eaten anything impure or unclean."
10:33	Now we are all here in the presence of God to listen to everything
10:33	Now we are all here in the presence of God to listen to everything
10:35	but accepts men from every nation who fear him and do what is
10:36	the good news of peace through Jesus Christ, who is Lord of all.
10:38	doing good and healing all who were under the power of the devil,
10:39	"We are witnesses of everything he did in the country of the Jews
10:41	He was not seen by all the people, but by witnesses whom God
10:43	All the prophets testify about him that everyone who believes in
10:43	All the prophets testify about him that everyone who believes in
10:44	these words, the Holy Spirit came on all who heard the message.
11:14	message through which you and all your household will be saved.'
11:23	and encouraged them all to remain true to the Lord with all their
12:11	and from everything the Jewish people were anticipating."
13:10	are a child of the devil and an enemy of everything that is right!
13:10	that is right! You are full of all kinds of deceit and trickery.
13:10	is right! You are full of all kinds of deceit and [RPG] trickery.
13:22	a man after my own heart; he will do everything I want him to do.'
13:24	John preached repentance and baptism to all the people of Israel.
13:27	the words of the prophets that are read every [+2848] Sabbath.
13:29	When they had carried out all that was written about him,
13:39	Through him everyone who believes is justified from everything
13:39	Through him everyone who believes is justified from everything
13:44	On the next Sabbath almost the whole city gathered to hear the
14:15	who made heaven and earth and sea and everything in them.
14:16	In the past, he let all nations go their own way.
15: 3	had been converted. This news made all the brothers very glad.
15:12	The whole assembly became silent as they listened to Barnabas
15:17	and all the Gentiles who bear my name, says the Lord, who does
15:21	the earliest times and is read in the synagogues on every Sabbath."
15:36	and visit the brothers in all the towns where we preached the word
16:26	At once all the prison doors flew open, and everybody's chains
16:26	the prison doors flew open, and everybody's chains came loose.
16:32	the word of the Lord to him and to all the others in his house.
16:33	then immediately he and all his family were baptized.
17: 7	They are all defying Caesar's decrees, saying that there is another
17:11	for they received the message with great eagerness and examined
17:17	as well as in the marketplace day by day [+2465+2848] with those

17:21	(All the Athenians and the foreigners who lived there spent their
17:22	"Men of Athens! I see that in every way you are very religious.
17:24	the world and everything in it is the Lord of heaven and earth
17:25	because he himself gives all men life and breath and everything
17:25	himself gives all men life and breath and everything [+3836] else.
17:26	From one man he made every nation of men, that they should
17:26	nation of men, that they should inhabit the whole [+4725] earth;
17:30	but now he commands all people everywhere to repent.
17:31	He has given proof of this to all men by raising him from the dead."
18: 2	because Claudius had ordered all the Jews to leave Rome.
18: 4	Every [+2848] Sabbath he reasoned in the synagogue, trying to
18:17	Then they all turned on Sosthenes the synagogue ruler and beat
18:23	the region of Galatia and Phrygia, strengthening all the disciples.
19: 7	There were about twelve men in all.
19:10	so that all the Jews and Greeks who lived in the province of Asia
19:17	When this became known to [RPG] the Jews and Greeks living in
19:17	and Greeks living in Ephesus, they were all seized with fear,
19:19	brought their scrolls together and burned them publicly [+1967].
19:26	here in Ephesus and in practically the whole province of Asia.
19:34	he was a Jew, they all shouted in unison for about two hours:
20:18	"You know how I lived the whole time I was with you,
20:19	I served the Lord with great humility and with tears, although I
20:25	"Now I know that none of you among whom I have gone about
20:26	I declare to you today that I am innocent of the blood of all men.
20:27	For I have not hesitated to proclaim to you the whole will of God.
20:28	and all the flock of which the Holy Spirit has made you overseers.
20:32	and give you an inheritance among all those who are sanctified.
20:35	In everything I did, I showed you that by this kind of hard work
20:36	When he had said this, he knelt down with all of them and prayed.
20:37	They all wept as they embraced him and kissed him.
21: 5	All the disciples and their wives and children accompanied us out
21:18	the rest of us went to see James, and all the elders were present.
21:20	of Jews have believed, and all of them are zealous for the law.
21:21	They have been informed that you teach all the Jews who live
21:24	Then everybody will know there is no truth in these reports about
21:27	at the temple. They stirred up the whole crowd and seized him,
21:28	This is the man who teaches all men everywhere against our
22: 3	and was just as zealous for God as any of you are today.
22: 5	as also the high priest and the Council can testify. I even
22:10	There you will be told all that you have been assigned to do.'
22:12	of the law and highly respected by all the Jews living there.
22:15	You will be his witness to all men of what you have seen
22:30	and ordered the chief priests and all the Sanhedrin to assemble.
23: 1	I have fulfilled my duty to God in all good conscience to this day."
24: 3	excellent Felix, we acknowledge this with profound gratitude.
24: 5	stirring up riots among the Jews all over the world.
24: 8	learn the truth about all these charges we are bringing against him."
24:14	I believe everything that agrees with the Law and that is written in
24:16	So I strive always [+1328] to keep my conscience clear before God
25:24	"King Agrippa, and all who are present with us, you see this man!
26: 2	today as I make my defense against all the accusations of the Jews,
26: 3	because you are well acquainted with all the Jewish customs
26: 4	"The Jews all know the way I have lived ever since I was a child,
26:11	I went from one synagogue to another [+2848+3836+5252] to
26:14	We all fell to the ground, and I heard a voice saying to me in
26:20	then to those in Jerusalem and in all Judea, and to the Gentiles
26:29	but all who are listening to me today may become what I am,
27:20	storm continued raging, we finally gave up all hope of being saved.
27:24	and God has graciously given you the lives of all who sail with
27:35	he took some bread and gave thanks to God in front of them all.
27:36	They were all encouraged and ate some food themselves.
27:37	Altogether [+3836] there were 276 of us on board.
27:44	on pieces of the ship. In this way everyone reached land in safety.
28: 2	They built a fire and welcomed us all because it was raining
28:30	in his own rented house and welcomed all who came to see him.
28:31	Boldly [+3552+4244] and without hindrance he preached the
Ro 1: 5	and apostleship to call people from among all the Gentiles to the
1: 7	To all in Rome who are loved by God and called to be saints:
1: 8	First, I thank my God through Jesus Christ for all of you,
1:16	because it is the power of God for the salvation of everyone who
1:18	The wrath of God is being revealed from heaven against all the
1:29	They have become filled with every kind of wickedness, evil,
2: 1	have no excuse, you who pass judgment on someone else,
2: 9	will be trouble and distress for every human being who does evil:
2:10	but glory, honor and peace for everyone who does good: first for
3: 2	Much in every way! First of all, they have been entrusted with the

3: 4 Not at all! Let God be true, and **every** man a liar. As it is written:
3: 9 made the charge that Jews and Gentiles alike are **all** under sin.
3:12 **All** have turned away, they have together become worthless;
3:19 so that **every** mouth may be silenced and the whole world held
3:19 may be silenced and the **whole** world held accountable to God.
3:20 Therefore no **one** [+4922] will be declared righteous in his sight by
3:22 from God comes through faith in Jesus Christ to **all** who believe.
3:23 for **all** have sinned and fall short of the glory of God,
4:11 he is the father *of* **all** who believe but have not been circumcised,
4:16 be by grace and may be guaranteed *to* **all** Abraham's offspring—
4:16 to those who are of the faith of Abraham. He is the father *of* us **all**.
5:12 and death through sin, and in this way death came to **all** men,
5:12 and in this way death came to all men, because **all** sinned—
5:18 just as the result of one trespass was condemnation for **all** men,
5:18 act of righteousness was justification that brings life for **all** men.
7: 8 the commandment, produced in me **every** *kind* of covetous desire.
8:22 We know that the **whole** creation has been groaning as in the pains
8:28 And we know that in **all** *things* God works for the good of those
8:32 He who did not spare his own Son, but gave him up for us **all**—
8:32 he not also, along with him, graciously give us **all** [+3836] **things**?
8:37 in **all** these things we are more than conquerors through him who
9: 5 the human ancestry of Christ, who is God over **all**, forever praised!
9: 6 had failed. For not **all** who are descended from Israel are Israel.
9: 7 because they are his descendants are *they* **all** Abraham's children.
9:17 in you and that my name might be proclaimed in **all** the earth."
10: 4 so that there may be righteousness *for* **everyone** who believes.
10:11 "**Anyone** who trusts in him will never be put to shame."
10:12 the same Lord is Lord *of* **all** and richly blesses all who call on him,
10:12 the same Lord is Lord of all and richly blesses **all** who call on him,
10:13 "**Everyone** who calls on the name of the Lord will be saved."
10:16 But not **all** the Israelites accepted the good news. For Isaiah says,
10:18 "Their voice has gone out into **all** the earth, their words to the ends
11:10 so they cannot see, and their backs be bent **forever** [+1328]."
11:26 And so **all** Israel will be saved, as it is written: "The deliverer will
11:32 For God has bound **all** *men* over to disobedience so that he may
11:32 men over to disobedience so that he may have mercy on them **all**.
11:36 For from him and through him and to him are **all** [+3836] **things**.
12: 3 For by the grace given me I say *to* **every** *one* of you: Do not think
12: 4 and these members do not **all** have the same function,
12:17 Be careful to do what is right in the eyes *of* **everybody** [+476].
12:18 as far as it depends on you, live at peace with **everyone** [+476].
13: 1 **Everyone** [+6034] must submit himself to the governing
13: 7 Give **everyone** what you owe him: If you owe taxes, pay taxes;
14: 2 One man's faith allows him to eat **everything**, but another man,
14: 5 more sacred than another; another man considers **every** day alike.
14:10 on your brother? For we will **all** stand before God's judgment seat.
14:11 surely as I live,' says the Lord, '**every** knee will bow before me;
14:11 knee will bow before me; **every** tongue will confess to God.' "
14:20 **All** *food* is clean, but it is wrong for a man to eat anything that
14:23 not from faith; and **everything** that does not come from faith is sin.
15:11 And again, "Praise the Lord, **all** you Gentiles, and sing praises to
15:11 the Lord, all you Gentiles, and sing praises to him, **all** you peoples."
15:13 May the God of hope fill you with **all** joy and peace as you trust in
15:14 **complete** [+4444] in knowledge and competent to instruct one
15:33 The God of peace be with you **all**. Amen.
16: 4 Not only I but **all** the churches of the Gentiles are grateful to them.
16:15 Nereus and his sister, and Olympas and **all** the saints with them.
16:16 another with a holy kiss. **All** the churches of Christ send greetings.
16:19 **Everyone** has heard about your obedience, so I am full of joy over
16:26 of the eternal God, so that **all** nations might believe and obey him—
1Co 1: 2 together with **all** those everywhere who call on the name of our
1: 2 together with **all** those **everywhere** [+5536] who call on the name
1: 5 For in him you have been enriched in **every** *way*—in all your
1: 5 in every way—in **all** your speaking and in all your knowledge—
1: 5 in every way—in all your speaking and in **all** your knowledge—
1:10 that **all** of you agree with one another so that there may be no
1:29 so that no **one** [+4922] may boast before him.
2:10 The Spirit searches **all** *things*, even the deep things of God.
2:15 The spiritual man makes judgments about **all** [+3836] **things**,
3:21 So then, no more boasting about men! **All** *things* are yours,
3:22 the world or life or death or the present or the future—**all** are yours,
4:13 we have become the scum of the earth, the refuse *of* **the world**s.
4:17 which agrees with what I teach everywhere in **every** church.
6:12 "**Everything** is permissible for me"—but not everything is
6:12 is permissible for me"—but not **everything** is beneficial.
6:12 "**Everything** is permissible for me"—but I will not be mastered by

6:18 **All** *other* sins a man commits are outside his body, but he who sins
7: 7 I wish that **all** men were as I am. But each man has his own gift
7:17 God has called him. This is the rule I lay down in **all** the churches.
8: 1 We know that we **all** possess knowledge. Knowledge puffs up,
8: 6 from whom **all** [+3836] **things** came and for whom we live;
8: 6 through whom **all** [+3836] **things** came and through whom we
8: 7 But not **everyone** knows this. Some people are still so accustomed
9:12 we put up with **anything** rather than hinder the gospel of Christ.
9:19 Though I am **free and belong to no man** [+1666+1801], I make
9:19 and belong to no man, I make myself a slave *to* **everyone**,
9:22 I have become **all** *things* to all men so that by all possible means I
9:22 I have become all things *to* **all** *men* so that by all possible means I
9:23 I do **all** *this* for the sake of the gospel, that I may share in its
9:24 Do you not know that in a race **all** the runners run, but only one
9:25 **Everyone** who competes in the games goes into strict training.
9:25 Everyone who competes in the games goes into **strict** training.
10: 1 that our forefathers were **all** under the cloud and that they all
10: 1 were all under the cloud and that they **all** passed through the sea.
10: 2 They were **all** baptized into Moses in the cloud and in the sea.
10: 3 They **all** ate the same spiritual food
10: 4 for they drank **[RPG]** from the spiritual rock that accompanied
10:17 who are many, are one body, for we **all** partake of the one loaf.
10:23 "**Everything** is permissible"—but not everything is beneficial.
10:23 "**Everything** is permissible"—but not **everything** is beneficial.
10:23 "**Everything** is permissible"—but not everything is constructive.
10:23 "**Everything** is permissible"—but not **everything** is constructive.
10:25 Eat **anything** sold in the meat market without raising questions of
10:27 eat **whatever** is put before you without raising questions of
10:31 or drink or whatever you do, do it **all** for the glory of God.
10:33 even as I try to please **everybody** in every way. For I am not
10:33 even as I try to please everybody *in* **every** *way*. For I am not
11: 2 I praise you for remembering me in **everything** and for holding to
11: 3 Now I want you to realize that the head *of* **every** man is Christ,
11: 4 **Every** man who prays or prophesies with his head covered
11: 5 And **every** woman who prays or prophesies with her head
11:12 man is born of woman. But **everything** [+3836] comes from God.
12: 6 but the same God works **all** [+3836] *of them* in all men.
12: 6 kinds of working, but the same God works all of them in **all** *men*.
12:11 **All** these are the work of one and the same Spirit, and he gives
12:12 many parts; and though **all** its parts are many, they form one body.
12:13 For we were **all** baptized by one Spirit into one body—
12:13 slave or free—and we were **all** given the one Spirit to drink.
12:19 If they were **all** [+3836] one part, where would the body be?
12:26 If one part suffers, **every** part suffers with it; if one part is honored,
12:26 suffers with it; if one part is honored, **every** part rejoices with it.
12:29 Are **all** apostles? Are all prophets? Are all teachers? Do all work
12:29 Are all apostles? Are **all** prophets? Are all teachers? Do all work
12:29 Are all apostles? Are all prophets? Are **all** teachers? Do all work
12:29 Are all prophets? Are all teachers? Do **all** work miracles?
12:30 Do **all** have gifts of healing? Do all speak in tongues? Do all
12:30 all have gifts of healing? Do **all** speak in tongues? Do all interpret?
12:30 all have gifts of healing? Do all speak in tongues? Do **all** interpret?
13: 2 gift of prophecy and can fathom **all** mysteries and all knowledge,
13: 2 gift of prophecy and can fathom all mysteries and **all** knowledge,
13: 2 and if I have **[RPG]** a faith that can move mountains, but have not
13: 3 If I give **all** I possess to the poor and surrender my body to the
13: 7 It **always** protects, always trusts, always hopes, always perseveres.
13: 7 It always protects, **always** trusts, always hopes, always perseveres.
13: 7 It always protects, always trusts, **always** hopes, always perseveres.
13: 7 It always protects, always trusts, always hopes, **always** perseveres.
14: 5 I would like **every** *one* of you to speak in tongues, but I would
14:18 I thank God that I speak in tongues more than **all** of you.
14:23 the whole church comes together and **everyone** speaks in tongues,
14:24 or someone who does not understand comes in while **everybody** is
14:24 he will be convinced by **all** that he is a sinner and will be judged by
14:24 be convinced by all that he is a sinner and will be judged by **all**,
14:26 **All** *of these* must be done for the strengthening of the church.
14:31 For you can **all** prophesy in turn so that everyone may be
14:31 in turn so that **everyone** may be instructed and encouraged.
14:31 so that everyone may be instructed and **[RPG]** encouraged.
14:33 of disorder but of peace. As in **all** the congregations of the saints,
14:40 But **everything** should be done in a fitting and orderly way.
15: 7 Then he appeared to James, then *to* **all** the apostles,
15: 8 and last *of* **all** he appeared to me also, as to one abnormally born.
15:10 No, I worked harder than **all** of them—yet not I, but the grace of
15:19 life we have hope in Christ, we are to be pitied more than **all** men.

15: 22   For as in Adam **all** die, so in Christ all will be made alive.
15: 22   For as in Adam all die, so in Christ **all** will be made alive.
15: 24   the kingdom to God the Father after he has destroyed **all** dominion,
15: 24   after he has destroyed all dominion, **[RPG]** authority and power.
15: 25   For he must reign until he has put **all** his enemies under his feet.
15: 27   For he "has put **everything** under his feet." Now when it says that
15: 27   Now when it says that "**everything**" has been put under him,
15: 27   include God himself, who put **everything** [+3836] under Christ.
15: 28   When he has done this^s [+3836], then the Son himself will be
15: 28   be made subject to him who put **everything** [+3836] under him,
15: 28   him who put everything under him, so that God may be **all** in all.
15: 28   him who put everything under him, so that God may be all in **all**.
15: 30   And as for us, why do we endanger ourselves **every** hour?
15: 39   **All** flesh is not the same: Men have one kind of flesh, animals have
15: 51   you a mystery: We will not **all** sleep, but we will all be changed—
15: 51   you a mystery: We will not all sleep, but we will **all** be changed—
16: 14   Do **everything** in love.
16: 16   to submit to such as these and to **everyone** who joins in the work,
16: 20   **All** the brothers here send you greetings. Greet one another with a
16: 24   My love to **all** of you in Christ Jesus. Amen.
2Co   1: 1   of God in Corinth, together with **all** the saints throughout Achaia:
1: 3   Jesus Christ, the Father of compassion and the God of **all** comfort,
1: 4   who comforts us in **all** our troubles,
1: 4   so that we can comfort those in **any** trouble with the comfort we
2: 3   I had confidence in **all** of you, that you would all share my joy.
2: 3   I had confidence in all of you, that you would **all** share my joy.
2: 5   he has not so much grieved me as he has grieved **all** of you,
2: 9   to see if you would stand the test and be obedient in **everything**.
2: 14   through us spreads **everywhere** [+1877+5536] the fragrance of the
3: 2   written on our hearts, known and read by **everybody** [+476].
3: 18   And we, who with unveiled faces **all** reflect the Lord's glory,
4: 2   by setting forth the truth plainly we commend ourselves to **every**
4: 8   We are hard pressed on **every** side, but not crushed; perplexed,
4: 15   **All** [+3836] this is for your benefit, so that the grace that is
5: 10   For we must **all** appear before the judgment seat of Christ,
5: 14   because we are convinced that one died for **all**, and therefore all
5: 14   we are convinced that one died for all, and therefore **all** died.
5: 15   And he died for **all**, that those who live should no longer live for
5: 18   **All** [+3836] this is from God, who reconciled us to himself
6: 4   Rather, as servants of God we commend ourselves in **every** way:
6: 10   making many rich; having nothing, and yet possessing **everything**.
7: 1   let us purify ourselves from **everything** that contaminates body
7: 4   greatly encouraged; in **all** our troubles my joy knows no bounds.
7: 5   this body of ours had no rest, but we were harassed at **every** turn—
7: 11   At **every** point you have proved yourselves to be innocent in this
7: 13   Titus was, because his spirit has been refreshed by **all** of you.
7: 14   But just as **everything** we said to you was true, so our boasting
7: 15   is all the greater when he remembers that you were **all** obedient,
7: 16   I am glad I can have **complete** [+1877] confidence in you.
8: 7   But just as you excel in **everything**—in faith, in speech, in
8: 7   in knowledge, in **complete** earnestness and in your love for us—
8: 18   who is praised by **all** the churches for his service to the gospel.
9: 8   And God is able to make **all** grace abound to you, so that in all
9: 8   so that in **all** things at all times, having all that you need, you will
9: 8   so that in all things at all times, having **all** that you need, you will
9: 8   having all that you need, you will abound in **every** good work.
9: 11   You will be made rich in **every** way so that you can be generous
9: 11   rich in every way so that you can be generous on **every** occasion,
9: 13   for your generosity in sharing with them and with **everyone** else.
10: 5   and **every** pretension that sets itself up against the knowledge of
10: 5   and we take captive **every** thought to make it obedient to Christ.
10: 6   And we will be ready to punish **every** act of disobedience,
11: 6   We have made this **perfectly** [+1877] clear to you in every way.
11: 6   We have made this perfectly clear to you in **every** way.
11: 9   I have kept myself from being a burden to you in **any** way,
11: 28   I face daily the pressure of my concern for **all** the churches.
12: 12   and miracles—were done among you with **great** perseverance.
12: 19   and **everything** [+3836] we do, dear friends, is for your
13: 1   "**Every** matter must be established by the testimony of two
13: 2   I will not spare those who sinned earlier or **any** of the others,
13: 13   **All** the saints send their greetings.
13: 14   love of God, and the fellowship of the Holy Spirit be with you **all**.
Gal   1: 2   and **all** the brothers with me, To the churches in Galatia:
2: 14   I said to Peter in front of them **all**, "You are a Jew, yet you live like
2: 16   because by observing the law no **one** [+4922] will be justified.
3: 8   in advance to Abraham: "**All** nations will be blessed through you."

3: 10   "Cursed is **everyone** who does not continue to do everything
3: 10   "Cursed is everyone who does not continue to do **everything**
3: 13   for it is written: "Cursed is **everyone** who is hung on a tree."
3: 22   But the Scripture declares that the **whole world** is a prisoner of sin,
3: 26   You are **all** sons of God through faith in Christ Jesus,
3: 28   slave nor free, male nor female, for you are **all** one in Christ Jesus.
4: 1   he is no different from a slave, although he owns **the whole** estate.
5: 3   Again I declare to **every** man who lets himself be circumcised that
5: 14   The **entire** law is summed up in a single command: "Love your
6: 6   Anyone who receives instruction in the word must share **all** good
6: 10   Therefore, as we have opportunity, let us do good to **all** people,
Eph   1: 3   who has blessed us in the heavenly realms with **every** spiritual
1: 8   that he lavished on us with **all** wisdom and understanding.
1: 10   will have reached their fulfillment—to bring **all** [+3836] **things**
1: 11   out **everything** [+3836] in conformity with the purpose of his will,
1: 15   about your faith in the Lord Jesus and your love for **all** the saints,
1: 21   far above **all** rule and authority, power and dominion, and every
1: 21   power and dominion, and **every** title that can be given,
1: 22   And God placed **all** things under his feet and appointed him to be
1: 22   and appointed him to be head over **everything** for the church,
1: 23   the fullness of him who fills **everything** [+3836] in every way.
1: 23   is his body, the fullness of him who fills everything in **every** way.
2: 3   **All** of us also lived among them at one time,
2: 21   In him the **whole** building is joined together and rises to become a
3: 8   Although I am less than the least of all of God's people, this grace
3: 9   and to make plain to **everyone** the administration of this mystery,
3: 9   ages past was kept hidden in God, who created **all** [+3836] **things**.
3: 15   from whom his **whole** family in heaven and on earth derives its
3: 18   may have power, together with **all** the saints, to grasp how wide
3: 19   that you may be filled to the measure of **all** the fullness of God.
3: 20   Now to him who is able to do immeasurably more than **all** we ask
3: 21   glory in the church and in Christ Jesus throughout **all** generations,
4: 2   Be **completely** humble and gentle; Be patient, bearing with one
4: 6   one God and Father of **all**, who is over all and through all
4: 6   and Father of all, who is over **all** and through all and in all.
4: 6   and Father of all, who is over all and through **all** and in all.
4: 6   and Father of all, who is over all and through all and in **all**.
4: 10   He who descended is the very one who ascended higher than **all**
4: 10   higher than all the heavens, in order to fill the **whole universe**.)
4: 13   until we **all** reach unity in the faith and in the knowledge of the
4: 14   and blown here and there by **every** wind of teaching and by the
4: 15   we will in **all** [+3836] **things** grow up into him who is the Head,
4: 16   From him the **whole** body, joined and held together by every
4: 16   joined and held together by **every** supporting ligament, grows
4: 19   over to sensuality so as to indulge in **every** kind of impurity,
4: 29   Do not let **any** unwholesome talk come out of your mouths,
4: 31   Get rid of **all** bitterness, rage and anger, brawling and slander,
4: 31   brawling and slander, along with **every** form of malice.
5: 3   or of **any** kind of impurity, or of greed, because these are improper
5: 5   **No** [+4024] immoral, impure or greedy person—such a man is an
5: 9   (for the fruit of the light consists in **all** goodness, righteousness
5: 13   But **everything** [+3836] exposed by the light becomes visible,
5: 14   for it is light that makes **everything** visible. This is why it is said:
5: 20   always giving thanks to God the Father for **everything**,
5: 24   so also wives should submit to their husbands in **everything**.
6: 16   In addition to all this, take up the shield of faith, with which you
6: 16   with which you can extinguish **all** the flaming arrows of the evil
6: 18   And pray in the Spirit on **all** occasions with all kinds of prayers
6: 18   And pray in the Spirit on all occasions with **all** kinds of prayers
6: 18   this in mind, be alert and **always** keep on praying for all the saints.
6: 18   this in mind, be alert and always keep on praying for **all** the saints.
6: 21   and faithful servant in the Lord, will tell you **everything**,
6: 24   Grace to **all** who love our Lord Jesus Christ with an undying love.
Php   1: 1   of Christ Jesus, To **all** the saints in Christ Jesus at Philippi,
1: 3   I thank my God **every** time I remember you.
1: 4   In **all** my prayers for all of you, I always pray with joy
1: 4   In all my prayers for **all** of you, I always pray with joy
1: 7   It is right for me to feel this way about **all** of you, since I have you
1: 7   confirming the gospel, **all** of you share in God's grace with me.
1: 8   God can testify how I long for **all** of you with the affection of
1: 9   may abound more and more in knowledge and **depth** of insight,
1: 13   palace guard and to **everyone** else that I am in chains for Christ.
1: 18   The important thing is that in **every** way, whether from false
1: 20   but will have **sufficient** courage so that now as always Christ will
1: 25   and I will continue with **all** of you for your progress and joy in the
2: 9   the highest place and gave him the name that is above **every** name,

2:10 that at the name of Jesus **every** knee should bow, in heaven
2:11 and **every** tongue confess that Jesus Christ is Lord, to the glory of
2:14 Do **everything** without complaining or arguing,
2:17 coming from your faith, I am glad and rejoice with **all** of you.
2:21 For **everyone** looks out for his own interests, not those of Jesus
2:26 For he longs for **all** of you and is distressed because you heard he
2:29 Welcome him in the Lord with **great** joy, and honor men like him,
3: 8 I consider **everything** a loss compared to the surpassing greatness
3: 8 Jesus my Lord, for whose sake I have lost **all** [+3836] **things**.
3:21 by the power that enables him to bring **everything** [+3836] under
4: 5 Let your gentleness be evident to **all** [+476]. The Lord is near.
4: 6 but in **everything**, by prayer and petition, with thanksgiving,
4: 7 which transcends **all** understanding, will guard your hearts
4:12 I have learned the secret of being content in **any** and every
4:12 learned the secret of being content in any and **every** *situation*,
4:13 I can do **everything** through him who gives me strength.
4:18 I have received **full** payment and even more; I am amply supplied,
4:19 And my God will meet **all** your needs according to his glorious
4:21 Greet **all** the saints in Christ Jesus. The brothers who are with me
4:22 **All** the saints send you greetings, especially those who belong to
Col 1: 4 faith in Christ Jesus and of the love you have for **all** the saints—
1: 6 **All over** the world this gospel is bearing fruit and growing,
1: 9 fill you with the knowledge of his will through **all** spiritual wisdom
1:10 live a life worthy of the Lord and may please him in **every** *way*:
1:10 bearing fruit in **every** good work, growing in the knowledge of
1:11 being strengthened with **all** power according to his glorious might
1:11 glorious might so that you may have **great** endurance and patience,
1:15 is the image of the invisible God, the firstborn *over* **all** creation.
1:16 For by him **all** [+3836] **things** were created: things in heaven
1:16 or rulers or authorities; **all** [+3836] **things** were created by him
1:17 He is before **all** *things*, and in him all things hold together.
1:17 is before all things, and in him **all** [+3836] **things** hold together.
1:18 the dead, so that in **everything** he might have the supremacy.
1:19 For God was pleased to have **all** his fullness dwell in him,
1:20 and through him to reconcile to himself **all** [+3836] **things**,
1:23 and that has been proclaimed to **every** creature under heaven,
1:28 admonishing **[RPG]** and teaching everyone with all wisdom,
1:28 admonishing and teaching **everyone** [+476] with all wisdom,
1:28 admonishing and teaching everyone with **all** wisdom,
1:28 so that we may present **everyone** [+476] perfect in Christ.
2: 2 so that they may have the **full** riches of complete understanding,
2: 3 in whom are hidden **all** the treasures of wisdom and knowledge.
2: 9 For in Christ **all** the fullness of the Deity lives in bodily form,
2:10 fullness in Christ, who is the head *over* **every** power and authority.
2:13 God made you alive with Christ. He forgave us **all** our sins,
2:19 from whom the **whole** body, supported and held together by its
2:22 These are **all** destined to perish with use, because they are based on
3: 8 But now you must rid yourselves of **all** [+3836] *such* **things** as
3:11 barbarian, Scythian, slave or free, but Christ is **all** [+3836],
3:11 barbarian, Scythian, slave or free, but Christ is all, and is in **all**.
3:14 And over **all** these virtues put on love, which binds them all
3:16 richly as you teach and admonish one another with **all** wisdom,
3:17 And **[RPG]** whatever you do, whether in word or deed, do it all in
3:17 whether in word or deed, do it **all** in the name of the Lord Jesus,
3:20 Children, obey your parents in **everything**, for this pleases the
3:22 Slaves, obey your earthly masters in **everything**; and do it,
4: 7 Tychicus will tell you **all** the news about me. He is a dear brother,
4: 9 is one of you. They will tell you **everything** that is happening here.
4:12 that you may stand firm in **all** the will of God, mature and fully
1Th 1: 2 We always thank God for **all** of you, mentioning you in our
1: 7 And so you became a model *to* **all** the believers in Macedonia.
1: 8 your faith in God has become known **everywhere** [+1877+5536].
2:15 also drove us out. They displease God and are hostile *to* **all** men
3: 7 in **all** our distress and persecution we were encouraged about you
3: 9 How can we thank God enough for you in return for **all** the joy we
3:12 love increase and overflow for each other and for **everyone** *else*,
3:13 and Father when our Lord Jesus comes with **all** his holy ones.
4: 6 The Lord will punish men for **all** such sins, as we have already told
4:10 And in fact, you do love **all** the brothers throughout Macedonia.
5: 5 You are **all** sons of the light and sons of the day. We do not belong
5:14 encourage the timid, help the weak, be patient with **everyone**.
5:15 but always try to be kind to each other and to **everyone** *else*.
5:18 give thanks in **all** *circumstances*, for this is God's will for you in
5:21 Test **everything**. Hold on to the good.
5:22 Avoid **every** kind of evil.
5:26 Greet **all** the brothers with a holy kiss.

5:27 I charge you before the Lord to have this letter read *to* **all** the
2Th 1: 3 and the love every one of you **[RPG]** has for each other is
1: 4 and faith in **all** the persecutions and trials you are enduring.
1:10 and to be marveled at among **all** those who have believed.
1:11 and that by his power he may fulfill **every** good purpose of yours
2: 4 and will exalt himself over **everything** that is called God
2: 9 the work of Satan displayed in **all** *kinds of* counterfeit miracles,
2:10 and in **every** *sort* of evil that deceives those who are perishing.
2:12 so that **all** will be condemned who have not believed the truth
2:17 your hearts and strengthen you in **every** good deed and word.
3: 2 be delivered from wicked and evil men, for not **everyone** has faith.
3: 6 to keep away from **every** brother who is idle and does not live
3:16 Now may the Lord of peace himself give you peace at **all** *times*
3:16 of peace himself give you peace at all times and in **every** way.
3:16 peace at all times and in every way. The Lord be with **all** of you.
3:17 in my own hand, which is the distinguishing mark in **all** my letters.
3:18 The grace of our Lord Jesus Christ be with you **all**.
1Ti 1:15 Here is a trustworthy saying that deserves **full** acceptance:
2: 1 I urge, then, first *of* **all**, that requests, prayers, intercession
2: 1 intercession and thanksgiving be made for **everyone** [+476]—
2: 2 for kings and **all** those in authority, that we may live peaceful
2: 2 we may live peaceful and quiet lives in **all** godliness and holiness.
2: 4 who wants **all** men to be saved and to come to a knowledge of the
2: 6 who gave himself as a ransom for **all** *men*—the testimony given in
2: 8 I want men **everywhere** [+1877+5536] to lift up holy hands in
2:11 A woman should learn in quietness and **full** submission.
3: 4 and see that his children obey him with **proper** respect.
3:11 not malicious talkers but temperate and trustworthy in **everything**.
4: 4 For **everything** God created is good, and nothing is to be rejected
4: 8 training is of some value, but godliness has value for **all** *things*,
4: 9 This is a trustworthy saying that deserves **full** acceptance
4:10 who is the Savior *of* **all** men, and especially of those who believe.
4:15 yourself wholly to them, so that **everyone** may see your progress.
5: 2 as mothers, and younger women as sisters, with **absolute** purity.
5:10 those in trouble and devoting herself *to* **all** *kinds* of good deeds.
5:20 Those who sin are to be rebuked **publicly** [+1967], so that the
6: 1 of slavery should consider their masters worthy *of* **full** respect,
6:10 For the love of money is a root *of* **all** *kinds* of evil. Some people,
6:13 In the sight of God, who gives life to **everything** [+3836],
6:17 who richly provides us with **everything** for our enjoyment.
2Ti 1:15 You know that **everyone** in the province of Asia has deserted me,
2: 7 what I am saying, for the Lord will give you insight into **all** *this*.
2:10 Therefore I endure **everything** for the sake of the elect, that they
2:19 "**Everyone** who confesses the name of the Lord must turn away
2:21 made holy, useful to the Master and prepared to do **any** good work.
2:24 instead, he must be kind to **everyone**, able to teach, not resentful.
3: 9 as in the case of those men, their folly will be clear *to* **everyone**.
3:11 persecutions I endured. Yet the Lord rescued me from **all** *of them*.
3:12 **everyone** who wants to live a godly life in Christ Jesus will be
3:16 **All** Scripture is God-breathed and is useful for teaching, rebuking,
3:17 so that the man of God may be thoroughly equipped for **every**
4: 2 with **great** patience [+3429] and careful instruction.
4: 5 But you, keep your head in **all** *situations*, endure hardship,
4: 8 not only to me, but also *to* **all** who have longed for his appearing.
4:16 no one came to my support, but **everyone** deserted me.
4:17 might be fully proclaimed and **all** the Gentiles might hear it.
4:18 The Lord will rescue me from **every** evil attack and will bring me
4:21 greets you, and so do Pudens, Linus, Claudia and **all** the brothers.
Tit 1:15 To the pure, **all** *things* are pure, but to those who are corrupted
1:16 are detestable, disobedient and unfit for doing **anything** good.
2: 7 In **everything** set them an example by doing what is good.
2: 9 Teach slaves to be subject to their masters in **everything**, to try to
2:10 to steal from them, but to show that they can be **fully** [+19] trusted,
2:10 so that in **every** *way* they will make the teaching about God our
2:11 For the grace of God that brings salvation has appeared *to* **all** men.
2:14 who gave himself for us to redeem us from **all** wickedness
2:15 Encourage and rebuke with **all** authority. Do not let anyone despise
3: 1 and authorities, to be obedient, to be ready to do **whatever** is good,
3: 2 and considerate, and to show **true** humility toward all men.
3: 2 and considerate, and to show true humility toward **all** men.
3:15 **Everyone** with me sends you greetings. Greet those who love us in
3:15 Greet those who love us in the faith. Grace be with you **all**.
Phm 1: 5 about your faith in the Lord Jesus and your love for **all** the saints.
1: 6 so that you will have a **full** understanding *of* **every** good thing we
Heb 1: 2 whom he appointed heir *of* **all** *things*, and through whom he made
1: 3 of his being, sustaining **all** [+3836] **things** by his powerful word.

1: 6 into the world, he says, "Let **all** God's angels worship him."
1: 11 will perish, but you remain; they will **all** wear out like a garment.
1: 14 Are not **all** angels ministering spirits sent to serve those who will
2: 2 and **every** violation and disobedience received its just punishment,
2: 8 put **everything** under his feet." In putting everything under him,
2: 8 In putting **everything** [+3836] under him, God left nothing that is
2: 8 Yet at present we do not see **everything** [+3836] subject to him.
2: 9 so that by the grace of God he might taste death for **everyone**.
2: 10 that God, for whom and through whom **[RPG]** everything exists,
2: 10 that God, for whom and through whom **everything** [+3836] exists,
2: 11 and those who are made holy **[RPG]** are of the same family.
2: 15 and free those who **all** their lives were held in slavery by their fear
2: 17 For this reason he had to be made like his brothers in **every** way,
3: 4 For **every** house is built by someone, but God is the builder of
3: 4 house is built by someone, but God is the builder *of* **everything**.
3: 16 and rebelled? Were they not **all** those Moses led out of Egypt?
4: 4 words: "And on the seventh day God rested from **all** his work."
4: 12 Sharper than **any** double-edged sword, it penetrates even to
4: 13 Nothing in all creation is hidden from God's sight **Everything** is
4: 15 but we have one who has been tempted in **every** way, just as we
5: 1 **Every** high priest is selected from among men and is appointed to
5: 9 he became the source of eternal salvation *for* **all** who obey him
5: 13 **Anyone** who lives on milk, being still an infant, is not acquainted
6: 16 and the oath confirms what is said and puts an end *to* **all** argument.
7: 2 and Abraham gave him a tenth of **everything**. First, his name
7: 7 And **without** [+6006] doubt the lesser person is blessed by the
8: 3 **Every** high priest is appointed to offer both gifts and sacrifices,
8: 5 "See to it that you make **everything** according to the pattern shown
8: 11 saying, 'Know the Lord,' because they will **all** know me,
9: 6 the priests entered **regularly** [+1328] into the outer room to carry
9: 19 When Moses had proclaimed **every** commandment of the law to all
9: 19 When Moses had proclaimed **every** commandment of the law *to* **all**
9: 19 and branches of hyssop, and sprinkled the scroll and **all** the people.
9: 21 tabernacle and **everything** [+3836+5007] used in its ceremonies.
9: 22 the law requires that nearly **everything** be cleansed with blood,
10: 11 Day after day **every** priest stands and performs his religious duties;
11: 13 **All** these people were still living by faith when they died. They did
11: 39 These were **all** commended for their faith, yet none of them
12: 1 let us throw off **everything** that hinders and the sin that so easily
12: 6 those he loves, and he punishes **everyone** he accepts as a son."
12: 8 If you are not disciplined (and **everyone** undergoes discipline),
12: 11 **No** [+4024] discipline seems pleasant at the time, but painful.
12: 14 Make **every** effort to live in peace with **all** *men* and to be holy;
12: 23 You have come to God, the judge of **all** *men*, to the spirits of
13: 4 Marriage should be honored by **all**, and the marriage bed kept pure,
13: 15 let us **continually** [+1328] offer to God a sacrifice of praise—
13: 18 have a clear conscience and desire to live honorably in **every** way.
13: 21 equip you with **everything** good for doing his will, and may he
13: 24 Greet **all** your leaders and all God's people. Those from Italy send
13: 24 Greet all your leaders and **all** God's people. Those from Italy send
13: 25 Grace be with you **all**.

Jas 1: 2 Consider it **pure** joy, my brothers, whenever you face trials of
1: 5 should ask God, who gives generously *to* **all** without finding fault,
1: 8 he is a double-minded man, unstable in **all** he does.
1: 17 **Every** good and perfect gift is from above, coming down from the
1: 17 Every good and **[RPG]** perfect gift is from above, coming down
1: 19 **Everyone** [+476] should be quick to listen, slow to speak
1: 21 get rid of **all** moral filth and the evil that is so prevalent
2: 10 and yet stumbles at just one point is guilty *of* breaking **all** of it.
3: 7 **All** kinds of animals, birds, reptiles and creatures of the sea are
3: 16 selfish ambition, there you find disorder and **every** evil practice.
4: 16 As it is, you boast and brag. **All** such boasting is evil.
5: 12 Above **all**, my brothers, do not swear—not by heaven or by earth

1Pe 1: 15 But just as he who called you is holy, so be holy in **all** you do;
1: 24 For, "**All** men are like grass, and all their glory is like the flowers
1: 24 are like grass, and **all** their glory is like the flowers of the field;
2: 1 Therefore, rid yourselves of **all** malice and all deceit, hypocrisy,
2: 1 Therefore, rid yourselves of all malice and **all** deceit, hypocrisy,
2: 1 and all deceit, hypocrisy, envy, and slander of **every** *kind*.
2: 13 Submit yourselves for the Lord's sake *to* **every** authority instituted
2: 17 Show proper respect to **everyone**: Love the brotherhood of
2: 18 Slaves, submit yourselves to your masters with **all** respect,
3: 8 Finally, **all** of you, live in harmony with one another;
3: 15 Always be prepared to give an answer *to* **everyone** who asks you
4: 7 The end *of* **all** *things* is near. Therefore be clear minded
4: 8 Above **all**, love each other deeply, because love covers over a

4: 11 so that in **all** *things* God may be praised through Jesus Christ.
5: 5 **All** of you, clothe yourselves with humility toward one another,
5: 7 Cast **all** your anxiety on him because he cares for you.
5: 10 And the God *of* **all** grace, who called you to his eternal glory in
5: 14 another with a kiss of love. Peace *to* **all** *of* you who are in Christ.

2Pe 1: 3 His divine power has given us **everything** we need for life
1: 5 this very reason, make **every** effort to add to your faith goodness;
1: 20 you must understand that **no** [+4024] prophecy of Scripture came
3: 4 **everything** goes on as it has since the beginning of creation."
3: 9 not wanting anyone to perish, but **everyone** to come to repentance.
3: 11 Since **everything** will be destroyed in this way, what kind of
3: 16 He writes the same way in **all** his letters, speaking in them of these

1Jn 1: 7 and the blood of Jesus, his Son, purifies us from **all** sin.
1: 9 and will forgive us our sins and purify us from **all** unrighteousness.
2: 16 For **everything** in the world—the cravings of sinful man, the lust
2: 19 but their going showed that **none** *of* them [+4024] belonged to us.
2: 20 an anointing from the Holy One, and **all** of you know the truth.
2: 21 you do know it and because **no** [+4024] lie comes from the truth.
2: 23 **No** [+4028] one who denies the Son has the Father;
2: 27 But as his anointing teaches you about **all** *things* and as that
2: 29 you know that **everyone** who does what is right has been born of
3: 3 **Everyone** who has this hope in him purifies himself, just as he is
3: 4 **Everyone** who sins breaks the law; in fact, sin is lawlessness.
3: 6 No **one** who lives in him keeps on sinning. No one who continues
3: 6 No **one** who continues to sin has either seen him or known him.
3: 9 No **one** who is born of God will continue to sin, because God's
3: 10 **Anyone** who does not do what is right is not a child of God;
3: 15 **Anyone** who hates his brother is a murderer, and you know that no
3: 15 and you know that **no** [+4024] murderer has eternal life in him.
3: 20 For God is greater than our hearts, and he knows **everything**.
4: 1 Dear friends, do not believe **every** spirit, but test the spirits to see
4: 2 **Every** spirit that acknowledges that Jesus Christ has come in the
4: 3 but **every** spirit that does not acknowledge Jesus is not from God.
4: 7 **Everyone** who loves has been born of God and knows God.
5: 1 **Everyone** who believes that Jesus is the Christ is born of God,
5: 1 and **everyone** who loves the father loves his child as well.
5: 4 for **everyone** born of God overcomes the world. This is the victory
5: 17 **All** wrongdoing is sin, and there is sin that does not lead to death.
5: 18 We know that **anyone** born of God does not continue to sin;

2Jn 1: 1 I love in the truth—and not I only, but also **all** who know the truth—
1: 9 **Anyone** who runs ahead and does not continue in the teaching of

3Jn 1: 2 that you may enjoy good health and that **all** may go well with you,
1: 12 Demetrius is well spoken of by **everyone**—and even by the truth

Jude 1: 3 although I was **very** eager to write to you about the salvation we
1: 5 Though you already know **all** *this*, I want to remind you that the
1: 15 to judge **everyone** [+2848], and to convict all the ungodly of all the
1: 15 and to convict **all** the ungodly of all the ungodly acts they have
1: 15 and to convict all the ungodly of **all** the ungodly acts they have
1: 15 and of **all** the harsh words ungodly sinners have spoken against
1: 25 Jesus Christ our Lord, before **all** ages, now and forevermore!
1: 25 before all ages, now and **forevermore** [+172+1650+3836]!

Rev 1: 7 and **every** eye will see him, even those who pierced him;
1: 7 and **all** the peoples of the earth will mourn because of him.
2: 23 Then **all** the churches will know that I am he who searches hearts
4: 11 and honor and power, for you created **all** [+3836] things,
5: 6 which are the seven spirits of God sent out into **all** the earth.
5: 9 and with your blood you purchased men for God from **every** tribe
5: 13 Then I heard **every** creature in heaven and on earth and under the
5: 13 and under the earth and on the sea, and **all** that is in them, singing:
6: 14 and **every** mountain and island was removed from its place.
6: 15 and **every** slave and every free man hid in caves and among the
7: 1 any wind from blowing on the land or on the sea or on **any** tree.
7: 4 of those who were sealed: 144,000 from **all** the tribes of Israel.
7: 9 from **every** nation, tribe, people and language, standing before the
7: 11 **All** the angels were standing around the throne and around the
7: 16 The sun will not beat upon them, nor **any** scorching heat.
7: 17 living water. And God will wipe away **every** tear from their eyes."
8: 3 was given much incense to offer, with the prayers *of* **all** the saints,
8: 7 of the trees were burned up, and **all** the green grass was burned up.
9: 4 were told not to harm the grass of the earth or **any** plant or tree,
9: 4 told not to harm the grass of the earth or any plant or **[RPG]** tree,
11: 6 and to strike the earth with **every** *kind* of plague as often as they
12: 5 a male child, who will rule **all** the nations with an iron scepter.
13: 7 And he was given authority over **every** tribe, people, language
13: 8 **All** inhabitants of the earth will worship the beast—all whose
13: 12 He exercised **all** the authority of the first beast on his behalf,

13:16 He also forced **everyone**, small and great, rich and poor, free
14: 6 who live on the earth—to **every** nation, tribe, language and people.
14: 8 which made **all** the nations drink the maddening wine of her
15: 4 **All** nations will come and worship before you, for your righteous
16: 3 like that of a dead man, and **every** living thing in the sea died.
16:20 **Every** island fled away and the mountains could not be found.
18: 2 has become a home for demons and a haunt *for* **every** evil spirit,
18: 2 for every evil spirit, a haunt *for* **every** unclean and detestable bird.
18: 2 bird [UBS+ *a haunt for every unclean and detestable beast.*]
18: 3 For **all** the nations have drunk the maddening wine of her
18:12 **every** *sort* of citron wood, and articles of every kind made of
18:12 and articles of **every** *kind* made of ivory, costly wood, bronze,
18:12 kind made of ivory, **[RPG]** costly wood, bronze, iron and marble;
18:14 **All** your riches and splendor have vanished, never to be
18:17 "**Every** sea captain, and all who travel by ship, the sailors,
18:17 "Every sea captain, and **all** who travel by ship, the sailors, and all
18:19 where **all** who had ships on the sea became rich through her
18:22 No **[RPG]** workman of any trade will ever be found in you again.
18:22 No workman *of* **any** trade will ever be found in you again.
18:23 great men. By your magic spell **all** the nations were led astray.
18:24 and of the saints, and *of* **all** who have been killed on the earth."
19: 5 "Praise our God, **all** you his servants, you who fear him, both small
19:17 who cried in a loud voice *to* **all** the birds flying in midair,
19:18 and the flesh of **all** *people*, frcc and slave, small and great."
19:21 on the horse, and **all** the birds gorged themselves on their flesh.
21: 4 He will wipe **every** tear from their eyes. There will be no more
21: 5 who was seated on the throne said, "I am making **everything** new!"
21: 8 those who practice magic arts, the idolaters and **all** liars—
21:19 The foundations of the city walls were decorated *with* **every** kind
21:27 enter it, nor will **anyone** who does what is shameful or deceitful,
22: 3 No longer will there be **any** curse. The throne of God and of the
22:15 the idolaters and **everyone** who loves and practices falsehood.
22:18 I warn **everyone** who hears the words of the prophecy of this book:
22:21 the Lord Jesus be with **God's** people. [UBS *be with all.*; NIV *41*]

4247 πάσχα, *pascha* [29]

Passover [25], Passover lamb [3], Passover Week [1]

Mt 26: 2 "As you know, the **Passover** is two days away—and the Son of
    26:17 do you want us to make preparations for you to eat the **Passover**?"
    26:18 I am going to celebrate the **Passover** with my disciples at your
    26:19 did as Jesus had directed them and prepared the **Passover**.
Mk 14: 1 Now the **Passover** and the Feast of Unleavened Bread were only
    14:12 when it was customary to sacrifice the **Passover lamb**,
    14:12 want us to go and make preparations for you to eat the **Passover**?"
    14:14 my guest room, where I may eat the **Passover** with my disciples?'
    14:16 things just as Jesus had told them. So they prepared the **Passover**.
Lk 2:41 year his parents went to Jerusalem for the Feast *of* the **Passover**.
    22: 1 Feast of Unleavened Bread, called the **Passover**, was approaching,
    22: 7 Bread on which the **Passover lamb** had to be sacrificed.
    22: 8 saying, "Go and make preparations for us to eat the **Passover**."
    22:11 the guest room, where I may eat the **Passover** with my disciples?'
    22:13 things just as Jesus had told them. So they prepared the **Passover**.
    22:15 "I have eagerly desired to eat this **Passover** with you before I suffer.
Jn 2:13 When it was almost time *for* the Jewish **Passover**, Jesus went up to
    2:23 Now while he was in Jerusalem at the **Passover** Feast,
    6: 4 The Jewish **Passover** Feast was near.
    11:55 When it was almost time *for* the Jewish **Passover**, many went up
    11:55 to Jerusalem for their ceremonial cleansing before the **Passover**.
    12: 1 Six days before the **Passover**, Jesus arrived at Bethany,
    13: 1 It was just before the **Passover** Feast. Jesus knew that the time had
    18:28 not enter the palace; they wanted to be able to eat the **Passover**.
    18:39 for me to release to you one prisoner at the time of the **Passover**.
    19:14 It was the day of Preparation *of* **Passover Week**, about the sixth
Ac 12: 4 Herod intended to bring him out for public trial after the **Passover**.
1Co 5: 7 you really are. For Christ, our **Passover lamb**, has been sacrificed.
Heb 11:28 By faith he kept the **Passover** and the sprinkling of blood,

4248 πάσχω, *paschō* [42 / 41] [→ *2801, 2802, 3584,*
3926, 4077, 4078, 4079, 4557, 4634, 5155, 5217, 5218, 5224]

suffer [21], suffered [14], suffering [5], suffers [1]

Mt 16:21 go to Jerusalem and **suffer** many things at the hands of the elders,
    17:12 In the same way the Son of Man is going to **suffer** at their hands."

17:15 on my son," he said. "He has seizures and *is* **suffering** greatly.
    27:19 for *I have* **suffered** a great deal today in a dream because of him."
Mk 5:26 *She had* **suffered** a great deal under the care of many doctors
    8:31 then began to teach them that the Son of Man must **suffer** many
    9:12 Why then is it written that the Son of Man *must* **suffer** much
Lk 9:22 "The Son of Man must **suffer** many things and be rejected by the
    13: 2 than all the other Galileans because *they* **suffered** this way?
    17:25 But first he must **suffer** many things and be rejected by this
    22:15 "I have eagerly desired to eat this Passover with you before I **suffer**.
    24:26 Did not the Christ have to **suffer** these things and then enter his
    24:46 The Christ *will* **suffer** and rise from the dead on the third day,
Ac 1: 3 After his **suffering**, he showed himself to these men and gave
    3:18 through all the prophets, saying that his Christ *would* **suffer**.
    9:16 I will show him how much he must **suffer** for my name."
    17: 3 explaining and proving that the Christ had to **suffer** and rise from
    28: 5 Paul shook the snake off into the fire and **suffered** no ill effects.
1Co 12:26 If one part **suffers**, every part suffers with it; if one part is honored,
2Co 1: 6 in you patient endurance of the same sufferings we **suffer**.
Gal 3: 4 *Have you* **suffered** so much for nothing—if it really was for
Php 1:29 of Christ not only to believe on him, but also *to* **suffer** for him,
1Th 2:14 You **suffered** from your own countrymen the same things those
2Th 1: 5 worthy of the kingdom of God, for which *you are* **suffering**
2Ti 1:12 That is why *I am* **suffering** as I am. Yet I am not ashamed,
Heb 2:18 Because *he* himself **suffered** when he was tempted, he is able to
    5: 8 he was a son, he learned obedience from what *he* **suffered**
    9:26 Then Christ would have had to **suffer** many times since the
    13:12 so Jesus also **suffered** outside the city gate to make the people holy
1Pe 2:19 commendable if a man bears up under the pain *of* unjust **suffering**
    2:20 But if *you* **suffer** for doing good and you endure it, this is
    2:21 To this you were called, because Christ **suffered** for you,
    2:23 he did not retaliate; *when he* **suffered**, he made no threats.
    3:14 But even if *you should* **suffer** for what is right, you are blessed.
    3:17 if it is God's will, *to* **suffer** for doing good than for doing evil.
    3:18 For Christ *died* [UBS *suffered*; NIV *633*] for sins once for all,
    4: 1 Therefore, *since* Christ **suffered** in his body, arm yourselves also
    4: 1 because he *who has* **suffered** in his body is done with sin.
    4:15 If you **suffer**, it should not be as a murderer or thief or any other
    4:19 those *who* **suffer** according to God's will should commit
    5:10 *after you have* **suffered** a little while, will himself restore you
Rev 2:10 Do not be afraid of what you are about to **suffer**. I tell you,

4249 Πάταρα, *Patara* [1]

Patara [1]

Ac 21: 1 The next day we went to Rhodes and from there to **Patara**.

4250 πατάσσω, *patassō* [10]

strike [4], struck [3], killing [1], strike down [1], struck down [1]

Mt 26:31 " '*I will* **strike** the shepherd, and the sheep of the flock will be
    26:51 drew it out and **struck** the servant of the high priest, cutting off his
Mk 14:27 " '*I will* **strike** the shepherd, and the sheep will be scattered.'
Lk 22:49 to happen, they said, "Lord, *should we* **strike** with our swords?"
    22:50 And one of them **struck** the servant of the high priest, cutting off
Ac 7:24 so he went to his defense and avenged him *by* **killing** the Egyptian
    12: 7 He **struck** Peter on the side and woke him up. "Quick, get up!"
    12:23 an angel of the Lord **struck** him **down**, and he was eaten by worms
Rev 11: 6 and *to* **strike** the earth with every kind of plague as often as they
    19:15 Out of his mouth comes a sharp sword with which to **strike down**

4251 πατέω, *pateō* [5] [→ *1853, 2922, 4344*]

trample on [1], trample [1], trampled on [1], trampled [1], treads
[1]

Lk 10:19 I have given you authority *to* **trample** on snakes and scorpions
    21:24 Jerusalem will be **trampled on** by the Gentiles until the times of
Rev 11: 2 to the Gentiles. *They will* **trample on** the holy city for 42 months.
    14:20 *They were* **trampled** in the winepress outside the city, and blood
    19:15 He **treads** the winepress of the fury of the wrath of God Almighty.

4252 πατήρ, **patēr** [413] [→ *525, 526, 574, 3093, 4254, 4255, 4256, 4257, 4258, 4259, 4260, 4261, 4262, 4635, 5396, 5399*]

human father[s] [153] Mt 2:22; 3:9; 4:21,22; 8:21; 10:21,35,37; 15:4,4,5,6; 19:5,19,29; 21:31; 23:9,30,32; Mk 1:20; 5:40; 7:10,10, 11,12; 9:21,24; 10:7,19,29; 11:10; 13:12; 15:21; Lk 1:17,32,55,59, 62,67,72,73; 2:33,48; 3:8; 6:23,26; 8:51; 9:42,59; 11:11,47,48; 12:53,53; 14:26; 15:12,12,17,18,18,20,20,21,22,27,28,29; 16:24, 27,27,30; 18:20; Jn 4:12,20,53; 6:31,42,49,58; 7:22; 8:19,38,39, 41,44,44,44,53,56; Ac 3:13,25; 4:25; 5:30; 7:2,2,4,11,12,14,15, 19,20,32,38,39,44,45,45,51,52; 13:17,32,36; 15:10; 16:1,3; 22:1, 14; 26:6; 28:8,25; Ro 4:11,12,12,16,17,18; 9:5,10; 11:28; 15:8; 1Co 4:15; 5:1; 10:1; Gal 4:2; Eph 5:31; 6:2,4; Php 2:22; Col 3:21; 1Th 2:11; 1Ti 5:1; Heb 1:1; 3:9; 7:10; 8:9; 11:23; 12:7,9; Jas 2:21; 2Pe 3:4; 1Jn 2:13,14

τὸ θέλημα τοῦ πατρός (the will of the Father) [5] Mt 7:21; 12:50; 21:31; Jn 6:40; Gal 1:4

θεός [καὶ] πατήρ (God [and] Father) [42] Jn 6:27; 8:42; Ro 1:7; 15:6; 1Co 1:3; 8:6; 15:24; 2Co 1:2,3; 11:31; Gal 1:1,3,4; Eph 1:2,3; 4:6; 5:20; 6:23; Php 1:2; 2:11; 4:20; Col 1:2,3; 3:17; 1Th 1:1,3; 3:11,13; 2Th 1:1,2; 2:16; 1Ti 1:2; 2Ti 1:2; Tit 1:4; Phm 1:3; Jas 1:27; 1Pe 1:2,3; 2Pe 1:17; 2Jn 1:3; Jude 1:1; Rev 1:6

οὐράνιος πατήρ (heavenly Father) [7] Mt 5:48; 6:14,26,32; 15:13; 18:35; 23:9

father [336], fathers [35], father's [21], forefathers [13], patriarchs [4], ancestor [2], parents [1], thems [+*1609+3836*] [1]

Mt	2:22	that Archelaus was reigning in Judea in place of his **father** Herod,
	3: 9	think you can say to yourselves, 'We have Abraham as our **father**.'
	4:21	They were in a boat with their **father** Zebedee, preparing their
	4:22	immediately they left the boat and their **father** and followed him.
	5:16	they may see your good deeds and praise your **Father** in heaven.
	5:45	that you may be sons *of* your **Father** in heaven. He causes his sun
	5:48	Be perfect, therefore, as your heavenly **Father** is perfect.
	6: 1	If you do, you will have no reward from your **Father** in heaven.
	6: 4	Then your **Father**, who sees what is done in secret, will reward
	6: 6	your room, close the door and pray *to* your **Father**, who is unseen.
	6: 6	Then your **Father**, who sees what is done in secret, will reward
	6: 8	for your **Father** knows what you need before you ask him.
	6: 9	you should pray: " 'Our **Father** in heaven, hallowed be your name,
	6:14	they sin against you, your heavenly **Father** will also forgive you.
	6:15	not forgive men their sins, your **Father** will not forgive your sins.
	6:18	men that you are fasting, but only *to* your **Father**, who is unseen;
	6:18	and your **Father**, who sees what is done in secret, will reward you.
	6:26	or store away in barns, and yet your heavenly **Father** feeds them.
	6:32	these things, and your heavenly **Father** knows that you need them.
	7:11	how much more will your **Father** in heaven give good gifts to
	7:21	but only he who does the will *of* my **Father** who is in heaven.
	8:21	disciple said to him, "Lord, first let me go and bury my **father**."
	10:20	you speaking, but the Spirit *of* your **Father** speaking through you.
	10:21	"Brother will betray brother to death, and a **father** his child;
	10:29	of them will fall to the ground apart from the will *of* your **Father**.
	10:32	I will also acknowledge him before my **Father** in heaven.
	10:33	me before men, I will disown him before my **Father** in heaven.
	10:35	For I have come to turn " 'a man against his **father**, a daughter
	10:37	"Anyone who loves his **father** or mother more than me is not
	11:25	time Jesus said, "I praise you, **Father**, Lord of heaven and earth,
	11:26	Yes, **Father**, for this was your good pleasure.
	11:27	"All things have been committed to me by my **Father**. No one
	11:27	No one knows the Son except the **Father**, and no one knows the
	11:27	and no one knows the **Father** except the Son and those to whom
	12:50	For whoever does the will *of* my **Father** in heaven is my brother
	13:43	righteous will shine like the sun in the kingdom *of* their **Father**.
	15: 4	'Honor your **father** and mother' and 'Anyone who curses his
	15: 4	your father and mother' and 'Anyone who curses his **father**
	15: 5	But you say that if a man says *to* his **father** or mother,
	15: 6	he is not to 'honor his **father**' with it. Thus you nullify the word of
	15:13	"Every plant that my heavenly **Father** has not planted will be
	16:17	this was not revealed to you by man, but *by* my **Father** in heaven.
	16:27	For the Son of Man is going to come in his **Father's** glory with his
	18:10	their angels in heaven always see the face *of* my **Father** in heaven.
	18:14	In the same way your **Father** in heaven is not willing that any of
	18:19	you ask for, it will be done for you by my **Father** in heaven.
	18:35	"This is how my heavenly **Father** will treat each of you unless you
	19: 5	'For this reason a man will leave his **father** and mother and be
	19:19	honor your **father** and mother,' and 'love your neighbor as
	19:29	left houses or brothers or sisters or **father** or mother or children
	20:23	belong to those for whom they have been prepared by my **Father**."
	21:31	"Which of the two did what his **father** wanted?" "The first,"
	23: 9	And do not call anyone on earth 'father,' for you have one Father,
	23: 9	on earth 'father,' for you have one **Father**, and he is in heaven.
	23:30	And you say, 'If we had lived in the days *of* our **forefathers**,
	23:32	Fill up, then, the measure of the sin *of* your **forefathers**!
	24:36	not even the angels in heaven, nor the Son, but only the **Father**.
	25:34	to those on his right, 'Come, you who are blessed *by* my **Father**;
	26:29	that day when I drink it anew with you in my **Father's** kingdom."
	26:39	He fell with his face to the ground and prayed, "My **Father**,
	26:42	He went away a second time and prayed, "My **Father**, if it is not
	26:53	Do you think I cannot call on my **Father**, and he will at once put at
	28:19	baptizing them in the name *of* the **Father** and of the Son and of the
Mk	1:20	and they left their **father** Zebedee in the boat with the hired men
	5:40	he took the child's **father** and mother and the disciples who were
	7:10	For Moses said, 'Honor your **father** and your mother,' and,
	7:10	'Anyone who curses his **father** or mother must be put to death.'
	7:11	But you say that if a man says *to* his **father** or mother:
	7:12	then you no longer let him do anything *for* his **father** or mother.
	8:38	of him when he comes in his **Father's** glory with the holy angels."
	9:21	Jesus asked the boy's **father**, "How long has he been like this?"
	9:24	Immediately the boy's **father** exclaimed, "I do believe; help me
	10: 7	'For this reason a man will leave his **father** and mother and be
	10:19	false testimony, do not defraud, honor your **father** and mother.' "
	10:29	or brothers or sisters or mother or **father** or children or fields for
	11:10	"Blessed is the coming kingdom *of* our **father** David!" "Hosanna in
	11:25	so that your **Father** in heaven may forgive you your sins."
	13:12	"Brother will betray brother to death, and a **father** his child.
	13:32	not even the angels in heaven, nor the Son, but only the **Father**.
	14:36	*Abba*, **Father**," he said, "everything is possible for you. Take this
	15:21	man from Cyrene, Simon, the **father** of Alexander and Rufus,
Lk	1:17	to turn the hearts *of* the **fathers** to their children
	1:32	The Lord God will give him the throne *of* his **father** David,
	1:55	and his descendants forever, even as he said to our **fathers**."
	1:59	and they were going to name him after his **father** Zechariah,
	1:62	Then they made signs *to* his **father**, to find out what he would like
	1:67	His **father** Zechariah was filled with the Holy Spirit
	1:72	to show mercy to our **fathers** and to remember his holy covenant,
	1:73	the oath he swore to our **father** Abraham:
	2:33	The child's **father** and mother marveled at what was said about
	2:48	Your **father** and I have been anxiously searching for you."
	2:49	he asked. "Didn't you know I had to be in my **Father's** house?"
	3: 8	not begin to say to yourselves, 'We have Abraham as our **father**.'
	6:23	in heaven. For that is how their **fathers** treated the prophets.
	6:26	well of you, for that is how their **fathers** treated the false prophets.
	6:36	Be merciful, just as your **Father** is merciful.
	8:51	except Peter, John and James, and the child's **father** and mother.
	9:26	in his glory and in the glory *of* the **Father** and of the holy angels.
	9:42	the evil spirit, healed the boy and gave him back *to* his **father**.
	9:59	But the man replied, "Lord, first let me go and bury my **father**."
	10:21	Holy Spirit, said, "I praise you, **Father**, Lord of heaven and earth,
	10:21	to little children. Yes, **Father**, for this was your good pleasure.
	10:22	"All things have been committed to me by my **Father**. No one
	10:22	No one knows who the Son is except the **Father**, and no one
	10:22	and no one knows who the **Father** is except the Son and those to
	11: 2	" 'Father, hallowed be your name, your kingdom come.
	11:11	"Which of you **fathers**, if your son asks for a fish, will give him a
	11:13	how much more will your **Father** in heaven give the Holy Spirit to
	11:47	for the prophets, and it was your **forefathers** who killed them.
	11:48	So you testify that you approve of what your **forefathers** did;
	12:30	after all such things, and your **Father** knows that you need them.
	12:32	for your **Father** has been pleased to give you the kingdom.
	12:53	They will be divided, **father** against son and son against father,
	12:53	They will be divided, father against son and son against **father**,
	14:26	"If anyone comes to me and does not hate his **father** and mother,
	15:12	The younger one said *to* his **father**, 'Father, give me my share of
	15:12	one said to his father, '**Father**, give me my share of the estate.'
	15:17	'How many *of* my **father's** hired men have food to spare,
	15:18	I will set out and go back to my **father** and say to him: Father,
	15:18	say to him: **Father**, I have sinned against heaven and against you.
	15:20	So he got up and went to his **father**. "But while he was still a long
	15:20	his **father** saw him and was filled with compassion for him;

15:21 "The son said to him, 'Father, I have sinned against heaven
15:22 "But the father said to his servants, 'Quick! Bring the best robe
15:27 'and your father has killed the fattened calf because he has him
15:28 and refused to go in. So his father went out and pleaded with him.
15:29 But he answered his father, 'Look! All these years I've been
16:24 'Father Abraham, have pity on me and send Lazarus to dip the tip
16:27 "He answered, 'Then I beg you, father, send Lazarus to my father's
16:27 'Then I beg you, father, send Lazarus to my father's house,
16:30 " 'No, father Abraham,' he said, 'but if someone from the dead
18:20 do not give false testimony, honor your father and mother.' "
22:29 confer on you a kingdom, just as my Father conferred one on me,
22:42 "Father, if you are willing, take this cup from me; yet not my will,
23:34 Jesus said, "Father, forgive them, for they do not know what they
23:46 Jesus called out with a loud voice, "Father, into your hands I
24:49 I am going to send you what my Father has promised; but stay in
Jn 1:14 the glory of the One and Only, who came from the Father,
1:18 but God the One and Only, who is at the Father's side, has made
2:16 out of here! How dare you turn my Father's house into a market!"
3:35 The Father loves the Son and has placed everything in his hands.
4:12 Are you greater than our father Jacob, who gave us the well
4:20 Our fathers worshiped on this mountain, but you Jews claim that
4:21 a time is coming when you will worship the Father neither on this
4:23 come when the true worshipers will worship the Father in spirit
4:23 and truth, for they are the kind of worshipers the Father seeks.
4:53 the father realized that this was the exact time at which Jesus
5:17 said to them, "My Father is always at his work to this very day,
5:18 but he was even calling God his own Father, making himself
5:19 he can do only what he sees his Father doing, because whatever
5:20 For the Father loves the Son and shows him all he does. Yes,
5:21 For just as the Father raises the dead and gives them life,
5:22 Moreover, the Father judges no one, but has entrusted all
5:23 that all may honor the Son just as they honor the Father. He who
5:23 He who does not honor the Son does not honor the Father,
5:26 For as the Father has life in himself, so he has granted the Son to
5:36 of John. For the very work that the Father has given me to finish,
5:36 and which I am doing, testifies that the Father has sent me.
5:37 And the Father who sent me has himself testified concerning me.
5:43 I have come in my Father's name, and you do not accept me;
5:45 "But do not think I will accuse you before the Father. Your accuser
6:27 give you. On him God the Father has placed his seal of approval."
6:31 Our forefathers ate the manna in the desert; as it is written:
6:32 but it is my Father who gives you the true bread from heaven.
6:37 All that the Father gives me will come to me, and whoever comes
6:40 For my Father's will is that everyone who looks to the Son
6:42 not Jesus, the son of Joseph, whose father and mother we know?
6:44 "No one can come to me unless the Father who sent me draws him,
6:45 Everyone who listens to the Father and learns from him comes to
6:46 No one has seen the Father except the one who is from God;
6:46 except the one who is from God; only he has seen the Father.
6:49 Your forefathers ate the manna in the desert, yet they died.
6:57 Just as the living Father sent me and I live because of the Father,
6:57 Just as the living Father sent me and I live because of the Father,
6:58 Your forefathers ate manna and died, but he who feeds on this
6:65 that no one can come to me unless the Father has enabled him."
7:22 but from the patriarchs), you circumcise a child on the Sabbath.
8:16 because I am not alone. I stand with the Father, who sent me.
8:18 testifies for myself; my other witness is the Father, who sent me."
8:19 Then they asked him, "Where is your father?" "You do not know
8:19 "You do not know me or my Father," Jesus replied. "If you knew
8:19 Jesus replied. "If you knew me, you would know my Father also."
8:27 They did not understand that he was telling them about his Father.
8:28 nothing on my own but speak just what the Father has taught me.
8:38 I am telling you what I have seen in the Father's presence,
8:38 and you do what you have heard from your father."
8:39 "Abraham is our father," they answered. "If you were Abraham's
8:41 You are doing the things your own father does." "We are not
8:41 they protested. "The only Father we have is God himself."
8:42 Jesus said to them, "If God were your Father, you would love me,
8:44 You belong to your father, the devil, and you want to carry out
8:44 the devil, and you want to carry out your father's desire.
8:44 he speaks his native language, for he is a liar and the father of lies.
8:49 a demon," said Jesus, "but I honor my Father and you dishonor me.
8:53 Are you greater than our father Abraham? He died, and so did the
8:54 My Father, whom you claim as your God, is the one who glorifies
8:56 Your father Abraham rejoiced at the thought of seeing my day;
10:15 just as the Father knows me and I know the Father—and I lay

10:15 just as the Father knows me and I know the Father—and I lay
10:17 The reason my Father loves me is that I lay down my life—
10:18 to take it up again. This command I received from my Father."
10:25 not believe. The miracles I do in my Father's name speak for me,
10:29 My Father, who has given them to me, is greater than all;
10:29 greater than all; no one can snatch them out of my Father's hand.
10:30 I and the Father are one."
10:32 to them, "I have shown you many great miracles from the Father.
10:36 what about the one whom the Father set apart as his very own
10:37 Do not believe me unless I do what my Father does.
10:38 that you may know and understand that the Father is in me,
10:38 and understand that the Father is in me, and I in the Father."
11:41 Then Jesus looked up and said, "Father, I thank you that you
12:26 servant also will be. My Father will honor the one who serves me.
12:27 'Father, save me from this hour'? No, it was for this very reason I
12:28 Father, glorify your name!" Then a voice came from heaven,
12:49 but the Father who sent me commanded me what to say and how
12:50 So whatever I say is just what the Father has told me to say."
13:1 time had come for him to leave this world and go to the Father.
13:3 Jesus knew that the Father had put all things under his power,
14:2 In my Father's house are many rooms; if it were not so, I would
14:6 and the life. No one comes to the Father except through me.
14:7 If you really knew me, you would know my Father as well.
14:8 "Lord, show us the Father and that will be enough for us."
14:9 Anyone who has seen me has seen the Father. How can you say,
14:9 me has seen the Father. How can you say, 'Show us the Father'?
14:10 Don't you believe that I am in the Father, and that the Father is in
14:10 you believe that I am in the Father, and that the Father is in me?
14:10 Rather, it is the Father, living in me, who is doing his work.
14:11 Believe me when I say that I am in the Father and the Father is in
14:11 me when I say that I am in the Father and the Father is in me;
14:12 even greater things than these, because I am going to the Father.
14:13 ask in my name, so that the Son may bring glory to the Father.
14:16 And I will ask the Father, and he will give you another Counselor
14:20 On that day you will realize that I am in my Father, and you are in
14:21 one who loves me. He who loves me will be loved by my Father,
14:23 My Father will love him, and we will come to him and make our
14:24 you hear are not my own; they belong to the Father who sent me.
14:26 the Holy Spirit, whom the Father will send in my name,
14:28 If you loved me, you would be glad that I am going to the Father,
14:28 glad that I am going to the Father, for the Father is greater than I.
14:31 but the world must learn that I love the Father and that I do
14:31 and that I do exactly what my Father has commanded me.
15:1 "I am the true vine, and my Father is the gardener.
15:8 This is to my Father's glory, that you bear much fruit, showing
15:9 "As the Father has loved me, so have I loved you. Now remain in
15:10 just as I have obeyed my Father's commands and remain in his
15:15 for everything that I learned from my Father I have made known
15:16 Then the Father will give you whatever you ask in my name.
15:23 He who hates me hates my Father as well.
15:24 these miracles, and yet they have hated both me and my Father.
15:26 the Counselor comes, whom I will send to you from the Father,
15:26 the Spirit of truth who goes out from the Father, he will testify
16:3 will do such things because they have not known the Father or me.
16:10 in regard to righteousness, because I am going to the Father,
16:15 All that belongs to the Father is mine. That is why I said the Spirit
16:17 while you will see me,' and 'Because I am going to the Father'?"
16:23 the truth, my Father will give you whatever you ask in my name.
16:25 this kind of language but will tell you plainly about my Father.
16:26 I am not saying that I will ask the Father on your behalf.
16:27 the Father himself loves you because you have loved me and have
16:28 I came from the Father and entered the world; now I am leaving
16:28 now I am leaving the world and going back to the Father."
16:32 leave me all alone. Yet I am not alone, for my Father is with me.
17:1 he looked toward heaven and prayed: "Father, the time has come.
17:5 And now, Father, glorify me in your presence with the glory I had
17:11 Holy Father, protect them by the power of your name—the name
17:21 them may be one, Father, just as you are in me and I am in you.
17:24 "Father, I want those you have given me to be with me where I
17:25 "Righteous Father, though the world does not know you, I know
18:11 sword away! Shall I not drink the cup the Father has given me?"
20:17 "Do not hold on to me, for I have not yet returned to the Father.
20:17 'I am returning to my Father and your Father, to my God
20:17 'I am returning to my Father and your Father, to my God
20:21 "Peace be with you! As the Father has sent me, I am sending you."
Ac 1:4 "Do not leave Jerusalem, but wait for the gift my Father promised,

1: 7 to know the times or dates the **Father** has set by his own authority.
2:33 he has received from the **Father** the promised Holy Spirit
3:13 The God of Abraham, Isaac and Jacob, the God *of* our **fathers**,
3:25 of the prophets and of the covenant God made with your **fathers**.
4:25 Holy Spirit through the mouth of your servant, our **father** David:
5:30 The God *of* our **fathers** raised Jesus from the dead—whom you
7: 2 To this he replied: "Brothers and **fathers**, listen to me! The God of
7: 2 The God of glory appeared *to* our **father** Abraham while he was
7: 4 After the death of his **father**, God sent him to this land where you
7:11 bringing great suffering, and our **fathers** could not find food.
7:12 there was grain in Egypt, he sent our **fathers** on their first visit.
7:14 After this, Joseph sent for his **father** Jacob and his whole family,
7:15 Then Jacob went down to Egypt, where he and our **fathers** died.
7:19 and oppressed our **forefathers** by forcing them to throw out their
7:20 For three months he was cared for in his **father's** house.
7:32 'I am the God *of* your **fathers**, the God of Abraham, Isaac
7:38 the angel who spoke to him on Mount Sinai, and *with* our **fathers**;
7:39 "But our **fathers** refused to obey him. Instead, they rejected him
7:44 "Our **forefathers** had the tabernacle of the Testimony with them in
7:45 our **fathers** under Joshua brought it with them when they took the
7:45 land from the nations God drove out before **them**⁵ [*+1609+3836*].
7:51 with uncircumcised hearts and ears! You are just like your **fathers**:
7:52 Was there ever a prophet your **fathers** did not persecute?
13:17 The God of the people of Israel chose our **fathers**; he made the
13:32 "We tell you the good news: What God promised our **fathers**
13:36 fell asleep; he was buried with his **fathers** and his body decayed.
15:10 a yoke that neither we nor our **fathers** have been able to bear?
16: 1 was a Jewess and a believer, but whose **father** was a Greek.
16: 3 lived in that area, for they all knew that his **father** was a Greek.
22: 1 "Brothers and **fathers**, listen now to my defense."
22:14 'The God *of* our **fathers** has chosen you to know his will and to
26: 6 because of my hope in what God has promised our **fathers** that I
28: 8 His **father** was sick in bed, suffering from fever and dysentery.
28:25 "The Holy Spirit spoke the truth to your **forefathers** when he said
Ro 1: 7 Grace and peace to you from God our **Father** and from the Lord
4:11 he is the **father** of all who believe but have not been circumcised,
4:12 And he is also the **father** of the circumcised who not only are
4:12 but who also walk in the footsteps of the faith that our **father**
4:16 to those who are of the faith of Abraham. He is the **father** of us all.
4:17 As it is written: "I have made you a **father** of many nations."
4:18 in hope believed and so became the **father** of many nations,
6: 4 as Christ was raised from the dead through the glory *of* the **Father**,
8:15 the Spirit of sonship. And by him we cry, "*Abba*, **Father**."
9: 5 Theirs are the **patriarchs**, and from them is traced the human
9:10 Rebekah's children had one and the same father, our **father** Isaac.
11:28 election is concerned, they are loved on account of the **patriarchs**,
15: 6 you may glorify the God and **Father** of our Lord Jesus Christ.
15: 8 of God's truth, to confirm the promises *made to* the **patriarchs**
1Co 1: 3 Grace and peace to you from God our **Father** and the Lord Jesus
4:15 ten thousand guardians in Christ, you do not have many **fathers**,
5: 1 does not occur even among pagans: A man has his **father's** wife.
8: 6 yet for us there is but one God, the **Father**, from whom all things
10: 1 that our **forefathers** were all under the cloud and that they all
15:24 when he hands over the kingdom *to* God the **Father** after he has
2Co 1: 2 Grace and peace to you from God our **Father** and the Lord Jesus
1: 3 Praise be to the God and **Father** of our Lord Jesus Christ,
1: 3 Jesus Christ, the **Father** of compassion and the God of all comfort,
6:18 "I will be a **Father** to you, and you will be my sons and daughters,
11:31 The God and **Father** of the Lord Jesus, who is to be praised
Gal 1: 1 not from men nor by man, but by Jesus Christ and God the **Father**,
1: 3 Grace and peace to you from God our **Father** and the Lord Jesus
1: 4 the present evil age, according to the will *of* our God and **Father**,
4: 2 is subject to guardians and trustees until the time set *by* his **father**.
4: 6 his Son into our hearts, the Spirit who calls out, "*Abba*, **Father**."
Eph 1: 2 Grace and peace to you from God our **Father** and the Lord Jesus
1: 3 Praise be to the God and **Father** of our Lord Jesus Christ,
1:17 the glorious **Father**, may give you the Spirit of wisdom
2:18 For through him we both have access to the **Father** by one Spirit.
3:14 For this reason I kneel before the **Father**,
4: 6 one God and **Father** of all, who is over all and through all
5:20 always giving thanks *to* God the **Father** for everything,
5:31 "For this reason a man will leave his **father** and mother and be
6: 2 "Honor your **father** and mother"—which is the first commandment
6: 4 **Fathers**, do not exasperate your children; instead, bring them up in
6:23 and love with faith from God the **Father** and the Lord Jesus Christ.
Php 1: 2 Grace and peace to you from God our **Father** and the Lord Jesus

2:11 confess that Jesus Christ is Lord, to the glory of God the **Father**.
2:22 because as a son *with* his **father** he has served with me in the work
4:20 To our God and **Father** be glory for ever and ever. Amen.
Col 1: 2 in Christ at Colosse: Grace and peace to you from God our **Father**.
1: 3 the **Father** of our Lord Jesus Christ, when we pray for you,
1:12 giving thanks *to* the **Father**, who has qualified you to share in the
3:17 of the Lord Jesus, giving thanks *to* God the **Father** through him.
3:21 **Fathers**, do not embitter your children, or they will become
1Th 1: 1 To the church of the Thessalonians in God the **Father** and the Lord
1: 3 before our God and **Father** your work produced by faith,
2:11 For you know that we dealt with each of you as a **father** deals with
3:11 Now may our God and **Father** himself and our Lord Jesus clear
3:13 and **Father** when our Lord Jesus comes with all his holy ones.
2Th 1: 1 To the church of the Thessalonians in God our **Father**
1: 2 Grace and peace to you from God the **Father** and the Lord Jesus
2:16 May our Lord Jesus Christ himself and God our **Father**, who loved
1Ti 1: 2 mercy and peace from God the **Father** and Christ Jesus our Lord.
5: 1 an older man harshly, but exhort him as if he were your **father**.
2Ti 1: 2 mercy and peace from God the **Father** and Christ Jesus our Lord.
Tit 1: 4 Grace and peace from God the **Father** and Christ Jesus our Savior.
Phm 1: 3 Grace to you and peace from God our **Father** and the Lord Jesus
Heb 1: 1 In the past God spoke *to* our **forefathers** through the prophets at
1: 5 Or again, "I will be his **Father**, and he will be my Son"?
3: 9 where your **fathers** tested and tried me and for forty years saw
7:10 met Abraham, Levi was still in the body *of* his **ancestor**.
8: 9 It will not be like the covenant I made *with* their **forefathers** when
11:23 By faith Moses' **parents** hid him for three months after he was
12: 7 treating you as sons. For what son is not disciplined *by* his **father**?
12: 9 we have all had human **fathers** who disciplined us and we
12: 9 How much more should we submit *to* the **Father** of our spirits
Jas 1:17 from above, coming down from the **Father** of the heavenly lights,
1:27 Religion that God our **Father** accepts as pure and faultless is this:
2:21 Was not our **ancestor** Abraham considered righteous for what he
3: 9 With the tongue we praise our Lord and **Father**, and with it we
1Pe 1: 2 been chosen according to the foreknowledge *of* God the **Father**,
1: 3 Praise be to the God and **Father** of our Lord Jesus Christ!
1:17 Since you call on a **Father** who judges each man's work
2Pe 1:17 and glory from God the **Father** when the voice came to him from
3: 4 Ever since our **fathers** died, everything goes on as it has since the
1Jn 1: 2 the eternal life, which was with the **Father** and has appeared to us.
1: 3 And our fellowship is with the **Father** and with his Son,
2: 1 does sin, we have one who speaks to the **Father** in our defense—
2:13 I write to you, **fathers**, because you have known him who is from
2:13 I write to you, dear children, because you have known the **Father**.
2:14 I write to you, **fathers**, because you have known him who is from
2:15 If anyone loves the world, the love *of* the **Father** is not in him.
2:16 and does—comes not from the **Father** but from the world.
2:22 Such a man is the antichrist—he denies the **Father** and the Son.
2:23 No one who denies the Son has the **Father**;
2:23 the Father; whoever acknowledges the Son has the **Father** also.
2:24 If it does, you also will remain in the Son and in the **Father**.
3: 1 How great is the love the **Father** has lavished on us, that we
4:14 and testify that the **Father** has sent his Son to be the Savior of the
2Jn 1: 3 mercy and peace from God the **Father** and from Jesus Christ,
1: 3 from God the Father and from Jesus Christ, the **Father's** Son,
1: 4 children walking in the truth, just as the **Father** commanded us.
1: 9 whoever continues in the teaching has both the **Father**
Jude 1: 1 who are loved by God the **Father** and kept by Jesus Christ:
Rev 1: 6 made us to be a kingdom and priests to serve his God and **Father**—
2:27 like pottery'—just as I have received authority from my **Father**.
3: 5 but will acknowledge his name before my **Father** and his angels.
3:21 just as I overcame and sat down with my **Father** on his throne.
14: 1 had his name and his **Father's** name written on their foreheads.

4253 Πάτμος, *Patmos* [1]

Patmos [1]

Rev 1: 9 was on the island of **Patmos** because of the word of God

4254 πατραλῷας, *patralōas* Not used in UBS/NIV

[√ *4252 + 262*]

4255 πατριά, *patria* [3] [√ *4252*]

family [1], line [1], peoples [1]

Lk   2: 4 of David, because he belonged to the house and **line** of David.
Ac   3:25 'Through your offspring all **peoples** on earth will be blessed.'
Eph 3:15 from whom his whole **family** in heaven and on earth derives its

4256 πατριάρχης, *patriarchēs* [4] [√ *4252 + 806*]

patriarch [2], patriarchs [2]

Ac   2:29 I can tell you confidently that the **patriarch** David died and was
      7: 8 of Jacob, and Jacob became the father of the twelve **patriarchs**.
      7: 9 "Because the **patriarchs** were jealous of Joseph, they sold him as a
Heb 7: 4 Even the **patriarch** Abraham gave him a tenth of the plunder!

4257 πατρικός, *patrikos* [1] [√ *4252*]

fathers [1]

Gal 1:14 and was extremely zealous for the traditions *of* my **fathers**.

4258 πατρίς, *patris* [8] [√ *4252*]

hometown [6], country of their own [1], country [1]

Mt 13:54 Coming to his **hometown**, he began teaching the people in their
    13:57 "Only in his **hometown** and in his own house is a prophet without
Mk 6: 1 Jesus left there and went to his **hometown**, accompanied by his
     6: 4 Jesus said to them, "Only in his **hometown**, among his relatives
Lk   4:23 Do here in your **hometown** what we have heard that you did in
     4:24 the truth," he continued, "no prophet is accepted in his **hometown**.
Jn   4:44 had pointed out that a prophet has no honor in his own **country**.)
Heb 11:14 such things show that they are looking for a **country of their own**.

4259 Πατροβᾶς, *Patrobas* [1] [√ *4252 + 1050*]

Patrobas [1]

Ro 16:14 Phlegon, Hermes, **Patrobas**, Hermas and the brothers with them.

4260 πατρολῴας, *patrolōas* [1] [√ *4252 + 262*]

kill their fathers [1]

1Ti 1: 9 *for those who* **kill their fathers** or mothers, for murderers,

4261 πατροπαράδοτος, *patroparadotos* [1]
[√ *4252 + 4123 + 1443*]

handed down from forefathers [1]

1Pe 1:18 the empty way of life **handed down** to you **from** your **forefathers**,

4262 πατρῷος, *patrōos* [3] [√ *4252*]

fathers [2], ancestors [1]

Ac 22: 3 Under Gamaliel I was thoroughly trained in the law *of* our **fathers**
   24:14 I admit that I worship the God *of* our **fathers** as a follower of the
   28:17 nothing against our people or against the customs *of* our **ancestors**,

4263 Παῦλος, *Paulos* [158]

Παῦλος ... Βαρναβᾶς (Paul ... Barnabas) [12] Ac 13:43,46,50;
   14:12,14; 15:2,2,12,22,25,35,36

Σέργιος Παῦλος (Serguis Paulus) [1] Ac 13:7

Paul [150], Paul's [6], himˢ [*+3836*] [1], Paulus [1]

Ac 13: 7 who was an attendant of the proconsul, Sergius **Paulus**.
   13: 9 Then Saul, who was also called **Paul**, filled with the Holy Spirit,
   13:13 **Paul** and his companions sailed to Perga in Pamphylia,
   13:16 Standing up, **Paul** motioned with his hand and said: "Men of Israel
   13:43 and devout converts to Judaism followed **Paul** and Barnabas,
   13:45 with jealousy and talked abusively against what **Paul** was saying.

13:46 Then **Paul** and Barnabas answered them boldly: "We had to speak
13:50 They stirred up persecution against **Paul** and Barnabas,
14: 9 He listened to **Paul** as he was speaking. Paul looked directly at
14:11 When the crowd saw what **Paul** had done, they shouted in the
14:12 and **Paul** they called Hermes because he was the chief speaker.
14:14 But when the apostles Barnabas and **Paul** heard of this, they tore
14:19 They stoned **Paul** and dragged him outside the city, thinking he
15: 2 This brought **Paul** and Barnabas into sharp dispute and debate with
15: 2 So **Paul** and Barnabas were appointed, along with some other
15:12 and **Paul** telling about the miraculous signs and wonders God had
15:22 their own men and send them to Antioch with **Paul** and Barnabas.
15:25 and send them to you with our dear friends Barnabas and **Paul**—
15:35 But **Paul** and Barnabas remained in Antioch, where they
15:36 Some time later **Paul** said to Barnabas, "Let us go back and visit the
15:38 but **Paul** did not think it wise to take him,
15:40 but **Paul** chose Silas and left, commended by the brothers to the
16: 3 **Paul** wanted to take him along on the journey, so he circumcised
16: 9 During the night **Paul** had a vision of a man of Macedonia
16:14 of God. The Lord opened her heart to respond to **Paul's** message.
16:17 This girl followed **Paul** and the rest of us, shouting, "These men are
16:18 Finally **Paul** became so troubled that he turned around and said to
16:19 they seized **Paul** and Silas and dragged them into the marketplace
16:25 About midnight **Paul** and Silas were praying and singing hymns to
16:28 But **Paul** shouted, "Don't harm yourself! We are all here!"
16:29 called for lights, rushed in and fell trembling before **Paul** and Silas.
16:36 The jailer told **Paul**, "The magistrates have ordered that you
16:37 But **Paul** said to the officers: "They beat us publicly without a trial,
17: 2 As his custom was, **Paul** went into the synagogue, and on three
17: 4 Some of the Jews were persuaded and joined **Paul** and Silas,
17:10 as it was night, the brothers sent **Paul** and Silas away to Berea.
17:13 When the Jews in Thessalonica learned that **Paul** was preaching
17:14 The brothers immediately sent **Paul** to the coast, but Silas
17:15 The men who escorted **Paul** brought him to Athens and then left
17:16 While **Paul** was waiting for them in Athens, he was greatly
17:22 **Paul** then stood up in the meeting of the Areopagus and said:
17:33 At that, **Paul** left the Council.
18: 5 from Macedonia, **Paul** devoted himself exclusively to preaching,
18: 9 One night the Lord spoke *to* **Paul** in a vision: "Do not be afraid;
18:12 the Jews made a united attack on **Paul** and brought him into court.
18:14 Just as **Paul** was about to speak, Gallio said to the Jews, "If you
18:18 **Paul** stayed on in Corinth for some time. Then he left the brothers
19: 1 **Paul** took the road through the interior and arrived at Ephesus.
19: 4 **Paul** said, "John's baptism was a baptism of repentance. He told the
19: 6 When **Paul** placed his hands on them, the Holy Spirit came on
19:11 God did extraordinary miracles through **Paul**,
19:13 They would say, "In the name of Jesus, whom **Paul** preaches,
19:15 "Jesus I know, and I know about **Paul**, but who are you?"
19:21 **Paul** decided to go to Jerusalem, passing through Macedonia
19:26 And you see and hear how this fellow **Paul** has convinced
19:29 and Aristarchus, **Paul's** traveling companions from Macedonia,
19:30 **Paul** wanted to appear before the crowd, but the disciples would
20: 1 **Paul** sent for the disciples and, after encouraging them,
20: 7 **Paul** spoke to the people and, because he intended to leave the next
20: 9 who was sinking into a deep sleep as **Paul** talked on and on.
20:10 **Paul** went down, threw himself on the young man and put his arms
20:13 and sailed for Assos, where we were going to take **Paul** aboard.
20:16 **Paul** had decided to sail past Ephesus to avoid spending time in
20:37 They all wept as they embraced himˢ [*+3836*] and kissed him.
21: 4 Through the Spirit they urged **Paul** not to go on to Jerusalem.
21:11 he took **Paul's** belt, tied his own hands and feet with it and said,
21:13 Then **Paul** answered, "Why are you weeping and breaking my
21:18 The next day **Paul** and the rest of us went to see James, and all the
21:26 The next day **Paul** took the men and purified himself along with
21:29 and assumed that **Paul** had brought him into the temple area.)
21:30 Seizing **Paul**, they dragged him from the temple, and immediately
21:32 saw the commander and his soldiers, they stopped beating **Paul**.
21:37 As the soldiers were about to take **Paul** into the barracks, he asked
21:39 **Paul** answered, "I am a Jew, from Tarsus in Cilicia, a citizen of no
21:40 **Paul** stood on the steps and motioned to the crowd.
22:25 him out to flog him, **Paul** said to the centurion standing there,
22:28 price for my citizenship." "But I was born a citizen," **Paul** replied.
22:30 to assemble. Then he brought **Paul** and had him stand before them.
23: 1 **Paul** looked straight at the Sanhedrin and said, "My brothers,
23: 3 Then **Paul** said to him, "God will strike you, you whitewashed
23: 5 **Paul** replied, "Brothers, I did not realize that he was the high priest;
23: 6 Then **Paul**, knowing that some of them were Sadducees

23:10 so violent that the commander was afraid **Paul** would be torn to
23:12 with an oath not to eat or drink until they had killed **Paul**.
23:14 taken a solemn oath not to eat anything until we have killed **Paul**.
23:16 But when the son *of* **Paul's** sister heard of this plot, he went into
23:16 sister heard of this plot, he went into the barracks and told them.
23:17 Then **Paul** called one of the centurions and said, "Take this young
23:18 "**Paul**, the prisoner, sent for me and asked me to bring this young
23:20 "The Jews have agreed to ask you to bring **Paul** before the
23:24 Provide mounts *for* **Paul** so that he may be taken safely to
23:31 took **Paul** with them during the night and brought him as far as
23:33 delivered the letter to the governor and handed **Paul** over to him.
24: 1 and they brought their charges against **Paul** before the governor.
24:10 When the governor motioned for him to speak, **Paul** replied.
24:24 He sent for **Paul** and listened to him as he spoke about faith in
24:26 At the same time he was hoping that **Paul** would offer him a bribe,
24:27 Felix wanted to grant a favor to the Jews, he left **Paul** in prison.
25: 2 appeared before him and presented the charges against **Paul**.
25: 4 Festus answered, "**Paul** is being held at Caesarea, and I myself am
25: 6 convened the court and ordered that **Paul** be brought before him.
25: 8 Then **Paul** made his defense: "I have done nothing wrong against
25: 9 Festus, wishing to do the Jews a favor, said *to* **Paul**, "Are you
25:10 **Paul** answered: "I am now standing before Caesar's court, where I
25:14 many days there, Festus discussed **Paul's** case with the king.
25:19 and about a dead man named Jesus who **Paul** claimed was alive.
25:21 When **Paul** made his appeal to be held over for the Emperor's
25:23 men of the city. At the command of Festus, **Paul** was brought in.
26: 1 Then Agrippa said to **Paul**, "You have permission to speak for
26: 1 So **Paul** motioned with his hand and began his defense:
26:24 "You are out of your mind, **Paul**!" he shouted. "Your great
26:25 "I am not insane, most excellent Festus," **Paul** replied. "What I am
26:28 Then Agrippa said to **Paul**, "Do you think that in such a short time
26:29 **Paul** replied, "Short time or long—I pray God that not only you
27: 1 **Paul** and some other prisoners were handed over to a centurion
27: 3 and Julius, in kindness *to* **Paul**, allowed him to go to his friends
27: 9 because by now it was after the Fast. So **Paul** warned them,
27:11 But the centurion, instead of listening to what **Paul** said,
27:21 a long time without food, **Paul** stood up before them and said:
27:24 and said, 'Do not be afraid, **Paul**. You must stand trial before
27:31 Then **Paul** said to the centurion and the soldiers, "Unless these men
27:33 Just before dawn **Paul** urged them all to eat. "For the last fourteen
27:43 But the centurion wanted to spare **Paul's** life and kept them from
28: 3 **Paul** gathered a pile of brushwood and, as he put it on the fire,
28: 8 **Paul** went in to see him and, after prayer, placed his hands on him
28:15 At the sight of these men **Paul** thanked God and was encouraged.
28:16 When we got to Rome, **Paul** was allowed to live by himself,
28:25 and began to leave after **Paul** had made this final statement:
Ro 1: 1 **Paul**, a servant of Christ Jesus, called to be an apostle and set apart
1Co 1: 1 **Paul**, called to be an apostle of Christ Jesus by the will of God,
1:12 One of you says, "I follow **Paul**"; another, "I follow Apollos";
1:13 Is Christ divided? Was **Paul** crucified for you? Were you baptized
1:13 Paul crucified for you? Were you baptized into the name *of* **Paul**?
3: 4 when one says, "I follow **Paul**," and another, "I follow Apollos,"
3: 5 What, after all, is Apollos? And what is **Paul**? Only servants,
3:22 whether **Paul** or Apollos or Cephas or the world or life or death
16:21 I, **Paul**, write this greeting in my own hand.
2Co 1: 1 **Paul**, an apostle of Christ Jesus by the will of God, and Timothy
10: 1 I, **Paul**, who am "timid" when face to face with you, but "bold"
Gal 1: 1 **Paul**, an apostle—sent not from men nor by man, but by Jesus
5: 2 I, **Paul**, tell you that if you let yourselves be circumcised,
Eph 1: 1 **Paul**, an apostle of Christ Jesus by the will of God, To the saints in
3: 1 For this reason I, **Paul**, the prisoner of Christ Jesus for the sake of
Php 1: 1 **Paul** and Timothy, servants of Christ Jesus, To all the saints in
Col 1: 1 **Paul**, an apostle of Christ Jesus by the will of God, and Timothy
1:23 under heaven, and of which I, **Paul**, have become a servant.
4:18 I, **Paul**, write this greeting in my own hand. Remember my chains.
1Th 1: 1 **Paul**, Silas and Timothy, To the church of the Thessalonians in
2:18 certainly I, **Paul**, did, again and again—but Satan stopped us.
2Th 1: 1 **Paul**, Silas and Timothy, To the church of the Thessalonians in
3:17 I, **Paul**, write this greeting in my own hand, which is the
1Ti 1: 1 **Paul**, an apostle of Christ Jesus by the command of God our Savior
2Ti 1: 1 **Paul**, an apostle of Christ Jesus by the will of God, according to
Tit 1: 1 **Paul**, a servant of God and an apostle of Jesus Christ for the faith
Phm 1: 1 **Paul**, a prisoner of Christ Jesus, and Timothy our brother,
1: 9 I then, as **Paul**—an old man and now also a prisoner of Christ
1:19 I, **Paul**, am writing this with my own hand. I will pay it back—
2Pe 3:15 just as our dear brother **Paul** also wrote you with the wisdom that

4264 παύω, *pauō* [15] [→ *187, 188, 398, 399, 2058, 2923, 2924, 5265*]

stopped [6], finished [2], done with [1], ended [1], keep [1], stilled [1], stop [1], stops [1], subsided [1]

Lk 5: 4 When *he had* **finished** speaking, he said to Simon, "Put out into
8:24 and the raging waters; the *storm* **subsided**, and all was calm.
11: 1 When *he* **finished**, one of his disciples said to him, "Lord, teach us
Ac 5:42 *they* never **stopped** teaching and proclaiming the good news that
6:13 "This fellow never **stops** speaking against this holy place
13:10 *Will you* never **stop** perverting the right ways of the Lord?
20: 1 When the uproar *had* **ended**, Paul sent for the disciples and,
20:31 Remember that for three years *I* never **stopped** warning each of
21:32 saw the commander and his soldiers, *they* **stopped** beating Paul.
1Co 13: 8 they will cease; where there are tongues, *they will be* **stilled**;
Eph 1:16 I *have* not **stopped** giving thanks for you, remembering you in my
Col 1: 9 we have not **stopped** praying for you and asking God to fill you
Heb 10: 2 If it could, would *they* not have **stopped** being offered? For the
1Pe 3:10 would love life and see good days *must* **keep** his tongue from evil
4: 1 because he who has suffered in his body *is* **done with** sin.

4265 Πάφος, *Paphos* [2]

Paphos [2]

Ac 13: 6 They traveled through the whole island until they came to **Paphos**.
13:13 From **Paphos**, Paul and his companions sailed to Perga in

4266 παχύνω, *pachynō* [2]

calloused [2]

Mt 13:15 For this people's heart *has become* **calloused**; they hardly hear
Ac 28:27 For this people's heart *has become* **calloused**; they hardly hear

4267 πέδη, *pedē* [3] [√ *4269*]

foot [2], irons on foot [1]

Mk 5: 4 For he had often been chained hand and **foot**, but he tore the chains
5: 4 but he tore the chains apart and broke the **irons on** his **feet**.
Lk 8:29 and though he was chained hand and **foot** and kept under guard,

4268 πεδινός, *pedinos* [1] [√ *4269*]

level [1]

Lk 6:17 He went down with them and stood on a **level** place. A large crowd

4269 πεζεύω, *pezeuō* [1] [→ *4267, 4268, 4270, 4271, 5134, 5135, 5136, 5544, 5545*]

going on foot [1]

Ac 20:13 He had made this arrangement because he was **going** there **on foot**.

4270 πεζῇ, *pezē* [2] [√ *4269*]

on foot [2]

Mt 14:13 Hearing of this, the crowds followed him **on foot** from the towns.
Mk 6:33 and ran **on foot** from all the towns and got there ahead of them.

4271 πεζός, *pezos* Not used in UBS/NIV [√ *4269*]

4272 πειθαρχέω, *peitharcheō* [4] [√ *4275 + 806*]

obey [2], obedient [1], taken advice [1]

Ac 5:29 the other apostles replied: "We must **obey** God rather than men!
5:32 so is the Holy Spirit, whom God has given *to* those *who* **obey** him."
27:21 "Men, you should have **taken** my **advice** not to sail from Crete;
Tit 3: 1 the people to be subject to rulers and authorities, *to be* **obedient**,

4273 πειθός, peithos [1] [√ 4275]

persuasive [1]

1Co 2: 4 and my preaching were not with wise and **persuasive** words,

4274 πειθώ, peithō   Not used in UBS/NIV [√ 4275]

4275 πείθω, peithō [52] [→ 400, 577, 578, 579, 2340, 4272, 4273, 4274, 4282, 4301, 4391, 4392; cf. 4412]

convinced [7], confident [5], persuaded [5], confidence [2], confident of [2], followers [2], persuade [2], put confidence [2], convince [1], convinced of [1], convinced that [1], dissuaded [1], encouraged [1], follow [1], fully convinced [+2779+3857] [1], give in [1], listening to [1], make obey [1], obey [1], obeying [1], persuasively [1], put trust [+1639] [1], rely [+1639] [1], satisfy [1], secured the support [1], set at rest [1], sure [1], trusted [1], trusts [1], trying to persuade [1], trying to win the approval of [1], urged [1], won over [1]

Mt 27:20 and the elders **persuaded** the crowd to ask for Barabbas
27:43 He **trusts** in God. Let God rescue him now if he wants him,
28:14 to the governor, we *will* **satisfy** him and keep you out of trouble."
Lk 11:22 he takes away the armor in which the *man* **trusted** and divides up
16:31 *they* will not *be* **convinced** even if someone rises from the dead.' "
18: 9 To some who *were* **confident** of their own righteousness
20: 6 will stone us, because they are **persuaded** that John was a prophet."
Ac 5:36 He was killed, all his **followers** were dispersed, and it all came to
5:37 in revolt. He too was killed, and all his **followers** were scattered.
5:40 His speech **persuaded** them. They called the apostles in and had
12:20 *Having* **secured the support** of Blastus, a trusted personal servant
13:43 talked with them and **urged** them to continue in the grace of God.
14:19 Jews came from Antioch and Iconium and **won** the crowd **over**.
17: 4 Some of the Jews *were* **persuaded** and joined Paul and Silas,
18: 4 reasoned in the synagogue, **trying to persuade** Jews and Greeks.
19: 8 for three months, arguing **persuasively** about the kingdom of God.
19:26 And you see and hear how this fellow Paul *has* **convinced**
21:14 When he *would* not *be* **dissuaded**, we gave up and said,
23:21 Don't **give in** to them, because more than forty of them are waiting
26:26 *I am* **convinced** that none of this has escaped his notice, because it
26:28 "Do you think that in such a short time *you can* **persuade** me to be
27:11 But the centurion, instead of **listening to** what Paul said,
28:23 and *tried to* **convince** them about Jesus from the Law of Moses
28:24 Some *were* **convinced** by what he said, but others would not
Ro 2: 8 *for* those who are self-seeking and who reject the truth and **follow**
2:19 if *you are* **convinced that** you are a guide for the blind, a light for
8:38 For *I am* **convinced** that neither death nor life, neither angels nor
14:14 *I am* **fully convinced** [+2779+3857] that no food is unclean in
15:14 I myself *am* **convinced**, my brothers, that you yourselves are full
2Co 1: 9 But this happened that *we might* not **rely** [+1639] on ourselves
1:15 *I had* **confidence** in all of you, that you would all share my joy.
5:11 we know what it is to fear the Lord, *we try to* **persuade** men.
10: 7 If anyone *is* **confident** that he belongs to Christ, he should consider
Gal 1:10 Am *I* now **trying to win the approval of** men, or of God?
5: 7 Who cut in on you and kept you from **obeying** the truth?
5:10 I *am* **confident** in the Lord that you will take no other view.
Php 1: 6 *being* **confident** *of* this, that he who began a good work in you will
1:14 most of the brothers in the Lord *have been* **encouraged** to speak
1:25 **Convinced of** this, I know that I will remain, and I will continue
2:24 And *I am* **confident** in the Lord that I myself will come soon.
3: 3 glory in Christ Jesus, and who **put** no **confidence** in the flesh—
3: 4 If anyone else thinks he has reasons to **put confidence** in the flesh,
2Th 3: 4 *We have* **confidence** in the Lord that you are doing and will
2Ti 1: 5 your mother Eunice and, *I am* **persuaded**, now lives in you also.
1:12 and *am* **convinced** that he is able to guard what I have entrusted to
Phm 1:21 **Confident** of your obedience, I write to you, knowing that you will
Heb 2:13 And again, "I *will* **put** *my* **trust** [+1639] in him." And again he
6: 9 dear friends, *we are* **confident of** better things in your case—
13:17 **Obey** your leaders and submit to their authority. They keep watch
13:18 *We are* **sure** that we have a clear conscience and desire to live
Jas 3: 3 When we put bits into the mouths of horses to **make** them **obey** us,
1Jn 3:19 to the truth, and how *we* **set** our hearts **at rest** in his presence

4276 Πειλᾶτος, Peilatos   Not used in UBS/NIV [√ 4397]

4277 πεινάω, peinaō [23] [→ 4698]

hungry [19], hunger [3], go hungry [1]

Mt 4: 2 After fasting forty days and forty nights, *he was* **hungry**.
5: 6 Blessed are those *who* **hunger** and thirst for righteousness,
12: 1 His disciples *were* **hungry** and began to pick some heads of grain
12: 3 read what David did when *he* and his companions *were* **hungry**?
21:18 as he was on his way back to the city, *he was* **hungry**.
25:35 For *I was* **hungry** and you gave me something to eat, I was thirsty
25:37 'Lord, when did we see you **hungry** and feed you, or thirsty
25:42 For *I was* **hungry** and you gave me nothing to eat, I was thirsty
25:44 when did we see you **hungry** or thirsty or a stranger or needing
Mk 2:25 David did when he and his companions *were* **hungry**, give in need?
11:12 The next day as they were leaving Bethany, Jesus *was* **hungry**.
Lk 1:53 He has filled the **hungry** with good things but has sent the rich
4: 2 nothing during those days, and at the end of them *he was* **hungry**.
6: 3 read what David did when he and his companions *were* **hungry**?
6:21 Blessed are you who **hunger** now, for you will be satisfied.
6:25 Woe to you who are well fed now, for *you will go* **hungry**.
Jn 6:35 He who comes to me *will* never *go* **hungry**, and he who believes in
Ro 12:20 "If your enemy *is* **hungry**, feed him; if he is thirsty, give him
1Co 4:11 To this very hour *we* **go hungry** and thirsty, we are in rags,
11:21 for anybody else. One remains **hungry**, another gets drunk.
11:34 If anyone *is* **hungry**, he should eat at home, so that when you meet
Php 4:12 content in any and every situation, whether well fed or **hungry**,
Rev 7:16 Never again *will they* **hunger**; never again will they thirst.

4278 πεῖρα, peira [2] [→ 585, 586, 1733, 4279, 4280, 4281]

faced [+3284] [1], tried to do [+3284] [1]

Heb 11:29 but *when* the Egyptians **tried** [+3284] **to do** so, they were
11:36 Some **faced** [+3284] jeers and flogging, while still others were

4279 πειράζω, peirazō [38] [√ 4278]

tempted [11], test [7], tested [7], tried [3], tempt [2], tempter [2], trying to trap [2], did$ [1], examine [1], tempting [1], trap [1]

Mt 4: 1 Then Jesus was led by the Spirit into the desert *to be* **tempted** by
4: 3 The **tempter** came to him and said, "If you are the Son of God,
16: 1 and **tested** him by asking him to show them a sign from heaven.
19: 3 Some Pharisees came to him *to* **test** him. They asked, "Is it lawful
22:18 evil intent, said, "You hypocrites, why *are you* **trying to trap** me?
22:35 One of them, an expert in the law, **tested** him with this question:
Mk 1:13 and he was in the desert forty days, *being* **tempted** by Satan.
8:11 *To* **test** him, they asked him for a sign from heaven.
10: 2 Some Pharisees came and **tested** him by asking, "Is it lawful for a
12:15 "Why *are you* **trying to trap** me?" he asked. "Bring me a denarius
Lk 4: 2 where for forty days *he was* **tempted** by the devil. He ate nothing
11:16 Others **tested** him by asking for a sign from heaven.
Jn 6: 6 He asked this *only* to **test** him, for he already had in mind what he
8: 6 They were using this question as a **trap**, in order to have a basis for
Ac 5: 9 said to her, "How could you agree to **test** the Spirit of the Lord?
9:26 When he came to Jerusalem, *he* **tried** to join the disciples,
15:10 why *do you try to* **test** God by putting on the necks of the
16: 7 they came to the border of Mysia, *they* **tried** to enter Bithynia,
24: 6 and even **tried** to desecrate the temple; so we seized him.
1Co 7: 5 Then come together again so that Satan *will* not **tempt** you
10: 9 We should not test the Lord, as some of them **did**$—and were
10:13 he will not let you *be* **tempted** beyond what you can bear.
2Co 13: 5 **Examine** yourselves to see whether you are in the faith;
Gal 6: 1 him gently. But watch yourself, or you also *may be* **tempted**.
1Th 3: 5 I was afraid that in some way the **tempter** might have tempted you
3: 5 I was afraid that in some way the tempter *might have* **tempted**
Heb 2:18 Because he himself suffered *when he was* **tempted**, he is able to
2:18 he was tempted, he is able to help those *who are being* **tempted**.
3: 9 where your fathers **tested** and tried me and for forty years saw
4:15 *but* we have one who has been **tempted** in every way, just as we
11:17 By faith Abraham, *when* God **tested** him, offered Isaac as a
Jas 1:13 *When* **tempted**, no one should say, "God is tempting me." For God
1:13 When tempted, no one should say, "God *is* **tempting** *me*." For God
1:13 For God cannot be tempted by evil, nor *does* he **tempt** anyone;
1:14 but each one *is* **tempted** when, by his own evil desire, he is

Rev 2: 2 that *you have* **tested** those who claim to be apostles but are not,
　　 2:10 I tell you, the devil will put some of you in prison to **test** *you*,
　　 3:10 to come upon the whole world *to* **test** those who live on the earth.

4280 πειρασμός, *peirasmos* [21] [√ *4278*]

temptation [8], trial [4], trials [4], testing [2], tempted [1], tempting [1], tested [1]

Mt 6:13 And lead us not into **temptation**, but deliver us from the evil one.'
　 26:41 "Watch and pray so that you will not fall into **temptation**.
Mk 14:38 Watch and pray so that you will not fall into **temptation**. The spirit
Lk 4:13 When the devil had finished all this **tempting**, he left him until an
　　 8:13 They believe for a while, but in the time *of* **testing** they fall away.
　 11: 4 everyone who sins against us. And lead us not into **temptation**.' "
　 22:28 You are those who have stood by me in my **trials**.
　 22:40 he said to them, "Pray that you will not fall into **temptation**."
　 22:46 "Get up and pray so that you will not fall into **temptation**."
Ac 20:19 with tears, although I was *severely* **tested** by the plots of the Jews.
1Co 10:13 No **temptation** has seized you except what is common to man.
　 10:13 But when you are **tempted**, he will also provide a way out
Gal 4:14 Even though my illness was a **trial** to you, you did not treat me
1Ti 6: 9 People who want to get rich fall into **temptation** and a trap
Heb 3: 8 as you did in the rebellion, during the time *of* **testing** in the desert,
Jas 1: 2 it pure joy, my brothers, whenever you face **trials** of many kinds,
　　 1:12 Blessed is the man who perseveres *under* **trial**, because when he
1Pe 1: 6 a little while you may have had to suffer grief in all kinds of **trials**.
　　 4:12 do not be surprised at the painful **trial** you are suffering,
2Pe 2: 9 then the Lord knows how to rescue godly men from **trials**
Rev 3:10 I will also keep you from the hour *of* **trial** that is going to come

4281 πειράω, *peiraō* [1] [√ *4278*]

tried [1]

Ac 26:21 is why the Jews seized me in the temple courts and **tried** to kill me.

4282 πεισμονή, *peismonē* [1] [√ *4275*]

persuasion [1]

Gal 5: 8 That kind of **persuasion** does not come from the one who calls

4283 πέλαγος, *pelagos* [2]

depths [1], open sea [1]

Mt 18: 6 hung around his neck and to be drowned in the **depths** of the sea.
Ac 27: 5 When we had sailed across the **open sea** off the coast of Cilicia

4284 πελεκίζω, *pelekizō* [1]

beheaded [1]

Rev 20: 4 And I saw the souls *of* those *who had been* **beheaded** because of

4285 πεμπταῖος, *pemptaios*　Not used in UBS/NIV [√ *4297*]

4286 πέμπτος, *pemptos* [4] [√ *4297*]

fifth [4]

Rev 6: 9 When he opened the **fifth** seal, I saw under the altar the souls of
　　 9: 1 The **fifth** angel sounded his trumpet, and I saw a star that had
　 16:10 The **fifth** angel poured out his bowl on the throne of the beast,
　 21:20 the **fifth** sardonyx, the sixth carnelian, the seventh chrysolite,

4287 πέμπω, *pempō* [79] [→ *402, 673, 1734, 1852, 3569, 4636, 5225*]

sent [44], send [20], sending [7], sent [+*4707*] [2], take [2], had beheaded [+*642*] [1], provide [1], send for [1], sends [1]

Mt 2: 8 He **sent** them to Bethlehem and said, "Go and make a careful
　 11: 2 John heard in prison what Christ was doing, *he* **sent** his disciples
　 14:10 and **had** John **beheaded** [+*642*] in the prison.

　 22: 7 He **sent** his army and destroyed those murderers and burned their
Mk 5:12 The demons begged Jesus, "**Send** us among the pigs; allow us to
Lk 4:26 Yet Elijah *was* not **sent** to any of them, but to a widow in
　　 7: 6 He was not far from the house *when* the centurion **sent** friends to
　　 7:10 Then the men *who had been* **sent** returned to the house and found
　　 7:19 *he* **sent** them to the Lord to ask, "Are you the one who was to
　 15:15 to a citizen of that country, *who* **sent** him to his fields to feed pigs.
　 16:24 pity on me and **send** Lazarus to dip the tip of his finger in water
　 16:27 'Then I beg you, father, **send** Lazarus to my father's house,
　 20:11 *He* **sent** [+*4707*] another servant,
　 20:12 *He* **sent** [+*4707*] still a third, and they wounded him and threw him
　 20:13 *I will* **send** my son, whom I love; perhaps they will respect him.'
Jn 1:22 are you? Give us an answer to take back *to* those *who* **sent** us.
　　 1:33 except that the one who **sent** me to baptize with water told me,
　　 4:34 "is to do the will *of* him *who* **sent** me and to finish his work.
　　 5:23 does not honor the Son does not honor the Father, who **sent** him.
　　 5:24 hears my word and believes him *who* **sent** me has eternal life
　　 5:30 is just, for I seek not to please myself but him *who* **sent** me.
　　 5:37 And the Father *who* **sent** me has himself testified concerning me.
　　 6:38 heaven not to do my will but to do the will *of* him *who* **sent** me.
　　 6:39 And this is the will *of* him *who* **sent** me, that I shall lose none of
　　 6:44 "No one can come to me unless the Father who **sent** me draws him,
　　 7:16 "My teaching is not my own. It comes *from* him *who* **sent** me.
　　 7:18 but he who works for the honor *of* the one who **sent** him is a man
　　 7:28 I am not here on my own, but he *who* **sent** me is true. You do not
　　 7:33 you for only a short time, and then I go to the one *who* **sent** me.
　　 8:16 because I am not alone. I stand with the Father, who **sent** me.
　　 8:18 testifies for myself; my other witness is the Father, who **sent** me."
　　 8:26 But he *who* **sent** me is reliable, and what I have heard from him I
　　 8:29 The one *who* **sent** me is with me; he has not left me alone,
　　 9: 4 As long as it is day, we must do the work *of* him *who* **sent** me.
　 12:44 he does not believe in me only, but in the one *who* **sent** me.
　 12:45 When he looks at me, he sees the one *who* **sent** me.
　 12:49 but the Father who **sent** me commanded me what to say and how
　 13:16 his master, nor is a messenger greater than the one *who* **sent** him.
　 13:20 I tell you the truth, whoever accepts anyone *I* **send** accepts me;
　 13:20 accepts me; and whoever accepts me accepts the one *who* **sent** me."
　 14:24 you hear are not my own; they belong to the Father *who* **sent** me.
　 14:26 the Holy Spirit, whom the Father *will* **send** in my name,
　 15:21 because of my name, for they do not know the One *who* **sent** me.
　 15:26 the Counselor comes, whom *I will* **send** to you from the Father,
　 16: 5 "Now I am going to him *who* **sent** me, yet none of you asks me,
　 16: 7 Counselor will not come to you; but if I go, *I will* **send** him to you.
　 20:21 "Peace be with you! As the Father has sent me, I *am* **sending** you."
Ac 10: 5 Now **send** men to Joppa to bring back a man named Simon who is
　 10:32 **Send** to Joppa *for* Simon who is called Peter. He is a guest in the
　 10:33 So *I* **sent** for you immediately, and it was good of you to come.
　 11:29 his ability, decided *to* **provide** help for the brothers living in Judea.
　 15:22 their own men and **send** them to Antioch with Paul and Barnabas.
　 15:25 and **send** them to you with our dear friends Barnabas and Paul—
　 19:31 **sent** him a *message* begging him not to venture into the theater.
　 20:17 From Miletus, Paul **sent** to Ephesus for the elders of the church.
　 23:30 a plot to be carried out against the man, *I* **sent** him to you at once.
　 25:25 because he made his appeal to the Emperor I decided to **send** him
　 25:27 For I think it is unreasonable *to* **send** on a prisoner without
Ro 8: 3 God did *by* **sending** his own Son in the likeness of sinful man to
1Co 4:17 For this reason *I am* **sending** to you Timothy, my son whom I
　 16: 3 *I will* give letters of introduction to the men you approve and **send**
2Co 9: 3 But *I am* **sending** the brothers in order that our boasting about you
Eph 6:22 *I am* **sending** him to you for this very purpose, that you may know
Php 2:19 I hope in the Lord Jesus *to* **send** Timothy to you soon, that I also
　　 2:23 therefore, *to* **send** him as soon as I see how things go with me.
　　 2:25 But I think it is necessary *to* **send** *back* to you Epaphroditus,
　　 2:28 Therefore I am all the more eager *to* **send** him, so that when you
　　 4:16 *you* **sent** me aid again and again when I was in need.
Col 4: 8 *I am* **sending** him to you for the express purpose that you may
1Th 3: 2 We **sent** Timothy, who is our brother and God's fellow worker in
　　 3: 5 when I could stand it no longer, *I* **sent** to find out about your faith.
2Th 2:11 For this reason God **sends** them a powerful delusion so that they
Tit 3:12 As soon as *I* **send** Artemas or Tychicus to you, do your best to
1Pe 2:14 *who are* **sent** by him to punish those who do wrong and to
Rev 1:11 "Write on a scroll what you see and **send** it to the seven churches:
　 11:10 will gloat over them and will celebrate by **sending** each other gifts,
　 14:15 "**Take** your sickle and reap, because the time to reap has come,
　 14:18 "**Take** your sharp sickle and gather the clusters of grapes from the
　 22:16 *have* **sent** my angel to give you this testimony for the churches.

4288 πένης, penēs [1] [→ 4293; cf. 4506]

poor [1]

2Co 9: 9 "He has scattered abroad his gifts *to* the **poor**; his righteousness

4289 πενθερά, penthera [6] [√ 4290]

mother-in-law [6]

Mt 8:14 he saw Peter's **mother-in-law** lying in bed with a fever.
     10:35 against her mother, a daughter-in-law against her **mother-in-law**—
Mk 1:30 Simon's **mother-in-law** was in bed with a fever, and they told
Lk 4:38 Now Simon's **mother-in-law** was suffering from a high fever,
    12:53 **mother-in-law** against daughter-in-law and daughter-in-law
    12:53 daughter-in-law and daughter-in-law against **mother-in-law**."

4290 πενθερός, pentheros [1] [→ 4289]

father-in-law [1]

Jn 18:13 who was the **father-in-law** of Caiaphas, the high priest that year.

4291 πενθέω, pentheō [10] [√ 4292]

mourn [6], mourning [2], filled with grief [1], grieved over [1]

Mt 5: 4 Blessed are those *who* **mourn**, for they will be comforted.
    9:15 "How can the guests of the bridegroom **mourn** while he is with
Mk 16:10 who had been with him and who *were* **mourning** and weeping.
Lk 6:25 Woe to you who laugh now, for *you will* **mourn** and weep.
1Co 5: 2 Shouldn't *you* rather *have been* **filled with grief** and have put out
2Co 12:21 and *I will be* **grieved over** many who have sinned earlier and have
Jas 4: 9 Grieve, **mourn** and wail. Change your laughter to mourning
Rev 18:11 "The merchants of the earth *will* weep and **mourn** over her
    18:15 stand far off, terrified at her torment. *They will* weep and **mourn**
    18:19 dust on their heads, and *with* weeping and **mourning** cry out:

4292 πένθος, penthos [5] [→ 4291]

mourning [3], grief [1], mourn [+3972] [1]

Jas 4: 9 Change your laughter to **mourning** and your joy to gloom.
Rev 18: 7 Give her as much torture and **grief** as the glory and luxury she
    18: 7 sit as queen; I am not a widow, and *I will* never **mourn** [+3972].'
    18: 8 death, **mourning** and famine. She will be consumed by fire,
    21: 4 There will be no more death or **mourning** or crying or pain,

4293 πενιχρός, penichros [1] [√ 4288]

poor [1]

Lk 21: 2 He also saw a **poor** widow put in two very small copper coins.

4294 πεντάκις, pentakis [1] [√ 4297]

five times [1]

2Co 11:24 **Five times** I received from the Jews the forty lashes minus one.

4295 πεντακισχίλιοι, pentakischilioi [6] [√ 4297 + 5943]

five thousand [6]

Mt 14:21 The number of those who ate was about **five thousand** men,
    16: 9 Don't you remember the five loaves *for* the **five thousand**,
Mk 6:44 The number of the men who had eaten was **five thousand**.
    8:19 When I broke the five loaves for the **five thousand**, how many
Lk 9:14 (About **five thousand** men were there.) But he said to his disciples,
Jn 6:10 in that place, and the men sat down, about **five thousand** of them.

4296 πεντακόσιοι, pentakosioi [2] [√ 4297]

five hundred [2]

Lk 7:41 One owed him **five hundred** denarii, and the other fifty.
1Co 15: 6 he appeared *to* more than **five hundred** of the brothers at the same

4297 πέντε, pente [38] [→ 1278, 4285, 4286, 4294, 4295, 4296, 4298, 4299, 4300]

five [35], fifty thousand [+3689] [1], seventy-five [+1573] [1], three or three and a half miles [+1633+2445+5084+5558] [1]

Mt 14:17 "We have here only **five** loaves of bread and two fish," they
    14:19 Taking the **five** loaves and the two fish and looking up to heaven,
    16: 9 Don't you remember the **five** loaves for the five thousand,
    25: 2 **Five** of them were foolish and five were wise.
    25: 2 Five of them were foolish and **five** were wise.
    25:15 To one he gave **five** talents of money, to another two talents,
    25:16 The man who had received the **five** talents went at once and put his
    25:16 went at once and put his money to work and gained **five** more.
    25:20 The man who had received the **five** talents brought the other five.
    25:20 The man who had received the five talents brought the other **five**.
    25:20 'Master,' he said, 'you entrusted me with **five** talents. See,
    25:20 'you entrusted me with five talents. See, I have gained **five** more.'
Mk 6:38 and see." When they found out, they said, "**Five**—and two fish."
    6:41 Taking the **five** loaves and the two fish and looking up to heaven,
    8:19 When I broke the **five** loaves for the five thousand, how many
Lk 1:24 became pregnant and *for* **five** months remained in seclusion.
    9:13 They answered, "We have only **five** loaves of bread and two fish—
    9:16 Taking the **five** loaves and the two fish and looking up to heaven,
    12: 6 Are not **five** sparrows sold for two pennies? Yet not one of them is
    12:52 From now on there will be **five** in one family divided against each
    14:19 "Another said, 'I have just bought **five** yoke of oxen, and I'm on my
    16:28 for I have **five** brothers. Let him warn them, so that they will not
    19:18 "The second came and said, 'Sir, your mina has earned **five** more.'
    19:19 "His master answered, 'You take charge of **five** cities.'
Jn 4:18 The fact is, you have had **five** husbands, and the man you now
    5: 2 and which is surrounded by **five** covered colonnades.
    6: 9 "Here is a boy with **five** small barley loaves and two small fish,
    6:13 and filled twelve baskets with the pieces of the **five** barley loaves
    6:19 rowed **three or three and a half miles** [+1633+2445+5084+5558]
Ac 4: 4 and the number of men grew to about **five** thousand.
    7:14 his father Jacob and his whole family, **seventy-five** [+1573] in all.
    19:19 of the scrolls, the total came to **fifty thousand** [+3689] drachmas.
    20: 6 and **five** days later joined the others at Troas, where we stayed
    24: 1 **Five** days later the high priest Ananias went down to Caesarea with
1Co 14:19 But in the church I would rather speak **five** intelligible words to
Rev 9: 5 given power to kill them, but only to torture them *for* **five** months.
    9:10 and in their tails they had power to torment people *for* **five** months.
    17:10 **Five** have fallen, one is, the other has not yet come; but when he

4298 πεντεκαιδέκατος, pentekaidekatos [1] [√ 4297 + 2779 + 1274]

fifteenth [1]

Lk 3: 1 In the **fifteenth** year of the reign of Tiberius Caesar—when Pontius

4299 πεντήκοντα, pentēkonta [7] [√ 4297]

fifty [3], 153 [+1669+5552] [1], 450 [+2779+5484] [1], fifties [1], four hundred [1]

Mk 6:40 So they sat down in groups of hundreds and **fifties**.
Lk 7:41 One owed him five hundred denarii, and the other **fifty**.
    9:14 to his disciples, "Have them sit down in groups of about **fifty** each."
    16: 6 'Take your bill, sit down quickly, and make it **four hundred**.'
Jn 8:57 "You are not yet **fifty** years old," the Jews said to him, "and you
    21:11 dragged the net ashore. It was full of large fish, **153** [+1669+5552],
Ac 13:20 All this took about **450** [+2779+5484] years. "After this, God gave

4300 πεντηκοστή, pentēkostē [3] [√ 4297]

Pentecost [3]

Ac 2: 1 When the day *of* **Pentecost** came, they were all together in one
    20:16 in a hurry to reach Jerusalem, if possible, by the day *of* **Pentecost**.
1Co 16: 8 But I will stay on at Ephesus until **Pentecost**,

4301 πεποίθησις, pepoithēsis [6] [√ 4275]

confidence [4], as [+3836] [1], confident of [1]

2Co 1:15 *Because I was* **confident of** this, I planned to visit you first

3: 4 Such **confidence** as this is ours through Christ before God.
8:22 and now even more so *because of* his great **confidence** in you.
10: 2 as[s] [+*3836*] I expect to be toward some people who think that we
Eph 3:12 faith in him we may approach God with freedom and **confidence**.
Php 3: 4 though I myself have reasons for such **confidence**. If anyone else

---

4302 -περ, -*per* Not used in UBS/NIV [→ *1478, 1570,*
1642, 2077, 2080, 2472, 2749, 2778, 2788, 4013, 6061, 6062]

4303 Πέραια, *Peraia* Not used in UBS/NIV [√ *4305*]

4304 περαιτέρω, *peraiterō* [1] [√ *4305*]

further [1]

Ac 19:39 If there is anything **further** you want to bring up, it must be settled

4305 πέραν, *peran* [23 / 22] [→ *527, 596, 1385, 4303,*
4304, 4306, 4373, 4405; cf. 4513]

other side [5], across [3], on the other side [3], other side of the
lake [2], across [+*1650+3836*] [1], across the lake [+*1650+3836*]
[1], along [1], crossed [1], on the opposite shore [1], region
across [1], regions across [1], to far shore [1], to other side [1]

Mt 4:15 and land of Naphtali, the way to the sea, **along** the Jordan,
4:25 Jerusalem, Judea and the **region across** the Jordan followed him.
8:18 around him, he gave orders to cross to the **other side of the lake**.
8:28 When he arrived at the **other side** in the region of the Gadarenes,
14:22 get into the boat and go on ahead of him to the **other side**,
16: 5 When they went **across** [+*1650+3836*] **the lake**, the disciples
19: 1 and went into the region of Judea **to** the **other side** of the Jordan.
Mk 3: 8 and the **regions across** the Jordan and around Tyre and Sidon.
4:35 he said to his disciples, "Let us go over to the **other side**."
5: 1 They went **across** [+*1650+3836*] the lake to the region of the
5:21 Jesus had again crossed over by boat to the **other side of the lake**,
6:45 and go on ahead of him [UBS+ *to the other side*] to Bethsaida,
8:13 he left them, got back into the boat and crossed to the **other side**.
10: 1 that place and went into the region of Judea and **across** the Jordan.
Lk 8:22 said to his disciples, "Let's go over to the **other side** of the lake."
Jn 1:28 This all happened at Bethany **on the other side** of the Jordan,
3:26 that man who was with you **on the other side** of the Jordan—
6: 1 Jesus crossed **to** the **far shore** of the Sea of Galilee (that is,
6:17 they got into a boat and set off **across** the lake for Capernaum.
6:22 The next day the crowd that had stayed **on the opposite shore** of
6:25 When they found him **on the other side** of the lake, they asked
10:40 Then Jesus went back **across** the Jordan to the place where John
18: 1 Jesus left with his disciples and **crossed** the Kidron Valley.

4306 πέρας, *peras* [4] [√ *4305*]

ends [3], end [1]

Mt 12:42 for she came from the **ends** of the earth to listen to Solomon's
Lk 11:31 for she came from the **ends** of the earth to listen to Solomon's
Ro 10:18 gone out into all the earth, their words to the **ends** of the world."
Heb 6:16 and the oath confirms what is said and puts an **end** to all argument.

4307 Πέργαμος, *Pergamos* [2]

Pergamum [2]

Rev 1:11 to Ephesus, Smyrna, **Pergamum**, Thyatira, Sardis, Philadelphia
2:12 "To the angel of the church in **Pergamum** write: These are the

4308 Πέργη, *Pergē* [3]

Perga [3]

Ac 13:13 Paul and his companions sailed to **Perga** in Pamphylia,
13:14 From **Perga** they went on to Pisidian Antioch. On the Sabbath they
14:25 and when they had preached the word in **Perga**, they went down to

---

4309 περί, *peri* [333 / 332]

[→ *597, 598, 1853, 2341, 2342, 4310, 4311, 4312, 4313, 4314,*
4315, 4316, 4317, 4318, 4319, 4320, 4321, 4322, 4323, 4324, 4325,
4326, 4327, 4328, 4329, 4330, 4331, 4332, 4333, 4334, 4335, 4336,
4337, 4338, 4339, 4340, 4341, 4342, 4343, 4344, 4345, 4346, 4347,
4348, 4349, 4350, 4351, 4352, 4362, 4363, 4364, 4365, 4366, 4367,
4368, 4369, 4370, 5226, 5227; cf. 4356]

about [133], for [52], *untranslated* [39], of [17], around [11],
concerning [11], in regard to [5], on [5], because [4], by [3], in
[3], to [3], with [3], against [2], as [2], from [2], meant [+*3306*]
[2], on behalf [+*281*] [2], sin offerings [+*281*] [2], tied around [RP*4329*] [2],
about [+*4005*] [1], about [+*6059*] [1], as for [1], as to [1], at [1],
besiege with questions [+*694+4498*] [1], companions [+*3836*]
[1], concerned [1], consider [+*3972*] [1], flashed around
[RP*4313*] [1], go with [1], how [+*3836*] [1], in case [1], in favor [1],
in that case [+*4005*] [1], interest in [1], my [+*1831+3836*] [1],
nearby [+*3836+5536*] [1], over the matter of [1], over [1],
regarding [1], surrounding [1], that [+*3836*] [1], to be[s] [1], to do
with [1], to help [1], to know [1], welfare [+*3836*] [1], what I meant
[+*4047*] [1]

Mt 2: 8 to Bethlehem and said, "Go and make a careful search **for** the child.
3: 4 made of camel's hair, and he had a leather belt **around** his waist.
4: 6 "'He will command his angels **concerning** you, and they will lift
6:28 "And why do you worry **about** clothes? See how the lilies of the
8:18 When Jesus saw the crowd **around** him, he gave orders to cross to
9:36 When he saw the crowds, he had compassion **on** them,
11: 7 were leaving, Jesus began to speak to the crowd **about** John:
11:10 This is the one **about** whom it is written: " 'I will send my
12:36 day of judgment for every careless word they have spoken. [NIE]
15: 7 You hypocrites! Isaiah was right when he prophesied **about** you:
16:11 How is it you don't understand that I was not talking to you **about**
17:13 Then the disciples understood that he was talking to them **about**
18: 6 it would be better for him to have a large millstone hung **around**
18:19 I tell you that if two of you on earth agree **about** anything you ask
19:17 "Why do you ask me **about** what is good?" Jesus replied. "There is
20: 3 "**About** the third hour he went out and saw others standing in the
20: 5 "He went out again **about** the sixth hour and the ninth hour
20: 6 **About** the eleventh hour he went out and found still others
20: 9 "The workers who were hired **about** the eleventh hour came
20:24 the ten heard about this, they were indignant **with** the two brothers.
21:45 heard Jesus' parables, they knew he was talking **about** them.
22:16 You aren't swayed by men, because you pay no attention to who
22:31 But **about** the resurrection of the dead—have you not read what
22:42 "What do you think **about** the Christ? Whose son is he?" "The son
24:36 "No one knows **about** that day or hour, not even the angels in
26:24 The Son of Man will go just as it is written **about** him. But woe to
26:28 which is poured out **for** many for the forgiveness of sins.
27:46 **About** the ninth hour Jesus cried out in a loud voice, "*Eloi,*
Mk 1: 6 with a leather belt **around** his waist, and he ate locusts and wild
1:30 was in bed with a fever, and they told Jesus **about** her.
1:44 and offer the sacrifices that Moses commanded **for** your cleansing,
3: 8 and the regions across the Jordan and **around** Tyre and Sidon.
3:32 A crowd was sitting **around** him, and they told him, "Your mother
3:34 Then he looked at those seated in a circle **around** him and said,
4:10 and the others **around** him asked him about the parables.
4:19 and the desires **for** other things come in and choke the word,
5:16 to the demon-possessed man—and told **about** the pigs as well.
5:27 When she heard **about** Jesus, she came up behind him in the crowd
6:48 **About** the fourth watch of the night he went out to them,
7: 6 "Isaiah was right when he prophesied **about** you hypocrites;
7:25 In fact, as soon as she heard **about** him, a woman whose little
8:30 Jesus warned them not to tell anyone **about** him.
9:14 they saw a large crowd **around** them and the teachers of the law
9:42 into the sea with a large millstone **tied around** [RP*4329*] his neck.
10:10 they were in the house again, the disciples asked Jesus **about** this.
10:41 ten heard about this, they became indignant **with** James and John.
12:14 You aren't swayed **by** men, because you pay no attention to who
12:26 Now **about** the dead rising—have you not read in the book of
13:32 "No one knows **about** that day or hour, not even the angels in
14:21 The Son of Man will go just as it is written **about** him. But woe to
16: S [UBS+ *commanded them they told briefly to those around Peter.*]
Lk 1: 1 Many have undertaken to draw up an account **of** the things that
1: 4 so that you may know the certainty **of** the things you have been

2:17 they spread [NIE] the word concerning what had been told them
2:17 they spread the word concerning what had been told them **about**
2:18 and all who heard it were amazed **at** what the shepherds said to
2:27 When the parents brought in the child Jesus to do **for** him what the
2:33 child's father and mother marveled at what was said **about** him.
2:38 and spoke **about** the child to all who were looking forward to the
3:15 and were all wondering in their hearts if [NIE] John might
3:19 But when John rebuked Herod the tetrarch **because** of Herodias,
3:19 brother's wife, and [RPG] all the other evil things he had done,
4:10 " 'He will command his angels **concerning** you to guard you
4:14 and news **about** him spread through the whole countryside.
4:37 And the news **about** him spread throughout the surrounding area.
4:38 was suffering from a high fever, and they asked Jesus **to help** her.
5:14 and offer the sacrifices that Moses commanded **for** your cleansing,
5:15 Yet the news **about** him spread all the more, so that crowds of
6:28 bless those who curse you, pray **for** those who mistreat you.
7: 3 The centurion heard **of** Jesus and sent some elders of the Jews to
7:17 This news **about** Jesus spread throughout Judea and the
7:18 John's disciples told him **about** all these things. Calling two of
7:24 messengers left, Jesus began to speak to the crowd **about** John:
7:27 This is the one **about** whom it is written: " 'I will send my
9: 9 Who, then, is this I hear such things **about** [+4005]?"
9:11 He welcomed them and spoke to them **about** the kingdom of God,
9:45 that they did not grasp it, and they were afraid to ask him **about** it.
10:40 But Martha was distracted **by** all the preparations that had to be
10:41 the Lord answered, "you are worried and upset **about** many things,
11:53 him fiercely and *to* besiege him **with questions** [+694+4498],
12:26 cannot do this very little thing, why do you worry **about** the rest?
13: 1 Now there were some present at that time who told Jesus **about** the
13: 8 it alone for one more year, and I'll dig **around** it and fertilize it.
16: 2 So he called him in and asked him, 'What is this I hear **about** you?
17: 2 **tied around** [RP4329] his neck than for him to cause one of these
19:37 to praise God in loud voices **for** all the miracles they had seen:
21: 5 Some of his disciples were remarking **about** how the temple was
22:32 But I have prayed **for** you, Simon, that your faith may not fail.
22:37 in me. Yes, what is written **about** me is reaching its fulfillment."
22:49 [NIE] they said, "Lord, should we strike with our swords?"
23: 8 From what he had heard **about** him, he hoped to see him perform
24: 4 While they were wondering **about** this, suddenly two men in
24:14 They were talking with each other **about** everything that had
24:19 "What things?" he asked. "**About** Jesus of Nazareth," they replied.
24:27 to them what was said in all the Scriptures **concerning** himself.
24:44 Everything must be fulfilled that is written **about** me in the Law of

Jn   1: 7 He came as a witness to testify **concerning** that light, so that
1: 8 himself was not the light; he came only as a witness **to** the light.
1:15 John testifies **concerning** him. He cries out, saying, "This was he of
1:22 take back to those who sent us. What do you say **about** yourself?"
1:47 he said **of** him, "Here is a true Israelite, in whom there is nothing
2:21 But the temple he had spoken **of** was his body.
2:25 He did not need man's testimony **about** man, for he knew what
3:25 and a certain Jew **over the matter of** ceremonial washing.
5:31 "If I testify **about** myself, my testimony is not valid.
5:32 There is another who testifies **in my favor**, and I know that his
5:32 in my favor, and I know that his testimony **about** me is valid.
5:36 and which I am doing, testifies [NIE] that the Father has sent me.
5:37 And the Father who sent me has himself testified **concerning** me.
5:39 possess eternal life. These are the Scriptures that testify **about** me,
5:46 believed Moses, you would believe me, for he wrote **about** me.
6:41 At this the Jews began to grumble **about** him because he said,
6:61 Aware that his disciples were grumbling **about** this, Jesus said to
7: 7 but it hates me because I testify [NIE] that what it does is evil.
7:12 Among the crowds there was widespread whispering **about** him.
7:13 But no one would say anything publicly **about** him for fear of the
7:17 he will find out whether [NIE] my teaching comes from God
7:32 The Pharisees heard the crowd whispering such things **about** him.
7:39 By this *he* meant [+3306] the Spirit, whom those who believed in
8:13 challenged him, "Here you are, appearing **as** your own witness;
8:14 Jesus answered, "Even if I testify **on** my own **behalf**, my testimony
8:18 I am one who testifies **for** myself; my other witness is the Father,
8:18 for myself; [RPG] my other witness is the Father, who sent me."
8:26 "I have much to say in judgment **of** you. But he who sent me is
8:46 Can any of you prove me guilty **of** sin? If I am telling the truth,
9:17 turned again to the blind man, "What have you to say **about** him?
9:18 The Jews still did not believe [NIE] that he had been blind
9:21 we don't know. Ask him. He is of age; he will speak **for** himself."
10:13 because he is a hired hand and cares nothing **for** the sheep.

10:25 not believe. The miracles I do in my Father's name speak **for** me,
10:33 "We are not stoning you **for** any of these," replied the Jews,
10:33 stoning you for any of these," replied the Jews, "but **for** blasphemy,
10:41 a miraculous sign, all that John said **about** this man was true."
11:13 Jesus had been speaking **of** his death, but his disciples thought he
11:13 but his disciples thought *he* meant [+3306] natural sleep.
11:19 to Martha and Mary to comfort them **in** *the loss* of their brother.
12: 6 He did not say this because he cared **about** the poor but because he
12:41 Isaiah said this because he saw Jesus' glory and spoke **about** him.
13:18 "I am not referring to all of you; I know those I have chosen.
13:22 stared at one another, at a loss **to know** which of them he meant.
13:24 to this disciple and said, "Ask him which [NIE] one he means."
15:22 be guilty of sin. Now, however, they have no excuse **for** their sin.
15:26 of truth who goes out from the Father, he will testify **about** me.
16: 8 he will convict the world of guilt **in regard to** sin
16: 8 of guilt in regard to sin and [RPG] righteousness and judgment:
16: 8 of guilt in regard to sin and righteousness and [RPG] judgment:
16: 9 **in regard to** sin, because men do not believe in me;
16:10 **in regard to** righteousness, because I am going to the Father,
16:11 and **in regard to** judgment, because the prince of this world now
16:19 "Are you asking one another **what I meant** [+4047] when I said,
16:25 this kind of language but will tell you plainly **about** my Father.
16:26 my name. I am not saying that I will ask the Father **on** your **behalf**.
17: 9 I pray **for** them. I am not praying for the world, but for those you
17: 9 I am not praying for the world, but for those you have given me,
17: 9 for the world, but **for** those you have given me, for they are yours.
17:20 "My prayer is not **for** them alone. I pray also for those who will
17:20 I pray also **for** those who will believe in me through their message,
18:19 the high priest questioned Jesus **about** his disciples and his
18:19 questioned Jesus about his disciples and [RPG] his teaching.
18:23 I said something wrong," Jesus replied, "testify **as to** what is wrong.
18:34 your own idea," Jesus asked, "or did others talk to you **about** me?"
19:24 they said to one another. "Let's decide by lot who will get [NIE] it."
21:24 This is the disciple who testifies **to** these things and who wrote

Ac   1: 1 Theophilus, I wrote **about** all that Jesus began to do and to teach
1: 3 over a period of forty days and spoke **about** the kingdom of God.
1:16 spoke long ago through the mouth of David **concerning** Judas,
2:29 I can tell you confidently that [NIE] the patriarch David died
2:31 Seeing what was ahead, he spoke **of** the resurrection of the Christ,
5:24 priests were puzzled, [NIE] wondering what would come of this.
7:52 They even killed those who predicted [NIE] the coming of the
8:12 But when they believed Philip as he preached the good news **of** the
8:15 they prayed **for** them that they might receive the Holy Spirit,
8:34 please, who is the prophet talking about, himself or someone else?"
8:34 who is the prophet talking about, [RPG] himself or someone else?"
8:34 who is the prophet talking about, himself or [RPG] someone else?"
9:13 "I have heard many reports **about** this man and all the harm he has
10: 3 One day at **about** [+6059] three in the afternoon he had a vision.
10: 9 **About** noon the following day as they were on their journey
10:19 While Peter was still thinking **about** the vision, the Spirit said to
11:22 News **of** this reached the ears of the church at Jerusalem, and they
12: 5 in prison, but the church was earnestly praying to God **for** him.
13:13 and his **companions** [+3836] sailed to Perga in Pamphylia,
13:29 When they had carried out all that was written **about** him,
15: 2 up to Jerusalem to see the apostles and elders **about** this question.
15: 6 The apostles and elders met to **consider** [+3972] this question.
17:32 but others said, "We want to hear you again **on** this subject."
18:15 But since it involves questions **about** words and names and your
18:25 and he spoke with great fervor and taught **about** Jesus accurately,
19: 8 for three months, arguing persuasively **about** the kingdom of God.
19:23 About that time there arose a great disturbance **about** the Way.
19:25 them together, along with the workmen **in** related trades, and said:
19:40 in danger of being charged with rioting **because** of today's events.
19:40 **In that case** [+4005] we would not be able to account for this
19:40 In that case we would not be able to account **for** this commotion,
21:21 They have been informed [NIE] that you teach all the Jews who
21:24 Then everybody will know there is no truth in these reports **about**
21:25 **As for** the Gentile believers, we have written to them our decision
22: 6 "**About** noon as I came near Damascus, suddenly a bright light
22: 6 suddenly a bright light from heaven **flashed around** [RP4313] me.
22:10 There you will be told [NIE] all that you have been assigned to
22:18 because they will not accept your testimony **about** me.'
23: 6 I stand on trial **because** of my hope in the resurrection of the dead."
23:11 As you have testified **about** me in Jerusalem, so you must also
23:15 the pretext of wanting more accurate information **about** his case.
23:20 on the pretext of wanting more accurate information **about** him.

23:29 I found that the accusation had **to do with** questions about their
24: 8 examining him yourself you will be able to learn the truth **about**
24:10 over this nation; so I gladly make **my** [+*1831+3836*] defense.
24:13 And they cannot prove to you [NIE] the charges they are now
24:21 unless it was [NIE] this one thing I shouted as I stood in their
24:21 'It is **concerning** the resurrection of the dead that I am on trial
24:22 Then Felix, who was well acquainted with [NIE] the Way,
24:24 and listened to him as he *spoke* **about** faith in Christ Jesus.
24:25 As Paul discoursed **on** righteousness, self-control and the judgment
25: 9 up to Jerusalem and stand trial before me there **on** these charges."
25:15 [NIE] When I went to Jerusalem, the chief priests and elders of
25:16 and has had an opportunity to defend himself **against** their charges.
25:18 they did not charge [NIE] him with any of the crimes I had
25:19 they had some points of dispute with him **about** their own religion
25:19 and **about** a dead man named Jesus who Paul claimed was alive.
25:20 I was at a loss how to investigate [NIE] such matters; so I asked
25:20 willing to go to Jerusalem and stand trial there **on** these charges.
25:24 The whole Jewish community has petitioned me **about** him in
25:26 But I have nothing definite to write to His Majesty **about** him.
26: 1 Agrippa said to Paul, "You have permission to speak **for** yourself."
26: 2 today as I make my defense **against** all the accusations of the Jews,
26: 7 O king, it is **because** of this hope that the Jews are accusing me.
26:26 The king is familiar **with** these things, and I can speak freely to
28: 7 There was an estate **nearby** [+*3836+5536*] that belonged to
28:15 The brothers there had heard **that** [+*3836*] we were coming,
28:21 "We have not received any letters from Judea **concerning** you,
28:21 have come from there has reported or said anything bad **about** you.
28:22 for we know that people everywhere are talking against [NIE]
28:23 and tried to convince them **about** Jesus from the Law of Moses
28:31 the kingdom of God and taught **about** the Lord Jesus Christ.
Ro   1: 3 **regarding** his Son, who as to his human nature was a descendant
   1: 8 First, I thank my God through Jesus Christ **for** all of you,
   8: 3 his own Son in the likeness of sinful man to be^s a sin offering.
  14:12 So then, each of us will give an account **of** himself to God.
  15:14 I myself am convinced, [NIE] my brothers, that you yourselves
  15:21 "Those who were not told **about** him will see, and those who have
1Co   1: 4 I always thank God **for** you because of his grace given you in
   1:11 some from Chloe's household have informed me [NIE] that there
   7: 1 Now for the matters you wrote **about**: It is good for a man not to
   7:25 Now **about** virgins: I have no command from the Lord, but I give a
   7:37 who is under no compulsion but has control **over** his own will,
   8: 1 Now **about** food sacrificed to idols: We know that we all possess
   8: 4 So then, **about** eating food sacrificed to idols: We know that an
  12: 1 Now **about** spiritual gifts, brothers, I do not want you to be
  16: 1 Now **about** the collection for God's people: Do what I told the
  16:12 Now **about** our brother Apollos: I strongly urged him to go to you
2Co   9: 1 There is no need for me to write to you **about** this service to the
  10: 8 For even if I boast somewhat freely **about** the authority the Lord
Eph   6:18 this in mind, be alert and always keep on praying **for** all the saints.
   6:22 that you may know **how** [+*3836*] we are, and that he may
Php   1:27 whether I come and see you or only hear **about** you in my absence,
   2:19 that I also may be cheered when I receive news **about** you.
   2:20 like him, who takes a genuine interest in your **welfare** [+*3836*].
   2:23 therefore, to send him as soon as I see how things **go with** me.
Col   1: 3 the Father of our Lord Jesus Christ, when we pray **for** you,
   4: 3 And pray **for** us, too, that God may open a door for our message,
   4: 8 the express purpose that you may know **about** our circumstances
   4:10 (You have received instructions **about** him; if he comes to you,
1Th   1: 2 We always thank God **for** all of you, mentioning you in our
   1: 9 for they themselves report what kind of reception you gave [NIE]
   3: 9 How can we thank God enough **for** you in return for all the joy we
   4: 6 The Lord will punish men **for** all such sins, as we have already told
   4: 9 Now **about** brotherly love we do not need to write to you,
   4:13 we do not want you to be ignorant **about** those who fall asleep,
   5: 1 brothers, **about** times and dates we do not need to write to you,
   5:25 Brothers, pray **for** us.
2Th   1: 3 We ought always to thank God **for** you, brothers, and rightly so,
   1:11 With this in mind, we constantly pray **for** you, that our God may
   2:13 But we ought always to thank God **for** you, brothers loved by the
   3: 1 pray **for** us that the message of the Lord may spread rapidly
1Ti   1: 7 they are talking about or [NIE] what they so confidently affirm.
   1:19 have rejected these and so have shipwrecked [NIE] their faith.
   6: 4 He has an unhealthy **interest in** controversies and quarrels about
   6:21 have professed and in so doing have wandered **from** the faith.
2Ti   1: 3 and day I constantly remember [NIE] you in my prayers.
   2:18 who have wandered away **from** the truth. They say that the

   3: 8 who, *as far as* the faith is **concerned**, are rejected.
Tit   2: 7 **In** everything set them an example by doing what is good.
   2: 8 may be ashamed because they have nothing bad to say **about** us.
   3: 8 And I want you to stress [NIE] these things, so that those who
Phm   1:10 I appeal to you **for** my son Onesimus, who became my son while I
Heb   2: 5 he has subjected the world to come, **about** which we are speaking.
   4: 4 For somewhere he has spoken **about** the seventh day in these
   4: 8 them rest, God would not have spoken later **about** another day.
   5: 3 This is why he has to offer sacrifices **for** his own sins, as well as
   5: 3 This is why he has to offer sacrifices for his own [RPG] sins,
   5: 3 sacrifices for his own sins, as well as **for** the sins of the people.
   5:11 We have much to say **about** this,
   6: 9 dear friends, we are confident of better things **in** your **case**—
   7:14 and in regard to that tribe Moses said nothing **about** priests.
   9: 5 But we cannot discuss [NIE] these things in detail now.
  10: 6 burnt offerings and **sin offerings** [+*281*] you were not pleased.
  10: 7 Then I said, 'Here I am—it is written **about** me in the scroll—
  10: 8 burnt offerings and **sin offerings** [+*281*] you did not desire,
  10:18 these have been forgiven, there is no longer any sacrifice **for** sin.
  10:26 received the knowledge of the truth, no sacrifice **for** sins is left,
  11: 7 By faith Noah, when warned **about** things not yet seen, in holy
  11:20 By faith Isaac blessed Jacob and Esau **in regard to** their future.
  11:22 spoke **about** the exodus of the Israelites from Egypt and gave
  11:22 of the Israelites from Egypt and gave instructions **about** his bones.
  11:32 I do not have time to tell **about** Gideon, Barak, Samson, Jephthah,
  11:40 God had planned something better **for** us so that only together with
  13:11 the blood of animals into the Most Holy Place **as** a sin offering,
  13:18 Pray **for** us. We are sure that we have a clear conscience and desire
1Pe   1:10 **Concerning** this salvation, the prophets, who spoke of the grace
   1:10 the prophets, who spoke **of** the grace that was to come to you,
   3:15 who asks you to give the reason **for** the hope that you have.
   3:18 For Christ died **for** sins once for all, the righteous for the
   5: 7 Cast all your anxiety on him because he cares **for** you.
2Pe   1:12 So I will always remind you **of** these things, even though you know
   3:16 the same way in all his letters, speaking in them **of** these matters.
1Jn   1: 1 have touched—this we proclaim **concerning** the Word of life.
   2: 2 He is the atoning sacrifice **for** our sins, and not only for ours
   2: 2 and not only for ours but also for the sins of the whole world.
   2: 2 and not only for ours but also **for** the sins of the whole world.
   2:26 I am writing these things to you **about** those who are trying to lead
   2:27 But as his anointing teaches you **about** all things and as that
   4:10 he loved us and sent his Son as an atoning sacrifice **for** our sins.
   5: 9 it is the testimony of God, which he has given **about** his Son.
   5:10 because he has not believed the testimony God has given **about** his
   5:16 that leads to death. I am not saying that he should pray **about** that.
3Jn   1: 2 may enjoy good health and that [NIE] all may go well with you,
Jude   1: 3 although I was very eager to write to you **about** the salvation we
   1: 7 and the **surrounding** towns gave themselves up to sexual
   1: 9 when he was disputing with the devil **about** the body of Moses,
   1:15 and to convict all the ungodly **of** all the ungodly acts they have
   1:15 and **of** all the harsh words ungodly sinners have spoken against
Rev 15: 6 shining linen and wore golden sashes **around** their chests.

4310 περιάγω, *periagō* [6] [√ *4309 + 72*]

groped about [1], take along [1], travel over [1], went around [1], went through [1], went [1]

Mt   4:23 Jesus **went** throughout Galilee, teaching in their synagogues,
   9:35 Jesus **went through** all the towns and villages, teaching in their
  23:15 *You* **travel over** land and sea to win a single convert, and when he
Mk   6: 6 Then Jesus **went around** teaching from village to village.
Ac 13:11 and darkness came over him, and he **groped about**,
1Co   9: 5 Don't we have the right *to* **take** a believing wife **along** *with* us,

4311 περιαιρέω, *periaireō* [5] [√ *4309 + 145*]

cutting loose [1], gave up [1], set sail [1], take away [1], taken away [1]

Ac 27:20 continued raging, we finally **gave up** all hope of being saved.
  27:40 **Cutting loose** the anchors, they left them in the sea and at the same
  28:13 From there we **set sail** and arrived at Rhegium. The next day the
2Co   3:16 But whenever anyone turns to the Lord, the veil *is* **taken away**.
Heb 10:11 he offers the same sacrifices, which can never **take away** sins.

4312 περιάπτω, *periaptō* [1] [√ 4309 + 721]

kindled [1]

Lk 22:55 But *when they had* **kindled** a fire in the middle of the courtyard

4313 περιαστράπτω, *periastraptō* [2] [√ 4309 + 847]

flashed around [RP4309] [1], flashed around [1]

Ac 9: 3 on his journey, suddenly a light from heaven **flashed around** him.
   22: 6 suddenly a bright light from heaven **flashed** [RP4309] **around** me.

4314 περιβάλλω, *periballō* [23] [√ 4309 + 965]

dressed in [4], wear [3], clothe [2], clothed in [2], dressed
[+2668] [2], dressed [2], clothed with [1], clothed [1], dressing in
[1], in [1], robed in [1], wearing nothing [+1218+2093] [1],
wearing [1], wrap around [1]

Mt 6:29 even Solomon in all his splendor *was* **dressed** like one of these.
    6:31 shall we eat?' or 'What shall we drink?' or 'What *shall we* **wear**?'
   25:36 I needed clothes and *you* **clothed** me, I was sick and you looked
   25:38 a stranger and invite you in, or needing clothes and **clothe** you?
   25:43 I needed clothes and *you did* not **clothe** me, I was sick and in
Mk 14:51 young man, **wearing** [+1218+2093] **nothing** but a linen garment,
   16: 5 they saw a young man **dressed in** a white robe sitting on the right
Lk 12:27 not even Solomon in all his splendor *was* **dressed** like one of
   23:11 **Dressing** him **in** an elegant robe, they sent him back to Pilate.
Jn 19: 2 and put it on his head. *They* **clothed** him **in** a purple robe
Ac 12: 8 "**Wrap** your cloak **around** *you* and follow me," the angel told him.
Rev 3: 5 He who overcomes *will*, like them, *be* **dressed** [+2668] in white.
    3:18 and white clothes to **wear**, so you can cover your shameful
    4: 4 *They were* **dressed** [+2668] in white and had crowns of gold on
    7: 9 *They were* **wearing** white robes and were holding palm branches
    7:13 Then one of the elders asked me, "These **in** white robes—who are
   10: 1 *He was* **robed in** a cloud, with a rainbow above his head;
   11: 3 and they will prophesy for 1,260 days, **clothed in** sackcloth."
   12: 1 a woman **clothed with** the sun, with the moon under her feet
   17: 4 The woman was **dressed in** purple and scarlet, and was glittering
   18:16 Woe, O great city, **dressed in** fine linen, purple and scarlet,
   19: 8 Fine linen, bright and clean, was given her to **wear**." (Fine linen
   19:13 *He is* **dressed in** a robe dipped in blood, and his name is the Word

4315 περιβλέπω, *periblepō* [7] [√ 4309 + 1063]

looked around at [3], looked around [2], looked at [1], looking
around [1]

Mk 3: 5 *He* **looked around at** them in anger and, deeply distressed at their
    3:34 Then *he* **looked at** those seated in a circle around him and said,
    5:32 But Jesus *kept* **looking around** to see who had done it.
    9: 8 Suddenly, *when they* **looked around**, they no longer saw anyone
   10:23 Jesus **looked around** and said to his disciples, "How hard it is for
   11:11 *He* **looked around at** everything, but since it was already late,
Lk 6:10 He **looked around at** them all, and then said to the man,

4316 περιβόλαιον, *peribolaion* [2] [√ 4309 + 965]

covering [1], robe [1]

1Co 11:15 it is her glory? For long hair is given to her as a **covering**.
Heb 1:12 You will roll them up like a **robe**; like a garment they will be

4317 περιδέω, *perideō* [1] [√ 4309 + 1313]

around [1]

Jn 11:44 and feet wrapped with strips of linen, and a cloth **around** his face.

4318 περιεργάζομαι, *periergazomai* [1]
[√ 4309 + 2240]

busybodies [1]

2Th 3:11 some among you are idle. They are not busy; *they are* **busybodies**.

4319 περίεργος, *periergos* [2] [√ 4309 + 2240]

busybodies [1], sorcery [1]

Ac 19:19 A number who had practiced **sorcery** brought their scrolls together
1Ti 5:13 but also gossips and **busybodies**, saying things they ought not to.

4320 περιέρχομαι, *perierchomai* [3] [√ 4309 + 2262]

going about [1], went about [1], went around [1]

Ac 19:13 Some Jews who **went around** driving out evil spirits tried to
1Ti 5:13 into the habit of being idle and **going about** from house to house.
Heb 11:37 *They* **went about** in sheepskins and goatskins, destitute,

4321 περιέχω, *periechō* [2] [√ 4309 + 2400]

astonished [+2502] [1], says [1]

Lk 5: 9 and all his companions *were* **astonished** [+2502] at the catch of
1Pe 2: 6 For in Scripture it **says**: "See, I lay a stone in Zion, a chosen

4322 περιζώννυμι, *perizōnnymi* [6] [√ 4309 + 2439]

around [1], buckled around waist [1], dress to serve [1], dressed
ready for service [+3836+4019] [1], get ready [1], wore [1]

Lk 12:35 "Be **dressed** [+3836+4019] **ready for service** and keep your lamps
   12:37 I tell you the truth, *he will* **dress** *himself* **to serve**, will have them
   17: 8 **get** *yourself* **ready** and wait on me while I eat and drink;
Eph 6:14 Stand firm then, with the belt of truth **buckled around** your **waist**,
Rev 1:13 reaching down to his feet and *with* a golden sash **around** his chest.
   15: 6 shining linen and **wore** golden sashes around their chests.

4323 περιζωννύω, *perizōnnyō* Not used in UBS/NIV
[√ 4309 + 2439]

4324 περίθεσις, *perithesis* [1] [√ 4309 + 5502]

wearing [1]

1Pe 3: 3 as braided hair and the **wearing** of gold jewelry and fine clothes.

4325 περιΐστημι, *periistēmi* [4] [√ 4309 + 2705]

avoid [2], standing here [1], stood around [1]

Jn 11:42 but I said this for the benefit of the people **standing here**,
Ac 25: 7 the Jews who had come down from Jerusalem **stood around** him,
2Ti 2:16 **Avoid** godless chatter, because those who indulge in it will become
Tit 3: 9 But **avoid** foolish controversies and genealogies and arguments

4326 περικάθαρμα, *perikatharma* [1] [√ 4309 + 2754]

scum [1]

1Co 4:13 Up to this moment we have become the **scum** of the earth,

4327 περικαθίζω, *perikathizō* Not used in UBS/NIV
[√ 4309 + 2767]

4328 περικαλύπτω, *perikalyptō* [3] [√ 4309 + 2821]

blindfolded [+3836+4725] [1], blindfolded [1], gold-covered
[+4119+5992] [1]

Mk 14:65 some began to spit at him; they **blindfolded** [+3836+4725] him,
Lk 22:64 They **blindfolded** him and demanded, "Prophesy! Who hit you?"
Heb 9: 4 incense and the **gold-covered** [+4119+5992] ark of the covenant.

4329 περίκειμαι, *perikeimai* [5] [√ 4309 + 3023]

tied around [RP4309] [2], bound [1], subject to [1], surrounded [1]

Mk 9:42 into the sea with a large millstone **tied** [RP4309] **around** his neck
Lk 17: 2 **tied** [RP4309] **around** his neck than for him to cause one of these
Ac 28:20 because of the hope of Israel that *I am* **bound** *with* this chain."
Heb 5: 2 and are going astray, since *he* himself *is* **subject to** weakness.
   12: 1 since we are **surrounded** by such a great cloud of witnesses,

4330 περικεφαλαία, *perikephalaia* [2]
[√ *4309 + 3051*]

helmet [2]

Eph 6:17 Take the **helmet** of salvation and the sword of the Spirit, which is
1Th 5: 8 and love as a breastplate, and the hope of salvation as a **helmet**.

4331 περικρατής, *perikratēs* [1] [√ *4309 + 3197*]

secure [1]

Ac 27:16 called Cauda, we were hardly able to make the lifeboat **secure**.

4332 περικρύβω, *perikrybō* [1] [√ *4309 + 3221*]

in seclusion [*+1571*] [1]

Lk 1:24 and for five months *remained* **in seclusion** [*+1571*].

4333 περικυκλόω, *perikykloō* [1] [√ *4309 + 3241*]

encircle [1]

Lk 19:43 against you and **encircle** you and hem you in on every side.

4334 περιλάμπω, *perilampō* [2] [√ *4309 + 3290*]

blazing around [1], shone around [1]

Lk 2: 9 and the glory of the Lord **shone around** them, and they were
Ac 26:13 brighter than the sun, **blazing around** me and my companions.

4335 περιλείπομαι, *perileipomai* [2] [√ *4309 + 3309*]

left [2]

1Th 4:15 that we who are still alive, who *are* **left** till the coming of the Lord,
     4:17 and *are* **left** will be caught up together with them in the clouds to

4336 περιλείχω, *perileichō* Not used in UBS/NIV
[√ *4309 + 3314*]

4337 περίλυπος, *perilypos* [5 / 4] [√ *4309 + 3383*]

overwhelmed with sorrow [2], greatly distressed [1], very sad [1]

Mt 26:38 "My soul is **overwhelmed with sorrow** to the point of death.
Mk 6:26 The king was **greatly distressed**, but because of his oaths
     14:34 "My soul is **overwhelmed with sorrow** to the point of death,"
Lk 18:23 When he heard this, he became **very sad**, because he was a man of
     18:24 Jesus looked at him [UBS+ *being* **very sad**] and said, "How hard it

4338 περιμένω, *perimenō* [1] [√ *4309 + 3531*]

wait for [1]

Ac 1: 4 "Do not leave Jerusalem, but **wait for** the gift my Father promised,

4339 πέριξ, *perix* [1] [√ *4309*]

around [1]

Ac 5:16 Crowds gathered also from the towns **around** Jerusalem,

4340 περιοικέω, *perioikeō* [1] [√ *4309 + 3875*]

neighbors [1]

Lk 1:65 The **neighbors** were all filled with awe, and throughout the hill

4341 περίοικος, *perioikos* [1] [√ *4309 + 3875*]

neighbors [1]

Lk 1:58 Her **neighbors** and relatives heard that the Lord had shown her

4342 περιούσιος, *periousios* [1] [√ *4309 + 1639*]

his very own [1]

Tit 2:14 and to purify for himself a people that are **his very own**,

4343 περιοχή, *periochē* [1] [√ *4309 + 2400*]

passage [1]

Ac 8:32 The eunuch was reading this **passage** of Scripture: "He was led like

4344 περιπατέω, *peripateō* [95] [√ *4309 + 4251*]

walk [25], live [17], walking [14], walks [4], live a life [3], walked [3], acting [2], walk around [2], act [1], behave [1], daily life [1], did^s [1], do [1], do^s [1], eat [1], followed [*+3552*] [1], go [1], idle [*+865*] [1], live lives [1], living [1], moved about [1], passing by [1], prowls around [1], retain the place in life [1], staying away from [*+1877+4024*] [1], the way act [1], use [*+1877*] [1], walk along [1], walked around [1], walking around [1], walks around [1], went around [1], went [1]

Mt 4:18 As Jesus *was* **walking** beside the Sea of Galilee, he saw two
     9: 5 to say, 'Your sins are forgiven,' or to say, 'Get up and **walk**'?
     11: 5 The blind receive sight, the lame **walk**, those who have leprosy are
     14:25 watch of the night Jesus went out to them, **walking** on the lake.
     14:26 When the disciples saw him **walking** on the lake, they were
     14:29 down out of the boat, **walked** on the water and came toward Jesus.
     15:31 the crippled made well, the lame **walking** and the blind seeing.
Mk 2: 9 sins are forgiven,' or to say, 'Get up, take your mat and **walk**'?
     5:42 the girl stood up and **walked around** (she was twelve years old).
     6:48 fourth watch of the night he went out to them, **walking** on the lake.
     6:49 but when they saw him **walking** on the lake, they thought he was a
     7: 5 "Why don't your disciples **live** according to the tradition of the
     8:24 and said, "I see people; they look like trees **walking around**."
     11:27 and *while* Jesus *was* **walking** in the temple courts, the chief
     12:38 They like *to* **walk around** in flowing robes and be greeted in the
     16:12 form to two of them *while they were* **walking** in the country.
Lk 5:23 to say, 'Your sins are forgiven,' or to say, 'Get up and **walk**'?
     7:22 The blind receive sight, the lame **walk**, those who have leprosy are
     11:44 like unmarked graves, which men **walk** over without knowing it."
     20:46 They like *to* **walk around** in flowing robes and love to be greeted
     24:17 them, "What are you discussing together *as you* **walk along**?"
Jn 1:36 When he saw Jesus **passing by**, he said, "Look, the Lamb of God!"
     5: 8 Then Jesus said to him, "Get up! Pick up your mat and **walk**."
     5: 9 At once the man was cured; he picked up his mat and **walked**.
     5:11 man who made me well said to me, 'Pick up your mat and **walk**.' "
     5:12 him, "Who is this fellow who told you to pick it up and **walk**?"
     6:19 they saw Jesus approaching the boat, **walking** on the water;
     6:66 of his disciples turned back and no longer **followed** [*+3552*] him.
     7: 1 After this, Jesus **went around** in Galilee, purposely staying away
     7: 1 purposely **staying away from** [*+1877+4024*] Judea
     8:12 Whoever follows me *will* never **walk** in darkness, but will have the
     10:23 and Jesus *was* in the temple area **walking** in Solomon's
     11: 9 A man *who* **walks** by day will not stumble, for he sees by this
     11:10 It is when he **walks** by night that he stumbles, for he has no light."
     11:54 Therefore Jesus no longer **moved about** publicly among the Jews.
     12:35 **Walk** while you have the light, before darkness overtakes you.
     12:35 The man *who* **walks** in the dark does not know where he is going.
     21:18 were younger you dressed yourself and **went** where you wanted;
Ac 3: 6 I have I give you. In the name of Jesus Christ of Nazareth, **walk**."
     3: 8 He jumped to his feet and *began to* **walk**. Then he went with them
     3: 8 into the temple courts, **walking** and jumping, and praising God.
     3: 9 When all the people saw him **walking** and praising God,
     3:12 as if by our own power or godliness we had made this man **walk**?
     14: 8 in his feet, who was lame from birth and *had* never **walked**.
     14:10 up on your feet!" At that, the *man* jumped up and *began to* **walk**.
     21:21 not to circumcise their children or **live** according to our customs.
Ro 6: 4 dead through the glory of the Father, we too *may* **live** a new life.
     8: 4 who *do* not **live** according to the sinful nature but according to the
     13:13 *Let us* **behave** decently, as in the daytime, not in orgies
     14:15 because of what you eat, *you are* no longer **acting** in love.
1Co 3: 3 are you not worldly? *Are you* not **acting** like mere men?
     7:17 each one *should* **retain the place in life** that the Lord assigned to
2Co 4: 2 *we do* not **use** [*+1877*] deception, nor do we distort the word of
     5: 7 *We* **live** by faith, not by sight.

          10: 2 some people who think that we **live** by the standards of this world.
          10: 3 For *though we* **live** in the world, we do not wage war as the world
          12:18 *Did we* not **act** in the same spirit and follow the same course?
Gal   5:16 So I say, **live** by the Spirit, and you will not gratify the desires of
Eph   2: 2 in which *you* used to **live** when you followed the ways of this
          2:10 to do good works, which God prepared in advance for *us to* **do**.
          4: 1 I urge you *to* **live a life** worthy of the calling you have received.
          4:17 on it in the Lord, that you *must* no longer **live** as the Gentiles do,
          4:17 in the Lord, that you must no longer live as the Gentiles **do**s,
          5: 2 and **live a life** of love, just as Christ loved us and gave himself up
          5: 8 but now you are light in the Lord. **Live** as children of light
          5:15 Be very careful, then, how *you* **live**—not as unwise but as wise,
Php   3:17 and take note of those *who* **live** according to the pattern we gave
          3:18 again even with tears, many **live** as enemies of the cross of Christ.
Col   1:10 And we pray this *in order that* you *may* **live a life** worthy of the
          2: 6 just as you received Christ Jesus as Lord, *continue to* **live** in him,
          3: 7 You used to **walk** in these ways, in the life you once lived.
          4: 5 Be wise *in* **the way** *you* **act** toward outsiders; make the most of
1Th   2:12 and urging you to **live** lives worthy of God,
          4: 1 brothers, we instructed you how *to* **live** in order to please God,
          4: 1 you how to live in order to please God, as in fact *you are* **living**.
          4:12 so that *your* **daily life** may win the respect of outsiders and
2Th   3: 6 and *does* not **live** according to the teaching you received from us.
          3:11 We hear that some among you *are* **idle** [+865]. They are not busy;
Heb 13: 9 by ceremonial foods, which are of no value to those *who* **eat** them.
1Pe   5: 8 Your enemy the devil **prowls around** like a roaring lion looking
1Jn   1: 6 If we claim to have fellowship with him yet **walk** in the darkness,
          1: 7 But if *we* **walk** in the light, as he is in the light, we have fellowship
          2: 6 Whoever claims to live in him must **walk** as Jesus did.
          2: 6 Whoever claims to live in him must walk as Jesus **did**s.
          2:11 his brother is in the darkness and **walks around** in the darkness;
2Jn   1: 4 It has given me great joy to find some of your children **walking** in
          1: 6 And this is love: that *we* **walk** in obedience to his commands.
          1: 6 heard from the beginning, his command is that *you* **walk** in love.
3Jn   1: 3 faithfulness to the truth and how you *continue to* **walk** in the truth.
          1: 4 I have no greater joy than to hear that my children *are* **walking** in
Rev   2: 1 in his right hand and **walks** among the seven golden lampstands:
          3: 4 *They will* **walk** with me, dressed in white, for they are worthy.
          9:20 bronze, stone and wood—idols that cannot see or hear or **walk**.
          16:15 with him, so that he *may* not **go** naked and be shamefully exposed."
          21:24 The nations *will* **walk** by its light, and the kings of the earth will

4345 περιπείρω, **peripeirō** [1] [√ *4309*]

pierced [1]

1Ti   6:10 wandered from the faith and **pierced** themselves with many griefs.

4346 περιπίπτω, **peripiptō** [3] [√ *4309 + 4406*]

face [1], fell into the hands of [1], struck [1]

Lk   10:30 from Jerusalem to Jericho, when *he* **fell into the hands of** robbers.
Ac   27:41 But the ship **struck** a sandbar and ran aground. The bow stuck fast
Jas   1: 2 it pure joy, my brothers, whenever *you* **face** trials of many kinds,

4347 περιποιέω, **peripoieō** [3] [√ *4309 + 4472*]

bought [1], gain [1], keep [1]

Lk   17:33 Whoever tries *to* **keep** his life will lose it, and whoever loses his
Ac   20:28 of the church of God, which *he* **bought** with his own blood.
1Ti   3:13 Those who have served well **gain** an excellent standing and great

4348 περιποίησις, **peripoiēsis** [5] [√ *4309 + 4472*]

belonging to God [+*1650*] [1], possession [1], receive [1], saved
[+*1650+6034*] [1], share [1]

Eph   1:14 until the redemption *of* those who are God's **possession**—
1Th   5: 9 suffer wrath but to **receive** salvation through our Lord Jesus Christ.
2Th   2:14 that you might **share** in the glory of our Lord Jesus Christ.
Heb 10:39 but of those who believe and are **saved** [+*1650+6034*].
1Pe   2: 9 a holy nation, a people **belonging** [+*1650*] **to God**,

4349 περιραίνω, **perirainō** Not used in UBS/NIV
[√ *4309 + 4817*]

4350 περιραντίζω, **perirantizō** Not used in UBS/NIV
[√ *4309 + 4817*]

4351 περιρήγνυμι, **perirēgnymi** [1] [√ *4309 + 4838*]

stripped [+*2668+3836*] [1]

Ac   16:22 and the magistrates ordered them *to be* **stripped** [+*2668+3836*]

4352 περισπάω, **perispaō** [1] [√ *4309 + 5060*]

distracted [1]

Lk   10:40 But Martha *was* **distracted** by all the preparations that had to be

4353 περισσεία, **perisseia** [4] [√ *4356*]

abundant provision [1], greatly [+*1650*] [1], overflowing [1],
prevalent [1]

Ro   5:17 much more will those who receive God's **abundant provision**
2Co   8: 2 their **overflowing** joy and their extreme poverty welled up in rich
          10:15 our area of activity among you will **greatly** [+*1650*] expand,
Jas   1:21 get rid of all moral filth and the evil that is so **prevalent**

4354 περίσσευμα, **perisseuma** [5] [√ *4356*]

overflow [2], plenty [2], left over [1]

Mt   12:34 For out of the **overflow** of the heart the mouth speaks.
Mk   8: 8 picked up seven basketfuls of broken pieces *that were* **left over**.
Lk   6:45 in his heart. For out of the **overflow** of his heart his mouth speaks.
2Co   8:14 At the present time your **plenty** will supply what they need,
          8:14 they need, so that in turn their **plenty** will supply what you need.

4355 περισσεύω, **perisseuō** [39] [√ *4356*]

left over [5], overflow [5], excel [3], abound [2], have an
abundance [2], overflowing [2], wealth [2], abundance [1], better
[1], do so more and more [+*3437*] [1], do this more and more
[+*3437*] [1], enhances [1], flow over [1], give fully [1], grew [1],
have to spare [1], is [1], lavished [1], living in plenty [1], make
abound [1], more [1], overflows [1], plenty [1], surpasses [+*4498*]
[1], welled up [1]

Mt   5:20 For I tell you that unless your righteousness **surpasses** [+*4498*]
          13:12 Whoever has will be given more, and *he will* **have an abundance**.
          14:20 picked up twelve basketfuls of broken pieces that *were* **left over**.
          15:37 picked up seven basketfuls of broken pieces that *were* **left over**.
          25:29 who has will be given more, and *he will* **have an abundance**.
Mk   12:44 They all gave out of their **wealth**;
Lk   9:17 picked up twelve basketfuls of broken pieces that *were* **left over**.
          12:15 a man's life does not consist in the **abundance** of his possessions."
          15:17 'How many of my father's hired men **have** food **to spare**,
          21: 4 All these people gave their gifts out of their **wealth**; but she out of
Jn   6:12 he said to his disciples, "Gather the pieces *that are* **left over**.
          6:13 pieces of the five barley loaves **left over** by those who had eaten.
Ac   16: 5 churches were strengthened in the faith and **grew** daily in numbers.
Ro   3: 7 "If my falsehood **enhances** God's truthfulness and so increases his
          5:15 by the grace of the one man, Jesus Christ, **overflow** to the many!
          5:15 so that *you may* **overflow** with hope by the power of the Holy
1Co   8: 8 to God; we are no worse if we do not eat, and no **better** if we do.
          14:12 to have spiritual gifts, try to **excel** *in* gifts that build up the church.
          15:58 Always **give** yourselves **fully** to the work of the Lord, because you
2Co   1: 5 For just as the sufferings of Christ **flow over** into our lives,
          1: 5 over into our lives, so also through Christ our comfort **overflows**.
          3: 9 how much more glorious *is* the ministry that brings righteousness!
          4:15 and more people *may cause* thanksgiving *to* **overflow** to the glory
          8: 2 and their extreme poverty **welled up** in rich generosity.
          8: 7 But just as *you* **excel** in everything—in faith, in speech, in
          8: 7 in your love for us—see that *you* also **excel** in this grace of giving.
          9: 8 And God is able *to* **make** all grace **abound** to you, so that in all
          9: 8 having all that you need, *you will* **abound** in every good work.
          9:12 but is also **overflowing** in many expressions of thanks to God.
Eph   1: 8 that *he* **lavished** on us with all wisdom and understanding.
Php   1: 9 that your love *may* **abound** more and more in knowledge
          1:26 you again your joy in Christ Jesus *will* **overflow** on account of me.

	4:12	know what it is to be in need, and I know what it is *to have* **plenty**.
	4:12	whether well fed or hungry, whether **living in plenty** or in want.
	4:18	I have received full payment and even **more**; I am amply supplied,
Col	2: 7	in the faith as you were taught, and **overflowing** with thankfulness.
1Th	3:12	*May* the Lord make your love increase and **overflow** for each
	4: 1	and urge you in the Lord Jesus to **do this more and more** [+*3437*].
	4:10	Yet we urge you, brothers, *to* **do so more and more** [+*3437*].

4356 περισσός, *perissos* [6] [→ *1735, 4353, 4354, 4355, 4357, 4358, 4359, 4360, 5655, 5656, 5668, 5669; cf. 4309*]

advantage [1], beyond [1], completely [+*1666*+*3336*] [1], more [1], no need [1], to the full [1]

Mt	5:37	your 'No,' 'No'; anything **beyond** this comes from the evil one.
	5:47	greet only your brothers, what are you doing **more** than others?
Mk	6:51	wind died down. They were **completely** [+*1666*+*3336*] amazed,
Jn	10:10	I have come that they may have life, and have it **to the full**.
Ro	3: 1	What **advantage**, then, is there in being a Jew, or what value is
2Co	9: 1	There is **no need** for me to write to you about this service to the

4357 περισσότερον, *perissoteron* Not used in UBS/NIV [√ *4356*]

4358 περισσότερος, *perissoteros* [16] [√ *4356*]

more than [2], more [2], most severely [2], special [2], excessive [1], freely [1], greater [1], harder than [1], more [+*3437*] [1], more important than [1], much more [1], very [1]

Mt	11: 9	go out to see? A prophet? Yes, I tell you, and **more than** a prophet.
Mk	7:36	the more he did so, the **more** [+*3437*] they kept talking about it.
	12:33	and to love your neighbor as yourself is **more important than** all
	12:40	make lengthy prayers. Such men will be punished **most severely**."
Lk	7:26	go out to see? A prophet? Yes, I tell you, and **more than** a prophet.
	12: 4	be afraid of those who kill the body and after that can do no **more**.
	12:48	one who has been entrusted with much, **much more** will be asked.
	20:47	make lengthy prayers. Such men will be punished **most severely**."
1Co	12:23	and the parts that we think are less honorable we treat with **special**
	12:23	And the parts that are unpresentable are treated with **special**
	12:24	of the body and has given **greater** honor to the parts that lacked it,
	15:10	No, I worked **harder than** all of them—yet not I, but the grace of
2Co	2: 7	so that he will not be overwhelmed *by* **excessive** sorrow.
	10: 8	For even if I boast somewhat **freely** about the authority the Lord
Heb	6:17	nature of his purpose **very** clear to the heirs of what was promised,
	7:15	And what we have said is even **more** clear if another priest like

4359 περισσοτέρως, *perissoterōs* [12] [√ *4356*]

more [2], depth [1], especially [+*3437*] [1], especially [1], every [1], extremely [1], greater [1], more careful [1], more frequently [1], much harder [1], particularly [1]

2Co	1:12	and **especially** in our relations with you, in the holiness
	2: 4	not to grieve you but to let you know the **depth** of my love for you.
	7:13	we were **especially** [+*3437*] delighted to see how happy Titus was,
	7:15	And his affection for you is all the **greater** when he remembers
	11:23	I have worked **much harder**, been in prison more frequently,
	11:23	I have worked much harder, been in prison **more frequently**,
	12:15	expend myself as well. If I love you **more**, will you love me less?
Gal	1:14	and was **extremely** zealous for the traditions of my fathers.
Php	1:14	been encouraged to speak the word of God **more** courageously
1Th	2:17	out of our intense longing we made **every** effort to see you.
Heb	2: 1	We must pay **more careful** attention, therefore, to what we have
	13:19	I **particularly** urge you to pray so that I may be restored to you

4360 περισσῶς, *perissōs* [4] [√ *4356*]

all the louder [2], even more [1], obsession [+*1841*] [1]

Mt	27:23	asked Pilate. But they shouted **all the louder**, "Crucify him!"
Mk	10:26	The disciples were **even more** amazed, and said to each other,
	15:14	asked Pilate. But they shouted **all the louder**, "Crucify him!"
Ac	26:11	*In my* **obsession against** [+*1841*] them, I even went to foreign

4361 περιστερά, *peristera* [10]

doves [5], dove [4], pigeons [1]

Mt	3:16	and he saw the Spirit of God descending like a **dove** and lighting
	10:16	Therefore be as shrewd as snakes and as innocent as **doves**.
	21:12	of the money changers and the benches of those selling **doves**.
Mk	1:10	being torn open and the Spirit descending on him like a **dove**.
	11:15	of the money changers and the benches of those selling **doves**,
Lk	2:24	in the Law of the Lord: "a pair of doves or two young **pigeons**."
	3:22	and the Holy Spirit descended on him in bodily form like a **dove**.
Jn	1:32	"I saw the Spirit come down from heaven as a **dove** and remain on
	2:14	sheep and **doves**, and others sitting at tables exchanging money.
	2:16	To those who sold **doves** he said, "Get these out of here! How dare

4362 περιτέμνω, *peritemnō* [17] [√ *4309* + *5533*]

circumcised [12], circumcise [4], circumcised [+*3284*] [1]

Lk	1:59	On the eighth day they came *to* **circumcise** the child, and they
	2:21	On the eighth day, when it was time *to* **circumcise** him, he was
Jn	7:22	but from the patriarchs), *you* **circumcise** a child on the Sabbath.
Ac	7: 8	the father of Isaac and **circumcised** him eight days after his birth.
	15: 1	"Unless *you are* **circumcised**, according to the custom taught by
	15: 5	"The Gentiles must *be* **circumcised** and required to obey the law of
	16: 3	so *he* **circumcised** [+*3284*] him because of the Jews who lived in
	21:21	telling them not *to* **circumcise** their children or live according to
1Co	7:18	Was a man *already* **circumcised** when he was called? He should
	7:18	when he was called? *He should* not *be* **circumcised**.
Gal	2: 3	even Titus, who was with me, was compelled *to be* **circumcised**,
	5: 2	I, Paul, tell you that if *you let yourselves be* **circumcised**,
	5: 3	Again I declare to every man *who lets himself be* **circumcised**
	6:12	impression outwardly are trying to compel you *to be* **circumcised**.
	6:13	Not even those *who are* **circumcised** obey the law, yet they want
	6:13	yet they want you *to be* **circumcised** that they may boast about
Col	2:11	In him *you were* also **circumcised**, in the putting off of the sinful

4363 περιτίθημι, *peritithēmi* [8] [√ *4309* + *5502*]

put on [4], put around [2], set on [1], treat with [1]

Mt	21:33	He **put** a wall **around** it, dug a winepress in it and built a
	27:28	*They* stripped him and **put** a scarlet robe **on** him,
	27:48	He filled it with wine vinegar, **put** it **on** a stick, and offered it to
Mk	12: 1	He **put** a wall **around** it, dug a pit for the winepress and built a
	15:17	on him, then twisted together a crown of thorns and **set** it **on** him.
	15:36	with wine vinegar, **put** it **on** a stick, and offered it to Jesus to drink.
Jn	19:29	**put** the sponge **on** a stalk of the hyssop plant, and lifted it to Jesus'
1Co	12:23	and the parts that we think are less honorable *we* **treat with** special

4364 περιτομή, *peritomē* [36] [√ *4309* + *5533*]

circumcision [16], circumcised [7], Jews [4], circumcised [+*1666*] [3], circumcision group [2], after*s* [+*1877*] [1], circumcised [+*3284*] [1], Jews [+*1666*] [1], you*s* [+*3836*] [1]

Jn	7:22	because Moses gave you **circumcision** (though actually it did not
	7:23	Now if a child *can be* **circumcised** [+*3284*] on the Sabbath
Ac	7: 8	Then he gave Abraham the covenant of **circumcision**.
	10:45	The **circumcised** [+*1666*] believers who had come with Peter were
	11: 2	up to Jerusalem, the **circumcised** [+*1666*] *believers* criticized him
Ro	2:25	**Circumcision** has value if you observe the law, but if you break
	2:25	but if you break the law, you*s* [+*3836*] have become as though you
	2:26	will they not be regarded as though they were **circumcised**?
	2:27	even though you have the written code and **circumcision**,
	2:28	one outwardly, nor is **circumcision** merely outward and physical.
	2:29	and **circumcision** is circumcision of the heart, by the Spirit,
	3: 1	is there in being a Jew, or what value is there *in* **circumcision**?
	3:30	who will justify the **circumcised** by faith and the uncircumcised
	4: 9	Is this blessedness only for the **circumcised**, or also for the
	4:10	Was it after he was **circumcised**, or before? It was not after,
	4:10	was circumcised, or before? It was not after*s* [+*1877*], but before!
	4:11	And he received the sign *of* **circumcision**, a seal of the
	4:12	And he is also the father *of* the **circumcised** who not only are
	4:12	father of the circumcised who not only are **circumcised** [+*1666*]
	15: 8	For I tell you that Christ has become a servant *of* the **Jews** on
1Co	7:19	**Circumcision** is nothing and uncircumcision is nothing.
Gal	2: 7	the gospel to the Gentiles, just as Peter had been *to* the **Jews**.

2: 8 who was at work in the ministry of Peter as an apostle *to* the **Jews**,
2: 9 agreed that we should go to the Gentiles, and they to the **Jews**.
2: 12 he was afraid of those who belonged to the **circumcision group**.
5: 6 For in Christ Jesus neither **circumcision** nor uncircumcision has
5: 11 Brothers, if I am still preaching **circumcision**, why am I still being
6: 15 Neither **circumcision** nor uncircumcision means anything;
Eph 2: 11 "the **circumcision**" (that done in the body by the hands of men)—
Php 3: 3 For it is we who are the **circumcision**, we who worship by the
3: 5 **circumcised** on the eighth day, of the people of Israel, of the tribe
Col 2: 11 not *with* a **circumcision** done by the hands of men but with the
2: 11 by the hands of men but with the **circumcision** done by Christ,
3: 11 Here there is no Greek or Jew, **circumcised** or uncircumcised,
4: 11 These are the only **Jews** [+*1666*] among my fellow workers for the
Tit 1: 10 and deceivers, especially those of the **circumcision group**.

4365 περιτρέπω, *peritrepō* [1] [√ *4309 + 5572*]

driving [1]

Ac 26: 24 Paul!" he shouted. "Your great learning *is* **driving** you insane."

4366 περιτρέχω, *peritrechō* [1] [√ *4309 + 5556*]

ran throughout [1]

Mk 6: 55 *They* **ran throughout** that whole region and carried the sick on

4367 περιφέρω, *peripherō* [3] [√ *4309 + 5770*]

blown here and there [1], carried [+*806*] [1], carry around [1]

Mk 6: 55 and **carried** [+*806*] the sick on mats to wherever they heard he
2Co 4: 10 We always **carry around** in our body the death of Jesus, so that
Eph 4: 14 and **blown here and there** by every wind of teaching and by the

4368 περιφρονέω, *periphroneō* [1] [√ *4309 + 5856*]

despise [1]

Tit 2: 15 and rebuke with all authority. *Do* not *let* anyone **despise** you.

4369 περίχωρος, *perichōros* [9] [√ *4309 + 6003*]

region [3], surrounding country [3], country around [1],
countryside [1], surrounding [1]

Mt 3: 5 from Jerusalem and all Judea and the whole **region** of the Jordan.
14: 35 recognized Jesus, they sent word to all the **surrounding country**.
Mk 1: 28 News about him spread quickly over the whole **region** of Galilee.
Lk 3: 3 He went into all the **country around** the Jordan, preaching a
4: 14 and news about him spread through the whole **countryside**.
4: 37 And the news about him spread throughout the **surrounding** area.
7: 17 Jesus spread throughout Judea and the **surrounding country**.
8: 37 Then all the people *of* the **region** of the Gerasenes asked Jesus to
Ac 14: 6 cities of Lystra and Derbe and to the **surrounding country**,

4370 περίψημα, *peripsēma* [1] [√ *4309 + 6041*]

refuse [1]

1Co 4: 13 we have become the scum of the earth, the **refuse** of the world.

4371 περπερεύομαι, *perpereuomai* [1]

boast [1]

1Co 13: 4 love is kind. It does not envy, it *does* not **boast**, it is not proud.

4372 Περσίς, *Persis* [1]

Persis [1]

Ro 16: 12 Greet my dear friend **Persis**, another woman who has worked very

4373 πέρυσι, *perysi* [2] [√ *4305*]

last year [2]

2Co 8: 10 **Last year** you were the first not only to give but also to have the

9: 2 telling them that since **last year** you in Achaia were ready to give;

4374 πετεινόν, *peteinon* [14] [√ *4375*]

birds [14]

Mt 6: 26 Look at the **birds** of the air; they do not sow or reap or store away
8: 20 Jesus replied, "Foxes have holes and **birds** of the air have nests,
13: 4 some fell along the path, and the **birds** came and ate it up.
13: 32 so that the **birds** of the air come and perch in its branches."
Mk 4: 4 some fell along the path, and the **birds** came and ate it up.
4: 32 with such big branches that the **birds** of the air can perch in its
Lk 8: 5 the path; it was trampled on, and the **birds** of the air ate it up.
9: 58 Jesus replied, "Foxes have holes and **birds** of the air have nests,
12: 24 God feeds them. And how much more valuable you are than **birds**!
13: 19 and became a tree, and the **birds** of the air perched in its branches."
Ac 10: 12 as well as reptiles of the earth and **birds** of the air.
11: 6 animals of the earth, wild beasts, reptiles, and **birds** of the air.
Ro 1: 23 made to look like mortal man and **birds** and animals and reptiles.
Jas 3: 7 All kinds *of* animals, **birds**, reptiles and creatures of the sea are

4375 πέτομαι, *petomai* [5] [→ *1736, 2925, 4374, 4762, 4763, 4764*]

flying [4], fly [1]

Rev 4: 7 the third had a face like a man, the fourth was like a **flying** eagle.
8: 13 I heard an eagle *that was* **flying** in midair call out in a loud voice:
12: 14 so that *she might* **fly** to the place prepared for her in the desert,
14: 6 Then I saw another angel **flying** in midair, and he had the eternal
19: 17 who cried in a loud voice *to* all the birds **flying** in midair,

4376 πέτρα, *petra* [15] [→ *4377, 4378*]

rock [12], rocks [3]

Mt 7: 24 into practice is like a wise man who built his house on the **rock**.
7: 25 yet it did not fall, because it had its foundation on the **rock**.
16: 18 tell you that you are Peter, and on this **rock** I will build my church,
27: 51 in two from top to bottom. The earth shook and the **rocks** split.
27: 60 and placed it in his own new tomb that he had cut out of the **rock**.
Mk 15: 46 wrapped it in the linen, and placed it in a tomb cut out of **rock**.
Lk 6: 48 a house, who dug down deep and laid the foundation on **rock**.
8: 6 Some fell on **rock**, and when it came up, the plants withered
8: 13 Those on the **rock** are the ones who receive the word with joy
Ro 9: 33 stone that causes men to stumble and a **rock** that makes them fall,
1Co 10: 4 for they drank from the spiritual **rock** that accompanied them,
10: 4 the spiritual **rock** that accompanied them, and that **rock** was Christ.
1Pe 2: 8 stone that causes men to stumble and a **rock** that makes them fall."
Rev 6: 15 every free man hid in caves and among the **rocks** of the mountains.
6: 16 They called *to* the mountains and the **rocks**, "Fall on us and hide us

4377 Πέτρος, *Petros* [156 / 155] [√ *4376*]

Πέτρος ... Ἰωάννης ... Ἰάκωβος (Peter ... John ... James)
[10] Mt 10:2; 17:1; Mk 5:37; 9:2; 13:3; 14:33; Lk 6:14; 8:51; 9:28; Ac 1:13

Σίμων Πέτρος (Simon Peter) [29] Mt 4:18; 10:2; 16:16; Mk 3:16; 14:37; Lk 5:8; 6:14; Jn 1:40; 6:8,68; 13:6,9,24,36; 18:10,15,25; 20:2,6; 21:2,3,7,11,15,17; Ac 10:5,18,32; 11:13

Συμεών Πέτρος (Simeon Peter) [1] 2Pe 1:1

Peter [150], Peter's [5]

Mt 4: 18 he saw two brothers, Simon called **Peter** and his brother Andrew.
8: 14 When Jesus came into **Peter's** house, he saw Peter's mother-in-law
10: 2 first, Simon (who is called **Peter**) and his brother Andrew;
14: 28 "Lord, if it's you," **Peter** replied, "tell me to come to you on the
14: 29 Then **Peter** got down out of the boat, walked on the water
15: 15 **Peter** said, "Explain the parable to us."
16: 16 Simon **Peter** answered, "You are the Christ, the Son of the living
16: 18 And I tell you that you are **Peter**, and on this rock I will build my
16: 22 **Peter** took him aside and began to rebuke him. "Never, Lord!"
16: 23 Jesus turned and said *to* **Peter**, "Get behind me, Satan! You are a
17: 1 After six days Jesus took with him **Peter**, James and John the
17: 4 **Peter** said to Jesus, "Lord, it is good for us to be here. If you wish,
17: 24 the collectors of the two-drachma tax came to **Peter** and asked,

18:21 Then **Peter** came to Jesus and asked, "Lord, how many times shall I
19:27 **Peter** answered him, "We have left everything to follow you!
26:33 **Peter** replied, "Even if all fall away on account of you, I never
26:35 But **Peter** declared, "Even if I have to die with you, I will never
26:37 He took **Peter** and the two sons of Zebedee along with him,
26:40 you men not keep watch with me for one hour?" he asked **Peter**.
26:58 But **Peter** followed him at a distance, right up to the courtyard of
26:69 Now **Peter** was sitting out in the courtyard, and a servant girl came
26:73 After a little while, those standing there went up to **Peter** and said,
26:75 Then **Peter** remembered the word Jesus had spoken: "Before the

Mk 3:16 twelve he appointed: Simon (to whom he gave the name **Peter**);
5:37 He did not let anyone follow him except **Peter**, James and John the
8:29 "Who do you say I am?" **Peter** answered, "You are the Christ."
8:32 about this, and **Peter** took him aside and began to rebuke him.
8:33 when Jesus turned and looked at his disciples, he rebuked **Peter**.
9:2 After six days Jesus took **Peter**, James and John with him
9:5 **Peter** said to Jesus, "Rabbi, it is good for us to be here. Let us put
10:28 **Peter** said to him, "We have left everything to follow you!"
11:21 **Peter** remembered and said to Jesus, "Rabbi, look! The fig tree you
13:3 the temple, **Peter**, James, John and Andrew asked him privately,
14:29 **Peter** declared, "Even if all fall away, I will not."
14:33 He took **Peter**, James and John along with him, and he began to be
14:37 found them sleeping. "Simon," he said *to* **Peter**, "are you asleep?
14:54 **Peter** followed him at a distance, right into the courtyard of the
14:66 While **Peter** was below in the courtyard, one of the servant girls of
14:67 When she saw **Peter** warming himself, she looked closely at him.
14:70 After a little while, those standing near said *to* **Peter**, "Surely you
14:72 Then **Peter** remembered the word Jesus had spoken to him:
16:7 But go, tell his disciples and **Peter**, 'He is going ahead of you into
16:S [UBS+ *commanded them they told briefly to those around* **Peter**.]

Lk 5:8 When Simon **Peter** saw this, he fell at Jesus' knees and said,
6:14 Simon (whom he named **Peter**), his brother Andrew, James,
8:45 When they all denied it, **Peter** said, "Master, the people are
8:51 he did not let anyone go in with him except **Peter**, John and James,
9:20 "Who do you say I am?" **Peter** answered, "The Christ of God."
9:28 he took **Peter**, John and James with him and went up onto a
9:32 **Peter** and his companions were very sleepy, but when they became
9:33 **Peter** said to him, "Master, it is good for us to be here."
12:41 **Peter** asked, "Lord, are you telling this parable to us, or to
18:28 **Peter** said to him, "We have left all we had to follow you!"
22:8 Jesus sent **Peter** and John, saying, "Go and make preparations for
22:34 Jesus answered, "I tell you, **Peter**, before the rooster crows today,
22:54 him into the house of the high priest. **Peter** followed at a distance.
22:55 and had sat down together, **Peter** sat down with them.
22:58 said, "You also are one of them." "Man, I am not!" **Peter** replied.
22:60 **Peter** replied, "Man, I don't know what you're talking about!"
22:61 The Lord turned and looked straight at **Peter**. Then Peter
22:61 Then **Peter** remembered the word the Lord had spoken to him:
24:12 **Peter**, however, got up and ran to the tomb. Bending over,

Jn 1:40 Andrew, Simon **Peter's** brother, was one of the two who heard
1:42 You will be called Cephas" (which, when translated, is **Peter**).
1:44 Philip, like Andrew and **Peter**, was from the town of Bethsaida.
6:8 of his disciples, Andrew, Simon **Peter's** brother, spoke up,
6:68 Simon **Peter** answered him, "Lord, to whom shall we go? You have
13:6 He came to Simon **Peter**, who said to him, "Lord, are you going to
13:8 "No," said **Peter**, "you shall never wash my feet." Jesus answered,
13:9 "Then, Lord," Simon **Peter** replied, "not just my feet but my hands
13:24 Simon **Peter** motioned to this disciple and said, "Ask him which
13:36 Simon **Peter** asked him, "Lord, where are you going?"
13:37 **Peter** asked, "Lord, why can't I follow you now? I will lay down
18:10 Then Simon **Peter**, who had a sword, drew it and struck the high
18:11 Jesus commanded **Peter**, "Put your sword away! Shall I not drink
18:15 Simon **Peter** and another disciple were following Jesus.
18:16 but **Peter** had to wait outside at the door. The other disciple,
18:16 came back, spoke to the girl on duty there and brought **Peter** in.
18:17 not one of his disciples, are you?" the girl at the door asked **Peter**.
18:18 keep warm. **Peter** also was standing with them, warming himself.
18:25 As Simon **Peter** stood warming himself, he was asked, "You are
18:26 a relative of the man whose ear **Peter** had cut off, challenged him,
18:27 Again **Peter** denied it, and at that moment a rooster began to crow.
20:2 So she came running to Simon **Peter** and the other disciple,
20:3 So **Peter** and the other disciple started for the tomb.
20:4 but the other disciple outran **Peter** and reached the tomb first.
20:6 Then Simon **Peter**, who was behind him, arrived and went into the
21:2 Simon **Peter**, Thomas (called Didymus), Nathanael from Cana in
21:3 Simon **Peter** told them, and they said, "We'll go with you."

21:7 Then the disciple whom Jesus loved said *to* **Peter**, "It is the Lord!"
21:7 As soon as Simon **Peter** heard him say, "It is the Lord," he wrapped
21:11 Simon **Peter** climbed aboard and dragged the net ashore. It was
21:15 had finished eating, Jesus said *to* Simon **Peter**, "Simon son of John,
21:17 **Peter** was hurt because Jesus asked him the third time, "Do you
21:20 **Peter** turned and saw that the disciple whom Jesus loved was
21:21 When **Peter** saw him, he asked, "Lord, what about him?"

Ac 1:13 Those present were **Peter**, John, James and Andrew; Philip
1:15 In those days **Peter** stood up among the believers (a group
2:14 Then **Peter** stood up with the Eleven, raised his voice
2:37 they were cut to the heart and said to **Peter** and the other apostles,
2:38 **Peter** replied, "Repent and be baptized, every one of you,
3:1 One day **Peter** and John were going up to the temple at the time of
3:3 When he saw **Peter** and John about to enter, he asked them for
3:4 **Peter** looked straight at him, as did John. Then Peter said,
3:6 Then **Peter** said, "Silver or gold I do not have, but what I have I
3:11 While the beggar held on to **Peter** and John, all the people were
3:12 When **Peter** saw this, he said to them: "Men of Israel, why does
4:8 Then **Peter**, filled with the Holy Spirit, said to them: "Rulers
4:13 When they saw the courage *of* **Peter** and John and realized that
4:19 But **Peter** and John replied, "Judge for yourselves whether it is
5:3 Then **Peter** said, "Ananias, how is it that Satan has so filled your
5:8 **Peter** asked her, "Tell me, is this the price you and Ananias got for
5:9 **Peter** said to her, "How could you agree to test the Spirit of the
5:15 so that at least **Peter's** shadow might fall on some of them as he
5:29 **Peter** and the other apostles replied: "We must obey God rather
8:14 had accepted the word of God, they sent **Peter** and John to them.
8:20 **Peter** answered: "May your money perish with you, because you
9:32 As **Peter** traveled about the country, he went to visit the saints in
9:34 "Aeneas," **Peter** said to him, "Jesus Christ heals you. Get up and
9:38 so when the disciples heard that **Peter** was in Lydda, they sent two
9:39 **Peter** went with them, and when he arrived he was taken upstairs
9:40 **Peter** sent them all out of the room; then he got down on his knees
9:40 "Tabitha, get up." She opened her eyes, and seeing **Peter** she sat
10:5 to Joppa to bring back a man named Simon who is called **Peter**.
10:9 and approaching the city, **Peter** went up on the roof to pray.
10:13 Then a voice told him, "Get up, **Peter**. Kill and eat."
10:14 "Surely not, Lord!" **Peter** replied. "I have never eaten anything
10:17 While **Peter** was wondering about the meaning of the vision,
10:18 asking if Simon who was known as **Peter** was staying there.
10:19 While **Peter** was still thinking about the vision, the Spirit said to
10:21 **Peter** went down and said to the men, "I'm the one you're looking
10:25 As **Peter** entered the house, Cornelius met him and fell at his feet
10:26 But **Peter** made him get up. "Stand up," he said, "I am only a man
10:32 Send to Joppa for Simon who is called **Peter**. He is a guest in the
10:34 Then **Peter** began to speak: "I now realize how true it is that God
10:44 While **Peter** was still speaking these words, the Holy Spirit came
10:45 The circumcised believers who had come with **Peter** were
10:46 heard them speaking in tongues and praising God. Then **Peter** said,
11:2 So when **Peter** went up to Jerusalem, the circumcised believers
11:4 **Peter** began and explained everything to them precisely as it had
11:7 Then I heard a voice telling me, 'Get up, **Peter**. Kill and eat.'
11:13 his house and say, 'Send to Joppa for Simon who is called **Peter**.
12:3 he saw that this pleased the Jews, he proceeded to seize **Peter** also.
12:5 So **Peter** was kept in prison, but the church was earnestly praying
12:6 **Peter** was sleeping between two soldiers, bound with two chains,
12:7 He struck **Peter** on the side and woke him up. "Quick, get up!"
12:11 Then **Peter** came to himself and said, "Now I know without a doubt
12:14 When she recognized **Peter's** voice, she was so overjoyed she ran
12:14 ran back without opening it and exclaimed, "**Peter** is at the door!"
12:16 But **Peter** kept on knocking, and when they opened the door
12:18 commotion among the soldiers as to what had become of **Peter**.
15:7 After much discussion, **Peter** got up and addressed them.

Gal 2:7 the gospel to the Gentiles, just as **Peter** had been to the Jews.
2:8 who was at work in the ministry of **Peter** as an apostle to the Jews,

1Pe 1:1 **Peter**, an apostle of Jesus Christ, To God's elect, strangers in the

2Pe 1:1 Simon **Peter**, a servant and apostle of Jesus Christ, To those who

4378 πετρώδης, *petrōdēs* [4] [√ *4376 + 1626*]

rocky places [4]

Mt 13:5 Some fell on **rocky places**, where it did not have much soil.
13:20 The one who received the seed that fell on **rocky places** is the man
Mk 4:5 Some fell on **rocky places**, where it did not have much soil.
4:16 Others, like seed sown on **rocky places**, hear the word and at once

4379 πήγανον, pēganon [1]

rue [1]

Lk   11:42 **rue** and all other kinds of garden herbs, but you neglect justice

4380 πηγή, pēgē [11]

springs [5], spring [2], well [2], *untranslated* [1], bleeding [+135+3836] [1]

Mk   5:29 Immediately her **bleeding** [+135+3836] stopped and she felt in her
Jn   4: 6 Jacob's **well** was there, and Jesus, tired as he was from the journey,
     4: 6 and Jesus, tired as he was from the journey, sat down by the **well**.
     4:14 the water I give him will become in him a **spring** of water welling
Jas   3:11 [RPG] Can both fresh water and salt water flow from the same
2Pe   2:17 These men are **springs** without water and mists driven by a storm.
Rev   7:17 will be their shepherd; he will lead them to **springs** of living water.
     8:10 from the sky on a third of the rivers and on the **springs** of water—
    14: 7 who made the heavens, the earth, the sea and the **springs** of water."
    16: 4 third angel poured out his bowl on the rivers and **springs** of water,
    21: 6 will give to drink without cost from the **spring** of the water of life.

4381 πήγνυμι, pēgnymi [1] [→ 4074, 4075, 4699, 5009]

set up [1]

Heb   8: 2 the sanctuary, the true tabernacle **set up** *by* the Lord, not by man.

4382 πηδάλιον, pēdalion [2]

rudder [1], rudders [1]

Ac   27:40 and at the same time untied the ropes that *held* the **rudders**.
Jas   3: 4 they are steered by a very small **rudder** wherever the pilot wants

4383 πηλίκος, pēlikos [2] [√ 2462]

how great [1], what large [1]

Gal   6:11 See **what large** letters I use as I write to you with my own hand!
Heb   7: 4 Just think **how great** he was: Even the patriarch Abraham gave

4384 πηλός, pēlos [6]

mud [4], *untranslated* [1], its [+3836] [1]

Jn   9: 6 said this, he spit on the ground, made *some* **mud** with the saliva,
     9: 6 some mud with the saliva, and put it^s [+3836] on the man's eyes.
     9:11 "The man they call Jesus made *some* **mud** and put it on my eyes.
     9:14 Now the day on which Jesus had made the **mud** and opened the
     9:15 "He put **mud** on my eyes," the man replied, "and I washed, and
Ro   9:21 Does not the potter [RPG] have the right to make out of the same

4385 πήρα, pēra [6]

bag [6]

Mt   10:10 take no **bag** for the journey, or extra tunic, or sandals or a staff;
Mk   6: 8 journey except a staff—no bread, no **bag**, no money in your belts.
Lk   9: 3 the journey—no staff, no **bag**, no bread, no money, no extra tunic.
     10: 4 Do not take a purse or **bag** or sandals; and do not greet anyone on
     22:35 I sent you without purse, **bag** or sandals, did you lack anything?"
     22:36 said to them, "But now if you have a purse, take it, and also a **bag**;

4386 πηρόω, pēroō   Not used in UBS/NIV [→ 401, 4387]

4387 πήρωσις, pērōsis   Not used in UBS/NIV [√ 4386]

4388 πῆχυς, pēchys [4]

hour [2], cubits [1], hundred yards [+1357] [1]

Mt   6:27 Who of you by worrying can add a single **hour** to his life?
Lk   12:25 Who of you by worrying can add a single **hour** to his life?
Jn   21: 8 for they were not far from shore, about a **hundred yards** [+1357].
Rev 21:17 He measured its wall and it was 144 **cubits** *thick*, by man's

4389 πιάζω, piazō [12] [√ 4390]

arrest [3], seize [3], caught [2], arresting [1], captured [1], seized [1], taking [1]

Jn   7:30 At this they tried *to* **seize** him, but no one laid a hand on him,
      7:32 chief priests and the Pharisees sent temple guards to **arrest** him.
      7:44 Some wanted *to* **seize** him, but no one laid a hand on him.
      8:20 Yet no one **seized** him, because his time had not yet come.
     10:39 Again they tried *to* **seize** him, but he escaped their grasp.
     11:57 where Jesus was, he should report it so that *they might* **arrest** him.
     21: 3 went out and got into the boat, but that night *they* **caught** nothing.
     21:10 Jesus said to them, "Bring some of the fish *you have* just **caught**."
Ac   3: 7 **Taking** him by the right hand, he helped him up, and instantly the
     12: 4 *After* **arresting** him, he put him in prison, handing him over to be
2Co 11:32 had the city of the Damascenes guarded *in order to* **arrest** me.
Rev 19:20 But the beast *was* **captured**, and with him the false prophet who

4390 πιέζω, piezō [1] [→ 4389]

pressed down [1]

Lk   6:38 A good measure, **pressed down**, shaken together and running over,

4391 πιθανολογία, pithanologia [1] [√ 4275 + 3306]

fine-sounding arguments [1]

Col   2: 4 so that no one may deceive you by **fine-sounding arguments**.

4392 πιθός, pithos   Not used in UBS/NIV [√ 4275]

4393 πικραίνω, pikrainō [4] [√ 4395]

bitter [1], harsh [1], turn sour [1], turned sour [1]

Col   3:19 Husbands, love your wives and *do* not *be* **harsh** with them.
Rev   8:11 and many people died from the waters that *had become* **bitter**.
     10: 9 It *will* **turn** your stomach **sour**, but in your mouth it will be as
     10:10 in my mouth, but when I had eaten it, my stomach **turned sour**.

4394 πικρία, pikria [4] [√ 4395]

bitterness [2], bitter [1], bitterness [+5958] [1]

Ac   8:23 For I see that you are full of **bitterness** [+5958] and captive to sin."
Ro   3:14 "Their mouths are full of cursing and **bitterness**."
Eph   4:31 Get rid of all **bitterness**, rage and anger, brawling and slander,
Heb 12:15 and that no **bitter** root grows up to cause trouble and defile many.

4395 πικρός, pikros [2] [→ 4176, 4177, 4393, 4394, 4396]

bitter [1], salt water [1]

Jas   3:11 Can both fresh water and **salt water** flow from the same spring?
      3:14 But if you harbor **bitter** envy and selfish ambition in your hearts,

4396 πικρῶς, pikrōs [2] [√ 4395]

bitterly [2]

Mt   26:75 disown me three times." And he went outside and wept **bitterly**.
Lk   22:62 And he went outside and wept **bitterly**.

4397 Πιλᾶτος, Pilatos [55] [→ 4276]

Pilate [54], Pilate's [1]

Mt   27: 2 led him away and handed him over *to* **Pilate**, the governor.
     27:13 Then **Pilate** asked him, "Don't you hear the testimony they are
     27:17 So when the crowd had gathered, **Pilate** asked them, "Which one do
     27:22 is called Christ?" **Pilate** asked. They all answered, "Crucify him!"
     27:24 When **Pilate** saw that he was getting nowhere,
     27:58 Going to **Pilate**, he asked for Jesus' body, and Pilate ordered that it
     27:58 he asked for Jesus' body, and **Pilate** ordered that it be given to him.
     27:62 Preparation Day, the chief priests and the Pharisees went to **Pilate**.
     27:65 "Take a guard," **Pilate** answered. "Go, make the tomb as secure as
Mk   15: 1 They bound Jesus, led him away and handed him over *to* **Pilate**.
     15: 2 king of the Jews?" asked **Pilate**. "Yes, it is as you say," Jesus

15: 4 So again **Pilate** asked him, "Aren't you going to answer? See how
15: 5 But Jesus still made no reply, and **Pilate** was amazed.
15: 9 you want me to release to you the king of the Jews?" asked **Pilate**,
15:12 with the one you call the king of the Jews?" **Pilate** asked them.
15:14 "Why? What crime has he committed?' asked **Pilate**. But they
15:15 Wanting to satisfy the crowd, **Pilate** released Barabbas to them.
15:43 kingdom of God, went boldly to **Pilate** and asked for Jesus' body.
15:44 **Pilate** was surprised to hear that he was already dead. Summoning
Lk 3: 1 when Pontius **Pilate** was governor of Judea, Herod tetrarch of
13: 1 the Galileans whose blood **Pilate** had mixed with their sacrifices.
23: 1 Then the whole assembly rose and led him off to **Pilate**.
23: 3 So **Pilate** asked Jesus, "Are you the king of the Jews?" "Yes,
23: 4 Then **Pilate** announced to the chief priests and the crowd,
23: 6 On hearing this, **Pilate** asked if the man was a Galilean.
23:11 Dressing him in an elegant robe, they sent him back *to* **Pilate**.
23:12 That day Herod and **Pilate** became friends—before this they had
23:13 **Pilate** called together the chief priests, the rulers and the people,
23:20 Wanting to release Jesus, **Pilate** appealed to them again.
23:24 So **Pilate** decided to grant their demand.
23:52 Going to **Pilate**, he asked for Jesus' body.
Jn 18:29 So **Pilate** came out to them and asked, "What charges are you
18:31 **Pilate** said, "Take him yourselves and judge him by your own law."
18:33 **Pilate** then went back inside the palace, summoned Jesus
18:35 "Am I a Jew?" **Pilate** replied. "It was your people and your chief
18:37 "You are a king, then!" said **Pilate**. Jesus answered, "You are right
18:38 "What is truth?" **Pilate** asked. With this he went out again to the
19: 1 Then **Pilate** took Jesus and had him flogged.
19: 4 Once more **Pilate** came out and said to the Jews, "Look, I am
19: 6 Crucify!" But **Pilate** answered, "You take him and crucify him.
19: 8 When **Pilate** heard this, he was even more afraid,
19:10 "Do you refuse to speak to me?" **Pilate** said. "Don't you realize I
19:12 From then on, **Pilate** tried to set Jesus free, but the Jews kept
19:13 When **Pilate** heard this, he brought Jesus out and sat down on the
19:15 **Pilate** asked. "We have no king but Caesar," the chief priests
19:19 **Pilate** had a notice prepared and fastened to the cross. It read:
19:21 The chief priests of the Jews protested *to* **Pilate**, "Do not write 'The
19:22 **Pilate** answered, "What I have written, I have written."
19:31 they asked **Pilate** to have the legs broken and the bodies taken
19:38 Later, Joseph of Arimathea asked **Pilate** for the body of Jesus.
19:38 With **Pilate's** permission, he came and took the body away.
Ac 3:13 handed him over to be killed, and you disowned him before **Pilate**,
4:27 Indeed Herod and Pontius **Pilate** met together with the Gentiles
13:28 for a death sentence, they asked **Pilate** to have him executed.
1Ti 6:13 who while testifying before Pontius **Pilate** made the good

4398 πίμπλημι, *pimplēmi* [24] [→ *1854, 1855, 1857, 1858, 4101, 4113, 4436, 4437, 4439, 4447, 4496*]

filled [15], completed [2], was [2], came [1], fulfillment [1], furious [+2596] [1], furious [+486] [1], time [1]

Mt 22:10 both good and bad, and the wedding hall *was* **filled** with guests.
27:48 *He* **filled** it with wine vinegar, put it on a stick, and offered it to
Lk 1:15 and *he will be* **filled** with the Holy Spirit even from birth.
1:23 When his time of service *was* **completed**, he returned home.
1:41 leaped in her womb, and Elizabeth *was* **filled** with the Holy Spirit.
1:57 When *it* **was** time for Elizabeth to have her baby, she gave birth to
1:67 His father Zechariah *was* **filled** with the Holy Spirit
2: 6 While they were there, the time **came** for the baby to be born,
2:21 On the eighth day, when *it was* **time** to circumcise him, he was
2:22 purification according to the Law of Moses *had been* **completed**,
4:28 All the people in the synagogue *were* **furious** [+2596] when they
5: 7 and *they* came and **filled** both boats so full that they began to sink.
5:26 *They were* **filled** with awe and said, "We have seen remarkable
6:11 But they *were* **furious** [+486] and began to discuss with one
21:22 For this is the time of punishment *in* **fulfillment** of all that has
Ac 2: 4 All of them *were* **filled** with the Holy Spirit and began to speak in
3:10 and *they were* **filled** with wonder and amazement at what had
4: 8 Then Peter, **filled** with the Holy Spirit, said to them: "Rulers
4:31 And *they were* all **filled** with the Holy Spirit and spoke the word
5:17 members of the party of the Sadducees, *were* **filled** with jealousy.
9:17 so that you may see again and *be* **filled** with the Holy Spirit."
13: 9 **filled** with the Holy Spirit, looked straight at Elymas and said,
13:45 *they were* **filled** with jealousy and talked abusively against what
19:29 Soon the whole city *was* in an uproar. The people seized Gaius

4399 πίμπρημι, *pimprēmi* [1] [→ *1856, 1859, 1868, 2926*]

swell up [1]

Ac 28: 6 The people expected him to **swell up** or suddenly fall dead,

4400 πινακίδιον, *pinakidion* [1] [√ *4402*]

writing tablet [1]

Lk 1:63 He asked for a **writing tablet**, and to everyone's astonishment he

4401 πινακίς, *pinakis* Not used in UBS/NIV [√ *4402*]

4402 πίναξ, *pinax* [5] [→ *4400, 4401*]

platter [4], dish [1]

Mt 14: 8 she said, "Give me here on a **platter** the head of John the Baptist."
14:11 His head was brought in on a **platter** and given to the girl,
Mk 6:25 you to give me right now the head of John the Baptist on a **platter**."
6:28 and brought back his head on a **platter**. He presented it to the girl,
Lk 11:39 "Now then, you Pharisees clean the outside *of* the cup and **dish**,

4403 πίνω, *pinō* [73] [→ *2927, 3884, 4503, 4530, 4539, 4540, 4542, 5228, 5234, 5235, 5621; cf. 4532*]

drink [46], drinking [10], drinks [8], drank [5], drink from [1], drinks in [1], drunk [1], take [1]

Mt 6:25 I tell you do not worry about your life, what you will eat or **drink**;
6:31 not worry, saying, 'What shall we eat?' or 'What *shall we* **drink**?'
11:18 For John came neither eating nor **drinking**, and they say, 'He has a
11:19 The Son of Man came eating and **drinking**, and they say,
20:22 "Can you **drink** the cup I am going to drink?" "We can,"
20:22 "Can you drink the cup I am going to **drink**?" "We can,"
20:23 Jesus said to them, "*You will* indeed **drink from** my cup,
24:38 people were eating and **drinking**, marrying and giving in marriage,
24:49 to beat his fellow servants and to eat and **drink** with drunkards.
26:27 and offered it to them, saying, "**Drink** from it, all of you.
26:29 *I will* not **drink** of this fruit of the vine from now on until that day
26:29 that day when *I* **drink** it anew with you in my Father's kingdom."
26:42 if it is not possible for this cup to be taken away unless *I* **drink** it,
27:34 There they offered Jesus wine *to* **drink**, mixed with gall; but after
27:34 mixed with gall; but after tasting it, he refused *to* **drink** it.
Mk 10:38 "Can you **drink** the cup I drink or be baptized with the baptism I
10:38 "Can you drink the cup I **drink** or be baptized with the baptism I
10:39 "*You will* **drink** the cup I drink and be baptized with the baptism I
10:39 "You will drink the cup I **drink** and be baptized with the baptism I
14:23 gave thanks and offered it to them, and *they* all **drank** from it.
14:25 *I will* not **drink** again of the fruit of the vine until that day when I
14:25 vine until that day when *I* **drink** it anew in the kingdom of God."
16:18 and when *they* **drink** deadly poison, it will not hurt them at all;
Lk 1:15 *He is* never *to* take wine or other fermented drink, and he will be
5:30 "Why do you eat and **drink** with tax collectors and 'sinners'?"
5:33 disciples of the Pharisees, but yours *go on* eating and **drinking**."
5:39 And no one *after* **drinking** old wine wants the new, for he says,
7:33 For John the Baptist came neither eating bread nor **drinking** wine,
7:34 The Son of Man came eating and **drinking**, and you say, 'Here is a
10: 7 Stay in that house, eating and **drinking** whatever they give you,
12:19 laid up for many years. Take life easy; eat, **drink** and be merry." '
12:29 And do not set your heart on what you will eat or **drink**; do not
12:45 and maidservants and *to* eat and **drink** and get drunk.
13:26 "Then you will say, '*We* ate and **drank** with you, and you taught in
17: 8 get yourself ready and wait on me while *I* eat and **drink**;
17: 8 on me while I eat and drink; after that you *may* eat and **drink**'?
17:27 *People were* eating, **drinking**, marrying and being given in
17:28 People were eating and **drinking**, buying and selling, planting
22:18 For I tell you *I will* not **drink** again of the fruit of the vine until the
22:30 may eat and **drink** at my table in my kingdom and sit on thrones,
Jn 4: 7 came to draw water, Jesus said to her, "Will you give me a **drink**?"
4: 9 and I am a Samaritan woman. How can you ask me for a **drink**?"
4:10 "If you knew the gift of God and who it is that asks you for a **drink**,
4:12 who gave us the well and **drank** from it himself, as did also his

4:13 "Everyone who **drinks** this water will be thirsty again,
4:14 but whoever **drinks** the water I give him will never thirst.
6:53 unless you eat the flesh of the Son of Man and **drink** his blood,
6:54 Whoever eats my flesh and **drinks** my blood has eternal life,
6:56 Whoever eats my flesh and **drinks** my blood remains in me,
7:37 in a loud voice, "If anyone is thirsty, let him come to me and **drink**.
18:11 sword away! *Shall I* not **drink** the cup the Father has given me?"
Ac 9: 9 For three days he was blind, and did not eat or **drink** anything.
23:12 and bound themselves with an oath not *to* eat or **drink** until they
23:21 have taken an oath not to eat or **drink** until they have killed him.
Ro 14:21 It is better not to eat meat or **drink** wine or to do anything else that
1Co 9: 4 Don't we have the right *to* food and **drink**?
10: 4 and **drank** the same spiritual drink; for they drank from the
10: 4 for *they* **drank** from the spiritual rock that accompanied them,
10: 7 "The people sat down *to* eat and **drink** and got up to indulge in
10:21 You cannot **drink** the cup of the Lord and the cup of demons too;
10:31 So whether you eat or **drink** or whatever you do, do it all for the
11:22 Don't you have homes to eat and **drink** in? Or do you despise the
11:25 my blood; do this, whenever *you* **drink** it, in remembrance of me."
11:26 For whenever you eat this bread and **drink** this cup, you proclaim
11:27 or **drinks** the cup of the Lord in an unworthy manner will be guilty
11:28 examine himself before he eats of the bread and **drinks** of the cup.
11:29 and **drinks** without recognizing the body of the Lord eats
11:29 the body of the Lord eats and **drinks** judgment on himself.
15:32 dead are not raised, "*Let us* eat and **drink**, for tomorrow we die."
Heb 6: 7 Land that **drinks in** the rain often falling on it and that produces a
Rev 14:10 he, too, *will* **drink** of the wine of God's fury, which has been
16: 6 and you have given them blood *to* **drink** as they deserve."
18: 3 For all the nations *have* **drunk** the maddening wine of her

4404 πιότης, *piotēs* [1]

nourishing [1]

Ro 11:17 the others and now share in the **nourishing** sap from the olive root,

4405 πιπράσκω, *pipraskō* [9] [√ *4305*]

sold [7], sales [1], selling [1]

Mt 13:46 *he* went away and **sold** everything he had and bought it.
18:25 and his children and all that he had *be* **sold** to repay the debt.
26: 9 "This perfume could have *been* **sold** at a high price and the money
Mk 14: 5 It could have *been* **sold** for more than a year's wages
Jn 12: 5 "Why wasn't this perfume **sold** and the money given to the poor?
Ac 2:45 **Selling** their possessions and goods, they gave to anyone as he had
4:34 or houses sold them, brought the money *from* the **sales**.
5: 4 And *after it was* **sold**, wasn't the money at your disposal?
Ro 7:14 that the law is spiritual; but I am unspiritual, **sold** as a slave to sin.

4406 πίπτω, *piptō* [90] [→ *404, 528, 674, 1206, 1479, 1738, 1860, 2158, 2928, 4178, 4183, 4346, 4637, 4700, 4773, 4774, 5229*]

fell [39], fall [13], fallen [8], falls [8], fell down [7], collapsed [2], *untranslated* [1], beat [1], bow down [1], bowed down [1], came [1], condemned [*+3213+5679*] [1], died [1], drop out [1], fails [1], fall [*+1639*] [1], fall down [*+2093+4725*] [1], fall down [1], threw himself [*+2093+4725*] [1]

Mt 2:11 with his mother Mary, and they **bowed down** and worshiped him.
4: 9 I will give you," he said, "if you will **bow down** and worship me."
7:25 yet *it did* not **fall**, because it had its foundation on the rock.
7:27 and beat against that house, and *it* **fell** with a great crash."
10:29 Yet not one of them *will* **fall** to the ground apart from the will of
13: 4 some **fell** along the path, and the birds came and ate it up.
13: 5 Some **fell** on rocky places, where it did not have much soil.
13: 7 Other seed **fell** among thorns, which grew up and choked the
13: 8 Still other seed **fell** on good soil, where it produced a crop—
15:14 If a blind man leads a blind man, both *will* **fall** into a pit."
15:27 even the dogs eat the crumbs that **fall** from their masters' table."
17: 6 the disciples heard this, *they* **fell** facedown to the ground, terrified.
17:15 is suffering greatly. *He* often **falls** into the fire or into the water.
18:26 "The servant **fell** on his knees before him. 'Be patient with me,'

18:29 "His fellow servant **fell** to his knees and begged him, 'Be patient
21:44 He *who* **falls** on this stone will be broken to pieces, but he on
21:44 will be broken to pieces, but he on whom *it* **falls** will be crushed."
24:29 the stars *will* **fall** from the sky, and the heavenly bodies will be
26:39 *he* **fell** with his face to the ground and prayed, "My Father,
Mk 4: 4 some **fell** along the path, and the birds came and ate it up.
4: 5 Some **fell** on rocky places, where it did not have much soil.
4: 7 Other seed **fell** among thorns, which grew up and choked the
4: 8 Still other seed **fell** on good soil. It came up, grew and produced a
5:22 named Jairus, came there. Seeing Jesus, *he* **fell** at his feet
9:20 He **fell** to the ground and rolled around, foaming at the mouth.
13:25 the stars *will* **fall** [*+1639*] from the sky, and the heavenly bodies
14:35 *he* **fell** to the ground and prayed that if possible the hour might
Lk 5:12 he **fell** with his face to the ground and begged him, "Lord, if you are
8: 5 As he was scattering the seed, some **fell** along the path; it was
8: 7 Other seed **fell** among thorns, which grew up with it and choked
8: 8 Still other seed **fell** on good soil. It came up and yielded a crop,
8:14 The seed *that* **fell** among thorns stands for those who hear,
8:41 named Jairus, a ruler of the synagogue, came and **fell** at Jesus' feet,
10:18 He replied, "I saw Satan **fall** like lightning from heaven.
11:17 itself will be ruined, and a house divided against itself *will* **fall**.
13: 4 Or those eighteen who died *when* the tower in Siloam **fell** on
14: 5 of you has a son or an ox that **falls** into a well on the Sabbath day,
16:17 and earth to disappear than for the least stroke of a pen *to* **drop out**
16:21 and longing to eat what **fell** from the rich man's table. Even the
17:16 *He* threw [*+2093+4725*] **himself** at Jesus' feet and thanked him—
20:18 Everyone who **falls** on that stone will be broken to pieces,
20:18 will be broken to pieces, but he on whom *it* **falls** will be crushed."
21:24 *They will* **fall** by the sword and will be taken as prisoners to all the
23:30 " 'they will say to the mountains, "**Fall** on us!" and to the hills,
Jn 11:32 where Jesus was and saw him, *she* **fell** at his feet and said, "Lord,
12:24 you the truth, unless a kernel of wheat **falls** to the ground and dies,
18: 6 When Jesus said, "I am he," they drew back and **fell** to the ground.
Ac 1:26 Then they cast lots, and the lot **fell** to Matthias; so he was added to
5: 5 When Ananias heard this, he **fell** down and died. And great fear
5:10 At that moment *she* **fell** down at his feet and died. Then the young
9: 4 He **fell** to the ground and heard a voice say to him, "Saul, Saul,
10:25 the house, Cornelius met him and **fell** at his feet in reverence.
13:11 Immediately mist and darkness **came** over him, and he groped
15:16 " 'After this I will return and rebuild David's **fallen** tent. Its ruins I
20: 9 *he* **fell** to the ground from the third story and was picked up dead.
22: 7 *I* **fell** to the ground and heard a voice say to me, 'Saul! Saul!
Ro 11:11 Did they stumble so as to **fall** *beyond recovery*? Not at all!
11:22 sternness to those *who* **fell**, but kindness to you, provided that you
14: 4 To his own master he stands or **falls**. And he will stand,
1Co 10: 8 of them did—and in one day twenty-three thousand of them **died**.
10:12 if you think you are standing firm, be careful that *you* don't **fall**!
13: 8 Love never **fails**. But where there are prophecies, they will cease;
14:25 So he will **fall** [*+2093+4725*] **down** and worship God, exclaiming,
Heb 3:17 Was it not with those who sinned, whose bodies **fell** in the desert?
4:11 so that no one *will* **fall** by following their example of disobedience.
11:30 By faith the walls of Jericho **fell**, after the people had marched
Jas 5:12 yes, and your "No," no, or *you will be* **condemned** [*+3213+5679*].
Rev 1:17 When I saw him, *I* **fell** at his feet as though dead. Then he placed
2: 5 Remember the height from which *you have* **fallen**! Repent
4:10 the twenty-four elders **fall down** before him who sits on the throne,
5: 8 and the twenty-four elders **fell down** before the Lamb.
5:14 creatures said, "Amen," and the elders **fell down** and worshiped.
6:13 and the stars in the sky **fell** to earth, as late figs drop from a fig tree
6:16 "**Fall** on us and hide us from the face of him who sits on the throne
7:11 *They* **fell down** on their faces before the throne and worshiped
7:16 The sun will not **beat** upon them, nor any scorching heat.
8:10 **fell** from the sky on a third of the rivers and on the springs of
8:10 fell from the sky [RPG] on a third of the rivers and on the springs
9: 1 and I saw a star *that had* **fallen** from the sky to the earth.
11:13 there was a severe earthquake and a tenth of the city **collapsed**.
11:16 on their thrones before God, **fell** on their faces and worshiped God,
14: 8 A second angel followed and said, "**Fallen**! Fallen is Babylon the
14: 8 **Fallen** is Babylon the Great, which made all the nations drink the
16:19 city split into three parts, and the cities of the nations **collapsed**.
17:10 Five *have* **fallen**, one is, the other has not yet come; but when he
18: 2 a mighty voice he shouted: "**Fallen**! Fallen is Babylon the Great!
18: 2 a mighty voice he shouted: "**Fallen**! **Fallen** is Babylon the Great!
19: 4 and the four living creatures **fell down** and worshiped God,
19:10 At this *I* **fell** at his feet to worship him. But he said to me,
22: 8 *I* **fell down** to worship at the feet of the angel who had been

4407 Πισιδία, *Pisidia* [1] [→ *4408*]

Pisidia [1]

Ac 14:24 After going through **Pisidia**, they came into Pamphylia,

4408 Πισίδιος, *Pisidios* [1] [√ *4407*]

Pisidian [1]

Ac 13:14 From Perga they went on to **Pisidian** Antioch. On the Sabbath they

4409 πιστεύω, *pisteuō* [241] [√ *4412*]

πιστεύω εἰς (believe in) [48] Mt 18:6; Mk 9:42; Jn 1:12; 2:11,23; 3:16,18,18,36; 4:39; 6:29,35,40; 7:5,31,38,39,48; 8:30; 9:35,36; 10:42; 11:25,26,45,48; 12:36,37,42,44,44,46; 14:1,1,12; 16:9; 17:20; Ac 10:43; 19:4; Ro 4:18; 10:10,14; Gal 2:16; Php 1:29; 1Pe 1:8; 1Jn 5:10,10,13

πιστεύω ἐπί (believe upon) [12] Mt 27:42; Lk 24:25; Ac 9:42; 11:17; 16:31; 22:19; Ro 4:5,24; 9:33; 10:11; 1Ti 1:16; 1Pe 2:6

believe [113], believed [58], believes [23], believers [8], put faith [5], trusts [5], trust [4], entrusted with [3], faith [3], believing [2], entrusted [2], put trust [2], believe [+*1639*] [1], believe [+*1877*] [1], believe in [1], believed on [1], come to believe [1], committed [1], did[s] [1], do[s] [1], entrust [1], putting faith [1], rely on [1], took at [+*4005*] [1], trusted [1]

Mt 8:13 to the centurion, "Go! It will be done just as *you* **believed** it would."
9:28 and he asked them, "*Do you* **believe** that I am able to do this?"
18:6 But if anyone causes one of these little ones who **believe** in me to
21:22 If *you* **believe**, you will receive whatever you ask for in prayer."
21:25 'From heaven,' he will ask, 'Then why didn't *you* **believe** him?'
21:32 and *you did* not **believe** him, but the tax collectors
21:32 did not believe him, but the tax collectors and the prostitutes **did**[s].
21:32 And even after you saw this, you did not repent and **believe** him.
24:23 'Look, here is the Christ!' or, 'There he is!' *do* not **believe** it.
24:26 do not go out; or, 'Here he is, in the inner rooms,' *do* not **believe** it.
27:42 him come down now from the cross, and *we will* **believe** in him.
Mk 1:15 of God is near. Repent and **believe** [+*1877*] the good news!"
5:36 Jesus told the synagogue ruler, "Don't be afraid; just **believe**."
9:23 can'?" said Jesus. "Everything is possible *for* him *who* **believes**."
9:24 Immediately the boy's father exclaimed, "*I do* **believe**; help me
9:42 "And if anyone causes one of these little ones who **believe** in me to
11:23 not doubt in his heart but **believes** that what he says will happen,
11:24 for in prayer, **believe** that you have received it, and it will be yours.
11:31 'From heaven,' he will ask, 'Then why didn't *you* **believe** him?'
13:21 here is the Christ!' or, 'Look, there he is!' *do* not **believe** it.
15:32 come down now from the cross, that we may see and **believe**."
16:13 and reported it to the rest; but *they did* not **believe** them either.
16:14 and their stubborn refusal *to* **believe** those who had seen him after
16:16 Whoever **believes** and is baptized will be saved, but whoever does
16:17 And these signs will accompany those *who* **believe**: In my name
Lk 1:20 because *you did* not **believe** my words, which will come true at
1:45 Blessed is she *who has* **believed** that what the Lord has said to her
8:12 word from their hearts, so that they may not **believe** and be saved.
8:13 They **believe** for a while, but in the time of testing they fall away.
8:50 to Jairus, "Don't be afraid; just **believe**, and she will be healed."
16:11 in handling worldly wealth, who *will* **trust** you with true riches?
20:5 'From heaven,' he will ask, 'Why didn't *you* **believe** him?'
22:67 "tell us." Jesus answered, "If I tell you, *you will* not **believe** me,
24:25 and how slow of heart *to* **believe** all that the prophets have spoken!
Jn 1:7 concerning that light, so that through him all men *might* **believe**.
1:12 Yet to all who received him, to those who **believed** in his name,
1:50 "*You* **believe** because I told you I saw you under the fig tree.
2:11 He thus revealed his glory, and his disciples **put** *their* **faith** in him.
2:22 Then *they* **believed** the Scripture and the words that Jesus had
2:23 saw the miraculous signs he was doing and **believed** in his name.
2:24 But Jesus *would* not **entrust** himself to them, for he knew all men.
3:12 I have spoken to you of earthly things and *you do* not **believe**;
3:12 how then *will you* **believe** if I speak of heavenly things?
3:15 that everyone who **believes** in him may have eternal life.
3:16 that whoever **believes** in him shall not perish but have eternal life.
3:18 Whoever **believes** in him is not condemned, but whoever does not
3:18 but whoever *does* not **believe** stands condemned already
3:18 because *he has* not **believed** in the name of God's one and only
3:36 Whoever **believes** in the Son has eternal life, but whoever rejects
4:21 Jesus declared, "**Believe** me, woman, a time is coming when you
4:39 Many of the Samaritans from that town **believed** in him because of
4:41 And because of his words many more *became* **believers**.
4:42 the woman, "*We* no longer **believe** just because of what you said;
4:48 and wonders," Jesus told him, "*you will* never **believe**."
4:50 The man **took** Jesus **at** [+*4005*] his word **[RPG]** and departed.
4:53 to him, "Your son will live." So he and all his household **believed**.
5:24 hears my word and **believes** him who sent me has eternal life
5:38 does his word dwell in you, for you *do* not **believe** the one he sent.
5:44 How can you **believe** if you accept praise from one another,
5:46 If *you* **believed** Moses, you would believe me, for he wrote about
5:46 believed Moses, *you* would **believe** me, for he wrote about me.
5:47 But since *you do* not **believe** what he wrote, how are you going to
5:47 believe what he wrote, how *are you going to* **believe** what I say?"
6:29 "The work of God is this: to **believe** in the one he has sent."
6:30 then will you give that we may see it and **believe** you?
6:35 never go hungry, and he *who* **believes** in me will never be thirsty.
6:36 But as I told you, you have seen me and still *you do* not **believe**.
6:40 who looks to the Son and **believes** in him shall have eternal life,
6:47 I tell you the truth, he *who* **believes** has everlasting life.
6:64 Yet there are some of you who *do* not **believe**." For Jesus had
6:64 known from the beginning which of them *did* not **believe** [+*1639*]
6:69 We **believe** and know that you are the Holy One of God."
7:5 For even his own brothers *did* not **believe** in him.
7:31 Still, many in the crowd **put** *their* **faith** in him. They said,
7:38 Whoever **believes** in me, as the Scripture has said, streams of
7:39 the Spirit, whom those *who* **believed** in him were later to receive.
7:48 "*Has* any of the rulers or of the Pharisees **believed** in him?
8:24 if *you do* not **believe** that I am ⌊the one I claim to be⌋, you will
8:30 Even as he spoke, many **put** *their* **faith** in him.
8:31 To the Jews *who had* **believed** him, Jesus said, "If you hold to my
8:45 Yet because I tell the truth, *you do* not **believe** me!
8:46 guilty of sin? If I am telling the truth, why don't you **believe** me?
9:18 The Jews still *did* not **believe** that he had been blind and had
9:35 when he found him, he said, "*Do* you **believe** in the Son of Man?"
9:36 is he, sir?" the man asked. "Tell me so that *I may* **believe** in him."
9:38 Then the man said, "Lord, *I* **believe**," and he worshiped him.
10:25 Jesus answered, "I did tell you, but *you do* not **believe**.
10:26 but you *do* not **believe** because you are not my sheep.
10:37 *Do* not **believe** me unless I do what my Father does.
10:38 But if I do it, even though *you do* not **believe** me,
10:38 **believe** the miracles, that you may know and understand that the
10:42 And in that place many **believed** in Jesus.
11:15 for your sake I am glad I was not there, so that *you may* **believe**.
11:25 and the life. He *who* **believes** in me will live, even though he dies;
11:26 and whoever lives and **believes** in me will never die. Do you
11:26 and believes in me will never die. *Do you* **believe** this?"
11:27 "Yes, Lord," she told him, "I **believe** that you are the Christ,
11:40 Then Jesus said, "Did I not tell you that if *you* **believed**, you would
11:42 the people standing here, that *they may* **believe** that you sent me."
11:45 to visit Mary, and had seen what Jesus did, **put** *their* **faith** in him.
11:48 everyone *will* **believe** in him, and then the Romans will come
12:11 the Jews were going over to Jesus and **putting** *their* **faith** *in* him.
12:36 **Put** *your* **trust** in the light while you have it, so that you may
12:37 signs in their presence, *they still would* not **believe** in him.
12:38 who *has* **believed** our message and to whom has the arm of the
12:39 For this reason they could not **believe**, because, as Isaiah says
12:42 Yet at the same time many even among the leaders **believed** in
12:44 Then Jesus cried out, "*When* a man **believes** in me, he does not
12:44 *he does* not **believe** in me only, but in the one who sent me.
12:46 so that no one who **believes** in me should stay in darkness.
13:19 so that when it does happen *you will* **believe** that I am He.
14:1 "Do not let your hearts be troubled. **Trust** in God; trust also in me.
14:1 "Do not let your hearts be troubled. Trust in God; **trust** also in me.
14:10 Don't *you* **believe** that I am in the Father, and that the Father is in
14:11 **Believe** me when I say that I am in the Father and the Father is in
14:11 or at least **believe** on the evidence of the miracles themselves.
14:12 anyone *who has* **faith** in me will do what I have been doing.
14:29 before it happens, so that when it does happen *you will* **believe**.
16:9 in regard to sin, because *men do* not **believe** in me;
16:27 you have loved me and *have* **believed** that I came from God.
16:30 ask you questions. This makes *us* **believe** that you came from God."
16:31 "*You* **believe** at last!" Jesus answered.
17:8 certainty that I came from you, and *they* **believed** that you sent me.
17:20 I pray also for those *who will* **believe** in me through their message,

17:21 also be in us so that the world *may* **believe** that you have sent me.
19:35 that he tells the truth, and he testifies so that you also *may* **believe**.
20: 8 had reached the tomb first, also went inside. He saw and **believed**.
20:25 the nails were, and put my hand into his side, *I will* not **believe** it."
20:29 Jesus told him, "Because you have seen me, *you have* **believed**;
20:29 blessed are those who have not seen and yet *have* **believed**."
20:31 But these are written that *you may* **believe** that Jesus is the Christ,
20:31 Son of God, and that *by* **believing** you may have life in his name.

Ac 2:44 All the **believers** were together and had everything in common.
 4: 4 But many who heard the message **believed**, and the number of men
 4:32 All the **believers** were one in heart and mind. No one claimed that
 5:14 more and more men and women **believed** in the Lord and were
 8:12 But when *they* **believed** Philip as he preached the good news of
 8:13 Simon himself **believed** and was baptized. And he followed Philip
 9:26 were all afraid of him, not **believing** that he really was a disciple.
 9:42 known all over Joppa, and many people **believed** in the Lord.
10:43 All the prophets testify about him that everyone who **believes** in
11:17 *who* **believed** in the Lord Jesus Christ, who was I to think that I
11:21 and a great number of people **believed** and turned to the Lord.
13:12 When the proconsul saw what had happened, *he* **believed**,
13:39 Through him everyone who **believes** is justified from everything
13:41 going to do something in your days that *you would* never **believe**,
13:48 of the Lord; and all who were appointed for eternal life **believed**.
14: 1 so effectively that a great number of Jews and Gentiles **believed**.
14:23 committed them to the Lord, in whom *they had* **put** *their* **trust**.
15: 5 Then some *of* the **believers** who belonged to the party of the
15: 7 might hear from my lips the message of the gospel and **believe**.
15:11 *We* **believe** it is through the grace of our Lord Jesus that we are
16:31 They replied, "**Believe** in the Lord Jesus, and you will be saved—
16:34 he was filled with joy *because he had* **come to believe** in God—
17:12 Many of the Jews **believed**, as did also a number of prominent
17:34 A few men became followers of Paul and **believed**. Among them
18: 8 the synagogue ruler, and his entire household **believed** in the Lord;
18: 8 and many of the Corinthians who heard him **believed** and were
18:27 he was a great help to those *who* by grace *had* **believed**.
19: 2 asked them, "Did you receive the Holy Spirit *when you* **believed**?"
19: 4 He told the people to **believe** in the one coming after him,
19:18 Many *of* those *who* **believed** now came and openly confessed their
21:20 "You see, brother, how many thousands of Jews *have* **believed**,
21:25 As for the Gentile **believers**, we have written to them our decision
22:19 to another to imprison and beat those *who* **believe** in you.
24:14 *I* **believe** everything that agrees with the Law and that is written in
26:27 King Agrippa, *do you* **believe** the prophets? I know you do."
26:27 King Agrippa, do you **believe** the prophets? I know *you* **do**ˢ."
27:25 for *I have* **faith** in God that it will happen just as he told me.

Ro 1:16 it is the power of God for the salvation *of* everyone who **believes**:
 3: 2 First of all, *they have been* **entrusted with** the very words of God.
 3:22 from God comes through faith in Jesus Christ to all who **believe**.
 4: 3 "Abraham **believed** God, and it was credited to him as
 4: 5 man who does not work but **trusts** God who justifies the wicked,
 4:11 he is the father *of* all who **believe** but have not been circumcised,
 4:17 He is our father in the sight of God, in whom *he* **believed**—
 4:18 Abraham in hope **believed** and so became the father of many
 4:24 for us *who* **believe** in him who raised Jesus our Lord from the
 6: 8 if we died with Christ, *we* **believe** that we will also live with him.
 9:33 and the one *who* **trusts** in him will never be put to shame."
10: 4 so that there may be righteousness for everyone who **believes**.
10: 9 and **believe** in your heart that God raised him from the dead,
10:10 For it is with your heart that *you* **believe** and are justified,
10:11 "Anyone who **trusts** in him will never be put to shame."
10:14 How, then, can they call on the one *they have* not **believed** in?
10:14 And how *can they* **believe** in the one of whom they have not
10:16 good news. For Isaiah says, "Lord, who *has* **believed** our message?"
13:11 because our salvation is nearer now than when *we first* **believed**.
14: 2 One man's **faith** allows him to eat everything, but another man,
15:13 the God of hope fill you with all joy and peace as you **trust** *in* him,

1Co 1:21 the foolishness of what was preached to save those *who* **believe**.
 3: 5 Only servants, through whom *you came to* **believe**—as the Lord
 9:17 I am simply discharging the trust **committed** to *me*.
11:18 there are divisions among you, and to some extent *I* **believe** it.
13: 7 It always protects, always **trusts**, always hopes, always perseveres.
14:22 Tongues, then, are a sign, not *for* **believers** but for unbelievers;
14:22 however, is *for* **believers**, not for unbelievers.
15: 2 the word I preached to you. Otherwise, *you have* **believed** in vain.
15:11 or they, this is what we preach, and this is what *you* **believed**.

2Co 4:13 It is written: "*I* **believed**; therefore I have spoken." With that same

---

 4:13 With that same spirit of faith we also **believe** and therefore speak,
Gal 2: 7 they saw that *I had been* **entrusted with** the task of preaching the
 2:16 *have* **put** *our* **faith** in Christ Jesus that we may be justified by faith
 3: 6 "*He* **believed** God, and it was credited to him as righteousness."
 3:22 through faith in Jesus Christ, might be given *to* those *who* **believe**.
Eph 1:13 *Having* **believed**, you were marked in him with a seal,
 1:19 and his incomparably great power for us who **believe**. That power
Php 1:29 been granted to you on behalf of Christ not only *to* **believe** on him,
1Th 1: 7 And so you became a model *to* all the **believers** in Macedonia
 2: 4 we speak as men approved by God *to be* **entrusted with** the
 2:10 righteous and blameless we were among you who **believed**.
 2:13 actually is, the word of God, which is at work in you who **believe**.
 4:14 *We* **believe** that Jesus died and rose again and so we believe that
2Th 1:10 and to be marveled at among all those *who have* **believed**.
 1:10 This includes you, because you **believed** our testimony to you.
 2:11 sends them a powerful delusion so that they *will* **believe** the lie
 2:12 so that all will be condemned who *have* not **believed** the truth
1Ti 1:11 the glorious gospel of the blessed God, which he **entrusted** to me.
 1:16 patience as an example for those who would **believe** on him
 3:16 the nations, *was* **believed on** in the world, was taken up in glory.
2Ti 1:12 Yet I am not ashamed, because I know whom *I have* **believed**,
Tit 1: 3 the preaching **entrusted** to me by the command of God our Savior,
 3: 8 so that those *who have* **trusted** in God may be careful to devote
Heb 4: 3 Now we who *have* **believed** enter that rest, just as God has said,
 11: 6 because anyone who comes to him must **believe** that he exists
Jas 2:19 You **believe** that there is one God. Good! Even the demons believe
 2:19 is one God. Good! Even the demons **believe** that—and shudder.
 2:23 And the scripture was fulfilled that says, "Abraham **believed** God,
1Pe 1: 8 *you* **believe** *in* him and are filled with an inexpressible
 2: 6 and the one *who* **trusts** in him will never be put to shame."
 2: 7 Now to you who **believe**, this stone is precious. But to those who
1Jn 3:23 to **believe** in the name of his Son, Jesus Christ, and to love one
 4: 1 Dear friends, *do* not **believe** every spirit, but test the spirits to see
 4:16 And so we know and **rely on** the love God has for us. God is love.
 5: 1 Everyone who **believes** that Jesus is the Christ is born of God,
 5: 5 the world? Only he *who* **believes** that Jesus is the Son of God.
 5:10 Anyone *who* **believes** in the Son of God has this testimony in his
 5:10 Anyone *who does* not **believe** God has made him out to be a liar,
 5:10 because *he has* not **believed** the testimony God has given about his
 5:13 I write these things to you who **believe** in the name of the Son of
Jude 1: 5 people out of Egypt, but later destroyed those *who did* not **believe**.

4410 πιστικός, *pistikos* [2] [√ *4412*]

pure [2]

Mk 14: 3 an alabaster jar of very expensive perfume, *made of* **pure** nard.
Jn 12: 3 Then Mary took about a pint *of* **pure** nard, an expensive perfume;

4411 πίστις, *pistis* [243] [√ *4412*]

δικαιοσύνη πίστεως (righteousness of faith) [6] Ro 4:11,13;
  9:30; 10:6; Gal 5:5; Php 3:9

ἐκ πίστεως (from/out of faith) [23] Ro 1:17,17; 3:26,30;
  4:16,16; 5:1; 9:30,32; 10:6; 14:23,23; Gal 2:16;
  3:7,8,9,11,12,22,24; 5:5; Heb 10:38; Jas 2:24

ἔχω πίστις (have faith) [13] Mt 17:20; 21:21; Mk 4:40; 11:22; Lk
  17:6; Ac 14:9; Ro 14:22; 1Co 13:2; 1Ti 1:19; Phm 1:5; Jas
  2:1,14,18

κατὰ πίστιν (according to faith) [6] Mt 9:29; Eph 1:15; Tit
  1:1,4; Heb 11:7,13

πίστις ... ἔργον (faith ... work) [22] Ro 3:27,28; 9:32; Gal
  2:16,16; 3:2,5; 1Th 1:3; 2Th 1:11; Heb 6:1; Jas
  2:14,14,17,18,18,18,20,22,22,24,26; Rev 2:19

faith [221], believe [4], faithfulness [4], faith from first to last
[+*1650*+*4411*] [2], have faith [+*1666*] [2], belief [1], believe
[+*1666*] [1], believe about [+*2400*] [1], believers [+*2400*+*3836*]
[1], believers [+*3836*] [1], believing [1], faithful [1], given proof
[+*4218*] [1], pledge [1], trusted [1]

Mt 8:10 the truth, I have not found anyone in Israel with such great **faith**.
 9: 2 When Jesus saw their **faith**, he said to the paralytic, "Take heart,
 9:22 "Take heart, daughter," he said, "your **faith** has healed you."
 9:29 and said, "According to your **faith** will it be done to you";

	15:28	Then Jesus answered, "Woman, you have great **faith**! Your request
	17:20	I tell you the truth, if you have **faith** as small as a mustard seed,
	21:21	"I tell you the truth, if you have **faith** and do not doubt,
	23:23	important matters of the law—justice, mercy and **faithfulness**.
Mk	2: 5	When Jesus saw their **faith**, he said to the paralytic, "Son, your sins
	4:40	his disciples, "Why are you so afraid? Do you still have no **faith**?"
	5:34	He said to her, "Daughter, your **faith** has healed you. Go in peace
	10:52	"Go," said Jesus, "your **faith** has healed you." Immediately he
	11:22	"Have **faith** in God," Jesus answered.
Lk	5:20	Jesus saw their **faith**, he said, "Friend, your sins are forgiven."
	7: 9	"I tell you, I have not found such great **faith** even in Israel."
	7:50	Jesus said to the woman, "Your **faith** has saved you; go in peace."
	8:25	"Where is your **faith**?" he asked his disciples. In fear and
	8:48	Then he said to her, "Daughter, your **faith** has healed you. Go in
	17: 5	The apostles said to the Lord, "Increase our **faith**!"
	17: 6	He replied, "If you have **faith** as small as a mustard seed, you can
	17:19	Then he said to him, "Rise and go; your **faith** has made you well."
	18: 8	when the Son of Man comes, will he find **faith** on the earth?"
	18:42	Jesus said to him, "Receive your sight; your **faith** has healed you."
	22:32	But I have prayed for you, Simon, that your **faith** may not fail.
Ac	3:16	By **faith** in the name of Jesus, this man whom you see and know
	3:16	and the **faith** that comes through him that has given this complete
	6: 5	They chose Stephen, a man full *of* **faith** and of the Holy Spirit;
	6: 7	and a large number of priests became obedient *to* the **faith**.
	11:24	He was a good man, full of the Holy Spirit and **faith**, and a great
	13: 8	opposed them and tried to turn the proconsul from the **faith**.
	14: 9	Paul looked directly at him, saw that he had **faith** to be healed
	14:22	the disciples and encouraging them to remain true to the **faith**.
	14:27	and how he had opened the door *of* **faith** to the Gentiles.
	15: 9	between us and them, for he purified their hearts *by* **faith**.
	16: 5	So the churches were strengthened *in* the **faith** and grew daily in
	17:31	He has **given proof** [+*4218*] of this to all men by raising him from
	20:21	must turn to God in repentance and have **faith** in our Lord Jesus.
	24:24	and listened to him as he spoke about **faith** in Christ Jesus.
	26:18	and a place among those who are sanctified *by* **faith** in me.'
Ro	1: 5	among all the Gentiles to the obedience that *comes from* **faith**.
	1: 8	all of you, because your **faith** is being reported all over the world.
	1:12	that you and I may be mutually encouraged by each other's **faith**.
	1:17	a righteousness that is by **faith** [+*1650*+*4411*] **from first to last**,
	1:17	a righteousness that is by **faith from first to last** [+*1650*+*4411*],
	1:17	first to last, just as it is written: "The righteous will live by **faith**."
	3: 3	not have faith? Will their lack of faith nullify God's **faithfulness**?
	3:22	This righteousness from God comes through **faith** in Jesus Christ
	3:25	him as a sacrifice of atonement, through **faith** in his blood.
	3:26	and the one who justifies those *who* **have faith** [+*1666*] in Jesus.
	3:27	On that of observing the law? No, but on that *of* **faith**.
	3:28	For we maintain that a man is justified *by* **faith** apart from
	3:30	who will justify the circumcised by **faith** and the uncircumcised
	3:30	by faith and the uncircumcised through that same **faith**.
	3:31	Do we, then, nullify the law by this **faith**? Not at all! Rather,
	4: 5	who justifies the wicked, his **faith** is credited as righteousness.
	4: 9	We have been saying that Abraham's **faith** was credited to him as
	4:11	a seal of the righteousness that he had *by* **faith** while he was still
	4:12	but who also walk in the footsteps *of* the **faith** that our father
	4:13	of the world, but through the righteousness that *comes by* **faith**.
	4:14	by law are heirs, **faith** has no value and the promise is worthless,
	4:16	Therefore, the promise comes by **faith**, so that it may be by grace
	4:16	are of the law but also to those who are of the **faith** of Abraham.
	4:19	Without weakening *in* his **faith**, he faced the fact that his body was
	4:20	of God, but was strengthened *in* his **faith** and gave glory to God,
	5: 1	Therefore, since we have been justified through **faith**, we have
	5: 2	through whom we have gained access *by* **faith** into this grace in
	9:30	have obtained it, a righteousness that is by **faith**;
	9:32	Because they pursued it not by **faith** but as if it were by works.
	10: 6	But the righteousness that is by **faith** says: "Do not say in your
	10: 8	and in your heart," that is, the word *of* **faith** we are proclaiming:
	10:17	Consequently, **faith** comes from hearing the message,
	11:20	they were broken off because of unbelief, and you stand *by* **faith**.
	12: 3	in accordance with the measure *of* **faith** God has given you.
	12: 6	man's gift is prophesying, let him use it in proportion *to* his **faith**.
	14: 1	Accept him whose **faith** is weak, without passing judgment on
	14:22	So whatever you **believe** [+*2400*] *about* these things keep between
	14:23	is condemned if he eats, because his eating is not from **faith**;
	14:23	not from faith; and everything that does not come from **faith** is sin.
	16:26	of the eternal God, so that all nations might **believe** and obey him—
1Co	2: 5	so that your **faith** might not rest on men's wisdom, but on God's
	12: 9	to another **faith** by the same Spirit, to another gifts of healing by
	13: 2	and if I have a **faith** that can move mountains, but have not love,
	13:13	And now these three remain: **faith**, hope and love. But the greatest
	15:14	has not been raised, our preaching is useless and so is your **faith**.
	15:17	And if Christ has not been raised, your **faith** is futile; you are still
	16:13	Be on your guard; stand firm in the **faith**; be men of courage;
2Co	1:24	Not that we lord it over your **faith**, but we work with you for your
	1:24	work with you for your joy, because it is *by* **faith** you stand firm.
	4:13	With that same spirit *of* **faith** we also believe and therefore speak,
	5: 7	We live by **faith**, not by sight.
	8: 7	*in* **faith**, in speech, in knowledge, in complete earnestness
	10:15	Our hope is that, as your **faith** continues to grow, our area of
	13: 5	Examine yourselves to see whether you are in the **faith**;
Gal	1:23	"The man who formerly persecuted us is now preaching the **faith**
	2:16	is not justified by observing the law, but by **faith** in Jesus Christ.
	2:16	have put our faith in Christ Jesus that we may be justified by **faith**
	2:20	I live by **faith** in the Son of God, who loved me and gave himself
	3: 2	the Spirit by observing the law, or by **believing** what you heard?
	3: 5	you observe the law, or because you **believe** what you heard?
	3: 7	then, that those who **believe** [+*1666*] are children of Abraham.
	3: 8	The Scripture foresaw that God would justify the Gentiles by **faith**,
	3: 9	So those who **have faith** [+*1666*] are blessed along with Abraham,
	3:11	before God by the law, because, "The righteous will live by **faith**."
	3:12	The law is not based on **faith**; on the contrary, "The man who does
	3:14	so that by **faith** we might receive the promise of the Spirit.
	3:22	that what was promised, being given through **faith** in Jesus Christ,
	3:23	Before this **faith** came, we were held prisoners by the law,
	3:23	held prisoners by the law, locked up until **faith** should be revealed.
	3:24	in charge to lead us to Christ that we might be justified by **faith**.
	3:25	Now that **faith** has come, we are no longer under the supervision
	3:26	You are all sons of God through **faith** in Christ Jesus,
	5: 5	But by **faith** we eagerly await through the Spirit the righteousness
	5: 6	The only thing that counts is **faith** expressing itself through love.
	5:22	is love, joy, peace, patience, kindness, goodness, **faithfulness**,
	6:10	especially to those who belong to the family *of* **believers** [+*3836*].
Eph	1:15	ever since I heard about your **faith** in the Lord Jesus and your love
	2: 8	For it is by grace you have been saved, through **faith**—and this not
	3:12	and through **faith** in him we may approach God with freedom
	3:17	so that Christ may dwell in your hearts through **faith**. And I pray
	4: 5	one Lord, one **faith**, one baptism;
	4:13	until we all reach unity *in* the **faith** and in the knowledge of the
	6:16	In addition to all this, take up the shield *of* **faith**, with which you
	6:23	and love with **faith** from God the Father and the Lord Jesus Christ.
Php	1:25	will continue with all of you for your progress and joy *in* the **faith**,
	1:27	in one spirit, contending as one man *for* the **faith** of the gospel
	2:17	drink offering on the sacrifice and service *coming from* your **faith**,
	3: 9	that comes from the law, but that which is through **faith** in Christ—
	3: 9	in Christ—the righteousness that comes from God and is by **faith**.
Col	1: 4	because we have heard *of* your **faith** in Christ Jesus and of the love
	1:23	if you continue in your **faith**, established and firm, not moved from
	2: 5	to see how orderly you are and how firm your **faith** in Christ is.
	2: 7	and built up in him, strengthened *in* the **faith** as you were taught,
	2:12	and raised with him through your **faith** in the power of God,
1Th	1: 3	before our God and Father your work *produced by* **faith**,
	1: 8	and Achaia—your **faith** in God has become known everywhere.
	3: 2	the gospel of Christ, to strengthen and encourage you in your **faith**,
	3: 5	when I could stand it no longer, I sent to find out about your **faith**.
	3: 6	us from you and has brought good news about your **faith** and love.
	3: 7	persecution we were encouraged about you because of your **faith**.
	3:10	we may see you again and supply what is lacking *in* your **faith**.
	5: 8	let us be self-controlled, putting on **faith** and love as a breastplate,
2Th	1: 3	and rightly so, because your **faith** is growing more and more,
	1: 4	and **faith** in all the persecutions and trials you are enduring.
	1:11	good purpose of yours and every act *prompted by* your **faith**.
	2:13	the sanctifying work of the Spirit and through **belief** in the truth.
	3: 2	be delivered from wicked and evil men, for not everyone has **faith**.
1Ti	1: 2	To Timothy my true son in the **faith**: Grace, mercy and peace from
	1: 4	promote controversies rather than God's work—which is by **faith**.
	1: 5	comes from a pure heart and a good conscience and a sincere **faith**.
	1:14	along with the **faith** and love that are in Christ Jesus.
	1:19	holding on to **faith** and a good conscience. Some have rejected
	1:19	Some have rejected these and so have shipwrecked their **faith**.
	2: 7	I am not lying—and a teacher of the true **faith** to the Gentiles.
	2:15	if they continue in **faith**, love and holiness with propriety.
	3: 9	They must keep hold of the deep truths *of* the **faith** with a clear
	3:13	standing and great assurance in their **faith** in Christ Jesus.

4: 1 Spirit clearly says that in later times some will abandon the **faith**
4: 6 brought up in the truths *of* the **faith** and of the good teaching that
4: 12 for the believers in speech, in life, in love, in **faith** and in purity.
5: 8 he has denied the **faith** and is worse than an unbeliever.
5: 12 on themselves, because they have broken their first **pledge**.
6: 10 have wandered from the **faith** and pierced themselves with many
6: 11 godliness, **faith**, love, endurance and gentleness.
6: 12 Fight the good fight *of* the **faith**. Take hold of the eternal life to
6: 21 have professed, and in so doing have wandered from the **faith**.

2Ti 1: 5 I have been reminded *of* your sincere **faith**, which first lived in
1: 13 the pattern of sound teaching, with **faith** and love in Christ Jesus.
2: 18 has already taken place, and they destroy the **faith** of some.
2: 22 desires of youth, and pursue righteousness, **faith**, love and peace,
3: 8 depraved minds, who, as far as the **faith** is concerned, are rejected.
3: 10 my way of life, my purpose, **faith**, patience, love, endurance,
3: 15 which are able to make you wise for salvation through **faith** in
4: 7 the good fight, I have finished the race, I have kept the **faith**.

Tit 1: 1 of God and an apostle of Jesus Christ for the **faith** of God's elect
1: 4 To Titus, my true son in our common **faith**: Grace and peace from
1: 13 rebuke them sharply, so that they will be sound in the **faith**
2: 2 self-controlled, and sound *in* **faith**, in love and in endurance.
2: 10 not to steal from them, but to show that they can be fully **trusted**,
3: 15 Greet those who love us in the **faith**. Grace be with you all.

Phm 1: 5 because I hear about your **faith** in the Lord Jesus and your love for
1: 6 I pray that you may be active in sharing your **faith**, so that you will

Heb 4: 2 to them, because those who heard did not combine it with **faith**.
6: 1 of repentance from acts that lead to death, and *of* **faith** in God,
6: 12 but to imitate those who through **faith** and patience inherit what
10: 22 us draw near to God with a sincere heart in full assurance of **faith**,
10: 38 But my righteous one will live by **faith**. And if he shrinks back,
10: 39 and are destroyed, but *of those who* **believe** and are saved.
11: 1 Now **faith** is being sure of what we hope for and certain of what
11: 3 *By* **faith** we understand that the universe was formed at God's
11: 4 *By* **faith** Abel offered God a better sacrifice than Cain did.
11: 5 *By* **faith** Enoch was taken from this life, so that he did not
11: 6 And without **faith** it is impossible to please God, because anyone
11: 7 *By* **faith** Noah, when warned about things not yet seen, in holy fear
11: 7 and became heir of the righteousness that comes by **faith**.
11: 8 *By* **faith** Abraham, when called to go to a place he would later
11: 9 *By* **faith** he made his home in the promised land like a stranger in a
11: 11 *By* **faith** Abraham, even though he was past age—and Sarah
11: 13 All these people were still living by **faith** when they died.
11: 17 *By* **faith** Abraham, when God tested him, offered Isaac as a
11: 20 *By* **faith** Isaac blessed Jacob and Esau in regard to their future.
11: 21 *By* **faith** Jacob, when he was dying, blessed each of Joseph's sons,
11: 22 *By* **faith** Joseph, when his end was near, spoke about the exodus of
11: 23 *By* **faith** Moses' parents hid him for three months after he was born,
11: 24 *By* **faith** Moses, when he had grown up, refused to be known as
11: 27 *By* **faith** he left Egypt, not fearing the king's anger; he persevered
11: 28 *By* **faith** he kept the Passover and the sprinkling of blood,
11: 29 *By* **faith** the people passed through the Red Sea as on dry land;
11: 30 *By* **faith** the walls of Jericho fell, after the people had marched
11: 31 *By* **faith** the prostitute Rahab, because she welcomed the spies,
11: 33 who through **faith** conquered kingdoms, administered justice,
11: 39 These were all commended for their **faith**, yet none of them
12: 2 Let us fix our eyes on Jesus, the author and perfecter *of* our **faith**,
13: 7 Consider the outcome of their way of life and imitate their **faith**.

Jas 1: 3 because you know that the testing *of* your **faith** develops
1: 6 But when he asks, *he must* **believe** and not doubt, because he who
2: 1 as **believers** [+*2400+3836*] in our glorious Lord Jesus Christ,
2: 5 those who are poor in the eyes of the world to be rich in **faith**
2: 14 my brothers, if a man claims to have **faith** but has no deeds?
2: 14 claims to have **faith** but has no deeds? Can such **faith** save him?
2: 17 In the same way, **faith** by itself, if it is not accompanied by action,
2: 18 But someone will say, "You have **faith**; I have deeds." Show me
2: 18 "You have **faith**; I have deeds." Show me your **faith** without deeds,
2: 18 **faith** without deeds, and I will show you my **faith** by what I do.
2: 20 do you want evidence that **faith** without deeds is useless?
2: 22 You see that his **faith** and his actions were working together,
2: 22 working together, and his **faith** was made complete by what he did.
2: 24 that a person is justified by what he does and not by **faith** alone.
2: 26 the body without the spirit is dead, so **faith** without deeds is dead.
5: 15 And the prayer *offered in* **faith** will make the sick person well;

1Pe 1: 5 who through **faith** are shielded by God's power until the coming of
1: 7 These have come so that your **faith**—of greater worth than gold,
1: 9 for you are receiving the goal *of* your **faith**, the salvation of your

1: 21 the dead and glorified him, and so your **faith** and hope are in God.
5: 9 Resist him, standing firm *in* the **faith**, because you know that your

2Pe 1: 1 and Savior Jesus Christ have received a **faith** as precious as ours:
1: 5 this very reason, make every effort to add to your **faith** goodness;

1Jn 5: 4 This is the victory that has overcome the world, even our **faith**.

Jude 1: 3 and urge you to contend *for* the **faith** that was once for all
1: 20 build yourselves up *in* your most holy **faith** and pray in the Holy

Rev 2: 13 You did not renounce your **faith** in me, even in the days of
2: 19 your deeds, your love and **faith**, your service and perseverance,
13: 10 for patient endurance and **faithfulness** on the part of the saints.
14: 12 who obey God's commandments and remain **faithful** to Jesus.

4412 πιστός, *pistos* [67] [→ *601, 602, 603, 3898, 3899,*
4409, 4410, 4411, 4413; cf. 4275]

faithful [36], trustworthy [13], believe [5], believer [4], believers
[3], can be trusted [2], believing [1], faith [1], reliable [1], sure [1]

Mt 24: 45 "Who then is the **faithful** and wise servant, whom the master has
25: 21 "His master replied, 'Well done, good and **faithful** servant!
25: 21 You have been **faithful** with a few things; I will put you in charge
25: 23 "His master replied, 'Well done, good and **faithful** servant!
25: 23 You have been **faithful** with a few things; I will put you in charge

Lk 12: 42 The Lord answered, "Who then is the **faithful** and wise manager,
16: 10 "Whoever **can be trusted** with very little can also be trusted with
16: 10 "Whoever can be trusted with very little **can** also **be trusted** with
16: 11 So if you have not been **trustworthy** in handling worldly wealth,
16: 12 And if you have not been **trustworthy** with someone else's
19: 17 'Because you have been **trustworthy** in a very small matter,

Jn 20: 27 out your hand and put it into my side. Stop doubting and **believe**."

Ac 10: 45 The circumcised **believers** who had come with Peter were
13: 34 " 'I will give you the holy and **sure** blessings promised to David.'
16: 1 whose mother was a Jewess and a **believer**, but whose father was a
16: 15 "If you consider me a **believer** in the Lord," she said, "come and

1Co 1: 9 you into fellowship with his Son Jesus Christ our Lord, is **faithful**.
4: 2 that those who have been given a trust must prove **faithful**.
4: 17 to you Timothy, my son whom I love, who is **faithful** in the Lord.
7: 25 I give a judgment as one who by the Lord's mercy is **trustworthy**.
10: 13 And God is **faithful**; he will not let you be tempted beyond what

2Co 1: 18 But as surely as God is **faithful**, our message to you is not "Yes"
6: 15 What does a **believer** have in common with an unbeliever?

Gal 3: 9 who have faith are blessed along with Abraham, the man *of* **faith**.

Eph 1: 1 will of God, To the saints in Ephesus, the **faithful** in Christ Jesus:
6: 21 Tychicus, the dear brother and **faithful** servant in the Lord,

Col 1: 2 *To* the holy and **faithful** brothers in Christ at Colosse: Grace
1: 7 fellow servant, who is a **faithful** minister of Christ on our behalf,
4: 7 is a dear brother, a **faithful** minister and fellow servant in the Lord.
4: 9 with Onesimus, our **faithful** and dear brother, who is one of you.

1Th 5: 24 The one who calls you is **faithful** and he will do it.

2Th 3: 3 But the Lord is **faithful**, and he will strengthen and protect you

1Ti 1: 12 who has given me strength, that he considered me **faithful**,
1: 15 Here is a **trustworthy** saying that deserves full acceptance:
3: 1 Here is a **trustworthy** saying: If anyone sets his heart on being an
3: 11 not malicious talkers but temperate and **trustworthy** in everything.
4: 3 created to be received with thanksgiving *by* those *who* **believe**
4: 9 This is a **trustworthy** saying that deserves full acceptance
4: 10 who is the Savior of all men, and especially *of those who* **believe**.
4: 12 but set an example *for* the **believers** in speech, in life, in love,
5: 16 If any woman who is a **believer** has widows in her family,
6: 2 Those who have **believing** masters are not to show less respect for
6: 2 because those who benefit from their service are **believers**,

2Ti 2: 2 entrust *to* **reliable** men who will also be qualified to teach others.
2: 11 Here is a **trustworthy** saying: If we died with him, we will also
2: 13 if we are faithless, he will remain **faithful**, for he cannot disown

Tit 1: 6 a man whose children **believe** and are not open to the charge of
1: 9 He must hold firmly to the **trustworthy** message as it has been
3: 8 This is a **trustworthy** saying. And I want you to stress these

Heb 2: 17 might become a merciful and **faithful** high priest in service to God,
3: 2 He was **faithful** to the one who appointed him, just as Moses was
3: 5 Moses was **faithful** as a servant in all God's house, testifying to
10: 23 to the hope we profess, for he who promised is **faithful**.
11: 11 because he considered him **faithful** who had made the promise.

1Pe 1: 21 Through him you **believe** in God, who raised him from the dead
4: 19 to God's will should commit themselves *to* their **faithful** Creator
5: 12 With the help of Silas, whom I regard as a **faithful** brother,

1Jn 1: 9 he is **faithful** and just and will forgive us our sins and purify us

3Jn 1: 5 you are **faithful** in what you are doing for the brothers,
Rev 1: 5 and from Jesus Christ, who is the **faithful** witness, the firstborn
      2:10 Be **faithful**, even to the point of death, and I will give you the
      2:13 even in the days of Antipas, my **faithful** witness, who was put to
      3:14 the **faithful** and true witness, the ruler of God's creation.
    17:14 and with him will be his called, chosen and **faithful** *followers*."
    19:11 me was a white horse, whose rider is called **Faithful** and True.
    21: 5 "Write this down, for these words are **trustworthy** and true."
    22: 6 The angel said to me, "These words are **trustworthy** and true.

4413 πιστόω, *pistoō* [1] [√ *4412*]

convinced [1]

2Ti 3:14 continue in what you have learned and *have become* **convinced** *of*,

4414 πλανάω, *planaō* [39] [√ *4415*]

deceived [9], deceive [6], deceives [3], going astray [3],
deceiving [2], in error [2], lead astray [2], wandered off [2],
deluded [1], leads astray [1], led astray [1], misleads [1], misled
[1], mistaken [1], wander off [1], wander [1], wandered [1],
wanders away [1]

Mt 18:12 If a man owns a hundred sheep, and one of them **wanders away**,
    18:12 on the hills and go to look for the one *that* **wandered off**?
    18:13 that one sheep than about the ninety-nine that *did* not **wander off**.
    22:29 "*You are* **in error** because you do not know the Scriptures
    24: 4 Jesus answered: "Watch out that no one **deceives** you.
    24: 5 in my name, claiming, 'I am the Christ,' and *will* **deceive** many.
    24:11 and many false prophets will appear and **deceive** many people.
    24:24 and perform great signs and miracles to **deceive** even the elect—
Mk 12:24 "*Are you* not **in error** because you do not know the Scriptures
    12:27 the God of the dead, but of the living. *You are* badly **mistaken**!"
    13: 5 Jesus said to them: "Watch out that no one **deceives** you.
    13: 6 will come in my name, claiming, 'I am he,' and *will* **deceive** many.
Lk 21: 8 He replied: "Watch out that *you are* not **deceived**. For many will
Jn 7:12 "He is a good man." Others replied, "No, *he* **deceives** the people."
    7:47 "You mean he *has* **deceived** you also?" the Pharisees retorted.
1Co 6: 9 wicked will not inherit the kingdom of God? *Do* not *be* **deceived**:
  15:33 *Do* not *be* **misled**: "Bad company corrupts good character."
Gal 6: 7 *Do* not *be* **deceived**: God cannot be mocked. A man reaps what he
2Ti 3:13 will go from bad to worse, **deceiving** and being deceived.
    3:13 will go from bad to worse, deceiving and *being* **deceived**.
Tit 3: 3 **deceived** and enslaved by all kinds of passions and pleasures.
Heb 3:10 and I said, 'Their hearts *are* always **going astray**, and they have
    5: 2 to deal gently *with* those who are ignorant and *are* **going astray**,
    11:38 *They* **wandered** in deserts and mountains, and in caves and holes
Jas 1:16 Don't *be* **deceived**, my dear brothers.
    5:19 if one of you *should* **wander** from the truth and someone should
1Pe 2:25 For you were like sheep **going astray**, but now you have returned
2Pe 2:15 and **wandered off** to follow the way of Balaam son of Beor,
1Jn 1: 8 to be without sin, *we* **deceive** ourselves and the truth is not in us.
    2:26 these things to you about those *who are trying to* **lead** you **astray**.
    3: 7 Dear children, *do* not *let* anyone **lead** you **astray**. He who does
Rev 2:20 By her teaching *she* **misleads** my servants *into* sexual immorality
    12: 9 called the devil, or Satan, who **leads** the whole world **astray**.
    13:14 behalf of the first beast, *he* **deceived** the inhabitants of the earth.
    18:23 great men. By your magic spell all the nations *were* **led astray**.
    19:20 With these signs *he had* **deluded** those who had received the mark
    20: 3 to keep *him* from **deceiving** the nations anymore until the
    20: 8 and will go out *to* **deceive** the nations in the four corners of the
    20:10 And the devil, who **deceived** them, was thrown into the lake of

4415 πλάνη, *planē* [10] [→ *675, 4414, 4416, 4417, 4418*]

error [5], deceitful [1], deception [1], delusion [1], falsehood [1],
perversion [1]

Mt 27:64 from the dead. This last **deception** will be worse than the first."
Ro 1:27 and received in themselves the due penalty *for* their **perversion**.
Eph 4:14 by the cunning and craftiness of men in their **deceitful** scheming.
1Th 2: 3 For the appeal we make does not spring from **error** or impure
2Th 2:11 For this reason God sends them a powerful **delusion** so that they
Jas 5:20 Whoever turns a sinner from the **error** of his way will save him
2Pe 2:18 entice people who are just escaping from those who live in **error**.
    3:17 so that you may not be carried away *by* the **error** of lawless men

1Jn 4: 6 is how we recognize the Spirit of truth and the spirit *of* **falsehood**.
Jude 1:11 the way of Cain; they have rushed for profit *into* Balaam's **error**;

4416 πλάνης, *planēs* Not used in UBS/NIV [√ *4415*]

4417 πλανήτης, *planētēs* [1] [√ *4415*]

wandering [1]

Jude 1:13 **wandering** stars, for whom blackest darkness has been reserved

4418 πλάνος, *planos* [5] [√ *4415*]

deceiver [2], deceivers [1], deceiving [1], impostors [1]

Mt 27:63 "we remember that while he was still alive that **deceiver** said,
2Co 6: 8 bad report and good report; genuine, yet regarded as **impostors**;
1Ti 4: 1 and follow **deceiving** spirits and things taught by demons.
2Jn 1: 7 Many **deceivers**, who do not acknowledge Jesus Christ as coming
    1: 7 into the world. Any such person is the **deceiver** and the antichrist.

4419 πλάξ, *plax* [3]

tablets [2], stone tablets [1]

2Co 3: 3 living God, not on **tablets** of stone but on tablets of human hearts.
    3: 3 living God, not on tablets of stone but on **tablets** of human hearts.
Heb 9: 4 staff that had budded, and the **stone tablets** of the covenant.

4420 πλάσμα, *plasma* [1] [√ *4421*]

formed [1]

Ro 9:20 "Shall what is **formed** say to him who formed it, 'Why did you

4421 πλάσσω, *plassō* [2] [→ *4420, 4422*]

formed [2]

Ro 9:20 "Shall what is formed say *to* him *who* **formed** it, 'Why did you
1Ti 2:13 For Adam *was* **formed** first, then Eve.

4422 πλαστός, *plastos* [1] [√ *4421*]

made up [1]

2Pe 2: 3 these teachers will exploit you *with* stories they have **made up**.

4423 πλατεῖα, *plateia* [9] [√ *4426*]

streets [5], great street [2], street [2]

Mt 6: 5 in the synagogues and on the **street** corners to be seen by men.
    12:19 will not quarrel or cry out; no one will hear his voice in the **streets**.
Lk 10:10 you enter a town and are not welcomed, go into its **streets** and say,
    13:26 'We ate and drank with you, and you taught in our **streets**.'
    14:21 'Go out quickly into the **streets** and alleys of the town and bring in
Ac 5:15 people brought the sick into the **streets** and laid them on beds
Rev 11: 8 Their bodies will lie in the **street** of the great city, which is
    21:21 The **great street** of the city was of pure gold, like transparent
    22: 2 down the middle *of* the **great street** of the city. On each side of the

4424 πλάτος, *platos* [4] [√ *4426*]

wide [3], breadth [1]

Eph 3:18 to grasp how **wide** and long and high and deep is the love of
Rev 20: 9 They marched across the **breadth** of the earth and surrounded the
    21:16 The city was laid out like a square, as long as it was **wide**.
    21:16 it to be 12,000 stadia in length, and as **wide** and high as it is long.

4425 πλατύνω, *platynō* [3] [√ *4426*]

make wide [1], open wide [1], opened wide [1]

Mt 23: 5 *They* **make** their phylacteries **wide** and the tassels on their
2Co 6:11 freely to you, Corinthians, and **opened wide** our hearts to you.
    6:13 I speak as to my children—**open wide** your hearts also.

4426 πλατύς, *platys* [1] [→ 4423, 4424, 4425]

wide [1]

Mt 7:13 For **wide** is the gate and broad is the road that leads to destruction,

4427 πλέγμα, *plegma* [1] [√ 4428]

braided hair [1]

1Ti 2: 9 not with **braided hair** or gold or pearls or expensive clothes,

4428 πλέκω, *plekō* [3] [→ 1861, 1862, 4427, 4451]

twisted together [3]

Mt 27:29 and then **twisted together** a crown of thorns and set it on his head.
Mk 15:17 then **twisted together** a crown of thorns and set it on him.
Jn 19: 2 The soldiers **twisted together** a crown of thorns and put it on his

4429 πλεονάζω, *pleonazō* [9] [√ 4444]

increase [2], increasing [2], credited [1], have too much [1], increased [1], make increase [1], reaching more and more [+1328+3836+4498] [1]

Ro 5:20 The law was added so that the trespass *might* **increase**. But where
     5:20 But where sin **increased**, grace increased all the more,
     6: 1 then? Shall we go on sinning so that grace *may* **increase**?
2Co 4:15 so that the grace that is **reaching** [+1328+3836+4498] **more and more** *people* may cause thanksgiving to overflow to the glory of
     8:15 "He who gathered much *did* not **have too much**, and he who
Php 4:17 but I am looking for what *may be* **credited** to your account.
1Th 3:12 *May* the Lord **make** your love **increase** and overflow for each
2Th 1: 3 and the love every one of you has for each other *is* **increasing**.
2Pe 1: 8 For if you possess these qualities *in* **increasing** *measure*,

4430 πλεονεκτέω, *pleonekteō* [5] [√ 4444 + 2400]

exploit [2], exploited [1], outwit [1], take advantage of [1]

2Co 2:11 in order that Satan *might* not **outwit** us. For we are not unaware of
     7: 2 no one, we have corrupted no one, *we have* **exploited** no one.
    12:17 *Did I* **exploit** you through any of the men I sent you?
    12:18 and I sent our brother with him. Titus *did* not **exploit** you, did he?
1Th 4: 6 matter no one should wrong his brother or **take advantage of** him.

4431 πλεονέκτης, *pleonektēs* [4] [√ 4444 + 2400]

greedy [3], greedy person [1]

1Co 5:10 world who are immoral, or the **greedy** and swindlers, or idolaters.
     5:11 who calls himself a brother but is sexually immoral or **greedy**,
     6:10 nor thieves nor the **greedy** nor drunkards nor slanderers nor
Eph 5: 5 No immoral, impure or **greedy person**—such a man is an

4432 πλεονεξία, *pleonexia* [10] [√ 4444 + 2400]

greed [8], lust for more [1], one grudgingly given [1]

Mk 7:22 **greed**, malice, deceit, lewdness, envy, slander, arrogance and folly.
Lk 12:15 Be on your guard against all kinds *of* **greed**; a man's life does not
Ro 1:29 filled with every kind of wickedness, evil, **greed** and depravity.
2Co 9: 5 it will be ready as a generous gift, not as **one grudgingly given**.
Eph 4:19 indulge in every kind of impurity, with a continual **lust for more**.
     5: 3 or of any kind of impurity, or *of* **greed**, because these are improper
Col 3: 5 impurity, lust, evil desires and **greed**, which is idolatry.
1Th 2: 5 never used flattery, nor did we put on a mask to cover up **greed**—
2Pe 2: 3 In their **greed** these teachers will exploit you with stories they have
     2:14 seduce the unstable; they are experts *in* **greed**—an accursed brood!

4433 πλευρά, *pleura* [5]

side [5]

Jn 19:34 Instead, one of the soldiers pierced Jesus' **side** with a spear,
   20:20 After he said this, he showed them his hands and **side**. The
   20:25 the nails were, and put my hand into his **side**, I will not believe it."
   20:27 see my hands. Reach out your hand and put it into my **side**.
Ac 12: 7 He struck Peter *on* the **side** and woke him up. "Quick, get up!"

4434 πλέω, *pleō* [6] [→ 676, 1095, 1386, 1739, 2929, 4179, 4449, 4450, 4452, 4453, 5709]

sail [2], sailed [2], sailing [1], travel by ship [+2093+5536] [1]

Lk 8:23 *As* they **sailed**, he fell asleep. A squall came down on the lake,
Ac 21: 3 and passing to the south of it, *we* **sailed** on to Syria.
   27: 2 We boarded a ship from Adramyttium about to **sail** for ports along
   27: 6 The centurion found an Alexandrian ship **sailing** for Italy
   27:24 and God has graciously given you the lives of all *who* **sail** with
Rev 18:17 sea captain, and all who **travel by ship** [+2093+5536], the sailors,

4435 πληγή, *plēgē* [22] [√ 4448]

plagues [10], plague [3], wound [2], beat [+2202] [1], beatings [1], flogged [+2202] [1], flogged [1], punishment [1], wounded [+2400+3836] [1], wounds [1]

Lk 10:30 They stripped him of his clothes, **beat** [+2202] him and went away,
   12:48 and does things deserving **punishment** will be beaten with few
Ac 16:23 *After they had been* severely **flogged** [+2202], they were thrown
   16:33 hour of the night the jailer took them and washed their **wounds**;
2Co 6: 5 in **beatings**, imprisonments and riots; in hard work, sleepless
    11:23 been in prison more frequently, been **flogged** more severely,
Rev 9:18 A third of mankind was killed by the three **plagues** of fire,
     9:20 The rest of mankind that were not killed by these **plagues** still did
    11: 6 and to strike the earth with every kind of **plague** as often as they
    13: 3 to have had a fatal **wound**, but the fatal **wound** had been healed.
    13:12 worship the first beast, whose fatal **wound** had been healed.
    13:14 honor of the beast who *was* **wounded** [+2400+3836] by the sword
    15: 1 seven angels with the seven last **plagues**—last, because with them
    15: 6 Out of the temple came the seven angels with the seven **plagues**,
    15: 8 and no one could enter the temple until the seven **plagues** of the
    16: 9 who had control over these **plagues**, but they refused to repent
    16:21 And they cursed God on account of the **plague** of hail,
    16:21 account of the plague of hail, because the **plague** was so terrible.
    18: 4 share in her sins, so that you will not receive any of her **plagues**;
    18: 8 Therefore in one day her **plagues** will overtake her: death,
    21: 9 who had the seven bowls full *of* the seven last **plagues** came
    22:18 to them, God will add to him the **plagues** described in this book.

4436 πλῆθος, *plēthos* [31] [√ 4398]

number [6], assembly [3], crowd [3], people [3], multitude [2], all disciples [+3412+3836] [1], all [1], assembled worshipers [+3295+3836] [1], church [1], crowd [+3295+3836] [1], crowds [1], great company [1], great number [1], group [1], Jewish community [+2681] [1], large number [1], numerous [1], pile [1], publicly [+1967+3836] [1]

Mk 3: 7 his disciples to the lake, and a large **crowd** from Galilee followed.
     3: 8 many **people** came to him from Judea, Jerusalem, Idumea,
Lk 1:10 all the **assembled** [+3295+3836] **worshipers** were praying outside.
     2:13 Suddenly a **great company** of the heavenly host appeared with the
     5: 6 they caught *such* a large **number** of fish that their nets began to
     6:17 was there and a great **number** of people from all over Judea,
     8:37 Then all the **people** of the region of the Gerasenes asked Jesus to
    19:37 the whole **crowd** of disciples began joyfully to praise God in loud
    23: 1 Then the whole **assembly** rose and led him off to Pilate.
    23:27 A large **number** of people followed him, including women who
Jn   5: 3 Here a **great number** of disabled people used to lie—the blind,
    21: 6 were unable to haul the net in because of the **large number** of fish.
Ac   2: 6 they heard this sound, a **crowd** came together in bewilderment,
     4:32 **All** the believers were one in heart and mind. No one claimed that
     5:14 and women believed in the Lord and were added to their **number**.
     5:16 **Crowds** gathered also from the towns around Jerusalem,
     6: 2 So the Twelve gathered **all** the **disciples** [+3412+3836] together
     6: 5 This proposal pleased the whole **group**. They chose Stephen,
    14: 1 There they spoke so effectively that a great **number** of Jews
    14: 4 The **people** of the city were divided; some sided with the Jews,
    15:12 The whole **assembly** became silent as they listened to Barnabas
    15:30 where they gathered the **church** together and delivered the letter.
    17: 4 as did a large **number** of God-fearing Greeks and not a few
    19: 9 refused to believe and **publicly** [+1967+3836] maligned the Way.
    21:36 The **crowd** [+3295+3836] that followed kept shouting, "Away with
    23: 7 the Pharisees and the Sadducees, and the **assembly** was divided.
    25:24 The whole **Jewish community** [+2681] has petitioned me about

28: 3 Paul gathered a **pile** of brushwood and, as he put it on the fire,
Heb 11:12 came descendants *as* **numerous** as the stars in the sky and as
Jas 5:20 way will save him from death and cover over a **multitude** of sins.
1Pe 4: 8 each other deeply, because love covers over a **multitude** of sins.

4437 πληθύνω, *plēthynō* [12] [√ *4398*]

abundance [3], give many descendants [+*4437*] [2], increase [2], greatly increased [+*889*+*2779*] [1], grew in numbers [1], increased [1], increasing [1], spread [1]

Mt 24:12 Because of the **increase** of wickedness, the love of most will grow
Ac 6: 1 In those days *when* the *number* of disciples *was* **increasing**,
 6: 7 The number of disciples in Jerusalem **increased** rapidly, and a
 7:17 *number* of our people in Egypt **greatly increased** [+*889*+*2779*].
 9:31 the Holy Spirit, *it* **grew in numbers**, living in the fear of the Lord.
 12:24 But the word of God continued to increase and **spread**.
2Co 9:10 and bread for food will also supply and **increase** your store of seed
Heb 6:14 "I will surely bless you and **give** you **many descendants** [+*4437*]."
 6:14 "I will surely bless you and **give** [+*4437*] you **many descendants**."
1Pe 1: 2 sprinkling by his blood: Grace and peace *be* yours *in* **abundance**.
2Pe 1: 2 and peace *be* yours *in* **abundance** through the knowledge of God
Jude 1: 2 Mercy, peace and love *be* yours *in* **abundance**.

4438 πλήκτης, *plēktēs* [2] [√ *4448*]

violent [2]

1Ti 3: 3 not **violent** but gentle, not quarrelsome, not a lover of money.
Tit 1: 7 not quick-tempered, not given to drunkenness, not **violent**,

4439 πλήμμυρα, *plēmmyra* [1] [√ *4398*]

flood [1]

Lk 6:48 When a **flood** came, the torrent struck that house but could not

4440 πλήν, *plēn* [31] [√ *4444*]

but [14], however [4], only [4], yet [4], *untranslated* [1], beyond [+*4498*] [1], except [1], important thing [1], in any case [1]

Mt 11:22 **But** I tell you, it will be more bearable for Tyre and Sidon on the
 11:24 **But** I tell you that it will be more bearable for Sodom on the day of
 18: 7 things must come, **but** woe to the man through whom they come!
 26:39 may this cup be taken from me. **Yet** not as I will, but as you will."
 26:64 "Yes, it is as you say," Jesus replied. "**But** I say to all of you:
Mk 12:32 are right in saying that God is one and there is no other **but** him.
Lk 6:24 "**But** woe to you who are rich, for you have already received your
 6:35 **But** love your enemies, do good to them, and lend to them without
 10:11 off against you. **Yet** be sure of this: The kingdom of God is near.'
 10:14 **But** it will be more bearable for Tyre and Sidon at the judgment
 10:20 **However**, do not rejoice that the spirits submit to you, but rejoice
 11:41 **But** give what is inside the dish, to the poor, and everything will
 12:31 **But** seek his kingdom, and these things will be given to you as
 13:33 **In any case**, I must keep going today and tomorrow and the next
 17: 1 bound to come, **but** woe to that person through whom they come.
 18: 8 **However**, when the Son of Man comes, will he find faith on the
 19:27 **But** those enemies of mine who did not want me to be king over
 22:21 **But** the hand of him who is going to betray me is with mine on the
 22:22 go as it has been decreed, **but** woe to that man who betrays him."
 22:42 take this cup from me; **yet** not my will, but yours be done."
 23:28 weep for me; [NIE] weep for yourselves and for your children.
Ac 8: 1 and all **except** the apostles were scattered throughout Judea
 15:28 and to us not to burden you with anything **beyond** [+*4498*] the
 20:23 I **only** know that in every city the Holy Spirit warns me that prison
 27:22 not one of you will be lost; **only** the ship will be destroyed.
1Co 11:11 In the Lord, **however**, woman is not independent of man, nor is
Eph 5:33 **However**, each one of you also must love his wife as he loves
Php 1:18 The **important thing** is that in every way, whether from false
 3:16 **Only** let us live up to what we have already attained.
 4:14 **Yet** it was good of you to share in my troubles.
Rev 2:25 **Only** hold on to what you have until I come.

4441 πλήρης, *plērēs* [16] [√ *4444*]

full [9], basketfuls [+*3186*] [2], always [1], basketfuls [+*5083*] [1], covered [1], fully [1], furious [+*2596*] [1]

Mt 14:20 and the disciples picked up twelve **basketfuls** [+*3186*] of broken
 15:37 Afterward the disciples picked up seven **basketfuls** [+*5083*] of
Mk 4:28 first the stalk, then the head, then the **full** kernel in the head.
 8:19 how many **basketfuls** [+*3186*] of pieces did you pick up?"
Lk 4: 1 Jesus, **full** of the Holy Spirit, returned from the Jordan and was led
 5:12 of the towns, a man came along who was **covered** with leprosy.
Jn 1:14 and Only, who came from the Father, **full** of grace and truth.
Ac 6: 3 choose seven men from among you who are known to be **full** of
 6: 5 They chose Stephen, a man **full** of faith and of the Holy Spirit;
 6: 8 Now Stephen, a man **full** of God's grace and power, did great
 7:55 But Stephen, **full** of the Holy Spirit, looked up to heaven and saw
 9:36 is Dorcas), who was **always** doing good and helping the poor.
 11:24 He was a good man, **full** of the Holy Spirit and faith, and a great
 13:10 that is right! You are **full** of all kinds of deceit and trickery.
 19:28 they heard this, they were **furious** [+*2596*] and began shouting:
2Jn 1: 8 what you have worked for, but that you may be rewarded **fully**.

4442 πληροφορέω, *plērophoreō* [6] [√ *4444* + *5770*]

discharge all [1], fulfilled [1], fully assured [1], fully convinced [1], fully persuaded [1], fully [1]

Lk 1: 1 up an account of the things *that have been* **fulfilled** among us,
Ro 4:21 *being* **fully persuaded** that God had power to do what he had
 14: 5 day alike. Each one *should be* **fully convinced** in his own mind.
Col 4:12 may stand firm in all the will of God, mature and **fully assured**.
2Ti 4: 5 work of an evangelist, **discharge all** the duties of your ministry.
 4:17 so that through me the message *might be* **fully** *proclaimed*

4443 πληροφορία, *plērophoria* [4] [√ *4444* + *5770*]

complete [1], conviction [1], full assurance [1], sure [1]

Col 2: 2 so that they may have the full riches *of* **complete** understanding,
1Th 1: 5 also with power, with the Holy Spirit and with deep **conviction**.
Heb 6:11 same diligence to the very end, in order to *make* your hope **sure**.
 10:22 let us draw near to God with a sincere heart in **full assurance** of

4444 πληρόω, *plēroō* [86] [→ *405*, *499*, *1740*, *1741*, *4429*, *4430*, *4431*, *4432*, *4440*, *4441*, *4442*, *4443*, *4445*, *4650*, *5230*, *5670*]

fulfilled [21], fulfill [11], complete [7], filled with [6], filled [6], fill with [3], come [2], completed [2], finished [2], full [2], after passed [1], amply supplied [1], bring to fulfillment [1], come true [1], complete [+*4246*] [1], completing [1], fill up [1], fill [1], filled in [1], fills [1], finds fulfillment [1], fully met [1], fully [1], given fullness [+*1639*] [1], gone by [1], greatly encouraged [+*4155*] [1], happened [1], make complete [+*1639*] [1], make complete [1], meet [1], passed [1], present in fullness [1], summed up [1], was [1]

Mt 1:22 All this took place to **fulfill** what the Lord had said through the
 2:15 so *was* **fulfilled** what the Lord had said through the prophet:
 2:17 Then what was said through the prophet Jeremiah *was* **fulfilled**:
 2:23 So *was* **fulfilled** what was said through the prophets: "He will be
 3:15 so now; it is proper for us to do this *to* **fulfill** all righteousness."
 4:14 to **fulfill** what was said through the prophet Isaiah:
 5:17 the Prophets; I have not come to abolish them but *to* **fulfill** them.
 8:17 This was to **fulfill** what was spoken through the prophet Isaiah:
 12:17 This was to **fulfill** what was spoken through the prophet Isaiah:
 13:35 So *was* **fulfilled** what was spoken through the prophet: "I will open /
 13:48 When it *was* **full**, the fishermen pulled it up on the shore.
 21: 4 This took place to **fulfill** what was spoken through the prophet:
 23:32 **Fill up**, then, the measure of the sin of your forefathers!
 26:54 then *would* the Scriptures *be* **fulfilled** that say it must happen in
 26:56 all taken place that the writings of the prophets *might be* **fulfilled**."
 27: 9 Then what was spoken by Jeremiah the prophet *was* **fulfilled**:
Mk 1:15 "The time *has* **come**," he said. "The kingdom of God is near.
 14:49 and you did not arrest me. But the Scriptures *must be* **fulfilled**."
Lk 1:20 not believe my words, which *will* **come true** at their proper time."
 2:40 *he was* **filled with** wisdom, and the grace of God was upon him.

3: 5 Every valley *shall be* **filled in**, every mountain and hill made low.
4:21 saying to them, "Today this scripture *is* **fulfilled** in your hearing."
7: 1 When Jesus *had* **finished** saying all this in the hearing of the
9:31 which he was about to **bring to fulfillment** at Jerusalem.
21:24 on by the Gentiles until the times of the Gentiles *are* **fulfilled**.
22:16 I will not eat it again until *it* **finds fulfillment** in the kingdom of
24:44 Everything must *be* **fulfilled** that is written about me in the Law of
Jn 3:29 the bridegroom's voice. That joy is mine, and *it is now* **complete**.
7: 8 up to this Feast, because for me the right time *has* not yet **come**."
12: 3 And the house *was* **filled** with the fragrance of the perfume.
12:38 This was to **fulfill** the word of Isaiah the prophet: "Lord, who has
13:18 I know those I have chosen. But this is to **fulfill** the scripture:
15:11 so that my joy may be in you and that your joy *may be* **complete**.
15:25 But this is to **fulfill** what is written in their Law: 'They hated me
16: 6 Because I have said these things, you *are* **filled with** grief.
16:24 Ask and you will receive, and your joy will be **complete**.
17:12 the one doomed to destruction so that Scripture *would be* **fulfilled**.
17:13 so that they may have the **full** *measure* of my joy within them.
18: 9 This happened so that the words he had spoken *would be* **fulfilled**:
18:32 indicating the kind of death he was going to die *would be* **fulfilled**.
19:24 This happened that the scripture *might be* **fulfilled** which said,
19:36 These things happened so that the scripture *would be* **fulfilled**:
Ac 1:16 the Scripture had to *be* **fulfilled** which the Holy Spirit spoke long
2: 2 from heaven and **filled** the whole house where they were sitting.
2:28 to me the paths of life; *you will* **fill me with** joy in your presence.'
3:18 But this is how God **fulfilled** what he had foretold through all the
5: 3 how is it that Satan *has* so **filled** your heart that you have lied to
5:28 "Yet *you have* **filled** Jerusalem with your teaching and are
7:23 "When Moses *was* forty years old, he decided to visit his fellow
7:30 "**After** forty years *had* **passed**, an angel appeared to Moses in the
9:23 After many days *had* **gone by**, the Jews conspired to kill him,
12:25 When Barnabas and Saul *had* **finished** their mission, they returned
13:25 As John *was* **completing** his work, he said: 'Who do you think I
13:27 yet in condemning him *they* **fulfilled** the words of the prophets
13:52 And the disciples *were* **filled with** joy and with the Holy Spirit.
14:26 to the grace of God for the work *they had now* **completed**.
19:21 After all this *had* **happened**, Paul decided to go to Jerusalem,
24:27 *When* two years *had* **passed**, Felix was succeeded by Porcius
Ro 1:29 *They have become* **filled with** every kind of wickedness,
8: 4 the righteous requirements of the law *might be* **fully met** in us,
13: 8 one another, for he who loves his fellowman *has* **fulfilled** the law.
15:13 *May* the God of hope **fill** you **with** all joy and peace as you trust in
15:14 **complete** [+*4246*] in knowledge and competent to instruct one
15:19 around to Illyricum, I *have* **fully** **proclaimed** the gospel of Christ.
2Co 7: 4 *I am* **greatly encouraged** [+*4155*]; in all our troubles my joy
10: 6 every act of disobedience, once your obedience *is* **complete**.
Gal 5:14 The entire law *is* **summed up** in a single command: "Love your
Eph 1:23 is his body, the fullness of him *who* **fills** everything in every way.
3:19 that *you may be* **filled** to the measure of all the fullness of God.
4:10 higher than all the heavens, in order to **fill** the whole universe.)
5:18 which leads to debauchery. Instead, *be* **filled** with the Spirit.
Php 1:11 **filled with** the fruit of righteousness that comes through Jesus
2: 2 then **make** my joy **complete** by being like-minded,
4:18 *I am* **amply supplied**, now that I have received from Epaphroditus
4:19 And my God *will* **meet** all your needs according to his glorious
Col 1: 9 asking God to **fill** *you* **with** the knowledge of his will through
1:25 God gave me *to* **present** to you the word of God **in its** **fullness**—
2:10 and *you have been* **given fullness** [+*1639*] in Christ, who is the
4:17 "See to it that *you* **complete** the work you have received in the
2Th 1:11 and that by his power *he may* **fulfill** every good purpose of yours
2Ti 1: 4 your tears, I long to see you, so that *I may be* **filled with** joy.
Jas 2:23 And the scripture *was* **fulfilled** that says, "Abraham believed God,
1Jn 1: 4 We write this to **make** our joy **complete** [+*1639*].
2Jn 1:12 and talk with you face to face, so that our joy may be **complete**.
Rev 3: 2 for I have not found your deeds **complete** in the sight of my God.
6:11 brothers who were to be killed as they had been *was* **completed**.

4445 πλήρωμα, *plērōma* [17] [√ *4444*]

fullness [6], fulfillment [2], basketfuls [+*3186*] [1], basketfuls [+*5083*] [1], everything [1], full measure [1], full number [1], fully [1], measure of fullness [1], patch [1], piece [1]

Mt 9:16 for the **patch** will pull away from the garment, making the tear
Mk 2:21 If he does, the new **piece** will pull away from the old, making the
6:43 and the disciples picked up twelve **basketfuls** [+*3186*] of broken

8:20 how many **basketfuls** [+*5083*] of pieces did you pick up?"
Jn 1:16 From the **fullness** of his grace we have all received one blessing
Ro 11:12 for the Gentiles, how much greater riches will their **fullness** bring!
11:25 Israel has experienced a hardening in part until the **full number** of
13:10 harm to its neighbor. Therefore love is the **fulfillment** of the law.
15:29 to you, I will come in the **full measure** of the blessing of Christ.
1Co 10:26 for, "The earth is the Lord's, and **everything** in it."
Gal 4: 4 But when the time had **fully** come, God sent his Son, born of a
Eph 1:10 put into effect when the times will have *reached* their **fulfillment**—
1:23 is his body, the **fullness** of him who fills everything in every way.
3:19 that you may be filled to the **measure of** all the **fullness** of God.
4:13 attaining to the whole measure *of* the **fullness** of Christ.
Col 1:19 For God was pleased to have all his **fullness** dwell in him,
2: 9 For in Christ all the **fullness** of the Deity lives in bodily form,

4446 πλησίον, *plēsion* [17] [→ *4180, 4181*]

neighbor [15], near [1], other [1]

Mt 5:43 heard that it was said, 'Love your **neighbor** and hate your enemy.'
19:19 your father and mother,' and 'love your **neighbor** as yourself.' "
22:39 And the second is like it: 'Love your **neighbor** as yourself.'
Mk 12:31 The second is this: 'Love your **neighbor** as yourself.' There is no
12:33 and to love your **neighbor** as yourself is more important than all
Lk 10:27 and with all your mind'; and, 'Love your **neighbor** as yourself.' "
10:29 to justify himself, so he asked Jesus, "And who is my **neighbor**?"
10:36 "Which of these three do you think was a **neighbor** to the man who
Jn 4: 5 **near** the plot of ground Jacob had given to his son Joseph.
Ac 7:27 "But the man who was mistreating the **other** pushed Moses aside
Ro 13: 9 are summed up in this one rule: "Love your **neighbor** as yourself."
13:10 Love does no harm *to* its **neighbor**. Therefore love is the
15: 2 Each of us should please his **neighbor** for his good, to build him
Gal 5:14 in a single command: "Love your **neighbor** as yourself."
Eph 4:25 of you must put off falsehood and speak truthfully to his **neighbor**,
Jas 2: 8 in Scripture, "Love your **neighbor** as yourself," you are doing right.
4:12 and destroy. But you—who are you to judge your **neighbor**?

4447 πλησμονή, *plēsmonē* [1] [√ *4398*]

indulgence [1]

Col 2:23 but they lack any value in restraining sensual **indulgence**.

4448 πλήσσω, *plēssō* [1] [→ *1742, 2159, 4435, 4438*]

struck [1]

Rev 8:12 and a third of the sun *was* **struck**, a third of the moon, and a third

4449 πλοιάριον, *ploiarion* [5] [√ *4434*]

boat [2], boats [2], small boat [1]

Mk 3: 9 Because of the crowd he told his disciples to have a **small boat**
Jn 6:22 shore of the lake realized that only one **boat** had been there,
6:23 Then some **boats** from Tiberias landed near the place where the
6:24 they got into the **boats** and went to Capernaum in search of Jesus.
21: 8 The other disciples followed *in* the **boat**, towing the net full of

4450 πλοῖον, *ploion* [67 / 68] [√ *4434*]

boat [39], ship [17], boats [5], ships [3], its [+*3836*] [2], on board [+*1877+3836*] [1], ship's [1]

Mt 4:21 They were in a **boat** with their father Zebedee, preparing their nets.
4:22 and immediately they left the **boat** and their father and followed
8:23 Then he got into the **boat** and his disciples followed him.
8:24 storm came up on the lake, so that the waves swept over the **boat**.
9: 1 Jesus stepped into a **boat**, crossed over and came to his own town.
13: 2 Such large crowds gathered around him that he got into a **boat**
14:13 had happened, he withdrew by **boat** privately to a solitary place.
14:22 Immediately Jesus made the disciples get into the **boat** and go on
14:24 but the **boat** was already a considerable distance from land,
14:29 Then Peter got down out of the **boat**, walked on the water
14:32 And when they climbed into the **boat**, the wind died down.
14:33 Then those who were in the **boat** worshiped him, saying, "Truly
15:39 he got into the **boat** and went to the vicinity of Magadan.
Mk 1:19 he saw James son of Zebedee and his brother John in a **boat**,

	1:20	and they left their father Zebedee in the **boat** with the hired men
	4: 1	so large that he got into a **boat** and sat in it out on the lake,
	4:36	the crowd behind, they took him along, just as he was, in the **boat**.
	4:36	just as he was, in the boat. There were also other **boats** with him.
	4:37	A furious squall came up, and the waves broke over the **boat**,
	4:37	broke over the boat, so that it^s [+3836] was nearly swamped.
	5: 2	When Jesus got out of the **boat**, a man with an evil spirit came
	5:18	As Jesus was getting into the **boat**, the man who had been
	5:21	When Jesus had again crossed over by **boat** to the other side of the
	6:32	So they went away by themselves in a **boat** to a solitary place.
	6:45	Immediately Jesus made his disciples get into the **boat** and go on
	6:47	When evening came, the **boat** was in the middle of the lake,
	6:51	Then he climbed into the **boat** with them, and the wind died down.
	6:54	As soon as they got out of the **boat**, people recognized Jesus.
	8:10	he got into the **boat** with his disciples and went to the region of
	8:13	got back into the **boat** [UBS-] and crossed to the other side.
	8:14	to bring bread, except for one loaf they had with them in the **boat**.
Lk	5: 2	he saw at the water's edge two **boats**, left there by the fishermen,
	5: 3	He got into one *of* the **boats**, the one belonging to Simon,
	5: 3	from shore. Then he sat down and taught the people from the **boat**.
	5: 7	So they signaled their partners in the other **boat** to come and help
	5: 7	and they came and filled both **boats** so full that they began to sink.
	5:11	So they pulled their **boats** up on shore, left everything
	8:22	to the other side of the lake." So they got into a **boat** and set out.
	8:37	they were overcome with fear. So he got into the **boat** and left.
Jn	6:17	where they got into a **boat** and set off across the lake for
	6:19	or three and a half miles, they saw Jesus approaching the **boat**,
	6:21	Then they were willing to take him into the **boat**, and immediately
	6:21	and immediately the **boat** reached the shore where they were
	6:22	and that Jesus had not entered it^s [+3836] with his disciples,
	21: 3	So they went out and got into the **boat**, but that night they caught
	21: 6	"Throw your net on the right side *of* the **boat** and you will find
Ac	20:13	We went on ahead to the **ship** and sailed for Assos, where we were
	20:38	never see his face again. Then they accompanied him to the **ship**.
	21: 2	We found a **ship** crossing over to Phoenicia, went on board
	21: 3	We landed at Tyre, where our **ship** was to unload its cargo.
	21: 6	to each other, we went aboard the **ship**, and they returned home.
	27: 2	We boarded a **ship** from Adramyttium about to sail for ports along
	27: 6	There the centurion found an Alexandrian **ship** sailing for Italy
	27:10	is going to be disastrous and bring great loss *to* **ship** and cargo,
	27:15	The **ship** was caught by the storm and could not head into the
	27:17	it aboard, they passed ropes under the **ship** itself to hold it together.
	27:19	they threw the **ship's** tackle overboard with their own hands.
	27:22	not one of you will be lost; only the **ship** will be destroyed.
	27:30	In an attempt to escape from the **ship**, the sailors let the lifeboat
	27:31	centurion and the soldiers, "Unless these men stay with the **ship**,
	27:37	Altogether there were 276 of us **on board** [+1877+3836].
	27:38	they lightened the **ship** by throwing the grain into the sea.
	27:39	where they decided to run the **ship** aground if they could.
	27:44	The rest were to get there on planks or on pieces of the **ship**.
	28:11	After three months we put out to sea in a **ship** that had wintered in
Jas	3: 4	Or take **ships** as an example. Although they are so large and are
Rev	8: 9	creatures in the sea died, and a third *of* the **ships** were destroyed.
	18:19	where all who had **ships** on the sea became rich through her

4451 πλοκή, *plokē*   Not used in UBS/NIV [√ *4428*]

4452 πλόος, *ploos* [3] [√ *4434*]

voyage [2], sailing [1]

Ac	21: 7	We continued our **voyage** from Tyre and landed at Ptolemais,
	27: 9	and **sailing** had already become dangerous because by now it was
	27:10	I can see that our **voyage** is going to be disastrous and bring great

4453 πλοῦς, *plous*   Not used in UBS/NIV [√ *4434*]

4454 πλούσιος, *plousios* [28] [√ *4458*]

rich [26], wealth [1], wealthy [1]

Mt	19:23	the truth, it is hard for a **rich** *man* to enter the kingdom of heaven.
	19:24	eye of a needle than for a **rich** *man* to enter the kingdom of God."
	27:57	there came a **rich** man from Arimathea, named Joseph,
Mk	10:25	eye of a needle than for a **rich** *man* to enter the kingdom of God."

	12:41	into the temple treasury. Many **rich** *people* threw in large amounts.
Lk	6:24	"But woe to you who are **rich**, for you have already received your
	12:16	"The ground *of* a certain **rich** man produced a good crop.
	14:12	your friends, your brothers or relatives, or your **rich** neighbors;
	16: 1	"There was a **rich** man whose manager was accused of wasting his
	16:19	"There was a **rich** man who was dressed in purple and fine linen
	16:21	and longing to eat what fell from the **rich** *man's* table. Even the
	16:22	him to Abraham's side. The **rich** *man* also died and was buried.
	18:23	he became very sad, because he was a *man of* great **wealth**.
	18:25	eye of a needle than for a **rich** *man* to enter the kingdom of God."
	19: 2	name of Zacchaeus; he was a chief tax collector and was **wealthy**.
	21: 1	Jesus saw the **rich** putting their gifts into the temple treasury.
2Co	8: 9	that though he was **rich**, yet for your sakes he became poor,
Eph	2: 4	because of his great love for us, God, who is **rich** in mercy,
1Ti	6:17	Command those who are **rich** in this present world not to be
Jas	1:10	But the one who is **rich** should take pride in his low position,
	1:11	the **rich** *man* will fade away even while he goes about his
	2: 5	those who are poor in the eyes of the world to be **rich** in faith
	2: 6	have insulted the poor. Is it not the **rich** who are exploiting you?
	5: 1	*you* **rich** *people*, weep and wail because of the misery that is
Rev	2: 9	I know your afflictions and your poverty—yet you are **rich**!
	3:17	You say, 'I am **rich**; I have acquired wealth and do not need a
	6:15	the princes, the generals, the **rich**, the mighty, and every slave
	13:16	forced everyone, small and great, **rich** and poor, free and slave,

4455 πλουσίως, *plousiōs* [4] [√ *4458*]

richly [2], generously [1], rich [1]

Col	3:16	Let the word of Christ dwell in you **richly** as you teach
1Ti	6:17	who **richly** provides us with everything for our enjoyment.
Tit	3: 6	whom he poured out on us **generously** through Jesus Christ our
2Pe	1:11	and you will receive a **rich** welcome into the eternal kingdom of

4456 πλουτέω, *plouteō* [12] [√ *4458*]

rich [8], acquired wealth [1], gained wealth [1], get rich [1], richly blesses [1]

Lk	1:53	the hungry with good things but has sent the **rich** away empty.
	12:21	who stores up things for himself but *is* not **rich** toward God."
Ro	10:12	the same Lord is Lord of all and **richly blesses** all who call on him,
1Co	4: 8	Already *you have become* **rich**! You have become kings—
2Co	8: 9	became poor, so that you through his poverty *might become* **rich**.
1Ti	6: 9	People who want *to* **get rich** fall into temptation and a trap
	6:18	*to be* **rich** in good deeds, and to be generous and willing to share.
Rev	3:17	'I am **rich**; *I have* **acquired wealth** and do not need a thing.'
	3:18	to buy from me gold refined in the fire, so *you can become* **rich**;
	18: 3	and the merchants of the earth *grew* **rich** from her excessive
	18:15	these things and **gained** their **wealth** from her will stand far off,
	18:19	where all who had ships on the sea *became* **rich** through her

4457 πλουτίζω, *ploutizō* [3] [√ *4458*]

enriched [1], made rich [1], making rich [1]

1Co	1: 5	For in him *you have been* **enriched** in every way—in all your
2Co	6:10	poor, yet **making** many **rich**; having nothing, and yet possessing
	9:11	*You will be* **made rich** in every way so that you can be generous

4458 πλοῦτος, *ploutos* [22] [→ *4454, 4455, 4456, 4457*]

riches [14], wealth [6], rich [1], value [1]

Mt	13:22	but the worries of this life and the deceitfulness *of* **wealth** choke it,
Mk	4:19	the deceitfulness *of* **wealth** and the desires for other things come in
Lk	8:14	by life's worries, **riches** and pleasures, and they do not mature.
Ro	2: 4	Or do you show contempt for the **riches** of his kindness, tolerance
	9:23	What if he did this to make the **riches** of his glory known to the
	11:12	But if their transgression means **riches** for the world, and their loss
	11:12	and their loss means **riches** for the Gentiles, how much greater
	11:33	the depth *of* the **riches** of the wisdom and knowledge of God!
2Co	8: 2	and their extreme poverty welled up in **rich** generosity.
Eph	1: 7	forgiveness of sins, in accordance with the **riches** of God's grace,
	1:18	has called you, the **riches** of his glorious inheritance in the saints,
	2: 7	coming ages he might show the incomparable **riches** of his grace,
	3: 8	to preach to the Gentiles the unsearchable **riches** of Christ,

3:16 I pray that out of his glorious **riches** he may strengthen you with
Php   4:19 all your needs according to his glorious **riches** in Christ Jesus.
Col   1:27 known among the Gentiles the glorious **riches** of this mystery,
       2: 2 so that they may have the full **riches** of complete understanding,
1Ti   6:17 present world not to be arrogant nor to put their hope in **wealth**,
Heb 11:26 He regarded disgrace for the sake of Christ as *of* greater **value** than
Jas   5: 2 Your **wealth** has rotted, and moths have eaten your clothes.
Rev   5:12 and **wealth** and wisdom and strength and honor and glory
      18:17 In one hour such great **wealth** has been brought to ruin!' "Every sea

4459 πλύνω, *plynō* [3] [→ *677*]

wash [1], washed [1], washing [1]

Lk   5: 2 left there by the fishermen, *who were* **washing** their nets.
Rev   7:14 they *have* **washed** their robes and made them white in the blood of
      22:14 "Blessed are those *who* **wash** their robes, that they may have the

4460 πνεῦμα, *pneuma* [379] [√ *4463*]

plural: spirits [34] Mt 8:16; 10:1; 12:45; Mk 1:27; 3:11; 5:13; 6:7;
    Lk 4:36; 6:18; 7:21; 8:2; 10:20; 11:26; Ac 5:16; 8:7; 19:12,13; 1Co
    12:10; 14:12,32; 1Ti 4:1; Heb 1:7,14; 12:9,23; 1Pe 3:19; 1Jn 4:1;
    Rev 1:4; 3:1; 4:5; 5:6; 16:13,14; 22:6

ἀκάθαρτος πνεῦμα (unclean spirit) [23] Mt 10:1; 12:43; Mk
    1:23,26,27; 3:11,30; 5:2,8,13; 6:7; 7:25; 9:25; Lk 4:33,36; 6:18;
    8:29; 9:42; 11:24; Ac 5:16; 8:7; Rev 16:13; 18:2

δύναμις [τοῦ ἁγίου] πνεύματος (power of [the Holy] Spirit)
    [4] Lk 4:14; Ac 1:8; Ro 15:13,19

ἐν πνεύματι (in/by the Spirit) [30] Mt 12:28; 22:43; Lk 1:17;
    2:27; 4:1; Jn 4:23,24; Ac 19:21; Ro 1:9; 2:29; 8:9; 1Co 6:11;
    12:3,13; 14:16; 2Co 6:6; Gal 6:1; Eph 2:18,22; 3:5; 5:18; 6:18;
    Php 1:27; Col 1:8; 1Th 1:5; 1Ti 3:16; Rev 1:10; 4:2; 17:3; 21:10

ἔχω πνεῦμα (have [the] spirit/Spirit) [9] Mk 3:30; 7:25; 9:17;
    Ac 8:7; 16:16; Ro 8:9; 1Co 7:40; Jude 1:19; Rev 3:1

πνεῦμα ἅγιος (Holy Spirit) [90] Mt 1:18,20; 3:11; 12:32; 28:19;
    Mk 1:8; 3:29; 12:36; 13:11; Lk 1:15,35,41,67; 2:25,26; 3:16,22;
    4:1; 10:21; 11:13; 12:10,12; Jn 1:33; 14:26; 20:22; Ac 1:2,5,8,16;
    2:4,33,38; 4:8,25,31; 5:3,32; 6:5; 7:51,55; 8:15,17,19; 9:17,31;
    10:38,44,45,47; 11:15,16,24; 13:2,4,9,52; 15:8,28; 16:6; 19:2,2,6;
    20:23,28; 21:11; 28:25; Ro 5:5; 9:1; 14:17; 15:13,16; 1Co 6:19;
    12:3; 2Co 6:6; 13:13; Eph 1:13; 4:30; 1Th 1:5,6; 4:8; 2Ti 1:14; Tit
    3:5; Heb 2:4; 3:7; 6:4; 9:8; 10:15; 1Pe 1:12; 2Pe 1:21; Jude 1:20

πνεῦμα [ἅγιος] καὶ δύναμις ([Holy] Spirit and power) [4]
    Lk 1:17; Ac 10:38; 1Co 2:4; Gal 3:5

πνεῦμα ... γράμμα (Spirit ... letter) [4] Ro 2:29; 7:6; 2Co 3:6,6

πνεῦμα θεοῦ (Spirit of God) [19] Mt 3:16; 12:28; Ro 8:9,14;
    15:19; 1Co 2:11,14; 3:16; 6:11; 7:40; 12:3; 2Co 3:3; Eph 4:30;
    Php 3:3; 1Pe 4:14; 1Jn 4:2; Rev 3:1; 4:5; 5:6

πνεῦμα Ἰησοῦ (Spirit of Jesus) [2] Ac 16:7; Php 1:19

πνεῦμα κυρίου (Spirit of the Lord) [5] Lk 4:18; Ac 5:9; 8:39;
    2Co 3:17,18

πνεῦμα ... σάρξ (spirit ... flesh) [33] Mt 26:41; Mk 14:38; Lk
    24:39; Jn 3:6,6; 6:63,63; Ac 2:17; Ro 8:4,5,5,6,9,9,9,13; 1Co 5:5;
    2Co 7:1; Gal 3:3; 4:29; 5:16,17,17; 6:8,8; Php 3:3; Col 2:5; 1Ti
    3:16; Heb 12:9; 1Pe 3:18; 4:6; 1Jn 4:2,2

πνεῦμα ... σῶμα (spirit ... body) [13] Ro 8:10,11,11,13,23; 1Co
    5:3; 6:19; 7:34; 12:13,13; Eph 4:4; 1Th 5:23; Jas 2:26

πνεῦμα Χριστοῦ (Spirit of Christ) [3] Ro 8:9; Php 1:19; 1Pe
    1:11

πονηρός πνεῦμα (evil spirit) [8] Mt 12:45; Lk 7:21; 8:2; 11:26;
    Ac 19:12,13,15,16

ὕδωρ ... πνεῦμα (water ... Spirit) [14] Mt 3:11,16; Mk 1:8,10; Lk
    3:16; Jn 1:33; 3:5; Ac 1:5; 8:39; 10:47; 11:16; 1Jn 5:6,8; Rev 22:17

ψυχή ... πνεῦμα (soul ... spirit) [6] Mt 12:18; Lk 1:47; 1Co
    15:45; Php 1:27; 1Th 5:23; Heb 4:12

Spirit/spirit [325], spirits [32], breath [3], ghost [2], Spirit's [2],
spiritual [2], attitude [1], decided [+*1877*+*3836*+*5502*] [1],
demon-possessed [+*2400*+*3836*+*3836*+*4505*] [1], gently

[+*1877*+*4559*] [1], he[s] [+*899*+*899*+*1877*+*3836*] [1], mind [1],
prophecy [1], sighed deeply [+*417*+*3836*] [1], spirit which
predicted the future [+*4780*] [1], whole heart [1], wind [1], winds
[1], with great fervor [+*2417*+*3836*] [1]

Mt   1:18 she was found to be with child through the Holy **Spirit**.
       1:20 because what is conceived in her is from the Holy **Spirit**.
       3:11 fit to carry. He will baptize you with the Holy **Spirit** and with fire.
       3:16 and he saw the **Spirit** of God descending like a dove and lighting
       4: 1 Then Jesus was led by the **Spirit** into the desert to be tempted by
       5: 3 "Blessed are the poor *in* **spirit**, for theirs is the kingdom of heaven.
       8:16 and he drove out the **spirits** with a word and healed all the sick.
      10: 1 and gave them authority to drive out evil **spirits** and to heal every
      10:20 you speaking, but the **Spirit** of your Father speaking through you.
      12:18 I will put my **Spirit** on him, and he will proclaim justice to the
      12:28 But if I drive out demons by the **Spirit** of God, then the kingdom
      12:31 but the blasphemy against the **Spirit** will not be forgiven.
      12:32 but anyone who speaks against the Holy **Spirit** will not be
      12:43 "When an evil **spirit** comes out of a man, it goes through arid
      12:45 and takes with it seven other **spirits** more wicked than itself,
      22:43 He said to them, "How is it then that David, speaking by the **Spirit**,
      26:41 not fall into temptation. The **spirit** is willing, but the body is weak."
      27:50 Jesus had cried out again in a loud voice, he gave up his **spirit**.
      28:19 in the name of the Father and of the Son and *of* the Holy **Spirit**,
Mk   1: 8 you with water, but he will baptize you with the Holy **Spirit**."
       1:10 being torn open and the **Spirit** descending on him like a dove.
       1:12 At once the **Spirit** sent him out into the desert,
       1:23 then a man in their synagogue who was possessed by an evil **spirit**
       1:26 The evil **spirit** shook the man violently and came out of him with a
       1:27 He even gives orders *to* evil **spirits** and they obey him."
       2: 8 Immediately Jesus knew *in* his **spirit** that this was what they were
       3:11 Whenever the evil **spirits** saw him, they fell down before him
       3:29 But whoever blasphemes against the Holy **Spirit** will never be
       3:30 He said this because they were saying, "He has an evil **spirit**."
       5: 2 a man with an evil **spirit** came from the tombs to meet him.
       5: 8 For Jesus had said to him, "Come out of this man, *you* evil **spirit**!"
       5:13 and the evil **spirits** came out and went into the pigs.
       6: 7 them out two by two and gave them authority over evil **spirits**.
       7:25 a woman whose little daughter was possessed by an evil **spirit**
       8:12 He **sighed deeply** [+*417*+*3836*] and said, "Why does this
       9:17 who is possessed by a **spirit** that has robbed him of speech.
       9:20 When the **spirit** saw Jesus, it immediately threw the boy into a
       9:25 that a crowd was running to the scene, he rebuked the evil **spirit**.
       9:25 "You deaf and mute **spirit**," he said, "I command you, come out of
      12:36 David himself, speaking by the Holy **Spirit**, declared: " 'The Lord
      13:11 you at the time, for it is not you speaking, but the Holy **Spirit**.
      14:38 not fall into temptation. The **spirit** is willing, but the body is weak."
Lk   1:15 and he will be filled *with* the Holy **Spirit** even from birth.
       1:17 he will go on before the Lord, in the **spirit** and power of Elijah,
       1:35 The angel answered, "The Holy **Spirit** will come upon you,
       1:41 leaped in her womb, and Elizabeth was filled *with* the Holy **Spirit**.
       1:47 and my **spirit** rejoices in God my Savior,
       1:67 His father Zechariah was filled *with* the Holy **Spirit**
       1:80 And the child grew and became strong *in* **spirit**; and he lived in the
       2:25 for the consolation of Israel, and the Holy **Spirit** was upon him.
       2:26 It had been revealed to him by the Holy **Spirit** that he would not
       2:27 Moved by the **Spirit**, he went into the temple courts. When the
       3:16 to untie. He will baptize you with the Holy **Spirit** and with fire.
       3:22 and the Holy **Spirit** descended on him in bodily form like a dove.
       4: 1 Jesus, full *of* the Holy **Spirit**, returned from the Jordan and was led
       4: 1 returned from the Jordan and was led by the **Spirit** in the desert,
       4:14 Jesus returned to Galilee in the power *of* the **Spirit**, and news
       4:18 "The **Spirit** of the Lord is on me,
       4:33 synagogue there was a man possessed by a demon, an evil **spirit**.
       4:36 With authority and power he gives orders *to* evil **spirits** and they
       6:18 healed of their diseases. Those troubled by evil **spirits** were cured,
       7:21 sicknesses and evil **spirits**, and gave sight to many who were blind.
       8: 2 and also some women who had been cured of evil **spirits**
       8:29 For Jesus had commanded the evil **spirit** to come out of the man.
       8:55 Her **spirit** returned, and at once she stood up. Then Jesus told them
       9:39 A **spirit** seizes him and he suddenly screams; it throws him into
       9:42 But Jesus rebuked the evil **spirit**, healed the boy and gave him
      10:20 However, do not rejoice that the **spirits** submit to you, but rejoice
      10:21 full of joy through the Holy **Spirit**, said, "I praise you, Father,
      11:13 how much more will your Father in heaven give the Holy **Spirit** to
      11:24 "When an evil **spirit** comes out of a man, it goes through arid

11:26 Then it goes and takes seven other **spirits** more wicked than itself,
12:10 but anyone who blasphemes against the Holy **Spirit** will not be
12:12 the Holy **Spirit** will teach you at that time what you should say."
13:11 and a woman was there who had been crippled by a **spirit** for
23:46 out with a loud voice, "Father, into your hands I commit my **spirit**,"
24:37 They were startled and frightened, thinking they saw a **ghost**.
24:39 and see; a **ghost** does not have flesh and bones, as you see I have."

Jn 1:32 "I saw the **Spirit** come down from heaven as a dove and remain on
1:33 'The man on whom you see the **Spirit** come down and remain is he
1:33 and remain is he who will baptize with the Holy **Spirit**.'
3: 5 enter the kingdom of God unless he is born of water and the **Spirit**.
3: 6 Flesh gives birth to flesh, but the **Spirit** gives birth to spirit.
3: 6 Flesh gives birth to flesh, but the Spirit gives birth to **spirit**.
3: 8 The **wind** blows wherever it pleases. You hear its sound, but you
3: 8 or where it is going. So it is with everyone born of the **Spirit**."
3:34 speaks the words of God, for God gives the **Spirit** without limit.
4:23 come when the true worshipers will worship the Father in **spirit**
4:24 God is **spirit**, and his worshipers must worship in spirit and in
4:24 is spirit, and his worshipers must worship in **spirit** and in truth."
6:63 The **Spirit** gives life; the flesh counts for nothing. The words I
6:63 The words I have spoken to you are **spirit** and they are life.
7:39 By this he meant the **Spirit**, whom those who believed in him were
7:39 Up to that time the **Spirit** had not been given, since Jesus had not
11:33 her also weeping, he was deeply moved *in* **spirit** and troubled.
13:21 Jesus was troubled *in* **spirit** and testified, "I tell you the truth,
14:17 the **Spirit** of truth. The world cannot accept him, because it neither
14:26 But the Counselor, the Holy **Spirit**, whom the Father will send in
15:26 the **Spirit** of truth who goes out from the Father, he will testify
16:13 But when he, the **Spirit** of truth, comes, he will guide you into all
19:30 is finished." With that, he bowed his head and gave up his **spirit**.
20:22 with that he breathed on them and said, "Receive the Holy **Spirit**.

Ac 1: 2 after giving instructions through the Holy **Spirit** to the apostles he
1: 5 but in a few days you will be *baptized with* the Holy **Spirit**."
1: 8 But you will receive power when the Holy **Spirit** comes on you;
1:16 the Scripture had to be fulfilled which the Holy **Spirit** spoke long
2: 4 All of them were filled *with* the Holy **Spirit** and began to speak in
2: 4 and began to speak in other tongues as the **Spirit** enabled them.
2:17 'In the last days, God says, I will pour out my **Spirit** on all people.
2:18 both men and women, I will pour out my **Spirit** in those days,
2:33 he has received from the Father the promised Holy **Spirit**
2:38 of your sins. And you will receive the gift *of* the Holy **Spirit**.
4: 8 Then Peter, filled *with* the Holy **Spirit**, said to them: "Rulers
4:25 You spoke by the Holy **Spirit** through the mouth of your servant,
4:31 And they were all filled *with* the Holy **Spirit** and spoke the word
5: 3 Satan has so filled your heart that you have lied to the Holy **Spirit**
5: 9 said to her, "How could you agree to test the **Spirit** of the Lord?
5:16 bringing their sick and those tormented by evil **spirits**, and all of
5:32 We are witnesses of these things, and so is the Holy **Spirit**,
6: 3 seven men from among you who are known to be full *of* the **Spirit**
6: 5 They chose Stephen, a man full of faith and *of* the Holy **Spirit**;
6:10 not stand up against his wisdom or the **Spirit** by whom he spoke.
7:51 You are just like your fathers: You always resist the Holy **Spirit**!
7:55 But Stephen, full *of* the Holy **Spirit**, looked up to heaven and saw
7:59 were stoning him, Stephen prayed, "Lord Jesus, receive my **spirit**."
8: 7 With shrieks, evil **spirits** came out of many, and many paralytics
8:15 they prayed for them that they might receive the Holy **Spirit**,
8:17 placed their hands on them, and they received the Holy **Spirit**.
8:18 When Simon saw that the **Spirit** was given at the laying on of the
8:19 everyone on whom I lay my hands may receive the Holy **Spirit**."
8:29 The **Spirit** told Philip, "Go to that chariot and stay near it."
8:39 out of the water, the **Spirit** of the Lord suddenly took Philip away,
9:17 so that you may see again and be filled *with* the Holy **Spirit**."
9:31 and encouraged *by* the Holy **Spirit**, it grew in numbers, living in
10:19 the **Spirit** said to him, "Simon, three men are looking for you.
10:38 how God anointed Jesus of Nazareth *with* the Holy **Spirit**
10:44 these words, the Holy **Spirit** came on all who heard the message.
10:45 gift *of* the Holy **Spirit** had been poured out even on the Gentiles.
10:47 with water? They have received the Holy **Spirit** just as we have."
11:12 The **Spirit** told me to have no hesitation about going with them.
11:15 the Holy **Spirit** came on them as he had come on us at the
11:16 with water, but you will be baptized with the Holy **Spirit**.'
11:24 He was a good man, full *of* the Holy **Spirit** and faith, and a great
11:28 and through the **Spirit** predicted that a severe famine would spread
13: 2 they were worshiping the Lord and fasting, the Holy **Spirit** said,
13: 4 The two of them, sent on their way by the Holy **Spirit**, went down
13: 9 filled *with* the Holy **Spirit**, looked straight at Elymas and said,

13:52 And the disciples were filled with joy and *with* the Holy **Spirit**.
15: 8 showed that he accepted them by giving the Holy **Spirit** to them,
15:28 It seemed good *to* the Holy **Spirit** and to us not to burden you with
16: 6 having been kept by the Holy **Spirit** from preaching the word in
16: 7 to enter Bithynia, but the **Spirit** of Jesus would not allow them to.
16:16 girl who had a **spirit** [+*4780*] by **which** she **predicted the future**.
16:18 so troubled that he turned around and said *to* the **spirit**,
17:16 in Athens, he^s [+*899+899+1877+3836*] was greatly distressed to
18:25 and he spoke **with great fervor** [+*2417+3836*] and taught about
19: 2 asked them, "Did you receive the Holy **Spirit** when you believed?"
19: 2 "No, we have not even heard that there is a Holy **Spirit**."
19: 6 the Holy **Spirit** came on them, and they spoke in tongues
19:12 and their illnesses were cured and the evil **spirits** left them.
19:13 those *who were* **demon-possessed** [+*2400+3836+3836+4505*].
19:15 ₁One day₂ the evil **spirit** answered them, "Jesus I know, and I know
19:16 Then the man who had the evil **spirit** jumped on them
19:21 Paul **decided** [+*1877+3836+5502*] to go to Jerusalem, passing
20:22 "And now, compelled *by* the **Spirit**, I am going to Jerusalem,
20:23 I only know that in every city the Holy **Spirit** warns me that prison
20:28 and all the flock of which the Holy **Spirit** has made you overseers.
21: 4 Through the **Spirit** they urged Paul not to go on to Jerusalem.
21:11 tied his own hands and feet with it and said, "The Holy **Spirit** says,
23: 8 and that there are neither angels nor **spirits**, but the Pharisees
23: 9 they said. "What if a **spirit** or an angel has spoken to him?"
28:25 "The Holy **Spirit** spoke the truth to your forefathers when he said

Ro 1: 4 and who through the **Spirit** of holiness was declared with power to
1: 9 whom I serve with my **whole heart** in preaching the gospel of his
2:29 is circumcision of the heart, by the **Spirit**, not by the written code.
5: 5 God has poured out into our hearts by the Holy **Spirit**,
7: 6 from the law so that we serve in the new way *of* the **Spirit**,
8: 2 because through Christ Jesus the law *of* the **Spirit** of life set me
8: 4 not live according to the sinful nature but according to the **Spirit**.
8: 5 but those who live in accordance with the **Spirit** have their minds
8: 5 with the Spirit have their minds set on what the **Spirit** desires.
8: 6 is death, but the mind *controlled by* the **Spirit** is life and peace;
8: 9 however, are controlled not by the sinful nature but by the **Spirit**,
8: 9 the sinful nature but by the Spirit, if the **Spirit** of God lives in you.
8: 9 And if anyone does not have the **Spirit** of Christ, he does not
8:10 because of sin, yet your **spirit** is alive because of righteousness.
8:11 And if the **Spirit** of him who raised Jesus from the dead is living in
8:11 dead will also give life to your mortal bodies through his **Spirit**,
8:13 but if *by* the **Spirit** you put to death the misdeeds of the body,
8:14 because those who are led *by* the **Spirit** of God are sons of God.
8:15 For you did not receive a **spirit** that makes you a slave again to
8:15 you a slave again to fear, but you received the **Spirit** of sonship.
8:16 The **Spirit** himself testifies with our spirit that we are God's
8:16 The Spirit himself testifies with our **spirit** that we are God's
8:23 only so, but we ourselves, who have the firstfruits *of* the **Spirit**,
8:26 In the same way, the **Spirit** helps us in our weakness. We do not
8:26 but the **Spirit** himself intercedes for us with groans that words
8:27 And he who searches our hearts knows the mind *of* the **Spirit**,
9: 1 I am not lying, my conscience confirms it in the Holy **Spirit**—
11: 8 "God gave them a **spirit** of stupor, eyes so that they could not see
12:11 be lacking in zeal, but keep your **spiritual** fervor, serving the Lord.
14:17 but of righteousness, peace and joy in the Holy **Spirit**,
15:13 that you may overflow with hope by the power *of* the Holy **Spirit**.
15:16 an offering acceptable to God, sanctified by the Holy **Spirit**.
15:19 the power of signs and miracles, through the power *of* the **Spirit**.
15:30 brothers, by our Lord Jesus Christ and by the love *of* the **Spirit**,

1Co 2: 4 persuasive words, but with a demonstration *of* the **Spirit's** power,
2:10 but God has revealed it to us by his **Spirit**. The Spirit searches all
2:10 The **Spirit** searches all things, even the deep things of God.
2:11 knows the thoughts of a man except the man's **spirit** within him?
2:11 way no one knows the thoughts of God except the **Spirit** of God.
2:12 We have not received the **spirit** of the world but the Spirit who is
2:12 not received the spirit of the world but the **Spirit** who is from God,
2:13 taught us by human wisdom but in words taught *by* the **Spirit**,
2:14 does not accept the things *that come from* the **Spirit** of God,
3:16 yourselves are God's temple and that God's **Spirit** lives in you?
4:21 I come to you with a whip, or in love and with a gentle **spirit**?
5: 3 Even though I am not physically present, I am with you *in* **spirit**.
5: 4 in the name of our Lord Jesus and I am with you in **spirit**,
5: 5 may be destroyed and his **spirit** saved on the day of the Lord.
6:11 in the name of the Lord Jesus Christ and by the **Spirit** of our God.
6:17 But he who unites himself with the Lord is one with him in **spirit**.
6:19 Do you not know that your body is a temple *of* the Holy **Spirit**,

7: 34 Her aim is to be devoted to the Lord *in* both body and **spirit**.
7: 40 if she stays as she is—and I think that I too have the **Spirit** of God.
12: 3 Therefore I tell you that no one who is speaking by the **Spirit** of
12: 3 and no one can say, "Jesus is Lord," except by the Holy **Spirit**.
12: 4 There are different kinds of gifts, but the same **Spirit**.
12: 7 Now to each one the manifestation *of* the **Spirit** is given for the
12: 8 To one there is given through the **Spirit** the message of wisdom,
12: 8 to another the message of knowledge by means of the same **Spirit**,
12: 9 to another faith by the same **Spirit**, to another gifts of healing by
12: 9 by the same Spirit, to another gifts of healing by that one **Spirit**,
12: 10 to another prophecy, to another distinguishing between **spirits**,
12: 11 All these are the work of one and the same **Spirit**, and he gives
12: 13 For we were all baptized by one **Spirit** into one body—
12: 13 slave or free—and we were all given the one **Spirit** to drink.
14: 2 no one understands him; he utters mysteries *with* his **spirit**.
14: 12 Since you are eager to have **spiritual** *gifts*, try to excel in gifts that
14: 14 For if I pray in a tongue, my **spirit** prays, but my mind is
14: 15 I will pray *with* my **spirit**, but I will also pray with my mind;
14: 15 I will sing *with* my **spirit**, but I will also sing with my mind.
14: 16 If you are praising God with your **spirit**, how can one who finds
14: 32 The **spirits** of prophets are subject to the control of prophets.
15: 45 Adam became a living being"; the last Adam, a life-giving **spirit**.
16: 18 For they refreshed my **spirit** and yours also. Such men deserve
2Co 1: 22 and put his **Spirit** in our hearts as a deposit, guaranteeing what is
2: 13 I still had no peace *of* **mind**,
3: 3 written not with ink but *with* the **Spirit** of the living God,
3: 6 not of the letter but *of* the **Spirit**; for the letter kills, but the Spirit
3: 6 but of the Spirit; for the letter kills, but the **Spirit** gives life.
3: 8 will not the ministry *of* the **Spirit** be even more glorious?
3: 17 Now the Lord is the **Spirit**, and where the Spirit of the Lord is,
3: 17 is the Spirit, and where the **Spirit** of the Lord is, there is freedom.
3: 18 which comes from the Lord, who is the **Spirit**.
4: 13 With that same **spirit** of faith we also believe and therefore speak,
5: 5 us for this very purpose and has given us the **Spirit** as a deposit,
6: 6 patience and kindness; in the Holy **Spirit** and in sincere love;
7: 1 ourselves from everything that contaminates body and **spirit**,
7: 13 Titus was, because his **spirit** has been refreshed by all of you.
11: 4 or if you receive a different **spirit** from the one you received,
12: 18 Did we not act *in* the same **spirit** and follow the same course?
13: 14 love of God, and the fellowship *of* the Holy **Spirit** be with you all.
Gal 3: 2 Did you receive the **Spirit** by observing the law, or by believing
3: 3 After beginning *with* the **Spirit**, are you now trying to attain your
3: 5 Does God give you his **Spirit** and work miracles among you
3: 14 so that by faith we might receive the promise *of* the **Spirit**.
4: 6 you are sons, God sent the **Spirit** of his Son into our hearts,
4: 29 ordinary way persecuted the son born by the power of the **Spirit**.
5: 5 But by faith we eagerly await *through* the **Spirit** the righteousness
5: 16 So I say, live *by* the **Spirit**, and you will not gratify the desires of
5: 17 For the sinful nature desires what is contrary to the **Spirit**,
5: 17 to the Spirit, and the **Spirit** what is contrary to the sinful nature.
5: 18 But if you are led *by* the **Spirit**, you are not under law.
5: 22 But the fruit *of* the **Spirit** is love, joy, peace, patience, kindness,
5: 25 Since we live *by* the **Spirit**, let us keep in step with the Spirit.
5: 25 Since we live by the Spirit, let us keep in step *with* the **Spirit**.
6: 1 you who are spiritual should restore him **gently** [*+1877+4559*].
6: 8 the one who sows to please the **Spirit**, from the Spirit will reap
6: 8 who sows to please the Spirit, from the **Spirit** will reap eternal life.
6: 18 The grace of our Lord Jesus Christ be with your **spirit**, brothers.
Eph 1: 13 you were marked in him with a seal, the promised Holy **Spirit**,
1: 17 glorious Father, may give you the **Spirit** of wisdom and revelation,
2: 2 the **spirit** who is now at work in those who are disobedient.
2: 18 For through him we both have access to the Father by one **Spirit**.
2: 22 together to become a dwelling in which God lives by his **Spirit**.
3: 5 as it has now been revealed by the **Spirit** to God's holy apostles
3: 16 strengthen you with power through his **Spirit** in your inner being,
4: 3 Make every effort to keep the unity *of* the **Spirit** through the bond
4: 4 There is one body and one **Spirit**—just as you were called to one
4: 23 to be made new *in* the **attitude** of your minds;
4: 30 And do not grieve the Holy **Spirit** of God, with whom you were
5: 18 which leads to debauchery. Instead, be filled with the **Spirit**.
6: 17 Take the helmet of salvation and the sword *of* the **Spirit**, which is
6: 18 And pray in the **Spirit** on all occasions with all kinds of prayers
Php 1: 19 your prayers and the help given *by* the **Spirit** of Jesus Christ,
1: 27 you in my absence, I will know that you stand firm in one **spirit**,
2: 1 if any fellowship *with* the **Spirit**, if any tenderness
3: 3 we who worship *by* the **Spirit** of God, who glory in Christ Jesus,
4: 23 The grace of the Lord Jesus Christ be with your **spirit**. Amen.
Col 1: 8 and who also told us of your love in the **Spirit**.
2: 5 I am present with you *in* **spirit** and delight to see how orderly you
1Th 1: 5 also with power, with the Holy **Spirit** and with deep conviction.
1: 6 you welcomed the message with the joy *given by* the Holy **Spirit**.
4: 8 does not reject man but God, who gives you his Holy **Spirit**.
5: 19 Do not put out the **Spirit's** fire;
5: 23 May your whole **spirit**, soul and body be kept blameless at the
2Th 2: 2 not to become easily unsettled or alarmed by *some* **prophecy**,*
2: 8 whom the Lord Jesus will overthrow *with* the **breath** of his mouth
2: 13 chose you to be saved through the sanctifying work *of* the **Spirit**
1Ti 3: 16 in a body, was vindicated by the **Spirit**, was seen by angels,
4: 1 The **Spirit** clearly says that in later times some will abandon the
4: 1 and follow deceiving **spirits** and things taught by demons.
2Ti 1: 7 For God did not give us a **spirit** of timidity, but a spirit of power,
1: 14 to you—guard it with the help *of* the Holy **Spirit** who lives in us.
4: 22 The Lord be with your **spirit**. Grace be with you.
Tit 3: 5 us through the washing of rebirth and renewal *by* the Holy **Spirit**,
Phm 1: 25 The grace of the Lord Jesus Christ be with your **spirit**.
Heb 1: 7 he says, "He makes his angels **winds**, his servants flames of fire."
1: 14 Are not all angels ministering **spirits** sent to serve those who will
2: 4 and gifts *of* the Holy **Spirit** distributed according to his will.
3: 7 So, as the Holy **Spirit** says: "Today, if you hear his voice,
4: 12 it penetrates even to dividing soul and **spirit**, joints and marrow;
6: 4 have tasted the heavenly gift, who have shared in the Holy **Spirit**,
9: 8 The Holy **Spirit** was showing by this that the way into the Most
9: 14 who through the eternal **Spirit** offered himself unblemished to
10: 15 The Holy **Spirit** also testifies to us about this. First he says:
10: 29 that sanctified him, and who has insulted the **Spirit** of grace?
12: 9 How much more should we submit to the Father *of* our **spirits**
12: 23 the judge of all men, *to* the **spirits** of righteous men made perfect,
Jas 2: 26 As the body without the **spirit** is dead, so faith without deeds is
4: 5 Or do you think Scripture says without reason that the **spirit** he
1Pe 1: 2 through the sanctifying *work of* the **Spirit**, for obedience to Jesus
1: 11 and circumstances to which the **Spirit** of Christ in them was
1: 12 preached the gospel to you by the Holy **Spirit** sent from heaven.
3: 4 of your inner self, the unfading beauty *of* a gentle and quiet **spirit**,
3: 18 He was put to death in the body but made alive *by* the **Spirit**,
3: 19 through whom also he went and preached *to* the **spirits** in prison
4: 6 to the body, but live according to God *in regard to* the **spirit**.
4: 14 you are blessed, for the **Spirit** of glory and of God rests on you.
2Pe 1: 21 spoke from God as they were carried along by the Holy **Spirit**.
1Jn 3: 24 we know that he lives in us: We know it by the **Spirit** he gave us.
4: 1 Dear friends, do not believe every **spirit**, but test the spirits to see
4: 1 every spirit, but test the **spirits** to see whether they are from God,
4: 2 This is how you can recognize the **Spirit** of God: Every spirit that
4: 2 Every **spirit** that acknowledges that Jesus Christ has come in the
4: 3 but every **spirit** that does not acknowledge Jesus is not from God.
4: 6 This is how we recognize the **Spirit** of truth and the spirit of
4: 6 is how we recognize the Spirit of truth and the **spirit** of falsehood.
4: 13 we live in him and he in us, because he has given us of his **Spirit**.
5: 6 And it is the **Spirit** who testifies, because the Spirit is the truth.
5: 6 And it is the Spirit who testifies, because the **Spirit** is the truth.
5: 8 the **Spirit**, the water and the blood; and the three are in agreement.
Jude 1: 19 who follow mere natural instincts and do not have the **Spirit**.
1: 20 yourselves up in your most holy faith and pray in the Holy **Spirit**.
Rev 1: 4 and who is to come, and from the seven **spirits** before his throne,
1: 10 On the Lord's Day I was in the **Spirit**, and I heard behind me a
2: 7 who has an ear, let him hear what the **Spirit** says to the churches.
2: 11 who has an ear, let him hear what the **Spirit** says to the churches.
2: 17 who has an ear, let him hear what the **Spirit** says to the churches.
2: 29 who has an ear, let him hear what the **Spirit** says to the churches.
3: 1 These are the words of him who holds the seven **spirits** of God
3: 6 who has an ear, let him hear what the **Spirit** says to the churches.
3: 13 who has an ear, let him hear what the **Spirit** says to the churches.
3: 22 who has an ear, let him hear what the **Spirit** says to the churches."
4: 2 At once I was in the **Spirit**, and there before me was a throne in
4: 5 seven lamps were blazing. These are the seven **spirits** of God.
5: 6 which are the seven **spirits** of God sent out into all the earth.
11: 11 the three and a half days a **breath** of life from God entered them,
13: 15 He was given power to give **breath** to the image of the first beast,
14: 13 "Yes," says the **Spirit**, "they will rest from their labor, for their
16: 13 Then I saw three evil **spirits** that looked like frogs; they came out
16: 14 They are **spirits** of demons performing miraculous signs, and they
17: 3 Then the angel carried me away in the **Spirit** into a desert.
18: 2 has become a home for demons and a haunt *for* every evil **spirit**,

19:10   Worship God! For the testimony of Jesus is the **spirit** of prophecy."
21:10   And he carried me away in the **Spirit** to a mountain great and high,
22: 6   The Lord, the God *of* the **spirits** of the prophets, sent his angel to
22:17   The **Spirit** and the bride say, "Come!" And let him who hears say,

4461 πνευματικός, *pneumatikos* [26] [√ *4463*]

spiritual [25], spiritually [1]

Ro   1:11   so that I may impart to you some **spiritual** gift to make you
    7:14   We know that the law is **spiritual**; but I am unspiritual, sold as a
  15:27   For if the Gentiles have shared *in* the Jews' **spiritual** blessings,
1Co   2:13   taught by the Spirit, expressing **spiritual** *truths* in spiritual words.
    2:13   taught by the Spirit, expressing spiritual truths *in* **spiritual** *words*.
    2:15   The **spiritual** *man* makes judgments about all things, but he
    3: 1   Brothers, I could not address you as **spiritual** but as worldly—
    9:11   If we have sown **spiritual** seed among you, is it too much if we
  10: 3   They all ate the same **spiritual** food
  10: 4   and drank the same **spiritual** drink; for they drank from the
  10: 4   for they drank from the **spiritual** rock that accompanied them,
  12: 1   Now about **spiritual** *gifts*, brothers, I do not want you to be
  14: 1   Follow the way of love and eagerly desire **spiritual** *gifts*,
  14:37   If anybody thinks he is a prophet or **spiritually** *gifted*, let him
  15:44   it is sown a natural body, it is raised a **spiritual** body. If there is a
  15:44   If there is a natural body, there is also a **spiritual** *body*.
  15:46   The **spiritual** did not come first, but the natural, and after that the
  15:46   did not come first, but the natural, and after that the **spiritual**.
Gal   6: 1   is caught in a sin, you who are **spiritual** should restore him gently.
Eph   1: 3   who has blessed us in the heavenly realms with every **spiritual**
    5:19   Speak to one another with psalms, hymns and **spiritual** songs.
    6:12   and against the **spiritual** *forces* of evil in the heavenly realms.
Col   1: 9   you with the knowledge of his will through all **spiritual** wisdom
    3:16   hymns and **spiritual** songs with gratitude in your hearts to God.
1Pe   2: 5   are being built into a **spiritual** house to be a holy priesthood,
    2: 5   offering **spiritual** sacrifices acceptable to God through Jesus

4462 πνευματικῶς, *pneumatikōs* [2] [√ *4463*]

figuratively [1], spiritually [1]

1Co   2:14   he cannot understand them, because they are **spiritually** discerned.
Rev 11: 8   which is **figuratively** called Sodom and Egypt, where also their

4463 πνέω, *pneō* [7] [→ *1743, 1863, 2535, 4460, 4461, 4462, 4466, 5710*]

blew [2], blows [2], blowing [1], from blowing [1], wind [1]

Mt   7:25   the streams rose, and the winds **blew** and beat against that house;
    7:27   the streams rose, and the winds **blew** and beat against that house,
Lk   12:55   And when the south wind **blows**, you say, 'It's going to be hot,'
Jn   3: 8   The wind **blows** wherever it pleases. You hear its sound, but you
    6:18   A strong wind *was* **blowing** and the waters grew rough.
Ac   27:40   Then they hoisted the foresail *to* the **wind** and made for the beach.
Rev   7: 1   winds of the earth to prevent any wind **from blowing** on the land

4464 πνίγω, *pnigō* [3] [→ *678, 4465, 5231*]

choke [1], choked [1], drowned [1]

Mt   13: 7   seed fell among thorns, which grew up and **choked** the plants.
  18:28   He grabbed him and *began to* **choke** him. 'Pay back what you owe
Mk   5:13   rushed down the steep bank into the lake and *were* **drowned**.

4465 πνικτός, *pniktos* [3] [√ *4464*]

meat of strangled animals [3]

Ac   15:20   from the **meat of strangled animals** and from blood.
  15:29   *from* the **meat of strangled animals** and from sexual immorality.
  21:25   from the **meat of strangled animals** and from sexual immorality."

4466 πνοή, *pnoē* [2] [√ *4463*]

breath [1], wind [1]

Ac   2: 2   Suddenly a sound like the blowing *of* a violent **wind** came from
  17:25   he himself gives all men life and **breath** and everything else.

4467 ποδαπός, *podapos*   Not used in UBS/NIV
[√ *608 + 4544*]

4468 ποδήρης, *podērēs* [1] [√ *4546*]

a robe reaching down to feet [1]

Rev   1:13   dressed in **a robe reaching down to** his **feet** and with a golden

4469 ποδονιπτήρ, *podoniptēr*   Not used in UBS/NIV
[√ *4546 + 3782*]

4470 πόθεν, *pothen* [29]

where from [16], where [7], how [2], *untranslated* [1], from which [1], what causes [1], why [1]

Mt   13:27   good seed in your field? **Where** then did the weeds come **from**?'
  13:54   "**Where** did this man get this wisdom and these miraculous
  13:56   his sisters with us? **Where** then did this man get all these things?"
  15:33   "**Where** could we get enough bread in this remote place to feed
  21:25   John's baptism—**where** did it come **from**? Was it from heaven,
Mk   6: 2   were amazed. "**Where** did this man get these things?" they asked.
    8: 4   "But **where** in this remote place can anyone get enough bread to
  12:37   David himself calls him 'Lord.' **How** then can he be his son?"
Lk   1:43   But **why** am I so favored, that the mother of my Lord should come
  13:25   "But he will answer, 'I don't know you or **where** you come **from**.'
  13:27   "But he will reply, 'I don't know you or **where** you come **from**.
  20: 7   So they answered, "We don't know **where** it was **from**."
Jn   1:48   "**How** do you know me?" Nathanael asked. Jesus answered,
    2: 9   He did not realize **where** it had come **from**, though the servants
    3: 8   but you cannot tell **where** it comes **from** or where it is going.
    4:11   and the well is deep. **Where** can you get this living water?
    6: 5   said to Philip, "**Where** shall we buy bread for these people to eat?"
    7:27   But we know **where** this man is **from**; when the Christ comes,
    7:27   when the Christ comes, no one will know **where** he is **from**."
    7:28   cried out, "Yes, you know me, and you know **where** I am **from**.
    8:14   is valid, for I know **where** I came **from** and where I am going.
    8:14   But you have no idea **where** I come **from** or where I am going.
    9:29   but as for this fellow, we don't even know **where** he comes **from**."
    9:30   You don't know **where** he comes **from**, yet he opened my eyes.
  19: 9   "**Where** do you come **from**?" he asked Jesus, but Jesus gave him
Jas   4: 1   **What causes** fights and quarrels among you? Don't they come
    4: 1   What causes fights and **[RPG]** quarrels among you? Don't they
Rev   2: 5   Remember the *height* **from which** you have fallen! Repent
    7:13   in white robes—who are they, and **where** did they come **from**?"

4471 ποία, *poia*   Not used in UBS/NIV   [√ *4478 (or) 4481*]

4472 ποιέω, *poieō* [568] [→ *16, 17, 18, 942, 1647, 1648, 2343, 2443, 2803, 2804, 2818, 3674, 3846, 4062, 4347, 4348, 4473, 4474, 4475, 4701, 5010, 5188, 5935*]

δικαιοσύνη ποιεῖν (to do righteousness) [5] Mt 6:1; 1Jn 2:29; 3:7,10; Rev 22:11

καλός ποιεῖν (to do good) [12] Mt 3:10; 7:17,18,19; 12:33,33; Lk 3:9; 6:43; Ro 7:21; 2Co 13:7; Gal 6:9; Jas 4:17

καλῶς ποιεῖν (to do well) [11] Mt 12:12; Mk 7:37; Lk 6:27; Ac 10:33; 1Co 7:37,38; Php 4:14; Jas 2:8,19; 2Pe 1:19; 3Jn 1:6

ποιεῖν ἁμαρτίαν (to do sin) [8] Jn 8:34; 2Co 5:21; 11:7; Jas 5:15; 1Pe 2:22; 1Jn 3:4,8,9

ποιεῖν ἐλεημοσύνη (to do alms) [5] Mt 6:2,3; Ac 9:36; 10:2; 24:17

ποιεῖν κακός (to do evil) [9] Mt 27:23; Mk 15:14; Lk 23:22; Jn 18:30; Ac 9:13; Ro 3:8; 13:4; 2Co 13:7; 1Pe 3:12

ποιεῖν καρπός (to produce fruit) [17] Mt 3:8,10; 7:17,17,18,18,19; 12:33; 13:26; 21:43; Lk 3:8,9; 6:43,43; 8:8; 13:9; Rev 22:2

do [159], doing [43], did [38], done [37], made [35], make [26], does [24], performed [7], produce [6], bear [5], committed [5], give [4], making [4], treated [4], appointed [3], bears [3], do with [3], put into practice [3], put up [3], was [3], *untranslated* [2], acted [2], be [2], bring [2], carry out [2], formed [2], give to the needy [+*1797*] [2], given [2], judge [+*3213*] [2], kept [2], makes [2], perform [2], performing [2], practice [2], practiced [2], practices [2], pray [+*1255*] [2], preparing [2], provide [2], put [2], puts into practice [2], remember [+*3644*] [2], sins [+*281*+*3836*] [2], spending [2], tell [+*5745*] [2], treat [2], work [2], accomplish [1], accomplished [1], accomplishing [1], act [1], acts [1], agreeing [+*1191*+*1651*] [1], are [1], attack [+*4483*] [1], avenged [+*1689*] [1], bearing [1], bears [+*1639*] [1], been [1], began [1], breaks law [+*490*] [1], bring about [1], business [+*5515*] [1], carrying out [1], cause [1], causes [1], celebrate [1], claim to be [+*4932*] [1], claimed to be [+*1571*] [1], claims to be [+*1571*] [1], commits [1], consider [1], created things [1], criminal [+*2805*] [1], delay [+*332*] [1], dividing into shares [+*3538*] [1], done [+*1639*] [1], duty [+*4005*+*4053*] [1], earned [1], exercise [1], exercised [1], following [1], forced [1], forcing [1], gain [1], gaining [1], gave to in need [+*1797*] [1], gave [1], get [1], gives away [+*1316*] [1], good [+*2822*] [1], grows [+*890*] [1], had [1], have [+*5618*] [1], held [1], help [+*2292*] [1], helping the poor [+*1797*] [1], involved in [1], keep [1], keeps [1], kept up [1], live by [1], lives by [1], made out to be [1], make out to be [1], mentioning [+*3644*] [1], mourned deeply [+*3157*+*3489*] [1], obey [1], peacemakers [+*1645*] [1], prays [+*4047*] [1], prepared [1], provided [1], put out of the synagogue [+*697*] [1], reached [1], redeemed [+*3391*] [1], remember [+*3647*] [1], remembering [+*3644*] [1], sacrificeds [+*4047*] [1], satisfy [+*2653*] [1], see [1], set up [1], show [1], sin [+*281*] [1], sinned [+*281*+*1639*] [1], spend [1], spent [1], stayed [1], stirring up [+*2180*] [1], sweep away with the torrent [+*4533*] [1], think about [+*4630*] [1], treat [+*1650*] [1], turn into [1], turned into [1], unite [+*3517*] [1], walked along [+*3847*] [1], wass [1], weeping [+*3081*] [1], who do you think you are [+*4932*+*5515*] [1], win [1], with [1], worked [1], wrote [1], yielded [1], yielding [1]

Mt 1:24 he **did** what the angel of the Lord had commanded him and took
3: 3 'Prepare the way for the Lord, **make** straight paths for him.' "
3: 8 **Produce** fruit in keeping with repentance.
3:10 and every tree that *does* not **produce** good fruit will be cut down
4:19 follow me," Jesus said, "and *I will* **make** you fishers of men."
5:19 but whoever **practices** and teaches these commands will be called
5:32 for marital unfaithfulness, **causes** her to become an adulteress,
5:36 by your head, for you cannot **make** even one hair white or black.
5:46 reward will you get? *Are* not even the tax collectors **doing** that?
5:47 greet only your brothers, what *are you* **doing** more than others?
5:47 what are you doing more than others? *Do* not even pagans **do** that?
6: 1 "Be careful not *to* **do** your 'acts of righteousness' before men,
6: 2 "So when *you* **give** [+*1797*] **to the needy**, do not announce it with
6: 2 as the hypocrites **do** in the synagogues and on the streets, to be
6: 3 But *when* you **give** [+*1797*] **to the needy**, do not let your left hand
6: 3 do not let your left hand know what your right hand *is* **doing**,
7:12 in everything, **do** to others what you would have them do to you,
7:12 in everything, do to others what you would have them **do** to you,
7:17 Likewise every good tree **bears** good fruit, but a bad tree bears bad
7:17 every good tree bears good fruit, but a bad tree **bears** bad fruit.
7:18 A good tree cannot **bear** bad fruit, and a bad tree cannot bear good
7:18 tree cannot bear bad fruit, and a bad tree cannot **bear** good fruit.
7:19 Every tree that *does* not **bear** good fruit is cut down and thrown
7:21 but only he *who* **does** the will of my Father who is in heaven.
7:22 and in your name drive out demons and **perform** many miracles?'
7:24 and **puts** them **into practice** is like a wise man who built his house
7:26 and *does* not **put** them **into practice** is like a foolish man who
8: 9 and he comes. I say to my servant, '**Do this**,' and he does it."
8: 9 and he comes. I say to my servant, 'Do this,' and *he* **does** it."
9:28 and he asked them, "Do you believe that I am able *to* **do** this?"
12: 2 Your disciples *are* **doing** what is unlawful on the Sabbath.
12: 2 Your disciples are doing what is unlawful **[RPG]** on the Sabbath.
12: 3 "Haven't you read what David **did** when he and his companions
12:12 than a sheep! Therefore it is lawful *to* **do** good on the Sabbath."
12:16 warning them not to **tell** [+*5745*] who he was.
12:33 "**Make** a tree good and its fruit will be good, or make a tree bad
12:33 its fruit will be good, or **make** a tree bad and its fruit will be bad,

12:50 For whoever **does** the will of my Father in heaven is my brother
13:23 a crop, **yielding** a hundred, sixty or thirty times what was sown."
13:26 When the wheat sprouted and **formed** heads, then the weeds also
13:28 " 'An enemy **did** this,' he replied. "The servants asked him, 'Do
13:41 out of his kingdom everything that causes sin and all who **do** evil.
13:58 And *he did* not **do** many miracles there because of their lack of
17: 4 If you wish, *I will* **put up** three shelters—one for you, one for
17:12 not recognize him, but *have* **done** to him everything they wished.
18:35 "This is how my heavenly Father *will* **treat** each of you unless you
19: 4 "that at the beginning the Creator '**made** them male and female,'
19:16 and asked, "Teacher, what good thing *must I* **do** to get eternal life?"
20: 5 about the sixth hour and the ninth hour and **did** the same thing.
20:12 'These men who were hired last **worked** only one hour,' they said,
20:12 'and *you have* **made** them equal to us who have borne the burden
20:15 Don't I have the right *to* **do** what I want with my own money?
20:32 and called them. "What do you want *me to* **do** for you?" he asked.
21: 6 The disciples went and **did** as Jesus had instructed them.
21:13 a house of prayer,' but you *are* **making** it a 'den of robbers.' "
21:15 and the teachers of the law saw the wonderful things *he* **did**
21:21 do not doubt, not only *can you* **do** what was done to the fig tree,
21:23 "By what authority *are you* **doing** these things?" they asked.
21:24 I will tell you by what authority *I am* **doing** these things.
21:27 "Neither will I tell you by what authority *I am* **doing** these things.
21:31 "Which of the two **did** what his father wanted?" "The first,"
21:36 than the first time, and the tenants **treated** them the same way.
21:40 the owner of the vineyard comes, what *will he* **do** to those tenants?"
21:43 away from you and given to a people *who will* **produce** its fruit.
22: 2 "The kingdom of heaven is like a king who **prepared** a wedding
23: 3 So you must obey them and **do** everything they tell you. But do not
23: 3 But *do* not **do** what they do, for they do not practice what they
23: 3 do not do what they do, for *they do* not **practice** what they preach.
23: 5 "Everything they do *is* **done** for men to see: They make their
23:15 You travel over land and sea *to* **win** a single convert, and when he
23:15 *you* **make** him twice as much a son of hell as you are.
23:23 You should have **practiced** the latter, without neglecting the
24:46 It will be good for that servant whose master finds him **doing**
25:40 whatever *you* **did** for one of the least of these brothers of mine,
25:40 did for one of the least of these brothers of mine, *you* **did** for me.'
25:45 you the truth, whatever *you did* not **do** for one of the least of these,
25:45 you did not do for one of the least of these, *you did* not **do** for me.'
26:12 this perfume on my body, *she* **did** it to prepare me for burial.
26:13 the world, what she *has* **done** will also be told, in memory of her."
26:18 *I am going to* **celebrate** the Passover with my disciples at your
26:19 So the disciples **did** as Jesus had directed them and prepared the
26:73 you are one of them, for your accent **gives** [+*1316*] you **away**."
27:22 "What *shall I* **do**, then, **with** Jesus who is called Christ?" Pilate
27:23 "Why? What crime *has he* **committed**?" asked Pilate. But they
28:14 to the governor, we will satisfy him and **keep** you out of trouble."
28:15 So the soldiers took the money and **did** as they were instructed.

Mk 1: 3 'Prepare the way for the Lord, **make** straight paths for him.' "
1:17 follow me," Jesus said, "and *I will* **make** you fishers of men."
2:23 and as his disciples **walked** [+*3847*] **along**, they began to pick
2:24 "Look, why *are they* **doing** what is unlawful on the Sabbath?"
2:25 "Have you never read what David **did** when he and his companions
3: 4 *to* **do** good or to do evil, to save life or to kill?" But they remained
3: 8 When they heard all *he was* **doing**, many people came to him from
3:12 But he gave them strict orders not to **tell** [+*5745*] who he was.
3:14 *He* **appointed** twelve—designating them apostles—that they might
3:16 These are the twelve *he* **appointed**: Simon (to whom he gave the
3:35 Whoever **does** God's will is my brother and sister and mother."
4:32 **with** such big branches that the birds of the air can perch in its
5:19 to your family and tell them how much the Lord *has* **done** for you,
5:20 and began to tell in the Decapolis how much Jesus *had* **done** for
5:32 But Jesus kept looking around to see who *had* **done** it.
6: 5 He could not **do** any miracles there, except lay his hands on a few
6:21 On his birthday Herod **gave** a banquet for his high officials
6:30 around Jesus and reported to him all *they had* **done** and taught.
7:12 then you no longer let him **do** anything for his father or mother.
7:13 that you have handed down. And *you* **do** many things like that."
7:37 "*He has* **done** everything well," they said. "He even makes the deaf
7:37 they said. "*He* even **makes** the deaf hear and the mute speak."
9: 5 *Let us* **put up** three shelters—one for you, one for Moses
9:13 has come, and *they have* **done** to him everything they wished,
9:39 "No one who **does** a miracle in my name can in the next moment
10: 6 "But at the beginning of creation God '**made** them male
10:17 "Good teacher," he asked, "what *must I* **do** to inherit eternal life?"

10:35	"Teacher," they said, "we want *you to* **do** for us whatever we ask."
10:36	"What do you want me *to* **do** for you?" he asked.
10:51	"What do you want *me to* **do** for you?" Jesus asked him. The blind
11: 3	If anyone asks you, 'Why *are you* **doing** this?' tell him, 'The Lord
11: 5	standing there asked, "What *are you* **doing**, untying that colt?"
11:17	prayer for all nations'? But you *have* **made** it 'a den of robbers.' "
11:28	"By what authority *are you* **doing** these things?" they asked.
11:28	things?" they asked. "And who gave you authority to **do** this?"
11:29	and I will tell you by what authority *I am* **doing** these things.
11:33	"Neither will I tell you by what authority *I am* **doing** these things."
12: 9	"What then *will* the owner of the vineyard **do**? He will come
14: 7	have with you, and you can **help** [+2292] them any time you want.
14: 8	*She* **did** what she could. She poured perfume on my body
14: 9	the world, what she *has* **done** will also be told, in memory of her."
15: 1	teachers of the law and the whole Sanhedrin, **reached** a decision.
15: 7	the insurrectionists who *had* **committed** murder in the uprising.
15: 8	came up and asked Pilate *to* **do** for them what he usually did.
15:12	"What *shall I* **do**, then, **with** the one you call the king of the Jews?"
15:14	"Why? What crime *has he* **committed**?" asked Pilate. But they
15:15	Wanting *to* **satisfy** [+2653] the crowd, Pilate released Barabbas to

Lk

1:25	"The Lord *has* **done** this for me," she said. "In these days he has
1:49	for the Mighty One *has* **done** great things for me—holy is his
1:51	*He has* **performed** mighty deeds with his arm; he has scattered
1:68	because he has come and *has* **redeemed** [+3391] his people.
1:72	*to* **show** mercy to our fathers and to remember his holy covenant,
2:27	When the parents brought in the child Jesus *to* **do** for him what the
2:48	His mother said to him, "Son, why *have you* **treated** us like this?
3: 4	'Prepare the way for the Lord, **make** straight paths for him.
3: 8	**Produce** fruit in keeping with repentance. And do not begin to say
3: 9	and every tree *that does* not **produce** good fruit will be cut down
3:10	"What *should we* **do** then?" the crowd asked.
3:11	him who has none, and the one who has food *should* **do** the same."
3:12	came to be baptized. "Teacher," they asked, "what *should we* **do**?"
3:14	Then some soldiers asked him, "And what *should* we **do**?" He
3:19	his brother's wife, and all the other evil things he *had* **done**,
4:23	**Do** here in your hometown what we have heard that you did in
5: 6	*When they had* **done** so, they caught such a large number of fish
5:29	Then Levi **held** a great banquet for Jesus at his house, and a large
5:33	"John's disciples often fast and **pray** [+1255], and so do the
5:34	"Can you **make** the guests of the bridegroom fast while he is with
6: 2	"Why *are you* **doing** what is unlawful on the Sabbath?"
6: 3	"Have you never read what David *did* when he and his companions
6:10	out your hand." He **did** so, and his hand was completely restored.
6:11	and began to discuss with one another what *they* might **do** to Jesus.
6:23	in heaven. For that is how their fathers **treated** the prophets.
6:26	well of you, for that is how their fathers **treated** the false prophets.
6:27	who hear me: Love your enemies, **do** good to those who hate you,
6:31	**Do** to others as you would have them do to you.
6:31	Do to others as you would have them **do** to you.
6:33	are good to you, what credit is that to you? Even 'sinners' **do** that.
6:43	"No good tree **bears** [+1639] bad fruit, nor does a bad tree bear
6:43	"No good tree bears bad fruit, nor *does* a bad tree **bear** good fruit.
6:46	"Why do you call me, 'Lord, Lord,' and *do* not **do** what I say?
6:47	comes to me and hears my words and **puts** them **into practice**.
6:49	and *does* not **put** them **into practice** is like a man who built a
7: 8	and he comes. I say to my servant, '**Do** this,' and he does it."
7: 8	and he comes. I say to my servant, 'Do this,' and *he* **does** it."
8: 8	It came up and **yielded** a crop, a hundred times more than was
8:21	brothers are those who hear God's word and **put** it **into practice**."
8:39	"Return home and tell how much God *has* **done** for you."
8:39	and told all over town how much Jesus *had* **done** for him.
9:10	the apostles returned, they reported to Jesus what *they had* **done**.
9:15	The disciples **did** so, and everybody sat down.
9:33	*Let us* **put up** three shelters—one for you, one for Moses
9:43	While everyone was marveling at all that Jesus *did*, he said to his
10:25	"Teacher," he asked, "what *must I* **do** to inherit eternal life?"
10:28	answered correctly," Jesus replied. "**Do** this and you will live."
10:37	The expert in the law replied, "The one *who* **had** mercy on him."
10:37	one who had mercy on him." Jesus told him, "Go and **do** likewise."
11:40	Did not the one *who* **made** the outside make the inside also?
11:40	*Did* not the one who made the outside **make** the inside also?
11:42	You should have **practiced** the latter without leaving the former
12: 4	be afraid of those who kill the body and after that can **do** no more.
12:17	He thought to himself, 'What *shall I* **do**? I have no place to store
12:18	"Then he said, 'This is what *I'll* **do**. I will tear down my barns
12:33	**Provide** purses for yourselves that will not wear out, a treasure in

12:43	It will be good for that servant whom the master finds **doing**
12:47	or *does* not **do** what his master wants will be beaten with many
12:48	and **does** things deserving punishment will be beaten with few
13: 9	If *it* **bears** fruit next year, fine! If not, then cut it down.' "
13:22	the towns and villages, teaching *as he* **made** his way to Jerusalem.
14:12	"When *you* **give** a luncheon or dinner, do not invite your friends,
14:13	But when *you* **give** a banquet, invite the poor, the crippled,
14:16	"A certain man *was* **preparing** a great banquet and invited many
15:19	to be called your son; **make** me like one of your hired men.'
16: 3	"The manager said to himself, 'What *shall I* **do** now? My master is
16: 4	I know what *I'll* **do** so that, when I lose my job here, people will
16: 8	the dishonest manager because *he had* **acted** shrewdly.
16: 9	I tell you, use worldly wealth *to* **gain** friends for yourselves,
17: 9	Would he thank the servant because *he* **did** what he was told to do?
17:10	when *you have* **done** everything you were told to do, should say,
17:10	'We are unworthy servants; *we have only* **done** our duty.' "
17:10	unworthy servants; we have only done our **duty** [+4005+4053].' "
18: 7	And *will* not God **bring about** justice for his chosen ones,
18: 8	I tell you, *he will* see that they **get** justice, and quickly. However,
18:18	asked him, "Good teacher, what *must I* **do** to inherit eternal life?"
18:41	"What do you want *me to* **do** for you?" "Lord, I want to see," he
19:18	"The second came and said, 'Sir, your mina *has* **earned** five more.'
19:46	be a house of prayer'; but you *have* **made** it 'a den of robbers.' "
19:48	Yet they could not find any way *to* **do** it, because all the people
20: 2	"Tell us by what authority *you are* **doing** these things," they said.
20: 8	"Neither will I tell you by what authority *I am* **doing** these things."
20:13	"Then the owner of the vineyard said, 'What *shall I* **do**? I will send
20:15	killed him. "What then *will* the owner of the vineyard **do** to them?
22:19	"This is my body given for you; **do** this in remembrance of me."
23:22	he spoke to them: "Why? What crime *has* this man **committed**?
23:31	For if *men* **do** these things when the tree is green, what will
23:34	"Father, forgive them, for they do not know what *they are* **doing**."

Jn

2: 5	His mother said to the servants, "**Do** whatever he tells you."
2:11	first of his miraculous signs, Jesus **performed** at Cana in Galilee.
2:15	So he **made** a whip out of cords, and drove all from the temple
2:16	out of here! How dare you **turn** my Father's house **into** a market!"
2:18	sign can you show us to prove your authority *to* **do** all this?"
2:23	many people saw the miraculous signs he *was* **doing** and believed
3: 2	For no one could **perform** the miraculous signs you are doing if
3: 2	For no one could perform the miraculous signs you *are* **doing** if
3:21	But whoever **lives by** the truth comes into the light, so that it may
4: 1	The Pharisees heard that Jesus *was* **gaining** and baptizing more
4:29	"Come, see a man who told me everything *I* ever **did**. Could this be
4:34	"is to **do** the will of him who sent me and to finish his work.
4:39	of the woman's testimony, "He told me everything *I ever* **did**."
4:45	They had seen all that *he had* **done** in Jerusalem at the Passover
4:46	visited Cana in Galilee, where *he had* **turned** the water **into** wine.
4:54	This was the second miraculous sign that Jesus **performed**,
5:11	But he replied, "The man *who* **made** me well said to me, 'Pick up
5:15	and told the Jews that it was Jesus who *had* **made** him well.
5:16	So, because Jesus was **doing** these things on the Sabbath,
5:18	even calling God his own Father, **making** himself equal with God.
5:19	"I tell you the truth, the Son can **do** nothing by himself; he can do
5:19	he can do only what he sees his Father **doing**, because whatever
5:19	Father doing, because whatever the Father **does** the Son also does.
5:19	Father doing, because whatever the Father does the Son also **does**.
5:20	For the Father loves the Son and shows him all he **does**. Yes,
5:27	And he has given him authority *to* **judge** [+3213] because he is the
5:29	those *who have* **done** good will rise to live, and those who have
5:30	By myself I can **do** nothing; I judge only as I hear, and my
5:36	and which *I am* **doing**, testifies that the Father has sent me.
6: 2	because they saw the miraculous signs he *had* **performed** on the
6: 6	to test him, for he already had in mind what he was going to **do**.
6:10	Jesus said, "**Have** the people sit down." There was plenty of grass
6:14	After the people saw the miraculous sign that Jesus **did**, they began
6:15	knowing that they intended to come and **make** him king by force,
6:28	they asked him, "What *must we* **do** to do the works God requires?"
6:30	then *will* you **give** that we may see it and believe you?
6:38	For I have come down from heaven not to **do** my will but to do the
7: 3	go to Judea, so that your disciples may see the miracles *you* **do**.
7: 4	No one who wants to become a public figure **acts** in secret.
7: 4	Since *you are* **doing** these things, show yourself to the world."
7:17	If anyone chooses *to* **do** God's will, he will find out whether my
7:19	Yet not one of you **keeps** the law. Why are you trying to kill me?"
7:21	Jesus said to them, "*I* **did** one miracle, and you are all astonished.
7:23	why are you angry with me for **healing** [+5618] the whole man on

7:31 the Christ comes, *will he* **do** more miraculous signs than this man?"
7:31 will he do more miraculous signs than this man?" **[RPG]**
7:51 anyone without first hearing him to find out what *he is* **doing**?"
8:28 and that *I* **do** nothing on my own but speak just what the Father has
8:29 he has not left me alone, for I always **do** what pleases him."
8:34 tell you the truth, everyone who **sins** [+281+3836] is a slave to sin.
8:38 and you **do** what you have heard from your father."
8:39 said Jesus, "then *you would* **do** the things Abraham did.
8:40 the truth that I heard from God. Abraham *did not* **do** such things.
8:41 You *are* **doing** the things your own father does." "We are not
8:44 the devil, and you want *to* **carry out** your father's desire.
8:53 so did the prophets. **Who do you think you are** [+4932+5515]?"
9: 6 said this, he spit on the ground, **made** some mud with the saliva,
9:11 "The man they call Jesus **made** some mud and put it on my eyes
9:14 Now the day on which Jesus *had* **made** the mud and opened the
9:16 But others asked, "How can a sinner **do** such miraculous signs?"
9:26 Then they asked him, "What *did he* **do** to you? How did he open
9:31 not listen to sinners. He listens to the godly man *who* **does** his will.
9:33 If this man were not from God, he could **do** nothing."
10:25 not believe. The miracles I **do** in my Father's name speak for me,
10:33 because you, a mere man, **claim** [+4932] **to be** God."
10:37 Do not believe me unless *I* **do** what my Father does.
10:38 But if *I* **do** it, even though you do not believe me,
10:41 They said, "Though John never **performed** a miraculous sign,
11:37 "Could not he who opened the eyes of the blind man *have* **kept** this
11:45 to visit Mary, and had seen what Jesus **did**, put their faith in him.
11:46 of them went to the Pharisees and told them what Jesus *had* **done**.
11:47 of the Sanhedrin. "What *are we* **accomplishing**?" they asked.
11:47 they asked. "Here *is* this man **performing** many miraculous signs.
12: 2 Here a dinner *was* **given** in Jesus' honor. Martha served,
12:16 been written about him and that *they had* **done** these things to him.
12:18 because they had heard that he *had* **given** this miraculous sign,
12:37 Even *after* Jesus *had* **done** all these miraculous signs in their
13: 7 Jesus replied, "You do not realize now what I *am* **doing**, but later
13:12 "Do you understand what I *have* **done** for you?" he asked them.
13:15 I have set you an example that you *should* **do** as I have done for
13:15 I have set you an example that you should do as I *have* **done** for
13:17 that you know these things, you will be blessed if *you* **do** them.
13:27 into him. "What *you are about to* **do**, do quickly," Jesus told him,
13:27 into him. "What you are about to **do**, **do** quickly," Jesus told him,
14:10 Rather, it is the Father, living in me, *who is* **doing** his work.
14:12 anyone who has faith in me *will* **do** what I have been doing.
14:12 anyone who has faith in me will do what I *have been* **doing**.
14:12 *He will* **do** even greater things than these, because I am going to
14:13 And *I will* **do** whatever you ask in my name, so that the Son may
14:14 You may ask me for anything in my name, and I *will* **do** it.
14:23 love him, and we will come to him and **make** our home with him.
14:31 and that *I* **do** exactly what my Father has commanded me.
15: 5 he will bear much fruit; apart from me you can **do** nothing.
15:14 You are my friends if *you* **do** what I command.
15:15 because a servant does not know his master's **business** [+5515].
15:21 *They will* **treat** [+1650] you this way because of my name,
15:24 If *I had* not **done** among them what no one else did, they would
15:24 If I had not done among them what no one else **did**, they would not
16: 2 *They will* **put** you **out of the synagogue** [+697]; in fact, a time is
16: 3 *They will* **do** such things because they have not known the Father
17: 4 you glory on earth by completing the work you gave me to **do**.
18:18 and officials stood around a fire *they had* **made** to keep warm.
18:30 "If he were not a **criminal** [+2805]," they replied, "we would not
18:35 priests who handed you over to me. What is it *you have* **done**?"
19: 7 he must die, because *he* **claimed** [+1571] **to be** the Son of God."
19:12 Anyone who **claims** [+1571] **to be** a king opposes Caesar."
19:23 they took his clothes, **dividing** them **into four shares** [+3538],
19:24 and cast lots for my clothing." So this is what the soldiers **did**.
20:30 Jesus **did** many other miraculous signs in the presence of his
21:25 Jesus **did** many other things as well. If every one of them were

Ac   1: 1 Theophilus, *I* **wrote** about all that Jesus began to do and to teach
1: 1 Theophilus, I wrote about all that Jesus began *to* **do** and to teach
2:22 wonders and signs, which God **did** among you through him,
2:36 God *has* **made** this Jesus, whom you crucified, both Lord
2:37 said to Peter and the other apostles, "Brothers, what *shall we* **do**?"
3:12 as if by our own power or godliness we *had* **made** this man walk?
4: 7 to question them: "By what power or what name *did* you **do** this?"
4:16 "What *are we* **to do with** these men?" they asked.
4:24 they said, "you **made** the heaven and the earth and the sea,
4:28 They **did** what your power and will had decided beforehand should

5:34 and ordered that the men *be* **put** outside for a little while.
6: 8 **did** great wonders and miraculous signs among the people.
7:19 and oppressed our forefathers *by* **forcing** them to throw out their
7:24 so *he* went to his defense and **avenged** [+1689] him by killing the
7:36 He led them out of Egypt and **did** wonders and miraculous signs in
7:40 They told Aaron, '**Make** us gods who will go before us. As for this
7:43 and the star of your god Rephan, the idols *you* **made** to worship.
7:44 It *had been* **made** as God directed Moses, according to the pattern
7:50 Has not my hand **made** all these things?'
8: 2 men buried Stephen and **mourned deeply** [+3157+3489] for him.
8: 6 the crowds heard Philip and saw the miraculous signs he **did**,
9: 6 and go into the city, and you will be told what you must **do**."
9:13 this man and all the harm he has **done** to your saints in Jerusalem.
9:36 who was always doing good and **helping the poor** [+1797].
9:39 and other clothing that Dorcas *had* **made** while she was still with
10: 2 he **gave** [+1797] generously to those in need and prayed to God
10:33 So I sent for you immediately, and *it* was good of you to come.
10:39 "We are witnesses of everything *he* **did** in the country of the Jews
11:30 This *they* **did**, sending their gift to the elders by Barnabas
12: 8 said to him, "Put on your clothes and sandals." And Peter **did** so.
13:22 a man after my own heart; he *will* **do** everything I want him to do.'
14:11 When the crowd saw what Paul *had* **done**, they shouted in the
14:15 "Men, why *are you* **doing** this? We too are only men, human like
14:15 who **made** heaven and earth and sea and everything in them.
14:27 church together and reported all that God *had* **done** through them
15: 3 had been converted. *This* news **made** all the brothers very glad.
15: 4 to whom they reported everything God *had* **done** through them.
15:12 and wonders God *had* **done** among the Gentiles through them.
15:17 who bear my name, says the Lord, *who* **does** these things'
15:33 *After* **spending** some time there, they were sent off by the brothers
16:18 She **kept** this **up** for many days. Finally Paul became so troubled
16:21 advocating customs unlawful for us Romans to accept or **practice**."
16:30 brought them out and asked, "Sirs, what must I **do** to be saved?"
17:24 "The God who **made** the world and everything in it is the Lord of
17:26 From one man he **made** every nation of men, that they should
18:23 *After* **spending** some time in Antioch, Paul set out from there
19:11 God **did** extraordinary miracles through Paul,
19:14 Seven sons of Sceva, a Jewish chief priest, were **doing** this.
19:24 silversmith named Demetrius, *who* **made** silver shrines of Artemis,
20: 3 where *he* **stayed** three months. Because the Jews made a plot
20:24 However, *I* **consider** my life worth nothing to me, if only I may
21:13 "Why *are you* **weeping** [+3081] and breaking my heart?
21:19 and reported in detail what God *had* **done** among the Gentiles
21:23 so **do** what we tell you. There are four men with us who have made
21:33 Then he asked who he was and what *he had* **done** [+1639].
22:10 " 'What *shall* I **do**, Lord?' I asked. " 'Get up,' the Lord said,
22:10 There you will be told all that you have been assigned *to* **do**.'
22:26 and reported it. "What are you going to **do**?" he asked.
23:12 The next morning the Jews **formed** a conspiracy and bound
23:13 More than forty men were **involved in** this plot.
24:12 or **stirring up** [+2180] a crowd in the synagogues or anywhere else
24:17 I came to Jerusalem *to* **bring** my people gifts for the poor
25: 3 *for they were* **preparing** an ambush to kill him along the way.
25:17 When they came here with me, *I did* not **delay the case** [+332],
26:10 And that is just what *I* **did** in Jerusalem. On the authority of the
26:28 "Do you think that in such a short time you can persuade me *to* **be** a
27:18 storm that the next day *they* **began** to throw the cargo overboard.
28:17 *although* I *have* **done** nothing against our people or against the

Ro   1: 9 his Son, is my witness how constantly *I* **remember** [+3644] you
1:28 them over to a depraved mind, *to* **do** what ought not to be done.
1:32 *they* not only *continue to* **do** these very things but also approve of
2: 3 a mere man, pass judgment on them and yet **do** the same things,
2:14 who do not have the law, **do** by nature things required by the law,
3: 8 as some claim that we say—"*Let us* **do** evil that good may result"?
3:12 become worthless; there is no one *who* **does** good, not even one."
4:21 being fully persuaded that God had power *to* **do** what he had
7:15 what I do. For what I want to do I do not do, but what I hate *I* **do**.
7:16 And if *I* **do** what I do not want to do, I agree that the law is good.
7:19 For what *I* **do** is not the good I want to do; no, the evil I do not
7:20 Now if *I* **do** what I do not want to do, it is no longer I who do it,
7:21 law at work: When I want *to* **do** good, evil is right there with me.
9:20 say to him who formed it, 'Why *did you* **make** me like this?' "
9:21 Does not the potter have the right *to* **make** out of the same lump of
9:28 For the Lord *will* **carry out** his sentence on earth with speed
10: 5 is by the law: "The man *who* **does** these things will live by them."
12:20 to drink. *In* **doing** this, you will heap burning coals on his head."

13: 3   one in authority? Then **do** what is right and he will commend you.
13: 4   But if *you* **do** wrong, be afraid, for he does not bear the sword for
13:14   and *do* not **think about** [*+4630*] how to gratify the desires of the
15:26   and Achaia were pleased *to* **make** a contribution for the poor
16:17   and **put** obstacles *in* your *way* that are contrary to the teaching you

1Co 6:15   *Shall I* then take the members of Christ and **unite** [*+3517*] them
6:18   All other sins a man **commits** are outside his body, but he who sins
7:36   and he feels he ought to marry, *he should* **do** as he wants.
7:37   mind not to marry the virgin—this *man* also **does** the right thing.
7:38   So then, he who marries the virgin **does** right, but he who does not
7:38   virgin does right, but he who does not marry her **does** even better.
9:23   *I* **do** all this for the sake of the gospel, that I may share in its
10:13   he will also **provide** a way out so that you can stand up under it.
10:31   So whether you eat or drink or whatever *you* **do**, do it all for
10:31   or drink or whatever you do, **do** it all for the glory of God.
11:24   "This is my body, which is for you; **do** this in remembrance of me."
11:25   my blood; **do** this, whenever you drink it, in remembrance of me.
15:29   no resurrection, what *will* those **do** who are baptized for the dead?
16: 1   for God's people: **Do** what I told the Galatian churches to do.

2Co 5:21   God **made** him who had no sin to be sin for us, so that in him we
8:10   Last year you were the first not only *to* **give** but also to have the
8:11   Now finish the **work**, so that your eager willingness to do it may
11: 7   **Was**ˢ *it* a sin for me to lower myself in order to elevate you by
11:12   And *I will keep on* **doing** what I am doing in order to cut the
11:12   And I will keep on doing what *I am* **doing** in order to cut the
11:25   times I was shipwrecked, *I* **spent** a night and a day in the open sea,
13: 7   Now we pray to God that you *will* not **do** anything wrong.
13: 7   but that you *will* **do** what is right even though we may seem to

Gal 2:10   continue to remember the poor, the very thing I was eager *to* **do**.
3:10   "Cursed is everyone who does not continue *to* **do** everything
3:12   the contrary, "The man *who* **does** these things will live by them."
5: 3   himself be circumcised that he is obligated *to* **obey** the whole law.
5:17   in conflict with each other, so that *you do* not **do** what you want.
6: 9   Let us not become weary *in* **doing** good, for at the proper time we

Eph 1:16   I have not stopped giving thanks for you, **remembering** [*+3644*]
2: 3   of our sinful nature and **following** its desires and thoughts.
2:14   who *has* **made** the two one and has destroyed the barrier,
2:15   create in himself one new man out of the two, thus **making** peace,
3:11   according to his eternal purpose which *he* **accomplished** in Christ
3:20   Now to him who is able *to* **do** immeasurably more than all we ask
4:16   and held together by every supporting ligament, **grows** [*+890*]
6: 6   but like slaves of Christ, **doing** the will of God from your heart.
6: 8   that the Lord will reward everyone for whatever good *he* **does**,
6: 9   And masters, **treat** your slaves in the same way. Do not threaten

Php 1: 4   In all my prayers for all of you, I always **pray** [*+1255*] with joy
2:14   **Do** everything without complaining or arguing,
4:14   Yet it **was** good of *you* to share in my troubles.

Col 3:17   And whatever *you* **do**, whether in word or deed, do it all in the
3:23   Whatever *you* **do**, work at it with all your heart, as working for the
4:16   **see** that it is also read in the church of the Laodiceans and that you

1Th 1: 2   We always thank God for all of you, **mentioning** [*+3644*] you in
4:10   And in fact, you **do** love all the brothers throughout Macedonia.
5:11   one another and build each other up, just as in fact *you are* **doing**.
5:24   The one who calls you is faithful and he *will* **do** it.

2Th 3: 4   We have confidence in the Lord that *you are* **doing** and will
3: 4   confidence in the Lord that *you* are doing and *will continue to* **do**

1Ti 1:13   I was shown mercy because *I* **acted** in ignorance and unbelief.
2: 1   prayers, intercession and thanksgiving be **made** for everyone—
4:16   Persevere in them, because *if you* **do**, you will save both yourself
5:21   instructions without partiality, and *to* **do** nothing out of favoritism.

2Ti 4: 5   in all situations, endure hardship, **do** the work of an evangelist,

Tit 3: 5   not because of righteous things we *had* **done**, but because of his

Phm 1: 4   I always thank my God *as* I **remember** [*+3644*] you in my prayers,
1:14   But I did not want *to* **do** anything without your consent, so that any
1:21   I write to you, knowing that *you will* **do** even more than I ask.

Heb 1: 2   heir of all things, and through whom *he* **made** the universe.
1: 3   *After he had* **provided** purification for sins, he sat down at the
1: 7   he says, "He **makes** his angels winds, his servants flames of fire."
3: 2   He was faithful *to* the one *who* **appointed** him, just as Moses was
6: 3   And God permitting, *we will* **do** so.
7:27   *He* **sacrificed**ˢ [*+4047*] for their sins once for all when he offered
8: 5   "See to it that *you* **make** everything according to the pattern shown
8: 9   It will not be like the covenant *I* **made** with their forefathers when
10: 7   about me in the scroll—I have come *to* **do** your will, O God.' "
10: 9   Then he said, "Here I am, I have come *to* **do** your will." He sets
10:36   need to persevere so that *when you have* **done** the will of God,

11:28   By faith *he* **kept** the Passover and the sprinkling of blood,
12:13   "**Make** level paths for your feet," so that the lame may not be
12:27   that is, **created things**—so that what cannot be shaken may
13: 6   Lord is my helper; I will not be afraid. What *can* man **do** to me?"
13:17   Obey them so that their work *will* **be** a joy, not a burden, for that
13:19   I particularly urge you *to* **pray**ˢ [*+4047*] so that I may be restored
13:21   equip you with everything good for **doing** his will, and may he
13:21   and *may he* **work** in us what is pleasing to him, through Jesus

Jas 2: 8   in Scripture, "Love your neighbor as yourself," *you are* **doing** right.
2:12   and **act** as those who are going to be judged by the law that gives
2:13   mercy will be shown *to* anyone *who has* not **been** merciful.
2:19   **Good** [*+2822*]! Even the demons believe that—and shudder.
3:12   My brothers, can a fig tree **bear** olives, or a grapevine bear figs?
3:12   grapevine bear figs? Neither can a salt spring **produce** fresh water.
3:18   **Peacemakers** [*+1645*] who sow in peace raise a harvest of
4:13   or tomorrow we will go to this or that city, **spend** a year there,
4:15   to say, "If it is the Lord's will, we will live and **do** this or that."
4:17   who knows the good *he ought to* **do** and doesn't do it, sins.
4:17   who knows the good he ought to do and doesn't **do** it, sins.
5:15   raise him up. If *he has* **sinned** [*+281+1639*], he will be forgiven.

1Pe 2:22   "He **committed** no sin, and no deceit was found in his mouth."
3:11   He must turn from evil and **do** good; he must seek peace
3:12   their prayer, but the face of the Lord is against *those who* **do** evil."

2Pe 1:10   be all the more eager *to* **make** your calling and election sure.
1:10   your calling and election sure. For *if you* **do** these things, you will
       never fall,
1:15   you will always be able *to* **remember** [*+3647*] these things.
1:19   and you *will* **do** well to pay attention to it, as to a light shining in a

1Jn 1: 6   him yet walk in the darkness, we lie and *do* not **live by** the truth.
1:10   *we* **make** him **out to be** a liar and his word has no place in our
2:17   pass away, but the *man who* **does** the will of God lives forever.
2:29   you know that everyone who **does** what is right has been born of
3: 4   Everyone who **sins** [*+281+3836*] breaks the law; in fact, sin is
3: 4   Everyone who **breaks the law** [*+490*]; in fact, sin is
3: 7   He *who* **does** what is right is righteous, just as he is righteous.
3: 8   He *who* **does** what is sinful is of the devil, because the devil has
3: 9   No one who is born of God *will continue to* **sin** [*+281*],
3:10   Anyone who *does* not **do** what is right is not a child of God;
3:22   because we obey his commands and **do** what pleases him.
5: 2   children of God: by loving God and **carrying out** his commands.
5:10   Anyone who does not believe God *has* **made** him **out to be** a liar,

3Jn 1: 5   *you* **are** faithful in what you are doing for the brothers,
1: 6   *You will* **do** well to send them on their way in a manner worthy of
1:10   So if I come, I will call attention to what *he is* **doing**,

Jude 1: 3   *although I* **was** very eager to write to you about the salvation we
1:15   *to* **judge** [*+3213*] everyone, and to convict all the ungodly of all

Rev 1: 6   and *has* **made** us to be a kingdom and priests to serve his God
2: 5   Repent and **do** the things you did at first. If you do not repent,
3: 9   *I will* **make** them come and fall down at your feet
3:12   Him who overcomes *I will* **make** a pillar in the temple of my God.
5:10   *You have* **made** them to be a kingdom and priests to serve our
11: 7   the beast that comes up from the Abyss *will* **attack** [*+4483*] them,
12:15   the woman and **sweep** her **away with the torrent** [*+4533*].
12:17   and went off *to* **make** war against the rest of her offspring—
13: 5   blasphemies and *to* **exercise** his authority for forty-two months.
13: 7   He was given power *to* **make** war against the saints and to conquer
13:12   He **exercised** all the authority of the first beast on his behalf,
13:12   and **made** the earth and its inhabitants worship the first beast,
13:13   And he **performed** great and miraculous signs, even causing fire
13:13   even **causing** fire to come down from heaven to earth in full view
13:14   Because of the signs he was given power *to* **do** on behalf of the
13:14   He ordered them *to* **set up** an image in honor of the beast who was
13:15   so that it *could* speak and **cause** all who refused to worship the
13:16   *He* also **forced** everyone, small and great, rich and poor, free
14: 7   Worship him *who* **made** the heavens, the earth, the sea
16:14   They are spirits of demons **performing** miraculous signs,
17:16   They *will* **bring** her to ruin and leave her naked; they will eat her
17:17   For God has put it into their hearts *to* **accomplish** his purpose by
17:17   *by* **agreeing** [*+1191+1651*] to give the beast their power to rule,
19:19   and their armies gathered together *to* **make** war against the rider on
19:20   and with him the false prophet who *had* **performed** the miraculous
21: 5   who was seated on the throne said, "*I am* **making** everything new!"
21:27   enter it, nor will anyone who **does** what is shameful or deceitful,
22: 2   **bearing** twelve crops of fruit, yielding its fruit every month.
22:11   continue to be vile; *let* him who does right continue *to* **do** right;
22:15   the idolaters and everyone who loves and **practices** falsehood.

4473 ποίημα, *poiēma* [2] [√ *4472*]

made [1], workmanship [1]

Ro 1:20 been clearly seen, being understood *from* what has been **made**,
Eph 2:10 For we are God's **workmanship**, created in Christ Jesus to do

4474 ποίησις, *poiēsis* [1] [√ *4472*]

does [1]

Jas 1:25 he has heard, but doing it—he will be blessed in what he **does**.

4475 ποιητής, *poiētēs* [6] [√ *4472*]

do [+*1181*] [1], do [1], doing [1], keeping [1], obey [1], poets [1]

Ac 17:28 As some *of* your own **poets** have said, 'We are his offspring.'
Ro 2:13 but it is those *who* **obey** the law who will be declared righteous.
Jas 1:22 to the word, and so deceive yourselves. **Do** [+*1181*] what it says.
     1:23 but does not **do** what it says is like a man who looks at his face in
     1:25 to do this, not forgetting what he has heard, but **doing** it—
     4:11 When you judge the law, you are not **keeping** it, but sitting in

4476 ποικίλος, *poikilos* [10] [→ *4497*]

all kinds of [4], various [3], many kinds [1], various forms [1], various kinds [1]

Mt 4:24 and people brought to him all who were ill *with* **various** diseases,
Mk 1:34 and Jesus healed many who had **various** diseases. He also drove
Lk 4:40 the people brought to Jesus all who had **various kinds** of sickness,
2Ti 3: 6 loaded down with sins and are swayed *by* **all kinds of** evil desires,
Tit 3: 3 deceived and enslaved *by* **all kinds of** passions and pleasures.
Heb 2: 4 God also testified to it *by* signs, wonders and **various** miracles,
    13: 9 Do not be carried away *by* **all kinds of** strange teachings.
Jas 1: 2 it pure joy, my brothers, whenever you face trials of **many kinds**,
1Pe 1: 6 a little while you may have had to suffer grief in **all kinds of** trials.
     4:10 faithfully administering God's grace in its **various forms**.

4477 ποιμαίνω, *poimainō* [11] [√ *4478*]

rule [3], be shepherds of [2], be shepherd of [1], be shepherd [1], looking after sheep [1], shepherds [1], take care of [1], tends [1]

Mt 2: 6 for out of you will come a ruler who *will* **be** the **shepherd of** my
Lk 17: 7 one of you had a servant plowing or **looking after the sheep**.
Jn 21:16 you know that I love you.' Jesus said, "**Take care of** my sheep."
Ac 20:28 **Be shepherds of** the church of God, which he bought with his own
1Co 9: 7 of its grapes? Who **tends** a flock and does not drink of the milk?
1Pe 5: 2 **Be shepherds of** God's flock that is under your care, serving as
Jude 1:12 without the slightest qualm—**shepherds** who feed only themselves.
Rev 2:27 '*He will* **rule** them with an iron scepter; he will dash them to
     7:17 For the Lamb at the center of the throne *will* **be** their **shepherd**;
    12: 5 a male child, who will **rule** all the nations with an iron scepter.
    19:15 "He *will* **rule** them with an iron scepter." He treads the winepress of

4478 ποιμήν, *poimēn* [18] [→ *799*, *4471*?, *4477*, *4479*, *4480*]

shepherd [13], shepherds [4], pastors [1]

Mt 9:36 they were harassed and helpless, like sheep without a **shepherd**.
   25:32 and he will separate the people one from another as a **shepherd**
   26:31 " 'I will strike the **shepherd**, and the sheep of the flock will be
Mk 6:34 on them, because they were like sheep without a **shepherd**.
  14:27 " 'I will strike the **shepherd**, and the sheep will be scattered.'
Lk 2: 8 And there were **shepherds** living out in the fields nearby,
    2:15 left them and gone into heaven, the **shepherds** said to one another,
    2:18 and all who heard it were amazed at what the **shepherds** said to
    2:20 The **shepherds** returned, glorifying and praising God for all the
Jn 10: 2 The man who enters by the gate is the **shepherd** of his sheep.
  10:11 "I am the good **shepherd**. The good shepherd lays down his life for
  10:11 The good **shepherd** lays down his life for the sheep.
  10:12 The hired hand is not the **shepherd** who owns the sheep. So when
  10:14 "I am the good **shepherd**; I know my sheep and my sheep know
  10:16 listen to my voice, and there shall be one flock and one **shepherd**.
Eph 4:11 some to be evangelists, and some to be **pastors** and teachers,
Heb 13:20 from the dead our Lord Jesus, that great **Shepherd** of the sheep,

1Pe 2:25 but now you have returned to the **Shepherd** and Overseer of your

4479 ποίμνη, *poimnē* [5] [√ *4478*]

flock [3], *untranslated* [1], flocks [1]

Mt 26:31 strike the shepherd, and the sheep *of* the **flock** will be scattered.'
Lk 2: 8 out in the fields nearby, keeping watch over their **flocks** at night.
Jn 10:16 listen to my voice, and there shall be one **flock** and one shepherd.
1Co 9: 7 of its grapes? Who tends a **flock** and does not drink of the milk?
    9: 7 Who tends a flock and does not drink of the milk? **[RPG]**

4480 ποίμνιον, *poimnion* [5] [√ *4478*]

flock [5]

Lk 12:32 "Do not be afraid, little **flock**, for your Father has been pleased to
Ac 20:28 and all the **flock** of which the Holy Spirit has made you overseers.
  20:29 wolves will come in among you and will not spare the **flock**.
1Pe 5: 2 Be shepherds of God's **flock** that is under your care, serving as
    5: 3 it over those entrusted to you, but being examples *to* the **flock**.

4481 ποῖος, *poios* [33] [√ *3888*, *4471*?]

what [21], which [4], kind of [3], what kind of [2], a way [1], how is it [1], the [1]

Mt 19:18 "**Which** *ones*?" the man inquired. Jesus replied, " 'Do not murder,
  21:23 "By **what** authority are you doing these things?" they asked.
  21:24 I will tell you by **what** authority I am doing these things.
  21:27 "Neither will I tell you by **what** authority I am doing these things.
  22:36 "Teacher, **which** is the greatest commandment in the Law?"
  24:42 because you do not know *on* **what** day your Lord will come.
  24:43 If the owner of the house had known *at* **what** time of night the
Mk 11:28 "By **what** authority are you doing these things?" they asked.
  11:29 and I will tell you by **what** authority I am doing these things.
  11:33 "Neither will I tell you by **what** authority I am doing these things."
  12:28 "Of all the commandments, **which** is the most important?"
Lk 5:19 When they could not find **a way** to do this because of the crowd,
    6:32 "If you love those who love you, **what** credit is that to you?
    6:33 do good to those who are good to you, **what** credit is that to you?
    6:34 from whom you expect repayment, **what** credit is that to you?
  12:39 If the owner of the house had known *at* **what** hour the thief was
  20: 2 "Tell us by **what** authority you are doing these things," they said.
  20: 8 "Neither will I tell you by **what** authority I am doing these things."
  24:19 "**What** *things*?" he asked. "About Jesus of Nazareth," they replied.
Jn 10:32 miracles from the Father. For **which** of these do you stone me?"
  12:33 He said this to show the **kind of** death he was going to die.
  18:32 so that the words Jesus had spoken indicating the **kind of** death he
  21:19 Jesus said this to indicate the **kind of** death by which Peter would
Ac 4: 7 to question them: "By **what** power or what name did you do this?"
    4: 7 to question them: "By what power or **what** name did you do this?"
    7:49 **What kind of** house will you build for me? says the Lord.
  23:34 The governor read the letter and asked **what** province he was from.
Ro 3:27 Where, then, is boasting? It is excluded. On **what** principle?
1Co 15:35 are the dead raised? *With* **what kind of** body will they come?"
Jas 4:14 **What** is your life? You are a mist that appears for a little while
1Pe 1:11 trying to find out **the** time and circumstances to which the Spirit of
    2:20 But **how is it** to your credit if you receive a beating for doing
Rev 3: 3 like a thief, and you will not know at **what** time I will come to you.

4482 πολεμέω, *polemeō* [7] [√ *4483*]

fight [2], fought [2], make war [2], makes war [1]

Jas 4: 2 You quarrel and **fight**. You do not have, because you do not ask
Rev 2:16 to you and *will* **fight** against them with the sword of my mouth.
  12: 7 Michael and his angels **fought** against the dragon, and the dragon
  12: 7 against the dragon, and the dragon and his angels **fought** *back*.
  13: 4 asked, "Who is like the beast? Who can **make war** against him?"
  17:14 They *will* **make war** against the Lamb, but the Lamb will
  19:11 is called Faithful and True. With justice *he* judges and **makes war**.

4483 πόλεμος, **polemos** [18] [→ *4482*]

battle [6], wars [5], war [4], attack [+*4472*] [1], fights [1], go war [+*5202*] [1]

Mt	24: 6	You will hear *of* wars and rumors of wars, but see to it that you are
	24: 6	You will hear *of* wars and rumors of wars, but see to it that you are
Mk	13: 7	When you hear *of* wars and rumors of wars, do not be alarmed.
	13: 7	When you hear of wars and rumors of wars, do not be alarmed.
Lk	14:31	"Or suppose a king is about *to* go to war [+*5202*] against another
	21: 9	When you hear of wars and revolutions, do not be frightened.
1Co	14: 8	trumpet does not sound a clear call, who will get ready for battle?
Heb	11:34	and who became powerful in battle and routed foreign armies.
Jas	4: 1	What causes fights and quarrels among you? Don't they come
Rev	9: 7	The locusts looked like horses prepared for battle. On their heads
	9: 9	like the thundering of many horses and chariots rushing into battle.
	11: 7	the beast that comes up from the Abyss *will* attack [+*4472*] them,
	12: 7	And there was war in heaven. Michael and his angels fought
	12:17	and went off to make war against the rest of her offspring—
	13: 7	He was given power to make war against the saints and to conquer
	16:14	to gather them for the battle on the great day of God Almighty.
	19:19	and their armies gathered together to make war against the rider on
	20: 8	corners of the earth—Gog and Magog—to gather them for battle.

4484 πόλις, **polis** [162] [→ *315, 1279, 2631, 3268, 3619, 3735, 3736, 3776, 4485, 4486, 4487, 4488, 4489, 5232*]

ἅγιος πόλις (holy city) [6] Mt 4:5; 27:53; Rev 11:2; 21:2,10; 22:19

πόλις θεοῦ (city of God) [2] Heb 12:22; Rev 3:12

city [86], town [51], towns [12], cities [8], city's [1], from town to town [+*3836*] [1], place [1], there^s [*+ 1877+3836+4047*] [1], village [1]

Mt	2:23	and he went and lived in a town called Nazareth. So was fulfilled
	4: 5	Then the devil took him to the holy city and had him stand on the
	5:14	"You are the light of the world. A city on a hill cannot be hidden.
	5:35	his footstool; or by Jerusalem, for it is the city of the Great King.
	8:33	tending the pigs ran off, went into the town and reported all this,
	8:34	Then the whole town went out to meet Jesus. And when they saw
	9: 1	Jesus stepped into a boat, crossed over and came to his own town.
	9:35	Jesus went through all the towns and villages, teaching in their
	10: 5	not go among the Gentiles or enter any town of the Samaritans.
	10:11	"Whatever town or village you enter, search for some worthy
	10:14	shake the dust off your feet when you leave that home or town.
	10:15	and Gomorrah on the day of judgment than *for* that town.
	10:23	When you are persecuted in one place, flee to another. I tell you
	10:23	you will not finish going through the cities of Israel before the Son
	11: 1	he went on from there to teach and preach in the towns of Galilee.
	11:20	Then Jesus began to denounce the cities in which most of his
	12:25	and every city or household divided against itself will not stand.
	14:13	Hearing of this, the crowds followed him on foot from the towns.
	21:10	the whole city was stirred and asked, "Who is this?"
	21:17	And he left them and went out of the city to Bethany, where he
	21:18	the morning, as he was on his way back to the city, he was hungry.
	22: 7	sent his army and destroyed those murderers and burned their city.
	23:34	you will flog in your synagogues and pursue from town to town.
	23:34	you will flog in your synagogues and pursue from town to town.
	26:18	He replied, "Go into the city to a certain man and tell him,
	27:53	and after Jesus' resurrection they went into the holy city
	28:11	some of the guards went into the city and reported to the chief
Mk	1:33	The whole town gathered at the door,
	1:45	Jesus could no longer enter a town openly but stayed outside in
	5:14	the pigs ran off and reported this in the town and countryside,
	6:33	and ran on foot from all the towns and got there ahead of them.
	6:56	And wherever he went—into villages, towns or countryside—
	11:19	When evening came, they went out *of* the city.
	14:13	So he sent two of his disciples, telling them, "Go into the city,
	14:16	went into the city and found things just as Jesus had told them.
Lk	1:26	God sent the angel Gabriel to Nazareth, a town in Galilee,
	1:39	Mary got ready and hurried to a town in the hill country of Judea,
	2: 3	And everyone went to his own town to register.
	2: 4	So Joseph also went up from the town of Nazareth in Galilee to
	2: 4	of Nazareth in Galilee to Judea, to Bethlehem the town of David,
	2:11	Today in the town of David a Savior has been born to you;
	2:39	the Lord, they returned to Galilee to their own town of Nazareth.

	4:29	They got up, drove him out *of* the town, and took him to the brow
	4:29	and took him to the brow of the hill on which the town was built,
	4:31	Then he went down to Capernaum, a town in Galilee, and on the
	4:43	the good news of the kingdom of God *to* the other towns also,
	5:12	While Jesus was in one *of* the towns, a man came along who was
	7:11	Soon afterward, Jesus went to a town called Nain, and his disciples
	7:12	As he approached the town gate, a dead person was being carried
	7:12	she was a widow. And a large crowd *from* the town was with her.
	7:37	When a woman who had lived a sinful life in that town learned
	8: 1	Jesus traveled about from one town and village to another,
	8: 4	and people were coming to Jesus from town after town,
	8:27	he was met by a demon-possessed man from the town.
	8:34	they ran off and reported this in the town and countryside,
	8:39	and told all over town how much Jesus had done for him.
	9: 5	shake the dust off your feet when you leave their town, as a
	9:10	and they withdrew by themselves to a town called Bethsaida.
	10: 1	and sent them two by two ahead of him to every town and place
	10: 8	"When you enter a town and are welcomed, eat what is set before
	10:10	But when you enter a town and are not welcomed, go into its
	10:11	'Even the dust of your town that sticks to our feet we wipe off
	10:12	it will be more bearable on that day for Sodom than *for* that town.
	13:22	Then Jesus went through the towns and villages, teaching as he
	14:21	into the streets and alleys *of* the town and bring in the poor,
	18: 2	"In a certain town there was a judge who neither feared God nor
	18: 3	And there was a widow in that town who kept coming to him with
	19:17	been trustworthy in a very small matter, take charge of ten cities.'
	19:19	"His master answered, 'You take charge of five cities.'
	19:41	As he approached Jerusalem and saw the city, he wept over it
	22:10	He replied, "As you enter the city, a man carrying a jar of water
	23:19	had been thrown into prison for an insurrection in the city,
	23:51	He came from the Judean town of Arimathea and he was waiting
	24:49	but stay in the city until you have been clothed with power from on
Jn	1:44	Philip, like Andrew and Peter, was from the town of Bethsaida.
	4: 5	So he came to a town in Samaria called Sychar, near the plot of
	4: 8	(His disciples had gone into the town to buy food.)
	4:28	water jar, the woman went back to the town and said to the people,
	4:30	They came out of the town and made their way toward him.
	4:39	Many of the Samaritans from that town believed in him because of
	11:54	to a village called Ephraim, where he stayed with his disciples.
	19:20	this sign, for the place where Jesus was crucified was near the city,
Ac	4:27	and the people of Israel in this city to conspire against your holy
	5:16	Crowds gathered also *from* the towns around Jerusalem,
	7:58	dragged him out *of* the city and began to stone him. Meanwhile,
	8: 5	Philip went down to a city in Samaria and proclaimed the Christ
	8: 8	So there was great joy in that city.
	8: 9	some time a man named Simon had practiced sorcery in the city
	8:40	preaching the gospel in all the towns until he reached Caesarea.
	9: 6	"Now get up and go into the city, and you will be told what you
	10: 9	day as they were on their journey and approaching the city,
	11: 5	"I was in the city of Joppa praying, and in a trance I saw a vision.
	12:10	and second guards and came to the iron gate leading to the city.
	13:44	On the next Sabbath almost the whole city gathered to hear the
	13:50	women of high standing and the leading men *of* the city.
	14: 4	The people *of* the city were divided; some sided with the Jews,
	14: 6	out about it and fled to the Lycaonian cities of Lystra and Derbe
	14:13	whose temple was just outside the city, brought bulls and wreaths
	14:19	They stoned Paul and dragged him outside the city, thinking he
	14:20	had gathered around him, he got up and went back into the city.
	14:21	They preached the good news in that city and won a large number
	15:21	For Moses has been preached in every city from the earliest times
	15:36	and visit the brothers in all the towns where we preached the word
	16: 4	As they traveled from town [+*3836*] to town, they delivered the
	16:12	a Roman colony and the leading city of that district of Macedonia.
	16:12	And we stayed there^s [+*1877+3836+4047*] several days.
	16:14	a dealer in purple cloth *from* the city of Thyatira, who was a
	16:20	"These men are Jews, and are throwing our city into an uproar
	16:39	escorted them from the prison, requesting them to leave the city.
	17: 5	from the marketplace, formed a mob and started a riot in the city.
	17:16	he was greatly distressed to see that the city was full of idols.
	18:10	to attack and harm you, because I have many people in this city."
	19:29	Soon the whole city was in an uproar. The people seized Gaius
	19:35	doesn't all the world know that the city of Ephesus is the guardian
	20:23	I only know that in every city the Holy Spirit warns me that prison
	21: 5	and their wives and children accompanied us out of the city,
	21:29	(They had previously seen Trophimus the Ephesian in the city with
	21:30	The whole city was aroused, and the people came running from all

21:39 "I am a Jew, from Tarsus in Cilicia, a citizen *of* no ordinary **city**.
22: 3 "I am a Jew, born in Tarsus of Cilicia, but brought up in this **city**,
24:12 stirring up a crowd in the synagogues or anywhere else in the **city**.
25:23 with the high ranking officers and the leading men *of* the **city**.
26:11 against them, I even went to foreign **cities** to persecute them.
27: 8 and came to a place called Fair Havens, near the **town** of Lasea.
Ro 16:23 Erastus, who is the **city's** director of public works, and our brother
2Co 11:26 in danger in the **city**, in danger in the country, in danger at sea;
11:32 In Damascus the governor under King Aretas had the **city** of the
Tit   1: 5 out what was left unfinished and appoint elders in every **town**,
Heb 11:10 For he was looking forward to the **city** with foundations,
11:16 ashamed to be called their God, for he has prepared a **city** for them.
12:22 Mount Zion, to the heavenly Jerusalem, the **city** of the living God.
13:14 For here we do not have an enduring **city**, but we are looking for
Jas   4:13 you who say, "Today or tomorrow we will go to this or that **city**,
2Pe 2: 6 if he condemned the **cities** of Sodom and Gomorrah by burning
Jude 1: 7 and the surrounding **towns** gave themselves up to sexual
Rev 3:12 on him the name of my God and the name *of* the **city** of my God,
11: 2 to the Gentiles. They will trample on the holy **city** for 42 months.
11: 8 Their bodies will lie in the street *of* the great **city**, which is
11:13 there was a severe earthquake and a tenth *of* the **city** collapsed.
14:20 They were trampled in the winepress outside the **city**, and blood
16:19 The great **city** split into three parts, and the cities of the nations
16:19 city split into three parts, and the **cities** of the nations collapsed.
17:18 The woman you saw is the great **city** that rules over the kings of
18:10 and cry: " 'Woe! Woe, O great **city**, O Babylon, city of power!
18:10 and cry: " 'Woe! Woe, O great city, O Babylon, **city** of power!
18:16 Woe, O great **city**, dressed in fine linen, purple and scarlet,
18:18 they will exclaim, 'Was there ever a city like this great **city**?'
18:19 Woe, O great **city**, where all who had ships on the sea became rich
18:21 "With such violence the great **city** of Babylon will be thrown down,
20: 9 and surrounded the camp of God's people, the **city** he loves.
21: 2 I saw the Holy **City**, the new Jerusalem, coming down out of
21:10 Spirit to a mountain great and high, and showed me the Holy **City**,
21:14 The wall *of* the **city** had twelve foundations, and on them were the
21:15 talked with me had a measuring rod of gold to measure the **city**,
21:16 The **city** was laid out like a square, as long as it was wide.
21:16 He measured the **city** with the rod and found it to be 12,000 stadia
21:18 wall was made of jasper, and the **city** of pure gold, as pure as glass.
21:19 The foundations *of* the **city** walls were decorated with every kind
21:21 The great street *of* the **city** was of pure gold, like transparent glass.
21:23 The **city** does not need the sun or the moon to shine on it,
22:14 right to the tree of life and may go through the gates into the **city**.
22:19 take away from him his share in the tree of life and in the holy **city**,

4485 πολιτάρχης, politarchēs [2] [√ 4484 + 806]

city officials [2]

Ac 17: 6 dragged Jason and some other brothers before the **city officials**,
17: 8 the crowd and the **city officials** were thrown into turmoil.

4486 πολιτεία, politeia [2] [√ 4484]

citizenship [2]

Ac 22:28 the commander said, "I had to pay a big price for my **citizenship**."
Eph 2:12 excluded *from* **citizenship** in Israel and foreigners to the covenants

4487 πολίτευμα, politeuma [1] [√ 4484]

citizenship [1]

Php 3:20 But our **citizenship** is in heaven. And we eagerly await a Savior

4488 πολιτεύομαι, politeuomai [2] [√ 4484]

conduct [1], fulfilled duty [1]

Ac 23: 1 I *have* **fulfilled** *my* **duty** to God in all good conscience to this day."
Php 1:27 **conduct** *yourselves* in a manner worthy of the gospel of Christ.

4489 πολίτης, politēs [4] [√ 4484]

citizen [2], neighbor [1], subjects [1]

Lk 15:15 So he went and hired himself out to a **citizen** of that country,
19:14 "But his **subjects** hated him and sent a delegation after him to say,

Ac 21:39 "I am a Jew, from Tarsus in Cilicia, a **citizen** of no ordinary city.
Heb 8:11 No longer will a man teach his **neighbor**, or a man his brother,

4490 πολλάκις, pollakis [18] [√ 4498]

often [10], again and again [2], many times [2], *untranslated* [1], constantly [1], many a time [1]

Mt 17:15 is suffering greatly. He **often** falls into the fire or into the water.
17:15 He often falls into the fire or **[RPG]** into the water.
Mk 5: 4 For he had **often** been chained hand and foot, but he tore the chains
9:22 "It has **often** thrown him into fire or water to kill him. But if you
Jn 18: 2 the place, because Jesus had **often** met there with his disciples.
Ac 26:11 **Many a time** I went from one synagogue to another to have them
Ro   1:13 that I planned **many times** to come to you (but have been
2Co 8:22 we are sending with them our brother who has **often** proved to us
11:23 more severely, and been exposed to death **again and again**.
11:26 I have been **constantly** on the move. I have been in danger from
11:27 I have labored and toiled and have **often** gone without sleep;
11:27 I have known hunger and thirst and have **often** gone without food;
Php 3:18 as I have **often** told you before and now say again even with tears,
2Ti   1:16 because he **often** refreshed me and was not ashamed of my chains.
Heb 6: 7 Land that drinks in the rain **often** falling on it and that produces a
9:25 Nor did he enter heaven to offer himself **again and again**,
9:26 Then Christ would have had to suffer **many times** since the
10:11 **again and again** he offers the same sacrifices, which can never

4491 πολλαπλασίων, pollaplasiōn [1] [√ 4498]

many times as much [1]

Lk 18:30 will fail to receive **many times as much** in this age and, in the age

4492 πολυεύσπλαγχνος, polyeusplanchnos Not used in UBS/NIV [√ 4498 + 2292 + 5073]

4493 πολύλαλος, polylalos Not used in UBS/NIV [√ 4498 + 3281]

4494 πολυλογία, polylogia [1] [√ 4498 + 3306]

many words [1]

Mt 6: 7 for they think they will be heard because of their **many words**.

4495 πολυμερῶς, polymerōs [1] [√ 4498 + 3538]

at many times [1]

Heb 1: 1 God spoke to our forefathers through the prophets **at many times**

4496 πολυπλήθεια, polyplētheia Not used in UBS/NIV [√ 4498 + 4398]

4497 πολυποίκιλος, polypoikilos [1] [√ 4498 + 4476]

manifold [1]

Eph 3:10 the **manifold** wisdom of God should be made known to the rulers

4498 πολύς, polys [416 / 413] [→ 4102, 4490, 4491, 4492, 4493, 4494, 4495, 4496, 4497, 4499, 4500, 4501, 4502]

many [194], great [35], large [29], much [27], more [19], how much [8], most [8], greater [6], very [5], rushing [3], all the more [+3437] [2], all [2], few [+4024] [2], great deal of [2], great deal [2], long [2], majority [2], number [2], plentiful [2], plenty [2], strict [2], a long time [+2093] [1], again and again [1], all silent [+4968] [1], any further [+2093] [1], badly [1], before very long [+3552+4024] [1], besiege with questions [+694+4309] [1], better [1], beyond [+4440] [1], big [1], bigger [1], bold [1], by far [1], considerable [1], crowds [1], deep [1], earnestly [1], even more so [+5080] [1], freely [1], further [1], generously [1], get very far [+2093+4621] [1], greatly [1], hard [1], high [1], intense [1], larger [1], late in the day [+6052] [1], long [*+2465*] [1], long period [1], long time [1], loudly [1], many [*+4725*] [1], more [*+4123*] [1], more and more [*+2093*] [1], most [*+3836*] [1], often [1], on and on [*+2093*] [1], on the contrary [*+247+3437*] [1], only [*+2445+4024*] [1], over [1], plenty of [1], powerful [*+2710*] [1], reaching more and more [*+1328+3836+4429*] [1], several [1], severe [1], severely [1], strong [1], strongly [1], surpasses [*+4355*] [1], urgently [*+3552+4155*] [1], very large [1], violent [1], violently [1], warmly [1], wept and wept [*+3081*] [1], widespread [1]

Mt	2:18 "A voice is heard in Ramah, weeping and **great** mourning,
	3: 7 But when he saw **many** of the Pharisees and Sadducees coming to
	4:25 **Large** crowds from Galilee, the Decapolis, Jerusalem, Judea
	5:12 Rejoice and be glad, because **great** is your reward in heaven,
	5:20 For I tell you that unless your righteousness **surpasses** [*+4355*]
	6:25 Is not life **more** *important than* food, and the body more
	6:30 the fire, will he not **much** more clothe you, O you of little faith?
	7:13 is the road that leads to destruction, and **many** enter through it.
	7:22 **Many** will say to me on that day, 'Lord, Lord, did we not prophesy
	7:22 and in your name drive out demons and perform **many** miracles?'
	8: 1 he came down from the mountainside, **large** crowds followed him.
	8:11 I say to you that **many** will come from the east and the west,
	8:16 **many** who were demon-possessed were brought to him,
	8:30 Some distance from them a **large** herd of pigs was feeding.
	9:10 **many** tax collectors and "sinners" came and ate with him and his
	9:14 the Pharisees fast [UBS+ *often*], but your disciples do not fast?"
	9:37 to his disciples, "The harvest is **plentiful** but the workers are few.
	10:31 So don't be afraid; you are worth more than **many** sparrows.
	11:20 Then Jesus began to denounce the cities in which **most** of his
	12:15 from that place. **Many** followed him, and he healed all their sick,
	12:41 at the preaching of Jonah, and now *one* **greater** *than* Jonah is here.
	12:42 to Solomon's wisdom, and now *one* **greater** *than* Solomon is here.
	13: 2 *Such* **large** crowds gathered around him that he got into a boat
	13: 3 Then he told them **many** *things* in parables, saying: "A farmer went
	13: 5 Some fell on rocky places, where it did not have **much** soil.
	13:17 **many** prophets and righteous men longed to see what you saw
	13:58 And he did not do **many** miracles there because of their lack of
	14:14 When Jesus landed and saw a **large** crowd, he had compassion on
	14:24 but the boat was already a **considerable** distance from land,
	15:30 **Great** crowds came to him, bringing the lame, the blind,
	15:30 the lame, the blind, the crippled, the mute and **many** others,
	16:21 go to Jerusalem and suffer **many** *things* at the hands of the elders,
	19: 2 **Large** crowds followed him, and he healed them there.
	19:22 man heard this, he went away sad, because he had **great** wealth.
	19:30 But **many** who are first will be last, and many who are last will be
	20:10 those came who were hired first, they expected to receive **more**.
	20:28 be served, but to serve, and to give his life as a ransom for **many**."
	20:29 his disciples were leaving Jericho, a **large** crowd followed him.
	21: 8 A **very large** crowd spread their cloaks on the road, while others
	21:36 Then he sent other servants to them, **more** *than* the first time,
	22:14 "For **many** are invited, but few are chosen."
	24: 5 For **many** will come in my name, claiming, 'I am the Christ,'
	24: 5 in my name, claiming, 'I am the Christ,' and will deceive **many**.
	24:10 At that time **many** will turn away from the faith and will betray
	24:11 and **many** false prophets will appear and deceive many people.
	24:11 and many false prophets will appear and deceive **many** *people*.
	24:12 of the increase of wickedness, the love *of* **most** will grow cold,
	24:30 Man coming on the clouds of the sky, with power and **great** glory.
	25:19 "After a **long** time the master of those servants returned and settled
	25:21 faithful with a few things; I will put you in charge of **many** *things*.
	25:23 faithful with a few things; I will put you in charge of **many** *things*.
	26: 9 "This perfume could have been sold *at* a **high** *price* and the money
	26:28 which is poured out for **many** for the forgiveness of sins.
	26:47 With him was a **large** crowd armed with swords and clubs,
	26:53 and he will at once put at my disposal **more** *than* twelve legions of
	26:60 they did not find any, though **many** false witnesses came forward.
	27:19 for I have suffered a **great deal** today in a dream because of him."
	27:52 and the bodies of **many** holy people who had died were raised to
	27:53 they went into the holy city and appeared *to* **many** *people*.
	27:55 **Many** women were there, watching from a distance. They had
Mk	1:34 and Jesus healed **many** who had various diseases. He also drove
	1:34 He also drove out **many** demons, but he would not let the demons
	1:45 Instead he went out and began to talk **freely**, spreading the news.
	2: 2 So **many** gathered that there was no room left, not even outside the
	2:15 **many** tax collectors and "sinners" were eating with him and his
	2:15 and his disciples, for there were **many** who followed him.
	3: 7 his disciples to the lake, and a **large** crowd from Galilee followed.
	3: 8 **many** people came to him from Judea, Jerusalem, Idumea,
	3:10 For he had healed **many**, so that those with diseases were pushing
	3:12 But he gave them **strict** orders not to tell who he was.
	4: 1 *so* **large** that he got into a boat and sat in it out on the lake,
	4: 2 He taught them **many** *things* by parables, and in his teaching said:
	4: 5 Some fell on rocky places, where it did not have **much** soil.
	4:33 *With* **many** similar parables Jesus spoke the word to them,
	5: 9 your name?" "My name is Legion," he replied, "for we are **many**."
	5:10 And he begged Jesus **again and again** not to send them out of the
	5:21 a **large** crowd gathered around him while he was by the lake.
	5:23 and pleaded **earnestly** with him, "My little daughter is dying.
	5:24 went with him. A **large** crowd followed and pressed around him.
	5:26 She had suffered a **great deal** under the care of many doctors
	5:26 She had suffered a great deal under the care *of* **many** doctors
	5:38 Jesus saw a commotion, with people crying and wailing **loudly**.
	5:43 He gave **strict** orders not to let anyone know about this, and told
	6: 2 to teach in the synagogue, and **many** who heard him were amazed.
	6:13 They drove out **many** demons and anointed many sick people with
	6:13 and anointed **many** sick people with oil and healed them.
	6:20 When Herod heard John, he was **greatly** puzzled; yet he liked to
	6:23 And he promised her with [UBS+ *many*] an oath, "Whatever you
	6:31 because *so* **many** *people* were coming and going that they did not
	6:33 But **many** who saw them leaving recognized them and ran on foot
	6:34 When Jesus landed and saw a **large** crowd, he had compassion on
	6:34 without a shepherd. So he began teaching them **many** *things*.
	6:35 By this time it was **late in the day** [*+6052*], so his disciples came
	6:35 "This is a remote place," they said, "and it's already **very** late.
	7: 4 And they observe **many** other traditions, such as the washing of
	7:13 that you have handed down. And you do **many** *things* like that."
	8: 1 During those days another **large** crowd gathered. Since they had
	8:31 began to teach them that the Son of Man must suffer **many** *things*
	9:12 Why then is it written that the Son of Man must suffer **much**
	9:14 they saw a **large** crowd around them and the teachers of the law
	9:26 The spirit shrieked, convulsed him **violently** and came out.
	9:26 The boy looked so much like a corpse that **many** said, "He's dead."
	10:22 man's face fell. He went away sad, because he had **great** wealth.
	10:31 But **many** who are first will be last, and the last first."
	10:45 be served, but to serve, and to give his life as a ransom for **many**."
	10:48 **Many** rebuked him and told him to be quiet,
	10:48 but he shouted **all the more** [*+3437*], "Son of David, have mercy
	11: 8 **Many** *people* spread their cloaks on the road, while others spread
	12: 5 He sent **many** others; some of them they beat, others they killed.
	12:27 not the God of the dead, but of the living. You are **badly** mistaken!"
	12:37 can he be his son?" The **large** crowd listened to him with delight.
	12:41 into the temple treasury. **Many** rich people threw in large amounts.
	12:41 the temple treasury. Many rich people threw in **large** *amounts*.
	12:43 this poor widow has put **more** into the treasury *than* all the others.
	13: 6 **Many** will come in my name, claiming, 'I am he,' and will deceive
	13: 6 come in my name, claiming, 'I am he,' and will deceive **many**.
	13:26 men will see the Son of Man coming in clouds with **great** power
	14:24 of the covenant, which is poured out for **many**," he said to them.
	14:56 **Many** testified falsely against him, but their statements did not
	15: 3 The chief priests accused him of **many** *things*.
	15:41 **Many** other *women* who had come up with him to Jerusalem were
Lk	1: 1 **Many** have undertaken to draw up an account of the things that
	1:14 and delight to you, and **many** will rejoice because of his birth,
	1:16 **Many** of the people of Israel will he bring back to the Lord their
	2:34 child is destined to cause the falling and rising *of* **many** in Israel,
	2:35 so that the thoughts of **many** hearts will be revealed. And a sword
	2:36 She was **very** old; she had lived with her husband seven years after
	3:13 "Don't collect any **more** [*+4123*] *than* you are required to,"
	3:18 And with **many** other words John exhorted the people
	4:25 I assure you that there were **many** widows in Israel in Elijah's
	4:27 And there were **many** in Israel with leprosy in the time of Elisha
	4:41 Moreover, demons came out of **many** *people*, shouting, "You are
	5: 6 they caught *such* a **large** number of fish that their nets began to
	5:15 so that **crowds** of people came to hear him and to be healed of
	5:29 and a **large** crowd of tax collectors and others were eating with
	6:17 A **large** crowd of his disciples was there and a great number of
	6:17 was there and a **great** number of people from all over Judea,
	6:23 and leap for joy, because **great** is your reward in heaven.
	6:35 Then your reward will be **great**, and you will be sons of the Most
	7:11 and his disciples and a **large** crowd went along with him.
	7:21 At that very time Jesus cured **many** who had diseases, sicknesses
	7:21 sicknesses and evil spirits, and gave sight *to* **many** who were blind.

7:42 the debts of both. Now which of them will love him **more**?"
7:43 "I suppose the one who had the **bigger** debt canceled."
7:47 Therefore, I tell you, her **many** sins have been forgiven—for she
7:47 I tell you, her many sins have been forgiven—for she loved **much**.
8: 3 the manager of Herod's household; Susanna; and **many** others.
8: 4 While a **large** crowd was gathering and people were coming to
8:29 **Many** times it had seized him, and though he was chained hand
8:30 "Legion," he replied, because **many** demons had gone into him.
9:13 "We have **only** [+2445+4024] five loaves of bread and two fish—
9:22 "The Son of Man must suffer **many** *things* and be rejected by the
9:37 when they came down from the mountain, a **large** crowd met him.
10: 2 He told them, "The harvest is **plentiful**, but the workers are few.
10:24 For I tell you that **many** prophets and kings wanted to see what
10:40 But Martha was distracted by **all** the preparations that had to be
10:41 the Lord answered, "you are worried and upset about **many** *things*,
11:31 to Solomon's wisdom, and now *one* **greater** *than* Solomon is here.
11:32 at the preaching of Jonah, and now *one* **greater** *than* Jonah is here.
11:53 him fiercely and *to* **besiege** him **with questions** [+694+4309],
12: 7 Don't be afraid; you are worth more than **many** sparrows.
12:19 to myself, "You have **plenty** of good things laid up for many years.
12:19 to myself, "You have plenty of good things laid up for **many** years.
12:23 Life is **more** *than* food, and the body more than clothes.
12:47 or does not do what his master wants will be beaten with **many**
12:48 From everyone who has been given **much**, much will be
12:48 everyone who has been given much, **much** will be demanded;
12:48 and from the one who has been entrusted with **much**, much more
13:24 because **many**, I tell you, will try to enter and will not be able to.
14:16 man was preparing a great banquet and invited **many** *guests*.
14:25 **Large** crowds were traveling with Jesus, and turning to them he
15:13 "Not **long** [+2465] after that, the younger son got together all he
16:10 can be trusted with very little can also be trusted with **much**,
16:10 is dishonest with very little will also be dishonest with **much**.
17:25 But first he must suffer **many** *things* and be rejected by this
18:39 but he shouted **all the more** [+3437], "Son of David, have mercy
21: 3 he said, "this poor widow has put in **more** *than* all the others.
21: 8 For **many** will come in my name, claiming, 'I am he,' and,
21:27 see the Son of Man coming in a cloud with power and **great** glory.
22:65 And they said **many** other insulting *things* to him.
23:27 A **large** number of people followed him, including women who

Jn 2:12 and his disciples. There they stayed *for* a **few** [+4024] days.
2:23 **many** *people* saw the miraculous signs he was doing and believed
3:23 baptizing at Aenon near Salim, because there was **plenty of** water,
4: 1 that Jesus was gaining and baptizing **more** disciples than John,
4:39 **Many** of the Samaritans from that town believed in him because of
4:41 And because of his words **many** more became believers.
4:41 And because of his words many more became **believers**.
5: 6 and learned that he had been in this condition *for* a **long** time,
6: 2 and a **great** crowd of people followed him because they saw the
6: 5 When Jesus looked up and saw a **great** crowd coming toward him,
6:10 There was **plenty** of grass in that place, and the men sat down,
6:60 On hearing it, **many** of his disciples said, "This is a hard teaching.
6:66 From this time **many** of his disciples turned back and no longer
7:12 Among the crowds there was **widespread** whispering about him.
7:31 Still, **many** in the crowd put their faith in him. They said,
7:31 the Christ comes, will he do **more** miraculous signs *than* this man?"
8:26 "I have **much** to say in judgment of you. But he who sent me is
8:30 Even as he spoke, **many** put their faith in him.
10:20 **Many** of them said, "He is demon-possessed and raving mad.
10:32 to them, "I have shown you **many** great miracles from the Father.
10:41 and **many** *people* came to him. They said, "Though John never
10:42 And in that place **many** believed in Jesus.
11:19 and **many** Jews had come to Martha and Mary to comfort them in
11:45 Therefore **many** of the Jews who had come to visit Mary,
11:47 they asked. "Here is this man performing **many** miraculous signs.
11:55 **many** went up from the country to Jerusalem for their ceremonial
12: 9 Meanwhile a **large** crowd of Jews found out that Jesus was there
12:11 for on account of him **many** of the Jews were going over to Jesus
12:12 The next day the **great** crowd that had come for the Feast heard
12:24 remains only a single seed. But if it dies, it produces **many** seeds.
12:42 Yet at the same time **many** even among the leaders believed in
14: 2 In my Father's house are **many** rooms; if it were not so, I would
14:30 I will not speak with you **much** longer, for the prince of this world
15: 2 that does bear fruit he prunes so that it will be even **more** fruitful.
15: 5 If a man remains in me and I in him, he will bear **much** fruit;
15: 8 This is to my Father's glory, that you bear **much** fruit, showing
16:12 "I have **much** more to say to you, more than you can now bear.

19:20 **Many** of the Jews read this sign, for the place where Jesus was
20:30 Jesus did **many** other miraculous signs in the presence of his
21:15 "Simon son of John, do you truly love me **more** *than* these?"
21:25 Jesus did **many** other things as well. If every one of them were

Ac 1: 3 to these men and gave **many** convincing proofs that he was alive.
1: 5 but in a **few** [+4024] days you will be baptized with the Holy
2:40 *With* **many** other words he warned them; and he pleaded with
2:43 and **many** wonders and miraculous signs were done by the
4: 4 But **many** who heard the message believed, and the number of
4:17 But to stop this thing from spreading **any further** [+2093] among
4:22 For the man who was miraculously healed was **over** forty years
5:12 The apostles performed **many** miraculous signs and wonders
6: 7 and a **large** number of priests became obedient to the faith.
8: 7 With shrieks, evil spirits came out of **many**, and many paralytics
8: 7 came out of many, and **many** paralytics and cripples were healed.
8: 8 So there was **great** joy in that city.
8:25 to Jerusalem, preaching the gospel *in* **many** Samaritan villages.
9:13 "I have heard **many** *reports* about this man and all the harm he has
9:42 known all over Joppa, and **many** *people* believed in the Lord.
10: 2 he gave **generously** to those in need and prayed to God regularly.
10:27 with him, Peter went inside and found a **large** gathering of people.
11:21 and a **great** number of people believed and turned to the Lord.
13:31 and for **many** days he was seen by those who had traveled with
13:43 **many** of the Jews and devout converts to Judaism followed Paul
14: 1 There they spoke so effectively that a **great** number of Jews
14:22 must go through **many** hardships to enter the kingdom of God,"
15: 7 After **much** discussion, Peter got up and addressed them: "Brothers,
15:28 and to us not to burden you with anything **beyond** [+4440] the
15:32 said **much** to encourage and strengthen the brothers.
15:35 where they and **many** others taught and preached the word of the
16:16 She earned a **great deal of** money for her owners by
16:18 She kept this up for **many** days. Finally Paul became so troubled
16:23 After they had been **severely** flogged, they were thrown into
17: 4 as did a **large** number of God-fearing Greeks and not a few
17:12 **Many** of the Jews believed, as did also a number of prominent
18: 8 and **many** of the Corinthians who heard him believed and were
18:10 to attack and harm you, because I have **many** people in this city."
18:20 When they asked him to spend **more** time with them, he declined.
18:27 he was a **great** help to those who by grace had believed.
19:18 **Many** of those who believed now came and openly confessed their
19:32 **Most** [+3836] of the *people* did not even know why they were
20: 2 speaking **many** words of encouragement to the people, and finally
20: 9 was sinking into a deep sleep as Paul talked **on** [+2093] **and on**.
21:10 After we had been there a **number** of days, a prophet named
21:40 When they were **all silent** [+4968], he said to them in Aramaic:
22:28 the commander said, "I had to pay a **big** price for my citizenship."
23:10 so **violent** that the commander was afraid Paul would be torn to
23:13 **More** *than* forty men were involved in this plot.
23:21 because **more** *than* forty of them are waiting in ambush for him.
24: 2 "We have enjoyed a **long period** of peace under you, and your
24: 4 But in order not to weary you **further**, I would request that you be
24:10 "I know that for a **number** of years you have been a judge over this
24:11 You can easily verify that no **more** *than* twelve days ago I went up
24:17 "After an absence *of* **several** years, I came to Jerusalem to bring my
25: 6 After spending [UBS+ *not more than*] eight or ten days with them,
25: 7 bringing **many** serious charges against him, which they could not
25:14 Since they were spending **many** days there, Festus discussed
25:23 The next day Agrippa and Bernice came with **great** pomp
26: 9 "I too was convinced that I ought to do **all** *that was possible* to
26:10 On the authority of the chief priests I put **many** of the saints in
26:24 Paul!" he shouted. "Your **great** learning is driving you insane."
27:10 is going to be disastrous and bring **great** loss to ship and cargo,
27:12 the **majority** decided that we should sail on, hoping to reach
27:14 **Before very** [+3552+4024] **long**, a wind of hurricane force,
27:20 When neither sun nor stars appeared for **many** days and the storm
27:21 After the men had gone a **long time** without food, Paul stood up
28: 6 but after waiting a **long** [+2093] **time** and seeing nothing unusual
28:10 They honored us *in* **many** ways and when we were ready to sail,
28:23 and came *in even* **larger** *numbers* to the place where he was

Ro 3: 2 **Much** in every way! First of all, they have been entrusted with the
4:17 As it is written: "I have made you a father *of* **many** nations."
4:18 in hope believed and so became the father *of* **many** nations,
5: 9 **how much** more shall we be saved from God's wrath through him!
5:10 **how much** more, having been reconciled, shall we be saved
5:15 For if the **many** died by the trespass of the one man, how much
5:15 **how much** more did God's grace and the gift that came by the

5: 15 by the grace of the one man, Jesus Christ, overflow to the **many**!
5: 16 but the gift followed **many** trespasses and brought justification.
5: 17 **how much** more will those who receive God's abundant provision
5: 19 For just as through the disobedience of the one man the **many** were
5: 19 so also through the obedience of the one man the **many** will be
8: 29 of his Son, that he might be the firstborn among **many** brothers.
9: 22 power known, bore with **great** patience the objects of his wrath—
12: 4 Just as each of us has one body with **many** members, and these
12: 5 so in Christ we who are **many** form one body, and each member
15: 22 This is why I have **often** been hindered from coming to you.
15: 23 and since I have been longing for **many** years to see you,
16: 2 for she has been a great help *to* **many** *people*, including me.
16: 6 Greet Mary, who worked **very** hard for you.
16: 12 another woman who has worked **very** hard in the Lord.
1Co 1: 26 Not **many** of you were wise by human standards; not many were
1: 26 not **many** were influential; not **many** were of noble birth.
1: 26 not many were influential; not **many** were of noble birth.
2: 3 I came to you in weakness and fear, and with **much** trembling.
4: 15 ten thousand guardians in Christ, you do not have **many** fathers,
8: 5 or on earth (as indeed there are **many** "gods" and many "lords"),
8: 5 or on earth (as indeed there are many "gods" and **many** "lords"),
9: 19 I make myself a slave to everyone, to win *as* **many** *as possible.*
10: 5 Nevertheless, God was not pleased with **most** of them; their bodies
10: 17 Because there is one loaf, we, who are **many**, are one body,
10: 33 For I am not seeking my own good but the good *of* **many**,
11: 30 That is why **many** among you are weak and sick, and a number of
12: 12 The body is a unit, though it is made up of **many** parts; and though
12: 12 many parts; and though all its parts are **many**, they form one body.
12: 14 Now the body is not made up of one part but of **many**.
12: 20 As it is, there are **many** parts, but one body.
12: 22 **On the contrary** [*+247+3437*], those parts of the body that seem
14: 27 If anyone speaks in a tongue, two—or at the **most** three—
15: 6 **most** of whom are still living, though some have fallen asleep.
16: 9 work has opened to me, and there are **many** who oppose me.
16: 12 I **strongly** urged him to go to you with the brothers.
16: 19 Aquila and Priscilla greet you **warmly** in the Lord, and so does the
2Co 1: 11 Then **many** [*+4725*] will give thanks on our behalf for the gracious
1: 11 for the gracious favor granted us in answer to the prayers *of* **many**.
2: 4 For I wrote you out of **great** distress and anguish of heart and with
2: 4 you out of great distress and anguish of heart and with **many** tears,
2: 6 The punishment inflicted on him by the **majority** is sufficient for
2: 17 Unlike *so* **many**, we do not peddle the word of God for profit.
3: 9 **how much** more glorious is the ministry that brings righteousness!
3: 11 with glory, **how much** greater is the glory of that which lasts!
3: 12 Therefore, since we have such a hope, we are **very** bold.
4: 15 so that the grace that *is* **reaching more and more people**
[*+1328+3836+4429*] may cause thanksgiving to overflow to the
6: 4 in **great** endurance; in troubles, hardships and distresses;
6: 10 poor, yet making **many** rich; having nothing, and yet possessing
7: 4 I have **great** confidence in you; I take great pride in you. I am
7: 4 I have great confidence in you; I take **great** pride in you. I am
8: 2 Out of the **most** severe trial, their overflowing joy and their
8: 4 they **urgently** [*+3552+4155*] pleaded with us for the privilege of
8: 15 "He who gathered **much** did not have too much, and he who
8: 22 who has often proved to us in **many** *ways* that he is zealous,
8: 22 and now **even more so**[s] [*+5080*] because of his great confidence
8: 22 and now even more so *because of* his **great** confidence in you.
9: 2 to give; and your enthusiasm has stirred **most** *of them* to action.
9: 12 but is also overflowing in **many** expressions of thanks to God.
11: 18 Since **many** are boasting in the way the world does, I too will
12: 21 and I will be grieved over **many** who have sinned earlier and have
Gal 1: 14 I was advancing in Judaism beyond **many** Jews of my own age
3: 16 meaning **many** *people*, but "and to your seed," meaning one person
4: 27 because **more** are the children of the desolate woman than of her
Eph 2: 4 But because of his **great** love for us, God, who is rich in mercy,
Php 1: 14 **most** of the brothers in the Lord have been encouraged to speak the
1: 23 I desire to depart and be with Christ, which is better **by far**;
2: 12 not only in my presence, but now **much** more in my absence—
3: 18 again even with tears, **many** live as enemies of the cross of Christ.
Col 4: 13 I vouch for him that he is working **hard** for you and for those at
1Th 1: 5 also with power, with the Holy Spirit and with **deep** conviction.
1: 6 in spite of **severe** suffering, you welcomed the message with the
2: 2 God we dared to tell you his gospel in spite of **strong** opposition.
2: 17 out of our **intense** longing we made every effort to see you.
1Ti 3: 8 to be men worthy of respect, sincere, not indulging *in* **much** wine,
3: 13 standing and **great** assurance in their faith in Christ Jesus.

6: 9 and a trap and into **many** foolish and harmful desires that plunge
6: 10 wandered from the faith and pierced themselves *with* **many** griefs.
6: 12 made your good confession in the presence *of* **many** witnesses.
2Ti 2: 2 And the things you have heard me say in the presence of **many**
2: 16 those who indulge in it will become **more** [*+2093*] **and more**
3: 9 But *they will* not **get very far** [*+2093+4621*] because, as in the
4: 14 Alexander the metalworker did me a **great deal of** harm. The Lord
Tit 1: 10 For there are **many** rebellious people, mere talkers and deceivers,
2: 3 not to be slanderers or addicted *to* **much** wine, but to teach what is
Phm 1: 7 Your love has given me **great** joy and encouragement,
1: 8 *although* in Christ I *could be* **bold** [*+2400+4244*] and order you to
Heb 2: 10 In bringing **many** sons to glory, it was fitting that God, for whom
3: 3 Jesus has been found worthy of **greater** honor than Moses,
3: 3 just as the builder of a house has **greater** honor *than* the house
5: 11 We have **much** to say about this,
7: 23 Now there have been **many** of those priests, since death prevented
9: 28 Christ was sacrificed once to take away the sins of **many** *people*;
10: 32 when you stood your ground in a **great** contest in the face of
11: 4 By faith Abel offered God a **better** sacrifice than Cain did.
12: 9 **How much** more should we submit to the Father of our spirits
12: 15 and that no bitter root grows up to cause trouble and defile **many**.
12: 25 **how much** less will we, if we turn away from him who warns us
Jas 3: 1 Not **many** of you should presume to be teachers, my brothers,
3: 2 We all stumble in **many** ways. If anyone is never at fault in what
5: 16 The prayer of a righteous man *is* **powerful** [*+2710*] and effective.
1Pe 1: 3 In his **great** mercy he has given us new birth into a living hope
2Pe 2: 2 **Many** will follow their shameful ways and will bring the way of
1Jn 2: 18 the antichrist is coming, even now **many** antichrists have come.
4: 1 because **many** false prophets have gone out into the world.
2Jn 1: 7 **Many** deceivers, who do not acknowledge Jesus Christ as coming
1: 12 I have **much** to write to you, but I do not want to use paper
3Jn 1: 13 I have **much** to write to you, but I do not want to do so with pen
Rev 1: 15 in a furnace, and his voice was like the sound *of* **rushing** waters.
2: 19 and that you are now doing **more** *than* you did at first.
5: 4 *I* **wept and wept** [*+3081*] because no one was found who was
5: 11 Then I looked and heard the voice *of* **many** angels, numbering
7: 9 and there before me was a **great** multitude that no one could count,
8: 3 He was given **much** incense to offer, with the prayers of all the
8: 11 and **many** people died from the waters that had become bitter.
9: 9 and the sound of their wings was like the thundering *of* **many**
10: 11 "You must prophesy again about **many** peoples, nations, languages
14: 2 And I heard a sound from heaven like the roar *of* **rushing** waters.
17: 1 the punishment of the great prostitute, who sits on **many** waters.
19: 1 After this I heard what sounded like the roar *of* a **great** multitude
19: 6 Then I heard what sounded like a **great** multitude, like the roar of
19: 6 like the roar *of* **rushing** waters and like loud peals of thunder,
19: 12 His eyes are like blazing fire, and on his head are **many** crowns.

4499 πολύσπλαγχνος, *polysplanchnos* [1]
[√ *4498 + 5073*]

full of compassion [1]

Jas 5: 11 finally brought about. The Lord is **full of compassion** and mercy.

4500 πολυτελής, *polytelēs* [3] [√ *4498 + 5465*]

expensive [1], great worth [1], very expensive [1]

Mk 14: 3 a woman came with an alabaster jar *of* **very expensive** perfume,
1Ti 2: 9 not with braided hair or gold or pearls or **expensive** clothes,
1Pe 3: 4 of a gentle and quiet spirit, which is of **great worth** in God's sight.

4501 πολύτιμος, *polytimos* [3] [√ *4498 + 5507*]

expensive [1], great value [1], greater worth [1]

Mt 13:46 When he found one *of* **great value**, he went away and sold
Jn 12: 3 Then Mary took about a pint of pure nard, an **expensive** perfume;
1Pe 1: 7 of **greater worth** *than* gold, which perishes even though refined

4502 πολυτρόπως, *polytropōs* [1] [√ *4498 + 5572*]

in various ways [1]

Heb 1: 1 through the prophets at many times and **in various ways**,

4503 πόμα, poma [2] [√ 4403]

drink [2]

1Co 10: 4 and drank the same spiritual **drink**; for they drank from the
Heb 9:10 They are only a matter of food and **drink** and various ceremonial

4504 πονηρία, ponēria [7] [√ 4505]

evil [3], wickedness [2], malice [1], wicked ways [1]

Mt 22:18 But Jesus, knowing their **evil** *intent*, said, "You hypocrites,
Mk 7:22 greed, **malice**, deceit, lewdness, envy, slander, arrogance and folly.
Lk 11:39 and dish, but inside you are full of greed and **wickedness**.
Ac 3:26 you to bless you by turning each of you from your **wicked ways**."
Ro 1:29 filled with every kind of wickedness, **evil**, greed and depravity.
1Co 5: 8 not with the old yeast, the yeast *of* malice and **wickedness**,
Eph 6:12 and against the spiritual forces *of* **evil** in the heavenly realms.

4505 πονηρός, ponēros [78] [→ 4504; cf. 4506]

ὁ πονηρός (the evil [one]) [18] Mt 5:37,39; 6:13; 13:19,38; Lk 6:45,45,45; Jn 17:15; Ro 12:9; 1Co 5:13; Eph 6:16; 2Th 3:3; 1Jn 2:13,14; 3:12; 5:18,19

καλός ... πονηρός (good ... evil) [3] Mt 7:17,18; 13:38

πονηρός ἔργον (evil deed) [6] Jn 3:19; 7:7; Col 1:21; 2Ti 4:18; 1Jn 3:12; 2Jn 1:11

πονηρός πνεῦμα (evil spirit) [8] Mt 12:45; Lk 7:21; 8:2; 11:26; Ac 19:12,13,15,16

evil [47], wicked [11], bad [7], more wicked [2], crimes [1], demon-possessed [+2400+3836+3836+4460] [1], envious [+1639+3836+4057] [1], envy [+4057] [1], evil one [1], evils [1], guilty conscience [+5287] [1], maliciously [+3364] [1], painful [1], serious [1], sinful [1]

Mt 5:11 persecute you and falsely say all kinds of **evil** against you
5:37 your 'No,' 'No'; anything beyond this comes from the **evil** one.
5:39 But I tell you, Do not resist an **evil** *person*. If someone strikes you
5:45 He causes his sun to rise on the **evil** and the good, and sends rain
6:13 And lead us not into temptation, but deliver us from the **evil** one.'
6:23 But if your eyes are **bad**, your whole body will be full of darkness.
7:11 If you, then, though you are **evil**, know how to give good gifts to
7:17 every good tree bears good fruit, but a bad tree bears **bad** fruit.
7:18 A good tree cannot bear **bad** fruit, and a bad tree cannot bear good
9: 4 Jesus said, "Why do you entertain **evil** thoughts in your hearts?
12:34 You brood of vipers, how can you who are **evil** say anything good?
12:35 The **evil** man brings evil things out of the evil stored up in him.
12:35 and the evil man brings **evil** *things* out of the evil stored up in him.
12:35 and the evil man brings evil things out of the **evil** stored up in him.
12:39 "A **wicked** and adulterous generation asks for a miraculous sign!
12:45 and takes with it seven other spirits **more wicked** *than* itself,
12:45 than the first. That is how it will be *with* this **wicked** generation."
13:19 the **evil** one comes and snatches away what was sown in his heart.
13:38 the sons of the kingdom. The weeds are the sons *of* the **evil** *one*,
13:49 The angels will come and separate the **wicked** from the righteous
15:19 For out of the heart come **evil** thoughts, murder, adultery,
16: 4 A **wicked** and adulterous generation looks for a miraculous sign,
18:32 'You **wicked** servant,' he said, 'I canceled all that debt of yours
20:15 Or are you **envious** [+1639+3836+4057] because I am generous?'
22:10 and gathered all the people they could find, both good and **bad**,
25:26 "His master replied, 'You **wicked**, lazy servant! So you knew that I
Mk 7:22 greed, malice, deceit, lewdness, **envy** [+4057], slander, arrogance
7:23 All these **evils** come from inside and make a man 'unclean.' "
Lk 3:19 his brother's wife, and all the other **evil** *things* he had done,
6:22 when they exclude you and insult you and reject your name as **evil**,
6:35 of the Most High, because he is kind to the ungrateful and **wicked**.
6:45 and the **evil** *man* brings evil things out of the evil stored up in his
6:45 and the evil man brings **evil** *things* out of the evil stored up in his
6:45 and the evil man brings evil things out of the **evil** stored up in his
7:21 sickness and **evil** spirits, and gave sight to many who were blind.
8: 2 and also some women who had been cured of **evil** spirits
11:13 If you then, though you are **evil**, know how to give good gifts to
11:26 Then it goes and takes seven other spirits **more wicked** *than* itself,
11:29 As the crowds increased, Jesus said, "This is a **wicked** generation.
11:34 But when they are **bad**, your body also is full of darkness.
19:22 'I will judge you by your own words, *you* **wicked** servant!

Jn 3:19 men loved darkness instead of light because their deeds were **evil**.
7: 7 hate you, but it hates me because I testify that what it does is **evil**.
17:15 them out of the world but that you protect them from the **evil** one.
Ac 17: 5 so they rounded up some **bad** characters from the marketplace,
18:14 making a complaint about some misdemeanor or **serious** crime,
19:12 and their illnesses were cured and the **evil** spirits left them.
19:13 those *who were* **demon-possessed** [+2400+3836+3836+4460].
19:15 ⌊One day⌋ the **evil** spirit answered them, "Jesus I know, and I know
19:16 Then the man who had the **evil** spirit jumped on them
25:18 they did not charge him with any *of* the **crimes** I had expected.
28:21 have come from there has reported or said anything **bad** about you.
Ro 12: 9 Love must be sincere. Hate what is **evil**; cling to what is good.
1Co 5:13 will judge those outside. "Expel the **wicked** *man* from among you."
Gal 1: 4 who gave himself for our sins to rescue us from the present **evil**
Eph 5:16 making the most of every opportunity, because the days are **evil**.
6:13 so that when the day *of* **evil** comes, you may be able to stand your
6:16 which you can extinguish all the flaming arrows *of* the **evil** one.
Col 1:21 and were enemies in your minds because of your **evil** behavior.
1Th 5:22 Avoid every kind *of* **evil**.
2Th 3: 2 And pray that we may be delivered from wicked and **evil** men,
3: 3 and he will strengthen and protect you from the **evil** one.
1Ti 6: 4 words that result in envy, strife, malicious talk, **evil** suspicions
2Ti 3:13 while **evil** men and impostors will go from bad to worse, deceiving
4:18 The Lord will rescue me from every **evil** attack and will bring me
Heb 3:12 See to it, brothers, that none of you has a **sinful**, unbelieving heart
10:22 hearts sprinkled to cleanse us from a **guilty conscience** [+5287]
Jas 2: 4 among yourselves and become judges *with* **evil** thoughts?
4:16 As it is, you boast and brag. All such boasting is **evil**.
1Jn 2:13 write to you, young men, because you have overcome the **evil** one.
2:14 the word of God lives in you, and you have overcome the **evil** one.
3:12 like Cain, who belonged to the **evil** one and murdered his brother.
3:12 Because his own actions were **evil** and his brother's were
5:18 born of God keeps him safe, and the **evil** one cannot harm him.
5:19 and that the whole world is under the control of the **evil** one.
2Jn 1:11 Anyone who welcomes him shares *in* his **wicked** work.
3Jn 1:10 to what he is doing, gossiping **maliciously** [+3364] about us.
Rev 16: 2 and **painful** sores broke out on the people who had the mark of the

4506 πόνος, ponos [4] [→ 1387, 2930; cf. 4288, 4505]

agony [1], pain [1], pains [1], working [1]

Col 4:13 I vouch for him that he is **working** hard for you and for those at
Rev 16:10 was plunged into darkness. Men gnawed their tongues in **agony**
16:11 cursed the God of heaven because of their **pains** and their sores,
21: 4 There will be no more death or mourning or crying or **pain**,

4507 Ποντικός, Pontikos [1] [√ 4509]

of Pontus [1]

Ac 18: 2 There he met a Jew named Aquila, a native **of Pontus**, who had

4508 Πόντιος, Pontios [3]

Pontius [3]

Lk 3: 1 when **Pontius** Pilate was governor of Judea, Herod tetrarch of
Ac 4:27 Indeed Herod and **Pontius** Pilate met together with the Gentiles
1Ti 6:13 who while testifying before **Pontius** Pilate made the good

4509 πόντος, pontos Not used in UBS/NIV [→ 2931, 4507, 4510]

4510 Πόντος, Pontos [2] [√ 4509]

Pontus [2]

Ac 2: 9 of Mesopotamia, Judea and Cappadocia, **Pontus** and Asia,
1Pe 1: 1 scattered throughout **Pontus**, Galatia, Cappadocia, Asia

4511 Πόπλιος, Poplios [2]

hisˢ [+3836] [1], Publius [1]

Ac 28: 7 There was an estate nearby that *belonged to* **Publius**, the chief
28: 8 **Hisˢ** [+3836] father was sick in bed, suffering from fever

4512 πορεία, *poreia* [2] [√ *4513*]

goes about his business [1], way [1]

Lk   13:22 the towns and villages, teaching as he made his **way** to Jerusalem.
Jas   1:11 rich man will fade away even while he **goes about his business**.

4513 πορεύομαι, *poreuomai* [153]

[→ *679, 680, 1388, 1389, 1660, 1744, 1864, 1865, 1866, 1867,
1989, 2164, 2344, 2345, 3844, 3845, 4182, 4512, 4515, 4516, 4638,
4702, 5233, 5294; cf. 4305*]

go [59], went [22], going [12], goes [7], *untranslated* [6], on way
[4], go back [3], follow [*+2848*] [2], follow [*+3958*] [2], gone [2],
living [2], went on way [2], went out [2], about [1], accompany
[*+5250*] [1], came [1], companions [*+3836+5250*] [1], continued
on way [1], depart [1], departed [1], enter [*+1650*] [1], following
[*+2848*] [1], go on way [1], going back [1], heading [1], hurried
[*+3552+5082*] [1], journey [1], leave [1], leaving [*+608*] [1],
leaving [1], left [*+608+4725*] [1], left [1], observing [*+1877*] [1],
set out [1], started out [1], taken [1], traveled [1], walking away
[1], walking [1], way [1], went along [1]

Mt   2: 8 and said, "**Go** and make a careful search for the child.
      2: 9 After they had heard the king, *they* **went on** their **way**, and the star
      2:20 "Get up, take the child and his mother and **go** to the land of Israel,
      8: 9 I tell this one, '**Go**,' and he goes; and that one, 'Come,' and he
      8: 9 I tell this one, '**Go**,' and he **goes**; and that one, 'Come,' and he
      9:13 But **go** and learn what this means: 'I desire mercy, not sacrifice.'
     10: 6 **Go** rather to the lost sheep of Israel.
     10: 7 *As* you **go**, preach this message: 'The kingdom of heaven is near.'
     11: 4 Jesus replied, "**Go back** and report to John what you hear and see:
     11: 7 *As* John's disciples *were* **leaving**, Jesus began to speak to the
     12: 1 At that time Jesus **went** through the grainfields on the Sabbath.
     12:45 Then it **goes** and takes with it seven other spirits more wicked than
     17:27 we may not offend them, **go** to the lake and throw out your line.
     18:12 on the hills and **go** to look for the one that wandered off?
     19:15 When he had placed his hands on them, *he* **went on** from there.
     21: 2 saying to them, "**Go** to the village ahead of you, and at once you
     21: 6 The disciples **went** and did as Jesus had instructed them.
     22: 9 **Go** to the street corners and invite to the banquet anyone you find.'
     22:15 Then the Pharisees **went out** and laid plans to trap him in his
     24: 1 and *was* **walking away** when his disciples came up to him to call
     25: 9 Instead, **go** to those who sell oil and buy some for yourselves.'
     25:16 The man who had received the five talents **went** at once and put his
     25:41 will say to those on his left, '**Depart** from me, you who are cursed,
     26:14 the one called Judas Iscariot—**went** to the chief priests
     27:66 So they **went** and made the tomb secure by putting a seal on the
     28: 7 Then **go** quickly and tell his disciples: 'He has risen from the dead
     28:11 *While* the women *were* **on** *their* **way**, some of the guards went
     28:16 Then the eleven disciples **went** to Galilee, to the mountain where
     28:19 Therefore **go** and make disciples of all nations, baptizing them in
Mk 16:10 She **went** and told those who had been with him and who were
     16:12 to two of them while they were walking [**RPG**] in the country.
     16:15 "**Go** into all the world and preach the good news to all creation.
Lk   1: 6 **observing** [*+1877*] all the Lord's commandments and regulations
      1:39 and **hurried** [*+3552+5082*] to a town in the hill country of Judea,
      2: 3 And everyone **went** to his own town to register.
      2:41 Every year his parents **went** to Jerusalem for the Feast of the
      4:30 But he walked right through the crowd and **went on** his **way**.
      4:42 At daybreak Jesus **went out** to a solitary place. The people were
      4:42 to where he was, they tried to keep him from **leaving** [*+608*] them.
      5:24 the paralyzed man, "I tell you, get up, take your mat and **go** home."
      7: 6 So Jesus **went** with them. He was not far from the house when the
      7: 8 I tell this one, '**Go**,' and he goes; and that one, 'Come,' and he
      7: 8 I tell this one, '**Go**,' and *he* **goes**; and that one, 'Come,' and he
      7:11 Soon afterward, Jesus **went** to a town called Nain, and his disciples
      7:22 "**Go back** and report to John what you have seen and heard:
      7:50 Jesus said to the woman, "Your faith has saved you; **go** in peace."
      8:14 but *as* they **go on** their **way** they are choked by life's worries,
      8:48 he said to her, "Daughter, your faith has healed you. **Go** in peace."
      9:12 so *they can* **go** to the surrounding villages and countryside
      9:13 and two fish—unless we **go** and buy food for all this crowd."
      9:51 to be taken up to heaven, Jesus resolutely **set out** for Jerusalem.
      9:52 [**RPG**] who went into a Samaritan village to get things ready for
      9:53 there did not welcome him, because he was **heading** for Jerusalem.

      9:56 and *they* **went** to another village.
      9:57 *As* they *were* **walking** along the road, a man said to him, "I will
     10:37 one who had mercy on him." Jesus told him, "**Go** and do likewise."
     10:38 As Jesus and his disciples *were* **on** their **way**, he came to a village
     11: 5 and *he* **goes** to him at midnight and says, 'Friend, lend me three
     11:26 Then *it* **goes** and takes seven other spirits more wicked than itself,
     13:31 to Jesus and said to him, "Leave this place and **go** somewhere else.
     13:32 He replied, "**Go** tell that fox, 'I will drive out demons and heal
     13:33 I must *keep* **going** today and tomorrow and the next day—
     14:10 But when you are invited, [**NIE**] take the lowest place, so that
     14:19 just bought five yoke of oxen, and I'm **on** my **way** to try them out.
     14:31 "Or suppose a king *is* **about** to go to war against another king.
     15: 4 in the open country and **go** after the lost sheep until he finds it?
     15:15 So he **went** and hired himself out to a citizen of that country,
     15:18 I *will* set out and **go back** to my father and say to him: Father,
     16:30 he said, 'but if someone from the dead **goes** to them, they will
     17:11 Now on his **way** to Jerusalem, Jesus traveled along the border
     17:14 When he saw them, he said, "**Go**, show yourselves to the priests."
     17:19 Then he said to him, "Rise and **go**; your faith has made you well."
     19:12 "A man of noble birth **went** to a distant country to have himself
     19:28 After Jesus had said this, *he* **went on** ahead, going up to Jerusalem.
     19:36 *As* he **went along**, people spread their cloaks on the road.
     21: 8 'I am he,' and, 'The time is near.' *Do* not **follow** [*+3958*] them.
     22: 8 saying, "**Go** and make preparations for us to eat the Passover."
     22:22 The Son of Man *will* **go** as it has been decreed, but woe to that man
     22:33 he replied, "Lord, I am ready *to* **go** with you to prison and to death."
     22:39 Jesus went out [**RPG**] as usual to the Mount of Olives, and his
     24:13 Now that same day two of them were **going** to a village called
     24:28 As they approached the village to which *they were* **going**,
     24:28 to which they were going, Jesus acted as if he *were* **going** farther.
Jn   4:50 Jesus replied, "You may **go**. Your son will live." The man took
      4:50 Your son will live." The man took Jesus at his word and **departed**.
      7:35 "Where does this man intend to **go** that we cannot find him?
      7:35 Will he **go** where our people live scattered among the Greeks,
      7:53 Then each **went** to his own home.
      8: 1 But Jesus **went** to the Mount of Olives.
      8:11 condemn you," Jesus declared. "**Go** now and leave your life of sin."
     10: 4 he **goes** on ahead of them, and his sheep follow him because they
     11:11 Lazarus has fallen asleep; but I *am* **going** there to wake him up."
     14: 2 I would have told you. I *am* **going** there to prepare a place for you.
     14: 3 And *if* I **go** and prepare a place for you, I will come back and take
     14:12 even greater things than these, because I *am* **going** to the Father.
     14:28 If you loved me, you would be glad that I *am* **going** to the Father,
     16: 7 Counselor will not come to you; but if I **go**, I will send him to you.
     16:28 now I am leaving the world and **going back** to the Father."
     20:17 **Go** instead to my brothers and tell them, 'I am returning to my
Ac   1:10 They were looking intently up into the sky *as* he *was* **going**,
      1:11 come back in the same way you have seen him **go** into heaven."
      1:25 this apostolic ministry, which Judas left *to* **go** where he belongs."
      5:20 "**Go**, stand in the temple courts," he said, "and tell the people the
      5:41 The apostles **left** [*+608+4725*] the Sanhedrin, rejoicing
      8:26 an angel of the Lord said to Philip, "**Go** south to the road—
      8:27 So *he* **started out**, and on his way he met an Ethiopian eunuch,
      8:36 As *they* **traveled** along the road, they came to some water
      8:39 the eunuch did not see him again, but **went** *on* his way rejoicing
      9: 3 As he neared Damascus on his **journey**, suddenly a light from
      9:11 "**Go** to the house of Judas on Straight Street and ask for a man
      9:15 But the Lord said to Ananias, "**Go**! This man is my chosen
      9:31 the Holy Spirit, it grew in numbers, **living** in the fear of the Lord.
     10:20 Do not hesitate to **go** with them, for I have sent them."
     12:17 the brothers about this," he said, and then *he* **left** for another place.
     14:16 In the past, he let all nations **go** their own way.
     16: 7 came to the border of Mysia, they tried *to* **enter** [*+1650*] Bithynia,
     16:16 Once *when* we *were* **going** to the place of prayer, we were met by
     16:36 that you and Silas be released. Now you can leave. **Go** in peace."
     17:14 The brothers immediately sent Paul [**RPG**] to the coast, but Silas
     18: 6 clear of my responsibility. From now on I *will* **go** to the Gentiles."
     19:21 Paul decided *to* **go** to Jerusalem, passing through Macedonia
     20: 1 said good-by and set out [**RPG**] for Macedonia
     20:22 "And now, compelled by the Spirit, I *am* **going** to Jerusalem,
     21: 5 But when our time was up, *we* left and **continued on** *our* **way**.
     22: 5 and **went** there to bring these people as prisoners to Jerusalem to
     22: 6 "About noon *as* I **came** near Damascus, suddenly a bright light
     22:10 Lord?' I asked. " 'Get up,' the Lord said, 'and **go** into Damascus.
     22:21 "Then the Lord said to me, '**Go**; I will send you far away to the
     23:23 and two hundred spearmen *to* **go** to Caesarea at nine tonight."

24: 25 Felix was afraid and said, "That's enough for now! *You may* **leave**.
25: 12 he declared: "You have appealed to Caesar. To Caesar *you will* **go**!"
25: 20 so I asked if he would be willing *to* **go** to Jerusalem and stand trial
26: 12 "On one of these journeys *I was* **going** to Damascus with the
26: 13 the sun, blazing around me and my **companions** [+3836+5250].
27: 3 allowed him *to* **go** to his friends so they might provide for his
28: 26 " 'Go to this people and say, "You will be ever hearing but never
Ro 15: 24 I plan to do so when *I* **go** to Spain. I hope to visit you while
15: 25 *I am on my* **way** to Jerusalem in the service of the saints there.
1Co 10: 27 If some unbeliever invites you to a meal and you want *to* **go**,
16: 4 If it seems advisable for me *to* **go** also, they will accompany me.
16: 4 advisable for me to go also, *they will* **accompany** [+5250] me.
16: 6 the winter, so that you can help me on my journey, wherever *I* **go**.
1Ti 1: 3 As I urged you *when I* **went** into Macedonia, stay there in Ephesus
2Ti 4: 10 he loved this world, has deserted me and *has* **gone** to Thessalonica.
Jas 4: 13 you who say, "Today or tomorrow *we will* **go** to this or that city,
1Pe 3: 19 through whom also he **went** and preached to the spirits in prison
3: 22 who *has* **gone** into heaven and is at God's right hand—with angels,
4: 3 **living** in debauchery, lust, drunkenness, orgies, carousing
2Pe 2: 10 This is especially true of those *who* **follow** [+3958] the corrupt
3: 3 will come, scoffing and **following** [+2848] their own evil desires.
Jude 1: 11 They have **taken** the way of Cain; they have rushed for profit into
1: 16 and faultfinders; *they* **follow** [+2848] their own evil desires;
1: 18 "In the last times there will be scoffers *who will* **follow** [+2848]

4514 πορθέω, portheō [3]

destroy [1], raised havoc [1], tried destroy [1]

Ac   9: 21 "Isn't he the man *who* **raised havoc** in Jerusalem among those who
Gal 1: 13 intensely I persecuted the church of God and *tried to* **destroy** it.
1: 23 persecuted us is now preaching the faith *he* once **tried** *to* **destroy**."

4515 πορία, poria Not used in UBS/NIV [√ 4513]

4516 πορισμός, porismos [2] [√ 4513]

gain [1], means to financial gain [1]

1Ti 6: 5 and who think that godliness is a **means to financial gain**.
6: 6 But godliness with contentment is great **gain**.

4517 Πόρκιος, Porkios [1]

Porcius [1]

Ac 24: 27 Felix was succeeded by **Porcius** Festus, but because Felix wanted

4518 πορνεία, porneia [25] [√ 4520]

sexual immorality [13], adulteries [5], immorality [2], marital
unfaithfulness [2], *untranslated* [1], illegitimate children
[+1164+1666] [1], sexual sin [1]

Mt   5: 32 except for **marital unfaithfulness**, causes her to become an
15: 19 murder, adultery, **sexual immorality**, theft, false testimony,
19: 9 anyone who divorces his wife, except for **marital unfaithfulness**,
Mk   7: 21 come evil thoughts, **sexual immorality**, theft, murder, adultery,
Jn   8: 41 "We *are* not **illegitimate children** [+1164+1666]," they protested.
Ac 15: 20 from **sexual immorality**, from the meat of strangled animals
15: 29 from the meat of strangled animals and from **sexual immorality**,
21: 25 from the meat of strangled animals and from **sexual immorality**."
1Co 5: 1 It is actually reported that there is **sexual immorality** among you,
5: 1 and of a kind [RPG] that does not occur even among pagans;
6: 13 The body is not *meant for* **sexual immorality**, but for the Lord,
6: 18 Flee from **sexual immorality**. All other sins a man commits are
7: 2 But since there is so much **immorality**, each man should have his
2Co 12: 21 **sexual sin** and debauchery in which they have indulged.
Gal 5: 19 nature are obvious: **sexual immorality**, impurity and debauchery;
Eph 5: 3 among you there must not be even a hint of **sexual immorality**,
Col 3: 5 **sexual immorality**, impurity, lust, evil desires and greed,
1Th 4: 3 should be sanctified: that you should avoid **sexual immorality**;
Rev 2: 21 I have given her time to repent of her **immorality**, but she is
9: 21 their magic arts, their **sexual immorality** or their thefts.
14: 8 made all the nations drink the maddening wine *of* her **adulteries**."
17: 2 of the earth were intoxicated with the wine *of* her **adulteries**."
17: 4 filled with abominable things and the filth *of* her **adulteries**.

18: 3 all the nations have drunk the maddening wine *of* her **adulteries**.
19: 2 the great prostitute who corrupted the earth by her **adulteries**.

4519 πορνεύω, porneuō [8] [√ 4520]

committed adultery [3], commit sexual immorality [1], committing
sexual immorality [1], did[s] [1], sexual immorality [1], sins sexually
[1]

1Co 6: 18 his body, but he *who* **sins sexually** sins against his own body.
10: 8 *We should* not **commit sexual immorality**, as some of them did—
10: 8 We should not commit sexual immorality, as some of them **did**[s]—
Rev 2: 14 food sacrificed to idols and *by* **committing sexual immorality**.
2: 20 By her teaching she misleads my servants into **sexual immorality**
17: 2 With her the kings of the earth **committed adultery**
18: 3 The kings of the earth **committed adultery** with her,
18: 9 "When the kings of the earth who **committed adultery** with her

4520 πόρνη, pornē [12] [→ 1745, 4518, 4519, 4521]

prostitute [8], prostitutes [4]

Mt 21: 31 and the **prostitutes** are entering the kingdom of God ahead of you.
21: 32 did not believe him, but the tax collectors and the **prostitutes** did.
Lk 15: 30 who has squandered your property with **prostitutes** comes home,
1Co 6: 15 then take the members of Christ and unite them *with* a **prostitute**?
6: 16 Do you not know that he who unites himself *with* a **prostitute** is
Heb 11: 31 By faith the **prostitute** Rahab, because she welcomed the spies,
Jas 2: 25 was not even Rahab the **prostitute** considered righteous for what
Rev 17: 1 "Come, I will show you the punishment *of* the great **prostitute**,
17: 5 OF **PROSTITUTES** AND OF THE ABOMINATIONS OF
17: 15 where the **prostitute** sits, are peoples, multitudes, nations
17: 16 The beast and the ten horns you saw will hate the **prostitute**.
19: 2 He has condemned the great **prostitute** who corrupted the earth by

4521 πόρνος, pornos [10] [√ 4520]

sexually immoral [7], immoral [2], adulterers [1]

1Co 5: 9 you in my letter not to associate with **sexually immoral** *people*—
5: 10 not at all meaning the people of this world who are **immoral**,
5: 11 who calls himself a brother but is **sexually immoral** or greedy,
6: 9 Neither the **sexually immoral** nor idolaters nor adulterers nor
Eph 5: 5 No **immoral**, impure or greedy person—such a man is an idolater—
1Ti 1: 10 *for* **adulterers** and perverts, for slave traders and liars
Heb 12: 16 See that no one is **sexually immoral**, or is godless like Esau,
13: 4 for God will judge the adulterer and all the **sexually immoral**.
Rev 21: 8 the unbelieving, the vile, the murderers, the **sexually immoral**,
22: 15 the **sexually immoral**, the murderers, the idolaters and everyone

4522 πόρρω, porrō [4] [√ 4574]

far [2], farther [1], long way off [1]

Mt 15: 8 people honor me with their lips, but their hearts are **far** from me.
Mk   7: 6 people honor me with their lips, but their hearts are **far** from me.
Lk 14: 32 he will send a delegation while the other is still a **long way off**
24: 28 to which they were going, Jesus acted as if he were going **farther**.

4523 πόρρωθεν, porrōthen [2] [√ 4574]

at a distance [1], from a distance [1]

Lk 17: 12 ten men who had leprosy met him. They stood **at a distance**
Heb 11: 13 they only saw them and welcomed them **from a distance**.

4524 πορρωτέρω, porrōterō Not used in UBS/NIV
[√ 4574]

4525 πορφύρα, porphyra [4] [→ 4526, 4527, 4528]

purple robe [2], purple [2]

Mk 15: 17 They put a **purple robe** on him, then twisted together a crown of
15: 20 they took off the **purple robe** and put his own clothes on him.
Lk 16: 19 "There was a rich man who was dressed in **purple** and fine linen
Rev 18: 12 *of* gold, silver, precious stones and pearls; fine linen, **purple**,

4526 πορφύρεος, *porphyreos* Not used in UBS/NIV
[√ *4525*]

4527 πορφυρόπωλις, *porphyropōlis* [1]
[√ *4525 + 4797*]

dealer in purple cloth [1]

Ac 16:14 a **dealer in purple cloth** from the city of Thyatira, who was a

4528 πορφυροῦς, *porphyrous* [4] [√ *4525*]

purple [4]

Jn   19: 2 and put it on his head. They clothed him in a **purple** robe
    19: 5 Jesus came out wearing the crown of thorns and the **purple** robe,
Rev 17: 4 The woman was dressed in **purple** and scarlet, and was glittering
    18:16 Woe, O great city, dressed in fine linen, **purple** and scarlet,

4529 ποσάκις, *posakis* [3] [√ *4005*]

how often [2], how many times [1]

Mt 18:21 **how many times** shall I forgive my brother when he sins against
    23:37 **how often** I have longed to gather your children together,
Lk 13:34 **how often** I have longed to gather your children together,

4530 πόσις, *posis* [3] [√ *4403*]

drink [2], drinking [1]

Jn   6:55 For my flesh is real food and my blood is real **drink**.
Ro 14:17 For the kingdom of God is not a *matter of* eating and **drinking**,
Col 2:16 Therefore do not let anyone judge you by what you eat or **drink**,

4531 πόσος, *posos* [27] [√ *4012*]

how much [11], how many [10], *untranslated* [1], even [+*3437*]
[1], how great [1], how much more [1], how [1], what [1]

Mt   6:23 then the light within you is darkness, **how great** is that darkness!
    7:11 **how much** more will your Father in heaven give good gifts to
  10:25 called Beelzebub, **how much** more the members of his household!
  12:12 **How much more** valuable is a man than a sheep! Therefore it is
  15:34 "**How many** loaves do you have?" Jesus asked. "Seven," they
  16: 9 for the five thousand, and **how many** basketfuls you gathered?
  16:10 for the four thousand, and **how many** basketfuls you gathered?
  27:13 "Don't you hear [RPG] the testimony they are bringing against
Mk   6:38 "**How many** loaves do you have?" he asked. "Go and see." When
    8: 5 "**How many** loaves do you have?" Jesus asked. "Seven," they
    8:19 five thousand, **how many** basketfuls of pieces did you pick up?"
    8:20 four thousand, **how many** basketfuls of pieces did you pick up?"
    9:21 Jesus asked the boy's father, "**How** long has he been like this?"
  15: 4 going to answer? See **how many** *things* they are accusing you of."
Lk 11:13 **how much** more will your Father in heaven give the Holy Spirit to
  12:24 God feeds them. And **how much** more valuable you are than birds!
  12:28 the fire, **how much** more will he clothe you, O you of little faith!
  15:17 '**How many** of my father's hired men have food to spare,
  16: 5 He asked the first, '**How much** do you owe my master?'
  16: 7 "Then he asked the second, 'And **how much** do you owe?'
Ac 21:20 "You see, brother, **how many** thousands of Jews have believed,
Ro 11:12 for the Gentiles, **how much** greater riches will their fullness bring!
  11:24 **how much** more readily will these, the natural branches, be grafted
2Co 7:11 See **what** this godly sorrow has produced in you: what earnestness,
Phm 1:16 He is very dear to me but **even** [+*3437*] dearer to you, both as a
Heb 9:14 **How much** more, then, will the blood of Christ, who through the
  10:29 **How much** more severely do you think a man deserves to be

4532 ποταμός, *potamos* [17] [→ *3544, 4533; cf. 4403*]

river [9], rivers [3], streams [3], torrent [2]

Mt   3: 6 their sins, they were baptized by him in the Jordan **River**.
    7:25 the **streams** rose, and the winds blew and beat against that house;
    7:27 the **streams** rose, and the winds blew and beat against that house,
Mk   1: 5 their sins, they were baptized by him in the Jordan **River**.
Lk   6:48 a flood came, the **torrent** struck that house but could not shake it,
    6:49 The moment the **torrent** struck that house, it collapsed and its

Jn   7:38 has said, **streams** of living water will flow from within him."
Ac 16:13 On the Sabbath we went outside the city gate to the **river**,
2Co 11:26 I have been in danger *from* **rivers**, in danger from bandits,
Rev 8:10 fell from the sky on a third *of* the **rivers** and on the springs of
    9:14 "Release the four angels who are bound at the great **river**
  12:15 Then from his mouth the serpent spewed water like a **river**,
  12:16 and swallowing the **river** that the dragon had spewed out of his
  16: 4 The third angel poured out his bowl on the **rivers** and springs of
  16:12 The sixth angel poured out his bowl on the great **river** Euphrates,
  22: 1 Then the angel showed me the **river** of the water of life, as clear as
  22: 2 On each side *of* the **river** stood the tree of life, bearing twelve

4533 ποταμοφόρητος, *potamophorētos* [1]
[√ *4532 + 5770*]

sweep away with the torrent [+*4472*] [1]

Rev 12:15 the woman and **sweep** [+*4472*] her **away with the torrent**.

4534 ποταπός, *potapos* [7] [√ *4544 + 608*]

what kind of [4], how great [1], what magnificent [1], what
massive [1]

Mt   8:27 The men were amazed and asked, "**What kind of** *man* is this?
Mk 13: 1 of his disciples said to him, "Look, Teacher! **What massive** stones!
  13: 1 Teacher! What massive stones! **What magnificent** buildings!"
Lk   1:29 at his words and wondered **what kind of** greeting this might be.
    7:39 know who is touching him and **what kind of** woman she is—
2Pe 3:11 be destroyed in this way, **what kind of** *people* ought you to be?
1Jn 3: 1 **How great** is the love the Father has lavished on us, that we should

4535 ποταπῶς, *potapōs* Not used in UBS/NIV
[√ *4544 + 608*]

4536 πότε, *pote* [19] [√ *4544*]

when [11], how long [+*2401*] [7], to return [+*380*] [1]

Mt 17:17 Jesus replied, "**how long** [+*2401*] shall I stay with you?
  17:17 "how long shall I stay with you? **How long** [+*2401*] shall I put up
  24: 3 "Tell us," they said, "**when** will this happen, and what will be the
  25:37 'Lord, **when** did we see you hungry and feed you, or thirsty
  25:38 **When** did we see you a stranger and invite you in, or needing
  25:39 **When** did we see you sick or in prison and go to visit you?'
  25:44 **when** did we see you hungry or thirsty or a stranger or needing
Mk   9:19 Jesus replied, "**how long** [+*2401*] shall I stay with you?
    9:19 **How long** [+*2401*] shall I put up with you? Bring the boy to me."
  13: 4 "Tell us, **when** will these things happen? And what will be the sign
  13:33 Be on guard! Be alert! You do not know **when** that time will come.
  13:35 because you do not know **when** the owner of the house will come
Lk   9:41 Jesus replied, "**how long** [+*2401*] shall I stay with you and put up
  12:36 like men waiting for their master **to return** [+*380*] from a wedding
  17:20 having been asked by the Pharisees **when** the kingdom of God
  21: 7 "Teacher," they asked, "**when** will these things happen? And what
Jn   6:25 side of the lake, they asked him, "Rabbi, **when** did you get here?"
  10:24 saying, "**How long** [+*2401*] will you keep us in suspense?
Rev 6:10 They called out in a loud voice, "**How long** [+*2401*], Sovereign

4537 ποτέ, *pote* [29] [√ *4544*]

once [6], at one time [3], ever [3], formerly [3], used to [2],
untranslated [1], at last [+*2453*] [1], had been [1], long ago [1],
never [+*3590+4024*] [1], never [+*4024*] [1], never [+*4046*] [1],
now at last [+*2453*] [1], of the past [1], previous [1], were [+*1639*]
[1], when [1]

Lk 22:32 And **when** you have turned back, strengthen your brothers."
Jn   9:13 They brought to the Pharisees the man who **had been** blind.
Ro   1:10 and I pray that **now at last** [+*2453*] by God's will the way may be
    7: 9 **Once** I was alive apart from law; but when the commandment
  11:30 Just as you who were **at one time** disobedient to God have now
1Co 9: 7 Who [NIE] serves as a soldier at his own expense? Who plants a
Gal 1:13 For you have heard of my **previous** way of life in Judaism,
    1:23 "The man who **formerly** persecuted us is now preaching the faith
    1:23 persecuted us is now preaching the faith he **once** tried to destroy."

	2: 6 whatever *they* were [*+1639*] makes no difference to me;
Eph	2: 2 in which you used to live when you followed the ways of this
	2: 3 All of us also lived among them at one time,
	2:11 remember that formerly you who are Gentiles by birth and called
	2:13 But now in Christ Jesus you who once were far away have been
	5: 8 For you were once darkness, but now you are light in the Lord.
	5:29 After all, no one ever hated his own body, but he feeds and cares
Php	4:10 I rejoice greatly in the Lord that at last [*+2453*] you have renewed
Col	1:21 Once you were alienated from God and were enemies in your
	3: 7 You used to walk in these ways, in the life you once lived.
1Th	2: 5 You know we never [*+4046*] used flattery, nor did we put on a
Tit	3: 3 At one time we too were foolish, disobedient, deceived
Phm	1:11 Formerly he was useless to you, but now he has become useful
Heb	1: 5 For to which of the angels did God ever say, "You are my Son;
	1:13 To which of the angels did God ever say, "Sit at my right hand until
1Pe	2:10 Once you were not a people, but now you are the people of God;
	3: 5 For this is the way the holy women of the past who put their hope
	3:20 who disobeyed long ago when God waited patiently in the days of
2Pe	1:10 For if you do these things, you will never [*+3590+4024*] fall,
	1:21 For prophecy never [*+4024*] had its origin in the will of man,

4538 πότερον, *poteron* [1] [√ *4544 + 2283*]

whether [1]

Jn   7:17 he will find out whether my teaching comes from God or whether

4539 ποτήριον, *potērion* [31] [√ *4403*]

cup [29], cups [1], gives a cup [*+4540*] [1]

Mt	10:42 And if anyone gives even a cup of cold water to one of these little
	20:22 "Can you drink the cup I am going to drink?" "We can,"
	20:23 Jesus said to them, "You will indeed drink from my cup, but to sit
	23:25 You clean the outside *of* the cup and dish, but inside they are full
	23:26 First clean the inside *of* the cup and dish, and then the outside also
	26:27 Then he took the cup, gave thanks and offered it to them, saying,
	26:39 "My Father, if it is possible, may this cup be taken from me.
Mk	7: 4 other traditions, such as the washing *of* cups, pitchers and kettles.)
	9:41 anyone *who* gives you a cup [*+4540*] of water in my name
	10:38 "Can you drink the cup I drink or be baptized with the baptism I am
	10:39 "You will drink the cup I drink and be baptized with the baptism I
	14:23 Then he took the cup, gave thanks and offered it to them, and they
	14:36 Take this cup from me. Yet not what I will, but what you will."
Lk	11:39 "Now then, you Pharisees clean the outside *of* the cup and dish,
	22:17 After taking the cup, he gave thanks and said, "Take this and divide
	22:20 In the same way, after the supper he took the cup, saying,
	22:20 saying, "This cup is the new covenant in my blood, which is poured
	22:42 "Father, if you are willing, take this cup from me; yet not my will,
Jn	18:11 sword away! Shall I not drink the cup the Father has given me?"
1Co	10:16 Is not the cup of thanksgiving for which we give thanks a
	10:21 You cannot drink the cup of the Lord and the cup of demons too;
	10:21 You cannot drink the cup of the Lord and the cup of demons too;
	11:25 In the same way, after supper he took the cup, saying, "This cup is
	11:25 he took the cup, saying, "This cup is the new covenant in my blood;
	11:26 For whenever you eat this bread and drink this cup, you proclaim
	11:27 or drinks the cup of the Lord in an unworthy manner will be guilty
	11:28 examine himself before he eats of the bread and drinks of the cup.
Rev	14:10 which has been poured full strength into the cup of his wrath.
	16:19 and gave her the cup filled with the wine of the fury of his wrath.
	17: 4 She held a golden cup in her hand, filled with abominable things
	18: 6 for what she has done. Mix her a double portion from her own cup.

4540 ποτίζω, *potizō* [15] [√ *4403*]

gave to drink [2], give to drink [2], offered to drink [2], waters [2], gave [1], give water [1], given to drink [1], gives a cup [*+4539*] [1], gives water to [1], made drink [1], watered [1]

Mt	10:42 And if anyone gives even a cup of cold water to one of these little
	25:35 I was thirsty and *you* gave me something to drink, I was a
	25:37 and feed you, or thirsty and *you* gave you something to drink?
	25:42 me nothing to eat, I was thirsty and *you* gave me nothing to drink,
	27:48 wine vinegar, put it on a stick, and offered it to Jesus to drink.
Mk	9:41 anyone *who* gives you a cup [*+4539*] of water in my name
	15:36 wine vinegar, put it on a stick, and offered it to Jesus to drink.
Lk	13:15 his ox or donkey from the stall and lead it out *to* give it water?

Ro	12:20 is hungry, feed him; if he is thirsty, give him something to drink.
1Co	3: 2 *I* gave you milk, not solid food, for you were not yet ready for it.
	3: 6 I planted the seed, Apollos watered it, but God made it grow.
	3: 7 So neither he who plants nor he *who* waters is anything, but only
	3: 8 The man who plants and the man *who* waters have one purpose,
	12:13 slave or free—and *we were* all given the one Spirit to drink.
Rev	14: 8 which made all the nations drink the maddening wine of her

4541 Ποτίολοι, *Potioloi* [1]

Puteoli [1]

Ac   28:13 south wind came up, and on the following day we reached Puteoli.

4542 πότος, *potos* [1] [√ *4403*]

carousing [1]

1Pe 4: 3 lust, drunkenness, orgies, carousing and detestable idolatry.

4543 πού, *pou* [4] [√ *4544*]

a place where [1], about [1], somewhere [1], that [*+3590*] [1]

Ac	27:29 Fearing that [*+3590*] we would be dashed against the rocks,
Ro	4:19 since he was about a hundred years old—and that Sarah's womb
Heb	2: 6 But there is a place where someone has testified: "What is man that
	4: 4 For somewhere he has spoken about the seventh day in these

4544 ποῦ, *pou* [48] [→ *1325, 1326, 1327, 1643, 3595, 3607, 3608, 3610, 3889, 3961, 3962, 3963, 3968, 4030, 4467, 4534, 4535, 4536, 4537, 4538, 4543*]

where [43], place [2], no place [*+4024*] [1], what has happened [*+4036*] [1], what [1]

Mt	2: 2 and asked, "Where is the one who has been born king of the Jews?
	2: 4 of the law, he asked them where the Christ was to be born.
	8:20 the air have nests, but the Son of Man has no place to lay his head."
	26:17 "Where do you want us to make preparations for you to eat the
Mk	14:12 "Where do you want us to go and make preparations for you to eat
	14:14 Where is my guest room, where I may eat the Passover with my
	15:47 and Mary the mother of Joses saw where he was laid.
Lk	8:25 "Where is your faith?" he asked his disciples. In fear
	9:58 the air have nests, but the Son of Man has no place to lay his head."
	12:17 'What shall I do? I have no place [*+4024*] to store my crops.'
	17:17 Jesus asked, "Were not all ten cleansed? Where are the other nine?
	17:37 "Where, Lord?" they asked. He replied, "Where there is a dead
	22: 9 "Where do you want us to prepare for it?" they asked.
	22:11 Where is the guest room, where I may eat the Passover with my
Jn	1:38 said, "Rabbi" (which means Teacher), "where are you staying?"
	1:39 So they went and saw where he was staying, and spent that day
	3: 8 but you cannot tell where it comes from or where it is going.
	7:11 the Jews were watching for him and asking, "Where is that man?"
	7:35 "Where does this man intend to go that we cannot find him?
	8:10 Jesus straightened up and asked her, "Woman, where are they?
	8:14 is valid, for I know where I came from and where I am going.
	8:14 But you have no idea where I come from or where I am going.
	8:19 Then they asked him, "Where is your father?" "You do not know
	9:12 "Where is this man?" they asked him. "I don't know," he said.
	11:34 "Where have you laid him?" he asked. "Come and see, Lord,"
	11:57 and Pharisees had given orders that if anyone found out where
	12:35 The man who walks in the dark does not know where he is going.
	13:36 Simon Peter asked him, "Lord, where are you going?"
	14: 5 Thomas said to him, "Lord, we don't know where you are going,
	16: 5 who sent me, yet none of you asks me, 'Where are you going?'
	20: 2 out of the tomb, and we don't know where they have put him!"
	20:13 Lord away," she said, "and I don't know where they have put him."
	20:15 if you have carried him away, tell me where you have put him,
Ro	3:27 Where, then, is boasting? It is excluded. On what principle?
1Co	1:20 Where is the wise man? Where is the scholar? Where is the
	1:20 Where is the wise man? Where is the scholar? Where is the
	1:20 Where is the scholar? Where is the philosopher of this age?
	12:17 the whole body were an eye, where would the sense of hearing be?
	12:17 If the whole body were an ear, where would the sense of smell be?
	12:19 If they were all one part, where would the body be?
	15:55 "Where, O death, is your victory? Where, O death, is your sting?"

15:55 "Where, O death, is your victory? **Where**, O death, is your sting?"
Gal 4:15 **What** [*+4036*] **has happened** *to* all your joy? I can testify that,
Heb 11: 8 and went, even though he did not know **where** he was going.
1Pe 4:18 to be saved, **what** will become of the ungodly and the sinner?"
2Pe 3: 4 They will say, "**Where** is this 'coming' he promised? Ever since
1Jn 2:11 he does not know **where** he is going, because the darkness has
Rev 2:13 I know **where** you live—where Satan has his throne. Yet you

4545 Πούδης, *Poudēs* [1]

Pudens [1]

2Ti 4:21 greets you, and so do **Pudens**, Linus, Claudia and all the brothers.

4546 πούς, *pous* [93] [→ *435, 3980, 4468, 4469, 5488, 5711*]

νίπτω πούς (wash feet) [8] Jn 13:5,6,8,10,12,14,14; 1Ti 5:10

feet [76], foot [8], *untranslated* [5], foot of ground [*+1037*] [1], legs [1], them^s [*+899+3836*] [1], under [*+3836+4123*] [1]

Mt 4: 6 their hands, so that you will not strike your **foot** against a stone.' "
   5:35 **[RPG]** or by Jerusalem, for it is the city of the Great King.
   7: 6 they may trample them under their **feet**, and then turn and tear you
 10:14 shake the dust off your **feet** when you leave that home or town.
 15:30 the crippled, the mute and many others, and laid them at his **feet**;
 18: 8 If your hand or your **foot** causes you to sin, cut it off and throw it
 18: 8 than to have two hands or two **feet** and be thrown into eternal fire.
 22:13 'Tie him hand and **foot**, and throw him outside, into the darkness,
 22:44 "Sit at my right hand until I put your enemies under your **feet**.' '
 28: 9 he said. They came to him, clasped his **feet** and worshiped him.
Mk 5:22 named Jairus, came there. Seeing Jesus, he fell at his **feet**
  6:11 or listen to you, shake the dust off your **feet** when you leave,
  7:25 daughter was possessed by an evil spirit came and fell at his **feet**.
  9:45 And if your **foot** causes you to sin, cut it off. It is better for you to
  9:45 It is better for you to enter life crippled than to have two **feet**
 12:36 "Sit at my right hand until I put your enemies under your **feet**." '
Lk 1:79 in the shadow of death, to guide our **feet** into the path of peace."
  4:11 their hands, so that you will not strike your **foot** against a stone.' "
  7:38 and as she stood behind him at his **feet** weeping, she began to wet
  7:38 him at his **feet** weeping, she began to wet his **feet** with her tears.
  7:38 kissed them^s [*+899+3836*] and poured perfume on them.
  7:44 You did not give me any water for my **feet**, but she wet my feet
  7:44 but she wet my **feet** with her tears and wiped them with her hair.
  7:45 from the time I entered, has not stopped kissing my **feet**.
  7:46 did not put oil on my head, but she has poured perfume on my **feet**.
  8:35 had gone out, sitting at Jesus' **feet**, dressed and in his right mind;
  8:41 named Jairus, a ruler of the synagogue, came and fell at Jesus' **feet**,
  9: 5 shake the dust off your **feet** when you leave their town, as a
 10:11 'Even the dust of your town that sticks to our **feet** we wipe off
 10:39 called Mary, who sat at the Lord's **feet** listening to what he said.
 15:22 and put it on him. Put a ring on his finger and sandals on his **feet**.
 17:16 He threw himself at Jesus' **feet** and thanked him—and he was a
 20:43 until I make your enemies a footstool *for* your **feet**." '
 24:39 Look at my hands and my **feet**. It is myself! Touch me and see;
 24:40 When he had said this, he showed them his hands and **feet**.
Jn 11: 2 who poured perfume on the Lord and wiped his **feet** with her hair.
 11:32 where Jesus was and saw him, she fell at his **feet** and said, "Lord,
 11:44 man came out, his hands and **feet** wrapped with strips of linen,
 12: 3 she poured it on Jesus' **feet** and wiped his feet with her hair.
 12: 3 she poured it on Jesus' **feet** and wiped his **feet** with her hair.
 13: 5 he poured water into a basin and began to wash his disciples' **feet**,
 13: 6 who said to him, "Lord, are you going to wash my **feet**?"
 13: 8 "No," said Peter, "you shall never wash my **feet**." Jesus answered,
 13: 9 Peter replied, "not just my **feet** but my hands and my head as well!"
 13:10 "A person who has had a bath needs only to wash his **feet**;
 13:12 When he had finished washing their **feet**, he put on his clothes
 13:14 Now that I, your Lord and Teacher, have washed your **feet**,
 13:14 have washed your feet, you also should wash one another's **feet**.
 20:12 Jesus' body had been, one at the head and the other at the **foot**.
Ac 2:35 until I make your enemies a footstool *for* your **feet**." '
  4:35 and put it at the apostles' **feet**, and it was distributed to anyone as
  4:37 he owned and brought the money and put it at the apostles' **feet**.
  5: 2 for himself, but brought the rest and put it at the apostles' **feet**.
  5: 9 The **feet** of the men who buried your husband are at the door,
  5:10 At that moment she fell down at his **feet** and died. Then the young

  7: 5 gave him no inheritance here, not even a **foot** [*+1037*] **of ground**.
  7:33 **[RPG]** the place where you are standing is holy ground.
  7:49 " 'Heaven is my throne, and the earth is my **[RPG]** footstool.
  7:58 the witnesses laid their clothes at the **feet** of a young man named
 10:25 the house, Cornelius met him and fell at his **feet** in reverence.
 13:25 coming after me, whose sandals **[RPG]** I am not worthy to untie.'
 13:51 So they shook the dust from their **feet** in protest against them
 14: 8 In Lystra there sat a man crippled *in* his **feet**, who was lame from
 14:10 and called out, "Stand up on your **feet**!" At that, the man jumped up
 16:24 he put them in the inner cell and fastened their **feet** in the stocks.
 21:11 he took Paul's belt, tied his own hands and **feet** with it and said,
 22: 3 **Under** [*+3836+4123*] Gamaliel I was thoroughly trained in the law
 26:16 'Now get up and stand on your **feet**. I have appeared to you to
Ro 3:15 "Their **feet** are swift to shed blood;
 10:15 "How beautiful are the **feet** of those who bring good news!"
 16:20 The God of peace will soon crush Satan under your **feet**. The grace
1Co 12:15 If the **foot** should say, "Because I am not a hand, I do not belong to
 12:21 need you!" And the head cannot say *to* the **feet**, "I don't need you!"
 15:25 For he must reign until he has put all his enemies under his **feet**.
 15:27 For he "has put everything under his **feet**." Now when it says that
Eph 1:22 And God placed all things under his **feet** and appointed him to be
  6:15 and with your **feet** fitted with the readiness that comes from the
1Ti 5:10 showing hospitality, washing the **feet** of the saints, helping those in
Heb 1:13 my right hand until I make your enemies a footstool *for* your **feet**"?
  2: 8 and put everything under his **feet**." In putting everything under him,
 10:13 time he waits for his enemies to be made his footstool, **[RPG]**
 12:13 "Make level paths *for* your **feet**," so that the lame may not be
Rev 1:15 His **feet** were like bronze glowing in a furnace, and his voice was
  1:17 When I saw him, I fell at his **feet** as though dead. Then he placed
  2:18 eyes are like blazing fire and whose **feet** are like burnished bronze.
  3: 9 I will make them come and fall down at your **feet**
 10: 1 his face was like the sun, and his **legs** were like fiery pillars.
 10: 2 He planted his right **foot** on the sea and his left foot on the land,
 11:11 and they stood on their **feet**, and terror struck those who saw them.
 12: 1 with the moon under her **feet** and a crown of twelve stars on her
 13: 2 but had **feet** like those of a bear and a mouth like that of a lion.
 19:10 At this I fell at his **feet** to worship him. But he said to me,
 22: 8 I fell down to worship at the **feet** of the angel who had been

4547 πρᾶγμα, *pragma* [11] [√ *4556*]

matter [2], things [2], anything [*+4246*] [1], dispute [1], help [1], practice [1], realities [*+1635+3836*] [1], thing [1], what [1]

Mt 18:19 I tell you that if two of you on earth agree about **anything** [*+4246*]
Lk 1: 1 Many have undertaken to draw up an account of the **things** that
Ac 5: 4 What made you think of doing such a **thing**? You have not lied to
Ro 16: 2 of the saints and to give her any **help** she may need from you,
1Co 6: 1 If any of you has a **dispute** with another, dare he take it before the
2Co 7:11 point you have proved yourselves to be innocent *in* this **matter**.
1Th 4: 6 and that in this **matter** no one should wrong his brother or take
Heb 6:18 by two unchangeable **things** in which it is impossible for God to
 10: 1 that are coming—not the **realities** [*+1635+3836*] themselves.
 11: 1 being sure of what we hope for and certain *of* **what** we do not see.
Jas 3:16 selfish ambition, there you find disorder and every evil **practice**.

4548 πραγματεία, *pragmateia* [1] [√ *4556*]

civilian affairs [*+1050*] [1]

2Ti 2: 4 one serving as a soldier gets involved in **civilian affairs** [*+1050*]—

4549 πραγματεύομαι, *pragmateuomai* [1] [√ *4556*]

put to work [1]

Lk 19:13 ten minas. '**Put** this money **to work**,' he said, 'until I come back.'

4550 πραιτώριον, *praitōrion* [8]

palace [4], Praetorium [2], palace guard [1], palace of the Roman governor [1]

Mt 27:27 Then the governor's soldiers took Jesus into the **Praetorium**
Mk 15:16 soldiers led Jesus away into the palace (that is, the **Praetorium**)
Jn 18:28 led Jesus from Caiaphas to the **palace of the Roman governor**.
 18:28 to avoid ceremonial uncleanness the Jews did not enter the **palace**;

18:33 Pilate then went back inside the **palace**, summoned Jesus
19: 9 and he went back inside the **palace**. "Where do you come from?"
Ac 23:35 Then he ordered that Paul be kept under guard in Herod's **palace**.
Php 1:13 it has become clear throughout the whole **palace guard** and to

4551 πράκτωρ, *praktōr* [2] [√ *4556*]

officer [2]

Lk 12:58 you off to the judge, and the judge turn you over *to* the **officer**,
   12:58 turn you over to the officer, and the **officer** throw you into prison.

4552 πρᾶξις, *praxis* [6] [√ *4556*]

action [1], deeds [1], function [1], has done [1], misdeeds [1], practices [1]

Mt 16:27 then he will reward each person according to what he **has done**.
Lk 23:51 who had not consented *to* their decision and **action**. He came from
Ac 19:18 who believed now came and openly confessed their *evil* **deeds**.
Ro 8:13 but if by the Spirit you put to death the **misdeeds** of the body,
   12: 4 and these members do not all have the same **function**,
Col 3: 9 since you have taken off your old self with its **practices**

4553 πρᾶος, *praos* Not used in UBS/NIV [√ *4558*]

4554 πραότης, *praotēs* Not used in UBS/NIV [√ *4558*]

4555 πρασιά, *prasia* [2] [→ *5995*]

groups [+*4555*] [2]

Mk 6:40 So they sat down in **groups** [+*4555*] of hundreds and fifties.
   6:40 So they sat down in **groups** [+*4555*] of hundreds and fifties.

4556 πράσσω, *prassō* [39] [→ *407, 1390, 4547, 4548,* *4549, 4551, 4552*]

do [9], done [6], doing [4], acted [1], collect [1], collected [1], deeds [1], defying [+*595*] [1], did [1], does [1], done [+*1639*] [1], harm [+*2805*] [1], indulged [1], live [1], mind business [1], observe [1], practice [1], practiced [1], preach[s] [1], prove by [+*545*] [1], put into practice [1], them[s] [+*3836+3836+5525*] [1], wrongdoer [+*2805*] [1]

Lk 3:13 "Don't **collect** any more than you are required to," he told them.
   19:23 so that when I came back, *I* could have **collected** it with interest?'
   22:23 among themselves which of them it might be who would **do** this.
   23:15 as you can see, he *has* **done** [+*1639*] nothing to deserve death.
   23:41 We are punished justly, for we are getting what our **deeds** deserve.
   23:41 what our deeds deserve. But this man *has* **done** nothing wrong.'
Jn 3:20 Everyone who **does** evil hates the light, and will not come into the
   5:29 to live, and those *who have* **done** evil will rise to be condemned.
Ac 3:17 "Now, brothers, I know that *you* **acted** in ignorance, as did your
   5:35 of Israel, consider carefully what you intend *to* **do** to these men.
   15:29 You *will* **do** well to avoid these things. Farewell.
   16:28 But Paul shouted, "Don't **harm** [+*2805*] yourself! We are all here!"
   17: 7 They *are* all **defying** [+*595*] Caesar's decrees, saying that there is
   19:19 A number who *had* **practiced** sorcery brought their scrolls
   19:36 are undeniable, you ought to be quiet and not **do** anything rash.
   25:11 If, however, I am guilty of **doing** anything deserving death,
   25:25 I found he *had* **done** nothing deserving of death, but because he
   26: 9 "I too was convinced that I ought *to* **do** all that was possible to
   26:20 and turn to God and **prove** [+*545*] their repentance **by** their deeds.
   26:26 of this has escaped his notice, because it was not **done** in a corner.
   26:31 "This man *is* not **doing** anything that deserves death
Ro 1:32 Although they know God's righteous decree that those *who* **do**
   1:32 do these very things but also approve of those *who* **practice** them.
   2: 1 because you who pass judgment **do** the same things.
   2: 2 Now we know that God's judgment against those *who* **do** such
   2: 3 a mere man, pass judgment on **them**[s] [+*3836+3836+5525*] and yet
   2:25 Circumcision has value if *you* **observe** the law, but if you break
   7:15 I do not understand what I do. For what I want to do *I do* not **do**,
   7:19 want to do; no, the evil I do not want to do—this *I keep on* **doing**.
   9:11 before the twins were born or *had* **done** anything good or bad—
   13: 4 an agent of wrath to bring punishment *on* the **wrongdoer** [+*2805*].

1Co 5: 2 and have put out of your fellowship the man *who did* this?
   9:17 If *I* **preach**[s] voluntarily, I have a reward; if not voluntarily,
2Co 5:10 that each one may receive what is due him for the things **done**
   12:21 sexual sin and debauchery in which *they have* **indulged**.
Gal 5:21 that those *who* **live** like this will not inherit the kingdom of God.
Eph 6:21 so that you also may know how I am and what *I am* **doing**.
Php 4: 9 or received or heard from me, or seen in me—**put** it **into practice**.
1Th 4:11 *to* **mind** your own **business** and to work with your hands,

4557 πραϋπαθία, *praupathia* [1] [√ *4558 + 4248*]

gentleness [1]

1Ti 6:11 godliness, faith, love, endurance and **gentleness**.

4558 πραΰς, *praus* [4] [→ *4553, 4554, 4557, 4559*]

gentle [3], meek [1]

Mt 5: 5 Blessed are the **meek**, for they will inherit the earth.
   11:29 upon you and learn from me, for I am **gentle** and humble in heart,
   21: 5 **gentle** and riding on a donkey, on a colt, the foal of a donkey.' "
1Pe 3: 4 of your inner self, the unfading beauty *of* a **gentle** and quiet spirit,

4559 πραΰτης, *prautēs* [11] [√ *4558*]

gentleness [3], gentle [2], humility [2], gently [+*1877+4460*] [1], gently [+*1877*] [1], humbly [+*1877*] [1], meekness [1]

1Co 4:21 I come to you with a whip, or in love and with a **gentle** spirit?
2Co 10: 1 By the **meekness** and gentleness of Christ, I appeal to you—
Gal 5:23 **gentleness** and self-control. Against such things there is no law.
   6: 1 you who are spiritual should restore him **gently** [+*1877+4460*].
Eph 4: 2 Be completely humble and **gentle**; be patient, bearing with one
Col 3:12 with compassion, kindness, humility, **gentleness** and patience.
2Ti 2:25 Those who oppose him he must **gently** [+*1877*] instruct,
Tit 3: 2 and considerate, and to show true **humility** toward all men.
Jas 1:21 so prevalent and **humbly** [+*1877*] accept the word planted in you,
   3:13 good life, by deeds done in the **humility** that comes from wisdom.
1Pe 3:15 for the hope that you have. But do this with **gentleness** and respect,

4560 πρέπω, *prepō* [7] [→ *2346, 2640, 3485*]

proper [2], appropriate [1], fitting [1], improper[s] [1], in accord [1], meets need [1]

Mt 3:15 so now; it is **proper** for us to do this to fulfill all righteousness."
1Co 11:13 Is it **proper** for a woman to pray to God with her head uncovered?
Eph 5: 3 or of greed, because *these are* **improper**[s] for God's holy people.
1Ti 2:10 good deeds, **appropriate** for women who profess to worship God.
Tit 2: 1 You must teach what *is* **in accord** with sound doctrine.
Heb 2:10 *it was* **fitting** that God, for whom and through whom everything
   7:26 Such a high priest **meets** our **need**—one who is holy, blameless,

4561 πρεσβεία, *presbeia* [2] [√ *4565*]

delegation [2]

Lk 14:32 he will send a **delegation** while the other is still a long way off
   19:14 "But his subjects hated him and sent a **delegation** after him to say,

4562 πρεσβευτής, *presbeutēs* Not used in UBS/NIV [√ *4565*]

4563 πρεσβεύω, *presbeuō* [2] [√ *4565*]

ambassador [1], ambassadors [1]

2Co 5:20 *We are* therefore Christ's **ambassadors**, as though God were
Eph 6:20 for which *I am an* **ambassador** in chains. Pray that I may declare

4564 πρεσβυτέριον, *presbyterion* [3] [√ *4565*]

body of elders [1], council of elders [1], council [1]

Lk 22:66 At daybreak the **council of** the **elders** of the people, both the chief
Ac 22: 5 as also the high priest and all the **Council** can testify. I even
1Ti 4:14 message when the **body of elders** laid their hands on you.

4565 πρεσβύτερος, *presbyteros* [66] [→ *4561, 4562, 4563, 4564, 4566, 4567, 5236*]

ἀπόστολοι καὶ πρεσβύτεροι (apostles and elders) [6] Ac 15:2,4,6,22,23; 16:4

οἱ ἀρχιερεῖς καὶ πρεσβύτεροι (the chief priests and elders) [17] Mt 16:21; 21:23; 26:3,47; 27:1,3,12,20; Mk 8:31; 11:27; 14:43,53; Lk 9:22; 22:52; Ac 4:23; 23:14; 25:15

γραμματεῖς ... πρεσβύτεροι teachers of the law ... elders [12] Mt 16:21; 26:57; 27:41; Mk 8:31; 11:27; 14:43,53; 15:1; Lk 9:22; 20:1; Ac 4:5; 6:12

παράδοσις πρεσβυτέρων (tradition of the elders) [3] Mt 15:2; Mk 7:3,5

elders [56], older [4], elder [3], ancients [1], old men [1], older man [1]

Mt 15: 2 "Why do your disciples break the tradition *of* the **elders**? They
16:21 go to Jerusalem and suffer many things at the hands of the **elders**,
21:23 the chief priests and the **elders** of the people came to him.
26: 3 and the **elders** of the people assembled in the palace of the high
26:47 and clubs, sent from the chief priests and the **elders** of the people.
26:57 where the teachers of the law and the **elders** had assembled.
27: 1 and the **elders** of the people came to the decision to put Jesus to
27: 3 returned the thirty silver coins to the chief priests and the **elders**.
27:12 When he was accused by the chief priests and the **elders**, he gave
27:20 and the **elders** persuaded the crowd to ask for Barabbas
27:41 chief priests, the teachers of the law and the **elders** mocked him.
28:12 When the chief priests had met with the **elders** and devised a plan,
Mk 7: 3 hands a ceremonial washing, holding to the tradition of the **elders**.
7: 5 *of* the **elders** instead of eating their food with 'unclean' hands?"
8:31 Son of Man must suffer many things and be rejected by the **elders**,
11:27 chief priests, the teachers of the law and the **elders** came to him.
14:43 sent from the chief priests, the teachers of the law, and the **elders**,
14:53 all the chief priests, **elders** and teachers of the law came together.
15: 1 the chief priests, with the **elders**, the teachers of the law
Lk 7: 3 centurion heard of Jesus and sent *some* **elders** of the Jews to him,
9:22 Son of Man must suffer many things and be rejected by the **elders**,
15:25 "Meanwhile, the **older** son was in the field. When he came near the
20: 1 the teachers of the law, together with the **elders**, came up to him.
22:52 and the **elders**, who had come for him, "Am I leading a rebellion,
Jn 8: 9 the **older** *ones* first, until only Jesus was left, with the woman still
Ac 2:17 your young men will see visions, your **old men** will dream dreams.
4: 5 day the rulers, **elders** and teachers of the law met in Jerusalem.
4: 8 with the Holy Spirit, said to them: "Rulers and **elders** of the people!
4:23 and reported all that the chief priests and **elders** had said to them.
6:12 stirred up the people and the **elders** and the teachers of the law.
11:30 they did, sending their gift to the **elders** by Barnabas and Saul.
14:23 and Barnabas appointed **elders** for them in each church and,
15: 2 up to Jerusalem to see the apostles and **elders** about this question.
15: 4 they were welcomed by the church and the apostles and **elders**,
15: 6 The apostles and **elders** met to consider this question.
15:22 Then the apostles and **elders**, with the whole church, decided to
15:23 The apostles and **elders**, your brothers, To the Gentile believers in
16: 4 by the apostles and **elders** in Jerusalem for the people to obey.
20:17 From Miletus, Paul sent to Ephesus for the **elders** of the church.
21:18 the rest of us went to see James, and all the **elders** were present.
23:14 They went to the chief priests and **elders** and said, "We have taken
24: 1 priest Ananias went down to Caesarea with some *of* the **elders**
25:15 chief priests and **elders** of the Jews brought charges against him
1Ti 5: 1 Do not rebuke an **older man** harshly, but exhort him as if he were
5: 2 **older** women as mothers, and younger women as sisters,
5:17 The **elders** who direct the affairs of the church well are worthy of
5:19 Do not entertain an accusation against an **elder** unless it is brought
Tit 1: 5 out what was left unfinished and appoint **elders** in every town,
Heb 11: 2 This is what the **ancients** were commended for.
Jas 5:14 He should call the **elders** of the church to pray over him and anoint
1Pe 5: 1 *To* the **elders** among you, I appeal as a fellow elder, a witness of
5: 5 in the same way be submissive *to those who* are **older**.
2Jn 1: 1 The **elder**, To the chosen lady and her children, whom I love in the
3Jn 1: 1 The **elder**, To my dear friend Gaius, whom I love in the truth.
Rev 4: 4 other thrones, and seated on them were twenty-four **elders**.
4:10 the twenty-four **elders** fall down before him who sits on the throne,
5: 5 Then one of the **elders** said to me, "Do not weep! See, the Lion of
5: 6 of the throne, encircled by the four living creatures and the **elders**.
5: 8 and the twenty-four **elders** fell down before the Lamb.

5:11 They encircled the throne and the living creatures and the **elders**.
5:14 creatures said, "Amen," and the **elders** fell down and worshiped.
7:11 the throne and around the **elders** and the four living creatures.
7:13 Then one of the **elders** asked me, "These in white robes—who are
11:16 And the twenty-four **elders**, who were seated on their thrones
14: 3 the throne and before the four living creatures and the **elders**.
19: 4 The twenty-four **elders** and the four living creatures fell down

4566 πρεσβύτης, *presbytēs* [3] [√ *4565*]

old man [2], older [1]

Lk 1:18 sure of this? I am an **old man** and my wife is well along in years."
Tit 2: 2 Teach the **older** *men* to be temperate, worthy of respect,
Phm 1: 9 as Paul—an **old man** and now also a prisoner of Christ Jesus—

4567 πρεσβῦτις, *presbytis* [1] [√ *4565*]

older [1]

Tit 2: 3 teach the **older** *women* to be reverent in the way they live,

4568 πρηνής, *prēnēs* [1]

fell headlong [+*1181*] [1]

Ac 1:18 there *he* **fell headlong** [+*1181*], his body burst open and all his

4569 πρίζω, *prizō* [1] [√ *4573*]

sawed in two [1]

Heb 11:37 They were stoned; *they were* **sawed in two**; they were put to death

4570 πρίν, *prin* [13] [√ *4574*]

before [8], before [+*2445*] [4], before [+*323+2445*] [1]

Mt 1:18 to be married to Joseph, but **before** [+*2445*] they came together,
26:34 Jesus answered, "this very night, **before** the rooster crows,
26:75 "**Before** the rooster crows, you will disown me three times."
Mk 14:30 **before** [+*2445*] the rooster crows twice you yourself will disown
14:72 "**Before** the rooster crows twice you will disown me three times."
Lk 2:26 would not die **before** [+*323+2445*] he had seen the Lord's Christ.
22:61 "**Before** the rooster crows today, you will disown me three times."
Jn 4:49 The royal official said, "Sir, come down **before** my child dies."
8:58 you the truth," Jesus answered, "**before** Abraham was born, I am!"
14:29 I have told you now **before** it happens, so that when it does happen
Ac 2:20 and the moon to blood **before** the coming of the great and glorious
7: 2 he was still in Mesopotamia, **before** [+*2445*] he lived in Haran.
25:16 to hand over any man **before** [+*2445*] he has faced his accusers

4571 Πρίσκα, *Priska* [6] [→ *4572*]

Priscilla [6]

Ac 18: 2 who had recently come from Italy with his wife **Priscilla**,
18:18 and sailed for Syria, accompanied by **Priscilla** and Aquila.
18:26 When **Priscilla** and Aquila heard him, they invited him to their
Ro 16: 3 Greet **Priscilla** and Aquila, my fellow workers in Christ Jesus.
1Co 16:19 Aquila and **Priscilla** greet you warmly in the Lord, and so does the
2Ti 4:19 Greet **Priscilla** and Aquila and the household of Onesiphorus.

4572 Πρίσκιλλα, *Priskilla* Not used in UBS/NIV [√ *4571*]

4573 πρίω, *priō* Not used in UBS/NIV [→ *1391, 4569*]

4574 πρό, *pro* [47]

[→ *4522, 4523, 4524, 4570, 4575, 4576, 4577, 4578, 4579, 4580, 4581, 4582, 4583, 4584, 4585, 4586, 4587, 4588, 4589, 4590, 4591, 4592, 4593, 4594, 4595, 4596, 4597, 4598, 4599, 4600, 4601, 4602, 4603, 4604, 4605, 4606, 4607, 4608, 4609, 4610, 4611, 4612, 4613, 4614, 4615, 4616, 4617, 4618, 4619, 4620, 4621, 4622, 4623, 4624, 4625, 4626, 4627, 4628, 4629, 4630, 4631, 4632, 4633, 4634, 4635, 4636, 4637, 4638, 4640, 4706, 4710, 4711, 4726, 4727, 4728, 4729,*

4730, 4731, 4732, 4733, 4734, 4735, 4740, 4741, 4742, 4743, 4749, 5864; cf. 4745, 4755]

before [21], before [+3836] [9], ahead [+4725] [4], at [3], above [2], some time ago [+2465+3836+4047] [2], ago [1], ahead [1], before [+4725] [1], chosen before [RP4589] [1], just outside [1], on ahead [+4725] [1]

Mt 5:12 for in the same way they persecuted the prophets who were **before**
6: 8 for your Father knows what you need **before** [+3836] you ask him.
8:29 "Have you come here to torture us **before** the appointed time?"
11:10 " 'I will send my messenger **ahead** [+4725] of you, who will
24:38 For in the days **before** the flood, people were eating and drinking,
Mk 1: 2 "I will send my messenger **ahead** [+4725] of you, who will prepare
Lk 2:21 the name the angel had given him **before** [+3836] he had been
7:27 " 'I will send my messenger **ahead** [+4725] of you, who will
9:52 And he sent messengers **on ahead** [+4725], who went into a
10: 1 and sent them two by two **ahead** [+4725] of him to every town
11:38 noticing that Jesus did not first wash **before** the meal,
21:12 "But **before** all this, they will lay hands on you and persecute you.
22:15 have eagerly desired to eat this Passover with you **before** [+3836]
Jn 1:48 "I saw you while you were still under the fig tree **before** [+3836]
5: 7 While I am trying to get in, someone else goes down **ahead** of me."
10: 8 All who ever came **before** me were thieves and robbers,
11:55 to Jerusalem for their ceremonial cleansing **before** the Passover.
12: 1 Six days **before** the Passover, Jesus arrived at Bethany,
13: 1 It was *just* **before** the Passover Feast. Jesus knew that the time had
13:19 "I am telling you now **before** [+3836] it happens, so that when it
17: 5 with the glory I had with you **before** [+3836] the world began.
17:24 given me because you loved me **before** the creation of the world.
Ac 5:36 **Some time ago** [+2465+3836+4047] Theudas appeared, claiming
12: 6 bound with two chains, and sentries stood guard **at** the entrance.
12:14 ran back without opening it and exclaimed, "Peter is **at** the door!"
13:24 **Before** [+4725] the coming of Jesus, John preached repentance
14:13 whose temple was **just outside** the city, brought bulls and wreaths
21:38 terrorists out into the desert **some time ago** [+2465+3836+4047]?"
23:15 his case. We are ready to kill him **before** [+3836] he gets here."
Ro 16: 7 among the apostles, and they were in Christ **before** I was.
1Co 2: 7 and that God destined for our glory **before** time *began.*
4: 5 Therefore judge nothing **before** the appointed time; wait till the
2Co 12: 2 I know a man in Christ who fourteen years **ago** was caught up to
Gal 1:17 nor did I go up to Jerusalem to see those who were apostles **before**
2:12 **Before** [+3836] certain men came from James, he used to eat with
3:23 **Before** [+3836] this faith came, we were held prisoners by the law,
Eph 1: 4 For he chose us in him **before** the creation of the world to be holy
Col 1:17 He is **before** all things, and in him all things hold together.
2Ti 1: 9 This grace was given us in Christ Jesus **before** the beginning of
4:21 Do your best to get here **before** winter. Eubulus greets you,
Tit 1: 2 who does not lie, promised **before** the beginning of time,
Heb 11: 5 For **before** he was taken, he was commended as one who pleased
Jas 5: 9 brothers, or you will be judged. The Judge is standing **at** the door!
5:12 **Above** all, my brothers, do not swear—not by heaven or by earth
1Pe 1:20 He was **chosen before** [RP4589] the creation of the world,
4: 8 **Above** all, love each other deeply, because love covers over a
Jude 1:25 Jesus Christ our Lord, **before** all ages, now and forevermore!

4575 προάγω, proagō [20] [√ 4574 + 72]

go ahead of [2], go on ahead of [2], going ahead of [2], went ahead of [2], bring out [1], bring to trial [1], brought before [1], brought [1], entering ahead of [1], former [1], leading the way [1], led the way [1], once made [1], reaching ahead of [1], runs ahead [1], went ahead [1]

Mt 2: 9 and the star they had seen in the east **went ahead of** them until it
14:22 get into the boat and **go on ahead of** him to the other side,
21: 9 The crowds that **went ahead of** him and those that followed
21:31 and the prostitutes *are* **entering** the kingdom of God **ahead of** you.
26:32 But after I have risen, I will **go ahead of** you into Galilee."
28: 7 'He has risen from the dead and *is* **going ahead of** you into
Mk 6:45 disciples get into the boat and **go on ahead of** him to Bethsaida,
10:32 with Jesus **leading the way**, and the disciples were astonished,
11: 9 Those *who* **went ahead** and those who followed shouted,
14:28 But after I have risen, I will **go ahead of** you into Galilee."
16: 7 tell his disciples and Peter, 'He is **going ahead of** you into Galilee.'
Lk 18:39 Those *who* **led the way** rebuked him and told him to be quiet,
Ac 12: 6 The night before Herod was to **bring** him **to trial**, Peter was

16:30 He then **brought** them out and asked, "Sirs, what must I do to be
17: 5 search of Paul and Silas *in order to* **bring** them **out** to the crowd.
25:26 Therefore *I have* **brought** him **before** all of you, and especially
1Ti 1:18 instruction in keeping with the prophecies **once made** about you,
5:24 men are obvious, **reaching** the place of judgment **ahead of** them;
Heb 7:18 The **former** regulation is set aside because it was weak
2Jn 1: 9 Anyone who **runs ahead** and does not continue in the teaching of

4576 προαιρέω, proaireō [1] [√ 4574 + 145]

decided [1]

2Co 9: 7 Each man should give what *he has* **decided** in his heart to give,

4577 προαιτιάομαι, proaitiaomai [1] [√ 4574 + 162]

already made the charge [1]

Ro 3: 9 *We have* **already made the charge** that Jews and Gentiles alike

4578 προακούω, proakouō [1] [√ 4574 + 201]

already heard about [1]

Col 1: 5 and that *you have* **already heard about** in the word of truth,

4579 προαμαρτάνω, proamartanō [2] [√ 4574 + 279]

sinned earlier [2]

2Co 12:21 and I will be grieved over many who *have* **sinned earlier**
13: 2 On my return I will not spare those *who* **sinned earlier** or any of

4580 προαύλιον, proaulion [1] [√ 4574 + 885]

entryway [1]

Mk 14:68 you're talking about," he said, and went out into the **entryway**.

4581 προβαίνω, probainō [5] [√ 4574 + 326]

well along [2], going on [1], gone farther [1], old [+1877+2465] [1]

Mt 4:21 **Going on** from there, he saw two other brothers, James son of
Mk 1:19 *When he had* **gone** a little **farther**, he saw James son of Zebedee
Lk 1: 7 Elizabeth was barren; and they were both **well along** in years.
1:18 sure of this? I am an old man and my wife *is* **well along** in years."
2:36 She *was* very **old** [+1877+2465]; she had lived with her husband

4582 προβάλλω, proballō [2] [√ 4574 + 965]

pushed to the front [1], sprout leaves [1]

Lk 21:30 When *they* **sprout leaves**, you can see for yourselves and know
Ac 19:33 The Jews **pushed** Alexander **to the front**, and some of the crowd

4583 προβατικός, probatikos [1] [√ 4574 + 326]

Sheep Gate [1]

Jn 5: 2 Now there is in Jerusalem near the **Sheep Gate** a pool, which in

4584 προβάτιον, probation Not used in UBS/NIV
[√ 4574 + 326]

4585 πρόβατον, probaton [39] [√ 4574 + 326]

sheep [38], sheep's [1]

Mt 7:15 They come to you in **sheep's** clothing, but inwardly they are
9:36 they were harassed and helpless, like **sheep** without a shepherd.
10: 6 Go rather to the lost **sheep** of Israel.
10:16 I am sending you out like **sheep** among wolves. Therefore be as
12:11 "If any of you has a **sheep** and it falls into a pit on the Sabbath,
12:12 How much more valuable is a man than a **sheep**! Therefore it is
15:24 He answered, "I was sent only to the lost **sheep** of Israel."
18:12 If a man owns a hundred **sheep**, and one of them wanders away,
25:32 one from another as a shepherd separates the **sheep** from the goats.
25:33 He will put the **sheep** on his right and the goats on his left.

26:31 strike the shepherd, and the **sheep** of the flock will be scattered.'
Mk   6:34 on them, because they were like **sheep** without a shepherd.
14:27 " 'I will strike the shepherd, and the **sheep** will be scattered.'
Lk   15: 4 "Suppose one of you has a hundred **sheep** and loses one of them.
15: 6 and says, 'Rejoice with me; I have found my lost **sheep**.'
Jn   2:14 **sheep** and doves, and others sitting at tables exchanging money.
2:15 and drove all from the temple area, both **sheep** and cattle;
10: 1 the truth, the man who does not enter the **sheep** pen by the gate,
10: 2 The man who enters by the gate is the shepherd *of* his **sheep**.
10: 3 watchman opens the gate for him, and the **sheep** listen to his voice.
10: 3 to his voice. He calls his own **sheep** by name and leads them out.
10: 4 of them, and his **sheep** follow him because they know his voice.
10: 7 Jesus said again, "I tell you the truth, I am the gate *for* the **sheep**.
10: 8 me were thieves and robbers, but the **sheep** did not listen to them.
10:11 The good shepherd lays down his life for the **sheep**.
10:12 The hired hand is not the shepherd who owns the **sheep**. So when
10:12 he sees the wolf coming, he abandons the **sheep** and runs away.
10:13 because he is a hired hand and cares nothing for the **sheep**.
10:15 and I know the Father—and I lay down my life for the **sheep**.
10:16 I have other **sheep** that are not of this sheep pen. I must bring them
10:26 but you do not believe because you are not my **sheep**.
10:27 My **sheep** listen to my voice; I know them, and they follow me.
21:16 you know that I love you." Jesus said, "Take care of my **sheep**."
21:17 all things; you know that I love you." Jesus said, "Feed my **sheep**.
Ac   8:32 "He was led like a **sheep** to the slaughter, and as a lamb before the
Ro   8:36 death all day long; we are considered as **sheep** to be slaughtered."
Heb 13:20 from the dead our Lord Jesus, that great Shepherd *of* the **sheep**,
1Pe   2:25 For you were like **sheep** going astray, but now you have returned
Rev 18:13 cattle and **sheep**; horses and carriages; and bodies and souls of

4586 προβιβάζω, *probibazō* [1] [√ *4574 + 326*]

prompted [1]

Mt   14: 8 **Prompted** by her mother, she said, "Give me here on a platter the

4587 προβλέπω, *problepō* [1] [√ *4574 + 1063*]

planned [1]

Heb 11:40 God *had* **planned** something better for us so that only together

4588 προγίνομαι, *proginomai* [1] [√ *4574 + 1181*]

committed beforehand [1]

Ro   3:25 he had left the sins **committed beforehand** unpunished—

4589 προγινώσκω, *proginōskō* [5] [√ *4574 + 1182*]

foreknew [2], already know [1], chosen before [*RP4574*] [1], known [1]

Ac 26: 5 *They have* **known** me for a long time and can testify, if they are
Ro   8:29 For those God **foreknew** he also predestined to be conformed to
11: 2 God did not reject his people, whom *he* **foreknew**. Don't you
1Pe   1:20 He was **chosen** [*RP4574*] **before** the creation of the world,
2Pe   3:17 Therefore, dear friends, *since* you **already know** this, be on your

4590 πρόγνωσις, *prognōsis* [2] [√ *4574 + 1182*]

foreknowledge [2]

Ac   2:23 was handed over to you *by* God's set purpose and **foreknowledge**;
1Pe   1: 2 who have been chosen according to the **foreknowledge** of God the

4591 πρόγονος, *progonos* [2] [√ *4574 + 1181*]

my forefathers [1], parents and grandparents [1]

1Ti   5: 4 their own family and so repaying their **parents and grandparents**,
2Ti   1: 3 I thank God, whom I serve, as **my forefathers** did, with a clear

4592 προγράφω, *prographō* [4] [√ *4574 + 1211*]

already written [1], portrayed [1], was written about [1], written in the past [1]

Ro   15: 4 For everything that *was* **written in the past** was written to teach

Gal   3: 1 Before your very eyes Jesus Christ *was clearly* **portrayed** as
Eph   3: 3 known to me by revelation, as *I have* **already written** briefly.
Jude   1: 4 For certain men whose condemnation **was written about** long ago

4593 πρόδηλος, *prodēlos* [3] [√ *4574 + 1316*]

obvious [2], clear [1]

1Ti   5:24 The sins of some men are **obvious**, reaching the place of judgment
5:25 In the same way, good deeds are **obvious**, and even those that are
Heb   7:14 For it is **clear** that our Lord descended from Judah, and in regard to

4594 προδίδωμι, *prodidōmi* [1] [√ *4574 + 1443*]

given [1]

Ro   11:35 "Who *has ever* **given** to God, that God should repay him?"

4595 προδότης, *prodotēs* [3] [√ *4574 + 1443*]

betrayed [*+1181*] [1], traitor [1], treacherous [1]

Lk   6:16 Judas son of James, and Judas Iscariot, who became a **traitor**.
Ac   7:52 And now you *have* **betrayed** [*+1181*] and murdered him—
2Ti   3: 4 **treacherous**, rash, conceited, lovers of pleasure rather than lovers

4596 πρόδρομος, *prodromos* [1] [√ *4574 + 5556*]

went before [1]

Heb   6:20 where Jesus, who **went before** us, has entered on our behalf.

4597 προεῖπον, *proeipon*   Not used in UBS/NIV [√ *4574 + 3306*]

4598 προελπίζω, *proelpizō* [1] [√ *4574 + 1828*]

first to hope [1]

Eph   1:12 in order that we, who were the **first to hope** in Christ, might be for

4599 προενάρχομαι, *proenarchomai* [2] [√ *4574 + 1877 + 806*]

earlier made a beginning [1], the first [1]

2Co   8: 6 So we urged Titus, since *he had* **earlier made a beginning**,
8:10 Last year you *were* **the first** not only to give but also to have the

4600 προεπαγγέλλω, *proepangellō* [2] [√ *4574 + 2093 + 34*]

promised beforehand [1], promised [1]

Ro   1: 2 the gospel *he* **promised beforehand** through his prophets in the
2Co   9: 5 finish the arrangements for the generous gift you *had* **promised**.

4601 προέρχομαι, *proerchomai* [9] [√ *4574 + 2262*]

going farther [2], went on ahead [2], go on [1], got there ahead of [1], leading [1], visit [*+1650*] [1], walked [1]

Mt 26:39 **Going** a little **farther**, he fell with his face to the ground
Mk   6:33 and ran on foot from all the towns and **got there ahead of** them.
14:35 **Going** a little **farther**, he fell to the ground and prayed that if
Lk   1:17 And he *will* **go on** before the Lord, in the spirit and power of
22:47 man who was called Judas, one of the Twelve, *was* **leading** them.
Ac 12:10 *When they had* **walked** the length of one street, suddenly the
20: 5 These men **went on ahead** and waited for us at Troas.
20:13 We **went on ahead** to the ship and sailed for Assos, where we
2Co   9: 5 So I thought it necessary to urge the brothers to **visit** [*+1650*] you

4602 προετοιμάζω, *proetoimazō* [2] [√ *4574 + 2289*]

prepared in advance [2]

Ro   9:23 objects of his mercy, whom *he* **prepared in advance** for glory—
Eph   2:10 to do good works, which God **prepared in advance** for us to do.

4603 προευαγγελίζομαι, *proeuangelizomai* [1]
[√ 4574 + 2292 + 34]

announced the gospel in advance [1]

Gal 3: 8 by faith, and **announced the gospel in advance** to Abraham:

4604 προέχω, *proechō* [1] [√ 4574 + 2400]

better [1]

Ro 3: 9 What shall we conclude then? *Are we any* **better**? Not at all!

4605 προηγέομαι, *proēgeomai* [1] [√ 4574 + 72]

above [1]

Ro 12:10 another in brotherly love. Honor one another **above** *yourselves.*

4606 πρόθεσις, *prothesis* [12] [√ 4574 + 5502]

purpose [5], consecrated [4], plan [1], true [1], wanted [1]

Mt 12: 4 of God, and he and his companions ate the **consecrated** bread—
Mk 2:26 he entered the house of God and ate the **consecrated** bread,
Lk 6: 4 He entered the house of God, and taking the **consecrated** bread,
Ac 11:23 and encouraged them all to remain **true** to the Lord with all their
27:13 began to blow, they thought they had obtained what they **wanted**;
Ro 8:28 who love him, who have been called according to his **purpose**.
9:11 or bad—in order that God's **purpose** in election might stand:
Eph 1:11 having been predestined according to the **plan** of him who works
3:11 according to his eternal **purpose** which he accomplished in Christ
2Ti 1: 9 anything we have done but because of his own **purpose** and grace.
3:10 my way of life, my **purpose**, faith, patience, love, endurance,
Heb 9: 2 room were the lampstand, the table and the **consecrated** bread;

4607 προθεσμία, *prothesmia* [1] [√ 4574 + 5502]

time set [1]

Gal 4: 2 is subject to guardians and trustees until the **time set** by his father.

4608 προθυμία, *prothymia* [5] [√ 4574 + 2596]

eagerness [3], eager [1], willingness [1]

Ac 17:11 for they received the message with great **eagerness** and examined
2Co 8:11 so that your **eager** willingness to do it may be matched by your
8:12 For if the **willingness** is there, the gift is acceptable according to
8:19 to honor the Lord himself and to show our **eagerness** *to help.*
9: 2 For I know your **eagerness** *to help,*

4609 πρόθυμος, *prothymos* [3] [√ 4574 + 2596]

willing [2], eager [1]

Mt 26:41 not fall into temptation. The spirit is **willing**, but the body is weak."
Mk 14:38 not fall into temptation. The spirit is **willing**, but the body is weak."
Ro 1:15 so **eager** to preach the gospel also to you who are at Rome.

4610 προθύμως, *prothymōs* [1] [√ 4574 + 2596]

eager [1]

1Pe 5: 2 as God wants you to be; not greedy for money, but **eager** *to serve*;

4611 πρόιμος, *proimos* [1] [√ 4574]

autumn rains [1]

Jas 5: 7 and how patient he is for the **autumn** and spring **rains**.

4612 προϊνός, *proinos* Not used in UBS/NIV [√ 4574]

4613 προΐστημι, *proistēmi* [8] [√ 4574 + 2705]

manage [2], devote to [1], devote [1], direct [1], leadership [1], manage and see that [1], over [1]

Ro 12: 8 if it is **leadership**, let him govern diligently; if it is showing mercy,

1Th 5:12 among you, *who are* **over** you in the Lord and who admonish you.
1Ti 3: 4 *He must* **manage** his own family well **and see that** his children
3: 5 (If anyone does not know how *to* **manage** his own family,
3:12 but one wife and *must* **manage** his children and his household
5:17 The elders *who* **direct** the *affairs* of the church well are worthy of
Tit 3: 8 God may be careful *to* **devote** *themselves* to doing what is good.
3:14 Our people must learn *to* **devote** *themselves* **to** doing what is

4614 προκαλέω, *prokaleō* [1] [√ 4574 + 2813]

provoking [1]

Gal 5:26 Let us not become conceited, **provoking** and envying each other.

4615 προκαταγγέλλω, *prokatangellō* [2]
[√ 4574 + 2848 + 34]

foretold [1], predicted [1]

Ac 3:18 But this is how God fulfilled what *he had* **foretold** through all the
7:52 They even killed those *who* **predicted** the coming of the Righteous

4616 προκαταρτίζω, *prokatartizō* [1]
[√ 4574 + 2848 + 785]

in advance finish the arrangements for [1]

2Co 9: 5 brothers to visit you **in advance** and **finish the arrangements for**

4617 προκατέχω, *prokatechō* Not used in UBS/NIV
[√ 4574 + 2848 + 2400]

4618 πρόκειμαι, *prokeimai* [5] [√ 4574 + 3023]

marked out [1], offered [1], serve as [1], set before [1], there [1]

2Co 8:12 For if the willingness *is* **there**, the gift is acceptable according to
Heb 6:18 we who have fled to take hold *of* the hope **offered** to us may be
12: 1 and let us run with perseverance the race **marked out** for us.
12: 2 who for the joy **set before** him endured the cross, scorning its
Jude 1: 7 *They* **serve as** an example of those who suffer the punishment of

4619 προκηρύσσω, *prokēryssō* [1] [√ 4574 + 3061]

preached [1]

Ac 13:24 John **preached** repentance and baptism to all the people of Israel.

4620 προκοπή, *prokopē* [3] [√ 4574 + 3164]

progress [2], advance [1]

Php 1:12 that what has happened to me has really served to **advance** the
1:25 and I will continue with all of you for your **progress** and joy in the
1Ti 4:15 yourself wholly to them, so that everyone may see your **progress**.

4621 προκόπτω, *prokoptō* [6] [√ 4574 + 3164]

advancing [1], get very far [+2093+4498] [1], go [1], grew [1], indulge [1], nearly over [1]

Lk 2:52 And Jesus **grew** in wisdom and stature, and in favor with God
Ro 13:12 The night *is* **nearly over**; the day is almost here. So let us put aside
Gal 1:14 *I was* **advancing** in Judaism beyond many Jews of my own age
2Ti 2:16 because *those who* **indulge** in it will become more and more
3: 9 But *they will* not **get** [+2093+4498] **very far** because, as in the
3:13 while evil men and impostors *will* **go** from bad to worse, deceiving

4622 πρόκριμα, *prokrima* [1] [√ 4574 + 3212]

partiality [1]

1Ti 5:21 and the elect angels, to keep these instructions without **partiality**,

4623 προκυρόω, *prokyroō* [1] [√ 4574 + 3263]

previously established [1]

Gal 3:17 does not set aside the covenant **previously established** by God

4624 προλαμβάνω, *prolambanō* [3] [√ *4574 + 3284*]

beforehand [1], caught [1], goes ahead [1]

Mk 14: 8 She poured perfume on my body **beforehand** to prepare for my
1Co 11: 21 each of you **goes ahead** without waiting for anybody else.
Gal 6: 1 Brothers, if someone *is* **caught** in a sin, you who are spiritual

4625 προλέγω, *prolegō* [15] [√ *4574 + 3306*]

said before [2], told ahead of time [2], already gave warning [1], already said [1], already told [1], did^s before [1], foretold [1], repeat [1], said previously [1], spoke long ago [1], spoken in the past [1], telling [1], warn [1]

Mt 24: 25 See, *I have* **told** you **ahead of time**.
Mk 13: 23 So be on your guard; *I have* **told** you everything **ahead of time**.
Ac 1: 16 **spoke long ago** through the mouth of David concerning Judas,
Ro 9: 29 It is just as Isaiah **said previously**: "Unless the Lord Almighty had
2Co 7: 3 *I have* **said before** that you have such a place in our hearts that we
13: 2 *I* **already gave** you a **warning** when I was with you the second
13: 2 *I now* **repeat** it while absent: On my return I will not spare those
Gal 1: 9 As *we have* **already said**, so now I say again: If anybody is
5: 21 *I* **warn** you, as I did before, that those who live like this will not
5: 21 I warn you, as *I* **did^s before**, that those who live like this will not
1Th 3: 4 were with you, *we kept* **telling** you that we would be persecuted.
4: 6 for all such sins, as *we have* **already told** you and warned you.
Heb 4: 7 a long time later he spoke through David, as *was* **said before**:
2Pe 3: 2 I want you to recall the words **spoken in the past** by the holy
Jude 1: 17 remember what the apostles of our Lord Jesus Christ **foretold**.

4626 προμαρτύρομαι, *promartyromai* [1]
[√ *4574 + 3459*]

predicted [1]

1Pe 1: 11 in them was pointing *when he* **predicted** the sufferings of Christ

4627 προμελετάω, *promeletaō* [1] [√ *4574 + 3508*]

worry beforehand [1]

Lk 21: 14 But make up your mind not *to* **worry beforehand** how you will

4628 προμεριμνάω, *promerimnaō* [1]
[√ *4574 + 3533*]

worry beforehand about [1]

Mk 13: 11 and brought to trial, *do* not **worry beforehand about** what to say.

4629 προνοέω, *pronoeō* [3] [√ *4574 + 3808*]

careful [1], provide for [1], taking pains [1]

Ro 12: 17 for evil. *Be* **careful** to do what is right in the eyes of everybody.
2Co 8: 21 For *we are* **taking pains** to do what is right, not only in the eyes of
1Ti 5: 8 If anyone *does* not **provide for** his relatives, and especially for his

4630 πρόνοια, *pronoia* [2] [√ *4574 + 3808*]

foresight [1], think about [+4472] [1]

Ac 24: 2 and your **foresight** has brought about reforms in this nation.
Ro 13: 14 and *do* not **think** [+4472] **about** how to gratify the desires of the

4631 πρόοιδα, *prooida* Not used in UBS/NIV
[√ *4574 + 3857*]

4632 προοράω, *prooraō* [4] [√ *4574 + 3972*]

foresaw [1], previously seen [+1639] [1], saw [1], seeing what was ahead [1]

Ac 2: 25 David said about him: " '*I* **saw** the Lord always before me.
2: 31 **Seeing what was ahead**, he spoke of the resurrection of the Christ,
21: 29 (*They had* **previously seen** [+1639] Trophimus the Ephesian in
Gal 3: 8 The Scripture **foresaw** that God would justify the Gentiles by faith,

4633 προορίζω, *proorizō* [6] [√ *4574 + 4000*]

predestined [4], decided beforehand [1], destined [1]

Ac 4: 28 your power and will *had* **decided beforehand** should happen.
Ro 8: 29 For those God foreknew *he* also **predestined** to be conformed to
8: 30 And those *he* **predestined**, he also called; those he called,
1Co 2: 7 and that God **destined** for our glory before time began.
Eph 1: 5 he **predestined** us to be adopted as his sons through Jesus Christ,
1: 11 *having been* **predestined** according to the plan of him who works

4634 προπάσχω, *propaschō* [1] [√ *4574 + 4248*]

previously suffered [1]

1Th 2: 2 *We had* **previously suffered** and been insulted in Philippi,

4635 προπάτωρ, *propatōr* [1] [√ *4574 + 4252*]

forefather [+2848+4922] [1]

Ro 4: 1 Abraham, our **forefather** [+2848+4922], discovered in this matter?

4636 προπέμπω, *propempō* [9] [√ *4574 + 4287*]

accompanied [2], send on way [2], assist on journey [1], help on journey [1], help on way [1], send on their way [1], sent on way [1]

Ac 15: 3 The church **sent** *them* **on** *their* **way**, and as they traveled through
20: 38 never see his face again. Then *they* **accompanied** him to the ship.
21: 5 and their wives and children **accompanied** us out of the city,
Ro 15: 24 passing through and to have you **assist** me **on** my **journey** there,
1Co 16: 6 the winter, so that you *can* **help** me **on** my **journey**, wherever I go.
16: 11 **Send** him **on** his **way** in peace so that he may return to me.
2Co 1: 16 and then to have you **send** me **on** my **way** to Judea.
Tit 3: 13 you can to **help** Zenas the lawyer and Apollos **on** *their* **way**
3Jn 1: 6 You will do well to **send** them **on their way** in a manner worthy of

4637 προπετής, *propetēs* [2] [√ *4574 + 4406*]

rash [2]

Ac 19: 36 are undeniable, you ought to be quiet and not do anything **rash**.
2Ti 3: 4 treacherous, **rash**, conceited, lovers of pleasure rather than lovers

4638 προπορεύομαι, *proporeuomai* [2]
[√ *4574 + 4513*]

go before [1], go on [1]

Lk 1: 76 for *you will* **go on** before the Lord to prepare the way for him,
Ac 7: 40 They told Aaron, 'Make us gods who *will* **go before** us. As for this

4639 πρός, *pros* [700 / 698]

[→ *717, 718, 1869, 2347, 2348, 4641, 4642, 4643, 4644, 4645, 4646, 4647, 4648, 4649, 4650, 4651, 4652, 4653, 4654, 4655, 4656, 4657, 4658, 4659, 4660, 4661, 4662, 4663, 4664, 4665, 4666, 4667, 4668, 4669, 4670, 4671, 4672, 4673, 4674, 4675, 4676, 4677, 4678, 4679, 4680, 4681, 4682, 4683, 4684, 4685, 4688, 4689, 4690, 4691, 4692, 4693, 4694, 4695, 4696, 4697, 4698, 4699, 4700, 4701, 4702, 4703, 4704, 4705, 4707, 4708, 4709, 4712, 4713, 4714, 4715, 4716, 4717, 4718, 4725; cf. 4686*]

to [374], *untranslated* [105], with [47], for [24], at [21], against [17], in [8], toward [8], before [7], to see [7], among [6], around [5], of [4], lead to [3], them [+899] [3], about [2], as [2], because [2], in order to [2], into [2], joined [+2262] [2], so that [2], together [+253] [2], united to [RP4681] [2], visit [+2262] [2], addressed [+3306] [1], answer [+2400] [1], approaching [+2262] [1], argued about [+253+1363] [1], begging [+1797+3836] [1], beside [1], between [1], bring [1], come to [RP4665] [1], comparing with [1], concerning [1], end [+1639] [1], for [+3836] [1], for a little while [+6052] [1], gave [+2400] [1], give [1], in approaching [1], in order to [+3836] [1], in restraining [1], intensely [+2160] [1], join [+2262] [1], leads to [1], lustfully [+2121+3836] [1], nearly [1], on [1], one another [+257+257] [1], outside [1], see [+2262] [1], so as to [1], so that [+3836] [1], talked the matter over [+253+1368]

[1], they [+899] [1], to give [1], to keep from [+3590+3836] [1], to show that [+3836] [1], told [+1181] [1], vicinity of [1], visit [+1181] [1], visited [+2262] [1]

Mt 2:12 And having been warned in a dream not to go back to Herod,
3: 5 People went out to him from Jerusalem and all Judea
3:10 The ax is already at the root of the trees, and every tree that does
3:13 came from Galilee to the Jordan to be baptized by [NIE] John.
3:14 saying, "I need to be baptized by you, and do you come to me?"
3:15 Jesus replied, "Let [NIE] it be so now; it is proper for us to do this
4: 6 their hands, so that you will not strike your foot against a stone.' "
5:28 lustfully [+2121+3836] has already committed adultery with her in
6: 1 to do your 'acts of righteousness' before men, to be seen by them.
7:15 They come to you in sheep's clothing, but inwardly they are
10: 6 Go rather to the lost sheep of Israel.
10:13 let your peace rest on it; if it is not, let your peace return to you.
11:28 "Come to me, all you who are weary and burdened,
13: 2 Such large crowds gathered around him that he got into a boat
13:30 First collect the weeds and tie them in bundles to be burned;
13:56 Aren't all his sisters with us? Where then did this man get all these
14:25 During the fourth watch of the night Jesus went out to them,
14:28 if it's you," Peter replied, "tell me to come to you on the water."
14:29 down out of the boat, walked on the water and came toward Jesus.
17:14 When they came to the crowd, a man approached Jesus and knelt
19: 8 you to divorce your wives because your hearts were hard.
19:14 Jesus said, "Let the little children come to me, and do not hinder
21:32 For John came to you to show you the way of righteousness,
21:34 he sent his servants to the tenants to collect his fruit.
21:37 Last of all, he sent his son to them. 'They will respect my son,'
23: 5 "Everything they do is done for [+3836] men to see: They make
23:34 Therefore I am sending [NIE] you prophets and wise men
23:37 Jerusalem, you who kill the prophets and stone those sent to you,
25: 9 Instead, go to those who sell oil and buy some for yourselves.'
25:36 you looked after me, I was in prison and you came to visit me.'
25:39 When did we see you sick or in prison and go to visit you?'
26:12 this perfume on my body, she did it to prepare me for burial.
26:14 the one called Judas Iscariot—went to the chief priests
26:18 He replied, "Go into the city to a certain man and tell him,
26:18 going to celebrate the Passover with my disciples at your house.' "
26:40 Then he returned to his disciples and found them sleeping.
26:45 Then he returned to the disciples and said to them, "Are you still
26:57 Those who had arrested Jesus took him to Caiaphas, the high
27: 4 "What is that to us?" they replied. "That's your responsibility."
27:14 But Jesus made no reply, not even to a single charge—to the great
27:19 sitting on the judge's seat, his wife sent [NIE] him this message:
27:62 Preparation Day, the chief priests and the Pharisees went to Pilate.

Mk 1: 5 and all the people of Jerusalem went out to him.
1:27 The people were all so amazed that they asked [NIE] each other,
1:32 That evening after sunset the people brought to Jesus all the sick
1:33 The whole town gathered at the door,
1:40 A man with leprosy came to him and begged him on his knees,
1:45 in lonely places. Yet the people still came to him from everywhere.
2: 2 not even outside the door, and he preached the word to them.
2: 3 Some men came, bringing to him a paralytic, carried by four of
2:13 the lake. A large crowd came to him, and he began to teach them.
3: 7 Jesus withdrew with his disciples to the lake, and a large crowd
3: 8 many people came to him from Judea, Jerusalem, Idumea,
3:13 and called to him those he wanted, and they came to him.
3:31 Standing outside, they sent someone in to call him.
4: 1 The crowd that gathered around him was so large that he got into
4: 1 while all the people were along the shore at the water's edge.
4:41 They were terrified and asked [NIE] each other, "Who is this?"
5:11 A large herd of pigs was feeding on the nearby hillside.
5:15 When they came to Jesus, they saw the man who had been
5:19 "Go home to your family and tell them how much the Lord has
5:22 named Jairus, came there. Seeing Jesus, he fell at his feet
6: 3 Joseph, Judas and Simon? Aren't his sisters here with us?"
6:25 At once the girl hurried in to the king with the request: "I want you
6:30 The apostles gathered around Jesus and reported to him all they
6:45 his disciples get into the boat and go on ahead of him to Bethsaida,
6:48 About the fourth watch of the night he went out to them,
6:51 Then he climbed into the boat with them, and the wind died down.
7: 1 of the law who had come from Jerusalem gathered around Jesus
7:25 daughter was possessed by an evil spirit came and fell at his feet.
8:16 They discussed this with one another and said, "It is because we
9:10 They kept the matter to themselves, discussing what "rising from

9:14 When they came to the other disciples, they saw a large crowd
9:14 crowd around them and the teachers of the law arguing with them.
9:16 "What are you arguing with them about?" he asked.
9:17 in the crowd answered, "Teacher, I brought [NIE] you my son,
9:19 Jesus replied, "how long shall I stay with you?
9:19 with you? How long shall I put up with you? Bring the boy to me."
9:20 [NIE] When the spirit saw Jesus, it immediately threw the boy
9:34 because on the way they had argued about [+253+1363] who was
10: 1 Again crowds of people came to him, and as was his custom,
10: 5 because your hearts were hard that Moses wrote you this law,"
10: 7 leave his father and mother and be united to [RP4681] his wife,
10:14 He said to them, "Let the little children come to me, and do not
10:26 more amazed, and said to each other, "Who then can be saved?"
10:50 Throwing his cloak aside, he jumped to his feet and came to Jesus.
11: 1 and came to Bethphage and Bethany at the Mount of Olives,
11: 4 They went and found a colt outside in the street, tied at a doorway.
11: 7 When they brought the colt to Jesus and threw their cloaks over it,
11:27 chief priests, the teachers of the law and the elders came to him.
11:31 They discussed it among themselves and said, "If we say,
12: 2 At harvest time he sent a servant to the tenants to collect from
12: 4 Then he sent another servant to them; they struck this man on the
12: 6 He sent him last of all, [NIE] saying, 'They will respect my son.'
12: 7 "But the tenants said to one another, 'This is the heir. Come,
12:12 because they knew he had spoken the parable against them.
12:13 of the Pharisees and Herodians to Jesus to catch him in his words.
12:18 who say there is no resurrection, came to him with a question.
13:22 will appear and perform signs and miracles to deceive the elect—
14: 4 Some of those present were saying indignantly to one another,
14:10 one of the Twelve, went to the chief priests to betray Jesus to them.
14:49 Every day I was with you, teaching in the temple courts, and you
14:53 They took Jesus to the high priest, and all the chief priests,
14:54 There he sat with the guards and warmed himself at the fire.
15:31 and the teachers of the law mocked him among themselves.
15:43 kingdom of God, went boldly to Pilate and asked for Jesus' body.
16: 3 and they asked [NIE] each other, "Who will roll the stone away

Lk 1:13 But the angel said to him: "Do not be afraid, Zechariah; your prayer
1:18 Zechariah asked [NIE] the angel, "How can I be sure of this?
1:19 and I have been sent to speak to you and to tell you this good
1:27 to a virgin pledged to be married to a man named Joseph,
1:28 The angel went to her and said, "Greetings, you who are highly
1:34 "How will this be," Mary asked [NIE] the angel, "since I am a
1:43 so favored, that the mother of my Lord should come to me?
1:55 and his descendants forever, even as he said to our fathers."
1:61 They said to her, "There is no one among your relatives who has
1:73 the oath he swore to our father Abraham,
1:80 and he lived in the desert until he appeared publicly to Israel.
2:15 left them and gone into heaven, the shepherds said to one another,
2:18 and all who heard it were amazed at what the shepherds said to
2:20 had heard and seen, which were just as they [+899] had been told.
2:34 Then Simeon blessed them and said to Mary, his mother: "This
2:48 His mother said to him, "Son, why have you treated us like this?
2:49 [NIE] "Didn't you know I had to be in my Father's house?"
3: 9 The ax is already at the root of the trees, and every tree that does
3:12 to be baptized. "Teacher," they asked, [NIE] "what should we do?"
3:13 collect any more than you are required to," he told them [+899].
4: 4 Jesus answered, [NIE] "It is written: 'Man does not live on bread
4:11 their hands, so that you will not strike your foot against a stone.' "
4:21 and he began by saying to them, "Today this scripture is fulfilled in
4:23 Jesus said to them, "Surely you will quote this proverb to me:
4:26 Yet Elijah was not sent to any of them, but to a widow in
4:26 to any of them, but to a widow in Zarephath in the region of Sidon.
4:36 All the people were amazed and said to each other, "What is this
4:40 the people brought to Jesus all who had various kinds of sickness,
4:43 [NIE] "I must preach the good news of the kingdom of God to the
5: 4 had finished speaking, he said to Simon, "Put out into deep water,
5:10 Then Jesus said to Simon, "Don't be afraid; from now on you will
5:22 [NIE] "Why are you thinking these things in your hearts?
5:30 of the law who belonged to their sect complained to his disciples
5:31 Jesus answered [NIE] them, "It is not the healthy who need a
5:33 They said to him, "John's disciples often fast and pray, and
5:34 [NIE] "Can you make the guests of the bridegroom fast while he is
5:36 He told [NIE] them this parable: "No one tears a patch from a new
6: 3 [NIE] "Have you never read what David did when he and his
6: 9 Then Jesus said to them, "I ask you, which is lawful on the Sabbath:
6:11 and began to discuss with one another what they might do to Jesus.
6:47 I will show you what he is like who comes to me and hears my

7: 3 centurion heard of Jesus and sent some elders of the Jews **to** him,
7: 4 When they came **to** Jesus, they pleaded earnestly with him,
7: 7 That is why I did not even consider myself worthy to come **to** you.
7:19 he sent them **to** the Lord to ask, "Are you the one who was to come,
7:20 When the men came **to** Jesus, they said, "John the Baptist sent us to
7:20 came **to** Jesus, they said, "John the Baptist sent us **to** you to ask,
7:24 messengers left, Jesus began to speak **to** the crowd about John:
7:40 Jesus answered [NIE] him, "Simon, I have something to tell you."
7:44 Then he turned **toward** the woman and said to Simon, "Do you see
7:50 Jesus said **to** the woman, "Your faith has saved you; go in peace."
8: 4 and people were coming **to** Jesus from town after town,
8:13 They believe **for** a while, but in the time of testing they fall away.
8:19 Now Jesus' mother and brothers came **to see** him, but they were not
8:21 [NIE] "My mother and brothers are those who hear God's word
8:22 One day Jesus said **to** his disciples, "Let's go over to the other side
8:25 In fear and amazement they asked [NIE] one another, "Who is
8:35 When they came **to** Jesus, they found the man from whom the
9: 3 He told **them** [+899]: "Take nothing for the journey—no staff,
9:13 He replied, [NIE] "You give them something to eat." They
9:14 But he said **to** his disciples, "Have them sit down in groups of about
9:23 Then he said **to** them all: "If anyone would come after me,
9:33 Peter said **to** him, "Master, it is good for us to be here.
9:41 Jesus replied, "how long shall I stay **with** you and put up with you?
9:43 was marveling at all that Jesus did, he said **to** his disciples,
9:50 Jesus said, [NIE] "for whoever is not against you is for you."
9:57 the road, a man said **to** him, "I will follow you wherever you go."
9:59 He said **to** another man, "Follow me." But the man replied, "Lord,
9:62 Jesus replied [UBS+ *to him*], "No one who puts his hand to the
10: 2 He told **them** [+899], "The harvest is plentiful, but the workers are
10:23 Then he turned **to** his disciples and said privately, "Blessed are the
10:26 is written in the Law?" he replied. [NIE] "How do you read it?"
10:29 so he asked [NIE] Jesus, "And who is my neighbor?"
10:39 called Mary, who sat **at** the Lord's feet listening to what he said.
11: 1 he finished, one of his disciples said **to** him, "Lord, teach us to pray,
11: 5 Then he said **to** them, "Suppose one of you has a friend, and he
11: 5 and he goes **to** him at midnight and says, 'Friend, lend me three
11: 6 because a friend of mine on a journey has come **to** me, and I have
11:39 Then the Lord said **to** him, "Now then, you Pharisees clean the
12: 1 on one another, Jesus began to speak first **to** his disciples, saying:
12: 3 and what you have whispered **in** the ear in the inner rooms will be
12:15 Then he said **to** them, "Watch out! Be on your guard against all
12:16 And he told [NIE] them this parable: "The ground of a certain rich
12:22 Then Jesus said **to** his disciples: "Therefore I tell you, do not worry
12:41 Peter asked, "Lord, are you telling this parable **to** us, or to
12:41 "Lord, are you telling this parable to us, or **to** everyone?"
12:47 or does not do [NIE] what his master wants will be beaten with
12:58 or he may drag you off **to** the judge, and the judge turn you over to
13: 7 So he said **to** the man who took care of the vineyard, 'For three
13:23 are only a few people going to be saved?" He said **to** them,
13:34 Jerusalem, you who kill the prophets and stone those sent **to** you,
14: 3 Jesus asked [NIE] the Pharisees and experts in the law, "Is it
14: 5 Then he asked [NIE] them, "If one of you has a son or an ox that
14: 6 And they had nothing to say. [NIE]
14: 7 the places of honor at the table, he told [NIE] them this parable:
14: 7 the places of honor at the table, he told them this parable: [NIE]
14:23 "Then the master told [NIE] his servant, 'Go out to the roads
14:25 crowds were traveling with Jesus, and turning **to** them he said:
14:26 "If anyone comes **to** me and does not hate his father and mother,
14:32 the other is still a long way off and will ask **for** terms of peace.
15: 3 Then Jesus told [NIE] them this parable:
15:18 I will set out and go back **to** my father and say to him: Father,
15:20 So he got up and went **to** his father. "But while he was still a long
15:22 "But the father said **to** his servants, 'Quick! Bring the best robe
16: 1 Jesus told [NIE] his disciples: "There was a rich man whose
16:20 **At** his gate was laid a beggar named Lazarus, covered with sores
16:26 been fixed, so that those who want to go from here **to** you cannot,
16:26 here to you cannot, nor can anyone cross over from there **to** us.'
16:30 he said, 'but if someone from the dead goes **to** them, they will
17: 1 Jesus said **to** his disciples: "Things that cause people to sin are
17: 4 and seven times comes back **to** you and says, 'I repent,'
17:22 Then he said **to** his disciples, "The time is coming when you will
18: 1 a parable **to** [+3836] **show** them **that** they should always pray
18: 3 And there was a widow in that town who kept coming **to** him with
18: 9 **To** some who were confident of their own righteousness
18:11 The Pharisee stood up and prayed **about** himself: 'God, I thank
18:16 the children to him and said, "Let the little children come **to** me,

18:31 Jesus took the Twelve aside and told [NIE] them, "We are going
18:40 Jesus stopped and ordered the man to be brought **to** him. When he
19: 5 he looked up and said **to** him, "Zacchaeus, come down
19: 8 But Zacchaeus stood up and said **to** the Lord, "Look, Lord!
19: 9 Jesus said **to** him, "Today salvation has come to this house,
19:13 'Put this money to work,' he said, [NIE] 'until I come back.'
19:29 and Bethany **at** the hill called the Mount of Olives,
19:33 As they were untying the colt, its owners asked [NIE] them,
19:35 They brought it **to** Jesus, threw their cloaks on the colt and put
19:37 When he came near [NIE] the place where the road goes down
19:39 Some of the Pharisees in the crowd said **to** Jesus, "Teacher,
19:42 had only known on this day what would **bring** you peace—
20: 2 these things," they said. [NIE] "Who gave you this authority?"
20: 3 He replied, [NIE] "I will also ask you a question. Tell me,
20: 5 They discussed it **among** themselves and said, "If we say,
20: 9 He went on to tell [NIE] the people this parable: "A man planted a
20:10 At harvest time he sent a servant **to** the tenants so they would give
20:14 the tenants saw him, *they* **talked the matter over** [+253+1368].
20:19 because they knew he had spoken this parable **against** them.
20:23 He saw through their duplicity and said **to** them,
20:25 He said **to** them, "Then give to Caesar what is Caesar's, and to God
20:41 Then Jesus said **to** them, "How is it that they say the Christ is the
21:38 and all the people came early in the morning [NIE] to hear him at
22:15 And he said **to** them, "I have eagerly desired to eat this Passover
22:23 They began to question **among** themselves which of them it might
22:45 When he rose from prayer and went back **to** the disciples,
22:52 Then Jesus said **to** the chief priests, the officers of the temple
22:56 A servant girl saw him seated there **in** the firelight. She looked
22:70 the Son of God?" He replied, [NIE] "You are right in saying I am."
23: 4 Then Pilate announced **to** the chief priests and the crowd,
23: 7 he sent him **to** Herod, who was also in Jerusalem at that time.
23:12 Pilate became friends—before this they had been enemies. [NIE]
23:14 and said **to** them, "You brought me this man as one who was
23:15 Neither has Herod, for he sent him back **to** us; as you can see,
23:22 For the third time he spoke to them: "Why? What crime has this
23:28 Jesus turned and said **to** them, "Daughters of Jerusalem, do not
24: 5 but the men said **to** them, "Why do you look for the living among
24:10 of James, and the others with them who told this **to** the apostles.
24:12 and he went away, wondering to himself what had happened.
24:14 They were talking **with** each other about everything that had
24:17 He asked [NIE] them, "What are you discussing together as you
24:17 "What are you discussing **together** [+253] as you walk along?"
24:18 One of them, named Cleopas, asked [NIE] him, "Are you only a
24:25 He said **to** them, "How foolish you are, and how slow of heart to
24:29 But they urged him strongly, "Stay with us, for it is **nearly** evening;
24:32 They asked [NIE] each other, "Were not our hearts burning within
24:44 He said **to** them, "This is what I told you while I was still with you:
24:44 to them, "This is what I told [NIE] you while I was still with you:
24:50 When he had led them out to the **vicinity of** Bethany, he lifted up
Jn 1: 1 the Word, and the Word was **with** God, and the Word was God.
1: 2 He was **with** God in the beginning.
1:19 testimony when the Jews of Jerusalem sent [UBS+ *to him*] priests
1:29 The next day John saw Jesus coming **toward** him and said,
1:42 And he brought him **to** Jesus. Jesus looked at him and said,
1:47 *When* Jesus saw Nathanael **approaching** [+2262], he said of him,
2: 3 was gone, Jesus' mother said **to** him, "They have no more wine."
3: 2 He came **to** Jesus at night and said, "Rabbi, we know you are a
3: 4 [NIE] "Surely he cannot enter a second time into his mother's
3:20 and will not come **into** the light for fear that his deeds will be
3:21 But whoever lives by the truth comes **into** the light, so that it may
3:26 They came **to** John and said to him, "Rabbi, that man who was with
3:26 well, he is baptizing, and everyone is going **to** him."
4:15 The woman said **to** him, "Sir, give me this water so that I won't get
4:30 They came out of the town and made their way **toward** him.
4:33 Then his disciples said **to** each other, "Could someone have brought
4:35 open your eyes and look at the fields! They are ripe **for** harvest.
4:40 So when the Samaritans came **to** him, they urged him to stay with
4:47 he went **to** him and begged him to come and heal his son,
4:48 people see miraculous signs and wonders," Jesus told [NIE] him,
4:49 The royal official said, [NIE] "Sir, come down before my child
5:33 "You have sent **to** John and he has testified to the truth.
5:35 and gave light, and you chose **for** a time to enjoy his light.
5:40 yet you refuse to come **to** me to have life.
5:45 "But do not think I will accuse you **before** the Father. Your accuser
6: 5 When Jesus looked up and saw a great crowd coming **toward** him,
6: 5 and saw a great crowd coming toward him, he said **to** Philip,

6:17 By now it was dark, and Jesus *had* not yet **joined** [+2262] them.
6:28 Then they asked [NIE] him, "What must we do to do the works
6:34 "Sir," they said, [NIE] "from now on give us this bread."
6:35 He who comes to me will never go hungry, and he who believes in
6:37 All that the Father gives me will come **to** me, and whoever comes
6:37 come to me, and whoever comes **to** me I will never drive away.
6:44 "No one can come **to** me unless the Father who sent me draws him,
6:45 who listens to the Father and learns from him comes **to** me.
6:52 Then the Jews began to argue sharply **among** themselves,
6:65 "This is why I told you that no one can come **to** me unless the
6:68 Simon Peter answered him, "Lord, **to** whom shall we go? You have
7: 3 Jesus' brothers said **to** him, "You ought to leave here and go to
7:33 you for only a short time, and then I go **to** the one who sent me.
7:35 The Jews said **to** one another, "Where does this man intend to go
7:37 in a loud voice, "If anyone is thirsty, let him come **to** me and drink.
7:45 Finally the temple guards went back **to** the chief priests
7:50 who had gone **to** Jesus earlier and who was one of their own
7:50 Jesus earlier and who was one of their own number, asked, [NIE]
8: 2 where all the people gathered **around** him, and he sat down to
8:31 **To** the Jews who had believed him, Jesus said, "If you hold to my
8:33 They answered [NIE] him, "We are Abraham's descendants
8:57 years old," the Jews said **to** him, "and you have seen Abraham!"
9:13 They brought **to** the Pharisees the man who had been blind.
10:35 If he called them 'gods,' **to** whom the word of God came—
10:41 and many people came **to** him. They said, "Though John never
11: 3 So the sisters sent word **to** Jesus, "Lord, the one you love is sick."
11: 4 heard this, Jesus said, "This sickness *will* not **end** [+1639] in death.
11:15 glad I was not there, so that you may believe. But let us go **to** him."
11:19 and many Jews had come **to** Martha and Mary to comfort them in
11:21 "Lord," Martha said **to** Jesus, "if you had been here, my brother
11:29 When Mary heard this, she got up quickly and went **to** him.
11:32 where Jesus was and saw him, she fell **at** his feet and said, "Lord,
11:45 Therefore many of the Jews who had come **to** *visit* Mary,
11:46 But some of them went **to** the Pharisees and told them what Jesus
12:19 So the Pharisees said **to** one another, "See, this is getting us
12:32 when I am lifted up from the earth, will draw all men **to** myself."
13: 1 the time had come for him to leave this world and *go* **to** the Father.
13: 3 and that he had come from God and was returning **to** God;
13: 6 He came **to** Simon Peter, who said to him, "Lord, are you going to
13:28 but no one at the meal understood [NIE] why Jesus said this to
14: 3 and take you to be **with** me that you also may be where I am.
14: 6 and the life. No one comes **to** the Father except through me.
14:12 do even greater things than these, because I am going **to** the Father.
14:18 I will not leave you as orphans; I will come **to** you.
14:23 love him, and we will come **to** him and make our home with him.
14:28 heard me say, 'I am going away and I am coming back **to** you.'
14:28 If you loved me, you would be glad that I am going **to** the Father,
16: 5 "Now I am going **to** him who sent me, yet none of you asks me,
16: 7 Unless I go away, the Counselor will not come **to** you; but if I go,
16: 7 Counselor will not come to you; but if I go, I will send him **to** you.
16:10 in regard to righteousness, because I am going **to** the Father,
16:17 Some of his disciples said **to** one another, "What does he mean by
16:17 while you will see me,' and 'Because I am going **to** the Father'?"
16:28 now I am leaving the world and going back **to** the Father."
17:11 no longer, but they are still in the world, and I am coming **to** you.
17:13 "I am coming **to** you now, but I say these things while I am still in
18:13 and brought him first **to** Annas, who was the father-in-law of
18:16 but Peter had to wait outside **at** the door. The other disciple,
18:24 Then Annas sent him, still bound, **to** Caiaphas the high priest.
18:29 So Pilate came out **to** them and asked, "What charges are you
18:38 With this he went out again **to** the Jews and said, "I find no basis for
19: 3 went up **to** him again and again, saying, "Hail, king of the Jews!"
19:24 "Let's not tear it," they said **to** one another. "Let's decide by lot
19:39 the man *who* earlier *had* **visited** [+2262] Jesus at night.
20: 2 So she came running **to** Simon Peter and the other disciple,
20: 2 she came running to Simon Peter and [RPG] the other disciple,
20:10 Then the disciples went back **to** their homes,
20:11 but Mary stood outside [NIE] the tomb crying. As she wept,
20:12 Jesus' body had been, one **at** the head and the other at the foot.
20:12 Jesus' body had been, one at the head and the other **at** the foot.
20:17 "Do not hold on to me, for I have not yet returned **to** the Father.
20:17 Go instead **to** my brothers and tell them, 'I am returning to my
20:17 'I am returning **to** my Father and your Father, to my God and your
21:22 "If I want him to remain alive until I return, what is that **to** you?
21:23 "If I want him to remain alive until I return, what is that **to** you?"
Ac   1: 7 He said **to** them: "It is not for you to know the times or dates the

2:12 Amazed and perplexed, they asked **one another** [+257+257],
2:29 I can tell [NIE] you confidently that the patriarch David died
2:37 they were cut to the heart and said **to** Peter and the other apostles,
2:38 Peter replied, [NIE] "Repent and be baptized, every one of you,
2:47 praising God and enjoying the favor **of** all the people.
3: 2 Now a man crippled from birth was being carried **to** the temple
3:10 to sit **begging** [+1797+3836] at the temple gate called Beautiful,
3:11 and came running **to** them in the place called Solomon's
3:12 When Peter saw this, he said **to** them: "Men of Israel, why does this
3:22 own people; you must listen to everything he tells [NIE] you.
3:25 of the prophets and of the covenant God made **with** your fathers.
3:25 He said **to** Abraham, 'Through your offspring all peoples on earth
4: 1 came up to Peter and John while they were speaking **to** the people.
4: 8 Then Peter, filled with the Holy Spirit, said **to** them: "Rulers
4:15 withdraw from the Sanhedrin and then conferred **together** [+253].
4:19 "Judge for yourselves [NIE] whether it is right in God's sight to
4:23 Peter and John went back **to** their own people and reported all that
4:23 and reported all that the chief priests and elders had said **to** them.
4:24 they heard this, they raised their voices together in prayer **to** God.
4:37 he owned and brought the money and put it **at** the apostles' feet.
5: 8 Peter asked [NIE] her, "Tell me, is this the price you and Ananias
5: 9 Peter said **to** her, "How could you agree to test the Spirit of the
5:10 At that moment she fell down **at** his feet and died. Then the young
5:10 her dead, carried her out and buried her **beside** her husband.
5:35 Then he addressed [NIE] them: "Men of Israel, consider carefully
6: 1 the Grecian Jews among them complained **against** the Hebraic
7: 3 God said, [NIE] 'and go to the land I will show you.'
8:14 had accepted the word of God, they sent Peter and John **to** them.
8:20 [NIE] "May your money perish with you, because you thought you
8:24 "Pray **to** the Lord for me so that nothing you have said may happen
8:26 Now an angel of the Lord said **to** Philip, "Go south to the road—
9: 2 and asked him for letters **to** the synagogues in Damascus,
9:10 The Lord called **to** him in a vision, "Ananias!" "Yes, Lord," he
9:11 The Lord told [NIE] him, "Go to the house of Judas on Straight
9:15 But the Lord said to Ananias, "Go! This man is my chosen
9:27 But Barnabas took him and brought him **to** the apostles. He told
9:29 He talked and debated **with** the Grecian Jews,
9:32 traveled about the country, he went **to** *visit* the saints in Lydda.
9:38 they sent two men **to** him and urged him, "Please come at once!"
9:40 Turning **toward** the dead woman, he said, "Tabitha, get up."
10: 3 saw an angel of God, who came **to** him and said, "Cornelius!"
10:13 Then a voice **told** [+1181] him, "Get up, Peter. Kill and eat."
10:15 The voice spoke **to** him a second time, "Do not call anything
10:21 Peter went down and said **to** the men, "I'm the one you're looking
10:28 He said **to** them: "You are well aware that it is against our law for a
10:33 So I sent **for** you immediately, and it was good of you to come.
11: 2 up to Jerusalem, the circumcised believers criticized [NIE] him
11: 3 "You went into the house [NIE] of uncircumcised men and ate
11:11 then three men who had been sent **to** me from Caesarea stopped at
11:14 He will bring [NIE] you a message through which you and all
11:20 and Cyrene, went to Antioch and began to speak **to** Greeks also,
11:30 This they did, sending their gift **to** the elders by Barnabas and Saul.
12: 5 in prison, but the church was earnestly praying **to** God for him.
12: 8 Then the angel said **to** him, "Put on your clothes and sandals."
12:15 "You're out of your mind," they told [NIE] her. When she kept
12:20 they now joined together and sought an audience **with** him.
12:21 sat on his throne and delivered a public address **to** the people.
13:15 the synagogue rulers sent word **to** them, saying, "Brothers,
13:15 "Brothers, if you have a message of encouragement **for** the people,
13:31 Galilee to Jerusalem. They are now his witnesses **to** our people.
13:32 tell you the good news: What God promised [NIE] our fathers
13:36 he fell asleep; he was buried **with** his fathers and his body decayed.
14:11 "The gods have come down **to** us in human form!"
15: 2 and Barnabas into sharp dispute and debate **with** them.
15: 2 to go up to Jerusalem **to** see the apostles and elders about this
15: 7 After much discussion, Peter got up and **addressed** [+3306] them:
15:25 and send them **to** you with our dear friends Barnabas and Paul—
15:33 with the blessing of peace to return **to** those who had sent them.
15:36 Some time later Paul said **to** Barnabas, "Let us go back and visit the
16:36 The jailer told [NIE] Paul, "The magistrates have ordered that you
16:37 But Paul said **to** the officers: "They beat us publicly without a trial,
16:40 and Silas came out of the prison, they went **to** Lydia's *house*,
17: 2 As his custom was, Paul went into [NIE] the synagogue,
17:15 and then left with instructions **for** Silas and Timothy to join him as
17:15 for Silas and Timothy to **join** [+2262] him as soon as possible.
17:17 as well as in the marketplace day by day **with** those who happened

18: 6   he shook out his clothes in protest and said **to** them,
18:14   Just as Paul was about to speak, Gallio said **to** the Jews, "If you
18:21   as he left, he promised, "I will come back [NIE] if it is God's will."
19: 2   and asked [NIE] them, "Did you receive the Holy Spirit when you
19: 2   They answered, [NIE] "No, we have not even heard that there is a
19:31   sent [NIE] him a message begging him not to venture into the
19:38   and his fellow craftsmen have a grievance **against** anybody,
20: 6   and five days later **joined** [+2262] the others at Troas, where we
20:18   When they arrived, [NIE] he said to them: "You know how I lived
21:11   Coming *over* **to** us, he took Paul's belt, tied his own hands
21:18   The next day Paul and the rest of us went **to see** James, and all the
21:37   he asked the commander, "May I say something **to** you?"
21:39   a citizen of no ordinary city. Please let me speak **to** the people."
22: 1   "Brothers and fathers, listen now to my defense." [NIE]
22: 5   I even obtained letters from them **to** their brothers in Damascus,
22: 8   Jesus of Nazareth, whom you are persecuting,' he replied. [NIE]
22:10   I asked. " 'Get up,' the Lord said, [NIE] 'and go into Damascus.
22:12   "A man named Ananias came **to see** me. He was a devout observer
22:15   You will be his witness **to** all men of what you have seen
22:21   "Then the Lord said **to** me, 'Go; I will send you far away to the
22:25   him out to flog him, Paul said **to** the centurion standing there,
23: 3   Then Paul said **to** him, "God will strike you, you whitewashed
23:17   the centurions and said, "Take this young man **to** the commander;
23:18   So he took him **to** the commander. The centurion said, "Paul,
23:18   sent for me and asked me to bring this young man **to** you
23:22   him, "Don't tell anyone that you have reported this **to** me."
23:24   mounts for Paul so that he may be taken safely **to** Governor Felix."
23:30   a plot to be carried out against the man, I sent him **to** you at once.
23:30   I also ordered his accusers to present to you their case **against** him.
24:12   My accusers did not find me arguing **with** anyone at the temple,
24:16   So I strive always to keep my conscience clear **before** God
24:19   before you and bring charges if they have anything **against** me.
25:16   "I told [NIE] them that it is not the Roman custom to hand over
25:19   they had some points of dispute **with** him about their own religion
25:21   I ordered him held until I could send him **to** Caesar."
25:22   Agrippa said **to** Festus, "I would like to hear this man myself."
26: 1   Then Agrippa said **to** Paul, "You have permission to speak for
26: 9   that was possible to oppose [NIE] the name of Jesus of Nazareth.
26:14   and I heard a voice saying to me in Aramaic, 'Saul, Saul,
26:14   do you persecute me? It is hard for you to kick **against** the goads.'
26:26   king is familiar with these things, and I can speak freely **to** him.
26:28   Then Agrippa said **to** Paul, "Do you think that in such a short time
26:31   They left the room, and while talking **with** one another, they said,
27: 3   allowed him to go **to** his friends so they might provide for his
27:12   Since the harbor was unsuitable **to** winter in, the majority decided
27:34   Now I urge you to take some food. You need it **to** survive.
28: 4   his hand, they said **to** each other, "This man must be a murderer,
28: 8   Paul went in **to see** him and, after prayer, placed his hands on him
28:10   to sail, they furnished us with the supplies [NIE] we needed.
28:17   When they had assembled, Paul said **to** them: "My brothers,
28:21   [NIE] "We have not received any letters from Judea concerning
28:23   and came [NIE] in even larger numbers to the place where he was
28:25   They disagreed **among** themselves and began to leave after Paul
28:25   "The Holy Spirit spoke the truth **to** your forefathers when he said
28:26   " 'Go **to** this people and say, "You will be ever hearing but never
28:30   in his own rented house and welcomed all who came **to see** him.

Ro   1:10   last by God's will the way may be opened for me to come **to** you.
1:13   that I planned many times to come **to** you (but have been prevented
3:26   he did it **to** demonstrate his justice at the present time, so as to be
4: 2   by works, he had something to boast about—but not **before** God.
5: 1   we have peace **with** God through our Lord Jesus Christ,
8:18   are not worth **comparing with** the glory that will be revealed in us.
8:31   What, then, shall we say *in response* **to** this? If God is for us,
10: 1   and prayer **to** God for the Israelites is that they may be saved.
10:21   But **concerning** Israel he says, "All day long I have held out my
10:21   "All day long I have held out my hands **to** a disobedient
15: 2   of us should please his neighbor for his good, **to** build him up.
15:17   Therefore I glory in Christ Jesus in my service **to** God.
15:22   This is why I have often been hindered from coming **to** you.
15:23   and since I have been longing for many years *to* **see** [+2262] you,
15:29   I know that when I come **to** you, I will come in the full measure of
15:30   of the Spirit, to join me in my struggle by praying **to** God for me.
15:32   so that by God's will I may come **to** you with joy and together with

1Co   2: 1   When I came **to** you, brothers, I did not come with eloquence
2: 3   I came **to** you in weakness and fear, and with much trembling.
4:18   Some of you have become arrogant, as if I were not coming **to** you.

4:19   But I will come **to** you very soon, if the Lord is willing, and
4:21   Shall I come **to** you with a whip, or in love and with a gentle
6: 1   If any of you has a dispute **with** another, dare he take it before the
6: 5   I say this **to** shame you. Is it possible that there is nobody among
7: 5   Do not deprive each other except by mutual consent and **for** a time,
7:35   I am saying this **for** your own good, not to restrict you, but that
7:35   but that you may *live* **in** a right way in undivided devotion to the
10:11   to them as examples and were written down **as** warnings for us,
12: 2   or other you were influenced and led astray **to** mute idols.
12: 7   Now to each one the manifestation of the Spirit is given **for** the
13:12   but a poor reflection as in a mirror; then we shall see face **to** face.
14: 6   Now, brothers, if I come **to** you and speak in tongues, what good
14:12   spiritual gifts, try to excel in gifts that [NIE] build up the church.
14:26   All of these must be done **for** the strengthening of the church.
15:34   there are some who are ignorant of God—I say this **to** your shame.
16: 5   After I go through Macedonia, I will come **to** you—for I will be
16: 6   Perhaps I will stay **with** you awhile, or even spend the winter,
16: 7   I hope to spend some time **with** you, if the Lord permits.
16:10   see to it that he has nothing to fear while he is **with** you,
16:11   Send him on his way in peace so that he may return **to** me.
16:12   I strongly urged him to go **to** you with the brothers.

2Co   1:12   and especially *in* our *relations* **with** you, in the holiness
1:15   I planned *to* **visit** [+2262] you first so that you might benefit twice.
1:16   my way to Macedonia and to come back **to** you from Macedonia,
1:18   as God is faithful, our message **to** you is not "Yes" and "No."
1:20   so through him the "Amen" is spoken by us **to** the glory of God.
2: 1   up my mind that I would not make another painful visit **to** you.
2:16   to the other, the fragrance of life. And who is equal **to** such a task?
3: 1   like some people, letters of recommendation **to** you or from you?
3: 4   Such confidence as this is ours through Christ **before** God.
3:13   **to** [+3590+3836] **keep** the Israelites **from** gazing at it while the
3:16   But whenever anyone turns **to** the Lord, the veil is taken away.
4: 2   by setting forth the truth plainly we commend ourselves **to** every
4: 6   made his light shine in our hearts **to give** us the light of the
5: 8   would prefer to be away from the body and at home **with** the Lord.
5:10   that each one may receive what is due him **for** the things done
5:12   so that *you can* **answer** [+2400] those who take pride in what is
6:11   We have spoken freely **to** you, Corinthians, and opened wide our
6:14   in common? Or what fellowship can light have **with** darkness?
6:15   What harmony is there **between** Christ and Belial? What does a
7: 3   I do not say this **to** condemn you; I have said before that you have
7: 4   I have great confidence **in** you; I take great pride in you. I am
7: 8   regret it—I see that my letter hurt you, but only **for** a little while—
7:12   but rather that before God you could see **for** yourselves how
8:17   but he is coming **to** you with much enthusiasm and on his own
8:19   which we administer **in order** to honor the Lord himself and to
10: 4   On the contrary, they have divine power **to** demolish strongholds.
11: 8   other churches by receiving support from them **so as to** serve you.
11: 9   And when I was **with** you and needed something, I was not a
12:14   Now I am ready *to* **visit** [+2262] you for the third time, and I will
12:17   Did I exploit you through any of the men I sent [NIE] you?
12:21   I am afraid that when I come again my God will humble me **before**
13: 1   This will be my third visit **to** you. "Every matter must be
13: 7   Now we pray **to** God that you will not do anything wrong.

Gal   1:17   nor did I go up to Jerusalem **to see** those who were apostles before
1:18   to get acquainted with Peter and stayed **with** him fifteen days.
2: 5   We did not give in to them **for** a moment, so that the truth of the
2: 5   a moment, so that the truth of the gospel might remain **with** you.
2:14   When I saw that they were not acting in line **with** the truth of the
4:18   is good, and to be so always and not just when I am **with** you.
4:20   how I wish I could be **with** you now and change my tone,
6:10   Therefore, as we have opportunity, let us do good **to** all people,
6:10   especially **to** those who belong to the family of believers.

Eph   2:18   For through him we both have access **to** the Father by one Spirit.
3: 4   In reading [NIE] this, then, you will be able to understand my
3:14   For this reason I kneel **before** the Father,
4:12   **to** prepare God's people for works of service, so that the body of
4:14   by the cunning and craftiness of men **in** their deceitful scheming.
4:29   but only what is helpful **for** building others up according to their
5:31   leave his father and mother and *be* **united to** [RP4681] his wife,
6: 9   And masters, treat your [NIE] slaves in the same way. Do not
6:11   **so that** [+3836] you can take your stand against the devil's
6:11   so that you can take your stand **against** the devil's schemes.
6:12   For our struggle is not **against** flesh and blood, but against the
6:12   our struggle is not against flesh and blood, but **against** the rulers,
6:12   and blood, but against the rulers, **against** the authorities,

6: 12 **against** the powers of this dark world and against the spiritual
6: 12 and **against** the spiritual forces of evil in the heavenly realms.
6: 22 I am sending him **to** you for this very purpose, that you may know

Php 1: 26 so that through my being **with** you again your joy in Christ Jesus
2: 25 But I think it is necessary to send back **to** you Epaphroditus,
2: 30 risking his life to make up for the help you could not give **[NIE]**
4: 6 and petition, with thanksgiving, present your requests **to** God.

Col 2: 23 but they lack any value in **restraining** sensual indulgence.
3: 13 and forgive whatever grievances you may have **against** one
3: 19 Husbands, love your wives and do not be harsh **with** them.
4: 5 Be wise in the way you act **toward** outsiders; make the most of
4: 8 I am sending him **to** you for the express purpose that you may
4: 10 instructions about him; if he comes **to** you, welcome him.)

1Th 1: 8 and Achaia—your faith **in** God has become known everywhere.
1: 9 they themselves report what kind of reception you **gave** [+*2400*]
1: 9 They tell how you turned **to** God from idols to serve the living
2: 1 You know, brothers, that our visit **to** you was not a failure.
2: 2 but with the help of our God we dared to tell **[NIE]** you his gospel
2: 9 and day **in order** not to [+*3836*] be a burden to anyone while we
2: 17 when we were torn away from you **for** a short time (in person,
2: 18 For we wanted to come **to** you—certainly I, Paul, did, again
3: 4 In fact, when we were **with** you, we kept telling you that we would
3: 6 But Timothy has just now come **to** us from you and has brought
3: 11 and our Lord Jesus clear the way for us to come **to** you.
4: 12 so that your daily life may win the respect **of** outsiders and
5: 14 encourage the timid, help the weak, be patient **with** everyone.

2Th 2: 5 Don't you remember that when I was **with** you I used to tell you
3: 1 Lord may spread rapidly and be honored, just as it was **with** you.
3: 8 and toiling **so that** we would not be a burden to any of you.
3: 10 For even when we were **with** you, we gave you this rule: "If a man

1Ti 1: 16 Christ Jesus might display his unlimited patience **as** an example for
3: 14 Although I hope to come **to** you soon, I am writing you these
4: 7 and old wives' tales; rather, train yourself **to** be godly.
4: 8 For physical training is **of** some value, but godliness has value for
4: 8 training is of some value, but godliness has value **for** all things,

2Ti 2: 24 instead, he must be kind **to** everyone, able to teach, not resentful.
3: 16 All Scripture is God-breathed and is useful **for** teaching, rebuking,
3: 16 **[RPG]** rebuking, correcting and training in righteousness,
3: 16 rebuking, **[RPG]** correcting and training in righteousness,
3: 16 rebuking, correcting and **[RPG]** training in righteousness,
3: 17 so that the man of God may be thoroughly equipped **for** every
4: 9 Do your best to come **to** me quickly,

Tit 1: 16 They are detestable, disobedient and unfit **for** doing anything good.
3: 1 and authorities, to be obedient, to be ready **to** do whatever is good,
3: 2 and considerate, and to show true humility **toward** all men.
3: 12 As soon as I send Artemas or Tychicus **to** you, do your best to
3: 12 or Tychicus to you, do your best to come **to** me at Nicopolis,

Phm 1: 5 because I hear about your faith **in** the Lord Jesus and your love for
1: 13 I would have liked to keep him **with** me so that he could take your
1: 15 **for a little while** [+*6052*] was that you might have him back for

Heb 1: 7 In speaking **of** the angels he says, "He makes his angels winds,
1: 8 But **about** the Son he says, "Your throne, O God, will last for ever
1: 13 **To** which of the angels did God ever say, "Sit at my right hand until
2: 17 might become a merciful and faithful high priest in service **to** God,
4: 13 and laid bare before the eyes of him **to** whom we must give
5: 1 and is appointed to represent them in matters *related* **to** God,
5: 5 But God said to him, "You are my Son; today I have become your
5: 7 loud cries and tears **to** the one who could save him from death,
5: 14 who by constant use have trained themselves **to** distinguish good
6: 11 same diligence to the very end, **in order to** make your hope sure.
7: 21 but he became a priest with an oath when God said **to** him:
9: 13 unclean sanctify them **so that** they are outwardly clean.
9: 20 of the covenant, which God has commanded **[NIE]** you to keep."
10: 16 "This is the covenant I will make **with** them after that time,
11: 18 even though God had said **to** him, "It is through Isaac that your
12: 1 In your struggle **against** sin, you have not yet resisted to the point
12: 10 Our fathers disciplined us **for** a little while as they thought best;
12: 11 No discipline seems pleasant **at** the time, but painful. Later on,
13: 13 Let us, then, go **to** him outside the camp, bearing the disgrace he

Jas 4: 5 that the spirit he caused to live in us envies **intensely** [+*2160*]?
4: 14 You are a mist that appears **for** a little while and then vanishes.

1Pe 2: 4 *As you* **come to** [RP*4665*] him, the living Stone—rejected by men
3: 15 Always be prepared *to* **give** an answer to everyone who asks you to
4: 12 do not be surprised at the painful **[NIE]** trial you are suffering,

2Pe 1: 3 His divine power has given us everything we need **for** life
3: 16 as they do the other Scriptures, **to** their own destruction.

1Jn 1: 2 the eternal life, which was **with** the Father and has appeared to us.
2: 1 does sin, we have one who speaks **to** the Father in our defense—
3: 21 if our hearts do not condemn us, we have confidence **before** God
5: 14 This is the confidence we have **in approaching** God: that if we ask
5: 16 If anyone sees his brother commit a sin that does not **lead to** death,
5: 16 will give him life. I refer to those whose sin does not **lead to** death.
5: 16 There is a sin that **leads to** death. I am not saying that he should
5: 17 All wrongdoing is sin, and there is sin that does not **lead to** death.

2Jn 1: 10 If anyone comes **to** you and does not bring this teaching, do not
1: 12 I hope *to* **visit** [+*1181*] you and talk with you face to face,
1: 12 Instead, I hope to visit you and talk with you face **to** face,

3Jn 1: 14 I hope to see you soon, and we will talk face **to** face. Peace to you.

Rev 1: 13 down to his feet and with a golden sash around **[NIE]** his chest.
1: 17 When I saw him, I fell **at** his feet as though dead. Then he placed
3: 20 the door, I will come **[NIE]** in and eat with him, and he with me.
10: 9 So I went to the angel and asked him to give me the little scroll.
12: 5 And her child was snatched up **to** God and to his throne.
12: 5 And her child was snatched up to God and **to** his throne.
12: 12 to the earth and the sea, because the devil has gone down **to** you!
13: 6 He opened his mouth to blaspheme **[NIE]** God, and to slander his

---

4640 προσάββατον, **prosabbaton** [1] [√ *4574 + 4879*]

day before the Sabbath [1]

Mk 15: 42 It was Preparation Day (that is, the **day before the Sabbath**).

4641 προσαγορεύω, **prosagoreuō** [1] [√ *4639 + 72*]

designated to be [1]

Heb 5: 10 and *was* **designated** by God **to be** high priest in the order of

---

4642 προσάγω, **prosagō** [4] [√ *4639 + 72*]

bring [2], approaching [1], brought before [1]

Lk 9: 41 shall I stay with you and put up with you? **Bring** your son here."
Ac 16: 20 They **brought** them **before** the magistrates and said, "These men
27: 27 when about midnight the sailors sensed they *were* **approaching**
1Pe 3: 18 once for all, the righteous for the unrighteous, to **bring** you to God.

4643 προσαγωγή, **prosagōgē** [3] [√ *4639 + 72*]

access [2], approach [+*2400*] [1]

Ro 5: 2 through whom we have gained **access** by faith into this grace in
Eph 2: 18 For through him we both have **access** to the Father by one Spirit.
3: 12 and through faith in him *we may* **approach** [+*2400*] God with

---

4644 προσαιτέω, **prosaiteō** [1 / 2] [√ *4639 + 160*]

beg [1], begging [1]

Mk 10: 46 Son of Timaeus), was sitting by the roadside **begging**. [UBS *4645*]
Jn 9: 8 begging asked, "Isn't this the same man who *used to* sit and **beg**?"

4645 προσαίτης, **prosaitēs** [2 / 1] [√ *4639 + 160*]

begging [1]

Mk 10: 46 was sitting by the roadside begging. [UBS *a beggar*; NIV *4644*]
Jn 9: 8 and those who had formerly seen him **begging** asked,

---

4646 προσαναβαίνω, **prosanabainō** [1]
[√ *4639 + 324 + 326*]

move [1]

Lk 14: 10 host comes, he will say to you, 'Friend, **move** up to a better place.'

4647 προσαναλαμβάνω, **prosanalambanō** Not
used in UBS/NIV [√ *4639 + 324 + 3284*]

4648 προσαναλίσκω, **prosanaliskō** Not used in
UBS/NIV [√ *4639 + 324 + 274*]

4649 προσαναλόω, ***prosanaloō*** [1 / 0]
[√ 4639 + 324 + 274]

Lk   8:43 [UBS+ *and she had* **spent** *all she had on doctors*] but no one could

4650 προσαναπληρόω, ***prosanaplēroō*** [2]
[√ 4639 + 324 + 4444]

supplied [1], supplying [1]

2Co 9:12 This service that you perform is not only **supplying** the needs of
   11: 9 for the brothers who came from Macedonia **supplied** what I

4651 προσανατίθημι, ***prosanatithēmi*** [2]
[√ 4639 + 324 + 5502]

added [1], consult [1]

Gal 1:16 I might preach him among the Gentiles, *I did* not **consult** any man,
    2: 6 by external appearance—those men **added** nothing to my message.

4652 προσανέχω, ***prosanechō***   Not used in UBS/NIV
[√ 4639 + 324 + 2400]

4653 προσαπειλέω, ***prosapeileō*** [1] [√ 4639 + 581]

further threats [1]

Ac   4:21 *After* **further threats** they let them go. They could not decide how

4654 προσαχέω, ***prosacheō***   Not used in UBS/NIV
[√ 4639 + 2491]

4655 προσδαπανάω, ***prosdapanao*** [1]
[√ 4639 + 1252]

extra expense [1]

Lk 10:35 I will reimburse you for any **extra expense** you may have.'

4656 προσδέομαι, ***prosdeomai*** [1] [√ 4639 + 1289]

needed [1]

Ac 17:25 *as if he* **needed** anything, because he himself gives all men life

4657 προσδέχομαι, ***prosdechomai*** [14]
[√ 4639 + 1312]

waiting for [5], wait for [2], *untranslated* [1], accepted [1], looking
forward to [1], receive [1], refused [+4024] [1], welcome [1],
welcomes [1]

Mk 15:43 who was himself **waiting for** the kingdom of God, went boldly to
Lk   2:25 *He was* **waiting for** the consolation of Israel, and the Holy Spirit
    2:38 and spoke about the child *to* all who *were* **looking forward to** the
  12:36 like men **waiting for** their master to return from a wedding
  15: 2 the law muttered, "This man **welcomes** sinners and eats with them."
  23:51 town of Arimathea and he *was* **waiting for** the kingdom of God.
Ac 23:21 They are ready now, **waiting for** your consent to their request."
  24:15 [RPG] that there will be a resurrection of both the righteous
Ro 16: 2 I ask *you* to **receive** her in the Lord in a way worthy of the saints
Php 2:29 **Welcome** him in the Lord with great joy, and honor men like him,
Tit   2:13 *while we* **wait for** the blessed hope—the glorious appearing of our
Heb 10:34 in prison and joyfully **accepted** the confiscation of your property,
  11:35 Others were tortured and **refused** [+4024] to be released, so that
Jude 1:21 Keep yourselves in God's love *as* you **wait for** the mercy of our

4658 προσδίδωμι, ***prosdidōmi***   Not used in UBS/NIV
[√ 4639 + 1443]

4659 προσδοκάω, ***prosdokaō*** [16] [√ 4639 + 1506]

expect [5], expecting [3], looking forward to [2], expected [1],
look forward to [1], suspense [1], waiting expectantly [1], waiting
for [1], waiting [1]

Mt 11: 3 you the one who was to come, or *should we* **expect** someone else?"
  24:50 of that servant will come on a day *when he does* not **expect** him
Lk   1:21 the people were **waiting for** Zechariah and wondering why he
    3:15 The people *were* **waiting expectantly** and were all wondering in
    7:19 you the one who was to come, or *should we* **expect** someone else?"
    7:20 the one who was to come, or *should we* **expect** someone else?' "
    8:40 a crowd welcomed him, for they were all **expecting** him.
  12:46 of that servant will come on a day when *he does* not **expect** him
Ac   3: 5 gave them his attention, **expecting** to get something from them.
  10:24 Cornelius was **expecting** them and had called together his relatives
  27:33 "you *have been in constant* **suspense** and have gone without food—
  28: 6 The people **expected** him to swell up or suddenly fall dead,
  28: 6 but *after* **waiting** a long time and seeing nothing unusual happen
2Pe 3:12 *as you* **look forward to** the day of God and speed its coming.
    3:13 But in keeping with his promise *we are* **looking forward to** a new
    3:14 So then, dear friends, *since* you *are* **looking forward to** this,

4660 προσδοκία, ***prosdokia*** [2] [√ 4639 + 1506]

anticipating [1], apprehensive [1]

Lk 21:26 faint from terror, **apprehensive** of what is coming on the world,
Ac 12:11 and from everything the Jewish people were **anticipating**."

4661 προσεάω, ***proseaō*** [1] [√ 4639 + 1572]

allow to hold course [1]

Ac 27: 7 *When* the wind *did* not **allow** us **to hold** our **course**, we sailed to

4662 προσεγγίζω, ***prosengizō***   Not used in UBS/NIV
[√ 4639 + 1584]

4663 προσεδρεύω, ***prosedreuō***   Not used in UBS/NIV
[√ 4639 + 1612]

4664 προσεργάζομαι, ***prosergazomai*** [1]
[√ 4639 + 2240]

earned more [1]

Lk 19:16 first one came and said, 'Sir, your mina *has* **earned** ten **more**.'

4665 προσέρχομαι, ***proserchomai*** [86]
[√ 4639 + 2262]

came to [34], came [10], went to [8], going to [4], came up [3],
come to [3], went [3], *untranslated* [2], came forward [2], came
up to [2], draw near [2], agree to [1], approach [1], approached
[1], came before [1], come to [RP4639] [1], comes [1], coming
[1], go to [1], stepped forward [1], visit [1], went over [1], went up
to [1], went up [1]

Mt   4: 3 The tempter **came to** him and said, "If you are the Son of God,
    4:11 Then the devil left him, and angels **came** and attended him.
    5: 1 up on a mountainside and sat down. His disciples **came to** him,
    8: 2 A man with leprosy **came** and knelt **before** him and said, "Lord,
    8: 5 had entered Capernaum, a centurion **came to** him, asking for help.
    8:19 Then a teacher of the law **came to** him and said, "Teacher,
    8:25 The disciples **went** and woke him, saying, "Lord, save us!
    9:14 Then John's disciples **came** and asked him, "How is it that we
    9:20 had been subject to bleeding for twelve years **came up** behind him
    9:28 had gone indoors, the blind men **came to** him, and he asked them,
  13:10 The disciples **came to** him and asked, "Why do you speak to the
  13:27 "The owner's servants **came to** him and said, 'Sir, didn't you sow
  13:36 His disciples **came to** him and said, "Explain to us the parable of
  14:12 John's disciples **came** and took his body and buried it. Then they
  14:15 the disciples **came to** him and said, "This is a remote place,
  15: 1 and teachers of the law **came to** Jesus from Jerusalem and asked,
  15:12 Then the disciples **came to** him and asked, "Do you know that the

15:23 So his disciples **came to** him and urged him, "Send her away,
15:30 Great crowds **came to** him, bringing the lame, the blind,
16: 1 The Pharisees and Sadducees **came to** Jesus and tested him by
17: 7 Jesus **came** and touched them. "Get up," he said. "Don't be afraid."
17:14 came to the crowd, a man **approached** Jesus and knelt before him.
17:19 Then the disciples **came to** Jesus in private and asked, "Why
17:24 the collectors of the two-drachma tax **came to** Peter and asked,
18: 1 At that time the disciples **came to** Jesus and asked, "Who is the
18:21 Then Peter **came to** Jesus and asked, "Lord, how many times shall I
19: 3 Some Pharisees **came to** him to test him. They asked, "Is it lawful
19:16 Now a man **came up to** Jesus and asked, "Teacher, what good thing
20:20 Then the mother of Zebedee's sons **came to** Jesus with her sons
21:14 The blind and the lame **came to** him at the temple, and he healed
21:23 the chief priests and the elders of the people **came to** him.
21:28 *He* **went to** the first and said, 'Son, go and work today in the
21:30 "Then the father **went to** the other son and said the same thing.
22:23 who say there is no resurrection, **came to** him with a question.
24: 1 and was walking away when his disciples **came up to** him to call
24: 3 sitting on the Mount of Olives, the disciples **came to** him privately.
25:20 The man who had received the five talents **[RPG]** brought the
25:22 "The man with the two talents also **came**. 'Master,' he said,
25:24 "Then the man who had received the one talent **came**. 'Master,'
26: 7 a woman **came to** him with an alabaster jar of very expensive
26:17 Feast of Unleavened Bread, the disciples **came to** Jesus and asked,
26:49 **Going** at once to Jesus, Judas said, "Greetings, Rabbi!" and kissed
26:50 Then the *men* **stepped forward**, seized Jesus and arrested him.
26:60 they did not find any, *though* many false witnesses **came forward.**
26:60 many false witnesses came forward. Finally two **came forward**
26:69 was sitting out in the courtyard, and a servant girl **came to** him.
26:73 After a little while, those standing there **went up to** Peter and said,
27:58 **Going to** Pilate, he asked for Jesus' body, and Pilate ordered that it
28: 2 heaven and, **going to** the tomb, rolled back the stone and sat on it.
28: 9 he said. They **came to** him, clasped his feet and worshiped him.
28:18 Then Jesus **came to** them and said, "All authority in heaven

Mk 1:31 So *he* **went to** her, took her hand and helped her up. The fever left
6:35 By this time it was late in the day, so his disciples **came to** him.
10: 2 Some Pharisees **came** and tested him by asking, "Is it lawful for a
12:28 One of the teachers of the law **came** and heard them debating.
14:45 Going at once to Jesus, **[RPG]** Judas said, "Rabbi!" and kissed him.

Lk 7:14 Then he **went up** and touched the coffin, and those carrying it
8:24 The disciples **went** and woke him, saying, "Master, Master,
8:44 She **came up** behind him and touched the edge of his cloak,
9:12 Late in the afternoon the Twelve **came to** him and said,
9:42 Even *while* the boy *was* **coming**, the demon threw him to the
10:34 *He* **went to** him and bandaged his wounds, pouring on oil
13:31 At that time some Pharisees **came to** Jesus and said to him,
20:27 who say there is no resurrection, **came to** Jesus with a question.
23:36 The soldiers also **came up** and mocked him. They offered him
23:52 **Going to** Pilate, he asked for Jesus' body.

Jn 12:21 They **came to** Philip, who was from Bethsaida in Galilee,
Ac 7:31 *As* he **went over** to look more closely, he heard the Lord's voice:
8:29 The Spirit told Philip, "**Go to** that chariot and stay near it."
9: 1 threats against the Lord's disciples. *He* **went to** the high priest
10:28 is against our law for a Jew to associate with a Gentile or **visit** him.
12:13 and a servant girl named Rhoda **came** to answer the door.
18: 2 had ordered all the Jews to leave Rome. Paul **went** to see them,
22:26 centurion heard this, *he* **went to** the commander and reported it.
22:27 The commander **went to** Paul and asked, "Tell me, are you a
23:14 They **went to** the chief priests and elders and said, "We have taken
28: 9 the rest of the sick on the island **came** and were cured.

1Ti 6: 3 and *does* not **agree to** the sound instruction of our Lord Jesus
Heb 4:16 *Let us* then **approach** the throne of grace with confidence,
7:25 Therefore he is able to save completely those *who* **come to** God
10: 1 year after year, make perfect those *who* **draw near** *to worship*.
10:22 *let us* **draw near** to God with a sincere heart in full assurance of
11: 6 because anyone *who* **comes** to him must believe that he exists
12:18 *You* have not **come to** a mountain that can be touched and that is
12:22 But *you* have **come to** Mount Zion, to the heavenly Jerusalem,
1Pe 2: 4 *As you* **come** [*RP4639*] **to** him, the living Stone—rejected by men

4666 προσευχή, *proseuchē* [36] [√ *4639 + 2377*]

prayer [16], prayers [12], place of prayer [2], pray [2], praying [2], prayed earnestly [*+4667*] [1], praying [*+1181*] [1]

Mt 21:13 he said to them, " 'My house will be called a house *of* **prayer**,'

21:22 If you believe, you will receive whatever you ask for in **prayer**."
Mk 9:29 He replied, "This kind can come out only by **prayer**."
11:17 " 'My house will be called a house *of* **prayer** for all nations'?
Lk 6:12 out to a mountainside to pray, and spent the night **praying** to God.
19:46 is written," he said to them, " 'My house will be a house *of* **prayer**';
22:45 When he rose from **prayer** and went back to the disciples,
Ac 1:14 They all joined together constantly *in* **prayer**, along with the
2:42 and to the fellowship, to the breaking of bread and to **prayer**.
3: 1 and John were going up to the temple at the time *of* **prayer**—
6: 4 and will give our attention *to* **prayer** and the ministry of the word."
10: 4 "Your **prayers** and gifts to the poor have come up as a memorial
10:31 God has heard your **prayer** and remembered your gifts to the poor.
12: 5 but the church was earnestly **praying** [*+1181*] to God for him.
16:13 city gate to the river, where we expected to find a **place of prayer**.
16:16 Once when we were going to the **place of prayer**, we were met by
Ro 1:10 in my **prayers** at all times; and I pray that now at last by God's
12:12 Be joyful in hope, patient in affliction, faithful *in* **prayer**.
15:30 of the Spirit, to join me in my struggle by **praying** to God for me.
1Co 7: 5 and for a time, so that you may devote yourselves *to* **prayer**.
Eph 1:16 stopped giving thanks for you, remembering you in my **prayers**.
6:18 And pray in the Spirit on all occasions with all kinds of **prayers**
Php 4: 6 but in everything, *by* **prayer** and petition, with thanksgiving,
Col 4: 2 Devote yourselves *to* **prayer**, being watchful and thankful.
4:12 He is always wrestling in **prayer** for you, that you may stand firm
1Th 1: 2 always thank God for all of you, mentioning you in our **prayers**.
1Ti 2: 1 **prayers**, intercession and thanksgiving are made for everyone—
5: 5 and continues night and day to **pray** and to ask God for help.
Phm 1: 4 I always thank my God as I remember you in my **prayers**,
1:22 because I hope to be restored to you in answer to your **prayers**.
Jas 5:17 *He* **prayed earnestly** [*+4667*] that it would not rain, and it did not
1Pe 3: 7 the gracious gift of life, so that nothing will hinder your **prayers**.
4: 7 be clear minded and self-controlled so that you can **pray**.
Rev 5: 8 golden bowls full of incense, which are the **prayers** of the saints,
8: 3 was given much incense to offer, *with* the **prayers** of all the saints,
8: 4 The smoke of the incense, *together with* the **prayers** of the saints,

4667 προσεύχομαι, *proseuchomai* [85] [√ *4639 + 2377*]

pray [42], prayed [17], praying [12], prayer [5], prays [3], make prayers [2], pray for [2], prayed earnestly [*+4666*] [1], praying to [1]

Mt 5:44 Love your enemies and **pray** for those who persecute you,
6: 5 "And when *you* **pray**, do not be like the hypocrites, for they love to
6: 5 for they love *to* **pray** standing in the synagogues and on the street
6: 6 But when you **pray**, go into your room, close the door and pray to
6: 6 your room, close the door and **pray** to your Father, who is unseen.
6: 7 And *when you* **pray**, do not keep on babbling like pagans,
6: 9 "This, then, is how you *should* **pray**: " 'Our Father in heaven,
14:23 dismissed them, he went up on a mountainside by himself *to* **pray**.
19:13 to Jesus for him to place his hands on them and **pray for** them.
24:20 **Pray** that your flight will not take place in winter or on the
26:36 and he said to them, "Sit here while *I* go over there and **pray**."
26:39 he fell with his face to the ground and **prayed**, "My Father,
26:41 Watch and **pray** so that you will not fall into temptation. The spirit
26:42 *He* went away a second time and **prayed**, "My Father, if it is not
26:44 he left them and went away once more and **prayed** the third time,
Mk 1:35 left the house and went off to a solitary place, where *he* **prayed**.
6:46 After leaving them, he went up on a mountainside *to* **pray**.
11:24 Therefore I tell you, whatever you ask for in **prayer**, believe that
11:25 And when you stand **praying**, if you hold anything against anyone,
12:40 devour widows' houses and for a show **make** lengthy **prayers**.
13:18 **Pray** that this will not take place in winter,
14:32 and Jesus said to his disciples, "Sit here while *I* **pray**."
14:35 and **prayed** that if possible the hour might pass from him.
14:38 Watch and **pray** so that you will not fall into temptation. The spirit
14:39 Once more *he* went away and **prayed** the same thing.
Lk 1:10 incense came, all the assembled worshipers were **praying** outside.
3:21 was baptized too. And *as he was* **praying**, heaven was opened
5:16 But Jesus often withdrew to lonely places and **prayed**.
6:12 One of those days Jesus went out to a mountainside *to* **pray**,
6:28 bless those who curse you, **pray** for those who mistreat you.
9:18 Once when he was **praying** in private and his disciples were
9:28 and James with him and went up onto a mountain *to* **pray**.
9:29 As he *was* **praying**, the appearance of his face changed, and his

11: 1 One day Jesus was **praying** in a certain place. When he finished,
11: 1 one of his disciples said to him, "Lord, teach us *to* **pray**,
11: 2 He said to them, "When *you* **pray**, say: " 'Father, hallowed be your
18: 1 his disciples a parable to show them that they should always **pray**
18:10 "Two men went up to the temple *to* **pray**, one a Pharisee
18:11 The Pharisee stood up and **prayed** about himself: 'God, I thank
20:47 devour widows' houses and for a show **make** lengthy **prayers**.
22:40 he said to them, "**Pray** that you will not fall into temptation."
22:41 about a stone's throw beyond them, knelt down and **prayed**,
22:44 And being in anguish, *he* **prayed** more earnestly, and his sweat
22:46 "Get up and **pray** so that you will not fall into temptation."
Ac   1:24 Then *they* **prayed**, "Lord, you know everyone's heart. Show us
6: 6 men to the apostles, *who* **prayed** and laid their hands on them.
8:15 they **prayed** for them that they might receive the Holy Spirit,
9:11 and ask for a man from Tarsus named Saul, for *he is* **praying**.
9:40 all out of the room; then he got down on his knees and **prayed**.
10: 9 and approaching the city, Peter went up on the roof *to* **pray**.
10:30 "Four days ago I was in my house **praying** at this hour, at three in
11: 5 "I was in the city of Joppa **praying**, and in a trance I saw a vision.
12:12 called Mark, where many people had gathered and *were* **praying**.
13: 3 So *after they had* fasted and **prayed**, they placed their hands on
14:23 with **prayer** and fasting, committed them to the Lord, in whom
16:25 midnight Paul and Silas *were* **praying** and singing hymns **to** God,
20:36 When he had said this, he knelt down with all of them and **prayed**.
21: 5 us out of the city, and there on the beach we knelt *to* **pray**.
22:17 "When I returned to Jerusalem and *was* **praying** at the temple,
28: 8 him and, *after* **prayer**, placed his hands on him and healed him.
Ro   8:26 We do not know what *we* ought *to* **pray for**, but the Spirit himself
1Co 11: 4 Every man *who* **prays** or prophesies with his head covered
11: 5 And every woman *who* **prays** or prophesies with her head
11:13 Is it proper for a woman *to* **pray** to God with her head uncovered?
14:13 For this reason anyone who speaks in a tongue *should* **pray** that he
14:14 For if *I* **pray** in a tongue, my spirit prays, but my mind is
14:14 For if I **pray** in a tongue, my spirit **prays**, but my mind is
14:15 *I will* **pray** with my spirit, but I will also pray with my mind;
14:15 I will **pray** with my spirit, but *I will* also pray with my mind;
Eph   6:18 And **pray** in the Spirit on all occasions with all kinds of prayers
Php   1: 9 And this *is my* **prayer**: that your love may abound more and more
Col   1: 3 the Father of our Lord Jesus Christ, *when we* **pray** for you,
1: 9 we have not stopped **praying** for you and asking God to fill you
4: 3 And **pray** for us, too, that God may open a door for our message,
1Th   5:17 **pray** continually;
5:25 Brothers, **pray** for us.
2Th   1:11 With this in mind, *we* constantly **pray** for you, that our God may
3: 1 **pray** for us that the message of the Lord may spread rapidly
1Ti   2: 8 I want men everywhere *to* lift up holy hands in **prayer**,
Heb 13:18 **Pray** for us. We are sure that we have a clear conscience
Jas   5:13 Is any one of you in trouble? *He should* **pray**. Is anyone happy?
5:14 He should call the elders of the church *to* **pray** over him and anoint
5:17 *He* **prayed** [+4666] **earnestly** that it would not rain, and it did not
5:18 Again he **prayed**, and the heavens gave rain, and the earth
Jude 1:20 yourselves up in your most holy faith and **pray** in the Holy Spirit.

4668 προσέχω, *prosechō* [24] [√ *4639* + *2400*]

on guard [4], careful [2], devote [2], pay attention [2], attention [1], beware [1], consider carefully [1], follow [1], followed [1], guard [1], indulging [1], keep watch over [1], paid close attention [1], pay attention to [1], respond to [1], served at [1], watch out [1], watch [1]

Mt   6: 1 "*Be* **careful** not to do your 'acts of righteousness' before men,
7:15 "**Watch out** for false prophets. They come to you in sheep's
10:17 "*Be on your* **guard** against men; they will hand you over to the
16: 6 "*Be on your* **guard** against the yeast of the Pharisees
16:11 But *be* **on** *your* **guard** against the yeast of the Pharisees
16:12 Then they understood that he was not telling them *to* **guard** against
Lk   12: 1 "*Be on your* **guard** against the yeast of the Pharisees, which is
17: 3 So **watch** yourselves. "If your brother sins, rebuke him, and if he
20:46 "**Beware** of the teachers of the law. They like to walk around in
21:34 "*Be* **careful**, or your hearts will be weighed down with dissipation,
Ac   5:35 of Israel, **consider carefully** what you intend to do to these men.
8: 6 signs he did, *they* all **paid close attention** to what he said.
8:10 both high and low, *gave* him *their* **attention** and exclaimed,
8:11 *They* **followed** him because he had amazed them for a long time
16:14 The Lord opened her heart *to* **respond to** Paul's message.

20:28 **Keep watch over** yourselves and all the flock of which the Holy
1Ti   1: 4 nor *to* **devote** *themselves* to myths and endless genealogies.
3: 8 to be men worthy of respect, sincere, not **indulging** in much wine,
4: 1 and **follow** deceiving spirits and things taught by demons.
4:13 **devote** *yourself* to the public reading of Scripture, to preaching
Tit   1:14 and *will* **pay** no **attention** to Jewish myths or to the commands of
Heb   2: 1 We must **pay** more careful **attention**, therefore, **to** what we have
7:13 and no one from that tribe *has ever* **served at** the altar.
2Pe   1:19 and you will do well to **pay attention** to it, as to a light shining in a

4669 προσηλόω, *prosēloō* [1] [√ *4639* + *2464*]

nailing [1]

Col   2:14 that stood opposed to us; he took it away, **nailing** it to the cross.

4670 προσήλυτος, *prosēlytos* [4] [√ *4639* + *2262*]

converts to Judaism [2], convert to Judaism [1], convert [1]

Mt   23:15 You travel over land and sea to win a single **convert**, and when he
Ac   2:11 (both Jews and **converts to Judaism**); Cretans and Arabs—
6: 5 Parmenas, and Nicolas from Antioch, a **convert to Judaism**.
13:43 many *of* the Jews and devout **converts to Judaism** followed Paul

4671 πρόσθεσις, *prosthesis* Not used in UBS/NIV [√ *4639* + *5502*]

4672 πρόσκαιρος, *proskairos* [4] [√ *4639* + *2789*]

only a short time [2], a short time [1], temporary [1]

Mt   13:21 But since he has no root, he lasts **only a short time**. When trouble
Mk   4:17 But since they have no root, they last **only a short time**.
2Co   4:18 For what is seen is **temporary**, but what is unseen is eternal.
Heb 11:25 of God rather than to enjoy the pleasures of sin *for* **a short time**.

4673 προσκαλέω, *proskaleō* [29] [√ *4639* + *2813*]

called [8], called to [7], called in [3], call [2], called together [2], calling to [2], sent for [2], calling [1], gathered together [1], summoning [1]

Mt   10: 1 *He* **called** his twelve disciples **to** him and gave them authority to
15:10 Jesus **called** the crowd *to* him and said, "Listen and understand.
15:32 Jesus **called** his disciples **to** him and said, "I have compassion for
18: 2 He **called** a little child and had him stand among them.
18:32 "Then the master **called** the servant **in**. 'You wicked servant,'
20:25 Jesus **called** them **together** and said, "You know that the rulers of
Mk   3:13 went up on a mountainside and **called to** him those he wanted,
3:23 So Jesus **called** them and spoke to them in parables: "How can
6: 7 **Calling** the Twelve **to** him, he sent them out two by two and gave
7:14 Again Jesus **called** the crowd *to* him and said, "Listen to me,
8: 1 they had nothing to eat, Jesus **called** his disciples *to* him and said,
8:34 Then *he* **called** the crowd to him along with his disciples and said:
10:42 Jesus **called** them **together** and said, "You know that those who are
12:43 **Calling** his disciples **to** him, Jesus said, "I tell you the truth,
15:44 **Summoning** the centurion, he asked him if Jesus had already died.
Lk   7:18 disciples told him about all these things. **Calling** Two of them,
15:26 So he **called** one of the servants and asked him what was going on.
16: 5 "So *he* **called in** each one of his master's debtors. He asked the
18:16 But Jesus **called** the children **to** him and said, "Let the little children
Ac   2:39 for all who are far off—for all whom the Lord our God *will* **call**."
5:40 persuaded them. *They* **called** the apostles **in** and had them flogged.
6: 2 So the Twelve **gathered** all the disciples **together** and said,
13: 2 me Barnabas and Saul for the work to which *I have* **called** them."
13: 7 **sent for** Barnabas and Saul because he wanted to hear the word of
16:10 concluding that God *had* **called** us to preach the gospel to them.
23:17 Then Paul **called** one of the centurions and said, "Take this young
23:18 **sent for** me and asked me to bring this young man to you
23:23 Then he **called** two of his centurions and ordered them, "Get ready
Jas   5:14 *He should* **call** the elders of the church to pray over him and anoint

4674 προσκαρτερέω, *proskartereō* [10]
[√ 4639 + 2846]

attendants [1], continued [1], devote [1], devoted to [+*1639*] [1], faithful [1], followed everywhere [1], give attention [1], give full time [1], joined constantly [+*1639*] [1], ready [1]

Mk 3: 9 the crowd he told his disciples to *have* a small boat **ready** for him,
Ac 1:14 They all **joined** [+*1639*] together **constantly** in prayer, along with
      2:42 *They* **devoted** [+*1639*] *themselves* **to** the apostles' teaching
      2:46 Every day *they* **continued** *to meet* together in the temple courts.
      6: 4 and *will* **give** our **attention** to prayer and the ministry of the word."
      8:13 And *he* **followed** Philip **everywhere**, astonished by the great signs
    10: 7 his servants and a devout soldier who *was one of* his **attendants**.
Ro 12:12 Be joyful in hope, patient in affliction, **faithful** in prayer.
    13: 6 are God's servants, *who* **give** *their* **full time** to governing.
Col 4: 2 **Devote** *yourselves* to prayer, being watchful and thankful.

4675 προσκαρτέρησις, *proskarterēsis* [1]
[√ 4639 + 2846]

keep on [1]

Eph 6:18 this in mind, be alert and always **keep on** praying for all the saints.

4676 προσκεφάλαιον, *proskephalaion* [1]
[√ 4639 + 3051]

cushion [1]

Mk 4:38 Jesus was in the stern, sleeping on a **cushion**. The disciples woke

4677 προσκληρόω, *prosklēroō* [1] [√ 4639 + 3102]

joined [1]

Ac 17: 4 Some of the Jews were persuaded and **joined** Paul and Silas,

4678 πρόσκλησις, *prosklēsis* Not used in UBS/NIV
[√ 4639 + 2813]

4679 προσκλίνω, *prosklinō* [1] [√ 4639 + 3111]

rallied [1]

Ac 5:36 to be somebody, and about four hundred men **rallied** to him.

4680 πρόσκλισις, *prosklisis* [1] [√ 4639 + 3111]

out of favoritism [+*2848*] [1]

1Ti 5:21 without partiality, and to do nothing **out of favoritism** [+*2848*].

4681 προσκολλάω, *proskollaō* [2] [√ 4639 + 3140]

united to [*RP4639*] [2]

Mk 10: 7 leave his father and mother and *be* **united** [*RP4639*] **to** his wife,
Eph 5:31 leave his father and mother and *be* **united** [*RP4639*] **to** his wife,

4682 πρόσκομμα, *proskomma* [6] [√ 4639 + 3164]

causes men to stumble [2], stumbling block [2], stumble [1], stumbling [1]

Ro 9:32 as if it were by works. They stumbled over the "**stumbling** stone."
      9:33 I lay in Zion a stone that **causes men to stumble** and a rock that
    14:13 make up your mind not to put any **stumbling block** or obstacle in
    14:20 for a man to eat anything that causes someone else to **stumble**.
1Co 8: 9 of your freedom does not become a **stumbling block** to the weak.
1Pe 2: 8 "A stone that **causes men to stumble** and a rock that makes them

4683 προσκοπή, *proskopē* [1] [√ 4639 + 3164]

stumbling block [1]

2Co 6: 3 We put no **stumbling block** in anyone's path, so that our ministry

4684 προσκόπτω, *proskoptō* [8] [√ 4639 + 3164]

strike [2], stumble [2], beat against [1], cause fall [1], stumbled over [1], stumbles [1]

Mt 4: 6 their hands, so that *you* will not **strike** your foot against a stone.' "
      7:27 the streams rose, and the winds blew and **beat against** that house,
Lk 4:11 their hands, so that *you* will not **strike** your foot against a stone.' "
Jn 11: 9 A man who walks by day *will* not **stumble**, for he sees by this
    11:10 It is when he walks by night that *he* **stumbles**, for he has no light."
Ro 9:32 as if it were by works. *They* **stumbled over** the "stumbling stone."
    14:21 or to do anything else that *will* **cause** your brother *to* **fall**.
1Pe 2: 8 They **stumble** because they disobey the message—which is also

4685 προσκυλίω, *proskyliō* [2] [√ 4639 + 3244]

rolled in front of [1], rolled [1]

Mt 27:60 *He* **rolled** a big stone **in front of** the entrance to the tomb
Mk 15:46 of rock. Then *he* **rolled** a stone against the entrance of the tomb.

4686 προσκυνέω, *proskyneō* [60] [→ 4687; cf. 4639]

worship [28], worshiped [17], knelt before [3], worshipers [3], fall down [1], fell on knees in front of [1], kneeling down [1], on knees before [1], paid homage [1], refused to worship [+*3590*] [1], reverence [1], worshiping [1], worships [1]

Mt 2: 2 We saw his star in the east and have come *to* **worship** him."
      2: 8 you find him, report to me, so that I too *may* go and **worship** him."
      2:11 with his mother Mary, and *they* bowed down and **worshiped** him.
      4: 9 I will give you," he said, "if *you* will bow down and **worship** me."
    4:10 it is written: '**Worship** the Lord your God, and serve him only.' "
      8: 2 A man with leprosy came and **knelt before** him and said, "Lord,
      9:18 he was saying this, a ruler came and **knelt before** him and said,
    14:33 Then those who were in the boat **worshiped** him, saying,
    15:25 The woman came and **knelt before** him. "Lord, help me!" she said.
    18:26 "The servant fell on *his* **knees before** him. 'Be patient with me,'
    20:20 to Jesus with her sons and, **kneeling down**, asked a favor of him.
    28: 9 he said. They came to him, clasped his feet and **worshiped** him.
    28:17 When they saw him, *they* **worshiped** him;
Mk 5: 6 Jesus from a distance, he ran and **fell on** his **knees in front of** him.
    15:19 and spit on him. Falling on their knees, *they* **paid homage** to him.
Lk 4: 7 So if you **worship** me, it will all be yours."
      4: 8 "It is written: '**Worship** the Lord your God and serve him only.' "
    24:52 Then they **worshiped** him and returned to Jerusalem with great
Jn 4:20 Our fathers **worshiped** on this mountain, but you Jews claim that
      4:20 but you Jews claim that the place where we must **worship** is in
      4:21 a time is coming when *you* will **worship** the Father neither on this
      4:22 You Samaritans **worship** what you do not know; we worship what
      4:22 we **worship** what we do know, for salvation is from the Jews.
      4:23 and has now come when the true worshipers *will* **worship** the
      4:23 and truth, for they are the kind of **worshipers** the Father seeks.
      4:24 is spirit, and his **worshipers** must worship in spirit and in truth."
      4:24 is spirit, and his worshipers must **worship** in spirit and in truth."
      9:38 Then the man said, "Lord, I believe," and *he* **worshiped** him.
    12:20 some Greeks among those who went up to **worship** at the Feast.
Ac 7:43 and the star of your god Rephan, the idols you made *to* **worship**.
      8:27 of the Ethiopians. This man had gone to Jerusalem *to* **worship**,
    10:25 the house, Cornelius met him and fell at his feet in **reverence**.
    24:11 no more than twelve days ago I went up to Jerusalem *to* **worship**.
1Co 14:25 So *he will* fall down and **worship** God, exclaiming, "God is really
Heb 1: 6 into the world, he says, "*Let* all God's angels **worship** him."
    11:21 Joseph's sons, and **worshiped** as he leaned on the top of his staff.
Rev 3: 9 I will make them come and **fall down** at your feet
      4:10 sits on the throne, and **worship** him who lives for ever and ever.
      5:14 creatures said, "Amen," and the elders fell down and **worshiped**.
      7:11 fell down on their faces before the throne and **worshiped** God,
      9:20 *they did* not stop **worshiping** demons, and idols of gold, silver,
    11: 1 the temple of God and the altar, and count the **worshipers** there.
    11:16 their thrones before God, fell on their faces and **worshiped** God,
    13: 4 *Men* **worshiped** the dragon because he had given authority to the
    13: 4 and they also **worshiped** the beast and asked, "Who is like the
    13: 8 All inhabitants of the earth *will* **worship** the beast—all whose
    13:12 and made the earth and its inhabitants **worship** the first beast,
    13:15 and cause all who **refused to worship** [+*3590*] the image to be
    14: 7 **Worship** him who made the heavens, the earth, the sea

14: 9 "If anyone **worships** the beast and his image and receives his mark
14: 11 rest day or night for those *who* **worship** the beast and his image,
15: 4 All nations will come and **worship** before you, for your righteous
16: 2 people who had the mark of the beast and **worshiped** his image.
19: 4 and the four living creatures fell down and **worshiped** God,
19: 10 At this I fell at his feet *to* **worship** him. But he said to me,
19: 10 **Worship** God! For the testimony of Jesus is the spirit of prophecy."
19: 20 who had received the mark of the beast and **worshiped** his image.
20: 4 They *had* not **worshiped** the beast or his image and had not
22: 8 I fell down *to* **worship** at the feet of the angel who had been
22: 9 and of all who keep the words of this book. **Worship** God!"

4687 προσκυνητής, *proskynētēs* [1] [√ 4686]

worshipers [1]

Jn   4:23 and has now come when the true **worshipers** will worship the

4688 προσλαλέω, *proslaleō* [2] [√ 4639 + 3281]

talk with [1], talked with [1]

Ac 13:43 who **talked with** them and urged them to continue in the grace of
   28:20 For this reason I have asked to see you and **talk with** you.

4689 προσλαμβάνω, *proslambanō* [12]
[√ 4639 + 3284]

accept [2], accepted [2], took aside [2], ate [1], eaten [1], invited
to home [1], rounded up [1], welcome [1], welcomed [1]

Mt 16:22 Peter **took** him **aside** and began to rebuke him. "Never, Lord!"
Mk 8:32 about this, and Peter **took** him **aside** and began to rebuke him.
Ac 17: 5 so *they* **rounded up** some bad characters from the marketplace,
   18:26 *they* **invited** him to *their* **home** and explained to him the way of
   27:33 and have gone without food—*you* haven't **eaten** anything.
   27:36 They were all encouraged and **ate** some food *themselves*.
   28: 2 *They* built a fire and **welcomed** us all because it was raining
Ro 14: 1 **Accept** him whose faith is weak, without passing judgment on
   14: 3 must not condemn the man who does, for God *has* **accepted** him.
   15: 7 **Accept** one another, then, just as Christ **accepted** you, in order to
   15: 7 **Accept** one another, then, just as Christ **accepted** you, in order to
Phm 1:17 consider me a partner, **welcome** him as you would welcome me.

4690 προσλέγω, *proslegō* Not used in UBS/NIV
[√ 4639 + 3306]

4691 πρόσλημψις, *proslēmpsis* [1] [√ 4639 + 3284]

acceptance [1]

Ro 11:15 of the world, what will their **acceptance** be but life from the dead?

4692 πρόσληψις, *proslēpsis* Not used in UBS/NIV
[√ 4639 + 3284]

4693 προσμένω, *prosmenō* [7] [√ 4639 + 3531]

with [2], continue in [1], continues [1], remain [1], stay [1], stayed
[1]

Mt 15:32 *they have* already *been* **with** me three days and have nothing to
Mk 8: 2 *they have* already *been* **with** me three days and have nothing to
Ac 11:23 and encouraged them all *to* **remain** true to the Lord with all their
   13:43 talked with them and urged them *to* **continue in** the grace of God.
   18:18 Paul **stayed** on in Corinth for some time. Then he left the brothers
1Ti 1: 3 **stay** there in Ephesus so that you may command certain men not
    5: 5 and **continues** night and day to pray and to ask God for help.

4694 προσορμίζω, *prosormizō* [1] [√ 4639 + 1649]

anchored [1]

Mk 6:53 had crossed over, they landed at Gennesaret and **anchored** there.

4695 προσοφείλω, *prosopheilō* [1] [√ 4639 + 4053]

owe [1]

Phm 1:19 I will pay it back—not to mention that *you* **owe** me your very self.

4696 προσοχθίζω, *prosochthizō* [2] [√ 4639]

angry [2]

Heb 3:10 That is why *I was* **angry** with that generation, and I said,
   3:17 And with *whom was he* **angry** for forty years? Was it not with

4697 προσπαίω, *prospaiō* Not used in UBS/NIV
[√ 4639 + 4091]

4698 πρόσπεινος, *prospeinos* [1] [√ 4639 + 4277]

hungry [1]

Ac 10:10 He became **hungry** and wanted something to eat, and while the

4699 προσπήγνυμι, *prospēgnymi* [1] [√ 4639 + 4381]

nailing to cross [1]

Ac 2:23 help of wicked men, put him to death *by* **nailing** him **to the cross.**

4700 προσπίπτω, *prospiptō* [8] [√ 4639 + 4406]

fell at feet [3], beat against [1], fell at [1], fell before [1], fell down
before [1], fell [1]

Mt 7:25 the streams rose, and the winds blew and **beat against** that house;
Mk 3:11 *they* **fell down before** him and cried out, "You are the Son of God."
    5:33 came and **fell at** his **feet** and, trembling with fear, told him the
    7:25 daughter was possessed by an evil spirit came and **fell at** his feet.
Lk 5: 8 saw this, he **fell at** Jesus' knees and said, "Go away from me, Lord;
    8:28 When he saw Jesus, he cried out and **fell at** his **feet**, shouting at the
    8:47 she could not go unnoticed, came trembling and **fell at** his **feet**.
Ac 16:29 called for lights, rushed in and **fell** trembling **before** Paul and Silas.

4701 προσποιέω, *prospoieō* [1] [√ 4639 + 4472]

acted as if [1]

Lk 24:28 to which they were going, Jesus **acted as if** he were going farther.

4702 προσπορεύομαι, *prosporeuomai* [1]
[√ 4639 + 4513]

came to [1]

Mk 10:35 Then James and John, the sons of Zebedee, **came to** him.

4703 προσρήγνυμι, *prosrēgnymi* [2] [√ 4639 + 4838]

struck [2]

Lk 6:48 a flood came, the torrent **struck** that house but could not shake it,
    6:49 The moment the torrent **struck** that house, it collapsed and its

4704 προσρήσσω, *prosrēssō* Not used in UBS/NIV
[√ 4639 + 4838]

4705 προστάσσω, *prostassō* [7] [√ 4639 + 5435]

commanded [5], ordered [1], set [1]

Mt 1:24 he did what the angel of the Lord *had* **commanded** him and took
    8: 4 show yourself to the priest and offer the gift Moses **commanded**,
Mk 1:44 and offer the sacrifices that Moses **commanded** for your cleansing,
Lk 5:14 and offer the sacrifices that Moses **commanded** for your cleansing,
Ac 10:33 to listen to everything the Lord *has* **commanded** you to tell us."
   10:48 So *he* **ordered** that they be baptized in the name of Jesus Christ.
   17:26 and he determined the times **set** for them and the exact places

4706 προστάτις, *prostatis* [1] [√ 4574 + 2705]

great help [1]

Ro 16: 2 for she has been a **great help** to many people, including me.

4707 προστίθημι, *prostithēmi* [18] [√ 4639 + 5502]

added [4], add [2], given [2], sent [+4287] [2], added to [1], and even more [+2779+5148] [1], brought [1], buried [1], further word spoken [+3364] [1], increase [1], proceeded [1], went on [1]

Mt 6:27 Who of you by worrying can **add** a single hour to his life?
  6:33 his righteousness, and all these things *will be* **given** to you as well.
Mk 4:24 it will be measured to you—**and even more** [+2779+5148].
Lk 3:20 Herod **added** this to them all: He locked John up in prison.
  12:25 Who of you by worrying can **add** a single hour to his life?
  12:31 seek his kingdom, and these things *will be* **given** to you as well.
  17: 5 The apostles said to the Lord, "**Increase** our faith!"
  19:11 While they were listening to this, he **went on** to tell them a parable,
  20:11 He **sent** [+4287] another servant,
  20:12 He **sent** [+4287] still a third, and they wounded him and threw him
Ac 2:41 and about three thousand *were* **added** *to* their *number* that day.
  2:47 And the Lord **added** to their number daily those who were being
  5:14 and women believed in the Lord and *were* **added to** their number.
  11:24 and faith, and a great number of people *were* **brought** to the Lord.
  12: 3 he saw that this pleased the Jews, *he* **proceeded** to seize Peter also.
  13:36 fell asleep; *he was* **buried** with his fathers and his body decayed.
Gal 3:19 *It was* **added** because of transgressions until the Seed to whom the
Heb 12:19 heard it begged that no **further word** *be* **spoken** [+3364] to them,

4708 προστρέχω, *prostrechō* [3] [√ 4639 + 5556]

ran up to [2], ran [1]

Mk 9:15 they were overwhelmed with wonder and **ran** to greet him.
  10:17 on his way, a man **ran up to** him and fell on his knees before him.
Ac 8:30 Then Philip **ran up to** the chariot and heard the man reading Isaiah

4709 προσφάγιον, *prosphagion* [1] [√ 4639 + 5741]

fish [1]

Jn 21: 5 He called out to them, "Friends, haven't you any **fish**?" "No,"

4710 πρόσφατος, *prosphatos* [1] [√ 4574 + 5777 (or) 5840]

new [1]

Heb 10:20 *by* a **new** and living way opened for us through the curtain,

4711 προσφάτως, *prosphatōs* [1] [√ 4574 + 5777 (or) 5840]

recently [1]

Ac 18: 2 who had **recently** come from Italy with his wife Priscilla,

4712 προσφέρω, *prospherō* [47] [√ 4639 + 5770]

brought [12], offered [8], offer [7], offer sacrifices [3], bringing [2], offering [2], bring [1], get [1], lifted [1], madeˢ [1], offered as a sacrifice [1], offered up [1], offering made [+4714] [1], offers [1], presented with [1], repeatedˢ [1], sacrifice [1], sacrificed [1], treating [1]

Mt 2:11 Then *they* opened their treasures and **presented** him **with** gifts of
  4:24 and *people* **brought** to him all who were ill with various diseases,
  5:23 if *you are* **offering** your gift at the altar and there remember that
  5:24 and be reconciled to your brother; then come and **offer** your gift.
  8: 4 show yourself to the priest and **offer** the gift Moses commanded,
  8:16 many who were demon-possessed *were* **brought** to him,
  9: 2 *Some men* **brought** to him a paralytic, lying on a mat. When Jesus
  9:32 was demon-possessed and could not talk *was* **brought** to Jesus.
  12:22 Then *they* **brought** him a demon-possessed man who was blind
  14:35 all the surrounding country. *People* **brought** all their sick to him
  17:16 *I* **brought** him to your disciples, but they could not heal him."
  18:24 a man who owed him ten thousand talents *was* **brought** to him.
  19:13 Then little children *were* **brought** to Jesus for him to place his
  22:19 me the coin used for paying the tax." They **brought** him a denarius,
  25:20 The man who had received the five talents **brought** the other five.
Mk 1:44 and **offer** the **sacrifices** that Moses commanded for your cleansing,
  2: 4 Since they could not **get** him to Jesus because of the crowd,
  10:13 *People were* **bringing** little children to Jesus to have him touch
Lk 5:14 and **offer** the **sacrifices** that Moses commanded for your cleansing,
  18:15 *People were* also **bringing** babies to Jesus to have him touch
  23:14 "*You* **brought** me this man as one who was inciting the people to
  23:36 also came up and mocked him. *They* **offered** him wine vinegar
Jn 16: 2 anyone who kills you will think he *is* **offering** a service to God.
  19:29 sponge in it, put the sponge on a stalk of the hyssop plant, and **lifted**
Ac 7:42 " '*Did you* **bring** me sacrifices and offerings forty years in the
  8:18 at the laying on of the apostles' hands, *he* **offered** them money
  21:26 and the **offering** [+4714] *would be* **made** for each of them.
Heb 5: 1 them in matters related to God, to **offer** gifts and sacrifices for sins.
  5: 3 This is why he has to **offer sacrifices** for his own sins, as well as
  5: 7 he **offered up** prayers and petitions with loud cries and tears to the
  8: 3 Every high priest is appointed to **offer** both gifts and sacrifices,
  8: 3 so it was necessary for this one also to have something *to* **offer**.
  8: 4 for there are already men *who* **offer** the gifts prescribed by the law.
  9: 7 which *he* **offered** for himself and for the sins the people had
  9: 9 and sacrifices *being* **offered** were not able to clear the conscience
  9:14 who through the eternal Spirit **offered** himself unblemished to
  9:25 Nor did he enter heaven to **offer** himself again and again, the way
  9:28 so Christ *was* **sacrificed** once to take away the sins of many
  10: 1 by the same sacrifices **repeated**ˢ endlessly year after year,
  10: 2 If it could, would they not have stopped *being* **offered**? For the
  10: 8 pleased with them" (although the law required them *to be* **made**ˢ).
  10:11 again and again *he* **offers** the same sacrifices, which can never take
  10:12 But *when* this priest *had* **offered** for all time one sacrifice for sins,
  11: 4 By faith Abel **offered** God a better sacrifice than Cain did.
  11:17 faith Abraham, when God tested him, **offered** Isaac **as a sacrifice**.
  11:17 He who had received the promises *was about to* **sacrifice** his one
  12: 7 Endure hardship as discipline; God *is* **treating** you as sons.

4713 προσφιλής, *prosphilēs* [1] [√ 4639 + 5813]

lovely [1]

Php 4: 8 is noble, whatever is right, whatever is pure, whatever is **lovely**,

4714 προσφορά, *prosphora* [9] [√ 4639 + 5770]

offering [3], sacrifice [3], offerings [2], offering made [+4712] [1]

Ac 21:26 and the **offering** *would be* **made** [+4712] for each of them.
  24:17 to bring my people gifts for the poor and to present **offerings**.
Ro 15:16 so that the Gentiles might become an **offering** acceptable to God,
Eph 5: 2 and gave himself up for us as a fragrant **offering** and sacrifice to
Heb 10: 5 "Sacrifice and **offering** you did not desire, but a body you prepared
  10: 8 First he said, "Sacrifices and **offerings**, burnt offerings and sin
  10:10 we have been made holy through the **sacrifice** of the body of Jesus
  10:14 because *by* one **sacrifice** he has made perfect forever those who
  10:18 these have been forgiven, there is no longer any **sacrifice** for sin.

4715 προσφωνέω, *prosphōneō* [7] [√ 4639 + 5889]

calling out [2], appealed [1], called forward [1], called to [1], said [1], speak [1]

Mt 11:16 like children sitting in the marketplaces and **calling out** to others:
Lk 6:13 he **called** his disciples **to** *him* and chose twelve of them,
  7:32 children sitting in the marketplace and **calling out** to each other:
  13:12 Jesus saw her, *he* **called** her **forward** and said to her, "Woman,
  23:20 Wanting to release Jesus, Pilate **appealed** to them again.
Ac 21:40 the crowd. When they were all silent, *he* **said** to them in Aramaic:
  22: 2 When they heard *him* **speak** to them in Aramaic, they became very

4716 προσχαίρω, *proschairō* Not used in UBS/NIV [√ 4639 + 5897]

4717 πρόσχυσις, *proschysis* [1] [√ 1772; cf. 4639]

sprinkling [1]

Heb 11:28 By faith he kept the Passover and the **sprinkling** of blood,

4718 προσψαύω, *prospsauō* [1] [√ *4639 + 6041*]

lift [1]

Lk 11:46 and *you* yourselves *will* not **lift** one finger to help them.

4719 προσωπολημπτέω, *prosōpolēmpteō* [1]
[√ *4725 + 3284*]

show favoritism [1]

Jas 2: 9 But if *you* **show favoritism**, you sin and are convicted by the law

4720 προσωπολήμπτης, *prosōpolēmptēs* [1]
[√ *4725 + 3284*]

show favoritism [*+1639*] [1]

Ac 10:34 realize how true it is that God *does* not **show favoritism** [*+1639*]

4721 προσωπολημψία, *prosōpolēmpsia* [4]
[√ *4725 + 3284*]

favoritism [2], show favoritism [*+1639*] [1], show favoritism
[*+1877*] [1]

Ro 2:11 For God *does* not **show favoritism** [*+1639*].
Eph 6: 9 and yours is in heaven, and there is no **favoritism** with him.
Col 3:25 wrong will be repaid for his wrong, and there is no **favoritism**.
Jas 2: 1 in our glorious Lord Jesus Christ, don't **show favoritism** [*+1877*].

4722 προσωπολ ηπτέω, *prosōpolēpteō* Not used in
UBS/NIV [√ *4725 + 3284*]

4723 προσωπολήπτης, *prosōpolēptēs* Not used in
UBS/NIV [√ *4725 + 3284*]

4724 προσωποληψία, *prosōpolēpsia* Not used in
UBS/NIV [√ *4725 + 3284*]

4725 πρόσωπον, *prosōpon* [76] [→ *719, 2349, 4719,
4720, 4721, 4722, 4723, 4724; cf. 4639 + 3972*]

face [22], faces [7], ahead [*+4574*] [4], presence [3], appearance
[2], me [*+1609+3836*] [2], pay attention who they are
[*+476+1063*] [2], sight [2], with face to the ground [*+2093*] [2],
you [*+3836+5148*] [2], before [*+2848*] [1], before [*+4574*] [1],
before [*+608*] [1], blindfolded [*+3836+4328*] [1], face to face
[*+2848*] [1], faced [*+2848*] [1], facedown to the ground [*+2093*]
[1], fall down [*+2093+4406*] [1], flatter [*+2513*] [1], from [*+608*]
[1], he [*+899+3836*] [1], in person [1], in presence [*+3552+3836*]
[1], its [*+899+3836*] [1], its^s [*+899+3836*] [1], judge by external
appearance [*+476+3284*] [1], left [*+608+4513*] [1], many [*+4498*]
[1], on ahead [*+4574*] [1], personally [1], reach [1], resolutely
[*+3836+5114*] [1], see [1], show partiality [*+3284*] [1], surface of
things [*+2848*] [1], threw himself [*+2093+4406*] [1], what is seen
[1], whole [*+4246*] [1]

Mt 6:16 for they disfigure their **faces** to show men they are fasting.
     6:17 But when you fast, put oil on your head and wash your **face**,
  11:10 'I will send my messenger **ahead** [*+4574*] of you, who will prepare
  16: 3 You know how to interpret the **appearance** of the sky, but you
  17: 2 His **face** shone like the sun, and his clothes became as white as the
  17: 6 heard this, they fell **facedown** [*+2093*] **to the ground**, terrified.
  18:10 For I tell you that their angels in heaven always see the **face** of my
  22:16 because *you* **pay** no **attention** to **who they are** [*+476+1063*].
  26:39 he fell **with** his **face** [*+2093*] **to the ground** and prayed, "My
  26:67 Then they spit in his **face** and struck him with their fists. Others
Mk 1: 2 "I will send my messenger **ahead** [*+4574*] of you, who will prepare
  12:14 because *you* **pay** no **attention** to **who they are** [*+476+1063*];
  14:65 some began to spit at him; they **blindfolded** [*+3836+4328*] him,
Lk 2:31 which you have prepared in the **sight** of all people,
  5:12 he fell **with** his **face** [*+2093*] **to the ground** and begged him,
  7:27 'I will send my messenger **ahead** [*+4574*] of you, who will prepare
  9:29 As he was praying, the appearance *of* his **face** changed, and his

  9:51 to heaven, Jesus **resolutely** [*+3836+5114*] set out for Jerusalem.
  9:52 And he sent messengers **on ahead** [*+4574*], who went into a
  9:53 welcome him, because **he** [*+899+3836*] was heading for Jerusalem.
  10: 1 and sent them two by two **ahead** [*+4574*] of him to every town
  12:56 You know how to interpret the **appearance** of the earth
  17:16 *He* threw himself [*+2093+4406*] at Jesus' feet and thanked him—
  20:21 and that *you do* not **show partiality** [*+3284*] but teach the way of
  21:35 For it will come upon all those who live on the **face** of the whole
  24: 5 In their fright the women bowed down with their **faces** to the
Ac 2:28 of life; you will fill me with joy in your **presence** [*+3552+3836*].'
  3:13 over to be killed, and you disowned him **before** [*+2848*] Pilate,
  3:19 that times of refreshing may come **from** [*+608*] the Lord,
  5:41 The apostles **left** [*+608+4513*] the Sanhedrin, rejoicing
  6:15 at Stephen, and they saw that his **face** was like the face of an angel.
  6:15 at Stephen, and they saw that his face was like the **face** of an angel.
  7:45 took the land from the nations God drove out **before** [*+608*] them.
  13:24 **Before** [*+4574*] the coming of Jesus, John preached repentance
  17:26 nation of men, that they should inhabit the **whole** [*+4246*] earth;
  20:25 preaching the kingdom will ever see **me** [*+1609+3836*] again.
  20:38 most was his statement that they would never see his **face** again.
  25:16 to hand over any man before he has **faced** [*+2848*] his accusers
1Co 13:12 but a poor reflection as in a mirror; then we shall see **face** to face.
  13:12 but a poor reflection as in a mirror; then we shall see face to **face**.
  14:25 So he will **fall down** [*+2093+4406*] and worship God, exclaiming,
2Co 1:11 Then **many** [*+4498*] will give thanks on our behalf for the gracious
  2:10 to forgive—I have forgiven in the **sight** of Christ for your sake,
  3: 7 so that the Israelites could not look steadily at the **face** of Moses
  3: 7 steadily at the face of Moses because of its^s [*+899+3836*] glory,
  3:13 who would put a veil over his **face** to keep the Israelites from
  3:18 And we, who with unveiled **faces** all reflect the Lord's glory,
  4: 6 the light of the knowledge of the glory of God in the **face** of Christ.
  5:12 so that you can answer those who take pride in **what is seen** rather
  8:24 and the reason for our pride in you, so that the churches can **see** it.
  10: 1 I, Paul, who am "timid" when **face** [*+2848*] **to face** with you,
  10: 7 You are looking only on the **surface** [*+2848*] **of things**. If anyone
  11:20 of you or pushes himself forward or slaps you in the **face**.
Gal 1:22 I was **personally** unknown to the churches of Judea that are in
  2: 6 God *does* not **judge by external appearance** [*+476+3284*]—
  2:11 When Peter came to Antioch, I opposed him to his **face**,
Col 2: 1 and for all who have not met **me** [*+1609+3836*] personally.
1Th 2:17 when we were torn away from you for a short time (**in person**,
  2:17 intense longing we made every effort to see **you** [*+3836+5148*].
  3:10 we pray most earnestly that we may see **you** [*+3836+5148*] again
2Th 1: 9 and shut out from the **presence** of the Lord and from the majesty
Heb 9:24 he entered heaven itself, now to appear for us *in* God's **presence**.
Jas 1:11 its blossom falls and its [*+899+3836*] beauty is destroyed.
  1:23 but does not do what it says is like a man who looks at his **face** in
1Pe 3:12 their prayer, but the **face** of the Lord is against those who do evil."
Jude 1:16 and **flatter** [*+2513*] others for their own advantage.
Rev 4: 7 the second was like an ox, the third had a **face** like a man,
  6:16 "Fall on us and hide us from the **face** of him who sits on the throne
  7:11 They fell down on their **faces** before the throne and worshiped
  9: 7 like crowns of gold, and their **faces** resembled human faces.
  9: 7 like crowns of gold, and their faces resembled human **faces**.
  10: 1 his **face** was like the sun, and his legs were like fiery pillars.
  11:16 on their thrones before God, fell on their **faces** and worshiped God,
  12:14 care of for a time, times and half a time, out of the serpent's **reach**.
  20:11 Earth and sky fled from his **presence**, and there was no place for
  22: 4 They will see his **face**, and his name will be on their foreheads.

4726 προτάσσω, *protassō* Not used in UBS/NIV
[√ *4574 + 5435*]

4727 προτείνω, *proteinō* [1] [√ *1753; cf. 4574*]

stretched out [1]

Ac 22:25 As *they* **stretched** him **out** to flog him, Paul said to the centurion

4728 πρότερος, *proteros* [11] [√ *4574*]

first [3], earlier [2], formerly [2], before [1], former [1], once [1],
when [1]

Jn 6:62 What if you see the Son of Man ascend to where he was **before**!
  7:50 who had gone to Jesus **earlier** and who was one of their own

9: 8 and those who had **formerly** seen him begging asked,
2Co 1: 15 I planned to visit you **first** so that you might benefit twice.
Gal 4: 13 because of an illness that I **first** preached the gospel to you.
Eph 4: 22 You were taught, with regard to your **former** way of life, to put off
1Ti 1: 13 Even though I was **once** a blasphemer and a persecutor and a
Heb 4: 6 and those who **formerly** had the gospel preached to them did not
7: 27 after day, **first** for his own sins, and then for the sins of the people.
10: 32 Remember those **earlier** days after you had received the light,
1Pe 1: 14 do not conform to the evil desires you had **when** you lived in

4729 προτίθημι, *protithēmi* [3] [√ 4574 + 5502]

planned [1], presented [1], purposed [1]

Ro 1: 13 that *I* **planned** many times to come to you (but have been
3: 25 God **presented** him as a sacrifice of atonement, through faith in his
Eph 1: 9 will according to his good pleasure, which *he* **purposed** in Christ,

4730 προτρέπω, *protrepō* [1] [√ 4574 + 5572]

encouraged [1]

Ac 18: 27 the brothers **encouraged** him and wrote to the disciples there to

4731 προτρέχω, *protrechō* [2] [√ 4574 + 5556]

outran [+5441] [1], ran [1]

Lk 19: 4 So he **ran** ahead and climbed a sycamore-fig tree to see him,
Jn 20: 4 but the other disciple **outran** [+5441] Peter and reached the tomb

4732 προϋπάρχω, *prouparchō* [2] [√ 4574 + 5679 + 806]

before this been [+1639] [1], for some time [1]

Lk 23: 12 became friends—**before this** *they had* **been** [+1639] enemies.
Ac 8: 9 Now **for some time** a man named Simon had practiced sorcery in

4733 πρόφασις, *prophasis* [6] [√ 4574 + 5743]

show [2], excuse [1], false motives [1], mask to cover up [1], pretending [1]

Mk 12: 40 They devour widows' houses and *for* a **show** make lengthy prayers.
Lk 20: 47 They devour widows' houses and *for* a **show** make lengthy prayers.
Jn 15: 22 be guilty of sin. Now, however, they have no **excuse** for their sin.
Ac 27: 30 **pretending** they were going to lower some anchors from the bow.
Php 1: 18 every way, whether *from* **false motives** or true, Christ is preached.
1Th 2: 5 never used flattery, nor did we put on a **mask to cover up** greed—

4734 προφέρω, *propherō* [2] [√ 4574 + 5770]

brings [2]

Lk 6: 45 The good man **brings** good things out of the good stored up in his
6: 45 and the evil man **brings** evil things out of the evil stored up in his

4735 προφητεία, *prophēteia* [19] [→ 4736, 4737, 4738, 4739, 6021; cf. 4574 + 5774]

prophecy [12], prophecies [3], prophesying [2], gift of prophecy [1], prophetic message [1]

Mt 13: 14 In them is fulfilled the **prophecy** of Isaiah: " 'You will be ever
Ro 12: 6 If a man's gift is **prophesying**, let him use it in proportion to his
1Co 12: 10 to another miraculous powers, to another **prophecy**, to another
13: 2 If I have the **gift of prophecy** and can fathom all mysteries
13: 8 But where there are **prophecies**, they will cease; where there are
14: 6 some revelation or knowledge or **prophecy** or word of instruction?
14: 22 **prophecy**, however, is for believers, not for unbelievers.
1Th 5: 20 do not treat **prophecies** with contempt.
1Ti 1: 18 I give you this instruction in keeping with the **prophecies** once
4: 14 which was given you through a **prophetic message** when the body
2Pe 1: 20 you must understand that no **prophecy** of Scripture came about by
1: 21 For **prophecy** never had its origin in the will of man, but men
Rev 1: 3 Blessed is the one who reads the words *of* this **prophecy**,
11: 6 so that it will not rain during the time they are **prophesying**;

19: 10 Worship God! For the testimony of Jesus is the spirit *of* **prophecy**."
22: 7 Blessed is he who keeps the words *of* the **prophecy** in this book."
22: 10 he told me, "Do not seal up the words *of* the **prophecy** of this book,
22: 18 I warn everyone who hears the words *of* the **prophecy** of this
22: 19 And if anyone takes words away from this book *of* **prophecy**,

4736 προφητεύω, *prophēteuō* [28] [√ 4735]

prophesy [12], prophesied [8], prophesies [5], prophecy [1], prophesying [1], spoke [1]

Mt 7: 22 to me on that day, 'Lord, Lord, *did we* not **prophesy** in your name,
11: 13 For all the Prophets and the Law **prophesied** until John.
15: 7 You hypocrites! Isaiah was right *when he* **prophesied** about you:
26: 68 and said, "**Prophesy** to us, Christ. Who hit you?"
Mk 7: 6 "Isaiah was right *when he* **prophesied** about you hypocrites;
14: 65 blindfolded him, struck him with their fists, and said, "**Prophesy**!"
Lk 1: 67 father Zechariah was filled with the Holy Spirit and **prophesied**:
22: 64 They blindfolded him and demanded, "**Prophesy**! Who hit you?"
Jn 11: 51 but as high priest that year *he* **prophesied** that Jesus would die for
Ac 2: 17 Your sons and daughters *will* **prophesy**, your young men will see
2: 18 I will pour out my Spirit in those days, and *they will* **prophesy**.
19: 6 Spirit came on them, and they spoke in tongues and **prophesied**.
21: 9 He had four unmarried daughters *who* **prophesied**.
1Co 11: 4 Every man *who* prays or **prophesies** with his head covered
11: 5 And every woman *who* prays or **prophesies** with her head
13: 9 For we know in part and *we* **prophesy** in part,
14: 1 and eagerly desire spiritual gifts, especially the gift of **prophecy**.
14: 3 But everyone *who* **prophesies** speaks to men for their
14: 4 a tongue edifies himself, but he *who* **prophesies** edifies the church.
14: 5 of you to speak in tongues, but I would rather have *you* **prophesy**.
14: 5 He *who* **prophesies** is greater than one who speaks in tongues,
14: 24 does not understand comes in while everybody *is* **prophesying**,
14: 31 For you can all **prophesy** in turn so that everyone may be
14: 39 Therefore, my brothers, be eager *to* **prophesy**, and do not forbid
1Pe 1: 10 the prophets, who **spoke** of the grace that was to come to you,
Jude 1: 14 Enoch, the seventh from Adam, **prophesied** about these men:
Rev 10: 11 "You must **prophesy** again about many peoples, nations, languages
11: 3 and *they will* **prophesy** for 1,260 days, clothed in sackcloth."

4737 προφήτης, *prophētēs* [144] [√ 4735]

ἀπόστολος ... προφήτης (apostle ... prophet) [8] Lk 11:49; 1Co 12:28, 29; Eph 2:20; 3:5; 4:11; 2Pe 3:2; Rev 18:20

διὰ τοῦ προφήτου, -τῶν (through the prophet[s]) [18] Mt 1:22; 2:5,15,17,23; 3:3; 4:14; 8:17; 12:17; 13:35; 21:4; 24:15; 27:9; Lk 1:70; 18:31; Ac 2:16; 28:25; Ro 1:2

νόμος ... προφήται (Law ... Prophets) [11] Mt 5:17; 7:12; 11:13; 22:40; Lk 16:16; 24:44; Jn 1:45; Ac 13:15; 24:14; 28:23; Ro 3:21

prophets [80], prophet [60], prophet's [2], him[s] [+3836] [1], prophet [+467] [1]

Mt 1: 22 took place to fulfill what the Lord had said through the **prophet**:
2: 5 in Judea," they replied, "for this is what the **prophet** has written:
2: 15 so was fulfilled what the Lord had said through the **prophet**:
2: 17 Then what was said through the **prophet** Jeremiah was fulfilled:
2: 23 So was fulfilled what was said through the **prophets**: "He will be
3: 3 This is he who was spoken of through the **prophet** Isaiah:
4: 14 to fulfill what was said through the **prophet** Isaiah:
5: 12 for in the same way they persecuted the **prophets** who were before
5: 17 "Do not think that I have come to abolish the Law or the **Prophets**;
7: 12 have them do to you, for this sums up the Law and the **Prophets**.
8: 17 This was to fulfill what was spoken through the **prophet** Isaiah:
10: 41 Anyone who receives a **prophet** because he is a prophet will
10: 41 a prophet because he is a **prophet** will receive a prophet's reward,
10: 41 a prophet because he is a **prophet** will receive a **prophet's** reward,
11: 9 go out to see? A **prophet**? Yes, I tell you, and more than a prophet.
11: 9 go out to see? A prophet? Yes, I tell you, and more than a **prophet**.
11: 13 For all the **Prophets** and the Law prophesied until John.
12: 17 This was to fulfill what was spoken through the **prophet** Isaiah:
12: 39 But none will be given it except the sign *of* the **prophet** Jonah:
13: 17 many **prophets** and righteous men longed to see what you see
13: 35 So was fulfilled what was spoken through the **prophet**: "I will open
13: 57 in his hometown and in his own house is a **prophet** without honor."

14: 5 was afraid of the people, because they considered him a **prophet**.
16: 14 others say Elijah; and still others, Jeremiah or one of the **prophets**."
21: 4 This took place to fulfill what was spoken through the **prophet**:
21: 11 "This is Jesus, the **prophet** from Nazareth in Galilee."
21: 26 are afraid of the people, for they all hold that John was a **prophet**."
21: 46 afraid of the crowd because the people held that he was a **prophet**.
22: 40 All the Law and the **Prophets** hang on these two commandments."
23: 29 You build tombs *for* the **prophets** and decorate the graves of the
23: 30 have taken part with them in shedding the blood *of* the **prophets**.'
23: 31 that you are the descendants of those who murdered the **prophets**.
23: 34 Therefore I am sending you **prophets** and wise men and teachers.
23: 37 Jerusalem, you who kill the **prophets** and stone those sent to you,
24: 15 that causes desolation,' spoken of through the **prophet** Daniel—
26: 56 But this has all taken place that the writings *of* the **prophets** might
27: 9 Then what was spoken by Jeremiah the **prophet** was fulfilled:
Mk 1: 2 It is written in Isaiah the **prophet**: "I will send my messenger ahead
6: 4 his relatives and in his own house is a **prophet** without honor."
6: 15 And still others claimed, "He is a **prophet**, like one of the prophets
6: 15 "He is a prophet, like one *of* the **prophets** *of long ago*."
8: 28 the Baptist; others say Elijah; and still others, one *of* the **prophets**."
11: 32 the people, for everyone held that John really was a **prophet**.)
Lk 1: 70 (as he said through his holy **prophets** of long ago),
1: 76 And you, my child, will be called a **prophet** of the Most High;
3: 4 As is written in the book of the words of Isaiah the **prophet**:
4: 17 The scroll of the **prophet** Isaiah was handed to him. Unrolling it,
4: 24 the truth," he continued, "no **prophet** is accepted in his hometown.
4: 27 were many in Israel with leprosy in the time of Elisha the **prophet**,
6: 23 in heaven. For that is how their fathers treated the **prophets**.
7: 16 praised God. "A great **prophet** has appeared among us," they said.
7: 26 go out to see? A **prophet**? Yes, I tell you, and more than a prophet.
7: 26 go out to see? A prophet? Yes, I tell you, and more than a **prophet**.
7: 39 he said to himself, "If this man were a **prophet**, he would know
9: 8 and still others that one *of* the **prophets** of long ago had come back
9: 19 that one *of* the **prophets** of long ago has come back to life."
10: 24 For I tell you that many **prophets** and kings wanted to see what
11: 47 "Woe to you, because you build tombs *for* the **prophets**, and it was
11: 49 God in his wisdom said, 'I will send them **prophets** and apostles,
11: 50 the **prophets** that has been shed since the beginning of the world,
13: 28 Isaac and Jacob and all the **prophets** in the kingdom of God,
13: 33 the next day—for surely no **prophet** can die outside Jerusalem!
13: 34 Jerusalem, you who kill the **prophets** and stone those sent to you,
16: 16 "The Law and the **Prophets** were proclaimed until John. Since that
16: 29 "Abraham replied, 'They have Moses and the **Prophets**; let them
16: 31 "He said to him, 'If they do not listen to Moses and the **Prophets**,
18: 31 and everything that is written by the **prophets** about the Son of
20: 6 will stone us, because they are persuaded that John was a **prophet**."
24: 19 "He was a **prophet** [+*467*], powerful in word and deed before God
24: 25 and how slow of heart to believe all that the **prophets** have
24: 27 And beginning with Moses and all the **Prophets**, he explained to
24: 44 about me in the Law of Moses, the **Prophets** and the Psalms."
Jn 1: 21 He said, "I am not." "Are you the **Prophet**?" He answered, "No."
1: 23 John replied in the words of Isaiah the **prophet**, "I am the voice of
1: 25 you baptize if you are not the Christ, nor Elijah, nor the **Prophet**?"
1: 45 wrote about in the Law, and about whom the **prophets** also wrote
4: 19 "Sir," the woman said, "I can see that you are a **prophet**.
4: 44 (Now Jesus himself had pointed out that a **prophet** has no honor in
6: 14 to say, "Surely this is the **Prophet** who is to come into the world."
6: 45 It is written in the **Prophets**: 'They will all be taught by God.'
7: 40 words, some of the people said, "Surely this man is the **Prophet**."
7: 52 and you will find that a **prophet** does not come out of Galilee."
8: 52 Abraham died and so did the **prophets**, yet you say that if anyone
8: 53 He died, and so did the **prophets**. Who do you think you are?"
9: 17 It was your eyes he opened." The man replied, "He is a **prophet**."
12: 38 This was to fulfill the word *of* Isaiah the **prophet**: "Lord, who has
Ac 2: 16 No, this is what was spoken by the **prophet** Joel:
2: 30 But he was a **prophet** and knew that God had promised him on
3: 18 is how God fulfilled what he had foretold through all the **prophets**,
3: 21 as he promised long ago through his holy **prophets**.
3: 22 'The Lord your God will raise up for you a **prophet** like me from
3: 23 Anyone who does not listen to him[s] [+*3836*] will be completely
3: 24 "Indeed, all the **prophets** from Samuel on, as many as have spoken,
3: 25 And you are heirs *of* the **prophets** and of the covenant God made
7: 37 'God will send you a **prophet** like me from your own people.'
7: 42 This agrees with what is written in the book *of* the **prophets**:
7: 48 High does not live in houses made by men. As the **prophet** says:
7: 52 Was there ever a **prophet** your fathers did not persecute?

8: 28 was sitting in his chariot reading the book of Isaiah the **prophet**.
8: 30 ran up to the chariot and heard the man reading Isaiah the **prophet**.
8: 34 please, who is the **prophet** talking about, himself or someone else?"
10: 43 All the **prophets** testify about him that everyone who believes in
11: 27 During this time *some* **prophets** came down from Jerusalem to
13: 1 In the church at Antioch there were **prophets** and teachers:
13: 15 After the reading *from* the Law and the **Prophets**, the synagogue
13: 20 God gave them judges until the time of Samuel the **prophet**.
13: 27 yet in condemning him they fulfilled the words *of* the **prophets**
13: 40 Take care that what the **prophets** have said does not happen to
15: 15 The words *of* the **prophets** are in agreement with this, as it is
15: 32 Judas and Silas, who themselves were **prophets**, said much to
21: 10 number of days, a **prophet** named Agabus came down from Judea.
24: 14 that agrees with the Law and that is written in the **Prophets**,
26: 22 I am saying nothing beyond what the **prophets** and Moses said
26: 27 King Agrippa, do you believe the **prophets**? I know you do."
28: 23 them about Jesus from the Law of Moses and from the **Prophets**.
28: 25 truth to your forefathers when he said through Isaiah the **prophet**:
Ro 1: 2 the gospel he promised beforehand through his **prophets** in the
3: 21 has been made known, to which the Law and the **Prophets** testify.
11: 3 they have killed your **prophets** and torn down your altars;
1Co 12: 28 second **prophets**, third teachers, then workers of miracles,
12: 29 Are all apostles? Are all **prophets**? Are all teachers? Do all work
14: 29 Two or three **prophets** should speak, and the others should weigh
14: 32 The spirits *of* **prophets** are subject to the control of prophets.
14: 32 The spirits of prophets are subject to the control *of* **prophets**.
14: 37 If anybody thinks he is a **prophet** or spiritually gifted, let him
Eph 2: 20 built on the foundation *of* the apostles and **prophets**, with Christ
3: 5 been revealed by the Spirit to God's holy apostles and **prophets**.
4: 11 some to be **prophets**, some to be evangelists, and some to be
1Th 2: 15 who killed the Lord Jesus and the **prophets** and also drove us out.
Tit 1: 12 Even one of their own **prophets** has said, "Cretans are always liars,
Heb 1: 1 In the past God spoke to our forefathers through the **prophets** at
11: 32 Barak, Samson, Jephthah, David, Samuel and the **prophets**,
Jas 5: 10 of suffering, take the **prophets** who spoke in the name of the Lord.
1Pe 1: 10 Concerning this salvation, the **prophets**, who spoke of the grace
2Pe 2: 16 spoke with a man's voice and restrained the **prophet's** madness.
3: 2 you to recall the words spoken in the past by the holy **prophets**
Rev 10: 7 just as he announced to his servants the **prophets**."
11: 10 because these two **prophets** had tormented those who live on the
11: 18 and for rewarding your servants the **prophets** and your saints
16: 6 for they have shed the blood of your saints and **prophets**,
18: 20 over her, O heaven! Rejoice, saints and apostles and **prophets**!
18: 24 In her was found the blood *of* **prophets** and of the saints, and of all
22: 6 The Lord, the God of the spirits *of* the **prophets**, sent his angel to
22: 9 am a fellow servant with you and with your brothers the **prophets**

4738 προφητικός, *prophētikos* [2] [√ *4735*]

of prophets [1], prophetic [1]

Ro 16: 26 and made known through the **prophetic** writings by the command
2Pe 1: 19 And we have the word **of** the **prophets** made more certain,

---

4739 προφῆτις, *prophētis* [2] [√ *4735*]

prophetess [2]

Lk 2: 36 There was also a **prophetess**, Anna, the daughter of Phanuel,
Rev 2: 20 You tolerate that woman Jezebel, who calls herself a **prophetess**.

4740 προφθάνω, *prophthanō* [1] [√ *4574* + *5777*]

first [1]

Mt 17: 25 When Peter came into the house, Jesus *was the* **first** to speak.

4741 προχειρίζω, *procheirizō* [3] [√ *4574* + *5931*]

appoint [1], appointed [1], chosen [1]

Ac 3: 20 that he may send the Christ, *who has been* **appointed** for you—
22: 14 'The God of our fathers *has* **chosen** you to know his will and to
26: 16 I have appeared to you to **appoint** you as a servant and as a

4742 προχειροτονέω, *procheirotoneō* [1] [√ 1753; cf. 4574 + 5931]

already chosen [1]

Ac 10:41 all the people, but *by* witnesses whom God *had* **already chosen**—

4743 Πρόχορος, *Prochoros* [1] [√ 4574 + 5962]

Procorus [1]

Ac 6: 5 also Philip, **Procorus**, Nicanor, Timon, Parmenas, and Nicolas

4744 πρύμνα, *prymna* [3]

stern [3]

Mk 4:38 Jesus was in the **stern**, sleeping on a cushion. The disciples woke
Ac 27:29 they dropped four anchors from the **stern** and prayed for daylight.
27:41 and the **stern** was broken to pieces by the pounding of the surf.

4745 πρωΐ, *prōi* [12] [→ 4746, 4747, 4748; cf. 4574]

early [3], early in the morning [2], in the morning [2], at dawn [1], early in the morning [+275] [1], early morning [1], morning [1], very early in the morning [+2317] [1]

Mt 16: 3 and **in the morning**, 'Today it will be stormy, for the sky is red
20: 1 **early** [+275] **in the morning** to hire men to work in his vineyard.
21:18 **Early in the morning**, as he was on his way back to the city,
Mk 1:35 Very **early in the morning**, while it was still dark, Jesus got up,
11:20 **In the morning**, as they went along, they saw the fig tree withered
13:35 the evening, or at midnight, or when the rooster crows, or **at dawn**,
15: 1 **Very early** [+2317] **in the morning**, the chief priests,
16: 2 Very **early** on the first day of the week, just after sunrise,
16: 9 When Jesus rose **early** on the first day of the week, he appeared
Jn 18:28 By now it was **early morning**, and to avoid ceremonial
20: 1 **Early** on the first day of the week, while it was still dark,
Ac 28:23 From **morning** till evening he explained and declared to them the

4746 πρωΐα, *prōia* [2] [√ 4745]

early in the morning [+1181] [1], early in the morning [1]

Mt 27: 1 **Early in the morning**, all the chief priests and the elders of the
Jn 21: 4 **Early** [+1181] **in the morning**, Jesus stood on the shore,

4747 πρώϊμος, *prōimos* Not used in UBS/NIV [√ 4745]

4748 πρωϊνός, *prōinos* [2] [√ 4745]

morning [2]

Rev 2:28 I will also give him the **morning** star.
22:16 and the Offspring of David, and the bright **Morning** Star."

4749 πρῷρα, *prōra* [2] [√ 4574]

bow [2]

Ac 27:30 pretending they were going to lower some anchors from the **bow**.
27:41 and ran aground. The **bow** stuck fast and would not move,

4750 πρωτεύω, *prōteuō* [1] [√ 4755]

supremacy [1]

Col 1:18 the dead, so that in everything he might have the **supremacy**.

4751 πρωτοκαθεδρία, *prōtokathedria* [4] [√ 4755 + 2757]

most important seats [4]

Mt 23: 6 at banquets and the **most important seats** in the synagogues;
Mk 12:39 and have the **most important seats** in the synagogues
Lk 11:43 because you love the **most important seats** in the synagogues
20:46 and have the **most important seats** in the synagogues

4752 πρωτοκλισία, *prōtoklisia* [5] [√ 4755 + 3111]

place of honor [2], places of honor [2], places of honor at the table [1]

Mt 23: 6 they love the **place of honor** at banquets and the most important
Mk 12:39 seats in the synagogues and the **places of honor** at banquets.
Lk 14: 7 he noticed how the guests picked the **places of honor at the table**,
14: 8 invites you to a wedding feast, do not take the **place of honor**,
20:46 seats in the synagogues and the **places of honor** at banquets.

4753 πρωτόμαρτυς, *prōtomartys* Not used in UBS/NIV [√ 4755 + 3459]

4754 πρῶτον, *prōton* [60] [√ 4755]

first [47], first of all [4], above all [+4047] [1], after [1], at first [1], begins [1], earlier [1], first of all [+4047] [1], in early days [1], in the first place [1], until [+1569+3590] [1]

Mt 5:24 in front of the altar. **First** go and be reconciled to your brother;
6:33 But seek **first** his kingdom and his righteousness, and all these
7: 5 **first** take the plank out of your own eye, and then you will see
8:21 disciple said to him, "Lord, **first** let me go and bury my father."
12:29 and carry off his possessions unless he **first** ties up the strong man?
13:30 **First** collect the weeds and tie them in bundles to be burned;
17:10 then do the teachers of the law say that Elijah must come **first**?"
23:26 **First** clean the inside of the cup and dish, and then the outside also
Mk 3:27 and carry off his possessions unless he **first** ties up the strong man.
4:28 **first** the stalk, then the head, then the full kernel in the head.
7:27 "**First** let the children eat all they want," he told her, "for it is not
9:11 "Why do the teachers of the law say that Elijah must come **first**?"
9:12 Jesus replied, "To be sure, Elijah does come **first**, and restores all
13:10 And the gospel must **first** be preached to all nations.
16: 9 he appeared **first** to Mary Magdalene, out of whom he had driven
Lk 6:42 **first** take the plank out of your eye, and then you will see clearly to
9:59 But the man replied, "Lord, **first** let me go and bury my father."
9:61 Lord; but **first** let me go back and say good-by to my family."
10: 5 "When you enter a house, **first** say, 'Peace to this house.'
11:38 noticing that Jesus did not **first** wash before the meal,
12: 1 on one another, Jesus began to speak **first** to his disciples, saying:
14:28 Will he not **first** sit down and estimate the cost to see if he has
14:31 Will he not **first** sit down and consider whether he is able with ten
17:25 But first he must suffer many things and be rejected by this
21: 9 These things must happen **first**, but the end will not come right
Jn 1:41 The **first** *thing* Andrew did was to find his brother Simon
2:10 "Everyone brings out the choice wine **first** and then the cheaper
7:51 "Does our law condemn anyone without **first** hearing him to find
10:40 to the place where John had been baptizing **in the early days**.
12:16 **At first** his disciples did not understand all this. Only after Jesus
15:18 "If the world hates you, keep in mind that it hated me **first**.
18:13 and brought him **first** to Annas, who was the father-in-law of
19:39 by Nicodemus, the man who **earlier** had visited Jesus at night.
Ac 3:26 he sent him **first** to you to bless you by turning each of you from
7:12 that there was grain in Egypt, he sent our fathers on their **first** *visit*.
13:46 "We had to speak the word of God to you **first**. Since you reject it
15:14 Simon has described to us how God *at* **first** showed his concern by
26:20 **First** to those in Damascus, then to those in Jerusalem and in all
Ro 1: 8 **First**, I thank my God through Jesus Christ for all of you,
1:16 of everyone who believes: **first** for the Jew, then for the Gentile.
2: 9 human being who does evil: **first** for the Jew, then for the Gentile;
2:10 for everyone who does good: **first** for the Jew, then for the Gentile.
3: 2 **First of all**, they have been entrusted with the very words of God.
15:24 my journey there, **after** I have enjoyed your company for a while.
1Co 11:18 **In the first place**, I hear that when you come together as a church,
12:28 And in the church God has appointed **first of all** apostles,
15:46 The spiritual did not come **first**, but the natural, and after that the
2Co 8: 5 but they gave themselves **first** to the Lord and then to us in
1Th 4:16 with the trumpet call of God, and the dead in Christ will rise **first**.
2Th 2: 3 for that day will not come, **until** [+1569+3590] the rebellion
1Ti 2: 1 I urge, then, first of all, that requests, prayers, intercession
3:10 They must **first** be tested; and then if there is nothing against them,
5: 4 these should learn **first of all** to put their religion into practice by
2Ti 1: 5 which **first** lived in your grandmother Lois and in your mother
2: 6 The hardworking farmer should be the **first** to receive a share of
Heb 7: 2 tenth of everything. **First**, his name means "king of righteousness";

Jas	3:17	But the wisdom that comes from heaven is **first of all** pure;
1Pe	4:17	and if it **begins** with us, what will the outcome be for those who do
2Pe	1:20	**Above** [+4047] **all**, you must understand that no prophecy of
	3: 3	**First** [+4047] **of all**, you must understand that in the last days

4755 πρῶτος, *prōtos* [95] [→ 1310, 4750, 4751, 4752, 4753, 4754, 4756, 4757, 4758, 4759, 5812; cf. 4574]

first [75], leading [3], before [2], leaders [2], most important [2], worst [2], as of first importance [+1877] [1], beginning [1], best [1], chief official [1], former [1], leaders [+1639] [1], old order of things [1], outer [1], prominent [1]

Mt	10: 2	**first**, Simon (who is called Peter) and his brother Andrew;
	12:45	And the final condition of that man is worse than the **first**.
	17:27	Take the **first** fish you catch; open its mouth and you will find a
	19:30	But many who are **first** will be last, and many who are last will be
	19:30	many who are first will be last, and many who are last will be **first**.
	20: 8	beginning with the last ones hired and going on to the **first**.'
	20:10	So when those came who were hired **first**, they expected to receive
	20:16	"So the last will be **first**, and the first will be last."
	20:16	"So the last will be first, and the **first** will be last."
	20:27	and whoever wants to be **first** must be your slave—
	21:28	He went to the **first** and said, 'Son, go and work today in the
	21:31	"The **first**," they answered. Jesus said to them, "I tell you the truth,
	21:36	Then he sent other servants to them, more than the **first** *time*,
	22:25	The **first** *one* married and died, and since he had no children,
	22:38	This is the **first** and greatest commandment.
	26:17	*On* the **first** *day* of the Feast of Unleavened Bread, the disciples
	27:64	from the dead. This last deception will be worse than the **first**."
Mk	6:21	*for* his high officials and military commanders and the **leading** *men*
	9:35	Jesus called the Twelve and said, "If anyone wants to be **first**,
	10:31	But many who are **first** will be last, and the last first."
	10:31	But many who are first will be last, and the last **first**."
	10:44	and whoever wants to be **first** must be slave of all.
	12:20	The **first** *one* married and died without leaving any children.
	12:28	"Of all the commandments, which is the **most important**?"
	12:29	"The **most important** *one*," answered Jesus, "is this: 'Hear,
	14:12	*On* the **first** day of the Feast of Unleavened Bread, when it was
	16: 9	When Jesus rose early *on* the **first** *day* of the week, he appeared
Lk	2: 2	(This was the **first** census that took place while Quirinius was
	11:26	And the final condition of that man is worse than the **first**."
	13:30	Indeed there are those who are last who will be **first**, and first who
	13:30	are those who are last who will be first, and **first** who will be last."
	14:18	The **first** said, 'I have just bought a field, and I must go and see it.
	15:22	said to his servants, 'Quick! Bring the **best** robe and put it on him.
	16: 5	He asked the **first**, 'How much do you owe my master?'
	19:16	"The **first** *one* came and said, 'Sir, your mina has earned ten more.'
	19:47	and the **leaders** among the people were trying to kill him.
	20:29	seven brothers. The **first** *one* married a woman and died childless.
Jn	1:15	comes after me has surpassed me because he was **before** me.' "
	1:30	who comes after me has surpassed me because he was **before** me.'
	8: 7	of you is without sin, let him be the **first** to throw a stone at her."
	19:32	and broke the legs *of* the **first** *man* who had been crucified with
	20: 4	but the other disciple outran Peter and reached the tomb **first**.
	20: 8	other disciple, who had reached the tomb **first**, also went inside.
Ac	1: 1	In my **former** book, Theophilus, I wrote about all that Jesus began
	12:10	They passed the **first** and second guards and came to the iron gate
	13:50	women of high standing and the **leading** *men* of the city.
	16:12	a Roman colony and the **leading** city of that district of Macedonia.
	17: 4	number of God-fearing Greeks and not a few **prominent** women.
	20:18	I was with you, from the **first** day I came into the province of Asia.
	25: 2	where the chief priests and Jewish **leaders** appeared before him
	26:23	that the Christ would suffer and, as the **first** to rise from the dead,
	27:43	He ordered those who could swim to jump overboard **first**
	28: 7	nearby that belonged to Publius, the **chief official** of the island.
	28:17	Three days later he called together the **leaders** [+1639] of the
Ro	10:19	**First**, Moses says, "I will make you envious by those who are not a
1Co	14:30	to someone who is sitting down, the **first** speaker should stop.
	15: 3	what I received I passed on to you **as of first** [+1877] **importance**:
	15:45	"The **first** man Adam became a living being"; the last Adam,
	15:47	The **first** man was of the dust of the earth, the second man from
Eph	6: 2	and mother"—which is the **first** commandment with a promise—
Php	1: 5	because of your partnership in the gospel from the **first** day until
1Ti	1:15	came into the world to save sinners—of whom I am the **worst**.
	1:16	very reason I was shown mercy so that in me, the **worst** of sinners,

	2:13	For Adam was formed **first**, then Eve.
	5:12	on themselves, because they have broken their **first** pledge.
2Ti	4:16	At my **first** defense, no one came to my support, but everyone
Heb	8: 7	For if there had been nothing wrong with that **first** covenant,
	8:13	By calling this covenant "new," he has made the **first** *one* obsolete;
	9: 1	Now the **first** covenant had regulations for worship and also an
	9: 2	In its **first** *room* were the lampstand, the table and the consecrated
	9: 6	the priests entered regularly into the **outer** room to carry on their
	9: 8	yet been disclosed as long as the **first** tabernacle was still standing.
	9:15	to set them free from the sins committed under the **first** covenant.
	9:18	This is why even the **first** *covenant* was not put into effect without
	10: 9	to do your will." He sets aside the **first** to establish the second.
2Pe	2:20	they are worse off at the end than they were at the **beginning**.
1Jn	4:19	We love because he **first** loved us.
Rev	1:17	hand on me and said: "Do not be afraid. I am the **First** and the Last.
	2: 4	Yet I hold this against you: You have forsaken your **first** love.
	2: 5	Repent and do the things you did at **first**. If you do not repent,
	2: 8	These are the words of him who is the **First** and the Last, who died
	2:19	and that you are now doing more than you did at **first**.
	4: 1	And the voice I had **first** heard speaking to me like a trumpet said,
	4: 7	The **first** living creature was like a lion, the second was like an ox,
	8: 7	The **first** angel sounded his trumpet, and there came hail and fire
	13:12	He exercised all the authority *of* the **first** beast on his behalf,
	13:12	and made the earth and its inhabitants worship the **first** beast,
	16: 2	The **first** angel went and poured out his bowl on the land,
	20: 5	until the thousand years were ended.) This is the **first** resurrection.
	20: 6	and holy are those who have part in the **first** resurrection.
	21: 1	new earth, for the **first** heaven and the first earth had passed away,
	21: 1	new earth, for the first heaven and the **first** earth had passed away,
	21: 4	or crying or pain, for the **old order of things** has passed away."
	21:19	The **first** foundation was jasper, the second sapphire, the third
	22:13	and the Omega, the **First** and the Last, the Beginning and the End.

4756 πρωτοστάτης, *prōtostatēs* [1] [√ 4755 + 2705]

ringleader [1]

Ac	24: 5	Jews all over the world. He is a **ringleader** of the Nazarene sect

4757 πρωτοτόκια, *prōtotokia* [1] [√ 4755 + 5503]

inheritance rights as the oldest son [1]

Heb	12:16	for a single meal sold his **inheritance rights as the oldest son**.

4758 πρωτότοκος, *prōtotokos* [8] [√ 4755 + 5503]

firstborn [8]

Lk	2: 7	and she gave birth to her **firstborn**, a son. She wrapped him in
Ro	8:29	of his Son, that he might be the **firstborn** among many brothers.
Col	1:15	is the image of the invisible God, the **firstborn** over all creation.
	1:18	he is the beginning and the **firstborn** from among the dead,
Heb	1: 6	And again, when God brings his **firstborn** into the world, he says,
	11:28	so that the destroyer of the **firstborn** would not touch the firstborn
	12:23	to the church *of* the **firstborn**, whose names are written in heaven.
Rev	1: 5	who is the faithful witness, the **firstborn** from the dead,

4759 πρώτως, *prōtōs* [1] [√ 4755]

first [1]

Ac	11:26	of people. The disciples were called Christians **first** at Antioch.

4760 πταίω, *ptaiō* [5] [→ 720]

at fault [1], fall [1], stumble in [1], stumble [1], stumbles [1]

Ro	11:11	*Did they* **stumble** so as to fall beyond recovery? Not at all!
Jas	2:10	and yet **stumbles** at just one point is guilty of breaking all of it.
	3: 2	*We* all **stumble in** many ways. If anyone is never at fault in what
	3: 2	If anyone *is* never **at fault** in what he says, he is a perfect man,
2Pe	1:10	and election sure. For if you do these things, *you will* never **fall**,

4761 πτέρνα, *pterna* [1]

heel [1]

Jn 13:18 'He who shares my bread has lifted up his **heel** against me.'

4762 πτερύγιον, *pterygion* [2] [√ 4375]

highest point [2]

Mt 4: 5 the holy city and had him stand on the **highest point** of the temple.
Lk 4: 9 to Jerusalem and had him stand on the **highest point** of the temple.

4763 πτέρυξ, *pteryx* [5] [√ 4375]

wings [5]

Mt 23:37 as a hen gathers her chicks under her **wings**, but you were not
Lk 13:34 as a hen gathers her chicks under her **wings**, but you were not
Rev 4: 8 Each of the four living creatures had six **wings** and was covered
9: 9 and the sound *of* their **wings** was like the thundering of many
12:14 The woman was given the two **wings** of a great eagle, so that she

4764 πτηνός, *ptēnos* [1] [√ 4375]

birds [1]

1Co 15:39 of flesh, animals have another, **birds** another and fish another.

4765 πτοέω, *ptoeō* [2] [→ 4766]

frightened [1], startled [1]

Lk 21: 9 When you hear of wars and revolutions, *do* not *be* **frightened**.
24:37 They were **startled** and frightened, thinking they saw a ghost.

4766 πτόησις, *ptoēsis* [1] [√ 4765]

give way [1]

1Pe 3: 6 her daughters if you do what is right and do not **give way** to fear.

4767 Πτολεμαΐς, *Ptolemais* [1]

Ptolemais [1]

Ac 21: 7 We continued our voyage from Tyre and landed at **Ptolemais**,

4768 πτύον, *ptyon* [2] [√ 4772]

winnowing fork [2]

Mt 3:12 His **winnowing fork** is in his hand, and he will clear his threshing
Lk 3:17 His **winnowing fork** is in his hand to clear his threshing floor

4769 πτύρω, *ptyrō* [1]

frightened [1]

Php 1:28 without *being* **frightened** in any way by those who oppose you.

4770 πτύσμα, *ptysma* [1] [√ 4772]

saliva [1]

Jn 9: 6 said this, he spit on the ground, made some mud with the **saliva**,

4771 πτύσσω, *ptyssō* [1] [→ 408]

rolled up [1]

Lk 4:20 Then *he* **rolled up** the scroll, gave it back to the attendant

4772 πτύω, *ptyō* [3] [→ 1746, 1870, 4768, 4770]

spit [3]

Mk 7:33 into the man's ears. Then he **spit** and touched the man's tongue.
8:23 *When he had* **spit** on the man's eyes and put his hands on him,
Jn 9: 6 Having said this, *he* **spit** on the ground, made some mud with the

4773 πτῶμα, *ptōma* [7] [√ 4406]

body [3], bodies [2], *untranslated* [1], carcass [1]

Mt 14:12 John's disciples came and took his **body** and buried it. Then they
24:28 Wherever there is a **carcass**, there the vultures will gather.
Mk 6:29 John's disciples came and took his **body** and laid it in a tomb.
15:45 from the centurion that it was so, he gave the **body** to Joseph.
Rev 11: 8 Their **bodies** will lie in the street of the great city, which is
11: 9 language and nation will gaze on their **bodies** and refuse them
11: 9 nation will gaze on their bodies and refuse [RPG] them burial.

4774 πτῶσις, *ptōsis* [2] [√ 4406]

crash [1], falling [1]

Mt 7:27 and beat against that house, and it fell with a great **crash**."
Lk 2:34 "This child is destined to cause the **falling** and rising of many in

4775 πτωχεία, *ptōcheia* [3] [√ 4777]

poverty [3]

2Co 8: 2 and their extreme **poverty** welled up in rich generosity.
8: 9 became poor, so that you *through* his **poverty** might become rich.
Rev 2: 9 I know your afflictions and your **poverty**—yet you are rich!

4776 πτωχεύω, *ptōcheuō* [1] [√ 4777]

poor [1]

2Co 8: 9 that though he was rich, yet for your sakes *he became* **poor**,

4777 πτωχός, *ptōchos* [34] [→ 4775, 4776]

poor [31], beggar [2], miserable [1]

Mt 5: 3 "Blessed are the **poor** in spirit, for theirs is the kingdom of heaven.
11: 5 the dead are raised, and the good news is preached to the **poor**.
19:21 want to be perfect, go, sell your possessions and give *to* the **poor**,
26: 9 have been sold at a high price and the money given *to* the **poor**."
26:11 The **poor** you will always have with you, but you will not always
Mk 10:21 "Go, sell everything you have and give *to* the **poor**, and you will
12:42 But a **poor** widow came and put in two very small copper coins,
12:43 this **poor** widow has put more into the treasury than all the others.
14: 5 for more than a year's wages and the money given *to* the **poor**."
14: 7 The **poor** you will always have with you, and you can help them
Lk 4:18 because he has anointed me to preach good news *to* the **poor**.
6:20 "Blessed are you who are **poor**, for yours is the kingdom of God.
7:22 the dead are raised, and the good news is preached to the **poor**.
14:13 give a banquet, invite the **poor**, the crippled, the lame, the blind,
14:21 into the streets and alleys of the town and bring in the **poor**,
16:20 At his gate was laid a **beggar** named Lazarus, covered with sores
16:22 "The time came when the **beggar** died and the angels carried him to
18:22 Sell everything you have and give *to* the **poor**, and you will have
19: 8 he said, "this **poor** widow has put in more than all the others.
21: 3 he said, "this **poor** widow has put in more than all the others.
Jn 12: 5 "Why wasn't this perfume sold and the money given *to* the **poor**?
12: 6 He did not say this because he cared about the **poor** but because he
12: 8 You will always have the **poor** among you, but you will not always
13:29 what was needed for the Feast, or to give something *to* the **poor**.
Ro 15:26 and Achaia were pleased to make a contribution for the **poor**
2Co 6:10 **poor**, yet making many rich; having nothing, and yet possessing
Gal 2:10 All they asked was that we should continue to remember the **poor**,
4: 9 that you are turning back to those weak and **miserable** principles?
Jas 2: 2 and fine clothes, and a **poor** *man* in shabby clothes also comes in.
2: 3 but say *to* the **poor** *man*, "You stand there" or "Sit on the floor by
2: 5 Has not God chosen those who are **poor** in the eyes of the world to
2: 6 But you have insulted the **poor**. Is it not the rich who are
Rev 3:17 do not realize that you are wretched, pitiful, **poor**, blind and naked.
13:16 forced everyone, small and great, rich and **poor**, free and slave,

4778 πυγμή, *pygmē* [1] [→ 4781, 4782]

ceremonial [1]

Mk 7: 3 Jews do not eat unless they give their hands a **ceremonial** washing,

4779 Πύθιος, *Pythios*   Not used in UBS/NIV

4780 πύθων, *python* [1]

spirit which predicted the future [*+4460*] [1]

Ac   16:16   girl who had a **spirit** by **which** she **predicted the future** [*+4460*].

4781 πυκνός, *pyknos* [3] [√ *4778*]

frequent [1], frequently [1], often [1]

Lk   5:33   "John's disciples **often** fast and pray, and so do the disciples of the
Ac   24:26   him a bribe, so he sent for him **frequently** and talked with him.
1Ti   5:23   a little wine because of your stomach and your **frequent** illnesses.

4782 πυκτεύω, *pykteuo* [1] [√ *4778*]

fight [1]

1Co   9:26   a man running aimlessly; *I do* not **fight** like a man beating the air.

4783 πύλη, *pyle* [10] [→ *4784*]

gate [6], city gate [2], city gates [1], gates [1]

Mt   7:13   "Enter through the narrow **gate**. For wide is the gate and broad is
     7:13   For wide is the **gate** and broad is the road that leads to destruction,
     7:14   But small is the **gate** and narrow the road that leads to life,
     16:18   will build my church, and the **gates** of Hades will not overcome it.
Lk   7:12   As he approached the town **gate**, a dead person was being carried
Ac   3:10   man who used to sit begging at the temple **gate** called Beautiful,
     9:24   and night they kept close watch on the **city gates** in order to kill
     12:10   and second guards and came to the iron **gate** leading to the city.
     16:13   On the Sabbath we went outside the **city gate** to the river,
Heb   13:12   so Jesus also suffered outside the **city gate** to make the people holy

4784 πυλών, *pylon* [18] [√ *4783*]

gates [7], *untranslated* [3], gate [3], city gates [1], door [1],
gateway [1], it's [*+3836*] [1], outer entrance [*+2598*] [1]

Mt   26:71   Then he went out to the **gateway**, where another girl saw him
Lk   16:20   At his **gate** was laid a beggar named Lazarus, covered with sores
Ac   10:17   found out where Simon's house was and stopped at the **gate**.
     12:13   Peter knocked at the **outer entrance** [*+2598*], and a servant girl
     12:14   she was so overjoyed she ran back without opening **it**'s [*+3836*]
     12:14   ran back without opening it and exclaimed, "Peter is at the **door**!"
     14:13   brought bulls and wreaths to the **city gates** because he
Rev   21:12   It had a great, high wall with twelve **gates**, and with twelve angels
     21:12   high wall with twelve gates, and with twelve angels at the **gates**.
     21:13   There were three **gates** on the east, three on the north, three on the
     21:13   three **[RPG]** on the north, three on the south and three on the
     21:13   on the north, three **[RPG]** on the south and three on the west.
     21:13   on the north, three on the south and three **[RPG]** on the west.
     21:15   a measuring rod of gold to measure the city, its **gates** and its walls.
     21:21   The twelve **gates** were twelve pearls, each gate made of a single
     21:21   twelve gates were twelve pearls, each **gate** made of a single pearl.
     21:25   On no day will its **gates** ever be shut, for there will be no night
     22:14   right to the tree of life and may go through the **gates** into the city.

4785 πυνθάνομαι, *pynthanomai* [12]

asked [5], ask [2], asking [1], information [1], inquired [1],
learning [1], question [1]

Mt   2:4   of the law, *he* **asked** them where the Christ was to be born.
Lk   15:26   So *he* called one of the servants and **asked** him what was going on.
     18:36   When he heard the crowd going by, *he* **asked** what was happening.
Jn   4:52   *When he* **inquired** as to the time when his son got better,
     13:24   motioned to this disciple and said, "**Ask** him which one he means."
Ac   4:7   and John brought before them and *began to* **question** them:
     10:18   **asking** if Simon who was known as Peter was staying there.
     10:29   without raising any objection. *May I* **ask** why you sent for me?"
     21:33   with two chains. Then *he* **asked** who he was and what he had done.
     23:19   drew him aside and **asked**, "What is it you want to tell me?"
     23:20   on the pretext of wanting more accurate **information** about him.
     23:34   what province he was from. **Learning** that he was from Cilicia,

4786 πῦρ, *pyr* [71] [→ *351, 1747, 4787, 4789, 4790, 4791, 4792, 4793, 4794, 4795, 4796*]

αἰώνιος πῦρ (eternal fire) [3]   Mt 18:8; 25:41; Jude 1:7
ἄσβεστος πῦρ (unquenchable fire)   [3]   Mt 3:12; Mk 9:43; Lk 3:17
γέεννα τοῦ πυρός (Gehenna of fire) [2]   Mt 5:22; 18:9
λίμνη πυρός (lake of fire) [6]   Rev 19:20; 20:10,14,14,15; 21:8
φλόξ πυρός (flame of fire) [6]   Ac 7:30; 2Th 1:8; Heb 1:7; Rev 1:14; 2:18; 19:12

fire [57], fiery [5], burning [4], flames [2], all ablaze [*+2794*] [1], blazing [*+2794*] [1], spark [1]

Mt   3:10   not produce good fruit will be cut down and thrown into the **fire**.
     3:11   fit to carry. He will baptize you with the Holy Spirit and with **fire**.
     3:12   into the barn and burning up the chaff *with* unquenchable **fire**."
     5:22   anyone who says, 'You fool!' will be in danger of the **fire** of hell.
     7:19   that does not bear good fruit is cut down and thrown into the **fire**.
     13:40   "As the weeds are pulled up and burned *in* the **fire**, so it will be at
     13:42   They will throw them into the **fiery** furnace, where there will be
     13:50   and throw them into the **fiery** furnace, where there will be weeping
     17:15   is suffering greatly. He often falls into the **fire** or into the water.
     18:8   than to have two hands or two feet and be thrown into eternal **fire**.
     18:9   one eye than to have two eyes and be thrown into the **fire** of hell.
     25:41   into the eternal **fire** prepared for the devil and his angels.
Mk   9:22   "It has often thrown him into **fire** or water to kill him. But if you
     9:43   than with two hands to go into hell, where the **fire** never goes out.
     9:48   where " 'their worm does not die, and the **fire** is not quenched.'
     9:49   Everyone will be salted with **fire**.
Lk   3:9   not produce good fruit will be cut down and thrown into the **fire**."
     3:16   to untie. He will baptize you with the Holy Spirit and with **fire**.
     3:17   into his barn, but he will burn up the chaff *with* unquenchable **fire**."
     9:54   do you want us to call **fire** down from heaven to destroy them?"
     12:49   "I have come to bring **fire** on the earth, and how I wish it were
     17:29   **fire** and sulfur rained down from heaven and destroyed them all.
     22:55   But when they had kindled a **fire** in the middle of the courtyard
Jn   15:6   such branches are picked up, thrown into the **fire** and burned.
Ac   2:3   They saw what seemed to be tongues *of* **fire** that separated
     2:19   and signs on the earth below, blood and **fire** and billows of smoke.
     7:30   an angel appeared to Moses in the flames *of* a **burning** bush in the
     28:5   But Paul shook the snake off into the **fire** and suffered no ill
Ro   12:20   to drink. In doing this, you will heap **burning** coals on his head."
1Co   3:13   It will be revealed with **fire**, and the fire will test the quality of
     3:13   with fire, and the **fire** will test the quality of each man's work.
     3:15   himself will be saved, but only as one escaping through the **flames**.
2Th   1:7   is revealed from heaven in blazing **fire** with his powerful angels.
Heb   1:7   he says, "He makes his angels winds, his servants flames *of* **fire**."
     10:27   and *of* raging **fire** that will consume the enemies of God.
     11:34   quenched the fury *of* the **flames**, and escaped the edge of the
     12:18   to a mountain that can be touched and that is burning *with* **fire**;
     12:29   for our "God is a consuming **fire**."
Jas   3:5   Consider what a great forest is set on fire by a small **spark**.
     3:6   The tongue also is a **fire**, a world of evil among the parts of the
     5:3   Their corrosion will testify against you and eat your flesh like **fire**.
1Pe   1:7   worth than gold, which perishes even though refined by **fire**—
2Pe   3:7   the same word the present heavens and earth are reserved *for* **fire**,
Jude   1:7   as an example of those who suffer the punishment *of* eternal **fire**.
     1:23   snatch others from the **fire** and save them; to others show mercy,
Rev   1:14   like wool, as white as snow, and his eyes were like blazing **fire**.
     2:18   whose eyes are like blazing **fire** and whose feet are like burnished
     3:18   I counsel you to buy from me gold refined in the **fire**, so you can
     4:5   of thunder. Before the throne, seven lamps *were* **blazing** [*+2794*].
     8:5   filled it with **fire** from the altar, and hurled it on the earth;
     8:7   his trumpet, and there came hail and **fire** mixed with blood,
     8:8   and something like a huge mountain, all ablaze [*+2794*],
     9:17   of lions, and out of their mouths came **fire**, smoke and sulfur.
     9:18   A third of mankind was killed by the three plagues of **fire**,
     10:1   his face was like the sun, and his legs were like **fiery** pillars.
     11:5   **fire** comes from their mouths and devours their enemies.
     13:13   even causing **fire** to come down from heaven to earth in full view
     14:10   He will be tormented with **burning** sulfur in the presence of the
     14:18   Still another angel, who had charge of the **fire**, came from the altar
     15:2   And I saw what looked like a sea of glass mixed *with* **fire** and,
     16:8   on the sun, and the sun was given power to scorch people with **fire**.
     17:16   and leave her naked; they will eat her flesh and burn her with **fire**.

18: 8 She will be consumed by **fire**, for mighty is the Lord God who
19: 12 His eyes are like blazing **fire**, and on his head are many crowns.
19: 20 The two of them were thrown alive into the **fiery** lake of burning
20: 9 city he loves. But **fire** came down from heaven and devoured them.
20: 10 was thrown into the lake *of* **burning** sulfur, where the beast
20: 14 Then death and Hades were thrown into the lake *of* **fire**. The lake
20: 14 thrown into the lake of fire. The lake *of* **fire** is the second death.
20: 15 written in the book of life, he was thrown into the lake *of* **fire**.
21: 8 and all liars—their place will be in the **fiery** lake of burning sulfur.

4787 πυρά, *pyra* [2] [√ *4786*]

fire [2]

Ac 28: 2 They built a **fire** and welcomed us all because it was raining
28: 3 as he put it on the **fire**, a viper, driven out by the heat,

4788 πύργος, *pyrgos* [4]

tower [2], watchtower [2]

Mt 21: 33 put a wall around it, dug a winepress in it and built a **watchtower**
Mk 12: 1 wall around it, dug a pit for the winepress and built a **watchtower**
Lk 13: 4 Or those eighteen who died when the **tower** in Siloam fell on
14: 28 "Suppose one of you wants to build a **tower**. Will he not first sit

4789 πυρέσσω, *pyressō* [2] [√ *4786*]

with a fever [2]

Mt 8: 14 he saw Peter's mother-in-law lying in bed **with a fever**.
Mk 1: 30 Simon's mother-in-law was in bed **with a fever**, and they told

4790 πυρετός, *pyretos* [6] [√ *4786*]

fever [6]

Mt 8: 15 He touched her hand and the **fever** left her, and she got up
Mk 1: 31 helped her up. The **fever** left her and she began to wait on them.
Lk 4: 38 Now Simon's mother-in-law was suffering *from* a high **fever**,
4: 39 So he bent over her and rebuked the **fever**, and it left her. She got
Jn 4: 52 they said to him, "The **fever** left him yesterday at the seventh hour."
Ac 28: 8 His father was sick in bed, suffering from **fever** and dysentery.

4791 πύρινος, *pyrinos* [1] [√ *4786*]

fiery red [1]

Rev 9: 17 Their breastplates were **fiery red**, dark blue, and yellow as sulfur.

4792 πυρόω, *pyroō* [6] [√ *4786*]

burn with passion [1], fire [1], flaming [1], glowing [1], inwardly
burn [1], refined [1]

1Co 7: 9 should marry, for it is better to marry than *to* **burn with passion**.
2Co 11: 29 not feel weak? Who is led into sin, and I *do* not **inwardly burn**?
Eph 6: 16 with which you can extinguish all the **flaming** arrows of the evil
2Pe 3: 12 That day will bring about the destruction of the heavens by **fire**,
Rev 1: 15 His feet were like bronze **glowing** in a furnace, and his voice was
3: 18 I counsel you to buy from me gold **refined** in the fire, so you can

4793 πυρράζω, *pyrrazō* [2] [√ *4786*]

red [2]

Mt 16: 2 evening comes, you say, 'It will be fair weather, for the sky *is* **red**,'
16: 3 'Today it will be stormy, for the sky *is* **red** and overcast.'

4794 πυρρός, *pyrros* [2] [√ *4786*]

fiery red [1], red [1]

Rev 6: 4 Then another horse came out, a **fiery red** *one*. Its rider was given
12: 3 an enormous **red** dragon with seven heads and ten horns and seven

4795 Πύρρος, *Pyrros* [1] [√ *4786*]

Pyrrhus [1]

Ac 20: 4 He was accompanied by Sopater *son of* **Pyrrhus** from Berea,

4796 πύρωσις, *pyrōsis* [3] [√ *4786*]

burning [2], painful [1]

1Pe 4: 12 do not be surprised *at* the **painful** trial you are suffering,
Rev 18: 9 with her and shared her luxury see the smoke *of* her **burning**,
18: 18 When they see the smoke *of* her **burning**, they will exclaim,

4797 πωλέω, *pōleō* [22] [→ *4527*]

sold [8], sell [7], selling [7]

Mt 10: 29 *Are* not two sparrows **sold** for a penny? Yet not one of them will
13: 44 and then in his joy went and **sold** all he had and bought that field.
19: 21 want to be perfect, go, **sell** your possessions and give to the poor,
21: 12 temple area and drove out all who *were* buying and **selling** there.
21: 12 of the money changers and the benches *of* those **selling** doves.
25: 9 Instead, go to those *who* **sell** oil and buy some for yourselves.'
Mk 10: 21 "Go, **sell** everything you have and give to the poor, and you will
11: 15 and began driving out those who were buying and **selling** there.
11: 15 of the money changers and the benches *of* those **selling** doves,
Lk 12: 6 *Are* not five sparrows **sold** for two pennies? Yet not one of them is
12: 33 **Sell** your possessions and give to the poor. Provide purses for
17: 28 and drinking, buying and **selling**, planting and building.
18: 22 **Sell** everything you have and give to the poor, and you will have
19: 45 the temple area and began driving out those *who were* **selling**.
22: 36 and if you don't have a sword, **sell** your cloak and buy one.
Jn 2: 14 In the temple courts he found men **selling** cattle, sheep and doves,
2: 16 *To* those *who* **sold** doves he said, "Get these out of here! How dare
Ac 4: 34 For *from time to time* those who owned lands or houses **sold**
4: 37 **sold** a field he owned and brought the money and put it at the
5: 1 together with his wife Sapphira, also **sold** a piece of property.
1Co 10: 25 Eat anything **sold** in the meat market without raising questions of
Rev 13: 17 so that no one could buy or **sell** unless he had the mark, which is

4798 πῶλος, *pōlos* [12]

colt [12]

Mt 21: 2 and at once you will find a donkey tied there, with her **colt** by her.
21: 5 gentle and riding on a donkey, on a **colt**, the foal of a donkey.' "
21: 7 They brought the donkey and the **colt**, placed their cloaks on them,
Mk 11: 2 and just as you enter it, you will find a **colt** tied there, which no
11: 4 They went and found a **colt** outside in the street, tied at a doorway.
11: 5 standing there asked, "What are you doing, untying that **colt**?"
11: 7 When they brought the **colt** to Jesus and threw their cloaks on it,
Lk 19: 30 and as you enter it, you will find a **colt** tied there, which no one has
19: 33 As they were untying the **colt**, its owners asked them, "Why are you
19: 33 the colt, its owners asked them, "Why are you untying the **colt**?"
19: 35 it to Jesus, threw their cloaks on the **colt** and put Jesus on it.
Jn 12: 15 of Zion; see, your king is coming, seated on a donkey's **colt**."

4799 πώποτε, *pōpote* [6]

ever [3], never [+3590+4024] [1], never [+4046] [1], never [1]

Lk 19: 30 you will find a colt tied there, which no one has **ever** ridden.
Jn 1: 18 No one has **ever** seen God, but God the One and Only, who is at
5: 37 You have **never** [+4046] heard his voice nor seen his form,
6: 35 and he who believes in me will **never** [+3590+4024] be thirsty.
8: 33 are Abraham's descendants and have **never** been slaves of anyone.
1Jn 4: 12 No one has **ever** seen God; but if we love one another, God lives in

4800 πωρόω, *pōroō* [5] [→ *4801*]

hardened [2], deadened [1], hardened [+2400] [1], made dull [1]

Mk 6: 52 had not understood about the loaves; their hearts were **hardened**.
8: 17 still not see or understand? *Are* your hearts **hardened** [+2400]?
Jn 12: 40 "He has blinded their eyes and **deadened** their hearts, so they can
Ro 11: 7 it did not obtain, but the elect did. The others were **hardened**,
2Co 3: 14 But their minds were **made dull**, for to this day the same veil

4801 πώρωσις, *pōrōsis* [3] [√ *4800*]

hardening [2], stubborn [1]

Mk   3: 5 deeply distressed at their **stubborn** hearts, said to the man,
Ro 11:25 Israel has experienced a **hardening** in part until the full number of
Eph   4:18 because of the ignorance that is in them due to the **hardening** of

4802 πῶς, *pōs* [103 / 102]

how [82], how is it [8], *untranslated* [3], what [3], some way [2],
even [1], under what circumstances [1], way [1], why [1]

Mt   6:28 See **how** the lilies of the field grow. They do not labor or spin.
    7: 4 **How** can you say to your brother, 'Let me take the speck out of
  10:19 they arrest you, do not worry about what to say or **how** to say it.
  12: 4 [NIE] He entered the house of God, and he and his companions
  12:26 he is divided against himself. **How** then can his kingdom stand?
  12:29 **how** can anyone enter a strong man's house and carry off his
  12:34 You brood of vipers, **how** can you who are evil say anything good?
  16:11 **How** is it you don't understand that I was not talking to you about
  21:20 were amazed. "**How** did the fig tree wither so quickly?" they asked.
  22:12 he asked, '**how** did you get in here without wedding clothes?'
  22:43 He said to them, "**How** is it then that David, speaking by the
  22:45 If then David calls him 'Lord,' **how** can he be his son?"
  23:33 brood of vipers! **How** will you escape being condemned to hell?
  26:54 But **how** then would the Scriptures be fulfilled that say it must
Mk   2:26 [UBS+ *How*] In the days of Abiathar the high priest, he entered
  3:23 and spoke to them in parables: "**How** can Satan drive out Satan?
  4:13 this parable? **How** then will you understand any parable?
  4:30 Again he said, "**What** shall we say the kingdom of God is like,
  5:16 Those who had seen it told the people **what** had happened to the
  9:12 **Why** then is it written that the Son of Man must suffer much
  10:23 "**How** hard it is for the rich to enter the kingdom of God!"
  10:24 said again, "Children, **how** hard it is to enter the kingdom of God!
  11:18 of the law heard this and began looking for a **way** to kill him,
  12:26 in the account of the bush, **how** God said to him, 'I am the God of
  12:35 "**How is it** that the teachers of the law say that the Christ is the son
  12:41 and watched [NIE] the crowd putting their money into the temple
  14: 1 and the teachers of the law were looking for **some** sly **way** to arrest
  14:11 So he watched for an opportunity [NIE] to hand him over.
Lk   1:34 "**How** will this be," Mary asked the angel, "since I am a virgin?"
  6:42 **How** can you say to your brother, 'Brother, let me take the speck
  8:18 Therefore consider carefully **how** you listen. Whoever has will be
  8:36 Those who had seen it told the people **how** the demon-possessed
  10:26 "What is written in the Law?" he replied. "**How** do you read it?"
  11:18 If Satan is divided against himself, **how** can his kingdom stand?
  12:11 do not worry about **how** you will defend yourselves or what you
  12:27 "Consider **how** the lilies grow. They do not labor or spin. Yet I tell
  12:50 baptism to undergo, and **how** distressed I am until it is completed!
  12:56 **How is it** that you don't know how to interpret this present time?
  14: 7 When he noticed **how** the guests picked the places of honor at the
  18:24 and said, "**How** hard it is for the rich to enter the kingdom of God!
  20:41 to them, "**How is it** that they say the Christ is the Son of David?
  20:44 David calls him 'Lord.' **How** then can he be his son?"
  22: 2 and the teachers of the law were looking for **some way** to get rid of
  22: 4 temple guard and discussed with them **how** he might betray Jesus.
Jn   3: 4 "**How** can a man be born when he is old?" Nicodemus asked.
  3: 9 "**How** can this be?" Nicodemus asked.
  3:12 **how** then will you believe if I speak of heavenly things?
  4: 9 and I am a Samaritan woman. **How** can you ask me for a drink?"
  5:44 **How** can you believe if you accept praise from one another,
  5:47 believe what he wrote, **how** are you going to believe what I say?"
  6:42 we know? **How** can he now say, 'I came down from heaven'?"
  6:52 among themselves, "**How** can this man give us his flesh to eat?"
  7:15 "**How** did this man get such learning without having studied?"
  8:33 been slaves of anyone. **How** can you say that we shall be set free?"
  9:10 "**How** then were your eyes opened?" they demanded.
  9:15 Therefore the Pharisees also asked him **how** he had received his
  9:16 But others asked, "**How** can a sinner do such miraculous signs?"
  9:19 the one you say was born blind? **How is it** that now he can see?"
  9:21 But **how** he can see now, or who opened his eyes, we don't know.
  9:26 asked him, "What did he do to you? **How** did he open your eyes?"
  11:36 Then the Jews said, "See **how** he loved him!"
  12:34 so **how** can you say, 'The Son of Man must be lifted up'?
  14: 5 don't know where you are going, so **how** can we know the way?"
  14: 9 me has seen the Father. **How** can you say, 'Show us the Father'?

Ac   2: 8 Then **how is it** that each of us hears them in his own native
  4:21 They could not decide **how** to punish them, because all the people
  8:31 "**How can I**," he said, "unless someone explains it to me?" So he
  9:27 He told them **how** Saul on his journey had seen the Lord and that
  9:27 and **how** in Damascus he had preached fearlessly in the name of
  11:13 He told us **how** he had seen an angel appear in his house and say,
  12:17 and described **how** the Lord had brought him out of prison.
  15:36 we preached the word of the Lord and see **how** they are doing."
  20:18 "You know **how** I lived the whole time I was with you,   .
Ro   3: 6 Certainly not! If that were so, **how** could God judge the world?
  4:10 **Under what circumstances** was it credited? Was it after he was
  6: 2 By no means! We died to sin; **how** can we live in it any longer?
  8:32 **how** will he not also, along with him, graciously give us all things?
  10:14 **How**, then, can they call on the one they have not believed in?
  10:14 And **how** can they believe in the one of whom they have not
  10:14 And **how** can they hear without someone preaching to them?
  10:15 And **how** can they preach unless they are sent? As it is written,
1Co   3:10 is building on it. But each one should be careful **how** he builds.
  7:32 is concerned about the Lord's affairs—**how** he can please the Lord.
  7:33 about the affairs of this world—**how** he can please his wife—
  7:34 about the affairs of this world—**how** she can please her husband.
  14: 7 **how** will anyone know what tune is being played unless there is a
  14: 9 with your tongue, **how** will anyone know what you are saying?
  14:16 **how** can one who finds himself among those who do not
  15:12 **how** can some of you say that there is no resurrection of the dead?
  15:35 But someone may ask, "**How** are the dead raised? With what kind
2Co   3: 8 will not the ministry of the Spirit be **even** more glorious?
Gal   2:14 **How is it**, then, that you force Gentiles to follow Jewish customs?
  4: 9 **how is it** that you are turning back to those weak and miserable
Eph   5:15 Be very careful, then, **how** you live—not as unwise but as wise,
Col   4: 6 seasoned with salt, so that you may know **how** to answer everyone.
1Th   1: 9 They tell **how** you turned to God from idols to serve the living
  4: 1 brothers, we instructed you **how** to live in order to please God,
2Th   3: 7 For you yourselves know **how** you ought to follow our example.
1Ti   3: 5 to manage his own family, **how** can he take care of God's church?)
  3:15 you will know **how** people ought to conduct themselves in God's
Heb   2: 3 **how** shall we escape if we ignore such a great salvation?
1Jn   3:17 but has no pity on him, **how** can the love of God be in him?
Rev   3: 3 Remember, therefore, **what** you have received and heard,

4803 πώς, *pōs* [15 / 14]

that [+*3590*] [3], so that [2], somehow [2], for [+*3590*] [1], for fear
that [+*3590*] [1], hoping [+*1538+1623*] [1], in some way [1],
somehow [+*1623*] [1], that [+*1623*] [1], that [1]

Ac 27:12 sail on, **hoping** [+*1538+1623*] to reach Phoenix and winter there.
Ro   1:10 and I pray **that** [+*1623*] now at last by God's will the way may be
  11:14 in the hope that I may **somehow** arouse my own people to envy
  11:21 branches, [UBS+ *perhaps* (+*3590*)] he will not spare you either.
1Co   8: 9 **that** the exercise of your freedom does not become a stumbling
  9:27 and make it my slave **so that** after I have preached to others,
2Co   2: 7 **so that** he will not be overwhelmed by excessive sorrow.
  9: 4 **For** [+*3590*] if any Macedonians come with me and find you
  11: 3 But I am afraid **that** [+*3590*] just as Eve was deceived by the
  12:20 For I am afraid **that** [+*3590*] when I come I may not find you as I
  12:20 I fear **that** [+*3590*] there may be quarreling, jealousy, outbursts of
Gal   2: 2 privately to those who seemed to be leaders, **for fear that** [+*3590*]
  4:11 I fear for you, that **somehow** I have wasted my efforts on you.
Php   3:11 and so, **somehow** [+*1623*], to attain to the resurrection from the
1Th   3: 5 I was afraid that **in some way** the tempter might have tempted you

P, R

4804 ρ, *r* Not used in UBS/NIV

4805 Ῥαάβ, *Rhaab* [2]

Rahab [2]

Heb 11:31 By faith the prostitute **Rahab**, because she welcomed the spies,
Jas   2:25 was not even **Rahab** the prostitute considered righteous for what

4806 ῥαββί, rhabbi [15] [→ 4807, 4808, 4809]

Rabbi [15]

Mt 23: 7 be greeted in the marketplaces and to have men call them 'Rabbi.'
23: 8 "But you are not to be called 'Rabbi,' for you have only one Master
26:25 the one who would betray him, said, "Surely not I, Rabbi?"
26:49 Going at once to Jesus, Judas said, "Greetings, Rabbi!" and kissed
Mk 9: 5 Peter said to Jesus, "Rabbi, it is good for us to be here. Let us put
11:21 Peter remembered and said to Jesus, "Rabbi, look! The fig tree
14:45 Going at once to Jesus, Judas said, "Rabbi!" and kissed him.
Jn 1:38 said, "Rabbi" (which means Teacher), "where are you staying?"
1:49 Then Nathanael declared, "Rabbi, you are the Son of God;
3: 2 He came to Jesus at night and said, "Rabbi, we know you are a
3:26 They came to John and said to him, "Rabbi, that man who was
4:31 Meanwhile his disciples urged him, "Rabbi, eat something."
6:25 side of the lake, they asked him, "Rabbi, when did you get here?"
9: 2 "Rabbi, who sinned, this man or his parents, that he was born
11: 8 "But Rabbi," they said, "a short while ago the Jews tried to stone

4807 ῥαββονί, rhabboni Not used in UBS/NIV [√ 4806]

4808 ῥαββουνί, rhabbouni [2] [√ 4806]

Rabbi [1], Rabboni [1]

Mk 10:51 Jesus asked him. The blind man said, "Rabbi, I want to see."
Jn 20:16 She turned toward him and cried out in Aramaic, "Rabboni!"

4809 ῥαββωνί, rhabbōni Not used in UBS/NIV [√ 4806]

4810 ῥαβδίζω, rhabdizō [2] [√ 4811]

beaten with rods [1], beaten [1]

Ac 16:22 and the magistrates ordered them to be stripped and beaten.
2Co 11:25 Three times I was beaten with rods, once I was stoned,

4811 ῥάβδος, rhabdos [12] [→ 4810, 4812, 4824, 4825]

staff [5], scepter [4], untranslated [1], measuring rod [1], whip [1]

Mt 10:10 take no bag for the journey, or extra tunic, or sandals or a staff;
Mk 6: 8 "Take nothing for the journey except a staff—no bread, no bag,
Lk 9: 3 the journey—no staff, no bag, no bread, no money, no extra tunic.
1Co 4:21 Shall I come to you with a whip, or in love and with a gentle
Heb 1: 8 and ever, and righteousness will be the scepter of your kingdom.
1: 8 and righteousness will be the scepter of your kingdom. [RPG]
9: 4 Aaron's staff that had budded, and the stone tablets of the
11:21 Joseph's sons, and worshiped as he leaned on the top of his staff.
Rev 2:27 'He will rule them with an iron scepter; he will dash them to
11: 1 I was given a reed like a measuring rod and was told, "Go
12: 5 a male child, who will rule all the nations with an iron scepter.
19:15 "He will rule them with an iron scepter." He treads the winepress of

4812 ῥαβδοῦχος, rhabdouchos [2] [√ 4811 + 2400]

officers [2]

Ac 16:35 the magistrates sent their officers to the jailer with the order:
16:38 The officers reported this to the magistrates, and when they heard

4813 ῥαβιθά, rhabitha Not used in UBS/NIV [√ cf. 5420]

4814 'Ραγαύ, Rhagau [1]

Reu [1]

Lk 3:35 the son of Serug, the son of Reu, the son of Peleg, the son of Eber,

4815 ῥαδιούργημα, rhadiourgēma [1] [√ 4816]

crime [1]

Ac 18:14 making a complaint about some misdemeanor or serious crime,

4816 ῥαδιουργία, rhadiourgia [1] [→ 4815; cf. 2240]

trickery [1]

Ac 13:10 that is right! You are full of all kinds of deceit and trickery.

4817 ῥαίνω, rhainō Not used in UBS/NIV [→ 4349, 4350, 4822, 4823]

4818 'Ραιφάν, Rhaiphan [1] [→ 4833, 4834, 4854]

Rephan [1]

Ac 7:43 lifted up the shrine of Molech and the star of your god Rephan,

4819 ῥακά, rhaka [1] [→ 4828]

Raca [1]

Mt 5:22 who says to his brother, 'Raca,' is answerable to the Sanhedrin.

4820 ῥάκος, rhakos [2]

cloth [2]

Mt 9:16 "No one sews a patch of unshrunk cloth on an old garment,
Mk 2:21 "No one sews a patch of unshrunk cloth on an old garment,

4821 'Ραμά, Rhama [1]

Ramah [1]

Mt 2:18 "A voice is heard in Ramah, weeping and great mourning,

4822 ῥαντίζω, rhantizō [4] [√ 4817]

sprinkled [2], sprinkled on [1], sprinkled to cleanse [1]

Heb 9:13 and the ashes of a heifer sprinkled on those who are ceremonially
9:19 branches of hyssop, and sprinkled the scroll and all the people.
9:21 he sprinkled with the blood both the tabernacle and everything
10:22 having our hearts sprinkled to cleanse us from a guilty

4823 ῥαντισμός, rhantismos [2] [√ 4817]

sprinkled [1], sprinkling [1]

Heb 12:24 and to the sprinkled blood that speaks a better word than the blood
1Pe 1: 2 for obedience to Jesus Christ and sprinkling by his blood:

4824 ῥαπίζω, rhapizō [2] [√ 4811]

slapped [1], strikes [1]

Mt 5:39 If someone strikes you on the right cheek, turn to him the other
26:67 spit in his face and struck him with their fists. Others slapped him

4825 ῥάπισμα, rhapisma [3] [√ 4811]

struck in the face [+1443] [2], beat [1]

Mk 14:65 and said, "Prophesy!" And the guards took him and beat him.
Jn 18:22 one of the officials nearby struck [+1443] him in the face.
19: 3 king of the Jews!" And they struck [+1443] him in the face.

4826 ῥάσσω, rhassō Not used in UBS/NIV [√ 4838]

4827 ῥαφίς, rhaphis [2] [→ 731, 2165]

needle [2]

Mt 19:24 it is easier for a camel to go through the eye of a needle than for a
Mk 10:25 It is easier for a camel to go through the eye of a needle than for a

4828 ῥαχά, rhacha Not used in UBS/NIV [√ 4819]

4829 Ῥαχάβ, *Rhachab* [1]

Rahab [1]

Mt   1: 5   whose mother was **Rahab**, Boaz the father of Obed, whose mother

4830 Ῥαχήλ, *Rhachēl* [1]

Rachel [1]

Mt   2:18   **Rachel** weeping for her children and refusing to be comforted,

4831 Ῥεβέκκα, *Rhebekka* [1]

Rebekah's [1]

Ro   9:10   Not only that, but **Rebekah's** children had one and the same father,

4832 ῥέδη, *rhedē* [1]

carriages [1]

Rev 18:13   cattle and sheep; horses and **carriages**; and bodies and souls of

4833 Ῥεμφάν, *Rhemphan* Not used in UBS/NIV
[√ *4818*]

4834 Ῥεφάν, *Rhephan* Not used in UBS/NIV [√ *4818*]

4835 ῥέω, *rheō* [1] [→ *137, 4184, 4868, 5929*]

flow [1]

Jn   7:38   has said, streams of living water *will* **flow** from within him."

4836 Ῥήγιον, *Rhēgion* [1]

Rhegium [1]

Ac   28:13   From there we set sail and arrived at **Rhegium**. The next day the

4837 ῥῆγμα, *rhēgma* [1] [√ *4838*]

destruction [1]

Lk   6:49   struck that house, it collapsed and its **destruction** was complete."

4838 ῥήγνυμι, *rhēgnymi* [7] [→ *1392, 1393, 1396, 4351, 4703, 4704, 4826, 4837, 4841, 5357*]

burst [3], break forth [1], tear to pieces [1], threw to the ground [1], throws to the ground [1]

Mt   7: 6   trample them under their feet, and then turn and **tear** you **to pieces**.
     9:17   If they do, the skins *will* **burst**, the wine will run out
Mk   2:22   If he does, the wine *will* **burst** the skins, and both the wine
     9:18   Whenever it seizes him, *it* **throws** him **to the ground**. He foams at
Lk   5:37   If he does, the new wine *will* **burst** the skins, the wine will run out
     9:42   was coming, the demon **threw** him **to the ground** in a convulsion.
Gal   4:27   **break forth** and cry aloud, you who have no labor pains;

4839 ῥῆμα, *rhēma* [68] [→ *394, 395, 777, 4244, 4245, 4842, 4843*]

ῥῆμα θεοῦ (word of God) [6] Lk 3:2; Jn 3:34; 8:47; Eph 6:17; Heb 6:5; 11:3

ῥῆμα κυρίου (word of the Lord) [3] Lk 22:61; Ac 11:16; 1Pe 1:25

word [16], words [16], things [6], say [4], what[s] [+*3836*] [4], *untranslated* [2], matter [2], meant [2], bring a message [+*3281*] [1], charge [1], command [1], final statement [+*1651*] [1], it[s] [+*3836+4047*] [1], meaning [1], message [1], nothing [+*4024+4246*] [1], promised [1], said [1], saying [1], sayings [1], says [1], thing [1], this[s] [+*3836+4047*] [1], what said [1]

Mt   4: 4   but on every **word** that comes from the mouth of God.' "
    12:36   on the day of judgment for every careless **word** they have spoken.
    18:16   so that 'every **matter** may be established by the testimony of two

    26:75   Then Peter remembered the **word** Jesus had spoken: "Before the
    27:14   But Jesus made no reply, not even to a single **charge**—to the great
Mk   9:32   But they did not understand what he **meant** and were afraid to ask
    14:72   Then Peter remembered the **word** Jesus had spoken to him:
Lk   1:37   For **nothing** [+*4024+4246*] is impossible with God."
    1:38   servant," Mary answered. "May it be to me as you have **said**.
    1:65   the hill country of Judea people were talking about all these **things**.
    2:15   "Let's go to Bethlehem and see this **thing** that has happened,
    2:17   they spread the **word** concerning what had been told them about
    2:19   But Mary treasured up all these **things** and pondered them in her
    2:29   "Sovereign Lord, as you have **promised**, you now dismiss your
    2:50   But they did not understand what[s] [+*3836*] he was saying to them.
    2:51   to them. But his mother treasured all these **things** in her heart.
    3: 2   the **word** of God came to John son of Zechariah in the desert.
    5: 5   caught anything. But because you **say** so, I will let down the nets."
    7: 1   When Jesus had finished **saying** all this in the hearing of the
    9:45   But they did not understand what this **meant**. It was hidden from
    9:45   grasp it, and they were afraid to ask him about it[s] [+*3836+4047*].
    18:34   Its **meaning** was hidden from them, and they did not know what he
    20:26   They were unable to trap him in **what** he had **said** there in public.
    22:61   Then Peter remembered the **word** the Lord had spoken to him:
    24: 8   Then they remembered his **words**.
    24:11   the women, because their **words** seemed to them like nonsense.
Jn   3:34   For the one whom God has sent speaks the **words** of God,
    5:47   believe what he wrote, how are you going to believe what I **say**?"
    6:63   The **words** I have spoken to you are spirit and they are life.
    6:68   to whom shall we go? You have the **words** of eternal life.
    8:20   He spoke these **words** while teaching in the temple area near the
    8:47   He who belongs to God hears what God **says**. The reason you do
    10:21   "These are not the **sayings** of a man possessed by a demon.
    12:47   "As for the person who hears my **words** but does not keep them,
    12:48   a judge for the one who rejects me and does not accept my **words**;
    14:10   The **words** I say to you are not just my own. Rather, it is the
    15: 7   If you remain in me and my **words** remain in you, ask whatever
    17: 8   For I gave them the **words** you gave me and they accepted them.
Ac   2:14   let me explain this to you; listen carefully to what I **say**.
    5:20   he said, "and tell the people the full **message** of this new life."
    5:32   We are witnesses *of* these **things**, and so is the Holy Spirit,
    6:11   "We have heard Stephen speak **words** of blasphemy against Moses
    6:13   "This fellow never stops speaking [RPG] against this holy place
    10:22   you come to his house so that he could hear what you have to **say**."
    10:37   You know what[s] [+*3836*] has happened throughout Judea,
    10:44   While Peter was still speaking these **words**, the Holy Spirit came
    11:14   He *will* **bring** you a **message** [+*3281*] through which you
    11:16   Then I remembered what[s] [+*3836*] the Lord had said: 'John
    13:42   the people invited them to speak further about these **things** on the
    16:38   The officers reported this[s] [+*3836+4047*] to the magistrates,
    26:25   Paul replied. "What I am saying is true and reasonable. [RPG]
    28:25   began to leave *after* Paul had made this **final statement** [+*1651*]:
Ro   10: 8   "The **word** is near you; it is in your mouth and in your heart,"
    10: 8   and in your heart," that is, the **word** of faith we are proclaiming:
    10:17   the message, and the message is heard through the **word** of Christ.
    10:18   gone out into all the earth, their **words** to the ends of the world."
2Co 12: 4   heard inexpressible things, **things** that man is not permitted to tell.
    13: 1   "Every **matter** must be established by the testimony of two
Eph   5:26   cleansing her by the washing with water through the **word**,
    6:17   of salvation and the sword of the Spirit, which is the **word** of God.
Heb   1: 3   of his being, sustaining all things *by* his powerful **word**.
    6: 5   who have tasted the goodness of the **word** of God and the powers
    11: 3   we understand that the universe was formed *at* God's **command**,
    12:19   or to such a voice *speaking* **words** that those who heard it begged
1Pe   1:25   but the **word** of the Lord stands forever." And this is the word that
    1:25   stands forever." And this is the **word** that was preached to you.
2Pe   3: 2   I want you to recall the **words** spoken in the past by the holy
Jude   1:17   remember what[s] [+*3836*] the apostles of our Lord Jesus Christ

4840 Ῥησά, *Rhēsa* [1]

Rhesa [1]

Lk   3:27   the son of Joanan, the son *of* **Rhesa**, the son of Zerubbabel,

4841 ῥήσσω, *rhēssō* Not used in UBS/NIV [√ *4838*]

4842 ῥήτωρ, rhētōr [1] [√ 4839]

lawyer [1]

Ac 24: 1 to Caesarea with some of the elders and a **lawyer** named Tertullus,

4843 ῥητῶς, rhētōs [1] [√ 4839]

clearly [1]

1Ti 4: 1 The Spirit **clearly** says that in later times some will abandon the

4844 ῥίζα, rhiza [17] [→ 1748, 4845]

root [16], roots [1]

Mt 3: 10 The ax is already at the **root** of the trees, and every tree that does
   13: 6 plants were scorched, and they withered because they had no **root**.
   13: 21 But since he has no **root**, he lasts only a short time. When trouble
Mk 4: 6 plants were scorched, and they withered because they had no **root**.
   4: 17 But since they have no **root**, they last only a short time.
   11: 20 as they went along, they saw the fig tree withered from the **roots**.
Lk 3: 9 The ax is already at the **root** of the trees, and every tree that does
   8: 13 receive the word with joy when they hear it, but they have no **root**.
Ro 11: 16 the whole batch is holy; if the **root** is holy, so are the branches.
   11: 17 the others and now share in the nourishing sap *from* the olive **root**,
   11: 18 You do not support the **root**, but the root supports you.
   11: 18 You do not support the **root**, but the **root** supports you.
   15: 12 And again, Isaiah says, "The **Root** of Jesse will spring up, one who
1Ti 6: 10 For the love of money is a **root** of all kinds of evil. Some people,
Heb 12: 15 and that no bitter **root** grows up to cause trouble and defile many.
Rev 5: 5 the Lion of the tribe of Judah, the **Root** of David, has triumphed.
   22: 16 I am the **Root** and the Offspring of David, and the bright Morning

4845 ῥιζόω, rhizoō [2] [√ 4844]

rooted [2]

Eph 3: 17 And I pray that you, *being* **rooted** and established in love,
Col 2: 7 **rooted** and built up in him, strengthened in the faith as you were

4846 ῥιπή, rhipē [1] [√ 4849]

twinkling [1]

1Co 15: 52 in a flash, in the **twinkling** of an eye, at the last trumpet.

4847 ῥιπίζω, rhipizō [1] [√ 4849]

tossed [1]

Jas 1: 6 doubts is like a wave of the sea, blown and **tossed** by the wind.

4848 ῥιπτέω, rhipteō [1] [√ 4849]

throwing off [1]

Ac 22: 23 *As* they *were* shouting and **throwing off** their cloaks and flinging

4849 ῥίπτω, rhiptō [7] [→ 681, 2166, 4846, 4847, 4848]

dropped [1], helpless [1], laid [1], threw down [1], threw
overboard [1], threw [1], thrown [1]

Mt 9: 36 had compassion on them, because they were harassed and **helpless**,
   15: 30 the crippled, the mute and many others, and **laid** them at his feet;
   27: 5 So Judas **threw** the money into the temple and left. Then he went
Lk 4: 35 Then the demon **threw** the man **down** before them all and came
   17: 2 It would be better for him *to be* **thrown** into the sea with a
Ac 27: 19 *they* **threw** the ship's tackle **overboard** with their own hands.
   27: 29 they **dropped** four anchors from the stern and prayed for daylight.

4850 Ῥοβοάμ, Rhoboam [2]

Rehoboam [2]

Mt 1: 7 Solomon the father of **Rehoboam**, Rehoboam the father of Abijah,
   1: 7 **Rehoboam** the father of Abijah, Abijah the father of Asa,

4851 Ῥόδη, Rhodē [1]

Rhoda [1]

Ac 12: 13 and a servant girl named **Rhoda** came to answer the door.

4852 Ῥόδος, Rhodos [1]

Rhodes [1]

Ac 21: 1 The next day we went to **Rhodes** and from there to Patara.

4853 ῥοιζηδόν, rhoizēdon [1]

with a roar [1]

2Pe 3: 10 The heavens will disappear **with a roar**; the elements will be

4854 Ῥομφά, Rhompha Not used in UBS/NIV [√ 4818]

4855 ῥομφαία, rhomphaia [7]

sword [7]

Lk 2: 35 will be revealed. And a **sword** will pierce your own soul too."
Rev 1: 16 and out of his mouth came a sharp double-edged **sword**.
   2: 12 are the words of him who has the sharp, double-edged **sword**.
   2: 16 to you and will fight against them with the **sword** of my mouth.
   6: 8 They were given power over a fourth of the earth to kill by **sword**,
   19: 15 Out of his mouth comes a sharp **sword** with which to strike down
   19: 21 The rest of them were killed with the **sword** that came out of the

4856 ῥοπή, rhopē Not used in UBS/NIV

4857 Ῥουβήν, Rhoubēn [1]

Reuben [1]

Rev 7: 5 from the tribe *of* **Reuben** 12,000, from the tribe of Gad 12,000,

4858 Ῥούθ, Rhouth [1]

Ruth [1]

Mt 1: 5 father of Obed, whose mother was **Ruth**, Obed the father of Jesse,

4859 Ῥοῦφος, Rhouphos [2]

Rufus [2]

Mk 15: 21 man from Cyrene, Simon, the father *of* Alexander and **Rufus**,
Ro 16: 13 Greet **Rufus**, chosen in the Lord, and his mother, who has been a

4860 ῥύμη, rhymē [4]

street [2], alleys [1], streets [1]

Mt 6: 2 as the hypocrites do in the synagogues and on the **streets**,
Lk 14: 21 into the streets and **alleys** of the town and bring in the poor,
Ac 9: 11 "Go to the house of Judas on Straight **Street** and ask for a man from
   12: 10 When they had walked the *length of* one **street**, suddenly the angel

4861 ῥύομαι, rhyomai [17]

rescue [5], rescued [4], deliver [3], delivered [3], deliverer [1],
rescues [1]

Mt 6: 13 And lead us not into temptation, but **deliver** us from the evil one.'
   27: 43 *Let* God **rescue** him now if he wants him, for he said, 'I am the
Lk 1: 74 *to* **rescue** us from the hand of our enemies, and to enable us to
Ro 7: 24 wretched man I am! Who *will* **rescue** me from this body of death?
   11: 26 "The **deliverer** will come from Zion; he will turn godlessness away
   15: 31 Pray that *I may be* **rescued** from the unbelievers in Judea
2Co 1: 10 He *has* **delivered** us from such a deadly peril, and he will deliver
   1: 10 has delivered us from such a deadly peril, and *he will* **deliver** us.
   1: 10 On him we have set our hope that *he will* continue to **deliver** us,
Col 1: 13 For he *has* **rescued** us from the dominion of darkness and brought
1Th 1: 10 from the dead—Jesus, who **rescues** us from the coming wrath.
2Th 3: 2 And pray that *we may be* **delivered** from wicked and evil men,

2Ti 3:11 persecutions I endured. Yet the Lord **rescued** me from all of them.
    4:17 Gentiles might hear it. And *I was* **delivered** from the lion's mouth.
    4:18 The Lord *will* **rescue** me from every evil attack and will bring me
2Pe 2: 7 and if *he* **rescued** Lot, a righteous man, who was distressed by the
    2: 9 then the Lord knows how *to* **rescue** godly men from trials

4862 ῥυπαίνω, *rhypainō* [1] [√ 4866]

vile [1]

Rev 22:11 *let* him who is vile continue *to be* **vile**; let him who does right

4863 ῥυπαρεύω, *rhypareuō* Not used in UBS/NIV
[√ 4866]

4864 ῥυπαρία, *rhyparia* [1] [√ 4866]

moral filth [1]

Jas 1:21 get rid of all **moral filth** and the evil that is so prevalent

4865 ῥυπαρός, *rhyparos* [2] [√ 4866]

shabby [1], vile [1]

Jas 2: 2 and fine clothes, and a poor man in **shabby** clothes also comes in.
Rev 22:11 let him who is **vile** continue to be vile; let him who does right

4866 ῥύπος, *rhypos* [1] [→ 4862, 4863, 4864, 4865, 4867]

dirt [1]

1Pe 3:21 not the removal *of* **dirt** from the body but the pledge of a good

4867 ῥυπόω, *rhypoō* Not used in UBS/NIV [√ 4866]

4868 ῥύσις, *rhysis* [3] [√ 4835]

subject to bleeding [+135+1877] [2], bleeding [ı 135 ı 3836] [1]

Mk 5:25 who had been **subject to bleeding** [+135+1877] for twelve years.
Lk 8:43 who had been **subject to bleeding** [+135+1877] for twelve years,
    8:44 of his cloak, and immediately her **bleeding** [+135+3836] stopped.

4869 ῥυτίς, *rhytis* [1]

wrinkle [1]

Eph 5:27 without stain or **wrinkle** or any other blemish, but holy

4870 Ῥωμαϊκός, *Rhōmaikos* Not used in UBS/NIV
[√ 4873]

4871 Ῥωμαῖος, *Rhōmaios* [12] [√ 4873]

Roman citizen [4], Romans [3], from Rome [1], Roman citizen [+476] [1], Roman citizens [+476] [1], Roman citizens [1], Roman [1]

Jn 11:48 and then the **Romans** will come and take away both our place
Ac 2:10 Egypt and the parts of Libya near Cyrene; visitors **from Rome**
    16:21 by advocating customs unlawful for us **Romans** to accept
    16:37 even though we are **Roman** [+476] **citizens**, and threw us into
    16:38 and when they heard that Paul and Silas were **Roman citizens**,
    22:25 "Is it legal for you to flog a **Roman** [+476] **citizen** who hasn't even
    22:26 are you going to do?" he asked. "This man is a **Roman citizen**."
    22:27 went to Paul and asked, "Tell me, are you a **Roman citizen**?"
    22:29 when he realized that he had put Paul, a **Roman citizen**, in chains.
    23:27 and rescued him, for I had learned that he is a **Roman citizen**.
    25:16 "I told them that it is not the **Roman** custom to hand over any man
    28:17 I was arrested in Jerusalem and handed over to the **Romans**.

4872 Ῥωμαϊστί, *Rhōmaisti* [1] [√ 4873]

in Latin [1]

Jn 19:20 the city, and the sign was written in Aramaic, **Latin** and Greek.

4873 Ῥώμη, *Rhōmē* [8] [→ 4870, 4871, 4872]

Rome [8]

Ac 18: 2 because Claudius had ordered all the Jews to leave **Rome**.
    19:21 "After I have been there," he said, "I must visit **Rome** also."
    23:11 testified about me in Jerusalem, so you must also testify in **Rome**."
    28:14 invited us to spend a week with them. And so we came to **Rome**.
    28:16 When we got to **Rome**, Paul was allowed to live by himself,
Ro 1: 7 To all in **Rome** who are loved by God and called to be saints:
    1:15 so eager to preach the gospel also to you who are at **Rome**.
2Ti 1:17 On the contrary, when he was in **Rome**, he searched hard for me

4874 ῥώννυμι, *rhōnnymi* [1] [→ 778, 779]

farewell [1]

Ac 15:29 You will do well to avoid these things. **Farewell**.

Σ, S

4875 σ, s Not used in UBS/NIV

4876 σαβαχθάνι, *sabachthani* [2] [√ cf. 2407]

sabachthani [2]

Mt 27:46 cried out in a loud voice, "*Eloi, Eloi, lama* **sabachthani**?"—
Mk 15:34 cried out in a loud voice, "*Eloi, Eloi, lama* **sabachthani**?"—

4877 Σαβαώθ, *Sabaōth* [2]

Almighty [2]

Ro 9:29 "Unless the Lord **Almighty** had left us descendants, we would have
Jas 5: 4 cries of the harvesters have reached the ears *of* the Lord **Almighty**.

4878 σαββατισμός, *sabbatismos* [1] [√ 4879]

Sabbath-rest [1]

Heb 4: 9 There remains, then, a **Sabbath-rest** for the people of God;

4879 σάββατον, *sabbaton* [68] [→ 4640, 4878]

plural [25] Mt 12:1,5,10,11,12; 28:1,1; Mk 1:21; 2:23,24; 3:2,4; 16:2; Lk 4:16,31; 6:2; 13:10; 24:1; Jn 20:1,19; Ac 13:14; 16:13; 17:2; 20:7; Col 2:16

ἡμέρα σάββατον (Sabbath day) [6] Lk 4:16; 13:14,16; 14:5; Ac 13:14; 16:13

κύριος σαββάτου (Lord of the Sabbath) [3] Mt 12:8; Mk 2:28; Lk 6:5

Sabbath [52], week [9], After the Sabbath [+4067] [1], day^s [1], one Sabbath [+1877+3836] [1], one Sabbath [+1877] [1], Sabbath day [1], Sabbath day's walk from [+1584+2400+3847] [1], Sabbath days [1]

Mt 12: 1 At that time Jesus went through the grainfields *on* the **Sabbath**.
    12: 2 Your disciples are doing what is unlawful on the **Sabbath**.
    12: 5 Or haven't you read in the Law that *on* the **Sabbath** the priests in
    12: 5 that on the Sabbath the priests in the temple desecrate the **day**^s
    12: 8 For the Son of Man is Lord *of* the **Sabbath**."
    12:10 accuse Jesus, they asked him, "Is it lawful to heal *on* the **Sabbath**?"
    12:11 "If any of you has a sheep and it falls into a pit *on* the **Sabbath**,
    12:12 than a sheep! Therefore it is lawful to do good *on* the **Sabbath**."
    24:20 that your flight will not take place in winter or *on* the **Sabbath**.
    28: 1 **After the Sabbath** [+4067], at dawn on the first day of the week,
    28: 1 at dawn on the first day *of* the **week**, Mary Magdalene
Mk 1:21 They went to Capernaum, and when the **Sabbath** came, Jesus went
    2:23 **One Sabbath** [+1877+3836] Jesus was going through the
    2:24 "Look, why are they doing what is unlawful on the **Sabbath**?"
    2:27 Then he said to them, "The **Sabbath** was made for man, not man
    2:27 "The Sabbath was made for man, not man for the **Sabbath**.
    2:28 So the Son of Man is Lord even *of* the **Sabbath**."
    3: 2 watched him closely to see if he would heal him *on* the **Sabbath**.

(margin handwriting: cultui / reject—)

3: 4 Then Jesus asked them, "Which is lawful *on* the **Sabbath**: to do
6: 2 When the **Sabbath** came, he began to teach in the synagogue,
16: 1 When the **Sabbath** was over, Mary Magdalene, Mary the mother
16: 2 Very early on the first day *of* the **week**, just after sunrise,
16: 9 When Jesus rose early on the first day *of* the **week**, he appeared

Lk 4:16 and on the **Sabbath** day he went into the synagogue, as was his
4:31 a town in Galilee, and on the **Sabbath** began to teach the people.
6: 1 **One Sabbath** [+*1877*] Jesus was going through the grainfields,
6: 2 "Why are you doing what is unlawful *on* the **Sabbath**?"
6: 5 Then Jesus said to them, "The Son of Man is Lord *of* the **Sabbath**."
6: 6 On another **Sabbath** he went into the synagogue and was teaching,
6: 7 they watched him closely to see if he would heal on the **Sabbath**.
6: 9 Jesus said to them, "I ask you, which is lawful *on* the **Sabbath**:
13:10 On a **Sabbath** Jesus was teaching in one of the synagogues,
13:14 Indignant because Jesus had healed *on* the **Sabbath**, the synagogue
13:14 So come and be healed on those days, not *on* the **Sabbath**."
13:15 Doesn't each of you *on* the **Sabbath** untie his ox or donkey from
13:16 long years, be set free *on* the **Sabbath** day from what bound her?"
14: 1 One **Sabbath**, when Jesus went to eat in the house of a prominent
14: 3 and experts in the law, "Is it lawful to heal *on* the **Sabbath** or not?"
14: 5 of you has a son or an ox that falls into a well on the **Sabbath** day,
18:12 I fast twice a **week** and give a tenth of all I get.'
23:54 It was Preparation Day, and the **Sabbath** was about to begin.
23:56 But they rested *on* the **Sabbath** in obedience to the commandment.
24: 1 On the first day *of* the **week**, very early in the morning, the women

Jn 5: 9 and walked. The day on which this took place was a **Sabbath**,
5:10 the Jews said to the man who had been healed, "It is the **Sabbath**;
5:16 So, because Jesus was doing these things on the **Sabbath**,
5:18 not only was he breaking the **Sabbath**, but he was even calling
7:22 but from the patriarchs), you circumcise a child on the **Sabbath**.
7:23 Now if a child can be circumcised on the **Sabbath** so that the law
7:23 are you angry with me for healing the whole man on the **Sabbath**?
9:14 had made the mud and opened the man's eyes on a **Sabbath**.
9:16 "This man is not from God, for he does not keep the **Sabbath**."
19:31 day of Preparation, and the next day was to be a special **Sabbath**.
19:31 did not want the bodies left on the crosses during the **Sabbath**,
20: 1 Early on the first day *of* the **week**, while it was still dark,
20:19 On the evening of that first day *of* the **week**, when the disciples

Ac 1:12 Olives, a **Sabbath** [+*1584+2400+3847*] **day's walk from** the city.
13:14 *On* the **Sabbath** they entered the synagogue and sat down.
13:27 fulfilled the words of the prophets that are read every **Sabbath**.
13:42 them to speak further about these things on the next **Sabbath**.
13:44 On the next **Sabbath** almost the whole city gathered to hear the
15:21 the earliest times and is read in the synagogues on every **Sabbath**."
16:13 *On* the **Sabbath** we went outside the city gate to the river,
17: 2 and on three **Sabbath days** he reasoned with them from the
18: 4 Every **Sabbath** he reasoned in the synagogue, trying to persuade
20: 7 On the first day *of* the **week** we came together to break bread.

1Co 16: 2 On the first day *of* every **week**, each one of you should set aside a
Col 2:16 to a religious festival, a New Moon celebration or a **Sabbath day**.

4880 σαγήνη, sagēnē [1]

net [1]

Mt 13:47 the kingdom of heaven is like a **net** that was let down into the lake

4881 Σαδδουκαῖος, Saddoukaios [14] [√ *cf. 4882*]

Sadducees [14]

Mt 3: 7 of the Pharisees and **Sadducees** coming to where he was baptizing,
16: 1 The Pharisees and **Sadducees** came to Jesus and tested him by
16: 6 on your guard against the yeast of the Pharisees and **Sadducees**."
16:11 be on your guard against the yeast *of* the Pharisees and **Sadducees**."
16:12 in bread, but against the teaching *of* the Pharisees and **Sadducees**.
22:23 That same day the **Sadducees**, who say there is no resurrection,
22:34 Hearing that Jesus had silenced the **Sadducees**, the Pharisees got

Mk 12:18 Then the **Sadducees**, who say there is no resurrection, came to him
Lk 20:27 Some *of* the **Sadducees**, who say there is no resurrection,
Ac 4: 1 captain of the temple guard and the **Sadducees** came up to Peter
5:17 his associates, who were members of the party *of* the **Sadducees**,
23: 6 knowing that some of them were **Sadducees** and the others
23: 7 a dispute broke out *between* the Pharisees and the **Sadducees**,
23: 8 (The **Sadducees** say there is no resurrection, and that there are

4882 Σαδώκ, Sadōk [2] [√ *cf. 4881*]

Zadok [2]

Mt 1:14 Azor the father of **Zadok**, Zadok the father of Akim, Akim the
1:14 of Zadok, **Zadok** the father of Akim, Akim the father of Eliud,

4883 σαίνω, sainō [1]

unsettled [1]

1Th 3: 3 so that no one *would be* **unsettled** by these trials. You know quite

4884 σάκκος, sakkos [4]

sackcloth [4]

Mt 11:21 they would have repented long ago in **sackcloth** and ashes.
Lk 10:13 they would have repented long ago, sitting in **sackcloth** and ashes.
Rev 6:12 The sun turned black like **sackcloth** made of goat hair, the whole
11: 3 and they will prophesy for 1,260 days, clothed in **sackcloth**."

4885 Σαλά, Sala [2 / 1]

Shelah [1]

Lk 3:32 the son of Boaz, the son *of* Salmon, [UBS *Sala*; NIV *4891*]
3:35 son of Reu, the son of Peleg, the son of Eber, the son *of* **Shelah**,

4886 Σαλαθιήλ, Salathiēl [3]

Shealtiel [3]

Mt 1:12 Jeconiah was the father of **Shealtiel**, Shealtiel the father of
1:12 was the father of Shealtiel, **Shealtiel** the father of Zerubbabel,
Lk 3:27 the son of Zerubbabel, the son *of* **Shealtiel**, the son of Neri,

4887 Σαλαμίς, Salamis [1]

Salamis [1]

Ac 13: 5 When they arrived at **Salamis**, they proclaimed the word of God in

4888 σαλεύω, saleuō [15] [→ *810, 4893; cf. 256*]

shaken [8], swayed [2], agitating [1], shake [1], shaken together [1], shook [1], unsettled [+*608+3808+3836*] [1]

Mt 11: 7 did you go out into the desert to see? A reed **swayed** by the wind?
24:29 will fall from the sky, and the heavenly bodies *will be* **shaken**.'
Mk 13:25 will fall from the sky, and the heavenly bodies *will be* **shaken**.'
Lk 6:38 good measure, pressed down, **shaken together** and running over,
6:48 a flood came, the torrent struck that house but could not **shake** it,
7:24 did you go out into the desert to see? A reed **swayed** by the wind?
21:26 is coming on the world, for the heavenly bodies *will be* **shaken**.
Ac 2:25 before me. Because he is at my right hand, *I will* not *be* **shaken**.
4:31 After they prayed, the place where they were meeting *was* **shaken**.
16:26 violent earthquake that the foundations of the prison *were* **shaken**.
17:13 they went there too, **agitating** the crowds and stirring them up.
2Th 2: 2 not *to become* easily **unsettled** [+*608+3808+3836*] or alarmed by
some prophecy, report or letter supposed to have come from us,
Heb 12:26 At that time his voice **shook** the earth, but now he has promised,
12:27 words "once more" indicate the removing of what *can be* **shaken**—
12:27 created things—so that what cannot *be* **shaken** may remain.

4889 Σαλήμ, Salēm [2]

Salem [2]

Heb 7: 1 This Melchizedek was king *of* **Salem** and priest of God Most High.
7: 2 righteousness"; then also, "king *of* **Salem**" means "king of peace."

4890 Σαλίμ, Salim [1]

Salim [1]

Jn 3:23 Now John also was baptizing at Aenon near **Salim**, because there

4891 Σαλμών, **Salmōn** [2 / 3]

Salmon [3]

Mt 1: 4 Amminadab the father of Nahshon, Nahshon the father of **Salmon**,
    1: 5 **Salmon** the father of Boaz, whose mother was Rahab, Boaz the
Lk 3:32 the son of Obed, the son of Boaz, the son *of* **Salmon**, [UBS *4885*]

4892 Σαλμώνη, **Salmōnē** [1]

Salmone [1]

Ac 27: 7 to hold our course, we sailed to the lee of Crete, opposite **Salmone**.

4893 σάλος, **salos** [1] [√ *4888*]

tossing [1]

Lk 21:25 be in anguish and perplexity at the roaring and **tossing** of the sea.

4894 σάλπιγξ, **salpinx** [11] [√ *4895*]

trumpet [7], trumpet call [2], trumpets [2]

Mt 24:31 And he will send his angels with a loud **trumpet call**, and they will
1Co 14: 8 Again, if the **trumpet** does not sound a clear call, who will get
    15:52 in a flash, in the twinkling of an eye, at the last **trumpet**.
1Th 4:16 with the voice of the archangel and with the **trumpet call** of God,
Heb 12:19 to a **trumpet** blast or to such a voice speaking words that those
Rev 1:10 in the Spirit, and I heard behind me a loud voice like a **trumpet**,
     4: 1 And the voice I had first heard speaking to me like a **trumpet** said,
     8: 2 who stand before God, and to them were given seven **trumpets**.
     8: 6 Then the seven angels who had the seven **trumpets** prepared to
     8:13 because of the **trumpet** blasts about to be sounded by the other
     9:14 It said to the sixth angel who had the **trumpet**, "Release the four

4895 σαλπίζω, **salpizō** [12] [→ *4894, 4896*]

sounded trumpet [7], announce with trumpets [1], sound trumpet [1], sound [1], sounded [1], trumpet sound [1]

Mt   6: 2 when you give to the needy, *do* not **announce** it **with trumpets**,
1Co 15:52 For the **trumpet** *will* **sound**, the dead will be raised imperishable,
Rev 8: 6 seven angels who had the seven trumpets prepared to **sound** them.
     8: 7 The first angel **sounded** *his* **trumpet**, and there came hail
     8: 8 The second angel **sounded** *his* **trumpet**, and something like a huge
     8:10 The third angel **sounded** *his* **trumpet**, and a great star, blazing like
     8:12 The fourth angel **sounded** *his* **trumpet**, and a third of the sun was
     8:13 because of the trumpet blasts about to *be* **sounded** by the other
     9: 1 The fifth angel **sounded** *his* **trumpet**, and I saw a star that had
     9:13 The sixth angel **sounded** *his* **trumpet**, and I heard a voice coming
    10: 7 in the days when the seventh angel is about to **sound** his **trumpet**,
    11:15 The seventh angel **sounded** *his* **trumpet**, and there were loud

4896 σαλπιστής, **salpistēs** [1] [√ *4895*]

trumpeters [1]

Rev 18:22 The music of harpists and musicians, flute players and **trumpeters**,

4897 Σαλώμη, **Salōmē** [2]

Salome [2]

Mk 15:40 Mary the mother of James the younger and of Joses, and **Salome**.
    16: 1 and **Salome** bought spices so that they might go to anoint Jesus'

4898 Σαλωμών, **Salōmōn** Not used in UBS/NIV
    [√ *5048*]

4899 Σαμάρεια, **Samareia** [11] [→ *4900, 4901, 4902*]

Samaria [10], Samaritan [1]

Lk 17:11 Jesus traveled along the border between **Samaria** and Galilee.
Jn 4: 4 Now he had to go through **Samaria**.
    4: 5 So he came to a town *in* **Samaria** called Sychar, near the plot of
    4: 7 When a **Samaritan** woman came to draw water, Jesus said to her,
Ac 1: 8 and in all Judea and **Samaria**, and to the ends of the earth."

8: 1 except the apostles were scattered throughout Judea and **Samaria**.
8: 5 Philip went down to a city *in* **Samaria** and proclaimed the Christ
8: 9 practiced sorcery in the city and amazed all the people *of* **Samaria**.
8:14 When the apostles in Jerusalem heard that **Samaria** had accepted
9:31 throughout Judea, Galilee and **Samaria** enjoyed a time of peace.
15: 3 on their way, and as they traveled through Phoenicia and **Samaria**,

4900 Σαμαρία, **Samaria** Not used in UBS/NIV [√ *4899*]

4901 Σαμαρίτης, **Samaritēs** [9] [√ *4899*]

Samaritan [5], Samaritans [4]

Mt 10: 5 not go among the Gentiles or enter any town *of* the **Samaritans**.
Lk 9:52 who went into a **Samaritan** village to get things ready for him;
    10:33 But a **Samaritan**, as he traveled, came where the man was;
    17:16 himself at Jesus' feet and thanked him—and he was a **Samaritan**.
Jn 4: 9 ask me for a drink?" (For Jews do not associate with **Samaritans**.)
    4:39 Many *of* the **Samaritans** from that town believed in him
    4:40 So when the **Samaritans** came to him, they urged him to stay with
    8:48 "Aren't we right in saying that you are a **Samaritan**
Ac 8:25 to Jerusalem, preaching the gospel in many **Samaritan** villages.

4902 Σαμαρῖτις, **Samaritis** [2] [√ *4899*]

Samaritan [2]

Jn 4: 9 The **Samaritan** woman said to him, "You are a Jew and I am a
    4: 9 woman said to him, "You are a Jew and I am a **Samaritan** woman.

4903 Σαμοθρᾴκη, **Samothrakē** [1]

Samothrace [1]

Ac 16:11 From Troas we put out to sea and sailed straight for **Samothrace**,

4904 Σάμος, **Samos** [1]

Samos [1]

Ac 20:15 The day after that we crossed over to **Samos**, and on the following

4905 Σαμουήλ, **Samouēl** [3]

Samuel [3]

Ac 3:24 "Indeed, all the prophets from **Samuel** on, as many as have spoken,
    13:20 God gave them judges until the time of **Samuel** the prophet.
Heb 11:32 Barak, Samson, Jephthah, David, **Samuel** and the prophets,

4906 Σαμφουρειν, **Samphourein** Not used in UBS/NIV

4907 Σαμψών, **Sampsōn** [1]

Samson [1]

Heb 11:32 Barak, **Samson**, Jephthah, David, Samuel and the prophets,

4908 σανδάλιον, **sandalion** [2]

sandals [+*5686*] [1], sandals [1]

Mk 6: 9 Wear **sandals** but not an extra tunic.
Ac 12: 8 the angel said to him, "Put on your clothes and **sandals** [+*5686*]."

4909 σανίς, **sanis** [1]

planks [1]

Ac 27:44 The rest were to get there on **planks** or on pieces of the ship.

4910 Σαούλ, **Saoul** [9]

Saul [9]

Ac 9: 4 heard a voice say to him, "**Saul**, Saul, why do you persecute me?"
    9: 4 heard a voice say to him, "Saul, **Saul**, why do you persecute me?"

     9:17 Placing his hands on Saul, he said, "Brother **Saul**, the Lord—
13:21 and he gave them **Saul** son of Kish, of the tribe of Benjamin,
22: 7 I fell to the ground and heard a voice say to me, '**Saul**! Saul!
22: 7 I fell to the ground and heard a voice say to me, 'Saul! **Saul**!
22:13 He stood beside me and said, 'Brother **Saul**, receive your sight!'
26:14 saying to me in Aramaic, '**Saul**, Saul, why do you persecute me?
26:14 saying to me in Aramaic, 'Saul, **Saul**, why do you persecute me?

4911 σαπρός, *sapros* [8] [√ 4960]

bad [7], unwholesome [1]

Mt   7:17 every good tree bears good fruit, but a **bad** tree bears bad fruit.
     7:18 tree cannot bear bad fruit, and a **bad** tree cannot bear good fruit.
   12:33 its fruit will be good, or make a tree **bad** and its fruit will be bad,
   12:33 its fruit will be good, or make a tree bad and its fruit will be **bad**,
   13:48 and collected the good fish in baskets, but threw the **bad** away.
Lk   6:43 "No good tree bears bad fruit, nor does a **bad** tree bear good fruit.
   6:43 "No good tree bears bad fruit, nor does a **bad** tree bear good fruit.
Eph   4:29 Do not let any **unwholesome** talk come out of your mouths,

4912 Σάπφιρα, *Sapphira* [1] [√ 4913]

Sapphira [1]

Ac   5: 1 Now a man named Ananias, together with his wife **Sapphira**,

4913 σάπφιρος, *sapphiros* [1] [→ 4912]

sapphire [1]

Rev 21:19 the second **sapphire**, the third chalcedony, the fourth emerald,

4914 σαργάνη, *sarganē* [1]

basket [1]

2Co 11:33 But I was lowered in a **basket** from a window in the wall

4915 Σάρδεις, *Sardeis* [3]

Sardis [3]

Rev   1:11 to Ephesus, Smyrna, Pergamum, Thyatira, **Sardis**, Philadelphia
   3: 1 "To the angel of the church in **Sardis** write: These are the words of
   3: 4 Yet you have a few people in **Sardis** who have not soiled their

4916 σάρδινος, *sardinos* Not used in UBS/NIV [√ 4917]

4917 σάρδιον, *sardion* [2] [→ 4916, 4918]

carnelian [2]

Rev   4: 3 the one who sat there had the appearance of jasper and **carnelian**.
   21:20 the fifth sardonyx, the sixth **carnelian**, the seventh chrysolite,

4918 σαρδόνυξ, *sardonyx* [1] [√ 4917]

sardonyx [1]

Rev 21:20 the fifth **sardonyx**, the sixth carnelian, the seventh chrysolite,

4919 Σάρεπτα, *Sarepta* [1]

Zarephath [1]

Lk   4:26 any of them, but to a widow in **Zarephath** in the region of Sidon.

4920 σαρκικός, *sarkikos* [7] [√ 4922]

worldly [3], material [2], of the world [1], sinful [1]

Ro 15:27 they owe it to the Jews to share with them their **material** *blessings.*
1Co   3: 3 You are still **worldly**. For since there is jealousy and quarreling
   3: 3 there is jealousy and quarreling among you, are you not **worldly**?
   9:11 among you, is it too much if we reap a **material** harvest from you?
2Co   1:12 We have done so not according to **worldly** wisdom but according
   10: 4 The weapons we fight with are not the weapons **of the world**.
1Pe   2:11 as aliens and strangers in the world, to abstain from **sinful** desires,

4921 σάρκινος, *sarkinos* [4] [√ 4922]

ancestry [1], of human [1], unspiritual [1], worldly [1]

Ro   7:14 that the law is spiritual; but I am **unspiritual**, sold as a slave to sin.
1Co   3: 1 Brothers, I could not address you as spiritual but as **worldly**—
2Co   3: 3 living God, not on tablets of stone but on tablets **of human** hearts.
Heb   7:16 become a priest not on the basis of a regulation as to his **ancestry**

4922 σάρξ, *sarx* [147] [→ 4920, 4921]

ἐν σαρκί (in/by the flesh) [26] Ro 2:28; 7:5,18; 8:3,8,9; 2Co 10:3; Gal 2:20; 4:14; 6:12,13; Eph 2:11,11,14; Php 1:22,24; 3:3, 4,4; Col 1:24; 2:1; 1Ti 3:16; Phm 1:16; 1Pe 4:2; 1Jn 4:2; 2Jn 1:7

κατὰ σάρκα (according to the flesh) [21] Jn 8:15; Ro 1:3; 4:1; 8:4,5,12,13; 9:3,5; 1Co 1:26; 10:18; 2Co 1:17; 5:16,16; 10:2,3; 11:18; Gal 4:23,29; Eph 6:5; Col 3:22

πνεῦμα ... σάρξ (spirit ... flesh) [33] Mt 26:41; Mk 14:38; Lk 24:39; Jn 3:6,6; 6:63,63; Ac 2:17; Ro 8:4,5,5,6,9,9,9,13; 1Co 5:5; 2Co 7:1; Gal 3:3; 4:29; 5:16,17,17; 6:8,8; Php 3:3; Col 2:5; 1Ti 3:16; Heb 12:9; 1Pe 3:18; 4:6; 1Jn 4:2,2

σάρξ καὶ αἷμα (flesh and blood) [5] Mt 16:17; 1Co 15:50; Gal 1:16; Eph 6:12; Heb 2:14

σάρξ ... νοῦς (flesh ... mind) [2] Ro 7:25; Col 2:18

flesh [33], sinful nature [23], body [20], *untranslated* [8], one [+4246] [5], human [3], people [3], sinful man [3], earthly [+2848] [2], in the ordinary way [+2848] [2], man [+135+2779] [2], nature [2], world [2], as a man [+1877] [1], birth [1], bodies [1], corrupted flesh [1], earthly [+1877] [1], external [1], forefather [+2848+4635] [1], human ancestry [+2848] [1], human effort [1], human nature [1], human standards [1], illness [+819+3836] [1], in this way[s] [+2848] [1], it[s] [1], its[s] [+3836] [1], life on earth [1], life [1], man [1], mankind [1], men [1], natural selves [1], natural [1], outwardly [+1877] [1], outwardly [1], people of Israel [+2702+2848] [1], personally [+1877] [1], perversion [+599+2283+3958] [1], physical [+1877] [1], physical [1], race [+2848+5150] [1], sensual [1], sinful human nature [1], sinful [1], such[s] [+1877] [1], the world [1], this world [1], unspiritual [1], worldly manner [1], worldly point of view [1]

Mt 16:17 of Jonah, for this was not revealed to you *by* **man** [+135+2779],
   19: 5 and be united to his wife, and the two will become one **flesh**'?
   19: 6 **[RPG]** Therefore what God has joined together, let man not
   24:22 those days had not been cut short, no **one** [+4246] would survive,
   26:41 not fall into temptation. The spirit is willing, but the **body** is weak."
Mk 10: 8 and the two will become one **flesh**.' So they are no longer two,
   10: 8 become one flesh.' So they are no longer two, but one. **[RPG]**
   13:20 Lord had not cut short those days, no **one** [+4246] would survive.
   14:38 not fall into temptation. The spirit is willing, but the **body** is weak."
Lk   3: 6 And all **mankind** will see God's salvation.' "
   24:39 and see; a ghost does not have **flesh** and bones, as you see I have."
Jn   1:13 nor of **human** decision or a husband's will, but born of God.
   1:14 The Word became **flesh** and made his dwelling among us.
   3: 6 **Flesh** gives birth to flesh,
   3: 6 Flesh gives birth to **flesh**,
   6:51 This bread is my **flesh**, which I will give for the life of the world."
   6:52 among themselves, "How can this man give us his **flesh** to eat?"
   6:53 unless you eat the **flesh** of the Son of Man and drink his blood,
   6:54 Whoever eats my **flesh** and drinks my blood has eternal life,
   6:55 For my **flesh** is real food and my blood is real drink.
   6:56 Whoever eats my **flesh** and drinks my blood remains in me,
   6:63 The Spirit gives life; the **flesh** counts for nothing. The words I have
   8:15 You judge by **human standards**; I pass judgment on no one.
   17: 2 For you granted him authority over all **people** that he might give
Ac   2:17 " 'In the last days, God says, I will pour out my Spirit on all **people**.
   2:26 is glad and my tongue rejoices; my **body** also will live in hope,
   2:31 he was not abandoned to the grave, nor did his **body** see decay.
Ro   1: 3 his Son, who as to his **human nature** was a descendant of David,
   2:28 nor is circumcision merely outward and **physical** [+1877].
   3:20 Therefore no **one** [+4246] will be declared righteous in his sight by
   4: 1 Abraham, our **forefather** [+2848+4635], discovered in this matter?
   6:19 this in human terms because you are weak *in* your **natural selves**.
   7: 5 For when we were controlled by the **sinful nature**, the sinful
   7:18 I know that nothing good lives in me, that is, in my **sinful nature**.
   7:25 to God's law, but *in* the **sinful nature** a slave to the law of sin.

8: 3 was powerless to do in that it was weakened by the **sinful nature**,
8: 3 God did by sending his own Son in the likeness *of* sinful **man** to be
8: 3 man to be a sin offering. And so he condemned sin in **sinful man**,
8: 4 who do not live according to the **sinful nature** but according to the
8: 5 Those who live according to the **sinful nature** have their minds set
8: 5 the sinful nature have their minds set on what that **nature** desires;
8: 6 The mind *of* **sinful man** is death, but the mind controlled by the
8: 7 the **sinful** mind is hostile to God. It does not submit to God's law,
8: 8 Those controlled by the **sinful nature** cannot please God.
8: 9 however, are controlled not by the **sinful nature** but by the Spirit,
8:12 but it is not *to* the **sinful nature**, to live according to it.
8:12 but it is not *to* the sinful nature, to live according to it's.
8:13 For if you live according to the **sinful nature**, you will die;
9: 3 for the sake of my brothers, those *of* my own **race** [+*2848*+*5150*],
9: 5 and from them is traced the **human** [+*2848*] **ancestry** of Christ,
9: 8 other words, it is not the **natural** children who are God's children,
11:14 in the hope that I may somehow arouse my own **people** to envy
13:14 do not think about how to gratify the desires *of* the **sinful nature**.
1Co 1:26 Not many of you were wise by **human** standards; not many were
    1:29 so that no **one** [+*4246*] may boast before him.
    5: 5 so that the **sinful nature** may be destroyed and his spirit saved on
    6:16 with her in body? For it is said, "The two will become one **flesh**."
    7:28 But those who marry will face many troubles *in* this **life**, and I
  10:18 Consider the **people of Israel** [+*2702*+*2848*]: Do not those who eat
  15:39 All **flesh** is not the same: Men have one kind of flesh, animals have
  15:39 **[RPG]** Men have one kind of flesh, animals have another,
  15:39 Men have one kind of **flesh**, animals have another, birds another
  15:39 animals have another, **[RPG]** birds another and fish another.
  15:50 brothers, that **flesh** and blood cannot inherit the kingdom of God,
2Co 1:17 Or do I make my plans in a **worldly manner** so that in the same
    4:11 for Jesus' sake, so that his life may be revealed in our mortal **body**.
    5:16 So from now on we regard no one from a **worldly point of view**.
    5:16 Though we once regarded Christ **in this way**s [+*2848*], we do
    7: 1 let us purify ourselves from everything that contaminates **body**
    7: 5 For when we came into Macedonia, this **body** of ours had no rest,
  10: 2 some people who think that we live by the standards of **this world**.
  10: 3 For though we live in the **world**, we do not wage war as the world
  10: 3 we live in the world, we do not wage war as **the world** does.
  11:18 Since many are boasting in the way the **world** does, I too will
  12: 7 there was given me a thorn *in* my **flesh**, a messenger of Satan,
Gal 1:16 him among the Gentiles, I did not consult any **man** [+*135*+*2779*],
    2:16 because by observing the law no **one** [+*4246*] will be justified.
    2:20 The life I live in the **body**, I live by faith in the Son of God,
    3: 3 the Spirit, are you now trying to attain your goal *by* **human effort**?
    4:13 because of an **illness** [+*819*+*3836*] that I first preached the gospel
    4:14 Even though my illness **[RPG]** was a trial to you, you did not
    4:23 son by the slave woman was born **in the ordinary** [+*2848*] **way**;
    4:29 At that time the son born **in the ordinary** [+*2848*] **way** persecuted
    5:13 But do not use your freedom to indulge the **sinful nature**;
    5:16 the Spirit, and you will not gratify the desires *of* the **sinful nature**.
    5:17 For the **sinful nature** desires what is contrary to the Spirit,
    5:17 to the Spirit, and the Spirit what is contrary to the **sinful nature**.
    5:19 The acts *of* the **sinful nature** are obvious: sexual immorality,
    5:24 Those who belong to Christ Jesus have crucified the **sinful nature**
    6: 8 The one who sows to please his **sinful nature**, from that nature
    6: 8 to please his sinful nature, from that **nature** will reap destruction;
    6:12 Those who want to make a good impression **outwardly** [+*1877*]
    6:13 want you to be circumcised that they may boast about your **flesh**.
Eph 2: 3 gratifying the cravings *of* our **sinful nature** and following its
    2: 3 our sinful nature and following its**s** [+*3836*] desires and thoughts.
    2:11 remember that formerly you who are Gentiles by **birth** and called
    2:11 "the circumcision" (that done in the **body** by the hands of men)—
    2:15 by abolishing in his **flesh** the law with its commandments
    5:29 After all, no one ever hated his own **body**, but he feeds and cares
    5:31 and be united to his wife, and the two will become one **flesh**."
    6: 5 Slaves, obey your **earthly** [+*1877*] masters with respect and fear,
    6:12 For our struggle is not against **flesh** and blood, but against the
Php 1:22 If I am to go on living in the **body**, this will mean fruitful labor for
    1:24 but it is more necessary for you that I remain in the **body**.
    3: 3 who glory in Christ Jesus, and who put no confidence in the **flesh**—
    3: 4 though I myself have reasons for **such**s [+*1877*] confidence.
    3: 4 If anyone else thinks he has reasons to put confidence in the **flesh**,
Col 1:22 But now he has reconciled you by Christ's **physical** body through
    1:24 and I fill up in my **flesh** what is still lacking in regard to Christ's
    2: 1 at Laodicea, and for all who have not met me **personally** [+*1877*]
    2: 5 For though I am absent from you in **body**, I am present with you in

2:11 you were also circumcised, in the putting off *of* the **sinful nature**,
2:13 dead in your sins and in the uncircumcision *of* your **sinful nature**,
2:18 has seen, and his **unspiritual** mind puffs him up with idle notions.
2:23 but they lack any value in restraining **sensual** indulgence.
3:22 Slaves, obey your **earthly** [+*2848*] masters in everything;
1Ti 3:16 He appeared in a **body**, was vindicated by the Spirit, was seen by
Phm 1:16 dearer to you, both **as a man** [+*1877*] and as a brother in the Lord.
Heb 2:14 Since the children have **flesh** and blood, he too shared in their
    5: 7 During the days of Jesus' **life on earth**, he offered up prayers
    9:10 **external** regulations applying until the time of the new order.
    9:13 unclean sanctify them so that they are **outwardly** clean.
  10:20 and living way opened for us through the curtain, that is, his **body**,
  12: 9 we have all had **human** fathers who disciplined us and we
Jas 5: 3 Their corrosion will testify against you and eat your **flesh** like fire.
1Pe 1:24 For, "All **men** are like grass, and all their glory is like the flowers of
    3:18 He was put to death in the **body** but made alive by the Spirit,
    3:21 not the removal of dirt from the **body** but the pledge of a good
    4: 1 Therefore, since Christ suffered *in* his **body**, arm yourselves also
    4: 1 because he who has suffered *in* his **body** is done with sin.
    4: 2 he does not live the rest of his **earthly** [+*1877*] life for evil human
    4: 6 that they might be judged according to men *in regard to* the **body**,
2Pe 2:10 true of those who follow the corrupt desire *of* the **sinful nature**
    2:18 by appealing to the lustful desires *of* **sinful human nature**,
1Jn 2:16 the cravings of **sinful man**, the lust of his eyes and the boasting of
    4: 2 acknowledges that Jesus Christ has come in the **flesh** is from God,
2Jn 1: 7 who do not acknowledge Jesus Christ as coming in the **flesh**,
Jude 1: 7 Sodom and Gomorrah and the surrounding towns gave themselves
           up to sexual immorality and **perversion** [+*599*+*2283*+*3958*].
    1: 8 these dreamers pollute their own **bodies**, reject authority
    1:23 with fear—hating even the clothing stained by **corrupted flesh**.
Rev 17:16 and leave her naked; they will eat her **flesh** and burn her with fire.
  19:18 so that you may eat the **flesh** of kings, generals, and mighty men,
  19:18 **[RPG]** generals, and mighty men, of horses and their riders,
  19:18 generals, and **[RPG]** mighty men, of horses and their riders,
  19:18 generals, and mighty men, **[RPG]** of horses and their riders,
  19:18 and the **flesh** of all people, free and slave, small and great."
  19:21 on the horse, and all the birds gorged themselves on their **flesh**.

4923 Σαρούχ, **Sarouch** Not used in UBS/NIV [√ *4952*]

4924 σαρόω, **saroō** [3]

swept clean [2], sweep [1]

Mt 12:44 it finds the house unoccupied, **swept clean** and put in order.
Lk 11:25 When it arrives, it finds the house **swept clean** and put in order.
  15: 8 a lamp, **sweep** the house and search carefully until she finds it?

4925 Σάρρα, **Sarra** [4]

Sarah [3], Sarah's [1]

Ro 4:19 about a hundred years old—and that **Sarah's** womb was also dead.
  9: 9 "At the appointed time I will return, and **Sarah** will have a son."
Heb 11:11 even though he was past age—and **Sarah** herself was barren—
1Pe 3: 6 like **Sarah**, who obeyed Abraham and called him her master.

4926 Σαρών, **Sarōn** [1] [√ cf. *838*]

Sharon [1]

Ac 9:35 who lived in Lydda and **Sharon** saw him and turned to the Lord.

4927 Σατάν, **Satan** Not used in UBS/NIV [→ *4928*]

4928 Σατανᾶς, **Satanas** [36] [√ *4927*]

Satan [35], Satan's [1]

Mt 4:10 Jesus said to him, "Away from me, **Satan**! For it is written:
  12:26 If **Satan** drives out Satan, he is divided against himself. How
  12:26 If Satan drives out **Satan**, he is divided against himself. How
  16:23 Jesus turned and said to Peter, "Get behind me, **Satan**! You are a
Mk 1:13 and he was in the desert forty days, being tempted by **Satan**.
  3:23 and spoke to them in parables: "How can **Satan** drive out Satan?
  3:23 and spoke to them in parables: "How can Satan drive out **Satan**?

3:26 And if **Satan** opposes himself and is divided, he cannot stand;
4:15 **Satan** comes and takes away the word that was sown in them.
8:33 at his disciples, he rebuked Peter. "Get behind me, **Satan**!" he said.
Lk 10:18 He replied, "I saw **Satan** fall like lightning from heaven.
    11:18 If **Satan** is divided against himself, how can his kingdom stand?
    13:16 of Abraham, whom **Satan** has kept bound for eighteen long years,
    22: 3 Then **Satan** entered Judas, called Iscariot, one of the Twelve.
    22:31 "Simon, Simon, **Satan** has asked to sift you as wheat.
Jn 13:27 As soon as Judas took the bread, **Satan** entered into him. "What you
Ac   5: 3 how is it that **Satan** has so filled your heart that you have lied to
    26:18 them from darkness to light, and from the power *of* **Satan** to God,
Ro 16:20 The God of peace will soon crush **Satan** under your feet. The grace
1Co 5: 5 hand this man over *to* **Satan**, so that the sinful nature may be
     7: 5 Then come together again so that **Satan** will not tempt you
2Co 2:11 in order that **Satan** might not outwit us. For we are not unaware of
    11:14 no wonder, for **Satan** himself masquerades as an angel of light.
    12: 7 me a thorn in my flesh, a messenger *of* **Satan**, to torment me.
1Th 2:18 certainly I, Paul, did, again and again—but **Satan** stopped us.
2Th 2: 9 the work *of* **Satan** displayed in all kinds of counterfeit miracles,
1Ti 1:20 whom I have handed over *to* **Satan** to be taught not to blaspheme.
     5:15 Some have in fact already turned away to follow **Satan**.
Rev 2: 9 who say they are Jews and are not, but are a synagogue *of* **Satan**.
     2:13 I know where you live—where **Satan** has his throne. Yet you
     2:13 who was put to death in your city—where **Satan** lives.
     2:24 and have not learned **Satan's** so-called deep secrets (I will not
     3: 9 I will make those who are of the synagogue *of* **Satan**, who claim to
    12: 9 called the devil, or **Satan**, who leads the whole world astray.
    20: 2 seized the dragon, that ancient serpent, who is the devil, or **Satan**,
    20: 7 the thousand years are over, **Satan** will be released from his prison

4929 σάτον, *saton* [2]

large amount [*+5552*] [1]

Mt 13:33 and mixed into a **large amount** of flour until it worked all through
Lk 13:21 and mixed into a **large amount** of flour until it worked all through

4930 Σαῦλος, *Saulos* [15]

Saul [15]

Ac   7:58 witnesses laid their clothes at the feet *of* a young man named **Saul**.
     8: 1 And **Saul** was there, giving approval to his death. On that day a
     8: 3 But **Saul** began to destroy the church. Going from house to house,
     9: 1 **Saul** was still breathing out murderous threats against the Lord's
     9: 8 **Saul** got up from the ground, but when he opened his eyes he
     9:11 on Straight Street and ask for a man from Tarsus named **Saul**,
     9:22 Yet **Saul** grew more and more powerful and baffled the Jews living
     9:24 but **Saul** learned of their plan. Day and night they kept close watch
    11:25 Then Barnabas went to Tarsus to look for **Saul**,
    11:30 they did, sending their gift to the elders by Barnabas and **Saul**.
    12:25 When Barnabas and **Saul** had finished their mission, they returned
    13: 1 (who had been brought up with Herod the tetrarch) and **Saul**.
    13: 2 me Barnabas and **Saul** for the work to which I have called them."
    13: 7 sent for Barnabas and **Saul** because he wanted to hear the word of
    13: 9 Then **Saul**, who was also called Paul, filled with the Holy Spirit,

4931 σβέννυμι, *sbennymi* [6] [→ *812, 2410*]

quenched [2], extinguish [1], going out [1], put out fire [1], snuff
out [1]

Mt 12:20 and a smoldering wick *he will* not **snuff out**, till he leads justice to
    25: 8 to the wise, 'Give us some of your oil; our lamps *are* **going out**.'
Mk   9:48 where " 'their worm does not die, and the fire *is* not **quenched**.'
Eph 6:16 with which you can **extinguish** all the flaming arrows of the evil
1Th 5:19 *Do* not **put out** the Spirit's **fire**;
Heb 11:34 **quenched** the fury of the flames, and escaped the edge of the

4932 σεαυτοῦ, *seautou* [43] [√ *5148 + 899*]

yourself [32], you [2], your own [2], *untranslated* [1], claim to be
[*+4472*] [1], take care of mat [*+5143*] [1], who do you think you
are [*+4472+5515*] [1], your life [1], your very self [1], your [1]

Mt   4: 6 "If you are the Son of God," he said, "throw **yourself** down. For it
     8: 4 show **yourself** to the priest and offer the gift Moses commanded,

19:19 your father and mother,' and 'love your neighbor as **yourself**.' "
22:39 And the second is like it: 'Love your neighbor as **yourself**.'
27:40 to destroy the temple and build it in three days, save **yourself**!
Mk   1:44 show **yourself** to the priest and offer the sacrifices that Moses
    12:31 The second is this: 'Love your neighbor as **yourself**.' There is no
    15:30 come down from the cross and save **yourself**!"
Lk   4: 9 "If you are the Son of God," he said, "throw **yourself** down from
     4:23 you will quote this proverb to me: 'Physician, heal **yourself**!
     5:14 show **yourself** to the priest and offer the sacrifices that Moses
    10:27 and with all your mind'; and, 'Love your neighbor as **yourself**.' "
    23:37 and said, "If you are the king of the Jews, save **yourself**."
    23:39 insults at him: "Aren't you the Christ? Save **yourself** and us!"
Jn   1:22 take back to those who sent us. What do you say about **yourself**?"
     7: 4 Since you are doing these things, show **yourself** to the world."
     8:13 challenged him, "Here you are, appearing as **your own** witness;
     8:53 so did the prophets. **Who do you think you are** [*+4472+5515*]?"
    10:33 because you, a mere man, **claim to be** [*+4472*] God."
    14:22 why do you intend to show **yourself** to us and not to the world?"
    17: 5 glorify me *in* **your** presence with the glory I had with you before
    18:34 "Is that **your own** *idea*," Jesus asked, "or did others talk to you
    21:18 when you were younger you dressed **yourself** and went where you
Ac   9:34 Christ heals you. Get up and **take care of** *your* **mat** [*+5143*]."
    16:28 But Paul shouted, "Don't harm **yourself**! We are all here!"
    26: 1 Agrippa said to Paul, "You have permission to speak for **yourself**."
Ro   2: 1 whatever point you judge the other, you are condemning **yourself**,
     2: 5 you are storing up wrath *against* **yourself** for the day of God's
     2:19 if you are convinced that **you** are a guide for the blind, a light for
     2:21 you, then, who teach others, do you not teach **yourself**? You who
    13: 9 are summed up in this one rule: "Love your neighbor as **yourself**."
    14:22 So whatever you believe about these things keep between **yourself**
Gal 5:14 in a single command: "Love your neighbor as **yourself**."
     6: 1 him gently. But watch **yourself**, or you also may be tempted.
1Ti 4: 7 and old wives' tales; rather, train **yourself** to be godly.
     4:16 Watch **your life** and doctrine closely. Persevere in them, because if
     4:16 because if you do, you will save both **yourself** and your hearers.
     5:22 and do not share in the sins of others. Keep **yourself** pure.
2Ti 2:15 Do your best to present **yourself** to God as one approved,
     4:11 Get Mark and bring him with **you**, because he is helpful to me in
Tit 2: 7 In everything set them **[RPG]** an example by doing what is good.
Phm 1:19 I will pay it back—not to mention that you owe me **your very self**.
Jas 2: 8 in Scripture, "Love your neighbor as **yourself**," you are doing right.

4933 σεβάζομαι, *sebazomai* [1] [√ *4936*]

worshiped [1]

Ro   1:25 and **worshiped** and served created things rather than the Creator—

4934 σέβασμα, *sebasma* [2] [√ *4936*]

objects of worship [1], worshiped [1]

Ac 17:23 I walked around and looked carefully at your **objects of worship**,
2Th 2: 4 exalt himself over everything that is called God or is **worshiped**,

4935 σεβαστός, *sebastos* [3] [√ *4936*]

Emperor [1], Emperor's [1], Imperial [1]

Ac 25:21 When Paul made his appeal to be held over for the **Emperor's**
    25:25 because he made his appeal to the **Emperor** I decided to send him
    27: 1 a centurion named Julius, who belonged to the **Imperial** Regiment.

4936 σέβω, *sebō* [10] [→ *813, 814, 815, 2354, 2355, 2356, 2357, 2537, 2538, 4933, 4934, 4935, 4948, 4949*]

worship [3], God-fearing [2], worshiper [2], devout [1],
God-fearing Greeks [1], worshiped [1]

Mt 15: 9 *They* **worship** me in vain; their teachings are but rules taught by
Mk   7: 7 *They* **worship** me in vain; their teachings are but rules taught by
Ac 13:43 many *of* the Jews and **devout** converts to Judaism followed Paul
    13:50 But the Jews incited the **God-fearing** women of high standing
    16:14 cloth from the city of Thyatira, *who was a* **worshiper** of God.
    17: 4 as did a large number *of* **God-fearing** Greeks and not a few
    17:17 in the synagogue *with* the Jews and the **God-fearing Greeks**,
    18: 7 and went next door to the house *of* Titius Justus, a **worshiper** of

18:13 "is persuading the people *to* **worship** God in ways contrary to the
19:27 who *is* **worshiped** throughout the province of Asia and the world,

4937 σειρά, *seira* [1 / 0] [√ *1649*]

2Pe   2: 4 into gloomy <u>dungeons</u> [UBS *into chains* of darkness; NIV *4987*]

4938 σειρός, *seiros*   Not used in UBS/NIV [√ *4987*]

4939 σεισμός, *seismos* [14] [√ *4940*]

earthquake [9], earthquakes [3], quake [1], storm [1]

Mt   8:24 Without warning, a furious **storm** came up on the lake, so that the
     24: 7 There will be famines and **earthquakes** in various places.
     27:54 and those with him who were guarding Jesus saw the **earthquake**
     28: 2 There was a violent **earthquake**, for an angel of the Lord came
Mk   13: 8 There will be **earthquakes** in various places, and famines.
Lk   21:11 There will be great **earthquakes**, famines and pestilences and
Ac   16:26 Suddenly there was such a violent **earthquake** that the foundations
Rev   6:12 as he opened the sixth seal. There was a great **earthquake**.
      8: 5 of thunder, rumblings, flashes of lightning and an **earthquake**.
     11:13 At that very hour there was a severe **earthquake** and a tenth of the
     11:13 Seven thousand people were killed in the **earthquake**,
     11:19 rumblings, peals of thunder, an **earthquake** and a great hailstorm.
     16:18 of lightning, rumblings, peals of thunder and a severe **earthquake**.
     16:18 since man has been on earth, so tremendous was the **quake**.

4940 σείω, *seiō* [5] [→ *411*, *1398*, *2167*, *2939*, *4939*]

shook [2], shake [1], shaken [1], stirred [1]

Mt   21:10 the whole city *was* **stirred** and asked, "Who is this?"
     27:51 in two from top to bottom. The earth **shook** and the rocks split.
     28: 4 The guards were so afraid of him that *they* **shook** and became like
Heb 12:26 "Once more I *will* **shake** not only the earth but also the heavens."
Rev   6:13 as late figs drop from a fig tree *when* **shaken** by a strong wind.

4941 Σεκοῦνδος, *Sekoundos* [1]

Secundus [1]

Ac   20: 4 Aristarchus and **Secundus** from Thessalonica, Gaius from Derbe,

4942 Σελεύκεια, *Seleukeia* [1]

Seleucia [1]

Ac   13: 4 went down to **Seleucia** and sailed from there to Cyprus.

4943 σελήνη, *selēnē* [9] [→ *4944*]

moon [9]

Mt   24:29 " 'the sun will be darkened, and the **moon** will not give its light;
Mk   13:24 " 'the sun will be darkened, and the **moon** will not give its light;
Lk   21:25 "There will be signs in the sun, **moon** and stars. On the earth,
Ac   2:20 and the **moon** to blood before the coming of the great and glorious
1Co 15:41 has one kind of splendor, the **moon** another and the stars another;
Rev   6:12 like sackcloth made of goat hair, the whole **moon** turned blood red,
      8:12 of the sun was struck, a third *of* the **moon**, and a third of the stars,
     12: 1 with the **moon** under her feet and a crown of twelve stars on her
     21:23 The city does not need the sun or the **moon** to shine on it,

4944 σεληνιάζομαι, *selēniazomai* [2] [√ *4943*]

seizures [2]

Mt   4:24 those *having* **seizures**, and the paralyzed, and he healed them.
     17:15 on my son," he said. "*He has* **seizures** and is suffering greatly.

4945 Σεμεΐ, *Semei*   Not used in UBS/NIV [√ *4946*]

4946 Σεμεΐν, *Semein* [1] [→ *4945*]

Semein [1]

Lk   3:26 the son *of* **Semein**, the son of Josech, the son of Joda,

4947 σεμίδαλις, *semidalis* [1]

fine flour [1]

Rev 18:13 and frankincense, of wine and olive oil, of **fine flour** and wheat;

4948 σεμνός, *semnos* [4] [√ *4936*]

worthy of respect [3], noble [1]

Php   4: 8 Finally, brothers, whatever is true, whatever is **noble**, whatever is
1Ti   3: 8 Deacons, likewise, are to be *men* **worthy of respect**, sincere,
      3:11 In the same way, their wives are to be *women* **worthy of respect**,
Tit   2: 2 **worthy of respect**, self-controlled, and sound in faith, in love

4949 σεμνότης, *semnotēs* [3] [√ *4936*]

holiness [1], respect [1], seriousness [1]

1Ti   2: 2 we may live peaceful and quiet lives in all godliness and **holiness**.
      3: 4 family well and see that his children obey him with proper **respect**.
Tit   2: 7 doing what is good. In your teaching show integrity, **seriousness**

4950 Σέργιος, *Sergios* [1]

Sergius [1]

Ac   13: 7 who was an attendant of the proconsul, **Sergius** Paulus.

4951 Σερούκ, *Serouk*   Not used in UBS/NIV [√ *4952*]

4952 Σερούχ, *Serouch* [1] [→ *4923*, *4951*]

Serug [1]

Lk   3:35 the son *of* **Serug**, the son of Reu, the son of Peleg, the son of Eber,

4953 Σήθ, *Sēth* [1]

Seth [1]

Lk   3:38 son of Enosh, the son *of* **Seth**, the son of Adam, the son of God.

4954 Σήμ, *Sēm* [1]

Shem [1]

Lk   3:36 the son *of* **Shem**, the son of Noah, the son of Lamech,

4955 σημαίνω, *sēmainō* [6] [√ *4956*]

indicate [1], indicating [1], made known [1], predicted [1], show
[1], specifying [1]

Jn   12:33 He said this *to* **show** the kind of death he was going to die.
     18:32 so that the words Jesus had spoken **indicating** the kind of death he
     21:19 Jesus said this *to* **indicate** the kind of death by which Peter would
Ac   11:28 and through the Spirit **predicted** that a severe famine would spread
     25:27 to send on a prisoner without **specifying** the charges against him."
Rev   1: 1 *He* **made** it **known** by sending his angel to his servant John,

4956 σημεῖον, *sēmeion* [77] [→ *817*, *2168*, *2358*, *4185*,
                                    4955, *4957*, *5361*]

σημεῖον Ἰωνᾶ (sign of Jonah) [3] Mt 12:39; 16:4; Lk 11:29

σημεῖον καὶ τέρας (signs and wonders) [16] Mt 24:24; Mk
13:22; Jn 4:48; Ac 2:19,22,43; 4:30; 5:12; 6:8; 7:36; 14:3; 15:12;
Ro 15:19; 2Co 12:12; 2Th 2:9; Heb 2:4

miraculous signs [23], sign [18], signs [15], miraculous sign [11], none[s] [+*4024*] [3], miracle [2], mark [1], miraculously [1], signal [1], the distinguishing mark [1], wondrous sign [1]

Mt	12:38	said to him, "Teacher, we want to see a **miraculous sign** from you."
	12:39	"A wicked and adulterous generation asks for a **miraculous sign**!
	12:39	But **none**[s] [+*4024*] will be given it except the sign of the prophet
	12:39	But none will be given it except the **sign** of the prophet Jonah.
	16: 1	and tested him by asking him to show them a **sign** from heaven.
	16: 3	of the sky, but you cannot interpret the **signs** of the times.
	16: 4	A wicked and adulterous generation looks for a **miraculous sign**,
	16: 4	but **none**[s] [+*4024*] will be given it except the sign of Jonah."
	16: 4	miraculous sign, but none will be given it except the **sign** of Jonah."
	24: 3	and what will be the **sign** of your coming and of the end of the
	24:24	false Christs and false prophets will appear and perform great **signs**
	24:30	"At that time the **sign** of the Son of Man will appear in the sky,
	26:48	Now the betrayer had arranged a **signal** with them: "The one I kiss
Mk	8:11	question Jesus. To test him, they asked him for a **sign** from heaven.
	8:12	and said, "Why does this generation ask for a **miraculous sign**?
	8:12	a miraculous sign? I tell you the truth, no **sign** will be given to it."
	13: 4	And what will be the **sign** that they are all about to be fulfilled?"
	13:22	For false Christs and false prophets will appear and perform **signs**
	16:17	And these **signs** will accompany those who believe: In my name
	16:20	and confirmed his word by the **signs** that accompanied it.
Lk	2:12	This will be a **sign** to you: You will find a baby wrapped in cloths
	2:34	of many in Israel, and to be a **sign** that will be spoken against,
	11:16	Others tested him by asking for a **sign** from heaven.
	11:29	It asks for a miraculous sign, but none will be given it except
	11:29	but **none**[s] [+*4024*] will be given it except the sign of Jonah.
	11:29	miraculous sign, but none will be given it except the **sign** of Jonah.
	11:30	For as Jonah was a **sign** to the Ninevites, so also will the Son of
	21: 7	And what will be the **sign** that they are about to take place?"
	21:11	in various places, and fearful events and great **signs** from heaven.
	21:25	"There will be **signs** in the sun, moon and stars. On the earth,
	23: 8	had heard about him, he hoped to see him perform some **miracle**.
Jn	2:11	This, the first *of* his **miraculous signs**, Jesus performed at Cana in
	2:18	"What **miraculous sign** can you show us to prove your authority to
	2:23	many people saw the **miraculous signs** he was doing and believed
	3: 2	For no one could perform the **miraculous signs** you are doing if
	4:48	"Unless you people see **miraculous signs** and wonders," Jesus told
	4:54	This was the second **miraculous sign** that Jesus performed,
	6: 2	because they saw the **miraculous signs** he had performed on the
	6:14	After the people saw the **miraculous sign** that Jesus did,
	6:26	not because you saw **miraculous signs** but because you ate the
	6:30	"What **miraculous sign** then will you give that we may see it
	7:31	Christ comes, will he do more **miraculous signs** than this man?"
	9:16	But others asked, "How can a sinner do such **miraculous signs**?"
	10:41	They said, "Though John never performed a **miraculous sign**,
	11:47	they asked. "Here is this man performing many **miraculous signs**.
	12:18	because they had heard that he had given this **miraculous sign**,
	12:37	Even after Jesus had done all these **miraculous signs** in their
	20:30	Jesus did many other **miraculous signs** in the presence of his
Ac	2:19	show wonders in the heaven above and **signs** on the earth below,
	2:22	a man accredited by God to you *by* miracles, wonders and **signs**,
	2:43	many wonders and **miraculous signs** were done by the apostles.
	4:16	living in Jerusalem knows they have done an outstanding **miracle**,
	4:22	For the man who was **miraculously** healed was over forty years
	4:30	Stretch out your hand to heal and perform **miraculous signs**
	5:12	The apostles performed many **miraculous signs** and wonders
	6: 8	did great wonders and **miraculous signs** among the people.
	7:36	out of Egypt and did wonders and **miraculous signs** in Egypt,
	8: 6	the crowds heard Philip and saw the **miraculous signs** he did,
	8:13	astonished *by* the great **signs** and miracles he saw.
	14: 3	the message of his grace by enabling them to do **miraculous signs**
	15:12	and Paul telling about the **miraculous signs** and wonders God had
Ro	4:11	And he received the **sign** of circumcision, a seal of the
	15:19	by the power *of* **signs** and miracles, through the power of the
1Co	1:22	Jews demand **miraculous signs** and Greeks look for wisdom,
	14:22	Tongues, then, are a **sign**, not for believers but for unbelievers;
2Co	12:12	The things that **mark** an apostle—signs, wonders and miracles—
	12:12	The things that mark an apostle—**signs**, wonders and miracles—
2Th	2: 9	displayed in all kinds of counterfeit miracles, **signs** and wonders,
	3:17	my own hand, which is **the distinguishing mark** in all my letters.
Heb	2: 4	God also testified to it *by* **signs**, wonders and various miracles,
Rev	12: 1	A great and **wondrous sign** appeared in heaven: a woman clothed
	12: 3	Then another **sign** appeared in heaven: an enormous red dragon

	13:13	And he performed great and **miraculous signs**, even causing fire to
	13:14	Because of the **signs** he was given power to do on behalf of the
	15: 1	I saw in heaven another great and marvelous **sign**: seven angels
	16:14	They are spirits of demons performing **miraculous signs**,
	19:20	prophet who had performed the **miraculous signs** on his behalf.

4957 σημειόω, *sēmeioō* [1] [√ *4956*]

take special note [1]

2Th	3:14	not obey our instruction in this letter, **take special note** of him.

4958 σήμερον, *sēmeron* [41] [√ *2465*]

today [32], day [2], very day [+*2465*] [2], day [+*2465*] [1], days [1], this day [1], today [+*2465+3836*] [1], today's [1]

Mt	6:11	Give us **today** our daily bread.
	6:30	which is here **today** and tomorrow is thrown into the fire,
	11:23	had been performed in Sodom, it would have remained to this **day**.
	16: 3	'**Today** it will be stormy, for the sky is red and overcast.'
	21:28	to the first and said, 'Son, go and work **today** in the vineyard.'
	27: 8	That is why it has been called the Field of Blood to this **day**.
	27:19	for I have suffered a great deal **today** in a dream because of him."
	28:15	been widely circulated among the Jews to this **very day** [+*2465*].
Mk	14:30	"I tell you the truth," Jesus answered, "**today**—yes, tonight—
Lk	2:11	**Today** in the town of David a Savior has been born to you;
	4:21	saying to them, "**Today** this scripture is fulfilled in your hearing."
	5:26	filled with awe and said, "We have seen remarkable things **today**."
	12:28	which is here **today**, and tomorrow is thrown into the fire,
	13:32	'I will drive out demons and heal people **today** and tomorrow,
	13:33	I must keep going **today** and tomorrow and the next day—
	19: 5	come down immediately. I must stay at your house **today**."
	19: 9	Jesus said to him, "**Today** salvation has come to this house,
	22:34	Jesus answered, "I tell you, Peter, before the rooster crows **today**,
	22:61	"Before the rooster crows **today**, you will disown me three times."
	23:43	"I tell you the truth, **today** you will be with me in paradise."
Ac	4: 9	If we are being called to account **today** for an act of kindness
	13:33	' 'You are my Son; **today** I have become your Father.'
	19:40	in danger of being charged with rioting because of **today's** events.
	20:26	I declare to you **today** [+*2465+3836*] that I am innocent of the
	22: 3	and was just as zealous for God as any of you are **today**.
	24:21	the resurrection of the dead that I am on trial before you **today**.' "
	26: 2	I consider myself fortunate to stand before you **today** as I make my
	26:29	but all who are listening to me **today** may become what I am,
	27:33	"For the last fourteen **days**," he said, "you have been in constant
Ro	11: 8	and ears so that they could not hear, to this **very day** [+*2465*]."
2Co	3:14	for to this **day** [+*2465*] the same veil remains when the old
	3:15	Even to **this day** when Moses is read, a veil covers their hearts.
Heb	1: 5	ever say, "You are my Son; **today** I have become your Father"?
	3: 7	So, as the Holy Spirit says: "**Today**, if you hear his voice,
	3:13	But encourage one another daily, as long as it is called **Today**,
	3:15	"**Today**, if you hear his voice, do not harden your hearts as you did
	4: 7	Therefore God again set a certain day, calling it **Today**, when a
	4: 7	"**Today**, if you hear his voice, do not harden your hearts."
	5: 5	said to him, "You are my Son; **today** I have become your Father."
	13: 8	Jesus Christ is the same yesterday and **today** and forever.
Jas	4:13	you who say, "**Today** or tomorrow we will go to this or that city,

4959 σημικίνθιον, *sēmikinthion*   Not used in UBS/NIV [√ *4980*]

4960 σήπω, *sēpō* [1] [→ *4911*]

rotted [1]

Jas	5: 2	Your wealth *has* **rotted**, and moths have eaten your clothes.

4961 σηρικός, *sērikos*   Not used in UBS/NIV

4962 σής, *sēs* [3] [→ *4963*]

moth [3]

Mt	6:19	where **moth** and rust destroy, and where thieves break in and steal.
	6:20	where **moth** and rust do not destroy, and where thieves do not

Lk 12:33 not be exhausted, where no thief comes near and no **moth** destroys.

4963 σητόβρωτος, **sētobrōtos** [1] [√ *4962 + 1048*]

moths have eaten [*+1181*] [1]

Jas 5: 2 wealth has rotted, and **moths** [*+1181*] **have eaten** your clothes.

4964 σθενόω, **sthenoō** [1] [→ *819, 820, 821, 822*]

make strong [1]

1Pe 5:10 *will* himself restore you and **make** you **strong**, firm and steadfast.

4965 σιαγών, **siagōn** [2]

cheek [2]

Mt 5:39 If someone strikes you on the right **cheek,** turn to him the other
Lk 6:29 If someone strikes you on one **cheek,** turn to him the other also.

4966 σιαίνομαι, **siainomai** Not used in UBS/NIV

4967 σιγάω, **sigaō** [10] [→ *4968*]

quiet [3], silent [3], finished [1], hidden [1], kept this to themselves [1], stop [1]

Lk 9:36 The disciples **kept this to themselves,** and told no one at that time
18:39 Those who led the way rebuked him and told him to *be* **quiet,**
20:26 there in public. And astonished by his answer, *they became* **silent.**
Ac 12:17 Peter motioned with his hand for them *to be* **quiet** and described
15:12 The whole assembly *became* **silent** as they listened to Barnabas
15:13 When they **finished,** James spoke up: "Brothers, listen to me.
Ro 16:25 according to the revelation of the mystery **hidden** for long ages
1Co 14:28 the speaker *should keep* **quiet** in the church and speak to himself
14:30 to someone who is sitting down, the first speaker *should* **stop.**
14:34 women *should remain* **silent** in the churches. They are not

4968 σιγή, **sigē** [2] [√ *4967*]

all silent [*+4498*] [1], silence [1]

Ac 21:40 When they were **all silent** [*+4498*], he said to them in Aramaic:
Rev 8: 1 seventh seal, there was **silence** in heaven for about half an hour.

4969 σιδήρεος, **sidēreos** Not used in UBS/NIV [√ *4970*]

4970 σίδηρος, **sidēros** [1] [→ *4969, 4971*]

iron [1]

Rev 18:12 every kind made of ivory, costly wood, bronze, **iron** and marble;

4971 σιδηροῦς, **sidērous** [5] [√ *4970*]

iron [4], of iron [1]

Ac 12:10 and second guards and came to the **iron** gate leading to the city.
Rev 2:27 'He will rule them with an **iron** scepter; he will dash them to
9: 9 They had breastplates like breastplates **of iron,** and the sound of
12: 5 a male child, who will rule all the nations with an **iron** scepter.
19:15 "He will rule them with an **iron** scepter." He treads the winepress

4972 Σιδών, **Sidōn** [9] [→ *4973*]

Sidon [9]

Mt 11:21 that were performed in you had been performed in Tyre and **Sidon,**
11:22 it will be more bearable *for* Tyre and **Sidon** on the day of
15:21 that place, Jesus withdrew to the region *of* Tyre and **Sidon.**
Mk 3: 8 and the regions across the Jordan and around Tyre and **Sidon.**
7:31 Then Jesus left the vicinity of Tyre and went through **Sidon,**
Lk 6:17 over Judea, from Jerusalem, and from the coast of Tyre and **Sidon,**
10:13 that were performed in you had been performed in Tyre and **Sidon,**
10:14 But it will be more bearable *for* Tyre and **Sidon** at the judgment
Ac 27: 3 The next day we landed at **Sidon;** and Julius, in kindness to Paul,

4973 Σιδώνιος, **Sidōnios** [2] [√ *4972*]

people of Sidon [1], region of Sidon [1]

Lk 4:26 any of them, but to a widow in Zarephath *in* the **region of Sidon.**
Ac 12:20 He had been quarreling *with* the **people of** Tyre and **Sidon;**

4974 σικάριος, **sikarios** [1] [√ *cf. 5000, 5001 [?]*]

terrorists [*+467+3836*] [1]

Ac 21:38 and led four thousand **terrorists** [*+467+3836*] out into the desert

4975 σίκερα, **sikera** [1]

fermented drink [1]

Lk 1:15 He is never to take wine or *other* **fermented drink,** and he will be

4976 Σίλας, **Silas** [12] [→ *4977*]

Silas [12]

Ac 15:22 and **Silas,** two men who were leaders among the brothers.
15:27 and **Silas** to confirm by word of mouth what we are writing.
15:32 Judas and **Silas,** who themselves were prophets, said much to
15:40 but Paul chose **Silas** and left, commended by the brothers to the
16:19 they seized Paul and **Silas** and dragged them into the marketplace
16:25 About midnight Paul and **Silas** were praying and singing hymns to
16:29 called for lights, rushed in and fell trembling before Paul and **Silas.**
17: 4 Some of the Jews were persuaded and joined Paul and **Silas,**
17:10 as it was night, the brothers sent Paul and **Silas** away to Berea.
17:14 sent Paul to the coast, but **Silas** and Timothy stayed at Berea.
17:15 and then left with instructions for **Silas** and Timothy to join him as
18: 5 When **Silas** and Timothy came from Macedonia, Paul devoted

4977 Σιλουανός, **Silouanos** [4] [√ *4976*]

Silas [4]

2Co 1:19 who was preached among you by me and **Silas** and Timothy,
1Th 1: 1 Paul, **Silas** and Timothy, To the church of the Thessalonians in
2Th 1: 1 Paul, **Silas** and Timothy, To the church of the Thessalonians in
1Pe 5:12 With the help of **Silas,** whom I regard as a faithful brother,

4978 Σιλωάμ, **Silōam** [3]

Siloam [3]

Lk 13: 4 Or those eighteen who died when the tower in **Siloam** fell on
Jn 9: 7 he told him, "wash in the Pool *of* **Siloam**" (this word means Sent).
9:11 He told me to go to **Siloam** and wash. So I went and washed,

4979 Σιμαίας, **Simaias** Not used in UBS/NIV

4980 σιμικίνθιον, **simikinthion** [1] [→ *4959*]

aprons [1]

Ac 19:12 and **aprons** that had touched him were taken to the sick,

4981 Σίμων, **Simōn** [75] [→ *5208*]

Simon [70], Simon's [4], his[s] [1]

Mt 4:18 he saw two brothers, **Simon** called Peter and his brother Andrew.
10: 2 first, **Simon** (who is called Peter) and his brother Andrew;
10: 4 **Simon** the Zealot and Judas Iscariot, who betrayed him.
13:55 and aren't his brothers James, Joseph, **Simon** and Judas?
16:16 **Simon** Peter answered, "You are the Christ, the Son of the living
16:17 Jesus replied, "Blessed are you, **Simon** son of Jonah, for this was
17:25 Jesus was the first to speak. "What do you think, **Simon**?"
26: 6 While Jesus was in Bethany in the home *of* a man known as **Simon**
27:32 they were going out, they met a man from Cyrene, named **Simon,**
Mk 1:16 he saw **Simon** and his brother Andrew casting a net into the lake,
1:16 he saw Simon and **his**[s] brother Andrew casting a net into the lake,
1:29 they went with James and John to the home *of* **Simon** and Andrew.
1:30 **Simon's** mother-in-law was in bed with a fever, and they told
1:36 **Simon** and his companions went to look for him,

　　3:16 the twelve he appointed: **Simon** (to whom he gave the name Peter);
　　3:18 Thomas, James son of Alphaeus, Thaddaeus, **Simon** the Zealot
　　6: 3 Mary's son and the brother *of* James, Joseph, Judas and **Simon**?
　14: 3 reclining at the table in the home *of* a man known as **Simon** the
　14:37 found them sleeping. "**Simon**," he said to Peter, "are you asleep?
　15:21 man from Cyrene, **Simon**, the father of Alexander and Rufus,
Lk　4:38 Jesus left the synagogue and went to the home *of* **Simon**.
　　4:38 Now **Simon's** mother-in-law was suffering from a high fever,
　　5: 3 He got into one of the boats, the one belonging to **Simon**,
　　5: 4 had finished speaking, he said to **Simon**, "Put out into deep water,
　　5: 5 **Simon** answered, "Master, we've worked hard all night and haven't
　　5: 8 When **Simon** Peter saw this, he fell at Jesus' knees and said,
　　5:10 so were James and John, the sons of Zebedee, **Simon's** partners.
　　5:10 Then Jesus said to **Simon**, "Don't be afraid; from now on you will
　　6:14 **Simon** (whom he named Peter), his brother Andrew, James,
　　6:15 James son of Alphaeus, **Simon** who was called the Zealot,
　　7:40 Jesus answered him, "**Simon**, I have something to tell you."
　　7:43 **Simon** replied, "I suppose the one who had the bigger debt
　　7:44 Then he turned toward the woman and said *to* **Simon**, "Do you see
　22:31 "**Simon**, Simon, Satan has asked to sift you as wheat.
　22:31 "Simon, **Simon**, Satan has asked to sift you as wheat.
　23:26 As they led him away, they seized **Simon** from Cyrene, who was
　24:34 "It is true! The Lord has risen and has appeared *to* **Simon**."
Jn　1:40 Andrew, **Simon** Peter's brother, was one of the two who heard
　　1:41 The first thing Andrew did was to find his brother **Simon** and tell
　　1:42 Jesus looked at him and said, "You are **Simon** son of John.
　　6: 8 Another of his disciples, Andrew, **Simon** Peter's brother, spoke up,
　　6:68 **Simon** Peter answered him, "Lord, to whom shall we go? You have
　　6:71 (He meant Judas, the *son of* **Simon** Iscariot, who, though one of
　13: 2 already prompted Judas Iscariot, *son of* **Simon**, to betray Jesus.
　13: 6 He came to **Simon** Peter, who said to him, "Lord, are you going to
　13: 9 "Then, Lord," **Simon** Peter replied, "not just my feet but my hands
　13:24 **Simon** Peter motioned to this disciple and said, "Ask him which
　13:26 the piece of bread, he gave it to Judas Iscariot, *son of* **Simon**.
　13:36 **Simon** Peter asked him, "Lord, where are you going?"
　18:10 Then **Simon** Peter, who had a sword, drew it and struck the high
　18:15 **Simon** Peter and another disciple were following Jesus.
　18:25 As **Simon** Peter stood warming himself, he was asked, "You are not
　20: 2 So she came running to **Simon** Peter and the other disciple,
　20: 6 Then **Simon** Peter, who was behind him, arrived and went into the
　21: 2 **Simon** Peter, Thomas (called Didymus), Nathanael from Cana in
　21: 3 to fish," **Simon** Peter told them, and they said, "We'll go with you."
　21: 7 As soon as **Simon** Peter heard him say, "It is the Lord," he wrapped
　21:11 **Simon** Peter climbed aboard and dragged the net ashore. It was full
　21:15 had finished eating, Jesus said *to* **Simon** Peter, "Simon son of John,
　21:15 finished eating, Jesus said to Simon Peter, "**Simon** son of John,
　21:16 Again Jesus said, "**Simon** son of John, do you truly love me?"
　21:17 third time he said to him, "**Simon** son of John, do you love me?"
Ac　1:13 James son of Alphaeus and **Simon** the Zealot, and Judas son of
　　8: 9 Now for some time a man named **Simon** had practiced sorcery in
　　8:13 **Simon** himself believed and was baptized. And he followed Philip
　　8:18 When **Simon** saw that the Spirit was given at the laying on of the
　　8:24 Then **Simon** answered, "Pray to the Lord for me so that nothing you
　　9:43 Peter stayed in Joppa for some time with a tanner named **Simon**.
　10: 5 Now send men to Joppa to bring back a man named **Simon** who is
　10: 6 He is staying with **Simon** the tanner, whose house is by the sea."
　10:17 the men sent by Cornelius found out where **Simon's** house was
　10:18 asking if **Simon** who was known as Peter was staying there.
　10:32 Send to Joppa for **Simon** who is called Peter. He is a guest in the
　10:32 He is a guest in the home *of* **Simon** the tanner, who lives by the
　11:13 in his house and say, 'Send to Joppa for **Simon** who is called Peter.

4982 Σινά, *Sina* [4]

Sinai [4]

Ac　7:30 in the flames of a burning bush in the desert *near* Mount **Sinai**.
　　7:38 with the angel who spoke to him on Mount **Sinai**, and with our
Gal　4:24 One covenant is from Mount **Sinai** and bears children who are to
　　4:25 Now Hagar stands for Mount **Sinai** in Arabia and corresponds to

4983 σίναπι, *sinapi* [5]

mustard [5]

Mt　13:31 "The kingdom of heaven is like a **mustard** seed, which a man took

　17:20 I tell you the truth, if you have faith as small as a **mustard** seed,
Mk　4:31 It is like a **mustard** seed, which is the smallest seed you plant in
Lk　13:19 It is like a **mustard** seed, which a man took and planted in his
　17: 6 He replied, "If you have faith as small as a **mustard** seed, you can

4984 σινδών, *sindōn* [6]

linen cloth [3], garment [1], linen garment [1], linen [1]

Mt　27:59 Joseph took the body, wrapped it in a clean **linen cloth**,
Mk　14:51 A young man, wearing nothing but a **linen garment**,
　14:52 he fled naked, leaving his **garment** behind.
　15:46 So Joseph bought *some* **linen cloth**, took down the body,
　15:46 some **linen cloth**, took down the body, wrapped it in the **linen**,
Lk　23:53 wrapped it *in* **linen cloth** and placed it in a tomb cut in the rock,

4985 σινιάζω, *siniazō* [1]

sift [1]

Lk　22:31 "Simon, Simon, Satan has asked *to* **sift** you as wheat.

4986 σιρικός, *sirikos* [1]

silk [1]

Rev　18:12 *of* gold, silver, precious stones and pearls; fine linen, purple, **silk**

4987 σιρός, *siros* [0 / 1] [→ *4938*]

dungeons [1]

2Pe　2: 4 putting them into gloomy **dungeons** [UBS *4937*] to be held for

4988 σιτευτός, *siteutos* [3] [√ *4992*]

fattened [3]

Lk　15:23 Bring the **fattened** calf and kill it. Let's have a feast and celebrate.
　15:27 'and your father has killed the **fattened** calf because he has him
　15:30 with prostitutes comes home, you kill the **fattened** calf for him!'

4989 σιτίον, *sition* [1] [√ *4992*]

grain [1]

Ac　7:12 When Jacob heard that there was **grain** in Egypt, he sent our

4990 σιτιστός, *sitistos* [1] [√ *4992*]

fattened cattle [1]

Mt　22: 4 My oxen and **fattened cattle** have been butchered, and everything

4991 σιτομέτριον, *sitometrion* [1] [√ *4992 + 3586*]

food allowance [1]

Lk　12:42 his servants to give them their **food allowance** at the proper time?

4992 σῖτος, *sitos* [14] [→ *826, 827, 2169, 4988, 4989,* *4990, 4991*]

wheat [11], grain [2], kernel [1]

Mt　3:12 gathering his **wheat** into the barn and burning up the chaff with
　13:25 his enemy came and sowed weeds among the **wheat**, and went
　13:29 you are pulling the weeds, you may root up the **wheat** with them.
　13:30 to be burned; then gather the **wheat** and bring it into my barn.' "
Mk　4:28 first the stalk, then the head, then the full **kernel** in the head.
Lk　3:17 to clear his threshing floor and to gather the **wheat** into his barn,
　12:18 bigger ones, and there I will store all my **grain** and my goods.
　16: 7 " 'A thousand bushels *of* **wheat**,' he replied. "He told him,
　22:31 "Simon, Simon, Satan has asked to sift you as **wheat**.
Jn　12:24 you the truth, unless a kernel *of* **wheat** falls to the ground and dies,
Ac　27:38 they lightened the ship by throwing the **grain** into the sea.
1Co　15:37 that will be, but just a seed, perhaps *of* **wheat** or of something else.
Rev　6: 6 saying, "A quart *of* **wheat** for a day's wages, and three quarts of
　18:13 and frankincense, of wine and olive oil, of fine flour and **wheat**;

4993 Σιχάρ, *Sichar*   Not used in UBS/NIV [√ *5373*]

4994 Σιών, *Siōn* [7]

Zion [7]

Mt 21: 5   "Say to the Daughter *of* **Zion**, 'See, your king comes to you,
Jn 12:15   "Do not be afraid, O Daughter *of* **Zion**; see, your king is coming,
Ro   9:33   I lay in **Zion** a stone that causes men to stumble and a rock that
     11:26   "The deliverer will come from **Zion**; he will turn godlessness away
Heb 12:22   But you have come to Mount **Zion**, to the heavenly Jerusalem,
1Pe 2: 6   "See, I lay a stone in **Zion**, a chosen and precious cornerstone,
Rev 14: 1   and there before me was the Lamb, standing on Mount **Zion**,

4995 σιωπάω, *siōpaō* [10] [→ *4996*]

quiet [5], silent [5]

Mt 20:31   The crowd rebuked them and told them to *be* **quiet**,
     26:63   But Jesus *remained* **silent**. The high priest said to him, "I charge
Mk   3: 4   or to do evil, to save life or to kill?" But they *remained* **silent**.
     4:39   He got up, rebuked the wind and said to the waves, "**Quiet!**
     9:34   But *they kept* **quiet** because on the way they had argued about
   10:48   Many rebuked him and told him to *be* **quiet**,
   14:61   But Jesus *remained* **silent** and gave no answer. Again the high
Lk   1:20   And now you will be **silent** and not able to speak until the day this
   19:40   "I tell you," he replied, "if they *keep* **quiet**, the stones will cry out."
Ac 18: 9   in a vision: "Do not be afraid; keep on speaking, *do* not *be* **silent**.

4996 σιωπῇ, *siōpē*   Not used in UBS/NIV [√ *4995*]

4997 σκανδαλίζω, *skandalizō* [29] [→ *4998*]

causes to sin [8], fall away [7], offend [2], took offense [2], cause to fall [1], cause to sin [1], causes fall into sin [1], causes sin [1], falls away [1], go astray [1], led into sin [1], offended [1], turn away from the faith [1], will[s] [1]

Mt   5:29   If your right eye **causes** you *to* **sin**, gouge it out and throw it away.
     5:30   And if your right hand **causes** you to **sin**, cut it off and throw it
   11: 6   Blessed is the man *who does* not **fall away** on account of me."
   13:21   or persecution comes because of the word, *he* quickly **falls away**.
   13:57   And they **took offense** at him. But Jesus said to them, "Only in his
   15:12   "Do you know that the Pharisees *were* **offended** when they heard
   17:27   "But so that *we may* not **offend** them, go to the lake and throw out
   18: 6   if anyone **causes** one of these little ones who believe in me **to sin**,
   18: 8   If your hand or your foot **causes** you **to sin**, cut it off and throw it
   18: 9   And if your eye **causes** you **to sin**, gouge it out and throw it away.
   24:10   At that time many *will* **turn away from the faith** and will betray
   26:31   "This very night you *will* all **fall away** on account of me, for it is
   26:33   Peter replied, "Even if all **fall away** on account of you, I never
   26:33   "Even if all fall away on account of you, I never **will[s]**."
Mk   4:17   or persecution comes because of the word, *they* quickly **fall away**.
    6: 3   Aren't his sisters here with us?" And *they* **took offense** at him.
    9:42   if anyone **causes** one of these little ones who believe in me **to sin**,
    9:43   If your hand **causes** you **to sin**, cut it off. It is better for you to
    9:45   And if your foot **causes** you **to sin**, cut it off. It is better for you to
    9:47   And if your eye **causes** you **to sin**, pluck it out. It is better for you
   14:27   "*You will* all **fall away**," Jesus told them, "for it is written: " 'I will
   14:29   Peter declared, "Even if all **fall away**, I will not."
Lk   7:23   Blessed is the man *who does* not **fall away** on account of me."
   17: 2   his neck than for him *to* **cause** one of these little ones to **sin**.
Jn   6:61   grumbling about this, Jesus said to them, "*Does* this **offend** you?
   16: 1   "All this I have told you so that *you will* not **go astray**.
1Co 8:13   Therefore, if what I eat **causes** my brother *to* **fall into sin**,
    8:13   I will never eat meat again, so that *I will* not **cause** him **to fall**.
2Co 11:29   do not feel weak? Who *is* **led into sin**, and I do not inwardly burn?

4998 σκάνδαλον, *skandalon* [15] [√ *4997*]

stumbling block [3], makes fall [2], causes sin [1], entice to sin [+*965+1967*] [1], make stumble [1], obstacle [1], obstacles [1], offense [1], such[s] things [+*3836*] [1], they[s] [+*3836*] [1], things that cause people to sin [1], things that cause to sin [1]

Mt 13:41   and they will weed out of his kingdom everything that **causes sin**
   16:23   You are a **stumbling block** to me; you do not have in mind the

---

   18: 7   "Woe to the world because of the **things that cause** people **to sin**!
   18: 7   of the things that cause people to sin! Such[s] [+*3836*] **things**
   18: 7   but woe to the man through whom **they[s]** [+*3836*] come!
Lk 17: 1   "**Things that cause people to sin** are bound to come, but woe to
Ro   9:33   stone that causes men to stumble and a rock *that* **makes** them **fall**,
   11: 9   a snare and a trap, a **stumbling block** and a retribution for them.
   14:13   not to put any stumbling block or **obstacle** in your brother's way.
   16:17   and put **obstacles** in your way that are contrary to the teaching you
1Co 1:23   a **stumbling block** to Jews and foolishness to Gentiles,
Gal 5:11   In that case the **offense** of the cross has been abolished.
1Pe 2: 8   stone that causes men to stumble and a rock *that* **makes** them **fall**."
1Jn 2:10   lives in the light, and there is nothing in him to **make** him **stumble**.
Rev 2:14   who taught Balak *to* **entice** the Israelites **to sin** [+*965+1967*] by

4999 σκάπτω, *skaptō* [3] [→ *2940, 5002*]

dig [2], dug [1]

Lk   6:48   a house, who **dug** down deep and laid the foundation on rock.
   13: 8   it alone for one more year, and *I'll* **dig** around it and fertilize it.
   16: 3   my job. I'm not strong enough *to* **dig**, and I'm ashamed to beg—

5000 Σκαριώθ, *Skariōth*   Not used in UBS/NIV [√ *2696*; cf. *4974* [?]]

5001 Σκαριώτης, *Skariōtēs*   Not used in UBS/NIV [√ *2696*; cf. *4974* [?]]

5002 σκάφη, *skaphē* [3] [√ *4999*]

lifeboat [3]

Ac 27:16   called Cauda, we were hardly able to make the **lifeboat** secure.
   27:30   escape from the ship, the sailors let the **lifeboat** down into the sea,
   27:32   So the soldiers cut the ropes that *held* the **lifeboat** and let it fall

5003 σκέλος, *skelos* [3]

legs [3]

Jn 19:31   they asked Pilate to have the **legs** broken and the bodies taken
   19:32   and broke the **legs** of the first man who had been crucified with
   19:33   and found that he was already dead, they did not break his **legs**.

5004 σκέπασμα, *skepasma* [1]

clothing [1]

1Ti 6: 8   But if we have food and **clothing**, we will be content with that.

5005 Σκευᾶς, *Skeuas* [1]

Sceva [1]

Ac 19:14   Seven sons *of* **Sceva**, a Jewish chief priest, were doing this.

5006 σκευή, *skeuē* [1] [√ *5007*]

tackle [1]

Ac 27:19   they threw the ship's **tackle** overboard with their own hands.

5007 σκεῦος, *skeuos* [23] [→ *412, 564, 683, 2171, 2941, 4186, 4187, 5006*]

articles [2], instrument [2], jar [2], objects [2], possessions [2], something [+*5516*] [1], *untranslated* [1], body [1], everything [+*3836+4246*] [1], goods [1], jars [1], merchandise [1], partner [1], pottery [+*3039*] [1], pottery [1], sea anchor [1], sheet [1]

Mt 12:29   and carry off his **possessions** unless he first ties up the strong man?
Mk   3:27   and carry off his **possessions** unless he first ties up the strong man.
   11:16   and would not allow anyone to carry **merchandise** through the
Lk   8:16   "No one lights a lamp and hides it *in* a **jar** or puts it under a bed.
   17:31   of his house, with his **goods** inside, should go down to get them.
Jn 19:29   A **jar** of wine vinegar was there,
Ac   9:15   This man is my chosen **instrument** to carry my name before the

10: 11　and **something** [+*5516*] like a large sheet being let down to earth
10: 16　three times, and immediately the **sheet** was taken back to heaven.
11:　5　I saw **something** [+*5516*] like a large sheet being let down from
27: 17　they lowered the **sea anchor** and let the ship be driven along.
Ro　9: 21　out of the same lump of clay some **pottery** for noble purposes
　　9: 22　power known, bore with great patience the **objects** of his wrath—
　　9: 23　to make the riches of his glory known to the **objects** of his mercy,
2Co　4:　7　But we have this treasure in **jars** of clay to show that this
1Th　4:　4　that each of you should learn to control his own **body** in a way that
2Ti　2: 20　In a large house there are **articles** not only of gold and silver,
　　2: 21　he will be an **instrument** for noble purposes, made holy, useful to
Heb　9: 21　tabernacle and **everything** [+*3836*+*4246*] used in its ceremonies.
1Pe　3:　7　and treat them with respect as the weaker **partner** and as heirs
Rev　2: 27　an iron scepter; he will dash them to pieces like **pottery'** [+*3039*]—
　　18: 12　and **articles** of every kind made of ivory, costly wood, bronze,
　　18: 12　kind made of ivory, **[RPG]** costly wood, bronze, iron and marble;

5008 σκηνή, *skēnē* [20] [→ *2172, 2942, 2943, 5009, 5010, 5011, 5012, 5013*]

tabernacle [9], shelters [3], room [2], dwelling place [1], dwelling [1], dwellings [1], shrine [1], tent [1], tents [1]

Mt　17:　4　If you wish, I will put up three **shelters**—one for you, one for
Mk　9:　5　Let us put up three **shelters**—one for you, one for Moses and one
Lk　9: 33　Let us put up three **shelters**—one for you, one for Moses and one
　　16:　9　that when it is gone, you will be welcomed into eternal **dwellings**.
Ac　7: 43　You have lifted up the **shrine** of Molech and the star of your god
　　7: 44　"Our forefathers had the **tabernacle** of the Testimony with them in
　　15: 16　" 'After this I will return and rebuild David's fallen **tent**. Its ruins I
Heb　8:　2　the sanctuary, the true **tabernacle** set up by the Lord, not by man.
　　8:　5　Moses was warned when he was about to build the **tabernacle**:
　　9:　2　A **tabernacle** was set up. In its first room were the lampstand,
　　9:　3　Behind the second curtain was a **room** called the Most Holy Place,
　　9:　6　the priests entered regularly into the outer **room** to carry on their
　　9:　8　been disclosed as long as the first **tabernacle** was still standing.
　　9: 11　been disclosed and more perfect **tabernacle** that is not man-made,
　　9: 21　he sprinkled with the blood both the **tabernacle** and everything
　　11:　9　he lived in **tents**, as did Isaac and Jacob, who were heirs with him
　　13: 10　We have an altar from which those who minister *at* the **tabernacle**
Rev　13:　6　and to slander his name and his **dwelling place** and those who live
　　15:　5　the temple, that is, the **tabernacle** of the Testimony, was opened.
　　21:　3　"Now the **dwelling** of God is with men, and he will live with them.

5009 σκηνοπηγία, *skēnopēgia* [1] [√ *5008 + 4381*]

Tabernacles [1]

Jn　7:　2　But when the Jewish Feast of **Tabernacles** was near,

5010 σκηνοποιός, *skēnopoios* [1] [√ *5008 + 4472*]

tentmaker [1]

Ac　18:　3　and because he was a **tentmaker** as they were, he stayed

5011 σκῆνος, *skēnos* [2] [√ *5008*]

tent [2]

2Co　5:　1　Now we know that if the earthly **tent** we live in is destroyed,
　　5:　4　For while we are in this **tent**, we groan and are burdened,

5012 σκηνόω, *skēnoō* [5] [√ *5008*]

live [2], dwell [1], made his dwelling [1], spread tent [1]

Jn　1: 14　The Word became flesh and **made his dwelling** among us.
Rev　7: 15　and he who sits on the throne *will* **spread** *his* **tent** over them.
　　12: 12　Therefore rejoice, you heavens and you *who* **dwell** in them!
　　13:　6　his name and his dwelling place and those *who* **live** in heaven.
　　21:　3　"Now the dwelling of God is with men, and *he will* **live** with them.

5013 σκήνωμα, *skēnōma* [3] [√ *5008*]

dwelling place [1], it^s [+*3836*] [1], tent [1]

Ac　7: 46　and asked that he might provide a **dwelling place** for the God of

2Pe　1: 13　to refresh your memory as long as I live in the **tent** of this body,
　　1: 14　because I know that I will soon put it^s [+*3836*] aside, as our Lord

5014 σκιά, *skia* [7] [→ *684, 2173, 2944*]

shadow [6], shade [1]

Mt　4: 16　on those living in the land of the **shadow** of death a light has
Mk　4: 32　such big branches that the birds of the air can perch in its **shade**."
Lk　1: 79　to shine on those living in darkness and in the **shadow** of death,
Ac　5: 15　so that at least Peter's **shadow** might fall on some of them as he
Col　2: 17　These are a **shadow** of the things that were to come; the reality,
Heb　8:　5　at a sanctuary that is a copy and **shadow** of what is in heaven.
　　10:　1　The law is *only* a **shadow** of the good things that are coming—

5015 σκιρτάω, *skirtaō* [3]

leaped [2], leap for joy [1]

Lk　1: 41　Elizabeth heard Mary's greeting, the baby **leaped** in her womb,
　　1: 44　greeting reached my ears, the baby in my womb **leaped** for joy.
　　6: 23　"Rejoice in that day and **leap for joy**,

5016 σκληροκαρδία, *sklērokardia* [3] [√ *5020 + 2840*]

hearts hard [2], stubborn [1]

Mt　19:　8　you to divorce your wives because your **hearts** were **hard**.
Mk　10:　5　because your **hearts** were **hard** that Moses wrote you this law,"
　　16: 14　and their **stubborn** refusal to believe those who had seen him after

5017 σκληρός, *sklēros* [5] [√ *5020*]

hard [3], harsh [1], strong [1]

Mt　25: 24　'Master,' he said, 'I knew that you are a **hard** man,
Jn　6: 60　On hearing it, many of his disciples said, "This is a **hard** teaching.
Ac　26: 14　do you persecute me? It is **hard** for you to kick against the goads.'
Jas　3:　4　Although they are so large and are driven by **strong** winds,
Jude　1: 15　and of all the **harsh** *words* ungodly sinners have spoken against

5018 σκληρότης, *sklērotēs* [1] [√ *5020*]

stubbornness [1]

Ro　2:　5　But because of your **stubbornness** and your unrepentant heart,

5019 σκληροτράχηλος, *sklērotrachēlos* [1] [√ *5020 + 5549*]

stiff-necked [1]

Ac　7: 51　"You **stiff-necked** *people*, with uncircumcised hearts and ears!

5020 σκληρύνω, *sklērynō* [6] [→ *5016, 5017, 5018, 5019*]

harden [3], hardened [1], hardens [1], obstinate [1]

Ac　19:　9　But some of them *became* **obstinate**; they refused to believe
Ro　9: 18　wants to have mercy, and *he* **hardens** whom he wants to harden.
Heb　3:　8　*do* not **harden** your hearts as you did in the rebellion,
　　3: 13　so that none of you *may be* **hardened** by sin's deceitfulness.
　　3: 15　his voice, *do* not **harden** your hearts as you did in the rebellion."
　　4:　7　"Today, if you hear his voice, *do* not **harden** your hearts."

5021 σκολιός, *skolios* [4]

crooked [2], corrupt [1], harsh [1]

Lk　3:　5　The **crooked** *roads* shall become straight, the rough ways smooth.
Ac　2: 40　pleaded with them, "Save yourselves from this **corrupt** generation."
Php　2: 15　children of God without fault in a **crooked** and depraved
1Pe　2: 18　who are good and considerate, but also *to* those who are **harsh**.

5022 σκόλοψ, *skolops* [1]

thorn [1]

2Co　12:　7　there was given me a **thorn** in my flesh, a messenger of Satan,

5023 σκοπέω, **skopeō** [6] [→ *258, 2170, 2174, 2175, 2176, 2945, 2946, 5024, 5297*]

fix eyes on [1], look to [1], see to it [1], take note of [1], watch out for [1], watch [1]

Lk   11:35   **See to it**, then, that the light within you is not darkness.
Ro   16:17   *to* **watch out for** those who cause divisions and put obstacles in
2Co   4:18   So *we* **fix** our **eyes** not **on** what is seen, but on what is unseen.
Gal   6: 1   him gently. But **watch** yourself, or you also may be tempted.
Php   2: 4   Each of you *should* **look** not only **to** your own interests, but also to
     3:17   and **take note of** those who live according to the pattern we gave

5024 σκοπός, **skopos** [1] [√ *5023*]

goal [1]

Php   3:14   I press on toward the **goal** to win the prize for which God has

5025 σκορπίζω, **skorpizō** [5] [→ *1399, 5026*]

scatters [3], scattered abroad [1], scattered [1]

Mt   12:30   me is against me, and he who does not gather with me **scatters**.
Lk   11:23   me is against me, and he who does not gather with me, **scatters**.
Jn   10:12   and runs away. Then the wolf attacks the flock and **scatters** it.
     16:32   "But a time is coming, and has come, when *you will be* **scattered**,
2Co   9: 9   "*He has* **scattered abroad** his gifts to the poor; his righteousness

5026 σκορπίος, **skorpios** [5] [√ *5025*]

scorpions [3], scorpion [2]

Lk   10:19   and **scorpions** and to overcome all the power of the enemy;
     11:12   Or if he asks for an egg, will give him a **scorpion**?
Rev   9: 3   the earth and were given power like that of **scorpions** of the earth.
     9: 5   was like that of the sting of *a* **scorpion** when it strikes a man.
     9:10   They had tails and stings like **scorpions**, and in their tails they had

5027 σκοτεινός, **skoteinos** [3] [√ *5030*]

full of darkness [2], dark [1]

Mt   6:23   But if your eyes are bad, your whole body will be **full of darkness**.
Lk   11:34   But when they are bad, your body also is **full of darkness**.
     11:36   is full of light, and no part of it **dark**, it will be completely lighted,

5028 σκοτία, **skotia** [16] [√ *5030*]

darkness [11], dark [5]

Mt   10:27   What I tell you in the **dark**, speak in the daylight; what is
Lk   12: 3   What you have said in the **dark** will be heard in the daylight,
Jn   1: 5   The light shines in the **darkness**, but the darkness has not
     1: 5   light shines in the darkness, but the **darkness** has not understood it.
     6:17   By now it was **dark**, and Jesus had not yet joined them.
     8:12   Whoever follows me will never walk in **darkness**, but will have
     12:35   Walk while you have the light, before **darkness** overtakes you.
     12:35   The man who walks in the **dark** does not know where he is going.
     12:46   so that no one who believes in me should stay in **darkness**.
     20: 1   Early on the first day of the week, while it was still **dark**,
1Jn   1: 5   and declare to you: God is light; in him there is no **darkness** at all.
     2: 8   because the **darkness** is passing and the true light is already
     2: 9   to be in the light but hates his brother is still in the **darkness**.
     2:11   But whoever hates his brother is in the **darkness** and walks around
     2:11   his brother is in the darkness and walks around in the **darkness**;
     2:11   know where he is going, because the **darkness** has blinded him.

5029 σκοτίζομαι, **skotizomai** [5] [√ *5030*]

darkened [4], turned dark [1]

Mt   24:29   after the distress of those days " 'the sun *will be* **darkened**,
Mk   13:24   in those days, following that distress, " 'the sun *will be* **darkened**,
Ro   1:21   thinking became futile and their foolish hearts *were* **darkened**.
     11:10   *May* their eyes *be* **darkened** so they cannot see, and their backs be
Rev   8:12   and a third of the stars, so that a third of them **turned dark**.

5030 σκότος, **skotos** [31] [→ *5027, 5028, 5029, 5031*]

darkness [29], dark [2]

Mt   4:16   the people living in **darkness** have seen a great light; on those
     6:23   If then the light within you is **darkness**, how great is that darkness!
     6:23   then the light within you is darkness, how great is that **darkness**!
     8:12   into the **darkness**, where there will be weeping and gnashing of
     22:13   'Tie him hand and foot, and throw him outside, into the **darkness**,
     25:30   into the **darkness**, where there will be weeping and gnashing of
     27:45   From the sixth hour until the ninth hour **darkness** came over all
Mk   15:33   At the sixth hour **darkness** came over the whole land until the
Lk   1:79   to shine on those living in **darkness** and in the shadow of death,
     11:35   See to it, then, that the light within you is not **darkness**.
     22:53   lay a hand on me. But this is your hour—when **darkness** reigns."
     23:44   and **darkness** came over the whole land until the ninth hour,
Jn   3:19   but men loved **darkness** instead of light because their deeds were
Ac   2:20   The sun will be turned to **darkness** and the moon to blood before
     13:11   Immediately mist and **darkness** came over him, and he groped
     26:18   to open their eyes and turn them from **darkness** to light, and from
Ro   2:19   you are a guide for the blind, a light for those who are in the **dark**,
     13:12   So let us put aside the deeds *of* **darkness** and put on the armor of
1Co   4: 5   He will bring to light what is hidden *in* **darkness** and will expose
2Co   4: 6   For God, who said, "Let light shine out of **darkness**," made his
     6:14   in common? Or what fellowship can light have with **darkness**?
Eph   5: 8   For you were once **darkness**, but now you are light in the Lord.
     5:11   Have nothing to do with the fruitless deeds *of* **darkness**, but rather
     6:12   against the powers of this **dark** world and against the spiritual
Col   1:13   For he has rescued us from the dominion *of* **darkness** and brought
1Th   5: 4   are not in **darkness** so that this day should surprise you like a thief.
     5: 5   sons of the day. We do not belong to the night or to the **darkness**.
1Pe   2: 9   of him who called you out of **darkness** into his wonderful light.
2Pe   2:17   mists driven by a storm. Blackest **darkness** is reserved for them.
1Jn   1: 6   If we claim to have fellowship with him yet walk in the **darkness**,
Jude   1:13   for whom blackest **darkness** has been reserved forever.

5031 σκοτόω, **skotoō** [3] [√ *5030*]

darkened [2], darkness [1]

Eph   4:18   They are **darkened** in their understanding and separated from the
Rev   9: 2   The sun and sky *were* **darkened** by the smoke from the Abyss.
     16:10   throne of the beast, and his kingdom was plunged into **darkness**.

5032 σκύβαλον, **skybalon** [1]

rubbish [1]

Php   3: 8   lost all things. I consider them **rubbish**, that I may gain Christ

5033 Σκύθης, **Skythēs** [1]

Scythian [1]

Col   3:11   barbarian, **Scythian**, slave or free, but Christ is all, and is in all.

5034 σκυθρωπός, **skythrōpos** [2] [√ *3972*]

downcast [1], look somber [+*1181*] [1]

Mt   6:16   "When you fast, *do* not **look somber** [+*1181*] as the hypocrites do,
Lk   24:17   together as you walk along?" They stood still, their *faces* **downcast**.

5035 σκύλλω, **skyllō** [4] [→ *5036*]

bother [2], harassed [1], trouble [1]

Mt   9:36   compassion on them, because they were **harassed** and helpless,
Mk   5:35   daughter is dead," they said. "Why **bother** the teacher any more?"
Lk   7: 6   "Lord, don't **trouble** *yourself*, for I do not deserve to have you
     8:49   "Your daughter is dead," he said. "Don't **bother** the teacher any

5036 σκῦλον, **skylon** [1] [√ *5035*]

spoils [1]

Lk   11:22   away the armor in which the man trusted and divides up the **spoils**.

5037 σκωληκόβρωτος, *skōlēkobrōtos* [1]

[√ *5038 + 1048*]

eaten by worms [1]

Ac 12:23 the Lord struck him down, and he was **eaten by worms** and died.

5038 σκώληξ, *skōlēx* [1] [→ *5037*]

worm [1]

Mk 9:48 where " 'their **worm** does not die, and the fire is not quenched.'

5039 σμαράγδινος, *smaragdinos* [1] [√ *5040*]

emerald [1]

Rev 4: 3 A rainbow, resembling an **emerald**, encircled the throne.

5040 σμάραγδος, *smaragdos* [1] [→ *5039*]

emerald [1]

Rev 21:19 the second sapphire, the third chalcedony, the fourth **emerald**,

5041 σμῆγμα, *smēgma* Not used in UBS/NIV

5042 σμίγμα, *smigma* Not used in UBS/NIV [√ *3502*]

5043 σμύρνα¹, *smyrna1* [2] [→ *2430, 5044, 5045, 5046*]

myrrh [2]

Mt 2:11 and presented him with gifts of gold and of incense and of **myrrh**.
Jn 19:39 Nicodemus brought a mixture *of* **myrrh** and aloes,

5044 Σμύρνα², *Smyrna2* [2] [√ *5043*]

Smyrna [2]

Rev 1:11 to Ephesus, **Smyrna**, Pergamum, Thyatira, Sardis, Philadelphia
2: 8 "To the angel of the church in **Smyrna** write: These are the words

5045 Σμυρναῖος, *Smyrnaios* Not used in UBS/NIV
[√ *5043*]

5046 σμυρνίζω, *smyrnizō* [1] [√ *5043*]

mixed with myrrh [1]

Mk 15:23 Then they offered him wine **mixed with myrrh**, but he did not

5047 Σόδομα, *Sodoma* [9]

Sodom [7], Sodom [*+1178*] [2]

Mt 10:15 it will be more bearable *for* **Sodom** [*+1178*] and Gomorrah on the
11:23 that were performed in you had been performed in **Sodom**,
11:24 But I tell you that it will be more bearable *for* **Sodom** [*+1178*] on
Lk 10:12 it will be more bearable on that day *for* **Sodom** than for that town.
17:29 But the day Lot left **Sodom**, fire and sulfur rained down from
Ro 9:29 we would have become like **Sodom**, we would have been like
2Pe 2: 6 if he condemned the cities *of* **Sodom** and Gomorrah by burning
Jude 1: 7 **Sodom** and Gomorrah and the surrounding towns gave themselves
Rev 11: 8 which is figuratively called **Sodom** and Egypt, where also their

5048 Σολομών, *Solomōn* [12] [→ *4898*]

Solomon [7], Solomon's [5]

Mt 1: 6 David was the father of **Solomon**, whose mother had been Uriah's
1: 7 **Solomon** the father of Rehoboam, Rehoboam the father of Abijah,
6:29 Yet I tell you that not even **Solomon** in all his splendor was
12:42 came from the ends of the earth to listen to **Solomon**'s wisdom,
12:42 to Solomon's wisdom, and now one greater than **Solomon** is here.
Lk 11:31 for she came from the ends of the earth to listen to **Solomon**'s
11:31 to Solomon's wisdom, and now one greater than **Solomon** is here.
12:27 not even **Solomon** in all his splendor was dressed like one of these.

Jn 10:23 and Jesus was in the temple area walking in **Solomon's** Colonnade.
Ac 3:11 and came running to them in the place called **Solomon's**
5:12 And all the believers used to meet together in **Solomon's**
7:47 But it was **Solomon** who built the house for him.

5049 σορός, *soros* [1]

coffin [1]

Lk 7:14 Then he went up and touched the **coffin**, and those carrying it

5050 σός, *sos* [27] [√ *5148*]

your [12], yours [6], *untranslated* [2], you [2], belongs to you [1], you have [*+3836*] [1], your family [*+3836*] [1], your own [1], yours [*+3836*] [1]

Mt 7: 3 brother's eye and pay no attention to the plank in **your own** eye?
7:22 to me on that day, 'Lord, Lord, did we not prophesy *in* **your** name,
7:22 *in* **your** name drive out demons and perform many miracles?'
7:22 and in your name drive out demons **[RPG]** and perform many
13:27 to him and said, 'Sir, didn't you sow good seed in **your** field?
20:14 Take **your** *pay* and go. I want to give the man who was hired last
24: 3 and what will be the sign *of* **your** coming and of the end of the
25:25 hid your talent in the ground. See, here is what belongs to **you**.'
Mk 2:18 and the disciples of the Pharisees are fasting, but **yours** are not?"
5:19 "Go home to **your** [*+3836*] **family** and tell them how much the
Lk 5:33 of the Pharisees, but **yours** [*+3836*] go on eating and drinking."
6:30 and if anyone takes what **belongs to you**, do not demand it back.
15:31 'you are always with me, and everything I have is **yours**.
22:42 take this cup from me; yet not my will, but **yours** be done."
Jn 4:42 to the woman, "We no longer believe just because of what **you** said;
17: 6 They were **yours**; you gave them to me and they have obeyed your
17: 9 for the world, but for those you have given me, for they are **yours**.
17:10 All I have is **yours**, and all you have is mine. And glory has come
17:10 All I have is yours, and all **you have** [*+3836*] is mine. And glory
17:17 Sanctify them by the truth; **your** word is truth.
18:35 "It was **your** people and your chief priests who handed you over to
Ac 5: 4 And after it was sold, wasn't the money at **your** disposal?
24: 2 and **your** foresight has brought about reforms in this nation.
24: 4 I would request that you be **[RPG]** kind enough to hear us briefly.
1Co 8:11 for whom Christ died, is destroyed by **your** knowledge.
14:16 those who do not understand say "Amen" to **your** thanksgiving,
Phm 1:14 But I did not want to do anything without **your** consent, so that any

5051 σουδάριον, *soudarion* [4]

burial cloth [1], cloth [1], handkerchiefs [1], piece of cloth [1]

Lk 19:20 here is your mina; I have kept it laid away in a **piece of cloth**.
Jn 11:44 and feet wrapped with strips of linen, and a **cloth** around his face.
20: 7 as well as the **burial cloth** that had been around Jesus' head.
Ac 19:12 so that even **handkerchiefs** and aprons that had touched him were

5052 Σουσάννα, *Sousanna* [1]

Susanna [1]

Lk 8: 3 the manager of Herod's household; **Susanna**; and many others.

5053 σοφία, *sophia* [51] [√ *5055*]

σοφία θεοῦ, (wisdom of God) [7] Lk 11:49; Ro 11:33; 1Co 1:21,24,30; 2:7; Eph 3:10

σοφία κοσμοῦ, (wisdom of the world) [3] 1Co 1:20,21; 3:19

wisdom [47], wise [2], human wisdom [1], superior wisdom [*+5667*] [1]

Mt 11:19 and "sinners." ' But **wisdom** is proved right by her actions."
12:42 came from the ends of the earth to listen to Solomon's **wisdom**,
13:54 "Where did this man get this **wisdom** and these miraculous
Mk 6: 2 "What's this **wisdom** that has been given him, that he even does
Lk 2:40 he was filled with **wisdom**, and the grace of God was upon him.
2:52 And Jesus grew *in* **wisdom** and stature, and in favor with God
7:35 But **wisdom** is proved right by all her children."
11:31 came from the ends of the earth to listen to Solomon's **wisdom**,
11:49 Because of this, God in his **wisdom** said, 'I will send them

	21:15	and **wisdom** that none of your adversaries will be able to resist
Ac	6: 3	among you who are known to be full of the Spirit and **wisdom**.
	6:10	but they could not stand up against his **wisdom** or the Spirit by
	7:10	He gave Joseph **wisdom** and enabled him to gain the goodwill of
	7:22	Moses was educated in all the **wisdom** of the Egyptians and was
Ro	11:33	the depth of the riches *of* the **wisdom** and knowledge of God!
1Co	1:17	not with words *of* **human wisdom**, lest the cross of Christ or
	1:19	"I will destroy the **wisdom** of the wise; the intelligence of the
	1:20	of this age? Has not God made foolish the **wisdom** of the world?
	1:21	For since in the **wisdom** of God the world through its wisdom did
	1:21	For since in the wisdom of God the world through its **wisdom** did
	1:22	Jews demand miraculous signs and Greeks look for **wisdom**,
	1:24	and Greeks, Christ the power of God and the **wisdom** of God.
	1:30	are in Christ Jesus, who has become for us **wisdom** from God—
	2: 1	I did not come with eloquence or **superior wisdom** [+*5667*] as I
	2: 4	My message and my preaching were not with **wise** and persuasive
	2: 5	so that your faith might not rest on men's **wisdom**, but on God's
	2: 6	We do, however, speak a message of **wisdom** among the mature,
	2: 6	but not the **wisdom** of this age or of the rulers of this age,
	2: 7	No, we speak of God's secret **wisdom**, a wisdom that has been
	2:13	not in words taught us *by* human **wisdom** but in words taught by
	3:19	For the **wisdom** of this world is foolishness in God's sight.
	12: 8	To one there is given through the Spirit the message *of* **wisdom**,
2Co	1:12	We have done so not according to worldly **wisdom** but according
Eph	1: 8	that he lavished on us with all **wisdom** and understanding.
	1:17	glorious Father, may give you the Spirit *of* **wisdom** and revelation,
	3:10	the manifold **wisdom** of God should be made known to the rulers
Col	1: 9	fill you with the knowledge of his will through all spiritual **wisdom**
	1:28	admonishing and teaching everyone with all **wisdom**,
	2: 3	in whom are hidden all the treasures *of* **wisdom** and knowledge.
	2:23	Such regulations indeed have an appearance *of* **wisdom**, with their
	3:16	richly as you teach and admonish one another with all **wisdom**,
	4: 5	Be **wise** in the way you act toward outsiders; make the most of
Jas	1: 5	If any of you lacks **wisdom**, he should ask God, who gives
	3:13	good life, by deeds done in the humility that *comes from* **wisdom**.
	3:15	Such "**wisdom**" does not come down from heaven but is earthly,
	3:17	But the **wisdom** that comes from heaven is first of all pure;
2Pe	3:15	just as our dear brother Paul also wrote you with the **wisdom** that
Rev	5:12	and wealth and **wisdom** and strength and honor and glory
	7:12	Praise and glory and **wisdom** and thanks and honor and power
	13:18	This calls for **wisdom**. If anyone has insight, let him calculate the
	17: 9	"This calls for a mind with **wisdom**. The seven heads are seven

5054 σοφίζω, *sophizō* [2] [√ *5055*]

cleverly invented [1], make wise [1]

2Ti	3:15	which are able *to* **make** you **wise** for salvation through faith in
2Pe	1:16	We did not follow **cleverly invented** stories when we told you

5055 σοφός, *sophos* [20] [→ *831, 2947, 5053, 5054, 5814, 5815*]

wise [18], expert [1], wiser [1]

Mt	11:25	because you have hidden these things from the **wise** and learned,
	23:34	Therefore I am sending you prophets and **wise** *men* and teachers.
Lk	10:21	because you have hidden these things from the **wise** and learned,
Ro	1:14	both to Greeks and non-Greeks, both *to* the **wise** and the foolish.
	1:22	Although they claimed to be **wise**, they became fools
	16:19	but I want you to be **wise** about what is good, and innocent about
	16:27	*to* the only **wise** God be glory forever through Jesus Christ!
1Co	1:19	"I will destroy the wisdom *of* the **wise**; the intelligence of the
	1:20	Where is the **wise** *man*? Where is the scholar? Where is the
	1:25	For the foolishness of God is **wiser** *than* man's wisdom,
	1:26	Not many of you were **wise** by human standards; not many were
	1:27	But God chose the foolish things of the world to shame the **wise**;
	3:10	grace God has given me, I laid a foundation as an **expert** builder,
	3:18	If any one of you thinks he is **wise** by the standards of this age,
	3:18	of this age, he should become a "fool" so that he may become **wise**.
	3:19	As it is written: "He catches the **wise** in their craftiness";
	3:20	again, "The Lord knows that the thoughts *of* the **wise** are futile."
	6: 5	Is it possible that there is nobody among you **wise** enough to judge
Eph	5:15	Be very careful, then, how you live—not as unwise but as **wise**,
Jas	3:13	Who is **wise** and understanding among you? Let him show it by his

5056 Σπανία, *Spania* [2]

Spain [2]

Ro	15:24	I plan to do so when I go to **Spain**. I hope to visit you while
	15:28	received this fruit, I will go to **Spain** and visit you on the way.

5057 σπαράσσω, *sparassō* [3] [√ *5060*]

convulsed [1], shook violently [1], throws into convulsions [1]

Mk	1:26	The evil spirit **shook** the man **violently** and came out of him with a
	9:26	The spirit shrieked, **convulsed** him violently and came out.
Lk	9:39	it **throws** him **into convulsions** so that he foams at the mouth.

5058 σπαργανόω, *sparganoō* [2]

wrapped in cloths [2]

Lk	2: 7	*She* **wrapped** him **in cloths** and placed him in a manger,
	2:12	You will find a baby **wrapped in cloths** and lying in a manger."

5059 σπαταλάω, *spatalaō* [2]

lived in self-indulgence [1], lives for pleasure [1]

1Ti	5: 6	But the widow *who* **lives for pleasure** is dead even while she
Jas	5: 5	You have **lived** on earth **in luxury** and **self-indulgence**.

5060 σπάω, *spaō* [2] [→ *413, 597, 685, 1400, 2177, 2341, 4352, 5057, 5360*]

drew [2]

Mk	14:47	Then one of those standing near **drew** his sword and struck the
Ac	16:27	*he* **drew** his sword and was about to kill himself because he

5061 σπεῖρα, *speira* [7]

company of soldiers [2], detachment of soldiers [2], regiment [2], Roman troops [1]

Mt	27:27	and gathered the whole **company of soldiers** around him.
Mk	15:16	and called together the whole **company of soldiers**.
Jn	18: 3	guiding a **detachment of soldiers** and some officials from the
	18:12	Then the **detachment of soldiers** with its commander
Ac	10: 1	a centurion in what was known as the Italian **Regiment**.
	21:31	news reached the commander *of* the **Roman troops** that the whole
	27: 1	centurion named Julius, *who belonged to* the Imperial **Regiment**.

5062 σπείρω, *speirō* [52] [→ *1401, 1402, 2178, 5065, 5066, 5076, 5077, 5078*]

sow [9], sown [9], sows [8], farmer [4], seed sown [4], received seed that fell [3], sower [3], plant [2], planted [2], scattering the seed [2], sow seed [2], sowed [2], scattering seed [1], sown seed [1]

Mt	6:26	*they do* not **sow** or reap or store away in barns, and yet your
	13: 3	things in parables, saying: "A **farmer** went out to sow his seed.
	13: 3	things in parables, saying: "A farmer went out *to* **sow** his **seed**.
	13: 4	As he *was* **scattering** the **seed**, some fell along the path,
	13:18	"Listen then to what the parable *of* the **sower** means:
	13:19	the evil one comes and snatches away what *was* **sown** in his heart.
	13:19	what was sown in his heart. This is the **seed sown** along the path.
	13:20	The one *who* **received** the **seed that fell** on rocky places is the
	13:22	The one *who* **received** the **seed that fell** among the thorns is the
	13:23	But the one *who* **received** the **seed that fell** on good soil is the
	13:24	"The kingdom of heaven is like a man *who* **sowed** good seed in his
	13:27	came to him and said, 'Sir, didn't *you* **sow** good seed in your field?
	13:31	is like a mustard seed, which a man took and **planted** in his field.
	13:37	"The one *who* **sowed** the good seed is the Son of Man.
	13:39	and the enemy who **sows** them is the devil. The harvest is the end
	25:24	harvesting where *you have* not **sown** and gathering where you
	25:26	So you knew that I harvest where *I have* not **sown** and gather
Mk	4: 3	"Listen! A **farmer** went out to sow his seed.
	4: 3	"Listen! A farmer went out *to* **sow** his seed.
	4: 4	As he *was* **scattering** the **seed**, some fell along the path,
	4:14	The **farmer** sows the word.

4:14 The farmer **sows** the word.
4:15 Some people are like seed along the path, where the word *is* **sown**.
4:15 Satan comes and takes away the word that *was* **sown** in them.
4:16 Others, like **seed sown** on rocky places, hear the word and at once
4:18 Still others, like **seed sown** among thorns, hear the word;
4:20 Others, like **seed sown** on good soil, hear the word, accept it,
4:31 a mustard seed, which is the smallest seed *you* **plant** in the ground.
4:32 Yet when **planted**, it grows and becomes the largest of all garden
Lk 8: 5 "A **farmer** went out to sow his seed. As he was scattering the seed,
8: 5 "A farmer went out *to* **sow** his seed. As he was scattering the seed,
8: 5 As he *was* **scattering the seed**, some fell along the path; it was
12:24 *They* do not **sow** or reap, they have no storeroom or barn;
19:21 take out what you did not put in and reap what *you did* not **sow**.'
19:22 taking out what I did not put in, and reaping what *I did* not **sow**?
Jn 4:36 eternal life, so that the **sower** and the reaper may be glad together.
4:37 Thus the saying 'One **sows** and another reaps' is true.
1Co 9:11 If we *have* **sown** spiritual seed among you, is it too much if we
15:36 How foolish! What you **sow** does not come to life unless it dies.
15:37 *When you* **sow**, you do not plant the body that will be, but just a
15:37 you sow, *you do* not **plant** the body that will be, but just a seed,
15:42 The body that *is* **sown** is perishable, it is raised imperishable;
15:43 *it is* **sown** in dishonor, it is raised in glory; it is sown in weakness,
15:43 it is raised in glory; *it is* **sown** in weakness, it is raised in power;
15:44 *it is* **sown** a natural body, it is raised a spiritual body. If there is a
2Co 9: 6 Whoever **sows** sparingly will also reap sparingly, and whoever
9: 6 and whoever **sows** generously will also reap generously.
9:10 Now he who supplies seed *to* the **sower** and bread for food will
Gal 6: 7 be deceived: God cannot be mocked. A man reaps what *he* **sows**.
6: 8 The one *who* **sows** to please his sinful nature, from that nature will
6: 8 the one *who* **sows** to please the Spirit, from the Spirit will reap
Jas 3:18 Peacemakers *who* **sow** in peace raise a harvest of righteousness.

5063 σπεκουλάτωρ, *spekoulatōr* [1]

executioner [1]

Mk 6:27 So he immediately sent an **executioner** with orders to bring John's

5064 σπένδω, *spendō* [2] [→ *836*]

poured out like a drink offering [2]

Php 2:17 But even if *I am being* **poured out like a drink offering** on the
2Ti 4: 6 For I *am* already *being* **poured out like a drink offering**,

5065 σπέρμα, *sperma* [43] [√ *5062*]

σπέρμα 'Ααβραάμ, (seed of Abraham) [11] Lk 1:55; Jn
8:33,37; Ac 3:25; Ro 4:13,16; 9:7; 11:1; 2Co 11:22; Gal 3:16; Heb
2:16

σπέρμα Δαυίδ, (seed of David) [3] Jn 7:42; Ro 1:3; 2Ti 2:8

seed [11], descendants [10], offspring [8], children [3],
descendant [2], have children [+*1985*] [2], seeds [2], become a
father [+*2856+3284*] [1], child [1], descended from [+*1666*] [1],
family [1], have children [+*482*] [1]

Mt 13:24 "The kingdom of heaven is like a man who sowed good **seed** in his
13:27 came to him and said, 'Sir, didn't you sow good **seed** in your field?
13:32 Though it is the smallest of all your **seeds**, yet when it grows,
13:37 "The one who sowed the good **seed** is the Son of Man.
13:38 is the world, and the good **seed** stands for the sons of the kingdom.
22:24 brother must marry the widow and **have children** [+*482*] for him.
22:25 The first one married and died, and since he had no **children**,
Mk 4:31 a mustard seed, which is the smallest **seed** you plant in the ground.
12:19 must marry the widow and **have children** [+*1985*] for his brother.
12:20 The first one married and died without leaving any **children**.
12:21 second one married the widow, but he also died, leaving no **child**.
12:22 In fact, none of the seven left any **children**. Last of all, the woman
Lk 1:55 *to* Abraham and his **descendants** forever, even as he said to our
20:28 must marry the widow and **have children** [+*1985*] for his brother.
Jn 7:42 not the Scripture say that the Christ will come from David's **family**
8:33 "We are Abraham's **descendants** and have never been slaves of
8:37 I know you are Abraham's **descendants**. Yet you are ready to kill
Ac 3:25 'Through your **offspring** all peoples on earth will be blessed.'
7: 5 him that he and his **descendants** after him would possess the land,
7: 6 'Your **descendants** will be strangers in a country not their own,

13:23 "From this man's **descendants** God has brought to Israel the Savior
Ro 1: 3 his Son, who as to his human nature was a **descendant** of David,
4:13 and his **offspring** received the promise that he would be heir of the
4:16 be by grace and may be guaranteed *to* all Abraham's **offspring**—
4:18 just as it had been said to him, "So shall your **offspring** be."
9: 7 because they are his **descendants** are they all Abraham's children.
9: 7 "It is through Isaac that your **offspring** will be reckoned."
9: 8 children of the promise who are regarded as Abraham's **offspring**.
9:29 "Unless the Lord Almighty had left us **descendants**, we would have
11: 1 I am an Israelite myself, a **descendant** of Abraham, from the tribe
1Co 15:38 he has determined, and to each kind *of* seed he gives its own body.
2Co 11:22 So am I. Are they Abraham's **descendants**? So am I.
Gal 3:16 The promises were spoken to Abraham and *to* his **seed**.
3:16 The Scripture does not say "and *to* **seeds**," meaning many people,
3:16 but "and *to* your **seed**," meaning one person, who is Christ.
3:19 because of transgressions until the **Seed** to whom the promise
3:29 If you belong to Christ, then you are Abraham's **seed**, and heirs
2Ti 2: 8 raised from the dead, descended [+*1666*] **from** David.
Heb 2:16 For surely it is not angels he helps, but Abraham's **descendants**.
11:11 was enabled to **become a father** [+*2856+3284*] because he
11:18 to him, "It is through Isaac that your **offspring** will be reckoned."
1Jn 3: 9 of God will continue to sin, because God's **seed** remains in him;
Rev 12:17 and went off to make war against the rest *of* her **offspring**—

5066 σπερμολόγος, *spermologos* [1] [√ *5062 + 3306*]

babbler [1]

Ac 17:18 Some of them asked, "What is this **babbler** trying to say?" Others

5067 σπεύδω, *speudō* [6] [→ *5079, 5080, 5081, 5082*]

at once [1], hurried off [+*2262*] [1], immediately [1], in a hurry [1],
quick [1], speed [1]

Lk 2:16 So *they* **hurried** [+*2262*] **off** and found Mary and Joseph,
19: 5 looked up and said to him, "Zacchaeus, come down **immediately**,
19: 6 So he came down **at once** and welcomed him gladly.
Ac 20:16 for *he was* **in a hurry** to reach Jerusalem, if possible, by the day of
22:18 and saw the Lord speaking. '**Quick**!' he said to me. 'Leave
2Pe 3:12 as you look forward to the day of God and **speed** its coming.

5068 σπήλαιον, *spēlaion* [6]

den [3], caves [2], cave [1]

Mt 21:13 called a house of prayer,' but you are making it a '**den** of robbers.' "
Mk 11:17 prayer for all nations'? But you have made it 'a **den** of robbers.' "
Lk 19:46 be a house of prayer'; but you have made it 'a **den** of robbers.' "
Jn 11:38 to the tomb. It was a **cave** with a stone laid across the entrance.
Heb 11:38 in deserts and mountains, and *in* **caves** and holes in the ground.
Rev 6:15 and every slave and every free man hid in **caves** and among the

5069 σπιλάς, *spilas* [1] [√ *5070*]

blemishes [1]

Jude 1:12 These men are **blemishes** at your love feasts, eating with you

5070 σπίλος, *spilos* [2] [→ *834, 5069, 5071*]

blots [1], stain [1]

Eph 5:27 without **stain** or wrinkle or any other blemish, but holy
2Pe 2:13 They are **blots** and blemishes, reveling in their pleasures while

5071 σπιλόω, *spiloō* [2] [√ *5070*]

corrupts [1], stained [1]

Jas 3: 6 It **corrupts** the whole person, sets the whole course of his life on
Jude 1:23 with fear—hating even the clothing **stained** by corrupted flesh.

5072 σπλαγχνίζομαι, *splanchnizomai* [12]
[√ *5073*]

had compassion [4], have compassion [2], took pity [2], filled with compassion for [1], filled with compassion [1], heart went out [1], take pity [1]

Mt   9:36 When he saw the crowds, *he* **had compassion** on them,
       14:14 a large crowd, *he* **had compassion** on them and healed their sick.
       15:32 disciples to him and said, "*I* **have compassion** for these people;
       18:27 The servant's master **took pity** *on* him, canceled the debt
       20:34 Jesus **had compassion** *on* them and touched their eyes.
Mk   1:41 **Filled with compassion**, Jesus reached out his hand and touched
       6:34 Jesus landed and saw a large crowd, *he* **had compassion** on them,
       8: 2 "*I* **have compassion** for these people; they have already been with
       9:22 kill him. But if you can do anything, **take pity** on us and help us."
Lk   7:13 Lord saw her, *his* **heart went out** to her and he said, "Don't cry."
      10:33 where the man was; and when he saw him, *he* **took pity** *on* him.
      15:20 his father saw him and *was* **filled with compassion for** him;

5073 σπλάγχνον, *splanchnon* [11] [→ *2359, 4492, 4499, 5072*]

affection [3], dearly [1], has no pity [+*3091+3836*] [1], heart [1], hearts [1], intestines [1], tender mercy [+*1799*] [1], tenderness [1], very heart [1]

Lk   1:78 because of the **tender mercy** [+*1799*] of our God, by which the
Ac   1:18 fell headlong, his body burst open and all his **intestines** spilled out.
2Co 6:12 We are not withholding our **affection** from you, but you are
      7:15 And his **affection** for you is all the greater when he remembers that
Php 1: 8 God can testify how I long for all of you with the **affection** of
      2: 1 any fellowship with the Spirit, if any **tenderness** and compassion,
Col   3:12 Therefore, as God's chosen people, holy and **dearly** loved,
Phm 1: 7 because you, brother, have refreshed the **hearts** of the saints.
      1:12 I am sending him—who is my **very heart**—back to you.
      1:20 some benefit from you in the Lord; refresh my **heart** in Christ.
1Jn 3:17 and sees his brother in need but **has no pity** [+*3091+3836*] on him,

5074 σπόγγος, *spongos* [3]

sponge [3]

Mt 27:48 Immediately one of them ran and got a **sponge**. He filled it with
Mk 15:36 One man ran, filled a **sponge** with wine vinegar, put it on a stick,
Jn 19:29 A jar of wine vinegar was there, so they soaked a **sponge** in it,

5075 σποδός, *spodos* [3]

ashes [3]

Mt 11:21 they would have repented long ago in sackcloth and **ashes**.
Lk 10:13 they would have repented long ago, sitting in sackcloth and **ashes**.
Heb 9:13 and the **ashes** of a heifer sprinkled on those who are ceremonially

5076 σπορά, *spora* [1] [√ *5062*]

seed [1]

1Pe 1:23 not of perishable **seed**, but of imperishable, through the living

5077 σπόριμος, *sporimos* [3] [√ *5062*]

grainfields [3]

Mt 12: 1 At that time Jesus went through the **grainfields** on the Sabbath.
Mk 2:23 One Sabbath Jesus was going through the **grainfields**, and as his
Lk 6: 1 One Sabbath Jesus was going through the **grainfields**, and his

5078 σπόρος, *sporos* [6] [√ *5062*]

seed [5], store of seed [1]

Mk 4:26 the kingdom of God is like. A man scatters **seed** on the ground.
      4:27 and day, whether he sleeps or gets up, the **seed** sprouts and grows,
Lk 8: 5 "A farmer went out to sow his **seed**. As he was scattering the seed,
      8:11 "This is the meaning of the parable: The **seed** is the word of God.
2Co 9:10 Now he who supplies **seed** to the sower and bread for food will
      9:10 and bread for food will also supply and increase your **store of seed**

5079 σπουδάζω, *spoudazō* [11] [√ *5067*]

do best [4], make every effort [4], eager [2], made effort [1]

Gal 2:10 continue to remember the poor, the very thing *I was* **eager** to do.
Eph 4: 3 **Make every effort** to keep the unity of the Spirit through the bond
1Th 2:17 out of our intense longing *we* **made** every **effort** to see you.
2Ti 2:15 **Do** *your* **best** to present yourself to God as one approved,
      4: 9 **Do** *your* **best** to come to me quickly,
      4:21 **Do** *your* **best** to get here before winter. Eubulus greets you,
Tit   3:12 or Tychicus to you, **do** *your* **best** to come to me at Nicopolis,
Heb 4:11 *Let us*, therefore, **make every effort** to enter that rest, so that no
2Pe 1:10 *be* all the more **eager** to make your calling and election sure.
      1:15 And *I will* **make every effort** *to see that* after my departure you
      3:14 since *you* are looking forward to this, **make every effort** to be

5080 σπουδαῖος, *spoudaios* [3] [√ *5067*]

enthusiasm [1], even more so[s] [+*4498*] [1], zealous [1]

2Co 8:17 but he is coming to you with *much* **enthusiasm** and on his own
      8:22 who has often proved to us in many ways that he is **zealous**,
      8:22 and now **even more so**[s] [+*4498*] because of his great confidence

5081 σπουδαίως, *spoudaiōs* [4] [√ *5067*]

all the more eager [1], earnestly [1], everything you can [1], hard [1]

Lk 7: 4 When they came to Jesus, they pleaded **earnestly** with him,
Php 2:28 Therefore I am **all the more eager** to send him, so that when you
2Ti 1:17 when he was in Rome, he searched **hard** for me until he found me.
Tit   3:13 *Do* **everything you can** to help Zenas the lawyer and Apollos on

5082 σπουδή, *spoudē* [12] [√ *5067*]

earnestness [3], concern [1], devoted [1], diligence [1], diligently [+*1877*] [1], eager [1], effort [1], hurried [+*3552+4513*] [1], hurried [+*3552*] [1], zeal [1]

Mk 6:25 At once the girl **hurried** [+*3552*] in to the king with the request:
Lk 1:39 and **hurried** [+*3552+4513*] to a town in the hill country of Judea,
Ro 12: 8 if it is leadership, let him govern **diligently** [+*1877*]; if it is
      12:11 Never be lacking *in* **zeal**, but keep your spiritual fervor,
2Co 7:11 what **earnestness**, what eagerness to clear yourselves,
      7:12 God you could see for yourselves how **devoted** to us you *are*.
      8: 7 in knowledge, *in* complete **earnestness** and in your love for us—
      8: 8 of your love by comparing it with the **earnestness** of others.
      8:16 who put into the heart of Titus the same **concern** I have for you.
Heb 6:11 We want each of you to show this same **diligence** to the very end,
2Pe 1: 5 this very reason, make every **effort** to add to your faith goodness;
Jude 1: 3 although I was very **eager** to write to you about the salvation we

5083 σπυρίς, *spyris* [5]

basketfuls [2], basket [1], basketfuls [+*4441*] [1], basketfuls [+*4445*] [1]

Mt 15:37 Afterward the disciples picked up seven **basketfuls** [+*4441*] of
      16:10 for the four thousand, and how many **basketfuls** you gathered?
Mk 8: 8 Afterward the disciples picked up seven **basketfuls** of broken
      8:20 how many **basketfuls** [+*4445*] of pieces did you pick up?"
Ac 9:25 and lowered him in a **basket** through an opening in the wall.

5084 στάδιον, *stadion* [7] [√ *2705*]

stadia [2], distance [1], less than two miles [+*608+1278+6055*] [1], race [1], seven miles [+*2008*] [1], three or three and a half miles [+*1633+2445+4297+5558*] [1]

Mt 14:24 but the boat was already a considerable **distance** from land,
Lk 24:13 called Emmaus, about **seven miles** [+*2008*] from Jerusalem.
Jn 6:19 rowed **three or three and a half miles** [+*1633+2445+4297+5558*]
      11:18 Bethany was **less than two miles** [+*608+1278+6055*] from Jerusalem,
1Co 9:24 Do you not know that in a **race** all the runners run, but only one
Rev 14:20 rising as high as the horses' bridles for a distance of 1,600 **stadia**.
      21:16 the city with the rod and found it to be 12,000 **stadia** in length,

5085 στάμνος, *stamnos* [1] [√ 2705]

jar [1]

Heb 9: 4 This ark contained the gold **jar** of manna, Aaron's staff that had

5086 στασιαστής, *stasiastēs* [1] [√ 2705]

insurrectionists [1]

Mk 15: 7 A man called Barabbas was in prison with the **insurrectionists**

5087 στάσις, *stasis* [9] [√ 2705]

dispute [3], insurrection [2], rioting [1], riots [1], standing [1], uprising [1]

Mk 15: 7 the insurrectionists who had committed murder in the **uprising**.
Lk 23:19 (Barabbas had been thrown into prison for an **insurrection** in the
23:25 the man who had been thrown into prison for **insurrection**
Ac 15: 2 This brought Paul and Barnabas into sharp **dispute** and debate with
19:40 we are in danger of being charged with **rioting** because of today's
23: 7 a **dispute** broke out between the Pharisees and the Sadducees,
23:10 The **dispute** became so violent that the commander was afraid Paul
24: 5 stirring up **riots** among the Jews all over the world.
Heb 9: 8 yet been disclosed as long as the first tabernacle was still **standing**.

5088 στατήρ, *statēr* [1] [√ 2705]

four-drachma coin [1]

Mt 17:27 you catch; open its mouth and you will find a **four-drachma coin**.

5089 σταυρός, *stauros* [27] [→ 416, 5090, 5365; cf. 2705]

cross [26], crosses [1]

Mt 10:38 and anyone who does not take his **cross** and follow me is not
16:24 he must deny himself and take up his **cross** and follow me.
27:32 named Simon, and they forced him to carry the **cross**.
27:40 Come down from the **cross**, if you are the Son of God!"
27:42 Let him come down now from the **cross**, and we will believe in
Mk 8:34 he must deny himself and take up his **cross** and follow me.
15:21 way in from the country, and they forced him to carry the **cross**.
15:30 come down from the **cross** and save yourself!"
15:32 come down now from the **cross**, that we may see and believe."
Lk 9:23 he must deny himself and take up his **cross** daily and follow me.
14:27 And anyone who does not carry his **cross** and follow me cannot be
23:26 and put the **cross** on him and made him carry it behind Jesus.
Jn 19:17 Carrying his own **cross**, he went out to the place of the Skull
19:19 Pilate had a notice prepared and fastened to the **cross**. It read:
19:25 Near the **cross** of Jesus stood his mother, his mother's sister,
19:31 Because the Jews did not want the bodies left on the **crosses** during
1Co 1:17 of human wisdom, lest the **cross** of Christ be emptied of its power.
1:18 For the message *of* the **cross** is foolishness to those who are
Gal 5:11 In that case the offense *of* the **cross** has been abolished.
6:12 they do this to avoid being persecuted *for* the **cross** of Christ.
6:14 May I never boast except in the **cross** of our Lord Jesus Christ,
Eph 2:16 this one body to reconcile both of them to God through the **cross**,
Php 2: 8 and became obedient to death—even death *on* a **cross**!
3:18 again even with tears, many live as enemies *of* the **cross** of Christ.
Col 1:20 in heaven, by making peace through his blood, *shed on* the **cross**.
2:14 that stood opposed to us; he took it away, nailing it *to* the **cross**.
Heb 12: 2 who for the joy set before him endured the **cross**, scorning its

5090 σταυρόω, *stauroō* [46] [√ 5089]

crucified [31], crucify [15]

Mt 20:19 him over to the Gentiles to *be* mocked and flogged and **crucified**
23:34 Some of them *you will* kill and **crucify**; others you will flog in
26: 2 and the Son of Man will be handed over to *be* **crucified**."
27:22 is called Christ?" Pilate asked. They all answered, "**Crucify** *him*!"
27:23 asked Pilate. But they shouted all the louder, "**Crucify** *him*!"
27:26 But he had Jesus flogged, and handed him over to *be* **crucified**.
27:31 his own clothes on him. Then they led him away to **crucify** him.
27:35 *When they had* **crucified** him, they divided up his clothes by
27:38 Two robbers *were* **crucified** with him, one on his right and one on
28: 5 for I know that you are looking for Jesus, who *was* **crucified**.

Mk 15:13 "**Crucify** him!" they shouted.
15:14 asked Pilate. But they shouted all the louder, "**Crucify** him!"
15:15 He had Jesus flogged, and handed him over to *be* **crucified**.
15:20 put his own clothes on him. Then they led him out to **crucify** him.
15:24 And *they* **crucified** him. Dividing up his clothes, they cast lots to
15:25 It was the third hour when *they* **crucified** him.
15:27 *They* **crucified** two robbers with him, one on his right and one on
16: 6 "You are looking for Jesus the Nazarene, who *was* **crucified**.
Lk 23:21 But they kept shouting, "**Crucify** him! Crucify him!"
23:21 But they kept shouting, "Crucify him! **Crucify** him!"
23:23 with loud shouts they insistently demanded that he *be* **crucified**,
23:33 the Skull, there *they* **crucified** him, along with the criminals—
24: 7 of sinful men, *be* **crucified** and on the third day be raised again.' "
24:20 handed him over to be sentenced to death, and *they* **crucified** him;
Jn 19: 6 chief priests and their officials saw him, they shouted, "**Crucify**!
19: 6 and their officials saw him, they shouted, "Crucify! **Crucify**!"
19: 6 Crucify!" But Pilate answered, "You take him and **crucify** him.
19:10 you realize I have power either to free you or *to* **crucify** you?"
19:15 But they shouted, "Take him away! Take him away! **Crucify** him!"
19:15 him away! Crucify him!" "*Shall I* **crucify** your king?" Pilate asked.
19:16 Finally Pilate handed him over to them to *be* **crucified**.
19:18 Here *they* **crucified** him, and with him two others—one on each
19:20 for the place where Jesus *was* **crucified** was near the city,
19:23 When the soldiers **crucified** Jesus, they took his clothes, dividing
19:41 At the place where Jesus *was* **crucified**, there was a garden,
Ac 2:36 has made this Jesus, whom you **crucified**, both Lord and Christ."
4:10 whom you **crucified** but whom God raised from the dead,
1Co 1:13 Is Christ divided? *Was* Paul **crucified** for you? Were you baptized
1:23 but we preach Christ **crucified**: a stumbling block to Jews
2: 2 while I was with you except Jesus Christ and him **crucified**.
2: 8 for if they had, *they* would not have **crucified** the Lord of glory.
2Co 13: 4 For to be sure, *he was* **crucified** in weakness, yet he lives by God's
Gal 3: 1 your very eyes Jesus Christ was clearly portrayed as **crucified**.
5:24 Those who belong to Christ Jesus *have* **crucified** the sinful nature
6:14 Jesus Christ, through which the world *has been* **crucified** to me,
Rev 11: 8 called Sodom and Egypt, where also their Lord *was* **crucified**.

5091 σταφυλή, *staphylē* [3]

grapes [3]

Mt 7:16 Do people pick **grapes** from thornbushes, or figs from thistles?
Lk 6:44 People do not pick figs from thornbushes, or **grapes** from briers.
Rev 14:18 of grapes from the earth's vine, because its **grapes** are ripe."

5092 στάχυς¹, *stachys¹* [5] [→ 5093]

heads of grain [3], head [2]

Mt 12: 1 were hungry and began to pick *some* **heads of grain** and eat them.
Mk 2:23 disciples walked along, they began to pick some **heads of grain**.
4:28 first the stalk, then the **head**, then the full kernel in the head.
4:28 first the stalk, then the head, then the full kernel in the **head**.
Lk 6: 1 and his disciples began to pick some **heads of grain**, rub them in

5093 Στάχυς², *Stachys²* [1] [√ 5092]

Stachys [1]

Ro 16: 9 our fellow worker in Christ, and my dear friend **Stachys**.

5094 στέγη, *stegē* [3] [√ 5095]

roof [3]

Mt 8: 8 "Lord, I do not deserve to have you come under my **roof**.
Mk 2: 4 of the crowd, they made an opening in the **roof** above Jesus and,
Lk 7: 6 for I do not deserve to have you come under my **roof**.

5095 στέγω, *stegō* [4] [→ 689, 5094, 5566]

stand [2], protects [1], put up with [1]

1Co 9:12 *we* **put up with** anything rather than hinder the gospel of Christ.
13: 7 *It* always **protects**, always trusts, always hopes, always perseveres.
1Th 3: 1 So *when we could* **stand** it no longer, we thought it best to be left
3: 5 For this reason, *when I could* **stand** it no longer, I sent to find out

5096 στεῖρα, steira [5] [√ *5104*]

barren [3], barren woman [1], barren women [1]

Lk   1: 7   But they had no children, because Elizabeth was **barren**; and they
    1:36   old age, and she who was said to be **barren** is in her sixth month.
   23:29   'Blessed are the **barren women**, the wombs that never bore
Gal   4:27   "Be glad, *O* **barren woman**, who bears no children; break forth
Heb 11:11   even though he was past age—and Sarah herself was **barren**—

5097 στέλλω, stellō [2] [→ *690, 1403, 1405, 2186, 2948,
2950, 5124, 5366, 5713, 5714*]

avoid [1], keep away [1]

2Co   8:20   *We want to* **avoid** any criticism of the way we administer this
2Th   3: 6   *to* **keep away** from every brother who is idle and does not live

5098 στέμμα, stemma [1] [√ *5110*]

wreaths [1]

Ac   14:13   brought bulls and **wreaths** to the city gates because he

5099 στεναγμός, stenagmos [2] [√ *5101*]

groaning [1], groans [1]

Ac   7:34   I have heard their **groaning** and have come down to set them free.
Ro   8:26   but the Spirit himself intercedes for us *with* **groans** that words

5100 στενάζω, stenazō [6] [√ *5101*]

groan [3], burden [1], grumble [1], with a deep sigh [1]

Mk   7:34   He looked up to heaven and **with a deep sigh** said to him,
Ro   8:23   **groan** inwardly as we wait eagerly for our adoption as sons,
2Co   5: 2   Meanwhile *we* **groan**, longing to be clothed with our heavenly
    5: 4   For while we are in this tent, *we* **groan** and are burdened,
Heb 13:17   Obey them so that their work will be a joy, not a **burden**,
Jas   5: 9   Don't **grumble** against each other, brothers, or you will be judged.

5101 στενός, stenos [3] [→ *417, 5099, 5100, 5102, 5103,
5367*]

narrow [2], small [1]

Mt   7:13   "Enter through the **narrow** gate. For wide is the gate and broad is
    7:14   But **small** is the gate and narrow the road that leads to life,
Lk   13:24   "Make every effort to enter through the **narrow** door,

5102 στενοχωρέω, stenochōreō [3] [√ *5101 + 6003*]

withholding [2], crushed [1]

2Co   4: 8   We are hard pressed on every side, but not **crushed**; perplexed,
    6:12   We *are* not **withholding** our affection *from you*, but you are
    6:12   our affection from you, but *you are* **withholding** yours *from* us.

5103 στενοχωρία, stenochōria [4] [√ *5101 + 6003*]

difficulties [1], distress [1], distresses [1], hardship [1]

Ro   2: 9   will be trouble and **distress** for every human being who does evil;
    8:35   Shall trouble or **hardship** or persecution or famine or nakedness
2Co   6: 4   in great endurance; in troubles, hardships and **distresses**;
   12:10   in insults, in hardships, in persecutions, *in* **difficulties**.

5104 στερεός, stereos [4] [→ *5096, 5105, 5106*]

solid [3], standing firm [1]

2Ti   2:19   Nevertheless, God's **solid** foundation stands firm, sealed with this
Heb   5:12   truths of God's word all over again. You need milk, not **solid** food!
    5:14   But **solid** food is for the mature, who by constant use have trained
1Pe   5: 9   Resist him, **standing firm** in the faith, because you know that your

5105 στερεόω, stereoō [3] [√ *5104*]

made strong [1], strengthened [1], strong [1]

Ac   3: 7   him up, and instantly the man's feet and ankles *became* **strong**.
    3:16   of Jesus, this man whom you see and know *was* **made strong**.
   16: 5   So the churches *were* **strengthened** in the faith and grew daily in

5106 στερέωμα, stereōma [1] [√ *5104*]

firm [1]

Col   2: 5   to see how orderly you are and how **firm** your faith in Christ is.

5107 Στεφανᾶς, Stephanas [3] [√ *5110*]

Stephanas [3]

1Co   1:16   (Yes, I also baptized the household *of* **Stephanas**; beyond that,
   16:15   You know that the household *of* **Stephanas** were the first converts
   16:17   I was glad when **Stephanas**, Fortunatus and Achaicus arrived,

5108 Στέφανος¹, Stephanos¹ [7] [√ *5110*]

Stephen [6], him$ [+*3836*] [1]

Ac   6: 5   They chose **Stephen**, a man full of faith and of the Holy Spirit;
    6: 8   Now **Stephen**, a man full of God's grace and power, did great
    6: 9   of Cilicia and Asia. These men began to argue with **Stephen**,
    7:59   While they were stoning **him**$ [+*3836*], Stephen prayed, "Lord
    8: 2   Godly men buried **Stephen** and mourned deeply for him.
   11:19   in connection with **Stephen** traveled as far as Phoenicia,
   22:20   And when the blood of your martyr **Stephen** was shed, I stood

5109 στέφανος², stephanos² [18] [√ *5110*]

crown [15], crowns [3]

Mt   27:29   and then twisted together a **crown** of thorns and set it on his head.
Mk   15:17   then twisted together a **crown** of thorns and set it on him.
Jn   19: 2   The soldiers twisted together a **crown** of thorns and put it on his
   19: 5   When Jesus came out wearing the **crown** of thorns and the purple
1Co   9:25   They do it to get a **crown** that will not last; but we do it to get a
Php   4: 1   my brothers, you whom I love and long for, my joy and **crown**,
1Th   2:19   or the **crown** in which we will glory in the presence of our Lord
2Ti   4: 8   Now there is in store for me the **crown** of righteousness,
Jas   1:12   he will receive the **crown** of life that God has promised to those
1Pe   5: 4   you will receive the **crown** of glory that will never fade away.
Rev   2:10   even to the point of death, and I will give you the **crown** of life.
    3:11   Hold on to what you have, so that no one will take your **crown**.
    4: 4   They were dressed in white and had **crowns** of gold on their heads.
    4:10   and ever. They lay their **crowns** before the throne and say,
    6: 2   Its rider held a bow, and he was given a **crown**, and he rode out as
    9: 7   On their heads they wore something like **crowns** of gold, and their
   12: 1   the moon under her feet and a **crown** of twelve stars on her head.
   14:14   and seated on the cloud was one "like a son of man" with a **crown**

5110 στεφανόω, stephanoō [3] [→ *5098, 5107, 5108,
5109*]

crowned [2], receive the victor's crown [1]

2Ti   2: 5   he does not **receive the victor's crown** unless he competes
Heb   2: 7   lower than the angels; *you* **crowned** him with glory and honor
    2: 9   now **crowned** with glory and honor because he suffered death,

5111 στῆθος, stēthos [5]

against [+*2093+3836*] [2], breast [1], breasts [1], chests [1]

Lk   18:13   but beat his **breast** and said, 'God, have mercy on me, a sinner.'
   23:48   sight saw what took place, they beat their **breasts** and went away.
Jn   13:25   Leaning back **against** [+*2093+3836*] Jesus, he asked him,
   21:20   (This was the one who had leaned back **against** [+*2093+3836*]
Rev   15: 6   shining linen and wore golden sashes around their **chests**.

5112 στήκω, stēkō [9] [√ 2705]

stand firm [5], stand [1], standing firm [1], standing [1], stands [1]

Mk	3:31	**Standing** outside, they sent someone in to call him.
	11:25	And when you **stand** praying, if you hold anything against anyone,
Ro	14: 4	To his own master he **stands** or falls. And he will stand,
1Co	16:13	Be on your guard; **stand firm** in the faith; be men of courage;
Gal	5: 1	**Stand firm**, then, and do not let yourselves be burdened again by a
Php	1:27	you in my absence, I will know that you **stand firm** in one spirit,
	4: 1	and crown, that is how you should **stand firm** in the Lord,
1Th	3: 8	For now we really live, since you are **standing firm** in the Lord.
2Th	2:15	**stand firm** and hold to the teachings we passed on to you,

5113 στηριγμός, stērigmos [1] [√ 5114]

secure position [1]

2Pe	3:17	by the error of lawless men and fall from your **secure position**.

5114 στηρίζω, stērizō [13] [→ 844, 2185, 5113]

strengthen [6], establish [1], firmly established [1], fixed [1], make firm [1], make strong [1], resolutely [+3836+4725] [1], stand firm [+2840+3836] [1]

Lk	9:51	Jesus **resolutely** [+3836+4725] set out for Jerusalem.
	16:26	besides all this, between us and you a great chasm has been **fixed**,
	22:32	And when you have turned back, **strengthen** your brothers."
Ro	1:11	that I may impart to you some spiritual gift to **make** you **strong**—
	16:25	Now to him who is able to **establish** you by my gospel
1Th	3: 2	gospel of Christ, to **strengthen** and encourage you in your faith,
	3:13	May he **strengthen** your hearts so that you will be blameless
2Th	2:17	your hearts and **strengthen** you in every good deed and word.
	3: 3	and he will **strengthen** and protect you from the evil one.
Jas	5: 8	You too, be patient and **stand** [+2840+3836] **firm**,
1Pe	5:10	will himself restore you and **make** you strong, **firm** and steadfast.
2Pe	1:12	know them and are **firmly established** in the truth you now have.
Rev	3: 2	**Strengthen** what remains and is about to die, for I have not found

5115 στιβάς, stibas [1]

branches [1]

Mk	11: 8	the road, while others spread **branches** they had cut in the fields.

5116 στίγμα, stigma [1] [→ 5117]

marks [1]

Gal	6:17	one cause me trouble, for I bear on my body the **marks** of Jesus.

5117 στιγμή, stigmē [1] [√ 5116]

instant [+5989] [1]

Lk	4: 5	and showed him in an **instant** [+5989] all the kingdoms of the

5118 στίλβω, stilbō [1]

dazzling [+3336] [1]

Mk	9: 3	His clothes became **dazzling** [+3336] white, whiter than anyone in

5119 στοά, stoa [4] [→ 5121, 5147; cf. 2705]

colonnade [3], covered colonnades [1]

Jn	5: 2	and which is surrounded by five **covered colonnades**.
	10:23	Jesus was in the temple area walking in Solomon's **Colonnade**.
Ac	3:11	came running to them in the place called Solomon's **Colonnade**.
	5:12	all the believers used to meet together in Solomon's **Colonnade**.

5120 στοιβάς, stoibas Not used in UBS/NIV

5121 Στοϊκός, Stoikos [1] [√ 5119]

Stoic [1]

Ac	17:18	A group of Epicurean and **Stoic** philosophers began to dispute with

5122 στοιχεῖον, stoicheion [7] [√ 5123]

basic principles [3], elements [2], elementary truths [+794+3836] [1], principles [1]

Gal	4: 3	we were in slavery under the **basic principles** of the world.
	4: 9	that you are turning back to those weak and miserable **principles**?
Col	2: 8	and the **basic principles** of this world rather than on Christ.
	2:20	Since you died with Christ to the **basic principles** of this world,
Heb	5:12	the **elementary** [+794+3836] **truths** of God's word all over again.
2Pe	3:10	the **elements** will be destroyed by fire, and the earth
	3:12	of the heavens by fire, and the **elements** will melt in the heat.

5123 στοιχέω, stoicheō [5] [→ 5122, 5368]

follow [1], keep in step [1], live up [1], living [1], walk [1]

Ac	21:24	about you, but that you yourself are **living** in obedience to the law.
Ro	4:12	but who also **walk** in the footsteps of the faith that our father
Gal	5:25	Since we live by the Spirit, let us **keep in step** with the Spirit.
	6:16	Peace and mercy to all who **follow** this rule, even to the Israel of
Php	3:16	Only let us **live up** to what we have already attained.

5124 στολή, stolē [9] [√ 5097]

robes [4], robe [3], flowing robes [2]

Mk	12:38	They like to walk around in **flowing robes** and be greeted in the
	16: 5	they saw a young man dressed in a white **robe** sitting on the right
Lk	15:22	said to his servants, 'Quick! Bring the best **robe** and put it on him.
	20:46	They like to walk around in **flowing robes** and love to be greeted
Rev	6:11	Then each of them was given a white **robe**, and they were told to
	7: 9	They were wearing white **robes** and were holding palm branches
	7:13	Then one of the elders asked me, "These in white **robes**—who are
	7:14	they have washed their **robes** and made them white in the blood of
	22:14	"Blessed are those who wash their **robes**, that they may have the

5125 στόμα, stoma [78] [→ 694, 1492, 2187, 5126]

ἀνοίγω τὸ στόμα, (to open the mouth) [11] Mt 5:2; 13:35; 17:27; Lk 1:64; Ac 8:32,35; 10:34; 18:14; 2Co 6:11; Rev 12:16; 13:6

διὰ στόματος, (by/through the mouth of) [6] Mt 4:4; Lk 1:70; Ac 1:16; 3:18,21; 15:7

mouth [42], mouths [9], lips [6], face [4], through [+1328] [3], testimony [2], words [2], untranslated [1], began to speak [+487+3306+3836] [1], began to teach [+487+1438+3836] [1], edge [1], say [+1666+3836] [1], speak [+487+3836] [1], spoken freely [+487+3836] [1], sword [+3479] [1], thats [1], theys [+899+3836] [1]

Mt	4: 4	but on every word that comes from the **mouth** of God.' "
	5: 2	and he **began to teach** [+487+1438+3836] them, saying:
	12:34	For out of the overflow of the heart the **mouth** speaks.
	13:35	"I will open my **mouth** in parables, I will utter things hidden since
	15:11	What goes into a man's **mouth** does not make him 'unclean,'
	15:11	but what comes out of his **mouth**, that is what makes him
	15:17	"Don't you see that whatever enters the **mouth** goes into the
	15:18	But the things that come out of the **mouth** come from the heart,
	17:27	you catch; open its **mouth** and you will find a four-drachma coin.
	18:16	so that 'every matter may be established by the **testimony** of two
	21:16	" 'From the **lips** of children and infants you have ordained praise'?"
Lk	1:64	Immediately his **mouth** was opened and his tongue was loosed,
	1:70	(as he said **through** [+1328] his holy prophets of long ago),
	4:22	and were amazed at the gracious words that came from his **lips**.
	6:45	in his heart. For out of the overflow of his heart his **mouth** speaks.
	11:54	waiting to catch him in something he might **say** [+1666+3836]
	19:22	"His master replied, 'I will judge you by your own **words**,
	21:15	For I will give you **words** and wisdom that none of your
	21:24	They will fall by the **sword** [+3479] and will be taken as prisoners
	22:71	we need any more **testimony**? We have heard it from his own **lips**."

Jn 19:29 the sponge on a stalk of the hyssop plant, and lifted it *to* Jesus' **lips**.
Ac 1:16 spoke long ago through the **mouth** of David concerning Judas,
3:18 fulfilled what he had foretold **through** [+*1328*] all the prophets,
3:21 as he promised long ago **through** [+*1328*] his holy prophets.
4:25 You spoke by the Holy Spirit *through* the **mouth** of your servant,
8:32 a lamb before the shearer is silent, so he did not open his **mouth**.
8:35 Then **[RPG]** Philip began with that very passage of Scripture
10:34 Then Peter **began to speak** [+*487+3306+3836*]: "I now realize
11:8 Lord! Nothing impure or unclean has ever entered my **mouth**.'
15:7 the Gentiles might hear from my **lips** the message of the gospel
18:14 Just as Paul was about to **speak** [+*487+3836*], Gallio said to the
22:14 and to see the Righteous One and to hear words from his **mouth**.
23:2 ordered those standing near Paul to strike him *on* the **mouth**.
Ro 3:14 "Their **mouths** are full of cursing and bitterness."
3:19 so that every **mouth** may be silenced and the whole world held
10:8 it is in your **mouth** and in your heart," that is, the word of faith we
10:9 That if you confess with your **mouth**, "Jesus is Lord," and believe
10:10 and it is *with* your **mouth** that you confess and are saved.
15:6 so that with one heart and **mouth** you may glorify the God
2Co 6:11 We **have spoken freely** [+*487+3836*] to you, Corinthians,
13:1 "Every matter must be established by the **testimony** of two
Eph 4:29 Do not let any unwholesome talk come out of your **mouths**,
6:19 Pray also for me, that whenever I open my **mouth**, words may be
Col 3:8 anger, rage, malice, slander, and filthy language from your **lips**.
2Th 2:8 whom the Lord Jesus will overthrow with the breath *of* his **mouth**
2Ti 4:17 Gentiles might hear it. And I was delivered from the lion's **mouth**.
Heb 11:33 and gained what was promised; who shut the **mouths** of lions,
11:34 the fury of the flames, and escaped the **edge** of the sword;
Jas 3:3 When we put bits into the **mouths** of horses to make them obey us,
3:10 Out of the same **mouth** come praise and cursing. My brothers,
1Pe 2:22 "He committed no sin, and no deceit was found in his **mouth**."
2Jn 1:12 Instead, I hope to visit you and talk with you **face** to face,
1:12 Instead, I hope to visit you and talk with you face to **face**,
3Jn 1:14 I hope to see you soon, and we will talk **face** to face. Peace to you.
1:14 I hope to see you soon, and we will talk face to **face**. Peace to you.
Jude 1:16 they follow their own evil desires; they^s [+*899+3836*] boast about
Rev 1:16 and out of his **mouth** came a sharp double-edged sword.
2:16 to you and will fight against them with the sword *of* my **mouth**.
3:16 neither hot nor cold—I am about to spit you out of my **mouth**.
9:17 of lions, and out of their **mouths** came fire, smoke and sulfur.
9:18 plagues of fire, smoke and sulfur that came out of their **mouths**.
9:19 The power of the horses was in their **mouths** and in their tails;
10:9 your stomach sour, but in your **mouth** it will be as sweet as honey."
10:10 It tasted as sweet as honey in my **mouth**, but when I had eaten it,
11:5 fire comes from their **mouths** and devours their enemies.
12:15 Then from his **mouth** the serpent spewed water like a river,
12:16 But the earth helped the woman by opening its **mouth**
12:16 swallowing the river that the dragon had spewed out of his **mouth**.
13:2 but had feet like those of a bear and a **mouth** like that of a lion.
13:2 but had feet like those of a bear and a mouth like that^s of a lion.
13:5 The beast was given a **mouth** to utter proud words
13:6 He opened his **mouth** to blaspheme God, and to slander his name
14:5 No lie was found in their **mouths**; they are blameless.
16:13 they came out of the **mouth** of the dragon, out of the mouth of the
16:13 out of the **mouth** of the beast and out of the mouth of the false
16:13 of the mouth of the beast and out of the **mouth** of the false prophet.
19:15 Out of his **mouth** comes a sharp sword with which to strike down
19:21 the sword that came out of the **mouth** of the rider on the horse,

5126 στόμαχος, *stomachos* [1] [√ *5125*]

stomach [1]

1Ti 5:23 and use a little wine because of your **stomach** and your frequent

5127 στρατεία, *strateia* [2] [√ *5131*]

fight [1], weapons fight with [+*3836+3960*] [1]

2Co 10:4 The **weapons** we **fight with** [+*3836+3960*] are not the weapons of
1Ti 1:18 about you, so that by following them you may fight the good **fight**,

5128 στράτευμα, *strateuma* [8] [√ *5131*]

troops [3], armies [2], army [2], soldiers [1]

Mt 22:7 He sent his **army** and destroyed those murderers and burned their

Lk 23:11 Then Herod and his **soldiers** ridiculed and mocked him.
Ac 23:10 He ordered the **troops** to go down and take him away from them
23:27 about to kill him, but I came with my **troops** and rescued him,
Rev 9:16 The number *of* the mounted **troops** was two hundred million.
19:14 The **armies** of heaven were following him, riding on white horses
19:19 and their **armies** gathered together to make war against the rider on
19:19 together to make war against the rider on the horse and his **army**.

5129 στρατεύομαι, *strateuomai* [7] [√ *5131*]

battle [1], fight [1], serves as a soldier [1], serving as a soldier [1], soldiers [1], wage war [1], war [1]

Lk 3:14 Then *some* **soldiers** asked him, "And what should we do?" He
1Co 9:7 Who **serves as a soldier** at his own expense? Who plants a
2Co 10:3 we live in the world, *we do* not **wage war** as the world does.
1Ti 1:18 about you, so that by following them *you may* **fight** the good fight,
2Ti 2:4 No one **serving as a soldier** gets involved in civilian affairs—
Jas 4:1 Don't they come from your desires that **battle** within you?
1Pe 2:11 to abstain from sinful desires, which **war** against your soul.

5130 στρατηγός, *stratēgos* [10] [√ *5131 + 72*]

magistrates [5], captain [3], officers of guard [1], officers of the temple guard [1]

Lk 22:4 went *to* the chief priests and the **officers of the temple guard**
22:52 the **officers of** the temple **guard**, and the elders, who had come for
Ac 4:1 The priests and the **captain** of the temple guard and the Sadducees
5:24 the **captain** of the temple guard and the chief priests were puzzled,
5:26 the **captain** went with his officers and brought the apostles.
16:20 They brought them before the **magistrates** and said, "These men
16:22 and the **magistrates** ordered them to be stripped and beaten.
16:35 the **magistrates** sent their officers to the jailer with the order:
16:36 "The **magistrates** have ordered that you and Silas be released.
16:38 The officers reported this *to* the **magistrates**, and when they heard

5131 στρατιά, *stralia* [2] [→ *529, 5127, 5128, 5129, 5130, 5132, 5133, 5134, 5135, 5136, 5369*]

bodies [1], host [1]

Lk 2:13 Suddenly a great company *of* the heavenly **host** appeared with the
Ac 7:42 and gave them over to the worship *of* the heavenly **bodies**.

5132 στρατιώτης, *stratiōtēs* [26] [√ *5131*]

soldiers [22], soldier [3], them^s [1]

Mt 8:9 For I myself am a man under authority, with **soldiers** under me.
27:27 Then the governor's **soldiers** took Jesus into the Praetorium
28:12 and devised a plan, they gave the **soldiers** a large sum of money,
Mk 15:16 The **soldiers** led Jesus away into the palace (that is,
Lk 7:8 For I myself am a man under authority, with **soldiers** under me.
23:36 The **soldiers** also came up and mocked him. They offered him
Jn 19:2 The **soldiers** twisted together a crown of thorns and put it on his
19:23 When the soldiers crucified Jesus, they took his clothes, dividing
19:23 his clothes, dividing them into four shares, one for each of **them**^{s}
19:24 and cast lots for my clothing." So this is what the **soldiers** did.
19:32 The **soldiers** therefore came and broke the legs of the first man
19:34 Instead, one *of* the **soldiers** pierced Jesus' side with a spear,
Ac 10:7 of his servants and a devout **soldier** who was one of his attendants.
12:4 handing him over to be guarded by four squads of four **soldiers**
12:6 Peter was sleeping between two **soldiers**, bound with two chains,
12:18 there was no small commotion among the **soldiers** as to what had
21:32 at once took some officers and **soldiers** and ran down to the crowd.
21:32 When the rioters saw the commander and his **soldiers**,
21:35 of the mob was so great he had to be carried by the **soldiers**.
23:23 "Get ready a *detachment of* two hundred **soldiers**, seventy
23:31 So the **soldiers**, carrying out their orders, took Paul with them
27:31 Then Paul said *to* the centurion and the **soldiers**, "Unless these men
27:32 So the **soldiers** cut the ropes that held the lifeboat and let it fall
27:42 The **soldiers** planned to kill the prisoners to prevent any of them
28:16 Paul was allowed to live by himself, with a **soldier** to guard him.
2Ti 2:3 Endure hardship with us like a good **soldier** of Christ Jesus.

5133 στρατολογέω, *stratologeō* [1] [√ 5131 + 3306]

commanding officer [1]

2Ti 2: 4 in civilian affairs—he wants to please his **commanding officer**.

5134 στρατοπεδάρχης, *stratopedarchēs* Not used in UBS/NIV [√ 5131 + 4269 + 806]

5135 στρατοπέδαρχος, *stratopedarchos* Not used in UBS/NIV [√ 5131 + 4269 + 806]

5136 στρατόπεδον, *stratopedon* [1] [√ 5131 + 4269]

armies [1]

Lk 21:20 "When you see Jerusalem being surrounded by **armies**, you will

5137 στρεβλόω, *strebloō* [1] [√ 5138]

distort [1]

2Pe 3:16 which ignorant and unstable people **distort**, as they do the other

5138 στρέφω, *strephō* [21] [→ 418, 419, 695, 1406, 1750, 2188, 2189, 2951, 2953, 3570, 5137, 5266, 5370, 5371, 5715]

turned [7], turn [5], turning [2], change [1], returned [1], turned around [+1650+3836+3958] [1], turned away [1], turned back [1], turned toward [1], turning around [1]

Mt 5:39 someone strikes you on the right cheek, **turn** to him the other also.
7: 6 trample them under their feet, and then **turn** and tear you to pieces.
9:22 Jesus **turned** and saw her. "Take heart, daughter," he said, "your
16:23 Jesus **turned** and said to Peter, "Get behind me, Satan! You are a
18: 3 you the truth, unless *you* **change** and become like little children,
27: 3 he was seized with remorse and **returned** the thirty silver coins to
Lk 7: 9 and **turning** to the crowd following him, he said, "I tell you,
7:44 Then he **turned** toward the woman and said to Simon, "Do you see
9:55 But Jesus **turned** and rebuked them,
10:23 Then he **turned** to his disciples and said privately, "Blessed are the
14:25 crowds were traveling with Jesus, and **turning** to them he said:
22:61 The Lord **turned** and looked straight at Peter. Then Peter
23:28 Jesus **turned** and said to them, "Daughters of Jerusalem, do not
Jn 1:38 **Turning around**, Jesus saw them following and asked, "What do
12:40 see with their eyes, nor understand with their hearts, nor **turn**—
20:14 At this, *she* **turned** [+1650+3836+3958] **around** and saw Jesus
20:16 She **turned toward** him and cried out in Aramaic, "Rabboni!"
Ac 7:39 they rejected him and in their hearts **turned back** to Egypt.
7:42 But God **turned away** and gave them over to the worship of the
13:46 yourselves worthy of eternal life, *we* now **turn** to the Gentiles.
Rev 11: 6 and they have power *to* **turn** the waters into blood and to strike the

5139 στρηνιάω, *strēniaō* [2] [√ 5140]

luxury gave [1], shared luxury [1]

Rev 18: 7 as much torture and grief as the glory and **luxury** she gave herself.
18: 9 with her and **shared** her **luxury** see the smoke of her burning,

5140 στρῆνος, *strēnos* [1] [→ 2952, 5139]

luxuries [1]

Rev 18: 3 the merchants of the earth grew rich from her excessive **luxuries**."

5141 στρουθίον, *strouthion* [4]

sparrows [4]

Mt 10:29 Are not two **sparrows** sold for a penny? Yet not one of them will
10:31 So don't be afraid; you are worth more than many **sparrows**.
Lk 12: 6 Are not five **sparrows** sold for two pennies? Yet not one of them is
12: 7 Don't be afraid; you are worth more than many **sparrows**.

5142 στρώννυμι, *strōnnymi* Not used in UBS/NIV [√ 5143]

5143 στρωννύω, *strōnnyō* [6] [→ 2954, 3346, 5142, 5716]

spread [3], furnished [2], take care of mat [+4932] [1]

Mt 21: 8 A very large crowd **spread** their cloaks on the road, while others
21: 8 others cut branches from the trees and **spread** them on the road.
Mk 11: 8 Many people **spread** their cloaks on the road, while others spread
14:15 He will show you a large upper room, **furnished** and ready.
Lk 22:12 He will show you a large upper room, all **furnished**.
Ac 9:34 Christ heals you. Get up and **take** [+4932] **care of** *your* **mat**."

5144 στυγητός, *stygētos* [1] [→ 696, 2539, 5145]

hated [1]

Tit 3: 3 We lived in malice and envy, being **hated** and hating one another.

5145 στυγνάζω, *stygnazō* [2] [√ 5144]

face fell [1], overcast [1]

Mt 16: 3 'Today it will be stormy, for the sky is red and **overcast**.'
Mk 10:22 At this the man's **face fell**. He went away sad, because he had great

5146 στῦλος, *stylos* [4]

pillar [2], pillars [2]

Gal 2: 9 those reputed to be **pillars**, gave me and Barnabas the right hand of
1Ti 3:15 the church of the living God, the **pillar** and foundation of the truth.
Rev 3:12 Him who overcomes I will make a **pillar** in the temple of my God.
10: 1 his face was like the sun, and his legs were like fiery **pillars**.

5147 Στωϊκός, *Stōikos* Not used in UBS/NIV [√ 5119]

5148 σύ, *sy* [2905 / 2900] See Index of Articles, Etc. [→ 4932, 5050, 5629]

you [1990], your [705], *untranslated* [130], yours [14], yourselves [12], your own [8], yes it is as you say [+3306] [4], home [+3875] [3], you [+2840+3836] [3], home [+1650+3836+3875] [2], listen carefully [+1650+3836+4044+5148+5502] [2], please [+1289] [2], please [+2263] [2], you [+3836+3950] [2], you [+3836+4725] [2], you [+3836+6034] [2], your own [+2848] [2], yourself [2], and even more [+2779+4707] [1], both of you [+899+2779] [1], does [+1877+3531] [1], the two of you [+899+2779] [1], them [+3517+3836] [1], yes [+3306] [1], you [+6034] [1], you can see [+595] [1], you're [1], your [+2848] [1], your hearts [1], yourselves [+2840+3836] [1], yourselves [+6034] [1]

5149 συγγένεια, *syngeneia* [3] [√ 5250 + 1181]

family [1], people [1], relatives [1]

Lk 1:61 "There is no one among your **relatives** who has that name."
Ac 7: 3 'Leave your country and your **people**,' God said,
7:14 After this, Joseph sent for his father Jacob and his whole **family**,

5150 συγγενής, *syngenēs* [11] [√ 5250 + 1181]

relatives [8], relative [2], race [+2848+4922] [1]

Mk 6: 4 among his **relatives** and in his own house is a prophet without
Lk 1:58 and **relatives** heard that the Lord had shown her great mercy,
2:44 Then they began looking for him among their **relatives**
14:12 or dinner, do not invite your friends, your brothers or **relatives**,
21:16 will be betrayed even by parents, brothers, **relatives** and friends,
Jn 18:26 a **relative** of the man whose ear Peter had cut off, challenged him,
Ac 10:24 and had called together his **relatives** and close friends.
Ro 9: 3 for the sake of my brothers, those *of* my own **race** [+2848+4922],
16: 7 and Junias, my **relatives** who have been in prison with me.
16:11 Greet Herodion, my **relative**. Greet those in the household of
16:21 greetings to you, as do Lucius, Jason and Sosipater, my **relatives**.

5151 συγγενίς, *syngenis* [1] [√ *5250 + 1181*]

relative [1]

Lk   1:36 Even Elizabeth your **relative** is going to have a child in her old

5152 συγγνώμη, *syngnōmē* [1] [√ *5250 + 1182*]

concession [1]

1Co 7: 6 I say this as a **concession**, not as a command.

5153 συγκάθημαι, *synkathēmai* [2] [√ *5250 + 2757*]

sat [+*1639*] [1], sitting with [1]

Mk 14:54 There he **sat** [+*1639*] with the guards and warmed himself at the
Ac 26:30 with him the governor and Bernice and those **sitting with** them.

5154 συγκαθίζω, *synkathizō* [2] [√ *5250 + 2767*]

sat down together [1], seated with [1]

Lk 22:55 a fire in the middle of the courtyard and *had* **sat down together**,
Eph 2: 6 and **seated** us **with** him in the heavenly realms in Christ Jesus,

5155 συγκακοπαθέω, *synkakopatheō* [2]
     [√ *5250 + 2805 + 4248*]

endure hardship with [1], join in suffering [1]

2Ti 1: 8 But **join** *with* me **in suffering** for the gospel, by the power of God,
     2: 3 **Endure hardship with** us like a good soldier of Christ Jesus.

5156 συγκακουχέομαι, *synkakoucheomai* [1]
     [√ *5250 + 2805 + 2400*]

mistreated along with [1]

Heb 11:25 He chose *to be* **mistreated along with** the people of God rather

5157 συγκαλέω, *synkaleō* [8] [√ *5250 + 2813*]

called together [6], calls together [2]

Mk 15:16 and **called together** the whole company of soldiers.
Lk   9: 1 *When* Jesus *had* **called** the Twelve **together**, he gave them power
    15: 6 Then *he* **calls** his friends and neighbors **together** and says,
    15: 9 *she* **calls** her friends and neighbors **together** and says,
    23:13 Pilate **called together** the chief priests, the rulers and the people,
Ac   5:21 and his associates arrived, *they* **called together** the Sanhedrin—
    10:24 and *had* **called together** his relatives and close friends.
    28:17 Three days later he **called together** the leaders of the Jews.

5158 συγκαλύπτω, *synkalyptō* [1] [√ *5250 + 2821*]

concealed [1]

Lk 12: 2 There is nothing **concealed** that will not be disclosed, or hidden

5159 συγκάμπτω, *synkamptō* [1] [√ *5250 + 2828*]

bent [1]

Ro 11:10 be darkened so they cannot see, and their backs *be* **bent** forever."

5160 συγκαταβαίνω, *synkatabainō* [1]
     [√ *5250 + 2848 + 326*]

come with [1]

Ac 25: 5 Let some of your leaders **come with** me and press charges against

5161 συγκατάθεσις, *synkatathesis* [1]
     [√ *5250 + 2848 + 5502*]

agreement [1]

2Co 6:16 What **agreement** is there between the temple of God and idols?

5162 συγκατανεύω, *synkataneuō* Not used in
     UBS/NIV [√ *5250 + 2848 + 3748*]

5163 συγκατατίθημι, *synkatatithēmi* [1]
     [√ *5250 + 2848 + 5502*]

consented [+*1639*] [1]

Lk 23:51 who *had* not **consented** [+*1639*] to their decision and action.

5164 συγκαταψηφίζομαι, *synkatapsēphizomai*
     [1] [√ *5250 + 2848 + 6029*]

added [1]

Ac   1:26 the lot fell to Matthias; so *he was* **added** to the eleven apostles.

5165 σύγκειμαι, *synkeimai* Not used in UBS/NIV
     [√ *5250 + 3023*]

5166 συγκεράννυμι, *synkerannymi* [2]
     [√ *5250 + 3042*]

combine with [1], combined [1]

1Co 12:24 But God *has* **combined** the members of the body and has given
Heb 4: 2 to them, because those who heard *did* not **combine** it **with** faith.

5167 συγκινέω, *synkineō* [1] [√ *5250 + 3075*]

stirred up [1]

Ac   6:12 So *they* **stirred up** the people and the elders and the teachers of

5168 συγκλείω, *synkleiō* [4] [√ *5250 + 3091*]

bound over [1], caught [1], declares a prisoner [1], locked up [1]

Lk   5: 6 *they* **caught** such a large number of fish that their nets began to
Ro 11:32 For God *has* **bound** all men **over** to disobedience so that he may
Gal 3:22 But the Scripture **declares** that the whole world *is* **a prisoner** of
     3:23 held prisoners by the law, **locked up** until faith should be revealed.

5169 συγκληρονόμος, *synklēronomos* [4]
     [√ *5250 + 3102 + 3795*]

heirs with [2], co-heirs with [1], heirs together with [1]

Ro   8:17 heirs of God and **co-heirs with** Christ, if indeed we share in his
Eph 3: 6 that through the gospel the Gentiles are **heirs together with** Israel,
Heb 11: 9 and Jacob, who were **heirs with** him of the same promise.
1Pe 3: 7 weaker partner and as **heirs with** you of the gracious gift of life,

5170 συγκοινωνέω, *synkoinōneō* [3] [√ *5250 + 3123*]

share [2], to do with [1]

Eph 5:11 *Have* nothing **to do with** the fruitless deeds of darkness, but rather
Php 4:14 Yet it was good of you *to* **share** in my troubles.
Rev 18: 4 "Come out of her, my people, so that *you* will not **share** in her sins,

5171 συγκοινωνός, *synkoinōnos* [4] [√ *5250 + 3123*]

share [+*1181*] [2], companion [1], share with [+*1639*] [1]

Ro 11:17 and now **share** [+*1181*] in the nourishing sap from the olive root,
1Co 9:23 the sake of the gospel, that *I may* **share** [+*1181*] *in* its *blessings*.
Php 1: 7 the gospel, all of you **share** [+*1639*] in God's grace **with** me.
Rev 1: 9 your brother and **companion** in the suffering and kingdom

5172 συγκομίζω, *synkomizō* [1] [√ *5250 + 3180*]

buried [1]

Ac   8: 2 Godly men **buried** Stephen and mourned deeply for him.

5173 συγκρίνω, **synkrinō** [3] [√ *5250 + 3212*]

compare [2], expressing [1]

1Co 2:13 taught by the Spirit, **expressing** spiritual truths in spiritual words.
2Co 10:12 or **compare** ourselves with some who commend themselves.
    10:12 by themselves and **compare** themselves with themselves,

5174 συγκύπτω, **synkyptō** [1] [√ *5250 + 3252*]

bent over [1]

Lk 13:11 She was **bent over** and could not straighten up at all.

5175 συγκυρία, **synkyria** [1] [√ *5250*]

happened [+2848] [1]

Lk 10:31 A priest **happened** [+2848] to be going down the same road,

5176 συγχαίρω, **synchairō** [7] [√ *5250 + 5897*]

rejoice with [4], rejoices with [2], shared joy [1]

Lk 1:58 that the Lord had shown her great mercy, and *they* **shared** her **joy**.
    15: 6 his friends and neighbors together and says, '**Rejoice with** me;
    15: 9 her friends and neighbors together and says, '**Rejoice with** me;
1Co 12:26 suffers with it; if one part is honored, every part **rejoices with** it.
    13: 6 Love does not delight in evil but **rejoices with** the truth.
Php 2:17 coming from your faith, *I* am glad and **rejoice with** all of you.
    2:18 So you too should be glad and **rejoice with** me.

5177 συγχέω, **syncheō** [5] [√ *1772; cf. 5250*]

baffled [1], bewilderment [1], confusion [1], in an uproar [1], stirred up [1]

Ac 2: 6 they heard this sound, a crowd came together in **bewilderment**,
    9:22 and **baffled** the Jews living in Damascus by proving that Jesus is
    19:32 The assembly was *in* **confusion**: Some were shouting one thing,
    21:27 at the temple. *They* **stirred up** the whole crowd and seized him,
    21:31 Roman troops that the whole city of Jerusalem *was* **in an uproar**.

5178 συγχράομαι, **synchraomai** [1] [√ *5250 + 5968*]

associate with [1]

Jn 4: 9 ask me for a drink?" (For Jews *do* not **associate with** Samaritans.)

5179 συγχύνω, **synchynō** Not used in UBS/NIV [√ *1772; cf. 5250*]

5180 σύγχυσις, **synchysis** [1] [√ *1772; cf. 5250*]

uproar [1]

Ac 19:29 Soon the whole city was *in* an **uproar**. The people seized Gaius

5181 συγχωρέω, **synchōreō** Not used in UBS/NIV [√ *5250 + 6003*]

5182 συζάω, **syzaō** [3] [√ *5250 + 2409*]

live with [3]

Ro 6: 8 if we died with Christ, we believe that *we will* also **live with** him.
2Co 7: 3 such a place in our hearts that we *would* **live** or die **with** you.
2Ti 2:11 If we died with him, *we will* also **live with** him;

5183 συζεύγνυμι, **syzeugnymi** [2] [√ *5250 + 2413*]

joined together [2]

Mt 19: 6 Therefore what God *has* **joined together**, let man not separate."
Mk 10: 9 Therefore what God *has* **joined together**, let man not separate."

5184 συζητέω, **syzēteō** [10] [√ *5250 + 2426*]

question [2], argue with [1], arguing about [1], arguing [1], asked [1], debated [1], debating [1], discussed [1], discussing [1]

Mk 1:27 The people were all so amazed that they **asked** each other,
    8:11 The Pharisees came and began *to* **question** Jesus. To test him,
    9:10 to themselves, **discussing** what "rising from the dead" meant.
    9:14 crowd around them and the teachers of the law **arguing** with them.
    9:16 "What *are you* **arguing** with them **about**?" he asked.
    12:28 One of the teachers of the law came and heard them **debating**.
Lk 22:23 They began *to* **question** among themselves which of them it might
    24:15 As they talked and **discussed** these things with each other,
Ac 6: 9 of Cilicia and Asia. *These men* began *to* **argue with** Stephen,
    9:29 He talked and **debated** with the Grecian Jews,

5185 συζήτησις, **syzētēsis** Not used in UBS/NIV [√ *5250 + 2426*]

5186 συζητητής, **syzētētēs** [1] [√ *5250 + 2426*]

philosopher [1]

1Co 1:20 Where is the scholar? Where is the **philosopher** of this age?

5187 σύζυγος, **syzygos** [1] [√ *5250 + 2413*]

yokefellow [1]

Php 4: 3 Yes, and I ask you, loyal **yokefellow**, help these women who have

5188 συζωοποιέω, **syzōopoieō** [2] [√ *5250 + 2409 + 4472*]

made alive with [RP5250] [1], made alive with [1]

Eph 2: 5 **made** us **alive with** Christ even when we were dead in
Col 2:13 of your sinful nature, God **made** you **alive** [RP5250] **with** Christ.

5189 συκάμινος, **sykaminos** [1]

mulberry tree [1]

Lk 17: 6 you can say *to* this **mulberry tree**, 'Be uprooted and planted in the

5190 συκῆ, **sykē** [16] [√ *5192*]

fig tree [14], figs [1], tree [1]

Mt 21:19 Seeing a **fig tree** by the road, he went up to it but found nothing on
    21:19 "May you never bear fruit again!" Immediately the **tree** withered.
    21:20 were amazed. "How did the **fig tree** wither so quickly?" they asked.
    21:21 do not doubt, not only can you do what was done *to* the **fig tree**,
    24:32 "Now learn this lesson from the **fig tree**: As soon as its twigs get
Mk 11:13 Seeing in the distance a **fig tree** in leaf, he went to find out if it had
    11:20 as they went along, they saw the **fig tree** withered from the roots.
    11:21 said to Jesus, "Rabbi, look! The **fig tree** you cursed has withered!"
    13:28 "Now learn this lesson from the **fig tree**: As soon as its twigs get
Lk 13: 6 "A man had a **fig tree**, planted in his vineyard, and he went to look
    13: 7 three years now I've been coming to look for fruit on this **fig tree**
    21:29 He told them this parable: "Look at the **fig tree** and all the trees.
Jn 1:48 "I saw you while you were still under the **fig tree** before Philip
    1:50 "You believe because I told you I saw you under the **fig tree**.
Jas 3:12 My brothers, can a **fig tree** bear olives, or a grapevine bear figs?
Rev 6:13 as late **figs** drop from a fig tree when shaken by a strong wind.

5191 συκομορέα, **sykomorea** [1] [√ *5192*]

sycamore-fig tree [1]

Lk 19: 4 So he ran ahead and climbed a **sycamore-fig tree** to see him,

5192 σῦκον, **sykon** [4] [→ *5190, 5191, 5193*]

figs [4]

Mt 7:16 Do people pick grapes from thornbushes, or **figs** from thistles?
Mk 11:13 he found nothing but leaves, because it was not the season *for* **figs**.
Lk 6:44 People do not pick **figs** from thornbushes, or grapes from briers.

Jas 3:12 My brothers, can a fig tree bear olives, or a grapevine bear **figs**?

5193 συκοφαντέω, **sykophanteō** [2] [√ 5192 + 5743]

accuse falsely [1], cheated out of [1]

Lk 3:14 He replied, "Don't extort money and don't **accuse** people **falsely**—
19: 8 and if *I have* **cheated** anybody **out of** anything, I will pay back

5194 συλαγωγέω, **sylagōgeō** [1] [√ 5195 + 72]

takes captive [+1639] [1]

Col 2: 8 See to it that no one **takes** you **captive** [+1639] through hollow

5195 συλάω, **sylaō** [1] [→ 2644, 2645, 5194]

robbed [1]

2Co 11: 8 *I* **robbed** other churches by receiving support from them so as to

5196 συλλαλέω, **syllaleō** [6] [√ 5250 + 3281]

talking with [3], conferred with [1], discussed with [1], said [1]

Mt 17: 3 there appeared before them Moses and Elijah, **talking with** Jesus.
Mk 9: 4 before them Elijah and Moses, who were **talking with** Jesus.
Lk 4:36 All the people were amazed and **said** to each other, "What is this
9:31 appeared in glorious splendor, **talking with** Jesus. They spoke
22: 4 temple guard and **discussed with** them how he might betray Jesus.
Ac 25:12 *After* Festus *had* **conferred with** his council, he declared:

5197 συλλαμβάνω, **syllambanō** [16] [√ 5250 + 3284]

arrested [2], capture [2], help [2], seized [2], conceived [+1877+3120+3836] [1], conceived [1], have [1], pregnant [1], seize [1], seizing [1], taken [1], with child [+1143+1877] [1]

Mt 26:55 that you have come out with swords and clubs *to* **capture** me?
Mk 14:48 "that you have come out with swords and clubs *to* **capture** me?
Lk 1:24 After this his wife Elizabeth *became* **pregnant** and for five months
1:31 *You will be* **with child** [+1143+1877] and give birth to a son,
1:36 Even Elizabeth your relative *is going to* **have** a child in her old
2:21 had given him before he *had been* **conceived** [+1877+3120+3836].
5: 7 So they signaled their partners in the other boat *to* come and **help**
5: 9 companions were astonished at the catch of fish *they had* **taken**,
22:54 Then **seizing** him, they led him away and took him into the house
Jn 18:12 with its commander and the Jewish officials **arrested** Jesus.
Ac 1:16 who served as guide *for* those *who* **arrested** Jesus—
12: 3 he saw that this pleased the Jews, he proceeded *to* **seize** Peter also.
23:27 This man *was* **seized** by the Jews and they were about to kill him,
26:21 That is why the Jews **seized** me in the temple courts and tried to
Php 4: 3 **help** these women who have contended at my side in the cause of
Jas 1:15 Then, *after* desire *has* **conceived**, it gives birth to sin; and sin,

5198 συλλέγω, **syllegō** [8] [√ 5250 + 3306]

pick [2], collect [1], collected [1], pull up [1], pulled up [1], pulling [1], weed [1]

Mt 7:16 *Do people* **pick** grapes from thornbushes, or figs from thistles?
13:28 "The servants asked him, 'Do you want *us* to go and **pull them up?'**
13:29 " 'No,' he answered, 'because *while you are* **pulling** the weeds,
13:30 First **collect** the weeds and tie them in bundles to be burned;
13:40 "As the weeds *are* **pulled up** and burned in the fire, so it will be at
13:41 and *they will* **weed** out of his kingdom everything that causes sin
13:48 Then *they* sat down and **collected** the good fish in baskets,
Lk 6:44 *People do* not **pick** figs from thornbushes, or grapes from briers.

5199 συλλογίζομαι, **syllogizomai** [1] [√ 5250 + 3306]

discussed [1]

Lk 20: 5 They **discussed** it among themselves and said, "If we say,

5200 συλλυπέω, **syllypeō** [1] [√ 5250 + 3383]

deeply distressed [1]

Mk 3: 5 **deeply distressed** at their stubborn hearts, said to the man,

5201 συμβαίνω, **symbainō** [8] [√ 5250 + 326]

happened [3], had to be [1], happen [1], happening [1], of them [+899] [1], was [1]

Mk 10:32 the Twelve aside and told them what was going to **happen** to him.
Lk 24:14 were talking with each other about everything that *had* **happened**.
Ac 3:10 filled with wonder and amazement at what *had* **happened** to him.
20:19 with tears, *although* I **was** severely tested by the plots of the Jews.
21:35 of the mob was so great he **had to be** carried by the soldiers.
1Co 10:11 These things **happened** to them as examples and were written
1Pe 4:12 as though something strange *were* **happening** to you.
2Pe 2:22 **Of them** [+899] the proverbs are true: "A dog returns to its vomit,"

5202 συμβάλλω, **symballō** [6] [√ 5250 + 965]

conferred [1], dispute with [1], go war [+4483] [1], help [1], met [1], pondered [1]

Lk 2:19 Mary treasured up all these things and **pondered** them in her heart.
14:31 "Or suppose a king is about *to* **go** to **war** [+4483] against another
Ac 4:15 them to withdraw from the Sanhedrin and then **conferred** together.
17:18 of Epicurean and Stoic philosophers *began to* **dispute with** him.
18:27 he *was a* great **help** to those who by grace had believed.
20:14 When *he* **met** us at Assos, we took him aboard and went on to

5203 συμβασιλεύω, **symbasileuō** [2] [√ 5250 + 995]

kings with [1], reign with [1]

1Co 4: 8 you really had become **kings with** you so that we *might be* you!
2Ti 2:12 if we endure, *we will* also **reign with** him. If we disown him,

5204 συμβιβάζω, **symbibazō** [7] [√ 5250 + 326]

held together [2], concluding [1], instruct [1], proving [1], shouted instructions [1], united [1]

Ac 9:22 and baffled the Jews living in Damascus *by* **proving** that Jesus is
16:10 **concluding** that God had called us to preach the gospel to them.
19:33 to the front, and some of the crowd **shouted instructions** to him.
1Co 2:16 "For who has known the mind of the Lord that he *may* **instruct**
Eph 4:16 joined and **held together** by every supporting ligament, grows
Col 2: 2 purpose is that they may be encouraged in heart and **united** in love,
2:19 supported and **held together** by its ligaments and sinews,

5205 συμβουλεύω, **symbouleuō** [4] [√ 5250 + 1089]

advised [1], conspired [1], counsel [1], plotted [1]

Mt 26: 4 and *they* **plotted** to arrest Jesus in some sly way and kill him.
Jn 18:14 Caiaphas was the one *who had* **advised** the Jews that it would be
Ac 9:23 After many days had gone by, the Jews **conspired** to kill him,
Rev 3:18 *I* **counsel** you to buy from me gold refined in the fire, so you can

5206 συμβούλιον, **symboulion** [8] [√ 5250 + 1089]

council [1], decided to [+3284] [1], decision [1], devised a plan [+3284] [1], laid plans [+3284] [1], plot [+1443] [1], plotted [+3284] [1], to the decision [+3284] [1]

Mt 12:14 Pharisees went out and **plotted** [+3284] how they might kill Jesus.
22:15 went out and **laid plans** [+3284] to trap him in his words.
27: 1 and the elders of the people came **to the decision** [+3284] to put
27: 7 So *they* **decided** [+3284] **to** use the money to buy the potter's field
28:12 chief priests had met with the elders and **devised a plan** [+3284],
Mk 3: 6 and *began to* **plot** [+1443] with the Herodians how they might kill
15: 1 teachers of the law and the whole Sanhedrin, reached a **decision**.
Ac 25:12 After Festus had conferred with his **council**, he declared: "You

5207 σύμβουλος, **symboulos** [1] [√ 5250 + 1089]

counselor [1]

Ro 11:34 has known the mind of the Lord? Or who has been his **counselor**?"

5208 Συμεών, **Symeōn** [7] [√ 4981]

Simeon [5], Simon [2]

Lk 2:25 Now there was a man in Jerusalem called **Simeon**, who was
2:34 Then **Simeon** blessed them and said to Mary, his mother: "This
3:30 the son *of* **Simeon**, the son of Judah, the son of Joseph, the son of
Ac 13: 1 Barnabas, **Simeon** called Niger, Lucius of Cyrene, Manaen (who
15:14 **Simon** has described to us how God at first showed his concern by
2Pe 1: 1 **Simon** Peter, a servant and apostle of Jesus Christ, To those who
Rev 7: 7 from the tribe *of* **Simeon** 12,000, from the tribe of Levi 12,000,

5209 συμμαθητής, **symmathētēs** [1] [√ 5250 + 3443]

rest of the disciples [1]

Jn 11:16 said *to* the **rest of the disciples**, "Let us also go, that we may die

5210 συμμαρτυρέω, **symmartyreō** [3] [√ 5250 + 3459]

bearing witness [1], confirms [1], testifies with [1]

Ro 2:15 their consciences also **bearing witness**, and their thoughts now
8:16 The Spirit himself **testifies with** our spirit that we are God's
9: 1 I am not lying, my conscience **confirms** it in the Holy Spirit—

5211 συμμερίζομαι, **symmerizomai** [1] [√ 5250 + 3538]

share [1]

1Co 9:13 and those who serve at the altar **share** in what is offered on the

5212 συμμέτοχος, **symmetochos** [2] [√ 5250 + 3552 + 2400]

partners with [1], sharers together in [1]

Eph 3: 6 of one body, and **sharers together in** the promise in Christ Jesus.
5: 7 Therefore do not be **partners with** them.

5213 συμμιμητής, **symmimētēs** [1] [√ 5250 + 3628]

join with others following example [+1181] [1]

Php 3:17 **Join with others** in **following** my **example** [+*1181*], brothers,

5214 συμμορφίζω, **symmorphizō** [1] [√ 5250 + 3671]

becoming like [1]

Php 3:10 of sharing in his sufferings, **becoming like** him in his death,

5215 σύμμορφος, **symmorphos** [2] [√ 5250 + 3671]

conformed [1], like [1]

Ro 8:29 For those God foreknew he also predestined to be **conformed** to
Php 3:21 our lowly bodies so that they will be **like** his glorious body.

5216 συμμορφόω, **symmorphoō** Not used in UBS/NIV [√ 5250 + 3671]

5217 συμπαθέω, **sympatheō** [2] [√ 5250 + 4248]

sympathize with [1], sympathized with [1]

Heb 4:15 For we do not have a high priest who is unable *to* **sympathize with**
10:34 *You* **sympathized with** those in prison and joyfully accepted the

5218 συμπαθής, **sympathēs** [1] [√ 5250 + 4248]

sympathetic [1]

1Pe 3: 8 be **sympathetic**, love as brothers, be compassionate and humble.

5219 συμπαραγίνομαι, **symparaginomai** [1] [√ 5250 + 4123 + 1181]

gathered [1]

Lk 23:48 When all the people *who had* **gathered** to witness this sight saw

5220 συμπαρακαλέω, **symparakaleō** [1] [√ 5250 + 4123 + 2813]

mutually encouraged [1]

Ro 1:12 and I *may be* **mutually encouraged** by each other's faith.

5221 συμπαραλαμβάνω, **symparalambanō** [4] [√ 5250 + 4123 + 3284]

take with [1], take [1], taking with [1], took along [1]

Ac 12:25 from Jerusalem, **taking with** *them* John, also called Mark.
15:37 Barnabas wanted *to* **take** John, also called Mark, **with** them,
15:38 but Paul did not think it wise *to* **take** him,
Gal 2: 1 to Jerusalem, this time with Barnabas. *I* **took** Titus **along** also.

5222 συμπαραμένω, **symparamenō** Not used in UBS/NIV [√ 5250 + 4123 + 3531]

5223 συμπάρειμι, **sympareimi** [1] [√ 5250 + 4123 + 1639]

present with [1]

Ac 25:24 "King Agrippa, and all who *are* **present with** us, you see this man!

5224 συμπάσχω, **sympaschō** [2] [√ 5250 + 4248]

share in sufferings [1], suffers with [1]

Ro 8:17 if indeed *we* **share in** his **sufferings** in order that we may also
1Co 12:26 If one part suffers, every part **suffers with** it; if one part is

5225 συμπέμπω, **sympempō** [2] [√ 5250 + 4287]

sending with [1], sending [1]

2Co 8:18 And *we are* **sending** along with him the brother who is praised by
8:22 *we are* **sending with** them our brother who has often proved to us

5226 συμπεριέχω, **symperiechō** Not used in UBS/NIV [√ 5250 + 4309 + 2400]

5227 συμπεριλαμβάνω, **symperilambanō** [1] [√ 5250 + 4309 + 3284]

put arms around [1]

Ac 20:10 threw himself on the young man and **put** *his* **arms around** him.

5228 συμπίνω, **sympinō** [1] [√ 5250 + 4403]

drank with [1]

Ac 10:41 by us who ate and **drank with** him after he rose from the dead.

5229 συμπίπτω, **sympiptō** [1] [√ 5250 + 4406]

collapsed [1]

Lk 6:49 struck that house, *it* **collapsed** and its destruction was complete."

5230 συμπληρόω, **sympleroō** [3] [√ *5250 + 4444*]

approached [1], came [1], swamped [1]

Lk   8:23   so that the boat *was being* **swamped**, and they were in great
     9:51   As the time **approached** for him to be taken up to heaven,
Ac   2: 1   When the day of Pentecost **came**, they were all together in one

5231 συμπνίγω, **sympnigō** [5] [√ *5250 + 4464*]

choke [2], choked [2], crushed [1]

Mt   13:22   but the worries of this life and the deceitfulness of wealth **choke** it,
Mk   4: 7   seed fell among thorns, which grew up and **choked** the plants,
     4:19   and the desires for other things come in and **choke** the word,
Lk   8:14   but as they go on their way *they are* **choked** by life's worries,
     8:42   As Jesus was on his way, the crowds *almost* **crushed** him.

5232 συμπολίτης, **sympolitēs** [1] [√ *5250 + 4484*]

fellow citizens with [1]

Eph   2:19   but **fellow citizens with** God's people and members of God's

5233 συμπορεύομαι, **symporeuomai** [4]
[√ *5250 + 4513*]

came [1], traveling with [1], walked along with [1], went along with [1]

Mk   10: 1   Again crowds of *people* **came** to him, and as was his custom,
Lk   7:11   and his disciples and a large crowd **went along with** him.
     14:25   Large crowds *were* **traveling with** Jesus, and turning to them he
     24:15   each other, Jesus himself came up and **walked along with** them;

5234 συμποσία, **symposia** Not used in UBS/NIV
[√ *5250 + 4403*]

5235 συμπόσιον, **symposion** [2] [√ *5250 + 4403*]

groups [+*5235*] [2]

Mk   6:39   have all the people sit down in **groups** [+*5235*] on the green grass.
     6:39   have all the people sit down in **groups** [+*5235*] on the green grass.

5236 συμπρεσβύτερος, **sympresbyteros** [1]
[√ *5250 + 4565*]

fellow elder [1]

1Pe   5: 1   To the elders among you, I appeal as a **fellow elder**, a witness of

5237 συμφέρω, **sympherō** [15] [√ *5250 + 5770*]

better [5], beneficial [2], good [2], best [1], brought together [1], common good [1], for good [1], gained [1], helpful [1]

Mt   5:29   *It is* **better** for you to lose one part of your body than for your
     5:30   *It is* **better** for you to lose one part of your body than for your
     18: 6   *it would be* **better** for him to have a large millstone hung around
     19:10   the situation between a husband and wife, *it is* **better** not to marry."
Jn   11:50   You do not realize that *it is* **better** for you that one man die for the
     16: 7   *It is* **for** your **good** that I am going away. Unless I go away,
     18:14   the Jews that *it would be* **good** if one man died for the people.
Ac   19:19   number who had practiced sorcery **brought** their scrolls **together**
     20:20   have not hesitated to preach anything that *would be* **helpful** to you
1Co   6:12   is permissible for me"—but not everything is **beneficial**.
     10:23   "Everything is permissible"—but not everything *is* **beneficial**.
     12: 7   one the manifestation of the Spirit is given for the **common good**.
2Co   8:10   And here is my advice about what *is* **best** for you in this matter:
     12: 1   *Although* there is nothing *to be* **gained**, I will go on to visions
Heb   12:10   but God disciplines us for our **good**, that we may share in his

5238 σύμφημι, **symphēmi** [1] [√ *5250 + 5774*]

agree [1]

Ro   7:16   And if I do what I do not want to do, *I* **agree** that the law is good.

5239 σύμφορος, **symphoros** [2] [√ *5250 + 5770*]

good [2]

1Co   7:35   I am saying this for your own **good**, not to restrict you, but that you
     10:33   For I am not seeking my own **good** but the good of many,

5240 συμφορτίζω, **symphortizō** Not used in
UBS/NIV [√ *5250 + 5770*]

5241 συμφυλέτης, **symphyletēs** [1] [√ *5250 + 5876*]

countrymen [1]

1Th   2:14   You suffered from your own **countrymen** the same things those

5242 σύμφυτος, **symphytos** [1] [√ *5250 + 5886*]

united [1]

Ro   6: 5   If we have been **united** with him like this in his death, we will

5243 συμφύω, **symphyō** [1] [√ *5250 + 5886*]

grew up with [1]

Lk   8: 7   fell among thorns, which **grew up with** it and choked the plants.

5244 συμφωνέω, **symphōneō** [6] [√ *5250 + 5889*]

agree [3], agreed [1], in agreement with [1], match [1]

Mt   18:19   I tell you that if two of you on earth **agree** about anything you ask
     20: 2   *He* **agreed** to pay them a denarius for the day and sent them into
     20:13   not being unfair to you. Didn't *you* **agree** to work for a denarius?
Lk   5:36   new garment, and the patch from the new *will* not **match** the old.
Ac   5: 9   said to her, "How *could you* **agree** to test the Spirit of the Lord?
     15:15   The words of the prophets *are* **in agreement with** this, as it is

5245 συμφώνησις, **symphōnēsis** [1] [√ *5250 + 5889*]

harmony [1]

2Co   6:15   What **harmony** is there between Christ and Belial? What does a

5246 συμφωνία, **symphōnia** [1] [√ *5250 + 5889*]

music [1]

Lk   15:25   When he came near the house, he heard **music** and dancing.

5247 σύμφωνος, **symphōnos** [1] [√ *5250 + 5889*]

mutual consent [1]

1Co   7: 5   Do not deprive each other except by **mutual consent** and for a

5248 συμψηφίζω, **sympsēphizō** [1] [√ *5250 + 6029*]

calculated [1]

Ac   19:19   When *they* **calculated** the value of the scrolls, the total came to

5249 σύμψυχος, **sympsychos** [1] [√ *5250 + 6038*]

spirit [1]

Php   2: 2   having the same love, being one in **spirit** and purpose.

5250 σύν, **syn** [128]

[→ *850, 851, 852, 853, 2190, 2192, 2194, 3568, 5149, 5150, 5151, 5152, 5153, 5154, 5155, 5156, 5157, 5158, 5159, 5160, 5161, 5162, 5163, 5164, 5165, 5166, 5167, 5168, 5169, 5170, 5171, 5172, 5173, 5174, 5175, 5176, 5177, 5178, 5179, 5180, 5181, 5182, 5183, 5184, 5185, 5186, 5187, 5188, 5196, 5197, 5198, 5199, 5200, 5201, 5202, 5203, 5204, 5205, 5206, 5207, 5209, 5210, 5211, 5212, 5213, 5214, 5215, 5216, 5217, 5218, 5219, 5220, 5221, 5222, 5223, 5224, 5225, 5226, 5227, 5228, 5229, 5230, 5231, 5232, 5233, 5234, 5235, 5236,*

5237, 5238, 5239, 5240, 5241, 5242, 5243, 5244, 5245, 5246, 5247,
5248, 5249, 5251, 5252, 5253, 5254, 5255, 5256, 5257, 5258, 5260,
5261, 5262, 5263, 5264, 5265, 5266, 5267, 5268, 5269, 5270, 5271,
5272, 5273, 5274, 5275, 5276, 5277, 5278, 5279, 5280, 5281, 5282,
5283, 5284, 5285, 5286, 5287, 5288, 5289, 5290, 5291, 5292, 5293,
5294, 5295, 5296, 5297, 5298, 5299, 5300, 5301, 5302, 5303, 5304,
5305, 5306, 5307, 5308, 5309, 5310, 5311, 5312, 5313, 5314, 5315,
5316, 5317, 5318, 5319, 5320, 5321, 5322, 5323, 5324, 5325, 5326,
5327, 5328, 5329, 5330, 5331, 5332, 5333, 5334, 5335, 5336, 5337,
5338, 5339, 5340, 5341, 5342, 5343, 5344, 5345, 5346, 5347, 5348,
5349, 5350, 5357, 5360, 5361, 5362, 5363, 5364, 5365, 5366, 5367,
5368, 5369, 5370, 5371, 5372]

with [76], and [13], together with [7], along with [6], companions
[+3836] [3], untranslated [2], associates [+3836] [2], companions
[+1639+3836] [2], crucified with [RP5365] [2], accompanied
[RP5302] [1], accompanied by [1], accompany [+4513] [1],
accompany [RP5292] [1], as [1], attendant of [1], companions
[+3836+4513] [1], fellow [+3836] [1], join in [1], made alive with
[RP5188] [1], on [1], take along [1], through [+5931] [1], what is
more [+4047+4246] [1], when [1]

Mt 25:27 so that when I returned I would have received it back **with** interest.
    26:35 But Peter declared, "Even if I have to die **with** you, I will never
    27:38 Two robbers were crucified **with** him, one on his right and one on
    27:44 In the same way the robbers who *were* **crucified with** [RP5365]
Mk 2:26 to eat. And he also gave some *to* his **companions** [+1639+3836]."
    4:10 **and** the others around him asked him about the parables.
    8:34 Then he called the crowd to him **along with** his disciples and said:
    9:4 And there appeared before them Elijah **and** Moses, who were
    15:27 They crucified two robbers **with** him, one on his right and one on
    15:32 Those **crucified with** [RP5365] him also heaped insults on him.
Lk 1:56 Mary stayed **with** Elizabeth for about three months and
    2:5 He went there to register **with** Mary, who was pledged to be
    2:13 Suddenly a great company of the heavenly host appeared **with** the
    5:9 and all his **companions** [+3836] were astonished at the catch of
    5:19 and lowered him **on** his mat through the tiles into the middle of the
    7:6 So Jesus went **with** them. He was not far from the house when the
    7:12 she was a widow. And a large crowd from the town was **with** her.
    8:1 the good news of the kingdom of God. The Twelve were **with** him,
    8:38 The man from whom the demons had gone out begged to go **with**
    8:51 he did not let anyone go in **with** him except Peter, John and James,
    9:32 Peter and his **companions** [+3836] were very sleepy, but when
    19:23 so that when I came back, I could have collected it **with** interest?'
    20:1 the teachers of the law, **together with** the elders, came up to him.
    22:14 the hour came, [NIE] Jesus and his apostles reclined at the table.
    22:56 She looked closely at him and said, "This man was **with** him."
    23:11 Then Herod **and** his soldiers ridiculed and mocked him.
    23:32 both criminals, were also led out **with** him to be executed.
    24:10 of James, and the others **with** them who told this to the apostles.
    24:21 And **what is more** [+4047+4246], it is the third day since all this
    24:24 Then some *of* our **companions** [+3836] went to the tomb
    24:29 the day is almost over." So he went in to stay **with** them.
    24:33 There they found the Eleven and those **with** them,
    24:44 He said to them, "This is what I told you while I was still **with** you:
Jn 12:2 while Lazarus was among those reclining at the table **with** him.
    18:1 Jesus left **with** his disciples and crossed the Kidron Valley.
    21:3 to fish," Simon Peter told them, and they said, "We'll go **with** you."
Ac 1:14 **along with** the women and Mary the mother of Jesus, and with his
    1:22 one of these must become a witness **with** us of his resurrection."
    2:14 Then Peter stood up **with** the Eleven, raised his voice
    3:4 Peter looked straight at him, **as** did John. Then Peter said,
    3:8 Then he went **with** them into the temple courts, walking
    4:13 and they took note that these men had been **with** Jesus.
    4:14 could see the man who had been healed standing there **with** them,
    4:27 Indeed Herod and Pontius Pilate met together **with** the Gentiles
    5:1 Now a man named Ananias, **together with** his wife Sapphira,
    5:17 Then the high priest and all his **associates** [+3836], who were
    5:21 When the high priest and his **associates** [+3836] arrived,
    5:26 the captain went **with** his officers and brought the apostles.
    7:35 **through** [+5931] the angel who appeared to him in the bush.
    8:20 "May your money perish **with** you, because you thought you could
    8:31 it to me?" So he invited Philip to come up and sit **with** him.
    10:2 He **and** all his family were devout and God-fearing; he gave

    10:20 Do not hesitate to go **with** them, for I have sent them."
    10:23 The next day Peter started out **with** them, and some of the brothers
    11:12 These six brothers also went **with** me, and we entered the man's
    13:7 who was an **attendant of** the proconsul, Sergius Paulus.
    14:4 were divided; some sided **with** the Jews, others with the apostles.
    14:4 were divided; some sided with the Jews, others **with** the apostles.
    14:5 afoot among the Gentiles and Jews, **together with** their leaders,
    14:13 because **he and** the crowd wanted to offer sacrifices to them.
    14:20 back into the city. The next day he **and** Barnabas left for Derbe.
    14:28 And they stayed there a long time **with** the disciples.
    15:22 Then the apostles and elders, **with** the whole church, decided to
    15:22 their own men and send them to Antioch **with** Paul and Barnabas.
    15:25 and send them to you **with** our dear friends Barnabas and Paul—
    16:3 Paul wanted to **take** him **along** on the journey, so he circumcised
    16:32 the word of the Lord to him **and** to all the others in his house.
    17:34 also a woman named Damaris, and a number of others. [NIE]
    18:8 the synagogue ruler, **and** his entire household believed in the Lord;
    18:18 and sailed for Syria, **accompanied by** Priscilla and Aquila.
    19:38 and his **fellow** [+3836] craftsmen have a grievance against
    20:36 When he had said this, he knelt down **with** all of them and prayed.
    21:5 All the disciples **and** their wives and children accompanied us out
    21:16 Some of the disciples from Caesarea **accompanied** [RP5302] us
    21:18 The next day Paul and the rest of us went to see James, and all the
    21:24 these men, **join in** their purification rites and pay their expenses,
    21:26 next day Paul took the men and purified himself **along with** them.
    21:29 (They had previously seen Trophimus the Ephesian in the city **with**
    22:9 My **companions** [+1639+3836] saw the light, but they did not
    23:15 **and** the Sanhedrin petition the commander to bring him before you
    23:27 were about to kill him, but I came **with** my troops and rescued him,
    23:32 The next day they let the cavalry go on **with** him, while they
    24:24 Several days later Felix came **with** his wife Drusilla, who was a
    25:23 and entered the audience room **with** the high ranking officers
    26:13 the sun, blazing around me and my **companions** [+3836+4513].
    27:2 Aristarchus, a Macedonian from Thessalonica, was **with** us.
    28:16 Paul was allowed to live by himself, **with** a soldier to guard him.
Ro 6:8 Now if we died **with** Christ, we believe that we will also live with
    8:32 how will he not also, **along with** him, graciously give us all
    16:14 Phlegon, Hermes, Patrobas, Hermas and the brothers **with** them.
    16:15 Nereus and his sister, and Olympas and all the saints **with** them.
1Co 1:2 **together with** all those everywhere who call on the name of our
    5:4 in the name of our Lord Jesus and I am **with** you in spirit,
    10:13 But **when** you are tempted, he will also provide a way out
    11:32 being disciplined so that we will not be condemned **with** the world.
    15:10 than all of them—yet not I, but the grace of God that was **with** me.
    16:4 advisable for me to go also, *they will* **accompany** [+4513] me.
    16:19 in the Lord, **and** so does the church that meets at their house.
2Co 1:1 of God in Corinth, **together with** all the saints throughout Achaia:
    1:21 Now it is God who makes both us **and** you stand firm in Christ.
    4:14 raised the Lord Jesus from the dead will also raise us **with** Jesus
    4:14 also raise us with Jesus and present us **with** you in his presence.
    8:19 he was chosen by the churches to **accompany** [RP5292] us as we
    9:4 For if any Macedonians come **with** me and find you unprepared,
    13:4 in him, yet by God's power we will live **with** him to serve you.
Gal 1:2 and all the brothers **with** me, To the churches in Galatia:
    2:3 Yet not even Titus, who was **with** me, was compelled to be
    3:9 So those who have faith are blessed **along with** Abraham,
    5:24 to Christ Jesus have crucified the sinful nature **with** its passions
Eph 3:18 may have power, **together with** all the saints, to grasp how wide
    4:31 and anger, brawling and slander, **along with** every form of malice.
Php 1:1 Christ Jesus at Philippi, **together with** the overseers and deacons:
    1:23 I desire to depart and be **with** Christ, which is better by far;
    2:22 because as a son with his father he has served **with** me in the work
    4:21 in Christ Jesus. The brothers who are **with** me send greetings.
Col 2:5 I am present **with** you in spirit and delight to see how orderly you
    2:13 of your sinful nature, God **made** you **alive with** [RP5188] Christ.
    2:20 Since you died **with** Christ to the basic principles of this world,
    3:3 For you died, and your life is now hidden **with** Christ in God.
    3:4 is your life, appears, then you also will appear **with** him in glory.
    3:9 since you have taken off your old self **with** its practices
    4:9 He is *coming* **with** Onesimus, our faithful and dear brother,
1Th 4:14 so we believe that God will bring **with** Jesus those who have fallen
    4:17 and are left will be caught up together **with** them in the clouds to
    4:17 meet the Lord in the air. And so we will be **with** the Lord forever.
    5:10 whether we are awake or asleep, we may live together **with** him.
Jas 1:11 For the sun rises **with** scorching heat and withers the plant;
2Pe 1:18 from heaven when we were **with** him on the sacred mountain.

5251 συνάγω, **synagō** [59] [√ *5250 + 72*]

gathered [12], gather [10], gathered together [5], met [5],
assembled [3], gathering [2], got together [2], invite in [2],
meeting [2], met together [2], store [2], bring together [1], called
meeting [1], called together [1], came together [1], caught [1],
come together [*+1639*] [1], gather together [1], harvests [1],
invited in [1], picked up [1], store away [1], went [1]

Mt   2: 4 *When* he had **called together** all the people's chief priests
     3:12 **gathering** his wheat into the barn and burning up the chaff with
     6:26 they do not sow or reap or **store away** in barns, and yet your
  12:30 me is against me, and he *who does* not **gather** with me scatters.
  13: 2 Such large crowds **gathered** around him that he got into a boat
  13:30 to be burned; then **gather** the wheat and bring it into my barn.' "
  13:47 a net that was let down into the lake and **caught** all kinds of fish.
  18:20 For where two or three **come** [*+1639*] **together** in my name,
  22:10 out into the streets and **gathered** all the people they could find,
  22:34 that Jesus had silenced the Sadducees, the Pharisees **got together**.
  22:41 *While* the Pharisees *were* **gathered together**, Jesus asked them,
  24:28 Wherever there is a carcass, there the vultures *will* **gather**.
  25:24 have not sown and **gathering** where you have not scattered seed.
  25:26 where I have not sown and **gather** where I have not scattered seed?
  25:32 All the nations *will be* **gathered** before him, and he will separate
  25:35 me something to drink, I was a stranger and *you* **invited** me **in**,
  25:38 When did we see you a stranger and **invite** you **in**, or needing
  25:43 I was a stranger and *you did* not **invite** me **in**, I needed clothes
  26: 3 and the elders of the people **assembled** in the palace of the high
  26:57 where the teachers of the law and the elders *had* **assembled**.
  27:17 So *when* the crowd *had* **gathered**, Pilate asked them, "Which one
  27:27 and **gathered** the whole company of soldiers around him.
  27:62 Preparation Day, the chief priests and the Pharisees **went** to Pilate.
  28:12 *When* the chief priests *had* **met** with the elders and devised a plan,

Mk 2: 2 So many **gathered** that there was no room left, not even outside
    4: 1 The crowd that **gathered** around him was so large that he got into
    5:21 a large crowd **gathered** around him while he was by the lake.
    6:30 The apostles **gathered** around Jesus and reported to him all they
    7: 1 of the law who had come from Jerusalem **gathered** around Jesus

Lk 3:17 to clean his threshing floor and *to* **gather** the wheat into his barn,
  11:23 me is against me, and he *who does* not **gather** with me, scatters.
  12:17 to himself, 'What shall I do? I have no place *to* **store** my crops.'
  12:18 bigger ones, and there *I will* **store** all my grain and my goods.
  15:13 "Not long after that, the younger son **got together** all he had,
  22:66 both the chief priests and teachers of the law, **met together**,

Jn 4:36 even now he **harvests** the crop for eternal life, so that the sower
    6:12 he said to his disciples, "**Gather** the pieces that are left over.
    6:13 So *they* **gathered** them and filled twelve baskets with the pieces of
  11:47 chief priests and the Pharisees **called** a **meeting** of the Sanhedrin.
  11:52 children of God, to **bring** them **together** and make them one.
  15: 6 such branches *are* **picked up**, thrown into the fire and burned.
  18: 2 the place, because Jesus *had* often **met** there with his disciples.

Ac 4: 5 day the rulers, elders and teachers of the law **met** in Jerusalem.
    4:26 and the rulers **gather** together against the Lord and against his
    4:27 Indeed Herod and Pontius Pilate **met together** with the Gentiles
    4:31 After they prayed, the place where they were **meeting** was shaken.
  11:26 So for a whole year Barnabas and Saul **met** with the church
  13:44 On the next Sabbath almost the whole city **gathered** to hear the
  14:27 they **gathered** the church **together** and reported all that God had
  15: 6 The apostles and elders **met** to consider this question.
  15:30 where *they* **gathered** the church **together** and delivered the letter.
  20: 7 On the first day of the week we **came together** to break bread.
  20: 8 were many lamps in the upstairs room where we were **meeting**.

1Co 5: 4 *When* you *are* **assembled** in the name of our Lord Jesus and I am

Rev 16:14 *to* **gather** them for the battle on the great day of God Almighty.
  16:16 Then *they* **gathered** the kings **together** to the place that in Hebrew
  19:17 in midair, "Come, **gather together** for the great supper of God,
  19:19 and their armies **gathered together** to make war against the rider
  20: 8 corners of the earth—Gog and Magog—*to* **gather** them for battle.

5252 συναγωγή, **synagōgē** [56 / 57] [→ *697, 801, 2191; cf. 5250 + 72*]

synagogue [31], synagogues [23], congregation [1], from one
synagogue to another [*+2848+3836+4246*] [1], meeting [1]

Mt 4:23 Jesus went throughout Galilee, teaching in their **synagogues**,
    6: 2 as the hypocrites do in the **synagogues** and on the streets,
    6: 5 for they love to pray standing in the **synagogues** and on the street
    9:35 through all the towns and villages, teaching in their **synagogues**,
  10:17 you over to the local councils and flog you in their **synagogues**.
  12: 9 Going on from that place, he went into their **synagogue**,
  13:54 he began teaching the people in their **synagogue**, and they were
  23: 6 honor at banquets and the most important seats in the **synagogues**;
  23:34 others you will flog in your **synagogues** and pursue from town to

Mk 1:21 Sabbath came, Jesus went into the **synagogue** and began to teach.
    1:23 then a man in their **synagogue** who was possessed by an evil spirit
    1:29 As soon as they left the **synagogue**, they went with James
    1:39 preaching in their **synagogues** and driving out demons.
    3: 1 Another time he went into the **synagogue**, and a man with a
    6: 2 When the Sabbath came, he began to teach in the **synagogue**,
  12:39 and have the most important seats in the **synagogues**
  13: 9 handed over to the local councils and flogged in the **synagogues**.

Lk 4:15 He taught in their **synagogues**, and everyone praised him.
    4:16 and on the Sabbath day he went into the **synagogue**, as was his
    4:20 The eyes of everyone in the **synagogue** were fastened on him,
    4:28 All the people in the **synagogue** were furious when they heard this.
    4:33 In the **synagogue** there was a man possessed by a demon,
    4:38 Jesus left the **synagogue** and went to the home of Simon.
    4:44 And he kept on preaching in the **synagogues** of Judea.
    6: 6 On another Sabbath he went into the **synagogue** and was teaching,
    7: 5 because he loves our nation and has built our **synagogue**."
    8:41 named Jairus, a ruler *of* the **synagogue**, came and fell at Jesus' feet,
  11:43 because you love the most important seats in the **synagogues**
  12:11 "When you are brought before **synagogues**, rulers and authorities,
  13:10 On a Sabbath Jesus was teaching in one *of* the **synagogues**,
  20:46 and have the most important seats in the **synagogues**
  21:12 They will deliver you to **synagogues** and prisons, and you will be

Jn 6:59 He said this while teaching in the **synagogue** in Capernaum.
  18:20 "I always taught in **synagogues** or at the temple, where all the Jews

Ac 6: 9 from members of the **Synagogue** of the Freedmen (as it was
    9: 2 and asked him for letters to the **synagogues** in Damascus,
    9:20 At once he began to preach in the **synagogues** that Jesus is the Son
  13: 5 they proclaimed the word of God in the Jewish **synagogues**.
  13:14 On the Sabbath they entered the **synagogue** and sat down.
  13:42 As Paul and Barnabas were leaving the **synagogue**, [UBS-]
  13:43 When the **congregation** was dismissed, many of the Jews
  14: 1 and Barnabas went as usual into the Jewish **synagogue**
  15:21 the earliest times and is read in the **synagogues** on every Sabbath."
  17: 1 they came to Thessalonica, where there was a Jewish **synagogue**.
  17:10 to Berea. On arriving there, they went to the Jewish **synagogue**.
  17:17 So he reasoned in the **synagogue** with the Jews
  18: 4 Every Sabbath he reasoned in the **synagogue**, trying to persuade
  18: 7 Then Paul left the **synagogue** and went next door to the house of
  18:19 He himself went into the **synagogue** and reasoned with the Jews.
  18:26 He began to speak boldly in the **synagogue**. When Priscilla
  19: 8 Paul entered the **synagogue** and spoke boldly there for three
  22:19 'these men know that I went from one **synagogue** to another to
  24:12 or stirring up a crowd in the **synagogues** or anywhere else in the
  26:11 I went **from one synagogue** [*+2848+3836+4246*] **to another** to

Jas 2: 2 Suppose a man comes into your **meeting** wearing a gold ring

Rev 2: 9 who say they are Jews and are not, but are a **synagogue** of Satan.
    3: 9 I will make those who are of the **synagogue** of Satan, who claim to

5253 συναγωνίζομαι, **synagōnizomai** [1] [√ *5250 + 74*]

join in struggle [1]

Ro 15:30 of the Spirit, *to* **join** me **in** my **struggle** by praying to God for me.

5254 συναθλέω, **synathleō** [2] [√ *5250 + 123*]

contended at side [1], contending as [1]

Php 1:27 in one spirit, **contending as** one man for the faith of the gospel
    4: 3 help these women who *have* **contended at** my **side** in the cause of

5255 συναθροίζω, **synathroizō** [2] [√ *5250 + 125*]

called together [1], gathered [1]

Ac 12:12 called Mark, where many people had **gathered** and were praying.
  19:25 He **called** them **together**, along with the workmen in related

5256 συναίρω, synairō [3] [√ 5250 + 149]

settle [1], settled accounts [+3364] [1], settlement [1]

Mt 18:23 the kingdom of heaven is like a king who wanted *to* **settle** accounts
    18:24 As he began the **settlement**, a man who owed him ten thousand
    25:19 of those servants returned and **settled accounts** [+3364] with them.

5257 συναιχμάλωτος, synaichmalōtos [3]
[√ 5250 + 171]

fellow prisoner [2], in prison with [1]

Ro 16: 7 and Junias, my relatives *who have been* **in prison with** me.
Col 4:10 My **fellow prisoner** Aristarchus sends you his greetings, as does
Phm 1:23 Epaphras, my **fellow prisoner** in Christ Jesus, sends you greetings.

5258 συνακολουθέω, synakoloutheō [3]
[√ 5250 + 199 [1.3]]

follow [1], followed [1], following [1]

Mk 5:37 He did not let anyone **follow** him except Peter, James and John the
    14:51 wearing nothing but a linen garment, *was* **following** Jesus.
Lk 23:49 including the women who *had* **followed** him from Galilee,

5259 συναλίζω, synalizō [1]

eating with [1]

Ac 1: 4 On one occasion, *while he was* **eating with** them, he gave them

5260 συναλίσκομαι, synaliskomai Not used in
UBS/NIV [√ 5250 + 274]

5261 συναλλάσσω, synallassō [1] [√ 5250 + 248]

reconcile [+1645+1650] [1]

Ac 7:26 *He tried to* **reconcile** [+1645+1650] them by saying, 'Men,

5262 συναναβαίνω, synanabainō [2]
[√ 5250 + 324 + 326]

come up with [1], traveled with [1]

Mk 15:41 Many other women who *had* **come up with** him to Jerusalem were
Ac 13:31 and for many days he was seen *by* those *who had* **traveled with**

5263 συνανάκειμαι, synanakeimai [7]
[√ 5250 + 324 + 3023]

dinner guests [2], at the table with [1], ate with [1], eating with [1],
fellow guests [1], guests [1]

Mt 9:10 collectors and "sinners" came and **ate with** him and his disciples.
    14: 9 was distressed, but because of his oaths and his **dinner guests**,
Mk 2:15 tax collectors and "sinners" *were* **eating with** him and his disciples,
    6:22 came in and danced, she pleased Herod and his **dinner guests**.
Lk 7:49 The other **guests** began to say among themselves, "Who is this who
    14:10 Then you will be honored in the presence of all your **fellow guests**.
    14:15 When one *of* those **at the table with** him heard this, he said to

5264 συναναμείγνυμι, synanameignymi [3]
[√ 5250 + 324 + 3502]

associate with [3]

1Co 5: 9 I have written you in my letter not *to* **associate with** sexually
    5:11 But now I am writing you that you *must* not **associate with**
2Th 3:14 *Do* not **associate with** him, in order that he may feel ashamed.

5265 συναναπαύομαι, synanapauomai [1]
[√ 5250 + 324 + 4264]

together refreshed [1]

Ro 15:32 I may come to you with joy and **together** with you *be* **refreshed**.

5266 συναναστρέφομαι, synanastrephomai Not
used in UBS/NIV [√ 5250 + 324 + 5138]

5267 συναντάω, synantaō [6] [√ 5250 + 505]

met [4], happen [1], meet [1]

Lk 9:37 when they came down from the mountain, a large crowd **met** him.
    22:10 "As you enter the city, a man carrying a jar of water *will* **meet** you.
Ac 10:25 the house, Cornelius **met** him and fell at his feet in reverence.
    20:22 am going to Jerusalem, not knowing what *will* **happen** to me there.
Heb 7: 1 He **met** Abraham returning from the defeat of the kings
    7:10 because when Melchizedek **met** Abraham, Levi was still in the

5268 συνάντησις, synantēsis Not used in UBS/NIV
[√ 5250 + 505]

5269 συναντιλαμβάνομαι, synantilambanomai
[2] [√ 5250 + 505 + 3284]

help [1], helps [1]

Lk 10:40 sister has left me to do the work by myself? Tell her to **help** me!"
Ro 8:26 In the same way, the Spirit **helps** us in our weakness. We do not

5270 συναπάγω, synapagō [3] [√ 5250 + 608 + 72]

carried away [1], led astray [1], willing to associate [1]

Ro 12:16 be proud, but *be* **willing to associate** with people of low position.
Gal 2:13 so that by their hypocrisy even Barnabas *was* **led astray**.
2Pe 3:17 so that you may not *be* **carried away** by the error of lawless men

5271 συναποθνήσκω, synapothnēskō [3]
[√ 5250 + 608 + 2569]

die with [2], died with [1]

Mk 14:31 "Even if I have to **die with** you, I will never disown you."
2Co 7: 3 you have such a place in our hearts that we *would* live or **die with**
2Ti 2:11 If *we* **died with** him, we will also live with him;

5272 συναπόλλυμι, synapollymi [1]
[√ 5250 + 608 + 3897]

killed with [1]

Heb 11:31 the spies, *was* not **killed with** those who were disobedient.

5273 συναποστέλλω, synapostellō [1] [√ 5250 + 690]

sent with [1]

2Co 12:18 I urged Titus to go to you and *I* **sent** our brother **with** him.

5274 συναρμολογέω, synarmologeō [2]
[√ 5250 + 764 + 3306]

joined together [2]

Eph 2:21 In him the whole building *is* **joined together** and rises to become a
    4:16 **joined** and held **together** by every supporting ligament, grows

5275 συναρπάζω, synarpazō [4] [√ 5250 + 773]

seized [3], caught [1]

Lk 8:29 Many times it *had* **seized** him, and though he was chained hand
Ac 6:12 *They* **seized** Stephen and brought him before the Sanhedrin.
    19:29 The *people* **seized** Gaius and Aristarchus, Paul's traveling
    27:15 The ship *was* **caught** *by* the storm and could not head into the

5276 συναυλίζομαι, synaulizomai Not used in
UBS/NIV [√ 5250 + 887]

5277 συναυξάνω, *synauxanō* [1] [√ 5250 + 889]

grow together [1]

Mt 13:30 Let both **grow together** until the harvest. At that time I will tell the

5278 σύνδεσμος, *syndesmos* [4] [√ 5250 + 1313]

binds together [+1639] [1], bond [1], captive [1], sinews [1]

Ac 8:23 For I see that you are full of bitterness and **captive** to sin."
Eph 4:3 Make every effort to keep the unity of the Spirit through the **bond**
Col 2:19 supported and held together by its ligaments and **sinews**,
    3:14 on love, which **binds** [+1639] them all **together** in perfect unity.

5279 συνδέω, *syndeō* [1] [√ 5250 + 1313]

fellow prisoners [1]

Heb 13:3 Remember those in prison as if you *were* their **fellow prisoners**,

5280 συνδοξάζω, *syndoxazō* [1] [√ 5250 + 1518]

share in glory [1]

Ro 8:17 in his sufferings in order that *we may* also **share in** his **glory**.

5281 σύνδουλος, *syndoulos* [10] [√ 5250 + 1528]

fellow servant [4], fellow servants [3], fellow servant with with [2], servants [1]

Mt 18:28 he found one *of* his **fellow servants** who owed him a hundred
    18:29 "His **fellow servant** fell to his knees and begged him, 'Be patient
    18:31 When the other **servants** saw what had happened, they were
    18:33 Shouldn't you have had mercy on your **fellow servant** just as I had
    24:49 and he then begins to beat his **fellow servants** and to eat and drink
Col 1:7 You learned it from Epaphras, our dear **fellow servant**, who is a
    4:7 is a dear brother, a faithful minister and **fellow servant** in the Lord.
Rev 6.11 until the number of their **fellow servants** and brothers who were to
    19:10 I am a **fellow servant with** you and **with** your brothers who hold
    22:9 I am a **fellow servant with** you and **with** your brothers the

5282 συνδρομή, *syndromē* [1] [√ 5250 + 5556]

running from all directions [1]

Ac 21:30 was aroused, and the people came **running from all directions**.

5283 συνεγείρω, *synegeirō* [3] [√ 5250 + 1586]

raised up with [1], raised with [1], raised [1]

Eph 2:6 And God **raised** us **up with** Christ and seated us with him in the
Col 2:12 and **raised** with him through your faith in the power of God,
    3:1 Since, then, *you have been* **raised with** Christ, set your hearts on

5284 συνέδριον, *synedrion* [22] [√ 5250 + 1612]

Sanhedrin [19], local councils [2], thems [+899+3836] [1]

Mt 5:22 who says to his brother, 'Raca,' is answerable *to* the **Sanhedrin**.
    10:17 they will hand you over to the **local councils** and flog you in their
    26:59 and the whole **Sanhedrin** were looking for false evidence against
Mk 13:9 You will be handed over to the **local councils** and flogged in the
    14:55 and the whole **Sanhedrin** were looking for evidence against Jesus
    15:1 with the elders, the teachers of the law and the whole **Sanhedrin**,
Lk 22:66 met together, and Jesus was led before thems [+899+3836].
Jn 11:47 chief priests and the Pharisees called a meeting of the **Sanhedrin**.
Ac 4:15 So they ordered them to withdraw from the **Sanhedrin** and
    5:21 and his associates arrived, they called together the **Sanhedrin**—
    5:27 they made them appear before the **Sanhedrin** to be questioned by
    5:34 stood up in the **Sanhedrin** and ordered that the men be put outside
    5:41 The apostles left the **Sanhedrin**, rejoicing because they had been
    6:12 They seized Stephen and brought him before the **Sanhedrin**.
    6:15 All who were sitting in the **Sanhedrin** looked intently at Stephen,
    22:30 and ordered the chief priests and all the **Sanhedrin** to assemble.
    23:1 Paul looked straight at the **Sanhedrin** and said, "My brothers,
    23:6 called out in the **Sanhedrin**, "My brothers, I am a Pharisee,
    23:15 and the **Sanhedrin** petition the commander to bring him before
    23:20 **Sanhedrin** tomorrow on the pretext of wanting more accurate
    23:28 why they were accusing him, so I brought him to their **Sanhedrin**.
    24:20 what crime they found in me when I stood before the **Sanhedrin**—

5285 συνέδριος, *synedrios* Not used in UBS/NIV
[√ 5250 + 1612]

5286 σύνεδρος, *synedros* Not used in UBS/NIV
[√ 5250 + 1612]

5287 συνείδησις, *syneidēsis* [30] [√ 5250 + 3857 (or) 3972]

conscience [23], consciences [4], conscious [1], guilty conscience [+4505] [1], guilty [1]

Ac 23:1 I have fulfilled my duty to God *in* all good **conscience** to this day."
    24:16 So I strive always to keep my **conscience** clear before God
Ro 2:15 their **consciences** also bearing witness, and their thoughts now
    9:1 I am not lying, my **conscience** confirms it in the Holy Spirit—
    13:5 because of possible punishment but also because of **conscience**.
1Co 8:7 to an idol, and since their **conscience** is weak, it is defiled.
    8:10 For if anyone with a weak **conscience** sees you who have this
    8:12 your brothers in this way and wound their weak **conscience**,
    10:25 sold in the meat market without raising questions of **conscience**,
    10:27 is put before you without raising questions of **conscience**.
    10:28 for the sake of the man who told you and for **conscience'** sake—
    10:29 the other man's **conscience**, I mean, not yours. For why should my
    10:29 For why should my freedom be judged by another's **conscience**?
2Co 1:12 Our **conscience** testifies that we have conducted ourselves in the
    4:2 commend ourselves to every man's **conscience** in the sight of God.
    5:11 are is plain to God, and I hope it is also plain to your **conscience**.
1Ti 1:5 comes from a pure heart and a good **conscience** and a sincere faith.
    1:19 holding on to faith and a good **conscience**. Some have rejected
    3:9 keep hold of the deep truths of the faith with a clear **conscience**.
    4:2 whose **consciences** have been seared as with a hot iron.
2Ti 1:3 with a clear **conscience**, as night and day I constantly remember
Tit 1:15 is pure. In fact, both their minds and **consciences** are corrupted.
Heb 9:9 and sacrifices being offered were not able to clear the **conscience**
    9:14 to God, cleanse our **consciences** from acts that lead to death,
    10:2 once for all, and would no longer have felt **guilty** for their sins.
    10:22 hearts sprinkled to cleanse us from a **guilty conscience** [+4505]
    13:18 We are sure that we have a clear **conscience** and desire to live
1Pe 2:19 under the pain of unjust suffering because he is **conscious** of God.
    3:16 keeping a clear **conscience**, so that those who speak maliciously
    3:21 from the body but the pledge *of* a good **conscience** toward God.

5288 συνείδω, *syneidō* Not used in UBS/NIV
[√ 5250 + 3857 (or) 3972]

5289 σύνειμι¹, *syneimi¹* [2] [√ 5250 + 1639]

companions [1], were with [1]

Lk 9:18 Jesus was praying in private and his disciples **were with** him,
Ac 22:11 My **companions** led me by the hand into Damascus,

5290 σύνειμι², *syneimi²* [1] [√ 5250 + 1640]

gathering [1]

Lk 8:4 *While* a large crowd *was* **gathering** and people were coming to

5291 συνεισέρχομαι, *syneiserchomai* [2]
[√ 5250 + 1650 + 2262]

entered [RP1650] [1], went with into [RP1650] [1]

Jn 6:22 and that Jesus *had* not **entered** [RP1650] it with his disciples,
    18:15 *he* **went** [RP1650] **with** Jesus **into** the high priest's courtyard,

5292 συνέκδημος, synekdēmos [2]
[√ 5250 + 1666 + 1322]

accompany [RP5250] [1], traveling companions [1]

Ac 19:29 and Aristarchus, Paul's **traveling companions** from Macedonia,
2Co 8:19 he was chosen by the churches to **accompany** [RP5250] us as we

5293 συνεκλεκτός, syneklektos [1]
[√ 5250 + 1666 + 3306]

chosen together with [1]

1Pe 5:13 She who is in Babylon, **chosen together with** you, sends you her

5294 συνεκπορεύομαι, synekporeuomai Not used
in UBS/NIV [√ 5250 + 1666 + 4513]

5295 συνελαύνω, synelaunō Not used in UBS/NIV
[√ 5250 + 1785]

5296 συνεπιμαρτυρέω, synepimartyreō [1]
[√ 5250 + 2093 + 3459]

also testified [1]

Heb 2:4 God **also testified** to it by signs, wonders and various miracles,

5297 συνεπίσκοπος, synepiskopos Not used in
UBS/NIV [√ 5250 + 2093 + 5023]

5298 συνεπιτίθημι, synepitithēmi [1]
[√ 5250 + 2093 + 5502]

joined in the accusation [1]

Ac 24:9 The Jews **joined in the accusation**, asserting that these things

5299 συνέπομαι, synepomai [1] [√ 5250]

accompanied by [1]

Ac 20:4 He *was* **accompanied by** Sopater son of Pyrrhus from Berea,

5300 συνεργέω, synergeō [5] [√ 5250 + 2240]

fellow workers [1], joins in the work [1], worked with [1], working together [1], works [1]

Mk 16:20 and the Lord **worked with** them and confirmed his word by the
Ro 8:28 And we know that in all things God **works** for the good of those
1Co 16:16 to submit to such as these and to everyone who **joins in the work**,
2Co 6:1 As God's **fellow workers** we urge you not to receive God's grace
Jas 2:22 You see that his faith and his actions *were* **working together**,

5301 συνεργός, synergos [13] [√ 5250 + 2240]

fellow worker [6], fellow workers [5], work together [+1181] [1], work with [+1639] [1]

Ro 16:3 Greet Priscilla and Aquila, my **fellow workers** in Christ Jesus.
16:9 Greet Urbanus, our **fellow worker** in Christ, and my dear friend
16:21 Timothy, my **fellow worker**, sends his greetings to you, as do
1Co 3:9 For we are God's **fellow workers**; you are God's field,
2Co 1:24 lord it over your faith, but *we* **work** [+1639] **with** you for your joy,
8:23 As for Titus, he is my partner and **fellow worker** among you;
Php 2:25 my brother, **fellow worker** and fellow soldier, who is also your
4:3 along with Clement and the rest *of* my **fellow workers**,
Col 4:11 These are the only Jews among my **fellow workers** for the
1Th 3:2 and God's **fellow worker** in spreading the gospel of Christ,
Phm 1:1 our brother, *To* Philemon our dear friend and **fellow worker**,
1:24 so do Mark, Aristarchus, Demas and Luke, my **fellow workers**.
3Jn 1:8 to such men so that *we may* **work** [+1181] **together** for the truth.

5302 συνέρχομαι, synerchomai [30] [√ 5250 + 2262]

come together [4], came together [3], gathered [3], accompanied [RP5250] [1], assemble [1], assembled [1], came with [1], came [1], come along with [1], come together [+899+2093+3836] [1], come with [+1639] [1], come with [1], comes together [+899+2093+3836] [1], continued with [1], gathering [1], going with [1], meet together [1], meetings [1], met together [1], there [1], went along [1], went with [1], with [1]

Mt 1:18 pledged to be married to Joseph, but before they **came together**,
Mk 3:20 and again a crowd **gathered**, so that he and his disciples were not
14:53 all the chief priests, elders and teachers of the law **came together**.
Lk 5:15 so that crowds of people **came** to hear him and to be healed of their
23:55 The women who *had* **come** [+1639] **with** Jesus from Galilee
Jn 11:33 and the Jews *who had* **come along with** her also weeping,
18:20 in synagogues or at the temple, where all the Jews **come together**.
Ac 1:6 So when they **met together**, they asked him, "Lord, are you at this
1:21 *of* the men who *have been* **with** us the whole time the Lord Jesus
2:6 they heard this sound, a crowd **came together** in bewilderment,
5:16 Crowds **gathered** also from the towns around Jerusalem,
9:39 Peter **went with** them, and when he arrived he was taken upstairs
10:23 out with them, and some of the brothers from Joppa **went along**.
10:27 with him, Peter went inside and found a large **gathering** *of people.*
10:45 The circumcised believers who *had* **come with** Peter were
11:12 The Spirit told me to have no hesitation about **going with** them.
15:38 them in Pamphylia and *had* not **continued with** them in the work.
16:13 and began to speak to the women *who had* **gathered** there.
19:32 Most of the people did not even know why *they were* **there**.
21:16 Some of the disciples from Caesarea **accompanied** [RP5250] us
22:30 and ordered the chief priests and all the Sanhedrin *to* **assemble**.
25:17 When they **came** here **with** me, I did not delay the case,
28:17 *When* they *had* **assembled**, Paul said to them: "My brothers,
1Co 11:17 no praise for you, for *your* **meetings** do more harm than good.
11:18 In the first place, I hear that *when* you **come together** as a church,
11:20 *When* you **come** [+899+2093+3836] **together**, it is not the Lord's
11:33 So then, my brothers, *when you* **come together** to eat, wait for
11:34 so that *when you* **meet together** it may not result in judgment.
14:23 So if the whole church **comes** [+899+2093+3836] **together** and
14:26 When you **come together**, everyone has a hymn, or a word of

5303 συνεσθίω, synesthiō [5] [√ 5250 + 2266]

ate with [2], eat [1], eats with [1], with eat [1]

Lk 15:2 muttered, "This man welcomes sinners and **eats with** them."
Ac 10:41 by us who **ate** and drank **with** him after he rose from the dead.
11:3 went into the house of uncircumcised men and **ate with** them."
1Co 5:11 a drunkard or a swindler. **With** such a man *do* not even **eat**.
Gal 2:12 certain men came from James, *he used to* **eat** with the Gentiles.

5304 σύνεσις, synesis [7] [√ 918; cf. 5250]

understanding [4], insight [2], intelligence [1]

Mk 12:33 your heart, with all your **understanding** and with all your strength,
Lk 2:47 Everyone who heard him was amazed at his **understanding**
1Co 1:19 of the wise; the **intelligence** of the intelligent I will frustrate."
Eph 3:4 you will be able to understand my **insight** into the mystery of
Col 1:9 of his will through all spiritual wisdom and **understanding**.
2:2 so that they may have the full riches *of* complete **understanding**,
2Ti 2:7 what I am saying, for the Lord will give you **insight** into all this.

5305 συνετός, synetos [4] [√ 918; cf. 5250]

intelligent [2], learned [2]

Mt 11:25 because you have hidden these things from the wise and **learned**,
Lk 10:21 because you have hidden these things from the wise and **learned**,
Ac 13:7 The proconsul, an **intelligent** man, sent for Barnabas and Saul
1Co 1:19 of the wise; the intelligence *of* the **intelligent** I will frustrate."

5306 συνευδοκέω, syneudokeō [6]
[√ 5250 + 2292 + 1506]

approve of [2], giving approval [2], willing [2]

Lk 11:48 So you testify that *you* **approve of** what your forefathers did;

Ac   8: 1   And Saul was there, **giving approval** to his death. On that day a
      22:20   I stood there **giving** my **approval** and guarding the clothes of those
Ro   1:32   do these very things but also **approve of** those who practice them.
1Co   7:12   has a wife who is not a believer and she *is* **willing** to live with him,
      7:13   a husband who is not a believer and he *is* **willing** to live with her,

5307 συνευωχέομαι, *syneuōcheomai* [2]
[√ *5250 + 2292 + 2400*]

eating with [1], feast with [1]

2Pe   2:13   reveling in their pleasures *while they* **feast with** you.
Jude 1:12   at your love feasts, **eating with** you without the slightest qualm—

5308 συνεφίστημι, *synephistēmi* [1]
[√ *5250 + 2093 + 2705*]

joined in the attack [1]

Ac   16:22   The crowd **joined in the attack** against Paul and Silas,

5309 συνέχω, *synechō* [12]   [√ *5250 + 2400*]

suffering [2], compels [1], covered [1], crowding against [1],
devoted [1], distressed [1], guarding [1], hem in [1], overcome
[1], suffering from [1], torn [1]

Mt   4:24   those **suffering** severe pain, the demon-possessed, those having
Lk   4:38   Now Simon's mother-in-law was **suffering** from a high fever,
      8:37   asked Jesus to leave them, because *they were* **overcome** with fear.
      8:45   "Master, the people *are* **crowding** and pressing **against** you."
     12:50   to undergo, and how **distressed** *I am* until it is completed!
     19:43   against you and encircle you and **hem** you **in** on every side.
     22:63   The men who *were* **guarding** Jesus began mocking and beating
Ac   7:57   At this *they* **covered** their ears and, yelling at the top of their
     18: 5   from Macedonia, Paul **devoted** *himself exclusively* to preaching,
     28: 8   His father was sick in bed, **suffering from** fever and dysentery.
2Co   5:14   For Christ's love **compels** us, because we are convinced that one
Php   1:23   *I am* **torn** between the two: I desire to depart and be with Christ,

5310 συνήδομαι, *synēdomai* [1]   [√ *5250 + 2454*]

delight [1]

Ro   7:22   For in my inner being *I* **delight** in God's law;

5311 συνήθεια, *synētheia* [3]   [√ *5250 + 1621*]

accustomed to [1], custom [1], practice [1]

Jn   18:39   But it is your **custom** for me to release to you one prisoner at the
1Co   8: 7   so **accustomed to** idols that when they eat such food they think of
     11:16   wants to be contentious about this, we have no other **practice**—

5312 συνηλικιώτης, *synēlikiōtēs* [1]   [√ *5250 + 2462*]

of own age [1]

Gal   1:14   I was advancing in Judaism beyond many Jews **of** my **own age**

5313 συνθάπτω, *synthaptō* [2]   [√ *5250 + 2507*]

buried with [2]

Ro   6: 4   *We were* therefore **buried with** him through baptism into death in
Col   2:12   *having been* **buried with** him in baptism and raised with him

5314 συνθλάω, *synthlaō* [2]   [√ *5250*]

broken to pieces [2]

Mt   21:44   He who falls on this stone *will be* **broken to pieces**, but he on
Lk   20:18   Everyone who falls on that stone *will be* **broken to pieces**,

5315 συνθλίβω, *synthlibō* [2]   [√ *5250 + 2567*]

crowding against [1], pressed around [1]

Mk   5:24   went with him. A large crowd followed and **pressed around** him.

      5:31   "You see the people **crowding against** you," his disciples

5316 συνθρύπτω, *synthryptō* [1]   [√ *5250 + 2586*]

breaking [1]

Ac   21:13   Paul answered, "Why are you weeping and **breaking** my heart?

5317 συνίημι, *syniēmi* [26]   [√ *918; cf. 5250*]

understand [14], understood [4], understanding [3], understands
[2], did[s] [1], realize [1], wise [1]

Mt   13:13   they do not see; though hearing, *they do* not hear or **understand**.
     13:14   " 'You will be ever hearing but never **understanding**; you will be
     13:15   hear with their ears, **understand** with their hearts and turn,
     13:19   hears the message about the kingdom and *does* not **understand** it,
     13:23   on good soil is the man who hears the word and **understands** it.
     13:51   "*Have you* **understood** all these things?" Jesus asked. "Yes,"
     15:10   Jesus called the crowd to him and said, "Listen and **understand**.
     16:12   Then *they* **understood** that he was not telling them to guard
     17:13   Then the disciples **understood** that he was talking to them about
Mk   4:12   but never perceiving, and ever hearing but never **understanding**;
      6:52   for *they had* not **understood** about the loaves; their hearts were
      7:14   to him and said, "Listen to me, everyone, and **understand** this.
      8:17   Do you still not see or **understand**? Are your hearts hardened?
      8:21   He said to them, "*Do you* still not **understand**?"
Lk   2:50   But they *did* not **understand** what he was saying to them.
      8:10   they may not see; though hearing, *they may* not **understand**.'
     18:34   The disciples *did* not **understand** any of this. Its meaning was
     24:45   he opened their minds *so* they *could* **understand** the Scriptures.
Ac   7:25   Moses thought that his own people *would* **realize** that God was
      7:25   realize that God was using him to rescue them, but they **did**[s] not.
     28:26   and say, "You will be ever hearing but never **understanding**;
     28:27   hear with their ears, **understand** with their hearts and turn,
Ro   3:11   there is no one *who* **understands**, no one who seeks God.
     15:21   will see, and those who have not heard *will* **understand**."
2Co 10:12   and compare themselves with themselves, *they are* not **wise**.
Eph   5:17   do not be foolish, but **understand** what the Lord's will is.

5318 συνιστάω, *synistaō*   Not used in UBS/NIV
[√ *5250 + 2705*]

5319 συνίστημι, *synistēmi* [16]   [√ *5250 + 2705*]

commend [6], commends [2], brings out more clearly [1],
commended [1], demonstrates [1], formed [1], hold together [1],
prove that [1], proved [1], standing with [1]

Lk   9:32   they saw his glory and the two men **standing with** him.
Ro   3: 5   our unrighteousness **brings out** God's righteousness **more clearly**,
      5: 8   But God **demonstrates** his own love for us in this: While we were
     16: 1   *I* **commend** to you our sister Phoebe, a servant of the church in
2Co   3: 1   Are we beginning *to* **commend** ourselves again? Or do we need,
      4: 2   by setting forth the truth plainly *we* **commend** ourselves to every
      5:12   *We are* not *trying to* **commend** ourselves to you again, but are
      6: 4   Rather, as servants of God *we* **commend** ourselves in every way:
      7:11   At every point *you have* **proved** yourselves to be innocent in this
     10:12   or compare ourselves with some who **commend** themselves.
     10:18   For it is not the one *who* **commends** himself who is approved,
     10:18   himself who is approved, but the one whom the Lord **commends**.
     12:11   I ought *to have been* **commended** by you, for I am not in the least
Gal   2:18   If I rebuild what I destroyed, *I* **prove that** I am a lawbreaker.
Col   1:17   He is before all things, and in him all things **hold together**.
2Pe   3: 5   and the earth *was* **formed** out of water and by water.

5320 συνίω, *syniō*   Not used in UBS/NIV   [√ *918; cf. 5250*]

5321 συνοδεύω, *synodeuō* [1]   [√ *5250 + 3847*]

traveling with [1]

Ac   9: 7   The men **traveling with** Saul stood there speechless; they heard

5322 συνοδία, *synodia* [1] [√ 5250 + 3847]

company [1]

Lk 2:44 Thinking he was in their **company**, they traveled on for a day.

5323 σύνοιδα, *synoida* [2] [√ 5250 + 3857]

conscience is clear [+4029] [1], full knowledge [1]

Ac 5: 2 *With* his wife's **full knowledge** he kept back part of the money for
1Co 4: 4 My **conscience** [+4029] **is clear**, but that does not make me

5324 συνοικέω, *synoikeō* [1] [√ 5250 + 3875]

live with [1]

1Pe 3: 7 in the same way be considerate *as you* **live with** your wives,

5325 συνοικοδομέω, *synoikodomeō* [1]
[√ 5250 + 3875 + 1560]

built together [1]

Eph 2:22 And in him you too *are being* **built together** to become a dwelling

5326 συνομιλέω, *synomileō* [1] [√ 5250 + 3917]

talking with [1]

Ac 10:27 **Talking with** him, Peter went inside and found a large gathering of

5327 συνομορέω, *synomoreō* [1]
[√ 5250 + 3927 + 4000]

next door [1]

Ac 18: 7 the synagogue and went **next door** to the house of Titius Justus,

5328 συνοράω, *synoraō* [2] [√ 5250 + 3972]

dawned on [1], found out about [1]

Ac 12:12 *When* this *had* **dawned on** him, he went to the house of Mary the
     14: 6 But *they* **found out about** it and fled to the Lycaonian cities of

5329 συνορία, *synoria* Not used in UBS/NIV
[√ 5250 + 4000]

5330 συνοχή, *synochē* [2] [√ 5250 + 2400]

anguish [2]

Lk 21:25 nations will be in **anguish** and perplexity at the roaring and tossing
2Co 2: 4 you out of great distress and **anguish** of heart and with many tears,

5331 συνταράσσω, *syntarassō* Not used in UBS/NIV
[√ 5250 + 5429]

5332 συντάσσω, *syntassō* [3] [√ 5250 + 5435]

commanded [1], directed [1], instructed [1]

Mt 21: 6 The disciples went and did as Jesus *had* **instructed** them.
     26:19 So the disciples did as Jesus *had* **directed** them and prepared the
     27:10 used them to buy the potter's field, as the Lord **commanded** me."

5333 συντέλεια, *synteleia* [6] [√ 5250 + 5465]

end [5], very end [1]

Mt 13:39 The harvest is the **end** of the age, and the harvesters are angels.
     13:40 pulled up and burned in the fire, so it will be at the **end** of the age.
     13:49 This is how it will be at the **end** of the age. The angels will come
     24: 3 what will be the sign of your coming and *of* the **end** of the age?"
     28:20 And surely I am with you always, to the **very end** of the age."
Heb 9:26 But now he has appeared once for all at the **end** of the ages to do

5334 συντελέω, *synteleō* [6] [√ 5250 + 5465]

end [1], finality [1], finished [1], fulfilled [1], make [1], over [1]

Mk 13: 4 And what will be the sign that they are all about to *be* **fulfilled**?"
Lk 4: 2 nothing during those days, and *at* the **end** of them he was hungry.
     4:13 *When* the devil *had* **finished** all this tempting, he left him until an
Ac 21:27 When the seven days *were* nearly **over**, some Jews from the
Ro 9:28 Lord will carry out his sentence on earth *with* speed and **finality**."
Heb 8: 8 when *I will* **make** a new covenant with the house of Israel

5335 συντέμνω, *syntemnō* [1] [√ 5250 + 5533]

speed [1]

Ro 9:28 For the Lord will carry out his sentence on earth *with* **speed**

5336 συντεχνίτης, *syntechnitēs* Not used in
UBS/NIV [√ 5250 + 5492]

5337 συντηρέω, *syntēreō* [3] [√ 5250 + 5498]

preserved [1], protected [1], treasured up [1]

Mt 9:17 they pour new wine into new wineskins, and both *are* **preserved**."
Mk 6:20 because Herod feared John and **protected** him, knowing him to be
Lk 2:19 But Mary **treasured up** all these things and pondered them in her

5338 συντίθημι, *syntithēmi* [3] [√ 5250 + 5502]

agreed [2], decided [1]

Lk 22: 5 They were delighted and **agreed** to give him money.
Jn 9:22 for already the Jews *had* **decided** that anyone who acknowledged
Ac 23:20 "The Jews *have* **agreed** to ask you to bring Paul before the

5339 συντόμως, *syntomōs* [2 / 1] [√ 5250 + 5533]

briefly [1]

Mk 16: S [UBS+ *commanded them they told* **briefly** *to those around Peter.*]
Ac 24: 4 I would request that you be kind enough to hear us **briefly**.

5340 συντρέχω, *syntrechō* [3] [√ 5250 + 5556]

came running [1], plunge with [1], ran [1]

Mk 6:33 and **ran** on foot from all the towns and got there ahead of them.
Ac 3:11 and **came running** to them in the place called Solomon's
1Pe 4: 4 They think it strange that you *do* not **plunge with** them into the

5341 συντρίβω, *syntribō* [7] [√ 5250 + 5561]

broke [2], broken [1], bruised [1], crush [1], dash to pieces [1],
destroying [1]

Mt 12:20 A **bruised** reed he will not break, and a smoldering wick he will
Mk 5: 4 but he tore the chains apart and **broke** the irons on his feet.
     14: 3 pure nard. She **broke** the jar and poured the perfume on his head.
Lk 9:39 at the mouth. It scarcely ever leaves him and *is* **destroying** him.
Jn 19:36 scripture would be fulfilled: "Not one of his bones *will be* **broken**,"
Ro 16:20 The God of peace *will* soon **crush** Satan under your feet. The grace
Rev 2:27 with an iron scepter; *he will* **dash** them **to pieces** like pottery'—

5342 σύντριμμα, *syntrimma* [1] [√ 5250 + 5561]

ruin [1]

Ro 3:16 **ruin** and misery mark their ways,

5343 σύντροφος, *syntrophos* [1] [√ 5250 + 5555]

brought up with [1]

Ac 13: 1 Manaen (who had been **brought up with** Herod the tetrarch)

5344 συντυγχάνω, **syntynchanō** [1] [√ *5250 + 5593*]

get near [1]

Lk   8: 19 but they were not able *to* **get near** him because of the crowd.

5345 Συντύχη, **Syntychē** [1] [√ *5250 + 5593*]

Syntyche [1]

Php   4: 2 and I plead with **Syntyche** to agree with each other in the Lord.

5346 συντυχία, **syntychia**   Not used in UBS/NIV
       [√ *5250 + 5593*]

5347 συνυποκρίνομαι, **synypokrinomai** [1]
       [√ *5250 + 5679 + 3212*]

joined in hypocrisy [1]

Gal   2: 13 The other Jews **joined** him **in** his **hypocrisy**, so that by their

5348 συνυπουργέω, **synypourgeō** [1]
       [√ *5250 + 5679 + 2240*]

help [1]

2Co   1: 11 *as* you **help** us by your prayers. Then many will give thanks on our

5349 συνωδίνω, **synōdinō** [1] [√ *5250 + 6047*]

in the pains of childbirth [1]

Ro   8: 22 groaning as **in the pains of childbirth** right up to the present time.

5350 συνωμοσία, **synōmosia** [1] [√ *5250 + 3923*]

plot [1]

Ac   23: 13 More than forty men were involved in this **plot**.

5351 Σύρα, **Syra**   Not used in UBS/NIV [√ *5354*]

5352 Συράκουσαι, **Syrakousai** [1]

Syracuse [1]

Ac   28: 12 We put in at **Syracuse** and stayed there three days.

5353 Συρία, **Syria** [8] [√ *5354*]

Syria [8]

Mt   4: 24 News about him spread all over **Syria**, and people brought to him
Lk   2: 2 first census that took place while Quirinius was governor *of* **Syria**.)
Ac   15: 23 To the Gentile believers in Antioch, **Syria** and Cilicia:
     15: 41 He went through **Syria** and Cilicia, strengthening the churches.
     18: 18 Then he left the brothers and sailed for **Syria**, accompanied by
     20: 3 Jews made a plot against him just as he was about to sail for **Syria**,
     21: 3 and passing to the south of it, we sailed on to **Syria**.
Gal   1: 21 Later I went to **Syria** and Cilicia.

5354 Σύρος, **Syros** [1] [→ *5351, 5353, 5355, 5356*]

Syrian [1]

Lk   4: 27 yet not one of them was cleansed—only Naaman the **Syrian**.''

5355 Συροφοινίκισσα, **Syrophoinikissa** [1]
       [√ *5354 + 5836*]

Syrian Phoenicia [1]

Mk   7: 26 The woman was a Greek, born in **Syrian Phoenicia**. She begged

5356 Συροφοίνισσα, **Syrophoinissa**   Not used in
       UBS/NIV [√ *5354 + 5836*]

5357 συρρήγνυμι, **syrrēgnymi**   Not used in UBS/NIV
       [√ *5250 + 4838*]

5358 Σύρτις, **Syrtis** [1] [√ *5359*]

sandbars of Syrtis [1]

Ac   27: 17 Fearing that they would run aground on the **sandbars of Syrtis**,

5359 σύρω, **syrō** [5] [→ *2955, 5358*]

dragged [2], dragged off [1], swept [1], towing [1]

Jn   21: 8 **towing** the net full of fish, for they were not far from shore,
Ac   8: 3 to house, *he* **dragged off** men and women and put them in prison.
     14: 19 *They* stoned Paul and **dragged** him outside the city, thinking he
     17: 6 *they* **dragged** Jason and some other brothers before the city
Rev 12: 4 His tail **swept** a third of the stars out of the sky and flung them to

5360 συσπαράσσω, **sysparassō** [2] [√ *5250 + 5060*]

in a convulsion [1], threw into a convulsion [1]

Mk   9: 20 spirit saw Jesus, *it* immediately **threw** the boy **into a convulsion**.
Lk   9: 42 was coming, the demon threw him to the ground **in a convulsion**.

5361 σύσσημον, **syssēmon** [1] [√ *5250 + 4956*]

signal [1]

Mk   14: 44 Now the betrayer had arranged a **signal** with them: ''The one I kiss

5362 σύσσωμος, **syssōmos** [1] [√ *5250 + 5393*]

members together of one body [1]

Eph   3: 6 **members together of one body**, and sharers together in the

5363 συστασιαστής, **systasiastēs**   Not used in
       UBS/NIV [√ *5250 + 2705*]

5364 συστατικός, **systatikos** [1] [√ *5250 + 2705*]

recommendation [1]

2Co   3: 1 like some people, letters *of* **recommendation** to you or from you?

5365 συσταυρόω, **systauroō** [5] [√ *5250 + 5089*]

crucified with [3], crucified with [*RP5250*] [2]

Mt   27: 44 In the same way the robbers who *were* **crucified** [*RP5250*] **with**
Mk   15: 32 Those **crucified** [*RP5250*] **with** him also heaped insults on him.
Jn   19: 32 and broke the legs of the first man who *had been* **crucified with**
Ro   6: 6 For we know that our old self *was* **crucified with** him so that the
Gal   2: 20 *I have been* **crucified with** Christ and I no longer live, but Christ

5366 συστέλλω, **systellō** [2] [√ *5250 + 5097*]

short [1], wrapped up [1]

Ac   5: 6 **wrapped up** his body, and carried him out and buried him.
1Co   7: 29 What I mean, brothers, is that the time is **short**. From now on those

5367 συστενάζω, **systenazō** [1] [√ *5250 + 5101*]

groaning [1]

Ro   8: 22 We know that the whole creation *has been* **groaning** as in the

5368 συστοιχέω, **systoicheō** [1] [√ *5250 + 5123*]

corresponds [1]

Gal   4: 25 Sinai in Arabia and **corresponds** to the present city of Jerusalem,

5369 συστρατιώτης, *systratiōtēs* [2] [√ 5250 + 5131]

fellow soldier [2]

Php 2:25 my brother, fellow worker and **fellow soldier**, who is also your
Phm 1: 2 *to* Archippus our **fellow soldier** and to the church that meets in

5370 συστρέφω, *systrephō* [2] [√ 5250 + 5138]

came together [1], gathered [1]

Mt 17:22 *When* they **came together** in Galilee, he said to them, "The Son of
Ac 28: 3 Paul **gathered** a pile of brushwood and, as he put it on the fire,

5371 συστροφή, *systrophē* [2] [√ 5250 + 5138]

commotion [1], conspiracy [1]

Ac 19:40 In that case we would not be able to account for this **commotion**,
    23:12 The next morning the Jews formed a **conspiracy** and bound

5372 συσχηματίζω, *syschēmatizō* [2] [√ 5250 + 5386]

conform to the pattern of [1], conform [1]

Ro 12: 2 *Do* not **conform** *any longer* **to the pattern of** this world,
1Pe 1:14 *do* not **conform** to the evil desires you had when you lived in

5373 Συχάρ, *Sychar* [1] [→ 4993]

Sychar [1]

Jn 4: 5 So he came to a town in Samaria called **Sychar**, near the plot of

5374 Συχέμ, *Sychem* [2]

Shechem [2]

Ac 7:16 Their bodies were brought back to **Shechem** and placed in the
    7:16 from the sons of Hamor at **Shechem** for a certain sum of money.

5375 σφαγή, *sphagē* [3] [√ 5377]

slaughter [2], slaughtered [1]

Ac 8:32 "He was led like a sheep to the **slaughter**, and as a lamb before the
Ro 8:36 death all day long; we are considered as sheep to be **slaughtered**."
Jas 5: 5 You have fattened yourselves in the day *of* **slaughter**.

5376 σφάγιον, *sphagion* [1] [√ 5377]

offerings [1]

Ac 7:42 you bring me sacrifices and **offerings** forty years in the desert,

5377 σφάζω, *sphazō* [10] [→ 2956, 2957, 5375, 5376]

slain [5], had a wound [1], killed [1], murder [1], murdered [1], slay [1]

1Jn 3:12 like Cain, who belonged to the evil one and **murdered** his brother.
    3:12 evil one and murdered his brother. And why *did he* **murder** him?
Rev 5: 6 Then I saw a Lamb, looking as if *it had been* **slain**, standing in the
    5: 9 to take the scroll and to open its seals, because *you were* **slain**,
    5:12 who *was* **slain**, to receive power and wealth and wisdom
    6: 4 to take peace from the earth and to make men **slay** each other.
    6: 9 I saw under the altar the souls *of* those *who had been* **slain**
    13: 3 One of the heads of the beast seemed *to have* **had a** fatal **wound**,
    13: 8 to the Lamb that *was* **slain** from the creation of the world.
    18:24 and of the saints, and *of* all who *have* been **killed** on the earth."

5378 σφάλλω, *sphallō*   Not used in UBS/NIV [→ 854, 855, 856, 857, 2195]

5379 σφόδρα, *sphodra* [11] [→ 5380]

greatly [2], terrified [+5828] [2], very [2], filled with grief [+3382] [1], great [1], overjoyed [+3489+5897+5915] [1], rapidly [1], so [1]

Mt 2:10 When they saw the star, *they were* **overjoyed** [+3489+5897+5915].
    17: 6 heard this, they fell facedown to the ground, **terrified** [+5828].
    17:23 be raised to life." And the disciples *were* **filled with grief** [+3382].
    18:31 they were **greatly** distressed and went and told their master
    19:25 they were **greatly** astonished and asked, "Who then can be saved?"
    26:22 They were **very** sad and began to say to him one after the other,
    27:54 and all that had happened, *they were* **terrified** [+5828],
Mk 16: 4 saw that the stone, which was **very** large, had been rolled away.
Lk 18:23 he became very sad, because he was a man of **great** wealth.
Ac 6: 7 The number of disciples in Jerusalem increased **rapidly**, and a
Rev 16:21 account of the plague of hail, because the plague was **so** terrible.

5380 σφοδρῶς, *sphodrōs* [1] [√ 5379]

such violent [1]

Ac 27:18 We took **such** a **violent** battering from the storm that the next day

5381 σφραγίζω, *sphragizō* [15] [√ 5382]

sealed [4], *untranslated* [2], seal up [2], certified [+3456+3836] [1], made sure that [1], marked with a seal [1], on placed seal of approval [1], put a seal [1], putting a seal on [1], set seal of ownership on [1]

Mt 27:66 they went and made the tomb secure *by* **putting a seal on** the stone
Jn 3:33 The man who has accepted it *has* **certified** [+3456+3836] that God
    6:27 give you. **On** him God the Father *has* **placed** *his* **seal of approval**."
Ro 15:28 So after *I* have completed this task and *have* **made sure that** they
2Co 1:22 **set** his **seal of ownership on** us, and put his Spirit in our hearts as
Eph 1:13 Having believed, *you were* **marked** in him **with a seal**,
    4:30 of God, with whom *you were* **sealed** for the day of redemption.
Rev 7: 3 or the trees until *we* **put a seal** on the foreheads of the servants of
    7: 4 Then I heard the number *of* those *who were* **sealed**: 144,000 from
    7: 4 who were sealed: 144,000 **[RPG]** from all the tribes of Israel.
    7: 5 From the tribe of Judah 12,000 *were* **sealed**, from the tribe of
    7: 8 of Joseph 12,000, from the tribe of Benjamin 12,000. **[RPG]**
    10: 4 "**Seal up** what the seven thunders have said and do not write it
    20: 3 He threw him into the Abyss, and locked and **sealed** it over him,
    22:10 told me, "*Do* not **seal up** the words of the prophecy of this book,

5382 σφραγίς, *sphragis* [16] [→ 2958, 5381]

seal [10], seals [5], sealed with [+2400+3836] [1]

Ro 4:11 a **seal** of the righteousness that he had by faith while he was still
1Co 9: 2 I am to you! For you are the **seal** of my apostleship in the Lord.
2Ti 2:19 God's solid foundation stands firm, **sealed** [+2400+3836] **with** this
Rev 5: 1 a scroll with writing on both sides and sealed *with* seven **seals**.
    5: 2 loud voice, "Who is worthy to break the **seals** and open the scroll?"
    5: 5 has triumphed. He is able to open the scroll and its seven **seals**."
    5: 9 "You are worthy to take the scroll and to open its **seals**, because you
    6: 1 I watched as the Lamb opened the first of the seven **seals**.
    6: 3 When the Lamb opened the second **seal**, I heard the second living
    6: 5 When the Lamb opened the third **seal**, I heard the third living
    6: 7 When the Lamb opened the fourth **seal**, I heard the voice of the
    6: 9 When he opened the fifth **seal**, I saw under the altar the souls of
    6:12 I watched as he opened the sixth **seal**. There was a great
    7: 2 angel coming up from the east, having the **seal** of the living God.
    8: 1 When he opened the seventh **seal**, there was silence in heaven for
    9: 4 but only those people who did not have the **seal** of God on their

5383 σφυδρόν, *sphydron* [1] [√ 5384]

ankles [1]

Ac 3: 7 him up, and instantly the man's feet and **ankles** became strong.

5384 σφυρόν, *sphyron*   Not used in UBS/NIV [→ 5383]

5385 σχεδόν, schedon [3] [√ 2400]

almost [1], nearly [1], practically [1]

Ac 13:44 On the next Sabbath **almost** the whole city gathered to hear the
    19:26 here in Ephesus and in **practically** the whole province of Asia.
Heb 9:22 the law requires that **nearly** everything be cleansed with blood,

5386 σχῆμα, schēma [2] [→ 858, 859, 860, 2360, 2361, 2362, 2363, 3571, 5372; cf. 2400]

form [1], in appearance [1]

1Co 7:31 in them. For this world in its *present* **form** is passing away.
Php 2: 8 And being found **in appearance** as a man, he humbled himself

5387 σχίζω, schizō [11] [→ 5388]

torn [5], divided [2], split [1], tear [1], tears [1], torn open [1]

Mt 27:51 At that moment the curtain of the temple *was* **torn** in two from top
    27:51 in two from top to bottom. The earth shook and the rocks **split**.
Mk 1:10 he saw heaven *being* **torn open** and the Spirit descending on him
    15:38 The curtain of the temple *was* **torn** in two from top to bottom.
Lk 5:36 "No one **tears** a patch from a new garment and sews it on an old
    5:36 If he does, *he will have* **torn** the new garment, and the patch from
    23:45 stopped shining. And the curtain of the temple *was* **torn** in two.
Jn 19:24 "*Let's* not **tear** it," they said to one another. "Let's decide by lot
    21:11 full of large fish, 153, but even with so many the net *was* not **torn**.
Ac 14: 4 The people of the city *were* **divided**; some sided with the Jews,
    23: 7 the Pharisees and the Sadducees, and the assembly *was* **divided**.

5388 σχίσμα, schisma [8] [√ 5387]

divided [3], divisions [2], tear [2], division [1]

Mt 9:16 the patch will pull away from the garment, making the **tear** worse.
Mk 2:21 the new piece will pull away from the old, making the **tear** worse.
Jn 7:43 Thus the people were **divided** because of Jesus.
    9:16 can a sinner do such miraculous signs?" So they were **divided**.
    10:19 At these words the Jews were again **divided**.
1Co 1:10 with one another so that there may be no **divisions** among you
    11:18 there are **divisions** among you, and to some extent I believe it.
    12:25 so that there should be no **division** in the body, but that its parts

5389 σχοινίον, schoinion [2]

cords [1], ropes [1]

Jn 2:15 So he made a whip out of **cords**, and drove all from the temple
Ac 27:32 So the soldiers cut the **ropes** that held the lifeboat and let it fall

5390 σχολάζω, scholazō [2] [√ 5391]

devote [1], unoccupied [1]

Mt 12:44 it finds the house **unoccupied**, swept clean and put in order.
1Co 7: 5 and for a time, so that *you may* **devote** *yourselves* to prayer.

5391 σχολή, scholē [1] [→ 5390]

lecture hall [1]

Ac 19: 9 and had discussions daily in the **lecture hall** of Tyrannus.

5392 σῴζω, sōzō [106] [→ 420, 861, 862, 1407, 1751, 5396, 5399, 5400, 5401, 5402, 5403]

saved [45], save [37], healed [13], saved [+1639] [2], survive [2], bring safely [1], cured [1], delivered [1], get better [1], made well [1], make well [1], saves [1]

Mt 1:21 the name Jesus, because he *will* **save** his people from their sins."
    8:25 The disciples went and woke him, saying, "Lord, **save** us!
    9:21 She said to herself, "If I only touch his cloak, *I will be* **healed**."
    9:22 "Take heart, daughter," he said, "your faith *has* **healed** you."
    9:22 *has* **healed** you." And the woman *was* **healed** from that moment.
    10:22 because of me, but he who stands firm to the end *will be* **saved**.
    14:30 he was afraid and, beginning to sink, cried out, "Lord, **save** me!"

    16:25 For whoever wants *to* **save** his life will lose it, but whoever loses
    19:25 they were greatly astonished and asked, "Who then can *be* **saved**?"
    24:13 but he who stands firm to the end *will be* **saved**.
    24:22 If those days had not been cut short, no one would **survive**,
    27:40 to destroy the temple and build it in three days, **save** yourself!
    27:42 "*He* **saved** others," they said, "but he can't save himself! He's the
    27:42 "*He* saved others," they said, "but he can't **save** himself! He's the
    27:49 "Now leave him alone. Let's see if Elijah comes *to* **save** him."
Mk 3: 4 to do good or to do evil, *to* **save** life or to kill?" But they remained
    5:23 and put your hands on her so that *she will be* **healed** and live."
    5:28 because she thought, "If I just touch his clothes, *I will be* **healed**."
    5:34 He said to her, "Daughter, your faith *has* **healed** you. Go in peace
    6:56 even the edge of his cloak, and all who touched him *were* **healed**.
    8:35 For whoever wants *to* **save** his life will lose it, but whoever loses
    8:35 but whoever loses his life for me and for the gospel *will* **save** it.
    10:26 more amazed, and said to each other, "Who then can *be* **saved**?"
    10:52 "Go," said Jesus, "your faith *has* **healed** you." Immediately he
    13:13 because of me, but he who stands firm to the end *will be* **saved**.
    13:20 If the Lord had not cut short those days, no one would **survive**.
    15:30 come down from the cross and **save** yourself!"
    15:31 "*He* **saved** others," they said, "but he can't save himself!
    15:31 "*He* saved others," they said, "but he can't **save** himself!
    16:16 Whoever believes and is baptized *will be* **saved**, but whoever does
Lk 6: 9 the Sabbath: to do good or to do evil, *to* **save** life or to destroy it?"
    7:50 Jesus said to the woman, "Your faith *has* **saved** you; go in peace."
    8:12 word from their hearts, so that *they may* not believe and *be* **saved**.
    8:36 it told the people how the demon-possessed man *had been* **cured**.
    8:48 Then he said to her, "Daughter, your faith *has* **healed** you.
    8:50 to Jairus, "Don't be afraid; just believe, and *she will be* **healed**."
    9:24 For whoever wants *to* **save** his life will lose it, but whoever loses
    9:24 his life will lose it, but whoever loses his life for me *will* **save** it.
    13:23 asked him, "Lord, *are* only a few people *going to be* **saved**?"
    17:19 Then he said to him, "Rise and go; your faith *has* **made** you **well**."
    18:26 Those who heard this asked, "Who then can *be* **saved**?"
    18:42 Jesus said to him, "Receive your sight; your faith *has* **healed** you."
    19:10 For the Son of Man came to seek and *to* **save** what was lost."
    23:35 They said, "*He* **saved** others; let him save himself if he is the
    23:35 *let him* **save** himself if he is the Christ of God, the Chosen One."
    23:37 and said, "If you are the king of the Jews, **save** yourself."
    23:39 insults at him: "Aren't you the Christ? **Save** yourself and us!"
Jn 3:17 world to condemn the world, but to **save** the world through him.
    5:34 I accept human testimony; but I mention it that you *may be* **saved**.
    10: 9 I am the gate; whoever enters through me *will be* **saved**. He will
    11:12 His disciples replied, "Lord, if he sleeps, *he will* **get better**."
    12:27 'Father, **save** me from this hour'? No, it was for this very reason I
    12:47 not judge him. For I did not come to judge the world, but to **save** it.
Ac 2:21 And everyone who calls on the name of the Lord *will be* **saved**.'
    2:40 pleaded with them, "**Save** *yourselves* from this corrupt generation."
    2:47 the Lord added to their number daily those *who were being* **saved**.
    4: 9 of kindness shown to a cripple and are asked how he *was* **healed**,
    4:12 name under heaven given to men by which we must *be* **saved**."
    11:14 message through which you and all your household *will be* **saved**.'
    14: 9 Paul looked directly at him, saw that he had faith *to be* **healed**
    15: 1 according to the custom taught by Moses, you cannot *be* **saved**."
    15:11 believe it is through the grace of our Lord Jesus that we *are* **saved**,
    16:30 brought them out and asked, "Sirs, what must I do to *be* **saved**?"
    16:31 They replied, "Believe in the Lord Jesus, and *you will be* **saved**—
    27:20 continued raging, we finally gave up all hope *of being* **saved**.
    27:31 "Unless these men stay with the ship, you cannot *be* **saved**."
Ro 5: 9 how much more *shall we be* **saved** from God's wrath through him!
    5:10 having been reconciled, *shall we be* **saved** through his life!
    8:24 For in this hope *we were* **saved**. But hope that is seen is no hope at
    9:27 be like the sand by the sea, only the remnant *will be* **saved**.
    10: 9 your heart that God raised him from the dead, *you will be* **saved**.
    10:13 "Everyone who calls on the name of the Lord *will be* **saved**."
    11:14 somehow arouse my own people to envy and **save** some of them.
    11:26 And so all Israel *will be* **saved**, as it is written: "The deliverer will
1Co 1:18 but *to us who are being* **saved** it is the power of God.
    1:21 the foolishness of what was preached to **save** those who believe.
    3:15 he himself *will be* **saved**, but only as one escaping through the
    5: 5 may be destroyed and his spirit **saved** on the day of the Lord.
    7:16 How do you know, wife, whether *you will* **save** your husband?
    7:16 how do you know, husband, whether *you will* **save** your wife?
    9:22 things to all men so that by all possible means *I might* **save** some.
    10:33 my own good but the good of many, so that *they may be* **saved**.
    15: 2 By this gospel *you are* **saved**, if you hold firmly to the word I

2Co	2:15	are to God the aroma of Christ among those *who are being* **saved**
Eph	2: 5	in transgressions—it is by grace *you have been* **saved** [*+1639*].
	2: 8	For it is by grace *you have been* **saved** [*+1639*], through faith—
1Th	2:16	keep us from speaking to the Gentiles so that *they may be* **saved**.
2Th	2:10	because they refused to love the truth and so *be* **saved**.
1Ti	1:15	Christ Jesus came into the world *to* **save** sinners—of whom I am
	2: 4	who wants all men *to be* **saved** and to come to a knowledge of the
	2:15	But women *will be* **saved** through childbearing—if they continue
	4:16	because if you do, *you will* **save** both yourself and your hearers.
2Ti	1: 9	who *has* **saved** us and called us to a holy life—not because of
	4:18	evil attack and *will* **bring** me **safely** to his heavenly kingdom.
Tit	3: 5	he **saved** us, not because of righteous things we had done,
Heb	5: 7	loud cries and tears to the one who could **save** him from death,
	7:25	Therefore he is able *to* **save** completely those who come to God
Jas	1:21	and humbly accept the word planted in you, which can **save** you.
	2:14	claims to have faith but has no deeds? Can such faith **save** him?
	4:12	one Lawgiver and Judge, the one who is able *to* **save** and destroy.
	5:15	And the prayer offered in faith *will* **make** the sick person **well**;
	5:20	Whoever turns a sinner from the error of his way *will* **save** him
1Pe	3:21	and this water symbolizes baptism that now **saves** you also—
	4:18	And, "If it is hard for the righteous *to be* **saved**, what will become
Jude	1: 5	I want to remind you that the Lord **delivered** his people out of
	1:23	snatch others from the fire and **save** them; to others show mercy,

5393 σῶμα, *sōma* [142] [→ *5362, 5394, 5395*]

ὅλος σῶμα, (whole body) [10] Mt 5:29,30; 6:22,23; Lk 11:34,36; 1Co 12:17; Jas 3:2,3,6

πνεῦμα ... σῶμα, (spirit ... body) [13] Ro 8:10,11,11,13,23; 1Co 5:3; 6:19; 7:34; 12:13,13; Eph 4:4; 1Th 5:23; Jas 2:26

σῶμα Ἰησοῦ, (body of Jesus) [13] Mt 26:26; 27:58; Mk 14:22; 15:43; Lk 23:52; 24:3; Jn 19:38,38,40; 20:12; Ro 8:11; 2Co 4:10; Heb 10:10

σῶμα ... ψυχη, (body ... soul) [8] Mt 6:25,25; 10:28,28; Lk 12:22,23; 1Th 5:23; Rev 18:13

body [115], bodies [14], *untranslated* [1], animal [1], dead body [1], dead [1], in person [*+3836+3836+4242*] [1], its[s] [*+3836*] [1], person [1], physical [1], physically [1], reality [1], sinful [*+3836*] [1], suffering[s] [*+1877*] [1], the parts [*+3836+4047*] [1]

Mt	5:29	part of your body than for your whole **body** to be thrown into hell.
	5:30	one part of your body than for your whole **body** to go into hell.
	6:22	"The eye is the lamp *of* the **body**. If your eyes are good, your whole
	6:22	If your eyes are good, your whole **body** will be full of light.
	6:23	But if your eyes are bad, your whole **body** will be full of darkness.
	6:25	you will eat or drink; or about your **body**, what you will wear.
	6:25	important than food, and the **body** more important than clothes?
	10:28	Do not be afraid of those who kill the **body** but cannot kill the soul.
	10:28	be afraid of the One who can destroy both soul and **body** in hell.
	26:12	When she poured this perfume on my **body**, she did it to prepare
	26:26	and gave it to his disciples, saying, "Take and eat; this is my **body**."
	27:52	and the **bodies** of many holy people who had died were raised to
	27:58	Going to Pilate, he asked for Jesus' **body**, and Pilate ordered that it
	27:59	Joseph took the **body**, wrapped it in a clean linen cloth,
Mk	5:29	and she felt *in* her **body** that she was freed from her suffering.
	14: 8	She poured perfume on my **body** beforehand to prepare for my
	14:22	and gave it to his disciples, saying, "Take it; this is my **body**."
	15:43	kingdom of God, went boldly to Pilate and asked for Jesus' **body**.
Lk	11:34	Your eye is the lamp *of* your **body**. When your eyes are good,
	11:34	When your eyes are good, your whole **body** also is full of light.
	11:34	But when they are bad, your **body** also is full of darkness.
	11:36	Therefore, if your whole **body** is full of light, and no part of it
	12: 4	do not be afraid of those who kill the **body** and after that can do no
	12:22	what you will eat; or about your **body**, what you will wear.
	12:23	Life is more than food, and the **body** more than clothes.
	17:37	He replied, "Where there is a **dead body**, there the vultures will
	22:19	and gave it to them, saying, "This is my **body** given for you;
	23:52	Going to Pilate, he asked for Jesus' **body**.
	23:55	followed Joseph and saw the tomb and how his **body** was laid in it.
	24: 3	when they entered, they did not find the **body** of the Lord Jesus.
	24:23	but didn't find his **body**. They came and told us that they had seen
Jn	2:21	But the temple he had spoken of was his **body**.
	19:31	Because the Jews did not want the **bodies** left on the crosses during
	19:38	Later, Joseph of Arimathea asked Pilate for the **body** of Jesus.

	19:38	With Pilate's permission, he came and took the **body** away.
	19:40	Taking Jesus' **body**, the two of them wrapped it, with the spices,
	20:12	seated where Jesus' **body** had been, one at the head and the other at
Ac	9:40	Turning toward the **dead woman**, he said, "Tabitha, get up."
Ro	1:24	sexual impurity for the degrading of their **bodies** with one another.
	4:19	in his faith, he faced the fact that his **body** was as good as dead—
	6: 6	with him so that the **body** of sin might be done away with,
	6:12	Therefore do not let sin reign in your mortal **body** so that you
	7: 4	my brothers, you also died to the law through the **body** of Christ,
	7:24	wretched man I am! Who will rescue me from this **body** of death?
	8:10	your **body** is dead because of sin, yet your spirit is alive because of
	8:11	dead will also give life *to* your mortal **bodies** through his Spirit,
	8:13	but if by the Spirit you put to death the misdeeds *of* the **body**,
	8:23	eagerly for our adoption as sons, the redemption *of* our **bodies**.
	12: 1	to offer your **bodies** as living sacrifices, holy and pleasing to God—
	12: 4	Just as each of us has one **body** with many members, and these
	12: 5	so in Christ we who are many form one **body**, and each member
1Co	5: 3	Even though I am not **physically** present, I am with you in spirit.
	6:13	The **body** is not meant for sexual immorality, but for the Lord,
	6:13	for sexual immorality, but for the Lord, and the Lord *for* the **body**.
	6:15	Do you not know that your **bodies** are members of Christ himself?
	6:16	he who unites himself with a prostitute is one with her in **body**?
	6:18	All other sins a man commits are outside his **body**, but he who sins
	6:18	his body, but he who sins sexually sins against his own **body**.
	6:19	Do you not know that your **body** is a temple of the Holy Spirit,
	6:20	you were bought at a price. Therefore honor God with your **body**.
	7: 4	The wife's **body** does not belong to her alone but also to her
	7: 4	the husband's **body** does not belong to him alone but also to his
	7:34	Her aim is to be devoted to the Lord *in* both **body** and spirit.
	9:27	I beat my **body** and make it my slave so that after I have preached
	10:16	And is not the bread that we break a participation *in* the **body** of
	10:17	Because there is one loaf, we, who are many, are one **body**,
	11:24	he broke it and said, "This is my **body**, which is for you;
	11:27	in an unworthy manner will be guilty of sinning against the **body**
	11:29	who eats and drinks without recognizing the **body** of the Lord eats
	12:12	The **body** is a unit, though it is made up of many parts; and though
	12:12	and though all its[s] [*+3836*] parts are many, they form one body.
	12:12	many parts; and though all its parts are many, they form one **body**.
	12:13	For we were all baptized by one Spirit into one **body**—
	12:14	Now the **body** is not made up of one part but of many.
	12:15	should say, "Because I am not a hand, I do not belong to the **body**,"
	12:15	the body," it would not for that reason cease to be part of the **body**.
	12:16	should say, "Because I am not an eye, I do not belong to the **body**,"
	12:16	the body," it would not for that reason cease to be part of the **body**.
	12:17	If the whole **body** were an eye, where would the sense of hearing
	12:18	But in fact God has arranged the parts in the **body**, every one of
	12:19	If they were all one part, where would the **body** be?
	12:20	As it is, there are many parts, but one **body**.
	12:22	those parts *of* the **body** that seem to be weaker are indispensable,
	12:23	and **the parts**[s] [*+3836+4047*] that we think are less honorable we
	12:24	But God has combined the members of the **body** and has given
	12:25	so that there should be no division in the **body**, but that its parts
	12:27	Now you are the **body** of Christ, and each one of you is a part of it.
	13: 3	give all I possess to the poor and surrender my **body** to the flames,
	15:35	are the dead raised? With what kind of **body** will they come?"
	15:37	you sow, you do not plant the **body** that will be, but just a seed,
	15:38	But God gives it a **body** as he has determined, and to each kind of
	15:38	he has determined, and to each kind of seed he gives its own **body**.
	15:40	There are also heavenly **bodies** and there are earthly bodies;
	15:40	There are also heavenly bodies and there are earthly **bodies**;
	15:44	it is sown a natural **body**, it is raised a spiritual body. If there is a
	15:44	it is sown a natural body, it is raised a spiritual **body**. If there is a
	15:44	If there is a natural **body**, there is also a spiritual body.
2Co	4:10	We always carry around in our **body** the death of Jesus, so that the
	4:10	so that the life of Jesus may also be revealed in our **body**.
	5: 6	and know that as long as we are at home in the **body** we are away
	5: 8	and would prefer to be away from the **body** and at home with the
	5:10	may receive what is due him for the things done while in the **body**,
	10:10	but **in person** [*+3836+3836+4242*] he is unimpressive and his
	12: 2	Whether it was in the **body** or out of the body I do not know—
	12: 2	Whether it was in the body or out of the **body** I do not know—
	12: 3	whether in the **body** or apart from the body I do not know,
	12: 3	whether in the body or apart from the **body** I do not know,
Gal	6:17	no one cause me trouble, for I bear on my **body** the marks of Jesus.
Eph	1:23	which is his **body**, the fullness of him who fills everything in every
	2:16	and in this one **body** to reconcile both of them to God through the

4: 4 There is one **body** and one Spirit—just as you were called to one
4: 12 for works of service, so that the **body** of Christ may be built up
4: 16 From him the whole **body**, joined and held together by every
4: 16 grows **[RPG]** and builds itself up in love, as each part does its
5: 23 is the head of the church, his **body**, of which he is the Savior.
5: 28 same way, husbands ought to love their wives as their own **bodies**.
5: 30 for we are members *of* his **body**.
Php 1: 20 so that now as always Christ will be exalted in my **body**,
3: 21 will transform our lowly **bodies** so that they will be like his
3: 21 our lowly bodies so that they will be like his glorious **body**.
Col 1: 18 And he is the head *of* the **body**, the church; he is the beginning
1: 22 But now he has reconciled you by Christ's physical **body** through
1: 24 Christ's afflictions, for the sake of his **body**, which is the church.
2: 11 also circumcised, in the putting off of the **sinful** [*+3836*] nature,
2: 17 things that were to come; the **reality**, however, is found in Christ.
2: 19 from whom the whole **body**, supported and held together by its
2: 23 their false humility and their harsh treatment *of* the **body**,
3: 15 since as members of one **body** you were called to peace.
1Th 5: 23 and **body** be kept blameless at the coming of our Lord Jesus Christ.
Heb 10: 5 and offering you did not desire, but a **body** you prepared for me;
10: 10 we have been made holy through the sacrifice *of* the **body** of Jesus
10: 22 guilty conscience and having our **bodies** washed with pure water.
13: 3 who are mistreated as if you yourselves were **suffering**⁵ [*+1877*].
13: 11 Place as a sin offering, but the **bodies** are burned outside the camp.
Jas 2: 16 and well fed," but does nothing about his **physical** needs,
2: 26 As the **body** without the spirit is dead, so faith without deeds is
3: 2 he is a perfect man, able to keep his whole **body** in check.
3: 3 of horses to make them obey us, we can turn the whole **animal**.
3: 6 It corrupts the whole **person**, sets the whole course of his life on
1Pe 2: 24 He himself bore our sins in his **body** on the tree, so that we might
Jude 1: 9 when he was disputing with the devil about the **body** of Moses,
Rev 18: 13 and sheep; horses and carriages; and **bodies** and souls of men.

5394 σωματικός, *sōmatikos* [2] [√ *5393*]

bodily [1], physical [1]

Lk 3: 22 and the Holy Spirit descended on him *in* **bodily** form like a dove.
1Ti 4: 8 For **physical** training is of some value, but godliness has value for

5395 σωματικῶς, *sōmatikōs* [1] [√ *5393*]

in bodily form [1]

Col 2: 9 For in Christ all the fullness of the Deity lives **in bodily form**,

5396 Σώπατρος, *Sōpatros* [1] [√ *5392 + 4252*]

Sopater [1]

Ac 20: 4 He was accompanied by **Sopater** son of Pyrrhus from Berea,

5397 σωρεύω, *sōreuō* [2] [→ *2197*]

heap [1], loaded down [1]

Ro 12: 20 to drink. In doing this, *you will* **heap** burning coals on his head."
2Ti 3: 6 *who are* **loaded down** with sins and are swayed by all kinds of

5398 Σωσθένης, *Sōsthenēs* [2]

Sosthenes [2]

Ac 18: 17 Then they all turned on **Sosthenes** the synagogue ruler and beat
1Co 1: 1 of Christ Jesus by the will of God, and our brother **Sosthenes**,

5399 Σωσίπατρος, *Sōsipatros* [1] [√ *5392 + 4252*]

Sosipater [1]

Ro 16: 21 greetings to you, as do Lucius, Jason and **Sosipater**, my relatives.

5400 σωτήρ, *sōtēr* [24] [√ *5392*]

Savior [24]

Lk 1: 47 and my spirit rejoices in God my **Savior**,

2: 11 Today in the town of David a **Savior** has been born to you;
Jn 4: 42 and we know that this man really is the **Savior** of the world."
Ac 5: 31 and **Savior** that he might give repentance and forgiveness of sins to
13: 23 "From this man's descendants God has brought to Israel the **Savior**
Eph 5: 23 is the head of the church, his body, of which he is the **Savior**.
Php 3: 20 And we eagerly await a **Savior** from there, the Lord Jesus Christ,
1Ti 1: 1 apostle of Christ Jesus by the command *of* God our **Savior** and *of*
2: 3 This is good, and pleases God our **Savior**,
4: 10 who is the **Savior** of all men, and especially of those who believe.
2Ti 1: 10 but it has now been revealed through the appearing *of* our **Savior**,
Tit 1: 3 the preaching entrusted to me by the command of God our **Savior**,
1: 4 and peace from God the Father and Christ Jesus our **Savior**.
2: 10 way they will make the teaching *about* God our **Savior** attractive.
2: 13 the glorious appearing *of* our great God and **Savior**, Jesus Christ,
3: 4 But when the kindness and love of God our **Savior** appeared,
3: 6 he poured out on us generously through Jesus Christ our **Savior**,
2Pe 1: 1 To those who through the righteousness *of* our God and **Savior**
1: 11 into the eternal kingdom of our Lord and **Savior** Jesus Christ.
2: 20 and **Savior** Jesus Christ and are again entangled in it
3: 2 and the command *given by* our Lord and **Savior** through your
3: 18 in the grace and knowledge *of* our Lord and **Savior** Jesus Christ.
1Jn 4: 14 and testify that the Father has sent his Son to be the **Savior** of the
Jude 1: 25 *to* the only God our **Savior** be glory, majesty, power and authority,

5401 σωτηρία, *sōtēria* [46 / 45] [√ *5392*]

salvation [36], saved [3], saved [*+1650*] [2], deliverance [1],
rescue [*+1443*] [1], save [1], survive [1]

Mk 16: S [UBS+ *holy and imperishable proclamation of eternal* **salvation**.]
Lk 1: 69 He has raised up a horn *of* **salvation** for us in the house of his
1: 71 **salvation** from our enemies and from the hand of all who hate us—
1: 77 to give his people the knowledge *of* **salvation** through the
19: 9 Jesus said to him, "Today **salvation** has come to this house,
Jn 4: 22 we worship what we do know, for **salvation** is from the Jews.
Ac 4: 12 **Salvation** is found in no one else, for there is no other name under
7: 25 would realize that God was using him to **rescue** [*+1443*] them,
13: 26 it is to us that this message *of* **salvation** has been sent.
13: 47 that you may bring **salvation** to the ends of the earth.' "
16: 17 of the Most High God, who are telling you the way to be **saved**."
27: 34 Now I urge you to take some food. You need it to **survive**.
Ro 1: 16 because it is the power of God for the **salvation** of everyone who
10: 1 prayer to God for the Israelites is that they may be **saved** [*+1650*].
10: 10 and it is with your mouth that you confess and are **saved** [*+1650*].
11: 11 **salvation** has come to the Gentiles to make Israel envious.
13: 11 because our **salvation** is nearer now than when we first believed.
2Co 1: 6 If we are distressed, it is for your comfort and **salvation**; if we are
6: 2 of my favor I heard you, and in the day *of* **salvation** I helped you."
6: 2 now is the time of God's favor, now is the day *of* **salvation**.
7: 10 Godly sorrow brings repentance that leads to **salvation** and leaves
Eph 1: 13 when you heard the word of truth, the gospel *of* your **salvation**.
Php 1: 19 what has happened to me will turn out for my **deliverance**.
1: 28 to them that they will be destroyed, but that you will be **saved**—
2: 12 continue to work out your **salvation** with fear and trembling,
1Th 5: 8 and love as a breastplate, and the hope *of* **salvation** as a helmet.
5: 9 but to receive **salvation** through our Lord Jesus Christ.
2Th 2: 13 because from the beginning God chose you to be **saved** through the
2Ti 2: 10 that they too may obtain the **salvation** that is in Christ Jesus,
3: 15 which are able to make you wise for **salvation** through faith in
Heb 1: 14 ministering spirits sent to serve those who will inherit **salvation**?
2: 3 how shall we escape if we ignore such a great **salvation**?
2: 10 should make the author *of* their **salvation** perfect through
5: 9 he became the source of eternal **salvation** for all who obey him
6: 9 of better things in your case—things that accompany **salvation**.
9: 28 to bear sin, but to bring **salvation** to those who are waiting for him.
11: 7 things not yet seen, in holy fear built an ark to **save** his family.
1Pe 1: 5 of the **salvation** that is ready to be revealed in the last time.
1: 9 are receiving the goal of your faith, the **salvation** of your souls.
1: 10 Concerning this **salvation**, the prophets, who spoke of the grace
2: 2 spiritual milk, so that by it you may grow up in your **salvation**,
2Pe 3: 15 Bear in mind that our Lord's patience means **salvation**, just as our
Jude 1: 3 although I was very eager to write to you about the **salvation** we
Rev 7: 10 "**Salvation** belongs to our God, who sits on the throne, and to the
12: 10 "Now have come the **salvation** and the power and the kingdom of
19: 1 "Hallelujah! **Salvation** and glory and power belong to our God,

5402 σωτήριον, *sōtērion* [4] [√ 5392]

salvation [4]

Lk   2:30 For my eyes have seen your **salvation**,
     3: 6 And all mankind will see God's **salvation**.' "
Ac 28:28 "Therefore I want you to know that God's **salvation** has been sent
Eph 6:17 Take the helmet *of* **salvation** and the sword of the Spirit, which is

5403 σωτήριος, *sōtērios* [1] [√ 5392]

salvation [1]

Tit   2:11 For the grace of God *that brings* **salvation** has appeared to all

5404 σωφρονέω, *sōphroneō* [6] [→ 5405, 5406, 5407, 5408, 5409; cf. 5856]

in right mind [3], clear minded [1], self-controlled [1], sober judgment [1]

Mk   5:15 the legion of demons, sitting there, dressed and **in** *his* **right mind**;
Lk   8:35 had gone out, sitting at Jesus' feet, dressed and **in** *his* **right mind**;
Ro 12: 3 than you ought, but rather think of yourself with **sober judgment**,
2Co 5:13 it is for the sake of God; if *we are* **in** *our* **right mind**, it is for you.
Tit   2: 6 Similarly, encourage the young men *to be* **self-controlled**.
1Pe 4: 7 Therefore *be* **clear minded** and self-controlled so that you can

5405 σωφρονίζω, *sōphronizō* [1] [√ 5404]

train [1]

Tit   2: 4 Then *they can* **train** the younger women to love their husbands

5406 σωφρονισμός, *sōphronismos* [1] [√ 5404]

self-discipline [1]

2Ti 1: 7 of timidity, but a spirit of power, of love and *of* **self-discipline**.

5407 σωφρόνως, *sōphronōs* [1] [√ 5404]

self-controlled [1]

Tit   2:12 and to live **self-controlled**, upright and godly lives in this present

5408 σωφροσύνη, *sōphrosynē* [3] [√ 5404]

propriety [2], reasonable [1]

Ac 26:25 Paul replied. "What I am saying is true and **reasonable**.
1Ti 2: 9 with decency and **propriety**, not with braided hair or gold
     2:15 if they continue in faith, love and holiness with **propriety**.

5409 σώφρων, *sōphrōn* [4] [√ 5404]

self-controlled [4]

1Ti 3: 2 but one wife, temperate, **self-controlled**, respectable, hospitable,
Tit   1: 8 what is good, *who* is **self-controlled**, upright, holy and disciplined.
     2: 2 worthy of respect, **self-controlled**, and sound in faith, in love
     2: 5 to be **self-controlled** and pure, to be busy at home, to be kind,

T, *T*

5410 τ, *t* Not used in UBS/NIV

5411 ταβέρναι, *tabernai* Not used in UBS/NIV [→ 5553]

5412 Ταβιθά, *Tabitha* [2] [√ cf. 2496]

Tabitha [2]

Ac   9:36 In Joppa there was a disciple named **Tabitha** (which,
     9:40 Turning toward the dead woman, he said, "**Tabitha**, get up."

5413 τάγμα, *tagma* [1] [√ 5435]

turn [1]

1Co 15:23 But each in his own **turn**: Christ, the firstfruits; then, when he

5414 τακτός, *taktos* [1] [√ 5435]

appointed [1]

Ac 12:21 *On* the **appointed** day Herod, wearing his royal robes, sat on his

5415 ταλαιπωρέω, *talaipōreō* [1] [√ 5417]

grieve [1]

Jas 4: 9 **Grieve**, mourn and wail. Change your laughter to mourning

5416 ταλαιπωρία, *talaipōria* [2] [√ 5417]

misery [2]

Ro   3:16 ruin and **misery** mark their ways,
Jas 5: 1 weep and wail because of the **misery** that is coming upon you.

5417 ταλαίπωρος, *talaipōros* [2] [→ 5415, 5416]

wretched [2]

Ro   7:24 What a **wretched** man I am! Who will rescue me from this body of
Rev 3:17 But you do not realize that you are **wretched**, pitiful, poor,

5418 ταλαντιαῖος, *talantiaios* [1] [√ 5419]

hundred pounds [1]

Rev 16:21 From the sky huge hailstones *of* about a **hundred pounds** each fell

5419 τάλαντον, *talanton* [14] [→ 5418]

talents [7], *untranslated* [3], talent [3], talents of money [1]

Mt 18:24 a man who owed him ten thousand **talents** was brought to him.
   25:15 To one he gave five **talents of money**, to another two talents,
   25:16 The man who had received the five **talents** went at once and put
   25:20 The man who had received the five **talents** brought the other five.
   25:20 **[RPG]** 'Master,' he said, 'you entrusted me with five talents.
   25:20 'Master,' he said, 'you entrusted me with five **talents**. See,
   25:20 me with five talents. See, I have gained five more.' **[RPG]**
   25:22 'The man with the two **talents** also came. 'Master,' he said,
   25:22 'Master,' he said, 'you entrusted me with two **talents**; see,
   25:22 me with two talents; see, I have gained two more.' **[RPG]**
   25:24 "Then the man who had received the one **talent** came. 'Master,'
   25:25 So I was afraid and went out and hid your **talent** in the ground.
   25:28 " 'Take the **talent** from him and give it to the one who has the ten
   25:28 the talent from him and give it to the one who has the ten **talents**.

5420 ταλιθά, *talitha* [1] [√ cf. 4813]

Talitha [1]

Mk   5:41 He took her by the hand and said to her, "*Talitha koum!*"

5421 ταμεῖον, *tameion* [4] [√ 5533]

inner rooms [2], room [1], storeroom [1]

Mt   6: 6 go into your **room**, close the door and pray to your Father,
   24:26 not go out; or, 'Here he is, in the **inner rooms**,' do not believe it.
Lk 12: 3 and what you have whispered in the ear in the **inner rooms** will be
   12:24 They do not sow or reap, they have no **storeroom** or barn;

5422 τανῦν, *tanyn* Not used in UBS/NIV [√ 3836 + 3814]

5423 τάξις, *taxis* [9] [√ 5435]

order [6], on duty [+1877+3836] [1], orderly way [+2848] [1], orderly [1]

Lk   1: 8 Once when Zechariah's division was **on duty** [+1877+3836]

1Co 14:40 everything should be done in a fitting and **orderly** [+2848] way.
Col 2: 5 present with you in spirit and delight to see how **orderly** you are
Heb 5: 6 "You are a priest forever, in the **order** of Melchizedek."
     5:10 and was designated by God to be high priest in the **order** of
     6:20 He has become a high priest forever, in the **order** of Melchizedek.
     7:11 one in the **order** of Melchizedek, not in the order of Aaron?
     7:11 one in the order of Melchizedek, not in the **order** of Aaron?
     7:17 is declared: "You are a priest forever, in the **order** of Melchizedek."

5424 ταπεινός, *tapeinos* [8] [→ 5425, 5426, 5427, 5428]

humble [4], downcast [1], in humble circumstances [1], of low
position [1], timid [1]

Mt 11:29 upon you and learn from me, for I am gentle and **humble** in heart,
Lk 1:52 down rulers from their thrones but has lifted up the **humble**.
Ro 12:16 be proud, but be willing to associate *with people* **of low position**.
2Co 7: 6 But God, who comforts the **downcast**, comforted us by the coming
    10: 1 I, Paul, who am "**timid**" when face to face with you, but "bold"
Jas 1: 9 The brother **in humble circumstances** ought to take pride in his
     4: 6 "God opposes the proud but gives grace *to* the **humble**."
1Pe 5: 5 because, "God opposes the proud but gives grace *to* the **humble**."

5425 ταπεινοφροσύνη, *tapeinophrosynē* [7]
[√ 5424 + 5856]

humility [6], humble [1]

Ac 20:19 I served the Lord with great **humility** and with tears, although I
Eph 4: 2 Be completely **humble** and gentle; be patient, bearing with one
Php 2: 3 but *in* **humility** consider others better than yourselves.
Col 2:18 Do not let anyone who delights in *false* **humility** and the worship
     2:23 their *false* **humility** and their harsh treatment of the body,
     3:12 with compassion, kindness, **humility**, gentleness and patience.
1Pe 5: 5 clothe yourselves with **humility** toward one another, because,

5426 ταπεινόφρων, *tapeinophrōn* [1] [√ 5424 + 5856]

humble [1]

1Pe 3: 8 be sympathetic, love as brothers, be compassionate and **humble**.

5427 ταπεινόω, *tapeinoō* [14] [√ 5424]

humbled [4], humbles [4], humble [3], lower [1], made low [1],
need [1]

Mt 18: 4 whoever **humbles** himself like this child is the greatest in the
   23:12 For whoever exalts himself *will be* **humbled**, and whoever
   23:12 will be humbled, and whoever **humbles** himself will be exalted.
Lk 3: 5 Every valley shall be filled in, every mountain and hill **made low**.
   14:11 For everyone who exalts himself *will be* **humbled**, and he who
   14:11 will be humbled, and he *who* **humbles** himself will be exalted."
   18:14 For everyone who exalts himself *will be* **humbled**, and he who
   18:14 will be humbled, and he *who* **humbles** himself will be exalted."
2Co 11: 7 Was it a sin for *me to* **lower** myself in order to elevate you by
   12:21 I am afraid that when I come again my God will **humble** me before
Php 2: 8 as a man, *he* **humbled** himself and became obedient to death—
     4:12 I know what it is *to be in* **need**, and I know what it is to have
Jas 4:10 **Humble** *yourselves* before the Lord, and he will lift you up.
1Pe 5: 6 **Humble** *yourselves*, therefore, under God's mighty hand,

5428 ταπείνωσις, *tapeinōsis* [4] [√ 5424]

humble state [1], humiliation [1], low position [1], lowly [1]

Lk 1:48 for he has been mindful of the **humble state** of his servant.
Ac 8:33 In his **humiliation** he was deprived of justice. Who can speak of
Php 3:21 will transform our **lowly** bodies so that they will be like his
Jas 1:10 But the one who is rich should take pride in his **low position**,

5429 ταράσσω, *tarassō* [17] [→ 1410, 1752, 5331, 5430, 5431]

troubled [6], disturbed [2], terrified [2], throwing into confusion
[2], frightened [1], startled [1], stirred [1], stirring up [1], thrown
into turmoil [1]

Mt 2: 3 When King Herod heard this *he was* **disturbed**, and all Jerusalem

14:26 the disciples saw him walking on the lake, *they were* **terrified**.
Mk 6:50 because *they* all saw him and *were* **terrified**. Immediately he
Lk 1:12 Zechariah saw him, *he was* **startled** and was gripped with fear.
   24:38 He said to them, "Why are you **troubled**, and why do doubts rise in
Jn 5: 7 "I have no one to help me into the pool when the water *is* **stirred**.
   11:33 her also weeping, he was deeply moved in spirit and **troubled**.
   12:27 "Now my heart *is* **troubled**, and what shall I say? 'Father, save me
   13:21 Jesus was **troubled** in spirit and testified, "I tell you the truth,
   14: 1 "*Do* not *let* your hearts *be* **troubled**. Trust in God; trust also in me.
   14:27 *Do* not *let* your hearts *be* **troubled** and do not be afraid.
Ac 15:24 went out from us without our authorization and **disturbed** you,
   17: 8 the crowd and the city officials *were* **thrown into turmoil**.
   17:13 they went there too, agitating the crowds and **stirring** them **up**.
Gal 1: 7 Evidently some people are **throwing** you **into confusion** and are
     5:10 The one *who is* **throwing** you **into confusion** will pay the penalty,
1Pe 3:14 you are blessed. "Do not fear what they fear; *do* not *be* **frightened**."

5430 ταραχή, *tarachē* Not used in UBS/NIV [√ 5429]

5431 τάραχος, *tarachos* [2] [√ 5429]

commotion [1], great disturbance [+3900+4024] [1]

Ac 12:18 there was no small **commotion** among the soldiers as to what had
   19:23 there arose a **great disturbance** [+3900+4024] about the Way.

5432 Ταρσεύς, *Tarseus* [2] [√ 5433]

from Tarsus [1], man from Tarsus [1]

Ac 9:11 on Straight Street and ask for a **man from Tarsus** named Saul,
   21:39 Paul answered, "I am a Jew, **from Tarsus** in Cilicia, a citizen of no

5433 Ταρσός, *Tarsos* [3] [→ 5432]

Tarsus [3]

Ac 9:30 they took him down to Caesarea and sent him off to **Tarsus**.
   11:25 Then Barnabas went to **Tarsus** to look for Saul,
   22: 3 "I am a Jew, born in **Tarsus** of Cilicia, but brought up in this city.

5434 ταρταρόω, *tartaroō* [1]

sent to hell [1]

2Pe 2: 4 God did not spare angels when they sinned, but **sent** them **to hell**,

5435 τάσσω, *tassō* [8] [→ 421, 530, 538, 698, 863, 864, 865, 1408, 1409, 1411, 2112, 2198, 2199, 4705, 4726, 5332, 5413, 5414, 5423, 5717, 5718]

appointed [2], *untranslated* [1], arranged [1], assigned [1],
devoted [1], established [1], told [1]

Mt 28:16 went to Galilee, to the mountain where Jesus *had* **told** them to go.
Lk 7: 8 myself am a man under authority, **[RPG]** with soldiers under me.
Ac 13:48 of the Lord; and all who were **appointed** for eternal life believed.
   15: 2 So Paul and Barnabas *were* **appointed**, along with some other
   22:10 There you will be told all that you *have been* **assigned** to do.'
   28:23 *They* **arranged** *to meet* Paul on a certain day, and came in even
Ro 13: 1 The authorities that exist have been **established** by God.
1Co 16:15 and *they have* **devoted** themselves to the service of the saints.

5436 ταῦρος, *tauros* [4]

bulls [3], oxen [1]

Mt 22: 4 My **oxen** and fattened cattle have been butchered, and everything
Ac 14:13 brought **bulls** and wreaths to the city gates because he
Heb 9:13 The blood of goats and **bulls** and the ashes of a heifer sprinkled on
    10: 4 because it is impossible for the blood *of* **bulls** and goats to take

5437 ταὐτά, *tauta* Not used in UBS/NIV [√ 3836 + 899]

5438 ταφή, **taphē** [1] [√ *5439*]

burial place [1]

Mt 27: 7 the money to buy the potter's field as a **burial place** for foreigners.

5439 τάφος, **taphos** [7] [→ *1946, 1947, 5438; cf. 2507*]

tomb [4], tombs [2], graves [1]

Mt 23:27 You are like whitewashed **tombs**, which look beautiful on the
     23:29 You build **tombs** for the prophets and decorate the graves of the
     27:61 and the other Mary were sitting there opposite the **tomb**.
     27:64 So give the order for the **tomb** to be made secure until the third
     27:66 they went and made the **tomb** secure by putting a seal on the stone
     28: 1 Mary Magdalene and the other Mary went to look at the **tomb**.
Ro   3:13 "Their throats are open **graves**; their tongues practice deceit."

5440 τάχα, **tacha** [2] [√ *5444*]

perhaps [1], possibly [1]

Ro   5: 7 though for a good man someone might **possibly** dare to die.
Phm 1:15 **Perhaps** the reason he was separated from you for a little while

5441 ταχέως, **tacheōs** [15] [√ *5444*]

quickly [6], soon [5], easily [1], hasty [1], outran [+4731] [1], very
soon [1]

Lk   14:21 'Go out **quickly** into the streets and alleys of the town and bring in
     16: 6 "The manager told him, 'Take your bill, sit down **quickly**,
Jn   11:31 comforting her, noticed how **quickly** she got up and went out,
     13:27 into him. "What you are about to do, do **quickly**," Jesus told him,
     20: 4 but the other disciple **outran** [+4731] Peter and reached the tomb
Ac   17:15 instructions for Silas and Timothy to join him as **soon** *as possible*.
1Co 4:19 But I will come to you **very soon**, if the Lord is willing, and
Gal 1: 6 so **quickly** deserting the one who called you by the grace of Christ
Php 2:19 I hope in the Lord Jesus to send Timothy to you **soon**, that I also
     2:24 And I am confident in the Lord that I myself will come **soon**.
2Th 2: 2 not to become **easily** unsettled or alarmed by some prophecy,
1Ti 5:22 Do not be **hasty** in the laying on of hands, and do not share in the
2Ti 4: 9 Do your best to come to me **quickly**,
Heb 13:19 particularly urge you to pray so that I may be restored to you **soon**.
     13:23 been released. If he arrives **soon**, I will come with him to see you.

5442 ταχινός, **tachinos** [2] [√ *5444*]

soon [1], swift [1]

2Pe 1:14 because I know that I will **soon** put it aside, as our Lord Jesus
     2: 1 Lord who bought them—bringing **swift** destruction on themselves.

5443 τάχος, **tachos** [8] [√ *5444*]

soon [+1877] [5], immediately [+1877] [1], quick [+1877] [1],
quickly [+1877] [1]

Lk   18: 8 I tell you, he will see that they get justice, and **quickly** [+1877].
Ac   12: 7 "**Quick** [+1877], get up!" he said, and the chains fell off Peter's
     22:18 'Leave Jerusalem **immediately** [+1877], because they will not
     25: 4 being held at Caesarea, and I myself am going there **soon** [+1877].
Ro   16:20 The God of peace will **soon** [+1877] crush Satan under your feet.
1Ti 3:14 Although I hope to come to you **soon** [+1877], I am writing you
Rev 1: 1 which God gave him to show his servants what must **soon** [+1877]
     22: 6 to show his servants the things that must **soon** [+1877] take place."

5444 ταχύς, **tachys** [13] [→ *5440, 5441, 5442, 5443*]

soon [6], quickly [3], quick [2], hurried [1], in the next moment [1]

Mt   5:25 "Settle matters **quickly** with your adversary who is taking you to
     28: 7 Then go **quickly** and tell his disciples: 'He has risen from the dead
     28: 8 So the women **hurried** away from the tomb, afraid yet filled with
Mk   9:39 "No one who does a miracle in my name can **in the next moment**
Lk   15:22 "But the father said to his servants, '**Quick**! Bring the best robe
Jn   11:29 When Mary heard this, she got up **quickly** and went to him.
Jas   1:19 Everyone should be **quick** to listen, slow to speak and slow to
Rev   2:16 I will **soon** come to you and will fight against them with the sword

---

3:11 I am coming **soon**. Hold on to what you have, so that no one will
11:14 The second woe has passed; the third woe is coming **soon**.
22: 7 "Behold, I am coming **soon**! Blessed is he who keeps the words of
22:12 "Behold, I am coming **soon**! My reward is with me, and I will give
22:20 He who testifies to these things says, "Yes, I am coming **soon**."

5445 τέ, **te** [215] See Index of Articles, Etc.

[→ *1664, 1668, 3612, 4020, 4021, 4030, 4046, 4121, 5538, 6063*]

untranslated [139], and [42], both [13], but [4], then [4], so [3],
and also [2], even [2], as [1], between [1], or [1], that is [1],
whether [1], yes [+2285] [1]

5446 τεῖχος, **teichos** [9] [→ *3546, 5526*]

wall [6], walls [3]

Ac   9:25 and lowered him in a basket through an opening in the **wall**.
2Co 11:33 But I was lowered in a basket from a window in the **wall**
Heb 11:30 By faith the **walls** of Jericho fell, after the people had marched
Rev 21:12 It had a great, high **wall** with twelve gates, and with twelve angels
     21:14 The **wall** of the city had twelve foundations, and on them were the
     21:15 a measuring rod of gold to measure the city, its gates and its **walls**.
     21:17 He measured its **wall** and it was 144 cubits thick, by man's
     21:18 The **wall** was made of jasper, and the city of pure gold, as pure as
     21:19 The foundations of the city **walls** were decorated with every kind

5447 τεκμήριον, **tekmērion** [1]

convincing proofs [1]

Ac   1: 3 to these men and gave many **convincing proofs** that he was alive.

5448 τεκνίον, **teknion** [8] [√ *5503*]

dear children [7], children [1]

Jn   13:33 "My **children**, I will be with you only a little longer. You will look
1Jn   2: 1 My **dear children**, I write this to you so that you will not sin.
     2:12 I write to you, **dear children**, because your sins have been
     2:28 And now, **dear children**, continue in him, so that when he appears
     3: 7 **Dear children**, do not let anyone lead you astray. He who does
     3:18 **Dear children**, let us not love with words or tongue but with
     4: 4 You, **dear children**, are from God and have overcome them,
     5:21 **Dear children**, keep yourselves from idols.

5449 τεκνογονέω, **teknogoneō** [1] [√ *5503 + 1181*]

have children [1]

1Ti   5:14 *to* **have children**, to manage their homes and to give the enemy no

5450 τεκνογονία, **teknogonia** [1] [√ *5503 + 1181*]

childbearing [1]

1Ti   2:15 But women will be saved through **childbearing**—if they continue

5451 τέκνον, **teknon** [99] [√ *5503*]

τέκνον θεοῦ, (child of God) [10] Jn 1:12; 11:52; Ro 8:16,21;
9:8; Php 2:15; 1Jn 3:1,2,10; 5:2

children [73], son [14], child [5], children's [2], brood [1],
daughters [1], dear children [1], objects [1], sons [1]

Mt   2:18 Rachel weeping for her **children** and refusing to be comforted,
     3: 9 I tell you that out of these stones God can raise up **children** for
     7:11 though you are evil, know how to give good gifts *to* your **children**,
     9: 2 Jesus saw their faith, he said to the paralytic, "Take heart, **son**;
     10:21 "Brother will betray brother to death, and a father his **child**;
     10:21 **children** will rebel against their parents and have them put to
     15:26 "It is not right to take the **children's** bread and toss it to their dogs."
     18:25 the master ordered that he and his wife and his **children** and all
     19:29 left houses or brothers or sisters or father or mother or **children**
     21:28 There was a man who had two **sons**. He went to the first and said,
     21:28 to the first and said, '**Son**, go and work today in the vineyard.'
     22:24 "Moses told us that if a man dies without having **children**,

23:37	how often I have longed to gather your **children** together,
27:25	the people answered, "Let his blood be on us and on our **children**!"

Mk 2: 5 their faith, he said to the paralytic, "**Son**, your sins are forgiven."
7:27 "First let the **children** eat all they want," he told her, "for it is not
7:27 "for it is not right to take the **children's** bread and toss it to their
10:24 But Jesus said again, "**Children**, how hard it is to enter the
10:29 or brothers or sisters or mother or father or **children** or fields for
10:30 age (homes, brothers, sisters, mothers, **children** and fields—
12:19 us that if a man's brother dies and leaves a wife but no **children**,
13:12 "Brother will betray brother to death, and a father his **child**.
13:12 **Children** will rebel against their parents and have them put to

Lk 1: 7 But they had no **children**, because Elizabeth was barren; and they
1:17 to turn the hearts of the fathers to their **children**
2:48 His mother said to him, "**Son**, why have you treated us like this?"
3: 8 For I tell you that out of these stones God can raise up **children** for
7:35 But wisdom is proved right by all her **children**."
11:13 though you are evil, know how to give good gifts *to* your **children**,
13:34 how often I have longed to gather your **children** together,
14:26 and mother, his wife and **children**, his brothers and sisters—
15:31 " 'My **son**,' the father said, 'you are always with me, and
16:25 "But Abraham replied, '**Son**, remember that in your lifetime you
18:29 or parents or **children** for the sake of the kingdom of God
19:44 dash you to the ground, you and the **children** within your walls.
20:31 and in the same way the seven died, leaving no **children**.
23:28 do not weep for me; weep for yourselves and for your **children**.

Jn 1:12 in his name, gave the right to become **children** or God—
8:39 "If you were Abraham's **children**," said Jesus, "then you would do
11:52 not only for that nation but also for the scattered **children** of God,

Ac 2:39 The promise is *for* you and your **children** and for all who are far
7: 5 possess the land, even though at that time Abraham had no **child**.
13:33 he has fulfilled for us, their **children**, by raising up Jesus.
21: 5 and their wives and **children** accompanied us out of the city,
21:21 telling them not to circumcise their **children** or live according to

Ro 8:16 Spirit himself testifies with our spirit that we are God's **children**.
8:17 Now if we are **children**, then we are heirs—heirs of God
8:21 and brought into the glorious freedom *of* the **children** of God.
9: 7 because they are his descendants are they all Abraham's **children**.
9: 8 other words, it is not the natural **children** who are God's children,
9: 8 other words, it is not the natural children who are God's **children**,
9: 8 but it is the **children** of the promise who are regarded as

1Co 4:14 writing this to shame you, but to warn you, as my dear **children**.
4:17 to you Timothy, my **son** whom I love, who is faithful in the Lord.
7:14 Otherwise your **children** would be unclean, but as it is, they are

2Co 6:13 As a fair exchange—I speak as *to* my **children**—open wide your
12:14 After all, **children** should not have to save up for their parents,
12:14 not have to save up for their parents, but parents *for* their **children**.

Gal 4:19 My **dear children**, for whom I am again in the pains of childbirth
4:25 city of Jerusalem, because she is in slavery with her **children**.
4:27 because more are the **children** of the desolate woman than of her
4:28 Now you, brothers, like Isaac, are **children** of promise.
4:31 Therefore, brothers, we are not **children** of the slave woman,

Eph 2: 3 and thoughts. Like the rest, we were by nature **objects** of wrath.
5: 1 Be imitators of God, therefore, as dearly loved **children**
5: 8 but now you are light in the Lord. Live as **children** of light
6: 1 **Children**, obey your parents in the Lord, for this is right.
6: 4 Fathers, do not exasperate your **children**; instead, bring them up in

Php 2:15 **children** of God without fault in a crooked and depraved
2:22 because as a **son** with his father he has served with me in the work

Col 3:20 **Children**, obey your parents in everything, for this pleases the
3:21 Fathers, do not embitter your **children**, or they will become

1Th 2: 7 gentle among you, like a mother caring for her *little* **children**.
2:11 we dealt with each of you as a father deals with his own **children**,

1Ti 1: 2 To Timothy my true **son** in the faith: Grace, mercy and peace from
1:18 Timothy, my **son**, I give you this instruction in keeping with the
3: 4 family well and see that his **children** obey him with proper respect.
3:12 but one wife and must manage his **children** and his household
5: 4 But if a widow has **children** or grandchildren, these should learn

2Ti 1: 2 *To* Timothy, my dear **son**: Grace, mercy and peace from God the
2: 1 You then, my **son**, be strong in the grace that is in Christ Jesus.

Tit 1: 4 To Titus, my true **son** in our common faith: Grace and peace from
1: 6 a man whose **children** believe and are not open to the charge of

Phm 1:10 I appeal to you for my **son** Onesimus, who became my son while I

1Pe 1:14 As obedient **children**, do not conform to the evil desires you had
3: 6 You are her **daughters** if you do what is right and do not give way

2Pe 2:14 seduce the unstable; they are experts in greed—an accursed **brood**!

1Jn 3: 1 has lavished on us, that we should be called **children** of God!

3: 2 Dear friends, now we are **children** of God, and what we will be
3:10 This is how we know who the **children** of God are and who the
3:10 who the children of God are and who the **children** of the devil are:
5: 2 This is how we know that we love the **children** of God: by loving

2Jn 1: 1 The elder, To the chosen lady and her **children**, whom I love in the
1: 4 It has given me great joy to find some of your **children** walking in
1:13 The **children** of your chosen sister send their greetings.

3Jn 1: 4 I have no greater joy than to hear that my **children** are walking in

Rev 2:23 I will strike her **children** dead. Then all the churches will know
12: 4 so that he might devour her **child** the moment it was born.
12: 5 And her **child** was snatched up to God and to his throne.

5452 τεκνοτροφέω, *teknotropheō* [1] [√ 5503 + 5555]

bringing up children [1]

1Ti 5:10 such as **bringing up children**, showing hospitality, washing the

5453 τεκνόω, *teknoō* Not used in UBS/NIV [√ 5503]

5454 τέκτων, *tektōn* [2] [√ 5492]

carpenter [1], carpenter's [1]

Mt 13:55 "Isn't this the **carpenter's** son? Isn't his mother's name Mary,
Mk 6: 3 Isn't this the **carpenter**? Isn't this Mary's son and the brother of

5455 τέλειος, *teleios* [19] [√ 5465]

perfect [9], mature [5], adults [1], finish [+*2400*] [1], mature [+*467*] [1], more perfect [1], perfection [1]

Mt 5:48 Be **perfect**, therefore, as your heavenly Father is perfect.
5:48 Be perfect, therefore, as your heavenly Father is **perfect**.
19:21 Jesus answered, "If you want to be **perfect**, go, sell your
Ro 12: 2 approve what God's will is—his good, pleasing and **perfect** will.
1Co 2: 6 however, speak a message of wisdom among the **mature**,
13:10 but when **perfection** comes, the imperfect disappears.
14:20 In regard to evil be infants, but in your thinking be **adults**.
Eph 4:13 in the knowledge of the Son of God and become **mature** [+*467*],
Php 3:15 All of us who are **mature** should take such a view of things.
Col 1:28 all wisdom, so that we may present everyone **perfect** in Christ.
4:12 may stand firm in all the will of God, **mature** and fully assured.
Heb 5:14 But solid food is *for* the **mature**, who by constant use have trained
9:11 the greater and **more perfect** tabernacle that is not man-made,
Jas 1: 4 Perseverance *must* **finish** [+*2400*] its work so that you may be
1: 4 must finish its work so that you may be **mature** and complete,
1:17 Every good and **perfect** gift is from above, coming down from the
1:25 But the man who looks intently into the **perfect** law that gives
3: 2 he is a **perfect** man, able to keep his whole body in check.
1Jn 4:18 But **perfect** love drives out fear, because fear has to do with

5456 τελειότης, *teleiotēs* [2] [√ 5465]

maturity [1], perfect [1]

Col 3:14 virtues put on love, which binds them all together *in* **perfect** *unity*.
Heb 6: 1 leave the elementary teachings about Christ and go on to **maturity**,

5457 τελειόω, *teleioō* [23] [√ 5465]

made perfect [8], made complete [4], finish [3], make perfect [2], clear [1], complete [1], completing [1], fulfilled [1], over [1], reach goal [1]

Lk 2:43 *After* the Feast *was* **over**, while his parents were returning home,
13:32 and tomorrow, and on the third day *I will* **reach** *my goal*.'
Jn 4:34 "is to do the will of him who sent me and *to* **finish** his work.
5:36 of John. For the very work that the Father has given me to **finish**,
17: 4 I have brought you glory on earth *by* **completing** the work you
17:23 May they be brought to **complete** unity to let the world know that
19:28 and so that the Scripture *would be* **fulfilled**, Jesus said, "I am
Ac 20:24 if only I *may* **finish** the race and complete the task the Lord Jesus
Php 3:12 have already obtained all this, or have already *been* **made perfect**,
Heb 2:10 *should* **make** the author of their salvation **perfect** through
5: 9 and, *once* **made perfect**, he became the source of eternal salvation
7:19 (for the law **made** nothing **perfect**), and a better hope is

    7:28 the law, appointed the Son, *who has been* **made perfect** forever.
    9: 9 and sacrifices being offered were not able *to* **clear** the conscience
  10: 1 year after year, **make perfect** those who draw near to worship.
  10:14 because by one sacrifice he has **made perfect** forever those who
  11:40 so that only together with us *would they be* **made perfect**.
  12:23 the judge of all men, to the spirits of righteous men **made perfect**,
Jas 2:22 and his faith was **made complete** by what he did.
1Jn 2: 5 anyone obeys his word, God's love *is* truly **made complete** in him.
  4:12 one another, God lives in us and his love is **made complete** in us.
  4:17 love *is* **made complete** among us so that we will have confidence
  4:18 with punishment. The one who fears *is* not **made perfect** in love.

5458 τελείως, *teleiōs* [1] [√ 5465]

fully [1]

1Pe 1:13 set your hope **fully** on the grace to be given you when Jesus Christ

5459 τελείωσις, *teleiōsis* [2] [√ 5465]

accomplished [1], perfection [1]

Lk   1:45 believed that what the Lord has said to her will be **accomplished**!"
Heb 7:11 If **perfection** could have been attained through the Levitical

5460 τελειωτής, *teleiōtēs* [1] [√ 5465]

perfecter [1]

Heb 12: 2 Let us fix our eyes on Jesus, the author and **perfecter** of our faith,

5461 τελεσφορέω, *telesphoreō* [1] [√ 5465 + 5770]

mature [1]

Lk   8:14 by life's worries, riches and pleasures, and *they do* not **mature**.

5462 τελευτάω, *teleutaō* [11] [→ 5463; cf. 5465]

died [5], die [2], put to death [+2505] [2], dead [1], end was near [1]

Mt   2:19 *After Herod* **died**, an angel of the Lord appeared in a dream to
    9:18 and knelt before him and said, "My daughter *has* just **died**.
  15: 4 who curses his father or mother *must be* **put to death** [+2505].'
  22:25 The first one married and **died**, and since he had no children,
Mk   7:10 who curses his father or mother *must be* **put to death** [+2505].'
    9:48 where " 'their worm *does* not **die**, and the fire is not quenched.'
Lk   7: 2 whom his master valued highly, was sick and about to **die**.
Jn 11:39 "But, Lord," said Martha, the sister *of* the **dead** *man*, "by this time
Ac 2:29 I can tell you confidently that the patriarch David **died** and was
  7:15 Then Jacob went down to Egypt, where he and our fathers **died**.
Heb 11:22 By faith Joseph, *when his* **end was near**, spoke about the exodus

5463 τελευτή, *teleutē* [1] [√ 5462]

death [1]

Mt   2:15 where he stayed until the **death** of Herod. And so was fulfilled

5464 τελέω, *teleō* [28] [√ 5465]

finished [8], completed [4], fulfilled [3], ended [2], pay [2], accomplished [1], carried out [1], done [1], finish [1], gratify [1], keep [1], made perfect [1], obeys [1], over [1]

Mt   7:28 When Jesus *had* **finished** saying these things, the crowds were
  10:23 *you will* not **finish** *going through* the cities of Israel before the
  11: 1 After Jesus *had* **finished** instructing his twelve disciples, he went
  13:53 When Jesus *had* **finished** these parables, he moved on from there.
  17:24 to Peter and asked, "Doesn't your teacher **pay** the temple tax?"
  19: 1 When Jesus *had* **finished** saying these things, he left Galilee
  26: 1 When Jesus *had* **finished** saying all these things, he said to his
Lk   2:39 and Mary *had* **done** everything required by the Law of the Lord,
  12:50 baptism to undergo, and how distressed I am until *it is* **completed**!
  18:31 is written by the prophets about the Son of Man *will be* **fulfilled**.
  22:37 the transgressors'; and I tell you that this must *be* **fulfilled** in me.
Jn 19:28 knowing that all *was* now **completed**, and so that the Scripture
  19:30 When he had received the drink, Jesus said, "*It is* **finished**."

Ac 13:29 When *they had* **carried out** all that was written about him,
Ro   2:27 and yet **obeys** the law will condemn you who,
  13: 6 This is also why *you* **pay** taxes, for the authorities are God's
2Co 12: 9 is sufficient for you, for my power *is* **made perfect** in weakness."
Gal 5:16 the Spirit, and *you will* not **gratify** the desires of the sinful nature.
2Ti 4: 7 the good fight, *I have* **finished** the race, I have kept the faith.
Jas 2: 8 If *you* really **keep** the royal law found in Scripture, "Love your
Rev 10: 7 the mystery of God *will be* **accomplished**, just as he announced to
  11: 7 Now when *they have* **finished** their testimony, the beast that
  15: 1 last plagues—last, because with them God's wrath *is* **completed**.
  15: 8 until the seven plagues of the seven angels *were* **completed**.
  17:17 give the beast their power to rule, until God's words *are* **fulfilled**.
  20: 3 the nations anymore until the thousand years *were* **ended**.
  20: 5 the dead did not come to life until the thousand years *were* **ended**.)
  20: 7 When the thousand years *are* **over**, Satan will be released from his

5465 τέλος, *telos* [40] [→ 269, 699, 1412, 1754, 2200, 3387, 3911, 4117, 4500, 5333, 5334, 5455, 5456, 5457, 5458, 5459, 5460, 5461, 5464; cf. 5462, 5467]

end [20], fulfillment [2], goal [2], outcome [2], result [2], revenue [2], destiny [1], duty [1], end [+2400] [1], eventually [+1650] [1], finally [+3836] [1], finally brought about [1], fully [+2401] [1], last [1], radianceˢ [1], the full extent of [+1650] [1]

Mt 10:22 because of me, but he who stands firm to the **end** will be saved.
  17:25 "From whom do the kings of the earth collect **duty** and taxes—
  24: 6 not alarmed. Such things must happen, but the **end** is still to come.
  24:13 but he who stands firm to the **end** will be saved.
  24:14 world as a testimony to all nations, and then the **end** will come.
  26:58 He entered and sat down with the guards to see the **outcome**.
Mk   3:26 opposes himself and is divided, he cannot stand; his **end** has come.
  13: 7 be alarmed. Such things must happen, but the **end** is still to come.
  13:13 because of me, but he who stands firm to the **end** will be saved.
Lk   1:33 reign over the house of Jacob forever; his kingdom will never **end**."
  18: 5 so that she won't **eventually** [+1650] wear me out with her
  21: 9 things must happen first, but the **end** will not come right away."
  22:37 in me. Yes, what is written about me is reaching its **fulfillment**."
Jn 13: 1 he now showed them **the full extent** [+1650] **of** his love.
Ro   6:21 the things you are now ashamed of? Those things **result** in death!
    6:22 the benefit you reap leads to holiness, and the **result** is eternal life.
  10: 4 Christ is the **end** of the law so that there may be righteousness for
  13: 7 if **revenue**, then revenue; if respect, then respect; if honor,
  13: 7 if revenue, then **revenue**; if respect, then respect; if honor,
1Co 1: 8 He will keep you strong to the **end**, so that you will be blameless
  10:11 as warnings for us, on whom the **fulfillment** of the ages has come.
  15:24 Then the **end** will come, when he hands over the kingdom to God
2Co 1:14 you will come to understand **fully** [+2401] that you can boast of us
    3:13 Israelites from gazing at it while the **radiance**ˢ was fading away.
  11:15 of righteousness. Their **end** will be what their actions deserve.
Php 3:19 Their **destiny** is destruction, their god is their stomach, and their
1Th 2:16 sins to the limit. The wrath of God has come upon them at **last**.
1Ti 1: 5 The **goal** of this command is love, which comes from a pure heart
Heb 3:14 We have come to share in Christ if we hold firmly till the **end**
  6: 8 and is in danger of being cursed. In the **end** it will be burned.
  6:11 We want each of you to show this same diligence to the very **end**,
  7: 3 without beginning of days or **end** [+2400] of life,
Jas 5:11 and have seen what the Lord **finally brought about**.
1Pe 1: 9 for you are receiving the **goal** of your faith, the salvation of your
  3: 8 **Finally** [+3836], all of you, live in harmony with one another;
  4: 7 The **end** of all things is near. Therefore be clear minded
  4:17 what will the **outcome** be for those who do not obey the gospel of
Rev 2:26 To him who overcomes and does my will to the **end**, I will give
  21: 6 I am the Alpha and the Omega, the Beginning and the **End**.
  22:13 and the Omega, the First and the Last, the Beginning and the **End**.

5466 τελωνεῖον, *telōneion* Not used in UBS/NIV [√ 5467]

5467 τελώνης, *telōnēs* [21] [→ 803, 5466, 5467, 5468; cf. 5465 + 6050]

tax collectors [15], tax collector [6]

Mt   5:46 reward will you get? Are not even the **tax collectors** doing that?

9: 10 many **tax collectors** and "sinners" came and ate with him and his
9: 11 "Why does your teacher eat with **tax collectors** and 'sinners'?"
10: 3 and Bartholomew; Thomas and Matthew the **tax collector**;
11: 19 a friend *of* **tax collectors** and "sinners." ' But wisdom is proved
18: 17 to the church, treat him as you would a pagan or a **tax collector**.
21: 31 the **tax collectors** and the prostitutes are entering the kingdom of
21: 32 did not believe him, but the **tax collectors** and the prostitutes did.
Mk 2: 15 many **tax collectors** and "sinners" were eating with him and his
2: 16 Pharisees saw him eating with the "sinners" and **tax collectors**,
2: 16 his disciples: "Why does he eat with **tax collectors** and 'sinners'?"
Lk 3: 12 **Tax collectors** also came to be baptized. "Teacher," they asked,
5: 27 and saw a **tax collector** by the name of Levi sitting at his tax
5: 29 and a large crowd *of* **tax collectors** and others were eating with
5: 30 "Why do you eat and drink with **tax collectors** and 'sinners'?"
7: 29 (All the people, even the **tax collectors**, when they heard Jesus'
7: 34 a glutton and a drunkard, a friend *of* **tax collectors** and "sinners." '
15: 1 Now the **tax collectors** and "sinners" were all gathering around to
18: 10 to the temple to pray, one a Pharisee and the other a **tax collector**.
18: 11 robbers, evildoers, adulterers—or even like this **tax collector**.
18: 13 "But the **tax collector** stood at a distance. He would not even look

5468 τελώνιον, *telōnion* [3] [√ 5467]

tax collector's booth [2], tax booth [1]

Mt 9: 9 he saw a man named Matthew sitting at the **tax collector's booth**.
Mk 2: 14 he saw Levi son of Alphaeus sitting at the **tax collector's booth**.
Lk 5: 27 saw a tax collector by the name of Levi sitting at his **tax booth**.

5469 τέρας, *teras* [16]

wonders [13], miracles [3]

Mt 24: 24 and perform great signs and **miracles** to deceive even the elect—
Mk 13: 22 will appear and perform signs and **miracles** to deceive the elect—
Jn 4: 48 "Unless you people see miraculous signs and **wonders**," Jesus told
Ac 2: 19 I will show **wonders** in the heaven above and signs on the earth
2: 22 was a man accredited by God to you *by* miracles, **wonders**
2: 43 and many **wonders** and miraculous signs were done by the
4: 30 and **wonders** through the name of your holy servant Jesus."
5: 12 performed many miraculous signs and **wonders** among the people.
6: 8 did great **wonders** and miraculous signs among the people.
7: 36 He led them out of Egypt and did **wonders** and miraculous signs in
14: 3 of his grace by enabling them to do miraculous signs and **wonders**.
15: 12 and **wonders** God had done among the Gentiles through them.
Ro 15: 19 by the power *of* signs and **miracles**, through the power of the
2Co 12: 12 The things that mark an apostle—signs, **wonders** and miracles—
2Th 2: 9 displayed in all kinds of counterfeit miracles, signs and **wonders**,
Heb 2: 4 God also testified to it *by* signs, **wonders** and various miracles,

5470 Τέρτιος, *Tertios* [1]

Tertius [1]

Ro 16: 22 I, **Tertius**, who wrote down this letter, greet you in the Lord.

5471 Τέρτουλλος, *Tertoullos*   Not used in UBS/NIV

5472 Τέρτυλλος, *Tertyllos* [2]

Tertullus [2]

Ac 24: 1 to Caesarea with some of the elders and a lawyer named **Tertullus**,
24: 2 Paul was called in, **Tertullus** presented his case before Felix:

5473 τεσσαράκοντα, *tessarakonta*   Not used in UBS/NIV [√ 5475]

5474 τεσσαρακονταετής, *tessarakontaetēs*   Not used in UBS/NIV [√ 5475 + 2291]

5475 τέσσαρες, *tessares* [41 / 40] [→ *1280, 5473, 5474, 5476, 5477, 5478, 5479, 5480, 5481, 5482, 5483, 5484, 5485, 5486, 5487, 5488, 5489, 5490, 5544, 5545*]

four [29], twenty-four [*+1633*] [6], 144,000 [*+1669+5477+5942*] [3], 144 [*+1669+5477*] [1], eighty-four [*+2291+3837*] [1]

Mt 24: 31 and they will gather his elect from the **four** winds, from one end of
Mk 2: 3 men came, bringing to him a paralytic, carried by **four** of them.
13: 27 he will send his angels and gather his elect from the **four** winds,
Lk 2: 37 and then was a widow until she was **eighty-four** [*+2291+3837*].
She never left the temple but worshiped night and day, fasting
Jn 11: 17 Jesus found that Lazarus had already been in the tomb *for* **four**
19: 23 they took his clothes, dividing them into **four** shares, one for each
Ac 10: 11 and something like a large sheet being let down to earth *by* its **four**
11: 5 like a large sheet being let down from heaven *by* its **four** corners,
12: 4 handing him over to be guarded by **four** squads of four soldiers
21: 9 He had **four** unmarried daughters who prophesied.
21: 23 we tell you. There are **four** men with us who have made a vow.
27: 29 they dropped **four** anchors from the stern and prayed for daylight.
Rev 4: 4 Surrounding the throne were **twenty-four** [*+1633*] other thrones,
4: 4 and seated on them were **twenty-four** [*+1633*] elders.
4: 6 In the center, around the throne, were **four** living creatures,
4: 8 Each of the **four** living creatures had six wings and was covered
4: 10 the **twenty-four** [*+1633*] elders fall down before him who sits on
5: 6 of the throne, encircled by the **four** living creatures and the elders.
5: 8 the **four** living creatures and the twenty-four elders fell down
5: 8 and the **twenty-four** [*+1633*] elders fell down before the Lamb.
5: 14 The **four** living creatures said, "Amen," and the elders fell down
6: 1 Then I heard one of the **four** living creatures say in a voice like
6: 6 Then I heard what sounded like a voice among the **four** living
7: 1 After this I saw four angels standing at the four corners of the
7: 1 After this I saw four angels standing at the **four** corners of the
7: 1 holding back the **four** winds of the earth to prevent any wind from
7: 2 He called out in a loud voice *to* the **four** angels who had been
7: 4 who were sealed: **144,000** [*+1669+5477+5942*] from all the tribes
7: 11 the throne and around the elders and the **four** living creatures.
9: 13 I heard a voice coming from the [UBS+ **four**] horns of the golden
9: 14 "Release the **four** angels who are bound at the great river
9: 15 And the **four** angels who had been kept ready for this very hour
11: 16 And the **twenty-four** [*+1633*] elders, who were seated on their
14: 1 and with him **144,000** [*+1669+5477+5942*] who had his name and
14: 3 the throne and before the **four** living creatures and the elders.
14: 3 could learn the song except the **144,000** [*+1669+5477+5942*]
15: 7 Then one of the **four** living creatures gave to the seven angels
19: 4 The **twenty-four** [*+1633*] elders and the four living creatures fell
19: 4 and the **four** living creatures fell down and worshiped God,
20: 8 and will go out to deceive the nations in the **four** corners of the
21: 17 He measured its wall and it was **144** [*+1669+5477*] cubits thick,

5476 τεσσαρεσκαιδέκατος, *tessareskaidekatos* [2] [√ *5475 + 2779 + 1274*]

fourteen [1], fourteenth [1]

Ac 27: 27 On the **fourteenth** night we were still being driven across the
27: 33 "For the last **fourteen** days," he said, "you have been in constant

5477 τεσσεράκοντα, *tesserakonta* [22] [√ *5475*]

forty [15], 144,000 [*+1669+5475+5942*] [3], 144 [*+1669+5475*] [1], 42 [*+1545+2779*] [1], forty-six [*+1971+2779*] [1], forty-two [*+1545+2779*] [1]

Mt 4: 2 After fasting **forty** days and forty nights, he was hungry.
4: 2 After fasting forty days and **forty** nights, he was hungry.
Mk 1: 13 and he was in the desert **forty** days, being tempted by Satan.
Lk 4: 2 where *for* **forty** days he was tempted by the devil. He ate nothing
Jn 2: 20 "It has taken **forty-six** [*+1971+2779*] years to build this temple,
Ac 1: 3 He appeared to them over a period *of* **forty** days and spoke about
4: 22 For the man who was miraculously healed was over **forty** years
7: 30 "After **forty** years had passed, an angel appeared to Moses in the
7: 36 signs in Egypt, at the Red Sea and *for* **forty** years in the desert.
7: 42 you bring me sacrifices and offerings **forty** years in the desert,
13: 21 Saul son of Kish, of the tribe of Benjamin, who ruled **forty** years.
23: 13 More than **forty** *men* were involved in this plot.
23: 21 because more than **forty** of them are waiting in ambush for him.

2Co 11:24 Five times I received from the Jews the **forty** *lashes* minus one.
Heb 3: 9 fathers tested and tried me and *for* **forty** years saw what I did.
3:17 And with whom was he angry *for* **forty** years? Was it not with
Rev 7: 4 who were sealed: **144,000** [*+1669+5475+5942*] from all the tribes
11: 2 They will trample on the holy city *for* **42** [*+1545+2779*] months.
13: 5 and to exercise his authority *for* **forty-two** [*+1545+2779*] months.
14: 1 and with him **144,000** [*+1669+5475+5942*] who had his name and
14: 3 could learn the song except the **144,000** [*+1669+5475+5942*] who
21:17 He measured its wall and it was **144** [*+1669+5475*] cubits thick,

5478 τεσσερακονταετής, *tesserakontaetēs* [2]
[√ *5475 + 2291*]

forty years [2]

Ac 7:23 "When Moses was **forty years** old, he decided to visit his fellow
13:18 he endured their conduct *for* about **forty years** in the desert,

5479 τεταρταῖος, *tetartaios* [1] [√ *5475*]

four days [1]

Jn 11:39 "by this time there is a bad odor, for he has been there **four days**."

5480 τέταρτος, *tetartos* [10] [√ *5475*]

fourth [9], four [1]

Mt 14:25 *During* the **fourth** watch of the night Jesus went out to them,
Mk 6:48 About the **fourth** watch of the night he went out to them,
Ac 10:30 "**Four** days ago I was in my house praying at this hour, at three in
Rev 4: 7 the third had a face like a man, the **fourth** was like a flying eagle.
6: 7 When the Lamb opened the **fourth** seal, I heard the voice of the
6: 7 I heard the voice *of* the **fourth** living creature say, "Come!"
6: 8 They were given power over a **fourth** of the earth to kill by sword,
8:12 The **fourth** angel sounded his trumpet, and a third of the sun was
16: 8 The **fourth** angel poured out his bowl on the sun, and the sun was
21:19 the second sapphire, the third chalcedony, the **fourth** emerald,

5481 τετράγωνος, *tetragōnos* [1] [√ *5475 + 1224*]

square [1]

Rev 21:16 The city was laid out like a **square**, as long as it was wide.

5482 τετράδιον, *tetradion* [1] [√ *5475*]

squads of four [1]

Ac 12: 4 handing him over to be guarded *by* four **squads of four** soldiers

5483 τετρακισχίλιοι, *tetrakischilioi* [5]
[√ *5475 + 5943*]

four thousand [5]

Mt 15:38 The number of those who ate was **four thousand**, besides women
16:10 Or the seven loaves *for* the **four thousand**, and how many
Mk 8: 9 About **four thousand** *men* were present. And having sent them
8:20 "And when I broke the seven loaves for the **four thousand**,
Ac 21:38 and led **four thousand** terrorists out into the desert some time ago?"

5484 τετρακόσιοι, *tetrakosioi* [4] [√ *5475*]

four hundred [2], 430 [*+2779+5558*] [1], 450 [*+2779+4299*] [1]

Ac 5:36 to be somebody, and about **four hundred** men rallied to him.
7: 6 and they will be enslaved and mistreated **four hundred** years.
13:20 All this took about **450** [*+2779+4299*] years. "After this, God gave
Gal 3:17 The law, introduced **430** [*+2779+5558*] years later, does not set

5485 τετράμηνος, *tetramēnos* [1] [√ *5475 + 3604*]

four months [1]

Jn 4:35 Do you not say, '**Four months** more and then the harvest'?

5486 τετραπλόος, *tetraploos* Not used in UBS/NIV
[√ *5475*]

5487 τετραπλοῦς, *tetraplous* [1] [√ *5475*]

four times [1]

Lk 19: 8 anybody out of anything, I will pay back **four times** the amount."

5488 τετράπους, *tetrapous* [3] [√ *5475 + 4546*]

four-footed animals [2], animals [1]

Ac 10:12 It contained all kinds of **four-footed animals**, as well as reptiles of
11: 6 I looked into it and saw **four-footed animals** of the earth,
Ro 1:23 made to look like mortal man and birds and **animals** and reptiles.

5489 τετραρχέω, *tetrarcheō* [3] [√ *5475 + 806*]

tetrarch [3]

Lk 3: 1 Herod **tetrarch** of Galilee, his brother Philip tetrarch of Iturea
3: 1 of Galilee, his brother Philip **tetrarch** of Iturea and Traconitis,
3: 1 of Iturea and Traconitis, and Lysanias **tetrarch** of Abilene—

5490 τετράρχης, *tetrarchēs* [4] [√ *5475 + 806*]

tetrarch [4]

Mt 14: 1 At that time Herod the **tetrarch** heard the reports about Jesus,
Lk 3:19 But when John rebuked Herod the **tetrarch** because of Herodias,
9: 7 Now Herod the **tetrarch** heard about all that was going on.
Ac 13: 1 Manaen (who had been brought up with Herod the **tetrarch**)

5491 τεφρόω, *tephroō* [1] [√ *5606*]

burning to ashes [1]

2Pe 2: 6 the cities of Sodom and Gomorrah *by* **burning** *them* **to ashes**,

5492 τέχνη, *technē* [3] [→ *802, 3937, 5336, 5454, 5493; cf. 5503*]

untranslated [1], skill [1], trade [1]

Ac 17:29 or silver or stone—an image made by man's design and **skill**.
18: 3 and because he was a tentmaker **[RPG]** as they were, he stayed
Rev 18:22 No workman *of* any **trade** will ever be found in you again.

5493 τεχνίτης, *technitēs* [4] [√ *5492*]

craftsmen [2], architect [1], workman [1]

Ac 19:24 shrines of Artemis, brought in no little business *for* the **craftsmen**.
19:38 and his fellow **craftsmen** have a grievance against anybody,
Heb 11:10 to the city with foundations, whose **architect** and builder is God.
Rev 18:22 No **workman** of any trade will ever be found in you again.

5494 τήκομαι, *tēkomai* [1]

melt [1]

2Pe 3:12 of the heavens by fire, and the elements *will* **melt** in the heat.

5495 τηλαυγῶς, *tēlaugōs* [1] [√ *879*]

clearly [1]

Mk 8:25 his sight was restored, and he saw everything **clearly**.

5496 τηλικοῦτος, *tēlikoutos* [4] [√ *2462 + 4047*]

so large [1], such great [1], such [1], tremendous [*+3489*] [1]

2Co 1:10 He has delivered us from **such** a deadly peril, and he will deliver
Heb 2: 3 how shall we escape if we ignore **such** a **great** salvation?
Jas 3: 4 Although they are **so large** and are driven by strong winds,
Rev 16:18 man has been on earth, so **tremendous** [*+3489*] was the quake.

5497 τηνικαῦτα, tēnikauta Not used in UBS/NIV

5498 τηρέω, tēreō [70 / 71] [→ 1413, 4190, 4191, 5337, 5499]

obey [16], keep [10], kept [10], keeps [5], held [3], obeyed [3], obeys [2], protect [2], reserved [2], do [1], do^s so [1], does [1], guard [1], guarding [1], guards [1], held over [1], hold [1], keep under guard [1], keeps safe [1], kept watch over [1], not marry [1], observe [1], protected [1], save [1], saved [1], stood [1], take to heart [1]

Mt 19:17 who is good. If you want to enter life, **obey** the commandments."
23: 3 So *you must* **obey** them and do everything they tell you. But do
27:36 And sitting down, *they* **kept watch over** him there.
27:54 and those with him *who were* **guarding** Jesus saw the earthquake
28: 4 The **guards** were so afraid of him that they shook and became like
28:20 and teaching them *to* **obey** everything I have commanded you.
Mk 7: 9 in order to **observe** [UBS *set up 2705*] your own traditions!
Jn 2:10 have had too much to drink; but you *have* **saved** the best till now."
8:51 I tell you the truth, if anyone **keeps** my word, he will never see
8:52 so did the prophets, yet you say that if anyone **keeps** your word,
8:55 I would be a liar like you, but I do know him and **keep** his word.
9:16 "This man is not from God, for *he does* not **keep** the Sabbath."
12: 7 "Lit was intended, that *she should* **save** this perfume for the day of
14:15 "If you love me, *you will* **obey** what I command.
14:21 Whoever has my commands and **obeys** them, he is the one who
14:23 Jesus replied, "If anyone loves me, *he will* **obey** my teaching.
14:24 He who does not love me *will* not **obey** my teaching. These words
15:10 If *you* **obey** my commands, you will remain in my love, just as I
15:10 just as I *have* **obeyed** my Father's commands and remain in his
15:20 you also. If *they* **obeyed** my teaching, they will obey yours also.
15:20 you also. If they **obeyed** my teaching, *they will* **obey** yours also.
17: 6 you gave them to me and *they have* **obeyed** your word.
17:11 Holy Father, **protect** them by the power of your name—the name
17:12 I **protected** them and kept them safe by that name you gave me.
17:15 them out of the world but *that you* **protect** them from the evil one.
Ac 12: 5 So Peter *was* **kept** in prison, but the church was earnestly praying
12: 6 bound with two chains, and sentries **stood** guard at the entrance.
15: 5 must be circumcised and required *to* **obey** the law of Moses."
16:23 and the jailer was commanded *to* **guard** them carefully.
24:23 He ordered the centurion *to* **keep** Paul **under guard** but to give
25: 4 Festus answered, "Paul *is being* **held** at Caesarea, and I myself am
25:21 When Paul made his appeal *to be* **held over** for the Emperor's
25:21 I ordered him **held** until I could send him to Caesar."
1Co 7:37 own will, and who has made up his mind **not** *to* **marry** the virgin—
2Co 11: 9 *I have* **kept** myself *from* being a burden to you in any way,
11: 9 being a burden to you in any way, and *will continue to* **do**^s so.
Eph 4: 3 Make every effort *to* **keep** the unity of the Spirit through the bond
1Th 5:23 *May* your whole spirit, soul and body *be* **kept** blameless at the
1Ti 5:22 and do not share in the sins of others. **Keep** yourself pure.
6:14 *to* **keep** this command without spot or blame until the appearing of
2Ti 4: 7 the good fight, I have finished the race, *I have* **kept** the faith.
Jas 1:27 their distress and *to* **keep** oneself from being polluted by the world.
2:10 For whoever **keeps** the whole law and yet stumbles at just one
1Pe 1: 4 that can never perish, spoil or fade—**kept** in heaven for you,
2Pe 2: 4 putting them into gloomy dungeons *to be* **held** for judgment;
2: 9 from trials and *to* **hold** the unrighteous for the day of judgment,
2:17 mists driven by a storm. Blackest darkness *is* **reserved** for them.
3: 7 *being* **kept** for the day of judgment and destruction of ungodly
1Jn 2: 3 We know that we have come to know him if *we* **obey** his
2: 4 says, "I know him," but *does* not **do** what he commands is a liar,
2: 5 But if anyone **obeys** his word, God's love is truly made complete
3:22 because *we* **obey** his commands and do what pleases him.
3:24 Those *who* **obey** his commands live in him, and he in them.
5: 3 This is love for God: to **obey** his commands. And his commands
5:18 the one who was born of God **keeps** him **safe**, and the evil one
Jude 1: 1 who are loved by God the Father and **kept** by Jesus Christ:
1: 6 And the angels *who did* not **keep** their positions of authority
1: 6 these *he has* **kept** in darkness, bound with everlasting chains for
1:13 for whom blackest darkness *has been* **reserved** forever.
1:21 **Keep** yourselves in God's love as you wait for the mercy of our
Rev 1: 3 are those who hear it and **take to heart** what is written in it,
2:26 To him who overcomes and *does* my will to the end, I will give
3: 3 therefore, what *you* have received and heard; **obey** it, and repent.
3: 8 yet *you have* **kept** my word and have not denied my name.

3:10 Since *you have* **kept** my command to endure patiently, I will also
3:10 I will also **keep** you from the hour of trial that is going to come
12:17 those *who* **obey** God's commandments and hold to the testimony
14:12 This calls for patient endurance on the part of the saints who **obey**
16:15 Blessed is he who stays awake and **keeps** his clothes *with* him,
22: 7 Blessed is he *who* **keeps** the words of the prophecy in this book."
22: 9 brothers the prophets and *of* all *who* **keep** the words of this book.

5499 τήρησις, tērēsis [3] [√ 5498]

jail [2], keeping [1]

Ac 4: 3 because it was evening, they put them in **jail** until the next day.
5:18 They arrested the apostles and put them in the public **jail**.
1Co 7:19 is nothing. **Keeping** God's commands is what counts.

5500 Τιβεριάς, Tiberias [3] [√ 5501]

Tiberias [3]

Jn 6: 1 to the far shore of the Sea of Galilee (that is, the Sea *of* **Tiberias**),
6:23 Then some boats from **Tiberias** landed near the place where the
21: 1 Jesus appeared again to his disciples, by the Sea *of* **Tiberias**.

5501 Τιβέριος, Tiberios [1] [→ 5500]

Tiberius [1]

Lk 3: 1 In the fifteenth year of the reign *of* **Tiberius** Caesar—when Pontius

5502 τίθημι, tithēmi [100]

[→ 118, 119, 120, 127, 292, 423, 460, 507, 509, 629, 700, 853, 1347, 1415, 1416, 1704, 1758, 1951, 2120, 2202, 2310, 2557, 2874, 2960, 3557, 3572, 3792, 3793, 3794, 3804, 3805, 3999, 4146, 4153, 4192, 4324, 4363, 4606, 4607, 4651, 4671, 4707, 4729, 5161, 5163, 5298, 5338, 5625, 5719; cf. 353, 2529, 2565, 2874]

put [21], laid [10], lay down [8], placed [7], appointed [5], made [5], lay [4], make [3], puts [3], assign [2], knelt down [+1205+3836] [2], put in [2], appoint [1], appointing [1], arranged [1], brings out [1], burial [+1650+3645] [1], committed [1], decided [+1877+3836+4460] [1], decided that [+1087] [1], destined [1], falling on [1], fastened [1], fell on [1], got down [1], knelt [+1205+3836] [1], laid down [1], laid in [1], lays down [1], lays [1], listen carefully [+1650+3836+4044+5148+5148] [1], made think [+1877+2840+3836] [1], make up mind [+1877+2840+3836] [1], offer [1], planted [1], set aside [+1571+4123] [1], set [1], took off [1], use [1], wondered about [+1877+2840+3836] [1]

Mt 5:15 Neither do people light a lamp and **put** it under a bowl.
12:18 *I will* **put** my Spirit on him, and he will proclaim justice to the
22:44 "Sit at my right hand until *I* **put** your enemies under your feet." '
24:51 will cut him to pieces and **assign** him a place with the hypocrites,
27:60 and **placed** it in his own new tomb that he had cut out of the rock.
Mk 4:21 to them, "Do you bring in a lamp to **put** it under a bowl or a bed?
4:21 put it under a bowl or a bed? Instead, don't *you* **put** it on its stand?
4:30 of God is like, or what parable *shall we* **use** to describe it?
6:29 John's disciples came and took his body and **laid** it in a tomb.
6:56 or countryside—*they* **placed** the sick in the marketplaces.
10:16 the children in his arms, **put** his hands on them and blessed them.
12:36 "Sit at my right hand until *I* **put** your enemies under your feet." '
15:19 and spit on him. **Falling** on their knees, they paid homage to him.
15:46 wrapped it in the linen, and **placed** it in a tomb cut out of rock.
15:47 and Mary the mother of Joses saw where *he was* **laid**.
16: 6 He has risen! He is not here. See the place where they **laid** him.
Lk 1:66 who heard this **wondered** [+1877+2840+3836] **about** it, asking,
5:18 and tried to take him into the house *to* **lay** him before Jesus.
6:48 a house, who dug down deep and **laid** the foundation on rock.
8:16 "No one lights a lamp and hides it in a jar or **puts** it under a bed.
8:16 Instead, *he* **puts** it on a stand, so that those who come in can see
9:44 "**Listen carefully to** [+1650+3836+4044+5148+5148] what I am
11:33 "No one lights a lamp and **puts** it in a place where it will be hidden,
12:46 will cut him to pieces and **assign** him a place with the unbelievers.

14:29 For if he **lays** the foundation and is not able to finish it,
19:21 You take out what *you did* not **put in** and reap what you did not
19:22 did you, that I am a hard man, taking out what *I did* not **put in**,
20:43 until *I* **make** your enemies a footstool for your feet." '
21:14 But **make up** your **mind** [*+1877+2840+3836*] not to worry
22:41 about a stone's throw beyond them, **knelt down** [*+1205+3836*]
23:53 wrapped it in linen cloth and **placed** it in a tomb cut in the rock,
23:55 followed Joseph and saw the tomb and how his body *was* **laid in** it.

Jn 2:10 "Everyone **brings out** the choice wine first and then the cheaper
10:11 The good shepherd **lays down** his life for the sheep.
10:15 and I know the Father—and *I* **lay down** my life for the sheep.
10:17 The reason my Father loves me is that I **lay down** my life—
10:18 No one takes it from me, but I **lay** it **down** of my own accord.
10:18 I have authority *to* **lay** it **down** and authority to take it up again.
11:34 "Where *have you* **laid** him?" he asked. "Come and see, Lord,"
13:4 so he got up from the meal, **took off** his outer clothing,
13:37 why can't I follow you now? *I will* **lay down** my life for you."
13:38 Then Jesus answered, *"Will you really* **lay down** your life for me?
15:13 love has no one than this, that he **lay down** his life for his friends.
15:16 but I chose you and **appointed** you to go and bear fruit—
19:19 Pilate had a notice prepared and **fastened** to the cross. It read:
19:41 and in the garden a new tomb, in which no one had ever been **laid**.
19:42 and since the tomb was nearby, *they* **laid** Jesus there.
20:2 out of the tomb, and we don't know where *they have* **put** him!"
20:13 Lord away," she said, "and I don't know where *they have* **put** him."
20:15 if you have carried him away, tell me where *you have* **put** him,

Ac 1:7 to know the times or dates the Father *has* **set** by his own authority.
2:35 until *I* **make** your enemies a footstool for your feet." '
3:2 where he *was* **put** every day to beg from those going into the
4:3 because it was evening, *they* **put** them in jail until the next day.
4:35 and **put** it at the apostles' feet, and it was distributed to anyone as
4:37 he owned and brought the money and **put** it at the apostles' feet.
5:2 for himself, but brought the rest and **put** it at the apostles' feet.
5:4 What **made** you **think** [*+1877+2840+3836*] of doing such a thing?
5:15 brought the sick into the streets and **laid** them on beds and mats
5:18 They arrested the apostles and **put** them in the public jail.
5:25 The men *you* **put** in jail are standing in the temple courts teaching
7:16 and **placed** in the tomb that Abraham had bought from the sons of
7:60 Then he **fell on** his knees and cried out, "Lord, do not hold this sin
9:37 and her body was washed and **placed** in an upstairs room.
9:40 all out of the room; then *he* **got down** on his knees and prayed.
12:4 After arresting him, *he* **put** him in prison, handing him over to be
13:29 *they* took him down from the tree and **laid** him in a tomb.
13:47 for ' *I have* **made** you a light for the Gentiles, that you may bring
19:21 Paul **decided** [*+1877+3836+4460*] to go to Jerusalem, passing
20:28 and all the flock of which the Holy Spirit *has* **made** you overseers.
20:36 When he had said this, he **knelt down** [*+1205+3836*] with all of
21:5 of the city, and there on the beach *we* **knelt** [*+1205+3836*] to pray.
27:12 the majority **decided that** [*+1087*] we should sail on, hoping to

Ro 4:17 As it is written: "*I have* **made** you a father of many nations."
9:33 *I* **lay** in Zion a stone that causes men to stumble and a rock that
14:13 not *to* **put** any stumbling block or obstacle *in* your brother's *way*.

1Co 3:10 grace God has given me, *I* **laid** a foundation as an expert builder,
3:11 For no one can **lay** any foundation other than the one already laid,
9:18 that in preaching the gospel *I may* **offer** it free of charge, and
12:18 But in fact God *has* **arranged** the parts in the body, every one of
12:28 And in the church God *has* **appointed** first of all apostles,
15:25 For he must reign until *he has* **put** all his enemies under his feet.
16:2 each one of you *should* **set** [*+1571+4123*] **aside** a sum of money in

2Co 3:13 *who would* **put** a veil over his face to keep the Israelites from
5:19 And *he has* **committed** to us the message of reconciliation.

1Th 5:9 For God *did* not **appoint** us to suffer wrath but to receive salvation

1Ti 1:12 that he considered me faithful, **appointing** me to his service.
2:7 And for this purpose I *was* **appointed** a herald and an apostle—

2Ti 1:11 And of this gospel I *was* **appointed** a herald and an apostle

Heb 1:2 whom *he* **appointed** heir of all things, and through whom he made
1:13 "Sit at my right hand until *I* **make** your enemies a footstool for your
10:13 Since that time he waits for his enemies *to be* **made** his footstool,

1Pe 2:6 "See, *I* **lay** a stone in Zion, a chosen and precious cornerstone,
2:8 disobey the message—which is also what *they were* **destined** for.

2Pe 2:6 and **made** an example of what is going to happen to the

1Jn 3:16 how we know what love is: Jesus Christ **laid down** his life for us.
3:16 life for us. And we ought *to* **lay down** our lives for our brothers.

Rev 1:17 Then *he* **placed** his right hand on me and said: "Do not be afraid.
10:2 *He* **planted** his right foot on the sea and his left foot on the land,
11:9 will gaze on their bodies and refuse them **burial** [*+1650+3645*].

5503 τίκτω, *tiktō* [18] [→ *866, 4757, 4758, 5448, 5449, 5450, 5451, 5452, 5453, 5527, 5817; cf. 5492*]

gave birth to [3], give birth to [3], born [2], baby to be born [1],
bears children [1], born to [1], give birth [*+6048*] [1], give birth
[1], given birth to [1], gives birth to [1], giving birth to a child [1],
have baby [1], produces [1]

Mt 1:21 She will **give birth to** a son, and you are to give him the name
1:23 "The virgin will be with child and *will* **give birth to** a son,
1:25 But he had no union with her until *she* **gave birth to** a son.
2:2 and asked, "Where is the one *who has been* **born** king of the Jews?
Lk 1:31 You will be with child and **give birth to** a son, and you are to give
1:57 When it was time for Elizabeth *to* **have** her **baby**, she gave birth to
2:6 While they were there, the time came for the **baby to be born**,
2:7 and *she* **gave birth to** her firstborn, a son. She wrapped him in
2:11 Today in the town of David a Savior *has been* **born to** you;
Jn 16:21 A woman **giving birth to a child** has pain because her time has
Gal 4:27 "Be glad, O barren woman, who **bears** no **children**; break forth
Heb 6:7 and that **produces** a crop useful to those for whom it is farmed
Jas 1:15 Then, after desire has conceived, *it* **gives birth to** sin; and sin,
Rev 12:2 and cried out in pain *as she was about to* **give birth** [*+6048*].
12:4 dragon stood in front of the woman who was about to **give birth**,
12:4 so that he might devour her child the moment *it was* **born**.
12:5 *She* **gave birth to** a son, a male child, who will rule all the nations
12:13 he pursued the woman who *had* **given birth to** the male child.

5504 τίλλω, *tillō* [3]

pick [3]

Mt 12:1 were hungry and began *to* **pick** some heads of grain and eat them.
Mk 2:23 disciples walked along, they began *to* **pick** some heads of grain.
Lk 6:1 and his disciples *began to* **pick** some heads of grain, rub them in

5505 Τιμαῖος, *Timaios* [1] [√ *5507*]

Timaeus [1]

Mk 10:46 the city, a blind man, Bartimaeus (that is, the Son *of* **Timaeus**),

5506 τιμάω, *timaō* [21] [√ *5507*]

honor [16], *untranslated* [1], give recognition to [1], honored
[*+5507*] [1], price set on [*+5507*] [1], show proper respect to [1]

Mt 15:4 '**Honor** your father and mother' and 'Anyone who curses his
15:6 he is not *to* '**honor** his father' with it. Thus you nullify the word of
15:8 " 'These people **honor** me with their lips, but their hearts are far
19:19 **honor** your father and mother,' and 'love your neighbor as
27:9 silver coins, the **price** [*+5507*] set on him by the people of Israel,
27:9 silver coins, the price set on him **[RPG]** by the people of Israel,
Mk 7:6 " 'These people **honor** me with their lips, but their hearts are far
7:10 For Moses said, '**Honor** your father and your mother,' and,
10:19 false testimony, do not defraud, **honor** your father and mother.' "
Lk 18:20 do not give false testimony, **honor** your father and mother.' "
Jn 5:23 that all *may* **honor** the Son just as they honor the Father. He who
5:23 that all may honor the Son just as *they* **honor** the Father. He who
5:23 He who does not **honor** the Son does not honor the Father,
5:23 He who does not honor the Son *does* not **honor** the Father,
8:49 a demon," said Jesus, "but *I* **honor** my Father and you dishonor me.
12:26 servant also will be. My Father *will* **honor** the one who serves me.
Ac 28:10 They **honored** [*+5507*] us in many ways and when we were ready
Eph 6:2 "**Honor** your father and mother"—which is the first commandment
1Ti 5:3 **Give** *proper* **recognition to** those widows who are really in need.
1Pe 2:17 **Show proper respect to** everyone: Love the brotherhood of
2:17 Love the brotherhood of believers, fear God, **honor** the king.

5507 τιμή, *timē* [41 / 42] [→ *869, 870, 871, 872, 873, 988, 1952, 2203, 2204, 2700, 4501, 5505, 5506, 5508, 5509, 5510, 5511, 5512, 5513, 5818*]

honor [23], money [3], noble purposes [3], price [2], respect [2],
value [2], blood money [*+135*] [1], honorable [1], honored
[*+5506*] [1], precious [1], price set on [*+5506*] [1], special
treatment [1], sum [1]

Mt 27:6 law to put this into the treasury, since it is **blood money** [*+135*]."

27: 9 silver coins, the **price set on** [+*5506*] him by the people of Israel,
Jn 4:44 (Now Jesus himself had pointed out that a prophet has no **honor** in
Ac 4:34 or houses sold them, brought the **money** from the sales
5: 2 With his wife's full knowledge he kept back part *of* the **money** for
5: 3 and have kept for yourself some *of* the **money** you received for the
7:16 from the sons of Hamor at Shechem *for* a *certain* **sum** of money.
19:19 When they calculated the **value** of the scrolls, the total came to
28:10 They **honored** [+*5506*] us in many ways and when we were ready
Ro 2: 7 good seek glory, **honor** and immortality, he will give eternal life.
2:10 but glory, **honor** and peace for everyone who does good: first for
9:21 out of the same lump of clay some pottery for **noble purposes**
12:10 another in brotherly love. **Honor** one another above yourselves.
13: 7 then revenue; if respect, then respect; if **honor**, then honor.
13: 7 then revenue; if respect, then respect; if honor, then **honor**.
1Co 6:20 you were bought *at* a **price**. Therefore honor God with your body.
7:23 You were bought *at* a **price**; do not become slaves of men.
12:23 parts that we think are less honorable we treat with special **honor**.
12:24 while our presentable parts need no **special** [UBS-] **treatment**.
12:24 of the body and has given greater **honor** to the parts that lacked it,
Col 2:23 but they lack any **value** in restraining sensual indulgence.
1Th 4: 4 learn to control his own body in a way that is holy and **honorable**,
1Ti 1:17 invisible, the only God, be **honor** and glory for ever and ever.
5:17 direct the affairs of the church well are worthy *of* double **honor**,
6: 1 of slavery should consider their masters worthy *of* full **respect**,
6:16 has seen or can see. To him be **honor** and might forever. Amen.
2Ti 2:20 and clay; some are for **noble purposes** and some for ignoble.
2:21 he will be an instrument for **noble purposes**, made holy, useful to
Heb 2: 7 lower than the angels; you crowned him *with* glory and **honor**
2: 9 now crowned *with* glory and **honor** because he suffered death,
3: 3 just as the builder of a house has greater **honor** than the house
5: 4 No one takes this **honor** upon himself; he must be called by God,
1Pe 1: 7 result in praise, glory and **honor** when Jesus Christ is revealed.
2: 7 Now to you who believe, this stone is **precious**. But to those who
3: 7 and treat them with **respect** as the weaker partner and as heirs with
2Pe 1:17 For he received **honor** and glory from God the Father when the
Rev 4: 9 **honor** and thanks to him who sits on the throne and who lives for
4:11 our Lord and God, to receive glory and **honor** and power,
5:12 and wisdom and strength and **honor** and glory and praise!"
5:13 and to the Lamb be praise and **honor** and glory and power,
7:12 Praise and glory and wisdom and thanks and **honor** and power
21:26 The glory and **honor** of the nations will be brought into it.

5508 τίμιος, *timios* [13] [√ *5507*]

precious [6], costly [2], honored [2], valuable [1], very precious [1], worth [1]

Ac 5:34 a teacher of the law, who was **honored** by all the people, stood up
20:24 However, I consider my life **worth** nothing to me, if only I may
1Co 3:12 If any man builds on this foundation *using* gold, silver, **costly**
Heb 13: 4 Marriage should be **honored** by all, and the marriage bed kept
Jas 5: 7 See how the farmer waits for the land to yield its **valuable** crop
1Pe 1:19 but *with* the **precious** blood of Christ, a lamb without blemish
2Pe 1: 4 these he has given us his very great and **precious** promises,
Rev 17: 4 and was glittering *with* gold, **precious** stones and pearls.
18:12 cargoes *of* gold, silver, **precious** stones and pearls; fine linen,
18:12 of every kind made of ivory, **costly** wood, bronze, iron and marble;
18:16 and scarlet, and glittering with gold, **precious** stones and pearls!
21:11 and its brilliance was like that of a **very precious** jewel, like a
21:19 of the city walls were decorated *with* every kind of **precious** stone.

5509 τιμιότης, *timiotēs* [1] [√ *5507*]

wealth [1]

Rev 18:19 all who had ships on the sea became rich through her **wealth**!

5510 Τιμόθεος, *Timotheos* [24] [√ *5507 + 2536*]

Timothy [24]

Ac 16: 1 and then to Lystra, where a disciple named **Timothy** lived,
17:14 sent Paul to the coast, but Silas and **Timothy** stayed at Berea.
17:15 instructions for Silas and **Timothy** to join him as soon as possible.
18: 5 When Silas and **Timothy** came from Macedonia, Paul devoted
19:22 He sent two of his helpers, **Timothy** and Erastus, to Macedonia,
20: 4 **Timothy** also, and Tychicus and Trophimus from the province of

Ro 16:21 **Timothy**, my fellow worker, sends his greetings to you, as do
1Co 4:17 For this reason I am sending to you **Timothy**, my son whom I love,
16:10 If **Timothy** comes, see to it that he has nothing to fear while he is
2Co 1: 1 and **Timothy** our brother, To the church of God in Corinth,
1:19 who was preached among you by me and Silas and **Timothy**,
Php 1: 1 Paul and **Timothy**, servants of Christ Jesus, To all the saints in
2:19 I hope in the Lord Jesus to send **Timothy** to you soon, that I also
Col 1: 1 of Christ Jesus by the will of God, and **Timothy** our brother,
1Th 1: 1 Paul, Silas and **Timothy**, To the church of the Thessalonians in
3: 2 We sent **Timothy**, who is our brother and God's fellow worker in
3: 6 But **Timothy** has just now come to us from you and has brought
2Th 1: 1 Paul, Silas and **Timothy**, To the church of the Thessalonians in
1Ti 1: 2 *To* **Timothy** my true son in the faith: Grace, mercy and peace from
1:18 **Timothy**, my son, I give you this instruction in keeping with the
6:20 **Timothy**, guard what has been entrusted to your care. Turn away
2Ti 1: 2 *To* **Timothy**, my dear son: Grace, mercy and peace from God the
Phm 1: 1 Paul, a prisoner of Christ Jesus, and **Timothy** our brother,
Heb 13:23 I want you to know that our brother **Timothy** has been released.

5511 Τίμων, *Timōn* [1] [√ *5507*]

Timon [1]

Ac 6: 5 also Philip, Procorus, Nicanor, **Timon**, Parmenas, and Nicolas

5512 τιμωρέω, *timōreō* [2] [√ *5507 + 149*]

punished [2]

Ac 22: 5 to bring these people as prisoners to Jerusalem to *be* **punished**.
26:11 I went from one synagogue to another *to have* them **punished**,

5513 τιμωρία, *timōria* [1] [√ *5507 + 149*]

punished [1]

Heb 10:29 to be **punished** who has trampled the Son of God under foot,

5514 τίνω, *tinō* [1] [→ *702*]

punished [+*1472*] [1]

2Th 1: 9 They *will be* **punished** [+*1472*] with everlasting destruction

5515 τίς, *tis* [556 / 554] See Index of Articles, Etc.

[→ *1414, 1484, 2672, 2776, 4022*]

what [221], who [122], why [73], why [+*1328*] [23], which [19], *untranslated* [9], whom [9], how [8], whose [6], what do want with [+*2779*] [5], how [+*1877*] [4], why [+*1650*] [4], how is it that [+*1328*] [3], suppose one [3], nothing [+*4024*] [2], something [2], was there ever [2], which [+*323*] [2], a [1], all the world [+*476+1639+4005*] [1], any [+*476*] [1], any way [+*3836*] [1], any [1], business [+*4472*] [1], each [1], how [+*2848*] [1], how far will they go [+*1639+4047*] [1], meaning [+*323+1639*] [1], my supper [+*1268*] [1], nothing [+*3590*] [1], one [1], some [1], suppose a [1], suppose one [+*476*] [1], the [1], those [1], what [+*1650*] [1], what [+*1877*] [1], what [+*323*] [1], what [+*4005*] [1], what about [1], what business is it of mine [+*1609*] [1], what does it matter [1], what going on [+*323+4047*] [1], what shall we do [+*1639+4036*] [1], what's [1], where [1], which [+*476*] [1], who do you think you are [+*4472+4932*] [1], whose [+*2400*] [1], why [+*162+3836*] [1], why [+*1915*] [1], why [+*3364*] [1], why [+*5920*] [1], why do involve [+*2779*] [1]

5516 τὶς, *tis* [533] See Index of Articles, Etc.

[→ *3614, 3615, 4015*]

some [104], a [84], anyone [78], one [36], *untranslated* [32], anything [31], any [25], someone [22], something [16], a certain [9], he [8], anybody [5], an [4], certain [3], one [+*1651*] [3], several [3], whatever [+*1569*] [3], any one [2], anyone [+*1569*] [2], anyone's [2], nothing [+*3590*] [2], nothing [+*4024*] [2], others [2], something [+*5007*] [2], that none [+*3607*] [2], whatever [+*1623*] [2], whatever [+*323+4005*] [2], whatever [+*323*] [2], who

[2], whoever [+1569] [2], a few [1], a kind of [1], and none [+4046] [1], and nothing [+4028] [1], another [+257] [1], any [+323+4005] [1], any other [1], anyone else [1], anything [+1569] [1], deadly poison [+2503] [1], ideas^s [1], important [1], in keeping with income [+1569+2338+4005] [1], it [+2240+3836] [1], man's^s [1], members^s [1], named [1], nobody [+3590] [1], nobody [+4024] [1], none [+3590] [1], nothing [+4046] [1], others [+1254] [1], person [1], persons [1], pieces [1], some [+3525] [1], some point [1], somebody [1], somewhat [1], the rest [+3538] [1], the [1], them [1], thing [1], what [+1623] [1], what [+2240+3836] [1], what [+323] [1], what [+4005] [1], what [1], whatever [+1569+4005] [1], whatever [1], who [+1569] [1]

5517 Τίτιος, *Titios* [1] [√ 5519]

Titius [1]

Ac 18: 7 the synagogue and went next door to the house *of* **Titius** Justus,

5518 τίτλος, *titlos* [2]

had a notice prepared [+1211] [1], sign [1]

Jn 19:19 Pilate **had a notice** [+1211] **prepared** and fastened to the cross.
19:20 Many of the Jews read this **sign**, for the place where Jesus was

5519 Τίτος, *Titos* [13] [→ 5517]

Titus [13]

2Co 2:13 no peace of mind, because I did not find my brother **Titus** there.
7: 6 who comforts the downcast, comforted us by the coming *of* **Titus**,
7:13 we were especially delighted to see how happy **Titus** was,
7:14 so our boasting about you to **Titus** has proved to be true as well.
8: 6 So we urged **Titus**, since he had earlier made a beginning,
8:16 who put into the heart *of* **Titus** the same concern I have for you.
8:23 As for **Titus**, he is my partner and fellow worker among you;
12:18 I urged **Titus** to go to you and I sent our brother with him.
12:18 and I sent our brother with him. **Titus** did not exploit you, did he?
Gal 2: 1 to Jerusalem, this time with Barnabas. I took **Titus** along also.
2: 3 Yet not even **Titus**, who was with me, was compelled to be
2Ti 4:10 Crescens has gone to Galatia, and **Titus** to Dalmatia.
Tit 1: 4 *To* **Titus**, my true son in our common faith: Grace and peace from

5520 τοί, *toi*   Not used in UBS/NIV [→ 2486, 2792, 2793, 3530, 5521, 5522, 5523]

5521 τοιγαροῦν, *toigaroun* [2] [√ 5520 + 1142 + 4036]

therefore [2]

1Th 4: 8 **Therefore**, he who rejects this instruction does not reject man
Heb 12: 1 **Therefore**, since we are surrounded by such a great cloud of

5522 τοίγε, *toige*   Not used in UBS/NIV [√ 5520 + 1145]

5523 τοίνυν, *toinyn* [3] [√ 5520 + 3814]

then [2], therefore [1]

Lk 20:25 He said to them, "**Then** give to Caesar what is Caesar's, and to
1Co 9:26 **Therefore** I do not run like a man running aimlessly; I do not fight
Heb 13:13 Let us, **then**, go to him outside the camp, bearing the disgrace he

5524 τοιόσδε, *toiosde* [1] [√ 3836]

untranslated [1]

2Pe 1:17 and glory from God the Father when the voice came to him **[NIE]**

5525 τοιοῦτος, *toioutos* [57] [√ 3836 + 4047]

such [22], *untranslated* [4], such as these [4], him [3], like this [2], so [2], such a man [2], this [2], blemish^s [*3836*] [1], he [1], man like that [1], men like him [1], of a kind [1], other [1], related^s trades [1], similar [1], such a [1], that [1], them

[+3836+3836+4556] [1], these [1], they are the kind [1], those^s who marry [+3836] [1], unequaled [+1181+3888+4024] [1], what [+3961] [1]

Mt 9: 8 and they praised God, who had given **such** authority to men.
18: 5 "And whoever welcomes a little child **like this** in my name
19:14 hinder them, for the kingdom of heaven belongs to **such as these**."
Mk 4:33 *With* many **similar** parables Jesus spoke the word to them,
6: 2 that has been given him, that he even does **[RPG]** miracles!
7:13 that you have handed down. And you do many things like **that**."
9:37 "Whoever welcomes one *of* **these** little children in my name
10:14 not hinder them, for the kingdom of God belongs to **such as these**.
13:19 those will be days of distress **unequaled** [+1181+3888+4024]
Lk 9: 9 "I beheaded John. Who, then, is this I hear **such** *things* about?"
18:16 not hinder them, for the kingdom of God belongs to **such as these**.
Jn 4:23 and truth, for **they are the kind** of worshipers the Father seeks.
8: 5 In the Law Moses commanded us to stone **such** *women*. Now what
9:16 But others asked, "How can a sinner do **such** miraculous signs?"
Ac 16:24 Upon receiving **such** orders, he put them in the inner cell
19:25 along with the workmen in **related**^{s} **trades**, and said:
22:22 Then they raised their voices and shouted, "Rid the earth of **him**!
26:29 but all who are listening to me today may become **what** [+3961] I
Ro 1:32 righteous decree that those who do **such** *things* deserve death,
2: 2 judgment against those who do **such** *things* is based on truth.
2: 3 a mere man, pass judgment on **them**^{s} [+3836+3836+4556] and yet
16:18 For **such** *people* are not serving our Lord Christ, but their own
1Co 5: 1 among you, and **of a kind** that does not occur even among pagans:
5: 5 hand **this** *man* over to Satan, so that the sinful nature may be
5:11 a drunkard or a swindler. With **such a man** do not even eat.
7:15 A believing man or woman is not bound in **such** *circumstances*;
7:28 But **those**^{s} [+3836] **who marry** will face many troubles in this
11:16 wants to be contentious about this, we have no **other** practice—
15:48 As was the earthly man, **so** are those who are of the earth;
15:48 as is the man from heaven, **so** also are those who are of heaven.
16:16 to submit *to* **such as these** and to everyone who joins in the work,
16:18 refreshed my spirit and yours also. **Such** *men* deserve recognition.
2Co 2: 6 The punishment *inflicted on* **him** by the majority is sufficient for
2: 7 so that **he** will not be overwhelmed by excessive sorrow.
3: 4 **Such** confidence as this is ours through Christ before God.
3:12 Therefore, since we have **such** a hope, we are very bold.
10:11 **Such** *people* should realize that what we are in our letters when we
10:11 are absent, **[RPG]** we will be in our actions when we are present.
11:13 For **such** *men* are false apostles, deceitful workmen,
12: 2 the body or out of the body I do not know—God knows. **[RPG]**
12: 3 And I know that **this** man—whether in the body or apart from the
12: 5 I will boast about a **man like that**, but I will not boast about
Gal 5:21 that those who live **like this** will not inherit the kingdom of God.
5:23 gentleness and self-control. Against **such** *things* there is no law.
6: 1 is caught in a sin, you who are spiritual should restore **him** gently.
Eph 5:27 without stain or wrinkle or any other **blemish**^{s} [+3836], but holy
Php 2:29 Welcome him in the Lord with great joy, and honor **men like him**,
2Th 3:12 **Such** *people* we command and urge in the Lord Jesus Christ to
Tit 3:11 You may be sure that **such a man** is warped and sinful; he is
Phm 1: 9 I then, **[RPG]** as Paul—an old man and now also a prisoner of
Heb 7:26 **Such** a high priest meets our need—one who is holy, blameless,
8: 1 We do have **such** a high priest, who sat down at the right hand of
11:14 People who say **such** *things* show that they are looking for a
12: 3 Consider him who endured **such** opposition from sinful men,
13:16 and to share with others, for *with* **such** sacrifices God is pleased.
Jas 4:16 As it is, you boast and brag. All **such** boasting is evil.
3Jn 1: 8 We ought therefore to show hospitality to **such** *men* so that we

5526 τοῖχος, *toichos* [1] [√ 5446]

wall [1]

Ac 23: 3 Then Paul said to him, "God will strike you, *you* whitewashed **wall**!

5527 τόκος, *tokos* [2] [√ 5503]

interest [2]

Mt 25:27 so that when I returned I would have received it back with **interest**.
Lk 19:23 so that when I came back, I could have collected it with **interest**?'

5528 τολμάω, *tolmaō* [16] [→ 703, 5529, 5530, 5531, 5532]

dare [6], dared [5], be^s [1], boldly [1], courageously [1], dares [1], venture [1]

Mt 22:46 and from that day on no one **dared** to ask him any more questions.
Mk 12:34 And from then on no one **dared** ask him any more questions.
  15:43 kingdom of God, went **boldly** to Pilate and asked for Jesus' body.
Lk 20:40 And no one **dared** to ask him any more questions.
Jn 21:12 None of the disciples **dared** ask him, "Who are you?"
Ac 5:13 No one else **dared** join them, even though they were highly
   7:32 and Jacob.' Moses trembled with fear and *did* not **dare** to look.
Ro 5: 7 though for a good man someone *might* possibly **dare** to die.
  15:18 *I will* not **venture** to speak of anything except what Christ has
1Co 6: 1 **dare** he take it before the ungodly for judgment instead of before
2Co 10: 2 *to* **be**^{s} toward some people who think that we live by the standards
  10:12 *We do* not **dare** to classify or compare ourselves with some who
  11:21 What anyone else **dares** to boast about—I am speaking as a fool—
  11:21 boast about—I am speaking as a fool—I also **dare** to boast about.
Php 1:14 been encouraged to speak the word of God more **courageously**
Jude 1: 9 *did* not **dare** to bring a slanderous accusation against him,

5529 τολμηρός, *tolmēros* [1] [√ 5528]

quite boldly [1]

Ro 15:15 I have written you **quite boldly** on some points, as if to remind you

5530 τολμηρότερον, *tolmēroteron* Not used in UBS/NIV [√ 5528]

5531 τολμηροτέρως, *tolmēroterōs* Not used in UBS/NIV [√ 5528]

5532 τολμητής, *tolmētēs* [1] [√ 5528]

bold [1]

2Pe 2:10 **Bold** and arrogant, these men are not afraid to slander celestial

5533 τομός, *tomos* [1] [→ 598, 704, 705, 875, 1497, 2961, 3982, 4362, 4364, 5335, 5339, 5421]

sharper [1]

Heb 4:12 **Sharper** than any double-edged sword, it penetrates even to

5534 τόξον, *toxon* [1] [→ 2962]

bow [1]

Rev 6: 2 Its rider held a **bow**, and he was given a crown, and he rode out as

5535 τοπάζιον, *topazion* [1]

topaz [1]

Rev 21:20 the eighth beryl, the ninth **topaz**, the tenth chrysoprase,

5536 τόπος, *topos* [94] [→ 876, 1954]

place [63], places [6], everywhere [+1877+4246] [3], room [3], area [2], *untranslated* [1], among [1], by itself [+1650+1651+3023+6006] [1], everywhere [+4246] [1], foothold [1], nearby [+3836+4309] [1], opportunity [1], ports [1], rocks [+5550] [1], sandbar [+1458] [1], seat [1], spot [1], take over [+3284+3836] [1], there [+1877+3836] [1], travel by ship [+2093+4434] [1], where [+1650+3836] [1], where [+1877+4005] [1]

Mt 12:43 it goes through arid **places** seeking rest and does not find it.
  14:13 had happened, he withdrew by boat privately to a solitary **place**.
  14:15 the disciples came to him and said, "This is a remote **place**,
  14:35 And when the men *of* that **place** recognized Jesus, they sent word
  24: 7 There will be famines and earthquakes in various **places**.
  24:15 "So when you see standing in the holy **place** 'the abomination that

  26:52 "Put your sword back in its **place**," Jesus said to him, "for all who
  27:33 They came to a **place** called Golgotha (which means The Place of
  27:33 They came to a place called Golgotha (which means The **Place** of
  28: 6 he has risen, just as he said. Come and see the **place** where he lay.
Mk 1:35 Jesus got up, left the house and went off to a solitary **place**,
   1:45 no longer enter a town openly but stayed outside in lonely **places**.
   6:11 And if any **place** will not welcome you or listen to you,
   6:31 "Come with me by yourselves to a quiet **place** and get some rest."
   6:32 So they went away by themselves in a boat to a solitary **place**.
   6:35 "This is a remote **place**," they said, "and it's already very late.
  13: 8 There will be earthquakes in various **places**, and famines.
  15:22 They brought Jesus to the **place** called Golgotha (which means The
  15:22 to the place called Golgotha (which means The **Place** of the Skull).
  16: 6 He has risen! He is not here. See the **place** where they laid him.
Lk 2: 7 him in a manger, because there was no **room** for them in the inn.
   4:17 handed to him. Unrolling it, he found the **place** where it is written:
   4:37 And the news about him spread throughout the surrounding **area**.
   4:42 At daybreak Jesus went out to a solitary **place**. The people were
   6:17 He went down with them and stood on a level **place**. A large
   9:12 and find food and lodging, because we are in a remote **place** here."
  10: 1 ahead of him to every town and **place** where he was about to go.
  10:32 So too, a Levite, when he came to the **place** and saw him,
  11: 1 One day Jesus was praying in a certain **place**. When he finished,
  11:24 it goes through arid **places** seeking rest and does not find it.
  14: 9 both of you will come and say to you, 'Give this man your **seat**.'
  14: 9 humiliated, you will have to take the least important **place**.
  14:10 But when you are invited, take the lowest **place**, so that when your
  14:22 'what you ordered has been done, but there is still **room**.'
  16:28 so that they will not also come to this **place** of torment.'
  19: 5 When Jesus reached the **spot**, he looked up and said to him,
  21:11 famines and pestilences in various **places**, and fearful events
  22:40 On reaching the **place**, he said to them, "Pray that you will not fall
  23:33 When they came to the **place** called the Skull, there they crucified
Jn 4:20 but you Jews claim that the **place** where we must worship is in
   5:13 had slipped away into the crowd that was **there** [+1877+3836].
   6:10 There was plenty of grass in that **place**, and the men sat down.
   6:23 Then some boats from Tiberias landed near the **place** where the
  10:40 Then Jesus went back across the Jordan to the **place** where John
  11: 6 was sick, he stayed **where** [+1877+4005] he was two more days.
  11:30 the village, but was still at the **place** where Martha had met him.
  11:48 Romans will come and take away both our **place** and our nation."
  14: 2 I would have told you. I am going there to prepare a **place** for you.
  14: 3 And if I go and prepare a **place** for you, I will come back and take
  18: 2 Now Judas, who betrayed him, knew the **place**, because Jesus had
  19:13 and sat down on the judge's seat at a **place** known as the Stone
  19:17 he went out to the **place** of the Skull (which in Aramaic is called
  19:20 for the **place** where Jesus was crucified was near the city,
  19:41 At the **place** where Jesus was crucified, there was a garden,
  20: 7 The cloth was folded up **by itself** [+1650+1651+3023+6006],
Ac 1:25 *to* **take over** [+3284+3836] this apostolic ministry, which Judas
   1:25 which Judas left to go **where** [+1650+3836] he belongs."
   4:31 After they prayed, the **place** where they were meeting was shaken.
   6:13 "This fellow never stops speaking against this holy **place**
   6:14 heard him say that this Jesus of Nazareth will destroy this **place**
   7: 7 they will come out of that country and worship me in this **place**.'
   7:33 off your sandals; the **place** where you are standing is holy ground.
   7:49 build for me? says the Lord. Or where will my resting **place** be?
  12:17 The brothers about this," he said, and then he left for another **place**.
  16: 3 so he circumcised him because of the Jews who lived in that **area**,
  21:28 all men everywhere against our people and our law and this **place**.
  21:28 brought Greeks into the temple area and defiled this holy **place**."
  25:16 and has had an **opportunity** to defend himself against their
  27: 2 We boarded a ship from Adramyttium about to sail for **ports** along
  27: 8 the coast with difficulty and came to a **place** called Fair Havens,
  27:29 Fearing that we would be dashed against the **rocks** [+5550],
  27:41 But the ship struck a **sandbar** [+1458] and ran aground. The bow
  28: 7 There was an estate **nearby** [+3836+4309] that belonged to
Ro 9:26 "It will happen that in the very **place** where it was said to them,
  12:19 my friends, but leave **room** for God's wrath, for it is written:
  15:23 But now that there is no more **place** for me to work in these
1Co 1: 2 together with all those **everywhere** [+4246] who call on the name
  14:16 how can one who finds himself **among** those who do not
2Co 2:14 through us spreads **everywhere** [+1877+4246] the fragrance of the
Eph 4:27 and do not give the devil a **foothold**.
1Th 1: 8 your faith in God has become known **everywhere** [+1877+4246].
1Ti 2: 8 I want men **everywhere** [+1877+4246] to lift up holy hands in

Heb	8: 7 that first covenant, no **place** would have been sought for another.
	11: 8 when called to go to a **place** he would later receive as his
	12: 17 He could bring about no [NIE] change of mind, though he sought
2Pe	1: 19 as to a light shining in a dark **place**, until the day dawns
Rev	2: 5 I will come to you and remove your lampstand from its **place**.
	6: 14 and every mountain and island was removed from its **place**.
	12: 6 The woman fled into the desert to a **place** prepared for her by God,
	12: 8 But he was not strong enough, and they lost their **place** in heaven.
	12: 14 so that she might fly to the **place** prepared for her in the desert,
	16: 16 Then they gathered the kings together to the **place** that in Hebrew
	18: 17 sea captain, and all who **travel by ship** [+2093+4434], the sailors,
	20: 11 and sky fled from his presence, and there was no **place** for them.

5537 τοσοῦτος, *tosoutos* [20] [√ 4047]

such great [4], as much [2], so many [2], such [2], this [2], all the more [+3437] [1], all these [1], all [1], enough [1], long [1], so much [1], that [1], these [1]

Mt	8: 10 the truth, I have not found anyone in Israel with **such great** faith.
	15: 33 "Where could we get **enough** bread in this remote place to feed
	15: 33 could we get enough bread in this remote place to feed **such**
Lk	7: 9 "I tell you, I have not found **such great** faith even in Israel."
	15: 29 *All* **these** years I've been slaving for you and never disobeyed your
Jn	6: 9 and two small fish, but how far will they go among **so many**?"
	12: 37 Even after Jesus had done **all these** miraculous signs in their
	14: 9 Philip, even after I have been among you **such** a long time?
	21: 11 full of large fish, 153, but even with **so many** the net was not torn.
Ac	5: 8 "Tell me, is **this** the *price* you and Ananias got for the land?"
	5: 8 and Ananias got for the land?" "Yes," she said, "**that** is the *price*."
1Co	14: 10 Undoubtedly there are **all** sorts of languages in the world,
Gal	3: 4 Have you suffered **so much** for nothing—if it really was for
Heb	1: 4 So he became **as much** superior to the angels as the name he has
	4: 7 calling it Today, when a **long** time later he spoke through David,
	7: 22 Because of **this** oath, Jesus has become the guarantee of a better
	10: 25 and **all the more** [+3437] as you see the Day approaching.
	12: 1 since we are surrounded *by* **such** a **great** cloud of witnesses,
Rev	18: 7 Give her **as much** torture and grief as the glory and luxury she
	18: 17 In one hour **such great** wealth has been brought to ruin!'

5538 τότε, *tote* [160] [√ 4005 + 5445]

then [105], *untranslated* [24], at that time [12], so [4], when [3], finally [+4036] [2], that time on [2], and [1], as soon as [1], at that [1], formerly [1], of that time [1], once [1], that time [1], then on [1]

Mt	2: 7 **Then** Herod called the Magi secretly and found out from them the
	2: 16 **When** Herod realized that he had been outwitted by the Magi,
	2: 17 **Then** what was said through the prophet Jeremiah was fulfilled:
	3: 5 [NIE] People went out to him from Jerusalem and all Judea
	3: 13 **Then** Jesus came from Galilee to the Jordan to be baptized by
	3: 15 for us to do this to fulfill all righteousness." **Then** John consented.
	4: 1 **Then** Jesus was led by the Spirit into the desert to be tempted by
	4: 5 **Then** the devil took him to the holy city and had him stand on the
	4: 10 [NIE] Jesus said to him, "Away from me, Satan! For it is written:
	4: 11 **Then** the devil left him, and angels came and attended him.
	4: 17 From **that time on** Jesus began to preach, "Repent, for the kingdom
	5: 24 and be reconciled to your brother; **then** come and offer your gift.
	7: 5 **then** you will see clearly to remove the speck from your brother's
	7: 23 **Then** I will tell them plainly, 'I never knew you. Away from me,
	8: 26 **Then** he got up and rebuked the winds and the waves, and it was
	9: 6 **Then** he said to the paralytic, "Get up, take your mat and go home."
	9: 14 **Then** John's disciples came and asked him, "How is it that we
	9: 15 when the bridegroom will be taken from them; **then** they will fast.
	9: 29 **Then** he touched their eyes and said, "According to your faith will
	9: 37 **Then** he said to his disciples, "The harvest is plentiful
	11: 20 **Then** Jesus began to denounce the cities in which most of his
	12: 13 **Then** he said to the man, "Stretch out your hand." So he stretched it
	12: 22 **Then** they brought him a demon-possessed man who was blind
	12: 29 unless he first ties up the strong man? **Then** he can rob his house.
	12: 38 **Then** some of the Pharisees and teachers of the law said to him,
	12: 44 **Then** it says, 'I will return to the house I left.' When it arrives,
	12: 45 **Then** it goes and takes with it seven other spirits more wicked than
	13: 26 wheat sprouted and formed heads, **then** the weeds also appeared.
	13: 36 **Then** he left the crowd and went into the house. His disciples came
	13: 43 **Then** the righteous will shine like the sun in the kingdom of their

	15: 1 **Then** some Pharisees and teachers of the law came to Jesus from
	15: 12 **Then** the disciples came to him and asked, "Do you know that the
	15: 28 **Then** Jesus answered, "Woman, you have great faith! Your request
	16: 12 **Then** they understood that he was not telling them to guard against
	16: 20 **Then** he warned his disciples not to tell anyone that he was the
	16: 21 From **that time on** Jesus began to explain to his disciples that he
	16: 24 **Then** Jesus said to his disciples, "If anyone would come after me,
	16: 27 **then** he will reward each person according to what he has done.
	17: 13 **Then** the disciples understood that he was talking to them about
	17: 19 **Then** the disciples came to Jesus in private and asked, "Why
	18: 21 **Then** Peter came to Jesus and asked, "Lord, how many times shall I
	18: 32 "**Then** the master called the servant in. 'You wicked servant,'
	19: 13 **Then** little children were brought to Jesus for him to place his
	19: 27 [NIE] Peter answered him, "We have left everything to follow
	20: 20 **Then** the mother of Zebedee's sons came to Jesus with her sons
	21: 1 on the Mount of Olives, [NIE] Jesus sent two disciples,
	22: 8 "**Then** he said to his servants, 'The wedding banquet is ready,
	22: 13 "**Then** the king told the attendants, 'Tie him hand and foot,
	22: 15 **Then** the Pharisees went out and laid plans to trap him in his
	22: 21 **Then** he said to them, "Give to Caesar what is Caesar's, and to God
	23: 1 **Then** Jesus said to the crowds and to his disciples:
	24: 9 "**Then** you will be handed over to be persecuted and put to death,
	24: 10 **At that time** many will turn away from the faith and will betray
	24: 14 world as a testimony to all nations, and **then** the end will come.
	24: 16 **then** let those who are in Judea flee to the mountains.
	24: 21 For **then** there will be great distress, unequaled from the beginning
	24: 23 **At that time** if anyone says to you, 'Look, here is the Christ!'
	24: 30 "**At that time** the sign of the Son of Man will appear in the sky,
	24: 30 in the sky, and [RPG] all the nations of the earth will mourn.
	24: 40 [NIE] Two men will be in the field; one will be taken
	25: 1 "**At that time** the kingdom of heaven will be like ten virgins who
	25: 7 "**Then** all the virgins woke up and trimmed their lamps.
	25: 31 angels with him, [NIE] he will sit on his throne in heavenly glory.
	25: 34 "**Then** the King will say to those on his right, 'Come, you who are
	25: 37 "**Then** the righteous will answer him, 'Lord, when did we see you
	25: 41 "**Then** he will say to those on his left, 'Depart from me, you who
	25: 44 "They also will [NIE] answer, 'Lord, when did we see you hungry
	25: 45 [NIE] "He will reply, 'I tell you the truth, whatever you did not do
	26: 3 **Then** the chief priests and the elders of the people assembled in the
	26: 14 **Then** one of the Twelve—the one called Judas Iscariot—went to
	26: 16 **then on** Judas watched for an opportunity to hand him over.
	26: 31 **Then** Jesus told them, "This very night you will all fall away on
	26: 36 **Then** Jesus went with his disciples to a place called Gethsemane,
	26: 38 **Then** he said to them, "My soul is overwhelmed with sorrow to the
	26: 45 **Then** he returned to the disciples and said to them, "Are you still
	26: 50 **Then** the men stepped forward, seized Jesus and arrested him.
	26: 52 "Put your sword back in its place," [NIE] Jesus said to him,
	26: 56 might be fulfilled." **Then** all the disciples deserted him and fled.
	26: 65 **Then** the high priest tore his clothes and said, "He has spoken
	26: 67 **Then** they spit in his face and struck him with their fists. Others
	26: 74 **Then** he began to call down curses on himself and he swore to
	27: 3 When Judas, who had betrayed him, saw that Jesus was
	27: 9 **Then** what was spoken by Jeremiah the prophet was fulfilled:
	27: 13 **Then** Pilate asked him, "Don't you hear the testimony they are
	27: 16 **At that time** they had a notorious prisoner, called Barabbas.
	27: 26 **Then** he released Barabbas to them. But he had Jesus flogged,
	27: 27 **Then** the governor's soldiers took Jesus into the Praetorium
	27: 38 [NIE] Two robbers were crucified with him, one on his right
	27: 58 he asked for Jesus' body, **and** Pilate ordered that it be given to him.
	28: 10 **Then** Jesus said to them, "Do not be afraid. Go and tell my brothers
Mk	2: 20 will be taken from them, and [NIE] on that day they will fast.
	3: 27 unless he first ties up the strong man. **Then** he can rob his house.
	13: 14 **then** let those who are in Judea flee to the mountains.
	13: 21 **At that time** if anyone says to you, 'Look, here is the Christ!'
	13: 26 "**At that time** men will see the Son of Man coming in clouds with
	13: 27 And [RPG] he will send his angels and gather his elect from the
Lk	5: 35 will be taken from them; [RPG] in those days they will fast."
	6: 42 **then** you will see clearly to remove the speck from your brother's
	11: 24 and does not find it. **Then** it says, 'I will return to the house I left.'
	11: 26 **Then** it goes and takes with it seven other spirits more wicked than itself,
	13: 26 "**Then** you will say, 'We ate and drank with you, and you taught in
	14: 9 **Then**, humiliated, you will have to take the least important place.
	14: 10 **Then** you will be honored in the presence of all your fellow guests.
	14: 21 **Then** the owner of the house became angry and ordered his
	16: 16 Since **that time**, the good news of the kingdom of God is being
	21: 10 **Then** he said to them: "Nation will rise against nation, and kingdom

21:20 by armies, [RPG] you will know that its desolation is near.
21:21 **Then** let those who are in Judea flee to the mountains, let those in
21:27 **At that time** they will see the Son of Man coming in a cloud with
23:30 **Then** " 'they will say to the mountains, "Fall on us!" and to the
24:45 **Then** he opened their minds so they could understand the
Jn 7:10 left for the Feast, [NIE] he went also, not publicly, but in secret.
8:28 **then** you will know that I am ᵼthe one I claim to beᴊ and that I do
10:22 **Then** came the Feast of Dedication at Jerusalem. It was winter,
11: 6 Lazarus was sick, [NIE] he stayed where he was two more days.
11:14 So **then** he told them plainly, "Lazarus is dead,
12:16 Only after Jesus was glorified [RPG] did they realize that these
13:27 As soon as Judas took the bread, Satan entered into him. "What you
19: 1 **Then** Pilate took Jesus and had him flogged.
19:16 **Finally** [+4036] Pilate handed him over to them to be crucified.
20: 8 **Finally** [+4036] the other disciple, who had reached the tomb first,
Ac 1:12 **Then** they returned to Jerusalem from the hill called the Mount of
4: 8 **Then** Peter, filled with the Holy Spirit, said to them: "Rulers
5:26 **At that,** the captain went with his officers and brought the
6:11 **Then** they secretly persuaded some men to say, "We have heard
7: 4 "**So** he left the land of the Chaldeans and settled in Haran.
8:17 **Then** Peter and John placed their hands on them, and they received
10:46 heard them speaking in tongues and praising God. **Then** Peter said,
10:48 **Then** they asked Peter to stay with them for a few days.
13: 3 **So** after they had fasted and prayed, they placed their hands on
13:12 **When** the proconsul saw what had happened, he believed,
15:22 **Then** the apostles and elders, with the whole church, decided to
17:14 [RPG] The brothers immediately sent Paul to the coast, but Silas
21:13 **Then** Paul answered, "Why are you weeping and breaking my
21:26 **Then** he went to the temple to give notice of the date when the
21:33 [NIE] The commander came up and arrested him and ordered him
23: 3 **Then** Paul said to him, "God will strike you, you whitewashed
25:12 [NIE] After Festus had conferred with his council, he declared:
26: 1 **So** Paul motioned with his hand and began his defense:
27:21 time without food, [NIE] Paul stood up before them and said:
27:32 **So** the soldiers cut the ropes that held the lifeboat and let it fall
28: 1 **Once** safely on shore, we found out that the island was called
Ro 6:21 What benefit did you reap **at that time** from the things you are
1Co 4: 5 men's hearts. **At that time** each will receive his praise from God.
13:12 but a poor reflection as in a mirror; **then** we shall see face to face.
13:12 I know in part; **then** I shall know fully, even as I am fully known.
15:28 **then** the Son himself will be made subject to him who put
15:54 with immortality, **then** the saying that is written will come true:
16: 2 so that when I come no collections will have to be made. [RPG]
2Co 12:10 in difficulties. For when I am weak, **then** I am strong.
Gal 4: 8 **Formerly,** when you did not know God, you were slaves to those
4:29 **At that time** the son born in the ordinary way persecuted the son
6: 4 **Then** he can take pride in himself, without comparing himself to
Col 3: 4 is your life, appears, **then** you also will appear with him in glory.
1Th 5: 3 and safety," [RPG] destruction will come on them suddenly,
2Th 2: 8 And **then** the lawless one will be revealed, whom the Lord Jesus
Heb 10: 7 **Then** I said, 'Here I am—it is written about me in the scroll—
10: 9 **Then** he said, "Here I am, I have come to do your will." He sets
12:26 **At that time** his voice shook the earth, but now he has promised,
2Pe 3: 6 By these waters also the world **of that time** was deluged

5539 τοὐναντίον, tounantion [3] [√ 3836 + 1882]

but [+1254+1883+3836] [1], instead [+1883+3437+3836] [1], on contrary [+247+1883] [1]

2Co 2: 7 Now **instead,** you ought to forgive and comfort him, so that he will
Gal 2: 7 **On** the **contrary,** they saw that I had been entrusted with the task
1Pe 3: 9 Do not repay evil with evil or insult with insult, **but** with blessing,

5540 τοὔνομα, tounoma [1] [√ 3836 + 3950]

named [1]

Mt 27:57 there came a rich man from Arimathea, [NIE] **named** Joseph,

5541 τοὐπίσω, toupisō Not used in UBS/NIV [√ 3836 + 3958]

5542 τουτέστιν, toutestin Not used in UBS/NIV [√ 4047 + 1639]

5543 τράγος, tragos [4 / 3] [√ 5592]

goats [3]

Heb 9:12 He did not enter by means of the blood *of* **goats** and calves;
9:13 The blood *of* **goats** and bulls and the ashes of a heifer sprinkled on
9:19 he took the blood of calves [UBS+ *and* **goats**], together with water,
10: 4 it is impossible for the blood of bulls and **goats** to take away sins.

5544 τράπεζα, trapeza [15] [√ 5475 + 4269]

table [9], tables [4], deposit [1], set a meal before [+4192] [1]

Mt 15:27 even the dogs eat the crumbs that fall from their masters' **table.**"
21:12 He overturned the **tables** of the money changers and the benches of
Mk 7:28 "but even the dogs under the **table** eat the children's crumbs."
11:15 He overturned the **tables** of the money changers and the benches of
Lk 16:21 and longing to eat what fell from the rich man's **table.** Even the
19:23 Why then didn't you put my money on **deposit,**
22:21 hand of him who is going to betray me is with mine on the **table.**
22:30 may eat and drink at my **table** in my kingdom and sit on thrones,
Jn 2:15 the coins of the money changers and overturned their **tables.**
Ac 6: 2 neglect the ministry of the word of God in order to wait on **tables.**
16:34 brought them into his house and **set a meal before** [+4192] them;
Ro 11: 9 "May their **table** become a snare and a trap, a stumbling block
1Co 10:21 you cannot have a part *in* both the Lord's **table** and the table of
10:21 have a part in both the Lord's table and the **table** of demons.
Heb 9: 2 first room were the lampstand, the **table** and the consecrated bread;

5545 τραπεζίτης, trapezitēs [1] [√ 5475 + 4269]

bankers [1]

Mt 25:27 you should have put my money on deposit *with* the **bankers,**

5546 τραῦμα, trauma [1] [→ 1765, 5547]

wounds [1]

Lk 10:34 He went to him and bandaged his **wounds,** pouring on oil

5547 τραυματίζω, traumatizō [2] [√ 5546]

bleeding [1], wounded [1]

Lk 20:12 He sent still a third, and they **wounded** him and threw him out.
Ac 19:16 such a beating that they ran out of the house naked and **bleeding.**

5548 τραχηλίζω, trachēlizō [1] [√ 5549]

laid bare [1]

Heb 4:13 and **laid bare** before the eyes of him to whom we must give

5549 τράχηλος, trachēlos [7] [→ 5019, 5548]

neck [3], embraced [+2093+2158+3836] [1], necks [1], risked lives [+3836+5719] [1], threw arms around [+2093+2158+3836] [1]

Mt 18: 6 be better for him to have a large millstone hung around his **neck**
Mk 9:42 be thrown into the sea with a large millstone tied around his **neck.**
Lk 15:20 **threw** *his* **arms around** [+2093+2158+3836] him and kissed him.
17: 2 his **neck** than for him to cause one of these little ones to sin.
Ac 15:10 why do you try to test God by putting on the **necks** of the disciples
20:37 They all wept as *they* **embraced** [+2093+2158+3836] him and
Ro 16: 4 They **risked** their **lives** [+3836+5719] for me. Not only I but all the

5550 τραχύς, trachys [2] [→ 5551]

rocks [+5536] [1], rough [1]

Lk 3: 5 The crooked roads shall become straight, the **rough** ways smooth.
Ac 27:29 Fearing that we would be dashed against the **rocks** [+5536],

5551 Τραχωνῖτις, Trachōnitis [1] [√ 5550]

Traconitis [+6001] [1]

Lk 3: 1 his brother Philip tetrarch *of* Iturea and **Traconitis** [+6001],

5552 τρεῖς, *treis* [68] [→ 804, 5553, 5558, 5559, 5560, 5562, 5564, 5565, 5566, 5567, 5568, 5569]

three [63], 153 [+*1669*+*4299*] [1], large amount [+*4929*] [1], twenty to thirty gallons [+*1545*+*2445*+*3583*] [1], twenty-three [+*1633*] [1]

Mt 12:40 For as Jonah was **three** days and three nights in the belly of a huge
   12:40 Jonah was three days and **three** nights in the belly of a huge fish,
   12:40 so the Son of Man will be **three** days and three nights in the heart
   12:40 of Man will be three days and **three** nights in the heart of the earth.
   13:33 and mixed into a **large amount** [+*4929*] of flour until it worked all
   15:32 they have already been with me **three** days and have nothing to
   17: 4 If you wish, I will put up **three** shelters—one for you, one for
   18:16 'every matter may be established by the testimony *of* two or **three**
   18:20 For where two or **three** come together in my name, there am I with
   26:61 am able to destroy the temple of God and rebuild it in **three** days.' "
   27:40 who are going to destroy the temple and build it in **three** days,
   27:63 still alive that deceiver said, 'After **three** days I will rise again.'
Mk 8: 2 they have already been with me **three** days and have nothing to
   8:31 and that he must be killed and after **three** days rise again.
   9: 5 Let us put up **three** shelters—one for you, one for Moses and one
   9:31 hands of men. They will kill him, and after **three** days he will rise."
   10:34 spit on him, flog him and kill him. **Three** days later he will rise."
   14:58 destroy this man-made temple and in **three** days will build another,
   15:29 You who are going to destroy the temple and build it in **three** days,
Lk 1:56 Mary stayed with Elizabeth *for* about **three** months and
   2:46 After **three** days they found him in the temple courts,
   4:25 when the sky was shut for **three** and a half years and there was a
   9:33 Let us put up **three** shelters—one for you, one for Moses and one
   10:36 "Which *of* these **three** do you think was a neighbor to the man who
   11: 5 him at midnight and says, 'Friend, lend me **three** loaves of bread,
   12:52 against each other, **three** against two and two against three.
   12:52 against each other, three against two and two against **three**.
   13: 7 '*For* **three** years now I've been coming to look for fruit on this fig
   13:21 and mixed into a **large amount** [+*4929*] of flour until it worked all
Jn 2: 6 each holding from **twenty to thirty gallons** [+*1545*+*2445*+*3583*].
   2:19 "Destroy this temple, and I will raise it again in **three** days."
   2:20 to build this temple, and you are going to raise it in **three** days?"
   21:11 dragged the net ashore. It was full of large fish, **153** [+*1669*+*4299*],
Ac 5: 7 About **three** hours later his wife came in, not knowing what had
   7:20 *For* **three** months he was cared for in his father's house.
   9: 9 *For* **three** days he was blind, and did not eat or drink anything.
   10:19 the Spirit said to him, "Simon, **three** men are looking for you.
   11:11 then **three** men who had been sent to me from Caesarea stopped at
   17: 2 and on **three** Sabbath days he reasoned with them from the
   19: 8 entered the synagogue and spoke boldly there for **three** months,
   20: 3 where he stayed **three** months. Because the Jews made a plot
   25: 1 **Three** days after arriving in the province, Festus went up from
   28: 7 us to his home and *for* **three** days entertained us hospitably.
   28:11 After **three** months we put out to sea in a ship that had wintered in
   28:12 We put in at Syracuse and stayed there **three** days.
   28:17 **Three** days later he called together the leaders of the Jews.
1Co 10: 8 and in one day **twenty-three** [+*1633*] thousand of them died.
   13:13 And now these **three** remain: faith, hope and love. But the greatest
   14:27 If anyone speaks in a tongue, two—or at the most **three**—
   14:29 Two or **three** prophets should speak, and the others should weigh
2Co 13: 1 must be established by the testimony of two or **three** witnesses."
Gal 1:18 Then after **three** years, I went up to Jerusalem to get acquainted
1Ti 5:19 against an elder unless it is brought by two or **three** witnesses.
Heb 10:28 died without mercy on the testimony of two or **three** witnesses.
Jas 5:17 not rain, and it did not rain on the land *for* **three** and a half years.
1Jn 5: 7 For there are **three** that testify:
   5: 8 the Spirit, the water and the blood; and the **three** are in agreement.
Rev 6: 6 and **three** quarts of barley for a day's wages, and do not damage
   8:13 the trumpet blasts about to be sounded by the other **three** angels!"
   9:18 A third of mankind was killed by the **three** plagues of fire,
   11: 9 *For* **three** and a half days men from every people, tribe, language
   11:11 But after the **three** and a half days a breath of life from God
   16:13 Then I saw **three** evil spirits that looked like frogs; they came out
   16:19 The great city split into **three** parts, and the cities of the nations
   21:13 There were **three** gates on the east, three on the north, three on the
   21:13 **three** on the north, three on the south and three on the west.
   21:13 three on the north, **three** on the south and three on the west.
   21:13 three on the north, three on the south and **three** on the west.

5553 Τρεῖς ταβέρναι, *Treis tabernai* [1]

[√ *5552* + *5411*]

Three Taverns [1]

Ac 28:15 as far as the Forum of Appius and the **Three Taverns** to meet us.

5554 τρέμω, *tremō* [3] [→ 1764, 1958, 5571]

trembling [2], afraid [1]

Mk 5:33 came and fell at his feet and, **trembling** with fear, told him the
Lk 8:47 she could not go unnoticed, came **trembling** and fell at his feet.
2Pe 2:10 and arrogant, *these men are* not **afraid** to slander celestial beings;

5555 τρέφω, *trephō* [9] [→ 427, 1418, 1485, 1763, 1957, 2576, 5343, 5452, 5575, 5576, 5577, 5578]

feeds [2], taken care of [2], brought up [1], fattened [1], feed [1], food supply [1], nursed [1]

Mt 6:26 or store away in barns, and yet your heavenly Father **feeds** them.
   25:37 'Lord, when did we see you hungry and **feed** you, or thirsty
Lk 4:16 He went to Nazareth, where he had been **brought up**, and on the
   12:24 or reap, they have no storeroom or barn; yet God **feeds** them.
   23:29 the wombs that never bore and the breasts that never **nursed**!'
Ac 12:20 because they depended on the king's country for their **food supply**.
Jas 5: 5 You have **fattened** yourselves in the day of slaughter.
Rev 12: 6 for her by God, where she *might be* **taken care of** for 1,260 days.
   12:14 where she *would be* **taken care of** for a time, times and half a

5556 τρέχω, *trechō* [20] [→ 1536, 1661, 2192, 2312, 2963, 4366, 4596, 4708, 4731, 5282, 5340, 5579, 5580, 5720]

ran [6], run [5], running [3], effort [1], run race [1], runners [1], running a [1], rushing [1], spread rapidly [1]

Mt 27:48 Immediately one of them **ran** and got a sponge. He filled it with
   28: 8 the tomb, afraid yet filled with joy, and **ran** to tell his disciples.
Mk 5: 6 Jesus from a distance, *he* **ran** and fell on his knees in front of him.
   15:36 One man **ran**, filled a sponge with wine vinegar, put it on a stick,
Lk 15:20 he **ran** to his son, threw his arms around him and kissed him.
   24:12 Peter, however, got up and **ran** to the tomb. Bending over,
Jn 20: 2 So *she* came **running** to Simon Peter and the other disciple,
   20: 4 Both *were* **running**, but the other disciple outran Peter and reached
Ro 9:16 It does not, therefore, depend on man's desire or **effort**, but on
1Co 9:24 Do you not know that in a race all the **runners** run, but only one
   9:24 Do you not know that in a race all the runners **run**, but only one
   9:24 but only one gets the prize? **Run** in such a way as to get the prize.
   9:26 Therefore I *do* not **run** like a man running aimlessly; I do not fight
Gal 2: 2 be leaders, for fear that *I was* **running** or had run my race in vain.
   2: 2 be leaders, for fear that I was running or *had* **run** *my* race in vain.
   5: 7 *You were* **running a** good race. Who cut in on you and kept you
Php 2:16 in order that I may boast on the day of Christ that *I did* not **run**
2Th 3: 1 I pray for us that the message of the Lord *may* **spread rapidly**
Heb 12: 1 and *let us* **run** with perseverance the race marked out for us.
Rev 9: 9 the thundering of many horses and chariots **rushing** into battle.

5557 τρῆμα, *trēma* [1]

eye [1]

Lk 18:25 it is easier for a camel to go through the **eye** of a needle than for a

5558 τριάκοντα, *triakonta* [11] [√ *5552*]

thirty [8], 430 [+*2779*+*5484*] [1], thirty-eight [+*2779*+*3893*] [1], three or three and a half miles [+*1633*+*2445*+*4297*+*5084*] [1]

Mt 13: 8 produced a crop—a hundred, sixty or **thirty** *times* what was sown.
   13:23 yielding a hundred, sixty or **thirty** *times* what was sown."
   26:15 him over to you?" So they counted out for him **thirty** silver coins.
   27: 3 and returned the **thirty** silver coins to the chief priests
   27: 9 "They took the **thirty** silver coins, the price set on him by the
Mk 4: 8 a crop, multiplying **thirty**, sixty, or even a hundred *times*."
   4:20 a crop—**thirty**, sixty or even a hundred *times* as much as was sown."
Lk 3:23 Now Jesus himself was about **thirty** years old when he began his
Jn 5: 5 had been an invalid *for* **thirty-eight** [+*2779*+*3893*] years.

6: 19   rowed **three or three and a half miles** [+*1633+2445+4297+5084*]
Gal   3: 17   The law, introduced **430** [+*2779+5484*] years later, does not set

5559   τριακόσιοι, *triakosioi*   [2]   [√ *5552*]

a year's wages [+*1324*] [1], the money worth a year's wages [+*1324*] [1]

Mk   14: 5   It could have been sold for more than **a year's** [+*1324*] **wages**
Jn   12: 5   **the money** given to the poor? It was **worth a year's wages** [+*1324*]."

5560   τρίβολος, *tribolos*   [2]   [√ *5552 + 965*]

thistles [2]

Mt   7: 16   Do people pick grapes from thornbushes, or figs from **thistles**?
Heb   6: 8   But land that produces thorns and **thistles** is worthless and is in

5561   τρίβος, *tribos*   [3]   [→ *1384, 1417, 4139, 5341, 5342, 5990*]

paths [3]

Mt   3: 3   'Prepare the way for the Lord, make straight **paths** for him.' "
Mk   1: 3   'Prepare the way for the Lord, make straight **paths** for him.' "
Lk   3: 4   'Prepare the way for the Lord, make straight **paths** for him.

5562   τριετία, *trietia*   [1]   [√ *5552 + 2291*]

three years [1]

Ac   20: 31   Remember that *for* **three years** I never stopped warning each of

5563   τρίζω, *trizō*   [1]

gnashes [1]

Mk   9: 18   He foams at the mouth, **gnashes** his teeth and becomes rigid.

5564   τρίμηνος, *trimēnos*   [1]   [√ *5552 + 3604*]

three months [1]

Heb   11: 23   By faith Moses' parents hid him *for* **three months** after he was

5565   τρίς, *tris*   [12]   [√ *5552*]

three times [12]

Mt   26: 34   before the rooster crows, you will disown me **three times**."
    26: 75   "Before the rooster crows, you will disown me **three times**."
Mk   14: 30   the rooster crows twice you yourself will disown me **three times**."
    14: 72   "Before the rooster crows twice you will disown me **three times**."
Lk   22: 34   rooster crows today, you will deny **three times** that you know me."
    22: 61   "Before the rooster crows today, you will disown me **three times**."
Jn   13: 38   before the rooster crows, you will disown me **three times**!
Ac   10: 16   This happened **three times**, and immediately the sheet was taken
    11: 10   This happened **three times**, and then it was all pulled up to heaven
2Co   11: 25   **Three times** I was beaten with rods, once I was stoned, three times
    11: 25   **three times** I was shipwrecked, I spent a night and a day in the
    12: 8   **Three times** I pleaded with the Lord to take it away from me.

5566   τρίστεγον, *tristegon*   [1]   [√ *5552 + 5095*]

third story [1]

Ac   20: 9   he fell to the ground from the **third story** and was picked up dead.

5567   τρισχίλιοι, *trischilioi*   [1]   [√ *5552 + 5943*]

three thousand [1]

Ac   2: 41   and about **three thousand** were added to their number that day.

5568   τρίτον, *triton*   [8]   [√ *5552*]

third time [6], third [2]

Mk   14: 41   Returning the **third time**, he said to them, "Are you still sleeping

Lk   23: 22   *For* the **third time** he spoke to them: "Why? What crime has this
Jn   21: 14   This was now the **third time** Jesus appeared to his disciples after
    21: 17   The **third time** he said to him, "Simon son of John, do you love
    21: 17   Peter was hurt because Jesus asked him the **third time**, "Do you
1Co   12: 28   second prophets, **third** teachers, then workers of miracles,
2Co   12: 14   Now I am ready to visit you *for* the **third time**, and I will not be a
    13: 1   This will be my **third** visit to you. "Every matter must be

5569   τρίτος, *tritos*   [48]   [√ *5552*]

third [45], nine [+*6052*] [1], nine in the morning [+*2465+3836+6052*] [1], third time [+*1666*] [1]

Mt   16: 21   and that he must be killed and *on* the **third** day be raised to life.
    17: 23   They will kill him, and *on* the **third** day he will be raised to life."
    20: 3   "About the **third** hour he went out and saw others standing in the
    20: 19   and crucified. *On* the **third** day he will be raised to life!"
    22: 26   The same thing happened to the second and **third** brother,
    26: 44   and went away once more and prayed the **third** [+*1666*] **time**,
    27: 64   So give the order for the tomb to be made secure until the **third**
Mk   12: 21   but he also died, leaving no child. It was the same with the **third**.
    15: 25   It was the **third** hour when they crucified him.
Lk   9: 22   and he must be killed and *on* the **third** day be raised to life."
    12: 38   even if he comes in the second or **third** watch of the night.
    13: 32   and tomorrow, and *on* the **third** day I will reach my goal.'
    18: 33   *On* the **third** day he will rise again."
    20: 12   He sent still a **third**, and they wounded him and threw him out.
    20: 31   and then the **third** married her, and in the same way the seven
    24: 7   of sinful men, be crucified and *on* the **third** day be raised again.' "
    24: 21   And what is more, it is the **third** day since all this took place.
    24: 46   The Christ will suffer and rise from the dead *on* the **third** day,
Jn   2: 1   *On* the **third** day a wedding took place at Cana in Galilee.
Ac   2: 15   It's *only* **nine** [+*2465+3836+6052*] **in the morning**!
    10: 40   but God raised him from the dead on the **third** day and caused him
    23: 23   and two hundred spearmen to go to Caesarea at **nine** [+*6052*]
    27: 19   *On* the **third** day, they threw the ship's tackle overboard with their
1Co   15: 4   that he was raised *on* the **third** day according to the Scriptures,
2Co   12: 2   Christ who fourteen years ago was caught up to the **third** heaven.
Rev   4: 7   the second was like an ox, the **third** had a face like a man,
    6: 5   When the Lamb opened the **third** seal, I heard the third living
    6: 5   opened the third seal, I heard the **third** living creature say, "Come!"
    8: 7   A **third** of the earth was burned up, a third of the trees were burned
    8: 7   of the earth was burned up, a **third** of the trees were burned up,
    8: 8   was thrown into the sea. A **third** of the sea turned into blood,
    8: 9   a **third** of the living creatures in the sea died, and a third of the
    8: 9   creatures in the sea died, and a **third** of the ships were destroyed.
    8: 10   The **third** angel sounded his trumpet, and a great star, blazing like
    8: 10   fell from the sky on a **third** of the rivers and on the springs of
    8: 11   A **third** of the waters turned bitter, and many people died from the
    8: 12   and a **third** of the sun was struck, a third of the moon, and a third
    8: 12   of the sun was struck, a **third** of the moon, and a third of the stars,
    8: 12   of the sun was struck, a third of the moon, and a **third** of the stars,
    8: 12   and a third of the stars, so that a **third** of them turned dark.
    8: 12   A **third** of the day was without light, and also a third of the night.
    9: 15   and month and year were released to kill a **third** of mankind.
    9: 18   A **third** of mankind was killed by the three plagues of fire,
    11: 14   The second woe has passed; the **third** woe is coming soon.
    12: 4   His tail swept a **third** of the stars out of the sky and flung them to
    14: 9   A **third** angel followed them and said in a loud voice: "If anyone
    16: 4   The **third** angel poured out his bowl on the rivers and springs of
    21: 19   the second sapphire, the **third** chalcedony, the fourth emerald,

5570   τρίχινος, *trichinos*   [1]   [√ *2582*]

made of hair [1]

Rev   6: 12   The sun turned black like sackcloth **made of** *goat* **hair**, the whole

5571   τρόμος, *tromos*   [5]   [√ *5554*]

trembling [3], fear [1], trembling [+*2400*] [1]

Mk   16: 8   **Trembling** [+*2400*] and bewildered, the women went out
1Co   2: 3   I came to you in weakness and fear, and with much **trembling**.
2Co   7: 15   that you were all obedient, receiving him with fear and **trembling**.
Eph   6: 5   Slaves, obey your earthly masters with respect and **fear**, and with
Php   2: 12   continue to work out your salvation with fear and **trembling**,

5572 τροπή, *tropē* [1] [→ *426, 706, 1762, 1956, 1959, 2205, 2206, 2207, 2208, 2365, 3573, 4365, 4502, 4730, 5573, 5574*]

shifting [1]

Jas 1:17 of the heavenly lights, who does not change like **shifting** shadows.

5573 τρόπος, *tropos* [13] [√ *5572*]

way [4], as [+4005] [3], in any way [+2848+3594] [1], in the same way [+4005] [1], just as [+2848+4005+4048] [1], just as [+2848+4005] [1], just as [+4005] [1], lives [1]

Mt 23:37 often I have longed to gather your children together, **as** [+4005]
Lk 13:34 often I have longed to gather your children together, **as** [+4005]
Ac 1:11 will come back **in the same** [+4005] **way** you have seen him go
   7:28 Do you want to kill me **as** [+4005] you killed the Egyptian
   15:11 our Lord Jesus that we are saved, **just as** [+2848+4005] they are."
   27:25 in God that it will happen **just as** [+2848+4005+4048] he told me.
Ro 3: 2 Much in every **way**! First of all, they have been entrusted with the
Php 1:18 The important thing is that *in* every **way**, whether from false
2Th 2: 3 Don't let anyone deceive you **in any way** [+2848+3594], for ιthat
   3:16 of peace himself give you peace at all times and in every **way**.
2Ti 3: 8 **Just as** [+4005] Jannes and Jambres opposed Moses, so also these
Heb 13: 5 Keep your **lives** free from the love of money and be content with
Jude 1: 7 In a similar **way**, Sodom and Gomorrah and the surrounding towns

5574 τροποφορέω, *tropophoreō* [1] [√ *5572 + 5570*]

endured conduct [1]

Ac 13:18 *he* **endured** their **conduct** for about forty years in the desert,

5575 τροφή, *trophē* [16] [√ *5555*]

food [12], ate [1], eat [+3561] [1], eaten as much as wanted [+3170] [1], keep [1]

Mt 3: 4 leather belt around his waist. His **food** was locusts and wild honey.
   6:25 Is not life more important than **food**, and the body more important
   10:10 extra tunic, or sandals or a staff; for the worker is worth his **keep**.
   24:45 in his household to give them their **food** at the proper time?
Lk 12:23 Life is more than **food**, and the body more than clothes.
Jn 4: 8 (His disciples had gone into the town to buy **food**.)
Ac 2:46 bread in their homes and **ate** together with glad and sincere hearts,
   9:19 and after taking *some* **food**, he regained his strength. Saul spent
   14:17 he provides you with plenty *of* **food** and fills your hearts with joy."
   27:33 Just before dawn Paul urged them all *to* **eat** [+3561]. "For the last
   27:34 Now I urge you to take *some* **food**. You need it to survive.
   27:36 They were all encouraged and ate *some* **food** themselves.
   27:38 *When they had* **eaten as much as** *they* **wanted** [+3170],
Heb 5:12 truths of God's word all over again. You need milk, not solid **food**!
   5:14 But solid **food** is for the mature, who by constant use have trained
Jas 2:15 Suppose a brother or sister is without clothes and daily **food**.

5576 Τρόφιμος, *Trophimos* [3] [√ *5555*]

Trophimus [3]

Ac 20: 4 and Tychicus and **Trophimus** from the province of Asia.
   21:29 (They had previously seen **Trophimus** the Ephesian in the city
2Ti 4:20 Erastus stayed in Corinth, and I left **Trophimus** sick in Miletus.

5577 τροφός, *trophos* [1] [√ *5555*]

mother [1]

1Th 2: 7 were gentle among you, like a **mother** caring for her little children.

5578 τροφοφορέω, *trophophoreō* Not used in UBS/NIV [√ *5555 + 5570*]

5579 τροχιά, *trochia* [1] [√ *5556*]

paths [1]

Heb 12:13 "Make level **paths** for your feet," so that the lame may not be

5580 τροχός, *trochos* [1] [√ *5556*]

course [1]

Jas 3: 6 corrupts the whole person, sets the *whole* **course** of his life on fire,

5581 τρύβλιον, *tryblion* [2]

bowl [2]

Mt 26:23 one who has dipped his hand into the **bowl** with me will betray
Mk 14:20 Twelve," he replied, "one who dips bread into the **bowl** with me.

5582 τρυγάω, *trygaō* [3]

untranslated [1], gather [1], gathered [1]

Lk 6:44 do not pick figs from thornbushes, or **[RPG]** grapes from briers.
Rev 14:18 and **gather** the clusters of grapes from the earth's vine,
   14:19 **gathered** its grapes and threw them into the great winepress of

5583 τρυγών, *trygōn* [1]

doves [1]

Lk 2:24 in the Law of the Lord: "a pair *of* **doves** or two young pigeons."

5584 τρυμαλιά, *trymalia* [1] [→ *5585*]

eye [1]

Mk 10:25 It is easier for a camel to go through the **eye** of a needle than for a

5585 τρύπημα, *trypēma* [1] [√ *5584*]

eye [1]

Mt 19:24 it is easier for a camel to go through the **eye** of a needle than for a

5586 Τρύφαινα, *Tryphaina* [1] [√ *5588*]

Tryphena [1]

Ro 16:12 Greet **Tryphena** and Tryphosa, those women who work hard in the

5587 τρυφάω, *tryphaō* [1] [√ *5588*]

lived in luxury [1]

Jas 5: 5 *You have* **lived** on earth **in luxury** and self-indulgence. You have

5588 τρυφή, *tryphē* [2] [→ *1960, 5586, 5587, 5589; cf. 2586*]

carouse [1], luxury [1]

Lk 7:25 who wear expensive clothes and indulge *in* **luxury** are in palaces.
2Pe 2:13 Their idea of pleasure is to **carouse** in broad daylight. They are

5589 Τρυφῶσα, *Tryphōsa* [1] [√ *5588*]

Tryphosa [1]

Ro 16:12 Greet Tryphena and **Tryphosa**, those women who work hard in the

5590 Τρῳάς, *Trōas* [6]

Troas [6]

Ac 16: 8 So they passed by Mysia and went down to **Troas**.
   16:11 From **Troas** we put out to sea and sailed straight for Samothrace,
   20: 5 These men went on ahead and waited for us at **Troas**.
   20: 6 and five days later joined the others at **Troas**, where we stayed
2Co 2:12 Now when I went to **Troas** to preach the gospel of Christ
2Ti 4:13 bring the cloak that I left with Carpus at **Troas**, and my scrolls,

5591 Τρωγύλλιον, *Trōgyllion* Not used in UBS/NIV

5592 τρώγω, **trōgō** [6] [→ *5543*]

eats [2], feeds on [2], eating [1], shares [1]

Mt 24:38 people were **eating** and drinking, marrying and giving in marriage,
Jn 6:54 Whoever **eats** my flesh and drinks my blood has eternal life,
     6:56 Whoever **eats** my flesh and drinks my blood remains in me,
     6:57 of the Father, so the one *who* **feeds on** me will live because of me.
     6:58 and died, but he *who* **feeds on** this bread will live forever."
    13:18 'He *who* **shares** my bread has lifted up his heel against me.'

5593 τυγχάνω, **tynchanō** [12] [→ *1950, 1961, 2209,
2366, 4193, 5344, 5345, 5346, 5608, 5659*]

enjoyed [1], extraordinary [+*3836*+*4024*] [1], gain [1], had [1],
obtain [1], perhaps [+*1623*] [1], perhaps [1], provide [1], received
[1], taking part [1], undoubtedly [+*1623*] [1], unusual [+*4024*] [1]

Lk 20:35 But those who are considered worthy of **taking part** in that age
Ac 19:11 God did **extraordinary** [+*3836*+*4024*] miracles through Paul,
    24: 2 "*We have* **enjoyed** a long period of peace under you, and your
    26:22 But *I have* **had** God's help to this very day,
    27: 3 him to go to his friends *so* they *might* **provide** for his needs.
    28: 2 The islanders showed us **unusual** [+*4024*] kindness. They built a
1Co 14:10 **Undoubtedly** [+*1623*] there are all sorts of languages in the world,
    15:37 but just a seed, **perhaps** [+*1623*] of wheat or of something else.
    16: 6 **Perhaps** I will stay with you awhile, or even spend the winter,
2Ti 2:10 that they too *may* **obtain** the salvation that is in Christ Jesus,
Heb 8: 6 But the ministry Jesus *has* **received** is as superior to theirs as the
    11:35 to be released, so that *they might* **gain** a better resurrection.

5594 τυμπανίζω, **tympanizō** [1] [√ *5597*]

tortured [1]

Heb 11:35 Others *were* **tortured** and refused to be released, so that they

5595 τυπικῶς, **typikōs** [1] [√ *5597*]

examples [1]

1Co 10:11 These things happened to them as **examples** and were written

5596 τύπος, **typos** [15] [√ *5597*]

pattern [4], example [2], examples [2], model [2], as follows
[+*2400*+*3836*+*4047*] [1], form [1], idols [1], marks [1], where[s]
[+*1650*+*3836*] [1]

Jn 20:25 "Unless I see the nail **marks** in his hands and put my finger where
    20:25 his hands and put my finger **where**[s] [+*1650*+*3836*] the nails were,
Ac 7:43 and the star of your god Rephan, the **idols** you made to worship.
     7:44 as God directed Moses, according to the **pattern** he had seen.
    23:25 He wrote a letter **as** [+*2400*+*3836*+*4047*] **follows**:
Ro 5:14 a command, as did Adam, who was a **pattern** of the one to come.
     6:17 you wholeheartedly obeyed the **form** of teaching to which you
1Co 10: 6 Now these things occurred as **examples** to keep us from setting our
Php 3:17 and take note of those who live according to the **pattern** we gave
1Th 1: 7 And so you became a **model** to all the believers in Macedonia
2Th 3: 9 but in order to make ourselves a **model** for you to follow.
1Ti 4:12 but set an **example** for the believers in speech, in life, in love,
Tit 2: 7 In everything set them an **example** by doing what is good.
Heb 8: 5 "See to it that you make everything according to the **pattern** shown
1Pe 5: 3 it over those entrusted to you, but being **examples** to the flock.

5597 τύπτω, **typtō** [13] [→ *531, 1963, 5594, 5595, 5596,
5721*]

beat [5], struck [3], strike [2], beating [1], strikes [1], wound [1]

Mt 24:49 and he then begins *to* **beat** his fellow servants and to eat and drink
    27:30 and took the staff and **struck** him on the head *again and again.*
Mk 15:19 *Again and again* they **struck** him on the head with a staff
Lk 6:29 *If* someone **strikes** you on one cheek, turn to him the other also.
    12:45 and he then begins *to* **beat** the menservants and maidservants
    18:13 but **beat** his breast and said, 'God, have mercy on me, a sinner.'
    23:48 sight saw what took place, they **beat** their breasts and went away.
Ac 18:17 Sosthenes the synagogue ruler and **beat** him in front of the court.

    21:32 saw the commander and his soldiers, they stopped **beating** Paul.
    23: 2 ordered those standing near Paul *to* **strike** him on the mouth.
    23: 3 Paul said to him, "God will **strike** you, you whitewashed wall!
    23: 3 yet you yourself violate the law by commanding that I *be* **struck**!"
1Co 8:12 your brothers in this way and **wound** their weak conscience,

5598 Τύραννος[1], **Tyrannos**[1] [1] [√ *5599*]

Tyrannus [1]

Ac 19: 9 and had discussions daily in the lecture hall *of* **Tyrannus.**

5599 Τύραννος[2], **tyrannos**[2] Not used in UBS/NIV
[→ *5598*]

5600 τυρβάζω, **tyrbazō** Not used in UBS/NIV

5601 Τύριος, **Tyrios** [1] [√ *5602*]

people of Tyre [1]

Ac 12:20 He had been quarreling *with* the **people of Tyre** and Sidon;

5602 Τύρος, **Tyros** [11] [→ *5601*]

Tyre [11]

Mt 11:21 miracles that were performed in you had been performed in **Tyre**
    11:22 it will be more bearable *for* **Tyre** and Sidon on the day of
    15:21 that place, Jesus withdrew to the region *of* **Tyre** and Sidon.
Mk 3: 8 and the regions across the Jordan and around **Tyre** and Sidon.
     7:24 Jesus left that place and went to the vicinity *of* **Tyre**. He entered a
     7:31 Then Jesus left the vicinity *of* **Tyre** and went through Sidon,
Lk 6:17 over Judea, from Jerusalem, and from the coast *of* **Tyre** and Sidon,
    10:13 miracles that were performed in you had been performed in **Tyre**
    10:14 But it will be more bearable *for* **Tyre** and Sidon at the judgment
Ac 21: 3 We landed at **Tyre**, where our ship was to unload its cargo.
    21: 7 We continued our voyage from **Tyre** and landed at Ptolemais,

5603 τυφλός, **typhlos** [50 / 49] [→ *5604*]

blind [49]

Mt 9:27 two **blind** *men* followed him, calling out, "Have mercy on us,
     9:28 had gone indoors, the **blind** *men* came to him, and he asked them,
    11: 5 The **blind** receive sight, the lame walk, those who have leprosy are
    12:22 Then they brought him a demon-possessed man who was **blind**
    15:14 Leave them; they are **blind** guides. If a blind man leads a blind
    15:14 Leave them; they are **blind** guides [UBS+ *of the blind*].
    15:14 If a **blind** *man* leads a blind man, both will fall into a pit."
    15:14 If a blind man leads a **blind** *man*, both will fall into a pit."
    15:30 the lame, the **blind**, the crippled, the mute and many others,
    15:31 the crippled made well, the lame walking and the **blind** seeing.
    20:30 Two **blind** *men* were sitting by the roadside, and when they heard
    21:14 The **blind** and the lame came to him at the temple, and he healed
    23:16 "Woe to you, **blind** guides! You say, 'If anyone swears by the
    23:17 *You* **blind** fools! Which is greater: the gold, or the temple that
    23:19 *You* **blind** men! Which is greater: the gift, or the altar that makes
    23:24 *You* **blind** guides! You strain out a gnat but swallow a camel.
    23:26 **Blind** Pharisee! First clean the inside of the cup and dish, and
Mk 8:22 and some people brought a **blind** *man* and begged Jesus to touch
     8:23 He took the **blind** *man* by the hand and led him outside the village.
    10:46 the city, a **blind** *man*, Bartimaeus (that is, the Son of Timaeus),
    10:49 and said, "Call him." So they called to the **blind** *man*, "Cheer up!
    10:51 Jesus asked him. The **blind** *man* said, "Rabbi, I want to see."
Lk 4:18 freedom for the prisoners and recovery of sight *for* the **blind**,
     6:39 He also told them this parable: "Can a **blind** *man* lead a blind man?
     6:39 He also told them this parable: "Can a blind man lead a **blind** *man*?
     7:21 sicknesses and evil spirits, and gave sight *to* many who were **blind**.
     7:22 The **blind** receive sight, the lame walk, those who have leprosy are
    14:13 give a banquet, invite the poor, the crippled, the lame, the **blind**,
    14:21 and bring in the poor, the crippled, the **blind** and the lame.'
    18:35 a **blind** *man* was sitting by the roadside begging.
Jn 5: 3 of disabled people used to lie—the **blind**, the lame, the paralyzed.
     9: 1 As he went along, he saw a man **blind** from birth.
     9: 2 who sinned, this man or his parents, that he was born **blind**?"

9:13 They brought to the Pharisees the man who had been **blind**.
9:17 Finally they turned again *to* the **blind** *man*, "What have you to say
9:18 The Jews still did not believe that he had been **blind** and had
9:19 this your son?" they asked. "Is this the one you say was born **blind**?
9:20 is our son," the parents answered, "and we know he was born **blind**.
9:24 A second time they summoned the man who had been **blind**.
9:25 I don't know. One thing I do know. I was **blind** but now I see!"
9:32 Nobody has ever heard of opening the eyes *of* a man born **blind**.
9:39 so that the blind will see and those who see will become **blind**."
9:40 with him heard him say this and asked, "What? Are we **blind** too?"
9:41 Jesus said, "If you were **blind**, you would not be guilty of sin;
10:21 possessed by a demon. Can a demon open the eyes *of* the **blind**?"
11:37 "Could not he who opened the eyes *of* the **blind** *man* have kept this
Ac 13:11 You are going to be **blind**, and for a time you will be unable to see
Ro   2:19 if you are convinced that you are a guide *for* the **blind**, a light for
2Pe 1: 9 But if anyone does not have them, he is nearsighted and **blind**,
Rev 3:17 do not realize that you are wretched, pitiful, poor, **blind** and naked.

5604 τυφλόω, *typhloō* [3] [√ 5603]

blinded [2], blinded [*+3836+4057*] [1]

Jn 12:40 "He has **blinded** their eyes and deadened their hearts, so they can
2Co 4: 4 The god of this age *has* **blinded** the minds of unbelievers,
1Jn 2:11 he is going, because the darkness *has* **blinded** [*+3836+4057*] him.

5605 τυφόομαι, *typhoomai* [3] [√ 5606]

conceited [3]

1Ti 3: 6 or *he may become* **conceited** and fall under the same judgment as
     6: 4 *he is* **conceited** and understands nothing. He has an unhealthy
2Ti 3: 4 treacherous, rash, **conceited**, lovers of pleasure rather than lovers

5606 τύφω, *typhō* [1] [→ 5491, 5605]

smoldering [1]

Mt 12:20 and a **smoldering** wick he will not snuff out, till he leads justice to

5607 τυφωνικός, *typhōnikos* [1]

of hurricane force [1]

Ac 27:14 Before very long, a wind **of hurricane force**, called the

5608 Τυχικός, *Tychikos* [5] [√ 5593]

Tychicus [5]

Ac 20: 4 and **Tychicus** and Trophimus from the province of Asia.
Eph 6:21 **Tychicus**, the dear brother and faithful servant in the Lord,
Col 4: 7 **Tychicus** will tell you all the news about me. He is a dear brother,
2Ti 4:12 I sent **Tychicus** to Ephesus.
Tit 3:12 As soon as I send Artemas or **Tychicus** to you, do your best to

Υ, υ

5609 υ, y Not used in UBS/NIV

5610 ὑακίνθινος, *hyakinthinos* [1] [√ 5611]

dark blue [1]

Rev 9:17 Their breastplates were fiery red, **dark blue**, and yellow as sulfur.

5611 ὑάκινθος, *hyakinthos* [1] [→ 5610]

jacinth [1]

Rev 21:20 the ninth topaz, the tenth chrysoprase, the eleventh **jacinth**,

5612 ὑάλινος, *hyalinos* [3] [√ 5613]

of glass [2], untranslated [1]

Rev 4: 6 Also before the throne there was what looked like a sea **of glass**,
     15: 2 And I saw what looked like a sea **of glass** mixed with fire and,
     15: 2 number of his name. [RPG] They held harps given them by God

5613 ὕαλος, *hyalos* [2] [→ 5612]

glass [2]

Rev 21:18 wall was made of jasper, and the city of pure gold, as pure as **glass**.
     21:21 The great street of the city was of pure gold, like transparent **glass**.

5614 ὑβρίζω, *hybrizō* [5] [√ 5615]

insult [2], insulted [1], mistreat [1], mistreated [1]

Mt 22: 6 The rest seized his servants, **mistreated** them and killed them.
Lk 11:45 "Teacher, when you say these things, *you* **insult** us also."
     18:32 will mock him, **insult** *him*, spit on him, flog him and kill him.
Ac 14: 5 together with their leaders, *to* **mistreat** them and stone them.
1Th 2: 2 *We had* previously suffered and *been* **insulted** in Philippi,

5615 ὕβρις, *hybris* [3] [→ 1964, 5614, 5616]

damage [1], disastrous [*+3552*] [1], insults [1]

Ac 27:10 I can see that our voyage is going to be **disastrous** [*+3552*]
     27:21 then you would have spared yourselves this **damage** and loss.
2Co 12:10 in **insults**, in hardships, in persecutions, in difficulties.

5616 ὑβριστής, *hybristēs* [2] [√ 5615]

insolent [1], violent man [1]

Ro   1:30 slanderers, God-haters, **insolent**, arrogant and boastful; they invent
1Ti 1:13 I was once a blasphemer and a persecutor and a **violent man**,

5617 ὑγιαίνω, *hygiainō* [12] [√ 5618]

sound [8], enjoy good health [1], healthy [1], safe and sound [1], well [1]

Lk   5:31 "It is not the **healthy** who need a doctor, but the sick.
     7:10 had been sent returned to the house and found the servant **well**.
     15:27 killed the fattened calf because he has him back **safe and sound**.'
1Ti 1:10 and for whatever else is contrary *to* the **sound** doctrine
     6: 3 and does not agree to the **sound** instruction of our Lord Jesus
2Ti 1:13 keep as the pattern *of* **sound** teaching, with faith and love in Christ
     4: 3 For the time will come when men will not put up with **sound**
Tit 1: 9 so that he can encourage others by **sound** doctrine and refute those
     1:13 rebuke them sharply, so that *they will be* **sound** in the faith
     2: 1 You must teach what is in accord *with* **sound** doctrine.
     2: 2 self-controlled, and **sound** in faith, in love and in endurance.
3Jn 1: 2 I pray that you *may* **enjoy good health** and that all may go well

5618 ὑγιής, *hygiēs* [11] [→ 5617]

well [4], cured [1], freed [1], healed [1], healing [*+4472*] [1], made well [1], sound [1], soundness [1]

Mt 12:13 and it was completely restored, just as **sound** as the other.
     15:31 the crippled **made well**, the lame walking and the blind seeing.
Mk   5:34 has healed you. Go in peace and be **freed** from your suffering."
Jn   5: 6 condition for a long time, he asked him, "Do you want to get **well**?"
     5: 9 At once the man was **cured**; he picked up his mat and walked.
     5:11 But he replied, "The man who made me **well** said to me, 'Pick up
     5:14 found him at the temple and said to him, "See, you are **well** again.
     5:15 and told the Jews that it was Jesus who had made him **well**.
     7:23 why are you angry with me for **healing** [*+4472*] the whole man on
Ac   4:10 God raised from the dead, that this man stands before you **healed**.
Tit 2: 8 and **soundness** of speech that cannot be condemned, so that those

5619 ὑγρός, *hygros* [1] [√ 5624]

green [1]

Lk 23:31 For if men do these things when the tree is **green**, what will

5620 ὑδρία, *hydria* [3] [√ 5623]

jars [1], water jar [1], water jars [1]

Jn   2: 6   Nearby stood six stone **water jars**, the kind used by the Jews for
     2: 7   Jesus said to the servants, "Fill the **jars** with water"; so they filled
     4:28   Then, leaving her **water jar**, the woman went back to the town

5621 ὑδροποτέω, *hydropoteō* [1] [√ 5623 + 4403]

drinking only water [1]

1Ti   5:23   Stop **drinking only water**, and use a little wine because of your

5622 ὑδρωπικός, *hydrōpikos* [1] [√ 5623]

suffering from dropsy [1]

Lk   14: 2   There in front of him was a man **suffering from dropsy**.

5623 ὕδωρ, *hydōr* [76] [→ 536, 5620, 5621, 5622; cf. 5624]

ζῶν ὕδωρ, (living water) [3] Jn 4:10,11; 7:38

ὕδωρ ζωῆς, (water of life) [4] Rev 7:17; 21:6; 22:1,17

ὕδωρ ... πνεῦμα, (water ... Spirit) [13] Mt 3:11,16; Mk 1:8,10; Lk 3:16; Jn 1:33; 3:5; Ac 1:5; 8:39; 10:47; 11:16; 1Jn 5:6,8

water [65], waters [10], deluged [+2885] [1]

Mt   3:11   "I baptize you with **water** for repentance. But after me will come
     3:16   As soon as Jesus was baptized, he went up out of the **water**.
     8:32   rushed down the steep bank into the lake and died in the **water**.
    14:28   if it's you," Peter replied, "tell me to come to you on the **water**."
    14:29   down out of the boat, walked on the **water** and came toward Jesus.
    17:15   is suffering greatly. He often falls into the fire or into the **water**.
    27:24   he took **water** and washed his hands in front of the crowd.
Mk   1: 8   I baptize you *with* **water**, but he will baptize you with the Holy
     1:10   As Jesus was coming up out of the **water**, he saw heaven being
     9:22   "It has often thrown him into fire or **water** to kill him. But if you
     9:41   anyone who gives you a cup of **water** in my name because you
    14:13   "Go into the city, and a man carrying a jar of **water** will meet you.
Lk   3:16   John answered them all, "I baptize you *with* **water**. But one more
     7:44   You did not give me any **water** for my feet, but she wet my feet
     8:24   He got up and rebuked the wind and the raging **waters**; the storm
     8:25   He commands even the winds and the **water**, and they obey him."
    16:24   pity on me and send Lazarus to dip the tip of his finger *in* **water**
    22:10   "As you enter the city, a man carrying a jar of **water** will meet you.
Jn   1:26   "I baptize with **water**," John replied, "but among you stands one
     1:31   but the reason I came baptizing with **water** was that he might be
     1:33   except that the one who sent me to baptize with **water** told me,
     2: 7   Jesus said to the servants, "Fill the jars *with* **water**"; so they filled
     2: 9   and the master of the banquet tasted the **water** that had been turned
     2: 9   come from, though the servants who had drawn the **water** knew.
     3: 5   no one can enter the kingdom of God unless he is born of **water**
     3:23   baptizing at Aenon near Salim, because there was plenty of **water**,
     4: 7   When a Samaritan woman came to draw **water**, Jesus said to her,
     4:10   would have asked him and he would have given you living **water**."
     4:11   and the well is deep. Where can you get this living **water**?
     4:13   "Everyone who drinks this **water** will be thirsty again,
     4:14   but whoever drinks the **water** I give him will never thirst.
     4:14   the **water** I give him will become in him a spring of water welling
     4:14   the water I give him will become in him a spring of **water** welling
     4:15   give me this **water** so that I won't get thirsty and have to keep
     4:46   visited Cana in Galilee, where he had turned the **water** into wine.
     5: 7   "I have no one to help me into the pool when the **water** is stirred.
     7:38   has said, streams *of* living **water** will flow from within him."
    13: 5   he poured **water** into a basin and began to wash his disciples' feet,
    19:34   side with a spear, bringing a sudden *flow of* blood and **water**.
Ac   1: 5   For John baptized *with* **water**, but in a few days you will be
     8:36   they came to some **water** and the eunuch said, "Look, here is water.
     8:36   they came to some water and the eunuch said, "Look, here is **water**.
     8:38   Then both Philip and the eunuch went down into the **water**
     8:39   When they came up out of the **water**, the Spirit of the Lord
    10:47   "Can anyone keep these people from being baptized *with* **water**?
    11:16   'John baptized *with* **water**, but you will be baptized with the Holy
Eph   5:26   cleansing her by the washing *with* **water** through the word,
Heb   9:19   together *with* **water**, scarlet wool and branches of hyssop,
    10:22   guilty conscience and having our bodies washed *with* pure **water**.

Jas   3:12   grapevine bear figs? Neither can a salt spring produce fresh **water**.
1Pe   3:20   In it only a few people, eight in all, were saved through **water**,
2Pe   3: 5   and the earth was formed out of **water** and by water.
     3: 5   and the earth was formed out of water and by **water**.
     3: 6   By these waters also the world of that time *was* **deluged** [+2885]
1Jn   5: 6   This is the one who came by **water** and blood—Jesus Christ.
     5: 6   He did not come by **water** only, but by water and blood.
     5: 6   He did not come by water only, but by **water** and blood.
     5: 8   the Spirit, the **water** and the blood; and the three are in agreement.
Rev   1:15   in a furnace, and his voice was like the sound *of* rushing **waters**.
     7:17   will be their shepherd; he will lead them to springs *of* living **water**.
     8:10   from the sky on a third of the rivers and on the springs *of* **water**—
     8:11   A third *of* the **waters** turned bitter, and many people died from the
     8:11   and many people died from the **waters** that had become bitter.
    11: 6   and they have power to turn the **waters** into blood and to strike the
    12:15   Then from his mouth the serpent spewed **water** like a river,
    14: 2   And I heard a sound from heaven like the roar *of* rushing **waters**
    14: 7   who made the heavens, the earth, the sea and the springs *of* **water**."
    16: 4   third angel poured out his bowl on the rivers and springs *of* **water**,
    16: 5   Then I heard the angel *in charge of* the **waters** say: "You are just in
    16:12   and its **water** was dried up to prepare the way for the kings from
    17: 1   the punishment of the great prostitute, who sits on many **waters**.
    17:15   "The **waters** you saw, where the prostitute sits, are peoples,
    19: 6   like the roar of rushing **waters** and like loud peals of thunder,
    21: 6   will give to drink without cost from the spring of the **water** of life.
    22: 1   Then the angel showed me the river *of* the **water** of life, as clear as
    22:17   and whoever wishes, let him take the free gift *of* the **water** of life.

5624 ὑετός, *hyetos* [5] [→ 5619; cf. 5623]

rain [3], it^s [1], raining [1]

Ac   14:17   He has shown kindness by giving you **rain** from heaven and crops
    28: 2   built a fire and welcomed us all because it was **raining** and cold.
Heb   6: 7   Land that drinks in the **rain** often falling on it and that produces a
Jas   5:18   Again he prayed, and the heavens gave **rain**, and the earth
Rev   11: 6   so that **it**^{s} will not rain during the time they are prophesying;

5625 υἱοθεσία, *huiothesia* [5] [√ 5626 + 5502]

adoption as sons [2], adopted as sons [1], full rights of sons [1], sonship [1]

Ro   8:15   you a slave again to fear, but you received the Spirit *of* **sonship**.
     8:23   groan inwardly as we wait eagerly for our **adoption as sons**,
     9: 4   Theirs is the **adoption as sons**; theirs the divine glory,
Gal   4: 5   those under law, that we might receive the **full rights of sons**.
Eph   1: 5   he predestined us to be **adopted as** his **sons** through Jesus Christ,

5626 υἱός, *huios* [377 / 376] [→ 5625]

μονογενὴς υἱός, (one and only son) [5] Lk 7:12; 9:38; Jn 3:16,18; 1Jn 4:9

υἱοὶ θεοῦ, (sons of God) [7] Mt 5:9; Lk 20:36; Ro 8:14,19; 9:26; Gal 3:26; 4:6

υἱός Ἀβραάμ, (son of Abraham) [4] Mt 1:1; Lk 19:9; Ac 13:26; Gal 3:7; 4:22

υἱός ἀγαπητός, (beloved son) [8] Mt 3:17; 17:5; Mk 1:11; 9:7; 12:6; Lk 3:22; 20:13; 2Pe 1:17

υἱὸς ἀνθρώπου [4] Jn 5:27; Heb 2:6; Rev 1:13; 14:14, (Son of Man)

ὁ υἱὸς τοῦ ἀνθρώπου, (the Son of Man) [82] Mt 8:20; 9:6; 10:23; 11:19; 12:8,32,40; 13:37,41; 16:13,27,28; 17:9,12,22; 19:28; 20:18,28; 24:27,30,30,37,39,44; 25:31; 26:2,24,24,45,64; Mk 2:10,28; 8:31,38; 9:9,12,31; 10:33,45; 13:26; 14:21,41,62; Lk 5:24; 6:5,22; 7:34; 9:22,26,44,58; 11:30; 12:8,10,40; 17:22,24,26,30; 18:8,31; 19:10; 21:27,36; 22:22,48,69; 24:7; Jn 1:51; 3:13,14; 6:27,53,62; 8:28; 9:35; 12:23,34,34; 13:31; Ac 7:56

υἱός Δαυίδ, (son of David) [15] Mt 1:1,20; 9:27; 12:23; 15:22; 20:30,31; 21:9,15; Mk 10:47,48; 12:35; Lk 18:38,39; 20:41; cf. Mt 22:42

υἱός θεοῦ, (son of God) [45] Mt 4:3,6; 8:29; 14:33; 16:16; 26:63; 27:40,43,54; Mk 1:1; 3:11; 5:7; 15:39; Lk 1:35; 4:3,9,41; 8:28; 22:70; Jn 1:34,49; 3:18; 5:25; 10:36; 11:4,27; 19:7; 20:31; Ac

9:20; Ro 1:4; 2Co 1:19; Gal 2:20; Eph 4:13; Heb 4:14; 6:6; 7:3;
10:29; 1Jn 3:8; 4:15; 5:5,10,12,13,20; Rev 2:18

υἱοὶ Ἰσραήλ, (sons of Israel) [14] Mt 27:9; Lk 1:16; Ac 5:21;
7:23,37; 9:15; 10:36; Ro 9:27; 2Co 3:7,13; Heb 11:22; Rev 2:14;
7:4; 21:12

υἱὸς ὑψίστου, (Son of the Most High) [3] Mk 5:7; Lk 1:32; 8:28

son [299], sons [36], people [8], Israelites [+2702] [7], children
[3], guests [3], Israel [+2702] [3], child [2], descendants [2], man
[2], men [+476+3836+3836] [2], those[s] who are [+3836] [2],
children [+1169] [1], foal [1], followers [1], heirs [1], one[s] [1],
subjects [1], whose[s] [1]

Mt 1: 1 A record of the genealogy of Jesus Christ the son of David,
    1: 1 genealogy of Jesus Christ the son of David, the son of Abraham:
    1:20 Lord appeared to him in a dream and said, "Joseph son of David,
    1:21 She will give birth to a son, and you are to give him the name
    1:23 "The virgin will be with child and will give birth to a son, and they
    1:25 But he had no union with her until she gave birth to a son.
    2:15 Lord had said through the prophet: "Out of Egypt I called my son."
    3:17 And a voice from heaven said, "This is my Son, whom I love;
    4: 3 The tempter came to him and said, "If you are the Son of God,
    4: 6 "If you are the Son of God," he said, "throw yourself down. For it is
    5: 9 Blessed are the peacemakers, for they will be called sons of God.
    5:45 that you may be sons of your Father in heaven. He causes his sun
    7: 9 "Which of you, if his son asks for bread, will give him a stone?
    8:12 But the subjects of the kingdom will be thrown outside,
    8:20 the air have nests, but the Son of Man has no place to lay his head."
    8:29 "What do you want with us, Son of God?" they shouted. "Have you
    9: 6 so that you may know that the Son of Man has authority on earth
    9:15 "How can the guests of the bridegroom mourn while he is with
    9:27 men followed him, calling out, "Have mercy on us, Son of David!"
   10:23 you will not finish going through the cities of Israel before the Son
   10:37 anyone who loves his son or daughter more than me is not worthy
   11:19 The Son of Man came eating and drinking, and they say, 'Here is a
   11:27 No one knows the Son except the Father, and no one knows the
   11:27 and no one knows the Father except the Son and those to whom the
   11:27 except the Son and those to whom the Son chooses to reveal him.
   12: 8 For the Son of Man is Lord of the Sabbath."
   12:23 people were astonished and said, "Could this be the Son of David?"
   12:27 demons by Beelzebub, by whom do your people drive them out?
   12:32 Anyone who speaks a word against the Son of Man will be
   12:40 so the Son of Man will be three days and three nights in the heart
   13:37 "The one who sowed the good seed is the Son of Man.
   13:38 is the world, and the good seed stands for the sons of the kingdom.
   13:38 the sons of the kingdom. The weeds are the sons of the evil one,
   13:41 The Son of Man will send out his angels, and they will weed out of
   13:55 "Isn't this the carpenter's son? Isn't his mother's name Mary,
   14:33 in the boat worshiped him, saying, "Truly you are the Son of God."
   15:22 came to him, crying out, "Lord, Son of David, have mercy on me!
   16:13 he asked his disciples, "Who do people say the Son of Man is?"
   16:16 Peter answered, "You are the Christ, the Son of the living God."
   16:27 For the Son of Man is going to come in his Father's glory with his
   16:28 taste death before they see the Son of Man coming in his kingdom."
   17: 5 and a voice from the cloud said, "This is my Son, whom I love;
   17: 9 you have seen, until the Son of Man has been raised from the dead."
   17:12 In the same way the Son of Man is going to suffer at their hands."
   17:15 "Lord, have mercy on my son," he said. "He has seizures and is
   17:22 "The Son of Man is going to be betrayed into the hands of men.
   17:25 earth collect duty and taxes—from their own sons or from others?"
   17:26 Peter answered. "Then the sons are exempt," Jesus said to him.
   19:28 of all things, when the Son of Man sits on his glorious throne,
   20:18 and the Son of Man will be betrayed to the chief priests
   20:20 Then the mother of Zebedee's sons came to Jesus with her sons
   20:20 Then the mother of Zebedee's sons came to Jesus with her sons
   20:21 "Grant that one of these two sons of mine may sit at your right
   20:28 just as the Son of Man did not come to be served, but to serve,
   20:30 going by, they shouted, "Lord, Son of David, have mercy on us!"
   20:31 shouted all the louder, "Lord, Son of David, have mercy on us!"
   21: 5 gentle and riding on a donkey, on a colt, the foal of a donkey.' "
   21: 9 and those that followed shouted, "Hosanna to the Son of David!"
   21:15 temple area, "Hosanna to the Son of David," they were indignant.
   21:37 Last of all, he sent his son to them. 'They will respect my son,'
   21:37 he sent his son to them. 'They will respect my son,' he said.
   21:38 "But when the tenants saw the son, they said to each other,
   22: 2 heaven is like a king who prepared a wedding banquet for his son.

       22:42 the Christ? Whose son is he?" "The son of David," they replied.
       22:45 If then David calls him 'Lord,' how can he be his son?"
       23:15 you make him twice as much a son of hell as you are.
       23:31 So you testify against yourselves that you are the descendants of
       23:35 from the blood of righteous Abel to the blood of Zechariah son of
       24:27 visible even in the west, so will be the coming of the Son of Man.
       24:30 "At that time the sign of the Son of Man will appear in the sky,
       24:30 They will see the Son of Man coming on the clouds of the sky,
       24:36 not even the angels in heaven, nor the Son, but only the Father.
       24:37 in the days of Noah, so it will be at the coming of the Son of Man.
       24:39 all away. That is how it will be at the coming of the Son of Man.
       24:44 because the Son of Man will come at an hour when you do not
       25:31 "When the Son of Man comes in his glory, and all the angels with
       26: 2 and the Son of Man will be handed over to be crucified."
       26:24 The Son of Man will go just as it is written about him. But woe to
       26:24 But woe to that man who betrays the Son of Man! It would be
       26:37 He took Peter and the two sons of Zebedee along with him,
       26:45 is near, and the Son of Man is betrayed into the hands of sinners.
       26:63 by the living God: Tell us if you are the Christ, the Son of God."
       26:64 In the future you will see the Son of Man sitting at the right hand
       27: 9 the thirty silver coins, the price set on him by the people of Israel,
       27:40 Come down from the cross, if you are the Son of God!"
       27:43 him now if he wants him, for he said, 'I am the Son of God.' "
       27:54 they were terrified, and exclaimed, "Surely he was the Son of God!"
       27:56 the mother of James and Joses, and the mother of Zebedee's sons.
       28:19 in the name of the Father and of the Son and of the Holy Spirit,
Mk   1: 1 The beginning of the gospel about Jesus Christ, the Son of God.
       1:11 "You are my Son, whom I love; with you I am well pleased."
       2:10 But that you may know that the Son of Man has authority on earth
       2:19 "How can the guests of the bridegroom fast while he is with them?
       2:28 So the Son of Man is Lord even of the Sabbath."
       3:11 they fell down before him and cried out, "You are the Son of God."
       3:17 them he gave the name Boanerges, which means Sons of Thunder);
       3:28 and blasphemies of men [+476+3836+3836] will be forgiven
       5: 7 "What do you want with me, Jesus, Son of the Most High God?
       6: 3 Isn't this Mary's son and the brother of James, Joseph, Judas
       8:31 then began to teach them that the Son of Man must suffer many
       8:38 the Son of Man will be ashamed of him when he comes in his
       9: 7 from the cloud: "This is my Son, whom I love. Listen to him!"
       9: 9 what they had seen until the Son of Man had risen from the dead.
       9:12 Why then is it written that the Son of Man must suffer much
       9:17 A man in the crowd answered, "Teacher, I brought you my son,
       9:31 "The Son of Man is going to be betrayed into the hands of men.
      10:33 "and the Son of Man will be betrayed to the chief priests
      10:35 Then James and John, the sons of Zebedee, came to him. "Teacher,"
      10:45 For even the Son of Man did not come to be served, but to serve,
      10:46 the city, a blind man, Bartimaeus (that is, the Son of Timaeus),
      10:47 he began to shout, "Jesus, Son of David, have mercy on me!"
      10:48 but he shouted all the more, "Son of David, have mercy on me!"
      12: 6 "He had one left to send, a son, whom he loved. He sent him last of
      12: 6 He sent him last of all, saying, 'They will respect my son.'
      12:35 "How is it that the teachers of the law say that the Christ is the son
      12:37 David himself calls him 'Lord.' How then can he be his son?"
      13:26 "At that time men will see the Son of Man coming in clouds with
      13:32 not even the angels in heaven, nor the Son, but only the Father.
      14:21 The Son of Man will go just as it is written about him. But woe to
      14:21 But woe to that man who betrays the Son of Man! It would be
      14:41 Look, the Son of Man is betrayed into the hands of sinners.
      14:61 priest asked him, "Are you the Christ, the Son of the Blessed One?"
      14:62 "And you will see the Son of Man sitting at the right hand of the
      15:39 saw how he died, he said, "Surely this man was the Son of God!"
Lk   1:13 Your wife Elizabeth will bear you a son, and you are to give him
       1:16 Many of the people of Israel will he bring back to the Lord their
       1:31 You will be with child and give birth to a son, and you are to give
       1:32 He will be great and will be called the Son of the Most High.
       1:35 So the holy one to be born will be called the Son of God.
       1:36 Even Elizabeth your relative is going to have a child in her old
       1:57 it was time for Elizabeth to have her baby, she gave birth to a son.
       2: 7 and she gave birth to her firstborn, a son. She wrapped him in
       3: 2 the word of God came to John son of Zechariah in the desert.
       3:22 "You are my Son, whom I love; with you I am well pleased."
       3:23 He was the son, so it was thought, of Joseph, the son of Heli,
       4: 3 The devil said to him, "If you are the Son of God, tell this stone to
       4: 9 "If you are the Son of God," he said, "throw yourself down from
       4:22 words that came from his lips. "Isn't this Joseph's son?" they asked.
       4:41 came out of many people, shouting, "You are the Son of God!"

5: 10 and so were James and John, the **sons** of Zebedee, Simon's
5: 24 But that you may know that the **Son** of Man has authority on earth
5: 34 "Can you make the **guests** of the bridegroom fast while he is with
6: 5 Then Jesus said to them, "The **Son** of Man is Lord of the Sabbath."
6: 22 insult you and reject your name as evil, because of the **Son** of Man.
6: 35 your reward will be great, and you will be **sons** of the Most High,
7: 12 carried out—the only **son** of his mother, and she was a widow.
7: 34 The **Son** of Man came eating and drinking, and you say, 'Here is a
8: 28 "What do you want with me, Jesus, **Son** of the Most High God?
9: 22 "The **Son** of Man must suffer many things and be rejected by the
9: 26 the **Son** of Man will be ashamed of him when he comes in his
9: 35 from the cloud, saying, "This is my **Son**, whom I have chosen;
9: 38 "Teacher, I beg you to look at my son, for he is my only child.
9: 41 shall I stay with you and put up with you? Bring your **son** here."
9: 44 The **Son** of Man is going to be betrayed into the hands of men."
9: 58 the air have nests, but the **Son** of Man has no place to lay his head."
10: 6 If a **man** of peace is there, your peace will rest on him; if not,
10: 22 No one knows who the **Son** is except the Father, and no one knows
10: 22 and no one knows who the Father is except the **Son** and those to
10: 22 except the Son and those to whom the **Son** chooses to reveal him."
11: 11 "Which of you fathers, if your **son** asks for a fish, will give him a
11: 19 by Beelzebub, by whom do your **followers** drive them out?
11: 30 to the Ninevites, so also will the **Son** of Man be to this generation.
12: 8 the **Son** of Man will also acknowledge him before the angels of
12: 10 And everyone who speaks a word against the **Son** of Man will be
12: 40 because the **Son** of Man will come at an hour when you do not
12: 53 They will be divided, father against **son** and son against father,
12: 53 They will be divided, father against son and son against **father**,
14: 5 "If one of you has a **son** or an ox that falls into a well on the
15: 11 Jesus continued: "There was a man who had two **sons**.
15: 13 "Not long after that, the younger **son** got together all he had,
15: 19 I am no longer worthy to be called your **son**; make me like one of
15: 21 "The **son** said to him, 'Father, I have sinned against heaven
15: 21 and against you. I am no longer worthy to be called your **son**.'
15: 24 For this **son** of mine was dead and is alive again; he was lost
15: 25 "Meanwhile, the older **son** was in the field. When he came near the
15: 30 But when this **son** of yours who has squandered your property with
16: 8 For the **people** of this world are more shrewd in dealing with their
16: 8 in dealing with their own kind than are the **people** of the light.
17: 22 when you will long to see one of the days *of* the **Son** of Man,
17: 24 For the **Son** of Man in his day will be like the lightning,
17: 26 the days of Noah, so also will it be in the days *of* the **Son** of Man.
17: 30 "It will be just like this on the day the **Son** of Man is revealed.
18: 8 However, when the **Son** of Man comes, will he find faith on the
18: 31 and everything that is written by the prophets *about* the **Son** of
18: 38 He called out, "Jesus, **Son** of David, have mercy on me!"
18: 39 but he shouted all the more, "**Son** of David, have mercy on me!"
19: 9 has come to this house, because this man, too, is a **son** of Abraham.
19: 10 For the **Son** of Man came to seek and to save what was lost."
20: 13 I will send my **son**, whom I love; perhaps they will respect him.'
20: 34 "The **people** of this age marry and are given in marriage.
20: 36 They are God's **children**, since they are children of the
20: 36 are God's children, since they are **children** of the resurrection.
20: 41 to them, "How is it that they say the Christ is the **Son** of David?
20: 44 David calls him 'Lord.' How then can he be his **son**?"
21: 27 At that time they will see the **Son** of Man coming in a cloud with
21: 36 and that you may be able to stand before the **Son** of Man."
22: 22 The **Son** of Man will go as it has been decreed, but woe to that
22: 48 asked him, "Judas, are you betraying the **Son** of Man with a kiss?"
22: 69 the **Son** of Man will be seated at the right hand of the mighty God."
22: 70 They all asked, "Are you then the **Son** of God?" He replied,
24: 7 'The **Son** of Man must be delivered into the hands of sinful men,

Jn   1: 34 I have seen and I testify that this is the **Son** of God."
1: 42 Jesus looked at him and said, "You are Simon **son** of John.
1: 45 the prophets also wrote—Jesus of Nazareth, the **son** of Joseph."
1: 49 Then Nathanael declared, "Rabbi, you are the **Son** of God;
1: 51 the angels of God ascending and descending on the **Son** of Man."
3: 13 heaven except the one who came from heaven—the **Son** of Man.
3: 14 up the snake in the desert, so the **Son** of Man must be lifted up,
3: 16 "For God so loved the world that he gave his one and only **Son**,
3: 17 For God did not send his **Son** into the world to condemn the world,
3: 18 he has not believed in the name of God's one and only **Son**.
3: 35 The Father loves the **Son** and has placed everything in his hands.
3: 36 Whoever believes in the **Son** has eternal life, but whoever rejects
3: 36 but whoever rejects the **Son** will not see life, for God's wrath
4: 5 near the plot of ground Jacob had given *to* his **son** Joseph.

4: 12 from it himself, as did also his **sons** and his flocks and herds?"
4: 46 And there was a certain royal official whose **son** lay sick at
4: 47 he went to him and begged him to come and heal his **son**,
4: 50 Jesus replied, "You may go. Your **son** will live." The man took
4: 53 the exact time at which Jesus had said to him, "Your **son** will live."
5: 19 "I tell you the truth, the **Son** can do nothing by himself; he can do
5: 19 Father doing, because whatever the Father does the **Son** also does.
5: 20 For the Father loves the **Son** and shows him all he does. Yes,
5: 21 even so the **Son** gives life to whom he is pleased to give it.
5: 22 Father judges no one, but has entrusted all judgment *to* the **Son**,
5: 23 that all may honor the **Son** just as they honor the Father. He who
5: 23 He who does not honor the **Son** does not honor the Father,
5: 25 and has now come when the dead will hear the voice *of* the **Son** of
5: 26 life in himself, so he has granted the **Son** to have life in himself.
5: 27 he has given him authority to judge because he is the **Son** of Man.
6: 27 that endures to eternal life, which the **Son** of Man will give you.
6: 40 For my Father's will is that everyone who looks to the **Son**
6: 42 not Jesus, the **son** of Joseph, whose father and mother we know?
6: 53 unless you eat the flesh *of* the **Son** of Man and drink his blood,
6: 62 What if you see the **Son** of Man ascend to where he was before!
8: 28 So Jesus said, "When you have lifted up the **Son** of Man, then you
8: 35 no permanent place in the family, but a **son** belongs to it forever.
8: 36 So if the **Son** sets you free, you will be free indeed.
9: 19 "Is this your **son**?" they asked. "Is this the one you say was born
9: 20 "We know he is our **son**," the parents answered, "and we know he
9: 35 when he found him, he said, "Do you believe in the **Son** of Man?"
10: 36 do you accuse me of blasphemy because I said, 'I am God's **Son**'?
11: 4 it is for God's glory so that God's **Son** may be glorified through it."
11: 27 she told him, "I believe that you are the Christ, the **Son** of God,
12: 23 "The hour has come for the **Son** of Man to be glorified.
12: 34 so how can you say, 'The **Son** of Man must be lifted up'?
12: 34 'The **Son** of Man must be lifted up'? Who is this 'Son of Man'?"
12: 36 the light while you have it, so that you may become **sons** of light."
13: 31 "Now is the **Son** of Man glorified and God is glorified in him.
14: 13 you ask in my name, so that the **Son** may bring glory to the Father.
17: 1 time has come. Glorify your **Son**, that your Son may glorify you.
17: 1 time has come. Glorify your Son, that your **Son** may glorify you.
17: 12 None has been lost except the one[s] doomed to destruction
19: 7 to that law he must die, because he claimed to be the **Son** of God."
19: 26 he said to his mother, "Dear woman, here is your **son**,"
20: 31 the **Son** of God, and that by believing you may have life in his

Ac   2: 17 Your **sons** and daughters will prophesy, your young men will see
3: 25 And you are **heirs** of the prophets and of the covenant God made
4: 36 whom the apostles called Barnabas (which means **Son** of
5: 21 the full assembly of the elders *of* **Israel** [+2702]—and sent to the
7: 16 and placed in the tomb that Abraham had bought from the **sons** of
7: 21 Pharaoh's daughter took him and brought him up as her own **son**.
7: 23 forty years old, he decided to visit his fellow **Israelites** [+2702].
7: 29 fled to Midian, where he settled as a foreigner and had two **sons**.
7: 37 "This is that Moses who told the **Israelites** [+2702], 'God will send
7: 56 open and the **Son** of Man standing at the right hand of God."
9: 15 before the Gentiles and their kings and before the **people** of Israel.
9: 20 At once he began to preach in the synagogues that Jesus is the **Son**
10: 36 You know the message God sent *to* the **people** of Israel,
13: 10 "You are a **child** of the devil and an enemy of everything that is
13: 21 and he gave them Saul **son** of Kish, of the tribe of Benjamin,
13: 26 "Brothers, **children** [+1169] of Abraham, and you God-fearing
13: 33 " 'You are my **Son**; today I have become your Father.'
16: 1 whose[s] mother was a Jewess and a believer, but whose father was
19: 14 Seven **sons** of Sceva, a Jewish chief priest, were doing this.
23: 6 the Sanhedrin, "My brothers, I am a Pharisee, the **son** of a Pharisee.
23: 16 But when the **son** of Paul's sister heard of this plot, he went into

Ro   1: 3 regarding his **Son**, who as to his human nature was a descendant of
1: 4 with power to be the **Son** of God by his resurrection from the dead:
1: 9 I serve with my whole heart in preaching the gospel *of* his **Son**,
5: 10 we were reconciled to him through the death *of* his **Son**, how much
8: 3 God did by sending his own **Son** in the likeness of sinful man to be
8: 14 because those who are led by the Spirit of God are **sons** of God.
8: 19 The creation waits in eager expectation for the **sons** of God to be
8: 29 he also predestined to be conformed to the likeness *of* his **Son**,
8: 32 He who did not spare his own **Son**, but gave him up for us all—
9: 9 "At the appointed time I will return, and Sarah will have a **son**."
9: 26 are not my people,' they will be called 'sons of the living God.' "

1Co   1: 9 who has called you into fellowship *with* his **Son** Jesus Christ our
15: 28 then the **Son** himself will be made subject to him who put

2Co	1:19	For the **Son** of God, Jesus Christ, who was preached among you by
3: 7	so that the **Israelites** [+2702] could not look steadily at the face of
3:13	who would put a veil over his face to keep the **Israelites** [+2702]
6:18	and you will be my **sons** and daughters, says the Lord Almighty."
Gal	1:16	to reveal his **Son** in me so that I might preach him among the
2:20	I live by faith *in* the **Son** of God, who loved me and gave himself
3: 7	Understand, then, that those who believe are **children** of Abraham.
3:26	You are all **sons** of God through faith in Christ Jesus,
4: 4	fully come, God sent his **Son**, born of a woman, born under law,
4: 6	Because you are **sons**, God sent the Spirit of his Son into our
4: 6	you are sons, God sent the Spirit *of* his **Son** into our hearts,
4: 7	So you are no longer a slave, but a **son**; and since you are a son,
4: 7	but a son; and since you are a **son**, God has made you also an heir.
4:22	For it is written that Abraham had two **sons**, one by the slave
4:30	"Get rid of the slave woman and her **son**, for the slave woman's son
4:30	for the slave woman's **son** will never share in the inheritance with
4:30	son will never share in the inheritance with the free woman's **son**."
Eph	2: 2	the spirit who is now at work in **those**ˢ [+3836] **who are**
3: 5	which was not made known *to* **men** [+476+3836+3836] in other
4:13	and in the knowledge *of* the **Son** of God and become mature,
5: 6	things God's wrath comes on **those**ˢ [+3836] **who are** disobedient.
Col	1:13	of darkness and brought us into the kingdom *of* the **Son** he loves,
3: 6	of God is coming [UBS+ *on* **those**ˢ (+3836) *who are disobedient*].
1Th	1:10	and to wait for his **Son** from heaven, whom he raised from the
5: 5	You are all **sons** of the light and sons of the day. We do not belong
5: 5	You are all sons of the light and **sons** of the day. We do not belong
2Th	2: 3	man of lawlessness is revealed, the **man** doomed to destruction.
Heb	1: 2	but in these last days he has spoken to us by his **Son**, whom he
1: 5	For to which of the angels did God ever say, "You are my **Son**;
1: 5	Or again, "I will be his Father, and he will be my **Son**"?
1: 8	But about the **Son** he says, "Your throne, O God, will last for ever
2: 6	that you are mindful of him, the **son** of man that you care for him?
2:10	In bringing many **sons** to glory, it was fitting that God, for whom
3: 6	But Christ is faithful as a **son** over God's house. And we are his
4:14	Jesus the **Son** of God, let us hold firmly to the faith we profess.
5: 5	But God said to him, "You are my **Son**; today I have become your
5: 8	Although he was a **son**, he learned obedience from what he
6: 6	because to their loss they are crucifying the **Son** of God all over
7: 3	or end of life, like the **Son** of God he remains a priest forever.
7: 5	Now the law requires the **descendants** of Levi who become priests
7:28	but the oath, which came after the law, appointed the **Son**,
10:29	to be punished who has trampled the **Son** of God under foot,
11:21	By faith Jacob, when he was dying, blessed each of Joseph's **sons**,
11:22	spoke about the exodus *of* the **Israelites** [+2702] from Egypt
11:24	grown up, refused to be known as the **son** of Pharaoh's daughter.
12: 5	forgotten that word of encouragement that addresses you as **sons**:
12: 5	"My **son**, do not make light of the Lord's discipline, and do not lose
12: 6	those he loves, and he punishes everyone he accepts as a **son**."
12: 7	Endure hardship as discipline; God is treating you as **sons**.
12: 7	treating you as sons. For what **son** is not disciplined by his father?
12: 8	then you are illegitimate children and not true **sons**.
Jas	2:21	for what he did when he offered his **son** Isaac on the altar?
1Pe	5:13	with you, sends you her greetings, and so does my **son** Mark.
2Pe	1:17	from the Majestic Glory, saying, "This is my **Son**, whom I love;
1Jn	1: 3	And our fellowship is with the Father and with his **Son**,
1: 7	and the blood *of* Jesus, his **Son**, purifies us from all sin.
2:22	Such a man is the antichrist—he denies the Father and the **Son**.
2:23	No one who denies the **Son** has the Father; whoever acknowledges
2:23	has the Father; whoever acknowledges the **Son** has the Father also.
2:24	If it does, you also will remain in the **Son** and in the Father.
3: 8	The reason the **Son** of God appeared was to destroy the devil's
3:23	to believe in the name *of* his **Son**, Jesus Christ, and to love one
4: 9	and only **Son** into the world that we might live through him.
4:10	he loved us and sent his **Son** as an atoning sacrifice for our sins.
4:14	testify that the Father has sent his **Son** to be the Savior of the
4:15	If anyone acknowledges that Jesus is the **Son** of God, God lives in
5: 5	the world? Only he who believes that Jesus is the **Son** of God.
5: 9	it is the testimony of God, which he has given about his **Son**.
5:10	Anyone who believes in the **Son** of God has this testimony in his
5:10	he has not believed the testimony God has given about his **Son**.
5:11	God has given us eternal life, and this life is in his **Son**.
5:12	He who has the **Son** has life; he who does not have the Son of God
5:12	has life; he who does not have the **Son** of God does not have life.
5:13	I write these things to you who believe in the name *of* the **Son** of
5:20	We know also that the **Son** of God has come and has given us
5:20	And we are in him who is true—even in his **Son** Jesus Christ.

2Jn	1: 3	peace from God the Father and from Jesus Christ, the Father's **Son**,
1: 9	whoever continues in the teaching has both the Father and the **Son**.
Rev	1:13	and among the lampstands was someone "like a **son** of man,"
2:14	who taught Balak to entice the **Israelites** [+2702] to sin by eating
2:18	These are the words of the **Son** of God, whose eyes are like blazing
7: 4	who were sealed: 144,000 from all the tribes *of* **Israel** [+2702].
12: 5	She gave birth to a **son**, a male child, who will rule all the nations
14:14	and seated on the cloud was one "like a **son** of man" with a crown
21: 7	will inherit all this, and I will be his God and he will be my **son**.
21:12	were written the names of the twelve tribes *of* **Israel** [+2702].

5627 ὕλη, hylē [1] [→ 1494]

forest [1]

Jas | 3: 5 | Consider what a great **forest** is set on fire by a small spark.

5628 Ὑμέναιος, Hymenaios [2]

Hymenaeus [2]

1Ti | 1:20 | Among them are **Hymenaeus** and Alexander, whom I have handed
2Ti | 2:17 | spread like gangrene. Among them are **Hymenaeus** and Philetus,

5629 ὑμέτερος, hymeteros [11] [√ 5148]

you [5], your own [2], your [2], yours [2]

Lk	6:20	"Blessed are you who are poor, for **yours** is the kingdom of God.
16:12	else's property, who will give you *property of* **your own**?
Jn	7: 6	"The right time for me has not yet come; for **you** any time is right.
8:17	In **your own** Law it is written that the testimony of two men is
15:20	you also. If they obeyed my teaching, they will obey **yours** also.
Ac	27:34	Now I urge you to take some food. **You** need it to survive.
Ro	11:31	they too may now receive mercy as a result of God's mercy *to* **you**.
1Co	15:31	just as surely as I glory over **you** in Christ Jesus our Lord.
16:17	because they have supplied what was lacking from **you**.
2Co | 8: 8 | but I want to test the sincerity *of* **your** love by comparing it with
Gal | 6:13 | they want you to be circumcised that they may boast about **your**

5630 ὑμνέω, hymneō [4] [√ 5631]

sung a hymn [2], sing praises [1], singing hymns [1]

Mt | 26:30 | *When they had* **sung a hymn**, they went out to the Mount of
Mk | 14:26 | *When they had* **sung a hymn**, they went out to the Mount of
Ac | 16:25 | midnight Paul and Silas *were* praying and **singing hymns** to God,
Heb | 2:12 | in the presence of the congregation *I will* **sing** your **praises**."

5631 ὕμνος, hymnos [2] [→ 5630]

hymns [2]

Eph | 5:19 | Speak to one another with psalms, **hymns** and spiritual songs.
Col | 3:16 | **hymns** and spiritual songs with gratitude in your hearts to God.

5632 ὑπάγω, hypagō [79] [√ 5679 + 72]

go [45], going [18], get [2], going away [2], went [2], away [1], goes [1], going back [1], going out [1], going over [1], heading [1], leave [1], leaving [1], on way [1], returning [1]

Mt	4:10	Jesus said to him, "**Away** from me, Satan! For it is written:
5:24	in front of the altar. First **go** and be reconciled to your brother;
5:41	If someone forces you to go one mile, **go** with him two miles.
8: 4	But **go**, show yourself to the priest and offer the gift Moses
8:13	Then Jesus said to the centurion, "**Go**! It will be done just as you
8:32	He said to them, "**Go**!" So they came out and went into the pigs,
9: 6	Then he said to the paralytic, "Get up, take your mat and **go** home."
13:44	and then in his joy **went** and sold all he had and bought that field.
16:23	Jesus turned and said to Peter, "**Get** behind me, Satan! You are a
18:15	**go** and show him his fault, just between the two of you.
19:21	want to be perfect, **go**, sell your possessions and give to the poor,
20: 4	He told them, 'You also **go** and work in my vineyard, and I will
20: 7	"He said to them, 'You also **go** and work in my vineyard.'
20:14	Take your pay and **go**. I want to give the man who was hired last
21:28	to the first and said, 'Son, **go** and work today in the vineyard.'
26:18	He replied, "**Go** into the city to a certain man and tell him,

	26:24	The Son of Man *will* **go** just as it is written about him. But woe to
	27:65	Pilate answered. "**Go**, make the tomb as secure as you know how."
	28:10	**Go** and tell my brothers to go to Galilee; there they will see me."
Mk	1:44	But **go**, show yourself to the priest and offer the sacrifices that
	2:11	"I tell you, get up, take your mat and **go** home."
	5:19	"**Go** home to your family and tell them how much the Lord has
	5:34	has healed you. **Go** in peace and be freed from your suffering."
	6:31	were coming and **going** that they did not even have a chance to eat,
	6:33	But many who saw them **leaving** recognized them and ran on foot
	6:38	he asked. "**Go** and see." When they found out, they said, "Five—
	7:29	Then he told her, "For such a reply, *you may* **go**; the demon has left
	8:33	at his disciples, he rebuked Peter. "**Get** behind me, Satan!" he said.
	10:21	"**Go**, sell everything you have and give to the poor, and you will
	10:52	"**Go**," said Jesus, "your faith has healed you." Immediately he
	11: 2	saying to them, "**Go** to the village ahead of you, and just as you
	14:13	So he sent two of his disciples, telling them, "**Go** into the city,
	14:21	The Son of Man *will* **go** just as it is written about him. But woe to
	16: 7	But **go**, tell his disciples and Peter, 'He is going ahead of you into
Lk	8:42	As Jesus *was* **on** his **way**, the crowds almost crushed him.
	10: 3	**Go**! I am sending you out like lambs among wolves.
	12:58	As *you are* **going** with your adversary to the magistrate, try hard to
	17:14	yourselves to the priests." And as they **went**, they were cleansed.
	19:30	"**Go** to the village ahead of you, and as you enter it, you will find a
Jn	3: 8	but you cannot tell where it comes from or where *it is* **going**.
	4:16	He told her, "**Go**, call your husband and come back."
	6:21	immediately the boat reached the shore where *they were* **heading**.
	6:67	"You do not want *to* **leave** too, do you?" Jesus asked the Twelve.
	7: 3	brothers said to him, "You ought to leave here and **go** to Judea,
	7:33	you for only a short time, and then *I* **go** to the one who sent me.
	8:14	is valid, for I know where I came from and where *I am* **going**.
	8:14	But you have no idea where I come from or where *I am* **going**.
	8:21	"I *am* **going away**, and you will look for me, and you will die in
	8:21	and you will die in your sin. Where *I* **go**, you cannot come."
	8:22	kill himself? Is that why he says, 'Where *I* **go**, you cannot come'?"
	9: 7	"**Go**," he told him, "wash in the Pool of Siloam" (this word means
	9:11	He told me *to* **go** to Siloam and wash. So I went and washed,
	11: 8	ago the Jews tried to stone you, and yet *you are* **going back** there?"
	11:31	followed her, supposing *she was* **going** to the tomb to mourn there.
	11:44	Jesus said to them, "Take off the grave clothes and let him **go**."
	12:11	for on account of him many of the Jews *were* **going over** to Jesus
	12:35	The man who walks in the dark does not know where *he is* **going**.
	13: 3	and that he had come from God and *was* **returning** to God;
	13:33	the Jews, so I tell you now: Where I *am* **going**, you cannot come.
	13:36	Simon Peter asked him, "Lord, where *are you* **going**?"
	13:36	Jesus replied, "Where I *am* **going**, you cannot follow now,
	14: 4	You know the way to the place where *I am* **going**."
	14: 5	Thomas said to him, "Lord, we don't know where *you are* **going**,
	14:28	heard me say, '*I am* **going away** and I am coming back to you.'
	15:16	but I chose you and appointed you to **go** and bear fruit—
	16: 5	"Now *I am* **going** to him who sent me, yet none of you asks me,
	16: 5	who sent me, yet none of you asks me, 'Where *are you* **going**?'
	16:10	in regard to righteousness, because *I am* **going** to the Father,
	16:17	while you will see me,' and 'Because *I am* **going** to the Father'?"
	18: 8	Jesus answered. "If you are looking for me, then let these men **go**."
	21: 3	"I'm **going out** to fish," Simon Peter told them, and they said,
Jas	2:16	If one of you says to him, "**Go**, I wish you well; keep warm
1Jn	2:11	he does not know where *he is* **going**, because the darkness has
Rev	10: 8	"**Go**, take the scroll that lies open in the hand of the angel who is
	13:10	If anyone is to go into captivity, into captivity *he will* **go**. If anyone
	14: 4	kept themselves pure. They follow the Lamb wherever *he* **goes**.
	16: 1	"**Go**, pour out the seven bowls of God's wrath on the earth."
	17: 8	and will come up out of the Abyss and **go** to his destruction.
	17:11	He belongs to the seven and *is* **going** to his destruction.

5633 ὑπακοή, *hypakoē* [15] [√ *5679 + 201*]

obedience [8], obedient [3], obey [3], obeying [1]

Ro	1: 5	among all the Gentiles to the **obedience** that comes from faith.
	5:19	so also through the **obedience** of the one man the many will be
	6:16	that when you offer yourselves to someone to **obey** him as slaves,
	6:16	you are slaves to sin, which leads to death, or to **obedience**,
	15:18	me in leading the Gentiles to **obey** God by what I have said
	16:19	Everyone has heard about your **obedience**, so I am full of joy over
	16:26	of the eternal God, so that all nations might believe and **obey** him—
2Co	7:15	is all the greater when he remembers that you were all **obedient**,

	10: 5	and we take captive every thought to make it **obedient** to Christ.
	10: 6	every act of disobedience, once your **obedience** is complete.
Phm	1:21	Confident of your **obedience**, I write to you, knowing that you will
Heb	5: 8	he was a son, he learned **obedience** from what he suffered
1Pe	1: 2	for **obedience** to Jesus Christ and sprinkling by his blood:
	1:14	As **obedient** children, do not conform to the evil desires you had
	1:22	Now that you have purified yourselves by **obeying** the truth

5634 ὑπακούω, *hypakouō* [21] [√ *5679 + 201*]

obey [14], obeyed [4], accepted [1], answer [1], obedient [1]

Mt	8:27	kind of man is this? Even the winds and the waves **obey** him!"
Mk	1:27	He even gives orders to evil spirits and *they* **obey** him."
	4:41	each other, "Who is this? Even the wind and the waves **obey** him!"
Lk	8:25	He commands even the winds and the water, and *they* **obey** him."
	17: 6	'Be uprooted and planted in the sea,' and *it will* **obey** you.
Ac	6: 7	and a large number of priests *became* **obedient** to the faith.
	12:13	and a servant girl named Rhoda came *to* **answer** the door.
Ro	6:12	let sin reign in your mortal body so that you **obey** its evil desires.
	6:16	to obey him as slaves, you are slaves to the one whom *you* **obey**—
	6:17	*you* wholeheartedly **obeyed** the form of teaching to which you
	10:16	But not all the Israelites **accepted** the good news. For Isaiah says,
Eph	6: 1	Children, **obey** your parents in the Lord, for this is right.
	6: 5	Slaves, **obey** your earthly masters with respect and fear, and with
Php	2:12	Therefore, my dear friends, as *you have* always **obeyed**—
Col	3:20	Children, **obey** your parents in everything, for this pleases the
	3:22	Slaves, **obey** your earthly masters in everything; and do it,
2Th	1: 8	do not know God and *do not* **obey** the gospel of our Lord Jesus.
	3:14	If anyone *does* not **obey** our instruction in this letter, take special
Heb	5: 9	he became the source of eternal salvation *for* all who **obey** him
	11: 8	**obeyed** and went, even though he did not know where he was
1Pe	3: 6	like Sarah, *who* **obeyed** Abraham and called him her master.

5635 ὕπανδρος, *hypandros* [1] [√ *5679 + 467*]

married [1]

Ro	7: 2	by law a **married** woman is bound to her husband as long as he is

5636 ὑπαντάω, *hypantaō* [10] [√ *5679 + 505*]

met [6], went out to meet [2], meet [1], oppose [1]

Mt	8:28	two demon-possessed men coming from the tombs **met** him.
	28: 9	Suddenly Jesus **met** them. "Greetings," he said. They came to him,
Mk	5: 2	a man with an evil spirit came from the tombs *to* **meet** him.
Lk	8:27	he *was* **met** by a demon-possessed man from the town.
	14:31	and consider whether he is able with ten thousand men *to* **oppose**
Jn	4:51	his servants **met** him with the news that his boy was living.
	11:20	was coming, *she* **went out to meet** him, but Mary stayed at home.
	11:30	the village, but was still at the place where Martha *had* **met** him.
	12:18	that he had given this miraculous sign, **went out to meet** him.
Ac	16:16	we *were* **met** by a slave girl who had a spirit by which she

5637 ὑπάντησις, *hypantēsis* [3] [√ *5679 + 505*]

meet [3]

Mt	8:34	Then the whole town went out to **meet** Jesus. And when they saw
	25: 1	virgins who took their lamps and went out to **meet** the bridegroom.
Jn	12:13	They took palm branches and went out to **meet** him, shouting,

5638 ὕπαρξις, *hyparxis* [2] [√ *5679 + 806*]

goods [1], possessions [1]

Ac	2:45	Selling their possessions and **goods**, they gave to anyone as he had
Heb	10:34	you knew that you yourselves had better and lasting **possessions**.

5639 ὑπάρχω, *hyparchō* [60] [√ *5679 + 806*]

was [10], possessions [9], are [8], is [7], *untranslated* [5], be [3], possess [2], property [2], baptized [*+966*] [1], being [1], contained [*+1877*] [1], gone [1], has [*+3836*] [1], have [1], indulge [1], loved money [+5795] [1], means [1], need [1], owned [+3230] [1], owned [1], that am [1], wasn't [1]

Mt 19:21 want to be perfect, go, sell your **possessions** and give to the poor,
   24:47 I tell you the truth, he will put him in charge of all his **possessions**.
   25:14 who called his servants and entrusted his **property** to them.
Lk 7:25 who wear expensive clothes and **indulge** in luxury are in palaces.
   8: 3 women were helping to support them out of their own **means**.
   8:41 [NIE] a ruler of the synagogue, came and fell at Jesus' feet,
   9:48 who sent me. For he *who* **is** least among you all—he is the greatest."
  11:13 If you then, *though you* are evil, know how to give good gifts to
  11:21 fully armed, guards his own house, his **possessions** are safe.
  12:15 a man's life does not consist in the abundance of his **possessions**."
  12:33 Sell your **possessions** and give to the poor. Provide purses for
  12:44 I tell you the truth, he will put him in charge of all his **possessions**.
  14:33 any of you who does not give up everything he **has** [+3836] cannot
  16: 1 rich man whose manager was accused of wasting his **possessions**.
  16:14 The Pharisees, *who* **loved money** [+5795], heard all this and were
  16:23 In hell, where *he* **was** in torment, he looked up and saw Abraham
  19: 8 Here and now I give half of my **possessions** to the poor, and if I
  23:50 Now *there* **was** a man named Joseph, a member of the Council,
Ac 2:30 But *he* **was** a prophet and knew that God had promised him on
  3: 2 Now a man [NIE] crippled from birth was being carried to the
  3: 6 Then Peter said, "Silver or gold I *do* not **have**, but what I have I
  4:32 No one claimed that any of his **possessions** was his own, but they
  4:34 For from time to time those *who* **owned** [+3230] lands or houses
  4:37 sold a field he **owned** and brought the money and put it at the
  5: 4 And after it was sold, **wasn't** the money at your disposal?
  7:55 But Stephen, [NIE] full of the Holy Spirit, looked up to heaven
  8:16 *they* had simply *been* **baptized** [+966] into the name of the Lord
  10:12 It **contained** [+1877] all kinds of four-footed animals, as well as
  16: 3 lived in that area, for they all knew that his father **was** a Greek.
  16:20 brought them before the magistrates and said, "These men **are** Jews,
  16:37 *even though we* **are** Roman citizens, and threw us into prison.
  17:24 made the world and everything in it **is** the Lord of heaven and earth
  17:27 out for him and find him, though *he* **is** not far from each one of us.
  17:29 "Therefore *since we* **are** God's offspring, we should not think that
  19:36 are **to** be quiet and not do anything rash.
  19:40 able to account for this commotion, *since there* **is** no reason for it."
  21:20 of Jews have believed, and all of them **are** zealous for the law.
  22: 3 and **was** just as zealous for God as any of you are today.
  27:12 *Since* the harbor **was** unsuitable to winter in, the majority decided
  27:21 *After* the men *had* **gone** a long time without food, Paul stood up
  27:34 Now I urge you to take some food. You **need** it to survive.
  28: 7 *There* **was** an estate nearby that belonged to Publius, the chief
  28:18 release me, because I **was** not guilty of any crime deserving death.
Ro 4:19 *since he* **was** about a hundred years old—and that Sarah's womb
1Co 7:26 I think [NIE] that it is good for you to remain as you are.
  11: 7 not to cover his head, *since he* **is** the image and glory of God;
  11:18 *there* **are** divisions among you, and to some extent I believe it.
  12:22 those parts of the body that seem *to* **be** weaker are indispensable,
  13: 3 If I give all I **possess** to the poor and surrender my body to the
2Co 8:17 to you with much enthusiasm and [NIE] on his own initiative.
  12:16 to you. Yet, crafty fellow **that** *I* **am**, I caught you by trickery!
Gal 1:14 and **was** extremely zealous for the traditions of my fathers.
  2:14 "You **are** a Jew, yet you live like a Gentile and not like a Jew.
Php 2: 6 Who, **being** in very nature God, did not consider equality with God
  3:20 But our citizenship **is** in heaven. And we eagerly await a Savior
Heb 10:34 in prison and joyfully accepted the confiscation *of* your **property**,
Jas 2:15 Suppose a brother or sister **is** without clothes and daily food.
2Pe 1: 8 For *if you* **possess** these qualities in increasing measure, they will
  2:19 them freedom, *while they* themselves **are** slaves of depravity—
  3:11 be destroyed in this way, what kind of people ought you *to* **be**?

5640 ὑπείκω, **hypeikō** [1] [√ 5679 + 1634]

submit [1]

Heb 13:17 Obey your leaders and **submit** *to* their *authority*. They keep watch

5641 ὑπεναντίος, **hypenantios** [2] [√ 5679 + 1882]

enemies [1], stood opposed [+1639] [1]

Col 2:14 that was against us and that **stood opposed** [+1639] to us;
Heb 10:27 and of raging fire that will consume the **enemies** of God.

5642 ὑπέρ, **hyper** [150]

[→ 5643, 5644, 5645, 5646, 5647, 5648, 5649, 5650, 5651, 5652, 5653, 5654, 5655, 5656, 5657, 5658, 5659, 5660, 5661, 5662, 5663, 5664, 5665, 5666, 5667, 5668, 5669, 5670, 5671, 5672, 5673]

for [92], about [8], in [6], above [4], beyond [4], for the sake of [4], more than [4], on behalf [4], *untranslated* [3], concerning [2], for sake [2], on behalf of [2], over [2], than [2], to [2], according to [1], as for [+1664] [1], because of [1], better than [1], brighter [+3288] [1], Christ's [+5986] [1], more than is warranted [1], more [1], take place [1]

Mt 5:44 Love your enemies and pray **for** those who persecute you,
  10:24 "A student is not **above** his teacher, nor a servant above his master.
  10:24 "A student is not above his teacher, nor a servant **above** his master.
  10:37 who loves his father or mother **more than** me is not worthy of me;
  10:37 who loves his son or daughter **more than** me is not worthy of me;
Mk 9:40 for whoever is not against us is **for** us.
  14:24 of the covenant, which is poured out **for** many," he said to them.
Lk 6:40 A student is not **above** his teacher, but everyone who is fully
  9:50 stop him," Jesus said, "for whoever is not against you is **for** you."
  16: 8 in dealing with their own kind **than** are the people of the light.
  22:19 and gave it to them, saying, "This is my body given **for** you;
  22:20 cup is the new covenant in my blood, which is poured out **for** you.
Jn 1:30 This is [NIE] the one I meant when I said, 'A man who comes
  6:51 This bread is my flesh, which I will give **for** the life of the world."
  10:11 The good shepherd lays down his life **for** the sheep.
  10:15 and I know the Father—and I lay down my life **for** the sheep.
  11: 4 it is **for** God's glory so that God's Son may be glorified through it."
  11:50 You do not realize that it is better for you that one man die **for** the
  11:51 but as high priest that year he prophesied that Jesus would die **for**
  11:52 and not only **for** that nation but also for the scattered children of
  13:37 why can't I follow you now? I will lay down my life **for** you."
  13:38 Then Jesus answered, "Will you really lay down your life **for** me?
  15:13 love has no one than this, that he lay down his life **for** his friends.
  17:19 **For** them I sanctify myself, that they too may be truly sanctified.
  18:14 the Jews that it would be good if one man died **for** the people.
Ac 5:41 because they had been counted worthy of suffering disgrace **for** the
  8:24 "Pray to the Lord **for** me so that nothing you have said may happen
  9:16 I will show him how much he must suffer **for** my name."
  15:26 men who have risked their lives **for** the name of our Lord Jesus
  21:13 but also to die in Jerusalem **for** the name of the Lord Jesus."
  21:26 would end and the offering would be made **for** each of them.
  26:13 I saw a light from heaven, **brighter than** [+3288] the sun,
Ro 1: 5 Through him and **for** his name's **sake**, we received grace
  5: 6 when we were still powerless, Christ died **for** the ungodly.
  5: 7 Very rarely will anyone die **for** a righteous man, though for a good
  5: 7 though **for** a good man someone might possibly dare to die.
  5: 8 love for us in this: While we were still sinners, Christ died **for** us.
  8:27 because the Spirit intercedes **for** the saints in accordance with
  8:31 we say in response to this? If God is **for** us, who can be against us?
  8:32 He who did not spare his own Son, but gave him up **for** us all—
  8:34 to life—is at the right hand of God and is also interceding **for** us.
  9: 3 were cursed and cut off from Christ **for the sake of** my brothers,
  9:27 Isaiah cries out **concerning** Israel: "Though the number of the
  10: 1 and prayer to God **for** the Israelites is that they may be saved.
  14:15 Do not by your eating destroy your brother **for** whom Christ died.
  15: 8 Christ has become a servant of the Jews **on behalf of** God's truth,
  15: 9 so that the Gentiles may glorify God **for** his mercy, as it is written:
  15:30 of the Spirit, to join me in my struggle by praying to God **for** me.
  16: 4 They risked their lives **for** me. Not only I but all the churches of
1Co 1:13 Is Christ divided? Was Paul crucified **for** you? Were you baptized
  4: 6 us the meaning of the saying, "Do not *go* **beyond** what is written."
  4: 6 Then you will not take pride **in** one man over against another.
  10:13 he will not let you be tempted **beyond** what you can bear.
  10:30 why am I denounced **because of** something I thank God for?
  11:24 he broke it and said, "This is my body, which is **for** you;
  12:25 but that its parts should have equal concern **for** each other.
  15: 3 that Christ died **for** our sins according to the Scriptures,
  15:29 no resurrection, what will those do who are baptized **for** the dead?
  15:29 If the dead are not raised at all, why are people baptized **for** them?
2Co 1: 6 If we are distressed, it is **for** your comfort and salvation; if we are
  1: 6 if we are comforted, it is **for** your comfort, which produces in you
  1: 7 And our hope **for** you is firm, because we know that just as you
  1: 8 brothers, **about** the hardships we suffered in the province of Asia.
  1: 8 We were under great pressure, *far* **beyond** our ability to endure,

1:11 as you help **[NIE]** us by your prayers. Then many will give thanks
1:11 Then many will give thanks **on** our **behalf** for the gracious favor
5:12 to you again, but are giving you an opportunity to take pride **in** us,
5:14 because we are convinced that one died **for** all, and therefore all
5:15 And he died **for** all, that those who live should no longer live for
5:15 but for him who died **for** them and was raised again.
5:20 We are therefore **Christ's [+5986]** ambassadors, as though God
5:20 We implore you **on** Christ's **behalf**: Be reconciled to God.
5:21 God made him who had no sin to be sin **for** us, so that in him we
7: 4 I have great confidence in you; I take great pride **in** you. I am
7: 7 your deep sorrow, your ardent concern **for** me, so that my joy was
7:12 God you could see for yourselves how devoted **to** us you are.
7:14 I had boasted to him **about** you, and you have not embarrassed me.
8:16 who put into the heart of Titus the same concern I have **for** you.
8:23 **As for [+1664]** Titus, he is my partner and fellow worker among
8:24 men the proof of your love and the reason for our pride **in** you,
9: 2 to help, and I have been boasting **about** it to the Macedonians,
9: 3 But I am sending the brothers in order that our boasting **about** you
9:14 And in their prayers **for** you their hearts will go out to you,
11:23 of Christ? (I am out of my mind to talk like this.) I am **more**.
12: 5 I will boast **about** a man like that, but I will not boast about
12: 5 but I will not boast **about** myself, except about my weaknesses.
12: 6 so no one will think **more** of me **than is warranted** by what I do
12: 8 **[NIE]** Three times I pleaded with the Lord to take it away from
12:10 That is why, **for** Christ's **sake**, I delight in weaknesses, in insults,
12:13 How were you inferior **to** the other churches, except that I was
12:15 So I will very gladly spend **for** you everything I have and expend
12:19 and everything we do, dear friends, is **for** your strengthening.
13: 8 For we cannot do anything against the truth, but only **for** the truth.
Gal 1: 4 who gave himself **for** our sins to rescue us from the present evil
1:14 I was advancing in Judaism **beyond** many Jews of my own age
2:20 by faith in the Son of God, who loved me and gave himself **for** me.
3:13 redeemed us from the curse of the law by becoming a curse **for** us,
Eph 1:16 I have not stopped giving thanks **for** you, remembering you in my
1:22 and appointed him to be head **over** everything for the church,
3: 1 the prisoner of Christ Jesus **for the sake of** you Gentiles—
3:13 therefore, not to be discouraged because of my sufferings **for** you,
3:20 Now to him who is able to do immeasurably **more than** all we ask
5: 2 and gave himself up **for** us as a fragrant offering and sacrifice to
5:20 always giving thanks to God the Father **for** everything, in the name
5:25 just as Christ loved the church and gave himself up **for** her
6:19 Pray also **for** me, that whenever I open my mouth, words may be
6:20 **for** which I am an ambassador in chains. Pray that I may declare it
Php 1: 4 In all my prayers **for** all of you, I always pray with joy
1: 7 It is right for me to feel this way **about** all of you, since I have you
1:29 For it has been granted to you **on behalf of** Christ not only to
1:29 of Christ not only to believe on him, but also to suffer **for** him,
2: 9 the highest place and gave him the name that is **above** every name,
2:13 works in you to will and to act **according to** his good purpose.
4:10 in the Lord that at last you have renewed your concern **for** me.
Col 1: 7 fellow servant, who is a faithful minister of Christ **on** our **behalf**,
1: 9 we have not stopped praying **for** you and asking God to fill you
1:24 Now I rejoice in what was suffered **for** you, and I fill up in my
1:24 Christ's afflictions, **for the sake of** his body, which is the church.
2: 1 I want you to know how much I am struggling **for** you and for
4:12 He is always wrestling in prayer **for** you, that you may stand firm
4:13 I vouch for him that he is working hard **for** you and for those at
1Th 3: 2 the gospel of Christ, to strengthen and encourage you **in** your faith,
5:10 He died **for** us so that, whether we are awake or asleep, we may
2Th 1: 4 among God's churches we boast **about** your perseverance.
1: 5 worthy of the kingdom of God, **for** which you are suffering.
2: 1 **Concerning** the coming of our Lord Jesus Christ and our being
1Ti 2: 1 prayers, intercession and thanksgiving be made **for** everyone—
2: 2 **for** kings and all those in authority, that we may live peaceful
2: 6 who gave himself as a ransom **for** all men—the testimony given in
Tit 2:14 who gave himself **for** us to redeem us from all wickedness
Phm 1:13 so that he could **take** your **place** in helping me while I am in
1:16 no longer as a slave, but **better than** a slave, as a dear brother.
1:21 I write to you, knowing that you will do even **more than** I ask.
Heb 2: 9 so that by the grace of God he might taste death **for** everyone.
4:12 Sharper **than** any double-edged sword, it penetrates even to
5: 1 and is appointed to *represent* them in matters related to God,
5: 1 them in matters related to God, to offer gifts and sacrifices **for** sins.
6:20 where Jesus, who went before us, has entered **on** our **behalf**.
7:25 to God through him, because he always lives to intercede **for** them.
7:27 after day, first **for** his own sins, and then for the sins of the people.

9: 7 which he offered **for** himself and for the sins the people had
9:24 he entered heaven itself, now to appear **for** us in God's presence.
10:12 But when this priest had offered for all time one sacrifice **for** sins,
13:17 They keep watch **over** you as men who must give an account.
Jas 5:16 to each other and pray **for** each other so that you may be healed.
1Pe 2:21 To this you were called, because Christ suffered **for** you,
3:18 once for all, the righteous **for** the unrighteous, to bring you to God.
1Jn 3:16 how we know what love is: Jesus Christ laid down his life **for** us.
3:16 life for us. And we ought to lay down our lives **for** our brothers.
3Jn 1: 7 It was **for the sake of** the Name that they went out, receiving no

5643 ὑπεραίρομαι, *hyperairomai* [3] [√ *5642 + 149*]

untranslated [1], conceited [1], exalt himself [1]

2Co 12: 7 To keep *me* from *becoming* **conceited** because of these
12: 7 a thorn in my flesh, a messenger of Satan, to torment me. **[RPG]**
2Th 2: 4 and *will* **exalt himself** over everything that is called God

5644 ὑπέρακμος, *hyperakmos* [1] [√ *5642 + 216*]

getting along in years [1]

1Co 7:36 and if she is **getting along in years** and he feels he ought to marry,

5645 ὑπεράνω, *hyperanō* [3] [√ *5642 + 539*]

above [1], far above [1], higher than [1]

Eph 1:21 **far above** all rule and authority, power and dominion, and every
4:10 He who descended is the very one who ascended **higher than** all
Heb 9: 5 **Above** the ark were the cherubim of the Glory,

5646 ὑπερασπίζω, *hyperaspizō* Not used in
UBS/NIV [√ *5642 + 835*]

5647 ὑπεραυξάνω, *hyperauxanō* [1] [√ *5642 + 889*]

growing more and more [1]

2Th 1: 3 and rightly so, because your faith *is* **growing more and more**,

5648 ὑπερβαίνω, *hyperbainō* [1] [√ *5642 + 326*]

wrong [1]

1Th 4: 6 and that in this matter no one *should* **wrong** his brother or take

5649 ὑπερβαλλόντως, *hyperballontōs* [1]
[√ *5642 + 965*]

more severely [1]

2Co 11:23 been in prison more frequently, been flogged **more severely**,

5650 ὑπερβάλλω, *hyperballō* [5] [√ *5642 + 965*]

surpassing [2], incomparable [1], incomparably [1], surpasses [1]

2Co 3:10 has no glory now in comparison with the **surpassing** glory.
9:14 go out to you, because of the **surpassing** grace God has given you.
Eph 1:19 and his **incomparably** great power for us who believe. That power
2: 7 in order that in the coming ages he might show the **incomparable**
3:19 and to know this love *that* **surpasses** knowledge—that you may be

5651 ὑπερβολή, *hyperbolē* [8] [√ *5642 + 965*]

that far outweighs them all [+*983+1650+2848+5651*] [2],
all-surpassing [1], great [+*2848*] [1], intensely [+*2848*] [1], most
excellent [+*2848*] [1], surpassingly great [1], utterly [+*2848*] [1]

Ro 7:13 the commandment sin might become **utterly** [+*2848*] sinful.
1Co 12:31 And now I will show you the **most excellent** [+*2848*] way.
2Co 1: 8 We were under **great** [+*2848*] pressure, far beyond our ability to
4: 7 in jars of clay to show that this **all-surpassing** power is from God
4:17 glory **that far outweighs them all** [+*983+1650+2848+5651*].
4:17 glory **that far outweighs them all** [+*983+1650+2848+5651*].
12: 7 *because of* these **surpassingly great** revelations,

Gal   1: 13 how **intensely** [+2848] I persecuted the church of God and tried to

5652 ὑπερεγώ, *hyperegō*   Not used in UBS/NIV
[√ 5642 + 1609]

5653 ὑπερείδω, *hypereidō*   Not used in UBS/NIV
[√ 5642 + 1626]

5654 ὑπερέκεινα, *hyperekeina*   [1]   [√ 5642 + 1695]
regions beyond [1]

2Co 10: 16 so that we can preach the gospel in the **regions beyond** you.

5655 ὑπερεκπερισσοῦ, *hyperekperissou*   [3]
[√ 5642 + 1666 + 4356]

highest regard [1], immeasurably [1], most earnestly [1]

Eph   3: 20 Now to him who is able to do **immeasurably** more than all we ask
1Th   3: 10 and day we pray **most earnestly** that we may see you again
         5: 13 Hold them *in* the **highest regard** in love because of their work.

5656 ὑπερεκπερισσῶς, *hyperekperissōs*   Not used
in UBS/NIV [√ 5642 + 1666 + 4356]

5657 ὑπερεκτείνω, *hyperekteinō*   [1]   [√ 1753; cf. 5642]
going too far [1]

2Co 10: 14 *We are* not **going too far** in our boasting, as would be the case if

5658 ὑπερεκχύννω, *hyperekchynnō*   [1]   [√ 1772; cf. 5642 + 1666]
running over [1]

Lk   6: 38 good measure, pressed down, shaken together and **running over**,

5659 ὑπερεντυγχάνω, *hyperentynchanō*   [1]
[√ 5642 + 1877 + 5593]
intercedes for [1]

Ro   8: 26 but the Spirit himself **intercedes for** us with groans that words

5660 ὑπερέχω, *hyperechō*   [5]   [√ 5642 + 2400]
better than [1], governing [1], supreme authority [1], surpassing greatness [1], transcends [1]

Ro   13: 1 Everyone must submit himself *to* the **governing** authorities,
Php   2: 3 but in humility consider others **better than** yourselves.
        3: 8 I consider everything a loss compared to the **surpassing greatness**
        4: 7 which **transcends** all understanding, will guard your hearts
1Pe   2: 13 among men: whether to the king, as the **supreme authority**,

5661 ὑπερηφανία, *hyperēphania*   [1]   [√ 5642 + 5743]
arrogance [1]

Mk   7: 22 malice, deceit, lewdness, envy, slander, **arrogance** and folly.

5662 ὑπερήφανος, *hyperēphanos*   [5]   [√ 5642 + 5743]
proud [4], arrogant [1]

Lk   1: 51 he has scattered *those who are* **proud** in their inmost thoughts.
Ro   1: 30 slanderers, God-haters, insolent, **arrogant** and boastful;
2Ti   3: 2 lovers of money, boastful, **proud**, abusive, disobedient to their
Jas   4: 6 "God opposes the **proud** but gives grace to the humble."
1Pe   5: 5 because, "God opposes the **proud** but gives grace to the humble."

5663 ὑπερλίαν, *hyperlian*   [2]   [√ 5642 + 3336]
super-apostles [+693] [2]

2Co 11: 5 not think I am in the least inferior to those "**super-apostles** [+693]."
     12: 11 for I am not in the least inferior to the "**super-apostles** [+693],"

5664 ὑπερνικάω, *hypernikaō*   [1]   [√ 5642 + 3772]
more than conquerors [1]

Ro   8: 37 in all these things *we are* **more than conquerors** through him who

5665 ὑπέρογκος, *hyperonkos*   [2]   [√ 5642 + 3839]
boast about [+3281] [1], boastful [1]

2Pe   2: 18 For they mouth empty, **boastful** words and, by appealing to the
Jude 1: 16 they **boast** [+3281] **about** themselves and flatter others for their

5666 ὑπεροράω, *hyperoraō*   [1]   [√ 5642 + 3972]
overlooked [1]

Ac 17: 30 In the past God **overlooked** such ignorance, but now he commands

5667 ὑπεροχή, *hyperochē*   [2]   [√ 5642 + 2400]
authority [1], superior wisdom [+5053] [1]

1Co   2: 1 I did not come with eloquence or **superior wisdom** [+5053] as I
1Ti   2: 2 for kings and all those in **authority**, that we may live peaceful

5668 ὑπερπερισσεύω, *hyperperisseuō*   [2]
[√ 5642 + 4356]
increased all the more [1], knows no bounds [1]

Ro   5: 20 But where sin increased, grace **increased all the more**,
2Co   7: 4 greatly encouraged; in all our troubles my joy **knows no bounds**.

5669 ὑπερπερισσῶς, *hyperperissōs*   [1]
[√ 5642 + 4356]
overwhelmed with amazement [+1742] [1]

Mk   7: 37 *People were* **overwhelmed with amazement** [+1742]. "He has

5670 ὑπερπλεονάζω, *hyperpleonazō*   [1]
[√ 5642 + 4444]
poured out abundantly [1]

1Ti   1: 14 The grace of our Lord *was* **poured out** on me **abundantly**,

5671 ὑπερυψόω, *hyperypsoō*   [1]   [√ 5642 + 5737]
exalted to the highest place [1]

Php   2: 9 Therefore God **exalted** him **to the highest place** and gave him the

5672 ὑπερφρονέω, *hyperphroneō*   [1]   [√ 5642 + 5856]
think highly [1]

Ro 12: 3 one of you: *Do* not **think** of yourself more **highly** than you ought,

5673 ὑπερῷον, *hyperōon*   [4]   [√ 5642]
upstairs room [3], room [1]

Ac   1: 13 they went **upstairs** to the **room** where they were staying.
      9: 37 and her body was washed and placed in an **upstairs room**.
      9: 39 with them, and when he arrived he was taken upstairs to the **room**.
     20: 8 There were many lamps in the **upstairs room** where we were

5674 ὑπέχω, *hypechō*   [1]   [√ 5679 + 2400]
suffer [1]

Jude 1: 7 They serve as an example of *those who* **suffer** the punishment of

5675 ὑπήκοος, hypēkoos [3] [√ 5679 + 201]

obedient [2], obey [+1181] [1]

Ac 7: 39 "But our fathers refused to **obey** [+1181] him. Instead, they rejected
2Co 2: 9 to see if you would stand the test and be **obedient** in everything.
Php 2: 8 as a man, he humbled himself and became **obedient** to death—

5676 ὑπηρετέω, hypēreteō [3] [√ 5677]

served [1], supplied [1], take care of needs [1]

Ac 13: 36 "For when David had **served** God's purpose in his own generation,
    20: 34 You yourselves know that these hands of mine have **supplied** my
    24: 23 some freedom and permit his friends to **take care of** his **needs**.

5677 ὑπηρέτης, hypēretēs [20] [→ 5676; cf. 5679]

officials [5], guards [4], servants [3], officers [2], temple guards
[2], attendant [1], helper [1], officer [1], servant [1]

Mt 5: 25 and the judge may hand you over to the **officer**, and you may be
    26: 58 He entered and sat down with the **guards** to see the outcome.
Mk 14: 54 There he sat with the **guards** and warmed himself at the fire.
    14: 65 and said, "Prophesy!" And the **guards** took him and beat him.
Lk 1: 2 who from the first were eyewitnesses and **servants** of the word.
    4: 20 he rolled up the scroll, gave it back to the **attendant** and sat down.
Jn 7: 32 chief priests and the Pharisees sent **temple guards** to arrest him.
    7: 45 Finally the **temple guards** went back to the chief priests
    7: 46 "No one ever spoke the way this man does," the **guards** declared.
    18: 3 of soldiers and some **officials** from the chief priests and Pharisees.
    18: 12 with its commander and the Jewish **officials** arrested Jesus.
    18: 18 and **officials** stood around a fire they had made to keep warm.
    18: 22 Jesus said this, one of the **officials** nearby struck him in the face.
    18: 36 my **servants** would fight to prevent my arrest by the Jews.
    19: 6 As soon as the chief priests and their **officials** saw him,
Ac 5: 22 But on arriving at the jail, the **officers** did not find them there.
    5: 26 the captain went with his **officers** and brought the apostles.
    13: 5 God in the Jewish synagogues. John was with them as their **helper**.
    26: 16 I have appeared to you to appoint you as a **servant** and as a
1Co 4: 1 men ought to regard us as **servants** of Christ and as those entrusted

5678 ὕπνος, hypnos [6] [→ 70, 71, 934, 1965, 1966, 2030, 2031]

untranslated [1], natural sleep [+3122+3836+3836] [1], sleep [1],
slumber [1], sound asleep [+608+2965+3836] [1], very sleepy
[+976] [1]

Mt 1: 24 [RPG] he did what the angel of the Lord had commanded him
Lk 9: 32 Peter and his companions were **very sleepy** [+976], but when they
Jn 11: 13 his disciples thought he meant **natural sleep** [+3122+3836+3836].
Ac 20: 9 who was sinking into a deep **sleep** as Paul talked on and on.
    20: 9 talked on and on. When he was **sound asleep** [+608+2965+3836],
           he fell to the ground from the third story and was picked up dead.
Ro 13: 11 The hour has come for you to wake up from your **slumber**,

5679 ὑπό, hypo [220]

[→ 537, 538, 4732, 5347, 5348, 5632, 5633, 5634, 5635, 5636,
5637, 5638, 5639, 5640, 5641, 5674, 5675, 5680, 5681, 5682, 5683,
5684, 5685, 5686, 5687, 5688, 5689, 5690, 5691, 5692, 5693, 5694,
5695, 5696, 5697, 5698, 5699, 5700, 5701, 5702, 5703, 5704, 5705,
5706, 5707, 5708, 5709, 5710, 5711, 5712, 5713, 5714, 5715, 5716,
5717, 5718, 5719, 5720, 5721, 5722, 5723, 5724; cf. 5677]

by [97], untranslated [53], under [37], from [7], have [3], of [3], in
[2], subject to [2], at their hands [+899] [1], at [1], condemned
[+3213+4406] [1], established [1], for [1], he [+899] [1], him
[+899] [1], on [1], placed under [RP5718] [1], put under [RP5718]
[1], result of [1], she [+899] [1], slave to [1], the way [1], they
[+899] [1], to [1]

Mt 1: 22 All this took place to fulfill what the [NIE] Lord had said through
    2: 15 so was fulfilled what [NIE] the Lord had said through the
    2: 16 When Herod realized that he had been outwitted **by** the Magi,
    3: 6 their sins, they were baptized **by** him in the Jordan River.
    3: 13 Then Jesus came from Galilee to the Jordan to be baptized **by**

    3: 14 saying, "I need to be baptized **by** you, and do you come to me?"
    4: 1 Then Jesus was led **by** the Spirit into the desert to be tempted by
    4: 1 Then Jesus was led **by** the Spirit into the desert to be tempted by
    5: 13 good for anything, except to be thrown out and trampled **by** men.
    5: 15 Neither do people light a lamp and put it **under** a bowl.
    6: 2 do in the synagogues and on the streets, to be honored **by** men.
    8: 8 "Lord, I do not deserve to have you come **under** my roof.
    8: 9 For I myself am a man **under** authority, with soldiers under me.
    8: 9 For I myself am a man under authority, with soldiers **under** me.
    8: 24 came up on the lake, so that [NIE] the waves swept over the boat.
    10: 22 [NIE] All men will hate you because of me, but he who stands
    11: 7 did you go out into the desert to see? A reed swayed **by** the wind?
    11: 27 "All things have been committed to me **by** my Father. No one
    14: 8 Prompted **by** her mother, she said, "Give me here on a platter the
    14: 24 from land, buffeted **by** the waves because the wind was against it.
    17: 12 the Son of Man is going to suffer **at their hands** [+899]."
    19: 12 they were born that way; others were made that way **by** men;
    20: 23 These places belong to those for whom they have been prepared **by**
    22: 31 of the dead—have you not read what [NIE] God said to you,
    23: 7 be greeted in the marketplaces and to **have** men call them 'Rabbi.'
    23: 37 as a hen gathers her chicks **under** her wings, but you were not
    24: 9 put to death, and you will be hated **by** all nations because of me.
    27: 12 When he was accused **by** the chief priests and the elders, he gave
Mk 1: 5 their sins, they were baptized **by** him in the Jordan River.
    1: 9 from Nazareth in Galilee and was baptized **by** John in the Jordan.
    1: 13 and he was in the desert forty days, being tempted **by** Satan.
    2: 3 men came, bringing to him a paralytic, carried **by** four of them.
    4: 21 to them, "Do you bring in a lamp to put it **under** a bowl or a bed?
    4: 21 "Do you bring in a lamp to put it under a bowl or [RPG] a bed?
    4: 32 with such big branches that the birds of the air can perch **in** its
    5: 4 but **he** [+899] tore the chains apart and broke the irons on his feet.
    5: 26 She had suffered a great deal **under** the care of many doctors
    8: 31 Son of Man must suffer many things and be rejected **by** the elders,
    13: 13 [NIE] All men will hate you because of me, but he who stands
    16: 11 they heard that Jesus was alive and that **she** [+899] had seen him,
Lk 2: 18 and all who heard it were amazed at what [NIE] the shepherds
    2: 21 the name [NIE] the angel had given him before he had been
    2: 26 It had been revealed to him **by** the Holy Spirit that he would not
    3: 7 John said to the crowds coming out to be baptized **by** him,
    3: 19 But when [NIE] John rebuked Herod the tetrarch because of
    4: 2 where for forty days he was tempted **by** the devil. He ate nothing
    4: 15 he taught in their synagogues, and [NIE] everyone praised him.
    7: 6 for I do not deserve to have you come **under** my roof.
    7: 8 For I myself am a man **under** authority, with soldiers under me.
    7: 8 For I myself am a man under authority, with soldiers **under** me.
    7: 24 did you go out into the desert to see? A reed swayed **by** the wind?
    7: 30 for themselves, because they had not been baptized **by** John.)
    8: 14 but as they go on their way they are choked **by** life's worries,
    8: 29 his chains and had been driven **by** the demon into solitary places.
    9: 7 because [NIE] some were saying that John had been raised from
    9: 8 [NIE] others that Elijah had appeared, and still others that one of
    10: 22 "All things have been committed to me **by** my Father. No one
    11: 33 and puts it in a place where it will be hidden, or **under** a bowl.
    13: 17 but the people were delighted with all the wonderful things [NIE]
    13: 34 as a hen gathers her chicks **under** her wings, but you were not
    14: 8 "When [NIE] someone invites you to a wedding feast, do not take
    14: 8 more distinguished than you may have been invited. [NIE]
    16: 22 beggar died and [NIE] the angels carried him to Abraham's side.
    17: 20 having been asked **by** the Pharisees when the kingdom of God
    17: 24 and lights up [NIE] the sky from one end to the other.
    17: 24 and lights up the sky from one end to the other. [NIE]
    21: 16 You will be betrayed even **by** parents, brothers, relatives
    21: 17 [NIE] All men will hate you because of me.
    21: 20 "When you see Jerusalem being surrounded **by** armies, you will
    21: 24 Jerusalem will be trampled on **by** the Gentiles until the times of the
    23: 8 about him, he hoped to see **him** [+899] perform some miracle.
Jn 1: 48 "I saw you while you were still **under** the fig tree before Philip
    14: 21 one who loves me. He who loves me will be loved **by** my Father,
Ac 2: 5 in Jerusalem God-fearing Jews from every nation **under** heaven.
    2: 24 because it was impossible **for** death to keep its hold on him.
    4: 11 He is " 'the stone [NIE] you builders rejected, which has become
    4: 12 for there is no other name **under** heaven given to men by which to
    5: 16 bringing their sick and those tormented **by** evil spirits, and all of
    5: 21 **At** daybreak they entered the temple courts, as they had been told,
    8: 6 When the crowds heard [NIE] Philip and saw the miraculous
    10: 17 the men sent **by** Cornelius found out where Simon's house was

10:22 and God-fearing man, who is respected **by** all the Jewish people.
10:22 **[NIE]** A holy angel told him to have you come to his house
10:33 listen to everything **[NIE]** the Lord has commanded you to tell us."
10:38 doing good and healing all who were under the power **of** the devil,
10:41 but by witnesses **[NIE]** whom God had already chosen—
10:42 and to testify that he is the one whom **[NIE]** God appointed as
12: 5 but **[NIE]** the church was earnestly praying to God for him.
13: 4 The two of them, sent on their way **by** the Holy Spirit, went down
13:45 and talked abusively against what **[NIE]** Paul was saying.
15: 3 **[NIE]** The church sent them on their way, and as they traveled
15:40 and left, commended **by** the brothers to the grace of the Lord.
16: 2 **[NIE]** The brothers at Lystra and Iconium spoke well of him.
16: 4 they delivered the decisions reached **by** the apostles and elders in
16: 6 having been kept **by** the Holy Spirit from preaching the word in the
16:14 The Lord opened her heart to respond to **[NIE]** Paul's message.
17:13 When the Jews in Thessalonica learned that **[NIE]** Paul was
17:19 "May we know what this new teaching is that **[NIE]** you are
17:25 And he is not served **by** human hands, as if he needed anything,
20: 3 Because **[NIE]** the Jews made a plot against him just as he was
21:35 of the mob was so great he had to be carried **by** the soldiers.
22:11 My **[NIE]** companions led me by the hand into Damascus,
22:12 of the law and highly respected **by** all the Jews living there.
22:30 to find out exactly why Paul was being accused **by** the Jews,
23:10 the commander was afraid Paul would be torn to pieces **by** them.
23:27 This man was seized **by** the Jews and they were about to kill him,
23:27 was seized by the Jews and **they** [+*899*] were about to kill him,
24:26 At the same time he was hoping that **[NIE]** Paul would offer him
25:14 "There is a man here whom **[NIE]** Felix left as a prisoner.
26: 2 today as I make my defense against all the accusations **of** the Jews,
26: 6 because of my hope in what **[NIE]** God has promised our fathers
26: 7 because of this hope that **[NIE]** the Jews are accusing me.
27:11 But the centurion, instead of listening to what **[NIE]** Paul said,
27:41 and the stern was broken to pieces **by** the pounding of the surf.
Ro 3: 9 made the charge that Jews and Gentiles alike are all **under** sin.
3:13 tongues practice deceit." "The poison of vipers is **on** their lips."
3:21 has been made known, **to** which the Law and the Prophets testify.
6:14 be your master, because you are not **under** law, but under grace.
6:14 be your master, because you are not under law, but **under** grace.
6:15 Shall we sin because we are not **under** law but under grace?
6:15 Shall we sin because we are not under law but **under** grace?
7:14 that the law is spiritual; but I am unspiritual, sold as a **slave to** sin.
12:21 Do not be overcome by evil, but overcome evil with good.
13: 1 for there is no authority except that which God has **established**.
13: 1 The authorities that exist have been established **by** God.
15:15 you of them again, because of the grace **[NIE]** God gave me
15:24 passing through and to **have** you assist me on my journey there,
16:20 The God of peace will soon crush Satan **under** your feet.
1Co 1:11 some **from** Chloe's household have informed me that there are
2:12 that we may understand what **[NIE]** God has freely given us.
2:15 all things, but he himself is not **subject to** any man's judgment:
4: 3 I care very little if I am judged **by** you or by any human court;
4: 3 I care very little if I am judged by you or **by** any human court;
6:12 is permissible for me"—but I will not be mastered **by** anything.
7:25 but I give a judgment as one who **by** the Lord's mercy is
8: 3 But the man who loves God is known **by** God.
9:20 To those **under** the law I became like one under the law (though I
9:20 To those under the law I became like one **under** the law (though I
9:20 like one under the law (though I myself am not **under** the law),
9:20 I myself am not under the law), so as to win those **under** the law.
10: 1 that our forefathers were all **under** the cloud and that they all
10: 9 not test the Lord, as some of them did—and were killed **by** snakes.
10:10 as some of them did—and were killed **by** the destroying angel.
10:29 For why should my freedom be judged **by** another's conscience?
11:32 When we are judged **by** the Lord, we are being disciplined
14:24 he will be convinced **by** all that he is a sinner and will be judged by
14:24 be convinced by all that he is a sinner and will be judged **by** all,
15:25 For he must reign until he has put all his enemies **under** his feet.
15:27 For *he* "has **put** evérything **under** [*RP5718*] his feet." Now when it
2Co 1: 4 trouble with the comfort we ourselves have received **from** God.
1:16 and then to **have** you send me on my way to Judea.
2: 6 The punishment inflicted on him **by** the majority is sufficient for
2:11 in order that **[NIE]** Satan might not outwit us. For we are not
3: 2 are our letter, written on our hearts, known and read **by** everybody.
3: 3 the **result of** our ministry, written not with ink but with the Spirit
5: 4 so that what is mortal may be swallowed up **by** life.
8:19 he was chosen **by** the churches to accompany us as we carry the

8:19 which **[NIE]** we administer in order to honor the Lord himself
8:20 We want to avoid any criticism of **the way** we administer this
11:24 Five times I received **from** the Jews the forty lashes minus one.
12:11 I ought to have been commended **by** you, for I am not in the least
Gal 1:11 that the gospel **[NIE]** I preached is not something that man made
3:10 All who rely on observing the law are **under** a curse, for it is
3:17 does not set aside the covenant previously established **by** God
3:22 But the Scripture declares that the whole world is a prisoner **of** sin,
3:23 Before this faith came, we were held prisoners **by** the law,
3:25 faith has come, we are no longer **under** the supervision of the law.
4: 2 He is **subject to** guardians and trustees until the time set by his
4: 3 we were in slavery **under** the basic principles of the world.
4: 4 fully come, God sent his Son, born of a woman, born **under** law,
4: 5 to redeem those **under** law, that we might receive the full rights of
4: 9 But now that you know God—or rather are known **by** God—
4:21 Tell me, you who want to be **under** the law, are you not aware of
5:15 each other, watch out or you will be destroyed **by** each other.
5:18 But if you are led by the Spirit, you are not **under** law.
Eph 1:22 And God **placed** all things **under** [*RP5718*] his feet and appointed
2:11 and called "uncircumcised" **by** those who call themselves "the
5:12 For it is shameful even to mention what the disobedient do **[NIE]**
5:13 But everything exposed **by** the light becomes visible,
Php 1:28 without being frightened in any way **by** those who oppose you.
3:12 but I press on to take hold of that for which **[NIE]** Christ Jesus
Col 1:23 and that has been proclaimed to every creature **under** heaven,
2:18 and his **[NIE]** unspiritual mind puffs him up with idle notions.
1Th 1: 4 For we know, brothers loved **by** God, that he has chosen you,
2: 4 we speak as men approved **by** God to be entrusted with the gospel.
2:14 You suffered **from** your own countrymen the same things those
2:14 the same things those churches suffered **from** the Jews,
2Th 2:13 we ought always to thank God for you, brothers loved **by** the Lord,
1Ti 6: 1 All who are **under** the yoke of slavery should consider their
2Ti 2:26 trap of the devil, who has taken them captive to do **[NIE]** his will.
Heb 2: 3 by the Lord, was confirmed to us **by** those who heard him.
3: 4 For every house is built **by** someone, but God is the builder of
5: 4 honor upon himself; he must be called **by** God, just as Aaron was.
5:10 and was designated **by** God to be high priest in the order of
7: 7 And without doubt the lesser person is blessed **by** the greater.
9:19 When **[NIE]** Moses had proclaimed every commandment of the
11:23 By faith Moses' **[NIE]** parents hid him for three months after he
12: 3 Consider him who endured such opposition **from** sinful men,
12: 5 and do not lose heart when **[NIE]** he rebukes you,
Jas 1:14 **by** his own evil desire, he is dragged away and enticed.
2: 3 to the poor man, "You stand there" or "Sit *on the floor* **by** my feet,"
2: 9 you sin and are convicted **by** the law as lawbreakers.
3: 4 Although they are so large and are driven **by** strong winds,
3: 4 they are steered **by** a very small rudder wherever the pilot wants to
3: 6 the whole course of his life on fire, and is itself set on fire **by** hell.
5:12 yes, and your "No," no, or *you will be* **condemned** [+*3213+4406*].
1Pe 2: 4 rejected **by** men but chosen by God and precious to him—
5: 6 Humble yourselves, therefore, **under** God's mighty hand,
2Pe 1:17 and glory from God the Father when the voice came to him **from**
1:21 but men spoke from God as they were carried along **by** the Holy
2: 7 who was distressed **by** the filthy lives of lawless men
2:17 These men are springs without water and mists driven **by** a storm.
3: 2 I want you to recall the words spoken in the past **by** the holy
3Jn 1:12 Demetrius is well spoken of **by** everyone—and even by the truth
1:12 is well spoken of by everyone—and even **by** the truth itself.
Jude 1: 6 these he has kept **in** darkness, bound with everlasting chains for
1:12 are clouds without rain, blown along **by** the wind;
1:17 remember what **[NIE]** the apostles of our Lord Jesus Christ
Rev 6: 8 **by** sword, famine and plague, and **by** the wild beasts of the earth.
6:13 as late figs drop from a fig tree when shaken **by** a strong wind.

5680 ὑποβάλλω, *hypoballō* [1] [√ *5679 + 965*]

secretly persuaded [1]

Ac 6:11 Then *they* **secretly persuaded** some men to say, "We have heard

5681 ὑπογραμμός, *hypogrammos* [1] [√ *5679 + 1211*]

example [1]

1Pe 2:21 because Christ suffered for you, leaving you an **example**,

5682 ὑπόδειγμα, **hypodeigma** [6] [√ 5679 + 1257]

example [4], copies [1], copy [1]

Jn 13:15 I have set you an **example** that you should do as I have done for
Heb 4:11 so that no one will fall by following their **example** of
8: 5 They serve at a sanctuary that is a **copy** and shadow of what is in
9:23 *for* the **copies** of the heavenly things to be purified with these
Jas 5:10 Brothers, as an **example** of patience in the face of suffering,
2Pe 2: 6 and made them an **example** of what is going to happen to the

5683 ὑποδείκνυμι, **hypodeiknymi** [6] [√ 5679 + 1259]

show [3], warned [2], showed [1]

Mt 3: 7 brood of vipers! Who **warned** you to flee from the coming wrath?
Lk 3: 7 brood of vipers! Who **warned** you to flee from the coming wrath?
6:47 *I will* **show** you what he is like who comes to me and hears my
12: 5 But *I will* **show** you whom you should fear: Fear him who,
Ac 9:16 *I will* **show** him how much he must suffer for my name."
20:35 *I* **showed** you that by this kind of hard work we must help the

5684 ὑποδεικνύω, **hypodeiknyō** Not used in UBS/NIV [√ 5679 + 1259]

5685 ὑποδέχομαι, **hypodechomai** [4] [√ 5679 + 1312]

gave lodging to [1], opened home to [1], welcomed into house [1], welcomed [1]

Lk 10:38 a village where a woman named Martha **opened** her **home to** him.
19: 6 So he came down at once and **welcomed** him gladly.
Ac 17: 7 and Jason *has* **welcomed** them *into his* house. They are all defying
Jas 2:25 righteous for what she did *when she* **gave lodging to** the spies

5686 ὑποδέω, **hypodeō** [3] [√ 5679 + 1313]

fitted [1], sandals [+4908] [1], wear [1]

Mk 6: 9 **Wear** sandals but not an extra tunic.
Ac 12: 8 the angel said to him, "Put on your clothes and **sandals** [+4908]."
Eph 6:15 and with your feet **fitted** with the readiness that comes from the

5687 ὑπόδημα, **hypodēma** [10] [√ 5679 + 1313]

sandals [10]

Mt 3:11 who is more powerful than I, whose **sandals** I am not fit to carry.
10:10 take no bag for the journey, or extra tunic, or **sandals** or a staff;
Mk 1: 7 the thongs of whose **sandals** I am not worthy to stoop down
Lk 3:16 I will come, the thongs of whose **sandals** I am not worthy to untie.
10: 4 Do not take a purse or bag or **sandals**; and do not greet anyone on
15:22 and put it on him. Put a ring on his finger and **sandals** on his feet.
22:35 I sent you without purse, bag or **sandals**, did you lack anything?"
Jn 1:27 after me, the thongs of whose **sandals** I am not worthy to untie."
Ac 7:33 "Then the Lord said to him, 'Take off your **sandals**; the place
13:25 he is coming after me, whose **sandals** I am not worthy to untie.'

5688 ὑπόδικος, **hypodikos** [1] [√ 5679 + 1472]

held accountable [+1181] [1]

Ro 3:19 and the whole world **held accountable** [+1181] to God.

5689 ὑποζύγιον, **hypozygion** [2] [√ 5679 + 2413]

donkey beast [1], donkey [1]

Mt 21: 5 gentle and riding on a donkey, on a colt, the foal *of* a **donkey.**' "
2Pe 2:16 But he was rebuked for his wrongdoing *by* a **donkey**—a beast

5690 ὑποζώννυμι, **hypozōnnymi** [1] [√ 5679 + 2439]

passed under to hold together [+5968] [1]

Ac 27:17 *they* **passed** [+5968] ropes **under** the ship itself **to hold** it **together.**

5691 ὑποκάτω, **hypokatō** [11] [√ 5679 + 2848]

under [9], *untranslated* [1], put under [RP5718] [1]

Mt 22:44 "Sit at my right hand until I put your enemies **under** your feet." '
Mk 6:11 listen to you, shake the dust off [NIE] your feet when you leave,
7:28 "but even the dogs **under** the table eat the children's crumbs."
12:36 "Sit at my right hand until I put your enemies **under** your feet." '
Lk 8:16 "No one lights a lamp and hides it in a jar or puts it **under** a bed.
Jn 1:50 "You believe because I told you I saw you **under** the fig tree.
Heb 2: 8 and **put** everything **under** [RP5718] his feet." In putting everything
Rev 5: 3 one in heaven or on earth or **under** the earth could open the scroll
5:13 creature in heaven and on earth and **under** the earth and on the sea,
6: 9 I saw **under** the altar the souls of those who had been slain
12: 1 with the moon **under** her feet and a crown of twelve stars on her

5692 ὑπόκειμαι, **hypokeimai** Not used in UBS/NIV [√ 5679 + 3023]

5693 ὑποκρίνομαι, **hypokrinomai** [1] [√ 5679 + 3212]

pretended [1]

Lk 20:20 a close watch on him, they sent spies, *who* **pretended** to be honest.

5694 ὑπόκρισις, **hypokrisis** [6] [√ 5679 + 3212]

hypocrisy [5], hypocritical [1]

Mt 23:28 but on the inside you are full *of* **hypocrisy** and wickedness.
Mk 12:15 Should we pay or shouldn't we?" But Jesus knew their **hypocrisy.**
Lk 12: 1 your guard against the yeast of the Pharisees, which is **hypocrisy.**
Gal 2:13 so that *by* their **hypocrisy** even Barnabas was led astray.
1Ti 4: 2 Such teachings come through **hypocritical** liars,
1Pe 2: 1 rid yourselves of all malice and all deceit, **hypocrisy,** envy,

5695 ὑποκριτής, **hypokritēs** [17] [√ 5679 + 3212]

hypocrites [15], hypocrite [2]

Mt 6: 2 as the **hypocrites** do in the synagogues and on the streets,
6: 5 "And when you pray, do not be like the **hypocrites,** for they love to
6:16 "When you fast, do not look somber as the **hypocrites** do, for they
7: 5 *You* **hypocrite,** first take the plank out of your own eye, and
15: 7 *You* **hypocrites!** Isaiah was right when he prophesied about you:
22:18 But Jesus, knowing their evil intent, said, "*You* **hypocrites,**
23:13 "Woe to you, teachers of the law and Pharisees, *you* **hypocrites!**
23:15 "Woe to you, teachers of the law and Pharisees, *you* **hypocrites!**
23:23 "Woe to you, teachers of the law and Pharisees, *you* **hypocrites!**
23:25 "Woe to you, teachers of the law and Pharisees, *you* **hypocrites!**
23:27 "Woe to you, teachers of the law and Pharisees, *you* **hypocrites!**
23:29 "Woe to you, teachers of the law and Pharisees, *you* **hypocrites!**
24:51 will cut him to pieces and assign him a place with the **hypocrites,**
Mk 7: 6 "Isaiah was right when he prophesied about you **hypocrites;**
Lk 6:42 *You* **hypocrite,** first take the plank out of your eye, and then you
12:56 **Hypocrites!** You know how to interpret the appearance of the
13:15 The Lord answered him, "*You* **hypocrites!** Doesn't each of you on

5696 ὑπολαμβάνω, **hypolambanō** [5] [√ 5679 + 3284]

suppose [2], hid [1], reply [1], show hospitality to [1]

Lk 7:43 "*I* **suppose** the one who had the bigger debt canceled."
10:30 *In* **reply** Jesus said: "A man was going down from Jerusalem to
Ac 1: 9 up before their very eyes, and a cloud **hid** him from their sight.
2:15 These men are not drunk, as you **suppose.** It's only nine in the
3Jn 1: 8 We ought therefore *to* **show hospitality to** such men so that we

5697 ὑπολαμπάς, **hypolampas** Not used in UBS/NIV [√ 5679 + 3290]

5698 ὑπόλειμμα, **hypoleimma** [1] [√ 5679 + 3309]

remnant [1]

Ro 9:27 be like the sand by the sea, *only* the **remnant** will be saved.

5699 ὑπολείπω, *hypoleipō* [1] [√ *5679 + 3309*]

left [1]

Ro 11: 3 your altars; I *am* the only one **left**, and they are trying to kill me"?

5700 ὑπολήνιον, *hypolēnion* [1] [√ *5679 + 3332*]

pit for the winepress [1]

Mk 12: 1 wall around it, dug a **pit for the winepress** and built a watchtower.

5701 ὑπολιμπάνω, *hypolimpanō* [1] [√ *5679 + 3309*]

leaving [1]

1Pe 2: 21 because Christ suffered for you, **leaving** you an example,

5702 ὑπομένω, *hypomenō* [17] [√ *5679 + 3531*]

endure [4], stands firm [3], endured [2], perseveres [2], endure hardship [1], patient [1], persevered [1], stayed behind [1], stayed [1], stood ground [1]

Mt 10: 22 because of me, but he *who* **stands firm** to the end will be saved.
    24: 13 but he *who* **stands firm** to the end will be saved.
Mk 13: 13 but he *who* **stands firm** to the end will be saved.
Lk   2: 43 the boy Jesus **stayed behind** in Jerusalem, but they were unaware
Ac 17: 14 sent Paul to the coast, but Silas and Timothy **stayed** at Berea.
Ro 12: 12 Be joyful in hope, **patient** in affliction, faithful in prayer.
1Co 13: 7 It always protects, always trusts, always hopes, always **perseveres**.
2Ti 2: 10 Therefore *I* **endure** everything for the sake of the elect, that they
    2: 12 if *we* **endure**, we will also reign with him. If we disown him,
Heb 10: 32 when *you* **stood** *your* **ground** in a great contest in the face of
    12: 2 who for the joy set before him **endured** the cross, scorning its
    12: 3 Consider him *who* **endured** such opposition from sinful men,
    12: 7 **Endure hardship** as discipline; God is treating you as sons.
Jas 1: 12 Blessed is the man who **perseveres** under trial, because when he
    5: 11 As you know, we consider blessed those *who have* **persevered**.
1Pe 2: 20 to your credit if *you* receive a beating for doing wrong and **endure**
    2: 20 But if you suffer for doing good and *you* **endure** it, this is

5703 ὑπομιμνῄσκω, *hypomimnēskō* [7]
[√ *5679 + 3648*]

remind [3], call attention to [1], remembered [1], remind of [1], reminding of [1]

Lk 22: 61 Then Peter **remembered** the word the Lord had spoken to him:
Jn 14: 26 all things and *will* **remind** you of everything I have said to you.
2Ti 2: 14 *Keep* **reminding** them of these things. Warn them before God
Tit 3: 1 **Remind** the people to be subject to rulers and authorities,
2Pe 1: 12 So I will always **remind** you of these things, even though you
3Jn 1: 10 So if I come, *I will* **call attention to** what he is doing,
Jude 1: 5 I want *to* **remind** you that the Lord delivered his people out of

5704 ὑπόμνησις, *hypomnēsis* [3] [√ *5679 + 3648*]

memory [1], reminded [*+3284*] [1], reminders [1]

2Ti 1: 5 *I have been* **reminded** [*+3284*] of your sincere faith, which first
2Pe 1: 13 I think it is right to refresh your **memory** as long as I live in the
    3: 1 I have written both of them as **reminders** to stimulate you to

5705 ὑπομονή, *hypomonē* [32] [√ *5679 + 3531*]

perseverance [13], endurance [8], patient endurance [4], patiently [*+1328*] [1], persevered [*+2400*] [1], persevering [1], persistence [1], standing firm [1], to endure patiently [1], to persevere [1]

Lk 8: 15 who hear the word, retain it, and by **persevering** produce a crop.
    21: 19 By **standing firm** you will gain life.
Ro 2: 7 To those who by **persistence** in doing good seek glory, honor
    5: 3 because we know that suffering produces **perseverance**;
    5: 4 **perseverance**, character; and character, hope.
    8: 25 hope for what we do not yet have, we wait for it **patiently** [*+1328*].
    15: 4 so that through **endurance** and the encouragement of the
    15: 5 May the God who *gives* **endurance** and encouragement give you a

2Co 1: 6 which produces in you **patient endurance** of the same sufferings
    6: 4 in great **endurance**; in troubles, hardships and distresses;
    12: 12 and miracles—were done among you with great **perseverance**.
Col 1: 11 so that you may have great **endurance** and patience,
1Th 1: 3 and your **endurance** inspired by hope in our Lord Jesus Christ.
2Th 1: 4 among God's churches we boast about your **perseverance**
    3: 5 Lord direct your hearts onto God's love and Christ's **perseverance**.
1Ti 6: 11 godliness, faith, love, **endurance** and gentleness.
2Ti 3: 10 my way of life, my purpose, faith, patience, love, **endurance**,
Tit 2: 2 self-controlled, and sound in faith, in love and *in* **endurance**.
Heb 10: 36 You need **to persevere** so that when you have done the will of
    12: 1 and let us run with **perseverance** the race marked out for us.
Jas 1: 3 you know that the testing of your faith develops **perseverance**.
    1: 4 **Perseverance** must finish its work so that you may be mature
    5: 11 You have heard of Job's **perseverance** and have seen what the
2Pe 1: 6 and to knowledge, self-control; and to self-control, **perseverance**;
    1: 6 and to self-control, perseverance; and to **perseverance**, godliness;
Rev 1: 9 and kingdom and **patient endurance** that are ours in Jesus,
    2: 2 I know your deeds, your hard work and your **perseverance**.
    2: 3 *You have* **persevered** [*+2400*] and have endured hardships for my
    2: 19 your deeds, your love and faith, your service and **perseverance**,
    3: 10 Since you have kept my command **to endure patiently**, I will also
    13: 10 This calls for **patient endurance** and faithfulness on the part of the
    14: 12 This calls for **patient endurance** on the part of the saints who

5706 ὑπονοέω, *hyponoeō* [3] [√ *5679 + 3808*]

expected [1], sensed [1], think [1]

Ac 13: 25 John was completing his work, he said: 'Who *do you* **think** I am?
    25: 18 they did not charge him with any of the crimes I *had* **expected**.
    27: 27 when about midnight the sailors **sensed** they were approaching

5707 ὑπόνοια, *hyponoia* [1] [√ *5679 + 3808*]

suspicions [1]

1Ti 6: 4 words that result in envy, strife, malicious talk, evil **suspicions**

5708 ὑποπιάζω, *hypopiazō* Not used in UBS/NIV
[√ *5679 + 3972*]

5709 ὑποπλέω, *hypopleō* [2] [√ *5679 + 4434*]

passed to the lee of [1], sailed to the lee of [1]

Ac 27: 4 From there *we* put out to sea again and **passed to the lee of**
    27: 7 hold our course, *we* **sailed to the lee of** Crete, opposite Salmone.

5710 ὑποπνέω, *hypopneō* [1] [√ *5679 + 4463*]

gentle blow [1]

Ac 27: 13 *When* a **gentle** south wind *began to* **blow**, they thought they had

5711 ὑποπόδιον, *hypopodion* [7] [√ *5679 + 4546*]

footstool [6], feet [1]

Mt 5: 35 or by the earth, for it is his **footstool**;
Lk 20: 43 until I make your enemies a **footstool** for your feet." '
Ac 2: 35 until I make your enemies a **footstool** for your feet." '
    7: 49 " 'Heaven is my throne, and the earth is my **footstool**. What kind of
Heb 1: 13 "Sit at my right hand until I make your enemies a **footstool** for your
    10: 13 Since that time he waits for his enemies to be made his **footstool**,
Jas 2: 3 to the poor man, "You stand there" or "Sit on the floor by my **feet**,"

5712 ὑπόστασις, *hypostasis* [5] [√ *5679 + 2705*]

being [1], confidence [1], confident [1], self-confident [1], sure [1]

2Co 9: 4 about you—would be ashamed of having been so **confident**.
    11: 17 In this **self-confident** boasting I am not talking as the Lord would,
Heb 1: 3 radiance of God's glory and the exact representation of his **being**,
    3: 14 Christ if we hold firmly till the end the **confidence** we had at first.
    11: 1 Now faith is *being* **sure** of what we hope for and certain of what

5713 ὑποστέλλω, *hypostellō* [4] [√ *5679 + 5097*]

hesitated [2], draw back [1], shrinks back [1]

Ac 20:20   You know that *I have* not **hesitated** to preach anything that would
     20:27   For *I have* not **hesitated** to proclaim to you the whole will of God.
Gal 2:12   he began *to* **draw back** and separate himself from the Gentiles
Heb 10:38   by faith. And if *he* **shrinks back**, I will not be pleased with him."

5714 ὑποστολή, *hypostolē* [1] [√ *5679 + 5097*]

shrink back [1]

Heb 10:39   But we are not *of those who* **shrink back** and are destroyed,

5715 ὑποστρέφω, *hypostrephō* [35] [√ *5679 + 5138*]

returned [18], return [4], came back [2], decay [*+1426+1650*] [1],
go back [1], home [1], left [1], on way home [*+1639*] [1], return
[*+1650*] [1], returning home [1], returning [1], turn their backs [1],
went away [1], went back [1]

Lk 1:56   with Elizabeth for about three months and then **returned** home.
     2:20   The shepherds **returned**, glorifying and praising God for all the
     2:43   After the Feast was over, while his parents *were* **returning home**,
     2:45   did not find him, *they* **went back** to Jerusalem to look for him.
     4: 1   **returned** from the Jordan and was led by the Spirit in the desert,
     4:14   Jesus **returned** to Galilee in the power of the Spirit, and news
     7:10   Then the men who had been sent **returned** to the house and found
     8:37   they were overcome with fear. So he got into the boat and **left**.
     8:39   "**Return** [*+1650*] home and tell how much God has done for you."
     8:40   Now when Jesus **returned**, a crowd welcomed him, for they were
     9:10   *When* the apostles **returned**, they reported to Jesus what they had
     10:17   The seventy-two **returned** with joy and said, "Lord,
     11:24   and does not find it. Then it says, '*I will* **return** to the house I left.'
     17:15   One of them, when he saw he was healed, **came back**,
     17:18   Was no one found to **return** and give praise to God except this
     19:12   distant country to have himself appointed king and then *to* **return**.
     23:48   sight saw what took place, *they* beat their breasts and **went away**.
     23:56   Then they *went* **home** and prepared spices and perfumes. But they
     24: 9   *When they* **came back** from the tomb, they told all these things to
     24:33   *They* got up and **returned** at once to Jerusalem. There they found
     24:52   they worshiped him and **returned** to Jerusalem with great joy.
Ac 1:12   Then *they* **returned** to Jerusalem from the hill called the Mount of
     8:25   the word of the Lord, Peter and John **returned** to Jerusalem,
     8:28   and on *his* **way** [*+1639*] **home** was sitting in his chariot reading the
     12:25   *they* **returned** from Jerusalem, taking with them John, also called
     13:13   Perga in Pamphylia, where John left them to **return** to Jerusalem.
     13:34   the dead, never *to* **decay** [*+1426+1650*], is stated in these words:
     14:21   of disciples. Then *they* **returned** to Lystra, Iconium and Antioch,
     20: 3   about to sail for Syria, he decided *to* **go back** through Macedonia.
     21: 6   to each other, we went aboard the ship, and they **returned** home.
     22:17   "*When* I **returned** to Jerusalem and was praying at the temple,
     23:32   the cavalry go on with him, *while they* **returned** to the barracks.
Gal 1:17   I went immediately into Arabia and later **returned** to Damascus.
Heb 7: 1   He met Abraham **returning** from the defeat of the kings
2Pe 2:21   then *to* **turn their backs** on the sacred command that was passed

5716 ὑποστρωννύω, *hypostrōnnyō* [1]
[√ *5679 + 5143*]

spread [1]

Lk 19:36   As he went along, *people* **spread** their cloaks on the road.

5717 ὑποταγή, *hypotagē* [4] [√ *5679 + 5435*]

give in [*+1634+3836*] [1], obedience [1], obey [*+2400*] [1],
submission [1]

2Co 9:13   men will praise God for the **obedience** that accompanies your
Gal 2: 5   *We did* not **give in** [*+1634+3836*] to them for a moment, so that
1Ti 2:11   A woman should learn in quietness and full **submission**.
     3: 4   and see that his children **obey** [*+2400*] him with proper respect.

5718 ὑποτάσσω, *hypotassō* [38] [√ *5679 + 5435*]

submit [13], subject [4], put under [3], subjected [3], submissive
[3], in submission [2], bring under control [1], done^s [1], made
subject [1], obedient [1], placed under [*RP5679*] [1], put under
[*RP5679*] [1], put under [*RP5691*] [1], putting under [1], subject to
the control [1], submits [1]

Lk 2:51   he went down to Nazareth with them and was **obedient** to them.
     10:17   and said, "Lord, even the demons **submit** to us in your name."
     10:20   However, do not rejoice that the spirits **submit** to you, but rejoice
Ro 8: 7   is hostile to God. *It does* not **submit** to God's law, nor can it do so.
     8:20   For the creation *was* **subjected** to frustration, not by its own
     8:20   own choice, but by the will of the one *who* **subjected** it, in hope
     10: 3   to establish their own, *they did* not **submit** to God's righteousness.
     13: 1   Everyone *must* **submit** *himself* to the governing authorities,
     13: 5   it is necessary *to* **submit** to the authorities, not only because of
1Co 14:32   The spirits of prophets *are* **subject to the control** of prophets.
     14:34   not allowed to speak, but *must be* **in submission**, as the Law says.
     15:27   For *he* "*has* **put** [*RP5679*] everything **under** his feet." Now when it
     15:27   Now when it says that "everything" *has been* **put under** him,
     15:27   does not include God himself, who **put** everything **under** Christ.
     15:28   When *he has* **done^s** this, then the Son himself will be made
     15:28   then the Son himself *will be* **made subject** to him who put
     15:28   will be made subject to him *who* **put** everything **under** him,
     16:16   to **submit** to such as these and to everyone who joins in the work,
Eph 1:22   And God **placed** [*RP5679*] all things **under** his feet and appointed
     5:21   **Submit** to one another out of reverence for Christ.
     5:24   Now as the church **submits** to Christ, so also wives should submit
Php 3:21   the power that enables him *to* **bring** everything **under** his **control**,
Col 3:18   Wives, **submit** to your husbands, as is fitting in the Lord.
Tit 2: 5   to be busy at home, to be kind, and to be **subject** to their husbands,
     2: 9   Teach slaves *to be* **subject** to their masters in everything,
     3: 1   Remind the people *to be* **subject** to rulers and authorities,
Heb 2: 5   It is not to angels *that he has* **subjected** the world to come,
     2: 8   and **put** everything **under** [*RP5691*] his feet." In putting everything
     2: 8   In **putting** everything **under** him, God left nothing that is not
     2: 8   to him. Yet at present we do not see everything **subject** to him.
     12: 9   How much more *should we* **submit** to the Father of our spirits
Jas 4: 7   **Submit** *yourselves*, then, to God. Resist the devil, and he will flee
1Pe 2:13   **Submit** *yourselves* for the Lord's sake to every authority instituted
     2:18   Slaves, **submit** *yourselves* to your masters with all respect,
     3: 1   Wives, in the same way *be* **submissive** to your husbands so that,
     3: 5   *They were* **submissive** to their own husbands,
     3:22   with angels, authorities and powers **in submission** to him.
     5: 5   in the same way *be* **submissive** to those who are older.

5719 ὑποτίθημι, *hypotithēmi* [2] [√ *5679 + 5502*]

point out [1], risked lives [*+3836+5549*] [1]

Ro 16: 4   They **risked** [*+3836+5549*] their **lives** for me. Not only I but all the
1Ti 4: 6   *If you* **point** these things **out** to the brothers, you will be a good

5720 ὑποτρέχω, *hypotrechō* [1] [√ *5679 + 5556*]

passed to the lee of [1]

Ac 27:16   *As we* **passed to the lee of** a small island called Cauda, we were

5721 ὑποτύπωσις, *hypotypōsis* [2] [√ *5679 + 5597*]

example [1], pattern [1]

1Ti 1:16   Christ Jesus might display his unlimited patience as an **example**
2Ti 1:13   keep as the **pattern** of sound teaching, with faith and love in Christ

5722 ὑποφέρω, *hypopherō* [3] [√ *5679 + 5770*]

bears up under [1], endured [1], stand up under [1]

1Co 10:13   he will also provide a way out so that you can **stand up under** it.
2Ti 3:11   to me in Antioch, Iconium and Lystra, the persecutions *I* **endured**.
1Pe 2:19   For it is commendable if a *man* **bears up under** the pain of unjust

5723 ὑποχωρέω, *hypochōreō* [2] [√ 5679 + 6003]

withdrew [+1639] [1], withdrew [1]

Lk 5:16 But Jesus *often* **withdrew** [+1639] to lonely places and prayed.
    9:10 and *they* **withdrew** by themselves to a town called Bethsaida,

5724 ὑπωπιάζω, *hypōpiazō* [2] [√ 5679 + 3972]

beat [1], wear out [1]

Lk 18: 5 so that *she* won't eventually **wear** me **out** with her coming!' "
1Co 9:27 *I* **beat** my body and make it my slave so that after I have preached

5725 ὗς, *hys* [1]

sow [1]

2Pe 2:22 "A **sow** that is washed goes back to her wallowing in the mud.'

5726 ὑσσός, *hyssos*   Not used in UBS/NIV

5727 ὕσσωπος, *hyssōpos* [2]

branches of hyssop [1], stalk of the hyssop plant [1]

Jn 19:29 put the sponge on a **stalk of the hyssop plant**, and lifted it to Jesus'
Heb 9:19 together with water, scarlet wool and **branches of hyssop**,

5728 ὑστερέω, *hystereō* [16] [√ 5731]

lack [4], inferior to [2], destitute [1], fall short [1], fallen short [1], gone [1], lacked [1], living in want [1], misses [1], need [1], needed [1], worse [1]

Mt 19:20 "All these I have kept," the young man said. "What *do I* still **lack**?"
Mk 10:21 "One thing you **lack**," he said. "Go, sell everything you have
Lk 15:14 a severe famine in that whole country, and he began *to be in* **need**.
   22:35 I sent you without purse, bag or sandals, *did you* **lack** anything?"
Jn 2: 3 *When* the wine *was* **gone**, Jesus' mother said to him, "They have no
Ro 3:23 for all have sinned and **fall short** of the glory of God,
1Co 1: 7 Therefore you *do* not **lack** any spiritual gift as you eagerly wait for
    8: 8 to God; *we are* no **worse** if we do not eat, and no better if we do.
   12:24 of the body and has given greater honor *to* the parts *that* **lacked** it,
2Co 11: 5 But I do not think I *am* in the least **inferior to** those
   11: 9 And when I was with you and **needed** *something*, I was not a
   12:11 for *I am* not in the least **inferior to** the "super-apostles," even
Php 4:12 whether well fed or hungry, whether **living** in plenty or **in want**.
Heb 4: 1 let us be careful that none of you be found *to have* **fallen short** of
   11:37 in sheepskins and goatskins, **destitute**, persecuted and mistreated—
   12:15 See to it that no one **misses** the grace of God and that no bitter root

5729 ὑστέρημα, *hysterēma* [9] [√ 5731]

lacking [3], need [2], could not give [1], needed [1], needs [1], poverty [1]

Lk 21: 4 but she out of her **poverty** put in all she had to live on."
1Co 16:17 because they have supplied what was **lacking** from you.
2Co 8:14 At the present time your plenty will supply what they **need**,
    8:14 they need, so that in turn their plenty will supply what you **need**.
    9:12 This service that you perform is not only supplying the **needs** of
   11: 9 the brothers who came from Macedonia supplied what I **needed**.
Php 2:30 risking his life to make up for the help you **could not give** me.
Col 1:24 and I fill up in my flesh what is still **lacking** in regard to Christ's
1Th 3:10 we may see you again and supply what is **lacking** in your faith.

5730 ὑστέρησις, *hysterēsis* [2] [√ 5731]

need [1], poverty [1]

Mk 12:44 but she, out of her **poverty**, put in everything—all she had to live
Php 4:11 I am not saying this because I am in **need**, for I have learned to be

5731 ὕστερος, *hysteros* [12 / 13] [→ 935, 5728, 5729, 5730]

later [5], finally [2], *untranslated* [1], after [1], finally [+4246] [1], last of all [1], later on [1], then [1]

Mt 4: 2 **After** fasting forty days and forty nights, he was hungry.
   21:29 " 'I will not,' he answered, but **later** he changed his mind and went.
   21:32 after you saw this, you did not repent and **[RPG]** believe him.
   21:37 **Last of all**, he sent his son to them. 'They will respect my son,'
   22:27 **Finally** [+4246], the woman died.
   25:11 "**Later** the others also came. 'Sir! Sir!' they said. 'Open the door
   26:60 many false witnesses came forward. **Finally** two came forward
Mk 16:14 **Later** Jesus appeared to the Eleven as they were eating; he rebuked
Lk 20:32 **Finally**, the woman died too.
Jn 13:36 I am going, you cannot follow now, but you will follow **later**."
1Ti 4: 1 The Spirit clearly says that in **later** times some will abandon the
Heb 10:17 **Then** [UBS-] he adds: "Their sins and lawless acts I will remember
   12:11 **Later on**, however, it produces a harvest of righteousness

5732 ὑφαίνω, *hyphainō*   Not used in UBS/NIV [→ 5733]

5733 ὑφαντός, *hyphantos* [1] [√ 5732]

woven [1]

Jn 19:23 garment was seamless, **woven** in one piece from top to bottom.

5734 ὑψηλός, *hypsēlos* [11 / 12] [√ 5737]

high [6], arrogant [+5858] [1], exalted above [1], heaven [1], highly valued [+3836] [1], mighty [1], proud [+3836+5858] [1]

Mt 4: 8 the devil took him to a very **high** mountain and showed him all the
   17: 1 brother of James, and led them up a **high** mountain by themselves.
Mk 9: 2 James and John with him and led them up a **high** mountain,
Lk 4: 5 The devil led him up to a **high** [UBS-] place and showed him in
   16:15 What is **highly** [+3836] **valued** among men is detestable in God's
Ac 13:17 stay in Egypt, with **mighty** power he led them out of that country,
Ro 11:20 of unbelief, and you stand by faith. *Do* not *be* **arrogant** [+5858],
   12:16 *Do* not *be* **proud** [+3836+5858], but be willing to associate with
Heb 1: 3 for sins, he sat down at the right hand of the Majesty in **heaven**.
    7:26 blameless, pure, set apart from sinners, **exalted above** the heavens.
Rev 21:10 And he carried me away in the Spirit to a mountain great and **high**,
   21:12 It had a great, **high** wall with twelve gates, and with twelve angels

5735 ὑψηλοφρονέω, *hypsēlophroneō* [1] [√ 5737 + 5856]

arrogant [1]

1Ti 6:17 present world not *to be* **arrogant** nor to put their hope in wealth,

5736 ὕψιστος, *hypsistos* [13] [√ 5737]

Most High [9], highest [4]

Mt 21: 9 he who comes in the name of the Lord!" "Hosanna in the **highest**!"
Mk 5: 7 "What do you want with me, Jesus, Son of the **Most High** God?
   11:10 coming kingdom of our father David!" "Hosanna in the **highest**!"
Lk 1:32 He will be great and will be called the Son *of* the **Most High**.
    1:35 upon you, and the power *of* the **Most High** will overshadow you.
    1:76 And you, my child, will be called a prophet *of* the **Most High**;
    2:14 "Glory to God in the **highest**, and on earth peace to men on whom
    6:35 your reward will be great, and you will be sons *of* the **Most High**,
    8:28 "What do you want with me, Jesus, Son of the **Most High** God?
   19:38 the name of the Lord!" "Peace in heaven and glory in the **highest**!"
Ac 7:48 "However, the **Most High** does not live in houses made by men.
   16:17 of us, shouting, "These men are servants *of* the **Most High** God,
Heb 7: 1 Melchizedek was king of Salem and priest of God **Most High**.

5737 ὕψος, *hypsos* [6] [→ 5671, 5734, 5735, 5736, 5738, 5739]

high [3], heaven [1], high position [1], on high [1]

Lk 1:78 of our God, by which the rising sun will come to us from **heaven**
   24:49 in the city until you have been clothed with power from **on high**."

Eph	3:18	to grasp how wide and long and **high** and deep is the love of
	4: 8	"When he ascended on **high**, he led captives in his train and gave
Jas	1: 9	in humble circumstances ought to take pride in his **high position**.
Rev	21:16	it to be 12,000 stadia in length, and as wide and **high** as it is long.

5738 ὑψόω, hypsoō [20] [√ *5737*]

lifted up [8], exalted [5], exalts [3], lift up [2], elevate [1], made prosper [1]

Mt	11:23	And you, Capernaum, *will you be* **lifted up** to the skies? No,
	23:12	For whoever **exalts** himself will be humbled, and whoever
	23:12	will be humbled, and whoever humbles himself *will be* **exalted**.
Lk	1:52	down rulers from their thrones but *has* **lifted up** the humble.
	10:15	And you, Capernaum, *will you be* **lifted up** to the skies? No,
	14:11	For everyone who **exalts** himself will be humbled, and he who
	14:11	and he who humbles himself *will be* **exalted**."
	18:14	For everyone who **exalts** himself will be humbled, and he who
	18:14	will be humbled, and he who humbles himself *will be* **exalted**."
Jn	3:14	Just as Moses **lifted up** the snake in the desert, so the Son of Man
	3:14	up the snake in the desert, so the Son of Man must *be* **lifted up**,
	8:28	So Jesus said, "When *you have* **lifted up** the Son of Man, then you
	12:32	But I, when *I am* **lifted up** from the earth, will draw all men to
	12:34	so how can you say, 'The Son of Man must *be* **lifted up**'?
Ac	2:33	**Exalted** to the right hand of God, he has received from the Father
	5:31	God **exalted** him to his own right hand as Prince and Savior that he
	13:17	he **made** the people **prosper** during their stay in Egypt, with
2Co	11: 7	Was it a sin for me to lower myself in order to **elevate** you by
Jas	4:10	Humble yourselves before the Lord, and *he will* **lift** you **up**.
1Pe	5: 6	under God's mighty hand, that *he may* **lift** you **up** in due time.

5739 ὕψωμα, hypsōma [2] [√ *5737*]

height [1], pretension [1]

Ro	8:39	neither **height** nor depth, nor anything else in all creation,
2Co	10: 5	and every **pretension** that sets itself up against the knowledge of

Φ, Ph

5740 φ, ph   Not used in UBS/NIV

5741 φάγος, phagos [2] [→ *4709; cf. 2266*]

glutton [+*476*] [2]

Mt	11:19	and they say, 'Here is a **glutton** [+*476*] and a drunkard,
Lk	7:34	and you say, 'Here is a **glutton** [+*476*] and a drunkard,

5742 φαιλόνης, phailonēs [1] [→ *5769*]

cloak [1]

2Ti	4:13	bring the **cloak** that I left with Carpus at Troas, and my scrolls,

5743 φαίνω, phainō [31] [→ *428, 905, 906, 907, 908, 1421, 1871, 1872, 2210, 2211, 2212, 2213, 2216, 2993, 4733, 5193, 5661, 5662, 5745, 5746, 5747, 5748, 5749, 5751, 5752, 5753, 5762?, 5763?, 5833, 5890, 5891, 5892, 5893, 5894, 5895*]

appeared [7], shine [3], shining [3], seen [2], visible [2], appear as [1], appear [1], appears [1], become [1], gave light [1], look [1], obvious [1], recognized [1], see [1], seemed [1], shines [1], show [1], think [1], without light [+*3590*] [1]

Mt	1:20	an angel of the Lord **appeared** to him in a dream and said,
	2: 7	and found out from them the exact time the star *had* **appeared**.
	2:13	had gone, an angel of the Lord **appeared** to Joseph in a dream.
	2:19	an angel of the Lord **appeared** in a dream to Joseph in Egypt
	6: 5	in the synagogues and on the street corners to *be* **seen** by men.
	6:16	for they disfigure their faces to **show** men they are fasting.
	6:18	so that *it will* not *be* **obvious** to men that you are fasting, but only
	9:33	and said, "Nothing like this *has* ever *been* **seen** in Israel."

	13:26	wheat sprouted and formed heads, then the weeds also **appeared**.
	23:27	which **look** beautiful on the outside but on the inside are full of
	23:28	on the outside you **appear** to people **as** righteous but on the inside
	24:27	For as lightning that comes from the east *is* **visible** even in the
	24:30	"At that time the sign of the Son of Man *will* **appear** in the sky,
Mk	14:64	"You have heard the blasphemy. What *do you* **think**?" They all
	16: 9	he **appeared** first to Mary Magdalene, out of whom he had driven
Lk	9: 8	others that Elijah *had* **appeared**, and still others that one of the
	24:11	the women, because their words **seemed** to them like nonsense.
Jn	1: 5	The light **shines** in the darkness, but the darkness has not
	5:35	John was a lamp that burned and **gave light**, and you chose for a
Ro	7:13	But in order that sin *might be* **recognized** as sin, it produced death
2Co	13: 7	Not *that people will* **see** that we have stood the test but that you
Php	2:15	depraved generation, in which *you* **shine** like stars in the universe
Heb	11: 3	so that what is seen was not made out of *what was* **visible**.
Jas	4:14	You are a mist that **appears** for a little while and then vanishes.
1Pe	4:18	to be saved, what *will* **become** of the ungodly and the sinner?'
2Pe	1:19	as to a light **shining** in a dark place, until the day dawns
1Jn	2: 8	the darkness is passing and the true light *is* already **shining**.
Rev	1:16	His face was like the sun **shining** in all its brilliance.
	8:12	A third of the day was **without light** [+*3590*], and also a third of
	18:23	The light of a lamp *will* never **shine** in you again. The voice of
	21:23	The city does not need the sun or the moon to **shine** on it,

5744 Φάλεκ, Phalek [1]

Peleg [1]

Lk	3:35	the son of Serug, the son of Reu, the son *of* **Peleg**, the son of Eber,

5745 φανερός, phaneros [18] [√ *5743*]

open [2], tell [+*4472*] [2], clear [1], disclosed [1], know [+*1639*] [1], knows [1], laid bare [1], learned about [+*1181*] [1], obvious [1], outward [+*1877+3836*] [1], outwardly [+*1877+3836*] [1], plain [1], see [1], show [+*1181*] [1], shown for what it is [1], well known [1]

Mt	12:16	warning them not to **tell** [+*4472*] who he was.
Mk	3:12	But he gave them strict orders not to **tell** [+*4472*] who he was.
	4:22	whatever is concealed is meant to be brought out into the **open**.
	6:14	Herod heard about this, for Jesus' name had become **well known**.
Lk	8:17	For there is nothing hidden that will not be **disclosed**, and nothing
	8:17	concealed that will not be known or brought out into the **open**.
Ac	4:16	"Everybody living in Jerusalem **knows** they have done an
	7:13	who he was, and Pharaoh **learned** [+*1181*] about Joseph's family.
Ro	1:19	since what may be known about God is **plain** to them,
	2:28	A man is not a Jew if he is only one **outwardly** [+*1877+3836*],
	2:28	nor is circumcision merely **outward** [+*1877+3836*] and physical.
1Co	3:13	his work will be **shown for what it is**, because the Day will bring
	11:19	No doubt there have to be differences among you to **show** [+*1181*]
	14:25	and the secrets of his heart will be **laid bare**. So he will fall down
Gal	5:19	The acts of the sinful nature are **obvious**: sexual immorality,
Php	1:13	it has become **clear** throughout the whole palace guard and to
1Ti	4:15	yourself wholly to them, so that everyone may **see** your progress.
1Jn	3:10	This is how we **know** [+*1639*] who the children of God are

5746 φανερόω, phaneroō [49] [√ *5743*]

appeared [9], revealed [9], appears [4], disclosed [3], appear [2], made known [2], plain [2], show [2], showed [2], appeared [+*1571*] [1], brought to light [1], cover [+*3590*] [1], displayed [1], expose [1], happened [1], made clear [1], made plain [1], makes visible [1], proclaim clearly [1], see [1], seen plainly [1], spreads [1], visible [1]

Mk	4:22	For whatever is hidden is meant to *be* **disclosed**, and whatever is
	16:12	Afterward Jesus **appeared** in a different form to two of them while
	16:14	Later Jesus **appeared** to the Eleven as they were eating;
Jn	1:31	came baptizing with water was that he might be **revealed** to Israel."
	2:11	He thus **revealed** his glory, and his disciples put their faith in him.
	3:21	so that *it may be* **seen plainly** that what he has done has been done
	7: 4	Since you are doing these things, **show** yourself to the world."
	9: 3	so that the work of God *might be* **displayed** in his life.
	17: 6	"*I have* **revealed** you to those whom you gave me out of the
	21: 1	Afterward Jesus **appeared** [+*1571*] again to his disciples,

21: 1 to his disciples, by the Sea of Tiberias. *It* **happened** this way:
21:14 This was now the third time Jesus **appeared** to his disciples after
Ro 1:19 God is plain to them, because God *has* made it **plain** to them.
3:21 apart from law, *has been* **made known**, to which the Law
16:26 but now **revealed** and made known through the prophetic writings
1Co 4: 5 is hidden in darkness and *will* **expose** the motives of men's hearts.
2Co 2:14 and through us **spreads** everywhere the fragrance of the
3: 3 *You* **show** that you are a letter from Christ, the result of our
4:10 so that the life of Jesus *may* also *be* **revealed** in our body.
4:11 for Jesus' sake, so that his life *may be* **revealed** in our mortal body.
5:10 For we must all **appear** before the judgment seat of Christ,
5:11 *What we are is* **plain** to God, and I hope it is also plain to your
5:11 are is plain to God, and I hope it *is* also **plain** to your conscience.
7:12 but rather that before God you *could* **see** for yourselves how
11: 6 *We have* **made** this perfectly **clear** to you in every way.
Eph 5:13 But everything exposed by the light *becomes* **visible**,
5:14 for it is light that **makes** everything **visible**. This is why it is said:
Col 1:26 hidden for ages and generations, but *is* now **disclosed** to the saints.
3: 4 When Christ, who is your life, **appears**, then you also will appear
3: 4 is your life, appears, then you also *will* **appear** with him in glory.
4: 4 Pray that *I may* **proclaim** it **clearly**, as I should.
1Ti 3:16 He **appeared** in a body, was vindicated by the Spirit, was seen by
2Ti 1:10 but *it has* now *been* **revealed** through the appearing of our Savior,
Tit 1: 3 and at his appointed season he **brought** his word **to light** through
Heb 9: 8 *had* not yet *been* **disclosed** as long as the first tabernacle was still
9:26 But now *he has* **appeared** once for all at the end of the ages to do
1Pe 1:20 of the world, but *was* **revealed** in these last times for your sake.
5: 4 And *when* the Chief Shepherd **appears**, you will receive the crown
1Jn 1: 2 The life **appeared**; we have seen it and testify to it, and we
1: 2 the eternal life, which was with the Father and *has* **appeared** to us.
2:19 with us; but their going **showed** that none of them belonged to us.
2:28 so that when *he* **appears** we may be confident and unashamed
3: 2 of God, and what we will be *has* not yet *been* **made known**.
3: 2 But we know that when *he* **appears**, we shall be like him,
3: 5 But you know that he **appeared** so that he might take away our
3: 8 The reason the Son of God **appeared** was to destroy the devil's
4: 9 This is how God **showed** his love among us: He sent his one
Rev 3:18 to wear, so *you can* **cover** [+*3590*] your shameful nakedness;
15: 4 worship before you, for your righteous acts *have been* **revealed**."

5747 φανερῶς, *phaneros* [3] [√ *5743*]

distinctly [1], openly [1], publicly [1]

Mk 1:45 Jesus could no longer enter a town **openly** but stayed outside in
Jn 7:10 had left for the Feast, he went also, not **publicly**, but in secret.
Ac 10: 3 He **distinctly** saw an angel of God, who came to him and said,

5748 φανέρωσις, *phanerōsis* [2] [√ *5743*]

manifestation [1], setting forth plainly [1]

1Co 12: 7 Now to each one the **manifestation** of the Spirit is given for the
2Co 4: 2 *by* **setting forth** the truth **plainly** we commend ourselves to every

5749 φανός, *phanos* [1] [√ *5743*]

torches [1]

Jn 18: 3 and Pharisees. They were carrying **torches**, lanterns and weapons.

5750 Φανουήλ, *Phanouēl* [1]

Phanuel [1]

Lk 2:36 a prophetess, Anna, the daughter *of* **Phanuel**, of the tribe of Asher.

5751 φαντάζω, *phantazō* [1] [√ *5743*]

sight [1]

Heb 12:21 The **sight** was so terrifying that Moses said, "I am trembling with

5752 φαντασία, *phantasia* [1] [√ *5743*]

pomp [1]

Ac 25:23 The next day Agrippa and Bernice came with great **pomp**

5753 φάντασμα, *phantasma* [2] [√ *5743*]

ghost [2]

Mt 14:26 walking on the lake, they were terrified. "It's a **ghost**," they said,
Mk 6:49 they saw him walking on the lake, they thought he was a **ghost**.

5754 φάραγξ, *pharanx* [1]

valley [1]

Lk 3: 5 Every **valley** shall be filled in, every mountain and hill made low.

5755 Φαραώ, *Pharaō* [5]

Pharaoh [3], Pharaoh's [2]

Ac 7:10 and enabled him to gain the goodwill *of* **Pharaoh** king of Egypt;
7:13 brothers who he was, and **Pharaoh** learned about Joseph's family.
7:21 **Pharaoh's** daughter took him and brought him up as her own son.
Ro 9:17 For the Scripture says *to* **Pharaoh**: "I raised you up for this very
Heb 11:24 grown up, refused to be known as the son *of* **Pharaoh's** daughter.

5756 Φαρές, *Phares* [3]

Perez [3]

Mt 1: 3 Judah the father of **Perez** and Zerah, whose mother was Tamar,
1: 3 was Tamar, **Perez** the father of Hezron, Hezron the father of Ram,
Lk 3:33 son of Ram, the son of Hezron, the son *of* **Perez**, the son of Judah,

5757 Φαρισαῖος, *Pharisaios* [98]

ἀρχιερεῖς καὶ Φαρισαῖοι, (chief priests and Pharisees) [7]
     Mt 21:45; 27:62; Jn 7:32,45; 11:47,57; 18:3

γραμματεῖς καὶ Φαρισαῖοι, (teachers of the law and
Pharisees) [19] Mt 5:20; 12:38; 15:1; 23:2,13,15,23,25,27,29; Mk
2:16; 7:1; Lk 5:21,30; 6:7; 11:53; 15:2; Jn 8:3; Ac 23:9

Φαρισαῖοι καὶ Σαδδουκαῖοι, (Pharisees and Sadducees) [6]
     Mt 3:7; 16:1,6,11,12; Ac 23:7

Pharisees [84], Pharisee [12], Pharisee's [2]

Mt 3: 7 But when he saw many *of* the **Pharisees** and Sadducees coming to
5:20 you that unless your righteousness surpasses that *of* the **Pharisees**
9:11 When the **Pharisees** saw this, they asked his disciples, "Why does
9:14 and asked him, "How is it that we and the **Pharisees** fast,
9:34 But the **Pharisees** said, "It is by the prince of demons that he drives
12: 2 When the **Pharisees** saw this, they said to him, "Look!
12:14 But the **Pharisees** went out and plotted how they might kill Jesus.
12:24 But when the **Pharisees** heard this, they said, "It is only by
12:38 Then some of the **Pharisees** and teachers of the law said to him,
15: 1 Then *some* **Pharisees** and teachers of the law came to Jesus from
15:12 "Do you know that the **Pharisees** were offended when they heard
16: 1 The **Pharisees** and Sadducees came to Jesus and tested him by
16: 6 "Be on your guard against the yeast *of* the **Pharisees**
16:11 But be on your guard against the yeast *of* the **Pharisees**
16:12 in bread, but against the teaching *of* the **Pharisees** and Sadducees.
19: 3 *Some* **Pharisees** came to him to test him. They asked, "Is it lawful
21:45 When the chief priests and the **Pharisees** heard Jesus' parables,
22:15 Then the **Pharisees** went out and laid plans to trap him in his
22:34 that Jesus had silenced the Sadducees, the **Pharisees** got together.
22:41 While the **Pharisees** were gathered together, Jesus asked them,
23: 2 "The teachers of the law and the **Pharisees** sit in Moses' seat.
23:13 "Woe to you, teachers of the law and **Pharisees**, you hypocrites!
23:15 "Woe to you, teachers of the law and **Pharisees**, you hypocrites!
23:23 "Woe to you, teachers of the law and **Pharisees**, you hypocrites!
23:25 "Woe to you, teachers of the law and **Pharisees**, you hypocrites!
23:26 Blind **Pharisee**! First clean the inside of the cup and dish,
23:27 "Woe to you, teachers of the law and **Pharisees**, you hypocrites!
23:29 "Woe to you, teachers of the law and **Pharisees**, you hypocrites!
27:62 Preparation Day, the chief priests and the **Pharisees** went to Pilate.
Mk 2:16 When the teachers of the law who were **Pharisees** saw him eating
2:18 Now John's disciples and the **Pharisees** were fasting. Some people
2:18 that John's disciples and the disciples *of* the **Pharisees** are fasting,
2:24 The **Pharisees** said to him, "Look, why are they doing what is
3: 6 Then the **Pharisees** went out and began to plot with the Herodians
7: 1 The **Pharisees** and some of the teachers of the law who had come

7: 3 (The **Pharisees** and all the Jews do not eat unless they give their
7: 5 So the **Pharisees** and teachers of the law asked Jesus, "Why don't
8:11 The **Pharisees** came and began to question Jesus. To test him,
8:15 "Watch out for the yeast *of* the **Pharisees** and that of Herod."
10: 2 *Some* **Pharisees** came and tested him by asking, "Is it lawful for a
12:13 Later they sent some *of* the **Pharisees** and Herodians to Jesus to
Lk 5:17 One day as he was teaching, **Pharisees** and teachers of the law,
5:21 The **Pharisees** and the teachers of the law began thinking to
5:30 But the **Pharisees** and the teachers of the law who belonged to
5:33 often fast and pray, and so do the disciples *of* the **Pharisees**,
6: 2 Some *of* the **Pharisees** asked, "Why are you doing what is unlawful
6: 7 The **Pharisees** and the teachers of the law were looking for a
7:30 But the **Pharisees** and experts in the law rejected God's purpose
7:36 Now one *of* the **Pharisees** invited Jesus to have dinner with him,
7:36 so he went to the **Pharisee's** house and reclined at the table.
7:37 in that town learned that Jesus was eating at the **Pharisee's** house,
7:39 When the **Pharisee** who had invited him saw this, he said to
11:37 had finished speaking, a **Pharisee** invited him to eat with him;
11:38 But the **Pharisee**, noticing that Jesus did not first wash before the
11:39 "Now then, you **Pharisees** clean the outside of the cup and dish,
11:42 "Woe to you **Pharisees**, because you give God a tenth of your mint,
11:43 "Woe to you **Pharisees**, because you love the most ʿimportant seats
11:53 the **Pharisees** and the teachers of the law began to oppose him
12: 1 "Be on your guard against the yeast *of* the **Pharisees**, which is
13:31 At that time some **Pharisees** came to Jesus and said to him,
14: 1 when Jesus went to eat in the house of a prominent **Pharisee**,
14: 3 Jesus asked the **Pharisees** and experts in the law, "Is it lawful to
15: 2 But the **Pharisees** and the teachers of the law muttered, "This man
16:14 The **Pharisees**, who loved money, heard all this and were sneering
17:20 having been asked by the **Pharisees** when the kingdom of God
18:10 to the temple to pray, one a **Pharisee** and the other a tax collector.
18:11 The **Pharisee** stood up and prayed about himself: 'God, I thank
19:39 Some *of the* **Pharisees** in the crowd said to Jesus, "Teacher,
Jn 1:24 Now some **Pharisees** who had been sent
3: 1 Now there was a man of the **Pharisees** named Nicodemus,
4: 1 The **Pharisees** heard that Jesus was gaining and baptizing more
7:32 The **Pharisees** heard the crowd whispering such things about him.
7:32 chief priests and the **Pharisees** sent temple guards to arrest him.
7:45 the temple guards went back to the chief priests and **Pharisees**,
7:47 "You mean he has deceived you also?" the **Pharisees** retorted.
7:48 "Has any of the rulers or of the **Pharisees** believed in him?"
8: 3 and the **Pharisees** brought in a woman caught in adultery.
8:13 The **Pharisees** challenged him, "Here you are, appearing as your
9:13 They brought to the **Pharisees** the man who had been blind.
9:15 Therefore the **Pharisees** also asked him how he had received his
9:16 Some of the **Pharisees** said, "This man is not from God, for he does
9:40 Some **Pharisees** who were with him heard him say this and asked,
11:46 But some of them went to the **Pharisees** and told them what Jesus
11:47 chief priests and the **Pharisees** called a meeting of the Sanhedrin.
11:57 and **Pharisees** had given orders that if anyone found out where
12:19 So the **Pharisees** said to one another, "See, this is getting us
12:42 because of the **Pharisees** they would not confess their faith for fear
18: 3 of soldiers and some officials from the chief priests and **Pharisees**.
Ac 5:34 But a **Pharisee** named Gamaliel, a teacher of the law, who was
15: 5 the believers who belonged to the party *of* the **Pharisees** stood up
23: 6 that some of them were Sadducees and the others **Pharisees**,
23: 6 the Sanhedrin, "My brothers, I am a **Pharisee**, the son of a Pharisee.
23: 6 the Sanhedrin, "My brothers, I am a Pharisee, the son *of* a **Pharisee**."
23: 7 a dispute broke out *between* the **Pharisees** and the Sadducees,
23: 8 neither angels nor spirits, but the **Pharisees** acknowledge them all.)
23: 9 and some of the teachers of the law who were **Pharisees** stood up
26: 5 according to the strictest sect of our religion, I lived as a **Pharisee**.
Php 3: 5 a Hebrew of Hebrews; in regard to the law, a **Pharisee**;

5758 φαρμακεία, *pharmakeia* [2] [√ 5760]

magic spell [1], witchcraft [1]

Gal 5:20 idolatry and **witchcraft**; hatred, discord, jealousy, fits of rage,
Rev 18:23 great men. By your **magic spell** all the nations were led astray.

5759 φαρμακεύς, *pharmakeus* Not used in UBS/NIV
[√ 5760]

5760 φάρμακον, *pharmakon* [1] [→ 5758, 5759, 5761]

magic arts [1]

Rev 9:21 their **magic arts**, their sexual immorality or their thefts.

5761 φάρμακος, *pharmakos* [2] [√ 5760]

practice magic arts [2]

Rev 21: 8 *those who* **practice magic arts**, the idolaters and all liars—
22:15 Outside are the dogs, those who **practice magic arts**, the sexually

5762 φάσις, *phasis* [1] [√ 5774 *(or)* 5743]

news [1]

Ac 21:31 **news** reached the commander of the Roman troops that the whole

5763 φάσκω, *phaskō* [3] [√ 5774 *(or)* 5743]

claimed [2], asserting that [1]

Ac 24: 9 joined in the accusation, **asserting that** these things were true.
25:19 and about a dead man named Jesus who Paul **claimed** was alive.
Ro 1:22 *Although they* **claimed** to be wise, they became fools

5764 φάτνη, *phatnē* [4]

manger [3], stall [1]

Lk 2: 7 She wrapped him in cloths and placed him in a **manger**,
2:12 You will find a baby wrapped in cloths and lying in a **manger**."
2:16 and Joseph, and the baby, who was lying in the **manger**.
13:15 his ox or donkey from the **stall** and lead it out to give it water?

5765 φαῦλος, *phaulos* [6]

bad [3], evil [3]

Jn 3:20 Everyone who does **evil** hates the light, and will not come into the
5:29 to live, and those who have done **evil** will rise to be condemned.
Ro 9:11 before the twins were born or had done anything good or **bad**—
2Co 5:10 him for the things done while in the body, whether good or **bad**.
Tit 2: 8 may be ashamed because they have nothing **bad** to say about us.
Jas 3:16 selfish ambition, there you find disorder and every **evil** practice.

5766 φέγγος, *phengos* [2]

light [2]

Mt 24:29 " 'the sun will be darkened, and the moon will not give its **light**;
Mk 13:24 " 'the sun will be darkened, and the moon will not give its **light**;

5767 φείδομαι, *pheidomai* [10] [→ 910, 5768]

spare [9], refrain [1]

Ac 20:29 wolves will come in among you and *will* not **spare** the flock.
Ro 8:32 He who *did* not **spare** his own Son, but gave him up for us all—
11:21 For if God *did* not **spare** the natural branches, he will not spare
11:21 did not spare the natural branches, *he will* not **spare** you either.
1Co 7:28 will face many troubles in this life, and I *want to* **spare** you this.
2Co 1:23 I call God as my witness that it was *in order to* **spare** you that I
12: 6 But *I* **refrain**, so no one will think more of me than is warranted by
13: 2 On my return *I will* not **spare** those who sinned earlier or any of
2Pe 2: 4 For if God *did* not **spare** angels when they sinned, but sent them to
2: 5 if *he did* not **spare** the ancient world when he brought the flood on

5768 φειδομένως, *pheidomenōs* [2] [√ 5767]

sparingly [2]

2Co 9: 6 Whoever sows **sparingly** will also reap sparingly, and whoever
9: 6 Whoever sows sparingly will also reap **sparingly**, and whoever

5769 φελόνης, *phelonēs* Not used in UBS/NIV [√ 5742]

5770 φέρω, pherō [66]

[→ *429, 708, 711, 1022, 1422, 1427, 1457, 1566, 1662, 1766, 2214, 2369, 2504, 2844, 2845, 2965, 3947, 4195, 4210, 4367, 4442, 4443, 4533, 4712, 4714, 4734, 5237, 5239, 5240, 5461, 5574, 5578, 5722, 5841, 5843, 5844, 5845, 5846, 5892*]

brought [16], bring [12], bear [6], bringing [3], came [2], carried [2], driven along [2], bearing [1], bears [1], blowing [1], bore [1], brought in [1], carrying [1], charge [+*162*] [1], did^s so [1], fruitful [+*2843*] [1], given [1], go on [1], lead [1], leading [1], made carry [1], multiplying [1], origin [1], produces [1], prove [1], put [1], reach out [1], sustaining [1], take [1], took [1]

Mt 14:11 His head *was* **brought in** on a platter and given to the girl,
    14:11 in on a platter and given to the girl, *who* **carried** it to her mother.
    14:18 "**Bring** them here to me," he said.
    17:17 How long shall I put up with you? **Bring** the boy here to me."
Mk   1:32 That evening after sunset the *people* **brought** to Jesus all the sick
     2: 3 Some men came, **bringing** to him a paralytic, carried by four of
     4: 8 It came up, grew and produced a crop, **multiplying** thirty, sixty,
     6:27 So he immediately sent an executioner with orders *to* **bring** John's
     6:28 and **brought** *back* his head on a platter. He presented it to the girl,
     7:32 There *some people* **brought** to him a man who was deaf and could
     8:22 and *some people* **brought** a blind man and begged Jesus to touch
     9:17 A man in the crowd answered, "Teacher, *I* **brought** you my son,
     9:19 with you? How long shall I put up with you? **Bring** the boy to me."
     9:20 So *they* **brought** him. When the spirit saw Jesus, it immediately
    11: 2 tied there, which no one has ever ridden. Untie it and **bring** it here.
    11: 7 When *they* **brought** the colt to Jesus and threw their cloaks over it,
    12:15 to trap me?" he asked. "**Bring** me a denarius and let me look at it."
    12:16 They **brought** the coin, and he asked them, "Whose portrait is this?
    15:22 *They* **brought** Jesus to the place called Golgotha (which means
Lk   5:18 Some men came **carrying** a paralytic on a mat and tried to take
    15:23 **Bring** the fattened calf and kill it. Let's have a feast and celebrate.
    23:26 and put the cross on him and **made** him **carry** it behind Jesus.
    24: 1 the women **took** the spices they had prepared and went to the
Jn   2: 8 "Now draw some out and **take** it to the master of the banquet."
     2: 8 some out and take it to the master of the banquet." They **did^s** so,
     4:33 said to each other, "Could someone *have* **brought** him food?"
    12:24 remains only a single seed. But if it dies, *it* **produces** many seeds.
    15: 2 He cuts off every branch in me *that* **bears** no fruit, while every
    15: 2 while every branch *that does* **bear** fruit he prunes so that it will be
    15: 2 bear fruit he prunes so that *it will be even* more **fruitful** [+*2843*].
    15: 4 No branch can **bear** fruit by itself; it must remain in the vine.
    15: 5 If a man remains in me and I in him, he *will* **bear** much fruit;
    15: 8 This is to my Father's glory, that *you* **bear** much fruit, showing
    15:16 but I chose you and appointed you to go and **bear** fruit—
    18:29 and asked, "What charges *are you* **bringing** against this man?"
    19:39 Nicodemus **brought** a mixture of myrrh and aloes,
    20:27 Then he said to Thomas, "**Put** your finger here; see my hands.
    20:27 see my hands. **Reach** out your hand and put it into my side.
    21:10 Jesus said to them, "**Bring** some of the fish you have just caught."
    21:18 else will dress you and **lead** you where you do not want to go."
Ac   2: 2 Suddenly a sound like the **blowing** of a violent wind came from
     4:34 or houses sold them, **brought** the money from the sales
     4:37 sold a field he owned and **brought** the money and put it at the
     5: 2 for himself, but **brought** the rest and put it at the apostles' feet.
     5:16 **bringing** their sick and those tormented by evil spirits, and all of
    12:10 and second guards and came to the iron gate **leading** to the city.
    14:13 **brought** bulls and wreaths to the city gates because he
    25:18 *they did* not **charge** him with [+*162*] any of the crimes I had
    27:15 head into the wind; so *we* gave way to it and *were* **driven along**.
    27:17 they lowered the sea anchor and *let* the ship *be* **driven along**.
Ro   9:22 power known, **bore** with great patience the objects of his wrath—
2Ti 4:13 When *you* come, **bring** the cloak that I left with Carpus at Troas,
Heb 1: 3 of his being, **sustaining** all things by his powerful word.
     6: 1 *let us* leave the elementary teachings about Christ and **go on**
     9:16 of a will, it is necessary *to* **prove** the death of the one who made it,
    12:20 because *they could* not **bear** what was commanded: "If even an
    13:13 go to him outside the camp, **bearing** the disgrace he bore.
1Pe 1:13 set your hope fully on the grace to be **given** you when Jesus Christ
2Pe 1:17 and glory from God the Father *when* the voice **came** to him from
     1:18 We ourselves heard this voice that **came** from heaven when we
     1:21 For prophecy never *had its* **origin** in the will of man, but men
     1:21 but men spoke from God *as they were* **carried** along by the Holy
     2:11 *do* not **bring** slanderous accusations against such beings in the

2Jn 1:10 If anyone comes to you and *does* not **bring** this teaching, do not
Rev 21:24 and the kings of the earth *will* **bring** their splendor into it.
    21:26 The glory and honor of the nations *will be* **brought** into it.

5771 φεύγω, pheugō [29] [→ *709, 1423, 1767, 2966, 5868, 5870*]

flee [9], fled [7], escape [3], ran off [3], flee from [2], elude [+*608*] [1], escaped [1], fled away [1], run away [1], runs away [1]

Mt   2:13 he said, "take the child and his mother and **escape** to Egypt.
     3: 7 brood of vipers! Who warned you *to* **flee** from the coming wrath?
     8:33 Those tending the pigs **ran off**, went into the town and reported all
    10:23 When you are persecuted in one place, **flee** to another. I tell you
    23:33 brood of vipers! How *will you* **escape** being condemned to hell?
    24:16 then *let* those who are in Judea **flee** to the mountains.
    26:56 might be fulfilled." Then all the disciples deserted him and **fled**.
Mk   5:14 Those tending the pigs **ran off** and reported this in the town
    13:14 then *let* those who are in Judea **flee** to the mountains.
    14:50 Then everyone deserted him and **fled**.
    14:52 he **fled** naked, leaving his garment behind.
    16: 8 and bewildered, the women went out and **fled** from the tomb.
Lk   3: 7 brood of vipers! Who warned you *to* **flee** from the coming wrath?
     8:34 *they* **ran off** and reported this in the town and countryside,
    21:21 then *let* those who are in Judea **flee** to the mountains, let those in
Jn 10: 5 *they will* **run away** from him because they do not recognize a
    10:12 he sees the wolf coming, he abandons the sheep and **runs away**.
Ac   7:29 When Moses heard this, *he* **fled** to Midian, where he settled as a
    27:30 In an attempt *to* **escape** from the ship, the sailors let the lifeboat
1Co 6:18 **Flee from** sexual immorality. All other sins a man commits are
    10:14 Therefore, my dear friends, **flee** from idolatry.
1Ti 6:11 But you, man of God, **flee from** all this, and pursue righteousness,
2Ti 2:22 **Flee** the evil desires of youth, and pursue righteousness, faith,
Heb 11:34 the fury of the flames, and **escaped** the edge of the sword;
Jas 4: 7 then, to God. Resist the devil, and *he will* **flee** from you.
Rev 9: 6 not find it; they will long to die, but death *will* **elude** [+*608*] them.
    12: 6 The woman **fled** into the desert to a place prepared for her by God,
    16:20 Every island **fled away** and the mountains could not be found.
    20:11 Earth and sky **fled** from his presence, and there was no place for

5772 Φῆλιξ, Phēlix [9]

Felix [9]

Ac 23:24 mounts for Paul so that he may be taken safely to Governor **Felix**."
    23:26 Claudius Lysias, *To His Excellency, Governor* **Felix**: *Greetings*.
    24: 3 Everywhere and in every way, most excellent **Felix**,
    24:22 Then **Felix**, who was well acquainted with the Way,
    24:24 Several days later **Felix** came with his wife Drusilla, who was a
    24:25 to come, **Felix** was afraid and said, "That's enough for now!
    24:27 **Felix** was succeeded by Porcius Festus, but because Felix wanted
    24:27 but because **Felix** wanted to grant a favor to the Jews, he left Paul
    25:14 He said: "There is a man here whom **Felix** left as a prisoner.

5773 φήμη, phēmē [2] [√ *5774*]

news [2]

Mt   9:26 **News** of this spread through all that region.
Lk   4:14 and **news** about him spread through the whole countryside.

5774 φημί, phēmi [66] [→ *1424, 2367, 2368, 4735, 5238, 5762?, 5763?, 5773, 5775; cf. 1059, 1555, 4735*]

said [25], replied [18], answered [7], *untranslated* [4], asked [3], declared [2], mean [2], say [2], claim [1], declare [1], shouted [+*3489+3836+5889*] [1]

Mt   4: 7 Jesus **answered** him, "It is also written: 'Do not put the Lord your
     8: 8 The centurion replied, [**RPG**] "Lord, I do not deserve to have you
    13:28 " 'An enemy did this,' he **replied**. "The servants asked him, 'Do
    13:29 " 'No,' he **answered**, 'because while you are pulling the weeds,
    14: 8 Prompted by her mother, she **said**, "Give me here on a platter the
    17:26 Peter answered. "Then the sons are exempt," Jesus **said** to him.
    19:21 Jesus **answered**, "If you want to be perfect, go, sell your
    21:27 Then he **said**, "Neither will I tell you by what authority I am doing
    22:37 Jesus **replied**: " 'Love the Lord your God with all your heart

	25:21	"His master **replied**, 'Well done, good and faithful servant!
	25:23	"His master **replied**, 'Well done, good and faithful servant!
	26:34	"I tell you the truth," Jesus **answered**, "this very night,
	26:61	and declared, "This fellow **said**, 'I am able to destroy the temple of
	27:11	you the king of the Jews?" "Yes, it is as you say," Jesus **replied**.
	27:23	"Why? What crime has he committed?" **asked** Pilate. But they
	27:65	"Take a guard," Pilate **answered**. "Go, make the tomb as secure as
Mk	9:12	Jesus **replied**, "To be sure, Elijah does come first, and restores all
	9:38	"Teacher," **said** John, "we saw a man driving out demons in your
	10:20	"Teacher," he **declared**, "all these I have kept since I was a boy."
	10:29	"I tell you the truth," Jesus **replied**, "no one who has left home
	12:24	Jesus **replied**, "Are you not in error because you do not know the
	14:29	Peter **declared**, "Even if all fall away, I will not."
Lk	7:40	"Simon, I have something to tell you." "Tell me, teacher," he **said**.
	7:44	Then *he* turned toward the woman and **said** to Simon, "Do you see
	15:17	"When he came to his senses, *he* **said**, 'How many of my father's
	22:58	A little later someone else saw him and **said**, "You also are one of
	22:58	said, "You also are one of them." "Man, I am not!" Peter **replied**.
	22:70	then the Son of God?" He **replied**, "You are right in saying I am."
	23:3	the king of the Jews?" "Yes, it is as you say," Jesus replied. **[RPG]**
	23:40	"Don't you fear God," he **said**, "since you are under the same
Jn	1:23	John **replied** in the words of Isaiah the prophet, "I am the voice of
	9:38	Then the man **said**, "Lord, I believe," and he worshiped him.
	18:29	So Pilate came out to them and **asked**, "What charges are you
Ac	2:38	Peter **replied**, "Repent and be baptized, every one of you,
	7:2	To this he **replied**: "Brothers and fathers, listen to me! The God of
	8:36	they came to some water and the eunuch **said**, "Look, here is water.
	10:28	*He* **said** to them: "You are well aware that it is against our law for a
	10:30	Cornelius **answered**: "Four days ago I was in my house praying at
	10:31	and **said**, 'Cornelius, God has heard your prayer and remembered
	16:30	He then brought them out and **asked**, "Sirs, what must I do to be
	16:37	But Paul **said** to the officers: "They beat us publicly without a trial,
	17:22	Paul then stood up in the meeting of the Areopagus and **said**:
	19:35	The city clerk quieted the crowd and **said**: "Men of Ephesus,
	21:37	"May I say something to you?" "Do you speak Greek?" he **replied**.
	22:2	speak to them in Aramaic, they became very quiet. Then Paul **said**:
	22:27	"Tell me, are you a Roman citizen?" "Yes, I am," he **answered**.
	22:28	price for my citizenship." "But I was born a citizen," Paul **replied**.
	23:5	Paul **replied**, "Brothers, I did not realize that he was the high priest;
	23:17	Then Paul called one of the centurions and **said**, "Take this young
	23:18	The centurion **said**, "Paul, the prisoner, sent for me and asked me to
	23:35	he **said**, "I will hear your case when your accusers get here."
	25:5	**[NIE]** Let some of your leaders come with me and press charges
	25:22	hear this man myself." He **replied**, "Tomorrow you will hear him."
	25:24	Festus **said**: "King Agrippa, and all who are present with us,
	26:1	Then Agrippa **said** to Paul, "You have permission to speak for
	26:24	are out of your mind, Paul!" he **shouted** [+*3489+3836+5889*].
	26:25	"I am not insane, most excellent Festus," Paul **replied**. "What I am
	26:32	Agrippa **said** to Festus, "This man could have been set free if he
Ro	3:8	slanderously reported as saying and as some **claim** that we say—
1Co	6:16	with her in body? For *it is* **said**, "The two will become one flesh."
	7:29	What *I* **mean**, brothers, is that the time is short. From now on those
	10:15	I speak to sensible people; judge for yourselves what *I* **say**.
	10:19	*Do* I **mean** then that a sacrifice offered to an idol is anything,
	15:50	I **declare** to you, brothers, that flesh and blood cannot inherit the
2Co	10:10	For some **say**, "His letters are weighty and forceful, but in person
Heb	8:5	"See to it **[NIE]** that you make everything according to the pattern

5775 φημίζω, *phēmizō*   Not used in UBS/NIV [√ *5774*]

5776 Φῆστος, *Phēstos* [13]

Festus [13]

Ac	24:27	Felix was succeeded by Porcius **Festus**, but because Felix wanted
	25:1	in the province, **Festus** went up from Caesarea to Jerusalem,
	25:4	**Festus** answered, "Paul is being held at Caesarea, and I myself am
	25:9	**Festus**, wishing to do the Jews a favor, said to Paul, "Are you
	25:12	After **Festus** had conferred with his council, he declared: "You
	25:13	and Bernice arrived at Caesarea to pay their respects to **Festus**.
	25:14	many days there, **Festus** discussed Paul's case with the king.
	25:22	Agrippa said to **Festus**, "I would like to hear this man myself."
	25:23	men of the city. At the command *of* **Festus**, Paul was brought in.
	25:24	**Festus** said: "King Agrippa, and all who are present with us,
	26:24	At this point **Festus** interrupted Paul's defense. "You are out of
	26:25	"I am not insane, most excellent **Festus**," Paul replied. "What I am
	26:32	Agrippa said *to* **Festus**, "This man could have been set free if he

5777 φθάνω, *phthanō* [7]   [→ *4710?, 4711?, 4740*]

come [3], attained [2], get [1], precede [1]

Mt	12:28	by the Spirit of God, then the kingdom of God *has* **come** upon you.
Lk	11:20	by the finger of God, then the kingdom of God *has* **come** to you.
Ro	9:31	but Israel, who pursued a law of righteousness, *has* not **attained** it.
2Co	10:14	come to you, for *we did* **get** as far as you with the gospel of Christ.
Php	3:16	Only let us live up to what *we have already* **attained**.
1Th	2:16	sins to the limit. The wrath of God *has* **come** upon them at last.
	4:15	the Lord, *will* certainly not **precede** those who have fallen asleep.

5778 φθαρτός, *phthartos* [6]   [√ *5780*]

perishable [4], mortal [1], not last [1]

Ro	1:23	of the immortal God for images made to look like **mortal** man
1Co	9:25	They do it to get a crown that will **not last**; but we do it to get a
	15:53	For the **perishable** must clothe itself with the imperishable,
	15:54	When the **perishable** has been clothed with the imperishable,
1Pe	1:18	For you know that it was not *with* **perishable** *things* such as silver
	1:23	not of **perishable** seed, but of imperishable, through the living

5779 φθέγγομαι, *phthengomai* [3]   [→ *710, 5782*]

mouth words [1], speak [1], spoke [1]

Ac	4:18	Then they called them in again and commanded them not *to* **speak**
2Pe	2:16	*who* **spoke** with a man's voice and restrained the prophet's
	2:18	For *they* **mouth** empty, boastful **words** and, by appealing to the

5780 φθείρω, *phtheirō* [9]   [→ *91, 914, 915, 917, 1425, 1426, 2967, 5778, 5781, 5785*]

corrupted [3], destroy [2], corrupts [1], destroys [1], led astray [1], perish [+*5785*] [1]

1Co	3:17	If anyone **destroys** God's temple, God will destroy him; for God's
	3:17	If anyone destroys God's temple, God *will* **destroy** him; for God's
	15:33	Do not be misled: "Bad company **corrupts** good character."
2Co	7:2	We have wronged no one, *we have* **corrupted** no one, we have
	11:3	your minds *may somehow be* **led astray** from your sincere
Eph	4:22	off your old self, which *is being* **corrupted** by its deceitful desires;
2Pe	2:12	and destroyed, and like beasts *they* too *will* **perish** [+*5785*].
Jude	1:10	unreasoning animals—these are the very things that **destroy** *them*.
Rev	19:2	He has condemned the great prostitute who **corrupted** the earth by

5781 φθινοπωρινός, *phthinopōrinos* [1]
[√ *5780 + 3967*]

autumn [1]

Jude	1:12	the wind; **autumn** trees, without fruit and uprooted—twice dead.

5782 φθόγγος, *phthongos* [2]   [√ *5779*]

notes [1], voice [1]

Ro	10:18	"Their **voice** has gone out into all the earth, their words to the ends
1Co	14:7	what tune is being played unless there is a distinction *in* the **notes**?

5783 φθονέω, *phthoneō* [1]   [√ *5784*]

envying [1]

Gal	5:26	Let us not become conceited, provoking and **envying** each other.

5784 φθόνος, *phthonos* [9]   [→ *916, 5783*]

envy [8], envies [1]

Mt	27:18	For he knew it was out of **envy** that they had handed Jesus over to
Mk	15:10	knowing it was out of **envy** that the chief priests had handed Jesus
Ro	1:29	They are full *of* **envy**, murder, strife, deceit and malice.
Gal	5:21	and **envy**; drunkenness, orgies, and the like. I warn you, as I did
Php	1:15	It is true that some preach Christ out of **envy** and rivalry, but others

1Ti 6: 4 in controversies and quarrels about words that result in **envy**,
Tit 3: 3 We lived in malice and **envy**, being hated and hating one another.
Jas 4: 5 reason that the spirit he caused to live in us **envies** intensely?
1Pe 2: 1 rid yourselves of all malice and all deceit, hypocrisy, **envy**,

5785 φθορά, *phthora* [9] [√ 5780]

corruption [1], decay [1], depravity [1], destroyed [1], destruction [1], perish [+5780] [1], perish [1], perishable [+1877] [1], perishable [1]

Ro   8:21 that the creation itself will be liberated from its bondage *to* **decay**
1Co 15:42 The body that is sown is **perishable** [+1877], it is raised
      15:50 kingdom of God, nor does the **perishable** inherit the imperishable.
Gal   6: 8 to please his sinful nature, from that nature will reap **destruction**;
Col   2:22 These are all destined to **perish** with use, because they are based
2Pe   1: 4 and escape the **corruption** in the world caused by evil desires.
      2:12 creatures of instinct, born only to be caught and **destroyed**,
      2:12 and destroyed, and like beasts *they* too *will* **perish** [+5780].
      2:19 them freedom, while they themselves are slaves *of* **depravity**—

5786 φιάλη, *phiale* [12]

bowl [7], bowls [5]

Rev   5: 8 one had a harp and they were holding golden **bowls** full of incense,
      15: 7 the seven angels seven golden **bowls** filled with the wrath of God,
      16: 1 "Go, pour out the seven **bowls** of God's wrath on the earth."
      16: 2 The first angel went and poured out his **bowl** on the land, and ugly
      16: 3 The second angel poured out his **bowl** on the sea, and it turned into
      16: 4 The third angel poured out his **bowl** on the rivers and springs of
      16: 8 The fourth angel poured out his **bowl** on the sun, and the sun was
      16:10 The fifth angel poured out his **bowl** on the throne of the beast,
      16:12 The sixth angel poured out his **bowl** on the great river Euphrates,
      16:17 The seventh angel poured out his **bowl** into the air, and out of the
      17: 1 One of the seven angels who had the seven **bowls** came and said to
      21: 9 One of the seven angels who had the seven **bowls** full of the seven

5787 φιλάγαθος, *philagathos* [1] [√ 5813 + 19]

loves what is good [1]

Tit   1: 8 *one who* **loves what is good**, who is self-controlled, upright,

5788 Φιλαδέλφεια, *Philadelpheia* [2]
[√ 5813 + 81 [1.3]]

Philadelphia [2]

Rev   1:11 Smyrna, Pergamum, Thyatira, Sardis, **Philadelphia** and Laodicea."
      3: 7 "To the angel of the church in **Philadelphia** write: These are the

5789 φιλαδελφία, *philadelphia* [6] [√ 5813 + 81 [1.3]]

brotherly kindness [2], brotherly love [2], love for brothers [1], loving each other as brothers [1]

Ro   12:10 Be devoted to one another *in* **brotherly love**. Honor one another
1Th   4: 9 Now about **brotherly love** we do not need to write to you,
Heb 13: 1 Keep on **loving each other as brothers**.
1Pe   1:22 obeying the truth so that you have sincere **love for** your **brothers**,
2Pe   1: 7 and to godliness, **brotherly kindness**; and to brotherly kindness,
      1: 7 to godliness, brotherly kindness; and to **brotherly kindness**, love.

5790 φιλάδελφος, *philadelphos* [1] [√ 5813 + 81 [1.3]]

love as brothers [1]

1Pe   3: 8 be sympathetic, **love as brothers**, be compassionate and humble.

5791 φίλανδρος, *philandros* [1] [√ 5813 + 467]

love their husbands [1]

Tit   2: 4 Then they can train the younger women to **love their husbands**

5792 φιλανθρωπία, *philanthropia* [2] [√ 5813 + 476]

kindness [1], love [1]

Ac   28: 2 The islanders showed us unusual **kindness**. They built a fire
Tit   3: 4 But when the kindness and **love** of God our Savior appeared,

5793 φιλανθρώπως, *philanthropos* [1] [√ 5813 + 476]

in kindness [+5968] [1]

Ac   27: 3 and Julius, **in kindness** [+5968] to Paul, allowed him to go to his

5794 φιλαργυρία, *philargyria* [1] [√ 5813 + 738]

love of money [1]

1Ti   6:10 For the **love of money** is a root of all kinds of evil. Some people,

5795 φιλάργυρος, *philargyros* [2] [√ 5813 + 738]

loved money [+5639] [1], lovers of money [1]

Lk   16:14 The Pharisees, *who* **loved** [+5639] **money**, heard all this and were
2Ti   3: 2 **lovers of money**, boastful, proud, abusive, disobedient to their

5796 φίλαυτος, *philautos* [1] [√ 5813 + 899]

lovers of themselves [1]

2Ti   3: 2 People will be **lovers of themselves**, lovers of money, boastful,

5797 φιλέω, *phileo* [25] [√ 5813]

love [13], loves [6], kiss [3], loved [3]

Mt   6: 5 for *they* **love** to pray standing in the synagogues and on the street
      10:37 "Anyone *who* **loves** his father or mother more than me is not worthy
      10:37 anyone *who* **loves** his son or daughter more than me is not worthy
      23: 6 *they* **love** the place of honor at banquets and the most important
      26:48 arranged a signal with them: "The one *I* **kiss** is the man; arrest him."
Mk   14:44 "The one *I* **kiss** is the man; arrest him and lead him away under
Lk   20:46 around in flowing robes and **love** to be greeted in the marketplaces
      22:47 of the Twelve, was leading them. He approached Jesus *to* **kiss** him,
Jn   5:20 For the Father **loves** the Son and shows him all he does. Yes,
      11: 3 So the sisters sent word to Jesus, "Lord, the one *you* **love** is sick."
      11:36 Then the Jews said, "See how *he* **loved** him!"
      12:25 The man *who* **loves** his life will lose it, while the man who hates
      15:19 If you belonged to the world, it would **love** you as its own.
      16:27 the Father himself **loves** you because you have loved me and have
      16:27 the Father himself loves you because you *have* **loved** me and have
      20: 2 Simon Peter and the other disciple, the one Jesus **loved**, and said,
      21:15 "Yes, Lord," he said, "you know that *I* **love** you." Jesus said, "Feed
      21:16 He answered, "Yes, Lord, you know that *I* **love** you." Jesus said,
      21:17 third time he said to him, "Simon son of John, *do you* **love** me?"
      21:17 because Jesus asked him the third time, "*Do you* **love** me?"
      21:17 He said, "Lord, you know all things; you know that *I* **love** you."
1Co 16:22 If anyone *does* not **love** the Lord—a curse be on him. Come,
Tit   3:15 Greet those *who* **love** us in the faith. Grace be with you all.
Rev   3:19 Those whom I **love** I rebuke and discipline. So be earnest,
      22:15 the idolaters and everyone *who* **loves** and practices falsehood.

5798 φιλήδονος, *philedonos* [1] [√ 5813 + 2454]

lovers of pleasure [1]

2Ti   3: 4 rash, conceited, **lovers of pleasure** rather than lovers of God—

5799 φίλημα, *philema* [7] [√ 5813]

kiss [7]

Lk   7:45 You did not give me a **kiss**, but this woman, from the time I
      22:48 asked him, "Judas, are you betraying the Son of Man *with* a **kiss**?"
Ro   16:16 Greet one another with a holy **kiss**. All the churches of Christ send
1Co 16:20 here send you greetings. Greet one another with a holy **kiss**.
2Co 13:12 Greet one another with a holy **kiss**.
1Th   5:26 Greet all the brothers with a holy **kiss**.
1Pe   5:14 Greet one another with a **kiss** of love. Peace to all of you who are

5800 **Φιλήμων,** *Philēmōn* [1] [√ *5813*]

Philemon [1]

Phm 1: 1 our brother, *To* **Philemon** our dear friend and fellow worker,

5801 **Φίλητος,** *Philētos* [1] [√ *5813*]

Philetus [1]

2Ti 2: 17 spread like gangrene. Among them are Hymenaeus and **Philetus,**

5802 **φιλία,** *philia* [1] [√ *5813*]

friendship [1]

Jas 4: 4 don't you know that **friendship** with the world is hatred toward

5803 **Φιλιππήσιος,** *Philippēsios* [1] [√ *5813 + 2691*]

Philippians [1]

Php 4: 15 Moreover, as you **Philippians** know, in the early days of your

5804 **Φίλιπποι,** *Philippoi* [4] [√ *5813 + 2691*]

Philippi [4]

Ac 16: 12 From there we traveled to **Philippi,** a Roman colony
    20: 6 But we sailed from **Philippi** after the Feast of Unleavened Bread,
Php 1: 1 of Christ Jesus, To all the saints in Christ Jesus at **Philippi,**
1Th 2: 2 We had previously suffered and been insulted in **Philippi,**

5805 **Φίλιππος,** *Philippos* [36] [√ *5813 + 2691*]

Philip [32], Philip's [2], Philippi [2]

Mt 10: 3 **Philip** and Bartholomew; Thomas and Matthew the tax collector;
    14: 3 put him in prison because of Herodias, his brother **Philip's** wife,
    16: 13 When Jesus came to the region *of* Caesarea **Philippi,** he asked his
Mk 3: 18 Andrew, **Philip,** Bartholomew, Matthew, Thomas, James son of
    6: 17 He did this because of Herodias, his brother **Philip's** wife,
    8: 27 and his disciples went on to the villages around Caesarea **Philippi.**
Lk 3: 1 of Galilee, his brother **Philip** tetrarch of Iturea and Traconitis,
    6: 14 his brother Andrew, James, John, **Philip,** Bartholomew,
Jn 1: 43 to leave for Galilee. Finding **Philip,** he said to him, "Follow me."
    1: 44 **Philip,** like Andrew and Peter, was from the town of Bethsaida.
    1: 45 **Philip** found Nathanael and told him, "We have found the one
    1: 46 come from there?" Nathanael asked. "Come and see," said **Philip.**
    1: 48 "I saw you while you were still under the fig tree before **Philip**
    6: 5 and saw a great crowd coming toward him, he said to **Philip,**
    6: 7 **Philip** answered him, "Eight months' wages would not buy enough
    12: 21 They came to **Philip,** who was from Bethsaida in Galilee,
    12: 22 **Philip** went to tell Andrew; Andrew and Philip in turn told Jesus.
    12: 22 Philip went to tell Andrew; Andrew and **Philip** in turn told Jesus.
    14: 8 **Philip** said, "Lord, show us the Father and that will be enough for
    14: 9 "Don't you know me, **Philip,** even after I have been among you
Ac 1: 13 and Andrew; **Philip** and Thomas, Bartholomew and Matthew;
    6: 5 also **Philip,** Procorus, Nicanor, Timon, Parmenas, and Nicolas
    8: 5 **Philip** went down to a city in Samaria and proclaimed the Christ
    8: 6 When the crowds heard **Philip** and saw the miraculous signs he
    8: 12 But when they believed **Philip** as he preached the good news of the
    8: 13 And he followed **Philip** everywhere, astonished by the great signs
    8: 26 Now an angel of the Lord said to **Philip,** "Go south to the road—
    8: 29 The Spirit told **Philip,** "Go to that chariot and stay near it."
    8: 30 Then **Philip** ran up to the chariot and heard the man reading Isaiah
    8: 31 it to me?" So he invited **Philip** to come up and sit with him.
    8: 34 The eunuch asked **Philip,** "Tell me, please, who is the prophet
    8: 35 Then **Philip** began with that very passage of Scripture and told him
    8: 38 Then both **Philip** and the eunuch went down into the water
    8: 39 out of the water, the Spirit of the Lord suddenly took **Philip** away,
    8: 40 **Philip,** however, appeared at Azotus and traveled about,
    21: 8 reached Caesarea and stayed at the house *of* **Philip** the evangelist,

5806 **φιλόθεος,** *philotheos* [1] [√ *5813 + 2536*]

lovers of God [1]

2Ti 3: 4 rash, conceited, lovers of pleasure rather than **lovers of God**—

5807 **Φιλόλογος,** *Philologos* [1] [√ *5813 + 3306*]

Philologus [1]

Ro 16: 15 Greet **Philologus,** Julia, Nereus and his sister, and Olympas

5808 **φιλονεικία,** *philoneikia* [1] [→ *5809; cf. 5813*]

dispute [1]

Lk 22: 24 Also a **dispute** arose among them as to which of them was

5809 **φιλόνεικος,** *philoneikos* [1] [√ *5808*]

contentious [1]

1Co 11: 16 If anyone wants to be **contentious** *about* this, we have no other

5810 **φιλοξενία,** *philoxenia* [2] [√ *5813 + 3828*]

entertain strangers [1], hospitality [1]

Ro 12: 13 Share with God's people who are in need. Practice **hospitality.**
Heb 13: 2 Do not forget *to* **entertain strangers,** for by so doing some people

5811 **φιλόξενος,** *philoxenos* [3] [√ *5813 + 3828*]

hospitable [2], hospitality [1]

1Ti 3: 2 temperate, self-controlled, respectable, **hospitable,** able to teach,
Tit 1: 8 Rather he must be **hospitable,** one who loves what is good,
1Pe 4: 9 Offer **hospitality** to one another without grumbling.

5812 **φιλοπρωτεύω,** *philoprōteuō* [1] [√ *5813 + 4755*]

loves to be first [1]

3Jn 1: 9 I wrote to the church, but Diotrephes, *who* **loves to be first,**

5813 **φίλος,** *philos* [29]

[→ *920, 921, 2541, 2968, 4713, 5787, 5788, 5789, 5790, 5791, 5792, 5793, 5794, 5795, 5796, 5797, 5798, 5799, 5800, 5801, 5802, 5803, 5804, 5805, 5806, 5807, 5810, 5811, 5812, 5814, 5815, 5816, 5817, 5818, 5819, 5820; cf. 5808*]

friends [17], friend [12]

Mt 11: 19 a **friend** of tax collectors and "sinners." ' But wisdom is proved
Lk 7: 6 He was not far from the house when the centurion sent **friends** to
    7: 34 a glutton and a drunkard, a **friend** of tax collectors and "sinners." '
    11: 5 Then he said to them, "Suppose one of you has a **friend,** and he
    11: 5 and he goes to him at midnight and says, '**Friend,** lend me three
    11: 6 because a **friend** of mine on a journey has come to me, and I have
    11: 8 he will not get up and give him the bread because he is his **friend,**
    12: 4 "I tell you, my **friends,** do not be afraid of those who kill the body
    14: 10 host comes, he will say to you, '**Friend,** move up to a better place.'
    14: 12 "When you give a luncheon or dinner, do not invite your **friends,**
    15: 6 Then he calls his **friends** and neighbors together and says,
    15: 9 she calls her **friends** and neighbors together and says,
    15: 29 gave me even a young goat so I could celebrate with my **friends.**
    16: 9 I tell you, use worldly wealth to gain **friends** for yourselves,
    21: 16 will be betrayed even by parents, brothers, relatives and **friends,**
    23: 12 That day Herod and Pilate became **friends**—before this they had
Jn 3: 29 The **friend** who attends the bridegroom waits and listens for him,
    11: 11 he went on to tell them, "Our **friend** Lazarus has fallen asleep;
    15: 13 love has no one than this, that he lay down his life for his **friends.**
    15: 14 You are my **friends** if you do what I command.
    15: 15 Instead, I have called you **friends,** for everything that I learned
    19: 12 kept shouting, "If you let this man go, you are no **friend** of Caesar.
Ac 10: 24 and had called together his relatives and close **friends.**
    19: 31 Even some of the officials of the province, **friends** of Paul,
    27: 3 allowed him to go to his **friends** so they might provide for his
Jas 2: 23 credited to him as righteousness," and he was called God's **friend.**
    4: 4 Anyone who chooses to be a **friend** of the world becomes an
3Jn 1: 14 face to face. Peace to you. The **friends** here send their greetings.
    1: 14 friends here send their greetings. Greet the **friends** there by name.

5814 φιλοσοφία, *philosophia* [1] [√ *5813 + 5055*]

philosophy [1]

Col 2: 8 one takes you captive through hollow and deceptive **philosophy**,

5815 φιλόσοφος, *philosophos* [1] [√ *5813 + 5055*]

philosophers [1]

Ac 17: 18 A group *of* Epicurean and Stoic **philosophers** began to dispute

5816 φιλόστοργος, *philostorgos* [1] [√ *5813*]

devoted [1]

Ro 12: 10 Be **devoted** to one another in brotherly love. Honor one another

5817 φιλότεκνος, *philoteknos* [1] [√ *5813 + 5503*]

love their children [1]

Tit 2: 4 can train the younger women to **love their** husbands and **children**,

5818 φιλοτιμέομαι, *philotimeomai* [3] [√ *5813 + 5507*]

ambition [1], make it ambition [1], make it goal [1]

Ro 15: 20 It *has always been my* **ambition** to preach the gospel where Christ
2Co 5: 9 So *we* **make it** *our* **goal** to please him, whether we are at home in
1Th 4: 11 **Make it** your **ambition** to lead a quiet life, to mind your own

5819 φιλοφρόνως, *philophronōs* [1] [√ *5813 + 5856*]

hospitably [1]

Ac 28: 7 us to his home and for three days entertained us **hospitably**.

5820 φιλόφρων, *philophrōn*   Not used in UBS/NIV [√ *5813 + 5856*]

5821 φιμόω, *phimoō* [7]

quiet [2], muzzle [1], silence talk [1], silenced [1], speechless [1], still [1]

Mt 22: 12 get in here without wedding clothes?' The man *was* **speechless**.
    22: 34 Hearing that Jesus *had* **silenced** the Sadducees, the Pharisees got
Mk 1: 25 "*Be* **quiet**!" said Jesus sternly. "Come out of him!"
    4: 39 got up, rebuked the wind and said to the waves, "Quiet! *Be* **still**!"
Lk 4: 35 "*Be* **quiet**!" Jesus said sternly. "Come out of him!" Then the demon
1Ti 5: 18 "*Do* not **muzzle** the ox while it is treading out the grain,"
1Pe 2: 15 doing good *you should* **silence** the ignorant **talk** of foolish men.

5822 φλαγελλόω, *phlagelloō*   Not used in UBS/NIV [√ *5848*]

5823 Φλέγων, *Phlegōn* [1] [√ *5825*]

Phlegon [1]

Ro 16: 14 **Phlegon**, Hermes, Patrobas, Hermas and the brothers with them.

5824 φλογίζω, *phlogizō* [2] [√ *5825*]

set on fire [1], sets on fire [1]

Jas 3: 6 corrupts the whole person, **sets** the whole course of his life **on fire**,
    3: 6 the whole course of his life on fire, and *is* itself **set on fire** by hell.

5825 φλόξ, *phlox* [7] [→ *5823, 5824*]

blazing [4], flames [2], fire [1]

Lk 16: 24 in water and cool my tongue, because I am in agony in this **fire**.'
Ac 7: 30 an angel appeared to Moses in the **flames** of a burning bush in the
2Th 1: 7 is revealed from heaven in **blazing** fire with his powerful angels.
Heb 1: 7 he says, "He makes his angels winds, his servants **flames** of fire."

Rev 1: 14 like wool, as white as snow, and his eyes were like **blazing** fire.
    2: 18 whose eyes are like **blazing** fire and whose feet are like burnished
    19: 12 His eyes are like **blazing** fire, and on his head are many crowns.

5826 φλυαρέω, *phlyareō* [1] [√ *5827*]

gossiping about [1]

3Jn 1: 10 call attention to what he is doing, **gossiping** maliciously **about** us.

5827 φλύαρος, *phlyaros* [1] [→ *3886, 5826*]

gossips [1]

1Ti 5: 13 but also **gossips** and busybodies, saying things they ought not to.

5828 φοβέομαι, *phobeomai* [95] [√ *5832*]

afraid [39], afraid of [14], fear [14], feared [5], alarmed [2], fearing [2], God-fearing [+*2536+3836*] [2], terrified [+*3489+5832*] [2], terrified [+*5379*] [2], careful [1], fear for [1], fearing that [+*3590*] [1], fears [1], filled with awe [1], free from fear of [+*3590*] [1], God-fearing Gentiles [+*2536+3836*] [1], in fear [1], respect [1], reverence for [1], reverence [1], terrified [1], worship [1]

Mt 1: 20 son of David, *do* not *be* **afraid** to take Mary home as your wife,
    2: 22 In Judea in place of his father Herod, *he was* **afraid** to go there.
    9: 8 When the crowd saw this, *they were* **filled with awe**; and they
    10: 26 "So *do* not *be* **afraid of** them. There is nothing concealed that will
    10: 28 *Do* not *be* **afraid** of those who kill the body but cannot kill the
    10: 28 *be* **afraid** of the One who can destroy both soul and body in hell.
    10: 31 So don't *be* **afraid**; you are worth more than many sparrows.
    14: 5 Herod wanted to kill John, but *he was* **afraid of** the people,
    14: 27 immediately said to them: "Take courage! It is I. Don't *be* **afraid**."
    14: 30 *he was* **afraid** and, beginning to sink, cried out, "Lord, save me!"
    17: 6 heard this, they fell facedown to the ground, **terrified** [+*5379*].
    17: 7 Jesus came and touched them. "Get up," he said. "Don't *be* **afraid**."
    21: 26 *we are* **afraid of** the people, for they all hold that John was a
    21: 46 but *they were* **afraid of** the crowd because the people held that he
    25: 25 So *I was* **afraid** and went out and hid your talent in the ground.
    27: 54 and all that had happened, *they were* **terrified** [+*5379*],
    28: 5 The angel said to the women, "*Do* not *be* **afraid**, for I know that
    28: 10 Then Jesus said to them, "*Do* not *be* **afraid**. Go and tell my
Mk 4: 41 *They were* **terrified** [+*3489+5832*] and asked each other,
    5: 15 sitting there, dressed and in his right mind; and *they were* **afraid**.
    5: 33 came and fell at his feet and, trembling with **fear**, told him the
    5: 36 what they said, Jesus told the synagogue ruler, "Don't *be* **afraid**;
    6: 20 because Herod **feared** John and protected him, knowing him to be
    6: 50 he spoke to them and said, "Take courage! It is I. Don't *be* **afraid**."
    9: 32 not understand what he meant and *were* **afraid** to ask him about it.
    10: 32 disciples were astonished, while those who followed *were* **afraid**.
    11: 18 and began looking for a way to kill him, for *they* **feared** him,
    11: 32 (*They* **feared** the people, for everyone held that John really was a
    12: 12 But *they were* **afraid of** the crowd; so they left him and went
    16: 8 the tomb. They said nothing to anyone, because *they were* **afraid**.
Lk 1: 13 "*Do* not *be* **afraid**, Zechariah; your prayer has been heard.
    1: 30 But the angel said to her, "*Do* not *be* **afraid**, Mary, you have
    1: 50 His mercy extends *to* those *who* **fear** him, from generation to
    2: 9 Lord shone around them, and *they were* **terrified** [+*3489+5832*]
    2: 10 But the angel said to them, "*Do* not *be* **afraid**. I bring you good
    5: 10 Then Jesus said to Simon, "Don't *be* **afraid**; from now on you will
    8: 25 **In fear** and amazement they asked one another, "Who is this?
    8: 35 at Jesus' feet, dressed and in his right mind; and *they were* **afraid**.
    8: 50 Hearing this, Jesus said to Jairus, "Don't *be* **afraid**; just believe,
    9: 34 enveloped them, and *they were* **afraid** as they entered the cloud.
    9: 45 that they did not grasp it, and *they were* **afraid** to ask him about it.
    12: 4 *do* not *be* **afraid** of those who kill the body and after that can do
    12: 5 But I will show you whom *you should* **fear**: Fear him who,
    12: 5 **Fear** him who, after the killing of the body, has power to throw
    12: 5 has power to throw you into hell. Yes, I tell you, **fear** him.
    12: 7 Don't *be* **afraid**; you are worth more than many sparrows.
    12: 32 "*Do* not *be* **afraid**, little flock, for your Father has been pleased to
    18: 2 "In a certain town *there* was a judge *who* neither **feared** God nor
    18: 4 said to himself, 'Even though *I* don't **fear** God or care about men,
    19: 21 *I was* **afraid of** you, because you are a hard man. You take out
    20: 19 this parable against them. But *they were* **afraid of** the people.
    22: 2 some way to get rid of Jesus, for *they were* **afraid of** the people.

	23:40	"Don't you **fear** God," he said, "since you are under the same
Jn	6:19	the boat, walking on the water; and *they were* **terrified**.
	6:20	But he said to them, "It is I; don't *be* **afraid**."
	9:22	His parents said this because *they were* **afraid of** the Jews,
	12:15	"*Do not be* **afraid**, O Daughter of Zion; see, your king is coming,
	19: 8	When Pilate heard this, *he was* even more **afraid**,
Ac	5:26	use force, because *they* **feared** that the people would stone them.
	9:26	he tried to join the disciples, but *they were* all **afraid of** him,
	10: 2	and all his family were devout and **God-fearing** [+2536+3836];
	10:22	He is a righteous and **God-fearing** [+2536+3836] man, who is
	10:35	but accepts men from every nation who **fear** him and do what is
	13:16	"Men of Israel and you *Gentiles who* **worship** God, listen to me!
	13:26	of Abraham, and you **God-fearing** [+2536+3836] **Gentiles**, it is to
	16:38	that Paul and Silas were Roman citizens, *they were* **alarmed**.
	18: 9	in a vision: "*Do not be* **afraid**; keep on speaking, do not be silent.
	22:29	The commander himself *was* **alarmed** when he realized that he
	23:10	so violent that the commander *was* **afraid** Paul would be torn to
	27:17	**Fearing** [+3590] **that** they would run aground on the sandbars of
	27:24	and said, '*Do not be* **afraid**, Paul. You must stand trial before
	27:29	**Fearing** that we would be dashed against the rocks, they dropped
Ro	11:20	and you stand by faith. Do not be arrogant, but *be* **afraid**.
	13: 3	Do you want *to be* **free from fear** [+3590] **of** the one in authority?
	13: 4	But if you do wrong, *be* **afraid**, for he does not bear the sword for
2Co	11: 3	But *I am* **afraid** that just as Eve was deceived by the serpent's
	12:20	For *I am* **afraid** that when I come I may not find you as I want you
Gal	2:12	*because he was* **afraid of** those who belonged to the circumcision
	4:11	*I* **fear** for you, that somehow I have wasted my efforts on you.
Eph	5:33	wife as he loves himself, and the wife must **respect** her husband.
Col	3:22	their favor, but with sincerity of heart and **reverence for** the Lord.
Heb	4: 1	*let us be* **careful** that none of you be found to have fallen short of
	11:23	no ordinary child, and *they were* not **afraid of** the king's edict.
	11:27	By faith he left Egypt, not **afraid** of the king's anger; he persevered
	13: 6	say with confidence, "The Lord is my helper; *I will* not *be* **afraid**.
1Pe	2:17	Love the brotherhood of believers, **fear** God, honor the king.
	3: 6	her daughters if you do what is right and *do* not give way to **fear**.
	3:14	you are blessed. "*Do not* **fear** what they **fear**; do not be frightened."
1Jn	4:18	with punishment. The *one who* **fears** is not made perfect in love.
Rev	1:17	Then he placed his right hand on me and said: "*Do not be* **afraid**.
	2:10	*Do not be* **afraid of** what you are about to suffer. I tell you,
	11:18	the prophets *and your saints and those who* **reverence** your name,
	14: 7	He said in a loud voice, "**Fear** God and give him glory,
	15: 4	Who *will* not **fear** you, O Lord, and bring glory to your name?
	19: 5	all you his servants, you *who* **fear** him, both small and great!"

5829 φοβερός, *phoberos* [3] [√ 5832]

dreadful [1], fearful [1], terrifying [1]

Heb	10:27	but only a **fearful** expectation of judgment and of raging fire that
	10:31	It is a **dreadful** *thing* to fall into the hands of the living God.
	12:21	The sight was so **terrifying** that Moses said, "I am trembling with

5830 φοβέω, *phobeō*   Not used in UBS/NIV [√ 5832]

5831 φόβητρον, *phobētron* [1] [√ 5832]

fearful events [1]

| Lk | 21:11 | in various places, and **fearful events** and great signs from heaven. |

5832 φόβος, *phobos* [47] [→ 925, 1768, 1769, 1873, 5828, 5829, 5830, 5831]

fear [20], respect [5], awe [3], reverence [3], terrified [+3489+5828] [2], terror [2], afraid [+3552] [1], afraid [1], alarm [1], fear [+3489] [1], feared [1], fears [1], filled with awe [+3284] [1], reverent fear [1], terrified [+1328] [1], terrified [1], terror [+3489] [1], warning [1]

Mt	14:26	they were **terrified**. "It's a ghost," they said, and cried out in **fear**.
	28: 4	The guards were so **afraid** of him that they shook and became like
	28: 8	So the women hurried away from the tomb, **afraid** [+3552] yet
Mk	4:41	*They were* **terrified** [+3489+5828] and asked each other,
Lk	1:12	Zechariah saw him, he was startled and was gripped with **fear**.
	1:65	The neighbors were all filled with **awe**, and throughout the hill
	2: 9	Lord shone around them, and *they were* **terrified** [+3489+5828].

	5:26	They were filled *with* **awe** and said, "We have seen remarkable
	7:16	They *were* all **filled with awe** [+3284] and praised God. "A great
	8:37	to leave them, because they were overcome *with* **fear** [+3489].
	21:26	Men will faint from **terror**, apprehensive of what is coming on the
Jn	7:13	But no one would say anything publicly about him for **fear** of the
	19:38	was a disciple of Jesus, but secretly because he **feared** the Jews.
	20:19	with the doors locked for **fear** of the Jews, Jesus came and stood
Ac	2:43	Everyone was filled with **awe**, and many wonders and miraculous
	5: 5	and died. And great **fear** seized all who heard what had happened.
	5:11	Great **fear** seized the whole church and all who heard about these
	9:31	the Holy Spirit, it grew in numbers, living *in* the **fear** of the Lord.
	19:17	and Greeks living in Ephesus, they were all seized with **fear**,
Ro	3:18	"There is no **fear** of God before their eyes."
	8:15	you did not receive a spirit that makes you a slave again to **fear**,
	13: 3	For rulers hold no **terror** for those who do right, but for those who
	13: 7	then revenue; if **respect**, then respect; if honor, then honor.
	13: 7	then revenue; if respect, then **respect**; if honor, then honor.
1Co	2: 3	I came to you in weakness and **fear**, and with much trembling.
2Co	5:11	Since, then, we know what it is to **fear** the Lord, we try to persuade
	7: 1	and spirit, perfecting holiness out of **reverence** for God.
	7: 5	were harassed at every turn—conflicts on the outside, **fears** within.
	7:11	what indignation, what **alarm**, what longing, what concern,
	7:15	that you were all obedient, receiving him with **fear** and trembling.
Eph	5:21	Submit to one another out of **reverence** for Christ.
	6: 5	Slaves, obey your earthly masters with **respect** and fear, and with
Php	2:12	continue to work out your salvation with **fear** and trembling,
1Ti	5:20	are to be rebuked publicly, so that the others may take **warning**.
Heb	2:15	and free those who all their lives were held in slavery *by* their **fear**
1Pe	1:17	work impartially, live your lives as strangers here in **reverent fear**.
	2:18	Slaves, submit yourselves to your masters with all **respect**,
	3: 2	when they see the purity and **reverence** of your lives.
	3:14	you are blessed. "Do not fear what they **fear**; do not be frightened."
	3:15	the hope that you have. But do this with gentleness and **respect**,
1Jn	4:18	There is no **fear** in love. But perfect love drives out fear,
	4:18	But perfect love drives out **fear**, because fear has to do with
	4:18	love drives out fear, because **fear** has to do with punishment.
Jude	1:23	the fire and save them; to others show mercy, mixed with **fear**—
Rev	11:11	stood on their feet, and **terror** [+3489] struck those who saw them.
	18:10	**Terrified** at her torment, they will stand far off and cry: "'Woe!
	18:15	gained their wealth from her will stand far off, **terrified** [+1328].

5833 Φοίβη, *Phoibē* [1] [√ 5743]

Phoebe [1]

| Ro | 16: 1 | I commend to you our sister **Phoebe**, a servant of the church in |

5834 Φοινίκη, *Phoinikē* [3] [√ 5836]

Phoenicia [3]

Ac	11:19	in connection with Stephen traveled as far as **Phoenicia**,
	15: 3	on their way, and as they traveled through **Phoenicia** and Samaria,
	21: 2	We found a ship crossing over to **Phoenicia**, went on board

5835 Φοινίκισσα, *Phoinikissa*   Not used in UBS/NIV [√ 5836]

5836 φοῖνιξ¹, *phoinix¹* [2] [→ 5355, 5356, 5834, 5835, 5837]

palm branches [1], palm [1]

| Jn | 12:13 | They took **palm** branches and went out to meet him, shouting, |
| Rev | 7: 9 | white robes and were holding **palm branches** in their hands. |

5837 Φοῖνιξ², *Phoinix²* [1] [√ 5836]

Phoenix [1]

| Ac | 27:12 | that we should sail on, hoping to reach **Phoenix** and winter there. |

5838 φονεύς, *phoneus* [7] [√ 5840]

murderers [3], murderer [2], murdered [1], murderer [+467] [1]

| Mt | 22: 7 | He sent his army and destroyed those **murderers** and burned their |

Ac   3:14 and asked that a **murderer** [+467] be released to you.
    7:52 Righteous One. And now you have betrayed and **murdered** him—
   28: 4 his hand, they said to each other, "This man must be a **murderer**;
1Pe   4:15 it should not be as a **murderer** or thief or any other kind of
Rev 21: 8 But the cowardly, the unbelieving, the vile, the **murderers**,
   22:15 the **murderers**, the idolaters and everyone who loves and practices

5839 φονεύω, **phoneuō** [12] [√ 5840]

murder [6], murdered [3], commit murder [1], kill [1], murders [1]

Mt   5:21 '*Do* not **murder**, and anyone who murders will be subject to
   5:21 and anyone *who* **murders** will be subject to judgment.'
  19:18 Jesus replied, " '*Do* not **murder**, do not commit adultery,
  23:31 that you are the descendants *of* those *who* **murdered** the prophets.
  23:35 whom *you* **murdered** between the temple and the altar.
Mk 10:19 '*Do* not **murder**, do not commit adultery, do not steal, do not give
Lk   18:20 '*Do* not commit adultery, *do* not **murder**, do not steal, do not give
Ro   13: 9 "*Do* not **murder**," "Do not steal," "Do not covet,"
Jas   2:11 who said, "Do not commit adultery," also said, "*Do* not **murder**."
   2:11 If you do not commit adultery but *do* **commit murder**, you have
   4: 2 *You* **kill** and covet, but you cannot have what you want.
   5: 6 *You have* condemned and **murdered** innocent men, who were not

5840 φόνος, **phonos** [9] [→ 439, 4710?, 4711?, 5838, 5839]

murder [6], murderous [1], murders [1], put to death [+633+1877] [1]

Mt   15:19 **murder**, adultery, sexual immorality, theft, false testimony,
Mk   7:21 come evil thoughts, sexual immorality, theft, **murder**, adultery,
  15: 7 the insurrectionists who had committed **murder** in the uprising.
Lk   23:19 thrown into prison for an insurrection in the city, and for **murder**.)
  23:25 who had been thrown into prison for insurrection and **murder**,
Ac   9: 1 Saul was still breathing out **murderous** threats against the Lord's
Ro   1:29 They are full *of* envy, **murder**, strife, deceit and malice.
Heb 11:37 sawed in two; *they were* **put to death** [+633+1877] by the sword.
Rev   9:21 Nor did they repent of their **murders**, their magic arts, their sexual

5841 φορέω, **phoreō** [6] [√ 5770]

bear [2], wearing [2], borne [1], wear [1]

Mt   11: 8 fine clothes? No, those *who* **wear** fine clothes are in kings' palaces.
Jn   19: 5 When Jesus came out **wearing** the crown of thorns and the purple
Ro   13: 4 do wrong, be afraid, for *he does* not **bear** the sword for nothing.
1Co 15:49 And just as *we have* **borne** the likeness of the earthly man,
  15:49 earthly man, so *shall we* **bear** the likeness of the man from heaven.
Jas   2: 3 If you show special attention to the man **wearing** fine clothes

5842 φόρον, **phoron** [1]

forum [1]

Ac   28:15 and they traveled as far as the **Forum** of Appius and the Three

5843 φόρος, **phoros** [5] [√ 5770]

taxes [5]

Lk   20:22 Is it right for us to pay **taxes** to Caesar or not?"
  23: 2 He opposes payment *of* **taxes** to Caesar and claims to be Christ,
Ro   13: 6 This is also why you pay **taxes**, for the authorities are God's
  13: 7 If you owe **taxes**, pay taxes; if revenue, then revenue; if respect,
  13: 7 If you owe taxes, pay **taxes**; if revenue, then revenue; if respect,

5844 φορτίζω, **phortizō** [2] [√ 5770]

burdened [1], load down [1]

Mt   11:28 "Come to me, all you who are weary and **burdened**,
Lk   11:46 because *you* **load** people **down** *with* burdens they can hardly

5845 φορτίον, **phortion** [6] [√ 5770]

burden [1], burdens [1], cargo [1], help [1], load [1], loads [1]

Mt   11:30 For my yoke is easy and my **burden** is light."
  23: 4 They tie up heavy **loads** and put them on men's shoulders,
Lk   11:46 because you load people down with **burdens** they can hardly carry,
  11:46 and you yourselves will not lift one finger *to* **help** them.
Ac   27:10 is going to be disastrous and bring great loss *to* ship and **cargo**,
Gal   6: 5 for each one should carry his own **load**.

5846 φόρτος, **phortos** Not used in UBS/NIV [√ 5770]

5847 Φορτουνᾶτος, **Phortounatos** [1]

Fortunatus [1]

1Co 16:17 I was glad when Stephanas, **Fortunatus** and Achaicus arrived,

5848 φραγέλλιον, **phragellion** [1] [→ 5822, 5849]

whip [1]

Jn   2:15 So he made a **whip** out of cords, and drove all from the temple

5849 φραγελλόω, **phragelloō** [2] [√ 5848]

had flogged [2]

Mt   27:26 But he **had** Jesus **flogged**, and handed him over to be crucified.
Mk   15:15 He **had** Jesus **flogged**, and handed him over to be crucified.·

5850 φραγμός, **phragmos** [4] [√ 5852]

wall [2], barrier [1], country lanes [1]

Mt   21:33 He put a **wall** around it, dug a winepress in it and built a
Mk   12: 1 He put a **wall** around it, dug a pit for the winepress and built a
Lk   14:23 'Go out to the roads and **country lanes** and make them come in,
Eph   2:14 who has made the two one and has destroyed the **barrier**,

5851 φράζω, **phrazō** [1]

explain [1]

Mt   15:15 Peter said, "**Explain** the parable to us."

5852 φράσσω, **phrassō** [3] [→ 5850]

shut [1], silenced [1], stop [1]

Ro   3:19 so that every mouth *may be* **silenced** and the whole world held
2Co 11:10 nobody in the regions of Achaia *will* **stop** this boasting of mine.
Heb 11:33 and gained what was promised; who **shut** the mouths of lions,

5853 φρέαρ, **phrear** [7]

well [3], *untranslated* [1], Abyss [1], it[s] [+3836] [1], shaft [1]

Lk   14: 5 of you has a son or an ox that falls into a **well** on the Sabbath day,
Jn   4:11 woman said, "you have nothing to draw with and the **well** is deep.
  4:12 who gave us the **well** and drank from it himself, as did also his
Rev   9: 1 to the earth. The star was given the key *to* the **shaft** of the Abyss.
  9: 2 When he opened [RPG] the Abyss, smoke rose from it like the
  9: 2 smoke rose from **it**[s] [+3836] like the smoke from a gigantic
  9: 2 The sun and sky were darkened by the smoke *from* the **Abyss**.

5854 φρεναπατάω, **phrenapataō** [1] [√ 5856 + 573]

deceives [1]

Gal   6: 3 thinks he is something when he is nothing, *he* **deceives** himself.

5855 φρεναπάτης, **phrenapatēs** [1] [√ 5856 + 573]

deceivers [1]

Tit   1:10 For there are many rebellious people, mere talkers and **deceivers**,

5856 φρήν, *phrēn* [2] [→ *932, 933, 3939, 4368, 5425, 5426, 5672, 5735, 5819, 5820, 5854, 5855, 5858, 5859, 5860, 5861, 5862, 5863; cf. 2370, 2969, 4196, 5404*]

thinking like [*+1181+3836*] [1], thinking [1]

1Co 14:20 Brothers, stop **thinking** [*+1181+3836*] like children. In regard to
　　14:20 In regard to evil be infants, but *in* your **thinking** be adults.

5857 φρίσσω, *phrissō* [1]

shudder [1]

Jas 2:19 is one God. Good! Even the demons believe that—and **shudder**.

5858 φρονέω, *phroneō* [26] [√ *5856*]

have in mind [2], *untranslated* [1], agree with each other
[*+899+3836*] [1], arrogant [*+5734*] [1], attitude [1], being
like-minded [*+899+3836*] [1], concern [1], concerned [1], does^s
so [1], feel [1], live in harmony [*+899+3836*] [1], mind on [1],
mind [1], minds set on [1], on think [1], proud [*+3836+5734*] [1],
purpose [1], regards as special [1], set minds on [1], spirit of
unity [*+899+3836*] [1], take a view of things [1], take view [1],
think [1], thought [1], views are [1]

Mt 16:23 *you do* not **have in mind** the things of God, but the things of men."
Mk 8:33 "*You do* not **have in mind** the things of God, but the things of
Ac 28:22 But we want to hear what *your* **views are**, for we know that people
Ro 8: 5 the sinful nature *have their* **minds set on** what that nature desires;
　　11:20 of unbelief, and you stand by faith. *Do* not *be* **arrogant** [*+5734*],
　　12: 3 **[RPG]** but rather think of yourself with sober judgment,
　　12: 3 than you ought, but rather **think** of yourself with sober judgment,
　　12:16 **Live in harmony** [*+899+3836*] with one another. Do not be proud,
　　12:16 *Do* not *be* **proud** [*+3836+5734*], but be willing to associate with
　　14: 6 He *who* **regards** one day **as special**, does so to the Lord. He who
　　14: 6 He who regards one day as special, **does**^s so to the Lord. He who
　　15: 5 and encouragement give you a **spirit of unity** [*+899+3836*] among
1Co 13:11 When I was a child, I talked like a child, *I* **thought** like a child,
2Co 13:11 for perfection, listen to my appeal, *be of* one **mind**, live in peace.
Gal 5:10 I am confident in the Lord that *you will* **take** no other view.
Php 1: 7 It is right for me *to* **feel** this way about all of you, since I have you
　　2: 2 then make my joy complete by **being like-minded** [*+899+3836*],
　　2: 2 having the same love, being one in spirit and **purpose**.
　　2: 5 Your **attitude** *should be* the same as that of Christ Jesus.
　　3:15 All of us who are mature *should* **take** such **a view of things**.
　　3:15 And if *on* some point *you* **think** differently, that too God will
　　3:19 and their glory is in their shame. Their **mind** *is* **on** earthly things.
　　4: 2 and I plead with Syntyche *to* **agree** [*+899+3836*] **with each other**
　　4:10 in the Lord that at last you have renewed your **concern** for me.
　　4:10 Indeed, *you have been* **concerned**, but you had no opportunity to
Col 3: 2 **Set** *your* **minds on** things above, not on earthly things.

5859 φρόνημα, *phronēma* [4] [√ *5856*]

mind [4]

Ro 8: 6 The **mind** of sinful man is death, but the mind controlled by the
　　8: 6 is death, but the **mind** controlled by the Spirit is life and peace;
　　8: 7 the sinful **mind** is hostile to God. It does not submit to God's law,
　　8:27 And he who searches our hearts knows the **mind** of the Spirit,

5860 φρόνησις, *phronēsis* [2] [√ *5856*]

understanding [1], wisdom [1]

Lk 1:17 their children and the disobedient to the **wisdom** of the righteous—
Eph 1: 8 that he lavished on us with all wisdom and **understanding**.

5861 φρόνιμος, *phronimos* [14] [√ *5856*]

wise [8], conceited [*+1571+4123*] [2], more shrewd [1], sensible
[1], shrewd [1], they^s [*+3836*] [1]

Mt 7:24 and puts them into practice is like a **wise** man who built his house
　　10:16 Therefore be as **shrewd** as snakes and as innocent as doves.
　　24:45 "Who then is the faithful and **wise** servant, whom the master has
　　25: 2 Five of them were foolish and five were **wise**.

25: 4 The **wise**, however, took oil in jars along with their lamps.
25: 8 The foolish ones said *to* the **wise**, 'Give us some of your oil;
25: 9 " 'No,' they^s [*+3836*] replied, 'there may not be enough for both us
Lk 12:42 The Lord answered, "Who then is the faithful and **wise** manager,
　　16: 8 For the people of this world are **more shrewd** in dealing with their
Ro 11:25 brothers, so that you may not be **conceited** [*+1571+4123*]:
　　12:16 with people of low position. Do not be **conceited** [*+1571+4123*].
1Co 4:10 We are fools for Christ, but you are so **wise** in Christ! We are
　　10:15 I speak *to* **sensible** *people*; judge for yourselves what I say.
2Co 11:19 You gladly put up with fools since you are so **wise**!

5862 φρονίμως, *phronimōs* [1] [√ *5856*]

shrewdly [1]

Lk 16: 8 the dishonest manager because he had acted **shrewdly**.

5863 φροντίζω, *phrontizō* [1] [√ *5856*]

careful [1]

Tit 3: 8 so that those who have trusted in God *may be* **careful** to devote

5864 φρουρέω, *phroureō* [4] [√ *4574 + 3972*]

guard [1], guarded [1], held prisoners [1], shielded [1]

2Co 11:32 had the city of the Damascenes **guarded** in order to arrest me.
Gal 3:23 Before this faith came, *we were* **held prisoners** by the law,
Php 4: 7 *will* **guard** your hearts and your minds in Christ Jesus.
1Pe 1: 5 who through faith *are* **shielded** by God's power until the coming

5865 φρυάσσω, *phryassō* [1]

rage [1]

Ac 4:25 " 'Why *do* the nations **rage** and the peoples plot in vain?

5866 φρύγανον, *phryganon* [1]

brushwood [1]

Ac 28: 3 Paul gathered a pile *of* **brushwood** and, as he put it on the fire,

5867 Φρυγία, *Phrygia* [3]

Phrygia [3]

Ac 2:10 **Phrygia** and Pamphylia, Egypt and the parts of Libya near Cyrene;
　　16: 6 and his companions traveled throughout the region of **Phrygia**
　　18:23 from place to place throughout the region of Galatia and **Phrygia**,

5868 φυγαδεύω, *phygadeuō* Not used in UBS/NIV
[√ *5771*]

5869 Φύγελος, *Phygelos* [1]

Phygelus [1]

2Ti 1:15 of Asia has deserted me, including **Phygelus** and Hermogenes.

5870 φυγή, *phygē* [1] [√ *5771*]

flight [1]

Mt 24:20 Pray that your **flight** will not take place in winter or on the

5871 φυλακή, *phylakē* [47 / 46] [√ *5875*]

prison [31], jail [3], haunt [2], watch [2], cell [1], guard [1], guards
[1], imprisonments [1], keeping watch [*+5875*] [1], prisons [1],
time of night [1], watch of the night [1]

Mt 5:25 hand you over to the officer, and you may be thrown into **prison**.
　　14: 3 and bound him and put him in **prison** because of Herodias,
　　14:10 and had John beheaded in the **prison**.
　　14:25 *During* the fourth **watch** of the night Jesus went out to them,
　　18:30 and had the man thrown into **prison** until he could pay the debt.
　　24:43 If the owner of the house had known *at* what **time of night** the

25:36 you looked after me, I was in **prison** and you came to visit me.'
25:39 When did we see you sick or in **prison** and go to visit you?'
25:43 clothe me, I was sick and in **prison** and you did not look after me.'
25:44 or thirsty or a stranger or needing clothes or sick or in **prison**,
Mk 6:17 to have John arrested, and he had him bound and put in **prison**.
6:27 to bring John's head. The man went, beheaded John in the **prison**,
6:48 About the fourth **watch** of the night he went out to them,
Lk 2: 8 fields nearby, **keeping watch** [+5875] over their flocks at night.
3:20 Herod added this to them all: He locked John up in **prison**.
12:38 even if he comes in the second or third **watch of the night**.
12:58 turn you over to the officer, and the officer throw you into **prison**.
21:12 They will deliver you to synagogues and **prisons**, and you will be
22:33 replied, "Lord, I am ready to go with you to **prison** and to death."
23:19 (Barabbas had been thrown into **prison** for an insurrection in the
23:25 He released the man who had been thrown into **prison** for
Jn 3:24 (This was before John was put in **prison**.)
Ac 5:19 during the night an angel of the Lord opened the doors *of* the **jail**
5:22 But on arriving at the **jail**, the officers did not find them there.
5:25 The men you put in **jail** are standing in the temple courts teaching
8: 3 to house, he dragged off men and women and put them in **prison**.
12: 4 After arresting him, he put him in **prison**, handing him over to be
12: 5 So Peter was kept in **prison**, but the church was earnestly praying
12: 6 bound with two chains, and sentries stood **guard** at the entrance.
12:10 They passed the first and second **guards** and came to the iron gate
12:17 and described how the Lord had brought him out of **prison**.
16:23 they had been severely flogged, they were thrown into **prison**,
16:24 he put them in the inner **cell** and fastened their feet in the stocks.
16:27 and when he saw the **prison** doors open, he drew his sword
16:37 even though we are Roman citizens, and threw us into **prison**.
16:40 After Paul and Silas came out of the **prison**, they went to Lydia's
22: 4 arresting both men and women and throwing them into **prison**,
26:10 the authority of the chief priests I put many of the saints in **prison**,
2Co 6: 5 in beatings, **imprisonments** and riots; in hard work, sleepless
11:23 I have worked much harder, been in **prison** more frequently,
Heb 11:36 and flogging, while still others were chained and put in **prison**.
1Pe 3:19 through whom also he went and preached to the spirits in **prison**
Rev 2:10 I tell you, the devil will put some of you in **prison** to test you,
18: 2 has become a home for demons and a **haunt** for every evil spirit,
18: 2 for every evil spirit, a **haunt** for every unclean and detestable bird.
18: 2 bird [UBS+ *a* **haunt** *for every unclean and detestable beast*].
20: 7 the thousand years are over, Satan will be released from his **prison**

5872 φυλακίζω, *phylakizō* [1] [√ 5875]

imprison [1]

Ac 22:19 men know that I went from one synagogue to another *to* **imprison**

5873 φυλακτήριον, *phylaktērion* [1] [√ 5875]

phylacteries [1]

Mt 23: 5 They make their **phylacteries** wide and the tassels on their

5874 φύλαξ, *phylax* [3] [√ 5875]

guards [2], sentries [1]

Ac 5:23 the jail securely locked, with the **guards** standing at the doors;
12: 6 bound with two chains, and **sentries** stood guard at the entrance.
12:19 he cross-examined the **guards** and ordered that they be executed.

5875 φυλάσσω, *phylassō* [31] [→ 1126, 1302, 1428, 5871, 5872, 5873, 5874]

keep [5], guard [4], kept [3], obey [3], kept under guard [2], on guard [2], abstain from [1], guarded [1], guarding [1], guards [1], in obedience to [1], keep from [1], keeping watch [+5871] [1], kept safe [1], obeyed [1], on guard against [1], protect [1], protected [1]

Mt 19:20 "All these *I have* **kept**," the young man said. "What do I still lack?"
Mk 10:20 "Teacher," he declared, "all these *I have* **kept** since I was a boy."
Lk 2: 8 fields nearby, **keeping watch** [+5871] over their flocks at night.
8:29 and though he was chained hand and foot and **kept under guard**,
11:21 "When a strong man, fully armed, **guards** his own house, his
11:28 "Blessed rather are those who hear the word of God and **obey** it."

12:15 *Be* **on** *your* **guard** against all kinds of greed; a man's life does not
18:21 "All these *I have* **kept** since I was a boy," he said.
Jn 12:25 while the man who hates his life in this world *will* **keep** it for
12:47 "As for the person who hears my words but *does* not **keep** them,
17:12 I protected them and **kept** them **safe** by that name you gave me.
Ac 7:53 law that was put into effect through angels but *have* not **obeyed** it."
12: 4 handing him over *to be* **guarded** by four squads of four soldiers
16: 4 by the apostles and elders in Jerusalem for the people *to* **obey**.
21:24 about you, but that you yourself are living **in obedience to** the law.
21:25 have written to them our decision that they *should* **abstain from**
22:20 and **guarding** the clothes of those who were killing him.'
23:35 Then he ordered that Paul *be* **kept under guard** in Herod's palace.
28:16 Paul was allowed to live by himself, with a soldier *to* **guard** him.
Ro 2:26 If those who are not circumcised **keep** the law's requirements,
Gal 6:13 Not even those who are circumcised **obey** the law, yet they want
2Th 3: 3 and he *will* strengthen and **protect** you from the evil one.
1Ti 5:21 the elect angels, to **keep** these instructions without partiality,
6:20 Timothy, **guard** what has been entrusted to your care. Turn away
2Ti 1:12 and am convinced that he is able *to* **guard** what I have entrusted to
1:14 **Guard** the good deposit that was entrusted to you—guard it with
4:15 You too *should be* **on** *your* **guard against** him, because he
2Pe 2: 5 but **protected** Noah, a preacher of righteousness, and seven others;
3:17 *be* **on** *your* **guard** so that you may not be carried away by the error
1Jn 5:21 Dear children, **keep** yourselves from idols.
Jude 1:24 To him who is able *to* **keep** you **from** falling and to present you

5876 φυλή, *phylē* [31] [→ 260, 1559, 5241; cf. 5886]

tribe [24], tribes [5], nations [1], peoples [1]

Mt 19:28 will also sit on twelve thrones, judging the twelve **tribes** of Israel.
24:30 will appear in the sky, and all the **nations** of the earth will mourn.
Lk 2:36 a prophetess, Anna, the daughter of Phanuel, of the **tribe** of Asher.
22:30 my kingdom and sit on thrones, judging the twelve **tribes** of Israel.
Ac 13:21 Saul son of Kish, of the **tribe** of Benjamin, who ruled forty years.
Ro 11: 1 a descendant of Abraham, *from* the **tribe** of Benjamin.
Php 3: 5 people of Israel, of the **tribe** of Benjamin, a Hebrew of Hebrews;
Heb 7:13 He of whom these things are said belonged to a different **tribe**,
7:14 and in regard to that **tribe** Moses said nothing about priests.
Jas 1: 1 Jesus Christ, *To* the twelve **tribes** scattered among the nations:
Rev 1: 7 and all the **peoples** of the earth will mourn because of him.
5: 5 See, the Lion of the **tribe** of Judah, the Root of David,
5: 9 and with your blood you purchased men for God from every **tribe**
7: 4 of those who were sealed: 144,000 from all the **tribes** of Israel.
7: 5 From the **tribe** of Judah 12,000 were sealed, from the tribe of
7: 5 from the **tribe** of Reuben 12,000, from the tribe of Gad 12,000,
7: 5 from the tribe of Reuben 12,000, from the **tribe** of Gad 12,000,
7: 6 from the **tribe** of Asher 12,000, from the tribe of Naphtali 12,000,
7: 6 from the tribe of Asher 12,000, from the **tribe** of Naphtali 12,000,
7: 6 the tribe of Naphtali 12,000, from the **tribe** of Manasseh 12,000,
7: 7 from the **tribe** of Simeon 12,000, from the tribe of Levi 12,000,
7: 7 from the tribe of Simeon 12,000, from the **tribe** of Levi 12,000,
7: 7 from the tribe of Levi 12,000, from the **tribe** of Issachar 12,000,
7: 8 from the **tribe** of Zebulun 12,000, from the tribe of Joseph 12,000,
7: 8 from the tribe of Zebulun 12,000, from the **tribe** of Joseph 12,000,
7: 8 the tribe of Joseph 12,000, from the **tribe** of Benjamin 12,000.
7: 9 from every nation, **tribe**, people and language, standing before the
11: 9 **tribe**, language and nation will gaze on their bodies and refuse
13: 7 And he was given authority over every **tribe**, people, language
14: 6 who live on the earth—to every nation, **tribe**, language and people.
21:12 On the gates were written the names *of* the twelve **tribes** of Israel.

5877 φύλλον, *phyllon* [6]

leaves [5], in leaf [+2400] [1]

Mt 21:19 by the road, he went up to it but found nothing on it except **leaves**.
24:32 As soon as its twigs get tender and its **leaves** come out, you know
Mk 11:13 Seeing in the distance a fig tree **in leaf** [+2400], he went to find out
11:13 When he reached it, he found nothing but **leaves**, because it was
13:28 As soon as its twigs get tender and its **leaves** come out, you know
Rev 22: 2 And the **leaves** of the tree are for the healing of the nations.

5878 φύραμα, *phyrama* [5]

batch of dough [2], batch [2], lump of clay [1]

Ro 9:21 out of the same **lump of clay** some pottery for noble purposes

11:16 dough offered as firstfruits is holy, then the *whole* **batch** is holy;
1Co 5: 6 know that a little yeast works through the whole **batch of dough**?
     5: 7 Get rid of the old yeast that you may be a new **batch** without
Gal 5: 9 "A little yeast works through the whole **batch of dough**."

5879 φυσικός, *physikos* [3] [√ *5886*]

natural [2], creatures of instinct [1]

Ro   1:26 Even their women exchanged **natural** relations for unnatural ones.
     1:27 In the same way the men also abandoned **natural** relations with
2Pe 2:12 **creatures of instinct**, born only to be caught and destroyed,

5880 φυσικῶς, *physikōs* [1] [√ *5886*]

instinct [1]

Jude 1:10 and what things they do understand *by* **instinct**, like unreasoning

5881 φυσιόω, *physioō* [7] [√ *5886*]

arrogant [2], proud [2], puffs up [2], take pride [1]

1Co 4: 6 Then *you* will not **take pride** in one man over against another.
     4:18 Some of you have become **arrogant**, as if I were not coming to
     4:19 then I will find out not only how these **arrogant** *people* are
     5: 2 And you are **proud**! Shouldn't you rather have been filled with
     8: 1 all possess knowledge. Knowledge **puffs up**, but love builds up.
    13: 4 love is kind. It does not envy, it does not boast, *it is* not **proud**.
Col 2:18 has seen, and his unspiritual mind **puffs** him **up** with idle notions.

5882 φύσις, *physis* [14] [√ *5886*]

nature [7], natural [+*2848*] [2], *untranslated* [1], birth [1], kinds
[1], physically [+*1666*] [1], unnatural ones [+*3836*+*4123*] [1]

Ro   1:26 exchanged natural relations for **unnatural** [+*3836*+*4123*] **ones**.
     2:14 who do not have the law, do *by* **nature** things required by the law,
     2:27 The one who is not circumcised **physically** [+*1666*] and yet obeys
    11:21 For if God did not spare the **natural** [+*2848*] branches, he will not
    11:24 if you were cut out of an olive tree that is wild by **nature**,
    11:24 and contrary to **nature** were grafted into a cultivated olive tree,
    11:24 how much more readily will these, the **natural** [+*2848*] branches,
1Co 11:14 Does not the very **nature** of things teach you that if a man has long
Gal 2:15 "We who are Jews *by* **birth** and not 'Gentile sinners'
     4: 8 know God, you were slaves to those who *by* **nature** are not gods.
Eph 2: 3 and thoughts. Like the rest, we were *by* **nature** objects of wrath.
Jas 3: 7 All **kinds** of animals, birds, reptiles and creatures of the sea are
     3: 7 of the sea are being tamed and have been tamed [RPG] by man,
2Pe 1: 4 so that through them you may participate in the divine **nature**

5883 φυσίωσις, *physiōsis* [1] [√ *5886*]

arrogance [1]

2Co 12:20 of anger, factions, slander, gossip, **arrogance** and disorder.

5884 φυτεία, *phyteia* [1] [√ *5886*]

plant [1]

Mt 15:13 "Every **plant** that my heavenly Father has not planted will be pulled

5885 φυτεύω, *phyteuō* [11] [√ *5886*]

planted [6], plants [3], planted the seed [1], planting [1]

Mt 15:13 "Every plant that my heavenly Father *has* not **planted** will be
    21:33 There was a landowner who **planted** a vineyard. He put a wall
Mk 12: 1 "A man **planted** a vineyard. He put a wall around it, dug a pit for
Lk 13: 6 "A man had a fig tree, **planted** in his vineyard, and he went to look
    17: 6 'Be uprooted and **planted** in the sea,' and it will obey you.
    17:28 and drinking, buying and selling, **planting** and building.
    20: 9 "A man **planted** a vineyard, rented it to some farmers and went
1Co 3: 6 I **planted the seed**, Apollos watered it, but God made it grow.
     3: 7 So neither he *who* **plants** nor he who waters is anything, but only
     3: 8 The man *who* **plants** and the man who waters have one purpose,
     9: 7 Who **plants** a vineyard and does not eat of its grapes? Who tends a

5886 φύω, *phyō* [3] [→ *1770, 1874, 1875, 3574, 3745, 4103, 5242, 5243, 5879, 5880, 5881, 5882, 5883, 5884, 5885*; *cf. 5876*]

came up [2], grows [1]

Lk   8: 6 Some fell on rock, and *when it* **came up**, the plants withered
     8: 8 *It* **came up** and yielded a crop, a hundred times more than was
Heb 12:15 and that no bitter root **grows** up to cause trouble and defile many.

5887 φωλεός, *phōleos* [2]

holes [2]

Mt   8:20 Jesus replied, "Foxes have **holes** and birds of the air have nests,
Lk   9:58 Jesus replied, "Foxes have **holes** and birds of the air have nests,

5888 φωνέω, *phōneō* [43 / 42] [√ *5889*]

called [9], crows [7], call [3], called out [3], calling [3], crowed
[3], called to [2], summoned [2], asking for [1], called in [1], calls
[1], crow [1], invite [1], said [1], sent for [+*3306*] [1], sent for [1],
shouted [+*3489*+*5889*] [1], shriek [+*3489*+*5889*] [1]

Mt 20:32 Jesus stopped and **called** them. "What do you want me to do for
    26:34 truth," Jesus answered, "this very night, before the rooster **crows**,
    26:74 to them, "I don't know the man!" Immediately a rooster **crowed**.
    26:75 "Before the rooster **crows**, you will disown me three times."
    27:47 of those standing there heard this, they said, "He's **calling** Elijah."
Mk   1:26 man violently and came out of him *with* a **shriek** [+*3489*+*5889*].
     9:35 Sitting down, Jesus **called** the Twelve and said, "If anyone wants to
    10:49 Jesus stopped and said, "**Call** him." So they **called** to the blind man,
    10:49 and said, "Call him." So *they* **called to** the blind man, "Cheer up!
    10:49 to the blind man, "Cheer up! On your feet! *He's* **calling** you."
    14:30 the rooster **crows** twice you yourself will disown me three times."
    14:68 went out into the entryway [UBS+ *and the rooster* **crowed**.].
    14:72 Immediately the rooster **crowed** the second time. Then Peter
    14:72 "Before the rooster **crows** twice you will disown me three times."
    15:35 standing near heard this, they said, "Listen, *he's* **calling** Elijah."
Lk   8: 8 When he said this, *he* **called out**, "He who has ears to hear,
     8:54 But he took her by the hand and **said**, "My child, get up!"
    14:12 "When you give a luncheon or dinner, *do* not **invite** your friends,
    16: 2 So he **called** him **in** and asked him, 'What is this I hear about you?
    16:24 So he **called to** him, 'Father Abraham, have pity on me and send
    19:15 Then *he* **sent** [+*3306*] **for** the servants to whom he had given the
    22:34 Jesus answered, "I tell you, Peter, before the rooster **crows** today,
    22:60 you're talking about!" Just as he was speaking, the rooster **crowed**.
    22:61 "Before the rooster **crows** today, you will disown me three times."
    23:46 Jesus **called out** with a loud voice, "Father, into your hands I
Jn   1:48 while you were still under the fig tree before Philip **called** you."
     2: 9 had drawn the water knew. Then he **called** the bridegroom *aside*
     4:16 He told her, "Go, **call** your husband and come back."
     9:18 and had received his sight until *they* **sent for** the man's parents.
     9:24 A second time *they* **summoned** the man who had been blind.
    10: 3 to his voice. He **calls** his own sheep by name and leads them out.
    11:28 she had said this, she went back and **called** her sister Mary aside.
    11:28 "The Teacher is here," she said, "and *is* **asking for** you."
    12:17 Now the crowd that was with him when *he* **called** Lazarus from
    13:13 "You **call** me 'Teacher' and 'Lord,' and rightly so, for that is what I
    13:38 I tell you the truth, before the rooster **crows**, you will disown me
    18:27 Again Peter denied it, and at that moment a rooster **began to crow**.
    18:33 **summoned** Jesus and asked him, "Are you the king of the Jews?"
Ac   9:41 Then he **called** the believers and the widows and presented her to
    10: 7 Cornelius **called** two of his servants and a devout soldier who was
    10:18 *They* **called out**, asking if Simon who was known as Peter was
    16:28 But Paul **shouted** [+*3489*+*5889*], "Don't harm yourself! We are all
Rev 14:18 and **called** in a loud voice to him who had the sharp sickle,

5889 φωνή, *phōnē* [139] [→ *231, 430, 851, 936, 1771, 1876, 2215, 2787, 2971, 3032, 4715, 5244, 5245, 5246, 5247, 5888*]

μέγας φωνή, (great voice) [40] Mt 27:46,50; Mk 1:26; 5:7;
15:34,37; Lk 4:33; 8:28; 17:15; 19:37; 23:23,46; Jn 11:43; Ac
7:57,60; 8:7; 14:10; 16:28; 26:24; Rev 1:10; 5:2,12; 6:10; 7:2,10;
8:13; 10:3; 11:12,15; 12:10; 14:2,7,9,15,18; 16:1,17; 19:1,17; 21:3

voice [85], sound [8], voices [5], rumblings [4], *untranslated* [2], roar [2], shouts [2], words [2], at the top of voice [*+3489*] [1], at the top of voices [*+3489*] [1], blasts [1], call [1], called out [*+2048*] [1], called out [*+3306+3489*] [1], called out in a loud voice [*+149*] [1], cried out [*+3189+3489*] [1], cry [1], gave a shout [*+3189*] [1], heard sound [*+1181*] [1], in unison [*+1181+1651*] [1], languages [1], me [*+1609+3836*] [1], music [1], peals [1], roar [*+3489*] [1], shouted [*+2048+3836*] [1], shouted [*+3489+3836+5774*] [1], shouted [*+3489+5888*] [1], shouting at the top of voice [*+3306+3489*] [1], shriek [*+3489+5888*] [1], shrieks [*+1066+3489*] [1], someone is saying [1], sounded [1], sounds [1], things [1], thundering [1], tone [1]

Mt 2:18 "A **voice** is heard in Ramah, weeping and great mourning,
3: 3 "A **voice** of one calling in the desert, 'Prepare the way for the Lord,
3:17 And a **voice** from heaven said, "This is my Son, whom I love;
12:19 will not quarrel or cry out; no one will hear his **voice** in the streets.
17: 5 and a **voice** from the cloud said, "This is my Son, whom I love;
27:46 About the ninth hour Jesus cried out *in* a loud **voice**, "*Eloi,*
27:50 And when Jesus had cried out again *in* a loud **voice**, he gave up his
Mk 1: 3 "a **voice** of one calling in the desert, 'Prepare the way for the Lord,
1:11 And a **voice** came from heaven: "You are my Son, whom I love;
1:26 man violently and came out of him *with* a **shriek** [*+3489+5888*].
5: 7 He shouted at the top of his **voice**, "What do you want with me,
9: 7 and enveloped them, and a **voice** came from the cloud:
15:34 And at the ninth hour Jesus cried out *in* a loud **voice**, "*Eloi,*
15:37 With a loud **cry**, Jesus breathed his last.
Lk 1:44 As soon as the **sound** of your greeting reached my ears, the baby in
3: 4 "A **voice** of one calling in the desert, 'Prepare the way for the Lord,
3:22 And a **voice** came from heaven: "You are my Son, whom I love;
4:33 an evil spirit. He cried out **at the top of** his **voice** [*+3489*],
8:28 and fell at his feet, **shouting at the top of** ***his*** **voice** [*+3306+3489*],
9:35 A **voice** came from the cloud, saying, "This is my Son, whom I
9:36 When the **voice** had spoken, they found that Jesus was alone.
11:27 was saying these things, a woman in the crowd **called** [*+2048*] **out**,
17:13 and **called out in a loud voice** [*+149*], "Jesus, Master, have pity on
17:15 he saw he was healed, came back, praising God in a loud **voice**.
19:37 to praise God *in* loud **voices** for all the miracles they had seen:
23:23 But *with* loud **shouts** they insistently demanded that he be
23:23 demanded that he be crucified, and their **shouts** prevailed.
23:46 Jesus called out *with* a loud **voice**, "Father, into your hands I
Jn 1:23 "I am the **voice** of one calling in the desert, 'Make straight the way
3: 8 You hear its **sound**, but you cannot tell where it comes from
3:29 for him, and is full of joy when he hears the bridegroom's **voice**.
5:25 and has now come when the dead will hear the **voice** of the Son of
5:28 time is coming when all who are in their graves will hear his **voice**
5:37 concerning me. You have never heard his **voice** nor seen his form,
10: 3 watchman opens the gate for him, and the sheep listen to his **voice**.
10: 4 of them, and his sheep follow him because they know his **voice**.
10: 5 away from him because they do not recognize a stranger's **voice**."
10:16 They too will listen to my **voice**, and there shall be one flock
10:27 My sheep listen to my **voice**; I know them, and they follow me.
11:43 he had said this, Jesus called *in* a loud **voice**, "Lazarus, come out!"
12:28 Then a **voice** came from heaven, "I have glorified it, and will glorify
12:30 Jesus said, "This **voice** was for your benefit, not mine.
18:37 Everyone on the side of truth listens to **me** [*+1609+3836*]."
Ac 2: 6 When they **heard** this **sound** [*+1181*], a crowd came together in
2:14 up with the Eleven, raised his **voice** and addressed the crowd:
4:24 they heard this, they raised their **voices** together in prayer to God.
7:31 As he went over to look more closely, he heard the Lord's **voice**:
7:57 yelling **at the top of** their **voices** [*+3489*], they all rushed at him,
7:60 Then *he* fell on his knees and **cried out** [*+3189+3489*], "Lord,
8: 7 *With* **shrieks** [*+1066+3489*], evil spirits came out of many,
9: 4 He fell to the ground and heard a **voice** say to him, "Saul, Saul,
9: 7 there speechless; they heard the **sound** but did not see anyone.
10:13 Then a **voice** told him, "Get up, Peter. Kill and eat."
10:15 The **voice** spoke to him a second time, "Do not call anything impure
11: 7 Then I heard a **voice** telling me, 'Get up, Peter. Kill and eat.'
11: 9 "The **voice** spoke from heaven a second time, 'Do not call anything
12:14 When she recognized Peter's **voice**, she was so overjoyed she ran
12:22 They shouted, "This is the **voice** of a god, not of a man."
13:27 yet in condemning him they fulfilled the **words** of the prophets that
14:10 and **called out** [*+3306+3489*], "Stand up on your feet!" At that,
14:11 had done, they **shouted** [*+2048+3836*] in the Lycaonian language,
16:28 But Paul **shouted** [*+3489+5888*], "Don't harm yourself! We are all
19:34 they all shouted **in unison** [*+1181+1651*] for about two hours:
22: 7 I fell to the ground and heard a **voice** say to me, 'Saul! Saul!
22: 9 but they did not understand the **voice** of him who was speaking to
22:14 and to see the Righteous One and to hear **words** from his mouth.
22:22 Then they raised their **voices** and shouted, "Rid the earth of him!
24:21 unless it was this one **thing**[s] I shouted as I stood in their presence:
26:14 and I heard a **voice** saying to me in Aramaic, 'Saul, Saul,
26:24 are out of your mind, Paul!" *he* **shouted** [*+3489+3836+5774*].
1Co 14: 7 Even in the case of lifeless things that make **sounds**, such as the
14: 8 Again, if the trumpet does not sound a clear **call**, who will get
14:10 Undoubtedly there are all sorts *of* **languages** in the world,
14:11 then I do not grasp the meaning *of* what **someone is saying**,
Gal 4:20 how I wish I could be with you now and change my **tone**,
1Th 4:16 with the **voice** of the archangel and with the trumpet call of God,
Heb 3: 7 So, as the Holy Spirit says: "Today, if you hear his **voice**,
3:15 "Today, if you hear his **voice**, do not harden your hearts as you did
4: 7 "Today, if you hear his **voice**, do not harden your hearts."
12:19 or *to* such a **voice** speaking words that those who heard it begged
12:26 At that time his **voice** shook the earth, but now he has promised,
2Pe 1:17 and glory from God the Father when the **voice** came to him from
1:18 We ourselves heard this **voice** that came from heaven when we
2:16 who spoke with a man's **voice** and restrained the prophet's
Rev 1:10 in the Spirit, and I heard behind me a loud **voice** like a trumpet,
1:12 I turned around to see the **voice** that was speaking to me.
1:15 in a furnace, and his **voice** was like the sound of rushing waters.
1:15 in a furnace, and his voice was like the **sound** of rushing waters.
3:20 If anyone hears my **voice** and opens the door, I will come in
4: 1 And the **voice** I had first heard speaking to me like a trumpet said,
4: 5 throne came flashes of lightning, **rumblings** and peals of thunder.
5: 2 And I saw a mighty angel proclaiming in a loud **voice**, "Who is
5:11 Then I looked and heard the **voice** of many angels, numbering
5:12 *In* a loud **voice** they sang: "Worthy is the Lamb, who was slain,
6: 1 Then I heard one of the four living creatures say in a **voice** like
6: 6 Then I heard what sounded like a **voice** among the four living
6: 7 I heard the **voice** of the fourth living creature say, "Come!"
6:10 They called out *in* a loud **voice**, "How long, Sovereign Lord,
7: 2 He called out *in* a loud **voice** to the four angels who had been
7:10 And they cried out *in* a loud **voice**: "Salvation belongs to our God,
8: 5 of thunder, **rumblings**, flashes of lightning and an earthquake.
8:13 I heard an eagle that was flying in midair call out *in* a loud **voice**:
8:13 because of the trumpet **blasts** about to be sounded by the other
9: 9 and the **sound** of their wings was like the thundering of many
9: 9 and the sound of their wings was like the **thundering** of many
9:13 and I heard a **voice** coming from the horns of the golden altar that
10: 3 and *he* **gave a** loud **shout** [*+3189*] like the roar of a lion. When he
10: 3 When he shouted, the **voices** of the seven thunders spoke.
10: 4 but I heard a **voice** from heaven say, "Seal up what the seven
10: 7 But in the days when the seventh **[RPG]** angel is about to sound
10: 8 Then the **voice** that I had heard from heaven spoke to me once
11:12 Then they heard a loud **voice** from heaven saying to them,
11:15 his trumpet, and there were loud **voices** in heaven, which said:
11:19 **rumblings**, peals of thunder, an earthquake and a great hailstorm.
12:10 Then I heard a loud **voice** in heaven say: "Now have come the
14: 2 And I heard a **sound** from heaven like the roar of rushing waters
14: 2 And I heard a sound from heaven like the **roar** of rushing waters
14: 2 the roar of rushing waters and like a **[RPG]** loud peal of thunder.
14: 2 The **sound** I heard was like that of harpists playing their harps.
14: 7 He said in a loud **voice**, "Fear God and give him glory,
14: 9 A third angel followed them and said in a loud **voice**: "If anyone
14:13 Then I heard a **voice** from heaven say, "Write: Blessed are the dead
14:15 and called in a loud **voice** to him who was sitting on the cloud,
14:18 and called *in* a loud **voice** to him who had the sharp sickle,
16: 1 Then I heard a loud **voice** from the temple saying to the seven
16:17 and out of the temple came a loud **voice** from the throne, saying,
16:18 of lightning, **rumblings**, peals of thunder and a severe earthquake.
18: 2 With a mighty **voice** he shouted: "Fallen! Fallen is Babylon the
18: 4 Then I heard another **voice** from heaven say: "Come out of her,
18:22 The **music** of harpists and musicians, flute players and trumpeters,
18:22 The **sound** of a millstone will never be heard in you again.
18:23 The **voice** of bridegroom and bride will never be heard in you
19: 1 After this I heard what sounded like the **roar** [*+3489*] of a great
19: 5 Then a **voice** came from the throne, saying: "Praise our God,
19: 6 Then I heard what **sounded** like a great multitude, like the roar of
19: 6 like the **roar** of rushing waters and like loud peals of thunder,
19: 6 like the roar of rushing waters and like loud **peals** of thunder,
19:17 who cried in a loud **voice** to all the birds flying in midair, "Come,
21: 3 And I heard a loud **voice** from the throne saying, "Now the dwelling

5890 φῶς, phōs [73] [√ 5743]

φῶς τοῦ κόσμου, (light of the world) [5] Mt 5:14; Jn 8:12; 9:5; 11:9; 12:46

light [66], daylight [2], lights [2], fire [1], firelight [1], its [+3836] [1]

Mt	4:16	the people living in darkness have seen a great **light**; on those
	4:16	on those living in the land of the shadow of death a **light** has
	5:14	"You are the **light** of the world. A city on a hill cannot be hidden.
	5:16	In the same way, let your **light** shine before men, that they may see
	6:23	If then the **light** within you is darkness, how great is that darkness!
	10:27	What I tell you in the dark, speak in the **daylight**; what is
	17:2	shone like the sun, and his clothes became as white as the **light**.
Mk	14:54	There he sat with the guards and warmed himself at the **fire**.
Lk	2:32	a **light** for revelation to the Gentiles and for glory to your people
	8:16	he puts it on a stand, so that those who come in can see the **light**.
	11:33	he puts it on its stand, so that those who come in may see the **light**.
	11:35	See to it, then, that the **light** within you is not darkness.
	12:3	What you have said in the dark will be heard in the **daylight**,
	16:8	in dealing with their own kind than are the people of the **light**.
	22:56	A servant girl saw him seated there in the **firelight**. She looked
Jn	1:4	In him was life, and that life was the **light** of men.
	1:5	The **light** shines in the darkness, but the darkness has not
	1:7	He came as a witness to testify concerning that **light**, so that
	1:8	He himself was not the **light**; he came only as a witness to the
	1:8	himself was not the light; he came only as a witness to the **light**.
	1:9	The true **light** that gives light to every man was coming into the
	3:19	**Light** has come into the world, but men loved darkness instead of
	3:19	but men loved darkness instead of **light** because their deeds were
	3:20	Everyone who does evil hates the **light**, and will not come into the
	3:20	and will not come into the **light** for fear that his deeds will be
	3:21	But whoever lives by the truth comes into the **light**, so that it may
	5:35	and gave light, and you chose for a time to enjoy his **light**.
	8:12	spoke again to the people, he said, "I am the **light** of the world.
	8:12	me will never walk in darkness, but will have the **light** of life."
	9:5	While I am in the world, I am the **light** of the world."
	11:9	walks by day will not stumble, for he sees by this world's **light**.
	11:10	It is when he walks by night that he stumbles, for he has no **light**."
	12:35	told them, "You are going to have the **light** just a little while longer.
	12:35	Walk while you have the **light**, before darkness overtakes you.
	12:36	Put your trust in the **light** while you have it, so that you may
	12:36	Put your trust in the light while you have it [+3836], so that you
	12:36	the light while you have it, so that you may become sons of **light**."
	12:46	I have come into the world as a **light**, so that no one who believes
Ac	9:3	on his journey, suddenly a **light** from heaven flashed around him.
	12:7	an angel of the Lord appeared and a **light** shone in the cell.
	13:47	"'I have made you a **light** for the Gentiles, that you may bring
	16:29	The jailer called for **lights**, rushed in and fell trembling before Paul
	22:6	suddenly a bright **light** from heaven flashed around me.
	22:9	My companions saw the **light**, but they did not understand the
	22:11	into Damascus, because the brilliance of the **light** had blinded me.
	26:13	O king, as I was on the road, I saw a **light** from heaven,
	26:18	to open their eyes and turn them from darkness to **light**, and from
	26:23	would proclaim **light** to his own people and to the Gentiles."
Ro	2:19	you are a guide for the blind, a **light** for those who are in the dark,
	13:12	let us put aside the deeds of darkness and put on the armor of **light**.
2Co	4:6	For God, who said, "Let **light** shine out of darkness," made his light
	6:14	in common? Or what fellowship can **light** have with darkness?
	11:14	no wonder, for Satan himself masquerades as an angel of **light**.
Eph	5:8	For you were once darkness, but now you are **light** in the Lord.
	5:8	but now you are light in the Lord. Live as children of **light**
	5:9	(for the fruit of the **light** consists in all goodness, righteousness
	5:13	But everything exposed by the **light** becomes visible,
	5:14	for it is **light** that makes everything visible. This is why it is said:
Col	1:12	you to share in the inheritance of the saints in the kingdom of **light**.
1Th	5:5	You are all sons of the **light** and sons of the day. We do not belong
1Ti	6:16	who alone is immortal and who lives in unapproachable **light**,
Jas	1:17	from above, coming down from the Father of the *heavenly* **lights**,
1Pe	2:9	of him who called you out of darkness into his wonderful **light**.
1Jn	1:5	and declare to you: God is **light**; in him there is no darkness at all.
	1:7	But if we walk in the **light**, as he is in the light, we have fellowship
	1:7	But if we walk in the light, as he is in the **light**, we have fellowship
	2:8	the darkness is passing and the true **light** is already shining.
	2:9	Anyone who claims to be in the **light** but hates his brother is still in
	2:10	Whoever loves his brother lives in the **light**, and there is nothing in
Rev	18:23	The **light** of a lamp will never shine in you again. The voice of
	21:24	The nations will walk by its **light**, and the kings of the earth will
	22:5	They will not need the **light** of a lamp or the light of the sun,
	22:5	They will not need the light of a lamp or the **light** of the sun,

5891 φωστήρ, phōstēr [2] [√ 5743]

brilliance [1], stars [1]

Php	2:15	depraved generation, in which you shine like **stars** in the universe
Rev	21:11	and its **brilliance** was like that of a very precious jewel, like a

5892 φωσφόρος, phōsphoros [1] [√ 5743 + 5770]

morning star [1]

2Pe	1:19	until the day dawns and the **morning star** rises in your hearts.

5893 φωτεινός, phōteinos [5] [√ 5743]

full of light [3], bright [1], lighted [1]

Mt	6:22	If your eyes are good, your whole body will be **full of light**.
	17:5	While he was still speaking, a **bright** cloud enveloped them,
Lk	11:34	When your eyes are good, your whole body also is **full of light**.
	11:36	Therefore, if your whole body is **full of light**, and no part of it
	11:36	is full of light, and no part of it dark, it will be completely **lighted**,

5894 φωτίζω, phōtizō [11] [√ 5743]

enlightened [2], bring to light [1], brought to light [1], give light [1], gives light to [1], gives light [1], illuminated [1], make plain to [1], received light [1], shines on [1]

Lk	11:36	be completely lighted, as when the light of a lamp **shines on** you."
Jn	1:9	The true light that **gives light to** every man was coming into the
1Co	4:5	He *will* **bring to light** what is hidden in darkness and will expose
Eph	1:18	I pray also that the eyes of your heart *may be* **enlightened** in order
	3:9	and *to* **make plain to** everyone the administration of this mystery,
2Ti	1:10	and *has* **brought** life and immortality to **light** through the gospel.
Heb	6:4	It is impossible for those *who have* once *been* **enlightened**,
	10:32	Remember those earlier days *after you had* **received** the **light**,
Rev	18:1	had great authority, and the earth *was* **illuminated** by his splendor.
	21:23	for the glory of God **gives** it **light**, and the Lamb is its lamp.
	22:5	or the light of the sun, for the Lord God *will* **give** them **light**.

5895 φωτισμός, phōtismos [2] [√ 5743]

light [2]

2Co	4:4	so that they cannot see the **light** of the gospel of the glory of
	4:6	made his light shine in our hearts to give us the **light** of the

X, Ch

5896 χ, ch Not used in UBS/NIV

5897 χαίρω, chairō [74] [→ 940, 2373, 2374, 2375, 4716, 5176, 5915, 5919, 5920, 5921, 5922, 5923]

rejoice [17], glad [14], greetings [6], delighted [4], hail [3], joy [3], rejoicing [3], delight [2], happy [2], joyful [2], joyfully [2], full of joy [+5915] [1], full of joy [1], gladly [1], gloat [1], good-by [1], happier [1], joy have [+5915] [1], make rejoice [1], overjoyed [+22] [1], overjoyed [+3489+5379+5915] [1], overjoyed [1], pleased [1], rejoices [1], welcome [+3306] [1], welcomes [+3306] [1], weres [1]

Mt	2:10	they saw the star, *they were* **overjoyed** [+3489+5379+5915].
	5:12	**Rejoice** and be glad, because great is your reward in heaven,
	18:13	*he is* **happier** about that one sheep than about the ninety-nine that
	26:49	Going at once to Jesus, Judas said, "**Greetings**, Rabbi!" and kissed
	27:29	front of him and mocked him. "**Hail**, king of the Jews!" they said.
	28:9	"**Greetings**," he said. They came to him, clasped his feet
Mk	14:11	They *were* **delighted** to hear this and promised to give him money.

15:18 And they began to call out to him, "**Hail**, king of the Jews!"
Lk 1:14 and delight to you, and many *will* **rejoice** because of his birth,
1:28 The angel went to her and said, "**Greetings**, you who are highly
6:23 "**Rejoice** in that day and leap for joy,
10:20 However, *do* not **rejoice** that the spirits submit to you, but rejoice
10:20 submit to you, but **rejoice** that your names are written in heaven."
13:17 but the people *were* **delighted** with all the wonderful things he was
15:5 And when he finds it, he **joyfully** puts it on his shoulders
15:32 But we had to celebrate and *be* **glad**, because this brother of yours
19:6 So he came down at once and welcomed him **gladly**.
19:37 the whole crowd of disciples began **joyfully** to praise God in loud
22:5 *They were* **delighted** and agreed to give him money.
23:8 When Herod saw Jesus, *he was* greatly **pleased**, because for a long
Jn 3:29 and *is* **full of joy** [+*5915*] when he hears the bridegroom's voice.
4:36 eternal life, so that the sower and the reaper *may be* **glad** together.
8:56 rejoiced at the thought of seeing my day; he saw it and *was* **glad**."
11:15 and for your sake *I am* **glad** I was not there, so that you may
14:28 If you loved me, *you* would *be* **glad** that I am going to the Father,
16:20 you the truth, you will weep and mourn while the world **rejoices**.
16:22 is your time of grief, but I will see you again and you *will* **rejoice**,
19:3 and went up to him again and again, saying, "**Hail**, king of the
20:20 and side. The disciples *were* **overjoyed** when they saw the Lord.
Ac 5:41 **rejoicing** because they had been counted worthy of suffering
8:39 the eunuch did not see him again, but went on his way **rejoicing**.
11:23 *he was* **glad** and encouraged them all to remain true to the Lord
13:48 heard this, *they were* **glad** and honored the word of the Lord;
15:23 To the Gentile believers in Antioch, Syria and Cilicia: **Greetings**.
15:31 The people read it and *were* **glad** for its encouraging message.
23:26 Claudius Lysias, To His Excellency, Governor Felix: **Greetings**.
Ro 12:12 *Be* **joyful** in hope, patient in affliction, faithful in prayer.
12:15 **Rejoice** with those who rejoice; mourn with those who mourn.
12:15 Rejoice with *those who* **rejoice**; mourn with those who mourn.
16:19 has heard about your obedience, so *I am* **full of joy** over you;
1Co 7:30 as if they did not; those *who are* **happy**, as if they were not;
7:30 as if they did not; those who are happy, as if *they* **were**[s] not;
13:6 Love *does* not **delight** in evil but rejoices with the truth.
16:17 *I was* **glad** when Stephanas, Fortunatus and Achaicus arrived,
2Co 2:3 I should not be distressed by those who ought *to* **make** me **rejoice**.
6:10 sorrowful, yet always **rejoicing**; poor, yet making many rich;
7:7 your ardent concern for me, so that my **joy** *was* greater than ever.
7:9 yet now *I am* **happy**, not because you were made sorry, but
7:13 *we were* especially **delighted** to see how happy Titus was,
7:16 *I am* **glad** I can have complete confidence in you.
13:9 *We are* **glad** whenever we are weak but you are strong; and our
13:11 Finally, brothers, **good-by**. Aim for perfection, listen to my appeal,
Php 1:18 And because of this *I* **rejoice**. Yes, and I will continue to rejoice,
1:18 because of this I rejoice. Yes, and *I will continue to* **rejoice**,
2:17 coming from your faith, *I am* **glad** and rejoice with all of you.
2:18 So you too *should be* **glad** and rejoice with me.
2:28 so that when you see him again *you may be* **glad** and I may have
3:1 Finally, my brothers, **rejoice** in the Lord! It is no trouble for me to
4:4 **Rejoice** in the Lord always. I will say it again: Rejoice!
4:4 Rejoice in the Lord always. I will say it again: **Rejoice**!
4:10 *I* **rejoice** greatly in the Lord that at last you have renewed your
Col 1:24 Now *I* **rejoice** in what was suffered for you, and I fill up in my
2:5 present with you in spirit and **delight** to see how orderly you are
1Th 3:9 return for all the **joy** *we* **have** [+*5915*] in the presence of our God
5:16 *Be* **joyful** always;
Jas 1:1 To the twelve tribes scattered among the nations: **Greetings**.
1Pe 4:13 But **rejoice** that you participate in the sufferings of Christ,
4:13 so that *you may be* **overjoyed** [+*22*] when his glory is revealed.
2Jn 1:4 *It has given me* great **joy** to find some of your children walking in
1:10 do not take him into your house or **welcome** [+*3306*] him.
1:11 Anyone *who* **welcomes** [+*3306*] him shares in his wicked work.
3Jn 1:3 *It gave me* great **joy** to have some brothers come and tell about
Rev 11:10 The inhabitants of the earth *will* **gloat** over them and will celebrate
19:7 *Let us* **rejoice** and be glad and give him glory! For the wedding of

5898 χάλαζα, *chalaza* [4]

hail [2], hailstones [1], hailstorm [1]

Rev 8:7 his trumpet, and there came **hail** and fire mixed with blood,
11:19 rumblings, peals of thunder, an earthquake and a great **hailstorm**.
16:21 From the sky huge **hailstones** of about a hundred pounds each fell
16:21 And they cursed God on account of the plague *of* **hail**,

5899 χαλάω, *chalaō* [7] [→ *5902, 5903, 5904*]

let down [3], lowered [3], lowered [+*2768*] [1]

Mk 2:4 through it, **lowered** the mat the paralyzed man was lying on.
Lk 5:4 "Put out into deep water, and **let down** the nets for a catch."
5:5 caught anything. But because you say so, *I will* **let down** the nets."
Ac 9:25 and **lowered** [+*2768*] him in a basket through an opening in the
27:17 *they* **lowered** the sea anchor and let the ship be driven along.
27:30 escape from the ship, the sailors **let** the lifeboat **down** into the sea,
2Co 11:33 But *I was* **lowered** in a basket from a window in the wall

5900 Χαλδαῖος, *Chaldaios* [1]

Chaldeans [1]

Ac 7:4 "So he left the land *of* the **Chaldeans** and settled in Haran.

5901 χαλεπός, *chalepos* [2]

so violent [+*3336*] [1], terrible [1]

Mt 8:28 They were **so violent** [+*3336*] that no one could pass that way.
2Ti 3:1 But mark this: There will be **terrible** times in the last days.

5902 χαλιναγωγέω, *chalinagōgeō* [2] [√ *5899 + 72*]

keep a tight rein on [1], keep in check [1]

Jas 1:26 himself religious and yet *does* not **keep a tight rein on** his tongue,
3:2 he is a perfect man, able *to* **keep** his whole body **in check**.

5903 χαλινός, *chalinos* [2] [√ *5899*]

bits [1], bridles [1]

Jas 3:3 When we put **bits** into the mouths of horses to make them obey us,
Rev 14:20 rising as high as the horses' **bridles** for a distance of 1,600 stadia.

5904 χαλινόω, *chalinoō* Not used in UBS/NIV [√ *5899*]

5905 χάλκεος, *chalkeos* Not used in UBS/NIV [√ *5910*]

5906 χαλκεύς, *chalkeus* [1] [√ *5910*]

metalworker [1]

2Ti 4:14 Alexander the **metalworker** did me a great deal of harm. The Lord

5907 χαλκηδών, *chalkēdōn* [1] [√ *5910*]

chalcedony [1]

Rev 21:19 the second sapphire, the third **chalcedony**, the fourth emerald,

5908 χαλκίον, *chalkion* [1] [√ *5910*]

kettles [1]

Mk 7:4 other traditions, such as the washing of cups, pitchers and **kettles**.)

5909 χαλκολίβανον, *chalkolibanon* [2] [√ *5910*]

bronze [1], burnished bronze [1]

Rev 1:15 His feet were like **bronze** glowing in a furnace, and his voice was
2:18 are like blazing fire and whose feet are like **burnished bronze**.

5910 χαλκός, *chalkos* [5] [→ *5905, 5906, 5907, 5908, 5909, 5911*]

money [2], bronze [1], copper [1], gong [1]

Mt 10:9 Do not take along any gold or silver or **copper** in your belts;
Mk 6:8 journey except a staff—no bread, no bag, no **money** in your belts.
12:41 and watched the crowd putting their **money** into the temple
1Co 13:1 have not love, I am *only* a resounding **gong** or a clanging cymbal.
Rev 18:12 every kind made of ivory, costly wood, **bronze**, iron and marble;

5911 χαλκοῦς, *chalkous* [1] [√ *5910*]

of bronze [1]

Rev 9:20 and idols **of** gold, silver, **bronze**, stone and wood—

5912 χαμαί, *chamai* [2]

on the ground [1], to the ground [1]

Jn   9: 6 Having said this, he spit **on the ground**, made some mud with the
18: 6 When Jesus said, "I am he," they drew back and fell **to the ground.**

5913 Χανάαν, *Chanaan* [2] [→ *5914*]

Canaan [+*1178*] [1], Canaan [1]

Ac   7:11 "Then a famine struck all Egypt and **Canaan**, bringing great
13:19 he overthrew seven nations in **Canaan** [+*1178*] and gave their land

5914 Χαναναῖος, *Chananaios* [1] [√ *5913*]

Canaanite [1]

Mt 15:22 A **Canaanite** woman from that vicinity came to him, crying out,

5915 χαρά, *chara* [59] [√ *5897*]

joy [44], happiness [2], joyfully [+*3552*] [2], rejoicing [2], filled
with joy [+*22*] [1], filled with joy [+*3489*] [1], full of joy [+*5897*] [1],
glad [1], happy [1], joy have [+*5897*] [1], overjoyed
[+*3489*+*5379*+*5897*] [1], overjoyed [1], pleasant [1]

Mt   2:10 When they saw the star, *they were* **overjoyed**
[+*3489*+*5379*+*5897*].
13:20 is the man who hears the word and at once receives it with **joy.**
13:44 and then in his **joy** went and sold all he had and bought that field.
25:21 charge of many things. Come and share your master's **happiness**!'
25:23 charge of many things. Come and share your master's **happiness**!'
28: 8 hurried away from the tomb, afraid yet **filled with joy** [+*3489*],
Mk   4:16 on rocky places, hear the word and at once receive it with **joy.**
Lk   1:14 He will be a **joy** and delight to you, and many will rejoice
2:10 I bring you good news of great **joy** that will be for all the people.
8:13 Those on the rock are the ones who receive the word with **joy**
10:17 The seventy-two returned with **joy** and said, "Lord,
15: 7 I tell you that in the same way there will be more **rejoicing** in
15:10 there is **rejoicing** in the presence of the angels of God over one
24:41 while they still did not believe it because of **joy** and amazement,
24:52 Then they worshiped him and returned to Jerusalem with great **joy.**
Jn   3:29 and is **full of joy** [+*5897*] when he hears the bridegroom's voice.
3:29 the bridegroom's voice. That **joy** is mine, and it is now complete.
15:11 I have told you this so that my **joy** may be in you and that your joy
15:11 so that my joy may be in you and that your **joy** may be complete.
16:20 the world rejoices. You will grieve, but your grief will turn to **joy.**
16:21 the anguish because of her **joy** that a child is born into the world.
16:22 you again and you will rejoice, and no one will take away your **joy.**
16:24 my name. Ask and you will receive, and your **joy** will be complete.
17:13 so that they may have the full measure of my **joy** within them.
Ac   8: 8 So there was great **joy** in that city.
12:14 she was so **overjoyed** she ran back without opening it
13:52 And the disciples were filled with **joy** and with the Holy Spirit.
15: 3 had been converted. This news made all the brothers very **glad.**
Ro 14:17 but *of* righteousness, peace and **joy** in the Holy Spirit,
15:13 May the God of hope fill you with all **joy** and peace as you trust in
15:32 so that by God's will I may come to you with **joy** and together with
2Co   1:24 that we lord it over your faith, but we work with you *for* your **joy,**
2: 3 I had confidence in all of you, that you would all share my **joy.**
7: 4 greatly encouraged; in all our troubles my **joy** knows no bounds.
7:13 we were especially delighted to see how **happy** Titus was.
8: 2 their overflowing **joy** and their extreme poverty welled up in rich
Gal   5:22 is love, **joy,** peace, patience, kindness, goodness, faithfulness,
Php   1: 4 In all my prayers for all of you, I always pray with **joy**
1:25 will continue with all of you for your progress and **joy** in the faith,
2: 2 then make my **joy** complete by being like-minded, having the same
2:29 Welcome him in the Lord with great **joy,** and honor men like him,
4: 1 my brothers, you whom I love and long for, my **joy** and crown,
Col   1:11 you may have great endurance and patience, and **joyfully** [+*3552*]
1Th   1: 6 you welcomed the message with the **joy** given by the Holy Spirit.

2:19 For what is our hope, our **joy,** or the crown in which we will glory
2:20 Indeed, you are our glory and **joy.**
3: 9 return for all the **joy** [+*5897*] we have in the presence of our God
2Ti   1: 4 your tears, I long to see you, so that I may be filled with **joy.**
Phm   1: 7 Your love has given me great **joy** and encouragement,
Heb 10:34 and **joyfully** [+*3552*] accepted the confiscation of your property,
12: 2 who for the **joy** set before him endured the cross, scorning its
12:11 No discipline seems **pleasant** at the time, but painful. Later on,
13:17 Obey them so that their work will be a **joy,** not a burden, for that
Jas   1: 2 Consider it pure **joy,** my brothers, whenever you face trials of
4: 9 Change your laughter to mourning and your **joy** to gloom.
1Pe   1: 8 and *are* filled with an inexpressible and glorious **joy** [+*22*],
1Jn   1: 4 We write this to make our **joy** complete.
2Jn   1:12 and talk with you face to face, so that our **joy** may be complete.
3Jn   1: 4 I have no greater **joy** than to hear that my children are walking in

5916 χάραγμα, *charagma* [8] [→ *5917, 5918, 5925*]

mark [7], image [1]

Ac 17:29 or silver or stone—an **image** made by man's design and skill.
Rev 13:16 and slave, to receive a **mark** on his right hand or on his forehead,
13:17 so that no one could buy or sell unless he had the **mark,** which is
14: 9 and his image and receives his **mark** on the forehead or on the
14:11 and his image, or for anyone who receives the **mark** of his name."
16: 2 and painful sores broke out on the people who had the **mark** of the
19:20 With these signs he had deluded those who had received the **mark**
20: 4 or his image and had not received his **mark** on their foreheads

5917 χαρακτήρ, *charaktēr* [1] [√ *5916*]

exact representation [1]

Hcb   1: 3 radiance of God's glory and the **exact representation** of his being,

5918 χάραξ, *charax* [1] [√ *5916*]

embankment [1]

Lk 19:43 you when your enemies will build an **embankment** against you

5919 χαρίζομαι, *charizomai* [23] [√ *5897*]

forgive [5], forgave [3], canceled [2], gave [2], hand over [2],
forgiven [1], forgiving [1], freely given [1], graciously give [1],
graciously given [1], granted [1], in grace gave [1], released [1],
restored [1]

Lk   7:21 sicknesses and evil spirits, and **gave** sight to many who were blind.
7:42 had the money to pay him back, so he **canceled** the debts of both.
7:43 "I suppose the one who *had* the bigger debt **canceled.**"
Ac   3:14 and Righteous One and asked that a murderer *be* **released** to you.
25:11 Jews are not true, no one has the right *to* **hand** me **over** to them.
25:16 "I told them that it is not the Roman custom *to* **hand over** any man
27:24 and God has **graciously given** you the lives of all who sail with
Ro   8:32 how *will* he not also, along with him, **graciously give** us all
1Co   2:12 from God, that we may understand what God *has* **freely given** us.
2Co   2: 7 Now instead, you ought *to* **forgive** and comfort him, so that he
2:10 If *you* **forgive** anyone, I also forgive him. And what I have
2:10 And what I *have* **forgiven**—if there was anything to forgive—
2:10 And what I have **forgiven**—if there was anything to **forgive**—
2:13 except that I was never a burden to you? **Forgive** me this wrong!'
Gal   3:18 but God **in** his **grace gave** it to Abraham through a promise.
Eph   4:32 **forgiving** each other, just as in Christ God forgave you.
4:32 forgiving each other, just as in Christ God **forgave** you.
Php   1:29 For *it has been* **granted** to you on behalf of Christ not only to
2: 9 the highest place and **gave** him the name that is above every name,
Col   2:13 God made you alive with Christ. *He* **forgave** us all our sins,
3:13 and **forgive** whatever grievances you may have against one
3:13 may have against one another. Forgive as the Lord **forgave** you.
Phm   1:22 because I hope *to be* **restored** to you in answer to your prayers.

5920 χάριν, *charin* [9] [√ *5897*]

for this reason [+*4047*] [2], for [2], because of [1], for the sake of
[1], the reason [+*4047*] [1], therefore [+*4005*] [1], why [+*5515*] [1]

Lk   7:47 **Therefore** [+*4005*], I tell you, her many sins have been forgiven—

Gal	3:19 **because of** transgressions until the Seed to whom the promise
Eph	3: 1 **For** [+4047] **this reason** I, Paul, the prisoner of Christ Jesus for
	3:14 **For** [+4047] **this reason** I kneel before the Father,
1Ti	5:14 their homes and to give the enemy no opportunity **for** slander.
Tit	1: 5 **The reason** [+4047] I left you in Crete was that you might
	1:11 they ought not to teach—and that **for the sake of** dishonest gain.
1Jn	3:12 and murdered his brother. And **why** [+5515] did he murder him?
Jude	1:16 boast about themselves and flatter others **for** their own advantage.

5921 χάρις, *charis* [155] [√ 5897]

κατὰ χάριν, (according to grace) [6] Ro 4:4,16; 12:6; 1Co 3:10; 2Th 1:12; 2Ti 1:9

ὑπὸ χάριν, (under grace) [2] Ro 6:14,15

χάρις καὶ εἰρήνη, (grace and peace) [17] Ro 1:7; 1Co 1:3; 2Co 1:2; Gal 1:3; Eph 1:2; Php 1:2; Col 1:2; 1Th 1:1; 2Th 1:2; 1Ti 1:2; 2Ti 1:2; Tit 1:4; Phm 1:3; 1Pe 1:2; 2Pe 1:2; 2Jn 1:3; Rev 1:4

χάρις ... ἔλεος, (grace ... mercy) [3] 1Ti 1:2; 2Ti 1:2; 2Jn 1:3

χάρις θεοῦ, (grace of God) [16] Lk 2:40; Ac 11:23; 13:43; 14:26; 1Co 3:10; 15:10,10; 2Co 8:1; 9:14; Gal 2:21; 2Th 1:12; Tit 2:11; Heb 2:9; 12:15; 1Pe 5:12; Jude 1:4

χάρις τῷ θεῷ, (grace with God) [9] Lk 1:30; Ro 6:17; 7:25; 1Co 15:57; 2Co 2:14; 8:16; 9:15; Col 3:16; 2Ti 1:3

χάρις κυρίου, (grace of the Lord) [15] Ac 15:11,40; Ro 16:20; 1Co 16:23; 2Co 8:9; 13:13; Gal 6:18; Php 4:23; 1Th 5:28; 2Th 1:12; 3:18; 1Ti 1:14; Phm 1:25; 2Pe 3:18; Rev 22:21

χάρις Χριστοῦ, (grace of Christ) [10] Ro 5:15; 2Co 8:9; 13:14; Gal 1:6; 6:18; Eph 4:7; Php 4:23; 1Th 5:28; 2Th 3:18; Phm 1:25

χάρις τῷ Χριστῷ, (grace to Christ) [1] 1Ti 1:12

grace [119], favor [7], thanks [5], credit [3], thank [+2400] [3], commendable [2], gift [2], act of grace [1], another^s [1], benefit [+1443] [1], benefit [+2400] [1], blessing [1], goodwill [1], gracious gift [1], gracious [1], gratitude [1], offering [1], privilege [1], thank [1], thankful [+2400] [1], thankfulness [1]

Lk	1:30 to her, "Do not be afraid, Mary, you have found **favor** with God.
	2:40 he was filled with wisdom, and the **grace** of God was upon him.
	2:52 Jesus grew in wisdom and stature, and *in* **favor** with God and men.
	4:22 and were amazed at the **gracious** words that came from his lips.
	6:32 "If you love those who love you, what **credit** is that to you?
	6:33 do good to those who are good to you, what **credit** is that to you?
	6:34 from whom you expect repayment, what **credit** is that to you?
	17: 9 *Would he* **thank** [+2400] the servant because he did what he was
Jn	1:14 and Only, who came from the Father, full *of* **grace** and truth.
	1:16 From the fullness of his grace we have all received one **blessing**
	1:16 of his grace we have all received one blessing after **another**^s.
	1:17 given through Moses; **grace** and truth came through Jesus Christ.
Ac	2:47 praising God and enjoying the **favor** of all the people.
	4:33 resurrection of the Lord Jesus, and much **grace** was upon them all.
	6: 8 Now Stephen, a man full *of God's* **grace** and power, did great
	7:10 and enabled him to gain the **goodwill** of Pharaoh king of Egypt;
	7:46 who enjoyed God's **favor** and asked that he might provide a
	11:23 When he arrived and saw the evidence of the **grace** of God,
	13:43 talked with them and urged them to continue in the **grace** of God.
	14: 3 who confirmed the message *of* his **grace** by enabling them to do
	14:26 where they had been committed *to* the **grace** of God for the work
	15:11 We believe it is through the **grace** of our Lord Jesus that we are
	15:40 and left, commended by the brothers *to* the **grace** of the Lord.
	18:27 he was a great help to those who by **grace** had believed.
	20:24 has given me—the task of testifying to the gospel *of* God's **grace**.
	20:32 "Now I commit you to God and to the word *of* his **grace**, which can
	24:27 but because Felix wanted to grant a **favor** to the Jews, he left Paul
	25: 3 They urgently requested Festus, as a **favor** to them, to have Paul
	25: 9 Festus, wishing to do the Jews a **favor**, said to Paul, "Are you
Ro	1: 5 we received **grace** and apostleship to call people from among all
	1: 7 **Grace** and peace to you from God our Father and from the Lord
	3:24 and are justified freely *by* his **grace** through the redemption that
	4: 4 his wages are not credited to him as a **gift**, but as an obligation.
	4:16 so that it may be by **grace** and may be guaranteed to all Abraham's
	5: 2 through whom we have gained access by faith into this **grace** in
	5:15 how much more did God's **grace** and the gift that came by the
	5:15 God's grace and the gift that came by the **grace** of the one man,
	5:17 more will those who receive God's abundant provision *of* **grace**

	5:20 But where sin increased, **grace** increased all the more,
	5:21 so also **grace** might reign through righteousness to bring eternal
	6: 1 then? Shall we go on sinning so that **grace** may increase?
	6:14 be your master, because you are not under law, but under **grace**.
	6:15 Shall we sin because we are not under law but under **grace**?
	6:17 But **thanks** be to God that, though you used to be slaves to sin,
	7:25 **Thanks** be to God—through Jesus Christ our Lord! So then,
	11: 5 So too, at the present time there is a remnant chosen by **grace**.
	11: 6 And if *by* **grace**, then it is no longer by works; if it were, grace
	11: 6 is no longer by works; if it were, grace **would** no longer be grace.
	11: 6 is no longer by works; if it were, grace would no longer be **grace**.
	12: 3 For by the **grace** given me I say to every one of you: Do not think
	12: 6 We have different gifts, according to the **grace** given us. If a man's
	15:15 if to remind you of them again, because of the **grace** God gave me
	16:20 Satan under your feet. The **grace** of our Lord Jesus be with you.
1Co	1: 3 **Grace** and peace to you from God our Father and the Lord Jesus
	1: 4 thank God for you because of his **grace** given you in Christ Jesus.
	3:10 By the **grace** God has given me, I laid a foundation as an expert
	10:30 If I take part in the meal *with* **thankfulness**, why am I denounced
	15:10 But *by* the **grace** of God I am what I am, and his grace to me was
	15:10 of God I am what I am, and his **grace** to me was not without effect.
	15:10 than all of them—yet not I, but the **grace** of God that was with me.
	15:57 But **thanks** be to God! He gives us the victory through our Lord
	16: 3 to the men you approve and send them with your **gift** to Jerusalem.
	16:23 The **grace** of the Lord Jesus be with you.
2Co	1: 2 **Grace** and peace to you from God our Father and the Lord Jesus
	1:12 so not according to worldly wisdom but according to God's **grace**.
	1:15 planned to visit you first so that *you might* **benefit** [+2400] twice.
	2:14 But **thanks** be to God, who always leads us in triumphal
	4:15 so that the **grace** that is reaching more and more people may cause
	6: 1 As God's fellow workers we urge you not to receive God's **grace**
	8: 1 we want you to know about the **grace** that God has given the
	8: 4 they urgently pleaded with us for the **privilege** of sharing in this
	8: 6 to bring also to completion this **act of grace** on your part.
	8: 7 in your love for us—see that you also excel in this **grace** *of giving*.
	8: 9 For you know the **grace** of our Lord Jesus Christ, that though he
	8:16 I **thank** God, who put into the heart of Titus the same concern I
	8:19 chosen by the churches to accompany us as we carry the **offering**,
	9: 8 And God is able to make all **grace** abound to you, so that in all
	9:14 go out to you, because of the surpassing **grace** God has given you.
	9:15 **Thanks** be to God for his indescribable gift!
	12: 9 But he said to me, "My **grace** is sufficient for you, for my power is
	13:14 May the **grace** of the Lord Jesus Christ, and the love of God,
Gal	1: 3 **Grace** and peace to you from God our Father and the Lord Jesus
	1: 6 so quickly deserting the one who called you by the **grace** of Christ
	1:15 who set me apart from birth and called me by his **grace**,
	2: 9 hand of fellowship when they recognized the **grace** given to me.
	2:21 I do not set aside the **grace** of God, for if righteousness could be
	5: 4 have been alienated from Christ; you have fallen away from **grace**.
	6:18 The **grace** of our Lord Jesus Christ be with your spirit, brothers.
Eph	1: 2 **Grace** and peace to you from God our Father and the Lord Jesus
	1: 6 to the praise *of* his glorious **grace**, which he has freely given us in
	1: 7 forgiveness of sins, in accordance with the riches *of* God's **grace**
	2: 5 were dead in transgressions—it is *by* **grace** you have been saved.
	2: 7 coming ages he might show the incomparable riches *of* his **grace**,
	2: 8 For it is *by* **grace** you have been saved, through faith—and this not
	3: 2 Surely you have heard about the administration *of* God's **grace**
	3: 7 I became a servant of this gospel by the gift of God's **grace** given
	3: 8 am less than the least of all God's people, this **grace** was given me:
	4: 7 But to each one of us **grace** has been given as Christ apportioned
	4:29 to their needs, that *it may* **benefit** [+1443] those who listen.
	6:24 **Grace** to all who love our Lord Jesus Christ with an undying love.
Php	1: 2 **Grace** and peace to you from God our Father and the Lord Jesus
	1: 7 confirming the gospel, all of you share *in* God's **grace** with me.
	4:23 The **grace** of the Lord Jesus Christ be with your spirit. Amen.
Col	1: 2 in Christ at Colosse: **Grace** and peace to you from God our Father.
	1: 6 the day you heard it and understood God's **grace** in all its truth.
	3:16 hymns and spiritual songs with **gratitude** in your hearts to God.
	4: 6 Let your conversation be always full of **grace**, seasoned with salt,
	4:18 in my own hand. Remember my chains. **Grace** be with you.
1Th	1: 1 God the Father and the Lord Jesus Christ: **Grace** and peace to you.
	5:28 The **grace** of our Lord Jesus Christ be with you.
2Th	1: 2 **Grace** and peace to you from God the Father and the Lord Jesus
	1:12 according to the **grace** of our God and the Lord Jesus Christ.
	2:16 who loved us and by his **grace** gave us eternal encouragement
	3:18 The **grace** of our Lord Jesus Christ be with you all.

1Ti 1: 2 **Grace**, mercy and peace from God the Father and Christ Jesus our
      1:12 *I* **thank** [+2400] Christ Jesus our Lord, who has given me strength,
      1:14 The **grace** of our Lord was poured out on me abundantly,
      6:21 so doing have wandered from the faith. **Grace** be with you.
2Ti 1: 2 **Grace**, mercy and peace from God the Father and Christ Jesus our
      1: 3 *I* **thank** [+2400] God, whom I serve, as my forefathers did,
      1: 9 anything we have done but because of his own purpose and **grace**.
      2: 1 You then, my son, be strong in the **grace** that is in Christ Jesus.
      4:22 The Lord be with your spirit. **Grace** be with you.
Tit 1: 4 **Grace** and peace from God the Father and Christ Jesus our Savior.
      2:11 For the **grace** of God that brings salvation has appeared to all men.
      3: 7 so that, having been justified *by* his **grace**, we might become heirs
      3:15 Greet those who love us in the faith. **Grace** be with you all.
Phm 1: 3 **Grace** to you and peace from God our Father and the Lord Jesus
      1:25 The **grace** of the Lord Jesus Christ be with your spirit.
Heb 2: 9 so that *by* the **grace** of God he might taste death for everyone.
      4:16 Let us then approach the throne of **grace** with confidence,
      4:16 may receive mercy and find **grace** to help us in our time of need.
    10:29 that sanctified him, and who has insulted the Spirit *of* **grace**?
    12:15 See to it that no one misses the **grace** of God and that no bitter root
    12:28 a kingdom that cannot be shaken, *let us be* **thankful** [+2400],
    13: 9 It is good for our hearts to be strengthened *by* **grace**, not by
    13:25 **Grace** be with you all.
Jas 4: 6 But he gives us more **grace**. That is why Scripture says: "God
      4: 6 "God opposes the proud but gives **grace** to the humble."
1Pe 1: 2 sprinkling by his blood: **Grace** and peace be yours in abundance.
      1:10 the prophets, who spoke of the **grace** that was to come to you,
      1:13 set your hope fully on the **grace** to be given you when Jesus Christ
      2:19 For it is **commendable** if a man bears up under the pain of unjust
      2:20 doing good and you endure it, this is **commendable** before God.
      3: 7 weaker partner and as heirs with you *of* the **gracious gift** of life,
      4:10 faithfully administering God's **grace** in its various forms.
      5: 5 because, "God opposes the proud but gives **grace** to the humble."
      5:10 And the God *of* all **grace**, who called you to his eternal glory in
      5:12 encouraging you and testifying that this is the true **grace** of God.
2Pe 1: 2 **Grace** and peace be yours in abundance through the knowledge of
      3:18 But grow in the **grace** and knowledge of our Lord and Savior Jesus
2Jn 1: 3 **Grace**, mercy and peace from God the Father and from Jesus
Jude 1: 4 who change the **grace** of our God into a license for immorality
Rev 1: 4 **Grace** and peace to you from him who is, and who was, and who
    22:21 The **grace** of the Lord Jesus be with God's people. Amen.

5922 χάρισμα, *charisma* [17] [√ 5897]

gift [8], gifts [7], gracious favor [1], spiritual gift [1]

Ro 1:11 that I may impart to you some spiritual **gift** to make you strong—
      5:15 But the **gift** is not like the trespass. For if the many died by the
      5:16 but the **gift** followed many trespasses and brought justification.
      6:23 but the **gift** of God is eternal life in Christ Jesus our Lord.
    11:29 for God's **gifts** and his call are irrevocable.
    12: 6 We have different **gifts**, according to the grace given us. If a man's
1Co 1: 7 Therefore you do not lack any **spiritual gift** as you eagerly wait
      7: 7 But each man has his own **gift** from God; one has this gift,
    12: 4 There are different kinds of **gifts**, but the same Spirit.
    12: 9 by the same Spirit, to another **gifts** of healing by that one Spirit,
    12:28 also those having **gifts** of healing, those able to help others,
    12:30 Do all have **gifts** of healing? Do all speak in tongues? Do all
    12:31 But eagerly desire the greater **gifts**. And now I will show you the
2Co 1:11 Then many will give thanks on our behalf for the **gracious favor**
1Ti 4:14 Do not neglect your **gift**, which was given you through a prophetic
2Ti 1: 6 For this reason I remind you to fan into flame the **gift** of God,
1Pe 4:10 Each one should use whatever **gift** he has received to serve others,

5923 χαριτόω, *charitoō* [2] [√ 5897]

freely given [1], highly favored [1]

Lk 1:28 went to her and said, "Greetings, *you who are* **highly favored**!
Eph 1: 6 glorious grace, which *he has* **freely given** us in the One he loves.

5924 Χαρράν, *Charran* [2]

Haran [2]

Ac 7: 2 while he was still in Mesopotamia, before he lived in **Haran**.
      7: 4 "So he left the land of the Chaldeans and settled in **Haran**.

5925 χάρτης, *chartēs* [1] [√ 5916]

paper [1]

2Jn 1:12 have much to write to you, but I do not want to use **paper** and ink.

5926 χάσμα, *chasma* [1]

chasm [1]

Lk 16:26 besides all this, between us and you a great **chasm** has been fixed,

5927 χεῖλος, *cheilos* [7]

lips [6], seashore [+2498+3836] [1]

Mt 15: 8 " 'These people honor me *with* their **lips**, but their hearts are far
Mk 7: 6 " 'These people honor me *with* their **lips**, but their hearts are far
Ro 3:13 tongues practice deceit." "The poison of vipers is on their **lips**."
1Co 14:21 and through the **lips** of foreigners I will speak to this people,
Heb 11:12 and as countless as the sand on the **seashore** [+2498+3836].
    13:15 to God a sacrifice of praise—the fruit *of* **lips** that confess his name.
1Pe 3:10 must keep his tongue from evil and his **lips** from deceitful speech.

5928 χειμάζω, *cheimazō* [1] [√ 5930]

took a battering from the storm [1]

Ac 27:18 We **took** such a violent **battering from the storm** that the next

5929 χείμαρρος, *cheimarros* [1] [√ 5930 + 4835]

valley [1]

Jn 18: 1 Jesus left with his disciples and crossed the Kidron **Valley**.

5930 χειμών, *cheimōn* [6] [→ 5928, 5929]

winter [4], storm [1], stormy [1]

Mt 16: 3 'Today it will be **stormy**, for the sky is red and overcast.'
    24:20 Pray that your flight will not take place in **winter** or on the
Mk 13:18 Pray that this will not take place in **winter**.
Jn 10:22 Then came the Feast of Dedication at Jerusalem. It was **winter**,
Ac 27:20 nor stars appeared for many days and the **storm** continued raging,
2Ti 4:21 Do your best to get here before **winter**. Eubulus greets you,

5931 χείρ, *cheir* [177] [→ 901, 942, 1429, 2217, 2218, 4741, 5932, 5933, 5934, 5935; cf. 4742, 5936]

χεὶρ θεοῦ, (hand of God) [2] Heb 10:31; 1Pe 5:6
χεὶρ κυρίου, (hand of the Lord) [3] Lk 1:66; Ac 11:21; 13:11; cf. Heb 1:10; 8:9
δεξιός χεῖρ, (right hand) [6] Mt 5:30; Lk 6:6; Ac 3:7; Rev 1:16; 10:5; 13:16
διὰ χειρῶν, (by the hands of) [11] Mk 6:2; Ac 2:23; 5:12; 7:25; 8:18; 11:30; 14:3; 15:23; 19:11,26; 2Ti 1:6
ἐκτείνω χεῖρα, (extend a hand) [14] Mt 8:3; 12:13,49; 14:31; 26:51; Mk 1:41; 3:5,5; Lk 5:13; 6:10; 22:53; Jn 21:18; Ac 4:30; 26:1
ἐπιτίθημι τὴν χεῖρα, (lay hands upon) [20] Mt 9:18; 19:13,15; Mk 5:23; 6:5; 7:32; 8:23,25; 16:18; Lk 4:40; 13:13; Ac 6:6; 8:17,19; 9:12,17; 13:3; 19:6; 28:8; 1Ti 5:22

hand [75], hands [70], motioned [+2939+3836] [2], seized [+2095+3836] [2], seized [+2095+3836] [2], arms [1], arrest [+2093+2095+3836] [1], arrested [+2093+2095+3836] [1], arrested [+2095+3836] [1], by [+1328] [1], by [+1877] [1], clutches [1], enabling [+1328+1443+3836] [1], finger [1], grasp [1], hand over to [+1650+4140] [1], handed over [+3836+4140] [1], help [1], help [+899+1328+3836] [1], man-made [+1181+1328] [1], on [+1666] [1], performed [+1181+1328+3836] [1], pointing [+1753+3836] [1], power [1], reached for [+1753+3836] [1], through [+1328+3836] [1], through [+5250] [1], under power [+1650] [1], using [+1328] [1], with [+1328] [1], wrists [1]

Mt 3:12 His winnowing fork is in his **hand**, and he will clear his threshing
    4: 6 his angels concerning you, and they will lift you up in their **hands**,

5:30 And if your right **hand** causes you to sin, cut it off and throw it
8: 3 Jesus reached out his **hand** and touched the man. "I am willing,"
8:15 He touched her **hand** and the fever left her, and she got up
9:18 just died. But come and put your **hand** on her, and she will live."
9:25 had been put outside, he went in and took the girl *by* the **hand**,
12:10 and a man with a shriveled **hand** was there. Looking for a reason
12:13 Then he said to the man, "Stretch out your **hand**." So he stretched it
12:49 **Pointing** [+*1753+3836*] to his disciples, he said, "Here are my
14:31 Immediately Jesus reached out his **hand** and caught him. "You of
15: 2 of the elders? They don't wash their **hands** before they eat!"
15:20 but eating *with* unwashed **hands** does not make him 'unclean.' "
17:22 "The Son of Man is going to be betrayed into the **hands** of men.
18: 8 If your **hand** or your foot causes you to sin, cut it off and throw it
18: 8 or crippled than to have two **hands** or two feet and be thrown into
19:13 children were brought to Jesus for him to place his **hands** on them
19:15 When he had placed his **hands** on them, he went on from there.
22:13 'Tie him **hand** and foot, and throw him outside, into the darkness,
26:23 "The one who has dipped his **hand** into the bowl with me will
26:45 and the Son of Man is betrayed into the **hands** of sinners.
26:50 forward, **seized** [+*2093+2095+3836*] Jesus and arrested him.
26:51 one of Jesus' companions **reached for** [+*1753+3836*] his sword,
27:24 he took water and washed his **hands** in front of the crowd.
Mk 1:31 So he went to her, took her **hand** and helped her up. The fever left
1:41 with compassion, Jesus reached out his **hand** and touched the man.
3: 1 into the synagogue, and a man with a shriveled **hand** was there.
3: 3 Jesus said to the man with the shriveled **hand**, "Stand up in front of
3: 5 at their stubborn hearts, said to the man, "Stretch out your **hand**."
3: 5 He stretched it out, and his **hand** was completely restored.
5:23 Please come and put your **hands** on her so that she will be healed
5:41 He took her *by* the **hand** and said to her, *"Talitha koum!"*
6: 2 been given him, that **he** [+*899+1328+3836*] even does miracles!
6: 5 except lay his **hands** on a few sick people and heal them.
7: 2 saw some of his disciples eating food *with* **hands** that were
7: 3 and all the Jews do not eat unless they give their **hands** a
7: 5 of the elders instead of eating their food *with* 'unclean' **hands**?"
7:32 hardly talk, and they begged him to place his **hand** on the man.
8:23 He took the blind man *by* the **hand** and led him outside the village.
8:23 When he had spit on the man's eyes and put his **hands** on him,
8:25 Once more Jesus put his **hands** on the man's eyes. Then his eyes
9:27 But Jesus took him *by* the **hand** and lifted him to his feet,
9:31 "The Son of Man is going to be betrayed into the **hands** of men.
9:43 If your **hand** causes you to sin, cut it off. It is better for you to
9:43 It is better for you to enter life maimed than with two **hands** to go
10:16 the children in his arms, put his **hands** on them and blessed them.
14:41 Look, the Son of Man is betrayed into the **hands** of sinners.
14:46 The men **seized** [+*2095+3836*] Jesus and arrested him.
16:18 they will pick up snakes with their **hands**;
16:18 they will place their **hands** on sick people, and they will get well."
Lk 1:66 then is this child going to be?" For the Lord's **hand** was with him.
1:71 salvation from our enemies and from the **hand** of all who hate us—
1:74 to rescue us from the **hand** of our enemies, and to enable us to
3:17 His winnowing fork is in his **hand** to clear his threshing floor
4:11 they will lift you up in their **hands**, so that you will not strike your
4:40 of sickness, and laying his **hands** on each one, he healed them.
5:13 Jesus reached out his **hand** and touched the man. "I am willing,"
6: 1 some heads of grain, rub them *in* their **hands** and eat the kernels.
6: 6 and a man was there whose right **hand** was shriveled.
6: 8 they were thinking and said to the man with the shriveled **hand**,
6:10 at them all, and then said to the man, "Stretch out your **hand**."
6:10 out your hand." He did so, and his **hand** was completely restored.
8:54 But he took her *by* the **hand** and said, "My child, get up!"
9:44 The Son of Man is going to be betrayed into the **hands** of men."
9:62 "No one who puts his **hand** to the plow and looks back is fit for
13:13 Then he put his **hands** on her, and immediately she straightened up
15:22 and put it on him. Put a ring on his **finger** and sandals on his feet.
20:19 looked for a way *to* **arrest** [+*2093+2095+3836*] him immediately,
21:12 "But before all this, they will lay **hands** on you and persecute you.
22:21 But the **hand** of him who is going to betray me is with mine on the
22:53 with you in the temple courts, and you did not lay a **hand** on me.
23:46 out with a loud voice, "Father, into your **hands** I commit my spirit."
24: 7 'The Son of Man must be delivered into the **hands** of sinful men,
24:39 Look at my **hands** and my feet. It is I myself! Touch me and see;
24:40 When he had said this, he showed them his **hands** and feet.
24:50 to the vicinity of Bethany, he lifted up his **hands** and blessed them.
Jn 3:35 The Father loves the Son and has placed everything in his **hands**.
7:30 At this they tried to seize him, but no one laid a **hand** on him,
7:44 Some wanted to seize him, but no one laid a **hand** on him.
10:28 they shall never perish; no one can snatch them out of my **hand**.
10:29 greater than all; no one can snatch them out of my Father's **hand**.
10:39 Again they tried to seize him, but he escaped their **grasp**.
11:44 man came out, his **hands** and feet wrapped with strips of linen,
13: 3 knew that the Father had put all things **under** his **power** [+*1650*],
13: 9 Peter replied, "not just my feet but my **hands** and my head as well!"
20:20 After he said this, he showed them his **hands** and side. The
20:25 "Unless I see the nail marks in his **hands** and put my finger where
20:25 the nails were, and put my **hand** into his side, I will not believe it."
20:27 Then he said to Thomas, "Put your finger here; see my **hands**.
20:27 see my hands. Reach out your **hand** and put it into my side.
21:18 but when you are old you will stretch out your **hands**,
Ac 2:23 and you, with the **help** of wicked men, put him to death by nailing
3: 7 Taking him by the right **hand**, he helped him up, and instantly the
4: 3 *They* **seized** [+*2095+3836*] Peter and John, and because it was
4:28 They did what your **power** and will had decided beforehand should
4:30 Stretch out your **hand** to heal and perform miraculous signs
5:12 The apostles **performed** [+*1181+1328+3836*] many miraculous
5:18 *They* **arrested** [+*2093+2095+3836*] the apostles and put them in
6: 6 men to the apostles, who prayed and laid their **hands** on them.
7:25 would realize that God was **using** [+*1328*] him to rescue them,
7:35 **through** [+*5250*] the angel who appeared to him in the bush.
7:41 and held a celebration in honor of what their **hands** had made.
7:50 Has not my **hand** made all these things?'
8:17 Then Peter and John placed their **hands** on them, and they received
8:18 that the Spirit was given at the laying on *of* the apostles' **hands**,
8:19 so that everyone on whom I lay my **hands** may receive the Holy
9:12 Ananias come and place his **hands** on him to restore his sight."
9:17 Placing his **hands** on Saul, he said, "Brother Saul, the Lord—
9:41 He took her *by* the **hand** and helped her to her feet. Then he called
11:21 The Lord's **hand** was with them, and a great number of people
11:30 sending their gift to the elders **by** [+*1328*] Barnabas and Saul.
12: 1 It was about this time that King Herod **arrested** [+*2095+3836*]
12: 7 "Quick, get up!" he said, and the chains fell off Peter's **wrists**.
12:11 that the Lord sent his angel and rescued me from Herod's **clutches**
12:17 Peter motioned *with* his **hand** for them to be quiet and described
13: 3 and prayed, they placed their **hands** on them and sent them off.
13:11 Now the **hand** of the Lord is against you. You are going to be
13:16 Standing up, Paul motioned *with* his **hand** and said: "Men of Israel
14: 3 *by* **enabling** [+*1328+1443+3836*] them to do miraculous signs and
15:23 **With** [+*1328*] them they sent the following letter: The apostles
17:25 And he is not served by human **hands**, as if he needed anything,
19: 6 When Paul placed his **hands** on them, the Holy Spirit came on
19:11 God did extraordinary miracles **through** [+*1328+3836*] Paul,
19:26 He says that **man-made** [+*1181+1328*] gods are no gods at all.
19:33 He **motioned** *for* **silence** [+*2939+3836*] in order to make a defense
20:34 You yourselves know that these **hands** of mine have supplied my
21:11 he took Paul's belt, tied his own **hands** and feet with it and said,
21:11 this belt and *will* **hand** him **over to** [+*1650+4140*] the Gentiles.' "
21:27 stirred up the whole crowd and **seized** [+*2093+2095+3836*] him,
21:40 Paul stood on the steps and **motioned** [+*2939+3836*] to the crowd.
23:19 The commander took the young man *by* the **hand**, drew him aside
26: 1 So Paul motioned with his **hand** and began his defense:
28: 3 a viper, driven out by the heat, fastened itself *on* his **hand**.
28: 4 When the islanders saw the snake hanging from his **hand**,
28: 8 see him and, after prayer, placed his **hands** on him and healed him.
28:17 *I was* arrested in Jerusalem and **handed over** [+*3836+4140*] to the
Ro 10:21 "All day long I have held out my **hands** to a disobedient
1Co 4:12 We work hard *with* our own **hands**. When we are cursed,
12:15 If the foot should say, "Because I am not a **hand**, I do not belong to
12:21 The eye cannot say *to* the **hand**, "I don't need you!" And the head
16:21 I, Paul, write this greeting *in* my own **hand**.
2Co 11:33 a basket from a window in the wall and slipped through his **hands**.
Gal 3:19 The law was put into effect through angels **by** [+*1877*] a mediator.
6:11 See what large letters I use as I write to you *with* my own **hand**!
Eph 4:28 but must work, doing something useful *with* his own **hands**,
Col 4:18 I, Paul, write this greeting *in* my own **hand**. Remember my chains.
1Th 4:11 to mind your own business and to work *with* your **hands**,
2Th 3:17 I, Paul, write this greeting *in* my own **hand**, which is the
1Ti 2: 8 I want men everywhere to lift up holy **hands** in prayer,
4:14 message when the body of elders laid their **hands** on you.
5:22 Do not be hasty in the laying on *of* **hands**, and do not share in the
2Ti 1: 6 gift of God, which is in you through the laying on *of* my **hands**.
Phm 1:19 I, Paul, am writing this *with* my own **hand**. I will pay it back—
Heb 1:10 of the earth, and the heavens are the work *of* your **hands**.

6: 2 instruction about baptisms, the laying on *of* **hands**, the resurrection
8: 9 when I took them *by* the **hand** to lead them out of Egypt,
10:31 It is a dreadful thing to fall into the **hands** of the living God.
12:12 Therefore, strengthen your feeble **arms** and weak knees.
Jas 4: 8 Wash your **hands**, you sinners, and purify your hearts,
1Pe 5: 6 Humble yourselves, therefore, under God's mighty **hand**,
1Jn 1: 1 our eyes, which we have looked at and our **hands** have touched—
Rev 1:16 In his right **hand** he held seven stars, and out of his mouth came a
6: 5 a black horse! Its rider was holding a pair of scales in his **hand**.
7: 9 white robes and were holding palm branches in their **hands**.
8: 4 prayers of the saints, went up before God from the angel's **hand**.
9:20 by these plagues still did not repent of the work *of* their **hands**;
10: 2 He was holding a little scroll, which lay open in his **hand**.
10: 5 standing on the sea and on the land raised his right **hand** to heaven.
10: 8 take the scroll that lies open in the **hand** of the angel who is
10:10 I took the little scroll from the angel's **hand** and ate it. It tasted as
13:16 and slave, to receive a mark on his right **hand** or on his forehead,
14: 9 his image and receives his mark on the forehead or on the **hand**,
14:14 with a crown of gold on his head and a sharp sickle in his **hand**.
17: 4 She held a golden cup in her **hand**, filled with abominable things
19: 2 He has avenged on [+1666] her the blood of his servants."
20: 1 having the key to the Abyss and holding in his **hand** a great chain.
20: 4 and had not received his mark on their foreheads or their **hands**.

5932 χειραγωγέω, cheiragōgeō [2] [√ 5931 + 72]

by the hand [1], led by the hand [1]

Ac 9: 8 he could see nothing. So they led him **by the hand** into Damascus.
22:11 My companions **led me by the hand** into Damascus,

5933 χειραγωγός, cheiragōgos [1] [√ 5931 + 72]

someone to lead by the hand [1]

Ac 13:11 and he groped about, seeking **someone to lead** him **by the hand**.

5934 χειρόγραφον, cheirographon [1] [√ 5931 + 1211]

written code [1]

Col 2:14 having canceled the **written code**, with its regulations, that was

5935 χειροποίητος, cheiropoiētos [6] [√ 5931 + 4472]

man-made [3], built by hands [1], done by the hands [1], made by men [1]

Mk 14:58 'I will destroy this **man-made** temple and in three days will build
Ac 7:48 "However, the Most High does not live in houses **made by men**.
17:24 of heaven and earth and does not live in temples **built by hands**.
Eph 2:11 "the circumcision" (that **done** in the body **by the hands** *of men*)—
Heb 9:11 the greater and more perfect tabernacle that is not **man-made**,
9:24 For Christ did not enter a **man-made** sanctuary that was only a

5936 χειροτονέω, cheirotoneō [2] [√ 1753; cf. 5931]

appointed [1], chosen [1]

Ac 14:23 and Barnabas **appointed** elders for them in each church and,
2Co 8:19 *he was* **chosen** by the churches to accompany us as we carry the

5937 χείρων, cheirōn [11]

worse than [4], worse [4], from bad to worse [+2093+3836] [1], more severely [1], worse off than [1]

Mt 9:16 the patch will pull away from the garment, making the tear **worse**.
12:45 And the final condition of that man is **worse than** the first.
27:64 from the dead. This last deception will be **worse than** the first."
Mk 2:21 the new piece will pull away from the old, making the tear **worse**.
5:26 had spent all she had, yet instead of getting better she grew **worse**.
Lk 11:26 And the final condition of that man is **worse than** the first."
Jn 5:14 well again. Stop sinning or something **worse** may happen to you."
1Ti 5: 8 he has denied the faith and is **worse than** an unbeliever.
2Ti 3:13 and impostors will go **from bad to worse** [+2093+3836],

Heb 10:29 How much **more severely** do you think a man deserves to be
2Pe 2:20 they are **worse off** at the end **than** they were at the beginning.

5938 Χερούβ, Cheroub [1]

cherubim [1]

Heb 9: 5 Above the ark were the **cherubim** of the Glory,

5939 χήρα, chēra [26]

widow [12], widows [12], *untranslated* [1], widow [+1222] [1]

Mk 12:40 They devour **widows**' houses and for a show make lengthy prayers.
12:42 But a poor **widow** came and put in two very small copper coins,
12:43 this poor **widow** has put more into the treasury than all the others.
Lk 2:37 and then was a **widow** until she was eighty-four. She never left the
4:25 I assure you that there were many **widows** in Israel in Elijah's
4:26 but to a **widow** [+1222] in Zarephath in the region of Sidon.
7:12 carried out—the only son of his mother, and she was a **widow**.
18: 3 And there was a **widow** in that town who kept coming to him with
18: 5 yet because this **widow** keeps bothering me, I will see that she gets
20:47 They devour **widows**' houses and for a show make lengthy prayers.
21: 2 He also saw a poor **widow** put in two very small copper coins.
21: 3 he said, "this poor **widow** has put in more than all the others.
Ac 6: 1 because their **widows** were being overlooked in the daily
9:39 All the **widows** stood around him, crying and showing him the
9:41 Then he called the believers and the **widows** and presented her to
1Co 7: 8 Now *to* the unmarried and the **widows** I say: It is good for them to
1Ti 5: 3 Give proper recognition to those **widows** who are really in need.
5: 3 recognition to those widows who are really in need. **[RPG]**
5: 4 But if a **widow** has children or grandchildren, these should learn
5: 5 The **widow** who is really in need and left all alone puts her hope in
5: 9 No **widow** may be put on the list of widows unless she is over
5:11 As for younger **widows**, do not put them on such a list. For when
5:16 If any woman who is a believer has **widows** in her family,
5:16 so that the church can help those **widows** who are really in need.
Jas 1:27 to look after orphans and **widows** in their distress and to keep
Rev 18: 7 'I sit as queen; I am not a **widow**, and I will never mourn.'

5940 χθές, chthes Not used in UBS/NIV [→ 2396]

5941 χιλίαρχος, chiliarchos [21] [√ 5943 + 806]

commander [17], generals [2], high ranking officers [1], military commanders [1]

Mk 6:21 gave a banquet *for* his high officials and **military commanders**
Jn 18:12 Then the detachment of soldiers with its **commander**
Ac 21:31 news reached the **commander** of the Roman troops that the whole
21:32 When the rioters saw the **commander** and his soldiers,
21:33 The **commander** came up and arrested him and ordered him to be
21:37 he asked the **commander**, "May I say something to you?"
22:24 the **commander** ordered Paul to be taken into the barracks.
22:26 centurion heard this, he went to the **commander** and reported it.
22:27 The **commander** went to Paul and asked, "Tell me, are you a
22:28 Then the **commander** said, "I had to pay a big price for my
22:29 The **commander** himself was alarmed when he realized that he
23:10 so violent that the **commander** was afraid Paul would be torn to
23:15 and the Sanhedrin petition the **commander** to bring him before
23:17 the centurions and said, "Take this young man to the **commander**;
23:18 So he took him to the **commander**. The centurion said, "Paul,
23:19 The **commander** took the young man by the hand, drew him aside
23:22 The **commander** dismissed the young man and cautioned him,
24:22 "When Lysias the **commander** comes," he said, "I will decide your
25:23 and entered the audience room with the **high ranking officers**
Rev 6:15 the princes, the **generals**, the rich, the mighty, and every slave
19:18 of kings, **generals**, and mighty men, of horses and their riders,

5942 χιλιάς, chilias [23] [√ 5943]

12,000 [+1557] [13], thousand [5], 144,000 [+1669+5475+5477] [3], thousands [2]

Lk 14:31 and consider whether he is able with ten **thousand** *men* to oppose
14:31 men to oppose the one coming against him with twenty **thousand**?
Ac 4: 4 and the number of men grew to about five **thousand**.

1Co 10: 8 of them did—and in one day twenty-three **thousand** of them died.
Rev 5:11 the voice of many angels, numbering **thousands** upon thousands,
     5:11 the voice of many angels, numbering thousands upon **thousands**,
     7: 4 who were sealed: **144,000** [+1669+5475+5477] from all the tribes
     7: 5 From the tribe of Judah **12,000** [+1557] were sealed, from the tribe
     7: 5 from the tribe of Reuben **12,000** [+1557], from the tribe of Gad
     7: 5 the tribe of Reuben 12,000, from the tribe of Gad **12,000** [+1557],
     7: 6 from the tribe of Asher **12,000** [+1557], from the tribe of Naphtali
     7: 6 tribe of Asher 12,000, from the tribe of Naphtali **12,000** [+1557],
     7: 6 of Naphtali 12,000, from the tribe of Manasseh **12,000** [+1557],
     7: 7 from the tribe of Simeon **12,000** [+1557], from the tribe of Levi
     7: 7 the tribe of Simeon 12,000, from the tribe of Levi **12,000** [+1557],
     7: 7 the tribe of Levi 12,000, from the tribe of Issachar **12,000** [+1557],
     7: 8 from the tribe of Zebulun **12,000** [+1557], from the tribe of Joseph
     7: 8 tribe of Zebulun 12,000, from the tribe of Joseph **12,000** [+1557],
     7: 8 tribe of Joseph 12,000, from the tribe of Benjamin **12,000** [+1557].
     11:13 Seven **thousand** people were killed in the earthquake,
     14: 1 and with him **144,000** [+1669+5475+5477] who had his name and
     14: 3 could learn the song except the **144,000** [+1669+5475+5477] who
     21:16 city with the rod and found it to be **12,000** [+1557] stadia in length,

5943 χίλιοι, chilioi [11] [→ 1493, 2233, 4295, 5483, 5567, 5941, 5942]

thousand [8], 1,260 [+1357+2008] [2], 1,600 [+1980] [1]

2Pe 3: 8 With the Lord a day is like a **thousand** years, and a thousand years
     3: 8 a day is like a thousand years, and a **thousand** years are like a day.
Rev 11: 3 and they will prophesy *for* **1,260** [+1357+2008] days, clothed in
     12: 6 where she might be taken care of *for* **1,260** [+1357+2008] days.
     14:20 rising as high as the horses' bridles for a distance of **1,600** [+1980]
     20: 2 who is the devil, or Satan, and bound him *for* a **thousand** years.
     20: 3 the nations anymore until the **thousand** years were ended.
     20: 4 They came to life and reigned with Christ a **thousand** years.
     20: 5 (The rest of the dead did not come to life until the **thousand** years
     20: 6 and of Christ and will reign with him *for* a **thousand** years.
     20: 7 When the **thousand** years are over, Satan will be released from his

5944 Χίος, Chios [1]

Kios [1]

Ac 20:15 The next day we set sail from there and arrived off **Kios**. The day

5945 χιτών, chitōn [11]

tunic [5], clothes [1], clothing [1], garment [1], robes [1], tunics [1], undergarment [1]

Mt 5:40 And if someone wants to sue you and take your **tunic**, let him have
     10:10 take no bag for the journey, or extra **tunic**, or sandals or a staff;
Mk 6: 9 Wear sandals but not an extra **tunic**.
     14:63 The high priest tore his **clothes**. "Why do we need any more
Lk 3:11 "The man with two **tunics** should share with him who has none,
     6:29 someone takes your cloak, do not stop him from taking your **tunic**.
     9: 3 the journey—no staff, no bag, no bread, no money, no extra **tunic**.
Jn 19:23 one for each of them, with the **undergarment** remaining.
     19:23 This **garment** was seamless, woven in one piece from top to
Ac 9:39 crying and showing him the **robes** and other clothing that Dorcas
Jude 1:23 with fear—hating even the **clothing** stained by corrupted flesh.

5946 χιών, chiōn [2] [→ 4199, 4200]

snow [2]

Mt 28: 3 appearance was like lightning, and his clothes were white as **snow**.
Rev 1:14 His head and hair were white like wool, as white as **snow**,

5947 χις', chi' Not used in UBS/NIV [√ cf. 5953]

5948 χλαμύς, chlamys [2]

robe [2]

Mt 27:28 They stripped him and put a scarlet **robe** on him,
     27:31 they took off the **robe** and put his own clothes on him.

5949 χλευάζω, chleuazō [1] [→ 1430]

sneered [1]

Ac 17:32 some of them **sneered**, but others said, "We want to hear you again

5950 χλιαρός, chliaros [1]

lukewarm [1]

Rev 3:16 So, because you are **lukewarm**—neither hot nor cold—I am about

5951 Χλόη, Chloē [1] [→ 5952]

Chloe's [1]

1Co 1:11 some from **Chloe's** household have informed me that there are

5952 χλωρός, chlōros [4] [√ 5951]

green [2], pale [1], plant [1]

Mk 6:39 them to have all the people sit down in groups on the **green** grass.
Rev 6: 8 I looked, and there before me was a **pale** horse! Its rider was
     8: 7 of the trees were burned up, and all the **green** grass was burned up.
     9: 4 were told not to harm the grass of the earth or any **plant** or tree,

5953 χξς', chx^' Not used in UBS/NIV [√ cf. 5947]

5954 χοϊκός, choikos [4] [√ 1772]

earthly [2], of dust [1], of earth [1]

1Co 15:47 The first man was **of the dust** of the earth, the second man from
     15:48 As was the **earthly** *man*, so are those who are of the earth;
     15:48 As was the earthly man, so are those who are **of the earth**;
     15:49 And just as we have borne the likeness *of* the **earthly** *man*,

5955 χοῖνιξ, choinix [2]

quart [1], quarts [1]

Rev 6: 6 saying, "A **quart** of wheat for a day's wages, and three quarts of
     6: 6 and three **quarts** of barley for a day's wages, and do not damage

5956 χοῖρος, choiros [12]

pigs [12]

Mt 7: 6 "Do not give dogs what is sacred; do not throw your pearls to **pigs**.
     8:30 Some distance from them a large herd *of* **pigs** was feeding.
     8:31 begged Jesus, "If you drive us out, send us into the herd *of* **pigs**."
     8:32 So they came out and went into the **pigs**, and the whole herd
Mk 5:11 A large herd *of* **pigs** was feeding on the nearby hillside.
     5:12 The demons begged Jesus, "Send us among the **pigs**; allow us to go
     5:13 and the evil spirits came out and went into the **pigs**.
     5:16 to the demon-possessed man—and told about the **pigs** as well.
Lk 8:32 A large herd *of* **pigs** was feeding there on the hillside. The demons
     8:33 When the demons came out of the man, they went into the **pigs**,
     15:15 to a citizen of that country, who sent him to his fields to feed **pigs**.
     15:16 He longed to fill his stomach with the pods that the **pigs** were

5957 χολάω, cholaō [1] [√ 5958]

angry [1]

Jn 7:23 why *are you* **angry** with me for healing the whole man on the

5958 χολή, cholē [2] [→ 5957]

bitterness [+4394] [1], gall [1]

Mt 27:34 There they offered Jesus wine to drink, mixed with **gall**; but after
Ac 8:23 For I see that you are full of **bitterness** [+4394] and captive to sin."

5959 χόος, choos Not used in UBS/NIV [√ 1772]

5960 Χοραζίν, Chorazin [2] [→ 6002]

Korazin [2]

Mt 11:21 "Woe to you, **Korazin**! Woe to you, Bethsaida! If the miracles that
Lk 10:13 "Woe to you, **Korazin**! Woe to you, Bethsaida! For if the miracles

5961 χορηγέω, chorēgeō [2] [√ 5962 + 72]

provides [1], supply [1]

2Co 9:10 and bread for food *will* also **supply** and increase your store of seed
1Pe 4:11 If anyone serves, he should do it with the strength God **provides**,

5962 χορός, choros [1] [→ 2220, 2221, 4743, 5961]

dancing [1]

Lk 15:25 When he came near the house, he heard music and **dancing**.

5963 χορτάζω, chortazō [16 / 15] [√ 5965]

satisfied [6], feed [2], well fed [2], eat all want [1], eat [1], fill [1],
filled [1], gorged [1]

Mt 5: 6 who hunger and thirst for righteousness, for they *will be* **filled**.
  14:20 *They* all ate and *were* **satisfied**, and the disciples picked up twelve
  15:33 could we get enough bread in this remote place to **feed** such
  15:37 *They* all ate and *were* **satisfied**. Afterward the disciples picked up
Mk 6:42 They all ate and *were* **satisfied**.
  7:27 "First let the children **eat all** they **want**," he told her, "for it is not
  8: 4 in this remote place can anyone *get enough* bread *to* **feed** them?"
  8: 8 The people ate and *were* **satisfied**. Afterward the disciples picked
Lk 6:21 Blessed are you who hunger now, for *you will be* **satisfied**.
  9:17 They all ate and *were* **satisfied**, and the disciples picked up twelve
  15:16 He longed *to* **fill** [UBS *to be* **filled with**; NIV *1153*] his stomach
  16:21 and longing *to* **eat** what fell from the rich man's table. Even the
Jn 6:26 miraculous signs but because you ate the loaves and *had your* **fill**.
Php 4:12 content in any and every situation, whether **well fed** or hungry,
Jas 2:16 *keep* warm and **well fed**," but does nothing about his physical
Rev 19:21 on the horse, and all the birds **gorged** *themselves* on their flesh.

5964 χόρτασμα, chortasma [1] [√ 5965]

food [1]

Ac 7:11 bringing great suffering, and our fathers could not find **food**.

5965 χόρτος, chortos [15] [→ 5963, 5964]

grass [9], field [1], hay [1], plant [1], stalk [1], wheat [1], wild [1]

Mt 6:30 If that is how God clothes the **grass** of the field, which is here
  13:26 When the **wheat** sprouted and formed heads, then the weeds also
  14:19 And he directed the people to sit down on the **grass**.
Mk 4:28 first the **stalk**, then the head, then the full kernel in the head.
  6:39 them to have all the people sit down in groups on the green **grass**.
Lk 12:28 If that is how God clothes the **grass** of the field, which is here
Jn 6:10 There was plenty *of* **grass** in that place, and the men sat down,
1Co 3:12 on this foundation *using* gold, silver, costly stones, wood, **hay**
Jas 1:10 in his low position, because he will pass away like a **wild** flower.
  1:11 For the sun rises with scorching heat and withers the **plant**.
1Pe 1:24 For, "All men are like **grass**, and all their glory is like the flowers
  1:24 are like grass, and all their glory is like the flowers *of* the **field**;
  1:24 like the flowers of the field; the **grass** withers and the flowers fall,
Rev 8: 7 of the trees were burned up, and all the green **grass** was burned up.
  9: 4 They were told not to harm the **grass** of the earth or any plant

5966 Χουζᾶς, Chouzas [1]

Cuza [1]

Lk 8: 3 Joanna the wife *of* **Cuza**, the manager of Herod's household;

5967 χοῦς, chous [2] [√ 1772]

dust [2]

Mk 6:11 or listen to you, shake the **dust** off your feet when you leave,
Rev 18:19 They will throw **dust** on their heads, and with weeping

5968 χράομαι, chraomai [11] [→ 712, 945, 946, 947, 2378, 2974, 3079, 4201, 4202, 5178, 5970, 5971, 5972, 5973, 5974, 5975, 5978, 5979, 5980, 5981, 5982, 5983; cf. 5969]

use [4], bold [+4244] [1], do so [+3437] [1], do [1], in kindness [+5793] [1], passed under to hold together [+5690] [1], used [1], uses [1]

Ac 27: 3 and Julius, **in kindness** [+5793] to Paul, allowed him to go to his
  27:17 *they* **passed** ropes **under** the ship itself **to hold** it **together** [+5690].
1Co 7:21 although if you can gain your freedom, **do** [+3437] **so**.
  7:31 those *who* **use** the things of the world, as if not engrossed in them.
  9:12 But *we did* not **use** this right. On the contrary, we put up with
  9:15 But I *have* not **used** any of these rights. And I am not writing this
2Co 1:17 When I planned this, *did I* **do** it lightly? Or do I make my plans in
  3:12 Therefore, since we have such a hope, *we are* very **bold** [+4244].
  13:10 that when I come *I may* not have to be harsh in *my* **use** of
1Ti 1: 8 We know that the law is good if one **uses** it properly.
  5:23 and **use** a little wine because of your stomach and your frequent

5969 χράω, chraō   Not used in UBS/NIV [→ 5976, 5977; cf. 3079, 5968]

5970 χρεία, chreia [49] [√ 5968]

need [+2400] [27], need [5], needs [+2400] [5], needs [4], needed [+2400] [2], needed [2], daily necessities [+338] [1], dependent on [+2400] [1], need [+1181+2400] [1], responsibility [1]

Mt 3:14 saying, "I **need** [+2400] to be baptized by you, and do you come to
  6: 8 for your Father knows what *you* **need** [+2400] before you ask him.
  9:12 Jesus said, "It is not the healthy *who* **need** [+2400] a doctor,
  14:16 Jesus replied, "*They* do not **need** [+2400] to go away. You give
  21: 3 says anything to you, tell him that the Lord **needs** [+2400] them,
  26:65 Why *do we* **need** [+2400] any more witnesses? Look, now you
Mk 2:17 "It is not the healthy *who* **need** [+2400] a doctor, but the sick.
  2:25 when he and his companions were hungry and *in* **need** [+2400]?
  11: 3 'The Lord **needs** [+2400] it and will send it back here shortly.' "
  14:63 "Why *do we* **need** [+2400] any more witnesses?" he asked.
Lk 5:31 "It is not the healthy *who* **need** [+2400] a doctor, but the sick.
  9:11 kingdom of God, and healed those *who* **needed** [+2400] healing.
  10:42 but only one thing is **needed**. Mary has chosen what is better,
  15: 7 ninety-nine righteous persons who *do* not **need** [+2400] to repent.
  19:31 'Why are you untying it?' tell him, 'The Lord **needs** [+2400] it.' "
  19:34 They replied, "The Lord **needs** [+2400] it."
  22:71 Then they said, "Why *do we* **need** [+2400] any more testimony?"
Jn 2:25 *He did* not **need** [+2400] man's testimony about man, for he knew
  13:10 "A person who has had a bath **needs** [+2400] only to wash his feet;
  13:29 was telling him to buy what *was* **needed** [+2400] for the Feast,
  16:30 and that *you do* not even **need** [+2400] to have anyone ask you
Ac 2:45 their possessions and goods, they gave to anyone as he had **need**.
  4:35 the apostles' feet, and it was distributed to anyone as he had **need**.
  6: 3 and wisdom. We will turn this **responsibility** over to them
  20:34 know that these hands of mine have supplied my own **needs**
  28:10 were ready to sail, they furnished us with the supplies we **needed**.
Ro 12:13 Share with God's people who are *in* **need**. Practice hospitality.
1Co 12:21 The eye cannot say to the hand, "I don't **need** [+2400] you!"
  12:21 And the head cannot say to the feet, "*I* don't **need** [+2400] you!"
  12:24 while our presentable parts **need** [+2400] no special treatment.
Eph 4:28 that he may have something to share with those *in* **need** [+2400].
  4:29 what is helpful for building others up *according to* their **needs**,
Php 2:25 is also your messenger, whom you sent to take care *of* my **needs**.
  4:16 you sent me aid again and again when I was in **need**.
  4:19 And my God will meet all your **needs** according to his glorious
1Th 1: 8 Therefore we *do* not **need** [+2400] to say anything about it,
  4: 9 Now about brotherly love *we do* not **need** [+2400] to write to you,
  4:12 and so that *you will* not *be* **dependent** [+2400] **on** anybody.
  5: 1 about times and dates *we do* not **need** [+2400] to write to you,
Tit 3:14 in order that they may provide for **daily necessities** [+338]
Heb 5:12 *you* **need** [+2400] someone to teach you the elementary truths of
  5:12 word all over again. You **need** [+1181+2400] milk, not solid food!
  7:11 the people), why was there still **need** for another priest to come—
  10:36 You **need** [+2400] to persevere so that when you have done the
1Jn 2:27 remains in you, and *you do* not **need** [+2400] anyone to teach you.
  3:17 and sees his brother *in* **need** [+2400] but has no pity on him,

Rev 3:17 am rich; I have acquired wealth and *do* not **need** [+2400] a thing.'
21:23 The city *does* not **need** [+2400] the sun or the moon to shine on it,
22: 5 *They will* not **need** [+2400] the light of a lamp or the light of the

5971 χρεοφειλέτης, *chreopheiletēs* [2]
[√ 5968 + 4053]

debtors [1], owed money to [+1639] [1]

Lk 7:41 "Two men **owed** [+1639] **money to** a certain moneylender.
16: 5 "So he called in each one *of* his master's **debtors**. He asked the

5972 χρεωφειλέτης, *chreōpheiletēs* Not used in
UBS/NIV [√ 5968 + 4053]

5973 χρή, *chrē* [1] [√ 5968]

should [1]

Jas 3:10 mouth come praise and cursing. My brothers, this **should** not be.

5974 χρῄζω, *chrēzō* [5] [√ 5968]

need [4], needs [1]

Mt 6:32 these things, and your heavenly Father knows that *you* **need** them.
Lk 11: 8 man's boldness he will get up and give him as much as *he* **needs**.
12:30 after all such things, and your Father knows that *you* **need** them.
Ro 16: 2 of the saints and to give her any help *she may* **need** from you,
2Co 3: 1 Or *do we* **need**, like some people, letters of recommendation to

5975 χρῆμα, *chrēma* [6] [√ 5968]

money [3], rich [+2400+3836] [2], bribe [1]

Mk 10:23 "How hard it is *for* the **rich** [+2400+3836] to enter the kingdom of
Lk 18:24 "How hard it is *for* the **rich** [+2400+3836] to enter the kingdom of
Ac 4:37 sold a field he owned and brought the **money** and put it at the
8:18 at the laying on of the apostles' hands, he offered them **money**
8:20 because you thought you could buy the gift of God with **money**!
24:26 At the same time he was hoping that Paul would offer him a **bribe**,

5976 χρηματίζω, *chrēmatizō* [9] [√ 5969]

warned [5], called [2], revealed [1], told [1]

Mt 2:12 And *having been* **warned** in a dream not to go back to Herod,
2:22 *Having been* **warned** in a dream, he withdrew to the district of
Lk 2:26 It had been **revealed** to him by the Holy Spirit that he would not
Ac 10:22 A holy angel **told** *him* to have you come to his house so that he
11:26 of people. The disciples *were* **called** Christians first at Antioch.
Ro 7: 3 man while her husband is still alive, *she is* **called** an adulteress.
Heb 8: 5 This is why Moses *was* **warned** when he was about to build the
11: 7 By faith Noah, *when* **warned** about things not yet seen, in holy
12:25 If they did not escape when they refused him *who* **warned** them on

5977 χρηματισμός, *chrēmatismos* [1] [√ 5969]

God's [1]

Ro 11: 4 And what was **God's** answer to him? "I have reserved for myself

5978 χρήσιμος, *chrēsimos* [1] [√ 5968]

value [1]

2Ti 2:14 about words; it is of no **value**, and only ruins those who listen.

5979 χρῆσις, *chrēsis* [2] [√ 5968]

relations [2]

Ro 1:26 Even their women exchanged natural **relations** for unnatural ones.
1:27 In the same way the men also abandoned natural **relations** with

5980 χρηστεύομαι, *chrēsteuomai* [1] [√ 5968]

kind [1]

1Co 13: 4 Love is patient, love *is* **kind**. It does not envy, it does not boast,

5981 χρηστολογία, *chrēstologia* [1] [√ 5968 + 3306]

smooth talk [1]

Ro 16:18 By **smooth talk** and flattery they deceive the minds of naive

5982 χρηστός, *chrēstos* [7] [√ 5968]

good [2], kind [2], better [1], easy [1], kindness [1]

Mt 11:30 For my yoke is **easy** and my burden is light."
Lk 5:39 drinking old wine wants the new, for he says, 'The old is **better**.' "
6:35 of the Most High, because he is **kind** to the ungrateful and wicked.
Ro 2: 4 not realizing that God's **kindness** leads you toward repentance?
1Co 15:33 Do not be misled: "Bad company corrupts **good** character."
Eph 4:32 Be **kind** and compassionate to one another, forgiving each other,
1Pe 2: 3 now that you have tasted that the Lord is **good**.

5983 χρηστότης, *chrēstotēs* [10] [√ 5968]

kindness [9], good [1]

Ro 2: 4 Or do you show contempt for the riches *of* his **kindness**, tolerance
3:12 become worthless; there is no one who does **good**, not even one."
11:22 Consider therefore the **kindness** and sternness of God: sternness to
11:22 sternness to those who fell, but **kindness** to you, provided that you
11:22 but kindness to you, provided that you continue in his **kindness**.
2Co 6: 6 in purity, understanding, patience and **kindness**; in the Holy Spirit
Gal 5:22 is love, joy, peace, patience, **kindness**, goodness, faithfulness,
Eph 2: 7 riches of his grace, expressed in his **kindness** to us in Christ Jesus.
Col 3:12 with compassion, **kindness**, humility, gentleness and patience.
Tit 3: 4 But when the **kindness** and love of God our Savior appeared,

5984 χρῖσμα, *chrisma* [3] [√ 5987]

anointing [3]

1Jn 2:20 But you have an **anointing** from the Holy One, and all of you
2:27 As for you, the **anointing** you received from him remains in you,
2:27 But as his **anointing** teaches you about all things and as that

5985 Χριστιανός, *Christianos* [3] [√ 5986]

Christian [2], Christians [1]

Ac 11:26 of people. The disciples were called **Christians** first at Antioch.
26:28 that in such a short time you can persuade me to be a **Christian**?"
1Pe 4:16 However, if you suffer as a **Christian**, do not be ashamed,

5986 Χριστός, *Christos* [529 / 528] [→ 532, 5985, 6023; cf. 5987]

ἀγάπη τοῦ Χριστοῦ, (love of Christ) [3] Ro 8:35; 2Co 5:14; Eph 3:19

ἀδελφοὶ ['Ιησοῦ Χριστοῦ], (brothers of [Jesus Christ]) [21] Mt 12:46,47,48,49; 13:55; 28:10; Mk 3:31,32,33,34,35; Lk 8:19,20,21; Jn 2:12; 7:3,5,10; 20:17; Ac 1:14; 1Co 9:5

αἷμα τοῦ Χριστοῦ, (the blood of Christ) [4] 1Co 10:16; Eph 2:13; Heb 9:14; 1Pe 1:19; cf. 1Pe 1:2; Rev 1:5

ἀνάστασις Χριστοῦ, (resurrection of Christ) [3] Ac 2:31; 1Pe 1:3; 3:21

ἀπόστολος Χριστοῦ, (apostle of Christ) [11] 1Co 1:1; 2Co 1:1; 11:13; Eph 1:1; Col 1:1; 1Th 2:7; 1Ti 1:1; 2Ti 1:1; Tit 1:1; 1Pe 1:1; 2Pe 1:1

βασιλεία τοῦ Χριστοῦ, (kingdom of Christ) [2] Eph 5:5; Rev 11:15

διὰ ['Ιησοῦ] Χριστοῦ, (by [Jesus] Christ) [18] Jn 1:17; Ac 10:36; Ro 1:8; 2:16; 5:21; 7:25; 16:27; 2Co 1:5; 3:4; 5:18; Gal 1:1; Eph 1:5; Php 1:11; Tit 3:6; Heb 13:21; 1Pe 2:5; 4:11; Jude 1:25

διάκονος Χριστοῦ, (minister of Christ) [3] 2Co 11:23; Col 1:7; 1Ti 4:6

δόξα [του] Χριστοῦ, (glory of Christ) [3] 2Co 4:4; 8:23; 2Th 2:14

δοῦλος Χριστοῦ, (slave of Christ) [9] Ro 1:1; 1Co 7:22; Gal 1:10; Eph 6:6; Php 1:1; Col 4:12; Jas 1:1; 2Pe 1:1; Jude 1:1

δέσμιος Χριστοῦ, (prisoner of Christ) [3] Eph 3:1; Phm 1:1,9

ἐν Χριστῷ, (in Christ) [84] Ro 3:24; 6:11,23; 8:1,2,39; 9:1; 12:5; 15:17; 16:3,7,9,10; 1Co 1:2,4,30; 3:1; 4:10,15,15,17; 15:18,19,22,31; 16:24; 2Co 2:14,17; 3:14; 5:17,19; 12:2,19; Gal 1:22; 2:4,17; 3:14,26,28; 5:6; Eph 1:1,3,10,12,20; 2:6,7,10,13; 3:6,11,21; 4:32; Php 1:1,13,26; 2:1,5; 3:3,14; 4:7,19,21; Col 1:2,4,28; 1Th 2:14; 4:16; 5:18; 1Ti 1:14; 3:13; 2Ti 1:1,9,13; 2:1,10; 3:12,15; Phm 1:8,20,23; 1Pe 3:16; 5:10,14

εὐαγγέλιον τοῦ Χρίστου, (the Gospel of Christ) [10] Mk 1:1; Ro 15:19; 1Co 9:12; 2Co 2:12; 4:4; 9:13; 10:14; Gal 1:7; Php 1:27; 1Th 3:2

ἡμέρα Χριστοῦ, (day of Christ) [4] 1Co 1:8; Php 1:6,10; 2:16

Ἰησοῦς Χριστός, (Jesus Christ) [136 / 135] Mt 1:1,18; Mk 1:1; Jn 1:17; 17:3; Ac 2:38; 3:6; 4:10; 8:12; 9:34; 10:36,48; 11:17; 15:26; 16:18; 28:31; Ro 1:4,6,7,8; 2:16[NIV]; 3:22; 5:1,11,15,17,21; 7:25; 13:14; 15:6,30; 16:25,27; 1Co 1:2,3,7,8,9,10; 2:2; 3:11; 6:11; 8:6; 15:57; 2Co 1:2,3,19; 4:5,6[UBS]; 8:9; 13:5[UBS],13; Gal 1:1,3,12; 2:16; 3:1,22; 6:14,18; Eph 1:2,3,5,17; 5:20; 6:23,24; Php 1:2,11, 19; 2:11,21; 3:20; 4:23; Col 1:3; 1Th 1:1,3; 5:9,23,28; 2Th 1:1,2, 12; 2:1,14,16; 3:6,12,18; 1Ti 6:3,14; 2Ti 2:8; Tit 1:1; 2:13; 3:6; Phm 1:3,25; Heb 10:10; 13:8,21; Jas 1:1; 2:1; 1Pe 1:1,2,3,3,7, 13; 2:5; 3:21; 4:11; 2Pe 1:1,1,8,11,14,16; 2:20; 3:18; 1Jn 1:3; 2:1; 3:23; 4:2; 5:6,20; 2Jn 1:3,7; Jude 1:1,1,4,17,21,25; Rev 1:1,2,5

κηρύσσω Χριστόν, (to preach Christ) [6] Ac 8:5; 1Co 1:23; 15:12; 2Co 4:5; 11:4; Php 1:15

κύριος Ἰησοῦς Χριστός, (Lord Jesus Christ) [69] Ac 10:36; 11:17; 15:26; 28:31; Ro 1:4,7; 5:1,11,21; 7:25; 13:14; 15:6,30; 1Co 1:2,3,7,8,9,10; 6:11; 8:6; 15:57; 2Co 1:2,3; 4:5; 8:9; 13:13; Gal 1:3; 6:14,18; Eph 1:2,3,17; 5:20; 6:23,24; Php 1:2; 2:11; 3:20; 4:23; Col 1:3; 2:6; 1Th 1:1,3; 5:9,23,28; 2Th 1:1,2,12; 2:1,14,16; 3:6,12,18; 1Ti 6:3,14; Phm 1:3,25; Jas 1:1; 2:1; 1Pe 1:3; 2Pe 1:8,14,16; Jude 1:17,21,25

κύριος Χριστός, (Lord Christ) [4] Lk 2:11; Ro 16:18; Col 3:24; 1Pe 3:15

λόγος Χριστοῦ, (word of Christ) [2] Col 3:16; Heb 6:1

μυστήριον τοῦ Χριστοῦ, (mystery of Christ) [5] Eph 3:4; 5:32; Col 1:27; 2:2; 4:3

ὄνομα Χριστοῦ, (name of Christ) [7] Ac 2:38; 3:6; 4:10; 8:12; 10:48; 16:18; 1Pe 4:14

πνεῦμα Χριστοῦ, (Spirit of Christ) [3] Ro 8:9; Php 1:19; 1Pe 1:11

σταυρός Χριστοῦ, (cross of Christ) [3] 1Co 1:17; Gal 6:12,14

ὑπέρ Χριστοῦ, (on behalf of Christ) [5] Ro 9:3; 2Co 5:20,20; 12:10; Php 1:29

χάρις Χριστοῦ, (grace of Christ) [10] Ro 5:15; 2Co 8:9; 13:13; Gal 1:6; 6:18; Eph 4:7; Php 4:23; 1Th 5:28; 2Th 3:18; Phm 1:25

Χριστός Ἰησοῦς, (Christ Jesus) [91 / 90] Ac 24:24; Ro 1:1; 2:16[UBS]; 3:24; 6:3,11,23; 8:1,2,34,39; 15:5,16,17; 16:3; 1Co 1:1,2,4,30; 4:15,17; 15:31; 16:24; 2Co 1:1; 13:5[NIV]; Gal 2:4,16; 3:14,26,28; 4:14; 5:6,24; Eph 1:1,1; 2:6,7,10,13,20; 3:1,6,11,21; Php 1:1,1, 6,8,26; 2:5; 3:3,8,12,14; 4:7,19,21; Col 1:1,4; 2:6; 4:12; 1Th 2:14; 5:18; 1Ti 1:1,1,2,12,14,15,16; 2:5; 3:13; 4:6; 5:21; 6:13; 2Ti 1:1,1,2,9,10,13; 2:1,3,10; 3:12,15; 4:1; Tit 1:4; Phm 1:1,9,23; 1Pe 5:10[UBS]

Χριστός κυρίου, (Christ the Lord) [1] Lk 2:26

Christ [516], Christ's [9], Anointed One [1], Christ's [+5642] [1], him^s [+3836] [1]

Mt   1: 1   A record of the genealogy *of* Jesus **Christ** the son of David,
     1:16   husband of Mary, of whom was born Jesus, who is called **Christ**.
     1:17   to the exile to Babylon, and fourteen from the exile to the **Christ**.
     1:18   This is how the birth *of* Jesus **Christ** came about: His mother Mary

     2: 4   of the law, he asked them where the **Christ** was to be born.
   11: 2   When John heard in prison what **Christ** was doing, he sent his
   16:16   Simon Peter answered, "You are the **Christ**, the Son of the living
   16:20   he warned his disciples not to tell anyone that he was the **Christ**.
   22:42   "What do you think about the **Christ**? Whose son is he?" "The son
   23:10   you to be called 'teacher,' for you have one Teacher, the **Christ**.
   24: 5   in my name, claiming, 'I am the **Christ**,' and will deceive many.
   24:23   At that time if anyone says to you, 'Look, here is the **Christ**!'
   26:63   by the living God: Tell us if you are the **Christ**, the Son of God."
   26:68   and said, "Prophesy to us, **Christ**. Who hit you?"
   27:17   me to release to you: Barabbas, or Jesus who is called **Christ**?"
   27:22   "What shall I do, then, with Jesus who is called **Christ**?" Pilate

Mk   1: 1   The beginning of the gospel *about* Jesus **Christ**, the Son of God.
    8:29   "Who do you say I am?" Peter answered, "You are the **Christ**."
    9:41   because you belong to **Christ** will certainly not lose his reward.
   12:35   "How is it that the teachers of the law say that the **Christ** is the son
   13:21   At that time if anyone says to you, 'Look, here is the **Christ**!'
   14:61   asked him, "Are you the **Christ**, the Son of the Blessed One?"
   15:32   Let this **Christ**, this King of Israel, come down now from the

Lk   2:11   of David a Savior has been born to you; he is **Christ** the Lord.
    2:26   Spirit that he would not die before he had seen the Lord's **Christ**.
    3:15   all wondering in their hearts if John might possibly be the **Christ**.
    4:41   not allow them to speak, because they knew he was the **Christ**.
    9:20   "Who do you say I am?" Peter answered, "The **Christ** of God."
   20:41   to them, "How is it that they say the **Christ** is the Son of David?
   22:67   "If you are the **Christ**," they said, "tell us." Jesus answered, "If I
   23: 2   He opposes payment of taxes to Caesar and claims to be **Christ**,
   23:35   let him save himself if he is the **Christ** of God, the Chosen One."
   23:39   insults at him: "Aren't you the **Christ**? Save yourself and us!"
   24:26   Did not the **Christ** have to suffer these things and then enter his
   24:46   The **Christ** will suffer and rise from the dead on the third day,

Jn   1:17   given through Moses; grace and truth came through Jesus **Christ**.
    1:20   did not fail to confess, but confessed freely, "I am not the **Christ**."
    1:25   "Why then do you baptize if you are not the **Christ**, nor Elijah,
    1:41   and tell him, "We have found the Messiah" (that is, the **Christ**).
    3:28   testify that I said, 'I am not the **Christ** but am sent ahead of him.'
    4:25   The woman said, "I know that Messiah" (called **Christ**) "is coming.
    4:29   who told me everything I ever did. Could this be the **Christ**?"
    7:26   Have the authorities really concluded that he is the **Christ**?
    7:27   when the **Christ** comes, no one will know where he is from."
    7:31   They said, "When the **Christ** comes, will he do more miraculous
    7:41   Others said, "He is the **Christ**." Still others asked, "How can the
    7:41   Still others asked, "How can the **Christ** come from Galilee?
    7:42   Does not the Scripture say that the **Christ** will come from David's
    9:22   that Jesus was the **Christ** would be put out of the synagogue.
   10:24   will you keep us in suspense? If you are the **Christ**, tell us plainly."
   11:27   "Yes, Lord," she told him, "I believe that you are the **Christ**,
   12:34   "We have heard from the Law that the **Christ** will remain forever,
   17: 3   the only true God, and Jesus **Christ**, whom you have sent.
   20:31   But these are written that you may believe that Jesus is the **Christ**,

Ac   2:31   Seeing what was ahead, he spoke of the resurrection *of* the **Christ**,
    2:36   has made this Jesus, whom you crucified, both Lord and **Christ**."
    2:38   in the name of Jesus **Christ** for the forgiveness of your sins.
    3: 6   I have I give you. In the name *of* Jesus **Christ** of Nazareth, walk."
    3:18   through all the prophets, saying that his **Christ** would suffer.
    3:20   and that he may send the **Christ**, who has been appointed for you—
    4:10   It is by the name of Jesus **Christ** of Nazareth, whom you crucified
    4:26   gather together against the Lord and against his **Anointed One**.'
    5:42   and proclaiming the good news that Jesus is the **Christ**.
    8: 5   went down to a city in Samaria and proclaimed the **Christ** there.
    8:12   good news of the kingdom of God and the name *of* Jesus **Christ**,
    9:22   the Jews living in Damascus by proving that Jesus is the **Christ**.
    9:34   "Aeneas," Peter said to him, "Jesus **Christ** heals you. Get up
   10:36   telling the good news of peace through Jesus **Christ**, who is Lord
   10:48   So he ordered that they be baptized in the name *of* Jesus **Christ**.
   11:17   who believed in the Lord Jesus **Christ**, who was I to think that I
   15:26   who have risked their lives for the name *of* our Lord Jesus **Christ**.
   16:18   "In the name *of* Jesus **Christ** I command you to come out of her!"
   17: 3   explaining and proving that the **Christ** had to suffer and rise from
   17: 3   "This Jesus I am proclaiming to you is the **Christ**," he said.
   18: 5   to preaching, testifying to the Jews that Jesus was the **Christ**.
   18:28   proving from the Scriptures that Jesus was the **Christ**.
   24:24   and listened to him as he spoke about faith in **Christ** Jesus.
   26:23   that the **Christ** would suffer and, as the first to rise from the dead,
   28:31   the kingdom of God and taught about the Lord Jesus **Christ**.

Ro   1: 1   Paul, a servant *of* **Christ** Jesus, called to be an apostle and set apart

1: 4 of God by his resurrection from the dead: Jesus **Christ** our Lord.
1: 6 you also are among those who are called to *belong to* Jesus **Christ**.
1: 7 peace to you from God our Father and from the Lord Jesus **Christ**.
1: 8 First, I thank my God through Jesus **Christ** for all of you,
2:16 the day when God will judge men's secrets through Jesus **Christ**,
3:22 This righteousness from God comes through faith *in* Jesus **Christ**
3:24 by his grace through the redemption that came by **Christ** Jesus.
5: 1 we have peace with God through our Lord Jesus **Christ**,
5: 6 when we were still powerless, **Christ** died for the ungodly.
5: 8 love for us in this: While we were still sinners, **Christ** died for us.
5:11 but we also rejoice in God through our Lord Jesus **Christ**,
5:15 and the gift that came by the grace *of* the one man, Jesus **Christ**,
5:17 of righteousness reign in life through the one man, Jesus **Christ**,
5:21 righteousness to bring eternal life through Jesus **Christ** our Lord.
6: 3 Or don't you know that all of us who were baptized into **Christ**
6: 4 just as **Christ** was raised from the dead through the glory of the
6: 8 Now if we died with **Christ**, we believe that we will also live with
6: 9 For we know that since **Christ** was raised from the dead, he cannot
6:11 count yourselves dead to sin but alive to God in **Christ** Jesus.
6:23 but the gift of God is eternal life in **Christ** Jesus our Lord.
7: 4 my brothers, you also died to the law through the body *of* **Christ**,
7:25 Thanks be to God—through Jesus **Christ** our Lord! So then,
8: 1 there is now no condemnation for those who are in **Christ** Jesus,
8: 2 because through **Christ** Jesus the law of the Spirit of life set me
8: 9 And if anyone does not have the Spirit *of* **Christ**, he does not
8:10 But if **Christ** is in you, your body is dead because of sin, yet your
8:11 he who raised **Christ** from the dead will also give life to your
8:17 heirs of God and co-heirs with **Christ**, if indeed we share in his
8:34 **Christ** Jesus, who died—more than that, who was raised to life—
8:35 Who shall separate us from the love *of* **Christ**? Shall trouble
8:39 will be able to separate us from the love of God that is in **Christ**
9: 1 I speak the truth in **Christ**—I am not lying, my conscience
9: 3 were cursed and cut off from **Christ** for the sake of my brothers,
9: 5 and from them is traced the human ancestry *of* **Christ**, who is God
10: 4 **Christ** is the end of the law so that there may be righteousness for
10: 6 'Who will ascend into heaven?' " (that is, to bring **Christ** down)
10: 7 descend into the deep?' " (that is, to bring **Christ** up from the dead).
10:17 the message, and the message is heard through the word *of* **Christ**.
12: 5 so in **Christ** we who are many form one body, and each member
13:14 Rather, clothe yourselves with the Lord Jesus **Christ**, and do not
14: 9 **Christ** died and returned to life so that he might be the Lord of
14:15 Do not by your eating destroy your brother for whom **Christ** died.
14:18 because anyone who serves **Christ** in this way is pleasing to God
15: 3 For even **Christ** did not please himself but, as it is written:
15: 5 you a spirit of unity among yourselves as you follow **Christ** Jesus,
15: 6 you may glorify the God and Father *of* our Lord Jesus **Christ**.
15: 7 Accept one another, then, just as **Christ** accepted you, in order to
15: 8 For I tell you that **Christ** has become a servant of the Jews on
15:16 to be a minister *of* **Christ** Jesus to the Gentiles with the priestly
15:17 Therefore I glory in **Christ** Jesus in my service to God.
15:18 I will not venture to speak of anything except what **Christ** has
15:19 around to Illyricum, I have fully proclaimed the gospel *of* **Christ**.
15:20 It has always been my ambition to preach the gospel where **Christ**
15:29 to you, I will come in the full measure of the blessing *of* **Christ**.
15:30 brothers, by our Lord Jesus **Christ** and by the love of the Spirit,
16: 3 Greet Priscilla and Aquila, my fellow workers in **Christ** Jesus.
16: 5 who was the first convert to **Christ** in the province of Asia.
16: 7 among the apostles, and they were in **Christ** before I was.
16: 9 Greet Urbanus, our fellow worker in **Christ**, and my dear friend
16:10 Greet Apelles, tested and approved in **Christ**. Greet those who
16:16 another with a holy kiss. All the churches *of* **Christ** send greetings.
16:18 For such people are not serving our Lord **Christ**, but their own
16:25 establish you by my gospel and the proclamation *of* Jesus **Christ**,
16:27 to the only wise God be glory forever through Jesus **Christ**!
1Co 1: 1 called to be an apostle *of* **Christ** Jesus by the will of God,
1: 2 to those sanctified in **Christ** Jesus and called to be holy,
1: 2 those everywhere who call on the name *of* our Lord Jesus **Christ**—
1: 3 and peace to you from God our Father and the Lord Jesus **Christ**.
1: 4 thank God for you because of his grace given you in **Christ** Jesus.
1: 6 because our testimony *about* **Christ** was confirmed in you.
1: 7 gift as you eagerly wait for our Lord Jesus **Christ** to be revealed.
1: 8 so that you will be blameless on the day *of* our Lord Jesus **Christ**.
1: 9 who has called you into fellowship with his Son Jesus **Christ** our
1:10 I appeal to you, brothers, in the name *of* our Lord Jesus **Christ**,
1:12 another, "I follow Cephas"; still another, "I follow **Christ**."
1:13 Is **Christ** divided? Was Paul crucified for you? Were you baptized

1:17 For **Christ** did not send me to baptize, but to preach the gospel—
1:17 of human wisdom, lest the cross *of* **Christ** be emptied of its power.
1:23 but we preach **Christ** crucified: a stumbling block to Jews
1:24 and Greeks, **Christ** the power of God and the wisdom of God.
1:30 It is because of him that you are in **Christ** Jesus, who has become
2: 2 resolved to know nothing while I was with you except Jesus **Christ**
2:16 Lord that he may instruct him?" But we have the mind *of* **Christ**.
3: 1 not address you as spiritual but as worldly—mere infants in **Christ**.
3:11 foundation other than the one already laid, which is Jesus **Christ**.
3:23 and you are *of* **Christ**, and **Christ** is of God.
3:23 and you are of Christ, and **Christ** is of God.
4: 1 men ought to regard us as servants *of* **Christ** and as those entrusted
4:10 We are fools for **Christ**, but you are so wise in Christ! We are
4:10 We are fools for Christ, but you are so wise in **Christ**! We are
4:15 Even though you have ten thousand guardians in **Christ**, you do
4:15 for in **Christ** Jesus I became your father through the gospel.
4:17 He will remind you of my way of life in **Christ** Jesus, which
5: 7 you really are. For **Christ**, our Passover lamb, has been sacrificed.
6:11 you were justified in the name *of* the Lord Jesus **Christ** and by the
6:15 Do you not know that your bodies are members *of* **Christ** himself?
6:15 Shall I then take the members *of* **Christ** and unite them with a
7:22 he who was a free man when he was called is **Christ's** slave.
8: 6 and there is but one Lord, Jesus **Christ**, through whom all things
8:11 So this weak brother, for whom **Christ** died, is destroyed by your
8:12 and wound their weak conscience, you sin against **Christ**.
9:12 we put up with anything rather than hinder the gospel *of* **Christ**.
9:21 (though I am not free from God's law but am under **Christ's** law),
10: 4 spiritual rock that accompanied them, and that rock was **Christ**.
10: 9 We should not test the Lord, [UBS *Christ*; NIV *3261*] as some of
10:16 for which we give thanks a participation in the blood *of* **Christ**?
10:16 is not the bread that we break a participation in the body *of* **Christ**?
11: 1 Follow my example, as I follow the example *of* **Christ**.
11: 3 Now I want you to realize that the head of every man is **Christ**,
11: 3 and the head of the woman is man, and the head *of* **Christ** is God.
12:12 all its parts are many, they form one body. So it is with **Christ**.
12:27 Now you are the body *of* **Christ**, and each one of you is a part of
15: 3 that **Christ** died for our sins according to the Scriptures,
15:12 But if it is preached that **Christ** has been raised from the dead,
15:13 no resurrection of the dead, then not even **Christ** has been raised.
15:14 And if **Christ** has not been raised, our preaching is useless
15:15 for we have testified about God that he raised **Christ** from the
15:16 if the dead are not raised, then **Christ** has not been raised either.
15:17 And if **Christ** has not been raised, your faith is futile; you are still
15:18 Then those also who have fallen asleep in **Christ** are lost.
15:19 If only for this life we have hope in **Christ**, we are to be pitied
15:20 But **Christ** has indeed been raised from the dead, the firstfruits of
15:22 For as in Adam all die, so in **Christ** all will be made alive.
15:23 **Christ**, the firstfruits; then, when he comes, those who belong to
15:23 then, when he comes, those who *belong to* him⁵ [*+3836*].
15:31 just as surely as I glory over you in **Christ** Jesus our Lord.
15:57 be to God! He gives us the victory through our Lord Jesus **Christ**.
16:24 My love to all of you in **Christ** Jesus. Amen.
2Co 1: 1 Paul, an apostle *of* **Christ** Jesus by the will of God, and Timothy
1: 2 and peace to you from God our Father and the Lord Jesus **Christ**.
1: 3 Praise be to the God and Father *of* our Lord Jesus **Christ**,
1: 5 For just as the sufferings *of* **Christ** flow over into our lives,
1: 5 over into our lives, so also through **Christ** our comfort overflows.
1:19 For the Son of God, Jesus **Christ**, who was preached among you
1:21 Now it is God who makes both us and you stand firm in **Christ**.
2:10 to forgive—I have forgiven in the sight *of* **Christ** for your sake,
2:12 Now when I went to Troas to preach the gospel *of* **Christ**
2:14 who always leads us in triumphal procession in **Christ** and through
2:15 For we are to God the aroma *of* **Christ** among those who are being
2:17 On the contrary, in **Christ** we speak before God with sincerity,
3: 3 You show that you are a letter *from* **Christ**, the result of our
3: 4 Such confidence as this is ours through **Christ** before God.
3:14 It has not been removed, because only in **Christ** is it taken away.
4: 4 that they cannot see the light of the gospel of the glory *of* **Christ**,
4: 5 For we do not preach ourselves, but Jesus **Christ** as Lord,
4: 6 light of the knowledge of the glory of God in the face *of* **Christ**.
5:10 For we must all appear before the judgment seat *of* **Christ**,
5:14 For **Christ's** love compels us, because we are convinced that one
5:16 Though we once regarded **Christ** in this way, we do so no longer.
5:17 Therefore, if anyone is in **Christ**, he is a new creation; the old has
5:18 who reconciled us to himself through **Christ** and gave us the
5:19 that God was reconciling the world to himself in **Christ**,

	5:20	We are therefore **Christ's** [+*5642*] ambassadors, as though God
	5:20	We implore you on **Christ's** behalf: Be reconciled to God.
	6:15	What harmony is there between **Christ** and Belial? What does a
	8: 9	For you know the grace *of* our Lord Jesus **Christ**, that though he
	8:23	they are representatives of the churches and an honor *to* **Christ**.
	9:13	that accompanies your confession of the gospel *of* **Christ**,
	10: 1	By the meekness and gentleness *of* **Christ**, I appeal to you—
	10: 5	and we take captive every thought to make it obedient *to* **Christ**.
	10: 7	If anyone is confident that he belongs *to* **Christ**, he should
	10: 7	he should consider again that we *belong to* **Christ** just as much as
	10:14	come to you, for we did get as far as you with the gospel *of* **Christ**.
	11: 2	I promised you to one husband, *to* **Christ**, so that I might present
	11: 3	be led astray from your sincere and pure devotion to **Christ**.
	11:10	As surely as the truth *of* **Christ** is in me, nobody in the regions of
	11:13	deceitful workmen, masquerading as apostles *of* **Christ**.
	11:23	Are they servants *of* **Christ**? (I am out of my mind to talk like
	12: 2	I know a man in **Christ** who fourteen years ago was caught up to
	12: 9	about my weaknesses, so that **Christ's** power may rest on me.
	12:10	That is why, for **Christ's** sake, I delight in weaknesses, in insults,
	12:19	We have been speaking in the sight of God as those in **Christ**;
	13: 3	since you are demanding proof that **Christ** is speaking through me.
	13: 5	Do you not realize that **Christ** Jesus is in you—unless, of course,
	13:14	May the grace *of* the Lord Jesus **Christ**, and the love of God,
Gal	1: 1	not from men nor by man, but by Jesus **Christ** and God the Father,
	1: 3	and peace to you from God our Father and the Lord Jesus **Christ**,
	1: 6	so quickly deserting the one who called you by the grace *of* **Christ**
	1: 7	you into confusion and are trying to pervert the gospel *of* **Christ**.
	1:10	were still trying to please men, I would not be a servant *of* **Christ**.
	1:12	I taught it; rather, I received it by revelation *from* Jesus **Christ**.
	1:22	personally unknown to the churches of Judea that are in **Christ**.
	2: 4	infiltrated our ranks to spy on the freedom we have in **Christ** Jesus
	2:16	is not justified by observing the law, but by faith *in* Jesus **Christ**.
	2:16	have put our faith in **Christ** Jesus that we may be justified by faith
	2:16	our faith in Christ Jesus that we may be justified by faith *in* **Christ**
	2:17	"If, while we seek to be justified in **Christ**, it becomes evident that
	2:17	we ourselves are sinners, does that mean that **Christ** promotes sin?
	2:20	I have been crucified with **Christ** and I no longer live, but Christ
	2:20	crucified with Christ and I no longer live, but **Christ** lives in me.
	2:21	could be gained through the law, **Christ** died for nothing!"
	3: 1	Before your very eyes Jesus **Christ** was clearly portrayed as
	3:13	**Christ** redeemed us from the curse of the law by becoming a curse
	3:14	to Abraham might come to the Gentiles through **Christ** Jesus,
	3:16	but "and to your seed," meaning one person, who is **Christ**.
	3:22	that what was promised, being given through faith *in* Jesus **Christ**,
	3:24	So the law was put in charge to lead us to **Christ** that we might be
	3:26	You are all sons of God through faith in **Christ** Jesus,
	3:27	for all of you who were baptized into **Christ** have clothed
	3:27	were baptized into Christ have clothed yourselves with **Christ**.
	3:28	slave nor free, male nor female, for you are all one in **Christ** Jesus.
	3:29	If you *belong to* **Christ**, then you are Abraham's seed, and heirs
	4:14	me as if I were an angel of God, as if I were **Christ** Jesus himself.
	4:19	for whom I am again in the pains of childbirth until **Christ** is
	5: 1	It is for freedom that **Christ** has set us free. Stand firm, then,
	5: 2	yourselves be circumcised, **Christ** will be of no value to you at all.
	5: 4	are trying to be justified by law have been alienated from **Christ**;
	5: 6	For in **Christ** Jesus neither circumcision nor uncircumcision has
	5:24	Those who *belong to* **Christ** Jesus have crucified the sinful nature
	6: 2	other's burdens, and in this way you will fulfill the law *of* **Christ**.
	6:12	they do this is to avoid being persecuted for the cross *of* **Christ**.
	6:14	May I never boast except in the cross *of* our Lord Jesus **Christ**,
	6:18	The grace *of* our Lord Jesus **Christ** be with your spirit, brothers.
Eph	1: 1	Paul, an apostle *of* **Christ** Jesus by the will of God, To the saints in
	1: 1	will of God, To the saints in Ephesus, the faithful in **Christ** Jesus:
	1: 2	and peace to you from God our Father and the Lord Jesus **Christ**.
	1: 3	Praise be to the God and Father *of* our Lord Jesus **Christ**,
	1: 3	us in the heavenly realms with every spiritual blessing in **Christ**.
	1: 5	he predestined us to be adopted as his sons through Jesus **Christ**,
	1:10	in heaven and on earth together under one head, even **Christ**.
	1:12	in order that we, who were the first to hope in **Christ**, might be for
	1:17	I keep asking that the God *of* our Lord Jesus **Christ**, the glorious
	1:20	which he exerted in **Christ** when he raised him from the dead
	2: 5	made us alive with **Christ** even when we were dead in
	2: 6	and seated us with him in the heavenly realms in **Christ** Jesus,
	2: 7	riches of his grace, expressed in his kindness to us in **Christ** Jesus.
	2:10	are God's workmanship, created in **Christ** Jesus to do good works,
	2:12	remember that at that time you were separate from **Christ**,

	2:13	But now in **Christ** Jesus you who once were far away have been
	2:13	were far away have been brought near through the blood *of* **Christ**.
	2:20	and prophets, with **Christ** Jesus himself as the chief cornerstone.
	3: 1	the prisoner *of* **Christ** Jesus for the sake of you Gentiles—
	3: 4	will be able to understand my insight into the mystery *of* **Christ**,
	3: 6	of one body, and sharers together in the promise in **Christ** Jesus.
	3: 8	to preach to the Gentiles the unsearchable riches *of* **Christ**,
	3:11	according to his eternal purpose which he accomplished in **Christ**
	3:17	so that **Christ** may dwell in your hearts through faith. And I pray
	3:18	grasp how wide and long and high and deep is the love *of* **Christ**,
	3:21	glory in the church and in **Christ** Jesus throughout all generations,
	4: 7	But to each one of us grace has been given as **Christ** apportioned
	4:12	for works of service, so that the body *of* **Christ** may be built up
	4:13	attaining to the whole measure of the fullness *of* **Christ**.
	4:15	will in all things grow up into him who is the Head, that is, **Christ**.
	4:20	You, however, did not come to know **Christ** that way.
	4:32	forgiving each other, just as in **Christ** God forgave you.
	5: 2	just as **Christ** loved us and gave himself up for us as a fragrant
	5: 5	has any inheritance in the kingdom *of* **Christ** and of God.
	5:14	O sleeper, rise from the dead, and **Christ** will shine on you."
	5:20	the Father for everything, in the name *of* our Lord Jesus **Christ**.
	5:21	Submit to one another out of reverence *for* **Christ**.
	5:23	For the husband is the head of the wife as **Christ** is the head of the
	5:24	Now as the church submits *to* **Christ**, so also wives should submit
	5:25	just as **Christ** loved the church and gave himself up for her
	5:29	but he feeds and cares for it, just as **Christ** does the church—
	5:32	a profound mystery—but I am talking about **Christ** and the church.
	6: 5	and with sincerity of heart, just as you would obey **Christ**.
	6: 6	but like slaves *of* **Christ**, doing the will of God from your heart.
	6:23	and love with faith from God the Father and the Lord Jesus **Christ**.
	6:24	Grace to all who love our Lord Jesus **Christ** with an undying love.
Php	1: 1	Paul and Timothy, servants *of* **Christ** Jesus, To all the saints in
	1: 1	*of* Christ Jesus, To all the saints in **Christ** Jesus at Philippi,
	1: 2	and peace to you from God our Father and the Lord Jesus **Christ**.
	1: 6	in you will carry it on to completion until the day *of* **Christ** Jesus.
	1: 8	testify how I long for all of you with the affection *of* **Christ** Jesus.
	1:10	is best and may be pure and blameless until the day *of* **Christ**,
	1:11	with the fruit of righteousness that comes through Jesus **Christ**—
	1:13	palace guard and to everyone else that I am in chains for **Christ**.
	1:15	It is true that some preach **Christ** out of envy and rivalry,
	1:17	The former preach **Christ** out of selfish ambition, not sincerely,
	1:18	every way, whether from false motives or true, **Christ** is preached.
	1:19	your prayers and the help given by the Spirit *of* Jesus **Christ**,
	1:20	so that now as always **Christ** will be exalted in my body,
	1:21	For to me, to live is **Christ** and to die is gain.
	1:23	I desire to depart and be with **Christ**, which is better by far;
	1:26	so that through my being with you again your joy in **Christ** Jesus
	1:27	conduct yourselves in a manner worthy of the gospel *of* **Christ**.
	1:29	For it has been granted to you on behalf *of* **Christ** not only to
	2: 1	If you have any encouragement from being united with **Christ**,
	2: 5	Your attitude should be the same as that of **Christ** Jesus:
	2:11	and every tongue confess that Jesus **Christ** is Lord, to the glory of
	2:16	in order that I may boast on the day *of* **Christ** that I did not run
	2:21	everyone looks out for his own interests, not those of Jesus **Christ**.
	2:30	because he almost died for the work *of* **Christ**, risking his life to
	3: 3	we who worship by the Spirit of God, who glory in **Christ** Jesus,
	3: 7	was to my profit I now consider loss for the sake *of* **Christ**.
	3: 8	to the surpassing greatness of knowing **Christ** Jesus my Lord,
	3: 8	lost all things. I consider them rubbish, that I may gain **Christ**
	3: 9	that comes from the law, but that which is through faith *in* **Christ**—
	3:12	but I press on to take hold of that for which **Christ** Jesus took hold
	3:14	the prize for which God has called me heavenward in **Christ** Jesus.
	3:18	again even with tears, many live as enemies of the cross *of* **Christ**.
	3:20	And we eagerly await a Savior from there, the Lord Jesus **Christ**,
	4: 7	will guard your hearts and your minds in **Christ** Jesus.
	4:19	all your needs according to his glorious riches in **Christ** Jesus.
	4:21	Greet all the saints in **Christ** Jesus. The brothers who are with me
	4:23	The grace *of* the Lord Jesus **Christ** be with your spirit. Amen.
Col	1: 1	Paul, an apostle *of* **Christ** Jesus by the will of God, and Timothy
	1: 2	To the holy and faithful brothers in **Christ** at Colosse: Grace
	1: 3	the Father *of* our Lord Jesus **Christ**, when we pray for you,
	1: 4	because we have heard of your faith in **Christ** Jesus and of the love
	1: 7	fellow servant, who is a faithful minister *of* **Christ** on our behalf,
	1:24	and I fill up in my flesh what is still lacking in regard to **Christ's**
	1:27	riches of this mystery, which is **Christ** in you, the hope of glory.
	1:28	all wisdom, so that we may present everyone perfect in **Christ**.

2: 2 in order that they may know the mystery of God, *namely,* **Christ**,
2: 5 to see how orderly you are and how firm your faith in **Christ** is.
2: 6 So then, just as you received **Christ** Jesus as Lord, continue to live
2: 8 and the basic principles of this world rather than on **Christ**.
2: 11 by the hands of men but with the circumcision done *by* **Christ**,
2: 17 things that were to come; the reality, however, is *found in* **Christ**.
2: 20 Since you died with **Christ** to the basic principles of this world,
3: 1 Since, then, you have been raised with **Christ**, set your hearts on
3: 1 on things above, where **Christ** is seated at the right hand of God.
3: 3 For you died, and your life is now hidden with **Christ** in God.
3: 4 When **Christ**, who is your life, appears, then you also will appear
3: 11 barbarian, Scythian, slave or free, but **Christ** is all, and is in all.
3: 15 Let the peace *of* **Christ** rule in your hearts, since as members of
3: 16 Let the word *of* **Christ** dwell in you richly as you teach
3: 24 from the Lord as a reward. It is the Lord **Christ** you are serving.
4: 3 so that we may proclaim the mystery *of* **Christ**, for which I am in
4: 12 Epaphras, who is one of you and a servant *of* **Christ** Jesus,
1Th 1: 1 of the Thessalonians in God the Father and the Lord Jesus **Christ**:
1: 3 and your endurance inspired by hope *in* our Lord Jesus **Christ**.
2: 6 As apostles *of* **Christ** we could have been a burden to you,
2: 14 imitators of God's churches in Judea, which are in **Christ** Jesus:
3: 2 and God's fellow worker in spreading the gospel *of* **Christ**,
4: 16 with the trumpet call of God, and the dead in **Christ** will rise first.
5: 9 but to receive salvation through our Lord Jesus **Christ**.
5: 18 in all circumstances, for this is God's will for you in **Christ** Jesus.
5: 23 body be kept blameless at the coming *of* our Lord Jesus **Christ**.
5: 28 The grace *of* our Lord Jesus **Christ** be with you.
2Th 1: 1 of the Thessalonians in God our Father and the Lord Jesus **Christ**:
1: 2 and peace to you from God the Father and the Lord Jesus **Christ**.
1: 12 according to the grace of our God and the Lord Jesus **Christ**.
2: 1 Concerning the coming *of* our Lord Jesus **Christ** and our being
2: 14 that you might share in the glory *of* our Lord Jesus **Christ**.
2: 16 May our Lord Jesus **Christ** himself and God our Father, who loved
3: 5 Lord direct your hearts into God's love and **Christ's** perseverance.
3: 6 In the name *of* the Lord Jesus **Christ**, we command you, brothers,
3: 12 we command and urge in the Lord Jesus **Christ** to settle down
3: 18 The grace *of* our Lord Jesus **Christ** be with you all.
1Ti 1: 1 an apostle *of* **Christ** Jesus by the command of God our Savior
1: 1 by the command of God our Savior and *of* **Christ** Jesus our hope,
1: 2 and peace from God the Father and **Christ** Jesus our Lord.
1: 12 I thank **Christ** Jesus our Lord, who has given me strength,
1: 14 along with the faith and love that are in **Christ** Jesus.
1: 15 **Christ** Jesus came into the world to save sinners—of whom I am
1: 16 **Christ** Jesus might display his unlimited patience as an example
2: 5 and one mediator between God and men, the man **Christ** Jesus,
3: 13 standing and great assurance in their faith in **Christ** Jesus.
4: 6 you will be a good minister *of* **Christ** Jesus, brought up in the
5: 11 when their sensual desires overcome their dedication to **Christ**,
5: 21 in the sight *of* God and **Christ** Jesus and the elect angels,
6: 3 does not agree to the sound instruction *of* our Lord Jesus **Christ**
6: 13 the sight of God, who gives life to everything, and *of* **Christ** Jesus,
6: 14 without spot or blame until the appearing *of* our Lord Jesus **Christ**,
2Ti 1: 1 Paul, an apostle *of* **Christ** Jesus by the will of God, according to
1: 1 will of God, according to the promise of life that is in **Christ** Jesus,
1: 2 and peace from God the Father and **Christ** Jesus our Lord.
1: 9 This grace was given us in **Christ** Jesus before the beginning of
1: 10 has now been revealed through the appearing *of* our Savior, **Christ**
1: 13 the pattern of sound teaching, with faith and love in **Christ** Jesus.
2: 1 You then, my son, be strong in the grace that is in **Christ** Jesus.
2: 3 Endure hardship with us like a good soldier *of* **Christ** Jesus.
2: 8 Remember Jesus **Christ**, raised from the dead, descended from
2: 10 that they too may obtain the salvation that is in **Christ** Jesus,
3: 12 everyone who wants to live a godly life in **Christ** Jesus will be
3: 15 able to make you wise for salvation through faith in **Christ** Jesus.
4: 1 In the presence of God and *of* **Christ** Jesus, who will judge the
Tit 1: 1 and an apostle *of* Jesus **Christ** for the faith of God's elect
1: 4 and peace from God the Father and **Christ** Jesus our Savior.
2: 13 the glorious appearing *of* our great God and Savior, Jesus **Christ**,
3: 6 whom he poured out on us generously through Jesus **Christ** our
Phm 1: 1 Paul, a prisoner *of* **Christ** Jesus, and Timothy our brother,
1: 3 and peace from God our Father and the Lord Jesus **Christ**.
1: 6 have a full understanding of every good thing we have in **Christ**.
1: 8 although in **Christ** I could be bold and order you to do what you
1: 9 as Paul—an old man and now also a prisoner *of* **Christ** Jesus—
1: 20 some benefit from you in the Lord; refresh my heart in **Christ**.
1: 23 Epaphras, my fellow prisoner in **Christ** Jesus, sends you greetings.
1: 25 The grace *of* the Lord Jesus **Christ** be with your spirit.
Heb 3: 6 But **Christ** is faithful as a son over God's house. And we are his
3: 14 We have come to share in **Christ** if we hold firmly till the end the
5: 5 So **Christ** also did not take upon himself the glory of becoming a
6: 1 Therefore let us leave the elementary teachings *about* **Christ**
9: 11 When **Christ** came as high priest of the good things that are
9: 14 How much more, then, will the blood *of* **Christ**, who through the
9: 24 For **Christ** did not enter a man-made sanctuary that was only a
9: 28 so **Christ** was sacrificed once to take away the sins of many
10: 10 holy through the sacrifice of the body *of* Jesus **Christ** once for all.
11: 26 He regarded disgrace *for the sake of* **Christ** as of greater value
13: 8 Jesus **Christ** is the same yesterday and today and forever.
13: 21 through Jesus **Christ**, to whom be glory for ever and ever.
Jas 1: 1 James, a servant of God and *of* the Lord Jesus **Christ**,
2: 1 My brothers, as believers *in* our glorious Lord Jesus **Christ**,
1Pe 1: 1 Peter, an apostle *of* Jesus **Christ**, To God's elect, strangers in the
1: 2 for obedience *to* Jesus **Christ** and sprinkling by his blood:
1: 3 Praise be to the God and Father *of* our Lord Jesus **Christ**!
1: 3 living hope through the resurrection *of* Jesus **Christ** from the dead,
1: 7 result in praise, glory and honor when Jesus **Christ** is revealed.
1: 11 and circumstances to which the Spirit *of* **Christ** in them was
1: 11 in them was pointing when he predicted the sufferings of **Christ**
1: 13 set your hope fully on the grace to be given you when Jesus **Christ**
1: 19 but with the precious blood *of* **Christ**, a lamb without blemish
2: 5 spiritual sacrifices acceptable to God through Jesus **Christ**.
2: 21 To this you were called, because **Christ** suffered for you,
3: 15 But in your hearts set apart **Christ** as Lord. Always be prepared to
3: 16 your good behavior in **Christ** may be ashamed of their slander.
3: 18 For **Christ** died for sins once for all, the righteous for the
3: 21 toward God. It saves you by the resurrection *of* Jesus **Christ**,
4: 1 Therefore, since **Christ** suffered in his body, arm yourselves also
4: 11 so that in all things God may be praised through Jesus **Christ**.
4: 13 But rejoice that you participate in the sufferings *of* **Christ**,
4: 14 If you are insulted because of the name *of* **Christ**, you are blessed,
5: 1 a witness of **Christ's** sufferings and one who also will share in the
5: 10 the God of all grace, who called you to his eternal glory in **Christ**,
5: 14 another with a kiss of love. Peace to all of you who are in **Christ**.
2Pe 1: 1 Simon Peter, a servant and apostle *of* Jesus **Christ**, To those who
1: 1 and Savior Jesus **Christ** have received a faith as precious as ours:
1: 8 and unproductive in your knowledge *of* our Lord Jesus **Christ**.
1: 11 into the eternal kingdom of our Lord and Savior Jesus **Christ**.
1: 14 soon put it aside, as our Lord Jesus **Christ** has made clear to me.
1: 16 we told you about the power and coming *of* our Lord Jesus **Christ**,
2: 20 and Savior Jesus **Christ** and are again entangled in it
3: 18 in the grace and knowledge *of* our Lord and Savior Jesus **Christ**.
1Jn 1: 3 our fellowship is with the Father and with his Son, Jesus **Christ**.
2: 1 to the Father in our defense—Jesus **Christ**, the Righteous One.
2: 22 Who is the liar? It is the man who denies that Jesus is the **Christ**.
3: 23 to believe in the name of his Son, Jesus **Christ**, and to love one
4: 2 Every spirit that acknowledges that Jesus **Christ** has come in the
5: 1 Everyone who believes that Jesus is the **Christ** is born of God,
5: 6 This is the one who came by water and blood—Jesus **Christ**.
5: 20 And we are in him who is true—even in his Son Jesus **Christ**.
2Jn 1: 3 mercy and peace from God the Father and from Jesus **Christ**,
1: 7 who do not acknowledge Jesus **Christ** as coming in the flesh,
1: 9 and does not continue in the teaching *of* **Christ** does not have God;
Jude 1: 1 Jude, a servant *of* Jesus **Christ** and a brother of James, To those
1: 1 who are loved by God the Father and kept *by* Jesus **Christ**:
1: 4 and deny Jesus **Christ** our only Sovereign and Lord.
1: 17 remember what the apostles *of* our Lord Jesus **Christ** foretold.
1: 21 for the mercy *of* our Lord Jesus **Christ** to bring you to eternal life.
1: 25 majesty, power and authority, through Jesus **Christ** our Lord,
Rev 1: 1 The revelation *of* Jesus **Christ**, which God gave him to show his
1: 2 that is, the word of God and the testimony *of* Jesus **Christ**.
1: 5 and from Jesus **Christ**, who is the faithful witness, the firstborn
11: 15 the world has become the kingdom of our Lord and *of* his **Christ**,
12: 10 and the kingdom of our God, and the authority *of* his **Christ**.
20: 4 They came to life and reigned with **Christ** a thousand years.
20: 6 but they will be priests of God and *of* **Christ** and will reign with

5987 χρίω, *chriō* [5] [→ *1608, 2222, 5984; cf. 5986*]

anointed [4], anointing [1]

Lk 4: 18 because *he has* **anointed** me to preach good news to the poor.
Ac 4: 27 to conspire against your holy servant Jesus, whom *you* **anointed**.

10: 38 how God **anointed** Jesus of Nazareth with the Holy Spirit
2Co 1: 21 who makes both us and you stand firm in Christ. *He* **anointed** us,
Heb 1: 9 has set you above your companions *by* **anointing** you with the oil

5988 χρονίζω, *chronizō* [5] [√ *5989*]

a long time in coming [1], delay [1], stayed so long [1], staying away a long time [1], taking a long time [1]

Mt 24: 48 and says to himself, 'My master *is* **staying away a long time**,'
     25: 5 The bridegroom *was* **a long time in coming**, and they all became
Lk   1: 21 for Zechariah and wondering why he **stayed so long** in the temple.
     12: 45 'My master *is* **taking a long time** in coming,' and he then begins
Heb 10: 37 a very little while, "He who is coming will come and *will* not **delay**.

5989 χρόνος, *chronos* [54] [→ *3432, 5988, 5990*]

time [26], times [5], as long as [+*2093+4012*] [2], beginning of time [+*173*] [2], long [2], some time [2], *untranslated* [1], a long time [+*3900+4024*] [1], delay [1], instant [+*5117*] [1], life [1], lives [1], longer [+*2285*] [1], old [1], only as long as [+*2093+4012*] [1], past [1], so long as [+*4012*] [1], spend time [+*2093+3531*] [1], spend time [+*2152*] [1], stayed a little longer [+*2091*] [1], while [1]

Mt   2: 7 and found out from them the exact **time** the star had appeared.
     2: 16 in accordance with the **time** he had learned from the Magi.
     25: 19 "After a long **time** the master of those servants returned and settled
Mk   2: 19 They cannot, **so long as** [+*4012*] they have him with them.
     9: 21 Jesus asked the boy's father, "How **long** has he been like this?"
Lk   1: 57 When it was **time** for Elizabeth to have her baby, she gave birth to
     4: 5 and showed him in an **instant** [+*5117*] all the kingdoms of the
     8: 27 *For* a long **time** this man had not worn clothes or lived in a house,
     8: 29 Many **times** it had seized him, and though he was chained hand
     18: 4 "For **some time** he refused. But finally he said to himself,
     20: 9 rented it to some farmers and went away *for* a long **time**.
     23: 8 because for a long **time** he had been wanting to see him.
Jn   5: 6 and learned that he had been in this condition *for* a long **time**,
     7: 33 "I am with you for only a short **time**, and then I go to the one who
     12: 35 told them, "You are going to have the light just a little **while** longer.
     14: 9 Philip, even after I have been among you such a *long* **time**?
Ac   1: 6 are you at this **time** going to restore the kingdom to Israel?"
     1: 7 "It is not for you to know the **times** or dates the Father has set by
     1: 21 men who have been with us the whole **time** the Lord Jesus went in
     3: 21 He must remain in heaven until the **time** comes for God to restore
     7: 17 "As the **time** drew near for God to fulfill his promise to Abraham,
     7: 23 "When Moses was forty years **old**, he decided to visit his fellow
     8: 11 because he had amazed them *for* a long **time** with his magic.
     13: 18 he endured their conduct for about forty years **[RPG]** in the
     14: 3 So Paul and Barnabas spent considerable **time** there,
     14: 28 And they stayed there **a long time** [+*3900+4024*] with the
     15: 33 After spending **some time** there, they were sent off by the brothers
     17: 30 In the **past** God overlooked such ignorance, but now he commands
     18: 20 When they asked him *to* **spend** more **time** [+*2093+3531*] with
     18: 23 After spending some **time** in Antioch, Paul set out from there
     19: 22 *while* he **stayed** in the province of Asia **a little longer** [+*2091*].
     20: 18 "You know how I lived the whole **time** I was with you,
     27: 9 Much **time** had been lost, and sailing had already become
Ro   7: 1 has authority over a man **only as long as** [+*2093+4012*] he lives?
     16: 25 according to the revelation of the mystery hidden *for* **long** ages
1Co 7: 39 A woman is bound to her husband **as long as** [+*2093+4012*] he
     16: 7 I hope *to* **spend** some **time** [+*2152*] with you, if the Lord permits.
Gal 4: 1 What I am saying is that **as long as** [+*2093+4012*] the heir is a
     4: 4 But when the **time** had fully come, God sent his Son, born of a
1Th 5: 1 brothers, about **times** and dates we do not need to write to you,
2Ti 1: 9 was given us in Christ Jesus before the **beginning of time** [+*173*],
Tit 1: 2 who does not lie, promised before the **beginning of time** [+*173*],
Heb 4: 7 calling it Today, when a long **time** later he spoke through David,
     5: 12 In fact, though by this **time** you ought to be teachers, you need
     11: 32 I do not have **time** to tell about Gideon, Barak, Samson, Jephthah,
1Pe 1: 17 work impartially, live your **lives** as strangers here in reverent fear.
     1: 20 of the world, but was revealed in these last **times** for your sake.
     4: 2 he does not live the rest of his earthly **life** for evil human desires,
     4: 3 For you have spent enough **time** in the past doing what pagans
Jude 1: 18 "In the last **times** there will be scoffers who will follow their own
Rev 2: 21 I have given her **time** to repent of her immorality, but she is
     6: 11 and they were told to wait a little **longer** [+*2285*], until the number

10: 6 and all that is in it, and said, "There will be no more **delay**!
20: 3 years were ended. After that, he must be set free *for* a short **time**.

5990 χρονοτριβέω, *chronotribeō* [1] [√ *5989 + 5561*]

spending time [+*1181*] [1]

Ac 20: 16 Ephesus to avoid **spending time** [+*1181*] in the province of Asia,

5991 χρύσεος, *chryseos*   Not used in UBS/NIV [√ *5996*]

5992 χρυσίον, *chrysion* [12] [√ *5996*]

gold [10], gold jewelry [1], gold-covered [+*4119+4328*] [1]

Ac   3: 6 Then Peter said, "Silver or **gold** I do not have, but what I have I
     20: 33 I have not coveted anyone's silver or **gold** or clothing.
1Ti 2: 9 not with braided hair or **gold** or pearls or expensive clothes,
Heb 9: 4 incense and the **gold-covered** [+*4119+4328*] ark of the covenant.
1Pe 1: 7 of greater worth than **gold**, which perishes even though refined by
     1: 18 or **gold** that you were redeemed from the empty way of life handed
     3: 3 as braided hair and the wearing *of* **gold jewelry** and fine clothes.
Rev 3: 18 I counsel you to buy from me **gold** refined in the fire, so you can
     17: 4 was dressed in purple and scarlet, and was glittering *with* **gold**,
     18: 16 purple and scarlet, and glittering with **gold**, precious stones
     21: 18 wall was made of jasper, and the city of pure **gold**, as pure as glass.
     21: 21 The great street of the city was of pure **gold**, like transparent glass.

5993 χρυσοδακτύλιος, *chrysodaktylios* [1]
[√ *5996 + 1235*]

wearing a gold ring [1]

Jas 2: 2 Suppose a man comes into your meeting **wearing a gold ring**

5994 χρυσόλιθος, *chrysolithos* [1] [√ *5996 + 3345*]

chrysolite [1]

Rev 21: 20 the seventh **chrysolite**, the eighth beryl, the ninth topaz,

5995 χρυσόπρασος, *chrysoprasos* [1] [√ *5996 + 4555*]

chrysoprase [1]

Rev 21: 20 the eighth beryl, the ninth topaz, the tenth **chrysoprase**,

5996 χρυσός, *chrysos* [10] [→ *5991, 5992, 5993, 5994, 5995, 5997, 5998*]

gold [10]

Mt   2: 11 and presented him with gifts of **gold** and of incense and of myrrh.
     10: 9 Do not take along any **gold** or silver or copper in your belts;
     23: 16 but if anyone swears by the **gold** of the temple, he is bound by his
     23: 17 is greater: the **gold**, or the temple that makes the gold sacred?
     23: 17 is greater: the gold, or the temple that makes the **gold** sacred?
Ac   17: 29 we should not think that the divine being is like **gold** or silver
1Co 3: 12 If any man builds on this foundation *using* **gold**, silver,
Jas 5: 3 Your **gold** and silver are corroded. Their corrosion will testify
Rev 9: 7 On their heads they wore something like crowns of **gold**, and their
     18: 12 cargoes *of* **gold**, silver, precious stones and pearls; fine linen,

5997 χρυσοῦς, *chrysous* [18] [√ *5996*]

golden [12], of gold [5], gold [1]

2Ti 2: 20 In a large house there are articles not only **of gold** and silver,
Heb 9: 4 which had the **golden** altar of incense and the gold-covered ark of
     9: 4 This ark contained the **gold** jar of manna, Aaron's staff that had
Rev 1: 12 to me. And when I turned I saw seven **golden** lampstands,
     1: 13 reaching down to his feet and with a **golden** sash around his chest.
     1: 20 saw in my right hand and of the seven **golden** lampstands is this:
     2: 1 in his right hand and walks among the seven **golden** lampstands:
     4: 4 They were dressed in white and had crowns **of gold** on their heads.
     5: 8 one had a harp and they were holding **golden** bowls full of incense,
     8: 3 who had a **golden** censer, came and stood at the altar.
     8: 3 the prayers of all the saints, on the **golden** altar before the throne.

9: 13　and I heard a voice coming from the horns *of* the **golden** altar that
9: 20　and idols **of gold**, silver, bronze, stone and wood—
14: 14　cloud was one "like a son of man" with a crown **of gold** on his head
15: 6　shining linen and wore **golden** sashes around their chests.
15: 7　the seven angels seven **golden** bowls filled with the wrath of God,
17: 4　She held a **golden** cup in her hand, filled with abominable things
21: 15　The angel who talked with me had a measuring rod **of gold** to

5998　χρυσόω, *chrysoō*　[2]　[√ *5996*]

glittering [2]

Rev 17: 4　was dressed in purple and scarlet, and *was* **glittering** with gold,
18: 16　purple and scarlet, and **glittering** with gold, precious stones

5999　χρώς, *chrōs*　[1]

that had touched [+*608*+*3836*] [1]

Ac　19: 12　and aprons **that had touched** [+*608*+*3836*] him were taken to the

6000　χωλός, *chōlos*　[14]

lame [10], crippled [3], cripples [1]

Mt　11: 5　The blind receive sight, the **lame** walk, those who have leprosy are
15: 30　bringing the **lame**, the blind, the crippled, the mute and many
15: 31　the crippled made well, the **lame** walking and the blind seeing.
18: 8　or **crippled** than to have two hands or two feet and be thrown into
21: 14　The blind and the **lame** came to him at the temple, and he healed
Mk　9: 45　It is better for you to enter life **crippled** than to have two feet
Lk　7: 22　The blind receive sight, the **lame** walk, those who have leprosy are
14: 13　give a banquet, invite the poor, the crippled, the **lame**, the blind,
14: 21　and bring in the poor, the crippled, the blind and the **lame**.'
Jn　5: 3　of disabled people used to lie—the blind, the **lame**, the paralyzed.
Ac　3: 2　Now a man **crippled** from birth was being carried to the temple
8: 7　came out of many, and many paralytics and **cripples** were healed.
14: 8　in his feet, who was **lame** from birth and had never walked.
Heb 12: 13　your feet," so that the **lame** may not be disabled, but rather healed.

6001　χώρα, *chōra*　[28]　[√ *6003*]

country [8], region [8], fields [3], Judea [+*2677*] [2], land [2], area [1], countryside [1], ground [1], they[s] [+*899*+*3836*] [1], Traconitis [+*5551*] [1]

Mt　2: 12　go back to Herod, they returned to their **country** by another route.
4: 16　on those living in the **land** of the shadow of death a light has
8: 28　When he arrived at the other side in the **region** of the Gadarenes,
Mk　1: 5　The whole Judean **countryside** and all the people of Jerusalem
5: 1　They went across the lake to the **region** of the Gerasenes.
5: 10　he begged Jesus again and again not to send them out *of* the **area**.
6: 55　They ran throughout that whole **region** and carried the sick on
Lk　2: 8　And there were shepherds living out in the **fields** nearby, keeping
3: 1　his brother Philip tetrarch *of* Iturea and **Traconitis** [+*5551*],
8: 26　They sailed to the **region** of the Gerasenes, which is across the lake
12: 16　"The **ground** of a certain rich man produced a good crop.
15: 13　set off for a distant **country** and there squandered his wealth in
15: 14　there was a severe famine in that whole **country**, and he began to
15: 15　So he went and hired himself out to a citizen *of* that **country**,
19: 12　"A man of noble birth went to a distant **country** to have himself
21: 21　in the city get out, and let those in the **country** not enter the city.
Jn　4: 35　then the harvest'? I tell you, open your eyes and look at the **fields**!
11: 54　Instead he withdrew to a **region** near the desert, to a village called
11: 55　many went up from the **country** to Jerusalem for their ceremonial
Ac　8: 1　all except the apostles were scattered throughout **Judea** [+*2677*]
10: 39　"We are witnesses of everything he did in the **country** of the Jews
12: 20　because they[s] [+*899*+*3836*] depended on the king's country for
13: 49　The word of the Lord spread through the whole **region**.
16: 6　and his companions traveled throughout the **region** of Phrygia
18: 23　and traveled from place to place throughout the **region** of Galatia
26: 20　then to those in Jerusalem and in all **Judea** [+*2677*], and to the
27: 27　about midnight the sailors sensed they were approaching **land**.
Jas　5: 4　The wages you failed to pay the workmen who mowed your **fields**

6002　Χωραζίν, *Chōrazin*　Not used in UBS/NIV

[√ *5960*]

6003　χωρέω, *chōreō*　[10]　[→ *432, 713, 1774, 2353, 4369, 5102, 5103, 5181, 5723, 6001, 6005*]

accept [3], have room for [2], come [1], goes [1], holding [1], make room for [1], room [1]

Mt　15: 17　"Don't you see that whatever enters the mouth **goes** into the
19: 11　Jesus replied, "Not everyone *can* **accept** this word, but only those to
19: 12　kingdom of heaven. The one who can **accept** this should accept it."
19: 12　kingdom of heaven. The one who can accept this *should* **accept** it."
Mk　2: 2　So many gathered that *there was* no **room** left, not even outside
Jn　2: 6　ceremonial washing, *each* **holding** from twenty to thirty gallons.
8: 37　you are ready to kill me, because you **have** no **room for** my word.
21: 25　I suppose that even the whole world would not **have room for** the
2Co　7: 2　**Make room for** us in your hearts. We have wronged no one,
2Pe　3: 9　not wanting anyone to perish, but everyone *to* **come** to repentance.

6004　χωρίζω, *chōrizō*　[13]　[√ *6006*]

separate [5], leave [2], do[s] so [1], does[s] [1], leaves [1], left [1], separated from [1], set apart [1]

Mt　19: 6　Therefore what God has joined together, *let* man not **separate**."
Mk　10: 9　Therefore what God has joined together, *let* man not **separate**."
Ac　1: 4　"*Do* not **leave** Jerusalem, but wait for the gift my Father promised,
18: 1　After this, Paul **left** Athens and went to Corinth.
18: 2　because Claudius had ordered all the Jews *to* **leave** Rome.
Ro　8: 35　Who *shall* **separate** us from the love of Christ? Shall trouble
8: 39　will be able *to* **separate** us from the love of God that is in Christ
1Co　7: 10　but the Lord): A wife *must* not **separate** from her husband.
7: 11　But if *she* **does**[s], she must remain unmarried or else be reconciled
7: 15　But if the unbeliever **leaves**, let him do so. A believing man
7: 15　But if the unbeliever leaves, *let him* **do**[s] so. A believing man
Phm　1: 15　Perhaps the reason *he was* **separated from** you for a little while
Heb　7: 26　one who is holy, blameless, pure, **set apart** from sinners, exalted

6005　χωρίον, *chōrion*　[10]　[√ *6003*]

field [3], land [2], place [2], estate [1], lands [1], plot of ground [1]

Mt　26: 36　Then Jesus went with his disciples to a **place** called Gethsemane,
Mk　14: 32　They went to a **place** called Gethsemane, and Jesus said to his
Jn　4: 5　near the **plot of ground** Jacob had given to his son Joseph.
Ac　1: 18　(With the reward he got for his wickedness, Judas bought a **field**;
1: 19　so they called that **field** in their language Akeldama, that is,
1: 19　that field in their language Akeldama, that is, **Field** of Blood.)
4: 34　from time to time those who owned **lands** or houses sold them,
5: 3　kept for yourself some of the money you received *for* the **land**?
5: 8　"Tell me, is this the price you and Ananias got *for* the **land**?"
28: 7　There was an **estate** nearby that belonged to Publius, the chief

6006　χωρίς, *chōris*　[41]　[→ *714, 1431, 6004, 6007*]

without [23], apart from [7], besides [2], independent of [2], not [2], besides everything else [+*3836*+*4211*] [1], by itself [+*1650*+*1651*+*3023*+*5536*] [1], separate from [1], together with [+*3590*] [1], without [+*4246*] [1]

Mt　13: 34　he did not say anything to them **without** *using* a parable.
14: 21　ate was about five thousand men, **besides** women and children.
15: 38　of those who ate was four thousand, **besides** women and children.
Mk　4: 34　He did not say anything to them **without** *using* a parable.
Lk　6: 49　like a man who built a house on the ground **without** a foundation.
Jn　1: 3　were made; **without** him nothing was made that has been made.
15: 5　he will bear much fruit; **apart from** me you can do nothing.
20: 7　The cloth was folded up **by itself** [+*1650*+*1651*+*3023*+*5536*],
Ro　3: 21　**apart from** law, has been made known, to which the Law
3: 28　For we maintain that a man is justified by faith **apart from**
4: 6　of the man to whom God credits righteousness **apart from** works:
7: 8　me every kind of covetous desire. For **apart from** law, sin is dead.
7: 9　Once I was alive **apart from** law; but when the commandment
10: 14　And how can they hear **without** someone preaching to them?
1Co　4: 8　have become rich! You have become kings—and that **without** us!
11: 11　In the Lord, however, woman is not **independent of** man,
11: 11　is not independent of man, nor is man **independent of** woman.
2Co　11: 28　**Besides** [+*3836*+*4211*] everything else, I face daily the pressure of
12: 3　whether in the body or **apart from** the body I do not know,
Eph　2: 12　remember that at that time you were **separate from** Christ,

Php 2:14 Do everything **without** complaining or arguing,
1Ti 2: 8 to lift up holy hands in prayer, **without** anger or disputing.
    5:21 and the elect angels, to keep these instructions **without** partiality,
Phm 1:14 But I did not want to do anything **without** your consent, so that
Heb 4:15 been tempted in every way, just as we are—yet was **without** sin.
    7: 7 And **without** [+4246] doubt the lesser person is blessed by the
    7:20 And it was not **without** an oath! Others became priests without any
    7:20 was not without an oath! Others became priests **without** any oath,
    9: 7 and that only once a year, and never **without** blood, which he
    9:18 This is why even the first covenant was not put into effect **without**
    9:22 and **without** the shedding of blood there is no forgiveness.
    9:28 and he will appear a second time, **not** to bear sin, but to bring
    10:28 Anyone who rejected the law of Moses died **without** mercy on the
    11: 6 And **without** faith it is impossible to please God, because anyone
    11:40 so that *only* **together** [+3590] **with** us would they be made perfect.
    12: 8 If you are **not** disciplined (and everyone undergoes discipline),
    12:14 and to be holy; **without** holiness no one will see the Lord.
Jas 2:18 "You have faith; I have deeds." Show me your faith **without** deeds,
    2:20 do you want evidence that faith **without** deeds is useless?
    2:26 As the body **without** the spirit is dead, so faith without deeds is
    2:26 the body without the spirit is dead, so faith **without** deeds is dead.

6007 χωρισμός, *chōrismos* Not used in UBS/NIV
[√ 6006]

6008 χῶρος, *chōros* [1]

northwest [1]

Ac 27:12 This was a harbor in Crete, facing both southwest and **northwest**.

Ψ, Ps

6009 ψ, *ps* Not used in UBS/NIV

6010 ψάλλω, *psallō* [5] [→ *6011*]

sing [2], make music [1], sing hymns [1], sing songs of praise [1]

Ro 15: 9 praise you among the Gentiles; *I will* **sing hymns** to your name."
1Co 14:15 *I will* **sing** with my spirit, but I will also sing with my mind.
    14:15 I will **sing** with my spirit, but *I will* also **sing** with my mind.
Eph 5:19 spiritual songs. Sing and **make music** in your heart to the Lord,
Jas 5:13 He should pray. Is anyone happy? *Let him* **sing songs of praise**.

6011 ψαλμός, *psalmos* [7] [√ *6010*]

psalms [5], hymn [1], Psalm [1]

Lk 20:42 David himself declares in the Book *of* **Psalms**: " 'The Lord said to
    24:44 about me in the Law of Moses, the Prophets and the **Psalms**."
Ac 1:20 "For," said Peter, "it is written in the book *of* **Psalms**, " 'May his
    13:33 As it is written in the second **Psalm**: " 'You are my Son; today I
1Co 14:26 everyone has a **hymn**, or a word of instruction, a revelation,
Eph 5:19 Speak to one another with **psalms**, hymns and spiritual songs.
Col 3:16 and as you sing **psalms**, hymns and spiritual songs with gratitude

6012 ψευδάδελφος, *pseudadelphos* [2] [√ *6017* + *81* [1.3]]

false brothers [2]

2Co 11:26 in the country, in danger at sea; and in danger from **false brothers**.
Gal 2: 4 because some **false brothers** had infiltrated our ranks to spy on the

6013 ψευδαπόστολος, *pseudapostolos* [1]
[√ *6017* + *690*]

false apostles [1]

2Co 11:13 For such men are **false apostles**, deceitful workmen,

6014 ψευδής, *pseudēs* [3] [√ *6017*]

false [2], liars [1]

Ac 6:13 They produced **false** witnesses, who testified, "This fellow never
Rev 2: 2 who claim to be apostles but are not, and have found them **false**.
    21: 8 those who practice magic arts, the idolaters and all **liars**—

6015 ψευδοδιδάσκαλος, *pseudodidaskalos* [1]
[√ *6017* + *1438*]

false teachers [1]

2Pe 2: 1 among the people, just as there will be **false teachers** among you.

6016 ψευδολόγος, *pseudologos* [1] [√ *6017* + *3306*]

liars [1]

1Ti 4: 2 Such teachings come through hypocritical **liars**,

6017 ψεύδομαι, *pseudomai* [12] [→ *950, 6012, 6013,*
6014, 6015, 6016, 6018, 6019, 6020, 6021, 6022, 6023, 6024,
6025, 6026]

lie [4], lying [3], deny [+2848] [1], falsely [1], liars [1], lied to [1],
lied [1]

Mt 5:11 persecute you and **falsely** say all kinds of evil against you
Ac 5: 3 Satan has so filled your heart *that* you *have* **lied to** the Holy Spirit
    5: 4 think of doing such a thing? *You have* not **lied** to men but to God."
Ro 9: 1 *I am* not **lying**, my conscience confirms it in the Holy Spirit—
2Co 11:31 who is to be praised forever, knows that *I am* not **lying**.
Gal 1:20 I assure you before God that what I am writing you *is* no **lie**.
Col 3: 9 *Do* not **lie** to each other, since you have taken off your old self
1Ti 2: 7 a herald and an apostle—I am telling the truth, *I am* not **lying**—
Heb 6:18 two unchangeable things in which it is impossible for God *to* **lie**,
Jas 3:14 in your hearts, do not boast about it or **deny** [+2848] the truth.
1Jn 1: 6 him yet walk in the darkness, *we* **lie** and do not live by the truth.
Rev 3: 9 of Satan, who claim to be Jews though *they* are not, but *are* **liars**—

6018 ψευδομαρτυρέω, *pseudomartyreō* [5]
[√ *6017* + *3459*]

give false testimony [3], gave false testimony [1], testified falsely
[1]

Mt 19:18 do not commit adultery, do not steal, *do* not **give false testimony**,
Mk 10:19 do not steal, *do* not **give false testimony**, do not defraud,
    14:56 Many **testified falsely** against him, but their statements did not
    14:57 Then some stood up and **gave** this **false testimony** against him:
Lk 18:20 do not murder, do not steal, *do* not **give false testimony**,

6019 ψευδομαρτυρία, *pseudomartyria* [2]
[√ *6017* + *3459*]

false evidence [1], false testimony [1]

Mt 15:19 adultery, sexual immorality, theft, **false testimony**, slander.
    26:59 and the whole Sanhedrin were looking for **false evidence** against

6020 ψευδόμαρτυς, *pseudomartys* [2]
[√ *6017* + *3459*]

false witnesses [2]

Mt 26:60 they did not find any, though many **false witnesses** came forward.
1Co 15:15 More than that, we are then found to be **false witnesses** about God,

6021 ψευδοπροφήτης, *pseudoprophētēs* [11]
[√ *6017* + *4735*]

false prophets [7], false prophet [4]

Mt 7:15 "Watch out for **false prophets**. They come to you in sheep's
    24:11 and many **false prophets** will appear and deceive many people.
    24:24 For false Christs and **false prophets** will appear and perform great
Mk 13:22 For false Christs and **false prophets** will appear and perform signs
Lk 6:26 well of you, for that is how their fathers treated the **false prophets**.

Ac 13: 6 they met a Jewish sorcerer and **false prophet** named Bar-Jesus,
2Pe 2: 1 But there were also **false prophets** among the people, just as there
1Jn 4: 1 because many **false prophets** have gone out into the world.
Rev 16: 13 the mouth of the beast and out of the mouth *of* the **false prophet**.
    19: 20 and with him the **false prophet** who had performed the miraculous
    20: 10 where the beast and the **false prophet** had been thrown.

6022 ψεῦδος, *pseudos* [10] [√ *6017*]

lie [4], counterfeit [2], falsehood [2], lies [+*3281*+*3836*] [1], what
is deceitful [1]

Jn 8: 44 When *he* **lies** [+*3281*+*3836*], he speaks his native language,
Ro 1: 25 They exchanged the truth of God for a **lie**, and worshiped
Eph 4: 25 Therefore each of you must put off **falsehood** and speak truthfully
2Th 2: 9 the work of Satan displayed in all kinds of **counterfeit** miracles,
    2: 11 sends them a powerful delusion so that they will believe the **lie**
1Jn 2: 21 because you do know it and because no **lie** comes from the truth.
    2: 27 you about all things and as that anointing is real, not **counterfeit**—
Rev 14: 5 No **lie** was found in their mouths; they are blameless.
    21: 27 enter it, nor will anyone who does **what is** shameful or **deceitful**,
    22: 15 the idolaters and everyone who loves and practices **falsehood**.

6023 ψευδόχριστος, *pseudochristos* [2] [√ *6017* + *5986*]

false Christs [2]

Mt 24: 24 For **false Christs** and false prophets will appear and perform great
Mk 13: 22 For **false Christs** and false prophets will appear and perform signs

6024 ψευδώνυμος, *pseudōnymos* [1] [√ *6017* + *3950*]

falsely called [1]

1Ti 6: 20 and the opposing ideas *of* what is **falsely called** knowledge,

6025 ψεῦσμα, *pseusma* [1] [√ *6017*]

falsehood [1]

Ro 3: 7 "If my **falsehood** enhances God's truthfulness and so increases his

6026 ψεύστης, *pseustēs* [10] [√ *6017*]

liar [8], liars [2]

Jn 8: 44 he speaks his native language, for he is a **liar** and the father of lies.
    8: 55 If I said I did not, I would be a **liar** like you, but I do know him
Ro 3: 4 Not at all! Let God be true, and every man a **liar**. As it is written:
1Ti 1: 10 and perverts, *for* slave traders and **liars** and perjurers—
Tit 1: 12 has said, "Cretans are always **liars**, evil brutes, lazy gluttons."
1Jn 1: 10 we make him out to be a **liar** and his word has no place in our
    2: 4 says, "I know him," but does not do what he commands is a **liar**,
    2: 22 Who is the **liar**? It is the man who denies that Jesus is the Christ.
    4: 20 If anyone says, "I love God," yet hates his brother, he is a **liar**.
    5: 10 Anyone who does not believe God has made him out to be a **liar**,

6027 ψηλαφάω, *psēlaphaō* [4] [√ *6041*]

touched [2], reach out for [1], touch [1]

Lk 24: 39 **Touch** me and see; a ghost does not have flesh and bones,
Ac 17: 27 men would seek him and perhaps **reach out for** him and find him,
Heb 12: 18 You have not come to a mountain that *can be* **touched** and that is
1Jn 1: 1 our eyes, which we have looked at and our hands *have* **touched**—

6028 ψηφίζω, *psēphizō* [2] [√ *6029*]

calculate [1], estimate [1]

Lk 14: 28 *Will he* not first sit down and **estimate** the cost to see if he has
Rev 13: 18 If anyone has insight, *let him* **calculate** the number of the beast,

6029 ψῆφος, *psēphos* [3] [→ *2975, 5164, 5248, 6028*; cf. *6041*]

it^s [+*3836*] [1], stone [1], vote [1]

Ac 26: 10 and when they were put to death, I cast my **vote** against them.
Rev 2: 17 I will also give him a white **stone** with a new name written on it,
    2: 17 give him a white stone with a new name written on it^s [+*3836*],

6030 ψιθυρισμός, *psithyrismos* [1] [→ *6031*]

gossip [1]

2Co 12: 20 of anger, factions, slander, **gossip**, arrogance and disorder.

6031 ψιθυριστής, *psithyristēs* [1] [√ *6030*]

gossips [1]

Ro 1: 29 full of envy, murder, strife, deceit and malice. They are **gossips**,

6032 ψίξ, *psix* Not used in UBS/NIV [→ *6033*]

6033 ψιχίον, *psichion* [2] [√ *6032*]

crumbs [2]

Mt 15: 27 even the dogs eat the **crumbs** that fall from their masters' table."
Mk 7: 28 "but even the dogs under the table eat the children's **crumbs**."

6034 ψυχή, *psychē* [103 / 102] [√ *6038*]

ἀπολλύειν ψυχή, (destroy the soul) [13] Mt 10:28,39,39;
    16:25,25; Mk 8:35,35; Lk 6:9; 9:24,24; 17:33,33; Jn 12:25
καρδία ... ψυχή ... διάνοια, (heart ... soul ... mind) [3] Mt
    22:37; Mk 12:30; Lk 10:27
σῶμα ... ψυχή, (body ... soul) [8] Mt 6:25,25; 10:28,28; Lk
    12:22,23; 1Th 5:23; Rev 18:13
τίθημι τὴν ψυχήν, (lay down the soul/life) [8] Jn
    10:11,15,17; 13:37,38; 15:13; 1Jn 3:16,16
ψυχή ... πνεῦμα, (soul ... spirit) [6] Mt 12:18; Lk 1:47; 1Co
    15:45; Php 1:27; 1Th 5:23; Heb 4:12

life [32], soul [19], souls [6], lives [5], heart [4], everyone [+*4246*]
[2], minds [2], you [+*3836*+*5148*] [2], *untranslated* [1], all [1],
anyone [+*4246*] [1], being [1], disciples [+*3412*] [1], he's
[+*899*+*1639*+*3836*] [1], him [+*899*] [1], human being [+*476*] [1], I
[+*1609*+*3836*] [1], I [+*1609*] [1], keep in suspense [+*149*+*3836*]
[1], living [+*2400*+*3836*] [1], longed for [+*2123*+*3836*] [1], man
[1], me [+*1609*+*3836*] [1], me [+*1609*] [1], mind [1], my [+*1847*]
[1], myself [+*1609*] [1], not one [+*4029*] [1], people [1], saved
[+*1650*+*4348*] [1], themselves [+*899*+*3836*] [1], thing [1], trying
to kill [+*2426*+*3836*] [1], unstable [+*844*] [1], us^s [1], you [+*5148*]
[1], you^s [1], yourselves [+*5148*] [1]

Mt 2: 20 for those who were trying to take the child's **life** are dead."
    6: 25 I tell you, do not worry about your **life**, what you will eat or drink;
    6: 25 Is not **life** more important than food, and the body more important
    10: 28 Do not be afraid of those who kill the body but cannot kill the **soul**.
    10: 28 be afraid of the One who can destroy both **soul** and body in hell.
    10: 39 Whoever finds his **life** will lose it, and whoever loses his life for
    10: 39 life will lose it, and whoever loses his **life** for my sake will find it.
    11: 29 and humble in heart, and you will find rest *for* your **souls**.
    12: 18 whom I have chosen, the one I love, in whom **I** [+*1609*] delight;
    16: 25 For whoever wants to save his **life** will lose it, but whoever loses
    16: 25 his life will lose it, but whoever loses his **life** for me will find it.
    16: 26 it be for a man if he gains the whole world, yet forfeits his **soul**?
    16: 26 forfeits his soul? Or what can a man give in exchange for his **soul**?
    20: 28 be served, but to serve, and to give his **life** as a ransom for many."
    22: 37 with all your heart and with all your **soul** and with all your mind.'
    26: 38 "My **soul** is overwhelmed with sorrow to the point of death.
Mk 3: 4 to do good or to do evil, to save **life** or to kill?" But they remained
    8: 35 For whoever wants to save his **life** will lose it, but whoever loses
    8: 35 but whoever loses his **life** for me and for the gospel will save it.
    8: 36 good is it for a man to gain the whole world, yet forfeit his **soul**?
    8: 37 Or what can a man give in exchange for his **soul**?
    10: 45 be served, but to serve, and to give his **life** as a ransom for many."

	12:30	and with all your **soul** and with all your mind and with all your
	14:34	"My **soul** is overwhelmed with sorrow to the point of death,"
Lk	1:46	And Mary said: "My **soul** glorifies the Lord
	2:35	will be revealed. And a sword will pierce your own **soul** too."
	6: 9	the Sabbath: to do good or to do evil, to save **life** or to destroy it?"
	9:24	For whoever wants to save his **life** will lose it, but whoever loses
	9:24	his life will lose it, but whoever loses his **life** for me will save it.
	10:27	and with all your **soul** and with all your strength and with all your
	12:19	And I'll say *to* **myself** [+1609], "You have plenty of good things
	12:19	"You^s have plenty of good things laid up for many years.
	12:20	'You fool! This very night your **life** will be demanded from you.
	12:22	I tell you, do not worry about your **life**, what you will eat;
	12:23	**Life** is more than food, and the body more than clothes.
	14:26	and children, his brothers and sisters—yes, even his own **life**—
	17:33	Whoever tries to keep his **life** will lose it, and whoever loses his
	21:19	By standing firm you will gain **life**.
Jn	10:11	good shepherd. The good shepherd lays down his **life** for the sheep.
	10:15	and I know the Father—and I lay down my **life** for the sheep.
	10:17	The reason my Father loves me is that I lay down my **life**—
	10:24	saying, "How long *will you* **keep** us **in suspense** [+149+3836]?
	12:25	The man who loves his **life** will lose it, while the man who hates
	12:25	while the man who hates his **life** in this world will keep it for
	12:27	"Now my **heart** is troubled, and what shall I say? 'Father, save me
	13:37	why can't I follow you now? I will lay down my **life** for you."
	13:38	Then Jesus answered, "Will you really lay down your **life** for me?
	15:13	love has no one than this, that he lay down his **life** for his friends.
Ac	2:27	because you will not abandon **me** [+1609+3836] to the grave,
	2:41	and about three thousand **[NIE]** were added to their number that
	2:43	**Everyone** [+4246] was filled with awe, and many wonders
	3:23	**Anyone** [+4246] who does not listen to him will be completely cut
	4:32	All the believers were one *in* heart and **mind**. No one claimed that
	7:14	sent for his father Jacob and his whole family, seventy-five in **all**.
	14: 2	up the Gentiles and poisoned their **minds** against the brothers.
	14:22	strengthening the **disciples** [+3412] and encouraging them to
	15:24	and disturbed you, troubling your **minds** by what they said.
	15:26	men who have risked their **lives** for the name of our Lord Jesus
	20:10	"Don't be alarmed," he said. "**He's** [+899+1639+3836] alive!"
	20:24	However, I consider my **life** worth nothing to me, if only I may
	27:10	and bring great loss to ship and cargo, and to our own **lives** also."
	27:22	keep up your courage, because **not one** [+4029] of you will be lost;
	27:37	Altogether there were 276 of **us**^s on board.
Ro	2: 9	and distress for every **human being** [+476] who does evil:
	11: 3	the only one left, and *they are* **trying to kill** [+2426+3836] me"?
	13: 1	**Everyone** [+4246] must submit himself to the governing
	16: 4	They risked their lives for **me** [+1609]. Not only I but all the
1Co	15:45	"The first man Adam became a living **being**"; the last Adam,
2Co	1:23	I call God as **my** [+1847] witness that it was in order to spare you
	12:15	So I will very gladly spend for **you** [+5148] everything I have and
Eph	6: 6	but like slaves of Christ, doing the will of God from your **heart**.
Php	1:27	in one spirit, contending as one **man** for the faith of the gospel
	2:30	risking his **life** to make up for the help you could not give me.
Col	3:23	Whatever you do, work at it with *all* your **heart**, as working for the
1Th	2: 8	to share with you not only the gospel of God but our **lives** as well
	5:23	**soul** and body be kept blameless at the coming of our Lord Jesus
Heb	4:12	it penetrates even to dividing **soul** and spirit, joints and marrow;
	6:19	We have this hope as an anchor *for* the **soul**, firm and secure.
	10:38	And if he shrinks back, I [+1609+3836] will not be pleased with
	10:39	but of those who believe and are **saved** [+1650+4348].
	12: 3	from sinful men, so that you will not grow weary and lose **heart**.
	13:17	They keep watch over **you** [+3836+5148] as men who must give
Jas	1:21	accept the word planted in you, which can save **you** [+3836+5148].
	5:20	a sinner from the error of his way will save **him** [+899] from death
1Pe	1: 9	you are receiving the goal of your faith, the salvation *of* your **souls**.
	1:22	Now that you have purified **yourselves** [+5148] by obeying
	2:11	to abstain from sinful desires, which war against your **soul**.
	2:25	you have returned to the Shepherd and Overseer *of* your **souls**.
	3:20	In it only a few **people**, eight in all, were saved through water,
	4:19	should commit **themselves** [+899+3836] to their faithful Creator
2Pe	2: 8	was tormented in his righteous **soul** by the lawless deeds he saw
	2:14	they never stop sinning; they seduce the **unstable** [+844];
1Jn	3:16	is how we know what love is: Jesus Christ laid down his **life** for us.
	3:16	his life for us. And we ought to lay down our **lives** for our brothers.
3Jn	1: 2	all may go well with you, even as your **soul** is getting along well.
Jude	1:15	convict all the ungodly [UBS+ *every* **person**] of all the ungodly acts
Rev	6: 9	I saw under the altar the **souls** of those who had been slain
	8: 9	a third of the **living** [+2400+3836] creatures in the sea died,

	12:11	they did not love their **lives** so much as to shrink from death.
	16: 3	like that of a dead man, and every living **thing** in the sea died.
	18:13	and sheep; horses and carriages; and bodies and **souls** of men.
	18:14	'The fruit you **longed for** [+2123+3836] is gone from you.
	20: 4	And I saw the **souls** of those who had been beheaded because of

6035 ψυχικός, *psychikos* [6] [√ 6038]

natural [3], follow mere natural instincts [1], unspiritual [1], without the Spirit [1]

1Co	2:14	The man **without the Spirit** does not accept the things that come
	15:44	it is sown a **natural** body, it is raised a spiritual body. If there is a
	15:44	If there is a **natural** body, there is also a spiritual body.
	15:46	did not come first, but the **natural**, and after that the spiritual.
Jas	3:15	come down from heaven but is earthly, **unspiritual**, of the devil.
Jude	1:19	who **follow mere natural instincts** and do not have the Spirit.

6036 ψῦχος, *psychos* [3] [√ 6038]

cold [3]

Jn	18:18	It was **cold**, and the servants and officials stood around a fire they
Ac	28: 2	built a fire and welcomed us all because it was raining and **cold**.
2Co	11:27	and have often gone without food; I have been **cold** and naked.

6037 ψυχρός, *psychros* [4] [√ 6038]

cold [3], one^s [1]

Mt	10:42	And if anyone gives even a cup *of* **cold** water to one of these little
Rev	3:15	I know your deeds, that you are neither **cold** nor hot. I wish you
	3:15	are neither cold nor hot. I wish you were either **one**^s or the other!
	3:16	So, because you are lukewarm—neither hot nor **cold**—I am about

6038 ψύχω, *psychō* [1] [→ 433, 434, 715, 953, 1500, 1775, 2379, 2701, 2976, 3901, 5249, 6034, 6035, 6036, 6037]

cold [1]

Mt	24:12	of the increase of wickedness, the love of most *will grow* **cold**,

6039 ψωμίζω, *psōmizō* [2] [√ 6040]

feed [1], give to the poor [1]

Ro	12:20	"If your enemy is hungry, **feed** him; if he is thirsty, give him
1Co	13: 3	If *I* **give** all I possess **to the poor** and surrender my body to the

6040 ψωμίον, *psōmion* [4] [→ 6039; cf. 6041]

bread [2], piece of bread [2]

Jn	13:26	"It is the one to whom I will give this **piece of bread** when I have
	13:26	Then, dipping the **piece of bread**, he gave it to Judas Iscariot,
	13:27	As soon as Judas took the **bread**, Satan entered into him. "What
	13:30	As soon as Judas had taken the **bread**, he went out. And it was

6041 ψώχω, *psōchō* [1] [→ 2223, 4370, 4718, 6027; cf. 6029, 6040]

rub [1]

Lk	6: 1	some heads of grain, **rub** them in their hands and eat the kernels.

Ω, W

6042 ῏Ω¹, Ō¹ [3]

Omega [3]

Rev	1: 8	"I am the Alpha and the **Omega**," says the Lord God, "who is,
	21: 6	I am the Alpha and the **Omega**, the Beginning and the End.
	22:13	I am the Alpha and the **Omega**, the First and the Last,

6043 ὦ², ὄ² [17]

untranslated [6], you [6], O [4], Oh [1]

Mt 15:28 Then Jesus answered, **[NIE]** "Woman, you have great faith!
　17:17 "**O** unbelieving and perverse generation," Jesus replied, "how long
Mk 9:19 "**O** unbelieving generation," Jesus replied, "how long shall I stay
Lk 9:41 "**O** unbelieving and perverse generation," Jesus replied, "how long
　24:25 He said to them, "How foolish **you** are, and how slow of heart to
Ac 1: 1 In my former book, **[NIE]** Theophilus, I wrote about all that Jesus
　13:10 "**You** are a child of the devil and an enemy of everything that is
　18:14 "If **you** Jews were making a complaint about some misdemeanor
　27:21 **[NIE]** "Men, you should have taken my advice not to sail from
Ro 2: 1 **[NIE]** You, therefore, have no excuse, you who pass judgment on
　2: 3 So when **you**, a mere man, pass judgment on them and yet do the
　9:20 But who are you, **O** man, to talk back to God? "Shall what is
　11:33 **Oh**, the depth of the riches of the wisdom and knowledge of God!
Gal 3: 1 **You** foolish Galatians! Who has bewitched you? Before your very
1Ti 6:11 But you, **[NIE]** man of God, flee from all this, and pursue
　6:20 **[NIE]** Timothy, guard what has been entrusted to your care.
Jas 2:20 **You** foolish man, do you want evidence that faith without deeds is

6044 Ὠβήδ, Ōbēd　Not used in UBS/NIV [√ 2725]

6045 ὧδε, hōde [61] [√ 3836]

here [48], this [4], *untranslated* [2], here [+2627] [2], here's [1], in
the one case [+3525] [1], now [+3370] [1], there [1], this calls for
[1]

Mt 8:29 "Have you come **here** to torture us before the appointed time?"
　12: 6 I tell you that one greater than the temple is **here**.
　12:41 at the preaching of Jonah, and now one greater than Jonah is **here**.
　12:42 to Solomon's wisdom, and now one greater than Solomon is **here**.
　14: 8 she said, "Give me **here** on a platter the head of John the Baptist."
　14:17 "We have **here** only five loaves of bread and two fish," they
　14:18 "Bring them **here** to me," he said.
　16:28 some who are standing **here** will not taste death before they see the
　17: 4 Peter said to Jesus, "Lord, it is good for us to be **here**. If you wish,
　17: 4 one **[RPG]** for you, one for Moses and one for Elijah."
　17:17 How long shall I put up with you? Bring the boy **here** to me."
　20: 6 'Why have you been standing **here** all day long doing nothing?'
　22:12 he asked, 'how did you get in **here** without wedding clothes?'
　24: 2 "I tell you the truth, not one stone **here** will be left on another;
　24:23 At that time if anyone says to you, 'Look, **here** is the Christ!'
　24:23 'Look, here is the Christ!' or, '**There** he is!' do not believe it.
　26:38 sorrow to the point of death. Stay **here** and keep watch with me."
　28: 6 He is not **here**; he has risen, just as he said. Come and see the place
Mk 6: 3 Joseph, Judas and Simon? Aren't his sisters **here** with us?"
　8: 4 "But where in **this** remote place can anyone get enough bread to
　9: 1 some who are standing **here** will not taste death before they see the
　9: 5 Peter said to Jesus, "Rabbi, it is good for us to be **here**. Let us put
　11: 3 tell him, 'The Lord needs it and will send it back **here** shortly.' "
　13: 2 "Not one stone **here** will be left on another; every one will be
　13:21 At that time if anyone says to you, 'Look, **here** is the Christ!'
　14:32 Jesus said to his disciples, "Sit **here** while I pray."
　14:34 to the point of death," he said to them. "Stay **here** and keep watch."
　16: 6 the Nazarene, who was crucified. He has risen! He is not **here**.
Lk 4:23 Do **here** in your hometown what we have heard that you did in
　9:12 and find food and lodging, because we are in a remote place **here**."
　9:33 Peter said to him, "Master, it is good for us to be **here**.
　9:41 shall I stay with you and put up with you? Bring your son **here**."
　11:31 to Solomon's wisdom, and now one greater than Solomon is **here**.
　11:32 at the preaching of Jonah, and now one greater than Jonah is **here**.
　14:21 into the streets and alleys of the town and bring in **[NIE]** the poor,
　15:17 hired men have food to spare, and **here** I am starving to death!
　16:25 bad things, but now he is comforted **here** and you are in agony.
　17:21 nor will people say, '**Here** [+2627] it is,' or 'There it is,'
　17:23 Men will tell you, 'There he is!' or '**Here** [+2627] he is!' Do not
　19:27 be king over them—bring them **here** and kill them in front of me.' "
　22:38 The disciples said, "See, Lord, **here** are two swords."
　23: 5 his teaching. He started in Galilee and has come all the way **here**."
　24: 6 He is not **here**; he has risen! Remember how he told you, while he
Jn 6: 9 "**Here** is a boy with five small barley loaves and two small fish,
　6:25 side of the lake, they asked him, "Rabbi, when did you get **here**?"
　11:21 "Lord," Martha said to Jesus, "if you had been **here**, my brother

　11:32 saw him, she fell at his feet and said, "Lord, if you had been **here**,
　20:27 Then he said to Thomas, "Put your finger **here**; see my hands.
Ac 9:14 And he has come **here** with authority from the chief priests to
　9:21 And hasn't he come **here** to take them as prisoners to the chief
1Co 4: 2 **Now** [+3370] it is required that those who have been given a trust
Col 4: 9 is one of you. They will tell you everything that is happening **here**.
Heb 7: 8 **In the one case** [+3525], the tenth is collected by men who die;
　13:14 For **here** we do not have an enduring city, but we are looking for
Jas 2: 3 the man wearing fine clothes and say, "**Here's** a good seat for you,"
Rev 4: 1 "Come up **here**, and I will show you what must take place after
　11:12 heard a loud voice from heaven saying to them, "Come up **here**."
　13:10 **This** calls for patient endurance and faithfulness on the part of the
　13:18 **This** calls for wisdom. If anyone has insight, let him calculate the
　14:12 **This** calls for patient endurance on the part of the saints who obey
　17: 9 "**This calls for** a mind with wisdom. The seven heads are seven

6046 ᾠδή, ōdē [7] [→ 106, 3069]

song [5], songs [2]

Eph 5:19 Speak to one another with psalms, hymns and spiritual **songs**.
Col 3:16 hymns and spiritual **songs** with gratitude in your hearts to God.
Rev 5: 9 And they sang a new **song**: "You are worthy to take the scroll
　14: 3 And they sang a new **song** before the throne and before the four
　14: 3 No one could learn the **song** except the 144,000 who had been
　15: 3 and sang the **song** of Moses the servant of God and the song of the
　15: 3 the song of Moses the servant of God and the **song** of the Lamb:

6047 ὠδίν, ōdin [4] [→ 5349, 6048]

birth pains [2], agony [1], labor pains [1]

Mt 24: 8 All these are the beginning *of* **birth pains**.
Mk 13: 8 and famines. These are the beginning *of* **birth pains**.
Ac 2:24 raised him from the dead, freeing him from the **agony** of death,
1Th 5: 3 as **labor pains** on a pregnant woman, and they will not escape.

6048 ὠδίνω, ōdinō [3] [√ 6047]

give birth [+5503] [1], have labor pains [1], in the pains of
childbirth [1]

Gal 4:19 for whom *I am* again **in the pains of childbirth** until Christ is
　4:27 break forth and cry aloud, you *who* **have** no **labor pains**;
Rev 12: 2 and cried out in pain *as she was about to* **give birth** [+5503].

6049 ὦμος, ōmos [2]

shoulders [2]

Mt 23: 4 They tie up heavy loads and put them on men's **shoulders**,
Lk 15: 5 And when he finds it, he joyfully puts it on his **shoulders**

6050 ὠνέομαι, ōneomai [1] [→ 4072; cf. 5467]

bought [1]

Ac 7:16 and placed in the tomb that Abraham *had* **bought** from the sons of

6051 ᾠόν, ōon [1]

egg [1]

Lk 11:12 Or if he asks for an **egg**, will give him a scorpion?

6052 ὥρα, hōra [106] [→ 2469, 2470, 6053]

ἐκεῖνος ὥρα, (that hour) [13] Mt 8:13; 9:22; 10:19; 15:28; 17:18;
18:1; 26:55; Mk 13:11; Lk 7:21; Jn 4:53; 19:27; Ac 16:33; Rev
11:13

ἔσχατος ὥρα, (last hour) [2] 1Jn 2:18,18

ὥρα ἔρχεται, (the hour is coming) [16] Mt 20:9; Mk 14:41; Jn
4:21,23; 5:25,28; 7:30; 8:20; 12:23; 13:1; 16:2,4,21,25,32; 17:1

hour [52], time [31], moment [6], hours [3], late [2], at hour
[+1181] [1], at once [+899+3836] [1], for a little while [+4639] [1],
immediately [+899+1877+3836] [1], its [+3836] [1], late in the
day [+4498] [1], little while [1], nine [+5569] [1], nine in the

morning [+2465+3836+5569] [1], noon [+1761] [1], short [1],
three in the afternoon [+1888+2465+3836] [1]

Mt   8:13   believed it would." And his servant was healed at that very **hour**.
     9:22   has healed you." And the woman was healed from that **moment**.
   10:19   or how to say it. At that **time** you will be given what to say,
   14:15   and said, "This is a remote place, and it's already getting **late**.
   15:28   is granted." And her daughter was healed from that very **hour**.
   17:18   and it came out of the boy, and he was healed from that **moment**.
   18: 1   At that **time** the disciples came to Jesus and asked, "Who is the
   20: 3   "About the third **hour** he went out and saw others standing in the
   20: 5   about the sixth **hour** and the ninth **hour** and did the same thing.
   20: 9   "The workers who were hired about the eleventh **hour** came
   20:12   'These men who were hired last worked only one **hour**,' they said,
   24:36   "No one knows about that day or **hour**, not even the angels in
   24:44   because the Son of Man will come *at* an **hour** when you do not
   24:50   when he does not expect him and at an **hour** he is not aware of.
   25:13   keep watch, because you do not know the day or the **hour**.
   26:40   "Could you men not keep watch with me *for* one **hour**?" he asked
   26:45   Look, the **hour** is near, and the Son of Man is betrayed into the
   26:55   At that **time** Jesus said to the crowd, "Am I leading a rebellion,
   27:45   From the sixth **hour** until the ninth hour darkness came over all the
   27:45   From the sixth hour until the ninth **hour** darkness came over all the
   27:46   About the ninth **hour** Jesus cried out in a loud voice, "*Eloi*,
Mk   6:35   By this time it was **late** [+4498] **in the day**, so his disciples came
   6:35   "This is a remote place," they said, "and it's already very **late**.
   11:11   around at everything, but since it^s [+3836] was already late,
   13:11   Just say whatever is given you at the **time**, for it is not you
   13:32   "No one knows about that day or **hour**, not even the angels in
   14:35   and prayed that if possible the **hour** might pass from him.
   14:37   to Peter, "are you asleep? Could you not keep watch *for* one **hour**?
   14:41   The **hour** has come. Look, the Son of Man is betrayed into the
   15:25   It was the third **hour** when they crucified him.
   15:33   **At** the sixth **hour** [+1181] darkness came over the whole land until
   15:33   sixth hour darkness came over the whole land until the ninth **hour**.
   15:34   And *at* the ninth **hour** Jesus cried out in a loud voice, "*Eloi*,
Lk   1:10   And *when* the **time** for the burning of incense *came*,
   2:38   Coming up to them *at* that very **moment**, she gave thanks to God
   7:21   At that very **time** Jesus cured many who had diseases, sicknesses
   10:21   At that **time** Jesus, full of joy through the Holy Spirit, said,
   12:12   for the Holy Spirit will teach you at that **time** what you should say."
   12:39   If the owner of the house had known *at* what **hour** the thief was
   12:40   because the Son of Man will come *at* an **hour** when you do not
   12:46   when he does not expect him and at an **hour** he is not aware of.
   13:31   At that **time** some Pharisees came to Jesus and said to him,
   14:17   *At* the **time** of the banquet he sent his servant to tell those who had
   20:19   looked for a way to arrest him **immediately** [+899+1877+3836],
   22:14   When the **hour** came, Jesus and his apostles reclined at the table.
   22:53   lay a hand on me. But this is your **hour**—when darkness reigns."
   22:59   About an **hour** later another asserted, "Certainly this fellow was
   23:44   It was now about the sixth **hour**, and darkness came over the
   23:44   and darkness came over the whole land until the ninth **hour**,
   24:33   They got up and returned **at once** [+899+3836] to Jerusalem.
Jn   1:39   and spent that day with him. It was about the tenth **hour**.
   2: 4   do you involve me?" Jesus replied. "My **time** has not yet come."
   4: 6   the journey, sat down by the well. It was about the sixth **hour**.
   4:21   a **time** is coming when you will worship the Father neither on this
   4:23   Yet a **time** is coming and has now come when the true worshipers
   4:52   When he inquired as to the **time** when his son got better, they said
   4:52   said to him, "The fever left him yesterday at the seventh **hour**."
   4:53   Then the father realized that this was the *exact* **time** at which Jesus
   5:25   a **time** is coming and has now come when the dead will hear the
   5:28   for a **time** is coming when all who are in their graves will hear his
   5:35   and gave light, and you chose for a **time** to enjoy his light.
   7:30   but no one laid a hand on him, because his **time** had not yet come.
   8:20   Yet no one seized him, because his **time** had not yet come.
   11: 9   Jesus answered, "Are there not twelve **hours** of daylight? A man
   12:23   "The **hour** has come for the Son of Man to be glorified.
   12:27   'Father, save me from this **hour**'? No, it was for this very reason I
   12:27   this **hour**'? No, it was for this very reason I came to this **hour**.
   13: 1   Jesus knew that the **time** had come for him to leave this world
   16: 2   a **time** is coming when anyone who kills you will think he is
   16: 4   so that when the **time** comes you will remember that I warned you.
   16:21   woman giving birth to a child has pain because her **time** has come;
   16:25   a **time** is coming when I will no longer use this kind of language
   16:32   "But a **time** is coming, and has come, when you will be scattered,

   17: 1   he looked toward heaven and prayed: "Father, the **time** has come.
   19:14   the day of Preparation of Passover Week, about the sixth **hour**.
   19:27   From that **time** on, this disciple took her into his home.
Ac   2:15   It's *only* **nine in the morning** [+2465+3836+5569]!
   3: 1   and John were going up to the temple at the **time** of prayer—
   5: 7   About three **hours** later his wife came in, not knowing what had
   10: 3   One day at about **three in the afternoon** [+1888+2465+3836] he
   10: 9   About **noon** [+1761] the following day as they were on their
   10:30   "Four days ago I was in my house praying at this **hour**, at three in
   16:18   you to come out of her!" *At* that **moment** the spirit left her.
   16:33   At that **hour** of the night the jailer took them and washed their
   19:34   he was a Jew, they all shouted in unison for about two **hours**:
   22:13   your sight!' And *at* that very **moment** I was able to see him.
   23:23   and two hundred spearmen to go to Caesarea at **nine** [+5569]
Ro   13:11   The **hour** has come for you to wake up from your slumber,
1Co   4:11   To this very **hour** we go hungry and thirsty, we are in rags,
   15:30   And as for us, why do we endanger ourselves every **hour**?
2Co   7: 8   regret it—I see that my letter hurt you, but only for a **little while**—
Gal   2: 5   We did not give in to them for a **moment**, so that the truth of the
1Th   2:17   when we were torn away from you for a **short** time (in person,
Phm   1:15   **for a little while** [+4639] was that you might have him back for
1Jn   2:18   Dear children, this is the last **hour**; and as you have heard that the
   2:18   antichrists have come. This is how we know it is the last **hour**.
Rev   3: 3   like a thief, and you will not know at what **time** I will come to you.
   3:10   I will also keep you from the **hour** of trial that is going to come
   9:15   And the four angels who had been kept ready for this very **hour**
   11:13   At that very **hour** there was a severe earthquake and a tenth of the
   14: 7   and give him glory, because the **hour** of his judgment has come.
   14:15   "Take your sickle and reap, because the **time** to reap has come,
   17:12   but who *for* one **hour** will receive authority as kings along with
   18:10   O Babylon, city of power! *In* one **hour** your doom has come!'
   18:17   *In* one **hour** such great wealth has been brought to ruin!' "Every sea
   18:19   rich through her wealth! *In* one **hour** she has been brought to ruin!

6053   ὡραῖος, *hōraios* [4] [√ 6052]

beautiful [4]

Mt   23:27   which look **beautiful** on the outside but on the inside are full of
Ac   3: 2   from birth was being carried to the temple gate called **Beautiful**,
   3:10   man who used to sit begging at the temple gate called **Beautiful**,
Ro   10:15   "How **beautiful** are the feet of those who bring good news!"

6054   ὠρύομαι, *ōryomai* [1]

roaring [1]

1Pe   5: 8   Your enemy the devil prowls around like a **roaring** lion looking

6055   ὡς, *hōs* [504 / 502] [→ 2777, 2778, 6056, 6058, 6059, 6061, 6062, 6063]

as [151], like [124], *untranslated* [45], when [33], about [18], just
as [17], as if [16], how [11], as though [6], that [6], while [5], after
[4], and [3], looked like [3], of [3], so [3], to [3], as small as [2],
meaning [2], on the pretext of [2], on [2], regarded as [2],
resembled [2], sounded like [2], when [+323] [2], according to
[1], and to which [1], are [1], as soon as [+323] [1], as soon as
[1], at [1], blood red [+135] [1], considered [+2400] [1], faithfully
[+2819] [1], for that [1], for [1], if only [1], in accordance with [1],
is [1], just like [1], just [1], less than two miles [+608+1278+5084]
[1], like [+1569] [1], one might even say [+2229+3306] [1],
saying^s [1], seem [1], seemed [1], since [1], so-called [+3306]
[1], somehow or other [+323] [1], something [1], supposed [1],
that is [1], the same as [+2779] [1], the same way [+2779] [1], the
size of [1], though [1], trying to [+323] [1], unlike [+4024] [1],
what [1]

Mt   1:24   he did **what** the angel of the Lord had commanded him and took
   5:48   Be perfect, therefore, **as** your heavenly Father is perfect.
   6: 5   "And when you pray, do not be **like** the hypocrites, for they love to
   6:10   your kingdom come, your will be done on earth **as** it is in heaven.
   6:12   Forgive us our debts, **as** we also have forgiven our debtors.
   6:16   "When you fast, do not look somber **as** the hypocrites do, for they
   6:29   not even Solomon in all his splendor was dressed **like** one of these.
   7:29   because he taught **as** one who had authority, and not as their

7:29 as one who had authority, and not **as** their teachers of the law.
8:13 the centurion, "Go! It will be done **just as** you believed it would."
10:16 I am sending you out **like** sheep among wolves. Therefore be as
10:16 Therefore be **as** shrewd as snakes and as innocent as doves.
10:16 Therefore be as shrewd as snakes and as innocent **as** doves.
10:25 It is enough for the student to be **like** his teacher, and the servant
10:25 the student to be like his teacher, and the servant **like** his master.
12:13 and it was completely restored, **just as** sound as the other.
13:43 Then the righteous will shine **like** the sun in the kingdom of their
14: 5 of the people, because *they* **considered** [+*2400*] him a prophet.
15:28 "Woman, you have great faith! Your **[NIE]** request is granted."
17: 2 His face shone **like** the sun, and his clothes became as white as the
17: 2 shone like the sun, and his clothes became as white **as** the light.
17:20 I tell you the truth, if you have faith **as small as** a mustard seed,
18: 3 you the truth, unless you change and become **like** little children,
18: 4 whoever humbles himself **like** this child is the greatest in the
18:33 Shouldn't you have had mercy on your fellow servant **just as** I had
19:19 your father and mother,' and 'love your neighbor **as** yourself.' "
20:14 I want to give the man who was hired last **the same as** [+*2779*] I
21:26 are afraid of the people, for they all hold **that** John was a prophet."
22:30 nor be given in marriage; they will be **like** the angels in heaven.
22:39 And the second is like it: 'Love your neighbor **as** yourself.'
24:38 For **[NIE]** in the days before the flood, people were eating
26:19 So the disciples did **as** Jesus had directed them and prepared the
26:39 may this cup be taken from me. Yet not **as** I will, but as you will."
26:39 may this cup be taken from me. Yet not as I will, but **as** you will."
26:55 **[NIE]** "Am I leading a rebellion, that you have come out with
27:65 Pilate answered. "Go, make the tomb as secure **as** you know how."
28: 3 His appearance was **like** lightning, and his clothes were white as
28: 3 appearance was like lightning, and his clothes were white **as** snow.
28: 4 so afraid of him that they shook and became **like** dead men.
28:15 So the soldiers took the money and did **as** they were instructed.
Mk 1:10 being torn open and the Spirit descending on him **like** a dove.
1:22 because he taught them **as** one who had authority, not as the
1:22 them as one who had authority, not **as** the teachers of the law.
4:26 He also said, "This is what the kingdom of God is **like**. A man
4:27 the seed sprouts and grows, **though** he does not know how.
4:31 It is **like** a mustard seed, which is the smallest seed you plant in the
4:36 the crowd behind, they took him along, **just as** he was, in the boat.
5:13 The herd, **about** two thousand in number, rushed down the steep
6:15 "He is a prophet, **like** one of the prophets of long ago."
6:34 on them, because they were **like** sheep without a shepherd.
7: 6 right when he prophesied about you hypocrites; **as** it is written:
8: 9 **About** four thousand men were present. And having sent them
8:24 and said, "I see people; they look **like** trees walking around."
9:21 Jesus asked the boy's father, "How long has he been **like** this?"
10: 1 of people came to him, and **as** was his custom, he taught them.
10:15 anyone who will not receive the kingdom of God **like** a little child
12:25 nor be given in marriage; they will be **like** the angels in heaven.
12:31 The second is this: 'Love your neighbor **as** yourself.' There is no
12:33 and to love your neighbor **as** yourself is more important than all
13:34 It's **like** a man going away: He leaves his house and puts his
14:48 **[NIE]** "Am I leading a rebellion," said Jesus, "that you have come
14:72 Then Peter remembered the word Jesus **[NIE]** had spoken to him:
Lk 1:23 **When** his time of service was completed, he returned home.
1:41 **When** Elizabeth heard Mary's greeting, the baby leaped in her
1:44 **As soon as** the sound of your greeting reached my ears, the baby in
1:56 Mary stayed with Elizabeth for **about** three months and
2:15 **When** the angels had left them and gone into heaven,
2:39 **When** Joseph and Mary had done everything required by the Law
3: 4 **As** is written in the book of the words of Isaiah the prophet:
3:22 and the Holy Spirit descended on him in bodily form **like** a dove.
3:23 He was the son, **so** it was thought, of Joseph, the son of Heli,
4:25 a half years **and** there was a severe famine throughout the land.
5: 4 **When** he had finished speaking, he said to Simon, "Put out into
6: 4 [UBS+ ***When***] He entered the house of God, and taking the
6:22 when they exclude you and insult you and reject your name **as** evil,
6:40 but everyone who is fully trained will be **like** his teacher.
7:12 **As** he approached the town gate, a dead person was being carried
8:42 because his only daughter, a girl of **about** twelve, was dying.
8:47 why she had touched him and **how** she had been instantly healed.
9:52 who went into a Samaritan village **to** get things ready for him;
10: 3 Go! I am sending you out **like** lambs among wolves.
10:18 He replied, "I saw Satan fall **like** lightning from heaven.
10:27 and with all your mind'; and, 'Love your neighbor **as** yourself.' "
11: 1 **When** he finished, one of his disciples said to him, "Lord, teach us
11:36 be completely lighted, **as** when the light of a lamp shines on you."
11:44 "Woe to you, because you are **like** unmarked graves, which men
12:27 not even Solomon in all his splendor was dressed **like** one of these.
12:58 **As** you are going with your adversary to the magistrate, try hard to
15:19 to be called your son; make me **like** one of your hired men.'
15:25 **When** he came near the house, he heard music and dancing.
16: 1 "There was a rich man whose manager was accused **of** wasting his
17: 6 He replied, "If you have faith **as small as** a mustard seed, you can
18:11 robbers, evildoers, adulterers—or even **like** this tax collector.
18:17 anyone who will not receive the kingdom of God **like** a little child
19: 5 **When** Jesus reached the spot, he looked up and said to him,
19:29 **As** he approached Bethphage and Bethany at the hill called the
19:41 **As** he approached Jerusalem and saw the city, he wept over it
20:37 **for** he calls the Lord 'the God of Abraham, and the God of Isaac,
21:34 of life, and that day will close on you unexpectedly **like** a trap.
22:26 Instead, the greatest among you should be **like** the youngest,
22:26 like the youngest, and the one who rules **like** the one who serves.
22:27 one who is at the table? But I am among you **as** one who serves.
22:31 "Simon, Simon, Satan has asked to sift you **as** wheat.
22:52 who had come for him, "Am I leading a **[NIE]** rebellion,
22:61 Then Peter remembered the word the Lord **[NIE]** had spoken to
22:66 **At** daybreak the council of the elders of the people, both the chief
23:14 "You brought me this man **as** one who was inciting the people to
23:26 **As** they led him away, they seized Simon from Cyrene, who was
23:55 followed Joseph and saw the tomb and **how** his body was laid in it.
24: 6 Remember **how** he told you, while he was still with you in Galilee:
24:32 "Were not our hearts burning within us **while** he talked with us on
24:32 with us on the road and **[RPG]** opened the Scriptures to us?"
24:35 and **how** Jesus was recognized by them when he broke the bread.
Jn 1:14 We have seen his glory, the glory **of** the One and Only, who came
1:32 "I saw the Spirit come down from heaven **as** a dove and remain on
1:39 and spent that day with him. It was **about** the tenth hour.
2: 9 and **[NIE]** the master of the banquet tasted the water that had
2:23 Now **while** he was in Jerusalem at the Passover Feast, many people
4: 3 **When** the Lord learned of this, he left Judea and went back once
4: 6 the journey, sat down by the well. It was **about** the sixth hour.
4:40 So **when** the Samaritans came to him, they urged him to stay with
6:10 in that place, and the men sat down, **about** five thousand of them.
6:12 **When** they had all had enough to eat, he said to his disciples,
6:16 **When** evening came, his disciples went down to the lake,
6:19 **When** they had rowed three or three and a half miles, they saw
7:10 However, **after** his brothers had left for the Feast, he went also,
7:10 left for the Feast, he went also, not publicly, but **[NIE]** in secret.
8: 7 **When** they kept on questioning him, he straightened up and said to
11: 6 Yet **when** he heard that Lazarus was sick, he stayed where he was
11:18 Bethany was **less than two miles** [+*608*+*1278*+*5084*] from Jerusalem,
11:20 **When** Martha heard that Jesus was coming, she went out to meet
11:29 **When** Mary heard this, she got up quickly and went to him.
11:32 **When** Mary reached the place where Jesus was and saw him,
11:33 **When** Jesus saw her weeping, and the Jews who had come along
12:35 Walk **while** you have the light, before darkness overtakes you.
12:36 Put your trust in the light **while** you have it, so that you may
15: 6 remain in me, he is **like** a branch that is thrown away and withers;
18: 6 **When** Jesus said, "I am he," they drew back and fell to the ground.
19:14 the day of Preparation of Passover Week, **about** the sixth hour.
19:33 But when they came to Jesus **and** found that he was already dead,
19:39 brought a mixture of myrrh and aloes, **about** seventy-five pounds.
20:11 the tomb crying. **As** she wept, she bent over to look into the tomb
21: 8 of fish, for they were not far from shore, **about** a hundred yards.
21: 9 **When** they landed, they saw a fire of burning coals there with fish
Ac 1:10 **[NIE]** They were looking intently up into the sky as he was going,
2:15 These men are not drunk, **as** you suppose. It's only nine in the
3:12 Why do you stare at us **as if** by our own power or godliness we had
3:22 'The Lord your God will raise up for you a prophet **like** me from
4: 4 and the number of men grew to **about** five thousand.
5: 7 **About** three hours later his wife came in, not knowing what had
5:24 **On** hearing this report, the captain of the temple guard
5:36 to be somebody, and **about** four hundred men rallied to him.
7:23 "**When** Moses was forty years old, he decided to visit his fellow
7:37 'God will send you a prophet **like** me from your own people.'
7:51 with uncircumcised hearts and ears! You are **just like** your fathers:
8:32 "He was led **like** a sheep to the slaughter, and as a lamb before the
8:32 and **as** a lamb before the shearer is silent, so he did not open his
8:36 **As** they traveled along the road, they came to some water
9:18 Immediately, *something* **like** scales fell from Saul's eyes,

9: 23 **After** many days had gone by, the Jews conspired to kill him,
10: 7 **When** the angel who spoke to him had gone, Cornelius called two
10: 11 and something **like** a large sheet being let down to earth by its four
10: 17 **While** Peter was wondering about the meaning of the vision,
10: 25 **As** Peter entered the house, Cornelius met him and fell at his feet
10: 28 "You are well aware **that** it is against our law for a Jew to associate
10: 38 **how** God anointed Jesus of Nazareth with the Holy Spirit
10: 47 with water? They have received the Holy Spirit **just** as we have."
11: 5 I saw something **like** a large sheet being let down from heaven by
11: 16 Then I remembered what the Lord [NIE] had said: 'John baptized
11: 17 So if God gave them the same gift **as** he gave us, who believed in
13: 18 he endured their conduct for **about** forty years in the desert,
13: 20 All this took **about** 450 years. "After this, God gave them judges
13: 25 **As** John was completing his work, he said: 'Who do you think I
13: 29 **When** they had carried out all that was written about him,
13: 33 **As** it is written in the second Psalm: " 'You are my Son; today I
14: 5 [NIE] There was a plot afoot among the Gentiles and Jews,
16: 4 **As** they traveled from town to town, they delivered the decisions
16: 10 **After** Paul had seen the vision, we got ready at once to leave for
16: 15 **When** she and the members of her household were baptized,
17: 13 **When** the Jews in Thessalonica learned that Paul was preaching
17: 15 instructions for Silas and Timothy to join him **as** soon as possible.
17: 22 "Men of Athens! I see that in every way you **are** very religious.
17: 28 **As** some of your own poets have said, 'We are his offspring.'
18: 5 **When** Silas and Timothy came from Macedonia, Paul devoted
19: 9 [NIE] But some of them became obstinate; they refused to
19: 21 **After** all this had happened, Paul decided to go to Jerusalem,
19: 34 he was a Jew, they all shouted in unison for **about** two hours:
20: 14 **When** he met us at Assos, we took him aboard and went on to
20: 18 **When** they arrived, he said to them: "You know how I lived the
20: 20 You know **that** I have not hesitated to preach anything that would
20: 24 **if only** I may finish the race and complete the task the Lord Jesus
21: 1 [NIE] After we had torn ourselves away from them, we put out to
21: 12 **When** we heard this, we and the people there pleaded with Paul
21: 27 **When** the seven days were nearly over, some Jews from the
22: 5 **as** also the high priest and all the Council can testify. I even
22: 11 because the brilliance of the light [NIE] had blinded me.
22: 25 **As** they stretched him out to flog him, Paul said to the centurion
23: 11 **As** you have testified about me in Jerusalem, so you must also
23: 15 **on the pretext of** wanting more accurate information about his
23: 20 **on the pretext of** wanting more accurate information about him.
25: 10 not done any wrong to the Jews, **as** you yourself know very well.
25: 14 **Since** they were spending many days there, Festus discussed Paul's
27: 1 [NIE] When it was decided that we would sail for Italy, Paul
27: 27 **On** the fourteenth night we were still being driven across the
27: 30 pretending they were going to lower some anchors [NIE] from
28: 4 **When** the islanders saw the snake hanging from his hand,
28: 19 not **that** I had any charge to bring against my own people.
Ro 1: 9 gospel of his Son, is my witness **how** constantly I remember you
1: 21 they neither glorified him **as** God nor gave thanks to him,
3: 7 so increases his glory, why am I still condemned **as** a sinner?"
4: 17 life to the dead and calls things that are not **as though** they were.
5: 15 But [NIE] the gift is not like the trespass. For if the many died by
5: 16 Again, the gift of God is not **like** the result of the one man's sin:
5: 18 **just as** the result of one trespass was condemnation for all men,
8: 36 death all day long; we are considered **as** sheep to be slaughtered."
9: 25 **As** he says in Hosea: "I will call them 'my people' who are not my
9: 27 "Though the number of the Israelites be **like** the sand by the sea,
9: 29 we would have become **like** Sodom, we would have been **like**
9: 29 become like Sodom, we would have been like [RPG] Gomorrah."
9: 32 Because they pursued it not by faith but **as if** it were by works.
10: 15 "**How** beautiful are the feet of those who bring good news!"
11: 2 the passage about Elijah—**how** he appealed to God against Israel:
11: 33 **How** unsearchable his judgments, and his paths beyond tracing
12: 3 **in accordance with** the measure of faith God has given you.
13: 9 are summed up in this one rule: "Love your neighbor **as** yourself."
13: 13 behave decently, **as** in the daytime, not in orgies and drunkenness,
15: 15 **as if** to remind you of them again, because of the grace God gave
15: 24 I plan to do so **when** [+323] I go to Spain. I hope to visit you while
1Co 3: 1 Brothers, I could not address you **as** spiritual but as worldly—
3: 1 Brothers, I could not address you **as** spiritual but as worldly—
3: 1 you as spiritual but as worldly—[RPG] mere infants in Christ.
3: 5 you came to believe—**as** the Lord has assigned to each his task.
3: 10 grace God has given me, I laid a foundation **as** an expert builder,
3: 15 himself will be saved, but only **as** one escaping through the flames.
4: 1 men ought to regard us **as** servants of Christ and as those entrusted

4: 7 And if you did receive it, why do you boast **as though** you did not?
4: 9 the end of the procession, **like** men condemned to die in the arena.
4: 13 [NIE] Up to this moment we have become the scum of the earth,
4: 14 writing this to shame you, but to warn you, **as** my dear children.
4: 18 Some of you have become arrogant, **as if** I were not coming to you.
5: 3 **And** I have already passed judgment on the one who did this,
7: 7 I wish that all men were **as** I am. But each man has his own gift
7: 8 the widows I say: It is good for them to stay unmarried, **as** I am.
7: 17 each one should retain the place in life **that** the Lord assigned to
7: 17 that the Lord assigned to him **and to which** God has called him.
7: 25 but I give a judgment **as** one who by the Lord's mercy is
7: 29 From now on those who have wives should live **as if** they had
7: 30 those who mourn, **as if** they did not; those who are happy,
7: 30 as if they did not; those who are happy, **as if** they were not;
7: 30 were not; those who buy something, **as if** it were not theirs to keep;
7: 31 those who use the things of the world, **as if** not engrossed in them.
8: 7 eat such food they think of it **as** having been sacrificed to an idol,
9: 5 **as** do the other apostles and the Lord's brothers and Cephas?
9: 20 To the Jews I became **like** a Jew, to win the Jews. To those under
9: 20 To those under the law I became **like** one under the law (though I
9: 21 To those not having the law I became **like** one not having the law
9: 26 Therefore I do not run **like** a man running aimlessly; I do not fight
9: 26 a man running aimlessly; I do not fight **like** a man beating the air.
10: 15 I speak [NIE] to sensible people; judge for yourselves what I say.
11: 2 And **when** [+323] I come I will give further directions.
12: 2 **somehow** [+323] **or other** you were influenced and led astray to
13: 11 When I was a child, I talked **like** a child, I thought like a child,
13: 11 When I was a child, I talked like a child, I thought **like** a child,
13: 11 I talked like a child, I thought like a child, I reasoned **like** a child.
14: 33 of disorder but of peace. **As** in all the congregations of the saints,
16: 10 with you, for he is carrying on the work of the Lord, **just as** I am.
2Co 1: 7 because we know that **just as** you share in our sufferings,
2: 17 **Unlike** [+4024] so many, we do not peddle the word of God for
2: 17 the contrary, in Christ we speak before God [NIE] with sincerity,
2: 17 we speak before God with sincerity, **like** men sent from God.
3: 1 Or do we need, **like** some people, letters of recommendation to you
3: 5 Not that we are competent in ourselves to claim anything [NIE]
5: 19 [NIE] that God was reconciling the world to himself in Christ,
5: 20 **as though** God were making his appeal through us.
6: 4 Rather, **as** servants of God we commend ourselves in every way:
6: 8 bad report and good report; genuine, yet **regarded as** impostors;
6: 9 known, yet **regarded as** unknown; dying, and yet we live on;
6: 9 [RPG] dying, and yet we live on; beaten, and yet not killed;
6: 9 dying, and yet we live on; [RPG] beaten, and yet not killed;
6: 10 [RPG] sorrowful, yet always rejoicing; poor, yet making many
6: 10 [RPG] poor, yet making many rich; having nothing, and yet
6: 10 many rich; [RPG] having nothing, and yet possessing everything.
6: 13 As a fair exchange—I speak **as** to my children—open wide your
7: 14 But **just as** everything we said to you was true, so our boasting
7: 15 were all obedient, receiving him [NIE] with fear and trembling.
9: 5 Then it will be ready **as** a generous gift, not as one grudgingly
9: 5 it will be ready as a generous gift, not **as** one grudgingly given.
10: 2 who think that we live [NIE] by the standards of this world.
10: 9 I do not want to seem to be **trying** [+323] **to** frighten you with my
10: 14 in our boasting, **as** would be the case if we had not come to you,
11: 3 But I am afraid that **just as** Eve was deceived by the serpent's
11: 15 then, if his servants masquerade **as** servants of righteousness.
11: 16 But if you do, then receive me **just as** you would a fool, so that I
11: 17 boasting I am not talking as the Lord would, but **as** a fool.
11: 21 To my shame I admit that we were too weak **for that!** What
13: 2 I already gave you a warning **when** I was with you the second
13: 7 but that you will do what is right even though we may **seem** to
Gal 1: 9 **As** we have already said, so now I say again: If anybody is
3: 16 **meaning** many people, but "and to your seed," meaning one
3: 16 but "and to your seed," **meaning** one person, who is Christ.
4: 12 I plead with you, brothers, become **like** me, for I became like you.
4: 12 I plead with you, brothers, become like me, for I became **like** you.
4: 14 Instead, you welcomed me **as if** I were an angel of God, as if I
4: 14 me as if I were an angel of God, **as if** I were Christ Jesus himself.
5: 14 in a single command: "Love your neighbor **as** yourself."
6: 10 Therefore, **as** we have opportunity, let us do good to all people,
Eph 2: 3 and thoughts. **Like** the rest, we were by nature objects of wrath.
3: 5 which was not made known to men in other generations **as** it has
5: 1 Be imitators of God, therefore, **as** dearly loved children
5: 8 but now you are light in the Lord. Live **as** children of light
5: 15 Be very careful, then, how you live—not **as** unwise but as wise,

5:15 Be very careful, then, how you live—not as unwise but **as** wise,
5:22 Wives, submit to your husbands **as** to the Lord.
5:23 For the husband is the head of the wife **as** Christ is the head of the
5:24 Now **as** the church submits to Christ, so also wives should submit
5:28 same way, husbands ought to love their wives **as** their own bodies.
5:33 each one of you also must love his wife **as** he loves himself,
6: 5 and with sincerity of heart, **just as** you would obey Christ.
6: 6 Obey them not only **to** win their favor when their eye is on you,
6: 6 but **like** slaves of Christ, doing the will of God from your heart.
6: 7 Serve wholeheartedly, **as if** you were serving the Lord, not men,
6:20 in chains. Pray that I may declare it fearlessly, **as** I should.

Php 1: 8 God can testify **how** I long for all of you with the affection of
1:20 so that now **as** always Christ will be exalted in my body,
2: 8 And being found in appearance **as** a man, he humbled himself
2:12 not only **[NIE]** in my presence, but now much more in my
2:15 depraved generation, in which you shine **like** stars in the universe
2:22 because **as** a son with his father he has served with me in the work
2:23 to send him **as** [+323] **soon as** I see how things go with me.

Col 2: 6 So then, **just as** you received Christ Jesus as Lord, continue to live
2:20 why, **as though** you still belonged to it, do you submit to its rules:
3:12 Therefore, **as** God's chosen people, holy and dearly loved,
3:18 Wives, submit to your husbands, **as** is fitting in the Lord.
3:22 and do it, not only when their eye is on you and **to** win their favor,
3:23 work at it with all your heart, **as** working for the Lord, not for men,
4: 4 Pray that I may proclaim it clearly, **as** I should.

1Th 2: 4 **[NIE]** We are not trying to please men but God, who tests our
2: 6 **As** apostles of Christ we could have been a burden to you,
2: 7 among you, **like** [+1569] a mother caring for her little children.
2:10 of **how** holy, righteous and blameless we were among you who
2:11 For you know **that** we *dealt with* each of you as a father deals
2:11 For you know that we dealt with each of you **as** a father *deals with*
5: 2 for you know very well that the day of the Lord will come **like** a
5: 4 are not in darkness so that this day should surprise you **like** a thief.
5: 6 So then, let us not be **like** others, who are asleep, but let us be alert

2Th 2: 2 by some prophecy, report or letter **supposed** to have come from us,
2: 2 come from us, **saying**ˢ that the day of the Lord has already come.
3:15 Yet do not regard him **as** an enemy, but warn him as a brother.
3:15 Yet do not regard him as an enemy, but warn him **as** a brother.

1Ti 5: 1 an older man harshly, but exhort him **as if** he were your father.
5: 1 him as if he were your father. Treat younger men **as** brothers,
5: 2 older women **as** mothers, and younger women as sisters,
5: 2 as mothers, and younger women **as** sisters, with absolute purity.

2Ti 1: 3 **as** night and day I constantly remember you in my prayers.
2: 3 Endure hardship with us **like** a good soldier of Christ Jesus.
2: 9 for which I am suffering even to the point of being chained **like** a
2:17 Their teaching will spread **like** gangrene. Among them are
3: 9 **as** in the case of those men, their folly will be clear to everyone.

Tit 1: 5 left unfinished and appoint elders in every town, **as** I directed you.
1: 7 Since an overseer **is** entrusted with God's work, he must be

Phm 1: 9 I then, **as** Paul—an old man and now also a prisoner of Christ
1:14 that any favor you do will be spontaneous and not **[NIE]** forced.
1:16 no longer **as** a slave, but better than a slave, as a dear brother.
1:17 consider me a partner, welcome him **as** you would welcome me.

Heb 1:11 will perish, but you remain; they will all wear out **like** a garment.
1:12 will roll them up like a robe; **like** a garment they will be changed.
3: 2 who appointed him, **just as** Moses was faithful in all God's house.
3: 5 Moses was faithful **as** a servant in all God's house, testifying to
3: 6 But Christ is faithful **as** a son over God's house. And we are his
3: 8 do not harden your hearts **as** you did in the rebellion,
3:11 **So** I declared on oath in my anger, 'They shall never enter my
3:15 his voice, do not harden your hearts **as** you did in the rebellion.'
4: 3 that rest, just as God has said, "**So** I declared on oath in my anger,
6:19 We have this hope **as** an anchor for the soul, firm and secure.
7: 9 **One might even say** [+2229+3306] that Levi, who collects the
11: 9 By faith he made his home in the promised land **like** a stranger in a
11:12 as the stars in the sky and as countless **as** the sand on the seashore.
11:27 he persevered because he **[NIE]** saw him who is invisible.
11:29 By faith the people passed through the Red Sea **as** on dry land;
12: 5 forgotten that word of encouragement that addresses you **as** sons:
12: 7 Endure hardship as discipline; God is treating you **as** sons.
12:16 See that no one is sexually immoral, or is godless **like** Esau,
12:27 **that is**, created things—so that what cannot be shaken may remain.
13: 3 Remember those in prison **as if** you were their fellow prisoners,
13: 3 and those who are mistreated **as if** you yourselves were suffering.
13:17 They keep watch over you **as** men who must give an account.

Jas 1:10 in his low position, because he will pass away **like** a wild flower.

2: 8 in Scripture, "Love your neighbor **as** yourself," you are doing right.
2: 9 you sin and are convicted by the law **as** lawbreakers.
2:12 and act **as** those who are going to be judged by the law that gives
5: 3 Their corrosion will testify against you and eat your flesh **like** fire.

1Pe 1:14 **As** obedient children, do not conform to the evil desires you had
1:19 precious blood of Christ, **[NIE]** a lamb without blemish or defect.
1:24 For, "All men are **like** grass, and all their glory is like the flowers of
1:24 are like grass, and all their glory is **like** the flowers of the field;
2: 2 **Like** newborn babies, crave pure spiritual milk, so that by it you
2: 5 you also, **like** living stones, are being built into a spiritual house to
2:11 Dear friends, I urge you, **as** aliens and strangers in the world,
2:12 though they accuse you **of** doing wrong, they may see your good
2:13 among men: whether to the king, **as** the supreme authority,
2:14 **[NIE]** who are sent by him to punish those who do wrong
2:16 Live **as** free men, but do not use your freedom as a cover-up for
2:16 as free men, but do not use your freedom **as** a cover-up for evil;
2:16 use your freedom as a cover-up for evil; live **as** servants of God.
2:25 For you were **like** sheep going astray, but now you have returned
3: 6 **like** Sarah, who obeyed Abraham and called him her master.
3: 7 and treat them with respect **as** the weaker partner and as heirs with
3: 7 the weaker partner and **as** heirs with you of the gracious gift of life,
4:10 whatever gift he has received to serve others, **faithfully** [+2819]
4:11 he should do it **as** one speaking the very words of God.
4:11 he should do it **[RPG]** with the strength God provides,
4:12 are suffering, **as though** something strange were happening to you.
4:15 it should not be **as** a murderer or thief or any other kind of
4:15 or thief or any other kind of criminal, or even **as** a meddler.
4:16 However, if you suffer **as** a Christian, do not be ashamed,
5: 3 not **[NIE]** lording it over those entrusted to you, but being
5: 8 Your enemy the devil prowls around **like** a roaring lion looking for
5:12 With the help of Silas, whom I regard **as** a faithful brother,

2Pe 1: 3 His divine **[NIE]** power has given us everything we need for life
1:19 **as** to a light shining in a dark place, until the day dawns
2: 1 among the people, **just as** there will be false teachers among you.
2:12 They are **like** brute beasts, creatures of instinct, born only to be
3: 8 With the Lord a day is **like** a thousand years, and a thousand years
3: 8 a day is like a thousand years, and a thousand years are **like** a day.
3: 9 is not slow in keeping his promise, **as** some understand slowness.
3:10 But the day of the Lord will come **like** a thief. The heavens will
3:16 He writes the **same** [+2779] **way** in all his letters, speaking in them
3:16 **as** they do the other Scriptures, to their own destruction.

1Jn 1: 7 But if we walk in the light, **as** he is in the light, we have fellowship
2:27 But **as** his anointing teaches you about all things and as that

2Jn 1: 5 I am not writing you **[NIE]** a new command but one we have had

Jude 1: 7 **[RPG]** In a similar way, Sodom and Gomorrah
1:10 things they do understand by instinct, **like** unreasoning animals—

Rev 1:10 in the Spirit, and I heard behind me a loud voice **like** a trumpet,
1:14 His head and hair were white **like** wool, as white as snow,
1:14 His head and hair were white like wool, as white **as** snow,
1:14 like wool, as white as snow, and his eyes were **like** blazing fire.
1:15 His feet were like bronze glowing **[NIE]** in a furnace, and his
1:15 in a furnace, and his voice was **like** the sound of rushing waters.
1:16 His face was **like** the sun shining in all its brilliance.
1:17 When I saw him, I fell at his feet **as though** dead. Then he placed
2:18 whose eyes are **like** blazing fire and whose feet are like burnished
2:24 and have not learned Satan's **so-called** [+3306] deep secrets (I will
2:27 with an iron scepter; he will dash them to pieces **like** pottery'—
2:27 like pottery'—**just as** I have received authority from my Father.
3: 3 But if you do not wake up, I will come **like** a thief, and you will
3:21 **just as** I overcame and sat down with my Father on his throne.
4: 1 And the voice I had first heard speaking to me **like** a trumpet said,
4: 6 Also before the throne there was what **looked like** a sea of glass,
4: 7 the second was like an ox, the third had a face **like** a man,
5: 6 Then I saw a Lamb, *looking* **as if** it had been slain, standing in the
6: 1 Then I heard one of the four living creatures say in a voice **like**
6: 6 Then I heard what **sounded like** a voice among the four living
6:11 and brothers who were to be killed **as** they had been was
6:12 The sun turned black **like** sackcloth made of goat hair, the whole
6:12 made of goat hair, the whole moon turned **blood red** [+135],
6:13 **as** late figs drop from a fig tree when shaken by a strong wind.
6:14 The sky receded **like** a scroll, rolling up, and every mountain
8: 1 seventh seal, there was silence in heaven for **about** half an hour.
8: 8 and *something* **like** a huge mountain, all ablaze, was thrown into
8:10 angel sounded his trumpet, and a great star, blazing **like** a torch,
9: 2 smoke rose from it **like** the smoke from a gigantic furnace.
9: 3 the earth and were given power **like** that of scorpions of the earth.

9: 5 And the agony they suffered was **like** that of the sting of a scorpion
9: 7 On their heads they wore **something** like crowns of gold, and their
9: 7 like crowns of gold, and their faces **resembled** human faces.
9: 8 Their hair was **like** women's hair, and their teeth were like lions'
9: 8 hair was like women's hair, and their teeth were **like** lions' teeth.
9: 9 They had breastplates **like** breastplates of iron, and the sound of
9: 9 and the sound of their wings was **like** the thundering of many
9:17 The heads of the horses **resembled** the heads of lions, and out of
10: 1 his face was **like** the sun, and his legs were like fiery pillars.
10: 1 his face was like the sun, and his legs were **like** fiery pillars.
10: 7 **just as** he announced to his servants the prophets."
10: 9 your stomach sour, but in your mouth it will be as sweet **as** honey."
10:10 It tasted as sweet **as** honey in my mouth, but when I had eaten it,
12:15 Then from his mouth the serpent spewed water **like** a river,
13: 2 but had feet **like** those of a bear and a mouth like that of a lion.
13: 2 but had feet like those of a bear and a mouth **like** that of a lion.
13: 3 One of the heads of the beast **seemed** to have had a fatal wound,
13:11 He had two horns like a lamb, but he spoke **like** a dragon.
14: 2 And I heard a sound from heaven **like** the roar of rushing waters
14: 2 like the roar of rushing waters and **like** a loud peal of thunder.
14: 2 The sound I heard was **like** that of harpists playing their harps.
14: 3 And they sang [UBS+ *as it were*] a new song before the throne
15: 2 And I saw what **looked like** a sea of glass mixed with fire and,
16: 3 and it turned into blood **like** that of a dead man, and every living
16:13 Then I saw three evil spirits that **looked like** frogs; they came out
16:15 "Behold, I come **like** a thief! Blessed is he who stays awake
16:21 From the sky huge hailstones of **about** a hundred pounds each fell
17:12 but who for one hour will receive authority **as** kings along with the
18: 6 Give back to her **as** she has given; pay her back double for what
18:21 Then a mighty angel picked up a boulder **the size of** a large
19: 1 After this I heard what **sounded like** the roar of a great multitude
19: 6 Then I heard what sounded **like** a great multitude, like the roar of
19: 6 **like** the roar of rushing waters and like loud peals of thunder,
19: 6 like the roar of rushing waters and **like** loud peals of thunder,
19:12 His eyes are **like** blazing fire, and on his head are many crowns.
20: 8 them for battle. In number they are **like** the sand on the seashore.
21: 2 from God, prepared **as** a bride beautifully dressed for her husband.
21:11 was like that of a very precious jewel, **like** a jasper, clear as crystal.
21:21 The great street of the city was of pure gold, **like** transparent glass.
22: 1 **as** clear as crystal, flowing from the throne of God and of the
22:12 and I will give to everyone **according to** what he has done.

6056 ὡσάν, *hōsan* Not used in UBS/NIV [√ *6055* + *323*]

6057 ὡσαννά, *hōsanna* [6]

Hosanna [6]

Mt 21: 9 and those that followed shouted, "**Hosanna** to the Son of David!"
21: 9 he who comes in the name of the Lord!" "**Hosanna** in the highest!"
21:15 temple area, "**Hosanna** to the Son of David," they were indignant.
Mk 11: 9 who went ahead and those who followed shouted, "**Hosanna!**"
11:10 coming kingdom of our father David!" "**Hosanna** in the highest!"
Jn 12:13 palm branches and went out to meet him, shouting, "**Hosanna!**"

6058 ὡσαύτως, *hōsautōs* [17] [√ *6055* + *899*]

in the same way [6], likewise [2], the same thing [2], the same [2], also [1], similarly [1], so also [1], the same way [1], too [1]

Mt 20: 5 about the sixth hour and the ninth hour and did **the same thing**.
21:30 "Then the father went to the other son and said **the same thing**.
21:36 than the first time, and the tenants treated them **the same way**.
25:17 **So also**, the one with the two talents gained two more.
Mk 12:21 but he also died, leaving no child. It was **the same** with the third.
14:31 I will never disown you." And all the others said **the same**.
Lk 13: 5 I tell you, no! But unless you repent, you **too** will all perish."
20:31 and **in the same way** the seven died, leaving no children.
22:20 **In the same way**, after the supper he took the cup, saying,
Ro 8:26 **In the same way**, the Spirit helps us in our weakness. We do not
1Co 11:25 **In the same way**, after supper he took the cup, saying, "This cup is
1Ti 2: 9 I **also** want women to dress modestly, with decency and propriety,
3: 8 Deacons, **likewise**, are to be men worthy of respect, sincere,
3:11 **In the same way**, their wives are to be women worthy of respect,
5:25 **In the same way**, good deeds are obvious, and even those that are
Tit 2: 3 **Likewise**, teach the older women to be reverent in the way they

2: 6 **Similarly**, encourage the young men to be self-controlled.

6059 ὡσεί, *hōsei* [21] [√ *6055* + *1623*]

about [11], like [6], about [+*4309*] [1], as [1], looked so much like [+*1181*] [1], what seemed to be [1]

Mt 3:16 and he saw the Spirit of God descending **like** a dove and lighting
9:36 they were harassed and helpless, **like** sheep without a shepherd.
14:21 The number of those who ate was **about** five thousand men,
Mk 9:26 The boy **looked so much like** [+*1181*] a corpse that many said,
Lk 3:23 Now Jesus himself was **about** thirty years old when he began his
9:14 (**About** five thousand men were there.) But he said to his disciples,
9:14 his disciples, "Have them sit down in groups of **about** fifty each."
9:28 **About** eight days after Jesus said this, he took Peter, John
22:41 He withdrew **about** a stone's throw beyond them, knelt down
22:44 and his sweat was **like** drops of blood falling to the ground.
22:59 **About** an hour later another asserted, "Certainly this fellow was
23:44 It was now **about** the sixth hour, and darkness came over the
24:11 the women, because their words seemed to them **like** nonsense.
Ac 1:15 stood up among the believers (a group numbering **about** a hundred
2: 3 They saw **what seemed to be** tongues of fire that separated
2:41 and **about** three thousand were added to their number that day.
6:15 at Stephen, and they saw that his face was **like** the face of an angel.
10: 3 One day at **about** [+*4309*] three in the afternoon he had a vision.
19: 7 There were **about** twelve men in all.
Ro 6:13 to God, **as** those who have been brought from death to life;
Heb 1:12 You will roll them up **like** a robe; like a garment they will be

6060 Ὡσηέ, *Hōsēe* [1]

Hosea [1]

Ro 9:25 As he says in **Hosea**: "I will call them 'my people' who are not my

6061 ὥσπερ, *hōsper* [36] [√ *6055* + *4302*]

as [15], just as [10], like [6], *untranslated* [1], as indeed [1], the way [1], unlike [1], what [1]

Mt 6: 2 **as** the hypocrites do in the synagogues and on the streets, to be
6: 7 And when you pray, do not keep on babbling **like** pagans,
12:40 For **as** Jonah was three days and three nights in the belly of a huge
13:40 "**As** the weeds are pulled up and burned in the fire, so it will be at
18:17 to the church, treat him **as** you would a pagan or a tax collector.
20:28 **just as** the Son of Man did not come to be served, but to serve,
24:27 For **as** lightning that comes from the east is visible even in the
24:37 **As** it was in the days of Noah, so it will be at the coming of the
25:14 "Again, it will be **like** a man going on a journey, who called his
25:32 and he will separate the people one from another **as** a shepherd
Lk 17:24 For the Son of Man in his day will be **like** the lightning,
18:11 'God, I thank you that I am not **like** other men—robbers, evildoers,
Jn 5:21 For **just as** the Father raises the dead and gives them life, even
5:26 For **as** the Father has life in himself, so he has granted the Son to
Ac 2: 2 Suddenly a sound **like** the blowing of a violent wind came from
3:17 brothers, I know that you acted in ignorance, **as** did your leaders.
11:15 the Holy Spirit came on them **as** he had come on us at the
Ro 5:12 Therefore, **just as** sin entered the world through one man,
5:19 For **just as** through the disobedience of the one man the many
5:21 so that, **just as** sin reigned in death, so also grace might reign
6: 4 **just as** Christ was raised from the dead through the glory of the
6:19 **Just as** you used to offer the parts of your body in slavery to
11:30 **Just as** you who were at one time disobedient to God have now
1Co 8: 5 or on earth (**as indeed** there are many "gods" and many "lords"),
10: 7 Do not be idolaters, as some of them were; **as** it is written:
11:12 For **as** woman came from man, so also man is born of woman.
15:22 For **as** in Adam all die, so in Christ all will be made alive.
16: 1 for God's people: Do **what** I told the Galatian churches to do.
2Co 8: 7 But **just as** you excel in everything—in faith, in speech, in
Gal 4:29 [NIE] At that time the son born in the ordinary way persecuted
1Th 5: 3 **as** labor pains on a pregnant woman, and they will not escape.
Heb 4:10 God's rest also rests from his own work, **just as** God did from his.
7:27 **Unlike** the other high priests, he does not need to offer sacrifices
9:25 **the way** the high priest enters the Most Holy Place every year with
Jas 2:26 **As** the body without the spirit is dead, so faith without deeds is
Rev 10: 3 and he gave a loud shout **like** the roar of a lion. When he shouted,

6062 ὡσπερεί, hōsperei [1] [√ 6055 + 4302 + 1623]

as [1]

1Co 15: 8 and last of all he appeared to me also, **as** to one abnormally born.

6063 ὥστε, hōste [83] [√ 6055 + 5445]

so [19], so that [17], therefore [13], that [12], *untranslated* [5], to [4], as a result [3], so then [3], now [2], and [1], consequently [1], in order to [1], such that [1], then [1]

Mt 8:24 storm came up on the lake, **so that** the waves swept over the boat.
    8:28 met him. They were so violent **that** no one could pass that way.
    10: 1 and gave them authority **to** drive out evil spirits and to heal every
    12:12 than a sheep! **Therefore** it is lawful to do good on the Sabbath."
    12:22 and mute, and Jesus healed him, **so that** he could both talk and see.
    13: 2 Such large crowds gathered around him **that** he got into a boat
    13:32 **so that** the birds of the air come and perch in its branches."
    13:54 teaching the people in their synagogue, **and** they were amazed.
    15:31 **[NIE]** The people were amazed when they saw the mute
    15:33 "Where could we get enough bread in this remote place **to** feed such
    19: 6 **So** they are no longer two, but one. Therefore what God has joined
    23:31 **So** you testify against yourselves that you are the descendants of
    24:24 and perform great signs and miracles **to** deceive even the elect—
    27: 1 of the people came to the decision to put Jesus **[NIE]** to death.
    27:14 even to a single charge—**to** the great amazement of the governor.
Mk 1:27 The people were all **so** amazed **that** they asked each other,
    1:45 **As a result**, Jesus could no longer enter a town openly but stayed
    2: 2 So many gathered **that** there was no room left, not even outside the
    2:12 **[NIE]** This amazed everyone and they praised God, saying,
    2:28 **So** the Son of Man is Lord even of the Sabbath."
    3:10 **so that** those with diseases were pushing forward to touch him.
    3:20 **so that** he and his disciples were not even able to eat.
    4: 1 so large **that** he got into a boat and sat in it out on the lake,
    4:32 with such big branches **that** the birds of the air can perch in its
    4:37 and the waves broke over the boat, **so that** it was nearly swamped.
    9:26 The boy looked so much like a corpse **that** many said, "He's dead."
    10: 8 the two will become one flesh.' **So** they are no longer two, but one.
    15: 5 But Jesus still made no reply, and **[NIE]** Pilate was amazed.
Lk 4:29 on which the town was built, **in order to** throw him down the cliff.
    5: 7 and they came and filled both boats so full **that** they began to sink.
    12: 1 **so that** they were trampling on one another, Jesus began to speak
    20:20 **so that** they might hand him over to the power and authority of the
Jn 3:16 "For God so loved the world **that** he gave his one and only Son,
Ac 1:19 **so** they called that field in their language Akeldama, that is,
    5:15 **As a result**, people brought the sick into the streets and laid them
    14: 1 There they spoke so effectively **that** a great number of Jews
    15:39 They had such a sharp disagreement **that** they parted company.
    16:26 Suddenly there was **such** a violent earthquake **that** the foundations
    19:10 **so that** all the Jews and Greeks who lived in the province of Asia
    19:12 **so that** even handkerchiefs and aprons that had touched him were
    19:16 He gave them such a beating **that** they ran out of the house naked
Ro 7: 4 **So**, my brothers, you also died to the law through the body of
    7: 6 from the law **so that** we serve in the new way of the Spirit,
    7:12 **So then**, the law is holy, and the commandment is holy, righteous
    13: 2 **Consequently**, he who rebels against the authority is rebelling
    15:19 **So** from Jerusalem all the way around to Illyricum, I have fully
1Co 1: 7 **Therefore** you do not lack any spiritual gift as you eagerly wait for
    3: 7 **So** neither he who plants nor he who waters is anything, but only
    3:21 **So** then, no more boasting about men! All things are yours,
    4: 5 **Therefore** judge nothing before the appointed time; wait till the
    5: 1 not occur even among pagans: **[NIE]** A man has his father's wife.
    5: 8 **Therefore** let us keep the Festival, not with the old yeast,
    7:38 **So** then he who marries the virgin does right, but he who does not
    10:12 **So**, if you think you are standing firm, be careful that you don't
    11:27 **Therefore**, whoever eats the bread or drinks the cup of the Lord in
    11:33 **So**, my brothers, when you come together to eat, wait for each
    13: 2 and if I have a faith **that** can move mountains, but have not love,
    14:22 Tongues, **then**, are a sign, not for believers but for unbelievers;
    14:39 **Therefore**, my brothers, be eager to prophesy, and do not forbid
    15:58 **Therefore**, my dear brothers, stand firm. Let nothing move you.
2Co 1: 8 far beyond our ability to endure, **so that** we despaired even of life.
    2: 7 **Now** instead, you ought to forgive and comfort him, so that he will
    3: 7 **so that** the Israelites could not look steadily at the face of Moses

    4:12 **So then**, death is at work in us, but life is at work in you.
    5:16 **So** from now on we regard no one from a worldly point of view.
    5:17 **Therefore**, if anyone is in Christ, he is a new creation; the old has
    7: 7 your ardent concern for me, **so that** my joy was greater than ever.
Gal 2:13 **so that** by their hypocrisy even Barnabas was led astray.
    3: 9 **So** those who have faith are blessed along with Abraham,
    3:24 **So** the law was put in charge to lead us to Christ that we might be
    4: 7 **So** you are no longer a slave, but a son; and since you are a son,
    4:16 Have I **now** become your enemy by telling you the truth?
Php 1:13 **As a result**, it has become clear throughout the whole palace guard
    2:12 **Therefore**, my dear friends, as you have always obeyed—
    4: 1 **Therefore**, my brothers, you whom I love and long for, my joy
1Th 1: 7 And **so** you became a model to all the believers in Macedonia
    1: 8 **Therefore** we do not need to say anything about it,
    4:18 **Therefore** encourage each other with these words.
2Th 1: 4 **Therefore**, among God's churches we boast about your
    2: 4 or is worshiped, **so that** he sets himself up in God's temple,
Heb 13: 6 **So** we say with confidence, "The Lord is my helper; I will not be
1Pe 1:21 the dead and glorified him, and **so** your faith and hope are in God.
    4:19 **So then**, those who suffer according to God's will should commit

6064 ὠτάριον, ōtarion [2] [√ 4044]

ear [2]

Mk 14:47 and struck the servant of the high priest, cutting off his **ear**.
Jn 18:10 and struck the high priest's servant, cutting off his right **ear**.

6065 ὠτίον, ōtion [3] [√ 4044]

ear [3]

Mt 26:51 and struck the servant of the high priest, cutting off his **ear**.
Lk 22:51 "No more of this!" And he touched the man's **ear** and healed him.
Jn 18:26 a relative of the man whose **ear** Peter had cut off, challenged him,

6066 ὠφέλεια, ōpheleia [2] [√ 6067]

advantage [1], value [1]

Ro 3: 1 is there in being a Jew, or what **value** is there in circumcision?
Jude 1:16 boast about themselves and flatter others for their own **advantage**.

6067 ὠφελέω, ōpheleō [15] [→ 543, 4055, 6066, 6068]

value [4], good [2], counts for [1], devoted to God [1], gain [1], getting better [1], getting nowhere [+4024+4029] [1], good for [1], good to [1], help received [1], was getting nowhere [+4029] [1]

Mt 15: 5 might otherwise have received from me *is* a gift **devoted to God**,'
    16:26 What **good** *will it be* for a man if he gains the whole world,
    27:24 When Pilate saw that *he* **was getting nowhere** [+4029],
Mk 5:26 had spent all she had, yet instead of **getting better** she grew worse.
    7:11 'Whatever **help** you *might* otherwise *have* **received** from me is
    8:36 What **good** *is it* for a man to gain the whole world, yet forfeit his
Lk 9:25 What **good** *is it* for a man to gain the whole world, and yet lose
Jn 6:63 The Spirit gives life; the flesh **counts for** nothing. The words I
    12:19 to one another, "See, *this is* **getting** [+4024+4029] us **nowhere**.
Ro 2:25 Circumcision **has value** if you observe the law, but if you break
1Co 13: 3 surrender my body to the flames, but have not love, *I* **gain** nothing.
    14: 6 if I come to you and speak in tongues, what **good** *will I be* **to** you,
Gal 5: 2 yourselves be circumcised, Christ *will be of* no **value** to you at all.
Heb 4: 2 but the message they heard *was of* no **value** to them, because those
    13: 9 by ceremonial foods, which *are* of no **value** to those who eat them.

6068 ὠφέλιμος, ōphelimos [4] [√ 6067]

value [2], profitable [1], useful [1]

1Ti 4: 8 For physical training is of some **value**, but godliness has value for
    4: 8 training is of some value, but godliness has **value** for all things,
2Ti 3:16 All Scripture is God-breathed and is **useful** for teaching, rebuking,
Tit 3: 8 is good. These things are excellent and **profitable** for everyone.

Index of Articles, Conjunctions, Particles, Prepositions and Pronouns

247 ἀλλά, *alla* [638]

Mt 4:4; 5:15, 17, 39; 6:13, 18; 7:21; 8:4, 8; 9:12, 13, 17, 18, 24; 10:20, 34; 11:8, 9; 13:21; 15:11; 16:12, 17, 23; 17:12; 18:22, 30; 19:6, 11; 20:23, 26, 28; 21:21; 22:30, 32; 24:6; 26:39; 27:24; Mk 1:44, 45; 2:17, 17, 22; 3:26, 27, 29; 4:17, 22; 5:19, 26, 39; 6:9, 52; 7:5, 15, 19, 25; 8:33; 9:8, 13, 22, 37; 10:8, 27, 40, 43, 45; 11:23, 32; 12:14, 25, 27; 13:7, 11, 11, 20, 24; 14:28, 29, 36, 36, 49; 16:7; Lk 1:60; 5:14, 31, 32, 38; 6:27; 7:7, 25, 26; 8:16, 27, 52; 11:33, 42; 12:7, 51; 13:3, 5; 14:10, 13; 16:21, 30; 17:8; 18:13; 20:21, 38; 21:9; 22:26, 36, 42, 53; 23:15; 24:6, 21, 22; Jn 1:8, 13, 31, 33; 3:8, 16, 17, 28, 36; 4:2, 14, 23; 5:18, 22, 24, 30, 34, 42; 6:9, 22, 26, 27, 32, 36, 38, 39, 64; 7:10, 12, 16, 22, 24, 27, 28, 44, 49; 8:12, 16, 26, 28, 37, 42, 49, 55; 9:3, 9, 31; 10:1, 5, 8, 18, 26, 33; 11:4, 11, 15, 22, 30, 42, 51, 52, 54; 12:6, 9, 16, 27, 30, 42, 44, 47, 49; 13:9, 10, 10, 18; 14:24, 31; 15:16, 19, 21, 25; 16:2, 4, 6, 7, 12, 13, 20, 25, 33; 17:9, 15, 20; 18:28, 40; 19:21, 24, 34; 20:7, 27; 21:8, 23; Ac 1:4, 8; 2:16; 4:17, 32; 5:4, 13; 7:39, 48; 9:6; 10:20, 35, 41; 13:25; 15:11, 20; 16:37; 18:9, 21; 19:2, 26, 27; 20:24; 21:13, 24; 26:16, 20, 25, 29; 27:10; Ro 1:21, 32; 2:13, 29, 29; 3:27, 31; 4:2, 4, 10, 12, 13, 16, 20, 24; 5:3, 11, 14, 15; 6:5, 13, 14, 15; 7:7, 13, 15, 17, 19, 20; 8:4, 9, 15, 20, 23, 26, 32, 37; 9:7, 8, 10, 12, 16, 24, 32; 10:2, 8, 16, 18, 19; 11:4, 11, 18, 20; 12:2, 3, 16, 19, 20, 21; 13:3, 5, 14; 14:13, 17, 20; 15:3, 21; 16:4, 18; 1Co 1:17, 27; 2:4, 5, 7, 9, 12, 13; 3:1, 2, 6, 7; 4:3, 4, 14, 15, 19, 20; 5:8; 6:6, 8, 11, 11, 11, 12, 12, 13; 7:4, 4, 7, 10, 19, 21, 35; 8:6, 7; 9:2, 12, 12, 21, 27; 10:5, 13, 20, 23, 23, 24, 29, 33; 11:8, 9, 17; 12:14, 22, 24, 25; 14:2, 17, 19, 20, 22, 22, 33, 34; 15:10, 10, 35, 37, 39, 40, 46, 46; 2Co 1:9, 9, 12, 13, 19, 24; 2:4, 5, 13, 17; 3:3, 3, 5, 6, 14, 15; 4:2, 2, 5, 8, 8, 9, 9, 16, 16, 18; 5:4, 12, 15, 16; 6:4; 7:5, 6, 7, 9, 11, 11, 11, 11, 11, 12, 14; 8:5, 7, 8, 10, 13, 19, 21; 9:12; 10:4, 12, 13, 18; 11:1, 6, 6, 17; 12:14, 14, 16; 13:3, 4, 4, 7, 8; Gal 1:1, 8, 12, 17; 2:3, 7, 14; 3:12, 16, 22; 4:2, 7, 8, 14, 17, 23, 29, 30, 31; 5:6, 13; 6:13, 15; Eph 1:21; 2:19; 4:29; 5:4, 15, 17, 18, 24, 27, 29; 6:4, 6, 12; Php 1:18, 20, 29; 2:3, 4, 7, 12, 17, 27, 27; 3:7, 8, 9; 4:6, 17; Col 2:5; 3:11, 22; 1Th 1:5, 8; 2:2, 4, 4, 7, 8, 13; 4:7, 8; 5:6, 9, 15; 2Th 2:12; 3:8, 9, 11, 15; 1Ti 1:13, 16; 2:10, 12; 3:3; 4:12; 5:1, 13, 23; 6:2, 4, 17; 2Ti 1:7, 8, 9, 12, 17; 2:9, 20, 24; 3:9; 4:3, 8, 16; Tit 1:8, 15; 2:10; 3:5; Phm 1:14, 16; Heb 2:16; 3:13, 16; 4:2; 5:4, 5; 7:16; 9:24; 10:3, 25, 39; 11:13; 12:11, 22, 26; 13:14; Jas 1:25, 26; 2:18; 3:15; 4:11; 1Pe 1:15, 19, 23; 2:16, 18, 20, 25; 3:4, 14, 15, 21; 4:2, 13; 5:2, 2, 3; 2Pe 1:16, 21; 2:4, 5; 3:9, 9; 1Jn 2:2, 7, 16, 19, 19, 21, 27; 3:18; 4:1, 10, 18; 5:6, 18; 2Jn 1:1, 5, 8, 12; 3Jn 1:9, 11, 13; Jude 1:6, 9; Rev 2:4, 6, 9, 9, 14, 20; 3:4, 9; 9:5; 10:7, 9; 17:12; 20:6

899 αὐτός, *autos* [5601 / 5593]

Mt 1:2, 11, 18, 18, 19, 19, 19, 20, 20, 20, 21, 21, 21, 21, 23, 24, 24, 25, 25; 2:2, 2, 3, 4, 5, 7, 8, 8, 9, 11, 11, 11, 11, 12, 13, 13, 13, 14, 16, 18, 20, 21, 22; 3:3, 4, 4, 4, 4, 5, 6, 6, 7, 7, 11, 12, 12, 12, 13, 14, 15, 15, 16ᵁ, 16; 4:3, 5, 5, 6, 8, 9, 9, 10, 11, 11, 11, 16, 18, 19, 20, 21, 21, 21, 21, 22, 22, 24, 24, 25; 5:1, 1, 1, 2, 3, 4, 5, 6, 7, 8, 9, 10, 15, 22, 22, 25, 28, 28, 28, 29, 30, 31, 32, 32, 35, 39, 40, 41, 45, 46, 47; 6:1, 2, 5, 7, 8, 8, 14, 15ᴺ, 16, 16, 26, 26, 27, 29, 33, 34; 7:6, 6, 9, 9, 10, 11, 12, 13, 14, 16, 16, 20, 20, 23, 24, 24, 26, 26, 27, 28, 29; 8:1, 1, 2, 3, 3, 4, 4, 4, 5, 5, 7, 7, 7, 9, 13, 14, 14, 15, 15, 16, 18, 18, 18, 19, 19, 20, 21, 22, 24, 25, 27, 28, 28, 28, 29, 30, 30, 31, 32, 32, 34, 35, 36, 37, 38; 10:1, 1, 1, 2, 4, 5, 6, 7, 7, 10, 11, 11, 12, 12, 13, 13, 14, 14, 15, 16, 17, 17, 18, 20, 21, 21, 23, 23, 24, 24, 24, 25, 25, 35, 36, 36, 37, 37, 37, 37, 38, 43, 43, 44, 44, 44, 44; 13:1, 1, 2, 3, 3, 5, 9, 12, 15, 16, 24, 24, 27, 28, 34, 34, 34; 14:1, 3, 3, 5, 5, 6, 6, 7, 9, 10, 10, 11, 11, 12, 12, 13, 13, 15, 16, 18, 19, 20, 21, 21, 22, 23, 23, 24, 25, 27, 29, 30, 32, 33, 34, 35, 37, 39, 40, 40, 40, 41, 43, 43, 44, 44, 45, 45; 16:1, 6, 6, 7, 7, 8, 10, 11, 12, 14, 14, 14, 15, 18, 19, 20, 21, 22, 22, 22, 23, 23, 24, 28, 34ᵁ, 34, 36, 37, 37, 37, 37, 38, 43, 43, 44, 44, 44; 13:1, 1, 1, 2, 3, 3, 5, 9, 12, 15, 16, 24, 24, 28, 34, 34, 34; 14:1, 3, 3, 5, 5, 6, 6, 7, 9, 10, 11, 11, 12, 12, 13, 13, 15, 16, 18, 19, 20, 21, 21, 22, 23, 23, 24, 25, 27, 29, 30, 32, 33, 34, 35, 37, 39, 40, 40, 40, 41, 43, 44, 46, 46, 46, 47; 48, 49, 49, 50; 13:2, 2, 4, 4, 7, 10, 10, 11ᵁ, 12, 13, 13, 13, 14, 16, 36, 36, 39, 41, 41, 42, 43, 44, 46, 50, 51ᴺ, 51, 52, 52, 54, 54, 54, 54, 55, 55, 56, 57, 57, 57, 58; 14:2, 2, 2, 3, 3, 4, 4, 5, 5, 7, 8, 11, 11, 12, 12, 13, 14, 14, 15, 16, 16, 17, 18, 22, 25, 26, 27, 28, 31, 31, 32, 33, 35, 35, 36, 36; 15:2, 3, 6, 8, 10, 12, 14, 15, 23, 23, 23, 23, 25, 27, 28, 30, 30, 30, 30, 32, 32, 33,

34; 16:1, 1, 2, 4, 4, 6, 13, 15, 17, 18, 20, 21, 21, 22, 22, 24, 24, 25, 25, 25, 25, 26, 26, 27, 27, 27, 28; 17:1, 1, 2, 2, 2, 3, 3, 5, 5, 5, 6, 7, 8, 8, 9, 9, 10, 12, 12, 12, 13, 14, 14, 16, 16, 17, 18, 18, 19, 20, 22, 22, 23, 24, 25, 25, 26, 27, 27, 27; 18:2, 2, 6, 6, 8, 9, 10, 12, 13, 13, 15, 15, 17, 19, 20, 21, 21, 22, 23, 24, 24, 25, 25, 26, 27, 27, 28, 28, 28, 29, 29, 30, 31, 32, 32, 32, 34, 34, 35; 19:2, 2, 3, 3, 3, 4, 5, 7, 7, 8, 9, 10, 10ᵁ, 11, 13, 13, 13, 14, 15, 16, 17, 18, 20, 21, 23, 26, 27, 28, 28; 20:1, 2, 2, 6, 7, 7, 8, 8, 10, 12, 13, 17, 18, 19, 20, 20, 20, 21, 21, 22, 23, 25, 25, 25, 28, 29, 29, 31, 32, 33, 34, 34, 34; 21:2, 2, 3, 3, 6, 7, 7, 9, 10, 13, 13, 14, 14, 16, 16, 17, 19, 19, 19, 21, 23, 23, 24, 25, 27, 27, 31, 32, 32, 32, 33, 33, 33, 34, 34, 35, 36, 37, 37, 38, 38, 39, 41, 41, 41, 41, 42, 43, 44, 45, 45, 46, 46; 22:1, 2, 3, 5, 6, 7, 7, 8, 12, 13, 13, 15, 16, 16, 18, 19, 20, 21, 21, 22, 23, 23, 24, 24, 24, 25, 25, 28, 29, 33, 34, 34, 35, 35, 37, 39, 41, 42, 43, 43, 45, 45, 46, 46; 23:1, 3, 4, 4, 4, 5, 5, 5ᴺ, 15, 18, 20, 20, 21, 21, 22, 26, 30, 34, 34, 37, 37; 24:1, 1, 2, 3, 4, 17, 18, 29, 31, 31, 31, 32, 43, 45, 45, 46, 47, 47, 48, 49, 51, 51; 25:2, 3, 6, 10, 10, 14, 14, 16, 18, 19, 21, 21, 23, 23, 26, 26, 28, 29, 31, 31, 31, 32, 32, 33, 34, 37, 40, 41, 44, 44, 45, 45; 26:1, 7, 7, 10, 13, 15, 15, 16, 18, 19, 21, 22, 24, 24, 25, 26, 27, 27, 27, 28, 31, 33, 34, 35, 36, 36, 38, 39, 40, 42, 43, 43, 44, 44, 45, 45; 2:2, 3, 4, 5, 6, 8, 8, 13, 13, 14, 14, 15, 15, 15, 16, 17, 18, 19, 19, 19, 20, 21, 23, 23, 24, 25, 25, 25, 26, 27; 3:2, 2, 2, 4, 5, 5, 6, 6, 7, 8, 9, 9, 9, 10, 10, 11, 11, 12, 12, 13, 13, 14, 14, 17, 19, 20, 21, 21, 23, 23, 27, 27, 31, 31, 31, 31, 32, 32, 33, 34; 4:1, 1, 2, 2, 2, 4, 7, 10, 10, 12, 13, 15, 15, 17, 19, 21, 24, 25, 27, 30, 32, 33, 34, 35, 36, 36, 38, 38, 40, 41; 5:2, 2, 3, 4, 4, 4, 6, 8, 9, 9, 10, 10, 12, 12, 13, 14, 16, 17, 17, 18, 18, 19, 19, 20, 21, 22, 22, 23, 23, 24, 25, 25, 26, 27; 6:1, 1, 1, 2, 3, 3, 4, 4, 6, 7, 7, 8, 10, 11, 14, 14, 17, 17, 17, 17, 19, 19, 20, 20, 20, 21, 21, 22, 23, 24, 24, 26, 27, 27, 28, 28, 28, 29, 29, 29, 30, 31, 31, 33, 33, 34, 34, 35, 36, 37, 37, 37, 37, 38, 39, 41, 41, 45, 45, 46, 47, 48, 48, 48, 48, 49, 50, 50, 50, 51, 52, 54, 54, 56, 56, 56; 7:1, 2, 5, 6, 6, 9, 12, 14, 15, 15, 17, 17, 18, 18, 19, 25, 25, 25, 26, 26, 27, 28, 29, 30, 32, 32, 33, 33, 34, 35, 36, 36, 36, 8:1, 3, 3, 4, 4, 5, 6, 7, 9, 10, 11, 11, 11, 12, 13, 15, 17, 19, 20, 21, 22, 22, 23, 23, 23, 23, 25, 26, 26, 27, 27, 28, 29, 29, 30, 30, 31, 32, 33, 34, 34, 35, 35, 36, 36, 37, 8:1, 3, 3, 4, 4, 5, 6, 7, 9, 10, 11, 11, 11, 12, 13, 15, 17, 19, 20, 21, 22, 22, 23, 23, 23, 25, 26, 26, 27, 27, 28, 29, 29, 30, 30, 31, 32, 33, 34, 34, 35, 35, 36, 37, 37, 38, 39, 41, 41, 45, 45, 46, 46, 47, 48, 48, 48, 48, 49, 50, 50, 50, 51, 52, 54, 54, 56, 56, 56; 9:1, 2, 2, 3, 4, 7, 7, 9, 11, 12, 13, 15, 16, 16, 17, 18, 18, 18, 19, 19, 20, 20, 20, 21, 21, 22, 22, 23, 25, 25, 25, 27, 27, 28, 28, 28, 29, 31, 31, 31, 32, 33, 35, 36, 36, 36, 36, 38, 38, 39, 41, 42, 42, 43, 45, 47, 48, 50; 10:1, 1, 2, 3, 5, 6, 7, 7, 10, 11, 11, 11, 12, 12, 13, 13, 14, 14, 15, 16, 16, 17, 17, 17, 18, 20, 21, 21, 21, 23, 24, 24, 24, 25, 25, 26, 27, 28, 34, 34, 35, 35, 36, 37, 37, 38, 43, 43, 44, 44, 44; 13:1, 1, 2, 3, 3, 5, 9, 12, 15, 16, 24, 24, 28, 34, 34, 34; 14:1, 3, 3, 5, 5, 6, 6, 7, 9, 10, 11, 11, 12, 12, 13, 13, 15, 16, 18, 19, 20, 21, 21, 22, 23, 23, 24, 25, 27, 29, 30, 32, 33, 34, 35, 37, 39, 41, 41, 41, 43, 44, 46, 46; 16:1, 6, 6, 7, 7, 8, 10, 11, 12, 14, 14, 14, 15, 18, 19, 20, 21, 22, 22, 22, 23, 23, 24, 28, 34ᵁ, 34, 36, 37, 37, 37, 37, 38, 43, 43, 44, 44, 44; Lk 1:5, 5, 7, 7, 8, 8, 11, 12, 13, 13, 14, 15, 16, 17, 17, 18, 19, 20, 21, 22, 22, 23, 23, 24, 28, 30, 31, 32, 32, 33, 35, 36, 36, 38, 41, 45, 48, 49, 50, 50, 51, 54, 55, 56, 57, 58, 59, 61, 61, 63, 64, 64, 65, 65, 65, 65, 67, 69, 69, 70, 72; 15:2, 2, 3, 4, 6, 8, 9, 10, 11, 12, 13, 14, 14, 15, 16, 17, 18, 19, 19, 20, 20, 20, 20, 20, 21, 22, 23, 24, 24, 25, 26, 27, 29, 29, 32, 32, 36, 36, 39, 41, 41, 41, 43, 44, 46, 46; 16:1, 6, 6, 7, 7, 8, 10, 11, 12, 14, 14, 14, 15, 18, 19, 20, 21, 22, 22, 22, 23, 23, 24, 28, 34ᵁ, 34, 36, 37, 37, 37, 37, 38, 43, 43, 44, 44, 44; 2:4, 5, 6, 6, 7, 7, 7, 8, 8, 9, 9, 10, 15, 17, 18, 19, 20, 21, 21, 21, 22, 22, 25, 26, 27, 27, 28, 28,

33, 33, 34, 34, 35, 36, 37, 38, 38, 40, 40, 41, 42, 43, 43, 44, 44, 45, 46, 46, 46, 47, 47, 48, 48, 48, 49, 50, 50, 51, 51, 51, 51; **3:**1, 4, 7, 10, 11, 12, 13, 14, 14, 15, 15, 16, 16, 17, 17, 17, 19, 19, 22, 23; **4:**2, 3, 4, 5, 5, 6, 6, 6, 8, 8, 9, 9, 10, 12, 13, 14, 14, 15, 15, 16, 16, 17, 17, 17, 22, 22, 23, 24, 26, 27, 29, 29, 29, 29, 30, 30, 31, 32, 32, 35, 35, 35, 35, 35, 37, 38, 38, 39, 39, 39, 40, 40, 40, 40, 41, 41, 42, 42, 42, 42, 43; **5:**1, 1, 2, 3, 6, 7, 7, 9, 9, 9, 11, 12, 12, 13, 13, 14, 14, 14, 15, 15, 16, 16, 17, 17, 18, 18, 18, 19, 19, 20, 22, 25, 25, 25, 27, 28, 29, 29, 29, 29, 30, 30, 31, 33, 34, 34, 35, 36, 37; **6:**1, 1, 3, 3, 3, 3, 4, 5, 6, 6, 7, 7, 8, 8, 9, 10, 10, 11, 12, 13, 13, 14, 17, 17, 18, 18, 19, 19, 20, 20, 20, 23, 23, 26, 26, 31, 32, 33, 35, 39, 40, 42, 45^N, 45, 47, 48, 48; **7:**1, 2, 3, 3, 3, 4, 5, 6, 6, 6, 9, 9, 11, 11, 12, 12, 12, 13, 13, 13, 15, 15, 16, 17, 18, 20, 22, 28, 30, 35, 36, 36, 38, 38, 38, 38, 39, 39, 40, 42, 42, 42, 43, 44, 47, 48; **8:**1, 1, 3, 3, 4, 5, 5, 5, 7, 9, 9, 12, 16, 18, 18, 19, 19, 19, 20, 21, 22, 22, 23, 24, 25, 25, 27, 28, 29, 30, 30, 31, 31, 32, 32, 32, 36, 37, 37, 37, 38, 38, 38, 39, 40, 40, 41, 41, 42, 42, 42, 42, 44, 44, 47, 47, 48, 49, 50, 51, 52, 53, 54, 54, 55, 55, 56, 56; **9:**1, 2, 3, 5, 9, 10, 10, 11, 11, 11, 12, 13, 13, 14, 14, 16, 17, 18, 18, 18, 20, 21, 23, 24, 24, 24, 26, 27, 29, 29, 29, 31, 31, 32, 32, 32, 33, 33, 34, 34, 34, 35, 36, 37, 37, 39, 39, 39, 39, 40, 42, 42, 42, 42, 43, 45, 45, 45, 46, 46, 47, 47, 48, 48, 53, 58; **13:**1, 1, 1, 2, 4, 4, 6, 6, 7, 8, 8, 8, 9, 12, 12, 13, 14, 15, 15, 17, 17, 17, 18, 19, 23, 23, 31, 31, 32, 34; **14:**1, 1, 1, 2, 4, 5, 7, 8, 9, 12, 12, 15, 16, 17, 18, 18, 19, 21, 21, 25, 25, 29, 29, 31, 32, 35; **15:**1, 1, 2, 3, 4, 4, 5, 6, 12, 12, 13, 14, 14, 15, 15, 16^N, 16, 18, 20, 20, 20, 20, 21, 22, 22, 22, 25, 27, 27, 28, 28, 29, 30, 31; **16:**1, 1, 2, 2, 4, 6, 7, 14, 15, 16, 18, 20, 21, 22, 23, 23, 24, 24, 27, 28, 28, 29, 30, 31; **17:**1, 2, 2, 3, 3, 4, 7, 8, 11, 12, 12, 13, 14, 14, 14, 15, 16, 16, 16, 19, 20, 24, 25, 30, 31, 31, 33, 33, 33, 35, 37, 37; **18:**1, 1, 3, 5, 5, 7, 7, 7, 8, 13, 14, 15, 15, 16, 16, 17, 18, 19, 22, 24, 29, 31, 31, 33, 33, 33, 35; **19:**2, 2, 4, 5, 6, 9, 9, 11, 11, 11, 13, 13, 14, 14, 14, 15, 15, 17, 22, 23, 24, 25, 27, 27, 30, 31, 32, 32, 33, 33, 33, 34, 34, 35, 35, 36, 36, 37, 39, 41, 46, 46, 47, 48; **20:**1, 2, 3, 5, 8, 9, 10, 10, 14, 14, 15, 15, 17, 18, 19, 19, 19, 20, 20, 21, 23, 23, 25, 26, 26, 27, 28, 29, 30, 31, 31, 33, 33, 33, 35, 37; **21:**1, 4, 4, 7, 8, 10, 12, 20, 21, 21, 29, 38, 38; **22:**2, 4, 4, 5, 6, 6, 9, 10, 10, 13, 14, 16, 19, 23, 23, 24, 24, 25, 25, 33, 35, 36, 36, 38, 39, 40, 41, 41, 43, 43, 44, 44, 45, 46, 47, 47, 47, 48, 49, 50, 50, 51, 52, 54, 55, 56, 56, 56, 57, 58, 58, 59, 60, 61, 63, 63, 64, 65, 66, 66, 67, 70, 71, 71; **23:**1, 1, 2, 3, 3, 7, 7, 8, 8, 8, 9, 9, 9, 10, 11, 11, 11, 12, 12, 14, 14, 15, 16, 20, 21, 22, 22, 23, 23, 24, 25, 26, 26, 27, 27, 28, 32, 33, 34, 34, 36, 36, 38, 39, 40, 40, 43, 49, 49, 51, 53, 53, 55, 55; **24:**4, 4, 5, 5, 8, 10, 11, 11, 13, 13, 14, 15, 15, 15, 16, 16, 17, 18^N, 18, 18, 19, 19, 20, 21, 22, 23, 23, 24, 25, 25, 26, 27, 28, 29, 29, 30, 30, 31, 31, 31, 31, 33, 33, 33, 35, 35, 36, 36, 36, 38, 39, 40, 41, 41, 42, 42, 44, 45, 46, 47, 50, 50, 50, 51, 51, 51, 52, 52; **Jn 1:**3, 3, 4, 5, 6, 7, 10, 10, 11, 12, 12, 12, 14, 15, 16, 19^U, 19, 21, 22, 25, 25, 26, 27, 29, 31, 32, 33, 33, 35, 37, 38, 38, 38, 39, 39, 40, 41, 42, 42, 43, 45, 45, 46, 46, 47, 47, 48, 48, 49, 50, 51; **2:**2, 3, 4, 5, 7, 7, 8, 10, 11, 11, 11, 12, 12, 12, 17, 18, 19, 19, 20, 23, 23, 24, 24, 24, 25; **3:**1, 2, 2, 2, 3, 4, 4, 8, 9, 10, 15, 16, 17, 18, 19, 20, 21, 22, 22, 26, 26, 27, 28, 29, 29, 30, 30, 31, 32, 32, 35, 38, 39, 43; **4:**4, 4, 4, 4, 5, 5, 5, 6, 6, 6, 7, 7, 11, 13, 14, 14, 18, 23, 25, 26, 27, 28, 29, 29, 30, 30, 30, 31, 33, 34, 34, 38, 39, 40, 41, 44, 45, 47, 47, 47, 48, 48, 49, 50, 50, 51, 51, 51, 52, 52, 53, 53, 54, 56, 60, 60, 61, 61, 64, 65, 66, 66, 68, 70, 71; **7:**1, 3, 3, 4, 5, 5, 6, 7, 7, 9, 10, 10, 11, 12, 13, 16, 17, 18, 18, 21, 26, 29, 29, 30, 30, 31, 32, 32, 35, 38, 39, 43, 44, 44, 44, 44, 45, 45, 46, 46, 47, 48, 50, 50, 50, 51, 52, 53, 53; **8:**2, 2, 3, 4, 6, 6, 9, 10, 12, 13, 14, 19, 20, 20, 21, 23, 28^U, 29, 30, 30, 31, 33, 33, 34, 38, 39, 39, 41, 44, 44, 48, 52, 55, 55, 55, 55, 57, 58, 59; **9:**2, 2, 3, 3, 6, 7, 7, 8, 9, 11, 11, 11, 12, 12, 12, 16, 16, 17, 18, 19, 20, 23, 24, 25, 27, 28, 29, 30, 31, 31, 32, 32, 33; **34:**35, 36, 37, 37, 37, 40, 40, 41, 41, 42, 47, 48, 48, 48, 49, 50; **13:**1, 1, 2, 3, 6, 7, 8, 9, 10, 11, 12, 12, 12, 16, 16, 16, 17, 18, 23, 25, 26, 27, 28, 29, 31, 32, 32, 32, 32, 36, 36^U; **14:**5, 6, 7, 7, 8, 9, 16, 17, 17, 21, 21, 21, 22, 23, 23, 23, 23, 23; **15:**2, 2, 5, 6, 6, **Ac 1:**3, 3, 4, 6, 7, 9, 9, 9, 9, 10, 10, 11, 14, 15, 18, 19, 20, 20, 22, 26; **2:**1, 3, 3, 4, 6, 11, 14, 14, 22, 22, 24, 24, 25, 29, 30, 30, 30, 31, 34, 36, 38, 40, 41, 44, 45, 47; **3:**2, 4, 4, 5, 7, 7, 8, 9, 10, 10, 10, 11, 12, 12, 12, 16, 16, 16, 18, 18, 21, 23, 24, 25, 26; **4:**1, 1, 2, 2, 5, 7, 7, 8, 13, 14, 15, 16, 17, 18, 19, 21, 21, 23, 24, 25, 26, 27, 27, 31, 32, 32, 33, 35, 36, 37, 37, 38, 39, 40; **5:**1, 6, 7, 8, 9, 10, 10, 10, 13, 13, 15; **6:**1, 1, 11, 12, 14, 15, 15; **7:**2, 3, 4, 4, 5, 5, 5, 5, 5, 5, 6^N, 6, 8, 8, 9, 10, 10, 10, 10, 13, 14,

15, 19, 21, 21, 21, 22, 23, 23, 23, 25, 25, 25, 26, 26, 27, 30, 31, 33, 34, 34, 35, 36, 38, 39, 40, 41, 42, 43, 44, 47, 54, 54, 57, 57, 58, 60; **8:**1, 2, 5, 6, 11, 11, 13, 14, 15, 16, 17, 18, 20, 27, 28, 30, 31, 32, 32, 33, 33, 33, 35, 35, 38, 39, 39, 40; **9:**2, 3, 3, 4, 7, 8, 8, 10, 11, 12, 15, 16, 16, 17, 18, 21, 23, 24, 24, 25, 25, 26, 27, 27, 27, 28, 29, 30, 30, 34, 35, 37, 37, 38, 38, 39, 39, 40, 41, 41, 41; **10:**2, 3, 3, 4, 4, 7, 7, 8, 8, 10, 10, 13, 15, 19, 20, 20, 22, 23, 23, 23, 24, 24, 25, 26, 26, 27, 28, 35, 35, 38, 38, 40, 41, 41, 43, 43, 46, 46, 48; **11:**2, 3, 4, 12, 13, 15, 17, 20, 21, 22, 26, 28, 29; **12:**4, 4, 5, 6, 7, 7, 8, 8, 8, 10, 10, 11, 13, 15, 15, 17, 17, 19, 20, 21, 23; **13:**2, 3, 4, 8, 8, 9, 11, 13, 14, 15, 17, 17, 19, 21, 22, 22, 24, 27, 28, 29, 30, 31, 31, 33, 34, 36, 42, 42, 43, 43, 46, 50, 50, 51; **14:**1, 1, 3, 3, 5, 8, 9, 11, 12, 14, 15, 16, 17, 18, 19, 20, 23, 23, 27; **15:**2, 2, 4, 5, 7, 8, 8^N, 9, 12, 13, 14, 16, 16, 17, 20, 21, 22, 22, 23, 26, 27, 27, 32, 33, 38, 38, 38, 39; **16:**3, 3, 3, 4, 7, 9, 10, 15, 16, 18, 18, 19, 20, 22, 22, 23, 23, 24, 24, 25, 30, 32, 32, 33, 33, 33, 34, 37, 37, 39; **17:**2, 2, 4, 5, 6, 9, 12, 15, 16, 16, 16, 18, 19, 24, 25, 26, 27, 28, 31, 33, 34, 34; **18:**2, 2, 3, 6, 6, 8, 11, 12, 13, 14, 15, 16, 17, 18, 19, 19, 20, 26, 26, 27, 27, 28, 35, 35, 38, 38, 40, 41, 41, 41; **10:**2, 3, 3, 4, 4, 7, 7, 8, 8, 8, 10, 13, 15, 19, 20, 21, 22, 30, 30, 32, 34, 35, 36, 36, 37, 38, 38; **20:**2, 3, 3, 4, 7, 10, 13, 14, 16, 16, 18, 18, 22, 30, 30, 32, 34, 35, 36, 36, 37, 38, 38; **21:**1, 3, 4, 7, 8, 12, 14, 19, 19, 20, 21, 24, 24, 24, 25, 26, 26, 26, 27, 27, 29, 30, 31, 32, 33, 34, 34, 35, 36, 40; **22:**2, 2, 3, 7, 9, 10, 10, 11, 13, 14, 15, 17, 18, 19, 22, 24; **23:**2, 3, 7, 13, 14, 14, 15, 15, 16, 16, 17; **7:**7, 11, 13, 14, 15, 15; **8:**2, 2, 2, 16, 18, 19, 22, 24; **9:**9, 13, 14, 15; **10:**1, 7, 12; **11:**3, 14, 15, 15, 33; **12:**13, 17, 18, 18; **13:**4, 4, 11; **Gal 1:**1, 12, 13, 15, 16, 16, 18; **2:**2, 9, 10, 11, 13, 13, 17; **3:**6, 10, 12, 12, 16; **4:**4, 6, 17, 25, 30; **6:**13, 16; **Eph 1:**4, 4, 5, 5, 6, 7, 7, 9, 9, 9, 9, 10, 11, 12, 14, 17, 18, 18, 19, 19, 20, 20, 22, 22, 23; **2:**4, 7, 10, 10, 14, 15, 15^U, 16, 18, 20; **3:**5, 7, 12, 16, 16, 21; **4:**10, 11, 15, 17, 18, 18, 21, 21, 25; **5:**7, 12, 23, 25, 26, 27, 29, 30, 31; **6:**4, 9, 9, 9, 9, 9, 10, 18, 20, 22; **Php 1:**6, 28, 29, 29, 30; **2:**2, 2, 9, 9, 18, 22, 24, 27, 27, 28, 28, 29; **3:**1, 9, 10, 10, 10, 16, 19, 21, 21, 21; **4:**2, 3, 19; **Col 1:**9, 11, 13, 16, 16, 16, 17, 17, 18, 18, 19, 20, 20, 20^U, 22, 22, 24, 26, 29; **2:**2, 6, 7, 9, 10, 12, 12, 13, 14, 14, 15, 18; **3:**4, 9, 10, 17, 19; **4:**2, 4, 8, 10, 13, 15, 17; **1Th 1:**9, 10; **2:**1, 14, 14, 16, 19, 19; **3:**3, 11, 13; **4:**6, 8, 9, 10, 14, 16, 17; **5:**2, 3, 10, 13, 13, 23; **2Th 1:**4, 7, 9, 10, 12; **2:**1, 4, 6, 8, 8, 10, 11, 11, 16; **3:**7, 14, 16; **1Ti 1:**8, 16, 18; **4:**16; **5:**16, 18; **2Ti 1:**8, 18; **2:**10, 17, 19, 25, 26; **3:**5, 9; **4:**1, 1, 8, 14, 14, 16, 18; **Tit 1:**3, 12, 12, 13, 15; **3:**1, 5, 13; **Phm 1:**12, 15, 17; **Heb 1:**3, 3, 4, 5, 5, 6, 7, 7, 11, 12, 12; **2:**4, 6, 6, 7, 7, 8, 8, 8, 8, 10, 10, 11, 13, 14, 14, 18; **3:**2, 2, 3, 5, 6, 7, 10, 10, 10, 11, 11, 11, 12, 12; **4:**1, 4, 6, 7, 8, 8, 10, 10, 10, 11, 13, 13; **5:**2, 3, 3, 5, 7, 7, 9; **6:**7, 10, 11, 14, 16, 17; **7:**1, 5, 6, 10, 11, 18, 21, 24, 25, 25; **8:**8, 9, 9, 9, 9, 10, 10, 10, 10, 11, 11, 11, 12, 12; **9:**5, 19, 23, 24, 26, 26, 28; **10:**1, 3, 11, 13, 16, 16, 16, 16, 17, 17, 20, 30, 38; **11:**4, 4, 5, 6, 7, 9, 11, 13, 16, 16, 16, 19, 21, 22, 23, 28, 35; **12:**2, 5, 10, 10, 11, 15, 17, 19; **13:**3, 5, 8, 13, 15, 15, 17, 21, 21; **Jas 1:**5, 8, 9, 10, 11, 11, 12, 13, 18, 23, 25, 26, 26, 27; **2:**5, 6, 7, 14, 16, 16, 21, 22, 23; **3:**3, 3, 3, 9, 9, 10, 11, 13; **4:**11, 17; **5:**3, 7, 14, 14, 15, 15, 18, 19, 20, 20; **1Pe 1:**3, 11, 12, 15, 21, 21, 21, 24; **2:**2, 5, 6, 9, 14, 21, 22, 24, 24; **3:**6, 11, 12, 12, 14, 22; **4:**1, 4, 10, 13, 19; **5:**7, 7, 9, 10, 10, 11; **2Pe 1:**3, 5, 9, 17, 18; **2:**1, 2, 3, 8, 11, 12, 13, 19, 19, 20, 21, 21, 22; **3:**3, 4, 5, 7, 10, 13, 14, 15, 16, 16, 18; **1Jn 1:**3, 5, 5, 6, 7, 7, 10, 10; **2:**2, 3, 3, 4, 4, 5, 5, 6, 6, 8, 9, 10, 10, 11, 11, 12, 15, 17, 21, 25, 27, 27, 27, 28, 28, 28, 29; **3:**1, 2, 2, 3, 5, 6, 6, 9, 9, 10, 12, 12, 12, 12, 15, 15, 16, 17, 17, 17, 17, 19, 22, 22, 23, 23, 24, 24, 24, 24; **4:**4, 5, 5, 9, 9, 10, 10, 12, 13, 13, 13, 15, 15, 16, 16, 18, 20, 20, 21, 21; **5:**1, 2, 3, 3, 9, 10, 10, 11, 14, 14, 15, 16, 16, 18, 18, 20, 20; **2Jn 1:**1, 6, 6, 10, 10, 11, 11; **3Jn 1:**9, 10, 10, 12; **Jude 1:**7, 11, 14, 15, 15, 16, 24; **Rev 1:**1, 1, 1, 3, 4, 5, 6, 6, 7, 7, 7, 14, 14, 15, 15, 16, 16, 16, 17, 17, 17, 18, 18, 21, 21, 22, 22, 23, 26, 27, 28; **3:**4, 5, 5, 8, 9, 12, 12, 20, 20, 20, 21, 21; **4:**4, 8, 10; **5:**2, 3, 4, 5, 9, 10, 11, 13; **6:**2, 2, 4, 4, 4, 5, 5, 8, 8, 8, 11, 11, 11, 11, 11, 14, 17; **7:**2, 3, 9, 9, 11, 14, 14, 14, 15, 15, 15, 16, 17, 17; **8:**2, 3, 5, 6, 12, 12; **9:**1, 3, 4, 5, 5, 5, 6, 6, 7, 7, 8, 9, 10, 10, 11, 11, 16, 16, 17, 17, 18, 19, 19, 19, 20, 21, 21, 21; **10:**1, 1, 1, 2, 2, 4, 5, 6, 6, 9, 9, 9, 10, 10; **11:**1, 2, 5, 5, 5, 5, 6, 6, 7, 7, 7, 8, 8, 9, 9, 10, 11, 11, 12, 12, 12, 15, 16, 16, 16, 19, 19; **12:**1, 3, 4, 4, 4, 4, 5, 6, 7, 7, 8, 9, 9, 10, 10, 11, 11, 11, 12, 14, 15, 15, 16, 16, 16, 17, 17; **13:**1, 1, 2, 2, 2, 2, 2, 3, 3, 4, 5, 5, 6, 6, 6, 7, 7, 7, 8, 8, 10, 12, 12, 12, 14, 16, 16, 17; **14:**1, 1, 1, 1, 2, 5, 7, 7, 8, 9, 9, 9, 9, 10, 10, 11, 11, 11, 11, 13, 13, 13, 14, 14, 16, 17, 18, 19; **15:**1, 2, 2, 8; **16:**2, 2, 3, 4, 6, 8, 8, 9, 10, 10, 10, 11, 11, 11, 12, 12, 14, 15, 16, 17, 19, 19, 21; **17:**2, 4, 4, 5, 6, 7, 9, 10, 11, 13, 14, 14, 16, 16, 16, 17, 17, 17, 18; **18:**1, 3, 3, 3, 4, 4, 4, 4, 5, 6, 6, 6, 6, 7, 7, 7, 8, 8, 9, 9, 10, 11, 11, 14, 14, 15, 18, 19, 19, 20, 24; **19:**2, 2, 2, 3, 5, 5, 7, 7, 8, 10, 10, 11, 12, 12, 13, 14, 15, 15, 15, 16, 18, 19, 20, 20, 20, 21; **20:**1, 2, 3, 3, 3, 4, 4, 4, 6, 7, 8, 8, 9, 10, 11, 11, 12, 13, 13; **21:**2, 3, 3, 3, 3, 3, 4, 7, 7, 8, 11, 14, 15, 15, 16, 16, 17, 18,

22, 22, 23, 23, 23, 24, 24, 24, 25, 26, 27; 22:2, 2, 3, 3, 3, 4, 4, 4, 5, 6, 6, 12, 14, 14, 18, 18, 19

1142 γάρ, gar [1041 / 1040]

Mt 1:20, 21; 2:2, 5, 6, 13, 20; 3:2, 3, 9, 15; 4:6, 10, 17, 18; 5:12, 18, 20, 29, 30, 46; 6:7, 8, 14, 16, 21, 24, 32, 32, 34; 7:2, 8, 12, 25, 29; 8:9; 9:5, 13, 16, 21, 24; 10:10, 17, 19, 20, 23, 26, 35; 11:13, 18, 30; 12:8, 33, 34, 37, 40, 50; 13:12, 15, 17; 14:3, 4, 24; 15:2, 4, 19, 27; 16:2, 3, 25, 26, 27; 17:15, 20; 18:7, 10, 20; 19:12, 14, 22; 20:1; 21:26, 32; 22:14, 16, 28, 30; 23:3, 5, 8, 9, 13, 17, 19, 39; 24:5, 6, 7, 21, 24, 27, 37, 38; 25:3, 14, 29, 35, 42; 26:9, 10, 11, 12, 28, 31, 43, 52, 73; 27:18, 19, 23, 43; 28:2, 5, 6; Mk 1:16, 22, 38; 2:15; 3:10, 21, 35; 4:22, 25; 5:8, 28, 42; 6:14, 17, 18, 20, 31, 48, 50, 52; 7:3, 10, 21, 27, 28[N]; 8:35, 36, 37, 38; 9:6, 6, 31, 34, 39, 40, 41, 49; 10:14, 22, 27, 45; 11:13, 18, 18, 32; 12:12, 14, 23, 25, 44; 13:8, 11, 19, 22, 33, 35; 14:2, 5, 7, 40, 56, 70; 15:10, 14; 16:4, 8, 8; Lk 1:15, 18, 30, 44, 48, 66, 76; 2:10; 3:8; 4:10; 5:9, 39; 6:23, 23, 26, 32, 33[U], 38, 43, 44, 44, 45; 7:5, 6, 8, 33; 8:17, 18, 29, 29, 40, 46, 52; 9:14, 24, 25, 26, 44, 48, 50; 10:7, 24, 42; 11:4, 10, 30; 12:12, 23, 30, 34, 52, 58; 14:14, 24, 28; 16:2, 13, 28; 17:21, 24; 18:16, 23, 25, 32; 19:5, 10, 21, 48; 20:6, 19, 33, 36, 36, 38, 40, 42; 21:4, 8, 9, 15, 23, 26, 35; 22:2, 16, 18, 27, 37, 37, 59, 71; 23:8, 12, 15, 22, 34, 41; Jn 2:25; 3:2, 16, 17, 19, 20, 24, 34, 34; 4:8, 9, 18, 23, 37, 42, 44, 45, 47; 5:13, 19, 20, 21, 22, 26, 36, 46, 46; 6:6, 27, 33, 40, 55, 64, 71; 7:1, 4, 5, 39, 41; 8:24, 42, 42; 9:22, 30; 11:39; 12:8, 43, 47; 13:11, 13, 15, 29; 14:30; 16:7, 13, 27; 18:13; 19:6, 31, 36; 20:9, 17; 21:7, 8; Ac 1:20; 2:15, 15, 25, 34, 39; 4:3, 12, 16, 20, 22, 27, 34, 34; 5:26, 36; 6:14; 7:33, 40; 8:7, 16, 21, 23, 31, 39; 9:11, 16; 10:46; 13:8, 27, 36, 47; 15:21, 28; 16:3, 28, 37; 17:20, 23, 28, 28; 18:3, 18, 28; 19:24, 32, 35, 37, 40; 20:10, 13, 16, 16, 27; 21:3, 13, 29, 36; 22:22, 26; 23:5, 8, 11, 17, 21; 24:5; 25:27; 26:16, 26, 26, 26; 27:22, 23, 25, 34, 34; 28:2, 20, 22, 27; Ro 1:9, 11, 16, 16, 17, 18, 19, 20, 26; 2:1, 1, 11, 12, 13, 14, 24, 25, 28; 3:2, 3, 9, 20, 22, 23, 28; 4:2, 3, 9, 13, 14, 15; 5:6, 7, 7, 10, 13, 15, 16, 17, 19; 6:5, 7, 10, 14, 14, 19, 20, 21, 23; 7:1, 2, 5, 7, 8, 11, 14, 15, 15, 18, 18, 19, 22; 8:2, 3, 5, 6, 7, 7, 13, 14, 15, 18, 19, 20, 22, 24, 24, 26, 38; 9:3, 6, 9, 11, 15, 17, 19, 28; 10:2, 3, 4, 5, 10, 11, 12, 12, 13, 16; 11:1, 15, 21, 23, 24, 25, 29, 30, 32, 34; 12:3, 4, 19, 20; 13:1, 3, 4, 4, 4, 6, 6, 8, 9, 11; 14:3, 4, 5[U], 6, 7, 8, 9, 10, 11, 15, 17, 18; 15:3, 4, 8, 18, 24, 26, 27, 27; 16:2, 18, 19; 1Co 1:11, 17, 18, 19, 21, 26; 2:2, 8, 10, 11, 14, 16; 3:2, 3, 3, 4, 9, 11, 13, 17, 19, 19, 21; 4:4, 7, 9, 15, 15, 20; 5:3, 7, 12; 6:16, 20; 7:9, 14, 16, 22, 31; 8:5, 10, 11; 9:2, 9, 10, 15, 16, 16, 16, 17, 19; 10:1, 4, 5, 17, 26, 29; 11:5, 6, 7, 8, 9, 12, 18, 19, 21, 22, 23, 26, 29; 12:8, 12, 13, 14; 13:9, 12; 14:2, 2, 8, 9, 14, 17, 31, 33, 34, 35; 15:3, 9, 16, 21, 22, 25, 27, 32, 34, 41, 52, 53; 16:5, 7, 7, 9, 10, 11, 18; 2Co 1:8, 12, 13, 19, 20, 24; 2:1, 2, 4, 9, 10, 11, 17; 3:6, 9, 10, 11, 14; 4:5, 11, 15, 17, 18; 5:1, 2, 4, 7, 10, 13, 14; 6:2, 14, 16; 7:3, 5, 8, 9, 10, 11; 8:9, 10, 12, 13, 21; 9:1, 2, 7; 10:3, 4, 8, 12, 14, 14, 18; 11:2, 2, 4, 5, 9, 13, 14, 19, 20; 12:6, 6, 9, 10, 11, 11, 13, 14, 14, 20; 13:4, 4, 8, 9; Gal 1:10, 11, 12, 13; 2:6, 8, 12, 18, 19, 21; 3:10, 10, 18, 21, 26, 27, 28; 4:15, 22, 24, 25, 27, 30; 5:5, 6, 13, 14, 17, 17; 6:3, 5, 7, 9, 13, 15, 17; Eph 2:8, 10, 14; 5:5, 6, 8, 9, 12, 14, 29; 6:1; Php 1:8, 18, 19, 21, 23; 2:13, 20, 21, 27; 3:3, 18, 20; 4:11; Col 2:1, 5; 3:3, 20, 25; 4:13; 1Th 1:8, 9; 2:1, 3, 5, 9, 14, 19, 20; 3:3, 4, 9; 4:2, 3, 7, 9, 10, 14, 15; 5:2, 5, 7, 18; 2Th 2:7; 3:2, 7, 10, 11; 1Ti 2:5, 13; 3:13; 4:5, 8, 10, 16; 5:4, 11, 15, 18; 6:7, 10; 2Ti 1:7, 12; 2:7, 11, 13, 16; 3:2, 6, 9; 4:3, 6, 10, 11, 15; Tit 1:7, 10; 2:11; 3:3, 9, 12; Phm 1:7, 15, 22; Heb 1:5; 2:2, 5, 8, 10, 11, 16, 18; 3:3, 4, 14, 16; 4:2, 3, 4, 8, 10, 12, 15; 5:1, 12, 13, 13; 6:4, 7, 10, 13, 16; 7:1, 10, 11, 12, 13, 14, 17, 18, 19, 20, 26, 27, 28; 8:3, 5, 7, 8; 9:2, 13, 16, 17, 19, 24; 10:1, 4, 14, 15, 23, 26, 30, 34, 36, 37; 11:2, 5, 6, 10, 14, 16, 26, 27, 32; 12:3, 6, 7, 10, 17, 17, 18, 20, 25, 29; 13:2, 4, 5, 9, 11, 14, 16, 17, 17, 18, 22; Jas 1:6, 7, 11, 13, 20, 24; 2:2, 10, 11, 13, 26; 3:2, 7, 16; 4:14; 1Pe 2:19, 20, 21, 25; 3:5, 10, 17; 4:3, 6, 15; 2Pe 1:8, 9, 10, 11, 16, 17, 21; 2:4, 8, 18, 19, 20, 21; 3:4, 5; 1Jn 2:19; 4:20; 5:3; 2Jn 1:11; 3Jn 1:3, 7; Jude 1:4; Rev 1:3; 3:2; 9:19, 19; 13:18; 14:4, 13; 16:14; 17:17; 19:8, 10; 21:1, 22, 23, 25; 22:10

1254 δέ, de [2792 / 2789]

Mt 1:2, 2, 3, 3, 3, 4, 4, 4, 5, 5, 5, 6, 6, 7, 7, 7, 8, 8, 8, 9, 9, 9, 10, 10, 10, 11, 12, 12, 13, 13, 13, 14, 14, 14, 15, 15, 15, 16, 18, 19, 20, 21, 22, 24; 2:1, 3, 5, 8, 9, 10, 13, 14, 19, 21, 22, 22; 3:1, 4, 4, 7, 10, 11, 12, 14, 15, 16; 4:4, 12, 18, 20, 22; 5:1, 13, 19, 21, 22, 22, 22, 28, 29, 31, 32, 33, 34, 37, 37, 39, 44; 6:1[U], 1, 3, 6, 7, 15, 16, 17, 20, 23, 27, 29, 30, 33; 7:3, 3, 14[N], 15, 17; 8:1, 5, 10, 11, 12, 16, 18, 20, 21, 22, 24, 27, 30, 31, 32, 33; 9:6, 8, 12, 13, 14, 15, 16, 17, 22, 25, 28, 31, 32, 34, 36, 37; 10:2, 6, 7, 11, 12, 13, 17, 18, 19, 21, 22, 23, 28, 28, 30, 33; 11:2, 7, 11, 12, 16; 12:1, 2, 3, 6, 7, 11, 14, 15, 24, 25, 28, 31, 32, 36, 39, 43, 47, 48; 13:5, 6, 7, 8, 8, 8, 11, 11, 12, 16, 20, 21, 21, 22, 23, 23, 23, 25, 26, 27, 28, 28, 29, 30, 32, 37, 38, 38, 38, 39, 39, 39, 46, 48, 52, 57; 14:6, 8, 13, 15, 16, 17, 18, 19, 21, 23, 24, 25, 26, 27, 28, 29, 30, 31, 33; 15:3, 5, 8, 9, 13, 14, 15, 16, 18, 20, 23, 24, 25, 26, 27, 32, 34, 36, 38; 16:2, 3, 6, 7, 8, 11, 13, 14, 14, 14, 15, 16, 17, 18, 23, 25, 26; 17:2, 4, 8, 11, 12, 17, 20, 22, 24, 26, 27; 18:6, 8, 15, 16, 17, 17, 24, 25, 27, 28, 30; 19:4, 8, 9, 11, 13, 14, 17, 17, 18, 22, 23, 24, 25, 26, 26, 28, 30; 20:2, 5, 5[U], 6, 8, 11, 13, 14, 21, 22, 23, 25, 31, 31, 34; 21:3, 4, 6, 8, 8, 9, 11, 13, 15, 16, 18, 21, 24, 25, 26, 28, 29, 29, 30, 30, 32, 32, 34, 35, 35, 37, 38, 44; 22:5, 5, 6, 7, 8, 11, 12, 14, 18, 19, 25, 27, 29, 31, 34, 37, 39, 41; 23:3, 4, 4, 5, 6, 8, 8, 11, 12, 13, 16, 18, 23[U], 24, 25, 27, 28; 24:2, 3, 6, 8, 13, 19, 20, 22, 29, 32, 35, 36, 43, 48, 49; 25:2, 4, 5, 6, 8, 9, 10, 11, 12, 15, 15, 18, 19, 22, 24, 26, 29, 31, 33, 38, 39, 46; 26:5, 6, 8, 10, 11, 15, 17, 18, 20, 23, 24, 25, 26, 29, 32, 33, 41, 48, 50, 56, 57, 58, 59, 60, 63, 66, 67, 69, 70, 71, 73; 27:1, 4, 6, 7, 11, 11, 15, 16, 19, 20, 20, 21, 21, 23, 23, 24, 26, 32, 35, 39, 44, 45, 46, 47, 49, 50, 54, 55, 57, 61, 62, 66; 28:1, 3, 4, 5, 9, 11, 15, 16, 17; Mk 1:8, 14, 30, 32, 45; 2:6, 10, 18, 20, 21, 22; 3:4, 29; 4:11, 15, 29, 34, 34; 5:11, 33, 34, 36, 40; 6:15, 15, 16, 19, 24, 37, 38, 49, 50; 7:6, 6, 7, 11, 20, 24, 26, 28, 36; 8:5, 9, 28, 28, 29, 33, 35; 9:12, 19, 21, 23, 25, 27, 32, 34, 39, 50; 10:3, 4, 5, 6, 13, 14, 18, 20, 21, 22, 24, 24, 26, 31, 32, 32, 36, 37, 38, 39, 39, 40, 43, 48, 50, 51; 11:6, 8, 17, 29; 12:5, 7, 15, 16, 16, 17, 26, 44; 13:5, 7, 9, 13, 14, 15[U], 17, 18, 23, 28, 31, 32, 37; 14:1, 4, 6, 7, 9, 11, 20, 21, 29, 31, 31, 38, 44, 46, 47, 52, 55, 61, 62, 63, 64, 68, 70, 71; 15:2, 4, 5, 6, 7, 9, 11, 12, 13, 14, 14, 15, 16, 23, 25, 36, 37, 39, 40, 44, 47; 16:6, 9, 12, 14, 16, 17, 20, S[U], S[U]; Lk 1:6, 8, 11, 13, 22, 24, 26, 29, 34, 38, 39, 56, 57, 62, 64, 76, 80; 2:1, 4, 6, 17, 19, 35, 40, 44, 47; 3:1, 1, 9, 11, 12, 13, 14, 15, 16, 17, 19, 21; 4:1, 3, 9, 21, 24, 25, 30, 38, 38, 39, 40, 40, 41, 42, 43; 5:1, 2, 3, 3, 4, 5, 6, 8, 10, 12, 15, 16, 22, 24, 33, 33, 34, 35, 36, 36, 37; 6:1, 2, 6, 7, 8, 8, 9, 10, 11, 12, 39, 40, 41, 41, 46, 48, 49; 7:2, 3, 4, 6, 6, 9, 12, 14, 16, 20, 24, 28, 30, 36, 39, 40, 41, 43, 44, 45, 46, 47, 48, 50; 8:4, 9, 10, 10, 11, 12, 13, 14, 15, 16, 19, 20, 21, 22, 23, 24, 24, 25, 25, 27, 28, 30, 30, 32, 33, 34, 35, 36, 37, 38, 38, 40, 42, 45, 46, 47, 48, 50, 51, 52, 52, 54, 56; 9:1, 6, 7, 8, 8, 9, 9, 11, 12, 12, 13, 13, 14, 16, 19, 19, 19, 20, 20, 20, 21, 23, 24, 25, 27, 28, 32, 32, 34, 34, 37, 41, 42, 42, 43, 43, 45, 46, 47, 49, 50, 51, 54, 55, 58, 59, 59, 60, 60, 61, 61, 62; 10:1, 2, 2, 5, 6, 7, 10, 16, 17, 18, 20, 26, 27, 28, 29, 30, 31, 32, 33, 34, 37, 37, 38, 38, 40, 40, 41, 42; 11:2, 11, 14, 15, 16, 17, 18, 19, 20, 22, 27, 28, 29, 34, 37, 37, 38, 39, 39, 42, 45, 46, 47, 48; 12:2, 4, 5, 8, 9, 10, 11, 13, 14, 15, 16, 20, 20, 22, 25, 27, 28, 30, 39, 41, 45, 47, 48, 48, 48, 50, 54, 56, 57; 13:1, 6, 7, 8, 9, 10, 12, 14, 15, 16, 23, 23, 28, 35[U]; 14:4, 7, 12, 15, 16, 25, 32, 34; 15:1, 3, 11, 12, 14, 17, 17, 20, 21, 22, 25, 27, 28, 28, 29, 30, 31, 32; 16:1, 3, 6, 6, 7, 7, 14, 15, 17, 19, 20, 22, 22, 25, 25, 25, 27, 29, 30, 31; 17:1, 6, 7, 15, 17, 17, 20, 22, 25, 29, 33, 35, 37; 18:1, 3, 4, 6, 7, 9, 13, 14, 15, 15, 16, 19, 21, 22, 23, 24, 26, 27, 28, 29, 31, 35, 36, 37, 39, 40, 40, 41; 19:8, 9, 11, 13, 14, 16, 19, 26, 32, 33, 34, 36, 37, 42, 46, 47; 20:3, 5, 6, 9, 10, 11, 12, 13, 14, 16, 17, 18, 23, 25, 25, 27, 31, 35, 37, 38, 39, 41, 45; 21:1, 2, 4, 7, 8, 9, 12, 16, 20, 28, 33, 34, 36, 37, 37; 22:1, 3, 7, 9, 10, 13, 24, 25, 26, 27, 28, 32, 33, 34, 35, 36, 38, 38, 39, 40, 43, 48, 49, 51, 52, 54, 54, 55, 56, 57, 58, 60, 67, 68, 69, 70, 70, 71; 23:2, 3, 3, 4, 5, 6, 8, 9, 9, 10, 11, 12, 13, 18, 18, 20, 21, 22, 23, 25, 25, 27, 28, 32, 33, 34, 34, 35, 36, 38, 39, 40, 41, 45, 46, 47, 49, 55, 56; 24:1, 2, 3, 5, 10, 12, 16, 17, 18, 19, 21, 24, 31, 36, 37, 41, 42, 44, 49, 50; Jn 1:12, 26[N], 38, 38, 44; 2:2, 6, 8, 9, 9, 21, 23, 24; 3:1, 18, 19, 21, 23, 29, 30, 36; 4:4, 6, 14, 32, 39, 43, 51, 54; 5:2, 5, 7, 9, 11, 13, 17, 29, 34, 35, 36, 47; 6:2, 3, 4, 6, 10, 12, 16, 20, 39, 51, 61, 71; 7:2, 6, 7, 9, 10, 12, 14, 18, 27, 31, 37, 39, 41, 44; 8:1, 2, 3, 5, 6, 6, 7, 9, 10, 11, 11, 14, 16, 17, 35, 35[N], 40, 45, 50, 55, 59; 9:14, 15, 16, 17, 21, 28, 29, 38, 41; 10:2, 5, 6, 20, 21[N], 38, 41; 11:1, 2, 4, 5, 10, 13, 13, 18, 19, 20, 29, 30, 37, 38, 41, 42, 46, 49, 51, 55, 57; 12:2, 3, 4, 6, 8, 10, 14, 20, 23, 24, 33, 37, 44; 13:1, 7, 20, 28, 30, 36; 14:2, 10, 11, 19, 21, 26; 15:15, 19, 22, 24, 27; 16:4, 5, 7, 10, 11, 13, 20, 21, 22; 17:3, 13, 20, 25; 18:2, 5, 7, 10, 14, 15, 15, 16, 18, 18, 22, 23, 25, 28, 36, 39, 40; 19:9, 12, 13, 14, 18, 19, 19, 23, 25, 33, 38, 38, 39, 41; 20:1, 4, 11, 17, 24, 25, 31; 21:1, 4, 6, 8, 12, 18, 19, 21, 23, 25; Ac 1:5, 7; 2:5, 6, 7, 12, 13, 14, 26, 34, 37, 38, 42, 43, 44, 47; 3:1, 4, 5, 6, 6, 7, 10, 11, 12, 14, 15, 18, 23, 24; 4:1, 4, 5, 13, 15, 19, 21, 23, 24, 32, 35, 36; 5:1, 3, 5, 6, 7, 8, 8, 9, 10, 10, 12, 13, 14, 16, 17, 19, 21, 21, 22, 22, 23, 24, 25, 27, 29, 33, 34, 39, 40; 6:1, 2, 3, 4, 8, 9; 7:1, 2, 6, 11, 12, 14, 17, 21, 22, 23, 25, 25, 27, 29, 31, 31, 32, 33, 42, 47, 49, 54, 55, 57, 60; 8:1, 1, 1, 2, 3, 5, 6, 7, 8, 9, 11, 12, 13, 14, 16, 18, 20, 24, 26, 29, 30, 31, 32, 34, 35, 36, 39, 40; 9:1, 3, 5, 5, 7, 7, 8, 8, 8, 10, 10, 11, 13, 15, 17, 19, 21, 22, 23, 24, 24, 25, 26, 27, 29, 30, 32, 33, 36, 37, 37, 38, 39, 40, 40, 41, 41, 42, 43; 10:1, 4, 4, 7, 9, 10, 10, 14, 16, 17, 19, 21, 22, 23, 24, 24, 25, 26, 34, 48; 11:1, 2, 4, 7, 8, 9, 10, 12, 12, 13, 15, 16, 16, 18, 20, 22, 25, 26, 27, 28, 29; 12:1, 2, 3, 3, 5, 6, 7, 8, 8, 9, 10, 13, 14, 15, 15, 15, 16, 16, 17, 18, 19, 20, 20, 21, 22, 23, 24, 25; 13:1, 2, 5, 6, 8, 9, 13, 13, 14, 15, 16, 25, 29, 30, 34, 37, 42, 43, 44, 45, 48, 49, 50, 51; 14:1, 2, 4, 4, 5, 12, 14, 19, 20, 23, 27, 28; 15:2, 4, 5, 7, 12, 13, 31, 33, 35, 36, 37, 38, 39, 40, 41; 16:1, 1, 4, 6, 7, 8, 10, 11, 11, 12, 15, 16, 18, 18, 19, 25, 25, 26, 26, 27, 28, 29, 31, 35, 36, 37, 38, 38, 40; 17:1, 2, 5, 6, 8, 10, 11, 13, 14, 15, 16, 18, 18, 21, 22, 32, 32, 34; 18:4, 5, 6, 8, 9, 11, 12, 14, 15, 17, 18, 19, 19, 20, 24, 26, 27; 19:1, 2, 3, 4, 5, 7, 8, 9, 10, 13, 14, 15, 15, 17, 19, 21, 22, 23, 27, 28, 30, 31, 33, 33, 34, 35, 39; 20:1, 2, 4, 4, 4, 5, 6, 7, 8, 9, 10, 11, 12, 13, 14, 15, 15, 17, 18, 37, 38; 21:1, 1, 3, 4, 5, 6, 7, 8, 9, 10, 12, 14, 15, 16, 17, 18, 20, 21, 25, 27, 32, 34, 34, 35, 37, 39, 39, 40, 40; 22:2, 3, 6, 8, 9, 9, 10, 10, 11, 12, 14, 17, 22, 25, 26, 27, 27, 28, 28, 28, 29, 30; 23:1, 2, 4, 6, 6, 7, 8, 9, 9, 10, 11, 12, 13, 15, 16, 17, 19, 20, 29, 30, 32, 34; 24:1, 2, 4, 9, 14, 17, 19, 22, 24, 25, 25, 27; 25:4, 6, 7, 9, 10, 11, 13, 14, 19, 20, 21, 22, 25, 25; 26:1, 15, 15, 24, 25, 28, 29, 32; 27:1, 2, 7, 9, 11, 12, 13, 14, 15, 16, 18, 20, 26, 27, 28, 30, 33, 35, 36, 37, 38, 39, 39, 41, 41, 42, 43, 44; 28:3, 4, 6, 6, 7, 8, 9, 11, 16, 17, 17, 19, 21, 22, 23, 24, 25, 30; Ro 1:12, 13, 17; 2:2, 3, 5, 8, 8, 10, 17, 25; 3:4, 4, 5, 7, 19, 21, 22; 4:3, 4, 5, 5, 15, 20, 23; 5:3, 4, 4, 5, 8, 11, 13, 16, 20, 20; 6:8, 10, 11, 17, 17, 18, 22, 22, 22, 23; 7:2, 3, 6, 8, 9, 9, 9, 14, 16, 17, 18, 20, 23, 25, 25; 8:5, 6, 8, 9, 9, 10, 10, 11, 13, 17, 17, 23, 24, 25, 26, 27, 28, 30, 30, 34; 9:6, 10, 13, 18, 21, 22, 27, 30, 31; 10:6, 10, 14, 14, 15, 17, 20, 21; 11:6, 7, 7, 12, 13, 16, 17, 17, 18, 20, 22, 23, 28, 30; 12:4, 5, 6; 13:1, 2, 3, 4, 12, 12; 14:1, 2, 3, 4, 5, 10, 23, 23; 15:1, 5, 9, 13, 14, 15, 20, 23, 23, 25, 29, 30, 33; 16:1, 17, 19, 19, 20, 25, 26; 1Co 1:10, 10, 12, 12, 12, 12, 16, 18, 23, 23, 24, 30; 2:6, 6, 10, 12, 14, 15, 15, 16; 3:4, 5, 8, 8, 10, 10, 12, 15, 15, 23, 23; 4:3, 4, 6, 7, 7, 10, 10, 10, 18, 19; 5:3, 11, 13; 6:13, 13, 14, 17, 18; 7:1, 2, 3, 4, 6, 7, 7, 8, 9, 10, 11, 12, 14, 15, 15, 25, 25, 28, 28, 29, 32, 33, 34, 35, 36, 37, 37, 39, 40, 40; 8:1, 1, 3, 7, 8, 9, 12; 9:15, 15, 17, 23, 24, 25, 25; 10:4, 6, 11, 11, 13, 20, 28, 29; 11:2, 3, 3, 3, 5, 6, 7, 12, 15, 16, 17, 21, 28, 31, 32, 34; 12:1, 4, 4, 6, 7, 8, 9, 10, 10, 10, 10, 11, 12, 18, 19, 20, 20, 21, 24, 27, 31; 13:1, 2, 3, 6, 8, 10, 12, 12, 13, 13; 14:1, 1, 2, 3, 4, 5, 5, 5, 6, 14, 15, 15, 20, 22, 23, 24, 24, 28, 28, 29, 30, 35, 38, 40; 15:1, 6, 8, 10, 10, 12, 13, 14, 15, 17, 20, 23, 27, 28, 35, 38, 39, 39, 39, 40, 50, 51, 54, 56, 56, 57; 16:1, 3, 4, 5, 6, 8, 10, 11, 12, 12, 15, 17; 2Co 1:6, 12, 13, 18, 21, 23; 2:5, 10, 12, 14, 16; 3:4, 6, 7, 16, 17, 17, 18; 4:3, 5, 7, 12, 13, 18; 5:5, 8, 11, 11, 18; 6:1, 10, 10, 12, 13, 15, 16; 7:7, 10, 13; 8:1, 11, 16, 17, 18, 19, 22, 22; 9:3, 6, 8, 10; 10:1, 1, 2, 10, 13, 15, 17; 11:3, 6, 12, 16, 21; 12:1, 5, 6, 15, 16, 19; 13:6,

7, 7, 9; Gal 1:15, 19, 20, 22, 23; 2:2, 2, 4, 6, 9, 11, 12, 16, 17, 20, 20, 20; 3:8, 11, 12, 16, 17, 18, 20, 20, 23, 25, 29; 4:1, 4, 6, 7, 9, 9, 13, 18, 20, 23, 25, 25, 26, 28; 5:3, 10, 11, 15, 16, 17, 18, 19, 22, 24; 6:4, 6, 8, 9, 10, 14; Eph 2:4, 13; 3:20; 4:7, 9, 11, 11, 11, 15, 20, 23, 28, 32; 5:3, 8, 11, 13, 32, 33; 6:21; Php 1:12, 15, 17, 22, 23, 24, 28; 2:8, 18, 19, 22, 24, 25, 25, 27; 3:1, 12, 13, 13, 18; 4:10, 10, 15, 18, 19, 20, 22; Col 1:22, 26; 2:17; 3:8, 14; 1Th 2:16, 17; 3:6, 11, 12; 4:9, 10, 13; 5:1, 4, 8, 12, 14, 21, 23; 2Th 2:1, 13, 16; 3:3, 4, 5, 6, 12, 13, 14, 16; 1Ti 1:5, 8, 9, 14, 17; 2:12, 14, 15; 3:5, 7, 10, 15; 4:1, 7, 7, 8; 5:4, 5, 6, 8, 11, 13, 13, 24; 6:2, 6, 8, 9, 11, 11; 2Ti 1:5, 10, 10; 2:5, 16, 20, 20, 22, 22, 23, 24; 3:1, 5, 8, 10, 12, 13, 14; 4:4, 5, 8, 12, 17, 20; Tit 1:1, 3, 15, 16; 2:1; 3:4, 9, 14; Phm 1:9, 11, 14, 16, 18, 22; Heb 1:6, 8, 11, 12, 13; 2:6, 8, 9; 3:4, 6, 10, 17, 18; 4:13, 15; 5:14; 6:8, 9, 11, 12; 7:2, 3, 4, 6, 7, 8, 19, 21, 24, 28; 8:1, 6, 13; 9:3, 5, 6, 7, 11, 12, 21, 23, 26, 27; 10:5, 12, 15, 18, 27, 32, 33, 38, 39; 11:1, 6, 16, 35, 36, 36; 12:6, 8, 9, 10, 11, 11, 13, 26, 27; 13:16, 19, 20, 22; Jas 1:4, 5, 6, 9, 10, 13, 14, 15, 19, 22, 25; 2:2, 3, 6, 9, 10, 11, 11, 14, 16, 16, 20, 23, 25; 3:3, 8, 14, 17, 18; 4:6, 6, 7, 11, 12, 16; 5:12, 12; 1Pe 1:7, 8, 12, 20, 25, 25; 2:4, 7, 9, 10, 10, 14, 23; 3:8, 9, 11, 12, 14, 15, 18; 4:6, 7, 16, 16, 17; 5:5, 5, 10; 2Pe 1:5, 5, 6, 6, 6, 7, 7, 13, 15; 2:1, 9, 10, 12, 16, 20; 3:7, 8, 10, 10, 13, 18; 1Jn 1:3, 7; 2:2, 5, 11, 17; 3:12, 17; 4:18; 5:5, 20; 3Jn 1:12, 14; Jude 1:1, 5, 8, 8, 9, 10, 10, 14, 17, 20, 23, 23, 24; Rev 1:14; 2:5, 16, 24; 10:2; 19:12; 21:8

1609 ἐγώ, egō [2667 / 2669]

Mt 1:23; 2:6, 8, 8, 15; 3:11, 11, 11, 14, 14, 15, 17; 4:9, 10[N], 19; 5:11, 22, 28, 32, 34, 39, 44; 6:9, 11, 11, 12, 12, 12, 12, 13, 13; 7:21, 21, 22, 23, 24, 26; 8:2, 6, 7, 8, 8, 9, 9, 17, 21, 21, 22, 25[N], 29, 29, 31, 31; 9:9, 14, 18, 27; 10:16, 18, 22, 32, 32, 32, 33, 33, 33, 37, 37, 37, 37, 38, 38, 39, 40, 40, 40; 11:6, 10, 10, 27, 27, 28, 28, 29, 29, 30, 30; 12:18, 18, 18, 18, 27, 28, 30, 30, 30, 44, 48, 48, 49, 49, 50, 50; 13:30, 35, 36, 56; 14:8, 18, 27, 28, 30; 15:5, 8, 8, 9, 13, 15, 22, 22, 23, 25, 32, 33; 16:15, 17, 18, 18, 23, 23, 24, 24, 25; 17:4, 5, 15, 17, 19, 27; 18:5, 5, 6, 10, 19, 21, 21, 26, 29, 32, 33, 35; 19:14, 17, 21, 27, 27, 28, 29; 20:7, 12, 13, 15, 15, 21, 22, 23, 23, 23, 30, 31, 33; 21:2, 13, 24, 24, 24, 25, 27, 30, 37, 42; 22:4, 4, 17, 18, 19, 25, 32, 44, 44; 23:30, 34, 39; 24:3, 5, 5, 9, 35, 48; 25:8, 8, 9, 11, 20, 22, 27, 27, 34, 35, 35, 35, 36, 36, 36, 40, 40, 41, 42, 42, 43, 43, 43, 45; 26:10, 11, 12, 12, 15, 15, 18, 18, 21, 22, 23, 23, 25, 26, 28, 29, 31, 32, 33, 34, 35, 38, 38, 39, 39, 39, 40, 42, 46, 53, 53, 55, 55, 63, 68, 75; 27:4, 10, 25, 25, 46, 46, 46; 28:10, 10, 13, 14, 18, 20; Mk 1:2, 7, 7, 8, 11, 17, 24, 24, 40; 2:14; 3:33, 33, 34, 34, 35; 5:7, 7, 9, 12, 23, 30, 31; 6:3, 16, 22, 23, 23, 25, 50; 7:6, 6, 7, 11, 14; 8:2, 27, 29, 33, 34, 34, 35, 38; 9:5, 7, 17, 19, 22, 22, 24, 25, 28, 37, 37, 37, 37, 37, 38, 39, 39, 40, 40, 42; 10:14, 18, 20, 21, 28, 29, 35, 36, 37, 38, 38, 39, 39, 40, 47, 48; 11:10, 17, 29, 30, 33; 12:6, 7, 11, 15, 15, 19, 26, 29, 36, 36; 13:4, 6, 6, 9, 13, 31; 14:6, 7, 8, 14, 14, 15, 18, 18, 19, 20, 22, 24, 28, 29, 30, 31, 34, 36, 36, 42, 48, 49, 58, 58, 62, 72; 15:34, 34, 34; 16:3, 17; Lk 1:1, 2, 3, 18, 18, 19, 20, 25, 25, 38, 43, 43, 43, 44, 44, 46, 47, 47, 48, 49, 55, 69, 71, 71, 72, 73, 74, 75, 78, 78, 79; 2:15, 30, 48, 48, 49, 49, 49; 3:14, 16, 16, 22; 4:6, 7, 18, 18, 18, 23, 34, 34, 43; 5:8, 12, 27; 6:46, 47, 47; 7:5, 5, 6, 7, 8, 8, 16, 20, 23, 27, 44, 44, 45, 45, 46, 46; 8:21, 21, 28, 28, 45, 46, 46, 46; 9:9, 13, 13, 18, 20, 23, 23, 24, 26, 33, 35, 38, 38, 48, 48, 48, 48, 49, 59, 59, 59, 61, 61; 10:11, 16, 16, 16, 16, 17, 22, 22, 29, 35, 35, 40, 40, 40; 11:1, 3, 3, 4, 4, 4, 4, 5, 6, 6, 7, 7, 7, 9, 18, 19, 20, 23, 23, 23, 24, 45; 12:4, 8, 9, 13, 13, 14, 17, 18, 18, 19, 41, 45; 13:25, 26, 27, 33, 35; 14:18, 19, 23, 24, 26, 26, 27, 27, 33; 15:6, 6, 9, 12, 17, 17, 18, 19, 24, 29, 29, 31; 16:3, 3, 4, 5, 9, 24, 24, 26, 26, 27; 17:5, 8, 13; 18:3, 3, 5, 5, 13, 16, 19, 22, 28, 38, 39; 19:5, 8, 14, 22, 23, 23, 27, 27, 27, 46; 20:2, 3, 3, 6, 8, 13, 14, 22, 24, 28, 42, 42; 21:8, 8, 12, 15, 17, 33; 22:8, 11, 15, 19, 20, 21, 21, 27, 28, 28, 29, 29, 29, 30, 30, 32, 34, 37, 37, 42, 42, 53, 53, 61, 67, 70; 23:2, 14, 14, 15, 18, 28, 30, 30, 39, 41, 42, 43, 46; 24:20, 21, 22, 22, 24, 29, 32, 32, 32, 32, 39, 39, 39, 39, 39, 44, 44, 49, 49; Jn 1:14, 15, 15, 15, 16, 20, 22, 23, 26, 27, 27, 30, 30, 30, 30, 31, 31, 33, 33, 33, 34, 43, 48; 2:4, 4, 16, 17, 18; 3:11, 28, 28, 30; 4:7, 9, 10, 12, 12, 14, 15, 20, 21, 22, 25, 26, 29, 32, 34, 38, 39, 49; 5:7, 7, 7, 11, 11, 17, 17, 24, 24, 30, 30, 31, 31, 32, 32, 34, 36, 36, 36, 36, 37, 37, 39, 40, 43, 43, 43, 45, 46, 46; 6:20, 26, 31, 32, 34, 35, 35, 35, 36, 37, 37, 37, 38, 39, 39, 40, 40, 41, 42, 44, 44, 44, 45, 48, 51, 51, 51, 52, 54, 54, 54, 55, 55, 56, 56, 56, 56, 57, 57, 57, 57, 63, 65, 69, 70; 7:7, 7, 8, 16, 17, 19, 23, 28, 28, 29, 29, 33, 34, 34, 34, 35, 36, 36, 36, 37, 38, 51; 8:5, 11, 12, 12, 14, 14, 15, 16, 16, 16, 18, 18, 18, 19, 19, 19, 19, 21, 21, 21, 22, 23, 23, 24, 26, 26, 28, 28, 29, 29, 29, 29, 31, 37, 38, 39, 40, 41, 42, 42, 42, 45, 45, 46, 46, 48, 49, 49, 49, 50, 50, 52, 53, 54, 54, 54, 54, 54, 55, 58; 9:4, 4, 9, 11, 11, 15, 20, 21, 24, 28, 29, 30, 34, 39, 40; 10:7, 8, 9, 9, 10, 11, 14, 14, 15, 15, 15, 16, 16, 17, 17, 17, 18, 18, 18, 24, 24, 25, 25, 25, 27, 27, 27, 28, 28, 29, 29, 30, 32, 34, 37, 37, 38, 38, 38; 11:11, 16, 21, 25, 25, 26, 27, 32, 41, 42, 42, 42, 48; 12:7, 8, 26, 26, 26, 26, 27, 27, 30, 32, 34, 38, 44, 44, 44, 45, 45, 46, 46, 47, 47, 48, 48, 49, 49, 49, 50, 50; 13:6, 7, 8, 8, 9, 13, 14, 15, 18, 18, 18, 19, 20, 20, 20, 21, 26, 33, 33, 36, 37, 38, 38; 14:1, 2, 3, 4, 6, 6, 7, 7, 8, 8, 9, 9, 9, 10, 10, 10, 10, 11, 11, 11, 12, 12, 12, 13, 14, 14, 14, 15, 16, 19, 19, 19, 20, 20, 20, 20, 21, 21, 21, 21, 21, 22, 23, 23, 23, 24, 24, 24, 26, 26, 27, 28, 28, 28, 30, 31; 15:1, 1, 2, 4, 4, 4, 5, 5, 5, 5, 6, 7, 7, 8, 8, 9, 9, 10, 10, 10, 10, 14, 14, 15, 16, 16, 16, 18, 19, 20, 20, 20, 21, 21, 23, 23, 24, 24, 25, 26, 26, 27; 16:3, 4, 5, 5, 7, 7, 9, 10, 14, 16, 16, 17, 17, 17, 19, 19, 23, 23, 24, 26, 26, 27, 27, 32, 32, 33, 33; 17:4, 4, 5, 6, 6, 7, 8, 8, 9, 9, 11, 11, 11, 12, 12, 14, 14, 16, 18, 18, 19, 20, 21, 21, 21, 21, 22, 22, 22, 23, 23, 23, 23, 24, 24, 24, 24, 24, 25, 25, 26, 26; 18:5, 6, 8, 8, 9, 11, 20, 20, 21, 21, 23, 26, 31, 34, 35, 35, 37, 37, 38; 19:6, 7, 10, 11, 11, 24, 24; 20:13, 15, 15, 17, 17, 17, 17, 21, 21, 25, 25, 27, 27, 28, 28, 29; 21:3, 15, 15, 16, 16, 17, 17, 17, 19, 22; Ac 1:4, 8, 17, 21, 21, 22, 22; 2:8, 8, 14, 17, 18, 18, 18, 25, 25, 26, 26, 26, 27, 28, 28, 29, 32, 34, 34, 39; 3:4, 6, 12, 13, 15, 22; 4:9, 12, 20, 25; 5:8, 28, 30, 32; 6:2, 4, 14; 7:2, 7, 7, 11, 12, 15, 19, 19, 27, 28, 32, 34, 37, 38, 38, 39, 40, 40, 40, 42, 44, 45, 45, 49, 49, 49, 49, 50, 59; 8:19, 24, 24, 31, 36; 9:4, 5, 10, 15, 15, 16, 16, 17, 38; 10:20, 21, 26, 28, 29, 30, 30, 33, 39, 41, 42, 47; 11:5, 5, 7, 8, 11, 12, 12, 13, 15, 15, 17, 17; 12:8, 11; 13:2, 17, 22, 22, 25, 25, 25, 26, 32, 33, 33, 33, 41, 47; 14:11, 15, 22; 15:7, 8, 9, 10, 10, 13, 17, 19, 24, 25, 25, 26, 28; 16:9, 10, 15, 15, 15, 16, 16, 17, 20, 21, 30, 37, 37, 37; 17:3, 20, 23, 27; 18:6, 10, 10, 15; 19:21, 21, 25, 27, 37; 20:5, 6, 7, 13, 14, 19, 21, 22, 22, 23, 23, 24, 25, 25, 29, 29, 34, 34; 21:1, 5, 5, 7, 11, 12, 13, 13, 16, 17, 17, 18, 23, 25, 37, 39, 39; 22:1, 3, 5, 6, 6, 7, 7, 8, 8, 8, 9, 9, 10, 11, 12, 13, 13, 14, 17, 17, 17, 18, 18, 19, 19, 21, 21, 27, 28, 28; 23:1, 3, 3, 6, 6, 11, 15, 18, 19, 22, 30; 24:4, 8, 11, 12, 13, 17, 18, 19, 20, 21; 25:9, 10, 11, 11, 15, 18, 20, 24, 24, 25, 27; 26:3, 4, 4, 5, 6, 7, 9, 10, 13, 13, 14, 14, 14, 15, 15, 16, 17, 18, 21, 28, 29, 29; 27:1, 2, 6, 7, 10, 18, 20, 21, 23, 23, 25, 26, 27; 28:2, 2, 7, 10, 15, 15, 17, 18, 18, 19, 21, 22; Ro 1:4, 7, 8, 9, 9, 10, 12, 15; 2:16; 3:5, 7, 8; 4:1, 12, 16, 24, 24, 25, 25; 5:1, 5, 5, 6, 8, 8, 8, 11, 21; 6:4, 6, 6, 23; 7:4, 5, 6, 8, 9, 9, 10, 11, 13, 13, 14, 17, 17, 18, 18, 18, 20, 20, 20, 21, 21, 23, 23, 23, 23, 24, 24, 25, 25; 8:2[N], 4, 16, 18, 23, 23, 26, 31, 31, 32, 32, 34, 35, 37, 39, 39; 9:1, 1, 2, 2, 3, 3, 3, 10, 17, 17, 19, 20, 24, 25, 25, 26, 29; 10:16, 19, 20, 20, 21; 11:1, 3, 3, 13, 13, 14, 19, 27; 12:3, 6, 19, 19; 13:11; 14:7, 11, 11, 12; 15:1, 2, 3, 6, 14, 14, 15, 16, 18, 19, 30, 30, 30, 31; 16:1, 2, 3, 4, 4, 5, 7, 7, 7, 8, 9, 9, 11, 13, 18, 20, 21, 21, 22, 23, 25; 1Co 1:2, 2, 3, 4, 7, 8, 9, 10, 11, 11, 12, 12, 12, 12, 17, 18, 23, 30; 2:1, 3, 4, 4, 7, 10, 12, 12, 16; 3:1, 4, 4, 6, 10; 4:1, 3, 4, 6, 8, 8, 9, 10, 10, 10, 14, 15, 16, 17, 17, 18; 5:3, 4, 4, 7, 12; 6:11, 12, 12, 12, 14; 7:8, 10, 12, 15[N], 28, 40; 8:6, 6, 6, 8, 13, 13; 9:1, 1, 2, 3, 6, 10, 10, 11, 11, 12, 15, 15, 15, 15, 16, 16, 16, 18, 18, 25, 26, 27; 10:1, 6, 6, 11, 14, 29, 30, 30, 33; 11:1, 1, 2, 16, 23, 24, 33; 12:13, 23, 24; 13:3, 3; 14:11, 14, 14, 19, 21, 39; 15:3, 8, 9, 10, 10, 10, 11, 14, 30, 31, 32, 52, 57, 57, 58; 16:4, 4, 6, 9, 10, 11, 24; 2Co 1:2, 3, 4, 4, 4, 5, 5, 6, 7, 8, 8, 10, 11, 11, 11, 12, 12, 14, 14, 14[U], 17, 18, 19, 19, 20, 21, 21, 22, 22, 23; 2:2, 2, 2, 3, 5, 10, 10, 12, 13, 13, 13, 14, 14; 3:2, 2, 3, 5, 6, 18; 4:3, 6, 7, 10, 11, 11, 12, 13, 14, 16, 16, 17, 17, 18; 5:1, 2, 5, 5, 10, 12, 14, 16, 18, 18, 19, 20, 21, 21; 6:11, 11, 12, 16, 16, 17, 18; 7:2, 3, 4, 4, 4, 5, 5, 6, 7, 7, 7, 9, 12, 13, 14; 8:4, 5, 6, 7[U], 7[N], 9, 19, 19, 19, 20, 20, 22, 23, 24; 9:1, 3, 4, 4, 11; 10:1, 2, 4, 7, 8, 13, 13, 15; 11:1, 1, 9, 10, 10, 12, 16, 16, 16, 18, 21, 21, 22, 22, 22, 23, 28, 29, 30, 32; 12:6, 6, 6, 7, 7, 8, 9, 9, 9, 9, 11, 11, 13, 13, 15, 16, 20, 21, 21, 21; 13:3, 4, 6, 7, 7, 9, 10; Gal 1:2, 3, 4, 4, 4, 8, 11, 12, 14, 14, 15, 15, 16, 17, 23, 24; 2:3, 4, 4, 6, 6, 8, 9, 9, 9, 15, 16, 19, 20, 20, 20, 20; 3:13, 13, 24; 4:3, 6, 12, 12, 12, 14, 14, 15, 18, 19, 20, 21, 26; 5:1, 2, 5, 10, 11; 6:14, 14, 14, 14, 17, 17, 17, 18; Eph 1:2, 3, 3, 4, 4, 5, 6, 8, 9, 12, 14, 15, 16, 17, 19; 2:3, 3, 4, 5, 7, 14; 3:1, 2, 3, 4, 7, 8, 11, 13, 14, 20; 4:1, 7; 5:2, 2, 20, 32; 6:12, 19, 19, 19, 20, 21, 22, 24; Php 1:2, 3, 4, 7, 7, 7, 7, 8, 12, 13, 14, 17, 19, 20, 20, 21, 22, 26, 30, 30; 2:2, 12, 12, 12, 16, 18, 19, 22, 23, 25, 25, 27, 28, 30; 3:1, 1, 3, 4, 4, 7, 8, 13, 17, 17, 20, 21; 4:1, 1, 3, 3, 9, 10, 11, 13, 14, 15, 16, 19, 20, 21; Col 1:2, 3, 7, 7[N], 8, 9, 13, 23, 24, 25, 25, 28, 29; 2:1, 13, 14, 14; 4:3, 3, 4, 7, 8, 10, 11, 18; 1Th 1:2, 3, 3, 5, 6, 8, 9, 10; 2:1, 2, 3, 4, 8, 9, 13, 13, 15, 16, 17, 18, 18, 19, 19, 20; 3:2, 5, 5, 6, 6, 6, 6, 6, 7, 9, 11, 11, 11, 12, 13, 13; 4:1, 7, 15, 17; 5:8, 9, 9, 10, 23, 25, 28; 2Th 1:1, 2[U], 4, 7, 8, 10, 11, 12, 12; 2:1, 1, 2, 13, 14, 14, 15, 16, 16, 16; 3:1, 6[U], 6, 7, 9, 14, 18; 1Ti 1:1, 1, 2, 11, 12, 12, 12, 14, 15, 16; 2:3, 7; 6:3, 14, 17; 2Ti 1:2, 3, 6, 7, 8, 8, 9, 9, 9, 10, 11, 12, 13, 14, 15, 16, 16, 17; 2:1, 2, 8, 12; 3:10, 11, 11; 4:6, 6, 8, 8, 8, 9, 10, 11, 11, 14, 16, 16, 16, 17, 17, 17, 18; Tit 1:3, 3, 4, 5; 2:8, 10, 12, 13, 14, 14; 3:3, 4, 5, 5, 6, 6, 12, 15, 15; Phm 1:1, 2, 3, 4, 4, 6, 11, 13, 13, 16, 17, 17, 18, 19, 19, 19, 20, 20, 22, 23, 24; Heb 1:2, 5, 5, 5, 5, 13; 2:1, 3, 3, 12, 13, 13, 13; 3:1, 6, 9, 10, 11, 11; 4:3, 3, 5, 13, 15; 5:5, 5, 11; 6:20; 7:14, 26; 8:9, 9, 9, 10, 10, 11; 9:14, 24; 10:5, 7, 15, 16, 20, 26, 30, 30, 38, 38, 39; 11:32, 40, 40; 12:1, 1, 1, 5, 9, 25, 26, 29; 13:6, 6, 6, 18, 20, 21, 23; Jas 1:2, 16, 18, 18, 19; 2:1, 1, 3, 5, 14, 18, 18, 18, 18, 21; 3:1, 3, 6, 10, 12; 4:5; 5:12, 17, 19; 1Pe 1:3, 3, 16; 2:24; 4:17; 5:13; 2Pe 1:1, 1, 2, 3, 3, 4, 8, 11, 14, 14, 14, 16, 17, 17, 17, 18; 2:20; 3:15, 15, 18; 1Jn 1:1, 1, 2, 3, 4, 4, 7, 8, 9, 9, 9, 10; 2:1, 2, 19, 19, 19, 19, 19, 25; 3:1, 1, 14, 16, 16, 19, 20, 20, 21, 23, 24, 24; 4:6, 6, 6, 9, 10, 10, 10, 11, 11, 12, 12, 13, 13, 14, 16, 16, 17, 17, 19, 19; 5:4, 11, 14, 15, 20; 2Jn 1:1, 1, 2, 2, 3, 12; 3Jn 1:1, 8, 9, 10, 12, 12; Jude 1:3, 4, 4, 17, 21, 25, 25; Rev 1:5, 5, 5, 6, 8, 9, 10, 12, 17, 17, 20; 2:3, 6, 13, 13, 13, 13, 16, 23, 26, 27, 27; 3:2, 4, 5, 8, 8, 9, 10, 10, 12, 12, 12, 12, 12, 16, 18, 19, 20, 20, 21, 21, 21, 21; 4:1, 11; 5:5, 10; 6:10, 16, 16; 7:3, 10, 12, 13, 14, 14; 10:8, 9, 9, 10, 10, 11; 11:1, 3, 15; 12:10, 10, 10; 17:1, 3, 7, 7, 15; 18:4; 19:1, 5, 6, 9, 9, 10; 21:6, 6, 6, 7, 9, 10, 10, 15; 22:1, 6, 8, 8, 9, 10, 12, 12, 13, 16, 16, 16, 18

1697 ἐκεῖνος, ekeinos [265 / 264]

Mt 3:1; 7:22, 25, 27; 8:13, 28; 9:22, 26, 31; 10:14, 15, 19; 11:25; 12:1, 45; 13:1, 11, 44; 14:1, 35, 35; 15:18, 22, 28; 17:18, 27; 18:1, 27, 28, 32; 20:4; 21:40; 22:7, 10, 23, 46; 23:23; 24:19, 22, 22, 29, 36, 38[U], 43, 46, 48, 50; 25:7, 19; 26:24, 24, 29, 55; 27:8, 19, 63; Mk 1:9; 2:20; 3:24, 25; 4:11, 20, 35; 6:55; 7:20; 8:1; 12:4, 5, 7; 13:11, 17, 19, 24, 24, 32; 14:21, 21, 25; 16:10, 11, 13, 13, 20; Lk 2:1; 4:2; 5:35; 6:23, 48, 49; 7:21; 8:32; 9:5, 36; 10:12, 12, 31; 11:7, 26, 42; 12:37, 38, 43, 45, 46, 47; 13:4; 14:24; 15:14, 15; 17:31; 18:3, 14; 19:4; 20:11, 18, 35; 21:23, 34; 22:12, 22; Jn 1:8, 18, 33, 39; 2:21; 3:28, 30; 4:25, 39, 53; 5:9, 11, 19, 35, 37, 38, 39, 43, 46, 47; 6:29, 57; 7:11, 29, 45; 8:42, 44; 9:9, 11, 12, 25, 28, 36, 37; 10:1, 6, 16, 35; 11:13, 29, 49, 51, 53; 12:48; 13:25, 26, 27, 30; 14:12, 20, 21, 26; 15:26; 16:8, 13, 14, 23, 26; 17:24; 18:13, 15, 17, 25; 19:15, 21, 27, 31, 35; 20:13, 15, 16, 19; 21:3, 7, 23; Ac 1:19; 2:18, 41; 3:13, 23; 5:37; 7:41; 8:1, 8; 9:37; 10:9; 12:1, 6; 14:21; 15:11; 16:3, 33, 35; 18:19; 19:16, 23; 20:2; 21:6; 22:11; 28:7; Ro 6:21; 11:23; 14:14, 15; 1Co 9:25; 10:6, 11, 28; 15:11; 2Co 7:8; 8:9, 14, 14; 10:18; Eph 2:12; 2Th 1:10; 2Ti 1:12, 18; 2:12, 13, 26; 3:9; 4:8; Tit 3:7; Heb 4:2, 2, 11; 6:7; 8:7, 10; 10:16; 11:15; 12:25; Jas 1:7; 4:15; 2Pe 1:16; 1Jn 2:6; 3:3, 5, 7, 16; 4:17; 5:16; Rev 9:6; 11:13

2445 ἤ, ē [343 / 341]

Mt 1:18; 5:17, 18, 36; 6:24, 24, 25, 31, 31; 7:4, 9, 10, 16; 9:5; 10:11, 14, 15, 19, 37, 37; 11:3, 22, 24; 12:5, 25, 29, 33, 33; 13:21; 15:4, 5; 16:14, 26; 17:25, 25; 18:8, 8, 8, 8, 9, 13, 16, 16, 20; 19:24, 29, 29, 29, 29, 29, 29; 20:15[U], 15; 21:25; 22:17; 23:17, 19; 24:23; 25:37, 38, 39, 44, 44, 44, 44, 44; 26:53; 27:17; Mk 2:9; 3:4, 4; 4:17, 21, 30; 6:56, 56; 7:10, 11, 12; 9:43, 45, 47; 10:25, 29, 29, 29, 29, 29, 29, 38, 40; 11:28, 30; 12:14, 15; 13:32, 35, 35, 35, 35; 14:30; Lk 2:24, 26; 5:23; 6:9, 9; 7:19, 20; 8:16; 9:13, 25; 10:12, 14; 11:12; 12:11[U], 11, 14, 41, 47, 51; 13:4, 15; 14:3, 5, 12, 31; 15:7, 8; 16:13, 13, 17; 17:2, 7, 21, 23; 18:11, 25, 29, 29, 29, 29; 20:2, 4, 22; 21:15; 22:27; Jn 2:6; 3:19; 4:1, 27; 6:19; 7:17, 48; 8:14; 9:2, 21; 13:29; 18:34; Ac 1:7; 3:12, 12; 4:7, 19, 34; 5:29, 38; 7:2, 49; 8:34; 10:28, 28; 11:8; 17:21, 21, 29, 29; 18:14; 19:12; 20:33, 33, 35; 23:9, 29; 24:12, 20, 21; 25:6, 16; 26:31; 27:11; 28:6, 17, 21; Ro 1:21; 2:4, 15; 3:1, 29; 4:9, 10, 13; 6:3, 16; 7:1; 8:35, 35, 35, 35, 35, 35; 9:11, 21; 10:7; 11:2, 34, 35; 13:11; 14:4, 10, 13; 1Co 1:13; 2:1; 4:3, 21; 5:10, 10, 11, 11, 11, 11, 11; 6:2, 9, 16, 19; 7:9, 11, 15, 16; 9:6, 7, 8, 10, 15; 10:19, 22; 11:4, 5, 6, 22, 27; 12:21; 13:1; 14:5, 6, 6, 6, 6, 7, 19, 23, 24, 27, 29, 36, 36, 37; 15:37; 16:6; 2Co 1:13, 13, 17; 3:1, 1; 6:14, 15; 9:7; 10:12; 11:4, 4, 7; 12:6; 13:5; Gal 1:8, 10, 10; 2:2; 3:2, 5, 15; 4:27; Eph 3:20; 5:3, 4, 5, 5, 27, 27; Php 3:12; Col 2:16, 16, 16; 3:17; 1Th 2:19, 19, 19; 2Th 2:4; 1Ti 1:4; 2:9, 9; 5:4, 19; 2Ti 3:4; Tit 1:6; 3:12; Phm 1:18; Heb 2:6; 10:28; 11:25; 12:16; Jas 1:17; 2:3, 15; 3:12; 4:5, 11, 13, 15; 1Pe 1:11, 18; 3:3, 9, 17; 4:15, 15, 15; 2Pe 2:21; 1Jn 4:4; Rev 3:15; 13:16, 17, 17; 14:9

2743 κἀγώ, kagō [84]

Mt 2:8; 10:32, 33; 11:28; 16:18; 18:33; 21:24, 24; 26:15; Lk 1:3; 2:48; 11:9; 19:23; 20:3; 22:29; Jn 1:31, 33, 34; 5:17; 6:44, 54, 56, 57; 7:28; 8:26; 10:15, 27, 28, 38; 12:32; 14:16, 20, 21; 15:4, 5, 9; 16:32; 17:6, 11, 18, 21, 22, 26; 20:15, 21; Ac 8:19; 10:28; 22:13, 19; Ro 3:7; 11:3; 1Co 2:1, 3; 3:1; 7:8, 40; 10:33; 11:1; 15:8; 16:4, 10; 2Co 2:10; 6:17; 11:16, 18, 21, 22, 22, 22; 12:20; Gal 4:12; 6:14; Eph 1:15; Php 2:19, 28; 1Th 3:5; Heb 8:9; Jas 2:18, 18; Rev 2:6, 27; 3:10, 21; 22:8

2779 καί, kai [9161 / 9140]

Mt 1:2, 3, 11, 17, 17, 19, 21, 23, 23, 24, 25, 25; 2:2, 3, 4, 4, 6, 8, 8, 9, 11, 11, 11, 11, 11, 12, 13, 13, 13, 14, 14, 15, 16, 16, 16, 18, 18, 20, 20, 21, 21, 23; 3:2, 4, 4, 5, 5, 6, 7, 9, 10, 11, 12, 12, 14, 16, 16, 16, 17; 4:2, 2, 3, 5, 6, 6, 8, 8, 9, 10, 11, 11, 13, 13, 15, 16, 16, 17, 18, 19, 19, 21, 21, 21, 22, 23, 23, 23, 23, 24, 24, 24, 24, 24, 24, 24, 25, 25, 25, 25, 25; 5:1, 2, 6, 11, 11, 12, 15, 15, 16, 18, 19, 19, 20, 23, 24, 24, 25, 25, 29, 29, 30, 30, 30, 32, 38, 39, 40, 40, 40, 41, 42, 43, 44, 45, 45, 45, 46, 47, 47; 6:2, 4, 5, 5, 6, 6, 10, 12, 12, 13, 14, 17, 18, 19, 19, 19, 20, 21, 24, 24, 24, 25, 26, 28, 30, 33, 33; 7:2, 4, 5, 6, 7, 7, 7, 8, 8, 10, 12, 12, 13, 13, 14, 14, 19, 22, 22, 23, 24, 25, 25, 25, 25, 25, 26, 26, 27, 27, 27, 27, 27, 27, 28, 29; 8:2, 3, 3, 4, 4, 6, 7, 8, 8, 9, 9, 9, 9, 9, 9, 9, 10, 11, 11, 11, 11, 12, 13, 13, 14, 14, 15, 15, 15, 15, 16, 16, 17, 19, 20, 20, 21, 22, 23, 24, 25, 26, 26, 26, 27, 27, 28, 29, 29, 32, 32, 32, 33, 33, 34, 34; 9:1, 1, 2, 2, 3, 4, 5, 6, 7, 8, 9, 9, 9, 10, 10[U], 10, 10, 11, 11, 13, 14, 15, 15, 16, 17, 17, 17, 18, 19, 19, 20, 22, 22, 23, 23, 23, 24, 25, 26, 27, 27, 28, 30, 30, 33, 33, 35, 35, 35, 35, 35, 36; 10:1, 1, 1, 2, 2, 2, 3, 3, 3, 4, 4, 5, 11, 13, 14, 15, 16, 17, 18, 18, 18, 21, 21, 21, 22, 25, 26, 27, 28, 28, 28, 29, 30, 32, 33, 35, 35, 36, 37, 38, 38, 39, 40, 41, 42; 11:1, 1, 4, 4, 5, 5, 5, 5, 6, 9, 12, 13, 14, 17, 17, 18, 19, 19, 19, 19, 19, 21, 21, 22, 23, 25, 25, 25, 27, 27, 28, 28, 29, 29, 29, 30; 12:1, 1, 3, 4, 5, 7, 9, 10, 10, 11, 11, 13, 13, 15, 15, 16, 18, 20, 21, 22, 22, 22, 23, 23, 25, 26, 27, 29, 29, 30, 31, 32, 33, 33, 35, 37, 38, 39, 39, 40, 40, 41, 41, 42, 42, 43, 44, 44, 45, 45, 45, 45, 46, 47, 48, 49, 49, 50, 50; 13:2, 2, 3, 4, 4, 5, 6, 7, 7, 8, 10, 12, 12, 13, 14, 14, 14, 14, 15, 15, 15, 15, 15, 15, 16, 17, 17, 17, 17, 19, 19, 20, 22, 22, 22, 23, 23, 25, 25, 26, 26, 30, 30, 32, 32, 34, 36, 40, 41, 41, 42, 42, 44, 44, 44, 46, 47, 48, 49, 50, 50, 52, 53, 54, 54, 54, 55, 55, 55, 55, 56, 57, 57, 58; 14:2, 2, 3, 5, 6, 9, 9, 10, 11, 11, 11, 12, 12, 12, 13, 14, 14, 14, 15, 17, 19, 19, 19, 20, 20, 20, 21, 22, 22, 23, 26, 29, 29, 30, 31, 32, 34, 35, 35, 36, 36; 15:1, 3, 4, 4, 6, 10, 10, 16, 17, 18, 21, 21, 22, 23, 26, 27, 28, 29, 29, 30, 30, 30, 30, 31, 31, 31, 32, 32, 33, 34, 34, 35, 36, 36, 36, 37, 37, 37, 38, 39, 39; 16:1, 1, 3, 4, 4, 4, 5, 6, 6, 9, 10, 11, 12, 17, 18, 18, 18, 19, 19, 21, 21, 21, 21, 21, 22, 24, 24, 27; 17:1, 1, 1, 1, 2, 2, 3, 3, 4, 4, 5, 6, 6, 7, 7, 7, 9, 10, 11, 12, 12, 14, 15, 15, 15, 16, 16, 17, 18, 18, 18, 20, 20, 23, 23, 23, 24, 25, 27, 27, 27; 18:2, 3, 3, 5, 6, 8, 9, 9, 12, 12, 13, 15, 17, 17, 18, 21, 25, 25, 25, 25, 26, 27, 28, 29, 31, 33, 33, 34, 35; 19:1, 1, 2, 2, 3, 3, 4, 5, 5, 5, 5, 7, 9, 12, 12, 13, 14, 15, 16, 19, 19, 21, 21, 21, 27, 28, 29, 29, 30; 20:3, 4, 4, 4, 5, 6, 7, 8, 9, 10, 10, 10, 12, 12, 14, 14, 16, 17, 17, 18, 18, 18, 19, 19, 19, 19, 20, 21, 23, 24, 25, 27, 28, 29, 30, 32, 32, 34, 34; 21:1, 1, 2, 2, 3, 5, 5, 6, 7, 7, 7, 8, 9, 10, 12, 12, 12, 12, 12, 13, 14, 14, 14, 15, 15, 15, 16, 16, 17, 17, 19, 19, 19, 19, 20, 21, 21, 21, 22, 23, 23, 23, 24, 24, 27, 27, 28, 30, 31, 32, 32, 33, 33, 33, 33, 33, 35, 36, 38, 39, 39, 41, 42, 43, 44, 45, 45, 46; 22:1, 3, 3, 4, 4, 6, 7, 7, 9, 10, 10, 10, 12, 13, 13, 16, 16, 16, 20, 20, 21, 22, 22, 23, 24, 25, 25, 26, 26, 32, 32, 33, 35, 37, 37, 38, 40, 46; 23:1, 2, 3, 3, 4[U], 4, 5, 6, 7, 7, 9, 12, 13, 15, 15, 15, 17, 18, 20, 21, 21, 22, 22, 23, 23, 23, 23, 23, 23, 23, 25, 25, 25, 26[N], 26, 27, 27, 28, 28, 29, 29, 30, 32, 34, 34, 34, 34, 34, 35, 37, 37; 24:1, 1, 3, 3, 4, 5, 6, 7, 7, 7, 9, 9, 10, 10, 10, 11, 11, 12, 14, 14, 18, 19, 22, 24, 24, 24, 24, 27, 29, 29, 29, 30, 30, 30, 30, 31, 31, 32, 33, 35, 36, 38, 38, 39, 39, 39[U], 40, 41, 43, 44, 45, 49, 49, 50, 51, 51, 51; 25:2, 5, 7, 9, 9, 10, 10, 11, 14, 15, 15, 16, 18, 19, 20, 21, 22, 23, 24, 24, 25, 26, 26, 27, 28, 29, 29, 30, 30, 31, 32, 32, 33, 35, 35, 35, 36, 36, 36, 37, 37, 38, 38, 39, 40, 41, 41, 42, 42, 43, 43, 43, 43, 44, 44, 46; 26:1, 2, 3, 4, 4, 7, 9, 13, 15, 16, 18, 19, 19, 21, 22, 26, 26, 27, 27, 30, 31, 35, 35, 36, 37, 37, 37, 38, 39, 39, 40, 40, 40, 41, 43, 44, 45, 45, 45, 47, 47, 47, 47, 49, 49, 50, 51, 51, 53, 55, 55, 57, 58, 59, 60, 61, 62, 63, 64, 67, 69, 69, 71, 72, 73, 73, 74, 74, 75, 75; 27:1, 2, 2, 3, 5, 5, 9, 10, 11, 12, 12, 14, 19, 20, 25, 25, 28, 29, 29, 29, 30, 30, 31, 31, 31, 33, 34, 36, 37, 38, 40, 40, 40[U], 41, 41, 42, 44, 48, 48, 48, 51, 51, 51, 52, 52, 53, 53, 54, 54, 56, 56, 56, 57, 59, 60, 60, 61, 62, 64, 64; 28:1, 2, 2, 2, 3, 4, 7, 7, 8, 8, 9, 9, 10, 12, 14, 14, 15, 17, 18, 18, 19, 19, 20; Mk 1:4, 5, 5, 5, 6, 6, 6, 6, 7, 9, 9, 10, 10, 11, 12, 13, 13, 13, 15, 15, 15, 16, 16, 17, 17, 18, 19, 19, 19, 20, 20, 21, 21, 22, 22, 23, 23, 24, 25, 25, 26, 26, 27, 27, 27, 28, 29, 29, 29, 30, 31, 31, 31, 32, 33, 34, 34, 34, 35, 35, 35, 36, 36, 37, 37, 38, 38, 39, 39, 40, 40, 40, 41, 41, 42, 42, 43, 44, 44, 45, 45; 2:1, 2, 2, 3, 4, 4, 5, 6, 8, 9, 9, 11, 12, 12, 12, 13, 13, 13, 14, 14, 14, 15, 15, 15, 15, 15, 16, 16, 16, 17, 18, 18, 18, 18, 18, 19, 20, 21, 22, 22, 22, 23, 23, 24, 25, 25, 25, 26, 26, 26, 27, 27, 28; 3:1, 1, 2, 3, 4, 5, 5, 5, 6, 7, 7, 8, 8, 8, 8, 8, 8, 9, 11, 11, 12, 13, 13, 13, 14, 14, 14, 15, 16, 16, 17, 17, 17, 18, 18, 18, 18, 18, 18, 18, 18, 19, 19, 20, 20, 21, 22, 22, 23, 24, 25, 26, 26, 27, 28, 31, 31, 31, 32, 32, 32, 32[U], 33, 33, 34, 34, 35, 35; 4:1, 1, 1, 2, 2, 4, 4, 4, 5, 5, 6, 6, 7, 7, 7, 7, 8, 8, 8, 8, 8, 8, 9, 10, 11, 12, 12, 12, 12, 13, 13, 15, 15, 16, 17, 18, 19, 19, 19, 19, 20, 20, 20, 20, 20, 21, 24, 24, 25, 25, 26, 27, 27, 27, 27, 27, 30, 32, 32, 32, 33, 35, 36, 36, 37, 37, 38, 38, 38, 39, 39, 39, 39, 40, 41, 41, 41, 41; 5:1, 2, 3, 4, 4, 4, 4, 5, 5, 5, 5, 6, 6, 7, 7, 9, 9, 10, 12, 13, 13, 13, 13, 14, 14, 14, 14, 15, 15, 15, 15, 16, 16, 17, 18, 19, 19, 19, 20, 20, 20, 21, 21, 22, 22, 23, 23, 24, 24, 24, 25, 26, 26, 26, 28, 29, 29, 30, 31, 31, 32, 33, 33, 33, 34, 37, 37, 37, 38, 38, 38, 38, 39, 39, 40, 40, 40, 40, 41, 42, 42, 42, 43, 43; 6:1, 1, 1, 2, 2, 2, 2, 3, 3, 3, 3, 3, 3, 4, 4, 4, 5, 6, 6, 7, 7, 7, 8, 9, 10, 11, 12, 13, 13, 13, 14, 14, 14, 17, 19, 19, 20, 20, 20, 20, 21, 21, 21, 22, 22, 22, 22, 23, 24, 25, 26, 26, 27, 27, 28, 28, 28, 29, 29, 29, 30, 30, 30, 31, 31, 31, 31, 32, 33, 33, 33, 33, 34, 34, 34, 35, 35, 36, 37, 37, 38, 38, 39, 40, 40, 41, 41, 41, 41, 41, 42, 42, 43, 43, 44, 45, 45, 46, 47, 47, 48, 48, 49, 50, 50, 51, 51, 51, 53, 53, 54, 55, 56, 56, 56, 56; 7:1, 1, 1, 3, 4, 4, 4, 4, 4[U], 5, 5, 9, 10, 10, 13, 14, 14, 17, 18, 18, 19, 23, 24, 24, 26, 27, 27, 28, 28, 29, 30, 30, 31, 32, 32, 32, 33, 33, 34, 34, 35, 35, 35, 36, 37, 37, 37; 8:1, 2, 3, 3, 4, 5, 6, 6, 6, 6, 7, 7, 7, 8, 8, 8, 9, 10, 11, 11, 12, 13, 14, 14, 15, 15, 16, 17, 18, 18, 20[N], 20, 21, 22, 22, 22, 23, 23, 24, 25, 25, 25, 26, 27, 27, 27, 28, 29, 30, 31, 31, 31, 31, 31, 31, 32, 32, 33, 33, 34, 34, 34, 35, 36, 38, 38, 38; 9:1, 2, 2, 2, 2, 2, 3, 4, 4, 5, 5, 5, 5, 7, 7, 8, 9, 10, 11, 12, 12, 13, 13, 14, 14, 15, 15, 16, 17, 18, 18, 18, 18, 18, 18, 20, 20, 20, 21, 22, 22, 22, 25, 25, 26, 26, 26, 27, 28, 29, 30, 30, 31, 31, 31, 32, 33, 33, 35, 35, 35, 36, 36, 37, 38, 39, 42, 42, 43, 45, 47, 48, 50; 10:1, 1, 1, 1, 2, 4, 6, 7, 7, 8, 10, 11, 11, 12, 13, 14, 16, 17, 17, 19, 21, 21, 21, 21, 23, 26, 28, 29, 30, 30, 30, 30, 30, 30, 31, 32, 32, 32, 33, 33, 33, 33, 34, 34, 34, 34, 34, 35, 35, 37, 39, 41, 41, 42, 42, 44, 45, 45, 46, 46, 46, 46, 47, 47, 48, 49, 49, 51, 52, 52, 52; 11:1, 1, 2, 2, 2, 3, 3, 4, 4, 4, 5, 6, 7, 7, 7, 8, 9, 9, 11, 11, 12, 13, 13, 14, 14, 15, 15, 15, 15, 15, 16, 17, 17, 18, 18, 18, 19, 20, 21, 22, 23, 23, 24, 24, 25, 25, 27, 27, 27, 27, 28, 29, 29, 31, 33, 33; 12:1, 1, 1, 1, 1, 1, 2, 3, 3, 4, 4, 4, 5, 5, 5, 7, 8, 8, 9, 9, 11, 12, 12, 12, 13, 13, 14, 14, 16, 16, 17, 17, 18, 18, 19, 19, 19, 20, 20, 21, 21, 21, 22, 22, 26, 26, 28, 30, 30, 30, 30, 32, 32, 33, 33, 33, 33, 33, 34, 34, 35, 37, 37, 38, 38, 39, 39, 40, 41, 41, 42, 43; 13:1, 1, 2, 3, 3, 3, 3, 4, 6, 7, 8, 9, 9, 9, 10, 11, 12, 12, 12, 12, 13, 16, 17, 19, 20, 21, 22, 22, 22, 24, 25, 25, 26, 26, 27, 27, 28, 29, 31, 34, 34; 14:1, 1, 1, 3, 5, 5, 7, 9, 10, 11, 11, 12, 13, 13, 13, 14, 15, 15, 16, 16, 16, 16, 17, 18, 18, 19, 22, 22, 22, 23, 23, 24, 26, 27, 27, 29, 30, 31, 32, 32, 33, 33, 33, 33, 33, 34, 34, 35, 35, 36, 37, 37, 37, 38, 39, 40, 40, 41, 41, 41, 43, 43, 43, 43, 43, 44, 45, 45, 46, 47, 48, 48, 49, 50, 51, 51, 53, 53, 53, 53, 54, 54, 54, 55, 55, 56, 57, 58, 59, 60, 61, 61, 62, 62, 65, 65, 65, 65, 65, 66, 67, 67, 68, 68[U], 69, 70, 70, 71, 72, 72, 72; 15:1, 1, 1, 1, 2, 3, 8, 15, 16, 17, 17, 18, 19, 19, 19, 20, 20, 20, 21, 21, 22, 23, 24, 24, 25, 26, 27, 27, 29, 29, 29, 31, 32, 32, 33, 34, 35, 36, 38, 40, 40, 40, 40, 40, 41, 41, 42, 43, 43, 44, 45, 46, 46, 46, 47; 16:1, 1, 1, 2, 3, 4, 5, 5, 7, 8, 8, 8, 10, 11, 11, 13, 14, 14, 15, 16, 18, 18, 18, 19, 20, S[U], S[U], S[U]; Lk 1:2, 3, 5, 5, 6, 7, 7, 10, 12, 12, 13, 13, 14, 14, 14, 15, 15, 15, 16, 17, 17, 17, 18, 18, 19, 19, 19, 20, 20, 21, 21, 22, 22, 22, 23, 24, 27, 28, 29, 30, 31, 31, 31, 32, 32, 33, 33, 35, 35, 35, 36, 36, 36, 38, 40, 40, 41, 41, 42, 42, 42, 43, 45, 46, 47, 49, 50, 50, 52, 53, 55, 56, 57, 58, 58, 58, 59, 59, 60, 61, 63, 63, 64, 64, 65, 65, 66, 66, 67, 67, 68, 69, 71, 72, 75, 76, 79, 80, 80; 2:3, 4, 4, 7, 7, 7, 8, 8, 9, 9, 9, 10, 12, 12, 13, 13, 14, 15, 15, 16, 16, 16, 16, 18, 20, 20, 20, 21, 21, 22, 24, 25, 25, 25, 25, 26, 27, 27, 28, 28, 28, 32, 33, 33, 34, 34, 34, 34, 35, 36, 37, 37, 37, 38, 38, 39, 40, 40, 41, 42, 43, 43, 44, 44, 45, 46, 46, 46, 47, 48, 48, 48, 49, 50, 51, 51, 51, 51, 52, 52, 52, 52; 3:1, 1, 1, 2, 3, 5, 5, 5, 5, 6, 8, 9, 9, 10, 11, 12, 12, 14, 14, 14, 14, 15, 16, 17, 18, 19, 20, 20, 21, 21, 22, 22, 23; 4:1, 2, 2, 4, 5, 6, 6, 6, 8, 8, 9, 9, 11, 12, 13, 14, 14, 15, 16, 16, 16, 17, 17, 18, 20, 20, 22, 22, 22, 23, 23, 25, 26, 27, 27, 28, 29, 29, 31, 31, 32, 33, 33, 34, 35, 35, 35, 36, 36, 36, 36, 37, 38, 39, 39, 41, 41, 41, 42, 42, 42, 43, 44; 5:1, 1, 2, 4, 5, 6, 7, 7, 7, 9, 10, 10, 10, 11, 12, 12, 13, 13, 14, 14, 15, 15, 16, 17, 17, 17, 17, 17, 17, 17, 18, 18, 18, 19, 20, 21, 21, 23, 24, 25, 26, 26, 26, 27, 27, 27, 28, 29, 29, 29, 30, 30, 30, 30, 31, 33, 33, 33, 35, 36, 36, 36, 37, 37, 37, 39; 6:1, 1, 3, 3, 4, 4, 5, 6, 6, 6, 7, 8, 8, 10, 10, 11, 12, 13, 13, 13, 14, 14, 14, 14, 14, 14, 15, 15, 15, 15, 16, 16, 17, 17, 17, 17, 17, 17, 18, 18, 19, 19, 20, 22, 22, 22, 23, 25, 29, 29, 29, 30, 31, 32, 32, 33, 33, 34, 34, 35, 35, 35, 35, 35, 36[U], 37, 37, 37, 37, 37, 38, 39, 42, 45, 46, 47, 47, 48, 48, 48, 49, 49, 49; 7:5, 7, 8, 8, 8, 8, 8, 8, 8, 9, 10, 11, 11, 11, 12, 12, 12, 13, 13, 14, 14, 15, 15, 15, 16, 16, 17, 17, 18, 18, 21, 21, 21, 22, 22, 22, 23, 25, 26, 29, 29, 30, 31, 32, 32, 32, 33, 34, 34, 34, 34, 35, 36, 37, 37, 38, 38, 38, 38, 39, 40, 44, 44, 49, 49; 8:1, 1, 1, 1, 1, 2, 2, 3, 3, 3, 4, 5, 5, 5, 6, 6, 7, 7, 8, 8, 10, 12, 13, 13, 14, 14, 14, 14, 15, 15, 17, 18, 18, 19, 19, 20, 21, 21, 22, 22, 22, 22, 23, 23, 23, 24, 24, 24, 25, 25, 25, 26, 27, 27, 28, 28, 29, 29, 29, 31, 32, 32, 33, 33, 34, 34, 35, 35, 35, 35, 37, 39, 39, 41, 41, 41, 42, 43, 44, 45, 45, 47, 47, 50, 51, 51, 51, 51, 52, 53, 55, 55, 55, 56; 9:1, 1, 2, 2, 3, 4, 4, 5, 6, 7, 9, 10, 10, 11, 11, 12, 12, 13, 15, 15, 16, 16, 16, 17, 17, 17, 18, 18, 22, 22, 22, 22, 22, 23, 23, 26, 26, 26, 28, 28, 28, 29, 29, 30, 30, 32, 32, 33, 33, 33, 33, 34, 35, 36, 36, 36, 38, 39, 39, 39, 39, 40, 40, 41, 41, 42, 42, 42, 45, 45, 48, 48, 49, 51, 52, 52, 53, 54, 54, 56, 57, 58, 58, 61, 62; 10:1, 1, 4, 6, 7, 8, 8, 9, 9, 10, 11, 13, 13, 14, 15, 16, 17, 19, 19, 19, 21, 21, 21, 21, 22, 22, 22, 23, 24, 24, 24, 24, 25, 27, 27, 27, 27, 28, 29, 30, 30, 30, 31, 32, 32, 33,

34, 34, 34, 35, 35, 35, 37, 39, 39, 41; **11:**1, 1, 4, 4, 4, 5, 5, 5, 6, 7, 7, 8, 9, 9, 9, 9, 10, 10, 11, 12, 14, 14, 14, 17, 18, 22, 23, 24, 25, 25, 26, 26, 26, 27, 28, 29, 30, 31, 31, 32, 32, 34, 34, 39, 39, 40, 41, 42, 42, 42, 42, 42, 43, 44, 45, 46, 46, 48, 49, 49, 49, 49, 51, 52, 53, 53, 53; **12:**2, 3, 4, 6, 7, 8, 10, 11, 11, 15, 17, 18, 18, 18, 18, 19, 21, 23, 24, 28, 29, 29, 29, 31, 33, 34, 35, 36, 36, 37, 37, 38, 38, 38, 40, 41, 42, 45, 45, 45, 45, 46, 46, 46, 47, 48, 49, 50, 52, 53, 53, 53, 54, 54, 55, 55, 56, 57, 58, 58, 59; **13:**2, 4, 6, 6, 7, 7, 8, 8, 9, 11, 11, 11, 12, 13, 13, 13, 14, 15, 15, 16, 17, 17, 18, 19, 19, 19, 20, 22, 22, 24, 25, 25, 25, 25, 26, 26, 27, 28, 28, 28, 28, 29, 29, 29, 29, 29, 30, 30, 31, 32, 32, 32, 32, 33, 33, 34, 34; **14:**1, 1, 2, 3, 3, 4, 4, 5, 5, 6, 9, 9, 9, 11, 12, 12, 12, 14, 16, 17, 18, 18, 19, 19, 20, 20, 21, 21, 21, 21, 21, 21, 22, 22, 23, 23, 23, 25, 26, 26, 26, 26, 26, 26, 26, 27N, 27, 29, 30, 34; **15:**1, 2, 2, 2, 4, 4, 5, 6, 6, 8, 8, 9, 9, 12, 13, 13, 14, 15, 15, 16, 16, 18, 18, 20, 20, 20, 20, 21, 22, 22, 22, 23, 23, 24, 24, 24, 25, 25, 26, 27, 28, 29, 29, 31, 32, 32, 32, 32; **16:**1, 1, 2, 5, 6, 7, 8, 9, 10, 10, 10, 12, 13, 13, 13, 14, 15, 16, 16, 17, 18, 18, 19, 19, 21, 21, 22, 22, 22, 23, 23, 24, 24, 24, 25, 26, 26, 28, 29, 31; **17:**2, 3, 4, 4, 5, 6, 6, 8, 8, 8, 8, 10, 11, 11, 11, 12, 13, 14, 14, 16, 16, 19, 20, 22, 23, 25, 26, 26, 27, 27, 29, 29, 31, 31, 34, 37, 37; **18:**1, 2, 3, 4, 4, 7, 7, 9, 9, 10, 11, 15, 16, 18, 20, 22, 22, 22, 26, 30, 31, 32, 32, 32, 32, 33, 34, 34, 34, 38, 39, 42, 43, 43, 43; **19:**1, 2, 2, 2, 3, 3, 4, 5, 6, 6, 7, 8, 9, 10, 11, 12, 13, 14, 15, 15, 17, 18, 19, 19, 20, 21, 22, 23, 23, 24, 24, 25, 26, 27, 28, 29, 29, 30, 31, 35, 35, 38, 39, 40, 41, 42, 43, 43, 43, 44, 44, 44, 45, 46, 47, 47, 47, 48; **20:**1, 1, 1, 2, 3, 3, 7, 8, 9, 9, 10, 11, 11, 11, 12, 12, 15, 16, 16, 19, 19, 19, 20, 20, 21, 21, 21, 24, 25, 26, 26, 28, 28, 29, 30, 31, 31, 31, 32, 34, 34, 35, 36, 37, 37, 37, 44, 46, 46, 46, 47; **21:**3, 5, 5, 7, 8, 9, 10, 11, 11, 11, 12, 12, 12, 15, 16, 16, 16, 16, 16, 17, 18, 21, 21, 23, 23, 24, 24, 24, 25, 25, 25, 25, 25, 26, 27, 27, 28, 29, 29, 31, 33, 34, 34, 34, 36, 38; **22:**2, 2, 4, 4, 5, 5, 6, 6, 8, 8, 11, 12, 13, 14, 14, 15, 17, 17, 19, 19, 20, 23, 24, 25, 26, 29, 30, 30, 32, 33, 33, 35, 35, 35, 35, 36, 36, 36, 37, 37, 39, 39, 41, 41, 44, 44, 45, 46, 47, 47, 50, 50, 51, 52, 52, 52, 53, 54, 55, 56, 56, 58, 58, 59, 59, 59, 60, 61, 61, 62, 63, 64, 65, 66, 66, 66; **23:**1, 2, 2, 4, 5, 7, 7, 8, 10, 11, 11, 12, 13, 13, 14, 15, 19, 23, 24, 25, 26, 27, 27, 28, 29, 29, 30, 32, 33, 33, 35, 35, 36, 37, 38, 39, 41, 42, 43, 44, 44, 46, 48, 49, 50, 50, 50, 51, 53, 53, 54, 54, 55, 56, 56; **24:**4, 4, 5, 7, 7, 8, 9, 9, 10, 10, 10, 11, 11, 12, 12, 13, 14, 15, 15, 15, 17, 18, 19, 19, 19, 20, 20, 21, 22, 23, 23, 24, 24, 24, 25, 25, 26, 27, 27, 28, 28, 29, 29, 29, 30, 30, 31, 31, 32, 33, 33, 33, 34, 35, 35, 36, 37, 38, 38, 39, 39, 39, 40, 40, 41, 43, 44, 44, 46, 46, 47, 47N, 49, 50, 51, 51, 52, 53; **Jn 1:**1, 1, 3, 4, 5, 5, 10, 10, 11, 14, 14, 14, 14, 15, 16, 17, 19, 19, 20, 20, 20, 21, 21, 21, 24, 25, 25, 29, 31, 32, 32, 33, 33, 34, 34, 35, 36, 37, 37, 38, 39, 39, 39, 40, 41, 43, 44, 45, 45, 46, 47, 48, 50, 51, 51, 51; **2:**1, 1, 2, 2, 3, 4, 4, 7, 8, 8, 9, 10, 10, 11, 11, 12, 12, 12, 12, 13, 13, 14, 14, 14, 14, 15, 15, 15, 15, 16, 18, 19, 19, 20, 20, 22, 22, 25; **3:**2, 3, 4, 5, 6, 8, 8, 9, 10, 10, 11, 11, 12, 13, 14, 19, 20, 22, 22, 22, 23, 23, 23, 26, 26, 26, 27, 29, 31, 32, 32, 35; **4:**1, 3, 10, 10, 10, 11, 12, 12, 12, 13, 16, 17, 18, 20, 23, 23, 23, 24, 24, 27, 27, 28, 28, 30, 34, 35, 35, 36, 36, 37, 38, 40, 41, 42, 45, 46, 47, 47, 48, 50, 53, 53; **5:**1, 5, 6, 8, 9, 9, 9, 10, 11, 12, 14, 15, 16, 17, 18, 19, 19, 20, 21, 21, 24, 24, 25, 25, 26, 27, 29, 30, 32, 33, 35, 37, 38, 39, 40, 43, 44; **6:**3, 5, 9, 11, 11, 13, 15, 17, 17, 17, 19, 19, 21, 22, 24, 25, 26, 26, 29, 30, 33, 35, 36, 36, 37, 40, 40, 42, 42, 43, 44, 45, 45, 49, 50, 51, 53, 54, 54, 55, 56, 56, 57, 57, 57, 58, 63, 64, 65, 66, 67, 69, 69, 70; **7:**1, 3, 3, 4, 10, 11, 12, 14, 16, 18, 19, 21, 21, 22, 26, 26, 28, 28, 28, 28, 29, 30, 31, 32, 32, 33, 34, 34, 35, 35, 36, 36, 37, 37, 42, 45, 45, 47, 51, 52, 52, 52, 53; **8:**2, 2, 3, 3, 7, 8, 9, 9, 11, 14, 14, 14, 16, 16, 17, 18, 19, 20, 21, 21, 23, 25, 26, 26, 28, 29, 32, 32, 33, 38, 39, 42, 44, 44, 44, 48, 48, 49, 50, 52, 52, 53, 55, 55, 55, 56, 56, 57, 59; **9:**1, 2, 6, 6, 7, 7, 7, 8, 8, 11, 11, 11, 11, 12, 14, 15, 15, 15, 16, 18, 19, 20, 20, 24, 27, 27, 28, 28, 30, 30, 31, 34, 34, 34, 35, 36, 36, 37, 37, 38, 39, 39, 40, 40; **10:**1, 3, 3, 3, 4, 8, 9, 9, 9, 10, 10, 10, 12, 12, 12, 12, 12, 13, 14, 14, 15, 15, 16, 16, 16, 16, 18, 20, 23, 24, 25, 27, 27, 28, 28, 28, 29, 30, 33, 35, 36, 38, 38, 38, 39, 40, 40, 41, 41, 42; **11:**1, 2, 5, 5, 8, 11, 15, 16, 19, 22, 25, 25, 26, 26, 28, 28, 28, 29, 31, 31, 33, 33, 34, 34, 37, 38, 41, 43, 44, 44, 44, 45, 46, 47, 47, 48, 48, 48, 48, 50, 52, 52, 54, 55, 56, 57; **12:**2, 3, 5, 6, 9, 9, 10, 11, 13, 13, 15, 17, 18U, 21, 22, 22, 22, 25, 26, 26, 27, 28, 28, 29, 30, 32, 34, 35, 36, 38, 40, 40, 40, 40, 41, 42, 44, 45, 47, 47, 48, 49, 50; **13:**2, 3, 3, 4, 4, 5, 5, 7, 9, 9, 10, 12U, 12, 13, 13, 14, 14, 15, 21, 21, 26, 26U, 27, 31, 32, 32, 33, 33, 34; **14:**1, 3, 3, 3, 3, 4, 6, 6, 7, 7, 7, 8, 9, 10, 11, 12, 12, 13, 16, 16, 17, 19, 19, 20, 20, 21, 21, 21, 22, 22, 22, 23, 23, 23, 23, 24, 26, 28, 29, 30, 31; **15:**1, 2, 4, 5, 6, 6, 6, 6, 7, 7, 8, 9, 10, 11, 16, 16, 16, 20, 20, 22, 23, 24, 24, 24, 24, 27; **16:**3, 5, 8, 8, 8, 10, 13, 14, 15, 16, 16, 16, 17, 17, 17, 17, 19, 19, 19, 19, 20, 22, 22, 22, 23, 24, 26, 27, 28, 28, 29, 30, 32, 32, 32; **17:**1, 3, 5, 6, 6, 8, 8, 8, 10, 10, 10, 11, 11, 11, 12, 12, 13, 14, 18, 19, 19, 20, 21, 21, 22, 23, 23, 24, 25, 25, 26, 26, 26; **18:**1, 2, 3, 3, 3, 3, 4, 5, 6, 10, 10, 12, 12, 12, 13, 15, 15, 16, 16, 17, 18, 18, 18, 19, 20, 20, 25, 25, 25, 27, 28, 29, 30, 31, 33, 33, 35, 37, 38, 38; **19:**1, 2, 2, 3, 3, 3, 4, 4, 5, 5, 6, 6, 7, 9, 10, 13, 14, 17, 18, 18, 19, 19, 20, 23, 23, 24, 25, 25, 26, 27, 30, 31, 32, 32, 34, 34, 35, 35, 35, 35, 37, 38, 38, 39, 39, 40, 41; **20:**1, 2, 2, 2, 2, 3, 3, 4, 4, 5, 6, 6, 6, 7, 8, 8, 8, 12, 12, 13, 13, 14, 14, 15, 17, 17, 17, 17, 18, 19, 19, 19, 20, 20, 21, 22, 22, 25, 25, 26, 26, 26, 26, 26, 27, 27, 27, 27, 28, 28, 29, 30, 31; **21:**2, 2, 2, 2, 3, 3, 3, 6, 6, 7, 9, 9, 11, 11, 13, 13, 13, 17, 18, 18, 18, 19, 20, 20, 24, 24, 25; **Ac 1:**1, 3, 3, 4, 8, 8, 8, 8, 9, 9, 10, 10, 11, 13, 13, 13, 13, 13, 13, 13, 13, 14, 14, 15, 17, 18, 18, 19, 20, 20, 21, 23, 23, 24, 25, 26, 26, 26; **2:**1, 2, 2, 3, 3, 4, 4, 6, 7, 8, 9, 9, 9, 9, 10, 10, 10, 11, 11, 12, 14, 14, 14, 17, 17, 17, 17, 17, 18, 18, 18, 19, 19, 19, 19, 20, 20, 21, 22, 22, 23, 26, 26, 29, 29, 30, 33U, 33, 36, 36, 37, 38, 38, 39, 39, 40, 41, 42, 42, 43, 44, 45, 45, 45, 46, 47; **3:**1, 2, 3, 6, 6U, 7, 7, 8, 8, 8, 8, 8, 9, 9, 10, 10, 11, 13, 13, 13, 14, 14, 16, 16, 16, 17, 17, 19, 20, 24, 24, 24, 25, 25; **4:**1, 1, 2, 3, 3, 4, 5, 5, 6, 6, 6, 6, 6, 7, 8, 10, 12, 13, 13, 13, 16, 18, 19, 20, 23, 23, 24, 24, 24, 24, 25, 26, 26, 27, 27, 28, 29, 29, 30, 30, 31, 31, 31, 32, 32, 33, 35, 37; **5:**2, 2, 2, 3, 4, 5, 6, 7, 9, 10, 10, 11, 11, 12, 12, 14, 15, 15, 15, 15, 16, 16, 17, 18, 18, 20, 21, 21, 21, 21, 23, 24, 25, 27, 28, 28, 29, 31, 31, 32, 32, 33, 36, 36, 37, 37, 37, 38, 38, 39, 40, 40, 42, 42; **6:**3, 4, 5, 5, 5, 5, 5, 5, 5, 5, 5, 6, 7, 7, 8, 8, 9, 9, 9, 9, 10, 10, 11, 12, 12, 12, 12, 13, 14, 15; **7:**2, 3,

3, 3, 4, 5, 5, 5, 6, 6, 7, 7, 7, 8, 8, 8, 8, 8, 9, 9, 10, 10, 10, 10, 10, 11, 11, 11, 13, 13, 14, 15, 15, 15, 16, 16, 17, 20, 21, 22, 22, 24, 24, 26, 27, 29, 30, 32, 32, 34, 34, 34, 35, 35U, 35, 36, 36, 36, 38, 39, 41, 41, 41, 42, 42, 43, 43, 43, 45, 46, 51, 51, 51, 52, 52, 53, 54, 55, 56, 56, 57, 58, 58, 59, 59, 60; **8:**1, 2, 3, 6, 7, 9, 12, 12, 13, 13, 13, 14, 17, 19, 22, 23, 25, 26, 27, 27, 28, 28, 29, 30, 32, 35, 36, 38, 38, 38, 38, 39, 40; **9:**1, 2, 4, 6, 6, 9, 9, 10, 11, 12, 12, 14, 15, 17, 17, 17, 18, 18, 19, 20, 21, 21, 22, 24, 24, 26, 27, 27, 27, 28, 28, 29, 30, 31, 31, 31, 31, 32, 34, 34, 34, 35, 35, 36, 39, 39, 39, 40, 40, 40, 41, 42; **10:**2, 2, 3, 4, 4, 5, 5, 7, 8, 9, 10, 11, 11, 12, 12, 13, 13, 14, 15, 16, 18, 20, 22, 22, 23, 24, 26, 27, 27, 28, 29, 30, 30, 31, 31, 32, 35, 38, 38, 39, 39, 39, 40, 41, 42, 42, 45, 45, 46, 47; **11:**1, 1, 3, 5, 5, 6, 6, 6, 6, 7, 7, 10, 11, 12, 12, 13, 13, 14, 15, 17, 18, 18, 19, 19, 20, 20, 21, 22, 23, 23, 23, 24, 24, 24, 26, 26, 26, 30, 30; **12:**3, 4, 7, 7, 7, 8, 8, 8, 9, 9, 10, 10, 10, 11, 11, 11, 12, 14, 16, 17, 17, 19, 19, 20, 20, 21, 22, 23, 24, 25; **13:**1, 1, 1, 1, 2, 2, 3, 3, 5, 5, 7, 9, 10, 11, 11, 11, 11, 14, 15, 16, 16, 17, 17, 18, 19, 20, 20, 21, 21, 22, 22, 26, 27, 27, 28, 32, 33, 35, 36, 36, 38, 41, 41, 43, 43, 45, 46, 46, 48, 48, 50, 50, 50, 50, 52; **14:**1, 1, 2, 3, 4, 5, 5, 6, 6, 7, 8, 9, 10, 10, 13, 14, 15, 15, 15, 15, 15, 17, 17, 18, 19, 19, 19, 20, 21, 21, 21, 22, 24, 25, 26, 27, 27; **15:**1, 2, 2, 2, 2, 2, 3, 3, 4, 4, 6, 7, 8, 8, 9, 9, 11, 12, 12, 12, 15, 16, 16, 16, 17, 20, 20, 20, 22, 22, 22, 23, 23, 23, 25, 27, 27, 28, 29, 29, 29, 30, 32, 32, 32, 35, 35, 35, 37, 38, 41; **16:**1, 1, 1, 2, 3, 4, 5, 6, 7, 9, 9, 9, 12, 13, 14, 15, 15, 17, 18, 18, 19, 20, 21, 22, 22, 24, 25, 26, 27, 29, 29, 30, 31, 31, 32, 33, 33, 33, 33, 34, 37, 39, 39, 40, 40; **17:**1, 2, 3, 3, 3, 4, 4, 4, 5, 5, 5, 6, 6, 7, 8, 9, 9, 10, 12, 12, 13, 13, 13, 14, 15, 15, 17, 17, 18, 18, 18, 18, 21, 23, 23, 24, 24, 25, 25, 26, 27, 27, 28, 28, 28, 28, 29, 32, 34, 34, 34; **18:**2, 2, 3, 3, 4, 5, 6, 7, 8, 8, 9, 10, 11, 12, 15, 15, 16, 17, 18, 18, 19, 21, 22, 22, 23, 23, 25, 25, 26, 26; **19:**1, 6, 6, 8, 9, 10, 12, 12, 13, 15, 16, 16, 17, 17, 17, 18, 19, 19, 20, 21, 21, 22, 25, 26, 26, 27, 27, 27, 28, 29, 29, 31, 32, 35, 36, 38, 38, 40, 41; **20:**1, 2, 4, 4, 4, 4, 6, 9, 10, 11, 11, 12, 15, 19, 19, 20, 20, 21, 21, 22, 23, 24, 25, 28, 30, 31, 32, 32, 32, 34, 36, 37; **21:**1, 2, 3, 3, 5, 5, 6, 7, 8, 11, 11, 11, 11, 12, 13, 13, 16, 19, 20, 24, 24, 24, 25, 25, 27, 27, 28, 28, 28, 28, 30, 30, 30, 32, 32, 33, 33, 33, 38; **22:**1, 2, 4, 4, 5, 5, 5, 5, 6, 7, 10, 13, 13, 14, 14, 15, 16, 16, 17, 18, 18, 19, 19, 20, 20, 20, 20, 21, 22, 23, 23, 25, 28, 29, 29, 30, 30, 30; **23:**3, 3, 6, 7, 7, 9, 11, 14, 16, 18, 19, 21, 23, 23, 23, 27, 30, 33, 33, 34, 34, 35; **24:**1, 2, 3, 5, 6, 6, 9, 12, 14, 15, 15, 16, 16, 17, 19, 23, 24, 25, 25, 26, 26; **25:**2, 3, 7, 10, 11, 13, 15, 19, 20, 22, 23, 23, 23, 23, 24, 24, 24, 26, 27; **26:**3, 6, 7, 10, 10, 11, 11, 12, 13, 16, 16, 17, 18, 18, 20, 20, 20, 22, 22, 23, 25, 26, 29, 29, 29, 29, 30, 30, 31; **27:**1, 4, 5, 6, 7, 9, 9, 10, 10, 10, 11, 12, 15, 19, 21, 22, 23, 24, 28, 28, 30, 31, 32, 35, 35, 36, 40, 40, 41, 44, 44; **28:**1, 2, 3, 6, 8, 8, 9, 9, 10, 10, 12, 13, 14, 15, 15, 20, 23, 24, 26, 26, 26, 26, 27, 27, 27, 27, 27, 27, 28, 30, 31; **Ro 1:**5, 6, 7, 7, 12, 13, 13, 13, 14, 14, 15, 16, 18, 20, 21, 23, 23, 23, 23, 25, 25, 27, 27, 28, 32; **2:**3, 4, 4, 5, 5, 7, 7, 8, 8, 9, 9, 10, 10, 10, 12, 12, 15, 15, 17, 17, 18, 18, 20, 27, 27, 29; **3:**4, 7, 8, 8, 9, 14, 16, 17, 19, 21, 23, 26, 29, 29, 30; **4:**3, 6, 7, 9, 11, 11U, 12, 12, 14, 16, 17, 19, 19, 21, 21, 22, 24, 25; **5:**2, 2, 3, 7, 11, 12, 12, 14, 15, 15, 16, 17, 18, 19, 21; **6:**4, 5, 8, 11, 13, 19; **7:**4, 6, 10, 11, 12, 12, 12, 23; **8:**2, 3, 6, 11, 17, 17, 21, 22, 23U, 23, 26, 29, 30, 30, 30, 30, 32, 34, 34; **9:**2, 4, 4, 4, 4, 5, 9, 10, 15, 17, 22, 23, 24, 24, 25, 25, 26, 28, 29, 29, 33, 33; **10:**1, 3, 8, 9, 12, 18, 20, 21; **11:**1, 3, 3, 5, 8, 9, 9, 9, 9, 10, 12, 14, 16, 16, 16, 17, 22, 22, 23, 24, 26, 27, 29, 31, 31, 33, 33, 33, 35, 36, 36; **12:**2, 2, 2, 14; **13:**3, 5, 6, 9, 11, 13, 13, 13, 14; **14:**6, 6, 6, 7, 9, 9, 9, 10, 11, 14, 17, 17, 17, 18, 19; **15:**1, 3, 4, 5, 6, 7, 9, 10, 11, 11, 12, 12, 13, 14, 14, 14, 18, 19, 19, 21, 22, 24, 26, 27, 27, 28, 30, 31; **16:**1, 2, 2, 2, 3, 4, 5, 7, 7, 7, 9, 12, 13, 13, 14, 15, 15, 15, 15, 17, 17, 18, 18, 21, 21, 21, 23, 23, 25; **1Co 1:**1, 2, 3, 3, 5, 8, 10, 10, 14, 16, 19, 22, 22, 24, 24, 25, 27, 28, 28, 30, 30; **2:**1, 2, 3, 3, 3, 4, 4, 4, 9, 9, 10, 11, 13, 14; **3:**1, 3, 3, 5, 8, 13, 16, 20; **4:**1, 5, 5, 5, 6, 7, 8, 9, 9, 11, 11, 11, 11, 11, 12, 17, 19; **5:**1, 2, 2, 4, 7, 8, 8, 10; **6:**1, 2, 6, 8, 8, 11, 11, 13, 13, 13, 13, 14, 14, 19; **7:**2, 3, 4, 5, 7, 8, 8, 11, 11, 12, 13, 13, 14, 17, 19, 21, 28, 28, 29, 30, 30, 30, 31, 34, 34, 34, 34, 34, 35, 36, 37, 38, 38, 40; **8:**4, 5, 5, 6, 6, 6, 7, 12; **9:**4, 5, 5, 5, 6, 7, 7, 8, 10, 14, 20, 27; **10:**1, 2, 2, 3, 4, 6, 7, 7, 8, 9, 10, 13, 20, 21, 21, 26, 27, 28, 32, 32, 32, 33; **11:**1, 2, 5, 6, 7, 9, 12, 18, 19, 19, 21, 22, 22, 23, 24, 24, 25, 26, 27, 28, 28, 29, 29, 30, 30; **12:**3, 5, 5, 6, 11, 12, 12, 13, 13, 14, 16, 23, 23, 26, 27, 28, 31; **13:**1, 2, 2, 2, 2, 3, 3, 9, 12; **14:**3, 3, 8, 9, 10, 11, 12, 15, 19, 21, 23, 25, 27, 28, 29, 31, 32, 34, 39, 40; **15:**1, 2, 3, 4, 4, 5, 8, 10, 11, 14, 14, 15, 18, 21, 22, 24, 24, 24, 28U, 29, 30, 32, 34, 37, 38, 40, 40, 41, 41, 42, 44, 45, 48, 48, 48, 49, 49, 50, 52, 52, 53, 54; **16:**1, 4, 6, 9, 9, 10, 12, 15, 16, 16, 16, 17, 17, 18, 19; **2Co 1:**1, 2, 2, 3, 3, 5, 6, 6, 7, 7, 8, 10, 10, 11, 12, 12U, 13, 14, 14, 15, 16, 16, 16, 17, 18, 19, 19, 19, 20, 21, 22, 22; **2:**2, 3, 4, 7, 9, 10, 10, 12, 14, 15, 16; **3:**2, 6, 10, 13; **4:**3, 7, 10, 11, 13, 13, 14, 14, 16, 16; **5:**2, 3, 4, 6, 8, 8, 9, 11, 12, 15, 15, 16, 18, 19; **6:**1, 2, 7, 8, 8, 8, 9, 9, 9, 10, 13, 14, 16, 16, 16, 17, 17, 17, 18, 18, 18; **7:**1, 3, 5, 7, 8, 8, 8, 12, 14, 15, 15; **8:**2, 3, 4, 5, 5, 6, 6, 7, 7, 7, 7, 7, 8, 10, 10, 11, 11, 14, 15, 19, 19, 21, 23, 24; **9:**2, 4, 5, 5, 6, 6, 6, 10, 10, 10, 10, 12, 13, 13, 14; **10:**1, 5, 5, 6, 7, 8, 10, 10, 11, 12, 13, 14; **11:**1, 3, 6, 9, 9, 9, 9, 12, 12, 14, 15, 16, 16, 18, 21, 22, 22, 22, 27, 27, 27, 29, 29, 31, 33, 33; **12:**1, 3, 4, 7, 9, 10, 11, 12, 12, 14, 15, 18, 20, 21, 21, 21, 21; **13:**1, 2, 2, 2, 4, 4, 9, 10, 11, 11, 14, 14; **Gal 1:**1, 2, 3, 3, 4, 7, 8, 9, 13, 14, 15, 16, 17, 18, 21, 24; **2:**1, 2, 8, 9, 9, 9, 10, 12, 13, 13U, 13, 14, 15, 16, 16, 17, 20; **3:**4, 5, 6, 16, 16, 16, 17, 28; **4:**2, 3, 7, 9, 10, 10, 10, 12, 14, 18, 20, 22, 27, 29, 30; **5:**1, 12, 15, 16, 21, 24, 25; **6:**1, 1, 2, 4, 4, 7, 14, 16, 16, 16; **Eph 1:**1, 2, 2, 3, 4, 8, 10, 11, 13, 13, 15, 15, 17, 19, 20, 21, 21, 21, 21, 21, 22, 22; **2:**1, 1, 3, 3, 3, 3, 5, 6, 6, 8, 12, 12, 14, 16, 17, 17, 19, 19, 20, 22; **3:**5, 6, 6, 9, 10, 12, 15, 17, 18, 18, 18, 21; **4:**2, 4, 4, 6, 6, 6, 9, 10, 11, 11, 13, 14, 16, 17, 17, 21, 24, 24, 26, 30, 31, 31, 31, 31, 32; **5:**2, 2, 2, 2, 3, 4, 4, 5, 9, 9, 11, 11, 12, 14, 14, 18, 19, 19, 19, 20, 23, 24, 25, 25, 27, 28, 29, 31, 31, 31, 32, 33; **6:**2, 3, 4, 4, 5, 7, 9, 9, 9, 10, 12, 13, 14, 15, 17, 17, 18, 18, 18, 19, 21, 21, 22, 23, 23; **Php 1:**1, 1, 2, 2, 7, 7, 9, 9, 9, 10, 11, 13, 14, 15, 15, 15, 18, 18, 19, 20, 20, 21, 22, 23, 25, 25, 25, 27, 28, 28, 29, 30; **2:**1, 4, 5, 8, 9, 9, 10, 10, 11, 12, 13, 13, 14, 15, 15, 17, 17, 17, 18, 18, 19, 24, 25, 25, 25, 26, 27, 27, 28, 29; **3:**3, 3, 4, 8, 8, 9, 10, 10, 12, 12, 15, 15, 17, 18, 19, 20, 21; **4:**1, 1, 2, 3, 3, 3, 6, 7, 7, 8, 9, 9, 9, 9, 9, 10, 12, 12, 12, 12, 12, 12, 12, 15, 15, 16, 16, 16, 18, 20; **Col 1:**1, 2, 2, 4, 6,

6, 6, 6, 8, 9, 9, 9, 10, 11, 13, 16, 16, 16, 17, 17, 18, 20, 21, 21, 22, 22, 23, 23, 24, 26, 28, 29; **2:**1, 1, 2, 3, 5, 5, 5, 7, 7, 8, 8, 10, 10, 11, 12, 13, 13, 14, 15, 16, 18, 19, 19, 19, 22, 23, 23; **3:**3, 4, 5, 7, 8, 10, 11, 11, 11, 12, 13, 13, 13, 15, 15, 15, 16, 17, 19, 23, 25; **4:**1, 1, 3, 3, 7, 7, 8, 9, 10, 11, 12, 13, 13, 14, 15, 15, 16, 16, 16, 16, 17; **1Th 1:**1, 1, 1, 1, 3, 3, 3, 5, 5, 5, 6, 6, 7, 8, 9, 9, 10; **2:**2, 8, 9, 9, 10, 10, 10, 12, 12, 12, 13, 13, 13, 14, 14, 15, 15, 15, 15, 15, 18, 18, 18, 19, 20; **3:**2, 2, 2, 4, 4, 4, 5, 5, 6, 6, 6, 6, 7, 10, 10, 11, 11, 12, 12, 12, 13; **4:**1, 1, 1, 4, 5, 6, 6, 6, 8, 10, 11, 11, 11, 12, 13, 14, 14, 16, 16, 17; **5:**1, 3, 3, 5, 6, 7, 8, 8, 11, 11, 12, 12, 13, 15, 15, 23, 23, 23, 24, 25; **2Th 1:**1, 1, 1, 2, 2, 3, 4, 4, 5, 7, 8, 9, 10, 11, 11, 11, 12, 12; **2:**1, 3, 4, 6, 8, 8, 9, 9, 10, 11, 13, 14, 15, 16, 16, 16, 17, 17; **3:**1, 1, 2, 2, 3, 4, 4, 5, 6, 8, 8, 10, 12, 15; **1Ti 1:**1, 2, 4, 5, 5, 9, 9, 9, 9, 10, 13, 13, 14, 15, 17, 19, 20; **2:**2, 2, 2, 3, 4, 5, 5, 7, 7, 8, 9, 9, 9, 14, 15, 15; **3:**7, 7, 10, 12, 13, 15, 16; **4:**1, 3, 4, 5, 6, 7, 8, 9, 10, 11, 16, 16, 16; **5:**4, 5, 5, 5, 5, 7, 8, 8, 13, 13, 13, 16, 17, 18, 20, 21, 21, 23, 24, 25, 25; **6:**1, 2, 2, 3, 3, 4, 5, 8, 9, 9, 9, 9, 10, 12, 13, 15, 15, 16, 20; **2Ti 1:**2, 3, 5, 5, 7, 7, 9, 9, 10, 11, 11, 12, 12, 13, 15, 16, 17, 18; **2:**2, 2, 5, 10, 11, 12, 12, 17, 17, 18, 19, 20, 20, 20, 20, 23, 26; **3:**5, 6, 7, 8, 8, 9, 11, 12, 13, 13, 14, 15, 16; **4:**1, 1, 1, 1, 2, 4, 6, 8, 10, 13, 15, 17, 17, 17, 18, 19, 19, 21, 21, 21, 21; **Tit 1:**1, 4, 4, 5, 9, 9, 10[U], 10, 14, 15, 15, 15, 16, 16; **2:**12, 12, 12, 13, 13, 14, 15, 15; **3:**3, 3, 3, 4, 5, 8, 8, 9, 9, 9, 9, 10, 11, 13, 14; **Phm 1:**1, 1, 2, 2, 2, 3, 3, 5, 5, 7, 9, 11, 11, 16, 16, 19, 21, 22; **Heb 1:**1, 2, 3, 5, 5, 6, 7, 7, 8, 9, 10, 10, 11, 12, 12, 12; **2:**2, 2, 4, 4, 4, 7, 9, 10, 11, 13, 13, 13, 14, 14, 15, 17; **3:**1, 2, 5, 6, 9, 10, 19; **4:**2, 2, 4, 5, 6, 10, 12, 12, 12, 12, 12, 12, 12, 13, 13, 16; **5:**1, 2, 2, 3, 3, 4, 4, 5, 6, 7, 7, 7, 9, 11, 12, 12, 12, 14; **6:**1, 2, 3, 4, 5, 6, 6, 7, 7, 8, 8, 9, 9, 10, 10, 12, 14, 15, 16, 19, 19; **7:**1, 2, 2, 4, 5, 6, 8, 9, 9, 11, 12, 15, 18, 20, 21, 22, 23, 25, 26, 26; **8:**2, 3, 3, 5, 6, 8, 8, 9, 10, 10, 10, 11, 11, 12, 13; **9:**1, 2, 2, 4, 4, 4, 7, 9, 10, 10, 11, 12, 13, 13, 15, 19[U], 19, 19, 19, 21, 21, 22, 22, 27, 28; **10:**4, 5, 6, 8, 8, 8, 11, 11, 15, 16, 17, 17, 20, 21, 22, 24, 24, 25, 27, 29, 29, 30, 33, 34, 34, 34, 37, 38; **11:**4, 5, 6, 7, 8, 9, 10, 11, 11, 12, 12, 12, 13, 13, 13, 15, 17, 19, 19, 20, 20, 21, 22, 23, 28, 32, 32, 32, 36, 36, 38, 38, 38, 39; **12:**1, 1, 2, 5, 8, 9, 9, 12, 13, 14, 15, 17, 18, 18, 18, 18, 19, 19, 20, 21, 21, 22, 22, 23, 23, 23, 24, 24, 26, 28, 29; **13:**3, 4, 4, 6, 8, 8, 9, 12, 16, 17, 17, 22, 24; **Jas 1:**1, 4, 5, 5, 6, 11, 11, 11, 11, 14, 17, 21, 22, 23, 24, 24, 25, 27, 27, 27; **2:**2, 3, 3, 4, 5, 6, 11, 12, 15, 16, 17, 18, 18, 19, 19, 22, 23, 23, 23, 24, 25, 25, 26; **3:**2, 3, 4, 4, 5, 5, 6, 6, 6, 7, 7, 7, 9, 9, 10, 11, 13, 14, 14, 16, 16, 17; **4:**1, 2, 2, 2, 2, 3, 7, 8, 8, 9, 9, 9, 10, 11, 12, 12, 13, 13, 13, 14, 15, 15, 17; **5:**2, 3, 3, 3, 4, 5, 7, 8, 10, 11, 11, 12, 14, 15, 15, 15, 16, 17, 17, 17, 18, 18, 18, 19, 20; **1Pe 1:**1, 2, 2, 3, 4, 4, 7, 7, 8, 10, 11, 15, 17, 19, 21, 21, 23, 24, 24; **2:**1, 1, 1, 1, 5, 6, 8, 8, 8, 11, 16, 18, 18, 20, 20, 21, 25; **3:**1, 3, 4, 5, 6, 7, 10, 10, 11, 11, 12, 13, 14, 15, 18, 19, 21, 22, 22; **4:**1, 3, 5, 6, 7, 11, 13, 14, 18, 18, 19; **5:**1, 1, 4, 12, 13; **2Pe 1:**1, 1, 2, 2, 3, 3, 4, 5, 8, 10, 11, 12, 14, 15, 16, 17, 18, 19, 19; **2:**1, 1, 1, 2, 3, 3, 5, 6, 6, 7, 8, 10, 11, 12, 12, 13, 14, 17, 20, 22; **3:**2, 2, 4, 5, 5, 7, 7, 8, 10, 10, 11, 12, 12, 13, 14, 15, 15, 16, 16, 16, 18, 18, 18, 18; **1Jn 1:**1, 2, 2, 2, 2, 2, 3, 3, 3, 3, 3, 4, 5, 5, 5, 6, 6, 7, 8, 9, 9, 10; **2:**1, 2, 2, 3, 4, 4, 6, 8, 8, 9, 10, 11, 11, 14, 14, 16, 16, 17, 17, 18, 18, 20, 20, 21, 22, 23, 24, 24, 25, 27, 27, 27, 27, 27, 28, 28, 29; **3:**1, 2, 3, 4, 4, 5, 5, 9, 10, 10, 12, 12, 13, 15, 16, 17, 17, 18, 19, 19, 20, 22, 22, 23, 23, 24, 24, 24; **4:**3, 3, 3, 4, 5, 6, 7, 7, 10, 11, 12, 13, 14, 14, 15, 16, 16, 16, 16, 17, 20, 21, 21; **5:**1, 1, 2, 3, 4, 6, 6, 6, 8, 8, 8, 11, 11, 14, 15, 16, 17, 18, 19, 20, 20, 20; **2Jn 1:**1, 1, 1, 2, 3, 3, 5, 6, 7, 9, 9, 9, 10, 10, 12, 12; **3Jn 1:**2, 3, 5, 10, 10, 10, 12, 12, 12, 13, 14; **Jude 1:**1, 2, 2, 4, 4, 7, 7, 7, 8, 11, 11, 14, 15, 15, 16, 22, 23, 24, 25, 25, 25; **Rev 1:**1, 2, 3, 3, 4, 4, 4, 4, 5, 5, 5, 6, 6, 6, 7, 7, 7, 8, 8, 8, 9, 9, 9, 9, 10, 11, 11, 11, 11, 11, 11, 11, 12, 12, 13, 13, 14, 14, 15, 15, 16, 16, 16, 17, 17, 17, 18, 18, 18, 18, 18, 19, 19, 20, 20; **2:**2, 2, 2, 2, 2, 2, 3, 3, 3, 5, 5, 5, 6, 8, 8, 8, 9, 9, 9, 10, 10, 12, 13, 13, 13, 14, 15, 16, 17, 17, 18, 18, 19, 19, 19, 19, 19, 20, 20, 20, 21, 21, 22, 23, 23, 23, 23, 26, 26, 27, 27, 28; **3:**1, 1, 1, 2, 3, 3, 3, 3, 4, 5, 5, 5, 7, 7, 7, 7, 8, 8, 9, 9, 9, 10, 12, 12, 12, 12, 14, 14, 16, 17, 17, 17, 17, 17, 17, 17, 18, 18, 18, 19, 19, 20, 20, 20, 20, 20, 21, 21; **4:**1, 1, 1, 2, 2, 3, 3, 3, 4, 4, 4, 5, 5, 5, 5, 6, 6, 6, 6, 7, 7, 7, 7, 8, 8, 8, 8, 8, 8, 9, 9, 9, 10, 10, 11, 11, 11, 11, 11; **5:**1, 1, 2, 2, 3, 4, 5, 5, 6, 6, 6, 6, 7, 7, 8, 8, 8, 9, 9, 9, 9, 9, 9, 10, 10, 10, 11, 11, 11, 11, 11, 11, 12, 12, 12, 12, 12, 12, 13, 13, 13, 13, 13, 13, 13, 13, 13, 14, 14, 14; **6:**1, 1, 2, 2, 2, 2, 2, 2, 3, 4, 4, 4, 4, 5, 5, 5, 5, 6, 6, 6, 6, 7, 8, 8, 8, 8, 8, 8, 8, 8, 9, 9, 10, 10, 10, 11, 11, 11, 11, 11, 12, 12, 12, 12, 13, 14, 14, 14, 15, 15, 15, 15, 15, 15, 15, 15, 16, 16, 16, 16, 17; **7:**2, 2, 2, 4, 9, 9, 9, 9, 9, 9, 10, 10, 11, 11, 11, 11, 11, 12, 12, 12, 12, 12, 12, 13, 13, 14, 14, 14, 14, 15, 15, 15, 17, 17; **8:**1, 2, 2, 3, 3, 3, 4, 5, 5, 5, 5, 5, 5, 5, 6, 7, 7, 7, 7, 7, 7, 7, 8, 8, 8, 9, 9, 10, 10, 10, 10, 11, 11, 11, 12, 12, 12, 12, 12, 12, 13, 13; **9:**1, 1, 1, 2, 2, 2, 2, 3, 3, 4, 5, 5, 6, 6, 6, 6, 7, 7, 7, 8, 8, 9, 9, 10, 10, 10, 11, 13, 13, 15, 15, 15, 15, 16, 17, 17, 17, 17, 17, 17, 17, 17, 18, 18, 19, 19, 20, 20, 20, 20, 20, 20, 21; **10:**1, 1, 1, 1, 2, 2, 3, 3, 4, 4, 4, 5, 5, 6, 6, 6, 6, 6, 6, 7, 8, 8, 8, 9, 9, 9, 9, 10, 10, 10, 10, 11, 11, 11, 11; **11:**1, 1, 1, 1, 2, 2, 2, 2, 3, 3, 4, 5, 5, 5, 6, 6, 7, 7, 7, 8, 8, 8, 9, 9, 9, 9, 9, 9, 10, 10, 10, 11, 11, 11, 11, 12, 12, 12, 13, 13, 13, 13, 13, 15, 15, 15, 15, 16, 16, 17, 17, 18, 18, 18, 18, 18, 18, 18, 18, 19, 19, 19, 19, 19, 19, 19; **12:**1, 1, 1, 2, 2, 2, 3, 3, 3, 3, 4, 4, 4, 5, 5, 5, 6, 7, 7, 7, 7, 8, 9, 9, 9, 10, 10, 10, 10, 10, 11, 11, 11, 12, 12, 13, 14, 14, 14, 15, 16, 16, 16, 17, 17, 17; **13:**1, 1, 1, 1, 1, 2, 2, 2, 2, 2, 2, 3, 3, 3, 4, 4, 4, 5, 5, 5, 5, 6, 6, 7, 7, 7, 7, 7, 7, 8, 10, 11, 11, 11, 12, 12, 12, 13, 13, 14, 14, 15, 15, 15, 16, 16, 16, 16, 16, 16, 17, 18; **14:**1, 1, 1, 1, 2, 2, 2, 3, 3, 3, 3, 4, 5, 6, 6, 6, 6, 6, 7, 7, 7, 7, 7, 8, 9, 9, 9, 10, 10, 10, 10, 11, 11, 11, 11, 11, 12, 13, 14, 14, 14, 14, 15, 15, 16, 16, 17, 17, 18, 18, 18, 19, 19, 19, 20, 20; **15:**1, 1, 2, 2, 2, 2, 3, 3, 3, 3, 4, 4, 5, 5, 6, 6, 7, 8, 8, 8; **16:**1, 1, 2, 2, 2, 2, 2, 3, 3, 3, 4, 4, 4, 5, 5, 6, 6, 7, 7, 8, 8, 9, 9, 9, 10, 10, 10, 11, 11, 11, 12, 12, 13, 13, 13, 15, 15, 16, 17, 17, 18, 18, 18, 18, 19, 19, 19, 20, 20, 21, 21; **17:**1, 1, 2, 3, 3, 3, 4, 4, 4, 4, 4, 4, 5, 5, 6, 6, 6, 7, 7, 7, 8, 8, 8, 8, 8, 8, 10, 10, 11, 11, 11, 11, 11, 12, 13, 13, 14, 14, 14, 14, 14, 15, 15, 15, 15, 16, 16, 16, 16, 16, 16, 17, 17, 18; **18:**1, 2, 2, 2, 2, 2, 2[U], 3, 3, 4, 4, 5, 6, 6, 7, 7, 7, 7, 8, 8, 8, 9, 9, 9, 11, 11, 12, 12, 12, 12, 12, 12, 12, 12, 12, 12, 12, 12, 12, 13, 13, 13, 13, 13, 13, 13, 13, 13, 13, 13, 13, 13, 13, 13, 14, 14, 14, 14, 15, 16, 16, 16, 16, 16, 17, 17, 17, 17, 18, 19, 19, 19, 20, 20, 20, 21, 21, 21, 22, 22, 22, 22, 22, 22, 23, 23, 23, 24, 24, 24; **19:**1, 1, 2, 2, 3, 3, 4, 4, 4, 5, 5, 5, 6, 6, 6, 7, 7, 7, 8, 9, 9, 10, 10, 10, 11, 11, 11, 11, 11, 11, 12, 13, 13, 14, 15, 15, 15, 16, 16, 16, 17, 17, 18, 18, 18, 18, 18, 18, 18, 18, 19, 19, 19, 19, 20, 20, 20, 21, 21; **20:**1, 1, 2, 2, 2, 3, 3, 3, 4, 4, 4, 4, 4, 4, 4, 4, 4, 4, 6, 6, 6, 7, 8, 8, 9, 9, 9, 9, 9, 10, 10, 10, 10, 10, 10, 11, 11, 11, 11, 12, 12, 12, 12, 12, 13, 13, 13, 13, 14, 14, 15; **21:**1, 1, 1, 1, 2, 3, 3, 3, 3, 4, 4, 5, 5, 5, 6, 6, 6, 7, 7, 8, 8, 8, 8, 8, 8, 8, 8, 9, 9, 10, 10, 10, 12, 12, 12, 13, 13, 13, 14, 14, 15, 15, 15, 16, 16, 16, 16, 16, 16, 17, 18, 18, 21, 21, 22, 22, 23, 23, 24, 24, 25, 26, 26, 27, 27, 27; **22:**1, 1, 2, 2, 2, 3, 3, 3, 3, 4, 4, 5, 5, 5, 5, 6, 6, 6, 7, 8, 8, 8, 8, 9, 9, 9, 10, 11, 11, 11, 12, 13, 13, 13, 14, 15, 15, 15, 15, 15, 15, 16, 17, 17, 17, 17, 19, 19

3590 μή, *mē* [1041 / 1040]

Mt **1:**19, 20; **2:**12; **3:**9, 10; **5:**13, 17, 18, 20, 20, 26, 29, 30, 34, 39, 42; **6:**1, 1, 2, 3, 7, 8, 13, 15, 16, 18, 19, 25, 31, 34; **7:**1, 1, 6, 9, 10, 19, 26; **8:**28; **9:**15, 17, 36; **10:**5, 5, 9, 10, 13, 14, 19, 23, 26, 28, 28, 31, 34, 42; **11:**6, 23, 27, 27; **12:**4, 16, 24, 29, 30, 30, 39; **13:**5, 6, 14, 14, 19, 57; **14:**17, 27; **15:**6, 24; **16:**4, 22, 28; **17:**7, 8, 27; **18:**3, 3, 10, 13, 16, 25, 35; **19:**6, 9, 14; **21:**19, 21; **22:**12, 23, 24, 25, 29; **23:**3, 8, 9, 23, 39; **24:**2, 4, 6, 17, 18, 20, 21, 22, 23, 26, 26, 34, 35, 36; **25:**9, 29; **26:**5, 5, 29, 35, 41, 42; **28:**5, 10; **Mk 2:**4, 7, 19, 21, 22, 26; **3:**9, 12, 20, 27; **4:**5, 6, 12, 12, 22; **5:**7, 10, 36, 37; **6:**4, 5, 8, 8, 8, 8, 9, 11, 34, 50; **7:**3, 4; **8:**1, 14; **9:**1, 9, 29, 39, 41; **10:**9, 14, 15, 15, 18, 19, 19, 19, 19, 19, 30; **11:**13, 23; **12:**15, 18, 19, 21, 24; **13:**2, 2, 5, 7, 11, 15, 16, 18, 19, 20, 21, 30, 31, 32, 36; **14:**2, 25, 31, 38; **16:**6, 18; **Lk 1:**13, 15, 20, 30; **2:**10, 26, 45; **3:**8, 9, 11; **4:**26, 27, 42; **5:**10, 19, 21, 34, 36, 37; **6:**4, 29, 30, 37, 37, 37, 37, 49; **7:**6, 13, 23, 30, 33, 42; **8:**6, 10, 10, 12, 17, 18, 28, 31, 50, 51, 52; **9:**5, 27, 33, 45, 50; **10:**4, 4, 4, 6, 7, 10, 15, 19, 20, 22, 22; **11:**4, 7, 23, 23, 24, 29, 35, 36, 42; **12:**4, 4, 7, 11, 21, 22, 29, 29, 32, 33, 47, 48, 59; **13:**3, 5, 9, 11, 14, 35; **14:**8, 12, 29, 32; **16:**26, 28; **17:**1, 9, 18, 23, 31, 31; **18:**1, 2, 2, 5, 7, 16, 17, 17, 19, 20, 20, 20, 20, 30; **19:**26, 27; **20:**7, 16, 27; **21:**8, 8, 9, 14, 18, 21, 32, 33; **22:**16, 18, 32, 35, 36, 40, 42, 46, 67, 68; **23:**28; **24:**16, 23; **Jn 2:**16; **3:**2, 3, 4, 5, 7, 13, 16, 18, 18, 20, 27; **4:**12, 14, 15, 33, 48, 48; **5:**14, 19, 23, 28, 45; **6:**12, 20, 22, 27, 35, 35, 37, 39, 43, 44, 46, 50, 53, 64, 65, 67; **7:**15, 23, 24, 31, 35, 41, 47, 48, 49, 51, 51, 52; **8:**12, 24, 51, 52, 53; **9:**27, 33, 39, 40; **10:**1, 5, 10, 21, 28, 37, 38; **11:**26, 37, 50, 56; **12:**15, 24, 35, 40, 42, 46, 47, 48; **13:**8, 8, 9, 10, 38; **14:**1, 2, 6, 11, 24, 27; **15:**2, 4, 4, 6, 22, 24; **16:**1, 7; **17:**12; **18:**11, 17, 25, 28, 30, 36, 40; **19:**11, 15, 21, 24, 31; **20:**17, 25, 25, 27, 29; **21:**5; **Ac 1:**4, 20; **2:**25; **3:**23; **4:**17, 18, 20; **5:**7, 26, 28, 40; **7:**19, 28, 42, 60; **8:**31; **9:**9, 26, 38; **10:**15, 47; **11:**9, 19; **12:**19; **13:**11, 40, 41; **14:**18; **15:**1, 19, 38, 38; **17:**6; **18:**9, 9; **19:**31; **20:**10, 16, 20, 22, 27, 29; **21:**4, 12, 14, 21, 34; **23:**8, 10, 21; **24:**4; **25:**24, 27; **26:**32; **27:**7, 15, 17, 21, 24, 29, 31, 42; **28:**26, 26; **Ro 1:**28; **2:**14, 14, 21, 22; **3:**3, 4, 5, 6, 8, 31; **4:**5, 8, 17, 19; **5:**13, 14; **6:**2, 12, 15; **7:**3, 7, 7, 7, 13; **8:**4; **9:**14, 14, 20, 29, 30; **10:**6, 15, 18, 19, 20, 20; **11:**1, 1, 8, 8, 10, 11, 11, 15, 18, 20, 21[U], 23, 25; **12:**2, 3, 11, 14, 16, 16, 19, 21; **13:**1, 3, 8, 13, 13, 13, 14; **14:**1, 3, 3, 3, 3, 6, 13, 14, 15, 16, 20, 21, 22; **15:**1, 20; **1Co 1:**7, 10, 13, 14, 15, 17, 28, 29; **2:**2, 5, 11, 11; **4:**5, 6, 6, 7, 18; **5:**8, 9, 11; **6:**9, 15; **7:**1, 5, 5, 10, 11, 12, 13, 17, 18, 18, 21, 23, 27, 27, 29, 30, 30, 30, 31, 37, 38; **8:**4, 8, 9, 13, 13; **9:**4, 5, 6, 8, 10, 12, 16, 18, 20, 21, 27; **10:**6, 12, 13, 22, 28, 33; **11:**22, 22, 29, 32, 34; **12:**3, 25, 29, 29, 29, 29, 30, 30, 30; **13:**1, 2, 3; **14:**5, 6, 7, 9, 11, 20, 28, 39; **15:**2, 33, 34, 36; **16:**2, 11; **2Co 1:**9; **2:**1, 2, 3, 5, 7, 11, 13; **3:**1, 7, 13, 14; **4:**2, 4, 7, 18, 18, 18; **5:**12, 19, 21; **6:**1, 3, 9, 14, 17; **8:**20; **9:**3, 4, 4, 5, 7; **10:**2, 9, 14; **11:**3, 16, 16; **12:**5, 6, 7, 7, 13, 17, 20, 20, 21, 21; **13:**7, 10; **Gal 1:**7, 19; **2:**2, 16, 17; **3:**21; **4:**8, 11, 18, 30; **5:**1, 7, 13, 15, 16, 17, 26; **6:**1, 7, 9, 9, 12, 14, 14; **Eph 2:**9, 12; **3:**13; **4:**9, 26, 26, 29, 30; **5:**7, 11, 15, 17, 18, 27; **6:**4, 6; **Php 1:**28; **2:**4, 12, 27; **3:**9; **4:**15; **Col 1:**23; **2:**8, 16, 21; **3:**2, 9, 19, 21, 21, 22; **1Th 1:**8; **2:**9, 15; **3:**5; **4:**5, 5, 6, 13, 13, 15; **5:**3, 6, 15, 19, 20; **2Th 1:**8, 8; **2:**2, 3, 3, 12; **3:**6, 8, 13, 14, 15; **1Ti 1:**3, 7, 20; **2:**9; **3:**3, 3, 6, 6, 7, 8, 8, 8, 11; **4:**14; **5:**1, 9, 13, 16, 19, 19; **6:**1, 2, 3, 17; **2Ti 1:**8; **2:**5, 14; **4:**16; **Tit 1:**6, 7, 7, 7, 7, 7, 11, 14; **2:**3, 5, 9, 10; **3:**14; **Phm 1:**14, 19; **Heb 3:**8, 13, 15, 18, 18; **4:**2, 7, 11, 15; **6:**1, 12; **7:**6; **8:**11, 12; **9:**9; **10:**17, 25, 35; **11:**3, 5, 8, 13, 27, 28, 40; **12:**3, 5, 13, 15, 15, 16, 19, 25, 27; **13:**2, 5, 5, 9, 16, 17; **Jas 1:**5, 7, 16, 22, 26; **2:**1, 11, 11, 13, 14, 14, 16, 17; **3:**1, 12, 14; **4:**2, 11, 17; **5:**9, 9, 12, 12, 17; **1Pe 1:**8, 14; **2:**6, 16; **3:**6, 7, 9, 10, 14; **4:**4, 12, 15, 16; **5:**2; **2Pe 1:**9, 10; **2:**21; **3:**8, 9, 17; **1Jn 2:**1, 4, 15, 22, 28; **3:**10, 10, 13, 14, 18, 21; **4:**1, 3, 8, 20; **5:**5, 10, 12, 16, 16; **2Jn 1:**7, 8, 9, 10, 10; **3Jn 1:**10, 11; **Jude 1:**5, 6, 19; **Rev 1:**17; **2:**5, 5, 11, 16, 17, 22; **3:**3, 3, 5, 12, 18; **5:**5; **6:**6; **7:**1, 3, 16; **8:**12; **9:**4, 4, 5, 6, 20; **10:**4; **11:**2, 6; **13:**15, 17, 17; **14:**3; **15:**4; **16:**15; **18:**4, 4, 7, 14, 21, 22, 22, 22, 23, 23; **19:**10, 12; **20:**3; **21:**25, 27, 27; **22:**9, 10

3836 ὁ, *ho* [19866 / 19867]

Mt **1:**2, 2, 2, 2, 3, 3, 3, 3, 3, 4, 4, 4, 5, 5, 5, 5, 5, 6, 6, 6, 6, 6, 7, 7, 7, 8, 8, 8, 9, 9, 9, 10, 10, 10, 11, 11, 11, 12, 12, 12, 13, 13, 13, 14, 14, 14, 15, 15, 15, 16, 16, 16, 17, 17, 17, 17, 18, 18, 18, 18, 19, 20, 20, 21, 21, 21, 22, 22, 23, 23, 23, 24, 24, 24, 24, 25; **2:**1, 1, 1, 2, 2, 2, 2, 3, 4, 4, 4, 5, 5, 5, 6, 6, 6, 7, 7, 7, 8, 9, 9, 9, 9, 9, 10, 11, 11, 11, 11, 12, 13, 13, 13, 13, 13, 14, 14, 14, 15, 15, 15, 15, 16, 16, 16, 16, 16, 16, 17, 17, 18, 19, 19, 20, 20, 20, 20, 20, 21, 21, 21, 22, 22, 22, 22, 23, 23; **3:**1, 1, 1, 1, 2, 2, 3, 3, 3, 3, 3, 4, 4, 4, 4, 5, 5, 5, 6, 6, 7, 7, 7, 8, 9, 9, 9, 9, 10, 10, 10, 11, 11, 12, 12, 12, 12, 12, 12, 13, 13, 13, 13, 13, 14, 15, 16, 16, 16, 16, 16, 17, 17, 17; **4:**1, 1, 1, 1, 3, 3, 3, 4, 4, 5, 5, 5, 5, 6, 6, 6, 7, 7, 8, 8, 8, 8, 10, 10, 11, 12, 13, 13, 14, 14, 15, 15, 16, 16, 16, 17, 17, 17, 18, 18, 18, 18, 18, 20, 20, 21, 21, 21, 21, 21, 21, 22, 22, 22, 23, 23, 23, 23, 23, 24, 24, 24, 25, 25; **5:**1, 1, 1, 2, 3, 3, 3, 3, 4, 5, 5, 6, 6, 7, 8, 8, 8, 9, 10, 10, 10, 12, 12, 12, 12, 13, 13, 13, 13, 14, 14, 15, 15, 15, 15, 16, 16, 16, 16, 16, 16, 17, 17, 18, 18, 18, 19, 19, 19, 19, 19, 19, 19, 20, 20, 20, 20, 21, 21, 22, 22, 22, 22, 22, 22, 22, 23, 23, 23, 24, 24, 24, 24, 25, 25, 25, 25, 25, 25, 26, 28, 28, 28, 29, 29, 29, 29, 30, 30, 30, 31, 32, 32, 33, 33, 33, 34, 34, 35, 35, 35, 36, 37, 37, 37, 39, 39, 39, 40, 40, 40, 42, 42, 43, 43, 44, 44, 45, 45, 45, 46, 46, 46,

47, 47, 47, 48, 48; **6:**1, 1, 1, 1, 1, 1, 2, 2, 2, 2, 2, 3, 3, 4, 4, 4, 4, 4, 5, 5, 5, 5, 5, 5, 6, 6, 6,
6, 6, 6, 6, 6, 7, 7, 8, 8, 9, 9, 9, 10, 10, 11, 11, 12, 12, 13, 14, 14, 14, 14, 15, 15[N], 15, 15,
16, 16, 16, 16, 17, 17, 18, 18, 18, 18, 18, 18, 18, 19, 21, 21, 22, 22, 22, 22, 22, 23, 23,
23, 23, 23, 24, 24, 24, 25, 25, 25, 25, 25, 25, 26, 26, 26, 26, 27, 28, 28, 29, 30, 30, 30,
32, 32, 32, 33, 33, 33, 34, 34, 34, 34; **7:**3, 3, 3, 3, 3, 3, 4, 4, 4, 4, 4, 5, 5, 5, 5, 5, 6, 6, 6,
6, 6, 8, 8, 8, 9, 11, 11, 11, 11, 11, 12, 12, 12, 13, 13, 13, 13, 13, 13, 14, 14, 14, 14, 14,
15, 16, 17, 20, 21, 21, 21, 21, 21, 21, 21, 21, 22, 22, 22, 22, 23, 23, 24, 24, 24, 25, 25,
25, 25, 25, 26, 26, 26, 26, 27, 27, 27, 27, 27, 28, 28, 28, 28, 29; **8:**1, 3, 3, 4, 4, 4, 6, 6, 8,
8, 8, 9, 10, 10, 10, 11, 11, 12, 12, 12, 12, 12, 12, 12, 13, 13, 13, 13, 14, 14, 14, 15, 15,
16, 16, 17, 17, 17, 17, 18, 18, 20, 20, 20, 20, 20, 20, 20, 21, 21, 22, 22, 22, 23, 23, 24,
24, 24, 26, 26, 27, 27, 27, 28, 28, 28, 28, 28, 29, 31, 31, 31, 32, 32, 32, 32, 32, 32, 33,
33, 33, 33, 34, 34, 34; **9:**1[N], 1, 2, 2, 2, 2, 3, 4, 4, 4, 5, 6, 6, 6, 6, 6, 6, 7, 8, 8, 8, 8, 9, 9,
10, 10, 10, 11, 11, 11, 11, 12, 12, 12, 14, 14, 14, 15, 15, 15, 15, 15, 16, 16, 17, 17, 17,
18, 18, 19, 19, 20, 20, 21, 22, 22, 22, 22, 23, 23, 23, 23, 23, 24, 25, 25, 25, 26, 26, 27,
28, 28, 28, 29, 29, 30, 30, 31, 31, 33, 33, 33, 33, 34, 34, 34, 34, 35, 35, 35, 35, 35, 35,
36, 37, 37, 37, 38, 38, 38; **10:**1, 2, 2, 2, 2, 2, 2, 2, 3, 3, 3, 4, 4, 4, 5, 5, 6, 6, 7, 7, 9, 10,
10, 12, 13, 13, 13, 14, 14, 14, 14, 14, 15, 16, 16, 17, 17, 18, 19, 20, 20, 20, 20, 22, 22,
23, 23, 23, 23[U], 23, 23, 24, 24, 25, 25, 25, 25, 25, 25, 27, 27, 27, 27, 28, 28, 28, 28, 29,
29, 30, 30, 32, 32, 32, 32[U], 33, 33, 33, 33[U], 34, 35, 35, 35, 36, 36, 37, 37, 38, 39, 39, 39,
39, 40, 40, 40, 41, 41, 42, 42; **11:**1, 1, 1, 1, 2, 2, 2, 2, 2, 3, 4, 7, 7, 7, 8, 8, 8, 8, 10, 10,
11, 11, 11, 11, 12, 12, 12, 12, 13, 13, 14, 15, 16, 16, 16, 19, 19, 19, 19, 20[N], 20, 20, 21,
21, 23, 23, 23, 25, 25, 25, 25, 26, 27, 27, 27, 27, 27, 27, 28, 29, 29, 29, 30, 30; **12:**1, 1, 1,
1, 1, 2, 2, 3, 3, 4, 4, 4, 4, 4, 4, 5, 5, 5, 5, 5, 6, 7, 8, 8, 8, 9, 10, 11, 11, 12, 13, 13, 13, 14,
15, 17, 17, 18, 18, 18, 18, 18, 19, 19, 20, 21, 22, 23, 23, 24, 24, 24, 24, 25, 26, 26, 26,
27, 27, 28, 28, 28, 29, 29, 29, 29, 29, 30, 30, 31, 31, 31, 32, 32, 32, 32, 32, 32, 33, 33,
33, 33, 33, 33, 34, 34, 34, 35, 35, 35, 35, 36, 37, 37, 38, 39, 39, 39, 40, 40, 40, 40, 40,
40, 41, 41, 41, 42, 42, 42, 42, 42, 43, 43, 44, 44[N], 45, 45, 45, 45, 45, 46, 46, 46, 47, 47,
48, 48, 48, 48, 49, 49, 49, 49, 50, 50, 50; **13:**1, 1, 1, 1, 2, 2, 3, 3, 4, 4, 4, 5, 5, 6, 7, 7, 8,
8, 9, 10, 11, 11, 11, 11, 14, 14, 15, 15, 15, 15, 15, 15, 15, 16, 16, 18, 18, 19, 19, 19, 19,
19, 19, 19, 20, 20, 20, 20, 21, 22, 22, 22, 22, 22, 22, 22, 22, 22, 23, 23, 23, 23, 24, 24,
24, 25, 25, 25, 25, 26, 26, 27, 27, 27, 28, 28, 29, 29, 29, 30, 30, 30, 30, 30, 30, 30, 31,
31, 31, 32, 32, 32, 32, 32, 33, 33, 34, 34, 35, 35, 35, 36, 36, 36, 36, 36, 36, 37, 37, 37,
37, 37, 38, 38, 38, 38, 38, 38, 38, 38, 39, 39, 39, 39, 39, 40, 40, 40, 41, 41, 41, 41, 41,
41, 41, 42, 42, 42, 42, 42, 43, 43, 43, 43, 43, 44, 44, 44, 44, 44, 45, 45, 47, 47, 47, 48,
48, 48, 49, 49, 49, 49, 49, 50, 50, 50, 50, 50, 51[N], 52, 52, 52, 52, 53, 53, 54, 54, 54, 54,
55, 55, 55, 55, 56, 57, 57, 57, 58; **14:**1, 1, 1, 2, 2, 2, 2, 3, 3, 3, 3, 4, 5, 6, 6, 6, 6, 6, 8, 8,
8, 8, 9, 9, 9, 10, 10, 11, 11, 11, 12, 12, 12, 13, 13, 13, 14, 15, 15, 15, 15, 15, 16, 17, 18,
19, 19, 19, 19, 19, 19, 19, 19, 19, 20, 20, 21, 22, 22, 22, 22, 23, 23, 24, 24, 24, 24, 25,
25, 26, 26, 26, 27, 28, 28, 29, 29, 29, 29, 29, 30, 31, 31, 32, 32, 33, 33, 34, 35, 35, 35,
35, 36, 36; **15:**1, 2, 2, 2, 2, 3, 3, 3, 3, 4, 4, 4, 4, 5, 5, 6, 6, 6, 6, 8, 8, 8, 10, 11, 11, 11, 11,
11, 11, 12, 12, 12, 13, 13, 13, 15, 15, 16, 17, 17, 17, 18, 18, 18, 18, 19, 20, 20, 20, 20,
21, 21, 22, 22, 23, 23, 24, 24, 24, 25, 26, 26, 26, 26, 27, 27, 27, 27, 27, 27, 28, 28, 28,
28, 29, 29, 29, 29, 30, 31, 31, 32, 32, 32, 32, 33, 34, 34, 35, 35, 36, 36, 36, 36, 36, 37,
37, 38, 39, 39, 39; **16:**1, 1, 2, 2, 3, 3, 3, 3, 3, 4, 5, 5, 6, 6, 6, 7, 8, 9, 9, 10, 10, 11, 11, 12,
12, 12, 12, 13, 13, 13, 13, 13, 13, 13, 14, 14, 14, 14, 16, 16, 16, 16, 17, 17, 17, 17, 18,
18, 19, 19, 19, 19, 19, 19, 19, 20, 20, 21, 21, 21, 21, 22, 23, 23, 23, 23, 23, 23, 24, 24,
24, 25, 25, 26, 26, 26, 27, 27, 27, 27, 27, 27, 28, 28, 28, 28; **17:**1, 1, 1, 2, 2, 2, 2, 4, 4, 5,
5, 5, 6, 7, 8, 9, 9, 9, 9, 9, 10, 10, 11, 12, 12, 13, 13, 14, 15, 15, 15, 16, 17, 18, 18, 18, 18,
19, 19, 20, 20, 20, 22, 22, 22, 22, 23, 24, 24, 24, 24, 24, 25, 25, 25, 25, 25, 25, 26, 26,
26, 27[N], 27, 27; **18:**1, 1, 1, 1, 1, 3, 3, 3, 4, 4, 4, 4, 5, 6, 6, 6, 6, 6, 7, 7, 7, 7, 7, 8, 8, 8, 8,
8, 9, 9, 9, 9, 10, 10, 10, 10, 10, 12, 12, 12, 13, 13, 14, 14, 14, 15, 15, 17, 17, 17, 17, 18,
18, 19, 19, 19, 20, 21, 21, 22, 23, 23, 23, 25, 25, 25, 26, 27, 27, 27, 28, 28, 29, 30, 30,
31, 31, 31, 31, 32, 32, 33, 34, 34, 34, 35, 35, 35, 35; **19:**1, 1, 1, 1, 1, 1, 3, 4, 4, 5, 5, 5, 5,
6, 8, 8, 9, 10, 10, 10, 10, 11, 11, 12, 12, 12, 12, 13, 13, 14, 14, 14, 14, 14, 15, 17, 17, 17,
17, 17, 18, 18, 19, 19, 19, 20, 21, 21, 21, 22, 22, 23, 23, 23, 23, 24, 24, 25, 26, 27, 28,
28, 28, 28, 28, 28, 28, 29; **20:**1, 1, 1, 2, 2, 2, 3, 4, 5, 6, 6, 7, 8, 8, 8, 8, 8, 8, 8, 9, 9, 10,
10, 11, 12, 12, 12, 12, 12, 13, 14, 14, 15, 15, 16, 16, 17, 17, 17[U], 18, 18, 18, 19, 19, 19,
20, 20, 20, 21, 21, 21, 22, 22, 23, 23, 23, 24, 24, 25, 25, 25, 25, 28, 28, 28, 30, 31, 31,
32, 33, 34, 34; **21:**1, 1, 2, 2, 3, 4, 4, 5, 5, 6, 6, 7, 7, 7, 8, 8, 8, 8, 8, 9, 9, 9, 9, 9, 9, 10, 11,
11, 11, 11, 12, 12, 12, 12, 12, 12, 12, 12, 13, 14, 15, 15, 15, 15, 15, 15, 15, 16, 17, 18,
19, 19, 19, 20, 20, 21, 21, 21, 21, 21, 22, 23, 23, 23, 23, 23, 24, 25, 25, 25, 26, 26, 27,
28, 28, 29, 30, 30, 31, 31, 31, 31, 31, 31, 31, 31, 31, 32, 32, 32, 34, 34, 34, 34, 34, 35,
35, 36, 37, 37, 38, 38, 38, 38, 39, 40, 40, 40, 41, 41, 41, 42, 42, 42, 43, 43, 43, 44, 44,
45, 45, 45, 46; **22:**1, 2, 2, 2, 3, 3, 3, 4, 4, 4, 4, 4, 5, 5, 5, 6, 6, 7, 7, 7, 7, 8, 8, 8, 9, 9, 9,
10, 10, 10, 11, 11, 12, 13, 13, 13, 13, 13, 13, 13, 15, 16, 16, 16, 16, 18, 18, 19, 19, 19,
20, 20, 21, 21, 21, 21, 23, 24, 24, 24, 25, 25, 25, 26, 26, 26, 27, 28, 28, 29, 29, 29, 29,
30, 30, 31, 31, 31, 31, 32, 32, 32, 32, 33, 33, 34, 34, 34, 36, 37, 37, 37, 37, 37, 38, 39,
40, 40, 40, 41, 41, 42, 42, 44, 44, 44, 46; **23:**1, 1, 1, 2, 2, 2, 3, 4, 4, 4, 5, 5, 5, 5, 5, 5[N], 6,
6, 6, 6, 7, 7, 7, 8, 9, 9, 9, 10, 11, 13, 13, 13, 13, 15, 15, 16, 16, 16, 16, 17, 17, 17, 17, 18,
18, 18, 19, 19, 19, 19, 20, 20, 20, 21, 21, 21, 22, 22, 22, 22, 22, 23, 23, 23, 23, 23, 23,
23, 23, 24, 24, 24, 25, 25, 25, 26, 26, 26[N], 26, 28, 29, 29, 29, 29, 30, 30, 30, 30, 31, 31,
32, 32, 33, 33, 34, 35, 35, 35, 35, 35, 35, 36, 37, 37, 37, 37, 37, 37, 38, 39; **24:**1, 1, 1, 1,
1, 2, 3, 3, 3, 3, 3, 3, 4, 5, 5, 6, 9, 9, 12, 12, 12, 12, 13, 14, 14, 14, 14, 14, 15, 15, 15, 15,
15, 16, 16, 16, 17, 17, 17, 17, 18, 18, 18, 19, 19, 19, 20, 21, 22, 22, 22, 23, 24, 26, 26,
27, 27, 27, 27, 28, 28, 29, 29, 29, 29, 29, 29, 29, 29, 29, 30, 30, 30, 30, 30, 30, 30, 30,
30, 31, 31, 31, 31, 32, 32, 32, 32, 32, 34, 35, 35, 35, 36, 36, 36, 36, 36, 37, 37, 37, 37,
37, 38, 38, 38, 38, 39, 39, 39, 39, 40, 41, 42, 43, 43, 43, 44, 44, 45, 45, 45, 45, 45, 46,
46, 47, 48, 48, 48, 49, 49, 50, 50, 51, 51, 51, 51, 51; **25:**1, 1, 1, 1, 3, 3, 4, 4, 4, 5, 6, 7, 7,
8, 8, 8, 8, 9, 9, 10, 10, 10, 10, 11, 12, 13, 13, 14, 14, 15, 16, 16, 17, 17, 18, 18, 18, 18,
19, 19, 20, 20, 21, 21, 21, 22, 22, 23, 23, 23, 24, 24, 25, 25, 25, 26, 27, 27, 27, 28, 28,
28, 29, 29, 30, 30, 30, 30, 30, 30, 31, 31, 31, 31, 32, 32, 32, 32, 33, 33, 34, 34, 34, 34,
34, 37, 40, 40, 40, 41, 41, 41, 41, 41, 41, 41, 45, 46; **26:**1, 1, 1, 2, 2, 2, 2, 3, 3, 3, 3, 3, 3,
4, 5, 5, 6, 6, 7, 8, 8, 9[N], 10, 10, 11, 12, 12, 12, 13, 13, 14, 14, 14, 15, 17, 17, 17, 17, 17,
18, 18, 18, 18, 18, 18, 18, 19, 19, 19, 20, 23, 23, 23, 23, 24, 24, 24, 24, 24, 24, 25, 26,
26, 26, 28, 28, 28, 29, 29, 29, 29, 29, 30, 30, 31, 31, 31, 31, 31, 32, 32, 33, 34, 34, 35,
35, 36, 36, 37, 37, 38, 39, 40, 40, 41, 41, 42, 43, 44, 45, 45, 45, 45, 45, 46, 47, 47, 47,
48, 49, 50, 50, 50, 51, 51, 51, 51, 51, 51, 52, 52, 52, 52, 53, 54, 55, 55, 55, 55, 56, 56,
56, 57, 57, 57, 57, 57, 58, 58, 58, 58, 58, 59, 59, 59, 61, 61, 62, 63, 63, 63, 63, 63, 63,
63, 64, 64, 64, 64, 64, 64, 65, 65, 65, 66, 67, 67, 68, 69, 69, 69, 70, 71, 71, 71, 72, 73,
73, 73, 74, 75, 75; **27:**1, 1, 1, 1, 2, 3, 3, 3, 4, 5, 5, 6, 6, 6, 7, 7, 7, 8, 8, 9, 9, 9, 9, 9, 10,
10, 11, 11, 11, 11, 11, 11, 12, 12, 13, 14, 15, 15, 17, 17[U], 17, 19, 19, 19, 20, 20, 20, 20,
20, 21, 21, 21, 21, 22, 22, 23, 23, 24, 24, 24, 24, 25, 25, 25, 26, 26, 27, 27, 27, 27, 27,
29, 29, 29, 30, 30, 31, 31, 31, 32, 35, 37, 37, 37, 37, 39, 39, 40, 40, 40, 40, 41, 41, 42,
43, 44, 44, 44, 45, 46, 46, 47, 49, 50, 50, 51, 51, 51, 51, 52, 52, 53, 53, 53, 54, 54, 54,
54, 54, 55, 55, 56, 56, 56, 56, 56, 57, 57, 58, 58, 58, 58, 59, 59, 60, 60, 60, 60, 61, 61,
61, 62, 62, 62, 62, 63, 64, 64, 64, 64, 64, 64, 64, 65, 66, 66, 66, 66; **28:**1, 1, 1, 1, 2, 3, 3,
4, 4, 5, 5, 5, 6, 7, 7, 7, 8, 8, 9, 9, 10, 10, 10, 11, 11, 11, 11, 12, 12, 13, 14, 15, 15, 15, 15,
16, 16, 16, 16, 17, 18, 18[U], 19, 19, 19, 19, 19, 20, 20, 20; **Mk 1:**1, 2, 2, 2, 2, 3, 3, 3, 4, 4,
5, 5, 5, 5, 6, 6, 7, 7, 7, 9, 9, 9, 10, 10, 10, 11, 11, 11, 12, 12, 13, 13, 13, 13, 14, 14, 14,
14, 14, 14, 15, 15, 15, 15, 16, 16, 16, 16, 17, 18, 19, 19, 19, 19, 19, 20, 20, 20, 21, 21,
22, 22, 23, 24, 24, 25, 26, 26, 27, 27, 28, 28, 28, 29, 29, 30, 31, 31, 32, 32, 32, 33, 33,
34, 36, 38, 39, 39, 39, 41, 42, 44, 44, 45, 45; **2:**2, 2, 2, 4, 4, 4, 4, 5, 5, 5, 5, 6, 6, 7, 8, 8,
8, 9, 9, 9, 10, 10, 10, 10, 11, 11, 12, 12, 13, 13, 14, 14, 14, 15, 15, 15, 16, 16, 16, 16, 16,
17, 17, 17, 18, 18, 18, 18, 18, 18, 19, 19, 19, 19, 19, 20, 20, 21, 21, 21, 22, 22, 22, 22,
23, 23, 23, 23, 24, 24, 25, 26, 26, 26, 26, 26, 26, 27, 27, 27, 27, 28, 28, 28; **3:**1, 1, 2, 3, 3,
3, 3, 4, 4, 5, 5, 5, 5, 5, 6, 6, 7, 7, 7, 7, 8, 8, 8[N], 8, 9, 9, 11, 11, 11, 11, 13, 15, 16, 16, 17,
17, 17, 17, 18, 18, 18, 20, 21, 22, 22, 22, 22, 22, 24, 25, 26, 27, 27, 27, 27, 27, 28, 28,
28, 28, 29, 29, 29, 31, 31, 32, 32, 32[U], 33, 33, 34, 34, 34, 35, 35; **4:**1, 1, 1, 1, 1, 2, 3, 4, 4,
4, 5, 5, 6, 6, 7, 7, 8, 8, 10, 10, 10, 11, 11, 11, 11, 11, 13, 13, 14, 14, 15, 15, 15, 15, 15,
15, 16, 16, 16, 17, 18, 18, 18, 18, 19, 19, 19, 19, 19, 19, 19, 20, 20, 20, 20, 21, 21, 21,
21, 26, 26, 26, 26, 27, 28, 28, 29, 29, 29, 30, 30, 31, 31, 31, 31, 32, 32, 32, 32, 33, 34,
35, 35, 36, 36, 37, 37, 37, 38, 38, 39, 39, 39, 41, 41; **5:**1, 1, 1, 1, 2, 2, 3, 3, 4, 4, 4, 5, 5,
6, 7, 7, 7, 8, 8, 8, 10, 11, 12, 13, 13, 13, 13, 13, 13, 13, 14, 14, 14, 14, 15, 15, 15, 15, 16,
16, 16, 17, 18, 18, 19, 19, 19, 20, 20, 21, 21, 21, 21, 22, 22, 23, 23, 26, 26, 27, 27, 27,
28, 29, 29, 29, 29, 30, 30, 30, 30, 31, 31, 32, 33, 33, 34, 34, 34, 35, 35, 35, 36, 36, 36,
37, 37, 38, 38, 39, 40, 40, 40, 40, 40, 41, 41, 41, 42; **6:**1, 1, 2, 2, 2, 2, 2, 3, 3, 3, 3, 4, 4,
4, 4, 5, 6, 6, 7, 7, 7, 8, 11, 11, 11, 14, 14, 14, 14, 15, 16, 17, 17, 17, 17, 18, 18, 18, 18,
19, 20, 20, 21, 21, 21, 21, 21, 22, 22, 22, 22, 22, 23, 24, 24, 24, 24, 25, 25, 25, 26, 26,
26, 27, 27, 27, 28, 28, 28, 28, 29, 29, 30, 30, 31, 31, 32, 33, 35, 35, 36, 37, 38, 39, 41,
41, 41, 41, 41, 41, 43, 44, 44[U], 45, 45, 45[U], 45, 46, 47, 47, 47, 48, 48, 48, 48, 49, 49, 50,
51, 51, 52, 52, 53, 54, 55, 55, 55, 56, 56, 56, 56; **7:**1, 1, 2, 2, 3, 3, 3, 3, 3, 5, 5, 5, 5, 5, 5,
6, 6, 6, 6, 6, 8, 8, 8, 8, 9, 9, 9, 10, 10, 10, 11, 11, 12, 12, 13, 13, 13, 14, 15, 15, 15, 15,
15, 17, 17[N], 17, 17, 18, 18, 19, 19, 19, 19, 20, 20, 20, 21, 21, 21, 21, 23, 23, 24, 25, 25,
26, 26, 26, 26, 27, 27, 27, 27, 28, 28, 28, 28, 28, 29, 29, 29, 30, 30, 30, 30, 31, 31, 31,
31, 32, 33, 33, 33, 33, 34, 35, 35, 35, 37, 37; **8:**1, 1, 2, 3, 4, 5, 6, 6, 6, 6, 6, 10, 10, 10,
11, 11, 12, 12, 12, 13[N], 13, 14, 15, 15, 15, 17[N], 17, 19, 19, 20, 20, 23, 23, 23, 23, 23, 24,
25, 25, 26, 27, 27, 27, 27, 27, 27, 27, 28, 28, 28, 29, 29, 31, 31, 31, 31, 31, 32, 32, 33,
33, 33, 33, 33, 33, 34, 34, 34, 35, 35, 35, 36, 36, 37, 38, 38, 38, 38, 38, 38, 38, 38, 38;
9:1, 1, 1, 2, 2, 2, 2, 3, 3, 4, 5, 5, 7, 7, 7, 8, 9, 9, 9, 10, 10, 11, 12, 12, 12, 14, 15, 17, 17,
18, 18, 19, 20, 20, 21, 21, 23, 23, 23, 24, 24, 24, 25, 25, 25, 25, 26, 27, 27, 28, 29, 30,
31, 31, 31, 32, 32, 33, 33, 34, 34, 35, 37, 37, 37, 38, 38, 39, 39, 41, 42, 42, 42, 42, 43,
43, 43, 43, 43, 43, 45, 45, 45, 45, 47, 47, 47, 47, 48, 48, 50, 50; **10:**1, 1, 1, 3, 4, 5, 5, 5,
7, 7, 7, 8, 9, 10, 10, 11, 12, 13, 14, 14, 14, 14, 14, 15, 15, 16, 18, 18, 19, 19, 19, 20, 21,
21, 22, 22, 23, 23, 23, 23, 23, 23, 24, 24, 24, 24, 24, 25, 25, 25, 25, 26, 27, 27, 28, 29,
29, 30, 30, 30, 31, 32, 32, 32, 32, 32, 33, 33, 33, 33, 33, 35, 36, 37, 37, 38, 38, 38, 39,
39, 39, 39, 40, 41, 42, 42, 42, 42, 45, 45, 45, 46, 46, 46, 47, 48, 49, 49, 50, 50, 50, 51,
51, 52, 52, 52; **11:**1, 1, 1, 2, 2, 3, 4, 5, 5, 6, 6, 7, 7, 7, 8, 8, 8, 9, 9, 9, 10, 10, 10, 11, 11,
11, 12, 13, 14, 14, 15, 15, 15, 15, 15, 15, 15, 15, 15, 16, 17, 17, 18, 18, 18, 18, 19, 20,
21, 21, 22, 23, 23, 23, 25, 25, 25, 25, 27, 27, 27, 27, 28, 29, 30, 30, 32, 32, 33, 33; **12:**2,
2, 2, 2, 2, 6, 7, 7, 7, 8, 9, 9, 9, 9, 10, 10, 12, 12, 13, 13, 14, 14, 15, 15, 16, 16, 16, 16, 17,
17, 17, 17, 17, 19, 19, 19, 20, 21, 21, 22, 22, 23, 23, 24, 24, 24, 24, 25, 26, 26, 26, 26,
26, 26, 26, 27[N], 28, 29, 29, 30, 30, 30, 30, 30, 31, 32, 33, 33, 33, 33, 33, 33, 33, 34, 34,
34, 35, 35, 35, 35, 36, 36, 36, 36, 36, 37, 38, 38, 38, 38, 39, 39, 40, 40, 40, 41, 41, 41,
43, 43, 43, 43, 43, 44, 44, 44; **13:**1, 1, 2, 2, 3, 3, 3, 4, 5, 6, 7, 10, 10, 11, 11, 11, 11, 13,
13, 14, 14, 14, 14, 14, 14, 15, 15, 15, 16, 16, 16, 16, 17, 17, 17, 19, 19, 19, 20, 20, 20,
21, 22, 22, 24, 24, 24, 24, 24, 25, 25, 25, 25, 25, 26, 26, 27, 27, 27, 28, 28, 28, 28, 28,
30, 31, 31, 31, 32, 32, 32, 32, 32, 33, 34, 34, 34, 34, 34, 35, 35; **14:**1, 1, 1, 1, 2, 2, 3, 3,
3, 3, 4, 4, 5, 5, 6, 7, 8, 8, 9, 9, 10, 10, 10, 11, 12, 12, 12, 12, 12, 13, 13, 14, 14, 14, 14,
14, 16, 16, 16, 17, 18, 18, 20, 20, 20, 20, 21, 21, 21, 21, 21, 21, 22[N], 22, 24, 24, 24, 25,
25, 25, 25, 25, 26, 26, 27, 27, 27, 28, 28, 29, 30, 30, 31, 32, 32, 33, 33[U], 33[U], 34, 35, 35,
36, 36, 37, 38, 38, 39, 40, 41, 41, 41, 41, 41, 41, 41, 42, 43, 43, 43, 43, 44, 46, 46, 47,
47, 47, 47, 47, 48, 49, 49, 52, 52, 53, 53, 53, 53, 53, 54, 54, 54, 54, 54, 55, 55, 55, 55,
56, 58, 58, 59, 60, 60, 61, 61, 61, 61, 61, 62, 62, 62, 62, 62, 62, 63, 63, 64, 64, 65, 65,
66, 66, 66, 66, 67, 67, 67, 68, 68, 69, 69, 70, 70, 70, 71, 71, 72, 72, 72; **15:**1, 1, 1, 1, 2, 2,
2, 2, 3, 4, 5, 5, 7, 7, 7, 8, 9, 9, 9, 10, 11, 11, 11, 12, 12, 12, 13, 14, 14, 15, 15, 15, 15, 15,
16, 16, 16, 18, 19, 19, 20, 20, 21, 21, 22, 24, 26, 26, 26, 26, 29, 29, 29, 29, 30, 31, 31,

32, 32, 32, 32, 33, 34, 34, 34, 34, 35, 37, 38, 38, 39, 39, 39, 40, 40, 40, 41, 41, 43, 43,
43, 43, 43, 43, 44, 44, 45, 45, 45, 46, 46, 46, 47, 47, 47; **16:**1, 1, 1, 1, 2, 2, 2, 2, 3, 3, 3,
4, 5, 5, 6, 6, 6, 6, 7, 7, 7, 8, 9, 10, 13, 14, 14, 14, 15, 15, 15, 16, 16, 17, 17, 18, 19, 19,
19, 19, 20, 20, 20, S[U], S[U], S[U], S[U], S[U], S[U]; **Lk 1:**1, 2, 2, 4, 5, 5, 5, 5, 6, 6, 6, 7, 7, 8, 8, 8, 8,
9, 9, 9, 9, 9, 10, 10, 10, 10, 11, 11, 13, 13, 13, 13, 14, 15, 16, 16, 18, 18, 18, 19, 19, 19,
20, 20, 21, 21, 21, 21, 22, 23, 23, 23, 24, 24, 26, 26, 26, 26, 26, 27, 27, 28[N], 28, 29, 29,
29, 30, 30, 31, 32, 32, 32, 33, 33, 33, 34, 35, 35, 36, 36, 37, 38, 38, 38, 39, 39, 40, 40,
41, 41, 41, 41, 41, 41, 42, 42, 43, 43, 44, 44, 44, 44, 44, 45, 45, 46, 46, 47, 47, 47, 48,
48, 48, 48, 49, 49, 50, 50, 55, 55, 55, 55, 56, 57, 57, 57, 58, 58, 58, 59, 59, 59, 59, 59,
60, 61, 61, 62, 62, 64, 64, 64, 65, 65, 65, 65, 66, 66, 66, 67, 68, 68, 68, 70, 71, 72, 73,
74, 75, 77, 77, 79, 79, 79, 80, 80, 80; **2:**1, 1, 2, 3, 4, 4, 4, 5, 6, 6, 6, 7, 7, 7, 8, 8, 8, 8, 10,
10, 12, 13, 13, 15, 15, 15, 15, 15, 15, 16, 16, 16, 16, 17, 17, 17, 18, 18, 18, 19, 19, 19,
20, 20, 21, 21, 21, 21, 21, 21, 22, 22, 22, 22, 23, 24, 24, 24, 25, 25, 26, 26, 26, 27, 27,
27, 27, 27, 27, 27, 27, 28, 28, 29, 29, 30, 30, 31, 33, 33, 33, 34, 34, 35, 36, 37, 38, 38,
38, 39, 39, 39, 40, 41, 41, 41, 42, 42, 43, 43, 43, 43, 44, 44, 44, 46, 46, 47, 47, 47, 48,
48, 49, 49, 50, 51, 51, 51, 52[U]; **3:**1, 1, 1, 1, 1, 1, 2, 2, 3, 3, 4, 4, 4, 4, 5, 5, 6, 6, 7, 7, 8, 8,
8, 8, 8, 9, 9, 9, 10, 11, 11, 11, 13, 13, 14, 15, 15, 15, 15, 16, 16, 16, 16, 17, 17, 17, 17,
17, 17, 18, 19, 19, 19, 19, 20, 20, 21, 21, 21, 22, 22, 22, 22, 23, 24, 24, 24, 24, 24, 25,
25, 25, 25, 25, 26, 26, 26, 26, 26, 27, 27, 27, 27, 27, 28, 28, 28, 28, 28, 29, 29, 29, 29,
29, 30, 30, 30, 30, 30, 31, 31, 31, 31, 31, 32, 32, 32, 32, 32, 33, 33, 33[U], 33, 33, 33, 34,
34, 34, 34, 34, 35, 35, 35, 35, 35, 36, 36, 36, 36, 36, 37, 37, 37, 37, 37, 38, 38, 38, 38;
4:1, 1, 1, 2, 2, 3, 3, 3, 4, 4, 5[N], 5, 5, 6, 6, 6, 8, 8, 9, 9, 9, 10, 10, 11, 12, 12, 13, 14, 14,
14, 14, 14, 15, 16, 16, 16, 16, 17, 17, 17, 20, 20, 20, 20, 21, 21, 22, 22, 22, 22, 23, 23,
23, 24, 25, 25, 25, 25, 26, 27, 27, 27, 28, 29, 29, 29, 31, 31, 32, 32, 33, 34, 34, 35, 35,
35, 36, 36, 37, 38, 38, 38, 39, 40, 40, 40, 41, 41, 41, 42, 42, 43, 43, 43, 43, 44, 44; **5:**1, 1,
1, 1, 1, 2, 2, 2, 3, 3, 3, 3, 4, 4, 4, 5, 5, 6, 7, 7, 7, 7, 8, 9, 9, 9, 10, 10, 10, 10, 11, 11, 12,
12, 12, 13, 13, 14, 14, 15, 15, 16, 17, 17, 17, 19, 19, 19, 19, 19, 19, 20, 20, 21, 21, 21,
22, 22, 22, 23, 24, 24, 24, 24, 24, 24, 25, 25, 26, 27, 29, 30, 30, 30, 30, 31, 31, 31, 33,
33, 33, 33, 33, 34, 34, 34, 34, 35, 35, 36, 36, 36, 36, 36, 37, 37, 37, 37, 39; **6:**1, 1, 1, 2, 2,
3, 3, 4, 4, 4, 4, 4, 4, 5, 5, 5, 6, 6, 6, 7, 7, 7, 8, 8, 8, 8, 8, 9, 9, 10, 10, 10, 11, 12, 12, 12,
12, 13, 14, 15, 17, 17, 17, 18, 18, 19, 20, 20, 20, 20, 21, 21, 22, 22, 22, 22, 23, 23,
23, 23, 23, 23, 24, 24, 25, 25, 26, 26, 26, 26, 27, 27, 27, 28, 28, 29, 29, 29, 29, 29, 29,
30, 30, 31, 32, 32, 32, 33, 33, 33, 34, 35, 35, 35, 36, 38, 40, 40, 41, 41, 41, 41, 41, 41,
41, 42, 42, 42, 42, 42, 42, 42, 42, 42, 42, 42, 42, 44, 45, 45, 45, 45, 45, 45, 45, 45[N], 45,
47, 47, 48, 48, 48, 48, 49, 49, 49, 49, 49; **7:**1, 1, 1, 3, 3, 3, 4, 4, 5, 5, 6, 6, 6, 6, 7, 8, 9, 9,
9, 10, 10, 10, 11, 11, 12, 12, 12, 12, 13, 14, 14, 15, 15, 16, 16, 16, 17, 17, 17, 18, 18, 18,
19, 19, 20, 20, 20, 21, 24, 24, 24, 25, 25, 27, 27, 28, 28, 28, 29, 29, 29, 29, 30, 30, 30,
30, 31, 31, 32, 33, 34, 34, 35, 35, 36, 36, 36, 37, 37, 37, 38, 38, 38, 38, 38, 38, 38, 39,
39, 39, 40, 40, 41, 41, 43, 43, 44, 44, 44, 44, 44, 44, 44, 45, 46, 46, 47, 47, 48, 49, 50,
50; **8:**1, 1, 1, 1, 2, 3, 4, 5, 5, 5, 5, 5, 5, 5, 6, 6, 7, 7, 8, 8, 8, 9, 9, 10, 10, 10, 10, 10, 11,
11, 11, 11, 12, 12, 12, 12, 12, 12, 13, 13, 13, 14, 14, 14, 14, 15, 15, 15, 16, 16, 19, 19,
19, 20, 20, 21, 21, 21, 21, 22, 22, 22, 22, 23, 24, 24, 24, 24, 25, 25, 25, 26, 26, 26, 27,
27, 27, 28, 28, 28, 29, 29, 29, 29, 29, 29, 30, 30, 31, 32, 33, 33, 33, 33, 33, 33, 34, 34,
34, 34, 35, 35, 35, 35, 35, 35, 36, 36, 37, 37, 37, 38, 38, 39, 39, 39, 39, 40, 40, 40, 41,
41, 41, 41, 42, 42, 43[U], 44, 44, 44, 44, 45, 45, 45, 45, 46, 47, 47, 48, 48, 49, 49, 49, 50,
51, 51, 51, 51, 52, 54, 54, 55, 56, 56, 56; **9:**1, 1, 2, 2, 2, 3, 5, 5, 5, 6, 7, 7, 7, 8, 10, 11,
11, 11, 11, 12, 12, 12, 12, 13, 13, 14, 16, 16, 16, 16, 16, 17, 18, 18, 18, 19, 19, 19, 20,
20, 21, 22, 22, 22, 22, 23, 24, 24, 25, 26, 26, 26, 26, 26, 27, 27, 27, 28, 28, 29, 29,
29, 29, 31, 32, 32, 32, 32, 32, 33, 33, 33, 34, 34, 35, 35, 35, 36, 36, 36, 37, 37, 38, 38,
40, 41, 41, 42, 42, 42, 42, 42, 42, 43, 43, 43, 44, 44, 44, 44, 45, 45, 45, 46, 47, 47, 47,
48, 48, 48, 48, 49, 50, 51, 51, 51, 51, 51, 53, 54, 54, 57, 58, 58, 58, 58, 58, 58, 58, 59,
59, 60, 60, 60, 60, 61, 61, 62, 62, 62, 62, 62; **10:**1, 2, 2, 2, 2, 2, 4, 5, 6, 7, 7, 7, 7, 8, 9, 9,
9, 10, 11, 11, 11, 11, 11, 11, 12, 12, 13, 13, 14, 15, 16, 16, 16, 16, 17, 17, 17, 18, 18, 19,
19, 19, 19, 20, 20, 20, 21, 21, 21, 21, 21, 21, 22, 22, 22, 22, 22, 22, 23, 23, 23, 26, 26,
27, 27, 27, 27, 27, 27, 27, 29, 29, 30, 31, 32, 34, 34, 35, 35, 35, 36, 36, 36, 37, 37, 37,
37, 38, 39, 39, 39, 40, 40, 41, 42; **11:**1, 1, 1, 2, 2, 3, 3, 3, 4, 7, 7, 7, 8, 8, 10, 10, 10, 11,
11, 13, 13, 13, 13, 14, 14, 14, 15, 15, 15, 17, 18, 18, 18, 19, 19, 20, 20, 20, 21, 21, 21,
22, 22, 23, 23, 24, 24, 24, 26, 26, 26, 27, 27, 27, 27, 28, 28, 28, 29, 29, 29, 30, 30, 30,
30, 31, 31, 31, 31, 31, 31, 32, 32, 32, 33, 33, 33, 33, 34, 34, 34, 34, 34, 34, 35, 35, 36,
36, 36, 37, 38, 38, 39, 39, 39, 39, 39, 39, 40, 40, 40, 41, 42, 42, 42, 42, 42, 42, 43, 43,
43, 43, 43, 44, 44, 44, 44, 45, 46, 46, 46, 46, 46, 47, 47, 47, 48, 48, 49, 49, 50, 50, 50,
50, 51[N], 51[N], 51, 51, 51, 51, 52, 52, 52, 52, 53, 53, 54; **12:**1, 1, 1, 1, 1, 3, 3, 3, 3, 3, 4, 4,
4, 5, 5, 5, 6, 7, 7, 8, 8, 8, 8, 8, 9, 9, 9, 9, 10, 10, 10, 10, 11, 11, 11, 12, 12, 13, 13, 13, 14,
15, 15, 15, 16, 17, 18, 18, 18, 19, 20, 20, 20, 21, 22, 22, 22, 23, 23, 23, 23, 24, 24, 24,
25, 26, 27, 27, 28, 28, 30, 30, 30, 31, 32, 32, 32, 33, 33, 34, 34, 35, 35, 36, 36, 37, 37,
38, 38, 39, 39, 39, 40, 40, 41, 41, 42, 42, 42, 42, 42, 42, 42, 43, 43, 44, 45, 45, 45, 45,
45, 46, 46, 46, 46, 47, 47, 47, 47, 47, 48, 49, 51, 52, 53, 53, 53, 53, 54, 54, 56, 56, 56,
56, 57, 58, 58, 58, 58, 58, 58, 59; **13:**1, 1, 1, 1, 2, 2, 4, 4, 4, 4, 4, 6, 6, 7, 7, 7, 8, 8, 9, 10,
10, 11, 12, 12, 13, 13, 14, 14, 14, 14, 14, 14, 15, 15, 15, 15, 15, 16, 16, 16, 16, 17, 17,
17, 17, 18, 18, 19, 19, 19, 20, 20, 23, 23, 24, 25, 25, 25, 26, 28, 28, 28, 28, 28, 28, 29,
29, 31, 32, 32, 33, 34, 34, 34, 34, 34, 34, 35, 35; **14:**1, 1, 1, 3, 3, 3, 4, 5, 7, 7, 8, 9, 9, 10,
10, 10, 11, 11, 12, 12, 12, 12, 14, 14, 15, 15, 15, 16, 17, 17, 17, 17, 18, 21, 21, 21, 21,
21, 21, 21, 22, 23, 23, 23, 23, 24, 24, 24, 26, 26, 26, 26, 26, 26, 26, 27, 28, 29, 30, 31,
32, 33, 34, 34, 35; **15:**1, 1, 2, 2, 3, 4, 4, 4, 5, 6, 6, 6, 6, 6, 7, 8, 9, 9, 10, 10, 12, 12, 12,
12, 12, 12, 13, 13, 14, 15, 15, 15, 16[N], 16, 16, 17, 18, 18, 19, 20, 20, 20, 21, 21, 22, 22,
22, 22, 22, 23, 23, 24, 25, 25, 25, 26, 27, 27, 27, 27, 27, 28, 29, 29, 29, 30, 30, 30, 30,
31, 31, 32; **16:**1, 1, 2, 2, 3, 3, 3, 4, 4, 5, 5, 5, 5, 6, 6, 6, 7, 7, 8, 8, 8, 8, 8, 8, 8, 8, 9, 9,
9, 10, 10, 11, 11, 12, 12, 13, 13, 13, 14, 15, 15, 15, 15, 15, 15, 16, 16, 16, 16, 17, 17, 17,
18, 18, 18, 20, 21, 21, 21, 21, 21, 22, 22, 22, 22, 23, 23, 23, 24, 24, 24, 24, 25, 25, 25,
26, 27, 27, 28, 28, 29, 30, 31; **17:**1, 1, 1, 2, 2, 2, 3, 4, 5, 5, 6, 6, 6, 7, 9, 9, 10, 11, 14, 14,
15, 16, 17, 17, 17, 18, 18, 19, 20, 20, 20, 20, 20, 21, 21, 22, 22, 22, 22, 24, 24, 24, 24,
24, 24, 24, 25, 26, 26, 26, 26, 27, 27, 28, 30, 30, 30, 31, 31, 31, 31, 31, 31, 32, 33, 34,
34, 34, 35, 35, 35, 37, 37, 37; **18:**1, 2, 3, 3, 4, 5, 5, 6, 6, 6, 7, 7, 7, 7, 8, 8, 8, 8, 8, 9, 9, 9,
10, 10, 10, 11, 11, 11, 11, 11, 12, 13, 13, 13, 13, 13, 13, 14, 14, 14, 15, 15, 16, 16, 16,
16, 16, 17, 17, 19, 19, 20, 20, 20, 21, 22, 22, 23, 24, 24, 24, 24, 24, 25, 25, 26, 27, 27,
27, 28, 28, 29, 29, 29, 30, 30, 30, 31, 31, 31, 31, 31, 32, 33, 33, 34, 34, 35, 35, 37, 39,
40, 41, 42, 42, 43, 43, 43; **19:**1, 3, 3, 3, 4, 5, 5, 5, 8, 8, 8, 8, 9, 9, 10, 10, 10, 11, 11, 11,
14, 15, 15, 15, 15, 16, 16, 18, 18, 20, 20, 22, 23, 24, 24, 24, 24, 26, 26, 27, 27, 29, 29,
29, 30, 31, 32, 33, 33, 33, 34, 34, 35, 35, 35, 35, 36, 36, 37, 37, 37, 37, 37, 37, 38, 38,
39, 39, 39, 40, 41, 42, 42, 43, 44, 44, 44, 45, 45, 46, 47, 47, 47, 47, 47, 47, 48, 48; **20:**1,
1, 1, 1, 1, 1, 2, 2, 4, 5, 6, 8, 9, 9, 10, 10, 10, 10, 11, 12, 13, 13, 13, 13, 14, 14, 14, 15, 15,
15, 16, 16, 17, 17, 17, 18, 18, 19, 19, 19, 19, 19, 19, 20, 20, 20, 21, 21, 23, 25, 25, 25,
25, 25, 25, 26, 26, 27, 27, 28, 28, 28, 29, 30, 31, 31, 32, 33, 33, 33, 34, 34, 34, 35, 35,
35, 35, 36, 37, 37, 37, 39, 41, 42, 43, 43, 45, 45, 46, 46, 46, 46, 46, 47, 47; **21:**1, 1, 1, 3,
3, 4, 4, 4, 4, 5, 7, 8, 8, 8, 9, 12, 12, 12, 14, 15, 17, 18, 19, 19, 20, 21, 21, 21, 21, 21, 21,
22, 22, 23, 23, 23, 23, 23, 24, 25, 26, 26, 26, 26, 27, 27, 28, 28, 29, 29, 30, 31, 31, 32,
33, 33, 33, 34, 34, 35, 35, 36, 36, 36, 37, 37, 37, 37, 37, 38, 38; **22:**1, 1, 1, 2, 2, 2, 2, 3,
3, 3, 4, 4, 6, 7, 7, 7, 8, 9, 10, 10, 10, 11, 11, 11, 11, 11, 11, 13, 14, 14, 15, 15, 16, 16, 18,
18, 18, 18, 18, 19, 19, 19, 20, 20, 20, 20, 20, 21, 21, 21, 22, 22, 22, 22, 23, 23, 24,
25, 25, 25, 25, 26, 26, 26, 26, 27, 27, 27, 27, 28, 28, 29, 30, 30, 30, 30, 31, 31, 31, 32,
32, 33, 34, 35, 36, 36, 36, 37, 37, 37, 38, 38, 39, 39, 39, 39, 40, 41, 42, 42, 42, 44, 44,
45, 45, 45, 47, 47, 47, 48, 48, 49, 49, 50, 50, 50, 50, 51, 51, 52, 52, 53, 53, 53, 53, 53,
54, 54, 54, 55, 55, 56, 57, 58, 60, 61, 61, 61, 61, 61, 63, 63, 64, 66, 66, 66, 67, 69, 69,
69, 69, 69, 70, 70, 70, 71, 71; **23:**1, 1, 2, 3, 3, 3, 3, 4, 4, 4, 4, 5, 5, 5, 5, 6, 7, 7, 8, 8, 8,
10, 10, 11, 11, 11, 12, 12, 12, 13, 13, 13, 14, 14, 14, 18, 19, 19, 20, 20, 21, 22, 23, 23,
24, 25, 25, 25, 26, 26, 27, 28, 28, 29, 29, 30, 30, 31, 31, 33, 33, 33, 34, 34, 35, 35, 35,
35, 35, 36, 37, 37, 38, 38, 39, 39, 40, 40, 40, 42, 43, 44, 45, 45, 45, 46, 46, 47, 47, 47,
47, 48, 48, 48, 48, 49, 49, 49, 51, 51, 51, 51, 51, 52, 52, 52, 55, 55, 55, 55, 56, 56; **24:**1,
1, 1, 2, 2, 3, 3, 4, 5, 5, 5, 5, 6, 7, 7, 7, 8, 9, 9, 9, 10, 10, 10, 10, 11, 12, 12, 12, 12, 13, 14,
15, 16, 16, 17, 18, 18, 19, 19, 19, 19, 19, 20, 20, 21, 21, 22, 23, 24, 24, 24, 25, 25, 25,
26, 26, 27, 27, 27, 28, 29, 29, 30, 30, 31, 32, 32, 32, 33, 33, 33, 34, 35, 35, 35, 35, 38,
39, 39, 40, 40, 41, 42, 44, 44, 44, 44, 45, 45, 45, 46, 46, 47, 47, 49, 49, 49, 50, 51, 51,
53, 53; **Jn 1:**1, 1, 1, 1, 2, 4, 4, 4, 5, 5, 5, 7, 8, 8, 9, 9, 9, 10, 10, 10, 11, 11, 12, 12, 14, 14,
15, 16, 17, 17, 17, 18, 18, 18, 19, 19, 19, 20, 21, 22, 23, 23, 23, 24, 25, 25, 26, 27, 27,
27, 28, 28, 29, 29, 29, 29, 29, 29, 29, 31, 32, 33, 33, 33, 34, 34, 35, 35, 35, 36, 36, 36,
37, 37, 38, 38, 39, 40, 40, 40, 41, 41, 41, 42, 42, 42, 43, 43, 43, 44, 44, 45, 45, 45, 45,
45, 46, 47, 47, 48, 48, 49, 49, 49, 50, 51, 51, 51, 51, 51; **2:**1, 1, 1, 1, 1, 2, 2, 2, 3, 3, 4, 4,
5, 5, 6, 6, 7, 7, 8, 8, 9, 9, 9, 9, 9, 9, 9, 10, 10, 10, 11, 11, 11, 11, 11, 12, 12, 12, 13, 13,
13, 14, 14, 14, 15, 15, 15, 15, 15, 15, 16, 16, 16, 16, 17, 17, 17, 18, 19, 20, 20, 21, 21,
22, 22, 22, 22, 23, 23, 23, 23, 23, 24, 25, 25; **3:**1, 1, 2, 2, 3, 3, 4, 4, 4, 5, 5, 6, 6, 6, 6, 8,
8, 8, 8, 10, 10, 11, 12, 12, 13, 13, 13, 13, 13, 14, 14, 14, 14, 15, 16, 16, 16, 16, 16, 17,
17, 17, 17, 17, 18, 18, 18, 18, 18, 19, 19, 19, 19, 19, 19, 19, 20, 20, 20, 20, 21, 21, 21,
21, 22, 22, 22, 23, 23, 24, 24, 25, 26, 26, 27, 28, 29, 29, 29, 29, 29, 29, 29, 29, 31,
31, 31, 31, 31, 31, 31, 32, 33, 33, 33, 34, 34, 34, 34, 35, 35, 35, 36, 36, 36, 36, 36, 36;
4:1, 2, 3, 3, 3, 4, 5, 5, 5, 5, 6, 6, 6, 6, 7, 7, 8, 8, 9, 9, 10, 10, 10, 11, 11, 11, 11, 12, 12,
12, 12, 13, 13, 14, 14, 14, 15, 15, 16, 17, 17, 19, 20, 20, 20, 21, 21, 21, 22, 22, 23, 23,
23, 23, 24, 24, 25, 25, 26, 26, 27, 28, 28, 28, 28, 29, 30, 31, 31, 32, 33, 34, 34, 34, 34,
35, 35, 35, 36, 36, 36, 37, 37, 37, 38, 39, 39, 39, 39, 40, 41, 42, 42, 42, 42, 43, 43, 44,
45, 45, 45, 45, 46, 46, 46, 46, 47, 47, 47, 48, 49, 49, 50, 50, 50, 50, 50, 51, 51, 52, 52,
53, 53, 53, 53, 53, 54, 54, 54; **5:**1, 2, 2, 2, 3, 5, 6, 7, 7, 7, 8, 8, 9, 9, 9, 10, 10, 10, 11, 11,
11, 12, 12, 13, 13, 13, 14, 14, 15, 15, 15, 16, 16, 17, 17, 18, 18, 18, 18, 19, 19, 19, 19,
20, 20, 21, 21, 21, 22, 22, 22, 23, 23, 23, 23, 23, 23, 24, 24, 24, 24, 24, 25, 25, 25, 25,
25, 26, 26, 28, 28, 28, 29, 29, 29, 29, 30, 30, 30, 30, 30, 30, 31, 32, 32, 33, 34, 35, 35,
35, 36, 36, 36, 36, 36, 36, 37, 38, 39, 39, 42, 42, 43, 43, 43, 43, 44, 44, 44, 45, 45, 47,
47; **6:**1, 1, 1, 1, 2, 2, 3, 3, 4, 4, 4, 5, 5, 7, 8, 8, 10, 10, 10, 10, 10, 11, 11, 11, 11, 12, 12,
13, 13, 13, 14, 14, 14, 14, 15, 16, 16, 17, 17, 18, 19, 19, 19, 20, 21, 21, 21, 22, 22, 22,
22, 22, 22, 22, 22, 23, 23, 23, 24, 24, 24, 24, 25, 26, 26, 27, 27, 27, 27, 27, 27, 27, 27,
28, 28, 29, 29, 29, 31, 31, 31, 31, 32, 32, 32, 32, 32, 32, 32, 33, 33, 33, 33, 33, 34, 35,
35, 35, 35, 35, 37, 37, 38, 38, 38, 38, 38, 39, 39, 39, 40, 40, 40, 40, 40, 41, 41, 41, 41,
42, 42, 42, 42, 44, 44, 44, 45, 45, 45, 46, 46, 46, 46, 47, 48, 48, 49, 49, 49, 50, 50, 50,
51, 51, 51, 51, 51, 51, 51, 51, 51, 51, 52, 52, 53, 53, 53, 53, 53, 54, 54, 54, 54, 55, 55,
56, 56, 56, 57, 57, 57, 58, 58, 58, 58[N], 58, 58, 58, 60, 60, 61, 61, 62, 62, 62, 63, 63, 63,
63, 64, 64, 64, 65, 66, 66, 67, 67, 69, 69, 70, 70, 71, 71; **7:**1, 1, 1, 1, 2, 2, 2, 3, 3, 3, 3, 4,
5, 6, 6, 6, 6, 6, 7, 7, 8, 8, 8, 9, 10, 10, 11, 11, 12, 12, 12, 13, 13, 14, 14, 15, 16, 16, 16,
17, 17, 17, 18, 18, 18, 18, 18, 18, 19, 19, 20, 22, 22, 22, 23, 24, 25, 26, 26, 27, 28, 28,
28, 30, 30, 31, 31, 32, 32, 32, 32, 33, 33, 35, 35, 35, 35, 36, 37, 37, 37, 37, 38, 38, 38,
39, 39, 40, 40, 40, 41, 41, 41, 41, 42, 42, 42, 42, 43, 44, 45, 45, 46, 47, 48, 48, 49, 49,
49, 50, 50, 51, 51, 52, 52, 53; **8:**1, 1, 2, 2, 3, 3, 4, 5, 5, 6, 6, 6, 7, 8, 9, 9, 9, 10, 11, 11,
11, 12, 12, 12, 12, 12, 12, 12, 13, 13, 14, 15, 16, 16, 16, 17, 17, 17, 18, 18, 19, 19, 19,
20, 20, 20, 20, 21, 22, 23, 23, 23, 23, 24, 24, 25, 25, 26, 26, 27, 28, 28, 28, 28, 29, 29,
31, 31, 31, 31, 32, 32, 34, 34, 34, 34, 35, 35, 35, 35, 35, 36, 37, 37, 38, 38, 39, 39, 39,
39, 39, 40, 40, 41, 41, 41, 42, 42, 42, 43, 43, 43, 43, 44, 44, 44, 44, 44, 44, 44, 44, 45,
47, 47, 47, 47, 47, 48, 49, 50, 50, 51, 51, 52, 52, 52, 52, 53, 53, 54, 54, 54, 55, 56, 56,
56, 57, 59; **9:**2, 2, 3, 3, 3, 4, 4, 5, 5, 6, 6, 6, 7, 7, 8, 8, 8, 8, 10, 11, 11, 11, 11, 13, 13, 14,
14, 14, 15, 15, 15, 16, 16, 16, 17, 17, 17, 18, 18, 18[U], 19, 20, 20, 21, 22, 22, 22, 23, 24,
24, 24, 26, 28, 29, 30, 30, 30, 31, 31, 32, 35, 35, 37, 37, 38, 39, 39, 39, 39, 40, 40, 41,

27, 27, 27, 27, 28, 28, 28, 32, 32, 32, 32, 32; **2:**1, 1, 1, 1, 2, 2, 2, 2, 3, 3, 3, 3, 3, 4, 4, 4, 4, 4, 4, 5, 5, 6, 7, 8, 8, 8, 9, 9, 10, 10, 11, 13, 13, 13, 14, 14, 14, 15, 15, 15, 15, 15, 16, 16, 16, 16, 18, 18, 18, 19, 20, 20, 20, 20, 21, 21, 22, 22, 22, 22, 23, 23, 23, 24, 24, 24, 25, 26, 26, 26, 26, 27, 27, 27, 27, 28, 28, 28, 28, 28, 29, 29, 29, 29; **3:**1, 1, 1, 1, 2, 2, 3, 3, 3, 4, 4, 4, 5, 5, 5, 6, 6, 7, 7, 7, 7, 8, 8, 8, 11, 11, 11, 12, 12, 13, 13, 14, 14, 15, 16, 18, 19, 19, 19, 19, 19, 21, 21, 22, 23, 23, 24, 24, 24, 25, 25, 25, 25, 25, 25, 25, 26, 26, 26, 26, 26, 27, 27, 29, 30, 30, 31; **4:**1, 3, 3, 4, 4, 5, 5, 5, 5, 6, 6, 6, 7, 7, 9, 9, 9, 9, 9, 11, 11, 11, 11, 11, 11, 11, 11, 12, 12, 12, 12, 12, 13, 13, 13, 14, 14, 14, 15, 16, 16, 16, 16, 16, 17, 17, 17, 18, 18, 18, 19, 19, 19, 19, 20, 20, 20, 20, 20, 24, 24, 24, 25, 25; **5:**1, 1, 2, 2, 2, 2, 2, 3, 3, 4, 4, 5, 5, 5, 5, 7, 8, 8, 9, 9, 10, 10, 10, 10, 11, 11, 11, 12, 12, 12, 12, 12, 14, 14, 14, 14, 14, 15, 15, 15, 15, 15, 15, 15, 15, 16, 16, 16, 17, 17, 17, 17, 17, 17, 17, 17, 17, 19, 19, 19, 19, 19, 20, 20, 20, 21, 21, 21, 21; **6:**1, 1, 2, 3, 4, 4, 4, 4, 5, 5, 5, 6, 6, 6, 6, 7, 7, 10, 10, 11, 11, 12, 12, 12, 12, 13, 13, 13, 13, 13, 17, 17, 18, 18, 19, 19, 19, 19, 19, 20, 20, 21, 22, 22, 22, 22, 23, 23, 23, 23, 23; **7:**1, 1, 2, 2, 2, 2, 2, 3, 3, 3, 4, 4, 4, 4, 4, 4, 5, 5, 5, 5, 5, 6, 7, 7, 7, 7, 8, 10, 10, 11, 11, 12, 12, 12, 12, 13, 13, 13, 13, 13, 17, 17, 18, 18, 19, 19, 19, 19, 19, 20, 20, 21, 22, 22, 22, 22, 23, 23, 23, 23, 23; **8:**1, 2, 2, 2, 2, 2, 2, 3, 3, 3, 3, 3, 3, 4, 4, 4, 4, 5, 5, 5, 5, 6, 6, 6, 6, 7, 7, 7, 7, 8, 10, 10, 11, 11, 11, 11, 11, 11, 12, 12, 13, 13, 15, 16, 16, 16, 18, 18, 19, 19, 19, 19, 20, 20, 20, 21, 21, 21, 21, 21, 22, 22, 23, 23, 25, 25, 25, 26, 27, 27, 27, 27, 27, 28, 30, 30, 32, 32, 33; **10:**1, 1, 1, 1, 3, 3, 3, 3, 4, 4, 5, 5, 5, 6, 6, 6, 7, 8, 8, 8, 8, 9, 9, 9, 9, 11, 11, 12, 12, 12, 13, 13, 15, 15, 15, 15, 16, 16, 17, 17, 18, 18, 18, 18, 18, 20, 20, 21, 21, 21; **11:**1, 1, 2, 2, 2, 2, 3, 3, 4, 4, 4, 5, 6, 7, 7, 8, 8, 8, 8, 9, 10, 10, 11, 11, 11, 12, 12, 12, 13, 13, 14, 15, 15, 16, 16, 16, 16, 17, 17, 17, 17, 18, 18, 18, 20, 20, 21, 21, 22, 22, 23, 23, 24, 24, 24, 25, 25, 25, 25, 25, 26, 27, 27, 28, 28, 28, 29, 29, 29, 30, 30, 31, 32, 32, 32, 33, 33, 36, 36; **12:**1, 1, 1, 1, 2, 2, 2, 2, 2, 2, 3, 3, 3, 3, 3, 4, 4, 5, 5, 6, 6, 6, 7, 7, 7, 8, 8, 8, 8, 9, 9, 10, 11, 11, 11, 12, 12, 13, 13, 14, 16, 16, 16, 18, 19, 20, 20, 21, 21, 21; **13:**1, 2, 2, 2, 2, 3, 3, 3, 3, 4, 4, 4, 4, 5, 5, 7, 7, 7, 7, 7, 7, 7, 7, 7, 7, 7, 7, 8, 8, 9, 9[U], 9, 10, 10, 10, 11, 11, 11, 12, 12, 12, 12, 12, 14, 14; **14:**1, 2, 3, 3, 3, 3, 3, 4, 4, 6, 6, 6, 6, 6, 6, 6, 8, 8, 10, 10, 10, 10, 11, 12, 13, 13, 14, 15, 15, 16, 17, 17, 18, 18, 18, 18, 19, 19, 19, 19, 19, 20, 20, 20, 20, 21, 21, 22, 22, 23; **15:**1, 1, 1, 2, 2, 3, 3, 3, 4, 4, 4, 4, 4, 5, 5, 5, 6, 6, 7, 7, 8, 8, 8, 9, 9, 9, 10, 11, 11, 11, 12, 12, 12, 13, 13, 13, 13, 13, 14, 15, 15, 16, 16, 16, 17, 17, 17, 17, 19, 19, 19, 22, 22, 23, 23, 24, 25, 26, 26, 26, 27, 27, 27, 27, 28, 30, 30, 30, 30, 30, 31, 31, 31, 31, 31, 33, 33; **16:**1, 1, 1, 2, 3, 4, 4, 4, 4, 5, 5, 7, 7, 8, 9, 9, 10, 10, 10, 11, 11, 11, 11, 12, 12, 12, 13, 13, 14, 14, 15, 15, 16, 16, 17, 17, 17, 17, 18, 18, 18, 18, 18, 18, 18, 18, 19, 19, 19, 19, 20, 20, 20, 20, 20, 21, 21, 22, 22, 23, 23, 23, 23, 25, 25, 25, 26, 26, 27, 27;
1Co 1:1, 2, 2, 2, 2, 2, 4, 4, 4, 6, 6, 7, 7, 8, 8, 9, 9, 9, 10, 10, 10, 10, 10, 11, 13, 13, 14[U], 15, 16, 17, 17, 18, 18, 18, 18, 18, 19, 19, 19, 19, 20, 20, 20, 20, 21, 21, 21, 21, 21, 21, 21, 24, 25, 25, 25, 25, 26, 27, 27, 27, 27, 27, 27, 27, 27, 27, 27, 28, 28, 28, 28, 28, 29, 31; **2:**1, 1, 4, 4, 5, 6, 6, 6, 6, 6, 7, 7, 7, 7, 8, 8, 8, 8, 9, 9, 10, 10, 10, 10, 11, 11, 11, 11, 11, 11, 11, 12, 12, 12, 12, 12, 12, 14, 14, 14, 15; **3:**5, 6, 7, 7, 8, 8, 8, 8, 10, 10, 10, 11, 12, 13, 13, 13, 13, 14, 15, 16, 16, 16, 17, 17, 17, 17, 17, 18, 19, 19, 19, 19, 19, 20, 20; **4:**2, 4, 5, 5, 5, 5, 5, 5, 6, 6, 6, 9, 9, 9, 11, 12, 13, 15, 17, 17, 19, 19, 19, 19, 20, 20; **5:**1, 2, 2, 3, 3, 4, 4, 4, 4, 4, 4, 5, 5, 5, 5, 6, 6, 7, 7, 9, 10, 10, 10, 10, 11, 12, 12, 13, 13, 13; **6:**1, 1, 1, 2, 2, 4, 4, 5, 11, 11, 11, 11, 13, 13, 13, 13, 13, 13, 13, 14, 14, 14, 15, 15, 15, 16, 16, 16, 17, 17, 18, 18, 18, 19, 20, 20; **7:**2, 2, 3, 3, 3, 3, 4, 4, 4, 4, 4, 5, 5, 5, 5, 16, 16, 17, 17, 19, 19, 20, 22, 22, 25, 26, 26, 28, 28, 28, 29, 29, 29, 30, 30, 30, 31, 31, 31, 31, 32, 32, 32, 32, 33, 33, 33, 34, 34, 34, 34, 34, 34, 34, 34, 34, 34, 34, 35, 35, 36, 37, 37, 37, 38, 38, 38, 39, 39, 40; **8:**1, 1, 1, 3, 4, 4, 6, 6, 6, 7, 7, 7, 7, 7, 8, 9, 9, 10, 10, 10, 10, 11, 11, 11, 12, 12, 13, 13, 13; **9:**1, 2, 2, 3, 3, 5, 5, 7, 7, 7, 8, 9, 9, 9, 10, 10, 10, 11, 11, 12, 12, 12, 13, 13, 13, 13, 13, 13, 14, 14, 14, 14, 14, 15, 16, 16, 18, 18, 18, 18, 19, 19, 20, 20, 20, 21, 21, 22, 22, 23, 24, 24, 25, 27; **10:**1, 1, 1, 2, 2, 2, 3, 4, 4, 4, 4, 5, 5, 5, 6, 7, 9, 9, 10, 11, 11, 12, 13, 13, 13, 13, 14, 16, 16, 16, 16, 16, 16, 17, 17, 17, 18, 18, 18, 18, 18, 20[N], 20, 22, 24, 24, 24, 25, 25, 26, 26, 26, 27, 27, 27, 28, 28, 29, 29, 29, 29[N], 32, 32, 33, 33; **11:**2, 3, 3, 3, 3, 3, 4, 4, 5, 5, 5, 5, 6, 6, 7, 7, 9, 9, 10, 10, 10, 12, 12, 12, 12, 12, 13, 14, 14, 15, 16, 16, 17, 17, 19, 20, 21, 21, 21, 22, 22, 22, 23, 23, 23, 24, 24, 24, 24, 25, 25, 25, 25, 26, 26, 26, 26, 27, 27, 27, 27, 27, 28, 28, 29, 29, 29[N], 32, 32, 33, 34; **12:**1, 2, 2, 4, 5, 6, 6, 6, 7, 7, 8, 8, 9, 9, 11, 11, 12, 12, 12, 12, 14, 14, 15, 15, 16, 16, 16, 17, 17, 17, 18, 18, 18, 19, 19, 19, 21, 21, 21, 21, 22, 22, 22, 23, 23, 24, 24, 24, 24, 24, 25, 25, 25, 26, 26, 26, 26, 31, 31; **13:**1, 1, 1, 2, 2, 2, 3, 3, 4, 4, 4, 5, 5, 6, 6, 8, 10, 11, 11, 13, 13; **14:**1, 1, 2, 3, 4, 4, 5, 5, 5, 7, 7, 7, 7, 9, 9, 11, 11, 11, 11, 12, 12, 13, 14, 14, 15, 15, 15, 15, 16, 16, 16, 16, 17, 17, 18, 19, 19, 20, 21, 21, 21, 22, 22, 22, 22, 23, 23, 24, 24, 24, 25, 25, 25, 25, 28, 29, 30, 33, 33, 33, 34, 34, 34, 35, 36, 36, 39, 39; **15:**1, 3, 3, 4, 4, 4, 5, 6, 7, 8, 9, 9, 9, 10, 10, 10, 10, 14, 14, 15, 15, 15, 17, 17, 18, 19, 20, 22, 22, 23, 23, 23, 24, 24, 24, 25, 25, 26, 27, 27, 27, 28, 28, 28, 28, 28, 28[U], 29, 29, 31, 31, 32, 35, 37, 37, 37, 38, 38, 39, 40, 40, 40, 42, 42, 45, 45, 46, 46, 46, 47, 47, 48, 48, 48, 49, 49, 49, 49, 50, 50, 52, 52, 53, 53, 54, 54, 54, 54, 54, 55, 55, 56, 56, 56, 56, 56, 57, 57, 57, 57, 58, 58, 58; **16:**1, 1, 1, 1, 3, 4, 7, 8, 10, 11, 12, 12, 13, 15, 15, 15, 16, 16, 17, 17, 18, 18, 19, 19, 19, 20, 21, 21, 22, 23, 23, 24; **2Co 1:**1, 1, 1, 1, 1, 1, 3, 3, 3, 3, 4, 4, 4, 4, 4, 4, 5, 5, 6, 6, 7, 7, 7, 8, 8, 8, 9, 9, 9, 9, 9, 11, 11, 12, 12, 12, 14, 14, 15, 16, 17, 17, 17, 18, 18, 18, 19, 19, 20, 20, 20, 21, 22, 22, 22, 23, 23, 24, 24, 24; **2:**1, 2, 2, 3, 4, 6, 6, 6, 6, 7, 7, 7, 9, 11, 11, 12, 12, 13, 13, 14, 14, 14, 14,

14, 15, 15, 15, 17, 17, 17; **3:**2, 2, 4, 4, 5, 5, 6, 6, 7, 7, 7, 7, 7, 7, 8, 8, 9, 9, 9, 9, 10, 10, 10, 11, 11, 13, 13, 13, 13, 13, 14, 14, 14, 14, 14, 15, 16, 17, 17, 17, 18, 18; **4:**1, 2, 2, 2, 2, 2, 2, 2, 3, 3, 4, 4, 4, 4, 4, 4, 4, 4, 6, 6, 6, 6, 6, 6, 7, 7, 7, 7, 7, 10, 10, 10, 10, 10, 10, 11, 11, 11, 12, 12, 12, 13, 13, 14, 14, 15, 16, 16, 17, 17, 18, 18; **5:**1, 1, 1, 2, 2, 2, 4, 4, 4, 4, 5, 5, 5, 6, 6, 8, 8, 8, 8, 10, 10, 10, 10, 11, 11, 11, 11, 12, 14, 14, 15, 16, 16, 16, 17, 17, 18, 18, 18, 19, 19, 19, 20, 20, 21; **6:**1, 1, 3, 7, 7, 7, 7, 8, 8, 9, 9, 9, 9, 10, 10, 10, 11, 11, 12, 14, 14, 15, 16, 16, 16, 17, 17, 18, 18, 18; **7:**1, 3, 3, 4, 4, 4, 5, 6, 6, 6, 6, 7, 7, 7, 7, 8, 8, 8, 10, 10, 10, 10, 11, 11, 11, 12, 12, 12, 12, 13, 13, 16; **8:**1, 1, 1, 1, 2, 2, 2, 2, 4, 4, 4, 4, 4, 5, 6, 7; **9:**1, 1, 1, 2, 2, 3, 5, 7, 8, 9, 10, 10, 10, 10, 10, 11, 12, 12, 13, 13, 13, 13, 13, 14, 15; **10:**1, 2, 2, 2, 4, 4, 5, 5, 5, 6, 7, 8, 8, 9, 10, 10, 10, 10, 11, 12, 12, 13, 13, 13, 14, 14, 15, 15, 16, 16; **11:**2, 3, 3, 3, 3, 4, 4, 5, 5, 5, 6, 7, 8, 8, 9, 10, 10, 10, 10, 11, 13, 13, 13, 13, 13, 14, 14, 14, 15, 15, 15, 16, 17, 17, 17, 18, 18, 18, 18, 19, 19, 19, 19, 20, 20, 21, 21, 21, 21; **4:**1, 1, 3, 3, 3, 3, 4, 6, 7, 7, 7, 7, 8, 9, 9, 10, 10, 10, 11, 11, 11, 11, 12, 12, 12, 13, 13, 13, 13, 13, 13, 13, 14, 14, 14, 14, 15, 15, 16, 16, 16, 16, 17, 17, 18, 18, 18, 18, 18, 18, 18, 19, 20, 20, 21, 22, 22, 22, 22, 23, 23, 23, 24, 24, 24, 25, 25, 26, 26, 27, 27, 28, 28, 28, 28, 28, 29, 29, 30, 30, 32; **5:**1, 2, 2, 5, 5, 6, 6, 6, 6, 9, 9, 9, 10, 11, 11, 11, 12, 13, 13, 14, 14, 14, 14, 15, 16, 17, 19, 19, 20, 20, 22, 22, 22, 23, 23, 23, 24, 24, 24, 25, 25, 25, 26, 26, 27, 27, 28, 28, 28, 28, 28, 29, 29, 29, 30, 31, 31, 31, 31, 32, 32, 33, 33, 33; **6:**1, 1, 2, 2, 3, 4, 4, 5, 5, 5, 6, 6, 7, 9, 9, 9, 9, 10, 10, 10, 11, 11, 11, 11, 11, 11, 11, 11, 12, 12, 12, 12, 12, 12, 13, 13, 14, 14, 15, 15, 16, 16, 16, 16, 17, 17, 17, 18, 19, 19, 19, 21, 21, 22, 23, 24, 24, 24; **Php 1:**1, 1, 3, 3, 4, 5, 5, 5, 5, 6, 7, 7, 7, 7, 7, 7, 7, 8, 9, 9, 10, 11, 12, 12, 13, 13, 13, 14, 14, 14, 14, 14[N], 15, 16, 17, 17, 17, 17, 19, 19, 19, 20, 20, 21, 21, 22, 23, 23, 23, 24, 24, 25, 25, 26, 26, 27, 27, 27, 27, 28, 29, 29, 29, 30; **2:**2, 2, 2, 2, 3, 4, 4, 6, 9, 9, 9, 10, 12, 12, 12, 13, 13, 13, 13, 17, 17, 18, 19, 20, 21, 21, 21, 22, 22, 23, 25, 25, 27, 29, 30, 30, 30, 30; **3:**1, 1, 2, 2, 2, 3, 3, 6, 6, 7, 8, 8, 8, 8, 9, 9, 9, 9, 10, 11, 11, 13, 13, 14, 14, 14, 14, 15, 15, 18, 18, 18, 19, 19, 19, 19, 19, 20, 21, 21, 21, 21, 21; **4:**2, 3, 3, 3, 5, 5, 6, 6, 6, 6, 7, 7, 7, 7, 8, 9, 10, 13, 14, 15, 16, 17, 17, 17, 18, 18, 19, 19, 20, 20, 20, 20, 21, 22, 22, 22, 23, 23, 23; **Col 1:**1, 2, 3, 3, 4, 4, 4, 5, 5, 5, 5, 5, 6, 6, 6, 6, 7, 7, 8, 9, 9, 10, 10, 10, 11, 11, 12, 12, 12, 12, 12, 13, 13, 13, 14, 14, 14, 15, 15, 16, 16, 16, 16, 16, 17, 17, 18, 18, 18, 19, 20, 20, 20, 20, 20, 20, 21, 21, 21, 22, 22, 23, 23, 23, 23, 23, 23, 24, 24, 24, 24, 24, 24, 25, 25, 25, 25, 26, 26, 26, 26, 27, 27, 27, 27, 27, 27, 29, 29; **2:**1, 1, 2, 2, 2, 2, 3, 3, 5, 5, 5, 5, 6, 6, 6, 7, 7, 8, 8, 8, 9, 9, 9, 10, 11, 11, 11, 11, 11, 11, 12, 12, 13, 13, 13, 14, 14, 14, 14, 15, 15, 17, 17, 17, 18, 18, 18, 19, 19, 19, 19, 19, 20, 20, 22, 22, 22, 22, 23; **3:**1, 1, 1, 2, 2, 3, 3, 3, 4, 4, 5, 5, 5, 5, 6, 6[U], 6[U], 8, 8, 9, 9, 10, 10, 10, 11, 12, 13, 14, 14, 15, 15, 15, 16, 16, 16, 16, 17, 18, 18, 19, 20, 20, 20, 21, 21, 21, 22, 22, 23, 23, 24, 24, 24, 25, 25, 25, 25; **4:**1, 1, 1, 1, 2, 3, 3, 3, 3, 3, 3, 5, 5, 6, 6, 7, 7, 7, 8, 9, 9, 10, 10, 11, 11, 11, 11, 12, 12, 12, 13, 13, 14, 14, 15, 15, 16, 16, 16, 17, 18, 18, 18, 18; **1Th 1:**1, 2, 3, 3, 3, 3, 3, 3, 3, 3, 4, 4, 5, 6, 6, 7, 7, 7, 8, 8, 8, 8, 8, 9, 9, 10, 10, 10, 10, 10; **2:**1, 1, 2, 2, 3, 4, 4, 4, 4, 7, 8, 8, 8, 9, 9, 9, 9, 10, 10, 10, 11, 12, 12, 12, 13, 13, 14, 14, 14, 14, 15, 15, 16, 16, 16, 16[N], 17, 18, 19, 19, 20, 20; **3:**2, 2, 2, 2, 2, 3, 3, 5, 5, 5, 5, 6, 6, 7, 7, 9, 9, 9, 10, 10, 10, 11, 11, 12, 12, 13, 13, 13, 13, 13, 13, 13; **4:**1, 2, 3, 3, 3, 4, 5, 5, 5, 6, 6, 6, 7, 8, 8, 8, 9, 9, 10, 10, 11, 12, 13, 14, 14, 14, 15, 15, 15, 15, 16, 16, 16, 16, 17, 17, 17, 17, 18; **5:**1, 1, 3, 3, 4, 6, 7, 7, 9, 10, 11, 12, 13, 14, 14, 14, 15, 19, 21, 23, 23, 23, 23, 23, 23, 24, 26, 27, 27, 28, 28; **2Th 1:**1, 3, 3, 3, 4, 4, 4, 4, 5, 5, 5, 5, 6, 7, 7, 7, 8, 8, 8, 8, 9, 9, 9, 10, 10, 10, 10, 11, 11, 12, 12, 12, 12; **2:**1, 1, 2, 2, 2, 3, 3, 3, 3, 4, 4, 4, 6, 6, 7, 7, 7, 7, 8, 8, 8, 8, 9, 9, 10, 10, 10, 11, 11, 11, 12, 12, 13, 13, 14, 14, 15, 16, 16, 16, 16, 16, 17, 17, 18, 18; **3:**1, 1, 1, 2, 3, 3, 3, 3, 5, 5, 5, 5, 5, 6, 6, 8, 9, 12, 12, 13, 14, 14, 14, 16, 16, 16, 16, 16, 16, 17, 18; **1Ti 1:**1, 2, 4, 5, 5, 8, 10, 11, 11, 11, 12, 12, 13, 14, 14, 14, 15, 15, 16, 16, 17, 17, 17, 17, 18, 18, 19, 20; **2:**2, 3, 6, 6, 8, 14, 15; **3:**1, 2, 4, 5, 6, 7, 7, 9, 9, 12, 13, 15, 15, 15, 16; **4:**1, 1, 2, 3, 3, 3, 6, 6, 6, 6, 7, 8, 8, 8, 8, 10, 10, 12, 13, 13, 14, 16; **5:**3, 4, 4, 4, 5, 5, 6, 8, 11, 12, 13, 13, 14, 15, 16, 16, 17, 17, 18, 18, 18, 20, 20, 21, 21, 23, 23, 24, 25, 25, 25; **6:**1, 1, 1, 1, 2, 2, 3, 3, 3, 5, 5, 5,

6, 7, 9, 9, 10, 10, 10, 12, 12, 12, 12, 13, 13, 13, 13, 13, 14, 14, 14, 15, 15, 15, 15, 16, 17,
17, 17, 19, 19, 20, 20, 20, 21, 21; **2Ti 1**:1, 2, 3, 3, 3, 4, 5, 5, 5, 6, 6, 6, 6, 7, 8, 8, 8, 8, 9,
9, 9, 10, 10, 10, 10, 12, 12, 13, 14, 14, 15, 15, 16, 16, 16, 18, 18; **2**:1, 1, 4, 4, 4, 6, 6, 7,
8, 9, 9, 10, 10, 11, 14, 14, 15, 15, 15, 16, 17, 18, 18, 18, 19, 19, 19, 19, 19, 19, 21, 22,
22, 22, 23, 25, 25, 26, 26, 26; **3**:2, 5, 6, 6, 8, 8, 8, 9, 9, 10, 10, 10, 10, 10, 10, 10, 11, 11,
11, 12, 13, 15, 15, 15, 16, 17, 17; **4**:1, 1, 1, 1, 2, 3, 3, 3, 4, 4, 4, 5, 6, 6, 7, 7, 7, 8, 8, 8, 8,
8, 8, 8, 10, 13, 13, 13, 14, 14, 14, 15, 16, 17, 17, 17, 18, 18, 18, 18, 18, 18, 19, 21, 22,
22, 22; **Tit 1**:1, 2, 3, 3, 4, 5, 7, 9, 9, 9, 9, 9, 10, 10, 13, 13, 14, 15, 15, 15, 15, 16; **2**:1, 2,
2, 2, 4, 5, 5, 5, 6, 7, 8, 10, 10, 10, 11, 11, 12, 12, 12, 13, 13, 13; **3**:4, 4, 4, 5, 5, 6, 7, 8, 8,
8, 11, 13, 14, 14, 15, 15, 15; **Phm 1**:1, 1, 2, 2, 2, 4, 4, 5, 5, 5, 5, 6, 6, 6, 7, 7, 7, 8, 9, 10,
10, 11, 12, 13, 13, 14, 14, 19, 20, 21, 22, 23, 24, 25, 25, 25; **Heb 1**:1, 1, 1, 2, 2, 3, 3, 3, 3,
3, 3, 3, 4, 5, 6, 6, 7, 7, 7, 7, 8, 8, 8, 8, 8, 8, 8, 8, 9, 9, 9, 10, 10, 10, 12, 12, 13, 13, 13, 14;
2:1, 2, 3, 3, 4, 4, 5, 5, 8, 8, 8, 8, 9, 9, 9, 10, 10, 10, 10, 11, 11, 12, 12, 13, 13, 14, 14, 14,
14, 14, 14, 14, 15, 17, 17, 17, 17, 17, 17, 18; **3**:1, 1, 2, 2, 3, 3, 4, 5, 5, 6, 6, 6, 6, 7, 7, 7,
8, 8, 8, 8, 8, 9, 9, 10, 10, 10, 10, 11, 11, 12, 13, 13, 14, 14, 14, 15, 15, 15, 15, 16, 17, 17, 17,
18, 18; **4**:1, 2, 2, 2, 2, 3, 3, 3, 3, 3, 4, 4, 4, 4, 4, 5, 6, 7, 7, 9, 9, 10, 10, 10, 10, 10, 11, 11,
11, 12, 12, 13, 13, 14, 14, 14, 14, 15, 16, 16; **5**:1, 1, 2, 3, 4, 4, 5, 5, 6, 6, 7, 7, 7, 7, 8, 9,
10, 10, 11, 11, 12, 12, 12, 12, 12, 12, 13, 14, 14, 14, 14; **6**:1, 1, 1, 1, 3, 4, 4, 4, 6, 6, 7, 7,
7, 8, 9, 10, 10, 10, 10, 10, 11, 11, 11, 12, 12, 13, 13, 15, 16, 16, 17, 17, 17, 17, 17, 18,
18, 18, 19, 19, 19, 20, 20; **7**:1, 1, 1, 1, 1, 1, 3, 3, 3, 4, 4, 5, 5, 5, 5, 5, 5, 6, 6, 6, 7, 7, 9,
10, 10, 11, 11, 11, 11, 12, 13, 14, 15, 17, 17, 18, 19, 19, 20, 21, 21, 21, 23, 23, 24, 24,
24, 24, 25, 25, 25, 25, 26, 26, 27, 27, 27, 27, 28, 28, 28, 28, 28, 28; **8**:1, 1, 1, 1, 2, 2, 2,
2, 3, 4, 4, 5, 5, 5, 5, 5, 7, 8, 8, 9, 9, 9, 9, 10, 10, 10, 10, 11, 11, 11, 12, 12, 13, 13, 13;
9:1, 1, 2, 2, 2, 2, 2, 3, 3, 4, 4, 4, 4, 4, 4, 4, 5, 6, 6, 7, 7, 7, 7, 7, 8, 8, 8, 8, 8, 9, 9, 9, 11,
11, 11, 12, 12, 13, 13, 13, 13, 14, 14, 14, 14, 14, 15, 15, 15, 15, 15, 16, 17, 18, 19, 19,
19, 19, 19[U], 19, 19, 20, 20, 20, 21, 21, 21, 21, 22, 23, 23, 23, 23, 24, 24, 24, 24, 25, 25,
26, 26[U], 26, 27, 28, 28, 28; **10**:1, 1, 1, 1, 1, 1, 1, 2, 2, 5, 7, 7, 7, 9, 9, 9, 9, 10, 10, 11, 12,
12, 13, 13, 13, 14, 14, 15, 15, 15, 16, 16, 16, 17, 17, 19, 19, 19, 20, 20, 21, 21, 22, 22,
23, 23, 23, 25, 25, 26, 26, 26, 27, 29, 29, 29, 29, 29, 29, 29, 30, 30, 31, 32, 33, 34, 34,
34, 35, 36, 36, 36, 37, 38, 38; **11**:2, 3, 3, 3, 4, 4, 4, 5, 5, 5, 5, 6, 6, 6, 7, 7, 7, 7, 9, 9, 9, 9,
10, 10, 10, 11, 12, 12, 12, 12, 12, 12, 12, 12, 13, 13, 14, 16, 17, 17, 17, 17, 19, 20, 20,
21, 21, 21, 22, 22, 22, 23, 23, 23, 23, 25, 25, 26, 26, 26, 26, 27, 27, 27, 28, 28, 28, 28,
28, 29, 29, 30, 31, 31, 31, 32, 32, 35, 35, 38, 38, 38, 39, 39, 40; **12**:1, 1, 2, 2, 2, 2, 2, 2, 3,
3, 3, 4, 5, 7, 9, 9, 9, 9, 10, 10, 10, 10, 10, 10, 10, 11, 11, 12, 12, 13, 13, 14, 14, 15, 15, 16,
17, 19, 20, 20, 21, 24, 25, 25, 25, 25, 26, 26, 26, 26, 27, 27, 27, 27, 28, 29; **13**:1, 2, 3, 3,
4, 4, 4, 5, 5, 7, 7, 7, 7, 7, 7, 8, 8, 9, 9, 10, 10, 11, 11, 11, 11, 11, 12, 12, 12, 13, 13, 14,
15, 15, 16, 16, 17, 17, 20, 20, 20, 20, 20, 20, 20, 21, 21, 21, 21, 21, 21, 22, 22, 23, 24,
24, 24, 24, 25; **Jas 1**:1, 1, 1, 3, 3, 4, 5, 6, 7, 7, 8, 9, 9, 9, 10, 10, 11, 11, 11, 11, 11, 11,
11, 11, 12, 12, 12, 13, 13, 14, 15, 15, 16, 17, 18, 18, 19, 19, 21, 21, 21, 23, 23, 25, 25, 25,
25, 26, 27, 27, 27; **2**:1, 1, 1, 3, 3, 3, 3, 3, 5, 5, 5, 5, 5, 6, 6, 7, 7, 8, 8, 9, 10, 11, 13, 13,
14, 14, 15, 16, 16, 16, 17, 18, 18, 18, 18, 19, 19, 20, 20, 21, 21, 21, 22, 22, 22, 22, 23,
23, 23, 25, 25, 26, 26; **3**:2, 3, 3, 3, 3, 3, 4, 4, 4, 5, 6, 6, 6, 6, 6, 6, 6, 6, 6, 6, 7, 7, 8, 9, 9,
9, 10, 11, 11, 11, 11, 13, 13, 14, 14, 15, 17, 18; **4**:1, 1, 1, 2, 3, 4, 4, 4, 4, 4, 5, 5, 6, 7, 7,
8, 9, 9, 11, 11, 12, 12, 12, 12, 13, 13, 14, 14, 14, 14, 15, 15, 16; **5**:1, 1, 1, 2, 2, 3, 3, 3, 3,
4, 4, 4, 4, 4, 4, 4, 4, 5, 5, 6, 7, 7, 7, 7, 7, 8, 8, 8, 9, 9, 10, 10, 10, 10, 11, 11, 11, 11, 12,
12, 12, 12, 14, 14, 14, 14, 15, 15, 15, 15, 16, 17, 17, 18, 18, 18, 19, 20; **1Pe 1**:3, 3, 3, 3,
5, 7, 7, 7, 9, 9, 10, 10, 11, 11, 11, 11, 12, 13, 13, 13, 14, 14, 15, 17, 17, 17, 17, 18, 20, 21,
21, 21, 22, 22, 22, 24, 24, 25, 25, 25, 25; **2**:2, 3, 5, 6, 7, 7, 7, 8, 9, 9, 9, 10, 11, 11, 12,
12, 12, 12, 13, 15, 15, 15, 16, 16, 17, 17, 17, 18, 18, 18, 18, 21, 22, 23, 24, 24, 24,
24, 24, 24, 25, 25; **3**:1, 1, 1, 1, 1, 2, 3, 4, 4, 4, 4, 4, 5, 5, 5, 6, 7, 7, 7, 7, 8, 9, 10, 10, 10,
13, 13, 14, 15, 15, 15, 15, 16, 16, 17, 17, 18, 19, 20, 20, 22; **4**:1, 1, 2, 2, 3, 3, 3, 4, 4, 5,
7, 8, 11, 11, 11, 11, 11, 11, 12, 13, 13, 13, 13, 14, 14, 14, 14, 16, 16, 17, 17, 17, 17, 17,
17, 17, 17, 17, 18, 18, 19, 19, 19, 19; **5**:1, 1, 1, 1, 1, 2, 2, 3, 3, 4, 4, 4, 5, 5, 6, 6, 7, 8, 9,
9, 9, 9, 9, 10, 10, 10, 11, 11, 11[N], 12, 12, 13, 13, 14; **2Pe 1**:1, 1, 2, 2, 3, 3, 3, 3, 4, 4, 4, 5,
5, 5, 5, 6, 6, 6, 6, 6, 6, 7, 7, 7, 7, 8, 8, 9, 9, 10, 11, 11, 11, 12, 13, 14, 14, 14, 15, 15, 16,
16, 16, 17, 17, 17, 18, 18, 19, 19; **2**:1, 1, 2, 2, 2, 3, 3, 4, 7, 7, 8, 10, 12, 13, 13, 15, 15,
15, 16, 16, 17, 17, 18, 18, 19, 20, 20, 20, 20, 20, 21, 21, 21, 22, 22, 22; **3**:1, 2, 2, 2, 2, 2,
3, 3, 4, 4, 4, 5, 5, 6, 7, 7, 7, 7, 9, 10, 10, 12, 12, 12, 13, 15, 15, 15, 15, 16, 16, 16, 17, 17,
17, 18, 18; **1Jn 1**:1, 1, 1, 1, 2, 2, 2, 2, 3, 3, 3, 3, 4, 5, 5, 6, 6, 7, 7, 7, 7, 8, 9, 9, 10; **2**:1, 2,
2, 2, 3, 4, 4, 4, 5, 5, 5, 6, 7, 7, 7, 8, 8, 8, 9, 9, 9, 9, 10, 10, 10, 10, 11, 11, 11, 11, 11, 11, 12,
12, 13, 13, 13, 14, 14, 14, 14, 15, 15, 15, 15, 15, 15, 16, 16, 16, 16, 16, 16, 16, 16, 16,
16, 17, 17, 17, 17, 17, 17, 20, 21, 21, 22, 22, 22, 22, 22, 22, 22, 23, 23, 23, 23, 23, 23,
24, 24, 25, 25, 25, 26, 27, 27, 28, 29, 29; **3**:1, 1, 3, 3, 4, 4, 4, 4, 4, 5, 6, 6, 7, 7, 8, 8, 8, 8,
8, 8, 8, 8, 9, 9, 9, 10, 10, 10, 10, 10, 10, 10, 10, 11, 12, 12, 12, 12, 13, 14, 14, 14, 14,
14, 15, 15, 16, 16, 16, 16, 17, 17, 17, 17, 17, 17, 18, 19, 19, 20, 20, 20, 21, 21, 22, 22,
23, 23, 23, 24, 24, 24; **4**:1, 1, 1, 2, 2, 2, 3, 3, 3, 3, 3, 4, 4, 4, 4, 5, 5, 5, 6, 6, 6, 6, 6, 6, 6,
6, 7, 7, 7, 7, 7, 8, 8, 8, 9, 9, 9, 9, 9, 9, 10, 10, 10, 10, 11, 12, 12, 13, 14, 14, 14, 15, 15,
15, 15, 16, 16, 16, 16, 16, 16, 17, 17, 17, 17, 18, 18, 18, 18, 18, 18, 20, 20, 20, 20,
20, 21, 21, 21, 21; **5**:1, 1, 1, 1, 1, 1, 2, 2, 2, 2, 3, 3, 3, 3, 4, 4, 4, 4, 4, 4, 5, 5, 5, 5, 6,
6, 6, 6, 6, 6, 6, 7, 8, 8, 8, 8, 8, 9, 9, 9, 9, 9, 9, 9, 10, 10, 10, 10, 10, 10, 10, 10, 10, 10, 11,
11, 11, 11, 12, 12, 12, 12, 12, 12, 13, 13, 13, 13, 14, 14, 15, 16, 16, 18, 18, 18, 18,
18, 19, 19, 19, 20, 20, 20, 20, 20, 20, 21; **2Jn 1**:1, 1, 1, 1, 2, 2, 2, 3, 3, 4, 4, 6, 6, 6, 7, 7,
7, 7, 9, 9, 9, 9, 9, 9, 9, 10, 11, 11, 11, 12, 13, 13, 13; **3Jn 1**:1, 1, 2, 3, 4, 4, 5, 6, 6, 7, 7, 8,
8, 9, 9, 10, 10, 10, 10, 11, 11, 11, 11, 11, 11, 12, 12, 14, 14; **Jude 1**:1, 3, 3, 3, 4, 4, 4, 4,
4, 5, 5, 5, 6, 6, 6, 7, 7, 9, 9, 9, 9, 10, 11, 11, 11, 11, 11, 11, 12, 12, 13, 13, 13, 15[N], 15,
15, 16, 16, 17, 17, 17, 17, 18, 18, 18, 19, 20, 21, 21, 23, 23, 23, 24, 24, 25, 25, 25; **Rev 1**:1,
1, 1, 1, 2, 2, 2, 3, 3, 3, 3, 3, 3, 4, 4, 4, 4, 4, 4, 4, 4, 5, 5, 5, 5, 5, 5, 5, 5, 5, 5, 6, 6, 6, 6, 6,
7, 7, 7, 8, 8, 8, 8, 8, 8, 8, 9, 9, 9, 9, 9, 9, 9, 10, 11, 12, 13, 13, 14, 14, 14, 15, 15, 16, 16,
16, 16, 16, 17, 17, 17, 17, 18, 18, 18, 18, 18, 18, 20, 20, 20, 20, 20, 20, 20, 20, 20; **2**:1, 1,
1, 1, 1, 1, 1, 1, 2, 2, 2, 2, 3, 4, 4, 5, 5, 5, 6, 6, 7, 7, 7, 7, 7, 7, 7, 7, 7, 8, 8, 8, 8, 9, 9, 9, 9, 9,
10, 10, 10, 11, 11, 11, 11, 11, 11, 12, 12, 12, 12, 12, 12, 13, 13, 13, 13, 13, 13, 13, 13,
14, 14, 14, 15, 15, 16, 16, 17, 17, 17, 17, 17, 17, 17, 17, 18, 18, 18, 18, 18, 18, 18, 19,
19, 19, 19, 19, 19, 19, 19, 20, 20, 20, 21, 22, 22, 22, 23, 23, 23, 23, 24, 24, 24, 24, 26,
26, 26, 26, 27, 27, 27, 28, 28, 29, 29, 29; **3**:1, 1, 1, 1, 1, 1, 1, 2, 2, 2, 4, 5, 5, 5, 5, 5, 5, 5,
6, 6, 6, 7, 7, 7, 7, 7, 7, 7, 8, 8, 8, 9, 9, 9, 9, 10, 10, 10, 10, 10, 10, 10, 10, 11, 12, 12, 12,
12, 12, 12, 12, 12, 12, 12, 12, 12, 12, 13, 13, 13, 14, 14, 14, 14, 14, 14, 14, 14, 15,
16, 17, 18, 18, 18, 20, 20, 20, 21, 21, 21, 21, 22, 22, 22; **4**:1, 1, 1, 2, 2, 3, 3, 4, 4, 4, 5, 5,
5, 5, 6, 6, 6, 7, 7, 7, 7, 7, 7, 8, 8, 8, 8, 8, 8, 9, 9, 9, 9, 9, 9, 10, 10, 10, 10, 10, 10, 10, 10, 10,
11, 11, 11, 11, 11, 11, 11; **5**:1, 1, 1, 2, 2, 3, 3, 3, 3, 4, 5, 5, 5, 5, 5, 5, 5, 6, 6, 6, 6, 6, 6, 7,
7, 7, 8, 8, 8, 8, 8, 9, 9, 9, 9, 9, 10, 10, 11, 11, 11, 11, 11, 12, 12, 12, 13, 13, 13, 13, 13, 13,
13, 13, 13, 13, 13, 13, 13, 13, 14, 14; **6**:1, 1, 1, 2, 3, 3, 3, 4, 4, 4, 5, 5, 5, 5, 5, 6, 6, 6, 7,
7, 7, 8, 8, 8, 8, 8, 8, 8, 9, 9, 9, 9, 9, 9, 9, 10, 10, 10, 10, 10, 11, 11, 11, 12, 12, 12, 12, 13,
13, 13, 13, 14, 14, 15, 15, 15, 15, 15, 15, 15, 15, 15, 16, 16, 16, 16, 16, 16, 17, 17, 17, 17;
7:1, 1, 1, 1, 1, 1, 2, 2, 2, 3, 3, 3, 3, 3, 3, 4, 4, 9, 9, 9, 10, 10, 10, 10, 10, 10, 11, 11, 11, 11,
11, 11, 11, 12, 12, 12, 12, 12, 12, 12, 12, 12, 13, 13, 13, 13, 14, 14, 14, 14, 14, 14,
15, 15, 15, 15, 15, 16, 17, 17, 17, 17, 17; **8**:1, 1, 1, 2, 2, 3, 3, 3, 3, 3, 3, 3, 4, 4, 4, 4, 4, 4,
5, 5, 5, 5, 5, 6, 6, 6, 7, 7, 7, 7, 7, 7, 8, 8, 8, 8, 9, 9, 9, 9, 9, 9, 9, 10, 10, 10, 10, 10, 10, 10, 11,
11, 11, 11, 11, 11, 11, 12, 12, 12, 12, 12, 12, 12, 12, 12, 12, 12, 13, 13, 13, 13, 13, 13;
9:1, 1, 1, 1, 1, 2, 2, 2, 2, 2, 2, 2, 3, 3, 3, 3, 4, 4, 4, 4, 4, 4, 5, 6, 6, 6, 6, 7, 7, 7, 7, 8, 9,
9, 10, 10, 10, 11, 11, 11, 12, 12, 13, 13, 13, 13, 13, 14, 14, 14, 14, 14, 14, 14, 15, 15,
15, 15, 15, 16, 16, 16, 16, 17, 17, 17, 17, 17, 17, 18, 18, 18, 18, 18, 18, 18, 18, 19, 19,
19, 19, 19, 20, 20, 20, 20, 20, 20, 20, 20, 20, 20, 20, 21, 21, 21, 21; **10**:1, 1, 1, 1, 1, 1,
2, 2, 2, 2, 2, 3, 3, 4, 4, 4, 5, 5, 5, 5, 5, 5, 6, 6, 6, 6, 6, 6, 6, 6, 6, 7, 7, 7, 7, 7, 7, 7, 7, 8, 8,
8, 8, 8, 8, 8, 8, 8, 9, 9, 9, 9, 10, 10, 10, 10, 10, 10; **11**:1, 1, 1, 1, 2, 2, 2, 2, 2, 2, 3, 4, 4, 4, 4,
4, 5, 5, 6, 6, 6, 6, 6, 6, 7, 7, 7, 7, 8, 8, 8, 8, 8, 8, 9, 9, 9, 10, 10, 10, 10, 10, 10, 11, 11, 11, 11,
12, 12, 12, 12, 13, 13, 13, 13, 13, 13, 13, 14, 14, 14, 14, 15, 15, 15, 15, 15, 15, 15, 15,
16, 16, 16, 16, 16, 16, 17, 17, 17, 17, 17, 17, 18, 18, 18, 18, 18, 18, 18, 18, 18, 18, 18,
18, 18, 18, 19, 19, 19, 19, 19, 19, 19; **12**:1, 1, 1, 1, 1, 3, 3, 4, 4, 4, 4, 4, 4, 4, 4, 4, 5, 5, 5,
5, 6, 6, 6, 7, 7, 7, 7, 7, 7, 8, 9, 9, 9, 9, 9, 9, 9, 9, 9, 10, 10, 10, 10, 10, 10, 10, 10, 10, 10,
10, 10, 11, 11, 11, 11, 11, 11, 12, 12, 12, 12, 12, 12, 13, 13, 13, 13, 14, 14, 14, 14, 14, 14,
15, 15, 15, 16, 16, 16, 16, 16, 16, 17, 17, 17, 17, 17, 17, 17, 17, 17; **13**:1, 1, 1, 1, 1, 2, 2,
2, 2, 2, 2, 3, 3, 3, 3, 3, 4, 4, 4, 4, 4, 6, 6, 6, 6, 6, 6, 7, 8, 8, 8, 8, 8, 8, 8, 10, 10, 10, 11, 12,
12, 12, 12, 12, 12, 12, 13, 13, 13, 14, 14, 14, 14, 14, 14, 14, 14, 14, 15, 15, 15, 15,
15, 15, 16, 16, 16, 16, 16, 16, 16, 17, 17, 17, 17, 17, 17, 18, 18, 18, 18, 18; **14**:1,
1, 1, 1, 1, 1, 2, 2, 2, 3, 3, 3, 3, 3, 3, 3, 4, 4, 4, 4, 4, 5, 6, 6, 7, 7, 7, 7, 7, 7, 8, 8, 8, 8, 8, 9,
9, 9, 9, 10, 10, 10, 10, 10, 10, 10, 11, 11, 11, 11, 11, 11, 11, 12, 12, 12, 12, 12, 12, 13,
13, 13, 13, 13, 13, 14, 14, 14, 15, 15, 15, 15, 15, 15, 15, 16, 16, 16, 16, 16, 17, 17, 17,
18, 18, 18, 18, 18, 18, 18, 18, 18, 18, 19, 19, 19, 19, 19, 19, 19, 19, 19, 19, 20, 20,
20, 20, 20; **15**:1, 1, 1, 1, 2, 2, 2, 2, 2, 2, 2, 2, 2, 3, 3, 3, 3, 3, 3, 3, 3, 3, 3, 3, 4, 4, 4, 5, 5, 5,
5, 6, 6, 6, 6, 6, 7, 7, 7, 7, 7, 7, 7, 8, 8, 8, 8, 8, 8, 8; **16**:1, 1, 1, 1, 1, 2, 2, 2, 2, 2, 2, 2, 2,
2, 3, 3, 3, 3, 3, 4, 4, 4, 4, 4, 5, 5, 5, 5, 5, 7, 7, 7, 7, 8, 8, 8, 8, 9, 9, 9, 9, 9, 9, 10, 10, 10,
10, 10, 10, 10, 11, 11, 11, 11, 11, 12, 12, 12, 12, 12, 12, 12, 12, 12, 13, 13, 13, 13, 13,
13, 14, 14, 14, 14, 14, 14, 14, 15, 15, 15, 16, 16, 17, 17, 17, 17, 17, 18, 19, 19, 19, 19,
19, 19, 19, 19, 19, 19, 21, 21, 21, 21, 21, 21, 21; **17**:1, 1, 1, 1, 1, 1, 1, 2, 2, 2, 2, 2, 2, 4,
4, 4, 4, 5, 5, 5, 5, 5, 5, 6, 6, 6, 6, 6, 7, 7, 7, 7, 7, 7, 7, 7, 8, 8, 8, 8, 8, 8, 8, 8, 9, 9, 9, 9, 10,
10, 10, 11, 11, 12, 12, 13, 13, 14, 14, 14, 15, 15, 16, 16, 16, 16, 17, 17, 17, 17, 17, 17,
17, 18, 18, 18, 18, 18, 18; **18**:1, 1, 2, 3, 3, 3, 3, 3, 3, 3, 3, 3, 3, 3, 4, 4, 4, 4, 5, 5, 5, 5, 6,
6, 6, 7, 8, 8, 8, 9, 9, 9, 9, 9, 10, 10, 10, 10, 10, 10, 10, 11, 11, 11, 11, 14, 14, 14, 14, 15,
15, 15, 15, 16, 16, 16, 17, 17, 17, 18, 18, 18, 18, 19, 19, 19, 19, 19, 19, 19, 20, 20, 20,
20, 20, 21, 21, 23, 23, 23, 23, 23, 24, 24; **19**:1, 1, 1, 1, 1, 2, 2, 2, 2, 2, 2, 2, 3, 3, 3, 4, 4,
4, 4, 4, 4, 5, 5, 5, 5, 5, 6, 6, 7, 7, 7, 7, 8, 8, 8, 9, 9, 9, 9, 9, 9, 10, 10, 10, 10, 10, 10, 10,
10, 11, 11, 12, 12, 13, 13, 13, 14, 14, 14, 15, 15, 15, 15, 15, 15, 15, 15, 16, 16, 17, 17,
17, 17, 17, 17, 18, 19, 19, 19, 19, 19, 19, 19, 19, 20, 20, 20, 20, 20, 20, 20, 20, 20, 20,
20, 20, 20, 21, 21, 21, 21, 21, 21, 21, 21; **20**:1, 1, 1, 1, 2, 2, 2, 2, 3, 3, 3, 4, 4, 4, 4, 4, 4,
4, 4, 4, 4, 4, 5, 5, 5, 5, 5, 6, 6, 6, 6, 6, 6, 6, 7, 7, 7, 8, 8, 8, 8, 8, 8, 8, 8, 8, 8, 9, 9, 9, 9, 9, 9,
9, 10, 10, 10, 10, 10, 10, 10, 10, 11, 11, 11, 11, 12, 12, 12, 12, 12, 12, 12, 12, 13, 13,
13, 13, 13, 13, 13, 13, 14, 14, 14, 14, 14, 14, 14, 14, 15, 15, 15, 15; **21**:1, 1, 1, 2, 2, 2, 2,
2, 3, 3, 3, 3, 3, 4, 4, 4, 5, 5, 5, 6, 6, 6, 6, 6, 6, 6, 6, 7, 8, 8, 8, 8, 8, 8, 8, 9, 9, 9, 9, 9, 9, 9,
9, 9, 10, 10, 10, 10, 11, 11, 11, 12, 12, 12, 14, 14, 14, 14, 15, 15, 15, 15, 16, 16, 16, 16,
16, 16, 16, 16, 17, 18, 18, 18, 19, 19, 19, 19, 19, 19, 19, 19, 20, 20, 20, 20, 20, 20, 20,
20, 21, 21, 21, 21, 22, 22, 22, 22, 23, 23, 23, 23, 23, 23, 23, 24, 24, 24, 24, 24, 25, 26,
26, 26, 27, 27, 27, 27, 27; **22**:1, 1, 1, 2, 2, 2, 2, 2, 2, 3, 3, 3, 3, 4, 4, 4, 5, 5, 5, 6, 6, 6, 6,
6, 6, 6, 7, 7, 7, 7, 8, 8, 8, 8, 9, 9, 9, 9, 9, 9, 9, 10, 10, 10, 10, 10, 11, 11, 11, 11, 12, 12, 13, 13,
13, 13, 13, 13, 14, 14, 14, 14, 14, 14, 14, 15, 15, 15, 15, 15, 16, 16, 16, 16, 16, 16, 16,
17, 17, 17, 17, 17, 18, 18, 18, 18, 18, 18, 18, 18, 19, 19, 19, 19, 19, 19, 19, 19, 19, 19,
19, 20, 21, 21, 21[N]

4005 ὅς, hos [1411]

Mt **1**:16, 23, 25; **2**:9, 16; **3**:11, 12, 17; **5**:19, 19, 21, 22, 22, 31, 32; **6**:8; **7**:2, 2, 9; **8**:4;
10:11, 14, 26, 26, 27, 27, 38, 42; **11**:4, 6, 10, 10, 16, 20, 27; **12**:2, 4, 11, 18, 18, 32, 32,
36; **13**:4, 8, 8, 8, 12, 17, 17, 23, 23, 23, 23, 31, 32, 33, 33, 44, 48; **14**:7, 22; **15**:5, 5, 13;
16:19, 19, 25, 25; **17**:5, 9; **18**:5, 6, 7, 19, 23, 28, 34; **19**:6, 9, 11; **20**:4, 15, 22, 23, 26, 27;
21:15, 24, 35, 35, 35, 42, 44; **22**:5, 5, 10; **23**:16, 16, 18, 18, 35, 37; **24**:2, 38, 44, 45, 46,
50, 50; **25**:15, 15, 15, 29; **26**:13, 24, 36, 48, 50; **27**:9, 15, 33, 56, 57, 60; **Mk 1**:2, 7, 44;
2:19, 24, 26; **3**:13, 14, 17, 19, 29, 35; **4**:4, 9, 16, 24, 25, 25, 25, 31; **5**:3, 33, 41; **6**:11, 16,

22, 23; 7:4, 11, 11, 13, 15, 25, 34; 8:35, 35, 38; 9:9, 37, 37, 39, 40, 41, 42; 10:9, 11, 15, 29, 35, 38, 38, 39, 39, 40, 43, 44; 11:2, 21, 23, 23; 12:5, 5, 10, 42; 13:2, 11, 19, 20, 30, 37; 14:8, 9, 21, 32, 44, 71; 15:6, 12, 16, 22, 23, 34, 40, 41, 42, 43, 46; 16:9; Lk 1:4, 20, 20, 25, 26, 27, 61, 73, 78; 2:11, 15, 20, 25, 31, 37, 50; 3:16, 17, 19; 4:6, 18, 29; 5:3, 9, 10, 17, 18, 21, 25, 29, 34; 6:2, 3, 4, 13, 14, 16, 18, 34, 38, 46, 48, 49; 7:2, 4, 22, 23, 27, 27, 32, 43, 45, 47, 47, 49; 8:2, 2, 5, 13, 13, 17, 17, 18, 18, 18, 35, 38, 41, 47; 9:4, 9, 24, 24, 26, 27, 31, 31, 33, 36, 43, 48, 48, 50; 10:5, 8, 10, 22, 23, 24, 24, 30, 35, 39; 11:6, 22, 27; 12:1, 2, 2, 3, 3, 8, 10, 12, 20, 24, 37, 40, 42, 43, 46, 46, 48, 48; 13:1, 4, 7, 14, 16, 19, 21, 21, 25, 30, 30, 34; 14:22, 33; 15:8, 9, 16; 16:1; 17:1, 7, 10, 12, 27, 29, 30, 31, 33, 33; 18:17, 29, 30; 19:13, 15, 20, 21, 21, 22, 22, 26, 30, 30, 37, 44; 20:17, 18, 47; 21:4, 6, 6, 6, 15, 24; 22:7, 10, 18, 22, 60; 23:14, 25, 27, 29, 29, 29, 33, 33, 41, 51; 24:1, 13, 17, 19, 21, 23, 25, 44, 49; Jn 1:3, 9, 13, 15, 26, 27, 30, 30, 33, 38, 41, 42, 45, 47; 2:5, 22, 23; 3:2, 11, 11, 26, 26, 32, 34; 4:5, 12, 14, 14, 14, 18, 22, 22, 29, 32, 38, 39, 46, 50, 52, 53; 5:7, 19, 20, 21, 28, 32, 36, 36, 38, 45; 6:2, 9, 13, 14, 21, 27, 29, 37, 39, 42, 51, 63, 64; 7:3, 25, 28, 31, 36, 39; 8:25, 26, 38, 38, 40, 40, 54; 9:7, 14, 19, 24; 10:6, 12, 16, 25, 29, 35, 36; 11:2, 3, 6, 45, 46; 12:1, 9, 38, 48, 50; 13:5, 7, 23, 24, 26, 27, 29, 38; 14:10, 12, 13, 17, 24, 26, 26; 15:3, 7, 14, 15, 16, 20, 24, 26, 26; 16:17, 18; 17:2, 3, 4, 5, 6, 8, 9, 11, 12, 22, 24, 24, 26; 18:1, 9, 9, 11, 13, 21, 26, 32; 19:17, 22, 26, 37, 41; 20:2, 7, 16, 30; 21:7, 10, 20, 20, 25; Ac 1:1, 2, 2, 3, 4, 7, 11, 11, 12, 16, 21, 22, 23, 24, 25; 2:8, 21, 22, 24, 32, 33, 36; 3:2, 3, 6, 13, 15, 15, 16, 18, 21, 21, 25; 4:10, 10, 12, 20, 22, 27, 31, 36; 5:25, 30, 32, 36, 36; 6:3, 6, 10, 14; 7:3, 4, 7, 16, 17, 18, 18, 20, 20, 28, 33, 35, 38, 39, 40, 40, 43, 44, 45, 45, 46, 52; 8:6, 10, 19, 24, 27, 27, 30, 32; 9:5, 6, 17, 33, 36, 36, 39; 10:5, 6, 12, 15, 17, 21, 21, 32, 36, 37, 38, 39, 39; 11:6, 9, 11, 14, 14, 23, 30; 12:4, 23; 13:2, 6, 7, 22, 22, 25, 31, 37, 39, 41; 14:8, 9, 11, 15, 16, 23, 26; 15:10, 11, 17, 24, 29, 36; 16:2, 14, 21, 24; 17:3, 7, 23, 23, 31, 31, 34; 18:7, 27; 19:13, 16, 25, 27, 35, 40; 20:18, 24, 25, 28, 28, 38; 21:11, 16, 19, 23, 24, 26, 29, 32; 22:4, 5, 8, 10, 15, 24; 23:12, 14, 19, 21, 28, 29; 24:6, 6, 8, 8, 11, 13, 14, 15, 18, 19, 21; 25:7, 11, 15, 16, 18, 18, 19, 21, 24, 26; 26:2, 7, 7, 10, 12, 15, 16, 16, 17, 22, 26; 27:8, 17, 23, 23, 25, 33, 39, 44, 44; 28:4, 7, 8, 10, 15, 22, 23; Ro 1:2, 5, 6, 9, 25, 27; 2:1, 6, 23, 29; 3:8, 14, 25, 30; 4:6, 7, 7, 8, 16, 17, 18, 21, 24, 25; 5:2, 2, 11, 12, 14; 6:10, 10, 16, 16, 17, 21; 7:6, 15, 15, 15, 16, 19, 19, 20; 8:3, 15, 24, 25, 26, 29, 30, 30, 30, 32, 34, 34; 9:4, 5, 5, 15, 15, 18, 18, 21, 21, 23, 24; 10:8, 13, 14, 14; 11:2, 7, 25; 12:3; 14:2, 5, 5, 15, 21, 22, 22, 23; 15:18, 21, 21; 16:2, 4, 5, 7, 17, 27; 1Co 1:8, 9, 30; 2:7, 8, 9, 9, 13, 16; 3:5, 11, 14; 4:5, 6, 7, 17, 17; 6:5, 18, 19; 7:1, 20, 24, 36, 37, 39; 8:6, 6, 11; 10:11, 13, 13, 15, 16, 16, 20, 30; 11:21, 21, 23, 23, 26, 27; 12:8, 23, 28; 14:37; 15:1, 1, 1, 2, 3, 6, 9, 10, 15, 25, 31, 36, 37; 16:2, 3; 2Co 1:4, 6, 10, 10, 13, 17; 2:3, 4, 10, 10, 16, 16; 3:6; 4:4, 4, 6; 5:4, 10; 7:7; 8:12, 12, 18, 22; 9:2; 10:1, 2, 8, 13, 18; 11:4, 4, 4, 12, 12, 15, 17, 21; 12:4, 6, 13, 17, 21; 13:3, 10; Gal 1:5, 7, 8, 9, 20, 23; 2:2, 4, 5, 10, 18, 20; 3:1, 10, 16, 19, 19; 4:9, 19, 19; 5:17, 21; 6:7, 14; Eph 1:6, 7, 8, 9, 11, 13, 13, 14, 20; 2:2, 3, 4, 10, 13, 21, 22; 3:4, 5, 7, 11, 12, 15, 20; 4:1, 15, 16, 30; 5:4, 5, 18; 6:16, 17, 20, 22; Php 2:5, 6, 15; 3:8, 12, 16, 18, 19, 19, 21; 4:3, 9, 10, 11; Col 1:4, 5, 6, 7, 9, 13, 14, 15, 18, 23, 23, 24, 25, 27, 27, 28, 29; 2:3, 10, 11, 12, 14, 17, 18, 19, 22; 3:6, 7, 14, 15, 17, 23, 25; 4:3, 8, 9, 10, 17; 1Th 1:10; 2:13; 3:9; 5:24; 2Th 1:4, 5, 11; 2:8, 9, 10, 14, 15; 3:3, 4, 6, 17; 1Ti 1:6, 7, 11, 15, 19, 20, 20; 2:4, 7, 10; 3:16; 4:3, 6, 10, 14; 6:4, 10, 12, 15, 16, 16, 21; 2Ti 1:3, 6, 6, 11, 12, 12, 13, 15; 2:2, 7, 9, 17, 20, 20; 3:8, 14; 4:8, 13, 15, 18; Tit 1:2, 3, 11, 11, 13; 2:1, 14; 3:5, 6; Phm 1:5, 10, 12, 13, 21; Heb 1:2, 2, 3; 2:5, 10, 10, 11, 13, 18; 3:6, 13, 17; 4:13; 5:7, 8, 11; 6:7, 8, 10, 17, 18, 19; 7:2, 2, 4, 13, 13, 14, 16, 19, 27; 8:1, 2, 3, 9, 10; 9:2, 4, 5, 7, 9, 14, 20; 10:1, 10, 16, 20, 29, 32; 11:4, 7, 8, 10, 15, 18, 29, 33, 38; 12:2, 6, 6, 7, 8, 14, 16, 19, 26, 28; 13:7, 9, 10, 11, 21, 23; Jas 1:12, 12, 17; 2:5; 4:4, 5; 5:10; 1Pe 1:6, 8, 8, 10, 12, 12, 12; 2:4, 7, 8, 8, 10, 12, 22, 23, 24, 24; 3:3, 4, 6, 16, 19, 20, 21, 22; 4:4, 5, 11, 11, 13; 5:9, 12; 2Pe 1:4, 9, 17, 19, 19; 2:2, 3, 12, 15, 17, 19; 3:1, 4, 6, 10, 12, 13, 16, 16; 1Jn 1:1, 1, 1, 1, 3, 5; 2:5, 7, 7, 8, 24, 24, 25, 27; 3:11, 17, 22, 24; 4:2, 3, 3, 6, 15, 16, 20, 20; 5:10, 14, 15, 15; 2Jn 1:1, 5, 8; 3Jn 1:1, 5, 6, 6, 10; Jude 1:13, 15, 15, 22, 23, 23; Rev 1:1, 1, 2, 4, 11, 19, 19, 19, 20; 2:6, 7, 8, 10, 13, 14, 17, 25, 25; 3:2, 4, 8, 11; 4:1, 1, 5; 5:6, 8, 13; 6:9; 7:2, 9; 8:2; 9:20, 20; 10:4, 5, 6, 8; 12:5, 16; 13:2, 8, 12, 14, 14; 14:2, 4, 8; 16:14, 18; 17:2, 8, 8, 11, 12, 15, 16, 18; 18:6, 19; 19:12, 20; 20:2, 8, 11, 12; 21:8, 12, 17; 22:6

4022 ὅτι, *hoti* [1296 / 1298]

Mt 2:16, 18, 22, 23; 3:9; 4:6, 12; 5:3, 4, 5, 6, 7, 8, 9, 10, 12, 17, 20, 21, 22, 23, 27, 28, 32, 33, 34, 35, 35, 36, 38, 43, 45; 6:5, 7, 26, 29, 32; 7:13, 14N, 23; 8:11, 27; 9:6, 18, 28, 36; 10:7, 34; 11:20, 21, 23, 24, 25, 26, 29; 12:5, 6, 36, 41, 42; 13:11, 13, 16, 16, 17; 14:5, 26; 15:12, 17, 23, 32; 16:7, 8, 11, 12, 17, 18, 20, 21, 23, 28; 17:10, 12, 13, 15; 18:10, 13, 19; 19:4, 8, 9, 23, 28; 20:7, 10, 15, 25, 30; 21:3, 16, 31, 43, 45; 22:16, 34; 23:10, 13, 15, 23, 25, 27, 29, 31; 24:32, 33, 34, 42, 43, 44, 47; 25:8, 13, 24, 26; 26:2, 21, 34, 53, 54, 72, 74, 75; 27:3, 18, 24, 43, 47, 63; 28:5, 7, 13; Mk 1:15, 34, 37, 40; 2:1, 8, 10, 12, 16, 16, 17; 3:11, 21, 22, 22, 28, 30; 4:29, 38, 41; 5:9, 23, 28, 29, 35; 6:4, 14, 15, 15, 17, 18, 34, 35, 49, 55; 7:2, 6, 18, 19, 20; 8:2, 4, 16, 17, 24, 28, 28, 31, 33; 9:1, 11, 11, 13, 25, 26, 28, 31, 38, 41, 41; 10:33, 42, 47; 11:17, 23, 23, 24, 32; 12:6, 7, 12, 14, 19, 26, 28, 29, 32, 34, 35, 43; 13:6, 28, 29, 30; 14:14, 18, 21, 25, 27, 27, 30, 58, 58, 69, 71, 72; 15:10, 39; 16:4, 7, 11, 14; Lk 1:22, 25, 37, 45, 48, 49, 58, 61, 68; 2:11, 23, 30, 49, 49; 3:8; 4:4, 6, 10, 11, 12, 21, 24, 32, 36, 41, 41, 43, 43; 5:8, 24, 26, 36; 6:19, 20, 21, 21, 24, 25, 25, 35; 7:4, 16, 16, 37, 39, 43, 47; 8:25, 30, 37, 42, 47, 49, 53; 9:7, 8, 8, 12, 19, 22, 38, 49, 53; 10:11, 12, 13, 20, 20, 21, 21, 24, 40; 11:18, 31, 32, 38, 42, 43, 44, 46, 47, 48, 52; 12:15, 17, 24, 30, 32, 37, 39, 40, 44, 51, 54, 55; 13:2, 2, 4, 14, 14, 24, 31, 33; 14:11, 14, 17, 24, 30; 15:2, 6, 7, 9, 24, 27, 27, 32; 16:3, 8, 8, 15, 24, 25; 17:9, 10, 15; 18:8, 9, 11, 14, 29, 37; 19:3, 4, 7, 9, 11, 17, 21, 22, 26, 31, 34, 42, 43; 20:5, 19, 21, 37; 21:3, 5, 20, 22, 30, 31, 32; 22:16, 18, 22, 37, 61, 70; 23:5, 7, 29, 31, 40; 24:7, 21, 29, 34, 39, 39, 44, 46; Jn 1:15, 16, 17, 20, 30, 32, 34, 50, 50; 2:17, 18, 22, 25; 3:2, 7, 11, 18, 19, 21, 23, 28, 28, 28, 33; 4:1, 1, 17, 19, 20, 21, 22, 25, 27, 35, 35, 37, 39, 42, 42, 44, 47, 51, 52, 53; 5:6, 15, 16, 18, 24, 25, 27, 28, 30, 32, 36, 38, 39, 42, 45; 6:2, 5, 14, 15, 22, 22, 24, 26, 26, 36, 38, 41, 42, 46, 61, 65, 69; 7:1, 7, 7, 8, 12, 22, 23, 26, 29, 30, 35, 39, 42, 52; 8:14, 16, 17, 20, 22, 24, 24, 27, 28, 29, 33, 34, 37, 37, 43, 44, 44, 45, 47, 48, 52, 54, 55; 9:8, 9, 9, 11, 16, 17, 17, 18, 19, 20, 20, 22, 23, 24, 25, 29, 30, 31, 32, 35, 41; 10:4, 5, 7, 13, 17, 26, 33, 34, 36, 36, 38, 41; 11:6, 9, 10, 13, 15, 20, 22, 24, 27, 31, 31, 40, 41, 42, 42, 47, 50, 51, 56; 12:6, 6, 9, 11, 12, 16, 18, 19, 34, 34, 39, 41, 49, 50; 13:1, 3, 3, 11, 19, 21, 29, 33, 35; 14:2, 10, 11, 12, 17, 17, 19, 20, 22, 28, 28, 28, 31; 15:5, 15, 15, 18, 19, 21, 25, 27; 16:3, 4, 4, 6, 9, 10, 11, 14, 15, 17, 19, 19, 20, 21, 21, 26, 27, 27, 30, 30, 32; 17:7, 8, 8, 8, 9, 14, 21, 23, 24, 25; 18:2, 8, 9, 14, 18, 37; 19:4, 7, 10, 20, 21, 28, 35, 42; 20:9, 13, 14, 15, 18, 29, 31; 21:4, 7, 12, 15, 16, 17, 17, 23, 23, 24; Ac 1:5, 17; 2:6, 13, 25, 27, 29, 30, 31, 36; 3:10, 17, 22; 4:10, 13, 13, 16, 21; 5:4, 9, 23, 25, 38, 41; 6:1, 11, 14; 7:6, 25; 8:14, 18, 20, 33; 9:15, 20, 22, 26, 27, 38; 10:14, 20, 34, 38, 42, 45; 11:1, 3, 8, 24; 12:3, 9, 11; 13:33, 34, 34, 38, 41; 14:9, 22, 27; 15:1, 5, 7, 24; 16:3, 10, 19, 36, 38; 17:3, 3, 6, 13, 18; 18:13; 19:21, 25, 26, 26, 34; 20:23, 23, 25, 26, 29, 31, 34, 35, 35, 38; 21:21, 22, 24, 29, 31; 22:2, 15, 19, 21, 29, 29; 23:5, 5, 6, 20, 22, 27, 34; 24:11, 14, 21, 26; 25:8, 16; 26:5, 27, 31; 27:10, 25; 28:1, 22, 25, 28; Ro 1:8, 13, 32; 2:2, 3, 4; 3:2, 8, 10, 19; 4:17, 21, 23; 5:3, 5, 8; 6:3, 6, 8, 9, 15, 16, 17; 7:1, 14, 16, 18, 21; 8:16, 18, 21, 22, 27, 28, 29, 36, 38; 9:2, 6, 7, 12, 17, 30, 32; 10:2, 5, 9, 9; 11:25, 36; 13:11; 14:11, 14, 23; 15:14, 29; 1Co 1:5, 11, 12, 14, 15, 25, 26; 2:14; 3:13, 16, 20; 4:9N, 9; 5:6; 6:2, 3, 7, 9, 15, 16, 19; 7:26; 8:1, 4, 4; 9:10, 13, 24; 10:1, 17, 19, 19, 20; 11:2, 3, 14, 15, 17, 23; 12:2, 3, 15, 16; 14:21, 23, 25, 37; 15:3, 4, 5, 12, 12, 15, 15, 27, 27, 50, 58; 16:15, 17; 2Co 1:5, 7, 8, 10, 12, 13, 14, 18, 23, 24; 2:3, 15; 3:3, 5, 14; 4:6, 14; 5:1, 6, 14, 19; 6:16; 7:3, 8, 8, 9, 9, 13, 14, 16; 8:2, 3, 9, 17; 9:2, 12; 10:7, 10, 11; 11:7, 10, 11, 21, 31; 12:4, 13, 19; 13:2, 5, 6, 6; Gal 1:6, 11, 13, 20, 23; 2:7, 11, 14, 16, 16; 3:7, 8, 8, 10, 11, 11, 13; 4:6, 12, 13, 15, 20, 22, 27; 5:2, 3, 10, 21; 6:8; Eph 2:11, 12, 18; 3:3; 4:9, 25; 5:5, 16, 23, 30; 6:8, 9, 12; Php 1:6, 12, 16, 18, 19, 20, 25, 27, 29; 2:11, 16, 22, 24, 26, 30; 3:12; 4:10, 11, 15, 16, 17; Col 1:16, 19; 2:9; 3:24; 4:1, 13; 1Th 1:5; 2:1, 13, 14; 3:3, 4, 6, 8; 4:14, 15, 16; 5:2, 9; 2Th 1:3, 10; 2:2, 3, 4, 5, 13; 3:4, 7, 9, 10; 1Ti 1:8, 9, 12, 13, 15; 4:1, 4, 10; 5:12; 6:2, 2, 7; 2Ti 1:5, 12, 15, 16; 2:23; 3:1, 15; Tit 3:11; Phm 1:7, 19, 21, 22; Heb 2:6, 6; 3:19; 7:8, 14, 17; 8:9, 10, 11, 12; 10:8; 11:6, 13, 14, 18, 19; 12:17; 13:18; Jas 1:3, 7, 10, 12, 13, 23; 2:19, 20, 22, 24; 3:1; 4:4, 5; 5:8, 11, 20; 1Pe 1:12, 16, 16, 18; 2:3, 15, 21; 3:9, 12, 18; 4:1, 8, 14, 17; 5:5, 7; 2Pe 1:14, 20; 3:3, 5, 8; 1Jn 1:5, 6, 8, 10; 2:3, 4, 5, 8, 11, 12, 13, 13, 13, 14, 14, 16, 18, 18, 19, 21, 21, 21, 22, 29, 29; 3:1, 2, 2, 5, 8, 9, 9, 11, 12, 14, 14, 15, 16, 19, 20, 20, 22, 24; 4:1, 3, 4, 7, 8, 9, 10, 10, 13, 13, 14, 15, 17, 18, 19, 20; 5:1, 2, 4, 5, 6, 7, 9, 9, 10, 11, 13, 14, 15, 15, 18, 19, 20; 2Jn 1:4, 7; 3Jn 1:12; Jude 1:5, 11, 18, 18; Rev 2:2, 4, 6, 14, 20, 23; 3:1, 1, 4, 8, 9, 10, 15, 16, 17, 17, 17; 4:11; 5:4, 9; 6:17; 7:17; 8:11; 10:6; 11:2, 10, 17; 12:10, 12, 12, 13; 13:4; 14:7, 15, 15, 18; 15:1, 4, 4, 4; 16:5, 6, 21; 17:8, 14; 18:3, 5, 7, 7, 8, 10, 11, 17, 19, 20, 23, 23; 19:2, 2, 6, 7; 21:4, 5; 22:5

4024 οὐ, *ou* [1623 / 1619]

Mt 1:25; 2:18, 18; 3:11; 4:4, 7; 5:14, 17, 18, 20, 21, 26, 27, 33, 36, 37, 37; 6:1, 5, 20, 24, 26, 26, 28, 30; 7:3, 18, 21, 22, 25, 29; 8:8, 20; 9:12, 13, 13, 14, 24; 10:20, 23, 24, 26, 26, 29, 34, 37, 37, 38, 38, 42; 11:11, 17, 17, 20; 12:2, 3, 4, 5, 7, 7, 19, 20, 20, 24, 25, 31, 32, 39, 43; 13:5, 11, 12, 13, 13, 14, 14, 17, 17, 21, 29, 55, 55, 57, 58; 14:4, 16, 17; 15:2, 6, 11, 13, 17, 20, 23, 24, 26, 32, 32; 16:3, 4, 7, 8, 11, 11, 12, 17, 18, 22, 23, 28; 17:12, 16, 19, 24; 18:3, 14, 22, 30, 33; 19:4, 8, 10, 11, 18, 18, 18, 18; 20:13, 15, 22, 23, 26, 28; 21:21, 25, 27, 29, 30, 32; 22:3, 8, 11, 16, 16, 17, 31, 32; 23:3, 4, 13, 30, 37, 39; 24:2, 2, 2, 21, 21, 22, 29, 34, 35, 39, 42, 43, 44, 50, 50; 25:3, 9, 12, 13, 24, 24, 26, 26, 42, 42, 43, 43, 43, 44, 45; 26:11, 24, 29, 35, 39, 40, 42, 53, 55, 60, 70, 72, 74; 27:6, 13, 14, 34, 42; 28:6; Mk 1:7, 22, 34; 2:17, 17, 18, 19, 24, 26, 27; 3:24, 25, 26, 27, 29; 4:5, 7, 13, 17, 21, 22, 25, 27, 34, 38; 5:19, 37, 39; 6:3, 3, 4, 5, 18, 19, 26, 52; 7:3, 4, 5, 18, 18, 19, 24, 27; 8:2, 14, 16, 17, 18, 18, 18, 33; 9:1, 3, 6, 18, 28, 30, 37, 38, 40, 41, 48, 48; 10:15, 27, 38, 40, 43, 45; 11:13, 16, 17, 31, 33; 12:14, 14, 14, 20, 22, 24, 26, 27, 31, 32, 34; 13:2, 2, 11, 14, 19, 19, 20, 24, 30, 31, 33, 35; 14:7, 21, 25, 29, 31, 36, 37, 40, 49, 55, 56, 60, 61, 71; 15:4, 23, 31; 16:6, 14, 18; Lk 1:7, 15, 20, 22, 33, 34, 37; 2:7, 37, 43, 49, 50; 3:16; 4:2, 4, 12, 41; 5:31, 32, 36; 6:2, 4, 37, 37, 40, 41, 42, 43, 44, 46, 48; 7:6, 6, 32, 32, 44, 45, 45, 46; 8:13, 14, 17, 17, 17, 19, 27, 27, 43, 47, 51, 52; 9:13, 27, 40, 49, 50, 53, 58; 10:19, 24, 24, 40, 42; 11:6, 7, 8, 29, 38, 40, 44, 46, 52; 12:2, 2, 6, 10, 15, 17, 24, 24, 27, 33, 39, 40, 46, 46, 56, 57, 59; 13:6, 7, 15, 16, 24, 25, 27, 33, 34, 35; 14:3, 5, 6, 14, 20, 26, 26, 27, 27, 30, 33, 33; 15:4, 7, 13, 28; 16:2, 3, 11, 12, 13, 31; 17:18, 20, 22; 18:4, 4, 7, 11, 13, 17, 34; 19:3, 14, 21, 21, 22, 22, 23, 44, 44, 48; 20:5, 21, 22, 26, 31, 38; 21:6, 6, 9, 15, 18, 32, 33; 22:16, 18, 26, 34, 53, 57, 58, 60, 67, 68; 23:29, 29, 34, 51, 53; 24:3, 6, 18, 24, 39; Jn 1:5, 8, 10, 11, 13, 20, 20, 21, 21, 25, 26, 27, 31, 33, 47; 2:3, 9, 12, 24, 25; 3:3, 5, 8, 10, 11, 12, 17, 18, 20, 27, 28, 34, 36; 4:2, 9, 14, 17, 17, 18, 22, 32, 35, 38, 44, 48; 5:7, 10, 13, 18, 19, 23, 24, 30, 30, 31, 34, 38, 38, 40, 41, 42, 43, 44, 47; 6:7, 22, 22, 24, 26, 32, 35, 35, 36, 37, 38, 42, 46, 53, 58, 63, 64, 70; 7:1, 7, 8U, 10, 12, 16, 18, 19, 22, 25, 28, 28, 34, 34, 35, 36, 36, 42, 45, 52; 8:12, 13, 14, 15, 16, 21, 22, 23, 27, 29, 35, 37, 40, 41, 43, 43, 44, 44, 45, 46, 47, 48, 49, 50, 51, 52, 55, 55; 9:8, 12, 16, 16, 18, 21, 21, 25, 27, 29, 30, 31, 32, 33, 41; 10:5, 5, 6, 8, 10, 12, 12, 13, 16, 21, 25, 26, 26, 28, 28, 33, 34, 35, 37; 11:4, 9, 10, 15, 21, 26, 32, 37, 40, 49, 51, 52, 56; 12:5, 6, 8, 9, 16, 19, 30, 35, 37, 39, 42, 44, 47, 47, 49; 13:7, 8, 8, 10, 16, 18, 33, 36, 37, 38; 14:5, 9, 10, 10, 17, 17, 18, 22, 24, 24, 27, 30; 15:4, 5, 15, 16, 19, 20, 21, 21, 22, 22, 24; 16:3, 4, 7, 9, 12, 13, 17, 18, 19, 23, 24, 26, 30, 32; 17:9, 14, 14, 15, 16, 16, 20, 25; 18:9, 11, 17, 25, 26, 28, 30, 31, 36, 36; 19:6, 9, 10, 10, 11, 12, 15, 33, 36; 20:2, 5, 7, 13, 14, 24, 25, 30; 21:4, 5, 8, 11, 18, 23, 23, 23; Ac 1:5, 7; 2:7, 15, 24, 27, 34; 3:6; 4:12, 16, 20; 5:4, 22, 26, 28U, 39, 42; 6:2, 10,

13; **7:**5, 5, 11, 18, 25, 32, 39, 40, 48, 52, 53; **8:**21, 21, 32, 39; **9:**9, 21; **10:**34, 41; **12:**9, 14, 18, 22, 23; **13:**10, 25, 35, 37, 39, 41, 46; **14:**17, 28; **15:**1, 2, 24; **16:**7, 21, 37; **17:**4, 12, 24, 27, 29; **18:**15, 20; **19:**11, 23, 24, 26, 26, 27, 30, 32, 35, 40; **20:**12, 27, 31; **21:**13, 38, 39; **22:**9, 11, 18, 22; **23:**5, 5; **24:**11, 18; **25:**6ᵁ, 7, 11, 16, 26; **26:**19, 25, 26, 26, 29; **27:**10, 14, 20, 31, 39; **28:**2, 4, 19, 26, 26; **Ro** 1:13, 16, 21, 28, 32; **2:**11, 13, 21, 26, 28, 29, 29; **3:**9, 10, 11, 11, 12, 12, 17, 18, 20, 22; **4:**2, 4, 8, 10, 12, 13, 15, 16, 20, 23; **5:**3, 5, 11, 13, 15, 16; **6:**14, 14, 15, 16; **7:**6, 7, 7, 7, 15, 15, 16, 18, 18, 19, 19, 20; **8:**7, 8, 9, 9, 12, 15, 18, 20, 23, 24, 25, 26, 32; **9:**1, 6, 6, 8, 10, 12, 16, 21, 24, 25, 25, 26, 31, 32, 33; **10:**2, 3, 11, 12, 14, 14, 16, 18, 19, 19; **11:**2, 2, 4, 7, 18, 21, 25; **12:**4; **13:**1, 3, 4, 5, 9, 9, 9, 9, 10; **14:**6, 17, 23, 23; **15:**3, 18, 18, 20, 21, 21; **16:**4, 18; **1Co** 1:16, 17, 17, 21, 26, 26, 26; **2:**1, 2, 4, 6, 8, 9, 9, 9, 12, 13, 14, 14; **3:**1, 2, 4, 6; **4:**4, 7, 14, 15, 19, 20; **5:**6, 6, 10; **6:**2, 3, 5, 9, 9, 10, 10, 10, 12, 12, 13, 15, 16, 19, 19; **7:**4, 4, 6, 9, 10, 12, 15, 25, 28, 28, 35, 36; **8:**7, 8, 13; **9:**1, 1, 1, 2, 6, 6, 7, 7, 8, 9, 9, 12, 12, 13, 15, 15, 16, 24, 26, 26; **10:**1, 5, 13, 13, 18, 20, 20, 21, 21, 23, 23; **11:**6, 7, 8, 9, 16, 17, 17, 20, 22, 22, 31; **12:**1, 14, 15, 15, 15, 15, 16, 16, 16, 16, 21, 21, 21, 24; **13:**4, 4, 4, 5, 5, 5, 5, 6; **14:**2, 16, 17, 22, 22, 23, 33, 34; **15:**9, 10, 10, 12, 13, 14, 15, 15, 16, 17, 29, 32, 36, 37, 39, 46, 50, 51, 58; **16:**7, 12, 22; **2Co** 1:8, 12, 13, 17, 17, 18, 18, 19, 19, 24; **2:**4, 5, 11, 13, 13, 17; **3:**3, 3, 5, 6, 10, 13; **4:**1, 5, 8, 8, 9, 9, 16; **5:**3, 4, 7, 12; **6:**12; **7:**3, 7, 8, 9, 12, 14; **8:**5, 8, 10, 12, 13, 15, 15, 19, 21; **9:**12; **10:**3, 4, 8, 8, 12, 12, 13, 14, 15, 16, 18; **11:**4, 4, 4, 6, 9, 10, 11, 14, 15, 17, 29, 29, 31; **12:**1, 2, 2, 3, 4, 5, 6, 13, 14, 14, 14, 16, 18, 18, 20, 20; **13:**2, 3, 5, 6, 7, 8, 10; **Gal** 1:1, 7, 10, 11, 16, 19, 20, 20; **2:**6, 14, 15, 16, 16, 16, 21; **3:**10, 16, 17, 20, 28, 28, 28; **4:**8, 14, 17, 21, 27, 27, 30, 31; **5:**8, 16, 18, 21, 23; **6:**4, 7; **Eph** 1:16, 21; **2:**8, 9; **3:**5; **4:**20; **5:**4, 5; **6:**7, 9, 12; **Php** 1:17, 22, 29; **2:**6, 16, 21, 27; **3:**1, 3, 12, 13ᵁ; **4:**11, 17; **Col** 1:9; **2:**1, 8, 19, 23; **3:**11, 23, 25; **1Th** 1:5; **8:**2:1, 3, 4, 8, 13, 17; **4:**7, 8, 9, 13, 15; **5:**1, 3, 4, 5, 9; **2Th** 2:5, 10; **3:**2, 7, 9, 9, 10, 14; **1Ti** 1:9; **2:**7, 12, 14; **3:**5; **5:**8, 13, 18, 25; **2Ti** 1:7, 9, 12, 16; **2:**5, 9, 13, 20, 24; **3:**9; **4:**3; **8:** **Tit** 3:5; **Heb** 1:12; **2:**5, 11, 16; **3:**10, 16, 19; **4:**2, 6, 8, 13, 15; **5:**4, 5, 12; **6:**10; **7:**11, 16, 20, 21, 27; **8:**2, 7, 9, 9, 12; **9:**5, 7, 11, 11, 22, 24; **10:**1, 2, 5, 6, 8, 17, 37, 38, 39; **11:**1, 5, 16, 23, 31, 35, 38, 39; **12:**7, 8, 9, 11, 17, 18, 20, 25, 26; **13:**5, 5, 6, 9, 9, 10, 14; **Jas** 1:17, 20, 23, 25; **2:**4, 5, 6, 7, 11, 21, 24, 25; **3:**2, 10, 15; **4:**1, 2, 2, 2, 3, 4, 11, 14; **5:**6, 12, 12, 17; **1Pe** 1:8; **2**, 12, 18, 23; **2:**6, 10, 10, 18, 22, 23, 23; **3:**3, 21; **2Pe** 1:8, 10, 16, 20, 21; **2:**3, 3, 4, 5, 10, 11; **3:**9; **1Jn** 1:5, 6, 8, 8, 10, 10; **2:**2, 4, 7, 10, 11, 15, 16, 19, 19, 21, 21, 21, 22, 27, 27; **3:**1, 1, 5, 6, 10, 18, 20, 20; **5:**3, 6, 10, 12, 16, 17, 18, 18; **2Jn** 1:1, 5, 9, 10, 12; **3Jn** 1:4, 9, 11, 13; **Jude** 1:9, 10; **Rev** 2:2, 2, 3, 9, 11, 13, 21, 24, 24, 24; **3:**2, 3, 4, 5, 8, 9, 12, 17; **4:**8; **6:**10; **7:**16; **9:**4, 6, 20, 21; **11:**9; **12:**8, 11; **13:**8; **14:**4, 5, 11; **15:**4; **16:**9, 11, 18, 20; **17:**8, 8, 8, 11; **18:**7, 7, 14, 21, 22, 22, 22, 23, 23; **20:**4, 4, 5, 6, 11, 15; **21:**1, 4, 4, 22, 23, 25, 25, 27; **22:**3, 5, 5

13, 14, 15, 19, 21, 21, 22, 23, 23, 24, 24, 24, 25, 25, 26, 31, 32, 33, 34, 36, 37, 38, 38[N], 40, 41, 41, 42, 44, 44, 46, 46, 47, 48, 49, 51, 52, 53, 54, 55, 56, 58; **9:**10, 17, 17, 19, 19, 26, 26, 27, 27, 28, 30, 34, 34, 35, 37, 41; **10:**1, 7, 24, 25, 26, 32, 33, 33, 34, 36; **11:**8, 15, 22, 23, 27, 28, 40, 41, 42, 49, 50, 56; **12:**15, 24, 28, 30, 34, 35, 35; **13:**6, 7, 8, 10, 12, 13, 14, 14, 15, 15, 15, 16, 18, 19, 20, 21, 21, 33, 33, 33, 34, 34, 34, 37, 37, 38, 38; **14:**1, 2, 2, 3, 3, 3, 9, 9, 10, 12, 16, 16, 17, 17, 17, 18, 18, 19, 19, 20, 20, 20, 25, 25, 26, 26, 26, 27, 27, 27, 27, 28, 28, 29, 30; **15:**3, 3, 4, 4, 5, 7, 7, 9, 11, 11, 11, 12, 14, 14, 15, 15, 15, 16, 16, 16, 16, 16, 16, 17, 18, 18[U], 19, 19, 20, 20, 21, 26, 27; **16:**1, 2, 2, 4, 4, 4, 4, 5, 6, 6, 7, 7, 7, 7, 12, 13, 13, 14, 15, 20, 20, 20, 20, 22, 22, 22, 22, 22, 23, 23, 24, 25, 25, 25, 26, 26, 27, 27, 30, 33; **17:**1, 1, 3, 4, 5, 5, 6, 6, 7, 8, 8, 11, 11, 12, 13, 14, 21, 21, 21, 23, 23, 25, 25, 25, 26; **18:**8, 17, 25, 26, 30, 31, 31, 33, 34, 34, 35, 37, 37, 39, 39, 39; **19:**4, 6, 9, 10, 10, 11, 11, 14, 15, 26, 27, 35; **20:**15, 17, 17, 19, 21, 21, 26, 27, 27; **21:**3, 12, 15, 15, 16, 16, 17, 17, 17, 18, 18, 18, 20, 22, 22, 23; **Ac 1:**5, 7, 8, 11, 24; **2:**14, 15, 17, 17, 17, 17, 22, 22, 27, 28, 29, 33, 35, 35, 36, 38, 38, 39, 39; **3:**6, 13, 14, 14, 16, 17, 19, 20, 22, 22, 22, 22, 25, 25, 25, 26, 26, 26; **4:**7, 10, 10, 10, 11, 19, 24, 25, 27, 28, 28, 29, 29, 30, 30, 30; **5:**3, 3, 4, 4, 9, 9, 9, 28, 28, 30, 38; **6:**3; **7:**3, 3, 3, 4, 27, 28, 32, 33, 34, 35, 37, 37, 43, 43, 51, 51, 51, 52, 52; **8:**20, 20, 21, 21, 22, 22, 22, 23, 24, 34; **9:**5, 6, 6, 13, 14, 17, 34; **10:**4, 4, 15, 19, 22, 22, 28, 31, 31, 33, 33, 33, 37; **11:**9, 14, 14, 14, 16; **12:**8, 8; **13:**11, 15, 26, 32, 33, 33, 34, 35, 38, 38, 41, 41, 46, 47, 47; **14:**10, 15, 15, 17, 17; **15:**7, 7, 24, 24, 25, 28; **16:**17, 18, 31, 31; **17:**3, 19, 22, 23, 23, 28, 32; **18:**6, 6, 10, 10, 10, 14, 15, 21; **19:**13, 15, 36; **20:**18, 18, 20, 20, 25, 26, 27, 28, 29, 30, 32, 35; **21:**21, 23, 24, 37, 38, 39; **22:**1, 3, 8, 10, 10, 14, 16, 18, 19, 20, 21, 25, 27; **23:**3, 3, 5, 11, 15, 15, 18, 18, 20, 21, 21, 30, 30, 35, 35; **24:**2, 4, 4, 10, 11, 13, 14, 19, 21, 22, 25; **25:**5, 10, 26, 26; **26:**1, 2, 3, 8, 14, 15, 16, 16, 16, 16, 17, 17, 24, 29; **27:**22, 22, 24, 24, 24, 31, 34, 34; **28:**20, 21, 21, 22, 25, 28; **Ro 1:**6, 7, 8, 8, 9, 10, 11, 11, 11, 12, 12, 13, 13, 13, 15; **2:**3, 4, 5, 17, 24, 25, 27; **3:**4, 4; **4:**17, 18; **6:**11, 12, 13, 13, 14, 19, 19, 19, 22; **7:**4, 4; **8:**2[U], 9, 9, 10, 11, 11, 11, 36; **9:**7, 17, 17, 20, 26; **10:**6, 8, 8, 8, 9, 9, 19, 19; **11:**3, 3, 13, 17, 18, 18, 20, 21, 22, 22, 24, 25, 28, 30; **12:**1, 1, 1, 2, 3, 14, 18, 20; **13:**4, 9, 11; **14:**4, 10, 10, 10, 10, 15, 15, 16, 21, 22; **15:**3, 5, 7, 9, 9, 13, 13, 14, 15, 15, 22, 23, 24, 24, 24, 28, 29, 30, 32, 32, 33; **16:**1, 2, 6, 16, 17, 17, 19, 19, 19, 20, 20, 21, 22, 23, 23, 25; **1Co 1:**3, 4, 4, 6, 7, 8, 10, 10, 11, 11, 12, 13, 14, 26, 30; **2:**1, 1, 2, 3, 5; **3:**1, 2, 3, 16, 17, 18, 21, 22, 23; **4:**3, 6, 7, 8, 10, 10, 10, 14, 15, 16, 17, 17, 18, 19, 21; **5:**1, 2, 2, 4, 6, 9, 11, 12, 13; **6:**1, 2, 5, 5, 7, 8, 15, 19, 19, 20; **7:**5, 5, 14, 15[U], 21, 28, 32, 35, 35; **8:**9, 10; **9:**1, 2, 2, 11, 11, 12; **10:**1, 13, 13, 15, 20, 27, 27, 28; **11:**2, 2, 3, 13, 14, 18, 18, 19, 19, 20, 22, 22, 23, 24, 30; **12:**1, 3, 21, 21, 27, 31; **14:**5, 6, 6, 6, 9, 12, 17, 18, 25, 36, 36, 37; **15:**1, 1, 2, 3, 12, 14, 17, 17, 34, 36, 51, 55, 55, 58; **16:**1, 2, 3, 5, 6, 6, 7, 7, 10, 12, 14, 15, 16, 18, 19, 19, 20, 23, 24; **2Co 1:**2, 6, 6, 7, 8, 11, 12, 13, 14, 14, 15, 16, 16, 16, 18, 19, 21, 23, 24, 24; **2:**1, 2, 3, 3, 4, 4, 5, 7, 8, 9, 10; **3:**1, 1, 2; **4:**5, 12, 14, 15; **5:**11, 12, 12, 13; **6:**1, 2, 2, 11, 12, 13, 17, 18, 18; **7:**4, 4, 7, 7, 7, 7, 8, 8, 11, 12, 12, 12, 13, 14, 14, 15, 15, 16; **8:**1, 6, 7[N], 7[U], 9, 9, 10, 13, 14, 14, 16, 17, 22, 23, 24, 24; **9:**1, 2, 2, 2, 3, 4, 4, 5, 5, 8, 10, 10, 13, 14, 14, 14; **10:**1, 1, 1, 6, 8, 9, 13, 14, 14, 15, 15, 16; **11:**2, 2, 3, 6, 7, 7, 8, 9, 9, 11, 20, 20; **12:**9, 11, 11, 12, 13, 14, 14, 14, 15, 15, 16, 16, 17, 17, 18, 19, 19, 20, 20, 21; **13:**1, 3, 3, 4, 5, 7, 7, 9, 9, 11, 13, 14; **Gal 1:**3, 6, 7, 8[U], 8, 9, 11, 20; **2:**5, 14; **3:**1, 2, 5, 5, 8, 16, 28, 29; **4:**11, 11, 12, 12, 13, 14, 15, 15, 15, 16, 16, 17, 17, 18, 19, 20, 20, 28; **5:**2, 2, 7, 8, 10, 10, 12, 13, 14, 21; **6:**1, 1, 11, 12, 13, 18; **Eph 1:**2, 13, 13, 15, 16, 17, 18, 18; **2:**1, 1, 8, 11, 13, 17, 22; **3:**1, 2, 13, 13, 16, 17; **4:**1, 4, 17, 20, 22, 23, 26, 29, 31, 32; **5:**3, 6, 14, 19, 33; **6:**1, 2, 3, 4, 5, 9, 11, 14, 21, 21, 22, 22; **Php 1:**2, 3, 4, 5, 6, 7, 7, 7, 8, 9, 10, 12, 19, 24, 25, 25, 26, 26, 27, 27, 28, 29; **2:**5, 13, 17, 17, 18, 19, 19, 20, 25, 25, 26, 30; **3:**1, 1, 15, 18; **4:**3, 5, 6, 7, 7, 9, 15, 15, 17, 18, 19, 21, 22, 23; **Col 1:**2, 3, 4, 5, 6, 6, 7[U], 8, 9, 12, 21, 22, 24, 25, 27; **2:**1, 1, 4, 5, 5, 5, 8, 13, 13, 13, 16, 18; **3:**3, 4, 4, 5[N], 7, 8, 8, 13, 13, 15, 16, 16, 21; **4:**1, 6, 6, 7, 8, 8, 9, 9, 10, 10, 12, 12, 12, 13, 14, 16, 16, 18; **1Th 1:**1, 2, 3, 4, 5, 5, 5, 6, 7, 8, 8, 9; **2:**1, 2, 6, 7, 8, 8, 9, 9, 10, 10, 11, 12, 12, 12, 13, 14, 14, 17, 17, 18, 19, 20; **3:**2, 2, 4, 4, 5, 5, 6, 6, 6, 7, 7, 8, 9, 9, 10, 10, 11, 12, 12, 13; **4:**1, 1, 2, 3, 3, 4, 6, 8, 9, 9, 10, 11, 11, 13, 15; **5:**1, 4, 4, 5, 12, 12, 12, 12, 14, 18, 23, 23, 24, 27, 28; **2Th 1:**2, 3, 3, 3, 4, 4, 4, 5, 6, 7, 10, 11, 11, 12, 12; **2:**1, 2, 3, 5, 5, 13, 13, 14, 17; **3:**1, 3, 4, 5, 6, 6, 7, 8, 9, 10, 10, 11, 13, 16, 16, 18; **1Ti 1:**3, 18, 18; **3:**14, 14; **4:**12, 14, 14, 15, 16; **5:**23; **6:**11, 13, 14, 21; **2Ti 1:**3, 4, 4, 5, 5, 5, 5, 6, 6, 18; **2:**1, 7; **3:**10, 14, 15; **4:**5, 5, 15, 21, 22, 22; **Tit 1:**5, 5; **2:**1, 15; **3:**8, 12, 15, 15; **Phm 1:**2, 3, 4, 5, 6, 7, 7, 8, 10, 11, 11, 12, 13, 14, 16, 18, 19, 20, 21, 21, 22, 22, 23, 25; **Heb 1:**5, 5, 8, 8, 9, 9, 9, 10, 10, 11, 12, 12, 13, 13; **2:**12, 12; **3:**8, 9, 12, 13, 15; **4:**1, 7; **5:**5, 5, 6, 12; **6:**9, 10, 11, 14, 14; **7:**17, 21; **8:**5; **9:**20; **10:**7, 9, 34, 35; **11:**18; **12:**3, 5, 7, 13; **13:**5, 5, 7, 7, 17, 17, 17, 19, 21, 22, 22, 23, 24, 24, 25; **Jas 1:**3, 5, 21; **2:**2, 3, 3, 6, 6, 6, 7, 8, 16, 18, 18, 18, 19; **3:**13, 14; **4:**1, 1, 1, 2, 3, 7, 8, 9, 10, 12, 14, 15, 16; **5:**1, 2, 2, 3, 3, 3, 4, 4, 5, 6, 8, 8, 12, 13, 14, 19; **1Pe 1:**2, 4, 7, 9, 10, 12, 12, 12, 13, 13, 14, 15, 17, 18, 20, 21, 22, 25; **2:**7, 9, 9, 12, 12, 21, 21, 25; **3:**2, 7, 13, 15, 15, 15, 16, 18, 21; **4:**1, 4, 12, 12, 12, 14, 15; **5:**1, 2, 6, 7, 7, 8, 9, 10, 12, 13, 14; **2Pe 1:**2, 5, 8, 10, 11, 12, 13, 15, 16, 19; **2:**1, 3, 13; **3:**1, 1, 2, 8, 9, 11, 15, 17; **1Jn 1:**2, 3, 3, 5; **2:**1, 7, 8, 8, 12, 12, 13, 13, 13, 14, 14, 14, 20, 21, 24, 24, 24, 24, 26, 26, 27, 27, 27, 27, 27; **3:**7, 13; **4:**4, 4; **5:**13; **2Jn 1:**4, 5, 5, 10, 12, 12, 13, 13; **3Jn 1:**2, 2, 3, 3, 6, 13, 13, 14, 14, 14; **Jude 1:**2, 3, 3, 5, 5, 9, 12, 17, 18, 20, 20, 24; **Rev 1:**4, 9; **2:**2, 2, 4, 4, 5, 5, 9, 10, 10, 13, 14, 15, 16, 19, 19, 19, 20, 23, 23, 24, 24; **3:**1, 2, 3, 8, 8, 9, 9, 10, 11, 15, 16, 17, 18, 18, 18; **4:**1, 11, 11; **5:**9; **7:**14; **10:**9, 9, 11; **11:**17, 17, 18, 18, 18; **12:**12; **14:**15, 18; **15:**3, 3, 4, 4, 4; **16:**7; **17:**1, 7; **18:**10, 14, 14, 14, 20, 22, 22, 22, 23, 23, 23, 23; **19:**10, 10; **21:**9; **22:**9, 9, 16

5445 τέ, *te* [215]

Mt **22:**10; **27:**48; **28:**12; **Lk 2:**16; **12:**45; **14:**26; **15:**2; **21:**11, 11; **22:**66; **23:**12; **24:**20; **Jn 2:**15; **4:**42; **6:**18; **Ac 1:**1, 8, 13, 15; **2:**9, 10, 11, 33, 37, 40, 43, 46, 46; **4:**13, 14, 27, 33; **5:**14, 19, 24, 35, 42; **6:**7, 12, 13; **7:**26; **8:**3, 12, 13, 25, 28, 31, 38; **9:**2, 3, 15, 15, 18, 24, 29; **10:**22, 28, 33, 39; **11:**21, 26; **12:**6, 12, 17; **13:**1, 1, 4, 11, 46, 52; **14:**1, 5, 11, 12, 13, 21; **15:**3, 4, 5, 6, 9, 32, 39; **16:**13, 23, 34; **17:**4, 4, 10, 14, 14, 19, 26; **18:**4, 5, 26; **19:**2, 3, 6, 10, 11, 12, 17, 18, 27, 29; **20:**3, 7, 11, 21, 35; **21:**12, 18, 20, 25, 28, 30, 31, 37; **22:**4, 7, 8, 23; **23:**5, 10, 24, 28; **24:**3, 5, 10, 15, 23, 27; **25:**2, 16, 23, 24; **26:**3, 4, 10, 10, 11, 14, 16, 16, 20, 20, 22, 22, 23, 30, 30; **27:**1, 3, 3, 5, 8, 17, 20, 21, 21, 29, 43; **28:**2, 23, 23; **Ro 1:**12, 14, 14, 16, 20, 26, 27; **2:**9, 10, 19; **3:**9; **7:**7; **10:**12; **14:**8, 8, 8, 8; **16:**26; **1Co 1:**24, 30; **4:**21; **2Co 10:**8; **12:**12; **Eph 3:**19; **Php 1:**7; **Heb 1:**3; **2:**4, 11; **4:**12; **5:**1, 7, 14; **6:**2, 2, 4, 5, 19; **8:**3; **9:**1, 2, 9, 19; **10:**33; **11:**32; **12:**2; **Jas 3:**7, 7; **Jude 1:**6; **Rev 19:**18

5515 τίς, *tis* [556 / 554]

Mt **3:**7; **5:**13, 46, 47; **6:**3, 25, 25, 25, 27, 28, 31, 31, 31; **7:**3, 9, 14[U]; **8:**26, 29; **9:**5, 11, 13, 14; **10:**11, 19, 19; **11:**7, 8, 9, 16; **12:**3, 7, 11, 27, 48, 48; **13:**10; **14:**31; **15:**2, 3, 32; **16:**8, 13, 15, 26, 26; **17:**10, 19, 25, 25; **18:**1, 12; **19:**7, 16, 17, 20, 25, 27; **20:**6, 21, 22, 32; **21:**10, 16, 23, 25, 28, 31, 40; **22:**17, 18, 20, 28, 42, 42; **23:**17, 19; **24:**3, 45; **26:**8, 10, 15, 62, 65, 66, 68, 70; **27:**4, 17, 21, 22, 23; **Mk 1:**24, 24, 27; **2:**7, 7, 8, 9, 18, 24, 25; **3:**33; **4:**24, 30, 40, 41; **5:**7, 9, 14, 30, 31, 35, 39; **6:**2, 24, 36; **7:**5; **8:**1, 2, 12, 17, 27, 29, 36, 37; **9:**6, 10, 16, 33, 34, 50; **10:**3, 17, 18, 26, 36, 38, 51; **11:**3, 5, 28, 31; **12:**9, 15, 16, 23; **13:**4, 11; **14:**4, 6, 36, 36, 40, 60, 63, 64, 68; **15:**12, 14, 24, 24, 34; **16:**3; **Lk 1:**18, 62, 66; **2:**48, 49; **3:**7, 10, 12, 14; **4:**34, 34, 36; **5:**21, 21, 22, 23, 30; **6:**2, 11, 41, 46, 47; **7:**24, 25, 26, 31, 31, 39, 42, 49; **8:**9, 25, 28, 30, 45; **9:**9, 18, 20, 25, 46; **10:**22, 22, 25, 26, 29, 36; **11:**5, 11, 19; **12:**5, 11[U], 11, 14, 17, 20, 22, 22, 25, 26, 29, 29, 42, 49, 57; **13:**18, 18, 20; **14:**5, 28, 31, 34; **15:**4, 8, 26; **16:**2, 3, 4, 11, 12; **17:**7, 8; **18:**6, 18, 19, 26, 36, 41; **19:**3, 15, 23, 31, 33, 48; **20:**2, 5, 13, 15, 17, 24, 33; **21:**7; **22:**23, 24, 27, 46, 64, 71; **23:**22, 31, 34; **24:**5, 17, 38, 38; **Jn 1:**19, 21, 22, 22, 25, 38; **2:**4, 18, 25; **4:**10, 27, 27; **5:**12, 13; **6:**6, 9, 28, 30, 30, 60, 64, 64, 68; **7:**19, 20, 36, 45, 51; **8:**5, 25, 43, 46, 46, 53; **9:**2, 17, 21, 26, 27, 36; **10:**6, 20; **11:**47, 56; **12:**5, 27, 34, 38, 38, 49, 49; **13:**12, 18, 22, 24, 25, 28, 37; **14:**22; **15:**15; **16:**17, 18, 18; **18:**4, 7, 21, 21, 23, 29, 35, 38; **19:**24; **20:**13, 15, 15; **21:**12, 20, 21, 22, 23; **Ac 1:**11; **2:**12, 37; **3:**12, 12; **4:**9, 16; **5:**3, 4, 9, 24, 35; **7:**27, 35, 40, 49, 52; **8:**33, 34, 36; **9:**4, 5, 6; **10:**4, 17, 21, 29; **11:**17; **12:**18; **13:**25; **14:**15; **15:**10; **16:**30; **17:**18, 19, 20; **19:**3, 15, 32, 35; **21:**13, 22, 33, 33; **22:**7, 8, 10, 16, 26, 30; **23:**19; **24:**20; **25:**26; **26:**8, 14, 15; **Ro 3:**1, 1, 3, 5, 7, 9; **4:**1, 3; **6:**1, 15, 21; **7:**7, 24; **8:**24, 26, 27, 31, 31, 33, 34, 35; **9:**14, 19, 19, 20, 20, 30, 32; **10:**6, 7, 8, 16; **11:**2, 4, 7, 15, 34, 34, 35; **12:**2; **14:**4, 10, 10; **1Co 2:**11, 16; **3:**5, 5; **4:**7, 7, 7, 21; **5:**12; **6:**7, 7; **7:**16, 16; **9:**7, 7, 7, 18; **10:**19, 30; **11:**22; **14:**6, 8, 15, 16, 26; **15:**2, 29, 29, 30, 32; **2Co 2:**2, 16; **6:**14, 14, 15, 15, 16; **11:**11, 29, 29; **12:**13; **Gal 3:**1, 19; **4:**30; **5:**7, 11; **Eph 1:**18, 18, 19; **3:**9, 18; **4:**9; **5:**10, 17; **6:**21; **Php 1:**18, 22; **Col 1:**27; **2:**20; **1Th 2:**19; **3:**9; **4:**2; **1Ti 1:**7; **2Ti 3:**14; **Heb 1:**5, 13; **2:**6; **3:**16, 17, 18; **7:**11; **11:**32; **12:**7; **13:**6; **Jas 2:**14, 16; **3:**13; **4:**12; **1Pe 1:**11; **3:**13; **4:**17; **1Jn 2:**22; **3:**2, 12; **5:**5; **Rev 2:**7, 11, 17, 29; **3:**6, 13, 22; **5:**2; **6:**17; **7:**13; **13:**4, 4; **15:**4; **17:**7; **18:**18

5516 τὶς, *tis* [533]

Mt **5:**23; **8:**28; **9:**3; **11:**27; **12:**19, 29, 38, 47; **16:**24, 28; **18:**12, 28; **20:**20; **21:**3, 3; **22:**24, 46; **24:**4, 23; **27:**47; **28:**11; **Mk 2:**6; **4:**23; **6:**23; **7:**1, 2; **8:**3, 4, 23, 34; **9:**1, 22, 30, 35, 38; **11:**3, 5, 13, 16, 25, 25; **12:**13, 19; **13:**5, 15, 21; **14:**4, 47, 51, 57, 65; **15:**21, 35, 36; **16:**18; **Lk 1:**5; **6:**2; **7:**2, 18, 36, 40, 41; **8:**2, 27, 46, 49, 51; **9:**7, 8, 8, 19, 23, 27, 49, 57; **10:**25, 30, 31, 33, 35, 38, 38; **11:**1, 1, 15, 27, 36, 45, 54; **12:**4, 13, 15, 16; **13:**1, 6, 23, 31; **14:**1, 2, 8, 15, 16, 26; **15:**11; **16:**1, 19, 20, 30, 31; **17:**12; **18:**2, 2, 9, 18, 35; **19:**8, 8, 12, 31, 39; **20:**9, 27, 28, 39; **21:**2, 5; **22:**35, 50, 56, 59; **23:**8, 19, 26; **24:**22, 24, 41; **Jn 1:**46; **2:**5, 25; **3:**3, 5; **4:**33, 46; **5:**5, 14, 19; **6:**7, 12, 46, 50, 51, 64; **7:**4, 17, 25, 37, 44, 48; **8:**25, 51, 52; **9:**16, 22, 31, 32; **10:**9, 28; **11:**1, 9, 10, 37, 46, 49, 57; **12:**20, 26, 26, 47; **13:**20, 29, 29; **14:**13, 14, 23; **15:**6, 13, 16; **16:**23, 30; **20:**23, 23; **21:**5; **Ac 2:**45; **3:**2, 5; **4:**32, 34, 35; **5:**1, 2, 15, 25, 34, 36; **6:**9; **7:**24; **8:**9, 9, 31, 34, 36; **9:**2, 10, 19, 33, 36, 43; **10:**1, 5, 6, 11, 23, 47, 48; **11:**5, 20, 29; **12:**1; **13:**6, 15, 41; **14:**8; **15:**1, 2, 5, 24, 36; **16:**1, 9, 12, 14, 16; **17:**4, 5, 6, 18, 18, 20, 21, 21, 25, 28, 34; **18:**2, 7, 14, 23, 24; **19:**1, 9, 13, 14, 24, 31, 32, 38, 39; **20:**9; **21:**10, 16, 34, 37; **22:**12; **23:**9, 17, 18, 20, 23; **24:**1, 1, 12, 19, 19, 24; **25:**5, 8, 11, 13, 14, 16, 19, 19, 26; **26:**26, 31; **27:**1, 8, 16, 26, 27, 39, 42, 44; **28:**3, 19, 21, 21; **Ro 1:**11, 13; **3:**3, 8; **5:**7, 7; **8:**9, 39; **9:**11; **11:**14, 17; **13:**9; **14:**14; **15:**18, 26; **1Co 1:**15, 16; **2:**2; **3:**4, 7, 12, 14, 15, 17, 18; **4:**2, 5, 18; **5:**1, 11; **6:**1, 11, 12; **7:**12, 13, 18, 18, 36; **8:**2, 2, 3, 7, 10; **9:**12, 22; **10:**7, 8, 9, 10, 19, 19, 27, 28, 31; **11:**16, 18, 34; **14:**24, 27, 35, 37, 38; **15:**6, 12, 34, 35, 37; **16:**2, 7, 11, 22; **2Co 2:**5, 10, 10; **3:**1, 5; **5:**17; **7:**14; **8:**20; **10:**2, 7, 8, 12; **11:**1, 16, 16, 20, 20, 20, 20, 20, 21; **12:**6, 6, 17; **13:**8; **Gal 1:**7, 9; **2:**6, 12; **5:**6; **6:**1, 3, 3, 15; **Eph 2:**9; **4:**29; **5:**27; **6:**8; **Php 1:**15, 15; **2:**1, 1, 1, 1; **3:**4, 15; **4:**8, 8; **Col 2:**8, 16, 23; **3:**13, 13, 17; **1Th 1:**8; **2:**9; **5:**15, 15; **2Th 2:**3; **3:**8, 8, 10, 11, 14; **1Ti 1:**3, 6, 8, 10, 19; **3:**1, 5; **4:**1; **5:**4, 8, 15, 16, 24, 24; **6:**3, 7, 10, 21; **2Ti 2:**5, 18, 21; **Tit 1:**6, 12; **Phm 1:**18; **Heb 2:**6, 7, 9; **3:**4, 12, 13; **4:**1, 6, 7, 11; **5:**4, 12; **8:**3; **10:**25, 27, 28; **11:**40; **12:**15, 15, 16; **13:**2; **Jas 1:**5, 7, 18, 23, 26; **2:**14, 16, 18; **3:**2; **5:**12, 13, 13, 14, 19, 19; **1Pe 2:**19; **3:**1; **4:**11, 11, 15; **5:**8; **2Pe 2:**19; **3:**9, 9, 16; **1Jn 2:**1, 15, 27; **4:**20; **5:**14, 16; **2Jn 1:**10; **3Jn 1:**9; **Jude 1:**4; **Rev 3:**20; **11:**5, 5; **13:**9, 10, 10, 17; **14:**9, 11; **20:**15; **22:**18, 19

KEY FEATURES OF THE GREEK-ENGLISH INDEX

NIV WORD
The indexed word exactly as it is spelled in the NIV. See the introduction, page xv.

NIV FREQUENCY
The total number of times this word occurs in the NIV New Testament. See the introduction, page xv.

AGAINST   [208]

GREEK FREQUENCY
The total number of times this word is translated by the entry word in the NIV New Testament. See the introduction, page xv.

against, *2848, kata* [47]

GREEK TRANSLATIONS
The Greek word or phrase translated by the entry word is indicated by G/K number and transliteration. See the introduction, pages vii, xv.

ABBREVIATIONS
NIV words that do not directly translate a Greek word are indicated by special codes. See the introduction, pages xii-xiii, xv.

against, *AIT* [15]
against, *RPE* [3]

stirred up against, *2074+2093, epiegeirō+epi* [1]

MULTIPLE WORD TRANSLATIONS
When more than one NIV word is used to translate a Greek word or phrase, all words in the NIV phrase appear on the index line. When more than one Greek word is translated by a word or phrase, all words in the Greek phrase are indicated by G/K number and transliteration. See the introduction, pages xii, xv.

pressing [against], *632, apothlibō* [1]

BRACKETS
When an NIV word is used more than once in a multiple word translation, it is in brackets to indicate it was counted only once in the NIV total frequency. See the introduction, page xv.

The

English-Greek Index

to the NIV

New Testament

42 [1]

42, *5477+2779+1545,
tesserakonta+kai+dyo* [1]

144 [1]

144, *1669+5477+5475,
hekaton+tesserakonta+tessares* [1]

153 [1]

153, *1669+4299+5552,
hekaton+pentēkonta+treis* [1]

276 [1]

276, *1357+1573+1971,
diakosioi+hebdomēkonta+hex* [1]

430 [1]

430, *5484+2779+5558,
tetrakosioi+kai+triakonta* [1]

450 [1]

450, *5484+2779+4299,
tetrakosioi+kai+pentēkonta* [1]

666 [1]

666, *1980+2008+1971,
hexakosioi+hexēkonta+hex* [1]

1,260 [3]

1,260, *5943+1357+2008,
chilioi+diakosioi+hexēkonta* [2]

1,600 [3]

1,600, *5943+1980, chilioi+hexakosioi* [1]

12,000 [13]

12,000 *1557+5942, dōdeka+chilias* [13]

144,000 [3]

144,000 *1669+5477+5475+5942,
hekaton+tesserakonta+tessares+chilias* [3]

A [2190]

a, *NIG* [1668]
a, *3836, ho* [169]
a, *5516, tis* [84]
a, *1651, heis* [17]

a, *AIT* [13]
a certain, *5516, tis* [9]
a little while, *3625, mikros* [7]
a single, *1651, heis* [6]
a, *RPE* [5]
basis for a charge, *162, aitia* [3]
looked for a way, *2426, zēteō* [3]
leading a rebellion, *3334, lēstēs* [3]
a man^s, *3836, ho* [3]
live a life, *4344, peripateō* [3]
as a result, *6063, hōste* [3]
in a manner worthy, *547, axiōs* [2]
not a believer, *603, apistos* [2]
give a tenth of, *620, apodekatoō* [2]
went away on a journey, *623, apodēmeō* [2]
at a loss, *679, aporeō* [2]
a day's wages, *1324, dēnarion* [2]
a man^s, *1667, hekastos* [2]
sang a dirge, *2577, thrēneō* [2]
produce a crop, *2844, karpophoreō* [2]
least stroke of a pen, *3037, keraia* [2]
a fraction of a penny, *3119, kodrantēs* [2]
at a distance, *3427, makrothen* [2]
a night and a day, *3819, nychthēmeron* [2]
only a short time, *4672, proskairos* [2]
with a fever, *4789, pyressō* [2]
poured out like a drink offering, *5064,
spendō* [2]
such a man, *5525, toioutos* [2]
sung a hymn, *5630, hymneō* [2]
a single, [1]
called out in a loud voice, *149+5889,
airō+phōnē* [1]
basis for a charge, *165, aitios* [1]
making a prisoner, *170, aichmalōtizō* [1]
without a trial, *185, akatakritos* [1]
without a doubt, *242, alēthōs* [1]
commit a sin, *279+281,
hamartanō+hamartia* [1]
casting a net, *311, amphiballō* [1]
one at a time, *324+3538, ana+meros* [1]
taken a solemn oath, *353+354,
anathema+anathematizō* [1]
am a virgin, *467+4024+1182,
anēr+ou+ginōskō* [1]
a, *467, anēr* [1]
owner of a house, *476+3867,
anthrōpos+oikodespotēs* [1]
for a long time, *540, anōthen* [1]
in a way worthy, *547, axiōs* [1]
for a distance of, *608, apo* [1]

give God a tenth of, *620, apodekatoō* [1]
going on a journey, *623, apodēmeō* [1]
sold as a slave, *625, apodidōmi* [1]
a revelation comes, *636, apokalyptō* [1]
a fig^s tree, *899, autos* [1]
a man's^s, *899, autos* [1]
not a lover of money, *921, aphilargyros* [1]
for a little while, *1099, brachys* [1]
get a taste, *1174, geuomai* [1]
had a notice prepared, *1211+5518,
graphō+titlos* [1]
possessed by a demon, *1227,
daimonizomai* [1]
lift a finger, *1235, daktylos* [1]
made a spectacle, *1258, deigmatizō* [1]
collected a tenth, *1282, dekatoō* [1]
delivered a public address, *1319, dēmēgoreō* [1]
a year's wages, *1324+5559,
dēnarion+triakosioi* [1]
eight months of a man's wages, *1324+1357,
dēnarion+diakosioi* [1]
a few days later, *1328+2465, dia+hēmera* [1]
over a period, *1328, dia* [1]
judge a dispute, *1359, diakrinō* [1]
stayed a while, *1417, diatribō* [1]
makes a slave, *1525, douleia* [1]
make a slave, *1530, douloō* [1]
expecting a child, *1607, enkyos* [1]
like a Gentile, *1619, ethnikōs* [1]
had taken part in a rebellion, *1639+3334,
eimi+lēstēs* [1]
have such a place, *1639, eimi* [1]
making a complaint^s about, *1639, eimi* [1]
as a result, *1650+3836, eis+ho* [1]
a unit, *1651, heis* [1]
one at a time, *1651+2848+1651,
heis+kata+heis* [1]
on a journey, *1666+3847, ek+hodos* [1]
made a choice, *1721, eklegomai* [1]
convinced that is a sinner, *1794, elenchō* [1]
a public figure, *1877+4244, en+parrēsia* [1]
as a fool, *1877+932, en+aphrosynē* [1]
as a man, *1877+4922, en+sarx* [1]
given a trust, *1877+3874, en+oikonomos* [1]
nursed a grudge against, *1923, enechō* [1]
make a search, *2004, exetazō* [1]
stayed a little longer, *2091+5989,
epechō+chronos* [1]
a long time, *2093+4498, epi+polys* [1]
a matter of, *2093, epi* [1]
a thorough search made for, *2118, epizēteō* [1]

written a letter, *2182, epistellō* [1]
gather a great number, *2197, episōreuō* [1]
work for a living, *2237, ergazomai* [1]
have a feast, *2266, esthiō* [1]
preach a gospel, *2294, euangelizō* [1]
preaching a gospel, *2294, euangelizō* [1]
have a chance, *2320, eukaireō* [1]
make a good impression, *2349, euprosōpeō* [1]
produced a good crop, *2369, euphoreō* [1]
held a celebration, *2370, euphrainō* [1]
collect a tenth from, *2400+620,*
    echō+apodekatoō [1]
what a great, *2462, hēlikos* [1]
lead a quiet life, *2483, hēsychazō* [1]
reap a harvest, *2545, therizō* [1]
like a Jew, *2680, Ioudaikōs* [1]
a while, *2789, kairos* [1]
produces a crop, *2844, karpophoreō* [1]
a follower of, *2848, kata* [1]
become a father, *2856+5065+3284,*
    katabolē+sperma+lambanō [1]
made a attack on, *2987, katephistamai* [1]
seared as with a hot iron, *3013, kaustēriazō* [1]
receive a beating, *3139, kolaphizō* [1]
a loud voice, *3189, krazō* [1]
gave a shout, *3189+5889, krazō+phōnē* [1]
in a circle, *3241, kyklō* [1]
bring a message, *3281+4839, laleō+rhēma* [1]
serve at a sanctuary, *3302, latreuō* [1]
about a pint, *3354, litra* [1]
had a bath, *3374, louō* [1]
become a disciple, *3411, mathēteuō* [1]
a week later, *3552+2465+3893,*
    meta+hēmera+oktō [1]
receive a share, *3561, metalambanō* [1]
have a part, *3576, metechō* [1]
a half, *3604+1971, mēn¹+hex* [1]
only a single, *3668, monos* [1]
made an idol in the form of a calf, *3674,*
    moschopoieō [1]
a short while ago, *3814, nyn* [1]
such a, *3836, ho* [1]
a short time, *3900, oligos* [1]
a hint of, *3951, onomazō* [1]
had a vision, *3969+3972, horama+horaō* [1]
a hundred and twenty feet deep, *3976+1633,*
    orgyia+eikosi [1]
dug a hole, *4002, oryssō* [1]
such a man'sˢ, *4005, hos* [1]
a manˢ, *4005, hos* [1]
such a man, *4005, hos* [1]
a, *4015, hostis* [1]
not a thing, *4029, oudeis* [1]
not a word, *4029, oudeis* [1]
such a man, *4047, houtos* [1]
in such a way, *4048, houtōs* [1]
formed a mob, *4062, ochlopoieō* [1]
breaking a command, *4126, parabasis* [1]
not put on such a list, *4148, paraiteomai* [1]
keeping a close watch, *4190, paratēreō* [1]
set a meal before, *4192+5544,*
    paratithēmi+trapeza [1]
a robe reaching down to feet, *4468, podērēs* [1]
a way, *4481, poios* [1]
many a time, *4490, pollakis* [1]
at a distance, *4523, porrōthen* [1]
from a distance, *4523, porrōthen* [1]
gives a cup, *4540+4539, potizō+potērion* [1]
a place where, *4543, pou* [1]
earlier made a beginning, *4599,*
    proenarchomai [1]
for a little while, *4639+6052, pros+hōra* [1]
a short time, *4672, proskairos* [1]
offered as a sacrifice, *4712, prospherō* [1]
with a roar, *4853, rhoizēdon* [1]
in a hurry, *5067, speudō* [1]

three or three and a half miles,
    5084+1633+4297+2445+5558,
    stadion+eikosi+pente+ē+triakonta [1]
with a deep sigh, *5100, stenazō* [1]
serves as a soldier, *5129, strateuomai* [1]
serving as a soldier, *5129, strateuomai* [1]
declares a prisoner, *5168, synkleiō* [1]
devised a plan, *5206+3284,*
    symboulion+lambanō [1]
in a convulsion, *5360, sysparassō* [1]
threw into a convulsion, *5360, sysparassō* [1]
had a wound, *5377, sphazō* [1]
marked with a seal, *5381, sphragizō* [1]
put a seal, *5381, sphragizō* [1]
putting a seal on, *5381, sphragizō* [1]
giving birth to a child, *5503, tiktō* [1]
a, *5515, tis* [1]
suppose a, *5515, tis* [1]
a few, *5516, tis* [1]
a kind of, *5516, tis* [1]
such a, *5525, toioutos* [1]
of a kind, *5525, toioutos* [1]
running a race, *5556, trechō* [1]
the money worth a year's wages, *5559+1324,*
    triakosioi+dēnarion [1]
take a view of things, *5858, phroneō* [1]
keep a tight rein on, *5902, chalinagōgeō* [1]
took a battering from the storm, *5928,*
    cheimazō [1]
a long time in coming, *5988, chronizō* [1]
staying away a long time, *5988, chronizō* [1]
taking a long time, *5988, chronizō* [1]
a long time, *5989+4024+3900,*
    chronos+ou+oligos [1]
wearing a gold ring, *5993, chrysodaktylios* [1]

AARON [4]

Aaron, *2, Aarōn* [4]

AARON'S [1]

Aaron's, *2, Aarōn* [1]

ABADDON [1]

Abaddon, *3, Abaddōn* [1]

ABANDON [2]

abandon, *923, aphistēmi* [1]
abandon, *1593, enkataleipō* [1]

ABANDONED [4]

abandoned, *1593, enkataleipō* [2]
abandoned, *657, apoleipō* [1]
abandoned, *918, aphiēmi* [1]

ABANDONS [1]

abandons, *918, aphiēmi* [1]

ABBA [3]

Abba, *5, abba* [3]

ABEL [4]

Abel, *6, Habel* [4]

ABHOR [1]

abhor, *1009, bdelyssomai* [1]

ABIATHAR [1]

Abiathar, *8, Abiathar* [1]

ABIJAH [3]

Abijah, *7, Abia* [3]

ABILENE [1]

Abilene, *9, Abilēnē* [1]

ABILITY [5]

ability, *1539, dynamis* [3]
ability, *2026, exousia* [1]
ability, *2344, euporeō* [1]

ABIUD [2]

Abiud, *10, Abioud* [2]

ABLAZE [1]

all ablaze, *4786+2794, pyr+kaiō* [1]

ABLE [49]

able, *1538, dynamai* [24]
able, *2710, ischyō* [5]
able, *AIT* [4]
able, *1543, dynatos* [4]
able to teach, *1434, didaktikos* [2]
able, *1542, dynateō* [2]
able, *2400, echō* [2]
able, *RPE* [1]
able to see, *329, anablepō* [1]
those able to help, *516, antilēmpsis* [1]
then will be able, *1650+3836, eis+ho* [1]
as much as were able, *2848+1539,*
    kata+dynamis [1]
able, *2996, katischyō* [1]

ABNORMALLY [1]

abnormally born, *1765, ektrōma* [1]

ABOARD [5]

hoisted aboard, *149, airō* [1]
climbed aboard, *326, anabainō* [1]
take aboard, *377, analambanō* [1]
took aboard, *377, analambanō* [1]
aboard, *1650, eis* [1]

ABOLISH [2]

abolish, *2907, katalyō* [2]

ABOLISHED [1]

abolished, *2934, katargeō* [1]

ABOLISHING [1]

abolishing, *2934, katargeō* [1]

ABOMINABLE [1]

abominable, *1007, bdelygma* [1]

ABOMINATION [2]

abomination, *1007, bdelygma* [2]

ABOMINATIONS [1]

abominations, *1007, bdelygma* [1]

ABOUND [3]

abound, *4355, perisseuō* [2]
make abound, *4355, perisseuō* [1]

ABOUT [396]

about, *4309, peri* [133]
about, *AIT* [35]
about to, *3516, mellō* [22]
about, *6055, hōs* [18]
about, *6059, hōsei* [11]
heard about, *201, akouō* [10]
about, *1877, en* [8]
about, *2093, epi* [8]

about, *5642, hyper* [8]
about, *NIG* [7]
talking about, *3306, legō* [7]
about, *1650, eis* [6]
about, *2848, kata* [6]
worry about, *3534, merimnaō* [5]
about, *RPE* [4]
concerned about, *3534, merimnaō* [4]
told about, *1192, gnōrizō* [2]
about, *4639, pros* [2]
hear about, *201, akouō* [1]
told about, *334, anangellō* [1]
makes judgments about, *373, anakrinō* [1]
tell about, *550, apangellō* [1]
about from, *600+608, apechō+apo* [1]
heard about, *919, aphikneomai* [1]
brought about, *1181, ginomai* [1]
came about, *1181, ginomai* [1]
find out about, *1182, ginōskō* [1]
knew about, *1182, ginōskō* [1]
know about, *1182, ginōskō* [1]
knows about, *1182, ginōskō* [1]
learned about, *1182, ginōskō* [1]
know about, *1192, gnōrizō* [1]
heard about, *1196+1181, gnōstos+ginomai* [1]
wrote about, *1211, graphō* [1]
bring about, *1259, deiknymi* [1]
bring about, *1328, dia* [1]
talking about, *1362, dialaleō* [1]
arguing about, *1368, dialogizomai* [1]
talking about, *1368, dialogizomai* [1]
spread the news about, *1424, diaphēmizō* [1]
gone about, *1451, dierchomai* [1]
traveled about, *1451+1328, dierchomai+dia* [1]
traveled about, *1451, dierchomai* [1]
traveled about, *1476, diodeuō* [1]
came about, *1639, eimi* [1]
making a complaint[s] about, *1639, eimi* [1]
moved about freely, *1660+2779+1744, eisporeuomai+kai+ekporeuomai* [1]
goes into great detail about, *1836, embateuō* [1]
wondering about, *1877+1571+1389, en+heautou+diaporeō* [1]
care about, *1956, entrepō* [1]
cared about, *1956, entrepō* [1]
telling about, *2007, exēgeomai* [1]
ask about, *2089, eperōtaō* [1]
asked about, *2089, eperōtaō* [1]
know about, *2179, epistamai* [1]
about to begin, *2216, epiphōskō* [1]
bring about, *2237, ergazomai* [1]
brought good news about, *2294, euangelizō* [1]
telling the good news about, *2294, euangelizō* [1]
told the good news about, *2294, euangelizō* [1]
bring about, *2351, heuriskō* [1]
about noon, *2465+3545, hēmera+mesos* [1]
say bad about, *2800, kakologeō* [1]
boast about, *3016, kauchaomai* [1]
brag about, *3016, kauchaomai* [1]
something to boast about, *3017, kauchēma* [1]
boasting about, *3018, kauchēsis* [1]
talking about, *3062, kēryssō* [1]
boast about, *3281+5665, laleō+hyperonkos* [1]
say about, *3281, laleō* [1]
speak about, *3281, laleō* [1]
spoke about, *3281, laleō* [1]
talking about, *3281, laleō* [1]
say about, *3306, legō* [1]
speak about, *3306, legō* [1]
spoke about, *3306, legō* [1]
telling about, *3306, legō* [1]
about a pint, *3354, litra* [1]
think about, *3357, logizomai* [1]
quarreling about words, *3362, logomacheō* [1]
quarrels about words, *3363, logomachia* [1]

inquire about, *3443, manthanō* [1]
tell about, *3455, martyreō* [1]
testified about, *3455, martyreō* [1]
testifies about, *3455, martyreō* [1]
told about, *3455, martyreō* [1]
anxious about, *3534, merimnaō* [1]
worry about, *3577, meteōrizomai* [1]
help speaking about, *3590+3281, mē+laleō* [1]
about law, *3788, nomikos* [1]
what am about to tell, *3836+3364+4047, ho+logos+houtos* [1]
knew about, *3857, oida* [1]
know about, *3857, oida* [1]
about, *4022, hoti* [1]
know all about, *4158, parakoloutheō* [1]
about, *4309+4005, peri+hos* [1]
groped about, *4310, periagō* [1]
going about, *4320, perierchomai* [1]
went about, *4320, perierchomai* [1]
moved about, *4344, peripateō* [1]
believe about, *4411+2400, pistis+echō* [1]
bring about, *4472, poieō* [1]
goes about his business, *4512, poreia* [1]
about, *4513, poreuomai* [1]
about, *4543, pou* [1]
already heard about, *4578, proakouō* [1]
was written about, *4592, prographō* [1]
worry beforehand about, *4628, promerimnaō* [1]
think about, *4630+4472, pronoia+poieō* [1]
argued about, *4639+253+1363, pros+allēlōn+dialegomai* [1]
arguing about, *5184, syzēteō* [1]
found out about, *5328, synoraō* [1]
finally brought about, *5465, telos* [1]
wondered about, *5502+1877+3836+2840, tithēmi+en+ho+kardia* [1]
what about, *5515, tis* [1]
learned about, *5745+1181, phaneros+ginomai* [1]
gossiping about, *5826, phlyareō* [1]
about, *6059+4309, hōsei+peri* [1]

ABOVE [28]

above, *539, anō* [5]
above, *5642, hyper* [4]
from above, *540, anōthen* [3]
above, *2062, epanō* [3]
above, *2093, epi* [2]
above, *4574, pro* [2]
above reproach, *455, anepilēmptos* [1]
above Jesus, *3963+1639, hopou+eimi* [1]
above all, *4047+4754, houtos+prōton* [1]
the passage above, *4047, houtos* [1]
above, *4123, para* [1]
above, *4605, proēgeomai* [1]
above, *5645, hyperanō* [1]
far above, *5645, hyperanō* [1]
exalted above, *5734, hypsēlos* [1]

ABRAHAM [72]

Abraham, *11, Abraam* [64]
Abraham, *RPE* [4]
Abraham[s], *899, autos* [3]
Abraham[s], *4005, hos* [1]

ABRAHAM'S [11]

Abraham's, *11, Abraam* [9]
Abraham's, *RPE* [1]
Abraham's[s], *3836, ho* [1]

ABROAD [1]

scattered abroad, *5025, skorpizō* [1]

ABSENCE [3]

absence, *NIG* [1]
in absence, *582, apeimi1* [1]
absence, *707, apousia* [1]

ABSENT [4]

absent, *582, apeimi1* [3]
absent from, *582, apeimi1* [1]

ABSOLUTE [1]

absolute, *4246, pas* [1]

ABSOLUTELY [2]

absolutely not, *3590+1181, mē+ginomai* [2]

ABSTAIN [5]

abstain from, *600, apechō* [4]
abstain from, *5875, phylassō* [1]

ABSTAINS [1]

abstains, *3590+2266, mē+esthiō* [1]

ABUNDANCE [6]

abundance, *4437, plēthynō* [3]
have an abundance, *4355, perisseuō* [2]
abundance, *4355, perisseuō* [1]

ABUNDANT [1]

abundant provision, *4353, perisseia* [1]

ABUNDANTLY [1]

poured out abundantly, *5670, hyperpleonazō* [1]

ABUSE [1]

heap abuse on, *1059, blasphēmeō* [1]

ABUSIVE [2]

abusive, *1059, blasphēmeō* [1]
abusive, *1061, blasphēmos* [1]

ABUSIVELY [2]

abusively, *1059, blasphēmeō* [1]
speak abusively against, *1059, blasphēmeō* [1]

ABYSS [9]

Abyss, *12, abyssos* [8]
Abyss, *5853, phrear* [1]

ACCENT [1]

accent, *3282, lalia* [1]

ACCEPT [22]

accept, *3284, lambanō* [9]
accept, *1312, dechomai* [3]
accept, *4138, paradechomai* [3]
accept, *6003, chōreō* [3]
accept, *4689, proslambanō* [2]
accept, *201, akouō* [1]
refuse to accept, *2024, exoutheneō* [1]

ACCEPTABLE [5]

acceptable, *2347, euprosdektos* [4]
acceptable, *1283, dektos* [1]

ACCEPTABLY [1]

acceptably, *2299, euarestōs* [1]

ACCEPTANCE [3]

acceptance, *628, apodochē* [2]

ACCEPTED [13]

acceptance, *4691, proslēmpsis* [1]

accepted, *1312, dechomai* [3]
accepted, *3284, lambanō* [2]
accepted, *4689, proslambanō* [2]
accepted, *622, apodechomai* [1]
accepted, *1283, dektos* [1]
showed that accepted, *3455, martyreō* [1]
accepted, *4161, paralambanō* [1]
accepted, *4657, prosdechomai* [1]
accepted, *5634, hypakouō* [1]

ACCEPTS [8]

accepts, *3284, lambanō* [5]
accepts, *1283+1639, dektos+eimi* [1]
accepts, *4123, para* [1]
accepts, *4138, paradechomai* [1]

ACCESS [2]

access, *4643, prosagōgē* [2]

ACCOMPANIED [10]

accompanied, *199, akoloutheō* [2]
accompanied, *4636, propempō* [2]
accompanied, *2051, epakoloutheō* [1]
accompanied by, *2262+2779, erchomai+kai* [1]
accompanied by, *2400, echō* [1]
accompanied by, *5250, syn* [1]
accompanied by, *5299, synepomai* [1]
accompanied, *5302+5250, synerchomai+syn* [1]

ACCOMPANIES [1]

accompanies, *AIT* [1]

ACCOMPANY [4]

that accompany, *2400, echō* [1]
accompany, *4158, parakoloutheō* [1]
accompany, *5250+4513, syn+poreuomai* [1]
accompany, *5292+5250, synekdēmos+syn* [1]

ACCOMPLISH [1]

accomplish, *4472, poieō* [1]

ACCOMPLISHED [5]

accomplished, *1181, ginomai* [1]
accomplished, *2981, katergazomai* [1]
accomplished, *4472, poieō* [1]
accomplished, *5459, teleiōsis* [1]
accomplished, *5464, teleō* [1]

ACCOMPLISHING [1]

accomplishing, *4472, poieō* [1]

ACCORD [3]

my own accord, *1831, emautou* [2]
in accord, *4560, prepō* [1]

ACCORDANCE [12]

in accordance with, *2848, kata* [6]
in accordance with, *2093, epi* [2]
in accordance with, *2777, kathōs* [2]
in accordance with, *1877, en* [1]
in accordance with, *6055, hōs* [1]

ACCORDING [58]

according to, *2848, kata* [44]
according, *AIT* [3]
according to, *1877, en* [3]
according to, *1666+3836, ek+ho* [1]
according to what, *2771+1569, katho+ean* [1]

according to what, *2771, katho* [1]
according to, *2777, kathōs* [1]
according to the rules, *3789, nomimōs* [1]
according to, *4048, houtōs* [1]
according to, *5642, hyper* [1]
according to, *6055, hōs* [1]

ACCOUNT [29]

account, *3364, logos* [6]
on account of, *1877, en* [5]
on account of, *1915, heneken* [4]
on account of, *1328, dia* [3]
in the account, *2093, epi* [2]
called to account, *373, anakrinō* [1]
account, *625+3364, apodidōmi+logos* [1]
give account for, *625+3364, apodidōmi+logos* [1]
write an account, *1211, graphō* [1]
on account, *1328, dia* [1]
account, *1456, diēgēsis* [1]
on account of, *1666, ek* [1]
taken into account, *1824, ellogeō* [1]
of little account, *2024, exoutheneō* [1]

ACCOUNTABLE [1]

held accountable, *5688+1181, hypodikos+ginomai* [1]

ACCOUNTS [2]

accounts, *3364, logos* [1]
settled accounts, *5256+3364, synairō+logos* [1]

ACCREDITED [1]

accredited, *617, apodeiknymi* [1]

ACCURATE [2]

more accurate, *209, akribōs* [2]

ACCURATELY [1]

accurately, *209, akribōs* [1]

ACCURSED [1]

accursed, *2932, katara* [1]

ACCUSATION [5]

free from accusation, *441, anenklētos* [1]
accusation, *1592, enkaleō* [1]
accusation, *2990, katēgoria* [1]
accusation, *3213, krisis* [1]
joined in the accusation, *5298, synepitithēmi* [1]

ACCUSATIONS [2]

accusations, *1592, enkaleō* [1]
accusations, *3213, krisis* [1]

ACCUSE [8]

accuse, *2989, katēgoreō* [5]
accuse, *2895, katalaleō* [1]
accuse, *3306, legō* [1]
accuse falsely, *5193, sykophanteō* [1]

ACCUSED [4]

accused, *2989, katēgoreō* [2]
accused, *1330, diaballō* [1]
accused of, *2989, katēgoreō* [1]

ACCUSER [2]

accuser, *2989, katēgoreō* [1]
accuser, *2992, katēgōr* [1]

ACCUSERS [5]

accusers, *2991, katēgoros* [3]
accusers, *RPE* [1]
accusers, *2400+3836+2991, echō+ho+katēgoros* [1]

ACCUSES [1]

accuses, *2989, katēgoreō* [1]

ACCUSING [6]

accusing, *2989, katēgoreō* [3]
accusing, *1592, enkaleō* [2]
accusing of, *2989, katēgoreō* [1]

ACCUSTOMED [1]

accustomed to, *5311, synētheia* [1]

ACHAIA [10]

Achaia, *938, Achaia* [10]

ACHAICUS [1]

Achaicus, *939, Achaikos* [1]

ACHIEVING [1]

achieving, *2981, katergazomai* [1]

ACKNOWLEDGE [10]

acknowledge, *3933, homologeō* [6]
acknowledge, *622, apodechomai* [1]
acknowledge, *1182, ginōskō* [1]
acknowledge, *2105, epiginōskō* [1]
acknowledge, *2106+2262, epignōsis+erchomai* [1]

ACKNOWLEDGED [2]

acknowledged that right, *1467, dikaioō* [1]
acknowledged that, *3933, homologeō* [1]

ACKNOWLEDGES [5]

acknowledges, *3933, homologeō* [4]
acknowledges that, *3933, homologeō* [1]

ACQUAINTANCE [1]

acquaintance, *AIT* [1]

ACQUAINTED [4]

not acquainted with, *586, apeiros* [1]
well acquainted with, *1195, gnōstēs* [1]
get acquainted with, *2707, historeō* [1]
acquainted with, *3857, oida* [1]

ACQUIRED [1]

acquired wealth, *4456, plouteō* [1]

ACQUITTED [1]

acquitted, *1467, dikaioō* [1]

ACROSS [12]

across, *4305, peran* [3]
across the lake, *527, antipera* [1]
sailed across, *1386, diapleō* [1]
across the lake, *1650+3836+4305, eis+ho+peran* [1]
across, *1650+3836+4305, eis+ho+peran* [1]
across, *1877, en* [1]
across, *2093, epi* [1]
laid across, *2130+2093, epikeimai+epi* [1]
region across, *4305, peran* [1]
regions across, *4305, peran* [1]

ı

ACT [11]

act of righteousness, *1468, dikaiōma* [1]
act, *1919, energeō* [1]
act, *2240, ergon* [1]
act of kindness shown to, *2307, euergesia* [1]
caught in the act, *2898+2093+900,
  katalambanō+epi+autophōros* [1]
act of worship, *3301, latreia* [1]
act of disobedience, *4157, parakoē* [1]
act, *4344, peripateō* [1]
the way act, *4344, peripateō* [1]
act, *4472, poieō* [1]
act of grace, *5921, charis* [1]

ACTED [4]

acted, *4472, poieō* [2]
acted, *4556, prassō* [1]
acted as if, *4701, prospoieō* [1]

ACTING [4]

acting, *4344, peripateō* [2]
acting improperly, *858, aschēmoneō* [1]
acting in line, *3980, orthopodeō* [1]

ACTION [5]

action, *2240, ergon* [2]
prepare for action, *350+3836+4019,
  anazōnnymi+ho+osphys* [1]
stirred to action, *2241, erethizō* [1]
action, *4552, praxis* [1]

ACTIONS [8]

actions, *2240, ergon* [7]
actions deserve, *2848+2240, kata+ergon* [1]

ACTIVE [2]

active, *1921, energēs* [2]

ACTIVITY [2]

activity, *2240, ergon* [1]
area of activity, *2834, kanōn* [1]

ACTS [10]

acts, *2240, ergon* [4]
righteous acts, *1468, dikaiōma* [2]
lawless acts, *490, anomia* [1]
indecent acts, *859, aschēmosynē* [1]
acts of righteousness, *1466, dikaiosynē* [1]
acts, *4472, poieō* [1]

ACTUALLY [4]

actually, *NIG* [1]
actually, *242, alēthōs* [1]
actually, *3914, holōs* [1]
though actually, *4022, hoti* [1]

ADAM [9]

Adam, *77, Adam* [9]

ADD [5]

add, *4707, prostithēmi* [2]
add to, *2112, epidiatassomai* [1]
add to, *2202+2093, epitithēmi+epi* [1]
add, *2220, epichorēgeō* [1]

ADDED [10]

added, *4707, prostithēmi* [4]
added, *3306, legō* [2]
added, *4209, pareiserchomai* [1]
added, *4651, prosanatithēmi* [1]
added to, *4707, prostithēmi* [1]
added, *5164, synkatapsēphizomai* [1]

ADDI [1]

Addi, *79, Addi* [1]

ADDICTED [1]

addicted, *1530, douloō* [1]

ADDITION [4]

in addition, *247+2779, alla+kai* [1]
in addition, *1254, de* [1]
in addition, *1877, en* [1]
in addition, *2093+1254, epi+de* [1]

ADDRESS [2]

delivered a public address, *1319, dēmēgoreō* [1]
address, *3281, laleō* [1]

ADDRESSED [3]

addressed, *710, apophthengomai* [1]
addressed, *3306+4639, legō+pros* [1]
addressed, *3306, legō* [1]

ADDRESSES [1]

addresses, *1363, dialegomai* [1]

ADDS [2]

adds to, *2202+2093, epitithēmi+epi* [1]
adds, *3306, legō* [1]

ADEQUATELY [1]

more adequately, *209, akribōs* [1]

ADJOURNED [1]

adjourned the proceedings, *327, anaballō* [1]

ADMINISTER [2]

administer, *1354, diakoneō* [2]

ADMINISTERED [1]

administered, *2237, ergazomai* [1]

ADMINISTERING [1]

administering, *3874, oikonomos* [1]

ADMINISTRATION [3]

administration, *3873, oikonomia* [2]
those with gifts of administration, *3236,
  kybernēsis* [1]

ADMIRABLE [1]

admirable, *2368, euphēmos* [1]

ADMIT [2]

admit, *3306, legō* [1]
admit, *3933, homologeō* [1]

ADMITTED [1]

admitted, *3933, homologeō* [1]

ADMONISH [2]

admonish, *3805, noutheteō* [2]

ADMONISHING [1]

admonishing, *3805, noutheteō* [1]

ADOPTED [1]

adopted as sons, *5625, huiothesia* [1]

ADOPTION [2]

adoption as sons, *5625, huiothesia* [2]

ADORNED [1]

adorned, *3175, kosmeō* [1]

ADORNMENT [1]

adornment, *3180, kosmos* [1]

ADRAMYTTIUM [1]

from Adramyttium, *101, Adramyttēnos* [1]

ADRIATIC [1]

Adriatic Sea, *102, Adrias* [1]

ADULTERER [1]

adulterer, *3659, moichos* [1]

ADULTERERS [3]

adulterers, *3659, moichos* [2]
adulterers, *4521, pornos* [1]

ADULTERESS [3]

adulteress, *3655, moichalis* [2]
become an adulteress, *3658, moicheuō* [1]

ADULTERIES [5]

adulteries, *4518, porneia* [5]

ADULTEROUS [4]

adulterous, *3655, moichalis* [4]

ADULTERY [25]

commit adultery, *3658, moicheuō* [10]
commits adultery, *3656, moichaō* [4]
adultery, *3657, moicheia* [3]
committed adultery, *4519, porneuō* [3]
commits adultery, *3658, moicheuō* [2]
adultery, *3655, moichalis* [1]
adultery, *3658, moicheuō* [1]
committed adultery with, *3658, moicheuō* [1]

ADULTS [1]

adults, *5455, teleios* [1]

ADVANCE [5]

prepared in advance, *4602, proetoimazō* [2]
announced the gospel in advance, *4603,
  proeuangelizomai* [1]
in advance finish the arrangements for, *4616,
  prokatartizō* [1]
advance, *4620, prokopē* [1]

ADVANCING [2]

forcefully advancing, *1041, biazō* [1]
advancing, *4621, prokoptō* [1]

ADVANTAGE [5]

no advantage, *269, alysitelēs* [1]
takes advantage of, *3284, lambanō* [1]
advantage, *4356, perissos* [1]
take advantage of, *4430, pleonekteō* [1]
advantage, *6066, ōpheleia* [1]

ADVERSARIES [1]

adversaries, *512, antikeimai* [1]

ADVERSARY [3]

adversary, *508, antidikos* [2]
adversary is taking to court, *508, antidikos* [1]

ADVICE [3]

advice, *RPE* [1]

advice, *1191, gnōmē* [1]
taken advice, *4272, peitharcheō* [1]

ADVISABLE [1]

advisable, *545+1639, axios+eimi* [1]

ADVISE [1]

advise, *3306, legō* [1]

ADVISED [1]

advised, *5205, symbouleuō* [1]

ADVOCATING [2]

advocating, *2858, katangeleus* [1]
advocating, *2859, katangellō* [1]

AENEAS [3]

Aeneas, *138, Aineas* [2]
Aeneas, *RPE* [1]

AENON [1]

Aenon, *143, Ainōn* [1]

AFFAIRS [6]

affairs, *3836, ho* [2]
affairs, *AIT* [1]
civilian affairs, *1050+4548,
   bios+pragmateia* [1]
the affairs[s], *3836, ho* [1]
the affairs, *3836, ho* [1]

AFFECTION [3]

affection, *5073, splanchnon* [3]

AFFIRM [1]

confidently affirm, *1331, diabebaioomai* [1]

AFFLICTION [1]

affliction, *2568, thlipsis* [1]

AFFLICTIONS [2]

afflictions, *2568, thlipsis* [2]

AFFORDED [2]

afforded by, *1328, dia* [2]

AFOOT [1]

plot afoot, *3995, hormē* [1]

AFRAID [62]

afraid, *5828, phobeomai* [39]
afraid of, *5828, phobeomai* [14]
afraid, *RPE* [1]
afraid, *1262, deiliaō* [1]
afraid, *1264, deilos* [1]
so afraid, *1264, deilos* [1]
afraid, *1873, emphobos* [1]
afraid, *3552+5832, meta+phobos* [1]
afraid[s] that, *3590, mē* [1]
afraid, *5554, tremō* [1]
afraid, *5832, phobos* [1]

AFTER [213]

after, *AIT* [72]
after, *3552, meta* [59]
after, *3958, opisō* [11]
after, *3552+3836, meta+ho* [9]
after, *4021, hote* [7]
after, *4020, hotan* [4]
after, *6055, hōs* [4]
after all, *1142, gar* [3]

then after, *4099, palin* [3]
after that, *2083, epeita* [2]
after, *2093, epi* [2]
look after, *2170, episkeptomai* [2]
day after day, *2848+2465, kata+hēmera* [2]
after, *NIG* [1]
just after sunrise, *422+3836+2463,
   anatellō+ho+hēlios* [1]
after, *505, anti* [1]
after marriage, *608+4220, apo+parthenia* [1]
after, *1181, ginomai* [1]
after this, *1254, de* [1]
after, *1328, dia* [1]
running off after, *1503, diōkō* [1]
one after the other, *1651+1667,
   heis+hekastos* [1]
after that, *1663, eita* [1]
after, *1666, ek* [1]
after this, *1877+3836+2759,
   en+ho+kathexēs* [1]
after[s], *1877+4364, en+peritomē* [1]
after, *1877, en* [1]
and after, *2083, epeita* [1]
run after, *2118, epizēteō* [1]
runs after, *2118, epizēteō* [1]
look after, *2150, epimeleomai* [1]
looked after, *2170, episkeptomai* [1]
day after, *2283, heteros* [1]
after, *2848, kata* [1]
from after town, *2848, kata* [1]
year after year, *2848+1929, kata+eniautos* [1]
some time after, *3552, meta* [1]
after, *3957, opisthen* [1]
after all, *4036, oun* [1]
after the Sabbath, *4067+4879,
   opse+sabbaton* [1]
after, *4216, parerchomai* [1]
day after day, *4246+2465, pas+hēmera* [1]
after passed, *4444, plēroō* [1]
looking after sheep, *4477, poimainō* [1]
after, *4754, prōton* [1]
after, *5731, hysteros* [1]

AFTERNOON [4]

three in the afternoon, *1888, enatos* [2]
late in afternoon, *2465+806+3111,
   hēmera+archō+klinō* [1]
three in the afternoon, *6052+1888+3836+2465,
   hōra+enatos+ho+hēmera* [1]

AFTERWARD [7]

afterward, *2779, kai* [2]
afterward, *3552+4047, meta+houtos* [2]
soon afterward, *1877+3836+2009,
   en+ho+hexēs* [1]
afterward, *3552, meta* [1]
afterward, *3575, metepeita* [1]

AGABUS [2]

Agabus, *13, Hagabos* [2]

AGAIN [169]

again, *4099, palin* [83]
again, *AIT* [13]
again, *2285, eti* [9]
again, *NIG* [6]
again and again, *4490, pollakis* [6]
rise again, *482, anistēmi* [4]
again, *2779, kai* [3]
see again, *329, anablepō* [2]
again, *540, anōthen* [2]
again, *562, hapax* [2]
again, *1489, dis* [2]
never again, *4024+3590, ou+mē* [2]

again, *4033, ouketi* [2]
again and again, *4498, polys* [2]
again, *247, alla* [1]
born again, *335, anagennaō* [1]
alive again, *348, anazaō* [1]
raised to life again, *414, anastasis* [1]
crucifying all over again, *416, anastauroō* [1]
raised again, *482, anistēmi* [1]
rose again, *482, anistēmi* [1]
again, *608+3836+3814, apo+ho+nyn* [1]
again, *608+785, apo+arti* [1]
again, *1142, gar* [1]
again, *1254, de* [1]
again, *1309, deuteron* [1]
raise again, *1586, egeirō* [1]
raised again, *1586, egeirō* [1]
rise again, *1586, egeirō* [1]
again, *1650+3836+172, eis+ho+aiōn* [1]
remind again, *2057, epanamimnēskō* [1]
alive again, *2409, zaō* [1]
or again, *2445, ē* [1]
again, *3600, mēketi* [1]
never again, *3600, mēketi* [1]
never again, *4024+3590+1650+3836+172,
   ou+mē+eis+ho+aiōn* [1]
not again, *4024+3590, ou+mē* [1]
cannot again, *4033, ouketi* [1]
ever again, *4033, ouketi* [1]
never again, *4033, ouketi* [1]
again, *4036, oun* [1]
again, *4099+1309, palin+deuteron* [1]
once again, *4099, palin* [1]
all over again, *4099+540, palin+anōthen* [1]
all over again, *4099, palin* [1]

AGAINST [208]

against, *2848, kata* [47]
against, *2093, epi* [32]
against, *1650, eis* [17]
against, *4639, pros* [17]
against, *AIT* [15]
against, *608, apo* [9]
against, *3552, meta* [8]
against, *1877, en* [4]
against, *1885, enantios* [4]
against, *RPE* [3]
testimony bringing against, *2909,
   katamartyreō* [3]
charge against, *162, aitia* [2]
against, *1967, enōpion* [2]
rebel against, *2060+2093, epanistēmi+epi* [2]
against, *2093+3836+5111, epi+ho+stēthos* [2]
speaks against, *2895, katalaleō* [2]
against, *3590, mē* [2]
against, *4309, peri* [2]
against law, *116, athemitos* [1]
nothing against them, *441, anenklētos* [1]
rebelling against, *468, anthistēmi* [1]
stand up against, *468, anthistēmi* [1]
spoken against, *515, antilegō* [1]
talked against, *515, antilegō* [1]
talking against, *515, antilegō* [1]
waging war against, *529, antistrateuomai* [1]
rebels against, *530, antitassō* [1]
pressing [against], *632, apothlibō* [1]
wipe off against, *669, apomassō* [1]
speak abusively against, *1059, blasphēmeō* [1]
blasphemy against, *1060, blasphēmia* [1]
nursed a grudge against, *1923, enechō* [1]
guilty of sinning against, *1944, enochos* [1]
stirred up against, *2074+2093, epegeirō+epi* [1]
speak maliciously against, *2092, epēreazō* [1]
bring against, *2214, epipherō* [1]
fighting against God, *2534, theomachos* [1]
over against, *2848, kata* [1]

bringing against, *2965, katapherō* [1]
cast against, *2965, katapherō* [1]
charge to bring against, *2989, katēgoreō* [1]
charges bringing against, *2989, katēgoreō* [1]
charges brought against, *2989, katēgoreō* [1]
charges making against, *2989, katēgoreō* [1]
press charges against, *2989, katēgoreō* [1]
against, *4024, ou* [1]
against, *4123, para* [1]
sin against, *4183, paraptōma* [1]
sins against, *4183, paraptōma* [1]
beat against, *4684, proskoptō* [1]
beat against, *4700, prospiptō* [1]
crowding against, *5309, synechō* [1]
crowding against, *5315, synthlibō* [1]
on guard against, *5875, phylassō* [1]

AGE [29]

age, *172, aiōn* [20]
of age, *2461, hēlikia* [2]
age, *2789, kairos* [2]
age, *AIT* [1]
age, *RPE* [1]
old age, *1179, gēras* [1]
age, *2789+2461, kairos+hēlikia* [1]
of own age, *5312, synēlikiōtēs* [1]

AGENT [1]

agent to bring punishment, *1690, ekdikos* [1]

AGES [9]

ages, *172, aiōn* [7]
ages past, *172, aiōn* [1]
ages past, *173, aiōnios* [1]

AGING [1]

aging, *1180, geraskō* [1]

AGITATING [1]

agitating, *4888, saleuō* [1]

AGITATORS [1]

agitators, *415, anastatoō* [1]

AGO [20]

long ago, *4093, palai* [3]
long ago, *792, archaios* [2]
people long ago, *792, archaios* [2]
some time ago, *4574+4047+3836+2465,
 pro+houtos+ho+hēmera* [2]
ago, *AIT* [1]
long ago, *172, aiōn* [1]
ago, *608+4005, apo+hos* [1]
ago, *608, apo* [1]
long ago, *608+172, apo+aiōn* [1]
some time ago, *608+2465+792,
 apo+hēmera+archaios* [1]
long ago, *1732, ekpalai* [1]
a short while ago, *3814, nyn* [1]
long ago, *4537, pote* [1]
ago, *4574, pro* [1]
spoke long ago, *4625, prolegō* [1]

AGONY [5]

in agony, *3849, odynaō* [2]
agony, *990, basanismos* [1]
agony, *4506, ponos* [1]
agony, *6047, ōdin* [1]

AGREE [9]

agree, *5244, symphōneō* [3]
agree, *2698, isos* [2]

agree with each other, *3836+899+5858,
 ho+autos+phroneō* [1]
agree with one another, *3836+899+3306,
 ho+autos+legō* [1]
agree to, *4665, proserchomai* [1]
agree, *5238, symphēmi* [1]

AGREED [5]

agreed, *5338, syntithēmi* [2]
agreed, *NIG* [1]
agreed, *1181+3924,
 ginomai+homothymadon* [1]
agreed, *5244, symphōneō* [1]

AGREEING [1]

agreeing, *4472+1651+1191,
 poieō+heis+gnōmē* [1]

AGREEMENT [3]

in agreement, *1650+3836+1651,
 eis+ho+heis* [1]
agreement, *5161, synkatathesis* [1]
in agreement with, *5244, symphōneō* [1]

AGREES [3]

this agrees with, *2777, kathōs* [1]
which agrees with, *2777, kathōs* [1]
agrees with, *2848, kata* [1]

AGRIPPA [11]

Agrippa, *68, Agrippas* [11]

AGROUND [4]

run aground, *1738, ekpiptō* [2]
run aground, *2034, exōtheō* [1]
ran aground, *2131, epikellō* [1]

AHAZ [2]

Ahaz, *937, Achaz* [2]

AHEAD [35]

ahead, *1869, emprosthen* [4]
ahead, *4574+4725, pro+prosōpon* [4]
ahead, *2978, katenanti* [3]
go ahead of, *4575, proagō* [2]
go on ahead of, *4575, proagō* [2]
going ahead of, *4575, proagō* [2]
went ahead of, *4575, proagō* [2]
went on ahead, *4601, proerchomai* [2]
told ahead of time, *4625, prolegō* [2]
ahead, *AIT* [1]
looking ahead, *611, apoblepō* [1]
on ahead, *1869, emprosthen* [1]
ahead, *4574, pro* [1]
on ahead, *4574+4725, pro+prosōpon* [1]
entering ahead of, *4575, proagō* [1]
reaching ahead of, *4575, proagō* [1]
runs ahead, *4575, proagō* [1]
went ahead, *4575, proagō* [1]
got there ahead of, *4601, proerchomai* [1]
goes ahead, *4624, prolambanō* [1]
seeing what was ahead, *4632, prooraō* [1]

AID [1]

aid, *RPE* [1]

AIM [2]

aim is to, *2671, hina* [1]
aim for perfection, *2936, katartizō* [1]

AIMLESSLY [1]

aimlessly, *85, adēlōs* [1]

AIR [15]

air, *4041, ouranos* [9]
air, *113, aēr* [6]

AKELDAMA [1]

Akeldama, *192, Hakeldamach* [1]

AKIM [2]

Akim, *943, Achim* [2]

ALABASTER [3]

alabaster jar, *223, alabastros* [3]

ALARM [1]

alarm, *5832, phobos* [1]

ALARMED [8]

alarmed, *2583, throeō* [3]
alarmed, *1701, ekthambeō* [2]
alarmed, *5828, phobeomai* [2]
alarmed, *2572, thorybeō* [1]

ALERT [4]

alert, *1213, grēgoreō* [2]
alert, *70, agrypneō* [1]
alert, *1063, blepō* [1]

ALEXANDER [5]

Alexander, *235, Alexandros* [5]

ALEXANDRIA [2]

of Alexandria, *233, Alexandreus* [2]

ALEXANDRIAN [2]

Alexandrian, *234, Alexandrinos* [2]

ALIENATE [1]

alienate, *1710, ekkleiō* [1]

ALIENATED [2]

alienated from, *558, apallotrioō* [1]
alienated, *2934, katargeō* [1]

ALIENS [3]

aliens, *4230, paroikos* [2]
aliens, *3828, xenos* [1]

ALIKE [4]

alike, *AIT* [2]
alike, *NIG* [1]
alike, *608+1651, apo+heis* [1]

ALIVE [28]

alive, *2409, zaō* [18]
alive, *AIT* [2]
alive again, *348, anazaō* [2]
made alive, *2443, zōopoieō* [2]
alive, *1877+899, en+autos* [1]
alive, *2437, zōē* [1]
made alive with, *5188+5250,
 syzōopoieō+syn* [1]
made alive with, *5188, syzōopoieō* [1]

ALL [912]

all, *4246, pas* [651]
all, *3910, holos* [34]
all, *AIT* [26]
all, *NIG* [24]
all, *570, hapas* [18]
all things, *3836+4246, ho+pas* [16]

all, *4012, hosos* [12]
all, *4246+4012, pas+hosos* [6]
all, *RPE* [4]
once for all, *562, hapax* [4]
once for all, *2384, ephapax* [4]
all the more, *3437, mallon* [4]
not at all, *3590+1181, mē+ginomai* [4]
all kinds of, *4476, poikilos* [4]
first of all, *4754, prōton* [4]
after all, *1142, gar* [3]
all, *3836+4246, ho+pas* [3]
all, *317, amphoteroi* [2]
all this, *3836+4246, ho+pas* [2]
all, *3836, ho* [2]
at all, *3914, holōs* [2]
all, *3924, homothymadon* [2]
all that, *4012, hosos* [2]
all who, *4012, hosos* [2]
not at all, *4024+3590, ou+mē* [2]
at all times, *4121, pantote* [2]
at all, *4122, pantōs* [2]
all over, *4246, pas* [2]
all the louder, *4360, perissōs* [2]
all the more, *4498+3437, polys+mallon* [2]
all, *4498, polys* [2]
all the others, *253, allēlōn* [1]
crucifying all over again, *416, anastauroō* [1]
lost all sensitivity, *556, apalgeō* [1]
all by itself, *897, automatos* [1]
by all this, *1328+4047, dia+houtos* [1]
all over, *1650+3910, eis+holos* [1]
at all, *1650+3836+4117, eis+ho+pantelēs* [1]
for all time, *1650+3836+1457,*
    eis+ho+diēnekēs [1]
all hope, *1828, elpis* [1]
last of all, *2274, eschatos* [1]
all the way, *2401, heōs* [1]
at all, *2773, katholou* [1]
all over, *2848+3910, kata+holos* [1]
all, *2848+2625, kata+idios* [1]
that far outweighs them all,
    2848+5651+1650+5651+983,
    kata+hyperbolē+eis+hyperbolē+baros [1]
have all you want, *3170+1639,*
    korennymi+eimi [1]
all around, *3239, kyklothen* [1]
all the harder, *3437, mallon* [1]
all the louder, *3505, meizōn* [1]
all the way to, *3588, mechri* [1]
all they asked was, *3667, monon* [1]
all alone, *3668, monos* [1]
left all alone, *3670, monoō* [1]
all along, *3836+794, ho+archē* [1]
all disciples, *3836+4436+3412,*
    ho+plēthos+mathētēs [1]
all had, *3836+2625, ho+idios* [1]
all long, *3910, holos* [1]
all over, *3910, holos* [1]
beyond all question, *3935,*
    homologoumenōs [1]
all of, *4012, hosos* [1]
all whom, *4012+323, hosos+an* [1]
all who, *4012+1569, hosos+ean* [1]
all, *4012+323, hosos+an* [1]
all, *4012+3910, hosos+holos* [1]
isn't at all, *4024+3590, ou+mē* [1]
nothing at all, *4024+4029, ou+oudeis* [1]
at all, *4029, oudeis* [1]
no at all, *4029, oudeis* [1]
after all, *4036, oun* [1]
above all, *4047+4754, houtos+prōton* [1]
first of all, *4047+4754, houtos+prōton* [1]
in all, *4047+1639, houtos+eimi* [1]
all along, *4093, palai* [1]
all over again, *4099+540, palin+anōthen* [1]
all over again, *4099, palin* [1]

by all possible means, *4122, pantōs* [1]
know all about, *4158, parakoloutheō* [1]
all, *4246+476, pas+anthrōpos* [1]
in all, *4246, pas* [1]
all, *4436, plēthos* [1]
discharge all, *4442, plērophoreō* [1]
all silent, *4498+4968, polys+sigē* [1]
all ablaze, *4786+2794, pyr+kaiō* [1]
all the more eager, *5081, spoudaiōs* [1]
running from all directions, *5282, syndromē* [1]
all the world, *5515+1639+476+4005,*
    tis+eimi+anthrōpos+hos [1]
all the more, *5537+3437, tosoutos+mallon* [1]
all these, *5537, tosoutos* [1]
all, *5537, tosoutos* [1]
increased all the more, *5668, hyperperisseuō* [1]
last of all, *5731, hysteros* [1]
eat all want, *5963, chortazō* [1]
all, *6034, psychē* [1]

ALL-SURPASSING   [1]

all-surpassing, *5651, hyperbolē* [1]

ALLEYS   [1]

alleys, *4860, rhymē* [1]

ALLOW   [6]

allow, *1572, eaō* [2]
allow, *AIT* [1]
allow, *918, aphiēmi* [1]
allow, *2671, hina* [1]
allow to hold course, *4661, proseaō* [1]

ALLOWANCE   [1]

food allowance, *4991, sitometrion* [1]

ALLOWED   [4]

allowed, *2205, epitrepō* [3]
allowed, *1572, eaō* [1]

ALLOWS   [1]

allows, *NIG* [1]

ALMIGHTY   [12]

Almighty, *4120, pantokratōr* [10]
Almighty, *4877, Sabaōth* [2]

ALMOST   [8]

almost time, *1584, engys* [2]
almost, *AIT* [1]
almost here, *1581, engizō* [1]
almost, *1581, engizō* [1]
almost, *2453, ēdē* [1]
almost, *4180, paraplēsios* [1]
almost, *5385, schedon* [1]

ALOES   [1]

aloes, *264, aloē* [1]

ALONE   [33]

alone, *3668, monos* [13]
leave alone, *918, aphiēmi* [5]
alone, *1651, heis* [3]
alone, *3667, monon* [3]
alone, *NIG* [2]
leave alone, *923+608, aphistēmi+apo* [1]
her alone, *2625, idios* [1]
him alone, *2625, idios* [1]
alone, *2848+2625, kata+idios* [1]
alone, *2848+3668, kata+monos* [1]
all alone, *3668, monos* [1]
left all alone, *3670, monoō* [1]

ALONG   [65]

along with, *3552, meta* [9]
along, *4123, para* [7]
along with, *5250, syn* [6]
along with, *2779, kai* [3]
along, *2848, kata* [3]
along, *1877, en* [2]
took along, *4161, paralambanō* [2]
well along, *4581, probainō* [2]
driven along, *5770, pherō* [2]
along, *AIT* [1]
along the shore, *839, asson* [1]
traveled along, *1451+1328, dierchomai+dia* [1]
along, *2093, epi* [1]
is getting along well, *2338, euodoō* [1]
came along, *2779+2627, kai+idou* [1]
take along, *3227, ktaomai* [1]
along, *3552, meta* [1]
all along, *3836+794, ho+archē* [1]
walked along, *3847+4472, hodos+poieō* [1]
all along, *4093, palai* [1]
walked along, *4135, paragō* [1]
went along, *4135, paragō* [1]
moved along, *4162, paralegomai* [1]
went along, *4182, paraporeuomai* [1]
blown along, *4195, parapherō* [1]
come along, *4216, parerchomai* [1]
along, *4305, peran* [1]
take along, *4310, periagō* [1]
walk along, *4344, peripateō* [1]
went along, *4513, poreuomai* [1]
mistreated along with, *5156,*
    synkakoucheomai [1]
took along, *5221, symparalambanō* [1]
walked along with, *5233, symporeuomai* [1]
went along with, *5233, symporeuomai* [1]
take along, *5250, syn* [1]
come along with, *5302, synerchomai* [1]
went along, *5302, synerchomai* [1]
getting along in years, *5644, hyperakmos* [1]

ALOUD   [1]

cry aloud, *1066, boaō* [1]

ALPHA   [3]

Alpha, *270, alpha* [3]

ALPHAEUS   [5]

Alphaeus, *271, Halphaios* [5]

ALREADY   [55]

already, *2453, ēdē* [33]
already, *AIT* [11]
already, *562, hapax* [1]
work already done, *2289, hetoimos* [1]
already, *4093, palai* [1]
already made the charge, *4577, proaitiaomai* [1]
already heard about, *4578, proakouō* [1]
already know, *4589, proginōskō* [1]
already written, *4592, prographō* [1]
already gave warning, *4625, prolegō* [1]
already said, *4625, prolegō* [1]
already told, *4625, prolegō* [1]
already chosen, *4742, procheirotoneō* [1]

ALSO   [288]

also, *2779, kai* [225]
also, *NIG* [17]
and also, *2779, kai* [14]
I also, *2743, kagō* [8]
also, *1254, de* [3]
me also, *2743, kagō* [3]
but also, *247, alla* [2]

also, *3931, homoiōs* [2]
and also, *5445, te* [2]
also, *2083, epeita* [1]
also me, *2743, kagō* [1]
but also, *2779, kai* [1]
but also, *2797, kakeinos* [1]
he also, *2797, kakeinos* [1]
them also, *2797, kakeinos* [1]
also, *2829, kan* [1]
also, *4005, hos* [1]
also, *4099, palin* [1]
also testified, *5296, synepimartyreō* [1]
so also, *6058, hōsautōs* [1]
also, *6058, hōsautōs* [1]

ALTAR [24]

altar, *2603, thysiastērion* [22]
altar, *1117, bōmos* [1]
altar of incense, *2593, thymiatērion* [1]

ALTARS [1]

altars, *2603, thysiastērion* [1]

ALTHOUGH [18]

although, *AIT* [12]
although, *NIG* [2]
although, *247+2779, alla+kai* [1]
although, *2788, kaiper* [1]
although in fact, *2793, kaitoige* [1]
although, *4022, hoti* [1]

ALTOGETHER [1]

altogether, *3836+4246, ho+pas* [1]

ALWAYS [57]

always, *4121, pantote* [35]
always, *107, aei* [7]
always, *4246, pas* [5]
always, *AIT* [3]
always, *1328+4246, dia+pas* [3]
always, *1668, hekastote* [1]
always, *1877+4246+2789, en+pas+kairos* [1]
always, *4246+3836+2465, pas+ho+hēmera* [1]
always, *4441, plērēs* [1]

AM [363]

am, *AIT* [173]
am, *1639, eimi* [130]
am, *NIG* [45]
am, *RPE* [4]
am, *2400, echō* [3]
am a virgin, *467+4024+1182,
    anēr+ou+ginōskō* [1]
am, *1181, ginomai* [1]
am present, *1639, eimi* [1]
am, *3516, mellō* [1]
what am about to tell, *3836+3364+4047,
    ho+logos+houtos* [1]
am with, *4205, pareimi* [1]
am, *4205, pareimi* [1]
that am, *5639, hyparchō* [1]

AMAZED [37]

amazed, *2513, thaumazō* [12]
amazed, *1742, ekplēssō* [9]
amazed, *2014, existēmi* [7]
amazed at, *2513, thaumazō* [3]
amazed, *2501, thambeō* [2]
amazed, *1703, ekthaumazō* [1]
amazed, *1749+3284, ekstasis+lambanō* [1]
utterly amazed, *2014+2513,
    existēmi+thaumazō* [1]
amazed, *2502, thambos* [1]

AMAZEMENT [6]

amazement, *2513, thaumazō* [4]
amazement, *1749, ekstasis* [1]
overwhelmed with amazement, *5669+1742,
    hyperperissōs+ekplēssō* [1]

AMBASSADOR [1]

ambassador, *4563, presbeuō* [1]

AMBASSADORS [1]

ambassadors, *4563, presbeuō* [1]

AMBITION [7]

selfish ambition, *2249, eritheia* [5]
make it ambition, *5818, philotimeomai* [1]
ambition, *5818, philotimeomai* [1]

AMBUSH [2]

ambush, *1909, enedra* [1]
waiting in ambush for, *1910, enedreuō* [1]

AMEN [30]

Amen, *297, amēn* [30]

AMETHYST [1]

amethyst, *287, amethystos* [1]

AMMINADAB [3]

Amminadab, *300, Aminadab* [3]

AMON [2]

Amon, *321, Amōn* [2]

AMONG [170]

among, *1877, en* [86]
among, *1877+3545, en+mesos* [14]
among, *AIT* [11]
among, *1650, eis* [11]
among, *3552, meta* [6]
among, *4639, pros* [6]
among, *NIG* [5]
from among, *1666, ek* [5]
among, *1666, ek* [3]
among, *1650+3836+3545, eis+ho+mesos* [2]
among, *2093, epi* [2]
among, *4123, para* [2]
among, *324+3545, ana+mesos* [1]
among men, *474, anthrōpinos* [1]
from among, *608, apo* [1]
divided among, *1374, diamerizō* [1]
scattered among the nations, *1402, diaspora* [1]
living among, *1594+1877, enkatoikeō+en* [1]
grafted in among, *1596+1877,
    enkentrizō+en* [1]
among, *1650+3847, eis+hodos* [1]
among, *1651+1666, heis+ek* [1]
come in among, *1656+1650,
    eiserchomai+eis* [1]
walk among, *1853, emperipateō* [1]
from among, *1877, en* [1]
work among, *1919+1877, energeō+en* [1]
among, *2848, kata* [1]
among, *3545, mesos* [1]
people live scattered among, *3836+1402,
    ho+diaspora* [1]
among, *5536, topos* [1]

AMOS [1]

Amos, *322, Amōs* [1]

AMOUNT [3]

amount, *AIT* [1]

large amount, *4929+5552, saton+treis* [1]

AMOUNTS [2]

amounts, *AIT* [1]
amounts to nothing, *2024, exoutheneō* [1]

AMPHIPOLIS [1]

Amphipolis, *315, Amphipolis* [1]

AMPLIATUS [1]

Ampliatus, *309, Ampliatos* [1]

AMPLY [1]

amply supplied, *4444, plēroō* [1]

AN [234]

an, *NIG* [190]
an, *3836, ho* [15]
an, *5516, tis* [4]
an, *AIT* [3]
an, *1651, heis* [3]
have an abundance, *4355, perisseuō* [2]
competes as an athlete, *123, athleō* [1]
bound with an oath, *354, anathematizō* [1]
taken an oath, *354, anathematizō* [1]
made an opening in, *689, apostegazō* [1]
ministry of an apostle, *692, apostolē* [1]
write an account, *1211, graphō* [1]
food sacrificed to an idol, *1628, eidōlothytos* [1]
sacrifice offered to an idol, *1628,
    eidōlothytos* [1]
throwing into an uproar, *1752, ektarassō* [1]
half an hour, *2469, hēmiōrion* [1]
or take as an example, *2627+2779, idou+kai* [1]
take an example, *3306, legō* [1]
become an adulteress, *3658, moicheuō* [1]
made an idol in the form of a calf, *3674,
    moschopoieō* [1]
promised with an oath, *3923, omnyō* [1]
sought an audience, *4205, pareimi* [1]
in an uproar, *5177, syncheō* [1]

ANANIAS [13]

Ananias, *393, Hananias* [11]
Ananias, *RPE* [1]
Ananias^s, *899, autos* [1]

ANCESTOR [2]

ancestor, *4252, patēr* [2]

ANCESTORS [1]

ancestors, *4262, patrōos* [1]

ANCESTRY [2]

human ancestry, *2848+4922, kata+sarx* [1]
ancestry, *4921, sarkinos* [1]

ANCHOR [3]

anchor, *46, ankyra* [1]
weighed anchor, *149, airō* [1]
sea anchor, *5007, skeuos* [1]

ANCHORED [1]

anchored, *4694, prosormizō* [1]

ANCHORS [3]

anchors, *46, ankyra* [3]

ANCIENT [3]

ancient, *792, archaios* [3]

ANCIENTS [1]

ancients, 4565, presbyteros [1]

AND [6719]

and, 2779, kai [4795]
and, NIG [1326]
and, 1254, de [254]
and, 5445, te [42]
and then, 2779, kai [25]
and I, 2743, kagō [24]
and also, 2779, kai [14]
and, 5250, syn [13]
and so, 2779, kai [11]
and yet, 2779, kai [11]
and, 1142, gar [9]
and, 2445, ē [9]
and, 2779+2627, kai+idou [9]
and, RPE [8]
and, 247, alla [6]
and even, 2779, kai [6]
and, 2671, hina [5]
and not, 3593, mēde [5]
one and only, 3666, monogenēs [5]
and, 4028, oude [5]
and, 4036, oun [5]
and, AIT [3]
Peter⁵ and John, 899, autos [3]
and yet, 1254, de [3]
and so, 1650+3836, eis+ho [3]
and no, 4028, oude [3]
again and again, 4490, pollakis [3]
and, 6055, hōs [3]
Jesus⁵ and his disciples, 899, autos [2]
Paul⁵ and Barnabas, 899, autos [2]
Paul⁵ and Silas, 899, autos [2]
come and share, 1656+1650,
　　eiserchomai+eis [2]
and I too, 2743, kagō [2]
and, 2777, kathōs [2]
and as well, 2779, kai [2]
and when, 2779, kai [2]
and there, 2795, kakei [2]
more and more, 3437, mallon [2]
and some, 4005+1254, hos+de [2]
and also, 5445, te [2]
and, 247+1145+2779, alla+ge+kai [1]
and, 247+2779, alla+kai [1]
and, 275, hama [1]
Barnabas⁵ and Saul, 899, autos [1]
Jesus and his disciples⁵, 899, autos [1]
he and his disciples, 899, autos [1]
what he has and does, 1050, bios [1]
and even, 1254, de [1]
and now, 1254, de [1]
and some, 1254, de [1]
and so, 1475, dio [1]
twin gods Castor and Pollux, 1483,
　　Dioskouroi [1]
test and approve, 1507, dokimazō [1]
tested and approved, 1511, dokimos [1]
and, 1623, ei [1]
and thus, 1650+3836, eis+ho [1]
one and the same, 1651, heis [1]
and, 1663, eita [1]
searched intently and with the greatest care,
　　1699+2779+2001,
　　ekzēteō+kai+exeraunaō [1]
free and belong to no man, 1801+1666+4246,
　　eleutheros+ek+pas [1]
appeared and presented the charges, 1872,
　　emphanizō [1]
and, 1877+3836, en+ho [1]
and after, 2083, epeita [1]
more and more, 2093+4498, epi+polys [1]
on and on, 2093+4498, epi+polys [1]

and, 2401+4015, heōs+hostis [1]
and, 2401, heōs [1]
flocks and herds, 2576, thremma [1]
and then, 2671, hina [1]
and I myself, 2743, kagō [1]
and me, 2743, kagō [1]
and, 2779+1181, kai+ginomai [1]
and as good as, 2779+4047, kai+houtos [1]
and both, 2779, kai [1]
and even more, 2779+4707+5148,
　　kai+prostithēmi+sy [1]
and indeed, 2779, kai [1]
and now, 2779, kai [1]
and others, 2779, kai [1]
and still, 2779, kai [1]
and though, 2779, kai [1]
and too, 2779, kai [1]
and up, 2779, kai [1]
and yet, 2792, kaitoi [1]
and at his house, 2795, kakei [1]
and from there, 2796, kakeithen [1]
Priscilla and Aquila, 2797, kakeinos [1]
and he, 2797, kakeinos [1]
and that, 2797, kakeinos [1]
and these, 2797, kakeinos [1]
and when, 2829, kan [1]
wept and wept, 3081+4498, klaiō+polys [1]
tossed back and forth by the waves, 3115,
　　klydōnizomai [1]
and as well, 3552, meta [1]
and, 3552, meta [1]
and don't, 3593, mēde [1]
and, 3593, mēde [1]
and not, 3612, mēte [1]
one and only son, 3666, monogenēs [1]
a night and a day, 3819, nychthēmeron [1]
Peter⁵ and John, 3836+3525, ho+men [1]
and seven⁵ others, 3838, ogdoos [1]
and so, 3854, hothen [1]
through and through, 3911, holotelēs [1]
a hundred and twenty feet deep, 3976+1633,
　　orgyia+eikosi [1]
and cannot, 4028+1538, oude+dynamai [1]
and not, 4028, oude [1]
and lost, 4028+2351, oude+heuriskō [1]
and nothing, 4028+5516, oude+tis [1]
and nothing, 4028, oude [1]
and none, 4046+5516, oute+tis [1]
and no, 4046, oute [1]
and, 4046, oute [1]
and, 4048, houtōs [1]
any and every, 4246, pas [1]
do so more and more, 4355+3437,
　　perisseuō+mallon [1]
do this more and more, 4355+3437,
　　perisseuō+mallon [1]
blown here and there, 4367, peripherō [1]
reaching more and more,
　　4429+1328+3836+4498,
　　pleonazō+dia+ho+polys [1]
again and again, 4498, polys [1]
parents and grandparents, 4591, progonos [1]
manage and see that, 4613, proistēmi [1]
three or three and a half miles,
　　5084+1633+4297+2445+5558,
　　stadion+eikosi+pente+ē+triakonta [1]
and, 5538, tote [1]
safe and sound, 5617, hygiainō [1]
growing more and more, 5647, hyperauxanō [1]
and to which, 6055, hōs [1]
and, 6063, hōste [1]

ANDREW [14]

Andrew, 436, Andreas [13]
Andrew⁵, 4047, houtos [1]

ANDRONICUS [1]

Andronicus, 438, Andronikos [1]

ANEW [2]

anew, 2785, kainos [2]

ANGEL [103]

angel, 34, angelos [86]
angel, RPE [16]
angel, AIT [1]

ANGEL'S [2]

angel's, 34, angelos [2]

ANGELS [83]

angels, 34, angelos [81]
angels, RPE [1]
like angels, 2694, isangelos [1]

ANGER [12]

anger, 3973, orgē [7]
anger, 2596, thymos [2]
anger, 3974, orgizō [2]
outbursts of anger, 2596, thymos [1]

ANGERED [1]

easily angered, 4236, paroxynō [1]

ANGRY [10]

angry, 3974, orgizō [4]
angry, 4696, prosochthizō [2]
angry, 3973, orgē [1]
make angry, 4239, parorgizō [1]
angry, 4240, parorgismos [1]
angry, 5957, cholaō [1]

ANGUISH [5]

anguish, 5330, synochē [2]
anguish, 75, agōnia [1]
anguish, 2568, thlipsis [1]
anguish, 3850, odynē [1]

ANIMAL [2]

animal, 2563, thērion [1]
animal, 5393, sōma [1]

ANIMALS [11]

meat of strangled animals, 4465, pniktos [3]
animals, 2442, zōon [2]
four-footed animals, 5488, tetrapous [2]
animals, 2563, thērion [1]
wild animals, 2563, thērion [1]
animals, 3229, ktēnos [1]
animals, 5488, tetrapous [1]

ANKLES [1]

ankles, 5383, sphydron [1]

ANNA [1]

Anna, 483, Hanna [1]

ANNAS [4]

Annas, 484, Hannas [4]

ANNOUNCE [1]

announce with trumpets, 4895, salpizō [1]

ANNOUNCED [4]

announced, 2294, euangelizō [1]
announced, 3284+3281, lambanō+laleō [1]

announced, *3306, legō* [1]
announced the gospel in advance, *4603,
    proeuangelizomai* [1]

ANNUAL [1]

annual, *2848+1929, kata+eniautos* [1]

ANOINT [2]

anoint, *230, aleiphō* [2]

ANOINTED [6]

anointed, *5987, chriō* [4]
anointed, *230, aleiphō* [1]
Anointed One, *5986, Christos* [1]

ANOINTING [5]

anointing, *5984, chrisma* [3]
anointing, *RPE* [1]
anointing, *5987, chriō* [1]

ANOTHER [163]

one another, *253, allēlōn* [46]
another, *257, allos* [35]
another, *2283, heteros* [29]
another, *257+1254, allos+de* [9]
one another, *1571, heautou* [7]
another, *4005+1254, hos+de* [6]
another[s], *3345, lithos* [4]
another, *AIT* [3]
another, *1254, de* [2]
from one to another, *2848, kata* [2]
another, *4099, palin* [2]
another, *RPE* [1]
another[s], *81, adelphos* [1]
another, *257+5516, allos+tis* [1]
one another, *257+4639+257,
    allos+pros+allos* [1]
another, *259, allotrios* [1]
one another, *899, autos* [1]
still another, *1254, de* [1]
another, *1311, deuteros* [1]
another, *1651, heis* [1]
from another place, *1949, enteuthen* [1]
another[s], *2465, hēmera* [1]
from one synagogue to another,
    *2848+4246+3836+5252,
    kata+pas+ho+synagōgē* [1]
agree with one another, *3836+899+3306,
    ho+autos+legō* [1]
another, *3836+1254, ho+de* [1]
another, *3836+2283, ho+heteros* [1]
another, *4015, hostis* [1]
another time, *4099, palin* [1]
another[s], *5921, charis* [1]

ANOTHER'S [2]

one another's, *253, allēlōn* [1]
another's, *257, allos* [1]

ANSWER [27]

answer, *646, apokrinomai* [9]
gave answer, *646, apokrinomai* [4]
answer, *647, apokrisis* [3]
going to answer, *646, apokrinomai* [2]
in answer to, *1328, dia* [2]
answer, *3306, legō* [2]
given answer, *646, apokrinomai* [1]
answer, *665, apologia* [1]
answer, *2400+4639, echō+pros* [1]
answer kindly, *4151, parakaleō* [1]
answer, *5634, hypakouō* [1]

ANSWERABLE [1]

answerable, *1944, enochos* [1]

ANSWERED [140]

answered, *646, apokrinomai* [80]
answered, *3306, legō* [52]
answered, *5774, phēmi* [7]
answered, *RPE* [1]

ANSWERS [2]

answers, *646, apokrinomai* [1]
answers, *647, apokrisis* [1]

ANTICHRIST [4]

antichrist, *532, antichristos* [4]

ANTICHRISTS [1]

antichrists, *532, antichristos* [1]

ANTICIPATING [1]

anticipating, *4660, prosdokia* [1]

ANTIOCH [21]

Antioch, *522, Antiocheia* [18]
Antioch, *RPE* [2]
from Antioch, *523, Antiocheus* [1]

ANTIPAS [1]

Antipas, *525, Antipas* [1]

ANTIPATRIS [1]

Antipatris, *526, Antipatris* [1]

ANXIETIES [1]

anxieties, *3533, merimna* [1]

ANXIETY [2]

less anxiety, *267, alypos* [1]
anxiety, *3533, merimna* [1]

ANXIOUS [1]

anxious about, *3534, merimnaō* [1]

ANXIOUSLY [1]

anxiously, *3849, odynaō* [1]

ANY [126]

any, *NIG* [25]
any, *5516, tis* [25]
any, *4246, pas* [17]
any, *AIT* [6]
not any, *4029, oudeis* [6]
any more, *2285, eti* [4]
any, *4029, oudeis* [3]
any more, *4033, ouketi* [3]
any longer, *2285, eti* [2]
not any, *3594, mēdeis* [2]
any, *3836, ho* [2]
any one, *5516, tis* [2]
any, *RPE* [1]
without raising any objection, *395,
    anantirrētōs* [1]
bring any charge, *1592, enkaleō* [1]
any, *1651, heis* [1]
any further, *2093+4498, epi+polys* [1]
any more than, *2777+4024, kathōs+ou* [1]
in any way, *2848+3594+5573,
    kata+mēdeis+tropos* [1]
don't any, *3594, mēdeis* [1]
any way, *3594, mēdeis* [1]
any, *3594, mēdeis* [1]

not any way, *3594, mēdeis* [1]
don't any more, *3600, mēketi* [1]
any longer, *3600, mēketi* [1]
any way, *3836+5515, ho+tis* [1]
any, *4005+323, hos+an* [1]
any, *4005+5516+323, hos+tis+an* [1]
if any, *4005+323, hos+an* [1]
any time, *4020, hotan* [1]
not by any means, *4024+3590, ou+mē* [1]
no any more, *4033, ouketi* [1]
not any, *4046, oute* [1]
any such person, *4047, houtos* [1]
any, *4121, pantote* [1]
any of, *4123, para* [1]
any and every, *4246, pas* [1]
in any case, *4440, plēn* [1]
any, *5515+476, tis+anthrōpos* [1]
any, *5515, tis* [1]
any other, *5516, tis* [1]

ANYBODY [7]

anybody, *5516, tis* [5]
anybody, *NIG* [1]
not anybody, *3594, mēdeis* [1]

ANYMORE [2]

anymore, *2285, eti* [1]
not anymore, *4033, ouketi* [1]

ANYONE [209]

anyone, *5516, tis* [78]
anyone, *3836, ho* [31]
anyone, *4005, hos* [18]
anyone, *4246, pas* [15]
not anyone, *3594, mēdeis* [13]
anyone, *4005+323, hos+an* [10]
anyone, *AIT* [7]
anyone, *4029, oudeis* [7]
don't anyone, *3594, mēdeis* [5]
anyone, *4005+1569, hos+ean* [5]
anyone, *NIG* [2]
anyone, *RPE* [2]
anyone, *1569+5516, ean+tis* [2]
not anyone, *4029, oudeis* [2]
anyone else, *257, allos* [1]
anyone[s], *1187, gnapheus* [1]
nor anyone, *1254+4029, de+oudeis* [1]
anyone, *1667, hekastos* [1]
anyone, *3594+476, mēdeis+anthrōpos* [1]
anyone, *3594, mēdeis* [1]
anyone[s], *3836+476, ho+anthrōpos* [1]
anyone[s], *3836, ho* [1]
anyone, *4012+1569, hosos+ean* [1]
anyone, *4015, hostis* [1]
anyone, *4246+6034, pas+psychē* [1]
anyone else, *5516, tis* [1]

ANYONE'S [4]

anyone's, *5516, tis* [2]
anyone's, *3594, mēdeis* [1]
not anyone's, *4029, oudeis* [1]

ANYTHING [79]

anything, *5516, tis* [31]
anything, *AIT* [11]
not anything, *3594, mēdeis* [5]
anything, *NIG* [4]
anything, *3836, ho* [4]
anything, *4246, pas* [4]
anything, *4029, oudeis* [3]
not anything, *4029, oudeis* [3]
anything, *4005+1569, hos+ean* [2]
anything, *RPE* [1]
anything, *257, allos* [1]

anything, *1569+5516, ean+tis* [1]
not anything, *3590+3594, mē+mēdeis* [1]
don't anything, *3594, mēdeis* [1]
haven't anything, *3594, mēdeis* [1]
without anything, *3594, mēdeis* [1]
anything that, *4005, hos* [1]
haven't anything, *4029, oudeis* [1]
no anything, *4029, oudeis* [1]
don't have anything to do with, *4148, paraiteomai* [1]
anything, *4246+4547, pas+pragma* [1]

ANYWHERE   [1]

anywhere else in, *2848, kata* [1]

APART   [17]

apart from, *6006, chōris* [7]
set apart, *928, aphorizō* [3]
apart from the law, *492, anomōs* [2]
set apart as very own, *39, hagiazō* [1]
set apart, *39, hagiazō* [1]
apart from, *459, aneu* [1]
tore apart, *1400, diaspaō* [1]
set apart, *6004, chōrizō* [1]

APELLES   [1]

Apelles, *593, Apellēs* [1]

APOLLONIA   [1]

Apollonia, *662, Apollōnia* [1]

APOLLOS   [11]

Apollos, *663, Apollōs* [10]
Apollos[s], *899, autos* [1]

APOLLYON   [1]

Apollyon, *661, Apollyōn* [1]

APOSTLE   [21]

apostle, *693, apostolos* [19]
apostle, *RPE* [1]
ministry of an apostle, *692, apostolē* [1]

APOSTLES   [62]

apostles, *693, apostolos* [56]
the apostles[s], *899, autos* [4]
the apostles[s], *3836+3525, ho+men* [1]
false apostles, *6013, pseudapostolos* [1]

APOSTLESHIP   [2]

apostleship, *692, apostolē* [2]

APOSTOLIC   [1]

apostolic, *692, apostolē* [1]

APPEAL   [13]

appeal to, *4151, parakaleō* [4]
appeal to, *2126, epikaleō* [2]
appeal, *4155, paraklēsis* [2]
made appeal to, *2126, epikaleō* [1]
made appeal, *2126, epikaleō* [1]
appeal, *4151, parakaleō* [1]
listen to appeal, *4151, parakaleō* [1]
making appeal, *4151, parakaleō* [1]

APPEALED   [4]

appealed, *1961, entynchanō* [1]
appealed to, *2126, epikaleō* [1]
appealed, *2126, epikaleō* [1]
appealed, *4715, prosphōneō* [1]

APPEALING   [1]

appealing, *AIT* [1]

APPEAR   [13]

appear, *1586, egeirō* [3]
appear, *5746, phaneroō* [2]
appear, *428, anaphainō* [1]
appear before, *1656+1650, eiserchomai+eis* [1]
appear, *1872, emphanizō* [1]
appear, *2705, histēmi* [1]
made appear, *2705, histēmi* [1]
appear, *3972, horaō* [1]
appear as, *5743, phainō* [1]
appear, *5743, phainō* [1]

APPEARANCE   [8]

appearance, *4725, prosōpon* [2]
appearance, *1624, eidea* [1]
appearance, *1626, eidos* [1]
appearance, *3364, logos* [1]
appearance, *3970, horasis* [1]
judge by external appearance, *4725+476+3284, prosōpon+anthrōpos+lambanō* [1]
in appearance, *5386, schēma* [1]

APPEARANCES   [1]

appearances, *4071, opsis* [1]

APPEARED   [53]

appeared, *3972, horaō* [17]
appeared, *5746, phaneroō* [9]
appeared, *5743, phainō* [7]
appeared, *1181, ginomai* [3]
appeared, *2210, epiphainō* [3]
appeared, *4134, paraginomai* [3]
appeared, *482, anistēmi* [2]
appeared, *2392, ephistēmi* [2]
appeared publicly, *345, anadeixis* [1]
appeared, *1586, egeirō* [1]
appeared and presented the charges, *1872, emphanizō* [1]
appeared, *1872, emphanizō* [1]
appeared, *2351, heuriskō* [1]
appeared, *3964, optanomai* [1]
appeared, *5746+1571, phaneroō+heautou* [1]

APPEARING   [6]

appearing, *2211, epiphaneia* [5]
appearing, *AIT* [1]

APPEARS   [6]

appears, *5746, phaneroō* [4]
appears, *482, anistēmi* [1]
appears, *5743, phainō* [1]

APPEASE   [1]

appease, *4151, parakaleō* [1]

APPETITES   [1]

appetites, *3120, koilia* [1]

APPHIA   [1]

Apphia, *722, Apphia* [1]

APPIUS   [1]

Appius, *716, Appios* [1]

APPLIED   [1]

applied, *3571, metaschēmatizō* [1]

APPLYING   [1]

applying, *2130, epikeimai* [1]

APPOINT   [4]

appoint as judges, *2767, kathizō* [1]
appoint, *2770, kathistēmi* [1]
appoint, *4741, procheirizō* [1]
appoint, *5502, tithēmi* [1]

APPOINTED   [27]

appointed, *5502, tithēmi* [5]
appointed, *2770, kathistēmi* [3]
appointed time, *2789, kairos* [3]
appointed, *4472, poieō* [3]
appointed, *3988, horizō* [2]
appointed, *5435, tassō* [2]
appointed, *RPE* [1]
appointed, *344, anadeiknymi* [1]
appointed, *1443, didōmi* [1]
appointed season, *2789, kairos* [1]
appointed, *3284, lambanō* [1]
appointed, *4047, houtos* [1]
appointed, *4741, procheirizō* [1]
appointed, *5414, taktos* [1]
appointed, *5936, cheirotoneō* [1]

APPOINTING   [1]

appointing, *5502, tithēmi* [1]

APPOINTS   [1]

appoints, *2770, kathistēmi* [1]

APPORTIONED   [1]

apportioned, *3586, metron* [1]

APPREHENSIVE   [1]

apprehensive, *4660, prosdokia* [1]

APPROACH   [2]

approach, *2400+4643, echō+prosagōgē* [1]
approach, *4665, proserchomai* [1]

APPROACHED   [14]

approached, *1581, engizō* [9]
approached, *1181, ginomai* [3]
approached, *4665, proserchomai* [1]
approached, *5230, symplēroō* [1]

APPROACHING   [7]

approaching, *1581, engizō* [3]
approaching, *1584+1181, engys+ginomai* [1]
approaching, *2262+4639, erchomai+pros* [1]
in approaching, *4639, pros* [1]
approaching, *4642, prosagō* [1]

APPROPRIATE   [1]

appropriate, *4560, prepō* [1]

APPROVAL   [5]

giving approval, *5306, syneudokeō* [2]
approval, *1511, dokimos* [1]
trying to win the approval of, *4275, peithō* [1]
on placed seal of approval, *5381, sphragizō* [1]

APPROVE   [5]

approve, *1507, dokimazō* [2]
approve of, *5306, syneudokeō* [2]
test and approve, *1507, dokimazō* [1]

APPROVED   [5]

approved, *1511, dokimos* [3]

approved, *1507, dokimazō* [1]
tested and approved, *1511, dokimos* [1]

APPROVES [1]

approves, *1507, dokimazō* [1]

APRONS [1]

aprons, *4980, simikinthion* [1]

AQUILA [7]

Aquila, *217, Akylas* [6]
Priscilla and Aquila, *2797, kakeinos* [1]

ARABIA [2]

Arabia, *728, Arabia* [2]

ARABS [1]

Arabs, *732, Araps* [1]

ARAMAIC [8]

in Aramaic, *1580, Hebraisti* [5]
in Aramaic, *1579+1365, Hebrais+dialektos* [3]

ARBITER [1]

arbiter, *3537, meristēs* [1]

ARCHANGEL [2]

archangel, *791, archangelos* [2]

ARCHELAUS [1]

Archelaus, *793, Archelaos* [1]

ARCHIPPUS [2]

Archippus, *800, Archippos* [2]

ARCHITECT [1]

architect, *5493, technitēs* [1]

ARDENT [1]

ardent concern, *2419, zēlos* [1]

ARE [1141]

are, *AIT* [470]
are, *1639, eimi* [369]
are, *NIG* [240]
are, *RPE* [17]
are, *2400, echō* [8]
are, *5639, hyparchō* [8]
are, *1181, ginomai* [5]
are from, *600+608, apechō+apo* [2]
pay attention who they are, *1063+4725+476, blepō+prosōpon+anthrōpos* [2]
those^s who are, *3836+5626, ho+huios* [2]
that are, *1181, ginomai* [1]
we are, *1609, egō* [1]
because are, *1639, eimi* [1]
are, *1650+1639, eis+eimi* [1]
hopes are set, *1827, elpizō* [1]
that are coming, *3516, mellō* [1]
not are you, *3590, mē* [1]
are mindful, *3630, mimnēskomai* [1]
what^s we are writing, *3836+899, ho+autos* [1]
who are here, *4047, houtos* [1]
as you are, *4048, houtōs* [1]
are here, *4205, pareimi* [1]
are present, *4205, pareimi* [1]
are, *4472, poieō* [1]
who do you think you are, *5515+4932+4472, tis+seautou+poieō* [1]
they are the kind, *5525, toioutos* [1]
views are, *5858, phroneō* [1]

are, *6055, hōs* [1]

AREA [16]

temple area, *2639, hieron* [10]
area, *5536, topos* [2]
area of activity, *2834, kanōn* [1]
area, *3538, meros* [1]
area, *3990, horion* [1]
area, *6001, chōra* [1]

AREN'T [9]

aren't, *4024, ou* [4]
aren't, *4024+1639, ou+eimi* [2]
aren't, *4049+1639, ouchi+eimi* [2]
aren't, *RPE* [1]

ARENA [1]

arena, *RPE* [1]

AREOPAGUS [3]

meeting of the Areopagus, *740, Areios pagos* [2]
member of the Areopagus, *741, Areopagitēs* [1]

ARETAS [1]

Aretas, *745, Haretas* [1]

ARGUE [3]

argue, *RPE* [1]
argue sharply, *3481, machomai* [1]
argue with, *5184, syzēteō* [1]

ARGUED [2]

argued vigorously, *1372, diamachomai* [1]
argued about, *4639+253+1363, pros+allēlōn+dialegomai* [1]

ARGUING [6]

arguing, *1363, dialegomai* [2]
arguing about, *1368, dialogizomai* [1]
arguing, *1369, dialogismos* [1]
arguing about, *5184, syzēteō* [1]
arguing, *5184, syzēteō* [1]

ARGUMENT [4]

argument, *517, antilogia* [1]
argument, *1369, dialogismos* [1]
argument, *2428, zētēsis* [1]
using argument, *3306, legō* [1]

ARGUMENTS [4]

arguments, *2251, eris* [1]
arguments, *2428, zētēsis* [1]
arguments, *3361, logismos* [1]
fine-sounding arguments, *4391, pithanologia* [1]

ARID [2]

arid, *536, anydros* [2]

ARIMATHEA [4]

Arimathea, *751, Harimathaia* [4]

ARISE [2]

arise, *482, anistēmi* [2]

ARISTARCHUS [5]

Aristarchus, *752, Aristarchos* [5]

ARISTOBULUS [1]

Aristobulus, *755, Aristoboulos* [1]

ARK [8]

ark, *3066, kibōtos* [6]
the ark^s, *899, autos* [1]
this ark^s, *4005, hos* [1]

ARM [3]

arm, *1098, brachiōn* [2]
arm, *3959, hoplizō* [1]

ARMAGEDDON [1]

Armageddon, *762, Harmagedōn* [1]

ARMED [3]

armed, *AIT* [2]
fully armed, *2774, kathoplizō* [1]

ARMIES [4]

armies, *5128, strateuma* [2]
armies, *4213, parembolē* [1]
armies, *5136, stratopedon* [1]

ARMOR [4]

full armor, *4110, panoplia* [2]
armor, *3960, hoplon* [1]
armor, *4110, panoplia* [1]

ARMS [6]

arms, *44, ankalē* [1]
taking in his arms, *1878, enankalizomai* [1]
took in arms, *1878, enankalizomai* [1]
threw arms around, *2158+2093+3836+5549, epipiptō+epi+ho+trachēlos* [1]
put arms around, *5227, symperilambanō* [1]
arms, *5931, cheir* [1]

ARMY [2]

army, *5128, strateuma* [2]

AROMA [1]

aroma, *2380, euōdia* [1]

AROSE [4]

arose, *NIG* [1]
opposition arose, *482, anistēmi* [1]
arose, *1181+1254, ginomai+de* [1]
arose, *1181, ginomai* [1]

AROUND [81]

around, *4309, peri* [11]
around, *4639, pros* [5]
around, *AIT* [4]
around, *2093, epi* [3]
turned around, *2188, epistrephō* [3]
around, *3241, kyklō* [3]
looked around at, *4315, periblepō* [3]
wrapped around, *1346, diazōnnymi* [2]
gathered around, *3240, kykloō* [2]
looked around, *4315, periblepō* [2]
tied around, *4329+4309, perikeimai+peri* [2]
walk around, *4344, peripateō* [2]
put around, *4363, peritithēmi* [2]
around, *RPE* [1]
walked around, *1451, dierchomai* [1]
went around, *1451, dierchomai* [1]
gathering around, *1581, engizō* [1]
crowding around, *2130, epikeimai* [1]
threw arms around, *2158+2093+3836+5549, epipiptō+epi+ho+trachēlos* [1]
all around, *3239, kyklothen* [1]
marched around, *3240, kykloō* [1]
rolled around, *3244, kyliō* [1]

wrapped around waist, *3284+1346*,
   lambanō+diazōnnymi [1]
move around, *3553*, *metabainō* [1]
standing around, *4225*, *paristēmi* [1]
stood around, *4225*, *paristēmi* [1]
went around, *4310*, *periagō* [1]
flashed around, *4313+4309*,
   periastraptō+peri [1]
flashed around, *4313*, *periastraptō* [1]
wrap around, *4314*, *periballō* [1]
looking around, *4315*, *periblepō* [1]
around, *4317*, *perideō* [1]
went around, *4320*, *perierchomai* [1]
around, *4322*, *perizōnnymi* [1]
buckled around waist, *4322*, *perizōnnymi* [1]
stood around, *4325*, *periistēmi* [1]
blazing around, *4334*, *perilampō* [1]
shone around, *4334*, *perilampō* [1]
around, *4339*, *perix* [1]
prowls around, *4344*, *peripateō* [1]
walked around, *4344*, *peripateō* [1]
walking around, *4344*, *peripateō* [1]
walks around, *4344*, *peripateō* [1]
went around, *4344*, *peripateō* [1]
carry around, *4367*, *peripherō* [1]
country around, *4369*, *perichōros* [1]
turning around, *5138*, *strephō* [1]
turned around, *5138+1650+3836+3958*,
   strephō+eis+ho+opisō [1]
put arms around, *5227*, *symperilambanō* [1]
pressed around, *5315*, *synthlibō* [1]

AROUSE [2]

arouse jealousy, *4143*, *parazēloō* [1]
arouse to envy, *4143*, *parazēloō* [1]

AROUSED [2]

aroused, *AIT* [1]
aroused, *3075*, *kineō* [1]

ARPHAXAD [1]

Arphaxad, *790*, *Arphaxad* [1]

ARRANGED [5]

arranged, *1443*, *didōmi* [2]
arranged, *2941*, *kataskeuazō* [1]
arranged, *5435*, *tassō* [1]
arranged, *5502*, *tithēmi* [1]

ARRANGEMENT [1]

made arrangement, *1411*, *diatassō* [1]

ARRANGEMENTS [1]

in advance finish the arrangements for, *4616*,
   prokatartizō [1]

ARREST [15]

arrest, *3195*, *krateō* [8]
arrest, *4389*, *piazō* [3]
arrest, *4140*, *paradidōmi* [2]
arrest, *1313*, *deō* [1]
arrest, *2095+2093+3836+5931*,
   epiballō+epi+ho+cheir [1]

ARRESTED [12]

arrested, *3195*, *krateō* [5]
arrested, *5197*, *syllambanō* [2]
arrested, *1300*, *desmios* [1]
arrested, *2095+3836+5931+2093*,
   epiballō+ho+cheir+epi [1]
arrested, *2095+3836+5931*,
   epiballō+ho+cheir [1]
arrested, *2138*, *epilambanomai* [1]

arrested, *4140*, *paradidōmi* [1]

ARRESTING [2]

arresting, *1297*, *desmeuō* [1]
arresting, *4389*, *piazō* [1]

ARRIVAL [1]

arrival, *2262*, *erchomai* [1]

ARRIVE [1]

arrive, *4134*, *paraginomai* [1]

ARRIVED [31]

arrived, *2262*, *erchomai* [13]
arrived, *2918*, *katantaō* [4]
arrived, *4134*, *paraginomai* [4]
arrived, *1181*, *ginomai* [2]
arrived in, *1656+1650*, *eiserchomai+eis* [2]
arrived, *1656+1650*, *eiserchomai+eis* [1]
arrived, *2262+1650*, *erchomai+eis* [1]
arrived, *2457*, *hēkō* [1]
arrived, *2849*, *katabainō* [1]
arrived, *2982*, *katerchomai* [1]
arrived, *3836+4242*, *ho+parousia* [1]

ARRIVES [3]

arrives, *2262*, *erchomai* [3]

ARRIVING [6]

arriving, *4134*, *paraginomai* [4]
arriving, *1181*, *ginomai* [1]
arriving in, *2094*, *epibainō* [1]

ARROGANCE [2]

arrogance, *5661*, *hyperēphania* [1]
arrogance, *5883*, *physiōsis* [1]

ARROGANT [6]

arrogant, *5881*, *physioō* [2]
arrogant, *881*, *authadēs* [1]
arrogant, *5662*, *hyperēphanos* [1]
arrogant, *5734+5858*, *hypsēlos+phroneō* [1]
arrogant, *5735*, *hypsēlophroneō* [1]

ARROWS [1]

arrows, *1018*, *belos* [1]

ARTEMAS [1]

Artemas, *782*, *Artemas* [1]

ARTEMIS [5]

Artemis, *783*, *Artemis* [5]

ARTICLES [2]

articles, *5007*, *skeuos* [2]

ARTS [3]

practice magic arts, *5761*, *pharmakos* [2]
magic arts, *5760*, *pharmakon* [1]

AS [999]

as, *6055*, *hōs* [151]
as, *NIG* [134]
as, *AIT* [114]
as, *2777*, *kathōs* [80]
just as, *2777*, *kathōs* [50]
as, *1650*, *eis* [26]
as, *1877+3836*, *en+ho* [17]
just as, *6055*, *hōs* [17]
as, *2848*, *kata* [16]
as if, *6055*, *hōs* [16]

as, *RPE* [15]
as, *6061*, *hōsper* [15]
as soon as, *2317*, *euthys1* [12]
as well as, *2779*, *kai* [12]
as, *2779*, *kai* [12]
just as, *6061*, *hōsper* [10]
as well, *2779*, *kai* [9]
even as, *2777*, *kathōs* [6]
as though, *6055*, *hōs* [6]
as, *1639*, *eimi* [5]
just as, *2749*, *kathaper* [5]
as, *3888*, *hoios* [5]
as, *4012*, *hosos* [5]
as far as, *948*, *achri* [4]
as long as, *2093+4012+5989*,
   epi+hosos+chronos [4]
as much as, *4012*, *hosos* [4]
as soon as, *4020+2317*, *hotan+euthys1* [4]
as soon as, *4020*, *hotan* [4]
as, *4021*, *hote* [4]
yes it is as you say, *5148+3306*, *sy+legō* [4]
such as these, *5525*, *toioutos* [4]
as small as, *6055*, *hōs* [4]
as, *1877*, *en* [3]
so as to, *2671*, *hina* [3]
as for, *2779*, *kai* [3]
as it is, *3814+1254*, *nyn+de* [3]
as, *4005+5573*, *hos+tropos* [3]
as a result, *6063*, *hōste* [3]
as for, *608*, *apo* [2]
as high as, *948*, *achri* [2]
as long as, *948+4005*, *achri+hos* [2]
as for, *1142*, *gar* [2]
as, *1142*, *gar* [2]
as, *1254*, *de* [2]
but as far as, *1254*, *de* [2]
as far as, *1650*, *eis* [2]
as soon as, *2054*, *epan* [2]
as long as, *2093+4012*, *epi+hosos* [2]
only as long as, *2093+4012+5989*,
   epi+hosos+chronos [2]
known as, *2126*, *epikaleō* [2]
as long as still, *2285*, *eti* [2]
as soon as, *2311*, *eutheōs* [2]
just as, *2317*, *euthys1* [2]
as long as, *2401*, *heōs* [2]
as far as, *2401*, *heōs* [2]
as surely as I live, *2409+1609*, *zaō+egō* [2]
as good as dead, *2453+3739*, *ēdē+nekroō* [2]
as precious as, *2700*, *isotimos* [2]
as much as, *2777*, *kathōs* [2]
as well as, *2777*, *kathōs* [2]
and as good as, *2779+4047*, *kai+houtos* [2]
and as well, *2779*, *kai* [2]
known as, *2813*, *kaleō* [2]
as for, *2848*, *kata* [2]
as much as were able, *2848+1539*,
   kata+dynamis [2]
just as, *2848+4012*, *kata+hosos* [2]
just as, *2848*, *kata* [2]
eaten as much as wanted, *3170+5575*,
   korennymi+trophē [2]
known as, *3306*, *legō* [2]
as far as, *3525*, *men* [2]
I mean that just as surely as, *3755*, *nē* [2]
as, *3927*, *homoios* [2]
as, *4005*, *hos* [2]
as often as, *4006+1569*, *hosakis+ean* [2]
as many as, *4012*, *hosos* [2]
as soon as, *4020+2453*, *hotan+ēdē* [2]
as soon as, *4021*, *hote* [2]
as, *4022*, *hoti* [2]
as, *4309*, *peri* [2]
as, *4639*, *pros* [2]
as much, *5537*, *tosoutos* [2]
as soon as, *5538*, *tote* [2]

adoption as sons, *5625, huiothesia* [2]
as soon as, *6055, hōs* [2]
as soon as, *6055+323, hōs+an* [2]
regarded as, *6055, hōs* [2]
set apart as very own, *39, hagiazō* [1]
competes as an athlete, *123, athleō* [1]
taken as prisoners, *170, aichmalōtizō* [1]
as, *505, anti* [1]
as, *608, apo* [1]
sold as a slave, *625, apodidōmi* [1]
as to, *726, ara* [1]
so much as, *948, achri* [1]
spoken of as evil, *1059, blasphēmeō* [1]
as for, *1254, de* [1]
just as, *1254, de* [1]
as the result of, *1328, dia* [1]
serve as deacons, *1354, diakoneō* [1]
as ought, *1469, dikaiōs* [1]
twice as much, *1487, diplous* [1]
serve as slaves, *1526, douleuō* [1]
as for, *1569, ean* [1]
such as, *1623, ei* [1]
be that as it may, *1639, eimi* [1]
as a result, *1650+3836, eis+ho* [1]
so as to, *1650, eis* [1]
so as, *1650+3836, eis+ho* [1]
just as though, *1651+2779+3836+899,*
    heis+kai+ho+autos [1]
as for, *1664+5642, eite+hyper* [1]
as for, *1664, eite* [1]
such as, *1664, eite* [1]
as, *1666, ek* [1]
as a fool, *1877+932, en+aphrosynē* [1]
as a man, *1877+4922, en+sarx* [1]
as members of, *1877, en* [1]
as of first importance, *1877+4755,*
    en+prōtos [1]
inasmuch as, *2093+4012+3525+4036,*
    epi+hosos+men+oun [1]
serving as overseers, *2174, episkopeō* [1]
as, *2285, eti* [1]
as, *2317, euthys1* [1]
as follows, *2400+3836+5596+4047,*
    echō+ho+typos+houtos [1]
as, *2453, ēdē* [1]
yellow as sulfur, *2523, theiōdēs* [1]
as know, *2627, idou* [1]
or take as an example, *2627+2779, idou+kai* [1]
serving as priest, *2634, hierateuō* [1]
as to, *2671, hina* [1]
as, *2671, hina* [1]
as, *2698, isos* [1]
as, *2745, katha* [1]
as, *2749, kathaper* [1]
precisely as it had happened, *2759, kathexēs* [1]
appoint as judges, *2767, kathizō* [1]
as, *2776+323, kathoti+an* [1]
as, *2776, kathoti* [1]
just as, *2778, kathōsper* [1]
as it is, *2779, kai* [1]
as can see, *2779+2627, kai+idou* [1]
as does, *2848, kata* [1]
as intended, *2848, kata* [1]
as to, *2848, kata* [1]
as usual, *2848+3836+1621, kata+ho+ethos* [1]
as usual, *2848+3836+899, kata+ho+autos* [1]
as was, *2848, kata* [1]
just as, *2848+3928, kata+homoiotēs* [1]
just as, *2848+4005+5573, kata+hos+tropos* [1]
gave to as inheritance, *2883,*
    kataklēronomeō [1]
seared as with a hot iron, *3013, kaustēriazō* [1]
clear as crystal, *3222, krystallizō* [1]
as, *3516, mellō* [1]
and as well, *3552, meta* [1]
as did⁵, *3552, meta* [1]

as it is, *3814, nyn* [1]
as it is, *3815+1254, nyni+de* [1]
as to, *3836, ho* [1]
as⁵, *3836+4301, ho+pepoithēsis* [1]
as one man, *3924, homothymadon* [1]
as, *3930, homoiōma* [1]
as, *3937, homotechnos* [1]
just as, *3940, homōs* [1]
just as, *4005+5573, hos+tropos* [1]
same as, *4005+2779, hos+kai* [1]
so long as, *4012+5989, hosos+chronos* [1]
as it is, *4022+1254, hoti+de* [1]
as, *4036, oun* [1]
as I did, *4047+899, houtos+autos* [1]
as, *4047, houtos* [1]
the same as, *4047, houtos* [1]
as it has, *4048, houtōs* [1]
as you are, *4048, houtōs* [1]
as⁵ is, *4048, houtōs* [1]
as, *4048, houtōs* [1]
just as if, *4048, houtōs* [1]
just as, *4048+2848+4005+5573,*
    houtōs+kata+hos+tropos [1]
as for, *4309, peri* [1]
as to, *4309, peri* [1]
many times as much, *4491, pollaplasiōn* [1]
serve as, *4618, prokeimai* [1]
so as to, *4639, pros* [1]
acted as if, *4701, prospoieō* [1]
offered as a sacrifice, *4712, prospherō* [1]
inheritance rights as the oldest son, *4757,*
    prōtotokia [1]
serves as a soldier, *5129, strateuomai* [1]
serving as a soldier, *5129, strateuomai* [1]
as, *5250, syn* [1]
contending as, *5254, synathleō* [1]
as, *5445, te* [1]
adopted as sons, *5625, huiothesia* [1]
appear as, *5743, phainō* [1]
loving each other as brothers, *5789,*
    philadelphia [1]
love as brothers, *5790, philadelphos* [1]
regards as special, *5858, phroneō* [1]
the same as, *6055+2779, hōs+kai* [1]
as, *6059, hōsei* [1]
as indeed, *6061, hōsper* [1]
as, *6062, hōsperei* [1]

ASA [2]

Asa, *809, Asa* [2]

ASCEND [3]

ascend, *326, anabainō* [3]

ASCENDED [3]

ascended, *326, anabainō* [3]

ASCENDING [1]

ascending, *326, anabainō* [1]

ASHAMED [21]

ashamed of, *2049, epaischynomai* [7]
ashamed, *159, aischynomai* [4]
ashamed, *2049, epaischynomai* [4]
ashamed of, *2875, kataischynō* [2]
ashamed, *RPE* [1]
does not need to be ashamed, *454,*
    anepaischyntos [1]
ashamed, *1956, entrepō* [1]
feel ashamed, *1956, entrepō* [1]

ASHER [2]

Asher, *818, Asēr* [2]

ASHES [4]

ashes, *5075, spodos* [3]
burning to ashes, *5491, tephroō* [1]

ASHORE [2]

ashore, *1650+3836+1178, eis+ho+gē* [1]
ashore, *2093+1178, epi+gē* [1]

ASIA [19]

province of Asia, *823, Asia* [15]
Asia, *823, Asia* [3]
from the province of Asia, *824, Asianos* [1]

ASIDE [21]

aside, *2848+2625, kata+idios* [3]
set aside, *119, atheteō* [2]
took aside, *4161, paralambanō* [2]
took aside, *4689, proslambanō* [2]
aside, *AIT* [1]
setting aside, *119, atheteō* [1]
set aside, *120, athetēsis* [1]
set aside, *218, akyroō* [1]
sets aside, *359, anaireō* [1]
throwing aside, *610, apoballō* [1]
put aside, *700, apotithēmi* [1]
pushed aside, *723, apōtheō* [1]
put aside, *1639+629, eimi+apothesis* [1]
turn aside, *1762, ektrepō* [1]
aside, *3277, lathra* [1]
set aside, *4123+1571+5502,*
    para+heautou+tithēmi [1]

ASK [83]

ask, *160, aiteō* [23]
ask, *2263, erōtaō* [18]
ask, *3306, legō* [15]
ask for, *160, aiteo* [8]
ask, *2089, eperōtaō* [5]
ask, *1289, deomai* [2]
ask questions, *2089, eperōtaō* [2]
ask for, *2426, zēteō* [2]
ask, *4785, pynthanomai* [2]
ask, *RPE* [1]
ask God for help, *1255, deēsis* [1]
ask, *2004, exetazō* [1]
ask about, *2089, eperōtaō* [1]
ask for, *2089, eperōtaō* [1]
ask questions, *2263, erōtaō* [1]

ASKED [260]

asked, *3306, legō* [153]
asked, *2089, eperōtaō* [35]
asked, *2263, erōtaō* [19]
asked, *646, apokrinomai* [17]
asked for, *160, aiteō* [9]
asked, *160, aiteō* [7]
asked, *4785, pynthanomai* [5]
asked, *5774, phēmi* [3]
asked, *RPE* [2]
asked favor, *160, aiteō* [1]
asked, *161+160, aitēma+aiteō* [1]
asked, *806+160, archō+aiteō* [1]
asked, *1977, exaiteō* [1]
asked about, *2089, eperōtaō* [1]
asked for, *2263, erōtaō* [1]
asked for, *2426, zēteō* [1]
all they asked was, *3667, monon* [1]
asked, *4151, parakaleō* [1]
asked, *5184, syzēteō* [1]

ASKING [16]

asking, *160, aiteō* [3]
asking, *3306, legō* [3]

asking, *2089, eperōtaō* [2]
asking, *RPE* [1]
asking questions, *2089, eperōtaō* [1]
asking, *2263, erōtaō* [1]
asking for, *2426, zēteō* [1]
asking, *2426, zēteō* [1]
asking for help, *4151, parakaleō* [1]
asking, *4785, pynthanomai* [1]
asking for, *5888, phōneō* [1]

ASKS [18]

asks, *160, aiteō* [6]
asks for, *160, aiteō* [4]
asks, *3306, legō* [3]
asks, *2263, erōtaō* [2]
asks for, *2118, epizēteō* [1]
asks for, *2426, zēteō* [1]
asks for, *3306, legō* [1]

ASLEEP [21]

fallen asleep, *3121, koimaō* [7]
asleep, *2761, katheudō* [6]
asleep, *3121, koimaō* [2]
fell asleep, *3121, koimaō* [2]
fell asleep, *934, aphypnoō* [1]
fell asleep, *2761, katheudō* [1]
sound asleep, *2965+608+3836+5678,
    katapherō+apo+ho+hypnos* [1]
fall asleep, *3121, koimaō* [1]

ASSEMBLE [1]

assemble, *5302, synerchomai* [1]

ASSEMBLED [6]

assembled, *5251, synagō* [3]
assembled together, *125, athroizō* [1]
assembled worshipers, *4436+3836+3295,
    plēthos+ho+laos* [1]
assembled, *5302, synerchomai* [1]

ASSEMBLY [9]

assembly, *1711, ekklēsia* [4]
assembly, *4436, plēthos* [3]
assembly of elders, *1172, gerousia* [1]
joyful assembly, *4108, panēgyris* [1]

ASSERTED [1]

asserted, *1462, diischyrizomai* [1]

ASSERTING [1]

asserting that, *5763, phaskō* [1]

ASSIGN [2]

assign, *5502, tithēmi* [2]

ASSIGNED [5]

assigned, *3532, merizō* [2]
assigned, *1443, didōmi* [1]
assigned task, *2240, ergon* [1]
assigned, *5435, tassō* [1]

ASSIST [1]

assist on journey, *4636, propempō* [1]

ASSOCIATE [6]

associate with, *5264, synanameignymi* [3]
associate with, *3140, kollaō* [1]
associate with, *5178, synchraomai* [1]
willing to associate, *5270, synapagō* [1]

ASSOCIATES [2]

associates, *3836+5250, ho+syn* [2]

ASSOS [2]

Assos, *840, Assos* [2]

ASSUMED [1]

assumed, *3787, nomizō* [1]

ASSURANCE [2]

assurance, *4244, parrēsia* [1]
full assurance, *4443, plērophoria* [1]

ASSURE [2]

assure, *2093+237+3306, epi+alētheia+legō* [1]
I assure you, *2627, idou* [1]

ASSURED [2]

assured, *857+1182, asphalōs+ginōskō* [1]
fully assured, *4442, plērophoreō* [1]

ASTONISHED [22]

astonished, *2513, thaumazō* [8]
astonished, *2014, existēmi* [6]
astonished, *1742, ekplēssō* [3]
astonished, *1702, ekthambos* [1]
astonished, *2014+1749, existēmi+ekstasis* [1]
astonished, *2501, thambeō* [1]
astonished, *2502+4321, thambos+periechō* [1]
astonished, *2513+2512, thaumazō+thauma* [1]

ASTONISHMENT [1]

astonishment, *2513, thaumazō* [1]

ASTRAY [12]

going astray, *4414, planaō* [3]
lead astray, *4414, planaō* [2]
led astray, *552, apagō* [1]
led astray, *3496, methistēmi* [1]
leads astray, *4414, planaō* [1]
led astray, *4414, planaō* [1]
go astray, *4997, skandalizō* [1]
led astray, *5270, synapagō* [1]
led astray, *5780, phtheirō* [1]

ASYNCRITUS [1]

Asyncritus, *850, Asynkritos* [1]

AT [579]

at, *1877, en* [133]
at, *AIT* [42]
at, *2093, epi* [39]
at, *1650, eis* [36]
at, *NIG* [23]
at, *4639, pros* [21]
at, *1666, ek* [20]
at that time, *5538, tote* [12]
at once, *2311, eutheōs* [8]
at once, *2317, euthys1* [8]
at, *608, apo* [7]
at, *2848, kata* [6]
at work in, *1919+1877, energeō+en* [5]
reclining at the table, *367, anakeimai* [4]
at, *1328, dia* [4]
looked at, *1838, emblepō* [4]
not at all, *3590+1181, mē+ginomai* [4]
at this, *4036, oun* [4]
at once, *4202, parachrēma* [4]
at, *RPE* [3]
hurled insults at, *1059, blasphēmeō* [3]
at this, *1254, de* [3]
at home, *1897, endēmeō* [3]
amazed at, *2513, thaumazō* [3]
laughed at, *2860, katagelaō* [3]

looked around at, *4315, periblepō* [3]
at one time, *4537, pote* [3]
at, *4574, pro* [3]
fell at feet, *4700, prospiptō* [3]
at the same time, *275, hama* [2]
at the table, *367, anakeimai* [2]
take places at the feast, *369, anaklinō* [2]
reclined at the table, *404, anapiptō* [2]
at a loss, *679, aporeō* [2]
look at, *1063, blepō* [2]
at, *1869, emprosthen* [2]
at work in, *1919, energeō* [2]
at once, *1994, exautēs* [2]
right at, *2093, epi* [2]
at that moment, *2779+2627, kai+idou* [2]
hurled insults at, *3366, loidoreō* [2]
at a distance, *3427, makrothen* [2]
at all, *3914, holōs* [2]
look at, *3972, horaō* [2]
looked at, *3972, horaō* [2]
not at all, *4024+3590, ou+mē* [2]
at all times, *4121, pantote* [2]
at all, *4122, pantōs* [2]
at, *324, ana* [1]
one at a time, *324+3538, ana+meros* [1]
looked carefully at, *355, anatheōreō* [1]
have recline at the table, *369, anaklinō* [1]
at the hands of, *608, apo* [1]
at last, *785, arti* [1]
at once, *785, arti* [1]
looked closely at, *867, atenizō* [1]
looked directly at, *867, atenizō* [1]
looked straight at, *867, atenizō* [1]
stare at, *867, atenizō* [1]
stared at, *867, atenizō* [1]
at once, *899+3836+6052, autos+ho+hōra* [1]
foaming at the mouth, *930, aphrizō* [1]
foams at the mouth, *930, aphrizō* [1]
foams at the mouth, *931, aphros* [1]
looks at, *1063, blepō* [1]
at daybreak, *1181+2465+2002,
    ginomai+hēmera+exerchomai* [1]
at hour, *1181+6052, ginomai+hōra* [1]
get at truth, *1182+855, ginōskō+asphalēs* [1]
or at least, *1623+1254+3590, ei+de+mē* [1]
at work, *1639, eimi* [1]
be at peace, *1644, eirēneuō* [1]
live at peace, *1644, eirēneuō* [1]
at all, *1650+3836+4117, eis+ho+pantelēs* [1]
one at a time, *1651+2848+1651,
    heis+kata+heis* [1]
at, *1656+1650, eiserchomai+eis* [1]
come at, *1656+1650, eiserchomai+eis* [1]
at Berea⁵, *1695, ekei* [1]
sneered at, *1727, ekmyktērizō* [1]
sneering at, *1727, ekmyktērizō* [1]
look at, *1838, emblepō* [1]
looked closely at, *1838, emblepō* [1]
looked directly at, *1838, emblepō* [1]
looked straight at, *1838, emblepō* [1]
spit at, *1870, emptyō* [1]
at the time of, *1877, en* [1]
at work in, *1877+1919, en+energeō* [1]
at, *1877+3836, en+ho* [1]
at work within, *1919+1877, en+energeō* [1]
at work, *1919, energeō* [1]
at, *1967, enōpion* [1]
at the time, *2093, epi* [1]
look at, *2098+2093, epiblepō+epi* [1]
shouting at, *2215, epiphōneō* [1]
at work, *2237, ergazomai* [1]
at this, *2311, eutheōs* [1]
at that moment, *2311, eutheōs* [1]
at this, *2317, euthys1* [1]
at the same time, *2384, ephapax* [1]
stopped at, *2392+2093, ephistēmi+epi* [1]

AVENGE [3]

avenge, *1689, ekdikēsis* [2]
avenge, *1688, ekdikeō* [1]

AVENGED [2]

avenged, *1688, ekdikeō* [1]
avenged, *4472+1689, poieō+ekdikēsis* [1]

AVOID [9]

avoid, *3590, mē* [3]
avoid, *4325, periistēmi* [2]
avoid, *600+608, apechō+apo* [1]
avoid, *608+600, apo+apechō* [1]
avoid, *1413, diatēreō* [1]
avoid, *5097, stellō* [1]

AWAIT [2]

eagerly await for, *587, apekdechomai* [1]
eagerly await, *587, apekdechomai* [1]

AWAKE [3]

awake, *1213, grēgoreō* [1]
stays awake, *1213, grēgoreō* [1]
fully awake, *1340, diagrēgoreō* [1]

AWARD [1]

award, *625, apodidōmi* [1]

AWARE [9]

aware, *1182, ginōskō* [4]
aware of, *1182, ginōskō* [2]
aware of, *201, akouō* [1]
well aware, *2179, epistamai* [1]
aware, *3857, oida* [1]

AWAY [207]

went away, *599, aperchomai* [18]
pass away, *4216, parerchomai* [10]
take away, *149, airō* [7]
send away, *668, apolyō* [7]
fall away, *4997, skandalizō* [7]
taken away, *149, airō* [4]
takes away, *149, airō* [4]
led away, *552, apagō* [4]
away, *608, apo* [4]
sent away, *668, apolyō* [4]
took away, *149, airō* [3]
go away, *599, aperchomai* [3]
sent away, *1990, exapostellō* [3]
away, *2032, exō* [3]
far away, *3426, makran* [3]
away with, *149, airō* [2]
pull away, *149, airō* [2]
passed away, *599, aperchomai* [2]
went away on a journey, *623, apodēmeō* [2]
rolled away, *653, apokyliō* [2]
turn away from, *695, apostrephō* [2]
carried away, *708, apopherō* [2]
take away, *904, aphaireō* [2]
go away, *2002, exerchomai* [2]
fading away, *2934, katargeō* [2]
away, *3552, meta* [2]
going away, *5632, hypagō* [2]
away, *AIT* [1]
away, *RPE* [1]
led away, *72, agō* [1]
do away, *120, athetēsis* [1]
never fade away, *277, amarantinos* [1]
turned away, *288, ameleō* [1]
take away, *429, anapherō* [1]
go away, *432, anachōreō* [1]
lead away, *552, apagō* [1]
away, *582, apeimi1* [1]

away from, *599+608, aperchomai+apo* [1]
goes away, *599, aperchomai* [1]
going away, *599, aperchomai* [1]
gone away, *599, aperchomai* [1]
far away, *608+3427, apo+makrothen* [1]
turn away from, *608+695, apo+apostrephō* [1]
throw away, *610, apoballō* [1]
went away, *623, apodēmeō* [1]
going away, *624, apodēmos* [1]
laid away, *641, apokeimai* [1]
roll away, *653, apokyliō* [1]
took away from, *655+608,
    apolambanō+apo* [1]
wash away, *666, apolouō* [1]
torn away from, *682+608,
    aporphanizō+apo* [1]
draw away, *685, apospaō* [1]
torn away, *685, apospaō* [1]
to turn away from, *686+608, apostasia+apo* [1]
sent away, *690, apostellō* [1]
turn away from, *695+608, apostrephō+apo* [1]
led away, *708, apopherō* [1]
away from, *713+608, apochōreō+apo* [1]
snatches away, *773, harpazō* [1]
suddenly took away, *773, harpazō* [1]
wandered away, *846, astocheō* [1]
take away from, *904, aphaireō* [1]
taken away from, *904, aphaireō* [1]
taken away, *904, aphaireō* [1]
takes away from, *904+608, aphaireō+apo* [1]
taking away, *904, aphaireō* [1]
away from, *923+608, aphistēmi+apo* [1]
fall away, *923, aphistēmi* [1]
take away from, *923+608, aphistēmi+apo* [1]
turn away from, *923+608, aphistēmi+apo* [1]
turns away from, *923+608, aphistēmi+apo* [1]
carried away, *1002, bastazō* [1]
gives away, *1316+4472, dēlos+poieō* [1]
wasting away, *1425, diaphtheirō* [1]
away[s], *1650+3836+2557, eis+ho+thēkē* [1]
away from, *1666+3545, ek+mesos* [1]
away, *1666+3836+3545, ek+ho+mesos* [1]
sent away, *1675, ekballō* [1]
away from, *1685+1666, ekdēmeō+ek* [1]
away from, *1685, ekdēmeō* [1]
away, *1685, ekdēmeō* [1]
away, *1712, ekklinō* [1]
turned away, *1712, ekklinō* [1]
swimming away, *1713, ekkolymbaō* [1]
slipped away, *1728, ekneuō* [1]
sent away, *1734, ekpempō* [1]
fall away, *1738, ekpiptō* [1]
fallen away from, *1738, ekpiptō* [1]
turn away from, *1762, ektrepō* [1]
turned away from, *1762, ektrepō* [1]
wandered away from, *1762, ektrepō* [1]
wipe away from, *1981+1666, exaleiphō+ek* [1]
dragged away, *1999, exelkō* [1]
slipping away from, *2002+1666,
    exerchomai+ek* [1]
right away, *2311, eutheōs* [1]
right away, *2317, euthys1* [1]
do away with, *2934, katargeō* [1]
done away with, *2934, katargeō* [1]
pass away, *2934, katargeō* [1]
taken away, *2934, katargeō* [1]
fade away, *3447, mainō* [1]
taken away, *3572, metatithēmi* [1]
staying away from, *4024+1877+4344,
    ou+en+peripateō* [1]
pass away, *4135, paragō* [1]
passing away, *4135, paragō* [1]
fall away, *4178, parapiptō* [1]
drift away, *4184, pararreō* [1]
carried away, *4195, parapherō* [1]
taken away, *4216, parerchomai* [1]

take away, *4311, periaireō* [1]
taken away, *4311, periaireō* [1]
wanders away, *4414, planaō* [1]
walking away, *4513, poreuomai* [1]
sweep away with the torrent, *4533+4472,
    potamophorētos+poieō* [1]
falls away, *4997, skandalizō* [1]
turn away from the faith, *4997, skandalizō* [1]
keep away, *5097, stellō* [1]
turned away, *5138, strephō* [1]
store away, *5251, synagō* [1]
carried away, *5270, synapagō* [1]
away, *5632, hypagō* [1]
went away, *5715, hypostrephō* [1]
fled away, *5771, pheugō* [1]
run away, *5771, pheugō* [1]
runs away, *5771, pheugō* [1]
staying away a long time, *5988, chronizō* [1]

AWE [6]

awe, *5832, phobos* [3]
awe, *1290, deos* [1]
filled with awe, *3284+5832,
    lambanō+phobos* [1]
filled with awe, *5828, phobeomai* [1]

AWHILE [1]

stay awhile, *4169, paramenō* [1]

AX [2]

ax, *544, axinē* [2]

AZOR [2]

Azor, *110, Azōr* [2]

AZOTUS [1]

Azotus, *111, Azōtos* [1]

BAAL [1]

Baal, *955, Baal* [1]

BABBLER [1]

babbler, *5066, spermologos* [1]

BABBLING [1]

babbling, *1006, battalogeō* [1]

BABIES [3]

babies, *1100, brephos* [2]
newborn babies, *1100, brephos* [1]

BABY [7]

baby, *1100, brephos* [4]
baby, *4086, paidion* [1]
baby to be born, *5503, tiktō* [1]
have baby, *5503, tiktō* [1]

BABYLON [11]

Babylon, *956, Babylōn* [11]

BACK [111]

back, *4099, palin* [7]
pay back, *625, apodidōmi* [6]
back, *AIT* [5]
went back, *599, aperchomai* [5]
back, *1650+3836+3958, eis+ho+opisō* [4]
came back, *2262, erchomai* [3]
come back, *2262, erchomai* [3]
went back, *2262, erchomai* [3]
go back, *4513, poreuomai* [3]
sent back, *402, anapempō* [2]
come back to life, *482, anistēmi* [2]

gave back, *625*, *apodidōmi* [2]
send back, *690*, *apostellō* [2]
came back, *5715*, *hypostrephō* [2]
back, *NIG* [1]
brought back, *343*, *anagō* [1]
brought back, *362*, *anakainizō* [1]
come back, *366*, *anakamptō* [1]
go back, *366*, *anakamptō* [1]
taken back, *377*, *analambanō* [1]
sending back, *402*, *anapempō* [1]
leaning back, *404*, *anapiptō* [1]
leaned back, *404*, *anapiptō* [1]
went back, *418*, *anastrephō* [1]
pay back, *500*, *antapodidōmi* [1]
talk back, *503*, *antapokrinomai* [1]
invite back, *511*, *antikaleō* [1]
talk back, *515*, *antilegō* [1]
expecting to get back, *594*, *apelpizō* [1]
turned back, *599+1650+3836+3958*,
    aperchomai+eis+ho+opisō [1]
have back, *600*, *apechō* [1]
demand back, *608+555*, *apo+apaiteō* [1]
give back, *625*, *apodidōmi* [1]
pays back, *625*, *apodidōmi* [1]
rolled back, *653*, *apokyliō* [1]
has back, *655*, *apolambanō* [1]
sailed back, *676*, *apopleō* [1]
put back, *695*, *apostrephō* [1]
pay back, *702*, *apotinō* [1]
take back, *1443*, *didōmi* [1]
pay back double, *1488+1487*,
    diploō+diplous [1]
went back into, *1656+1650*, *eiserchomai+eis* [1]
ran back, *1661*, *eistrechō* [1]
back, *1666*, *ek* [1]
come back to senses, *1729*, *eknēphō* [1]
back, *1924*, *enthade* [1]
came back, *2002*, *exerchomai* [1]
on way back, *2056*, *epanagō* [1]
bring back to, *2188+2093*, *epistrephō+epi* [1]
bring back, *2188*, *epistrephō* [1]
comes back, *2188*, *epistrephō* [1]
go back, *2188*, *epistrephō* [1]
turned back, *2188*, *epistrephō* [1]
turning back to, *2188+2093*, *epistrephō+epi* [1]
coming back, *2262*, *erchomai* [1]
holding back, *2988*, *katechō* [1]
holds back, *2988*, *katechō* [1]
tossed back and forth by the waves, *3115*,
    klydōnizomai [1]
receive back, *3152*, *komizō* [1]
received back, *3152*, *komizō* [1]
holding back, *3195*, *krateō* [1]
bring back, *3569*, *metapempō* [1]
brought back, *3572*, *metatithēmi* [1]
paid back, *3635*, *misthos* [1]
kept back, *3802*, *nosphizō* [1]
in back, *3957*, *opisthen* [1]
back, *3958*, *opisō* [1]
came back, *4134*, *paraginomai* [1]
going back, *4513*, *poreuomai* [1]
turned back, *5138*, *strephō* [1]
going back, *5632*, *hypagō* [1]
draw back, *5713*, *hypostellō* [1]
shrinks back, *5713*, *hypostellō* [1]
shrink back, *5714*, *hypostolē* [1]
go back, *5715*, *hypostrephō* [1]
went back, *5715*, *hypostrephō* [1]

BACKS [2]

backs, *3822*, *nōtos* [1]
turn their backs, *5715*, *hypostrephō* [1]

BAD [23]

bad, *4505*, *ponēros* [7]
bad, *4911*, *sapros* [7]
bad, *5765*, *phaulos* [3]
bad, *2805*, *kakos* [2]
bad report, *1556*, *dysphēmia* [1]
from bad to worse, *2093+3836+5937*,
    epi+ho+cheirōn [1]
say bad about, *2800*, *kakologeō* [1]
bad odor, *3853*, *ozō* [1]

BADLY [1]

badly, *4498*, *polys* [1]

BAFFLED [1]

baffled, *5177*, *syncheō* [1]

BAG [7]

bag, *4385*, *pēra* [6]
money bag, *1186*, *glōssokomon* [1]

BALAAM [2]

Balaam, *962*, *Balaam* [2]

BALAAM'S [1]

Balaam's, *962*, *Balaam* [1]

BALAK [1]

Balak, *963*, *Balak* [1]

BAND [1]

band of people, *3295*, *laos* [1]

BANDAGED [1]

bandaged, *2866*, *katadeō* [1]

BANDITS [1]

bandits, *3334*, *lēstēs* [1]

BANK [3]

steep bank, *3204*, *krēmnos* [3]

BANKERS [1]

bankers, *5545*, *trapezitēs* [1]

BANQUET [15]

wedding banquet, *1141*, *gamos* [5]
banquet, *1270*, *deipnon* [4]
master of the banquet, *804*, *architriklinos* [2]
banquet, *1141*, *gamos* [2]
banquet, *1531*, *dochē* [2]

BANQUETS [3]

banquets, *1270*, *deipnon* [3]

BAPTISM [20]

baptism, *967*, *baptisma* [16]
baptism receive, *966*, *baptizō* [1]
baptism, *966*, *baptizō* [1]
baptism undergo, *967+966*,
    baptisma+baptizō [1]
baptism, *968*, *baptismos* [1]

BAPTISMS [1]

baptisms, *968*, *baptismos* [1]

BAPTIST [14]

Baptist, *969*, *baptistēs* [12]
Baptist, *966*, *baptizō* [2]

BAPTIZE [12]

baptize, *966*, *baptizō* [12]

BAPTIZED [50]

baptized, *966*, *baptizō* [48]
baptized, *966+5639*, *baptizō+hyparchō* [1]
baptized, *966+967*, *baptizō+baptisma* [1]

BAPTIZING [9]

baptizing, *966*, *baptizō* [8]
baptizing, *967*, *baptisma* [1]

BAR-JESUS [1]

Bar-Jesus, *979*, *Bariēsous* [1]

BARABBAS [12]

Barabbas, *972*, *Barabbas* [11]
Barabbas^s, *4015*, *hostis* [1]

BARAK [1]

Barak, *973*, *Barak* [1]

BARBARIAN [1]

barbarian, *975*, *barbaros* [1]

BARE [3]

laid bare, *2351*, *heuriskō* [1]
laid bare, *5548*, *trachēlizō* [1]
laid bare, *5745*, *phaneros* [1]

BARLEY [3]

barley, *3208*, *krithē* [1]
barley, *3209*, *krithinos* [1]
small barley, *3209*, *krithinos* [1]

BARN [4]

barn, *630*, *apothēkē* [4]

BARNABAS [34]

Barnabas, *982*, *Barnabas* [28]
Barnabas, *RPE* [3]
Paul^s and Barnabas, *899*, *autos* [2]
Barnabas^s and Saul, *899*, *autos* [1]

BARNS [2]

barns, *630*, *apothēkē* [2]

BARRACKS [6]

barracks, *4213*, *parembolē* [6]

BARREN [5]

barren, *5096*, *steira* [3]
barren woman, *5096*, *steira* [1]
barren women, *5096*, *steira* [1]

BARRIER [1]

barrier, *5850*, *phragmos* [1]

BARSABBAS [2]

Barsabbas, *984*, *Barsabbas* [2]

BARTHOLOMEW [4]

Bartholomew, *978*, *Bartholomaios* [4]

BARTIMAEUS [1]

Bartimaeus, *985*, *Bartimaios* [1]

BASED [4]

based on, *2848*, *kata* [3]
based on, *1666*, *ek* [1]

BASIC [3]

basic principles, *5122, stoicheion* [3]

BASIN [1]

basin, *3781, niptēr* [1]

BASIS [10]

basis for a charge, *162, aitia* [3]
on the basis of, *2848, kata* [2]
basis, *AIT* [1]
basis for a charge, *165, aitios* [1]
basis, *165, aitios* [1]
on the basis of, *1328, dia* [1]
on the basis of, *2093, epi* [1]

BASKET [2]

basket, *4914, sarganē* [1]
basket, *5083, spyris* [1]

BASKETFULS [9]

basketfuls, *3186+4441, kophinos+plērēs* [2]
basketfuls, *3186, kophinos* [2]
basketfuls, *5083, spyris* [2]
basketfuls, *3186+4445, kophinos+plērōma* [1]
basketfuls, *5083+4441, spyris+plērēs* [1]
basketfuls, *5083+4445, spyris+plērōma* [1]

BASKETS [2]

baskets, *35, angos* [1]
baskets, *3186, kophinos* [1]

BATCH [4]

batch of dough, *5878, phyrama* [2]
batch, *5878, phyrama* [2]

BATH [1]

had a bath, *3374, louō* [1]

BATTERING [1]

took a battering from the storm, *5928, cheimazō* [1]

BATTLE [7]

battle, *4483, polemos* [6]
battle, *5129, strateuomai* [1]

BAY [1]

bay, *3146, kolpos* [1]

BE [1419]

be, *AIT* [827]
be, *1639, eimi* [262]
be, *NIG* [189]
be, *1181, ginomai* [48]
be, *RPE* [16]
be, *1639+1650, eimi+eis* [6]
be done, *1181, ginomai* [4]
peace be with, *1645, eirēnē* [4]
be, *2400, echō* [3]
pledged to be married, *3650, mnēsteuō* [3]
be, *5639, hyparchō* [3]
to be, *3516, mellō* [2]
to be sure, *3525, men* [2]
cease to be, *4024+1639, ou+eimi* [2]
can be trusted, *4412, pistos* [2]
be, *4472, poieō* [2]
be shepherds of, *4477, poimainō* [2]
cannot be condemned, *183, akatagnōstos* [1]
does not need to be ashamed, *454, anepaischyntos* [1]
census be taken of, *616, apographō* [1]
something to be grasped, *772, harpagmos* [1]

cannot be shaken, *810, asaleutos* [1]
let be, *918, aphiēmi* [1]
jailers to be tortured, *991, basanistēs* [1]
be, *1063, blepō* [1]
must be poured, *1064, blēteos* [1]
for to be sure, *1142, gar* [1]
proved to be, *1181, ginomai* [1]
should be, *1256, dei* [1]
preparations to be made, *1355, diakonia* [1]
seemed to be leaders, *1506, dokeō* [1]
claimed to be, *1571+4472, heautou+poieō* [1]
claims to be, *1571+4472, heautou+poieō* [1]
be diligent, *1639, eimi* [1]
be that as it may, *1639, eimi* [1]
be at peace, *1644, eirēneuō* [1]
then will be able, *1650+3836, eis+ho* [1]
be, *1931, enistēmi* [1]
found to be, *2093, epi* [1]
ought to be done, *2763, kathēkō* [1]
said to be, *2813, kaleō* [1]
be, *3531, menō* [1]
so shall it be, *3721, nai* [1]
be, *4005, hos* [1]
to be, *4022, hoti* [1]
happened to be there, *4193, paratynchanō* [1]
be, *4205, pareimi* [1]
to be*, *4309, peri* [1]
claim to be, *4472+4932, poieō+seautou* [1]
made out to be, *4472, poieō* [1]
make out to be, *4472, poieō* [1]
be shepherd of, *4477, poimainō* [1]
be shepherd, *4477, poimainō* [1]
designated to be, *4641, prosagoreuō* [1]
had to be, *5201, symbainō* [1]
baby to be born, *5503, tiktō* [1]
be*, *5528, tolmaō* [1]
loves to be first, *5812, philoprōteuō* [1]
what seemed to be, *6059, hōsei* [1]

BEACH [3]

beach, *129, aigialos* [2]
sandy beach, *129, aigialos* [1]

BEAR [32]

bear, *5770, pherō* [6]
bear, *4472, poieō* [5]
bear, *1002, bastazō* [3]
bear, *RPE* [2]
bear with, *462, anechomai* [2]
bear, *5841, phoreō* [2]
bear, *759, arkos* [1]
bear with, *1002, bastazō* [1]
bear, *1164, gennaō* [1]
bear, *1181, ginomai* [1]
bear, *1443, didōmi* [1]
bear, *1538, dynamai* [1]
bear, *1877, en* [1]
bear, *2093+2126+2093, epi+epikaleō+epi* [1]
bear in mind, *2451, hēgeomai* [1]
child bear, *2843+3836+3120, karpos+ho+koilia* [1]
bear fruit, *2844, karpophoreō* [1]
bear* fruit, *4048, houtōs* [1]

BEARABLE [5]

more bearable, *445, anektos* [5]

BEARING [6]

bearing fruit, *2844, karpophoreō* [2]
bearing with, *462, anechomai* [1]
bearing, *4472, poieō* [1]
bearing witness, *5210, symmartyreō* [1]
bearing, *5770, pherō* [1]

BEARS [8]

bears, *4472, poieō* [3]
bears children, *1164, gennaō* [1]
bears, *1639+4472, eimi+poieō* [1]
bears children, *5503, tiktō* [1]
bears up under, *5722, hypopherō* [1]
bears, *5770, pherō* [1]

BEAST [40]

beast, *2563, thērion* [35]
the beast*, *899, autos* [4]
donkey beast, *5689, hypozygion* [1]

BEASTS [5]

wild beasts, *2563, thērion* [2]
beasts*, *899, autos* [1]
beasts, *2442, zōon* [1]
fought wild beasts, *2562, thēriomacheō* [1]

BEAT [18]

beat, *1296, derō* [7]
beat, *5597, typtō* [5]
beat, *4406, piptō* [1]
beat, *4435+2202, plēgē+epitithēmi* [1]
beat against, *4684, proskoptō* [1]
beat against, *4700, prospiptō* [1]
beat, *4825, rhapisma* [1]
beat, *5724, hypōpiazō* [1]

BEATEN [5]

beaten with blows, *1296, derō* [2]
beaten, *4084, paideuō* [1]
beaten with rods, *4810, rhabdizō* [1]
beaten, *4810, rhabdizō* [1]

BEATING [5]

beating, *1296, derō* [2]
gave beating, *2710, ischyō* [1]
receive a beating, *3139, kolaphizō* [1]
beating, *5597, typtō* [1]

BEATINGS [1]

beatings, *4435, plēgē* [1]

BEAUTIFUL [8]

beautiful, *6053, hōraios* [4]
beautiful, *2819, kalos* [3]
make beautiful, *3175, kosmeō* [1]

BEAUTIFULLY [1]

beautifully dressed, *3175, kosmeō* [1]

BEAUTY [3]

beauty, *AIT* [1]
beauty, *RPE* [1]
beauty, *2346, euprepeia* [1]

BECAME [64]

became, *1181, ginomai* [26]
became, *AIT* [23]
became, *RPE* [6]
became, *1181+1650, ginomai+eis* [2]
became, *NIG* [1]
became, *806, archō* [1]
became father, *1164, gennaō* [1]
became son*, *1164, gennaō* [1]
became the father of, *1164, gennaō* [1]
became, *1639+1181, eimi+ginomai* [1]
became, *4218, parechō* [1]

BECAUSE [532]

because, *4022, hoti* [205]

began, *1887, enarchomai* [1]
began destroy, *3381, lymainō* [1]
began, *4472, poieō* [1]

BEGGAR [3]

beggar, *4777, ptōchos* [2]
the beggar^s, *899, autos* [1]

BEGGED [20]

begged, *4151, parakaleō* [13]
begged, *1289, deomai* [3]
begged, *2263, erōtaō* [2]
begged, *3306, legō* [1]
begged, *4148, paraiteomai* [1]

BEGGING [6]

begging, *4151, parakaleō* [2]
begging, *2050, epaiteō* [1]
begging, *4639+3836+1797,*
  pros+ho+eleēmosynē [1]
begging, *4644, prosaiteō* [1]
begging, *4645, prosaitēs* [1]

BEGIN [5]

begin, *806, archō* [3]
begin, *AIT* [1]
about to begin, *2216, epiphōskō* [1]

BEGINNING [45]

beginning, *794, archē* [31]
beginning, *806, archō* [7]
beginning of time, *5989+173,*
  chronos+aiōnios [2]
from the beginning, *540, anōthen* [1]
beginning, *1887, enarchomai* [1]
beginning, *2856, katabolē* [1]
earlier made a beginning, *4599,*
  proenarchomai [1]
beginning, *4755, prōtos* [1]

BEGINS [3]

begins, *806, archō* [2]
begins, *4754, prōton* [1]

BEGUN [1]

begun, *AIT* [1]

BEHALF [11]

on behalf, *5642, hyper* [4]
on behalf, *1967, enōpion* [3]
on behalf, *4309, peri* [2]
on behalf of, *5642, hyper* [2]

BEHAVE [1]

behave, *4344, peripateō* [1]

BEHAVIOR [3]

behavior, *419, anastrophē* [2]
behavior, *2240, ergon* [1]

BEHEADED [5]

beheaded, *642, apokephalizō* [3]
beheaded, *4284, pelekizō* [1]
had beheaded, *4287+642,*
  pempō+apokephalizō [1]

BEHIND [18]

behind, *3958, opisō* [5]
behind, *3957, opisthen* [4]
behind, *AIT* [1]
behind, *199, akoloutheō* [1]
following behind, *199, akoloutheō* [1]

---

leaving behind, *918, aphiēmi* [1]
trail behind, *2051, epakoloutheō* [1]
leaving behind, *2901, kataleipō* [1]
put behind, *2934, katargeō* [1]
behind, *3552, meta* [1]
stayed behind, *5702, hypomenō* [1]

BEHOLD [4]

behold, *2627, idou* [4]

BEING [94]

being, *AIT* [64]
being, *NIG* [11]
being, *476, anthrōpos* [2]
being, *1181, ginomai* [2]
being, *1639, eimi* [2]
have being, *1639, eimi* [2]
from being polluted, *834, aspilos* [1]
divine being, *2521, theios* [1]
being cursed, *2932, katara* [1]
get into the habit of being, *3443, manthanō* [1]
being like-minded, *3836+899+5858,*
  ho+autos+phroneō [1]
sets heart on being, *3977, oregō* [1]
being, *4242, parousia* [1]
being, *5639, hyparchō* [1]
being, *5712, hypostasis* [1]
being, *6034, psychē* [1]
human being, *6034+476, psychē+anthrōpos* [1]

BEINGS [3]

celestial beings, *1518, doxa* [2]
such beings, *899, autos* [1]

BELIAL [1]

Belial, *1016, Beliar* [1]

BELIEF [1]

belief, *4411, pistis* [1]

BELIEVE [139]

believe, *4409, pisteuō* [113]
not believe, *601, apisteō* [6]
believe, *4412, pistos* [5]
believe, *4411, pistis* [4]
refused to believe, *578, apeitheō* [2]
believe, *RPE* [1]
do not believe, *578, apeitheō* [1]
not believe, *603, apistos* [1]
believe, *1639+4409, eimi+pisteuō* [1]
believe, *1666+4411, ek+pistis* [1]
believe in, *4409, pisteuō* [1]
believe, *4409+1877, pisteuō+en* [1]
come to believe, *4409, pisteuō* [1]
believe about, *4411+2400, pistis+echō* [1]

BELIEVED [59]

believed, *4409, pisteuō* [58]
believed on, *4409, pisteuō* [1]

BELIEVER [6]

believer, *4412, pistos* [4]
not a believer, *603, apistos* [2]

BELIEVERS [21]

believers, *4409, pisteuō* [8]
believers, *81, adelphos* [3]
believers, *4412, pistos* [3]
believers, *AIT* [2]
believers, *41, hagios* [1]
brotherhood of believers, *82, adelphotēs* [1]
believers^s, *1666+899, ek+autos* [1]

---

believers, *2400+3836+4411,*
  echō+ho+pistis [1]
believers, *3836+4411, ho+pistis* [1]

BELIEVES [23]

believes, *4409, pisteuō* [23]

BELIEVING [7]

believing, *4409, pisteuō* [2]
[believing] woman, *80, adelphē* [1]
believing wife, *80+1222, adelphē+gynē* [1]
believing husband, *81, adelphos* [1]
believing man, *81, adelphos* [1]
believing, *4411, pistis* [1]
believing, *4412, pistos* [1]

BELLY [1]

belly, *3120, koilia* [1]

BELONG [32]

belong, *AIT* [9]
belong to, *1639, eimi* [5]
belong to, *1666+1639, ek+eimi* [4]
belong to, *1666, ek* [4]
belong to, *2027, exousiazō* [2]
belong, *1181, ginomai* [1]
belong, *1256, dei* [1]
belong to, *1639+1666, eimi+ek* [1]
free and belong to no man, *1801+1666+4246,*
  eleutheros+ek+pas [1]
belong to, *1877, en* [1]
belong, *2126+2093, epikaleō+epi* [1]
belong, *3531, menō* [1]
belong to family, *3858, oikeios* [1]

BELONGED [15]

belonged, *AIT* [3]
belonged to, *1666, ek* [3]
belonged to, *608, apo* [2]
belonged to, *1639+1666, eimi+ek* [2]
belonged to, *1666+1639, ek+eimi* [2]
belonged to, *1639, eimi* [1]
belonged, *2409, zaō* [1]
belonged to, *3576, metechō* [1]

BELONGING [3]

belonging, *AIT* [1]
belonging to, *1639, eimi* [1]
belonging to God, *1650+4348,*
  eis+peripoiēsis [1]

BELONGS [16]

belongs, *AIT* [3]
belongs to, *1639, eimi* [3]
belongs to, *2400, echō* [3]
belongs to, *1666+1639, ek+eimi* [2]
belongs to, *1639+1666, eimi+ek* [1]
belongs, *1639, eimi* [1]
belongs, *2625, idios* [1]
belongs, *3531, menō* [1]
belongs to you, *5050, sos* [1]

BELOW [3]

below, *3004, katō* [3]

BELT [5]

belt, *2438, zōnē* [4]
belt, *4019, osphys* [1]

BELTS [2]

belts, *2438, zōnē* [2]

BENCHES [2]

benches, *2756, kathedra* [2]

BENDING [1]

bending over, *4160, parakyptō* [1]

BENEFACTORS [1]

Benefactors, *2309, euergetēs* [1]

BENEFICIAL [2]

beneficial, *5237, sympherō* [2]

BENEFIT [10]

for benefit, *1328, dia* [3]
benefit, *2843, karpos* [2]
benefit, *514, antilambanō* [1]
for the benefit of, *1328, dia* [1]
benefit, *1443+5921, didōmi+charis* [1]
benefit, *3949, oninēmi* [1]
benefit, *5921+2400, charis+echō* [1]

BENEFITS [1]

reaped the benefits of, *1650+1656,
  eis+eiserchomai* [1]

BENJAMIN [4]

Benjamin, *1021, Beniamin* [4]

BENT [7]

bent, *2392, ephistēmi* [1]
bent on, *2671, hina* [1]
bent, *3252, kyptō* [1]
bent over to look, *4160, parakyptō* [1]
bent over, *4160, parakyptō* [1]
bent, *5159, synkamptō* [1]
bent over, *5174, synkyptō* [1]

BEOR [1]

Beor, *1027, Beōr* [1]

BEREA [4]

Berea, *1023, Beroia* [2]
from Berea, *1024, Beroiaios* [1]
at Berea⁵, *1695, ekei* [1]

BEREANS [1]

the Bereans⁵, *4047, houtos* [1]

BEREKIAH [1]

Berekiah, *974, Barachias* [1]

BERNICE [3]

Bernice, *1022, Bernikē* [3]

BERYL [1]

beryl, *1039, bēryllos* [1]

BESIDE [10]

beside, *4123, para* [3]
stood beside, *2392, ephistēmi* [2]
stood beside, *4225, paristēmi* [2]
beside, *2093, epi* [1]
walked beside, *4135+4123, paragō+para* [1]
beside, *4639, pros* [1]

BESIDES [6]

besides, *6006, chōris* [2]
besides, *275, hama* [1]
besides, *1877, en* [1]
besides, *2285, eti* [1]

besides everything else, *6006+3836+4211,
  chōris+ho+parektos* [1]

BESIEGE [1]

besiege with questions, *694+4309+4498,
  apostomatizō+peri+polys* [1]

BEST [10]

do best, *5079, spoudazō* [4]
best, *AIT* [1]
best, *1422, diapherō* [1]
thought it best, *2305, eudokeō* [1]
best, *2819, kalos* [1]
best, *4755, prōtos* [1]
best, *5237, sympherō* [1]

BETHANY [12]

Bethany, *1029, Bēthania* [12]

BETHESDA [1]

Bethesda, *1031, Bēthesda* [1]

BETHLEHEM [8]

Bethlehem, *1033, Bēthleem* [8]

BETHPHAGE [3]

Bethphage, *1036, Bēthphagē* [3]

BETHSAIDA [7]

Bethsaida, *1034, Bēthsaida* [7]

BETRAY [17]

betray, *4140, paradidōmi* [16]
betray, *1639+4140, eimi+paradidōmi* [1]

BETRAYED [15]

betrayed, *4140, paradidōmi* [14]
betrayed, *4595+1181, prodotēs+ginomai* [1]

BETRAYER [4]

betrayer, *4140, paradidōmi* [4]

BETRAYING [1]

betraying, *4140, paradidōmi* [1]

BETRAYS [3]

betrays, *4140, paradidōmi* [3]

BETTER [43]

better, *3202, kreittōn* [14]
better, *2819, kalos* [9]
better, *5237, sympherō* [5]
better, *NIG* [2]
better, *19, agathos* [1]
know better, *2106, epignōsis* [1]
better, *3153, kompsoteron* [1]
better, *3387, lysiteleō* [1]
better, *3437+3202, mallon+kreittōn* [1]
better, *4355, perisseuō* [1]
better, *4498, polys* [1]
better, *4604, proechō* [1]
get better, *5392, sōzō* [1]
better than, *5642, hyper* [1]
better than, *5660, hyperechō* [1]
better, *5982, chrēstos* [1]
getting better, *6067, ōpheleō* [1]

BETWEEN [21]

between, *3568, metaxy* [6]
between, *3552, meta* [3]
between, *AIT* [1]

between, *324+3545, ana+mesos* [1]
divided between, *1349, diaireō* [1]
distinguishing between, *1360, diakrisis* [1]
constant friction between, *1384, diaparatribē* [1]
between, *1666, ek* [1]
between, *1967, enōpion* [1]
between, *2093, epi* [1]
mediator between, *3542, mesitēs* [1]
between, *3545, mesos* [1]
between, *4639, pros* [1]
between, *5445, te* [1]

BEWARE [1]

beware, *4668, prosechō* [1]

BEWILDERED [1]

bewildered, *1749, ekstasis* [1]

BEWILDERMENT [1]

bewilderment, *5177, syncheō* [1]

BEWITCHED [1]

bewitched, *1001, baskainō* [1]

BEYOND [17]

beyond, *5642, hyper* [4]
beyond, *AIT* [1]
beyond limits, *296, ametros* [1]
beyond tracing out, *453, anexichniastos* [1]
beyond, *608, apo* [1]
beyond, *1650, eis* [1]
beyond, *1760, ektos* [1]
beyond, *2084, epekeina* [1]
beyond that, *3370, loipos* [1]
beyond all question, *3935,
  homologoumenōs* [1]
beyond, *4123, para* [1]
beyond, *4356, perissos* [1]
beyond, *4498+4440, polys+plēn* [1]
regions beyond, *5654, hyperekeina* [1]

BIG [3]

big, *3489, megas* [2]
big, *4498, polys* [1]

BIGGER [2]

bigger, *3505, meizōn* [1]
bigger, *4498, polys* [1]

BILL [2]

bill, *1207, gramma* [2]

BILLOWS [1]

billows, *874, atmis* [1]

BIND [4]

bind, *1313, deō* [4]

BINDING [1]

binding, *1010, bebaios* [1]

BINDS [1]

binds together, *1639+5278,
  eimi+syndesmos* [1]

BIRD [1]

bird, *3997, orneon* [1]

BIRDS [17]

birds, *4374, peteinon* [14]
birds, *3997, orneon* [2]

BIRTH [33]

birds, *4764, ptēnos* [1]

birth, *3120+3613, koilia+mētēr* [4]
gave birth to, *5503, tiktō* [3]
give birth to, *5503, tiktō* [3]
birth, *1161, genesis* [2]
gives birth to, *1164, gennaō* [2]
birth pains, *6047, ōdin* [2]
birth, *NIG* [1]
given new birth, *335, anagennaō* [1]
give birth, *652, apokyeō* [1]
gives birth to, *652, apokyeō* [1]
gave birth, *1002, bastazō* [1]
birth, *1162, genetē* [1]
birth, *1164, gennaō* [1]
gave birth to, *1164, gennaō* [1]
noble birth, *2302, eugenēs* [1]
of noble birth, *2302, eugenēs* [1]
birth, *4922, sarx* [1]
give birth, *5503, tiktō* [1]
given birth to, *5503, tiktō* [1]
gives birth to, *5503, tiktō* [1]
giving birth to a child, *5503, tiktō* [1]
birth, *5882, physis* [1]
give birth, *6048+5503, ōdinō+tiktō* [1]

BIRTHDAY [2]

birthday, *1160, genesia* [2]

BITE [1]

bite, *1099, brachys* [1]

BITHYNIA [2]

Bithynia, *1049, Bithynia* [2]

BITING [1]

biting, *1231, daknō* [1]

BITS [1]

bits, *5903, chalinos* [1]

BITTER [4]

bitter, *952, apsinthos* [1]
bitter, *4393, pikrainō* [1]
bitter, *4394, pikria* [1]
bitter, *4395, pikros* [1]

BITTERLY [2]

bitterly, *4396, pikrōs* [2]

BITTERNESS [3]

bitterness, *4394, pikria* [2]
bitterness, *5958+4394, cholē+pikria* [1]

BLACK [3]

black, *3506, melas* [3]

BLACKEST [2]

blackest, *2432, zophos* [2]

BLAME [3]

without blame, *455, anepilēmptos* [1]
no open to blame, *455, anepilēmptos* [1]
blame, *3522, memphomai* [1]

BLAMELESS [13]

blameless, *320, amōmos* [3]
blameless, *441, anenklētos* [3]
blameless, *289, amemptos* [2]
blameless, *290, amemptōs* [2]

blameless, *179, akakos* [1]
blameless, *318, amōmētos* [1]
blameless, *718, aproskopos* [1]

BLAMELESSLY [1]

blamelessly, *289, amemptos* [1]

BLASPHEME [4]

blaspheme, *1059, blasphēmeō* [3]
blaspheme, *1060, blasphēmia* [1]

BLASPHEMED [2]

blasphemed, *1059, blasphēmeō* [2]

BLASPHEMER [1]

blasphemer, *1061, blasphēmos* [1]

BLASPHEMES [2]

blasphemes, *1059, blasphēmeō* [2]

BLASPHEMIES [2]

blasphemies, *1060+1059,
    blasphēmia+blasphēmeō* [1]
blasphemies, *1060, blasphēmia* [1]

BLASPHEMING [2]

blaspheming, *1059, blasphēmeō* [2]

BLASPHEMOUS [2]

blasphemous, *1060, blasphēmia* [2]

BLASPHEMY [9]

blasphemy, *1060, blasphēmia* [5]
blasphemy, *1059, blasphēmeō* [1]
spoken blasphemy, *1059, blasphēmeō* [1]
blasphemy against, *1060, blasphēmia* [1]
blasphemy, *1061, blasphēmos* [1]

BLAST [1]

blast, *2491, ēchos1* [1]

BLASTS [1]

blasts, *5889, phōnē* [1]

BLASTUS [1]

Blastus, *1058, Blastos* [1]

BLAZING [7]

blazing, *5825, phlox* [4]
blazing, *2794, kaiō* [1]
blazing around, *4334, perilampō* [1]
blazing, *4786+2794, pyr+kaiō* [1]

BLEACH [1]

bleach, *3326, leukainō* [1]

BLEEDING [6]

subject to bleeding, *1877+4868+135,
    en+rhysis+haima* [2]
subject to bleeding, *137, haimorroeō* [1]
bleeding, *4380+3836+135,
    pēgē+ho+haima* [1]
bleeding, *4868+3836+135,
    rhysis+ho+haima* [1]
bleeding, *5547, traumatizō* [1]

BLEMISH [3]

without blemish, *320, amōmos* [2]
blemish[s], *3836+5525, ho+toioutos* [1]

BLEMISHES [2]

blemishes, *3700, mōmos* [1]
blemishes, *5069, spilas* [1]

BLESS [6]

bless, *2328, eulogeō* [5]
bless, *2328+2328, eulogeō+eulogeō* [1]

BLESSED [71]

blessed, *3421, makarios* [44]
blessed, *2328, eulogeō* [19]
blessed, *RPE* [2]
blessed through, *1922+1877, eneulogeō+en* [1]
blessed, *1922, eneulogeō* [1]
blessed, *2329, eulogētos* [1]
blessed, *2986, kateulogeō* [1]
call blessed, *3420, makarizō* [1]
consider blessed, *3420, makarizō* [1]

BLESSEDNESS [2]

blessedness, *3422, makarismos* [2]

BLESSES [1]

richly blesses, *4456, plouteō* [1]

BLESSING [11]

blessing, *2330, eulogia* [6]
blessing, *2328, eulogeō* [2]
the blessing[s], *899, autos* [1]
blessing of power, *2434, charis* [1]
blessing, *5921, charis* [1]

BLESSINGS [4]

blessings, *AIT* [3]
holy blessings promised, *4008, hosios* [1]

BLEW [2]

blew, *4463, pneō* [2]

BLIND [51]

blind, *5603, typhlos* [49]
blind, *3590+1063, mē+blepō* [2]

BLINDED [4]

blinded, *5604, typhloō* [2]
blinded, *4024+1838, ou+emblepō* [1]
blinded, *5604+3836+4057,
    typhloō+ho+ophthalmos* [1]

BLINDFOLDED [2]

blindfolded, *4328+3836+4725,
    perikalyptō+ho+prosōpon* [1]
blindfolded, *4328, perikalyptō* [1]

BLOCK [6]

stumbling block, *4998, skandalon* [3]
stumbling block, *4682, proskomma* [2]
stumbling block, *4683, proskopē* [1]

BLOOD [92]

blood, *135, haima* [86]
shedding blood, *135, haima* [2]
blood, *RPE* [1]
shedding of blood, *136, haimatekchysia* [1]
blood money, *5507+135, timē+haima* [1]
blood red, *6055+135, hōs+haima* [1]

BLOSSOM [1]

blossom, *470, anthos* [1]

BLOT [1]

blot out from, *1981+1666, exaleiphō+ek* [1]

BLOTS [1]

blots, *5070, spilos* [1]

BLOW [1]

gentle blow, *5710, hypopneō* [1]

BLOWING [3]

blowing, *4463, pneō* [1]
from blowing, *4463, pneō* [1]
blowing, *5770, pherō* [1]

BLOWN [3]

blown by the wind, *448, anemizō* [1]
blown along, *4195, parapherō* [1]
blown here and there, *4367, peripherō* [1]

BLOWS [4]

beaten with blows, *1296, derō* [2]
blows, *4463, pneō* [2]

BLUE [1]

dark blue, *5610, hyakinthinos* [1]

BOANERGES [1]

Boanerges, *1065, Boanērges* [1]

BOARD [3]

put on board, *1837+1650+899,*
    embibazō+eis+autos [1]
on board, *1877+3836+4450, en+ho+ploion* [1]
went on board, *2094, epibainō* [1]

BOARDED [1]

boarded, *2094, epibainō* [1]

BOAST [34]

boast, *3016, kauchaomai* [17]
boast, *3017, kauchēma* [4]
boast, *RPE* [3]
boast, *1595, enkauchaomai* [1]
boast over, *2878, katakauchaomai* [1]
boast, *2878, katakauchaomai* [1]
boast about, *3016, kauchaomai* [1]
boast of, *3016, kauchaomai* [1]
boast, *3017+1639, kauchēma+eimi* [1]
something to boast about, *3017, kauchēma* [1]
boast, *3018, kauchēsis* [1]
boast about, *3281+5665, laleō+hyperonkos* [1]
boast, *4371, perpereuomai* [1]

BOASTED [2]

boasted, *3016, kauchaomai* [1]
boasted, *3306, legō* [1]

BOASTFUL [3]

boastful, *225, alazōn* [2]
boastful, *5665, hyperonkos* [1]

BOASTING [16]

boasting, *3016, kauchaomai* [5]
boasting, *3018, kauchēsis* [4]
boasting, *RPE* [2]
boasting, *3017, kauchēma* [2]
boasting, *224, alazoneia* [1]
boasting of, *3016, kauchaomai* [1]
boasting about, *3018, kauchēsis* [1]

BOASTS [4]

boasts, *3016, kauchaomai* [2]
makes boasts, *902, aucheō* [1]
boasts, *3306, legō* [1]

BOAT [43]

boat, *4450, ploion* [39]
boat, *4449, ploiarion* [2]
boat, *RPE* [1]
small boat, *4449, ploiarion* [1]

BOATS [7]

boats, *4450, ploion* [5]
boats, *4449, ploiarion* [2]

BOAZ [3]

Boaz, *1067, Boes* [2]
Boaz, *1078, Boos* [1]

BODIES [28]

bodies, *5393, sōma* [14]
bodies, *RPE* [3]
bodies, *1539, dynamis* [3]
bodies, *AIT* [2]
bodies, *4773, ptōma* [2]
bodies, *3265, kōlon* [1]
bodies, *3517, melos* [1]
bodies, *4922, sarx* [1]
bodies, *5131, stratia* [1]

BODILY [2]

bodily, *5394, sōmatikos* [1]
in bodily form, *5395, sōmatikōs* [1]

BODY [168]

body, *5393, sōma* [115]
body, *4922, sarx* [20]
body, *AIT* [5]
body, *RPE* [5]
parts of body, *3517, melos* [3]
body, *4773, ptōma* [3]
the body's, *899, autos* [2]
part of body, *3517, melos* [2]
one body, *253, allēlōn* [1]
Jesus' body, *899, autos* [1]
out of his body, *1650+3836+909+1744,*
    eis+ho+aphedrōn+ekporeuomai [1]
out of the body, *1650+909+1675,*
    eis+aphedrōn+ekballō [1]
members of body, *3517, melos* [1]
part of the body, *3517, melos* [1]
parts of the body, *3517, melos* [1]
body decayed, *3972+1426,*
    horaō+diaphthora [1]
body, *4019, osphys* [1]
body of elders, *4564, presbyterion* [1]
body, *5007, skeuos* [1]
members together of one body, *5362,*
    syssōmos [1]
dead body, *5393, sōma* [1]

BOLD [5]

bold, *2509, tharreō* [2]
bold, *4244+5968, parrēsia+chraomai* [1]
bold, *4498+4244+2400,*
    polys+parrēsia+echō [1]
bold, *5532, tolmētēs* [1]

BOLDLY [10]

speaking boldly, *4245, parrēsiazomai* [2]
boldly, *703, apotolmaō* [1]
boldly, *3552+4246+4244,*
    meta+pas+parrēsia [1]

boldly, *3552+4244, meta+parrēsia* [1]
boldly, *4245, parrēsiazomai* [1]
speak boldly, *4245, parrēsiazomai* [1]
spoke boldly, *4245, parrēsiazomai* [1]
boldly, *5528, tolmaō* [1]
quite boldly, *5529, tolmēros* [1]

BOLDNESS [2]

boldness, *357, anaideia* [1]
boldness, *4244, parrēsia* [1]

BOND [2]

post bond, *2653, hikanos* [1]
bond, *5278, syndesmos* [1]

BONDAGE [1]

bondage, *1525, douleia* [1]

BONES [4]

bones, *4014, osteon* [4]

BOOK [24]

book, *1046, biblion* [13]
book, *1047, biblos* [8]
book, *RPE* [1]
book of Isaiah, *2480, Ēsaias* [1]
book, *3364, logos* [1]

BOOKS [3]

books, *1046, biblion* [3]

BOOTH [3]

tax collector's booth, *5468, telōnion* [2]
tax booth, *5468, telōnion* [1]

BORDER [2]

border, *AIT* [2]

BORE [6]

bore, *RPE* [1]
bore, *429, anapherō* [1]
bore, *1164, gennaō* [1]
bore fruit, *2844, karpophoreō* [1]
bore testimony, *3459, martys* [1]
bore, *5770, pherō* [1]

BORN [53]

born, *1164, gennaō* [37]
born, *RPE* [3]
born, *1181, ginomai* [3]
born, *1168, gennētos* [2]
born, *5503, tiktō* [2]
born, *AIT* [1]
born again, *335, anagennaō* [1]
born, *1169, genos* [1]
abnormally born, *1765, ektrōma* [1]
baby to be born, *5503, tiktō* [1]
born to, *5503, tiktō* [1]

BORNE [2]

borne, *1002, bastazō* [1]
borne, *5841, phoreō* [1]

BORROW [1]

borrow, *1247, danizō* [1]

BOTH [59]

both, *2779, kai* [14]
both, *5445, te* [13]
both, *NIG* [11]
both, *317, amphoteroi* [11]

both, *AIT* [1]
both, *RPE* [1]
both, *608, apo* [1]
both of them, *1877+4005, en+hos* [1]
on both sides, *2277+2779+3957,*
esōthen+kai+opisthen [1]
and both, *2779, kai* [1]
both, *2779+4047, kai+houtos* [1]
both, *2848, kata* [1]
both, *3836+1545+3938, ho+dyo+homou* [1]
both of you, *5148+2779+899, sy+kai+autos* [1]

BOTHER [3]

bother, *5035, skyllō* [2]
bother, *3160+4218, kopos+parechō* [1]

BOTHERING [3]

bothering, *3160+4218, kopos+parechō* [2]
bothering, *4218+3160, parechō+kopos* [1]

BOTTOM [3]

bottom, *3004, katō* [2]
to bottom, *1328+3910, dia+holos* [1]

BOUGHT [12]

bought, *60, agorazō* [9]
bought, *3227, ktaomai* [1]
bought, *4347, peripoieō* [1]
bought, *6050, ōneomai* [1]

BOULDER [1]

boulder, *3345, lithos* [1]

BOUND [26]

bound, *1313, deō* [16]
bound by his oath, *4053, opheilō* [2]
bound, *AIT* [1]
bound with an oath, *354, anathematizō* [1]
bound to come, *450+3590+2262,*
anendektos+mē+erchomai [1]
bound, *1301, desmos* [1]
bound, *1530, douloō* [1]
bound, *2988, katechō* [1]
bound, *4329, perikeimai* [1]
bound over, *5168, synkleiō* [1]

BOUNDS [1]

knows no bounds, *5668, hyperperisseuō* [1]

BOW [6]

bow, *2828, kamptō* [2]
bow, *4749, prōra* [2]
bow down, *4406, piptō* [1]
bow, *5534, toxon* [1]

BOWED [4]

bowed, *2828, kamptō* [1]
bowed down, *3111, klinō* [1]
bowed, *3111, klinō* [1]
bowed down, *4406, piptō* [1]

BOWL [12]

bowl, *5786, phialē* [7]
bowl, *3654, modios* [3]
bowl, *5581, tryblion* [2]

BOWLS [5]

bowls, *5786, phialē* [5]

BOY [12]

the boy[g], *899, autos* [4]
boy, *4090, pais* [4]

boy, *3744, neotēs* [2]
boy, *RPE* [1]
boy, *4081, paidarion* [1]

BOY'S [2]

boy's[s], *899, autos* [1]
boy's, *4086, paidion* [1]

BOYS [1]

boys, *4090, pais* [1]

BRAG [3]

brag, *1877+3836+224, en+ho+alazoneia* [1]
brag about, *3016, kauchaomai* [1]
brag, *3016, kauchaomai* [1]

BRAIDED [2]

braided, *1862, emplokē* [1]
braided hair, *4427, plegma* [1]

BRANCH [4]

branch, *3097, klēma* [3]
branch, *RPE* [1]

BRANCHES [16]

branches, *3080, klados* [9]
branches, *RPE* [2]
branches, *961, baion* [1]
branches, *3097, klēma* [1]
branches, *5115, stibas* [1]
branches of hyssop, *5727, hyssōpos* [1]
palm branches, *5836, phoinix1* [1]

BRAWLING [1]

brawling, *3199, kraugē* [1]

BREAD [83]

bread, *788, artos* [64]
bread, *RPE* [4]
Feast of Unleavened Bread, *109, azymos* [4]
loaves of bread, *788, artos* [3]
Unleavened Bread, *109, azymos* [2]
bread, *6040, psōmion* [2]
piece of bread, *6040, psōmion* [2]
bread without yeast, *109, azymos* [1]
Feast of Unleavened Bread, *2465+109,*
hēmera+azymos [1]

BREADTH [1]

breadth, *4424, platos* [1]

BREAK [13]

break in, *1482, dioryssō* [2]
break, *2862, katagnymi* [2]
break, *3089, klaō* [2]
break, *4124, parabainō* [2]
break, *1396, diarrēgnymi* [1]
break oath, *2155, epiorkeō* [1]
break, *3395, lyō* [1]
break, *4127+1639, parabatēs+eimi* [1]
break forth, *4838, rhēgnymi* [1]

BREAKFAST [1]

breakfast, *753, aristaō* [1]

BREAKING [6]

breaking, *RPE* [1]
breaking, *3082, klasis* [1]
breaking, *3395, lyō* [1]
breaking a command, *4126, parabasis* [1]
breaking, *4126, parabasis* [1]
breaking, *5316, synthryptō* [1]

BREAKS [2]

breaks law, *490+4472, anomia+poieō* [1]
breaks, *3395, lyō* [1]

BREAST [1]

breast, *5111, stēthos* [1]

BREASTPLATE [2]

breastplate, *2606, thōrax* [2]

BREASTPLATES [3]

breastplates, *2606, thōrax* [3]

BREASTS [2]

breasts, *3466, mastos* [1]
breasts, *5111, stēthos* [1]

BREATH [5]

breath, *4460, pneuma* [3]
breath, *AIT* [1]
breath, *4466, pnoē* [1]

BREATHED [3]

breathed last, *1743, ekpneō* [2]
breathed on, *1874, emphysaō* [1]

BREATHING [1]

breathing out, *1863, empneō* [1]

BRIBE [1]

bribe, *5975, chrēma* [1]

BRIDE [6]

bride, *3811, nymphē* [5]
bride, *1222, gynē* [1]

BRIDEGROOM [14]

bridegroom, *3812, nymphios* [11]
bridegroom, *3813, nymphōn* [3]

BRIDEGROOM'S [1]

bridegroom's, *3812, nymphios* [1]

BRIDLES [1]

bridles, *5903, chalinos* [1]

BRIEFLY [3]

briefly, *1328+3900, dia+oligos* [1]
briefly, *1877+3900, en+oligos* [1]
briefly, *5339, syntomōs* [1]

BRIERS [1]

briers, *1003, batos1* [1]

BRIGHT [5]

bright, *3287, lampros* [2]
bright, *2653, hikanos* [1]
bright, *3328, leukos* [1]
bright, *5893, phōteinos* [1]

BRIGHTER [1]

brighter, *5642+3288, hyper+lamprotēs* [1]

BRILLIANCE [3]

brilliance, *1518, doxa* [1]
brilliance, *1539, dynamis* [1]
brilliance, *5891, phōstēr* [1]

BRIM [1]

the brim, *539, anō* [1]

BRING [88]

bring, *5770, pherō* [12]
bring, *72, agō* [10]
bring, *965, ballō* [3]
bring glory to, *1519, doxazō* [3]
bring, *3284, lambanō* [3]
to bring, *1650, eis* [2]
bring, *2864, katagō* [2]
bring, *4472, poieō* [2]
bring, *4642, prosagō* [2]
bring, *NIG* [1]
bring, *RPE* [1]
bring out for trial, *343, anagō* [1]
bring up, *343, anagō* [1]
bring together under one head, *368,*
   anakephalaioō [1]
bring to end, *660, apollymi* [1]
bring into disrepute, *1059, blasphēmeō* [1]
bring about, *1259, deiknymi* [1]
bring to light, *1317, dēloō* [1]
bring about, *1328, dia* [1]
bring, *1443, didōmi* [1]
bring any charge, *1592, enkaleō* [1]
bring, *1639+1650, eimi+eis* [1]
bring into, *1650, eis* [1]
bring to, *1650, eis* [1]
in order to bring, *1650, eis* [1]
intended to bring, *1650, eis* [1]
bring in, *1652, eisagō* [1]
agent to bring punishment, *1690, ekdikos* [1]
bring up, *1763, ektrephō* [1]
bring, *1766, ekpherō* [1]
want to bring up, *2118, epizēteō* [1]
bring back to, *2188+2093, epistrephō+epi* [1]
bring back, *2188, epistrephō* [1]
bring to completion, *2200, epiteleō* [1]
bring against, *2214, epipherō* [1]
bring about, *2237, ergazomai* [1]
bring in, *2262, erchomai* [1]
bring good news, *2294, euangelizō* [1]
bring news, *2294, euangelizō* [1]
bring about, *2351, heuriskō* [1]
bring, *2400, echō* [1]
bring down, *2864, katagō* [1]
bring charges, *2989, katēgoreō* [1]
charge to bring against, *2989, katēgoreō* [1]
bring a message, *3281+4839, laleō+rhēma* [1]
bring, *3281, laleō* [1]
bring back, *3569, metapempō* [1]
bring near, *4225, paristēmi* [1]
bring to fulfillment, *4444, plēroō* [1]
bring about, *4472, poieō* [1]
bring out, *4575, proagō* [1]
bring to trial, *4575, proagō* [1]
bring, *4639, pros* [1]
bring, *4712, prospherō* [1]
bring together, *5251, synagō* [1]
bring safely, *5392, sōzō* [1]
bring under control, *5718, hypotassō* [1]
bring to light, *5894, phōtizō* [1]

BRINGING [20]

testimony bringing against, *2909,*
   katamartyreō [3]
bringing, *5770, pherō* [3]
bringing, *72, agō* [2]
bringing, *4712, prospherō* [2]
bringing, *RPE* [1]
bringing to, *1662+1650, eispherō+eis* [1]
bringing, *2002, exerchomai* [1]
bringing on, *2042, epagō* [1]

bringing, *2214, epipherō* [1]
bringing good news, *2294, euangelizō* [1]
bringing, *2400+3552+1571,*
   echō+meta+heautou [1]
bringing against, *2965, katapherō* [1]
charges bringing against, *2989, katēgoreō* [1]
bringing up children, *5452, teknotropheō* [1]

BRINGS [14]

brings, *AIT* [2]
brings out of, *1666+1675, ek+ekballō* [2]
brings, *2981, katergazomai* [2]
brings, *4734, prophero* [2]
brings into, *1652+1650, eisagō+eis* [1]
brings out of, *1675+1666, ekballō+ek* [1]
brings, *2237, ergazomai* [1]
brings life, *2437, zōē* [1]
brings out more clearly, *5319, synistēmi* [1]
brings out, *5502, tithēmi* [1]

BROAD [2]

broad, *2353, eurychōros* [1]
broad daylight, *2465, hēmera* [1]

BROILED [1]

broiled, *3966, optos* [1]

BROKE [25]

broke, *3089, klaō* [12]
broke out, *1181, ginomai* [3]
broke, *2880, kataklaō* [2]
broke, *5341, syntribō* [2]
broke, *RPE* [1]
broke open, *487, anoigō* [1]
broke down, *2095, epiballō* [1]
broke, *2095, epiballō* [1]
broke, *2862, katagnymi* [1]
broke, *3082, klasis* [1]

BROKEN [19]

broken pieces, *3083, klasma* [5]
broken off, *1709, ekklaō* [3]
broken into, *1482, dioryssō* [2]
broken, *3395, lyō* [2]
broken to pieces, *5314, synthlaō* [2]
broken, *119, atheteō* [1]
broken, *1396, diarrēgnymi* [1]
broken, *2862, katagnymi* [1]
broken to pieces, *3395, lyō* [1]
broken, *5341, syntribō* [1]

BRONZE [4]

bronze, *5909, chalkolibanon* [1]
burnished bronze, *5909, chalkolibanon* [1]
bronze, *5910, chalkos* [1]
of bronze, *5911, chalkous* [1]

BROOD [5]

brood, *1165, gennēma* [4]
brood, *5451, teknon* [1]

BROTHER [108]

brother, *81, adelphos* [104]
brother, *RPE* [3]
your brother$, *1697, ekeinos* [1]

BROTHER'S [8]

brother's, *81, adelphos* [8]

BROTHERHOOD [1]

brotherhood of believers, *82, adelphotēs* [1]

BROTHERLY [4]

brotherly kindness, *5789, philadelphia* [2]
brotherly love, *5789, philadelphia* [2]

BROTHERS [223]

brothers, *81, adelphos* [203]
brothers, *467+81, anēr+adelphos* [13]
false brothers, *6012, pseudadelphos* [2]
brothers, *RPE* [1]
brothers, *82, adelphotēs* [1]
love for brothers, *5789, philadelphia* [1]
loving each other as brothers, *5789,*
   philadelphia [1]
love as brothers, *5790, philadelphos* [1]

BROUGHT [114]

brought, *72, agō* [21]
brought, *5770, pherō* [16]
brought, *4712, prospherō* [12]
brought, *AIT* [4]
brought in, *72, agō* [3]
brought, *1650, eis* [3]
brought, *343, anagō* [2]
brought up, *427, anatrephō* [2]
brought, *1181, ginomai* [2]
brought in, *1652, eisagō* [2]
brought charges, *1872, emphanizō* [2]
brought to ruin, *2246, erēmoō* [2]
brought out, *2262, erchomai* [2]
brought, *2864, katagō* [2]
brought, *RPE* [1]
brought home, *72, agō* [1]
brought to trial, *72, agō* [1]
brought back, *343, anagō* [1]
brought back, *362, anakainizō* [1]
brought, *552, apagō* [1]
brought about, *1181, ginomai* [1]
brought glory, *1519, doxazō* [1]
brought into, *1650+1652, eis+eisagō* [1]
brought into, *1652+1650, eisagō+eis* [1]
brought, *1652, eisagō* [1]
brought into, *1662+1650, eispherō+eis* [1]
brought, *1662, eispherō* [1]
brought out, *1675, ekballō* [1]
brought, *1766, ekpherō* [1]
brought up, *1957, entrephō* [1]
brought out of, *1974+1666, exagō+ek* [1]
brought out, *1974, exagō* [1]
brought on, *2042, epagō* [1]
brought good news about, *2294, euangelizō* [1]
brought to life, *2409, zaō* [1]
brought, *2705, histēmi* [1]
brought down, *2747, kathaireō* [1]
charges brought against, *2989, katēgoreō* [1]
brought, *3152, komizō* [1]
brought, *3496, methistēmi* [1]
brought back, *3572, metatithēmi* [1]
brought in, *4218, parechō* [1]
brought before, *4575, proagō* [1]
brought, *4575, proagō* [1]
brought before, *4642, prosagō* [1]
brought, *4707, prostithēmi* [1]
brought together, *5237, sympherō* [1]
brought up with, *5343, syntrophos* [1]
finally brought about, *5465, telos* [1]
brought up, *5555, trephō* [1]
brought to light, *5746, phaneroō* [1]
brought in, *5770, pherō* [1]
brought to light, *5894, phōtizō* [1]

BROW [1]

brow, *4059, ophrys* [1]

BRUISED [1]

bruised, *5341, syntribō* [1]

BRUSHWOOD [1]

brushwood, *5866, phryganon* [1]

BRUTAL [1]

brutal, *466, anēmeros* [1]

BRUTALLY [1]

brutally treated, *3139, kolaphizō* [1]

BRUTE [1]

brute, *263, alogos* [1]

BRUTES [1]

brutes, *2563, thērion* [1]

BUCKLED [1]

buckled around waist, *4322, perizōnnymi* [1]

BUDDED [1]

budded, *1056, blastanō* [1]

BUFFETED [1]

buffeted, *989, basanizō* [1]

BUILD [19]

build, *3868, oikodomeō* [12]
build up, *3868, oikodomeō* [2]
build up, *3869, oikodomē* [2]
build, *2200, epiteleō* [1]
build up, *2224, epoikodomeō* [1]
build, *4212, paremballō* [1]

BUILDER [4]

builder, *2941, kataskeuazō* [2]
builder, *802, architektōn* [1]
builder, *1321, dēmiourgos* [1]

BUILDERS [5]

builders, *3868, oikodomeō* [4]
builders, *3871, oikodomos* [1]

BUILDING [10]

building, *3868, oikodomeō* [3]
building up, *3869, oikodomē* [3]
building, *3869, oikodomē* [3]
building on, *2224, epoikodomeō* [1]

BUILDINGS [3]

buildings, *3869, oikodomē* [3]

BUILDS [4]

builds on, *2224+2093, epoikodomeō+epi* [1]
builds, *2224, epoikodomeō* [1]
builds up, *3868, oikodomeō* [1]
builds up, *3869, oikodomē* [1]

BUILT [21]

built, *3868, oikodomeō* [10]
built, *2941, kataskeuazō* [3]
built, *721, haptō* [1]
not built by human hands, *942, acheiropoiētos* [1]
built on, *2224+2093, epoikodomeō+epi* [1]
built up, *2224, epoikodomeō* [1]
built, *2224, epoikodomeō* [1]
built up, *3869, oikodomē* [1]
built together, *5325, synoikodomeō* [1]

BULLS [3]

built by hands, *5935, cheiropoiētos* [1]

BULLS [3]

bulls, *5436, tauros* [3]

BUNDLES [1]

bundles, *1299, desmē* [1]

BURDEN [13]

burden, *983, baros* [3]
burden to, *2096, epibareō* [2]
burden, *2915, katanarkaō* [2]
burden, *4, aharēs* [1]
to burden, *2202+983, epitithēmi+baros* [1]
burden to, *2851, katabareō* [1]
burden to, *2915, katanarkaō* [1]
burden, *5100, stenazō* [1]
burden, *5845, phortion* [1]

BURDENED [4]

burdened, *976, bareō* [2]
burdened, *1923, enechō* [1]
burdened, *5844, phortizō* [1]

BURDENS [2]

burdens, *983, baros* [1]
burdens, *5845, phortion* [1]

BURDENSOME [1]

burdensome, *987, barys* [1]

BURIAL [7]

burial, *1947, entaphiasmos* [2]
burial, *1946, entaphiazō* [1]
prepare for burial, *1946, entaphiazō* [1]
burial cloth, *5051, soudarion* [1]
burial place, *5438, taphē* [1]
burial, *5502+1650+3645, tithēmi+eis+mnēma* [1]

BURIED [11]

buried, *2507, thaptō* [7]
buried with, *5313, synthaptō* [2]
buried, *4707, prostithēmi* [1]
buried, *5172, synkomizō* [1]

BURN [5]

burn incense, *2594, thymiaō* [1]
burn up, *2876, katakaiō* [1]
burn, *2876, katakaiō* [1]
burn with passion, *4792, pyroō* [1]
inwardly burn, *4792, pyroō* [1]

BURNED [12]

burned up, *2876, katakaiō* [4]
burned, *2876, katakaiō* [4]
burned, *2794, kaiō* [2]
burned, *1856, empimprēmi* [1]
burned, *3011, kausis* [1]

BURNING [15]

burning, *2794, kaiō* [5]
burning, *4786, pyr* [4]
burning, *4796, pyrōsis* [2]
fire of burning coals, *471, anthrakia* [1]
burning of incense, *2592, thymiama* [1]
burning up, *2876, katakaiō* [1]
burning to ashes, *5491, tephroō* [1]

BURNISHED [1]

burnished bronze, *5909, chalkolibanon* [1]

BURNT [3]

burnt offerings, *3906, holokautōma* [3]

BURST [4]

burst, *4838, rhēgnymi* [3]
burst, *3279, lakaō* [1]

BURY [4]

bury, *2507, thaptō* [4]

BUSH [4]

bush, *1003, batos1* [4]

BUSHELS [1]

thousand bushels, *1669+3174, hekaton+koros* [1]

BUSINESS [8]

business, *2238, ergasia* [2]
carry on business, *1864, emporeuomai* [1]
business, *1865, emporia* [1]
goes about his business, *4512, poreia* [1]
mind business, *4556, prassō* [1]
what business is it of mine, *5515+1609, tis+egō* [1]
business, *5515+4472, tis+poieō* [1]

BUSY [2]

busy, *2237, ergazomai* [1]
busy at home, *3877, oikourgos* [1]

BUSYBODIES [2]

busybodies, *4318, periergazomai* [1]
busybodies, *4319, periergos* [1]

BUT [1423]

but, *1254, de* [664]
but, *247, alla* [406]
but, *2779, kai* [172]
but, *NIG* [84]
but, *4440, plēn* [14]
but, *1142, gar* [11]
but, *1623+3590, ei+mē* [11]
but only, *247, alla* [6]
but, *4036, oun* [6]
but rather, *247, alla* [4]
but, *3530, mentoi* [4]
but, *5445, te* [4]
but, *247+2779, alla+kai* [3]
but only, *1623+3590, ei+mē* [3]
but, *3667, monon* [3]
but also, *247, alla* [2]
but when, *1254, de* [2]
but even, *2779, kai* [2]
but, *RPE* [1]
but instead, *247, alla* [1]
but, *247+2445, alla+ē* [1]
but even, *1254, de* [1]
but as far as, *1254, de* [1]
but, *1569+3590, ean+mē* [1]
but if, *1623+3590, ei+mē* [1]
but only, *1623+2779, ei+kai* [1]
but in the other case, *1695+1254, ekei+de* [1]
but, *2445, ē* [1]
but, *2627, idou* [1]
but I, *2743, kagō* [1]
but me, *2743, kagō* [1]
but also, *2779, kai* [1]
but still, *2779, kai* [1]
but that also, *2797, kakeinos* [1]
but, *3437+1254, mallon+de* [1]
but, *3529, menounge* [1]
but, *4022+1254, hoti+de* [1]

but, *4024+2777, ou+kathōs* [1]
but not either, *4028, oude* [1]
but, *5539+1254, tounantion+de* [1]

BUTCHERED [1]

butchered, *2604, thyō* [1]

BUY [16]

buy, *60, agorazō* [13]
buy, *AIT* [1]
buy, *1443, didōmi* [1]
buy, *3227, ktaomai* [1]

BUYING [3]

buying, *60, agorazō* [3]

BUYS [1]

buys, *60, agorazō* [1]

BY [813]

by, *AIT* [241]
by, *1877, en* [139]
by, *5679, hypo* [97]
by, *1328, dia* [79]
by, *1666, ek* [53]
by, *2848, kata* [34]
by, *608, apo* [23]
by, *2093, epi* [12]
by, *4123, para* [11]
by, *NIG* [6]
by, *RPE* [5]
possessed by, *2400, echō* [5]
by no means, *3590+1181, mē+ginomai* [4]
by, *4309, peri* [3]
passed by on the other side, *524,*
    antiparerchomai [2]
afforded by, *1328, dia* [2]
by, *1877+3836, en+ho* [2]
by now, *2453, ēdē* [2]
by this time, *2453, ēdē* [2]
by, *3552, meta* [2]
swear by, *3923, omnyō* [2]
by, *4022, hoti* [2]
bound by his oath, *4053, opheilō* [2]
passed by, *4182, paraporeuomai* [2]
two by two, *324+1545+1545, ana+dyo+dyo* [1]
blown by the wind, *448, anemizō* [1]
prove by, *545+4556, axios+prassō* [1]
take by force, *773, harpazō* [1]
all by itself, *897, automatos* [1]
by itself, *897, automatos* [1]
by himself, *899+3668, autos+monos* [1]
not built by human hands, *942,*
    acheiropoiētos [1]
not done by the hands of men, *942,*
    acheiropoiētos [1]
not made by man, *942, acheiropoiētos* [1]
possessed by a demon, *1227, daimonizomai* [1]
possessed by demons, *1227, daimonizomai* [1]
by now, *1254, de* [1]
by, *1254, de* [1]
by all this, *1328+4047, dia+houtos* [1]
by comparing with, *1328, dia* [1]
by means of, *1328, dia* [1]
by the authority of, *1328, dia* [1]
by, *1328+5931, dia+cheir* [1]
going by, *1388, diaporeuomai* [1]
two by two, *1545+1545, dyo+dyo* [1]
by, *1650, eis* [1]
pulled up by the roots, *1748, ekrizoō* [1]
by its own choice, *1776, hekōn* [1]
by the power of, *1877, en* [1]
by, *1877+5931, en+cheir* [1]
caused by, *1877, en* [1]

done by, *1877, en* [1]
encircled[s] by, *1877+3545, en+mesos* [1]
by, *1967, enōpion* [1]
travel by ship, *2093+5536+4434,*
    epi+topos+pleō [1]
accompanied by, *2262+2779, erchomai+kai* [1]
passed by, *2262, erchomai* [1]
put religion into practice by caring for, *2355,*
    eusebeō [1]
accompanied by, *2400, echō* [1]
surrounded by, *2400, echō* [1]
taught by God, *2531, theodidaktos* [1]
by, *2671, hina* [1]
by, *2779, kai* [1]
by means of, *2848, kata* [1]
by standards, *2848, kata* [1]
by the standards of, *2848, kata* [1]
day by day, *2848+4246+2465,*
    kata+pas+hēmera [1]
prescribed by, *2848, kata* [1]
required by, *2848, kata* [1]
by itself, *3023+6006+1650+1651+5536,*
    keimai+chōris+eis+heis+topos [1]
tossed back and forth by the waves, *3115,*
    klydōnizomai [1]
side by side, *3128, koinōnos* [1]
chosen by lot, *3275, lanchanō* [1]
decide by lot, *3275, lanchanō* [1]
by myself, *3668, monos* [1]
by ourselves, *3668, monos* [1]
by themselves, *3668, monos* [1]
by[s], *4005+3306, hos+legō* [1]
by, *4020, hotan* [1]
not by any means, *4024+3590, ou+mē* [1]
by no means, *4027, oudamōs* [1]
by this kind, *4048, houtōs* [1]
by all possible means, *4122, pantōs* [1]
going by, *4135, paragō* [1]
passing by, *4135, paragō* [1]
by the lake, *4144, parathalassios* [1]
pass by, *4216, parerchomai* [1]
passed by, *4216, parerchomai* [1]
passing by, *4216, parerchomai* [1]
standing by, *4225, paristēmi* [1]
passing by, *4344, peripateō* [1]
gone by, *4444, plēroō* [1]
live by, *4472, poieō* [1]
lives by, *4472, poieō* [1]
by far, *4498, polys* [1]
judge by external appearance, *4725+476+3284,*
    prosōpon+anthrōpos+lambanō [1]
eaten by worms, *5037, skōlēkobrōtos* [1]
accompanied by, *5250, syn* [1]
accompanied by, *5299, synepomai* [1]
by the hand, *5932, cheiragōgeō* [1]
led by the hand, *5932, cheiragōgeō* [1]
someone to lead by the hand, *5933,*
    cheiragōgos [1]
built by hands, *5935, cheiropoiētos* [1]
done by the hands, *5935, cheiropoiētos* [1]
made by men, *5935, cheiropoiētos* [1]

CAESAR [20]

Caesar, *2790, Kaisar* [20]

CAESAR'S [9]

Caesar's, *2790, Kaisar* [9]

CAESAREA [19]

Caesarea, *2791, Kaisareia* [17]
Caesarea, *RPE* [2]

CAIAPHAS [9]

Caiaphas, *2780, Kaiaphas* [9]

CAIN [3]

Cain, *2782, Kain* [3]

CAINAN [1]

Cainan, *2783, Kainam* [1]

CALCULATE [1]

calculate, *6028, psēphizō* [1]

CALCULATED [1]

calculated, *5248, sympsēphizō* [1]

CALF [4]

calf, *3675, moschos* [3]
made an idol in the form of a calf, *3674,*
    moschopoieō [1]

CALL [52]

call, *2813, kaleō* [12]
call, *3306, legō* [9]
call on, *2126, epikaleō* [7]
call, *5888, phōneō* [3]
call impure, *3124, koinoō* [2]
call, *4673, proskaleō* [2]
trumpet call, *4894, salpinx* [2]
call, *AIT* [1]
call, *RPE* [1]
call down curses, *354, anathematizō* [1]
call out to, *832, aspazomai* [1]
call attention to, *2109, epideiknymi* [1]
call, *2126+2093, epikaleō+epi* [1]
call, *2226, eponomazō* [1]
call, *2813+3836+3950, kaleō+ho+onoma* [1]
call down curses, *2874, katathematizō* [1]
call, *3104, klēsis* [1]
call out, *3306, legō* [1]
call blessed, *3420, makarizō* [1]
call on, *4151, parakaleō* [1]
call attention to, *5703, hypomimnēskō* [1]
call, *5889, phōnē* [1]

CALLED [208]

called, *2813, kaleō* [84]
called, *3306, legō* [31]
called, *3105, klētos* [9]
called, *5888, phōneō* [9]
called, *2126, epikaleō* [8]
called, *4673, proskaleō* [8]
called to, *4673, proskaleō* [7]
called together, *5157, synkaleō* [6]
called, *NIG* [4]
called, *3104, klēsis* [4]
called out, *3189, krazō* [3]
called in, *4673, proskaleō* [3]
called out, *5888, phōneō* [3]
called out, *1066, boaō* [2]
called together, *4673, proskaleō* [2]
called to, *5888, phōneō* [2]
called, *5976, chrēmatizō* [2]
called, *RPE* [1]
called out in a loud voice, *149+5889,*
    airō+phōnē [1]
called for, *160, aiteō* [1]
called to account, *373, anakrinō* [1]
called out, *2048+5889, epairō+phōnē* [1]
called, *2141, epilegō* [1]
called in, *2813, kaleō* [1]
called, *3189, krazō* [1]
called, *3198, kraugazō* [1]
called out, *3306+3489+5889,*
    legō+megas+phōnē [1]
called out, *3306, legō* [1]
called, *3950, onoma* [1]

called, *4005+3836+3950, hos+ho+onoma* [1]
called, *4005+3950, hos+onoma* [1]
called forward, *4715, prosphōneō* [1]
called to, *4715, prosphōneō* [1]
called meeting, *5251, synagō* [1]
called together, *5251, synagō* [1]
called together, *5255, synathroizō* [1]
called in, *5888, phōneō* [1]
falsely called, *6024, pseudōnymos* [1]

CALLING [21]

calling, *1066, boaō* [4]
calling, *3104, klēsis* [3]
calling, *5888, phōneō* [3]
calling, *3306, legō* [2]
calling to, *4673, proskaleō* [2]
calling out, *4715, prosphōneō* [2]
calling, *NIG* [1]
calling on, *2126, epikaleō* [1]
calling received, *3104+2813, klēsis+kaleō* [1]
calling out, *3189, krazō* [1]
calling, *4673, proskaleō* [1]

CALLOUSED [2]

calloused, *4266, pachynō* [2]

CALLS [22]

calls, *2813, kaleō* [8]
calls for, *1639, eimi* [3]
calls, *3306, legō* [3]
calls on, *2126, epikaleō* [2]
calls together, *5157, synkaleō* [2]
calls out, *3189, krazō* [1]
calls, *3951, onomazō* [1]
calls, *5888, phōneō* [1]
this calls for, *6045, hōde* [1]

CALM [3]

calm, *1132, galēnē* [3]

CALVES [2]

calves, *3675, moschos* [2]

CAME [386]

came, *2262, erchomai* [128]
came, *1181, ginomai* [41]
came to, *4665, proserchomai* [34]
came, *AIT* [16]
came out, *2002, exerchomai* [14]
came, *4134, paraginomai* [14]
came down, *2849, katabainō* [12]
came, *4665, proserchomai* [10]
came, *2002, exerchomai* [8]
came out of, *2002+1666, exerchomai+ek* [6]
came in, *1656, eiserchomai* [4]
came down, *2982, katerchomai* [4]
came up, *326, anabainō* [3]
came back, *2262, erchomai* [3]
came up, *4665, proserchomai* [3]
came together, *5302, synerchomai* [3]
came, *NIG* [2]
came up, *422, anatellō* [2]
came up, *1181, ginomai* [2]
came near, *1581, engizō* [2]
came up, *1581, engizō* [2]
came into, *1656+1650, eiserchomai+eis* [2]
out of came, *1666+1744, ek+ekporeuomai* [2]
out of came, *2002+1666, exerchomai+ek* [2]
came on, *2158+2093, epipiptō+epi* [2]
came up, *2392, ephistēmi* [2]
came, *2392, ephistēmi* [2]
came to life, *2409, zaō* [2]
came, *2918, katantaō* [2]
came forward, *4665, proserchomai* [2]

came up to, *4665, proserchomai* [2]
came back, *5715, hypostrephō* [2]
came, *5770, pherō* [2]
came up, *5886, phyō* [2]
came, *RPE* [1]
came loose, *479, aniēmi* [1]
came forward, *482, anistēmi* [1]
came, *599, aperchomai* [1]
came descendants, *1164, gennaō* [1]
the time came when, *1181+1254, ginomai+de* [1]
came about, *1181, ginomai* [1]
came, *1451, dierchomai* [1]
came about, *1639, eimi* [1]
came to, *1656+1650, eiserchomai+eis* [1]
came, *1656, eiserchomai* [1]
came, *1660, eisporeuomai* [1]
from came, *1666+1744, ek+ekporeuomai* [1]
came from, *1666+2002, ek+exerchomai* [1]
out of came, *1666+2002, ek+exerchomai* [1]
came from, *1744+1666, ekporeuomai+ek* [1]
came out of, *1744+1666, ekporeuomai+ek* [1]
came back, *2002, exerchomai* [1]
came out of, *2002, exerchomai* [1]
came, *2088, eperchomai* [1]
came, *2094, epibainō* [1]
came up, *2104, epiginomai* [1]
came home, *2262, erchomai* [1]
came up, *2262, erchomai* [1]
came to, *2351, heuriskō* [1]
came up, *2627, idou* [1]
came to rest, *2767, kathizō* [1]
came along, *2779+2627, kai+idou* [1]
came, *2849, katabainō* [1]
came, *2982, katerchomai* [1]
came upon, *3972, horaō* [1]
came early in the morning, *3983, orthrizō* [1]
came back, *4134, paraginomai* [1]
came to support, *4134, paraginomai* [1]
came for, *4205, pareimi* [1]
came, *4398, pimplēmi* [1]
came, *4406, piptō* [1]
came, *4513, poreuomai* [1]
came before, *4665, proserchomai* [1]
came to, *4702, prosporeuomai* [1]
came, *5230, symplēroō* [1]
came, *5233, symporeuomai* [1]
came together, *5251, synagō* [1]
came with, *5302, synerchomai* [1]
came, *5302, synerchomai* [1]
came running, *5340, syntrechō* [1]
came together, *5370, systrephō* [1]

CAMEL [4]

camel, *2823, kamēlos* [4]

CAMEL'S [2]

camel's, *2823, kamēlos* [2]

CAMP [3]

camp, *4213, parembolē* [3]

CAN [209]

can, *AIT* [102]
can, *1538, dynamai* [84]
can, *NIG* [8]
can, *RPE* [2]
can be trusted, *4412, pistos* [2]
[that can never] fade, *278, amarantos* [1]
[that can never] spoil, *299, amiantos* [1]
you can see, *595+5148, apenanti+sy* [1]
that can never perish, *915, aphthartos* [1]
can do, *1538, dynamai* [1]
can, *1543+1639, dynatos+eimi* [1]

can, *1896, endechomai* [1]
can, *2003, exesti* [1]
can^s, *2400, echō* [1]
can do, *2710, ischyō* [1]
as can see, *2779+2627, kai+idou* [1]
can, *3614, mēti* [1]
everything you can, *5081, spoudaiōs* [1]

CAN'T [5]

can't, *4024+1538, ou+dynamai* [5]

CANA [4]

Cana, *2830, Kana* [4]

CANAAN [2]

Canaan, *1178+5913, gē+Chanaan* [1]
Canaan, *5913, Chanaan* [1]

CANAANITE [1]

Canaanite, *5914, Chananaios* [1]

CANCELED [5]

canceled, *918, aphiēmi* [2]
canceled, *5919, charizomai* [2]
canceled, *1981, exaleiphō* [1]

CANDACE [1]

Candace, *2833, Kandakē* [1]

CANNOT [67]

cannot, *4024+1538, ou+dynamai* [40]
cannot, *4024, ou* [6]
cannot, *3590+1538, mē+dynamai* [3]
cannot, *3590, mē* [3]
cannot, *RPE* [2]
cannot, *4024+1639, ou+eimi* [2]
cannot be condemned, *183, akatagnōstos* [1]
words cannot express, *227, alalētos* [1]
cannot, *247+2445, alla+ē* [1]
cannot tempted, *585, apeirastos* [1]
cannot be shaken, *810, asaleutos* [1]
cannot do, *4024+1538, ou+dynamai* [1]
cannot^s, *4024+2400, ou+echō* [1]
and cannot, *4028+1538, oude+dynamai* [1]
cannot do, *4028+1538, oude+dynamai* [1]
cannot again, *4033, ouketi* [1]
cannot, *4046+1538, oute+dynamai* [1]

CAPERNAUM [16]

Capernaum, *3019, Kapharnaoum* [16]

CAPPADOCIA [2]

Cappadocia, *2838, Kappadokia* [2]

CAPSTONE [5]

capstone, *3051+1224, kephalē+gōnia* [5]

CAPTAIN [4]

captain, *5130, stratēgos* [3]
sea captain, *3237, kybernētēs* [1]

CAPTIVE [4]

take captive, *170, aichmalōtizō* [1]
takes captive, *1639+5194, eimi+sylagōgeō* [1]
taken captive, *2436, zōgreō* [1]
captive, *5278, syndesmos* [1]

CAPTIVES [1]

led captives in his train, *169+168, aichmalōteuō+aichmalōsia* [1]

charge, *2026, exousia* [2]
charge, *AIT* [1]
free of charge, *78, adapanos* [1]
charge, *162+5770, aitia+pherō* [1]
basis for a charge, *165, aitios* [1]
charge, *1371, diamartyromai* [1]
give charge, *1371, diamartyromai* [1]
free of charge, *1562, dōrean* [1]
bring any charge, *1592, enkaleō* [1]
charge, *1598, enklēma* [1]
in charge of, *1639+2093, eimi+epi* [1]
charge, *1823, ellogaō* [1]
charge before, *1941, enorkizō* [1]
charge under oath, *2019, exorkizō* [1]
in charge, *2026, exousia* [1]
take charge of, *2062+1181, epanō+ginomai* [1]
had charge of, *2400, echō* [1]
puts in charge, *2770, kathistēmi* [1]
charge to bring against, *2989, katēgoreō* [1]
charge, *2990, katēgoria* [1]
take charge of, *3195, krateō* [1]
put in charge to lead, *4080, paidagōgos* [1]
charge, *4133, parangellō* [1]
took charge of, *4161, paralambanō* [1]
already made the charge, *4577, proaitiaomai* [1]
charge, *4839, rhēma* [1]

CHARGED [2]

charged with, *1592, enkaleō* [1]
charged, *3306, legō* [1]

CHARGES [17]

charges, *AIT* [3]
brought charges, *1872, emphanizō* [2]
charges, *162, aitia* [1]
charges, *166, aitiōma* [1]
press charges, *1592, enkaleō* [1]
charges, *1598, enklēma* [1]
appeared and presented the charges, *1872, emphanizō* [1]
bring charges, *2989, katēgoreō* [1]
charges bringing against, *2989, katēgoreō* [1]
charges brought against, *2989, katēgoreō* [1]
charges making against, *2989, katēgoreō* [1]
charges, *2989, katēgoreō* [1]
press charges against, *2989, katēgoreō* [1]
charges, *2990, katēgoria* [1]

CHARIOT [4]

chariot, *761, harma* [3]
chariot, *RPE* [1]

CHARIOTS [1]

chariots, *761, harma* [1]

CHASM [1]

chasm, *5926, chasma* [1]

CHATTER [2]

chatter, *3032, kenophōnia* [2]

CHEAPER [1]

cheaper, *1781, elassōn* [1]

CHEAT [1]

cheat, *691, apostereō* [1]

CHEATED [2]

cheated, *691, apostereō* [1]
cheated out of, *5193, sykophanteō* [1]

CHECK [1]

keep in check, *5902, chalinagōgeō* [1]

CHEEK [2]

cheek, *4965, siagōn* [2]

CHEER [1]

cheer up, *2510, tharseō* [1]

CHEERED [1]

cheered, *2379, eupsycheō* [1]

CHEERFUL [1]

cheerful, *2659, hilaros* [1]

CHEERFULLY [1]

cheerfully, *1877+2660, en+hilarotēs* [1]

CHERUBIM [1]

cherubim, *5938, Cheroub* [1]

CHEST [1]

chest, *3466, mastos* [1]

CHESTS [1]

chests, *5111, stēthos* [1]

CHICKS [2]

chicks, *3799, nossia* [1]
chicks, *3800, nossion* [1]

CHIEF [71]

chief priests, *797, archiereus* [64]
chief, *RPE* [1]
chief cornerstone, *214, akrogōniaios* [1]
chief priest, *797, archiereus* [1]
Chief Shepherd, *799, archipoimēn* [1]
chief tax collector, *803, architelōnēs* [1]
chief, *2451, hēgeomai* [1]
chief official, *4755, prōtos* [1]

CHILD [61]

child, *4086, paidion* [21]
little child, *4086, paidion* [7]
child, *3758, nēpios* [5]
child, *5451, teknon* [5]
child, *AIT* [4]
child, *476, anthrōpos* [3]
the child's, *899, autos* [2]
with child, *1877+1143+2400, en+gastēr+echō* [2]
child, *5626, huios* [2]
child, *RPE* [1]
child, *1164, gennaō* [1]
expecting a child, *1607, enkyos* [1]
child bear, *2843+3836+3120, karpos+ho+koilia* [1]
only child, *3666, monogenēs* [1]
child, *3744, neotēs* [1]
child, *4090, pais* [1]
child, *5065, sperma* [1]
with child, *5197+1877+1143, syllambanō+en+gastēr* [1]
giving birth to a child, *5503, tiktō* [1]

CHILD'S [4]

child's, *4086, paidion* [2]
child's's, *899, autos* [1]
child's, *4090, pais* [1]

CHILDBEARING [1]

childbearing, *5450, teknogonia* [1]

CHILDBIRTH [2]

in the pains of childbirth, *5349, synōdinō* [1]
in the pains of childbirth, *6048, ōdinō* [1]

CHILDHOOD [1]

childhood, *4085, paidiothen* [1]

CHILDISH [1]

childish, *3758, nēpios* [1]

CHILDLESS [1]

childless, *866, ateknos* [1]

CHILDREN [128]

children, *5451, teknon* [73]
children, *4086, paidion* [8]
little children, *4086, paidion* [7]
dear children, *5448, teknion* [7]
children, *5065, sperma* [3]
children, *5626, huios* [3]
children, *AIT* [2]
the children's, *899, autos* [2]
have children, *1985+5065, exanistēmi+sperma* [2]
children, *3758, nēpios* [2]
little children, *3758, nēpios* [2]
dear children, *4086, paidion* [2]
children, *RPE* [1]
have children, *482+5065, anistēmi+sperma* [1]
no children, *866, ateknos* [1]
bears children, *1164, gennaō* [1]
illegitimate children, *1666+4518+1164, ek+porneia+gennaō* [1]
illegitimate children, *3785, nothos* [1]
children's, *4005, hos* [1]
children, *4090, pais* [1]
children, *5448, teknion* [1]
have children, *5449, teknogoneō* [1]
dear children, *5451, teknon* [1]
bringing up children, *5452, teknotropheō* [1]
bears children, *5503, tiktō* [1]
children, *5626+1169, huios+genos* [1]
love their children, *5817, philoteknos* [1]

CHILDREN'S [3]

children's, *5451, teknon* [2]
children's, *4086, paidion* [1]

CHLOE'S [1]

Chloe's, *5951, Chloē* [1]

CHOICE [3]

made a choice, *1721, eklegomai* [1]
by its own choice, *1776, hekōn* [1]
choice, *2819, kalos* [1]

CHOKE [3]

choke, *5231, sympnigō* [2]
choke, *4464, pnigō* [1]

CHOKED [4]

choked, *5231, sympnigō* [2]
choked, *678, apopnigō* [1]
choked, *4464, pnigō* [1]

CHOOSE [8]

choose, *1721, eklegomai* [3]
choose, *AIT* [1]
choose, *145, haireomai* [1]

CHOOSE

choose, *1088, boulēma* [1]
choose, *2170, episkeptomai* [1]
choose, *2527, thelō* [1]

CHOOSES [4]

chooses, *1089, boulomai* [3]
chooses, *2527, thelō* [1]

CHOOSING [1]

choosing, *2527, thelō* [1]

CHOSE [14]

chose, *1721, eklegomai* [8]
chose, *145, haireomai* [2]
chose, *RPE* [1]
chose, *1089, boulomai* [1]
chose, *2141, epilegō* [1]
chose, *2527, thelō* [1]

CHOSEN [35]

chosen, *1723, eklektos* [12]
chosen, *1721, eklegomai* [9]
chosen, *1724, eklogē* [3]
chosen, *2527, thelō* [2]
chosen, *RPE* [1]
chosen, *147, hairetizō* [1]
chosen, *3103, klēroō* [1]
chosen by lot, *3275, lanchanō* [1]
chosen before, *4589+4574, proginōskō+pro* [1]
chosen, *4741, procheirizō* [1]
already chosen, *4742, procheirotoneō* [1]
chosen together with, *5293, syneklektos* [1]
chosen, *5936, cheirotoneō* [1]

CHRIST [530]

Christ, *5986, Christos* [516]
Christ's, *899, autos* [9]
Christ, *RPE* [3]
Jesus' Christ, *1697, ekeinos* [1]
Christ's, *4005, hos* [1]

CHRIST'S [11]

Christ's, *5986, Christos* [9]
Christ's's, *899, autos* [1]
Christ's, *5642+5986, hyper+Christos* [1]

CHRISTIAN [2]

Christian, *5985, Christianos* [2]

CHRISTIANS [1]

Christians, *5985, Christianos* [1]

CHRISTS [2]

false Christs, *6023, pseudochristos* [2]

CHRYSOLITE [1]

chrysolite, *5994, chrysolithos* [1]

CHRYSOPRASE [1]

chrysoprase, *5995, chrysoprasos* [1]

CHURCH [79]

church, *1711, ekklēsia* [74]
church, *RPE* [4]
church, *4436, plēthos* [1]

CHURCHES [35]

churches, *1711, ekklēsia* [34]
churches, *RPE* [1]

CILICIA [8]

Cilicia, *3070, Kilikia* [7]
provinces of Cilicia, *3070, Kilikia* [1]

CINNAMON [1]

cinnamon, *3077, kinnamōmon* [1]

CIRCLE [1]

in a circle, *3241, kyklō* [1]

CIRCULATED [1]

widely circulated, *1424, diaphēmizō* [1]

CIRCUMCISE [4]

circumcise, *4362, peritemnō* [4]

CIRCUMCISED [29]

circumcised, *4362, peritemnō* [12]
circumcised, *4364, peritomē* [7]
not circumcised, *213, akrobystia* [4]
circumcised, *1666+4364, ek+peritomē* [3]
before circumcised, *1877+213, en+akrobystia* [1]
circumcised, *3284+4362, lambanō+peritemnō* [1]
circumcised, *4364+3284, peritomē+lambanō* [1]

CIRCUMCISION [19]

circumcision, *4364, peritomē* [16]
circumcision group, *4364, peritomē* [2]
circumcision, *RPE* [1]

CIRCUMSTANCES [7]

circumstances, *AIT* [4]
circumstances, *3836, ho* [1]
under what circumstances, *4802, pōs* [1]
in humble circumstances, *5424, tapeinos* [1]

CITIES [8]

cities, *4484, polis* [8]

CITIZEN [8]

Roman citizen, *4871, Rhōmaios* [4]
citizen, *4489, politēs* [2]
citizen, *RPE* [1]
Roman citizen, *476+4871, anthrōpos+Rhōmaios* [1]

CITIZENS [3]

Roman citizens, *476+4871, anthrōpos+Rhōmaios* [1]
Roman citizens, *4871, Rhōmaios* [1]
fellow citizens with, *5232, sympolitēs* [1]

CITIZENSHIP [3]

citizenship, *4486, politeia* [2]
citizenship, *4487, politeuma* [1]

CITRON [1]

citron, *2591, thyinos* [1]

CITY [105]

city, *4484, polis* [86]
the city's, *899, autos* [5]
city, *RPE* [2]
city of Jerusalem, *2647, Ierousalēm* [2]
city officials, *4485, politarchēs* [2]
city gate, *4783, pylē* [2]
city, *AIT* [1]
city clerk, *1208, grammateus* [1]

the city's, *2637, Ierichō* [1]
the city's, *2647, Ierousalēm* [1]
city gates, *4783, pylē* [1]
city gates, *4784, pylōn* [1]

CITY'S [1]

city's, *4484, polis* [1]

CIVILIAN [1]

civilian affairs, *1050+4548, bios+pragmateia* [1]

CLAIM [15]

claim, *3306, legō* [7]
claim, *NIG* [2]
claim, *3306+1571, legō+heautou* [2]
claim, *3357, logizomai* [1]
claim, *3933, homologeō* [1]
claim to be, *4472+4932, poieō+seautou* [1]
claim, *5774, phēmi* [1]

CLAIMED [7]

claimed, *3306, legō* [4]
claimed, *5763, phaskō* [2]
claimed to be, *1571+4472, heautou+poieō* [1]

CLAIMING [5]

claiming, *3306, legō* [3]
claiming, *3281, laleō* [1]
claiming, *3306+1571, legō+heautou* [1]

CLAIMS [5]

claims, *3306, legō* [3]
claims to be, *1571+4472, heautou+poieō* [1]
claims, *3306+1571, legō+heautou* [1]

CLANGING [1]

clanging, *226, alalazō* [1]

CLASPED [1]

clasped, *3195, krateō* [1]

CLASSIFY [1]

classify, *1605, enkrinō* [1]

CLAUDIA [1]

Claudia, *3086, Klaudia* [1]

CLAUDIUS [3]

Claudius, *3087, Klaudios* [3]

CLAY [3]

clay, *4017, ostrakinos* [1]
of clay, *4017, ostrakinos* [1]
lump of clay, *5878, phyrama* [1]

CLEAN [27]

clean, *2754, katharos* [11]
clean, *2751, katharizō* [7]
make clean, *2751, katharizō* [3]
made clean, *2751, katharizō* [2]
swept clean, *4924, saroō* [2]
ceremonially clean, *49, hagnizō* [1]
clean, *2755, katharotēs* [1]

CLEANSE [3]

cleanse, *2751, katharizō* [2]
sprinkled to cleanse, *4822, rhantizō* [1]

CLEANSED [6]

cleansed, *2751, katharizō* [5]

CLEANSED *2752, katharismos* [1]

CLEANSES [1]

cleanses, *1705, ekkathairō* [1]

CLEANSING [4]

cleansing, *2752, katharismos* [2]
ceremonial cleansing, *49, hagnizō* [1]
cleansing, *2751, katharizō* [1]

CLEAR [27]

clear, *2754, katharos* [2]
clear, *AIT* [1]
clear, *19, agathos* [1]
not clear, *83, adēlos* [1]
make clear, *636, apokalyptō* [1]
eagerness to clear, *665, apologia* [1]
clear, *718, aproskopos* [1]
made clear, *1317, dēloō* [1]
clear, *1316, dēlos* [1]
clear, *1350, diakathairō* [1]
clear, *1351, diakatharizō* [1]
clear, *1684, ekdēlos* [1]
make clear, *2109, epideiknymi* [1]
clear of responsibility, *2754, katharos* [1]
clear, *2819, kalos* [1]
clear, *2867, katadēlos* [1]
clear, *2985, kateuthynō* [1]
clear as crystal, *3222, krystallizō* [1]
clear, *3287, lampros* [1]
not clear, *4024+1182, ou+ginōskō* [1]
conscience is clear, *4029+5323,
    oudeis+synoida* [1]
clear, *4593, prodēlos* [1]
clear minded, *5404, sōphroneō* [1]
clear, *5457, teleioō* [1]
clear, *5745, phaneros* [1]
made clear, *5746, phaneroō* [1]

CLEARLY [11]

see clearly, *1332, diablepō* [2]
clearly, *AIT* [1]
clearly, *1316, dēlos* [1]
clearly, *1877+4244, en+parrēsia* [1]
clearly seen, *2775, kathoraō* [1]
clearly in the wrong, *2861, kataginōskō* [1]
clearly, *4843, rhētōs* [1]
brings out more clearly, *5319, synistēmi* [1]
clearly, *5495, tēlaugōs* [1]
proclaim clearly, *5746, phaneroō* [1]

CLEMENT [1]

Clement, *3098, Klēmēs* [1]

CLEOPAS [1]

Cleopas, *3093, Kleopas* [1]

CLERK [1]

city clerk, *1208, grammateus* [1]

CLEVERLY [1]

cleverly invented, *5054, sophizō* [1]

CLIFF [1]

throw down the cliff, *2889, katakrēmnizō* [1]

CLIMBED [4]

climbed, *326, anabainō* [3]
climbed aboard, *326, anabainō* [1]

CLIMBS [1]

climbs in, *326, anabainō* [1]

CLING [1]

cling, *3140, kollaō* [1]

CLOAK [14]

cloak, *2668, himation* [13]
cloak, *5742, phailonēs* [1]

CLOAKS [7]

cloaks, *2668, himation* [7]

CLOPAS [1]

Clopas, *3116, Klōpas* [1]

CLOSE [8]

close, *338, anankaios* [1]
close, *2392, ephistēmi* [1]
close, *3091, kleiō* [1]
close to, *3516, mellō* [1]
close, *3552, meta* [1]
keeping a close watch, *4190, paratēreō* [1]
kept close watch on, *4190, paratēreō* [1]
paid close attention, *4668, prosechō* [1]

CLOSED [2]

closed, *2826, kammyō* [2]

CLOSELY [6]

watched closely, *4190, paratēreō* [2]
looked closely at, *867, atenizō* [1]
looked closely at, *1838, emblepō* [1]
watch closely, *2091, epechō* [1]
look more closely, *2917, katanoeō* [1]

CLOSES [1]

closes, *643, apokleiō* [1]

CLOTH [11]

linen cloth, *4984, sindōn* [3]
cloth, *4820, rhakos* [2]
cloth, *RPE* [1]
dealer in purple cloth, *4527, porphyropōlis* [1]
burial cloth, *5051, soudarion* [1]
cloth, *5051, soudarion* [1]
piece of cloth, *5051, soudarion* [1]
scarlet cloth, *3132, kokkinos* [1]

CLOTHE [8]

clothe with, *1907, endyō* [3]
clothe, *RPE* [2]
clothe, *4314, periballō* [2]
clothe with, *1599, enkomboomai* [1]

CLOTHED [10]

clothed with, *1907, endyō* [3]
clothed with, *2086, ependyomai* [2]
clothed in, *4314, periballō* [2]
clothed, *1907, endyō* [1]
clothed with, *4314, periballō* [1]
clothed, *4314, periballō* [1]

CLOTHES [51]

clothes, *2668, himation* [22]
clothes, *1903, endyma* [7]
clothes, *2264, esthēs* [5]
clothes, *2669, himatismos* [3]
needed clothes, *1218, gymnos* [2]
needing clothes, *1218, gymnos* [2]
fine clothes, *3434, malakos* [2]
clothes, *RPE* [1]
clothes, *313, amphiezō* [1]
clothes, *314, amphiennymi* [1]
without clothes, *1218, gymnos* [1]
stripped of clothes, *1694, ekdyō* [1]
fine clothes, *1906+2668, endysis+himation* [1]
put on clothes, *2439, zōnnymi* [1]
clothes, *5945, chitōn* [1]

CLOTHING [8]

clothing, *2669, himatismos* [2]
wore clothing, *1639+1907, eimi+endyō* [1]
clothing, *1903, endyma* [1]
clothing, *2668, himation* [1]
outer clothing, *2668, himation* [1]
clothing, *5004, skepasma* [1]
clothing, *5945, chitōn* [1]

CLOTHS [2]

wrapped in cloths, *5058, sparganoō* [2]

CLOUD [19]

cloud, *3749, nephelē* [18]
cloud, *3751, nephos* [1]

CLOUDS [7]

clouds, *3749, nephelē* [7]

CLUBS [5]

clubs, *3833, xylon* [5]

CLUSTERS [1]

clusters of grapes, *1084, botrys* [1]

CLUTCHES [1]

clutches, *5931, cheir* [1]

CNIDUS [1]

Cnidus, *3118, Knidos* [1]

CO-HEIRS [1]

co-heirs with, *5169, synklēronomos* [1]

COALS [2]

fire of burning coals, *471, anthrakia* [1]
coals, *472, anthrax* [1]

COARSE [1]

coarse joking, *2365, eutrapelia* [1]

COAST [5]

coast, *AIT* [2]
the coast[s], *899, autos* [1]
coast, *2498, thalassa* [1]
coast, *4163, paralios* [1]

CODE [4]

written code, *1207, gramma* [3]
written code, *5934, cheirographon* [1]

COFFIN [1]

coffin, *5049, soros* [1]

COIN [4]

coin, *RPE* [1]
coin, *1534, drachmē* [1]
coin, *3790, nomisma* [1]
four-drachma coin, *5088, statēr* [1]

COINS [9]

silver coins, *736, argyrion* [3]
very small copper coins, *3321, leptos* [2]
coins, *736, argyrion* [1]
silver coins, *1324, dēnarion* [1]
silver coins, *1534, drachmē* [1]

coins, *3047, kerma* [1]

COLD [7]

cold, *6036, psychos* [3]
cold, *6037, psychros* [3]
cold, *6038, psychō* [1]

COLLAPSE [2]

collapse, *1725, eklyō* [2]

COLLAPSED [3]

collapsed, *4406, piptō* [2]
collapsed, *5229, sympiptō* [1]

COLLECT [6]

collect, *3284, lambanō* [3]
collect a tenth from, *2400+620, echō+apodekatoō* [1]
collect, *4556, prassō* [1]
collect, *5198, syllegō* [1]

COLLECTED [4]

collected a tenth, *1282, dekatoō* [1]
collected, *3284, lambanō* [1]
collected, *4556, prassō* [1]
collected, *5198, syllegō* [1]

COLLECTION [1]

collection, *3356, logeia* [1]

COLLECTIONS [1]

collections, *3356, logeia* [1]

COLLECTOR [7]

tax collector, *5467, telōnēs* [6]
chief tax collector, *803, architelōnēs* [1]

COLLECTOR'S [2]

tax collector's booth, *5468, telōnion* [2]

COLLECTORS [16]

tax collectors, *5467, telōnēs* [15]
collectors of tax, *3284, lambanō* [1]

COLLECTS [1]

collects, *3284, lambanō* [1]

COLONNADE [3]

Colonnade, *5119, stoa* [3]

COLONNADES [1]

covered colonnades, *5119, stoa* [1]

COLONY [1]

Roman colony, *3149, kolōnia* [1]

COLOSSE [1]

Colosse, *3145, Kolossai* [1]

COLT [12]

colt, *4798, pōlos* [12]

COMBINE [1]

combine with, *5166, synkerannymi* [1]

COMBINED [1]

combined, *5166, synkerannymi* [1]

COME [442]

come, *2262, erchomai* [194]

---

come, *2457, hēkō* [18]
come, *1639, eimi* [15]
come down, *2849, katabainō* [14]
come, *1307, deute* [12]
come, *AIT* [11]
come, *NIG* [9]
come out, *2002, exerchomai* [9]
come, *RPE* [8]
to come, *3516, mellō* [8]
come, *1306, deuro* [7]
come, *4205, pareimi* [7]
come, *1181, ginomai* [6]
come up, *326, anabainō* [5]
come in, *1656, eiserchomai* [5]
come out of, *2002+1666, exerchomai+ek* [4]
come, *2002, exerchomai* [4]
come together, *5302, synerchomai* [4]
come, *1656, eiserchomai* [3]
come in, *1660, eisporeuomai* [3]
out of come, *1666+2002, ek+exerchomai* [3]
come back, *2262, erchomai* [3]
come, *4134, paraginomai* [3]
come to, *4665, proserchomai* [3]
come, *5777, phthanō* [3]
come back to life, *482, anistēmi* [2]
deposit guaranteeing what is to come, *775, arrabōn* [2]
come near, *1581, engizō* [2]
come, *1586, egeirō* [2]
come and share, *1656+1650, eiserchomai+eis* [2]
come out, *1770, ekphyō* [2]
come, *2400, echō* [2]
has come, *2457, hēkō* [2]
have come, *2457, hēkō* [2]
still to come, *4037, oupō* [2]
come, *4444, plēroō* [2]
come, *199, akoloutheō* [1]
come back, *366, anakamptō* [1]
come to senses, *392, ananēphō* [1]
bound to come, *450+3590+2262, anendektos+mē+erchomai* [1]
come, *482, anistēmi* [1]
come of, *1181, ginomai* [1]
come true, *1181, ginomai* [1]
come over, *1329, diabainō* [1]
come, *1451, dierchomai* [1]
glory come to, *1519, doxazō* [1]
come together, *1639+5251, eimi+synagō* [1]
come upon, *1639+2093+2158, eimi+epi+epipiptō* [1]
come with, *1639+5302, eimi+synerchomai* [1]
come, *1639+2262, eimi+erchomai* [1]
come at, *1656+1650, eiserchomai+eis* [1]
come in among, *1656+1650, eiserchomai+eis* [1]
come to, *1656+1650, eiserchomai+eis* [1]
come from, *1666+2002, ek+exerchomai* [1]
come out of, *1666+1744, ek+ekporeuomai* [1]
out of come, *1666+1744, ek+ekporeuomai* [1]
come back to senses, *1729, eknēphō* [1]
come out of, *1744+1666, ekporeuomai+ek* [1]
come out, *1744, ekporeuomai* [1]
come, *1744, ekporeuomai* [1]
come, *1931, enistēmi* [1]
come out, *2002+1666, exerchomai+ek* [1]
come upon, *2082+2093, epeiserchomai+epi* [1]
come upon, *2088+2093, eperchomai+epi* [1]
come to understand, *2105, epiginōskō* [1]
come to help, *2170, episkeptomai* [1]
come to, *2170, episkeptomai* [1]
come, *2170, episkeptomai* [1]
come, *2391, ephikneomai* [1]
come on, *2392, ephistēmi* [1]
come, *2392, ephistēmi* [1]
come to life, *2409, zaō* [1]

---

come to life, *2443, zōopoieō* [1]
has come, *2453, ēdē* [1]
come, *2849, katabainō* [1]
come, *2918, katantaō* [1]
come down, *2982, katerchomai* [1]
come under judgment, *3212, krinō* [1]
to come, *3516+2262, mellō+erchomai* [1]
come, *3569, metapempō* [1]
command to come out, *3991, horkizō* [1]
come out of, *4047+2002, houtos+exerchomai* [1]
come from, *4134, paraginomai* [1]
come along, *4216, parerchomai* [1]
come, *4216, parerchomai* [1]
come, *4225, paristēmi* [1]
come to believe, *4409, pisteuō* [1]
come true, *4444, plēroō* [1]
come to, *4639+4665, pros+proserchomai* [1]
come with, *5160, synkatabainō* [1]
come up with, *5262, synanabainō* [1]
come along with, *5302, synerchomai* [1]
come together, *5302+2093+3836+899, synerchomai+epi+ho+autos* [1]
come with, *5302, synerchomai* [1]
come, *6003, chōreō* [1]

COME LORD [1]

come Lord, *3448, marana tha* [1]

COMES [121]

comes, *2262, erchomai* [58]
comes, *AIT* [19]
comes, *1639, eimi* [8]
comes, *NIG* [3]
comes, *1181, ginomai* [3]
comes in, *1656, eiserchomai* [3]
comes, *4242, parousia* [3]
comes, *1581, engizō* [2]
comes out of, *1666+1744, ek+ekporeuomai* [2]
comes out, *2002, exerchomai* [2]
comes down, *2849, katabainō* [2]
comes, *RPE* [1]
comes up, *326, anabainō* [1]
a revelation comes, *636, apokalyptō* [1]
comes near, *1581, engizō* [1]
comes into, *1656+1650, eiserchomai+eis* [1]
out of comes, *1666+1744, ek+ekporeuomai* [1]
comes from, *1744+1666, ekporeuomai+ek* [1]
comes out of, *1744+1666, ekporeuomai+ek* [1]
comes, *1744, ekporeuomai* [1]
comes, *2002, exerchomai* [1]
comes on, *2088+2093, eperchomai+epi* [1]
comes back, *2188, epistrephō* [1]
comes home, *2262, erchomai* [1]
comes, *2849, katabainō* [1]
comes, *4665, proserchomai* [1]
comes together, *5302+2093+3836+899, synerchomai+epi+ho+autos* [1]

COMFORT [14]

comfort, *4155, paraklēsis* [8]
comfort, *4151, parakaleō* [2]
comfort, *4170, paramytheomai* [1]
comfort, *4171, paramythia* [1]
comfort, *4172, paramythion* [1]
comfort, *4219, parēgoria* [1]

COMFORTED [6]

comforted, *4151, parakaleō* [6]

COMFORTING [2]

comforting, *4170, paramytheomai* [2]

COMFORTS [2]

comforts, *4151, parakaleō* [2]

COMING [118]

coming, *2262, erchomai* [58]
coming, *4242, parousia* [17]
coming down, *2849, katabainō* [9]
coming, *3516, mellō* [4]
coming, *AIT* [3]
coming, *NIG* [2]
coming up, *326, anabainō* [2]
coming, *326, anabainō* [2]
coming, *1451, dierchomai* [2]
coming, *2002, exerchomai* [2]
coming, *1658, eisodos* [1]
coming from, *1666+2002, ek+exerchomai* [1]
coming out, *1744, ekporeuomai* [1]
coming, *1803, eleusis* [1]
coming on, *2088, eperchomai* [1]
coming upon, *2088, eperchomai* [1]
coming, *2088, eperchomai* [1]
coming, *2164, epiporeuomai* [1]
coming, *2175, episkopē* [1]
coming back, *2262, erchomai* [1]
coming of, *2262, erchomai* [1]
coming up, *2392, ephistēmi* [1]
coming to nothing, *2934, katargeō* [1]
that are coming, *3516, mellō* [1]
coming, *4134, paraginomai* [1]
coming, *4665, proserchomai* [1]
a long time in coming, *5988, chronizō* [1]

COMMAND [47]

command, *1953, entolē* [17]
command, *4133, parangellō* [7]
command, *1948, entellō* [6]
command, *2198, epitagē* [5]
command, *3364, logos* [2]
command, *RPE* [1]
command, *2199, epitassō* [1]
loud command, *3026, keleusma* [1]
command, *3027, keleuō* [1]
command to come out, *3991, horkizō* [1]
breaking a command, *4126, parabasis* [1]
command, *4132, parangelia* [1]
gave command, *4133, parangellō* [1]
give this command, *4133, parangellō* [1]
command, *4839, rhēma* [1]

COMMANDED [22]

commanded, *4705, prostassō* [5]
commanded, *1948, entellō* [4]
commanded, *4133, parangellō* [4]
commanded, *1403, diastellō* [2]
commanded, *1411, diatassō* [1]
commanded, *1443+1953, didōmi+entolē* [1]
commanded to keep, *1948, entellō* [1]
commanded, *1953+1443, entolē+didōmi* [1]
commanded, *1953+3284, entolē+lambanō* [1]
commanded, *3306, legō* [1]
commanded, *5332, syntassō* [1]

COMMANDER [19]

commander, *5941, chiliarchos* [17]
commander, *RPE* [1]
the commander^s, *899, autos* [1]

COMMANDER'S [1]

the commander's^s, *899, autos* [1]

COMMANDERS [1]

military commanders, *5941, chiliarchos* [1]

COMMANDING [3]

commanding, *2848+2198+3306,*
kata+epitagē+legō [1]
commanding, *3027, keleuō* [1]
commanding officer, *5133, stratologeō* [1]

COMMANDMENT [14]

commandment, *1953, entolē* [13]
the commandment^s, *899, autos* [1]

COMMANDMENTS [11]

commandments, *1953, entolē* [10]
commandments, *RPE* [1]

COMMANDS [19]

commands, *1953, entolē* [15]
commands, *AIT* [1]
commands, *1945, entalma* [1]
commands, *2199, epitassō* [1]
commands, *4133, parangellō* [1]

COMMEND [8]

commend, *5319, synistēmi* [6]
commend, *2047, epainos* [1]
commend, *2400+2047, echō+epainos* [1]

COMMENDABLE [2]

commendable, *5921, charis* [2]

COMMENDED [7]

commended, *3455, martyreō* [4]
commended, *2046, epaineō* [1]
commended, *4140, paradidōmi* [1]
commended, *5319, synistēmi* [1]

COMMENDS [2]

commends, *5319, synistēmi* [2]

COMMISSION [2]

commission, *2207, epitropē* [1]
commission, *3873, oikonomia* [1]

COMMIT [16]

commit adultery, *3658, moicheuō* [10]
commit, *4192, paratithēmi* [3]
commit a sin, *279+281,*
hamartanō+hamartia [1]
commit sexual immorality, *4519, porneuō* [1]
commit murder, *5839, phoneuō* [1]

COMMITS [7]

commits adultery, *3656, moichaō* [4]
commits adultery, *3658, moicheuō* [2]
commits, *4472, poieō* [1]

COMMITTED [19]

committed, *4472, poieō* [5]
committed, *4140, paradidōmi* [3]
committed adultery, *4519, porneuō* [3]
committed, *AIT* [1]
sins committed in ignorance, *52, agnoēma* [1]
committed, *2981, katergazomai* [1]
committed adultery with, *3658, moicheuō* [1]
committed, *4192, paratithēmi* [1]
committed, *4409, pisteuō* [1]
committed beforehand, *4588, proginomai* [1]
committed, *5502, tithēmi* [1]

COMMITTING [1]

committing sexual immorality, *4519,*
porneuō [1]

COMMON [7]

common to man, *474, anthrōpinos* [1]
common use, *871, atimia* [1]
common, *3123, koinos* [1]
in common, *3123, koinos* [1]
in common, *3535, meris* [1]
in common, *3580, metochē* [1]
common good, *5237, sympherō* [1]

COMMOTION [4]

commotion, *2572, thorybeō* [1]
commotion, *2573, thorybos* [1]
commotion, *5371, systrophē* [1]
commotion, *5431, tarachos* [1]

COMMUNITY [1]

Jewish community, *4436+2681,*
plēthos+Ioudaios [1]

COMPANION [1]

companion, *5171, synkoinōnos* [1]

COMPANIONS [19]

companions, *3836+3552, ho+meta* [5]
companions, *3836+5250, ho+syn* [3]
companions, *3836+5250+1639,*
ho+syn+eimi [2]
companions, *RPE* [1]
companions, *3552, meta* [1]
companions, *3581, metochos* [1]
companions, *3836+1639+3552,*
ho+eimi+meta [1]
companions, *3836+3552+1639,*
ho+meta+eimi [1]
companions, *3836+4309, ho+peri* [1]
companions, *3836+5250+4513,*
ho+syn+poreuomai [1]
companions, *5289, syneimi1* [1]
traveling companions, *5292, synekdēmos* [1]

COMPANY [7]

company of soldiers, *5061, speira* [2]
parted company, *714+608+253,*
apochōrizō+apo+allēlōn [1]
enjoyed company, *1855, empimplēmi* [1]
company, *3918, homilia* [1]
great company, *4436, plēthos* [1]
company, *5322, synodia* [1]

COMPARE [6]

compare, *3929, homoioō* [4]
compare, *5173, synkrinō* [2]

COMPARED [1]

compared to, *1328, dia* [1]

COMPARING [3]

comparing, *AIT* [1]
by comparing with, *1328, dia* [1]
comparing with, *4639, pros* [1]

COMPARISON [1]

in comparison with,
1877+4047+3836+3538+1641,
en+houtos+ho+meros+heineken [1]

COMPASSION [14]

had compassion, *5072, splanchnizomai* [4]
compassion, *3880, oiktirmos* [3]
have compassion, *3882, oiktirō* [2]
have compassion, *5072, splanchnizomai* [2]
full of compassion, *4499, polysplanchnos* [1]

filled with compassion, *5072, splanchnizomai* [1]
filled with compassion for, *5072, splanchnizomai* [1]

COMPASSIONATE [2]

compassionate, *2359, eusplanchnos* [2]

COMPEL [1]

compel, *337, anankazō* [1]

COMPELLED [4]

compelled, *337, anankazō* [2]
compelled, *340+2130, anankē+epikeimai* [1]
compelled, *1313, deō* [1]

COMPELS [1]

compels, *5309, synechō* [1]

COMPETENCE [1]

competence, *2654, hikanotēs* [1]

COMPETENT [4]

not competent, *396, anaxios* [1]
competent, *1538, dynamai* [1]
competent, *2653, hikanos* [1]
made competent, *2655, hikanoō* [1]

COMPETES [3]

competes in the games, *76, agōnizomai* [1]
competes as an athlete, *123, athleō* [1]
competes, *123, athleō* [1]

COMPLAINED [2]

complained, *1181+1198, ginomai+gongysmos* [1]
complained, *1197, gongyzō* [1]

COMPLAINING [1]

complaining, *1198, gongysmos* [1]

COMPLAINT [1]

making a complaint^s about, *1639, eimi* [1]

COMPLETE [23]

complete, *4444, plēroō* [7]
made complete, *5457, teleioō* [4]
complete, *RPE* [1]
complete, *568, apartismos* [1]
make complete, *1639+4444, eimi+plēroō* [1]
complete, *1877+4246, en+pas* [1]
complete, *3489, megas* [1]
complete healing, *3907, holoklēria* [1]
complete, *3908, holoklēros* [1]
complete, *4246, pas* [1]
complete, *4443, plērophoria* [1]
complete, *4444+4246, plēroō+pas* [1]
make complete, *4444, plēroō* [1]
complete, *5457, teleioō* [1]

COMPLETED [9]

completed, *5464, teleō* [4]
completed, *4398, pimplēmi* [2]
completed, *4444, plēroō* [2]
completed, *2200, epiteleō* [1]

COMPLETELY [12]

completely restored, *635, apokathistēmi* [3]
completely, *3489, megas* [3]
completely, *1650+3836+4117, eis+ho+pantelēs* [1]

completely cut off from, *2017+1666, exolethreuō+ek* [1]
completely, *3336+1666+4356, lian+ek+perissos* [1]
completely, *3910, holos* [1]
completely, *3914, holōs* [1]
completely, *4246, pas* [1]

COMPLETING [2]

completing, *4444, plēroō* [1]
completing, *5457, teleioō* [1]

COMPLETION [3]

bring to completion, *2200, epiteleō* [1]
carry it on to completion, *2200, epiteleō* [1]
completion, *2200, epiteleō* [1]

COMPULSION [2]

compulsion, *340, ananke* [2]

CONCEALED [4]

concealed, *649, apokryphos* [2]
concealed, *2821, kalyptō* [1]
concealed, *5158, synkalyptō* [1]

CONCEIT [1]

vain conceit, *3029, kenodoxia* [1]

CONCEITED [7]

conceited, *5605, typhoomai* [3]
conceited, *3030, kenodoxos* [1]
conceited, *4123+1571+5861, para+heautou+phronimos* [1]
conceited, *5643, hyperairomai* [1]
conceited, *5861+4123+1571, phronimos+para+heautou* [1]

CONCEIVED [4]

conceived, *326, anabainō* [1]
conceived, *1164, gennaō* [1]
conceived, *5197+1877+3836+3120, syllambanō+en+ho+koilia* [1]
conceived, *5197, syllambanō* [1]

CONCERN [9]

free from concern, *291, amerimnos* [1]
showed concern, *2170, episkeptomai* [1]
ardent concern, *2419, zēlos* [1]
concern, *2419, zēlos* [1]
showed concern, *3508, melei* [1]
concern, *3533, merimna* [1]
have concern, *3534, merimnaō* [1]
concern, *5082, spoudē* [1]
concern, *5858, phroneō* [1]

CONCERNED [9]

concerned about, *3534, merimnaō* [4]
is concerned, *2848, kata* [2]
concerned, *3508, melei* [1]
concerned, *4309, peri* [1]
concerned, *5858, phroneō* [1]

CONCERNING [16]

concerning, *4309, peri* [11]
concerning, *AIT* [2]
concerning, *5642, hyper* [2]
concerning, *4639, pros* [1]

CONCESSION [1]

concession, *5152, syngnōmē* [1]

CONCLUDE [1]

conclude then, *4036, oun* [1]

CONCLUDED [1]

concluded, *1182, ginōskō* [1]

CONCLUDING [1]

concluding, *5204, symbibazō* [1]

CONDEMN [17]

condemn, *2891, katakrinō* [7]
condemn, *3212, krinō* [6]
condemn, *2861, kataginōskō* [2]
condemn, *2868, katadikazō* [1]
condemn, *2892, katakrisis* [1]

CONDEMNATION [6]

condemnation, *2890, katakrima* [3]
condemnation, *3210, krima* [3]

CONDEMNED [28]

condemned, *2891, katakrinō* [9]
condemned, *3212, krinō* [6]
condemned, *2868, katadikazō* [4]
eternally condemned, *353, anathema* [2]
condemned, *3213, krisis* [2]
cannot be condemned, *183, akatagnōstos* [1]
condemned, *1650+3213+2262, eis+krisis+erchomai* [1]
condemned to die, *2119, epithanatios* [1]
condemned, *2869, katadikē* [1]
condemned, *5679+3213+4406, hypo+krisis+piptō* [1]

CONDEMNING [2]

condemning, *2891, katakrinō* [1]
condemning, *3212, krinō* [1]

CONDEMNS [2]

condemns, *2891, katakrinō* [1]
condemns, *2892, katakrisis* [1]

CONDITION [3]

condition, *AIT* [2]
in this condition, *2400, echō* [1]

CONDUCT [3]

conduct, *418, anastrephō* [1]
conduct, *4488, politeuomai* [1]
endured conduct, *5574, tropophoreō* [1]

CONDUCTED [1]

conducted, *418, anastrephō* [1]

CONFER [1]

confer, *1416, diatithēmi* [1]

CONFERRED [3]

conferred, *1416, diatithēmi* [1]
conferred with, *5196, syllaleō* [1]
conferred, *5202, symballō* [1]

CONFESS [10]

confess, *3933, homologeō* [5]
confess, *2018, exomologeō* [3]
confess faith, *3933, homologeō* [1]
confess, *3934, homologia* [1]

CONFESSED [2]

openly confessed, *2018+334, exomologeō+anangellō* [1]

confessed, *3933, homologeō* [1]

CONFESSES [1]

confesses, *3951, onomazō* [1]

CONFESSING [2]

confessing, *2018, exomologeō* [2]

CONFESSION [3]

made confession, *3933+3934,*
    homologeō+homologia [1]
confession, *3934, homologia* [1]
made confession, *3934, homologia* [1]

CONFIDENCE [18]

confidence, *4244, parrēsia* [7]
confidence, *4301, pepoithēsis* [4]
confidence, *4275, peithō* [2]
put confidence, *4275, peithō* [2]
have confidence, *2509, tharreō* [1]
with confidence, *2509, tharreō* [1]
confidence, *5712, hypostasis* [1]

CONFIDENT [12]

confident, *4275, peithō* [5]
confident, *2509, tharreō* [2]
confident of, *4275, peithō* [2]
confident, *2400+4244, echō+parrēsia* [1]
confident of, *4301, pepoithēsis* [1]
confident, *5712, hypostasis* [1]

CONFIDENTLY [2]

confidently affirm, *1331, diabebaioomai* [1]
confidently, *3552+4244, meta+parrēsia* [1]

CONFINE [1]

confine, *AIT* [1]

CONFIRM [2]

confirm, *550, apangellō* [1]
confirm, *1011, bebaioō* [1]

CONFIRMED [5]

confirmed, *1011, bebaioō* [3]
confirmed, *3455, martyreō* [1]
confirmed, *3541, mesiteuō* [1]

CONFIRMING [1]

confirming, *1012, bebaiōsis* [1]

CONFIRMS [2]

confirms, *1650+1012, eis+bebaiōsis* [1]
confirms, *5210, symmartyreō* [1]

CONFISCATION [1]

confiscation, *771, harpagē* [1]

CONFLICT [1]

in conflict, *512, antikeimai* [1]

CONFLICTS [1]

conflicts, *3480, machē* [1]

CONFORM [2]

conform to the pattern of, *5372,*
    syschēmatizō [1]
conform, *5372, syschēmatizō* [1]

CONFORMED [1]

conformed, *5215, symmorphos* [1]

CONFORMITY [1]

in conformity with, *2848, kata* [1]

CONFORMS [1]

conforms to, *2848, kata* [1]

CONFUSION [3]

throwing into confusion, *5429, tarassō* [2]
confusion, *5177, syncheō* [1]

CONGREGATION [2]

congregation, *1711, ekklēsia* [1]
congregation, *5252, synagōgē* [1]

CONGREGATIONS [1]

congregations, *1711, ekklēsia* [1]

CONNECTION [2]

in connection with, *2093, epi* [1]
lost connection with, *4024+3195, ou+krateō* [1]

CONQUER [1]

conquer, *3771, nikaō* [1]

CONQUERED [1]

conquered, *2865, katagōnizomai* [1]

CONQUEROR [1]

conqueror, *3771, nikaō* [1]

CONQUERORS [1]

more than conquerors, *5664, hypernikaō* [1]

CONQUEST [1]

conquest, *3771, nikaō* [1]

CONSCIENCE [25]

conscience, *5287, syneidēsis* [23]
conscience is clear, *4029+5323,*
    oudeis+synoida [1]
guilty conscience, *5287+4505,*
    syneidēsis+ponēros [1]

CONSCIENCES [4]

consciences, *5287, syneidēsis* [4]

CONSCIOUS [2]

conscious, *2106, epignōsis* [1]
conscious, *5287, syneidēsis* [1]

CONSECRATED [6]

consecrated, *4606, prothesis* [4]
consecrated, *39, hagiazō* [1]
consecrated, *41+2813, hagios+kaleō* [1]

CONSENT [3]

consent, *1191, gnōmē* [1]
consent, *2039, epangelia* [1]
mutual consent, *5247, symphōnos* [1]

CONSENTED [3]

consented, *918, aphiēmi* [1]
consented, *1639+5163,*
    eimi+synkatatithēmi [1]
consented, *2018, exomologeō* [1]

CONSEQUENTLY [4]

consequently, *726+4036, ara+oun* [2]
consequently, *726, ara* [1]
consequently, *6063, hōste* [1]

CONSIDER [35]

consider, *2451, hēgeomai* [8]
consider, *2917, katanoeō* [3]
consider, *3212, krinō* [3]
consider, *3357, logizomai* [3]
consider, *NIG* [2]
consider carefully, *1063, blepō* [2]
consider, *355, anatheōreō* [1]
consider, *382, analogizomai* [1]
consider worthy, *546, axioō* [1]
consider, *1063, blepō* [1]
consider, *1086, bouleuō* [1]
consider, *2078+2093, epeidon+epi* [1]
consider, *2400, echō* [1]
consider, *2623, ide* [1]
consider, *2627, idou* [1]
consider[s], *2777, kathōs* [1]
consider blessed, *3420, makarizō* [1]
consider, *3972+4309, horaō+peri* [1]
consider, *4472, poieō* [1]
consider carefully, *4668, prosechō* [1]

CONSIDERABLE [2]

considerable, *2653, hikanos* [1]
considerable, *4498, polys* [1]

CONSIDERATE [4]

considerate, *2117, epieikēs* [3]
considerate, *2848+1194, kata+gnōsis* [1]

CONSIDERED [10]

considered righteous, *1467, dikaioō* [2]
considered, *2451, hēgeomai* [2]
considered, *1506, dokeō* [1]
considered, *1926, enthymeomai* [1]
considered, *2351, heuriskō* [1]
considered worthy of, *2921, kataxioō* [1]
considered, *3357, logizomai* [1]
considered, *6055+2400, hōs+echō* [1]

CONSIDERS [3]

considers, *3212, krinō* [2]
considers himself, *1506, dokeō* [1]

CONSIST [1]

consist, *1639, eimi* [1]

CONSISTS [1]

consists, *AIT* [1]

CONSOLATION [1]

consolation, *4155, paraklēsis* [1]

CONSPIRACY [1]

conspiracy, *5371, systrophē* [1]

CONSPIRE [1]

conspire, *AIT* [1]

CONSPIRED [1]

conspired, *5205, symbouleuō* [1]

CONSTANT [3]

constant, *AIT* [1]
constant friction between, *1384, diaparatribē* [1]
constant use, *2011, hexis* [1]

CONSTANTLY [6]

constantly, *AIT* [1]
constantly, *89, adialeiptos* [1]
constantly, *90, adialeiptōs* [1]

CONSTRUCTIVE

joined constantly, *1639+4674,*
eimi+proskartereō [1]
constantly, *4121, pantote* [1]
constantly, *4490, pollakis* [1]

CONSTRUCTIVE [1]

constructive, *3868, oikodomeō* [1]

CONSULT [1]

consult, *4651, prosanatithēmi* [1]

CONSUME [2]

consume, *2266, esthiō* [1]
consume, *2983, katesthiō* [1]

CONSUMED [1]

consumed, *2876, katakaiō* [1]

CONSUMING [1]

consuming, *2914, katanaliskō* [1]

CONTAIN [1]

contain, *1877, en* [1]

CONTAINED [2]

contained, *1877+2400, en+echō* [1]
contained, *1877+5639, en+hyparchō* [1]

CONTAMINATES [1]

that contaminates, *3663, molysmos* [1]

CONTEMPT [3]

treat with contempt, *2024, exoutheneō* [2]
show contempt for, *2969, kataphroneō* [1]

CONTEND [1]

contend, *2043, epagōnizomai* [1]

CONTENDED [1]

contended at side, *5254, synathleō* [1]

CONTENDING [1]

contending as, *5254, synathleō* [1]

CONTENT [5]

content, *758, arkeō* [3]
content, *RPE* [1]
content, *895, autarkēs* [1]

CONTENTIOUS [1]

contentious, *5809, philoneikos* [1]

CONTENTMENT [1]

contentment, *894, autarkeia* [1]

CONTEST [1]

contest, *124, athlēsis* [1]

CONTINUAL [1]

continual, *AIT* [1]

CONTINUALLY [5]

continually, *90, adialeiptōs* [3]
continually, *1328+4246, dia+pas* [2]

CONTINUE [28]

continue, *AIT* [13]
continue, *2285, eti* [5]
continue, *3531, menō* [4]
continue in, *2152, epimenō* [2]

continue, *1844, emmenō* [1]
continue, *1877, en* [1]
continue with, *4169, paramenō* [1]
continue in, *4693, prosmenō* [1]

CONTINUED [13]

continued, *3306, legō* [4]
continued, *AIT* [3]
continued, *1382, dianyō* [1]
continued, *1639, eimi* [1]
continued raging, *4024+3900+2130,*
ou+oligos+epikeimai [1]
continued on way, *4513, poreuomai* [1]
continued, *4674, proskartereō* [1]
continued with, *5302, synerchomai* [1]

CONTINUES [5]

continues, *AIT* [2]
continues, *3531, menō* [1]
continues, *4169, paramenō* [1]
continues, *4693, prosmenō* [1]

CONTINUING [3]

continuing, *AIT* [1]
continuing, *NIG* [1]
continuing, *4169, paramenō* [1]

CONTRADICT [1]

contradict, *515, antilegō* [1]

CONTRARY [18]

on the contrary, *247, alla* [10]
contrary to, *4123, para* [3]
contrary to, *2848, kata* [2]
on contrary, *247+5539, alla+tounantion* [1]
on the contrary, *247+4498+3437,*
alla+polys+mallon [1]
contrary, *512, antikeimai* [1]

CONTRIBUTING [1]

contributing to the needs of others, *3556,*
metadidōmi [1]

CONTRIBUTION [1]

contribution, *3126, koinōnia* [1]

CONTROL [9]

control, *2026, exousia* [2]
control, *AIT* [1]
gain control over, *170, aichmalōtizō* [1]
control, *1603, enkrateuomai* [1]
under the control, *3023, keimai* [1]
control, *3227, ktaomai* [1]
bring under control, *5718, hypotassō* [1]
subject to the control, *5718, hypotassō* [1]

CONTROLLED [4]

controlled, *AIT* [2]
controlled, *1639, eimi* [2]

CONTROVERSIES [4]

controversies, *2428, zētēsis* [2]
controversies, *1700, ekzētēsis* [1]
controversies, *2427, zētēma* [1]

CONVENED [2]

convened the court, *2767+2093+3836+1037,*
kathizō+epi+ho+bēma [1]
convened, *2767, kathizō* [1]

CONVENIENT [1]

find convenient, *2789+3561,*
kairos+metalambanō [1]

CONVERSATION [1]

conversation, *3364, logos* [1]

CONVERT [4]

first convert, *569, aparchē* [1]
recent convert, *3745, neophytos* [1]
convert to Judaism, *4670, prosēlytos* [1]
convert, *4670, prosēlytos* [1]

CONVERTED [1]

converted, *2189, epistrophē* [1]

CONVERTS [3]

converts to Judaism, *4670, prosēlytos* [2]
first converts, *569, aparchē* [1]

CONVICT [2]

convict of guilt, *1794, elenchō* [1]
convict, *1794, elenchō* [1]

CONVICTED [1]

convicted, *1794, elenchō* [1]

CONVICTION [1]

conviction, *4443, plērophoria* [1]

CONVINCE [1]

convince, *4275, peithō* [1]

CONVINCED [15]

convinced, *4275, peithō* [7]
convinced, *1506+1831, dokeō+emautou* [1]
convinced that is a sinner, *1794, elenchō* [1]
convinced, *3212, krinō* [1]
fully convinced, *3857+2779+4275,*
oida+kai+peithō [1]
convinced of, *4275, peithō* [1]
convinced that, *4275, peithō* [1]
convinced, *4413, pistoō* [1]
fully convinced, *4442, plērophoreō* [1]

CONVINCING [1]

convincing proofs, *5447, tekmērion* [1]

CONVULSED [1]

convulsed, *5057, sparassō* [1]

CONVULSION [2]

in a convulsion, *5360, sysparassō* [1]
threw into a convulsion, *5360, sysparassō* [1]

CONVULSIONS [1]

throws into convulsions, *5057, sparassō* [1]

COOL [1]

cool, *2976, katapsychō* [1]

COPIES [1]

copies, *5682, hypodeigma* [1]

COPPER [3]

very small copper coins, *3321, leptos* [2]
copper, *5910, chalkos* [1]

COPY [2]

copy, *531, antitypos* [1]

copy, *5682, hypodeigma* [1]

CORBAN [1]

Corban, *3167, korban* [1]

CORDS [1]

cords, *5389, schoinion* [1]

CORINTH [7]

Corinth, *3172, Korinthos* [6]
Corinth, *RPE* [1]

CORINTHIANS [2]

Corinthians, *3171, Korinthios* [2]

CORNELIUS [10]

Cornelius, *3173, Kornēlios* [8]
Cornelius, *RPE* [1]
Cornelius[s], *3836+1254, ho+de* [1]

CORNER [1]

corner, *1224, gōnia* [1]

CORNERS [6]

corners, *1224, gōnia* [3]
corners, *794, archē* [2]
corners, *1447, diexodos* [1]

CORNERSTONE [2]

chief cornerstone, *214, akrogōniaios* [1]
cornerstone, *214, akrogōniaios* [1]

CORPSE [1]

corpse, *3738, nekros* [1]

CORRECT [1]

correct, *1794, elenchō* [1]

CORRECTING [1]

correcting, *2061, epanorthōsis* [1]

CORRECTLY [3]

correctly, *3987, orthōs* [2]
correctly handles, *3982, orthotomeō* [1]

CORRESPONDS [1]

corresponds, *5368, systoicheō* [1]

CORRODED [1]

corroded, *2995, katioō* [1]

CORROSION [1]

corrosion, *2675, ios* [1]

CORRUPT [3]

corrupt, *1425, diaphtheirō* [1]
corrupt, *3622, miasmos* [1]
corrupt, *5021, skolios* [1]

CORRUPTED [6]

corrupted, *5780, phtheirō* [3]
corrupted, *3620, miainō* [2]
corrupted flesh, *4922, sarx* [1]

CORRUPTION [2]

corruption, *3621, miasma* [1]
corruption, *5785, phthora* [1]

CORRUPTS [2]

corrupts, *5071, spiloō* [1]

corrupts, *5780, phtheirō* [1]

COS [1]

Cos, *3271, Kōs* [1]

COSAM [1]

Cosam, *3272, Kōsam* [1]

COST [2]

cost, *1252, dapanē* [1]
without cost, *1562, dōrean* [1]

COSTLY [2]

costly, *5508, timios* [2]

COULD [95]

could, *AIT* [38]
could, *1538, dynamai* [31]
could, *2710, ischyō* [8]
could have, *1538, dynamai* [4]
could, *NIG* [2]
could, *1543, dynatos* [2]
could, *3614, mēti* [2]
could have, *323, an* [1]
could have done so, *1543, dynatos* [1]
if it could, *2075, epei* [1]
could, *2400, echō* [1]
could not talk, *3273, kōphos* [1]
could, *3590, mē* [1]
could hardly talk, *3652, mogilalos* [1]
could not give, *5729, hysterēma* [1]

COULDN'T [2]

couldn't, *4024+1538, ou+dynamai* [2]

COUNCIL [7]

member of the Council, *1085, bouleutēs* [2]
ruling council, *807, archōn* [1]
the Council[s], *899, autos* [1]
Council, *4564, presbyterion* [1]
council of elders, *4564, presbyterion* [1]
council, *5206, symboulion* [1]

COUNCILS [2]

local councils, *5284, synedrion* [2]

COUNSEL [2]

counsel, *1089, boulomai* [1]
counsel, *5205, symbouleuō* [1]

COUNSELOR [5]

Counselor, *4156, paraklētos* [4]
counselor, *5207, symboulos* [1]

COUNT [5]

count, *3357, logizomai* [2]
count, *RPE* [1]
count worthy, *546, axioō* [1]
count, *749, arithmeō* [1]

COUNTED [3]

counted worthy, *2921, kataxioō* [2]
counted out, *2705, histēmi* [1]

COUNTERFEIT [2]

counterfeit, *6022, pseudos* [2]

COUNTING [1]

counting, *3357, logizomai* [1]

COUNTLESS [1]

countless, *410, anarithmētos* [1]

COUNTRY [32]

country, *6001, chōra* [8]
country, *69, agros* [3]
surrounding country, *4369, perichōros* [3]
country, *AIT* [2]
country, *1178, gē* [2]
hill country, *3978, oreinos* [2]
country, *RPE* [1]
that country[s], *899, autos* [1]
king's country, *997, basilikos* [1]
country, *1620, ethnos* [1]
the country[s], *1697, ekeinos* [1]
country, *2244, erēmia* [1]
open country, *2245, erēmos* [1]
the country[s], *4246, pas* [1]
country of their own, *4258, patris* [1]
country, *4258, patris* [1]
country around, *4369, perichōros* [1]
country lanes, *5850, phragmos* [1]

COUNTRYMEN [2]

countrymen, *1169, genos* [1]
countrymen, *5241, symphyletēs* [1]

COUNTRYSIDE [8]

countryside, *69, agros* [5]
countryside, *1178, gē* [1]
countryside, *4369, perichōros* [1]
countryside, *6001, chōra* [1]

COUNTS [4]

the only thing that counts, *247, alla* [1]
what counts[s], *247, alla* [1]
what counts, *247, alla* [1]
counts for, *6067, ōpheleō* [1]

COURAGE [9]

take courage, *2510, tharseō* [3]
courage, *4244, parrēsia* [3]
keep up courage, *2313, euthymeō* [2]
men of courage, *437, andrizomai* [1]

COURAGEOUSLY [1]

courageously, *5528, tolmaō* [1]

COURSE [5]

course, *NIG* [1]
course, *2717, ichnos* [1]
of course, *3529, menounge* [1]
allow to hold course, *4661, proseaō* [1]
course, *5580, trochos* [1]

COURT [10]

court, *1037, bēma* [4]
adversary is taking to court, *508, antidikos* [1]
court, *885, aulē* [1]
court, *2093+1037, epi+bēma* [1]
court, *2465, hēmera* [1]
convened the court, *2767+2093+3836+1037, kathizō+epi+ho+bēma* [1]
court, *3215, kritērion* [1]

COURTS [24]

temple courts, *2639, hieron* [23]
courts, *61, agoraios* [1]

COURTYARD [6]

courtyard, *885, aulē* [6]

COUSIN [1]

cousin, *463, anepsios* [1]

COVENANT [33]

covenant, *1347, diathēkē* [25]
covenant, *RPE* [4]
covenant make, *1347+1416,*
   diathēkē+diatithēmi [2]
covenant, *AIT* [1]
covenant made, *1347+1416,*
   diathēkē+diatithēmi [1]

COVENANTS [3]

covenants, *1347, diathēkē* [3]

COVER [8]

cover, *2877, katakalyptō* [3]
atonement cover, *2663, hilastērion* [1]
cover, *2821, kalyptō* [1]
cover over, *2821, kalyptō* [1]
cover, *3590+5746, mē+phaneroō* [1]
mask to cover up, *4733, prophasis* [1]

COVER-UP [1]

cover-up, *2127, epikalymma* [1]

COVERED [9]

covered with, *1154, gemō* [3]
covered with sores, *1815, helkoō* [1]
covered, *2128, epikalyptō* [1]
covered, *2848+2400, kata+echō* [1]
covered, *4441, plērēs* [1]
covered colonnades, *5119, stoa* [1]
covered, *5309, synechō* [1]

COVERING [1]

covering, *4316, peribolaion* [1]

COVERS [2]

covers, *2093+3023, epi+keimai* [1]
covers over, *2821, kalyptō* [1]

COVET [3]

covet, *2121, epithymeō* [2]
covet, *2420, zēloō* [1]

COVETED [1]

coveted, *2121, epithymeō* [1]

COVETING [1]

coveting, *2123, epithymia* [1]

COVETOUS [1]

covetous desire, *2123, epithymia* [1]

COWARDLY [1]

cowardly, *1264, deilos* [1]

CRAFTINESS [2]

craftiness, *4111, panourgia* [2]

CRAFTSMEN [2]

craftsmen, *5493, technitēs* [2]

CRAFTY [1]

crafty, *4112, panourgos* [1]

CRASH [1]

crash, *4774, ptōsis* [1]

CRAVE [1]

crave, *2160, epipotheō* [1]

CRAVINGS [2]

cravings, *2123, epithymia* [2]

CREATE [1]

create, *3231, ktizō* [1]

CREATED [15]

created, *3231, ktizō* [11]
created, *3233, ktisma* [2]
created things, *3232, ktisis* [1]
created things, *4472, poieō* [1]

CREATION [24]

creation, *3232, ktisis* [15]
creation, *2856, katabolē* [9]

CREATOR [4]

Creator, *3231, ktizō* [3]
Creator, *3234, ktistēs* [1]

CREATURE [6]

living creature, *2442, zōon* [4]
creature, *3232, ktisis* [1]
creature, *3233, ktisma* [1]

CREATURES [16]

living creatures, *2442, zōon* [13]
creatures of sea, *1879, enalios* [1]
creatures, *3233, ktisma* [1]
creatures of instinct, *5879, physikos* [1]

CREDIT [5]

credit, *5921, charis* [3]
credit, *3094, kleos* [1]
credit, *3357, logizomai* [1]

CREDITED [11]

credited, *3357, logizomai* [10]
credited, *4429, pleonazō* [1]

CREDITS [1]

credits, *3357, logizomai* [1]

CRESCENS [1]

Crescens, *3206, Krēskēs* [1]

CRETANS [2]

Cretans, *3205, Krēs* [2]

CRETE [5]

Crete, *3207, Krētē* [5]

CRIED [19]

cried out, *3189, krazō* [8]
cried out, *371, anakrazō* [5]
cried out, *331, anaboaō* [1]
cried out, *1066, boaō* [1]
cried out, *3189+5889+3489,*
   krazō+phōnē+megas [1]
cried, *3189, krazō* [1]
cried out, *3306, legō* [1]
cried, *3306, legō* [1]

CRIES [4]

cries out, *3189, krazō* [2]
cries, *1068, boē* [1]
cries, *3199, kraugē* [1]

CRIME [6]

crime, *2805, kakos* [3]
crime, *93, adikēma* [1]
guilty of crime, *162, aitia* [1]
crime, *4815, rhadiourgēma* [1]

CRIMES [2]

crimes, *93, adikēma* [1]
crimes, *4505, ponēros* [1]

CRIMINAL [4]

criminal, *RPE* [1]
criminal, *2804, kakopoios* [1]
criminal, *2805+4472, kakos+poieō* [1]
criminal, *2806, kakourgos* [1]

CRIMINALS [3]

criminals, *2806, kakourgos* [3]

CRIPPLE [1]

cripple, *476+822, anthrōpos+asthenēs* [1]

CRIPPLED [9]

crippled, *6000, chōlos* [3]
crippled, *401, anapeiros* [2]
crippled, *3245, kyllos* [2]
crippled, *105, adynatos* [1]
crippled, *2400+819, echō+astheneia* [1]

CRIPPLES [1]

cripples, *6000, chōlos* [1]

CRISIS [1]

crisis, *340, anankē* [1]

CRISPUS [2]

Crispus, *3214, Krispos* [2]

CRITICISM [1]

criticism, *3699, mōmaomai* [1]

CRITICIZED [1]

criticized, *1359, diakrinō* [1]

CROOKED [2]

crooked, *5021, skolios* [2]

CROP [11]

crop, *2843, karpos* [6]
produce a crop, *2844, karpophoreō* [2]
crop, *1083, botanē* [1]
produced a good crop, *2369, euphoreō* [1]
produces a crop, *2844, karpophoreō* [1]

CROPS [5]

crops, *2843, karpos* [3]
crops, *AIT* [1]
crops, *2845, karpophoros* [1]

CROSS [30]

cross, *5089, stauros* [26]
cross, *599, aperchomai* [1]
the cross*s*, *899, autos* [1]
cross over, *1385, diaperaō* [1]
nailing to cross, *4699, prospēgnymi* [1]

CROSS-EXAMINED [1]

cross-examined, *373, anakrinō* [1]

CROSSED [9]

crossed over, *1385, diaperaō* [4]
crossed, *599, aperchomai* [2]
crossed over, *3553, metabainō* [1]
crossed over, *4125, paraballō* [1]
crossed, *4305, peran* [1]

CROSSES [1]

crosses, *5089, stauros* [1]

CROSSING [1]

crossing over, *1385, diaperaō* [1]

CROW [1]

crow, *5888, phōneō* [1]

CROWD [121]

crowd, *4063, ochlos* [106]
the crowdˢ, *899, autos* [4]
crowd, *4436, plēthos* [3]
crowd, *RPE* [2]
crowd, *1322, dēmos* [2]
crowd, *3295, laos* [2]
crowd of people, *4063, ochlos* [1]
crowd, *4436+3836+3295, plēthos+ho+laos* [1]

CROWDING [4]

crowding around, *2130, epikeimai* [1]
crowding, *2567, thlibō* [1]
crowding against, *5309, synechō* [1]
crowding against, *5315, synthlibō* [1]

CROWDS [27]

crowds, *4063, ochlos* [25]
crowds, *4436, plēthos* [1]
crowds, *4498, polys* [1]

CROWED [3]

crowed, *5888, phōneō* [3]

CROWN [17]

crown, *5109, stephanos2* [15]
crown, *RPE* [1]
receive the victor's crown, *5110, stephanoō* [1]

CROWNED [2]

crowned, *5110, stephanoō* [2]

CROWNS [6]

crowns, *1343, diadēma* [3]
crowns, *5109, stephanos2* [3]

CROWS [8]

crows, *5888, phōneō* [7]
when the rooster crows, *231, alektorophōnia* [1]

CRUCIFIED [36]

crucified, *5090, stauroō* [31]
crucified with, *5365, systauroō* [3]
crucified with, *5365+5250, systauroō+syn* [2]

CRUCIFY [15]

crucify, *5090, stauroō* [15]

CRUCIFYING [1]

crucifying all over again, *416, anastauroō* [1]

CRUMBS [2]

crumbs, *6033, psichion* [2]

CRUSH [1]

crush, *5341, syntribō* [1]

CRUSHED [4]

crushed, *3347, likmaō* [2]
crushed, *5102, stenochōreō* [1]
crushed, *5231, sympnigō* [1]

CRY [14]

cry out, *3189, krazō* [3]
cry, *3081, klaiō* [2]
cry, *3189, krazō* [2]
cry aloud, *1066, boaō* [1]
cry out, *1066, boaō* [1]
cry out, *3198, kraugazō* [1]
cry, *3199, kraugē* [1]
cry out, *3306, legō* [1]
cry, *3306, legō* [1]
cry, *5889, phōnē* [1]

CRYING [9]

crying, *3081, klaiō* [5]
crying out, *3189, krazō* [3]
crying, *3199, kraugē* [1]

CRYSTAL [3]

crystal, *3223, krystallos* [2]
clear as crystal, *3222, krystallizō* [1]

CUBITS [1]

cubits, *4388, pēchys* [1]

CULTIVATED [1]

cultivated olive tree, *2814, kallielaios* [1]

CUMMIN [1]

cummin, *3248, kyminon* [1]

CUNNING [2]

cunning, *3235, kybeia* [1]
cunning, *4111, panourgia* [1]

CUP [31]

cup, *4539, potērion* [29]
cup, *RPE* [1]
gives a cup, *4540+4539, potizō+potērion* [1]

CUPS [1]

cups, *4539, potērion* [1]

CURE [1]

cure, *2543, therapeuō* [1]

CURED [11]

cured, *2751, katharizō* [4]
cured, *2543, therapeuō* [3]
cured, *557+608, apallassō+apo* [1]
cured, *1639+2543, eimi+therapeuō* [1]
cured, *5392, sōzō* [1]
cured, *5618, hygiēs* [1]

CURSE [9]

curse, *2932, katara* [3]
curse, *2933, kataraomai* [3]
curse, *353, anathema* [1]
curse on, *2063, eparatos* [1]
curse, *2873, katathema* [1]

CURSED [11]

cursed, *1059, blasphēmeō* [3]
cursed, *353, anathema* [2]
cursed, *2129, epikataratos* [2]
cursed, *2933, kataraomai* [2]
being cursed, *2932, katara* [1]
cursed, *3366, loidoreō* [1]

CURSES [4]

curses, *2800, kakologeō* [2]
call down curses, *354, anathematizō* [1]
call down curses, *2874, katathematizō* [1]

CURSING [2]

cursing, *725, ara* [1]
cursing, *2932, katara* [1]

CURTAIN [6]

curtain, *2925, katapetasma* [6]

CUSHION [1]

cushion, *4676, proskephalaion* [1]

CUSTOM [11]

custom, *1621, ethos* [4]
custom, *1665, eiōtha* [4]
custom, *AIT* [1]
custom, *1616, ethizō* [1]
custom, *5311, synētheia* [1]

CUSTOMARY [1]

customary, *AIT* [1]

CUSTOMS [7]

customs, *1621, ethos* [6]
follow Jewish customs, *2678, ioudaizō* [1]

CUT [31]

cut down, *1716, ekkoptō* [5]
cut off, *644, apokoptō* [3]
cut off, *1716, ekkoptō* [3]
cut to pieces, *1497, dichotomeō* [2]
cut off, *3025, keirō* [2]
cut short, *3143, koloboō* [2]
cut, *3164, koptō* [2]
cut off from, *608, apo* [1]
cut, *644, apokoptō* [1]
cut in on, *1601, enkoptō* [1]
cut, *1639+3300, eimi+latomeō* [1]
cut out of, *1666+1716, ek+ekkoptō* [1]
cut from under, *1716, ekkoptō* [1]
completely cut off from, *2017+1666,*
    exolethreuō+ek [1]
cut, *2888, katakoptō* [1]
cut to, *2920, katanyssomai* [1]
hair cut, *3025, keirō* [1]
cut in the rock, *3292, laxeutos* [1]
cut out, *3300, latomeō* [1]

CUTS [1]

cuts off, *149, airō* [1]

CUTTING [5]

cutting off, *904, aphaireō* [3]
cutting off, *644, apokoptō* [1]
cutting loose, *4311, periaireō* [1]

CUZA [1]

Cuza, *5966, Chouzas* [1]

CYMBAL [1]

cymbal, *3247, kymbalon* [1]

CYPRUS [8]

Cyprus, *3251, Kypros* [5]
from Cyprus, *3250, Kyprios* [3]

CYRENE [7]

from Cyrene, *3254, Kyrēnaios* [4]
of Cyrene, *3254, Kyrēnaios* [2]
Cyrene, *3255, Kyrēnē* [1]

DAILY [12]

daily, *2848+2465, kata+hēmera* [5]
daily, *2157, epiousios* [2]
daily necessities, *338+5970, anankaios+chreia* [1]
daily, *2390, ephēmeros* [1]
daily, *2766, kathēmerinos* [1]
daily, *2848+1667+2465, kata+hekastos+hēmera* [1]
daily life, *4344, peripateō* [1]

DALMANUTHA [1]

Dalmanutha, *1236, Dalmanoutha* [1]

DALMATIA [1]

Dalmatia, *1237, Dalmatia* [1]

DAMAGE [2]

damage, *92, adikeō* [1]
damage, *5615, hybris* [1]

DAMARIS [1]

Damaris, *1240, Damaris* [1]

DAMASCENES [1]

the Damascenes, *1241, Damaskēnos* [1]

DAMASCUS [15]

Damascus, *1242, Damaskos* [15]

DANCE [2]

dance, *4004, orcheomai* [2]

DANCED [2]

danced, *4004, orcheomai* [2]

DANCING [1]

dancing, *5962, choros* [1]

DANGER [14]

danger, *3074, kindynos* [9]
in danger of, *1584, engys* [1]
in danger, *1944, enochos* [1]
danger that, *3073, kindyneuō* [1]
in danger of, *3073, kindyneuō* [1]
in great danger, *3073, kindyneuō* [1]

DANGEROUS [1]

dangerous, *2195, episphalēs* [1]

DANIEL [1]

Daniel, *1248, Daniēl* [1]

DARE [9]

dare, *5528, tolmaō* [6]
dare, *AIT* [2]
how dare you, *3590, mē* [1]

DARED [6]

dared, *5528, tolmaō* [5]
dared, *4245, parrēsiazomai* [1]

DARES [1]

dares, *5528, tolmaō* [1]

DARK [12]

dark, *5028, skotia* [5]
dark, *5030, skotos* [2]
dark, *903, auchmēros* [1]
while it was still dark, *1939, ennychos* [1]
dark, *5027, skoteinos* [1]
turned dark, *5029, skotizomai* [1]
dark blue, *5610, hyakinthinos* [1]

DARKENED [6]

darkened, *5029, skotizomai* [4]
darkened, *5031, skotoō* [2]

DARKNESS [45]

darkness, *5030, skotos* [29]
darkness, *5028, skotia* [11]
full of darkness, *5027, skoteinos* [2]
darkness, *1190, gnophos* [1]
darkness, *2432, zophos* [1]
darkness, *5031, skotoō* [1]

DASH [2]

dash to the ground, *1610, edaphizō* [1]
dash to pieces, *5341, syntribō* [1]

DASHED [1]

dashed, *1738, ekpiptō* [1]

DATE [1]

date, *AIT* [1]

DATES [2]

dates, *2789, kairos* [2]

DAUGHTER [25]

daughter, *2588, thygatēr* [23]
little daughter, *2589, thygatrion* [2]

DAUGHTER-IN-LAW [3]

daughter-in-law, *3811, nymphē* [3]

DAUGHTERS [5]

daughters, *2588, thygatēr* [4]
daughters, *5451, teknon* [1]

DAVID [57]

David, *1253, Dauid* [57]

DAVID'S [2]

David's, *1253, Dauid* [2]

DAWN [4]

dawn, *2216, epiphōskō* [1]
dawn, *2465+3516+1181, hēmera+mellō+ginomai* [1]
dawn, *3986, orthros* [1]
at dawn, *4745, prōi* [1]

DAWNED [2]

dawned, *422, anatellō* [1]
dawned on, *5328, synoraō* [1]

DAWNS [1]

dawns, *1419, diaugazō* [1]

DAY [260]

day, *2465, hēmera* [181]

next day, *2069, epaurion* [15]
day, *AIT* [12]
day, *RPE* [5]
day after day, *2848+2465, kata+hēmera* [4]
day, *NIG* [3]
next day, *892, aurion* [3]
next day, *2079, epeimi* [3]
day of Preparation, *4187, paraskeuē* [3]
following day, *2069, epaurion* [2]
every day, *2848+2465, kata+hēmera* [2]
day by day, *2848+4246+2465, kata+pas+hēmera* [2]
Preparation Day, *4187, paraskeuē* [2]
day after day, *4246+2465, pas+hēmera* [2]
day, *4958, sēmeron* [2]
very day, *4958+2465, sēmeron+hēmera* [2]
this very day, *785, arti* [1]
one day, *1181+1254, ginomai+de* [1]
on the following day, *1308, deuteraios* [1]
day after, *2283, heteros* [1]
next day, *2400, echō* [1]
one day, *2779+1181, kai+ginomai* [1]
the next day, *3552+1651+2465, meta+heis+hēmera* [1]
a night and a day, *3819, nychthēmeron* [1]
each day, *3836+2465, ho+hēmera* [1]
eighth day, *3892, oktaēmeros* [1]
that day[s], *4005, hos* [1]
day before the Sabbath, *4640, prosabbaton* [1]
Sabbath day, *4879, sabbaton* [1]
day[s], *4879, sabbaton* [1]
day, *4958+2465, sēmeron+hēmera* [1]
this day, *4958, sēmeron* [1]
late in the day, *6052+4498, hōra+polys* [1]

DAY'S [3]

a day's wages, *1324, dēnarion* [2]
Sabbath day's walk from, *1584+4879+2400+3847, engys+sabbaton+echō+hodos* [1]

DAYBREAK [3]

at daybreak, *1181+2465+2002, ginomai+hēmera+exerchomai* [1]
daybreak, *1181+2465, ginomai+hēmera* [1]
daybreak, *3986, orthros* [1]

DAYLIGHT [8]

daylight, *2465, hēmera* [4]
daylight, *5890, phōs* [2]
daylight, *879, augē* [1]
broad daylight, *2465, hēmera* [1]

DAYS [122]

days, *2465, hēmera* [114]
days, *AIT* [1]
days, *RPE* [1]
a few days later, *1328+2465, dia+hēmera* [1]
in the days of, *2093, epi* [1]
in early days, *4754, prōton* [1]
Sabbath days, *4879, sabbaton* [1]
days, *4958, sēmeron* [1]
four days, *5479, tetartaios* [1]

DAYTIME [1]

daytime, *2465, hēmera* [1]

DAZZLING [1]

dazzling, *5118+3336, stilbō+lian* [1]

DEACON [1]

deacon, *1356, diakonos* [1]

DEACONS [3]

deacons, *1356, diakonos* [2]
serve as deacons, *1354, diakoneō* [1]

DEAD [156]

dead, *3738, nekros* [123]
dead, *633, apothnēskō* [9]
dead, *2569, thnēskō* [9]
raised from the dead, *1586, egeirō* [6]
raised from the dead, *482, anistēmi* [1]
strike dead, *650+1877+2505,*
    apokteinō+en+thanatos [1]
as good as dead, *2453+3739, ēdē+nekroō* [1]
half dead, *2467, hēmithanēs* [1]
dead, *3739, nekroō* [1]
dead, *3740, nekrōsis* [1]
dead body, *5393, sōma* [1]
dead, *5393, sōma* [1]
dead, *5462, teleutaō* [1]

DEADENED [1]

deadened, *4800, pōroō* [1]

DEADLY [3]

deadly poison, *2503+5516, thanasimos+tis* [1]
deadly, *2504, thanatēphoros* [1]
deadly peril, *2505, thanatos* [1]

DEAF [5]

deaf, *3273, kōphos* [4]
man who was deaf, *3273, kōphos* [1]

DEAL [5]

great deal of, *4498, polys* [2]
great deal, *4498, polys* [2]
deal gently, *3584, metriopatheō* [1]

DEALER [1]

dealer in purple cloth, *4527, porphyropōlis* [1]

DEALING [2]

dealing, *AIT* [1]
in dealing with, *1650, eis* [1]

DEALS [1]

deals, *AIT* [1]

DEALT [2]

dealt, *AIT* [1]
dealt treacherously with, *2947,*
    katasophizomai [1]

DEAR [59]

dear friends, *28, agapētos* [22]
dear, *28, agapētos* [13]
dear friend, *28, agapētos* [9]
dear children, *5448, teknion* [7]
dear woman, *1222, gynē* [2]
dear children, *4086, paidion* [2]
dear, *RPE* [1]
so dear, *28, agapētos* [1]
dear lady, *3257, kyria* [1]
dear children, *5451, teknon* [1]

DEARER [1]

dearer, *RPE* [1]

DEARLY [2]

dearly loved, *28, agapētos* [1]
dearly, *5073, splanchnon* [1]

DEATH [141]

death, *2505, thanatos* [104]
put to death, *2506, thanatoō* [8]
put to death, *359, anaireō* [4]
put to death, *650, apokteinō* [4]
death, *3738, nekros* [3]
death, *633, apothnēskō* [2]
put to death, *2505+5462, thanatos+teleutaō* [2]
death, *AIT* [1]
grounds for the death penalty, *165+2505,*
    aitios+thanatos [1]
death, *358, anairesis* [1]
death[s], *899, autos* [1]
put to death, *1877+5840+633,*
    en+phonos+apothnēskō [1]
death sentence, *2505, thanatos* [1]
exposed to death, *2505, thanatos* [1]
face death, *2506, thanatoō* [1]
starving to death, *3350+660,*
    limos+apollymi [1]
put to death, *3739, nekroō* [1]
death, *3740, nekrōsis* [1]
from death[s], *3854, hothen* [1]
the death[s], *4005, hos* [1]
death, *5463, teleutē* [1]

DEBATE [2]

debate, *AIT* [1]
debate, *2428, zētēsis* [1]

DEBATED [1]

debated, *5184, syzēteō* [1]

DEBATING [1]

debating, *5184, syzēteō* [1]

DEBAUCHERY [5]

debauchery, *816, aselgeia* [4]
debauchery, *861, asōtia* [1]

DEBT [7]

debt, *RPE* [2]
repay the debt, *625, apodidōmi* [1]
debt, *1245, daneion* [1]
debt, *4051, opheilē* [1]
debt remain outstanding, *4053, opheilō* [1]
debt, *4053, opheilō* [1]

DEBTORS [2]

debtors, *4050, opheiletēs* [1]
debtors, *5971, chreopheiletēs* [1]

DEBTS [2]

debts, *RPE* [1]
debts, *4052, opheilēma* [1]

DECAPOLIS [3]

Decapolis, *1279, Dekapolis* [3]

DECAY [6]

decay, *1426, diaphthora* [4]
decay, *5715+1650+1426,*
    hypostrephō+eis+diaphthora [1]
decay, *5785, phthora* [1]

DECAYED [1]

body decayed, *3972+1426,*
    horaō+diaphthora [1]

DECEIT [6]

deceit, *1515, dolos* [5]
practice deceit, *1514, dolioō* [1]

DECEITFUL [5]

deceitful, *573, apatē* [1]
deceitful, *1513, dolios* [1]
deceitful, *1515, dolos* [1]
deceitful, *4415, planē* [1]
what is deceitful, *6022, pseudos* [1]

DECEITFULNESS [3]

deceitfulness, *573, apatē* [3]

DECEIVE [13]

deceive, *4414, planaō* [6]
deceive, *1987, exapataō* [3]
deceive, *4165, paralogizomai* [2]
deceive, *572, apataō* [1]
deceive, *675, apoplanaō* [1]

DECEIVED [13]

deceived, *4414, planaō* [9]
deceived, *1987, exapataō* [3]
deceived, *572, apataō* [1]

DECEIVER [2]

deceiver, *4418, planos* [2]

DECEIVERS [2]

deceivers, *4418, planos* [1]
deceivers, *5855, phrenapatēs* [1]

DECEIVES [6]

deceives, *4414, planaō* [3]
deceives, *572, apataō* [1]
deceives, *573, apatē* [1]
deceives, *5854, phrenapataō* [1]

DECEIVING [3]

deceiving, *4414, planaō* [2]
deceiving, *4418, planos* [1]

DECENCY [1]

decency, *133, aidōs* [1]

DECENTLY [1]

decently, *2361, euschēmonōs* [1]

DECEPTION [2]

deception, *4111, panourgia* [1]
deception, *4415, planē* [1]

DECEPTIVE [1]

deceptive, *573, apatē* [1]

DECIDE [3]

decide, *1336, diaginōskō* [1]
decide, *2351, heuriskō* [1]
decide by lot, *3275, lanchanō* [1]

DECIDED [18]

decided, *3212, krinō* [4]
decided, *326+2093+3836+2840,*
    anabainō+epi+ho+kardia [1]
decided, *1086, bouleuō* [1]
decided, *1181+1191, ginomai+gnōmē* [1]
decided, *1506, dokeō* [1]
decided, *2137, epikrinō* [1]
decided, *2527, thelō* [1]
decided that, *3212, krinō* [1]
decided, *3988, horizō* [1]
decided, *4576, proaireō* [1]
decided beforehand, *4633, proorizō* [1]

decided to, *5206+3284,*
   symboulion+lambanō [1]
decided, *5338, syntithēmi* [1]
decided that, *5502+1087, tithēmi+boulē* [1]
decided, *5502+1877+3836+4460,*
   tithēmi+en+ho+pneuma [1]

DECISION [6]

decision, *1087, boulē* [1]
decision, *1338, diagnōsis* [1]
decision, *2525, thelēma* [1]
decision that, *3212, krinō* [1]
decision, *5206, symboulion* [1]
to the decision, *5206+3284,*
   symboulion+lambanō [1]

DECISIONS [2]

decisions, *1504, dogma* [1]
decisions, *3213, krisis* [1]

DECLARE [7]

declare, *3458, martyromai* [2]
declare, *334, anangellō* [1]
declare, *550, apangellō* [1]
declare, *1972, exangellō* [1]
declare, *3281, laleō* [1]
declare, *5774, phēmi* [1]

DECLARED [23]

declared, *3306, legō* [8]
declared, *646, apokrinomai* [3]
declared, *1371, diamartyromai* [2]
declared righteous, *1467, dikaioō* [2]
declared, *3455, martyreō* [2]
declared on oath, *3923, omnyō* [2]
declared, *5774, phēmi* [2]
declared, *NIG* [1]
declared, *3988, horizō* [1]

DECLARES [6]

declares, *3306, legō* [4]
declares, *AIT* [1]
declares a prisoner, *5168, synkleiō* [1]

DECLARING [1]

declaring, *3281, laleō* [1]

DECLINED [1]

declined, *4024+2153, ou+epineuō* [1]

DECORATE [1]

decorate, *3175, kosmeō* [1]

DECORATED [1]

decorated, *3175, kosmeō* [1]

DECREE [2]

righteous decree, *1468, dikaiōma* [1]
decree, *1504, dogma* [1]

DECREED [1]

decreed, *3988, horizō* [1]

DECREES [1]

decrees, *1504, dogma* [1]

DEDICATED [1]

gifts dedicated to God, *356, anathēma* [1]

DEDICATION [2]

Feast of Dedication, *1589, enkainia* [1]

sensual desires overcome their dedication to,
   2952, katastrēniaō [1]

DEED [3]

deed, *2240, ergon* [3]

DEEDS [32]

deeds, *2240, ergon* [29]
mighty deeds, *3197, kratos* [1]
deeds, *4552, praxis* [1]
deeds, *4556, prassō* [1]

DEEP [14]

deep, *960, bathys* [3]
deep, *958, bathos* [2]
deep, *12, abyssos* [1]
deep water, *958, bathos* [1]
down deep, *959, bathynō* [1]
deep truths, *3696, mystērion* [1]
deep sorrow, *3851, odyrmos* [1]
a hundred and twenty feet deep, *3976+1633,*
   orgyia+eikosi [1]
ninety feet deep, *3976+1278,*
   orgyia+dekapente [1]
deep, *4498, polys* [1]
with a deep sigh, *5100, stenazō* [1]

DEEPLY [8]

deeply moved, *1839, embrimaomai* [2]
sighed deeply, *417+3836+4460,*
   anastenazō+ho+pneuma [1]
deeply distressed, *1701, ekthambeō* [1]
deeply, *1756, ektenēs* [1]
deeply, *1757, ektenōs* [1]
mourned deeply, *4472+3157+3489,*
   poieō+kopetos+megas [1]
deeply distressed, *5200, syllypeō* [1]

DEFEAT [1]

defeat, *3158, kopē* [1]

DEFEATED [1]

defeated, *2488, hēttēma* [1]

DEFECT [1]

without defect, *834, aspilos* [1]

DEFEND [3]

defend, *664, apologeomai* [2]
defend, *665, apologia* [1]

DEFENDING [3]

defending ourselves, *664, apologeomai* [1]
defending, *664, apologeomai* [1]
defending, *665, apologia* [1]

DEFENSE [12]

defense, *665, apologia* [4]
make defense, *664, apologeomai* [3]
defense, *664, apologeomai* [2]
went to defense, *310, amynomai* [1]
made defense, *664, apologeomai* [1]
speaks in defense, *4156, paraklētos* [1]

DEFILE [2]

defile, *3620, miainō* [1]
defile, *3662, molynō* [1]

DEFILED [2]

defiled, *3124, koinoō* [1]
defiled, *3662, molynō* [1]

DEFINITE [1]

definite, *855, asphalēs* [1]

DEFRAUD [1]

defraud, *691, apostereō* [1]

DEFYING [1]

defying, *595+4556, apenanti+prassō* [1]

DEGRADING [1]

degrading of, *869, atimazō* [1]

DEITY [1]

Deity, *2540, theotēs* [1]

DELAY [4]

delay, *332+4472, anabolē+poieō* [1]
without delay, *2317, euthys1* [1]
delay, *5988, chronizō* [1]
delay, *5989, chronos* [1]

DELAYED [1]

delayed, *1094, bradynō* [1]

DELEGATION [2]

delegation, *4561, presbeia* [2]

DELIBERATELY [2]

deliberately, *1731, hekousiōs* [1]
deliberately, *2527, thelō* [1]

DELIGHT [7]

delight, *2305, eudokeō* [2]
delight, *5897, chairō* [2]
delight, *21, agalliasis* [1]
with delight, *2452, hēdeōs* [1]
delight, *5310, synēdomai* [1]

DELIGHTED [6]

delighted, *5897, chairō* [4]
delighted, *2305, eudokeō* [2]

DELIGHTS [1]

delights, *2527, thelō* [1]

DELIVER [4]

deliver, *4861, rhyomai* [3]
deliver, *4140, paradidōmi* [1]

DELIVERANCE [1]

deliverance, *5401, sōtēria* [1]

DELIVERED [10]

delivered, *4861, rhyomai* [3]
delivered, *4140, paradidōmi* [2]
delivered, *347, anadidōmi* [1]
delivered a public address, *1319, dēmēgoreō* [1]
delivered, *2113, epididōmi* [1]
delivered over, *4140, paradidōmi* [1]
delivered, *5392, sōzō* [1]

DELIVERER [2]

deliverer, *3392, lytrōtēs* [1]
deliverer, *4861, rhyomai* [1]

DELUDED [1]

deluded, *4414, planaō* [1]

DELUGED [1]

deluged, *5623+2885, hydōr+kataklyzō* [1]

DELUSION [1]

delusion, *4415, planē* [1]

DEMAND [3]

demand, *160, aiteō* [1]
demand, *161, aitēma* [1]
demand back, *608+555, apo+apaiteō* [1]

DEMANDED [8]

demanded, *3306, legō* [3]
demanded, *160, aiteō* [1]
demanded from, *555+608, apaiteō+apo* [1]
demanded, *646, apokrinomai* [1]
demanded, *2089, eperōtaō* [1]
demanded, *2426, zēteō* [1]

DEMANDING [1]

demanding, *2426, zēteō* [1]

DEMAS [3]

Demas, *1318, Dēmas* [3]

DEMETRIUS [3]

Demetrius, *1320, Dēmētrios* [3]

DEMOLISH [2]

demolish, *2746, kathairesis* [1]
demolish, *2747, kathaireō* [1]

DEMON [16]

demon, *1228, daimonion* [15]
possessed by a demon, *1227, daimonizomai* [1]

DEMON-POSSESSED [16]

demon-possessed, *1227, daimonizomai* [10]
demon-possessed, *1228+2400,
    daimonion+echō* [4]
demon-possessed, *2400+1228,
    echō+daimonion* [1]
demon-possessed,
    *2400+3836+4460+3836+4505,
    echō+ho+pneuma+ho+ponēros* [1]

DEMON-POSSESSION [1]

suffering from demon-possession, *1227,
    daimonizomai* [1]

DEMONS [47]

demons, *1228, daimonion* [42]
demons, *RPE* [2]
demons, *794, archē* [1]
possessed by demons, *1227, daimonizomai* [1]
demons, *1230, daimōn* [1]

DEMONSTRATE [2]

demonstrate, *1893, endeixis* [2]

DEMONSTRATES [1]

demonstrates, *5319, synistēmi* [1]

DEMONSTRATION [1]

demonstration, *618, apodeixis* [1]

DEN [3]

den, *5068, spēlaion* [3]

DENARII [2]

denarii, *1324, dēnarion* [2]

DENARIUS [7]

denarius, *1324, dēnarion* [7]

DENIED [10]

denied, *766, arneomai* [10]

DENIES [3]

denies, *766, arneomai* [3]

DENOUNCE [1]

denounce, *3943, oneidizō* [1]

DENOUNCED [1]

denounced, *1059, blasphēmeō* [1]

DENY [8]

deny, *766, arneomai* [4]
deny, *565, aparneomai* [3]
deny, *6017+2848, pseudomai+kata* [1]

DENYING [2]

denying, *766, arneomai* [2]

DEPART [2]

depart, *386, analyō* [1]
depart, *4513, poreuomai* [1]

DEPARTED [1]

departed, *4513, poreuomai* [1]

DEPARTURE [3]

departure, *2016, exodos* [2]
departure, *385, analysis* [1]

DEPEND [1]

depend, *AIT* [1]

DEPENDED [1]

depended on, *608, apo* [1]

DEPENDENT [1]

dependent on, *5970+2400, chreia+echō* [1]

DEPENDS [4]

depends on, *1666, ek* [3]
depends on, *2848, kata* [1]

DEPOSIT [6]

deposit guaranteeing what is to come, *775,
    arrabōn* [2]
deposit guaranteeing, *775, arrabōn* [1]
put on deposit, *965, ballō* [1]
deposit entrusted to, *4146, parathēkē* [1]
deposit, *5544, trapeza* [1]

DEPRAVED [3]

depraved, *99, adokimos* [1]
depraved, *1406, diastrephō* [1]
depraved, *2967, kataphtheirō* [1]

DEPRAVITY [2]

depravity, *2798, kakia* [1]
depravity, *5785, phthora* [1]

DEPRIVE [2]

deprive, *691, apostereō* [1]
deprive, *3033, kenoō* [1]

DEPRIVED [1]

deprived, *149, airō* [1]

DEPTH [4]

depth, *958, bathos* [2]
depth, *4246, pas* [1]
depth, *4359, perissoterōs* [1]

DEPTHS [3]

depths, *87, hadēs* [2]
depths, *4283, pelagos* [1]

DERBE [4]

Derbe, *1292, Derbē* [3]
from Derbe, *1291, Derbaios* [1]

DERIVES [1]

derives name, *3951, onomazō* [1]

DESCEND [1]

descend, *2849, katabainō* [1]

DESCENDANT [4]

descendant, *5065, sperma* [2]
descendant, *1666+3836+2588,
    ek+ho+thygatēr* [1]
descendant, *1666+3875, ek+oikos* [1]

DESCENDANTS [16]

descendants, *5065, sperma* [10]
descendants, *5626, huios* [2]
descendants, *1155, genea* [1]
came descendants, *1164, gennaō* [1]
descendants, *2843+3836+4019,
    karpos+ho+osphys* [1]
give many descendants, *4437+4437,
    plēthynō+plēthynō* [1]

DESCENDED [7]

descended, *2849, katabainō* [3]
descended, *422, anatellō* [1]
descended from, *1666+5065, ek+sperma* [1]
descended from, *1666, ek* [1]
descended from, *2002+1666+3836+4019,
    exerchomai+ek+ho+osphys* [1]

DESCENDING [3]

descending, *2849, katabainō* [3]

DESCENT [2]

natural descent, *135, haima* [1]
trace descent, *1156, genealogeō* [1]

DESCRIBE [1]

describe, *RPE* [1]

DESCRIBED [4]

described, *1211, graphō* [2]
described, *1455, diēgeomai* [1]
described, *2007, exēgeomai* [1]

DESCRIBES [1]

describes, *1211, graphō* [1]

DESECRATE [2]

desecrate, *1014, bebēloō* [2]

DESERT [33]

desert, *2245, erēmos* [32]
desert region, *2245, erēmos* [1]

DESERTED [7]

deserted, *918, aphiēmi* [2]
deserted, *1593, enkataleipō* [2]
deserted, *695, apostrephō* [1]
deserted, *923+608, aphistēmi+apo* [1]
deserted, *2245, erēmos* [1]

DESERTING [1]

deserting, *3572+608, metatithēmi+apo* [1]

DESERTS [1]

deserts, *2244, erēmia* [1]

DESERVE [10]

deserve, *545+1639, axios+eimi* [2]
deserve, *545, axios* [2]
deserve, *AIT* [1]
deserve, *1639+2653, eimi+hikanos* [1]
deserve, *1639+545, eimi+axios* [1]
deserve, *2653+1639, hikanos+eimi* [1]
deserve, *2653, hikanos* [1]
actions deserve, *2848+2240, kata+ergon* [1]

DESERVED [2]

deserved, *545, axios* [1]
deserved, *1899, endikos* [1]

DESERVES [7]

deserves, *545, axios* [5]
deserves, *545+1639, axios+eimi* [1]
deserves, *546, axioō* [1]

DESERVING [5]

deserving, *545, axios* [4]
deserving, *AIT* [1]

DESIGN [1]

design, *1927, enthymēsis* [1]

DESIGNATED [2]

designated, *3951, onomazō* [1]
designated to be, *4641, prosagoreuō* [1]

DESIGNATING [1]

designating, *3951, onomazō* [1]

DESIRE [18]

desire, *2527, thelō* [8]
desire, *2123, epithymia* [3]
eagerly desire, *2420, zēloō* [2]
desire, *NIG* [1]
covetous desire, *2123, epithymia* [1]
desire, *2123+2400, epithymia+echō* [1]
evil desire, *2123, epithymia* [1]
desire, *2306, eudokia* [1]

DESIRED [1]

eagerly desired, *2123+2121,
epithymia+epithymeō* [1]

DESIRES [29]

desires, *2123, epithymia* [11]
evil desires, *2123, epithymia* [8]
desires, *2121, epithymeō* [2]
what desires*s*, *3836, ho* [2]
desires, *AIT* [1]
lustful desires, *2123+816,
epithymia+aselgeia* [1]
sinful desires, *2123, epithymia* [1]
desires, *2454, hēdonē* [1]
desires, *2525, thelēma* [1]

sensual desires overcome their dedication to,
2952, katastrēniaō [1]

DESOLATE [3]

desolate, *2245, erēmos* [3]

DESOLATION [3]

desolation, *2247, erēmōsis* [3]

DESPAIR [1]

in despair, *1989, exaporeō* [1]

DESPAIRED [1]

despaired, *1989, exaporeō* [1]

DESPISE [5]

despise, *2969, kataphroneō* [4]
despise, *4368, periphroneō* [1]

DESPISED [1]

despised, *2024, exoutheneō* [1]

DESTINED [6]

destined, *3023, keimai* [2]
destined, *AIT* [1]
destined, *641, apokeimai* [1]
destined, *4633, proorizō* [1]
destined, *5502, tithēmi* [1]

DESTINY [1]

destiny, *5465, telos* [1]

DESTITUTE [1]

destitute, *5728, hystereō* [1]

DESTROY [29]

destroy, *660, apollymi* [8]
destroy, *2907, katalyō* [6]
destroy, *2934, katargeō* [3]
destroy, *906, aphanizō* [2]
destroy, *3395, lyō* [2]
destroy, *5780, phtheirō* [2]
destroy, *384, analoō* [1]
destroy, *426, anatrepō* [1]
destroy, *1425, diaphtheirō* [1]
began destroy, *3381, lymainō* [1]
destroy, *4514, portheō* [1]
tried destroy, *4514, portheō* [1]

DESTROYED [24]

destroyed, *660, apollymi* [9]
destroyed, *2934, katargeō* [3]
destroyed, *3395, lyō* [3]
destroyed, *2907, katalyō* [2]
destroyed, *RPE* [1]
destroyed, *384, analoō* [1]
destroyed, *724, apōleia* [1]
destroyed, *1425, diaphtheirō* [1]
destroyed, *1650+724, eis+apōleia* [1]
destroyed, *3897, olethros* [1]
destroyed, *5785, phthora* [1]

DESTROYER [1]

destroyer, *3905, olothreuō* [1]

DESTROYING [3]

destroying, *1425, diaphtheirō* [1]
destroying, *3904, olothreutēs* [1]
destroying, *5341, syntribō* [1]

DESTROYS [2]

destroys, *1425, diaphtheirō* [1]
destroys, *5780, phtheirō* [1]

DESTRUCTION [17]

destruction, *724, apōleia* [10]
doomed to destruction, *724, apōleia* [2]
destruction, *3897, olethros* [2]
destruction, *3395, lyō* [1]
destruction, *4837, rhēgma* [1]
destruction, *5785, phthora* [1]

DESTRUCTIVE [1]

destructive, *724, apōleia* [1]

DETACHMENT [3]

detachment of soldiers, *5061, speira* [2]
detachment, *AIT* [1]

DETAIL [3]

detail, *1651+1667, heis+hekastos* [1]
goes into great detail about, *1836, embateuō* [1]
detail, *3538, meros* [1]

DETER [1]

deter, *1361, diakōlyō* [1]

DETERMINED [4]

determined, *1089, boulomai* [1]
determined, *2426, zēteō* [1]
determined, *2527, thelō* [1]
determined, *3988, horizō* [1]

DETERMINES [1]

determines, *1089, boulomai* [1]

DETESTABLE [4]

detestable, *116, athemitos* [1]
detestable, *1007, bdelygma* [1]
detestable, *1008, bdelyktos* [1]
detestable, *3631, miseō* [1]

DEVELOPED [1]

developed, *1181, ginomai* [1]

DEVELOPS [1]

develops, *2981, katergazomai* [1]

DEVIL [33]

devil, *1333, diabolos* [31]
devil, *RPE* [1]
of the devil, *1229, daimoniōdēs* [1]

DEVIL'S [3]

devil's, *1333, diabolos* [3]

DEVISED [1]

devised a plan, *5206+3284,
symboulion+lambanō* [1]

DEVOTE [6]

devote, *4668, prosechō* [2]
devote to, *4613, proistēmi* [1]
devote, *4613, proistēmi* [1]
devote, *4674, proskartereō* [1]
devote, *5390, scholazō* [1]

DEVOTED [10]

devoted to, *504, antechō* [2]
devoted to the Lord, *41, hagios* [1]

gift devoted to God, *1565, dōron* [1]
devoted to, *1639+4674, eimi+proskartereō* [1]
devoted, *5082, spoudē* [1]
devoted, *5309, synechō* [1]
devoted, *5435, tassō* [1]
devoted, *5816, philostorgos* [1]
devoted to God, *6067, ōpheleō* [1]

DEVOTING [1]

devoting, *2051, epakoloutheō* [1]

DEVOTION [2]

sincere devotion, *605, haplotēs* [1]
devotion, *2339, euparedros* [1]

DEVOUR [4]

devour, *2983, katesthiō* [3]
devour, *2927, katapinō* [1]

DEVOURED [1]

devoured, *2983, katesthiō* [1]

DEVOURING [1]

devouring, *2983, katesthiō* [1]

DEVOURS [1]

devours, *2983, katesthiō* [1]

DEVOUT [5]

devout, *2327, eulabēs* [2]
devout, *2356, eusebēs* [2]
devout, *4936, sebō* [1]

DID [379]

did, *ΛΙΤ* [262]
did, *4472, poieō* [38]
did, *RPE* [31]
did, *NIG* [17]
did, *1639, eimi* [2]
did, *2240, ergon* [2]
what he did, *2240, ergon* [2]
did wrong, *92, adikeō* [1]
did⁵, *965, ballō* [1]
did, *1181, ginomai* [1]
did⁵, *1197, gongyzō* [1]
did⁵ so, *1403, diastellō* [1]
did, *1892, endeiknymi* [1]
did⁵, *2121, epithymeō* [1]
did⁵, *2209, epitynchanō* [1]
what she did, *2240, ergon* [1]
what usually did, *2777, kathōs* [1]
did, *2981, katergazomai* [1]
did⁵, *3081, klaiō* [1]
did⁵, *3284, lambanō* [1]
as did⁵, *3552, meta* [1]
did⁵, *3857, oida* [1]
as I did, *4047+899, houtos+autos* [1]
did⁵ so, *4192, paratithēmi* [1]
did⁵, *4279, peirazō* [1]
did⁵, *4344, peripateō* [1]
did⁵, *4409, pisteuō* [1]
did⁵, *4519, porneuō* [1]
did, *4556, prassō* [1]
did⁵ before, *4625, prolegō* [1]
did⁵, *5317, syniēmi* [1]
did⁵ so, *5770, pherō* [1]

DIDN'T [12]

didn't, *4024, ou* [8]
didn't, *4049, ouchi* [3]
didn't, *3590, mē* [1]

DIDYMUS [3]

Didymus, *1441, Didymos* [3]

DIE [45]

die, *633, apothnēskō* [34]
die, *660, apollymi* [2]
die with, *5271, synapothnēskō* [2]
die, *5462, teleutaō* [2]
die, *614, apoginomai* [1]
die, *650, apokteinō* [1]
condemned to die, *2119, epithanatios* [1]
die, *3590+2441, mē+zōogoneō* [1]
die, *3972+2505, horaō+thanatos* [1]

DIED [72]

died, *633, apothnēskō* [49]
died, *5462, teleutaō* [5]
died, *1775, ekpsychō* [3]
died down, *3156, kopazō* [3]
died, *2505, thanatos* [2]
died, *3121, koimaō* [2]
died, *650, apokteinō* [1]
died, *1181+3738, ginomai+nekros* [1]
died, *1743, ekpneō* [1]
died, *2093+3738, epi+nekros* [1]
died, *2505+1181, thanatos+ginomai* [1]
died, *2506, thanatoō* [1]
died, *4406, piptō* [1]
died with, *5271, synapothnēskō* [1]

DIES [12]

dies, *633, apothnēskō* [11]
dies, *3121, koimaō* [1]

DIFFERENCE [3]

difference, *1405, diastolē* [2]
makes difference, *1422, diapherō* [1]

DIFFERENCES [1]

differences, *146, hairesis* [1]

DIFFERENT [14]

different, *2283, heteros* [4]
different kinds, *1348, diairesis* [3]
different kinds, *1169, genos* [2]
different from, *2283, heteros* [2]
makes different, *1359, diakrinō* [1]
different from, *1422, diapherō* [1]
different, *1427, diaphoros* [1]

DIFFERENTLY [1]

differently, *2284, heterōs* [1]

DIFFERS [1]

differs, *1422, diapherō* [1]

DIFFICULT [1]

make it difficult for, *4214, parenochleō* [1]

DIFFICULTIES [1]

difficulties, *5103, stenochōria* [1]

DIFFICULTY [3]

difficulty, *3660, molis* [2]
with difficulty, *3660, molis* [1]

DIG [2]

dig, *4999, skaptō* [2]

DIGGING [1]

digging through, *2021, exoryssō* [1]

DILIGENCE [1]

diligence, *5082, spoudē* [1]

DILIGENT [1]

be diligent, *1639, eimi* [1]

DILIGENTLY [2]

diligently, *1877+5082, en+spoudē* [1]
diligently study, *2236, eraunaō* [1]

DILL [1]

dill, *464, anēthon* [1]

DINNER [9]

dinner, *1270, deipnon* [2]
dinner guests, *5263, synanakeimai* [2]
dinner guests, *367, anakeimai* [1]
having dinner, *367, anakeimai* [1]
dinner, *756, ariston* [1]
have dinner, *2266, esthiō* [1]
dinner, *2879, katakeimai* [1]

DIONYSIUS [1]

Dionysius, *1477, Dionysios* [1]

DIOTREPHES [1]

Diotrephes, *1485, Diotrephēs* [1]

DIP [1]

dip, *970, baptō* [1]

DIPPED [3]

dipped, *970, baptō* [2]
dipped, *1835, embaptō* [1]

DIPPING [1]

dipping, *970, baptō* [1]

DIPS [1]

dips, *1835, embaptō* [1]

DIRECT [2]

direct, *2985, kateuthynō* [1]
direct, *4613, proistēmi* [1]

DIRECTED [6]

directed, *1411, diatassō* [2]
directed, *2199, epitassō* [1]
directed, *3027, keleuō* [1]
directed, *3306, legō* [1]
directed, *5332, syntassō* [1]

DIRECTION [1]

direction, *3847, hodos* [1]

DIRECTIONS [2]

give directions, *1411, diatassō* [1]
running from all directions, *5282, syndromē* [1]

DIRECTIVES [1]

directives, *4133, parangellō* [1]

DIRECTLY [2]

looked directly at, *867, atenizō* [1]
looked directly at, *1838, emblepō* [1]

DIRECTOR [1]

director of public works, *3874, oikonomos* [1]

DIRGE [2]

sang a dirge, *2577, thrēneō* [2]

DIRT [1]

dirt, *4866, rhypos* [1]

DISABLED [2]

disabled, *820, astheneō* [1]
disabled, *1762, ektrepō* [1]

DISAGREED [1]

disagreed, *851+1639, asymphōnos+eimi* [1]

DISAGREEMENT [1]

sharp disagreement, *4237, paroxysmos* [1]

DISAPPEAR [5]

disappear, *4216, parerchomai* [4]
disappear, *907, aphanismos* [1]

DISAPPEARED [1]

disappeared, *908+1181, aphantos+ginomai* [1]

DISAPPEARS [1]

disappears, *2934, katargeō* [1]

DISAPPOINT [1]

disappoint, *2875, kataischynō* [1]

DISARMED [1]

disarmed, *588, apekdyomai* [1]

DISASTROUS [1]

disastrous, *3552+5615, meta+hybris* [1]

DISCERN [1]

discern, *1507, dokimazō* [1]

DISCERNED [1]

discerned, *373, anakrinō* [1]

DISCHARGE [1]

discharge all, *4442, plērophoreō* [1]

DISCHARGING [1]

discharging, *NIG* [1]

DISCIPLE [28]

disciple, *3412, mathētēs* [24]
disciple, *AIT* [1]
disciple, *RPE* [1]
become a disciple, *3411, mathēteuō* [1]
disciple, *3413, mathētria* [1]

DISCIPLES [266]

disciples, *3412, mathētēs* [222]
disciples, *RPE* [16]
his disciples[s], *899, autos* [7]
the disciples[s], *899, autos* [5]
disciples, *AIT* [2]
Jesus[s] and his disciples, *899, autos* [2]
the disciples[s], *3836+1254, ho+de* [2]
Jesus and his disciples[s], *899, autos* [1]
he and his disciples, *899, autos* [1]
his disciples[s], *1697, ekeinos* [1]
the disciples[s], *1697, ekeinos* [1]
make disciples, *3411, mathēteuō* [1]
won disciples, *3411, mathēteuō* [1]
all disciples, *3836+4436+3412,
ho+plēthos+mathētēs* [1]

John's disciples[s], *4047, houtos* [1]
rest of the disciples, *5209, symmathētēs* [1]
disciples, *6034+3412, psychē+mathētēs* [1]

DISCIPLINE [5]

discipline, *4082, paideia* [3]
discipline[s], *4005, hos* [1]
discipline, *4084, paideuō* [1]

DISCIPLINED [6]

disciplined, *4084, paideuō* [3]
disciplined, *1604, enkratēs* [1]
disciplined, *4082, paideia* [1]
disciplined, *4083, paideutēs* [1]

DISCIPLINES [2]

disciplines, *RPE* [1]
disciplines, *4084, paideuō* [1]

DISCLOSED [6]

disclosed, *5746, phaneroō* [3]
disclosed, *636, apokalyptō* [2]
disclosed, *5745, phaneros* [1]

DISCORD [1]

discord, *2251, eris* [1]

DISCOURAGED [2]

become discouraged, *126, athymeō* [1]
discouraged, *1591, enkakeō* [1]

DISCOURSED [1]

discoursed, *1363, dialegomai* [1]

DISCOVER [1]

discover, *1182, ginōskō* [1]

DISCOVERED [1]

discovered, *2351, heuriskō* [1]

DISCREDITED [2]

discredited, *1650+4029+3357,
eis+oudeis+logizomai* [1]
discredited, *3699, mōmaomai* [1]

DISCRIMINATED [1]

discriminated, *1359, diakrinō* [1]

DISCUSS [2]

discuss, *1362, dialaleō* [1]
discuss, *3306, legō* [1]

DISCUSSED [8]

discussed, *1368, dialogizomai* [4]
discussed, *423, anatithēmi* [1]
discussed, *5184, syzēteō* [1]
discussed with, *5196, syllaleō* [1]
discussed, *5199, syllogizomai* [1]

DISCUSSING [2]

discussing, *506, antiballō* [1]
discussing, *5184, syzēteō* [1]

DISCUSSION [3]

discussion, *RPE* [2]
discussion, *2428, zētēsis* [1]

DISCUSSIONS [1]

had discussions, *1363, dialegomai* [1]

DISEASE [3]

disease, *3798, nosos* [3]

DISEASES [8]

diseases, *3798, nosos* [5]
diseases, *819, astheneia* [1]
diseases, *2809+3798, kakōs+nosos* [1]
diseases, *3465, mastix* [1]

DISFIGURE [1]

disfigure, *906, aphanizō* [1]

DISGRACE [9]

disgrace, *3944, oneidismos* [3]
disgrace, *156, aischros* [1]
suffering disgrace, *869, atimazō* [1]
disgrace, *871, atimia* [1]
expose to public disgrace, *1258, deigmatizō* [1]
disgrace, *3945, oneidos* [1]
subjecting to public disgrace, *4136,
paradeigmatizō* [1]

DISGRACEFUL [1]

disgraceful, *156, aischros* [1]

DISH [5]

dish, *4243, paropsis* [2]
dish, *AIT* [1]
dish, *NIG* [1]
dish, *4402, pinax* [1]

DISHONEST [6]

dishonest, *96, adikos* [2]
pursuing dishonest gain, *153, aischrokerdēs* [2]
dishonest, *94, adikia* [1]
dishonest, *156, aischros* [1]

DISHONOR [4]

dishonor, *869, atimazō* [2]
dishonor, *871, atimia* [2]

DISHONORED [1]

dishonored, *872, atimos* [1]

DISHONORS [2]

dishonors, *2875, kataischynō* [2]

DISMISS [1]

dismiss, *668, apolyō* [1]

DISMISSED [6]

dismissed, *668, apolyō* [5]
dismissed, *3395, lyō* [1]

DISOBEDIENCE [7]

disobedience, *577, apeitheia* [4]
disobedience, *4157, parakoē* [2]
act of disobedience, *4157, parakoē* [1]

DISOBEDIENT [13]

disobedient, *579, apeithēs* [5]
disobedient, *578, apeitheō* [4]
disobedient, *577, apeitheia* [2]
disobedient, *538, anypotaktos* [1]
the disobedient[s], *899, autos* [1]

DISOBEY [2]

disobey, *578, apeitheō* [1]
disobey, *579, apeithēs* [1]

DISOBEYED [3]

disobeyed, *578, apeitheō* [2]
disobeyed, *4216, parerchomai* [1]

DISORDER [3]

disorder, *189, akatastasia* [3]

DISOWN [12]

disown, *565, aparneomai* [7]
disown, *766, arneomai* [5]

DISOWNED [3]

disowned, *766, arneomai* [2]
disowned, *565, aparneomai* [1]

DISOWNS [2]

disowns, *766, arneomai* [2]

DISPERSED [1]

dispersed, *1370, dialyō* [1]

DISPLAY [3]

display, *1892, endeiknymi* [2]
put on display, *617, apodeiknymi* [1]

DISPLAYED [2]

displayed, *AIT* [1]
displayed, *5746, phaneroō* [1]

DISPLEASE [1]

displease, *3590+743, mē+areskō* [1]

DISPOSAL [2]

disposal, *2026, exousia* [1]
put at disposal, *4225, paristēmi* [1]

DISPUTABLE [1]

disputable, *1369, dialogismos* [1]

DISPUTE [8]

dispute, *5087, stasis* [3]
judge a dispute, *1359, diakrinō* [1]
points of dispute, *2427, zētēma* [1]
dispute, *4547, pragma* [1]
dispute with, *5202, symballō* [1]
dispute, *5808, philoneikia* [1]

DISPUTES [1]

disputes, *3215, kritērion* [1]

DISPUTING [2]

disputing, *1359+1363, diakrinō+dialegomai* [1]
disputing, *1369, dialogismos* [1]

DISQUALIFIED [1]

disqualified, *99, adokimos* [1]

DISQUALIFY [1]

disqualify for the prize, *2857, katabrabeuō* [1]

DISREPUTE [1]

bring into disrepute, *1059, blasphēmeō* [1]

DISSENSION [1]

dissension, *2251, eris* [1]

DISSENSIONS [1]

dissensions, *1496, dichostasia* [1]

DISSIPATION [2]

dissipation, *861, asōtia* [1]
dissipation, *3190, kraipalē* [1]

DISSUADED [1]

dissuaded, *4275, peithō* [1]

DISTANCE [15]

distance, *3427, makrothen* [7]
at a distance, *3427, makrothen* [2]
for a distance of, *608, apo* [1]
some distance, *3426, makran* [1]
long distance, *3427, makrothen* [1]
at a distance, *4523, porrōthen* [1]
from a distance, *4523, porrōthen* [1]
distance, *5084, stadion* [1]

DISTANT [2]

distant, *3431, makros* [2]

DISTINCTION [2]

made distinction, *1359, diakrinō* [1]
distinction, *1405, diastolē* [1]

DISTINCTLY [1]

distinctly, *5747, phanerōs* [1]

DISTINGUISH [1]

distinguish from, *1360, diakrisis* [1]

DISTINGUISHED [1]

person more distinguished, *1952, entimos* [1]

DISTINGUISHING [2]

distinguishing between, *1360, diakrisis* [1]
the distinguishing mark, *4956, sēmeion* [1]

DISTORT [3]

distort, *1516, doloō* [1]
distort the truth, *3281+1406, laleō+diastrephō* [1]
distort, *5137, strebloō* [1]

DISTRACTED [1]

distracted, *4352, perispaō* [1]

DISTRESS [9]

distress, *2568, thlipsis* [6]
distress, *340, anankē* [2]
distress, *5103, stenochōria* [1]

DISTRESSED [12]

distressed, *3382, lypeō* [3]
distressed, *86, adēmoneō* [1]
deeply distressed, *1701, ekthambeō* [1]
distressed, *2567, thlibō* [1]
distressed, *2930, kataponeō* [1]
distressed, *3383+2400, lypē+echō* [1]
greatly distressed, *4236, paroxynō* [1]
greatly distressed, *4337, perilypos* [1]
deeply distressed, *5200, syllypeō* [1]
distressed, *5309, synechō* [1]

DISTRESSES [1]

distresses, *5103, stenochōria* [1]

DISTRIBUTE [1]

distribute, *4192, paratithēmi* [1]

DISTRIBUTED [3]

distributed, *1344, diadidōmi* [2]
gifts distributed, *3536, merismos* [1]

DISTRIBUTION [1]

distribution, *1355, diakonia* [1]

DISTRICT [2]

district, *3535, meris* [1]
district, *3538, meros* [1]

DISTURBANCE [2]

disturbance, *2573, thorybos* [1]
great disturbance, *5431+4024+3900, tarachos+ou+oligos* [1]

DISTURBED [3]

disturbed, *5429, tarassō* [2]
greatly disturbed, *1387, diaponeomai* [1]

DIVIDE [3]

divide, *626, apodiorizō* [1]
divide, *1374, diamerizō* [1]
divide, *3532, merizō* [1]

DIVIDED [23]

divided, *3532, merizō* [9]
divided, *1374, diamerizō* [4]
divided, *5388, schisma* [3]
divided up, *1374, diamerizō* [2]
divided, *5387, schizō* [2]
divided, *RPE* [1]
divided between, *1349, diaireō* [1]
divided among, *1374, diamerizō* [1]

DIVIDES [1]

divides up, *1344, diadidōmi* [1]

DIVIDING [4]

dividing up, *1374, diamerizō* [1]
dividing, *3536, merismos* [1]
dividing wall, *3546, mesotoichon* [1]
dividing into shares, *4472+3538, poieō+meros* [1]

DIVINE [8]

divine, *2521, theios* [2]
divine, *2536, theos* [2]
divine glory, *1518, doxa* [1]
divine being, *2521, theios* [1]
divine nature, *2522, theiotēs* [1]
divine majesty, *3484, megaleiotēs* [1]

DIVISION [4]

division, *1375, diamerismos* [1]
division, *2389, ephēmeria* [1]
priestly division, *2389, ephēmeria* [1]
division, *5388, schisma* [1]

DIVISIONS [3]

divisions, *5388, schisma* [2]
divisions, *1496, dichostasia* [1]

DIVISIVE [1]

divisive, *148, hairetikos* [1]

DIVORCE [11]

divorce, *668, apolyō* [4]
divorce, *918, aphiēmi* [3]
divorce, *687, apostasion* [2]
certificate of divorce, *687, apostasion* [1]

divorce, *3386, lysis* [1]

DIVORCED [2]

divorced, *668+608+467, apolyō+apo+anēr* [1]
divorced, *668, apolyō* [1]

DIVORCES [6]

divorces, *668, apolyō* [6]

DO [911]

do, *AIT* [558]
do, *4472, poieō* [159]
do, *RPE* [48]
do, *NIG* [27]
do, *4556, prassō* [9]
do, *2237, ergazomai* [6]
do, *2240, ergon* [6]
do, *1181, ginomai* [5]
do, *1639, eimi* [5]
what do want with, *5515+2779, tis+kai* [5]
do best, *5079, spoudazō* [4]
do good, *16, agathopoieō* [3]
told to do, *1411, diatassō* [3]
do, *2981, katergazomai* [3]
do^s, *3590+1145, mē+ge* [3]
do with, *4472, poieō* [3]
do wrong, *92, adikeō* [2]
to do, *1650, eis* [2]
do^s, *2266, esthiō* [2]
do evil, *2803, kakopoieō* [2]
if you do, *3607, mēpote* [2]
do^s it, *3972, horaō* [2]
have nothing to do with, *4148, paraiteomai* [2]
do good, *14, agathoergeō* [1]
do what is right, *16, agathopoieō* [1]
do good, *17, agathopoiia* [1]
do right, *18, agathopoios* [1]
do harm, *92, adikeō* [1]
do away, *120, athetēsis* [1]
do, *419, anastrophē* [1]
ought to do, *465, anēkō* [1]
do so^s, *468, anthistēmi* [1]
do not believe, *578, apeitheō* [1]
have nothing to do with, *706, apotrepō* [1]
do^s, *1063, blepō* [1]
do, *1181+4475, ginomai+poiētēs* [1]
do^s so, *1182, ginōskō* [1]
do^s so, *1211, graphō* [1]
do the work, *1354, diakoneō* [1]
can do, *1538, dynamai* [1]
do^s, *1650, eis* [1]
do^s this, *1662, eispherō* [1]
have to do with, *2110, epidechomai* [1]
do, *2239, ergatēs* [1]
do good, *2343, eupoiia* [1]
has to do with, *2400, echō* [1]
can do, *2710, ischyō* [1]
do wrong, *2804, kakopoios* [1]
do^s, *2878, katakauchaomai* [1]
do away with, *2934, katargeō* [1]
do, *2960, katatithēmi* [1]
do so, *3437+5968, mallon+chraomai* [1]
so do, *3931, homoiōs* [1]
cannot do, *4024+1538, ou+dynamai* [1]
cannot do, *4028+1538, oude+dynamai* [1]
don't have anything to do with, *4148, paraiteomai* [1]
do, *4218, parechō* [1]
tried to do, *4278+3284, peira+lambanō* [1]
to do with, *4309, peri* [1]
do^s, *4344, peripateō* [1]
do, *4344, peripateō* [1]
do so more and more, *4355+3437, perisseuō+mallon* [1]

do this more and more, *4355+3437, perisseuō+mallon* [1]
do^s, *4409, pisteuō* [1]
do, *4475, poiētēs* [1]
to do with, *5170, synkoinōneō* [1]
do^s so, *5498, tēreō* [1]
do, *5498, tēreō* [1]
what shall we do, *5515+4036+1639, tis+oun+eimi* [1]
who do you think you are, *5515+4932+4472, tis+seautou+poieō* [1]
why do involve, *5515+2779, tis+kai* [1]
do, *5968, chraomai* [1]
do^s so, *6004, chōrizō* [1]

DOCTOR [4]

doctor, *2620, iatros* [4]

DOCTORS [1]

doctors, *2620, iatros* [1]

DOCTRINE [5]

doctrine, *1436, didaskalia* [5]

DOCTRINES [2]

teach false doctrines, *2281, heterodidaskaleō* [1]
teaches false doctrines, *2281, heterodidaskaleō* [1]

DOES [239]

does, *AIT* [158]
does, *4472, poieō* [24]
does, *NIG* [12]
does, *RPE* [12]
does wrong, *92, adikeō* [2]
if he does, *1623+1254+3590, ei+de+mē* [2]
does, *2237, ergazomai* [2]
does, *2240, ergon* [2]
does^s, *2266, esthiō* [2]
does^s, *3590+1145, mē+ge* [2]
does what is good, *16, agathopoieō* [1]
does not need to be ashamed, *454, anepaischyntos* [1]
does that mean that, *727, ara* [1]
what he has and does, *1050, bios* [1]
does^s, *1181+4048, ginomai+houtōs* [1]
does, *1181, ginomai* [1]
does, *1443, didōmi* [1]
does^s, *1877+5148+3531, en+sy+menō* [1]
does, *1928, eni* [1]
what he does, *2240, ergon* [1]
does what is evil, *2803, kakopoieō* [1]
as does, *2848, kata* [1]
does, *2981, katergazomai* [1]
does^s, *3836+3847, ho+hodos* [1]
does^s so, *4024+2266, ou+esthiō* [1]
does, *4474, poiēsis* [1]
does, *4556, prassō* [1]
does, *5498, tēreō* [1]
what does it matter, *5515, tis* [1]
does^s so, *5858, phroneō* [1]
does^s, *6004, chōrizō* [1]

DOESN'T [7]

doesn't, *4024, ou* [5]
doesn't, *3590, mē* [2]

DOG [1]

dog, *3264, kyōn* [1]

DOGS [8]

dogs, *3249, kynarion* [4]

dogs, *3264, kyōn* [4]

DOING [82]

doing, *4472, poieō* [43]
doing, *2240, ergon* [8]
doing, *RPE* [5]
doing, *4556, prassō* [4]
doing good, *16, agathopoieō* [3]
doing, *NIG* [2]
doing nothing, *734, argos* [2]
doing, *2237, ergazomai* [2]
doing, *AIT* [1]
doing wrong, *279, hamartanō* [1]
doing^s that, *462, anechomai* [1]
doing, *1181, ginomai* [1]
doing, *1650, eis* [1]
doing good, *2308, euergeteō* [1]
doing, *2400, echō* [1]
doing evil, *2803, kakopoieō* [1]
doing wrong, *2804, kakopoios* [1]
doing what is right, *2818, kalopoieō* [1]
doing, *2981, katergazomai* [1]
so doing^s, *4047, houtos* [1]
doing, *4475, poiētēs* [1]

DOMINION [3]

dominion, *794, archē* [1]
dominion, *2026, exousia* [1]
dominion, *3262, kyriotēs* [1]

DON'T [100]

don't, *4024, ou* [55]
don't, *3590, mē* [24]
don't anyone, *3594, mēdeis* [5]
don't, *3590+4024, mē+ou* [3]
don't, *3594, mēdeis* [2]
don't, *4028, oude* [1]
don't know, *51, agnoeō* [1]
don't, *3593, mēde* [1]
and don't, *3593, mēde* [1]
don't anything, *3594, mēdeis* [1]
don't any, *3594, mēdeis* [1]
don't this, *3594, mēdeis* [1]
don't any more, *3600, mēketi* [1]
don't, *4046, oute* [1]
don't have anything to do with, *4148, paraiteomai* [1]

DONE [108]

done, *4472, poieō* [37]
done, *1181, ginomai* [13]
done, *2240, ergon* [10]
done, *RPE* [7]
done, *4556, prassō* [6]
be done, *1181, ginomai* [4]
done wrong, *92, adikeō* [3]
done, *1639, eimi* [2]
done, *2237, ergazomai* [2]
well done, *2292, eu* [2]
done, *2981, katergazomai* [2]
harm done, *92, adikeō* [1]
done wrong, *279, hamartanō* [1]
done in ungodly way, *814, asebeō* [1]
not done by the hands of men, *942, acheiropoiētos* [1]
could have done so, *1543, dynatos* [1]
done, *1639+2237, eimi+ergazomai* [1]
done, *1639+4472, eimi+poieō* [1]
done, *1639+4556, eimi+prassō* [1]
readiness to see justice done, *1689, ekdikēsis* [1]
done by, *1877, en* [1]
work already done, *2289, hetoimos* [1]
well done, *2301, euge* [1]
ought to be done, *2763, kathēkō* [1]

done away with, *2934, katargeō* [1]
done hard work, *3159, kopiaō* [1]
done with, *4264, pauō* [1]
has done, *4552, praxis* [1]
done, *5464, teleō* [1]
done[s], *5718, hypotassō* [1]
done by the hands, *5935, cheiropoiētos* [1]

DONKEY [8]

donkey, *3952, onos* [4]
donkey, *3229, ktēnos* [1]
young donkey, *3942, onarion* [1]
donkey beast, *5689, hypozygion* [1]
donkey, *5689, hypozygion* [1]

DONKEY'S [1]

donkey's, *3952, onos* [1]

DOOM [1]

doom, *3213, krisis* [1]

DOOMED [2]

doomed to destruction, *724, apōleia* [2]

DOOR [33]

door, *2598, thyra* [21]
door, *AIT* [5]
door, *RPE* [3]
door, *2601, thyrōros* [1]
one at the door, *2601, thyrōros* [1]
door, *4784, pylōn* [1]
next door, *5327, synomoreō* [1]

DOORS [6]

doors, *2598, thyra* [6]

DOORWAY [1]

doorway, *2598, thyra* [1]

DORCAS [2]

Dorcas, *1520, Dorkas* [2]

DOUBLE [3]

double, *1487, diplous* [2]
pay back double, *1488+1487,*
    diploō+diplous [1]

DOUBLE-EDGED [3]

double-edged, *1492, distomos* [3]

DOUBLE-MINDED [2]

double-minded, *1500, dipsychos* [2]

DOUBT [8]

doubt, *1359, diakrinō* [4]
without a doubt, *242, alēthōs* [1]
doubt, *517, antilogia* [1]
no doubt, *1142, gar* [1]
doubt, *1491, distazō* [1]

DOUBTED [1]

doubted, *1491, distazō* [1]

DOUBTING [1]

doubting, *1181+603, ginomai+apistos* [1]

DOUBTS [3]

doubts, *1359, diakrinō* [2]
doubts, *1369, dialogismos* [1]

DOUGH [5]

worked through the dough, *2435, zymoō* [2]
batch of dough, *5878, phyrama* [2]
dough, *AIT* [1]

DOVE [4]

dove, *4361, peristera* [4]

DOVES [6]

doves, *4361, peristera* [5]
doves, *5583, trygōn* [1]

DOWN [219]

sat down, *2767, kathizō* [15]
come down, *2849, katabainō* [14]
went down, *2849, katabainō* [13]
came down, *2849, katabainō* [12]
coming down, *2849, katabainō* [9]
lay down, *5502, tithēmi* [8]
fell down, *4406, piptō* [7]
go down, *2849, katabainō* [6]
cut down, *1716, ekkoptō* [5]
sat down, *2764, kathēmai* [4]
came down, *2982, katerchomai* [4]
went down, *2982, katerchomai* [4]
sit down, *404, anapiptō* [3]
took down, *2747, kathaireō* [3]
sit down, *2767, kathizō* [3]
down, *2848, kata* [3]
thrown down, *2907, katalyō* [3]
down, *3004, katō* [3]
died down, *3156, kopazō* [3]
handed down, *4140, paradidōmi* [3]
let down, *5899, chalaō* [3]
sat down, *404, anapiptō* [2]
hurled down, *965, ballō* [2]
write down, *1211, graphō* [2]
written down, *1211, graphō* [2]
wrote down, *1211, graphō* [2]
down upon, *1650, eis* [2]
look down on, *2024, exoutheneō* [2]
sitting down, *2764, kathēmai* [2]
comes down, *2849, katabainō* [2]
down, *2849, katabainō* [2]
goes down, *2849, katabainō* [2]
going down, *2849, katabainō* [2]
look down on, *2969, kataphroneō* [2]
knelt down, *5502+3836+1205,*
    tithēmi+ho+gony [2]
down, *AIT* [1]
taken down, *149, airō* [1]
call down curses, *354, anathematizō* [1]
have sit down, *369, anaklinō* [1]
sit down, *369, anaklinō* [1]
sit down to eat, *404, anapiptō* [1]
down from, *608, apo* [1]
down deep, *959, bathynō* [1]
let down, *965, ballō* [1]
thrown down, *965, ballō* [1]
weighed down, *976, bareō* [1]
the rule lay down, *1411, diatassō* [1]
down, *1877, en* [1]
looked down on, *2024, exoutheneō* [1]
broke down, *2095, epiballō* [1]
go down, *2115+2093, epidyō+epi* [1]
right on down to, *2401, heōs* [1]
pulling down, *2746, kathairesis* [1]
tearing down, *2746, kathairesis* [1]
brought down, *2747, kathaireō* [1]
take down, *2747, kathaireō* [1]
tear down, *2747, kathaireō* [1]
sat down, *2757, kathezomai* [1]
sitting down, *2767, kathizō* [1]
let down, *2768, kathiēmi* [1]

down from, *2848, kata* [1]
gone down, *2849, katabainō* [1]
got down, *2849, katabainō* [1]
let down, *2849, katabainō* [1]
struck down, *2850, kataballō* [1]
place where the road goes down, *2853,*
    katabasis [1]
bring down, *2864, katagō* [1]
took down, *2864, katagō* [1]
call down curses, *2874, katathematizō* [1]
sat down, *2884, kataklinō* [1]
sit down, *2884, kataklinō* [1]
throw down the cliff, *2889, katakrēmnizō* [1]
stooped down, *2893, katakyptō* [1]
torn down, *2940, kataskaptō* [1]
ran down, *2963, katatrechō* [1]
come down, *2982, katerchomai* [1]
bowed down, *3111, klinō* [1]
stoop down, *3252, kyptō* [1]
settle down, *3552+2484, meta+hēsychia* [1]
strike down, *4250, patassō* [1]
struck down, *4250, patassō* [1]
handed down from forefathers, *4261,*
    patroparadotos [1]
pressed down, *4390, piezō* [1]
bow down, *4406, piptō* [1]
bowed down, *4406, piptō* [1]
fall down, *4406+2093+4725,*
    piptō+epi+prosōpon [1]
fall down, *4406, piptō* [1]
a robe reaching down to feet, *4468, podērēs* [1]
fall down, *4686, proskyneō* [1]
kneeling down, *4686, proskyneō* [1]
fell down before, *4700, prospiptō* [1]
threw down, *4849, rhiptō* [1]
sat down together, *5154, synkathizō* [1]
loaded down, *5397, sōreuō* [1]
got down, *5502, tithēmi* [1]
laid down, *5502, tithēmi* [1]
lays down, *5502, tithēmi* [1]
load down, *5844, phortizō* [1]

DOWNCAST [2]

downcast, *5034, skythrōpos* [1]
downcast, *5424, tapeinos* [1]

DOWNSTAIRS [1]

go downstairs, *2849, katabainō* [1]

DRACHMAS [1]

drachmas, *736, argyrion* [1]

DRAG [1]

drag off, *2955, katasyrō* [1]

DRAGGED [8]

dragged, *1816, helkyō* [3]
dragged, *5359, syrō* [2]
dragged, *1675, ekballō* [1]
dragged away, *1999, exelkō* [1]
dragged off, *5359, syrō* [1]

DRAGGING [1]

dragging, *1816, helkyō* [1]

DRAGON [14]

dragon, *1532, drakōn* [13]
dragon, *RPE* [1]

DRANK [6]

drank, *4403, pinō* [5]
drank with, *5228, sympinō* [1]

DRAW [12]

draw near, *4665, proserchomai* [2]
draw up, *421, anatassomai* [1]
draw out, *533, antleō* [1]
draw water, *533, antleō* [1]
draw, *533, antleō* [1]
to draw with, *534, antlēma* [1]
draw away, *685, apospaō* [1]
draw near, *1581, engizō* [1]
draw, *1816, helkyō* [1]
draw, *3284, lambanō* [1]
draw back, *5713, hypostellō* [1]

DRAWING [1]

drawing near, *1581, engizō* [1]

DRAWN [1]

drawn, *533, antleō* [1]

DRAWS [2]

draws, *1816, helkyō* [1]
draws, *3284, lambanō* [1]

DREADFUL [4]

how dreadful, *4026, ouai* [3]
dreadful, *5829, phoberos* [1]

DREAM [7]

dream, *3941, onar* [6]
dream, *1965, enypniazomai* [1]

DREAMERS [1]

dreamers, *1965, enypniazomai* [1]

DREAMS [1]

dreams, *1966, enypnion* [1]

DRESS [3]

dress, *2439, zōnnymi* [1]
dress, *3175, kosmeō* [1]
dress to serve, *4322, perizōnnymi* [1]

DRESSED [21]

dressed in, *4314, periballō* [4]
dressed in, *1907, endyō* [3]
dressed, *314, amphiennymi* [2]
dressed, *2667, himatizō* [2]
dressed, *4314+2668, periballō+himation* [2]
dressed, *4314, periballō* [2]
dressed, *AIT* [1]
dressed in, *1898, endidyskō* [1]
dressed, *2264, esthēs* [1]
dressed, *2439, zōnnymi* [1]
beautifully dressed, *3175, kosmeō* [1]
dressed ready for service, *3836+4019+4322,*
   ho+osphys+perizōnnymi [1]

DRESSING [1]

dressing in, *4314, periballō* [1]

DREW [7]

drew, *5060, spaō* [2]
drew, *432, anachōreō* [1]
drew, *599, aperchomai* [1]
drew out, *685, apospaō* [1]
drew near, *1581, engizō* [1]
drew, *1816, helkyō* [1]

DRIED [1]

dried up, *3830, xērainō* [1]

DRIFT [1]

drift away, *4184, pararreō* [1]

DRINK [66]

drink, *4403, pinō* [46]
drink, *4503, poma* [2]
drink, *4530, posis* [2]
gave to drink, *4540, potizō* [2]
give to drink, *4540, potizō* [2]
offered to drink, *4540, potizō* [2]
poured out like a drink offering, *5064,*
   spendō [2]
drink, *AIT* [1]
drink, *2266, esthiō* [1]
had too much to drink, *3499, methyskō* [1]
drink, *3954, oxos* [1]
drink from, *4403, pinō* [1]
given to drink, *4540, potizō* [1]
made drink, *4540, potizō* [1]
fermented drink, *4975, sikera* [1]

DRINKING [12]

drinking, *4403, pinō* [10]
drinking, *4530, posis* [1]
drinking only water, *5621, hydropoteō* [1]

DRINKS [9]

drinks, *4403, pinō* [8]
drinks in, *4403, pinō* [1]

DRIVE [22]

drive out, *1675, ekballō* [19]
drive out, *1675+1666, ekballō+ek* [1]
drive, *1675, ekballō* [1]
drive out, *2093, epi* [1]

DRIVEN [10]

driven, *1785, elaunō* [3]
driven, *1675, ekballō* [2]
driven along, *5770, pherō* [2]
driven, *1422, diapherō* [1]
driven out, *1675, ekballō* [1]
driven out, *2002, exerchomai* [1]

DRIVES [4]

drives out, *1675, ekballō* [3]
drives, *965, ballō* [1]

DRIVING [10]

driving out, *1675, ekballō* [8]
driving out evil spirits, *2020, exorkistēs* [1]
driving, *4365, peritrepō* [1]

DROP [2]

drop, *965, ballō* [1]
drop out, *4406, piptō* [1]

DROPPED [1]

dropped, *4849, rhiptō* [1]

DROPS [1]

drops, *2584, thrombos* [1]

DROPSY [1]

suffering from dropsy, *5622, hydrōpikos* [1]

DROVE [9]

drove out, *1675, ekballō* [5]
drove to it, *337, anankazō* [1]
drove from, *1675+1666, ekballō+ek* [1]
drove out, *1691, ekdiōkō* [1]

drove out, *2034, exōtheō* [1]

DROWN [3]

drown, *660, apollymi* [3]

DROWNED [4]

drowned, *678, apopnigō* [1]
drowned, *2927, katapinō* [1]
drowned, *2931, katapontizō* [1]
drowned, *4464, pnigō* [1]

DROWSY [1]

drowsy, *3818, nystazō* [1]

DRUNK [8]

get drunk, *3499, methyskō* [3]
drunk, *3501, methyō* [2]
get drunk, *3501, methyō* [1]
gets drunk, *3501, methyō* [1]
drunk, *4403, pinō* [1]

DRUNKARD [3]

drunkard, *3884, oinopotēs* [2]
drunkard, *3500, methysos* [1]

DRUNKARDS [2]

drunkards, *3500, methysos* [1]
drunkards, *3501, methyō* [1]

DRUNKENNESS [6]

drunkenness, *3494, methē* [3]
given to drunkenness, *4232, paroinos* [2]
drunkenness, *3886, oinophlygia* [1]

DRUSILLA [1]

Drusilla, *1537, Drousilla* [1]

DRY [2]

dry, *3831, xēros* [2]

DRYING [1]

drying, *1726, ekmassō* [1]

DUE [4]

due, *1256, dei* [1]
due to, *1328, dia* [1]
due time, *2789, kairos* [1]
receive what is due, *3152, komizō* [1]

DUG [4]

dug, *4002, oryssō* [2]
dug a hole, *4002, oryssō* [1]
dug, *4999, skaptō* [1]

DULL [3]

dull, *852, asynetos* [2]
made dull, *4800, pōroō* [1]

DULY [1]

duly established, *3263, kyroō* [1]

DUNGEONS [1]

dungeons, *4987, siros* [1]

DUPLICITY [1]

duplicity, *4111, panourgia* [1]

DURING [21]

during, *1877, en* [10]
during, *AIT* [4]

during, *1328*, *dia* [3]
during, *2093*, *epi* [2]
during, *2465*, *hēmera* [1]
during, *2848*, *kata* [1]

DUST [8]

dust, *3155*, *koniortos* [5]
dust, *5967*, *chous* [2]
of dust, *5954*, *choikos* [1]

DUTIES [2]

duties, *RPE* [1]
performs religious duties, *3310*, *leitourgeō* [1]

DUTY [7]

on duty, *1877+3836+5423*, *en+ho+taxis* [1]
girl on duty, *2601*, *thyrōros* [1]
priestly duty, *2646*, *hierourgeō* [1]
duty, *4005+4053+4472*,
    hos+opheilō+poieō [1]
duty, *4051*, *opheilē* [1]
fulfilled duty, *4488*, *politeuomai* [1]
duty, *5465*, *telos* [1]

DWELL [6]

dwell, *2997*, *katoikeō* [3]
dwell in, *1940+1877*, *enoikeō+en* [1]
dwell, *2400+3531*, *echō+menō* [1]
dwell, *5012*, *skēnoō* [1]

DWELLING [7]

dwelling, *RPE* [1]
dwelling, *2999*, *katoikētērion* [1]
dwelling, *3863*, *oikētērion* [1]
dwelling place, *5008*, *skēnē* [1]
dwelling, *5008*, *skēnē* [1]
made his dwelling, *5012*, *skēnoō* [1]
dwelling place, *5013*, *skēnōma* [1]

DWELLINGS [1]

dwellings, *5008*, *skēnē* [1]

DWELLS [1]

dwells in, *2997*, *katoikeō* [1]

DYING [6]

dying, *633*, *apothnēskō* [5]
dying, *2275*, *eschatōs* [1]

DYSENTERY [1]

dysentery, *1548*, *dysenterion* [1]

EACH [127]

each, *1667*, *hekastos* [55]
each other, *253*, *allēlōn* [32]
each other, *1571*, *heautou* [7]
each, *1651+1667*, *heis+hekastos* [5]
each, *NIG* [3]
each, *3836*, *ho* [3]
each, *AIT* [2]
each other's, *253*, *allēlōn* [2]
each, *324*, *ana* [2]
each, *RPE* [1]
each, *324+1651+1667*, *ana+heis+hekastos* [1]
each, *1651+2848+1651*, *heis+kata+heis* [1]
each other, *1651+3836+1651*, *heis+ho+heis* [1]
each, *1651*, *heis* [1]
each of, *1667*, *hekastos* [1]
on each side, *1949+2779+1696*,
    enteuthen+kai+ekeithen [1]
one on each side, *1949+2779+1949*,
    enteuthen+kai+enteuthen [1]

each, *2848*, *kata* [1]
in each, *2848*, *kata* [1]
each one's, *3517*, *melos* [1]
each day, *3836+2465*, *ho+hēmera* [1]
agree with each other, *3836+899+5858*,
    ho+autos+phroneō [1]
each one, *3836+324*, *ho+ana* [1]
each, *5515*, *tis* [1]
loving each other as brothers, *5789*,
    philadelphia [1]

EAGER [13]

eager, *2421*, *zēlōtēs* [3]
eager, *5079*, *spoudazō* [2]
eager expectation for, *638*, *apokaradokia* [1]
eager, *2420*, *zēloō* [1]
eager for, *3977*, *oregō* [1]
eager, *4608*, *prothymia* [1]
eager, *4609*, *prothymos* [1]
eager, *4610*, *prothymōs* [1]
all the more eager, *5081*, *spoudaiōs* [1]
eager, *5082*, *spoudē* [1]

EAGERLY [8]

eagerly desire, *2420*, *zēloō* [2]
eagerly await for, *587*, *apekdechomai* [1]
eagerly await, *587*, *apekdechomai* [1]
eagerly wait for, *587*, *apekdechomai* [1]
wait eagerly for, *587*, *apekdechomai* [1]
eagerly expect, *638*, *apokaradokia* [1]
eagerly desired, *2123+2121*,
    epithymia+epithymeō [1]

EAGERNESS [4]

eagerness, *4608*, *prothymia* [3]
eagerness to clear, *665*, *apologia* [1]

EAGLE [3]

eagle, *108*, *aetos* [3]

EAR [19]

ear, *4044*, *ous* [13]
ear, *6065*, *ōtion* [3]
ear, *6064*, *ōtarion* [2]
ear, *198*, *akoē* [1]

EARLIER [6]

sinned earlier, *4579*, *proamartanō* [2]
earlier, *4728*, *proteros* [2]
earlier made a beginning, *4599*,
    proenarchomai [1]
earlier, *4754*, *prōton* [1]

EARLIEST [1]

earliest, *792*, *archaios* [1]

EARLY [16]

early, *4745*, *prōi* [3]
early in the morning, *4745*, *prōi* [2]
early in the morning, *275+4745*, *hama+prōi* [1]
early, *792*, *archaios* [1]
early, *794*, *archē* [1]
very early in the morning, *2317+4745*,
    euthys[1]+prōi [1]
came early in the morning, *3983*, *orthrizō* [1]
early morning, *3984*, *orthrinos* [1]
very early in the morning, *3986+960*,
    orthros+bathys [1]
early morning, *4745*, *prōi* [1]
early in the morning, *4746+1181*,
    prōia+ginomai [1]
early in the morning, *4746*, *prōia* [1]
in early days, *4754*, *prōton* [1]

EARN [2]

earn living, *2237*, *ergazomai* [1]
earn, *2237*, *ergazomai* [1]

EARNED [3]

earned, *4218*, *parechō* [1]
earned, *4472*, *poieō* [1]
earned more, *4664*, *prosergazomai* [1]

EARNEST [1]

earnest, *2418*, *zēleuō* [1]

EARNESTLY [9]

earnestly seek, *1699*, *ekzēteō* [1]
earnestly, *1757*, *ektenōs* [1]
more earnestly, *1757*, *ektenōs* [1]
earnestly, *1877+1755*, *en+ekteneia* [1]
sought so earnestly, *2118*, *epizēteō* [1]
earnestly, *4498*, *polys* [1]
prayed earnestly, *4666+4667*,
    proseuchē+proseuchomai [1]
earnestly, *5081*, *spoudaiōs* [!]
most earnestly, *5655*, *hyperekperissou* [1]

EARNESTNESS [3]

earnestness, *5082*, *spoudē* [3]

EARS [25]

ears, *4044*, *ous* [21]
ears, *198*, *akoē* [4]

EARTH [156]

earth, *1178*, *gē* [151]
on earth, *2103*, *epigeios* [1]
under the earth, *2973*, *katachthonios* [1]
earth, *3180*, *kosmos* [1]
life on earth, *4922*, *sarx* [1]
of earth, *5954*, *choikos* [1]

EARTH'S [1]

earth's, *1178*, *gē* [1]

EARTHLY [15]

earthly, *2103*, *epigeios* [4]
earthly, *2093+3836+1178*, *epi+ho+gē* [2]
earthly things, *2103*, *epigeios* [2]
earthly, *2848+4922*, *kata+sarx* [2]
earthly, *5954*, *choikos* [2]
earthly, *1178*, *gē* [1]
earthly, *1877+4922*, *en+sarx* [1]
earthly, *3176*, *kosmikos* [1]

EARTHQUAKE [10]

earthquake, *4939*, *seismos* [9]
earthquake, *RPE* [1]

EARTHQUAKES [3]

earthquakes, *4939*, *seismos* [3]

EASIER [7]

easier, *2324*, *eukopos* [7]

EASILY [5]

easily, *AIT* [1]
easily entangles, *2342*, *euperistatos* [1]
easily, *2822*, *kalōs* [1]
easily angered, *4236*, *paroxynō* [1]
easily, *5441*, *tacheōs* [1]

EAST [9]

east, *424*, *anatolē* [7]

east, *424+2463*, *anatolē+hēlios* [2]

EASY   [2]

take life easy, *399*, *anapauō* [1]
easy, *5982*, *chrēstos* [1]

EAT   [109]

eat, *2266*, *esthiō* [92]
what eat, *1109*, *brōma* [2]
eat, *1174*, *geuomai* [2]
eat, *AIT* [1]
sit down to eat, *404*, *anapiptō* [1]
eat, *753*, *aristaō* [1]
to eat, *1110*, *brōsimos* [1]
eat, *1111*, *brōsis* [1]
eat, *1268*, *deipneō* [1]
eat, *2983*, *katesthiō* [1]
eat, *3561+5575*, *metalambanō+trophē* [1]
eat, *4344*, *peripateō* [1]
with eat, *5303*, *synesthiō* [1]
eat, *5303*, *synesthiō* [1]
eat all want, *5963*, *chortazō* [1]
eat, *5963*, *chortazō* [1]

EATEN   [9]

eaten, *2266*, *esthiō* [4]
eaten, *1048*, *bibrōskō* [1]
eaten as much as wanted, *3170+5575*,
   korennymi+trophē [1]
eaten, *4689*, *proslambanō* [1]
moths have eaten, *4963+1181*,
   sētobrōtos+ginomai [1]
eaten by worms, *5037*, *skōlēkobrōtos* [1]

EATING   [33]

eating, *2266*, *esthiō* [19]
eating, *2879*, *katakeimai* [3]
eating, *AIT* [1]
eating, *RPE* [1]
eating, *367*, *anakeimai* [1]
eating, *753*, *aristaō* [1]
eating, *1109*, *brōma* [1]
eating, *1111*, *brōsis* [1]
eating of, *2266*, *esthiō* [1]
eating with, *5259*, *synalizō* [1]
eating with, *5263*, *synanakeimai* [1]
eating with, *5307*, *syneuōcheomai* [1]
eating, *5592*, *trōgō* [1]

EATS   [13]

eats, *2266*, *esthiō* [10]
eats, *5592*, *trōgō* [2]
eats with, *5303*, *synesthiō* [1]

EBER   [1]

Eber, *1576*, *Eber* [1]

EDGE   [7]

edge, *3192*, *kraspedon* [4]
edge, *AIT* [1]
water's edge, *2498*, *thalassa* [1]
edge, *5125*, *stoma* [1]

EDICT   [1]

edict, *1409*, *diatagma* [1]

EDIFICATION   [1]

edification, *3869*, *oikodomē* [1]

EDIFIED   [2]

edified, *3868*, *oikodomeō* [1]
edified, *3869+3284*, *oikodomē+lambanō* [1]

EDIFIES   [2]

edifies, *3868*, *oikodomeō* [2]

EDUCATED   [1]

educated, *4084*, *paideuō* [1]

EFFECT   [6]

put into effect, *1408*, *diatagē* [1]
put into effect, *1411*, *diatassō* [1]
put into effect, *1590*, *enkainizō* [1]
takes effect, *2710*, *ischyō* [1]
without effect, *3031*, *kenos* [1]
put into effect, *3873*, *oikonomia* [1]

EFFECTIVE   [2]

effective, *1919*, *energeō* [1]
effective work, *1921*, *energēs* [1]

EFFECTIVELY   [1]

effectively, *AIT* [1]

EFFECTS   [1]

ill effects, *2805*, *kakos* [1]

EFFORT   [13]

make every effort, *5079*, *spoudazō* [4]
make every effort, *1503*, *diōkō* [2]
effort, *NIG* [1]
make every effort, *76*, *agōnizomai* [1]
make effort to obtain, *2426*, *zēteō* [1]
human effort, *4922*, *sarx* [1]
made effort, *5079*, *spoudazō* [1]
effort, *5082*, *spoudē* [1]
effort, *5556*, *trechō* [1]

EFFORTS   [2]

efforts, *3159*, *kopiaō* [1]
efforts, *3160*, *kopos* [1]

EGG   [1]

egg, *6051*, *ōon* [1]

EGYPT   [27]

Egypt, *131*, *Aigyptos* [20]
Egypt, *1178+131*, *gē+Aigyptos* [5]
Egypt, *RPE* [2]

EGYPTIAN   [4]

Egyptian, *130*, *Aigyptios* [3]
Egyptian, *RPE* [1]

EGYPTIANS   [2]

Egyptians, *130*, *Aigyptios* [2]

EIGHT   [9]

eight, *3893*, *oktō* [4]
eight months of a man's wages, *1324+1357*,
   dēnarion+diakosioi [1]
eight months wages, *1357+1324*,
   diakosioi+dēnarion [1]
eight hundred gallons, *1669+1004*,
   hekaton+batos² [1]
eight hundred, *3837*, *ogdoēkonta* [1]
eight, *3838*, *ogdoos* [1]

EIGHTEEN   [3]

eighteen, *1277*, *dekaoktō* [2]
eighteen, *1274+2779+3893*, *deka+kai+oktō* [1]

EIGHTH   [5]

eighth, *3838*, *ogdoos* [3]

eighth day, *3892*, *oktaēmeros* [1]
eighth, *3893*, *oktō* [1]

EIGHTY-FOUR   [1]

eighty-four, *2291+3837+5475*,
   etos+ogdoēkonta+tessares [1]

EITHER   [10]

either, *RPE* [3]
either, *2445*, *ē* [2]
not either, *4028*, *oude* [2]
either, *3612*, *mēte* [1]
but not either, *4028*, *oude* [1]
either, *4046*, *oute* [1]

EJECTED   [1]

ejected from, *590+608*, *apelaunō+apo* [1]

ELAMITES   [1]

Elamites, *1780*, *Elamitēs* [1]

ELDER   [5]

elder, *4565*, *presbyteros* [3]
elder, *RPE* [1]
fellow elder, *5236*, *sympresbyteros* [1]

ELDERS   [59]

elders, *4565*, *presbyteros* [56]
assembly of elders, *1172*, *gerousia* [1]
body of elders, *4564*, *presbyterion* [1]
council of elders, *4564*, *presbyterion* [1]

ELEAZAR   [2]

Eleazar, *1789*, *Eleazar* [2]

ELECT   [11]

elect, *1723*, *eklektos* [9]
God's elect, *1723*, *eklektos* [1]
elect, *1724*, *eklogē* [1]

ELECTION   [3]

election, *1724*, *eklogē* [3]

ELEGANT   [1]

elegant, *3287*, *lampros* [1]

ELEMENTARY   [2]

elementary, *794*, *archē* [1]
elementary truths, *5122+3836+794*,
   stoicheion+ho+archē [1]

ELEMENTS   [2]

elements, *5122*, *stoicheion* [2]

ELEVATE   [1]

elevate, *5738*, *hypsoō* [1]

ELEVEN   [6]

eleven, *1894*, *hendeka* [6]

ELEVENTH   [3]

eleventh, *1895*, *hendekatos* [3]

ELIAKIM   [3]

Eliakim, *1806*, *Eliakim* [3]

ELIEZER   [1]

Eliezer, *1808*, *Eliezer* [1]

ELIJAH [28]

Elijah, *2460, Ēlias* [28]

ELIJAH'S [1]

Elijah's, *2460, Ēlias* [1]

ELISHA [1]

Elisha, *1811, Elisaios* [1]

ELIUD [2]

Eliud, *1809, Elioud* [2]

ELIZABETH [10]

Elizabeth, *1810, Elisabet* [9]
Elizabeth⁵, *899, autos* [1]

ELMADAM [1]

Elmadam, *1825, Elmadam* [1]

ELOI [4]

Eloi, *1830, elōi* [4]

ELOQUENCE [1]

eloquence, *3364, logos* [1]

ELSE [38]

someone else, *257, allos* [6]
else, *NIG* [5]
else, *257, allos* [5]
else, *AIT* [4]
else, *2283, heteros* [3]
else, *3370, loipos* [3]
someone else, *2283, heteros* [2]
else, *RPE* [1]
somewhere else, *250, allachou* [1]
anyone else, *257, allos* [1]
somebody else, *2283, heteros* [1]
or else, *2445, ē* [1]
anywhere else in, *2848, kata* [1]
everybody else, *3370, loipos* [1]
no one else, *4029, oudeis* [1]
anyone else, *5516, tis* [1]
besides everything else, *6006+3836+4211,*
  chōris+ho+parektos [1]

ELSE'S [3]

someone else's, *259, allotrios* [3]

ELSEWHERE [2]

elsewhere, *1877+2283, en+heteros* [1]
elsewhere, *4099, palin* [1]

ELUDE [1]

elude, *5771+608, pheugō+apo* [1]

ELYMAS [2]

Elymas⁵, *899, autos* [1]
Elymas, *1829, Elymas* [1]

EMASCULATE [1]

emasculate, *644, apokoptō* [1]

EMBANKMENT [1]

embankment, *5918, charax* [1]

EMBARRASSED [1]

embarrassed, *2875, kataischynō* [1]

EMBITTER [1]

embitter, *2241, erethizō* [1]

EMBODIMENT [1]

embodiment, *3673, morphōsis* [1]

EMBOLDENED [1]

emboldened, *3868, oikodomeō* [1]

EMBRACED [1]

embraced, *2158+2093+3836+5549,*
  epipiptō+epi+ho+trachēlos [1]

EMERALD [2]

emerald, *5039, smaragdinos* [1]
emerald, *5040, smaragdos* [1]

EMMAUS [1]

Emmaus, *1843, Emmaous* [1]

EMPEROR [1]

Emperor, *4935, sebastos* [1]

EMPEROR'S [1]

Emperor's, *4935, sebastos* [1]

EMPHATICALLY [1]

emphatically, *1735, ekperissōs* [1]

EMPTIED [1]

emptied, *3033, kenoō* [1]

EMPTY [4]

empty, *3031, kenos* [2]
empty, *3469, mataios* [1]
empty, *3470, mataiotēs* [1]

EMPTY-HANDED [3]

empty-handed, *3031, kenos* [3]

ENABLE [2]

enable, *1443, didōmi* [2]

ENABLED [4]

enabled, *NIG* [1]
enabled, *1443+710,*
  didōmi+apophthengomai [1]
enabled, *1539, dynamis* [1]
enabled, *1639+1443, eimi+didōmi* [1]

ENABLES [1]

enables, *1538, dynamai* [1]

ENABLING [1]

enabling, *1443+1328+3836+5931,*
  didōmi+dia+ho+cheir [1]

ENCIRCLE [1]

encircle, *4333, perikykloō* [1]

ENCIRCLED [3]

encircled⁵ by, *1877+3545, en+mesos* [1]
encircled, *3239, kyklothen* [1]
encircled, *3241, kyklō* [1]

ENCOURAGE [15]

encourage, *4151, parakaleō* [13]
encourage, *4155, paraklēsis* [1]
encourage, *4170, paramytheomai* [1]

ENCOURAGED [14]

encouraged, *4151, parakaleō* [6]

encouraged, *2314, euthymos* [1]
encouraged, *3284+2511, lambanō+tharsos* [1]
encouraged, *4155+2400, paraklēsis+echō* [1]
encouraged, *4155, paraklēsis* [1]
encouraged, *4275, peithō* [1]
greatly encouraged, *4444+4155,*
  plēroō+paraklēsis [1]
encouraged, *4730, protrepō* [1]
mutually encouraged, *5220, symparakaleō* [1]

ENCOURAGEMENT [11]

encouragement, *4155, paraklēsis* [10]
speaking encouragement to, *4151, parakaleō* [1]

ENCOURAGING [6]

encouraging, *4151, parakaleō* [5]
encouraging message, *4155, paraklēsis* [1]

END [39]

end, *5465, telos* [20]
end, *5333, synteleia* [5]
end, *2274, eschatos* [2]
end, *AIT* [1]
end, *216, akron* [1]
bring to end, *660, apollymi* [1]
end, *1639+4639, eimi+pros* [1]
to this end, *1650+4005, eis+hos* [1]
end, *1722, ekleipō* [1]
end, *1741, ekplērōsis* [1]
end, *4306, peras* [1]
very end, *5333, synteleia* [1]
end, *5334, synteleō* [1]
end was near, *5462, teleutaō* [1]
end, *5465+2400, telos+echō* [1]

ENDANGER [1]

endanger, *3073, kindyneuō* [1]

ENDED [3]

ended, *5464, teleō* [2]
ended, *4264, pauō* [1]

ENDLESS [1]

endless, *596, aperantos* [1]

ENDLESSLY [1]

endlessly, *1650+3836+1457,*
  eis+ho+diēnekēs [1]

ENDS [7]

ends, *4306, peras* [3]
ends, *216, akron* [2]
ends, *2274, eschatos* [2]

ENDURANCE [12]

endurance, *5705, hypomonē* [8]
patient endurance, *5705, hypomonē* [4]

ENDURE [10]

endure, *5702, hypomenō* [4]
endure, *AIT* [1]
endure, *462, anechomai* [1]
endure hardship, *2802, kakopatheō* [1]
endure hardship with, *5155, synkakopatheō* [1]
endure hardship, *5702, hypomenō* [1]
to endure patiently, *5705, hypomonē* [1]

ENDURED [5]

endured, *5702, hypomenō* [2]
endured hardships, *1002, bastazō* [1]
endured conduct, *5574, tropophoreō* [1]
endured, *5722, hypopherō* [1]

ENDURES [2]

endures, *3531, menō* [2]

ENDURING [3]

enduring, *3531, menō* [2]
enduring, *462, anechomai* [1]

ENEMIES [23]

enemies, *2398, echthros* [21]
enemies, *1877+2397, en+echthra* [1]
enemies, *5641, hypenantios* [1]

ENEMY [13]

enemy, *2398, echthros* [10]
enemy, *508, antidikos* [1]
enemy, *512, antikeimai* [1]
enemy, *2398+476, echthros+anthrōpos* [1]

ENERGY [1]

energy, *1918, energeia* [1]

ENGAGED [1]

engaged, *NIG* [1]

ENGRAVED [1]

engraved, *1963, entypoō* [1]

ENGROSSED [1]

engrossed in, *2974, katachraomai* [1]

ENHANCES [1]

enhances, *4355, perisseuō* [1]

ENJOY [5]

enjoy, *NIG* [1]
enjoy, *22, agalliaō* [1]
enjoy, *1639, eimi* [1]
enjoy, *2400, echō* [1]
enjoy good health, *5617, hygiainō* [1]

ENJOYED [4]

enjoyed company, *1855, empimplēmi* [1]
enjoyed, *2351, heuriskō* [1]
enjoyed, *2400, echō* [1]
enjoyed, *5593, tynchanō* [1]

ENJOYING [1]

enjoying, *2400, echō* [1]

ENJOYMENT [1]

enjoyment, *656, apolausis* [1]

ENLARGE [1]

enlarge, *889, auxanō* [1]

ENLIGHTENED [2]

enlightened, *5894, phōtizō* [2]

ENOCH [3]

Enoch, *1970, Henōch* [3]

ENORMOUS [1]

enormous, *3489, megas* [1]

ENOSH [1]

Enosh, *1968, Enōs* [1]

ENOUGH [21]

enough, *AIT* [8]

enough, *757, arketos* [3]
enough, *758, arkeō* [3]
enough, *600, apechō* [1]
enough, *1538, dynamai* [1]
had enough, *1855, empimplēmi* [1]
has enough, *2400+1650, echō+eis* [1]
enough, *2653, hikanos* [1]
enough for now, *3836+3814+2400, ho+nyn+echō* [1]
enough, *5537, tosoutos* [1]

ENRAGED [2]

enraged, *3974, orgizō* [2]

ENRICHED [1]

enriched, *4457, ploutizō* [1]

ENSLAVED [3]

enslaved, *1526, douleuō* [2]
enslaved, *1530, douloō* [1]

ENSLAVES [1]

enslaves, *2871, katadouloō* [1]

ENTANGLED [1]

entangled in, *1861, emplekō* [1]

ENTANGLES [1]

easily entangles, *2342, euperistatos* [1]

ENTER [63]

enter, *1656+1650, eiserchomai+eis* [32]
enter, *1650+1656, eis+eiserchomai* [14]
enter, *1656, eiserchomai* [7]
enter, *RPE* [1]
enter, *1639+1656, eimi+eiserchomai* [1]
enter into, *1650+1656, eis+eiserchomai* [1]
enter, *1650+1656+1650, eis+eiserchomai+eis* [1]
enter, *1650+1658, eis+eisodos* [1]
enter, *1650+1660, eis+eisporeuomai* [1]
enter, *1650+4513, eis+poreuomai* [1]
enter, *1655, eiseimi* [1]
enter, *1660+1650, eisporeuomai+eis* [1]
enter, *1660, eisporeuomai* [1]

ENTERED [46]

entered, *1656+1650, eiserchomai+eis* [25]
entered, *1656, eiserchomai* [8]
entered, *2262+1650, erchomai+eis* [5]
entered, *RPE* [3]
entered, *1181+1656, ginomai+eiserchomai* [1]
entered into, *1650+1655, eis+eiseimi* [1]
entered, *1650+1656, eis+eiserchomai* [1]
entered into, *1656+1650, eiserchomai+eis* [1]
entered, *5291+1650, syneiserchomai+eis* [1]

ENTERING [3]

entering, *1656+1650, eiserchomai+eis* [1]
entering, *1656, eiserchomai* [1]
entering ahead of, *4575, proagō* [1]

ENTERS [9]

enters, *1656+1650, eiserchomai+eis* [3]
enters, *1656, eiserchomai* [3]
enters, *1660+1650, eisporeuomai+eis* [2]
enters, *1650+1660, eis+eisporeuomai* [1]

ENTERTAIN [3]

entertain thoughts, *1926, enthymeomai* [1]
entertain, *4138, paradechomai* [1]
entertain strangers, *5810, philoxenia* [1]

ENTERTAINED [2]

entertained, *3826, xenizō* [2]

ENTHUSIASM [2]

enthusiasm, *2419, zēlos* [1]
enthusiasm, *5080, spoudaios* [1]

ENTICE [2]

entice to sin, *965+4998+1967, ballō+skandalon+enōpion* [1]
entice, *1284, deleazō* [1]

ENTICED [1]

enticed, *1284, deleazō* [1]

ENTIRE [4]

entire, *3910, holos* [2]
entire, *4246, pas* [2]

ENTIRELY [1]

entirely on own, *882, authairetos* [1]

ENTRANCE [7]

entrance, *2598, thyra* [4]
the entrance[s], *899, autos* [1]
outer entrance, *2598+4784, thyra+pylōn* [1]
entrance[s], *3646, mnēmeion* [1]

ENTRUST [2]

entrust, *4192, paratithēmi* [1]
entrust, *4409, pisteuō* [1]

ENTRUSTED [19]

entrusted, *4140, paradidōmi* [6]
entrusted with, *4409, pisteuō* [3]
entrusted, *4409, pisteuō* [2]
entrusted, *1443, didōmi* [1]
entrusted to, *3102, klēros* [1]
entrusted with work, *3874, oikonomos* [1]
those entrusted with, *3874, oikonomos* [1]
deposit entrusted to, *4146, parathēkē* [1]
entrusted to care, *4146, parathēkē* [1]
entrusted to, *4146, parathēkē* [1]
entrusted with, *4192, paratithēmi* [1]

ENTRYWAY [1]

entryway, *4580, proaulion* [1]

ENVELOPED [3]

enveloped, *2173, episkiazō* [3]

ENVIES [1]

envies, *5784, phthonos* [1]

ENVIOUS [3]

make envious, *4143, parazēloō* [2]
envious, *3836+4057+4505+1639, ho+ophthalmos+ponēros+eimi* [1]

ENVY [13]

envy, *5784, phthonos* [8]
envy, *2419, zēlos* [2]
envy, *2420, zēloō* [1]
envy, *4057+4505, ophthalmos+ponēros* [1]
arouse to envy, *4143, parazēloō* [1]

ENVYING [1]

envying, *5783, phthoneō* [1]

EPAPHRAS [3]

Epaphras, *2071*, *Epaphras* [3]

EPAPHRODITUS [2]

Epaphroditus, *2073*, *Epaphroditos* [2]

EPENETUS [1]

Epenetus, *2045*, *Epainetos* [1]

EPHESIAN [1]

Ephesian, *2386*, *Ephesios* [1]

EPHESIANS [2]

Ephesians, *2386*, *Ephesios* [2]

EPHESUS [18]

Ephesus, *2387*, *Ephesos* [16]
of Ephesus, *2386*, *Ephesios* [2]

EPHPHATHA [1]

Ephphatha, *2395*, *ephphatha* [1]

EPHRAIM [1]

Ephraim, *2394*, *Ephraim* [1]

EPICUREAN [1]

Epicurean, *2134*, *Epikoureios* [1]

EQUAL [5]

equal, *2698*, *isos* [2]
equal, *2653*, *hikanos* [1]
equal with, *2777+2779*, *kathōs+kai* [1]
equal, *3836+899*, *ho+autos* [1]

EQUALED [2]

equaled, *RPE* [1]
equaled, *1181*, *ginomai* [1]

EQUALITY [3]

equality, *2699*, *isotēs* [2]
equality, *3836+1639+2698*, *ho+eimi+isos* [1]

EQUIP [1]

equip, *2936*, *katartizō* [1]

EQUIPPED [1]

equipped, *1992*, *exartizō* [1]

ER [1]

Er, *2474*, *Ēr* [1]

ERASTUS [3]

Erastus, *2235*, *Erastos* [3]

ERROR [7]

error, *4415*, *planē* [5]
in error, *4414*, *planaō* [2]

ESAU [3]

Esau, *2481*, *Ēsau* [3]

ESCAPE [10]

escape, *1767*, *ekpheugō* [5]
escape, *5771*, *pheugō* [3]
escape, *AIT* [1]
escape, *709*, *apopheugō* [1]

ESCAPED [6]

escaped, *709*, *apopheugō* [1]

escaped, *1407*, *diasōzō* [1]
escaped, *1767*, *ekpheugō* [1]
escaped, *2002+1666*, *exerchomai+ek* [1]
escaped notice, *3291*, *lanthanō* [1]
escaped, *5771*, *pheugō* [1]

ESCAPING [3]

escaping, *AIT* [1]
escaping from, *709*, *apopheugō* [1]
escaping, *1423*, *diapheugō* [1]

ESCORT [1]

escort out, *1974*, *exagō* [1]

ESCORTED [2]

escorted from, *1974*, *exagō* [1]
escorted, *2770*, *kathistēmi* [1]

ESLI [1]

Esli, *2268*, *Hesli* [1]

ESPECIALLY [13]

especially, *3436*, *malista* [9]
especially so, *3436*, *malista* [1]
especially, *3437+1254*, *mallon+de* [1]
especially, *4359+3437*, *perissoterōs+mallon* [1]
especially, *4359*, *perissoterōs* [1]

ESTABLISH [3]

establish, *2705*, *histēmi* [2]
establish, *5114*, *stērizō* [1]

ESTABLISHED [9]

established, *2530*, *themelioō* [2]
established, *2705*, *histēmi* [2]
duly established, *3263*, *kyroō* [1]
previously established, *4623*, *prokyroō* [1]
firmly established, *5114*, *stērizō* [1]
established, *5435*, *tassō* [1]
established, *5679*, *hypo* [1]

ESTATE [3]

estate, *AIT* [1]
estate, *4045*, *ousia* [1]
estate, *6005*, *chōrion* [1]

ESTIMATE [1]

estimate, *6028*, *psēphizō* [1]

ETERNAL [66]

eternal, *173*, *aiōnios* [63]
eternal, *172*, *aiōn* [2]
eternal, *132*, *aidios* [1]

ETERNALLY [2]

eternally condemned, *353*, *anathema* [2]

ETHIOPIAN [1]

Ethiopian, *467+134*, *anēr+Aithiops* [1]

ETHIOPIANS [1]

Ethiopians, *134*, *Aithiops* [1]

EUBULUS [1]

Eubulus, *2300*, *Euboulos* [1]

EUNICE [1]

Eunice, *2332*, *Eunikē* [1]

EUNUCH [6]

eunuch, *2336*, *eunouchos* [5]

eunuch, *RPE* [1]

EUNUCHS [1]

eunuchs, *2336*, *eunouchos* [1]

EUODIA [1]

Euodia, *2337*, *Euodia* [1]

EUPHRATES [2]

Euphrates, *2371*, *Euphratēs* [2]

EUTYCHUS [1]

Eutychus, *2366*, *Eutychos* [1]

EVANGELIST [2]

evangelist, *2296*, *euangelistēs* [2]

EVANGELISTS [1]

evangelists, *2296*, *euangelistēs* [1]

EVE [2]

Eve, *2293*, *Heua* [2]

EVEN [223]

even, *2779*, *kai* [91]
even, *AIT* [19]
not even, *4028*, *oude* [17]
even, *NIG* [16]
even as, *2777*, *kathōs* [6]
and even, *2779*, *kai* [6]
not even, *3593*, *mēde* [4]
not even, *4024*, *ou* [4]
even, *1254*, *de* [3]
even, *2285*, *eti* [3]
even though, *2779*, *kai* [3]
even if, *2829*, *kan* [3]
even if, *1569*, *ean* [2]
even, *2401*, *heōs* [2]
yet even, *2779*, *kai* [2]
but even, *2779*, *kai* [2]
or even, *2779*, *kai* [2]
even though, *2788*, *kaiper* [2]
even though, *2829*, *kan* [2]
even not, *4028*, *oude* [2]
even, *5445*, *te* [2]
even, *247+2779*, *alla+kai* [1]
even, *247*, *alla* [1]
even though, *247*, *alla* [1]
even to the point of, *948*, *achri* [1]
even to, *948*, *achri* [1]
and even, *1254*, *de* [1]
but even, *1254*, *de* [1]
even though, *1254*, *de* [1]
even though, *1569*, *ean* [1]
even though, *1623*, *ei* [1]
or even, *2445*, *ē* [1]
even now, *2453*, *ēdē* [1]
even, *2779+1145*, *kai+ge* [1]
even, *2779+2627*, *kai+idou* [1]
and even more, *2779+4707+5148*,
    kai+prostithēmi+sy [1]
even when, *2779*, *kai* [1]
if even, *2829*, *kan* [1]
even, *2829*, *kan* [1]
even though, *3525+1142*, *men+gar* [1]
even to the point of, *3588*, *mechri* [1]
even, *3667*, *monon* [1]
even in the case of, *3940*, *homōs* [1]
yet even, *3963*, *hopou* [1]
not even, *4024+4028*, *ou+oude* [1]
or even, *4046*, *oute* [1]
even more, *4360*, *perissōs* [1]

even more so[s], *4498+5080,*
　　polys+spoudaios [1]
even, *4531+3437, posos+mallon* [1]
even, *4802, pōs* [1]
one might even say, *6055+2229+3306,*
　　hōs+epos+legō [1]

EVENING [21]

evening, *4068, opsia* [12]
evening, *2270, hespera* [3]
evening meal, *1270, deipnon* [1]
on the evening, *1639+4068, eimi+opsia* [1]
evening, *3816, nyx* [1]
evening, *4067, opse* [1]
in the evening, *4067, opse* [1]
that evening, *4068+1181, opsia+ginomai* [1]

EVENTS [3]

events, *AIT* [2]
fearful events, *5831, phobētron* [1]

EVENTUALLY [1]

eventually, *1650+5465, eis+telos* [1]

EVER [81]

ever, *172, aiōn* [44]
ever, *AIT* [6]
ever seeing, *1063+1063, blepō+blepō* [3]
ever, *4537, pote* [3]
ever, *4799, pōpote* [3]
ever hearing, *198+201, akoē+akouō* [2]
ever since, *608+4005, apo+hos* [2]
nothing ever, *4030, oudepote* [2]
was there ever, *5515, tis* [2]
ever hearing, *201+201, akouō+akouō* [1]
ever, *1650+3836+172, eis+ho+aiōn* [1]
ever, *1666+3836+172, ek+ho+aiōn* [1]
greater than ever, *3437, mallon* [1]
nothing ever, *3590, mē* [1]
ever, *3590, mē* [1]
scarcely ever, *3653, mogis* [1]
ever, *4012, hosos* [1]
who ever, *4012, hosos* [1]
no ever, *4024+3590, ou+mē* [1]
no one ever, *4030, oudepote* [1]
ever, *4031, oudepō* [1]
ever again, *4033, ouketi* [1]
ever, *4037, oupō* [1]

EVER-INCREASING [2]

ever-increasing wickedness,
　　490+1650+3836+490,
　　anomia+eis+ho+anomia [1]
with ever-increasing glory,
　　608+1518+1650+1518,
　　apo+doxa+eis+doxa [1]

EVERLASTING [3]

everlasting, *173, aiōnios* [2]
everlasting, *132, aidios* [1]

EVERY [168]

every, *4246, pas* [127]
every, *2848, kata* [11]
every, *AIT* [5]
make every effort, *5079, spoudazō* [4]
every, *1667, hekastos* [3]
in every, *2848, kata* [3]
every, *RPE* [2]
make every effort, *1503, diōkō* [2]
every day, *2848+2465, kata+hēmera* [2]
every, *2848+4246, kata+pas* [2]
make every effort, *76, agōnizomai* [1]

every one, *1667, hekastos* [1]
every[s], *3836, ho* [1]
in every way, *4118, pantē* [1]
on every side, *4119, pantothen* [1]
any and every, *4246, pas* [1]
every, *4359, perissoterōs* [1]

EVERYBODY [8]

everybody, *4246, pas* [4]
everybody, *4246+476, pas+anthrōpos* [2]
everybody, *570, hapas* [1]
everybody else, *3370, loipos* [1]

EVERYBODY'S [1]

everybody's, *4246, pas* [1]

EVERYDAY [1]

from everyday life, *2848+476,*
　　kata+anthrōpos [1]

EVERYONE [116]

everyone, *4246, pas* [93]
everyone, *4246+476, pas+anthrōpos* [6]
everyone, *1667, hekastos* [3]
everyone, *476, anthrōpos* [2]
everyone, *570, hapas* [2]
front of everyone, *3836+3545, ho+mesos* [2]
everyone, *4246+6034, pas+psychē* [2]
everyone, *1569, ean* [1]
everyone, *1651+1667, heis+hekastos* [1]
everyone, *2848+4246, kata+pas* [1]
everyone, *3836, ho* [1]
everyone, *4246+1667, pas+hekastos* [1]
everyone, *4246+3836, pas+ho* [1]

EVERYONE'S [2]

everyone's, *4246, pas* [2]

EVERYTHING [147]

everything, *4246, pas* [101]
everything, *3836+4246, ho+pas* [14]
everything, *570, hapas* [7]
everything, *4012, hosos* [5]
everything, *RPE* [4]
everything, *4246+4012, pas+hosos* [4]
spend everything, *1251, dapanaō* [1]
have everything need, *3594+3309,*
　　mēdeis+leipō [1]
everything[s], *3836+2240, ho+ergon* [1]
everything that, *4012, hosos* [1]
everything, *4047, houtos* [1]
in everything, *4246, pas* [1]
everything, *4246+3836+5007,*
　　pas+ho+skeuos [1]
everything, *4246+4012+1569,*
　　pas+hosos+ean [1]
everything, *4246+4012+323, pas+hosos+an* [1]
everything, *4445, plērōma* [1]
everything you can, *5081, spoudaiōs* [1]
besides everything else, *6006+3836+4211,*
　　chōris+ho+parektos [1]

EVERYWHERE [13]

everywhere, *4116, pantachou* [6]
everywhere, *1877+4246+5536,*
　　en+pas+topos [1]
everywhere, *4114, pantachē* [1]
from everywhere, *4119, pantothen* [1]
everywhere, *4246+5536, pas+topos* [1]
followed everywhere, *4674, proskartereō* [1]

EVIDENCE [6]

evidence, *NIG* [1]

evidence, *1182, ginōskō* [1]
on the evidence of, *1328, dia* [1]
evidence, *1891, endeigma* [1]
evidence, *3456, martyria* [1]
false evidence, *6019, pseudomartyria* [1]

EVIDENT [2]

evident, *1182, ginōskō* [1]
evident, *2351, heuriskō* [1]

EVIDENTLY [1]

evidently, *1623+3590, ei+mē* [1]

EVIL [127]

evil, *4505, ponēros* [47]
evil, *2805, kakos* [25]
evil, *176, akathartos* [23]
evil desires, *2123, epithymia* [8]
evil, *94, adikia* [4]
evil, *2798, kakia* [3]
evil, *4504, ponēria* [3]
evil, *5765, phaulos* [3]
do evil, *2803, kakopoieō* [2]
evil, *AIT* [1]
evil, *490, anomia* [1]
spoken of as evil, *1059, blasphēmeō* [1]
driving out evil spirits, *2020, exorkistēs* [1]
evil desire, *2123, epithymia* [1]
does what is evil, *2803, kakopoieō* [1]
doing evil, *2803, kakopoieō* [1]
evil, *2809, kakōs* [1]
evil one, *4505, ponēros* [1]

EVILDOERS [3]

evildoers, *96, adikos* [1]
evildoers, *2237+3836+490,*
　　ergazomai+ho+anomia [1]
evildoers, *2239+94, ergatēs+adikia* [1]

EVILS [1]

evils, *4505, ponēros* [1]

EXACT [4]

exact, *AIT* [1]
found out exact, *208, akriboō* [1]
exact places, *3999, horothesia* [1]
exact representation, *5917, charaktēr* [1]

EXACTLY [2]

exactly, *855, asphalēs* [1]
exactly, *4048, houtōs* [1]

EXALT [1]

exalt himself, *5643, hyperairomai* [1]

EXALTED [8]

exalted, *5738, hypsoō* [5]
exalted, *3486, megalynō* [1]
exalted to the highest place, *5671,*
　　hyperypsoō [1]
exalted above, *5734, hypsēlos* [1]

EXALTS [3]

exalts, *5738, hypsoō* [3]

EXAMINE [2]

examine, *1507, dokimazō* [1]
examine, *4279, peirazō* [1]

EXAMINED [3]

examined, *373, anakrinō* [3]

EXAMINING [1]

examining, *373, anakrinō* [1]

EXAMPLE [16]

example, *5682, hypodeigma* [4]
example, *5596, typos* [2]
example, *RPE* [1]
for example, *1142, gar* [1]
example, *1257, deigma* [1]
or take as an example, *2627+2779, idou+kai* [1]
take an example, *3306, legō* [1]
follow example, *3628, mimeomai* [1]
follow example, *3629+1181,
   mimētēs+ginomai* [1]
join with others following example, *5213+1181,
   symmimētēs+ginomai* [1]
example, *5681, hypogrammos* [1]
example, *5721, hypotypōsis* [1]

EXAMPLES [3]

examples, *5596, typos* [2]
examples, *5595, typikōs* [1]

EXASPERATE [1]

exasperate, *4239, parorgizō* [1]

EXCEL [3]

excel, *4355, perisseuō* [3]

EXCELLENCY [1]

excellency, *3196, kratistos* [1]

EXCELLENT [7]

most excellent, *3196, kratistos* [3]
excellent, *2819, kalos* [2]
excellent, *746, aretē* [1]
most excellent, *2848+5651, kata+hyperbolē* [1]

EXCEPT [45]

except, *1623+3590, ei+mē* [36]
except, *NIG* [1]
except that, *247, alla* [1]
except, *247, alla* [1]
except for, *1623+3590, ei+mē* [1]
except, *1623+3614+323, ei+mēti+an* [1]
except, *3590, mē* [1]
except for, *4211+3364, parektos+logos* [1]
except for, *4211, parektos* [1]
except, *4440, plēn* [1]

EXCESSIVE [2]

excessive, *1539, dynamis* [1]
excessive, *4358, perissoteros* [1]

EXCHANGE [3]

in exchange for, *498, antallagma* [2]
exchange, *521, antimisthia* [1]

EXCHANGED [3]

exchanged, *3563, metallassō* [2]
exchanged, *248, allassō* [1]

EXCHANGING [1]

exchanging money, *3048, kermatistēs* [1]

EXCLAIM [1]

exclaim, *3189, krazō* [1]

EXCLAIMED [7]

exclaimed, *3306, legō* [4]
exclaimed, *430, anaphōneō* [1]

exclaimed, *550, apangellō* [1]
exclaimed, *3189, krazō* [1]

EXCLAIMING [1]

exclaiming, *550, apangellō* [1]

EXCLUDE [2]

exclude, *928, aphorizō* [1]
exclude, *1675, ekballō* [1]

EXCLUDED [2]

excluded, *558, apallotrioō* [1]
excluded, *1710, ekkleiō* [1]

EXCLUSIVELY [1]

exclusively, *AIT* [1]

EXCUSE [5]

excuse, *2400+4148, echō+paraiteomai* [2]
no excuse, *406, anapologētos* [1]
without excuse, *406, anapologētos* [1]
excuse, *4733, prophasis* [1]

EXCUSES [1]

make excuses, *4148, paraiteomai* [1]

EXECUTE [1]

execute, *650, apokteinō* [1]

EXECUTED [4]

executed, *359, anaireō* [2]
executed, *552, apagō* [1]
executed, *660, apollymi* [1]

EXECUTIONER [1]

executioner, *5063, spekoulatōr* [1]

EXEMPT [1]

exempt, *1801, eleutheros* [1]

EXERCISE [5]

exercise authority over, *2980, katexousiazō* [2]
exercise of freedom, *2026, exousia* [1]
exercise authority over, *2027, exousiazō* [1]
exercise, *4472, poieō* [1]

EXERCISED [1]

exercised, *4472, poieō* [1]

EXERTED [1]

exerted in, *1919+1877, energeō+en* [1]

EXHAUSTED [2]

exhausted, *AIT* [1]
not exhausted, *444, anekleiptos* [1]

EXHORT [1]

exhort, *4151, parakaleō* [1]

EXHORTATION [1]

exhortation, *4155, paraklēsis* [1]

EXHORTED [1]

exhorted, *4151, parakaleō* [1]

EXILE [5]

exile, *3578, metoikesia* [4]
send into exile, *3579, metoikizō* [1]

EXIST [1]

exist, *1639, eimi* [1]

EXISTED [1]

existed, *1639, eimi* [1]

EXISTS [2]

exists, *NIG* [1]
exists, *1639, eimi* [1]

EXODUS [1]

exodus, *2016, exodos* [1]

EXPAND [1]

expand, *3486, megalynō* [1]

EXPECT [10]

expect, *4659, prosdokaō* [5]
expect, *1506, dokeō* [2]
eagerly expect, *638, apokaradokia* [1]
expect, *1827, elpizō* [1]
expect, *3357, logizomai* [1]

EXPECTANTLY [1]

waiting expectantly, *4659, prosdokaō* [1]

EXPECTATION [2]

eager expectation for, *638, apokaradokia* [1]
expectation, *1693, ekdochē* [1]

EXPECTED [5]

expected, *3787, nomizō* [2]
expected, *1827, elpizō* [1]
expected, *4659, prosdokaō* [1]
expected, *5706, hyponoeō* [1]

EXPECTING [7]

expecting, *4659, prosdokaō* [3]
expecting to get back, *594, apelpizō* [1]
expecting a child, *1607, enkyos* [1]
expecting, *1683, ekdechomai* [1]
expecting to, *2671, hina* [1]

EXPEL [1]

expel, *1976, exairō* [1]

EXPELLED [1]

expelled, *1675, ekballō* [1]

EXPEND [1]

expend, *1682, ekdapanaō* [1]

EXPENSE [2]

expense, *4072, opsōnion* [1]
extra expense, *4655, prosdapanaō* [1]

EXPENSES [1]

pay expenses, *1251, dapanaō* [1]

EXPENSIVE [5]

very expensive, *988, barytimos* [1]
expensive, *1902, endoxos* [1]
expensive, *4500, polytelēs* [1]
very expensive, *4500, polytelēs* [1]
expensive, *4501, polytimos* [1]

EXPERIENCE [1]

experience, *3972, horaō* [1]

EXPERIENCED [1]

experienced, *1181, ginomai* [1]

EXPERT [4]

expert in the law, *3788, nomikos* [2]
the expert in the law^s, *3836+1254, ho+de* [1]
expert, *5055, sophos* [1]

EXPERTS [6]

experts in the law, *3788, nomikos* [5]
experts, *2840+1214, kardia+gymnazō* [1]

EXPLAIN [7]

explain, *334, anangellō* [1]
explain, *1196+1639, gnōstos+eimi* [1]
explain, *1259, deiknymi* [1]
explain, *1397, diasapheō* [1]
hard to explain, *1549, dysermēneutos* [1]
explain, *3306, legō* [1]
explain, *5851, phrazō* [1]

EXPLAINED [5]

explained, *1758, ektithēmi* [3]
explained what said, *1450, diermēneuō* [1]
explained, *2147, epilyō* [1]

EXPLAINING [1]

explaining, *1380, dianoigō* [1]

EXPLAINS [1]

explains to, *3842, hodēgeō* [1]

EXPLOIT [3]

exploit, *4430, pleonekteō* [2]
exploit, *1864, emporeuomai* [1]

EXPLOITED [1]

exploited, *4430, pleonekteō* [1]

EXPLOITING [1]

exploiting, *2872, katadynasteuō* [1]

EXPLOITS [1]

exploits, *2983, katesthiō* [1]

EXPOSE [3]

expose to public disgrace, *1258, deigmatizō* [1]
expose, *1794, elenchō* [1]
expose, *5746, phaneroō* [1]

EXPOSED [5]

exposed, *1794, elenchō* [2]
exposed, *1063, blepō* [1]
exposed to death, *2505, thanatos* [1]
publicly exposed, *2518, theatrizō* [1]

EXPRESS [2]

words cannot express, *227, alalētos* [1]
for the express purpose, *1650+899+4047, eis+autos+houtos* [1]

EXPRESSED [1]

expressed, *AIT* [1]

EXPRESSING [2]

expressing, *1919, energeō* [1]
expressing, *5173, synkrinō* [1]

EXPRESSIONS [1]

expressions of thanks, *2374, eucharistia* [1]

EXTENDS [1]

extends, *NIG* [1]

EXTENT [3]

to some extent, *247+608+3538, alla+apo+meros* [1]
the full extent of, *1650+5465, eis+telos* [1]
extent, *3538, meros* [1]

EXTERNAL [2]

judge by external appearance, *4725+476+3284, prosōpon+anthrōpos+lambanō* [1]
external, *4922, sarx* [1]

EXTINGUISH [1]

extinguish, *4931, sbennymi* [1]

EXTORT [1]

extort money, *1398, diaseiō* [1]

EXTRA [4]

extra, *1545, dyo* [2]
extra, *324+1545, ana+dyo* [1]
extra expense, *4655, prosdapanaō* [1]

EXTRAORDINARY [1]

extraordinary, *4024+3836+5593, ou+ho+tynchanō* [1]

EXTREME [1]

extreme, *2848+958, kata+bathos* [1]

EXTREMELY [1]

extremely, *4359, perissoterōs* [1]

EYE [32]

eye, *4057, ophthalmos* [25]
one eye, *3669, monophthalmos* [2]
eye is on, *4056, ophthalmodoulia* [2]
eye, *5557, trēma* [1]
eye, *5584, trymalia* [1]
eye, *5585, trypēma* [1]

EYES [72]

eyes, *4057, ophthalmos* [60]
in the eyes, *1967, enōpion* [4]
eyes, *3921, omma* [2]
eyes, *NIG* [1]
fix eyes, *927, aphoraō* [1]
before eyes, *1063, blepō* [1]
eyes opened, *1332, diablepō* [1]
open eyes, *2048+3836+4057, epairō+ho+ophthalmos* [1]
fix eyes on, *5023, skopeō* [1]

EYEWITNESSES [2]

eyewitnesses, *898, autoptēs* [1]
eyewitnesses, *2228, epoptēs* [1]

FACE [43]

face, *4725, prosōpon* [22]
face, *5125, stoma* [4]
face, *AIT* [3]
struck in the face, *1443+4825, didōmi+rhapisma* [2]
with face to the ground, *2093+4725, epi+prosōpon* [2]
face to face, *2848+4725, kata+prosōpon* [2]
face, *4071, opsis* [2]
face, *NIG* [1]
to face, *2093, epi* [1]

face, *2400, echō* [1]
face death, *2506, thanatoō* [1]
face, *4346, peripiptō* [1]
face fell, *5145, stygnazō* [1]

FACED [3]

faced, *2848+4725, kata+prosōpon* [1]
faced the fact, *2917, katanoeō* [1]
faced, *4278+3284, peira+lambanō* [1]

FACEDOWN [1]

facedown to the ground, *2093+4725, epi+prosōpon* [1]

FACES [9]

faces, *4725, prosōpon* [7]
faces, *AIT* [1]
in faces, *1869, emprosthen* [1]

FACING [2]

facing, *1063, blepō* [1]
facing, *3531, menō* [1]

FACT [28]

in fact, *2779, kai* [8]
in fact, *247, alla* [5]
in fact, *1142, gar* [4]
fact, *NIG* [2]
the fact is, *1142, gar* [1]
if in fact, *1642+726, eiper+ara* [1]
in fact, *2779+1142, kai+gar* [1]
although in fact, *2793, kaitoige* [1]
faced the fact, *2917, katanoeō* [1]
in fact, *3815, nyni* [1]
the fact^s, *4005, hos* [1]
the fact that, *4022, hoti* [1]
the very fact that, *4022, hoti* [1]

FACTIONS [2]

factions, *146, hairesis* [1]
factions, *2249, eritheia* [1]

FACTS [1]

facts, *AIT* [1]

FADE [3]

never fade away, *277, amarantinos* [1]
that can never fade, *278, amarantos* [1]
fade away, *3447, marainō* [1]

FADING [3]

fading away, *2934, katargeō* [2]
fading, *2934, katargeō* [1]

FAIL [9]

fail, *4024, ou* [3]
fail the test, *99+1639, adokimos+eimi* [1]
fail, *766, arneomai* [1]
fail, *1569+3590, ean+mē* [1]
fail, *1722, ekleipō* [1]
fail, *2907, katalyō* [1]
fail, *4049+3590, ouchi+mē* [1]

FAILED [4]

to have failed, *99+1639, adokimos+eimi* [1]
failed to pay, *691, apostereō* [1]
failed the test, *1639+99, eimi+adokimos* [1]
failed, *1738, ekpiptō* [1]

FAILINGS [1]

failings, *821, asthenēma* [1]

FAILS [1]

fails, *4406, piptō* [1]

FAILURE [1]

failure, *3031, kenos* [1]

FAINT [1]

faint, *715, apopsychō* [1]

FAIR [3]

fair, *899, autos* [1]
fair weather, *2304, eudia* [1]
fair, *2699, isotēs* [1]

FAIR HAVENS [1]

Fair Havens, *2816, Kaloi limenes* [1]

FAITH [254]

faith, *4411, pistis* [221]
of little faith, *3899, oligopistos* [5]
put faith, *4409, pisteuō* [5]
lack of faith, *602, apistia* [4]
faith, *RPE* [3]
faith, *4409, pisteuō* [3]
have faith, *1666+4411, ek+pistis* [2]
not have faith, *601, apisteō* [1]
faith⁵, *899, autos* [1]
little faith, *3898, oligopistia* [1]
confess faith, *3933, homologeō* [1]
faith we profess, *3934, homologia* [1]
faith⁵, *4005, hos* [1]
his faith⁵, *4005, hos* [1]
putting faith, *4409, pisteuō* [1]
faith from first to last, *4411+1650+4411,*
  pistis+eis+pistis [1]
faith, *4412, pistos* [1]
turn away from the faith, *4997, skandalizō* [1]

FAITHFUL [42]

faithful, *4412, pistos* [36]
faithful, *RPE* [2]
faithful to her husband, *1651+467+1222,*
  heis+anēr+gynē [1]
remain faithful to, *1844+1877, emmenō+en* [1]
faithful, *4411, pistis* [1]
faithful, *4674, proskartereō* [1]

FAITHFULLY [1]

faithfully, *6055+2819, hōs+kalos* [1]

FAITHFULNESS [5]

faithfulness, *4411, pistis* [4]
faithfulness, *NIG* [1]

FAITHLESS [2]

faithless, *601, apisteō* [1]
faithless, *853, asynthetos* [1]

FALL [48]

fall, *4406, piptō* [13]
fall away, *4997, skandalizō* [7]
fall, *1860, empiptō* [5]
fall into, *1656+1650, eiserchomai+eis* [3]
makes fall, *4998, skandalon* [2]
fall away, *923, aphistēmi* [1]
fall, *1639+4406, eimi+piptō* [1]
fall away, *1738, ekpiptō* [1]
fall from, *1738, ekpiptō* [1]
fall, *1738, ekpiptō* [1]
fall on, *2173, episkiazō* [1]
fall, *2262, erchomai* [1]
fall, *2928, katapiptō* [1]

fall asleep, *3121, koimaō* [1]
fall away, *4178, parapiptō* [1]
fall down, *4406+2093+4725,*
  piptō+epi+prosōpon [1]
fall down, *4406, piptō* [1]
cause fall, *4684, proskoptō* [1]
fall down, *4686, proskyneō* [1]
fall, *4760, ptaiō* [1]
cause to fall, *4997, skandalizō* [1]
causes fall into sin, *4997, skandalizō* [1]
fall short, *5728, hystereō* [1]

FALLEN [18]

fallen, *4406, piptō* [8]
fallen asleep, *3121, koimaō* [7]
fallen away from, *1738, ekpiptō* [1]
fallen on, *2158+2093, epipiptō+epi* [1]
fallen short, *5728, hystereō* [1]

FALLING [5]

falling, *720, aptaistos* [1]
falling, *2262, erchomai* [1]
falling, *2849, katabainō* [1]
falling, *4774, ptōsis* [1]
falling on, *5502, tithēmi* [1]

FALLS [11]

falls, *4406, piptō* [8]
falls, *1738, ekpiptō* [1]
falls, *1860, empiptō* [1]
falls away, *4997, skandalizō* [1]

FALSE [34]

false prophets, *6021, pseudoprophētēs* [7]
false prophet, *6021, pseudoprophētēs* [4]
give false testimony, *6018, pseudomartyreō* [3]
false, *AIT* [2]
false brothers, *6012, pseudadelphos* [2]
false, *6014, pseudēs* [2]
false witnesses, *6020, pseudomartys* [2]
false Christs, *6023, pseudochristos* [2]
nothing false, *94+4024, adikia+ou* [2]
false, *1515, dolos* [1]
teach false doctrines, *2281,*
  heterodidaskaleō [1]
teaches false doctrines, *2281,*
  heterodidaskaleō [1]
false motives, *4733, prophasis* [1]
false apostles, *6013, pseudapostolos* [1]
false teachers, *6015, pseudodidaskalos* [1]
gave false testimony, *6018, pseudomartyreō* [1]
false evidence, *6019, pseudomartyria* [1]
false testimony, *6019, pseudomartyria* [1]

FALSEHOOD [4]

falsehood, *6022, pseudos* [2]
falsehood, *4415, planē* [1]
falsehood, *6025, pseusma* [1]

FALSELY [4]

accuse falsely, *5193, sykophanteō* [1]
falsely, *6017, pseudomai* [1]
testified falsely, *6018, pseudomartyreō* [1]
falsely called, *6024, pseudōnymos* [1]

FAMILIAR [1]

familiar, *2179, epistamai* [1]

FAMILY [22]

family, *3875, oikos* [7]
family, *AIT* [2]
family, *1169, genos* [2]
family, *3836+3875, ho+oikos* [1]

family, *3836+4123, ho+para* [1]
family, *3836, ho* [1]
your family, *3836+5050, ho+sos* [1]
belong to family, *3858, oikeios* [1]
immediate family, *3858, oikeios* [1]
family, *3864, oikia* [1]
whole family, *4109, panoikei* [1]
family, *4255, patria* [1]
family, *5065, sperma* [1]
family, *5149, syngeneia* [1]

FAMINE [7]

famine, *3350, limos* [7]

FAMINES [3]

famines, *3350, limos* [3]

FAN [1]

fan into flame, *351, anazōpyreō* [1]

FAR [30]

far, *3426, makran* [4]
far, *AIT* [3]
far off, *608+3427, apo+makrothen* [3]
far away, *3426, makran* [3]
as far as, *948, achri* [2]
far, *4522, porrō* [2]
far away, *608+3427, apo+makrothen* [1]
but as far as, *1254, de* [1]
as far as, *1650, eis* [1]
far off, *1650+3426, eis+makran* [1]
as far as, *2401, heōs* [1]
that far outweighs them all,
  2848+5651+1650+5651+983,
  kata+hyperbolē+eis+hyperbolē+baros [1]
as far as, *3525, men* [1]
how far will they go, *4047+5515+1639,*
  houtos+tis+eimi [1]
to far shore, *4305, peran* [1]
by far, *4498, polys* [1]
get very far, *4621+2093+4498,*
  prokoptō+epi+polys [1]
far above, *5645, hyperanō* [1]
going too far, *5657, hyperekteinō* [1]

FAREWELL [1]

farewell, *4874, rhōnnymi* [1]

FARMED [1]

farmed, *1175, geōrgeō* [1]

FARMER [6]

farmer, *5062, speirō* [4]
farmer, *1177, geōrgos* [2]

FARMERS [3]

farmers, *1177, geōrgos* [3]

FARTHER [4]

going farther, *4601, proerchomai* [2]
farther, *4522, porrō* [1]
gone farther, *4581, probainō* [1]

FAST [14]

fast, *3764, nēsteuō* [11]
stuck fast, *2242, ereidō* [1]
stand fast, *2705, histēmi* [1]
fast, *3763, nēsteia* [1]

FASTED [1]

fasted, *3764, nēsteuō* [1]

FASTENED [4]

fastened, *856, asphalizō* [1]
fastened, *867, atenizō* [1]
fastened, *2750, kathaptō* [1]
fastened, *5502, tithēmi* [1]

FASTING [8]

fasting, *3764, nēsteuō* [6]
fasting, *3763, nēsteia* [2]

FATAL [3]

fatal, *2505, thanatos* [3]

FATHER [390]

father, *4252, patēr* [336]
father, *1164, gennaō* [40]
father, *RPE* [4]
become father, *1164, gennaō* [3]
without father, *574, apatōr* [1]
became father, *1164, gennaō* [1]
became the father of, *1164, gennaō* [1]
father's, *1666+3130, ek+koitē* [1]
the father's, *1697, ekeinos* [1]
become a father, *2856+5065+3284,
   katabolē+sperma+lambanō* [1]
the father's, *3836+1254, ho+de* [1]

FATHER'S [21]

father's, *4252, patēr* [21]

FATHER-IN-LAW [1]

father-in-law, *4290, pentheros* [1]

FATHERS [40]

fathers, *4252, patēr* [35]
fathers, *4262, patrōos* [2]
our fathers', *3836+3525, ho+men* [1]
fathers, *4257, patrikos* [1]
kill their fathers, *4260, patrolōas* [1]

FATHOM [1]

fathom, *3857, oida* [1]

FATTENED [5]

fattened, *4988, siteutos* [3]
fattened cattle, *4990, sitistos* [1]
fattened, *5555, trephō* [1]

FAULT [6]

without fault, *320, amōmos* [2]
show fault, *1794, elenchō* [1]
found fault with, *3522, memphomai* [1]
finding fault, *3943, oneidizō* [1]
at fault, *4760, ptaiō* [1]

FAULTFINDERS [1]

faultfinders, *3523, mempsimoiros* [1]

FAULTLESS [2]

faultless, *299, amiantos* [1]
faultless, *1181+289, ginomai+amemptos* [1]

FAVOR [19]

favor, *5921, charis* [7]
win favor, *473, anthrōpareskos* [2]
favor, *1283, dektos* [2]
favor, *AIT* [1]
favor, *19, agathos* [1]
asked favor, *160, aiteō* [1]
shown favor, *2078, epeidon* [1]
on whom favor rests, *2306, eudokia* [1]

favor, *2347, euprosdektos* [1]
in favor, *4309, peri* [1]
gracious favor, *5922, charisma* [1]

FAVORED [2]

so favored^s, *4047, houtos* [1]
highly favored, *5923, charitoō* [1]

FAVORITISM [7]

favoritism, *4721, prosōpolēmpsia* [2]
show favoritism, *1639+4720,
   eimi+prosōpolēmptēs* [1]
show favoritism, *1639+4721,
   eimi+prosōpolēmpsia* [1]
show favoritism, *1877+4721,
   en+prosōpolēmpsia* [1]
out of favoritism, *2848+4680,
   kata+prosklisis* [1]
show favoritism, *4719, prosōpolēmpteō* [1]

FEAR [50]

fear, *5832, phobos* [20]
fear, *5828, phobeomai* [14]
fear, *RPE* [1]
nothing to fear, *925, aphobōs* [1]
without fear, *925, aphobōs* [1]
with fear, *1769, ekphobos* [1]
in fear, *1873+1181, emphobos+ginomai* [1]
trembled with fear, *1958+1181,
   entromos+ginomai* [1]
holy fear, *2326, eulabeomai* [1]
for fear that, *2671+3590, hina+mē* [1]
for fear, *2671+3590, hina+mē* [1]
for fear that, *3590+4803, mē+pōs* [1]
free from fear of, *3590+5828,
   mē+phobeomai* [1]
fear, *5571, tromos* [1]
in fear, *5828, phobeomai* [1]
fear for, *5828, phobeomai* [1]
fear, *5832+3489, phobos+megas* [1]
reverent fear, *5832, phobos* [1]

FEARED [6]

feared, *5828, phobeomai* [5]
feared, *5832, phobos* [1]

FEARFUL [2]

fearful, *5829, phoberos* [1]
fearful events, *5831, phobētron* [1]

FEARING [3]

fearing, *5828, phobeomai* [2]
fearing that, *5828+3590, phobeomai+mē* [1]

FEARLESSLY [4]

fearlessly, *925, aphobōs* [1]
fearlessly, *1877+4244, en+parrēsia* [1]
fearlessly, *4245, parrēsiazomai* [1]
preached fearlessly, *4245, parrēsiazomai* [1]

FEARS [2]

fears, *5828, phobeomai* [1]
fears, *5832, phobos* [1]

FEAST [36]

feast, *2038, heortē* [22]
Feast of Unleavened Bread, *109, azymos* [4]
take places at the feast, *369, anaklinō* [2]
feast, *756, ariston* [1]
wedding feast, *1141, gamos* [1]
Feast of Dedication, *1589, enkainia* [1]
Passover Feast, *2038, heortē* [1]
have a feast, *2266, esthiō* [1]

Feast of Unleavened Bread, *2465+109,
   hēmera+azymos* [1]
Feast, *2465, hēmera* [1]
feast with, *5307, syneuōcheomai* [1]

FEASTS [1]

love feasts, *27, agapē* [1]

FED [3]

well fed, *5963, chortazō* [2]
well fed, *1855, empimplēmi* [1]

FEEBLE [1]

feeble, *4223, pariēmi* [1]

FEED [8]

feed, *1081, boskō* [3]
feed, *5963, chortazō* [2]
feed, *RPE* [1]
feed, *5555, trephō* [1]
feed, *6039, psōmizō* [1]

FEEDING [3]

feeding, *1081, boskō* [3]

FEEDS [5]

feeds, *5555, trephō* [2]
feeds on, *5592, trōgō* [2]
feeds, *1763, ektrephō* [1]

FEEL [3]

feel weak, *820, astheneō* [1]
feel ashamed, *1956, entrepō* [1]
feel, *5858, phroneō* [1]

FEELS [1]

feels, *AIT* [1]

FEET [90]

feet, *4546, pous* [76]
fell at feet, *4700, prospiptō* [3]
jumped to his feet, *403, anapēdaō* [1]
helped to her feet, *482, anistēmi* [1]
feet, *1000, basis* [1]
on your feet, *1586, egeirō* [1]
lifted to his feet, *1586, egeirō* [1]
feet, *2705, histēmi* [1]
a hundred and twenty feet deep, *3976+1633,
   orgyia+eikosi* [1]
ninety feet deep, *3976+1278,
   orgyia+dekapente* [1]
irons on feet, *4267, pedē* [1]
a robe reaching down to feet, *4468, podērēs* [1]
feet, *5711, hypopodion* [1]

FELIX [10]

Felix, *5772, Phēlix* [9]
Felix, *RPE* [1]

FELL [75]

fell, *4406, piptō* [39]
fell down, *4406, piptō* [7]
fell at feet, *4700, prospiptō* [3]
received seed that fell, *5062, speirō* [3]
fell, *2928, katapiptō* [2]
fell asleep, *3121, koimaō* [2]
fell, *674, apopiptō* [1]
fell asleep, *934, aphypnoō* [1]
fell into trance, *1181+2093+1749,
   ginomai+epi+ekstasis* [1]
fell, *1181, ginomai* [1]
fell on knees before, *1206, gonypeteō* [1]

image which fell from heaven, *1479,*
diopetēs [1]
fell off, *1738+1666, ekpiptō+ek* [1]
fell, *1860, empiptō* [1]
fell asleep, *2761, katheudō* [1]
fell, *2849, katabainō* [1]
fell into the hands of, *4346, peripiptō* [1]
fell headlong, *4568+1181, prēnēs+ginomai* [1]
fell on knees in front of, *4686, proskyneō* [1]
fell at, *4700, prospiptō* [1]
fell before, *4700, prospiptō* [1]
fell down before, *4700, prospiptō* [1]
fell, *4700, prospiptō* [1]
face fell, *5145, stygnazō* [1]
fell on, *5502, tithēmi* [1]

FELLOW [47]

fellow, *AIT* [13]
fellow worker, *5301, synergos* [6]
fellow workers, *5301, synergos* [5]
fellow servant, *5281, syndoulos* [4]
fellow, *476, anthrōpos* [3]
fellow servants, *5281, syndoulos* [3]
fellow prisoner, *5257, synaichmalōtos* [2]
fellow servant with with, *5281, syndoulos* [2]
fellow soldier, *5369, systratiōtēs* [2]
fellow, *81, adelphos* [1]
fellow, *3836+5250, ho+syn* [1]
fellow citizens with, *5232, sympolitēs* [1]
fellow elder, *5236, sympresbyteros* [1]
fellow guests, *5263, synanakeimai* [1]
fellow prisoners, *5279, syndeō* [1]
fellow workers, *5300, synergeō* [1]

FELLOW'S [1]

fellow's, *AIT* [1]

FELLOWMAN [1]

his fellowman[s], *3836+2283, ho+heteros* [1]

FELLOWSHIP [12]

fellowship, *3126, koinōnia* [10]
fellowship of sharing, *3126, koinōnia* [1]
fellowship, *3545, mesos* [1]

FELT [4]

felt, *2400, echō* [3]
felt, *1182, ginōskō* [1]

FEMALE [3]

female, *2559, thēlys* [3]

FERMENTED [1]

fermented drink, *4975, sikera* [1]

FEROCIOUS [1]

ferocious, *774, harpax* [1]

FERTILIZE [1]

fertilize, *965+3162, ballō+koprion* [1]

FERVOR [2]

fervor, *2417, zeō* [1]
with great fervor, *2417+3836+4460,*
zeō+ho+pneuma [1]

FESTIVAL [2]

keep the Festival, *2037, heortazō* [1]
religious festival, *2038, heortē* [1]

FESTUS [14]

Festus, *5776, Phēstos* [13]

Festus[s], *899, autos* [1]

FEVER [8]

fever, *4790, pyretos* [6]
with a fever, *4789, pyressō* [2]

FEW [21]

few, *3900, oligos* [15]
few, *AIT* [2]
few, *4024+4498, ou+polys* [2]
a few days later, *1328+2465, dia+hēmera* [1]
a few, *5516, tis* [1]

FIELD [31]

field, *69, agros* [22]
field, *6005, chōrion* [3]
harvest field, *2546, therismos* [2]
field, *1176, geōrgion* [1]
field, *3586+3836+2834, metron+ho+kanōn* [1]
field, *3586, metron* [1]
field, *5965, chortos* [1]

FIELDS [8]

fields, *69, agros* [5]
fields, *6001, chōra* [3]

FIERCELY [1]

fiercely, *1267, deinōs* [1]

FIERY [7]

fiery, *4786, pyr* [5]
fiery red, *4791, pyrinos* [1]
fiery red, *4794, pyrros* [1]

FIFTEEN [1]

fifteen, *1278, dekapente* [1]

FIFTEENTH [1]

fifteenth, *4298, pentekaidekatos* [1]

FIFTH [4]

fifth, *4286, pemptos* [4]

FIFTIES [1]

fifties, *4299, pentēkonta* [1]

FIFTY [4]

fifty, *4299, pentēkonta* [3]
fifty thousand, *3689+4297, myrias+pente* [1]

FIG [15]

fig tree, *5190, sykē* [14]
a fig[s] tree, *899, autos* [1]

FIGHT [10]

fight, *74, agōn* [2]
fight, *76, agōnizomai* [2]
fight, *4482, polemeō* [2]
weapons fight with, *3960+3836+5127,*
hoplon+ho+strateia [1]
fight, *4782, pykteuō* [1]
fight, *5127, strateia* [1]
fight, *5129, strateuomai* [1]

FIGHTING [2]

fighting against God, *2534, theomachos* [1]
fighting, *3481, machomai* [1]

FIGHTS [1]

fights, *4483, polemos* [1]

FIGS [5]

figs, *5192, sykon* [4]
figs, *5190, sykē* [1]

FIGURATIVELY [4]

taken figuratively, *251, allēgoreō* [1]
figuratively speaking, *1877+4130,*
en+parabolē [1]
figuratively, *1877+4231, en+paroimia* [1]
figuratively, *4462, pneumatikōs* [1]

FIGURE [2]

a public figure, *1877+4244, en+parrēsia* [1]
figure of speech, *4231, paroimia* [1]

FIGUREHEAD [1]

figurehead, *4185, parasēmos* [1]

FIGURES [1]

figures of speech, *4231, paroimia* [1]

FILL [9]

fill with, *4444, plēroō* [3]
fill, *1153, gemizō* [2]
fill up, *499, antanaplēroō* [1]
fill up, *4444, plēroō* [1]
fill, *4444, plēroō* [1]
fill, *5963, chortazō* [1]

FILLED [50]

filled, *4398, pimplēmi* [15]
filled with, *4444, plēroō* [6]
filled, *4444, plēroō* [6]
filled, *1153, gemizō* [5]
filled, *AIT* [2]
filled, *1154, gemō* [2]
filled with joy, *22+5915, agalliaō+chara* [1]
filled with joy, *22, agalliaō* [1]
was filled with, *1181, ginomai* [1]
filled, *1855, empimplēmi* [1]
filled with, *2400, echō* [1]
filled with awe, *3284+5832,*
lambanō+phobos [1]
filled with grief, *3382+5379,*
lypeō+sphodra [1]
filled with grief, *4291, pentheō* [1]
filled in, *4444, plēroō* [1]
filled with compassion, *5072,*
splanchnizomai [1]
filled with compassion for, *5072,*
splanchnizomai [1]
filled with awe, *5828, phobeomai* [1]
filled with joy, *5915+3489, chara+megas* [1]
filled, *5963, chortazō* [1]

FILLS [2]

fills with joy, *2372, euphrosynē* [1]
fills, *4444, plēroō* [1]

FILTH [2]

filth, *176, akathartos* [1]
moral filth, *4864, rhyparia* [1]

FILTHY [2]

filthy language, *155, aischrologia* [1]
filthy, *816, aselgeia* [1]

FINAL [3]

final, *2274, eschatos* [2]
final statement, *4839+1651, rhēma+heis* [1]

FINALITY [1]

finality, *5334, synteleō* [1]

FINALLY [22]

finally, *3836+3370, ho+loipos* [5]
finally, *3370, loipos* [3]
finally, *4036, oun* [3]
finally, *5538+4036, tote+oun* [2]
finally, *5731, hysteros* [2]
finally, *AIT* [1]
finally, *1254, de* [1]
finally, *2779, kai* [1]
finally, *3552+4047, meta+houtos* [1]
finally, *3836+5465, ho+telos* [1]
finally brought about, *5465, telos* [1]
finally, *5731+4246, hysteros+pas* [1]

FINANCIAL [1]

means to financial gain, *4516, porismos* [1]

FIND [70]

find, *2351, heuriskō* [53]
find out, *1182, ginōskō* [5]
find, *NIG* [2]
find out about, *1182, ginōskō* [1]
find out, *1507, dokimazō* [1]
find, *1639+2351, eimi+heuriskō* [1]
find, *1639, eimi* [1]
find out, *2105, epiginōskō* [1]
trying to find out, *2236, eraunaō* [1]
find out, *2351, heuriskō* [1]
find, *2623, ide* [1]
find convenient, *2789+3561,
    kairos+metalambanō* [1]
to find[s], *4022, hoti* [1]

FINDING [4]

finding, *2351, heuriskō* [2]
finding, *461, aneuriskō* [1]
finding fault, *3943, oneidizō* [1]

FINDS [16]

finds, *2351, heuriskō* [13]
finds himself, *405, anaplēroō* [1]
finds, *1181+2351, ginomai+heuriskō* [1]
finds fulfillment, *4444, plēroō* [1]

FINE [17]

fine linen, *1115, byssinos* [5]
fine, *2819, kalos* [2]
fine, *3287, lampros* [2]
fine clothes, *3434, malakos* [2]
fine linen, *1116, byssos* [1]
fine clothes, *1906+2668, endysis+himation* [1]
fine way, *2822, kalōs* [1]
fine, *3434, malakos* [1]
fine, *3525, men* [1]
fine flour, *4947, semidalis* [1]

FINE-SOUNDING [1]

fine-sounding arguments, *4391, pithanologia* [1]

FINGER [8]

finger, *1235, daktylos* [6]
lift a finger, *1235, daktylos* [1]
finger, *5931, cheir* [1]

FINGERS [1]

fingers, *1235, daktylos* [1]

FINISH [9]

finish, *5457, teleioō* [3]

finish, *1754, ekteleō* [2]
finish, *2200, epiteleō* [1]
in advance finish the arrangements for, *4616,
    prokatartizō* [1]
finish, *5455+2400, teleios+echō* [1]
finish, *5464, teleō* [1]

FINISHED [20]

finished, *5464, teleō* [8]
finished, *AIT* [5]
finished, *4264, pauō* [2]
finished, *4444, plēroō* [2]
finished, *1181, ginomai* [1]
finished, *4967, sigaō* [1]
finished, *5334, synteleō* [1]

FIRE [71]

fire, *4786, pyr* [57]
fire, *3106, klibanos* [2]
fire, *4787, pyra* [2]
set on fire, *409, anaptō* [1]
fire of burning coals, *471, anthrakia* [1]
fire, *471, anthrakia* [1]
fire, *3012, kausoō* [1]
fire, *4792, pyroō* [1]
put out fire, *4931, sbennymi* [1]
set on fire, *5824, phlogizō* [1]
sets on fire, *5824, phlogizō* [1]
fire, *5825, phlox* [1]
fire, *5890, phōs* [1]

FIRELIGHT [1]

firelight, *5890, phōs* [1]

FIRM [25]

stand firm, *5112, stēkō* [5]
stand firm, *2705, histēmi* [3]
stands firm, *5702, hypomenō* [3]
firm, *855, asphalēs* [1]
firm, *1010, bebaios* [1]
makes stand firm, *1011, bebaioō* [1]
firm, *1612, hedraios* [1]
stand firm, *1612+1181, hedraios+ginomai* [1]
standing firm, *2705, histēmi* [1]
stands firm, *2705, histēmi* [1]
firm, *2819, kalos* [1]
standing firm, *5104, stereos* [1]
firm, *5106, stereōma* [1]
standing firm, *5112, stēkō* [1]
make firm, *5114, stērizō* [1]
stand firm, *5114+3836+2840,
    stērizō+ho+kardia* [1]
standing firm, *5705, hypomonē* [1]

FIRMLY [5]

hold firmly to, *504, antechō* [1]
firmly, *1010, bebaios* [1]
hold firmly, *2988, katechō* [1]
hold firmly to, *3195, krateō* [1]
firmly established, *5114, stērizō* [1]

FIRST [161]

first, *4755, prōtos* [75]
first, *4754, prōton* [47]
first, *1651, heis* [9]
first, *794, archē* [5]
first of all, *4754, prōton* [4]
first, *AIT* [3]
first, *4728, proteros* [3]
first, *542, anōteros* [1]
first converts, *569, aparchē* [1]
first convert, *569, aparchē* [1]
first, *806, archō* [1]

as of first importance, *1877+4755,
    en+prōtos* [1]
first, *3552+3836, meta+ho* [1]
first of all, *4047+4754, houtos+prōton* [1]
faith from first to last, *4411+1650+4411,
    pistis+eis+pistis* [1]
first to hope, *4598, proelpizō* [1]
the first, *4599, proenarchomai* [1]
first, *4740, prophthanō* [1]
at first, *4754, prōton* [1]
in the first place, *4754, prōton* [1]
first, *4759, prōtōs* [1]
loves to be first, *5812, philoprōteuō* [1]

FIRSTBORN [10]

firstborn, *4758, prōtotokos* [8]
the firstborn[s] of Israel, *899, autos* [1]
firstborn, *1380+3616, dianoigō+mētra* [1]

FIRSTFRUITS [6]

firstfruits, *569, aparchē* [6]

FISH [31]

fish, *2716, ichthys* [19]
fish, *4066, opsarion* [4]
small fish, *2715, ichthydion* [2]
fish, *AIT* [1]
fish, *RPE* [1]
fish, *244, halieuō* [1]
huge fish, *3063, kētos* [1]
small fish, *4066, opsarion* [1]
fish, *4709, prosphagion* [1]

FISHERMEN [4]

fishermen, *243, halieus* [3]
fishermen, *RPE* [1]

FISHERS [2]

fishers, *243, halieus* [2]

FISTS [2]

struck with fists, *3139, kolaphizō* [2]

FIT [4]

fit for service, *2310, euthetos* [1]
fit, *2310, euthetos* [1]
fit, *2653, hikanos* [1]
fit, *2763, kathēkō* [1]

FITS [1]

fits of rage, *2596, thymos* [1]

FITTED [1]

fitted, *5686, hypodeō* [1]

FITTING [3]

fitting, *465, anēkō* [1]
fitting, *2361, euschēmonōs* [1]
fitting, *4560, prepō* [1]

FIVE [44]

five, *4297, pente* [35]
five thousand, *4295, pentakischilioi* [6]
five hundred, *4296, pentakosioi* [2]
five times, *4294, pentakis* [1]

FIX [3]

fix eyes, *927, aphoraō* [1]
fix thoughts on, *2917, katanoeō* [1]
fix eyes on, *5023, skopeō* [1]

FIXED [1]

fixed, *5114, stērizō* [1]

FLAME [1]

fan into flame, *351, anazōpyreō* [1]

FLAMES [5]

flames, *4786, pyr* [2]
flames, *5825, phlox* [2]
flames, *2794, kaiō* [1]

FLAMING [1]

flaming, *4792, pyroō* [1]

FLASH [2]

flash, *875, atomos* [1]
flash of lightning, *1993, exastraptō* [1]

FLASHED [2]

flashed around, *4313+4309,*
  periastraptō+peri [1]
flashed around, *4313, periastraptō* [1]

FLASHES [5]

flashes of lightning, *847, astrapē* [4]
which flashes, *848, astraptō* [1]

FLATTER [1]

flatter, *2513+4725, thaumazō+prosōpon* [1]

FLATTERY [2]

flattery, *2330, eulogia* [1]
flattery, *3364+3135, logos+kolakeia* [1]

FLED [10]

fled, *5771, pheugō* [7]
fled, *2966, katapheugō* [2]
fled away, *5771, pheugō* [1]

FLEE [11]

flee, *5771, pheugō* [9]
flee from, *5771, pheugō* [2]

FLESH [35]

flesh, *4922, sarx* [33]
mutilators of the flesh, *2961, katatomē* [1]
corrupted flesh, *4922, sarx* [1]

FLEW [1]

flew open, *487, anoigō* [1]

FLIGHT [1]

flight, *5870, phygē* [1]

FLINGING [1]

flinging, *965, ballō* [1]

FLOCK [9]

flock, *4480, poimnion* [5]
flock, *4479, poimnē* [3]
the flock's, *899, autos* [1]

FLOCKS [2]

flocks and herds, *2576, thremma* [1]
flocks, *4479, poimnē* [1]

FLOG [6]

flog, *3463, mastigoō* [4]
flog, *2666, hinıas* [1]
flog, *3464, mastizō* [1]

FLOGGED [9]

flogged, *1296, derō* [2]
flogged, *3463, mastigoō* [2]
had flogged, *5849, phragelloō* [2]
flogged, *2202+4435, epitithēmi+plēgē* [1]
flogged, *3465, mastix* [1]
flogged, *4435, plēgē* [1]

FLOGGING [1]

flogging, *3465, mastix* [1]

FLOOD [6]

flood, *2886, kataklysmos* [4]
flood, *431, anachysis* [1]
flood, *4439, plēmmyra* [1]

FLOOR [3]

threshing floor, *272, halōn* [2]
floor, *AIT* [1]

FLOUR [3]

flour, *236, aleuron* [2]
fine flour, *4947, semidalis* [1]

FLOW [4]

flow, *AIT* [1]
flow, *1108, bryō* [1]
flow over, *4355, perisseuō* [1]
flow, *4835, rheō* [1]

FLOWED [1]

flowed out of, *2002+1666, exerchomai+ek* [1]

FLOWER [1]

flower, *470, anthos* [1]

FLOWERS [2]

flowers, *470, anthos* [2]

FLOWING [3]

flowing robes, *5124, stolē* [2]
flowing from, *1744+1666, ekporeuomai+ek* [1]

FLUNG [1]

flung, *965, ballō* [1]

FLUTE [5]

played the flute, *884, auleō* [2]
flute players, *886, aulētēs* [2]
flute, *888, aulos* [1]

FLY [1]

fly, *4375, petomai* [1]

FLYING [4]

flying, *4375, petomai* [4]

FOAL [1]

foal, *5626, huios* [1]

FOAMING [2]

foaming at the mouth, *930, aphrizō* [1]
foaming up, *2072, epaphrizō* [1]

FOAMS [2]

foams at the mouth, *930, aphrizō* [1]
foams at the mouth, *931, aphros* [1]

FOLDED [1]

folded up, *1962, entylissō* [1]

FOLLOW [65]

follow, *199, akoloutheō* [32]
follow, *RPE* [6]
follow, *1979, exakoloutheō* [3]
follow, *3958, opisō* [3]
follow, *1639, eimi* [2]
follow, *2848+4513, kata+poreuomai* [2]
follow, *199+3958, akoloutheō+opisō* [1]
follow, *1503, diōkō* [1]
follow, *2051, epakoloutheō* [1]
follow, *2262+3958, erchomai+opisō* [1]
follow Jewish customs, *2678, ioudaizō* [1]
follow, *2848, kata* [1]
that would follow, *3552+4047,*
  meta+houtos [1]
follow example, *3628, mimeomai* [1]
follow, *3628, mimeomai* [1]
follow example, *3629+1181,*
  mimētēs+ginomai [1]
follow, *3958+4513, opisō+poreuomai* [1]
follow, *4275, peithō* [1]
follow, *4513+3958, poreuomai+opisō* [1]
follow, *4668, prosechō* [1]
follow, *5123, stoicheō* [1]
follow, *5258, synakoloutheō* [1]
follow mere natural instincts, *6035,*
  psychikos [1]

FOLLOWED [56]

followed, *199, akoloutheō* [41]
followed, *1666, ek* [2]
followed, *2887, katakoloutheō* [2]
followed, *RPE* [1]
followed, *599+3958, aperchomai+opisō* [1]
followed out, *2002+199,*
  exerchomai+akoloutheō [1]
followed, *2262, erchomai* [1]
followed, *2848, kata* [1]
followed, *3552+4344, meta+peripateō* [1]
followed, *3958, opisō* [1]
followed, *4158, parakoloutheō* [1]
followed, *4668, prosechō* [1]
followed everywhere, *4674, proskartereō* [1]
followed, *5258, synakoloutheō* [1]

FOLLOWER [1]

a follower of, *2848, kata* [1]

FOLLOWERS [8]

followers, *AIT* [2]
followers, *4275, peithō* [2]
Jesus followers', *1254+3836, de+ho* [1]
followers of, *3140, kollaō* [1]
followers, *3412, mathētēs* [1]
followers, *5626, huios* [1]

FOLLOWING [23]

following, *199, akoloutheō* [6]
following, *AIT* [3]
following day, *2069, epaurion* [2]
following behind, *199, akoloutheō* [1]
on the following day, *1308, deuteraios* [1]
following, *1877, en* [1]
following, *2079, epeimi* [1]
following, *2400, echō* [1]
following, *2848+4513, kata+poreuomai* [1]
following, *3552, meta* [1]
in the following, *4047, houtos* [1]
following, *4047, houtos* [1]
following, *4472, poieō* [1]
join with others following example, *5213+1181,*
  symmimētēs+ginomai [1]
following, *5258, synakoloutheō* [1]

FOLLOWS [2]

follows, *199, akoloutheō* [1]
as follows, *2400+3836+5596+4047,*
  echō+ho+typos+houtos [1]

FOLLY [2]

folly, *486, anoia* [1]
folly, *932, aphrosynē* [1]

FOOD [54]

food, *5575, trophē* [12]
food, *1109, brōma* [10]
food, *1111, brōsis* [6]
food sacrificed to idols, *1628, eidōlothytos* [5]
food, *AIT* [4]
food, *788, artos* [4]
food, *2266, esthiō* [2]
without food, *826, asitia* [1]
gone without food, *827, asitos* [1]
solid food, *1109, brōma* [1]
food, *1418, diatrophē* [1]
food sacrificed to an idol, *1628, eidōlothytos* [1]
food, *2169, episitismos* [1]
get food, *2266, esthiō* [1]
gone without food, *3763, nēsteia* [1]
food allowance, *4991, sitometrion* [1]
food supply, *5555, trephō* [1]
food, *5964, chortasma* [1]

FOODS [3]

foods, *1109, brōma* [3]

FOOL [9]

fool, *933, aphrōn* [5]
fool, *3704, mōros* [2]
fool, *932, aphrosynē* [1]
as a fool, *1877+932, en+aphrosynē* [1]

FOOLISH [22]

foolish, *3704, mōros* [7]
foolish, *485, anoētos* [6]
foolish, *933, aphrōn* [5]
foolish, *852, asynetos* [1]
foolish, *3031, kenos* [1]
made foolish, *3701, mōrainō* [1]
foolish talk, *3703, mōrologia* [1]

FOOLISHNESS [7]

foolishness, *3702, mōria* [5]
foolishness, *932, aphrosynē* [1]
foolishness, *3704, mōros* [1]

FOOLS [4]

fools, *3704, mōros* [2]
fools, *933, aphrōn* [1]
fools, *3701, mōrainō* [1]

FOOT [16]

foot, *4546, pous* [8]
foot, *4267, pedē* [2]
on foot, *4270, pezē* [2]
foot, *RPE* [1]
foot of ground, *1037+4546, bēma+pous* [1]
trampled under foot, *2922, katapateō* [1]
going on foot, *4269, pezeuō* [1]

FOOTHOLD [1]

foothold, *5536, topos* [1]

FOOTSTEPS [1]

footsteps, *2717, ichnos* [1]

FOOTSTOOL [6]

footstool, *5711, hypopodion* [6]

FOR [1979]

for, *1142, gar* [501]
for, *AIT* [415]
for, *4022, hoti* [145]
for, *1650, eis* [143]
for, *NIG* [98]
for, *5642, hyper* [92]
for, *4309, peri* [52]
for, *2093, epi* [33]
for, *1328, dia* [29]
for, *4639, pros* [24]
for, *RPE* [19]
looking for, *2426, zēteō* [18]
for, *1877, en* [16]
for, *2671, hina* [12]
look for, *2426, zēteō* [10]
asked for, *160, aiteō* [9]
for, *505, anti* [9]
for, *608, apo* [9]
for this reason, *1328+4047, dia+houtos* [9]
ask for, *160, aiteō* [8]
for sake, *1328, dia* [8]
for the sake of, *1328, dia* [8]
for, *1484, dioti* [6]
for, *1666, ek* [6]
stands for, *1639, eimi* [5]
looking for, *2118, epizēteō* [5]
for, *2848, kata* [5]
sent for, *3569, metapempō* [5]
waiting for, *4657, prosdechomai* [5]
asks for, *160, aiteō* [4]
once for all, *562, hapax* [4]
for purpose, *1650, eis* [4]
for, *1915, heneken* [4]
once for all, *2384, ephapax* [4]
for the sake of, *5642, hyper* [4]
basis for a charge, *162, aitia* [3]
for benefit, *1328, dia* [3]
for nothing, *1632, eikē* [3]
calls for, *1639, eimi* [3]
for me, *1847, emos* [3]
looked for a way, *2426, zēteō* [3]
watched for, *2426, zēteō* [3]
as for, *2779, kai* [3]
look for, *349, anazēteō* [2]
in exchange for, *498, antallagma* [2]
as for, *608, apo* [2]
as for, *1142, gar* [2]
for, *1254, de* [2]
for, *1328+3836, dia+ho* [2]
for, *1650+3836, eis+ho* [2]
held responsible for, *1699, ekzēteō* [2]
hope for, *1827, elpizō* [2]
for reason, *1915, heneken* [2]
for the sake, *1915, heneken* [2]
for, *2401, heōs* [2]
ask for, *2426, zēteō* [2]
searching for, *2426, zēteō* [2]
for, *2777, kathōs* [2]
than for, *2779+3590, kai+mē* [2]
as for, *2848, kata* [2]
for this reason, *4047+5920, houtos+charin* [2]
for that reason, *4123+4047, para+houtos* [2]
wait for, *4657, prosdechomai* [2]
pray for, *4667, proseuchomai* [2]
sent for, *4673, proskaleō* [2]
for sake, *5642, hyper* [2]
for, *5920, charin* [2]
have room for, *6003, chōreō* [2]
account for, [1]
longed for, *26, agapaō* [1]
for, *72, agō* [1]

greedy for money, *154, aischrokerdōs* [1]
called for, *160, aiteō* [1]
basis for a charge, *165, aitios* [1]
grounds for the death penalty, *165+2505,*
  aitios+thanatos [1]
for good, *173, aiōnios* [1]
for, *247, alla* [1]
necessary for, *338, anankaios* [1]
bring out for trial, *343, anagō* [1]
looking for, *349, anazēteō* [1]
prepare for action, *350+3836+4019,*
  anazōnnymi+ho+osphys [1]
wait for, *388, anamenō* [1]
make up for, *405, anaplēroō* [1]
cared for, *427, anatrephō* [1]
for this reason, *505+4047, anti+houtos* [1]
for a long time, *540, anōthen* [1]
eagerly await for, *587, apekdechomai* [1]
eagerly wait for, *587, apekdechomai* [1]
wait eagerly for, *587, apekdechomai* [1]
wait for, *587, apekdechomai* [1]
waiting for, *587, apekdechomai* [1]
for a distance of, *608, apo* [1]
eager expectation for, *638, apokaradokia* [1]
kept hidden for, *648+608+608,*
  apokryptō+apo+apo [1]
sent for, *690+3559, apostellō+metakaleō* [1]
license for immorality, *816, aselgeia* [1]
for this very reason, *899+4047,*
  autos+houtos [1]
for, *948, achri* [1]
watch out for, *1063, blepō* [1]
for a little while, *1099, brachys* [1]
for example, *1142, gar* [1]
for to be sure, *1142, gar* [1]
as for, *1254, de* [1]
ask God for help, *1255, deēsis* [1]
for sakes, *1328, dia* [1]
for that very reason, *1328+4047, dia+houtos* [1]
for the benefit of, *1328, dia* [1]
for this very reason, *1328+4047, dia+houtos* [1]
care for needs, *1354, diakoneō* [1]
cared for needs, *1354, diakoneō* [1]
for this reason, *1475, dio* [1]
thirst for, *1498, dipsaō* [1]
take for, *1506+1639, dokeō+eimi* [1]
for nothing, *1562, dōrean* [1]
without paying for it, *1562, dōrean* [1]
as for, *1569, ean* [1]
except for, *1623+3590, ei+mē* [1]
for all time, *1650+3836+1457,*
  eis+ho+diēnekēs [1]
for the express purpose, *1650+899+4047,*
  eis+autos+houtos [1]
for this reason, *1650+4047, eis+houtos* [1]
as for, *1664+5642, eite+hyper* [1]
as for, *1664, eite* [1]
wait for, *1683, ekdechomai* [1]
waiting for, *1683, ekdechomai* [1]
waits for, *1683, ekdechomai* [1]
reached for, *1753+3836+5931,*
  ekteinō+ho+cheir [1]
gifts for the poor, *1797, eleēmosynē* [1]
hopes for, *1827, elpizō* [1]
for work, *1877+4005+1256+2237,*
  en+hos+dei+ergazomai [1]
for, *1877+3836+3545, en+ho+mesos* [1]
waiting in ambush for, *1910, enedreuō* [1]
for sake, *1915, heneken* [1]
prepare for burial, *1946, entaphiazō* [1]
lawful for, *2003, exesti* [1]
search for, *2004, exetazō* [1]
for, *2076, epeidē* [1]
ask for, *2089, eperōtaō* [1]
a thorough search made for, *2118, epizēteō* [1]
asks for, *2118, epizēteō* [1]

looks for, *2118, epizēteō* [1]
longed for, *2123+3836+6034,*
    epithymia+ho+psychē [1]
for needs, *2149, epimeleia* [1]
long for, *2160, epipotheō* [1]
longs for, *2160+1639, epipotheō+eimi* [1]
longing for, *2161, epipothēsis* [1]
long for, *2162, epipothētos* [1]
care for, *2170, episkeptomai* [1]
work for a living, *2237, ergazomai* [1]
work for, *2237, ergazomai* [1]
worked for, *2237, ergazomai* [1]
asked for, *2263, erōtaō* [1]
fit for service, *2310, euthetos* [1]
gave thanks for, *2328, eulogeō* [1]
way opened for, *2338, euodoō* [1]
were looking for, *2351, heuriskō* [1]
put religion into practice by caring for, *2355,*
    eusebeō [1]
give thanks for, *2373, eucharisteō* [1]
thank for, *2373, eucharisteō* [1]
prayed for, *2377, euchomai* [1]
prayer for, *2377, euchomai* [1]
jealous for, *2420, zēloō* [1]
zealous for, *2420, zēloō* [1]
zealous for, *2421, zēlōtēs* [1]
asked for, *2426, zēteō* [1]
asking for, *2426, zēteō* [1]
asks for, *2426, zēteō* [1]
looks out for, *2426, zēteō* [1]
search for, *2426, zēteō* [1]
searched for, *2426, zēteō* [1]
sought for, *2426, zeteo* [1]
watching for, *2426, zēteō* [1]
works for, *2426, zēteō* [1]
cares for, *2499, thalpō* [1]
caring for, *2499, thalpō* [1]
wailed for, *2577, thrēneō* [1]
make atonement for, *2661, hilaskomai* [1]
for fear that, *2671+3590, hina+mē* [1]
for fear, *2671+3590, hina+mē* [1]
for, *2749, kathaper* [1]
for, *2776, kathoti* [1]
for, *2779, kai* [1]
peddle for profit, *2836, kapēleuō* [1]
for reasons, *2848, kata* [1]
disqualify for the prize, *2857, katabrabeuō* [1]
to look for, *2870, katadiōkō* [1]
aim for perfection, *2936, katartizō* [1]
show contempt for, *2969, kataphroneō* [1]
weeping for, *3081, klaiō* [1]
worked for, *3159, kopiaō* [1]
pay for, *3227, ktaomai* [1]
asks for, *3306, legō* [1]
sent for, *3306+5888, legō+phōneō* [1]
waiting for, *3516, mellō* [1]
for, *3525+1142, men+gar* [1]
waited for, *3531, menō* [1]
for, *3559, metakaleō* [1]
send for, *3559, metakaleō* [1]
for, *3569, metapempō* [1]
for, *3590+4803, mē+pōs* [1]
for fear that, *3590+4803, mē+pōs* [1]
for, *3590+1142, mē+gar* [1]
for, *3607, mēpote* [1]
dressed ready for service, *3836+4019+4322,*
    ho+osphys+perizōnnymi [1]
enough for now, *3836+3814+2400,*
    ho+nyn+echō [1]
for this reason, *3854, hothen* [1]
eager for, *3977, oregō* [1]
longing for, *3977, oregō* [1]
lawful for, *4024+2003, ou+exesti* [1]
asking for help, *4151, parakaleō* [1]
came for, *4205, pareimi* [1]
except for, *4211+3364, parektos+logos* [1]

except for, *4211, parektos* [1]
make it difficult for, *4214, parenochleō* [1]
send for, *4287, pempō* [1]
as for, *4309, peri* [1]
wait for, *4338, perimenō* [1]
lust for more, *4432, pleonexia* [1]
in advance finish the arrangements for, *4616,*
    prokatartizō [1]
provide for, *4629, pronoeō* [1]
for a little while, *4639+6052, pros+hōra* [1]
for, *4639+3836, pros+ho* [1]
waiting for, *4659, prosdokaō* [1]
for some time, *4732, prouparchō* [1]
leap for joy, *5015, skirtaō* [1]
watch out for, *5023, skopeō* [1]
lives for pleasure, *5059, spatalaō* [1]
filled with compassion for, *5072,*
    splanchnizomai [1]
for good, *5237, sympherō* [1]
intercedes for, *5659, hyperentynchanō* [1]
for, *5679, hypo* [1]
pit for the winepress, *5700, hypolēnion* [1]
shown for what it is, *5745, phaneros* [1]
love for brothers, *5789, philadelphia* [1]
fear for, *5828, phobeomai* [1]
reverence for, *5828, phobeomai* [1]
asking for, *5888, phōneō* [1]
sent for, *5888, phōneō* [1]
for the sake of, *5920, charin* [1]
make room for, *6003, chōreō* [1]
reach out for, *6027, psēlaphaō* [1]
this calls for, *6045, hōde* [1]
for that, *6055, hōs* [1]
for, *6055, hōs* [1]
counts for, *6067, ōpheleō* [1]
good for, *6067, ōpheleō* [1]

FORBEARANCE [1]

forbearance, *496, anochē* [1]

FORBID [2]

forbid, *3266, kōlyō* [2]

FORBIDS [1]

the law forbids, *4024+2003, ou+exesti* [1]

FORCE [7]

force, *337, anankazō* [2]
force, *773, harpazō* [1]
take by force, *773, harpazō* [1]
in force, *1010, bebaios* [1]
use force, *3552+1040, meta+bia* [1]
of hurricane force, *5607, typhōnikos* [1]

FORCED [4]

forced, *30, angareuō* [2]
forced, *2848+340, kata+anankē* [1]
forced, *4472, poieō* [1]

FORCEFUL [2]

forceful, *1043, biastēs* [1]
forceful, *2708, ischyros* [1]

FORCEFULLY [1]

forcefully advancing, *1041, biazō* [1]

FORCES [2]

forces, *AIT* [1]
forces, *30, angareuō* [1]

FORCING [2]

forcing way, *1041, biazō* [1]
forcing, *4472, poieō* [1]

FOREFATHER [1]

forefather, *4635+2848+4922,*
    propatōr+kata+sarx [1]

FOREFATHERS [15]

forefathers, *4252, patēr* [13]
handed down from forefathers, *4261,*
    patroparadotos [1]
my forefathers, *4591, progonos* [1]

FOREHEAD [3]

forehead, *3587, metōpon* [3]

FOREHEADS [5]

foreheads, *3587, metōpon* [5]

FOREIGN [4]

foreign, *AIT* [1]
foreign, *259, allotrios* [1]
foreign, *2032, exō* [1]
foreign, *3828, xenos* [1]

FOREIGNER [4]

foreigner, *975, barbaros* [2]
foreigner, *254, allogenēs* [1]
foreigner, *4230, paroikos* [1]

FOREIGNERS [5]

foreigners, *3828, xenos* [4]
foreigners, *2283, heteros* [1]

FOREKNEW [2]

foreknew, *4589, proginōskō* [2]

FOREKNOWLEDGE [2]

foreknowledge, *4590, prognōsis* [2]

FOREMAN [1]

foreman, *2208, epitropos* [1]

FORESAIL [1]

foresail, *784, artemōn* [1]

FORESAW [1]

foresaw, *4632, prooraō* [1]

FORESIGHT [1]

foresight, *4630, pronoia* [1]

FOREST [1]

forest, *5627, hylē* [1]

FORETOLD [3]

foretold, *2859, katangellō* [1]
foretold, *4615, prokatangellō* [1]
foretold, *4625, prolegō* [1]

FOREVER [31]

forever, *1650+3836+172, eis+ho+aiōn* [23]
forever, *1650+3836+1457,*
    eis+ho+diēnekēs [2]
forever, *173, aiōnios* [1]
last forever, *915, aphthartos* [1]
forever, *1328+4246, dia+pas* [1]
forever, *1650+172, eis+aiōn* [1]
forever, *1650+2465+172, eis+hēmera+aiōn* [1]
forever, *4121, pantote* [1]

FOREVERMORE [1]

forevermore, *1650+4246+3836+172, eis+pas+ho+aiōn* [1]

FORFEIT [2]

forfeit, *2423, zēmioō* [2]

FORFEITS [1]

forfeits, *2423, zēmioō* [1]

FORGAVE [3]

forgave, *5919, charizomai* [3]

FORGET [5]

forget, *2140, epilanthanomai* [3]
forget, *3291, lanthanō* [2]

FORGETS [2]

forgets, *2140, epilanthanomai* [1]
forgets, *4033+3648, ouketi+mnēmoneuō* [1]

FORGETTING [2]

forgetting, *2140, epilanthanomai* [1]
forgetting, *2144, epilēsmonē* [1]

FORGIVE [32]

forgive, *918, aphiēmi* [22]
forgive, *5919, charizomai* [5]
forgive, *RPE* [2]
forgive, *668, apolyō* [1]
forgive, *2664+1639, hileōs+eimi* [1]
not forgive, *3195, krateō* [1]

FORGIVEN [28]

forgiven, *918, aphiēmi* [22]
forgiven, *RPE* [1]
forgiven, *668, apolyō* [1]
forgiven, *912, aphesis* [1]
forgiven, *2400+912, echō+aphesis* [1]
not forgiven, *3195, krateō* [1]
forgiven, *5919, charizomai* [1]

FORGIVENESS [13]

forgiveness, *912, aphesis* [13]

FORGIVES [1]

forgives, *918, aphiēmi* [1]

FORGIVING [1]

forgiving, *5919, charizomai* [1]

FORGOT [1]

forgot, *2140, epilanthanomai* [1]

FORGOTTEN [4]

forgotten, *2140, epilanthanomai* [2]
forgotten, *1720, eklanthanomai* [1]
forgotten that, *3330+3284, lēthē+lambanō* [1]

FORK [2]

winnowing fork, *4768, ptyon* [2]

FORM [12]

form, *1626, eidos* [2]
form, *1639, eimi* [2]
form, *AIT* [1]
form, *3671, morphē* [1]
form, *3673, morphōsis* [1]
made an idol in the form of a calf, *3674, moschopoieō* [1]

form, *3929, homoioō* [1]
form, *5386, schēma* [1]
in bodily form, *5395, sōmatikōs* [1]
form, *5596, typos* [1]

FORMED [9]

formed, *4421, plassō* [2]
formed, *4472, poieō* [2]
formed, *2936, katartizō* [1]
formed, *3672, morphoō* [1]
formed a mob, *4062, ochlopoieō* [1]
formed, *4420, plasma* [1]
formed, *5319, synistēmi* [1]

FORMER [6]

the former, *2797, kakeinos* [2]
former, *1254, de* [1]
former, *4575, proagō* [1]
former, *4728, proteros* [1]
former, *4755, prōtos* [1]

FORMERLY [6]

formerly, *4537, pote* [3]
formerly, *4728, proteros* [2]
formerly, *5538, tote* [1]

FORMS [1]

various forms, *4476, poikilos* [1]

FORSAKE [1]

forsake, *1593, enkataleipō* [1]

FORSAKEN [3]

forsaken, *1593, enkataleipō* [2]
forsaken, *918, aphiēmi* [1]

FORTH [3]

tossed back and forth by the waves, *3115, klydōnizomai* [1]
break forth, *4838, rhēgnymi* [1]
setting forth plainly, *5748, phanerōsis* [1]

FORTUNATE [1]

fortunate, *3421, makarios* [1]

FORTUNATUS [1]

Fortunatus, *5847, Phortounatos* [1]

FORTUNE-TELLING [1]

fortune-telling, *3446, manteuomai* [1]

FORTY [17]

forty, *5477, tesserakonta* [15]
forty years, *5478, tesserakontaetēs* [2]

FORTY-SIX [1]

forty-six, *5477+2779+1971, tesserakonta+kai+hex* [1]

FORTY-TWO [1]

forty-two, *5477+2779+1545, tesserakonta+kai+dyo* [1]

FORUM [1]

Forum, *5842, phoron* [1]

FORWARD [12]

looking forward to, *4659, prosdokaō* [2]
came forward, *4665, proserchomai* [2]
came forward, *482, anistēmi* [1]
looking forward to, *1683, ekdechomai* [1]

pushes forward, *2048, epairō* [1]
pushing forward, *2158, epipiptō* [1]
looking forward to, *4657, prosdechomai* [1]
look forward to, *4659, prosdokaō* [1]
stepped forward, *4665, proserchomai* [1]
called forward, *4715, prosphōneō* [1]

FOUGHT [4]

fought, *4482, polemeō* [2]
fought, *76, agōnizomai* [1]
fought wild beasts, *2562, thēriomacheō* [1]

FOUND [104]

found, *2351, heuriskō* [84]
found out, *1182, ginōskō* [3]
found, *AIT* [1]
found, *NIG* [1]
hasn't found guilty, *185, akatakritos* [1]
found out exact, *208, akriboō* [1]
found, *461, aneuriskō* [1]
found worthy of, *546, axioō* [1]
found out, *1452, dierōtaō* [1]
found, *1506, dokeō* [1]
found, *1639, eimi* [1]
found to be, *2093, epi* [1]
found out, *2105, epiginōskō* [1]
found that, *2351, heuriskō* [1]
found in, *2848, kata* [1]
found, *2898, katalambanō* [1]
found fault with, *3522, memphomai* [1]
found, *3972, horaō* [1]
found out about, *5328, synoraō* [1]

FOUNDATION [14]

foundation, *2529, themelios* [12]
foundation, *1613, hedraiōma* [1]
foundation, *2530, themelioō* [1]

FOUNDATIONS [5]

foundations, *2529, themelios* [3]
foundations, *2528, themelion* [1]
laid the foundations of, *2530, themelioō* [1]

FOUNDED [1]

founded, *3793, nomotheteō* [1]

FOUR [42]

four, *5475, tessares* [29]
four thousand, *5483, tetrakischilioi* [5]
four hundred, *5484, tetrakosioi* [2]
four hundred, *4299, pentēkonta* [1]
four days, *5479, tetartaios* [1]
four, *5480, tetartos* [1]
squads of four, *5482, tetradion* [1]
four months, *5485, tetramēnos* [1]
four times, *5487, tetraplous* [1]

FOUR-DRACHMA [1]

four-drachma coin, *5088, statēr* [1]

FOUR-FOOTED [2]

four-footed animals, *5488, tetrapous* [2]

FOURTEEN [6]

fourteen, *1280, dekatessares* [5]
fourteen, *5476, tessareskaidekatos* [1]

FOURTEENTH [1]

fourteenth, *5476, tessareskaidekatos* [1]

FOURTH [9]

fourth, *5480, tetartos* [9]

FOX [1]

fox, *273, alōpēx* [1]

FOXES [2]

foxes, *273, alōpēx* [2]

FRACTION [1]

a fraction of a penny, *3119, kodrantēs* [1]

FRAGRANCE [3]

fragrance, *4011, osmē* [3]

FRAGRANT [2]

fragrant, *4011+2380, osmē+euōdia* [2]

FRANKINCENSE [1]

frankincense, *3337, libanos* [1]

FREE [44]

free, *1801, eleutheros* [18]
set free, *1802, eleutheroō* [5]
set free, *668, apolyō* [3]
set free, *3395, lyō* [2]
free, *AIT* [1]
free of charge, *78, adapanos* [1]
free from concern, *291, amerimnos* [1]
free from accusation, *441, anenklētos* [1]
free from law, *491, anomos* [1]
free, *557, apallassō* [1]
free, *668, apolyō* [1]
free from the love of money, *921, aphilargyros* [1]
free gift, *1562, dōrean* [1]
free of charge, *1562, dōrean* [1]
free, *1800, eleutheria* [1]
free and belong to no man, *1801+1666+4246, eleutheros+ek+pas* [1]
set free, *1801, eleutheros* [1]
sets free, *1802, eleutheroō* [1]
set free, *1975, exaireō* [1]
free from fear of, *3590+5828, mē+phobeomai* [1]

FREED [4]

freed, *1467, dikaioō* [1]
freed, *2615, iaomai* [1]
freed, *3395, lyō* [1]
freed, *5618, hygiēs* [1]

FREEDMAN [1]

freedman, *592, apeleutheros* [1]

FREEDMEN [1]

Freedmen, *3339, Libertinos* [1]

FREEDOM [15]

freedom, *1800, eleutheria* [10]
freedom, *457, anesis* [1]
freedom, *912, aphesis* [1]
gain freedom, *1801+1181, eleutheros+ginomai* [1]
exercise of freedom, *2026, exousia* [1]
freedom, *4244, parrēsia* [1]

FREEING [1]

freeing, *3395, lyō* [1]

FREELY [11]

freely, *1562, dōrean* [3]
freely, *AIT* [1]

moved about freely, *1660+2779+1744, eisporeuomai+kai+ekporeuomai* [1]
spoken freely, *3836+5125+487, ho+stoma+anoigō* [1]
freely, *4245, parrēsiazomai* [1]
freely, *4358, perissoteros* [1]
freely, *4498, polys* [1]
freely given, *5919, charizomai* [1]
freely given, *5923, charitoō* [1]

FREQUENT [1]

frequent, *4781, pyknos* [1]

FREQUENTLY [2]

more frequently, *4359, perissoterōs* [1]
frequently, *4781, pyknos* [1]

FRESH [2]

fresh water, *1184, glykys* [1]
fresh, *1184, glykys* [1]

FRICTION [1]

constant friction between, *1384, diaparatribē* [1]

FRIEND [25]

friend, *5813, philos* [12]
dear friend, *28, agapētos* [9]
friend, *2279, hetairos* [3]
friend, *476, anthrōpos* [1]

FRIENDS [43]

dear friends, *28, agapētos* [22]
friends, *5813, philos* [17]
friends, *28, agapētos* [1]
friends, *1196, gnōstos* [1]
friends, *2625, idios* [1]
friends, *4086, paidion* [1]

FRIENDSHIP [1]

friendship, *5802, philia* [1]

FRIGHT [1]

fright, *1873+1181, emphobos+ginomai* [1]

FRIGHTEN [1]

frighten, *1768, ekphobeō* [1]

FRIGHTENED [5]

so frightened, *1769, ekphobos* [1]
frightened, *1873, emphobos* [1]
frightened, *4765, ptoeō* [1]
frightened, *4769, ptyrō* [1]
frightened, *5429, tarassō* [1]

FROGS [1]

frogs, *1005, batrachos* [1]

FROM [1073]

from, *608, apo* [334]
from, *1666, ek* [313]
from, *AIT* [74]
from, *4123, para* [47]
where from, *4470, pothen* [16]
from, *RPE* [14]
from, *NIG* [10]
from there, *1696, ekeithen* [8]
from, *1328, dia* [7]
from, *5679, hypo* [7]
apart from, *6006, chōris* [7]
raised from the dead, *1586, egeirō* [6]
from among, *1666, ek* [5]
abstain from, *600, apechō* [4]

from, *1877, en* [4]
from there, *2796, kakeithen* [4]
from Cyrene, *3254, Kyrēnaios* [4]
from, *3590, mē* [4]
from above, *540, anōthen* [3]
taken from, *554+608, apairō+apo* [3]
from, *2093, epi* [3]
from Cyprus, *3250, Kyprios* [3]
apart from the law, *492, anomōs* [2]
from heaven, *540, anōthen* [2]
are from, *600+608, apechō+apo* [2]
turn away from, *695, apostrephō* [2]
went out from, *1666+2002, ek+exerchomai* [2]
from that place, *1696, ekeithen* [2]
from here, *1925, enthen* [2]
from, *2032, exō* [2]
different from, *2283, heteros* [2]
from Thessalonica, *2552, Thessalonikeus* [2]
from house to house, *2848+3875, kata+oikos* [2]
from one to another, *2848, kata* [2]
keep from, *3266, kōlyō* [2]
kept from, *3266, kōlyō* [2]
prevented from, *3266, kōlyō* [2]
keep from, *3590, mē* [2]
from heaven, *4040, ouranothen* [2]
from, *4309, peri* [2]
flee from, *5771, pheugō* [2]
from Adramyttium, *101, Adramyttēnos* [1]
heard from, *201, akouō* [1]
free from concern, *291, amerimnos* [1]
from, *324, ana* [1]
free from accusation, *441, anenklētos* [1]
apart from, *459, aneu* [1]
raised from the dead, *482, anistēmi* [1]
free from law, *491, anomos* [1]
from Antioch, *523, Antiocheus* [1]
from the beginning, *540, anōthen* [1]
demanded from, *555+608, apaiteō+apo* [1]
alienated from, *558, apallotrioō* [1]
absent from, *582, apeimi1* [1]
ejected from, *590+608, apelaunō+apo* [1]
away from, *599+608, aperchomai+apo* [1]
gone from, *599+608, aperchomai+apo* [1]
left from, *599+608, aperchomai+apo* [1]
about from, *600+608, apechō+apo* [1]
was from, *600+608, apechō+apo* [1]
cut off from, *608, apo* [1]
down from, *608, apo* [1]
from among, *608, apo* [1]
from the time, *608+4005, apo+hos* [1]
from, *608+4725, apo+prosōpon* [1]
receive from, *608+655, apo+apolambanō* [1]
turn away from, *608+695, apo+apostrephō* [1]
was from, *608+600, apo+apechō* [1]
removal from, *629, apothesis* [1]
hidden from, *648+608, apokryptō+apo* [1]
took away from, *655+608, apolambanō+apo* [1]
wandered from, *675+608, apoplanaō+apo* [1]
torn away from, *682+608, aporphanizō+apo* [1]
to turn away from, *686+608, apostasia+apo* [1]
turn away from, *695+608, apostrephō+apo* [1]
turning from, *695+608, apostrephō+apo* [1]
escaping from, *709, apopheugō* [1]
away from, *713+608, apochōreō+apo* [1]
from the province of Asia, *824, Asianos* [1]
from being polluted, *834, aspilos* [1]
take away from, *904, aphaireō* [1]
taken away from, *904, aphaireō* [1]
takes away from, *904+608, aphaireō+apo* [1]
hidden from, *905, aphanēs* [1]
free from the love of money, *921, aphilargyros* [1]
away from, *923+608, aphistēmi+apo* [1]

take away from, *923+608, aphistēmi+apo* [1]
turn away from, *923+608, aphistēmi+apo* [1]
turns away from, *923+608, aphistēmi+apo* [1]
from Berea, *1024, Beroiaios* [1]
suffering from demon-possession, *1227,
   daimonizomai* [1]
from Derbe, *1291, Derbaios* [1]
distinguish from, *1360, diakrisis* [1]
different from, *1422, diapherō* [1]
image which fell from heaven, *1479,
   diopetēs* [1]
Sabbath day's walk from,
   *1584+4879+2400+3847,
   engys+sabbaton+echō+hodos* [1]
from, *1584, engys* [1]
hindered from, *1601, enkoptō* [1]
from, *1650, eis* [1]
from came, *1666+1744, ek+ekporeuomai* [1]
from then on, *1666+4047, ek+houtos* [1]
away from, *1666+3545, ek+mesos* [1]
came from, *1666+2002, ek+exerchomai* [1]
come from, *1666+2002, ek+exerchomai* [1]
coming from, *1666+2002, ek+exerchomai* [1]
descended from, *1666+5065, ek+sperma* [1]
descended from, *1666, ek* [1]
from, *1666+3545, ek+mesos* [1]
gone out from, *1666+2002, ek+exerchomai* [1]
drove from, *1675+1666, ekballō+ek* [1]
remove from, *1675+1666, ekballō+ek* [1]
remove from, *1675, ekballō* [1]
away from, *1685+1666, ekdēmeō+ek* [1]
away from, *1685, ekdēmeō* [1]
cut from under, *1716, ekkoptō* [1]
fall from, *1738, ekpiptō* [1]
fallen away from, *1738, ekpiptō* [1]
came from, *1744+1666, ekporeuomai+ek* [1]
comes from, *1744+1666, ekporeuomai+ek* [1]
flowing from, *1744+1666, ekporeuomai+ek* [1]
went out from, *1744, ekporeuomai* [1]
shook from, *1759, ektinassō* [1]
turn away from, *1762, ektrepō* [1]
wandered away from, *1762, ektrepō* [1]
from among, *1877, en* [1]
from another place, *1949, enteuthen* [1]
from here, *1949, enteuthen* [1]
from, *1949, enteuthen* [1]
redeemed from, *1973+1666, exagorazō+ek* [1]
escorted from, *1974, exagō* [1]
blot out from, *1981+1666, exaleiphō+ek* [1]
wipe away from, *1981+1666, exaleiphō+ek* [1]
wipe from, *1981+1666, exaleiphō+ek* [1]
descended from, *2002+1666+3836+4019,
   exerchomai+ek+ho+osphys* [1]
set out from, *2002, exerchomai* [1]
slipping away from, *2002+1666,
   exerchomai+ek* [1]
completely cut off from, *2017+1666,
   exolethreuō+ek* [1]
from outward, *2033, exōthen* [1]
from the outside, *2033, exōthen* [1]
from bad to worse, *2093+3836+5937,
   epi+ho+cheirōn* [1]
from inside, *2277, esōthen* [1]
from within, *2277, esōthen* [1]
collect a tenth from, *2400+620,
   echō+apodekatoō* [1]
from, *2671+3590, hina+mē* [1]
to keep from, *2671+3590, hina+mē* [1]
from place to place, *2759, kathexēs* [1]
from, *2796, kakeithen* [1]
down from, *2848, kata* [1]
from after town, *2848, kata* [1]
from everyday life, *2848+476,
   kata+anthrōpos* [1]
from house to house, *2848+3836+3875,
   kata+ho+oikos* [1]

from human point of view, *2848+476,
   kata+anthrōpos* [1]
from one synagogue to another,
   *2848+4246+3836+5252,
   kata+pas+ho+synagōgē* [1]
from village to village, *2848+3836+3267,
   kata+ho+kōmē* [1]
from, *2848, kata* [1]
kept from, *3195+3590, krateō+mē* [1]
stop from taking, *3266, kōlyō* [1]
from village to village, *3267+3241,
   kōmē+kyklō* [1]
from Macedonia, *3424, Makedōn* [1]
from, *3545, mesos* [1]
taken from, *3572, metatithēmi* [1]
free from fear of, *3590+5828,
   mē+phobeomai* [1]
kept from, *3590, mē* [1]
from now on, *3836+3370, ho+loipos* [1]
from house to house, *3836+3864, ho+oikia* [1]
from town to town, *3836+4484, ho+polis* [1]
from there, *3854, hothen* [1]
from death[s], *3854, hothen* [1]
from, *3958, opisō* [1]
from, *4024, ou* [1]
separate from, *4024+3552, ou+meta* [1]
staying away from, *4024+1877+4344,
   ou+en+peripateō* [1]
from then on, *4033, ouketi* [1]
from heaven, *4039, ouranios* [1]
from everywhere, *4119, pantothen* [1]
from now on, *4121, pantote* [1]
come from, *4134, paraginomai* [1]
received from, *4161+4123,
   paralambanō+para* [1]
handed down from forefathers, *4261,
   patroparadotos* [1]
drink from, *4403, pinō* [1]
faith from first to last, *4411+1650+4411,
   pistis+eis+pistis* [1]
from blowing, *4463, pneō* [1]
from which, *4470, pothen* [1]
from a distance, *4523, porrōthen* [1]
to keep from, *4639+3836+3590,
   pros+ho+mē* [1]
from Rome, *4871, Rhōmaios* [1]
turn away from the faith, *4997, skandalizō* [1]
running from all directions, *5282, syndromē* [1]
suffering from, *5309, synechō* [1]
from Tarsus, *5432, Tarseus* [1]
man from Tarsus, *5432, Tarseus* [1]
suffering from dropsy, *5622, hydrōpikos* [1]
abstain from, *5875, phylassō* [1]
keep from, *5875, phylassō* [1]
took a battering from the storm, *5928,
   cheimazō* [1]
separated from, *6004, chōrizō* [1]
separate from, *6006, chōris* [1]

FRONT   [20]

in front of, *1869, emprosthen* [7]
in front, *1967, enōpion* [4]
front of everyone, *3836+3545, ho+mesos* [2]
in front of, *595, apenanti* [1]
in front of, *1666+1885, ek+enantios* [1]
in front, *1869, emprosthen* [1]
in front of, *2093, epi* [1]
pushed to the front, *4582, proballō* [1]
rolled in front of, *4685, proskyliō* [1]
fell on knees in front of, *4686, proskyneō* [1]

FRUIT   [52]

fruit, *2843, karpos* [41]
fruit, *1163, genēma* [3]
bearing fruit, *2844, karpophoreō* [2]

fruit, *AIT* [1]
without fruit, *182, akarpos* [1]
bear fruit, *2844, karpophoreō* [1]
bore fruit, *2844, karpophoreō* [1]
fruit, *3967, opōra* [1]
bear[s] fruit, *4048, houtōs* [1]

FRUITFUL   [2]

fruitful, *2843+5770, karpos+pherō* [1]
fruitful, *2843, karpos* [1]

FRUITLESS   [1]

fruitless, *182, akarpos* [1]

FRUSTRATE   [1]

frustrate, *119, atheteō* [1]

FRUSTRATION   [1]

frustration, *3470, mataiotēs* [1]

FULFILL   [14]

fulfill, *4444, plēroō* [11]
fulfill, *AIT* [1]
fulfill, *405, anaplēroō* [1]
fulfill, *625, apodidōmi* [1]

FULFILLED   [31]

fulfilled, *4444, plēroō* [21]
fulfilled, *5464, teleō* [3]
fulfilled, *405, anaplēroō* [1]
fulfilled, *1740, ekplēroō* [1]
see fulfilled, *2918, katantaō* [1]
fulfilled, *4442, plērophoreō* [1]
fulfilled duty, *4488, politeuomai* [1]
fulfilled, *5334, synteleō* [1]
fulfilled, *5457, teleioō* [1]

FULFILLMENT   [7]

fulfillment, *4445, plērōma* [2]
fulfillment, *5465, telos* [2]
fulfillment, *4398, pimplēmi* [1]
bring to fulfillment, *4444, plēroō* [1]
finds fulfillment, *4444, plēroō* [1]

FULL   [65]

full, *4441, plērēs* [9]
full, *4246, pas* [8]
full, *3550, mestos* [7]
full, *1154, gemō* [5]
received in full, *600, apechō* [3]
full of light, *5893, phōteinos* [3]
full armor, *4110, panoplia* [2]
full, *4444, plēroō* [2]
full of darkness, *5027, skoteinos* [2]
full, *AIT* [1]
full, *RPE* [1]
full of joy, *22, agalliaō* [1]
full strength, *204, akratos* [1]
full, *1153, gemizō* [1]
full of, *1154, gemō* [1]
full of, *1650, eis* [1]
the full extent of, *1650+5465, eis+telos* [1]
in full view of, *1869, emprosthen* [1]
full of, *1877, en* [1]
in full view, *1967, enōpion* [1]
full understanding, *2106, epignōsis* [1]
full of idols, *2977, kateidōlos* [1]
in full, *3836+2698, ho+isos* [1]
to the full, *4356, perissos* [1]
full assurance, *4443, plērophoria* [1]
full measure, *4445, plērōma* [1]
full number, *4445, plērōma* [1]
full of compassion, *4499, polysplanchnos* [1]

give full time, *4674, proskartereō* [1]
full knowledge, *5323, synoida* [1]
full rights of sons, *5625, huiothesia* [1]
full of joy, *5897, chairō* [1]
full of joy, *5915+5897, chara+chairō* [1]

FULL-GROWN　[1]

full-grown, *699, apoteleō* [1]

FULLNESS　[9]

fullness, *4445, plērōma* [6]
given fullness, *1639+4444, eimi+plēroō* [1]
present in fullness, *4444, plēroō* [1]
measure of fullness, *4445, plērōma* [1]

FULLY　[18]

fully awake, *1340, diagrēgoreō* [1]
fully known, *2105, epiginōskō* [1]
know fully, *2105, epiginōskō* [1]
fully, *2401+5465, heōs+telos* [1]
fully armed, *2774, kathoplizō* [1]
fully trained, *2936, katartizō* [1]
fully convinced, *3857+2779+4275,*
　oida+kai+peithō [1]
fully, *4246+19, pas+agathos* [1]
give fully, *4355, perisseuō* [1]
fully, *4441, plērēs* [1]
fully assured, *4442, plērophoreō* [1]
fully convinced, *4442, plērophoreō* [1]
fully persuaded, *4442, plērophoreō* [1]
fully, *4442, plērophoreō* [1]
fully met, *4444, plēroō* [1]
fully, *4444, plēroō* [1]
fully, *4445, plērōma* [1]
fully, *5458, teleiōs* [1]

FUN　[1]

made fun of, *1430, diachleuazō* [1]

FUNCTION　[1]

function, *4552, praxis* [1]

FURIOUS　[8]

furious, *3489, megas* [2]
furious, *1391+3836+2840,*
　diapriō+ho+kardia [1]
furious, *1391, diapriō* [1]
furious, *2597+3336, thymoō+lian* [1]
furious, *4398+2596, pimplēmi+thymos* [1]
furious, *4398+486, pimplēmi+anoia* [1]
furious, *4441+2596, plērēs+thymos* [1]

FURNACE　[4]

furnace, *2825, kaminos* [4]

FURNISHED　[3]

furnished, *5143, strōnnyō* [2]
furnished with, *2202, epitithēmi* [1]

FURTHER　[8]

further, *AIT* [2]
any further, *2093+4498, epi+polys* [1]
further, *3370, loipos* [1]
further, *4304, peraiterō* [1]
further, *4498, polys* [1]
further threats, *4653, prosapeileō* [1]
further word spoken, *4707+3364,*
　prostithēmi+logos [1]

FURTHERMORE　[1]

furthermore, *2779, kai* [1]

FURY　[5]

fury, *2596, thymos* [3]
fury, *1539, dynamis* [1]
fury, *2596+3489, thymos+megas* [1]

FUTILE　[3]

futile, *3469, mataios* [2]
futile, *3471, mataioō* [1]

FUTILITY　[1]

futility, *3470, mataiotēs* [1]

FUTURE　[6]

the future, *3516, mellō* [2]
future, *AIT* [1]
in the future, *608+785, apo+arti* [1]
future, *3516, mellō* [1]
spirit which predicted the future, *4460+4780,*
　pneuma+pythōn [1]

GABBATHA　[1]

Gabbatha, *1119, Gabbatha* [1]

GABRIEL　[2]

Gabriel, *1120, Gabriēl* [2]

GAD　[1]

Gad, *1122, Gad* [1]

GADARENES　[1]

Gadarenes, *1123, Gadarēnos* [1]

GAIN　[18]

gain, *3045, kerdainō* [3]
pursuing dishonest gain, *153, aischrokerdēs* [2]
gain, *3046, kerdos* [2]
gain, *RPE* [1]
gain control over, *170, aichmalōtizō* [1]
gain freedom, *1801+1181,*
　eleutheros+ginomai [1]
gain, *2426, zēteō* [1]
gain, *3227, ktaomai* [1]
gain, *4347, peripoieō* [1]
gain, *4472, poieō* [1]
gain, *4516, porismos* [1]
means to financial gain, *4516, porismos* [1]
gain, *5593, tynchanō* [1]
gain, *6067, ōpheleō* [1]

GAINED　[11]

gained, *3045, kerdainō* [4]
gained, *AIT* [1]
gained, *1390, diapragmateuomai* [1]
gained, *2209, epitynchanō* [1]
gained, *2400, echō* [1]
gained, *4055, ophelos* [1]
gained wealth, *4456, plouteō* [1]
gained, *5237, sympherō* [1]

GAINING　[1]

gaining, *4472, poieō* [1]

GAINS　[1]

gains, *3045, kerdainō* [1]

GAIUS　[5]

Gaius, *1127, Gaios* [5]

GALATIA　[5]

Galatia, *1130, Galatia* [3]
Galatia, *1131, Galatikos* [1]

of Galatia, *1131, Galatikos* [1]

GALATIAN　[1]

Galatian, *1130, Galatia* [1]

GALATIANS　[1]

Galatians, *1129, Galatēs* [1]

GALILEAN　[4]

Galilean, *1134, Galilaios* [4]

GALILEANS　[5]

Galileans, *1134, Galilaios* [5]

GALILEE　[64]

Galilee, *1133, Galilaia* [61]
Galilee's, *899, autos* [1]
Galilee, *1134, Galilaios* [1]
of Galilee, *1134, Galilaios* [1]

GALL　[1]

gall, *5958, cholē* [1]

GALLIO　[3]

Gallio, *1136, Galliōn* [3]

GALLONS　[2]

eight hundred gallons, *1669+1004,*
　hekaton+batos² [1]
twenty to thirty gallons,
　3583+1545+2445+5552,
　metrētēs+dyo+ē+treis [1]

GAMALIEL　[2]

Gamaliel, *1137, Gamaliēl* [2]

GAMES　[1]

competes in the games, *76, agōnizomai* [1]

GANGRENE　[1]

gangrene, *1121, gangraina* [1]

GARDEN　[6]

garden, *3057, kēpos* [3]
garden plants, *3303, lachanon* [2]
garden herbs, *3303, lachanon* [1]

GARDENER　[2]

gardener, *1177, geōrgos* [1]
gardener, *3058, kēpouros* [1]

GARMENT　[11]

garment, *2668, himation* [6]
garment, *RPE* [1]
outer garment, *2087, ependytēs* [1]
garment, *4984, sindōn* [1]
linen garment, *4984, sindōn* [1]
garment, *5945, chitōn* [1]

GARMENTS　[2]

garments, *2668, himation* [2]

GATE　[18]

gate, *4783, pylē* [6]
gate, *2598, thyra* [5]
gate, *4784, pylōn* [3]
city gate, *4783, pylē* [2]
gate, *RPE* [1]
Sheep Gate, *4583, probatikos* [1]

GATES [12]

gates, *4784, pylōn* [7]
gates, *RPE* [1]
gates, *2598, thyra* [1]
city gates, *4783, pylē* [1]
gates, *4783, pylē* [1]
city gates, *4784, pylōn* [1]

GATEWAY [1]

gateway, *4784, pylōn* [1]

GATHER [18]

gather, *5251, synagō* [10]
gather, *2190, episynagō* [3]
gather together, *2190, episynagō* [2]
gather a great number, *2197, episōreuō* [1]
gather together, *5251, synagō* [1]
gather, *5582, trygaō* [1]

GATHERED [36]

gathered, *5251, synagō* [12]
gathered together, *5251, synagō* [5]
gathered, *5302, synerchomai* [3]
gathered, *AIT* [2]
gathered around, *3240, kykloō* [2]
gathered, *3284, lambanō* [2]
gathered, *1639+2190, eimi+episynagō* [1]
gathered, *1639, eimi* [1]
gathered, *2190, episynagō* [1]
gathered to, *2191+2093, episynagōgē+epi* [1]
gathered, *2262, erchomai* [1]
gathered together, *4673, proskaleō* [1]
gathered, *5219, symparaginomai* [1]
gathered, *5255, synathroizō* [1]
gathered, *5370, systrephō* [1]
gathered, *5582, trygaō* [1]

GATHERING [5]

gathering, *5251, synagō* [2]
gathering around, *1581, engizō* [1]
gathering, *5290, syneimi2* [1]
gathering, *5302, synerchomai* [1]

GATHERS [2]

gathers, *RPE* [1]
gathers, *2190, episynagō* [1]

GAVE [166]

gave, *1443, didōmi* [74]
gave thanks, *2373, eucharisteō* [7]
gave thanks, *2328, eulogeō* [6]
gave, *RPE* [4]
gave answer, *646, apokrinomai* [4]
gave over, *4140, paradidōmi* [4]
gave, *AIT* [3]
gave up, *4140, paradidōmi* [3]
gave birth to, *5503, tiktō* [3]
gave back, *625, apodidōmi* [2]
gave orders, *1403, diastellō* [2]
gave up, *1443, didōmi* [2]
gave, *2202, epitithēmi* [2]
gave permission, *2205, epitrepō* [2]
gave orders, *3027, keleuō* [2]
gave, *4140, paradidōmi* [2]
gave to drink, *4540, potizō* [2]
gave, *5919, charizomai* [2]
gave thanks, *469, anthomologeomai* [1]
gave orders, *690, apostellō* [1]
gave up, *918, aphiēmi* [1]
gave, *965+1650, ballō+eis* [1]
gave, *965, ballō* [1]
gave birth, *1002, bastazō* [1]
gave birth to, *1164, gennaō* [1]

gave, *1374, diamerizō* [1]
gave praise to, *1519, doxazō* [1]
glory gave, *1519, doxazō* [1]
gave, *1563, dōreomai* [1]
gave up to sexual immorality, *1745, ekporneuō* [1]
gave[s], *1877, en* [1]
gave strength, *1904, endynamoō* [1]
gave instructions, *1948, entellō* [1]
gave way, *2113, epididōmi* [1]
gave, *2113, epididōmi* [1]
gave orders, *2203, epitimaō* [1]
gave thanks for, *2328, eulogeō* [1]
gave, *2400+4639, echō+pros* [1]
gave, *2400, echō* [1]
gave up, *2483, hēsychazō* [1]
gave beating, *2710, ischyō* [1]
gave, *2813, kaleō* [1]
gave to as inheritance, *2883, kataklēronomeō* [1]
gave a shout, *3189+5889, krazō+phōnē* [1]
gave testimony, *3455, martyreō* [1]
gave, *3532, merizō* [1]
gave strict orders, *4132+4133, parangelia+parangellō* [1]
gave command, *4133, parangellō* [1]
gave rule, *4133, parangellō* [1]
gave up, *4311, periaireō* [1]
gave to in need, *4472+1797, poieō+eleēmosynē* [1]
gave, *4472, poieō* [1]
gave, *4540, potizō* [1]
already gave warning, *4625, prolegō* [1]
gave lodging to, *5685, hypodechomai* [1]
luxury [gave], *5139, strēniō* [1]
gave light, *5743, phainō* [1]
in grace gave, *5919, charizomai* [1]
gave false testimony, *6018, pseudomartyreō* [1]

GAZA [1]

Gaza, *1124, Gaza1* [1]

GAZE [1]

gaze on, *1063, blepō* [1]

GAZING [1]

gazing, *867, atenizō* [1]

GENEALOGIES [2]

genealogies, *1157, genealogia* [2]

GENEALOGY [2]

without genealogy, *37, agenealogētos* [1]
genealogy, *1161, genesis* [1]

GENERALS [2]

generals, *5941, chiliarchos* [2]

GENERATION [29]

generation, *1155, genea* [29]

GENERATIONS [5]

generations, *1155, genea* [5]

GENEROSITY [3]

generosity, *605, haplotēs* [2]
your generosity[s], *4015, hostis* [1]

GENEROUS [5]

generous gift, *2330, eulogia* [2]
generous, *19, agathos* [1]
generous, *605, haplotēs* [1]

generous, *2331, eumetadotos* [1]

GENEROUSLY [6]

generously, *2093+2330, epi+eulogia* [2]
generously, *607, haplōs* [1]
generously, *1877+605, en+haplotēs* [1]
generously, *4455, plousiōs* [1]
generously, *4498, polys* [1]

GENNESARET [3]

Gennesaret, *1166, Gennēsaret* [3]

GENTILE [9]

Gentile, *1818, Hellēn* [4]
Gentile, *1620, ethnos* [2]
Gentile, *260, allophylos* [1]
like a Gentile, *1619, ethnikōs* [1]
Gentile, *1666+1620, ek+ethnos* [1]

GENTILES [88]

Gentiles, *1620, ethnos* [81]
Gentiles, *1818, Hellēn* [2]
Gentiles, *AIT* [1]
Gentiles, *RPE* [1]
Gentiles, *213, akrobystia* [1]
the Gentiles[s], *899, autos* [1]
God-fearing Gentiles, *5828+3836+2536, phobeomai+ho+theos* [1]

GENTLE [8]

gentle, *4558, praus* [3]
gentle, *4559, prautēs* [2]
gentle, *2117, epieikēs* [1]
gentle, *2473, ēpios* [1]
gentle blow, *5710, hypopneō* [1]

GENTLENESS [6]

gentleness, *4559, prautēs* [3]
gentleness, *2116, epieikeia* [1]
gentleness, *2117, epieikēs* [1]
gentleness, *4557, praupathia* [1]

GENTLY [3]

gently, *1877+4460+4559, en+pneuma+prautēs* [1]
gently, *1877+4559, en+prautēs* [1]
deal gently, *3584, metriopatheō* [1]

GENUINE [3]

genuine, *239, alēthēs* [1]
genuine, *1189, gnēsiōs* [1]
proved genuine, *1510, dokimion* [1]

GERASENES [3]

Gerasenes, *1170, Gerasēnos* [3]

GET [103]

get up, *1586, egeirō* [15]
get up, *482, anistēmi* [13]
get, *NIG* [6]
get, *149, airō* [5]
get, *2400, echō* [5]
get, *1181, ginomai* [4]
get ready, *2286, hetoimazō* [3]
get drunk, *3499, methyskō* [3]
get, *AIT* [2]
get, *1639, eimi* [2]
get rid of, *1675, ekballō* [2]
get, *1832, embainō* [2]
get out, *2002, exerchomai* [2]
get, *3284, lambanō* [2]
get, *5632, hypagō* [2]

get, *RPE* [1]
get out, *149, airō* [1]
get rid of, *149, airō* [1]
get rid of, *359, anaireō* [1]
get, *377, analambanō* [1]
get rest, *399, anapauō* [1]
expecting to get back, *594, apelpizō* [1]
get rid of, *700, apotithēmi* [1]
get married, *1138, gameō* [1]
get a taste, *1174, geuomai* [1]
get at truth, *1182+855, ginōskō+asphalēs* [1]
get learning, *1207+3857, gramma+oida* [1]
made get up, *1586, egeirō* [1]
get in, *1656, eiserchomai* [1]
get rid of, *1705, ekkathairō* [1]
get out, *1774, ekchōreō* [1]
get, *1996, exeimi1* [1]
get here, *2262, erchomai* [1]
get in, *2262, erchomai* [1]
get food, *2266, esthiō* [1]
get acquainted with, *2707, historeō* [1]
get the prize, *2898, katalambanō* [1]
get, *3227, ktaomai* [1]
get into the habit of being, *3443, manthanō* [1]
get drunk, *3501, methyō* [1]
get here, *4134, paraginomai* [1]
get ready, *4186, paraskeuazō* [1]
get ready, *4322, perizōnnymi* [1]
get rich, *4456, plouteō* [1]
get, *4472, poieō* [1]
get very far, *4621+2093+4498, prokoptō+epi+polys* [1]
get, *4712, prospherō* [1]
get near, *5344, syntynchanō* [1]
get better, *5392, sōzō* [1]
get, *5777, phthanō* [1]

GETHSEMANE [2]

Gethsemane, *1149, Gethsēmani* [2]

GETS [8]

gets up, *1586, egeirō* [2]
gets, *AIT* [1]
gets, *201, akouō* [1]
gets here, *1581, engizō* [1]
see that gets justice, *1688, ekdikeō* [1]
gets, *3284, lambanō* [1]
gets drunk, *3501, methyō* [1]

GETTING [8]

getting, *655, apolambanō* [1]
getting, *1832, embainō* [1]
is getting along well, *2338, euodoō* [1]
getting nowhere, *4024+6067+4029, ou+ōpheleō+oudeis* [1]
was getting nowhere, *4029+6067, oudeis+ōpheleō* [1]
getting, *4216, parerchomai* [1]
getting along in years, *5644, hyperakmos* [1]
getting better, *6067, ōpheleō* [1]

GHOST [4]

ghost, *4460, pneuma* [2]
ghost, *5753, phantasma* [2]

GIDEON [1]

Gideon, *1146, Gedeōn* [1]

GIFT [46]

gift, *1561, dōrea* [10]
gift, *1565, dōron* [8]
gift, *5922, charisma* [8]
gift, *RPE* [5]
gift, *AIT* [2]

gift, *1564, dōrēma* [2]
generous gift, *2330, eulogia* [2]
gift, *5921, charis* [2]
gift, *NIG* [1]
gift, *1517, doma* [1]
free gift, *1562, dōrean* [1]
gift devoted to God, *1565, dōron* [1]
gift of prophecy, *4735, prophēteia* [1]
gracious gift, *5921, charis* [1]
spiritual gift, *5922, charisma* [1]

GIFTED [1]

gifted, *AIT* [1]

GIFTS [31]

gifts, *1565, dōron* [8]
gifts, *5922, charisma* [7]
gifts, *AIT* [3]
gifts, *RPE* [3]
gifts, *1517, doma* [3]
gifts to the poor, *1797, eleēmosynē* [2]
gifts dedicated to God, *356, anathēma* [1]
gifts, *1443, didōmi* [1]
gifts for the poor, *1797, eleēmosynē* [1]
those with gifts of administration, *3236, kybernēsis* [1]
gifts distributed, *3536, merismos* [1]

GIGANTIC [1]

gigantic, *3489, megas* [1]

GIRL [19]

girl, *3166, korasion* [6]
servant girl, *4087, paidiskē* [4]
girl, *AIT* [2]
girl, *RPE* [1]
girlˢ, *899, autos* [1]
the slave girlˢ, *899, autos* [1]
girl on duty, *2601, thyrōros* [1]
little girl, *3166, korasion* [1]
girl, *4087, paidiskē* [1]
slave girl, *4087, paidiskē* [1]

GIRLS [1]

servant girls, *4087, paidiskē* [1]

GIVE [213]

give, *1443, didōmi* [115]
give, *625, apodidōmi* [9]
give, *RPE* [6]
give, *NIG* [5]
give, *2113, epididōmi* [5]
give, *4472, poieō* [4]
give, *2813, kaleō* [3]
give birth to, *5503, tiktō* [3]
give false testimony, *6018, pseudomartyreō* [3]
give a tenth of, *620, apodekatoō* [2]
give the right, *1443, didōmi* [2]
give to the poor, *1443+1797, didōmi+eleēmosynē* [2]
give thanks, *2373, eucharisteō* [2]
give to the needy, *4472+1797, poieō+eleēmosynē* [2]
give to drink, *4540, potizō* [2]
give, *AIT* [1]
give rest, *399, anapauō* [1]
give God a tenth of, *620, apodekatoō* [1]
give back, *625, apodidōmi* [1]
give account for, *625+3364, apodidōmi+logos* [1]
give share of, *625, apodidōmi* [1]
give birth, *652, apokyeō* [1]
give up, *698, apotassō* [1]
give greetings to, *832, aspazomai* [1]

give greeting, *832, aspazomai* [1]
give, *1328, dia* [1]
give notice of, *1334, diangellō* [1]
give, *1344, diadidōmi* [1]
give charge, *1371, diamartyromai* [1]
give directions, *1411, diatassō* [1]
give up, *1591, enkakeō* [1]
give up, *1593, enkataleipō* [1]
give in, *1634+3836+5717, eikō+ho+hypotagē* [1]
give up, *1725, eklyō* [1]
give, *2220, epichorēgeō* [1]
give thanks, *2328, eulogeō* [1]
give thanks for, *2373, eucharisteō* [1]
give, *2400, echō* [1]
give life, *2443, zōopoieō* [1]
give order, *3027, keleuō* [1]
give testimony, *3455, martyreō* [1]
give yourself wholly to, *3509, meletaō* [1]
whatever give, *3836, ho* [1]
give instructions, *4133, parangellō* [1]
give this command, *4133, parangellō* [1]
give, *4192, paratithēmi* [1]
give, *4225, paristēmi* [1]
give in, *4275, peithō* [1]
give fully, *4355, perisseuō* [1]
give many descendants, *4437+4437, plēthynō+plēthynō* [1]
give water, *4540, potizō* [1]
give, *4639, pros* [1]
to give, *4639, pros* [1]
give attention, *4674, proskartereō* [1]
give full time, *4674, proskartereō* [1]
give way, *4766, ptoēsis* [1]
give birth, *5503, tiktō* [1]
give recognition to, *5506, timaō* [1]
could not give, *5729, hysterēma* [1]
give light, *5894, phōtizō* [1]
graciously give, *5919, charizomai* [1]
give to the poor, *6039, psōmizō* [1]
give birth, *6048+5503, ōdinō+tiktō* [1]

GIVEN [168]

given, *1443, didōmi* [107]
given, *AIT* [5]
given in marriage, *1139, gamizō* [4]
given thanks, *2373, eucharisteō* [4]
given, *NIG* [2]
given, *625, apodidōmi* [2]
given, *1563, dōreomai* [2]
givenˢ, *3455, martyreō* [2]
given over, *4140, paradidōmi* [2]
given to drunkenness, *4232, paroinos* [2]
given, *4472, poieō* [2]
given, *4707, prostithēmi* [2]
given, *RPE* [2]
given new birth, *335, anagennaō* [1]
given answer, *646, apokrinomai* [1]
given orders, *690, apostellō* [1]
given in marriage, *1140, gamiskō* [1]
given, *1181, ginomai* [1]
given authority, *1443, didōmi* [1]
given fullness, *1639+4444, eimi+plēroō* [1]
given a trust, *1877+3874, en+oikonomos* [1]
given strength, *1904, endynamoō* [1]
given, *2093, epi* [1]
help given, *2221, epichorēgia* [1]
given, *2400+608, echō+apo* [1]
given, *2400, echō* [1]
given, *2813, kaleō* [1]
given rest, *2924, katapauō* [1]
given, *3284, lambanō* [1]
given testimony, *3455, martyreō* [1]
given, *3532, merizō* [1]
law was given, *3793, nomotheteō* [1]

title given, *3950+3951, onoma+onomazō* [1]
given, *4140, paradidōmi* [1]
given, *4151, parakaleō* [1]
given proof, *4411+4218, pistis+parechō* [1]
one grudgingly given, *4432, pleonexia* [1]
given to drink, *4540, potizō* [1]
given, *4594, prodidōmi* [1]
given birth to, *5503, tiktō* [1]
given, *5770, pherō* [1]
freely given, *5919, charizomai* [1]
graciously given, *5919, charizomai* [1]
freely given, *5923, charitoō* [1]

GIVER [1]

giver, *1522, dotēs* [1]

GIVES [39]

gives, *1443, didōmi* [13]
gives life, *2443, zōopoieō* [4]
gives, *AIT* [3]
gives birth to, *1164, gennaō* [2]
gives orders, *2199, epitassō* [2]
gives thanks, *2373, eucharisteō* [2]
gives, *RPE* [1]
gives birth to, *652, apokyeō* [1]
gives away, *1316+4472, dēlos+poieō* [1]
gives, *1349, diaireō* [1]
gives life, *1639+2443, eimi+zōopoieō* [1]
gives strength, *1904, endynamoō* [1]
gives life to, *2441, zōogoneō* [1]
gives light, *3290, lampō* [1]
gives a cup, *4540+4539, potizō+potērion* [1]
gives water to, *4540, potizō* [1]
gives birth to, *5503, tiktō* [1]
gives light to, *5894, phōtizō* [1]
gives light, *5894, phōtizō* [1]

GIVING [16]

giving thanks, *2373, eucharisteō* [5]
giving, *1443, didōmi* [3]
giving approval, *5306, syneudokeō* [2]
giving, *AIT* [1]
giving in marriage, *1139, gamizō* [1]
giving, *1521, dosis* [1]
giving, *1797, eleēmosynē* [1]
giving instructions, *1948, entellō* [1]
giving birth to a child, *5503, tiktō* [1]

GLAD [21]

glad, *5897, chairō* [14]
glad, *22, agalliaō* [2]
glad, *2370, euphrainō* [2]
glad, *21, agalliasis* [1]
make glad, *2370, euphrainō* [1]
glad, *5915, chara* [1]

GLADLY [5]

gladly, *2452, hēdeōs* [2]
gladly, *2315, euthymōs* [1]
very gladly, *2452, hēdeōs* [1]
gladly, *5897, chairō* [1]

GLASS [4]

of glass, *5612, hyalinos* [2]
glass, *5613, hyalos* [2]

GLEAMED [1]

that gleamed like lightning, *848, astraptō* [1]

GLITTERING [2]

glittering, *5998, chrysoō* [2]

GLOAT [1]

gloat, *5897, chairō* [1]

GLOOM [2]

gloom, *2432, zophos* [1]
gloom, *2993, katēpheia* [1]

GLOOMY [1]

gloomy, *2432, zophos* [1]

GLORIES [1]

glories, *1518, doxa* [1]

GLORIFIED [14]

glorified, *1519, doxazō* [11]
glorified, *1901, endoxazomai* [2]
glorified, *1518+1443, doxa+didōmi* [1]

GLORIFIES [2]

glorifies, *1519, doxazō* [1]
glorifies, *3486, megalynō* [1]

GLORIFY [13]

glorify, *1519, doxazō* [12]
glorify, *1443+1518, didōmi+doxa* [1]

GLORIFYING [1]

glorifying, *1519, doxazō* [1]

GLORIOUS [21]

glorious, *1518, doxa* [15]
glorious, *1519, doxazō* [2]
glorious presence, *1518, doxa* [1]
glorious splendor, *1518, doxa* [1]
glorious, *1877+1518, en+doxa* [1]
glorious, *2212, epiphanēs* [1]

GLORY [130]

glory, *1518, doxa* [112]
bring glory to, *1519, doxazō* [3]
glory, *RPE* [1]
with ever-increasing glory,
    608+1518+1650+1518,
    apo+doxa+eis+doxa [1]
divine glory, *1518, doxa* [1]
brought glory, *1519, doxazō* [1]
glory come to, *1519, doxazō* [1]
glory gave, *1519, doxazō* [1]
glory, *1519, doxazō* [1]
has glory, *1519, doxazō* [1]
take glory, *1519, doxazō* [1]
glory in, *2400+3018, echō+kauchēsis* [1]
glory, *3016, kauchaomai* [1]
glory over, *3018+2400, kauchēsis+echō* [1]
glory, *3018, kauchēsis* [1]
the glory's, *4005, hos* [1]
share in glory, *5280, syndoxazō* [1]

GLOWING [1]

glowing, *4792, pyroō* [1]

GLUTTON [2]

glutton, *476+5741, anthrōpos+phagos* [2]

GLUTTONS [1]

gluttons, *1143, gastēr* [1]

GNASHED [1]

gnashed, *1107, brychō* [1]

GNASHES [1]

gnashes, *5563, trizō* [1]

GNASHING [7]

gnashing, *1106, brygmos* [7]

GNAT [1]

gnat, *3270, kōnōps* [1]

GNAWED [1]

gnawed, *3460, masaomai* [1]

GO [271]

go, *4513, poreuomai* [59]
go, *5632, hypagō* [45]
go, *599, aperchomai* [22]
go out, *2002, exerchomai* [11]
go, *2262, erchomai* [10]
go, *AIT* [9]
go, *72, agō* [6]
let go, *668, apolyō* [6]
go in, *1656, eiserchomai* [6]
go down, *2849, katabainō* [6]
go, *NIG* [4]
go up, *326, anabainō* [4]
go, *2002, exerchomai* [4]
go, *RPE* [3]
go away, *599, aperchomai* [3]
go into, *1650+1656, eis+eiserchomai* [3]
go into, *1656+1650, eiserchomai+eis* [3]
go, *2188, epistrephō* [3]
go back, *4513, poreuomai* [3]
go, *149, airō* [2]
let go, *918, aphiēmi* [2]
go through, *1328+1451, dia+dierchomai* [2]
go over, *1451, dierchomai* [2]
go, *1451, dierchomai* [2]
go, *1639, eimi* [2]
go away, *2002, exerchomai* [2]
go ahead of, *4575, proagō* [2]
go on ahead of, *4575, proagō* [2]
go, *326, anabainō* [1]
go back, *366, anakamptō* [1]
go away, *432, anachōreō* [1]
go up, *456, anerchomai* [1]
go on, *599, aperchomai* [1]
go over, *599, aperchomai* [1]
let go of, *918, aphiēmi* [1]
let go on, *918, aphiēmi* [1]
go, *1181, ginomai* [1]
go, *1306, deuro* [1]
go through, *1328, dia* [1]
go, *1329, diabainō* [1]
go through, *1451+1328, dierchomai+dia* [1]
go through, *1451, dierchomai* [1]
go, *1586, egeirō* [1]
go's, *1650, eis* [1]
go through into, *1656+1650,*
    eiserchomai+eis [1]
go, *1656, eiserchomai* [1]
go into, *1660+1650+1650,*
    eisporeuomai+eis+eis [1]
go out, *1744, ekporeuomai* [1]
go on, *2094, epibainō* [1]
go down, *2115+2093, epidyō+epi* [1]
go on, *2152, epimenō* [1]
hearts go out to, *2160, epipotheō* [1]
go back, *2188, epistrephō* [1]
go, *2316, euthynō* [1]
go well, *2338, euodoō* [1]
go downstairs, *2849, katabainō* [1]
go unnoticed, *3291, lanthanō* [1]
how far will they go, *4047+5515+1639,*
    houtos+tis+eimi [1]

go hungry, *4277, peinaō* [1]
go with, *4309, peri* [1]
go, *4344, peripateō* [1]
go on way, *4513, poreuomai* [1]
go on, *4601, proerchomai* [1]
go, *4621, prokoptō* [1]
go before, *4638, proporeuomai* [1]
go on, *4638, proporeuomai* [1]
go to, *4665, proserchomai* [1]
go astray, *4997, skandalizō* [1]
go war, *5202+4483, symballō+polemos* [1]
go back, *5715, hypostrephō* [1]
go on, *5770, pherō* [1]

GOADS [1]

goads, *3034, kentron* [1]

GOAL [6]

goal, *5465, telos* [2]
attain goal, *2200, epiteleō* [1]
goal, *5024, skopos* [1]
reach goal, *5457, teleioō* [1]
make it goal, *5818, philotimeomai* [1]

GOAT [2]

goat, *AIT* [1]
young goat, *2253, eriphos* [1]

GOATS [5]

goats, *5543, tragos* [3]
goats, *2252, eriphion* [1]
goats, *2253, eriphos* [1]

GOATSKINS [1]

goatskins, *128+1293, aigeios+derma* [1]

GOD [1244]

god, *2536, theos* [1154]
God, *RPE* [62]
God's, *899, autos* [5]
God's, *3836, ho* [5]
God, *NIG* [3]
without God, *117, atheos* [1]
gifts dedicated to God, *356, anathēma* [1]
give God a tenth of, *620, apodekatoō* [1]
ask God for help, *1255, deēsis* [1]
justified before God, *1467, dikaioō* [1]
gift devoted to God, *1565, dōron* [1]
belonging to God, *1650+4348,
      eis+peripoiēsis* [1]
taught by God, *2531, theodidaktos* [1]
fighting against God, *2534, theomachos* [1]
of God, *2536, theos* [1]
worship God, *2537, theosebeia* [1]
God's, *3836+3281, ho+laleō* [1]
God's, *4005, hos* [1]
lovers of God, *5806, philotheos* [1]
devoted to God, *6067, ōpheleō* [1]

GOD'S [162]

God's, *2536, theos* [125]
God's's, *899, autos* [18]
God's people, *41, hagios* [8]
God's's, *3836, ho* [6]
God's, *RPE* [5]
God's, *NIG* [2]
God's, *AIT* [1]
God's holy people, *41, hagios* [1]
God's elect, *1723, eklektos* [1]
God's people, *4246, pas* [1]
God's, *5977, chrēmatismos* [1]

GOD-BREATHED [1]

God-breathed, *2535, theopneustos* [1]

GOD-FEARING [7]

God-fearing, *4936, sebō* [2]
God-fearing, *5828+3836+2536,
      phobeomai+ho+theos* [2]
God-fearing, *2327, eulabēs* [1]
God-fearing Greeks, *4936, sebō* [1]
God-fearing Gentiles, *5828+3836+2536,
      phobeomai+ho+theos* [1]

GOD-HATERS [1]

God-haters, *2539, theostygēs* [1]

GODDESS [3]

goddess, *RPE* [1]
goddess, *2516, thea* [1]
goddess, *2536, theos* [1]

GODLESS [5]

godless, *1013, bebēlos* [4]
godless, *815, asebēs* [1]

GODLESSNESS [2]

godlessness, *813, asebeia* [2]

GODLINESS [12]

godliness, *2354, eusebeia* [12]

GODLY [11]

godly, *2354, eusebeia* [2]
godly, *2357, eusebōs* [2]
godly, *2848+2536, kata+theos* [2]
godly, *2327, eulabēs* [1]
godly, *2356, eusebēs* [1]
godly, *2536, theos* [1]
godly man, *2538, theosebēs* [1]
godly, *2848+2354, kata+eusebeia* [1]

GODS [11]

gods, *2536, theos* [8]
gods, *1228, daimonion* [1]
twin gods Castor and Pollux, *1483,
      Dioskouroi* [1]
gods's, *3836, ho* [1]

GOES [27]

goes, *4513, poreuomai* [7]
goes through, *1451+1328, dierchomai+dia* [2]
goes down, *2849, katabainō* [2]
goes, *AIT* [1]
goes up, *326, anabainō* [1]
goes away, *599, aperchomai* [1]
never goes out, *812, asbestos* [1]
goes on, *1373, diamenō* [1]
goes into training, *1603, enkrateuomai* [1]
goes into, *1656+1650, eiserchomai+eis* [1]
goes out, *1744, ekporeuomai* [1]
goes into great detail about, *1836, embateuō* [1]
goes, *2262, erchomai* [1]
place where the road goes down, *2853,
      katabasis* [1]
goes to law, *3212, krinō* [1]
goes about his business, *4512, poreia* [1]
goes ahead, *4624, prolambanō* [1]
goes, *5632, hypagō* [1]
goes, *6003, chōreō* [1]

GOG [1]

Gog, *1223, Gōg* [1]

GOING [140]

going, *AIT* [30]
going to, *3516, mellō* [18]
going, *5632, hypagō* [18]
going, *4513, poreuomai* [12]
going up, *326, anabainō* [7]
going to, *4665, proserchomai* [4]
going, *2262, erchomai* [3]
going astray, *4414, planaō* [3]
going to answer, *646, apokrinomai* [2]
going through, *1451, dierchomai* [2]
going into, *1660+1650, eisporeuomai+eis* [2]
going out, *2002, exerchomai* [2]
going down, *2849, katabainō* [2]
going ahead of, *4575, proagō* [2]
going farther, *4601, proerchomai* [2]
going away, *5632, hypagō* [2]
going, *RPE* [1]
going away, *599, aperchomai* [1]
going on a journey, *623, apodēmeō* [1]
going away, *624, apodēmos* [1]
was going on, *1181, ginomai* [1]
going by, *1388, diaporeuomai* [1]
going through, *1388+1328,
      diaporeuomai+dia* [1]
going into, *1656+1650, eiserchomai+eis* [1]
going, *1660, eisporeuomai* [1]
going, *1744, ekporeuomai* [1]
going to happen, *2262, erchomai* [1]
since going through, *2400, echō* [1]
going on to, *2401, heōs* [1]
going to happen to, *3516, mellō* [1]
going on, *3553, metabainō* [1]
going to rain, *3915+2262,
      ombros+erchomai* [1]
going by, *4135, paragō* [1]
going, *4182, paraporeuomai* [1]
going on foot, *4269, pezeuō* [1]
going about, *4320, perierchomai* [1]
going back, *4513, poreuomai* [1]
going on, *4581, probainō* [1]
going out, *4931, sbennymi* [1]
going with, *5302, synerchomai* [1]
what going on, *5515+323+4047,
      tis+an+houtos* [1]
going back, *5632, hypagō* [1]
going out, *5632, hypagō* [1]
going over, *5632, hypagō* [1]
going too far, *5657, hyperekteinō* [1]

GOLD [28]

gold, *5992, chrysion* [10]
gold, *5996, chrysos* [10]
of gold, *5997, chrysous* [5]
gold jewelry, *5992, chrysion* [1]
wearing a gold ring, *5993, chrysodaktylios* [1]
gold, *5997, chrysous* [1]

GOLD-COVERED [1]

gold-covered, *4328+4119+5992,
      perikalyptō+pantothen+chrysion* [1]

GOLDEN [12]

golden, *5997, chrysous* [12]

GOLGOTHA [3]

Golgotha, *1201, Golgotha* [3]

GOMORRAH [4]

Gomorrah, *1202, Gomorra* [4]

GONE [39]

gone out, *2002, exerchomai* [6]

gone, *599, aperchomai* [3]
gone, *2002, exerchomai* [3]
gone, *2262, erchomai* [3]
gone, *RPE* [2]
gone, *1656, eiserchomai* [2]
gone, *4513, poreuomai* [2]
gone without sleep, *71, agrypnia* [1]
gone, *326, anabainō* [1]
gone, *432, anachōreō* [1]
gone away, *599, aperchomai* [1]
gone from, *599+608, aperchomai+apo* [1]
gone without food, *827, asitos* [1]
gone about, *1451, dierchomai* [1]
gone through, *1451, dierchomai* [1]
gone into, *1656+1650, eiserchomai+eis* [1]
gone out from, *1666+2002, ek+exerchomai* [1]
gone, *1722, ekleipō* [1]
gone down, *2849, katabainō* [1]
gone without food, *3763, nēsteia* [1]
gone, *4216, parerchomai* [1]
gone by, *4444, plēroō* [1]
gone farther, *4581, probainō* [1]
gone, *5639, hyparchō* [1]
gone, *5728, hystereō* [1]

GONG [1]

gong, *5910, chalkos* [1]

GOOD [247]

good, *19, agathos* [89]
good, *2819, kalos* [61]
good, *2822, kalōs* [8]
good news, *2295, euangelion* [6]
what is good, *2819, kalos* [4]
good, *3421, makarios* [4]
good, *RPE* [3]
do good, *16, agathopoieō* [3]
doing good, *16, agathopoieō* [3]
preached the good news, *2294, euangelizō* [3]
good pleasure, *2306, eudokia* [3]
good, *606, haplous* [2]
seemed good, *1506, dokeō* [2]
preach the good news, *2294, euangelizō* [2]
proclaiming the good news, *2294,*
    euangelizō [2]
the good news preached, *2294, euangelizō* [2]
good, *4055, ophelos* [2]
good, *5237, sympherō* [2]
good, *5239, symphoros* [2]
good, *5982, chrēstos* [2]
good, *6067, ōpheleō* [2]
good, *AIT* [1]
do good, *14, agathoergeō* [1]
does what is good, *16, agathopoieō* [1]
good, *16, agathopoieō* [1]
do good, *17, agathopoiia* [1]
good, *20, agathōsynē* [1]
for good, *173, aiōnios* [1]
not lovers of good, *920, aphilagathos* [1]
lose good name, *1650+591+2262,*
    eis+apelegmos+erchomai [1]
bring good news, *2294, euangelizō* [1]
bringing good news, *2294, euangelizō* [1]
brought good news about, *2294, euangelizō* [1]
preach good news, *2294, euangelizō* [1]
preaching the good news, *2294, euangelizō* [1]
tell good news, *2294, euangelizō* [1]
tell the good news, *2294, euangelizō* [1]
telling the good news about, *2294,*
    euangelizō [1]
telling the good news, *2294, euangelizō* [1]
the good news is preached, *2294, euangelizō* [1]
told the good news about, *2294, euangelizō* [1]
good purpose, *2306, eudokia* [1]
doing good, *2308, euergeteō* [1]

do good, *2343, eupoiia* [1]
good income, *2345, euporia* [1]
make a good impression, *2349, euprosōpeō* [1]
good report, *2367, euphēmia* [1]
produced a good crop, *2369, euphoreō* [1]
as good as dead, *2453+3739, ēdē+nekroō* [1]
good, *2710, ischyō* [1]
and as good as, *2779+4047, kai+houtos* [1]
teach what is good, *2815, kalodidaskalos* [1]
good, *2822+4472, kalōs+poieō* [1]
good, *3202, kreittōn* [1]
common good, *5237, sympherō* [1]
for good, *5237, sympherō* [1]
enjoy good health, *5617, hygiainō* [1]
loves what is good, *5787, philagathos* [1]
good, *5983, chrēstotēs* [1]
good for, *6067, ōpheleō* [1]
good to, *6067, ōpheleō* [1]

GOOD-BY [5]

saying good-by to, *571, apaspazomai* [1]
said good-by, *698, apotassō* [1]
say good-by, *698, apotassō* [1]
said good-by, *832, aspazomai* [1]
good-by, *5897, chairō* [1]

GOODNESS [7]

goodness, *20, agathōsynē* [3]
goodness, *746, aretē* [3]
goodness, *2819, kalos* [1]

GOODS [3]

goods, *19, agathos* [1]
goods, *5007, skeuos* [1]
goods, *5638, hyparxis* [1]

GOODWILL [2]

goodwill, *2306, eudokia* [1]
goodwill, *5921, charis* [1]

GORGED [1]

gorged, *5963, chortazō* [1]

GOSPEL [96]

gospel, *2295, euangelion* [60]
preach the gospel, *2294, euangelizō* [7]
preaching the gospel, *2294, euangelizō* [5]
this gospel^s, *4005, hos* [3]
gospel, *RPE* [2]
preached the gospel, *2294, euangelizō* [2]
the gospel preached, *2294, euangelizō* [2]
preaching gospel, *2295, euangelion* [2]
gospel^s, *257, allos* [1]
the gospel^s, *899, autos* [1]
had the gospel preached, *2294, euangelizō* [1]
preach a gospel, *2294, euangelizō* [1]
preaching a gospel, *2294, euangelizō* [1]
gospel preached, *2295+2294,*
    euangelion+euangelizō [1]
gospel proclaim, *2295+2294,*
    euangelion+euangelizō [1]
preach gospel, *2295, euangelion* [1]
preaching the gospel, *2295+2294,*
    euangelion+euangelizō [1]
proclaiming gospel, *2295, euangelion* [1]
spreading gospel, *2295, euangelion* [1]
the gospel^s, *4005, hos* [1]
announced the gospel in advance, *4603,*
    proeuangelizomai [1]

GOSSIP [1]

gossip, *6030, psithyrismos* [1]

GOSSIPING [1]

gossiping about, *5826, phlyareō* [1]

GOSSIPS [2]

gossips, *5827, phlyaros* [1]
gossips, *6031, psithyristēs* [1]

GOT [58]

got up, *482, anistēmi* [15]
got up, *1586, egeirō* [11]
got, *1832, embainō* [10]
got up, *1444, diegeirō* [2]
got into, *1832, embainō* [2]
got out of, *2002+1666, exerchomai+ek* [2]
got up, *2705, histēmi* [2]
got together, *5251, synagō* [2]
got, *NIG* [1]
got ready, *482, anistēmi* [1]
got, *625, apodidōmi* [1]
got married, *1222+1138, gynē+gameō* [1]
got to, *1656+1650, eiserchomai+eis* [1]
got ready, *2171, episkeuazomai* [1]
got, *2400, echō* [1]
got ready, *2426, zēteō* [1]
got down, *2849, katabainō* [1]
got, *3284, lambanō* [1]
got there ahead of, *4601, proerchomai* [1]
got down, *5502, tithēmi* [1]

GOUGE [2]

gouge out, *1975, exaireō* [2]

GOVERN [1]

govern, *RPE* [1]

GOVERNING [2]

governing^s, *899+4047, autos+houtos* [1]
governing, *5660, hyperechō* [1]

GOVERNOR [18]

governor, *2450, hēgemōn* [13]
governor, *2448, hēgemoneuō* [2]
governor, *RPE* [1]
governor, *1617, ethnarchēs* [1]
palace of the Roman governor, *4550,*
    praitōrion [1]

GOVERNOR'S [2]

governor's, *2450, hēgemōn* [2]

GOVERNORS [4]

governors, *2450, hēgemōn* [4]

GRABBED [1]

grabbed, *3195, krateō* [1]

GRACE [123]

grace, *5921, charis* [119]
grace, *RPE* [2]
in grace gave, *5919, charizomai* [1]
act of grace, *5921, charis* [1]

GRACIOUS [3]

gracious gift, *5921, charis* [1]
gracious, *5921, charis* [1]
gracious favor, *5922, charisma* [1]

GRACIOUSLY [2]

graciously given, *5919, charizomai* [1]
graciously give, *5919, charizomai* [1]

GRAFT [1]

graft in, *1596, enkentrizō* [1]

GRAFTED [5]

grafted in, *1596, enkentrizō* [2]
grafted in among, *1596+1877,*
enkentrizō+en [1]
grafted into, *1596, enkentrizō* [1]
grafted, *1596, enkentrizō* [1]

GRAIN [12]

heads of grain, *5092, stachys1* [3]
treading out the grain, *262, aloaō* [2]
grain, *2843, karpos* [2]
grain, *4992, sitos* [2]
grinding grain, *241, alēthō* [1]
produces grain, *2844, karpophoreō* [1]
grain, *4989, sition* [1]

GRAINFIELDS [3]

grainfields, *5077, sporimos* [3]

GRANDCHILDREN [1]

grandchildren, *1681, ekgonos* [1]

GRANDMOTHER [1]

grandmother, *3439, mammē* [1]

GRANDPARENTS [1]

parents and grandparents, *4591, progonos* [1]

GRANT [8]

grant, *1443, didōmi* [4]
grant, *AIT* [1]
grant, *1181, ginomai* [1]
grant, *2960, katatithēmi* [1]
grant, *3306, legō* [1]

GRANTED [8]

granted, *1443, didōmi* [4]
granted, *1181, ginomai* [1]
granted, *1650, eis* [1]
granted, *2822, kalōs* [1]
granted, *5919, charizomai* [1]

GRAPES [6]

grapes, *5091, staphylē* [3]
grapes, *306, ampelos* [1]
clusters of grapes, *1084, botrys* [1]
grapes, *2843, karpos* [1]

GRAPEVINE [1]

grapevine, *306, ampelos* [1]

GRASP [4]

grasp, *150, aisthanomai* [1]
grasp, *2898, katalambanō* [1]
grasp the meaning, *3857+3836+1539,*
oida+ho+dynamis [1]
grasp, *5931, cheir* [1]

GRASPED [1]

something to be grasped, *772, harpagmos* [1]

GRASS [9]

grass, *5965, chortos* [9]

GRATEFUL [1]

grateful, *2373, eucharisteō* [1]

GRATIFY [2]

how to gratify, *1650, eis* [1]
gratify, *5464, teleō* [1]

GRATIFYING [1]

gratifying^s, *1877, en* [1]

GRATITUDE [2]

gratitude, *2374, eucharistia* [1]
gratitude, *5921, charis* [1]

GRAVE [3]

grave, *87, hadēs* [2]
grave, *RPE* [1]

GRAVES [4]

graves, *3646, mnēmeion* [3]
graves, *5439, taphos* [1]

GREAT [172]

great, *3489, megas* [90]
great, *4498, polys* [35]
great, *4246, pas* [6]
such great, *5537, tosoutos* [4]
great, *3336, lian* [3]
great, *2653, hikanos* [2]
great street, *4423, plateia* [2]
great deal of, *4498, polys* [2]
great deal, *4498, polys* [2]
great, *NIG* [1]
great joy, *21, agalliasis* [1]
goes into great detail about, *1836, embateuō* [1]
gather a great number, *2197, episōreuō* [1]
with great fervor, *2417+3836+4460,*
zeō+ho+pneuma [1]
what a great, *2462, hēlikos* [1]
great, *2819, kalos* [1]
great, *2848+5651, kata+hyperbolē* [1]
in great danger, *3073, kindyneuō* [1]
shown great, *3486, megalynō* [1]
great, *3490, megethos* [1]
great, *3491, megistan* [1]
very great, *3492, megistos* [1]
great patience, *4246+3429,*
pas+makrothymia [1]
how great, *4383, pēlikos* [1]
great company, *4436, plēthos* [1]
great number, *4436, plēthos* [1]
great worth, *4500, polytelēs* [1]
great value, *4501, polytimos* [1]
how great, *4531, posos* [1]
how great, *4534, potapos* [1]
great help, *4706, prostatis* [1]
great, *5379, sphodra* [1]
great disturbance, *5431+4024+3900,*
tarachos+ou+oligos [1]
such great, *5496, tēlikoutos* [1]
surpassingly great, *5651, hyperbolē* [1]

GREATER [45]

greater than, *3505, meizōn* [20]
greater, *3505, meizōn* [10]
greater, *4498, polys* [6]
greater, *3437, mallon* [2]
become greater, *889, auxanō* [1]
greater, *3202, kreittōn* [1]
greater than ever, *3437, mallon* [1]
one greater than, *3505, meizōn* [1]
greater, *4358, perissoteros* [1]
greater, *4359, perissoterōs* [1]
greater worth, *4501, polytimos* [1]

GREATEST [14]

greatest, *3505, meizōn* [8]
greatest, *3489, megas* [5]
searched intently and with the greatest care,
1699+2779+2001,
ekzēteō+kai+exeraunaō [1]

GREATLY [17]

greatly, *5379, sphodra* [2]
greatly rejoice, *22, agalliaō* [1]
greatly increased, *889+2779+4437,*
auxanō+kai+plēthynō [1]
greatly disturbed, *1387, diaponeomai* [1]
greatly troubled, *1410, diatarassō* [1]
greatly, *1650+4353, eis+perisseia* [1]
greatly, *2708, ischyros* [1]
greatly, *2809, kakōs* [1]
greatly, *3336, lian* [1]
greatly, *3487, megalōs* [1]
greatly, *3489, megas* [1]
greatly, *4024+3585, ou+metriōs* [1]
greatly distressed, *4236, paroxynō* [1]
greatly distressed, *4337, perilypos* [1]
greatly encouraged, *4444+4155,*
plēroō+paraklēsis [1]
greatly, *4498, polys* [1]

GREATNESS [2]

greatness, *3484, megaleiotēs* [1]
surpassing greatness, *5660, hyperechō* [1]

GRECIAN [2]

Grecian Jews, *1821, Hellēnistēs* [2]

GREECE [1]

Greece, *1817, Hellas* [1]

GREED [10]

greed, *4432, pleonexia* [8]
greed, *771, harpagē* [2]

GREEDY [5]

greedy, *4431, pleonektēs* [3]
greedy for money, *154, aischrokerdōs* [1]
greedy person, *4431, pleonektēs* [1]

GREEK [11]

Greek, *1818, Hellēn* [5]
Greek, *1820, Hellēnis* [2]
Greek, *RPE* [1]
Greek, *1819, Hellēnikos* [1]
Greek, *1822, Hellēnisti* [1]
in Greek, *1822, Hellēnisti* [1]

GREEKS [16]

Greeks, *1818, Hellēn* [15]
God-fearing Greeks, *4936, sebō* [1]

GREEN [3]

green, *5952, chlōros* [2]
green, *5619, hygros* [1]

GREET [31]

greet, *832, aspazomai* [30]
greet, *RPE* [1]

GREETED [7]

greeted, *832, aspazomai* [4]
greeted, *833, aspasmos* [3]

GREETING [7]

greeting, *833, aspasmos* [6]
give greeting, *832, aspazomai* [1]

GREETINGS [27]

send greetings, *832, aspazomai* [11]
sends greetings, *832, aspazomai* [6]
greetings, *5897, chairō* [6]
greetings, *RPE* [1]
give greetings to, *832, aspazomai* [1]
sends greetings to, *832, aspazomai* [1]
greetings, *833, aspasmos* [1]

GREETS [1]

greets, *832, aspazomai* [1]

GREW [16]

grew, *889, auxanō* [4]
grew, *AIT* [3]
grew up, *326, anabainō* [2]
grew, *1181, ginomai* [1]
grew, *1650+3836+2262, eis+ho+erchomai* [1]
grew, *2710, ischyō* [1]
grew, *4355, perisseuō* [1]
grew in numbers, *4437, plēthynō* [1]
grew, *4621, prokoptō* [1]
grew up with, *5243, symphyō* [1]

GRIEF [8]

grief, *3383, lypē* [3]
caused grief, *3382, lypeō* [1]
filled with grief, *3382+5379,*
lypeō+sphodra [1]
suffer grief, *3382, lypeō* [1]
filled with grief, *4291, pentheō* [1]
grief, *4292, penthos* [1]

GRIEFS [1]

griefs, *3850, odynē* [1]

GRIEVANCE [1]

grievance, *3364, logos* [1]

GRIEVANCES [1]

grievances, *3664, momphē* [1]

GRIEVE [6]

grieve, *3382, lypeō* [5]
grieve, *5415, talaipōreō* [1]

GRIEVED [5]

grieved, *3382, lypeō* [2]
grieved, *RPE* [1]
grieved, *3849, odynaō* [1]
grieved over, *4291, pentheō* [1]

GRINDING [2]

grinding grain, *241, alēthō* [1]
grinding, *241, alēthō* [1]

GRIPPED [1]

gripped with, *2158+2093, epipiptō+epi* [1]

GROAN [3]

groan, *5100, stenazō* [3]

GROANING [2]

groaning, *5099, stenagmos* [1]
groaning, *5367, systenazō* [1]

GROANS [1]

groans, *5099, stenagmos* [1]

GROPED [1]

groped about, *4310, periagō* [1]

GROUND [37]

ground, *1178, gē* [20]
with face to the ground, *2093+4725,*
epi+prosōpon [2]
proper ground, *162, aitia* [1]
stand your ground, *468, anthistēmi* [1]
ground, *929, aphormē* [1]
foot of ground, *1037+4546, bēma+pous* [1]
dash to the ground, *1610, edaphizō* [1]
ground, *1611, edaphos* [1]
facedown to the ground, *2093+4725,*
epi+prosōpon [1]
to the ground, *3004, katō* [1]
threw to the ground, *4838, rhēgnymi* [1]
throws to the ground, *4838, rhēgnymi* [1]
stood ground, *5702, hypomenō* [1]
on the ground, *5912, chamai* [1]
to the ground, *5912, chamai* [1]
ground, *6001, chōra* [1]
plot of ground, *6005, chōrion* [1]

GROUNDS [2]

grounds for the death penalty, *165+2505,*
aitios+thanatos [1]
temple grounds, *2639, hieron* [1]

GROUP [6]

circumcision group, *4364, peritomē* [2]
group, *AIT* [1]
before the group, *1877+3545, en+mesos* [1]
group, *4063+3950, ochlos+onoma* [1]
group, *4436, plēthos* [1]

GROUPS [3]

groups, *3112, klisia* [1]
groups, *4555+4555, prasia+prasia* [1]
groups, *5235+5235, symposion+symposion* [1]

GROVE [3]

olive grove, *3057, kēpos* [2]
to the grove⁸, *1695, ekei* [1]

GROW [12]

grow, *889, auxanō* [4]
grow, *AIT* [2]
grow up, *889, auxanō* [2]
made grow, *889, auxanō* [1]
makes grow, *889, auxanō* [1]
causes to grow, *890, auxēsis* [1]
grow together, *5277, synauxanō* [1]

GROWING [3]

growing, *889, auxanō* [2]
growing more and more, *5647, hyperauxanō* [1]

GROWN [2]

grown, *AIT* [1]
grown up, *3489+1181, megas+ginomai* [1]

GROWS [6]

grows, *889, auxanō* [2]
grows, *326, anabainō* [1]
grows, *890+4472, auxēsis+poieō* [1]
grows, *3602, mēkynō* [1]
grows, *5886, phyō* [1]

GRUDGE [1]

nursed a grudge against, *1923, enechō* [1]

GRUDGINGLY [1]

one grudgingly given, *4432, pleonexia* [1]

GRUMBLE [4]

grumble, *1197, gongyzō* [3]
grumble, *5100, stenazō* [1]

GRUMBLERS [1]

grumblers, *1199, gongystēs* [1]

GRUMBLING [3]

grumbling, *1197, gongyzō* [2]
grumbling, *1198, gongysmos* [1]

GUARANTEE [1]

guarantee, *1583, engyos* [1]

GUARANTEED [1]

guaranteed, *1010, bebaios* [1]

GUARANTEEING [3]

deposit guaranteeing what is to come, *775,*
arrabōn [2]
deposit guaranteeing, *775, arrabōn* [1]

GUARD [33]

on guard, *4668, prosechō* [4]
guard, *5875, phylassō* [4]
on guard, *1213, grēgoreō* [2]
temple guard, *2639, hieron* [2]
guard, *3184, koustōdia* [2]
kept under guard, *5875, phylassō* [2]
on guard, *5875, phylassō* [2]
guard, *RPE* [1]
on guard, *70, agrypneō* [1]
under guard, *857, asphalōs* [1]
on guard, *1063, blepō* [1]
on your guard, *1063, blepō* [1]
guard carefully, *1428, diaphylassō* [1]
palace guard, *4550, praitōrion* [1]
guard, *4668, prosechō* [1]
officers of guard, *5130, stratēgos* [1]
officers of the temple guard, *5130, stratēgos* [1]
guard, *5498, tēreō* [1]
keep under guard, *5498, tēreō* [1]
guard, *5864, phroureō* [1]
guard, *5871, phylakē* [1]
on guard against, *5875, phylassō* [1]

GUARDED [2]

guarded, *5864, phroureō* [1]
guarded, *5875, phylassō* [1]

GUARDIAN [1]

guardian of the temple, *3753, neōkoros* [1]

GUARDIANS [2]

guardians, *2208, epitropos* [1]
guardians, *4080, paidagōgos* [1]

GUARDING [3]

guarding, *5309, synechō* [1]
guarding, *5498, tēreō* [1]
guarding, *5875, phylassō* [1]

GUARDS [12]

guards, *5677, hypēretēs* [4]
temple guards, *5677, hypēretēs* [2]

GUARDS

guards, *5874, phylax* [2]
guards, *3184, koustōdia* [1]
guards, *5498, tēreō* [1]
guards, *5871, phylakē* [1]
guards, *5875, phylassō* [1]

GUEST [5]

guest room, *2906, katalyma* [2]
guest, *2907, katalyō* [1]
guest room, *3825, xenia* [1]
guest, *3826, xenizō* [1]

GUESTS [14]

guests, *5626, huios* [3]
guests, *AIT* [1]
guests, *367, anakeimai* [2]
dinner guests, *5263, synanakeimai* [2]
dinner guests, *367, anakeimai* [1]
guests, *2813, kaleō* [1]
guests, *3826, xenizō* [1]
fellow guests, *5263, synanakeimai* [1]
guests, *5263, synanakeimai* [1]

GUIDE [4]

guide, *3843, hodēgos* [2]
guide, *2985, kateuthynō* [1]
guide, *3842, hodēgeō* [1]

GUIDES [3]

guides, *3843, hodēgos* [3]

GUIDING [1]

guiding, *3284, lambanō* [1]

GUILT [2]

guilt, *281, hamartia* [1]
convict of guilt, *1794, elenchō* [1]

GUILTY [15]

guilty of sin, *281+2400, hamartia+echō* [2]
guilty, *1944, enochos* [2]
guilty, *92, adikeō* [1]
guilty of crime, *162, aitia* [1]
hasn't found guilty, *185, akatakritos* [1]
prove guilty, *1794, elenchō* [1]
guilty of sinning against, *1944, enochos* [1]
make guilty of, *2042+2093, epagō+epi* [1]
guilty of sin, *2400+281, echō+hamartia* [1]
guilty, *2400, echō* [1]
guilty, *4050, opheiletēs* [1]
guilty conscience, *5287+4505, syneidēsis+ponēros* [1]
guilty, *5287, syneidēsis* [1]

HA [1]

Ha, *1568, ea* [1]

HABIT [2]

in the habit of, *1621, ethos* [1]
get into the habit of being, *3443, manthanō* [1]

HAD [731]

had, *AIT* [540]
had, *2400, echō* [74]
had, *NIG* [37]
had to, *1256, dei* [8]
had, *RPE* [4]
had compassion, *5072, splanchnizomai* [4]
had mercy on, *1796, eleeō* [3]
had, *1181, ginomai* [2]
had, *1639+2400, eimi+echō* [2]

had, *1877+1639, en+eimi* [2]
had, *1877, en* [2]
man who had been mute, *3273, kōphos* [2]
had flogged, *5849, phragelloō* [2]
had no opportunity, *177, akaireomai* [1]
had, *323+2400, an+echō* [1]
had to, *340, anankē* [1]
that had touched, *608+3836+5999, apo+ho+chrōs* [1]
had in mind, *1089, boulomai* [1]
had, *1164, gennaō* [1]
had*ˢ*, *1182, ginōskō* [1]
had, *1182, ginōskō* [1]
had a notice prepared, *1211+5518, graphō+titlos* [1]
had to, *1256+1639, dei+eimi* [1]
had discussions, *1363, dialegomai* [1]
had taken part in a rebellion, *1639+3334, eimi+lēstēs* [1]
had to, *1639+338, eimi+anankaios* [1]
had*ˢ*, *1796, eleeō* [1]
had enough, *1855, empimplēmi* [1]
what had been promised, *2039, epangelia* [1]
had the gospel preached, *2294, euangelizō* [1]
had charge of, *2400, echō* [1]
had been, *2453, ēdē* [1]
had no objections, *2483, hēsychazō* [1]
had, *2710, ischyō* [1]
precisely as it had happened, *2759, kathexēs* [1]
had, *3284, lambanō* [1]
had leprosy, *3320, lepros* [1]
had a bath, *3374, louō* [1]
had too much to drink, *3499, methyskō* [1]
had too much, *3551+1639, mestoō+eimi* [1]
all had, *3836+2625, ho+idios* [1]
had*ˢ*, *3836+4123, ho+para* [1]
what had happened to, *3836, ho* [1]
had idea, *3857, oida* [1]
had a vision, *3969+3972, horama+horaō* [1]
had to, *4053, opheilō* [1]
had beheaded, *4287+642, pempō+apokephalizō* [1]
had, *4472, poieō* [1]
had been, *4537, pote* [1]
had to be, *5201, symbainō* [1]
had a wound, *5377, sphazō* [1]
had, *5593, tynchanō* [1]

HADES [5]

Hades, *87, hadēs* [5]

HAGAR [2]

Hagar, *29, Hagar* [2]

HAIL [5]

hail, *5897, chairō* [3]
hail, *5898, chalaza* [2]

HAILSTONES [1]

hailstones, *5898, chalaza* [1]

HAILSTORM [1]

hailstorm, *5898, chalaza* [1]

HAIR [21]

hair, *2582, thrix* [13]
has long hair, *3150, komaō* [2]
hair, *RPE* [1]
hair cut, *3025, keirō* [1]
hair, *3051, kephalē* [1]
long hair, *3151, komē* [1]
braided hair, *4427, plegma* [1]
made of hair, *5570, trichinos* [1]

HAIRS [2]

hairs, *2582, thrix* [2]

HALF [11]

half, *2468, hēmisys* [5]
half, *3604+1971, mēn¹+hex* [2]
half dead, *2467, hēmithanēs* [1]
half an hour, *2469, hēmiōrion* [1]
a half, *3604+1971, mēn¹+hex* [1]
three or three and a half miles, *5084+1633+4297+2445+5558, stadion+eikosi+pente+ē+triakonta* [1]

HALFWAY [1]

halfway through, *3548, mesoō* [1]

HALL [2]

wedding hall, *1141, gamos* [1]
lecture hall, *5391, scholē* [1]

HALLELUJAH [4]

hallelujah, *252, hallēlouia* [4]

HALLOWED [2]

hallowed, *39, hagiazō* [2]

HAMOR [1]

Hamor, *1846, Hemmōr* [1]

HAND [128]

hand, *5931, cheir* [75]
right hand, *1288, dexios* [31]
hand over, *4140, paradidōmi* [9]
hired hand, *3638, misthōtos* [2]
hand over, *5919, charizomai* [2]
hand, *RPE* [1]
chained hand, *268+1313, halysis+deō* [1]
left hand, *754, aristeros* [1]
chained hand, *1297+268, desmeuō+halysis* [1]
hand mill, *3685, mylos* [1]
hand over to, *4140+1650+5931, paradidōmi+eis+cheir* [1]
by the hand, *5932, cheiragōgeō* [1]
led by the hand, *5932, cheiragōgeō* [1]
someone to lead by the hand, *5933, cheiragōgos* [1]

HANDED [26]

handed over, *4140, paradidōmi* [18]
handed down, *4140, paradidōmi* [3]
handed over, *1692, ekdotos* [1]
handed, *2113, epididōmi* [1]
handed over, *4140+3836+5931, paradidōmi+ho+cheir* [1]
handed over, *4225, paristēmi* [1]
handed down from forefathers, *4261, patroparadotos* [1]

HANDING [1]

handing over, *4140, paradidōmi* [1]

HANDKERCHIEFS [1]

handkerchiefs, *5051, soudarion* [1]

HANDLE [1]

handle, *721, haptō* [1]

HANDLES [1]

correctly handles, *3982, orthotomeō* [1]

HANDLING   [1]

handling, *AIT* [1]

HANDS   [80]

hands, *5931, cheir* [70]
hands, *AIT* [1]
at the hands of, *608, apo* [1]
with own hands, *901, autocheir* [1]
not built by human hands, *942,*
   acheiropoiētos [1]
not done by the hands of men, *942,*
   acheiropoiētos [1]
hands over, *4140, paradidōmi* [1]
fell into the hands of, *4346, peripiptō* [1]
at their hands, *5679+899, hypo+autos* [1]
built by hands, *5935, cheiropoiētos* [1]
done by the hands, *5935, cheiropoiētos* [1]

HANG   [1]

hang, *3203, kremannymi* [1]

HANGED   [1]

hanged, *551, apanchō* [1]

HANGING   [4]

hanging, *3203, kremannymi* [3]
hanging over, *4024+733, ou+argeō* [1]

HAPPEN   [29]

happen, *1181, ginomai* [13]
happen, *1639, eimi* [7]
happen, *NIG* [2]
happen, *RPE* [1]
happen to, *2088+2093, eperchomai+epi* [1]
happen to, *2088, eperchomai* [1]
going to happen, *2262, erchomai* [1]
going to happen to, *3516, mellō* [1]
happen, *5201, symbainō* [1]
happen, *5267, synantaō* [1]

HAPPENED   [52]

happened, *1181, ginomai* [28]
happened, *NIG* [9]
happened, *5201, symbainō* [3]
happened, *RPE* [1]
happened, *1639+1181, eimi+ginomai* [1]
happened, *1639, eimi* [1]
precisely as it had happened, *2759, kathexēs* [1]
happened, *2848+5175, kata+synkyria* [1]
what had happened to, *3836, ho* [1]
what has happened to, *3836+2848, ho+kata* [1]
what happened⁸, *4047, houtos* [1]
happened to be there, *4193, paratynchanō* [1]
happened, *4444, plēroō* [1]
what has happened, *4544+4036, pou+oun* [1]
happened, *5746, phaneroō* [1]

HAPPENING   [6]

happening, *1181, ginomai* [3]
happening, *NIG* [1]
happening⁸, *4047, houtos* [1]
happening, *5201, symbainō* [1]

HAPPENS   [4]

happens, *1181, ginomai* [3]
whatever happens, *3667, monon* [1]

HAPPIER   [2]

happier, *3421, makarios* [1]
happier, *5897, chairō* [1]

HAPPINESS   [2]

happiness, *5915, chara* [2]

HAPPY   [4]

happy, *5897, chairō* [2]
happy, *2313, euthymeō* [1]
happy, *5915, chara* [1]

HARAN   [2]

Haran, *5924, Charran* [2]

HARASSED   [2]

harassed, *2567, thlibō* [1]
harassed, *5035, skyllō* [1]

HARBOR   [3]

harbor, *3348, limēn* [2]
harbor, *2400, echō* [1]

HARD   [29]

hard, *1552, dyskolōs* [3]
worked hard, *3159, kopiaō* [3]
hard, *5017, sklēros* [3]
hard, *893, austēros* [2]
work hard, *3159, kopiaō* [2]
hearts hard, *5016, sklērokardia* [2]
try hard, *1443+2238, didōmi+ergasia* [1]
hard to explain, *1549, dysermēneutos* [1]
hard, *1551, dyskolos* [1]
hard to understand, *1554, dysnoētos* [1]
hard pressed, *2567, thlibō* [1]
hard pressed, *2568, thlipsis* [1]
done hard work, *3159, kopiaō* [1]
hard work, *3159, kopiaō* [1]
work hard, *3159+2237, kopiaō+ergazomai* [1]
hard, *3660, molis* [1]
hard, *4498, polys* [1]
hard, *5081, spoudaiōs* [1]

HARDEN   [4]

harden, *5020, sklērynō* [3]
harden, *RPE* [1]

HARDENED   [4]

hardened, *4800, pōroō* [2]
hardened, *4800+2400, pōroō+echō* [1]
hardened, *5020, sklērynō* [1]

HARDENING   [2]

hardening, *4801, pōrōsis* [2]

HARDENS   [1]

hardens, *5020, sklērynō* [1]

HARDER   [3]

all the harder, *3437, mallon* [1]
harder than, *4358, perissoteros* [1]
much harder, *4359, perissoterōs* [1]

HARDLY   [5]

hardly, *977, bareōs* [2]
hardly carry, *1546, dysbastaktos* [1]
could hardly talk, *3652, mogilalos* [1]
hardly, *3660, molis* [1]

HARDSHIP   [5]

endure hardship, *2802, kakopatheō* [1]
hardship, *3677, mochthos* [1]
hardship, *5103, stenochōria* [1]
endure hardship with, *5155, synkakopatheō* [1]

endure hardship, *5702, hypomenō* [1]

HARDSHIPS   [6]

hardships, *2568, thlipsis* [3]
hardships, *340, anankē* [2]
endured hardships, *1002, bastazō* [1]

HARDWORKING   [1]

hardworking, *3159, kopiaō* [1]

HARM   [16]

harm, *92, adikeō* [5]
harm, *2805, kakos* [3]
harm, *2808, kakoō* [2]
do harm, *92, adikeō* [1]
harm done, *92, adikeō* [1]
harm, *94, adikia* [1]
harm, *721, haptō* [1]
harm, *2482, hēssōn* [1]
harm, *4556+2805, prassō+kakos* [1]

HARMED   [1]

harmed, *2423, zēmioō* [1]

HARMFUL   [1]

harmful, *1054, blaberos* [1]

HARMONY   [3]

live in harmony, *3836+899+5858,*
   ho+autos+phroneō [1]
live in harmony with, *3939, homophrōn* [1]
harmony, *5245, symphōnēsis* [1]

HARP   [2]

harp, *3067, kithara* [2]

HARPISTS   [2]

harpists, *3069, kitharōdos* [2]

HARPS   [2]

harps, *3067, kithara* [2]

HARSH   [5]

harsh, *705, apotomōs* [1]
harsh treatment, *910, apheidia* [1]
harsh, *4393, pikrainō* [1]
harsh, *5017, sklēros* [1]
harsh, *5021, skolios* [1]

HARSHLY   [2]

rebuked harshly, *1839, embrimaomai* [1]
rebuke harshly, *2159, epiplēssō* [1]

HARVEST   [24]

harvest, *2546, therismos* [10]
harvest, *2843, karpos* [4]
harvest time, *2789, kairos* [3]
harvest field, *2546, therismos* [2]
harvest, *AIT* [1]
harvest, *1163, genēma* [1]
harvest, *2545, therizō* [1]
reap a harvest, *2545, therizō* [1]
reap harvest, *2545, therizō* [1]

HARVESTED   [1]

harvested, *2545, therizō* [1]

HARVESTERS   [3]

harvesters, *2547, theristēs* [2]
harvesters, *2545, therizō* [1]

HARVESTING [1]

harvesting, *2545, therizō* [1]

HARVESTS [1]

harvests, *5251, synagō* [1]

HAS [691]

has, *AIT* [522]
has, *2400, echō* [89]
has, *NIG* [40]
has, *RPE* [7]
has, *1639, eimi* [4]
has come, *2457, hēkō* [2]
has long hair, *3150, komaō* [2]
has back, *655, apolambanō* [1]
what he has and does, *1050, bios* [1]
has*, *1063, blepō* [1]
has, *1181, ginomai* [1]
has glory, *1519, doxazō* [1]
has the right, *1538, dynamai* [1]
has mercy on, *1796, eleeō* [1]
has promised, *2039, epangelia* [1]
what has been promised, *2039, epangelia* [1]
has served, *2262, erchomai* [1]
has the opportunity, *2320, eukaireō* [1]
has enough, *2400+1650, echō+eis* [1]
has hold, *2400, echō* [1]
has to do with, *2400, echō* [1]
has come, *2453, ēdē* [1]
has*, *2813, kaleō* [1]
has no pity, *3091+3836+5073,*
   kleiō+ho+splanchnon [1]
has authority over, *3259, kyrieuō* [1]
has mastery over, *3259, kyrieuō* [1]
has, *3836+5639, ho+hyparchō* [1]
what has happened to, *3836+2848, ho+kata* [1]
as it has, *4048, houtōs* [1]
has to, *4053, opheilō* [1]
what has happened, *4544+4036, pou+oun* [1]
has done, *4552, praxis* [1]

HASN'T [2]

hasn't, *AIT* [1]
hasn't found guilty, *185, akatakritos* [1]

HASTY [1]

hasty, *5441, tacheōs* [1]

HATE [17]

hate, *3631, miseō* [13]
hate, *1639+3631, eimi+miseō* [3]
hate, *696, apostygeō* [1]

HATED [10]

hated, *3631, miseō* [9]
hated, *5144, stygētos* [1]

HATES [12]

hates, *3631, miseō* [12]

HATING [2]

hating, *3631, miseō* [2]

HATRED [2]

hatred, *2397, echthra* [2]

HAUL [1]

haul in, *1816, helkyō* [1]

HAUNT [2]

haunt, *5871, phylakē* [2]

HAVE [1190]

have, *AIT* [746]
have, *2400, echō* [207]
have, *NIG* [67]
would have, *323, an* [24]
have, *1639, eimi* [16]
have, *RPE* [14]
have mercy on, *1796, eleeō* [11]
have to, *1256, dei* [8]
should have, *1256, dei* [4]
could have, *1538, dynamai* [4]
have, *1877, en* [4]
have, *2671, hina* [3]
have leprosy, *3320, lepros* [3]
have, *5679, hypo* [3]
have being, *1639, eimi* [2]
have faith, *1666+4411, ek+pistis* [2]
have pity, *1796, eleeō* [2]
have children, *1985+5065,*
   exanistēmi+sperma [2]
have come, *2457, hēkō* [2]
I have, *3836+1847, ho+emos* [2]
have compassion, *3882, oiktirō* [2]
have nothing to do with, *4148, paraiteomai* [2]
have, *4205, pareimi* [2]
have an abundance, *4355, perisseuō* [2]
have compassion, *5072, splanchnizomai* [2]
have in mind, *5858, phroneō* [2]
have room for, *6003, chōreō* [2]
to have failed, *99+1639, adokimos+eimi* [1]
could have, *323, an* [1]
have recline at the table, *369, anaklinō* [1]
have sit down, *369, anaklinō* [1]
have children, *482+5065, anistēmi+sperma* [1]
have back, *600, apechō* [1]
not have faith, *601, apisteō* [1]
have nothing to do with, *706, apotrepō* [1]
have authority over, *883, authenteō* [1]
let have, *918, aphiēmi* [1]
have*, *1063, blepō* [1]
have, *1181, ginomai* [1]
could have done so, *1543, dynatos* [1]
have such a place, *1639, eimi* [1]
have too little, *1782, elattoneō* [1]
have hope, *1827+1639, elpizō+eimi* [1]
have right, *2003, exesti* [1]
have the right, *2003, exesti* [1]
have praise, *2046, epaineō* [1]
have to do with, *2110, epidechomai* [1]
not have, *2142, epileipō* [1]
have, *2209, epitynchanō* [1]
have a feast, *2266, esthiō* [1]
have dinner, *2266, esthiō* [1]
have a chance, *2320, eukaireō* [1]
have confidence, *2509, tharreō* [1]
have, *3125, koinōneō* [1]
have all you want, *3170+1639,*
   korennymi+eimi [1]
have, *3284, lambanō* [1]
have concern, *3534, merimnaō* [1]
have transferred, *3569, metapempō* [1]
have a part, *3576, metechō* [1]
have, *3576, metechō* [1]
have everything need, *3594+3309,*
   mēdeis+leipō [1]
have, *3836+2400, ho+echō* [1]
you have, *3836+5050, ho+sos* [1]
shouldn't have, *4024+1256, ou+dei* [1]
have*, *4024, ou* [1]
have to, *4053, opheilō* [1]
should have, *4053, opheilō* [1]
have, *4123, para* [1]
don't have anything to do with, *4148,*
   paraiteomai [1]
have, *4154, parakeimai* [1]
now have, *4205, pareimi* [1]
have to spare, *4355, perisseuō* [1]
have too much, *4429, pleonazō* [1]
have, *4472, poieō* [1]
moths have eaten, *4963+1181,*
   sētobrōtos+ginomai [1]
have, *5197, syllambanō* [1]
have children, *5449, teknogoneō* [1]
have baby, *5503, tiktō* [1]
have, *5639, hyparchō* [1]
joy have, *5915+5897, chara+chairō* [1]
have labor pains, *6048, ōdinō* [1]

HAVEN'T [8]

haven't, *4024, ou* [4]
haven't, *3590+2400, mē+echō* [1]
haven't anything, *3594, mēdeis* [1]
haven't, *4028, oude* [1]
haven't anything, *4029, oudeis* [1]

HAVING [47]

having, *AIT* [27]
having, *2400, echō* [11]
having, *NIG* [4]
not having the law, *491, anomos* [3]
having dinner, *367, anakeimai* [1]
having, *2848, kata* [1]

HAVOC [1]

raised havoc, *4514, portheō* [1]

HAY [1]

hay, *5965, chortos* [1]

HE [2800]

he, *AIT* [1996]
he, *899, autos* [221]
he, *RPE* [179]
he, *3836, ho* [144]
he, *3836+1254, ho+de* [70]
he, *4005, hos* [44]
he, *4047, houtos* [42]
he, *1697, ekeinos* [25]
he, *NIG* [8]
he, *5516, tis* [8]
he*, *3836+2652, ho+Iēsous* [7]
he*, *3836+2536, ho+theos* [5]
he himself, *899, autos* [3]
he, *1571, heautou* [3]
because he* is, *1650+3950, eis+onoma* [3]
he*, *3836+3812, ho+nymphios* [3]
if he does, *1623+1254+3590, ei+de+mē* [2]
he himself, *1697, ekeinos* [2]
what he did, *2240, ergon* [2]
he, *2779, kai* [2]
he*, *3836+476, ho+anthrōpos* [2]
he and his disciples, *899, autos* [1]
what he has and does, *1050, bios* [1]
he, *1328+3836+5931+899,*
   dia+ho+cheir+autos [1]
what he does, *2240, ergon* [1]
he*, *2476, Hērōdēs* [1]
he*, *2652, Iēsous* [1]
he too, *2797, kakeinos* [1]
and he, *2797, kakeinos* [1]
he also, *2797, kakeinos* [1]
he*, *3836+235, ho+Alexandros* [1]
he*, *3836+3261, ho+kyrios* [1]
so he, *3836+1254, ho+de* [1]
he that, *3836, ho* [1]
he*, *3836+1333, ho+diabolos* [1]
he*, *3836+2989, ho+katēgoreō* [1]
he*, *3836+3273, ho+kōphos* [1]

he[s], *3836+3281, ho+laleō* [1]
he[s], *3836+3707, ho+Mōysēs* [1]
he[s], *3836+4460+899+1877+899,*
   ho+pneuma+autos+en+autos [1]
he[s], *3836+467, ho+anēr* [1]
he[s], *3836+508, ho+antidikos* [1]
he[s], *3836+804, ho+architriklinos* [1]
he[s], *3836+995, ho+basileus* [1]
he, *3836+3525, ho+men* [1]
he, *3836+4725+899, ho+prosōpon+autos* [1]
he, *4015, hostis* [1]
he, *5525, toioutos* [1]
he, *5679+899, hypo+autos* [1]

HE'S [8]

he's, *AIT* [4]
he's, *899, autos* [1]
he's, *1639, eimi* [1]
he's, *3836+6034+899+1639,*
   ho+psychē+autos+eimi [1]
he's, *4047, houtos* [1]

HEAD [61]

head, *3051, kephalē* [50]
head, *RPE* [4]
head, *5092, stachys1* [2]
bring together under one head, *368,*
   anakephalaioō [1]
head into, *535, antophthalmeō* [1]
struck on the head, *3052, kephalioō* [1]
keep head, *3768, nēphō* [1]
head of the house, *3867, oikodespotēs* [1]

HEADING [2]

heading, *4513, poreuomai* [1]
heading, *5632, hypagō* [1]

HEADLONG [1]

fell headlong, *4568+1181, prēnēs+ginomai* [1]

HEADS [22]

heads, *3051, kephalē* [18]
heads of grain, *5092, stachys1* [3]
heads, *2843, karpos* [1]

HEADWAY [1]

made slow headway, *1095, bradyploeō* [1]

HEAL [21]

heal, *2543, therapeuō* [12]
heal, *2615, iaomai* [6]
heal, *1407, diasōzō* [1]
heal people, *2617+699, iasis+apoteleō* [1]
heal, *2617, iasis* [1]

HEALED [54]

healed, *2543, therapeuō* [22]
healed, *2615, iaomai* [16]
healed, *5392, sōzō* [13]
healed, *1407, diasōzō* [1]
healed, *2617, iasis* [1]
healed, *5618, hygiēs* [1]

HEALING [12]

healing, *2543, therapeuō* [3]
healing, *2611, iama* [3]
healing, *2542, therapeia* [2]
healing, *2615, iaomai* [2]
complete healing, *3907, holoklēria* [1]
healing, *5618+4472, hygiēs+poieō* [1]

HEALS [1]

heals, *2615, iaomai* [1]

HEALTH [1]

enjoy good health, *5617, hygiainō* [1]

HEALTHY [3]

healthy, *2710, ischyō* [2]
healthy, *5617, hygiainō* [1]

HEAP [3]

heap up to the limit, *405, anaplēroō* [1]
heap abuse on, *1059, blasphēmeō* [1]
heap, *5397, sōreuō* [1]

HEAPED [2]

heaped insults on, *3943, oneidizō* [2]

HEAR [105]

hear, *201, akouō* [99]
hear, *NIG* [1]
hear, *RPE* [1]
hear about, *201, akouō* [1]
hear, *212, akroatēs* [1]
hear case, *1358, diakouō* [1]
hear, *1639+201, eimi+akouō* [1]

HEARD [232]

heard, *201, akouō* [197]
heard about, *201, akouō* [10]
heard of, *201, akouō* [4]
heard, *1653, eisakouō* [4]
heard, *198, akoē* [3]
what heard, *198, akoē* [2]
heard, *NIG* [1]
heard, *RPE* [1]
heard from, *201, akouō* [1]
heard, *201+1639, akouō+eimi* [1]
heard, *212+1181, akroatēs+ginomai* [1]
heard about, *919, aphikneomai* [1]
heard sound, *1181+5889, ginomai+phōnē* [1]
heard[s], *1181, ginomai* [1]
heard about, *1196+1181, gnōstos+ginomai* [1]
heard, *2052, epakouō* [1]
heard, *3364, logos* [1]
already heard about, *4578, proakouō* [1]

HEARERS [1]

hearers, *201, akouō* [1]

HEARING [21]

hearing, *201, akouō* [14]
ever hearing, *198+201, akoē+akouō* [2]
hearing, *RPE* [1]
hearing, *198, akoē* [1]
sense of hearing, *198, akoē* [1]
ever hearing, *201+201, akouō+akouō* [1]
hearing, *4044, ous* [1]

HEARS [19]

hears, *201, akouō* [18]
hears, *NIG* [1]

HEART [81]

heart, *2840, kardia* [60]
heart, *6034, psychē* [4]
take heart, *2510, tharseō* [3]
lose heart, *1591, enkakeō* [2]
his heart, *1571, heautou* [1]
lose heart, *1725, eklyō* [1]
set heart on, *2426, zēteō* [1]
know heart, *2841, kardiognōstēs* [1]

knows heart, *2841, kardiognōstēs* [1]
heart, *3924, homothymadon* [1]
sets heart on being, *3977, oregō* [1]
whole heart, *4460, pneuma* [1]
heart went out, *5072, splanchnizomai* [1]
heart, *5073, splanchnon* [1]
very heart, *5073, splanchnon* [1]
take to heart, *5498, tēreō* [1]

HEART'S [1]

heart's, *2840, kardia* [1]

HEARTLESS [1]

heartless, *845, astorgos* [1]

HEARTS [80]

hearts, *2840, kardia* [69]
hearts hard, *5016, sklērokardia* [2]
hearts, *RPE* [1]
our hearts, *1571, heautou* [1]
their hearts, *1571, heautou* [1]
your hearts, *1571, heautou* [1]
setting hearts on, *2122, epithymētēs* [1]
hearts go out to, *2160, epipotheō* [1]
set hearts on, *2426, zēteō* [1]
hearts, *5073, splanchnon* [1]
your hearts, *5148, sy* [1]

HEAT [6]

heat, *2549, thermē* [1]
heat, *3008, kauma* [1]
scorching heat, *3008, kauma* [1]
heat, *3012, kausoō* [1]
heat, *3014, kausōn* [1]
scorching heat, *3014, kausōn* [1]

HEATHEN [1]

heathen, *1620, ethnos* [1]

HEAVEN [236]

heaven, *4041, ouranos* [219]
heaven, *2230, epouranios* [3]
heaven, *AIT* [2]
from heaven, *540, anōthen* [2]
in heaven, *2230, epouranios* [2]
from heaven, *4040, ouranothen* [2]
heaven, *RPE* [1]
image which fell from heaven, *1479,*
   diopetēs [1]
from heaven, *4039, ouranios* [1]
in heaven, *4039, ouranios* [1]
heaven, *5734, hypsēlos* [1]
heaven, *5737, hypsos* [1]

HEAVENLY [30]

heavenly, *2230, epouranios* [7]
heavenly, *4039, ouranios* [7]
heavenly realms, *2230, epouranios* [5]
heavenly, *4041, ouranos* [3]
heavenly, *AIT* [2]
heavenly things, *2230, epouranios* [2]
heavenly, *RPE* [1]
heavenly, *1666+4041, ek+ouranos* [1]
heavenly things, *1877+3836+4041,*
   en+ho+ouranos [1]
heavenly, *1877+3836+4041,*
   en+ho+ouranos [1]

HEAVENS [15]

heavens, *4041, ouranos* [15]

HEAVENWARD [1]

heavenward, *539, anō* [1]

HEAVY [3]

heavy, *976, bareō* [1]
heavy, *987, barys* [1]
heavy, *2852, katabarynō* [1]

HEBRAIC [1]

Hebraic Jews, *1578, Hebraios* [1]

HEBREW [3]

in Hebrew, *1580, Hebraisti* [2]
Hebrew, *1578, Hebraios* [1]

HEBREWS [2]

Hebrews, *1578, Hebraios* [2]

HEEL [1]

heel, *4761, pterna* [1]

HEIFER [1]

heifer, *1239, damalis* [1]

HEIGHT [2]

height, *AIT* [1]
height, *5739, hypsōma* [1]

HEIR [8]

heir, *3101, klēronomos* [8]

HEIRS [10]

heirs, *3101, klēronomos* [6]
heirs with, *5169, synklēronomos* [2]
heirs together with, *5169, synklēronomos* [1]
heirs, *5626, huios* [1]

HELD [26]

held, *2400, echō* [6]
held, *AIT* [3]
held, *5498, tēreō* [3]
held responsible for, *1699, ekzēteō* [2]
held together, *5204, symbibazō* [2]
held out, *1736, ekpetannymi* [1]
held, *1944, enochos* [1]
held a celebration, *2370, euphrainō* [1]
held on to, *3195, krateō* [1]
held, *3357, logizomai* [1]
held in high honor, *3486, megalynō* [1]
held, *4472, poieō* [1]
held over, *5498, tēreō* [1]
held accountable, *5688+1181,
    hypodikos+ginomai* [1]
held prisoners, *5864, phroureō* [1]

HELI [1]

Heli, *2459, Ēli2* [1]

HELL [14]

hell, *1147, geenna* [12]
hell, *87, hadēs* [1]
sent to hell, *5434, tartaroō* [1]

HELMET [2]

helmet, *4330, perikephalaia* [2]

HELP [46]

help, *1070, boētheō* [6]
help, *AIT* [4]
help, *1354, diakoneō* [2]
help, *2064, eparkeō* [2]
help, *5197, syllambanō* [2]
help, *RPE* [1]
help, *504, antechō* [1]

help, *514, antilambanō* [1]
those able to help, *516, antilēmpsis* [1]
help, *965, ballō* [1]
help himself to, *1002, bastazō* [1]
help, *1069, boētheia* [1]
ask God for help, *1255, deēsis* [1]
with the help of, *1328, dia* [1]
help, *1355, diakonia* [1]
help, *1565, dōron* [1]
with the help of, *1877, en* [1]
help, *2135, epikouria* [1]
come to help, *2170, episkeptomai* [1]
help given, *2221, epichorēgia* [1]
help, *2292+4472, eu+poieō* [1]
help, *3311, leitourgia* [1]
help speaking about, *3590+3281, mē+laleō* [1]
asking for help, *4151, parakaleō* [1]
to help, *4309, peri* [1]
help, *4547, pragma* [1]
help on journey, *4636, propempō* [1]
help on way, *4636, propempō* [1]
great help, *4706, prostatis* [1]
help, *5202, symballō* [1]
help, *5269, synantilambanomai* [1]
help, *5348, synypourgeō* [1]
help, *5845, phortion* [1]
help, *5931, cheir* [1]
help received, *6067, ōpheleō* [1]

HELPED [8]

helped, *1070, boētheō* [2]
helped, *1354, diakoneō* [2]
helped up, *1586, egeirō* [2]
helped to her feet, *482, anistēmi* [1]
helped, *514, antilambanō* [1]

HELPER [2]

helper, *1071, boēthos* [1]
helper, *5677, hypēretēs* [1]

HELPERS [1]

helpers, *1354, diakoneō* [1]

HELPFUL [3]

helpful, *19, agathos* [1]
helpful, *2378, euchrēstos* [1]
helpful, *5237, sympherō* [1]

HELPING [4]

helping to support, *1354, diakoneō* [1]
helping, *1354, diakoneō* [1]
helping the poor, *1797+4472,
    eleēmosynē+poieō* [1]
helping, *2064, eparkeō* [1]

HELPLESS [1]

helpless, *4849, rhiptō* [1]

HELPS [2]

helps, *2138, epilambanomai* [1]
helps, *5269, synantilambanomai* [1]

HEM [1]

hem in, *5309, synechō* [1]

HEN [2]

hen, *3998, ornis* [2]

HER [280]

her, *899, autos* [199]
her, *RPE* [35]
her, *3836, ho* [27]

her, *AIT* [6]
her, *4005, hos* [3]
her, *1571, heautou* [2]
helped to her feet, *482, anistēmi* [1]
her own, *1571, heautou* [1]
faithful to her husband, *1651+467+1222,
    heis+anēr+gynē* [1]
her alone, *2625, idios* [1]
her own, *2625, idios* [1]
her own, *3836, ho* [1]
herˢ, *3836+4086, ho+paidion* [1]
her, *4015, hostis* [1]

HERALD [2]

herald, *3061, kēryx* [2]

HERBS [1]

garden herbs, *3303, lachanon* [1]

HERD [7]

herd, *36, agelē* [7]

HERDS [1]

flocks and herds, *2576, thremma* [1]

HERE [129]

here, *6045, hōde* [48]
here, *NIG* [16]
here, *2627, idou* [12]
here, *1924, enthade* [6]
here, *2623, ide* [6]
here, *AIT* [5]
here, *899, autos* [2]
here, *1695, ekei* [2]
from here, *1925, enthen* [2]
here, *2627+6045, idou+hōde* [2]
stand here, *2705, histēmi* [2]
here, *3963, hopou* [2]
here, *RPE* [1]
almost here, *1581, engizō* [1]
gets here, *1581, engizō* [1]
here, *1877+4047, en+houtos* [1]
here, *1877+1609, en+egō* [1]
here, *1877+899, en+autos* [1]
from here, *1949, enteuthen* [1]
here, *1949, enteuthen* [1]
of here, *1949, enteuthen* [1]
get here, *2262, erchomai* [1]
here, *2262, erchomai* [1]
here, *2457, hēkō* [1]
here is, *2627, idou* [1]
put here, *3023, keimai* [1]
here, *4022, hoti* [1]
here, *4047, houtos* [1]
see here, *4047+2555, houtos+theōreō* [1]
who are here, *4047, houtos* [1]
get here, *4134, paraginomai* [1]
are here, *4205, pareimi* [1]
here, *4205, pareimi* [1]
is here, *4205, pareimi* [1]
standing here, *4325, periistēmi* [1]
blown here and there, *4367, peripherō* [1]

HERE'S [2]

here's, *2627, idou* [1]
here's, *6045, hōde* [1]

HERESIES [1]

heresies, *146, hairesis* [1]

HERMAS [1]

Hermas, *2254, Hermas* [1]

HERMES [2]

Hermes, *2258, Hermēs* [2]

HERMOGENES [1]

Hermogenes, *2259, Hermogenēs* [1]

HEROD [43]

Herod, *2476, Hērōdēs* [37]
Herod, *RPE* [6]

HEROD'S [5]

Herod's, *2476, Hērōdēs* [5]

HERODIANS [3]

Herodians, *2477, Hērōdianoi* [3]

HERODIAS [6]

Herodias, *2478, Hērōdias* [6]

HERODION [1]

Herodion, *2479, Hērōdiōn* [1]

HERSELF [7]

herself, *1571, heautou* [3]
herself, *899, autos* [2]
herself, *AIT* [1]
herself, *RPE* [1]

HESITATE [1]

hesitate, *1359, diakrinō* [1]

HESITATED [2]

hesitated, *5713, hypostellō* [2]

HESITATION [1]

hesitation, *1359, diakrinō* [1]

HEZEKIAH [2]

Hezekiah, *1614, Hezekias* [2]

HEZRON [3]

Hezron, *2272, Hesrōm* [3]

HID [8]

hid, *3221, kryptō* [7]
hid, *5696, hypolambanō* [1]

HIDDEN [23]

hidden, *3221, kryptō* [9]
hidden, *3220, kryptos* [5]
hidden from, *648+608, apokryptō+apo* [1]
hidden, *648+608, apokryptō+apo* [1]
hidden, *648, apokryptō* [1]
kept hidden for, *648+608+608,*
    apokryptō+apo+apo [1]
hidden, *649, apokryphos* [1]
hidden from, *905, aphanēs* [1]
place hidden, *3219, kryptē* [1]
hidden, *4152, parakalyptō* [1]
hidden, *4967, sigaō* [1]

HIDE [1]

hide, *3221, kryptō* [1]

HIDES [1]

hides, *2821, kalyptō* [1]

HIERAPOLIS [1]

Hierapolis, *2631, Hierapolis* [1]

HIGH [88]

high priest, *797, archiereus* [51]
Most High, *5736, hypsistos* [9]
high, *5734, hypsēlos* [6]
high priest's, *797, archiereus* [3]
high, *5737, hypsos* [3]
high priests, *797, archiereus* [2]
high officials, *3489, megas* [2]
high, *3489, megas* [2]
high priest's, *796, archieratikos* [1]
high priesthood, *797, archiereus* [1]
as high as, *948, achri* [1]
high standing, *2363, euschēmōn* [1]
held in high honor, *3486, megalynō* [1]
high officials, *3491, megistan* [1]
high, *4498, polys* [1]
high position, *5737, hypsos* [1]
on high, *5737, hypsos* [1]
high ranking officers, *5941, chiliarchos* [1]

HIGHER [1]

higher than, *5645, hyperanō* [1]

HIGHEST [8]

highest, *5736, hypsistos* [4]
highest point, *4762, pterygion* [2]
highest regard, *5655, hyperekperissou* [1]
exalted to the highest place, *5671,*
    hyperypsoō [1]

HIGHLY [6]

valued highly, *1639+1952, eimi+entimos* [1]
highly respected, *3455, martyreō* [1]
highly regarded, *3486, megalynō* [1]
highly valued, *3836+5734, ho+hypsēlos* [1]
think highly, *5672, hyperphroneō* [1]
highly favored, *5923, charitoō* [1]

HILL [8]

hill, *4001, oros* [5]
hill country, *3978, oreinos* [2]
hill, *1090, bounos* [1]

HILLS [4]

hills, *4001, oros* [3]
hills, *1090, bounos* [1]

HILLSIDE [2]

hillside, *4001, oros* [2]

HIM [1928]

him, *899, autos* [1388]
him, *RPE* [270]
him, *3836, ho* [77]
him, *AIT* [64]
him, *4005, hos* [58]
him, *4047, houtos* [25]
him[s], *3836+2536, ho+theos* [7]
him, *1697, ekeinos* [6]
him[s], *3836+2652, ho+Iēsous* [6]
him[s], *3836+476, ho+anthrōpos* [5]
him, *5525, toioutos* [3]
him[s], *3836+81+899, ho+adelphos+autos* [2]
robbed him of speech, *228, alalos* [1]
him, *1571, heautou* [1]
him, *1667, hekastos* [1]
him alone, *2625, idios* [1]
him[s], *3812, nymphios* [1]
him[s], *3836+2930, ho+kataponeō* [1]
him[s], *3836+4263, ho+Paulos* [1]
him[s], *3836+467, ho+anēr* [1]
him[s], *3836+4737, ho+prophētēs* [1]
him[s], *3836+5108, ho+Stephanos[1]* [1]

him[s], *3836+5986, ho+Christos* [1]
him[s], *3836+81+1609, ho+adelphos+egō* [1]
him, *3836+3950+899, ho+onoma+autos* [1]
him, *4123+4005, para+hos* [1]
men like him, *5525, toioutos* [1]
him, *5679+899, hypo+autos* [1]
him, *6034+899, psychē+autos* [1]

HIMSELF [167]

himself, *1571, heautou* [77]
himself, *899, autos* [37]
himself, *AIT* [20]
himself, *RPE* [13]
he himself, *899, autos* [3]
he himself, *1697, ekeinos* [2]
himself, *2625, idios* [2]
himself, *3836+2840+899, ho+kardia+autos* [2]
finds himself, *405, anaplēroō* [1]
by himself, *899+3668, autos+monos* [1]
help himself to, *1002, bastazō* [1]
considers himself, *1506, dokeō* [1]
himself, *1697, ekeinos* [1]
to himself, *1877+1571, en+heautou* [1]
threw himself on, *2158, epipiptō* [1]
himself, *2840+899, kardia+autos* [1]
himself[s], *3836+3950+899,*
    ho+onoma+autos [1]
threw himself, *4406+2093+4725,*
    piptō+epi+prosōpon [1]
exalt himself, *5643, hyperairomai* [1]

HINDER [5]

hinder, *3266, kōlyō* [3]
hinder, *1600+1443, enkopē+didōmi* [1]
hinder, *1601, enkoptō* [1]

HINDERED [2]

hindered from, *1601, enkoptō* [1]
hindered, *3266, kōlyō* [1]

HINDERS [1]

hinders, *3839, onkos* [1]

HINDRANCE [1]

without hindrance, *219, akōlytōs* [1]

HINT [1]

a hint of, *3951, onomazō* [1]

HIRE [1]

hire, *3636, misthoō* [1]

HIRED [12]

hired, *RPE* [5]
hired men, *3634, misthios* [2]
hired hand, *3638, misthōtos* [2]
hired out to, *3140, kollaō* [1]
hired, *3636, misthoō* [1]
hired men, *3638, misthōtos* [1]

HIS [1468]

his, *899, autos* [902]
his, *3836, ho* [203]
his, *RPE* [146]
his, *AIT* [60]
his own, *2625, idios* [37]
his own, *1571, heautou* [17]
his, *1571, heautou* [14]
his own, *899, autos* [13]
his, *2625, idios* [10]
his disciples[s], *899, autos* [7]
his, *4005, hos* [6]
his[s], *3836+2536, ho+theos* [4]

his, *1697, ekeinos* [3]
Jesus⁵ and his disciples, *899, autos* [2]
his master⁵, *899, autos* [2]
his own, *3836, ho* [2]
bound by his oath, *4053, opheilō* [2]
his, *NIG* [1]
led captives in his train, *169+168,*
  aichmalōteuō+aichmalōsia [1]
not his own, *259, allotrios* [1]
jumped to his feet, *403, anapēdaō* [1]
Jesus and his disciples⁵, *899, autos* [1]
he and his disciples, *899, autos* [1]
his parents⁵, *899, autos* [1]
his heart, *1571, heautou* [1]
his senses, *1571, heautou* [1]
his very self, *1571, heautou* [1]
lifted to his feet, *1586, egeirō* [1]
out of his body, *1650+3836+909+1744,*
  eis+ho+aphedrōn+ekporeuomai [1]
his native language, *1666+3836+2625,*
  ek+ho+idios [1]
his, *1667, hekastos* [1]
his disciples⁵, *1697, ekeinos* [1]
taking in his arms, *1878, enankalizomai* [1]
in his sight, *1967+899, enōpion+autos* [1]
on his way, *2262, erchomai* [1]
his relatives, *2625, idios* [1]
at his house, *2795, kakei* [1]
His Majesty, *3261, kyrios* [1]
his⁵, *3836+4511, ho+Poplios* [1]
his fellowman⁵, *3836+2283, ho+heteros* [1]
his home, *3836+2625, ho+idios* [1]
his own home, *3836+2625, ho+idios* [1]
his son⁵, *3836, ho* [1]
his⁵, *3836+2610, ho+Iakōbos* [1]
his⁵, *3836+2652, ho+Iēsous* [1]
his⁵, *3836+476+4047,*
  ho+anthrōpos+houtos [1]
his⁵, *3836+899, ho+autos* [1]
his letters⁵, *4005, hos* [1]
his faith⁵, *4005, hos* [1]
his master⁵, *4047, houtos* [1]
his, *4047, houtos* [1]
his very own, *4342, periousios* [1]
goes about his business, *4512, poreia* [1]
his⁵, *4981, Simōn* [1]
made his dwelling, *5012, skēnoō* [1]

HIT [2]

hit, *1639+4091, eimi+paiō* [2]

HOARDED [1]

hoarded wealth, *2564, thēsaurizō* [1]

HOISTED [2]

hoisted aboard, *149, airō* [1]
hoisted, *2048, epairō* [1]

HOLD [41]

hold, *2400, echō* [4]
hold to, *2400, echō* [3]
hold to, *3195, krateō* [3]
take hold, *2138, epilambanomai* [2]
hold on to, *2988, katechō* [2]
hold on to, *3195, krateō* [2]
hold firmly to, *504, antechō* [1]
hold on to, *721, haptō* [1]
lay hold of, *773, harpazō* [1]
hold, *1639, eimi* [1]
hold out, *2091, epechō* [1]
taking hold of, *2138, epilambanomai* [1]
has hold, *2400, echō* [1]
keep hold of, *2400, echō* [1]
hold, *2451, hēgeomai* [1]

hold, *2705, histēmi* [1]
take hold, *2898, katalambanō* [1]
taken hold of, *2898, katalambanō* [1]
took hold of, *2898, katalambanō* [1]
hold firmly, *2988, katechō* [1]
hold to, *2988, katechō* [1]
hold, *2988, katechō* [1]
hold firmly to, *3195, krateō* [1]
hold on, *3195, krateō* [1]
take hold of, *3195, krateō* [1]
take hold, *3195, krateō* [1]
hold, *3531, menō* [1]
allow to hold course, *4661, proseaō* [1]
hold together, *5319, synistēmi* [1]
hold, *5498, tēreō* [1]
passed under to hold together, *5968+5690,*
  chraomai+hypozōnnymi [1]

HOLDING [14]

holding, *2400, echō* [3]
holding, *AIT* [1]
holding, *RPE* [1]
holding in, *2093, epi* [1]
holding on to, *2400, echō* [1]
holding, *2705, histēmi* [1]
holding back, *2988, katechō* [1]
holding to, *2988, katechō* [1]
holding back, *3195, krateō* [1]
holding on to, *3195, krateō* [1]
holding to, *3195, krateō* [1]
holding, *6003, chōreō* [1]

HOLDS [5]

holds, *2400, echō* [3]
holds back, *2988, katechō* [1]
holds, *3195, krateō* [1]

HOLE [1]

dug a hole, *4002, oryssō* [1]

HOLES [3]

holes, *5887, phōleos* [2]
holes, *3956, opē* [1]

HOLINESS [12]

holiness, *40, hagiasmos* [4]
holiness, *42, hagiotēs* [2]
holiness, *43, hagiōsynē* [2]
holiness, *4009, hosiotēs* [2]
holiness⁵, *4005, hos* [1]
holiness, *4949, semnotēs* [1]

HOLLOW [2]

hollow, *3031, kenos* [1]
prove hollow, *3033, kenoō* [1]

HOLY [193]

holy, *41, hagios* [155]
holy, *4008, hosios* [7]
Most Holy Place, *41, hagios* [5]
made holy, *39, hagiazō* [3]
holy, *RPE* [2]
make holy, *39, hagiazō* [2]
holy, *40, hagiasmos* [2]
holy people, *41, hagios* [2]
holy, *39, hagiazō* [1]
made holy, *39+1639, hagiazō+eimi* [1]
makes holy, *39, hagiazō* [1]
holy life, *40, hagiasmos* [1]
God's holy people, *41, hagios* [1]
Holy One, *41, hagios* [1]
Holy Place, *41, hagios* [1]
Most Holy Place, *41+41, hagios+hagios* [1]

holy ones, *41, hagios* [1]
most holy, *41, hagios* [1]
holy, *1877+43, en+hagiōsynē* [1]
holy fear, *2326, eulabeomai* [1]
holy, *2641, hieros* [1]
holy blessings promised, *4008, hosios* [1]
holy, *4010, hosiōs* [1]

HOMAGE [1]

paid homage, *4686, proskyneō* [1]

HOME [59]

home, *3864, oikia* [11]
home, *3875, oikos* [9]
home, *3875+899, oikos+autos* [5]
at home, *1897, endēmeō* [3]
home, *3875+5148, oikos+sy* [3]
home, *1650+3836+3875+5148,*
  eis+ho+oikos+sy [2]
home, *3836+3875+899, ho+oikos+autos* [2]
home, *RPE* [1]
brought home, *72, agō* [1]
took home, *72, agō* [1]
welcomed home, *346, anadechomai* [1]
on way home, *1639+5715,*
  eimi+hypostrephō [1]
home, *1650+3836+3875+899,*
  eis+ho+oikos+autos [1]
returned home, *2059, epanerchomai* [1]
came home, *2262, erchomai* [1]
comes home, *2262, erchomai* [1]
home, *2997, katoikeō* [1]
home, *2999, katoikētērion* [1]
home, *3665, monē* [1]
his home, *3836+2625, ho+idios* [1]
his own home, *3836+2625, ho+idios* [1]
home, *3836+2625, ho+idios* [1]
home, *3863, oikētērion* [1]
busy at home, *3877, oikourgos* [1]
take home, *4161, paralambanō* [1]
took home, *4161, paralambanō* [1]
made home, *4228, paroikeō* [1]
invited to home, *4689, proslambanō* [1]
opened home to, *5685, hypodechomai* [1]
home, *5715, hypostrephō* [1]
returning home, *5715, hypostrephō* [1]

HOMELESS [1]

homeless, *841, astateō* [1]

HOMES [6]

homes, *3864, oikia* [3]
their homes⁵, *899, autos* [1]
in homes, *2848+3875, kata+oikos* [1]
manage homes, *3866, oikodespoteō* [1]

HOMETOWN [6]

hometown, *4258, patris* [6]

HOMOSEXUAL [1]

homosexual offenders, *780, arsenokoitēs* [1]

HONEST [1]

honest, *1465, dikaios* [1]

HONEY [4]

honey, *3510, meli* [4]

HONOR [57]

honor, *5507, timē* [23]
honor, *5506, timaō* [16]
honor, *1518, doxa* [5]
honor, *AIT* [3]

without honor, *872, atimos* [2]
place of honor, *4752, prōtoklisia* [2]
places of honor, *4752, prōtoklisia* [2]
honor, *1519, doxazō* [1]
honor, *1952+2400, entimos+echō* [1]
held in high honor, *3486, megalynō* [1]
places of honor at the table, *4752, prōtoklisia* [1]

HONORABLE [2]

less honorable, *872, atimos* [1]
honorable, *5507, timē* [1]

HONORABLY [1]

honorably, *2822, kalōs* [1]

HONORED [9]

honored, *1519, doxazō* [4]
honored, *5508, timios* [2]
honored, *1518, doxa* [1]
honored, *1902, endoxos* [1]
honored, *5507+5506, timē+timaō* [1]

HOPE [80]

hope, *1828, elpis* [51]
hope, *1827, elpizō* [11]
put hope, *1827, elpizō* [4]
hope for, *1827, elpizō* [2]
set hope, *1827, elpizō* [2]
hope, *RPE* [1]
in the hope that, *1623, ei* [1]
have hope, *1827+1639, elpizō+eimi* [1]
puts hope, *1827, elpizō* [1]
all hope, *1828, elpis* [1]
in the hope that, *2671, hina* [1]
in the hope that, *3607, mēpote* [1]
this hope^s, *4005, hos* [1]
I hope, *4054, ophelon* [1]
first to hope, *4598, proelpizō* [1]

HOPED [3]

hoped, *1827, elpizō* [2]
hoped, *2671, hina* [1]

HOPES [3]

hopes are set, *1827, elpizō* [1]
hopes for, *1827, elpizō* [1]
hopes, *1827, elpizō* [1]

HOPING [3]

hoping, *1827, elpizō* [2]
hoping, *1623+4803+1538,
    ei+pōs+dynamai* [1]

HORN [1]

horn, *3043, keras* [1]

HORNS [10]

horns, *3043, keras* [10]

HORSE [7]

horse, *2691, hippos* [7]

HORSEMEN [1]

horsemen, *2689, hippeus* [1]

HORSES [10]

horses, *2691, hippos* [10]

HOSANNA [6]

hosanna, *6057, hōsanna* [6]

HOSEA [1]

Hosea, *6060, Hōsēe* [1]

HOSPITABLE [2]

hospitable, *5811, philoxenos* [2]

HOSPITABLY [1]

hospitably, *5819, philophronōs* [1]

HOSPITALITY [5]

showing hospitality, *3827, xenodocheō* [1]
hospitality, *3828, xenos* [1]
show hospitality to, *5696, hypolambanō* [1]
hospitality, *5810, philoxenia* [1]
hospitality, *5811, philoxenos* [1]

HOST [4]

host, *2813, kaleō* [2]
host invited, *2813, kaleō* [1]
host, *5131, stratia* [1]

HOSTILE [2]

hostile, *1885, enantios* [1]
hostile, *2397, echthra* [1]

HOSTILITY [2]

hostility, *2397, echthra* [2]

HOT [4]

hot, *2412, zestos* [2]
seared as with a hot iron, *3013, kaustēriazō* [1]
hot, *3014, kausōn* [1]

HOUR [58]

hour, *6052, hōra* [52]
hour, *RPE* [2]
hour, *4388, pēchys* [2]
at hour, *1181+6052, ginomai+hōra* [1]
half an hour, *2469, hēmiōrion* [1]

HOURS [3]

hours, *6052, hōra* [3]

HOUSE [159]

house, *3864, oikia* [66]
house, *3875, oikos* [59]
house, *RPE* [8]
house, *AIT* [5]
owner of the house, *3867, oikodespotēs* [5]
from house to house, *2848+3875,
    kata+oikos* [4]
from house to house, *2848+3836+3875,
    kata+ho+oikos* [2]
from house to house, *3836+3864, ho+oikia* [2]
owner of a house, *476+3867,
    anthrōpos+oikodespotēs* [1]
house, *885, aulē* [1]
roof of house, *1560, dōma* [1]
at his house, *2795, kakei* [1]
rented house, *3637, misthōma* [1]
house, *3836, ho* [1]
head of the house, *3867, oikodespotēs* [1]
welcomed into house, *5685, hypodechomai* [1]

HOUSEHOLD [21]

household, *3875, oikos* [8]
household, *3864, oikia* [4]
household, *3836, ho* [2]
members of household, *3865, oikiakos* [2]
household, *AIT* [1]
manager of household, *2208, epitropos* [1]
members of household, *3858, oikeios* [1]

servants in household, *3859, oiketeia* [1]
members of household, *3875, oikos* [1]

HOUSEHOLDS [1]

households, *3875, oikos* [1]

HOUSES [6]

houses, *3864, oikia* [4]
houses, *RPE* [1]
houses, *3875, oikos* [1]

HOW [254]

how, *4802, pōs* [82]
how, *NIG* [11]
how much, *4531, posos* [11]
how, *6055, hōs* [11]
how many, *4531, posos* [10]
this is how, *4048, houtōs* [8]
how much, *4498, polys* [8]
how is it, *4802, pōs* [8]
how, *5515, tis* [8]
how long, *2401+4536, heōs+pote* [7]
know how, *3857, oida* [7]
this is how, *1877+4047, en+houtos* [6]
how, *4022, hoti* [6]
how much, *4012, hosos* [5]
that is how, *4048, houtōs* [5]
how, *AIT* [4]
how, *RPE* [4]
how, *1877+5515, en+tis* [4]
how is it that, *1328+5515, dia+tis* [3]
how dreadful, *4026, ouai* [3]
how, *1877, en* [2]
how, *2777, kathōs* [2]
that is how, *2848+3836+899,
    kata+ho+autos* [2]
how, *3590, mē* [2]
how, *3968, hopōs* [2]
how many, *4012, hosos* [2]
how, *4470, pothen* [2]
how often, *4529, posakis* [2]
know how, *1182, ginōskō* [1]
how to gratify, *1650, eis* [1]
this is how, *1666+4047, ek+houtos* [1]
told how, *1687, ekdiēgeomai* [1]
how true, *2093+237, epi+alētheia* [1]
how much, *2462, hēlikos* [1]
look how, *2623, ide* [1]
see how, *2627, idou* [1]
how, *2848+5515, kata+tis* [1]
how dare you, *3590, mē* [1]
how, *3590+1142, mē+gar* [1]
how much more, *3615, mētige* [1]
how, *3836+2848, ho+kata* [1]
how, *3836+4309, ho+peri* [1]
this is how, *3854, hothen* [1]
knows how, *3857, oida* [1]
how, *3888, hoios* [1]
how far will they go, *4047+5515+1639,
    houtos+tis+eimi* [1]
how, *4048, houtōs* [1]
how I wish that, *4054, ophelon* [1]
how great, *4383, pēlikos* [1]
how is it, *4481, poios* [1]
how many times, *4529, posakis* [1]
how much more, *4531, posos* [1]
how, *4531, posos* [1]
how great, *4531, posos* [1]
how great, *4534, potapos* [1]

HOWEVER [32]

however, *1254, de* [23]
however, *4440, plēn* [4]
however, *247, alla* [3]

however, *NIG* [1]
however, *4036, oun* [1]

HUGE [3]

huge, *3489, megas* [2]
huge fish, *3063, kētos* [1]

HUMAN [29]

human, *476, anthrōpos* [10]
human, *474, anthrōpinos* [3]
human, *4922, sarx* [3]
human, *RPE* [1]
in human terms, *474, anthrōpinos* [1]
not built by human hands, *942, acheiropoiētos* [1]
from human point of view, *2848+476, kata+anthrōpos* [1]
human ancestry, *2848+4922, kata+sarx* [1]
human, *2848+476, kata+anthrōpos* [1]
of human, *4921, sarkinos* [1]
human effort, *4922, sarx* [1]
human nature, *4922, sarx* [1]
human standards, *4922, sarx* [1]
sinful human nature, *4922, sarx* [1]
human wisdom, *5053, sophia* [1]
human being, *6034+476, psychē+anthrōpos* [1]

HUMANITY [1]

humanity, *AIT* [1]

HUMBLE [11]

humble, *5424, tapeinos* [4]
humble, *5427, tapeinoō* [3]
in humble circumstances, *5424, tapeinos* [1]
humble, *5425, tapeinophrosynē* [1]
humble, *5426, tapeinophrōn* [1]
humble state, *5428, tapeinōsis* [1]

HUMBLED [4]

humbled, *5427, tapeinoō* [4]

HUMBLES [4]

humbles, *5427, tapeinoō* [4]

HUMBLY [1]

humbly, *1877+4559, en+prautēs* [1]

HUMILIATE [1]

humiliate, *2875, kataischynō* [1]

HUMILIATED [2]

humiliated, *2875, kataischynō* [1]
humiliated, *3552+158, meta+aischynē* [1]

HUMILIATION [1]

humiliation, *5428, tapeinōsis* [1]

HUMILITY [8]

humility, *5425, tapeinophrosynē* [6]
humility, *4559, prautēs* [2]

HUNDRED [25]

hundred, *1669, hekaton* [8]
hundred times, *1671, hekatontaplasiōn* [3]
two hundred, *1357, diakosioi* [2]
five hundred, *4296, pentakosioi* [2]
four hundred, *5484, tetrakosioi* [2]
two hundred million, *1490+3689, dismyrias+myrias* [1]
eight hundred gallons, *1669+1004, hekaton+batos²* [1]
hundred years old, *1670, hekatontaetēs* [1]

eight hundred, *3837, ogdoēkonta* [1]
a hundred and twenty feet deep, *3976+1633, orgyia+eikosi* [1]
four hundred, *4299, pentēkonta* [1]
hundred yards, *4388+1357, pēchys+diakosioi* [1]
hundred pounds, *5418, talantiaios* [1]

HUNDREDS [1]

hundreds, *1669, hekaton* [1]

HUNG [4]

hung, *3203, kremannymi* [3]
hung on, *1717, ekkremannymi* [1]

HUNGER [5]

hunger, *4277, peinaō* [3]
hunger, *3350, limos* [1]
hunger, *3763, nēsteia* [1]

HUNGRY [23]

hungry, *4277, peinaō* [19]
hungry, *3765, nēstis* [2]
go hungry, *4277, peinaō* [1]
hungry, *4698, prospeinos* [1]

HURLED [11]

hurled, *965, ballō* [4]
hurled insults at, *1059, blasphēmeō* [3]
hurled down, *965, ballō* [2]
hurled insults at, *3366, loidoreō* [2]

HURRICANE [1]

of hurricane force, *5607, typhōnikos* [1]

HURRIED [4]

hurried off, *2262+5067, erchomai+speudō* [1]
hurried, *3552+5082, meta+spoudē* [1]
hurried, *4513+3552+5082, poreuomai+meta+spoudē* [1]
hurried, *5444, tachys* [1]

HURRY [1]

in a hurry, *5067, speudō* [1]

HURT [5]

hurt, *92, adikeō* [2]
hurt, *3382, lypeō* [2]
hurt, *1055, blaptō* [1]

HUSBAND [39]

husband, *467, anēr* [36]
believing husband, *81, adelphos* [1]
husband, *476, anthrōpos* [1]
faithful to her husband, *1651+467+1222, heis+anēr+gynē* [1]

HUSBAND'S [2]

husband's, *467, anēr* [2]

HUSBANDS [13]

husbands, *467, anēr* [12]
love their husbands, *5791, philandros* [1]

HYMENAEUS [2]

Hymenaeus, *5628, Hymenaios* [2]

HYMN [3]

sung a hymn, *5630, hymneō* [2]
hymn, *6011, psalmos* [1]

HYMNS [4]

hymns, *5631, hymnos* [2]
singing hymns, *5630, hymneō* [1]
sing hymns, *6010, psallō* [1]

HYPOCRISY [6]

hypocrisy, *5694, hypokrisis* [5]
joined in hypocrisy, *5347, synypokrinomai* [1]

HYPOCRITE [2]

hypocrite, *5695, hypokritēs* [2]

HYPOCRITES [15]

hypocrites, *5695, hypokritēs* [15]

HYPOCRITICAL [1]

hypocritical, *5694, hypokrisis* [1]

HYSSOP [2]

branches of hyssop, *5727, hyssōpos* [1]
stalk of the hyssop plant, *5727, hyssōpos* [1]

I [2253]

I, *AIT* [1572]
I, *1609, egō* [435]
I, *RPE* [133]
I, *2743, kagō* [28]
and I, *2743, kagō* [24]
I, *NIG* [8]
I also, *2743, kagō* [8]
I myself, *1609, egō* [5]
so I, *2743, kagō* [5]
I, *1847, emos* [4]
I, *899, autos* [3]
I too, *2743, kagō* [3]
I, *1831, emautou* [2]
and I too, *2743, kagō* [2]
I have, *3836+1847, ho+emos* [2]
I wish, *4054, ophelon* [2]
as surely as I live, *2409+1609, zaō+egō* [1]
I assure you, *2627, idou* [1]
I tell you, *2627, idou* [1]
but I, *2743, kagō* [1]
I myself, *2743, kagō* [1]
and I myself, *2743, kagō* [1]
if I, *2743, kagō* [1]
so that I, *2743, kagō* [1]
I mean that just as surely as, *3755, nē* [1]
I, *3836+6034+1609, ho+psychē+egō* [1]
I, *4005, hos* [1]
as I did, *4047+899, houtos+autos* [1]
how I wish that, *4054, ophelon* [1]
I hope, *4054, ophelon* [1]
what I meant, *4309+4047, peri+houtos* [1]
I, *6034+1609, psychē+egō* [1]

I'LL [5]

I'll, *AIT* [5]

I'M [5]

I'm, *AIT* [3]
I'm, *RPE* [1]
I'm, *1609+1639, egō+eimi* [1]

I'VE [2]

I've, *AIT* [2]

ICONIUM [6]

Iconium, *2658, Ikonion* [6]

IDEA [5]

idea, *3857, oida* [2]
idea, *AIT* [1]
idea, *2451, hēgeomai* [1]
had idea, *3857, oida* [1]

IDEAS [3]

ideas, *AIT* [1]
opposing ideas, *509, antithesis* [1]
ideas^s, *5516, tis* [1]

IDLE [6]

idle, *734, argos* [1]
idle, *863, atakteō* [1]
idle, *864, ataktos* [1]
idle, *865, ataktōs* [1]
with idle notions, *1632, eikē* [1]
idle, *4344+865, peripateō+ataktōs* [1]

IDLERS [1]

idlers, *734, argos* [1]

IDOL [5]

idol, *1631, eidōlon* [2]
food sacrificed to an idol, *1628, eidōlothytos* [1]
sacrifice offered to an idol, *1628, eidōlothytos* [1]
made an idol in the form of a calf, *3674, moschopoieō* [1]

IDOL'S [1]

idol's temple, *1627, eidōleion* [1]

IDOLATER [2]

idolater, *1629, eidōlolatrēs* [2]

IDOLATERS [5]

idolaters, *1629, eidōlolatrēs* [5]

IDOLATRY [4]

idolatry, *1630, eidōlolatria* [4]

IDOLS [18]

idols, *1631, eidōlon* [8]
food sacrificed to idols, *1628, eidōlothytos* [5]
sacrificed to idols, *1628, eidōlothytos* [2]
idols, *RPE* [1]
full of idols, *2977, kateidōlos* [1]
idols, *5596, typos* [1]

IDUMEA [1]

Idumea, *2628, Idoumaia* [1]

IF [653]

if, *1623, ei* [303]
if, *1569, ean* [197]
if, *AIT* [31]
if, *323, an* [17]
as if, *6055, hōs* [16]
if, *1664, eite* [11]
if, *NIG* [9]
if, *RPE* [9]
if, *1623+3525, ei+men* [7]
if, *2779, kai* [7]
if, *2829, kan* [4]
even if, *2829, kan* [3]
if not, *247, alla* [2]
even if, *1569, ean* [2]
if, *1570, eanper* [2]
if he does, *1623+1254+3590, ei+de+mē* [2]
if, *1642, eiper* [2]
if you do, *3607, mēpote* [2]

if, *3607, mēpote* [2]
if, *247, alla* [1]
if, *1142, gar* [1]
see if, *1182, ginōskō* [1]
if, *1254, de* [1]
but if, *1623+3590, ei+mē* [1]
what if, *1623, ei* [1]
if, *1623+1145, ei+ge* [1]
if, *1623+726, ei+ara* [1]
to see if, *1623, ei* [1]
if in fact, *1642+726, eiper+ara* [1]
if indeed, *1642, eiper* [1]
if it could, *2075, epei* [1]
if that were so, *2075, epei* [1]
now if, *2075, epei* [1]
if it were, *2075, epei* [1]
if, *2671, hina* [1]
if I, *2743, kagō* [1]
if so, *2779, kai* [1]
what if, *2779, kai* [1]
if even, *2829, kan* [1]
if any, *4005+323, hos+an* [1]
if, *4022, hoti* [1]
just as if, *4048, houtōs* [1]
acted as if, *4701, prospoieō* [1]
if only, *6055, hōs* [1]

IGNOBLE [1]

ignoble, *871, atimia* [1]

IGNORANCE [6]

ignorance, *53, agnoia* [4]
ignorance, *51, agnoeō* [1]
sins committed in ignorance, *52, agnoēma* [1]

IGNORANT [8]

ignorant, *51, agnoeō* [5]
ignorant, *57, agnōsia* [2]
ignorant, *276, amathēs* [1]

IGNORE [1]

ignore, *288, ameleō* [1]

IGNORED [1]

ignored, *51, agnoeō* [1]

IGNORES [1]

ignores, *51, agnoeō* [1]

IGNORING [1]

ignoring, *4159, parakouō* [1]

ILL [4]

ill, *820, astheneō* [2]
ill effects, *2805, kakos* [1]
ill, *2809+2400, kakōs+echō* [1]

ILLEGITIMATE [2]

illegitimate children, *1666+4518+1164, ek+porneia+gennaō* [1]
illegitimate children, *3785, nothos* [1]

ILLNESS [2]

illness, *RPE* [1]
illness, *819+3836+4922, astheneia+ho+sarx* [1]

ILLNESSES [2]

illnesses, *819, astheneia* [1]
illnesses, *3798, nosos* [1]

ILLUMINATED [1]

illuminated, *5894, phōtizō* [1]

ILLUSTRATION [1]

illustration, *4130, parabolē* [1]

ILLYRICUM [1]

Illyricum, *2665, Illyrikon* [1]

IMAGE [15]

image, *1635, eikōn* [13]
image which fell from heaven, *1479, diopetēs* [1]
image, *5916, charagma* [1]

IMAGES [1]

images, *1635, eikōn* [1]

IMAGINE [1]

imagine, *3783, noeō* [1]

IMITATE [4]

imitate, *3628, mimeomai* [2]
imitate, *3629+1181, mimētēs+ginomai* [1]
imitate, *3629, mimētēs* [1]

IMITATORS [3]

imitators, *3629, mimētēs* [3]

IMMANUEL [1]

Immanuel, *1842, Emmanouēl* [1]

IMMEASURABLY [1]

immeasurably, *5655, hyperekperissou* [1]

IMMEDIATE [1]

immediate family, *3858, oikeios* [1]

IMMEDIATELY [46]

immediately, *2311, eutheōs* [19]
immediately, *2317, euthys1* [13]
immediately, *4202, parachrēma* [9]
immediately, *AIT* [1]
immediately, *1877+5443, en+tachos* [1]
immediately, *1877+899+3836+6052, en+autos+ho+hōra* [1]
immediately, *1994, exautēs* [1]
immediately, *5067, speudō* [1]

IMMORAL [9]

sexually immoral, *4521, pornos* [7]
immoral, *4521, pornos* [2]

IMMORALITY [21]

sexual immorality, *4518, porneia* [13]
immorality, *4518, porneia* [2]
license for immorality, *816, aselgeia* [1]
gave up to sexual immorality, *1745, ekporneuō* [1]
sexual immorality, *3130, koitē* [1]
commit sexual immorality, *4519, porneuō* [1]
committing sexual immorality, *4519, porneuō* [1]
sexual immorality, *4519, porneuō* [1]

IMMORTAL [3]

immortal, *915, aphthartos* [2]
immortal, *114, athanasia* [1]

IMMORTALITY [4]

immortality, *114, athanasia* [2]
immortality, *914, aphtharsia* [2]

IMPART [2]

impart life, *2443, zōopoieō* [1]
impart, *3556, metadidōmi* [1]

IMPARTIAL [1]

impartial, *88, adiakritos* [1]

IMPARTIALLY [1]

impartially, *719, aprosōpolēmptōs* [1]

IMPERFECT [1]

imperfect, *1666+3538, ek+meros* [1]

IMPERIAL [1]

Imperial, *4935, sebastos* [1]

IMPERISHABLE [6]

imperishable, *914, aphtharsia* [3]
imperishable, *915, aphthartos* [2]
imperishable, *1877+914, en+aphtharsia* [1]

IMPLORE [1]

implore, *1289, deomai* [1]

IMPORTANCE [1]

as of first importance, *1877+4755,*
    en+prōtos [1]

IMPORTANT [14]

most important seats, *4751, prōtokathedria* [4]
most important, *4755, prōtos* [2]
important, *AIT* [1]
important, *RPE* [1]
more important matters, *987, barys* [1]
important official, *1541, dynastēs* [1]
least important, *2274, eschatos* [1]
more important than, *4358, perissoteros* [1]
important thing, *4440, plēn* [1]
important, *5516, tis* [1]

IMPOSE [1]

impose, *965, ballō* [1]

IMPOSSIBLE [10]

impossible, *105, adynatos* [7]
impossible, *104, adynateō* [2]
impossible, *4024+1543, ou+dynatos* [1]

IMPOSTORS [2]

impostors, *1200, goēs* [1]
impostors, *4418, planos* [1]

IMPRESSION [1]

make a good impression, *2349, euprosōpeō* [1]

IMPRISON [1]

imprison, *5872, phylakizō* [1]

IMPRISONMENT [2]

imprisonment, *1301, desmos* [2]

IMPRISONMENTS [1]

imprisonments, *5871, phylakē* [1]

IMPROPER [1]

improper[s], *4560, prepō* [1]

IMPROPERLY [1]

acting improperly, *858, aschēmoneō* [1]

IMPURE [9]

impure, *3123, koinos* [4]
impure, *174, akatharsia* [2]
call impure, *3124, koinoō* [2]
impure, *176, akathartos* [1]

IMPURITY [7]

impurity, *174, akatharsia* [6]
sexual impurity, *174, akatharsia* [1]

IN [2905]

in, *1877, en* [1412]
in, *AIT* [375]
in, *1650, eis* [165]
in, *NIG* [106]
in, *2093, epi* [73]
in, *2848, kata* [42]
in, *1666, ek* [17]
in order that, *2671, hina* [16]
in, *1328, dia* [13]
in, *608, apo* [11]
in the same way, *4048, houtōs* [11]
in, *RPE* [10]
in order to, *2671, hina* [10]
in the same way, *3931, homoiōs* [10]
in the presence, *1967, enōpion* [9]
in fact, *2779, kai* [8]
in this way, *4048, houtōs* [8]
in, *4639, pros* [8]
went in, *1656, eiserchomai* [7]
in front of, *1869, emprosthen* [7]
go in, *1656, eiserchomai* [6]
in accordance with, *2848, kata* [6]
in, *5642, hyper* [6]
in the same way, *6058, hōsautōs* [6]
in fact, *247, alla* [5]
in Aramaic, *1580, Hebraisti* [5]
come in, *1656, eiserchomai* [5]
at work in, *1919+1877, energeō+en* [5]
in the sight, *1967, enōpion* [5]
put in charge, *2770, kathistēmi* [5]
experts in the law, *3788, nomikos* [5]
in regard to, *4309, peri* [5]
put in, *965, ballō* [4]
given in marriage, *1139, gamizō* [4]
in fact, *1142, gar* [4]
came in, *1656, eiserchomai* [4]
in front, *1967, enōpion* [4]
in the eyes, *1967, enōpion* [4]
dressed in, *4314, periballō* [4]
brought in, *72, agō* [3]
received in full, *600, apechō* [3]
in Aramaic, *1579+1365, Hebrais+dialektos* [3]
in order that, *1650+3836, eis+ho* [3]
comes in, *1656, eiserchomai* [3]
come in, *1660, eisporeuomai* [3]
in the presence, *1869, emprosthen* [3]
while in, *1877, en* [3]
dressed in, *1907, endyō* [3]
in sight, *1967, enōpion* [3]
in turn, *2779, kai* [3]
in every, *2848, kata* [3]
in keeping with, *2848, kata* [3]
in various, *2848, kata* [3]
in, *3552, meta* [3]
really in need, *3953, ontōs* [3]
in, *4309, peri* [3]
called in, *4673, proskaleō* [3]
in right mind, *5404, sōphroneō* [3]
in exchange for, *498, antallagma* [2]
in keeping with, *545, axios* [2]

in a manner worthy, *547, axiōs* [2]
in part, *608+3538, apo+meros* [2]
speaking in tongues, *1185, glōssa* [2]
in prison, *1300, desmios* [2]
in prison, *1313, deō* [2]
in answer to, *1328, dia* [2]
struck in the face, *1443+4825,*
    didōmi+rhapisma [2]
break in, *1482, dioryssō* [2]
in slavery, *1529, doulos2* [2]
in Hebrew, *1580, Hebraisti* [2]
grafted in, *1596, enkentrizō* [2]
live in peace, *1644, eirēneuō* [2]
brought in, *1652, eisagō* [2]
arrived in, *1656+1650, eiserchomai+eis* [2]
in presence, *1869, emprosthen* [2]
in spite of, *1877, en* [2]
in, *1877+3545, en+mesos* [2]
three in the afternoon, *1888, enatos* [2]
at work in, *1919, energeō* [2]
works in, *1919+1877, energeō+en* [2]
lives in, *1940+1877, enoikeō+en* [2]
in presence, *1967, enōpion* [2]
in accordance with, *2093, epi* [2]
in the account, *2093, epi* [2]
continue in, *2152, epimenō* [2]
in heaven, *2230, epouranios* [2]
in search of, *2426, zēteō* [2]
in accordance with, *2777, kathōs* [2]
in obedience to, *2848, kata* [2]
in the ordinary way, *2848+4922, kata+sarx* [2]
in the sight, *2978, katenanti* [2]
in sight, *2979, katenōpion* [2]
in, *2997, katoikeō* [2]
lived in, *2997, katoikeō* [2]
living in, *2997, katoikeō* [2]
in vain, *3031, kenos* [2]
put in order, *3175, kosmeō* [2]
in vain, *3472, matēn* [2]
share in, *3581, metochos* [2]
expert in the law, *3788, nomikos* [2]
in, *3836, ho* [2]
in agony, *3849, odynaō* [2]
in the same way, *4048+2779, houtōs+kai* [2]
in these words, *4048, houtōs* [2]
in sight, *4123, para* [2]
put in prison, *4140, paradidōmi* [2]
clothed in, *4314, periballō* [2]
in error, *4414, planaō* [2]
prepared in advance, *4602, proetoimazō* [2]
in order to, *4639, pros* [2]
early in the morning, *4745, prōi* [2]
in the morning, *4745, prōi* [2]
wrapped in cloths, *5058, sparganoō* [2]
invite in, *5251, synagō* [2]
put in, *5502, tithēmi* [2]
in, *5679, hypo* [2]
in submission, *5718, hypotassō* [2]
have in mind, *5858, phroneō* [2]
sins committed in ignorance, *52, agnoēma* [1]
competes in the games, *76, agōnizomai* [1]
called out in a loud voice, *149+5889,*
    airō+phōnē [1]
led captives in his train, *169+168,*
    aichmalōteuō+aichmalōsia [1]
in addition, *247+2779, alla+kai* [1]
early in the morning, *275+4745, hama+prōi* [1]
climbs in, *326, anabainō* [1]
sit in judgment on, *373, anakrinō* [1]
in human terms, *474, anthrōpinos* [1]
in return, *500, antapodidōmi* [1]
in place, *505, anti* [1]
in conflict, *512, antikeimai* [1]
in a way worthy, *547, axiōs* [1]
in absence, *582, apeimi1* [1]
in front of, *595, apenanti* [1]

in the future, *608+785, apo+arti* [1]
in store, *641, apokeimai* [1]
in reply, *646, apokrinomai* [1]
say in reply, *646, apokrinomai* [1]
made an opening in, *689, apostegazō* [1]
in that case, *726, ara* [1]
done in ungodly way, *814, asebeō* [1]
in same way, *899, autos* [1]
led in revolt, *923+3958, aphistēmi+opisō* [1]
lying in bed, *965, ballō* [1]
threw in, *965, ballō* [1]
in force, *1010, bebaios* [1]
looked in, *1063, blepō* [1]
had in mind, *1089, boulomai* [1]
giving in marriage, *1139, gamizō* [1]
given in marriage, *1140, gamiskō* [1]
in, *1142, gar* [1]
in the morning, *1181+2465,*
    ginomai+hēmera [1]
participate in, *1181+3128,*
    ginomai+koinōnos [1]
keep in mind, *1182, ginōskō* [1]
in rags, *1217, gymniteuō* [1]
in addition, *1254, de* [1]
in chains, *1313, deō* [1]
in keeping with, *1328, dia* [1]
in the presence of, *1328, dia* [1]
in view of, *1328, dia* [1]
in the service of, *1354, diakoneō* [1]
in safety, *1407, diasōzō* [1]
in slavery, *1526, douleuō* [1]
in slavery, *1530, douloō* [1]
written in, *1582+1877, engraphō+en* [1]
in danger of, *1584, engys* [1]
graft in, *1596, enkentrizō* [1]
grafted in among, *1596+1877,*
    enkentrizō+en [1]
cut in on, *1601, enkoptō* [1]
in the habit of, *1621, ethos* [1]
in the hope that, *1623, ei* [1]
in vain, *1632, eikē* [1]
give in, *1634+3836+5717,*
    eikō+ho+hypotagē [1]
had taken part in a rebellion, *1639+3334,*
    eimi+lēstēs [1]
in charge of, *1639+2093, eimi+epi* [1]
put in chains, *1639+1313, eimi+deō* [1]
if in fact, *1642+726, eiper+ara* [1]
in this way, *1650+3836, eis+ho* [1]
with this in mind, *1650+899, eis+autos* [1]
in agreement, *1650+3836+1651,*
    eis+ho+heis [1]
in dealing with, *1650, eis* [1]
in order that, *1650, eis* [1]
in order to bring, *1650, eis* [1]
in regard to, *1650, eis* [1]
result in, *1650, eis* [1]
bring in, *1652, eisagō* [1]
come in among, *1656+1650,*
    eiserchomai+eis [1]
get in, *1656, eiserchomai* [1]
in, *1656, eiserchomai* [1]
rushed in, *1659, eispēdaō* [1]
went in, *1660, eisporeuomai* [1]
in front of, *1666+1885, ek+enantios* [1]
result in, *1666+1181, ek+ginomai* [1]
but in the other case, *1695+1254, ekei+de* [1]
in that place, *1695, ekei* [1]
in, *1695, ekei* [1]
[in] Greek, *1822, Hellēnisti* [1]
haul in, *1816, helkyō* [1]
stayed in, *1844+1877, emmenō+en* [1]
entangled in, *1861, emplekō* [1]
involved in, *1861, emplekō* [1]
in faces, *1869, emprosthen* [1]
in front, *1869, emprosthen* [1]

in full view of, *1869, emprosthen* [1]
in fear, *1873+1181, emphobos+ginomai* [1]
planted in, *1875, emphytos* [1]
in addition, *1877, en* [1]
at work in, *1877+1919, en+energeō* [1]
in accordance with, *1877, en* [1]
in comparison with,
    1877+4047+3836+3538+1641,
    en+houtos+ho+meros+heineken [1]
in presence, *1877, en* [1]
in the cause of, *1877, en* [1]
taking in his arms, *1878, enankalizomai* [1]
took in arms, *1878, enankalizomai* [1]
in public, *1883+3836+3295,*
    enantion+ho+laos [1]
in the sight, *1883, enantion* [1]
dressed in, *1898, endidyskō* [1]
in place, *1907, endyō* [1]
waiting in ambush for, *1910, enedreuō* [1]
wrapped in, *1912, eneileō* [1]
exerted in, *1919+1877, energeō+en* [1]
produces in, *1919+1877, energeō+en* [1]
dwell in, *1940+1877, enoikeō+en* [1]
lived in, *1940+1877, enoikeō+en* [1]
in danger, *1944, enochos* [1]
in full view, *1967, enōpion* [1]
in his sight, *1967+899, enōpion+autos* [1]
in despair, *1989, exaporeō* [1]
in charge, *2026, exousia* [1]
in that case, *2075+726, epei+ara* [1]
in addition, *2093+1254, epi+de* [1]
in the days of, *2093, epi* [1]
holding in, *2093, epi* [1]
in connection with, *2093, epi* [1]
in front of, *2093, epi* [1]
in one place, *2093+3836+899,*
    epi+ho+autos [1]
in the time of, *2093, epi* [1]
arriving in, *2094, epibainō* [1]
trap in, *2138, epilambanomai* [1]
persevere in, *2152, epimenō* [1]
persist in, *2152, epimenō* [1]
bring in, *2262, erchomai* [1]
get in, *2262, erchomai* [1]
on way in, *2262, erchomai* [1]
in, *2276, esō* [1]
very early in the morning, *2317+4745,*
    euthys¹+prōi [1]
in season, *2323, eukairōs* [1]
glory in, *2400+3018, echō+kauchēsis* [1]
in leaf, *2400+5877, echō+phyllon* [1]
in this condition, *2400, echō* [1]
bear in mind, *2451, hēgeomai* [1]
late in afternoon, *2465+806+3111,*
    hēmera+archō+klinō [1]
in order to, *2527, thelō* [1]
those in trouble, *2567, thlibō* [1]
leads in triumphal procession, *2581,*
    thriambeuō [1]
offered in sacrifice, *2638, hierothytos* [1]
in the hope that, *2671, hina* [1]
puts in charge, *2770, kathistēmi* [1]
in the words*, *2777, kathōs* [1]
in fact, *2779+1142, kai+gar* [1]
although in fact, *2793, kaitoige* [1]
called in, *2813, kaleō* [1]
anywhere else in, *2848, kata* [1]
found in, *2848, kata* [1]
in any way, *2848+3594+5573,*
    kata+mēdeis+tropos [1]
in conformity with, *2848, kata* [1]
in each, *2848, kata* [1]
in homes, *2848+3875, kata+oikos* [1]
in regard to, *2848, kata* [1]
in response to, *2848, kata* [1]
in the way, *2848, kata* [1]

in this way*, *2848+4922, kata+sarx* [1]
in turn, *2848+1651, kata+heis* [1]
in whole, *2848, kata* [1]
clearly in the wrong, *2861, kataginōskō* [1]
put in, *2864, katagō* [1]
in bed, *2879, katakeimai* [1]
sick in bed, *2879, katakeimai* [1]
caught in the act, *2898+2093+900,*
    katalambanō+epi+autophōros [1]
engrossed in, *2974, katachraomai* [1]
result in, *2981, katergazomai* [1]
instructed in, *2994, katēcheō* [1]
receives instruction in, *2994, katēcheō* [1]
dwells in, *2997, katoikeō* [1]
live in, *2997, katoikeō* [1]
in danger of, *3073, kindyneuō* [1]
in great danger, *3073, kindyneuō* [1]
share in the inheritance, *3099, klēronomeō* [1]
in common, *3123, koinos* [1]
sitting in judgment, *3216, kritēs* [1]
in a circle, *3241, kyklō* [1]
in luxury, *3289, lamprōs* [1]
cut in the rock, *3292, laxeutos* [1]
in Lycaonian language, *3378, Lykaonisti* [1]
held in high honor, *3486, megalynō* [1]
in common, *3535, meris* [1]
in two, *3545, mesos* [1]
in, *3545, mesos* [1]
in presence, *3552+3836+4725,*
    meta+ho+prosōpon [1]
involved in, *3552, meta* [1]
share in, *3561, metalambanō* [1]
turn in repentance, *3567, metanoia* [1]
shared in, *3576, metechō* [1]
sharing in, *3576, metechō* [1]
in common, *3580, metochē* [1]
shared in, *3581+1181, metochos+ginomai* [1]
not in the least, *3594, mēdeis* [1]
in the hope that, *3607, mēpote* [1]
made an idol in the form of a calf, *3674,*
    moschopoieō [1]
in fact, *3815, nyni* [1]
live in harmony, *3836+899+5858,*
    ho+autos+phroneō [1]
the expert in the law*, *3836+1254, ho+de* [1]
in full, *3836+2698, ho+isos* [1]
in person, *3836+4242+3836+5393,*
    ho+parousia+ho+sōma [1]
in the present case, *3836+3814, ho+nyn* [1]
keep in suspense, *3836+6034+149,*
    ho+psychē+airō [1]
in mind, *3857, oida* [1]
servants in household, *3859, oiketeia* [1]
lives in, *3861, oikeō* [1]
live in, *3864, oikia* [1]
live in harmony with, *3939, homophrōn* [1]
even in the case of, *3940, homōs* [1]
in back, *3957, opisthen* [1]
in the case of, *3963, hopou* [1]
in order to, *3968, hopōs* [1]
acting in line, *3980, orthopodeō* [1]
came early in the morning, *3983, orthrizō* [1]
very early in the morning, *3986+960,*
    orthros+bathys [1]
in keeping with income,
    4005+5516+1569+2338,
    hos+tis+ean+euodoō [1]
in the same way, *4005+5573, hos+tropos* [1]
in these, *4005, hos* [1]
in this, *4022, hoti* [1]
one in which, *4023, hou* [1]
not in the least, *4029, oudeis* [1]
in heaven, *4039, ouranios* [1]
in other words, *4047+1639, houtos+eimi* [1]
in the following, *4047, houtos* [1]
in all, *4047+1639, houtos+eimi* [1]

INASMUCH [1]

INCENSE [9]

INCITED [1]

INCITING [1]

INCLUDE [1]

INCLUDED [1]

INCLUDES [1]

INCLUDING [5]

INCOME [2]

INCOMPARABLE [1]

INCOMPARABLY [1]

INCREASE [7]

INCREASED [5]

INCREASES [1]

INCREASING [3]

INCREDIBLE [1]

INDECENT [1]

INDEED [24]

INDEPENDENT [2]

INDESCRIBABLE [1]

INDESTRUCTIBLE [1]

INDICATE [2]

INDICATING [2]

INDIGNANT [6]

INDIGNANTLY [1]

saying indignantly, *24, aganakteō* [1]

INDIGNATION [1]

indignation, *25, aganaktēsis* [1]

INDISPENSABLE [1]

indispensable, *338, anankaios* [1]

INDOORS [2]

indoors, *1650+3836+3864, eis+ho+oikia* [1]
indoors, *1650+3875, eis+oikos* [1]

INDULGE [5]

indulge, *929, aphormē* [1]
indulge, *2238, ergasia* [1]
indulge in pagan revelry, *4089, paizō* [1]
indulge, *4621, prokoptō* [1]
indulge, *5639, hyparchō* [1]

INDULGED [1]

indulged, *4556, prassō* [1]

INDULGENCE [1]

indulgence, *4447, plēsmonē* [1]

INDULGING [1]

indulging, *4668, prosechō* [1]

INEFFECTIVE [1]

ineffective, *734, argos* [1]

INEXPRESSIBLE [2]

inexpressible, *443, aneklalētos* [1]
inexpressible, *777, arrētos* [1]

INFANCY [1]

infancy, *1100, brephos* [1]

INFANT [1]

infant, *3758, nēpios* [1]

INFANTS [5]

infants, *3758, nēpios* [3]
infants, *2558, thēlazō* [1]
infants, *3757, nēpiazō* [1]

INFERIOR [3]

inferior to, *5728, hystereō* [2]
inferior, *2273, hessoomai* [1]

INFILTRATED [1]

infiltrated ranks, *4207+4209,*
    pareisaktos+pareiserchomai [1]

INFIRMITIES [1]

infirmities, *819, astheneia* [1]

INFIRMITY [1]

infirmity, *819, astheneia* [1]

INFLAMED [1]

inflamed, *1706, ekkaiō* [1]

INFLICT [1]

inflict injury, *92, adikeō* [1]

INFLICTED [1]

inflicted, *AIT* [1]

INFLUENCED [1]

influenced, *72, agō* [1]

INFLUENTIAL [1]

influential, *1543, dynatos* [1]

INFORMATION [2]

information, *1336, diaginōskō* [1]
information, *4785, pynthanomai* [1]

INFORMED [3]

informed, *1317, dēloō* [1]
informed, *2994, katēcheō* [1]
informed, *3606, mēnyō* [1]

INHABIT [1]

inhabit, *2997, katoikeō* [1]

INHABITANTS [8]

inhabitants, *2997, katoikeō* [7]
inhabitants of, *2997, katoikeō* [1]

INHERIT [16]

inherit, *3099, klēronomeō* [15]
inherit, *3101, klēronomos* [1]

INHERITANCE [19]

inheritance, *3100, klēronomia* [14]
gave to as inheritance, *2883,*
    kataklēronomeō [1]
share in the inheritance, *3099, klēronomeō* [1]
take inheritance, *3099, klēronomeō* [1]
inheritance, *3102, klēros* [1]
inheritance rights as the oldest son, *4757,*
    prōtotokia [1]

INHERITED [1]

inherited, *3099, klēronomeō* [1]

INITIATIVE [1]

on own initiative, *882, authairetos* [1]

INJURED [1]

injured, *92, adikeō* [1]

INJURING [1]

injuring, *1055, blaptō* [1]

INJURY [1]

inflict injury, *92, adikeō* [1]

INK [3]

ink, *3506, melas* [3]

INMOST [1]

inmost, *2840, kardia* [1]

INN [2]

inn, *2906, katalyma* [1]
inn, *4106, pandocheion* [1]

INNER [8]

inner, *2276, esō* [2]
inner, *2278, esōteros* [2]
inner rooms, *5421, tameion* [2]
inner, *1311, deuteros* [1]
inner, *3220, kryptos* [1]

INNKEEPER [1]

innkeeper, *4107, pandocheus* [1]

INNOCENT [11]

innocent, *127, athōos* [2]
innocent, *193, akeraios* [2]
innocent, *360, anaitios* [2]
innocent, *1465, dikaios* [2]
innocent, *54, hagnos* [1]
make innocent, *1467, dikaioō* [1]
innocent, *2754, katharos* [1]

INQUIRE [1]

inquire about, *3443, manthanō* [1]

INQUIRED [2]

inquired, *3306, legō* [1]
inquired, *4785, pynthanomai* [1]

INSANE [2]

insane, *3419, mainomai* [1]
insane, *3444, mania* [1]

INSCRIPTION [5]

inscription, *2107, epigraphē* [3]
inscription, *AIT* [1]
this inscription, *4005+2108, hos+epigraphō* [1]

INSIDE [18]

inside, *2277, esōthen* [4]
went inside, *1656+1650, eiserchomai+eis* [3]
inside, *AIT* [2]
inside, *2276, esō* [2]
on the inside, *2277, esōthen* [2]
went inside, *1656, eiserchomai* [1]
inside, *1877, en* [1]
inside, *1913, eneimi* [1]
inside, *1955, entos* [1]
from inside, *2277, esōthen* [1]

INSIGHT [4]

insight, *5304, synesis* [2]
insight, *151, aisthēsis* [1]
insight, *3808, nous* [1]

INSIST [1]

insist on it, *3458, martyromai* [1]

INSISTED [4]

insisted, *646, apokrinomai* [1]
insisted, *2196, epischyō* [1]
insisted, *3281, laleō* [1]
insisted, *3306, legō* [1]

INSISTENTLY [1]

insistently, *2130, epikeimai* [1]

INSISTING [1]

insisting that, *1462, diischyrizomai* [1]

INSOLENT [1]

insolent, *5616, hybristēs* [1]

INSPIRED [1]

inspired, *AIT* [1]

INSTANT [1]

instant, *5117+5989, stigmē+chronos* [1]

INSTANTLY [2]

instantly, *4202, parachrēma* [2]

INSTEAD [41]

instead, *247, alla* [20]
instead, *1254, de* [6]
instead, *3437, mallon* [3]
instead, *505, anti* [2]
instead of, *3437+2445, mallon+ē* [2]
but instead, *247, alla* [1]
instead, *247+3437, alla+mallon* [1]
instead of, *247, alla* [1]
instead, *2671, hina* [1]
instead of, *2779+4049, kai+ouchi* [1]
instead of, *3594, mēdeis* [1]
instead, *3814+1254, nyn+de* [1]
instead, *5539+3437, tounantion+mallon* [1]

INSTINCT [2]

creatures of instinct, *5879, physikos* [1]
instinct, *5880, physikōs* [1]

INSTINCTS [1]

follow mere natural instincts, *6035,
    psychikos* [1]

INSTITUTED [2]

instituted, *AIT* [1]
instituted, *1408, diatagē* [1]

INSTRUCT [4]

instruct, *2994, katēcheō* [1]
instruct, *3805, noutheteō* [1]
instruct, *4084, paideuō* [1]
instruct, *5204, symbibazō* [1]

INSTRUCTED [8]

instructed, *1438, didaskō* [1]
instructed, *1948, entellō* [1]
instructed in, *2994, katēcheō* [1]
instructed, *2994, katēcheō* [1]
instructed, *3411, mathēteuō* [1]
instructed, *3443, manthanō* [1]
instructed, *4161+4123, paralambanō+para* [1]
instructed, *5332, syntassō* [1]

INSTRUCTING [1]

instructing, *1411, diatassō* [1]

INSTRUCTION [10]

word of instruction, *1439, didachē* [2]
instruction, *3364, logos* [2]
instruction, *RPE* [1]
careful instruction, *1439, didachē* [1]
instruction, *1439, didachē* [1]
receives instruction in, *2994, katēcheō* [1]
instruction, *3804, nouthesia* [1]
instruction, *4132, parangelia* [1]

INSTRUCTIONS [11]

instructions, *AIT* [2]
instructions, *4133, parangellō* [2]
gave instructions, *1948, entellō* [1]
giving instructions, *1948, entellō* [1]
instructions, *1953, entolē* [1]
with instructions, *3284+1953,
    lambanō+entolē* [1]
instructions, *4132, parangelia* [1]
give instructions, *4133, parangellō* [1]
shouted instructions, *5204, symbibazō* [1]

INSTRUCTOR [2]

instructor, *2994, katēcheō* [1]
instructor, *4083, paideutēs* [1]

INSTRUMENT [2]

instrument, *5007, skeuos* [2]

INSTRUMENTS [2]

instruments, *3960, hoplon* [2]

INSULT [9]

insult, *3943, oneidizō* [3]
insult, *3367, loidoria* [2]
insult, *5614, hybrizō* [2]
insult, *3366, loidoreō* [1]
insult, *3944, oneidismos* [1]

INSULTED [4]

insulted, *869, atimazō* [1]
insulted, *1964, enybrizō* [1]
insulted, *3943, oneidizō* [1]
insulted, *5614, hybrizō* [1]

INSULTING [1]

insulting, *1059, blasphēmeō* [1]

INSULTS [9]

hurled insults at, *1059, blasphēmeō* [3]
hurled insults at, *3366, loidoreō* [2]
heaped insults on, *3943, oneidizō* [2]
insults, *3944, oneidismos* [1]
insults, *5615, hybris* [1]

INSURRECTION [2]

insurrection, *5087, stasis* [2]

INSURRECTIONISTS [1]

insurrectionists, *5086, stasiastēs* [1]

INTEGRITY [3]

integrity, *239, alēthēs* [2]
integrity, *917, aphthoria* [1]

INTELLIGENCE [1]

intelligence, *5304, synesis* [1]

INTELLIGENT [2]

intelligent, *5305, synetos* [2]

INTELLIGIBLE [2]

intelligible, *2358, eusēmos* [1]
intelligible, *3836+3808, ho+nous* [1]

INTEND [3]

intend to, *3516, mellō* [2]
intend, *3516, mellō* [1]

INTENDED [6]

intended to, *3516, mellō* [2]
intended, *NIG* [1]
intended, *1089, boulomai* [1]
intended to bring, *1650, eis* [1]
as intended, *2848, kata* [1]

INTENDING [1]

intending, *AIT* [1]

INTENSE [2]

intense, *3489, megas* [1]
intense, *4498, polys* [1]

INTENSELY [3]

intensely, *2848+5651, kata+hyperbolē* [1]
intensely, *3489, megas* [1]

intensely, *4639+2160, pros+epipotheō* [1]

INTENT [2]

intent, *AIT* [1]
intent that, *2671, hina* [1]

INTENTLY [4]

looked intently, *867, atenizō* [1]
looking intently up, *867, atenizō* [1]
searched intently and with the greatest care,
    *1699+2779+2001,
    ekzēteō+kai+exeraunaō* [1]
looks intently, *4160, parakyptō* [1]

INTERCEDE [1]

intercede, *1961, entynchanō* [1]

INTERCEDES [2]

intercedes, *1961, entynchanō* [1]
intercedes for, *5659, hyperentynchanō* [1]

INTERCEDING [1]

interceding, *1961, entynchanō* [1]

INTERCESSION [1]

intercession, *1950, enteuxis* [1]

INTEREST [4]

interest, *5527, tokos* [2]
takes interest, *3534, merimnaō* [1]
interest in, *4309, peri* [1]

INTERESTS [4]

interests, *3836, ho* [2]
interests, *AIT* [1]
the interests, *3836, ho* [1]

INTERIOR [1]

interior, *541+3538, anōterikos+meros* [1]

INTERPRET [7]

interpret, *1450, diermēneuō* [3]
interpret, *1507, dokimazō* [2]
interpret, *RPE* [1]
interpret, *1359, diakrinō* [1]

INTERPRETATION [3]

interpretation, *2255, hermēneia* [2]
interpretation, *2146, epilysis* [1]

INTERPRETER [1]

interpreter, *1449, diermēneutēs* [1]

INTERPRETS [1]

interprets, *1450, diermēneuō* [1]

INTERRUPTED [1]

interrupted, *RPE* [1]

INTESTINES [1]

intestines, *5073, splanchnon* [1]

INTO [376]

into, *1650, eis* [248]
went into, *1656+1650, eiserchomai+eis* [13]
into, *1877, en* [10]
into, *AIT* [8]
into, *RPE* [3]
go into, *1650+1656, eis+eiserchomai* [3]
fall into, *1656+1650, eiserchomai+eis* [3]
go into, *1656+1650, eiserchomai+eis* [3]

put into practice, *4472, poieō* [3]
turned into, *1181, ginomai* [2]
broken into, *1482, dioryssō* [2]
came into, *1656+1650, eiserchomai+eis* [2]
went into, *1656, eiserchomai* [2]
going into, *1660+1650, eisporeuomai+eis* [2]
lead into, *1662+1650, eispherō+eis* [2]
got into, *1832, embainō* [2]
into, *2093, epi* [2]
puts into practice, *4472, poieō* [2]
into, *4639, pros* [2]
throwing into confusion, *5429, tarassō* [2]
into, *324+3545, ana+mesos* [1]
fan into flame, *351, anazōpyreō* [1]
head into, *535, antophthalmeō* [1]
bring into disrepute, *1059, blasphēmeō* [1]
been turned into, *1181, ginomai* [1]
fell into trance, *1181+2093+1749,*
   ginomai+epi+ekstasis [1]
plunged into, *1181, ginomai* [1]
put into effect, *1408, diatagē* [1]
put into effect, *1411, diatassō* [1]
put into effect, *1590, enkainizō* [1]
grafted into, *1596, enkentrizō* [1]
goes into training, *1603, enkrateuomai* [1]
bring into, *1650, eis* [1]
brought into, *1650+1652, eis+eisagō* [1]
enter into, *1650+1656, eis+eiserchomai* [1]
entered into, *1650+1655, eis+eiseimi* [1]
went into, *1650+1656, eis+eiserchomai* [1]
brings into, *1652+1650, eisagō+eis* [1]
brought into, *1652+1650, eisagō+eis* [1]
led into, *1652+1650, eisagō+eis* [1]
take into, *1652+1650, eisagō+eis* [1]
taken into, *1652+1650, eisagō+eis* [1]
took into, *1652+1650, eisagō+eis* [1]
comes into, *1656+1650, eiserchomai+eis* [1]
entered into, *1656+1650, eiserchomai+eis* [1]
go through into, *1656+1650,*
   eiserchomai+eis [1]
goes into, *1656+1650, eiserchomai+eis* [1]
going into, *1656+1650, eiserchomai+eis* [1]
gone into, *1656+1650, eiserchomai+eis* [1]
went back into, *1656+1650,*
   eiserchomai+eis [1]
invited into, *1657, eiskaleomai* [1]
welcome into, *1658+1650, eisodos+eis* [1]
go into, *1660+1650+1650,*
   eisporeuomai+eis+eis [1]
went into, *1660+1650, eisporeuomai+eis* [1]
brought into, *1662+1650, eispherō+eis* [1]
take into, *1662, eispherō* [1]
throwing into an uproar, *1752, ektarassō* [1]
taken into account, *1824, ellogeō* [1]
goes into great detail about, *1836, embateuō* [1]
look into, *2236, eraunaō* [1]
into, *2276, esō* [1]
put religion into practice by caring for, *2355,*
   eusebeō [1]
right into, *2401+2276+1650, heōs+esō+eis* [1]
get into the habit of being, *3443, manthanō* [1]
transformed into, *3565, metamorphoō* [1]
send into exile, *3579, metoikizō* [1]
put into effect, *3873, oikonomia* [1]
putting into, *4140, paradidōmi* [1]
fell into the hands of, *4346, peripiptō* [1]
dividing into shares, *4472+3538,*
   poieō+meros [1]
turn into, *4472, poieō* [1]
turned into, *4472, poieō* [1]
put into practice, *4556, prassō* [1]
causes fall into sin, *4997, skandalizō* [1]
led into sin, *4997, skandalizō* [1]
throws into convulsions, *5057, sparassō* [1]
went with into, *5291+1650,*
   syneiserchomai+eis [1]

threw into a convulsion, *5360, sysparassō* [1]
thrown into turmoil, *5429, tarassō* [1]
welcomed into house, *5685, hypodechomai* [1]

INTOXICATED [1]

intoxicated, *3499, methyskō* [1]

INTRODUCE [1]

secretly introduce, *4206, pareisagō* [1]

INTRODUCED [2]

introduced, *1181, ginomai* [1]
introduced, *2081, epeisagōgē* [1]

INTRODUCTION [1]

introduction, *AIT* [1]

INVALID [2]

invalid, *820, astheneō* [1]
invalid, *2400+1877+3836+819,*
   echō+en+ho+astheneia [1]

INVENT [1]

invent, *2388, epheuretēs* [1]

INVENTED [1]

cleverly invented, *5054, sophizō* [1]

INVESTIGATE [1]

investigate, *2428, zētēsis* [1]

INVESTIGATED [1]

investigated, *4158, parakoloutheō* [1]

INVESTIGATION [1]

investigation, *374, anakrisis* [1]

INVISIBLE [5]

invisible, *548, aoratos* [5]

INVITE [6]

invite, *2813, kaleō* [2]
invite in, *5251, synagō* [2]
invite back, *511, antikaleō* [1]
invite, *5888, phōneō* [1]

INVITED [22]

invited, *2813, kaleō* [11]
invited, *4151, parakaleō* [4]
invited, *2263, erōtaō* [2]
invited into, *1657, eiskaleomai* [1]
host invited, *2813, kaleō* [1]
invited, *3105, klētos* [1]
invited to home, *4689, proslambanō* [1]
invited in, *5251, synagō* [1]

INVITES [2]

invites, *2813, kaleō* [2]

INVOKE [1]

invoke the name, *3951+3950,*
   onomazō+onoma [1]

INVOLVE [1]

why do involve, *5515+2779, tis+kai* [1]

INVOLVED [3]

involved in, *1861, emplekō* [1]
involved in, *3552, meta* [1]
involved in, *4472, poieō* [1]

INVOLVES [1]

involves, *1639, eimi* [1]

INWARDLY [5]

inwardly, *1877+1571, en+heautou* [1]
inwardly, *1877+3836+3220,*
   en+ho+kryptos [1]
inwardly, *2277, esōthen* [1]
inwardly, *3836+2276, ho+esō* [1]
inwardly burn, *4792, pyroō* [1]

IRON [7]

iron, *4971, sidērous* [4]
seared as with a hot iron, *3013, kaustēriazō* [1]
iron, *4970, sidēros* [1]
of iron, *4971, sidērous* [1]

IRONS [1]

irons on feet, *4267, pedē* [1]

IRRELIGIOUS [1]

irreligious, *1013, bebēlos* [1]

IRREVOCABLE [1]

irrevocable, *294, ametamelētos* [1]

IS [2194]

is, *1639, eimi* [702]
is, *NIG* [645]
is, *AIT* [620]
is, *RPE* [31]
is, *1181, ginomai* [13]
is, *2400, echō* [13]
this is how, *4048, houtōs* [8]
how is it, *4802, pōs* [8]
is, *5639, hyparchō* [7]
this is how, *1877+4047, en+houtos* [6]
this is what, *4048, houtōs* [6]
that is why, *1328+4047, dia+houtos* [5]
what is right, *1466, dikaiosynē* [5]
that is why, *1475, dio* [5]
that is how, *4048, houtōs* [5]
this is why, *1328+4047, dia+houtos* [4]
this is why, *1475, dio* [4]
what is good, *2819, kalos* [4]
yes it is as you say, *5148+3306, sy+legō* [4]
how is it that, *1328+5515, dia+tis* [3]
because he[s] is, *1650+3950, eis+onoma* [3]
is, *1928, eni* [3]
is, *3306, legō* [3]
as it is, *3814+1254, nyn+de* [3]
deposit guaranteeing what is to come, *775,*
   arrabōn [2]
is[s], *1443, didōmi* [2]
prayer is, *2263, erōtaō* [2]
is concerned, *2848, kata* [2]
that is how, *2848+3836+899,*
   kata+ho+autos [2]
is, *3023, keimai* [2]
eye is on, *4056, ophthalmodoulia* [2]
do what is right, *16, agathopoieō* [1]
does what is good, *16, agathopoieō* [1]
olive tree that is wild, *66, agrielaios* [1]
is, *72, agō* [1]
is one of us, *199+3552+1609,*
   akoloutheō+meta+egō [1]
what is more, *247+3529+2779,*
   alla+menounge+kai [1]
what is sinful, *281, hamartia* [1]
adversary is taking to court, *508, antidikos* [1]
what is shameful, *1007, bdelygma* [1]
the fact is, *1142, gar* [1]
that is why, *1328+4005+162, dia+hos+aitia* [1]

this is why, *1328+899, dia+autos* [1]
is now, *1639, eimi* [1]
is, *1639+3493, eimi+methermēneuō* [1]
that is why, *1650+4047, eis+houtos* [1]
this is the reason, *1650+4047, eis+houtos* [1]
this is how, *1666+4047, ek+houtos* [1]
convinced that is a sinner, *1794, elenchō* [1]
that is why, *2093+4047, epi+houtos* [1]
the good news is preached, *2294, euangelizō* [1]
is getting along well, *2338, euodoō* [1]
is ours, *2400, echō* [1]
is under, *2400, echō* [1]
here is, *2627, idou* [1]
there is, *2627, idou* [1]
aim is to, *2671, hina* [1]
is, *2705, histēmi* [1]
this is why, *2777, kathōs* [1]
as it is, *2779, kai* [1]
it is true, *2779, kai* [1]
does what is evil, *2803, kakopoieō* [1]
is*, *2813, kaleō* [1]
teach what is good, *2815, kalodidaskalos* [1]
doing what is right, *2818, kalopoieō* [1]
what is right, *2819, kalos* [1]
this is, *2848+3836, kata+ho* [1]
the point is this, *3049, kephalaion* [1]
receive what is due, *3152, komizō* [1]
as it is, *3814, nyn* [1]
as it is, *3815+1254, nyni+de* [1]
that is, *3836, ho* [1]
what is, *3836, ho* [1]
this is how, *3854, hothen* [1]
this is why, *3854, hothen* [1]
say is like, *3929, homoioō* [1]
it is true, *3953, ontōs* [1]
what is right, *3987, orthōs* [1]
as it is, *4022+1254, hoti+de* [1]
is that why, *4022, hoti* [1]
is it possible that, *4024, ou* [1]
what is more, *4024+3667+1254+247+2779,*
    ou+monon+de+alla+kai [1]
conscience is clear, *4029+5323,*
    oudeis+synoida [1]
it is the same, *4048+2779, houtōs+kai* [1]
that is why, *4048, houtōs* [1]
this is, *4048, houtōs* [1]
as* is, *4048, houtōs* [1]
this is the way, *4048, houtōs* [1]
is here, *4205, pareimi* [1]
is, *4355, perisseuō* [1]
how is it, *4481, poios* [1]
what is seen, *4725, prosōpon* [1]
what is more, *5250+4246+4047,*
    syn+pas+houtos [1]
that is, *5445, te* [1]
what business is it of mine, *5515+1609,*
    tis+egō [1]
more than is warranted, *5642, hyper* [1]
shown for what it is, *5745, phaneros* [1]
loves what is good, *5787, philagathos* [1]
someone is saying, *5889, phōnē* [1]
[what is] deceitful, *6022, pseudos* [1]
is, *6055, hōs* [1]
that is, *6055, hōs* [1]

ISAAC [21]

Isaac, *2693, Isaak* [20]
Isaac*, *899, autos* [1]

ISAIAH [22]

Isaiah, *2480, Ēsaias* [21]
book of Isaiah, *2480, Ēsaias* [1]

ISCARIOT [11]

Iscariot, *2697, Iskariōtēs* [11]

ISLAND [11]

island, *3762, nēsos* [9]
the island*, *899, autos* [1]
small island, *3761, nēsion* [1]

ISLANDERS [2]

islanders, *975, barbaros* [2]

ISN'T [9]

isn't, *4024+1639, ou+eimi* [5]
isn't, *RPE* [1]
isn't at all, *4024+3590, ou+mē* [1]
isn't, *4024, ou* [1]
isn't, *4049+1639, ouchi+eimi* [1]

ISRAEL [69]

Israel, *2702, Israēl* [53]
of Israel, *2703, Israēlitēs* [6]
Israel, *3875+2702, oikos+Israēl* [3]
Israel, *5626+2702, huios+Israēl* [3]
Israel, *RPE* [1]
Israel*, *899, autos* [1]
the firstborn* of Israel, *899, autos* [1]
people of Israel, *2702+2848+4922,*
    Israēl+kata+sarx [1]

ISRAEL'S [1]

Israel's, *2702, Israēl* [1]

ISRAELITE [2]

Israelite, *2703, Israēlitēs* [2]

ISRAELITES [11]

Israelites, *5626+2702, huios+Israēl* [7]
Israelites, *RPE* [1]
the Israelites*, *899, autos* [1]
two Israelites*, *899, autos* [1]
Israelites, *2703, Israēlitēs* [1]

ISSACHAR [1]

Issachar, *2704, Issachar* [1]

ISSUED [1]

issued, *2002, exerchomai* [1]

IT [1348]

it, *AIT* [471]
it, *RPE* [343]
it, *NIG* [202]
it, *899, autos* [185]
it, *4005, hos* [14]
it, *4047, houtos* [12]
how is it, *4802, pōs* [8]
see to it, *1063, blepō* [5]
it, *3836, ho* [4]
it, *4015, hostis* [4]
yes it is as you say, *5148+3306, sy+legō* [4]
how is it that, *1328+5515, dia+tis* [3]
as it is, *3814+1254, nyn+de* [3]
it*, *3836+3180, ho+kosmos* [3]
make it, *1211, graphō* [2]
lord it over, *2894, katakyrieuō* [2]
lord it over, *3259, kyrieuō* [2]
it*, *3795, nomos* [2]
it*, *3836+1046, ho+biblion* [2]
it*, *3836+229, ho+halas* [2]
it*, *3836+4450, ho+ploion* [2]
do* it, *3972, horaō* [2]
see to it, *3972, horaō* [2]
drove to it, *337, anankazō* [1]
think it wise, *546, axioō* [1]
taken it off, *1218, gymnos* [1]

it*, *1466, dikaiosynē* [1]
think it worthwhile, *1507, dokimazō* [1]
without paying for it, *1562, dōrean* [1]
it, *1571, heautou* [1]
be that as it may, *1639, eimi* [1]
it*, *1650+3795, eis+nomos* [1]
it, *1697, ekeinos* [1]
while it was still dark, *1939, ennychos* [1]
if it could, *2075, epei* [1]
if it were, *2075, epei* [1]
put it too severely, *2096, epibareō* [1]
see to it, *2174, episkopeō* [1]
carry it on to completion, *2200, epiteleō* [1]
it*, *2240, ergon* [1]
thought it best, *2305, eudokeō* [1]
precisely as it had happened, *2759, kathexēs* [1]
as it is, *2779, kai* [1]
it is true, *2779, kai* [1]
lording it over, *2894, katakyrieuō* [1]
it*, *3180, kosmos* [1]
insist on it, *3458, martyromai* [1]
so shall it be, *3721, nai* [1]
as it is, *3814, nyn* [1]
as it is, *3815+1254, nyni+de* [1]
think it strange, *3826, xenizō* [1]
it*, *3836+3693, ho+myron* [1]
it that, *3836, ho* [1]
it*, *3836+1155+4047, ho+genea+houtos* [1]
it*, *3836+1561, ho+dōrea* [1]
it*, *3836+1631, ho+eidōlon* [1]
it*, *3836+1635+3836+2563,*
    ho+eikōn+ho+thērion [1]
it*, *3836+1847, ho+emos* [1]
it*, *3836+2295, ho+euangelion* [1]
it*, *3836+2585, ho+thronos* [1]
it*, *3836+27, ho+agapē* [1]
it*, *3836+2819, ho+kalos* [1]
it*, *3836+3364, ho+logos* [1]
it*, *3836+3954, ho+oxos* [1]
it*, *3836+4384, ho+pēlos* [1]
it*, *3836+4784, ho+pylōn* [1]
it*, *3836+4839+4047, ho+rhēma+houtos* [1]
it*, *3836+5013, ho+skēnōma* [1]
it*, *3836+5853, ho+phrear* [1]
it*, *3836+5890, ho+phōs* [1]
it*, *3836+6029, ho+psēphos* [1]
it*, *3836+6052, ho+hōra* [1]
it*, *3836+69, ho+agros* [1]
it*, *3836+993+3836+1847,*
    ho+basileia+ho+emos [1]
it is true, *3953, ontōs* [1]
it⁶, *4005+608+794+201,*
    hos+apo+archē+akouō [1]
as it is, *4022+1254, hoti+de* [1]
is it possible that, *4024, ou* [1]
what it says, *4047, houtos* [1]
it is the same, *4048+2779, houtōs+kai* [1]
as it has, *4048, houtōs* [1]
make it difficult for, *4214, parenochleō* [1]
how is it, *4481, poios* [1]
it*, *4922, sarx* [1]
see to it, *5023, skopeō* [1]
what business is it of mine, *5515+1609,*
    tis+egō [1]
what does it matter, *5515, tis* [1]
it*, *5516+3836+2240, tis+ho+ergon* [1]
it*, *5624, hyetos* [1]
shown for what it is, *5745, phaneros* [1]
make it ambition, *5818, philotimeomai* [1]
make it goal, *5818, philotimeomai* [1]

IT'S [8]

it's, *AIT* [3]
it's, *1639, eimi* [3]
it's, *NIG* [1]

it's, *RPE* [1]

ITALIAN [1]
Italian, *2713, Italikos* [1]

ITALY [4]
Italy, *2712, Italia* [4]

ITCHING [1]
itching, *3117, knēthō* [1]

ITS [110]
its, *899, autos* [48]
its, *3836, ho* [21]
its, *RPE* [20]
its, *AIT* [3]
its own, *2625, idios* [3]
its, *2625, idios* [2]
loses its saltiness, *3701, mōrainō* [2]
its, *4005, hos* [2]
its own, *899, autos* [1]
by its own choice, *1776, hekōn* [1]
its, *1877+899, en+autos* [1]
its^s, *3836+1178, ho+gē* [1]
its^s, *3836+2639, ho+hieron* [1]
its^s, *3836+4725+899, ho+prosōpon+autos* [1]
its^s, *3836+4922, ho+sarx* [1]
its^s, *3836+5393, ho+sōma* [1]
its, *3836+4725+899, ho+prosōpon+autos* [1]

ITSELF [26]
itself, *1571, heautou* [12]
itself, *899, autos* [4]
itself, *AIT* [3]
itself, *RPE* [3]
all by itself, *897, automatos* [1]
by itself, *897, automatos* [1]
by itself, *3023+6006+1650+1651+5536,
   keimai+chōris+eis+heis+topos* [1]
itself^s, *3875, oikos* [1]

ITUREA [1]
Iturea, *2714, Itouraios* [1]

IVORY [1]
made of ivory, *1804, elephantinos* [1]

JACINTH [1]
jacinth, *5611, hyakinthos* [1]

JACOB [26]
Jacob, *2609, Iakōb* [26]

JACOB'S [1]
Jacob's, *2609, Iakōb* [1]

JAIL [7]
jail, *5871, phylakē* [3]
jail, *1303, desmōtērion* [2]
jail, *5499, tērēsis* [2]

JAILER [7]
jailer, *RPE* [4]
jailer, *1302, desmophylax* [3]

JAILERS [1]
jailers to be tortured, *991, basanistēs* [1]

JAIRUS [6]
Jairus, *RPE* [3]
Jairus, *2608, Iairos* [2]

Jairus^s, *899, autos* [1]

JAMBRES [1]
Jambres, *2612, Iambrēs* [1]

JAMES [42]
James, *2610, Iakōbos* [41]
James^s, *899, autos* [1]

JANNAI [1]
Jannai, *2613, Iannai* [1]

JANNES [1]
Jannes, *2614, Iannēs* [1]

JAR [10]
alabaster jar, *223, alabastros* [3]
jar, *3040, keramion* [2]
jar, *5007, skeuos* [2]
jar, *223, alabastros* [1]
jar, *5085, stamnos* [1]
water jar, *5620, hydria* [1]

JARED [1]
Jared, *2616, Iaret* [1]

JARS [4]
jars, *31, angeion* [1]
jars, *5007, skeuos* [1]
jars, *5620, hydria* [1]
water jars, *5620, hydria* [1]

JASON [4]
Jason, *2619, Iasōn* [4]

JASON'S [1]
Jason's, *2619, Iasōn* [1]

JASPER [4]
jasper, *2618, iaspis* [3]
jasper, *3345+2618, lithos+iaspis* [1]

JEALOUS [3]
jealous for, *2420, zēloō* [1]
jealous of, *2420, zēloō* [1]
jealous, *2420, zēloō* [1]

JEALOUSY [8]
jealousy, *2419, zēlos* [7]
arouse jealousy, *4143, parazēloō* [1]

JECONIAH [2]
Jeconiah, *2651, Iechonias* [2]

JEERS [1]
jeers, *1849, empaigmos* [1]

JEHORAM [2]
Jehoram, *2732, Iōram* [2]

JEHOSHAPHAT [2]
Jehoshaphat, *2734, Iōsaphat* [2]

JEPHTHAH [1]
Jephthah, *2650, Iephthae* [1]

JEREMIAH [3]
Jeremiah, *2635, Ieremias* [3]

JERICHO [6]
Jericho, *2637, Ierichō* [6]

JERUSALEM [142]
Jerusalem, *2647, Ierousalēm* [136]
people of Jerusalem, *2643, Hierosolymitēs* [2]
city of Jerusalem, *2647, Ierousalēm* [2]
Jerusalem, *NIG* [1]
Jerusalem, *RPE* [1]

JESSE [5]
Jesse, *2649, Iessai* [5]

JESUS [1274]
Jesus, *2652, Iēsous* [897]
Jesus, *RPE* [177]
Jesus^s, *899, autos* [156]
Jesus^s, *3836+1254, ho+de* [25]
Jesus^s, *3836, ho* [5]
Jesus^s, *4047, houtos* [4]
Jesus^s and his disciples, *899, autos* [2]
Jesus, *NIG* [1]
Jesus and his disciples^s, *899, autos* [1]
Jesus^s body, *899, autos* [1]
Jesus followers^s, *1254+3836, de+ho* [1]
Jesus^s Christ, *1697, ekeinos* [1]
Jesus^s, *1697, ekeinos* [1]
above Jesus, *3963+1639, hopou+eimi* [1]
the Jesus^s, *4005, hos* [1]

JEW [22]
Jew, *2681, Ioudaios* [18]
Jew, *467+2681, anēr+Ioudaios* [2]
Jew, *476+2681, anthrōpos+Ioudaios* [1]
like a Jew, *2680, Ioudaikōs* [1]

JEWEL [1]
jewel, *3345, lithos* [1]

JEWELRY [1]
gold jewelry, *5992, chrysion* [1]

JEWESS [2]
Jewess, *2681, Ioudaios* [2]

JEWISH [22]
Jewish, *2681, Ioudaios* [18]
Jewish, *AIT* [1]
follow Jewish customs, *2678, ioudaizō* [1]
Jewish, *2679, Ioudaikos* [1]
Jewish community, *4436+2681,
   plēthos+Ioudaios* [1]

JEWS [170]
Jews, *2681, Ioudaios* [149]
the Jews^s, *899, autos* [5]
Jews, *RPE* [4]
Jews, *4364, peritomē* [4]
Grecian Jews, *1821, Hellēnistēs* [2]
Jews, *AIT* [1]
Jews, *467+2681, anēr+Ioudaios* [1]
Jews^s, *899, autos* [1]
Hebraic Jews, *1578, Hebraios* [1]
Jews, *1666+4364, ek+peritomē* [1]
Jews, *1877+3836+1169+1609,
   en+ho+genos+egō* [1]

JEZEBEL [1]
Jezebel, *2630, Iezabel* [1]

JOANAN [1]
Joanan, *2720, Iōanan* [1]

JOANNA [2]

Joanna, *2721, Iōanna* [2]

JOB [2]

job, *3873, oikonomia* [2]

JOB'S [1]

Job's, *2724, Iōb* [1]

JODA [1]

Joda, *2726, Iōda* [1]

JOEL [1]

Joel, *2727, Iōēl* [1]

JOHN [138]

John, *2722, Iōannēs* [119]
John, *RPE* [8]
John[s], *899, autos* [6]
Peter[s] and John, *899, autos* [3]
John[s], *1697, ekeinos* [1]
Peter[s] and John, *3836+3525, ho+men* [1]

JOHN'S [19]

John's, *2722, Iōannēs* [14]
John's[s], *899, autos* [3]
John's, *2722+899, Iōannēs+autos* [1]
John's disciples[s], *4047, houtos* [1]

JOIN [7]

join, *3140, kollaō* [2]
join, *2262+4639, erchomai+pros* [1]
join in suffering, *5155, synkakopatheō* [1]
join with others following example, *5213+1181, symmimētēs+ginomai* [1]
join in, *5250, syn* [1]
join in struggle, *5253, synagōnizomai* [1]

JOINED [12]

joined, *2262+4639, erchomai+pros* [2]
joined together, *5183, syzeugnymi* [2]
joined together, *5274, synarmologeō* [2]
joined constantly, *1639+4674, eimi+proskartereō* [1]
joined together, *3924, homothymadon* [1]
joined, *4677, prosklēroō* [1]
joined in the accusation, *5298, synepitithēmi* [1]
joined in the attack, *5308, synephistēmi* [1]
joined in hypocrisy, *5347, synypokrinomai* [1]

JOINS [1]

joins in the work, *5300, synergeō* [1]

JOINTS [1]

joints, *765, harmos* [1]

JOKING [1]

coarse joking, *2365, eutrapelia* [1]

JONAH [10]

Jonah, *2731, Iōnas* [9]
son of Jonah, *980, Bariōna* [1]

JONAM [1]

Jonam, *2729, Iōnam* [1]

JOPPA [10]

Joppa, *2673, Ioppē* [10]

JORDAN [15]

Jordan, *2674, Iordanēs* [15]

JORIM [1]

Jorim, *2733, Iōrim* [1]

JOSECH [1]

Josech, *2738, Iōsēch* [1]

JOSEPH [38]

Joseph, *2737, Iōsēph* [31]
Joseph, *RPE* [4]
Joseph[s], *899, autos* [2]
Joseph, *2736, Iōsēs* [1]

JOSEPH'S [3]

Joseph's, *2737, Iōsēph* [3]

JOSES [3]

Joses, *2736, Iōsēs* [3]

JOSHUA [3]

Joshua, *2652, Iēsous* [3]

JOSIAH [2]

Josiah, *2739, Iōsias* [2]

JOTHAM [2]

Jotham, *2718, Iōatham* [2]

JOURNEY [15]

journey, *3847, hodos* [4]
went away on a journey, *623, apodēmeō* [2]
going on a journey, *623, apodēmeō* [1]
went on journey, *623, apodēmeō* [1]
on a journey, *1666+3847, ek+hodos* [1]
on the journey, *2002, exerchomai* [1]
on their journey, *3844, hodoiporeō* [1]
journey, *3845, hodoiporia* [1]
journey, *4513, poreuomai* [1]
assist on journey, *4636, propempō* [1]
help on journey, *4636, propempō* [1]

JOURNEYS [1]

one of these journeys[s], *4005, hos* [1]

JOY [63]

joy, *5915, chara* [44]
joy, *5897, chairō* [3]
joy, *21, agalliasis* [2]
great joy, *21, agalliasis* [1]
filled with joy, *22+5915, agalliaō+chara* [1]
filled with joy, *22, agalliaō* [1]
full of joy, *22, agalliaō* [1]
fills with joy, *2372, euphrosynē* [1]
joy, *2372, euphrosynē* [1]
joy, *3017, kauchēma* [1]
joy, *3422, makarismos* [1]
leap for joy, *5015, skirtaō* [1]
shared joy, *5176, synchairō* [1]
full of joy, *5897, chairō* [1]
filled with joy, *5915+3489, chara+megas* [1]
full of joy, *5915+5897, chara+chairō* [1]
joy have, *5915+5897, chara+chairō* [1]

JOYFUL [3]

joyful, *5897, chairō* [2]
joyful assembly, *4108, panēgyris* [1]

JOYFULLY [4]

joyfully, *3552+5915, meta+chara* [2]

joyfully, *5897, chairō* [2]

JUDAH [10]

Judah, *2683, Ioudas* [10]

JUDAISM [5]

Judaism, *2682, Ioudaismos* [2]
converts to Judaism, *4670, prosēlytos* [2]
convert to Judaism, *4670, prosēlytos* [1]

JUDAS [41]

Judas, *2683, Ioudas* [32]
Judas, *RPE* [7]
Judas[s], *1697, ekeinos* [1]
Judas[s], *4047, houtos* [1]

JUDE [1]

Jude, *2683, Ioudas* [1]

JUDEA [44]

Judea, *2677, Ioudaia* [41]
Judea, *6001+2677, chōra+Ioudaia* [2]
Judea, *2683, Ioudas* [1]

JUDEAN [3]

Judean, *2681, Ioudaios* [3]

JUDGE [62]

judge, *3212, krinō* [38]
judge, *3216, kritēs* [14]
judge, *1471, dikastēs* [2]
judge, *373, anakrinō* [1]
judge a dispute, *1359, diakrinō* [1]
judge, *3210, krima* [1]
judge, *3213+4472, krisis+poieō* [1]
judge cases, *3215, kritērion* [1]
until judge, *4024+3212, ou+krinō* [1]
judge, *4472+3213, poieō+krisis* [1]
judge by external appearance, *4725+476+3284, prosōpon+anthrōpos+lambanō* [1]

JUDGE'S [2]

judge's seat, *1037, bēma* [2]

JUDGED [18]

judged, *3212, krinō* [14]
judged, *373, anakrinō* [2]
judged, *1359, diakrinō* [1]
judged, *3210+3284, krima+lambanō* [1]

JUDGES [14]

judges, *3212, krinō* [7]
judges, *3216, kritēs* [4]
judges, *373, anakrinō* [1]
appoint as judges, *2767, kathizō* [1]
judges, *3217, kritikos* [1]

JUDGING [4]

judging, *3212, krinō* [4]

JUDGMENT [61]

judgment, *3213, krisis* [28]
judgment, *3210, krima* [12]
pass judgment on, *3212, krinō* [3]
judgment seat, *1037, bēma* [2]
judgment, *1191, gnōmē* [2]
judgment, *373, anakrinō* [1]
sit in judgment on, *373, anakrinō* [1]
passing judgment, *1360, diakrisis* [1]
righteous judgment, *1464, dikaiokrisia* [1]
come under judgment, *3212, krinō* [1]
judgment that, *3212, krinō* [1]

judgment, *3212, krinō* [1]
pass judgment, *3212, krinō* [1]
passed judgment on, *3212, krinō* [1]
passing judgment on, *3212, krinō* [1]
take judgment, *3212, krinō* [1]
make judgment, *3213+3212, krisis+krinō* [1]
sitting in judgment, *3216, kritēs* [1]
sober judgment, *5404, sōphroneō* [1]

JUDGMENTS [5]

judgments, *3213, krisis* [2]
judgments, *AIT* [1]
makes judgments about, *373, anakrinō* [1]
judgments, *3210, krima* [1]

JULIA [1]

Julia, *2684, Ioulia* [1]

JULIUS [2]

Julius, *2685, Ioulios* [2]

JUMP [1]

jump overboard, *681, aporiptō* [1]

JUMPED [5]

jumped up, *256, hallomai* [1]
jumped to his feet, *403, anapēdaō* [1]
jumped, *965+1571, ballō+heautou* [1]
jumped, *1982, exallomai* [1]
jumped on, *2383+2093, ephallomai+epi* [1]

JUMPING [1]

jumping, *256, hallomai* [1]

JUNIAS [1]

Junias, *2687, Iounias* [1]

JURISDICTION [1]

jurisdiction, *2026, exousia* [1]

JUST [156]

just as, *2777, kathōs* [50]
just as, *6055, hōs* [17]
just, *NIG* [12]
just as, *6061, hōsper* [10]
just, *1465, dikaios* [8]
just, *AIT* [7]
just, *3667, monon* [6]
just as, *2749, kathaper* [5]
just then, *2779+2627, kai+idou* [2]
just as, *2848+4012, kata+hosos* [2]
just as, *2848, kata* [2]
just, *247, alla* [1]
just after sunrise, *422+3836+2463,*
   anatellō+ho+hēlios [1]
just now, *785, arti* [1]
just, *785, arti* [1]
just before, *948+4005, achri+hos* [1]
just⁵, *1218, gymnos* [1]
just as, *1254, de* [1]
just, *1254, de* [1]
just as though, *1651+2779+3836+899,*
   heis+kai+ho+autos [1]
just, *1899, endikos* [1]
just then, *2093+4047, epi+houtos* [1]
just then, *2317, euthys1* [1]
just what, *2777, kathōs* [1]
just, *2777, kathōs* [1]
just as, *2778, kathōsper* [1]
just, *2829, kan* [1]
just as, *2848+3928, kata+homoiotēs* [1]
just as, *2848+4005+5573, kata+hos+tropos* [1]

just like this, *2848+3836+899,*
   kata+ho+autos [1]
just, *3668, monos* [1]
I mean that just as surely as, *3755, nē* [1]
just, *3814, nyn* [1]
just, *3903, oligōs* [1]
just like, *3926, homoiopathēs* [1]
just as, *3940, homōs* [1]
just as, *4005+5573, hos+tropos* [1]
just one, *4047+3667, houtos+monon* [1]
just as if, *4048, houtōs* [1]
just as, *4048+2848+4005+5573,*
   houtōs+kata+hos+tropos [1]
just, *4202, parachrēma* [1]
just outside, *4574, pro* [1]
just like, *6055, hōs* [1]
just, *6055, hōs* [1]

JUSTICE [16]

justice, *1466, dikaiosynē* [5]
justice, *3213, krisis* [5]
justice, *1689, ekdikēsis* [2]
justice, *1472, dikē* [1]
justice, *1688, ekdikeō* [1]
see that gets justice, *1688, ekdikeō* [1]
readiness to see justice done, *1689, ekdikēsis* [1]

JUSTIFICATION [3]

justification, *1470, dikaiōsis* [2]
justification, *1468, dikaiōma* [1]

JUSTIFIED [21]

justified, *1467, dikaioō* [19]
justified before God, *1467, dikaioō* [1]
justified, *1650+1466, eis+dikaiosynē* [1]

JUSTIFIES [3]

justifies, *1467, dikaioō* [3]

JUSTIFY [4]

justify, *1467, dikaioō* [4]

JUSTLY [2]

justly, *1469, dikaiōs* [2]

JUSTUS [3]

Justus, *2688, Ioustos* [3]

KEEP [83]

keep, *AIT* [17]
keep, *5498, tēreō* [10]
keep watch, *1213, grēgoreō* [8]
keep, *5875, phylassō* [5]
keep, *2400, echō* [3]
keep, *NIG* [2]
keep up courage, *2313, euthymeō* [2]
keep, *2988, katechō* [2]
keep from, *3266, kōlyō* [2]
keep from, *3590, mē* [2]
keep watch, *70, agrypneō* [1]
keep, *625, apodidōmi* [1]
keep strong, *1011, bebaioō* [1]
keep in mind, *1182, ginōskō* [1]
keep, *1639, eimi* [1]
commanded to keep, *1948, entellō* [1]
keep the Festival, *2037, heortazō* [1]
keep hold of, *2400, echō* [1]
keep warm, *2548, thermainō* [1]
to keep from, *2671+3590, hina+mē* [1]
keep, *2770, kathistēmi* [1]
theirs to keep, *2988, katechō* [1]
keep secret, *3291, lanthanō* [1]
keep on, *3531, menō* [1]

keep head, *3768, nēphō* [1]
keep in suspense, *3836+6034+149,*
   ho+psychē+airō [1]
keep, *4264, pauō* [1]
keep, *4347, peripoieō* [1]
keep, *4472, poieō* [1]
to keep from, *4639+3836+3590,*
   pros+ho+mē [1]
keep watch over, *4668, prosechō* [1]
keep on, *4675, proskarterēsis* [1]
keep away, *5097, stellō* [1]
keep in step, *5123, stoicheō* [1]
keep, *5464, teleō* [1]
keep under guard, *5498, tēreō* [1]
keep, *5575, trophē* [1]
keep from, *5875, phylassō* [1]
keep a tight rein on, *5902, chalinagōgeō* [1]
keep in check, *5902, chalinagōgeō* [1]

KEEPER [1]

keeper, *2400, echō* [1]

KEEPING [14]

in keeping with, *2848, kata* [3]
in keeping with, *545, axios* [2]
keeping, *AIT* [1]
in keeping with, *1328, dia* [1]
keeping, *2400, echō* [1]
keeping, *2924, katapauō* [1]
in keeping with income,
   4005+5516+1569+2338,
   hos+tis+ean+euodoō [1]
keeping a close watch, *4190, paratēreō* [1]
keeping, *4475, poiētēs* [1]
keeping, *5499, tērēsis* [1]
keeping watch, *5875+5871,*
   phylassō+phylakē [1]

KEEPS [11]

keeps, *5498, tēreō* [5]
keeps, *AIT* [4]
keeps, *4472, poieō* [1]
keeps safe, *5498, tēreō* [1]

KENAN [1]

Kenan, *2783, Kainam* [1]

KEPT [53]

kept, *AIT* [13]
kept, *5498, tēreō* [10]
kept, *5875, phylassō* [3]
kept, *1639, eimi* [2]
kept on, *2152, epimenō* [2]
kept from, *3266, kōlyō* [2]
kept, *4472, poieō* [2]
kept under guard, *5875, phylassō* [2]
kept, *NIG* [1]
kept hidden for, *648+608+608,*
   apokryptō+apo+apo [1]
kept watch, *1213, grēgoreō* [1]
kept on, *1639, eimi* [1]
kept ready, *2286, hetoimazō* [1]
kept, *2400, echō* [1]
kept from, *3195+3590, krateō+mē* [1]
kept, *3195, krateō* [1]
kept from, *3590, mē* [1]
kept back, *3802, nosphizō* [1]
kept, *3802, nosphizō* [1]
kept on, *4189, parateinō* [1]
kept close watch on, *4190, paratēreō* [1]
kept up, *4472, poieō* [1]
kept this to themselves, *4967, sigaō* [1]
kept watch over, *5498, tēreō* [1]
kept safe, *5875, phylassō* [1]

KERNEL [2]

kernel, *3133, kokkos* [1]
kernel, *4992, sitos* [1]

KERNELS [1]

kernels, *RPE* [1]

KETTLES [1]

kettles, *5908, chalkion* [1]

KEY [4]

key, *3090, kleis* [4]

KEYS [2]

keys, *3090, kleis* [2]

KICK [1]

kick, *3280, laktizō* [1]

KIDRON [1]

Kidron, *3022, Kedrōn* [1]

KILL [61]

kill, *650, apokteinō* [34]
kill, *359, anaireō* [9]
kill, *660, apollymi* [8]
kill, *2604, thyō* [5]
kill, *1429, diacheirizō* [1]
trying to kill, *2426+3836+6034,*
    zēteō+ho+psyche [1]
kill, *2956, katasphazō* [1]
[kill their] mothers, *3618, mētrolōas* [1]
kill their fathers, *4260, patrolōas* [1]
kill, *5839, phoneuō* [1]

KILLED [40]

killed, *650, apokteinō* [26]
killed, *359, anaireō* [4]
killed, *660, apollymi* [4]
killed, *AIT* [1]
killed, *1429, diacheirizō* [1]
killed, *2506, thanatoō* [1]
killed, *2604, thyō* [1]
killed with, *5272, synapollymi* [1]
killed, *5377, sphazō* [1]

KILLING [3]

killing, *359, anaireō* [1]
killing, *650, apokteinō* [1]
killing, *4250, patassō* [1]

KILLS [2]

kills, *650, apokteinō* [2]

KIND [42]

kind, *AIT* [12]
what kind of, *4534, potapos* [4]
kind of, *4481, poios* [3]
kind, *19, agathos* [2]
what kind of, *4481, poios* [2]
kind, *5982, chrēstos* [2]
kind, *RPE* [1]
one kind, *257+3525, allos+men* [1]
one kind, *257, allos* [1]
kind, *1155, genea* [1]
kind, *1169, genos* [1]
kind, *1626, eidos* [1]
the kind⁸, *1666, ek* [1]
this⁸ kind of, *1877+4231, en+paroimia* [1]
kind, *2116, epieikeia* [1]
one kind, *2283, heteros* [1]
kind, *2473, ēpios* [1]

what kind of, *3961, hopoios* [1]
by this kind, *4048, houtōs* [1]
a kind of, *5516, tis* [1]
of a kind, *5525, toioutos* [1]
they are the kind, *5525, toioutos* [1]
kind, *5980, chrēsteuomai* [1]

KINDLED [2]

kindled, *409, anaptō* [1]
kindled, *4312, periaptō* [1]

KINDLY [1]

answer kindly, *4151, parakaleō* [1]

KINDNESS [16]

kindness, *5983, chrēstotēs* [9]
brotherly kindness, *5789, philadelphia* [2]
shown kindness, *14, agathoergeō* [1]
act of kindness shown to, *2307, euergesia* [1]
kindness, *5792, philanthrōpia* [1]
in kindness, *5793+5968,*
    philanthrōpōs+chraomai [1]
kindness, *5982, chrēstos* [1]

KINDS [23]

kinds, *AIT* [9]
all kinds of, *4476, poikilos* [4]
different kinds, *1348, diairesis* [3]
different kinds, *1169, genos* [2]
kinds, *1169, genos* [1]
what kinds of, *3888, hoios* [1]
many kinds, *4476, poikilos* [1]
various kinds, *4476, poikilos* [1]
kinds, *5882, physis* [1]

KING [89]

king, *995, basileus* [82]
king, *476+995, anthrōpos+basileus* [2]
king, *996, basileuō* [2]
king, *RPE* [1]
king, *993, basileia* [1]
made king, *3284+3836+993,*
    lambanō+ho+basileia [1]

KING'S [3]

king's, *995, basileus* [2]
king's country, *997, basilikos* [1]

KINGDOM [157]

kingdom, *993, basileia* [154]
kingdom, *RPE* [2]
kingdom, *2026, exousia* [1]

KINGDOMS [3]

kingdoms, *993, basileia* [3]

KINGS [33]

kings, *995, basileus* [28]
kings, *996, basileuō* [3]
the kings⁸, *899, autos* [1]
kings with, *5203, symbasileuō* [1]

KIOS [1]

Kios, *5944, Chios* [1]

KISH [1]

Kish, *3078, Kis* [1]

KISS [10]

kiss, *5799, philēma* [7]
kiss, *5797, phileō* [3]

KISSED [5]

kissed, *2968, kataphileō* [5]

KISSING [1]

kissing, *2968, kataphileō* [1]

KNEE [3]

knee, *1205, gony* [3]

KNEEL [1]

kneel, *2828+3836+1205, kamptō+ho+gony* [1]

KNEELING [1]

kneeling down, *4686, proskyneō* [1]

KNEES [10]

knees, *1205, gony* [5]
knees, *RPE* [1]
fell on knees before, *1206, gonypeteō* [1]
on knees, *1206, gonypeteō* [1]
fell on knees in front of, *4686, proskyneō* [1]
on knees before, *4686, proskyneō* [1]

KNELT [8]

knelt before, *4686, proskyneō* [3]
knelt down, *5502+3836+1205,*
    tithēmi+ho+gony [2]
knelt before, *1206, gonypeteō* [1]
knelt, *1206, gonypeteō* [1]
knelt, *5502+3836+1205, tithēmi+ho+gony* [1]

KNEW [37]

knew, *3857, oida* [20]
knew, *1182, ginōskō* [11]
knew, *2105, epiginōskō* [2]
knew about, *1182, ginōskō* [1]
knew, *1196, gnōstos* [1]
knew, *2179, epistamai* [1]
knew about, *3857, oida* [1]

KNOCK [3]

knock, *3218, krouō* [3]

KNOCKED [1]

knocked at, *3218, krouō* [1]

KNOCKING [2]

knocking, *3218, krouō* [2]

KNOCKS [3]

knocks, *3218, krouō* [3]

KNOW [365]

know, *3857, oida* [219]
know, *1182, ginōskō* [90]
know, *RPE* [9]
know how, *3857, oida* [7]
know, *2179, epistamai* [6]
know, *2105, epiginōskō* [5]
not know, *51, agnoeō* [2]
know that, *1182, ginōskō* [2]
know, *1192, gnōrizō* [2]
know, *1196+1639, gnōstos+eimi* [2]
know, *1196, gnōstos* [2]
know, *NIG* [1]
don't know, *51, agnoeō* [1]
know about, *1182, ginōskō* [1]
know how, *1182, ginōskō* [1]
know about, *1192, gnōrizō* [1]
know fully, *2105, epiginōskō* [1]
know better, *2106, epignōsis* [1]

KNOWING

know, *2106*, *epignōsis* [1]
know about, *2179*, *epistamai* [1]
know that, *2179*, *epistamai* [1]
as know, *2627*, *idou* [1]
know heart, *2841*, *kardiognōstēs* [1]
know, *3443*, *manthanō* [1]
know, *3783*, *noeō* [1]
know about, *3857*, *oida* [1]
know all about, *4158*, *parakoloutheō* [1]
to know, *4309*, *peri* [1]
already know, *4589*, *proginōskō* [1]
know, *5745+1639*, *phaneros+eimi* [1]

KNOWING [19]

knowing, *3857*, *oida* [12]
knowing, *1182*, *ginōskō* [4]
knowing, *1194*, *gnōsis* [1]
knowing, *2106*, *epignōsis* [1]
without knowing, *3291*, *lanthanō* [1]

KNOWLEDGE [44]

knowledge, *1194*, *gnōsis* [25]
knowledge, *2106*, *epignōsis* [14]
knowledge, *1182*, *ginōskō* [2]
knowledge, *RPE* [1]
thorough knowledge, *1543*, *dynatos* [1]
full knowledge, *5323*, *synoida* [1]

KNOWN [68]

known, *1182*, *ginōskō* [15]
made known, *1192*, *gnōrizō* [8]
known, *3857*, *oida* [7]
known, *1196*, *gnōstos* [6]
make known, *1192*, *gnōrizō* [5]
known, *NIG* [3]
known, *2105*, *epiginōskō* [3]
made known, *1182*, *ginōskō* [2]
known as, *2126*, *epikaleō* [2]
known as, *2813*, *kaleō* [2]
known as, *3306*, *legō* [2]
made known, *5746*, *phaneroō* [2]
make known, *334*, *anangellō* [1]
making known, *334*, *anangellō* [1]
known, *2002*, *exerchomai* [1]
made known, *2007*, *exēgeomai* [1]
fully known, *2105*, *epiginōskō* [1]
known, *3455*, *martyreō* [1]
well known, *3455*, *martyreō* [1]
known, *3951*, *onomazō* [1]
known, *4589*, *proginōskō* [1]
made known, *4955*, *sēmainō* [1]
well known, *5745*, *phaneros* [1]

KNOWS [37]

knows, *3857*, *oida* [14]
knows, *1182*, *ginōskō* [12]
knows, *2105*, *epiginōskō* [2]
knows, *RPE* [1]
knows about, *1182*, *ginōskō* [1]
knows thoughts, *1182*, *ginōskō* [1]
knows, *1194*, *gnōsis* [1]
knows heart, *2841*, *kardiognōstēs* [1]
knows how, *3857*, *oida* [1]
knows thoughts, *3857*, *oida* [1]
knows no bounds, *5668*, *hyperperisseuō* [1]
knows, *5745*, *phaneros* [1]

KORAH'S [1]

Korah's, *3169*, *Kore* [1]

KORAZIN [2]

Korazin, *5960*, *Chorazin* [2]

KOUM [1]

koum, *3182*, *koum* [1]

LABOR [13]

labor, *3159*, *kopiaō* [5]
labor, *3160*, *kopos* [5]
labor, *2240*, *ergon* [1]
labor pains, *6047*, *ōdin* [1]
have labor pains, *6048*, *ōdinō* [1]

LABORED [1]

labored, *3160*, *kopos* [1]

LABORING [1]

laboring, *3160*, *kopos* [1]

LABORS [1]

labors, *3159*, *kopiaō* [1]

LACK [11]

lack of faith, *602*, *apistia* [4]
lack, *5728*, *hystereō* [4]
lack of self-control, *202*, *akrasia* [1]
lack, *3309*, *leipō* [1]
lack, *4024*, *ou* [1]

LACKED [1]

lacked, *5728*, *hystereō* [1]

LACKING [5]

lacking, *5729*, *hysterēma* [3]
lacking, *3309*, *leipō* [1]
lacking, *3891*, *oknēros* [1]

LACKS [1]

lacks, *3309*, *leipō* [1]

LADY [2]

dear lady, *3257*, *kyria* [1]
lady, *3257*, *kyria* [1]

LAID [30]

laid, *5502*, *tithēmi* [10]
laid on, *2095+2093*, *epiballō+epi* [2]
laid, *3023*, *keimai* [2]
laid away, *641*, *apokeimai* [1]
laid, *700*, *apotithēmi* [1]
laid, *965*, *ballō* [1]
laid on, *2120*, *epithesis* [1]
laid across, *2130+2093*, *epikeimai+epi* [1]
laid on, *2202*, *epitithēmi* [1]
laid bare, *2351*, *heuriskō* [1]
laid the foundations of, *2530*, *themelioō* [1]
laid out, *3023*, *keimai* [1]
laid up, *3023*, *keimai* [1]
laid, *4849*, *rhiptō* [1]
laid plans, *5206+3284*,
    symboulion+lambanō [1]
laid down, *5502*, *tithēmi* [1]
laid in, *5502*, *tithēmi* [1]
laid bare, *5548*, *trachēlizō* [1]
laid bare, *5745*, *phaneros* [1]

LAKE [38]

lake, *2498*, *thalassa* [23]
lake, *3349*, *limnē* [10]
other side of the lake, *4305*, *peran* [2]
across the lake, *527*, *antipera* [1]
across the lake, *1650+3836+4305*,
    eis+ho+peran [1]
by the lake, *4144*, *parathalassios* [1]

LAMA [2]

lama, *3316*, *lema* [2]

LAMB [38]

lamb, *768*, *arnion* [28]
lamb, *303*, *amnos* [4]
lamb, *RPE* [3]
Passover lamb, *4247*, *pascha* [3]

LAMB'S [1]

lamb's, *768*, *arnion* [1]

LAMBS [2]

lambs, *748*, *arēn* [1]
lambs, *768*, *arnion* [1]

LAME [10]

lame, *6000*, *chōlos* [10]

LAMECH [1]

Lamech, *3285*, *Lamech* [1]

LAMP [12]

lamp, *3394*, *lychnos* [12]

LAMPS [8]

lamps, *3286*, *lampas* [7]
lamps, *3394*, *lychnos* [1]

LAMPSTAND [2]

lampstand, *3393*, *lychnia* [2]

LAMPSTANDS [6]

lampstands, *3393*, *lychnia* [6]

LAND [40]

land, *1178*, *gē* [31]
land, *RPE* [3]
land, *6001*, *chōra* [2]
land, *6005*, *chōrion* [2]
the land^s, *899*, *autos* [1]
land, *3831*, *xēros* [1]

LANDED [11]

landed, *2982*, *katerchomai* [3]
landed, *2002*, *exerchomai* [2]
landed, *609+1650+3836+1178*,
    apobainō+eis+ho+gē [1]
landed, *2093+3836+1178+2262*,
    epi+ho+gē+erchomai [1]
landed, *2262+2093+3836+1178*,
    erchomai+epi+ho+gē [1]
landed, *2262*, *erchomai* [1]
landed, *2864*, *katagō* [1]
landed, *2918*, *katantaō* [1]

LANDOWNER [3]

landowner, *476+3867*,
    anthrōpos+oikodespotēs [2]
landowner, *3867*, *oikodespotēs* [1]

LANDS [1]

lands, *6005*, *chōrion* [1]

LANES [1]

country lanes, *5850*, *phragmos* [1]

LANGUAGE [13]

language, *1185*, *glōssa* [5]
language, *1365*, *dialektos* [3]

filthy language, *155, aischrologia* [1]
his native language, *1666+3836+2625,*
   ek+ho+idios [1]
use language, *3281, laleō* [1]
language, *3282, lalia* [1]
in Lycaonian language, *3378, Lykaonisti* [1]

LANGUAGES [3]

languages, *1185, glōssa* [2]
languages, *5889, phōnē* [1]

LANTERNS [1]

lanterns, *3286, lampas* [1]

LAODICEA [6]

Laodicea, *3293, Laodikeia* [6]

LAODICEANS [1]

Laodiceans, *3294, Laodikeus* [1]

LAP [1]

lap, *3146, kolpos* [1]

LARGE [54]

large, *4498, polys* [29]
large, *3489, megas* [10]
large, *2653, hikanos* [4]
large millstone, *3685+3948, mylos+onikos* [2]
large amount, *4929+5552, saton+treis* [2]
large number, *2653, hikanos* [1]
large sum, *2653, hikanos* [1]
large, *4246, pas* [1]
what large, *4383, pēlikos* [1]
large number, *4436, plēthos* [1]
very large, *4498, polys* [1]
so large, *5496, tēlikoutos* [1]

LARGER [1]

larger, *4498, polys* [1]

LARGEST [2]

largest, *3505, meizōn* [2]

LASEA [1]

Lasea, *3297, Lasaia* [1]

LASHES [1]

lashes, *AIT* [1]

LAST [61]

last, *2274, eschatos* [42]
breathed last, *1743, ekpneō* [2]
last year, *4373, perysi* [2]
last, *NIG* [1]
last, *RPE* [1]
at last, *785, arti* [1]
last forever, *915, aphthartos* [1]
last, *1412, diateleō* [1]
last, *1639, eimi* [1]
last of all, *2274, eschatos* [1]
at last, *2453+4537, ēdē+pote* [1]
now at last, *2453+4537, ēdē+pote* [1]
last, *3531, menō* [1]
last night, *4047+3836+3816,*
   houtos+ho+nyx [1]
faith from first to last, *4411+1650+4411,*
   pistis+eis+pistis [1]
last, *5465, telos* [1]
last of all, *5731, hysteros* [1]
not last, *5778, phthartos* [1]

LASTING [1]

lasting, *3531, menō* [1]

LASTS [2]

lasts, *1639, eimi* [1]
lasts, *3531, menō* [1]

LATE [6]

late, *6052, hōra* [2]
late in afternoon, *2465+806+3111,*
   hēmera+archō+klinō [1]
late, *3913, olynthos* [1]
late, *4070, opsios* [1]
late in the day, *6052+4498, hōra+polys* [1]

LATER [38]

later, *3552, meta* [7]
later, *3552+4047, meta+houtos* [6]
later, *5731, hysteros* [5]
later, *3516, mellō* [4]
later, *1460, diistēmi* [2]
later, *2083, epeita* [2]
later, *2779, kai* [2]
later, *948, achri* [1]
later, *1309, deuteron* [1]
a few days later, *1328+2465, dia+hēmera* [1]
later, *1335, diaginomai* [1]
later, *1404, diastēma* [1]
a week later, *3552+2465+3893,*
   meta+hēmera+oktō [1]
some time later, *3552+4047, meta+houtos* [1]
when later, *3552, meta* [1]
later, *4099, palin* [1]
later on, *5731, hysteros* [1]

LATEST [1]

latest, *2785, kainos* [1]

LATIN [1]

in Latin, *4872, Rhōmaisti* [1]

LATTER [4]

the latter[s], *4047, houtos* [3]
latter, *3525, men* [1]

LAUGH [2]

laugh, *1151, gelaō* [2]

LAUGHED [3]

laughed at, *2860, katagelaō* [3]

LAUGHTER [1]

laughter, *1152, gelōs* [1]

LAVISHED [2]

lavished, *1443, didōmi* [1]
lavished, *4355, perisseuō* [1]

LAW [272]

law, *3795, nomos* [182]
teachers of the law, *1208, grammateus* [57]
experts in the law, *3788, nomikos* [5]
law, *RPE* [3]
not having the law, *491, anomos* [3]
apart from the law, *492, anomōs* [2]
teacher of the law, *1208, grammateus* [2]
expert in the law, *3788, nomikos* [2]
teachers of the law, *3791, nomodidaskalos* [2]
against law, *116, athemitos* [1]
breaks law, *490+4472, anomia+poieō* [1]
free from law, *491, anomos* [1]
under law, *1937, ennomos* [1]

law, *1953, entolē* [1]
the law, *2003, exesti* [1]
goes to law, *3212, krinō* [1]
about law, *3788, nomikos* [1]
teacher of the law, *3791, nomodidaskalos* [1]
receiving of the law, *3792, nomothesia* [1]
law was given, *3793, nomotheteō* [1]
the expert in the law[s], *3836+1254, ho+de* [1]
the law forbids, *4024+2003, ou+exesti* [1]
violate the law, *4174, paranomeō* [1]

LAW'S [1]

law's, *3795, nomos* [1]

LAWBREAKER [3]

lawbreaker, *4127+3795, parabatēs+nomos* [2]
lawbreaker, *4127, parabatēs* [1]

LAWBREAKERS [2]

lawbreakers, *491, anomos* [1]
lawbreakers, *4127, parabatēs* [1]

LAWFUL [12]

lawful, *2003, exesti* [10]
lawful for, *2003, exesti* [1]
lawful for, *4024+2003, ou+exesti* [1]

LAWGIVER [1]

Lawgiver, *3794, nomothetēs* [1]

LAWLESS [6]

lawless, *118, athesmos* [2]
lawless, *491, anomos* [2]
lawless acts, *490, anomia* [1]
the lawless[s] one, *4005, hos* [1]

LAWLESSNESS [3]

lawlessness, *490, anomia* [3]

LAWS [2]

laws, *3795, nomos* [2]

LAWSUITS [1]

lawsuits, *3210, krima* [1]

LAWYER [2]

lawyer, *3788, nomikos* [1]
lawyer, *4842, rhētōr* [1]

LAY [26]

lay down, *5502, tithēmi* [8]
lay, *5502, tithēmi* [4]
lay sick, *820, astheneō* [2]
lay, *3111, klinō* [2]
lay open, *487, anoigō* [1]
lay up treasure, *631, apothēsaurizō* [1]
lay hold of, *773, harpazō* [1]
lay, *965, ballō* [1]
the rule lay down, *1411, diatassō* [1]
lay, *1753, ekteinō* [1]
lay on, *2095+2093, epiballō+epi* [1]
lay on, *2202, epitithēmi* [1]
on lay, *2202, epitithēmi* [1]
lay, *3023, keimai* [1]

LAYING [6]

laying on, *2120, epithesis* [3]
laying on, *2202, epitithēmi* [2]
laying, *2850, kataballō* [1]

LAYS [2]

lays down, *5502, tithēmi* [1]
lays, *5502, tithēmi* [1]

LAZARUS [18]

Lazarus, *3276, Lazaros* [15]
Lazarus^s, *899, autos* [2]
Lazarus, *RPE* [1]

LAZY [3]

lazy, *734, argos* [1]
lazy, *3821, nōthros* [1]
lazy, *3891, oknēros* [1]

LEAD [18]

lead to, *4639, pros* [3]
lead, *AIT* [2]
lead into, *1662+1650, eispherō+eis* [2]
lead, *3842, hodēgeō* [2]
lead astray, *4414, planaō* [2]
lead away, *552, apagō* [1]
lead out, *552, apagō* [1]
lead out of, *1974+1666, exagō+ek* [1]
lead a quiet life, *2483, hēsychazō* [1]
put in charge to lead, *4080, paidagōgos* [1]
lead, *5770, pherō* [1]
someone to lead by the hand, *5933,
    cheiragōgos* [1]

LEADERS [12]

leaders, *2451, hēgeomai* [4]
leaders, *807, archōn* [3]
leaders, *4755, prōtos* [2]
seemed to be leaders, *1506, dokeō* [1]
leaders, *1543, dynatos* [1]
leaders, *1639+4755, eimi+prōtos* [1]

LEADERSHIP [2]

place of leadership, *2175, episkopē* [1]
leadership, *4613, proistēmi* [1]

LEADING [13]

leading to, *1650, eis* [3]
leading a rebellion, *3334, lēstēs* [3]
leading, *4755, prōtos* [3]
leading, *2029, exochē* [1]
leading the way, *4575, proagō* [1]
leading, *4601, proerchomai* [1]
leading, *5770, pherō* [1]

LEADS [17]

leads to, *1650, eis* [4]
leads, *552, apagō* [2]
leads to, *1639, eimi* [2]
leads, *AIT* [1]
leads, *72, agō* [1]
leads, *1675, ekballō* [1]
leads out, *1974, exagō* [1]
leads in triumphal procession, *2581,
    thriambeuō* [1]
leads to, *2848, kata* [1]
leads, *3842, hodēgeō* [1]
leads astray, *4414, planaō* [1]
leads to, *4639, pros* [1]

LEAF [1]

in leaf, *2400+5877, echō+phyllon* [1]

LEANED [2]

leaned, *AIT* [1]
leaned back, *404, anapiptō* [1]

LEANING [1]

leaning back, *404, anapiptō* [1]

LEAP [1]

leap for joy, *5015, skirtaō* [1]

LEAPED [2]

leaped, *5015, skirtaō* [2]

LEARN [14]

learn, *3443, manthanō* [10]
learn, *198, akoē* [1]
learn, *1182, ginōskō* [1]
learn the truth, *2105, epiginōskō* [1]
learn, *3857, oida* [1]

LEARNED [25]

learned, *3443, manthanō* [8]
learned, *1182, ginōskō* [6]
learned, *2105, epiginōskō* [3]
learned, *5305, synetos* [2]
learned, *201, akouō* [1]
learned, *208, akriboō* [1]
learned about, *1182, ginōskō* [1]
learned, *3360, logios* [1]
learned the secret, *3679, myeō* [1]
learned about, *5745+1181,
    phaneros+ginomai* [1]

LEARNING [4]

get learning, *1207+3857, gramma+oida* [1]
learning, *1207, gramma* [1]
learning, *3443, manthanō* [1]
learning, *4785, pynthanomai* [1]

LEARNS [1]

learns, *3443, manthanō* [1]

LEAST [18]

least, *1788, elachistos* [7]
least, *3625, mikros* [4]
least stroke of a pen, *3037, keraia* [2]
or at least, *1623+1254+3590, ei+de+mē* [1]
least important, *2274, eschatos* [1]
at least, *2829, kan* [1]
not in the least, *3594, mēdeis* [1]
not in the least, *4029, oudeis* [1]

LEATHER [2]

leather, *1294, dermatinos* [2]

LEAVE [50]

leave, *918, aphiēmi* [8]
leave, *2002, exerchomai* [8]
leave alone, *918, aphiēmi* [5]
leave, *2901, kataleipō* [4]
leave, *599+608, aperchomai+apo* [3]
leave, *3553, metabainō* [3]
leave, *6004, chōrizō* [2]
leave, *NIG* [1]
leave, *72, agō* [1]
leave, *479, aniēmi* [1]
leave, *668, apolyō* [1]
leave, *922, aphixis* [1]
leave alone, *923+608, aphistēmi+apo* [1]
leave, *1443, didōmi* [1]
leave, *1666+2002, ek+exerchomai* [1]
leave, *1744, ekporeuomai* [1]
leave, *1996, exeimi1* [1]
leave, *2002+1666+1666,
    exerchomai+ek+ek* [1]
leave, *2002+1666, exerchomai+ek* [1]

leave, *2002+2032, exerchomai+exō* [1]
leave, *2032+2002, exō+exerchomai* [1]
leave your life of sin, *3600+279,
    mēketi+hamartanō* [1]
leave, *4513, poreuomai* [1]
leave, *5632, hypagō* [1]

LEAVES [12]

leaves, *5877, phyllon* [5]
leaves, *NIG* [1]
leaves, *713+608, apochōreō+apo* [1]
leaves, *918, aphiēmi* [1]
leaves, *2400, echō* [1]
leaves, *2901, kataleipō* [1]
sprout leaves, *4582, proballō* [1]
leaves, *6004, chōrizō* [1]

LEAVING [23]

leaving, *918, aphiēmi* [4]
leaving, *2002, exerchomai* [3]
leaving, *2901, kataleipō* [3]
leaving, *698, apotassō* [1]
leaving behind, *918, aphiēmi* [1]
leaving, *1431, diachōrizō* [1]
leaving, *1744+1666, ekporeuomai+ek* [1]
leaving, *1744+608, ekporeuomai+apo* [1]
leaving, *1744, ekporeuomai* [1]
leaving, *1996, exeimi1* [1]
leaving behind, *2901, kataleipō* [1]
leaving undone, *4223, pariēmi* [1]
leaving, *4513+608, poreuomai+apo* [1]
leaving, *4513, poreuomai* [1]
leaving, *5632, hypagō* [1]
leaving, *5701, hypolimpanō* [1]

LECTURE [2]

lecture, *1438, didaskō* [1]
lecture hall, *5391, scholē* [1]

LED [39]

led, *72, agō* [6]
led away, *552, apagō* [4]
led out, *1974, exagō* [4]
led out of, *1974+1666, exagō+ek* [2]
led away, *72, agō* [1]
led off, *72, agō* [1]
led out, *72, agō* [1]
led captives in his train, *169+168,
    aichmalōteuō+aichmalōsia* [1]
led up, *343, anagō* [1]
led, *343, anagō* [1]
led up, *429, anapherō* [1]
led, *429, anapherō* [1]
led astray, *552, apagō* [1]
led, *552, apagō* [1]
led away, *708, apopherō* [1]
led in revolt, *923+3958, aphistēmi+opisō* [1]
led to, *1650, eis* [1]
led into, *1652+1650, eisagō+eis* [1]
led, *1766, ekpherō* [1]
led out of, *2002+1666, exerchomai+ek* [1]
led astray, *3496, methistēmi* [1]
led astray, *4414, planaō* [1]
led the way, *4575, proagō* [1]
led into sin, *4997, skandalizō* [1]
led astray, *5270, synapagō* [1]
led astray, *5780, phtheirō* [1]
led by the hand, *5932, cheiragōgeō* [1]

LEE [3]

passed to the lee of, *5709, hypopleō* [1]
sailed to the lee of, *5709, hypopleō* [1]
passed to the lee of, *5720, hypotrechō* [1]

LEFT [139]

left, *918, aphiēmi* [36]
left, *2002, exerchomai* [18]
left, *2901, kataleipō* [11]
left, *2381, euōnymos* [8]
left over, *4355, perisseuō* [5]
left, *599+608, aperchomai+apo* [4]
left, *657, apoleipō* [4]
left, *2002+1666, exerchomai+ek* [4]
left, *432, anachōreō* [3]
left, *754, aristeros* [3]
left, *923+608, aphistēmi+apo* [3]
left, *599, aperchomai* [2]
left, *698, apotassō* [2]
left, *3553, metabainō* [2]
left, *4335, perileipomai* [2]
left, *AIT* [1]
left, *NIG* [1]
left, *326, anabainō* [1]
left, *482+608, anistēmi+apo* [1]
left from, *599+608, aperchomai+apo* [1]
left, *608+609, apo+apobainō* [1]
left, *608, apo* [1]
left, *713+608, apochōreō+apo* [1]
left hand, *754, aristeros* [1]
left, *923, aphistēmi* [1]
left, *1460, diistēmi* [1]
left, *1572, eaō* [1]
left, *1593, enkataleipō* [1]
left, *1666+2002, ek+exerchomai* [1]
left, *1674, ekbainō* [1]
left, *1744, ekporeuomai* [1]
left, *1996, exeimi1* [1]
left, *2285, eti* [1]
left, *3309, leipō* [1]
left, *3531, menō* [1]
left, *3558, metairō* [1]
left all alone, *3670, monoō* [1]
left, *4124, parabainō* [1]
left unpunished, *4217, paresis* [1]
left over, *4354, perisseuma* [1]
left, *4513+608+4725, poreuomai+apo+prosōpon* [1]
left, *4513, poreuomai* [1]
left, *5699, hypoleipō* [1]
left, *5715, hypostrephō* [1]
left, *6004, chōrizō* [1]

LEGAL [2]

legal, *1937, ennomos* [1]
legal, *2003, exesti* [1]

LEGALISTIC [1]

legalistic, *1877+3795, en+nomos* [1]

LEGION [3]

legion, *3305, legiōn* [3]

LEGIONS [1]

legions, *3305, legiōn* [1]

LEGS [4]

legs, *5003, skelos* [3]
legs, *4546, pous* [1]

LEND [4]

lend, *1247, danizō* [3]
lend, *3079, kichrēmi* [1]

LENGTH [2]

length, *AIT* [1]
length, *RPE* [1]

LENGTHY [2]

lengthy, *3431, makros* [2]

LEOPARD [1]

leopard, *4203, pardalis* [1]

LEPER [2]

Leper, *3320, lepros* [2]

LEPROSY [11]

leprosy, *3319, lepra* [4]
have leprosy, *3320, lepros* [3]
man with leprosy, *3320, lepros* [2]
had leprosy, *3320, lepros* [1]
with leprosy, *3320, lepros* [1]

LESS [8]

less, *AIT* [1]
less anxiety, *267, alypos* [1]
less honorable, *872, atimos* [1]
less, *1783, elattoō* [1]
less, *2482, hēssōn* [1]
show less respect, *2969, kataphroneō* [1]
less, *3437, mallon* [1]
less than two miles, *6055+608+5084+1278, hōs+apo+stadion+dekapente* [1]

LESSER [1]

lesser, *1781, elassōn* [1]

LESSON [2]

lesson, *4130, parabolē* [2]

LEST [1]

lest, *2671+3590, hina+mē* [1]

LET [206]

let, *AIT* [136]
let, *918, aphiēmi* [18]
let, *NIG* [10]
let go, *668, apolyō* [6]
let, *1572, eaō* [6]
to let, *2671, hina* [6]
let, *2205, epitrepō* [5]
let, *1443, didōmi* [3]
let down, *5899, chalaō* [3]
let go, *918, aphiēmi* [2]
let, *2671, hina* [2]
let, *RPE* [1]
let be, *918, aphiēmi* [1]
let go of, *918, aphiēmi* [1]
let go on, *918, aphiēmi* [1]
let have, *918, aphiēmi* [1]
let down, *965, ballō* [1]
let down, *2768, kathiēmi* [1]
let down, *2849, katabainō* [1]
let, *3968, hopōs* [1]

LET'S [10]

let's, *AIT* [10]

LETS [1]

lets, *AIT* [1]

LETTER [22]

letter, *2186, epistolē* [15]
letter, *1207, gramma* [2]
letter, *AIT* [1]
letter, *RPE* [1]
sent the letter, *1211, graphō* [1]
written a letter, *2182, epistellō* [1]
smallest letter, *2740, iōta* [1]

LETTERS [13]

letters, *2186, epistolē* [9]
letters, *1207, gramma* [3]
his letters[s], *4005, hos* [1]

LEVEL [2]

level, *3981, orthos* [1]
level, *4268, pedinos* [1]

LEVI [12]

Levi, *3322, Leui* [8]
Levi, *RPE* [3]
Levi[s], *899, autos* [1]

LEVI'S [1]

Levi's[s], *899, autos* [1]

LEVITE [2]

Levite, *3324, Leuitēs* [2]

LEVITES [1]

Levites, *3324, Leuitēs* [1]

LEVITICAL [1]

Levitical, *3325, Leuitikos* [1]

LEWDNESS [1]

lewdness, *816, aselgeia* [1]

LIAR [8]

liar, *6026, pseustēs* [8]

LIARS [5]

liars, *6026, pseustēs* [2]
liars, *6014, pseudēs* [1]
liars, *6016, pseudologos* [1]
liars, *6017, pseudomai* [1]

LIBERAL [1]

liberal, *103, hadrotēs* [1]

LIBERATED [1]

liberated, *1802, eleutheroō* [1]

LIBYA [1]

Libya, *3340, Libyē* [1]

LICENSE [1]

license for immorality, *816, aselgeia* [1]

LICKED [1]

licked, *2143, epileichō* [1]

LIE [11]

lie, *6017, pseudomai* [4]
lie, *6022, pseudos* [4]
lie, *AIT* [1]
not lie, *950, apseudēs* [1]
lie, *2879, katakeimai* [1]

LIED [2]

lied to, *6017, pseudomai* [1]
lied, *6017, pseudomai* [1]

LIES [4]

lies, *AIT* [1]
lies[s], *899, autos* [1]
lies, *965, ballō* [1]
lies, *3281+3836+6022, laleō+ho+pseudos* [1]

LIFE [234]

life, *2437, zōē* [128]
life, *6034, psychē* [32]
raised to life, *1586, egeirō* [7]
life, *RPE* [4]
way of life, *419, anastrophē* [4]
gives life, *2443, zōopoieō* [4]
life, *AIT* [3]
the life⁵, *4005, hos* [3]
live a life, *4344, peripateō* [3]
life, *419, anastrophē* [2]
come back to life, *482, anistēmi* [2]
take life, *650, apokteinō* [2]
came to life, *2409, zaō* [2]
life, *2461, hēlikia* [2]
holy life, *40, hagiasmos* [1]
way of life, *73, agōgē* [1]
life, *172, aiōn* [1]
sinful life, *283, hamartōlos* [1]
sprang to life, *348, anazaō* [1]
take life easy, *399, anapauō* [1]
raised to life again, *414, anastasis* [1]
raised to life, *482, anistēmi* [1]
life, *1050, bios* [1]
of life, *1053, biōtikos* [1]
of this life, *1053, biōtikos* [1]
life, *1161, genesis* [1]
spare life, *1407, diasōzō* [1]
righteous life, *1466, dikaiosynē* [1]
gives life, *1639+2443, eimi+zōopoieō* [1]
brought to life, *2409, zaō* [1]
come to life, *2409, zaō* [1]
life, *2409, zaō* [1]
returned to life, *2409, zaō* [1]
brings life, *2437, zōē* [1]
gives life to, *2441, zōogoneō* [1]
come to life, *2443, zōopoieō* [1]
give life, *2443, zōopoieō* [1]
impart life, *2443, zōopoieō* [1]
lead a quiet life, *2483, hēsychazō* [1]
from everyday life, *2848+476,
    kata+anthrōpos* [1]
life, *3104, klēsis* [1]
long life, *3432, makrochronios* [1]
leave your life of sin, *3600+279,
    mēketi+hamartanō* [1]
way of life, *3847, hodos* [1]
daily life, *4344, peripateō* [1]
retain the place in life, *4344, peripateō* [1]
life on earth, *4922, sarx* [1]
life, *4922, sarx* [1]
your life, *4932, seautou* [1]
life, *5989, chronos* [1]

LIFE'S [1]

life's, *1050, bios* [1]

LIFE-GIVING [1]

life-giving, *2443, zōopoieō* [1]

LIFEBOAT [3]

lifeboat, *5002, skaphē* [3]

LIFELESS [1]

lifeless, *953, apsychos* [1]

LIFETIME [1]

lifetime, *2437, zōē* [1]

LIFT [9]

lift up, *149, airō* [2]
lift up, *2048, epairō* [2]
lift up, *5738, hypsoō* [2]

lift a finger, *1235, daktylos* [1]
lift out, *1586, egeirō* [1]
lift, *4718, prospsauō* [1]

LIFTED [13]

lifted up, *5738, hypsoō* [8]
lifted up, *2048, epairō* [2]
lifted up, *377, analambanō* [1]
lifted to his feet, *1586, egeirō* [1]
lifted, *4712, prospherō* [1]

LIGAMENT [1]

ligament, *913, haphē* [1]

LIGAMENTS [1]

ligaments, *913, haphē* [1]

LIGHT [93]

light, *5890, phōs* [66]
full of light, *5893, phōteinos* [3]
light, *1787, elaphros* [2]
light, *5766, phengos* [2]
light, *5895, phōtismos* [2]
light, *RPE* [1]
light, *721, haptō* [1]
light, *847, astrapē* [1]
bring to light, *1317, dēloō* [1]
light of the sun, *2463, hēlios* [1]
light, *2794, kaiō* [1]
gives light, *3290, lampō* [1]
light, *3394, lychnos* [1]
without light, *3590+5743, mē+phainō* [1]
make light of, *3902, oligōreō* [1]
gave light, *5743, phainō* [1]
brought to light, *5746, phaneroō* [1]
bring to light, *5894, phōtizō* [1]
brought to light, *5894, phōtizō* [1]
give light, *5894, phōtizō* [1]
gives light to, *5894, phōtizō* [1]
gives light, *5894, phōtizō* [1]
received light, *5894, phōtizō* [1]

LIGHTED [1]

lighted, *5893, phōteinos* [1]

LIGHTENED [1]

lightened, *3185, kouphizō* [1]

LIGHTING [1]

lighting, *2262, erchomai* [1]

LIGHTLY [1]

lightly, *1786, elaphria* [1]

LIGHTNING [10]

flashes of lightning, *847, astrapē* [4]
lightning, *847, astrapē* [4]
that gleamed like lightning, *848, astraptō* [1]
flash of lightning, *1993, exastraptō* [1]

LIGHTS [5]

lights, *721, haptō* [2]
lights, *5890, phōs* [2]
lights up, *3290, lampō* [1]

LIKE [260]

like, *6055, hōs* [124]
like, *3927, homoios* [37]
like, *3929, homoioō* [8]
like this, *4048, houtōs* [7]
like, *6059, hōsei* [6]

like, *6061, hōsper* [6]
like, *2848, kata* [5]
like, *NIG* [4]
like, *RPE* [3]
like, *2777, kathōs* [3]
like, *4048, houtōs* [3]
looked like, *6055, hōs* [3]
like, *2036, eoika* [2]
like, *2749, kathaper* [2]
like that, *4048, houtōs* [2]
poured out like a drink offering, *5064,
    spendō* [2]
like this, *5525, toioutos* [2]
sounded like, *6055, hōs* [2]
like, *AIT* [1]
that gleamed like lightning, *848, astraptō* [1]
like, *926, aphomoioō* [1]
like, *1089, boulomai* [1]
looked so much like, *1181+6059,
    ginomai+hōsei* [1]
thinking like, *1181+3836+5856,
    ginomai+ho+phrēn* [1]
like a Gentile, *1619, ethnikōs* [1]
looks like, *1639, eimi* [1]
like a Jew, *2680, Ioudaikōs* [1]
like angels, *2694, isangelos* [1]
like, *2701, isopsychos* [1]
just like this, *2848+3836+899,
    kata+ho+autos* [1]
like, *3888, hoios* [1]
just like, *3926, homoiopathēs* [1]
like, *3926, homoiopathēs* [1]
like, *3927+4047, homoios+houtos* [1]
like, *3928, homoiotēs* [1]
made like, *3929, homoioō* [1]
say is like, *3929, homoioō* [1]
like, *3930, homoiōma* [1]
look like, *3930, homoiōma* [1]
looked like, *3930+3927,
    homoiōma+homoios* [1]
like, *3931, homoiōs* [1]
looked like this, *4048, houtōs* [1]
like, *4234, paromoiazō* [1]
like, *4235, paromoios* [1]
becoming like, *5214, symmorphizō* [1]
like, *5215, symmorphos* [1]
man like that, *5525, toioutos* [1]
men like him, *5525, toioutos* [1]
just like, *6055, hōs* [1]
like, *6055+1569, hōs+ean* [1]

LIKE-MINDED [1]

being like-minded, *3836+899+5858,
    ho+autos+phroneō* [1]

LIKED [2]

liked, *1089, boulomai* [1]
liked, *2452, hēdeōs* [1]

LIKENESS [7]

likeness, *1635, eikōn* [4]
likeness, *3930, homoiōma* [2]
likeness, *3932, homoiōsis* [1]

LIKEWISE [9]

likewise, *3931, homoiōs* [3]
likewise, *4048, houtōs* [2]
likewise, *6058, hōsautōs* [2]
likewise, *2779, kai* [1]
likewise, *4048+2779, houtōs+kai* [1]

LILIES [2]

lilies, *3211, krinon* [2]

LIMIT [2]

heap up to the limit, *405, anaplēroō* [1]
limit, *3586, metron* [1]

LIMITS [2]

beyond limits, *296, ametros* [1]
limits, *296, ametros* [1]

LINE [3]

line, *45, ankistron* [1]
acting in line, *3980, orthopodeō* [1]
line, *4255, patria* [1]

LINEN [18]

fine linen, *1115, byssinos* [5]
strips of linen, *3856, othonion* [4]
linen cloth, *4984, sindōn* [3]
fine linen, *1116, byssos* [1]
strips of linen, *3024, keiria* [1]
linen, *3351, linon* [1]
linen, *3166, othonion* [1]
linen garment, *4984, sindōn* [1]
linen, *4984, sindōn* [1]

LINUS [1]

Linus, *3352, Linos* [1]

LION [5]

lion, *3329, leōn* [5]

LION'S [1]

lion's, *3329, leōn* [1]

LIONS [3]

lions, *3329, leōn* [3]

LIPS [12]

lips, *5125, stoma* [6]
lips, *5927, cheilos* [6]

LIST [2]

put on the list, *2899, katalegō* [1]
not put on such a list, *4148, paraiteomai* [1]

LISTEN [52]

listen, *201, akouō* [39]
listen, *72, agō* [2]
refuses to listen, *4159, parakouō* [2]
listen, *201+2627, akouō+idou* [1]
listen, *212, akroatēs* [1]
listen, *462, anechomai* [1]
listen, *1653, eisakouō* [1]
listen carefully, *1969, enōtizomai* [1]
listen, *2623, ide* [1]
listen, *2627, idou* [1]
listen to appeal, *4151, parakaleō* [1]
listen carefully,
  *5502+5148+1650+3836+4044+5148,
  tithēmi+sy+eis+ho+ous+sy* [1]

LISTENED [5]

listened, *201, akouō* [5]

LISTENING [10]

listening, *201, akouō* [8]
listening, *2053, epakroaomai* [1]
listening to, *4275, peithō* [1]

LISTENS [10]

listens, *201, akouō* [9]
listens, *212+1639, akroatēs+eimi* [1]

LITTLE [81]

little, *3625, mikros* [20]
little, *3900, oligos* [8]
a little while, *3625, mikros* [7]
little children, *4086, paidion* [7]
little child, *4086, paidion* [7]
of little faith, *3899, oligopistos* [5]
little while, *3900, oligos* [4]
little scroll, *1044, biblaridion* [3]
little, *1099, brachys* [3]
very little, *1788, elachistos* [3]
little daughter, *2589, thygatrion* [2]
little children, *3758, nēpios* [2]
little, *AIT* [1]
for a little while, *1099, brachys* [1]
care very little, *1650+1788+1639,
  eis+elachistos+eimi* [1]
have too little, *1782, elattoneō* [1]
of little account, *2024, exoutheneō* [1]
stayed a little longer, *2091+5989,
  epechō+chronos* [1]
little girl, *3166, korasion* [1]
little faith, *3898, oligopistia* [1]
for a little while, *4639+6052, pros+hōra* [1]
little while, *6052, hōra* [1]

LIVE [135]

live, *2409, zaō* [50]
live, *4344, peripateō* [17]
live, *2997, katoikeō* [7]
live, *AIT* [5]
live, *1639, eimi* [4]
live, *3531, menō* [4]
live, *RPE* [3]
live, *418, anastrephō* [3]
live a life, *4344, peripateō* [3]
live with, *5182, syzaō* [3]
live, *NIG* [2]
to live on, *1050, bios* [2]
live in peace, *1644, eirēneuō* [2]
live, *2764, kathēmai* [2]
live, *3861, oikeō* [2]
live, *5012, skēnoō* [2]
live, *419, anastrophē* [1]
live, *1051, bioō* [1]
live, *1341, diagō* [1]
live at peace, *1644, eirēneuō* [1]
live, *1877, en* [1]
live with, *1940+1877, enoikeō+en* [1]
live, *2400, echō* [1]
as surely as I live, *2409+1609, zaō+egō* [1]
live on, *2409, zaō* [1]
live, *2437, zōē* [1]
live, *2942, kataskēnoō* [1]
way live, *2949, katastēma* [1]
live in, *2997, katoikeō* [1]
live, *3000, katoikia* [1]
caused to live, *3001, katoikizō* [1]
live in harmony, *3836+899+5858,
  ho+autos+phroneō* [1]
people live scattered among, *3836+1402,
  ho+diaspora* [1]
live in, *3864, oikia* [1]
live in harmony with, *3939, homophrōn* [1]
live lives, *4344, peripateō* [1]
live by, *4472, poieō* [1]
live, *4556, prassō* [1]
live up, *5123, stoicheō* [1]
live with, *5324, synoikeō* [1]

LIVED [30]

lived, *1639, eimi* [6]
lived, *2409, zaō* [4]
lived, *2997, katoikeō* [4]
lived, *1181, ginomai* [2]
lived in, *2997, katoikeō* [2]
lived, *AIT* [1]
lived, *RPE* [1]
lived, *418, anastrephō* [1]
way lived, *1052, biōsis* [1]
lived, *1341, diagō* [1]
lived, *1639+1695, eimi+ekei* [1]
lived in, *1940+1877, enoikeō+en* [1]
lived there, *2111, epidēmeō* [1]
lived, *2370, euphrainō* [1]
lived, *3531, menō* [1]
lived, *3836+2998+2400,
  ho+katoikēsis+echō* [1]
[lived in] self-indulgence, *5059, spatalaō* [1]
lived in luxury, *5587, tryphaō* [1]

LIVES [60]

lives, *2409, zaō* [15]
lives, *3531, menō* [12]
lives, *AIT* [7]
lives, *6034, psychē* [5]
lives, *419, anastrophē* [3]
lives, *3861, oikeō* [3]
lives, *RPE* [2]
lives in, *1940+1877, enoikeō+en* [2]
lives, *2997, katoikeō* [2]
lives, *1050, bios* [1]
lives on, *3576, metechō* [1]
risked lives, *3836+5549+5719,
  ho+trachēlos+hypotithēmi* [1]
lives in, *3861, oikeō* [1]
live lives, *4344, peripateō* [1]
lives by, *4472, poieō* [1]
lives for pleasure, *5059, spatalaō* [1]
lives, *5573, tropos* [1]
lives, *5989, chronos* [1]

LIVING [88]

living, *2409, zaō* [42]
living creatures, *2442, zōon* [13]
living, *2997, katoikeō* [5]
living creature, *2442, zōon* [4]
living, *2764, kathēmai* [3]
living, *3861, oikeō* [3]
living, *2437, zōē* [2]
living in, *2997, katoikeō* [2]
living, *3531, menō* [2]
living, *4513, poreuomai* [2]
living, *AIT* [1]
living out, *64, agrauleō* [1]
living among, *1594+1877, enkatoikeō+en* [1]
earn living, *2237, ergazomai* [1]
work for a living, *2237, ergazomai* [1]
receive living, *2409, zaō* [1]
living, *3836+2400+6034, ho+echō+psychē* [1]
living, *4344, peripateō* [1]
living in plenty, *4355, perisseuō* [1]
living, *5123, stoicheō* [1]
[living] in want, *5728, hystereō* [1]

LOAD [2]

load down, *5844, phortizō* [1]
load, *5845, phortion* [1]

LOADED [1]

loaded down, *5397, sōreuō* [1]

LOADS [1]

loads, *5845, phortion* [1]

LOAF [3]

loaf, *788, artos* [3]

LOAVES [22]

loaves, *788, artos* [18]
loaves of bread, *788, artos* [3]
loaves, *RPE* [1]

LOCAL [2]

local councils, *5284, synedrion* [2]

LOCKED [7]

locked, *3091, kleiō* [5]
locked up, *2881, katakleiō* [1]
locked up, *5168, synkleiō* [1]

LOCUSTS [4]

locusts, *210, akris* [4]

LODGING [2]

lodging, *2907, katalyō* [1]
gave lodging to, *5685, hypodechomai* [1]

LOIS [1]

Lois, *3396, Lōis* [1]

LONELY [2]

lonely places, *2245, erēmos* [1]
lonely, *2245, erēmos* [1]

LONG [78]

long, *AIT* [7]
how long, *2401+4536, heōs+pote* [7]
long, *2653, hikanos* [4]
long, *2121, epithymeō* [3]
long, *2160, epipotheō* [3]
long, *3601, mēkos* [3]
long ago, *4093, palai* [3]
long ago, *792, archaios* [2]
people long ago, *792, archaios* [2]
as long as, *2093+4012+5989,*
   epi+hosos+chronos [2]
has long hair, *3150, komaō* [2]
long, *4498, polys* [2]
long, *5989, chronos* [2]
long, *RPE* [1]
long ago, *172, aiōn* [1]
for a long time, *540, anōthen* [1]
long ago, *608+172, apo+aiōn* [1]
as long as, *948+4005, achri+hos* [1]
long ago, *1732, ekpalai* [1]
long, *1732, ekpalai* [1]
a long time, *2093+4498, epi+polys* [1]
as long as, *2093+4012, epi+hosos* [1]
only as long as, *2093+4012+5989,*
   epi+hosos+chronos [1]
long for, *2160, epipotheō* [1]
long for, *2162, epipothētos* [1]
before long, *2285+3625, eti+mikros* [1]
as long as still, *2285, eti* [1]
as long as, *2401, heōs* [1]
long hair, *3151, komē* [1]
long way off, *3426, makran* [1]
long distance, *3427, makrothen* [1]
long life, *3432, makrochronios* [1]
long, *3486, megalynō* [1]
long, *3489, megas* [1]
before very long, *3552+4024+4498,*
   meta+ou+polys [1]
all long, *3910, holos* [1]
so long as, *4012+5989, hosos+chronos* [1]
long period, *4498, polys* [1]
long time, *4498, polys* [1]
long, *4498+2465, polys+hēmera* [1]
long way off, *4522, porrō* [1]
long ago, *4537, pote* [1]

spoke long ago, *4625, prolegō* [1]
long, *5537, tosoutos* [1]
a long time in coming, *5988, chronizō* [1]
stayed so long, *5988, chronizō* [1]
staying away a long time, *5988, chronizō* [1]
taking a long time, *5988, chronizō* [1]
a long time, *5989+4024+3900,*
   chronos+ou+oligos [1]

LONGED [6]

longed, *2121, epithymeō* [2]
longed, *2527, thelō* [2]
longed for, *26, agapaō* [1]
longed for, *2123+3836+6034,*
   epithymia+ho+psychē [1]

LONGER [53]

no longer, *4033, ouketi* [27]
no longer, *3600, mēketi* [9]
longer, *2285, eti* [7]
longer, *AIT* [3]
any longer, *2285, eti* [2]
stayed a little longer, *2091+5989,*
   epechō+chronos [1]
longer, *2285+5989, eti+chronos* [1]
any longer, *3600, mēketi* [1]
no longer, *4024+3590, ou+mē* [1]
not longer, *4033, ouketi* [1]

LONGING [7]

longing, *2121, epithymeō* [1]
longing, *2123, epithymia* [1]
longing, *2160, epipotheō* [1]
longing for, *2161, epipothēsis* [1]
longing, *2161, epipothēsis* [1]
longing, *2163+2400, epipothia+echō* [1]
longing for, *3977, oregō* [1]

LONGS [1]

longs for, *2160+1639, epipotheō+eimi* [1]

LOOK [71]

look, *2627, idou* [14]
look for, *2426, zēteō* [10]
look, *2623, ide* [9]
look, *3972, horaō* [4]
look, *1063, blepō* [3]
look for, *349, anazēteō* [2]
look at, *1063, blepō* [2]
look down on, *2024, exoutheneō* [2]
look after, *2170, episkeptomai* [2]
look down on, *2969, kataphroneō* [2]
look at, *3972, horaō* [2]
look steadily, *867, atenizō* [1]
look somber, *1181+5034,*
   ginomai+skythrōpos [1]
look at, *1838, emblepō* [1]
look at, *2098+2093, epiblepō+epi* [1]
look after, *2150, epimeleomai* [1]
look into, *2236, eraunaō* [1]
look at, *2517, theaomai* [1]
look at, *2555, theōreō* [1]
look how, *2623, ide* [1]
to look for, *2870, katadiōkō* [1]
look more closely, *2917, katanoeō* [1]
look, *2917, katanoeō* [1]
look up, *3836+4057+2048,*
   ho+ophthalmos+epairō [1]
look like, *3930, homoiōma* [1]
bent over to look, *4160, parakyptō* [1]
look, *4160, parakyptō* [1]
look forward to, *4659, prosdokaō* [1]
look to, *5023, skopeō* [1]
look, *5743, phainō* [1]

LOOKED [57]

looked, *3972, horaō* [9]
looked up, *329, anablepō* [5]
looked at, *1838, emblepō* [4]
looked up, *2048+3836+4057,*
   epairō+ho+ophthalmos [3]
looked for a way, *2426, zēteō* [3]
looked around at, *4315, periblepō* [3]
looked like, *6055, hōs* [3]
looked straight, *867, atenizō* [2]
looked at, *3972, horaō* [2]
looked around, *4315, periblepō* [2]
looked, *149+3836+4057,*
   airō+ho+ophthalmos [1]
looked carefully at, *355, anatheōreō* [1]
looked closely at, *867, atenizō* [1]
looked directly at, *867, atenizō* [1]
looked intently at, *867, atenizō* [1]
looked straight at, *867, atenizō* [1]
looked up, *867, atenizō* [1]
looked, *867+2917, atenizō+katanoeō* [1]
looked in, *1063, blepō* [1]
looked so much like, *1181+6059,*
   ginomai+hōsei [1]
looked closely at, *1838, emblepō* [1]
looked directly at, *1838, emblepō* [1]
looked straight at, *1838, emblepō* [1]
looked down on, *2024, exoutheneō* [1]
looked, *2048+3836+4057,*
   epairō+ho+ophthalmos [1]
looked after, *2170, episkeptomai* [1]
looked at, *2517, theaomai* [1]
looked on, *2555, theōreō* [1]
looked like, *3930+3927,*
   homoiōma+homoios [1]
looked like this, *4048, houtōs* [1]
looked at, *4315, periblepō* [1]

LOOKING [43]

looking for, *2426, zēteō* [18]
looking for, *2118, epizēteō* [5]
looking, *AIT* [3]
looking up, *329, anablepō* [3]
looking forward to, *4659, prosdokaō* [2]
looking for, *349, anazēteō* [1]
looking ahead, *611, apoblepō* [1]
looking intently up, *867, atenizō* [1]
looking on, *1063, blepō* [1]
looking forward to, *1683, ekdechomai* [1]
looking, *1838, emblepō* [1]
looking, *2048+3836+4057,*
   epairō+ho+ophthalmos [1]
were looking for, *2351, heuriskō* [1]
looking at, *2917, katanoeō* [1]
looking around, *4315, periblepō* [1]
looking after sheep, *4477, poimainō* [1]
looking forward to, *4657, prosdechomai* [1]

LOOKS [10]

looks at, *1063, blepō* [1]
looks, *1063, blepō* [1]
looks like, *1639, eimi* [1]
looks, *1639, eimi* [1]
looks for, *2118, epizēteō* [1]
looks out for, *2426, zēteō* [1]
looks at, *2555, theōreō* [1]
looks, *2555, theōreō* [1]
looks at, *2917, katanoeō* [1]
looks intently, *4160, parakyptō* [1]

LOOSE [4]

loose, *3395, lyō* [2]
came loose, *479, aniēmi* [1]
cutting loose, *4311, periaireō* [1]

LOOSED [3]

loosed, *3395, lyō* [2]
loosed, *RPE* [1]

LOOSENED [1]

loosened, *3395, lyō* [1]

LORD [617]

Lord, *3261, kyrios* [601]
Lord, *RPE* [4]
sovereign Lord, *1305, despotēs* [4]
the Lord's, *899, autos* [2]
lord it over, *2894, katakyrieuō* [2]
lord it over, *3259, kyrieuō* [2]
devoted to the Lord, *41, hagios* [1]
Lord, *3259, kyrieuō* [1]

LORD'S [34]

Lord's, *3261, kyrios* [32]
Lord's, *3258, kyriakos* [2]

LORDING [1]

lording it over, *2894, katakyrieuō* [1]

LORDS [4]

lords, *3261, kyrios* [3]
lords, *3259, kyrieuō* [1]

LOSE [20]

lose, *660, apollymi* [14]
lose heart, *1591, enkakeō* [2]
lose good name, *1650+591+2262,
    eis+apelegmos+erchomai* [1]
lose heart, *1725, eklyō* [1]
lose, *1725, eklyō* [1]
lose, *3496+1666, methistēmi+ek* [1]

LOSES [10]

loses, *660, apollymi* [7]
loses its saltiness, *3701, mōrainō* [2]
loses saltiness, *383+1181, analos+ginomai* [1]

LOSS [10]

loss, *2422, zēmia* [4]
loss, *AIT* [2]
at a loss, *679, aporeō* [2]
suffer loss, *2423, zēmioō* [1]
loss, *2488, hēttēma* [1]

LOST [18]

lost, *660, apollymi* [12]
lost all sensitivity, *556, apalgeō* [1]
lost, *613, apobolē* [1]
lost, *1335, diaginomai* [1]
lost, *2423, zēmioō* [1]
lost connection with, *4024+3195, ou+krateō* [1]
and lost, *4028+2351, oude+heuriskō* [1]

LOT [6]

Lot, *3397, Lōt* [3]
lot, *3102, klēros* [1]
chosen by lot, *3275, lanchanō* [1]
decide by lot, *3275, lanchanō* [1]

LOT'S [1]

Lot's, *3397, Lōt* [1]

LOTS [5]

lots, *3102, klēros* [5]

LOUD [36]

loud, *3489, megas* [31]
loud, *2708, ischyros* [2]
called out in a loud voice, *149+5889,
    airō+phōnē* [1]
loud command, *3026, keleusma* [1]
a loud voice, *3189, krazō* [1]

LOUDER [3]

all the louder, *4360, perissōs* [2]
all the louder, *3505, meizōn* [1]

LOUDLY [1]

loudly, *4498, polys* [1]

LOVE [232]

love, *27, agapē* [109]
love, *26, agapaō* [74]
love, *5797, phileō* [13]
love, *28, agapētos* [11]
love, *RPE* [6]
truly love, *26, agapaō* [2]
love, *27+2400, agapē+echō* [2]
love, *27+26, agapē+agapaō* [2]
love's, *899, autos* [1]
brotherly love, *5789, philadelphia* [2]
showed love, *26, agapaō* [1]
love feasts, *27, agapē* [1]
without love, *845, astorgos* [1]
free from the love of money, *921,
    aphilargyros* [1]
love for brothers, *5789, philadelphia* [1]
love as brothers, *5790, philadelphos* [1]
love their husbands, *5791, philandros* [1]
love, *5792, philanthrōpia* [1]
love of money, *5794, philargyria* [1]
[love their] children, *5817, philoteknos* [1]

LOVED [49]

loved, *26, agapaō* [40]
loved, *28, agapētos* [3]
loved, *5797, phileō* [3]
dearly loved, *28, agapētos* [1]
loved, *3916, homeiromai* [1]
loved money, *5795+5639,
    philargyros+hyparchō* [1]

LOVELY [1]

lovely, *4713, prosphilēs* [1]

LOVER [1]

not a lover of money, *921, aphilargyros* [1]

LOVERS [5]

not lovers of good, *920, aphilagathos* [1]
lovers of money, *5795, philargyros* [1]
lovers of themselves, *5796, philautos* [1]
lovers of pleasure, *5798, philēdonos* [1]
lovers of God, *5806, philotheos* [1]

LOVES [32]

loves, *26, agapaō* [22]
loves, *5797, phileō* [6]
loves, *RPE* [1]
loves, *27, agapē* [1]
loves what is good, *5787, philagathos* [1]
loves to be first, *5812, philoprōteuō* [1]

LOVING [2]

loving, *26, agapaō* [1]
loving each other as brothers, *5789,
    philadelphia* [1]

LOW [4]

low, *3625, mikros* [1]
of low position, *5424, tapeinos* [1]
made low, *5427, tapeinoō* [1]
low position, *5428, tapeinōsis* [1]

LOWER [5]

made lower, *1783, elattoō* [2]
lower, *1753, ekteinō* [1]
lower, *3005, katōteros* [1]
lower, *5427, tapeinoō* [1]

LOWERED [5]

lowered, *5899, chalaō* [3]
lowered, *2768+5899, kathiēmi+chalaō* [1]
lowered, *2768, kathiēmi* [1]

LOWEST [1]

lowest, *2274, eschatos* [1]

LOWLY [2]

lowly, *38, agenēs* [1]
lowly, *5428, tapeinōsis* [1]

LOYAL [1]

loyal, *1188, gnēsios* [1]

LUCIUS [2]

Lucius, *3372, Loukios* [2]

LUKE [3]

Luke, *3371, Loukas* [3]

LUKEWARM [1]

lukewarm, *5950, chliaros* [1]

LUMP [1]

lump of clay, *5878, phyrama* [1]

LUNCHEON [1]

luncheon, *756, ariston* [1]

LUST [6]

lust, *2123, epithymia* [2]
lust, *4079, pathos* [2]
lust, *3979, orexis* [1]
lust for more, *4432, pleonexia* [1]

LUSTFUL [1]

lustful desires, *2123+816,
    epithymia+aselgeia* [1]

LUSTFULLY [1]

lustfully, *4639+3836+2121,
    pros+ho+epithymeō* [1]

LUSTS [1]

lusts, *4079, pathos* [1]

LUXURIES [1]

luxuries, *5140, strēnos* [1]

LUXURY [5]

in luxury, *3289, lamprōs* [1]
luxury gave, *5139, strēniaō* [1]
shared luxury, *5139, strēniaō* [1]
lived in luxury, *5587, tryphaō* [1]
luxury, *5588, tryphē* [1]

LYCAONIAN [2]

Lycaonian, *3377, Lykaonia* [1]
in Lycaonian language, *3378, Lykaonisti* [1]

LYCIA [1]

Lycia, *3379, Lykia* [1]

LYDDA [4]

Lydda, *3375, Lydda* [3]
Lydda[s], *899, autos* [1]

LYDIA [1]

Lydia, *3376, Lydia* [1]

LYDIA'S [1]

Lydia's, *3376, Lydia* [1]

LYING [14]

lying, *3023, keimai* [4]
lying, *6017, pseudomai* [3]
lying, *965, ballō* [2]
lying, *2879, katakeimai* [2]
lying, *NIG* [1]
lying in bed, *965, ballō* [1]
lying on, *2879, katakeimai* [1]

LYSANIAS [1]

Lysanias, *3384, Lysanias* [1]

LYSIAS [2]

Lysias, *3385, Lysias* [2]

LYSTRA [6]

Lystra, *3388, Lystra* [6]

MAATH [1]

Maath, *3399, Maath* [1]

MACEDONIA [23]

Macedonia, *3423, Makedonia* [21]
from Macedonia, *3424, Makedōn* [1]
of Macedonia, *3424, Makedōn* [1]

MACEDONIAN [2]

Macedonian, *3423, Makedonia* [1]
Macedonian, *3424, Makedōn* [1]

MACEDONIANS [2]

Macedonians, *3424, Makedōn* [2]

MAD [1]

raving mad, *3419, mainomai* [1]

MADDENING [2]

maddening, *2596, thymos* [2]

MADE [201]

made, *4472, poieō* [35]
made, *1181, ginomai* [11]
made known, *1192, gnōrizō* [8]
made perfect, *5457, teleioō* [8]
made, *AIT* [5]
made, *2770, kathistēmi* [5]
made, *5502, tithēmi* [5]
made, *NIG* [4]
made complete, *5457, teleioō* [4]
made holy, *39, hagiazō* [3]
made, *337, anankazō* [2]
made reply, *646, apokrinomai* [2]
made secure, *856, asphalizō* [2]

made known, *1182, ginōskō* [2]
made, *1416, diatithēmi* [2]
made lower, *1783, elattoō* [2]
made promise, *2040, epangellomai* [2]
made, *2400, echō* [2]
made alive, *2443, zōopoieō* [2]
made clean, *2751, katharizō* [2]
made known, *5746, phaneroō* [2]
made, *RPE* [1]
made holy, *39+1639, hagiazō+eimi* [1]
made salty, *245, halizō* [1]
made new, *391, ananeoomai* [1]
made threats, *580, apeileō* [1]
made defense, *664, apologeomai* [1]
made an opening in, *689, apostegazō* [1]
made salty, *789, artyō* [1]
made grow, *889, auxanō* [1]
not made by man, *942, acheiropoiētos* [1]
made plans, *1086, bouleuō* [1]
made slow headway, *1095, bradyploeō* [1]
made a spectacle, *1258, deigmatizō* [1]
made clear, *1317, dēloō* [1]
covenant made, *1347+1416,
   diathēkē+diatithēmi* [1]
preparations to be made, *1355, diakonia* [1]
made distinction, *1359, diakrinō* [1]
made arrangement, *1411, diatassō* [1]
made fun of, *1430, diachleuazō* [1]
made get up, *1586, egeirō* [1]
made, *1586, egeirō* [1]
made up of, *1639, eimi* [1]
made, *1639, eimi* [1]
made a choice, *1721, eklegomai* [1]
made of ivory, *1804, elephantinos* [1]
made of, *1908, endōmēsis* [1]
made signs, *1935, enneuō* [1]
made known, *2007, exēgeomai* [1]
a thorough search made for, *2118, epizēteō* [1]
made appeal to, *2126, epikaleō* [1]
made appeal, *2126, epikaleō* [1]
made, *2240, ergon* [1]
made their way, *2262, erchomai* [1]
made ready, *2286, hetoimazō* [1]
made[s] that way, *2336+2335,
   eunouchos+eunouchizō* [1]
made up of, *2400, echō* [1]
made competent, *2655, hikanoō* [1]
made appear, *2705, histēmi* [1]
made stand, *2705, histēmi* [1]
something man made up, *2848+476,
   kata+anthrōpos* [1]
made, *2981, katergazomai* [1]
made a attack on, *2987, katephistamai* [1]
made, *2988, katechō* [1]
made, *3023, keimai* [1]
made nothing, *3033, kenoō* [1]
made up mind, *3212, krinō* [1]
made up, *3212, krinō* [1]
made king, *3284+3836+993,
   lambanō+ho+basileia* [1]
made, *3284, lambanō* [1]
made shine, *3290, lampō* [1]
made, *3306, legō* [1]
made white, *3326, leukainō* [1]
made sorry, *3382, lypeō* [1]
made an idol in the form of a calf, *3674,
   moschopoieō* [1]
made foolish, *3701, mōrainō* [1]
made like, *3929, homoioō* [1]
made confession, *3933+3934,
   homologeō+homologia* [1]
made confession, *3934, homologia* [1]
this made, *4036, oun* [1]
made obsolete, *4096, palaioō* [1]
made home, *4228, paroikeō* [1]
made up, *4422, plastos* [1]

made rich, *4457, ploutizō* [1]
made out to be, *4472, poieō* [1]
made, *4473, poiēma* [1]
made drink, *4540, potizō* [1]
once made, *4575, proagō* [1]
already made the charge, *4577, proaitiaomai* [1]
earlier made a beginning, *4599,
   proenarchomai* [1]
made[s], *4712, prospherō* [1]
offering made, *4712+4714,
   prospherō+prosphora* [1]
made dull, *4800, pōroō* [1]
made known, *4955, sēmainō* [1]
made his dwelling, *5012, skēnoō* [1]
made effort, *5079, spoudazō* [1]
made strong, *5105, stereoō* [1]
made alive with, *5188+5250,
   syzōopoieō+syn* [1]
made alive with, *5188, syzōopoieō* [1]
made sure that, *5381, sphragizō* [1]
made well, *5392, sōzō* [1]
made low, *5427, tapeinoō* [1]
made perfect, *5464, teleō* [1]
made think, *5502+1877+3836+2840,
   tithēmi+en+ho+kardia* [1]
made of hair, *5570, trichinos* [1]
made well, *5618, hygiēs* [1]
made subject, *5718, hypotassō* [1]
made prosper, *5738, hypsoō* [1]
made clear, *5746, phaneroō* [1]
made plain, *5746, phaneroō* [1]
made carry, *5770, pherō* [1]
made by men, *5935, cheiropoiētos* [1]

MADNESS [1]

madness, *4197, paraphronia* [1]

MAGADAN [1]

Magadan, *3400, Magadan* [1]

MAGDALENE [12]

Magdalene, *3402, Magdalēnē* [12]

MAGI [4]

Magi, *3407, magos* [4]

MAGIC [5]

practice magic arts, *5761, pharmakos* [2]
magic, *3404, mageia* [1]
magic spell, *5758, pharmakeia* [1]
magic arts, *5760, pharmakon* [1]

MAGISTRATE [1]

magistrate, *807, archōn* [1]

MAGISTRATES [5]

magistrates, *5130, stratēgos* [5]

MAGNIFICENT [1]

what magnificent, *4534, potapos* [1]

MAGOG [1]

Magog, *3408, Magōg* [1]

MAHALALEL [1]

Mahalalel, *3435, Maleleēl* [1]

MAIDSERVANTS [1]

maidservants, *4087, paidiskē* [1]

MAIMED [2]

maimed, *3245, kyllos* [2]

MAINTAIN [1]

maintain, *3357, logizomai* [1]

MAINTAINED [1]

maintained, *2400, echō* [1]

MAJESTIC [1]

Majestic, *3485, megaloprepēs* [1]

MAJESTY [7]

majesty, *3488, megalōsynē* [3]
majesty, *1518, doxa* [1]
His Majesty, *3261, kyrios* [1]
divine majesty, *3484, megaleiotēs* [1]
majesty, *3484, megaleiotēs* [1]

MAJORITY [2]

majority, *4498, polys* [2]

MAKE [141]

make, *4472, poieō* [26]
make unclean, *3124, koinoō* [7]
make known, *1192, gnōrizō* [5]
make preparations, *2286, hetoimazō* [5]
make every effort, *5079, spoudazō* [4]
make defense, *664, apologeomai* [3]
make clean, *2751, katharizō* [3]
make, *5502, tithēmi* [3]
make, *AIT* [2]
make, *NIG* [2]
make holy, *39, hagiazō* [2]
make it, *1211, graphō* [2]
covenant make, *1347+1416, diathēkē+diatithēmi* [2]
make, *1443, didōmi* [2]
make every effort, *1503, diōkō* [2]
make envious, *4143, parazēloō* [2]
make war, *4482, polemeō* [2]
make prayers, *4667, proseuchomai* [2]
make perfect, *5457, teleioō* [2]
make every effort, *76, agōnizomai* [1]
make known, *334, anangellō* [1]
make, *337, anankazō* [1]
make up for, *405, anaplēroō* [1]
make clear, *636, apokalyptō* [1]
make salty, *789, artyō* [1]
make secure, *856, asphalizō* [1]
make plans, *1086, bouleuō* [1]
make, *1181, ginomai* [1]
make, *1442, didō* [1]
make innocent, *1467, dikaioō* [1]
make much of, *1519, doxazō* [1]
make slave, *1524, doulagōgeō* [1]
make a slave, *1530, douloō* [1]
make complete, *1639+4444, eimi+plēroō* [1]
make, *1650, eis* [1]
make⁵, *1877, en* [1]
make a search, *2004, exetazō* [1]
make guilty of, *2042+2093, epagō+epi* [1]
make clear, *2109, epideiknymi* [1]
make visit, *2262, erchomai* [1]
make ready, *2286, hetoimazō* [1]
make straight, *2316, euthynō* [1]
make a good impression, *2349, euprosōpeō* [1]
make glad, *2370, euphrainō* [1]
make effort to obtain, *2426, zēteō* [1]
[make] steadfast, *2530, themelioō* [1]
make atonement for, *2661, hilaskomai* [1]
to make, *2671, hina* [1]
make stand, *2705, histēmi* [1]
make slaves, *2871, katadouloō* [1]
make use of, *2974, katachraomai* [1]
make money, *3045, kerdainō* [1]

make attractive, *3175, kosmeō* [1]
make beautiful, *3175, kosmeō* [1]
make up mind, *3212, krinō* [1]
make judgment, *3213+3212, krisis+krinō* [1]
make disciples, *3411, mathēteuō* [1]
make the most of opportunity, *3836+2789+1973, ho+kairos+exagorazō* [1]
make light of, *3902, oligōreō* [1]
make sure that, *3972, horaō* [1]
make excuses, *4148, paraiteomai* [1]
make, *4210, pareispherō* [1]
make it difficult for, *4214, parenochleō* [1]
make angry, *4239, parorgizō* [1]
make obey, *4275, peithō* [1]
make abound, *4355, perisseuō* [1]
make wide, *4425, platynō* [1]
make increase, *4429, pleonazō* [1]
make complete, *4444, plēroō* [1]
make out to be, *4472, poieō* [1]
make strong, *4964, sthenoō* [1]
make stumble, *4998, skandalon* [1]
make wise, *5054, sophizō* [1]
[make] firm, *5114, stērizō* [1]
make strong, *5114, stērizō* [1]
make, *5334, synteleō* [1]
make well, *5392, sōzō* [1]
make up mind, *5502+1877+3836+2840, tithēmi+en+ho+kardia* [1]
make it ambition, *5818, philotimeomai* [1]
make it goal, *5818, philotimeomai* [1]
make plain to, *5894, phōtizō* [1]
make rejoice, *5897, chairō* [1]
make room for, *6003, chōreō* [1]
make music, *6010, psallō* [1]

MAKES [20]

makes sacred, *39, hagiazō* [2]
makes unclean, *3124, koinoō* [2]
makes, *4472, poieō* [2]
makes fall, *4998, skandalon* [2]
makes holy, *39, hagiazō* [1]
makes judgments about, *373, anakrinō* [1]
makes grow, *889, auxanō* [1]
makes boasts, *902, aucheō* [1]
makes stand firm, *1011, bebaioō* [1]
makes different, *1359, diakrinō* [1]
makes difference, *1422, diapherō* [1]
makes a slave, *1525, douleia* [1]
this makes, *1877+4047, en+houtos* [1]
what makes unclean, *3124, koinoō* [1]
makes war, *4482, polemeō* [1]
makes visible, *5746, phaneroō* [1]

MAKING [18]

making, *1181, ginomai* [4]
making, *4472, poieō* [4]
making a prisoner, *170, aichmalōtizō* [1]
making known, *334, anangellō* [1]
making signs, *1377, dianeuō* [1]
making a complaint⁵ about, *1639, eimi* [1]
making peace, *1647, eirēnopoieō* [1]
making the most of, *1973, exagorazō* [1]
making money, *2238, ergasia* [1]
charges making against, *2989, katēgoreō* [1]
making appeal, *4151, parakaleō* [1]
making rich, *4457, ploutizō* [1]

MALCHUS [1]

Malchus, *3438, Malchos* [1]

MALE [7]

male, *781, arsēn* [6]
male prostitutes, *3434, malakos* [1]

MALICE [7]

malice, *2798, kakia* [5]
malice, *2799, kakoētheia* [1]
malice, *4504, ponēria* [1]

MALICIOUS [2]

malicious talk, *1060, blasphēmia* [1]
malicious talkers, *1333, diabolos* [1]

MALICIOUSLY [2]

speak maliciously against, *2092, epēreazō* [1]
maliciously, *3364+4505, logos+ponēros* [1]

MALIGN [1]

malign, *1059, blasphēmeō* [1]

MALIGNED [1]

maligned, *2800, kakologeō* [1]

MALTA [1]

Malta, *3514, Melitē* [1]

MAN [661]

man, *476, anthrōpos* [277]
man, *AIT* [212]
man, *467, anēr* [63]
the man⁵, *899, autos* [15]
man, *RPE* [13]
young man, *3734, neaniskos* [7]
man, *1651, heis* [4]
the man⁵, *3836+1254, ho+de* [4]
man, *NIG* [3]
young man, *3733, neanias* [3]
a man⁵, *3836, ho* [3]
the man⁵, *3836, ho* [3]
the man⁵, *4005, hos* [3]
sinful man, *4922, sarx* [3]
man, *81, adelphos* [2]
the young man⁵, *899, autos* [2]
a man⁵, *1667, hekastos* [2]
the man⁵, *1697, ekeinos* [2]
man who had been mute, *3273, kōphos* [2]
man with leprosy, *3320, lepros* [2]
old man, *4566, presbytēs* [2]
man, *4922+2779+135, sarx+kai+haima* [2]
such a man, *5525, toioutos* [2]
man, *5626, huios* [2]
this man, *AIT* [1]
believing man, *81, adelphos* [1]
common to man, *474, anthrōpinos* [1]
man, *474, anthrōpinos* [1]
this man⁵, *899, autos* [1]
not made by man, *942, acheiropoiētos* [1]
man⁵, *1208, grammateus* [1]
free and belong to no man, *1801+1666+4246, eleutheros+ek+pas* [1]
as a man, *1877+4922, en+sarx* [1]
godly man, *2538, theosebēs* [1]
something man made up, *2848+476, kata+anthrōpos* [1]
man who was deaf, *3273, kōphos* [1]
this man⁵, *3836, ho* [1]
man⁵, *3836, ho* [1]
as one man, *3924, homothymadon* [1]
this man⁵, *4005, hos* [1]
a man⁵, *4005, hos* [1]
man, *4005+1569, hos+ean* [1]
such a man, *4005, hos* [1]
the man⁵, *4005+1569, hos+ean* [1]
such a man, *4047, houtos* [1]
young man, *4090, pais* [1]
older man, *4565, presbyteros* [1]
man, *4922, sarx* [1]

man from Tarsus, *5432, Tarseus* [1]
man like that, *5525, toioutos* [1]
violent man, *5616, hybristēs* [1]
man, *6034, psychē* [1]

MAN'S [47]

man's, *AIT* [15]
man's, *476, anthrōpos* [12]
the man'sˢ, *899, autos* [10]
man's, *RPE* [2]
man's, *467, anēr* [2]
a man'sˢ, *899, autos* [1]
eight months of a man's wages, *1324+1357,
    dēnarion+diakosioi* [1]
man'sˢ, *3836, ho* [1]
the man'sˢ, *3836+1254, ho+de* [1]
such a man'sˢ, *4005, hos* [1]
man'sˢ, *5516, tis* [1]

MAN-MADE [4]

man-made, *5935, cheiropoiētos* [3]
man-made, *1328+5931+1181,
    dia+cheir+ginomai* [1]

MANAEN [1]

Manaen, *3441, Manaēn* [1]

MANAGE [4]

manage, *4613, proistēmi* [2]
manage homes, *3866, oikodespoteō* [1]
manage and see that, *4613, proistēmi* [1]

MANAGEMENT [1]

management, *3873, oikonomia* [1]

MANAGER [7]

manager, *3874, oikonomos* [4]
manager of household, *2208, epitropos* [1]
the managerˢ, *3836+1254, ho+de* [1]
manager, *3872, oikonomeō* [1]

MANASSEH [3]

Manasseh, *3442, Manassēs* [3]

MANGER [3]

manger, *5764, phatnē* [3]

MANIFESTATION [1]

manifestation, *5748, phanerōsis* [1]

MANIFOLD [1]

manifold, *4497, polypoikilos* [1]

MANKIND [4]

mankind, *476, anthrōpos* [3]
mankind, *4922, sarx* [1]

MANNA [5]

manna, *3445, manna* [5]

MANNER [4]

in a manner worthy, *547, axiōs* [2]
unworthy manner, *397, anaxiōs* [1]
worldly manner, *4922, sarx* [1]

MANURE [1]

manure pile, *3161, kopria* [1]

MANY [229]

many, *4498, polys* [194]
how many, *4531, posos* [10]

many, *2653, hikanos* [5]
how many, *4012, hosos* [2]
many times, *4490, pollakis* [2]
so many, *5537, tosoutos* [2]
many, *RPE* [1]
many troubles, *2568, thlipsis* [1]
many thousands, *3689, myrias* [1]
as many as, *4012, hosos* [1]
many, *4024+3900, ou+oligos* [1]
many people, *4063, ochlos* [1]
give many descendants, *4437+4437,
    plēthynō+plēthynō* [1]
many kinds, *4476, poikilos* [1]
many a time, *4490, pollakis* [1]
many times as much, *4491, pollaplasiōn* [1]
many words, *4494, polylogia* [1]
at many times, *4495, polymerōs* [1]
many, *4498+4725, polys+prosōpon* [1]
how many times, *4529, posakis* [1]

MARBLE [1]

marble, *3454, marmaros* [1]

MARCHED [2]

marched, *326, anabainō* [1]
marched around, *3240, kykloō* [1]

MARITAL [3]

marital unfaithfulness, *4518, porneia* [2]
marital, *AIT* [1]

MARK [20]

Mark, *3453, Markos* [8]
mark, *5916, charagma* [7]
mark, *1182, ginōskō* [1]
mark, *1877, en* [1]
mark my words, *2623, ide* [1]
mark, *4956, sēmeion* [1]
the distinguishing mark, *4956, sēmeion* [1]

MARKED [2]

marked out, *4618, prokeimai* [1]
marked with a seal, *5381, sphragizō* [1]

MARKET [2]

meat market, *3425, makellon* [1]
market, *3875+1866, oikos+emporion* [1]

MARKETPLACE [6]

marketplace, *59, agora* [5]
marketplace, *61, agoraios* [1]

MARKETPLACES [6]

marketplaces, *59, agora* [6]

MARKS [2]

marks, *5116, stigma* [1]
marks, *5596, typos* [1]

MARRIAGE [11]

given in marriage, *1139, gamizō* [4]
marriage, *467, anēr* [1]
after marriage, *608+4220, apo+parthenia* [1]
giving in marriage, *1139, gamizō* [1]
given in marriage, *1140, gamiskō* [1]
marriage, *1141, gamos* [1]
renounced marriage, *2336+2335+1571,
    eunouchos+eunouchizō+heautou* [1]
marriage bed, *3130, koitē* [1]

MARRIED [19]

married, *1138, gameō* [5]

married, *3284, lambanō* [3]
pledged to be married, *3650, mnēsteuō* [3]
married to, *2400, echō* [2]
get married, *1138, gameō* [1]
got married, *1222+1138, gynē+gameō* [1]
married to, *1222, gynē* [1]
married, *1313+1222, deō+gynē* [1]
married, *3284+1222, lambanō+gynē* [1]
married, *5635, hypandros* [1]

MARRIES [10]

marries, *1138, gameō* [7]
marries, *1181, ginomai* [2]
marries, *1139, gamizō* [1]

MARROW [1]

marrow, *3678, myelos* [1]

MARRY [20]

marry, *1138, gameō* [12]
marry, *3284, lambanō* [2]
marry, *1139, gamizō* [1]
marry, *1222+721, gynē+haptō* [1]
marry, *2102, epigambreuō* [1]
thoseˢ who marry, *3836+5525, ho+toioutos* [1]
to marryˢ, *4048+1181, houtōs+ginomai* [1]
not marry, *5498, tēreō* [1]

MARRYING [2]

marrying, *1138, gameō* [2]

MARTHA [13]

Martha, *3450, Martha* [13]

MARTYR [1]

martyr, *3459, martys* [1]

MARVELED [2]

marveled, *1639+2513, eimi+thaumazō* [1]
marveled at, *2513, thaumazō* [1]

MARVELING [1]

marveling, *2513, thaumazō* [1]

MARVELOUS [4]

marvelous, *2515, thaumastos* [4]

MARY [57]

Mary, *3451, Maria* [51]
Mary, *RPE* [3]
Maryˢ, *899, autos* [1]
Maryˢ, *1697, ekeinos* [1]
Maryˢ, *3836+1254, ho+de* [1]

MARY'S [2]

Mary's, *3451, Maria* [2]

MASK [1]

mask to cover up, *4733, prophasis* [1]

MASQUERADE [1]

masquerade, *3571, metaschēmatizō* [1]

MASQUERADES [1]

masquerades, *3571, metaschēmatizō* [1]

MASQUERADING [1]

masquerading, *3571, metaschēmatizō* [1]

MASSIVE [1]

what massive, *4534, potapos* [1]

MASTER [53]

master, *3261, kyrios* [35]
master, *2181, epistatēs* [7]
master, *RPE* [3]
master of the banquet, *804, architriklinos* [2]
his master⁵, *899, autos* [2]
master, *1305, despotēs* [1]
master, *1437, didaskalos* [1]
master, *3259, kyrieuō* [1]
his master⁵, *4047, houtos* [1]

MASTER'S [6]

master's, *3261, kyrios* [6]

MASTERED [2]

mastered, *2027, exousiazō* [1]
mastered, *2487, hēttaomai* [1]

MASTERS [11]

masters, *3261, kyrios* [7]
masters, *1305, despotēs* [4]

MASTERY [1]

has mastery over, *3259, kyrieuō* [1]

MAT [14]

mat, *3187, krabattos* [8]
mat, *3109, klinē* [3]
mat, *3110, klinidion* [2]
take care of mat, *5143+4932,*
    strōnnyō+seautou [1]

MATCH [1]

match, *5244, symphōneō* [1]

MATCHED [1]

matched, *4048+2779, houtōs+kai* [1]

MATERIAL [3]

material, *4920, sarkikos* [2]
material, *3180, kosmos* [1]

MATS [2]

mats, *3187, krabattos* [2]

MATTATHA [1]

Mattatha, *3477, Mattatha* [1]

MATTATHIAS [2]

Mattathias, *3478, Mattathias* [1]
of Mattathias, *3478, Mattathias* [1]

MATTER [20]

matter, *NIG* [4]
matter, *AIT* [3]
matter, *3364, logos* [2]
matter, *4547, pragma* [2]
matter, *4839, rhēma* [2]
talked the matter over, *1368+4639+253,*
    dialogizomai+pros+allēlōn [1]
a matter of, *2093, epi* [1]
settled the matter, *2705+1612,*
    histēmi+hedraios [1]
matter, *3538, meros* [1]
settle the matter, *3972, horaō* [1]
over the matter of, *4309, peri* [1]
what does it matter, *5515, tis* [1]

MATTERS [10]

matters, *AIT* [4]
more important matters, *987, barys* [1]

such⁵ matters, *1053, biōtikos* [1]
settle matters, *1639+2333, eimi+eunoeō* [1]
matters, *3836, ho* [1]
matters, *4005, hos* [1]
the matters, *4005, hos* [1]

MATTHAN [2]

Matthan, *3474, Matthan* [2]

MATTHAT [2]

Matthat, *3415, Maththat* [2]

MATTHEW [6]

Matthew, *3414, Maththaios* [5]
Matthew, *RPE* [1]

MATTHEW'S [1]

Matthew's, *RPE* [1]

MATTHIAS [2]

Matthias, *3416, Maththias* [2]

MATURE [7]

mature, *5455, teleios* [5]
mature, *467+5455, anēr+teleios* [1]
mature, *5461, telesphoreō* [1]

MATURITY [1]

maturity, *5456, teleiotēs* [1]

MAY [314]

may, *AIT* [281]
may, *NIG* [25]
may, *RPE* [2]
may, *1538, dynamai* [1]
be that as it may, *1639, eimi* [1]
may, *1639, eimi* [1]
may, *2003, exesti* [1]
may never, *3590+1181, mē+ginomai* [1]
may this never, *3590, mē* [1]

ME [846]

me, *1609, egō* [734]
me, *RPE* [50]
me, *AIT* [30]
me, *1831, emautou* [4]
me, *1847, emos* [4]
me, *3836+3950+1609, ho+onoma+egō* [4]
for me, *1847, emos* [3]
me also, *2743, kagō* [3]
me, *2743, kagō* [3]
me, *NIG* [2]
me, *3836+4725+1609, ho+prosōpon+egō* [2]
me, *1609+3836+5889, egō+ho+phōnē* [1]
but me, *2743, kagō* [1]
also me, *2743, kagō* [1]
and me, *2743, kagō* [1]
me, *3836+6034+1609, ho+psychē+egō* [1]
me say, *4123+1609, para+egō* [1]
me, *6034+1609, psychē+egō* [1]

MEAL [9]

meal, *AIT* [2]
meal, *RPE* [1]
meal, *756, ariston* [1]
meal, *1111, brōsis* [1]
evening meal, *1270, deipnon* [1]
meal, *1270, deipnon* [1]
at the meal, *3836+367, ho+anakeimai* [1]
set a meal before, *4192+5544,*
    paratithēmi+trapeza [1]

MEAN [16]

mean, *1639, eimi* [5]
mean, *3306, legō* [3]
mean, *2527+1639, thelō+eimi* [2]
mean, *5774, phēmi* [2]
mean, *NIG* [1]
does that mean that, *727, ara* [1]
you mean, *3590, mē* [1]
I mean that just as surely as, *3755, nē* [1]

MEANING [10]

meaning, *AIT* [2]
meaning, *1639, eimi* [2]
meaning, *6055, hōs* [2]
without meaning, *936, aphōnos* [1]
grasp the meaning, *3857+3836+1539,*
    oida+ho+dynamis [1]
meaning, *4839, rhēma* [1]
meaning, *5515+323+1639, tis+an+eimi* [1]

MEANINGLESS [1]

meaningless talk, *3467, mataiologia* [1]

MEANS [38]

means, *1639, eimi* [10]
means, *1639+3493, eimi+methermēneuō* [5]
means, *NIG* [4]
by no means, *3590+1181, mē+ginomai* [4]
means, *2257, hermēneuō* [2]
means, *3306, legō* [2]
by means of, *1328, dia* [1]
means, *1639+3306, eimi+legō* [1]
means, *2400, echō* [1]
by means of, *2848, kata* [1]
means, *3306+3493, legō+methermēneuō* [1]
means, *3493, methermēneuō* [1]
not by any means, *4024+3590, ou+mē* [1]
by no means, *4027, oudamōs* [1]
by all possible means, *4122, pantōs* [1]
means to financial gain, *4516, porismos* [1]
means, *5639, hyparchō* [1]

MEANT [13]

meant, *1639, eimi* [2]
meant to, *2671, hina* [1]
meant, *3306, legō* [2]
meant, *4839, rhēma* [2]
meant, *AIT* [1]
meant, *NIG* [1]
meant, *3306+4309, legō+peri* [1]
meant, *4309+3306, peri+legō* [1]
what I meant, *4309+4047, peri+houtos* [1]

MEANWHILE [12]

meanwhile, *1254, de* [5]
meanwhile, *2779, kai* [2]
meanwhile, *4036, oun* [2]
meanwhile, *1877+3836+3568,*
    en+ho+metaxy [1]
meanwhile, *1877+4005, en+hos* [1]
meanwhile, *1877+4047, en+houtos* [1]

MEASURE [15]

measure, *3586, metron* [6]
measure, *3582, metreō* [4]
measure, *AIT* [2]
whole measure, *3586+2461, metron+hēlikia* [1]
full measure, *4445, plērōma* [1]
measure of fullness, *4445, plērōma* [1]

MEASURED [5]

measured, *3582, metreō* [4]
measured, *520, antimetreō* [1]

MEASUREMENT [1]

measurement, *3586, metron* [1]

MEASURING [2]

measuring, *3586, metron* [1]
measuring rod, *4811, rhabdos* [1]

MEAT [7]

meat of strangled animals, *4465, pniktos* [3]
meat, *3200, kreas* [2]
meat, *NIG* [1]
meat market, *3425, makellon* [1]

MEDDLER [1]

meddler, *258, allotriepiskopos* [1]

MEDES [1]

Medes, *3597, Mēdos* [1]

MEDIATOR [6]

mediator, *3542, mesitēs* [5]
mediator between, *3542, mesitēs* [1]

MEEK [1]

meek, *4558, praus* [1]

MEEKNESS [1]

meekness, *4559, prautēs* [1]

MEET [16]

meet, *561, apantēsis* [3]
meet, *5637, hypantēsis* [3]
meet, *AIT* [2]
went out to meet, *5636, hypantaō* [2]
meet, *560, apantaō* [1]
meet, *1639, eimi* [1]
meet, *4444, plēroō* [1]
meet, *5267, synantaō* [1]
meet together, *5302, synerchomai* [1]
meet, *5636, hypantaō* [1]

MEETING [7]

meeting of the Areopagus, *740, Areios pagos* [2]
meeting, *5251, synagō* [2]
meeting together, *2191, episynagōgē* [1]
called meeting, *5251, synagō* [1]
meeting, *5252, synagōgē* [1]

MEETINGS [1]

meetings, *5302, synerchomai* [1]

MEETS [4]

meets, *AIT* [3]
meets need, *4560, prepō* [1]

MELCHIZEDEK [8]

Melchizedek, *3519, Melchisedek* [8]

MELEA [1]

Melea, *3507, Melea* [1]

MELKI [2]

Melki, *3518, Melchi* [2]

MELT [1]

melt, *5494, tēkomai* [1]

MEMBER [5]

member of the Council, *1085, bouleutēs* [2]
member, *AIT* [1]

member of the Areopagus, *741, Areopagitēs* [1]
member, *3836+2848+3517, ho+kata+melos* [1]

MEMBERS [17]

members, *3517, melos* [7]
members, *AIT* [2]
members of household, *3865, oikiakos* [2]
as members of, *1877, en* [1]
members of body, *3517, melos* [1]
members of household, *3858, oikeios* [1]
members of household, *3875, oikos* [1]
members together of one body, *5362, syssōmos* [1]
members^s, *5516, tis* [1]

MEMORIAL [1]

memorial offering, *3649, mnēmosynon* [1]

MEMORIES [1]

memories, *3644, mneia* [1]

MEMORY [3]

memory, *3649, mnēmosynon* [2]
memory, *5704, hypomnēsis* [1]

MEN [368]

men, *476, anthrōpos* [136]
men, *AIT* [118]
men, *467, anēr* [64]
men, *RPE* [6]
men, *NIG* [5]
young men, *3734, neaniskos* [4]
men, *781, arsēn* [3]
the men^s, *899, autos* [2]
hired men, *3634, misthios* [2]
the men^s, *3836+1254, ho+de* [2]
men^s, *3836, ho* [2]
men, *3836+5626+3836+476, ho+huios+ho+anthrōpos* [2]
causes men to stumble, *4682, proskomma* [2]
men of courage, *437, andrizomai* [1]
among men, *474, anthrōpinos* [1]
men^s, *899, autos* [1]
these men^s, *899, autos* [1]
not done by the hands of men, *942, acheiropoiētos* [1]
men^s, *1506, dokeō* [1]
servants men, *1528, doulos^1* [1]
men to work, *2239, ergatēs* [1]
hired men, *3638, misthōtos* [1]
the men^s, *3836+3525, ho+men* [1]
the men^s, *4005+1569, hos+ean* [1]
the men^s, *4005, hos* [1]
these men^s, *4005, hos* [1]
men^s, *4029, oudeis* [1]
men, *4029, oudeis* [1]
men^s, *4047, houtos* [1]
old men, *4565, presbyteros* [1]
men, *4922, sarx* [1]
men like him, *5525, toioutos* [1]
made by men, *5935, cheiropoiētos* [1]

MEN'S [8]

men's, *476, anthrōpos* [5]
men's, *AIT* [1]
men's^s, *899, autos* [1]
men's, *3836, ho* [1]

MENNA [1]

Menna, *3527, Menna* [1]

MENSERVANTS [1]

menservants, *4090, pais* [1]

MENTION [3]

mention, *3306, legō* [3]

MENTIONING [1]

mentioning, *3644+4472, mneia+poieō* [1]

MERCHANDISE [1]

merchandise, *5007, skeuos* [1]

MERCHANT [1]

merchant, *476+1867, anthrōpos+emporos* [1]

MERCHANTS [4]

merchants, *1867, emporos* [4]

MERCIFUL [7]

merciful, *1798, eleēmōn* [2]
merciful, *1799, eleos* [2]
merciful, *3881, oiktirmōn* [2]
merciful to, *1790, eleaō* [1]

MERCY [59]

mercy, *1799, eleos* [24]
have mercy on, *1796, eleeō* [11]
had mercy on, *1796, eleeō* [3]
mercy, *1796, eleeō* [3]
received mercy, *1796, eleeō* [3]
shown mercy, *1796, eleeō* [3]
mercy, *3880, oiktirmos* [2]
mercy, *RPE* [1]
without mercy, *447, aneleos* [1]
mercy, *1790, eleaō* [1]
to show mercy, *1790, eleaō* [1]
has mercy on, *1796, eleeō* [1]
receive mercy, *1796, eleeō* [1]
showing mercy, *1796, eleeō* [1]
mercy on, *2661, hilaskomai* [1]
mercy, *3881, oiktirmōn* [1]
tender mercy, *5073+1799, splanchnon+eleos* [1]

MERE [8]

mere, *AIT* [6]
mere talkers, *3468, mataiologos* [1]
follow mere natural instincts, *6035, psychikos* [1]

MERELY [4]

merely, *NIG* [3]
merely, *3667, monon* [1]

MERRY [1]

merry, *2370, euphrainō* [1]

MESOPOTAMIA [2]

Mesopotamia, *3544, Mesopotamia* [2]

MESSAGE [47]

message, *3364, logos* [29]
message, *198, akoē* [4]
message, *AIT* [2]
message, *32, angelia* [2]
message, *RPE* [1]
sent message, *690, apostellō* [1]
message, *3060, kērygma* [1]
message, *3062, kēryssō* [1]
bring a message, *3281+4839, laleō+rhēma* [1]
message, *3281, laleō* [1]
this message, *3306, legō* [1]
encouraging message, *4155, paraklēsis* [1]
prophetic message, *4735, prophēteia* [1]
message, *4839, rhēma* [1]

MESSENGER [6]

messenger, *34, angelos* [4]
messenger, *693, apostolos* [2]

MESSENGERS [3]

messengers, *34, angelos* [2]
the messengers', *899, autos* [1]

MESSIAH [2]

Messiah, *3549, Messias* [2]

MET [27]

met, *5636, hypantaō* [6]
met, *5251, synagō* [5]
met, *5267, synantaō* [4]
met, *2351, heuriskō* [3]
met together, *5251, synagō* [2]
met, *560, apantaō* [1]
met, *2779+2627, kai+idou* [1]
met with, *3972, horaō* [1]
met, *3972, horaō* [1]
fully met, *4444, plēroō* [1]
met, *5202, symballō* [1]
met together, *5302, synerchomai* [1]

METALWORKER [1]

metalworker, *5906, chalkeus* [1]

METHUSELAH [1]

Methuselah, *3417, Mathousala* [1]

MICHAEL [2]

Michael, *3640, Michaēl* [2]

MIDAIR [3]

midair, *3547, mesouranēma* [3]

MIDDLE [5]

middle, *3545, mesos* [5]

MIDIAN [1]

Midian, *1178+3409, gē+Madiam* [1]

MIDNIGHT [6]

midnight, *3543, mesonyktion* [3]
at midnight, *3543, mesonyktion* [1]
at midnight, *3545+3816, mesos+nyx* [1]
midnight, *3545+3836+3816,
   mesos+ho+nyx* [1]

MIGHT [99]

might, *AIT* [88]
might, *NIG* [7]
might, *3197, kratos* [2]
might, *323, an* [1]
one might even say, *6055+2229+3306,
   hōs+epos+legō* [1]

MIGHTY [16]

mighty, *2708, ischyros* [7]
mighty, *1539, dynamis* [2]
mighty, *2709, ischys* [2]
Mighty One, *1539, dynamis* [1]
mighty, *1543, dynatos* [1]
mighty, *3193, krataios* [1]
mighty deeds, *3197, kratos* [1]
mighty, *5734, hypsēlos* [1]

MILE [1]

mile, *3627, milion* [1]

MILES [4]

miles, *RPE* [1]
seven miles, *5084+2008,
   stadion+hexēkonta* [1]
three or three and a half miles,
   *5084+1633+4297+2445+5558,
   stadion+eikosi+pente+ē+triakonta* [1]
less than two miles, *6055+608+5084+1278,
   hōs+apo+stadion+dekapente* [1]

MILETUS [3]

Miletus, *3626, Milētos* [3]

MILITARY [1]

military commanders, *5941, chiliarchos* [1]

MILK [5]

milk, *1128, gala* [5]

MILL [1]

hand mill, *3685, mylos* [1]

MILLION [1]

two hundred million, *1490+3689,
   dismyrias+myrias* [1]

MILLSTONE [5]

large millstone, *3685+3948, mylos+onikos* [2]
millstone, *3345+3683, lithos+mylikos* [1]
millstone, *3684, mylinos* [1]
millstone, *3685, mylos* [1]

MINA [4]

mina, *3641, mna* [4]

MINAS [2]

minas, *3641, mna* [2]

MIND [53]

mind, *3808, nous* [15]
mind, *5859, phronēma* [4]
mind, *1379, dianoia* [3]
mind, *2840, kardia* [3]
out of mind, *3419, mainomai* [3]
in right mind, *5404, sōphroneō* [3]
out of mind, *2014, existēmi* [2]
have in mind, *5858, phroneō* [2]
mind, *AIT* [1]
had in mind, *1089, boulomai* [1]
keep in mind, *1182, ginōskō* [1]
with this in mind, *1650+899, eis+autos* [1]
bear in mind, *2451, hēgeomai* [1]
made up mind, *3212, krinō* [1]
make up mind, *3212, krinō* [1]
change mind, *3564, metamelomai* [1]
changed mind, *3564, metamelomai* [1]
change of mind, *3567, metanoia* [1]
in mind, *3857, oida* [1]
out of mind, *4196, paraphroneō* [1]
mind, *4460, pneuma* [1]
mind business, *4556, prassō* [1]
make up mind, *5502+1877+3836+2840,
   tithēmi+en+ho+kardia* [1]
mind on, *5858, phroneō* [1]
mind, *5858, phroneō* [1]
mind, *6034, psychē* [1]

MINDED [1]

clear minded, *5404, sōphroneō* [1]

MINDFUL [2]

mindful of, *2098+2093, epiblepō+epi* [1]

are mindful, *3630, mimnēskomai* [1]

MINDS [21]

minds, *1379, dianoia* [4]
minds, *3784, noēma* [4]
minds, *3808, nous* [4]
minds, *2840, kardia* [2]
minds, *6034, psychē* [2]
minds, *RPE* [1]
changed minds, *3554, metaballō* [1]
minds, *3752, nephros* [1]
set minds on, *5858, phroneō* [1]
minds set on, *5858, phroneō* [1]

MINE [19]

mine, *1609, egō* [11]
mine, *1847, emos* [5]
mine, *RPE* [1]
of mine, *1650+1609, eis+egō* [1]
what business is it of mine, *5515+1609,
   tis+egō* [1]

MINISTER [5]

minister, *1356, diakonos* [3]
minister, *3302, latreuō* [1]
minister, *3313, leitourgos* [1]

MINISTERING [1]

ministering, *3312, leitourgikos* [1]

MINISTERS [1]

ministers, *1356, diakonos* [1]

MINISTRY [22]

ministry, *1355, diakonia* [14]
ministry, *RPE* [2]
ministry, *NIG* [1]
ministry of an apostle, *692, apostolē* [1]
ministry, *1354, diakoneō* [1]
ministry, *3301, latreia* [1]
ministry, *3311, leitourgia* [1]
ministry, *3364, logos* [1]

MINT [2]

mint, *2455, hēdyosmon* [1]
spices mint, *2455, hēdyosmon* [1]

MINUS [1]

minus, *4123, para* [1]

MIRACLE [4]

miracle, *4956, sēmeion* [2]
miracle, *1539, dynamis* [1]
miracle, *2240, ergon* [1]

MIRACLES [27]

miracles, *1539, dynamis* [16]
miracles, *2240, ergon* [6]
miracles, *5469, teras* [3]
work miracles, *1539, dynamis* [1]
workers of miracles, *1539, dynamis* [1]

MIRACULOUS [38]

miraculous signs, *4956, sēmeion* [23]
miraculous sign, *4956, sēmeion* [11]
miraculous powers, *1539, dynamis* [3]
miraculous powers, *1920+1539,
   energēma+dynamis* [1]

MIRACULOUSLY [1]

miraculously, *4956, sēmeion* [1]

MIRROR [2]

mirror, *2269, esoptron* [2]

MISDEEDS [1]

misdeeds, *4552, praxis* [1]

MISDEMEANOR [1]

misdemeanor, *93, adikēma* [1]

MISERABLE [1]

miserable, *4777, ptōchos* [1]

MISERY [2]

misery, *5416, talaipōria* [2]

MISLEADS [1]

misleads, *4414, planaō* [1]

MISLED [1]

misled, *4414, planaō* [1]

MISSES [1]

misses, *5728, hystereō* [1]

MISSION [1]

mission, *1355, diakonia* [1]

MIST [2]

mist, *874, atmis* [1]
mist, *944, achlys* [1]

MISTAKEN [1]

mistaken, *4414, planaō* [1]

MISTREAT [2]

mistreat, *2092, epēreazō* [1]
mistreat, *5614, hybrizō* [1]

MISTREATED [6]

mistreated, *2807, kakoucheō* [2]
mistreated, *92, adikeō* [1]
mistreated, *2808, kakoō* [1]
mistreated along with, *5156, synkakoucheomai* [1]
mistreated, *5614, hybrizō* [1]

MISTREATING [1]

mistreating, *92, adikeō* [1]

MISTS [1]

mists, *3920, homichlē* [1]

MITYLENE [1]

Mitylene, *3639, Mitylēnē* [1]

MIX [1]

mix, *3042, kerannymi* [1]

MIXED [8]

mixed, *3502, meignymi* [4]
mixed, *1606, enkryptō* [2]
mixed, *AIT* [1]
mixed with myrrh, *5046, smyrnizō* [1]

MIXTURE [1]

mixture, *3623, migma* [1]

MNASON [1]

Mnason, *3643, Mnasōn* [1]

MOB [3]

mob, *4063, ochlos* [2]
formed a mob, *4062, ochlopoieō* [1]

MOCK [2]

mock, *1850, empaizō* [2]

MOCKED [9]

mocked, *1850, empaizō* [8]
mocked, *3682, myktērizō* [1]

MOCKING [1]

mocking, *1850, empaizō* [1]

MODEL [2]

model, *5596, typos* [2]

MODESTLY [1]

modestly, *1877+2950+3177, en+katastolē+kosmios* [1]

MODESTY [1]

modesty, *2362, euschēmosynē* [1]

MOISTURE [1]

moisture, *2657, ikmas* [1]

MOLECH [1]

Molech, *3661, Moloch* [1]

MOMENT [14]

moment, *6052, hōra* [6]
at that moment, *2779+2627, kai+idou* [2]
this moment, *785, arti* [1]
at that moment, *2311, eutheōs* [1]
the moment, *2317, euthys¹* [1]
the moment, *4020, hotan* [1]
at that moment, *4202, parachrēma* [1]
in the next moment, *5444, tachys* [1]

MOMENTARY [1]

momentary, *4194, parautika* [1]

MONEY [54]

money, *736, argyrion* [12]
money, *RPE* [5]
money changers, *3142, kollybistēs* [3]
money, *5507, timē* [3]
money, *5975, chrēma* [3]
money, *3440, mamōnas* [2]
money, *5910, chalkos* [2]
money, *AIT* [1]
money, *NIG* [1]
greedy for money, *154, aischrokerdōs* [1]
money⁵, *899, autos* [1]
the money⁵, *899, autos* [1]
free from the love of money, *921, aphilargyros* [1]
not a lover of money, *921, aphilargyros* [1]
money bag, *1186, glōssokomon* [1]
money, *1186, glōssokomon* [1]
extort money, *1398, diaseiō* [1]
money, *1797, eleēmosynē* [1]
making money, *2238, ergasia* [1]
money, *2238, ergasia* [1]
sum of money, *2564, thēsaurizō* [1]
make money, *3045, kerdainō* [1]
exchanging money, *3048, kermatistēs* [1]
money, *3836, ho* [1]
talents of money, *5419, talanton* [1]
blood money, *5507+135, timē+haima* [1]

the money worth a year's wages, *5559+1324, triakosioi+dēnarion* [1]
love of money, *5794, philargyria* [1]
loved money, *5795+5639, philargyros+hyparchō* [1]
lovers of money, *5795, philargyros* [1]
owed money to, *5971+1639, chreopheiletēs+eimi* [1]

MONEYLENDER [1]

moneylender, *1250, danistēs* [1]

MONTH [4]

month, *3604, mēn¹* [4]

MONTHS [15]

months, *3604, mēn¹* [11]
eight months of a man's wages, *1324+1357, dēnarion+diakosioi* [1]
eight months wages, *1357+1324, diakosioi+dēnarion* [1]
four months, *5485, tetramēnos* [1]
three months, *5564, trimēnos* [1]

MOON [10]

moon, *4943, selēnē* [9]
New Moon celebration, *3741, neomēnia* [1]

MORAL [1]

moral filth, *4864, rhyparia* [1]

MORE [194]

more, *3437, mallon* [21]
more, *4498, polys* [19]
more, *2285, eti* [9]
once more, *4099, palin* [9]
more, *NIG* [5]
more bearable, *445, anektos* [5]
more, *257, allos* [4]
any more, *2285, eti* [4]
all the more, *3437, mallon* [4]
no more, *4024, ou* [4]
more than, *5642, hyper* [4]
more, *AIT* [3]
more, *RPE* [3]
more powerful, *2708, ischyros* [3]
more and more, *3437, mallon* [3]
more, *3505, meizōn* [3]
any more, *4033, ouketi* [3]
more accurate, *209, akribōs* [2]
worth more than, *1422, diapherō* [2]
more than, *2062, epanō* [2]
more and more, *2093+4498, epi+polys* [2]
more than, *3437, mallon* [2]
no more, *4033, ouketi* [2]
more than, *4123, para* [2]
do so more and more, *4355+3437, perisseuō+mallon* [2]
do this more and more, *4355+3437, perisseuō+mallon* [2]
more than, *4358, perissoteros* [2]
more, *4358, perissoteros* [2]
more, *4359, perissoterōs* [2]
reaching more and more, *4429+1328+3836+4498, pleonazō+dia+ho+polys* [2]
all the more, *4498+3437, polys+mallon* [2]
more wicked, *4505, ponēros* [2]
growing more and more, *5647, hyperauxanō* [2]
and more, [1]
more adequately, *209, akribōs* [1]
what is more, *247+3529+2779, alla+menounge+kai* [1]
more than, *247, alla* [1]

some more, *257, allos* [1]
one thing more, *275, hama* [1]
more necessary, *338, anankaios* [1]
more important matters, *987, barys* [1]
more certain, *1010, bebaios* [1]
more valuable than, *1422, diapherō* [1]
no more, *1572+2401, eaō+heōs* [1]
more earnestly, *1757, ektenōs* [1]
pitied more than, *1795, eleeinos* [1]
person more distinguished, *1952, entimos* [1]
of more noble character, *2302, eugenēs* [1]
more than, *2445, ē* [1]
any more than, *2777+4024, kathōs+ou* [1]
more than that, *2779, kai* [1]
and even more, *2779+4707+5148,*
   kai+prostithēmi+sy [1]
look more closely, *2917, katanoeō* [1]
more than that, *3437+1254, mallon+de* [1]
more, *3437+4358, mallon+perissoteros* [1]
no more, *3594, mēdeis* [1]
don't any more, *3600, mēketi* [1]
no more, *3600, mēketi* [1]
how much more, *3615, mētige* [1]
more[s], *3641, mna* [1]
more, *4012, hosos* [1]
what is more, *4024+3667+1254+247+2779,*
   ou+monon+de+alla+kai [1]
more than, *4024, ou* [1]
no any more, *4033, ouketi* [1]
one[s] more, *4047, houtos* [1]
more, *4355, perisseuō* [1]
more, *4356, perissos* [1]
more important than, *4358, perissoteros* [1]
much more, *4358, perissoteros* [1]
more careful, *4359, perissoterōs* [1]
more frequently, *4359, perissoterōs* [1]
even more, *4360, perissōs* [1]
lust for more, *4432, pleonexia* [1]
even more so[s], *4498+5080,*
   polys+spoudaios [1]
more, *4498+4123, polys+para* [1]
how much more, *4531, posos* [1]
earned more, *4664, prosergazomai* [1]
all the more eager, *5081, spoudaiōs* [1]
what is more, *5250+4246+4047,*
   syn+pas+houtos [1]
brings out more clearly, *5319, synistēmi* [1]
more perfect, *5455, teleios* [1]
all the more, *5537+3437, tosoutos+mallon* [1]
more than is warranted, *5642, hyper* [1]
more, *5642, hyper* [1]
more severely, *5649, hyperballontōs* [1]
more than conquerors, *5664, hypernikaō* [1]
increased all the more, *5668, hyperperisseuō* [1]
more shrewd, *5861, phronimos* [1]
more severely, *5937, cheirōn* [1]

MOREOVER [4]

moreover, *1254, de* [2]
moreover, *1142, gar* [1]
moreover, *1663+3525, eita+men* [1]

MORNING [20]

early in the morning, *4745, prōi* [2]
in the morning, *4745, prōi* [2]
morning, *4748, prōinos* [2]
early in the morning, *275+4745, hama+prōi* [1]
in the morning, *1181+2465,*
   ginomai+hēmera [1]
the next morning, *1181+2465,*
   ginomai+hēmera [1]
very early in the morning, *2317+4745,*
   euthys[1]+prōi [1]
morning, *2465, hēmera* [1]
came early in the morning, *3983, orthrizō* [1]

early morning, *3984, orthrinos* [1]
very early in the morning, *3986+960,*
   orthros+bathys [1]
early morning, *4745, prōi* [1]
morning, *4745, prōi* [1]
early in the morning, *4746+1181,*
   prōia+ginomai [1]
early in the morning, *4746, prōia* [1]
morning star, *5892, phōsphoros* [1]
nine in the morning, *6052+5569+3836+2465,*
   hōra+tritos+ho+hēmera [1]

MORTAL [7]

mortal, *2570, thnētos* [6]
mortal, *5778, phthartos* [1]

MOSES [85]

Moses, *3707, Mōysēs* [79]
Moses, *RPE* [3]
Moses[s], *899, autos* [3]

MOST [41]

Most High, *5736, hypsistos* [9]
most, *4498, polys* [8]
Most Holy Place, *41, hagios* [5]
most important seats, *4751, prōtokathedria* [4]
most excellent, *3196, kratistos* [3]
most severely, *4358, perissoteros* [2]
most important, *4755, prōtos* [2]
Most Holy Place, *41+41, hagios+hagios* [1]
most holy, *41, hagios* [1]
making the most of, *1973, exagorazō* [1]
most excellent, *2848+5651, kata+hyperbolē* [1]
most, *3436, malista* [1]
most, *3836+4498, ho+polys* [1]
make the most of opportunity,
   3836+2789+1973,
   ho+kairos+exagorazō [1]
most earnestly, *5655, hyperekperissou* [1]

MOTH [3]

moth, *4962, sēs* [3]

MOTHER [85]

mother, *3613, mētēr* [73]
whose mother was, *1666, ek* [3]
mother, *3836, ho* [3]
mother, *RPE* [1]
without mother, *298, amētōr* [1]
mother, *1222, gynē* [1]
whose mother, *1666, ek* [1]
mother, *3120, koilia* [1]
mother, *5577, trophos* [1]

MOTHER'S [3]

mother's, *3613, mētēr* [3]

MOTHER-IN-LAW [6]

mother-in-law, *4289, penthera* [6]

MOTHERS [6]

nursing mothers, *2558, thēlazō* [3]
mothers, *3613, mētēr* [2]
kill their mothers, *3618, mētrolōas* [1]

MOTHS [1]

moths have eaten, *4963+1181,*
   sētobrōtos+ginomai [1]

MOTIONED [7]

motioned, *2939+3836+5931,*
   kataseiō+ho+cheir [2]

motioned, *2939, kataseiō* [2]
motioned, *3748, neuō* [2]
motioned with, *1753, ekteinō* [1]

MOTIVES [4]

motives, *AIT* [1]
motives, *1087, boulē* [1]
with wrong motives, *2809, kakōs* [1]
false motives, *4733, prophasis* [1]

MOUNT [18]

Mount, *4001, oros* [15]
Mount of Olives, *1779, elaiōn* [3]

MOUNTAIN [22]

mountain, *4001, oros* [22]

MOUNTAINS [9]

mountains, *4001, oros* [9]

MOUNTAINSIDE [8]

mountainside, *4001, oros* [8]

MOUNTED [1]

mounted, *2690, hippikos* [1]

MOUNTS [1]

mounts, *3229, ktēnos* [1]

MOURN [16]

mourn, *4291, pentheō* [6]
mourn, *3081, klaiō* [4]
mourn, *3164, koptō* [4]
mourn, *2577, thrēneō* [1]
mourn, *4292+3972, penthos+horaō* [1]

MOURNED [2]

mourned, *3164, koptō* [1]
mourned deeply, *4472+3157+3489,*
   poieō+kopetos+megas [1]

MOURNING [7]

mourning, *4292, penthos* [3]
mourning, *4291, pentheō* [2]
mourning, *3164, koptō* [1]
mourning, *3851, odyrmos* [1]

MOUTH [48]

mouth, *5125, stoma* [42]
word of mouth, *3364, logos* [2]
foaming at the mouth, *930, aphrizō* [1]
foams at the mouth, *930, aphrizō* [1]
foams at the mouth, *931, aphros* [1]
mouth words, *5779, phthengomai* [1]

MOUTHS [9]

mouths, *5125, stoma* [9]

MOVE [10]

move, *3075, kineō* [2]
move, *3553, metabainō* [2]
nothing move, *293, ametakinētos* [1]
move, *3496, methistēmi* [1]
not move, *3531+810, menō+asaleutos* [1]
move around, *3553, metabainō* [1]
on the move, *3845, hodoiporia* [1]
move, *4646, prosanabainō* [1]

MOVED [8]

deeply moved, *1839, embrimaomai* [2]
moved, *AIT* [1]

moved about freely, *1660+2779+1744,*
eisporeuomai+kai+ekporeuomai [1]
moved on, *3558, metairō* [1]
moved, *3560, metakineō* [1]
moved along, *4162, paralegomai* [1]
moved about, *4344, peripateō* [1]

MOWED [1]

mowed, *286, amaō* [1]

MUCH [85]

much, *4498, polys* [27]
how much, *4531, posos* [11]
much, *NIG* [5]
how much, *4012, hosos* [5]
much, *AIT* [2]
much, *3489, megas* [2]
as much as, *4012, hosos* [2]
as much, *5537, tosoutos* [2]
much, *RPE* [1]
so much as, *948, achri* [1]
looked so much like, *1181+6059,*
ginomai+hōsei [1]
twice as much, *1487, diplous* [1]
make much of, *1519, doxazō* [1]
how much, *2462, hēlikos* [1]
much, *2653, hikanos* [1]
as much as, *2777, kathōs* [1]
as much as were able, *2848+1539,*
kata+dynamis [1]
eaten as much as wanted, *3170+5575,*
korennymi+trophē [1]
much, *3437, mallon* [1]
had too much to drink, *3499, methyskō* [1]
had too much, *3551+1639, mestoō+eimi* [1]
how much more, *3615, mētige* [1]
so much, *4048, houtōs* [1]
much more, *4358, perissoteros* [1]
much harder, *4359, perissoterōs* [1]
have too much, *4429, pleonazō* [1]
many times as much, *4491, pollaplasiōn* [1]
how much more, *4531, posos* [1]
so much, *5537, tosoutos* [1]

MUD [5]

mud, *4384, pēlos* [4]
mud, *1079, borboros* [1]

MULBERRY [1]

mulberry tree, *5189, sykaminos* [1]

MULTIPLYING [1]

multiplying, *5770, pherō* [1]

MULTITUDE [5]

multitude, *4063, ochlos* [3]
multitude, *4436, plēthos* [2]

MULTITUDES [1]

multitudes, *4063, ochlos* [1]

MURDER [14]

murder, *5839, phoneuō* [6]
murder, *5840, phonos* [6]
murder, *5377, sphazō* [1]
commit murder, *5839, phoneuō* [1]

MURDERED [5]

murdered, *5839, phoneuō* [3]
murdered, *5377, sphazō* [1]
murdered, *5838, phoneus* [1]

MURDERER [6]

murderer, *475, anthrōpoktonos* [3]
murderer, *5838, phoneus* [2]
murderer, *467+5838, anēr+phoneus* [1]

MURDERERS [4]

murderers, *5838, phoneus* [3]
murderers, *439, androphonos* [1]

MURDEROUS [1]

murderous, *5840, phonos* [1]

MURDERS [2]

murders, *5839, phoneuō* [1]
murders, *5840, phonos* [1]

MUSIC [3]

music, *5246, symphōnia* [1]
music, *5889, phōnē* [1]
make music, *6010, psallō* [1]

MUSICIANS [1]

musicians, *3676, mousikos* [1]

MUST [159]

must, *AIT* [81]
must, *1256, dei* [57]
must, *RPE* [7]
must, *NIG* [4]
must, *340, anankē* [2]
must, *4053, opheilō* [2]
must, *339, anankastōs* [1]
must be poured, *1064, blēteos* [1]
must, *2400+2026, echō+exousia* [1]
must, *2400+340, echō+anankē* [1]
must, *2671, hina* [1]
must, *4122, pantōs* [1]

MUSTARD [5]

mustard, *4983, sinapi* [5]

MUTE [9]

mute, *3273, kōphos* [4]
mute, *228, alalos* [2]
man who had been mute, *3273, kōphos* [2]
mute, *936, aphōnos* [1]

MUTILATORS [1]

mutilators of the flesh, *2961, katatomē* [1]

MUTTER [1]

mutter, *1339, diagongyzō* [1]

MUTTERED [1]

muttered, *1339, diagongyzō* [1]

MUTUAL [2]

mutual, *253, allēlōn* [1]
mutual consent, *5247, symphōnos* [1]

MUTUALLY [1]

mutually encouraged, *5220, symparakaleō* [1]

MUZZLE [2]

muzzle, *3055, kēmoō* [1]
muzzle, *5821, phimoō* [1]

MY [674]

my, *1609, egō* [478]
my, *RPE* [51]

my, *1847, emos* [44]
my, *3836, ho* [41]
my, *AIT* [22]
my own, *1847, emos* [9]
my own, *1831, emautou* [7]
my, *NIG* [6]
my own, *1609, egō* [5]
my, *1831, emautou* [3]
my own accord, *1831, emautou* [2]
my, *1847+6034, emos+psychē* [1]
mark my words, *2623, ide* [1]
my, *3836+3950+1609, ho+onoma+egō* [1]
my, *3836+4309+1831, ho+peri+emautou* [1]
my forefathers, *4591, progonos* [1]
my supper, *5515+1268, tis+deipneō* [1]

MYRA [1]

Myra, *3688, Myra* [1]

MYRRH [4]

myrrh, *5043, smyrna¹* [2]
myrrh, *3693, myron* [1]
mixed with myrrh, *5046, smyrnizō* [1]

MYSELF [42]

myself, *1831, emautou* [17]
myself, *899, autos* [8]
I myself, *1609, egō* [5]
myself, *AIT* [2]
myself, *RPE* [2]
I myself, *2743, kagō* [2]
I myself, *899, autos* [1]
myself, *1571, heautou* [1]
myself, *1609, egō* [1]
myself, *1847, emos* [1]
by myself, *3668, monos* [1]
myself, *6034+1609, psychē+egō* [1]

MYSIA [2]

Mysia, *3695, Mysia* [2]

MYSTERIES [2]

mysteries, *3696, mystērion* [2]

MYSTERY [19]

mystery, *3696, mystērion* [18]
mystery, *RPE* [1]

MYTHS [4]

myths, *3680, mythos* [4]

NAAMAN [1]

Naaman, *3722, Naiman* [1]

NAGGAI [1]

Naggai, *3710, Nangai* [1]

NAHOR [1]

Nahor, *3732, Nachōr* [1]

NAHSHON [3]

Nahshon, *3709, Naassōn* [3]

NAHUM [1]

Nahum, *3725, Naoum* [1]

NAIL [1]

nail, *2464, hēlos* [1]

NAILING [2]

nailing, *4669, prosēloō* [1]

nailing to cross, *4699, prospēgnymi* [1]

NAILS [1]

nails, *2464, hēlos* [1]

NAIN [1]

Nain, *3723, Nain* [1]

NAIVE [1]

naive, *179, akakos* [1]

NAKED [7]

naked, *1218, gymnos* [6]
naked, *1219, gymnotēs* [1]

NAKEDNESS [2]

nakedness, *1219, gymnotēs* [2]

NAME [168]

name, *3950, onoma* [156]
name, *AIT* [2]
name, *RPE* [2]
name, *3306, legō* [2]
lose good name, *1650+591+2262,*
   eis+apelegmos+erchomai [1]
name, *2813+3836+3950, kaleō+ho+onoma* [1]
name, *2813, kaleō* [1]
derives name, *3951, onomazō* [1]
invoke the name, *3951+3950,*
   onomazō+onoma [1]
the name^s, *4005, hos* [1]

NAME'S [1]

name's, *3950, onoma* [1]

NAMED [44]

named, *3950, onoma* [30]
named, *NIG* [6]
named, *3950+899, onoma+autos* [2]
named, *2813+3836+3950,*
   kaleō+ho+onoma [1]
named, *2813, kaleō* [1]
named, *3306, legō* [1]
named, *3951, onomazō* [1]
named, *5516, tis* [1]
named, *5540, tounoma* [1]

NAMELY [1]

namely, *AIT* [1]

NAMES [11]

names, *3950, onoma* [9]
names, *AIT* [1]
names, *NIG* [1]

NAPHTALI [3]

Naphtali, *3750, Nephthalim* [3]

NARCISSUS [1]

Narcissus, *3727, Narkissos* [1]

NARD [2]

nard, *3726, nardos* [2]

NARROW [3]

narrow, *5101, stenos* [2]
narrow, *2567, thlibō* [1]

NATHAN [1]

Nathan, *3718, Natham* [1]

NATHANAEL [6]

Nathanael, *3720, Nathanaēl* [6]

NATION [26]

nation, *1620, ethnos* [26]

NATIONS [39]

nations, *1620, ethnos* [37]
scattered among the nations, *1402, diaspora* [1]
nations, *5876, phylē* [1]

NATIVE [4]

native, *1169, genos* [2]
his native language, *1666+3836+2625,*
   ek+ho+idios [1]
native, *1877+4005+1164, en+hos+gennaō* [1]

NATURAL [12]

natural, *6035, psychikos* [3]
natural, *2848+5882, kata+physis* [2]
natural, *5879, physikos* [2]
natural descent, *135, haima* [1]
natural sleep, *3836+3122+3836+5678,*
   ho+koimēsis+ho+hypnos [1]
natural selves, *4922, sarx* [1]
natural, *4922, sarx* [1]
follow mere natural instincts, *6035,*
   psychikos [1]

NATURE [39]

sinful nature, *4922, sarx* [22]
nature, *5882, physis* [7]
nature, *3671, morphē* [2]
nature, *4922, sarx* [?]
nature, *AIT* [1]
divine nature, *2522, theiotēs* [1]
nature, *3517, melos* [1]
human nature, *4922, sarx* [1]
sinful human nature, *4922, sarx* [1]
sinful nature, *5393+3836+4922,*
   sōma+ho+sarx [1]

NAZARENE [4]

Nazarene, *3716, Nazarēnos* [2]
Nazarene, *3717, Nazōraios* [2]

NAZARETH [27]

Nazareth, *3714, Nazareth* [12]
of Nazareth, *3717, Nazōraios* [11]
of Nazareth, *3716, Nazarēnos* [4]

NEAPOLIS [1]

Neapolis, *3735, Nea polis* [1]

NEAR [61]

near, *1584, engys* [22]
near, *1581, engizō* [12]
standing near, *4225, paristēmi* [5]
came near, *1581, engizō* [2]
come near, *1581, engizō* [2]
draw near, *4665, proserchomai* [2]
near, *AIT* [1]
comes near, *1581, engizō* [1]
draw near, *1581, engizō* [1]
drawing near, *1581, engizō* [1]
drew near, *1581, engizō* [1]
near, *1581+2093, engizō+epi* [1]
near, *1877, en* [1]
near, *2093, epi* [1]
stood near, *2392, ephistēmi* [1]
near, *2848, kata* [1]
stay near, *3140, kollaō* [1]

near, *4123, para* [1]
bring near, *4225, paristēmi* [1]
near, *4446, plēsion* [1]
get near, *5344, syntynchanō* [1]
end was near, *5462, teleutaō* [1]

NEARBY [8]

nearby, *1695, ekei* [2]
nearby, *1584, engys* [1]
nearby, *2400, echō* [1]
nearby, *3836+899, ho+autos* [1]
nearby, *4225, paristēmi* [1]
standing nearby, *4225, paristēmi* [1]
nearby, *4309+3836+5536, peri+ho+topos* [1]

NEARED [1]

neared, *1181+1581, ginomai+engizō* [1]

NEARER [1]

nearer, *1584, engys* [1]

NEARLY [5]

nearly, *2453, ēdē* [1]
nearly, *3516, mellō* [1]
nearly over, *4621, prokoptō* [1]
nearly, *4639, pros* [1]
nearly, *5385, schedon* [1]

NEARSIGHTED [1]

nearsighted, *3697, myōpazō* [1]

NECESSARY [8]

necessary, *340, anankē* [3]
necessary, *338, anankaios* [2]
more necessary, *338, anankaios* [1]
necessary for, *338, anankaios* [1]
necessary, *1256, dei* [1]

NECESSITIES [1]

daily necessities, *338+5970,*
   anankaios+chreia [1]

NECK [3]

neck, *5549, trachēlos* [3]

NECKS [1]

necks, *5549, trachēlos* [1]

NEED [55]

need, *5970+2400, chreia+echō* [24]
need, *5970, chreia* [5]
need, *5974, chrēzō* [4]
need, *2400+5970, echō+chreia* [3]
really in need, *3953, ontōs* [3]
need, *5729, hysterēma* [2]
need, *NIG* [1]
does not need to be ashamed, *454,*
   anepaischyntos [1]
need, *894, autarkeia* [1]
need, *1181+5970+2400,*
   ginomai+chreia+echō [1]
time of need, *2322, eukairos* [1]
need, *2400+340, echō+anankē* [1]
have everything need, *3594+3309,*
   mēdeis+leipō [1]
no need, *4356, perissos* [1]
gave to in need, *4472+1797,*
   poieō+eleēmosynē [1]
meets need, *4560, prepō* [1]
need, *5427, tapeinoō* [1]
need, *5639, hyparchō* [1]
need, *5728, hystereō* [1]

need, *5730, hysterēsis* [1]

NEEDED [9]

needed clothes, *1218, gymnos* [2]
needed, *5970+2400, chreia+echō* [2]
needed, *5970, chreia* [2]
needed, *4656, prosdeomai* [1]
needed, *5728, hystereō* [1]
needed, *5729, hysterēma* [1]

NEEDING [2]

needing clothes, *1218, gymnos* [2]

NEEDLE [3]

needle, *4827, rhaphis* [2]
needle, *1017, belonē* [1]

NEEDS [18]

needs, *5970+2400, chreia+echō* [4]
needs, *5970, chreia* [4]
needs, *RPE* [1]
care for needs, *1354, diakoneō* [1]
cared for needs, *1354, diakoneō* [1]
for needs, *2149, epimeleia* [1]
needs, *2201, epitēdeios* [1]
needs, *2400+5970, echō+chreia* [1]
contributing to the needs of others, *3556,
    metadidōmi* [1]
take care of needs, *5676, hypēreteō* [1]
needs, *5729, hysterēma* [1]
needs, *5974, chrēzō* [1]

NEEDY [3]

give to the needy, *4472+1797,
    poieō+eleēmosynē* [2]
needy, *1890, endeēs* [1]

NEGLECT [3]

neglect, *288, ameleō* [1]
neglect, *2901, kataleipō* [1]
neglect, *4216, parerchomai* [1]

NEGLECTED [1]

neglected, *918, aphiēmi* [1]

NEGLECTING [1]

neglecting, *918, aphiēmi* [1]

NEIGHBOR [16]

neighbor, *4446, plēsion* [15]
neighbor, *4489, politēs* [1]

NEIGHBORS [6]

neighbors, *1150, geitōn* [4]
neighbors, *4340, perioikeō* [1]
neighbors, *4341, perioikos* [1]

NEITHER [40]

neither, *4046, oute* [19]
neither, *4028, oude* [8]
neither, *4024, ou* [5]
neither, *3590, mē* [4]
neither, *3612, mēte* [3]
neither, *2779+4024, kai+ou* [1]

NEREUS [1]

Nereus, *3759, Nēreus* [1]

NERI [1]

Neri, *3760, Nēri* [1]

NESTS [2]

nests, *2943, kataskēnōsis* [2]

NET [8]

net, *1473, diktyon* [4]
casting a net, *311, amphiballō* [1]
net, *312, amphiblēstron* [1]
the net[s], *899, autos* [1]
net, *4880, sagēnē* [1]

NETS [8]

nets, *1473, diktyon* [8]

NEVER [104]

never, *4024+3590, ou+mē* [33]
never, *4024, ou* [16]
never, *4030, oudepote* [13]
never, *3590, mē* [5]
never, *4024+3590+1650+3836+172,
    ou+mē+eis+ho+aiōn* [5]
never, *1623, ei* [3]
never again, *4024+3590, ou+mē* [2]
never, *4024+1650+3836+172,
    ou+eis+ho+aiōn* [2]
never, *4028, oude* [2]
never stop, *188, akatapaustos* [1]
never fade away, *277, amarantinos* [1]
[that can never] fade, *278, amaranthos* [1]
[that can never] spoil, *299, amiantos* [1]
never goes out, *812, asbestos* [1]
that can never perish, *915, aphthartos* [1]
never, *2664, hileōs* [1]
may never, *3590+1181, mē+ginomai* [1]
may this never, *3590, mē* [1]
never, *3590+1181, mē+ginomai* [1]
never, *3595, mēdepote* [1]
never again, *3600, mēketi* [1]
never, *3600+3516, mēketi+mellō* [1]
never, *3600, mēketi* [1]
never, *3607, mēpote* [1]
never again, *4024+3590+1650+3836+172,
    ou+mē+eis+ho+aiōn* [1]
never, *4024+3590+4537, ou+mē+pote* [1]
never, *4024+3590+4799, ou+mē+pōpote* [1]
never, *4024+4537, ou+pote* [1]
never, *4029, oudeis* [1]
never again, *4033, ouketi* [1]
never, *4033+4024+3590, ouketi+ou+mē* [1]
never, *4046+4537, oute+pote* [1]
never, *4046+4799, oute+pōpote* [1]
never, *4799, pōpote* [1]

NEVERTHELESS [8]

nevertheless, *247, alla* [4]
nevertheless, *1254, de* [2]
nevertheless, *1623+3590, ei+mē* [1]
nevertheless, *3530, mentoi* [1]

NEW [58]

new, *2785, kainos* [39]
new, *3742, neos* [11]
new, *AIT* [1]
given new birth, *335, anagennaō* [1]
made new, *391, ananeoomai* [1]
the new order, *1481, diorthōsis* [1]
new way, *2786, kainotēs* [1]
new, *2786, kainotēs* [1]
New Moon celebration, *3741, neomēnia* [1]
new, *4710, prosphatos* [1]

NEWBORN [2]

newborn, *786, artigennētos* [1]
newborn babies, *1100, brephos* [1]

NEWS [43]

good news, *2295, euangelion* [6]
news, *3364, logos* [4]
preached the good news, *2294, euangelizō* [3]
news, *198, akoē* [2]
preach the good news, *2294, euangelizō* [2]
proclaiming the good news, *2294,
    euangelizō* [2]
the good news preached, *2294, euangelizō* [2]
news, *5773, phēmē* [2]
news, *RPE* [1]
with the news, *33, angellō* [1]
receive news, *1182, ginōskō* [1]
spread the news about, *1424, diaphēmizō* [1]
bring good news, *2294, euangelizō* [1]
bring news, *2294, euangelizō* [1]
bringing good news, *2294, euangelizō* [1]
brought good news about, *2294, euangelizō* [1]
preach good news, *2294, euangelizō* [1]
preaching the good news, *2294, euangelizō* [1]
tell good news, *2294, euangelizō* [1]
tell the good news, *2294, euangelizō* [1]
telling the good news about, *2294,
    euangelizō* [1]
telling the good news, *2294, euangelizō* [1]
the good news is preached, *2294, euangelizō* [1]
told the good news about, *2294, euangelizō* [1]
news, *2491, ēchos[1]* [1]
with the news, *3306, legō* [1]
the news[s], *3836, ho* [1]
news, *5762, phasis* [1]

NEXT [38]

next day, *2069, epaurion* [15]
next, *2009, hexēs* [4]
next day, *892, aurion* [3]
next day, *2079, epeimi* [3]
the next morning, *1181+2465,
    ginomai+hēmera* [1]
next, *1650+3836+3516, eis+ho+mellō* [1]
next, *1697, ekeinos* [1]
next to, *1877+3836+3146, en+ho+kolpos* [1]
next, *2079, epeimi* [1]
next, *2262, erchomai* [1]
next, *2283, heteros* [1]
next day, *2400, echō* [1]
next, *2400, echō* [1]
the next day, *3552+1651+2465,
    meta+heis+hēmera* [1]
next, *3568, metaxy* [1]
next door, *5327, synomoreō* [1]
in the next moment, *5444, tachys* [1]

NICANOR [1]

Nicanor, *3770, Nikanōr* [1]

NICODEMUS [6]

Nicodemus, *3773, Nikodēmos* [5]
Nicodemus, *RPE* [1]

NICOLAITANS [2]

Nicolaitans, *3774, Nikolaitēs* [2]

NICOLAS [1]

Nicolas, *3775, Nikolaos* [1]

NICOPOLIS [1]

Nicopolis, *3776, Nikopolis* [1]

NIGER [1]

Niger, *3769, Niger* [1]

NIGHT [59]

night, *3816, nyx* [51]
spend the night, *887, aulizomai* [1]
spent the night, *887, aulizomai* [1]
night, *1328+4246+3816, dia+pas+nyx* [1]
spent the night, *1639+1381,
    eimi+dianyktereuō* [1]
a night and a day, *3819, nychthēmeron* [1]
last night, *4047+3836+3816,
    houtos+ho+nyx* [1]
time of night, *5871, phylakē* [1]
watch of the night, *5871, phylakē* [1]

NIGHTS [4]

nights, *3816, nyx* [3]
sleepless nights, *71, agrypnia* [1]

NINE [3]

nine, *1933, ennea* [1]
nine, *5569+6052, tritos+hōra* [1]
nine in the morning, *6052+5569+3836+2465,
    hōra+tritos+ho+hēmera* [1]

NINETY [1]

ninety feet deep, *3976+1278,
    orgyia+dekapente* [1]

NINETY-NINE [4]

ninety-nine, *1916+1933,
    enenēkonta+ennea* [4]

NINEVEH [2]

of Nineveh, *3780, Nineuitēs* [2]

NINEVITES [1]

Ninevites, *3780, Nineuitēs* [1]

NINTH [7]

ninth, *1888, enatos* [7]

NO [480]

no, *4024, ou* [146]
no one, *4029, oudeis* [89]
no, *3590, mē* [58]
no longer, *4033, ouketi* [27]
no, *4029, oudeis* [23]
no, *247, alla* [14]
no one, *3594, mēdeis* [9]
no, *3594, mēdeis* [9]
no longer, *3600, mēketi* [9]
no, *4028, oude* [7]
no, *4049, ouchi* [7]
no, *3612, mēte* [5]
no, *4246+4024, pas+ou* [5]
by no means, *3590+1181, mē+ginomai* [4]
no more, *4024, ou* [4]
no, *NIG* [3]
no, *RPE* [3]
no, *2627, idou* [3]
no one, *4024+4029, ou+oudeis* [3]
and no, *4028, oude* [3]
no, *4024+3590, ou+mē* [2]
no more, *4033, ouketi* [2]
had no opportunity, *177, akaireomai* [1]
no advantage, *269, alysitelēs* [1]
paid no attention, *288, ameleō* [1]
no regret, *294, ametamelētos* [1]
no excuse, *406, anapologētos* [1]
no open to blame, *455, anepilēmptos* [1]
say no to, *766, arneomai* [1]
no ordinary, *842+3836+2536,
    asteios+ho+theos* [1]
no ordinary, *842, asteios* [1]

no understanding, *852, asynetos* [1]
no children, *866, ateknos* [1]
when no was present, *868, ater* [1]
no doubt, *1142, gar* [1]
no, *1142, gar* [1]
no more, *1572+2401, eaō+heōs* [1]
no, *1623, ei* [1]
free and belong to no man, *1801+1666+4246,
    eleutheros+ek+pas* [1]
had no objections, *2483, hēsychazō* [1]
no value, *3033, kenoō* [1]
has no pity, *3091+3836+5073,
    kleiō+ho+splanchnon* [1]
no more, *3594, mēdeis* [1]
no more, *3600, mēketi* [1]
no, *3600, mēketi* [1]
no, *3607, mēpote* [1]
no longer, *4024+3590, ou+mē* [1]
no ever, *4024+3590, ou+mē* [1]
no place, *4024+4544, ou+pou* [1]
no, *4024+4029, ou+oudeis* [1]
by no means, *4027, oudamōs* [1]
no anything, *4029, oudeis* [1]
no at all, *4029, oudeis* [1]
no one else, *4029, oudeis* [1]
no truth, *4029, oudeis* [1]
no way, *4029, oudeis* [1]
no whatever, *4029, oudeis* [1]
no one ever, *4030, oudepote* [1]
no any more, *4033, ouketi* [1]
no, *4033, ouketi* [1]
still no, *4033, ouketi* [1]
still no, *4037, oupō* [1]
and no, *4046, oute* [1]
no, *4046, oute* [1]
no, *4246+4028, pas+oude* [1]
no need, *4356, perissos* [1]
knows no bounds, *5668, hyperperisseuō* [1]

NOAH [8]

Noah, *3820, Nōe* [8]

NOBLE [10]

noble, *2819, kalos* [3]
noble purposes, *5507, timē* [3]
noble birth, *2302, eugenēs* [1]
of more noble character, *2302, eugenēs* [1]
of noble birth, *2302, eugenēs* [1]
noble, *4948, semnos* [1]

NOBODY [5]

nobody, *3590+5516, mē+tis* [1]
nobody, *3594, mēdeis* [1]
nobody, *4024+5516, ou+tis* [1]
nobody, *4024, ou* [1]
nobody, *4029, oudeis* [1]

NOISY [1]

noisy, *2572, thorybeō* [1]

NON-GREEKS [1]

non-Greeks, *975, barbaros* [1]

NONE [24]

none, *4029, oudeis* [7]
none, *3590, mē* [3]
none, *4024, ou* [3]
none[s], *4956+4024, sēmeion+ou* [3]
that none, *3607+5516, mēpote+tis* [2]
none, *3590+5516, mē+tis* [1]
none, *4024+4029, ou+oudeis* [1]
none, *4024+4246, ou+pas* [1]
none, *4024+570, ou+hapas* [1]
and none, *4046+5516, oute+tis* [1]

none, *4246, pas* [1]

NONSENSE [1]

nonsense, *3333, lēros* [1]

NOON [3]

about noon, *2465+3545, hēmera+mesos* [1]
noon, *3540, mesēmbria* [1]
noon, *6052+1761, hōra+hektos* [1]

NOR [81]

nor, *4046, oute* [30]
nor, *4028, oude* [28]
nor, *2779, kai* [5]
nor, *3593, mēde* [5]
nor, *3612, mēte* [4]
nor, *2779+4024, kai+ou* [3]
nor, *4024, ou* [3]
nor anyone, *1254+4029, de+oudeis* [1]
nor, *2445, ē* [1]
nor, *2779+3590, kai+mē* [1]

NORTH [2]

north, *1080, borras* [2]

NORTHEASTER [1]

the northeaster, *2350, eurakylōn* [1]

NORTHWEST [1]

northwest, *6008, chōros* [1]

NOT [1891]

not, *4024, ou* [1026]
not, *3590, mē* [525]
not, *4049, ouchi* [37]
not, *4024+3590, ou+mē* [29]
not even, *4028, oude* [17]
not, *4028, oude* [16]
not yet, *4037, oupō* [16]
not anyone, *3594, mēdeis* [13]
not, *3593, mēde* [11]
not, *3594, mēdeis* [8]
certainly not, *4024+3590, ou+mē* [7]
not, *4046, oute* [7]
not, *RPE* [6]
not believe, *601, apisteō* [6]
not any, *4029, oudeis* [6]
and not, *3593, mēde* [5]
not anything, *3594, mēdeis* [5]
not one, *4029, oudeis* [5]
not circumcised, *213, akrobystia* [4]
not at all, *3590+1181, mē+ginomai* [4]
not even, *3593, mēde* [4]
not even, *4024, ou* [4]
not, *NIG* [3]
not understand, *51, agnoeō* [3]
not having the law, *491, anomos* [3]
not understand, *2626, idiōtēs* [3]
not only, *3590, mē* [3]
so that not, *3607, mēpote* [3]
not, *3612, mēte* [3]
surely not, *3614, mēti* [3]
not anything, *4029, oudeis* [3]
still not, *4037, oupō* [3]
not know, *51, agnoeō* [2]
if not, *247, alla* [2]
not a believer, *603, apistos* [2]
absolutely not, *3590+1181, mē+ginomai* [2]
certainly not, *3590+1181, mē+ginomai* [2]
surely not, *3592, mēdamōs* [2]
not any, *3594, mēdeis* [2]
not at all, *4024+3590, ou+mē* [2]
even not, *4028, oude* [2]

not either, *4028, oude* [2]
not anyone, *4029, oudeis* [2]
not, *4029, oudeis* [2]
not yet, *4031, oudepō* [2]
not, *6006, chōris* [2]
not realizing, *51, agnoeō* [1]
not recognize, *51, agnoeō* [1]
not clear, *83, adēlos* [1]
not voluntarily, *220, akōn* [1]
not his own, *259, allotrios* [1]
not their own, *259, allotrios* [1]
not, *261, allōs* [1]
not quarrelsome, *285, amachos* [1]
not competent, *396, anaxios* [1]
not exhausted, *444, anekleiptos* [1]
not resentful, *452, anexikakos* [1]
does not need to be ashamed, *454,*
     anepaischyntos [1]
not, *479, aniēmi* [1]
not subject, *538, anypotaktos* [1]
do not believe, *578, apeitheō* [1]
not obey, *578, apeitheō* [1]
not present, *582, apeimi¹* [1]
not acquainted with, *586, apeiros* [1]
not have faith, *601, apisteō* [1]
not believe, *603, apistos* [1]
not cause to stumble, *718, aproskopos* [1]
not lovers of good, *920, aphilagathos* [1]
not a lover of money, *921, aphilargyros* [1]
not built by human hands, *942,*
     acheiropoiētos [1]
not done by the hands of men, *942,*
     acheiropoiētos [1]
not made by man, *942, acheiropoiētos* [1]
not lie, *950, apseudēs* [1]
whether or not, *1623, ei* [1]
not include, *1760, ektos* [1]
not have, *2142, epileipō* [1]
not until, *2453+1254, ēdē+de* [1]
not trained, *2626, idiōtēs* [1]
not forgiven, *3195, krateō* [1]
not forgive, *3195, krateō* [1]
could not talk, *3273, kōphos* [1]
not move, *3531+810, menō+asaleutos* [1]
not anything, *3590+3594, mē+mēdeis* [1]
not are you, *3590, mē* [1]
not, *3590+4024, mē+ou* [1]
not any way, *3594, mēdeis* [1]
not anybody, *3594, mēdeis* [1]
not in the least, *3594, mēdeis* [1]
not yet, *3596, mēdepō* [1]
not, *3600, mēketi* [1]
not yet, *3609, mēpō* [1]
and not, *3612, mēte* [1]
not, *3614, mēti* [1]
not one, *4024+3590, ou+mē* [1]
not again, *4024+3590, ou+mē* [1]
not by any means, *4024+3590, ou+mē* [1]
not clear, *4024+1182, ou+ginōskō* [1]
not even, *4024+4028, ou+oude* [1]
not yet, *4024, ou* [1]
and not, *4028, oude* [1]
but not either, *4028, oude* [1]
not a thing, *4029, oudeis* [1]
not a word, *4029, oudeis* [1]
not anyone's, *4029, oudeis* [1]
not in the least, *4029, oudeis* [1]
not, *4029+3590, oudeis+mē* [1]
still not, *4031, oudepō* [1]
not anymore, *4033, ouketi* [1]
not longer, *4033, ouketi* [1]
not, *4033, ouketi* [1]
up to that time not, *4037, oupō* [1]
yet not, *4037, oupō* [1]
not any, *4046, oute* [1]
not put on such a list, *4148, paraiteomai* [1]

not marry, *5498, tēreō* [1]
could not give, *5729, hysterēma* [1]
not last, *5778, phthartos* [1]
not one, *6034+4029, psychē+oudeis* [1]

NOTE   [4]

took note, *2105, epiginōskō* [1]
take note of, *3857, oida* [1]
take special note, *4957, sēmeioō* [1]
take note of, *5023, skopeō* [1]

NOTES   [1]

notes, *5782, phthongos* [1]

NOTHING   [113]

nothing, *4029, oudeis* [37]
nothing, *4024, ou* [14]
nothing, *3594, mēdeis* [11]
nothing, *3590, mē* [6]
nothing, *4024+4029, ou+oudeis* [5]
for nothing, *1632, eikē* [3]
doing nothing, *734, argos* [2]
nothing, *3590+5516, mē+tis* [2]
nothing, *4024+5515, ou+tis* [2]
nothing ever, *4030, oudepote* [2]
have nothing to do with, *4148, paraiteomai* [2]
nothing false, *94+4024, adikia+ou* [1]
nothing wrong with, *289, amemptos* [1]
nothing move, *293, ametakinētos* [1]
nothing against them, *441, anenklētos* [1]
have nothing to do with, *706, apotrepō* [1]
nothing to fear, *925, aphobōs* [1]
for nothing, *1562, dōrean* [1]
amounts to nothing, *2024, exoutheneō* [1]
coming to nothing, *2934, katargeō* [1]
nothing, *3031, kenos* [1]
made nothing, *3033, kenoō* [1]
nothing ever, *3590, mē* [1]
nothing, *3590+5515, mē+tis* [1]
nothing at all, *4024+4029, ou+oudeis* [1]
nothing, *4024+4005, ou+hos* [1]
nothing, *4024+4246+4839, ou+pas+rhēma* [1]
nothing, *4024+5516, ou+tis* [1]
and nothing, *4028+5516, oude+tis* [1]
and nothing, *4028, oude* [1]
nothing, *4028+1651, oude+heis* [1]
nothing, *4029+3364, oudeis+logos* [1]
nothing, *4029+4024+3590, oudeis+ou+mē* [1]
nothing, *4046+5516, oute+tis* [1]
nothing, *4046, oute* [1]
nothing, *4246+4024, pas+ou* [1]
wearing nothing, *4314+2093+1218,*
     periballō+epi+gymnos [1]
nothing, *5516+4024, tis+ou* [1]

NOTICE   [5]

written notice, *2107, epigraphē* [2]
had a notice prepared, *1211+5518,*
     graphō+titlos [1]
give notice of, *1334, diangellō* [1]
escaped notice, *3291, lanthanō* [1]

NOTICED   [3]

noticed, *3972, horaō* [2]
noticed, *2091, epechō* [1]

NOTICING   [2]

noticing, *3972, horaō* [2]

NOTIONS   [1]

with idle notions, *1632, eikē* [1]

NOTORIOUS   [1]

notorious, *2168, episēmos* [1]

NOURISHING   [1]

nourishing, *4404, piotēs* [1]

NOW   [365]

now, *3814, nyn* [101]
now, *1254, de* [82]
now, *AIT* [31]
now, *785, arti* [20]
now, *3815, nyni* [16]
now, *4036, oun* [12]
now, *2779, kai* [11]
now, *2627, idou* [9]
now, *1142, gar* [7]
now, *3836+3814, ho+nyn* [7]
now on, *3836+3814, ho+nyn* [6]
now, *NIG* [5]
now, *2453, ēdē* [5]
now, *2779+2627, kai+idou* [4]
now, *247, alla* [3]
now on, *785, arti* [3]
now, *RPE* [3]
by now, *2453, ēdē* [2]
now, *2627+3814, idou+nyn* [2]
now, *2779+3814+2627, kai+nyn+idou* [2]
now then, *4036, oun* [2]
now, *6063, hōste* [2]
now, *608+3836+3814, apo+ho+nyn* [1]
now, *608+4005, apo+hos* [1]
now, *608+785, apo+arti* [1]
just now, *785, arti* [1]
and now, *1254, de* [1]
by now, *1254, de* [1]
now that, *1254, de* [1]
now, *1306, deuro* [1]
now, *1475, dio* [1]
now that, *1623, ei* [1]
is now, *1639, eimi* [1]
right now, *1994, exautēs* [1]
now if, *2075, epei* [1]
now, *2274, eschatos* [1]
now, *2285, eti* [1]
now, *2311, eutheōs* [1]
now, *2445, ē* [1]
even now, *2453, ēdē* [1]
now at last, *2453+4537, ēdē+pote* [1]
now, *2779+1181, kai+ginomai* [1]
and now, *2779, kai* [1]
now, *3370, loipos* [1]
now, *3525, men* [1]
now then, *3814, nyn* [1]
now, *3814+2627, nyn+idou* [1]
from now on, *3836+3370, ho+loipos* [1]
enough for now, *3836+3814+2400,*
     ho+nyn+echō [1]
now, *4099, palin* [1]
from now on, *4121, pantote* [1]
now have, *4205, pareimi* [1]
now, *6045+3370, hōde+loipos* [1]

NOWHERE   [2]

getting nowhere, *4024+6067+4029,*
     ou+ōpheleō+oudeis [1]
was getting nowhere, *4029+6067,*
     oudeis+ōpheleō [1]

NULLIFY   [5]

nullify, *2934, katargeō* [3]
nullify, *218, akyroō* [2]

NUMBER [44]

number, *750, arithmos* [13]
number, *AIT* [8]
number, *4436, plēthos* [6]
number, *NIG* [3]
number, *2653, hikanos* [2]
number, *4498, polys* [2]
their own number, *899, autos* [1]
to their number, *2093+3836+899,*
  epi+ho+autos [1]
gather a great number, *2197, episōreuō* [1]
large number, *2653, hikanos* [1]
number, *2935, katarithmeō* [1]
number of people, *4063, ochlos* [1]
number, *4063, ochlos* [1]
great number, *4436, plēthos* [1]
large number, *4436, plēthos* [1]
full number, *4445, plērōma* [1]

NUMBERED [3]

numbered, *749, arithmeō* [2]
numbered, *3357, logizomai* [1]

NUMBERING [2]

numbering, *1639+750, eimi+arithmos* [1]
numbering, *1639, eimi* [1]

NUMBERS [5]

numbers of people, *4063, ochlos* [2]
numbers, *AIT* [1]
numbers, *750, arithmos* [1]
grew in numbers, *4437, plēthynō* [1]

NUMEROUS [1]

numerous, *4436, plēthos* [1]

NURSED [3]

nursed a grudge against, *1923, enechō* [1]
nursed, *2558, thēlazō* [1]
nursed, *5555, trephō* [1]

NURSING [3]

nursing mothers, *2558, thēlazō* [3]

NYMPHA [1]

Nympha, *3809, Nymphan* [1]

O [28]

O, *AIT* [16]
O, *3836, ho* [7]
O, *6043, ō²* [4]
O, *NIG* [1]

OARS [1]

the oarsˢ, *1785, elaunō* [1]

OATH [21]

oath, *3992, horkos* [6]
oath, *3993, horkōmosia* [4]
declared on oath, *3923, omnyō* [2]
bound by his oath, *4053, opheilō* [2]
oath, *RPE* [1]
taken a solemn oath, *353+354,*
  anathema+anathematizō [1]
bound with an oath, *354, anathematizō* [1]
taken an oath, *354, anathematizō* [1]
charge under oath, *2019, exorkizō* [1]
break oath, *2155, epiorkeō* [1]
promised with an oath, *3923, omnyō* [1]

OATHS [3]

oaths, *3992, horkos* [3]

OBED [3]

Obed, *2725, lōbēd* [3]

OBEDIENCE [12]

obedience, *5633, hypakoē* [8]
in obedience to, *2848, kata* [2]
obedience, *5717, hypotagē* [1]
in obedience to, *5875, phylassō* [1]

OBEDIENT [8]

obedient, *5633, hypakoē* [3]
obedient, *5675, hypēkoos* [2]
obedient, *4272, peitharcheō* [1]
obedient, *5634, hypakouō* [1]
obedient, *5718, hypotassō* [1]

OBEY [49]

obey, *5498, tēreō* [16]
obey, *5634, hypakouō* [14]
obey, *RPE* [3]
obey, *5633, hypakoē* [3]
obey, *5875, phylassō* [3]
obey, *4272, peitharcheō* [2]
obey, *201, akouō* [1]
not obey, *578, apeitheō* [1]
obey, *2400+5717, echō+hypotagē* [1]
obey, *4275, peithō* [1]
make obey, *4275, peithō* [1]
obey, *4472, poieō* [1]
obey, *4475, poiētēs* [1]
obey, *5675+1181, hypēkoos+ginomai* [1]

OBEYED [8]

obeyed, *5634, hypakouō* [4]
obeyed, *5498, tēreō* [3]
obeyed, *5875, phylassō* [1]

OBEYING [2]

obeying, *4275, peithō* [1]
obeying, *5633, hypakoē* [1]

OBEYS [3]

obeys, *5498, tēreō* [2]
obeys, *5464, teleō* [1]

OBJECTED [3]

objected, *3306, legō* [2]
objected, *515, antilegō* [1]

OBJECTION [1]

without raising any objection, *395,*
  anantirrētōs [1]

OBJECTIONS [1]

had no objections, *2483, hēsychazō* [1]

OBJECTS [4]

objects, *5007, skeuos* [2]
objects of worship, *4934, sebasma* [1]
objects, *5451, teknon* [1]

OBLIGATED [2]

obligated, *4050, opheiletēs* [2]

OBLIGATION [2]

obligation, *4050, opheiletēs* [1]
obligation, *4052, opheilēma* [1]

OBSCENITY [1]

obscenity, *157, aischrotēs* [1]

OBSERVATION [1]

careful observation, *4191, paratērēsis* [1]

OBSERVE [4]

observe, *2240, ergon* [1]
observe, *3195, krateō* [1]
observe, *4556, prassō* [1]
observe, *5498, tēreō* [1]

OBSERVER [1]

observerˢ, *2848, kata* [1]

OBSERVING [10]

observing, *2240, ergon* [8]
observing, *4190, paratēreō* [1]
observing, *4513+1877, poreuomai+en* [1]

OBSESSION [1]

obsession, *4360+1841,*
  perissōs+emmainomai [1]

OBSOLETE [2]

made obsolete, *4096, palaioō* [1]
obsolete, *4096, palaioō* [1]

OBSTACLE [1]

obstacle, *4998, skandalon* [1]

OBSTACLES [1]

obstacles, *4998, skandalon* [1]

OBSTINATE [2]

obstinate, *515, antilegō* [1]
obstinate, *5020, sklērynō* [1]

OBTAIN [3]

obtain, *2209, epitynchanō* [1]
make effort to obtain, *2426, zēteō* [1]
obtain, *5593, tynchanō* [1]

OBTAINED [5]

obtained, *1312, dechomai* [1]
obtained, *2351, heuriskō* [1]
obtained, *2898, katalambanō* [1]
obtained, *3195, krateō* [1]
obtained, *3284, lambanō* [1]

OBVIOUS [4]

obvious, *4593, prodēlos* [2]
obvious, *5743, phainō* [1]
obvious, *5745, phaneros* [1]

OCCASION [3]

occasion, *AIT* [1]
on one occasion, *2779+2627, kai+idou* [1]
on one occasion, *2779, kai* [1]

OCCASIONS [1]

occasions, *2789, kairos* [1]

OCCUR [1]

occur, *NIG* [1]

OCCURRED [2]

occurred, *1181, ginomai* [2]

OCCURS [1]

occurs, *2262, erchomai* [1]

ODOR [1]

bad odor, *3853, ozō* [1]

OF [4684]

of, *AIT* [3151]
of, *NIG* [301]
of, *1666, ek* [160]
because of, *1328, dia* [65]
teachers of the law, *1208, grammateus* [57]
out of, *1666, ek* [49]
of, *608, apo* [35]
of, *1877, en* [26]
of, *2093, epi* [21]
of, *4309, peri* [17]
province of Asia, *823, Asia* [15]
afraid of, *5828, phobeomai* [14]
of Nazareth, *3717, Nazōraios* [11]
some of, *1666, ek* [10]
one of, *1666, ek* [9]
for the sake of, *1328, dia* [8]
in front of, *1869, emprosthen* [7]
ashamed of, *2049, epaischynomai* [7]
of, *RPE* [6]
of, *1650, eis* [6]
because of, *1877, en* [6]
came out of, *2002+1666, exerchomai+ek* [6]
of Israel, *2703, Israēlitēs* [6]
because of, *608, apo* [5]
on account of, *1877, en* [5]
because of, *2093, epi* [5]
because of, *2848, kata* [5]
owner of the house, *3867, oikodespotēs* [5]
of little faith, *3899, oligopistos* [5]
of gold, *5997, chrysous* [5]
Feast of Unleavened Bread, *109, azymos* [4]
heard of, *201, akouō* [4]
way of life, *419, anastrophē* [4]
lack of faith, *602, apistia* [4]
flashes of lightning, *847, astrapē* [4]
peals of thunder, *1103, brontē* [4]
out of, *1328, dia* [4]
out of, *1877, en* [4]
come out of, *2002+1666, exerchomai+ek* [4]
of Nazareth, *3716, Nazarēnos* [4]
strips of linen, *3856, othonion* [4]
all kinds of, *4476, poikilos* [4]
what kind of, *4534, potapos* [4]
of, *4639, pros* [4]
first of all, *4754, prōton* [4]
for the sake of, *5642, hyper* [4]
out of, *608, apo* [3]
loaves of bread, *788, artos* [3]
on account of, *1328, dia* [3]
the result of, *1328, dia* [3]
because of, *1666, ek* [3]
out of come, *1666+2002, ek+exerchomai* [3]
Mount of Olives, *1779, elaiōn* [3]
of, *2848, kata* [3]
spoken of, *3306, legō* [3]
out of mind, *3419, mainomai* [3]
parts of body, *3517, melos* [3]
day of Preparation, *4187, paraskeuē* [3]
meat of strangled animals, *4465, pniktos* [3]
kind of, *4481, poios* [3]
worthy of respect, *4948, semnos* [3]
heads of grain, *5092, stachys[1]* [3]
of, *5679, hypo* [3]
full of light, *5893, phōteinos* [3]
of, *6055, hōs* [3]
of thorns, *181, akanthinos* [2]
of Alexandria, *233, Alexandreus* [2]
guilty of sin, *281+2400, hamartia+echō* [2]
give a tenth of, *620, apodekatoō* [2]
put out of the synagogue, *697,*
    aposynagōgos [2]

rid of, *700, apotithēmi* [2]
[of] silver, *739, argyrous* [2]
meeting of the Areopagus, *740, Areios pagos* [2]
master of the banquet, *804, architriklinos* [2]
member of the Council, *1085, bouleutēs* [2]
aware of, *1182, ginōskō* [2]
sure of, *1182, ginōskō* [2]
teacher of the law, *1208, grammateus* [2]
word of instruction, *1439, didachē* [2]
brings out of, *1666+1675, ek+ekballō* [2]
comes out of, *1666+1744, ek+ekporeuomai* [2]
out of came, *1666+1744, ek+ekporeuomai* [2]
part of, *1666, ek* [2]
get rid of, *1675, ekballō* [2]
in spite of, *1877, en* [2]
led out of, *1974+1666, exagō+ek* [2]
got out of, *2002+1666, exerchomai+ek* [2]
out of came, *2002+1666, exerchomai+ek* [2]
went out of, *2002, exerchomai* [2]
out of mind, *2014, existēmi* [2]
out of, *2032, exō* [2]
of Ephesus, *2386, Ephesios* [2]
in search of, *2426, zēteō* [2]
of age, *2461, hēlikia* [2]
people of Jerusalem, *2643, Hierosolymitēs* [2]
city of Jerusalem, *2647, Ierousalēm* [2]
speck of sawdust, *2847, karphos* [2]
on the basis of, *2848, kata* [2]
out of, *2848, kata* [2]
ashamed of, *2875, kataischynō* [2]
least stroke of a pen, *3037, keraia* [2]
of Cyrene, *3254, Kyrēnaios* [2]
speak of, *3306, legō* [2]
of stone, *3343, lithinos* [2]
word of mouth, *3364, logos* [2]
instead of, *3437+2445, mallon+ē* [2]
spoke well of, *3455, martyreō* [2]
part of body, *3517, melos* [2]
of Nineveh, *3780, Nineuitēs* [2]
teachers of the law, *3791, nomodidaskalos* [2]
of wood, *3832, xylinos* [2]
front of everyone, *3836+3545, ho+mesos* [2]
members of household, *3865, oikiakos* [2]
of clay, *4017, ostrakinos* [2]
of, *4022, hoti* [2]
numbers of people, *4063, ochlos* [2]
of, *4123, para* [2]
confident of, *4275, peithō* [2]
other side of the lake, *4305, peran* [2]
be shepherds of, *4477, poimainō* [2]
what kind of, *4481, poios* [2]
great deal of, *4498, polys* [2]
go ahead of, *4575, proagō* [2]
go on ahead of, *4575, proagō* [2]
going ahead of, *4575, proagō* [2]
went ahead of, *4575, proagō* [2]
told ahead of time, *4625, prolegō* [2]
place of prayer, *4666, proseuchē* [2]
place of honor, *4752, prōtoklisia* [2]
places of honor, *4752, prōtoklisia* [2]
full of darkness, *5027, skoteinos* [2]
company of soldiers, *5061, speira* [2]
detachment of soldiers, *5061, speira* [2]
approve of, *5306, syneudokeō* [2]
taken care of, *5555, trephō* [2]
of glass, *5612, hyalinos* [2]
on behalf of, *5642, hyper* [2]
batch of dough, *5878, phyrama* [2]
beginning of time, *5989+173,*
    chronos+aiōnios [2]
independent of, *6006, chōris* [2]
piece of bread, *6040, psōmion* [2]
on the pretext of, *6055, hōs* [2]
full of joy, *22, agalliaō* [1]
way of life, *73, agōgē* [1]
free of charge, *78, adapanos* [1]

brotherhood of believers, *82, adelphotēs* [1]
shedding of blood, *136, haimatekchysia* [1]
get rid of, *149, airō* [1]
rid of, *149+608, airō+apo* [1]
guilty of crime, *162, aitia* [1]
out of season, *178, akairōs* [1]
sense of hearing, *198, akoē* [1]
is one of us, *199+3552+1609,*
    akoloutheō+meta+egō [1]
one of, *199, akoloutheō* [1]
aware of, *201, akouō* [1]
lack of self-control, *202, akrasia* [1]
robbed him of speech, *228, alalos* [1]
instead of, *247, alla* [1]
out of trouble, *291, amerimnos* [1]
took care of the vineyard, *307, ampelourgos* [1]
recovery of sight, *330, anablepsis* [1]
get rid of, *359, anaireō* [1]
remind of, *389, anamimnēskō* [1]
men of courage, *437, andrizomai* [1]
owner of, *467+4005, anēr+hos* [1]
fire of burning coals, *471, anthrakia* [1]
owner of a house, *476+3867,*
    anthrōpos+oikodespotēs [1]
found worthy of, *546, axioō* [1]
in front of, *595, apenanti* [1]
at the hands of, *608, apo* [1]
for a distance of, *608, apo* [1]
census be taken of, *616, apographō* [1]
give God a tenth of, *620, apodekatoō* [1]
give share of, *625, apodidōmi* [1]
certificate of divorce, *687, apostasion* [1]
ministry of an apostle, *692, apostolē* [1]
put out of the synagogue, *697+4472,*
    aposynagōgos+poieō [1]
get rid of, *700, apotithēmi* [1]
member of the Areopagus, *741, Areopagitēs* [1]
lay hold of, *773, harpazō* [1]
positions of authority, *794, archē* [1]
from the province of Asia, *824, Asianos* [1]
officials of the province, *825, Asiarchēs* [1]
degrading of, *869, atimazō* [1]
of the scrolls[s], *899, autos* [1]
the firstborn[6] of Israel, *899, autos* [1]
let go of, *918, aphiēmi* [1]
not lovers of good, *920, aphilagathos* [1]
free from the love of money, *921,*
    aphilargyros [1]
not a lover of money, *921, aphilargyros* [1]
not done by the hands of men, *942,*
    acheiropoiētos [1]
even to the point of, *948, achri* [1]
son of Jonah, *980, Bariōna* [1]
foot of ground, *1037+4546, bēma+pous* [1]
of life, *1053, biōtikos* [1]
of this life, *1053, biōtikos* [1]
spoken of as evil, *1059, blasphēmeō* [1]
clusters of grapes, *1084, botrys* [1]
peal of thunder, *1103, brontē* [1]
of Galatia, *1131, Galatikos* [1]
of Galilee, *1134, Galilaios* [1]
because of, *1142, gar* [1]
full of, *1154, gemō* [1]
became the father of, *1164, gennaō* [1]
assembly of elders, *1172, gerousia* [1]
become of, *1181, ginomai* [1]
come of, *1181, ginomai* [1]
remind of, *1192, gnōrizō* [1]
of the devil, *1229, daimoniōdēs* [1]
told of, *1317, dēloō* [1]
eight months of a man's wages, *1324+1357,*
    dēnarion+diakosioi [1]
with the help of, *1328, dia* [1]
as the result of, *1328, dia* [1]
by means of, *1328, dia* [1]
by the authority of, *1328, dia* [1]

for the benefit of, *1328, dia* [1]
in the presence of, *1328, dia* [1]
in view of, *1328, dia* [1]
of, *1328, dia* [1]
on the basis of, *1328, dia* [1]
on the evidence of, *1328, dia* [1]
give notice of, *1334, diangellō* [1]
in the service of, *1354, diakoneō* [1]
made fun of, *1430, diachleuazō* [1]
speak of, *1455, diēgeomai* [1]
acts of righteousness, *1466, dikaiosynē* [1]
act of righteousness, *1468, dikaiōma* [1]
make much of, *1519, doxazō* [1]
workers of miracles, *1539, dynamis* [1]
roof of house, *1560, dōma* [1]
free of charge, *1562, dōrean* [1]
in danger of, *1584, engys* [1]
Feast of Dedication, *1589, enkainia* [1]
tire of, *1591, enkakeō* [1]
in the habit of, *1621, ethos* [1]
in charge of, *1639+2093, eimi+epi* [1]
made up of, *1639, eimi* [1]
one of, *1639+1666, eimi+ek* [1]
blessing of peace, *1645, eirēnē* [1]
full of, *1650, eis* [1]
of mine, *1650+1609, eis+egō* [1]
out of his body, *1650+3836+909+1744, eis+ho+aphedrōn+ekporeuomai* [1]
out of the body, *1650+909+1675, eis+aphedrōn+ekballō* [1]
reaped the benefits of, *1650+1656, eis+eiserchomai* [1]
the full extent of, *1650+5465, eis+telos* [1]
the placeˢ of, *1650, eis* [1]
out of comes, *1666+1744, ek+ekporeuomai* [1]
come out of, *1666+1744, ek+ekporeuomai* [1]
cut out of, *1666+1716, ek+ekkoptō* [1]
in front of, *1666+1885, ek+enantios* [1]
on account of, *1666, ek* [1]
out of came, *1666+2002, ek+exerchomai* [1]
out of come, *1666+1744, ek+ekporeuomai* [1]
puts out of, *1666+1675, ek+ekballō* [1]
each of, *1667, hekastos* [1]
brings out of, *1675+1666, ekballō+ek* [1]
take out of, *1675+1666, ekballō+ek* [1]
take out of, *1675, ekballō* [1]
stripped of clothes, *1694, ekdyō* [1]
get rid of, *1705, ekkathairō* [1]
came out of, *1744+1666, ekporeuomai+ek* [1]
come out of, *1744+1666, ekporeuomai+ek* [1]
comes out of, *1744+1666, ekporeuomai+ek* [1]
out of, *1760, ektos* [1]
take out of, *1766, ekpherō* [1]
ran out of, *1767+1666, ekpheugō+ek* [1]
convict of guilt, *1794, elenchō* [1]
made of ivory, *1804, elephantinos* [1]
in full view of, *1869, emprosthen* [1]
as members of, *1877, en* [1]
as of first importance, *1877+4755, en+prōtos* [1]
at the time of, *1877, en* [1]
both of them, *1877+4005, en+hos* [1]
by the power of, *1877, en* [1]
full of, *1877, en* [1]
in the cause of, *1877, en* [1]
thisˢ kind of, *1877+4231, en+paroimia* [1]
with the help of, *1877, en* [1]
creatures of sea, *1879, enalios* [1]
made of, *1908, endōmēsis* [1]
of, *1915, heneken* [1]
guilty of sinning against, *1944, enochos* [1]
of here, *1949, enteuthen* [1]
making the most of, *1973, exagorazō* [1]
brought out of, *1974+1666, exagō+ek* [1]
lead out of, *1974+1666, exagō+ek* [1]
flash of lightning, *1993, exastraptō* [1]

came out of, *2002, exerchomai* [1]
flowed out of, *2002+1666, exerchomai+ek* [1]
led out of, *2002+1666, exerchomai+ek* [1]
of little account, *2024, exoutheneō* [1]
exercise of freedom, *2026, exousia* [1]
sign of authority, *2026, exousia* [1]
make guilty of, *2042+2093, epagō+epi* [1]
of, *2062, epanō* [1]
take charge of, *2062+1181, epanō+ginomai* [1]
in the days of, *2093, epi* [1]
a matter of, *2093, epi* [1]
in front of, *2093, epi* [1]
in the time of, *2093, epi* [1]
on the basis of, *2093, epi* [1]
mindful of, *2098+2093, epiblepō+epi* [1]
taking hold of, *2138, epilambanomai* [1]
take care of, *2150, epimeleomai* [1]
took care of, *2150, epimeleomai* [1]
place of leadership, *2175, episkopē* [1]
manager of household, *2208, epitropos* [1]
coming of, *2262, erchomai* [1]
eating of, *2266, esthiō* [1]
last of all, *2274, eschatos* [1]
of more noble character, *2302, eugenēs* [1]
of noble birth, *2302, eugenēs* [1]
act of kindness shown to, *2307, euergesia* [1]
time of need, *2322, eukairos* [1]
expressions of thanks, *2374, eucharistia* [1]
south of, *2381, euōnymos* [1]
guilty of sin, *2400+281, echō+hamartia* [1]
had charge of, *2400, echō* [1]
keep hold of, *2400, echō* [1]
made up of, *2400, echō* [1]
jealous of, *2420, zēloō* [1]
points of dispute, *2427, zētēma* [1]
pair of scales, *2433, zygos* [1]
light of the sun, *2463, hēlios* [1]
Feast of Unleavened Bread, *2465+109, hēmera+azymos* [1]
book of Isaiah, *2480, Ēsaias* [1]
laid the foundations of, *2530, themelioō* [1]
of God, *2536, theos* [1]
sum of money, *2564, thēsaurizō* [1]
burning of incense, *2592, thymiama* [1]
altar of incense, *2593, thymiatērion* [1]
fits of rage, *2596, thymos* [1]
outbursts of anger, *2596, thymos* [1]
sacrifice of atonement, *2663, hilastērion* [1]
people of Israel, *2702+2848+4922, Israēl+kata+sarx* [1]
clear of responsibility, *2754, katharos* [1]
in the wordsˢ of, *2777, kathōs* [1]
instead of, *2779+4049, kai+ouchi* [1]
ofˢ, *2813, kaleō* [1]
area of activity, *2834, kanōn* [1]
a follower of, *2848, kata* [1]
by means of, *2848, kata* [1]
by the standards of, *2848, kata* [1]
from human point of view, *2848+476, kata+anthrōpos* [1]
out of favoritism, *2848+4680, kata+prosklisis* [1]
surface of things, *2848+4725, kata+prosōpon* [1]
taken hold of, *2898, katalambanō* [1]
took hold of, *2898, katalambanō* [1]
considered worthy of, *2921, kataxioō* [1]
mutilators of the flesh, *2961, katatomē* [1]
make use of, *2974, katachraomai* [1]
full of idols, *2977, kateidōlos* [1]
accused of, *2989, katēgoreō* [1]
accusing of, *2989, katēgoreō* [1]
inhabitants of, *2997, katoikeō* [1]
residents of, *2997, katoikeō* [1]
boast of, *3016, kauchaomai* [1]
boasting of, *3016, kauchaomai* [1]

strips of linen, *3024, keiria* [1]
provinces of Cilicia, *3070, Kilikia* [1]
in danger of, *3073, kindyneuō* [1]
bed of suffering, *3109, klinē* [1]
a fraction of a penny, *3119, kodrantēs* [1]
fellowship of sharing, *3126, koinōnia* [1]
followers of, *3140, kollaō* [1]
powers of world, *3179, kosmokratōr* [1]
take charge of, *3195, krateō* [1]
take hold of, *3195, krateō* [1]
piece of property, *3228, ktēma* [1]
those with gifts of administration, *3236, kybernēsis* [1]
collectors of tax, *3284, lambanō* [1]
takes advantage of, *3284, lambanō* [1]
band of people, *3295, laos* [1]
act of worship, *3301, latreia* [1]
speaks of, *3306, legō* [1]
record of, *3357, logizomai* [1]
of Macedonia, *3424, Makedōn* [1]
get into the habit of being, *3443, manthanō* [1]
speak well of, *3455, martyreō* [1]
well spoken of, *3455, martyreō* [1]
of Mattathias, *3478, Mattathias* [1]
at the top of, *3489, megas* [1]
members of body, *3517, melos* [1]
part of the body, *3517, melos* [1]
parts of the body, *3517, melos* [1]
of course, *3529, menounge* [1]
contributing to the needs of others, *3556, metadidōmi* [1]
change of mind, *3567, metanoia* [1]
even to the point of, *3588, mechri* [1]
to the point of, *3588, mechri* [1]
free from fear of, *3590+5828, mē+phobeomai* [1]
instead of, *3594, mēdeis* [1]
leave your life of sin, *3600+279, mēketi+hamartanō* [1]
made an idol in the form of a calf, *3674, moschopoieō* [1]
owner of the ship, *3729, nauklēros* [1]
guardian of the temple, *3753, neōkoros* [1]
of youth, *3754, neōterikos* [1]
teacher of the law, *3791, nomodidaskalos* [1]
receiving of the law, *3792, nomothesia* [1]
make the most of opportunity, *3836+2789+1973, ho+kairos+exagorazō* [1]
spirit of unity, *3836+899+5858, ho+autos+phroneō* [1]
way of life, *3847, hodos* [1]
take note of, *3857, oida* [1]
members of household, *3858, oikeios* [1]
head of the house, *3867, oikodespotēs* [1]
director of public works, *3874, oikonomos* [1]
members of household, *3875, oikos* [1]
what kinds of, *3888, hoios* [1]
make light of, *3902, oligōreō* [1]
of, *3927, homoios* [1]
even in the case of, *3940, homōs* [1]
a hint of, *3951, onomazō* [1]
what kind of, *3961, hopoios* [1]
in the case of, *3963, hopou* [1]
seen of, *3972, horaō* [1]
the sight of, *3972, horaō* [1]
one of these journeysˢ, *4005, hos* [1]
all of, *4012, hosos* [1]
sense of smell, *4018, osphrēsis* [1]
out of place, *4024+465, ou+anēkō* [1]
because of, *4036, oun* [1]
first of all, *4047+4754, houtos+prōton* [1]
come out of, *4047+2002, houtos+exerchomai* [1]
crowd of people, *4063, ochlos* [1]
number of people, *4063, ochlos* [1]

any of, *4123, para* [1]
act of disobedience, *4157, parakoē* [1]
took charge of, *4161, paralambanō* [1]
out of mind, *4196, paraphroneō* [1]
figure of speech, *4231, paroimia* [1]
figures of speech, *4231, paroimia* [1]
country of their own, *4258, patris* [1]
convinced of, *4275, peithō* [1]
trying to win the approval of, *4275, peithō* [1]
confident of, *4301, pepoithēsis* [1]
over the matter of, *4309, peri* [1]
fell into the hands of, *4346, peripiptō* [1]
take advantage of, *4430, pleonekteō* [1]
measure of fullness, *4445, plērōma* [1]
take care of, *4477, poimainō* [1]
be shepherd of, *4477, poimainō* [1]
plenty of, *4498, polys* [1]
full of compassion, *4499, polysplanchnos* [1]
of Pontus, *4507, Pontikos* [1]
of the past, *4537, pote* [1]
palace of the Roman governor, *4550,*
    praitōrion [1]
body of elders, *4564, presbyterion* [1]
council of elders, *4564, presbyterion* [1]
entering ahead of, *4575, proagō* [1]
reaching ahead of, *4575, proagō* [1]
got there ahead of, *4601, proerchomai* [1]
vicinity of, *4639, pros* [1]
rolled in front of, *4685, proskyliō* [1]
fell on knees in front of, *4686, proskyneō* [1]
gift of prophecy, *4735, prophēteia* [1]
of prophets, *4738, prophētikos* [1]
places of honor at the table, *4752, prōtoklisia* [1]
old order of things, *4755, prōtos* [1]
of the world, *4920, sarkikos* [1]
of human, *4921, sarkinos* [1]
worldly point of view, *4922, sarx* [1]
objects of worship, *4934, sebasma* [1]
of iron, *4971, sidērous* [1]
[people of] Sidon, *4973, Sidōnios* [1]
region of Sidon, *4973, Sidōnios* [1]
take note of, *5023, skopeō* [1]
piece of cloth, *5051, soudarion* [1]
store of seed, *5078, sporos* [1]
officers of guard, *5130, stratēgos* [1]
officers of the temple guard, *5130, stratēgos* [1]
take care of mat, *5143+4932,*
    strōnnyō+seautou [1]
both of you, *5148+2779+899, sy+kai+autos* [1]
the two of you, *5148+2779+899,*
    sy+kai+autos [1]
cheated out of, *5193, sykophanteō* [1]
of them, *5201+899, symbainō+autos* [1]
rest of the disciples, *5209, symmathētēs* [1]
attendant of, *5250, syn* [1]
of own age, *5312, synēlikiōtēs* [1]
in the pains of childbirth, *5349, synōdinō* [1]
sandbars of Syrtis, *5358, Syrtis* [1]
members together of one body, *5362,*
    syssōmos [1]
conform to the pattern of, *5372,*
    syschēmatizō [1]
on placed seal of approval, *5381, sphragizō* [1]
set seal of ownership on, *5381, sphragizō* [1]
talents of money, *5419, talanton* [1]
of low position, *5424, tapeinos* [1]
squads of four, *5482, tetradion* [1]
what business is it of mine, *5515+1609,*
    tis+egō [1]
a kind of, *5516, tis* [1]
of a kind, *5525, toioutos* [1]
of that time, *5538, tote* [1]
made of hair, *5570, trichinos* [1]
people of Tyre, *5601, Tyrios* [1]
of hurricane force, *5607, typhōnikos* [1]
full rights of sons, *5625, huiothesia* [1]

because of, *5642, hyper* [1]
take care of needs, *5676, hypēreteō* [1]
result of, *5679, hypo* [1]
remind of, *5703, hypomimnēskō* [1]
reminding of, *5703, hypomimnēskō* [1]
passed to the lee of, *5709, hypopleō* [1]
sailed to the lee of, *5709, hypopleō* [1]
passed to the lee of, *5720, hypotrechō* [1]
branches of hyssop, *5727, hyssōpos* [1]
stalk of the hyssop plant, *5727, hyssōpos* [1]
last of all, *5731, hysteros* [1]
love of money, *5794, philargyria* [1]
lovers of money, *5795, philargyros* [1]
lovers of themselves, *5796, philautos* [1]
lovers of pleasure, *5798, philēdonos* [1]
lovers of God, *5806, philotheos* [1]
take a view of things, *5858, phroneō* [1]
time of night, *5871, phylakē* [1]
watch of the night, *5871, phylakē* [1]
lump of clay, *5878, phyrama* [1]
creatures of instinct, *5879, physikos* [1]
at the top of voices, *5889+3489,*
    phōnē+megas [1]
at the top of voice, *5889+3489,*
    phōnē+megas [1]
shouting at the top of voice, *5889+3489+3306,*
    phōnē+megas+legō [1]
full of joy, *5897, chairō* [1]
[of] bronze, *5911, chalkous* [1]
full of joy, *5915+5897, chara+chairō* [1]
because of, *5920, charin* [1]
for the sake of, *5920, charin* [1]
act of grace, *5921, charis* [1]
of dust, *5954, choikos* [1]
of earth, *5954, choikos* [1]
plot of ground, *6005, chōrion* [1]
sing songs of praise, *6010, psallō* [1]
in the pains of childbirth, *6048, ōdinō* [1]
the size of, *6055, hōs* [1]

OFF   [73]

went off, *599, aperchomai* [5]
far off, *608+3427, apo+makrothen* [3]
cut off, *644, apokoptō* [3]
sent off, *668, apolyō* [3]
cutting off, *904, aphaireō* [3]
broken off, *1709, ekklaō* [3]
cut off, *1716, ekkoptō* [3]
ran off, *5771, pheugō* [3]
put off, *700, apotithēmi* [2]
took off, *1694, ekdyō* [2]
shake off, *1759, ektinassō* [2]
off, *2848, kata* [2]
cut off, *3025, keirō* [2]
take off, *3395, lyō* [2]
wandered off, *4414, planaō* [2]
led off, *72, agō* [1]
cuts off, *149, airō* [1]
off, *513, antikrys* [1]
taken off, *588, apekdyomai* [1]
putting off, *589, apekdysis* [1]
cut off from, *608, apo* [1]
shake off, *608+701, apo+apotinassō* [1]
set off, *623, apodēmeō* [1]
cutting off, *644, apokoptō* [1]
wipe off against, *669, apomassō* [1]
throw off, *700, apotithēmi* [1]
shook off, *701, apotinassō* [1]
carry off, *773, harpazō* [1]
taken it off, *1218, gymnos* [1]
carry off, *1395, diarpazō* [1]
running off after, *1503, diōkō* [1]
far off, *1650+3426, eis+makran* [1]
sent off, *1675, ekballō* [1]
fell off, *1738+1666, ekpiptō+ek* [1]

sent off, *1990, exapostellō* [1]
completely cut off from, *2017+1666,*
    exolethreuō+ek [1]
hurried off, *2262+5067, erchomai+speudō* [1]
set off, *2262, erchomai* [1]
drag off, *2955, katasyrō* [1]
long way off, *3426, makran* [1]
putting off, *3428, makrothymeō* [1]
shaved off, *3834, xyraō* [1]
wander off, *4414, planaō* [1]
long way off, *4522, porrō* [1]
throwing off, *4848, rhipteō* [1]
dragged off, *5359, syrō* [1]
took off, *5502, tithēmi* [1]
worse off than, *5937, cheirōn* [1]

OFFEND   [2]

offend, *4997, skandalizō* [2]

OFFENDED   [1]

offended, *4997, skandalizō* [1]

OFFENDERS   [1]

homosexual offenders, *780, arsenokoitēs* [1]

OFFENSE   [3]

took offense, *4997, skandalizō* [2]
offense, *4998, skandalon* [1]

OFFER   [25]

offer, *4712, prospherō* [7]
offer, *4225, paristēmi* [6]
offer, *1443, didōmi* [3]
offer sacrifices, *4712, prospherō* [3]
offer, *429, anapherō* [2]
offer, *AIT* [1]
offer, *RPE* [1]
offer sacrifices, *2604, thyō* [1]
offer, *5502, tithēmi* [1]

OFFERED   [26]

offered, *4712, prospherō* [8]
offered, *1443, didōmi* [4]
offered, *AIT* [3]
offered, *429, anapherō* [2]
offered to drink, *4540, potizō* [2]
offered, *RPE* [1]
sacrifice offered to an idol, *1628,*
    eidōlothytos [1]
offered, *2604, thyō* [1]
offered in sacrifice, *2638, hierothytos* [1]
offered, *4618, prokeimai* [1]
offered as a sacrifice, *4712, prospherō* [1]
offered up, *4712, prospherō* [1]

OFFERING   [14]

offering, *4714, prosphora* [3]
sin offering, *281, hamartia* [2]
offering, *4712, prospherō* [2]
poured out like a drink offering, *5064,*
    spendō [2]
offering, *429, anapherō* [1]
offering, *2602, thysia* [1]
memorial offering, *3649, mnēmosynon* [1]
offering made, *4712+4714,*
    prospherō+prosphora [1]
offering, *5921, charis* [1]

OFFERINGS   [11]

burnt offerings, *3906, holokautōma* [3]
place where the offerings were put, *1126,*
    gazophylakion [2]
sin offerings, *4309+281, peri+hamartia* [2]

offerings, *4714, prosphora* [2]
offerings, *1565, dōron* [1]
offerings, *5376, sphagion* [1]

OFFERS [1]

offers, *4712, prospherō* [1]

OFFICE [1]

office, *AIT* [1]

OFFICER [4]

officer, *4551, praktōr* [2]
commanding officer, *5133, stratologeō* [1]
officer, *5677, hypēretēs* [1]

OFFICERS [9]

officers, *4812, rhabdouchos* [2]
officers, *5677, hypēretēs* [2]
the officers', *899, autos* [1]
officers, *1672, hekatontarchēs* [1]
officers of guard, *5130, stratēgos* [1]
officers of the temple guard, *5130, stratēgos* [1]
high ranking officers, *5941, chiliarchos* [1]

OFFICIAL [4]

royal official, *997, basilikos* [2]
important official, *1541, dynastēs* [1]
chief official, *4755, prōtos* [1]

OFFICIALS [11]

officials, *5677, hypēretēs* [5]
high officials, *3489, megas* [2]
city officials, *4485, politarchēs* [2]
officials of the province, *825, Asiarchēs* [1]
high officials, *3491, megistan* [1]

OFFSPRING [11]

offspring, *5065, sperma* [8]
offspring, *1169, genos* [3]

OFTEN [16]

often, *4490, pollakis* [10]
how often, *4529, posakis* [2]
often, *AIT* [1]
as often as, *4006+1569, hosakis+ean* [1]
often, *4498, polys* [1]
often, *4781, pyknos* [1]

OH [1]

Oh, *6043, ō²* [1]

OIL [14]

oil, *1778, elaion* [9]
oil, *RPE* [2]
olive oil, *1778, elaion* [2]
put oil on, *230, aleiphō* [1]

OLD [39]

old, *4094, palaios* [19]
years old, *2291, etos* [3]
old, *AIT* [2]
old man, *4566, presbytēs* [2]
old, *NIG* [1]
old, *792, archaios* [1]
old, *1173, gerōn* [1]
old age, *1179, gēras* [1]
old, *1180, gēraskō* [1]
old wives tales, *1212, graōdēs* [1]
two years old, *1453, dietēs* [1]
hundred years old, *1670, hekatontaetēs* [1]
old way, *4095, palaiotēs* [1]
old men, *4565, presbyteros* [1]

old, *4581+1877+2465, probainō+en+hēmera* [1]
old order of things, *4755, prōtos* [1]
old, *5989, chronos* [1]

OLDER [9]

older, *4565, presbyteros* [4]
older, *RPE* [1]
older, *3505, meizōn* [1]
older man, *4565, presbyteros* [1]
older, *4566, presbytēs* [1]
older, *4567, presbytis* [1]

OLDEST [1]

inheritance rights as the oldest son, *4757, prōtotokia* [1]

OLIVE [10]

olive oil, *1778, elaion* [2]
olive grove, *3057, kēpos* [2]
olive tree that is wild, *66, agrielaios* [1]
wild olive shoot, *66, agrielaios* [1]
olive trees, *1777, elaia* [1]
olive tree, *1777, elaia* [1]
olive, *1777, elaia* [1]
cultivated olive tree, *2814, kallielaios* [1]

OLIVES [13]

olives, *1777, elaia* [10]
Mount of Olives, *1779, elaiōn* [3]

OLYMPAS [1]

Olympas, *3912, Olympas* [1]

OMEGA [3]

Omega, *6042, Ō¹* [3]

ON [1050]

on, *2093, epi* [258]
on, *AIT* [125]
on, *1877, en* [92]
on, *1650, eis* [48]
on, *NIG* [21]
on, *608, apo* [12]
on, *1666, ek* [12]
have mercy on, *1796, eleeō* [11]
on the contrary, *247, alla* [10]
on, *RPE* [9]
put on, *1907, endyō* [7]
on, *2062, epanō* [7]
call on, *2126, epikaleō* [7]
wait on, *1354, diakoneō* [6]
now on, *3836+3814, ho+nyn* [6]
on account of, *1877, en* [5]
put on, *2202+2093, epitithēmi+epi* [5]
put on, *2202, epitithēmi* [5]
on, *4309, peri* [5]
poured on, *230, aleiphō* [4]
on account, *1915, heneken* [4]
placed on, *2202, epitithēmi* [4]
on, *2848, kata* [4]
passed on, *4140, paradidōmi* [4]
put on, *4363, peritithēmi* [4]
on way, *4513, poreuomai* [4]
on guard, *4668, prosechō* [4]
on behalf, *5642, hyper* [4]
now on, *785, arti* [3]
on account of, *1328, dia* [3]
on, *1328, dia* [3]
depends on, *1666, ek* [3]
had mercy on, *1796, eleeō* [3]
spit on, *1870, emptyō* [3]
on behalf, *1967, enōpion* [3]

laying on, *2120, epithesis* [3]
place on, *2202, epitithēmi* [3]
based on, *2848, kata* [3]
pass judgment on, *3212, krinō* [3]
on the other side, *4305, peran* [3]
passed by on the other side, *524, antiparerchomai* [2]
went away on a journey, *623, apodēmeō* [2]
to live on, *1050, bios* [2]
on guard, *1213, grēgoreō* [2]
press on, *1503, diōkō* [2]
on to, *1650, eis* [2]
on, *1877+3836, en+ho* [2]
went on, *2002, exerchomai* [2]
look down on, *2024, exoutheneō* [2]
on the outside, *2033, exōthen* [2]
on and on, *2093+4498, epi+polys* [2]
write on, *2093+2108, epi+epigraphō* [2]
laid on, *2095+2093, epiballō+epi* [2]
sews on, *2095+2093, epiballō+epi* [2]
calls on, *2126, epikaleō* [2]
kept on, *2152, epimenō* [2]
came on, *2158+2093, epipiptō+epi* [2]
laying on, *2202, epitithēmi* [2]
placed on, *2202+2093, epitithēmi+epi* [2]
on the inside, *2277, esōthen* [2]
on the basis of, *2848, kata* [2]
look down on, *2969, kataphroneō* [2]
hold on to, *2988, katechō* [2]
hold on to, *3195, krateō* [2]
on, *3552, meta* [2]
declared on oath, *3923, omnyō* [2]
heaped insults on, *3943, oneidizō* [2]
eye is on, *4056, ophthalmodoulia* [2]
went on, *4135, paragō* [2]
on foot, *4270, pezē* [2]
on behalf, *4309, peri* [2]
went on way, *4513, poreuomai* [2]
go on ahead of, *4575, proagō* [2]
went on ahead, *4601, proerchomai* [2]
send on way, *4636, propempō* [2]
that time on, *5538, tote* [2]
feeds on, *5592, trōgō* [2]
on behalf of, *5642, hyper* [2]
on guard, *5875, phylassō* [2]
on, *6055, hōs* [2]
on the pretext of, *6055, hōs* [2]
on guard, *70, agrypneō* [1]
on the watch, *70, agrypneō* [1]
put oil on, *230, aleiphō* [1]
put on, *230, aleiphō* [1]
on contrary, *247+5539, alla+tounantion* [1]
on the contrary, *247+4498+3437, alla+polys+mallon* [1]
sit in judgment on, *373, anakrinō* [1]
put on, *377, analambanō* [1]
set on fire, *409, anaptō* [1]
go on, *599, aperchomai* [1]
on their way, *599, aperchomai* [1]
depended on, *608, apo* [1]
put on display, *617, apodeiknymi* [1]
going on a journey, *623, apodēmeō* [1]
went on journey, *623, apodēmeō* [1]
hold on to, *721, haptō* [1]
went on, *806, archō* [1]
entirely on own, *882, authairetos* [1]
on own initiative, *882, authairetos* [1]
let go on, *918, aphiēmi* [1]
put on deposit, *965, ballō* [1]
heap abuse on, *1059, blasphēmeō* [1]
gaze on, *1063, blepō* [1]
looking on, *1063, blepō* [1]
on guard, *1063, blepō* [1]
on your guard, *1063, blepō* [1]
on, *1181, ginomai* [1]
was going on, *1181, ginomai* [1]

went on, *1181, ginomai* [1]
fell on knees before, *1206, gonypeteō* [1]
on knees, *1206, gonypeteō* [1]
on, *1254, de* [1]
on the following day, *1308, deuteraios* [1]
on account, *1328, dia* [1]
on the basis of, *1328, dia* [1]
on the evidence of, *1328, dia* [1]
visit on the way, *1328, dia* [1]
visit on way, *1328+1451, dia+dierchomai* [1]
goes on, *1373, diamenō* [1]
passed on, *1438, didaskō* [1]
pass on, *1443, didōmi* [1]
went on, *1451+4134,
    dierchomai+paraginomai [1]
on, *1569, ean* [1]
written on, *1582+1877, engraphō+en* [1]
on your feet, *1586, egeirō* [1]
cut in on, *1601, enkoptō* [1]
put on, *1608, enchriō* [1]
on the evening, *1639+4068, eimi+opsia* [1]
kept on, *1639, eimi* [1]
on the side, *1639, eimi* [1]
on way home, *1639+5715,
    eimi+hypostrephō [1]
spur on, *1650+4237, eis+paroxysmos* [1]
from then on, *1666+4047, ek+houtos* [1]
based on, *1666, ek* [1]
on a journey, *1666+3847, ek+hodos* [1]
on account of, *1666, ek* [1]
on, *1666+5931, ek+cheir* [1]
rely on, *1666+1639, ek+eimi* [1]
on, *1696, ekeithen* [1]
hung on, *1717, ekkremannymi* [1]
sent on way, *1734, ekpempō* [1]
has mercy on, *1796, eleeō* [1]
put on board, *1837+1650+899,
    embibazō+eis+autos [1]
carry on business, *1864, emporeuomai* [1]
on ahead, *1869, emprosthen* [1]
breathed on, *1874, emphysaō* [1]
on board, *1877+3836+4450, en+ho+ploion* [1]
on duty, *1877+3836+5423, en+ho+taxis* [1]
put on, *1877, en* [1]
put on, *1898, endidyskō* [1]
putting on, *1907, endyō* [1]
on each side, *1949+2779+1696,
    enteuthen+kai+ekeithen [1]
one on each side, *1949+2779+1949,
    enteuthen+kai+enteuthen [1]
on the journey, *2002, exerchomai* [1]
looked down on, *2024, exoutheneō* [1]
on authority, *2026+3284, exousia+lambanō* [1]
bringing on, *2042, epagō* [1]
brought on, *2042, epagō* [1]
on way back, *2056, epanagō* [1]
rely on, *2058, epanapauomai* [1]
rest on, *2058+2093, epanapauomai+epi* [1]
curse on, *2063, eparatos* [1]
comes on, *2088+2093, eperchomai+epi* [1]
coming on, *2088, eperchomai* [1]
on the basis of, *2093, epi* [1]
place on, *2093+2202, epi+epitithēmi* [1]
put on, *2093+2097, epi+epibibazō* [1]
resting on, *2093, epi* [1]
go on, *2094, epibainō* [1]
went on board, *2094, epibainō* [1]
lay on, *2095+2093, epiballō+epi* [1]
put on, *2097+2093, epibibazō+epi* [1]
on earth, *2103, epigeios* [1]
laid on, *2120, epithesis* [1]
setting hearts on, *2122, epithymētēs* [1]
calling on, *2126, epikaleō* [1]
on, *2130, epikeimai* [1]
turned on, *2138, epilambanomai* [1]
go on, *2152, epimenō* [1]

stay on, *2152, epimenō* [1]
fallen on, *2158+2093, epipiptō+epi* [1]
threw himself on, *2158, epipiptō* [1]
cast on, *2166+2093, epiriptō+epi* [1]
threw on, *2166, epiriptō* [1]
rest on, *2172+2093, episkēnoō+epi* [1]
fall on, *2173, episkiazō* [1]
carry it on to completion, *2200, epiteleō* [1]
carry on, *2200, epiteleō* [1]
placing on, *2202+2093, epitithēmi+epi* [1]
laid on, *2202, epitithēmi* [1]
lay on, *2202, epitithēmi* [1]
on lay, *2202, epitithēmi* [1]
puts on, *2202+2093, epitithēmi+epi* [1]
putting on, *2202+2093, epitithēmi+epi* [1]
set on, *2202+2093, epitithēmi+epi* [1]
shine on, *2210, epiphainō* [1]
shine on, *2213, epiphauskō* [1]
pouring on, *2219, epicheō* [1]
put on, *2222+2093, epichriō+epi* [1]
put on, *2222, epichriō* [1]
building on, *2224, epoikodomeō* [1]
builds on, *2224+2093, epoikodomeō+epi* [1]
built on, *2224+2093, epoikodomeō+epi* [1]
carrying on, *2237, ergazomai* [1]
on his way, *2262, erchomai* [1]
on their way, *2262, erchomai* [1]
on way in, *2262, erchomai* [1]
on way, *2262, erchomai* [1]
traveled on, *2262+3847, erchomai+hodos* [1]
went on, *2262, erchomai* [1]
on both sides, *2277+2779+3957,
    esōthen+kai+opisthen [1]
on, *2285, eti* [1]
on whom favor rests, *2306, eudokia* [1]
jumped on, *2383+2093, ephallomai+epi* [1]
come on, *2392, ephistēmi* [1]
holding on to, *2400, echō* [1]
going on to, *2401, heōs* [1]
right on down to, *2401, heōs* [1]
live on, *2409, zaō* [1]
set heart on, *2426, zēteō* [1]
set hearts on, *2426, zēteō* [1]
put on clothes, *2439, zōnnymi* [1]
looked on, *2555, theōreō* [1]
girl on duty, *2601, thyrōros* [1]
mercy on, *2661, hilaskomai* [1]
bent on, *2671, hina* [1]
on trial, *2705+3212, histēmi+krinō* [1]
on one occasion, *2779+2627, kai+idou* [1]
on one occasion, *2779, kai* [1]
on, *2779, kai* [1]
on, *2779+3836+2759, kai+ho+kathexēs* [1]
depends on, *2848, kata* [1]
on the way, *2849, katabainō* [1]
lying on, *2879, katakeimai* [1]
put on the list, *2899, katalegō* [1]
fix thoughts on, *2917, katanoeō* [1]
trampled on, *2922, katapateō* [1]
trampling on, *2922, katapateō* [1]
spy on, *2945, kataskopeō* [1]
poured on, *2972, katacheō* [1]
made a attack on, *2987, katephistamai* [1]
struck on the head, *3052, kephalioō* [1]
held on to, *3195, krateō* [1]
hold on, *3195, krateō* [1]
holding on to, *3195, krateō* [1]
on trial, *3212, krinō* [1]
passed judgment on, *3212, krinō* [1]
passing judgment on, *3212, krinō* [1]
stand on trial, *3212, krinō* [1]
put on, *3284, lambanō* [1]
went on, *3306, legō* [1]
insist on it, *3458, martyromai* [1]
keep on, *3531, menō* [1]
going on, *3553, metabainō* [1]

went on, *3553, metabainō* [1]
moved on, *3558, metairō* [1]
lives on, *3576, metechō* [1]
poured perfume on to prepare, *3690, myrizō* [1]
reflect on, *3783, noeō* [1]
from now on, *3836+3370, ho+loipos* [1]
on their journey, *3844, hodoiporeō* [1]
on the move, *3845, hodoiporia* [1]
on[s] the other side, *3963, hopou* [1]
sets heart on being, *3977, oregō* [1]
from then on, *4033, ouketi* [1]
on every side, *4119, pantothen* [1]
from now on, *4121, pantote* [1]
on, *4123, para* [1]
not put on such a list, *4148, paraiteomai* [1]
call on, *4151, parakaleō* [1]
kept on, *4189, parateinō* [1]
kept close watch on, *4190, paratēreō* [1]
trample on, *4251, pateō* [1]
trampled on, *4251, pateō* [1]
irons on feet, *4267, pedē* [1]
going on foot, *4269, pezeuō* [1]
on the opposite shore, *4305, peran* [1]
set on, *4363, peritithēmi* [1]
believed on, *4409, pisteuō* [1]
rely on, *4409, pisteuō* [1]
continued on way, *4513, poreuomai* [1]
go on way, *4513, poreuomai* [1]
on ahead, *4574+4725, pro+prosōpon* [1]
going on, *4581, probainō* [1]
go on, *4601, proerchomai* [1]
assist on journey, *4636, propempō* [1]
help on journey, *4636, propempō* [1]
help on way, *4636, propempō* [1]
send on their way, *4636, propempō* [1]
sent on way, *4636, propempō* [1]
go on, *4638, proporeuomai* [1]
on, *4639, pros* [1]
keep on, *4675, proskarterēsis* [1]
fell on knees in front of, *4686, proskyneō* [1]
on knees before, *4686, proskyneō* [1]
went on, *4707, prostithēmi* [1]
sprinkled on, *4822, rhantizō* [1]
life on earth, *4922, sarx* [1]
fix eyes on, *5023, skopeō* [1]
on, *5250, syn* [1]
dawned on, *5328, synoraō* [1]
on placed seal of approval, *5381, sphragizō* [1]
putting a seal on, *5381, sphragizō* [1]
set seal of ownership on, *5381, sphragizō* [1]
falling on, *5502, tithēmi* [1]
fell on, *5502, tithēmi* [1]
price set on, *5507+5506, timē+timaō* [1]
what going on, *5515+323+4047,
    tis+an+houtos [1]
then on, *5538, tote* [1]
on way, *5632, hypagō* [1]
on, *5679, hypo* [1]
later on, *5731, hysteros* [1]
on high, *5737, hypsos* [1]
go on, *5770, pherō* [1]
set on fire, *5824, phlogizō* [1]
sets on fire, *5824, phlogizō* [1]
set minds on, *5858, phroneō* [1]
mind on, *5858, phroneō* [1]
minds set on, *5858, phroneō* [1]
on think, *5858, phroneō* [1]
on guard against, *5875, phylassō* [1]
shines, *5894, phōtizō* [1]
keep a tight rein on, *5902, chalinagōgeō* [1]
on the ground, *5912, chamai* [1]
dependent on, *5970+2400, chreia+echō* [1]

ONCE [78]

once more, *4099, palin* [9]

at once, *2311, eutheōs* [8]
at once, *2317, euthys¹* [8]
once, *562, hapax* [7]
once, *AIT* [6]
once, *4537, pote* [6]
once for all, *562, hapax* [4]
once for all, *2384, ephapax* [4]
at once, *4202, parachrēma* [4]
once, *1181+1254, ginomai+de* [2]
at once, *1994, exautēs* [2]
once, *4021, hote* [2]
once, *RPE* [1]
once, *608+4005+323, apo+hos+an* [1]
at once, *785, arti* [1]
at once, *899+3836+6052, autos+ho+hōra* [1]
once, *1254, de* [1]
once, *1651, heis* [1]
once, *2779+1181, kai+ginomai* [1]
once, *2779, kai* [1]
at once, *3590+3890, mē+okneō* [1]
at once, *4020+2317, hotan+euthys¹* [1]
once, *4020, hotan* [1]
once again, *4099, palin* [1]
once made, *4575, proagō* [1]
once, *4728, proteros* [1]
at once, *5067, speudō* [1]
once, *5538, tote* [1]

ONE [870]

one, *1651, heis* [243]
one, *AIT* [205]
no one, *4029, oudeis* [89]
one another, *253, allēlōn* [46]
one, *5516, tis* [36]
one, *3836, ho* [25]
one, *NIG* [24]
one, *RPE* [22]
the one, *4005, hos* [18]
one of, *1666, ek* [9]
no one, *3594, mēdeis* [9]
one, *4005+3525, hos+men* [8]
one another, *1571, heautou* [7]
one and only, *3666, monogenēs* [5]
one, *4005, hos* [5]
not one, *4029, oudeis* [5]
one, *4246+4922, pas+sarx* [5]
one, *4246, pas* [4]
one, *1651+5516, heis+tis* [3]
no one, *4024+4029, ou+oudeis* [3]
at one time, *4537, pote* [3]
suppose one, *5515, tis* [3]
that one, *AIT* [2]
that one, *257, allos* [2]
one, *476, anthrōpos* [2]
from one to another, *2848, kata* [2]
one eye, *3669, monophthalmos* [2]
the One, *3836, ho* [2]
the one, *4005+323, hos+an* [2]
this one, *4047, houtos* [2]
any one, *5516, tis* [2]
Holy One, *41, hagios* [1]
is one of us, *199+3552+1609, akoloutheō+meta+egō* [1]
one of, *199, akoloutheō* [1]
one another's, *253, allēlōn* [1]
one, *257, allos* [1]
one another, *257+4639+257, allos+pros+allos* [1]
one kind, *257+3525, allos+men* [1]
one kind, *257, allos* [1]
one thing more, *275, hama* [1]
one at a time, *324+3538, ana+meros* [1]
bring together under one head, *368, anakephalaioō* [1]

one⁵, *476, anthrōpos* [1]
one another, *899, autos* [1]
that one sheep⁵, *899, autos* [1]
the one⁵, *899, autos* [1]
the very one, *899, autos* [1]
one day, *1181+1254, ginomai+de* [1]
Mighty One, *1539, dynamis* [1]
one of, *1639+1666, eimi+ek* [1]
one, *1639, eimi* [1]
one after the other, *1651+1667, heis+hekastos* [1]
one and the same, *1651, heis* [1]
one at a time, *1651+2848+1651, heis+kata+heis* [1]
the one, *1651, heis* [1]
one, *1667, hekastos* [1]
every one, *1667, hekastos* [1]
the one, *1697, ekeinos* [1]
one Sabbath, *1877+3836+4879, en+ho+sabbaton* [1]
one Sabbath, *1877+4879, en+sabbaton* [1]
one on each side, *1949+2779+1949, enteuthen+kai+enteuthen* [1]
one⁵, *1953, entolē* [1]
in one place, *2093+3836+899, epi+ho+autos* [1]
one kind, *2283, heteros* [1]
one at the door, *2601, thyrōros* [1]
one⁵, *2668, himation* [1]
on one occasion, *2779+2627, kai+idou* [1]
on one occasion, *2779, kai* [1]
one day, *2779+1181, kai+ginomai* [1]
then the one, *2797, kakeinos* [1]
from one synagogue to another, *2848+4246+3836+5252, kata ı pas+ho+synagōgē* [1]
one greater than, *3505, meizōn* [1]
each one⁵, *3517, melos* [1]
one⁵, *3538, meros* [1]
one and only son, *3666, monogenēs* [1]
agree with one another, *3836+899+3306, ho+autos+legō* [1]
each one, *3836+324, ho+ana* [1]
one, *3836+1651, ho+heis* [1]
one, *3836+3525, ho+men* [1]
one, *3836+899, ho+autos* [1]
as one man, *3924, homothymadon* [1]
one of these journeys⁵, *4005, hos* [1]
the lawless⁵ one, *4005, hos* [1]
the one, *4005+3525, hos+men* [1]
the one, *4015, hostis* [1]
one in which, *4023, hou* [1]
not one, *4024+3590, ou+mē* [1]
no one else, *4029, oudeis* [1]
one, *4029, oudeis* [1]
no one ever, *4030, oudepote* [1]
just one, *4047+3667, houtos+monon* [1]
one⁵ more, *4047, houtos* [1]
one, *4047, houtos* [1]
with one voice, *4101, pamplēthei* [1]
one grudgingly given, *4432, pleonexia* [1]
evil one, *4505, ponēros* [1]
members together of one body, *5362, syssōmos* [1]
suppose one, *5515+476, tis+anthrōpos* [1]
one, *5515, tis* [1]
one⁵, *5626, huios* [1]
Anointed One, *5986, Christos* [1]
not one, *6034+4029, psychē+oudeis* [1]
one⁵, *6037, psychros* [1]
in the one case, *6045+3525, hōde+men* [1]
one might even say, *6055+2229+3306, hōs+epos+legō* [1]

ONES [21]

ones, *AIT* [19]

holy ones, *41, hagios* [1]
unnatural ones, *3836+4123+5882, ho+para+physis* [1]

ONESELF [1]

oneself, *1571, heautou* [1]

ONESIMUS [2]

Onesimus, *3946, Onēsimos* [2]

ONESIPHORUS [2]

Onesiphorus, *3947, Onēsiphoros* [2]

ONLY [171]

only, *3667, monon* [41]
only, *AIT* [34]
only, *3668, monos* [22]
only, *NIG* [9]
only, *1623+3590, ei+mē* [9]
but only, *247, alla* [6]
only, *247, alla* [6]
one and only, *3666, monogenēs* [5]
only, *4024+1623+3590, ou+ei+mē* [4]
only, *4440, plēn* [4]
but only, *1623+3590, ei+mē* [3]
not only, *3590, mē* [3]
only, *1623, ei* [2]
only, *3666, monogenēs* [2]
only a short time, *4672, proskairos* [2]
the only thing that counts, *247, alla* [1]
only, *1569+3590, ean+mē* [1]
but only, *1623+2779, ei+kai* [1]
only, *1623+3590+3667, ei+mē+monon* [1]
only, *1623+3590+3668, ei+mē+monos* [1]
the only, *1651, heis* [1]
only as long as, *2093+4012+5989, epi+hosos+chronos* [1]
only, *2285, eti* [1]
only, *2671, hina* [1]
only, *3607, mēpote* [1]
one and only son, *3666, monogenēs* [1]
only child, *3666, monogenēs* [1]
only a single, *3668, monos* [1]
only, *4024+4498+2445, ou+polys+ē* [1]
only, *4028+1651, oude+heis* [1]
only to, *4029+1623+3590, oudeis+ei+mē* [1]
only, *4048, houtōs* [1]
drinking only water, *5621, hydropoteō* [1]
if only, *6055, hōs* [1]

ONTO [1]

onto, *1650, eis* [1]

OPEN [40]

open, *487, anoigō* [21]
standing open, *487, anoigō* [2]
open, *5745, phaneros* [2]
open, *72, agō* [1]
no open to blame, *455, anepilēmptos* [1]
broke open, *487, anoigō* [1]
flew open, *487, anoigō* [1]
lay open, *487, anoigō* [1]
open, *489, anoixis* [1]
open sea, *1113, bythos* [1]
open, *1380, dianoigō* [1]
open to, *1877, en* [1]
open eyes, *2048+3836+4057, epairō+ho+ophthalmos* [1]
open country, *2245, erēmos* [1]
open, *3545, mesos* [1]
open sea, *4283, pelagos* [1]
open wide, *4425, platynō* [1]
torn open, *5387, schizō* [1]

OPENED   [48]

opened, *487, anoigō* [38]
opened, *1380, dianoigō* [5]
eyes opened, *1332, diablepō* [1]
opened, *1590, enkainizō* [1]
way opened for, *2338, euodoō* [1]
opened wide, *4425, platynō* [1]
opened home to, *5685, hypodechomai* [1]

OPENING   [5]

opening, *487, anoigō* [3]
opening, *AIT* [1]
made an opening in, *689, apostegazō* [1]

OPENLY   [3]

openly confessed, *2018+334,*
  exomologeō+anangellō [1]
openly, *4244, parrēsia* [1]
openly, *5747, phanerōs* [1]

OPENS   [3]

opens, *487, anoigō* [3]

OPINION   [1]

opinion, *1506, dokeō* [1]

OPPONENTS   [1]

opponents, *512, antikeimai* [1]

OPPORTUNE   [2]

opportune, *2322, eukairos* [1]
opportune time, *2789, kairos* [1]

OPPORTUNITY   [15]

opportunity, *929, aphormē* [5]
opportunity, *2789, kairos* [3]
opportunity, *2321, eukairia* [2]
had no opportunity, *177, akaireomai* [1]
has the opportunity, *2320, eukaireō* [1]
opportunity, *2323, eukairōs* [1]
make the most of opportunity,
  3836+2789+1973,
  ho+kairos+exagorazō [1]
opportunity, *5536, topos* [1]

OPPOSE   [11]

oppose, *512, antikeimai* [3]
oppose, *468, anthistēmi* [1]
oppose, *507, antidiatithēmi* [1]
oppose, *515, antilegō* [1]
oppose, *1666+1885, ek+enantios* [1]
oppose, *1885, enantios* [1]
oppose, *1923, enechō* [1]
oppose, *3266, kōlyō* [1]
oppose, *5636, hypantaō* [1]

OPPOSED   [7]

opposed, *468, anthistēmi* [4]
opposed, *530, antitassō* [1]
stood opposed, *1639+5641,*
  eimi+hypenantios [1]
opposed to, *2848, kata* [1]

OPPOSES   [5]

opposes, *530, antitassō* [2]
opposes, *482+2093, anistēmi+epi* [1]
opposes, *515, antilegō* [1]
opposes, *3266, kōlyō* [1]

OPPOSING   [2]

opposing ideas, *509, antithesis* [1]
opposing, *530, antitassō* [1]

OPPOSITE   [5]

opposite, *2978, katenanti* [2]
opposite, *595, apenanti* [1]
opposite, *2848, kata* [1]
on the opposite shore, *4305, peran* [1]

OPPOSITION   [3]

opposition, *74, agōn* [1]
opposition arose, *482, anistēmi* [1]
opposition, *517, antilogia* [1]

OPPRESSED   [2]

oppressed, *2575, thrauō* [1]
oppressed, *2808, kakoō* [1]

OPPRESSION   [1]

oppression, *2810, kakōsis* [1]

OR   [466]

or, *2445, ē* [241]
or, *2779, kai* [56]
or, *4028, oude* [35]
or, *1664, eite* [29]
or, *3593, mēde* [26]
or, *4046, oute* [14]
or, *3612, mēte* [13]
or, *NIG* [9]
or, *2671+3590, hina+mē* [8]
or, *3607, mēpote* [5]
or, *1623, ei* [4]
or, *3590, mē* [4]
or, *RPE* [2]
or, *1254, de* [2]
or even, *2779, kai* [2]
or, *4005+1254, hos+de* [2]
or, *1142, gar* [1]
whether or not, *1623, ei* [1]
or at least, *1623+1254+3590, ei+de+mē* [1]
or again, *2445, ē* [1]
or else, *2445, ē* [1]
or even, *2445, ē* [1]
or take as an example, *2627+2779, idou+kai* [1]
or, *2779+4024, kai+ou* [1]
or, *2829, kan* [1]
this or that, *3840+3836, hode+ho* [1]
or even, *4046, oute* [1]
three or three and a half miles,
  5084+1633+4297+2445+5558,
  stadion+eikosi+pente+ē+triakonta [1]
or, *5445, te* [1]
somehow or other, *6055+323, hōs+an* [1]

ORDAINED   [1]

ordained, *2936, katartizō* [1]

ORDER   [59]

in order that, *2671, hina* [16]
in order to, *2671, hina* [10]
order, *AIT* [7]
order, *5423, taxis* [6]
in order that, *1650+3836, eis+ho* [3]
order, *2199, epitassō* [2]
put in order, *3175, kosmeō* [2]
in order to, *4639, pros* [2]
order, *RPE* [1]
the new order, *1481, diorthōsis* [1]
in order that, *1650, eis* [1]
in order to bring, *1650, eis* [1]
in order to, *2527, thelō* [1]
give order, *3027, keleuō* [1]
order, *3306, legō* [1]
in order to, *3968, hopōs* [1]
in order to, *4639+3836, pros+ho* [1]

old order of things, *4755, prōtos* [1]
in order to, *6063, hōste* [1]

ORDERED   [31]

ordered, *3027, keleuō* [18]
ordered, *4133, parangellō* [4]
ordered, *3306, legō* [3]
ordered, *1411, diatassō* [2]
ordered, *2199, epitassō* [2]
ordered, *690, apostellō* [1]
ordered, *4705, prostassō* [1]

ORDERLY   [3]

orderly, *2759, kathexēs* [1]
orderly way, *2848+5423, kata+taxis* [1]
orderly, *5423, taxis* [1]

ORDERS   [15]

gave orders, *1403, diastellō* [2]
orders, *1953, entolē* [2]
gives orders, *2199, epitassō* [2]
gave orders, *3027, keleuō* [2]
gave orders, *690, apostellō* [1]
given orders, *690, apostellō* [1]
orders, *1411, diatassō* [1]
orders, *2199, epitassō* [1]
gave orders, *2203, epitimaō* [1]
gave strict orders, *4132+4133,*
  parangelia+parangellō [1]
orders, *4132, parangelia* [1]

ORDINARY   [6]

in the ordinary way, *2848+4922, kata+sarx* [2]
ordinary, *817, asēmos* [1]
no ordinary, *842+3836+2536,*
  asteios+ho+theos [1]
no ordinary, *842, asteios* [1]
ordinary, *2626, idiōtēs* [1]

ORGIES   [3]

orgies, *3269, kōmos* [3]

ORIGIN   [2]

origin, *AIT* [1]
origin, *5770, pherō* [1]

ORIGINATE   [1]

originate, *2002, exerchomai* [1]

ORPHANS   [2]

orphans, *4003, orphanos* [2]

OTHER   [177]

other, *257, allos* [34]
each other, *253, allēlōn* [32]
other, *2283, heteros* [29]
other, *AIT* [19]
other, *3370, loipos* [9]
each other, *1571, heautou* [7]
the other^s, *1651, heis* [6]
other side, *4305, peran* [5]
on the other side, *4305, peran* [3]
passed by on the other side, *524,*
  antiparerchomai [2]
the other, *4005+1254, hos+de* [2]
other than, *4123, para* [2]
other side of the lake, *4305, peran* [2]
other, *NIG* [1]
other, *RPE* [1]
other^s, *216, akron* [1]
other way, *249, allachothen* [1]
other, *257+1254, allos+de* [1]
other than, *257, allos* [1]

the other, *899, autos* [1]
each other, *1651+3836+1651, heis+ho+heis* [1]
one after the other, *1651+1667,*
   heis+hekastos [1]
but in the other case, *1695+1254, ekei+de* [1]
the other, *1697, ekeinos* [1]
other, *2285, eti* [1]
the other[s], *2412, zestos* [1]
agree with each other, *3836+899+5858,*
   ho+autos+phroneō [1]
on[s] the other side, *3963, hopou* [1]
other, *4012, hosos* [1]
other[s], *4041, ouranos* [1]
in other words, *4047+1639, houtos+eimi* [1]
at other times, *4047+1254, houtos+de* [1]
to other side, *4305, peran* [1]
other, *4446, plēsion* [1]
any other, *5516, tis* [1]
other, *5525, toioutos* [1]
loving each other as brothers, *5789,*
   philadelphia [1]
somehow or other, *6055+323, hōs+an* [1]

OTHER'S [2]

each other's, *253, allēlōn* [2]

OTHERS [109]

others, *257, allos* [31]
others, *2283, heteros* [14]
others, *3370, loipos* [9]
others, *NIG* [7]
others, *AIT* [5]
others, *257+1254, allos+de* [5]
others, *259, allotrios* [4]
others, *899, autos* [4]
others, *3836+1254, ho+de* [3]
others, *3836, ho* [3]
others, *4005+1254, hos+de* [3]
others, *476, anthrōpos* [2]
others, *4015, hostis* [2]
others, *5516, tis* [2]
others, *RPE* [1]
all the others, *253, allēlōn* [1]
others, *253, allēlōn* [1]
the others, *899, autos* [1]
others[s], *965, ballō* [1]
others, *1571, heautou* [1]
others, *1697, ekeinos* [1]
and others, *2779, kai* [1]
contributing to the needs of others, *3556,*
   metadidōmi [1]
others, *3836+3525, ho+men* [1]
still others, *3836+1254, ho+de* [1]
and seven[s] others, *3838, ogdoos* [1]
others, *4047, houtos* [1]
join with others following example, *5213+1181,*
   symmimētēs+ginomai [1]
others, *5516+1254, tis+de* [1]

OTHERWISE [10]

otherwise, *3607, mēpote* [4]
otherwise, *NIG* [2]
otherwise, *1623+1254+3590, ei+de+mē* [1]
otherwise, *1760+1623+3590, ektos+ei+mē* [1]
otherwise, *2075+726, epei+ara* [1]
otherwise, *2075, epei* [1]

OUGHT [38]

ought, *1256, dei* [13]
ought, *4053, opheilō* [13]
ought, *AIT* [7]
ought, *RPE* [1]
ought to do, *465, anēkō* [1]
ought to, *1256, dei* [1]

as ought, *1469, dikaiōs* [1]
ought to be done, *2763, kathēkō* [1]

OUR [405]

our, *1609, egō* [290]
our, *3836, ho* [55]
our, *RPE* [30]
our, *AIT* [15]
our, *2466, hēmeteros* [4]
our, *NIG* [2]
our, *1571, heautou* [2]
our own, *1609, egō* [2]
our own, *2625, idios* [2]
our hearts, *1571, heautou* [1]
our own, *2466, hēmeteros* [1]
our fathers[s], *3836+3525, ho+men* [1]

OURS [9]

ours, *1609, egō* [6]
ours, *NIG* [1]
is ours, *2400, echō* [1]
ours, *2466, hēmeteros* [1]

OURSELVES [25]

ourselves, *1571, heautou* [15]
ourselves, *899, autos* [4]
ourselves, *RPE* [2]
ourselves, *AIT* [1]
defending ourselves, *664, apologeomai* [1]
ourselves, *1609, egō* [1]
by ourselves, *3668, monos* [1]

OUT [538]

out of, *1666, ek* [49]
went out, *2002, exerchomai* [38]
drive out, *1675, ekballō* [19]
out, *2032, exō* [17]
came out, *2002, exerchomai* [14]
poured out, *1772, ekcheō* [11]
go out, *2002, exerchomai* [11]
come out, *2002, exerchomai* [9]
driving out, *1675, ekballō* [8]
cried out, *3189, krazō* [8]
watch out, *1063, blepō* [6]
came out of, *2002+1666, exerchomai+ek* [6]
gone out, *2002, exerchomai* [6]
out, *AIT* [5]
put out to sea, *343, anagō* [5]
cried out, *371, anakrazō* [5]
find out, *1182, ginōskō* [5]
drove out, *1675, ekballō* [5]
stretch out, *1753, ekteinō* [5]
out of, *1328, dia* [4]
reached out, *1753, ekteinō* [4]
out of, *1877, en* [4]
led out, *1974, exagō* [4]
come out of, *2002+1666, exerchomai+ek* [4]
went out, *2262, erchomai* [4]
out, *NIG* [3]
out of, *608, apo* [3]
sent out, *690, apostellō* [3]
broke out, *1181, ginomai* [3]
found out, *1182, ginōskō* [3]
out of come, *1666+2002, ek+exerchomai* [3]
drives out, *1675, ekballō* [3]
pour out, *1772, ekcheō* [3]
poured out, *1773, ekchynnomai* [3]
set out, *2002, exerchomai* [3]
called out, *3189, krazō* [3]
cry out, *3189, krazō* [3]
crying out, *3189, krazō* [3]
out of mind, *3419, mainomai* [3]
called out, *5888, phōneō* [3]
treading out the grain, *262, aloaō* [2]

send out, *690, apostellō* [2]
sending out, *690, apostellō* [2]
put out of the synagogue, *697,*
   aposynagōgos [2]
called out, *1066, boaō* [2]
brings out of, *1666+1675, ek+ekballō* [2]
comes out of, *1666+1744, ek+ekporeuomai* [2]
out of came, *1666+1744, ek+ekporeuomai* [2]
went out from, *1666+2002, ek+exerchomai* [2]
send out, *1675, ekballō* [2]
take out, *1675+1666, ekballō+ek* [2]
threw out, *1675, ekballō* [2]
stretched out, *1753, ekteinō* [2]
carried out, *1766, ekpherō* [2]
come out, *1770, ekphyō* [2]
run out, *1772, ekcheō* [2]
led out of, *1974+1666, exagō+ek* [2]
gouge out, *1975, exaireō* [2]
comes out, *2002, exerchomai* [2]
get out, *2002, exerchomai* [2]
going out, *2002, exerchomai* [2]
got out of, *2002+1666, exerchomai+ek* [2]
out of came, *2002+1666, exerchomai+ek* [2]
went out of, *2002, exerchomai* [2]
out of mind, *2014, existēmi* [2]
out of, *2032, exō* [2]
put out, *2056, epanagō* [2]
brought out, *2262, erchomai* [2]
out of, *2848, kata* [2]
cries out, *3189, krazō* [2]
wear out, *4096, palaioō* [2]
carry out, *4472, poieō* [2]
went out, *4513, poreuomai* [2]
calling out, *4715, prosphōneō* [2]
poured out like a drink offering, *5064,*
   spendō [2]
went out to meet, *5636, hypantaō* [2]
living out, *64, agrauleō* [1]
led out, *72, agō* [1]
get out, *149, airō* [1]
called out in a loud voice, *149+5889,*
   airō+phōnē [1]
take out, *149, airō* [1]
taking out, *149, airō* [1]
out of season, *178, akairōs* [1]
found out exact, *208, akriboō* [1]
out of trouble, *291, amerimnos* [1]
cried out, *331, anaboaō* [1]
bring out for trial, *343, anagō* [1]
set out, *343, anagō* [1]
pull out, *413, anaspaō* [1]
beyond tracing out, *453, anexichniastos* [1]
set out, *482, anistēmi* [1]
draw out, *533, antleō* [1]
lead out, *552, apagō* [1]
went out, *599, aperchomai* [1]
turn out, *609, apobainō* [1]
drew out, *685, apospaō* [1]
put out of the synagogue, *697+4472,*
   aposynagōgos+poieō [1]
sent out, *806+690, archō+apostellō* [1]
never goes out, *812, asbestos* [1]
call out to, *832, aspazomai* [1]
throw out, *965, ballō* [1]
watch out for, *1063, blepō* [1]
watch out, *1063+1571, blepō+heautou* [1]
cried out, *1066, boaō* [1]
cry out, *1066, boaō* [1]
rang out, *1181, ginomai* [1]
turned out, *1181, ginomai* [1]
find out about, *1182, ginōskō* [1]
found out, *1452, dierōtaō* [1]
strain out, *1494, diylizō* [1]
find out, *1507, dokimazō* [1]
try out, *1507, dokimazō* [1]
lift out, *1586, egeirō* [1]

carried out, *1639, eimi* [1]
out of his body, *1650+3836+909+1744,*
   eis+ho+aphedrōn+ekporeuomai [1]
out of the body, *1650+909+1675,*
   eis+aphedrōn+ekballō [1]
out of comes, *1666+1744, ek+ekporeuomai* [1]
come out of, *1666+1744, ek+ekporeuomai* [1]
cut out of, *1666+1716, ek+ekkoptō* [1]
gone out from, *1666+2002, ek+exerchomai* [1]
out of came, *1666+2002, ek+exerchomai* [1]
out of come, *1666+1744, ek+ekporeuomai* [1]
out, *1666, ek* [1]
puts out of, *1666+1675, ek+ekballō* [1]
brings out of, *1675+1666, ekballō+ek* [1]
brought out, *1675, ekballō* [1]
drive out, *1675+1666, ekballō+ek* [1]
driven out, *1675, ekballō* [1]
pluck out, *1675, ekballō* [1]
put out, *1675, ekballō* [1]
sent out, *1675, ekballō* [1]
take out of, *1675+1666, ekballō+ek* [1]
take out of, *1675, ekballō* [1]
took out, *1675, ekballō* [1]
way out, *1676, ekbasis* [1]
drove out, *1691, ekdiōkō* [1]
throw out, *1704, ekthetos* [1]
carried out, *1714, ekkomizō* [1]
held out, *1736, ekpetannymi* [1]
rushed out, *1737, ekpēdaō* [1]
came out of, *1744+1666, ekporeuomai+ek* [1]
come out of, *1744+1666, ekporeuomai+ek* [1]
come out, *1744, ekporeuomai* [1]
comes out of, *1744+1666, ekporeuomai+ek* [1]
coming out, *1744, ekporeuomai* [1]
go out, *1744, ekporeuomai* [1]
goes out, *1744, ekporeuomai* [1]
went out from, *1744, ekporeuomai* [1]
went out, *1744, ekporeuomai* [1]
shook out, *1759, ektinassō* [1]
out of, *1760, ektos* [1]
carry out, *1766, ekpherō* [1]
take out of, *1766, ekpherō* [1]
ran out of, *1767+1666, ekpheugō+ek* [1]
spilled out, *1772, ekcheō* [1]
get out, *1774, ekchōreō* [1]
breathing out, *1863, empneō* [1]
works out, *1919, energeō* [1]
brought out of, *1974+1666, exagō+ek* [1]
brought out, *1974, exagō* [1]
escort out, *1974, exagō* [1]
lead out of, *1974+1666, exagō+ek* [1]
leads out, *1974, exagō* [1]
blot out from, *1981+1666, exaleiphō+ek* [1]
wiped out, *1981, exaleiphō* [1]
came out of, *2002, exerchomai* [1]
come out, *2002+1666, exerchomai+ek* [1]
driven out, *2002, exerchomai* [1]
flowed out of, *2002+1666, exerchomai+ek* [1]
followed out, *2002+199,*
   exerchomai+akoloutheō [1]
led out of, *2002+1666, exerchomai+ek* [1]
out, *2002, exerchomai* [1]
rode out, *2002, exerchomai* [1]
set out from, *2002, exerchomai* [1]
started out, *2002, exerchomai* [1]
walked out, *2002, exerchomai* [1]
went out, *2002+2032, exerchomai+exō* [1]
rang out, *2010, exēcheō* [1]
driving out evil spirits, *2020, exorkistēs* [1]
torn out, *2021, exoryssō* [1]
drove out, *2034, exōtheō* [1]
called out, *2048+5889, epairō+phōnē* [1]
hold out, *2091, epechō* [1]
drive out, *2093, epi* [1]
find out, *2105, epiginōskō* [1]
found out, *2105, epiginōskō* [1]

straighten out, *2114, epidiorthoō* [1]
hearts go out to, *2160, epipotheō* [1]
trying to find out, *2236, eraunaō* [1]
find out, *2351, heuriskō* [1]
looks out for, *2426, zēteō* [1]
counted out, *2705, histēmi* [1]
carrying out, *2848, kata* [1]
out of favoritism, *2848+4680,*
   kata+prosklisis [1]
carry out, *2981, katergazomai* [1]
work out, *2981, katergazomai* [1]
laid out, *3023, keimai* [1]
hired out to, *3140, kollaō* [1]
calling out, *3189, krazō* [1]
calls out, *3189, krazō* [1]
cried out, *3189+5889+3489,*
   krazō+phōnē+megas [1]
cry out, *3198, kraugazō* [1]
cut out, *3300, latomeō* [1]
call out, *3306, legō* [1]
called out, *3306+3489+5889,*
   legō+megas+phōnē [1]
called out, *3306, legō* [1]
cried out, *3306, legō* [1]
cry out, *3306, legō* [1]
pointed out, *3455, martyreō* [1]
watch out, *3972, horaō* [1]
command to come out, *3991, horkizō* [1]
out of place, *4024+465, ou+anēkō* [1]
come out of, *4047+2002,*
   houtos+exerchomai [1]
out, *4123, para* [1]
out of mind, *4196, paraphroneō* [1]
drop out, *4406, piptō* [1]
carrying out, *4472, poieō* [1]
made out to be, *4472, poieō* [1]
make out to be, *4472, poieō* [1]
set out, *4513, poreuomai* [1]
started out, *4513, poreuomai* [1]
bring out, *4575, proagō* [1]
marked out, *4618, prokeimai* [1]
watch out, *4668, prosechō* [1]
stretched out, *4727, proteinō* [1]
going out, *4931, sbennymi* [1]
put out fire, *4931, sbennymi* [1]
snuff out, *4931, sbennymi* [1]
watch out for, *5023, skopeō* [1]
heart went out, *5072, splanchnizomai* [1]
cheated out of, *5193, sykophanteō* [1]
brings out more clearly, *5319, synistēmi* [1]
found out about, *5328, synoraō* [1]
carried out, *5464, teleō* [1]
brings out, *5502, tithēmi* [1]
going out, *5632, hypagō* [1]
poured out abundantly, *5670,*
   hyperpleonazō [1]
point out, *5719, hypotithēmi* [1]
wear out, *5724, hypōpiazō* [1]
reach out, *5770, pherō* [1]
reach out for, *6027, psēlaphaō* [1]

OUTBURSTS   [1]

outbursts of anger, *2596, thymos* [1]

OUTCOME   [3]

outcome, *5465, telos* [2]
outcome, *1676, ekbasis* [1]

OUTER   [5]

outer, *2033, exōthen* [1]
outer garment, *2087, ependytēs* [1]
outer entrance, *2598+4784, thyra+pylōn* [1]
outer clothing, *2668, himation* [1]
outer, *4755, prōtos* [1]

OUTRAN   [1]

outran, *4731+5441, protrechō+tacheōs* [1]

OUTSIDE   [43]

outside, *2032, exō* [25]
outside, *2033, exōthen* [6]
outside, *2035, exōteros* [3]
outside, *1760, ektos* [2]
on the outside, *2033, exōthen* [2]
put outside, *1675, ekballō* [1]
placed outside, *1758, ektithēmi* [1]
from the outside, *2033, exōthen* [1]
just outside, *4574, pro* [1]
outside, *4639, pros* [1]

OUTSIDERS   [3]

outsiders, *3836+2032, ho+exō* [2]
outsiders, *2033, exōthen* [1]

OUTSTANDING   [3]

outstanding, *1196, gnōstos* [1]
outstanding, *2168, episēmos* [1]
debt remain outstanding, *4053, opheilō* [1]

OUTWARD   [2]

outward, *1877+3836+5745,*
   en+ho+phaneros [1]
from outward, *2033, exōthen* [1]

OUTWARDLY   [4]

outwardly, *1877+3836+5745,*
   en+ho+phaneros [1]
outwardly, *1877+4922, en+sarx* [1]
outwardly, *3836+2032+476,*
   ho+exō+anthrōpos [1]
outwardly, *4922, sarx* [1]

OUTWEIGHS   [1]

that far outweighs them all,
   2848+5651+1650+5651+983,
   kata+hyperbolē+eis+hyperbolē+baros [1]

OUTWIT   [1]

outwit, *4430, pleonekteō* [1]

OUTWITTED   [1]

outwitted, *1850, empaizō* [1]

OVER   [190]

over, *2093, epi* [38]
handed over, *4140, paradidōmi* [18]
hand over, *4140, paradidōmi* [9]
over, *AIT* [6]
left over, *4355, perisseuō* [5]
crossed over, *1385, diaperaō* [4]
over, *2062, epanō* [4]
over, *2848, kata* [4]
gave over, *4140, paradidōmi* [4]
go over, *1451, dierchomai* [2]
over, *1650, eis* [2]
over, *1666, ek* [2]
over, *1877, en* [2]
authority over, *2026, exousia* [2]
lord it over, *2894, katakyrieuō* [2]
exercise authority over, *2980,*
   katexousiazō [2]
won over, *3045, kerdainō* [2]
lord it over, *3259, kyrieuō* [2]
given over, *4140, paradidōmi* [2]
turn over, *4140, paradidōmi* [2]
all over, *4246, pas* [2]
over, *5642, hyper* [2]

hand over, *5919, charizomai* [2]
over, *RPE* [1]
gain control over, *170, aichmalōtizō* [1]
crucifying all over again, *416, anastauroō* [1]
go over, *599, aperchomai* [1]
rule over, *806, archō* [1]
have authority over, *883, authenteō* [1]
over a period, *1328, dia* [1]
come over, *1329, diabainō* [1]
was over, *1335, diaginomai* [1]
talked the matter over, *1368+4639+253,
    dialogizomai+pros+allēlōn* [1]
cross over, *1385, diaperaō* [1]
crossing over, *1385, diaperaō* [1]
all over, *1650+3910, eis+holos* [1]
handed over, *1692, ekdotos* [1]
unless over, *1781, elassōn* [1]
exercise authority over, *2027, exousiazō* [1]
threw over, *2095, epiballō* [1]
triumphing over, *2581, thriambeuō* [1]
turn over to, *2770, kathistēmi* [1]
cover over, *2821, kalyptō* [1]
covers over, *2821, kalyptō* [1]
swept over, *2821, kalyptō* [1]
all over, *2848+3910, kata+holos* [1]
over against, *2848, kata* [1]
boast over, *2878, katakauchaomai* [1]
triumphs over, *2878, katakauchaomai* [1]
lording it over, *2894, katakyrieuō* [1]
glory over, *3018+2400,
    kauchēsis+echō* [1]
over, *3111, klinō* [1]
has authority over, *3259, kyrieuō* [1]
has mastery over, *3259, kyrieuō* [1]
take over, *3284+3836+5536,
    lambanō+ho+topos* [1]
crossed over, *3553, metabainō* [1]
all over, *3910, holos* [1]
hanging over, *4024+733, ou+argeō* [1]
all over again, *4099+540, palin+anōthen* [1]
all over again, *4099, palin* [1]
crossed over, *4125, paraballō* [1]
delivered over, *4140, paradidōmi* [1]
hand over to, *4140+1650+5931,
    paradidōmi+eis+cheir* [1]
handed over, *4140+3836+5931,
    paradidōmi+ho+cheir* [1]
handing over, *4140, paradidōmi* [1]
hands over, *4140, paradidōmi* [1]
turned over, *4140, paradidōmi* [1]
bending over, *4160, parakyptō* [1]
bent over to look, *4160, parakyptō* [1]
bent over, *4160, parakyptō* [1]
handed over, *4225, paristēmi* [1]
won over, *4275, peithō* [1]
grieved over, *4291, pentheō* [1]
over the matter of, *4309, peri* [1]
over, *4309, peri* [1]
travel over, *4310, periagō* [1]
left over, *4354, perisseuma* [1]
flow over, *4355, perisseuō* [1]
over, *4498, polys* [1]
over, *4613, proistēmi* [1]
nearly over, *4621, prokoptō* [1]
went over, *4665, proserchomai* [1]
keep watch over, *4668, prosechō* [1]
stumbled over, *4684, proskoptō* [1]
bound over, *5168, synkleiō* [1]
bent over, *5174, synkyptō* [1]
over, *5334, synteleō* [1]
over, *5457, teleioō* [1]
over, *5464, teleō* [1]
held over, *5498, tēreō* [1]
kept watch over, *5498, tēreō* [1]
going over, *5632, hypagō* [1]
running over, *5658, hyperekchynnō* [1]

OVERBEARING   [1]

overbearing, *881, authadēs* [1]

OVERBOARD   [3]

jump overboard, *681, aporiptō* [1]
throw the cargo overboard, *1678, ekbolē* [1]
threw overboard, *4849, rhiptō* [1]

OVERCAME   [2]

overcame, *3771, nikaō* [2]

OVERCAST   [1]

overcast, *5145, stygnazō* [1]

OVERCOME   [14]

overcome, *3771, nikaō* [8]
overcome, *AIT* [1]
to overcome, *2093, epi* [1]
overcome, *2487, hēttaomai* [1]
sensual desires overcome their dedication to,
    2952, katastrēniaō [1]
overcome, *2996, katischyō* [1]
overcome, *5309, synechō* [1]

OVERCOMES   [10]

overcomes, *3771, nikaō* [10]

OVERFLOW   [7]

overflow, *4355, perisseuō* [5]
overflow, *4354, perisseuma* [2]

OVERFLOWING   [3]

overflowing, *4355, perisseuō* [2]
overflowing, *4353, perisseia* [1]

OVERFLOWS   [1]

overflows, *4355, perisseuō* [1]

OVERJOYED   [4]

overjoyed, *5897+22, chairō+agalliaō* [1]
overjoyed, *5897+5915+3489+5379,
    chairō+chara+megas+sphodra* [1]
overjoyed, *5897, chairō* [1]
overjoyed, *5915, chara* [1]

OVERLOOKED   [2]

overlooked, *4145, paratheōreō* [1]
overlooked, *5666, hyperoraō* [1]

OVERPOWER   [1]

overpower, *3771, nikaō* [1]

OVERPOWERED   [1]

overpowered, *2894, katakyrieuō* [1]

OVERPOWERS   [1]

overpowers, *3771, nikaō* [1]

OVERSEER   [4]

overseer, *2176, episkopos* [3]
overseer, *2175, episkopē* [1]

OVERSEERS   [3]

overseers, *2176, episkopos* [2]
serving as overseers, *2174, episkopeō* [1]

OVERSHADOW   [1]

overshadow, *2173, episkiazō* [1]

OVERSHADOWING   [1]

overshadowing, *2944, kataskiazō* [1]

OVERTAKE   [2]

overtake, *2457, hēkō* [1]
overtake, *3958, opisō* [1]

OVERTAKES   [1]

overtakes, *2898, katalambanō* [1]

OVERTHREW   [1]

overthrew, *2747, kathaireō* [1]

OVERTHROW   [1]

overthrow, *359, anaireō* [1]

OVERTURNED   [3]

overturned, *2951, katastrephō* [2]
overturned, *426, anatrepō* [1]

OVERWHELMED   [5]

overwhelmed with sorrow, *4337, perilypos* [2]
overwhelmed with wonder, *1701,
    ekthambeō* [1]
overwhelmed, *2927, katapinō* [1]
overwhelmed with amazement, *5669+1742,
    hyperperissōs+ekplēssō* [1]

OWE   [8]

owe, *4053, opheilō* [4]
owe, *RPE* [1]
owe, *4050+1639, opheiletēs+eimi* [1]
owe, *4051, opheilē* [1]
owe, *4695, prosopheilō* [1]

OWED   [5]

owed, *4053, opheilō* [3]
owed, *4050, opheiletēs* [1]
owed money to, *5971+1639,
    chreopheiletēs+eimi* [1]

OWES   [1]

owes, *4053, opheilō* [1]

OWN   [175]

his own, *2625, idios* [37]
his own, *1571, heautou* [17]
his own, *899, autos* [13]
their own, *2625, idios* [11]
their own, *1571, heautou* [9]
my own, *1847, emos* [9]
your own, *5148, sy* [8]
my own, *1831, emautou* [7]
my own, *1609, egō* [5]
their own, *899, autos* [4]
own, *RPE* [3]
own, *899, autos* [3]
its own, *2625, idios* [3]
own, *2625, idios* [3]
own, *AIT* [2]
own people, *81, adelphos* [2]
your own, *1571, heautou* [2]
our own, *1609, egō* [2]
my own accord, *1831, emautou* [2]
our own, *2625, idios* [2]
your own, *2625, idios* [2]
your own, *2848+5148, kata+sy* [2]
his own, *3836, ho* [2]
your own, *4932, seautou* [2]
your own, *5629, hymeteros* [2]
set apart as very own, *39, hagiazō* [1]
not his own, *259, allotrios* [1]

OWNED

not their own, *259, allotrios* [1]
entirely on own, *882, authairetos* [1]
on own initiative, *882, authairetos* [1]
its own, *899, autos* [1]
their own number, *899, autos* [1]
with own hands, *901, autocheir* [1]
her own, *1571, heautou* [1]
by its own choice, *1776, hekōn* [1]
our own, *2466, hēmeteros* [1]
her own, *2625, idios* [1]
her own, *3836, ho* [1]
his own home, *3836+2625, ho+idios* [1]
own, *3836, ho* [1]
your own, *3836+2625, ho+idios* [1]
your own, *3836, ho* [1]
country of their own, *4258, patris* [1]
his very own, *4342, periousios* [1]
your own, *5050, sos* [1]
of own age, *5312, synēlikiōtēs* [1]

OWNED [2]

owned, *3230+5639, ktētōr+hyparchō* [1]
owned, *5639, hyparchō* [1]

OWNER [15]

owner, *3261, kyrios* [6]
owner of the house, *3867, oikodespotēs* [5]
owner of, *467+4005, anēr+hos* [1]
owner of a house, *476+3867,
    anthrōpos+oikodespotēs* [1]
owner of the ship, *3729, nauklēros* [1]
owner, *3867, oikodespotēs* [1]

OWNER'S [1]

owner's, *3867, oikodespotēs* [1]

OWNERS [3]

owners, *3261, kyrios* [3]

OWNERSHIP [1]

set seal of ownership on, *5381, sphragizō* [1]

OWNS [3]

owns, *1181, ginomai* [1]
owns, *1639+2625, eimi+idios* [1]
owns, *3261+1639, kyrios+eimi* [1]

OX [5]

ox, *1091, bous* [4]
ox, *3675, moschos* [1]

OXEN [3]

oxen, *1091, bous* [2]
oxen, *5436, tauros* [1]

PAGAN [3]

pagan, *1618, ethnikos* [1]
pagan, *1620, ethnos* [1]
indulge in pagan revelry, *4089, paizō* [1]

PAGANS [9]

pagans, *1620, ethnos* [6]
pagans, *1618, ethnikos* [3]

PAID [7]

paid, *625, apodidōmi* [2]
paid no attention, *288, ameleō* [1]
paid the tenth, *1282, dekatoō* [1]
paid back, *3635, misthos* [1]
paid close attention, *4668, prosechō* [1]
paid homage, *4686, proskyneō* [1]

PAIN [5]

pain, *3383, lypē* [2]
pain, *989, basanizō* [1]
severe pain, *992, basanos* [1]
pain, *4506, ponos* [1]

PAINFUL [4]

painful, *1877+3383, en+lypē* [1]
painful, *3383, lypē* [1]
painful, *4505, ponēros* [1]
painful, *4796, pyrōsis* [1]

PAINS [8]

birth pains, *6047, ōdin* [2]
pains, *4506, ponos* [1]
taking pains, *4629, pronoeō* [1]
in the pains of childbirth, *5349, synōdinō* [1]
labor pains, *6047, ōdin* [1]
have labor pains, *6048, ōdinō* [1]
in the pains of childbirth, *6048, ōdinō* [1]

PAIR [2]

pair, *2414, zeugos* [1]
pair of scales, *2433, zygos* [1]

PALACE [9]

palace, *4550, praitōrion* [4]
palace, *885, aulē* [2]
palace, *3875, oikos* [1]
palace guard, *4550, praitōrion* [1]
palace of the Roman governor, *4550,
    praitōrion* [1]

PALACES [2]

palaces, *994, basileios* [1]
palaces, *3875, oikos* [1]

PALE [1]

pale, *5952, chlōros* [1]

PALM [2]

palm branches, *5836, phoinix[1]* [1]
palm, *5836, phoinix[1]* [1]

PAMPHYLIA [5]

Pamphylia, *4103, Pamphylia* [5]

PAPER [1]

paper, *5925, chartēs* [1]

PAPHOS [2]

Paphos, *4265, Paphos* [2]

PARABLE [30]

parable, *4130, parabolē* [30]

PARABLES [15]

parables, *4130, parabolē* [15]

PARADISE [3]

paradise, *4137, paradeisos* [3]

PARALYTIC [9]

paralytic, *4166, paralytikos* [7]
paralytic, *476+4168, anthrōpos+paralyō* [1]
paralytic, *1639+4168, eimi+paralyō* [1]

PARALYTICS [1]

paralytics, *4168, paralyō* [1]

PARALYZED [5]

paralyzed, *4166, paralytikos* [3]
paralyzed, *3831, xēros* [1]
paralyzed, *4168, paralyō* [1]

PARCHMENTS [1]

parchments, *3521, membrana* [1]

PARENTS [23]

parents, *1204, goneus* [19]
parents, *RPE* [1]
his parents[s], *899, autos* [1]
parents, *4252, patēr* [1]
parents and grandparents, *4591, progonos* [1]

PARMENAS [1]

Parmenas, *4226, Parmenas* [1]

PART [33]

part, *3538, meros* [8]
part, *3517, melos* [6]
part, *AIT* [5]
in part, *608+3538, apo+meros* [2]
part of, *1666, ek* [2]
part of body, *3517, melos* [2]
part, *608, apo* [1]
had taken part in a rebellion, *1639+3334,
    eimi+lēstēs* [1]
taken part, *1639+3128, eimi+koinōnos* [1]
part of the body, *3517, melos* [1]
part, *3535, meris* [1]
have a part, *3576, metechō* [1]
take part, *3576, metechō* [1]
taking part, *5593, tynchanō* [1]

PARTAKE [1]

partake, *3576, metechō* [1]

PARTED [1]

parted company, *714+608+253,
    apochōrizō+apo+allēlōn* [1]

PARTHIANS [1]

Parthians, *4222, Parthoi* [1]

PARTIALITY [2]

show partiality, *3284+4725,
    lambanō+prosōpon* [1]
partiality, *4622, prokrima* [1]

PARTICIPANTS [1]

participants, *3128, koinōnos* [1]

PARTICIPATE [3]

participate in, *1181+3128,
    ginomai+koinōnos* [1]
participate, *3125, koinōneō* [1]
participate, *3128+1639, koinōnos+eimi* [1]

PARTICIPATION [2]

participation, *3126, koinōnia* [2]

PARTICULARLY [1]

particularly, *4359, perissoterōs* [1]

PARTNER [3]

partner, *3128, koinōnos* [2]
partner, *5007, skeuos* [1]

PARTNERS [3]

partners, *3128, koinōnos* [1]

partners, *3581, metochos* [1]
partners with, *5212, symmetochos* [1]

PARTNERSHIP [1]

partnership, *3126, koinōnia* [1]

PARTS [16]

parts, *3517, melos* [6]
parts of body, *3517, melos* [3]
parts, *RPE* [2]
parts, *3538, meros* [2]
parts of the body, *3517, melos* [1]
parts, *3836, ho* [1]
the parts[s], *3836+5393+4047,
    ho+sōma+houtos* [1]

PARTY [4]

party, *AIT* [2]
party, *146, hairesis* [2]

PASS [20]

pass away, *4216, parerchomai* [10]
pass judgment on, *3212, krinō* [3]
pass, *4216, parerchomai* [2]
pass on, *1443, didōmi* [1]
pass away, *2934, katargeō* [1]
pass judgment, *3212, krinō* [1]
pass away, *4135, paragō* [1]
pass by, *4216, parerchomai* [1]

PASSAGE [4]

passage, *AIT* [2]
the passage above, *4047, houtos* [1]
passage, *4343, periochē* [1]

PASSED [26]

passed on, *4140, paradidōmi* [4]
passed by on the other side, *524,
    antiparerchomai* [2]
passed away, *599, aperchomai* [2]
passed by, *4182, paraporeuomai* [2]
passed, *599, aperchomai* [1]
passed through, *1328+1451,
    dia+dierchomai* [1]
passed through, *1329, diabainō* [1]
passed on, *1438, didaskō* [1]
passed, *1451, dierchomai* [1]
passed through, *1476, diodeuō* [1]
passed by, *2262, erchomai* [1]
passed judgment on, *3212, krinō* [1]
passed, *3553, metabainō* [1]
passed, *4182, paraporeuomai* [1]
passed by, *4216, parerchomai* [1]
after passed, *4444, plēroō* [1]
passed, *4444, plēroō* [1]
passed to the lee of, *5709, hypopleō* [1]
passed to the lee of, *5720, hypotrechō* [1]
passed under to hold together, *5968+5690,
    chraomai+hypozōnnymi* [1]

PASSING [12]

passing through, *1451, dierchomai* [2]
passing judgment, *1360, diakrisis* [1]
passing through, *1388, diaporeuomai* [1]
passing, *2901, kataleipō* [1]
passing judgment on, *3212, krinō* [1]
passing away, *4135, paragō* [1]
passing by, *4135, paragō* [1]
passing, *4135, paragō* [1]
passing by, *4216, parerchomai* [1]
passing visit, *4227, parodos* [1]
passing by, *4344, peripateō* [1]

PASSION [1]

burn with passion, *4792, pyroō* [1]

PASSIONATE [1]

passionate, *2123, epithymia* [1]

PASSIONS [4]

passions, *2123, epithymia* [2]
passions, *4077, pathēma* [2]

PASSOVER [30]

Passover, *4247, pascha* [25]
Passover lamb, *4247, pascha* [3]
Passover Feast, *2038, heortē* [1]
Passover Week, *4247, pascha* [1]

PAST [13]

ages past, *172, aiōn* [1]
ages past, *173, aiōnios* [1]
past, *599, aperchomai* [1]
in the past, *4093, palai* [1]
past, *4093, palai* [1]
past, *4123, para* [1]
sail past, *4179, parapleō* [1]
past, *4216, parerchomai* [1]
past, *4233+1155, paroichomai+genea* [1]
of the past, *4537, pote* [1]
written in the past, *4592, prographō* [1]
spoken in the past, *4625, prolegō* [1]
past, *5989, chronos* [1]

PASTORS [1]

pastors, *4478, poimēn* [1]

PASTURE [1]

pasture, *3786, nomē* [1]

PATARA [1]

Patara, *4249, Patara* [1]

PATCH [5]

patch, *2099, epiblēma* [4]
patch, *4445, plērōma* [1]

PATH [8]

path, *3847, hodos* [7]
path, *AIT* [1]

PATHS [6]

paths, *5561, tribos* [3]
paths, *3847, hodos* [2]
paths, *5579, trochia* [1]

PATIENCE [12]

patience, *3429, makrothymia* [11]
great patience, *4246+3429,
    pas+makrothymia* [1]

PATIENT [14]

patient, *3428, makrothymeō* [8]
patient endurance, *5705, hypomonē* [4]
patient, *3429, makrothymia* [1]
patient, *5702, hypomenō* [1]

PATIENTLY [5]

patiently, *1328+5705, dia+hypomonē* [1]
waiting patiently, *3428, makrothymeō* [1]
patiently, *3429, makrothymia* [1]
patiently, *3430, makrothymōs* [1]
to endure patiently, *5705, hypomonē* [1]

PATMOS [1]

Patmos, *4253, Patmos* [1]

PATRIARCH [2]

patriarch, *4256, patriarchēs* [2]

PATRIARCHS [6]

patriarchs, *4252, patēr* [4]
patriarchs, *4256, patriarchēs* [2]

PATROBAS [1]

Patrobas, *4259, Patrobas* [1]

PATTERN [6]

pattern, *5596, typos* [4]
conform to the pattern of, *5372,
    syschēmatizō* [1]
pattern, *5721, hypotypōsis* [1]

PAUL [202]

Paul, *4263, Paulos* [150]
Paul, *RPE* [26]
Paul[s], *899, autos* [19]
Paul[s] and Barnabas, *899, autos* [2]
Paul[s] and Silas, *899, autos* [2]
Paul[s], *3836+3525, ho+men* [1]
Paul[s], *4005, hos* [1]
what Paul said[s], *4047, houtos* [1]

PAUL'S [7]

Paul's, *4263, Paulos* [6]
Paul's[s], *899, autos* [1]

PAULUS [1]

Paulus, *4263, Paulos* [1]

PAVEMENT [1]

Stone Pavement, *3346, lithostrōtos* [1]

PAY [35]

pay back, *625, apodidōmi* [6]
pay, *1443, didōmi* [5]
pay, *625, apodidōmi* [3]
pay attention who they are, *1063+4725+476,
    blepō+prosōpon+anthrōpos* [2]
pay attention to, *2917, katanoeō* [2]
pay attention, *4668, prosechō* [2]
pay, *5464, teleō* [2]
pay, *AIT* [1]
pay, *RPE* [1]
pay back, *500, antapodidōmi* [1]
failed to pay, *691, apostereō* [1]
pay back, *702, apotinō* [1]
pay respects to, *832, aspazomai* [1]
pay, *1002, bastazō* [1]
pay expenses, *1251, dapanaō* [1]
pay back double, *1488+1487,
    diploō+diplous* [1]
to pay, *1666, ek* [1]
pay for, *3227, ktaomai* [1]
pay, *4072, opsōnion* [1]
pay attention to, *4668, prosechō* [1]

PAYING [2]

paying, *AIT* [1]
without paying for it, *1562, dōrean* [1]

PAYMENT [2]

received payment, *600, apechō* [1]
payment, *1443, didōmi* [1]

PAYS [1]

pays back, *625, apodidōmi* [1]

PEACE [95]

peace, *1645, eirēnē* [82]
peace be with, *1645, eirēnē* [4]
live in peace, *1644, eirēneuō* [2]
peace, *457, anesis* [1]
be at peace, *1644, eirēneuō* [1]
live at peace, *1644, eirēneuō* [1]
blessing of peace, *1645, eirēnē* [1]
peace, *1646, eirēnikos* [1]
making peace, *1647, eirēnopoieō* [1]
peace⁵, *4005, hos* [1]

PEACE-LOVING [1]

peace-loving, *1646, eirēnikos* [1]

PEACEABLE [1]

peaceable, *285, amachos* [1]

PEACEFUL [1]

peaceful, *2475, ēremos* [1]

PEACEMAKERS [2]

peacemakers, *1648, eirēnopoios* [1]
peacemakers, *4472+1645, poieō+eirēnē* [1]

PEAL [1]

peal of thunder, *1103, brontē* [1]

PEALS [5]

peals of thunder, *1103, brontē* [4]
peals, *5889, phōnē* [1]

PEARL [1]

pearl, *3449, margaritēs* [1]

PEARLS [7]

pearls, *3449, margaritēs* [7]

PEDDLE [1]

peddle for profit, *2836, kapēleuō* [1]

PELEG [1]

Peleg, *5744, Phalek* [1]

PEN [5]

least stroke of a pen, *3037, keraia* [2]
pen, *885, aulē* [1]
sheep pen, *885, aulē* [1]
pen, *2812, kalamos* [1]

PENALTY [3]

grounds for the death penalty, *165+2505,
   aitios+thanatos* [1]
penalty, *521, antimisthia* [1]
penalty, *3210, krima* [1]

PENETRATES [1]

penetrates, *1459, diikneomai* [1]

PENNIES [1]

pennies, *837, assarion* [1]

PENNY [4]

penny, *837, assarion* [1]
a fraction of a penny, *3119, kodrantēs* [1]
penny, *3119, kodrantēs* [1]
penny, *3321, leptos* [1]

PENTECOST [3]

Pentecost, *4300, pentēkostē* [3]

PEOPLE [397]

people, *3295, laos* [126]
people, *AIT* [125]
people, *4063, ochlos* [29]
people, *476, anthrōpos* [18]
the people⁵, *899, autos* [17]
God's people, *41, hagios* [9]
people, *5626, huios* [8]
people, *NIG* [7]
people, *1620, ethnos* [6]
people, *3836, ho* [5]
people, *RPE* [4]
people, *1169, genos* [3]
people, *4436, plēthos* [3]
people, *4922, sarx* [3]
holy people, *41, hagios* [2]
own people, *81, adelphos* [2]
people long ago, *792, archaios* [2]
people of Jerusalem, *2643, Hierosolymitēs* [2]
numbers of people, *4063, ochlos* [2]
God's holy people, *41, hagios* [1]
people, *41, hagios* [1]
people, *81, adelphos* [1]
people, *1322, dēmos* [1]
people there, *1954, entopios* [1]
heal people, *2617+699, iasis+apoteleō* [1]
people of Israel, *2702+2848+4922,
   Israēl+kata+sarx* [1]
people, *2997, katoikeō* [1]
people, *3180, kosmos* [1]
band of people, *3295, laos* [1]
the people⁵, *3836+1254, ho+de* [1]
people live scattered among, *3836+1402,
   ho+diaspora* [1]
people, *3950+476, onoma+anthrōpos* [1]
people, *3950, onoma* [1]
the people⁵, *4005, hos* [1]
people, *4012, hosos* [1]
the people⁵, *4015, hostis* [1]
many people, *4063, ochlos* [1]
crowd of people, *4063, ochlos* [1]
number of people, *4063, ochlos* [1]
[people of] Sidon, *4973, Sidōnios* [1]
things that cause people to sin, *4998,
   skandalon* [1]
people, *5149, syngeneia* [1]
people of Tyre, *5601, Tyrios* [1]
people, *6034, psychē* [1]

PEOPLE'S [3]

people's, *3295, laos* [3]

PEOPLES [6]

peoples, *3295, laos* [4]
peoples, *4255, patria* [1]
peoples, *5876, phylē* [1]

PERCEIVING [3]

perceiving, *3972, horaō* [3]

PERCH [2]

perch, *2942, kataskēnoō* [2]

PERCHED [1]

perched, *2942, kataskēnoō* [1]

PEREZ [3]

Perez, *5756, Phares* [3]

PERFECT [22]

perfect, *5455, teleios* [9]
made perfect, *5457, teleioō* [8]
make perfect, *5457, teleioō* [2]
more perfect, *5455, teleios* [1]
perfect, *5456, teleiotēs* [1]
made perfect, *5464, teleō* [1]

PERFECTER [1]

perfecter, *5460, teleiōtēs* [1]

PERFECTING [1]

perfecting, *2200, epiteleō* [1]

PERFECTION [4]

aim for perfection, *2936, katartizō* [1]
perfection, *2937, katartisis* [1]
perfection, *5455, teleios* [1]
perfection, *5459, teleiōsis* [1]

PERFECTLY [2]

perfectly, *1877+4246, en+pas* [1]
perfectly united, *2936+3836+899,
   katartizō+ho+autos* [1]

PERFORM [7]

perform, *1181, ginomai* [2]
perform, *1443, didōmi* [2]
perform, *4472, poieō* [2]
service that perform, *1355+3836+3311+4047,
   diakonia+ho+leitourgia+houtos* [1]

PERFORMED [15]

performed, *1181, ginomai* [7]
performed, *4472, poieō* [7]
performed, *1328+3836+5931+1181,
   dia+ho+cheir+ginomai* [1]

PERFORMING [2]

performing, *4472, poieō* [2]

PERFORMS [1]

performs religious duties, *3310, leitourgeō* [1]

PERFUME [15]

perfume, *3693, myron* [12]
the perfume⁵, *899, autos* [1]
this perfume⁵, *899, autos* [1]
poured perfume on to prepare, *3690, myrizō* [1]

PERFUMES [1]

perfumes, *3693, myron* [1]

PERGA [3]

Perga, *4308, Pergē* [3]

PERGAMUM [2]

Pergamum, *4307, Pergamos* [2]

PERHAPS [6]

perhaps, *1623+726, ei+ara* [1]
perhaps, *1623+5593, ei+tynchanō* [1]
perhaps, *1623+726+1145, ei+ara+ge* [1]
perhaps, *2711, isōs* [1]
perhaps, *5440, tacha* [1]
perhaps, *5593, tynchanō* [1]

PERIL [1]

deadly peril, *2505, thanatos* [1]

PERIOD [2]

over a period, *1328, dia* [1]
long period, *4498, polys* [1]

PERISH [15]

perish, *660, apollymi* [9]
perish, *RPE* [1]
perish, *906, aphanizō* [1]
that can never perish, *915, aphthartos* [1]
perish, *1639+1650+724, eimi+eis+apōleia* [1]
perish, *5785+5780, phthora+phtheirō* [1]
perish, *5785, phthora* [1]

PERISHABLE [6]

perishable, *5778, phthartos* [4]
perishable, *1877+5785, en+phthora* [1]
perishable, *5785, phthora* [1]

PERISHES [1]

perishes, *660, apollymi* [1]

PERISHING [4]

perishing, *660, apollymi* [4]

PERJURERS [1]

perjurers, *2156, epiorkos* [1]

PERMANENT [2]

permanent, *563, aparabatos* [1]
permanent place, *3531, menō* [1]

PERMISSIBLE [4]

permissible, *2003, exesti* [4]

PERMISSION [5]

gave permission, *2205, epitrepō* [2]
permission, *2205, epitrepō* [2]
received permission, *2205, epitrepō* [1]

PERMIT [2]

permit, *2205, epitrepō* [1]
permit, *3594+3266, mēdeis+kōlyō* [1]

PERMITS [1]

permits, *2205, epitrepō* [1]

PERMITTED [3]

permitted, *2205, epitrepō* [2]
permitted, *2003, exesti* [1]

PERMITTING [1]

permitting, *2205, epitrepō* [1]

PERPLEXED [4]

perplexed, *679, aporeō* [2]
perplexed, *1389, diaporeō* [2]

PERPLEXITY [1]

perplexity, *680, aporia* [1]

PERSECUTE [12]

persecute, *1503, diōkō* [11]
persecute, *2808, kakoō* [1]

PERSECUTED [18]

persecuted, *1503, diōkō* [15]
persecuted, *2567, thlibō* [2]
persecuted, *2568, thlipsis* [1]

PERSECUTING [4]

persecuting, *1503, diōkō* [4]

PERSECUTION [9]

persecution, *1501, diōgmos* [5]
persecution, *2568, thlipsis* [3]
suffer persecution, *2400+2568,
   echō+thlipsis* [1]

PERSECUTIONS [5]

persecutions, *1501, diōgmos* [5]

PERSECUTOR [1]

persecutor, *1502, diōktēs* [1]

PERSEVERANCE [13]

perseverance, *5705, hypomonē* [13]

PERSEVERE [2]

persevere in, *2152, epimenō* [1]
to persevere, *5705, hypomonē* [1]

PERSEVERED [3]

persevered, *2846, kartereō* [1]
persevered, *5702, hypomenō* [1]
persevered, *5705+2400, hypomonē+echō* [1]

PERSEVERES [2]

perseveres, *5702, hypomenō* [2]

PERSEVERING [1]

persevering, *5705, hypomonē* [1]

PERSIS [1]

Persis, *4372, Persis* [1]

PERSIST [1]

persist in, *2152, epimenō* [1]

PERSISTENCE [1]

persistence, *5705, hypomonē* [1]

PERSON [21]

person, *AIT* [10]
person, *476, anthrōpos* [2]
person, *RPE* [1]
person more distinguished, *1952, entimos* [1]
in person, *3836+4242+3836+5393,
   ho+parousia+ho+sōma* [1]
person, *3836, ho* [1]
any such person, *4047, houtos* [1]
greedy person, *4431, pleonektēs* [1]
in person, *4725, prosōpon* [1]
person, *5393, sōma* [1]
person, *5516, tis* [1]

PERSONAL [1]

trusted personal servant, *2093+3836+3131,
   epi+ho+koitōn* [1]

PERSONALLY [2]

personally, *1877+4922, en+sarx* [1]
personally, *4725, prosōpon* [1]

PERSONS [2]

persons, *AIT* [1]
persons, *5516, tis* [1]

PERSUADE [3]

persuade, *4275, peithō* [2]

trying to persuade, *4275, peithō* [1]

PERSUADED [8]

persuaded, *4275, peithō* [5]
persuaded, *4128, parabiazomai* [1]
fully persuaded, *4442, plērophoreō* [1]
secretly persuaded, *5680, hypoballō* [1]

PERSUADING [1]

persuading, *400, anapeithō* [1]

PERSUASION [1]

persuasion, *4282, peismonē* [1]

PERSUASIVE [1]

persuasive, *4273, peithos* [1]

PERSUASIVELY [1]

persuasively, *4275, peithō* [1]

PERVERSE [2]

perverse, *1406, diastrephō* [2]

PERVERSION [2]

perversion, *599+3958+4922+2283,
   aperchomai+opisō+sarx+heteros* [1]
perversion, *4415, planē* [1]

PERVERT [1]

pervert, *3570, metastrephō* [1]

PERVERTING [1]

perverting, *1406, diastrephō* [1]

PERVERTS [1]

perverts, *780, arsenokoitēs* [1]

PESTILENCES [1]

pestilences, *3369, loimos* [1]

PETER [176]

Peter, *4377, Petros* [150]
Peter, *RPE* [13]
Peter, *3064, Kēphas* [5]
Peter[s] and John, *899, autos* [3]
Peter[s], *899, autos* [3]
Peter[s] and John, *3836+3525, ho+men* [1]
Peter[s], *3836, ho* [1]

PETER'S [7]

Peter's, *4377, Petros* [5]
Peter's[s], *899, autos* [2]

PETITION [2]

petition, *1255, deēsis* [1]
petition, *1872, emphanizō* [1]

PETITIONED [1]

petitioned, *1961, entynchanō* [1]

PETITIONS [1]

petitions, *2656, hiketēria* [1]

PHANUEL [1]

Phanuel, *5750, Phanouēl* [1]

PHARAOH [3]

Pharaoh, *5755, Pharaō* [3]

PHARAOH'S [2]

Pharaoh's, *5755, Pharaō* [2]

PHARISEE [12]

Pharisee, *5757, Pharisaios* [12]

PHARISEE'S [2]

Pharisee's, *5757, Pharisaios* [2]

PHARISEES [84]

Pharisees, *5757, Pharisaios* [84]

PHILADELPHIA [2]

Philadelphia, *5788, Philadelpheia* [2]

PHILEMON [1]

Philemon, *5800, Philēmōn* [1]

PHILETUS [1]

Philetus, *5801, Philētos* [1]

PHILIP [34]

Philip, *5805, Philippos* [32]
Philip, *RPE* [2]

PHILIP'S [2]

Philip's, *5805, Philippos* [2]

PHILIPPI [6]

Philippi, *5804, Philippoi* [4]
Philippi, *5805, Philippos* [2]

PHILIPPIANS [1]

Philippians, *5803, Philippēsios* [1]

PHILOLOGUS [1]

Philologus, *5807, Philologos* [1]

PHILOSOPHER [1]

philosopher, *5186, syzētētēs* [1]

PHILOSOPHERS [1]

philosophers, *5815, philosophos* [1]

PHILOSOPHY [1]

philosophy, *5814, philosophia* [1]

PHLEGON [1]

Phlegon, *5823, Phlegōn* [1]

PHOEBE [1]

Phoebe, *5833, Phoibē* [1]

PHOENICIA [3]

Phoenicia, *5834, Phoinikē* [3]

PHOENIX [1]

Phoenix, *5837, Phoinix²* [1]

PHRYGIA [3]

Phrygia, *5867, Phrygia* [3]

PHYGELUS [1]

Phygelus, *5869, Phygelos* [1]

PHYLACTERIES [1]

phylacteries, *5873, phylaktērion* [1]

PHYSICAL [4]

physical, *1877+4922, en+sarx* [1]
physical, *4922, sarx* [1]
physical, *5393, sōma* [1]
physical, *5394, sōmatikos* [1]

PHYSICALLY [2]

physically, *1666+5882, ek+physis* [1]
physically, *5393, sōma* [1]

PHYSICIAN [1]

Physician, *2620, iatros* [1]

PICK [11]

pick up, *149, airō* [6]
pick, *5504, tillō* [3]
pick, *5198, syllegō* [2]

PICKED [13]

picked up, *149, airō* [9]
picked up, *1002, bastazō* [1]
picked, *1721, eklegomai* [1]
picked up, *3284, lambanō* [1]
picked up, *5251, synagō* [1]

PIECE [7]

piece of bread, *6040, psōmion* [2]
piece, *RPE* [1]
piece of property, *3228, ktēma* [1]
piece, *3538, meros* [1]
piece, *4445, plērōma* [1]
piece of cloth, *5051, soudarion* [1]

PIECES [18]

broken pieces, *3083, klasma* [5]
pieces, *3083, klasma* [4]
cut to pieces, *1497, dichotomeō* [2]
broken to pieces, *5314, synthlaō* [2]
torn to pieces, *1400, diaspaō* [1]
broken to pieces, *3395, lyō* [1]
tear to pieces, *4838, rhēgnymi* [1]
dash to pieces, *5341, syntribō* [1]
pieces, *5516, tis* [1]

PIERCE [1]

pierce, *1451, dierchomai* [1]

PIERCED [4]

pierced, *1708, ekkenteō* [2]
pierced, *3817, nyssō* [1]
pierced, *4345, peripeirō* [1]

PIGEONS [1]

pigeons, *4361, peristera* [1]

PIGS [15]

pigs, *5956, choiros* [12]
pigs, *RPE* [2]
the pigs⁵, *899, autos* [1]

PILATE [61]

Pilate, *4397, Pilatos* [54]
Pilate, *RPE* [5]
Pilate⁵, *899, autos* [1]
Pilate⁵, *3836+1254, ho+de* [1]

PILATE'S [1]

Pilate's, *4397, Pilatos* [1]

PILE [2]

manure pile, *3161, kopria* [1]

pile, *4436, plēthos* [1]

PILED [1]

piled up, *3140, kollaō* [1]

PILLAR [2]

pillar, *5146, stylos* [2]

PILLARS [2]

pillars, *5146, stylos* [2]

PILOT [2]

pilot, *3237, kybernētēs* [1]
pilot, *3995, hormē* [1]

PINT [1]

about a pint, *3354, litra* [1]

PISIDIA [1]

Pisidia, *4407, Pisidia* [1]

PISIDIAN [1]

Pisidian, *4408, Pisidios* [1]

PIT [4]

pit, *1073, bothynos* [3]
pit for the winepress, *5700, hypolēnion* [1]

PITCHERS [1]

pitchers, *3829, xestēs* [1]

PITIED [1]

pitied more than, *1795, eleeinos* [1]

PITIFUL [1]

pitiful, *1795, eleeinos* [1]

PITY [6]

have pity, *1796, eleeō* [2]
took pity, *5072, splanchnizomai* [2]
has no pity, *3091+3836+5073,*
    kleiō+ho+splanchnon [1]
take pity, *5072, splanchnizomai* [1]

PLACE [151]

place, *5536, topos* [63]
take place, *1181, ginomai* [8]
Most Holy Place, *41, hagios* [5]
took place, *1181, ginomai* [5]
place, *AIT* [3]
place, *NIG* [3]
that place, *1696, ekeithen* [3]
place on, *2202, epitithēmi* [3]
place, *3538, meros* [3]
place where the offerings were put, *1126,*
    gazophylakion [2]
taken place, *1181, ginomai* [2]
from that place, *1696, ekeithen* [2]
remote place, *2244, erēmia* [2]
from place to place, *2759, kathexēs* [2]
place, *4544, pou* [2]
place of prayer, *4666, proseuchē* [2]
place of honor, *4752, prōtoklisia* [2]
place, *6005, chōrion* [2]
place, *RPE* [1]
Holy Place, *41, hagios* [1]
Most Holy Place, *41+41, hagios+hagios* [1]
returned to place, *404+4099,*
    anapiptō+palin [1]
in place, *505, anti* [1]
have such a place, *1639, eimi* [1]

place, *1639*, *eimi* [1]
the place' of, *1650*, *eis* [1]
in that place, *1695*, *ekei* [1]
in place, *1907*, *endyō* [1]
from another place, *1949*, *enteuthen* [1]
this place, *1949*, *enteuthen* [1]
place, *2068*, *epaulis* [1]
in one place, *2093+3836+899*,
   epi+ho+autos [1]
place on, *2093+2202*, *epi+epitithēmi* [1]
place of leadership, *2175*, *episkopē* [1]
place, *2767*, *kathizō* [1]
that place, *2796*, *kakeithen* [1]
place where the road goes down, *2853*,
   katabasis [1]
place, *3102*, *klēros* [1]
place hidden, *3219*, *kryptē* [1]
permanent place, *3531*, *menō* [1]
place where staying, *3825*, *xenia* [1]
the place where, *3963*, *hopou* [1]
place, *4001*, *oros* [1]
the place where, *4023*, *hou* [1]
no place, *4024+4544*, *ou+pou* [1]
out of place, *4024+465*, *ou+anēkō* [1]
retain the place in life, *4344*, *peripateō* [1]
place, *4484*, *polis* [1]
a place where, *4543*, *pou* [1]
in the first place, *4754*, *prōton* [1]
dwelling place, *5008*, *skēnē* [1]
dwelling place, *5013*, *skēnōma* [1]
burial place, *5438*, *taphē* [1]
take place, *5642*, *hyper* [1]
exalted to the highest place, *5671*,
   hyperypsoō [1]

PLACED [20]

placed, *5502*, *tithēmi* [7]
placed on, *2202*, *epitithēmi* [4]
placed, *1443*, *didōmi* [2]
placed on, *2202+2093*, *epitithēmi+epi* [2]
placed, *369*, *anaklinō* [1]
placed outside, *1758*, *ektithēmi* [1]
placed, *2202*, *epitithēmi* [1]
on placed seal of approval, *5381*, *sphragizō* [1]
placed under, *5718+5679*, *hypotassō+hypo* [1]

PLACES [20]

places, *5536*, *topos* [6]
rocky places, *4378*, *petrōdēs* [4]
places, RPE [2]
take places at the feast, *369*, *anaklinō* [2]
places of honor, *4752*, *prōtoklisia* [2]
lonely places, *2245*, *erēmos* [1]
solitary places, *2245*, *erēmos* [1]
exact places, *3999*, *horothesia* [1]
places of honor at the table, *4752*, *prōtoklisia* [1]

PLACING [1]

placing on, *2202+2093*, *epitithēmi+epi* [1]

PLAGUE [4]

plague, *4435*, *plēgē* [3]
plague, *2505*, *thanatos* [1]

PLAGUES [10]

plagues, *4435*, *plēgē* [10]

PLAIN [5]

plain, *5746*, *phaneroō* [2]
plain, *5745*, *phaneros* [1]
made plain, *5746*, *phaneroō* [1]
make plain to, *5894*, *phōtizō* [1]

PLAINLY [8]

plainly, *4244*, *parrēsia* [4]
tell plainly, *3933*, *homologeō* [1]
plainly, *3987*, *orthōs* [1]
seen plainly, *5746*, *phaneroō* [1]
setting forth plainly, *5748*, *phanerōsis* [1]

PLAN [5]

plan, NIG [1]
plan, *1088*, *boulēma* [1]
plan, *2101*, *epiboulē* [1]
plan, *4606*, *prothesis* [1]
devised a plan, *5206+3284*,
   symboulion+lambanō [1]

PLANK [6]

plank, *1512*, *dokos* [6]

PLANKS [1]

planks, *4909*, *sanis* [1]

PLANNED [6]

planned, *1089*, *boulomai* [2]
planned, RPE [1]
planned, *1087+1181*, *boulē+ginomai* [1]
planned, *4587*, *problepō* [1]
planned, *4729*, *protithēmi* [1]

PLANS [3]

made plans, *1086*, *bouleuō* [1]
make plans, *1086*, *bouleuō* [1]
laid plans, *5206+3284*,
   symboulion+lambanō [1]

PLANT [6]

plant, *5062*, *speirō* [2]
stalk of the hyssop plant, *5727*, *hyssōpos* [1]
plant, *5884*, *phyteia* [1]
plant, *5952*, *chlōros* [1]
plant, *5965*, *chortos* [1]

PLANTED [12]

planted, *5885*, *phyteuō* [6]
planted, *5062*, *speirō* [2]
planted, *965*, *ballō* [1]
planted in, *1875*, *emphytos* [1]
planted, *5502*, *tithēmi* [1]
planted the seed, *5885*, *phyteuō* [1]

PLANTING [1]

planting, *5885*, *phyteuō* [1]

PLANTS [11]

plants, AIT [3]
the plants', *899*, *autos* [3]
plants, *5885*, *phyteuō* [3]
garden plants, *3303*, *lachanon* [2]

PLATTER [4]

platter, *4402*, *pinax* [4]

PLAYED [3]

played the flute, *884*, *auleō* [2]
tune played, *884+2445+3068*,
   auleō+ē+kitharizō [1]

PLAYERS [2]

flute players, *886*, *aulētēs* [2]

PLAYING [1]

playing, *3068*, *kitharizō* [1]

PLEA [1]

with the plea, *3306*, *legō* [1]

PLEAD [4]

plead with, *4151*, *parakaleō* [3]
plead, *1289*, *deomai* [1]

PLEADED [8]

pleaded with, *4151*, *parakaleō* [7]
pleaded with, *1289*, *deomai* [1]

PLEADING [2]

pleading, *3306*, *legō* [1]
pleading with, *4151*, *parakaleō* [1]

PLEASANT [2]

pleasant, *19*, *agathos* [1]
pleasant, *5915*, *chara* [1]

PLEASE [27]

please, *743*, *areskō* [10]
please, AIT [4]
trying to please, *743*, *areskō* [2]
please, *1289+5148*, *deomai+sy* [2]
please, *2263+5148*, *erōtaō+sy* [2]
please, *742*, *areskeia* [1]
try to please, *743*, *areskō* [1]
please, *2297*, *euaresteō* [1]
please, *2298+1639*, *euarestos+eimi* [1]
please, *2298*, *euarestos* [1]
please, *2525*, *thelēma* [1]
please, *2671*, *hina* [1]

PLEASED [23]

pleased, *2305*, *eudokeō* [8]
well pleased, *2305*, *eudokeō* [5]
pleased, *743*, *areskō* [3]
pleased, *2297*, *euaresteō* [2]
pleased, *744+1639*, *arestos+eimi* [1]
pleased with, *2305*, *eudokeō* [1]
with pleased, *2305*, *eudokeō* [1]
pleased, *2527*, *thelō* [1]
pleased, *5897*, *chairō* [1]

PLEASES [6]

pleases, *744*, *arestos* [2]
pleases, *621*, *apodektos* [1]
pleases, *1639+2298*, *eimi+euarestos* [1]
pleases, *2298+1639*, *euarestos+eimi* [1]
pleases, *2527*, *thelō* [1]

PLEASING [6]

pleasing, *2298*, *euarestos* [5]
pleasing, *621*, *apodektos* [1]

PLEASURE [7]

good pleasure, *2306*, *eudokia* [3]
pleasure, *2306*, *eudokia* [1]
pleasure, *2454*, *hēdonē* [1]
lives for pleasure, *5059*, *spatalaō* [1]
lovers of pleasure, *5798*, *philēdonos* [1]

PLEASURES [5]

pleasures, *2454*, *hēdonē* [3]
pleasures, *573*, *apatē* [1]
pleasures, *656*, *apolausis* [1]

PLEDGE [2]

pledge, *2090*, *eperōtēma* [1]
pledge, *4411*, *pistis* [1]

PLEDGED [3]

pledged to be married, *3650, mnēsteuō* [3]

PLENTIFUL [2]

plentiful, *4498, polys* [2]

PLENTY [8]

plenty, *4354, perisseuma* [2]
plenty, *4498, polys* [2]
provides with plenty, *1855, empimplēmi* [1]
living in plenty, *4355, perisseuō* [1]
plenty, *4355, perisseuō* [1]
plenty of, *4498, polys* [1]

PLIED [1]

plied, *2089, eperōtaō* [1]

PLOT [8]

plot, *2101, epiboulē* [2]
plot, *1909, enedra* [1]
plot, *3509, meletaō* [1]
plot afoot, *3995, hormē* [1]
plot, *5206+1443, symboulion+didōmi* [1]
plot, *5350, synōmosia* [1]
plot of ground, *6005, chōrion* [1]

PLOTS [1]

plots, *2101, epiboulē* [1]

PLOTTED [3]

plotted, *1086, bouleuō* [1]
plotted, *5205, symbouleuō* [1]
plotted, *5206+3284, symboulion+lambanō* [1]

PLOW [1]

plow, *770, arotron* [1]

PLOWING [1]

plowing, *769, arotriaō* [1]

PLOWMAN [1]

plowman, *769, arotriaō* [1]

PLOWS [1]

plows, *769, arotriaō* [1]

PLUCK [1]

pluck out, *1675, ekballō* [1]

PLUNDER [1]

plunder, *215, akrothinion* [1]

PLUNGE [2]

plunge, *1112, bythizō* [1]
plunge with, *5340, syntrechō* [1]

PLUNGED [1]

plunged into, *1181, ginomai* [1]

PODS [1]

pods, *3044, keration* [1]

POETS [1]

poets, *4475, poiētēs* [1]

POINT [17]

point, *AIT* [3]
to the point, *2401, heōs* [2]
highest point, *4762, pterygion* [2]
even to the point of, *948, achri* [1]

from human point of view, *2848+476, kata+anthrōpos* [1]
the point is this, *3049, kephalaion* [1]
even to the point of, *3588, mechri* [1]
to the point of, *3588, mechri* [1]
at that point, *4036, oun* [1]
at this point, *4047+1254, houtos+de* [1]
worldly point of view, *4922, sarx* [1]
some point, *5516, tis* [1]
point out, *5719, hypotithēmi* [1]

POINTED [1]

pointed out, *3455, martyreō* [1]

POINTING [2]

pointing, *1317, dēloō* [1]
pointing, *1753+3836+5931, ekteinō+ho+cheir* [1]

POINTS [2]

points of dispute, *2427, zētēma* [1]
points, *3538, meros* [1]

POISON [3]

poison, *2675, ios* [2]
deadly poison, *2503+5516, thanasimos+tis* [1]

POISONED [1]

poisoned, *2808, kakoō* [1]

POLLUTE [1]

pollute, *3620, miainō* [1]

POLLUTED [2]

polluted, *246, alisgēma* [1]
from being polluted, *834, aspilos* [1]

POLLUX [1]

twin gods Castor and Pollux, *1483, Dioskouroi* [1]

POMP [1]

pomp, *5752, phantasia* [1]

PONDERED [1]

pondered, *5202, symballō* [1]

PONTIUS [3]

Pontius, *4508, Pontios* [3]

PONTUS [3]

Pontus, *4510, Pontos* [2]
of Pontus, *4507, Pontikos* [1]

POOL [3]

pool, *3148, kolymbēthra* [3]

POOR [42]

poor, *4777, ptōchos* [31]
give to the poor, *1443+1797, didōmi+eleēmosynē* [2]
gifts to the poor, *1797, eleēmosynē* [2]
poor reflection, *141, ainigma* [1]
gifts for the poor, *1797, eleēmosynē* [1]
helping the poor, *1797+4472, eleēmosynē+poieō* [1]
poor, *4288, penēs* [1]
poor, *4293, penichros* [1]
poor, *4776, ptōcheuō* [1]
give to the poor, *6039, psōmizō* [1]

PORCIUS [1]

Porcius, *4517, Porkios* [1]

PORTION [1]

portion, *AIT* [1]

PORTRAIT [3]

portrait, *1635, eikōn* [3]

PORTRAYED [1]

portrayed, *4592, prographō* [1]

PORTS [1]

ports, *5536, topos* [1]

POSITION [4]

secure position, *5113, stērigmos* [1]
of low position, *5424, tapeinos* [1]
low position, *5428, tapeinōsis* [1]
high position, *5737, hypsos* [1]

POSITIONS [1]

positions of authority, *794, archē* [1]

POSSESS [5]

possess, *2400, echō* [2]
possess, *5639, hyparchō* [2]
possess, *1650+2959, eis+kataschesis* [1]

POSSESSED [8]

possessed by, *2400, echō* [5]
possessed, *AIT* [1]
possessed by a demon, *1227, daimonizomai* [1]
possessed by demons, *1227, daimonizomai* [1]

POSSESSING [1]

possessing, *2988, katechō* [1]

POSSESSION [1]

possession, *4348, peripoiēsis* [1]

POSSESSIONS [15]

possessions, *5639, hyparchō* [9]
possessions, *5007, skeuos* [2]
possessions, *1050, bios* [1]
possessions, *3228, ktēma* [1]
possessions, *3836, ho* [1]
possessions, *5638, hyparxis* [1]

POSSIBLE [18]

possible, *1543, dynatos* [10]
possible, *AIT* [3]
possible, *NIG* [1]
possible, *1538, dynamai* [1]
possible, *1543+1639, dynatos+eimi* [1]
is it possible that, *4024, ou* [1]
by all possible means, *4122, pantōs* [1]

POSSIBLY [2]

possibly, *AIT* [1]
possibly, *5440, tacha* [1]

POST [1]

post bond, *2653, hikanos* [1]

POSTING [1]

posting, *3552, meta* [1]

POTTER [1]

potter, *3038, kerameus* [1]

POTTER'S [2]

potter's, *3038, kerameus* [2]

POTTERY [2]

pottery, *5007+3039, skeuos+keramikos* [1]
pottery, *5007, skeuos* [1]

POUNDING [1]

pounding, *1040, bia* [1]

POUNDS [2]

seventy-five pounds, *3354+1669,*
  litra+hekaton [1]
hundred pounds, *5418, talantiaios* [1]

POUR [5]

pour out, *1772, ekcheō* [3]
pour, *965, ballō* [2]

POURED [29]

poured out, *1772, ekcheō* [11]
poured on, *230, aleiphō* [4]
poured out, *1773, ekchynnomai* [3]
poured, *965, ballō* [2]
poured out like a drink offering, *5064,*
  spendō [2]
must be poured, *1064, blēteos* [1]
poured, *1443, didōmi* [1]
poured on, *2972, katacheō* [1]
poured, *2972, katacheō* [1]
poured, *3042, kerannymi* [1]
poured perfume on to prepare, *3690, myrizō* [1]
poured out abundantly, *5670,*
  hyperpleonazō [1]

POURING [1]

pouring on, *2219, epicheō* [1]

POURS [3]

pours, *965, ballō* [2]
pours, *RPE* [1]

POVERTY [5]

poverty, *4775, ptōcheia* [3]
poverty, *5729, hysterēma* [1]
poverty, *5730, hysterēsis* [1]

POWER [121]

power, *1539, dynamis* [73]
power, *2026, exousia* [11]
power, *NIG* [8]
power, *3197, kratos* [8]
power, *RPE* [4]
power, *1543, dynatos* [3]
power, *AIT* [2]
power, *794, archē* [2]
power, *1918, energeia* [2]
power, *1098, brachiōn* [1]
under power, *1650+5931, eis+cheir* [1]
by the power of, *1877, en* [1]
power, *2015, exischyō* [1]
power, *2708, ischyros* [1]
power, *2709, ischys* [1]
under the power, *2872, katadynasteuō* [1]
power, *5931, cheir* [1]

POWERFUL [13]

powerful, *1539, dynamis* [3]
more powerful, *2708, ischyros* [3]
powerful, *1543, dynatos* [2]
powerful, *1542, dynateō* [1]
powerful, *1904, endynamoō* [1]

powerful, *1918, energeia* [1]
powerful, *2708, ischyros* [1]
powerful, *4498+2710, polys+ischyō* [1]

POWERFULLY [1]

so powerfully, *1877+1539, en+dynamis* [1]

POWERLESS [2]

powerless, *105, adynatos* [1]
powerless, *822, asthenēs* [1]

POWERS [10]

miraculous powers, *1539, dynamis* [3]
powers, *1539, dynamis* [3]
powers, *794, archē* [1]
miraculous powers, *1920+1539,*
  energēma+dynamis [1]
powers of world, *3179, kosmokratōr* [1]
powers, *3262, kyriotēs* [1]

PRACTICALLY [1]

practically, *5385, schedon* [1]

PRACTICE [16]

put into practice, *4472, poieō* [3]
practice, *4472, poieō* [2]
puts into practice, *4472, poieō* [2]
practice magic arts, *5761, pharmakos* [2]
practice, *1503, diōkō* [1]
practice deceit, *1514, dolioō* [1]
put religion into practice by caring for, *2355,*
  eusebeō [1]
practice, *4547, pragma* [1]
practice, *4556, prassō* [1]
put into practice, *4556, prassō* [1]
practice, *5311, synētheia* [1]

PRACTICED [4]

practiced, *4472, poieō* [2]
practiced sorcery, *3405, mageuō* [1]
practiced, *4556, prassō* [1]

PRACTICES [4]

practices, *4472, poieō* [2]
practices, *2240, ergon* [1]
practices, *4552, praxis* [1]

PRAETORIUM [2]

Praetorium, *4550, praitōrion* [2]

PRAISE [41]

praise, *1518, doxa* [9]
praise, *2047, epainos* [7]
praise, *2329, eulogētos* [4]
praise, *2330, eulogia* [4]
praise, *140, aineō* [3]
praise, *1519, doxazō* [3]
praise, *2018, exomologeō* [3]
praise, *2046, epaineō* [2]
praise, *139, ainesis* [1]
praise, *142, ainos* [1]
gave praise to, *1519, doxazō* [1]
have praise, *2046, epaineō* [1]
praise, *2328, eulogeō* [1]
sing songs of praise, *6010, psallō* [1]

PRAISED [17]

praised, *1519, doxazō* [11]
praised, *2329, eulogētos* [3]
praised, *1443+142, didōmi+ainos* [1]
praised, *2047, epainos* [1]
praised, *2328, eulogeō* [1]

PRAISES [3]

praises, *746, aretē* [1]
sing praises to, *2046, epaineō* [1]
sing praises, *5630, hymneō* [1]

PRAISEWORTHY [1]

praiseworthy, *2047, epainos* [1]

PRAISING [13]

praising, *140, aineō* [5]
praising, *1519, doxazō* [4]
praising, *2328, eulogeō* [3]
praising, *3486, megalynō* [1]

PRAY [73]

pray, *4667, proseuchomai* [42]
pray, *RPE* [12]
pray, *1289, deomai* [5]
pray, *2377, euchomai* [3]
pray, *1255+4472, deēsis+poieō* [2]
pray, *2263, erōtaō* [2]
pray, *4666, proseuchē* [2]
pray for, *4667, proseuchomai* [2]
pray, *160, aiteō* [1]
pray, *2377+323, euchomai+an* [1]
pray^s, *4047+4472, houtos+poieō* [1]

PRAYED [24]

prayed, *4667, proseuchomai* [17]
prayed, *1289, deomai* [2]
prayed to, *1289, deomai* [1]
prayed, *2126, epikaleō* [1]
prayed for, *2377, euchomai* [1]
prayed, *3306, legō* [1]
prayed earnestly, *4666+4667,*
  proseuchē+proseuchomai [1]

PRAYER [33]

prayer, *4666, proseuchē* [16]
prayer, *4667, proseuchomai* [5]
prayer, *1255, deēsis* [4]
prayer is, *2263, erōtaō* [2]
place of prayer, *4666, proseuchē* [2]
prayer, *AIT* [1]
prayer, *1950, enteuxis* [1]
prayer, *2376, euchē* [1]
prayer for, *2377, euchomai* [1]

PRAYERS [21]

prayers, *4666, proseuchē* [12]
prayers, *1255, deēsis* [6]
make prayers, *4667, proseuchomai* [2]
prayers, *RPE* [1]

PRAYING [20]

praying, *4667, proseuchomai* [12]
praying, *1255, deēsis* [2]
praying, *4666, proseuchē* [2]
praying, *2263, erōtaō* [1]
praying, *3306, legō* [1]
praying, *4666+1181, proseuchē+ginomai* [1]
praying to, *4667, proseuchomai* [1]

PRAYS [3]

prays, *4667, proseuchomai* [3]

PREACH [37]

preach, *3062, kēryssō* [17]
preach the gospel, *2294, euangelizō* [7]
preach the good news, *2294, euangelizō* [2]
preach, *2294, euangelizō* [2]
preach, *2859, katangellō* [2]

preach, *RPE* [1]
preach, *334, anangellō* [1]
preach a gospel, *2294, euangelizō* [1]
preach good news, *2294, euangelizō* [1]
preach gospel, *2295, euangelion* [1]
preach, *3306, legō* [1]
preach[s], *4556, prassō* [1]

PREACHED   [44]

preached, *3062, kēryssō* [16]
preached, *2294, euangelizō* [7]
preached the good news, *2294, euangelizō* [3]
preached the gospel, *2294, euangelizō* [2]
the good news preached, *2294, euangelizō* [2]
the gospel preached, *2294, euangelizō* [2]
preached, *2859, katangellō* [2]
preached, *3281, laleō* [2]
preached, *550, apangellō* [1]
had the gospel preached, *2294, euangelizō* [1]
the good news is preached, *2294, euangelizō* [1]
gospel preached, *2295+2294,
    euangelion+euangelizō* [1]
what was preached, *3060, kērygma* [1]
preached, *3062+2400, kēryssō+echō* [1]
preached fearlessly, *4245, parrēsiazomai* [1]
preached, *4619, prokēryssō* [1]

PREACHER   [1]

preacher, *3061, kēryx* [1]

PREACHES   [2]

preaches, *3062, kēryssō* [2]

PREACHING   [32]

preaching, *3062, kēryssō* [10]
preaching the gospel, *2294, euangelizō* [5]
preaching, *3060, kērygma* [5]
preaching gospel, *2295, euangelion* [2]
preaching, *1877+3364, en+logos* [1]
preaching a gospel, *2294, euangelizō* [1]
preaching the good news, *2294, euangelizō* [1]
preaching, *2294, euangelizō* [1]
preaching the gospel, *2295+2294,
    euangelion+euangelizō* [1]
preaching, *2295, euangelion* [1]
preaching, *2859, katangellō* [1]
preaching, *3281, laleō* [1]
preaching, *3836+3364, ho+logos* [1]
preaching, *4155, paraklēsis* [1]

PRECEDE   [1]

precede, *5777, phthanō* [1]

PRECIOUS   [11]

precious, *5508, timios* [6]
precious, *1952, entimos* [2]
as precious as, *2700, isotimos* [1]
precious, *5507, timē* [1]
very precious, *5508, timios* [1]

PRECISELY   [1]

precisely as it had happened, *2759, kathexēs* [1]

PREDESTINED   [4]

predestined, *4633, proorizō* [4]

PREDICTED   [4]

spirit which predicted the future, *4460+4780,
    pneuma+pythōn* [1]
predicted, *4615, prokatangellō* [1]
predicted, *4626, promartyromai* [1]
predicted, *4955, sēmainō* [1]

PREFER   [2]

prefer, *2305+3437, eudokeō+mallon* [1]
prefer, *2527, thelō* [1]

PREGNANT   [6]

pregnant women, *1877+1143+2400,
    en+gastēr+echō* [3]
pregnant woman, *1877+1143+2400,
    en+gastēr+echō* [1]
pregnant, *1877+1143+2400,
    en+gastēr+echō* [1]
pregnant, *5197, syllambanō* [1]

PREPARATION   [6]

day of Preparation, *4187, paraskeuē* [3]
Preparation Day, *4187, paraskeuē* [2]
Preparation, *4187, paraskeuē* [1]

PREPARATIONS   [6]

make preparations, *2286, hetoimazō* [5]
preparations to be made, *1355, diakonia* [1]

PREPARE   [17]

prepare, *2286, hetoimazō* [10]
prepare, *2941, kataskeuazō* [3]
prepare for action, *350+3836+4019,
    anazōnnymi+ho+osphys* [1]
prepare for burial, *1946, entaphiazō* [1]
prepare, *2938, katartismos* [1]
poured perfume on to prepare, *3690, myrizō* [1]

PREPARED   [30]

prepared, *2286, hetoimazō* [19]
prepared, *2936, katartizō* [2]
prepared in advance, *4602, proetoimazō* [2]
prepared, *RPE* [1]
had a notice prepared, *1211+5518,
    graphō+titlos* [1]
prepared, *2289, hetoimos* [1]
prepared, *2392, ephistēmi* [1]
prepared, *2941, kataskeuazō* [1]
prepared, *4186, paraskeuazō* [1]
prepared, *4472, poieō* [1]

PREPARING   [4]

preparing, *2936, katartizō* [2]
preparing, *4472, poieō* [2]

PRESCRIBED   [1]

prescribed by, *2848, kata* [1]

PRESENCE   [30]

in the presence, *1967, enōpion* [9]
in the presence, *1869, emprosthen* [3]
presence, *4725, prosōpon* [3]
in presence, *1869, emprosthen* [2]
in presence, *1967, enōpion* [2]
presence, *NIG* [1]
presence, *RPE* [1]
in the presence of, *1328, dia* [1]
glorious presence, *1518, doxa* [1]
in presence, *1877, en* [1]
presence, *3545, mesos* [1]
in presence, *3552+3836+4725,
    meta+ho+prosōpon* [1]
in presence, *4123, para* [1]
in the presence, *4123, para* [1]
presence, *4123, para* [1]
presence, *4242, parousia* [1]

PRESENT   [47]

present, *3814, nyn* [9]

present, *4225, paristēmi* [7]
present, *1931, enistēmi* [3]
present, *AIT* [2]
the present, *1931, enistēmi* [2]
present time, *2789, kairos* [2]
present, *NIG* [1]
present, *RPE* [1]
not present, *582, apeimi[1]* [1]
when no was present, *868, ater* [1]
present, *1192, gnōrizō* [1]
am present, *1639, eimi* [1]
present, *1639, eimi* [1]
was present, *1639, eimi* [1]
present, *2705, histēmi* [1]
present, *3306, legō* [1]
at present, *3814, nyn* [1]
present time, *3814, nyn* [1]
those[s] present, *3836, ho* [1]
in the present case, *3836+3814, ho+nyn* [1]
present, *3836+3814+2789, ho+nyn+kairos* [1]
present, *4047, houtos* [1]
present, *4134, paraginomai* [1]
are present, *4205, pareimi* [1]
present, *4205, pareimi* [1]
were present, *4205, pareimi* [1]
present in fullness, *4444, plēroō* [1]
present with, *5223, sympareimi* [1]

PRESENTABLE   [1]

presentable, *2363, euschēmōn* [1]

PRESENTED   [7]

presented case, *806+2989, archō+katēgoreō* [1]
presented, *1443, didōmi* [1]
appeared and presented the charges, *1872,
    emphanizō* [1]
presented, *2705, histēmi* [1]
presented, *4225, paristēmi* [1]
presented with, *4712, prospherō* [1]
presented, *4729, protithēmi* [1]

PRESENTING   [1]

presenting, *3281, laleō* [1]

PRESERVE   [1]

preserve, *2441, zōogoneō* [1]

PRESERVED   [1]

preserved, *5337, syntēreō* [1]

PRESS   [5]

press on, *1503, diōkō* [2]
press charges, *1592, enkaleō* [1]
press charges against, *2989, katēgoreō* [1]
press, *3332, lēnos* [1]

PRESSED   [4]

hard pressed, *2567, thlibō* [1]
hard pressed, *2568, thlipsis* [1]
pressed down, *4390, piezō* [1]
pressed around, *5315, synthlibō* [1]

PRESSING   [1]

pressing against, *632, apothlibō* [1]

PRESSURE   [2]

under pressure, *976, bareō* [1]
pressure, *2180, epistasis* [1]

PRESUME   [1]

presume, *AIT* [1]

PRETENDED [1]

pretended, *5693, hypokrinomai* [1]

PRETENDING [1]

pretending, *4733, prophasis* [1]

PRETENSION [1]

pretension, *5739, hypsōma* [1]

PRETEXT [2]

on the pretext of, *6055, hōs* [2]

PREVAIL [1]

prevail, *3771, nikaō* [1]

PREVAILED [1]

prevailed, *2996, katischyō* [1]

PREVALENT [1]

prevalent, *4353, perisseia* [1]

PREVENT [3]

prevent, *3590, mē* [2]
to prevent, *3590, mē* [1]

PREVENTED [2]

prevented from, *3266, kōlyō* [2]

PREVIOUS [1]

previous, *4537, pote* [1]

PREVIOUSLY [4]

previously seen, *1639+4632, eimi+prooraō* [1]
previously established, *4623, prokyroō* [1]
said previously, *4625, prolegō* [1]
previously suffered, *4634, propaschō* [1]

PRICE [7]

price, *AIT* [3]
price, *5507, timē* [2]
price, *3049, kephalaion* [1]
price set on, *5507+5506, timē+timaō* [1]

PRIDE [8]

take pride, *3016, kauchaomai* [2]
pride, *3017, kauchēma* [2]
pride, *3018, kauchēsis* [2]
pride, *RPE* [1]
take pride, *5881, physioō* [1]

PRIEST [72]

high priest, *797, archiereus* [51]
priest, *2636, hiereus* [16]
priest, *RPE* [3]
chief priest, *797, archiereus* [1]
serving as priest, *2634, hierateuō* [1]

PRIEST'S [4]

high priest's, *797, archiereus* [3]
high priest's, *796, archieratikos* [1]

PRIESTHOOD [7]

priesthood, *2648, hierōsynē* [3]
priesthood, *2633, hierateuma* [2]
high priesthood, *797, archiereus* [1]
priesthood, *2632, hierateia* [1]

PRIESTLY [2]

priestly division, *2389, ephēmeria* [1]
priestly duty, *2646, hierourgeō* [1]

PRIESTS [83]

chief priests, *797, archiereus* [64]
priests, *2636, hiereus* [15]
high priests, *797, archiereus* [2]
priests, *RPE* [1]
priests, *2632, hierateia* [1]

PRINCE [8]

prince, *807, archōn* [7]
prince, *795, archēgos* [1]

PRINCES [1]

princes, *3491, megistan* [1]

PRINCIPLE [1]

principle, *3795, nomos* [1]

PRINCIPLES [4]

basic principles, *5122, stoicheion* [3]
principles, *5122, stoicheion* [1]

PRISCILLA [7]

Priscilla, *4571, Priska* [6]
Priscilla and Aquila, *2797, kakeinos* [1]

PRISON [44]

prison, *5871, phylakē* [31]
prison, *RPE* [3]
in prison, *1300, desmios* [2]
prison, *1303, desmōtērion* [2]
in prison, *1313, deō* [2]
put in prison, *4140, paradidōmi* [2]
prison, *1301, desmos* [1]
in prison with, *5257, synaichmalōtos* [1]

PRISONER [16]

prisoner, *1300, desmios* [11]
fellow prisoner, *5257, synaichmalōtos* [2]
prisoner, *AIT* [1]
making a prisoner, *170, aichmalōtizō* [1]
declares a prisoner, *5168, synkleiō* [1]

PRISONERS [11]

prisoners, *1300, desmios* [2]
prisoners, *1304, desmōtēs* [2]
prisoners, *1313, deō* [2]
taken as prisoners, *170, aichmalōtizō* [1]
prisoners, *171, aichmalōtos* [1]
prisoners, *1639+1313, eimi+deō* [1]
fellow prisoners, *5279, syndeō* [1]
held prisoners, *5864, phroureō* [1]

PRISONS [1]

prisons, *5871, phylakē* [1]

PRIVATE [2]

private, *2625, idios* [1]
private, *3668, monos* [1]

PRIVATELY [6]

privately, *2848+2625, kata+idios* [6]

PRIVILEGE [1]

privilege, *5921, charis* [1]

PRIZE [5]

prize, *1092, brabeion* [2]
prize, *AIT* [1]
disqualify for the prize, *2857, katabrabeuō* [1]
get the prize, *2898, katalambanō* [1]

PROCEEDED [1]

proceeded, *4707, prostithēmi* [1]

PROCEEDINGS [1]

adjourned the proceedings, *327, anaballō* [1]

PROCESSION [2]

procession, *AIT* [1]
leads in triumphal procession, *2581, thriambeuō* [1]

PROCLAIM [16]

proclaim, *2859, katangellō* [4]
proclaim, *550, apangellō* [3]
proclaim, *3062, kēryssō* [3]
proclaim, *NIG* [1]
proclaim, *334, anangellō* [1]
proclaim, *1334, diangellō* [1]
gospel proclaim, *2295+2294, euangelion+euangelizō* [1]
proclaim, *3281, laleō* [1]
proclaim clearly, *5746, phaneroō* [1]

PROCLAIMED [12]

proclaimed, *2859, katangellō* [3]
proclaimed, *3062, kēryssō* [3]
proclaimed, *AIT* [2]
proclaimed, *3281, laleō* [2]
proclaimed, *NIG* [1]
proclaimed, *1334, diangellō* [1]

PROCLAIMING [9]

proclaiming, *3062, kēryssō* [3]
proclaiming the good news, *2294, euangelizō* [2]
proclaiming, *2859, katangellō* [2]
proclaiming, *617, apodeiknymi* [1]
proclaiming gospel, *2295, euangelion* [1]

PROCLAMATION [1]

proclamation, *3060, kērygma* [1]

PROCONSUL [5]

proconsul, *478, anthypatos* [4]
proconsul, *RPE* [1]

PROCONSULS [1]

proconsuls, *478, anthypatos* [1]

PROCORUS [1]

Procorus, *4743, Prochoros* [1]

PRODUCE [9]

produce, *4472, poieō* [6]
produce a crop, *2844, karpophoreō* [2]
produce, *1164, gennaō* [1]

PRODUCED [9]

produced, *2981, katergazomai* [3]
produced, *1443, didōmi* [2]
produced, *AIT* [1]
produced, *1056, blastanō* [1]
produced a good crop, *2369, euphoreō* [1]
produced, *2705, histēmi* [1]

PRODUCES [8]

produces, *625, apodidōmi* [1]
produces, *1766, ekpherō* [1]
produces in, *1919+1877, energeō+en* [1]
produces a crop, *2844, karpophoreō* [1]
produces grain, *2844, karpophoreō* [1]

PROFESS [3]

produces, *2981, katergazomai* [1]
produces, *5503, tiktō* [1]
produces, *5770, pherō* [1]

PROFESS [3]

profess, *2040, epangellomai* [1]
faith we profess, *3934, homologia* [1]
profess, *3934, homologia* [1]

PROFESSED [1]

professed, *2040, epangellomai* [1]

PROFIT [3]

peddle for profit, *2836, kapēleuō* [1]
profit, *3046, kerdos* [1]
profit, *3635, misthos* [1]

PROFITABLE [1]

profitable, *6068, ōphelimos* [1]

PROFOUND [2]

profound, *3489, megas* [1]
profound, *4246, pas* [1]

PROGRESS [2]

progress, *4620, prokopē* [2]

PROMINENT [4]

prominent, *2363, euschēmōn* [2]
prominent, *807, archōn* [1]
prominent, *4755, prōtos* [1]

PROMISE [29]

promise, *2039, epangelia* [23]
made promise, *2040, epangellomai* [2]
promise, *2040, epangellomai* [2]
promise, *2041, epangelma* [1]
the promise⁵, *4005, hos* [1]

PROMISED [37]

promised, *2039, epangelia* [9]
promised, *2040, epangellomai* [8]
promised, *2039+1181, epangelia+ginomai* [2]
what was promised, *3836+2039,*
     ho+epangelia [2]
promised, *764, harmozō* [1]
has promised, *2039, epangelia* [1]
promised, *2039+2040,*
     epangelia+epangellomai [1]
was promised, *2039, epangelia* [1]
what had been promised, *2039, epangelia* [1]
what has been promised, *2039, epangelia* [1]
what was promised, *2039, epangelia* [1]
promised, *3281, laleō* [1]
promised, *3306, legō* [1]
promised with an oath, *3923, omnyō* [1]
promised, *3923, omnyō* [1]
promised, *3933, homologeō* [1]
holy blessings promised, *4008, hosios* [1]
promised beforehand, *4600, proepangellō* [1]
promised, *4600, proepangellō* [1]
promised, *4839, rhēma* [1]

PROMISES [10]

promises, *2039, epangelia* [9]
promises, *2041, epangelma* [1]

PROMOTE [1]

promote, *4218, parechō* [1]

PROMOTES [1]

promotes sin, *281+1356,*
     hamartia+diakonos [1]

PROMPTED [4]

prompted, *AIT* [2]
prompted, *965+1650+3836+2840,*
     ballō+eis+ho+kardia [1]
prompted, *4586, probibazō* [1]

PROOF [3]

proof, *1509, dokimē* [1]
proof, *1893, endeixis* [1]
given proof, *4411+4218, pistis+parechō* [1]

PROOFS [1]

convincing proofs, *5447, tekmērion* [1]

PROPER [13]

proper time, *2789, kairos* [4]
proper, *AIT* [2]
proper, *4560, prepō* [2]
proper ground, *162, aitia* [1]
proper, *1571, heautou* [1]
proper, *2625, idios* [1]
proper, *4246, pas* [1]
show proper respect to, *5506, timaō* [1]

PROPERLY [1]

properly, *3789, nomimōs* [1]

PROPERTY [7]

property, *AIT* [2]
property, *1050, bios* [2]
property, *5639, hyparchō* [2]
piece of property, *3228, ktēma* [1]

PROPHECIES [3]

prophecies, *4735, prophēteia* [3]

PROPHECY [15]

prophecy, *4735, prophēteia* [12]
prophecy, *4460, pneuma* [1]
gift of prophecy, *4735, prophēteia* [1]
prophecy, *4736, prophēteuō* [1]

PROPHESIED [8]

prophesied, *4736, prophēteuō* [8]

PROPHESIES [5]

prophesies, *4736, prophēteuō* [5]

PROPHESY [12]

prophesy, *4736, prophēteuō* [12]

PROPHESYING [3]

prophesying, *4735, prophēteia* [2]
prophesying, *4736, prophēteuō* [1]

PROPHET [65]

prophet, *4737, prophētēs* [60]
false prophet, *6021, pseudoprophētēs* [4]
prophet, *467+4737, anēr+prophētēs* [1]

PROPHET'S [3]

prophet's, *4737, prophētēs* [2]
prophet's, *RPE* [1]

PROPHETESS [2]

prophetess, *4739, prophētis* [2]

PROPHETIC [2]

prophetic message, *4735, prophēteia* [1]
prophetic, *4738, prophētikos* [1]

PROPHETS [89]

prophets, *4737, prophētēs* [80]
false prophets, *6021, pseudoprophētēs* [7]
the prophets⁵, *899, autos* [1]
of prophets, *4738, prophētikos* [1]

PROPORTION [1]

proportion, *381, analogia* [1]

PROPOSAL [1]

proposal, *3364, logos* [1]

PROPOSED [1]

proposed, *2705, histēmi* [1]

PROPRIETY [2]

propriety, *5408, sōphrosynē* [2]

PROSPER [1]

made prosper, *5738, hypsoō* [1]

PROSTITUTE [8]

prostitute, *4520, pornē* [8]

PROSTITUTES [5]

prostitutes, *4520, pornē* [4]
male prostitutes, *3434, malakos* [1]

PROTECT [3]

protect, *5498, tēreō* [2]
protect, *5875, phylassō* [1]

PROTECTED [3]

protected, *5337, syntēreō* [1]
protected, *5498, tēreō* [1]
protected, *5875, phylassō* [1]

PROTECTS [1]

protects, *5095, stegō* [1]

PROTEST [2]

protest, *AIT* [2]

PROTESTED [2]

protested, *3306, legō* [2]

PROUD [8]

proud, *5662, hyperēphanos* [4]
proud, *5881, physioō* [2]
proud, *3489, megas* [1]
proud, *3836+5734+5858,*
     ho+hypsēlos+phroneō [1]

PROVE [9]

prove by, *545+4556, axios+prassō* [1]
prove, *617, apodeiknymi* [1]
show to prove, *1259, deiknymi* [1]
prove guilty, *1794, elenchō* [1]
prove, *2351, heuriskō* [1]
prove hollow, *3033, kenoō* [1]
prove, *4225, paristēmi* [1]
prove that, *5319, synistēmi* [1]
prove, *5770, pherō* [1]

PROVED [10]

proved right, *1467, dikaioō* [3]

proved, *1509, dokimē* [2]
proved to be, *1181, ginomai* [1]
proved, *1181, ginomai* [1]
proved, *1507, dokimazō* [1]
proved genuine, *1510, dokimion* [1]
proved, *5319, synistēmi* [1]

PROVERB [1]

proverb, *4130, parabolē* [1]

PROVERBS [1]

proverbs, *4231, paroimia* [1]

PROVIDE [9]

provide, *4472, poieō* [2]
provide, *AIT* [1]
provide, *2351, heuriskō* [1]
provide with, *4218, parechō* [1]
provide, *4225, paristēmi* [1]
provide, *4287, pempō* [1]
provide for, *4629, pronoeō* [1]
provide, *5593, tynchanō* [1]

PROVIDED [3]

provided, *NIG* [1]
provided that, *1569, ean* [1]
provided, *4472, poieō* [1]

PROVIDES [3]

provides with plenty, *1855, empimplēmi* [1]
provides with, *4218, parechō* [1]
provides, *5961, chorēgeō* [1]

PROVINCE [19]

province of Asia, *823, Asia* [15]
province, *2065, eparcheia* [2]
from the province of Asia, *824, Asianos* [1]
officials of the province, *825, Asiarchēs* [1]

PROVINCES [1]

provinces of Cilicia, *3070, Kilikia* [1]

PROVING [3]

proving, *2109, epideiknymi* [1]
proving, *4192, paratithēmi* [1]
proving, *5204, symbibazō* [1]

PROVISION [1]

abundant provision, *4353, perisseia* [1]

PROVOKING [1]

provoking, *4614, prokaleō* [1]

PROWLS [1]

prowls around, *4344, peripateō* [1]

PRUNES [1]

prunes, *2748, kathairō* [1]

PSALM [1]

Psalm, *6011, psalmos* [1]

PSALMS [5]

psalms, *6011, psalmos* [5]

PTOLEMAIS [1]

Ptolemais, *4767, Ptolemais* [1]

PUBLIC [11]

public, *1323, dēmosios* [2]
public reading, *342, anagnōsis* [1]

expose to public disgrace, *1258, deigmatizō* [1]
delivered a public address, *1319, dēmēgoreō* [1]
a public figure, *1877+4244, en+parrēsia* [1]
in public, *1883+3836+3295,*
  enantion+ho+laos [1]
public, *3295, laos* [1]
director of public works, *3874, oikonomos* [1]
subjecting to public disgrace, *4136,*
  paradeigmatizō [1]
public, *4244, parrēsia* [1]

PUBLICLY [11]

publicly, *4244, parrēsia* [3]
publicly, *1323, dēmosios* [2]
publicly, *1967+4246, enōpion+pas* [2]
appeared publicly, *345, anadeixis* [1]
publicly, *1967+3836+4436,*
  enōpion+ho+plēthos [1]
publicly exposed, *2518, theatrizō* [1]
publicly, *5747, phaneros* [1]

PUBLIUS [1]

Publius, *4511, Poplios* [1]

PUDENS [1]

Pudens, *4545, Poudēs* [1]

PUFFS [2]

puffs up, *5881, physioō* [2]

PULL [4]

pull away, *149, airō* [2]
pull out, *413, anaspaō* [1]
pull up, *5198, syllegō* [1]

PULLED [5]

pulled up, *328, anabibazō* [1]
pulled up, *413, anaspaō* [1]
pulled up by the roots, *1748, ekrizoō* [1]
pulled up, *2864, katagō* [1]
pulled up, *5198, syllegō* [1]

PULLING [2]

pulling down, *2746, kathairesis* [1]
pulling, *5198, syllegō* [1]

PUNISH [7]

punish, *1443+1689, didōmi+ekdikēsis* [1]
punish, *1688, ekdikeō* [1]
punish, *1689, ekdikēsis* [1]
punish, *1690, ekdikos* [1]
punish, *3134, kolazō* [1]
punish, *3212, krinō* [1]
punish, *4084, paideuō* [1]

PUNISHED [8]

punished, *3284+3210, lambanō+krima* [2]
punished, *5512, timōreō* [2]
punished, *RPE* [1]
punished, *1472+5514, dikē+tinō* [1]
punished, *4084, paideuō* [1]
punished, *5513, timōria* [1]

PUNISHES [1]

punishes, *3463, mastigoō* [1]

PUNISHMENT [11]

punishment, *3136, kolasis* [2]
punishment, *1472, dikē* [1]
punishment, *1689, ekdikēsis* [1]
agent to bring punishment, *1690, ekdikos* [1]
punishment, *2204, epitimia* [1]

punishment, *3134, kolazō* [1]
punishment, *3210, krima* [1]
punishment, *3632, misthapodosia* [1]
punishment, *3973, orgē* [1]
punishment, *4435, plēgē* [1]

PURCHASED [2]

purchased, *60, agorazō* [2]

PURE [27]

pure, *2754, katharos* [11]
pure, *54, hagnos* [6]
pure, *299, amiantos* [2]
pure, *4410, pistikos* [2]
pure, *55, hagnotēs* [1]
pure, *100, adolos* [1]
pure, *193, akeraios* [1]
pure, *1637, eilikrinēs* [1]
pure, *4221, parthenos* [1]
pure, *4246, pas* [1]

PURIFICATION [4]

purification, *2752, katharismos* [2]
purification rites, *49, hagnizō* [1]
purification, *50, hagnismos* [1]

PURIFIED [4]

purified, *49, hagnizō* [2]
purified, *2751, katharizō* [2]

PURIFIES [2]

purifies, *49, hagnizō* [1]
purifies, *2751, katharizō* [1]

PURIFY [4]

purify, *2751, katharizō* [3]
purify, *49, hagnizō* [1]

PURITY [4]

purity, *48, hagneia* [2]
purity, *54, hagnos* [1]
purity, *55, hagnotēs* [1]

PURPLE [9]

purple, *4528, porphyrous* [4]
purple robe, *4525, porphyra* [2]
purple, *4525, porphyra* [2]
dealer in purple cloth, *4527, porphyropōlis* [1]

PURPOSE [26]

purpose, *1087, boulē* [6]
purpose, *4606, prothesis* [5]
for purpose, *1650, eis* [4]
purpose, *1191, gnōmē* [2]
purpose, *AIT* [1]
purpose, *NIG* [1]
for the express purpose, *1650+899+4047,*
  eis+autos+houtos [1]
purpose, *1877, en* [1]
good purpose, *2306, eudokia* [1]
purpose, *2306, eudokia* [1]
purpose that, *2671, hina* [1]
purpose, *2671, hina* [1]
purpose, *5858, phroneō* [1]

PURPOSED [1]

purposed, *4729, protithēmi* [1]

PURPOSELY [1]

purposely, *2527, thelō* [1]

QUESTION

question, *3306, legō* [1]
beyond all question, *3935,*
   homologoumenōs [1]
question, *4785, pynthanomai* [1]

QUESTIONED [5]

questioned, *2089, eperōtaō* [2]
questioned, *2263, erōtaō* [2]
questioned, *458, anetazō* [1]

QUESTIONING [1]

questioning, *2263, erōtaō* [1]

QUESTIONS [11]

raising questions, *373, anakrinō* [2]
ask questions, *2089, eperōtaō* [2]
questions, *2427, zētēma* [2]
besiege with questions, *694+4309+4498,*
   apostomatizō+peri+polys [1]
asking questions, *2089, eperōtaō* [1]
ask questions, *2263, erōtaō* [1]
questions, *3364, logos* [1]
questions⁵, *4029, oudeis* [1]

QUICK [4]

quick, *5444, tachys* [2]
quick, *1877+5443, en+tachos* [1]
quick, *5067, speudō* [1]

QUICK-TEMPERED [1]

quick-tempered, *3975, orgilos* [1]

QUICKLY [16]

quickly, *5441, tacheōs* [6]
quickly, *2317, euthys¹* [4]
quickly, *5444, tachys* [3]
quickly, *1877+5443, en+tachos* [1]
quickly, *2311, eutheōs* [1]
so quickly, *4202, parachrēma* [1]

QUIET [16]

quiet, *4995, siōpaō* [5]
quiet, *4967, sigaō* [3]
quiet, *2485, hēsychios* [2]
quiet, *5821, phimoō* [2]
quiet, *2245, erēmos* [1]
lead a quiet life, *2483, hēsychazō* [1]
quiet, *2484, hēsychia* [1]
quiet, *2948, katastello* [1]

QUIETED [1]

quieted, *2948, katastellō* [1]

QUIETLY [2]

quietly, *3277, lathra* [2]

QUIETNESS [1]

quietness, *2484, hēsychia* [1]

QUIRINIUS [1]

Quirinius, *3256, Kyrēnios* [1]

QUITE [4]

quite, *AIT* [2]
quite, *4122, pantōs* [1]
quite boldly, *5529, tolmēros* [1]

QUOTE [1]

quote, *3306, legō* [1]

RABBI [16]

Rabbi, *4806, rhabbi* [15]
Rabbi, *4808, rhabbouni* [1]

RABBONI [1]

Rabboni, *4808, rhabbouni* [1]

RACA [1]

Raca, *4819, rhaka* [1]

RACE [7]

race, *1536, dromos* [2]
a race, [1]
race, *74, agōn* [1]
race, *5084, stadion* [1]
race, *5150+2848+4922,*
   syngenēs+kata+sarx [1]
run race, *5556, trechō* [1]

RACHEL [1]

Rachel, *4830, Rhachēl* [1]

RADIANCE [2]

radiance, *575, apaugasma* [1]
radiance⁵, *5465, telos* [1]

RADIANT [1]

radiant, *1902, endoxos* [1]

RAGE [4]

rage, *2596, thymos* [2]
fits of rage, *2596, thymos* [1]
rage, *5865, phryassō* [1]

RAGING [3]

raging, *2419, zēlos* [1]
raging, *3114, klydōn* [1]
continued raging, *4024+3900+2130,*
   ou+oligos+epikeimai [1]

RAGS [1]

in rags, *1217, gymniteuō* [1]

RAHAB [3]

Rahab, *4805, Rhaab* [2]
Rahab, *4829, Rhachab* [1]

RAIN [11]

rain, *1101, brechō* [3]
rain, *5624, hyetos* [3]
rain, *1104, brochē* [2]
without rain, *536, anydros* [1]
sends rain, *1101, brechō* [1]
going to rain, *3915+2262,*
   ombros+erchomai [1]

RAINBOW [2]

rainbow, *2692, iris* [2]

RAINED [1]

rained, *1101, brechō* [1]

RAINING [1]

raining, *5624, hyetos* [1]

RAINS [1]

spring [rains], *4069, opsimos* [1]
autumn rains, *4611, proimos* [1]

RAISE [16]

raise up, *482, anistēmi* [5]
raise, *1586, egeirō* [5]
raise up, *1586, egeirō* [3]
raise, *NIG* [1]
raise again, *1586, egeirō* [1]
raise, *1995, exegeirō* [1]

RAISED [75]

raised, *1586, egeirō* [45]
raised to life, *1586, egeirō* [7]
raised from the dead, *1586, egeirō* [6]
raised, *149, airō* [2]
raised, *2048, epairō* [2]
raised to life again, *414, anastasis* [1]
raised again, *482, anistēmi* [1]
raised from the dead, *482, anistēmi* [1]
raised to life, *482, anistēmi* [1]
raised up, *482, anistēmi* [1]
raised, *482, anistēmi* [1]
raised again, *1586, egeirō* [1]
raised up, *1586, egeirō* [1]
raised up, *1995, exegeirō* [1]
raised havoc, *4514, portheō* [1]
raised up with, *5283, synegeirō* [1]
raised with, *5283, synegeirō* [1]
raised, *5283, synegeirō* [1]

RAISES [3]

raises, *1586, egeirō* [3]

RAISING [5]

raising questions, *373, anakrinō* [2]
without raising any objection, *395,*
   anantirrētōs [1]
raising up, *482, anistēmi* [1]
raising, *482, anistēmi* [1]

RALLIED [1]

rallied, *4679, prosklinō* [1]

RAM [3]

Ram, *730, Aram* [3]

RAMAH [1]

Ramah, *4821, Rhama* [1]

RAN [19]

ran, *5556, trechō* [6]
ran off, *5771, pheugō* [3]
ran up to, *4708, prostrechō* [2]
ran back, *1661, eistrechō* [1]
ran out of, *1767+1666, ekpheugō+ek* [1]
ran aground, *2131, epikellō* [1]
ran down, *2963, katatrechō* [1]
ran throughout, *4366, peritrechō* [1]
ran, *4708, prostrechō* [1]
ran, *4731, protrechō* [1]
ran, *5340, syntrechō* [1]

RANG [2]

rang out, *1181, ginomai* [1]
rang out, *2010, exēcheō* [1]

RANKING [1]

high ranking officers, *5941, chiliarchos* [1]

RANKS [1]

infiltrated ranks, *4207+4209,*
   pareisaktos+pareiserchomai [1]

RANSOM [4]

ransom, *3389, lytron* [2]
ransom, *519, antilytron* [1]
ransom, *667, apolytrōsis* [1]

RAPIDLY [2]

rapidly, *5379, sphodra* [1]
spread rapidly, *5556, trechō* [1]

RARELY [1]

very rarely, *3660, molis* [1]

RASH [2]

rash, *4637, propetēs* [2]

RATHER [42]

rather, *3437, mallon* [14]
rather, *247, alla* [11]
but rather, *247, alla* [4]
rather, *1254+3437, de+mallon* [2]
rather, *1254, de* [2]
rather than, *2779+4024, kai+ou* [2]
rather than, *4123, para* [2]
rather, *1142, gar* [1]
would rather, *2527, thelō* [1]
rather than, *2671+3590, hina+mē* [1]
rather than, *2779+3590, kai+mē* [1]
rather, *3528, menoun* [1]

RAVENS [1]

ravens, *3165, korax* [1]

RAVING [1]

raving mad, *3419, mainomai* [1]

REACH [7]

reach, *2918, katantaō* [2]
reach, *1181+1650, ginomai+eis* [1]
reach, *4725, prosōpon* [1]
reach goal, *5457, teleioō* [1]
reach out, *5770, pherō* [1]
reach out for, *6027, psēlaphaō* [1]

REACHED [24]

reached out, *1753, ekteinō* [4]
reached, *2262+1650, erchomai+eis* [4]
reached, *1181+2093, ginomai+epi* [2]
reached, *2262+2093, erchomai+epi* [2]
reached, *2262, erchomai* [2]
reached, *AIT* [1]
reached, *201+1650, akouō+eis* [1]
reached, *326, anabainō* [1]
reached, *1181, ginomai* [1]
reached, *1650+1656, eis+eiserchomai* [1]
reached for, *1753+3836+5931,*
*   ekteinō+ho+cheir* [1]
reached, *2093, epi* [1]
reached, *2918, katantaō* [1]
reached, *3212, krinō* [1]
reached, *4472, poieō* [1]

REACHES [1]

reaches, *2391, ephikneomai* [1]

REACHING [6]

reaching, *1181+2093, ginomai+epi* [1]
reaching, *2262+1650, erchomai+eis* [1]
reaching, *2400, echō* [1]
reaching more and more,
*   4429+1328+3836+4498,*
*   pleonazō+dia+ho+polys* [1]
a robe reaching down to feet, *4468, podērēs* [1]

reaching ahead of, *4575, proagō* [1]

READ [28]

read, *336, anaginōskō* [24]
read, *NIG* [1]
read, *342, anagnōsis* [1]
read, *1639+1211, eimi+graphō* [1]
read, *1639+2108, eimi+epigraphō* [1]

READER [2]

reader, *336, anaginōskō* [2]

READILY [1]

readily, *AIT* [1]

READINESS [2]

readiness to see justice done, *1689, ekdikēsis* [1]
readiness, *2288, hetoimasia* [1]

READING [7]

reading, *336, anaginōskō* [5]
public reading, *342, anagnōsis* [1]
reading, *342, anagnōsis* [1]

READS [1]

reads, *336, anaginōskō* [1]

READY [37]

ready, *2289, hetoimos* [14]
get ready, *2286, hetoimazō* [3]
ready, *2290, hetoimōs* [3]
ready, *1538, dynamai* [2]
ready, *4186, paraskeuazō* [2]
ready, *AIT* [1]
got ready, *482, anistēmi* [1]
got ready, *2171, episkeuazomai* [1]
kept ready, *2286, hetoimazō* [1]
made ready, *2286, hetoimazō* [1]
make ready, *2286, hetoimazō* [1]
got ready, *2426, zēteō* [1]
ready, *2426, zēteō* [1]
dressed ready for service, *3836+4019+4322,*
*   ho+osphys+perizōnnymi* [1]
ready[s], *4048, houtōs* [1]
get ready, *4186, paraskeuazō* [1]
get ready, *4322, perizōnnymi* [1]
ready, *4674, proskartereō* [1]

REAFFIRM [1]

reaffirm, *3263, kyroō* [1]

REAL [3]

real, *239, alēthēs* [3]

REALITIES [1]

realities, *1635+3836+4547,*
*   eikōn+ho+pragma* [1]

REALITY [1]

reality, *5393, sōma* [1]

REALIZE [15]

realize, *3857, oida* [8]
realize, *3357, logizomai* [2]
realize, *1182, ginōskō* [1]
realize, *2105, epiginōskō* [1]
realize, *2898, katalambanō* [1]
realize, *3630, mimnēskomai* [1]
realize, *5317, syniēmi* [1]

REALIZED [10]

realized, *3972, horaō* [4]
realized, *2105, epiginōskō* [3]
realized, *1182, ginōskō* [1]
realized that, *2105, epiginōskō* [1]
realized, *2898, katalambanō* [1]

REALIZING [1]

not realizing, *51, agnoeō* [1]

REALLY [21]

really, *AIT* [7]
really, *242, alēthōs* [3]
really in need, *3953, ontōs* [3]
really, *1145, ge* [2]
really, *3953, ontōs* [2]
really, *NIG* [1]
really, *239, alēthēs* [1]
really, *3437, mallon* [1]
really, *3530, mentoi* [1]

REALMS [5]

heavenly realms, *2230, epouranios* [5]

REAP [14]

reap, *2545, therizō* [10]
reap, *2400, echō* [2]
reap a harvest, *2545, therizō* [1]
reap harvest, *2545, therizō* [1]

REAPED [1]

reaped the benefits of, *1650+1656,*
*   eis+eiserchomai* [1]

REAPER [2]

reaper, *2545, therizō* [2]

REAPING [1]

reaping, *2545, therizō* [1]

REAPS [2]

reaps, *2545, therizō* [2]

REASON [45]

for this reason, *1328+4047, dia+houtos* [9]
the reason, *1328+4047, dia+houtos* [5]
reason, *162, aitia* [3]
reason, *2671, hina* [3]
reason, *NIG* [2]
the reason, *1650+4047, eis+houtos* [2]
for reason, *1915, heneken* [2]
for this reason, *4047+5920, houtos+charin* [2]
for that reason, *4123+4047, para+houtos* [2]
reason, *AIT* [1]
reason, *165, aitios* [1]
for this reason, *505+4047, anti+houtos* [1]
for this very reason, *899+4047,*
*   autos+houtos* [1]
for that very reason, *1328+4047, dia+houtos* [1]
for this very reason, *1328+4047, dia+houtos* [1]
for this reason, *1475, dio* [1]
without reason, *1562, dōrean* [1]
for this reason, *1650+4047, eis+houtos* [1]
this is the reason, *1650+4047, eis+houtos* [1]
this very reason, *1650+4047, eis+houtos* [1]
without reason, *3036, kenōs* [1]
reason, *3364, logos* [1]
for this reason, *3854, hothen* [1]
the reason, *4047+5920, houtos+charin* [1]

REASONABLE [2]

reasonable, *2848+3364, kata+logos* [1]

reasonable, *5408, sōphrosynē* [1]

REASONED [6]

reasoned, *1363, dialegomai* [4]
reasoned, *3357, logizomai* [2]

REASONS [3]

reasons, *AIT* [2]
for reasons, *2848, kata* [1]

REBEKAH'S [1]

Rebekah's, *4831, Rhebekka* [1]

REBEL [2]

rebel against, *2060+2093, epanistēmi+epi* [2]

REBELLED [1]

rebelled, *4176, parapikrainō* [1]

REBELLING [1]

rebelling against, *468, anthistēmi* [1]

REBELLION [9]

leading a rebellion, *3334, lēstēs* [3]
rebellion, *4177, parapikrasmos* [2]
rebellion, *517, antilogia* [1]
rebellion, *686, apostasia* [1]
inciting to rebellion, *695, apostrephō* [1]
had taken part in a rebellion, *1639+3334,
   eimi+lēstēs* [1]

REBELLIOUS [1]

rebellious, *538, anypotaktos* [1]

REBELS [2]

rebels against, *530, antitassō* [1]
rebels, *538, anypotaktos* [1]

REBIRTH [1]

rebirth, *4098, palingenesia* [1]

REBUILD [4]

rebuild, *488, anoikodomeō* [2]
rebuild, *3868, oikodomeō* [1]
rebuild, *4099+3868, palin+oikodomeō* [1]

REBUKE [10]

rebuke, *2203, epitimaō* [6]
rebuke, *1794, elenchō* [3]
rebuke harshly, *2159, epiplēssō* [1]

REBUKED [22]

rebuked, *2203, epitimaō* [17]
rebuked, *1794, elenchō* [2]
rebuked, *1792, elenxis* [1]
rebuked harshly, *1839, embrimaomai* [1]
rebuked, *3943, oneidizō* [1]

REBUKES [1]

rebukes, *1794, elenchō* [1]

REBUKING [1]

rebuking, *1791, elegmos* [1]

RECALL [1]

recall, *3630, mimnēskomai* [1]

RECALLED [1]

recalled, *3630, mimnēskomai* [1]

RECALLING [1]

recalling, *3630, mimnēskomai* [1]

RECEDED [1]

receded, *714, apochōrizō* [1]

RECEIVE [72]

receive, *3284, lambanō* [38]
receive, *1312, dechomai* [6]
receive sight, *329, anablepō* [4]
receive, *655, apolambanō* [2]
receive, *3152, komizō* [2]
receive, *4161, paralambanō* [2]
receive from, *608+655, apo+apolambanō* [1]
baptism receive, *966, baptizō* [1]
receive, *1181, ginomai* [1]
receive news, *1182, ginōskō* [1]
receive, *1443, didōmi* [1]
receive, *1639, eimi* [1]
receive, *1650, eis* [1]
receive, *1654, eisdechomai* [1]
receive mercy, *1796, eleeō* [1]
receive, *2220, epichorēgeō* [1]
receive living, *2409, zaō* [1]
receive a beating, *3139, kolaphizō* [1]
receive back, *3152, komizō* [1]
receive what is due, *3152, komizō* [1]
receive a share, *3561, metalambanō* [1]
receive, *4348, peripoiēsis* [1]
receive, *4657, prosdechomai* [1]
receive the victor's crown, *5110, stephanoō* [1]

RECEIVED [89]

received, *3284, lambanō* [37]
received, *4161, paralambanō* [7]
received sight, *329, anablepō* [5]
received, *1312, dechomai* [5]
received, *NIG* [3]
received in full, *600, apechō* [3]
received mercy, *1796, eleeō* [3]
received seed that fell, *5062, speirō* [3]
received, *RPE* [2]
received, *655, apolambanō* [2]
received, *346, anadechomai* [1]
received payment, *600, apechō* [1]
received, *600, apechō* [1]
received, *622, apodechomai* [1]
received, *1342, diadechomai* [1]
received permission, *2205, epitrepō* [1]
received, *2209, epitynchanō* [1]
received, *2400, echō* [1]
calling received, *3104+2813, klēsis+kaleō* [1]
received back, *3152, komizō* [1]
received, *3152, komizō* [1]
received, *3275, lanchanō* [1]
received with, *3562+3552,
   metalēmpsis+meta* [1]
received[8], *3931, homoiōs* [1]
received, *4151, parakaleō* [1]
received from, *4161+4123,
   paralambanō+para* [1]
received, *5593, tynchanō* [1]
received light, *5894, phōtizō* [1]
help received, *6067, ōpheleō* [1]

RECEIVES [15]

receives, *3284, lambanō* [7]
receives, *1312, dechomai* [6]
receives instruction in, *2994, katēcheō* [1]
receives, *3561, metalambanō* [1]

RECEIVING [8]

receiving, *3284, lambanō* [3]

receiving, *1312, dechomai* [1]
receiving, *3152, komizō* [1]
receiving, *3331, lēmpsis* [1]
receiving of the law, *3792, nomothesia* [1]
receiving, *4161, paralambanō* [1]

RECENT [1]

recent convert, *3745, neophytos* [1]

RECENTLY [1]

recently, *4711, prosphatōs* [1]

RECEPTION [1]

reception, *1658, eisodos* [1]

RECKONED [2]

reckoned, *2813, kaleō* [2]

RECLINE [1]

have recline at the table, *369, anaklinō* [1]

RECLINED [3]

reclined at the table, *404, anapiptō* [2]
reclined at the table, *2884, kataklinō* [1]

RECLINING [6]

reclining at the table, *367, anakeimai* [4]
reclining, *367, anakeimai* [1]
reclining at the table, *2879, katakeimai* [1]

RECOGNITION [2]

recognition, *2105, epiginōskō* [1]
give recognition to, *5506, timaō* [1]

RECOGNIZE [10]

recognize, *1182, ginōskō* [4]
recognize, *2105, epiginōskō* [4]
not recognize, *51, agnoeō* [1]
recognize, *3857, oida* [1]

RECOGNIZED [11]

recognized, *2105, epiginōskō* [6]
recognized, *1182, ginōskō* [4]
recognized, *5743, phainō* [1]

RECOGNIZING [2]

recognizing, *1359, diakrinō* [1]
recognizing, *2105, epiginōskō* [1]

RECOMMENDATION [1]

recommendation, *5364, systatikos* [1]

RECONCILE [3]

reconcile, *639, apokatallassō* [2]
reconcile, *5261+1650+1645,
   synallassō+eis+eirēnē* [1]

RECONCILED [8]

reconciled, *2904, katallassō* [5]
reconciled to, *557+608, apallassō+apo* [1]
reconciled, *639, apokatallassō* [1]
reconciled, *1367, diallassomai* [1]

RECONCILIATION [4]

reconciliation, *2903, katallagē* [4]

RECONCILING [1]

reconciling, *2904, katallassō* [1]

RECORD [2]

record, *1047, biblos* [1]
record of, *3357, logizomai* [1]

RECORDED [2]

recorded, *1211, graphō* [2]

RECOVERED [1]

recovered, *2351, heuriskō* [1]

RECOVERY [2]

recovery, *AIT* [1]
recovery of sight, *330, anablepsis* [1]

RED [8]

red, *2261, erythros* [2]
red, *4793, pyrrazō* [2]
fiery red, *4791, pyrinos* [1]
fiery red, *4794, pyrros* [1]
red, *4794, pyrros* [1]
blood red, *6055+135, hōs+haima* [1]

REDEEM [3]

redeem, *3390, lytroō* [2]
redeem, *1973, exagorazō* [1]

REDEEMED [5]

redeemed, *RPE* [1]
redeemed, *60, agorazō* [1]
redeemed from, *1973+1666, exagorazō+ek* [1]
redeemed, *3390, lytroō* [1]
redeemed, *4472+3391, poieō+lytrōsis* [1]

REDEMPTION [10]

redemption, *667, apolytrōsis* [8]
redemption, *3391, lytrōsis* [2]

REED [4]

reed, *2812, kalamos* [4]

REFER [1]

refer, *AIT* [1]

REFERRED [1]

referred, *AIT* [1]

REFERRING [1]

referring, *3306, legō* [1]

REFINED [2]

refined, *1507, dokimazō* [1]
refined, *4792, pyroō* [1]

REFLECT [2]

reflect, *3002, katoptrizō* [1]
reflect on, *3783, noeō* [1]

REFLECTION [1]

poor reflection, *141, ainigma* [1]

REFORMS [1]

reforms, *1480, diorthōma* [1]

REFRAIN [1]

refrain, *5767, pheidomai* [1]

REFRESH [2]

refresh, *399, anapauō* [1]
refresh, *1444, diegeirō* [1]

REFRESHED [5]

refreshed, *399, anapauō* [3]
refreshed, *434, anapsychō* [1]
together refreshed, *5265, synanapauomai* [1]

REFRESHING [1]

refreshing, *433, anapsyxis* [1]

REFUSAL [1]

refusal, *4024, ou* [1]

REFUSE [8]

refuse, *4148, paraiteomai* [2]
refuse, *119, atheteō* [1]
refuse to accept, *2024, exoutheneō* [1]
refuse, *4024+2527, ou+thelō* [1]
refuse, *4024+918, ou+aphiēmi* [1]
refuse, *4024, ou* [1]
refuse, *4370, peripsēma* [1]

REFUSED [15]

refused, *4024+2527, ou+thelō* [6]
refused to believe, *578, apeitheō* [2]
refused to repent, *4024+3566,
   ou+metanoeō* [2]
refused, *766, arneomai* [1]
refused to worship, *3590+4686,
   mē+proskyneō* [1]
refused, *4024+1312, ou+dechomai* [1]
refused, *4024+4657, ou+prosdechomai* [1]
refused, *4148, paraiteomai* [1]

REFUSES [3]

refuses to listen, *4159, parakouō* [2]
refuses to, *4046, oute* [1]

REFUSING [1]

refusing, *4024+2527, ou+thelō* [1]

REFUTE [1]

refute, *1794, elenchō* [1]

REFUTED [1]

refuted, *1352, diakatelenchomai* [1]

REGAINED [1]

regained strength, *1932, enischyō* [1]

REGARD [18]

in regard to, *4309, peri* [5]
regard, *AIT* [4]
regard, *3357, logizomai* [2]
in regard to, *1650, eis* [1]
with regard to, *1877+3538, en+meros* [1]
regard, *2451, hēgeomai* [1]
in regard to, *2848, kata* [1]
with regard to, *2848, kata* [1]
regard, *3857, oida* [1]
highest regard, *5655, hyperekperissou* [1]

REGARDED [8]

regarded, *3357, logizomai* [2]
regarded as, *6055, hōs* [2]
regarded, *1182, ginōskō* [1]
regarded, *1506, dokeō* [1]
regarded, *2451, hēgeomai* [1]
highly regarded, *3486, megalynō* [1]

REGARDING [2]

regarding, *1650, eis* [1]
regarding, *4309, peri* [1]

REGARDS [2]

regards, *3357, logizomai* [1]
regards as special, *5858, phroneō* [1]

REGIMENT [2]

regiment, *5061, speira* [2]

REGION [25]

region, *6001, chōra* [8]
region, *3990, horion* [6]
region, *3538, meros* [3]
region, *4369, perichōros* [3]
region, *1178, gē* [2]
desert region, *2245, erēmos* [1]
region across, *4305, peran* [1]
region of Sidon, *4973, Sidōnios* [1]

REGIONS [5]

regions, *3107, klima* [2]
regions, *3538, meros* [1]
regions across, *4305, peran* [1]
regions beyond, *5654, hyperekeina* [1]

REGISTER [2]

register, *616, apographō* [2]

REGRET [3]

regret, *3564, metamelomai* [2]
no regret, *294, ametamelētos* [1]

REGULARLY [2]

regularly, *1328+4246, dia+pas* [2]

REGULATION [2]

regulation, *1953, entolē* [1]
regulation, *3795+1953, nomos+entolē* [1]

REGULATIONS [6]

regulations, *1468, dikaiōma* [3]
regulations, *1504, dogma* [2]
such regulations[s], *4015, hostis* [1]

REHOBOAM [2]

Rehoboam, *4850, Rhoboam* [2]

REIGN [13]

reign, *996, basileuō* [10]
reign, *AIT* [1]
reign, *2449, hēgemonia* [1]
reign with, *5203, symbasileuō* [1]

REIGNED [4]

reigned, *996, basileuō* [4]

REIGNING [1]

reigning, *996, basileuō* [1]

REIGNS [2]

reigns, *996, basileuō* [1]
reigns, *2026, exousia* [1]

REIMBURSE [1]

reimburse, *625, apodidōmi* [1]

REIN [1]

keep a tight rein on, *5902, chalinagōgeō* [1]

REJECT [8]

reject, *723, apōtheō* [3]
reject, *119, atheteō* [2]

reject, *578, apeitheō* [1]
reject, *695, apostrephō* [1]
reject, *1675, ekballō* [1]

REJECTED [18]

rejected, *627, apodokimazō* [9]
rejected, *119, atheteō* [2]
rejected, *723, apōtheō* [2]
rejected, *99, adokimos* [1]
rejected, *612, apoblētos* [1]
rejected, *766, arneomai* [1]
rejected, *2022, exoudeneō* [1]
rejected, *2024, exoutheneō* [1]

REJECTION [1]

rejection, *613, apobolē* [1]

REJECTS [7]

rejects, *119, atheteō* [6]
rejects, *578, apeitheō* [1]

REJOICE [30]

rejoice, *5897, chairō* [17]
rejoice with, *5176, synchairō* [4]
rejoice, *2370, euphrainō* [3]
rejoice, *3016, kauchaomai* [3]
rejoice, *RPE* [1]
greatly rejoice, *22, agalliaō* [1]
make rejoice, *5897, chairō* [1]

REJOICED [1]

rejoiced, *22, agalliaō* [1]

REJOICES [5]

rejoices, *22, agalliaō* [2]
rejoices with, *5176, synchairō* [2]
rejoices, *5897, chairō* [1]

REJOICING [5]

rejoicing, *5897, chairō* [3]
rejoicing, *5915, chara* [2]

RELATED [2]

related, *AIT* [1]
related⁸ trades, *5525, toioutos* [1]

RELATIONS [3]

relations, *5979, chrēsis* [2]
relations, *AIT* [1]

RELATIONSHIP [1]

relationship to, *1877, en* [1]

RELATIVE [3]

relative, *5150, syngenēs* [2]
relative, *5151, syngenis* [1]

RELATIVES [10]

relatives, *5150, syngenēs* [8]
his relatives, *2625, idios* [1]
relatives, *5149, syngeneia* [1]

RELEASE [17]

release, *668, apolyō* [15]
release, *690+1877+912,*
  apostellō+en+aphesis [1]
release, *3395, lyō* [1]

RELEASED [13]

released, *668, apolyō* [5]
released, *3395, lyō* [3]

released, *2934, katargeō* [2]
released, *667, apolytrōsis* [1]
released, *1801, eleutheros* [1]
released, *5919, charizomai* [1]

RELIABLE [2]

reliable, *239, alēthēs* [1]
reliable, *4412, pistos* [1]

RELIEF [1]

relief, *457, anesis* [1]

RELIEVED [1]

relieved, *457, anesis* [1]

RELIGION [5]

religion, *2579, thrēskeia* [3]
religion, *1272, deisidaimonia* [1]
put religion into practice by caring for, *2355,*
  eusebeō [1]

RELIGIOUS [4]

very religious, *1273, deisidaimōn* [1]
religious festival, *2038, heortē* [1]
religious, *2580, thrēskos* [1]
performs religious duties, *3310, leitourgeō* [1]

RELUCTANTLY [1]

reluctantly, *1666+3383, ek+lypē* [1]

RELY [4]

rely on, *1666+1639, ek+eimi* [1]
rely on, *2058, epanapauomai* [1]
rely, *4275+1639, peithō+eimi* [1]
rely on, *4409, pisteuō* [1]

REMAIN [39]

remain, *3531, menō* [24]
remain, *1639, eimi* [3]
remain, *RPE* [2]
remain, *1373, diamenō* [2]
remain, *AIT* [1]
remain, *1312, dechomai* [1]
remain faithful to, *1844+1877, emmenō+en* [1]
remain true to, *1844, emmenō* [1]
remain, *2152, epimenō* [1]
remain true to, *3195, krateō* [1]
debt remain outstanding, *4053, opheilō* [1]
remain, *4693, prosmenō* [1]

REMAINED [10]

remained, *AIT* [6]
remained, *3531, menō* [2]
remained, *1373, diamenō* [1]
remained, *1417, diatribō* [1]

REMAINING [1]

remaining, *NIG* [1]

REMAINS [15]

remains, *3531, menō* [11]
remains, *657, apoleipō* [2]
remains, *AIT* [1]
remains, *3370, loipos* [1]

REMARKABLE [2]

remarkable, *2515, thaumastos* [1]
remarkable, *4141, paradoxos* [1]

REMARKED [1]

remarked, *RPE* [1]

REMARKING [1]

remarking, *3306, legō* [1]

REMEMBER [36]

remember, *3648, mnēmoneuō* [16]
remember, *3630, mimnēskomai* [10]
remember, *3644+4472, mneia+poieō* [2]
remember, *RPE* [1]
remember, *389, anamimnēskō* [1]
remember, *1182, ginōskō* [1]
remember, *2400+3644, echō+mneia* [1]
remember, *3644, mneia* [1]
remember, *3647+4472, mnēmē+poieō* [1]
remember, *3857, oida* [1]
remember this, *4047+1254, houtos+de* [1]

REMEMBERED [10]

remembered, *3630, mimnēskomai* [6]
remembered, *389, anamimnēskō* [2]
remembered, *3648, mnēmoneuō* [1]
remembered, *5703, hypomimnēskō* [1]

REMEMBERING [4]

remembering, *3630, mimnēskomai* [2]
remembering, *3644+4472, mneia+poieō* [1]
remembering, *3648, mnēmoneuō* [1]

REMEMBERS [1]

remembers, *389, anamimnēskō* [1]

REMEMBRANCE [3]

remembrance, *390, anamnēsis* [3]

REMIND [8]

remind, *5703, hypomimnēskō* [3]
remind of, *389, anamimnēskō* [1]
remind, *389, anamimnēskō* [1]
remind of, *1192, gnōrizō* [1]
remind again, *2057, epanamimnēskō* [1]
remind of, *5703, hypomimnēskō* [1]

REMINDED [1]

reminded, *5704+3284,*
  hypomnēsis+lambanō [1]

REMINDER [1]

reminder, *390, anamnēsis* [1]

REMINDERS [1]

reminders, *5704, hypomnēsis* [1]

REMINDING [1]

reminding of, *5703, hypomimnēskō* [1]

REMNANT [3]

remnant, *2905, kataloipos* [1]
remnant, *3307, leimma* [1]
remnant, *5698, hypoleimma* [1]

REMORSE [1]

seized with remorse, *3564, metamelomai* [1]

REMOTE [5]

remote, *2245, erēmos* [3]
remote place, *2244, erēmia* [2]

REMOVAL [1]

removal from, *629, apothesis* [1]

REMOVE [3]

remove from, *1675+1666, ekballō+ek* [1]
remove from, *1675, ekballō* [1]
remove, *3075, kineō* [1]

REMOVED [3]

removed, *149, airō* [1]
removed, *365, anakalyptō* [1]
removed, *3075, kineō* [1]

REMOVING [2]

removing, *3496, methistēmi* [1]
removing, *3557, metathesis* [1]

RENEWAL [2]

renewal, *364, anakainōsis* [1]
renewal, *4098, palingenesia* [1]

RENEWED [3]

renewed, *363, anakainoō* [2]
renewed, *352, anathallō* [1]

RENEWING [1]

renewing, *364, anakainōsis* [1]

RENOUNCE [1]

renounce, *766, arneomai* [1]

RENOUNCED [2]

renounced, *584, apeipon* [1]
renounced marriage, *2336+2335+1571,*
eunouchos+eunouchizō+heautou [1]

RENT [1]

rent, *1686, ekdidōmi* [1]

RENTED [4]

rented, *1686, ekdidōmi* [3]
rented house, *3637, misthōma* [1]

REPAID [4]

repaid, *500, antapodidōmi* [1]
repaid, *501, antapodoma* [1]
repaid, *655, apolambanō* [1]
repaid, *3152, komizō* [1]

REPAY [9]

repay, *500, antapodidōmi* [4]
repay, *625, apodidōmi* [3]
repay the debt, *625, apodidōmi* [1]
repay, *1443, didōmi* [1]

REPAYING [1]

repaying, *304+625, amoibē+apodidōmi* [1]

REPAYMENT [1]

repayment, *3284, lambanō* [1]

REPEAT [2]

repeat, *4099+3306, palin+legō* [1]
repeat, *4625, prolegō* [1]

REPEATED [1]

repeated[s], *4712, prospherō* [1]

REPEATEDLY [1]

repeatedly, *AIT* [1]

REPENT [27]

repent, *3566, metanoeō* [23]

refused to repent, *4024+3566,*
ou+metanoeō [2]
repent, *3564, metamelomai* [1]
repent, *3567, metanoia* [1]

REPENTANCE [20]

repentance, *3567, metanoia* [19]
turn in repentance, *3567, metanoia* [1]

REPENTED [5]

repented, *3566, metanoeō* [5]

REPENTS [3]

repents, *3566, metanoeō* [3]

REPHAN [1]

Rephan, *4818, Rhaiphan* [1]

REPLIED [176]

replied, *3306, legō* [92]
replied, *646, apokrinomai* [63]
replied, *5774, phēmi* [18]
replied, *NIG* [2]
replied, *RPE* [1]

REPLY [9]

made reply, *646, apokrinomai* [2]
reply, *646, apokrinomai* [2]
in reply, *646, apokrinomai* [1]
say in reply, *646, apokrinomai* [1]
reply, *3306, legō* [1]
reply, *3364, logos* [1]
reply, *5696, hypolambanō* [1]

REPORT [11]

report, *550, apangellō* [4]
report, *AIT* [2]
report, *3364, logos* [1]
bad report, *1556, dysphēmia* [1]
good report, *2367, euphēmia* [1]
report, *3606, mēnyō* [1]

REPORTED [20]

reported, *550, apangellō* [12]
reported, *334, anangellō* [2]
reported, *201, akouō* [1]
slanderously reported, *1059, blasphēmeō* [1]
reported, *1455, diēgeomai* [1]
reported, *1872, emphanizō* [1]
reported, *2007, exēgeomai* [1]
reported, *2859, katangellō* [1]

REPORTS [3]

reports, *AIT* [1]
reports, *198, akoē* [1]
reports, *2994, katēcheō* [1]

REPRESENT [3]

represent, *1639, eimi* [2]
represent, *AIT* [1]

REPRESENTATION [1]

exact representation, *5917, charaktēr* [1]

REPRESENTATIVES [1]

representatives, *693, apostolos* [1]

REPROACH [1]

above reproach, *455, anepilēmptos* [1]

REPTILES [4]

reptiles, *2260, herpeton* [4]

REPUTATION [2]

reputation, *3456, martyria* [1]
reputation, *3950, onoma* [1]

REPUTED [1]

reputed, *1506, dokeō* [1]

REQUEST [6]

request, *AIT* [1]
request, *RPE* [1]
request, *160, aiteō* [1]
request, *2263, erōtaō* [1]
request, *2527, thelō* [1]
request that, *4151, parakaleō* [1]

REQUESTED [2]

requested, *4148, paraiteomai* [1]
urgently requested, *4151+160,*
parakaleō+aiteō [1]

REQUESTING [1]

requesting, *2263, erōtaō* [1]

REQUESTS [3]

requests, *1255, deēsis* [2]
requests, *161, aitēma* [1]

REQUIRED [7]

required, *2848, kata* [2]
required, *AIT* [1]
required, *1411, diatassō* [1]
required, *2426, zēteō* [1]
required by, *2848, kata* [1]
required, *4133, parangellō* [1]

REQUIREMENTS [4]

requirements, *1468, dikaiōma* [1]
righteous requirements, *1468, dikaiōma* [1]
requirements, *2055, epanankes* [1]
requirements, *2240, ergon* [1]

REQUIRES [3]

requires, *AIT* [1]
requires, *1953, entolē* [1]
requires, *2848, kata* [1]

RESCUE [8]

rescue, *4861, rhyomai* [5]
rescue, *1975, exaireō* [2]
rescue, *1443+5401, didōmi+sōtēria* [1]

RESCUED [7]

rescued, *4861, rhyomai* [4]
rescued, *1975, exaireō* [3]

RESCUES [1]

rescues, *4861, rhyomai* [1]

RESEMBLED [3]

resembled, *6055, hōs* [2]
resembled, *1639+3927, eimi+homoios* [1]

RESEMBLING [1]

resembling, *3927+3970, homoios+horasis* [1]

RESENTFUL [1]

not resentful, *452, anexikakos* [1]

RESERVED [4]

reserved, 5498, tēreō [2]
reserved, 2564, thēsaurizō [1]
reserved, 2901, kataleipō [1]

RESIDENTS [1]

residents of, 2997, katoikeō [1]

RESIST [5]

resist, 468, anthistēmi [4]
resist, 528, antipiptō [1]

RESISTED [1]

resisted, 510, antikathistēmi [1]

RESISTS [1]

resists, 468, anthistēmi [1]

RESOLUTELY [1]

resolutely, 3836+4725+5114,
    ho+prosōpon+stērizō [1]

RESOLVED [1]

resolved, 3212, krinō [1]

RESOUNDING [1]

resounding, 2490, ēcheō [1]

RESPECT [19]

respect, 5832, phobos [5]
respect, 1956, entrepō [3]
worthy of respect, 4948, semnos [3]
respect, 5507, timē [2]
win the respect, 2361, euschēmonōs [1]
show less respect, 2969, kataphroneō [1]
respect, 3857, oida [1]
respect, 4949, semnotēs [1]
show proper respect to, 5506, timaō [1]
respect, 5828, phobeomai [1]

RESPECTABLE [1]

respectable, 3177, kosmios [1]

RESPECTED [3]

respected, 1956, entrepō [1]
highly respected, 3455, martyreō [1]
respected, 3455, martyreō [1]

RESPECTS [1]

pay respects to, 832, aspazomai [1]

RESPOND [2]

respond, 3306, legō [1]
respond to, 4668, prosechō [1]

RESPONDED [1]

responded, 646, apokrinomai [1]

RESPONSE [2]

response, AIT [1]
in response to, 2848, kata [1]

RESPONSIBILITY [4]

responsibility, 3972, horaō [2]
clear of responsibility, 2754, katharos [1]
responsibility, 5970, chreia [1]

RESPONSIBLE [3]

held responsible for, 1699, ekzēteō [2]
responsible, AIT [1]

REST [44]

rest, 3370, loipos [15]
rest, 2923, katapausis [8]
rest, 398, anapausis [4]
rest, AIT [2]
get rest, 399, anapauō [1]
give rest, 399, anapauō [1]
rest, 399, anapauō [1]
rest, 457, anesis [1]
that rest⁵, 899, autos [1]
rest, 1639, eimi [1]
rest on, 2058+2093, epanapauomai+epi [1]
rest, 2145, epiloipos [1]
rest on, 2172+2093, episkēnoō+epi [1]
rest, 2262, erchomai [1]
came to rest, 2767, kathizō [1]
given rest, 2924, katapauō [1]
the rest, 3538+5516, meros+tis [1]
set at rest, 4275, peithō [1]
rest of the disciples, 5209, symmathētēs [1]

RESTED [2]

rested, 2483, hēsychazō [1]
rested, 2924, katapauō [1]

RESTING [4]

resting, 399, anapauō [2]
resting on, 2093, epi [1]
resting, 2923, katapausis [1]

RESTLESS [1]

restless, 190, akatastatos [1]

RESTORE [7]

restore, 635, apokathistēmi [2]
restore, 2936, katartizō [2]
restore sight, 329, anablepō [1]
restore, 494, anorthoō [1]
restore, 640, apokatastasis [1]

RESTORED [7]

completely restored, 635, apokathistēmi [3]
restored, 635, apokathistēmi [2]
restored, 487, anoigō [1]
restored, 5919, charizomai [1]

RESTORES [1]

restores, 635, apokathistēmi [1]

RESTRAINED [1]

restrained, 3266, kōlyō [1]

RESTRAINING [1]

in restraining, 4639, pros [1]

RESTRICT [1]

restrict, 1105+2095, brochos+epiballō [1]

RESTS [3]

rests, 399, anapauō [1]
on whom favor rests, 2306, eudokia [1]
rests, 2924, katapauō [1]

RESULT [22]

result, AIT [3]
the result of, 1328, dia [3]
as a result, 6063, hōste [3]
result, 5465, telos [2]
result, 609, apobainō [1]
result, 1181, ginomai [1]
as the result of, 1328, dia [1]
as a result, 1650+3836, eis+ho [1]

result in, 1650, eis [1]
result, 1650+3836, eis+ho [1]
result in, 1666+1181, ek+ginomai [1]
result, 2262, erchomai [1]
result, 2351, heuriskō [1]
result in, 2981, katergazomai [1]
result of, 5679, hypo [1]

RESURRECTION [40]

resurrection, 414, anastasis [37]
resurrection, RPE [1]
resurrection, 1587, egersis [1]
resurrection, 1983, exanastasis [1]

RETAIN [3]

retain, 2400, echō [1]
retain, 2988, katechō [1]
retain the place in life, 4344, peripateō [1]

RETALIATE [1]

retaliate, 518, antiloidoreō [1]

RETORTED [1]

retorted, 646, apokrinomai [1]

RETRIBUTION [1]

retribution, 501, antapodoma [1]

RETURN [20]

return, 2262, erchomai [5]
return, 5715, hypostrephō [4]
return, 366, anakamptō [2]
return, 2188, epistrephō [2]
return, RPE [1]
return, 418, anastrephō [1]
in return, 500, antapodidōmi [1]
return, 2059, epanerchomai [1]
return, 2262+1650+3836+4099,
    erchomai+eis+ho+palin [1]
to return, 4536+386, pote+analyō [1]
return, 5715+1650, hypostrephō+eis [1]

RETURNED [36]

returned, 5715, hypostrephō [18]
returned, 2262, erchomai [6]
returned, 432, anachōreō [2]
returned, 599, aperchomai [2]
returned, 2188, epistrephō [2]
returned, 326, anabainō [1]
returned to place, 404+4099,
    anapiptō+palin [1]
returned home, 2059, epanerchomai [1]
returned to, 2188+2093, epistrephō+epi [1]
returned to life, 2409, zaō [1]
returned, 5138, strephō [1]

RETURNING [5]

returning, 326, anabainō [1]
returning, 2262, erchomai [1]
returning, 5632, hypagō [1]
returning home, 5715, hypostrephō [1]
returning, 5715, hypostrephō [1]

RETURNS [3]

returns, 2262, erchomai [2]
returns to, 2188+2093, epistrephō+epi [1]

REU [1]

Reu, 4814, Rhagau [1]

REUBEN [1]

Reuben, 4857, Rhoubēn [1]

REVEAL [3]

reveal, *636, apokalyptō* [3]

REVEALED [37]

revealed, *636, apokalyptō* [19]
revealed, *5746, phaneroō* [9]
revealed, *637, apokalypsis* [7]
revealed, *1871+1181, emphanēs+ginomai* [1]
revealed, *5976, chrēmatizō* [1]

REVELATION [10]

revelation, *637, apokalypsis* [9]
a revelation comes, *636, apokalyptō* [1]

REVELATIONS [2]

revelations, *637, apokalypsis* [2]

REVELING [1]

reveling, *1960, entryphaō* [1]

REVELRY [1]

indulge in pagan revelry, *4089, paizō* [1]

REVENGE [1]

take revenge, *1571+1688, heautou+ekdikeō* [1]

REVENUE [2]

revenue, *5465, telos* [2]

REVERENCE [7]

reverence, *5832, phobos* [3]
reverence, *2325, eulabeia* [1]
reverence, *4686, proskyneō* [1]
reverence for, *5828, phobeomai* [1]
reverence, *5828, phobeomai* [1]

REVERENT [3]

reverent submission, *2325, eulabeia* [1]
reverent, *2640, hieroprepēs* [1]
reverent fear, *5832, phobos* [1]

REVOLT [2]

revolt, *415, anastatoō* [1]
led in revolt, *923+3958, aphistēmi+opisō* [1]

REVOLUTIONS [1]

revolutions, *189, akatastasia* [1]

REWARD [24]

reward, *3635, misthos* [17]
reward, *625, apodidōmi* [4]
reward, *502, antapodosis* [1]
reward, *3152, komizō* [1]
reward, *3632, misthapodosia* [1]

REWARDED [3]

rewarded, *3632, misthapodosia* [1]
rewarded, *3635+3284, misthos+lambanō* [1]
rewarded, *3635+655, misthos+apolambanō* [1]

REWARDING [1]

rewarding, *1443+3836+3635,*
   didōmi+ho+misthos [1]

REWARDS [1]

rewards, *3633+1181,*
   misthapodotēs+ginomai [1]

RHEGIUM [1]

Rhegium, *4836, Rhēgion* [1]

RHESA [1]

Rhesa, *4840, Rhēsa* [1]

RHODA [1]

Rhoda, *4851, Rhodē* [1]

RHODES [1]

Rhodes, *4852, Rhodos* [1]

RICH [41]

rich, *4454, plousios* [26]
rich, *4456, plouteō* [8]
rich, *3836+5975+2400, ho+chrēma+echō* [2]
rich, *4455, plousios* [1]
get rich, *4456, plouteō* [1]
made rich, *4457, ploutizō* [1]
making rich, *4457, ploutizō* [1]
rich, *4458, ploutos* [1]

RICHES [17]

riches, *4458, ploutos* [14]
riches, *RPE* [2]
riches, *3353, liparos* [1]

RICHLY [4]

richly, *4455, plousiōs* [2]
richly, *3489, megas* [1]
richly blesses, *4456, plouteō* [1]

RID [9]

rid of, *700, apotithēmi* [2]
get rid of, *1675, ekballō* [2]
get rid of, *149, airō* [1]
rid of, *149+608, airō+apo* [1]
get rid of, *359, anaireō* [1]
get rid of, *700, apotithēmi* [1]
get rid of, *1705, ekkathairō* [1]

RIDDEN [2]

ridden, *2767, kathizō* [2]

RIDER [7]

rider, *2764+2093, kathēmai+epi* [6]
rider, *2764+2062, kathēmai+epanō* [1]

RIDERS [2]

riders, *2764+2093, kathēmai+epi* [2]

RIDES [1]

rides, *1002, bastazō* [1]

RIDICULE [1]

ridicule, *1850, empaizō* [1]

RIDICULED [1]

ridiculed, *2024, exoutheneō* [1]

RIDING [2]

riding, *AIT* [1]
riding, *2094, epibainō* [1]

RIGHT [139]

right hand, *1288, dexios* [31]
right, *1288, dexios* [21]
right, *1465, dikaios* [11]
right, *2026, exousia* [9]
right, *2822, kalōs* [6]
what is right, *1466, dikaiosynē* [5]
right, *2819, kalos* [4]
right, *AIT* [3]
proved right, *1467, dikaioō* [3]
right, *2003, exesti* [3]
right time, *2789, kairos* [3]
in right mind, *5404, sōphroneō* [3]
right, *19, agathos* [2]
right side, *1288, dexios* [2]
give the right, *1443, didōmi* [2]
right, *1466, dikaiosynē* [2]
right at, *2093, epi* [2]
right, *2318, euthys²* [2]
do what is right, *16, agathopoieō* [1]
do right, *18, agathopoios* [1]
right, *240, alēthinos* [1]
right, *744, arestos* [1]
right up to, *948, achri* [1]
walked right through, *1451+1328+3545,*
   dierchomai+dia+mesos [1]
acknowledged that right, *1467, dikaioō* [1]
has the right, *1538, dynamai* [1]
right then, *1994, exautēs* [1]
right now, *1994, exautēs* [1]
have right, *2003, exesti* [1]
have the right, *2003, exesti* [1]
right, *2093+237, epi+alētheia* [1]
right, *2289, hetoimos* [1]
right away, *2311, eutheōs* [1]
right away, *2317, euthys¹* [1]
right, *2363, euschēmōn* [1]
right into, *2401+2276+1650, heōs+esō+eis* [1]
right on down to, *2401, heōs* [1]
right up to, *2401, heōs* [1]
doing what is right, *2818, kalopoieō* [1]
what is right, *2819, kalos* [1]
the right thing, *2822, kalōs* [1]
what is right, *3987, orthōs* [1]
right there, *4154, parakeimai* [1]

RIGHTEOUS [65]

righteous, *1465, dikaios* [53]
considered righteous, *1467, dikaioō* [2]
declared righteous, *1467, dikaioō* [2]
righteous acts, *1468, dikaiōma* [2]
righteous judgment, *1464, dikaiokrisia* [1]
righteous life, *1466, dikaiosynē* [1]
righteous decree, *1468, dikaiōma* [1]
righteous requirements, *1468, dikaiōma* [1]
righteous, *1469, dikaiōs* [1]
righteous, *1877+1466, en+dikaiosynē* [1]

RIGHTEOUSNESS [80]

righteousness, *1466, dikaiosynē* [74]
righteousness, *RPE* [2]
righteousness, *1465, dikaios* [1]
acts of righteousness, *1466, dikaiosynē* [1]
act of righteousness, *1468, dikaiōma* [1]
righteousness, *2319, euthytēs* [1]

RIGHTLY [2]

rightly so, *545+1639, axios+eimi* [1]
rightly so, *2822, kalōs* [1]

RIGHTS [4]

rights, *AIT* [1]
rights, *2026, exousia* [1]
inheritance rights as the oldest son, *4757,*
   prōtotokia [1]
full rights of sons, *5625, huiothesia* [1]

RIGID [1]

becomes rigid, *3830, xērainō* [1]

RING [2]

ring, *1234, daktylios* [1]
wearing a gold ring, *5993, chrysodaktylios* [1]

RINGLEADER [1]

ringleader, *4756, prōtostatēs* [1]

RIOT [3]

riot, *1639+2573, eimi+thorybos* [1]
riot, *2572, thorybeō* [1]
riot, *2573, thorybos* [1]

RIOTERS [1]

the rioters⁵, *3836+1254, ho+de* [1]

RIOTING [1]

rioting, *5087, stasis* [1]

RIOTS [2]

riots, *189, akatastasia* [1]
riots, *5087, stasis* [1]

RIPE [4]

ripe, *196, akmazō* [1]
ripe, *3328, leukos* [1]
ripe, *3830, xērainō* [1]
ripe, *4140, paradidōmi* [1]

RISE [27]

rise, *482, anistēmi* [9]
rise, *1586, egeirō* [8]
rise again, *482, anistēmi* [4]
rise, *414, anastasis* [3]
rise, *326, anabainō* [1]
causes to rise, *422, anatellō* [1]
rise again, *1586, egeirō* [1]

RISEN [11]

risen, *1586, egeirō* [10]
risen, *482, anistēmi* [1]

RISES [5]

rises, *422, anatellō* [2]
rises, *326, anabainō* [1]
rises, *482, anistēmi* [1]
rises, *889, auxanō* [1]

RISING [6]

rising, *RPE* [1]
rising, *414, anastasis* [1]
rising, *422, anatellō* [1]
rising sun, *424, anatolē* [1]
rising, *482, anistēmi* [1]
rising, *1586, egeirō* [1]

RISKED [2]

risked lives, *3836+5549+5719,
    ho+trachēlos+hypotithēmi* [1]
risked, *4140, paradidōmi* [1]

RISKING [1]

risking, *4129, paraboleuomai* [1]

RITES [1]

purification rites, *49, hagnizō* [1]

RIVALRY [1]

rivalry, *2251, eris* [1]

RIVER [9]

river, *4532, potamos* [9]

RIVERS [3]

rivers, *4532, potamos* [3]

ROAD [20]

road, *3847, hodos* [17]
road, *RPE* [1]
took the road through, *1451, dierchomai* [1]
place where the road goes down, *2853,
    katabasis* [1]

ROADS [2]

roads, *AIT* [1]
roads, *3847, hodos* [1]

ROADSIDE [3]

roadside, *3847, hodos* [3]

ROAR [5]

roar, *5889, phōnē* [2]
roar, *3681, mykaomai* [1]
with a roar, *4853, rhoizēdon* [1]
roar, *5889+3489, phōnē+megas* [1]

ROARING [2]

roaring, *2492, ēchos²* [1]
roaring, *6054, ōryomai* [1]

ROB [3]

rob, *1395, diarpazō* [2]
rob temples, *2644, hierosyleō* [1]

ROBBED [5]

robbed him of speech, *228, alalos* [1]
robbed, *691, apostereō* [1]
robbed temples, *2645, hierosylos* [1]
robbed, *2747, kathaireō* [1]
robbed, *5195, sylaō* [1]

ROBBER [1]

robber, *3334, lēstēs* [1]

ROBBERS [10]

robbers, *3334, lēstēs* [9]
robbers, *774, harpax* [1]

ROBE [14]

robe, *2668, himation* [4]
robe, *5124, stolē* [3]
purple robe, *4525, porphyra* [2]
robe, *5948, chlamys* [2]
robe, *2264, esthēs* [1]
robe, *4316, peribolaion* [1]
a robe reaching down to feet, *4468, podērēs* [1]

ROBED [1]

robed in, *4314, periballō* [1]

ROBES [8]

robes, *5124, stolē* [4]
flowing robes, *5124, stolē* [2]
robes, *2264, esthēs* [1]
robes, *5945, chitōn* [1]

ROCK [13]

rock, *4376, petra* [12]
cut in the rock, *3292, laxeutos* [1]

ROCKS [4]

rocks, *4376, petra* [3]
rocks, *5550+5536, trachys+topos* [1]

ROCKY [4]

rocky places, *4378, petrōdēs* [4]

ROD [3]

rod, *2812, kalamos* [2]
measuring rod, *4811, rhabdos* [1]

RODE [1]

rode out, *2002, exerchomai* [1]

RODS [1]

beaten with rods, *4810, rhabdizō* [1]

ROLL [2]

roll away, *653, apokyliō* [1]
roll up, *1813, helissō* [1]

ROLLED [7]

rolled away, *653, apokyliō* [2]
rolled back, *653, apokyliō* [1]
rolled around, *3244, kyliō* [1]
rolled in front of, *4685, proskyliō* [1]
rolled, *4685, proskyliō* [1]
rolled up, *4771, ptyssō* [1]

ROLLING [1]

rolling up, *1813, helissō* [1]

ROMAN [13]

Roman citizen, *4871, Rhōmaios* [4]
Roman world, *3876, oikoumenē* [2]
Roman citizens, *476+4871,
    anthrōpos+Rhōmaios* [1]
Roman citizen, *476+4871,
    anthrōpos+Rhōmaios* [1]
Roman colony, *3149, kolōnia* [1]
palace of the Roman governor, *4550,
    praitōrion* [1]
Roman citizens, *4871, Rhōmaios* [1]
Roman, *4871, Rhōmaios* [1]
Roman troops, *5061, speira* [1]

ROMANS [3]

Romans, *4871, Rhōmaios* [3]

ROME [10]

Rome, *4873, Rhōmē* [8]
Rome, *RPE* [1]
from Rome, *4871, Rhōmaios* [1]

ROOF [8]

roof, *1560, dōma* [4]
roof, *5094, stegē* [3]
roof of house, *1560, dōma* [1]

ROOFS [2]

roofs, *1560, dōma* [2]

ROOM [24]

room, *AIT* [3]
room, *5536, topos* [3]
upstairs room, *5673, hyperōon* [3]
upper room, *333, anagaion* [2]
guest room, *2906, katalyma* [2]
room, *5008, skēnē* [2]
have room for, *6003, chōreō* [2]
room, *RPE* [1]
audience room, *211, akroatērion* [1]
guest room, *3825, xenia* [1]
room, *5421, tameion* [1]
room, *5673, hyperōon* [1]
make room for, *6003, chōreō* [1]
room, *6003, chōreō* [1]

ROOMS [3]

inner rooms, *5421, tameion* [2]
rooms, *3665, monē* [1]

ROOSTER [12]

rooster, *232, alektōr* [11]
when the rooster crows, *231, alektorophōnia* [1]

ROOT [17]

root, *4844, rhiza* [16]
root up, *1748, ekrizoō* [1]

ROOTED [2]

rooted, *4845, rhizoō* [2]

ROOTS [2]

pulled up by the roots, *1748, ekrizoō* [1]
roots, *4844, rhiza* [1]

ROPES [3]

ropes, *1069, boētheia* [1]
ropes, *2415, zeuktēria* [1]
ropes, *5389, schoinion* [1]

ROSE [9]

rose, *482, anistēmi* [5]
rose, *2262, erchomai* [2]
rose, *326, anabainō* [1]
rose again, *482, anistēmi* [1]

ROTTED [1]

rotted, *4960, sēpō* [1]

ROUGH [2]

rough, *1444, diegeirō* [1]
rough, *5550, trachys* [1]

ROUNDED [1]

rounded up, *4689, proslambanō* [1]

ROUTE [1]

route, *3847, hodos* [1]

ROUTED [1]

routed, *3111, klinō* [1]

ROWED [1]

rowed, *1785, elaunō* [1]

ROYAL [5]

royal official, *997, basilikos* [2]
royal, *997, basilikos* [2]
royal, *994, basileios* [1]

RUB [1]

rub, *6041, psōchō* [1]

RUBBISH [1]

rubbish, *5032, skybalon* [1]

RUDDER [1]

rudder, *4382, pēdalion* [1]

RUDDERS [1]

rudders, *4382, pēdalion* [1]

RUDE [1]

rude, *858, aschēmoneō* [1]

RUE [1]

rue, *4379, pēganon* [1]

RUFUS [2]

Rufus, *4859, Rhouphos* [2]

RUIN [5]

brought to ruin, *2246, erēmoō* [2]
ruin, *2246, erēmoō* [1]
ruin, *3897, olethros* [1]
ruin, *5342, syntrimma* [1]

RUINED [5]

ruined, *660, apollymi* [3]
ruined, *2246, erēmoō* [2]

RUINING [1]

ruining, *426, anatrepō* [1]

RUINS [2]

ruins, *2940, kataskaptō* [1]
ruins, *2953, katastrophē* [1]

RULE [11]

rule, *4477, poimainō* [3]
rule, *794, archē* [1]
rule over, *806, archō* [1]
rule, *993, basileia* [1]
rule, *1093, brabeuō* [1]
the rule lay down, *1411, diatassō* [1]
rule, *2834, kanōn* [1]
rule, *3364, logos* [1]
gave rule, *4133, parangellō* [1]

RULED [1]

ruled, *RPE* [1]

RULER [21]

ruler, *807, archōn* [9]
synagogue ruler, *801, archisynagōgos* [7]
ruler, *2451, hēgeomai* [2]
ruler, *482, anistēmi* [1]
ruler, *794, archē* [1]
ruler, *1541, dynastēs* [1]

RULER'S [1]

ruler's, *807, archōn* [1]

RULERS [22]

rulers, *807, archōn* [12]
rulers, *794, archē* [5]
synagogue rulers, *801, archisynagōgos* [2]
rulers, *806, archō* [1]
rulers, *1541, dynastēs* [1]
rulers, *2450, hēgemōn* [1]

RULES [6]

rules, *1945, entalma* [2]
submit to rules, *1505, dogmatizō* [1]
rules, *2400+993, echō+basileia* [1]
rules, *2451, hēgeomai* [1]
according to the rules, *3789, nomimōs* [1]

RULING [1]

ruling council, *807, archōn* [1]

RUMBLINGS [4]

rumblings, *5889, phōnē* [4]

RUMOR [1]

rumor, *3364, logos* [1]

RUMORS [2]

rumors, *198, akoē* [2]

RUN [13]

run, *5556, trechō* [5]
run aground, *1738, ekpiptō* [2]
run out, *1772, ekcheō* [2]
run aground, *2034, exōtheō* [1]
run after, *2118, epizēteō* [1]
run race, *5556, trechō* [1]
run away, *5771, pheugō* [1]

RUNNERS [1]

runners, *5556, trechō* [1]

RUNNING [10]

running, *5556, trechō* [3]
running, *RPE* [1]
running off after, *1503, diōkō* [1]
running, *2192, episyntrechō* [1]
running from all directions, *5282, syndromē* [1]
came running, *5340, syntrechō* [1]
running a race, *5556, trechō* [1]
running over, *5658, hyperekchynnō* [1]

RUNS [4]

runs, *RPE* [1]
runs after, *2118, epizēteō* [1]
runs ahead, *4575, proagō* [1]
runs away, *5771, pheugō* [1]

RUSHED [9]

rushed, *3994, hormaō* [5]
rushed in, *1659, eispēdaō* [1]
rushed out, *1737, ekpēdaō* [1]
rushed, *1772, ekcheō* [1]
rushed to, *2392, ephistēmi* [1]

RUSHING [4]

rushing, *4498, polys* [3]
rushing, *5556, trechō* [1]

RUST [2]

rust, *1111, brōsis* [2]

RUTH [1]

Ruth, *4858, Rhouth* [1]

RUTHLESS [1]

ruthless, *446, aneleēmōn* [1]

SABACHTHANI [2]

sabachthani, *4876, sabachthani* [2]

SABBATH [59]

Sabbath, *4879, sabbaton* [52]
Sabbath day's walk from,
    1584+4879+2400+3847,
    engys+sabbaton+echō+hodos [1]
one Sabbath, *1877+3836+4879,*
    en+ho+sabbaton [1]
one Sabbath, *1877+4879, en+sabbaton* [1]
after the Sabbath, *4067+4879,*
    opse+sabbaton [1]
day before the Sabbath, *4640, prosabbaton* [1]
Sabbath days, *4879, sabbaton* [1]
Sabbath day, *4879, sabbaton* [1]

SABBATH-REST [1]

Sabbath-rest, *4878, sabbatismos* [1]

SACKCLOTH [4]

sackcloth, *4884, sakkos* [4]

SACRED [7]

sacred, *41, hagios* [4]
makes sacred, *39, hagiazō* [2]
sacred, *AIT* [1]

SACRIFICE [23]

sacrifice, *2602, thysia* [11]
sacrifice, *4714, prosphora* [3]
atoning sacrifice, *2662, hilasmos* [2]
sacrifice, *RPE* [1]
sacrifice offered to an idol, *1628, eidōlothytos* [1]
sacrifice, *2604, thyō* [1]
offered in sacrifice, *2638, hierothytos* [1]
sacrifice of atonement, *2663, hilastērion* [1]
offered as a sacrifice, *4712, prospherō* [1]
sacrifice, *4712, prospherō* [1]

SACRIFICED [12]

food sacrificed to idols, *1628, eidōlothytos* [5]
sacrificed to idols, *1628, eidōlothytos* [2]
sacrificed, *2604, thyō* [2]
food sacrificed to an idol, *1628, eidōlothytos* [1]
sacrificed[s], *4047+4472, houtos+poieō* [1]
sacrificed, *4712, prospherō* [1]

SACRIFICES [23]

sacrifices, *2602, thysia* [16]
offer sacrifices, *4712, prospherō* [3]
sacrifices, *AIT* [1]
sacrifices, *RPE* [1]
offer sacrifices, *2604, thyō* [1]
the sacrifices[s], *4005, hos* [1]

SACRIFICING [1]

sacrificing, *2604, thyō* [1]

SAD [4]

sad, *3382, lypeō* [3]
very sad, *4337, perilypos* [1]

SADDENED [1]

saddened, *806+3382, archō+lypeō* [1]

SADDUCEES [14]

Sadducees, *4881, Saddoukaios* [14]

SAFE [4]

safe, *1877+1645, en+eirēnē* [1]
keeps safe, *5498, tēreō* [1]
safe and sound, *5617, hygiainō* [1]
kept safe, *5875, phylassō* [1]

SAFEGUARD [1]

safeguard, *855, asphalēs* [1]

SAFELY [3]

safely, *1407, diasōzō* [2]
bring safely, *5392, sōzō* [1]

SAFETY [2]

safety, *854, asphaleia* [1]
in safety, *1407, diasōzō* [1]

SAID [892]

said, *3306, legō* [784]
said, *3281, laleō* [26]
said, *5774, phēmi* [25]

said, *RPE* [13]
said, *646, apokrinomai* [10]
said, *NIG* [6]
said, *3364, logos* [5]
said, *806+3306, archō+legō* [4]
said before, *4625, prolegō* [2]
said, *550, apangellō* [1]
said good-by, *698, apotassō* [1]
said good-by, *832, aspazomai* [1]
explained what said, *1450, diermēneuō* [1]
said to be, *2813, kaleō* [1]
well said, *2822, kalōs* [1]
said, *3282, lalia* [1]
something said, *3364, logos* [1]
what said, *3364, logos* [1]
what Paul said[s], *4047, houtos* [1]
already said, *4625, prolegō* [1]
said previously, *4625, prolegō* [1]
said, *4715, prosphōneō* [1]
said, *4839, rhēma* [1]
what said, *4839, rhēma* [1]
said, *5196, syllaleō* [1]
said, *5888, phōneō* [1]

SAIL [12]

sail, *343, anagō* [4]
set sail, *343, anagō* [2]
sail, *4434, pleō* [2]
sail, *676, apopleō* [1]
set sail, *676, apopleō* [1]
sail past, *4179, parapleō* [1]
set sail, *4311, periaireō* [1]

SAILED [16]

sailed, *1739, ekpleō* [3]
sailed, *343, anagō* [2]
sailed straight, *2312, euthydromeō* [2]
sailed, *4434, pleō* [2]
sailed, *RPE* [1]
sailed back, *676, apopleō* [1]
sailed, *676, apopleō* [1]
sailed across, *1386, diapleō* [1]
sailed, *2929, katapleō* [1]
sailed, *4162, paralegomai* [1]
sailed to the lee of, *5709, hypopleō* [1]

SAILING [2]

sailing, *4434, pleō* [1]
sailing, *4452, ploos* [1]

SAILORS [3]

sailors, *3731, nautēs* [3]

SAINTS [45]

saints, *41, hagios* [45]

SAKE [31]

for sake, *1328, dia* [8]
for the sake of, *1328, dia* [8]
for the sake of, *5642, hyper* [4]
sake, *AIT* [2]
for the sake, *1915, heneken* [2]
sake, *1915, heneken* [2]
for sake, *5642, hyper* [2]
sake, *RPE* [1]
for sake, *1915, heneken* [1]
for the sake of, *5920, charin* [1]

SAKES [1]

for sakes, *1328, dia* [1]

SALAMIS [1]

Salamis, *4887, Salamis* [1]

SALEM [2]

Salem, *4889, Salēm* [2]

SALES [1]

sales, *4405, pipraskō* [1]

SALIM [1]

Salim, *4890, Salim* [1]

SALIVA [1]

saliva, *4770, ptysma* [1]

SALMON [3]

Salmon, *4891, Salmōn* [3]

SALMONE [1]

Salmone, *4892, Salmōnē* [1]

SALOME [2]

Salome, *4897, Salōmē* [2]

SALT [8]

salt, *229, halas* [6]
salt spring, *266, halykos* [1]
salt water, *4395, pikros* [1]

SALTED [1]

salted, *245, halizō* [1]

SALTINESS [3]

loses its saltiness, *3701, mōrainō* [2]
loses saltiness, *383+1181, analos+ginomai* [1]

SALTY [3]

made salty, *245, halizō* [1]
made salty, *789, artyō* [1]
make salty, *789, artyō* [1]

SALVATION [42]

salvation, *5401, sōtēria* [36]
salvation, *5402, sōtērion* [4]
salvation, *RPE* [1]
salvation, *5403, sōtērios* [1]

SALVE [1]

salve, *3141, kollourion* [1]

SAMARIA [10]

Samaria, *4899, Samareia* [10]

SAMARITAN [8]

Samaritan, *4901, Samaritēs* [5]
Samaritan, *4902, Samaritis* [2]
Samaritan, *4899, Samareia* [1]

SAMARITANS [5]

Samaritans, *4901, Samaritēs* [4]
Samaritans, *RPE* [1]

SAME [111]

same, *899, autos* [38]
in the same way, *4048, houtōs* [11]
in the same way, *3931, homoiōs* [10]
in the same way, *6058, hōsautōs* [6]
same, *AIT* [4]
the same, *3931, homoiōs* [4]
at the same time, *275, hama* [2]
that same, *1697, ekeinos* [2]
in the same way, *4048+2779, houtōs+kai* [2]
the same thing, *6058, hōsautōs* [2]

the same, *6058*, *hōsautōs* [2]
same, *NIG* [1]
in same way, *899*, *autos* [1]
same things, *899*, *autos* [1]
same way, *899*, *autos* [1]
that same, *899*, *autos* [1]
the same, *899*, *autos* [1]
one and the same, *1651*, *heis* [1]
the same, *1651*, *heis* [1]
same, *1697*, *ekeinos* [1]
at the same time, *2384*, *ephapax* [1]
same, *2698*, *isos* [1]
the same thing, *2749*, *kathaper* [1]
the same way[s], *3210*, *krima* [1]
that same, *3836*, *ho* [1]
the same thing, *3931*, *homoiōs* [1]
the same, *3931+2777*, *homoiōs+kathōs* [1]
at the same time, *3940*, *homōs* [1]
in the same way, *4005+5573*, *hos+tropos* [1]
same as, *4005+2779*, *hos+kai* [1]
this same, *4047*, *houtos* [1]
the same as, *4047*, *houtos* [1]
the same, *4047*, *houtos* [1]
in this same way, *4048+2779*, *houtōs+kai* [1]
it is the same, *4048+2779*, *houtōs+kai* [1]
the same, *4048*, *houtōs* [1]
the same as, *6055+2779*, *hōs+kai* [1]
the same way, *6055+2779*, *hōs+kai* [1]
the same way, *6058*, *hōsautōs* [1]

SAMOS [1]

Samos, *4904*, *Samos* [1]

SAMOTHRACE [1]

Samothrace, *4903*, *Samothrakē* [1]

SAMSON [1]

Samson, *4907*, *Sampsōn* [1]

SAMUEL [3]

Samuel, *4905*, *Samouēl* [3]

SANCTIFIED [10]

sanctified, *39*, *hagiazō* [7]
sanctified, *1639+39*, *eimi+hagiazō* [2]
sanctified, *40*, *hagiasmos* [1]

SANCTIFY [4]

sanctify, *39*, *hagiazō* [4]

SANCTIFYING [2]

sanctifying, *40*, *hagiasmos* [2]

SANCTUARY [6]

sanctuary, *41*, *hagios* [3]
sanctuary, *AIT* [1]
serve at a sanctuary, *3302*, *latreuō* [1]
sanctuary, *3875*, *oikos* [1]

SAND [4]

sand, *302*, *ammos* [4]

SANDALS [12]

sandals, *5687*, *hypodēma* [10]
sandals, *4908*, *sandalion* [1]
sandals, *5686+4908*, *hypodeō+sandalion* [1]

SANDBAR [1]

sandbar, *5536+1458*, *topos+dithalassos* [1]

SANDBARS [1]

sandbars of Syrtis, *5358*, *Syrtis* [1]

SANDY [1]

sandy beach, *129*, *aigialos* [1]

SANG [6]

sang, *106*, *adō* [3]
sang a dirge, *2577*, *thrēneō* [2]
sang, *3306*, *legō* [1]

SANHEDRIN [19]

Sanhedrin, *5284*, *synedrion* [19]

SAP [1]

sap, *AIT* [1]

SAPPHIRA [1]

Sapphira, *4912*, *Sapphira* [1]

SAPPHIRE [1]

sapphire, *4913*, *sapphiros* [1]

SARAH [3]

Sarah, *4925*, *Sarra* [3]

SARAH'S [1]

Sarah's, *4925*, *Sarra* [1]

SARDIS [3]

Sardis, *4915*, *Sardeis* [3]

SARDONYX [1]

sardonyx, *4918*, *sardonyx* [1]

SASH [1]

sash, *2438*, *zōnē* [1]

SASHES [1]

sashes, *2438*, *zōnē* [1]

SAT [42]

sat down, *2767*, *kathizō* [15]
sat, *2764*, *kathēmai* [8]
sat down, *2764*, *kathēmai* [4]
sat, *2767*, *kathizō* [4]
sat up, *361*, *anakathizō* [2]
sat down, *404*, *anapiptō* [2]
sat, *1639+5153*, *eimi+synkathēmai* [1]
sat, *2125*, *epikathizō* [1]
sat down, *2757*, *kathezomai* [1]
sat, *2757*, *kathezomai* [1]
sat down, *2884*, *kataklinō* [1]
sat, *4149*, *parakathezomai* [1]
sat down together, *5154*, *synkathizō* [1]

SATAN [35]

Satan, *4928*, *Satanas* [35]

SATAN'S [1]

Satan's, *4928*, *Satanas* [1]

SATISFIED [7]

satisfied, *5963*, *chortazō* [6]
satisfied, *758*, *arkeō* [1]

SATISFY [2]

satisfy, *2653+4472*, *hikanos+poieō* [1]
satisfy, *4275*, *peithō* [1]

SAUL [32]

Saul, *4930*, *Saulos* [15]
Saul, *4910*, *Saoul* [9]

Saul, *RPE* [4]
Saul[s], *899*, *autos* [3]
Barnabas[s] and Saul, *899*, *autos* [1]

SAUL'S [1]

Saul's[s], *899*, *autos* [1]

SAVAGE [1]

savage, *987*, *barys* [1]

SAVE [40]

save, *5392*, *sōzō* [37]
save up, *2564*, *thēsaurizō* [1]
save, *5401*, *sōtēria* [1]
save, *5498*, *tēreō* [1]

SAVED [56]

saved, *5392*, *sōzō* [45]
saved, *5401*, *sōtēria* [3]
saved, *1639+5392*, *eimi+sōzō* [2]
saved, *1650+5401*, *eis+sōtēria* [2]
saved, *RPE* [1]
saved through, *1407+1328*, *diasōzō+dia* [1]
saved, *1650+4348+6034*,
    eis+peripoiēsis+psychē [1]
saved, *5498*, *tēreō* [1]

SAVES [2]

saves, *RPE* [1]
saves, *5392*, *sōzō* [1]

SAVING [1]

saving, *NIG* [1]

SAVIOR [24]

Savior, *5400*, *sōtēr* [24]

SAW [226]

saw, *3972*, *horaō* [182]
saw, *2555*, *theōreō* [18]
saw, *1063*, *blepō* [8]
saw, *2517*, *theaomai* [7]
saw, *RPE* [2]
saw, *1838*, *emblepō* [2]
saw, *1062*, *blemma* [1]
saw that, *1063*, *blepō* [1]
saw, *1182*, *ginōskō* [1]
saw through, *2917*, *katanoeō* [1]
saw, *2917*, *katanoeō* [1]
saw that, *3972*, *horaō* [1]
saw, *4632*, *prooraō* [1]

SAWDUST [2]

speck of sawdust, *2847*, *karphos* [2]

SAWED [1]

sawed in two, *4569*, *prizō* [1]

SAY [250]

say, *3306*, *legō* [183]
say, *3281*, *laleō* [16]
say, *RPE* [12]
say, *NIG* [10]
say, *4839*, *rhēma* [4]
yes it is as you say, *5148+3306*, *sy+legō* [4]
say, *515*, *antilegō* [2]
say, *646*, *apokrinomai* [2]
say, *5774*, *phēmi* [2]
say, *201+1666*, *akouō+ek* [1]
say, *503*, *antapokrinomai* [1]
say in reply, *646*, *apokrinomai* [1]
say good-by, *698*, *apotassō* [1]

say no to, *766, arneomai* [1]
say, *1639+4123, eimi+para* [1]
say, *1639, eimi* [1]
say, *1666+3836+5125, ek+ho+stoma* [1]
say bad about, *2800, kakologeō* [1]
say about, *3281, laleō* [1]
say about, *3306, legō* [1]
say, *3364, logos* [1]
say is like, *3929, homoioō* [1]
me say, *4123+1609, para+egō* [1]
one might even say, *6055+2229+3306, hōs+epos+legō* [1]

SAYING [107]

saying, *3306, legō* [79]
saying, *3364, logos* [10]
saying, *3281, laleō* [6]
saying, *RPE* [4]
saying, *NIG* [2]
saying indignantly, *24, aganakteō* [1]
saying good-by to, *571, apaspazomai* [1]
saying, *710, apophthengomai* [1]
saying, *4839, rhēma* [1]
someone is saying, *5889, phōnē* [1]
saying[s], *6055, hōs* [1]

SAYINGS [1]

sayings, *4839, rhēma* [1]

SAYS [98]

says, *3306, legō* [83]
says, *RPE* [7]
says, *NIG* [2]
says, *3281, laleō* [2]
what says, *3364, logos* [1]
what it says, *4047, houtos* [1]
says, *4321, periechō* [1]
says, *4839, rhēma* [1]

SCALES [2]

pair of scales, *2433, zygos* [1]
scales, *3318, lepis* [1]

SCARCELY [1]

scarcely ever, *3653, mogis* [1]

SCARLET [6]

scarlet, *3132, kokkinos* [5]
scarlet cloth, *3132, kokkinos* [1]

SCATTERED [17]

scattered, *1399, diaskorpizō* [5]
scattered, *1401, diaspeirō* [3]
scattered seed, *1399, diaskorpizō* [2]
scattered among the nations, *1402, diaspora* [1]
scattered throughout, *1402, diaspora* [1]
scattered, *1772, ekcheō* [1]
scattered, *2954, katastrōnnymi* [1]
people live scattered among, *3836+1402, ho+diaspora* [1]
scattered abroad, *5025, skorpizō* [1]
scattered, *5025, skorpizō* [1]

SCATTERING [3]

scattering the seed, *5062, speirō* [2]
scattering seed, *5062, speirō* [1]

SCATTERS [4]

scatters, *5025, skorpizō* [3]
scatters, *965, ballō* [1]

SCENE [1]

scene, *NIG* [1]

SCEPTER [4]

scepter, *4811, rhabdos* [4]

SCEVA [1]

Sceva, *5005, Skeuas* [1]

SCHEMES [2]

schemes, *3497, methodeia* [1]
schemes, *3784, noēma* [1]

SCHEMING [1]

scheming, *3497, methodeia* [1]

SCHOLAR [1]

scholar, *1208, grammateus* [1]

SCOFFERS [3]

scoffers, *1851, empaiktēs* [2]
scoffers, *2970, kataphronētēs* [1]

SCOFFING [1]

scoffing, *1848, empaigmonē* [1]

SCORCH [1]

scorch, *3009, kaumatizō* [1]

SCORCHED [2]

scorched, *3009, kaumatizō* [2]

SCORCHING [2]

scorching heat, *3008, kauma* [1]
scorching heat, *3014, kausōn* [1]

SCORN [1]

treat with scorn, *1746, ekptyō* [1]

SCORNING [1]

scorning, *2969, kataphroneō* [1]

SCORPION [2]

scorpion, *5026, skorpios* [2]

SCORPIONS [3]

scorpions, *5026, skorpios* [3]

SCREAMS [1]

screams, *3189, krazō* [1]

SCRIPTURE [33]

scripture, *1210, graphē* [30]
scripture, *AIT* [3]

SCRIPTURES [20]

Scriptures, *1210, graphē* [18]
Scriptures, *RPE* [1]
Scriptures, *1207, gramma* [1]

SCROLL [17]

scroll, *1046, biblion* [12]
little scroll, *1044, biblaridion* [3]
scroll, *RPE* [1]
scroll, *3053+1046, kephalis+biblion* [1]

SCROLLS [3]

of the scroll[s], *899, autos* [1]
scrolls, *1046, biblion* [1]

scrolls, *1047, biblos* [1]

SCUM [1]

scum, *4326, perikatharma* [1]

SCYTHIAN [1]

Scythian, *5033, Skythēs* [1]

SEA [68]

sea, *2498, thalassa* [56]
put out to sea, *343, anagō* [5]
sea, *RPE* [1]
Adriatic Sea, *102, Adrias* [1]
open sea, *1113, bythos* [1]
creatures of sea, *1879, enalios* [1]
sea captain, *3237, kybernētēs* [1]
open sea, *4283, pelagos* [1]
sea anchor, *5007, skeuos* [1]

SEAL [17]

seal, *5382, sphragis* [10]
seal up, *5381, sphragizō* [2]
on placed seal of approval, *5381, sphragizō* [1]
marked with a seal, *5381, sphragizō* [1]
put a seal, *5381, sphragizō* [1]
putting a seal on, *5381, sphragizō* [1]
set seal of ownership on, *5381, sphragizō* [1]

SEALED [6]

sealed, *5381, sphragizō* [4]
sealed with, *2400+3836+5382, echo+ho+sphragis* [1]
sealed, *2958, katasphragizō* [1]

SEALS [5]

seals, *5382, sphragis* [5]

SEAMLESS [1]

seamless, *731, araphos* [1]

SEARCH [7]

in search of, *2426, zēteō* [2]
make a search, *2004, exetazō* [1]
search for, *2004, exetazō* [1]
a thorough search made for, *2118, epizēteō* [1]
search for, *2426, zēteō* [1]
search, *2426, zēteō* [1]

SEARCHED [2]

searched intently and with the greatest care, *1699+2779+2001, ekzēteō+kai+exeraunaō* [1]
searched for, *2426, zēteō* [1]

SEARCHES [3]

searches, *2236, eraunaō* [3]

SEARCHING [2]

searching for, *2426, zēteō* [2]

SEARED [2]

seared, *3009, kaumatizō* [1]
seared as with a hot iron, *3013, kaustēriazō* [1]

SEASHORE [2]

seashore, *2498, thalassa* [1]
seashore, *5927+3836+2498, cheilos+ho+thalassa* [1]

SEASON [4]

out of season, *178, akairōs* [1]

in season, *2323*, *eukairōs* [1]
appointed season, *2789*, *kairos* [1]
season, *2789*, *kairos* [1]

SEASONED [1]

seasoned, *789*, *artyō* [1]

SEASONS [2]

seasons, *2789*, *kairos* [2]

SEAT [7]

judge's seat, *1037*, *bēma* [2]
judgment seat, *1037*, *bēma* [2]
seat, *2756*, *kathedra* [1]
seat, *2764*, *kathēmai* [1]
seat, *5536*, *topos* [1]

SEATED [18]

seated, *2764*, *kathēmai* [12]
seated, *2757*, *kathezomai* [2]
seated, *2767*, *kathizō* [2]
seated, *367*, *anakeimai* [1]
seated with, *5154*, *synkathizō* [1]

SEATS [4]

most important seats, *4751*, *prōtokathedria* [4]

SECLUSION [1]

in seclusion, *4332+1571*,
   perikrybō+heautou [1]

SECOND [38]

second, *1311*, *deuteros* [27]
second time, *1666+1311*, *ek+deuteros* [6]
second time, *1309*, *deuteron* [2]
second, *1309*, *deuteron* [1]
second time, *1311*, *deuteros* [1]
the second^s, *2283*, *heteros* [1]

SECRET [15]

secret, *3220*, *kryptos* [7]
secret, *3696*, *mystērion* [3]
secret, *1877+3696*, *en+mystērion* [1]
secret, *3224*, *kryphaios* [1]
secret, *3225*, *kryphē* [1]
keep secret, *3291*, *lanthanō* [1]
learned the secret, *3679*, *myeō* [1]

SECRETLY [5]

secretly, *3221*, *kryptō* [1]
secretly, *3277*, *lathra* [1]
secretly introduce, *4206*, *pareisagō* [1]
secretly slipped in, *4208*, *pareisdyō* [1]
secretly persuaded, *5680*, *hypoballō* [1]

SECRETS [5]

secrets, *3220*, *kryptos* [2]
secrets, *3696*, *mystērion* [2]
secrets, *AIT* [1]

SECT [5]

sect, *146*, *hairesis* [4]
sect, *AIT* [1]

SECUNDUS [1]

Secundus, *4941*, *Sekoundos* [1]

SECURE [6]

made secure, *856*, *asphalizō* [2]
make secure, *856*, *asphalizō* [1]
secure, *1010*, *bebaios* [1]

secure, *4331*, *perikratēs* [1]
secure position, *5113*, *stērigmos* [1]

SECURED [1]

secured the support, *4275*, *peithō* [1]

SECURELY [1]

securely, *1877+4246+854*,
   en+pas+asphaleia [1]

SEDUCE [1]

seduce, *1284*, *deleazō* [1]

SEE [279]

see, *3972*, *horaō* [112]
see, *1063*, *blepō* [50]
see, *2555*, *theōreō* [23]
see, *2623*, *ide* [10]
see, *2627*, *idou* [10]
see, *NIG* [9]
to see, *4639*, *pros* [7]
see to it, *1063*, *blepō* [5]
see, *RPE* [4]
see, *2517*, *theaomai* [4]
see, *329*, *anablepō* [3]
see, *3783*, *noeō* [3]
see that, *3972*, *horaō* [3]
see, *AIT* [2]
see again, *329*, *anablepō* [2]
see clearly, *1332*, *diablepō* [2]
see, *2227*, *epopteuō* [2]
see to it, *3972*, *horaō* [2]
able to see, *329*, *anablepō* [1]
you can see, *595+5148*, *apenanti+sy* [1]
see, *878*, *augazō* [1]
see, *927*, *aphoraō* [1]
you see, *1142*, *gar* [1]
see if, *1182*, *ginōskō* [1]
to see if, *1623*, *ei* [1]
see that gets justice, *1688*, *ekdikeō* [1]
readiness to see justice done, *1689*, *ekdikēsis* [1]
to see, *2093*, *epi* [1]
see to it, *2174*, *episkopeō* [1]
see, *2262+4639*, *erchomai+pros* [1]
see how, *2627*, *idou* [1]
see that, *2671*, *hina* [1]
as can see, *2779+2627*, *kai+idou* [1]
see, *2908*, *katamanthanō* [1]
see fulfilled, *2918*, *katantaō* [1]
see, *3857*, *oida* [1]
see here, *4047+2555*, *houtos+theōreō* [1]
see, *4472*, *poieō* [1]
manage and see that, *4613*, *proistēmi* [1]
see, *4725*, *prosōpon* [1]
see to it, *5023*, *skopeō* [1]
see, *5743*, *phainō* [1]
see, *5745*, *phaneros* [1]
see, *5746*, *phaneroō* [1]

SEED [50]

seed, *5065*, *sperma* [11]
seed, *RPE* [9]
seed, *3133*, *kokkos* [6]
seed, *5078*, *sporos* [5]
seed sown, *5062*, *speirō* [4]
received seed that fell, *5062*, *speirō* [3]
scattered seed, *1399*, *diaskorpizō* [2]
scattering the seed, *5062*, *speirō* [2]
sow seed, *5062*, *speirō* [2]
seed^s, *3836*, *ho* [1]
scattering seed, *5062*, *speirō* [1]
sown seed, *5062*, *speirō* [1]
seed, *5076*, *spora* [1]
store of seed, *5078*, *sporos* [1]

planted the seed, *5885*, *phyteuō* [1]

SEEDS [3]

seeds, *5065*, *sperma* [2]
seeds, *2843*, *karpos* [1]

SEEING [17]

seeing, *3972*, *horaō* [7]
seeing, *1063*, *blepō* [5]
ever seeing, *1063+1063*, *blepō+blepō* [3]
seeing, *2555*, *theōreō* [1]
seeing what was ahead, *4632*, *prooraō* [1]

SEEK [16]

seek, *2426*, *zēteō* [14]
earnestly seek, *1699*, *ekzēteō* [1]
seek, *1699*, *ekzēteō* [1]

SEEKING [5]

seeking, *2426*, *zēteō* [5]

SEEKS [5]

seeks, *2426*, *zēteō* [4]
seeks, *1699*, *ekzēteō* [1]

SEEM [3]

seem, *1506*, *dokeō* [2]
seem, *6055*, *hōs* [1]

SEEMED [7]

seemed good, *1506*, *dokeō* [2]
seemed to be leaders, *1506*, *dokeō* [1]
seemed, *1506*, *dokeō* [1]
seemed, *5743*, *phainō* [1]
seemed, *6055*, *hōs* [1]
what seemed to be, *6059*, *hōsei* [1]

SEEMS [4]

seems, *1506*, *dokeō* [3]
seems, *AIT* [1]

SEEN [89]

seen, *3972*, *horaō* [62]
seen, *2517*, *theaomai* [8]
seen, *1063*, *blepō* [6]
seen, *5743*, *phainō* [2]
seen, *AIT* [1]
seen, *RPE* [1]
previously seen, *1639+4632*, *eimi+prooraō* [1]
seen, *1871*, *emphanēs* [1]
seen, *2555*, *theōreō* [1]
clearly seen, *2775*, *kathoraō* [1]
seen, *3969*, *horama* [1]
indeed seen, *3972+3972*, *horaō+horaō* [1]
seen of, *3972*, *horaō* [1]
what is seen, *4725*, *prosōpon* [1]
seen plainly, *5746*, *phaneroō* [1]

SEES [12]

sees, *1063*, *blepō* [5]
sees, *2555*, *theōreō* [5]
sees, *3972*, *horaō* [2]

SEIZE [4]

seize, *4389*, *piazō* [3]
seize, *5197*, *syllambanō* [1]

SEIZED [23]

seized, *3195*, *krateō* [4]
seized, *3284*, *lambanō* [3]
seized, *5275*, *synarpazō* [3]
seized, *1181+2093*, *ginomai+epi* [2]

seized, *2095+3836+5931,*
  epiballō+ho+cheir [2]
seized, *2138, epilambanomai* [2]
seized, *5197, syllambanō* [2]
seized, *2095+2093+3836+5931,*
  epiballō+epi+ho+cheir [1]
seized, *2095+3836+5931+2093,*
  epiballō+ho+cheir+epi [1]
seized with, *2158+2093, epipiptō+epi* [1]
seized with remorse, *3564, metamelomai* [1]
seized, *4389, piazō* [1]

SEIZES   [2]

seizes, *2898, katalambanō* [1]
seizes, *3284, lambanō* [1]

SEIZING   [4]

seizing, *3284, lambanō* [2]
seizing, *2138, epilambanomai* [1]
seizing, *5197, syllambanō* [1]

SEIZURES   [2]

seizures, *4944, selēniazomai* [2]

SELECTED   [1]

selected, *3284, lambanō* [1]

SELEUCIA   [1]

Seleucia, *4942, Seleukeia* [1]

SELF   [8]

self, *476, anthrōpos* [4]
self, *RPE* [1]
his very self, *1571, heautou* [1]
self, *3836+2840+476,*
  ho+kardia+anthrōpos [1]
your very self, *4932, seautou* [1]

SELF-CONDEMNED   [1]

self-condemned, *896, autokatakritos* [1]

SELF-CONFIDENT   [1]

self-confident, *5712, hypostasis* [1]

SELF-CONTROL   [6]

self-control, *1602, enkrateia* [4]
lack of self-control, *202, akrasia* [1]
without self-control, *203, akratēs* [1]

SELF-CONTROLLED   [11]

self-controlled, *3768, nēphō* [5]
self-controlled, *5409, sōphrōn* [4]
self-controlled, *5404, sōphroneō* [1]
self-controlled, *5407, sōphronōs* [1]

SELF-DISCIPLINE   [1]

self-discipline, *5406, sōphronismos* [1]

SELF-IMPOSED   [1]

self-imposed worship, *1615, ethelothrēskia* [1]

SELF-INDULGENCE   [2]

self-indulgence, *202, akrasia* [1]
lived in self-indulgence, *5059, spatalaō* [1]

SELF-SEEKING   [2]

self-seeking, *2249, eritheia* [1]
self-seeking, *2426+3836+1571,*
  zēteō+ho+heautou [1]

SELFISH   [5]

selfish ambition, *2249, eritheia* [5]

SELL   [7]

sell, *4797, pōleō* [7]

SELLING   [8]

selling, *4797, pōleō* [7]
selling, *4405, pipraskō* [1]

SELVES   [1]

natural selves, *4922, sarx* [1]

SEMEIN   [1]

Semein, *4946, Semein* [1]

SEND   [70]

send, *4287, pempō* [20]
send, *690, apostellō* [15]
send greetings, *832, aspazomai* [11]
send away, *668, apolyō* [7]
send back, *690, apostellō* [2]
send out, *690, apostellō* [2]
send out, *1675, ekballō* [2]
send on way, *4636, propempō* [2]
send, *RPE* [1]
send, *402, anapempō* [1]
send, *482, anistēmi* [1]
send, *668, apolyō* [1]
send, *1990, exapostellō* [1]
send for, *3559, metakaleō* [1]
send into exile, *3579, metoikizō* [1]
send for, *4287, pempō* [1]
send on their way, *4636, propempō* [1]

SENDING   [17]

sending, *4287, pempō* [7]
sending, *690, apostellō* [5]
sending out, *690, apostellō* [2]
sending back, *402, anapempō* [1]
sending with, *5225, sympempō* [1]
sending, *5225, sympempō* [1]

SENDS   [10]

sends greetings, *832, aspazomai* [6]
sends, *RPE* [1]
sends greetings to, *832, aspazomai* [1]
sends rain, *1101, brechō* [1]
sends, *4287, pempō* [1]

SENSE   [2]

sense of hearing, *198, akoē* [1]
sense of smell, *4018, osphrēsis* [1]

SENSED   [1]

sensed, *5706, hyponoeō* [1]

SENSELESS   [1]

senseless, *852, asynetos* [1]

SENSES   [3]

come to senses, *392, ananēphō* [1]
his senses, *1571, heautou* [1]
come back to senses, *1729, eknēphō* [1]

SENSIBLE   [1]

sensible, *5861, phronimos* [1]

SENSITIVITY   [1]

lost all sensitivity, *556, apalgeō* [1]

SENSUAL   [2]

sensual desires overcome their dedication to,
  2952, katastrēniaō [1]
sensual, *4922, sarx* [1]

SENSUALITY   [1]

sensuality, *816, aselgeia* [1]

SENT   [195]

sent, *690, apostellō* [92]
sent, *4287, pempō* [44]
sent, *1990, exapostellō* [7]
sent for, *3569, metapempō* [5]
sent, *AIT* [4]
sent away, *668, apolyō* [4]
sent off, *668, apolyō* [3]
sent out, *690, apostellō* [3]
sent away, *1990, exapostellō* [3]
sent, *RPE* [2]
sent back, *402, anapempō* [2]
sent word, *690, apostellō* [2]
sent for, *4673, proskaleō* [2]
sent, *4707+4287, prostithēmi+pempō* [2]
sent, *402, anapempō* [1]
sent away, *690, apostellō* [1]
sent for, *690+3559, apostellō+metakaleō* [1]
sent message, *690, apostellō* [1]
sent out, *806+690, archō+apostellō* [1]
sent the letter, *1211, graphō* [1]
sent away, *1675, ekballō* [1]
sent off, *1675, ekballō* [1]
sent out, *1675, ekballō* [1]
sent, *1675, ekballō* [1]
sent away, *1734, ekpempō* [1]
sent on way, *1734, ekpempō* [1]
sent off, *1990, exapostellō* [1]
sent for, *3306+5888, legō+phōneō* [1]
sent, *3579, metoikizō* [1]
sent[s], *4123, para* [1]
sent on way, *4636, propempō* [1]
sent with, *5273, synapostellō* [1]
sent to hell, *5434, tartaroō* [1]
sent for, *5888, phōneō* [1]

SENTENCE   [4]

sentence, *645, apokrima* [1]
death sentence, *2505, thanatos* [1]
sentence, *3210, krima* [1]
sentence, *3364, logos* [1]

SENTENCED   [1]

sentenced, *3210, krima* [1]

SENTRIES   [1]

sentries, *5874, phylax* [1]

SEPARATE   [11]

separate, *6004, chōrizō* [5]
separate, *928, aphorizō* [4]
separate from, *4024+3552, ou+meta* [1]
separate from, *6006, chōris* [1]

SEPARATED   [3]

separated, *558, apallotrioō* [1]
separated, *1374, diamerizō* [1]
separated from, *6004, chōrizō* [1]

SEPARATES   [1]

separates, *928, aphorizō* [1]

SERGIUS   [1]

Sergius, *4950, Sergios* [1]

SERIOUS [2]

serious, *987, barys* [1]
serious, *4505, ponēros* [1]

SERIOUSNESS [1]

seriousness, *4949, semnotēs* [1]

SERPENT [3]

serpent, *4058, ophis* [3]

SERPENT'S [2]

serpent's, *4058+899, ophis+autos* [1]
serpent's, *4058, ophis* [1]

SERUG [1]

Serug, *4952, Serouch* [1]

SERVANT [100]

servant, *1528, doulos¹* [54]
servant, *1356, diakonos* [13]
servant, *4090, pais* [12]
servant girl, *4087, paidiskē* [4]
fellow servant, *5281, syndoulos* [4]
the servantˢ, *899, autos* [2]
servant, *1527, doulē* [2]
servant, *3860, oiketēs* [2]
fellow servant with with, *5281, syndoulos* [2]
servant, *AIT* [1]
trusted personal servant, *2093+3836+3131,
  epi+ho+koitōn* [1]
servant, *2544, therapōn* [1]
servant girls, *4087, paidiskē* [1]
servant, *5677, hypēretēs* [1]

SERVANT'S [2]

servant's, *1528, doulos¹* [2]

SERVANTS [60]

servants, *1528, doulos¹* [37]
servants, *1356, diakonos* [7]
fellow servants, *5281, syndoulos* [3]
servants, *5677, hypēretēs* [3]
servants, *3313, leitourgos* [2]
servants, *RPE* [1]
the servantsˢ, *899, autos* [1]
[servants] women, *1527, doulē* [1]
servants men, *1528, doulos¹* [1]
servants, *2542, therapeia* [1]
servants in household, *3859, oiketeia* [1]
servants, *3860, oiketēs* [1]
servants, *4090, pais* [1]
servants, *5281, syndoulos* [1]

SERVE [36]

serve, *1526, douleuō* [10]
serve, *3302, latreuō* [10]
serve, *AIT* [3]
serve, *1354, diakoneō* [3]
serve, *1355, diakonia* [3]
serve as deacons, *1354, diakoneō* [1]
serve as slaves, *1526, douleuō* [1]
to serve, *1650, eis* [1]
serve at a sanctuary, *3302, latreuō* [1]
serve at, *4204, paredreuō* [1]
dress to serve, *4322, perizōnnymi* [1]
serve as, *4618, prokeimai* [1]

SERVED [13]

served, *1354, diakoneō* [4]
served, *1181, ginomai* [2]
served, *1526, douleuō* [2]
has served, *2262, erchomai* [1]

served, *2543, therapeuō* [1]
served, *3302, latreuō* [1]
served at, *4668, prosechō* [1]
served, *5676, hypēreteō* [1]

SERVES [9]

serves, *1354, diakoneō* [6]
serves, *1526, douleuō* [1]
serves, *3313, leitourgos* [1]
serves as a soldier, *5129, strateuomai* [1]

SERVICE [20]

service, *1355, diakonia* [9]
service, *3311, leitourgia* [2]
serviceˢ, *3836, ho* [2]
service, *AIT* [1]
in the service of, *1354, diakoneō* [1]
service that perform, *1355+3836+3311+4047,
  diakonia+ho+leitourgia+houtos* [1]
service, *2307, euergesia* [1]
fit for service, *2310, euthetos* [1]
service, *3301, latreia* [1]
dressed ready for service, *3836+4019+4322,
  ho+osphys+perizōnnymi* [1]

SERVING [9]

serving, *1526, douleuō* [3]
serving, *RPE* [1]
serving, *1354, diakoneō* [1]
serving, *1355, diakonia* [1]
serving as overseers, *2174, episkopeō* [1]
serving as priest, *2634, hierateuō* [1]
serving as a soldier, *5129, strateuomai* [1]

SET [73]

set free, *1802, eleutheroō* [5]
set before, *4192, paratithēmi* [5]
set free, *668, apolyō* [3]
set apart, *928, aphorizō* [3]
set out, *2002, exerchomai* [3]
set, *AIT* [2]
set aside, *119, atheteō* [2]
set sail, *343, anagō* [2]
set hope, *1827, elpizō* [2]
set free, *3395, lyō* [2]
set, *3988, horizō* [2]
set, *RPE* [1]
set apart as very own, *39, hagiazō* [1]
set apart, *39, hagiazō* [1]
set aside, *120, athetēsis* [1]
set aside, *218, akyroō* [1]
set out, *343, anagō* [1]
set on fire, *409, anaptō* [1]
set before, *423, anatithēmi* [1]
set out, *482, anistēmi* [1]
set off, *623, apodēmeō* [1]
set sail, *676, apopleō* [1]
set, *1181, ginomai* [1]
set, *1443, didōmi* [1]
set free, *1801, eleutheros* [1]
hopes are set, *1827, elpizō* [1]
set free, *1975, exaireō* [1]
set out from, *2002, exerchomai* [1]
set on, *2202+2093, epitithēmi+epi* [1]
set off, *2262, erchomai* [1]
set heart on, *2426, zēteō* [1]
set hearts on, *2426, zēteō* [1]
set, *2705, histēmi* [1]
set up, *2941, kataskeuazō* [1]
set aside, *4123+1571+5502,
  para+heautou+tithēmi* [1]
set a meal before, *4192+5544,
  paratithēmi+trapeza* [1]
set, *4218, parechō* [1]

set at rest, *4275, peithō* [1]
set sail, *4311, periaireō* [1]
set on, *4363, perititithēmi* [1]
set up, *4381, pēgnymi* [1]
set up, *4472, poieō* [1]
set out, *4513, poreuomai* [1]
time set, *4607, prothesmia* [1]
set before, *4618, prokeimai* [1]
set, *4705, prostassō* [1]
set seal of ownership on, *5381, sphragizō* [1]
set, *5502, tithēmi* [1]
price set on, *5507+5506, timē+timaō* [1]
set on fire, *5824, phlogizō* [1]
set minds on, *5858, phroneō* [1]
minds set on, *5858, phroneō* [1]
set apart, *6004, chōrizō* [1]

SETH [1]

Seth, *4953, sēth* [1]

SETS [6]

sets aside, *359, anaireō* [1]
sets free, *1802, eleutheroō* [1]
sets up, *2048, epairō* [1]
sets up, *2767, kathizō* [1]
sets heart on being, *3977, oregō* [1]
sets on fire, *5824, phlogizō* [1]

SETTING [4]

setting aside, *119, atheteō* [1]
setting, *1544, dynō* [1]
setting hearts on, *2122, epithymētēs* [1]
setting forth plainly, *5748, phanerōsis* [1]

SETTLE [4]

settle matters, *1639+2333, eimi+eunoeō* [1]
settle down, *3552+2484, meta+hēsychia* [1]
settle the matter, *3972, horaō* [1]
settle, *5256, synairō* [1]

SETTLED [5]

settled, *1181, ginomai* [1]
settled, *2147, epilyō* [1]
settled the matter, *2705+1612,
  histēmi+hedraios* [1]
settled, *2997, katoikeō* [1]
settled accounts, *5256+3364, synairō+logos* [1]

SETTLEMENT [1]

settlement, *5256, synairō* [1]

SEVEN [92]

seven, *2231, hepta* [85]
seven times, *2232, heptakis* [4]
seven thousand, *2233, heptakischilioi* [1]
and sevenˢ others, *3838, ogdoos* [1]
seven miles, *5084+2008,
  stadion+hexēkonta* [1]

SEVENTH [10]

seventh, *1575, hebdomos* [9]
seventh, *2231, hepta* [1]

SEVENTY [1]

seventy, *1573, hebdomēkonta* [1]

SEVENTY-FIVE [2]

seventy-five, *1573+4297,
  hebdomēkonta+pente* [1]
seventy-five pounds, *3354+1669,
  litra+hekaton* [1]

SEVENTY-SEVEN [1]

seventy-seven times, *1574+2231, hebdomēkontakis+hepta* [1]

SEVENTY-TWO [2]

seventy-two, *1573+1545, hebdomēkonta+dyo* [2]

SEVERAL [4]

several, *5516, tis* [3]
several, *4498, polys* [1]

SEVERE [8]

severe, *3489, megas* [4]
severe pain, *992, basanos* [1]
severe trial, *1509+2568, dokimē+thlipsis* [1]
severe, *2708, ischyros* [1]
severe, *4498, polys* [1]

SEVERELY [7]

most severely, *4358, perissoteros* [2]
severely, *AIT* [1]
put it too severely, *2096, epibareō* [1]
severely, *4498, polys* [1]
more severely, *5649, hyperballontōs* [1]
more severely, *5937, cheirōn* [1]

SEWS [3]

sews on, *2095+2093, epiballō+epi* [2]
sews, *2165, epiraptō* [1]

SEXUAL [20]

sexual immorality, *4518, porneia* [13]
sexual impurity, *174, akatharsia* [1]
gave up to sexual immorality, *1745, ekporneuō* [1]
sexual immorality, *3130, koitē* [1]
sexual sin, *4518, porneia* [1]
commit sexual immorality, *4519, porneuō* [1]
committing sexual immorality, *4519, porneuō* [1]
sexual immorality, *4519, porneuō* [1]

SEXUALLY [8]

sexually immoral, *4521, pornos* [7]
sins sexually, *4519, porneuō* [1]

SHABBY [1]

shabby, *4865, rhyparos* [1]

SHADE [1]

shade, *5014, skia* [1]

SHADOW [6]

shadow, *5014, skia* [6]

SHADOWS [1]

shadows, *684, aposkiasma* [1]

SHAFT [1]

shaft, *5853, phrear* [1]

SHAKE [5]

shake off, *1759, ektinassō* [2]
shake off, *608+701, apo+apotinassō* [1]
shake, *4888, saleuō* [1]
shake, *4940, seiō* [1]

SHAKEN [11]

shaken, *4888, saleuō* [8]
cannot be shaken, *810, asaleutos* [1]

shaken together, *4888, saleuō* [1]
shaken, *4940, seiō* [1]

SHAKING [2]

shaking, *3075, kineō* [2]

SHALL [75]

shall, *AIT* [70]
shall, *NIG* [3]
so shall it be, *3721, nai* [1]
what shall we do, *5515+4036+1639, tis+oun+eimi* [1]

SHALLOW [2]

shallow, *3590+958, mē+bathos* [2]

SHAME [12]

shame, *158, aischynē* [3]
put to shame, *2875, kataischynō* [3]
shame, *1959, entropē* [2]
shame, *2875, kataischynō* [2]
shame, *871, atimia* [1]
shame, *1956, entrepō* [1]

SHAMEFUL [6]

shameful, *158, aischynē* [2]
shameful, *156, aischros* [1]
shameful, *816, aselgeia* [1]
shameful, *871, atimia* [1]
what is shameful, *1007, bdelygma* [1]

SHAMEFULLY [3]

treated shamefully, *869, atimazo* [2]
shamefully, *859, aschēmosynē* [1]

SHARE [35]

come and share, *1656+1650, eiserchomai+eis* [2]
share, *3125, koinōneō* [2]
share with, *3556, metadidōmi* [2]
share in, *3581, metochos* [2]
share, *5170, synkoinōneō* [2]
share, *5171+1181, synkoinōnos+ginomai* [2]
share, *RPE* [1]
give share of, *625, apodidōmi* [1]
share, *1639, eimi* [1]
share, *2095+3538, epiballō+meros* [1]
share in the inheritance, *3099, klēronomeō* [1]
share, *3102, klēros* [1]
share, *3123, koinos* [1]
share with, *3125, koinōneō* [1]
share, *3126, koinōnia* [1]
willing to share, *3127, koinōnikos* [1]
share, *3128+1639, koinōnos+eimi* [1]
share, *3128, koinōnos* [1]
share, *3310, leitourgeō* [1]
share, *3535, meris* [1]
share, *3538, meros* [1]
share, *3556, metadidōmi* [1]
receive a share, *3561, metalambanō* [1]
share in, *3561, metalambanō* [1]
share, *4348, peripoiēsis* [1]
share with, *5171+1639, synkoinōnos+eimi* [1]
share, *5211, symmerizomai* [1]
share in sufferings, *5224, sympaschō* [1]
share in glory, *5280, syndoxazō* [1]

SHARED [8]

shared, *3125, koinōneō* [2]
shared, *3123, koinos* [1]
shared, *3275+3836+3102, lanchanō+ho+klēros* [1]
shared in, *3576, metechō* [1]

shared in, *3581+1181, metochos+ginomai* [1]
shared luxury, *5139, strēniaō* [1]
shared joy, *5176, synchairō* [1]

SHARERS [1]

sharers together in, *5212, symmetochos* [1]

SHARES [3]

shares, *3125, koinōneō* [1]
dividing into shares, *4472+3538, poieō+meros* [1]
shares, *5592, trōgō* [1]

SHARING [5]

sharing, *3126, koinōnia* [3]
fellowship of sharing, *3126, koinōnia* [1]
sharing in, *3576, metechō* [1]

SHARON [1]

Sharon, *4926, Sarōn* [1]

SHARP [9]

sharp, *3955, oxys* [7]
sharp, *4024+3900, ou+oligos* [1]
sharp disagreement, *4237, paroxysmos* [1]

SHARPER [1]

sharper, *5533, tomos* [1]

SHARPLY [2]

sharply, *705, apotomōs* [1]
argue sharply, *3481, machomai* [1]

SHAVED [3]

shaved, *3834, xyraō* [2]
shaved off, *3834, xyraō* [1]

SHE [196]

she, *AIT* [139]
she, *899, autos* [16]
she, *RPE* [9]
she, *4047, houtos* [9]
she, *3836+1254, ho+de* [8]
she, *1697, ekeinos* [3]
she, *3836, ho* [2]
she, *4015, hostis* [2]
she[s], *1222, gynē* [1]
what she did, *2240, ergon* [1]
she[s], *3836+1222, ho+gynē* [1]
she[s], *3836+3166, ho+korasion* [1]
she[s], *3836+3451, ho+Maria* [1]
she, *3840, hode* [1]
she, *4005, hos* [1]
she, *5679+899, hypo+autos* [1]

SHEALTIEL [3]

Shealtiel, *4886, Salathiēl* [3]

SHEARER [1]

shearer, *3025, keirō* [1]

SHECHEM [2]

Shechem, *5374, Sychem* [2]

SHED [6]

shed, *1772, ekcheō* [3]
shed, *1773, ekchynnomai* [2]
shed, *AIT* [1]

SHEDDING [3]

shedding blood, *135, haima* [2]

shedding of blood, *136, haimatekchysia* [1]

SHEEP [45]

sheep, *4585, probaton* [38]
sheep, *AIT* [2]
sheep, *RPE* [1]
sheep pen, *885, aulē* [1]
that one sheep⁶, *899, autos* [1]
looking after sheep, *4477, poimainō* [1]
Sheep Gate, *4583, probatikos* [1]

SHEEP'S [1]

sheep's, *4585, probaton* [1]

SHEEPSKINS [1]

sheepskins, *3603, mēlōtē* [1]

SHEET [3]

sheet, *3855, othonē* [2]
sheet, *5007, skeuos* [1]

SHELAH [1]

Shelah, *4885, Sala* [1]

SHELTERS [3]

shelters, *5008, skēnē* [3]

SHEM [1]

Shem, *4954, sēm* [1]

SHEPHERD [16]

shepherd, *4478, poimēn* [13]
Chief Shepherd, *799, archipoimēn* [1]
be shepherd of, *4477, poimainō* [1]
be shepherd, *4477, poimainō* [1]

SHEPHERDS [7]

shepherds, *4478, poimēn* [4]
be shepherds of, *4477, poimainō* [2]
shepherds, *4477, poimainō* [1]

SHIELD [1]

shield, *2599, thyreos* [1]

SHIELDED [1]

shielded, *5864, phroureō* [1]

SHIFTING [1]

shifting, *5572, tropē* [1]

SHINE [9]

shine, *5743, phainō* [3]
shine, *3290, lampō* [2]
shine, *1719, eklampō* [1]
shine on, *2210, epiphainō* [1]
shine on, *2213, epiphauskō* [1]
made shine, *3290, lampō* [1]

SHINES [2]

shines, *5743, phainō* [1]
shines on, *5894, phōtizō* [1]

SHINING [6]

shining, *5743, phainō* [3]
shining, *3287, lampros* [2]
stopped shining, *1722, ekleipō* [1]

SHIP [22]

ship, *4450, ploion* [17]
ship, *RPE* [2]

travel by ship, *2093+5536+4434,*
  epi+topos+pleō [1]
owner of the ship, *3729, nauklēros* [1]
ship, *3730, naus* [1]

SHIP'S [1]

ship's, *4450, ploion* [1]

SHIPS [3]

ships, *4450, ploion* [3]

SHIPWRECKED [2]

shipwrecked, *3728, nauageō* [2]

SHONE [4]

shone, *3290, lampō* [2]
shone with, *2400, echō* [1]
shone around, *4334, perilampō* [1]

SHOOK [7]

shook, *4940, seiō* [2]
shook off, *701, apotinassō* [1]
shook from, *1759, ektinassō* [1]
shook out, *1759, ektinassō* [1]
shook, *4888, saleuō* [1]
shook violently, *5057, sparassō* [1]

SHOOT [1]

wild olive shoot, *66, agrielaios* [1]

SHORE [13]

shore, *1178, gē* [5]
shore, *129, aigialos* [3]
shore, *RPE* [1]
shore, *302, ammos* [1]
along the shore, *839, asson* [1]
on the opposite shore, *4305, peran* [1]
to far shore, *4305, peran* [1]

SHORT [18]

cut short, *3143, koloboō* [2]
short, *3625, mikros* [2]
only a short time, *4672, proskairos* [2]
short time, *1099, brachys* [1]
short, *1328+1099, dia+brachys* [1]
a short while ago, *3814, nyn* [1]
short, *3836+2461+3625,*
  ho+hēlikia+mikros [1]
short time, *3900, oligos* [1]
a short time, *3900, oligos* [1]
short, *3900, oligos* [1]
a short time, *4672, proskairos* [1]
short, *5366, systellō* [1]
fall short, *5728, hystereō* [1]
fallen short, *5728, hystereō* [1]
short, *6052, hōra* [1]

SHORTENED [2]

shortened, *3143, koloboō* [2]

SHORTLY [1]

shortly, *2317, euthys¹* [1]

SHOULD [155]

should, *AIT* [127]
should, *NIG* [11]
should, *1256, dei* [5]
should have, *1256, dei* [4]
should, *RPE* [2]
should, *4053, opheilō* [2]
should be, *1256, dei* [1]
should, *3516, mellō* [1]

should have, *4053, opheilō* [1]
should, *5973, chrē* [1]

SHOULDERS [2]

shoulders, *6049, ōmos* [2]

SHOULDN'T [5]

shouldn't, *3266, kōlyō* [1]
shouldn't, *3590, mē* [1]
shouldn't have, *4024+1256, ou+dei* [1]
shouldn't, *4024, ou* [1]
shouldn't, *4049, ouchi* [1]

SHOUT [2]

gave a shout, *3189+5889, krazō+phōnē* [1]
shout, *3189, krazō* [1]

SHOUTED [26]

shouted, *3189, krazō* [15]
shouted, *3198, kraugazō* [3]
shouted, *2215, epiphōneō* [2]
shouted, *3306, legō* [2]
shouted, *2048+3836+5889,*
  epairō+ho+phōnē [1]
shouted, *3489+3836+5889+5774,*
  megas+ho+phōnē+phēmi [1]
shouted instructions, *5204, symbibazō* [1]
shouted, *5888+3489+5889,*
  phōneō+megas+phōnē [1]

SHOUTING [18]

shouting, *3189, krazō* [7]
shouting, *3198, kraugazō* [4]
shouting, *1066, boaō* [2]
shouting, *3306, legō* [2]
shouting at, *2215, epiphōneō* [1]
shouting, *2215, epiphōneō* [1]
shouting at the top of voice, *5889+3489+3306,*
  phōnē+megas+legō [1]

SHOUTS [2]

shouts, *5889, phōnē* [2]

SHOW [67]

show, *1259, deiknymi* [19]
show, *1892, endeiknymi* [5]
show, *1872, emphanizō* [3]
show, *2109, epideiknymi* [3]
show, *5683, hypodeiknymi* [3]
show, *AIT* [2]
show, *1443, didōmi* [2]
show that, *1892, endeiknymi* [2]
show, *4733, prophasis* [2]
show, *5746, phaneroō* [2]
show, *NIG* [1]
show, *RPE* [1]
show, *344, anadeiknymi* [1]
show to prove, *1259, deiknymi* [1]
show favoritism, *1639+4720,*
  eimi+prosōpolēmptēs [1]
show favoritism, *1639+4721,*
  eimi+prosōpolēmpsia [1]
to show mercy, *1790, eleaō* [1]
show fault, *1794, elenchō* [1]
show favoritism, *1877+4721,*
  en+prosōpolēmpsia [1]
to show, *1877, en* [1]
show special attention to, *2098+2093,*
  epiblepō+epi [1]
to show that, *2671, hina* [1]
show contempt for, *2969, kataphroneō* [1]
show less respect, *2969, kataphroneō* [1]

show partiality, *3284+4725*,
  lambanō+prosōpon [1]
show, *3972*, *horaō* [1]
show, *4472*, *poieō* [1]
to show that, *4639+3836*, *pros+ho* [1]
show favoritism, *4719*, *prosōpolēmpteō* [1]
show, *4955*, *sēmainō* [1]
show proper respect to, *5506*, *timaō* [1]
show hospitality to, *5696*, *hypolambanō* [1]
show, *5743*, *phainō* [1]
show, *5745+1181*, *phaneros+ginomai* [1]

SHOWED [16]

showed, *1259*, *deiknymi* [6]
showed, *5746*, *phaneroō* [2]
showed love, *26*, *agapaō* [1]
showed concern, *2170*, *episkeptomai* [1]
showed that accepted, *3455*, *martyreō* [1]
showed concern, *3508*, *melei* [1]
showed, *3606*, *mēnyō* [1]
showed, *4218*, *parechō* [1]
showed, *4225*, *paristēmi* [1]
showed, *5683*, *hypodeiknymi* [1]

SHOWING [6]

showing, *AIT* [1]
showing, *1259*, *deiknymi* [1]
showing, *1317*, *dēloō* [1]
showing mercy, *1796*, *eleeō* [1]
showing, *2109*, *epideiknymi* [1]
showing hospitality, *3827*, *xenodocheō* [1]

SHOWN [13]

shown, *1259*, *deiknymi* [3]
shown mercy, *1796*, *eleeō* [3]
shown, *NIG* [1]
shown kindness, *14*, *agathoergeō* [1]
shown, *1892*, *endeiknymi* [1]
shown favor, *2078*, *epeidon* [1]
act of kindness shown to, *2307*, *euergesia* [1]
shown great, *3486*, *megalynō* [1]
shown for what it is, *5745*, *phaneros* [1]

SHOWS [1]

shows, *1259*, *deiknymi* [1]

SHREWD [2]

more shrewd, *5861*, *phronimos* [1]
shrewd, *5861*, *phronimos* [1]

SHREWDLY [1]

shrewdly, *5862*, *phronimōs* [1]

SHRIEK [1]

shriek, *5888+5889+3489*,
  phōneō+phōnē+megas [1]

SHRIEKED [1]

shrieked, *3189*, *krazō* [1]

SHRIEKS [1]

shrieks, *1066+5889+3489*,
  boaō+phōnē+megas [1]

SHRINE [1]

shrine, *5008*, *skēnē* [1]

SHRINES [1]

shrines, *3724*, *naos* [1]

SHRINK [2]

shrink, *AIT* [1]

shrink back, *5714*, *hypostolē* [1]

SHRINKS [1]

shrinks back, *5713*, *hypostellō* [1]

SHRIVELED [5]

shriveled, *3831*, *xēros* [4]
shriveled, *3830*, *xērainō* [1]

SHUDDER [1]

shudder, *5857*, *phrissō* [1]

SHUT [10]

shut, *3091*, *kleiō* [8]
shut, *AIT* [1]
shut, *5852*, *phrassō* [1]

SHUTS [1]

shuts, *3091*, *kleiō* [1]

SICK [39]

sick, *820*, *astheneō* [12]
sick, *2809+2400*, *kakōs+echō* [8]
sick, *822*, *asthenēs* [6]
sick, *779*, *arrōstos* [5]
sick, *AIT* [2]
lay sick, *820*, *astheneō* [2]
sick, *RPE* [1]
sick, *2400+819*, *echō+astheneia* [1]
sick, *2827*, *kamnō* [1]
sick in bed, *2879*, *katakeimai* [1]

SICKLE [8]

sickle, *1535*, *drepanon* [8]

SICKNESS [5]

sickness, *3433*, *malakia* [3]
sickness, *819*, *astheneia* [1]
sickness, *820+3798*, *astheneō+nosos* [1]

SICKNESSES [2]

sicknesses, *819*, *astheneia* [1]
sicknesses, *3465*, *mastix* [1]

SIDE [34]

other side, *4305*, *peran* [5]
side, *4433*, *pleura* [5]
side, *3146*, *kolpos* [3]
on the other side, *4305*, *peran* [3]
passed by on the other side, *524*,
  antiparerchomai [2]
right side, *1288*, *dexios* [2]
side by side, *3128*, *koinōnos* [2]
other side of the lake, *4305*, *peran* [2]
side, *AIT* [1]
on the side, *1639*, *eimi* [1]
on each side, *1949+2779+1696*,
  enteuthen+kai+ekeithen [1]
one on each side, *1949+2779+1949*,
  enteuthen+kai+enteuthen [1]
side, *3538*, *meros* [1]
on⁵ the other side, *3963*, *hopou* [1]
on every side, *4119*, *pantothen* [1]
stood at side, *4225*, *paristēmi* [1]
to other side, *4305*, *peran* [1]
contended at side, *5254*, *synathleō* [1]

SIDED [1]

sided, *1639*, *eimi* [1]

SIDES [1]

on both sides, *2277+2779+3957*,
  esōthen+kai+opisthen [1]

SIDON [11]

Sidon, *4972*, *Sidōn* [9]
people Sidon, *4973*, *Sidōnios* [1]
region of Sidon, *4973*, *Sidōnios* [1]

SIFT [1]

sift, *4985*, *siniazō* [1]

SIGH [1]

with a deep sigh, *5100*, *stenazō* [1]

SIGHED [1]

sighed deeply, *417+3836+4460*,
  anastenazō+ho+pneuma [1]

SIGHT [41]

received sight, *329*, *anablepō* [5]
in the sight, *1967*, *enōpion* [5]
receive sight, *329*, *anablepō* [4]
in sight, *1967*, *enōpion* [3]
in the sight, *2978*, *katenanti* [2]
in sight, *2979*, *katenōpion* [2]
sight, *4057*, *ophthalmos* [2]
in sight, *4123*, *para* [2]
sight, *4725*, *prosōpon* [2]
sight, *AIT* [1]
sight, *RPE* [1]
restore sight, *329*, *anablepō* [1]
recovery of sight, *330*, *anablepsis* [1]
sight, *487+3836+4057*,
  anoigō+ho+ophthalmos [1]
sight, *1063*, *blepō* [1]
sight, *1626*, *eidos* [1]
in the sight, *1883*, *enantion* [1]
in his sight, *1967+899*, *enōpion+autos* [1]
sight, *1967*, *enōpion* [1]
sight, *2556*, *theōria* [1]
sight, *3969*, *horama* [1]
the sight of, *3972*, *horaō* [1]
sight, *5751*, *phantazō* [1]

SIGHTING [1]

sighting, *428*, *anaphainō* [1]

SIGN [34]

sign, *4956*, *sēmeion* [18]
miraculous sign, *4956*, *sēmeion* [11]
sign, *RPE* [1]
sign, *1893*, *endeixis* [1]
sign of authority, *2026*, *exousia* [1]
wondrous sign, *4956*, *sēmeion* [1]
sign, *5518*, *titlos* [1]

SIGNAL [2]

signal, *4956*, *sēmeion* [1]
signal, *5361*, *syssēmon* [1]

SIGNALED [1]

signaled, *2916*, *kataneuō* [1]

SIGNS [41]

miraculous signs, *4956*, *sēmeion* [23]
signs, *4956*, *sēmeion* [15]
signs, *RPE* [1]
making signs, *1377*, *dianeuō* [1]
made signs, *1935*, *enneuō* [1]

SILAS [21]

Silas, *4976, Silas* [12]
Silas, *4977, Silouanos* [4]
Silas, *RPE* [3]
Paul[s] and Silas, *899, autos* [2]

SILENCE [3]

silence, *AIT* [1]
silence, *4968, sigē* [1]
silence talk, *5821, phimoō* [1]

SILENCED [3]

silenced, *2187, epistomizō* [1]
silenced, *5821, phimoō* [1]
silenced, *5852, phrassō* [1]

SILENT [12]

silent, *4995, siōpaō* [5]
silent, *4967, sigaō* [3]
silent, *936, aphōnos* [1]
silent, *2483, hēsychazō* [1]
silent, *2484, hēsychia* [1]
all silent, *4498+4968, polys+sigē* [1]

SILK [1]

silk, *4986, sirikos* [1]

SILOAM [3]

Siloam, *4978, Silōam* [3]

SILVER [16]

silver, *738, argyros* [5]
silver coins, *736, argyrion* [3]
silver, *736, argyrion* [3]
of silver, *739, argyrous* [2]
silver, *739, argyrous* [1]
silver coins, *1324, dēnarion* [1]
silver coins, *1534, drachmē* [1]

SILVERSMITH [1]

silversmith, *737, argyrokopos* [1]

SIMEON [6]

Simeon, *5208, Symeōn* [5]
Simeon[s], *899, autos* [1]

SIMILAR [2]

similar, *3927, homoios* [1]
similar, *5525, toioutos* [1]

SIMILARLY [3]

similarly, *1254, de* [1]
similarly, *3931, homoiōs* [1]
similarly, *6058, hōsautōs* [1]

SIMON [74]

Simon, *4981, Simōn* [70]
Simon, *RPE* [2]
Simon, *5208, Symeōn* [2]

SIMON'S [4]

Simon's, *4981, Simōn* [4]

SIMPLY [4]

simply, *3667, monon* [2]
simply, *NIG* [1]
simply, *1254, de* [1]

SIN [127]

sin, *281, hamartia* [75]
sin, *279, hamartanō* [14]

causes to sin, *4997, skandalizō* [8]
sin, *RPE* [2]
guilty of sin, *281+2400, hamartia+echō* [2]
sin offering, *281, hamartia* [2]
sin offerings, *4309+281, peri+hamartia* [2]
sin, *94, adikia* [1]
commit a sin, *279+281, hamartanō+hamartia* [1]
sin, *280, hamartēma* [1]
promotes sin, *281+1356, hamartia+diakonos* [1]
sin, *281+2237, hamartia+ergazomai* [1]
sin, *281+4472, hamartia+poieō* [1]
what sin was, *281, hamartia* [1]
without sin, *281+4024, hamartia+ou* [1]
without sin, *387, anamartētos* [1]
entice to sin, *965+4998+1967, ballō+skandalon+enōpion* [1]
guilty of sin, *2400+281, echō+hamartia* [1]
leave your life of sin, *3600+279, mēketi+hamartanō* [1]
sin against, *4183, paraptōma* [1]
sin, *4183, paraptōma* [1]
sexual sin, *4518, porneia* [1]
cause to sin, *4997, skandalizō* [1]
causes fall into sin, *4997, skandalizō* [1]
causes sin, *4997, skandalizō* [1]
led into sin, *4997, skandalizō* [1]
things that cause people to sin, *4998, skandalon* [1]
causes sin, *4998, skandalon* [1]
things that cause to sin, *4998, skandalon* [1]

SIN'S [1]

sin's, *281, hamartia* [1]

SINAI [4]

Sinai, *4982, Sina* [4]

SINCE [108]

since, *AIT* [43]
since, *608, apo* [11]
since, *1623, ei* [10]
since, *2075, epei* [9]
since, *4022, hoti* [5]
since, *1142, gar* [4]
since, *2076, epeidē* [4]
since, *1666, ek* [3]
since, *2777, kathōs* [3]
ever since, *608+4005, apo+hos* [2]
since, *608+4005, apo+hos* [2]
since, *1328+3836, dia+ho* [2]
since, *RPE* [1]
since, *1328, dia* [1]
since, *1484, dioti* [1]
since, *1569, ean* [1]
since, *1642, eiper* [1]
since going through, *2400, echō* [1]
since, *2779, kai* [1]
since that time, *3836+3370, ho+loipos* [1]
since, *3963, hopou* [1]
since, *6055, hōs* [1]

SINCERE [10]

sincere, *537, anypokritos* [6]
sincere, *240, alēthinos* [1]
sincere devotion, *605, haplotēs* [1]
sincere, *911, aphelotēs* [1]
sincere, *3590+1474, mē+dilogos* [1]

SINCERELY [1]

sincerely, *56, hagnōs* [1]

SINCERITY [6]

sincerity, *1636, eilikrineia* [3]
sincerity, *605, haplotēs* [2]
sincerity, *1188, gnēsios* [1]

SINEWS [1]

sinews, *5278, syndesmos* [1]

SINFUL [42]

sinful nature, *4922, sarx* [22]
sinful, *283, hamartōlos* [6]
sinful man, *4922, sarx* [3]
sinful, *281, hamartia* [2]
sinful, *279, hamartanō* [1]
what is sinful, *281, hamartia* [1]
sinful life, *283, hamartōlos* [1]
sinful desires, *2123, epithymia* [1]
sinful, *4505, ponēros* [1]
sinful, *4920, sarkikos* [1]
sinful human nature, *4922, sarx* [1]
sinful, *4922, sarx* [1]
sinful nature, *5393+3836+4922, sōma+ho+sarx* [1]

SING [8]

sing, *106, adō* [2]
sing, *6010, psallō* [2]
sing praises to, *2046, epaineō* [1]
sing praises, *5630, hymneō* [1]
sing hymns, *6010, psallō* [1]
sing songs of praise, *6010, psallō* [1]

SINGING [2]

singing, *3306, legō* [1]
singing hymns, *5630, hymneō* [1]

SINGLE [9]

a single, *1651, heis* [7]
single, *AIT* [1]
only a single, *3668, monos* [1]

SINK [2]

sink, *1112, bythizō* [1]
sink, *2931, katapontizō* [1]

SINKING [1]

sinking, *2965, katapherō* [1]

SINNED [15]

sinned, *279, hamartanō* [12]
sinned earlier, *4579, proamartanō* [2]
sinned, *281+1639+4472, hamartia+eimi+poieō* [1]

SINNER [13]

sinner, *283, hamartōlos* [9]
sinner, *283+467, hamartōlos+anēr* [1]
sinner, *476+283, anthrōpos+hamartōlos* [1]
convinced that is a sinner, *1794, elenchō* [1]
sinner, *4126, parabasis* [1]

SINNERS [30]

sinners, *283, hamartōlos* [29]
sinners, *RPE* [1]

SINNING [10]

sinning, *279, hamartanō* [7]
sinning, *281, hamartia* [2]
guilty of sinning against, *1944, enochos* [1]

SINS [103]

sins, *281, hamartia* [74]
sins, *4183, paraptōma* [7]
sins, *RPE* [5]
sins, *279, hamartanō* [5]
sins, *280, hamartēma* [3]
sins, *4472+3836+281, poieō+ho+hamartia* [2]
sins committed in ignorance, *52, agnoēma* [1]
sins, *281+1639, hamartia+eimi* [1]
such sins[s], *4047, houtos* [1]
sins, *4053, opheilō* [1]
sins, *4126, parabasis* [1]
sins against, *4183, paraptōma* [1]
sins sexually, *4519, porneuō* [1]

SIR [23]

sir, *3261, kyrios* [23]

SIRS [1]

sirs, *3261, kyrios* [1]

SISTER [15]

sister, *80, adelphē* [15]

SISTERS [8]

sisters, *80, adelphē* [8]

SIT [33]

sit, *2764, kathēmai* [12]
sit, *2767, kathizō* [10]
sit down, *404, anapiptō* [3]
sit down, *2767, kathizō* [3]
have sit down, *369, anaklinō* [1]
sit down, *369, anaklinō* [1]
sit in judgment on, *373, anakrinō* [1]
sit down to eat, *404, anapiptō* [1]
sit down, *2884, kataklinō* [1]

SITS [11]

sits, *2764, kathēmai* [10]
sits, *2767, kathizō* [1]

SITTING [35]

sitting, *2764, kathēmai* [28]
sitting, *2757, kathezomai* [2]
sitting down, *2764, kathēmai* [2]
sitting down, *2767, kathizō* [1]
sitting in judgment, *3216, kritēs* [1]
sitting with, *5153, synkathēmai* [1]

SITUATION [4]

situation, *AIT* [1]
situation, *162, aitia* [1]
situation, *3104, klēsis* [1]
the situation, *4005, hos* [1]

SITUATIONS [1]

situations, *AIT* [1]

SIX [7]

six, *1971, hex* [7]

SIXTH [13]

sixth, *1761, hektos* [13]

SIXTY [5]

sixty, *2008, hexēkonta* [4]
sixty, *2291+2008, etos+hexēkonta* [1]

SIZE [1]

the size of, *6055, hōs* [1]

SKIES [2]

skies, *4041, ouranos* [2]

SKILL [1]

skill, *5492, technē* [1]

SKINS [3]

skins, *829, askos* [3]

SKULL [4]

Skull, *3191, kranion* [4]

SKY [22]

sky, *4041, ouranos* [21]
sky, *113, aēr* [1]

SLAIN [5]

slain, *5377, sphazō* [5]

SLANDER [14]

slander, *1060, blasphēmia* [5]
slander, *1059, blasphēmeō* [4]
slander, *2895, katalaleō* [2]
slander, *2896, katalalia* [2]
slander, *3367, loidoria* [1]

SLANDERED [2]

slandered, *1059, blasphēmeō* [1]
slandered, *1555, dysphēmeō* [1]

SLANDERER [1]

slanderer, *3368, loidoros* [1]

SLANDERERS [3]

slanderers, *1333, diabolos* [1]
slanderers, *2897, katalalos* [1]
slanderers, *3368, loidoros* [1]

SLANDERING [1]

slandering, *1059, blasphēmeō* [1]

SLANDEROUS [3]

slanderous, *1060, blasphēmia* [1]
slanderous, *1061, blasphēmos* [1]
slanderous, *1333, diabolos* [1]

SLANDEROUSLY [1]

slanderously reported, *1059, blasphēmeō* [1]

SLAPPED [1]

slapped, *4824, rhapizō* [1]

SLAPS [1]

slaps, *1296, derō* [1]

SLAUGHTER [2]

slaughter, *5375, sphagē* [2]

SLAUGHTERED [1]

slaughtered, *5375, sphagē* [1]

SLAVE [34]

slave, *1528, doulos[1]* [18]
slave woman, *4087, paidiskē* [4]
slave, *RPE* [1]
slave traders, *435, andrapodistēs* [1]
sold as a slave, *625, apodidōmi* [1]
the slave girl[s], *899, autos* [1]
make slave, *1524, doulagōgeō* [1]
makes a slave, *1525, douleia* [1]

slave, *1526, douleuō* [1]
make a slave, *1530, douloō* [1]
slave, *1530, douloō* [1]
slave girl, *4087, paidiskē* [1]
slave woman's, *4087, paidiskē* [1]
slave to, *5679, hypo* [1]

SLAVERY [7]

slavery, *1525, douleia* [2]
in slavery, *1529, doulos[2]* [2]
in slavery, *1526, douleuō* [1]
slavery, *1528, doulos[1]* [1]
in slavery, *1530, douloō* [1]

SLAVES [22]

slaves, *1528, doulos[1]* [11]
slaves, *1526, douleuō* [3]
become slaves, *1530, douloō* [2]
slaves, *RPE* [1]
your slaves[s], *899, autos* [1]
slaves, *1525, douleia* [1]
serve as slaves, *1526, douleuō* [1]
make slaves, *2871, katadouloō* [1]
slaves, *3860, oiketēs* [1]

SLAVING [1]

slaving, *1526, douleuō* [1]

SLAY [1]

slay, *5377, sphazō* [1]

SLEEP [6]

sleep, *2761, katheudō* [2]
gone without sleep, *71, agrypnia* [1]
sleep, *3121, koimaō* [1]
natural sleep, *3836+3122+3836+5678, ho+koimēsis+ho+hypnos* [1]
sleep, *5678, hypnos* [1]

SLEEPER [1]

sleeper, *2761, katheudō* [1]

SLEEPING [13]

sleeping, *2761, katheudō* [11]
sleeping, *3121, koimaō* [1]
sleeping, *3818, nystazō* [1]

SLEEPLESS [1]

sleepless nights, *71, agrypnia* [1]

SLEEPS [2]

sleeps, *2761, katheudō* [1]
sleeps, *3121, koimaō* [1]

SLEEPY [1]

very sleepy, *976+5678, bareō+hypnos* [1]

SLIGHTEST [1]

without the slightest qualm, *925, aphobōs* [1]

SLIPPED [3]

slipped away, *1728, ekneuō* [1]
slipped through, *1767, ekpheugō* [1]
secretly slipped in, *4208, pareisdyō* [1]

SLIPPING [1]

slipping away from, *2002+1666, exerchomai+ek* [1]

SLOW [6]

slow, *1096, bradys* [3]

slow, *1094, bradynō* [1]
made slow headway, *1095, bradyploeō* [1]
slow, *3821, nōthros* [1]

SLOWNESS [1]

slowness, *1097, bradytēs* [1]

SLUMBER [1]

slumber, *5678, hypnos* [1]

SLY [2]

sly way, *1515, dolos* [1]
sly, *1877+1515, en+dolos* [1]

SMALL [22]

small, *3625, mikros* [7]
very small, *1788, elachistos* [2]
small fish, *2715, ichthydion* [2]
very small copper coins, *3321, leptos* [2]
as small as, *6055, hōs* [2]
small, *2462, hēlikos* [1]
small barley, *3209, krithinos* [1]
small island, *3761, nēsion* [1]
small, *3900, oligos* [1]
small fish, *4066, opsarion* [1]
small boat, *4449, ploiarion* [1]
small, *5101, stenos* [1]

SMALLEST [3]

smallest, *3625, mikros* [2]
smallest letter, *2740, iōta* [1]

SMELL [2]

smell, *4011, osmē* [1]
sense of smell, *4018, osphrēsis* [1]

SMOKE [13]

smoke, *2837, kapnos* [13]

SMOLDERING [1]

smoldering, *5606, typhō* [1]

SMOOTH [2]

smooth, *3308, leios* [1]
smooth talk, *5981, chrēstologia* [1]

SMYRNA [2]

Smyrna, *5044, Smyrna²* [2]

SNAKE [5]

snake, *4058, ophis* [3]
snake, *2563, thērion* [2]

SNAKES [6]

snakes, *4058, ophis* [6]

SNARE [1]

snare, *4075, pagis* [1]

SNATCH [3]

snatch, *773, harpazō* [3]

SNATCHED [1]

snatched up, *773, harpazō* [1]

SNATCHES [1]

snatches away, *773, harpazō* [1]

SNEERED [2]

sneered at, *1727, ekmyktērizō* [1]

sneered, *5949, chleuazō* [1]

SNEERING [1]

sneering at, *1727, ekmyktērizō* [1]

SNOW [2]

snow, *5946, chiōn* [2]

SNUFF [1]

snuff out, *4931, sbennymi* [1]

SO [798]

so that, *2671, hina* [197]
so, *2779, kai* [89]
so, *NIG* [68]
so, *4048, houtōs* [65]
so, *4036, oun* [62]
so, *1254, de* [36]
so, *6063, hōste* [19]
so that, *6063, hōste* [17]
so, *AIT* [15]
so that, *1650+3836, eis+ho* [15]
so that, *3968, hopōs* [15]
so, *RPE* [13]
so, *2671, hina* [12]
so, *1475, dio* [11]
and so, *2779, kai* [11]
so that, *1650, eis* [10]
so, *726, ara* [8]
so that, *2779, kai* [8]
so that, *3836, ho* [6]
so I, *2743, kagō* [5]
so, *1328+4047, dia+houtos* [4]
so, *5538, tote* [4]
and so, *1650+3836, eis+ho* [3]
so as to, *2671, hina* [3]
so that not, *3607, mēpote* [3]
so, *3968, hopōs* [3]
so, *4047, houtos* [3]
so, *5445, te* [3]
so, *6055, hōs* [3]
so then, *6063, hōste* [3]
so, *247, alla* [2]
so, *1142, gar* [2]
so then, *1328+4047, dia+houtos* [2]
so that, *3968+323, hopōs+an* [2]
so then, *4036, oun* [2]
so that, *4639, pros* [2]
so that, *4803, pōs* [2]
so, *5525, toioutos* [2]
so many, *5537, tosoutos* [2]
so dear, *28, agapētos* [1]
do soˢ, *468, anthistēmi* [1]
rightly so, *545+1639, axios+eimi* [1]
so then, *726, ara* [1]
so much as, *948, achri* [1]
so, *1181+1254, ginomai+de* [1]
looked so much like, *1181+6059,
   ginomai+hōsei* [1]
doˢ so, *1182, ginōskō* [1]
doˢ so, *1211, graphō* [1]
so afraid, *1264, deilos* [1]
so, *1328+4005+162, dia+hos+aitia* [1]
so, *1328+4005, dia+hos* [1]
didˢ so, *1403, diastellō* [1]
and so, *1475, dio* [1]
so then, *1475, dio* [1]
so, *1484, dioti* [1]
soˢ, *1506, dokeō* [1]
could have done so, *1543, dynatos* [1]
so then, *1650+3836, eis+ho* [1]
so, *1650+3836, eis+ho* [1]
so as to, *1650, eis* [1]
so as, *1650+3836, eis+ho* [1]

so frightened, *1769, ekphobos* [1]
so powerfully, *1877+1539, en+dynamis* [1]
if that were so, *2075, epei* [1]
so, *2075, epei* [1]
sought so earnestly, *2118, epizēteō* [1]
so, *2627, idou* [1]
so that I, *2743, kagō* [1]
if so, *2779, kai* [1]
so too, *2779, kai* [1]
rightly so, *2822, kalōs* [1]
soˢ, *3031, kenos* [1]
especially so, *3436, malista* [1]
do so, *3437+5968, mallon+chraomai* [1]
so shall it be, *3721, nai* [1]
so he, *3836+1254, ho+de* [1]
so they, *3836+1254, ho+de* [1]
so, *3836, ho* [1]
so then, *3854, hothen* [1]
and so, *3854, hothen* [1]
so do, *3931, homoiōs* [1]
so, *3931, homoiōs* [1]
so long as, *4012+5989, hosos+chronos* [1]
doesˢ so, *4024+2266, ou+esthiō* [1]
so, *4025, oua* [1]
so doingˢ, *4047, houtos* [1]
so favoredˢ, *4047, houtos* [1]
so then, *4048, houtōs* [1]
so much, *4048, houtōs* [1]
didˢ so, *4192, paratithēmi* [1]
so quickly, *4202, parachrēma* [1]
do so more and more, *4355+3437,
   perisseuō+mallon* [1]
even more soˢ, *4498+5080,
   polys+spoudaios* [1]
so as to, *4639, pros* [1]
so that, *4639+3836, pros+ho* [1]
so, *5379, sphodra* [1]
so large, *5496, tēlikoutos* [1]
doˢ so, *5498, tēreō* [1]
so much, *5537, tosoutos* [1]
didˢ so, *5770, pherō* [1]
doesˢ so, *5858, phroneō* [1]
so violent, *5901+3336, chalepos+lian* [1]
stayed so long, *5988, chronizō* [1]
doˢ so, *6004, chōrizō* [1]
so also, *6058, hōsautōs* [1]

SO-CALLED [2]

so-called, *3306, legō* [1]
so-called, *6055+3306, hōs+legō* [1]

SOAKED [1]

soaked, *3550, mestos* [1]

SOBER [1]

sober judgment, *5404, sōphroneō* [1]

SODOM [9]

Sodom, *5047, Sodoma* [7]
Sodom, *1178+5047, gē+Sodoma* [2]

SOIL [13]

soil, *1178, gē* [13]

SOILED [1]

soiled, *3662, molynō* [1]

SOLD [19]

sold, *4797, pōleō* [8]
sold, *4405, pipraskō* [7]
sold, *RPE* [2]
sold as a slave, *625, apodidōmi* [1]
sold, *625, apodidōmi* [1]

SOLDIER [7]

soldier, *5132, stratiōtēs* [3]
fellow soldier, *5369, systratiōtēs* [2]
serves as a soldier, *5129, strateuomai* [1]
serving as a soldier, *5129, strateuomai* [1]

SOLDIERS [31]

soldiers, *5132, stratiōtēs* [22]
company of soldiers, *5061, speira* [2]
detachment of soldiers, *5061, speira* [2]
soldiers, *AIT* [1]
soldiers, *RPE* [1]
the soldiers', *3836, ho* [1]
soldiers, *5128, strateuma* [1]
soldiers, *5129, strateuomai* [1]

SOLEMN [1]

taken a solemn oath, *353+354,
  anathema+anathematizō* [1]

SOLID [4]

solid, *5104, stereos* [3]
solid food, *1109, brōma* [1]

SOLITARY [5]

solitary, *2245, erēmos* [4]
solitary places, *2245, erēmos* [1]

SOLOMON [7]

Solomon, *5048, Solomōn* [7]

SOLOMON'S [5]

Solomon's, *5048, Solomōn* [5]

SOMBER [1]

look somber, *1181+5034,
  ginomai+skythrōpos* [1]

SOME [237]

some, *5516, tis* [104]
some, *AIT* [46]
some of, *1666, ek* [10]
some, *RPE* [6]
some, *3836, ho* [6]
some, *4005+3525, hos+men* [6]
some, *608, apo* [5]
some, *3836+3525, ho+men* [5]
some, *257, allos* [4]
some, *NIG* [3]
some, *2283, heteros* [3]
some, *3525, men* [3]
some, *257+1254, allos+de* [2]
some, *1254, de* [2]
some, *2653, hikanos* [2]
some, *3900, oligos* [2]
and some, *4005+1254, hos+de* [2]
some, *4015, hostis* [2]
some time ago, *4574+4047+3836+2465,
  pro+houtos+ho+hēmera* [2]
some way, *4802, pōs* [2]
some time, *5989, chronos* [2]
to some extent, *247+608+3538,
  alla+apo+meros* [1]
some more, *257, allos* [1]
some time ago, *608+2465+792,
  apo+hēmera+archaios* [1]
and some, *1254, de* [1]
spent some time, *1417, diatribō* [1]
some, *1666, ek* [1]
some, *2445, ē* [1]
some, *2779, kai* [1]
some distance, *3426, makran* [1]
some time after, *3552, meta* [1]

some time later, *3552+4047, meta+houtos* [1]
some, *3836+1651+3538, ho+heis+meros* [1]
some, *4047, houtos* [1]
for some time, *4732, prouparchō* [1]
in some way, *4803, pōs* [1]
some, *5515, tis* [1]
some point, *5516, tis* [1]
some, *5516+3525, tis+men* [1]

SOMEBODY [3]

somebody, *NIG* [1]
somebody else, *2283, heteros* [1]
somebody, *5516, tis* [1]

SOMEHOW [5]

somehow, *4803, pōs* [2]
somehow, *NIG* [1]
somehow, *1623+4803, ei+pōs* [1]
somehow or other, *6055+323, hōs+an* [1]

SOMEONE [56]

someone, *5516, tis* [22]
someone, *NIG* [6]
someone else, *257, allos* [6]
someone, *3836, ho* [5]
someone, *AIT* [4]
someone else's, *259, allotrios* [3]
someone else, *2283, heteros* [2]
someone, *4015, hostis* [2]
someone, *257, allos* [1]
someone's, *476, anthrōpos* [1]
someone, *1651, heis* [1]
someone, *4005, hos* [1]
someone is saying, *5889, phōnē* [1]
someone to lead by the hand, *5933,
  cheiragōgos* [1]

SOMETHING [48]

something, *5516, tis* [16]
something, *AIT* [10]
something, *RPE* [8]
something, *NIG* [2]
something, *5007+5516, skeuos+tis* [2]
something, *5515, tis* [2]
something to be grasped, *772, harpagmos* [1]
something, *2240, ergon* [1]
something man made up, *2848+476,
  kata+anthrōpos* [1]
something to boast about, *3017, kauchēma* [1]
something said, *3364, logos* [1]
something, *3836, ho* [1]
something, *4005, hos* [1]
something, *6055, hōs* [1]

SOMETIMES [1]

sometimes, *4047+3525, houtos+men* [1]

SOMEWHAT [1]

somewhat, *5516, tis* [1]

SOMEWHERE [3]

somewhere, *RPE* [1]
somewhere else, *250, allachou* [1]
somewhere, *4543, pou* [1]

SON [422]

son, *5626, huios* [299]
the son, *3836, ho* [75]
son, *5451, teknon* [14]
son, *AIT* [11]
son, *3836, ho* [9]
son, *RPE* [4]
the son', *3836, ho* [2]

the Son', *899, autos* [1]
son of Jonah, *980, Bariōna* [1]
became son', *1164, gennaō* [1]
one and only son, *3666, monogenēs* [1]
his son', *3836, ho* [1]
son', *3836+3525, ho+men* [1]
the Son', *4005, hos* [1]
inheritance rights as the oldest son, *4757,
  prōtotokia* [1]

SONG [5]

song, *6046, ōdē* [5]

SONGS [3]

songs, *6046, ōdē* [2]
sing songs of praise, *6010, psallō* [1]

SONS [42]

sons, *5626, huios* [36]
adoption as sons, *5625, huiothesia* [2]
sons, *AIT* [1]
sons, *5451, teknon* [1]
adopted as sons, *5625, huiothesia* [1]
full rights of sons, *5625, huiothesia* [1]

SONSHIP [1]

sonship, *5625, huiothesia* [1]

SOON [40]

as soon as, *2317, euthys[1]* [6]
soon, *5444, tachys* [6]
soon, *1877+5443, en+tachos* [5]
soon, *5441, tacheōs* [5]
as soon as, *4020+2317, hotan+euthys[1]* [2]
as soon as, *4020, hotan* [2]
soon, *AIT* [1]
soon, *1584, engys* [1]
soon afterward, *1877+3836+2009,
  en+ho+hexēs* [1]
as soon as, *2054, epan* [1]
as soon as, *2311, eutheōs* [1]
soon, *2311, eutheōs* [1]
soon, *2779, kai* [1]
as soon as, *4020+2453, hotan+ēdē* [1]
as soon as, *4021, hote* [1]
very soon, *5441, tacheōs* [1]
soon, *5442, tachinos* [1]
as soon as, *5538, tote* [1]
as soon as, *6055, hōs* [1]
as soon as, *6055+323, hōs+an* [1]

SOPATER [1]

Sopater, *5396, sōpatros* [1]

SORCERER [2]

sorcerer, *3407, magos* [2]

SORCERY [2]

practiced sorcery, *3405, mageuō* [1]
sorcery, *4319, periergos* [1]

SORES [4]

sores, *1814, helkos* [3]
covered with sores, *1815, helkoō* [1]

SORROW [13]

sorrow, *3383, lypē* [7]
sorrow, *3382, lypeō* [2]
overwhelmed with sorrow, *4337, perilypos* [2]
caused sorrow, *3382, lypeō* [1]
deep sorrow, *3851, odyrmos* [1]

SORROWFUL [3]

sorrowful, *3382, lypeō* [3]

SORRY [1]

made sorry, *3382, lypeō* [1]

SORT [2]

sort, *AIT* [2]

SORTS [1]

sorts, *1169, genos* [1]

SOSIPATER [1]

Sosipater, *5399, sōsipatros* [1]

SOSTHENES [2]

Sosthenes, *5398, sōsthenēs* [2]

SOUGHT [5]

sought, *1699, ekzēteō* [1]
sought so earnestly, *2118, epizēteō* [1]
sought for, *2426, zēteō* [1]
sought, *2426, zēteō* [1]
sought an audience, *4205, pareimi* [1]

SOUL [19]

soul, *6034, psychē* [19]

SOULS [6]

souls, *6034, psychē* [6]

SOUND [25]

sound, *5617, hygiainō* [8]
sound, *5889, phōnē* [8]
heard sound, *1181+5889, ginomai+phōnē* [1]
sound, *1443, didōmi* [1]
sound, *2491, ēchos¹* [1]
sound asleep, *2965+608+3836+5678, katapherō+apo+ho+hypnos* [1]
sound trumpet, *4895, salpizō* [1]
sound, *4895, salpizō* [1]
trumpet sound, *4895, salpizō* [1]
safe and sound, *5617, hygiainō* [1]
sound, *5618, hygiēs* [1]

SOUNDED [11]

sounded trumpet, *4895, salpizō* [7]
sounded like, *6055, hōs* [2]
sounded, *4895, salpizō* [1]
sounded, *5889, phōnē* [1]

SOUNDINGS [2]

took soundings, *1075, bolizō* [2]

SOUNDNESS [1]

soundness, *5618, hygiēs* [1]

SOUNDS [1]

sounds, *5889, phōnē* [1]

SOUR [2]

turn sour, *4393, pikrainō* [1]
turned sour, *4393, pikrainō* [1]

SOURCE [1]

source, *165, aitios* [1]

SOUTH [9]

south, *3803, notos* [4]
south wind, *3803, notos* [3]

south of, *2381, euōnymos* [1]
south, *3540, mesēmbria* [1]

SOUTHWEST [1]

southwest, *3355, lips* [1]

SOVEREIGN [5]

sovereign Lord, *1305, despotēs* [4]
Sovereign, *1305, despotēs* [1]

SOW [12]

sow, *5062, speirō* [9]
sow seed, *5062, speirō* [2]
sow, *5725, hys* [1]

SOWED [3]

sowed, *5062, speirō* [2]
sowed, *2178, epispeirō* [1]

SOWER [3]

sower, *5062, speirō* [3]

SOWN [18]

sown, *5062, speirō* [9]
sown, *RPE* [4]
seed sown, *5062, speirō* [4]
sown seed, *5062, speirō* [1]

SOWS [8]

sows, *5062, speirō* [8]

SPAIN [2]

Spain, *5056, Spania* [2]

SPARE [12]

spare, *5767, pheidomai* [9]
spare life, *1407, diasōzō* [1]
spare, *3590+2400, mē+echō* [1]
have to spare, *4355, perisseuō* [1]

SPARED [1]

spared, *3045, kerdainō* [1]

SPARINGLY [2]

sparingly, *5768, pheidomenōs* [2]

SPARK [1]

spark, *4786, pyr* [1]

SPARROWS [4]

sparrows, *5141, strouthion* [4]

SPEAK [96]

speak, *3281, laleō* [62]
speak, *3306, legō* [12]
speak, *NIG* [3]
speak of, *3306, legō* [2]
speak, *RPE* [1]
began to speak, *487+3836+5125+3306, anoigō+ho+stoma+legō* [1]
speak, *487+3836+5125, anoigō+ho+stoma* [1]
speak abusively against, *1059, blasphēmeō* [1]
speak, *1182, ginōskō* [1]
speak, *1443, didōmi* [1]
speak of, *1455, diēgeomai* [1]
speak maliciously against, *2092, epēreazō* [1]
unable to speak, *3273, kōphos* [1]
speak about, *3281, laleō* [1]
speak about, *3306, legō* [1]
speak, *3364, logos* [1]
speak well of, *3455, martyreō* [1]

speak, *3455, martyreō* [1]
speak boldly, *4245, parrēsiazomai* [1]
speak, *4715, prosphōneō* [1]
speak, *5779, phthengomai* [1]

SPEAKER [5]

speaker, *RPE* [2]
speaker, *3364, logos* [2]
speaker, *3281, laleō* [1]

SPEAKING [58]

speaking, *3281, laleō* [38]
speaking, *3306, legō* [6]
speaking, *RPE* [3]
speaking in tongues, *1185, glōssa* [2]
speaking, *3364, logos* [2]
speaking boldly, *4245, parrēsiazomai* [2]
speaking, *AIT* [1]
speaking truth, *238, alētheuō* [1]
figuratively speaking, *1877+4130, en+parabolē* [1]
help speaking about, *3590+3281, mē+laleō* [1]
speaking encouragement to, *4151, parakaleō* [1]

SPEAKS [25]

speaks, *3281, laleō* [18]
speaks, *3306, legō* [3]
speaks against, *2895, katalaleō* [2]
speaks of, *3306, legō* [1]
speaks in defense, *4156, paraklētos* [1]

SPEAR [1]

spear, *3365, lonchē* [1]

SPEARMEN [1]

spearmen, *1287, dexiolabos* [1]

SPECIAL [8]

special, *4358, perissoteros* [2]
special, *AIT* [1]
show special attention to, *2098+2093, epiblepō+epi* [1]
special, *3489, megas* [1]
take special note, *4957, sēmeioō* [1]
special treatment, *5507, timē* [1]
regards as special, *5858, phroneō* [1]

SPECIFYING [1]

specifying, *4955, sēmainō* [1]

SPECK [6]

speck, *2847, karphos* [4]
speck of sawdust, *2847, karphos* [2]

SPECTACLE [2]

made a spectacle, *1258, deigmatizō* [1]
spectacle, *2519, theatron* [1]

SPEECH [11]

speech, *3364, logos* [5]
speech, *RPE* [1]
robbed him of speech, *228, alalos* [1]
without speech, *936, aphōnos* [1]
speech, *3281, laleō* [1]
figure of speech, *4231, paroimia* [1]
figures of speech, *4231, paroimia* [1]

SPEECHLESS [2]

speechless, *1917, eneos* [1]
speechless, *5821, phimoō* [1]

SPEED [2]

speed, *5067, speudō* [1]
speed, *5335, syntemnō* [1]

SPELL [1]

magic spell, *5758, pharmakeia* [1]

SPEND [9]

spend, *60, agorazō* [1]
spend the night, *887, aulizomai* [1]
spend everything, *1251, dapanaō* [1]
spend, *1251, dapanaō* [1]
spend time, *2093+5989+3531,*
   epi+chronos+menō [1]
spend, *2152, epimenō* [1]
spend the winter, *4199, paracheimazō* [1]
spend, *4472, poieō* [1]
spend time, *5989+2152, chronos+epimenō* [1]

SPENDING [5]

spending, *1417, diatribō* [2]
spending, *4472, poieō* [2]
spending time, *1181+5990,*
   ginomai+chronotribeō [1]

SPENT [11]

spent, *1251, dapanaō* [2]
spent, *AIT* [1]
spent the night, *887, aulizomai* [1]
spent, *1181, ginomai* [1]
spent some time, *1417, diatribō* [1]
spent, *1417, diatribō* [1]
spent the night, *1639+1381,*
   eimi+dianyktereuō [1]
spent time, *2320, eukaireō* [1]
spent, *3531, menō* [1]
spent, *4472, poieō* [1]

SPEWED [2]

spewed, *965, ballō* [2]

SPICE [1]

spice, *319, amōmon* [1]

SPICES [5]

spices, *808, arōma* [4]
spices mint, *2455, hēdyosmon* [1]

SPIES [4]

spies, *RPE* [1]
spies, *34, angelos* [1]
spies, *1588, enkathetos* [1]
spies, *2946, kataskopos* [1]

SPILLED [1]

spilled out, *1772, ekcheō* [1]

SPIN [2]

spin, *3756, nēthō* [2]

SPIRIT [338]

spirit, *4460, pneuma* [325]
spirit, *RPE* [8]
the spiritˢ, *899, autos* [1]
spirit of unity, *3836+899+5858,*
   ho+autos+phroneō [1]
spirit which predicted the future, *4460+4780,*
   pneuma+pythōn [1]
spirit, *5249, sympsychos* [1]
without the Spirit, *6035, psychikos* [1]

SPIRIT'S [2]

Spirit's, *4460, pneuma* [2]

SPIRITS [33]

spirits, *4460, pneuma* [32]
driving out evil spirits, *2020, exorkistēs* [1]

SPIRITUAL [30]

spiritual, *4461, pneumatikos* [25]
spiritual, *3358, logikos* [2]
spiritual, *4460, pneuma* [2]
spiritual gift, *5922, charisma* [1]

SPIRITUALLY [2]

spiritually, *4461, pneumatikos* [1]
spiritually, *4462, pneumatikōs* [1]

SPIT [10]

spit on, *1870, emptyō* [3]
spit, *4772, ptyō* [3]
spit, *1870, emptyō* [2]
spit, *1840, emeō* [1]
spit at, *1870, emptyō* [1]

SPITE [2]

in spite of, *1877, en* [2]

SPLENDOR [13]

splendor, *1518, doxa* [9]
splendor, *RPE* [1]
glorious splendor, *1518, doxa* [1]
splendor, *2211, epiphaneia* [1]
splendor, *3287, lampros* [1]

SPLIT [2]

split, *1181, ginomai* [1]
split, *5387, schizō* [1]

SPOIL [1]

that can never spoil, *299, amiantos* [1]

SPOILS [2]

spoils, *660, apollymi* [1]
spoils, *5036, skylon* [1]

SPOKE [63]

spoke, *3281, laleō* [33]
spoke, *3306, legō* [9]
spoke up, *646, apokrinomai* [3]
spoke, *RPE* [2]
spoke well of, *3455, martyreō* [2]
spoke, *AIT* [1]
spoke, *NIG* [1]
spoke, *646, apokrinomai* [1]
spoke to, *1363, dialegomai* [1]
spoke about, *3281, laleō* [1]
spoke about, *3306, legō* [1]
spoke well, *3455, martyreō* [1]
spoke, *3648, mnēmoneuō* [1]
spoke boldly, *4245, parrēsiazomai* [1]
spoke long ago, *4625, prolegō* [1]
spoke, *4736, prophēteuō* [1]
spoke, *5779, phthengomai* [1]

SPOKEN [46]

spoken, *3281, laleō* [17]
spoken, *3306, legō* [17]
spoken of, *3306, legō* [3]
spoken, *AIT* [1]
spoken against, *515, antilegō* [1]
spoken blasphemy, *1059, blasphēmeō* [1]

spoken of as evil, *1059, blasphēmeō* [1]
spoken, *1181, ginomai* [1]
well spoken of, *3455, martyreō* [1]
spoken freely, *3836+5125+487,*
   ho+stoma+anoigō [1]
spoken in the past, *4625, prolegō* [1]
further word spoken, *4707+3364,*
   prostithēmi+logos [1]

SPONGE [4]

sponge, *5074, spongos* [3]
sponge, *RPE* [1]

SPONTANEOUS [1]

spontaneous, *2848+1730, kata+hekousios* [1]

SPOT [2]

without spot, *834, aspilos* [1]
spot, *5536, topos* [1]

SPOTLESS [1]

spotless, *834, aspilos* [1]

SPRANG [3]

sprang up, *1984, exanatellō* [2]
sprang to life, *348, anazaō* [1]

SPREAD [24]

spread, *2002, exerchomai* [5]
spread, *5143, strōnnyō* [3]
spread, *RPE* [2]
spread, *599, aperchomai* [1]
spread widely, *889, auxanō* [1]
spread, *889, auxanō* [1]
spread, *1192, gnōrizō* [1]
spread, *1422, diapherō* [1]
spread the news about, *1424, diaphēmizō* [1]
spread, *1451, dierchomai* [1]
spread, *1639, eimi* [1]
spread, *1744, ekporeuomai* [1]
spread the word, *3455, martyreō* [1]
spread, *3786+2400, nomē+echō* [1]
spread, *4437, plēthynō* [1]
spread tent, *5012, skēnoō* [1]
spread rapidly, *5556, trechō* [1]
spread, *5716, hypostrōnnyō* [1]

SPREADING [3]

spreading, *1376, dianemō* [1]
spreading, *1424, diaphēmizō* [1]
spreading gospel, *2295, euangelion* [1]

SPREADS [1]

spreads, *5746, phaneroō* [1]

SPRING [8]

spring, *AIT* [2]
spring, *4380, pēgē* [2]
salt spring, *266, halykos* [1]
spring up, *1639, eimi* [1]
spring, *3956, opē* [1]
spring rains, *4069, opsimos* [1]

SPRINGS [5]

springs, *4380, pēgē* [5]

SPRINKLED [5]

sprinkled, *4822, rhantizō* [2]
sprinkled on, *4822, rhantizō* [1]
sprinkled to cleanse, *4822, rhantizō* [1]
sprinkled, *4823, rhantismos* [1]

SPRINKLING [2]

sprinkling, *4717, proschysis* [1]
sprinkling, *4823, rhantismos* [1]

SPROUT [1]

sprout leaves, *4582, proballō* [1]

SPROUTED [1]

sprouted, *1056, blastanō* [1]

SPROUTS [1]

sprouts, *1056, blastanō* [1]

SPUR [1]

spur on, *1650+4237, eis+paroxysmos* [1]

SPY [1]

spy on, *2945, kataskopeō* [1]

SQUADS [1]

squads of four, *5482, tetradion* [1]

SQUALL [2]

squall, *3278+449, lailaps+anemos* [2]

SQUANDERED [2]

squandered, *1399, diaskorpizō* [1]
squandered, *2983, katesthiō* [1]

SQUARE [1]

square, *5481, tetragōnos* [1]

STACHYS [1]

Stachys, *5093, Stachys²* [1]

STADIA [2]

stadia, *5084, stadion* [2]

STAFF [8]

staff, *4811, rhabdos* [5]
staff, *2812, kalamos* [3]

STAIN [1]

stain, *5070, spilos* [1]

STAINED [1]

stained, *5071, spiloō* [1]

STALK [2]

stalk of the hyssop plant, *5727, hyssōpos* [1]
stalk, *5965, chortos* [1]

STALL [1]

stall, *5764, phatnē* [1]

STAND [75]

stand, *2705, histēmi* [30]
stand firm, *5112, stēkō* [5]
stand, *3393, lychnia* [4]
stand up, *482, anistēmi* [3]
stand firm, *2705, histēmi* [3]
stand, *AIT* [2]
stand here, *2705, histēmi* [2]
stand trial, *3212, krinō* [2]
stand, *5095, stegō* [2]
stand up, *376, anakyptō* [1]
stand up against, *468, anthistēmi* [1]
stand your ground, *468, anthistēmi* [1]
stand up, *482+3981, anistēmi+orthos* [1]
makes stand firm, *1011, bebaioō* [1]

would stand the test, *1509, dokimē* [1]
stand up, *1586, egeirō* [1]
stand firm, *1612+1181, hedraios+ginomai* [1]
stand fast, *2705, histēmi* [1]
made stand, *2705, histēmi* [1]
make stand, *2705, histēmi* [1]
take stand, *2705, histēmi* [1]
taken stand, *2705, histēmi* [1]
stand on trial, *3212, krinō* [1]
stand, *3531, menō* [1]
stand before, *4225, paristēmi* [1]
stand trial before, *4225, paristēmi* [1]
stand, *4225, paristēmi* [1]
take stand, *4225, paristēmi* [1]
stand, *5112, stēkō* [1]
stand firm, *5114+3836+2840,*
  stērizō+ho+kardia [1]
stand up under, *5722, hypopherō* [1]

STANDARDS [4]

standards, *AIT* [1]
by standards, *2848, kata* [1]
by the standards of, *2848, kata* [1]
human standards, *4922, sarx* [1]

STANDING [62]

standing, *2705, histēmi* [34]
standing there, *2705, histēmi* [5]
standing near, *4225, paristēmi* [5]
standing open, *487, anoigō* [2]
standing up, *482, anistēmi* [1]
standing, *957, bathmos* [1]
standing, *1639+2705, eimi+histēmi* [1]
standing, *1639, eimi* [1]
high standing, *2363, euschēmōn* [1]
standing firm, *2705, histēmi* [1]
standing around, *4225, paristēmi* [1]
standing by, *4225, paristēmi* [1]
standing nearby, *4225, paristēmi* [1]
standing here, *4325, periistēmi* [1]
standing, *5087, stasis* [1]
standing firm, *5104, stereos* [1]
standing, *5112, stēkō* [1]
standing firm, *5112, stēkō* [1]
standing with, *5319, synistēmi* [1]
standing firm, *5705, hypomonē* [1]

STANDS [17]

stands for, *1639, eimi* [5]
stands firm, *5702, hypomenō* [3]
stands, *AIT* [2]
stands, *2705, histēmi* [2]
stands firm, *2705, histēmi* [1]
stands, *2901, kataleipō* [1]
stands, *3531, menō* [1]
stands, *4225, paristēmi* [1]
stands, *5112, stēkō* [1]

STAR [14]

star, *843, astēr* [11]
star, *849, astron* [1]
the star⁵, *899, autos* [1]
morning star, *5892, phōsphoros* [1]

STARE [1]

stare at, *867, atenizō* [1]

STARED [2]

stared at, *867, atenizō* [1]
stared, *1063, blepō* [1]

STARS [17]

stars, *843, astēr* [13]

stars, *849, astron* [3]
stars, *5891, phōstēr* [1]

STARTED [9]

started, *AIT* [3]
started, *806, archō* [1]
started, *1656, eiserchomai* [1]
started, *1744, ekporeuomai* [1]
started out, *2002, exerchomai* [1]
started, *2002, exerchomai* [1]
started out, *4513, poreuomai* [1]

STARTING [1]

starting, *1181, ginomai* [1]

STARTLED [2]

startled, *4765, ptoeō* [1]
startled, *5429, tarassō* [1]

STARVING [1]

starving to death, *3350+660,*
  limos+apollymi [1]

STATE [2]

state, *3306, legō* [1]
humble state, *5428, tapeinōsis* [1]

STATED [3]

stated, *3306, legō* [2]
stated, *3364, logos* [1]

STATEMENT [2]

statement, *3364, logos* [1]
final statement, *4839+1651, rhēma+heis* [1]

STATEMENTS [1]

statements, *3456, martyria* [1]

STATURE [1]

stature, *2461, hēlikia* [1]

STAY [26]

stay, *3531, menō* [14]
stay, *1639, eimi* [4]
stay on, *2152, epimenō* [1]
stay, *2152, epimenō* [1]
stay, *2767, kathizō* [1]
stay near, *3140, kollaō* [1]
stay, *3826, xenizō* [1]
stay awhile, *4169, paramenō* [1]
stay, *4229, paroikia* [1]
stay, *4693, prosmenō* [1]

STAYED [33]

stayed, *3531, menō* [11]
stayed, *1639, eimi* [4]
stayed, *2152, epimenō* [3]
stayed, *1417, diatribō* [2]
stayed a while, *1417, diatribō* [1]
stayed, *1639+1417, eimi+diatribō* [1]
stayed in, *1844+1877, emmenō+en* [1]
stayed a little longer, *2091+5989,*
  epechō+chronos [1]
stayed, *2705, histēmi* [1]
stayed, *2757, kathezomai* [1]
stayed, *2767, kathizō* [1]
stayed, *3531+1695, menō+ekei* [1]
stayed, *4472, poieō* [1]
stayed, *4693, prosmenō* [1]
stayed behind, *5702, hypomenō* [1]
stayed, *5702, hypomenō* [1]
stayed so long, *5988, chronizō* [1]

STAYING [10]

staying, *3531*, *menō* [2]
staying, *3826*, *xenizō* [2]
staying, *AIT* [1]
staying, *2910*, *katamenō* [1]
staying, *2997*, *katoikeō* [1]
place where staying, *3825*, *xenia* [1]
staying away from, *4024+1877+4344*,
  ou+en+peripateō [1]
staying away a long time, *5988*, *chronizō* [1]

STAYS [2]

stays awake, *1213*, *grēgoreō* [1]
stays, *3531*, *menō* [1]

STEADFAST [1]

make steadfast, *2530*, *themelioō* [1]

STEADILY [1]

look steadily, *867*, *atenizō* [1]

STEAL [11]

steal, *3096*, *kleptō* [10]
steal, *3802*, *nosphizō* [1]

STEALING [2]

stealing, *3096*, *kleptō* [2]

STEEP [3]

steep bank, *3204*, *krēmnos* [3]

STEEPED [1]

steeped, *3910*, *holos* [1]

STEERED [1]

steered, *3555*, *metagō* [1]

STEP [1]

keep in step, *5123*, *stoicheō* [1]

STEPHANAS [3]

Stephanas, *5107*, *Stephanas* [3]

STEPHEN [11]

Stephen, *5108*, *Stephanos¹* [6]
Stephen's, *899*, *autos* [3]
Stephen, *RPE* [2]

STEPPED [3]

stepped, *1832*, *embainō* [1]
stepped, *2002*, *exerchomai* [1]
stepped forward, *4665*, *proserchomai* [1]

STEPS [3]

steps, *325*, *anabathmos* [2]
steps, *2717*, *ichnos* [1]

STERN [3]

stern, *4744*, *prymna* [3]

STERNLY [3]

sternly, *2203*, *epitimaō* [2]
warned sternly, *1839*, *embrimaomai* [1]

STERNNESS [2]

sternness, *704*, *apotomia* [2]

STICK [2]

stick, *2812*, *kalamos* [2]

STICKS [1]

sticks, *3140*, *kollaō* [1]

STIFF-NECKED [1]

stiff-necked, *5019*, *sklērotrachēlos* [1]

STILL [105]

still, *AIT* [32]
still, *2285*, *eti* [31]
still, *2779*, *kai* [7]
still, *NIG* [4]
still, *2401+785*, *heōs+arti* [3]
still not, *4037*, *oupō* [3]
still, *1254*, *de* [2]
stood still, *2705*, *histēmi* [2]
still, *3836+3370*, *ho+loipos* [2]
still to come, *4037*, *oupō* [2]
still, *197*, *akmēn* [1]
still another, *1254*, *de* [1]
while it was still dark, *1939*, *ennychos* [1]
as long as still, *2285*, *eti* [1]
still, *2285+3814*, *eti+nyn* [1]
while still, *2285*, *eti* [1]
while still, *2401+4015*, *heōs+hostis* [1]
still, *2453*, *ēdē* [1]
and still, *2779*, *kai* [1]
but still, *2779*, *kai* [1]
still, *3531*, *menō* [1]
still others, *3836+1254*, *ho+de* [1]
still not, *4031*, *oudepō* [1]
still no, *4033*, *ouketi* [1]
still, *4036*, *oun* [1]
still no, *4037*, *oupō* [1]
still, *5821*, *phimoō* [1]

STILLED [1]

stilled, *4264*, *pauō* [1]

STIMULATE [1]

stimulate to, *1444*, *diegeirō* [1]

STING [3]

sting, *3034*, *kentron* [2]
sting, *990*, *basanismos* [1]

STINGS [1]

stings, *3034*, *kentron* [1]

STIR [1]

stir up, *1586*, *egeirō* [1]

STIRRED [8]

stirred up, *411*, *anaseiō* [1]
stirred up against, *2074+2093*, *epegeirō+epi* [1]
stirred up, *2074*, *epegeirō* [1]
stirred to action, *2241*, *erethizō* [1]
stirred, *4940*, *seiō* [1]
stirred up, *5167*, *synkineō* [1]
stirred up, *5177*, *syncheō* [1]
stirred, *5429*, *tarassō* [1]

STIRRING [3]

stirring up, *2180+4472*, *epistasis+poieō* [1]
stirring up, *3075*, *kineō* [1]
stirring up, *5429*, *tarassō* [1]

STIRS [1]

stirs up, *411*, *anaseiō* [1]

STOCKS [1]

stocks, *3833*, *xylon* [1]

STOIC [1]

Stoic, *5121*, *Stoikos* [1]

STOLE [1]

stole, *3096*, *kleptō* [1]

STOMACH [9]

stomach, *3120*, *koilia* [8]
stomach, *5126*, *stomachos* [1]

STONE [53]

stone, *3345*, *lithos* [35]
stone, *3342*, *lithazō* [5]
stone, *3344*, *lithoboleō* [4]
of stone, *3343*, *lithinos* [2]
stone, *RPE* [1]
stone, *965+2093*, *ballō+epi* [1]
stone, *2902*, *katalithazō* [1]
stone, *3343*, *lithinos* [1]
Stone Pavement, *3346*, *lithostrōtos* [1]
stone tablets, *4419*, *plax* [1]
stone, *6029*, *psēphos* [1]

STONE'S [1]

stone's, *3345*, *lithos* [1]

STONED [5]

stoned, *3342*, *lithazō* [3]
stoned, *3344*, *lithoboleō* [2]

STONES [14]

stones, *3345*, *lithos* [14]

STONING [2]

stoning, *3342*, *lithazō* [1]
stoning, *3344*, *lithoboleō* [1]

STOOD [69]

stood, *2705*, *histēmi* [26]
stood up, *482*, *anistēmi* [13]
stood up, *2705*, *histēmi* [5]
stood, *1181*, *ginomai* [2]
stood beside, *2392*, *ephistēmi* [2]
stood still, *2705*, *histēmi* [2]
stood beside, *4225*, *paristēmi* [2]
stood, *NIG* [1]
stood there, *482*, *anistēmi* [1]
stood, *1373*, *diamenō* [1]
stood the test, *1511*, *dokimos* [1]
stood opposed, *1639+5641*,
  eimi+hypenantios [1]
stood there, *1639+2392*, *eimi+ephistēmi* [1]
stood, *1639+2705*, *eimi+histēmi* [1]
stood, *1639+3023*, *eimi+keimai* [1]
stood up, *1985*, *exanistēmi* [1]
stood near, *2392*, *ephistēmi* [1]
stood there, *2705*, *histēmi* [1]
stood around, *4225*, *paristēmi* [1]
stood at side, *4225*, *paristēmi* [1]
stood there, *4225*, *paristēmi* [1]
stood around, *4325*, *periistēmi* [1]
stood, *5498*, *tēreō* [1]
stood ground, *5702*, *hypomenō* [1]

STOOP [1]

stoop down, *3252*, *kyptō* [1]

STOOPED [1]

stooped down, *2893*, *katakyptō* [1]

STOP [23]

stop, *3590*, *mē* [7]

stop, *3266, kōlyō* [3]
stop, *3600, mēketi* [3]
stop, *RPE* [1]
never stop, *188, akatapaustos* [1]
stop, *398+2400, anapausis+echō* [1]
stop, *2705, histēmi* [1]
stop, *2907, katalyō* [1]
stop from taking, *3266, kōlyō* [1]
told to stop, *3266, kōlyō* [1]
stop, *4264, pauō* [1]
stop, *4967, sigaō* [1]
stop, *5852, phrassō* [1]

STOPPED [17]

stopped, *4264, pauō* [6]
stopped, *2705, histēmi* [5]
stopped, *1364, dialeipō* [1]
stopped, *1601, enkoptō* [1]
stopped shining, *1722, ekleipō* [1]
stopped at, *2392+2093, ephistēmi+epi* [1]
stopped, *2392, ephistēmi* [1]
stopped, *3830, xērainō* [1]

STOPS [2]

stops, *3266, kōlyō* [1]
stops, *4264, pauō* [1]

STORE [7]

store up, *2564, thēsaurizō* [2]
store, *5251, synagō* [2]
in store, *641, apokeimai* [1]
store of seed, *5078, sporos* [1]
store away, *5251, synagō* [1]

STORED [5]

stored up, *2565, thēsauros* [4]
stored up, *641, apokeimai* [1]

STOREROOM [2]

storeroom, *2565, thēsauros* [1]
storeroom, *5421, tameion* [1]

STORES [1]

stores up, *2564, thēsaurizō* [1]

STORIES [2]

stories, *3364, logos* [1]
stories, *3680, mythos* [1]

STORING [1]

storing up, *2564, thēsaurizō* [1]

STORM [7]

storm, *AIT* [1]
storm, *RPE* [1]
storm, *2590, thyella* [1]
storm, *3278, lailaps* [1]
storm, *4939, seismos* [1]
took a battering from the storm, *5928, cheimazō* [1]
storm, *5930, cheimōn* [1]

STORMY [1]

stormy, *5930, cheimōn* [1]

STORY [2]

story, *3364, logos* [1]
third story, *5566, tristegon* [1]

STRAIGHT [13]

straight, *2318, euthys²* [6]
looked straight, *867, atenizō* [2]

sailed straight, *2312, euthydromeō* [2]
looked straight at, *867, atenizō* [1]
looked straight at, *1838, emblepō* [1]
make straight, *2316, euthynō* [1]

STRAIGHTEN [2]

straighten up, *376, anakyptō* [1]
straighten out, *2114, epidiorthoō* [1]

STRAIGHTENED [3]

straightened up, *376, anakyptō* [2]
straightened up, *494, anorthoō* [1]

STRAIN [1]

strain out, *1494, diylizō* [1]

STRAINING [2]

straining, *989, basanizō* [1]
straining toward, *2085, epekteinomai* [1]

STRANGE [5]

strange, *3828, xenos* [2]
strange tongues, *2280, heteroglōssos* [1]
strange, *3826, xenizō* [1]
think it strange, *3826, xenizō* [1]

STRANGER [6]

stranger, *3828, xenos* [4]
stranger, *259, allotrios* [2]

STRANGER'S [1]

stranger's, *259, allotrios* [1]

STRANGERS [7]

strangers, *4215, parepidēmos* [3]
strangers, *3828, xenos* [1]
strangers, *4229, paroikia* [1]
strangers, *4230, paroikos* [1]
entertain strangers, *5810, philoxenia* [1]

STRANGLED [3]

meat of strangled animals, *4465, pniktos* [3]

STRAW [1]

straw, *2811, kalamē* [1]

STREAMS [3]

streams, *4532, potamos* [3]

STREET [8]

great street, *4423, plateia* [2]
street, *4423, plateia* [2]
street, *4860, rhymē* [2]
street, *316, amphodon* [1]
street, *3847, hodos* [1]

STREETS [7]

streets, *4423, plateia* [5]
streets, *3847, hodos* [1]
streets, *4860, rhymē* [1]

STRENGTH [15]

strength, *2709, ischys* [6]
strength, *RPE* [1]
full strength, *204, akratos* [1]
strength, *1539, dynamis* [1]
turned to strength, *1540, dynamoō* [1]
gave strength, *1904, endynamoō* [1]
given strength, *1904, endynamoō* [1]
gives strength, *1904, endynamoō* [1]
regained strength, *1932, enischyō* [1]

strength, *3197, kratos* [1]

STRENGTHEN [9]

strengthen, *5114, stērizō* [6]
strengthen, *494, anorthoō* [1]
strengthen, *1443+3194, didōmi+krataioō* [1]
strengthen, *2185, epistērizō* [1]

STRENGTHENED [7]

strengthened, *1011, bebaioō* [2]
strengthened, *1540, dynamoō* [1]
strengthened, *1904, endynamoō* [1]
strengthened, *1932, enischyō* [1]
strengthened, *3868, oikodomeō* [1]
strengthened, *5105, stereoō* [1]

STRENGTHENING [6]

strengthening, *2185, epistērizō* [3]
strengthening, *3869, oikodomē* [3]

STRESS [1]

stress, *1331, diabebaioomai* [1]

STRETCH [5]

stretch out, *1753, ekteinō* [5]

STRETCHED [3]

stretched out, *1753, ekteinō* [2]
stretched out, *4727, proteinō* [1]

STRICT [4]

strict, *4498, polys* [2]
gave strict orders, *4132+4133, parangelia+parangellō* [1]
strict, *4246, pas* [1]

STRICTEST [1]

strictest, *207, akribēs* [1]

STRICTLY [2]

strictly, *AIT* [1]
strictly warned, *2203+4133, epitimaō+parangellō* [1]

STRIFE [2]

strife, *2251, eris* [2]

STRIKE [11]

strike, *4250, patassō* [4]
strike, *4684, proskoptō* [2]
strike, *5597, typtō* [2]
strike dead, *650+1877+2505, apokteinō+en+thanatos* [1]
strike, *1296, derō* [1]
strike down, *4250, patassō* [1]

STRIKES [3]

strikes, *4091, paiō* [1]
strikes, *4824, rhapizō* [1]
strikes, *5597, typtō* [1]

STRIPPED [3]

stripped of clothes, *1694, ekdyō* [1]
stripped, *1694, ekdyō* [1]
stripped, *4351+3836+2668, perirēgnymi+ho+himation* [1]

STRIPS [5]

strips of linen, *3856, othonion* [4]
strips of linen, *3024, keiria* [1]

STRIVE   [2]

strive, *76, agōnizomai* [1]
strive, *828, askeō* [1]

STROKE   [2]

least stroke of a pen, *3037, keraia* [2]

STRONG   [29]

strong, *2708, ischyros* [8]
strong, *1543, dynatos* [3]
strong, *2710, ischyō* [3]
strong, *3194, krataioō* [3]
strong, *1904, endynamoō* [2]
strong, *3489, megas* [2]
keep strong, *1011, bebaioō* [1]
strong warning, *1839, embrimaomai* [1]
strong, *4498, polys* [1]
make strong, *4964, sthenoō* [1]
strong, *5017, sklēros* [1]
made strong, *5105, stereoō* [1]
strong, *5105, stereoō* [1]
make strong, *5114, stērizō* [1]

STRONGER   [4]

stronger, *2708, ischyros* [3]
stronger, *2709, ischys* [1]

STRONGHOLDS   [1]

strongholds, *4065, ochyrōma* [1]

STRONGLY   [3]

strongly, *3336, lian* [1]
urged strongly, *4128, parabiazomai* [1]
strongly, *4498, polys* [1]

STRUCK   [21]

struck, *4250, patassō* [3]
struck, *5597, typtō* [3]
struck in the face, *1443+4825, didōmi+rhapisma* [2]
struck with fists, *3139, kolaphizō* [2]
struck, *4091, paiō* [2]
struck, *4703, prosrēgnymi* [2]
struck, *2158+2093, epipiptō+epi* [1]
struck, *2262+2093, erchomai+epi* [1]
struck down, *2850, kataballō* [1]
struck on the head, *3052, kephalioō* [1]
struck down, *4250, patassō* [1]
struck, *4346, peripiptō* [1]
struck, *4448, plēssō* [1]

STRUGGLE   [4]

struggle, *74, agōn* [1]
struggle, *497, antagōnizomai* [1]
struggle, *4097, palē* [1]
join in struggle, *5253, synagōnizomai* [1]

STRUGGLING   [2]

struggling, *74, agōn* [1]
struggling, *76, agōnizomai* [1]

STUBBORN   [2]

stubborn, *4801, pōrōsis* [1]
stubborn, *5016, sklērokardia* [1]

STUBBORNNESS   [1]

stubbornness, *5018, sklērotēs* [1]

STUCK   [1]

stuck fast, *2242, ereidō* [1]

STUDENT   [3]

student, *3412, mathētēs* [3]

STUDIED   [1]

studied, *3443, manthanō* [1]

STUDY   [1]

diligently study, *2236, eraunaō* [1]

STUMBLE   [9]

causes men to stumble, *4682, proskomma* [2]
stumble, *4684, proskoptō* [2]
not cause to stumble, *718, aproskopos* [1]
stumble, *4682, proskomma* [1]
stumble in, *4760, ptaiō* [1]
stumble, *4760, ptaiō* [1]
make stumble, *4998, skandalon* [1]

STUMBLED   [1]

stumbled over, *4684, proskoptō* [1]

STUMBLES   [2]

stumbles, *4684, proskoptō* [1]
stumbles, *4760, ptaiō* [1]

STUMBLING   [7]

stumbling block, *4998, skandalon* [3]
stumbling block, *4682, proskomma* [2]
stumbling, *4682, proskomma* [1]
stumbling block, *4683, proskopē* [1]

STUPID   [1]

stupid, *553, apaideutos* [1]

STUPOR   [1]

stupor, *2919, katanyxis* [1]

SUBDUE   [1]

subdue, *1238, damazō* [1]

SUBJECT   [16]

subject, *5718, hypotassō* [4]
subject to bleeding, *1877+4868+135, en+rhysis+haima* [2]
subject, *1944, enochos* [2]
subject to, *5679, hypo* [2]
subject, *AIT* [1]
subject to bleeding, *137, haimorroeō* [1]
not subject, *538, anypotaktos* [1]
subject to, *4329, perikeimai* [1]
made subject, *5718, hypotassō* [1]
subject to the control, *5718, hypotassō* [1]

SUBJECTED   [3]

subjected, *5718, hypotassō* [3]

SUBJECTING   [1]

subjecting to public disgrace, *4136, paradeigmatizō* [1]

SUBJECTS   [2]

subjects, *4489, politēs* [1]
subjects, *5626, huios* [1]

SUBMISSION   [4]

in submission, *5718, hypotassō* [2]
reverent submission, *2325, eulabeia* [1]
submission, *5717, hypotagē* [1]

SUBMISSIVE   [4]

submissive, *5718, hypotassō* [3]
submissive, *2340, eupeithēs* [1]

SUBMIT   [17]

submit, *5718, hypotassō* [13]
submit, *RPE* [2]
submit to rules, *1505, dogmatizō* [1]
submit, *5640, hypeikō* [1]

SUBMITS   [1]

submits, *5718, hypotassō* [1]

SUBSIDED   [1]

subsided, *4264, pauō* [1]

SUBVERTING   [1]

subverting, *1406, diastrephō* [1]

SUCCEEDED   [1]

succeeded, *3284+1345, lambanō+diadochos* [1]

SUCH   [94]

such, *5525, toioutos* [22]
such, *4047, houtos* [15]
such, *NIG* [9]
such, *AIT* [6]
such, *RPE* [4]
such as these, *5525, toioutos* [4]
such great, *5537, tosoutos* [4]
such, *3836, ho* [2]
such a man, *5525, toioutos* [2]
such, *5537, tosoutos* [2]
such beings, *899, autos* [1]
such, *899, autos* [1]
such[s] matters, *1053, biōtikos* [1]
such as, *1623, ei* [1]
have such a place, *1639, eimi* [1]
such as, *1664, eite* [1]
such[s], *1877+4922, en+sarx* [1]
such[s] things, *3836+4998, ho+skandalon* [1]
such a, *3836, ho* [1]
such a man's[s], *4005, hos* [1]
such a man, *4005, hos* [1]
such regulations[s], *4015, hostis* [1]
any such person, *4047, houtos* [1]
such a man, *4047, houtos* [1]
such sins[s], *4047, houtos* [1]
with such, *4048, houtōs* [1]
in such a way, *4048, houtōs* [1]
such things, *4048, houtōs* [1]
not put on such a list, *4148, paraiteomai* [1]
such violent, *5380, sphodrōs* [1]
such great, *5496, tēlikoutos* [1]
such, *5496, tēlikoutos* [1]
such a, *5525, toioutos* [1]
such that, *6063, hōste* [1]

SUDDEN   [1]

sudden, *2317, euthys[1]* [1]

SUDDENLY   [17]

suddenly, *1978, exaiphnēs* [5]
suddenly, *2779+2627, kai+idou* [4]
suddenly, *924, aphnō* [3]
suddenly, *167, aiphnidios* [1]
suddenly took away, *773, harpazō* [1]
suddenly, *1988, exapina* [1]
suddenly, *2311, eutheōs* [1]
suddenly, *2627, idou* [1]

SUE [1]

sue, *3212, krinō* [1]

SUFFER [29]

suffer, *4248, paschō* [21]
suffer, *AIT* [1]
suffer, *RPE* [1]
suffer persecution, *2400+2568,
   echō+thlipsis* [1]
suffer loss, *2423, zēmioō* [1]
suffer, *2568, thlipsis* [1]
suffer grief, *3382, lypeō* [1]
suffer, *4078, pathētos* [1]
suffer, *5674, hypechō* [1]

SUFFERED [20]

suffered, *4248, paschō* [14]
suffered, *4077, pathēma* [2]
suffered, *AIT* [1]
suffered, *1181, ginomai* [1]
suffered^s, *2777, kathōs* [1]
previously suffered, *4634, propaschō* [1]

SUFFERING [26]

suffering, *4248, paschō* [5]
suffering, *2568, thlipsis* [4]
suffering, *3465, mastix* [2]
suffering, *4077, pathēma* [2]
suffering, *5309, synechō* [2]
suffering disgrace, *869, atimazō* [1]
suffering, *989, basanizō* [1]
suffering, *1181, ginomai* [1]
suffering from demon-possession, *1227,
   daimonizomai* [1]
suffering^s, *1877+5393, en+sōma* [1]
suffering, *2801, kakopatheia* [1]
suffering, *2802, kakopatheō* [1]
bed of suffering, *3109, klinē* [1]
join in suffering, *5155, synkakopatheō* [1]
suffering from, *5309, synechō* [1]
suffering from dropsy, *5622, hydrōpikos* [1]

SUFFERINGS [13]

sufferings, *4077, pathēma* [10]
sufferings, *2568, thlipsis* [2]
share in sufferings, *5224, sympaschō* [1]

SUFFERS [2]

suffers, *4248, paschō* [1]
suffers with, *5224, sympaschō* [1]

SUFFICIENT [3]

sufficient, *758, arkeō* [1]
sufficient, *2653, hikanos* [1]
sufficient, *4246, pas* [1]

SUIT [1]

to suit, *2848, kata* [1]

SULFUR [8]

sulfur, *2520, theion* [7]
yellow as sulfur, *2523, theiōdēs* [1]

SUM [3]

sum of money, *2564, thēsaurizō* [1]
large sum, *2653, hikanos* [1]
sum, *5507, timē* [1]

SUMMED [2]

summed up, *368, anakephalaioō* [1]
summed up, *4444, plēroō* [1]

SUMMER [3]

summer, *2550, theros* [3]

SUMMONED [2]

summoned, *5888, phōneō* [2]

SUMMONING [1]

summoning, *4673, proskaleō* [1]

SUMS [1]

sums up, *1639, eimi* [1]

SUN [30]

sun, *2463, hēlios* [27]
rising sun, *424, anatolē* [1]
the sun^s, *899, autos* [1]
light of the sun, *2463, hēlios* [1]

SUNG [2]

sung a hymn, *5630, hymneō* [2]

SUNRISE [1]

just after sunrise, *422+3836+2463,
   anatellō+ho+hēlios* [1]

SUNSET [1]

sunset, *1544+2463, dynō+hēlios* [1]

SUPER-APOSTLES [2]

super-apostles, *5663+693,
   hyperlian+apostolos* [2]

SUPERIOR [6]

superior, *1427, diaphoros* [2]
superior to, *3202, kreittōn* [2]
superior, *1422, diapherō* [1]
superior wisdom, *5667+5053,
   hyperochē+sophia* [1]

SUPERVISION [1]

supervision, *4080, paidagōgos* [1]

SUPPER [7]

supper, *1270, deipnon* [4]
supper, *1268, deipneō* [2]
my supper, *5515+1268, tis+deipneō* [1]

SUPPLIED [4]

supplied, *405, anaplēroō* [1]
amply supplied, *4444, plēroō* [1]
supplied, *4650, prosanaplēroō* [1]
supplied, *5676, hypēreteō* [1]

SUPPLIES [2]

supplies, *AIT* [1]
supplies, *2220, epichorēgeō* [1]

SUPPLY [5]

supply, *1181, ginomai* [1]
supply, *1650, eis* [1]
supply, *2936, katartizō* [1]
food supply, *5555, trephō* [1]
supply, *5961, chorēgeō* [1]

SUPPLYING [1]

supplying, *4650, prosanaplēroō* [1]

SUPPORT [6]

support, *AIT* [1]
support, *1002, bastazō* [1]
helping to support, *1354, diakoneō* [1]
support, *4072, opsōnion* [1]
came to support, *4134, paraginomai* [1]
secured the support, *4275, peithō* [1]

SUPPORTED [1]

supported, *2220, epichorēgeō* [1]

SUPPORTING [1]

supporting, *2221, epichorēgia* [1]

SUPPORTS [1]

supports, *RPE* [1]

SUPPOSE [14]

suppose, *1569, ean* [5]
suppose one, *5515, tis* [3]
suppose, *5696, hypolambanō* [2]
suppose, *3787, nomizō* [1]
suppose, *3887, oiomai* [1]
suppose one, *5515+476, tis+anthrōpos* [1]
suppose a, *5515, tis* [1]

SUPPOSED [1]

supposed, *6055, hōs* [1]

SUPPOSING [2]

supposing, *1506, dokeō* [1]
supposing, *3887, oiomai* [1]

SUPPRESS [1]

suppress, *2988, katechō* [1]

SUPREMACY [1]

supremacy, *4750, prōteuō* [1]

SUPREME [1]

supreme authority, *5660, hyperechō* [1]

SURE [14]

sure of, *1182, ginōskō* [2]
to be sure, *3525, men* [2]
sure, *1010, bebaios* [1]
for to be sure, *1142, gar* [1]
sure, *3857+1182, oida+ginōskō* [1]
sure, *3857, oida* [1]
make sure that, *3972, horaō* [1]
sure, *4275, peithō* [1]
sure, *4412, pistos* [1]
sure, *4443, plērophoria* [1]
made sure that, *5381, sphragizō* [1]
sure, *5712, hypostasis* [1]

SURELY [28]

surely, *242, alēthōs* [6]
surely, *NIG* [4]
surely not, *3614, mēti* [3]
surely, *1623+1145, ei+ge* [2]
surely not, *3592, mēdamōs* [2]
surely, *4122, pantōs* [2]
surely, *247+1145, alla+ge* [1]
surely, *1142, gar* [1]
surely, *1327, dēpou* [1]
surely, *1623+3605, ei+mēn^2* [1]
as surely as I live, *2409+1609, zaō+egō* [1]
surely, *2623, ide* [1]
surely, *2627, idou* [1]
I mean that just as surely as, *3755, nē* [1]
surely, *3953, ontōs* [1]

SURF [1]

surf, *3246, kyma* [1]

SURFACE [1]

surface of things, *2848+4725, kata+prosōpon* [1]

SURPASSED [2]

surpassed, *1869+1181, emprosthen+ginomai* [2]

SURPASSES [2]

surpasses, *4355+4498, perisseuō+polys* [1]
surpasses, *5650, hyperballō* [1]

SURPASSING [3]

surpassing, *5650, hyperballō* [2]
surpassing greatness, *5660, hyperechō* [1]

SURPASSINGLY [1]

surpassingly great, *5651, hyperbolē* [1]

SURPRISE [2]

surprise, *2513, thaumazō* [1]
surprise, *2898, katalambanō* [1]

SURPRISED [6]

surprised, *2513, thaumazō* [5]
surprised, *3826, xenizō* [1]

SURPRISING [1]

surprising, *3489, megas* [1]

SURRENDER [1]

surrender, *4140, paradidōmi* [1]

SURRENDERED [1]

surrendered, *4140, paradidōmi* [1]

SURROUNDED [4]

surrounded by, *2400, echō* [1]
surrounded, *3238, kykleuō* [1]
surrounded, *3240, kykloō* [1]
surrounded, *4329, perikeimai* [1]

SURROUNDING [8]

surrounding country, *4369, perichōros* [3]
surrounding, *3241, kyklō* [2]
surrounding, *3239, kyklothen* [1]
surrounding, *4309, peri* [1]
surrounding, *4369, perichōros* [1]

SURVIVE [3]

survive, *5392, sōzō* [2]
survive, *5401, sōtēria* [1]

SURVIVES [1]

survives, *3531, menō* [1]

SURVIVORS [1]

survivors, *3370, loipos* [1]

SUSANNA [1]

Susanna, *5052, Sousanna* [1]

SUSPENSE [2]

keep in suspense, *3836+6034+149, ho+psychē+airō* [1]
suspense, *4659, prosdokaō* [1]

SUSPICIONS [1]

suspicions, *5707, hyponoia* [1]

SUSTAINING [1]

sustaining, *5770, pherō* [1]

SWALLOW [1]

swallow, *2927, katapinō* [1]

SWALLOWED [2]

swallowed up, *2927, katapinō* [2]

SWALLOWING [1]

swallowing, *2927, katapinō* [1]

SWAMPED [2]

swamped, *1153, gemizō* [1]
swamped, *5230, symplēroō* [1]

SWAYED [5]

swayed, *3508, melei* [2]
swayed, *4888, saleuō* [2]
swayed, *72, agō* [1]

SWEAR [7]

swear, *3923, omnyō* [4]
swear by, *3923, omnyō* [2]
swear, *3991, horkizō* [1]

SWEARS [10]

swears, *3923, omnyō* [10]

SWEAT [1]

sweat, *2629, hidrōs* [1]

SWEEP [2]

sweep away with the torrent, *4533+4472, potamophorētos+poieō* [1]
sweep, *4924, saroō* [1]

SWEET [2]

sweet, *1184, glykys* [2]

SWELL [1]

swell up, *4399, pimprēmi* [1]

SWEPT [5]

swept clean, *4924, saroō* [2]
swept, *965, ballō* [1]
swept over, *2821, kalyptō* [1]
swept, *5359, syrō* [1]

SWIFT [2]

swift, *3955, oxys* [1]
swift, *5442, tachinos* [1]

SWIM [1]

swim, *3147, kolymbaō* [1]

SWIMMING [1]

swimming away, *1713, ekkolymbaō* [1]

SWINDLER [1]

swindler, *774, harpax* [1]

SWINDLERS [2]

swindlers, *774, harpax* [2]

SWORD [29]

sword, *3479, machaira* [21]
sword, *4855, rhomphaia* [7]
sword, *5125+3479, stoma+machaira* [1]

SWORDS [7]

swords, *3479, machaira* [7]

SWORE [5]

swore, *3923, omnyō* [5]

SWORN [1]

sworn, *3923, omnyō* [1]

SWUNG [2]

swung, *965, ballō* [2]

SYCAMORE-FIG [1]

sycamore-fig tree, *5191, sykomorea* [1]

SYCHAR [1]

Sychar, *5373, Sychar* [1]

SYMBOLIZES [1]

symbolizes, *531, antitypos* [1]

SYMPATHETIC [1]

sympathetic, *5218, sympathēs* [1]

SYMPATHIZE [1]

sympathize with, *5217, sympatheō* [1]

SYMPATHIZED [1]

sympathized with, *5217, sympatheo* [1]

SYNAGOGUE [45]

synagogue, *5252, synagōgē* [31]
synagogue ruler, *801, archisynagōgos* [7]
put out of the synagogue, *697, aposynagōgos* [2]
synagogue rulers, *801, archisynagōgos* [2]
put out of the synagogue, *697+4472, aposynagōgos+poieō* [1]
the synagogue's, *899, autos* [1]
from one synagogue to another, *2848+4246+3836+5252, kata+pas+ho+synagōgē* [1]

SYNAGOGUES [23]

synagogues, *5252, synagōgē* [23]

SYNTYCHE [1]

Syntyche, *5345, Syntychē* [1]

SYRACUSE [1]

Syracuse, *5352, Syrakousai* [1]

SYRIA [8]

Syria, *5353, Syria* [8]

SYRIAN [1]

Syrian, *5354, Syros* [1]

SYRIAN PHOENICIA [1]

Syrian Phoenicia, *5355, Syrophoinikissa* [1]

SYRTIS [1]

sandbars of Syrtis, *5358, Syrtis* [1]

TABERNACLE [10]

tabernacle, *5008, skēnē* [9]
the tabernacle's, *4005, hos* [1]

TALK [20]

talk, *3281, laleō* [6]
talk, *3364, logos* [2]
talk back, *503, antapokrinomai* [1]
talk back, *515, antilegō* [1]
malicious talk, *1060, blasphēmia* [1]
talk, *3062, kēryssō* [1]
could not talk, *3273, kōphos* [1]
talk, *3306, legō* [1]
meaningless talk, *3467, mataiologia* [1]
could hardly talk, *3652, mogilalos* [1]
foolish talk, *3703, mōrologia* [1]
talk with, *4688, proslaleō* [1]
silence talk, *5821, phimoō* [1]
smooth talk, *5981, chrēstologia* [1]

TALKED [10]

talked, *3281, laleō* [4]
talked, *3917, homileō* [2]
talked against, *515, antilegō* [1]
talked, *1363, dialegomai* [1]
talked the matter over, *1368+4639+253, dialogizomai+pros+allēlōn* [1]
talked with, *4688, proslaleō* [1]

TALKERS [2]

malicious talkers, *1333, diabolos* [1]
mere talkers, *3468, mataiologos* [1]

TALKING [32]

talking about, *3306, legō* [7]
talking, *3306, legō* [7]
talking, *3281, laleō* [4]
talking with, *5196, syllaleō* [3]
talking, *3364, logos* [2]
talking, *3917, homileō* [2]
talking against, *515, antilegō* [1]
talking about, *1362, dialaleō* [1]
talking about, *1368, dialogizomai* [1]
talking, *1368, dialogizomai* [1]
talking about, *3062, kēryssō* [1]
talking about, *3281, laleō* [1]
talking with, *5326, synomileō* [1]

TAMAR [1]

Tamar, *2500, Thamar* [1]

TAME [1]

tame, *1238, damazō* [1]

TAMED [2]

tamed, *1238, damazō* [2]

TANNER [3]

tanner, *1114, byrseus* [3]

TARSUS [5]

Tarsus, *5433, Tarsos* [3]
from Tarsus, *5432, Tarseus* [1]
man from Tarsus, *5432, Tarseus* [1]

TASK [8]

task, *AIT* [3]
task, *RPE* [2]
task, *1355, diakonia* [1]
assigned task, *2240, ergon* [1]
task, *2240, ergon* [1]

TASSELS [1]

tassels, *3192, kraspedon* [1]

TASTE [7]

taste, *1174, geuomai* [6]
get a taste, *1174, geuomai* [1]

TASTED [5]

tasted, *1174, geuomai* [4]
tasted, *1639, eimi* [1]

TASTING [1]

tasting, *1174, geuomai* [1]

TAUGHT [35]

taught, *1438, didaskō* [20]
taught, *RPE* [3]
taught, *1435, didaktos* [3]
taught, *1439, didachē* [2]
taught, *1639+1438, eimi+didaskō* [2]
taught, *AIT* [1]
things taught, *1436, didaskalia* [1]
taught by God, *2531, theodidaktos* [1]
taught, *2994, katēcheō* [1]
taught, *4084, paideuō* [1]

TAX [29]

tax collectors, *5467, telōnēs* [15]
tax collector, *5467, telōnēs* [6]
tax collector's booth, *5468, telōnion* [2]
tax, *RPE* [1]
chief tax collector, *803, architelōnēs* [1]
temple tax, *1440, didrachmon* [1]
tax, *3056, kēnsos* [1]
collectors of tax, *3284, lambanō* [1]
tax booth, *5468, telōnion* [1]

TAXES [8]

taxes, *5843, phoros* [5]
taxes, *3056, kēnsos* [3]

TEACH [48]

teach, *1438, didaskō* [34]
teach, *RPE* [5]
able to teach, *1434, didaktikos* [2]
teach, *1436, didaskalia* [2]
teach, *3281, laleō* [2]
began to teach, *487+3836+5125+1438, anoigō+ho+stoma+didaskō* [1]
teach false doctrines, *2281, heterodidaskaleō* [1]
teach what is good, *2815, kalodidaskalos* [1]

TEACHER [55]

teacher, *1437, didaskalos* [50]
teacher of the law, *1208, grammateus* [2]
teacher, *2762, kathēgētēs* [2]
teacher of the law, *3791, nomodidaskalos* [1]

TEACHERS [70]

teachers of the law, *1208, grammateus* [57]
teachers, *1437, didaskalos* [8]
teachers of the law, *3791, nomodidaskalos* [2]
teachers, *RPE* [1]
teachers, *1208, grammateus* [1]
false teachers, *6015, pseudodidaskalos* [1]

TEACHES [6]

teaches, *1438, didaskō* [4]
teaches false doctrines, *2281, heterodidaskaleō* [1]
teaches, *4084, paideuō* [1]

TEACHING [74]

teaching, *1438, didaskō* [31]

teaching, *1439, didachē* [23]
teaching, *1436, didaskalia* [10]
teaching, *3364, logos* [9]
teaching, *4142, paradosis* [1]

TEACHINGS [8]

teachings, *1438+1436, didaskō+didaskalia* [2]
teachings, *4142, paradosis* [2]
teachings, *RPE* [1]
teachings, *1436, didaskalia* [1]
teachings, *1439, didachē* [1]
teachings, *3364, logos* [1]

TEAR [7]

tear, *1232, dakryon* [2]
tear, *5388, schisma* [2]
tear down, *2747, kathaireō* [1]
tear to pieces, *4838, rhēgnymi* [1]
tear, *5387, schizō* [1]

TEARING [1]

tearing down, *2746, kathairesis* [1]

TEARS [10]

tears, *1232, dakryon* [8]
with tears, *3081, klaiō* [1]
tears, *5387, schizō* [1]

TEETH [11]

teeth, *3848, odous* [10]
teeth, *RPE* [1]

TELL [255]

tell, *3306, legō* [216]
tell, *550, apangellō* [6]
tell, *3281, laleō* [5]
tell, *1192, gnōrizō* [4]
tell, *RPE* [3]
tell, *1455, diēgeomai* [3]
tell, *NIG* [2]
tell, *5745+4472, phaneros+poieō* [2]
tell, *334, anangellō* [1]
tell about, *550, apangellō* [1]
tell, *646, apokrinomai* [1]
tell, *1718, eklaleō* [1]
tell good news, *2294, euangelizō* [1]
tell the good news, *2294, euangelizō* [1]
I tell you, *2627, idou* [1]
tell, *2813, kaleō* [1]
tell, *3027, keleuō* [1]
tell, *3062, kēryssō* [1]
tell about, *3455, martyreō* [1]
what am about to tell, *3836+3364+4047, ho+logos+houtos* [1]
tell, *3857, oida* [1]
tell plainly, *3933, homologeō* [1]

TELLING [23]

telling, *3306, legō* [10]
telling, *RPE* [3]
telling, *3281, laleō* [3]
telling truth, *238, alētheuō* [1]
telling about, *2007, exēgeomai* [1]
telling the good news about, *2294, euangelizō* [1]
telling the good news, *2294, euangelizō* [1]
telling, *2859, katangellō* [1]
telling about, *3306, legō* [1]
telling, *4625, prolegō* [1]

TELLS [5]

tells, *3306, legō* [3]
tells, *1948, entellō* [1]

tells, *3281, laleō* [1]

TEMPERATE [3]

temperate, *3767, nēphalios* [3]

TEMPLE [121]

temple, *3724, naos* [42]
temple, *2639, hieron* [31]
temple courts, *2639, hieron* [23]
temple area, *2639, hieron* [10]
temple treasury, *1126, gazophylakion* [2]
temple guard, *2639, hieron* [2]
temple guards, *5677, hypēretēs* [2]
temple tax, *1440, didrachmon* [1]
idol's temple, *1627, eidōleion* [1]
temple grounds, *2639, hieron* [1]
temple, *2641, hieros* [1]
temple worship, *3301, latreia* [1]
guardian of the temple, *3753, neōkoros* [1]
whose temple⁵, *3836, ho* [1]
that temple⁵, *4015, hostis* [1]
officers of the temple guard, *5130, stratēgos* [1]

TEMPLES [3]

rob temples, *2644, hierosyleō* [1]
robbed temples, *2645, hierosylos* [1]
temples, *3724, naos* [1]

TEMPORARY [1]

temporary, *4672, proskairos* [1]

TEMPT [2]

tempt, *4279, peirazō* [2]

TEMPTATION [8]

temptation, *4280, peirasmos* [8]

TEMPTED [13]

tempted, *4279, peirazō* [11]
cannot tempted, *585, apeirastos* [1]
tempted, *4280, peirasmos* [1]

TEMPTER [2]

tempter, *4279, peirazō* [2]

TEMPTING [2]

tempting, *4279, peirazō* [1]
tempting, *4280, peirasmos* [1]

TEN [29]

ten, *1274, deka* [24]
ten thousand, *3689, myrias* [2]
ten thousand, *3692, myrios* [2]
ten thousand, *3691, myrioi* [1]

TENANTS [13]

tenants, *1177, geōrgos* [12]
tenants, *RPE* [1]

TENDER [3]

tender, *559, hapalos* [2]
tender mercy, *5073+1799, splanchnon+eleos* [1]

TENDERNESS [1]

tenderness, *5073, splanchnon* [1]

TENDING [3]

tending, *1081, boskō* [3]

TENDS [1]

tends, *4477, poimainō* [1]

TENT [5]

tent, *5011, skēnos* [2]
tent, *5008, skēnē* [1]
spread tent, *5012, skēnoō* [1]
tent, *5013, skēnōma* [1]

TENTH [13]

tenth, *1281, dekatos* [7]
give a tenth of, *620, apodekatoō* [2]
give God a tenth of, *620, apodekatoō* [1]
collected a tenth, *1282, dekatoō* [1]
paid the tenth, *1282, dekatoō* [1]
collect a tenth from, *2400+620, echō+apodekatoō* [1]

TENTMAKER [1]

tentmaker, *5010, skēnopoios* [1]

TENTS [1]

tents, *5008, skēnē* [1]

TERAH [1]

Terah, *2508, Thara* [1]

TERMS [2]

in human terms, *474, anthrōpinos* [1]
terms, *3836, ho* [1]

TERRIBLE [3]

terrible, *1267, deinōs* [1]
terrible, *3489, megas* [1]
terrible, *5901, chalepos* [1]

TERRIBLY [1]

terribly, *2809, kakōs* [1]

TERRIFIED [10]

terrified, *5429, tarassō* [2]
terrified, *5828+5379, phobeomai+sphodra* [2]
terrified, *5828+5832+3489, phobeomai+phobos+megas* [2]
terrified, *1328+5832, dia+phobos* [1]
terrified, *1873, emphobos* [1]
terrified, *5828, phobeomai* [1]
terrified, *5832, phobos* [1]

TERRIFYING [1]

terrifying, *5829, phoberos* [1]

TERRITORY [1]

territory, *2834, kanōn* [1]

TERROR [3]

terror, *5832, phobos* [2]
terror, *5832+3489, phobos+megas* [1]

TERRORISTS [1]

terrorists, *467+3836+4974, anēr+ho+sikarios* [1]

TERTIUS [1]

Tertius, *5470, Tertios* [1]

TERTULLUS [2]

Tertullus, *5472, Tertyllos* [2]

TEST [23]

test, *4279, peirazō* [7]
test, *1507, dokimazō* [6]
put to the test, *1733, ekpeirazō* [2]
test, *1733, ekpeirazō* [2]
fail the test, *99+1639, adokimos+eimi* [1]
test and approve, *1507, dokimazō* [1]
would stand the test, *1509, dokimē* [1]
stood the test, *1511, dokimos* [1]
test, *1511, dokimos* [1]
failed the test, *1639+99, eimi+adokimos* [1]

TESTED [10]

tested, *4279, peirazō* [7]
tested, *1507, dokimazō* [1]
tested and approved, *1511, dokimos* [1]
tested, *4280, peirasmos* [1]

TESTIFIED [12]

testified, *3455, martyreō* [5]
testified, *1371, diamartyromai* [3]
testified, *3306, legō* [1]
testified about, *3455, martyreō* [1]
also testified, *5296, synepimartyreō* [1]
testified falsely, *6018, pseudomartyreō* [1]

TESTIFIES [13]

testifies, *3455, martyreō* [6]
testifies to, *3455, martyreō* [3]
testifies, *RPE* [1]
testifies about, *3455, martyreō* [1]
testifies, *3457, martyrion* [1]
testifies with, *5210, symmartyreō* [1]

TESTIFY [31]

testify, *3455, martyreō* [22]
testify to, *3455, martyreō* [2]
testify to, *625+3457, apodidōmi+martyrion* [1]
testify, *1371, diamartyromai* [1]
testify, *3457+1639, martyrion+eimi* [1]
testify, *3457, martyrion* [1]
testify, *3458, martyromai* [1]
testify, *3459+1639, martys+eimi* [1]
testify, *3459, martys* [1]

TESTIFYING [5]

testifying to, *1371, diamartyromai* [1]
testifying, *1371, diamartyromai* [1]
testifying that, *2148, epimartyreō* [1]
testifying, *3455, martyreō* [1]
testifying, *3457, martyrion* [1]

TESTIMONY [62]

testimony, *3456, martyria* [31]
testimony, *3457, martyrion* [12]
testimony bringing against, *2909, katamartyreō* [3]
give false testimony, *6018, pseudomartyreō* [3]
testimony, *5125, stoma* [2]
without testimony, *282, amartyros* [1]
testimony, *3364+3455, logos+martyreō* [1]
gave testimony, *3455, martyreō* [1]
give testimony, *3455, martyreō* [1]
given testimony, *3455, martyreō* [1]
testimony, *3455, martyreō* [1]
testimony, *3456+4005+3455, martyria+hos+martyreō* [1]
bore testimony, *3459, martys* [1]
testimony, *3459, martys* [1]
gave false testimony, *6018, pseudomartyreō* [1]
false testimony, *6019, pseudomartyria* [1]

TESTING [3]

testing, *4280, peirasmos* [2]
testing, *1510, dokimion* [1]

TESTS [1]

tests, *1507, dokimazō* [1]

TETRARCH [7]

tetrarch, *5490, tetrarchēs* [4]
tetrarch, *5489, tetrarcheō* [3]

THADDAEUS [2]

Thaddaeus, *2497, Thaddaios* [2]

THAN [151]

than, *AIT* [31]
than, *2445, ē* [30]
greater than, *3505, meizōn* [20]
than, *4123, para* [9]
more than, *5642, hyper* [4]
worse than, *5937, cheirōn* [4]
than, *NIG* [2]
than, *RPE* [2]
worth more than, *1422, diapherō* [2]
more than, *2062, epanō* [2]
rather than, *2779+4024, kai+ou* [2]
than for, *2779+3590, kai+mē* [2]
more than, *3437, mallon* [2]
than, *3437+2445, mallon+ē* [2]
more than, *4123, para* [2]
other than, *4123, para* [2]
rather than, *4123, para* [2]
more than, *4358, perissoteros* [2]
than, *5642, hyper* [2]
more than, *247, alla* [1]
other than, *257, allos* [1]
more valuable than, *1422, diapherō* [1]
valuable than, *1422, diapherō* [1]
pitied more than, *1795, eleeinos* [1]
more than, *2445, ē* [1]
than, *2472, ēper* [1]
rather than, *2671+3590, hina+mē* [1]
any more than, *2777+4024, kathōs+ou* [1]
more than that, *2779, kai* [1]
rather than, *2779+3590, kai+mē* [1]
than that, *2779+3590, kai+mē* [1]
greater than ever, *3437, mallon* [1]
more than that, *3437+1254, mallon+de* [1]
one greater than, *3505, meizōn* [1]
weightier than, *3505, meizōn* [1]
than, *3888, hoios* [1]
more than, *4024, ou* [1]
harder than, *4358, perissoteros* [1]
more important than, *4358, perissoteros* [1]
better than, *5642, hyper* [1]
more than is warranted, *5642, hyper* [1]
higher than, *5645, hyperanō* [1]
better than, *5660, hyperechō* [1]
more than conquerors, *5664, hypernikaō* [1]
worse off than, *5937, cheirōn* [1]
less than two miles, *6055+608+5084+1278,
    hōs+apo+stadion+dekapente* [1]

THANK [18]

thank, *2373, eucharisteō* [12]
thank, *5921+2400, charis+echō* [2]
thank for, *2373, eucharisteō* [1]
thank, *2374, eucharistia* [1]
thank, *2400+5921, echō+charis* [1]
thank, *5921, charis* [1]

THANKED [2]

thanked, *2373, eucharisteō* [2]

THANKFUL [4]

thankful, *2373, eucharisteō* [1]
thankful, *2374, eucharistia* [1]
thankful, *2375, eucharistos* [1]
thankful, *2400+5921, echō+charis* [1]

THANKFULNESS [2]

thankfulness, *2374, eucharistia* [1]
thankfulness, *5921, charis* [1]

THANKS [38]

gave thanks, *2373, eucharisteō* [7]
gave thanks, *2328, eulogeō* [6]
giving thanks, *2373, eucharisteō* [5]
thanks, *5921, charis* [5]
given thanks, *2373, eucharisteō* [4]
give thanks, *2373, eucharisteō* [2]
gives thanks, *2373, eucharisteō* [2]
thanks, *2374, eucharistia* [2]
gave thanks, *469, anthomologeomai* [1]
gave thanks for, *2328, eulogeō* [1]
give thanks, *2328, eulogeō* [1]
give thanks for, *2373, eucharisteō* [1]
expressions of thanks, *2374, eucharistia* [1]

THANKSGIVING [9]

thanksgiving, *2374, eucharistia* [8]
thanksgiving, *2330, eulogia* [1]

THAT [2065]

that, *4022, hoti* [491]
that, *NIG* [379]
so that, *2671, hina* [197]
that, *3836, ho* [150]
that, *2671, hina* [116]
that, *1697, ekeinos* [95]
that, *4005, hos* [79]
that, *AIT* [64]
that, *RPE* [45]
that, *4047, houtos* [38]
so that, *6063, hōste* [17]
in order that, *2671, hina* [16]
so that, *1650+3836, eis+ho* [15]
so that, *3968, hopōs* [15]
at that time, *5538, tote* [12]
that, *6063, hōste* [12]
so that, *1650, eis* [10]
that, *899, autos* [8]
so that, *2779, kai* [8]
that, *3968, hopōs* [8]
that, *1650+3836, eis+ho* [7]
that, *1623, ei* [6]
so that, *3836, ho* [6]
that, *6055, hōs* [6]
that is why, *1328+4047, dia+houtos* [5]
that is why, *1475, dio* [5]
that very, *1697, ekeinos* [5]
that, *4015, hostis* [5]
that is how, *4048, houtōs* [5]
that, *2779, kai* [4]
that, *4012, hosos* [4]
how is it that, *1328+5515, dia+tis* [3]
in order that, *1650+3836, eis+ho* [3]
that place, *1696, ekeithen* [3]
that, *3590+4803, mē+pōs* [3]
that, *3590, mē* [3]
so that not, *3607, mēpote* [3]
that which, *3836, ho* [3]
that, *3836+899, ho+autos* [3]
see that, *3972, horaō* [3]
received seed that fell, *5062, speirō* [3]
that one, *257, allos* [2]
does that mean that, *727, ara* [2]
that very, *899, autos* [2]

know that, *1182, ginōskō* [2]
that, *1254, de* [2]
that was why, *1328+4047, dia+houtos* [2]
think that, *1506, dokeō* [2]
that, *1650, eis* [2]
from that place, *1696, ekeithen* [2]
that town, *1696, ekeithen* [2]
that same, *1697, ekeinos* [2]
show that, *1892, endeiknymi* [2]
after that, *2083, epeita* [2]
at that moment, *2779+2627, kai+idou* [2]
that is how, *2848+3836+899,
    kata+ho+autos* [2]
that none, *3607+5516, mēpote+tis* [2]
those that, *3836, ho* [2]
so that, *3968+323, hopōs+an* [2]
that, *3968+323, hopōs+an* [2]
that which, *4005, hos* [2]
all that, *4012, hosos* [2]
that, *4020, hotan* [2]
like that, *4048, houtōs* [2]
that way, *4048, houtōs* [2]
that, *4048, houtōs* [2]
for that reason, *4123+4047, para+houtos* [2]
so that, *4639, pros* [2]
so that, *4803, pōs* [2]
that time on, *5538, tote* [2]
olive tree that is wild, *66, agrielaios* [1]
the only thing that counts, *247, alla* [1]
except that, *247, alla* [1]
[that can never] fade, *278, amaranthos* [1]
[that can never] spoil, *299, amiantos* [1]
doing^s that, *462, anechomai* [1]
that had touched, *608+3836+5999,
    apo+ho+chrōs* [1]
in that case, *726, ara* [1]
that gleamed like lightning, *848, astraptō* [1]
that country^s, *899, autos* [1]
that one sheep^s, *899, autos* [1]
that rest^s, *899, autos* [1]
that same, *899, autos* [1]
that can never perish, *915, aphthartos* [1]
careful that, *1063, blepō* [1]
saw that, *1063, blepō* [1]
that are, *1181, ginomai* [1]
now that, *1254, de* [1]
that is why, *1328+4005+162, dia+hos+aitia* [1]
for that very reason, *1328+4047, dia+houtos* [1]
service that perform, *1355+3836+3311+4047,
    diakonia+ho+leitourgia+houtos* [1]
insisting that, *1462, diischyrizomai* [1]
acknowledged that right, *1467, dikaioō* [1]
provided that, *1569, ean* [1]
in the hope that, *1623, ei* [1]
now that, *1623, ei* [1]
that, *1623+4803, ei+pōs* [1]
be that as it may, *1639, eimi* [1]
that is why, *1650+4047, eis+houtos* [1]
in order that, *1650, eis* [1]
after that, *1663, eita* [1]
see that gets justice, *1688, ekdikeō* [1]
in that place, *1695, ekei* [1]
convinced that is a sinner, *1794, elenchō* [1]
that was the time, *1877+3836+2465+1697,
    en+ho+hēmera+ekeinos* [1]
that, *1877+3836, en+ho* [1]
that, *1915, heneken* [1]
if that were so, *2075, epei* [1]
in that case, *2075+726, epei+ara* [1]
that is why, *2093+4047, epi+houtos* [1]
realized that, *2105, epiginōskō* [1]
testifying that, *2148, epimartyreō* [1]
know that, *2179, epistamai* [1]
at that moment, *2311, eutheōs* [1]
made^s that way, *2336+2335,
    eunouchos+eunouchizō* [1]

found that, *2351, heuriskō* [1]
that accompany, *2400, echō* [1]
wish that, *2527, thelō* [1]
that, *2627, idou* [1]
for fear that, *2671+3590, hina+mē* [1]
in the hope that, *2671, hina* [1]
intent that, *2671, hina* [1]
purpose that, *2671, hina* [1]
see that, *2671, hina* [1]
to show that, *2671, hina* [1]
so that, *2743, kagō* [1]
that, *2771, katho* [1]
that way, *2777, kathōs* [1]
that, *2777, kathōs* [1]
at that, *2779, kai* [1]
more than that, *2779, kai* [1]
with that, *2779+2627, kai+idou* [1]
with that, *2779, kai* [1]
than that, *2779+3590, kai+mē* [1]
that place, *2796, kakeithen* [1]
and that, *2797, kakeinos* [1]
but that also, *2797, kakeinos* [1]
indicating that, *2848+4005, kata+hos* [1]
that far outweighs them all,
   2848+5651+1650+5651+983,
   kata+hyperbolē+eis+hyperbolē+baros [1]
danger that, *3073, kindyneuō* [1]
decided that, *3212, krinō* [1]
decision that, *3212, krinō* [1]
judgment that, *3212, krinō* [1]
forgotten that, *3330+3284, lēthē+lambanō* [1]
think that, *3357, logizomai* [1]
beyond that, *3370, loipos* [1]
more than that, *3437+1254, mallon+de* [1]
showed that accepted, *3455, martyreō* [1]
that are coming, *3516, mellō* [1]
that would follow, *3552+4047,*
   meta+houtos [1]
afraid^s that, *3590, mē* [1]
for fear that, *3590+4803, mē+pōs* [1]
that, *3590+4543, mē+pou* [1]
in the hope that, *3607, mēpote* [1]
that contaminates, *3663, molysmos* [1]
I mean that just as surely as, *3755, nē* [1]
that^s, *3795, nomos* [1]
since that time, *3836+3370, ho+loipos* [1]
he that, *3836, ho* [1]
it that, *3836, ho* [1]
that is, *3836, ho* [1]
that same, *3836, ho* [1]
that^s, *3836+2434, ho+zymē* [1]
that^s, *3836+2546, ho+therismos* [1]
that, *3836+4309, ho+peri* [1]
this or that, *3840+3836, hode+ho* [1]
that, *3854, hothen* [1]
acknowledged that, *3933, homologeō* [1]
acknowledges that, *3933, homologeō* [1]
make sure that, *3972, horaō* [1]
saw that, *3972, horaō* [1]
that day^s, *4005, hos* [1]
anything that, *4005, hos* [1]
that tribe^s, *4005, hos* [1]
everything that, *4012, hosos* [1]
that temple^s, *4015, hostis* [1]
is that why, *4022, hoti* [1]
the fact that, *4022, hoti* [1]
the very fact that, *4022, hoti* [1]
is it possible that, *4024, ou* [1]
at that point, *4036, oun* [1]
that, *4036, oun* [1]
up to that time not, *4037, oupō* [1]
that very, *4047, houtos* [1]
with that, *4047+3306, houtos+legō* [1]
at that, *4048, houtōs* [1]
that is why, *4048, houtōs* [1]
how I wish that, *4054, ophelon* [1]

that evening, *4068+1181, opsia+ginomai* [1]
request that, *4151, parakaleō* [1]
at that moment, *4202, parachrēma* [1]
convinced that, *4275, peithō* [1]
in that case, *4309+4005, peri+hos* [1]
manage and see that, *4613, proistēmi* [1]
so that, *4639+3836, pros+ho* [1]
to show that, *4639+3836, pros+ho* [1]
that, *4803, pōs* [1]
things that cause people to sin, *4998,*
   skandalon [1]
things that cause to sin, *4998, skandalon* [1]
that^s, *5125, stoma* [1]
prove that, *5319, synistēmi* [1]
made sure that, *5381, sphragizo* [1]
that is, *5445, te* [1]
decided that, *5502+1087, tithēmi+boulē* [1]
man like that, *5525, toioutos* [1]
that, *5525, toioutos* [1]
that, *5537, tosoutos* [1]
at that, *5538, tote* [1]
of that time, *5538, tote* [1]
that time, *5538, tote* [1]
that am, *5639, hyparchō* [1]
asserting that, *5763, phaskō* [1]
fearing that, *5828+3590, phobeomai+mē* [1]
for that, *6055, hōs* [1]
that is, *6055, hōs* [1]
such that, *6063, hōste* [1]

THAT'S   [2]

that's, *AIT* [1]
that's, *NIG* [1]

THE   [10888]

the, *3836, ho* [7564]
the, *NIG* [2130]
the, *RPE* [83]
the, *AIT* [75]
the son, *3836, ho* [75]
the truth, *297, amēn* [74]
teachers of the law, *1208, grammateus* [57]
the, *4005, hos* [19]
the one, *4005, hos* [18]
the people^s, *899, autos* [17]
the man^s, *899, autos* [15]
in the same way, *4048, houtōs* [11]
on the contrary, *247, alla* [10]
the man's^s, *899, autos* [10]
in the same way, *3931, homoiōs* [10]
in the presence, *1967, enōpion* [9]
for the sake of, *1328, dia* [8]
preach the gospel, *2294, euangelizō* [7]
raised from the dead, *1586, egeirō* [6]
the other^s, *1651, heis* [6]
in the same way, *6058, hōsautōs* [6]
the Jews^s, *899, autos* [5]
the city^s, *899, autos* [5]
the disciples^s, *899, autos* [5]
the reason, *1328+4047, dia+houtos* [5]
in the sight, *1967, enōpion* [5]
preaching the gospel, *2294, euangelizō* [5]
experts in the law, *3788, nomikos* [5]
owner of the house, *3867, oikodespotēs* [5]
reclining at the table, *367, anakeimai* [4]
the apostles^s, *899, autos* [4]
the beast^s, *899, autos* [4]
the boy^s, *899, autos* [4]
the crowd^s, *899, autos* [4]
in the eyes, *1967, enōpion* [4]
all the more, *3437, mallon* [4]
the man^s, *3836+1254, ho+de* [4]
the same, *3931, homoiōs* [4]
for the sake of, *5642, hyper* [4]
not having the law, *491, anomos* [3]

the plants^s, *899, autos* [3]
the women^s, *899, autos* [3]
the result of, *1328, dia* [3]
the, *1651, heis* [3]
in the presence, *1869, emprosthen* [3]
preached the good news, *2294, euangelizō* [3]
the man^s, *3836, ho* [3]
the life^s, *4005, hos* [3]
the man^s, *4005, hos* [3]
the latter^s, *4047, houtos* [3]
on the other side, *4305, peran* [3]
treading out the grain, *262, aloaō* [2]
at the same time, *275, hama* [2]
at the table, *367, anakeimai* [2]
take places at the feast, *369, anaklinō* [2]
reclined at the table, *404, anapiptō* [2]
apart from the law, *492, anomōs* [2]
passed by on the other side, *524,*
   antiparerchomai [2]
put out of the synagogue, *697,*
   aposynagōgos [2]
meeting of the Areopagus, *740, Areios pagos* [2]
master of the banquet, *804, architriklinos* [2]
played the flute, *884, auleō* [2]
the Lord^s, *899, autos* [2]
the body^s, *899, autos* [2]
the child^s, *899, autos* [2]
the children^s, *899, autos* [2]
the men^s, *899, autos* [2]
the servant^s, *899, autos* [2]
the vineyard^s, *899, autos* [2]
the young man^s, *899, autos* [2]
member of the Council, *1085, bouleutēs* [2]
place where the offerings were put, *1126,*
   gazophylakion [2]
teacher of the law, *1208, grammateus* [2]
give the right, *1443, didōmi* [2]
give to the poor, *1443+1797,*
   didōmi+eleēmosynē [2]
struck in the face, *1443+4825,*
   didōmi+rhapisma [2]
the reason, *1650+4047, eis+houtos* [2]
the man^s, *1697, ekeinos* [2]
the, *1697, ekeinos* [2]
put to the test, *1733, ekpeirazō* [2]
gifts to the poor, *1797, eleēmosynē* [2]
three in the afternoon, *1888, enatos* [2]
for the sake, *1915, heneken* [2]
the present, *1931, enistēmi* [2]
on the outside, *2033, exōthen* [2]
in the account, *2093, epi* [2]
with face to the ground, *2093+4725,*
   epi+prosōpon [2]
on the inside, *2277, esōthen* [2]
preach the good news, *2294, euangelizō* [2]
preached the gospel, *2294, euangelizō* [2]
proclaiming the good news, *2294,*
   euangelizō [2]
the good news preached, *2294, euangelizō* [2]
the gospel preached, *2294, euangelizō* [2]
to the point, *2401, heōs* [2]
worked through the dough, *2435, zymoō* [2]
the former, *2797, kakeinos* [2]
the truth, *2822, kalōs* [2]
in the ordinary way, *2848+4922, kata+sarx* [2]
on the basis of, *2848, kata* [2]
in the sight, *2978, katenanti* [2]
the future, *3516, mellō* [2]
expert in the law, *3788, nomikos* [2]
teachers of the law, *3791, nomodidaskalos* [2]
the disciples^s, *3836+1254, ho+de* [2]
the expert in the law^s, *3836+1254, ho+de* [2]
the men^s, *3836+1254, ho+de* [2]
the one, *3836, ho* [2]
the son^s, *3836, ho* [2]
the one, *4005+323, hos+an* [2]

the same thing, *2749, kathaper* [1]
convened the court, *2767+2093+3836+1037,*
   kathizō+epi+ho+bēma [1]
in the words[s] of, *2777, kathōs* [1]
the one, *2797, kakeinos* [1]
the right thing, *2822, kalōs* [1]
by the standards of, *2848, kata* [1]
in the way, *2848, kata* [1]
on the way, *2849, katabainō* [1]
place where the road goes down, *2853,*
   katabasis [1]
disqualify for the prize, *2857, katabrabeuō* [1]
clearly in the wrong, *2861, kataginōskō* [1]
under the power, *2872, katadynasteuō* [1]
reclining at the table, *2879, katakeimai* [1]
at the table, *2884, kataklinō* [1]
reclined at the table, *2884, kataklinō* [1]
throw down the cliff, *2889, katakrēmnizō* [1]
caught in the act, *2898+2093+900,*
   katalambanō+epi+autophōros [1]
get the prize, *2898, katalambanō* [1]
put on the list, *2899, katalegō* [1]
faced the fact, *2917, katanoeō* [1]
mutilators of the flesh, *2961, katatomē* [1]
under the earth, *2973, katachthonios* [1]
to the ground, *3004, katō* [1]
under the control, *3023, keimai* [1]
the point is this, *3049, kephalaion* [1]
struck on the head, *3052, kephalioō* [1]
share in the inheritance, *3099, klēronomeō* [1]
tossed back and forth by the waves, *3115,*
   klydōnizomai [1]
the same way[s], *3210, krima* [1]
distort the truth, *3281+1406,*
   laleō+diastrephō [1]
cut in the rock, *3292, laxeutos* [1]
with the news, *3306, legō* [1]
with the plea, *3306, legō* [1]
with the words, *3306, legō* [1]
all the harder, *3437, mallon* [1]
get into the habit of being, *3443, manthanō* [1]
spread the word, *3455, martyreō* [1]
at the top of, *3489, megas* [1]
all the louder, *3505, meizōn* [1]
part of the body, *3517, melos* [1]
parts of the body, *3517, melos* [1]
the rest, *3538+5516, meros+tis* [1]
the next day, *3552+1651+2465,*
   meta+heis+hēmera [1]
contributing to the needs of others, *3556,*
   metadidōmi [1]
all the way to, *3588, mechri* [1]
even to the point of, *3588, mechri* [1]
to the point of, *3588, mechri* [1]
not in the least, *3594, mēdeis* [1]
in the hope that, *3607, mēpote* [1]
made an idol in the form of a calf, *3674,*
   moschopoieō [1]
learned the secret, *3679, myeō* [1]
owner of the ship, *3729, nauklēros* [1]
guardian of the temple, *3753, neōkoros* [1]
according to the rules, *3789, nomimōs* [1]
teacher of the law, *3791, nomodidaskalos* [1]
receiving of the law, *3792, nomothesia* [1]
the apostles[s], *3836+3525, ho+men* [1]
the manager[s], *3836+1254, ho+de* [1]
the men[s], *3836+3525, ho+men* [1]
the people[s], *3836+1254, ho+de* [1]
at the meal, *3836+367, ho+anakeimai* [1]
in the present case, *3836+3814, ho+nyn* [1]
make the most of opportunity,
   3836+2789+1973,
   ho+kairos+exagorazō [1]
the affairs[s], *3836, ho* [1]
the affairs, *3836, ho* [1]
the father[s], *3836+1254, ho+de* [1]

the interests, *3836, ho* [1]
the man's[s], *3836+1254, ho+de* [1]
the news[s], *3836, ho* [1]
the parts[s], *3836+5393+4047,*
   ho+sōma+houtos [1]
the rioters[s], *3836+1254, ho+de* [1]
the soldiers[s], *3836, ho* [1]
the very, *3836, ho* [1]
the wife, *3836, ho* [1]
on the move, *3845, hodoiporia* [1]
grasp the meaning, *3857+3836+1539,*
   oida+ho+dynamis [1]
head of the house, *3867, oikodespotēs* [1]
the, *3888, hoios* [1]
the same thing, *3931, homoiōs* [1]
the same, *3931+2777, homoiōs+kathōs* [1]
even in the case of, *3940, homōs* [1]
at the same time, *3940, homōs* [1]
invoke the name, *3951+3950,*
   onomazō+onoma [1]
the quality, *3961, hopoios* [1]
in the case of, *3963, hopou* [1]
on[s] the other side, *3963, hopou* [1]
the place where, *3963, hopou* [1]
settle the matter, *3972, horaō* [1]
the sight of, *3972, horaō* [1]
came early in the morning, *3983, orthrizō* [1]
very early in the morning, *3986+960,*
   orthros+bathys [1]
the Son[s], *4005, hos* [1]
the death[s], *4005, hos* [1]
in the same way, *4005+5573, hos+tropos* [1]
the Jesus[s], *4005, hos* [1]
the authority[s], *4005, hos* [1]
the fact[s], *4005, hos* [1]
the glory[s], *4005, hos* [1]
the gospel[s], *4005, hos* [1]
the lawless[s] one, *4005, hos* [1]
the man[s], *4005+1569, hos+ean* [1]
the matters, *4005, hos* [1]
the men[s], *4005+1569, hos+ean* [1]
the men[s], *4005, hos* [1]
the name[s], *4005, hos* [1]
the one, *4005+3525, hos+men* [1]
the people[s], *4005, hos* [1]
the promise[s], *4005, hos* [1]
the sacrifices[s], *4005, hos* [1]
the situation, *4005, hos* [1]
the tabernacle[s], *4005, hos* [1]
the whom, *4005, hos* [1]
the cavalry[s], *4015, hostis* [1]
the one, *4015, hostis* [1]
the people[s], *4015, hostis* [1]
the moment, *4020, hotan* [1]
the fact that, *4022, hoti* [1]
the very fact that, *4022, hoti* [1]
the place where, *4023, hou* [1]
the law forbids, *4024+2003, ou+exesti* [1]
not in the least, *4029, oudeis* [1]
in the following, *4047, houtos* [1]
the reason, *4047+5920, houtos+charin* [1]
the Bereans[s], *4047, houtos* [1]
the passage above, *4047, houtos* [1]
the same as, *4047, houtos* [1]
the same, *4047, houtos* [1]
the women[s], *4047, houtos* [1]
it is the same, *4047+2779, houtōs+kai* [1]
the same, *4048, houtōs* [1]
the way, *4048, houtōs* [1]
this is the way, *4048, houtōs* [1]
this the way, *4048, houtōs* [1]
after the Sabbath, *4067+4879,*
   opse+sabbaton [1]
in the evening, *4067, opse* [1]
in the past, *4093, palai* [1]
in the presence, *4123, para* [1]

by the lake, *4144, parathalassios* [1]
violate the law, *4174, paranomeō* [1]
spend the winter, *4199, paracheimazō* [1]
the country[s], *4246, pas* [1]
the whole, *4246, pas* [1]
the world[s], *4246, pas* [1]
secured the support, *4275, peithō* [1]
trying to win the approval of, *4275, peithō* [1]
on the opposite shore, *4305, peran* [1]
over the matter of, *4309, peri* [1]
retain the place in life, *4344, peripateō* [1]
the way act, *4344, peripateō* [1]
fell into the hands of, *4346, peripiptō* [1]
to the full, *4356, perissos* [1]
spirit which predicted the future, *4460+4780,*
   pneuma+pythōn [1]
the, *4481, poios* [1]
sweep away with the torrent, *4533+4472,*
   potamophorētos+poieō [1]
of the past, *4537, pote* [1]
palace of the Roman governor, *4550,*
   praitōrion [1]
leading the way, *4575, proagō* [1]
led the way, *4575, proagō* [1]
already made the charge, *4577, proaitiaomai* [1]
pushed to the front, *4582, proballō* [1]
written in the past, *4592, prographō* [1]
the first, *4599, proenarchomai* [1]
announced the gospel in advance, *4603,*
   proeuangelizomai [1]
in advance finish the arrangements for, *4616,*
   prokatartizō [1]
spoken in the past, *4625, prolegō* [1]
day before the Sabbath, *4640, prosabbaton* [1]
early in the morning, *4746+1181,*
   prōia+ginomai [1]
early in the morning, *4746, prōia* [1]
places of honor at the table, *4752, prōtoklisia* [1]
in the first place, *4754, prōton* [1]
inheritance rights as the oldest son, *4757,*
   prōtotokia [1]
threw to the ground, *4838, rhēgnymi* [1]
throws to the ground, *4838, rhēgnymi* [1]
of the world, *4920, sarkikos* [1]
the world, *4922, sarx* [1]
the distinguishing mark, *4956, sēmeion* [1]
turn away from the faith, *4997, skandalizō* [1]
all the more eager, *5081, spoudaiōs* [1]
receive the victor's crown, *5110, stephanoō* [1]
officers of the temple guard, *5130, stratēgos* [1]
the two of you, *5148+2779+899,*
   sy+kai+autos [1]
to the decision, *5206+3284,*
   symboulion+lambanō [1]
rest of the disciples, *5209, symmathētēs* [1]
at the table with, *5263, synanakeimai* [1]
joined in the accusation, *5298, synepitithēmi* [1]
joins in the work, *5300, synergeō* [1]
joined in the attack, *5308, synephistēmi* [1]
in the pains of childbirth, *5349, synōdinō* [1]
conform to the pattern of, *5372,*
   syschēmatizō [1]
in the next moment, *5444, tachys* [1]
all the world, *5515+1639+476+4005,*
   tis+eimi+anthrōpos+hos [1]
the, *5515, tis* [1]
the, *5516, tis* [1]
they are the kind, *5525, toioutos* [1]
all the more, *5537+3437, tosoutos+mallon* [1]
the money worth a year's wages, *5559+1324,*
   triakosioi+dēnarion [1]
increased all the more, *5668, hyperperisseuō* [1]
exalted to the highest place, *5671,*
   hyperypsoō [1]
the way, *5679, hypo* [1]
pit for the winepress, *5700, hypolēnion* [1]

passed to the lee of, *5709, hypopleō* [1]
sailed to the lee of, *5709, hypopleō* [1]
subject to the control, *5718, hypotassō* [1]
passed to the lee of, *5720, hypotrechō* [1]
stalk of the hyssop plant, *5727, hyssōpos* [1]
watch of the night, *5871, phylakē* [1]
planted the seed, *5885, phyteuō* [1]
at the top of voices, *5889+3489,*
   phōnē+megas [1]
at the top of voice, *5889+3489,*
   phōnē+megas [1]
shouting at the top of voice, *5889+3489+3306,*
   phōnē+megas+legō [1]
on the ground, *5912, chamai* [1]
to the ground, *5912, chamai* [1]
for the sake of, *5920, charin* [1]
took a battering from the storm, *5928,*
   cheimazō [1]
by the hand, *5932, cheiragōgeō* [1]
led by the hand, *5932, cheiragōgeō* [1]
someone to lead by the hand, *5933,*
   cheiragōgos [1]
done by the hands, *5935, cheiropoiētos* [1]
without the Spirit, *6035, psychikos* [1]
give to the poor, *6039, psōmizō* [1]
in the one case, *6045+3525, hōde+men* [1]
in the pains of childbirth, *6048, ōdinō* [1]
late in the day, *6052+4498, hōra+polys* [1]
nine in the morning, *6052+5569+3836+2465,*
   hōra+tritos+ho+hēmera [1]
three in the afternoon, *6052+1888+3836+2465,*
   hōra+enatos+ho+hēmera [1]
the same as, *6055+2779, hōs+kai* [1]
the same way, *6055+2779, hōs+kai* [1]
the size of, *6055, hōs* [1]
the same way, *6058, hōsautōs* [1]
the way, *6061, hōsper* [1]

THEATER   [2]

theater, *2519, theatron* [2]

THEFT   [2]

theft, *3113, klopē* [2]

THEFTS   [1]

thefts, *3092, klemma* [1]

THEIR   [569]

their, *899, autos* [281]
their, *3836, ho* [96]
their, *RPE* [80]
their, *AIT* [45]
their, *1571, heautou* [12]
their own, *2625, idios* [11]
their own, *1571, heautou* [9]
their, *4005, hos* [7]
their own, *899, autos* [4]
their, *2625, idios* [3]
their, *1697, ekeinos* [2]
not their own, *259, allotrios* [1]
on their way, *599, aperchomai* [1]
their homes[s], *899, autos* [1]
their own number, *899, autos* [1]
their hearts, *1571, heautou* [1]
to their number, *2093+3836+899,*
   epi+ho+autos [1]
made their way, *2262, erchomai* [1]
on their way, *2262, erchomai* [1]
their, *2779, kai* [1]
sensual desires overcome their dedication to,
   2952, katastrēniaō [1]
[kill their] mothers, *3618, mētrolōas* [1]
on their journey, *3844, hodoiporeō* [1]
their work[s], *4047, houtos* [1]

their, *4047, houtos* [1]
country of their own, *4258, patris* [1]
kill their fathers, *4260, patrolōas* [1]
send on their way, *4636, propempō* [1]
at their hands, *5679+899, hypo+autos* [1]
turn their backs, *5715, hypostrephō* [1]
love their husbands, *5791, philandros* [1]
[love their] children, *5817, philoteknos* [1]

THEIRS   [8]

theirs, *899, autos* [3]
theirs, *4005, hos* [2]
theirs, *NIG* [1]
theirs, *RPE* [1]
theirs to keep, *2988, katechō* [1]

THEM   [1176]

them, *899, autos* [814]
them, *RPE* [235]
them, *AIT* [39]
them, *4005, hos* [24]
them, *4047, houtos* [15]
them, *1571, heautou* [6]
them, *1697, ekeinos* [6]
them[s], *3836+3412+899,*
   ho+mathētēs+autos [3]
them, *4015, hostis* [3]
them, *4639+899, pros+autos* [3]
them[s], *3836+476, ho+anthrōpos* [2]
them, *3836, ho* [2]
them, *NIG* [1]
them, *253, allēlōn* [1]
nothing against them, *441, anenklētos* [1]
them[s], *476, anthrōpos* [1]
before them, *1650+3545, eis+mesos* [1]
both of them, *1877+4005, en+hos* [1]
them also, *2797, kakeinos* [1]
that far outweighs them all,
   2848+5651+1650+5651+983,
   kata+hyperbolē+eis+hyperbolē+baros [1]
them[s], *3836+1177, ho+geōrgos* [1]
them[s], *3836+2239, ho+ergatēs* [1]
them[s], *3836+2465, ho+hēmera* [1]
them[s], *3836+2585, ho+thronos* [1]
them[s], *3836+2997+2093+3836+1178,*
   ho+katoikeō+epi+ho+gē [1]
them[s], *3836+3295, ho+laos* [1]
them[s], *3836+3412, ho+mathētēs* [1]
them[s], *3836+3517+5148, ho+melos+sy* [1]
them[s], *3836+3836+5525+4556,*
   ho+ho+toioutos+prassō [1]
them[s], *3836+4063, ho+ochlos* [1]
them[s], *3836+4252+1609, ho+patēr+egō* [1]
them[s], *3836+4546+899, ho+pous+autos* [1]
them[s], *3836+5284+899,*
   ho+synedrion+autos [1]
them[s], *5132, stratiōtēs* [1]
of them, *5201+899, symbainō+autos* [1]
them, *5516, tis* [1]

THEMSELVES   [68]

themselves, *1571, heautou* [30]
themselves, *AIT* [13]
themselves, *899, autos* [6]
themselves, *RPE* [5]
themselves, *253, allēlōn* [3]
themselves, *2625, idios* [3]
they themselves, *899, autos* [2]
themselves, *152, aisthētērion* [1]
by themselves, *3668, monos* [1]
themselves, *3836+2840+899,*
   ho+kardia+autos [1]
themselves, *3836+6034+899,*
   ho+psychē+autos [1]
kept this to themselves, *4967, sigaō* [1]

lovers of themselves, *5796, philautos* [1]

THEN   [707]

then, *2779, kai* [227]
then, *4036, oun* [110]
then, *5538, tote* [105]
then, *1254, de* [89]
then, *NIG* [55]
and then, *2779, kai* [25]
then, *726, ara* [12]
then, *1663, eita* [10]
then, *2083, epeita* [10]
then, *2671, hina* [6]
then, *5445, te* [4]
then, *4048, houtōs* [3]
then after, *4099, palin* [3]
so then, *6063, hōste* [3]
so then, *1328+4047, dia+houtos* [2]
just then, *2779+2627, kai+idou* [2]
then, *2779+2627, kai+idou* [2]
now then, *4036, oun* [2]
so then, *4036, oun* [2]
then, *4099, palin* [2]
then, *5523, toinyn* [2]
then, *247, alla* [1]
so then, *726, ara* [1]
then, *726+1145, ara+ge* [1]
then, *948+4005, achri+hos* [1]
then, *1145, ge* [1]
so then, *1475, dio* [1]
then, *1475, dio* [1]
so then, *1650+3836, eis+ho* [1]
then will be able, *1650+3836, eis+ho* [1]
from then on, *1666+4047, ek+houtos* [1]
right then, *1994, exautēs* [1]
then, *2075, epei* [1]
just then, *2093+4047, epi+houtos* [1]
just then, *2317, euthys[1]* [1]
then, *2317, euthys[1]* [1]
and then, *2671, hina* [1]
then, *2796, kakeithen* [1]
then the one, *2797, kakeinos* [1]
then, *3437, mallon* [1]
then, *3525, men* [1]
now then, *3814, nyn* [1]
so then, *3854, hothen* [1]
then, *3968, hopōs* [1]
from then on, *4033, ouketi* [1]
then, *4034, oukoun* [1]
well then, *4036, oun* [1]
conclude then, *4036, oun* [1]
so then, *4048, houtōs* [1]
then on, *5538, tote* [1]
then, *5731, hysteros* [1]
then, *6063, hōste* [1]

THEOPHILUS   [2]

Theophilus, *2541, Theophilos* [2]

THERE   [465]

there, *AIT* [195]
there, *RPE* [70]
there, *1695, ekei* [66]
there, *NIG* [56]
there before, *2627, idou* [9]
from there, *1696, ekeithen* [8]
standing there, *2705, histēmi* [5]
there, *1877+899, en+autos* [4]
there, *2795, kakei* [3]
from there, *2796, kakeithen* [3]
there, *899, autos* [2]
there, *1696, ekeithen* [2]
there[s], *1877+3836+2639, en+ho+hieron* [2]
there, *2627, idou* [2]
there, *2705, histēmi* [2]

and there, *2795, kakei* [2]
there, *2796, kakeithen* [2]
there, *3023, keimai* [2]
there, *4023, hou* [2]
was there ever, *5515, tis* [2]
stood there, *482, anistēmi* [1]
stood there, *1639+2392, eimi+ephistēmi* [1]
there[s], *1650+3836+2038, eis+ho+heortē* [1]
there, *1698, ekeise* [1]
there[s], *1877+4047+3836+4484,*
   en+houtos+ho+polis [1]
there, *1877+3545, en+mesos* [1]
there, *1877+3836+5536, en+ho+topos* [1]
there, *1924, enthade* [1]
people there, *1954, entopios* [1]
lived there, *2111, epidēmeō* [1]
been there, *2152, epimenō* [1]
there is, *2627, idou* [1]
stood there, *2705, histēmi* [1]
was there, *2705, histēmi* [1]
there, *2779+2627, kai+idou* [1]
there too, *2795, kakei* [1]
and from there, *2796, kakeithen* [1]
from there, *3854, hothen* [1]
right there, *4154, parakeimai* [1]
happened to be there, *4193, paratynchanō* [1]
stood there, *4225, paristēmi* [1]
blown here and there, *4367, peripherō* [1]
got there ahead of, *4601, proerchomai* [1]
there, *4618, prokeimai* [1]
there, *5302, synerchomai* [1]
there, *6045, hōde* [1]

THEREFORE   [159]

therefore, *4036, oun* [71]
therefore, *1475, dio* [27]
therefore, *1328+4047, dia+houtos* [23]
therefore, *6063, hōste* [13]
therefore, *726+4036, ara+oun* [5]
therefore, *NIG* [2]
therefore, *726, ara* [2]
therefore, *1478, dioper* [2]
therefore, *1484, dioti* [2]
therefore, *2671, hina* [2]
therefore, *2779, kai* [2]
therefore, *3854, hothen* [2]
therefore, *5521, toigaroun* [2]
therefore, *1314, dē* [1]
therefore, *1328+4005+162, dia+hos+aitia* [1]
therefore, *4005+5920, hos+charin* [1]
therefore, *5523, toinyn* [1]

THESE   [292]

these, *4047, houtos* [207]
these, *4005, hos* [14]
these, *AIT* [10]
these, *NIG* [10]
these, *3836, ho* [10]
these, *899, autos* [8]
these, *3840, hode* [7]
such as these, *5525, toioutos* [4]
these, *RPE* [3]
these, *4015, hostis* [3]
in these words, *4048, houtōs* [2]
these men[s], *899, autos* [1]
these very, *899, autos* [1]
these, *1697, ekeinos* [1]
these, *2797, kakeinos* [1]
and these, *2797, kakeinos* [1]
these[s], *2819+2240, kalos+ergon* [1]
in these, *4005, hos* [1]
one of these journeys[s], *4005, hos* [1]
these men[s], *4005, hos* [1]
these waters[s], *4005, hos* [1]
these very, *4047, houtos* [1]

these, *5525, toioutos* [1]
all these, *5537, tosoutos* [1]
these, *5537, tosoutos* [1]

THESSALONIANS   [3]

Thessalonians, *2552, Thessalonikeus* [2]
Thessalonians, *1877+2553,*
   en+Thessalonikē [1]

THESSALONICA   [6]

Thessalonica, *2553, Thessalonikē* [4]
from Thessalonica, *2552, Thessalonikeus* [2]

THEUDAS   [1]

Theudas, *2554, Theudas* [1]

THEY   [1767]

they, *AIT* [1339]
they, *899, autos* [127]
they, *RPE* [125]
they, *3836+1254, ho+de* [49]
they, *3836, ho* [24]
they, *4015, hostis* [23]
they, *4047, houtos* [22]
they, *4005, hos* [13]
they, *1697, ekeinos* [10]
they, *2797, kakeinos* [5]
they themselves, *899, autos* [2]
pay attention who they are, *1063+4725+476,*
   blepō+prosōpon+anthrōpos [2]
they, *1571, heautou* [2]
they[s], *3836+3412, ho+mathētēs* [2]
they[s], *3836+476, ho+anthrōpos* [2]
they, *NIG* [1]
they[s], *899+2779+3836+3412+899,*
   autos+kai+ho+mathētēs+autos [1]
they[s], *899+3836+6001, autos+ho+chōra* [1]
they, *1328+899, dia+autos* [1]
all they asked was, *3667, monon* [1]
so they, *3836+1254, ho+de* [1]
they[s], *3836+1322, ho+dēmos* [1]
they[s], *3836+1204+899, ho+goneus+autos* [1]
they[s], *3836+213, ho+akrobystia* [1]
they[s], *3836+3412+899, ho+mathētēs+autos* [1]
they[s], *3836+4998, ho+skandalon* [1]
they[s], *3836+5125+899, ho+stoma+autos* [1]
they[s], *3836+5861, ho+phronimos* [1]
they, *3836+3525, ho+men* [1]
they, *3836+4057+899,*
   ho+ophthalmos+autos [1]
how far will they go, *4047+5515+1639,*
   houtos+tis+eimi [1]
they, *4123+899, para+autos* [1]
they, *4639+899, pros+autos* [1]
they are the kind, *5525, toioutos* [1]
they, *5679+899, hypo+autos* [1]

THICK   [1]

thick, *AIT* [1]

THIEF   [12]

thief, *3095, kleptēs* [12]

THIEVES   [4]

thieves, *3095, kleptēs* [4]

THIGH   [1]

thigh, *3611, mēros* [1]

THING   [36]

thing, *AIT* [17]
thing, *2240, ergon* [2]
thing, *3364, logos* [2]

the same thing, *6058, hōsautōs* [2]
the only thing that counts, *247, alla* [1]
one thing more, *275, hama* [1]
the same thing, *2749, kathaper* [1]
the right thing, *2822, kalōs* [1]
the same thing, *3931, homoiōs* [1]
not a thing, *4029, oudeis* [1]
thing, *4047, houtos* [1]
important thing, *4440, plēn* [1]
thing, *4547, pragma* [1]
thing, *4839, rhēma* [1]
thing, *5516, tis* [1]
thing[s], *5889, phōnē* [1]
thing, *6034, psychē* [1]

THINGS   [276]

things, *AIT* [204]
all things, *3836+4246, ho+pas* [16]
things, *NIG* [10]
things, *3836, ho* [10]
things, *4839, rhēma* [6]
things, *2240, ergon* [5]
things, *RPE* [4]
earthly things, *2103, epigeios* [2]
heavenly things, *2230, epouranios* [2]
things, *4547, pragma* [2]
same things, *899, autos* [1]
things, *899, autos* [1]
things taught, *1436, didaskalia* [1]
heavenly things, *1877+3836+4041,*
   en+ho+ouranos [1]
surface of things, *2848+4725,*
   kata+prosōpon [1]
created things, *3232, ktisis* [1]
things, *3364, logos* [1]
such[s] things, *3836+4998, ho+skandalon* [1]
things, *4005, hos* [1]
such things, *4048, houtōs* [1]
created things, *4472, poieō* [1]
old order of things, *4755, prōtos* [1]
things that cause people to sin, *4998,*
   skandalon [1]
things that cause to sin, *4998, skandalon* [1]
take a view of things, *5858, phroneō* [1]

THINK   [50]

think, *1506, dokeō* [20]
think, *3787, nomizō* [4]
think, *NIG* [3]
think, *3357, logizomai* [3]
think that, *1506, dokeō* [2]
think, *2451, hēgeomai* [2]
think it wise, *546, axioō* [1]
think, *1063, blepō* [1]
think it worthwhile, *1507, dokimazō* [1]
think, *2555, theōreō* [1]
think about, *3357, logizomai* [1]
think that, *3357, logizomai* [1]
think it strange, *3826, xenizō* [1]
think, *3887, oiomai* [1]
think about, *4630+4472, pronoia+poieō* [1]
made think, *5502+1877+3836+2840,*
   tithēmi+en+ho+kardia [1]
who do you think you are, *5515+4932+4472,*
   tis+seautou+poieō [1]
think highly, *5672, hyperphroneō* [1]
think, *5706, hyponoeō* [1]
think, *5743, phainō* [1]
on think, *5858, phroneō* [1]
think, *5858, phroneō* [1]

THINKING   [19]

thinking, *1368, dialogizomai* [5]
thinking, *1369, dialogismos* [3]
thinking, *1506, dokeō* [3]

thinking, *3787, nomizō* [2]
thinking like, *1181+3836+5856,*
   ginomai+ho+phrēn [1]
thinking, *1379, dianoia* [1]
thinking, *1445, dienthymeomai* [1]
thinking, *3648, mnēmoneuō* [1]
thinking, *3808, nous* [1]
thinking, *5856, phrēn* [1]

THINKS   [7]

thinks, *1506, dokeō* [6]
thinks, *3787, nomizō* [1]

THIRD   [57]

third, *5569, tritos* [45]
third time, *5568, triton* [6]
third, *5568, triton* [2]
third, *RPE* [1]
third time, *1666+5569, ek+tritos* [1]
third[s], *4005, hos* [1]
third story, *5566, tristegon* [1]

THIRST   [4]

thirst, *1498, dipsaō* [2]
thirst for, *1498, dipsaō* [1]
thirst, *1499, dipsos* [1] ·

THIRSTY   [13]

thirsty, *1498, dipsaō* [13]

THIRTY   [9]

thirty, *5558, triakonta* [8]
twenty to thirty gallons,
   3583+1545+2445+5552,
   metrētēs+dyo+ē+treis [1]

THIRTY-EIGHT   [1]

thirty-eight, *5558+2779+3893,*
   triakonta+kai+oktō [1]

THIS   [1133]

this, *4047, houtos* [621]
this, *NIG* [104]
this, *RPE* [93]
this, *3836, ho* [76]
this, *AIT* [24]
this, *4005, hos* [14]
for this reason, *1328+4047, dia+houtos* [9]
this[s], *3836+3364, ho+logos* [9]
this, *1697, ekeinos* [8]
in this way, *4048, houtōs* [8]
this is how, *4048, houtōs* [8]
this, *4048, houtōs* [8]
like this, *4048, houtōs* [7]
this is how, *1877+4047, en+houtos* [6]
this is what, *4048, houtōs* [6]
this, *4015, hostis* [5]
this is why, *1328+4047, dia+houtos* [4]
this is why, *1475, dio* [4]
at this, *4036, oun* [4]
this very, *4047, houtos* [4]
this, *6045, hōde* [4]
this, *899, autos* [3]
at this, *1254, de* [3]
this gospel[s], *4005, hos* [3]
this, *4022, hoti* [3]
by this time, *2453, ēdē* [2]
all this, *3836+4246, ho+pas* [2]
this[s], *3836+2465, ho+hēmera* [2]
for this reason, *4047+5920, houtos+charin* [2]
this one, *4047, houtos* [2]
this way, *4048, houtōs* [2]
like this, *4525, toioutos* [2]

this, *5525, toioutos* [2]
this, *5537, tosoutos* [2]
for this reason, *505+4047, anti+houtos* [1]
this moment, *785, arti* [1]
this very day, *785, arti* [1]
this very, *785, arti* [1]
for this very reason, *899+4047,*
   autos+houtos [1]
this man[s], *899, autos* [1]
this perfume[s], *899, autos* [1]
of this life, *1053, biōtikos* [1]
after this, *1254, de* [1]
by all this, *1328+4047, dia+houtos* [1]
this is why, *1328+899, dia+autos* [1]
for this very reason, *1328+4047, dia+houtos* [1]
for this reason, *1475, dio* [1]
in this way, *1650+3836, eis+ho* [1]
to this end, *1650+4005, eis+hos* [1]
with this in mind, *1650+899, eis+autos* [1]
for this reason, *1650+4047, eis+houtos* [1]
this is the reason, *1650+4047, eis+houtos* [1]
this very reason, *1650+4047, eis+houtos* [1]
do[s] this, *1662, eispherō* [1]
this is how, *1666+4047, ek+houtos* [1]
after this, *1877+3836+2759,*
   en+ho+kathexēs [1]
this makes, *1877+4047, en+houtos* [1]
this[s] kind of, *1877+4231, en+paroimia* [1]
this place, *1949, enteuthen* [1]
at this, *2311, eutheōs* [1]
at this, *2317, euthys[1]* [1]
in this condition, *2400, echō* [1]
this agrees with, *2777, kathōs* [1]
this is why, *2777, kathōs* [1]
at this, *2779+2627, kai+idou* [1]
at this, *2779, kai* [1]
to this, *2779, kai* [1]
this, *2797, kakeinos* [1]
this is, *2848+3836, kata+ho* [1]
in this way[s], *2848+4922, kata+sarx* [1]
just like this, *2848+3836+899,*
   kata+ho+autos [1]
the point is this, *3049, kephalaion* [1]
this message, *3306, legō* [1]
may this never, *3590, mē* [1]
don't this, *3594, mēdeis* [1]
this man[s], *3836, ho* [1]
this very, *3836, ho* [1]
this[s], *3836+2240+4047, ho+ergon+houtos* [1]
this[s], *3836+3364+4047, ho+logos+houtos* [1]
this[s], *3836+3814, ho+nyn* [1]
this[s], *3836+4246, ho+pas* [1]
this[s], *3836+4839+4047, ho+rhēma+houtos* [1]
this or that, *3840+3836, hode+ho* [1]
for this reason, *3854, hothen* [1]
this is how, *3854, hothen* [1]
this is why, *3854, hothen* [1]
this ark[s], *4005, hos* [1]
this man[s], *4005, hos* [1]
this hope[s], *4005, hos* [1]
this inscription, *4005+2108, hos+epigraphō* [1]
in this, *4022, hoti* [1]
this made, *4036, oun* [1]
at this point, *4047+1254, houtos+de* [1]
at this, *4047+3306, houtos+legō* [1]
remember this, *4047+1254, houtos+de* [1]
this same, *4047, houtos* [1]
with this, *4047+3306, houtos+legō* [1]
this way, *4047+4246, houtos+pas* [1]
in this same way, *4048+2779, houtōs+kai* [1]
this is, *4048, houtōs* [1]
by this kind, *4048, houtōs* [1]
looked like this, *4048, houtōs* [1]
this is the way, *4048, houtōs* [1]
this the way, *4048, houtōs* [1]
give this command, *4133, parangellō* [1]

do this more and more, *4355+3437,*
   perisseuō+mallon [1]
before this been, *4732+1639,*
   prouparchō+eimi [1]
this world, *4922, sarx* [1]
this day, *4958, sēmeron* [1]
kept this to themselves, *4967, sigaō* [1]
this calls for, *6045, hōde* [1]

THISTLES   [2]

thistles, *5560, tribolos* [2]

THOMAS   [11]

Thomas, *2605, Thōmas* [11]

THONGS   [3]

thongs, *2666, himas* [3]

THORN   [1]

thorn, *5022, skolops* [1]

THORNBUSHES   [2]

thornbushes, *180, akantha* [2]

THORNS   [11]

thorns, *180, akantha* [9]
of thorns, *181, akanthinos* [2]

THOROUGH   [2]

thorough knowledge, *1543, dynatos* [1]
a thorough search made for, *2118, epizēteō* [1]

THOROUGHLY   [2]

thoroughly, *787, artios* [1]
thoroughly, *2848+205, kata+akribeia* [1]

THOSE   [480]

those, *3836, ho* [344]
those, *AIT* [32]
those, *1697, ekeinos* [27]
those, *NIG* [11]
those, *4005, hos* [10]
those, *RPE* [8]
those, *899, autos* [8]
those, *4047, houtos* [7]
those who, *4005, hos* [5]
those, *4012, hosos* [4]
those, *3836+1254, ho+de* [3]
those that, *3836, ho* [2]
those[s] who are, *3836+5626, ho+huios* [2]
those, *4015, hostis* [2]
those[s], *476, anthrōpos* [1]
those able to help, *516, antilēmpsis* [1]
those in trouble, *2567, thlibō* [1]
those, *2797, kakeinos* [1]
those with gifts of administration, *3236,*
   kybernēsis [1]
those[s] present, *3836, ho* [1]
those who, *3836, ho* [1]
those[s] who marry, *3836+5525, ho+toioutos* [1]
those[s], *3836+3295, ho+laos* [1]
those[s], *3836+476, ho+anthrōpos* [1]
those entrusted with, *3874, oikonomos* [1]
those whom, *4005+1569, hos+ean* [1]
those, *4005+3525, hos+men* [1]
those whom, *4012+1569, hosos+ean* [1]
those, *5515, tis* [1]

THOUGH   [90]

though, *AIT* [37]
as though, *6055, hōs* [6]
though, *1623, ei* [5]

THOUGHT

though, *NIG* [4]
though, *1623+2779, ei+kai* [4]
though, *2779, kai* [4]
even though, *2779, kai* [3]
though, *1254, de* [2]
though, *1639, eimi* [2]
even though, *2788, kaiper* [2]
though, *2788, kaiper* [2]
even though, *2829, kan* [2]
though, *3525, men* [2]
though, *247+1623+2779, alla+ei+kai* [1]
even though, *247, alla* [1]
though, *247, alla* [1]
though, *1142, gar* [1]
even though, *1254, de* [1]
even though, *1569, ean* [1]
though, *1569, ean* [1]
even though, *1623, ei* [1]
just as though, *1651+2779+3836+899, heis+kai+ho+autos* [1]
and though, *2779, kai* [1]
though, *2779+1145, kai+ge* [1]
even though, *3525+1142, men+gar* [1]
though actually, *4022, hoti* [1]
though, *4022, hoti* [1]
though, *6055, hōs* [1]

THOUGHT [21]

thought, *1506, dokeō* [7]
thought, *3787, nomizō* [4]
thought, *NIG* [1]
thought, *1191, gnōmē* [1]
thought, *1368, dialogizomai* [1]
thought, *2154, epinoia* [1]
thought it best, *2305, eudokeō* [1]
thought, *2451, hēgeomai* [1]
thought, *2840, kardia* [1]
thought, *3306, legō* [1]
thought, *3784, noēma* [1]
thought, *5858, phroneō* [1]

THOUGHTS [17]

thoughts, *1369, dialogismos* [5]
thoughts, *1927, enthymēsis* [3]
thoughts, *1379, dianoia* [2]
knows thoughts, *1182, ginōskō* [1]
thoughts, *1369+3836+2840, dialogismos+ho+kardia* [1]
thoughts, *1378, dianoēma* [1]
entertain thoughts, *1926, enthymeomai* [1]
fix thoughts on, *2917, katanoeō* [1]
thoughts, *3361, logismos* [1]
knows thoughts, *3857, oida* [1]

THOUSAND [34]

thousand, *5943, chilioi* [8]
five thousand, *4295, pentakischilioi* [6]
four thousand, *5483, tetrakischilioi* [5]
thousand, *5942, chilias* [5]
ten thousand, *3689, myrias* [2]
ten thousand, *3692, myrios* [2]
two thousand, *1493, dischilioi* [1]
thousand bushels, *1669+3174, hekaton+koros* [1]
seven thousand, *2233, heptakischilioi* [1]
fifty thousand, *3689+4297, myrias+pente* [1]
ten thousand, *3691, myrioi* [1]
three thousand, *5567, trischilioi* [1]

THOUSANDS [8]

thousands upon thousands, *3689, myrias* [4]
thousands, *5942, chilias* [2]
many thousands, *3689, myrias* [1]
thousands, *3689, myrias* [1]

THREATEN [1]

threaten, *581, apeilē* [1]

THREATS [4]

threats, *581, apeilē* [2]
made threats, *580, apeileō* [1]
further threats, *4653, prosapeileō* [1]

THREE [83]

three, *5552, treis* [63]
three times, *5565, tris* [12]
three in the afternoon, *1888, enatos* [2]
three or three and a half miles,
    *5084+1633+4297+2445+5558,
    stadion+eikosi+pente+ē+triakonta* [2]
three years, *5562, trietia* [1]
three months, *5564, trimēnos* [1]
three thousand, *5567, trischilioi* [1]
three in the afternoon, *6052+1888+3836+2465,
    hōra+enatos+ho+hēmera* [1]

THREE TAVERNS [1]

Three Taverns, *5553, Treis tabernai* [1]

THRESHER [1]

thresher, *262, aloaō* [1]

THRESHES [1]

threshes, *RPE* [1]

THRESHING [2]

threshing floor, *272, halōn* [2]

THREW [21]

threw, *965, ballō* [5]
threw, *1675, ekballō* [3]
threw out, *1675, ekballō* [2]
threw in, *965, ballō* [1]
threw over, *2095, epiballō* [1]
threw arms around, *2158+2093+3836+5549,
    epipiptō+epi+ho+trachēlos* [1]
threw himself on, *2158, epipiptō* [1]
threw on, *2166, epiriptō* [1]
threw himself, *4406+2093+4725,
    piptō+epi+prosōpon* [1]
threw to the ground, *4838, rhēgnymi* [1]
threw down, *4849, rhiptō* [1]
threw overboard, *4849, rhiptō* [1]
threw, *4849, rhiptō* [1]
threw into a convulsion, *5360, sysparassō* [1]

THROATS [1]

throats, *3296, larynx* [1]

THRONE [53]

throne, *2585, thronos* [52]
throne, *1037, bēma* [1]

THRONES [7]

thrones, *2585, thronos* [7]

THROUGH [275]

through, *1328, dia* [176]
through, *1877, en* [34]
through, *AIT* [7]
through, *1666, ek* [4]
through, *1328+5125, dia+stoma* [3]
traveled through, *1451, dierchomai* [3]
through, *2848, kata* [3]
go through, *1328+1451, dia+dierchomai* [2]
goes through, *1451+1328, dierchomai+dia* [2]
going through, *1451, dierchomai* [2]

passing through, *1451, dierchomai* [2]
through, *1650, eis* [2]
worked through the dough, *2435, zymoō* [2]
works through, *2435, zymoō* [2]
through, *3552, meta* [2]
through and through, *3911, holotelēs* [2]
through, *NIG* [1]
through, *RPE* [1]
go through, *1328, dia* [1]
passed through, *1328+1451,
    dia+dierchomai* [1]
through, *1328+3836+5931, dia+ho+cheir* [1]
passed through, *1329, diabainō* [1]
going through, *1388+1328,
    diaporeuomai+dia* [1]
passing through, *1388, diaporeuomai* [1]
went through, *1388, diaporeuomai* [1]
saved through, *1407+1328, diasōzō+dia* [1]
go through, *1451+1328, dierchomai+dia* [1]
go through, *1451, dierchomai* [1]
gone through, *1451, dierchomai* [1]
took the road through, *1451, dierchomai* [1]
walked right through, *1451+1328+3545,
    dierchomai+dia+mesos* [1]
went through, *1451, dierchomai* [1]
passed through, *1476, diodeuō* [1]
go through into, *1656+1650,
    eiserchomai+eis* [1]
slipped through, *1767, ekpheugō* [1]
blessed through, *1922+1877, eneulogeō+en* [1]
went through, *2002, exerchomai* [1]
digging through, *2021, exoryssō* [1]
since going through, *2400, echō* [1]
saw through, *2917, katanoeō* [1]
halfway through, *3548, mesoō* [1]
went through, *4310, periagō* [1]
through, *5250+5931, syn+cheir* [1]

THROUGHOUT [22]

throughout, *1877+3910, en+holos* [6]
traveled throughout, *1451, dierchomai* [2]
throughout, *1650+3910, eis+holos* [2]
throughout, *1877, en* [2]
throughout, *2848+3910, kata+holos* [2]
throughout, *2848, kata* [2]
scattered throughout, *1402, diaspora* [1]
throughout, *1650+4246, eis+pas* [1]
throughout, *1650, eis* [1]
throughout, *2093+4246, epi+pas* [1]
throughout, *3910, holos* [1]
ran throughout, *4366, peritrechō* [1]

THROW [25]

throw, *965, ballō* [15]
throw, *1675, ekballō* [2]
throw away, *610, apoballō* [1]
throw off, *700, apotithēmi* [1]
throw out, *965, ballō* [1]
throw, *1074, bolē* [1]
throw the cargo overboard, *1678, ekbolē* [1]
throw out, *1704, ekthetos* [1]
throw, *1833, emballō* [1]
throw down the cliff, *2889, katakrēmnizō* [1]

THROWING [7]

throwing into confusion, *5429, tarassō* [2]
throwing aside, *610, apoballō* [1]
throwing, *1675, ekballō* [1]
throwing into an uproar, *1752, ektarassō* [1]
throwing, *4140, paradidōmi* [1]
throwing off, *4848, rhipteō* [1]

THROWN [36]

thrown, *965, ballō* [26]

THROWN

thrown, *1675, ekballō* [3]
thrown down, *2907, katalyō* [3]
thrown, *RPE* [1]
thrown down, *965, ballō* [1]
thrown, *4849, rhiptō* [1]
thrown into turmoil, *5429, tarassō* [1]

THROWS [2]

throws to the ground, *4838, rhēgnymi* [1]
throws into convulsions, *5057, sparassō* [1]

THUNDER [8]

peals of thunder, *1103, brontē* [4]
thunder, *1103, brontē* [3]
peal of thunder, *1103, brontē* [1]

THUNDERED [1]

thundered, *1103, brontē* [1]

THUNDERING [1]

thundering, *5889, phōnē* [1]

THUNDERS [3]

thunders, *1103, brontē* [3]

THUS [10]

thus, *NIG* [3]
thus, *2779, kai* [2]
thus, *4036, oun* [2]
thus, *726+1145, ara+ge* [1]
and thus, *1650+3836, eis+ho* [1]
thus, *1877+4047, en+houtos* [1]

THYATIRA [4]

Thyatira, *2587, Thyateira* [4]

TIBERIAS [3]

Tiberias, *5500, Tiberias* [3]

TIBERIUS [1]

Tiberius, *5501, Tiberios* [1]

TIE [3]

tie, *1313, deō* [2]
tie up, *1297, desmeuō* [1]

TIED [7]

tied, *1313, deō* [5]
tied around, *4329+4309, perikeimai+peri* [2]

TIES [2]

ties up, *1313, deō* [2]

TIGHT [1]

keep a tight rein on, *5902, chalinagōgeō* [1]

TILES [1]

tiles, *3041, keramos* [1]

TILL [7]

till, *2401, heōs* [3]
till, *2401+323, heōs+an* [2]
till, *1650, eis* [1]
till, *3588, mechri* [1]

TIMAEUS [1]

Timaeus, *5505, Timaios* [1]

TIME [257]

time, *2789, kairos* [42]

time, *2465, hēmera* [32]
time, *6052, hōra* [31]
time, *5989, chronos* [26]
at that time, *5538, tote* [12]
time, *AIT* [11]
second time, *1666+1311, ek+deuteros* [6]
third time, *5568, triton* [6]
proper time, *2789, kairos* [4]
time, *NIG* [3]
appointed time, *2789, kairos* [3]
harvest time, *2789, kairos* [3]
right time, *2789, kairos* [3]
at one time, *4537, pote* [3]
at the same time, *275, hama* [2]
second time, *1309, deuteron* [2]
almost time, *1584, engys* [2]
by this time, *2453, ēdē* [2]
present time, *2789, kairos* [2]
some time ago, *4574+4047+3836+2465, pro+houtos+ho+hēmera* [2]
told ahead of time, *4625, prolegō* [2]
only a short time, *4672, proskairos* [2]
that time on, *5538, tote* [2]
beginning of time, *5989+173, chronos+aiōnios* [2]
some time, *5989, chronos* [2]
time, *172, aiōn* [1]
one at a time, *324+3538, ana+meros* [1]
for a long time, *540, anōthen* [1]
from the time, *608+4005, apo+hos* [1]
some time ago, *608+2465+792, apo+hēmera+archaios* [1]
short time, *1099, brachys* [1]
the time came when, *1181+1254, ginomai+de* [1]
spending time, *1181+5990, ginomai+chronotribeō* [1]
second time, *1311, deuteros* [1]
spent some time, *1417, diatribō* [1]
for all time, *1650+3836+1457, eis+ho+diēnekēs* [1]
one at a time, *1651+2848+1651, heis+kata+heis* [1]
third time, *1666+5569, ek+tritos* [1]
that was the time, *1877+3836+2465+1697, en+ho+hēmera+ekeinos* [1]
at the time of, *1877, en* [1]
a long time, *2093+4498, epi+polys* [1]
at the time, *2093, epi* [1]
in the time of, *2093, epi* [1]
spend time, *2093+5989+3531, epi+chronos+menō* [1]
spent time, *2320, eukaireō* [1]
time of need, *2322, eukairos* [1]
at the same time, *2384, ephapax* [1]
due time, *2789, kairos* [1]
opportune time, *2789, kairos* [1]
some time after, *3552, meta* [1]
some time later, *3552+4047, meta+houtos* [1]
present time, *3814, nyn* [1]
since that time, *3836+3370, ho+loipos* [1]
short time, *3900, oligos* [1]
a short time, *3900, oligos* [1]
at the same time, *3940, homōs* [1]
any time, *4020, hotan* [1]
up to that time not, *4037, oupō* [1]
another time, *4099, palin* [1]
time, *4205, pareimi* [1]
time, *4398, pimplēmi* [1]
many a time, *4490, pollakis* [1]
long time, *4498, polys* [1]
time set, *4607, prothesmia* [1]
a short time, *4672, proskairos* [1]
give full time, *4674, proskartereō* [1]
for some time, *4732, prouparchō* [1]
of that time, *5538, tote* [1]

that time, *5538, tote* [1]
time of night, *5871, phylakē* [1]
a long time in coming, *5988, chronizō* [1]
staying away a long time, *5988, chronizō* [1]
taking a long time, *5988, chronizō* [1]
a long time, *5989+4024+3900, chronos+ou+oligos* [1]
spend time, *5989+2152, chronos+epimenō* [1]

TIMES [50]

three times, *5565, tris* [12]
times, *2789, kairos* [8]
times, *AIT* [5]
times, *5989, chronos* [5]
seven times, *2232, heptakis* [4]
hundred times, *1671, hekatontaplasiōn* [3]
at all times, *4121, pantote* [2]
many times, *4490, pollakis* [2]
times, *NIG* [1]
times, *1155, genea* [1]
seventy-seven times, *1574+2231, hebdomēkontakis+hepta* [1]
at other times, *4047+1254, houtos+de* [1]
five times, *4294, pentakis* [1]
many times as much, *4491, pollaplasiōn* [1]
at many times, *4495, polymerōs* [1]
how many times, *4529, posakis* [1]
four times, *5487, tetraplous* [1]

TIMID [2]

timid, *3901, oligopsychos* [1]
timid, *5424, tapeinos* [1]

TIMIDITY [1]

timidity, *1261, deilia* [1]

TIMON [1]

Timon, *5511, Timōn* [1]

TIMOTHY [25]

Timothy, *5510, Timotheos* [24]
Timothy's, *899, autos* [1]

TIP [1]

tip, *216, akron* [1]

TIRE [1]

tire of, *1591, enkakeō* [1]

TIRED [1]

tired, *3159, kopiaō* [1]

TITIUS [1]

Titius, *5517, Titios* [1]

TITLE [2]

title given, *3950+3951, onoma+onomazō* [1]
title, *3950, onoma* [1]

TITUS [14]

Titus, *5519, Titos* [13]
Titus, *RPE* [1]

TO [5563]

to, *AIT* [3028]
to, *1650, eis* [462]
to, *4639, pros* [374]
to, *NIG* [323]
to, *2671, hina* [179]
to, *2093, epi* [73]
to, *RPE* [48]
according to, *2848, kata* [44]

to, *1877, en* [39]
came to, *4665, proserchomai* [34]
to, *2401, heōs* [31]
about to, *3516, mellō* [22]
to, *1650+3836, eis+ho* [21]
going to, *3516, mellō* [18]
to, *3968, hopōs* [17]
to, *3552, meta* [11]
to, *948, achri* [10]
in order to, *2671, hina* [10]
had to, *1256, dei* [8]
put to death, *2506, thanatoō* [8]
to come, *3516, mellō* [8]
went to, *4665, proserchomai* [8]
causes to sin, *4997, skandalizō* [8]
raised to life, *1586, egeirō* [7]
to, *2848, kata* [7]
to see, *4639, pros* [7]
called to, *4673, proskaleō* [7]
to let, *2671, hina* [6]
put out to sea, *343, anagō* [5]
see to it, *1063, blepō* [5]
food sacrificed to idols, *1628, eidōlothytos* [5]
belong to, *1639, eimi* [5]
in regard to, *4309, peri* [5]
put to death, *359, anaireō* [4]
put to death, *650, apokteinō* [4]
have to, *1256, dei* [4]
leads to, *1650, eis* [4]
went to, *1656+1650, eiserchomai+eis* [4]
belong to, *1666+1639, ek+eimi* [4]
belong to, *1666, ek* [4]
to, *1967, enōpion* [4]
to, *3588, mechri* [4]
to, *4123, para* [4]
appeal to, *4151, parakaleō* [4]
going to, *4665, proserchomai* [4]
to, *6063, hōste* [4]
told to do, *1411, diatassō* [3]
bring glory to, *1519, doxazō* [3]
belongs to, *1639, eimi* [3]
leading to, *1650, eis* [3]
belonged to, *1666, ek* [3]
according to, *1877, en* [3]
turn to, *2188+2093, epistrephō+epi* [3]
belongs to, *2400, echō* [3]
hold to, *2400, echō* [3]
up to, *2401, heōs* [3]
so as to, *2671, hina* [3]
put to shame, *2875, kataischynō* [3]
hold to, *3195, krateō* [3]
testifies to, *3455, martyreō* [3]
pledged to be married, *3650, mnēsteuō* [3]
contrary to, *4123, para* [3]
to, *4309, peri* [3]
lead to, *4639, pros* [3]
come to, *4665, proserchomai* [3]
gave birth to, *5503, tiktō* [3]
give birth to, *5503, tiktō* [3]
to, *6055, hōs* [3]
come back to life, *482, anistēmi* [2]
devoted to, *504, antechō* [2]
refused to believe, *578, apeitheō* [2]
belonged to, *608, apo* [2]
going to answer, *646, apokrinomai* [2]
doomed to destruction, *724, apōleia* [2]
trying to please, *743, areskō* [2]
deposit guaranteeing what is to come, *775, arrabōn* [2]
up to, *948, achri* [2]
to live on, *1050, bios* [2]
gives birth to, *1164, gennaō* [2]
in answer to, *1328, dia* [2]
able to teach, *1434, didaktikos* [2]
give to the poor, *1443+1797, didōmi+eleēmosynē* [2]

cut to pieces, *1497, dichotomeō* [2]
sacrificed to idols, *1628, eidōlothytos* [2]
belonged to, *1639+1666, eimi+ek* [2]
leads to, *1639, eimi* [2]
on to, *1650, eis* [2]
to bring, *1650, eis* [2]
to do, *1650, eis* [2]
belonged to, *1666+1639, ek+eimi* [2]
belongs to, *1666+1639, ek+eimi* [2]
put to the test, *1733, ekpeirazō* [2]
gifts to the poor, *1797, eleēmosynē* [2]
subject to bleeding, *1877+4868+135, en+rhysis+haima* [2]
belong to, *2027, exousiazō* [2]
with face to the ground, *2093+4725, epi+prosōpon* [2]
burden to, *2096, epibareō* [2]
appeal to, *2126, epikaleō* [2]
turned to, *2188+2093, epistrephō+epi* [2]
brought to ruin, *2246, erēmoō* [2]
married to, *2400, echō* [2]
to the point, *2401, heōs* [2]
came to life, *2409, zaō* [2]
put to death, *2505+5462, thanatos+teleutaō* [2]
meant to, *2671, hina* [2]
according to, *2771, katho* [2]
contrary to, *2848, kata* [2]
from house to house, *2848+3875, kata+oikos* [2]
from one to another, *2848, kata* [2]
in obedience to, *2848, kata* [2]
pay attention to, *2917, katanoeō* [2]
hold on to, *2988, katechō* [2]
hold on to, *3195, krateō* [2]
superior to, *3202, kreittōn* [2]
testify to, *3455, martyreō* [2]
going to happen to, *3516, mellō* [2]
intend to, *3516, mellō* [2]
intended to, *3516, mellō* [2]
to be, *3516, mellō* [2]
to be sure, *3525, men* [2]
see to it, *3972, horaō* [2]
cease to be, *4024+1639, ou+eimi* [2]
refused to repent, *4024+3566, ou+metanoeō* [2]
still to come, *4037, oupō* [2]
have nothing to do with, *4148, paraiteomai* [2]
refuses to listen, *4159, parakouō* [2]
given to drunkenness, *4232, paroinos* [2]
trying to trap, *4279, peirazō* [2]
give to the needy, *4472+1797, poieō+eleēmosynē* [2]
used to, *4537, pote* [2]
gave to drink, *4540, potizō* [2]
give to drink, *4540, potizō* [2]
offered to drink, *4540, potizō* [2]
in order to, *4639, pros* [2]
looking forward to, *4659, prosdokaō* [2]
came up to, *4665, proserchomai* [2]
converts to Judaism, *4670, prosēlytos* [2]
calling to, *4673, proskaleō* [2]
united to, *4681+4639, proskollaō+pros* [2]
causes men to stumble, *4682, proskomma* [2]
ran up to, *4708, prostrechō* [2]
broken to pieces, *5314, synthlaō* [2]
went out to meet, *5636, hypantaō* [2]
to, *5642, hyper* [2]
subject to, *5679, hypo* [2]
inferior to, *5728, hystereō* [2]
called to, *5888, phōneō* [2]
devoted to the Lord, *41, hagios* [1]
brought to trial, *72, agō* [1]
to have failed, *99+1639, adokimos+eimi* [1]
subject to bleeding, *137, haimorroeō* [1]
to some extent, *247+608+3538, alla+apo+meros* [1]

went to defense, *310, amynomai* [1]
able to see, *329, anablepō* [1]
drove to it, *337, anankazō* [1]
had to, *340, anankē* [1]
sprang to life, *348, anazaō* [1]
gifts dedicated to God, *356, anathēma* [1]
called to account, *373, anakrinō* [1]
come to senses, *392, ananēphō* [1]
jumped to his feet, *403, anapēdaō* [1]
returned to place, *404+4099, anapiptō+palin* [1]
sit down to eat, *404, anapiptō* [1]
heap up to the limit, *405, anaplēroō* [1]
raised to life again, *414, anastasis* [1]
causes to rise, *422, anatellō* [1]
bound to come, *450+3590+2262, anendektos+mē+erchomai* [1]
does not need to be ashamed, *454, anepaischyntos* [1]
no open to blame, *455, anepilēmptos* [1]
ought to do, *465, anēkō* [1]
common to man, *474, anthrōpinos* [1]
helped to her feet, *482, anistēmi* [1]
raised to life, *482, anistēmi* [1]
began to speak, *487+3836+5125+3306, anoigō+ho+stoma+legō* [1]
began to teach, *487+3836+5125+1438, anoigō+ho+stoma+didaskō* [1]
hold firmly to, *504, antechō* [1]
adversary is taking to court, *508, antidikos* [1]
those able to help, *516, antilēmpsis* [1]
to draw with, *534, antlēma* [1]
reconciled to, *557+608, apallassō+apo* [1]
saying good-by to, *571, apaspazomai* [1]
expecting to get back, *594, apelpizō* [1]
to, *608, apo* [1]
testify to, *625+3457, apodidōmi+martyrion* [1]
gives birth to, *652, apokyeō* [1]
bring to end, *660, apollymi* [1]
eagerness to be clear, *665, apologia* [1]
to turn away from, *686+608, apostasia+apo* [1]
failed to pay, *691, apostereō* [1]
inciting to rebellion, *695, apostrephō* [1]
have nothing to do with, *706, apotrepō* [1]
not cause to stumble, *718, aproskopos* [1]
hold on to, *721, haptō* [1]
as to, *726, ara* [1]
try to please, *743, areskō* [1]
say no to, *766, arneomai* [1]
something to be grasped, *772, harpagmos* [1]
give greetings to, *832, aspazomai* [1]
call out to, *832, aspazomai* [1]
pay respects to, *832, aspazomai* [1]
sends greetings to, *832, aspazomai* [1]
causes to grow, *890, auxēsis* [1]
nothing to fear, *925, aphobōs* [1]
even to the point of, *948, achri* [1]
even to, *948, achri* [1]
right up to, *948, achri* [1]
to where, *948, achri* [1]
entice to sin, *965+4998+1967, ballō+skandalon+enōpion* [1]
jailers to be tortured, *991, basanistēs* [1]
help himself to, *1002, bastazō* [1]
to eat, *1110, brōsimos* [1]
for to be sure, *1142, gar* [1]
gave birth to, *1164, gennaō* [1]
proved to be, *1181, ginomai* [1]
married to, *1222, gynē* [1]
had to, *1256+1639, dei+eimi* [1]
ought to, *1256, dei* [1]
expose to public disgrace, *1258, deigmatizō* [1]
show to prove, *1259, deiknymi* [1]
prayed to, *1289, deomai* [1]
bring to light, *1317, dēloō* [1]
compared to, *1328, dia* [1]

due to, *1328, dia* [1]
to bottom, *1328+3910, dia+holos* [1]
helping to support, *1354, diakoneō* [1]
preparations to be made, *1355, diakonia* [1]
spoke to, *1363, dialegomai* [1]
testifying to, *1371, diamartyromai* [1]
torn to pieces, *1400, diaspaō* [1]
stimulate to, *1444, diegeirō* [1]
submit to rules, *1505, dogmatizō* [1]
seemed to be leaders, *1506, dokeō* [1]
gave praise to, *1519, doxazō* [1]
glory come to, *1519, doxazō* [1]
turned to strength, *1540, dynamoō* [1]
hard to explain, *1549, dysermēneutos* [1]
hard to understand, *1554, dysnoētos* [1]
gift devoted to God, *1565, dōron* [1]
claimed to be, *1571+4472, heautou+poieō* [1]
claims to be, *1571+4472, heautou+poieō* [1]
lifted to his feet, *1586, egeirō* [1]
dash to the ground, *1610, edaphizō* [1]
to see if, *1623, ei* [1]
food sacrificed to an idol, *1628, eidōlothytos* [1]
sacrifice offered to an idol, *1628, eidōlothytos* [1]
belong to, *1639+1666, eimi+ek* [1]
belonged to, *1639, eimi* [1]
belonging to, *1639, eimi* [1]
belongs to, *1639+1666, eimi+ek* [1]
devoted to, *1639+4674, eimi+proskartereō* [1]
had to, *1639+338, eimi+anankaios* [1]
to, *1639, eimi* [1]
to this end, *1650+4005, eis+hos* [1]
attaining to, *1650, eis* [1]
belonging to God, *1650+4348, eis+peripoiēsis* [1]
bring to, *1650, eis* [1]
how to gratify, *1650, eis* [1]
in order to bring, *1650, eis* [1]
in regard to, *1650, eis* [1]
intended to bring, *1650, eis* [1]
led to, *1650, eis* [1]
so as to, *1650, eis* [1]
to cause, *1650, eis* [1]
to serve, *1650, eis* [1]
to, *1650+4047, eis+houtos* [1]
faithful to her husband, *1651+467+1222, heis+anēr+gynē* [1]
went to, *1655+1650, eiseimi+eis* [1]
came to, *1656+1650, eiserchomai+eis* [1]
come to, *1656+1650, eiserchomai+eis* [1]
got to, *1656+1650, eiserchomai+eis* [1]
trying⁸ to, *1656, eiserchomai* [1]
went to, *1660+1650, eisporeuomai+eis* [1]
bringing to, *1662+1650, eispherō+eis* [1]
according to, *1666+3836, ek+ho* [1]
to pay, *1666, ek* [1]
looking forward to, *1683, ekdechomai* [1]
readiness to see justice done, *1689, ekdikēsis* [1]
agent to bring punishment, *1690, ekdikos* [1]
to the grove⁸, *1695, ekei* [1]
come back to senses, *1729, eknēphō* [1]
gave up to sexual immorality, *1745, ekporneuō* [1]
merciful to, *1790, eleaō* [1]
to show mercy, *1790, eleaō* [1]
free and belong to no man, *1801+1666+4246, eleutheros+ek+pas* [1]
remain faithful to, *1844+1877, emmenō+en* [1]
remain true to, *1844, emmenō* [1]
to, *1869, emprosthen* [1]
belong to, *1877, en* [1]
next to, *1877+3836+3146, en+ho+kolpos* [1]
open to, *1877, en* [1]
put to death, *1877+5840+633, en+phonos+apothnēskō* [1]
relationship to, *1877, en* [1]

to himself, *1877+1571, en+heautou* [1]
to show, *1877, en* [1]
trying to, *1877, en* [1]
with regard to, *1877+3538, en+meros* [1]
commanded to keep, *1948, entellō* [1]
amounts to nothing, *2024, exoutheneō* [1]
refuse to accept, *2024, exoutheneō* [1]
sing praises to, *2046, epaineō* [1]
happen to, *2088+2093, eperchomai+epi* [1]
happen to, *2088, eperchomai* [1]
facedown to the ground, *2093+4725, epi+prosōpon* [1]
found to be, *2093, epi* [1]
from bad to worse, *2093+3836+5937, epi+ho+cheirōn* [1]
to face, *2093, epi* [1]
to overcome, *2093, epi* [1]
to see, *2093, epi* [1]
to their number, *2093+3836+899, epi+ho+autos* [1]
to where, *2093, epi* [1]
puts to, *2095+2093, epiballō+epi* [1]
show special attention to, *2098+2093, epiblepō+epi* [1]
come to understand, *2105, epiginōskō* [1]
call attention to, *2109, epideiknymi* [1]
have to do with, *2110, epidechomai* [1]
add to, *2112, epidiatassomai* [1]
want to bring up, *2118, epizēteō* [1]
condemned to die, *2119, epithanatios* [1]
appealed to, *2126, epikaleō* [1]
made appeal to, *2126, epikaleō* [1]
hearts go out to, *2160, epipotheō* [1]
come to help, *2170, episkeptomai* [1]
come to, *2170, episkeptomai* [1]
see to it, *2174, episkopeō* [1]
bring back to, *2188+2093, epistrephō+epi* [1]
returned to, *2188+2093, epistrephō+epi* [1]
returns to, *2188+2093, epistrephō+epi* [1]
turn to, *2188, epistrephō* [1]
turning back to, *2188+2093, epistrephō+epi* [1]
turning to, *2188+2093, epistrephō+epi* [1]
gathered to, *2191+2093, episynagōgē+epi* [1]
bring to completion, *2200, epiteleō* [1]
carry it on to completion, *2200, epiteleō* [1]
add to, *2202+2093, epitithēmi+epi* [1]
adds to, *2202+2093, epitithēmi+epi* [1]
to burden, *2202+983, epitithēmi+baros* [1]
about to begin, *2216, epiphōskō* [1]
trying to find out, *2236, eraunaō* [1]
put to work, *2237, ergazomai* [1]
men to work, *2239, ergatēs* [1]
stirred to action, *2241, erethizō* [1]
going to happen, *2262, erchomai* [1]
act of kindness shown to, *2307, euergesia* [1]
came to, *2351, heuriskō* [1]
rushed to, *2392, ephistēmi* [1]
has to do with, *2400, echō* [1]
holding on to, *2400, echō* [1]
going on to, *2401, heōs* [1]
right on down to, *2401, heōs* [1]
right up to, *2401, heōs* [1]
to where, *2401, heōs* [1]
brought to life, *2409, zaō* [1]
come to life, *2409, zaō* [1]
returned to life, *2409, zaō* [1]
make effort to obtain, *2426, zēteō* [1]
trying to kill, *2426+3836+6034, zēteō+ho+psychē* [1]
trying to take, *2426, zēteō* [1]
gives life to, *2441, zōogoneō* [1]
come to life, *2443, zōopoieō* [1]
exposed to death, *2505, thanatos* [1]
in order to, *2527, thelō* [1]
want to, *2527, thelō* [1]
wants to, *2527, thelō* [1]

aim is to, *2671, hina* [1]
as to, *2671, hina* [1]
expecting to, *2671, hina* [1]
to keep from, *2671+3590, hina+mē* [1]
to make, *2671, hina* [1]
to show that, *2671, hina* [1]
from place to place, *2759, kathexēs* [1]
ought to be done, *2763, kathēkō* [1]
came to rest, *2767, kathizō* [1]
turn over to, *2770, kathistēmi* [1]
according to, *2777, kathōs* [1]
to this, *2779, kai* [1]
said to be, *2813, kaleō* [1]
as to, *2848, kata* [1]
conforms to, *2848, kata* [1]
face to face, *2848+4725, kata+prosōpon* [1]
from house to house, *2848+3836+3875, kata+ho+oikos* [1]
from one synagogue to another, *2848+4246+3836+5252, kata+pas+ho+synagōgē* [1]
from village to village, *2848+3836+3267, kata+ho+kōmē* [1]
in regard to, *2848, kata* [1]
in response to, *2848, kata* [1]
leads to, *2848, kata* [1]
opposed to, *2848, kata* [1]
to suit, *2848, kata* [1]
with regard to, *2848, kata* [1]
burden to, *2851, katabareō* [1]
to look for, *2870, katadiōkō* [1]
gave to as inheritance, *2883, kataklēronomeō* [1]
burden to, *2915, katanarkaō* [1]
cut to, *2920, katanyssomai* [1]
coming to nothing, *2934, katargeō* [1]
sensual desires overcome their dedication to, *2952, katastrēniaō* [1]
hold to, *2988, katechō* [1]
holding to, *2988, katechō* [1]
theirs to keep, *2988, katechō* [1]
charge to bring against, *2989, katēgoreō* [1]
caused to live, *3001, katoikizō* [1]
to the ground, *3004, katō* [1]
something to boast about, *3017, kauchēma* [1]
entrusted to, *3102, klēros* [1]
willing to share, *3127, koinōnikos* [1]
hired out to, *3140, kollaō* [1]
united to, *3140, kollaō* [1]
held on to, *3195, krateō* [1]
hold firmly to, *3195, krateō* [1]
holding on to, *3195, krateō* [1]
holding to, *3195, krateō* [1]
remain true to, *3195, krateō* [1]
goes to law, *3212, krinō* [1]
told to stop, *3266, kōlyō* [1]
from village to village, *3267+3241, kōmē+kyklō* [1]
unable to speak, *3273, kōphos* [1]
starving to death, *3350+660, limos+apollymi* [1]
broken to pieces, *3395, lyō* [1]
had too much to drink, *3499, methyskō* [1]
give yourself wholly to, *3509, meletaō* [1]
close to, *3516, mellō* [1]
to come, *3516+2262, mellō+erchomai* [1]
to, *3516, mellō* [1]
was to, *3516, mellō* [1]
contributing to the needs of others, *3556, metadidōmi* [1]
belonged to, *3576, metechō* [1]
twenty to thirty gallons, *3583+1545+2445+5552, metrētēs+dyo+ē+treis* [1]
all the way to, *3588, mechri* [1]
even to the point of, *3588, mechri* [1]

TODAY   [34]

TODAY'S   [1]

TOGETHER   [97]

sat down together, *5154, synkathizō* [1]
heirs together with, *5169, synklēronomos* [1]
sharers together in, *5212, symmetochos* [1]
brought together, *5237, sympherō* [1]
bring together, *5251, synagō* [1]
called together, *5251, synagō* [1]
came together, *5251, synagō* [1]
gather together, *5251, synagō* [1]
called together, *5255, synathroizō* [1]
together refreshed, *5265, synanapauomai* [1]
grow together, *5277, synauxanō* [1]
chosen together with, *5293, syneklektos* [1]
working together, *5300, synergeō* [1]
work together, *5301+1181,*
   synergos+ginomai [1]
come together, *5302+2093+3836+899,*
   synerchomai+epi+ho+autos [1]
comes together, *5302+2093+3836+899,*
   synerchomai+epi+ho+autos [1]
meet together, *5302, synerchomai* [1]
met together, *5302, synerchomai* [1]
hold together, *5319, synistēmi* [1]
built together, *5325, synoikodomeō* [1]
members together of one body, *5362,*
   syssōmos [1]
came together, *5370, systrephō* [1]
passed under to hold together, *5968+5690,*
   chraomai+hypozōnnymi [1]

TOIL [1]

toil, *3160, kopos* [1]

TOILED [1]

toiled, *3677, mochthos* [1]

TOILING [1]

toiling, *3677, mochthos* [1]

TOLD [165]

told, *3306, legō* [91]
told, *3281, laleō* [16]
told, *550, apangellō* [13]
told, *RPE* [6]
told, *334, anangellō* [3]
told to do, *1411, diatassō* [3]
told, *4133, parangellō* [3]
told about, *1192, gnōrizō* [2]
told, *1455, diēgeomai* [2]
told, *2007, exēgeomai* [2]
told, *4192+3306, paratithēmi+legō* [2]
told ahead of time, *4625, prolegō* [2]
told, *NIG* [1]
told, *201, akouō* [1]
told about, *334, anangellō* [1]
told, *341, anagnōrizō* [1]
told, *646, apokrinomai* [1]
told, *806+3306, archō+legō* [1]
told, *1181+4639, ginomai+pros* [1]
told of, *1317, dēloō* [1]
told, *1397, diasapheō* [1]
told, *1411, diatassō* [1]
told how, *1687, ekdiēgeomai* [1]
told, *1687, ekdiēgeomai* [1]
told the good news about, *2294, euangelizō* [1]
told, *3062, kēryssō* [1]
told to stop, *3266, kōlyō* [1]
told about, *3455, martyreō* [1]
told, *3606, mēnyō* [1]
already told, *4625, prolegō* [1]
told, *5435, tassō* [1]
told, *5976, chrēmatizō* [1]

TOLERANCE [1]

tolerance, *496, anochē* [1]

TOLERATE [2]

tolerate, *918, aphiēmi* [1]
tolerate, *1002, bastazō* [1]

TOMB [41]

tomb, *3646, mnēmeion* [31]
tomb, *3645, mnēma* [4]
tomb, *5439, taphos* [4]
tomb, *RPE* [2]

TOMBS [11]

tombs, *3646, mnēmeion* [5]
tombs, *3645, mnēma* [3]
tombs, *5439, taphos* [2]
tombs, *RPE* [1]

TOMORROW [11]

tomorrow, *892, aurion* [11]

TONE [1]

tone, *5889, phōnē* [1]

TONGUE [22]

tongue, *1185, glōssa* [21]
the tongue[s], *899, autos* [1]

TONGUES [22]

tongues, *1185, glōssa* [19]
speaking in tongues, *1185, glōssa* [2]
strange tongues, *2280, heteroglōssos* [1]

TONIGHT [2]

tonight, *3816, nyx* [1]
tonight, *4047+3836+3816, houtos+ho+nyx* [1]

TOO [54]

too, *2779, kai* [29]
I too, *2743, kagō* [3]
too, *AIT* [2]
too, *NIG* [2]
and too, *2743, kagō* [2]
too, *3931, homoiōs* [2]
have too little, *1782, elattoneō* [1]
put it too severely, *2096, epibareō* [1]
so too, *2779, kai* [1]
and too, *2779, kai* [1]
there too, *2795, kakei* [1]
he too, *2797, kakeinos* [1]
had too much to drink, *3499, methyskō* [1]
had too much, *3551+1639, mestoō+eimi* [1]
too, *3836+899+2779, ho+autos+kai* [1]
too, *4036, oun* [1]
too, *4181, paraplēsiōs* [1]
have too much, *4429, pleonazō* [1]
going too far, *5657, hyperekteinō* [1]
too, *6058, hōsautōs* [1]

TOOK [135]

took, *3284, lambanō* [38]
took, *4161, paralambanō* [12]
took, *149, airō* [6]
took, *2138, epilambanomai* [6]
took place, *1181, ginomai* [5]
took, *3195, krateō* [5]
took, *NIG* [4]
took with, *4161, paralambanō* [4]
took away, *149, airō* [3]
took down, *2747, kathaireō* [3]
took, *RPE* [2]
took, *72, agō* [2]
took, *552, apagō* [2]
took soundings, *1075, bolizō* [2]

took off, *1694, ekdyō* [2]
took along, *4161, paralambanō* [2]
took aside, *4161, paralambanō* [2]
took aside, *4689, proslambanō* [2]
took offense, *4997, skandalizō* [2]
took pity, *5072, splanchnizomai* [2]
took home, *72, agō* [1]
took care of the vineyard, *307, ampelourgos* [1]
took, *343, anagō* [1]
took, *359, anaireō* [1]
took aboard, *377, analambanō* [1]
took, *377, analambanō* [1]
took away from, *655+608,*
   apolambanō+apo [1]
suddenly took away, *773, harpazō* [1]
took, *928, aphorizō* [1]
took, *1312, dechomai* [1]
took, *1443, didōmi* [1]
took the road through, *1451, dierchomai* [1]
took into, *1652+1650, eisagō+eis* [1]
took out, *1675, ekballō* [1]
took in arms, *1878, enankalizomai* [1]
took note, *2105, epiginōskō* [1]
took care of, *2150, epimeleomai* [1]
took down, *2864, katagō* [1]
took hold of, *2898, katalambanō* [1]
took, *2959, kataschesis* [1]
took up, *3284, lambanō* [1]
took charge of, *4161, paralambanō* [1]
took home, *4161, paralambanō* [1]
took, *4161+72, paralambanō+agō* [1]
took at, *4409+4005, pisteuō+hos* [1]
took along, *5221, symparalambanō* [1]
took off, *5502, tithēmi* [1]
took, *5770, pherō* [1]
took a battering from the storm, *5928,*
   cheimazō [1]

TOOTH [2]

tooth, *3848, odous* [2]

TOP [8]

top, *540, anōthen* [3]
top, *216, akron* [1]
at the top of, *3489, megas* [1]
at the top of voices, *5889+3489,*
   phōnē+megas [1]
at the top of voice, *5889+3489,*
   phōnē+megas [1]
shouting at the top of voice, *5889+3489+3306,*
   phōnē+megas+legō [1]

TOPAZ [1]

topaz, *5535, topazion* [1]

TORCH [1]

torch, *3286, lampas* [1]

TORCHES [1]

torches, *5749, phanos* [1]

TORE [4]

tore, *1396, diarrēgnymi* [3]
tore apart, *1400, diaspaō* [1]

TORMENT [7]

torment, *990, basanismos* [3]
torment, *992, basanos* [2]
torment, *92, adikeō* [1]
torment, *3139, kolaphizō* [1]

TORMENTED [5]

tormented, *989, basanizō* [4]

tormented, *4061*, *ochleō* [1]

TORN [12]

torn, *5387*, *schizō* [5]
torn away from, *682+608*,
    aporphanizō+apo [1]
torn away, *685*, *apospaō* [1]
torn to pieces, *1400*, *diaspaō* [1]
torn out, *2021*, *exoryssō* [1]
torn down, *2940*, *kataskaptō* [1]
torn, *5309*, *synechō* [1]
torn open, *5387*, *schizō* [1]

TORRENT [3]

torrent, *4532*, *potamos* [2]
sweep away with the torrent, *4533+4472*,
    potamophorētos+poieō [1]

TORTURE [5]

torture, *989*, *basanizō* [4]
torture, *990*, *basanismos* [1]

TORTURED [2]

jailers to be tortured, *991*, *basanistēs* [1]
tortured, *5594*, *tympanizō* [1]

TOSS [2]

toss, *965*, *ballō* [2]

TOSSED [2]

tossed back and forth by the waves, *3115*,
    klydōnizomai [1]
tossed, *4847*, *rhipizō* [1]

TOSSING [1]

tossing, *4893*, *salos* [1]

TOTAL [1]

total, *RPE* [1]

TOUCH [13]

touch, *721*, *haptō* [10]
touch, *2566*, *thinganō* [2]
touch, *6027*, *psēlaphaō* [1]

TOUCHED [23]

touched, *721*, *haptō* [20]
touched, *6027*, *psēlaphaō* [2]
that had touched, *608+3836+5999*,
    apo+ho+chrōs [1]

TOUCHES [1]

touches, *2566*, *thinganō* [1]

TOUCHING [1]

touching, *721*, *haptō* [1]

TOWARD [20]

toward, *4639*, *pros* [8]
toward, *1650*, *eis* [4]
toward, *AIT* [3]
toward, *2093*, *epi* [2]
straining toward, *2085*, *epekteinomai* [1]
toward, *2848*, *kata* [1]
turned toward, *5138*, *strephō* [1]

TOWEL [2]

towel, *3317*, *lention* [2]

TOWER [2]

tower, *4788*, *pyrgos* [2]

TOWING [1]

towing, *5359*, *syrō* [1]

TOWN [57]

town, *4484*, *polis* [51]
that town, *1696*, *ekeithen* [2]
from town to town, *3836+4484*, *ho+polis* [2]
from after town, *2848*, *kata* [1]
town, *3267*, *kōmē* [1]

TOWNS [12]

towns, *4484*, *polis* [12]

TRACE [1]

trace descent, *1156*, *genealogeō* [1]

TRACED [1]

traced, *NIG* [1]

TRACING [1]

beyond tracing out, *453*, *anexichniastos* [1]

TRACONITIS [1]

Traconitis, *5551+6001*, *Trachōnitis+chōra* [1]

TRADE [2]

trade, *3538*, *meros* [1]
trade, *5492*, *technē* [1]

TRADERS [1]

slave traders, *435*, *andrapodistēs* [1]

TRADES [1]

relatedˢ trades, *5525*, *toioutos* [1]

TRADITION [7]

tradition, *4142*, *paradosis* [7]

TRADITIONS [4]

traditions, *4142*, *paradosis* [3]
traditions, *4161*, *paralambanō* [1]

TRAIL [1]

trail behind, *2051*, *epakoloutheō* [1]

TRAIN [3]

led captives in his train, *169+168*,
    aichmalōteuō+aichmalōsia [1]
train, *1214*, *gymnazō* [1]
train, *5405*, *sōphronizō* [1]

TRAINED [5]

trained, *1214+2400*, *gymnazō+echō* [1]
trained, *1214*, *gymnazō* [1]
not trained, *2626*, *idiōtēs* [1]
fully trained, *2936*, *katartizō* [1]
trained, *4084*, *paideuō* [1]

TRAINING [4]

training, *4082*, *paideia* [2]
training, *1215*, *gymnasia* [1]
goes into training, *1603*, *enkrateuomai* [1]

TRAITOR [2]

traitor, *4140*, *paradidōmi* [1]
traitor, *4595*, *prodotēs* [1]

TRAMPLE [3]

trample, *2922*, *katapateō* [1]
trample on, *4251*, *pateō* [1]

trample, *4251*, *pateō* [1]

TRAMPLED [5]

trampled on, *2922*, *katapateō* [1]
trampled under foot, *2922*, *katapateō* [1]
trampled, *2922*, *katapateō* [1]
trampled on, *4251*, *pateō* [1]
trampled, *4251*, *pateō* [1]

TRAMPLING [1]

trampling on, *2922*, *katapateō* [1]

TRANCE [3]

trance, *1749*, *ekstasis* [2]
fell into trance, *1181+2093+1749*,
    ginomai+epi+ekstasis [1]

TRANSCENDS [1]

transcends, *5660*, *hyperechō* [1]

TRANSFERRED [1]

have transferred, *3569*, *metapempō* [1]

TRANSFIGURED [2]

transfigured, *3565*, *metamorphoō* [2]

TRANSFORM [1]

transform, *3571*, *metaschēmatizō* [1]

TRANSFORMED [2]

transformed into, *3565*, *metamorphoō* [1]
transformed, *3565*, *metamorphoō* [1]

TRANSGRESSION [3]

transgression, *4183*, *paraptōma* [2]
transgression, *4126*, *parabasis* [1]

TRANSGRESSIONS [4]

transgressions, *4183*, *paraptōma* [2]
transgressions, *490*, *anomia* [1]
transgressions, *4126*, *parabasis* [1]

TRANSGRESSORS [1]

transgressors, *491*, *anomos* [1]

TRANSLATED [2]

translated, *1450*, *diermēneuō* [1]
translated, *2257*, *hermēneuō* [1]

TRANSPARENT [1]

transparent, *1420*, *diaugēs* [1]

TRAP [10]

trap, *4075*, *pagis* [4]
trying to trap, *4279*, *peirazō* [2]
trap in, *2138*, *epilambanomai* [1]
trap, *2560*, *thēra* [1]
trap, *4074*, *pagideuō* [1]
trap, *4279*, *peirazō* [1]

TRAVEL [2]

travel by ship, *2093+5536+4434*,
    epi+topos+pleō [1]
travel over, *4310*, *periagō* [1]

TRAVELED [18]

traveled through, *1451*, *dierchomai* [3]
traveled throughout, *1451*, *dierchomai* [2]
traveled, *2262*, *erchomai* [2]
traveled, *AIT* [1]
traveled, *1388*, *diaporeuomai* [1]

traveled about, *1451+1328, dierchomai+dia* [1]
traveled about, *1451, dierchomai* [1]
traveled along, *1451+1328, dierchomai+dia* [1]
traveled, *1451, dierchomai* [1]
traveled about, *1476, diodeuō* [1]
traveled on, *2262+3847, erchomai+hodos* [1]
traveled, *3841, hodeuō* [1]
traveled, *4513, poreuomai* [1]
traveled with, *5262, synanabainō* [1]

TRAVELING [3]

traveling with, *5233, symporeuomai* [1]
traveling companions, *5292, synekdēmos* [1]
traveling with, *5321, synodeuō* [1]

TREACHEROUS [1]

treacherous, *4595, prodotēs* [1]

TREACHEROUSLY [1]

dealt treacherously with, *2947,
   katasophizomai* [1]

TREADING [2]

treading out the grain, *262, aloaō* [2]

TREADS [1]

treads, *4251, pateō* [1]

TREASURE [9]

treasure, *2565, thēsauros* [8]
lay up treasure, *631, apothēsaurizō* [1]

TREASURED [2]

treasured, *1413, diatēreō* [1]
treasured up, *5337, syntēreō* [1]

TREASURES [6]

treasures, *2565, thēsauros* [5]
treasures, *AIT* [1]

TREASURY [5]

temple treasury, *1126, gazophylakion* [2]
treasury, *1125, gaza²* [1]
treasury, *1126, gazophylakion* [1]
treasury, *3168, korbanas* [1]

TREAT [9]

treat with contempt, *2024, exoutheneō* [2]
treat, *4472, poieō* [2]
treat, *RPE* [1]
treat, *671, aponemō* [1]
treat, *1639, eimi* [1]
[treat with] scorn, *1746, ekptyō* [1]
treat with, *4363, peritithēmi* [1]
treat, *4472+1650, poieō+eis* [1]

TREATED [11]

treated, *4472, poieō* [4]
treated shamefully, *869, atimazō* [2]
treated, *418, anastrephō* [1]
treated with, *2400, echō* [1]
treated, *2451, hēgeomai* [1]
brutally treated, *3139, kolaphizō* [1]
way treated^s, *3210, krima* [1]

TREATING [1]

treating, *4712, prospherō* [1]

TREATMENT [2]

special treatment, [1]
harsh treatment, *910, apheidia* [1]

TREE [50]

tree, *1285, dendron* [17]
fig tree, *5190, sykē* [14]
tree, *3833, xylon* [11]
olive tree that is wild, *66, agrielaios* [1]
a fig^s tree, *899, autos* [1]
the tree^s, *899, autos* [1]
olive tree, *1777, elaia* [1]
cultivated olive tree, *2814, kallielaios* [1]
mulberry tree, *5189, sykaminos* [1]
tree, *5190, sykē* [1]
sycamore-fig tree, *5191, sykomorea* [1]

TREES [9]

trees, *1285, dendron* [8]
olive trees, *1777, elaia* [1]

TREMBLED [1]

trembled with fear, *1958+1181,
   entromos+ginomai* [1]

TREMBLING [8]

trembling, *5571, tromos* [3]
trembling, *5554, tremō* [2]
trembling, *1958+1181, entromos+ginomai* [1]
trembling, *1958, entromos* [1]
trembling, *2400+5571, echō+tromos* [1]

TREMENDOUS [1]

tremendous, *5496+3489, tēlikoutos+megas* [1]

TRESPASS [5]

trespass, *4183, paraptōma* [5]

TRESPASSES [1]

trespasses, *4183, paraptoma* [1]

TRIAL [15]

trial, *4280, peirasmos* [4]
stand trial, *3212, krinō* [2]
brought to trial, *72, agō* [1]
without a trial, *185, akatakritos* [1]
bring out for trial, *343, anagō* [1]
severe trial, *1509+2568, dokimē+thlipsis* [1]
on trial, *2705+3212, histēmi+krinō* [1]
on trial, *3212, krinō* [1]
stand on trial, *3212, krinō* [1]
stand trial before, *4225, paristēmi* [1]
bring to trial, *4575, proagō* [1]

TRIALS [6]

trials, *4280, peirasmos* [4]
trials, *2568, thlipsis* [2]

TRIBE [25]

tribe, *5876, phylē* [24]
that tribe^s, *4005, hos* [1]

TRIBES [6]

tribes, *5876, phylē* [5]
twelve tribes, *1559, dōdekaphylon* [1]

TRIBULATION [1]

tribulation, *2568, thlipsis* [1]

TRICK [1]

trick, *1515, dolos* [1]

TRICKERY [2]

trickery, *1515, dolos* [1]
trickery, *4816, rhadiourgia* [1]

TRIED [26]

tried, *2426, zēteō* [9]
tried, *AIT* [7]
tried, *4279, peirazō* [3]
tried, *2217, epicheireō* [2]
tried, *1508, dokimasia* [1]
tried, *3212, krinō* [1]
tried to do, *4278+3284, peira+lambanō* [1]
tried, *4281, peiraō* [1]
tried destroy, *4514, portheō* [1]

TRIES [2]

tries, *2426, zēteō* [1]
tries, *2527, thelō* [1]

TRIMMED [1]

trimmed, *3175, kosmeō* [1]

TRIUMPHAL [1]

leads in triumphal procession, *2581,
   thriambeuō* [1]

TRIUMPHED [1]

triumphed, *3771, nikaō* [1]

TRIUMPHING [1]

triumphing over, *2581, thriambeuō* [1]

TRIUMPHS [1]

triumphs over, *2878, katakauchaomai* [1]

TRIVIAL [1]

trivial, *1788, elachistos* [1]

TROAS [6]

Troas, *5590, Trōas* [6]

TROOPS [4]

troops, *5128, strateuma* [3]
Roman troops, *5061, speira* [1]

TROPHIMUS [3]

Trophimus, *5576, Trophimos* [3]

TROUBLE [19]

trouble, *2568, thlipsis* [8]
out of trouble, *291, amerimnos* [1]
caused trouble, *415, anastatoō* [1]
cause trouble, *1943, enochleō* [1]
those in trouble, *2567, thlibō* [1]
trouble, *2567, thlibō* [1]
trouble, *2798, kakia* [1]
trouble, *2802, kakopatheō* [1]
trouble, *3160, kopos* [1]
trouble, *3508, melei* [1]
trouble, *3891, oknēros* [1]
trouble, *5035, skyllō* [1]

TROUBLED [12]

troubled, *5429, tarassō* [6]
troubled, *86, adēmoneō* [2]
troubled, *1387, diaponeomai* [1]
greatly troubled, *1410, diatarassō* [1]
troubled, *1943, enochleō* [1]
troubled, *2567, thlibō* [1]

TROUBLEMAKER [1]

troublemaker, *3369, loimos* [1]

TROUBLES [7]

troubles, *2568, thlipsis* [6]

many troubles, *2568, thlipsis* [1]

TROUBLING [1]

troubling, *412, anaskeuazō* [1]

TRUE [59]

true, *240, alēthinos* [26]
true, *239, alēthēs* [9]
true, *237, alētheia* [5]
true, *4048, houtōs* [3]
true, *NIG* [2]
true, *1188, gnēsios* [2]
true, *AIT* [1]
true, *242, alēthōs* [1]
come true, *1181, ginomai* [1]
remain true to, *1844, emmenō* [1]
true, *1877+237, en+alētheia* [1]
how true, *2093+237, epi+alētheia* [1]
it is true, *2779, kai* [1]
remain true to, *3195, krateō* [1]
it is true, *3953, ontōs* [1]
true, *4246, pas* [1]
come true, *4444, plēroō* [1]
true, *4606, prothesis* [1]

TRULY [6]

truly love, *26, agapaō* [2]
truly, *242, alēthōs* [2]
truly, *1877+237, en+alētheia* [1]
truly, *3953, ontōs* [1]

TRUMPET [18]

trumpet, *4894, salpinx* [7]
sounded trumpet, *4895, salpizō* [7]
trumpet call, *4894, salpinx* [2]
sound trumpet, *4895, salpizō* [1]
trumpet sound, *4895, salpizō* [1]

TRUMPETERS [1]

trumpeters, *4896, salpistēs* [1]

TRUMPETS [3]

trumpets, *4894, salpinx* [2]
announce with trumpets, *4895, salpizō* [1]

TRUST [10]

trust, *4409, pisteuō* [4]
put trust, *4409, pisteuō* [2]
put trust, *1639+4275, eimi+peithō* [1]
trust, *1827, elpizō* [1]
given a trust, *1877+3874, en+oikonomos* [1]
trust, *3873, oikonomia* [1]

TRUSTED [6]

can be trusted, *4412, pistos* [2]
trusted personal servant, *2093+3836+3131,
   epi+ho+koitōn* [1]
trusted, *4275, peithō* [1]
trusted, *4409, pisteuō* [1]
trusted, *4411, pistis* [1]

TRUSTEES [1]

trustees, *3874, oikonomos* [1]

TRUSTS [6]

trusts, *4409, pisteuō* [5]
trusts, *4275, peithō* [1]

TRUSTWORTHY [13]

trustworthy, *4412, pistos* [13]

TRUTH [183]

truth, *237, alētheia* [94]
the truth, *297, amēn* [74]
truth, *239, alēthēs* [3]
truth, *242, alēthōs* [3]
the truth, *2822, kalōs* [2]
truth, *RPE* [1]
speaking truth, *238, alētheuō* [1]
telling truth, *238, alētheuō* [1]
get at truth, *1182+855, ginōskō+asphalēs* [1]
learn the truth, *2105, epiginōskō* [1]
distort the truth, *3281+1406,
   laleō+diastrephō* [1]
no truth, *4029, oudeis* [1]

TRUTHFUL [2]

truthful, *237, alētheia* [1]
truthful, *239, alēthēs* [1]

TRUTHFULLY [1]

truthfully, *237, alētheia* [1]

TRUTHFULNESS [1]

truthfulness, *237, alētheia* [1]

TRUTHS [4]

truths, *AIT* [1]
truths, *3364, logos* [1]
deep truths, *3696, mystērion* [1]
elementary truths, *5122+3836+794,
   stoicheion+ho+archē* [1]

TRY [9]

try, *AIT* [2]
try, *2426, zēteō* [2]
try to please, *743, areskō* [1]
try hard, *1443+2238, didōmi+ergasia* [1]
try, *1503, diōkō* [1]
try out, *1507, dokimazō* [1]
try, *1639, eimi* [1]

TRYING [27]

trying, *AIT* [7]
trying, *2426, zēteō* [6]
trying to please, *743, areskō* [2]
trying, *2527, thelō* [2]
trying to trap, *4279, peirazō* [2]
trying$ to, *1656, eiserchomai* [1]
trying to, *1877, en* [1]
trying to find out, *2236, eraunaō* [1]
trying to kill, *2426+3836+6034,
   zēteō+ho+psychē* [1]
trying to take, *2426, zēteō* [1]
trying to persuade, *4275, peithō* [1]
trying to win the approval of, *4275, peithō* [1]
trying to, *6055+323, hōs+an* [1]

TRYPHENA [1]

Tryphena, *5586, Tryphaina* [1]

TRYPHOSA [1]

Tryphosa, *5589, Tryphōsa* [1]

TUNE [1]

tune played, *884+2445+3068,
   auleō+ē+kitharizō* [1]

TUNIC [5]

tunic, *5945, chitōn* [5]

TUNICS [1]

tunics, *5945, chitōn* [1]

TURMOIL [1]

thrown into turmoil, *5429, tarassō* [1]

TURN [43]

turn, *5138, strephō* [5]
turn, *2188, epistrephō* [4]
turn to, *2188+2093, epistrephō+epi* [3]
in turn, *2779, kai* [3]
turn away from, *695, apostrephō* [2]
turn over, *4140, paradidōmi* [2]
turn, *AIT* [1]
turn, *NIG* [1]
turn away from, *608+695, apo+apostrephō* [1]
turn out, *609, apobainō* [1]
to turn away from, *686+608, apostasia+apo* [1]
turn away from, *695+608, apostrephō+apo* [1]
turn away from, *923+608, aphistēmi+apo* [1]
turn, *1181, ginomai* [1]
turn, *1406, diastrephō* [1]
turn, *1495, dichazō* [1]
turn, *1712, ekklinō* [1]
turn away from, *1762, ektrepō* [1]
turn aside, *1762, ektrepō* [1]
turn to, *2188, epistrephō* [1]
turn over to, *2770, kathistēmi* [1]
in turn, *2848+1651, kata+heis* [1]
turn, *3555, metagō* [1]
turn in repentance, *3567, metanoia* [1]
turn, *4218, parechō* [1]
turn sour, *4393, pikrainō* [1]
turn into, *4472, poieō* [1]
turn away from the faith, *4997, skandalizō* [1]
turn, *5413, tagma* [1]
turn their backs, *5715, hypostrephō* [1]

TURNED [41]

turned, *5138, strephō* [7]
turned, *2188, epistrephō* [4]
turned around, *2188, epistrephō* [3]
turned into, *1181, ginomai* [2]
turned, *1181, ginomai* [2]
turned to, *2188+2093, epistrephō+epi* [2]
turned away, *288, ameleō* [1]
turned back, *599+1650+3836+3958,
   aperchomai+eis+ho+opisō* [1]
turned, *846, astocheō* [1]
been turned into, *1181, ginomai* [1]
turned out, *1181, ginomai* [1]
turned, *1181+1650, ginomai+eis* [1]
turned to strength, *1540, dynamoō* [1]
turned away, *1712, ekklinō* [1]
turned away, *1762, ektrepō* [1]
turned on, *2138, epilambanomai* [1]
turned back, *2188, epistrephō* [1]
turned, *3306, legō* [1]
turned, *3570, metastrephō* [1]
turned over, *4140, paradidōmi* [1]
turned sour, *4393, pikrainō* [1]
turned into, *4472, poieō* [1]
turned dark, *5029, skotizomai* [1]
turned around, *5138+1650+3836+3958,
   strephō+eis+ho+opisō* [1]
turned away, *5138, strephō* [1]
turned back, *5138, strephō* [1]
turned toward, *5138, strephō* [1]

TURNING [8]

turning, *5138, strephō* [2]
turning, *AIT* [1]
turning from, *695+608, apostrephō+apo* [1]
turning, *2188, epistrephō* [1]
turning back to, *2188+2093, epistrephō+epi* [1]
turning to, *2188+2093, epistrephō+epi* [1]
turning around, *5138, strephō* [1]

TURNS [3]

turns, *2188, epistrephō* [2]
turns away from, *923+608, aphistēmi+apo* [1]

TWELFTH [1]

twelfth, *1558, dōdekatos* [1]

TWELVE [62]

twelve, *1557, dōdeka* [60]
twelve tribes, *1559, dōdekaphylon* [1]
twelve, *2291+1557, etos+dōdeka* [1]

TWENTY [4]

twenty, *1633, eikosi* [2]
twenty to thirty gallons,
   3583+1545+2445+5552,
   metrētēs+dyo+ē+treis [1]
a hundred and twenty feet deep, *3976+1633,*
   orgyia+eikosi [1]

TWENTY-FOUR [6]

twenty-four, *1633+5475, eikosi+tessares* [6]

TWENTY-THREE [1]

twenty-three, *1633+5552, eikosi+treis* [1]

TWICE [6]

twice, *1489, dis* [4]
twice, *1311, deuteros* [1]
twice as much, *1487, diplous* [1]

TWIGS [2]

twigs, *3080, klados* [2]

TWIN [1]

twin gods Castor and Pollux, *1483,*
   Dioskouroi [1]

TWINKLING [1]

twinkling, *4846, rhipē* [1]

TWINS [1]

twins, *AIT* [1]

TWISTED [3]

twisted together, *4428, plekō* [3]

TWO [143]

two, *1545, dyo* [122]
two, *NIG* [2]
two by two, *324+1545+1545,*
   ana+dyo+dyo [2]
two hundred, *1357, diakosioi* [2]
two years, *1454, dietia* [2]
two by two, *1545+1545, dyo+dyo* [2]
two, *AIT* [1]
two, *317, amphoteroi* [1]
the two$, *899, autos* [1]
two Israelites$, *899, autos* [1]
two years old, *1453, dietēs* [1]
two hundred million, *1490+3689,*
   dismyrias+myrias [1]
two thousand, *1493, dischilioi* [1]
in two, *3545, mesos* [1]
sawed in two, *4569, prizō* [1]
the two of you, *5148+2779+899,*
   sy+kai+autos [1]
less than two miles, *6055+608+5084+1278,*
   hōs+apo+stadion+dekapente [1]

TWO-DRACHMA [1]

two-drachma, *1440, didrachmon* [1]

TYCHICUS [5]

Tychicus, *5608, Tychikos* [5]

TYRANNUS [1]

Tyrannus, *5598, Tyrannos¹* [1]

TYRE [12]

Tyre, *5602, Tyros* [11]
people of Tyre, *5601, Tyrios* [1]

UGLY [1]

ugly, *2805, kakos* [1]

UNABLE [6]

unable to speak, *3273, kōphos* [1]
unable, *3590+1538, mē+dynamai* [1]
unable, *3590, mē* [1]
unable, *4024+1538, ou+dynamai* [1]
unable, *4024+2710, ou+ischyō* [1]
unable, *4033+2710, ouketi+ischyō* [1]

UNAPPROACHABLE [1]

unapproachable, *717, aprositos* [1]

UNASHAMED [1]

unashamed, *3590+159, mē+aischynomai* [1]

UNAWARE [3]

unaware, *51, agnoeō* [2]
unaware, *4024+1182, ou+ginōskō* [1]

UNBELIEF [6]

unbelief, *602, apistia* [6]

UNBELIEVER [5]

unbeliever, *603, apistos* [5]

UNBELIEVERS [8]

unbelievers, *603, apistos* [7]
unbelievers, *578, apeitheō* [1]

UNBELIEVING [7]

unbelieving, *603, apistos* [6]
unbelieving, *602, apistia* [1]

UNBLEMISHED [1]

unblemished, *320, amōmos* [1]

UNCEASING [1]

unceasing, *89, adialeiptos* [1]

UNCERTAIN [1]

uncertain, *84, adēlotēs* [1]

UNCHANGEABLE [1]

unchangeable, *292, ametathetos* [1]

UNCHANGING [1]

unchanging, *292, ametathetos* [1]

UNCIRCUMCISED [9]

uncircumcised, *213, akrobystia* [5]
uncircumcised, *213+2400, akrobystia+echō* [1]
uncircumcised, *598, aperitmētos* [1]
uncircumcised, *1877+213, en+akrobystia* [1]
become uncircumcised, *2177, epispaomai* [1]

UNCIRCUMCISION [4]

uncircumcision, *213, akrobystia* [4]

UNCLEAN [23]

make unclean, *3124, koinoō* [7]
unclean, *176, akathartos* [6]
unclean, *3123, koinos* [5]
makes unclean, *3124, koinoō* [2]
unclean, *174, akatharsia* [1]
ceremonially unclean, *3124, koinoō* [1]
what makes unclean, *3124, koinoō* [1]

UNCLEANNESS [1]

ceremonial uncleanness, *3620, miainō* [1]

UNCLOTHED [1]

unclothed, *1694, ekdyō* [1]

UNCOVERED [3]

uncovered, *184, akatakalyptos* [2]
uncovered, *1218, gymnos* [1]

UNDENIABLE [1]

undeniable, *394, anantirrētos* [1]

UNDER [90]

under, *5679, hypo* [37]
under, *5691, hypokatō* [9]
under, *1877, en* [5]
put under, *5718, hypotassō* [3]
under, *AIT* [2]
under, *1666, ek* [2]
kept under guard, *5875, phylassō* [2]
bring together under one head, *368,*
   anakephalaioō [1]
under guard, *857, asphalōs* [1]
under pressure, *976, bareō* [1]
under, *1328, dia* [1]
under power, *1650+5931, eis+cheir* [1]
under, *1650, eis* [1]
cut from under, *1716, ekkoptō* [1]
under law, *1937, ennomos* [1]
charge under oath, *2019, exorkizō* [1]
under, *2093, epi* [1]
under, *2277, esōthen* [1]
is under, *2400, echō* [1]
under the power, *2872, katadynasteuō* [1]
trampled under foot, *2922, katapateō* [1]
under the earth, *2973, katachthonios* [1]
under, *3006, katōterō* [1]
under the control, *3023, keimai* [1]
come under judgment, *3212, krinō* [1]
under, *3552, meta* [1]
under, *4123+3836+4546, para+ho+pous* [1]
under what circumstances, *4802, pōs* [1]
keep under guard, *5498, tēreō* [1]
bring under control, *5718, hypotassō* [1]
placed under, *5718+5679, hypotassō+hypo* [1]
put under, *5718+5679, hypotassō+hypo* [1]
put under, *5718+5691,*
   hypotassō+hypokatō [1]
putting under, *5718, hypotassō* [1]
bears up under, *5722, hypopherō* [1]
stand up under, *5722, hypopherō* [1]
passed under to hold together, *5968+5690,*
   chraomai+hypozōnnymi [1]

UNDERGARMENT [1]

undergarment, *5945, chitōn* [1]

UNDERGO [1]

baptism undergo, *967+966,*
   baptisma+baptizō [1]

UNDERGOES [1]

undergoes, *3581+1181, metochos+ginomai* [1]

UNDERGOING [1]

undergoing, *2200, epiteleō* [1]

UNDERSTAND [57]

understand, *1182, ginōskō* [17]
understand, *5317, syniēmi* [14]
understand, *3783, noeō* [7]
understand, *3857, oida* [5]
not understand, *51, agnoeō* [3]
not understand, *2626, idiōtēs* [3]
understand, *201, akouō* [2]
understand, *2179, epistamai* [2]
hard to understand, *1554, dysnoētos* [1]
come to understand, *2105, epiginōskō* [1]
understand, *2105, epiginōskō* [1]
understand, *2451, hēgeomai* [1]

UNDERSTANDING [16]

understanding, *5304, synesis* [4]
understanding, *5317, syniēmi* [3]
understanding, *1379, dianoia* [2]
no understanding, *852, asynetos* [1]
understanding, *1194, gnōsis* [1]
full understanding, *2106, epignōsis* [1]
understanding, *2184, epistēmōn* [1]
understanding, *3808, nous* [1]
understanding, *3857, oida* [1]
understanding, *5860, phronēsis* [1]

UNDERSTANDS [4]

understands, *5317, syniēmi* [2]
understands, *201, akouō* [1]
understands, *2179, epistamai* [1]

UNDERSTOOD [10]

understood, *5317, syniēmi* [4]
understood, *1182, ginōskō* [2]
understood, *2105, epiginōskō* [2]
understood, *2898, katalambanō* [1]
understood, *3783, noeō* [1]

UNDERTAKEN [1]

undertaken, *2217, epicheireō* [1]

UNDIVIDED [1]

undivided, *597, aperispastōs* [1]

UNDONE [1]

leaving undone, *4223, pariēmi* [1]

UNDOUBTEDLY [1]

undoubtedly, *1623+5593, ei+tynchanō* [1]

UNDYING [1]

undying, *914, aphtharsia* [1]

UNEQUALED [2]

unequaled, *3888+4024+1181+5525,
    hoios+ou+ginomai+toioutos* [1]
unequaled, *3888+4024+1181,
    hoios+ou+ginomai* [1]

UNEXPECTEDLY [1]

unexpectedly, *167, aiphnidios* [1]

UNFADING [1]

unfading, *915, aphthartos* [1]

UNFAIR [1]

unfair, *92, adikeō* [1]

UNFAITHFULNESS [2]

marital unfaithfulness, *4518, porneia* [2]

UNFINISHED [1]

unfinished, *AIT* [1]

UNFIT [1]

unfit, *99, adokimos* [1]

UNFORGIVING [1]

unforgiving, *836, aspondos* [1]

UNFRUITFUL [3]

unfruitful, *182, akarpos* [3]

UNGODLINESS [1]

ungodliness, *813, asebeia* [1]

UNGODLY [13]

ungodly, *815, asebēs* [8]
ungodly, *813, asebeia* [3]
ungodly, *96, adikos* [1]
done in ungodly way, *814, asebeō* [1]

UNGRATEFUL [2]

ungrateful, *940, acharistos* [2]

UNHEALTHY [1]

unhealthy, *3796, noseō* [1]

UNHOLY [3]

unholy, *495, anosios* [2]
unholy, *3123, koinos* [1]

UNIMPRESSIVE [1]

unimpressive, *822, asthenēs* [1]

UNINFORMED [1]

uninformed, *51, agnoeō* [1]

UNION [1]

union with, *1182, ginōskō* [1]

UNISON [1]

in unison, *5889+1181+1651,
    phōnē+ginomai+heis* [1]

UNIT [1]

a unit, *1651, heis* [1]

UNITE [1]

unite, *4472+3517, poieō+melos* [1]

UNITED [9]

united to, *4681+4639, proskollaō+pros* [2]
united, *RPE* [1]
united with, *1877, en* [1]
perfectly united, *2936+3836+899,
    katartizō+ho+autos* [1]
united to, *3140, kollaō* [1]
united, *3924, homothymadon* [1]
united, *5204, symbibazō* [1]
united, *5242, symphytos* [1]

UNITES [2]

unites, *3140, kollaō* [2]

UNITY [5]

unity, *1942, henotēs* [2]
unity, *AIT* [1]
unity, *1651, heis* [1]
spirit of unity, *3836+899+5858,
    ho+autos+phroneō* [1]

UNIVERSE [5]

universe, *172, aiōn* [2]
universe, *3180, kosmos* [1]
whole universe, *3180, kosmos* [1]
whole universe, *4246, pas* [1]

UNJUST [5]

unjust, *94, adikia* [2]
unjust, *96, adikos* [2]
unjust, *97, adikōs* [1]

UNKNOWN [4]

unknown, *51, agnoeō* [3]
unknown, *58, agnōstos* [1]

UNLAWFUL [4]

unlawful, *4024+2003, ou+exesti* [4]

UNLEAVENED [7]

Feast of Unleavened Bread, *109, azymos* [4]
Unleavened Bread, *109, azymos* [2]
Feast of Unleavened Bread, *2465+109,
    hēmera+azymos* [1]

UNLESS [40]

unless, *1569+3590, ean+mē* [31]
unless, *1623+3590, ei+mē* [2]
unless, *1623+3614, ei+mēti* [2]
unless, *1760+1623+3590, ektos+ei+mē* [2]
unless, *1623+4024, ei+ou* [1]
unless over, *1781, elassōn* [1]
unless, *2445, ē* [1]

UNLIKE [2]

unlike, *4024+6055, ou+hōs* [1]
unlike, *6061, hōsper* [1]

UNLIMITED [1]

unlimited, *570, hapas* [1]

UNLOAD [1]

unload, *711, apophortizomai* [1]

UNMARKED [1]

unmarked, *83, adēlos* [1]

UNMARRIED [7]

unmarried, *23, agamos* [4]
unmarried, *RPE* [1]
unmarried, *3395+608+1222, lyō+apo+gynē* [1]
unmarried, *4221, parthenos* [1]

UNNATURAL [1]

unnatural ones, *3836+4123+5882,
    ho+para+physis* [1]

UNNOTICED [1]

go unnoticed, *3291, lanthanō* [1]

UNOCCUPIED [1]

unoccupied, *5390, scholazō* [1]

UNPREPARED [1]

unprepared, *564, aparaskeuastos* [1]

UNPRESENTABLE [1]

unpresentable, *860, aschēmōn* [1]

UNPRODUCTIVE [2]

unproductive, *182, akarpos* [2]

UNPROFITABLE [1]

unprofitable, *543, anōphelēs* [1]

UNPUNISHED [1]

left unpunished, *4217, paresis* [1]

UNQUENCHABLE [2]

unquenchable, *812, asbestos* [2]

UNREASONABLE [1]

unreasonable, *263, alogos* [1]

UNREASONING [1]

unreasoning, *263, alogos* [1]

UNREPENTANT [1]

unrepentant, *295, ametanoētos* [1]

UNRIGHTEOUS [3]

unrighteous, *96, adikos* [3]

UNRIGHTEOUSNESS [2]

unrighteousness, *94, adikia* [2]

UNROLLING [1]

unrolling, *408, anaptyssō* [1]

UNSCHOOLED [1]

unschooled, *63, agrammatos* [1]

UNSEARCHABLE [2]

unsearchable, *451, anexeraunētos* [1]
unsearchable, *453, anexichniastos* [1]

UNSEEN [4]

unseen, *3590+1063, mē+blepō* [2]
unseen, *1877+3836+3220, en+ho+kryptos* [1]
unseen, *1877+3836+3224,
en+ho+kryphaios* [1]

UNSETTLED [2]

unsettled, *4883, sainō* [1]
unsettled, *4888+608+3836+3808,
saleuō+apo+ho+nous* [1]

UNSHRUNK [2]

unshrunk, *47, agnaphos* [2]

UNSPIRITUAL [3]

unspiritual, *4921, sarkinos* [1]
unspiritual, *4922, sarx* [1]
unspiritual, *6035, psychikos* [1]

UNSTABLE [3]

unstable, *190, akatastatos* [1]
unstable, *844, astēriktos* [1]
unstable, *6034+844, psychē+astēriktos* [1]

UNSUITABLE [1]

unsuitable, *460, aneuthetos* [1]

UNSWERVINGLY [1]

unswervingly, *195, aklinēs* [1]

UNTIE [8]

untie, *3395, lyō* [8]

UNTIED [2]

untied, *479, aniēmi* [1]
untied, *3395, lyō* [1]

UNTIL [102]

until, *2401, heōs* [29]
until, *948, achri* [16]
until, *2401+323, heōs+an* [14]
until, *2401+4005, heōs+hos* [13]
until, *948+4005, achri+hos* [5]
until, *1650, eis* [5]
until, *3588, mechri* [5]
until, *2401+4015, heōs+hostis* [3]
until, *2779, kai* [3]
until, *3588+4005, mechri+hos* [2]
until, *948+4005+323, achri+hos+an* [1]
until, *1569+3590+4754, ean+mē+prōton* [1]
until, *1623+3590+4020, ei+mē+hotan* [1]
until, *1877+4005, en+hos* [1]
until, *2401+2465, heōs+hēmera* [1]
not until, *2453+1254, ēdē+de* [1]
until judge, *4024+3212, ou+krinō* [1]

UNTO [1]

unto, *1650, eis* [1]

UNTYING [4]

untying, *3395, lyō* [4]

UNUSUAL [2]

unusual, *876, atopos* [1]
unusual, *4024+5593, ou+tynchanō* [1]

UNVEILED [1]

unveiled, *365, anakalyptō* [1]

UNWASHED [2]

unwashed, *481, aniptos* [2]

UNWHOLESOME [1]

unwholesome, *4911, sapros* [1]

UNWILLING [2]

unwilling, *4024+2525, ou+thelēma* [1]
unwilling, *4024+2527, ou+thelō* [1]

UNWISE [1]

unwise, *831, asophos* [1]

UNWORTHY [2]

unworthy manner, *397, anaxiōs* [1]
unworthy, *945, achreios* [1]

UP [439]

went up, *326, anabainō* [23]
got up, *482, anistēmi* [15]
get up, *1586, egeirō* [15]
get up, *482, anistēmi* [13]
stood up, *482, anistēmi* [13]
got up, *1586, egeirō* [11]
picked up, *149, airō* [9]
put up with, *462, anechomai* [8]
lifted up, *5738, hypsoō* [8]
going up, *326, anabainō* [7]
pick up, *149, airō* [6]

come up, *326, anabainō* [5]
looked up, *329, anablepō* [5]
raise up, *482, anistēmi* [5]
stood up, *2705, histēmi* [5]
go up, *326, anabainō* [4]
taken up, *377, analambanō* [4]
burned up, *2876, katakaiō* [4]
take up, *149, airō* [3]
came up, *326, anabainō* [3]
looking up, *329, anablepō* [3]
stand up, *482, anistēmi* [3]
spoke up, *646, apokrinomai* [3]
caught up, *773, harpazō* [3]
raise up, *1586, egeirō* [3]
woke up, *1586, egeirō* [3]
looked up, *2048+3836+4057,
epairō+ho+ophthalmos* [3]
up to, *2401, heōs* [3]
stored up, *2565, thēsauros* [3]
ate up, *2983, katesthiō* [3]
building up, *3869, oikodomē* [3]
gave up, *4140, paradidōmi* [3]
put up, *4472, poieō* [3]
came up, *4665, proserchomai* [3]
up, *NIG* [2]
lift up, *149, airō* [2]
coming up, *326, anabainō* [2]
grew up, *326, anabainō* [2]
sat up, *361, anakathizō* [2]
straightened up, *376, anakyptō* [2]
came up, *422, anatellō* [2]
brought up, *427, anatrephō* [2]
went up, *456, anerchomai* [2]
up, *539, anō* [2]
grow up, *889, auxanō* [2]
up to, *948, achri* [2]
came up, *1181, ginomai* [2]
ties up, *1313, deō* [2]
divided up, *1374, diamerizō* [2]
gave up, *1443, didomi* [2]
got up, *1444, diegeirō* [2]
came up, *1581, engizō* [2]
gets up, *1586, egeirō* [2]
helped up, *1586, egeirō* [2]
wake up, *1586, egeirō* [2]
sprang up, *1984, exanatellō* [2]
lift up, *2048, epairō* [2]
lifted up, *2048, epairō* [2]
went up, *2262, erchomai* [2]
keep up courage, *2313, euthymeō* [2]
came up, *2392, ephistēmi* [2]
store up, *2564, thēsaurizō* [2]
got up, *2705, histēmi* [2]
swallowed up, *2927, katapinō* [2]
take up, *3284, lambanō* [2]
spoke up, *3306, legō* [2]
build up, *3868, oikodomeō* [2]
build up, *3869, oikodomē* [2]
came up to, *4665, proserchomai* [2]
ran up to, *4708, prostrechō* [2]
seal up, *5381, sphragizō* [2]
lift up, *5738, hypsoō* [2]
puffs up, *5881, physioō* [2]
came up, *5886, phyō* [2]
stored up, [1]
jumped up, *256, hallomai* [1]
welling up, *256, hallomai* [1]
comes up, *326, anabainō* [1]
goes up, *326, anabainō* [1]
pulled up, *328, anabibazō* [1]
bring up, *343, anagō* [1]
led up, *343, anagō* [1]
summed up, *368, anakephalaioō* [1]
stand up, *376, anakyptō* [1]
straighten up, *376, anakyptō* [1]
lifted up, *377, analambanō* [1]

take up, *377, analambanō* [1]
taken up, *378, analēmpsis* [1]
heap up to the limit, *405, anaplēroō* [1]
make up for, *405, anaplēroō* [1]
stirred up, *411, anaseiō* [1]
stirs up, *411, anaseiō* [1]
pulled up, *413, anaspaō* [1]
draw up, *421, anatassomai* [1]
led up, *429, anapherō* [1]
taken up, *429, anapherō* [1]
go up, *456, anerchomai* [1]
stand up against, *468, anthistēmi* [1]
stand up, *482+3981, anistēmi+orthos* [1]
standing up, *482, anistēmi* [1]
raised up, *482, anistēmi* [1]
raising up, *482, anistēmi* [1]
straightened up, *494, anorthoō* [1]
fill up, *499, antanaplēroō* [1]
up, *542, anōteros* [1]
went up, *599, aperchomai* [1]
lay up treasure, *631, apothēsaurizō* [1]
stored up, *641, apokeimai* [1]
give up, *698, apotassō* [1]
snatched up, *773, harpazō* [1]
looked up, *867, atenizō* [1]
looking intently up, *867, atenizō* [1]
gave up, *918, aphiēmi* [1]
right up to, *948, achri* [1]
picked up, *1002, bastazō* [1]
wake up, *1181+1213, ginomai+grēgoreō* [1]
wake up, *1213, grēgoreō* [1]
tie up, *1297, desmeuō* [1]
divides up, *1344, diadidōmi* [1]
dividing up, *1374, diamerizō* [1]
stand up, *1586, egeirō* [1]
made get up, *1586, egeirō* [1]
raised up, *1586, egeirō* [1]
stir up, *1586, egeirō* [1]
give up, *1591, enkakeō* [1]
give up, *1593, enkataleipō* [1]
made up of, *1639, eimi* [1]
spring up, *1639, eimi* [1]
sums up, *1639, eimi* [1]
were up, *1639+326, eimi+anabainō* [1]
up, *1650, eis* [1]
give up, *1725, eklyō* [1]
gave up to sexual immorality, *1745, ekporneuō* [1]
pulled up by the roots, *1748, ekrizoō* [1]
root up, *1748, ekrizoō* [1]
bring up, *1763, ektrephō* [1]
roll up, *1813, helissō* [1]
rolling up, *1813, helissō* [1]
brought up, *1957, entrephō* [1]
folded up, *1962, entylissō* [1]
stood up, *1985, exanistēmi* [1]
up, *1992, exartizō* [1]
raised up, *1995, exegeirō* [1]
wake up, *2030, exypnizō* [1]
woke up, *2031+1181, exypnos+ginomai* [1]
sets up, *2048, epairō* [1]
taken up, *2048, epairō* [1]
foaming up, *2072, epaphrizō* [1]
stirred up against, *2074+2093, epegeirō+epi* [1]
stirred up, *2074, epegeirō* [1]
came up, *2104, epiginomai* [1]
want to bring up, *2118, epizēteō* [1]
stirring up, *2180+4472, epistasis+poieō* [1]
build up, *2224, epoikodomeō* [1]
built up, *2224, epoikodomeō* [1]
came up, *2262, erchomai* [1]
coming up, *2392, ephistēmi* [1]
made up of, *2400, echō* [1]
right up to, *2401, heōs* [1]
gave up, *2483, hēsychazō* [1]
cheer up, *2510, tharseō* [1]

save up, *2564, thēsaurizō* [1]
stores up, *2564, thēsaurizō* [1]
storing up, *2564, thēsaurizō* [1]
came up, *2627, idou* [1]
sets up, *2767, kathizō* [1]
and up, *2779, kai* [1]
something man made up, *2848+476, kata+anthrōpos* [1]
pulled up, *2864, katagō* [1]
burn up, *2876, katakaiō* [1]
burning up, *2876, katakaiō* [1]
locked up, *2881, katakleiō* [1]
use up, *2934, katargeō* [1]
set up, *2941, kataskeuazō* [1]
laid up, *3023, keimai* [1]
stirring up, *3075, kineō* [1]
piled up, *3140, kollaō* [1]
made up mind, *3212, krinō* [1]
made up, *3212, krinō* [1]
make up mind, *3212, krinō* [1]
picked up, *3284, lambanō* [1]
took up, *3284, lambanō* [1]
lights up, *3290, lampō* [1]
grown up, *3489+1181, megas+ginomai* [1]
dried up, *3830, xērainō* [1]
look up, *3836+4057+2048, ho+ophthalmos+epairō* [1]
builds up, *3868, oikodomeō* [1]
builds up, *3869, oikodomē* [1]
built up, *3869, oikodomē* [1]
up to that time not, *4037, oupō* [1]
gave up, *4311, periaireō* [1]
welled up, *4355, perisseuō* [1]
set up, *4381, pēgnymi* [1]
swell up, *4399, pimprēmi* [1]
made up, *4422, plastos* [1]
fill up, *4444, plēroō* [1]
summed up, *4444, plēroō* [1]
kept up, *4472, poieō* [1]
set up, *4472, poieō* [1]
went up to, *4665, proserchomai* [1]
went up, *4665, proserchomai* [1]
rounded up, *4689, proslambanō* [1]
offered up, *4712, prospherō* [1]
mask to cover up, *4733, prophasis* [1]
rolled up, *4771, ptyssō* [1]
put up with, *5095, stegō* [1]
live up, *5123, stoicheō* [1]
stirred up, *5167, synkineō* [1]
locked up, *5168, synkleiō* [1]
stirred up, *5177, syncheō* [1]
pull up, *5198, syllegō* [1]
pulled up, *5198, syllegō* [1]
grew up with, *5243, symphyō* [1]
picked up, *5251, synagō* [1]
come up with, *5262, synanabainō* [1]
raised up with, *5283, synegeirō* [1]
treasured up, *5337, syntēreō* [1]
brought up with, *5343, syntrophos* [1]
wrapped up, *5366, systellō* [1]
stirring up, *5429, tarassō* [1]
bringing up children, *5452, teknotropheō* [1]
make up mind, *5502+1877+3836+2840, tithēmi+en+ho+kardia* [1]
brought up, *5555, trephō* [1]
bears up under, *5722, hypopherō* [1]
stand up under, *5722, hypopherō* [1]

UPHOLD [1]

uphold, *2705, histēmi* [1]

UPON [27]

upon, *2093, epi* [14]
upon, *AIT* [3]
down upon, *1650, eis* [2]

thousands upon thousands, *3689, myrias* [2]
upon, *NIG* [1]
come upon, *1639+2093+2158, eimi+epi+epipiptō* [1]
come upon, *2082+2093, epeiserchomai+epi* [1]
come upon, *2088+2093, eperchomai+epi* [1]
coming upon, *2088, eperchomai* [1]
came upon, *3972, horaō* [1]

UPPER [2]

upper room, *333, anagaion* [2]

UPRIGHT [4]

upright, *1465, dikaios* [3]
upright, *1469, dikaiōs* [1]

UPRISING [1]

uprising, *5087, stasis* [1]

UPROAR [7]

uproar, *2573, thorybos* [3]
throwing into an uproar, *1752, ektarassō* [1]
uproar, *3199, kraugē* [1]
in an uproar, *5177, syncheō* [1]
uproar, *5180, synchysis* [1]

UPROOTED [2]

uprooted, *1748, ekrizoō* [2]

UPSET [1]

upset, *2571, thorybazō* [1]

UPSTAIRS [5]

upstairs room, *5673, hyperōon* [3]
went upstairs, *326, anabainō* [1]
taken upstairs, *343, anagō* [1]

URBANUS [1]

Urbanus, *4042, Ourbanos* [1]

URGE [21]

urge, *4151, parakaleō* [20]
urge, *4147, paraineō* [1]

URGED [12]

urged, *4151, parakaleō* [6]
urged, *2263, erōtaō* [3]
urged, *3306, legō* [1]
urged strongly, *4128, parabiazomai* [1]
urged, *4275, peithō* [1]

URGENTLY [2]

urgently, *3552+4498+4155, meta+polys+paraklēsis* [1]
urgently requested, *4151+160, parakaleō+aiteō* [1]

URGING [1]

urging, *3458, martyromai* [1]

URIAH'S [1]

Uriah's, *4043, Ourias* [1]

US [481]

us, *1609, egō* [365]
us, *AIT* [59]
us, *RPE* [50]
us, *NIG* [3]
is one of us, *199+3552+1609, akoloutheō+meta+egō* [1]
us, *2466, hēmeteros* [1]

us, *3836, ho* [1]
us^s, *6034, psychē* [1]

USE [24]

use, *NIG* [4]
use, *5968, chraomai* [4]
use^s, *3582, metreō* [3]
use, *AIT* [1]
use, *712, apochrēsis* [1]
common use, *871, atimia* [1]
use, *1328, dia* [1]
use, *1666, ek* [1]
constant use, *2011, hexis* [1]
use, *2400, echō* [1]
use up, *2934, katargeō* [1]
make use of, *2974, katachraomai* [1]
use language, *3281, laleō* [1]
use force, *3552+1040, meta+bia* [1]
use, *4344+1877, peripateō+en* [1]
use, *5502, tithēmi* [1]

USED [20]

used, *AIT* [14]
used to, *4537, pote* [2]
used, *NIG* [1]
used, *1181, ginomai* [1]
used, *3306, legō* [1]
used, *5968, chraomai* [1]

USEFUL [5]

useful, *2378, euchrēstos* [2]
useful, *19, agathos* [1]
useful, *2310, euthetos* [1]
useful, *6068, ōphelimos* [1]

USELESS [6]

useless, *3031, kenos* [2]
useless, *543, anōphelēs* [1]
useless, *734, argos* [1]
useless, *947, achrēstos* [1]
useless, *3469, mataios* [1]

USES [1]

uses, *5968, chraomai* [1]

USING [7]

using, *AIT* [3]
using, *NIG* [1]
using, *1328+5931, dia+cheir* [1]
using, *1639, eimi* [1]
using argument, *3306, legō* [1]

USUAL [2]

as usual, *2848+3836+1621, kata+ho+ethos* [1]
as usual, *2848+3836+899, kata+ho+autos* [1]

USUALLY [1]

what usually did, *2777, kathōs* [1]

UTTER [2]

utter, *2243, ereugomai* [1]
utter, *3281, laleō* [1]

UTTERLY [2]

utterly amazed, *2014+2513,*
   existēmi+thaumazō [1]
utterly, *2848+5651, kata+hyperbolē* [1]

UTTERS [1]

utters, *3281, laleō* [1]

UZZIAH [2]

Uzziah, *3852, Ozias* [2]

VAIN [8]

in vain, *3031, kenos* [2]
vain, *3031, kenos* [2]
in vain, *3472, matēn* [2]
in vain, *1632, eikē* [1]
vain conceit, *3029, kenodoxia* [1]

VALID [5]

valid, *239, alēthēs* [5]

VALLEY [2]

valley, *5754, pharanx* [1]
valley, *5929, cheimarros* [1]

VALUABLE [4]

more valuable than, *1422, diapherō* [1]
valuable than, *1422, diapherō* [1]
valuable, *1422, diapherō* [1]
valuable, *5508, timios* [1]

VALUE [14]

value, *6067, ōpheleō* [4]
value, *5507, timē* [2]
value, *6068, ōphelimos* [2]
value, *2710, ischyō* [1]
no value, *3033, kenoō* [1]
value, *4458, ploutos* [1]
great value, *4501, polytimos* [1]
value, *5978, chrēsimos* [1]
value, *6066, ōpheleia* [1]

VALUED [2]

valued highly, *1639+1952, eimi+entimos* [1]
highly valued, *3836+5734, ho+hypsēlos* [1]

VANISHED [1]

vanished, *660+608, apollymi+apo* [1]

VANISHES [1]

vanishes, *906, aphanizō* [1]

VARIOUS [10]

in various, *2848, kata* [3]
various, *4476, poikilos* [3]
various, *1427, diaphoros* [1]
various forms, *4476, poikilos* [1]
various kinds, *4476, poikilos* [1]
in various ways, *4502, polytropōs* [1]

VEGETABLES [1]

vegetables, *3303, lachanon* [1]

VEHEMENTLY [1]

vehemently, *2364, eutonōs* [1]

VEIL [4]

veil, *2820, kalymma* [4]

VEILED [2]

veiled, *2821, kalyptō* [2]

VENTURE [2]

venture, *1443+1571, didōmi+heautou* [1]
venture, *5528, tolmaō* [1]

VERDICT [1]

verdict, *3213, krisis* [1]

VERIFY [1]

verify, *2105, epiginōskō* [1]

VERY [93]

very, *NIG* [10]
that very, *1697, ekeinos* [5]
very, *4498, polys* [5]
very, *899, autos* [4]
this very, *4047, houtos* [4]
very little, *1788, elachistos* [3]
very, *3336, lian* [3]
that very, *899, autos* [2]
very small, *1788, elachistos* [2]
very small copper coins, *3321, leptos* [2]
very, *4246, pas* [2]
very day, *4958+2465, sēmeron+hēmera* [2]
very, *5379, sphodra* [2]
very, *AIT* [1]
set apart as very own, *39, hagiazō* [1]
very careful, *209, akribōs* [1]
very well, *209, akribōs* [1]
this very day, *785, arti* [1]
this very, *785, arti* [1]
for this very reason, *899+4047,*
   autos+houtos [1]
the very one, *899, autos* [1]
the very, *899, autos* [1]
these very, *899, autos* [1]
very sleepy, *976+5678, bareō+hypnos* [1]
very expensive, *988, barytimos* [1]
very well, *1019, beltiōn* [1]
very religious, *1273, deisidaimōn* [1]
for that very reason, *1328+4047, dia+houtos* [1]
for this very reason, *1328+4047, dia+houtos* [1]
his very self, *1571, heautou* [1]
care very little, *1650+1788+1639,*
   eis+elachistos+eimi [1]
this very reason, *1650+4047, eis+houtos* [1]
very while, *2285+4012+4012,*
   eti+hosos+hosos [1]
very early in the morning, *2317+4745,*
   euthys¹+prōi [1]
very gladly, *2452, hēdeōs* [1]
very well, *2822, kalōs* [1]
very, *3436, malista* [1]
very, *3437, mallon* [1]
very, *3489, megas* [1]
very great, *3492, megistos* [1]
very, *3530, mentoi* [1]
before very long, *3552+4024+4498,*
   meta+ou+polys [1]
very rarely, *3660, molis* [1]
the very, *3836, ho* [1]
this very, *3836, ho* [1]
very early in the morning, *3986+960,*
   orthros+bathys [1]
the very fact that, *4022, hoti* [1]
that very, *4047, houtos* [1]
these very, *4047, houtos* [1]
very sad, *4337, perilypos* [1]
his very own, *4342, periousios* [1]
very, *4358, perissoteros* [1]
very large, *4498, polys* [1]
very expensive, *4500, polytelēs* [1]
get very far, *4621+2093+4498,*
   prokoptō+epi+polys [1]
your very self, *4932, seautou* [1]
very heart, *5073, splanchnon* [1]
very end, *5333, synteleia* [1]
very soon, *5441, tacheōs* [1]
very precious, *5508, timios* [1]

VICINITY [6]

vicinity, *3990, horion* [5]

vicinity of, *4639, pros* [1]

VICTOR'S [1]

receive the victor's crown, *5110, stephanoō* [1]

VICTORIOUS [1]

victorious, *3771, nikaō* [1]

VICTORY [5]

victory, *3777, nikos* [4]
victory, *3772, nikē* [1]

VIEW [8]

view, *NIG* [1]
in view of, *1328, dia* [1]
in full view of, *1869, emprosthen* [1]
in full view, *1967, enōpion* [1]
from human point of view, *2848+476, kata+anthrōpos* [1]
worldly point of view, *4922, sarx* [1]
take a view of things, *5858, phroneō* [1]
take view, *5858, phroneō* [1]

VIEWPOINT [1]

viewpoint, *AIT* [1]

VIEWS [1]

views are, *5858, phroneō* [1]

VIGOROUSLY [2]

argued vigorously, *1372, diamachomai* [1]
vigorously, *2364, eutonōs* [1]

VILE [3]

vile, *1009, bdelyssomai* [1]
vile, *4862, rhypainō* [1]
vile, *4865, rhyparos* [1]

VILLAGE [21]

village, *3267, kōmē* [16]
from village to village, *2848+3836+3267, kata+ho+kōmē* [2]
from village to village, *3267+3241, kōmē+kyklō* [2]
village, *4484, polis* [1]

VILLAGES [9]

villages, *3267, kōmē* [8]
villages, *3268, kōmopolis* [1]

VINDICATED [1]

vindicated, *1467, dikaioō* [1]

VINE [7]

vine, *306, ampelos* [7]

VINEGAR [4]

wine vinegar, *3954, oxos* [4]

VINEYARD [26]

vineyard, *308, ampelōn* [23]
the vineyard's, *899, autos* [2]
took care of the vineyard, *307, ampelourgos* [1]

VIOLATE [1]

violate the law, *4174, paranomeō* [1]

VIOLATION [1]

violation, *4126, parabasis* [1]

VIOLENCE [2]

violence, *1040, bia* [1]
violence, *3996, hormēma* [1]

VIOLENT [9]

violent, *3489, megas* [2]
violent, *4438, plēktēs* [2]
violent, *1042, biaios* [1]
violent, *4498, polys* [1]
such violent, *5380, sphodrōs* [1]
violent man, *5616, hybristēs* [1]
so violent, *5901+3336, chalepos+lian* [1]

VIOLENTLY [2]

violently, *4498, polys* [1]
shook violently, *5057, sparassō* [1]

VIPER [1]

viper, *2399, echidna* [1]

VIPERS [5]

vipers, *2399, echidna* [4]
vipers, *835, aspis* [1]

VIRGIN [9]

virgin, *4221, parthenos* [8]
am a virgin, *467+4024+1182, anēr+ou+ginōskō* [1]

VIRGIN'S [1]

virgin's, *4221, parthenos* [1]

VIRGINS [4]

virgins, *4221, parthenos* [3]
virgins, *RPE* [1]

VIRTUES [1]

virtues, *AIT* [1]

VISIBLE [5]

visible, *5743, phainō* [2]
visible, *3971, horatos* [1]
makes visible, *5746, phaneroō* [1]
visible, *5746, phaneroō* [1]

VISION [14]

vision, *3969, horama* [8]
vision, *3965, optasia* [3]
had a vision, *3969+3972, horama+horaō* [1]
vision, *3969+3972, horama+horaō* [1]
vision, *3970, horasis* [1]

VISIONS [2]

visions, *3965, optasia* [1]
visions, *3970, horasis* [1]

VISIT [21]

visit, *AIT* [6]
visit, *2170, episkeptomai* [2]
visit, *1181+4639, ginomai+pros* [1]
visit on the way, *1328, dia* [1]
visit on way, *1328+1451, dia+dierchomai* [1]
visit, *1658, eisodos* [1]
make visit, *2262, erchomai* [1]
visit, *2262+4639, erchomai+pros* [1]
visit, *2262, erchomai* [1]
visit, *2517, theaomai* [1]
visit, *3972, horaō* [1]
passing visit, *4227, parodos* [1]
visit, *4601+1650, proerchomai+eis* [1]
visit, *4639+2262, pros+erchomai* [1]

visit, *4665, proserchomai* [1]

VISITED [2]

visited, *2262+1650, erchomai+eis* [1]
visited, *2262+4639, erchomai+pros* [1]

VISITOR [1]

visitor to, *4228, paroikeō* [1]

VISITORS [1]

visitors, *2111, epidēmeō* [1]

VISITS [1]

visits, *2175, episkopē* [1]

VOICE [92]

voice, *5889, phōnē* [85]
called out in a loud voice, *149+5889, airō+phōnē* [1]
a loud voice, *3189, krazō* [1]
voice, *3199, kraugē* [1]
with one voice, *4101, pamplēthei* [1]
voice, *5782, phthongos* [1]
at the top of voice, *5889+3489, phōnē+megas* [1]
shouting at the top of voice, *5889+3489+3306, phōnē+megas+legō* [1]

VOICES [6]

voices, *5889, phōnē* [5]
at the top of voices, *5889+3489, phōnē+megas* [1]

VOLUNTARILY [2]

not voluntarily, *220, akōn* [1]
voluntarily, *1776, hekōn* [1]

VOMIT [1]

vomit, *2000, exerama* [1]

VOTE [1]

vote, *6029, psēphos* [1]

VOUCH [1]

vouch, *3455, martyreō* [1]

VOW [2]

vow, *2376, euchē* [2]

VOYAGE [2]

voyage, *4452, ploos* [2]

VULTURES [2]

vultures, *108, aetos* [2]

WAGE [1]

wage war, *5129, strateuomai* [1]

WAGES [14]

wages, *3635, misthos* [7]
a day's wages, *1324, dēnarion* [2]
a year's wages, *1324+5559, dēnarion+triakosioi* [1]
eight months of a man's wages, *1324+1357, dēnarion+diakosioi* [1]
eight months wages, *1357+1324, diakosioi+dēnarion* [1]
wages, *4072, opsōnion* [1]
the money worth a year's wages, *5559+1324, triakosioi+dēnarion* [1]

WAGING   [1]

waging war against, *529, antistrateuomai* [1]

WAIL   [2]

wail, *3081, klaiō* [1]
wail, *3909, ololyzō* [1]

WAILED   [1]

wailed for, *2577, thrēneō* [1]

WAILING   [4]

wailing, *3081, klaiō* [3]
wailing, *226, alalazō* [1]

WAIST   [4]

waist, *4019, osphys* [2]
wrapped around waist, *3284+1346,
   lambanō+diazōnnymi* [1]
buckled around waist, *4322, perizōnnymi* [1]

WAIT   [17]

wait on, *1354, diakoneō* [6]
wait for, *4657, prosdechomai* [2]
wait, *NIG* [1]
wait for, *388, anamenō* [1]
wait, *399, anapauō* [1]
eagerly wait for, *587, apekdechomai* [1]
wait eagerly for, *587, apekdechomai* [1]
wait for, *587, apekdechomai* [1]
wait for, *1683, ekdechomai* [1]
wait, *2705, histēmi* [1]
wait for, *4338, perimenō* [1]

WAITED   [2]

waited, *587, apekdechomai* [1]
waited for, *3531, menō* [1]

WAITING   [16]

waiting for, *4657, prosdechomai* [5]
waiting, *NIG* [1]
waiting for, *587, apekdechomai* [1]
waiting for, *1683, ekdechomai* [1]
waiting in ambush for, *1910, enedreuō* [1]
waiting, *1910, enedreuō* [1]
waiting, *2426, zēteō* [1]
waiting patiently, *3428, makrothymeō* [1]
waiting for, *3516, mellō* [1]
waiting expectantly, *4659, prosdokaō* [1]
waiting for, *4659, prosdokaō* [1]
waiting, *4659, prosdokaō* [1]

WAITS   [4]

waits, *587, apekdechomai* [1]
waits for, *1683, ekdechomai* [1]
waits, *1683, ekdechomai* [1]
waits, *2705, histēmi* [1]

WAKE   [5]

wake up, *1586, egeirō* [2]
wake up, *1181+1213, ginomai+grēgoreō* [1]
wake up, *1213, grēgoreō* [1]
wake up, *2030, exypnizō* [1]

WALK   [31]

walk, *4344, peripateō* [25]
walk around, *4344, peripateō* [2]
Sabbath day's walk from,
   *1584+4879+2400+3847,
   engys+sabbaton+echō+hodos* [1]
walk among, *1853, emperipateō* [1]
walk along, *4344, peripateō* [1]
walk, *5123, stoicheō* [1]

WALKED   [12]

walked, *4344, peripateō* [3]
walked around, *1451, dierchomai* [1]
walked right through, *1451+1328+3545,
   dierchomai+dia+mesos* [1]
walked out, *2002, exerchomai* [1]
walked along, *3847+4472, hodos+poieō* [1]
walked along, *4135, paragō* [1]
walked beside, *4135+4123, paragō+para* [1]
walked around, *4344, peripateō* [1]
walked, *4601, proerchomai* [1]
walked along with, *5233, symporeuomai* [1]

WALKING   [17]

walking, *4344, peripateō* [14]
walking around, *4344, peripateō* [1]
walking away, *4513, poreuomai* [1]
walking, *4513, poreuomai* [1]

WALKS   [5]

walks, *4344, peripateō* [4]
walks around, *4344, peripateō* [1]

WALL   [10]

wall, *5446, teichos* [6]
wall, *5850, phragmos* [2]
dividing wall, *3546, mesotoichon* [1]
wall, *5526, toichos* [1]

WALLOWING   [1]

wallowing, *3243, kylismos* [1]

WALLS   [4]

walls, *5446, teichos* [3]
walls, *AIT* [1]

WANDER   [2]

wander off, *4414, planaō* [1]
wander, *4414, planaō* [1]

WANDERED   [7]

wandered off, *4414, planaō* [2]
wandered from, *675+608, apoplanaō+apo* [1]
wandered away, *846, astocheō* [1]
wandered, *846, astocheō* [1]
wandered away from, *1762, ektrepō* [1]
wandered, *4414, planaō* [1]

WANDERING   [1]

wandering, *4417, planētēs* [1]

WANDERS   [1]

wanders away, *4414, planaō* [1]

WANT   [127]

want, *2527, thelō* [74]
want, *AIT* [14]
want, *1089, boulomai* [9]
want, *2426, zēteō* [5]
want, *2671, hina* [5]
what do want with, *5515+2779, tis+kai* [5]
want, *NIG* [2]
want, *RPE* [2]
want, *2121, epithymeō* [2]
want, *546, axioō* [1]
want, *1639, eimi* [1]
want to bring up, *2118, epizēteō* [1]
want, *2400, echō* [1]
want, *2525, thelēma* [1]
want to, *2527, thelō* [1]
have all you want, *3170+1639,
   korennymi+eimi* [1]

living in want, *5728, hystereō* [1]
eat all want, *5963, chortazō* [1]

WANTED   [32]

wanted, *2527, thelō* [17]
wanted, *1089, boulomai* [9]
wanted, *AIT* [1]
wanted, *2118, epizēteō* [1]
wanted, *2426, zēteō* [1]
wanted, *2525, thelēma* [1]
eaten as much as wanted, *3170+5575,
   korennymi+trophē* [1]
wanted, *4606, prothesis* [1]

WANTING   [9]

wanting, *2527, thelō* [3]
wanting, *1089, boulomai* [2]
wanting, *2426, zēteō* [2]
wanting, *3516, mellō* [2]

WANTS   [26]

wants, *2527, thelō* [19]
wants, *NIG* [1]
wants, *1089, boulomai* [1]
wants, *1506, dokeō* [1]
wants, *2426, zēteō* [1]
wants, *2525, thelēma* [1]
wants to, *2527, thelō* [1]
wants, *2671, hina* [1]

WAR   [11]

war, *4483, polemos* [4]
make war, *4482, polemeō* [2]
waging war against, *529, antistrateuomai* [1]
makes war, *4482, polemeō* [1]
wage war, *5129, strateuomai* [1]
war, *5129, strateuomai* [1]
go war, *5202+4483, symballō+polemos* [1]

WARM   [2]

keep warm, *2548, thermainō* [1]
warm, *2548, thermainō* [1]

WARMED   [1]

warmed, *2548, thermainō* [1]

WARMING   [3]

warming, *2548, thermainō* [3]

WARMLY   [2]

warmly, *830, asmenōs* [1]
warmly, *4498, polys* [1]

WARN   [10]

warn, *3805, noutheteō* [3]
warn, *1371, diamartyromai* [2]
warn, *RPE* [1]
warn, *580, apeileō* [1]
warn, *3455, martyreō* [1]
warn, *3804, nouthesia* [1]
warn, *4625, prolegō* [1]

WARNED   [16]

warned, *5976, chrēmatizō* [5]
warned, *1371, diamartyromai* [2]
warned, *2203, epitimaō* [2]
warned, *5683, hypodeiknymi* [2]
warned, *1403, diastellō* [1]
warned sternly, *1839, embrimaomai* [1]
strictly warned, *2203+4133,
   epitimaō+parangellō* [1]
warned, *3306, legō* [1]

warned, *4147, paraineō* [1]

WARNING [6]

strong warning, *1839, embrimaomai* [1]
warning, *2203, epitimaō* [1]
without warning, *2779+2627, kai+idou* [1]
warning, *3805, noutheteō* [1]
already gave warning, *4625, prolegō* [1]
warning, *5832, phobos* [1]

WARNINGS [1]

warnings, *3804, nouthesia* [1]

WARNS [2]

warns, *RPE* [1]
warns, *1371, diamartyromai* [1]

WARPED [1]

warped, *1750, ekstrephō* [1]

WARRANTED [1]

more than is warranted, *5642, hyper* [1]

WARS [5]

wars, *4483, polemos* [5]

WAS [1363]

was, *AIT* [706]
was, *1639, eimi* [300]
was, *NIG* [226]
was, *1181, ginomai* [54]
was, *2400, echō* [10]
was, *5639, hyparchō* [10]
was, *RPE* [8]
whose mother was, *1666, ek* [3]
was, *4472, poieō* [3]
that was why, *1328+4047, dia+houtos* [2]
what was promised, *3836+2039,*
   ho+epangelia [2]
was, *4398, pimplēmi* [2]
was there ever, *5515, tis* [2]
what sin was, *281, hamartia* [1]
was from, *600+608, apechō+apo* [1]
was, *600, apechō* [1]
was from, *608+600, apo+apechō* [1]
when no was present, *868, ater* [1]
was filled with, *1181, ginomai* [1]
was going on, *1181, ginomai* [1]
was over, *1335, diaginomai* [1]
was present, *1639, eimi* [1]
was, *1639+1181, eimi+ginomai* [1]
that was the time, *1877+3836+2465+1697,*
   en+ho+hēmera+ekeinos [1]
while it was still dark, *1939, ennychos* [1]
was promised, *2039, epangelia* [1]
what was promised, *2039, epangelia* [1]
was, *2351, heuriskō* [1]
was, *2392, ephistēmi* [1]
was, *2527, thelō* [1]
was there, *2705, histēmi* [1]
as was, *2848, kata* [1]
was, *3023, keimai* [1]
what was preached, *3060, kērygma* [1]
man who was deaf, *3273, kōphos* [1]
was to, *3516, mellō* [1]
was, *3516, mellō* [1]
all they asked was, *3667, monon* [1]
law was given, *3793, nomotheteō* [1]
was getting nowhere, *4029+6067,*
   oudeis+ōpheleō [1]
was with, *4205, pareimi* [1]
was, *4205, pareimi* [1]
was, *4444, plēroō* [1]

was[s], *4472, poieō* [1]
was written about, *4592, prographō* [1]
seeing what was ahead, *4632, prooraō* [1]
was, *5201, symbainō* [1]
end was near, *5462, teleutaō* [1]

WASH [15]

wash, *3782, niptō* [10]
wash, *966, baptizō* [2]
wash away, *666, apolouō* [1]
wash, *2751, katharizō* [1]
wash, *4459, plynō* [1]

WASHED [11]

washed, *3374, louō* [4]
washed, *3782, niptō* [4]
washed, *666, apolouō* [1]
washed, *672, aponiptō* [1]
washed, *4459, plynō* [1]

WASHING [9]

washing, *3782, niptō* [3]
ceremonial washing, *2752, katharismos* [2]
washing, *3373, loutron* [2]
washing, *968, baptismos* [1]
washing, *4459, plynō* [1]

WASHINGS [1]

ceremonial washings, *968, baptismos* [1]

WASN'T [2]

wasn't, *4024, ou* [1]
wasn't, *5639, hyparchō* [1]

WASTE [2]

waste, *724+1181, apōleia+ginomai* [1]
waste, *724, apōleia* [1]

WASTED [2]

wasted, *660, apollymi* [1]
wasted, *1632, eikē* [1]

WASTING [2]

wasting, *1399, diaskorpizō* [1]
wasting away, *1425, diaphtheirō* [1]

WATCH [36]

keep watch, *1213, grēgoreō* [8]
watch out, *1063, blepō* [6]
watch, *1213, grēgoreō* [3]
watch, *5871, phylakē* [2]
keep watch, *70, agrypneō* [1]
on the watch, *70, agrypneō* [1]
watch out for, *1063, blepō* [1]
watch out, *1063+1571, blepō+heautou* [1]
kept watch, *1213, grēgoreō* [1]
watch closely, *2091, epechō* [1]
watch out, *3972, horaō* [1]
keeping a close watch, *4190, paratēreō* [1]
kept close watch on, *4190, paratēreō* [1]
keep watch over, *4668, prosechō* [1]
watch out, *4668, prosechō* [1]
watch, *4668, prosechō* [1]
watch out for, *5023, skopeō* [1]
watch, *5023, skopeō* [1]
kept watch over, *5498, tēreō* [1]
watch of the night, *5871, phylakē* [1]
keeping watch, *5875+5871,*
   phylassō+phylakē [1]

WATCHED [10]

watched for, *2426, zēteō* [3]

watched, *3972, horaō* [3]
watched closely, *4190, paratēreō* [2]
watched, *2555, theōreō* [1]
carefully watched, *4190, paratēreō* [1]

WATCHFUL [1]

watchful, *1213, grēgoreō* [1]

WATCHING [6]

watching, *2555, theōreō* [3]
watching, *1213, grēgoreō* [1]
watching for, *2426, zēteō* [1]
watching, *3972, horaō* [1]

WATCHMAN [1]

watchman, *2601, thyrōros* [1]

WATCHTOWER [2]

watchtower, *4788, pyrgos* [2]

WATER [79]

water, *5623, hydōr* [65]
water, *2498, thalassa* [2]
water, *AIT* [1]
water, *RPE* [1]
draw water, *533, antleō* [1]
without water, *536, anydros* [1]
deep water, *958, bathos* [1]
fresh water, *1184, glykys* [1]
salt water, *4395, pikros* [1]
give water, *4540, potizō* [1]
gives water to, *4540, potizō* [1]
water jars, *5620, hydria* [1]
water jar, *5620, hydria* [1]
drinking only water, *5621, hydropoteō* [1]

WATER'S [2]

water's edge, *2498, thalassa* [1]
water's, *3349, limnē* [1]

WATERED [1]

watered, *4540, potizō* [1]

WATERS [14]

waters, *5623, hydōr* [10]
waters, *4540, potizō* [2]
waters, *2498, thalassa* [1]
these waters[s], *4005, hos* [1]

WAVE [1]

wave, *3114, klydōn* [1]

WAVER [1]

waver, *1359, diakrinō* [1]

WAVES [9]

waves, *2498, thalassa* [4]
waves, *3246, kyma* [4]
tossed back and forth by the waves, *3115,*
   klydōnizomai [1]

WAY [218]

way, *3847, hodos* [50]
way, *AIT* [23]
in the same way, *4048, houtōs* [11]
in the same way, *3931, homoiōs* [10]
in this way, *4048, houtōs* [8]
in the same way, *6058, hōsautōs* [6]
way, *NIG* [5]
way of life, *419, anastrophē* [4]
on way, *4513, poreuomai* [4]
way, *5573, tropos* [4]

looked for a way, *2426, zēteō* [3]
in the ordinary way, *2848+4922, kata+sarx* [2]
in the same way, *4048+2779, houtōs+kai* [2]
that way, *4048, houtōs* [2]
this way, *4048, houtōs* [2]
went on way, *4513, poreuomai* [2]
send on way, *4636, propempō* [2]
some way, *4802, pōs* [2]
way of life, *73, agōgē* [1]
other way, *249, allachothen* [1]
in a way worthy, *547, axiōs* [1]
on their way, *599, aperchomai* [1]
done in ungodly way, *814, asebeō* [1]
in same way, *899, autos* [1]
same way, *899, autos* [1]
forcing way, *1041, biazō* [1]
way lived, *1052, biōsis* [1]
visit on the way, *1328, dia* [1]
visit on way, *1328+1451, dia+dierchomai* [1]
sly way, *1515, dolos* [1]
on way home, *1639+5715, eimi+hypostrephō* [1]
in this way, *1650+3836, eis+ho* [1]
way out, *1676, ekbasis* [1]
sent on way, *1734, ekpempō* [1]
worm way, *1905, endynō* [1]
on way back, *2056, epanagō* [1]
gave way, *2113, epididōmi* [1]
made their way, *2262, erchomai* [1]
on his way, *2262, erchomai* [1]
on their way, *2262, erchomai* [1]
on way in, 2262, *erchomai* [1]
on way, 2262, *erchomai* [1]
made$ that way, *2336+2335, eunouchos+eunouchizō* [1]
way opened for, *2338, euodoō* [1]
all the way, *2401, heōs* [1]
that way, *2777, kathōs* [1]
new way, *2786, kainotēs* [1]
fine way, *2822, kalōs* [1]
in any way, *2848+3594+5573, kata+mēdeis+tropos* [1]
in the way, *2848, kata* [1]
in this way$, *2848+4922, kata+sarx* [1]
orderly way, *2848+5423, kata+taxis* [1]
on the way, *2849, katabainō* [1]
way live, *2949, katastēma* [1]
the same way$, *3210, krima* [1]
way treated$, *3210, krima* [1]
long way off, *3426, makran* [1]
way, *3545, mesos* [1]
all the way to, *3588, mechri* [1]
any way, *3594, mēdeis* [1]
not any way, *3594, mēdeis* [1]
any way, *3836+5515, ho+tis* [1]
way of life, *3847, hodos* [1]
in the same way, *4005+5573, hos+tropos* [1]
no way, *4029, oudeis* [1]
this way, *4047+4246, houtos+pas* [1]
in this same way, *4048+2779, houtōs+kai* [1]
in such a way, *4048, houtōs* [1]
in way, *4048, houtōs* [1]
the way, *4048, houtōs* [1]
this is the way, *4048, houtōs* [1]
this the way, *4048, houtōs* [1]
old way, *4095, palaiotēs* [1]
in every way, *4118, pantē* [1]
the way act, *4344, peripateō* [1]
a way, *4481, poios* [1]
way, *4512, poreia* [1]
continued on way, *4513, poreuomai* [1]
go on way, *4513, poreuomai* [1]
way, *4513, poreuomai* [1]
long way off, *4522, porrō* [1]
leading the way, *4575, proagō* [1]
led the way, *4575, proagō* [1]

help on way, *4636, propempō* [1]
send on their way, *4636, propempō* [1]
sent on way, *4636, propempō* [1]
give way, *4766, ptoēsis* [1]
way, *4802, pōs* [1]
in some way, *4803, pōs* [1]
on way, *5632, hypagō* [1]
the way, *5679, hypo* [1]
the same way, *6055+2779, hōs+kai* [1]
the same way, *6058, hōsautōs* [1]
the way, *6061, hōsper* [1]

WAYS [19]

ways, *AIT* [9]
ways, *3847, hodos* [5]
ways, *172, aiōn* [1]
ways, *2240, ergon* [1]
ways$, *3836, ho* [1]
in various ways, *4502, polytropōs* [1]
wicked ways, *4504, ponēria* [1]

WE [943]

we, *AIT* [690]
we, *1609, egō* [177]
we, *RPE* [61]
we, *3836, ho* [5]
we, *899, autos* [3]
we, *NIG* [1]
we, *1571, heautou* [1]
we are, *1609, egō* [1]
what$ we are writing, *3836+899, ho+autos* [1]
faith we profess, *3934, homologia* [1]
we, *4015, hostis* [1]
what shall we do, *5515+4036+1639, tis+oun+eimi* [1]

WE'LL [1]

we'll, *1609, egō* [1]

WE'RE [2]

we're, *AIT* [2]

WE'VE [1]

we've, *AIT* [1]

WEAK [30]

weak, *822, asthenēs* [14]
weak, *820, astheneō* [11]
weak, *819, astheneia* [2]
weak, *105, adynatos* [1]
feel weak, *820, astheneō* [1]
weak, *4168, paralyō* [1]

WEAK-WILLED [1]

weak-willed women, *1220, gynaikarion* [1]

WEAKENED [1]

weakened, *820, astheneō* [1]

WEAKENING [1]

weakening, *820, astheneō* [1]

WEAKER [2]

weaker, *822, asthenēs* [2]

WEAKNESS [9]

weakness, *819, astheneia* [8]
weakness, *822, asthenēs* [1]

WEAKNESSES [4]

weaknesses, *819, astheneia* [4]

WEALTH [18]

wealth, *4458, ploutos* [6]
wealth, *3228, ktēma* [2]
wealth, *3440, mamōnas* [2]
wealth, *4355, perisseuō* [2]
hoarded wealth, *2564, thēsaurizō* [1]
wealth, *4045, ousia* [1]
wealth, *4454, plousios* [1]
acquired wealth, *4456, plouteō* [1]
gained wealth, *4456, plouteō* [1]
wealth, *5509, timiotēs* [1]

WEALTHY [1]

wealthy, *4454, plousios* [1]

WEAPONS [4]

weapons, *3960, hoplon* [2]
weapons, *RPE* [1]
weapons fight with, *3960+3836+5127, hoplon+ho+strateia* [1]

WEAR [11]

wear, *4314, periballō* [3]
wear, *1907, endyō* [2]
wear out, *4096, palaioō* [2]
wear, *1877, en* [1]
wear, *5686, hypodeō* [1]
wear out, *5724, hypōpiazō* [1]
wear, *5841, phoreō* [1]

WEARING [8]

wearing, *1907, endyō* [2]
wearing, *5841, phoreō* [2]
wearing nothing, *4314+2093+1218, periballō+epi+gymnos* [1]
wearing, *4314, periballō* [1]
wearing, *4324, perithesis* [1]
wearing a gold ring, *5993, chrysodaktylios* [1]

WEARY [5]

weary, *3159, kopiaō* [2]
become weary, *1591, enkakeō* [1]
weary, *1601, enkoptō* [1]
weary, *2827, kamnō* [1]

WEATHER [1]

fair weather, *2304, eudia* [1]

WEDDING [13]

wedding, *1141, gamos* [6]
wedding banquet, *1141, gamos* [5]
wedding feast, *1141, gamos* [1]
wedding hall, *1141, gamos* [1]

WEED [1]

weed, *5198, syllegō* [1]

WEEDS [8]

weeds, *2429, zizanion* [8]

WEEK [12]

week, *4879, sabbaton* [9]
week, *2465+2231, hēmera+hepta* [1]
a week later, *3552+2465+3893, meta+hēmera+oktō* [1]
Passover Week, *4247, pascha* [1]

WEEP [10]

weep, *3081, klaiō* [10]

WEEPING [15]

weeping, *3088, klauthmos* [7]
weeping, *3081, klaiō* [5]
weeping for, *3081, klaiō* [1]
weeping, *3836+3088, ho+klauthmos* [1]
weeping, *4472+3081, poieō+klaiō* [1]

WEIGH [1]

weigh carefully, *1359, diakrinō* [1]

WEIGHED [2]

weighed anchor, *149, airō* [1]
weighed down, *976, bareō* [1]

WEIGHTIER [1]

weightier than, *3505, meizōn* [1]

WEIGHTY [1]

weighty, *987, barys* [1]

WELCOME [14]

welcome, *1312, dechomai* [7]
welcome, *RPE* [1]
welcome, *622, apodechomai* [1]
welcome into, *1658+1650, eisodos+eis* [1]
welcome, *2110, epidechomai* [1]
welcome, *4657, prosdechomai* [1]
welcome, *4689, proslambanō* [1]
welcome, *5897+3306, chairō+legō* [1]

WELCOMED [17]

welcomed, *1312, dechomai* [7]
welcomed, *622, apodechomai* [3]
welcomed home, *346, anadechomai* [1]
welcomed, *832, aspazomai* [1]
welcomed, *1312+3552+1645,*
   dechomai+meta+eirēnē [1]
welcomed, *4138, paradechomai* [1]
welcomed, *4689, proslambanō* [1]
welcomed into house, *5685, hypodechomai* [1]
welcomed, *5685, hypodechomai* [1]

WELCOMES [11]

welcomes, *1312, dechomai* [9]
welcomes, *3306+5897, legō+chairō* [1]
welcomes, *4657, prosdechomai* [1]

WELFARE [1]

welfare, *3836+4309, ho+peri* [1]

WELL [83]

well, *2822, kalōs* [12]
as well, *2779, kai* [9]
as well as, *2779, kai* [6]
well pleased, *2305, eudokeō* [5]
well, *5618, hygiēs* [4]
well, *NIG* [3]
well, *5853, phrear* [3]
well, *AIT* [2]
well done, *2292, eu* [2]
well, *2292, eu* [2]
and as well, *2779, kai* [2]
spoke well of, *3455, martyreō* [2]
well, *4380, pēgē* [2]
well along, *4581, probainō* [2]
well fed, *5963, chortazō* [2]
very well, *209, akribōs* [1]
well, *209, akribōs* [1]
very well, *1019, beltiōn* [1]
well acquainted with, *1195, gnōstēs* [1]
well fed, *1855, empimplēmi* [1]
wish well, *1877+1645, en+eirēnē* [1]

well aware, *2179, epistamai* [1]
well done, *2301, euge* [1]
go well, *2338, euodoō* [1]
is getting along well, *2338, euodoō* [1]
well, *2623, ide* [1]
as well as, *2777, kathōs* [1]
well said, *2822, kalōs* [1]
very well, *2822, kalōs* [1]
speak well of, *3455, martyreō* [1]
spoke well, *3455, martyreō* [1]
well known, *3455, martyreō* [1]
well spoken of, *3455, martyreō* [1]
and as well, *3552, meta* [1]
well then, *4036, oun* [1]
made well, *5392, sōzō* [1]
make well, *5392, sōzō* [1]
well, *5617, hygiainō* [1]
made well, *5618, hygiēs* [1]
well known, *5745, phaneros* [1]

WELLED [1]

welled up, *4355, perisseuō* [1]

WELLING [1]

welling up, *256, hallomai* [1]

WENT [356]

went, *2262, erchomai* [45]
went out, *2002, exerchomai* [38]
went, *599, aperchomai* [24]
went up, *326, anabainō* [23]
went, *4513, poreuomai* [22]
went away, *599, aperchomai* [18]
went into, *1656+1650, eiserchomai+eis* [13]
went down, *2849, katabainō* [13]
went to, *4665, proserchomai* [8]
went in, *1656, eiserchomai* [7]
went, *2002, exerchomai* [6]
went, *AIT* [5]
went back, *599, aperchomai* [5]
went off, *599, aperchomai* [5]
went, *326, anabainō* [4]
went to, *1656+1650, eiserchomai+eis* [4]
went down, *2982, katerchomai* [4]
went, *NIG* [3]
went inside, *1656+1650, eiserchomai+eis* [3]
went, *1656, eiserchomai* [3]
went back, *2262, erchomai* [3]
went out, *2262, erchomai* [3]
went, *4665, proserchomai* [3]
went up, *456, anerchomai* [2]
went out, *599, aperchomai* [2]
went away on a journey, *623, apodēmeō* [2]
went, *1181, ginomai* [2]
went, *1451, dierchomai* [2]
went into, *1656, eiserchomai* [2]
went out from, *1666+2002, ek+exerchomai* [2]
went on, *2002, exerchomai* [2]
went out of, *2002, exerchomai* [2]
went up, *2262, erchomai* [2]
went, *2982, katerchomai* [2]
went on, *4135, paragō* [2]
went on way, *4513, poreuomai* [2]
went out, *4513, poreuomai* [2]
went ahead of, *4575, proagō* [2]
went on ahead, *4601, proerchomai* [2]
went, *5632, hypagō* [2]
went out to meet, *5636, hypantaō* [2]
went, *RPE* [1]
went with, *199, akoloutheō* [1]
went to defense, *310, amynomai* [1]
went upstairs, *326, anabainō* [1]
went back, *418, anastrephō* [1]
went, *583, apeimi²* [1]
went up, *599, aperchomai* [1]

went away, *623, apodēmeō* [1]
went on journey, *623, apodēmeō* [1]
went on, *806, archō* [1]
went on, *1181, ginomai* [1]
went through, *1388, diaporeuomai* [1]
went around, *1451, dierchomai* [1]
went on, *1451+4134,*
   dierchomai+paraginomai [1]
went through, *1451, dierchomai* [1]
went, *1639, eimi* [1]
went into, *1650+1656, eis+eiserchomai* [1]
went to, *1655+1650, eiseimi+eis* [1]
went, *1655, eiseimi* [1]
went back into, *1656+1650,*
   eiserchomai+eis [1]
went inside, *1656, eiserchomai* [1]
went into, *1660+1650, eisporeuomai+eis* [1]
went in, *1660, eisporeuomai* [1]
went to, *1660+1650, eisporeuomai+eis* [1]
went out from, *1744, ekporeuomai* [1]
went out, *1744, ekporeuomai* [1]
went, *1744, ekporeuomai* [1]
went out, *2002+2032, exerchomai+exō* [1]
went through, *2002, exerchomai* [1]
went on board, *2094, epibainō* [1]
went on, *2262, erchomai* [1]
went, *2849, katabainō* [1]
went on, *3306, legō* [1]
went on, *3553, metabainō* [1]
went along, *4135, paragō* [1]
went along, *4182, paraporeuomai* [1]
went around, *4310, periagō* [1]
went through, *4310, periagō* [1]
went, *4310, periagō* [1]
went about, *4320, perierchomai* [1]
went around, *4320, perierchomai* [1]
went around, *4344, peripateō* [1]
went, *4344, peripateō* [1]
went along, *4513, poreuomai* [1]
went ahead, *4575, proagō* [1]
went before, *4596, prodromos* [1]
went over, *4665, proserchomai* [1]
went up to, *4665, proserchomai* [1]
went up, *4665, proserchomai* [1]
went on, *4707, prostithēmi* [1]
heart went out, *5072, splanchnizomai* [1]
went along with, *5233, symporeuomai* [1]
went, *5251, synagō* [1]
went with into, *5291+1650,*
   syneiserchomai+eis [1]
went along, *5302, synerchomai* [1]
went with, *5302, synerchomai* [1]
went away, *5715, hypostrephō* [1]
went back, *5715, hypostrephō* [1]

WEPT [9]

wept, *3081, klaiō* [5]
wept and wept, *3081+4498, klaiō+polys* [2]
wept, *1233, dakryō* [1]
wept, *2653+3088+1181,*
   hikanos+klauthmos+ginomai [1]

WERE [733]

were, *AIT* [473]
were, *1639, eimi* [129]
were, *NIG* [91]
were, *1181, ginomai* [20]
were, *RPE* [6]
were, *2400, echō* [3]
place where the offerings were put, *1126,*
   gazophylakion [1]
were up, *1639+326, eimi+anabainō* [1]
if that were so, *2075, epei* [1]
if it were, *2075, epei* [1]
were looking for, *2351, heuriskō* [1]

as much as were able, *2848+1539,
    kata+dynamis* [1]
were present, *4205, pareimi* [1]
were, *4537+1639, pote+eimi* [1]
were with, *5289, syneimi¹* [1]
were[s], *5897, chairō* [1]

WEST [5]

west, *1553, dysmē* [5]

WET [2]

wet, *1101, brechō* [2]

WHAT [793]

what, *5515, tis* [221]
what, *3836, ho* [183]
what, *4005, hos* [129]
what, *NIG* [61]
what, *4481, poios* [21]
what, *AIT* [10]
what, *RPE* [9]
what, *247, alla* [7]
what, *4012, hosos* [6]
what, *4047, houtos* [6]
this is what, *4048, houtōs* [6]
what is right, *1466, dikaiosynē* [5]
what do want with, *5515+2779, tis+kai* [5]
what is good, *2819, kalos* [4]
what[s], *3836+4839, ho+rhēma* [4]
what kind of, *4534, potapos* [4]
what, *4005+1569, hos+ean* [3]
what, *4802, pōs* [3]
what heard, *198, akoē* [2]
deposit guaranteeing what is to come, *775,
    arrabōn* [2]
what eat, *1109, brōma* [2]
what he did, *2240, ergon* [2]
what, *2777, kathōs* [2]
what desires[s], *3836, ho* [2]
what was promised, *3836+2039,
    ho+epangelia* [2]
what[s], *3836+2240, ho+ergon* [2]
what kind of, *4481, poios* [2]
do what is right, *16, agathopoieō* [1]
does what is good, *16, agathopoieō* [1]
what is more, *247+3529+2779,
    alla+menounge+kai* [1]
what counts[s], *247, alla* [1]
what counts, *247, alla* [1]
what is sinful, *281, hamartia* [1]
what sin was, *281, hamartia* [1]
what is shameful, *1007, bdelygma* [1]
what he has and does, *1050, bios* [1]
explained what said, *1450, diermēneuō* [1]
what if, *1623, ei* [1]
what, *1623+5516, ei+tis* [1]
what, *1650+5515, eis+tis* [1]
what, *1697, ekeinos* [1]
what, *1877+4005+1254+323,
    en+hos+de+an* [1]
what, *1877+5515, en+tis* [1]
what had been promised, *2039, epangelia* [1]
what has been promised, *2039, epangelia* [1]
what was promised, *2039, epangelia* [1]
what, *2093+4005, epi+hos* [1]
what he does, *2240, ergon* [1]
what she did, *2240, ergon* [1]
what a great, *2462, hēlikos* [1]
according to what, *2771+1569, katho+ean* [1]
according to what, *2771, katho* [1]
just what, *2777, kathōs* [1]
what usually did, *2777, kathōs* [1]
what if, *2779, kai* [1]
does what is evil, *2803, kakopoieō* [1]
teach what is good, *2815, kalodidaskalos* [1]

doing what is right, *2818, kalopoieō* [1]
what is right, *2819, kalos* [1]
what was preached, *3060, kērygma* [1]
what makes unclean, *3124, koinoō* [1]
receive what is due, *3152, komizō* [1]
what said, *3364, logos* [1]
what says, *3364, logos* [1]
what[s], *3535, meris* [1]
what am about to tell, *3836+3364+4047,
    ho+logos+houtos* [1]
what had happened to, *3836, ho* [1]
what has happened to, *3836+2848, ho+kata* [1]
what is, *3836, ho* [1]
what[s] we are writing, *3836+899, ho+autos* [1]
what[s], *3836+2843, ho+karpos* [1]
what[s], *3836+3306, ho+legō* [1]
what[s], *3836+3364, ho+logos* [1]
what kinds of, *3888, hoios* [1]
what, *3888, hoios* [1]
what kind of, *3961, hopoios* [1]
what, *3961, hopoios* [1]
what is right, *3987, orthōs* [1]
what, *4005+5515, hos+tis* [1]
what, *4005+5516, hos+tis* [1]
what, *4012+1569, hosos+ean* [1]
what, *4022, hoti* [1]
what is more, *4024+3667+1254+247+2779,
    ou+monon+de+alla+kai* [1]
what Paul said[s], *4047, houtos* [1]
what happened[s], *4047, houtos* [1]
what it says, *4047, houtos* [1]
what I meant, *4309+4047, peri+houtos* [1]
what large, *4383, pēlikos* [1]
what causes, *4470, pothen* [1]
what, *4531, posos* [1]
what magnificent, *4534, potapos* [1]
what massive, *4534, potapos* [1]
what has happened, *4544+4036, pou+oun* [1]
what, *4544, pou* [1]
what, *4547, pragma* [1]
seeing what was ahead, *4632, prooraō* [1]
what is seen, *4725, prosōpon* [1]
under what circumstances, *4802, pōs* [1]
what said, *4839, rhēma* [1]
what is more, *5250+4246+4047,
    syn+pas+houtos* [1]
what business is it of mine, *5515+1609,
    tis+egō* [1]
what shall we do, *5515+4036+1639,
    tis+oun+eimi* [1]
what, *5515+323, tis+an* [1]
what about, *5515, tis* [1]
what does it matter, *5515, tis* [1]
what going on, *5515+323+4047,
    tis+an+houtos* [1]
what[s], *5516+3836+2240, tis+ho+ergon* [1]
what, *5516+323, tis+an* [1]
what, *5516, tis* [1]
what, *5525+3961, toioutos+hopoios* [1]
shown for what it is, *5745, phaneros* [1]
loves what is good, *5787, philagathos* [1]
[what is] deceitful, *6022, pseudos* [1]
what, *6055, hōs* [1]
what seemed to be, *6059, hōsei* [1]
what, *6061, hōsper* [1]

WHAT'S [1]

what's, *5515, tis* [1]

WHATEVER [58]

whatever, *4005+1569, hos+ean* [11]
whatever, *4005, hos* [7]
whatever, *4012, hosos* [7]
whatever, *1569+5516, ean+tis* [2]
whatever, *1623+5516, ei+tis* [2]

whatever, *2093+4012, epi+hosos* [2]
whatever, *4005+323, hos+an* [2]
whatever, *4005+5516+323, hos+tis+an* [2]
whatever, *4012+1569, hosos+ean* [2]
whatever, *4246+4012, pas+hosos* [2]
whatever, *4246, pas* [2]
whatever, *RPE* [1]
whatever, *323+5516, an+tis* [1]
whatever, *1569, ean* [1]
whatever, *2777, kathōs* [1]
whatever happens, *3667, monon* [1]
whatever give, *3836, ho* [1]
whatever, *3836, ho* [1]
whatever, *3961, hopoios* [1]
whatever, *4005+5516+1569, hos+tis+ean* [1]
whatever, *4012+323, hosos+an* [1]
whatever, *4012+3525, hosos+men* [1]
whatever, *4015, hostis* [1]
no whatever, *4029, oudeis* [1]
whatever, *4246+3836, pas+ho* [1]
whatever, *5516+1569, tis+ean* [1]
whatever, *5516+323, tis+an* [1]
whatever, *5516, tis* [1]

WHEAT [12]

wheat, *4992, sitos* [11]
wheat, *5965, chortos* [1]

WHEN [825]

when, *AIT* [462]
when, *4020, hotan* [94]
when, *4021, hote* [83]
when, *6055, hōs* [33]
when, *2779, kai* [22]
when, *1877+3836, en+ho* [15]
when, *1877, en* [15]
when, *1254, de* [12]
when, *4036, oun* [11]
when, *4536, pote* [11]
when, *NIG* [10]
when, *1877+4005, en+hos* [7]
when, *1569, ean* [4]
when, *4005, hos* [3]
when, *5538, tote* [3]
but when, *1254, de* [2]
when, *1623, ei* [2]
when, *2054, epan* [2]
when, *2093, epi* [2]
when, *2671, hina* [2]
and when, *2779, kai* [2]
when, *3552+3836, meta+ho* [2]
when, *4005+323, hos+an* [2]
when, *6055+323, hōs+an* [2]
when the rooster crows, *231, alektorophōnia* [1]
when, *323, an* [1]
when no was present, *868, ater* [1]
the time came when, *1181+1254,
    ginomai+de* [1]
when, *1328, dia* [1]
when, *1663, eita* [1]
when, *1877+2465, en+hēmera* [1]
when, *2076, epeidē* [1]
when, *2317, euthys¹* [1]
when, *2401+4005, heōs+hos* [1]
when, *2471+323, hēnika+an* [1]
when, *2779+2627, kai+idou* [1]
even when, *2779, kai* [1]
and when, *2829, kan* [1]
when, *2848, kata* [1]
when later, *3552, meta* [1]
when, *3552, meta* [1]
when, *4020+2453, hotan+ēdē* [1]
when, *4022, hoti* [1]
when, *4537, pote* [1]
when, *4728, proteros* [1]

whole world, *4246, pas* [1]
whole, *4246+4725, pas+prosōpon* [1]
whole heart, *4460, pneuma* [1]

WHOLEHEARTEDLY [2]

wholeheartedly, *1666+2840, ek+kardia* [1]
wholeheartedly, *3552+2334, meta+eunoia* [1]

WHOLESOME [1]

wholesome, *1637, eilikrinēs* [1]

WHOLLY [1]

give yourself wholly to, *3509, meletaō* [1]

WHOM [166]

whom, *4005, hos* [114]
whom, *3836, ho* [13]
whom, *RPE* [12]
whom, *5515, tis* [9]
whom, *4005+323, hos+an* [5]
whom, *899, autos* [4]
whom, *AIT* [3]
on whom favor rests, *2306, eudokia* [1]
the whom, *4005, hos* [1]
those whom, *4005+1569, hos+ean* [1]
whom, *4005+1569, hos+ean* [1]
those whom, *4012+1569, hosos+ean* [1]
all whom, *4012+323, hosos+an* [1]

WHOSE [60]

whose, *4005, hos* [23]
whose, *RPE* [7]
whose, *5515, tis* [6]
whose, *AIT* [5]
whose, *899, autos* [5]
whose mother was, *1666, ek* [3]
whose, *3836, ho* [3]
whose mother, *1666, ek* [1]
whose⁵, *2400, echō* [1]
whose, *2400+899, echō+autos* [1]
whose, *2625, idios* [1]
whose temple⁵, *3836, ho* [1]
whose, *4005+2400, hos+echō* [1]
whose, *5515+2400, tis+echō* [1]
whose⁵, *5626, huios* [1]

WHY [156]

why, *5515, tis* [73]
why, *1328+5515, dia+tis* [23]
why, *NIG* [6]
why, *2672, hinati* [6]
that is why, *1328+4047, dia+houtos* [5]
that is why, *1475, dio* [5]
this is why, *1328+4047, dia+houtos* [4]
this is why, *1475, dio* [4]
why, *1650+5515, eis+tis* [4]
why, *1142, gar* [3]
that was why, *1328+4047, dia+houtos* [2]
why, *1328+4005+162, dia+hos+aitia* [2]
that is why, *1328+4005+162, dia+hos+aitia* [1]
this is why, *1328+899, dia+autos* [1]
that is why, *1650+4047, eis+houtos* [1]
why, *1915, heneken* [1]
that is why, *2093+4047, epi+houtos* [1]
wondering why, *2513, thaumazō* [1]
this is why, *2777, kathōs* [1]
why, *3836+162+1328+4005,
   ho+aitia+dia+hos* [1]
this is why, *3854, hothen* [1]
is that why, *4022, hoti* [1]
why, *4022, hoti* [1]
that is why, *4048, houtōs* [1]
why, *4470, pothen* [1]
why, *4802, pōs* [1]

why, *5515+3836+162, tis+ho+aitia* [1]
why do involve, *5515+2779, tis+kai* [1]
why, *5515+1915, tis+heneken* [1]
why, *5515+3364, tis+logos* [1]
why, *5920+5515, charin+tis* [1]

WICK [1]

wick, *3351, linon* [1]

WICKED [21]

wicked, *4505, ponēros* [11]
wicked, *96, adikos* [2]
wicked, *2805, kakos* [2]
more wicked, *4505, ponēros* [2]
wicked, *491, anomos* [1]
wicked, *815, asebēs* [1]
wicked, *876, atopos* [1]
wicked ways, *4504, ponēria* [1]

WICKEDNESS [18]

wickedness, *94, adikia* [9]
wickedness, *490, anomia* [5]
wickedness, *4504, ponēria* [2]
ever-increasing wickedness,
   *490+1650+3836+490,
   anomia+eis+ho+anomia* [1]
wickedness, *2798, kakia* [1]

WIDE [7]

wide, *4424, platos* [3]
make wide, *4425, platynō* [1]
open wide, *4425, platynō* [1]
opened wide, *4425, platynō* [1]
wide, *4426, platys* [1]

WIDELY [2]

spread widely, *889, auxanō* [1]
widely circulated, *1424, diaphemizo* [1]

WIDESPREAD [1]

widespread, *4498, polys* [1]

WIDOW [18]

widow, *5939, chēra* [12]
widow, *1222, gynē* [3]
widow, *RPE* [1]
the widow⁵, *899, autos* [1]
widow, *1222+5939, gynē+chēra* [1]

WIDOWS [14]

widows, *5939, chēra* [12]
widows, *RPE* [2]

WIFE [63]

wife, *1222, gynē* [59]
wife, *RPE* [1]
believing wife, *80+1222, adelphē+gynē* [1]
the wife, *3836, ho* [1]
wife, *3836, ho* [1]

WIFE'S [2]

wife's, *1222, gynē* [2]

WILD [12]

wild, *67, agrios* [3]
wild beasts, *2563, thērion* [2]
olive tree that is wild, *66, agrielaios* [1]
wild olive shoot, *66, agrielaios* [1]
wild, *861, asōtia* [1]
wild, *862, asōtōs* [1]
fought wild beasts, *2562, thēriomacheō* [1]
wild animals, *2563, thērion* [1]

wild, *5965, chortos* [1]

WILL [1774]

will, *AIT* [1588]
will, *NIG* [77]
will, *2525, thelēma* [52]
will, *3516, mellō* [17]
will, *RPE* [15]
will, *2527, thelō* [7]
will, *806, archō* [5]
will, *1087, boulē* [2]
will, *1347, diathēkē* [2]
will, *1088, boulēma* [1]
will, *1089, boulomai* [1]
will, *1639, eimi* [1]
then will be able, *1650+3836, eis+ho* [1]
will, *2240, ergon* [1]
will, *2526, thelēsis* [1]
will, *2527+2525, thelō+thelēma* [1]
how far will they go, *4047+5515+1639,
   houtos+tis+eimi* [1]
will⁵, *4997, skandalizō* [1]

WILLING [25]

willing, *2527, thelō* [15]
willing, *1089, boulomai* [2]
willing, *4609, prothymos* [2]
willing, *5306, syneudokeō* [2]
willing, *1731, hekousiōs* [1]
willing, *2525, thelēma* [1]
willing to share, *3127, koinōnikos* [1]
willing to associate, *5270, synapagō* [1]

WILLINGNESS [2]

willingness, *2527, thelō* [1]
willingness, *4608, prothymia* [1]

WIN [12]

win, *3045, kerdainō* [5]
win, *AIT* [2]
win favor, *473, anthrōpareskos* [2]
win the respect, *2361, euschēmonōs* [1]
trying to win the approval of, *4275, peithō* [1]
win, *4472, poieō* [1]

WIND [26]

wind, *449, anemos* [19]
south wind, *3803, notos* [3]
blown by the wind, *448, anemizō* [1]
wind, *4460, pneuma* [1]
wind, *4463, pneō* [1]
wind, *4466, pnoē* [1]

WINDOW [2]

window, *2600, thyris* [2]

WINDS [11]

winds, *449, anemos* [10]
winds, *4460, pneuma* [1]

WINE [40]

wine, *3885, oinos* [32]
wine vinegar, *3954, oxos* [4]
wine, *RPE* [2]
the wine⁵, *899, autos* [1]
wine, *1183, gleukos* [1]

WINEPRESS [5]

winepress, *3332, lēnos* [3]
winepress, *3332+3836+3885,
   lēnos+ho+oinos* [1]
pit for the winepress, *5700, hypolēnion* [1]

WINESKINS [9]

wineskins, 829, askos [9]

WINGS [6]

wings, 4763, pteryx [5]
wings, RPE [1]

WINNOWING [2]

winnowing fork, 4768, ptyon [2]

WINTER [8]

winter, 5930, cheimōn [4]
winter, 4199, paracheimazō [2]
spend the winter, 4199, paracheimazō [1]
winter in, 4200, paracheimasia [1]

WINTERED [1]

wintered, 4199, paracheimazō [1]

WIPE [3]

wipe off against, 669, apomassō [1]
wipe away from, 1981+1666, exaleiphō+ek [1]
wipe from, 1981+1666, exaleiphō+ek [1]

WIPED [5]

wiped, 1726, ekmassō [4]
wiped out, 1981, exaleiphō [1]

WISDOM [52]

wisdom, 5053, sophia [47]
wisdom, RPE [2]
human wisdom, 5053, sophia [1]
superior wisdom, 5667+5053,
    hyperochē+sophia [1]
wisdom, 5860, phronēsis [1]

WISE [31]

wise, 5055, sophos [18]
wise, 5861, phronimos [8]
wise, 5053, sophia [2]
think it wise, 546, axioō [1]
make wise, 5054, sophizō [1]
wise, 5317, syniēmi [1]

WISELY [1]

wisely, 3807, nounechōs [1]

WISER [1]

wiser, 5055, sophos [1]

WISH [13]

wish, 2527, thelō [6]
I wish, 4054, ophelon [2]
wish well, 1877+1645, en+eirēnē [1]
wish, 2377, euchomai [1]
wish that, 2527, thelō [1]
wish, 3721, nai [1]
how I wish that, 4054, ophelon [1]

WISHED [2]

wished, 2527, thelō [2]

WISHES [2]

wishes, 2527, thelō [2]

WISHING [1]

wishing, 2527, thelō [1]

WITCHCRAFT [1]

witchcraft, 5758, pharmakeia [1]

WITH [1355]

with, 3552, meta [263]
with, AIT [249]
with, 1877, en [150]
with, 5250, syn [76]
with, 4639, pros [47]
with, 2779, kai [34]
with, NIG [28]
with, 4123, para [26]
with, 2400, echō [24]
with, 1666, ek [18]
with, RPE [15]
with, 1328, dia [14]
along with, 3552, meta [9]
put up with, 462, anechomai [8]
with, 608, apo [8]
with, 2093, epi [8]
pleaded with, 4151, parakaleō [7]
together with, 5250, syn [7]
with, 1650, eis [6]
in accordance with, 2848, kata [6]
filled with, 4444, plēroō [6]
along with, 5250, syn [6]
what do want with, 5515+2779, tis+kai [5]
with, 1639, eimi [4]
peace be with, 1645, eirēnē [4]
with, 2848, kata [4]
took with, 4161, paralambanō [4]
rejoice with, 5176, synchairō [4]
fellow servant with with, 5281, syndoulos [4]
covered with, 1154, gemō [3]
clothe with, 1907, endyō [3]
clothed with, 1907, endyō [3]
along with, 2779, kai [3]
in keeping with, 2848, kata [3]
plead with, 4151, parakaleō [3]
with, 4309, peri [3]
entrusted with, 4409, pisteuō [3]
fill with, 4444, plēroō [3]
do with, 4472, poieō [3]
talking with, 5196, syllaleō [3]
associate with, 5264, synanameignymi [3]
crucified with, 5365, systauroō [3]
away with, 149, airō [2]
bear with, 462, anechomai [2]
with, 505, anti [2]
in keeping with, 545, axios [2]
beaten with blows, 1296, derō [2]
with child, 1877+1143+2400,
    en+gastēr+echō [2]
withˢ, 1907, endyō [2]
treat with contempt, 2024, exoutheneō [2]
clothed with, 2086, ependyomai [2]
in accordance with, 2093, epi [2]
with face to the ground, 2093+4725,
    epi+prosōpon [2]
in accordance with, 2777, kathōs [2]
struck with fists, 3139, kolaphizō [2]
man with leprosy, 3320, lepros [2]
share with, 3556, metadidōmi [2]
have nothing to do with, 4148, paraiteomai [2]
overwhelmed with sorrow, 4337, perilypos [2]
with, 4693, prosmenō [2]
with a fever, 4789, pyressō [2]
heirs with, 5169, synklēronomos [2]
rejoices with, 5176, synchairō [2]
live with, 5182, syzaō [2]
die with, 5271, synapothnēskō [2]
ate with, 5303, synesthiō [2]
buried with, 5313, synthaptō [2]
crucified with, 5365+5250, systauroō+syn [2]
filled with joy, 22+5915, agalliaō+chara [1]
filled with joy, 22, agalliaō [1]
with the news, 33, angellō [1]
went with, 199, akoloutheō [1]

with certainty, 242, alēthōs [1]
with, 275, hama [1]
nothing wrong with, 289, amemptos [1]
bound with an oath, 354, anathematizō [1]
bearing with, 462, anechomai [1]
to draw with, 534, antlēma [1]
not acquainted with, 586, apeiros [1]
with ever-increasing glory,
    608+1518+1650+1518,
    apo+doxa+eis+doxa [1]
besiege with questions, 694+4309+4498,
    apostomatizō+peri+polys [1]
have nothing to do with, 706, apotrepō [1]
with, 708, apopherō [1]
with own hands, 901, autocheir [1]
withˢ, 918, aphiēmi [1]
bear with, 1002, bastazō [1]
was filled with, 1181, ginomai [1]
union with, 1182, ginōskō [1]
well acquainted with, 1195, gnōstēs [1]
with writing, 1211, graphō [1]
pleaded with, 1289, deomai [1]
with the help of, 1328, dia [1]
with, 1328+5931, dia+cheir [1]
by comparing with, 1328, dia [1]
in keeping with, 1328, dia [1]
charged with, 1592, enkaleō [1]
clothe with, 1599, enkomboomai [1]
with idle notions, 1632, eikē [1]
come with, 1639+5302, eimi+synerchomai [1]
with this in mind, 1650+899, eis+autos [1]
in dealing with, 1650, eis [1]
with, 1650+3836, eis+ho [1]
searched intently and with the greatest care,
    1699+2779+2001,
    ekzēteō+kai+exeraunaō [1]
overwhelmed with wonder, 1701,
    ekthambeō [1]
[treat with] scorn, 1746, ekptyō [1]
motioned with, 1753, ekteinō [1]
with fear, 1769, ekphobos [1]
covered with sores, 1815, helkoō [1]
provides with plenty, 1855, empimplēmi [1]
in accordance with, 1877, en [1]
in comparison with,
    1877+4047+3836+3538+1641,
    en+houtos+ho+meros+heineken [1]
united with, 1877, en [1]
while with, 1877, en [1]
with regard to, 1877+3538, en+meros [1]
with the help of, 1877, en [1]
with, 1877+3545, en+mesos [1]
with, 1877+3836, en+ho [1]
live with, 1940+1877, enoikeō+en [1]
trembled with fear, 1958+1181,
    entromos+ginomai [1]
with, 1967, enōpion [1]
in connection with, 2093, epi [1]
have to do with, 2110, epidechomai [1]
gripped with, 2158+2093, epipiptō+epi [1]
seized with, 2158+2093, epipiptō+epi [1]
furnished with, 2202, epitithēmi [1]
pleased with, 2305, eudokeō [1]
with pleased, 2305, eudokeō [1]
fills with joy, 2372, euphrosynē [1]
filled with, 2400, echō [1]
has to do with, 2400, echō [1]
sealed with, 2400+3836+5382,
    echō+ho+sphragis [1]
shone with, 2400, echō [1]
treated with, 2400, echō [1]
with great fervor, 2417+3836+4460,
    zeō+ho+pneuma [1]
with delight, 2452, hēdeōs [1]
with confidence, 2509, tharreō [1]
get acquainted with, 2707, historeō [1]

this agrees with, *2777, kathōs* [1]
equal with, *2777+2779, kathōs+kai* [1]
which agrees with, *2777, kathōs* [1]
with that, *2779+2627, kai+idou* [1]
with that, *2779, kai* [1]
together with rods, *4779, kai* [1]
with wrong motives, *2809, kakōs* [1]
agrees with, *2848, kata* [1]
in conformity with, *2848, kata* [1]
with regard to, *2848, kata* [1]
do away with, *2934, katargeō* [1]
done away with, *2934, katargeō* [1]
dealt treacherously with, *2947,*
   katasophizomai [1]
seared as with a hot iron, *3013, kaustēriazō* [1]
with tears, *3081, klaiō* [1]
share with, *3125, koinōneō* [1]
associate with, *3140, kollaō* [1]
those with gifts of administration, *3236,*
   kybernēsis [1]
filled with awe, *3284+5832,*
   lambanō+phobos [1]
with instructions, *3284+1953,*
   lambanō+entolē [1]
with the news, *3306, legō* [1]
with the plea, *3306, legō* [1]
with the words, *3306, legō* [1]
with leprosy, *3320, lepros* [1]
filled with grief, *3382+5379, lypeō+sphodra* [1]
found fault with, *3522, memphomai* [1]
with, *3545, mesos* [1]
together with, *3552, meta* [1]
received with, *3562+3552,*
   metalēmpsis+meta [1]
seized with remorse, *3564, metamelomai* [1]
together with, *3590+6006, mē+chōris* [1]
committed adultery with, *3658, moicheuō* [1]
with difficulty, *3660, molis* [1]
agree with each other, *3836+899+5858,*
   ho+autos+phroneō [1]
agree with one another, *3836+899+3306,*
   ho+autos+legō [1]
acquainted with, *3857, oida* [1]
entrusted with work, *3874, oikonomos* [1]
those entrusted with, *3874, oikonomos* [1]
promised with an oath, *3923, omnyō* [1]
live in harmony with, *3939, homophrōn* [1]
weapons fight with, *3960+3836+5127,*
   hoplon+ho+strateia [1]
met with, *3972, horaō* [1]
in keeping with income,
   4005+5516+1569+2338,
   hos+tis+ean+euodoō [1]
lost connection with, *4024+3195, ou+krateō* [1]
with this, *4047+3306, houtos+legō* [1]
with that, *4047+3306, houtos+legō* [1]
with such, *4048, houtōs* [1]
with one voice, *4101, pamplēthei* [1]
don't have anything to do with, *4148,*
   paraiteomai [1]
pleading with, *4151, parakaleō* [1]
continue with, *4169, paramenō* [1]
entrusted with, *4192, paratithēmi* [1]
am with, *4205, pareimi* [1]
was with, *4205, pareimi* [1]
provide with, *4218, parechō* [1]
provides with, *4218, parechō* [1]
done with, *4264, pauō* [1]
filled with grief, *4291, pentheō* [1]
go with, *4309, peri* [1]
to do with, *4309, peri* [1]
clothed with, *4314, periballō* [1]
treat with, *4363, peritithēmi* [1]
with, *4472, poieō* [1]
sweep away with the torrent, *4533+4472,*
   potamophorētos+poieō [1]

comparing with, *4639, pros* [1]
talk with, *4688, proslaleō* [1]
talked with, *4688, proslaleō* [1]
presented with, *4712, prospherō* [1]
burn with passion, *4792, pyroō* [1]
beaten with rods, *4810, rhabdizō* [1]
with a roar, *4853, rhoizēdon* [1]
announce with trumpets, *4895, salpizō* [1]
mixed with myrrh, *5046, smyrnizō* [1]
filled with compassion, *5072,*
   splanchnizomai [1]
filled with compassion for, *5072,*
   splanchnizomai [1]
put up with, *5095, stegō* [1]
with a deep sigh, *5100, stenazō* [1]
sitting with, *5153, synkathēmai* [1]
seated with, *5154, synkathizō* [1]
endure hardship with, *5155, synkakopatheō* [1]
mistreated along with, *5156,*
   synkakoucheomai [1]
come with, *5160, synkatabainō* [1]
combine with, *5166, synkerannymi* [1]
co-heirs with, *5169, synklēronomos* [1]
heirs together with, *5169, synklēronomos* [1]
to do with, *5170, synkoinōneō* [1]
share with, *5171+1639, synkoinōnos+eimi* [1]
associate with, *5178, synchraomai* [1]
live [with], *5182, syzaō* [1]
argue with, *5184, syzēteō* [1]
made alive with, *5188+5250,*
   syzōopoieō+syn [1]
made alive with, *5188, syzōopoieō* [1]
conferred with, *5196, syllaleō* [1]
discussed with, *5196, syllaleō* [1]
with child, *5197+1877+1143,*
   syllambanō+en+gastēr [1]
dispute with, *5202, symballō* [1]
kings with, *5203, symbasileuō* [1]
reign with, *5203, symbasileuō* [1]
testifies with, *5210, symmartyreō* [1]
partners with, *5212, symmetochos* [1]
join with others following example, *5213+1181,*
   symmimētēs+ginomai [1]
sympathize with, *5217, sympatheō* [1]
sympathized with, *5217, sympatheō* [1]
take with, *5221, symparalambanō* [1]
taking with, *5221, symparalambanō* [1]
present with, *5223, sympareimi* [1]
suffers with, *5224, sympaschō* [1]
sending with, *5225, sympempō* [1]
drank [with], *5228, sympinō* [1]
fellow citizens with, *5232, sympolitēs* [1]
traveling with, *5233, symporeuomai* [1]
walked along with, *5233, symporeuomai* [1]
went along with, *5233, symporeuomai* [1]
grew up with, *5243, symphyō* [1]
in agreement with, *5244, symphōneō* [1]
in prison with, *5257, synaichmalōtos* [1]
eating with, *5259, synalizō* [1]
come up with, *5262, synanabainō* [1]
traveled with, *5262, synanabainō* [1]
at the table with, *5263, synanakeimai* [1]
ate with, *5263, synanakeimai* [1]
eating with, *5263, synanakeimai* [1]
died with, *5271, synapothnēskō* [1]
killed with, *5272, synapollymi* [1]
sent with, *5273, synapostellō* [1]
raised up with, *5283, synegeirō* [1]
raised with, *5283, synegeirō* [1]
were with, *5289, syneimi¹* [1]
went with into, *5291+1650,*
   syneiserchomai+eis [1]
chosen together with, *5293, syneklektos* [1]
worked with, *5300, synergeō* [1]
work with, *5301+1639, synergos+eimi* [1]
came with, *5302, synerchomai* [1]

come along with, *5302, synerchomai* [1]
come with, *5302, synerchomai* [1]
continued with, *5302, synerchomai* [1]
going with, *5302, synerchomai* [1]
went with, *5302, synerchomai* [1]
with, *5302, synerchomai* [1]
with eat, *5303, synesthiō* [1]
eats with, *5303, synesthiō* [1]
eating with, *5307, syneuōcheomai* [1]
feast with, *5307, syneuōcheomai* [1]
standing with, *5319, synistēmi* [1]
traveling with, *5321, synodeuō* [1]
live with, *5324, synoikeō* [1]
talking with, *5326, synomileō* [1]
plunge with, *5340, syntrechō* [1]
brought up with, *5343, syntrophos* [1]
marked with a seal, *5381, sphragizō* [1]
overwhelmed with amazement, *5669+1742,*
   hyperperissōs+ekplēssō [1]
filled with awe, *5828, phobeomai* [1]
filled with joy, *5915+3489, chara+megas* [1]
in accordance with, *6055, hōs* [1]

WITHDRAW [1]

withdraw, *599, aperchomai* [1]

WITHDREW [11]

withdrew, *432, anachōreō* [6]
withdrew, *599, aperchomai* [1]
withdrew, *685, apospaō* [1]
withdrew, *923+608, aphistēmi+apo* [1]
withdrew, *1639+5723, eimi+hypochōreō* [1]
withdrew, *5723, hypochōreō* [1]

WITHER [1]

wither, *3830, xērainō* [1]

WITHERED [6]

withered, *3830, xērainō* [6]

WITHERS [3]

withers, *3830, xērainō* [3]

WITHHOLDING [2]

withholding, *5102, stenochōreō* [2]

WITHIN [14]

within, *1877, en* [8]
within, *1877+3836+3517, en+ho+melos* [1]
at work within, *1919+1877, energeō+en* [1]
within, *1955, entos* [1]
from within, *2277, esōthen* [1]
within, *2277, esōthen* [1]
within, *3120, koilia* [1]

WITHOUT [101]

without, *6006, chōris* [23]
without, *3590, mē* [8]
without, *3590+2400, mē+echō* [5]
without, *4024, ou* [4]
without, *3594, mēdeis* [3]
without blemish, *320, amōmos* [2]
without fault, *320, amōmos* [2]
without, *459, aneu* [2]
without honor, *872, atimos* [2]
without, *NIG* [1]
without genealogy, *37, agenealogētos* [1]
gone without sleep, *71, agrypnia* [1]
bread without yeast, *109, azymos* [1]
without yeast, *109, azymos* [1]
without God, *117, atheos* [1]
without fruit, *182, akarpos* [1]
without a trial, *185, akatakritos* [1]

without self-control, *203, akratēs* [1]
without hindrance, *219, akōlytōs* [1]
without a doubt, *242, alēthōs* [1]
without sin, *281+4024, hamartia+ou* [1]
without testimony, *282, amartyros* [1]
[without] mother, *298, amētōr* [1]
without sin, *387, anamartētos* [1]
without raising any objection, *395,*
   anantirrētōs [1]
without excuse, *406, anapologētos* [1]
without mercy, *447, aneleos* [1]
[without] mercy, *455, anepliēmptos* [1]
without rain, *536, anydros* [1]
without water, *536, anydros* [1]
without father, *574, apatōr* [1]
without food, *826, asitia* [1]
gone without food, *827, asitos* [1]
[without] defect, *834, aspilos* [1]
without spot, *834, aspilos* [1]
without love, *845, astorgos* [1]
without, *868, ater* [1]
without fear, *925, aphobōs* [1]
without the slightest qualm, *925, aphobōs* [1]
without meaning, *936, aphōnos* [1]
without speech, *936, aphōnos* [1]
without clothes, *1218, gymnos* [1]
without cost, *1562, dōrean* [1]
without paying for it, *1562, dōrean* [1]
without reason, *1562, dōrean* [1]
without, *1569+3590, ean+mē* [1]
without delay, *2317, euthys*[1] [1]
without warning, *2779+2627, kai+idou* [1]
without, *2779+3590, kai+mē* [1]
without, *2779+4024, kai+ou* [1]
without effect, *3031, kenos* [1]
without reason, *3036, kenōs* [1]
without knowing, *3291, lanthanō* [1]
without light, *3590+5743, mē+phainō* [1]
without, *3590+1650, mē+eis* [1]
without anything, *3594, mēdeis* [1]
without, *3612, mēte* [1]
gone without food, *3763, nēsteia* [1]
without, *4024+1666, ou+ek* [1]
without, *4029, oudeis* [1]
without, *6006+4246, chōris+pas* [1]
without the Spirit, *6035, psychikos* [1]

WITNESS [16]

witness, *3459, martys* [10]
witness, *3455, martyreō* [3]
witness, *AIT* [1]
witness, *3456, martyria* [1]
bearing witness, *5210, symmartyreō* [1]

WITNESSES [26]

witnesses, *3459, martys* [20]
witnesses, *3457, martyrion* [3]
false witnesses, *6020, pseudomartys* [2]
witnesses, *RPE* [1]

WIVES [14]

wives, *1222, gynē* [12]
old wives tales, *1212, graōdēs* [1]
wives, *1221, gynaikeios* [1]

WOE [42]

woe, *4026, ouai* [42]

WOES [1]

woes, *4026, ouai* [1]

WOKE [7]

woke up, *1586, egeirō* [3]
woke, *1586, egeirō* [2]

woke, *1444, diegeirō* [1]
woke up, *2031+1181, exypnos+ginomai* [1]

WOLF [2]

wolf, *3380, lykos* [2]

WOLVES [4]

wolves, *3380, lykos* [4]

WOMAN [117]

woman, *1222, gynē* [91]
woman, *AIT* [16]
slave woman, *4087, paidiskē* [4]
dear woman, *1222, gynē* [2]
woman, *RPE* [1]
woman, *80, adelphē* [1]
pregnant woman, *1877+1143+2400,*
   en+gastēr+echō [1]
barren woman, *5096, steira* [1]

WOMAN'S [3]

woman's, *AIT* [1]
woman's, *1222, gynē* [1]
slave woman's, *4087, paidiskē* [1]

WOMB [4]

womb, *3120, koilia* [3]
womb, *3616, mētra* [1]

WOMBS [1]

wombs, *3120, koilia* [1]

WOMEN [59]

women, *1222, gynē* [30]
women, *AIT* [14]
women, *RPE* [3]
the women's, *899, autos* [3]
pregnant women, *1877+1143+2400,*
   en+gastēr+echō [3]
women, *2559, thēlys* [2]
weak-willed women, *1220, gynaikarion* [1]
servants women, *1527, doulē* [1]
the women's, *4047, houtos* [1]
barren women, *5096, steira* [1]

WOMEN'S [1]

women's, *1222, gynē* [1]

WON [4]

won over, *3045, kerdainō* [2]
won disciples, *3411, mathēteuō* [1]
won over, *4275, peithō* [1]

WON'T [4]

won't, *3590, mē* [3]
won't, *4049, ouchi* [1]

WONDER [4]

overwhelmed with wonder, *1701,*
   ekthambeō [1]
wonder, *2502, thambos* [1]
wonder, *2512, thauma* [1]
wonder, *2513, thaumazō* [1]

WONDERED [2]

wondered, *1368, dialogizomai* [1]
wondered about, *5502+1877+3836+2840,*
   tithēmi+en+ho+kardia [1]

WONDERFUL [3]

wonderful, *1902, endoxos* [1]

wonderful, *2514, thaumasios* [1]
wonderful, *2515, thaumastos* [1]

WONDERING [6]

wondering, *RPE* [1]
wondering, *679, aporeō* [1]
wondering, *1368, dialogizomai* [1]
wondering about, *1877+1571+1389,*
   en+heautou+diaporeō [1]
wondering why, *2513, thaumazō* [1]
wondering, *2513, thaumazō* [1]

WONDERS [14]

wonders, *5469, teras* [13]
wonders, *3483, megaleios* [1]

WONDROUS [1]

wondrous sign, *4956, sēmeion* [1]

WOOD [5]

wood, *3833, xylon* [3]
of wood, *3832, xylinos* [2]

WOOL [2]

wool, *2250, erion* [2]

WORD [155]

word, *3364, logos* [125]
word, *4839, rhēma* [16]
word, *AIT* [3]
sent word, *690, apostellō* [2]
word of instruction, *1439, didachē* [2]
word of mouth, *3364, logos* [2]
word, *3306, legō* [1]
word, *3359, logion* [1]
spread the word, *3455, martyreō* [1]
not a word, *4029, oudeis* [1]
further word spoken, *4707+3364,*
   prostithēmi+logos [1]

WORDS [106]

words, *3364, logos* [53]
words, *4839, rhēma* [16]
words, *AIT* [8]
words, *3306, legō* [8]
words, *3359, logion* [3]
words, *RPE* [2]
in these words, *4048, houtōs* [2]
words, *5125, stoma* [2]
words, *5889, phōnē* [2]
words, *201, akouō* [1]
words cannot express, *227, alalētos* [1]
mark my words, *2623, ide* [1]
in the words of, *2777, kathōs* [1]
with the words, *3306, legō* [1]
quarreling about words, *3362, logomacheō* [1]
quarrels about words, *3363, logomachia* [1]
in other words, *4047+1639, houtos+eimi* [1]
many words, *4494, polylogia* [1]
mouth words, *5779, phthengomai* [1]

WORE [3]

wore, *AIT* [1]
wore clothing, *1639+1907, eimi+endyō* [1]
wore, *4322, perizōnnymi* [1]

WORK [100]

work, *2240, ergon* [35]
work, *2237, ergazomai* [7]
work, *AIT* [5]
at work in, *1919+1877, energeō+en* [5]
work, *RPE* [4]
work, *NIG* [2]

work, *1918, energeia* [2]
at work in, *1919, energeō* [2]
work hard, *3159, kopiaō* [2]
work, *3159, kopiaō* [2]
hard work, *3160, kopos* [2]
work, *4472, poieō* [2]
do the work, *1354, diakoneō* [1]
work, *1355, diakonia* [1]
work, *1536, dromos* [1]
work miracles, *1539, dynamis* [1]
at work, *1639, eimi* [1]
at work in, *1877+1919, en+energeō* [1]
for work, *1877+4005+1256+2237,*
   en+hos+dei+ergazomai [1]
at work within, *1919+1877, energeō+en* [1]
at work, *1919, energeō* [1]
work among, *1919+1877, energeō+en* [1]
work, *1919, energeō* [1]
effective work, *1921, energēs* [1]
at work, *2237, ergazomai* [1]
put to work, *2237, ergazomai* [1]
work for a living, *2237, ergazomai* [1]
work for, *2237, ergazomai* [1]
men to work, *2239, ergatēs* [1]
work already done, *2289, hetoimos* [1]
work out, *2981, katergazomai* [1]
done hard work, *3159, kopiaō* [1]
hard work, *3159, kopiaō* [1]
work hard, *3159+2237, kopiaō+ergazomai* [1]
work, *3160, kopos* [1]
work, *3873, oikonomia* [1]
entrusted with work, *3874, oikonomos* [1]
their work*, *4047, houtos* [1]
put to work, *4549, pragmateuomai* [1]
joins in the work, *5300, synergeō* [1]
work together, *5301+1181,*
   synergos+ginomai [1]
work with, *5301+1639, synergos+eimi* [1]

WORKED   [14]

worked, *2237, ergazomai* [3]
worked hard, *3159, kopiaō* [3]
worked through the dough, *2435, zymoō* [2]
worked for, *2237, ergazomai* [1]
worked for, *3159, kopiaō* [1]
worked, *3159, kopiaō* [1]
worked, *3160, kopos* [1]
worked, *4472, poieō* [1]
worked with, *5300, synergeō* [1]

WORKER   [9]

fellow worker, *5301, synergos* [6]
worker, *2239, ergatēs* [3]

WORKERS   [13]

workers, *2239, ergatēs* [5]
fellow workers, *5301, synergos* [5]
workers, *RPE* [1]
workers of miracles, *1539, dynamis* [1]
fellow workers, *5300, synergeō* [1]

WORKING   [7]

working, *1918, energeia* [2]
working, *RPE* [1]
working, *1920, energēma* [1]
working, *2237, ergazomai* [1]
working, *4506, ponos* [1]
working together, *5300, synergeō* [1]

WORKMAN   [2]

workman, *2239, ergatēs* [1]
workman, *5493, technitēs* [1]

WORKMANSHIP   [1]

workmanship, *4473, poiēma* [1]

WORKMEN   [3]

workmen, *2239, ergatēs* [3]

WORKS   [19]

works, *2240, ergon* [9]
works in, *1919+1877, energeō+en* [2]
works through, *2435, zymoō* [2]
works out, *1919, energeō* [1]
works, *1919, energeō* [1]
works, *2237, ergazomai* [1]
works for, *2426, zēteō* [1]
director of public works, *3874, oikonomos* [1]
works, *5300, synergeō* [1]

WORLD   [206]

world, *3180, kosmos* [173]
world, *3876, oikoumenē* [13]
world, *172, aiōn* [4]
world, *AIT* [2]
world, *1178, gē* [2]
Roman world, *3876, oikoumenē* [2]
world, *4922, sarx* [2]
powers of world, *3179, kosmokratōr* [1]
world, *3232, ktisis* [1]
the world*, *4246, pas* [1]
whole world, *4246, pas* [1]
of the world, *4920, sarkikos* [1]
the world, *4922, sarx* [1]
this world, *4922, sarx* [1]
all the world, *5515+1639+476+4005,*
   tis+eimi+anthrōpos+hos [1]

WORLD'S   [2]

world's, *1178, gē* [1]
world's, *3180, kosmos* [1]

WORLDLY   [10]

worldly, *4920, sarkikos* [3]
worldly, *94, adikia* [1]
worldly, *96, adikos* [1]
worldly, *3176, kosmikos* [1]
worldly, *3836+3180, ho+kosmos* [1]
worldly, *4921, sarkinos* [1]
worldly manner, *4922, sarx* [1]
worldly point of view, *4922, sarx* [1]

WORM   [2]

worm way, *1905, endynō* [1]
worm, *5038, skōlēx* [1]

WORMS   [1]

eaten by worms, *5037, skōlēkobrōtos* [1]

WORMWOOD   [1]

Wormwood, *952, apsinthos* [1]

WORN   [1]

worn, *1907, endyō* [1]

WORRIED   [1]

worried, *3534, merimnaō* [1]

WORRIES   [3]

worries, *3533, merimna* [3]

WORRY   [12]

worry about, *3534, merimnaō* [5]
worry, *3534, merimnaō* [4]

worry about, *3577, meteōrizomai* [1]
worry beforehand, *4627, promeletaō* [1]
worry beforehand about, *4628,*
   promerimnaō [1]

WORRYING   [2]

worrying, *3534, merimnaō* [2]

WORSE   [12]

worse than, *5937, cheirōn* [4]
worse, *5937, cheirōn* [4]
worse, *AIT* [1]
from bad to worse, *2093+3836+5937,*
   epi+ho+cheirōn [1]
worse, *5728, hystereō* [1]
worse off than, *5937, cheirōn* [1]

WORSHIP   [47]

worship, *4686, proskyneō* [28]
worship, *3302, latreuō* [5]
worship, *4936, sebō* [3]
worship, *AIT* [1]
self-imposed worship, *1615, ethelothrēskia* [1]
worship, *2355, eusebeō* [1]
worship God, *2537, theosebeia* [1]
worship, *2579, thrēskeia* [1]
act of worship, *3301, latreia* [1]
temple worship, *3301, latreia* [1]
worship, *3301, latreia* [1]
refused to worship, *3590+4686,*
   mē+proskyneō [1]
objects of worship, *4934, sebasma* [1]
worship, *5828, phobeomai* [1]

WORSHIPED   [21]

worshiped, *4686, proskyneō* [17]
worshiped, *3302, latreuō* [1]
worshiped, *4933, sebazomai* [1]
worshiped, *4934, sebasma* [1]
worshiped, *4936, sebō* [1]

WORSHIPER   [3]

worshiper, *4936, sebō* [2]
worshiper, *3302, latreuō* [1]

WORSHIPERS   [6]

worshipers, *4686, proskyneō* [3]
worshipers, *3302, latreuō* [1]
assembled worshipers, *4436+3836+3295,*
   plēthos+ho+laos [1]
worshipers, *4687, proskynētēs* [1]

WORSHIPING   [2]

worshiping, *3310, leitourgeō* [1]
worshiping, *4686, proskyneō* [1]

WORSHIPS   [1]

worships, *4686, proskyneō* [1]

WORST   [2]

worst, *4755, prōtos* [2]

WORTH   [9]

worth, *545, axios* [2]
worth more than, *1422, diapherō* [2]
worth, *4005+1639, hos+eimi* [1]
great worth, *4500, polytelēs* [1]
greater worth, *4501, polytimos* [1]
worth, *5508, timios* [1]
the money worth a year's wages, *5559+1324,*
   triakosioi+dēnarion [1]

WORTHLESS [6]

worthless, *3469, mataios* [2]
worthless, *99, adokimos* [1]
worthless, *945, achreios* [1]
become worthless, *946, achreioō* [1]
worthless, *2934, katargeō* [1]

WORTHWHILE [1]

think it worthwhile, *1507, dokimazō* [1]

WORTHY [37]

worthy, *545, axios* [17]
worthy, *547, axiōs* [3]
worthy of respect, *4948, semnos* [3]
in a manner worthy, *547, axiōs* [2]
worthy, *1944, enochos* [2]
worthy, *2653, hikanos* [2]
counted worthy, *2921, kataxioō* [2]
consider worthy, *546, axioō* [1]
count worthy, *546, axioō* [1]
found worthy of, *546, axioō* [1]
worthy, *546, axioō* [1]
in a way worthy, *547, axiōs* [1]
considered worthy of, *2921, kataxioō* [1]

WOULD [195]

would, *AIT* [118]
would have, *323, an* [24]
would, *323, an* [17]
would, *NIG* [15]
would, *3516, mellō* [8]
would, *2527, thelō* [7]
would, *RPE* [1]
would stand the test, *1509, dokimē* [1]
would, *1639, eimi* [1]
would rather, *2527, thelō* [1]
would, *2829, kan* [1]
that would follow, *3552+4047,*
    meta+houtos [1]

WOUND [4]

wound, *4435, plēgē* [2]
had a wound, *5377, sphazō* [1]
wound, *5597, typtō* [1]

WOUNDED [2]

wounded, *2400+3836+4435,*
    echō+ho+plēgē [1]
wounded, *5547, traumatizō* [1]

WOUNDS [3]

wounds, *3698, mōlōps* [1]
wounds, *4435, plēgē* [1]
wounds, *5546, trauma* [1]

WOVEN [1]

woven, *5733, hyphantos* [1]

WRAP [1]

wrap around, *4314, periballō* [1]

WRAPPED [11]

wrapped, *1313, deō* [2]
wrapped around, *1346, diazōnnymi* [2]
wrapped, *1962, entylissō* [2]
wrapped in cloths, *5058, sparganoō* [2]
wrapped in, *1912, eneileō* [1]
wrapped around waist, *3284+1346,*
    lambanō+diazōnnymi [1]
wrapped up, *5366, systellō* [1]

WRATH [31]

wrath, *3973, orgē* [27]
wrath, *2596, thymos* [4]

WREATHS [1]

wreaths, *5098, stemma* [1]

WRESTLING [1]

wrestling, *76, agōnizomai* [1]

WRETCHED [3]

wretched, *5417, talaipōros* [2]
wretched, *2809, kakōs* [1]

WRETCHES [1]

wretches, *2805, kakos* [1]

WRINKLE [1]

wrinkle, *4869, rhytis* [1]

WRISTS [1]

wrists, *5931, cheir* [1]

WRITE [51]

write, *1211, graphō* [40]
write, *NIG* [2]
write, *RPE* [2]
write down, *1211, graphō* [2]
write on, *2093+2108, epi+epigraphō* [2]
write an account, *1211, graphō* [1]
write, *2182, epistellō* [1]
write, *2863, katagraphō* [1]

WRITES [1]

writes, *RPE* [1]

WRITING [14]

writing, *1211, graphō* [11]
with writing, *1211, graphō* [1]
what^s we are writing, *3836+899, ho+autos* [1]
writing tablet, *4400, pinakidion* [1]

WRITINGS [2]

writings, *1210, graphē* [2]

WRITTEN [125]

written, *1211, graphō* [105]
written code, *1207, gramma* [3]
written down, *1211, graphō* [2]
written notice, *2107, epigraphē* [2]
written, *RPE* [1]
written, *616, apographō* [1]
written, *1209, graptos* [1]
written in, *1582+1877, engraphō+en* [1]
written on, *1582+1877, engraphō+en* [1]
written, *1582, engraphō* [1]
written, *2108, epigraphō* [1]
written a letter, *2182, epistellō* [1]
written, *2182, epistellō* [1]
already written, *4592, prographō* [1]
was written about, *4592, prographō* [1]
written in the past, *4592, prographō* [1]
written code, *5934, cheirographon* [1]

WRONG [29]

wrong, *2805, kakos* [8]
done wrong, *92, adikeō* [3]
do wrong, *92, adikeō* [2]
does wrong, *92, adikeō* [2]
wrong, *876, atopos* [2]
did wrong, *92, adikeō* [1]

wrong, *92, adikeō* [1]
wrong, *94, adikia* [1]
doing wrong, *279, hamartanō* [1]
done wrong, *279, hamartanō* [1]
nothing wrong with, *289, amemptos* [1]
do wrong, *2804, kakopoios* [1]
doing wrong, *2804, kakopoios* [1]
with wrong motives, *2809, kakōs* [1]
wrong, *2809, kakōs* [1]
clearly in the wrong, *2861, kataginōskō* [1]
wrong, *5648, hyperbainō* [1]

WRONGDOER [1]

wrongdoer, *2805+4556, kakos+prassō* [1]

WRONGDOING [2]

wrongdoing, *94, adikia* [1]
wrongdoing, *4175, paranomia* [1]

WRONGED [2]

wronged, *92, adikeō* [2]

WRONGS [1]

wrongs, *2805, kakos* [1]

WROTE [21]

wrote, *1211, graphō* [15]
wrote down, *1211, graphō* [2]
wrote, *RPE* [1]
wrote, *1207, gramma* [1]
wrote about, *1211, graphō* [1]
wrote, *4472, poieō* [1]

YARDS [1]

hundred yards, *4388+1357,*
    pēchys+diakosioi [1]

YEAR [18]

year, *1929, eniautos* [10]
year, *2291, etos* [3]
year after year, *2848+1929, kata+eniautos* [2]
last year, *4373, perysi* [2]
year, *RPE* [1]

YEAR'S [2]

a year's wages, *1324+5559,*
    dēnarion+triakosioi [1]
the money worth a year's wages, *5559+1324,*
    triakosioi+dēnarion [1]

YEARS [55]

years, *2291, etos* [40]
years old, *2291, etos* [3]
two years, *1454, dietia* [2]
years, *1929, eniautos* [2]
years, *2465, hēmera* [2]
forty years, *5478, tesserakontaetēs* [2]
two years old, *1453, dietēs* [1]
hundred years old, *1670, hekatontaetēs* [1]
three years, *5562, trietia* [1]
getting along in years, *5644, hyperakmos* [1]

YEAST [14]

yeast, *2434, zymē* [12]
bread without yeast, *109, azymos* [1]
without yeast, *109, azymos* [1]

YELLING [1]

yelling, *3189, krazō* [1]

YELLOW [1]

yellow as sulfur, *2523, theiōdēs* [1]

YES [46]

yes, *3721, nai* [32]
yes it is as you say, *5148+3306, sy+legō* [4]
yes, *NIG* [3]
yes, *1142, gar* [2]
yes, *247, alla* [1]
yes, *1254, de* [1]
yes, *2285+5445, eti+te* [1]
yes, *2627+1609, idou+egō* [1]
yes, *5148+3306, sy+legō* [1]

YESTERDAY [3]

yesterday, *2396, echthes* [3]

YET [136]

yet, *2779, kai* [35]
yet, *1254, de* [17]
not yet, *4037, oupō* [16]
yet, *247, alla* [15]
yet, *NIG* [12]
and yet, *2779, kai* [11]
yet, *4440, plēn* [4]
and yet, *1254, de* [3]
yet, *1145, ge* [2]
yet even, *2779, kai* [2]
not yet, *4031, oudepō* [2]
yet, *247+3437, alla+mallon* [1]
yet, *1142, gar* [1]
yet, *2627, idou* [1]
yet, *2779+2627, kai+idou* [1]
and yet, *2792, kaitoi* [1]
yet, *2792, kaitoi* [1]
yet, *3530, mentoi* [1]
yet, *3552+4047, meta+houtos* [1]
not yet, *3596, mēdepō* [1]
yet before, *3609, mēpō* [1]
not yet, *3609, mēpō* [1]
yet even, *3963, hopou* [1]
not yet, *4024, ou* [1]
yet, *4024+4037, ou+oupō* [1]
yet, *4036, oun* [1]
yet not, *4037, oupō* [1]
yet, *4099, palin* [1]

YIELD [1]

yield, *NIG* [1]

YIELDED [1]

yielded, *4472, poieō* [1]

YIELDING [2]

yielding, *625, apodidōmi* [1]
yielding, *4472, poieō* [1]

YOKE [6]

yoke, *2433, zygos* [5]
yoke, *2414, zeugos* [1]

YOKED [1]

yoked together, *2282, heterozygeō* [1]

YOKEFELLOW [1]

yokefellow, *5187, syzygos* [1]

YOU [4002]

you, *5148, sy* [1990]
you, *AIT* [1633]
you, *RPE* [273]
you, *3836, ho* [17]
you, *NIG* [16]
you, *899, autos* [8]
you, *1571, heautou* [7]

you, *6043, ō²* [6]
you, *5629, hymeteros* [5]
yes it is as you say, *5148+3306, sy+legō* [4]
you, *4015, hostis* [3]
you^s, *476, anthrōpos* [2]
if you do, *3607, mēpote* [2]
you, *3836+6034+5148, ho+psychē+sy* [2]
you, *4932, seautou* [2]
you, *5050, sos* [2]
you, *5148+3836+2840, sy+ho+kardia* [2]
who do you think you are, *5515+4932+4472, tis+seautou+poieō* [2]
you, *467, anēr* [1]
you can see, *595+5148, apenanti+sy* [1]
you see, *1142, gar* [1]
you, *2625, idios* [1]
I assure you, *2627, idou* [1]
I tell you, *2627, idou* [1]
have all you want, *3170+1639, korennymi+eimi* [1]
how dare you, *3590, mē* [1]
you mean, *3590, mē* [1]
not are you, *3590, mē* [1]
you have, *3836+5050, ho+sos* [1]
you^s, *3836+4364, ho+peritomē* [1]
you, *3836+2840+5148, ho+kardia+sy* [1]
you, *3836+3950+5148, ho+onoma+sy* [1]
you, *3836+4725+5148, ho+prosōpon+sy* [1]
you, *4005, hos* [1]
as you are, *4048, houtōs* [1]
you, *4246, pas* [1]
belongs to you, *5050, sos* [1]
everything you can, *5081, spoudaiōs* [1]
both of you, *5148+2779+899, sy+kai+autos* [1]
the two of you, *5148+2779+899, sy+kai+autos* [1]
you, *5148+3836+3950, sy+ho+onoma* [1]
you, *5148+3836+4725, sy+ho+prosōpon* [1]
you^s, *6034, psychē* [1]
you, *6034+5148, psychē+sy* [1]

YOU'RE [6]

you're, *AIT* [5]
you're, *5148, sy* [1]

YOUNG [24]

young man, *3734, neaniskos* [7]
young men, *3734, neaniskos* [4]
young man, *3733, neanias* [3]
young, *3742, neos* [3]
the young man^s, *899, autos* [2]
young goat, *2253, eriphos* [1]
young, *3744, neotēs* [1]
young, *3801, nossos* [1]
young donkey, *3942, onarion* [1]
young man, *4090, pais* [1]

YOUNGER [10]

younger, *3742, neos* [8]
younger, *1781, elassōn* [1]
younger, *3625, mikros* [1]

YOUNGEST [1]

youngest, *3742, neos* [1]

YOUR [944]

your, *5148, sy* [705]
your, *3836, ho* [80]
your, *RPE* [51]
your, *AIT* [47]
your, *5050, sos* [12]
your own, *5148, sy* [8]
your, *899, autos* [3]
your, *2625, idios* [3]

your own, *1571, heautou* [2]
your, *1571, heautou* [2]
your, *1609, egō* [2]
your own, *2625, idios* [2]
your own, *2848+5148, kata+sy* [2]
your own, *4932, seautou* [2]
your own, *5629, hymeteros* [2]
your, *5629, hymeteros* [2]
your, *NIG* [1]
stand your ground, *468, anthistēmi* [1]
your slaves^s, *899, autos* [1]
on your guard, *1063, blepō* [1]
your hearts, *1571, heautou* [1]
on your feet, *1586, egeirō* [1]
your brother^s, *1697, ekeinos* [1]
your, *2848+5148, kata+sy* [1]
leave your life of sin, *3600+279, mēketi+hamartanō* [1]
your family, *3836+5050, ho+sos* [1]
your own, *3836+2625, ho+idios* [1]
your own, *3836, ho* [1]
your, *4005, hos* [1]
your generosity^s, *4015, hostis* [1]
your life, *4932, seautou* [1]
your very self, *4932, seautou* [1]
your, *4932, seautou* [1]
your own, *5050, sos* [1]
your hearts, *5148, sy* [1]

YOURS [25]

yours, *5148, sy* [14]
yours, *5050, sos* [6]
yours, *5629, hymeteros* [2]
yours, *RPE* [1]
yours, *1571, heautou* [1]
yours, *3836+5050, ho+sos* [1]

YOURSELF [50]

yourself, *4932, seautou* [32]
yourself, *AIT* [8]
yourself, *899, autos* [3]
yourself, *RPE* [2]
yourself, *5148, sy* [2]
yourself, *1571, heautou* [1]
yourself, *1667, hekastos* [1]
give yourself wholly to, *3509, meletaō* [1]

YOURSELVES [85]

yourselves, *1571, heautou* [30]
yourselves, *AIT* [25]
yourselves, *5148, sy* [12]
yourselves, *899, autos* [10]
yourselves, *RPE* [3]
yourselves, *253, allēlōn* [2]
yourselves, *2625, idios* [1]
yourselves, *3836+2840+5148, ho+kardia+sy* [1]
yourselves, *6034+5148, psychē+sy* [1]

YOUTH [1]

of youth, *3754, neōterikos* [1]

ZACCHAEUS [3]

Zacchaeus, *2405, Zakchaios* [3]

ZADOK [2]

Zadok, *4882, Sadōk* [2]

ZAREPHATH [1]

Zarephath, *4919, Sarepta* [1]

ZEAL [4]

zeal, *2419, zēlos* [2]

zeal, *RPE* [1]
zeal, *5082, spoudē* [1]

ZEALOT [4]

Zealot, *2421, zēlōtēs* [2]
Zealot, *2831, Kananaios* [2]

ZEALOUS [8]

zealous, *2420, zēloō* [2]
zealous, *2421, zēlōtēs* [2]
zealous, *2419, zēlos* [1]
zealous for, *2420, zēloō* [1]
zealous for, *2421, zēlōtēs* [1]
zealous, *5080, spoudaios* [1]

ZEBEDEE [10]

Zebedee, *2411, Zebedaios* [10]

ZEBEDEE'S [2]

Zebedee's, *2411, Zebedaios* [2]

ZEBULUN [3]

Zebulun, *2404, Zaboulōn* [3]

ZECHARIAH [10]

Zechariah, *2408, Zacharias* [10]

ZECHARIAH'S [2]

Zechariah's[s], *899, autos* [1]
Zechariah's, *2408, Zacharias* [1]

ZENAS [1]

Zenas, *2424, Zēnas* [1]

ZERAH [1]

Zerah, *2406, Zara* [1]

ZERUBBABEL [3]

Zerubbabel, *2431, Zorobabel* [3]

ZEUS [2]

Zeus, *2416, Zeus* [2]

ZION [7]

Zion, *4994, Siōn* [7]

KEY FEATURES OF THE GREEK-ENGLISH DICTIONARY

GREEK WORD
Each entry begins with three designations for the Greek word: the G/K number, the word in Greek, and in transliteration. See the introduction, page xvi.

DEFINITION
The concise definition is always in italics and is preceded and followed by periods. See the introduction, page xvi.

4 ἀβαρής, *abarēs*, a. *not burdensome.* S: *4*, BAGD: 1B, CB: –

11 Ἀβραάμ, *Abraam*, n.pr., "father of many." *Abraham.* S: *11*, BAGD: 1D, CB: 339A

PART OF SPEECH
The fourth element in each entry is the Greek part of speech. See the introduction, page xvi, and the abbreviation table below.

RESOURCE REFERENCES
Each word is referenced to Strong's numbering system and the dictionaries of Bauer, Arndt, Gingrich, and Danker, and of Colin Brown. A dash (–) means there is no reference. See the introduction, pages xvi-xvii.

PROPER NAME "DEFINITION"
If the Greek word is a proper name that has a meaning in Greek or Hebrew, the probable definition is offered in quotation marks. If sources differ in "definitions," they are cited by abbreviation. See the introduction, page xvi, and the abbreviation table below.

DICTIONARY ABBREVIATIONS

& ....and	disj. ....disjunctive	num. ....numeral
? ....uncertain	emph. .... emphatic	p. ....pronoun
+ ....plus	excl. ....exclamation	pers. .... personal
a. ....adjective	g. ....gentilic	pl. ....plural
adv. ....adverb	IDB .... *Interpreter's Dictionary*	poss. .... possessive
adver. ....adversative	*of the Bible*	pp. ....preposition
aff. ....affirmative	imper. ....impersonal	pp.* .... improper preposition
art. .... article	indef. ....indefinite	pr. ....proper [noun]
BAGD:.... Bauer, Arndt, Gingrich & Danker,	infer. ....inferential	pt. ....particle
Greek-English Lexicon	inten. ....intensive	recip. ....reciprocal
BDB .... Brown, Driver & Briggs,	inter. ....interrogative	reflex. ....reflexive
Hebrew and English Lexicon	interj. ....interjection	rel. ....relative
c. ....conjunction	ISBE .... *International Standard*	S: .... Strong's number
CB:...........................Colin Brown,	*Bible Encyclopedia*	super. .... superlative
New International Dictionary	KB ....Koehler and Baumgartner	temp. ....temporal
of New Testament Theology	*Lexicon in Veteris Testamenti Libros*	trans. ....transitional
comp. ....comparative	l. ....loanword	v. ....verb
cond. .... conditional	letter .... letter of the alphabet	ZPBE .... *Zondervan Pictorial*
contr. .... contraction	n. .... noun	*Bible Encyclopedia*
demo. ....demonstrative	neg. ....negative	

A Concise

Greek-English Dictionary

to the

New Testament

1 α, a , letter. *1) letter of the Greek alphabet; 2) inseparable prefix: 1.1 alpha privative (as non- or un- in English), 1.2 prefix of intensity, 1.3 prefix of similarity, collectivity or association.* S: *1*, BAGD: 1A, CB: 339A

2 Ἀαρών, *Aarōn*, n.pr. *Aaron.* S: *2*, BAGD: 1A, CB: –

3 Ἀβαδδών, *Abaddōn*, n.pr., "destruction." *Abaddon.* S: *3*, BAGD: 1A, CB: –

4 ἀβαρής, *abarēs*, a. *not burdensome.* S: *4*, BAGD: 1B, CB: –

5 ἀββά, *abba*, l.[n.]. *father.* S: *5**, BAGD: 1B, CB: 339A

6 Ἅβελ, *Habel*, n.pr., "morning mist." *Abel.* S: *6**, BAGD: 1C, CB: –

7 Ἀβιά, *Abia*, n.pr., "[my] father is Yahweh." *Abijah.* S: *7*, BAGD: 1C, CB: –

8 Ἀβιαθάρ, *Abiathar*, n.pr., "[my] father give abundance" *or* "the father is preeminent." *Abiathar.* S: *8**, BAGD: 1C, CB: –

9 Ἀβιληνή, *Abilēnē*, n.pr., *probably* "meadow." *Abilene.* S: *9*, BAGD: 1D, CB: –

10 Ἀβιούδ, *Abioud*, n.pr., "[my] father has majesty." *Abiud.* S: *10*, BAGD: 1D, CB: –

11 Ἀβραάμ, *Abraam*, n.pr., "father of many." *Abraham.* S: *11*, BAGD: 1D, CB: 339A

12 ἄβυσσος, *abyssos*, n., "unfathomable depth." *Abyss, the deep place.* S: *12*, BAGD: 2B, CB: 339A

13 Ἅγαβος, *Hagabos*, n.pr. *Agabus.* S: *13**, BAGD: 2B, CB: –

14 ἀγαθοεργέω, *agathoergeō*, v. *to do good.* S: *14*, BAGD: 2B, CB: 339B

15 ἀγαθοεργός, *agathoergos*, a. variant: *one who does good.* S: *18 + 2041*, BAGD: 2B, CB: –

16 ἀγαθοποιέω, *agathopoieō*, v. *to do good.* S: *15*, BAGD: 2C, CB: 339B

17 ἀγαθοποιΐα, *agathopoiia*, n. *doing good.* S: *16*, BAGD: 2C, CB: 339B

18 ἀγαθοποιός, *agathopoios*, a. *one who does good.* S: *17*, BAGD: 2C, CB: 339B

19 ἀγαθός, *agathos*, a. *good.* S: *18*, BAGD: 2D, CB: 339B

20 ἀγαθωσύνη, *agathōsynē*, n. *goodness.* S: *19*, BAGD: 3D, CB: 339B

21 ἀγαλλίασις, *agalliasis*, n. *delight, great joy.* S: *20*, BAGD: 3D, CB: 339B

22 ἀγαλλιάω, *agalliaō*, v. *to be filled with delight, with great joy.* S: *21*, BAGD: 3D, CB: 339B

23 ἄγαμος, *agamos*, n. *unmarried.* S: *22*, BAGD: 4B, CB: 339B

24 ἀγανακτέω, *aganakteō*, v. *to be indignant.* S: *23*, BAGD: 4B, CB: –

25 ἀγανάκτησις, *aganaktēsis*, n. *indignation.* S: *24*, BAGD: 4B, CB: –

26 ἀγαπάω, *agapaō*, v. *to love.* S: *25*, BAGD: 4B, CB: 339B

27 ἀγάπη, *agapē*, n. *love, love feast.* S: *26*, BAGD: 5B, CB: 339B

28 ἀγαπητός, *agapētos*, a. *dearly loved one.* S: *27*, BAGD: 6B, CB: 339B

29 Ἀγάρ, *Hagar*, n.pr. *Hagar.* S: *28**, BAGD: 6D, CB: –

30 ἀγγαρεύω, *angareuō*, v. *to force, compel.* S: *29*, BAGD: 6D, CB: –

31 ἀγγεῖον, *angeion*, n. *jar.* S: *30*, BAGD: 6D, CB: –

32 ἀγγελία, *angelia*, n. *message.* S: *31*, BAGD: 7A, CB: 341C

33 ἀγγέλλω, *angellō*, v. *to bring news, be a messenger.* S: *518**, BAGD: 7A, CB: 341C

34 ἄγγελος, *angelos*, n. *angel, messenger.* S: *32*, BAGD: 7A, CB: 341C

35 ἄγγος, *angos*, n. *basket.* S: *30**, BAGD: 8B, CB: –

36 ἀγέλη, *agelē*, n. *herd.* S: *34*, BAGD: 8B, CB: –

37 ἀγενεαλόγητος, *agenealogētos*, a. *without genealogy.* S: *35*, BAGD: 8C, CB: 339B

38 ἀγενής, *agenēs*, a. *lowly, insignificant.* S: *36*, BAGD: 8C, CB: –

39 ἁγιάζω, *hagiazō*, v. *to sanctify, set apart, make holy.* S: *37*, BAGD: 8C, CB: 355A

40 ἁγιασμός, *hagiasmos*, n. *holiness.* S: *38*, BAGD: 9A, CB: 355A

41 ἅγιος, *hagios*, a. *holy, saint.* S: *40 & 39*, BAGD: 9B, CB: 355A

42 ἁγιότης, *hagiotēs*, n. *holiness.* S: *41*, BAGD: 10B, CB: 355A

43 ἁγιωσύνη, hagiōsynē, n. *holiness.* S: *42*, BAGD: 10B, CB: 355A

44 ἀγκάλη, ankalē, n. *arm.* S: *43*, BAGD: 10C, CB: 341C

45 ἄγκιστρον, ankistron, n. *fish-hook, fish line with a hook on it.* S: *44*, BAGD: 10C, CB: –

46 ἄγκυρα, ankyra, n. *anchor.* S: *45*, BAGD: 10C, CB: –

47 ἄγναφος, agnaphos, a. *unshrunk.* S: *46*, BAGD: 10D, CB: –

48 ἁγνεία, hagneia, n. *purity.* S: *47*, BAGD: 10D, CB: 355A

49 ἁγνίζω, hagnizō, v. *to purify, ceremonially cleanse.* S: *48*, BAGD: 11A, CB: 355A

50 ἁγνισμός, hagnismos, n. *purification.* S: *49*, BAGD: 11A, CB: 355A

51 ἀγνοέω, agnoeō, v. *to be ignorant, not know, not understand.* S: *50*, BAGD: 11B, CB: 339B

52 ἀγνόημα, agnoēma, n. *sin committed in ignorance.* S: *51*, BAGD: 11C, CB: 339B

53 ἄγνοια, agnoia, n. *ignorance.* S: *52*, BAGD: 11D, CB: 339B

54 ἁγνός, hagnos, a. *pure, innocent.* S: *53*, BAGD: 11D, CB: 355A

55 ἁγνότης, hagnotēs, n. *purity.* S: *54*, BAGD: 12A, CB: 355A

56 ἁγνῶς, hagnōs, adv. *sincerely, purely.* S: *55*, BAGD: 12A, CB: 355A

57 ἀγνωσία, agnōsia, n. *ignorance.* S: *56*, BAGD: 12B, CB: 339C

58 ἄγνωστος, agnōstos, a. *unknown.* S: *57*, BAGD: 12B, CB: 339C

59 ἀγορά, agora, n. *marketplace.* S: *58*, BAGD: 12C, CB: 339C

60 ἀγοράζω, agorazō, v. *to buy, purchase.* S: *59*, BAGD: 12D, CB: 339C

61 ἀγοραῖος, agoraios, a. *marketplace, place where the courts meet.* S: *60*, BAGD: 13A, CB: 339C

62 ἄγρα, agra, n. #catch *(of fish).* S: *61*, BAGD: 13A, CB: –

63 ἀγράμματος, agrammatos, a. *unschooled.* S: *62*, BAGD: 13B, CB: 339C

64 ἀγραυλέω, agrauleō, v. *to live outdoors.* S: *63*, BAGD: 13B, CB: –

65 ἀγρεύω, agreuō, v. *to catch.* S: *64*, BAGD: 13B, CB: –

66 ἀγριέλαιος, agrielaios, n. *wild olive tree.* S: *65*, BAGD: 13B, CB: 339C

67 ἄγριος, agrios, a. *wild.* S: *66*, BAGD: 13C, CB: 339C

68 Ἀγρίππας, Agrippas, n.pr., "wild horse." *Agrippa.* S: *67*, BAGD: 13D, CB: –

69 ἀγρός, agros, n. *field, countryside.* S: *68*, BAGD: 13D, CB: 339C

70 ἀγρυπνέω, agrypneō, v. *to keep awake, keep alert.* S: *69*, BAGD: 14A, CB: 339C

71 ἀγρυπνία, agrypnia, n. *sleeplessness, wakefulness.* S: *70*, BAGD: 14A, CB: 339C

72 ἄγω, agō, v. *to bring, lead.* S: *71 & 33*, BAGD: 14B, CB: 339C

73 ἀγωγή, agōgē, n. *way of life.* S: *72*, BAGD: 14D, CB: 339C

74 ἀγών, agōn, n. *struggle, fight.* S: *73*, BAGD: 15A, CB: 339C

75 ἀγωνία, agōnia, n. *anguish, anxiety.* S: *74*, BAGD: 15A, CB: 339C

76 ἀγωνίζομαι, agōnizomai, v. *to fight, struggle.* S: *75*, BAGD: 15B, CB: 339C

77 Ἀδάμ, Adam, n.pr., "[red] earth" *or* "[ruddy] skin color." *Adam.* S: *76*, BAGD: 15C, CB: 339A

78 ἀδάπανος, adapanos, a. *free of charge.* S: *77*, BAGD: 15C, CB: –

79 Ἀδδί, Addi, n.pr., *poss.* "my witness" *or* "adorned." *Addi.* S: *78*, BAGD: 15D, CB: –

80 ἀδελφή, adelphē, n. *sister.* S: *79*, BAGD: 15D, CB: 339A

81 ἀδελφός, adelphos, n. *brother.* S: *80*, BAGD: 15D, CB: 339A

82 ἀδελφότης, adelphotēs, n. *brotherhood.* S: *81*, BAGD: 16C, CB: 339A

83 ἄδηλος, adēlos, a. *not clear.* S: *82*, BAGD: 16C, CB: –

84 ἀδηλότης, adēlotēs, n. *uncertainty.* S: *83*, BAGD: 16D, CB: –

85 ἀδήλως, adēlōs, adv. *aimlessly, uncertainly.* S: *84*, BAGD: 16D, CB: 339A

86 ἀδημονέω, adēmoneō, v. *to be troubled, distressed.* S: *85*, BAGD: 16D, CB: –

87 ᾅδης, hadēs, n., "the underworld." *Hades, the grave.* S: *86*, BAGD: 16D, CB: 354C

88 ἀδιάκριτος, adiakritos, a. *impartial.* S: *87*, BAGD: 17A, CB: 339A

89 ἀδιάλειπτος, adialeiptos, a. *constant, unceasing.* S: *88*, BAGD: 17B, CB: 339A

90 ἀδιαλείπτως, adialeiptōs, adv. *constantly, unceasingly.* S: *89*, BAGD: 17B, CB: 339A

91 ἀδιαφθορία, adiaphthoria, n. variant: *sincerity, integrity.* S: *90*, BAGD: 17B, CB: –

92 ἀδικέω, adikeō, v. *to do wrong, mistreat.* S: *91*, BAGD: 17C, CB: 339A

93 ἀδίκημα, adikēma, n. *crime.* S: *92*, BAGD: 17D, CB: 339A

94 ἀδικία, adikia, n. *wickedness, evil, wrongdoing.* S: *93*, BAGD: 17D, CB: 339A

95 ἀδικοκρίτης, adikokritēs, n. variant: *unjust judge.* S: *94 + 2923*, BAGD: 18B, CB: –

96 ἄδικος, adikos, a. *unjust, unrighteous.* S: *94*, BAGD: 18B, CB: 339A

97 ἀδίκως, adikōs, adv. variant: *unjustly.* S: *95*, BAGD: 18B, CB: 339A

98 Ἀδμίν, Admin, n.pr. variant: *Admin.* S: *689**, BAGD: 18C, CB: –

99 ἀδόκιμος, adokimos, a. *failing the test, rejected.* S: *96*, BAGD: 18C, CB: 339A

100 ἄδολος, adolos, a. *pure.* S: *97*, BAGD: 18D, CB: 339A

101 Ἀδραμυττηνός, Adramyttēnos, a.pr.g., "of Adramyttium." *of Adramyttium.* S: *98*, BAGD: 18D, CB: –

102 Ἀδρίας, Adrias, n.pr. *Adriatic Sea.* S: *99*, BAGD: 18D, CB: –

103 ἁδρότης, hadrotēs, n. *liberal gift, liberality.* S: *100*, BAGD: 18D, CB: –

104 ἀδυνατέω, adynateō, v. *to be impossible.* S: *101*, BAGD: 19A, CB: –

105 ἀδύνατος, adynatos, a. *impossible, powerless.* S: *102*, BAGD: 19A, CB: 339A

106 ᾄδω, adō, v. *to sing.* S: *103*, BAGD: 19B, CB: 339A

107 ἀεί, aei, adv. *always.* S: *104*, BAGD: 19C, CB: 339A

108 ἀετός, *aetos*, n. *eagle, vulture.* S: *105*, BAGD: 19D, CB: 339B

109 ἄζυμος, *azymos*, a. *unleavened, made without yeast.* S: *106*, BAGD: 19D, CB: 344B

110 Ἀζώρ, *Azōr*, n.pr. *Azor.* S: *107*, BAGD: 20A, CB: –

111 Ἄζωτος, *Azōtos*, n.pr. *Azotus.* S: *108*, BAGD: 20A, CB: –

112 ἀηδία, *aēdia*, n. variant: *enmity.* S: *150*, BAGD: 20A, CB: –

113 ἀήρ, *aēr*, n. *air, sky.* S: *109*, BAGD: 20B, CB: 339A

114 ἀθανασία, *athanasia*, n. *immortality.* S: *110*, BAGD: 20C, CB: 344A

115 ἀθάνατος, *athanatos*, a. variant: *immortal.* S: *2288 + 1*, BAGD: 20C, CB: 344A

116 ἀθέμιτος, *athemitos*, a. *unlawful, detestable.* S: *111*, BAGD: 20D, CB: –

117 ἄθεος, *atheos*, a. *without God.* S: *112*, BAGD: 20D, CB: 344A

118 ἄθεσμος, *athesmos*, a. *lawless.* S: *113*, BAGD: 21A, CB: –

119 ἀθετέω, *atheteō*, v. *to reject, set aside.* S: *114*, BAGD: 21A, CB: 344A

120 ἀθέτησις, *athetēsis*, n. *setting aside, doing away with.* S: *115*, BAGD: 21B, CB: 344A

121 Ἀθῆναι, *Athēnai*, n.pr. *Athens.* S: *116*, BAGD: 21B, CB: –

122 Ἀθηναῖος, *Athēnaios*, a.pr.g. *Athenian.* S: *117*, BAGD: 21B, CB: –

123 ἀθλέω, *athleō*, v. *to compete in a contest.* S: *118*, BAGD: 21B, CB: 344A

124 ἄθλησις, *athlēsis*, n. *contest.* S: *119*, BAGD: 21C, CB: 344A

125 ἀθροίζω, *athroizō*, v. *to assemble together.* S: *4867**, BAGD: 21C, CB: 344B

126 ἀθυμέω, *athymeō*, v. *to be discouraged.* S: *120*, BAGD: 21C, CB: –

127 ἀθῷος, *athōos*, a. *innocent.* S: *121**, BAGD: 21D, CB: –

128 αἴγειος, *aigeios*, a. *of a goat.* S: *122*, BAGD: 21D, CB: –

129 αἰγιαλός, *aigialos*, n. *shore, beach.* S: *123*, BAGD: 21D, CB: –

130 Αἰγύπτιος, *Aigyptios*, a.pr.g., "of Egypt." *Egyptian.* S: *124*, BAGD: 21D, CB: 339C

131 Αἴγυπτος, *Aigyptos*, n.pr. *Egypt.* S: *125*, BAGD: 22A, CB: 339C

132 ἀΐδιος, *aidios*, a. *eternal.* S: *126*, BAGD: 22A, CB: 339C

133 αἰδώς, *aidōs*, n. *decency, modesty.* S: *127*, BAGD: 22B, CB: 339C

134 Αἰθίοψ, *Aithiops*, n.pr.g. *Ethiopian.* S: *128*, BAGD: 22B, CB: –

135 αἷμα, *haima*, n. *blood.* S: *129*, BAGD: 22C, CB: 355A

136 αἱματεκχυσία, *haimatekchysia*, n. *shedding, pouring out of blood.* S: *130*, BAGD: 23B, CB: 355A

137 αἱμορροέω, *haimorroeō*, v. *to be subject to bleeding.* S: *131*, BAGD: 23C, CB: –

138 Αἰνέας, *Aineas*, n.pr., *poss.* "praise." *Aeneas.* S: *132*, BAGD: 23C, CB: –

139 αἴνεσις, *ainesis*, n. *praise.* S: *133*, BAGD: 23C, CB: 340A

140 αἰνέω, *aineō*, v. *to praise.* S: *134*, BAGD: 23C, CB: 339C

141 αἴνιγμα, *ainigma*, n. *poor reflection, indistinct image.* S: *135*, BAGD: 23C, CB: 340A

142 αἶνος, *ainos*, n. *praise.* S: *136*, BAGD: 23D, CB: 340A

143 Αἰνών, *Ainōn*, n.pr., "spring." *Aenon.* S: *137*, BAGD: 23D, CB: –

144 αἴξ, *aix*, n. variant: *goat.* S: *2056**, BAGD: 23D, CB: –

145 αἱρέομαι, *haireomai*, v. *to choose.* S: *138*, BAGD: 24A cf. -έω, CB: 355A

146 αἵρεσις, *hairesis*, n. *sect (religious party), faction, heresy.* S: *139*, BAGD: 23D, CB: 355A

147 αἱρετίζω, *hairetizō*, v. *to choose.* S: *140*, BAGD: 24A, CB: 355A

148 αἱρετικός, *hairetikos*, a. *divisive.* S: *141*, BAGD: 24A, CB: 355A

149 αἴρω, *airō*, v. *to take up, take away.* S: *142*, BAGD: 24B, CB: 340A

150 αἰσθάνομαι, *aisthanomai*, v. *to grasp, understand.* S: *143*, BAGD: 24D, CB: 340A

151 αἴσθησις, *aisthēsis*, n. *insight.* S: *144*, BAGD: 25A, CB: 340A

152 αἰσθητήριον, *aisthētērion*, n. *sense, faculty.* S: *145*, BAGD: 25A, CB: 340A

153 αἰσχροκερδής, *aischrokerdēs*, a. *pursuing dishonest gain.* S: *146*, BAGD: 25A, CB: 340A

154 αἰσχροκερδῶς, *aischrokerdōs*, adv. *in greediness for money.* S: *147*, BAGD: 25B, CB: –

155 αἰσχρολογία, *aischrologia*, n. *filthy language.* S: *148*, BAGD: 25B, CB: 340A

156 αἰσχρός, *aischros*, a. *disgraceful, shameful.* S: *150 & 149*, BAGD: 25B, CB: 340A

157 αἰσχρότης, *aischrotēs*, n. *obscenity.* S: *151*, BAGD: 25B, CB: 340A

158 αἰσχύνη, *aischynē*, n. *shamefulness.* S: *152*, BAGD: 25B, CB: 340A

159 αἰσχύνομαι, *aischynomai*, v. *to be ashamed.* S: *153*, BAGD: 25C, CB: 340A

160 αἰτέω, *aiteō*, v. *ask, ask for.* S: *154*, BAGD: 25D, CB: 340A

161 αἴτημα, *aitēma*, n. *request.* S: *155*, BAGD: 26B, CB: 340A

162 αἰτία, *aitia*, n. *(legal) charge; reason, cause.* S: *156*, BAGD: 26B, CB: 340A

163 αἰτίαμα, *aitiama*, n. variant: *charge, complaint.* S: *157*, BAGD: 26B, CB: 340A

164 αἰτιάομαι, *aitiaomai*, v. variant: *to charge.* S: *4256**, BAGD: 26C, CB: –

165 αἴτιος, *aitios*, a. *basis, cause (for legal charges), source.* S: *159 & 158*, BAGD: 26D, CB: 340A

166 αἰτίωμα, *aitiōma*, n. *(legal) charge.* S: *157**, BAGD: 26D, CB: 340A

167 αἰφνίδιος, *aiphnidios*, a. *sudden, unexpected.* S: *160*, BAGD: 26D, CB: –

168 αἰχμαλωσία, *aichmalōsia*, n. *captivity.* S: *161*, BAGD: 26D, CB: 339C

169 αἰχμαλωτεύω, *aichmalōteuō*, v. *to take captive.* S: *162*, BAGD: 26D, CB: 339C

170 αἰχμαλωτίζω, *aichmalōtizō*, v. *to take captive, take prisoner.* S: *163*, BAGD: 27A, CB: 339C

171 αἰχμάλωτος, *aichmalōtos*, n. *prisoner.* S: *164*, BAGD: 27A, CB: 339C

172 αἰών, *aiōn*, n. *eternity, age (time period).* S: *165*, BAGD: 27B, CB: 340A

173 αἰώνιος, *aiōnios*, a. *eternal, long ago.* S: *166*, BAGD: 28B, CB: 340A

174 ἀκαθαρσία, *akatharsia*, n. *impurity.* S: *167*, BAGD: 28D, CB: 340B

175 ἀκαθάρτης, *akathartēs*, n. variant: *uncleanness.* S: *168*, BAGD: 29A, CB: –

176 ἀκάθαρτος, *akathartos*, a. *unclean, evil.* S: *169*, BAGD: 29A, CB: 340B

177 ἀκαιρέομαι, *akaireomai*, v. *to have no opportunity, have no time.* S: *170*, BAGD: 29B, CB: 340A

178 ἀκαίρως, *akairōs*, adv. *out of season.* S: *171*, BAGD: 29B, CB: 340A

179 ἄκακος, *akakos*, a. *blameless, innocent, unsuspecting.* S: *172*, BAGD: 29B, CB: 340A

180 ἄκανθα, *akantha*, n. *thorn, thornbush.* S: *173*, BAGD: 29C, CB: 340A

181 ἀκάνθινος, *akanthinos*, a. *of thorns, thorny.* S: *174*, BAGD: 29C, CB: 340A

182 ἄκαρπος, *akarpos*, a. *unfruitful, unproductive.* S: *175*, BAGD: 29D, CB: 340A

183 ἀκατάγνωστος, *akatagnōstos*, a. *not condemned.* S: *176*, BAGD: 29D, CB: –

184 ἀκατακάλυπτος, *akatakalyptos*, a. *uncovered.* S: *177*, BAGD: 29D, CB: 340A

185 ἀκατάκριτος, *akatakritos*, a. *uncondemned, without a proper trial.* S: *178*, BAGD: 29D, CB: –

186 ἀκατάλυτος, *akatalytos*, a. *indestructible.* S: *179*, BAGD: 30A, CB: 340A

187 ἀκατάπαστος, *akatapastos*, a. variant: *unceasing, restless.* S: *180**, BAGD: 30A, CB: –

188 ἀκατάπαυστος, *akatapaustos*, a. *never stopping.* S: *180*, BAGD: 30A, CB: –

189 ἀκαταστασία, *akatastasia*, n. *disorder, rebellion, riot.* S: *181*, BAGD: 30A, CB: 340B

190 ἀκατάστατος, *akatastatos*, a. *unstable, restless.* S: *182*, BAGD: 30B, CB: –

191 ἀκατάσχετος, *akataschetos*, a. variant: *uncontrollable.* S: *183*, BAGD: 30B, CB: –

192 Ἀκελδαμάχ, *Hakeldamach*, n.pr., "field of blood." *Akeldama.* S: *184**, BAGD: 30B, CB: 340B

193 ἀκέραιος, *akeraios*, a. *innocent, pure.* S: *185*, BAGD: 30B, CB: –

194 ἀκηδεμονέω, *akēdemoneō*, v. variant: *be in distress, troubled.* S: *85**, BAGD: 30C, CB: –

195 ἀκλινής, *aklinēs*, a. *unswerving, without wavering.* S: *186*, BAGD: 30C, CB: –

196 ἀκμάζω, *akmazō*, v. *to be or become ripe.* S: *187*, BAGD: 30D, CB: 340B

197 ἀκμήν, *akmēn*, adv. *still, even yet.* S: *188*, BAGD: 30D, CB: 340B cf. *akmē*

198 ἀκοή, *akoē*, n. *(act of) hearing, what is heard.* S: *189*, BAGD: 30D, CB: 340B

199 ἀκολουθέω, *akoloutheō*, v. *to follow.* S: *190*, BAGD: 31A, CB: 340B

200 ἀκουστός, *akoustos*, a. variant: *audible.* S: *191*, BAGD: 31D, CB: 340B

201 ἀκούω, *akouō*, v. *to hear, obey.* S: *191*, BAGD: 31D, CB: 340B

202 ἀκρασία, *akrasia*, n. *lack of self-control.* S: *192*, BAGD: 33A, CB: 340B

203 ἀκρατής, *akratēs*, a. *without self-control.* S: *193*, BAGD: 33A, CB: 340B

204 ἄκρατος, *akratos*, a. *undiluted.* S: *194*, BAGD: 33A, CB: –

205 ἀκρίβεια, *akribeia*, n. *thoroughness, strictness.* S: *195*, BAGD: 33A, CB: –

206 ἀκριβέστατος, *akribestatos*, a. variant: *strictest.* S: *196*, BAGD: 33A, CB: –

207 ἀκριβής, *akribēs*, a. *strict.* S: *196**, BAGD: 33B, CB: –

208 ἀκριβόω, *akriboō*, v. *to find out exactly.* S: *198*, BAGD: 33B, CB: –

209 ἀκριβῶς, *akribōs*, adv. *accurately, carefully, well.* S: *199*, BAGD: 33B, CB: –

210 ἀκρίς, *akris*, n. *locust.* S: *200*, BAGD: 33C, CB: 340B

211 ἀκροατήριον, *akroatērion*, n. *audience room.* S: *201*, BAGD: 33C, CB: –

212 ἀκροατής, *akroatēs*, n. *hearer.* S: *202*, BAGD: 33C, CB: 340B

213 ἀκροβυστία, *akrobystia*, n. *uncircumcision.* S: *203*, BAGD: 33D, CB: 340B

214 ἀκρογωνιαῖος, *akrogōniaios*, a. *cornerstone.* S: *204*, BAGD: 33D, CB: 340B

215 ἀκροθίνιον, *akrothinion*, n. *plunder, booty.* S: *205*, BAGD: 33D, CB: –

216 ἄκρον, *akron*, n. *end, top.* S: *206*, BAGD: 34A, CB: –

217 Ἀκύλας, *Akylas*, n.pr., "eagle." *Aquila.* S: *207*, BAGD: 34A, CB: –

218 ἀκυρόω, *akyroō*, v. *to nullify, make void.* S: *208*, BAGD: 34B, CB: –

219 ἀκωλύτως, *akōlytōs*, adv. *without hinderance.* S: *209*, BAGD: 34B, CB: –

220 ἄκων, *akōn*, a. *not voluntary, unwilling.* S: *210*, BAGD: 34B, CB: –

221 ἅλα, *hala*, n. variant: *salt.* S: *217**, BAGD: 34B, CB: –

222 ἀλάβαστρον, *alabastron*, n. variant: *alabaster jar.* S: *211*, BAGD: 34C, CB: –

223 ἀλάβαστρος, *alabastros*, n. *alabaster jar.* S: *211*, BAGD: 34C, CB: –

224 ἀλαζονεία, *alazoneia*, n. *boasting.* S: *212*, BAGD: 34C, CB: 340B

225 ἀλαζών, *alazōn*, n. *boaster, braggart.* S: *213*, BAGD: 34D, CB: 340B

226 ἀλαλάζω, *alalazō*, v. *to clang, wail.* S: *214*, BAGD: 34D, CB: –

227 ἀλάλητος, *alaletos*, a. *inexpressible, unspeakable.* S: *215*, BAGD: 34D, CB: 340B

228 ἄλαλος, alalos, a. *mute, unable to speak.* S: *216*, BAGD: 34D, CB: 340B

229 ἅλας, halas, n. *salt.* S: *217*, BAGD: 35A, CB: 355A

230 ἀλείφω, aleiphō, v. *to pour on, anoint.* S: *218*, BAGD: 35B, CB: 340B

231 ἀλεκτοροφωνία, alektorophōnia, n. *crowing of a rooster.* S: *219*, BAGD: 35B, CB: 340B

232 ἀλέκτωρ, alektōr, n. *rooster.* S: *220*, BAGD: 35C, CB: –

233 Ἀλεξανδρεύς, Alexandreus, n.pr.g., "of Alexandria." *Alexandrian.* S: *221*, BAGD: 35C, CB: –

234 Ἀλεξανδρῖνος, Alexandrinos, a.pr.g., "of Alexandria." *Alexandrian.* S: *222*, BAGD: 35C, CB: –

235 Ἀλέξανδρος, Alexandros, n.pr., "defender of men." *Alexander.* S: *223*, BAGD: 35C, CB: –

236 ἄλευρον, aleuron, n. *flour.* S: *224*, BAGD: 35D, CB: –

237 ἀλήθεια, alētheia, n. *truth, truthfulness.* S: *225*, BAGD: 35D, CB: 340B

238 ἀληθεύω, alētheuō, v. *to be truthful, tell the truth.* S: *226*, BAGD: 36C, CB: 340B

239 ἀληθής, alēthēs, a. *true, genuine.* S: *227*, BAGD: 36D, CB: 340B

240 ἀληθινός, alēthinos, a. *true, genuine.* S: *228*, BAGD: 37A, CB: 340B

241 ἀλήθω, alēthō, v. *to grind grain.* S: *229*, BAGD: 37B, CB: –

242 ἀληθῶς, alēthōs, adv. *truly, surely.* S: *230*, BAGD: 37B, CB: 340B

243 ἀλιεύς, halieus, n. *fisherman.* S: *231*, BAGD: 37C, CB: –

244 ἀλιεύω, halieuō, v. *to fish.* S: *232*, BAGD: 37D, CB: –

245 ἁλίζω, halizō, v. *to salt, make salty.* S: *233*, BAGD: 37D, CB: 355A

246 ἀλίσγημα, alisgēma, n. *pollution, ritually defiled.* S: *234*, BAGD: 37D, CB: 340C cf. -mata

247 ἀλλά, alla, pt.adver. *but, instead, yet, except.* S: *235*, BAGD: 38A, CB: –

248 ἀλλάσσω, allassō, v. *to change, exchange.* S: *236*, BAGD: 39A, CB: 340C

249 ἀλλαχόθεν, allachothen, adv.pl. *from another way.* S: *237*, BAGD: 39B, CB: –

250 ἀλλαχοῦ, allachou, adv.pl. *elsewhere, somewhere else.* S: *150*, BAGD: 39B, CB: –

251 ἀλληγορέω, allēgoreō, v. *to take figuratively, speak allegorically.* S: *238*, BAGD: 39B, CB: 340C

252 ἀλληλουϊά, hallēlouia, l.[v.+n.pr.]. *hallelujah, praise the LORD.* S: *239*, BAGD: 39C, CB: 355A

253 ἀλλήλων, allēlōn, p.recip. *one another, each other.* S: *240*, BAGD: 39C, CB: 340C

254 ἀλλογενής, allogenēs, a. *foreign.* S: *241*, BAGD: 39C, CB: 340C

255 ἀλλοιόω, alloioō, v. variant: *to change.* S: *2087**, BAGD: 39C, CB: –

256 ἅλλομαι, hallomai, v. *to jump up, well up.* S: *242*, BAGD: 39D, CB: 355A

257 ἄλλος, allos, a. & n. *another, other.* S: *243*, BAGD: 39D, CB: 340C

258 ἀλλοτριεπίσκοπος, allotriepiskopos, n. *meddler, busybody.* S: *244*, BAGD: 40C, CB: 340C

259 ἀλλότριος, allotrios, a. *belonging to another.* S: *245*, BAGD: 40C, CB: 340C

260 ἀλλόφυλος, allophylos, a. *Gentile, foreigner.* S: *246*, BAGD: 41A, CB: 340C

261 ἄλλως, allōs, adv. *differently.* S: *247*, BAGD: 41A, CB: 340C

262 ἀλοάω, aloaō, v. *to tread, thresh.* S: *248*, BAGD: 41A, CB: –

263 ἄλογος, alogos, a. *unreasonable, without reason.* S: *249*, BAGD: 41A, CB: 340C

264 ἀλόη, aloē, n. *aloes.* S: *250*, BAGD: 41B, CB: –

265 ἅλς, hals, n. variant: *salt.* S: *251*, BAGD: 41B, CB: 355A

266 ἁλυκός, halykos, a. *salt spring, salty.* S: *252*, BAGD: 41B, CB: 355A

267 ἄλυπος, alypos, a. *free from anxiety.* S: *253**, BAGD: 41C, CB: –

268 ἅλυσις, halysis, n. *chain.* S: *254*, BAGD: 41C, CB: –

269 ἀλυσιτελής, alysitelēs, a. *unadvantageous.* S: *255*, BAGD: 41C, CB: –

270 ἄλφα, alpha, n.pr., "First" or "Beginning." *Alpha.* S: *1**, BAGD: 41C, CB: –

271 Ἀλφαῖος, Halphaios, n.pr. *Alphaeus.* S: *256**, BAGD: 41C, CB: –

272 ἅλων, halōn, n. *threshing floor.* S: *257*, BAGD: 41D, CB: 355A

273 ἀλώπηξ, alōpēx, n. *fox.* S: *258*, BAGD: 41D, CB: 340C

274 ἅλωσις, halōsis, n. *capture, catch.* S: *259*, BAGD: 42A, CB: 355A

275 ἅμα, hama, adv. & pp.*. *together, at the same time.* S: *260*, BAGD: 42A, CB: 355A

276 ἀμαθής, amathēs, a. *ignorant.* S: *261*, BAGD: 42B, CB: –

277 ἀμαράντινος, amarantinos, a. *unfading.* S: *262*, BAGD: 42B, CB: –

278 ἀμάραντος, amarantos, a. *never fading.* S: *263*, BAGD: 42B, CB: –

279 ἁμαρτάνω, hamartanō, v. *to sin, do wrong.* S: *264*, BAGD: 42B, CB: 355A

280 ἁμάρτημα, hamartēma, n. *sin, wrongdoing.* S: *265*, BAGD: 42D, CB: 355B

281 ἁμαρτία, hamartia, n. *sin, wrongdoing.* S: *266*, BAGD: 43A, CB: 355B

282 ἀμάρτυρος, amartyros, a. *without testimony, without witness.* S: *267*, BAGD: 44A, CB: –

283 ἁμαρτωλός, hamartōlos, a. *sinful, sinner.* S: *268*, BAGD: 44A, CB: 355B

284 Ἀμασίας, Amasias, n.pr., "Yahweh is powerful." variant: *Amaziah.* S: *150*, BAGD: 44C, CB: –

285 ἄμαχος, amachos, a. *peaceable, not quarrelsome.* S: *269*, BAGD: 44C, CB: 340C

286 ἀμάω, amaō, v. *to mow, cut down.* S: *270*, BAGD: 44C, CB: –

287 ἀμέθυστος, amethystos, n. *amethyst.* S: *271*, BAGD: 44C, CB: 340C

288 ἀμελέω, ameleō, v. *to neglect, ignore.* S: *272*, BAGD: 44D, CB: –

289 ἄμεμπτος, amemptos, a. *blameless, faultless.* S: *273*, BAGD: 45A, CB: 340C

290 ἀμέμπτως, amemptōs, adv. *blamelessly.* S: *274*, BAGD: 45A, CB: 340C

291 ἀμέριμνος, amerimnos, a. *free from concern, free from care.* S: *275*, BAGD: 45B, CB: 340C

292 ἀμετάθετος, ametathetos, a. *unchangeable, unchanging.* S: *276*, BAGD: 45B, CB: 340C cf. *-ton*

293 ἀμετακίνητος, ametakinētos, a. *not moveable, immovable.* S: *277*, BAGD: 45C, CB: –

294 ἀμεταμέλητος, ametamelētos, a. *without regret, so, not revocable.* S: *278*, BAGD: 45C, CB: 340C

295 ἀμετανόητος, ametanoētos, a. *unrepentant.* S: *279*, BAGD: 45C, CB: 340C

296 ἄμετρος, ametros, a. *beyond limits, immeasurable.* S: *280*, BAGD: 45C, CB: 340C

297 ἀμήν, amēn, l.[adv.]. *amen, the truth.* S: *281*, BAGD: 45C, CB: 340C

298 ἀμήτωρ, amētōr, a. *without a mother.* S: *282*, BAGD: 46A, CB: 340C

299 ἀμίαντος, amiantos, a. *pure.* S: *283*, BAGD: 46B, CB: 340C

300 Ἀμιναδάβ, Aminadab, n.pr., "my people are generous." *Amminadab.* S: *284*, BAGD: 46B, CB: –

301 ἄμμον, ammon, n. variant: *sand.* S: *150*, BAGD: 46B, CB: –

302 ἄμμος, ammos, n. *sand.* S: *285*, BAGD: 46B, CB: –

303 ἀμνός, amnos, n. *lamb.* S: *286*, BAGD: 46C, CB: 340C

304 ἀμοιβή, amoibē, n. *repayment, recompense.* S: *287*, BAGD: 46C, CB: –

305 ἄμορφος, amorphos, a. variant: *misshapen, ugly.* S: *880*, BAGD: 46C, CB: –

306 ἄμπελος, ampelos, n. *vine, grapevine.* S: *288*, BAGD: 46D, CB: 340C

307 ἀμπελουργός, ampelourgos, n. *one who takes care of a vineyard.* S: *289*, BAGD: 47A, CB: 340C

308 ἀμπελών, ampelōn, n. *vineyard.* S: *290*, BAGD: 47A, CB: 340C

309 Ἀμπλιᾶτος, Ampliatos, n.pr. *Ampliatus.* S: *291**, BAGD: 47A, CB: –

310 ἀμύνομαι, amynomai, v. *to defend, help, come to the aid of.* S: *292*, BAGD: 47A, CB: –

311 ἀμφιβάλλω, amphiballō, v. *to cast a fishnet.* S: *906** + *293*, BAGD: 47B, CB: 340C

312 ἀμφίβληστρον, amphiblēstron, n. *casting net, fishing net.* S: *293*, BAGD: 47B, CB: –

313 ἀμφιέζω, amphiezō, v. *to clothe, dress.* S: *294**, BAGD: 47C, CB: –

314 ἀμφιέννυμι, amphiennymi, v. *to dress, clothe.* S: *294*, BAGD: 47C, CB: –

315 Ἀμφίπολις, Amphipolis, n.pr., "a city surrounded" *or* "a city conspicuous." *Amphipolis.* S: *295*, BAGD: 47C, CB: –

316 ἄμφοδον, amphodon, n. *street.* S: *296*, BAGD: 47C, CB: –

317 ἀμφότεροι, amphoteroi, a. *both, all.* S: *297**, BAGD: 47C, CB: 340C cf. *-ros*

318 ἀμώμητος, amōmētos, a. *blameless, unblemished.* S: *298*, BAGD: 47D, CB: 340C

319 ἄμωμον, amōmon, n. *spice.* S: *150*, BAGD: 47D, CB: 340C cf. *-mos*

320 ἄμωμος, amōmos, a. *unblemished, blameless.* S: *299*, BAGD: 47D, CB: 340C

321 Ἀμών, Amōn, n.pr., "trustworthy." *Amon.* S: *300*, BAGD: 48A, CB: –

322 Ἀμώς, Amōs, n.pr., "burden bearer." *Amos.* S: *301*, BAGD: 48A, CB: –

323 ἄν, an, pt. *not easily translated: indicates potential or condition.* S: *302*, BAGD: 48B, CB: –

324 ἀνά, ana, pp. *each, in turn, among.* S: *303*, BAGD: 49D, CB: 341A

325 ἀναβαθμός, anabathmos, n. *step.* S: *304*, BAGD: 50A, CB: –

326 ἀναβαίνω, anabainō, v. *to go up, rise.* S: *305*, BAGD: 50A, CB: 341A

327 ἀναβάλλω, anaballō, v. *to adjourn a proceeding.* S: *306**, BAGD: 50C, CB: –

328 ἀναβιβάζω, anabibazō, v. *to pull up, bring up.* S: *307*, BAGD: 50D, CB: –

329 ἀναβλέπω, anablepō, v. *to look up, receive sight.* S: *308*, BAGD: 50D, CB: 341A

330 ἀνάβλεψις, anablepsis, n. *recovery of sight.* S: *309*, BAGD: 51A, CB: –

331 ἀναβοάω, anaboaō, v. *to cry out.* S: *310*, BAGD: 51A, CB: 341A

332 ἀναβολή, anabolē, n. *delay, postponement.* S: *311*, BAGD: 51A, CB: –

333 ἀνάγαιον, anagaion, n. *upper room.* S: *508**, BAGD: 51A, CB: –

334 ἀναγγέλλω, anangellō, v. *to tell, report, announce.* S: *312*, BAGD: 51B, CB: 341B

335 ἀναγεννάω, anagennaō, v. *to give new birth, cause to be born again.* S: *313*, BAGD: 51C, CB: 341A

336 ἀναγινώσκω, anaginōskō, v. *to read, read aloud.* S: *314*, BAGD: 51C, CB: 341A

337 ἀναγκάζω, anankazō, v. *to compel, force.* S: *315*, BAGD: 52A, CB: 341B

338 ἀναγκαῖος, anankaios, a. *necessary, indispensable.* S: *316*, BAGD: 52B, CB: 341B

339 ἀναγκαστῶς, anankastōs, adv. *a must, by compulsion.* S: *317*, BAGD: 52B, CB: 341B

340 ἀνάγκη, anankē, n. *necessity; distress, hardship.* S: *318*, BAGD: 52B, CB: 341B

341 ἀναγνωρίζω, anagnōrizō, v. *to tell, make known again.* S: *319**, BAGD: 52D, CB: –

342 ἀνάγνωσις, anagnōsis, n. *reading, public reading.* S: *320*, BAGD: 52D, CB: 341A

343 ἀνάγω, anagō, v. *to lead up, bring up; (mid.) to put out to sea.* S: *321*, BAGD: 53A, CB: 339C cf. *agō*

344 ἀναδείκνυμι, anadeiknymi, v. *to show, appoint.* S: *322*, BAGD: 53B, CB: 341A

345 ἀνάδειξις, anadeixis, n. *public appearance.* S: *323*, BAGD: 53C, CB: 341A

346 ἀναδέχομαι, *anadechomai*, v. *to receive, welcome.* S: *324*, BAGD: 53C, CB: –

347 ἀναδίδωμι, *anadidōmi*, v. *to deliver, hand over.* S: *325*, BAGD: 53C, CB: –

348 ἀναζάω, *anazaō*, v. *to become alive again.* S: *326*, BAGD: 53D, CB: 341B

349 ἀναζητέω, *anazēteō*, v. *to look for, search for.* S: *327*, BAGD: 53D, CB: –

350 ἀναζώννυμι, *anazōnnymi*, v. *to gird, bind (to prepare for action).* S: *328*, BAGD: 53D, CB: 379C cf. *zōnnymi*

351 ἀναζωπυρέω, *anazōpyreō*, v. *to fan a flame, rekindle.* S: *329*, BAGD: 54A, CB: –

352 ἀναθάλλω, *anathallō*, v. *to renew, cause to grow or bloom again.* S: *330*, BAGD: 54A, CB: –

353 ἀνάθεμα, *anathema*, n. *curse, oath; one cursed.* S: *331*, BAGD: 54A, CB: 341B

354 ἀναθεματίζω, *anathematizō*, v. *to bind with an oath.* S: *332*, BAGD: 54C, CB: 341B

355 ἀναθεωρέω, *anatheōreō*, v. *to look carefully at.* S: *333*, BAGD: 54C, CB: 378A cf. *theōreō*

356 ἀνάθημα, *anathēma*, n. *gifts dedicated to God.* S: *334*, BAGD: 54C, CB: 341B

357 ἀναίδεια, *anaideia*, n. *boldness.* S: *335*, BAGD: 54C, CB: –

358 ἀναίρεσις, *anairesis*, n. *death.* S: *336*, BAGD: 54D, CB: –

359 ἀναιρέω, *anaireō*, v. *to kill, put to death; (mid.) take for oneself.* S: *337*, BAGD: 54D, CB: –

360 ἀναίτιος, *anaitios*, a. *innocent.* S: *338*, BAGD: 55B, CB: 341A

361 ἀνακαθίζω, *anakathizō*, v. *to sit up.* S: *339*, BAGD: 55B, CB: –

362 ἀνακαινίζω, *anakainizō*, v. *to bring back, restore.* S: *340*, BAGD: 55B, CB: 341A

363 ἀνακαινόω, *anakainoō*, v. *to renew.* S: *341*, BAGD: 55C, CB: 341A

364 ἀνακαίνωσις, *anakainōsis*, n. *renewal.* S: *342*, BAGD: 55C, CB: 341A

365 ἀνακαλύπτω, *anakalyptō*, v. *to unveil, uncover.* S: *343*, BAGD: 55C, CB: 341A

366 ἀνακάμπτω, *anakamptō*, v. *to return, come back.* S: *344*, BAGD: 55C, CB: –

367 ἀνάκειμαι, *anakeimai*, v. *to recline for a meal, dine.* S: *345*, BAGD: 55D, CB: 341A

368 ἀνακεφαλαιόω, *anakephalaioō*, v. *to bring together under one head, summarize.* S: *346**, BAGD: 55D, CB: 341A cf. *-oomai*

369 ἀνακλίνω, *anaklinō*, v. *to cause to lie down, recline (to eat).* S: *347*, BAGD: 56A, CB: 341A cf. *-omai*

370 ἀνακόπτω, *anakoptō*, v. variant: *to hinder, restrain.* S: *348*, BAGD: 56B, CB: –

371 ἀνακράζω, *anakrazō*, v. *to cry out.* S: *349*, BAGD: 56B, CB: –

372 ἀνακραυγάζω, *anakraugazō*, v. variant: *to cry out.* S: *150*, BAGD: 56B, CB: –

373 ἀνακρίνω, *anakrinō*, v. *to examine, judge.* S: *350*, BAGD: 56B, CB: 341A

374 ἀνάκρισις, *anakrisis*, n. *investigation.* S: *351*, BAGD: 56C, CB: –

375 ἀνακυλίω, *anakyliō*, v. variant: *to roll away.* S: *617*, BAGD: 56C, CB: –

376 ἀνακύπτω, *anakyptō*, v. *to straighten up, stand erect.* S: *352*, BAGD: 56C, CB: –

377 ἀναλαμβάνω, *analambanō*, v. *to take up, lift up, bring up.* S: *353*, BAGD: 56D, CB: 341A

378 ἀνάλημψις, *analēmpsis*, n. *taking up, ascension.* S: *354**, BAGD: 57A, CB: –

379 ἀναλίσκω, *analiskō*, v. variant: *to consume, destroy.* S: *355*, BAGD: 57A, CB: –

380 ἀνάλλομαι, *anallomai*, v. variant: *to jump up.* S: *242*, BAGD: 57B, CB: –

381 ἀναλογία, *analogia*, n. *proportion, right relationship.* S: *356*, BAGD: 57B, CB: 341A

382 ἀναλογίζομαι, *analogizomai*, v. *to consider, think carefully.* S: *357*, BAGD: 57B, CB: 363A cf. *logizomai*

383 ἄναλος, *analos*, a. *not salty.* S: *358*, BAGD: 57B, CB: 341A

384 ἀναλόω, *analoō*, v. *to destroy, consume.* S: *355*, BAGD: 57B, CB: –

385 ἀνάλυσις, *analysis*, n. *departure (i.e., death).* S: *359*, BAGD: 57B, CB: –

386 ἀναλύω, *analyō*, v. *to depart (i.e., die), return.* S: *360*, BAGD: 57C, CB: 341A

387 ἀναμάρτητος, *anamartētos*, a. *without sin.* S: *361*, BAGD: 57C, CB: –

388 ἀναμένω, *anamenō*, v. *to wait for, expect.* S: *362*, BAGD: 57D, CB: 341A

389 ἀναμιμνήσκω, *anamimnēskō*, v. *to remember, remind.* S: *363**, BAGD: 57D, CB: 341A

390 ἀνάμνησις, *anamnēsis*, n. *reminder, remembrance.* S: *364*, BAGD: 58A, CB: 341A

391 ἀνανεόομαι, *ananeoomai*, v. *to be made new, renewed.* S: *365**, BAGD: 58A, CB: 341B

392 ἀνανήφω, *ananēphō*, v. *to come to one's senses.* S: *366*, BAGD: 58B, CB: 341B

393 Ἀνανίας, *Hananias*, n.pr., "Yahweh is gracious." *Ananias.* S: *367**, BAGD: 58B, CB: –

394 ἀναντίρρητος, *anantirrētos*, a. *undeniable, indisputable.* S: *368*, BAGD: 58C, CB: –

395 ἀναντιρρήτως, *anantirrētōs*, adv. *without raising any objection, indisputable.* S: *369*, BAGD: 58C, CB: –

396 ἀνάξιος, *anaxios*, a. *not competent, unworthy.* S: *370*, BAGD: 58C, CB: 341B

397 ἀναξίως, *anaxiōs*, adv. *in an unworthy manner.* S: *371*, BAGD: 58D, CB: 341B

398 ἀνάπαυσις, *anapausis*, n. *rest, resting place.* S: *372*, BAGD: 58D, CB: 341B

399 ἀναπαύω, *anapauō*, v. *to rest, be refreshed; (act.) to give rest.* S: *373*, BAGD: 58D, CB: 341B

400 ἀναπείθω, *anapeithō*, v. *to persuade.* S: *374*, BAGD: 59B, CB: –

401 ἀνάπειρος, *anapeiros*, a. *crippled.* S: *376**, BAGD: 59B, CB: –

402 ἀναπέμπω, *anapempō*, v. *to send.* S: *375*, BAGD: 59B, CB: –

403 ἀναπηδάω, *anapēdaō*, v. *jump up, stand up.* S: *450**, BAGD: 59C, CB: –

404 ἀναπίπτω, *anapiptō*, v. *recline, sit down, lie down.* S: *377*, BAGD: 59C, CB: 341B

405 ἀναπληρόω, *anaplēroō*, v. *to fulfill, make complete.* S: *378*, BAGD: 59C, CB: 341B

406 ἀναπολόγητος, *anapologētos*, a. *without excuse.* S: *379*, BAGD: 60A, CB: 341B

407 ἀναπράσσω, *anaprassō*, v. variant: *to demand.* S: *4238**, BAGD: 60A, CB: –

408 ἀναπτύσσω, *anaptyssō*, v. *to unroll.* S: *380*, BAGD: 60A, CB: –

409 ἀνάπτω, *anaptō*, v. *to set on fire.* S: *381*, BAGD: 60A, CB: –

410 ἀναρίθμητος, *anarithmētos*, a. *countless.* S: *382*, BAGD: 60A, CB: –

411 ἀνασείω, *anaseiō*, v. *to stir up, incite.* S: *383*, BAGD: 60A, CB: 341B

412 ἀνασκευάζω, *anaskeuazō*, v. *to trouble, upset.* S: *384*, BAGD: 60A, CB: –

413 ἀνασπάω, *anaspaō*, v. *to pull up, draw out.* S: *385*, BAGD: 60B, CB: –

414 ἀνάστασις, *anastasis*, n. *resurrection, rising to life.* S: *386*, BAGD: 60B, CB: 341B

415 ἀναστατόω, *anastatoō*, v. *to cause trouble, start a revolt.* S: *387*, BAGD: 61A, CB: –

416 ἀνασταυρόω, *anastauroō*, v. *to crucify again.* S: *388*, BAGD: 61A, CB: 341B

417 ἀναστενάζω, *anastenazō*, v. *to sigh deeply.* S: *389*, BAGD: 61B, CB: –

418 ἀναστρέφω, *anastrephō*, v. *to conduct oneself, live (in a certain way); to return.* S: *390*, BAGD: 61B, CB: 341B

419 ἀναστροφή, *anastrophē*, n. *way of life, behavior.* S: *391*, BAGD: 61C, CB: 341B

420 ἀνασῴζω, *anasōzō*, v. variant: *to save.* S: *150*, BAGD: 61D, CB: –

421 ἀνατάσσομαι, *anatassomai*, v. *to draw up (an account), compile.* S: *392*, BAGD: 61D, CB: 341B

422 ἀνατέλλω, *anatellō*, v. *to rise, dawn.* S: *393*, BAGD: 62A, CB: 341B

423 ἀνατίθημι, *anatithēmi*, v. *to set before, declare before.* S: *394**, BAGD: 62B, CB: –

424 ἀνατολή, *anatolē*, n. *east, rising of the sun.* S: *395*, BAGD: 62B, CB: 341B

425 ἀνατολικός, *anatolikos*, a. variant: *eastern.* S: *510*, BAGD: 62C, CB: 341B cf. *anatolē*

426 ἀνατρέπω, *anatrepō*, v. *to overturn, destroy.* S: *396*, BAGD: 62C, CB: –

427 ἀνατρέφω, *anatrephō*, v. *to bring up, care for.* S: *397*, BAGD: 62D, CB: –

428 ἀναφαίνω, *anaphainō*, v. *to appear.* S: *398*, BAGD: 63A, CB: 369C cf. *phainō*

429 ἀναφέρω, *anapherō*, v. *to lead up, offer (a sacrifice), bear (sin).* S: *399*, BAGD: 63A, CB: 341B

430 ἀναφωνέω, *anaphōneō*, v. *to exclaim, cry out loudly.* S: *400*, BAGD: 63B, CB: –

431 ἀνάχυσις, *anachysis*, n. *flood, wide stream.* S: *401*, BAGD: 63C, CB: –

432 ἀναχωρέω, *anachōreō*, v. *to withdraw, leave.* S: *402*, BAGD: 63C, CB: 341A

433 ἀνάψυξις, *anapsyxis*, n. *refreshment, relaxation, relief.* S: *403*, BAGD: 63C, CB: 341B

434 ἀναψύχω, *anapsychō*, v. *to refresh, revive.* S: *404*, BAGD: 63D, CB: 341B

435 ἀνδραποδιστής, *andrapodistēs*, n. *slave trader, kidnapper.* S: *405*, BAGD: 63D, CB: 341B

436 Ἀνδρέας, *Andreas*, n.pr., "manly." *Andrew.* S: *406*, BAGD: 63D, CB: –

437 ἀνδρίζομαι, *andrizomai*, v. *to act courageously.* S: *407*, BAGD: 64A, CB: –

438 Ἀνδρόνικος, *Andronikos*, n.pr., "victor over men." *Andronicus.* S: *408*, BAGD: 64A, CB: –

439 ἀνδροφόνος, *androphonos*, n. *murderer.* S: *409*, BAGD: 64A, CB: –

440 ἀνεγκλησία, *anenklēsia*, n. variant: *blamelessness.* S: *507 + 2821*, BAGD: 64A, CB: –

441 ἀνέγκλητος, *anenklētos*, a. *blameless, free from accusation.* S: *410*, BAGD: 64B, CB: 341C

442 ἀνεκδιήγητος, *anekdiēgētos*, a. *indescribable.* S: *411*, BAGD: 64B, CB: –

443 ἀνεκλάλητος, *aneklalētos*, a. *inexpressible.* S: *412*, BAGD: 64B, CB: –

444 ἀνέκλειπτος, *anekleiptos*, a. *not exhaustible, unfailing.* S: *413*, BAGD: 64B, CB: –

445 ἀνεκτός, *anektos*, a. *bearable, tolerable.* S: *414**, BAGD: 64C, CB: 341C

446 ἀνελεήμων, *aneleēmōn*, a. *ruthless, merciless.* S: *415*, BAGD: 64C, CB: 341C

447 ἀνέλεος, *aneleos*, a. *merciless.* S: *448**, BAGD: 64C, CB: 341C

448 ἀνεμίζω, *anemizō*, v. *to be moved by the wind.* S: *416*, BAGD: 64C, CB: –

449 ἄνεμος, *anemos*, n. *wind, gale.* S: *417*, BAGD: 64D, CB: 341C

450 ἀνένδεκτος, *anendektos*, a. *impossible.* S: *418*, BAGD: 65A, CB: –

451 ἀνεξεραύνητος, *anexeraunētos*, a. *unsearchable, inscrutable.* S: *419**, BAGD: 65A, CB: 341C

452 ἀνεξίκακος, *anexikakos*, a. *not resentful, patient.* S: *420*, BAGD: 65A, CB: –

453 ἀνεξιχνίαστος, *anexichniastos*, a. *unsearchable, incomprehensible.* S: *421*, BAGD: 65A, CB: –

454 ἀνεπαίσχυντος, *anepaischyntos*, a. *unashamed.* S: *422*, BAGD: 65A, CB: –

455 ἀνεπίλημπτος, *anepilēmptos*, a. *above reproach, not open to blame.* S: *423**, BAGD: 65B, CB: 341C cf. *-ēmptos*

456 ἀνέρχομαι, *anerchomai*, v. *to go up.* S: *424*, BAGD: 65B, CB: –

457 ἄνεσις, *anesis*, n. *rest, relaxation, relief.* S: *425*, BAGD: 65B, CB: –

458 ἀνετάζω, *anetazō*, v. *to question, examine, interrogate.* S: *426*, BAGD: 65C, CB: –

459 ἄνευ, *aneu*, pp.*. *without, apart from.* S: *427*, BAGD: 65C, CB: –

460 ἀνεύθετος, *aneuthetos*, a. *unsuitable, poor.* S: *428*, BAGD: 65C, CB: –

461 ἀνευρίσκω, *aneuriskō*, v. *to find.* S: *429*, BAGD: 65D, CB: –

462 ἀνέχομαι, *anechomai*, v. *to put up with, endure.* S: *430*, BAGD: 65D, CB: 341B

463 ἀνεψιός, *anepsios*, n. *cousin.* S: *431*, BAGD: 66A, CB: –

464 ἄνηθον, *anēthon*, n. *dill.* S: *432*, BAGD: 66A, CB: 341C

465 ἀνήκω, *anēkō*, v. *to be fitting, proper; to do one's duty.* S: *433*, BAGD: 66B, CB: 341C

466 ἀνήμερος, *anēmeros*, a. *brutal, savage.* S: *434*, BAGD: 66C, CB: –

467 ἀνήρ, *anēr*, n. *man, male.* S: *435*, BAGD: 66C, CB: 341C

468 ἀνθίστημι, *anthistēmi*, v. *to resist, oppose, rebel, withstand.* S: *436*, BAGD: 67B, CB: –

469 ἀνθομολογέομαι, *anthomologeomai*, v. *to give thanks, praise.* S: *437*, BAGD: 67B, CB: –

470 ἄνθος, *anthos*, n. *flower, blossom.* S: *438*, BAGD: 67C, CB: 342A

471 ἀνθρακιά, *anthrakia*, n. *charcoal fire.* S: *439*, BAGD: 67C, CB: 342A cf. *-rach*

472 ἄνθραξ, *anthrax*, n. *coal, charcoal.* S: *440*, BAGD: 67C, CB: 342A

473 ἀνθρωπάρεσκος, *anthrōpareskos*, a. *one who wins favor, who pleases people.* S: *441*, BAGD: 67D, CB: 342A

474 ἀνθρώπινος, *anthrōpinos*, a. *human, common to mankind.* S: *442*, BAGD: 67D, CB: 342A

475 ἀνθρωποκτόνος, *anthrōpoktonos*, n. *murderer.* S: *443*, BAGD: 68A, CB: –

476 ἄνθρωπος, *anthrōpos*, n. *human being, person, mankind.* S: *444*, BAGD: 68B, CB: 342A

477 ἀνθυπατεύω, *anthypateuō*, v. variant: *to be proconsul.* S: *445*, BAGD: 69C, CB: –

478 ἀνθύπατος, *anthypatos*, n. *proconsul.* S: *446*, BAGD: 69C, CB: 342A

479 ἀνίημι, *aniēmi*, v. *loosen, untie; leave, abandon.* S: *447*, BAGD: 69D, CB: –

480 ἀνίλεως, *anileōs*, a. variant: *merciless.* S: *448*, BAGD: 69D, CB: 341C

481 ἄνιπτος, *aniptos*, a. *unwashed.* S: *449*, BAGD: 69D, CB: 341C

482 ἀνίστημι, *anistēmi*, v. *to get up, stand up, come back to life.* S: *450*, BAGD: 70A, CB: 341C

483 Ἄννα, *Hanna*, n.pr., "grace." *Anna.* S: *451**, BAGD: 70C, CB: –

484 Ἄννας, *Hannas*, n.pr., "grace." *Annas.* S: *452**, BAGD: 70C, CB: –

485 ἀνόητος, *anoētos*, a. *foolish, senseless.* S: *453*, BAGD: 70D, CB: 341C

486 ἄνοια, *anoia*, n. *folly, senselessness; fury.* S: *454*, BAGD: 70D, CB: 341C

487 ἀνοίγω, *anoigō*, v. *to open.* S: *455*, BAGD: 70D, CB: 341C

488 ἀνοικοδομέω, *anoikodomeō*, v. *to rebuild.* S: *456*, BAGD: 71C, CB: 366B cf. *oikodomeō*

489 ἄνοιξις, *anoixis*, n. *(the act of) opening.* S: *457*, BAGD: 71C, CB: 341C

490 ἀνομία, *anomia*, n. *wickedness, lawlessness, lawless deed.* S: *458*, BAGD: 71D, CB: 341C

491 ἄνομος, *anomos*, a. *without law, transgressing law.* S: *459*, BAGD: 72A, CB: 341C

492 ἀνόμως, *anomōs*, adv. *apart from law, without law.* S: *460*, BAGD: 72B, CB: 341C

493 ἀνόνητος, *anonētos*, a. variant: *useless.* S: *453**, BAGD: 72B, CB: –

494 ἀνορθόω, *anorthoō*, v. *to restore, rebuild, strengthen.* S: *461*, BAGD: 72C, CB: –

495 ἀνόσιος, *anosios*, a. *unholy, wicked.* S: *462*, BAGD: 72C, CB: 341C

496 ἀνοχή, *anochē*, n. *tolerance, forbearance, clemency.* S: *463*, BAGD: 72C, CB: 341C

497 ἀνταγωνίζομαι, *antagōnizomai*, v. *to struggle against.* S: *464*, BAGD: 72D, CB: 342A

498 ἀντάλλαγμα, *antallagma*, n. *something given in exchange.* S: *465*, BAGD: 72D, CB: 342A

499 ἀνταναπληρόω, *antanaplēroō*, v. *to fill up, complete.* S: *466*, BAGD: 72D, CB: 342A

500 ἀνταποδίδωμι, *antapodidōmi*, v. *to repay, return.* S: *467*, BAGD: 73A, CB: 342A

501 ἀνταπόδομα, *antapodoma*, n. *repayment, retribution.* S: *468*, BAGD: 73A, CB: 342A

502 ἀνταπόδοσις, *antapodosis*, n. *reward, repayment.* S: *469*, BAGD: 73A, CB: 342A

503 ἀνταποκρίνομαι, *antapokrinomai*, v. *to talk back, answer.* S: *470*, BAGD: 73B, CB: –

504 ἀντέχω, *antechō*, v. *to be devoted, hold firmly to; pay attention to.* S: *472**, BAGD: 73B, CB: –

505 ἀντί, *anti*, pp. *in exchange for, in place of, instead of, (one) after (another).* S: *473*, BAGD: 73C, CB: 342A

506 ἀντιβάλλω, *antiballō*, v. *to discuss, exchange (words).* S: *474*, BAGD: 74A, CB: –

507 ἀντιδιατίθημι, *antidiatithēmi*, v. *to oppose.* S: *475**, BAGD: 74A, CB: –

508 ἀντίδικος, *antidikos*, n. *enemy, opponent.* S: *476*, BAGD: 74A, CB: 342A

509 ἀντίθεσις, *antithesis*, n. *opposition, objection.* S: *477*, BAGD: 74B, CB: –

510 ἀντικαθίστημι, *antikathistēmi*, v. *to resist, oppose, contest against.* S: *478*, BAGD: 74B, CB: –

511 ἀντικαλέω, *antikaleō*, v. *to invite in reciprocation.* S: *479*, BAGD: 74B, CB: 359B cf. *kaleō*

512 ἀντίκειμαι, *antikeimai*, v. *to be an opponent, in conflict.* S: *480*, BAGD: 74B, CB: –

513 ἄντικρυς, *antikrys*, adv. *opposite of, in proximity to.* S: *481**, BAGD: 74C, CB: –

514 ἀντιλαμβάνω, *antilambanō*, v. *to help, come to the aid of, benefit.* S: *482**, BAGD: 74C, CB: –

515 ἀντιλέγω, *antilegō*, v. *to speak against, talk back, contradict.* S: *483 & 471*, BAGD: 74D, CB: –

516 ἀντίλημψις, antilēmpsis, n. help, ability to aid. S: 484*, BAGD: 75A, CB: –

517 ἀντιλογία, antilogia, n. argument, opposition, rebellion. S: 485, BAGD: 75A, CB: –

518 ἀντιλοιδορέω, antiloidoreō, v. to retaliate. S: 486, BAGD: 75A, CB: 342A

519 ἀντίλυτρον, antilytron, n. ransom. S: 487, BAGD: 75B, CB: 342A

520 ἀντιμετρέω, antimetreō, v. to measure in return. S: 488, BAGD: 75B, CB: –

521 ἀντιμισθία, antimisthia, n. an exchange; penalty. S: 489, BAGD: 75B, CB: 342A

522 Ἀντιόχεια, Antiocheia, n.pr. Antioch. S: 490, BAGD: 75B, CB: –

523 Ἀντιοχεύς, Antiocheus, n.pr.g., "of Antioch." from Antioch. S: 491, BAGD: 75C, CB: 342A

524 ἀντιπαρέρχομαι, antiparerchomai, v. to pass by on the opposite side. S: 492, BAGD: 75C, CB: –

525 Ἀντιπᾶς, Antipas, n.pr. Antipas. S: 493, BAGD: 75D, CB: –

526 Ἀντιπατρίς, Antipatris, n.pr. Antipatris. S: 494, BAGD: 75D, CB: –

527 ἀντιπέρα, antipera, adv. across from, opposite of. S: 495*, BAGD: 75D, CB: –

528 ἀντιπίπτω, antipiptō, v. to resist, oppose. S: 496, BAGD: 75D, CB: –

529 ἀντιστρατεύομαι, antistrateuomai, v. to wage war against. S: 497, BAGD: 75D, CB: –

530 ἀντιτάσσω, antitassō, v. to oppose, rebel, resist. S: 498*, BAGD: 76A, CB: –

531 ἀντίτυπος, antitypos, a. copy, representation. S: 499*, BAGD: 76A, CB: 342A

532 ἀντίχριστος, antichristos, n. antichrist. S: 500, BAGD: 76B, CB: 342A

533 ἀντλέω, antleō, v. to draw (water). S: 501, BAGD: 76C, CB: –

534 ἄντλημα, antlēma, n. container to draw water with. S: 502, BAGD: 76C, CB: –

535 ἀντοφθαλμέω, antophthalmeō, v. to head into, face (the wind). S: 503, BAGD: 76C, CB: –

536 ἄνυδρος, anydros, a. arid, without water. S: 504, BAGD: 76C, CB: –

537 ἀνυπόκριτος, anypokritos, a. sincere, genuine, without hypocrisy. S: 505, BAGD: 76D, CB: –

538 ἀνυπότακτος, anypotaktos, a. rebellious, disobedient; not made subject to, independent. S: 506, BAGD: 76D, CB: –

539 ἄνω, anō, adv.pl. above, upward, heavenward, top. S: 507, BAGD: 76D, CB: 341C

540 ἄνωθεν, anōthen, adv.pl. from above; from the begininning; again, anew. S: 509, BAGD: 77A, CB: 342A

541 ἀνωτερικός, anōterikos, a. interior, upper (regions). S: 510, BAGD: 77C, CB: –

542 ἀνώτερος, anōteros, a. higher (standing, place); first, earlier. S: 511, BAGD: 77C, CB: –

543 ἀνωφελής, anōphelēs, a. unprofitable, useless. S: 512*, BAGD: 77C, CB: –

544 ἀξίνη, axinē, n. ax. S: 513, BAGD: 77D, CB: –

545 ἄξιος, axios, a. worthy, deserving, in keeping with, corresponding to. S: 514, BAGD: 78A, CB: 344B

546 ἀξιόω, axioō, v. to consider worthy, consider wise or fitting. S: 515, BAGD: 78C, CB: 344B

547 ἀξίως, axiōs, adv. in a worthy manner, suitably. S: 516, BAGD: 78D, CB: 344B

548 ἀόρατος, aoratos, a. invisible, not seen. S: 517, BAGD: 79A, CB: 342A

549 Ἀουλία, Aoulia, n.pr., "of Julian [the family of Julius Caesar]." variant: Julia. S: 2456*, BAGD: 380B cf. Ἰουλία, CB: –

550 ἀπαγγέλλω, apangellō, v. to tell, report, proclaim, announce. S: 518, BAGD: 79B, CB: 342B

551 ἀπάγχω, apanchō, v. to hang (oneself). S: 519*, BAGD: 79C, CB: –

552 ἀπάγω, apagō, v. to lead away, bring before (an official). S: 520, BAGD: 79C, CB: 339C cf. agō

553 ἀπαίδευτος, apaideutos, a. stupid, uneducated. S: 521, BAGD: 79D, CB: 342A

554 ἀπαίρω, apairō, v. to take away. S: 522, BAGD: 79D, CB: –

555 ἀπαιτέω, apaiteō, v. to demand back. S: 523, BAGD: 80A, CB: 342B

556 ἀπαλγέω, apalgeō, v. to lose all sensitivity, become callous. S: 524, BAGD: 80A, CB: –

557 ἀπαλλάσσω, apallassō, v. (act.) to set free, release; (pass.) to be reconciled, come to a settlement (in court); to be cured. S: 525, BAGD: 80A, CB: 342B

558 ἀπαλλοτριόω, apallotrioō, v. to be excluded, separated, alienated. S: 526, BAGD: 80B, CB: 342B

559 ἀπαλός, hapalos, a. tender. S: 527, BAGD: 80B, CB: –

560 ἀπαντάω, apantaō, v. to meet, encounter. S: 528, BAGD: 80C, CB: 342B

561 ἀπάντησις, apantēsis, n. (the act of) meeting, encountering. S: 529, BAGD: 80C, CB: 342B

562 ἅπαξ, hapax, adv. once, once more, once for all. S: 530, BAGD: 80C, CB: 355B

563 ἀπαράβατος, aparabatos, a. permanent, unchangeable. S: 531, BAGD: 80D, CB: 342B

564 ἀπαρασκεύαστος, aparaskeuastos, a. unprepared, unready. S: 532, BAGD: 80D, CB: 342B

565 ἀπαρνέομαι, aparneomai, v. to disown, deny, repudiate. S: 533, BAGD: 81A, CB: 342B

566 ἀπαρτί, aparti, adv. variant: exactly, certainly. S: 575 + 737, BAGD: 81A, CB: –

567 ἀπάρτι, aparti, adv. [pp.+adv.]. variant: from now on, again. S: 534, BAGD: 110B cf. ἄρτι 3., CB: –

568 ἀπαρτισμός, apartismos, n. completion, finishing. S: 535, BAGD: 81B, CB: –

569 ἀπαρχή, aparchē, n. firstfruits. S: 536, BAGD: 81B, CB: 342B

570 ἅπας, hapas, a. all, every, whole. S: 537, BAGD: 81D, CB: 355B

571 ἀπασπάζομαι, apaspazomai, v. to say farewell. S: 782, BAGD: 81D, CB: –

572 ἀπατάω, *apataō*, v. *to deceive, cheat, trick.* S: *538*, BAGD: 81D, CB: 342B

573 ἀπάτη, *apatē*, n. *deception, deceitfulness.* S: *539*, BAGD: 82A, CB: 342B

574 ἀπάτωρ, *apatōr*, a. *fatherless.* S: *540*, BAGD: 82B, CB: 342B

575 ἀπαύγασμα, *apaugasma*, n. *radiance, brilliance.* S: *541*, BAGD: 82B, CB: 342B

576 ἀπαφρίζω, *apaphrizō*, v. variant: *to cast off like foam.* S: *1890*, BAGD: 82C, CB: –

577 ἀπείθεια, *apeitheia*, n. *disobedience.* S: *543*, BAGD: 82C, CB: 342B

578 ἀπειθέω, *apeitheō*, v. *to disobey, be disobedient.* S: *544*, BAGD: 82C, CB: 342B

579 ἀπειθής, *apeithēs*, a. *disobedient.* S: *545*, BAGD: 82D, CB: 342B

580 ἀπειλέω, *apeileō*, v. *to threaten, warn.* S: *546*, BAGD: 82D, CB: –

581 ἀπειλή, *apeilē*, n. *threat.* S: *547*, BAGD: 83A, CB: –

582 ἄπειμι[1], *apeimi*[1], v. *to be absent.* S: *548**, BAGD: 83A, CB: –

583 ἄπειμι[2], *apeimi*[2], v. *to go away.* S: *549**, BAGD: 83A, CB: –

584 ἀπεῖπον, *apeipon*, v. *to renounce, disown.* S: *550** & *561*, BAGD: 83B, CB: 343A cf. *apolegō*

585 ἀπείραστος, *apeirastos*, a. *incapable of being tempted, without temptation.* S: *551*, BAGD: 83B, CB: 342B

586 ἄπειρος, *apeiros*, a. *not acquainted with.* S: *552*, BAGD: 83B cf. ἄπειρος I., CB: 342B

587 ἀπεκδέχομαι, *apekdechomai*, v. *wait eagerly for.* S: *553*, BAGD: 83C, CB: 342B

588 ἀπεκδύομαι, *apekdyomai*, v. *to take off, disarm.* S: *554*, BAGD: 83C, CB: 342B

589 ἀπέκδυσις, *apekdysis*, n. *removal, putting off.* S: *555*, BAGD: 83C, CB: 342B

590 ἀπελαύνω, *apelaunō*, v. *to eject from (court), drive away.* S: *556*, BAGD: 83C, CB: –

591 ἀπελεγμός, *apelegmos*, n. *disrepute, discredit.* S: *557*, BAGD: 83D, CB: –

592 ἀπελεύθερος, *apeleutheros*, n. *freedman, one no longer a slave.* S: *558*, BAGD: 83D, CB: 342B

593 Ἀπελλῆς, *Apellēs*, n.pr. *Apelles.* S: *559*, BAGD: 83D, CB: –

594 ἀπελπίζω, *apelpizō*, v. *to expect nothing in return.* S: *560*, BAGD: 83D, CB: 342B

595 ἀπέναντι, *apenanti*, pp.*. *opposite, in front of, against (opposition to).* S: *561*, BAGD: 84A, CB: –

596 ἀπέραντος, *aperantos*, a. *endless, unlimited.* S: *562*, BAGD: 84A, CB: –

597 ἀπερισπάστως, *aperispastōs*, adv. *undividable, without distraction.* S: *563*, BAGD: 84B, CB: –

598 ἀπερίτμητος, *aperitmētos*, a. *uncircumcised.* S: *564*, BAGD: 84B, CB: 342B

599 ἀπέρχομαι, *aperchomai*, v. *to go away, withdraw.* S: *565*, BAGD: 84C, CB: 342B

600 ἀπέχω, *apechō*, v. *to receive (in full); to be distant; (mid.) to abstain, avoid.* S: *568* & *566* & *567*, BAGD: 84D, CB: 342B

601 ἀπιστέω, *apisteō*, v. *to disbelieve, be faithless, unfaithful.* S: *569*, BAGD: 85B, CB: 342C

602 ἀπιστία, *apistia*, n. *unbelief, lack of faith.* S: *570*, BAGD: 85C, CB: 342C

603 ἄπιστος, *apistos*, a. *unbelieving, doubting; incredible, unbelievable.* S: *571*, BAGD: 85D, CB: 342C

604 ἁπλόος, *haploos*, a. *good.* S: *573**, BAGD: 86A cf. ἁπλοῦς, CB: 355B

605 ἁπλότης, *haplotēs*, n. *generosity, sincerity.* S: *572*, BAGD: 85D, CB: 355B

606 ἁπλοῦς, *haplous*, a. *good.* S: *573*, BAGD: 86A, CB: 355B

607 ἁπλῶς, *haplōs*, adv. *generously, without reserve.* S: *574*, BAGD: 86B, CB: 355B

608 ἀπό, *apo*, pp. *from, away from; by means of; out of; against.* S: *575*, BAGD: 86C, CB: 342C

609 ἀποβαίνω, *apobainō*, v. *to leave, get out; to result in, turn to, lead to.* S: *576*, BAGD: 88C, CB: –

610 ἀποβάλλω, *apoballō*, v. *to throw away.* S: *577*, BAGD: 88D, CB: –

611 ἀποβλέπω, *apoblepō*, v. *to look ahead, pay attention.* S: *578*, BAGD: 89A, CB: 342C

612 ἀπόβλητος, *apoblētos*, a. *rejected.* S: *579*, BAGD: 89A, CB: –

613 ἀποβολή, *apobolē*, n. *rejection; loss.* S: *580*, BAGD: 89A, CB: –

614 ἀπογίνομαι, *apoginomai*, v. *to die.* S: *581**, BAGD: 89B, CB: 342C

615 ἀπογραφή, *apographē*, n. *census, registration.* S: *582*, BAGD: 89B, CB: –

616 ἀπογράφω, *apographō*, v. *to take a census, register, record.* S: *583*, BAGD: 89B, CB: 342C

617 ἀποδείκνυμι, *apodeiknymi*, v. *to display, exhibit, proclaim; prove, accredit, attest.* S: *584*, BAGD: 89C, CB: 342C

618 ἀπόδειξις, *apodeixis*, n. *demonstration, proof.* S: *585*, BAGD: 89D, CB: 342C

619 ἀποδεκατεύω, *apodekateuō*, v. variant: *to tithe, give one-tenth of.* S: *586**, BAGD: 89D, CB: 342C

620 ἀποδεκατόω, *apodekatoō*, v. *to give a tenth, tithe; collect a tithe.* S: *586*, BAGD: 89D, CB: 342C

621 ἀπόδεκτος, *apodektos*, a. *pleasing, pleasant.* S: *587*, BAGD: 90A, CB: 342C

622 ἀποδέχομαι, *apodechomai*, v. *to welcome, accept, receive; acknowledge, acclaim.* S: *588*, BAGD: 90A, CB: 342C

623 ἀποδημέω, *apodēmeō*, v. *to go away on a journey.* S: *589*, BAGD: 90A, CB: 342C

624 ἀπόδημος, *apodēmos*, a. *going away on a journey.* S: *590*, BAGD: 90B, CB: –

625 ἀποδίδωμι, *apodidōmi*, v. *give, give away; pay, pay back.* S: *591*, BAGD: 90B, CB: 342C

626 ἀποδιορίζω, *apodiorizō*, v. *to divide, separate, cause a division.* S: *592*, BAGD: 90D, CB: –

627 ἀποδοκιμάζω, *apodokimazō*, v. *to reject.* S: *593*, BAGD: 90D, CB: 342C

628 ἀποδοχή, *apodochē*, n. *acceptance, approval.* S: *594*, BAGD: 91A, CB: 342C

629 ἀπόθεσις, *apothesis*, n. *removal, putting aside, getting rid of.* S: *595*, BAGD: 91A, CB: 343B

630 ἀποθήκη, *apothēkē*, n. *barn, storehouse.* S: *596*, BAGD: 91A, CB: −

631 ἀποθησαυρίζω, *apothēsaurizō*, v. *to store up treasure.* S: *597*, BAGD: 91B, CB: −

632 ἀποθλίβω, *apothlibō*, v. *to press against, crowd up to.* S: *598*, BAGD: 91B, CB: −

633 ἀποθνήσκω, *apothnēskō*, v. *to die.* S: *599**, BAGD: 91B, CB: 343B

634 ἀποκαθιστάνω, *apokathistanō*, v. variant: *to restore, re-establish, cure.* S: *600**, BAGD: 91D, CB: 343A

635 ἀποκαθίστημι, *apokathistēmi*, v. *to (completely) restore.* S: *600*, BAGD: 91D, CB: 343A

636 ἀποκαλύπτω, *apokalyptō*, v. *to reveal, disclose.* S: *601*, BAGD: 92A, CB: 342C

637 ἀποκάλυψις, *apokalypsis*, n. *revelation, what is revealed, disclosure.* S: *602*, BAGD: 92B, CB: 342C

638 ἀποκαραδοκία, *apokaradokia*, n. *eager expectation.* S: *603*, BAGD: 92C, CB: 342C

639 ἀποκαταλλάσσω, *apokatallassō*, v. *to reconcile, reunite.* S: *604*, BAGD: 92C, CB: 343A

640 ἀποκατάστασις, *apokatastasis*, n. *restoration.* S: *605*, BAGD: 92D, CB: 343A

641 ἀπόκειμαι, *apokeimai*, v. *to be stored up, destined.* S: *606*, BAGD: 92D, CB: −

642 ἀποκεφαλίζω, *apokephalizō*, v. *to behead.* S: *607*, BAGD: 93A, CB: −

643 ἀποκλείω, *apokleiō*, v. *to close.* S: *608*, BAGD: 93A, CB: −

644 ἀποκόπτω, *apokoptō*, v. *to cut off; emasculate.* S: *609*, BAGD: 93A, CB: 343A

645 ἀπόκριμα, *apokrima*, n. *sentence, verdict.* S: *610*, BAGD: 93B, CB: −

646 ἀποκρίνομαι, *apokrinomai*, v. *to answer, ask.* S: *611*, BAGD: 93B, CB: −

647 ἀπόκρισις, *apokrisis*, n. *answer.* S: *612*, BAGD: 93D, CB: −

648 ἀποκρύπτω, *apokryptō*, v. *to hide, conceal.* S: *613*, BAGD: 93D, CB: 343A

649 ἀπόκρυφος, *apokryphos*, a. *concealed, hidden, secret.* S: *614*, BAGD: 93D, CB: 343A

650 ἀποκτείνω, *apokteinō*, v. *to kill.* S: *615*, BAGD: 93D, CB: 343A

651 ἀποκτέννω, *apoktennō*, v. variant: *to kill.* S: *615**, BAGD: 93D, CB: 343A cf. *apokteinō*

652 ἀποκυέω, *apokyeō*, v. *to give birth to, bring into being.* S: *616*, BAGD: 94A, CB: 343A

653 ἀποκυλίω, *apokyliō*, v. *to roll away, roll back.* S: *617*, BAGD: 94B, CB: −

654 ἀπολαλέω, *apolaleō*, v. variant: *to speak about freely.* S: *2980**, BAGD: 94B, CB: −

655 ἀπολαμβάνω, *apolambanō*, v. *to receive, be repaid.* S: *618*, BAGD: 94B, CB: 343A

656 ἀπόλαυσις, *apolausis*, n. *enjoyment, pleasure.* S: *619*, BAGD: 94D, CB: −

657 ἀπολείπω, *apoleipō*, v. *to leave behind.* S: *620*, BAGD: 94D, CB: 360A cf. *kataleipō*

658 ἀπολείχω, *apoleichō*, v. variant: *lick, lick off.* S: *621*, BAGD: 95A, CB: −

659 ἀπολιμπάνω, *apolimpanō*, v. variant: *leave behind.* S: *5277**, BAGD: 95A, CB: −

660 ἀπόλλυμι, *apollymi*, v. *to destroy, kill, cause to lose.* S: *622*, BAGD: 95A, CB: 343A

661 Ἀπολλύων, *Apollyōn*, n.pr., "destroyer." *Apollyon.* S: *623*, BAGD: 95C, CB: −

662 Ἀπολλωνία, *Apollōnia*, n.pr. *Apollonia.* S: *624*, BAGD: 95C, CB: −

663 Ἀπολλῶς, *Apollōs*, n.pr. *Apollos.* S: *625**, BAGD: 95D, CB: 343A cf. *-ōn*

664 ἀπολογέομαι, *apologeomai*, v. *to defend oneself, speak in one's own behalf.* S: *626*, BAGD: 95D, CB: 343A

665 ἀπολογία, *apologia*, n. *defense; answer or reply (of reason or accounting).* S: *627*, BAGD: 96A, CB: 343A

666 ἀπολούω, *apolouō*, v. *to wash away.* S: *628*, BAGD: 96A, CB: 343A

667 ἀπολύτρωσις, *apolytrōsis*, n. *redemption, ransom, release.* S: *629*, BAGD: 96B, CB: 343A

668 ἀπολύω, *apolyō*, v. *to release (forgive, grant clemency); divorce, send away.* S: *630*, BAGD: 96C, CB: 343A

669 ἀπομάσσω, *apomassō*, v. *to wipe off.* S: *631**, BAGD: 96D, CB: −

670 ἀπομένω, *apomenō*, v. variant: *to remain behind.* S: *5278**, BAGD: 97A, CB: −

671 ἀπονέμω, *aponemō*, v. *to treat with, show, pay (respect).* S: *632*, BAGD: 97A, CB: −

672 ἀπονίπτω, *aponiptō*, v. *to wash off.* S: *633*, BAGD: 97A, CB: −

673 ἀποπέμπω, *apopempō*, v. variant: *to send out.* S: *575 + 3992*, BAGD: 97B, CB: −

674 ἀποπίπτω, *apopiptō*, v. *to fall away, drop off.* S: *634*, BAGD: 97B, CB: −

675 ἀποπλανάω, *apoplanaō*, v. *to deceive, mislead; (pass.) to wander.* S: *635*, BAGD: 97B, CB: 343A

676 ἀποπλέω, *apopleō*, v. *to sail away from.* S: *636*, BAGD: 97C, CB: −

677 ἀποπλύνω, *apoplynō*, v. variant: *to wash off, wash out.* S: *637*, BAGD: 97C, CB: −

678 ἀποπνίγω, *apopnigō*, v. *to choke, smother; (pass.) to be drowned, choked (with water).* S: *638*, BAGD: 97C, CB: 343A

679 ἀπορέω, *aporeō*, v. *to be puzzled, at a loss, in wonder.* S: *639*, BAGD: 97C, CB: −

680 ἀπορία, *aporia*, n. *perplexity, consternation.* S: *640*, BAGD: 97D, CB: −

681 ἀπορίπτω, *aporiptō*, v. *to jump into, throw oneself into.* S: *641*, BAGD: 97D, CB: −

682 ἀπορφανίζω, *aporphanizō*, v. *to make an orphan of.* S: *642*, BAGD: 98A, CB: 367B cf. *orphanos*

683 ἀποσκευάζω, *aposkeuazō*, v. variant: *to pack up.* S: *643*, BAGD: 98A, CB: −

684 ἀποσκίασμα, *aposkiasma*, n. *shadow.* S: *644*, BAGD: 98A, CB: 343A

685 ἀποσπάω, *apospaō*, v. *to draw out, draw away, attract; (pass.) to withdraw.* S: *645*, BAGD: 98A, CB: –

686 ἀποστασία, *apostasia*, n. *turning away, rebellion, abandonment, apostasy.* S: *646*, BAGD: 98B, CB: 343A

687 ἀποστάσιον, *apostasion*, n. *divorce.* S: *647*, BAGD: 98B, CB: 343A

688 ἀποστάτης, *apostatēs*, n. variant: *deserter, apostate.* S: *3848**, BAGD: 98C, CB: 343A

689 ἀποστεγάζω, *apostegazō*, v. *to make an opening in a roof, remove a roof.* S: *648*, BAGD: 98C, CB: –

690 ἀποστέλλω, *apostellō*, v. *to send, send out, send away.* S: *649*, BAGD: 98C, CB: 343A

691 ἀποστερέω, *apostereō*, v. *to defraud, cheat, steal; deprive, deny, withhold.* S: *650*, BAGD: 99A, CB: 343A

692 ἀποστολή, *apostolē*, n. *apostleship, ministry / office of an apostle.* S: *651*, BAGD: 99B, CB: 343A

693 ἀπόστολος, *apostolos*, n. *apostle, representative, messenger, envoy.* S: *652*, BAGD: 99C, CB: 343A

694 ἀποστοματίζω, *apostomatizō*, v. *to besiege with questions, interrogate closely.* S: *653*, BAGD: 100B, CB: –

695 ἀποστρέφω, *apostrephō*, v. *to turn away from, rebel, mislead; to desert, reject; to return, put back.* S: *654*, BAGD: 100B, CB: 343A

696 ἀποστυγέω, *apostygeō*, v. *to hate, abhor, loathe.* S: *655*, BAGD: 100C, CB: –

697 ἀποσυνάγωγος, *aposynagōgos*, a. *put out of the synagogue, excommunicated.* S: *656*, BAGD: 100D, CB: 343B

698 ἀποτάσσω, *apotassō*, v. *to say good-by, leave; give up, renounce, forsake.* S: *657**, BAGD: 100D, CB: –

699 ἀποτελέω, *apoteleō*, v. *to bring to completion; (pass.) to be full-grown, mature, completed.* S: *658*, BAGD: 100D, CB: –

700 ἀποτίθημι, *apotithēmi*, v. *to put aside, get rid of.* S: *659*, BAGD: 101A, CB: 343B

701 ἀποτινάσσω, *apotinassō*, v. *to shake off, stomp off.* S: *660*, BAGD: 101B, CB: 343B

702 ἀποτίνω, *apotinō*, v. *to pay back, make restitution.* S: *661*, BAGD: 101B, CB: –

703 ἀποτολμάω, *apotolmaō*, v. *to bring forth boldly.* S: *662*, BAGD: 101B, CB: –

704 ἀποτομία, *apotomia*, n. *sternness, severity.* S: *663*, BAGD: 101C, CB: –

705 ἀποτόμως, *apotomōs*, adv. *harshly, sharply, severely, rigorously.* S: *664*, BAGD: 101C, CB: –

706 ἀποτρέπω, *apotrepō*, v. *to have nothing to do with, turn away from completely, avoid.* S: *665*, BAGD: 101C, CB: 343B

707 ἀπουσία, *apousia*, n. *absence.* S: *666*, BAGD: 101D, CB: –

708 ἀποφέρω, *apopherō*, v. *to carry away, lead away.* S: *667*, BAGD: 101D, CB: 370A cf. *pherō*

709 ἀποφεύγω, *apopheugō*, v. *to escape (from).* S: *668*, BAGD: 101D, CB: 343A

710 ἀποφθέγγομαι, *apophthengomai*, v. *to say, speak out, address, declare.* S: *669*, BAGD: 102A, CB: 343A cf. *-esthai*

711 ἀποφορτίζομαι, *apophortizomai*, v. *to unload.* S: *670*, BAGD: 102A, CB: –

712 ἀπόχρησις, *apochrēsis*, n. *using up, consumption.* S: *671*, BAGD: 102A, CB: –

713 ἀποχωρέω, *apochōreō*, v. *to go away from, leave.* S: *672*, BAGD: 102A, CB: –

714 ἀποχωρίζω, *apochōrizō*, v. *to part company, be separated; to recede, be split.* S: *673*, BAGD: 102B, CB: –

715 ἀποψύχω, *apopsychō*, v. *to faint.* S: *674*, BAGD: 102B, CB: –

716 Ἄππιος, *Appios*, n.pr. *Appius.* S: *675*, BAGD: 102B, CB: –

717 ἀπρόσιτος, *aprositos*, a. *unapproachable.* S: *676*, BAGD: 102C, CB: –

718 ἀπρόσκοπος, *aproskopos*, a. *blameless, clear; not causing one to stumble, not giving offense.* S: *677*, BAGD: 102C, CB: 343B

719 ἀπροσωπολήμπτως, *aprosōpolēmptōs*, adv. *impartially, without prejudice.* S: *678**, BAGD: 102C, CB: 343B cf. *-tēs*

720 ἄπταιστος, *aptaistos*, a. *without falling, without stumbling.* S: *679*, BAGD: 102C, CB: –

721 ἅπτω, *haptō*, v. *to touch, hold, handle; (act.) to start a fire.* S: *681 & 680*, BAGD: 102D, CB: 355B

722 Ἀπφία, *Apphia*, n.pr. *Apphia.* S: *682*, BAGD: 103B, CB: –

723 ἀπωθέω, *apōtheō*, v. *to reject, repudiate, push aside.* S: *683**, BAGD: 103B, CB: –

724 ἀπώλεια, *apōleia*, n. *destruction, ruin, waste.* S: *684*, BAGD: 103B, CB: 343A

725 ἀρά, *ara*, n. *curse.* S: *685*, BAGD: 103D, CB: 343B

726 ἄρα, *ara*, pt.infer. *then, so, therefore, consequently.* S: *686*, BAGD: 103D, CB: 343B

727 ἆρα, *ara*, pt.inter. *difficult to translate directly: introduces direct questions, showing anxiety or impatience.* S: *687*, BAGD: 104A, CB: 343B

728 Ἀραβία, *Arabia*, n.pr., "desert" *or* "steppe." *Arabia.* S: *688*, BAGD: 104A, CB: –

729 Ἄραβοι, *Araboi*, n.pr.g., "desert dwellers." variant: *Arabs.* S: *150*, BAGD: 104B, CB: –

730 Ἀράμ, *Aram*, n.pr., "high, exalted." *Ram, Aram.* S: *689*, BAGD: 104B, CB: –

731 ἄραφος, *araphos*, a. *seamless.* S: *729**, BAGD: 104B, CB: –

732 Ἄραψ, *Araps*, n.pr.g., "desert dweller." *Arab.* S: *690*, BAGD: 104C, CB: –

733 ἀργέω, *argeō*, v. *to be idle, grow weary.* S: *691*, BAGD: 104C, CB: –

734 ἀργός, *argos*, a. *idle, lazy; useless, ineffective; careless.* S: *692*, BAGD: 104C, CB: 343C

735 ἀργύρεος, *argyreos*, a. *(made of) silver.* S: *693*, BAGD: 105A cf. *-οῦς*, CB: 343C cf. *-ous*

736 ἀργύριον, *argyrion*, n. *silver.* S: *694*, BAGD: 104D, CB: 343C

737 ἀργυροκόπος, *argyrokopos*, n. *silversmith.* S: *695*, BAGD: 105A, CB: –

738 ἄργυρος, *argyros*, n. *silver.* S: *696*, BAGD: 105A, CB: 343C

739 ἀργυροῦς, *argyrous*, a. *(made of) silver.* S: *693**, BAGD: 105A, CB: 343C cf. *-ous*

740 Ἄρειος πάγος, *Areios pagos*, n.pr., "hill of the Greek god Ares." *meeting of the Areopagus.* S: *697*, BAGD: 105B, CB: 367B cf. *pagos*

741 Ἀρεοπαγίτης, *Areopagitēs*, n.pr.g., "of the Areopagus." *member of the Areopagus.* S: *698*, BAGD: 105B, CB: –

742 ἀρεσκεία, *areskeia*, n. *pleasing, striving to please.* S: *699**, BAGD: 105C, CB: 343C

743 ἀρέσκω, *areskō*, v. *to please, accommodate.* S: *700*, BAGD: 105C, CB: 343C

744 ἀρεστός, *arestos*, a. *pleasing, desirable, right.* S: *701*, BAGD: 105D, CB: 343C

745 Ἀρέτας, *Haretas*, n.pr., "virtuous." *Aretas.* S: *702**, BAGD: 105D, CB: –

746 ἀρετή, *aretē*, n. *goodness, excellence, virtue.* S: *703*, BAGD: 105D, CB: 343C

747 Ἀρηί, *Arēi*, n.pr. variant: *Arei.* S: *150*, BAGD: 108B cf. Ἀρνί, CB: –

748 ἀρήν, *arēn*, n. *lamb.* S: *704*, BAGD: 106A, CB: 343C

749 ἀριθμέω, *arithmeō*, v. *to count.* S: *705*, BAGD: 106B, CB: 343C

750 ἀριθμός, *arithmos*, n. *number.* S: *706*, BAGD: 106B, CB: 343C

751 Ἀριμαθαία, *Harimathaia*, n.pr. *Arimathea.* S: *707**, BAGD: 106C, CB: –

752 Ἀρίσταρχος, *Aristarchos*, n.pr., "best ruler." *Aristarchus.* S: *708*, BAGD: 106C, CB: –

753 ἀριστάω, *aristaō*, v. *to eat (breakfast).* S: *709*, BAGD: 106C, CB: –

754 ἀριστερός, *aristeros*, a. *left, left hand.* S: *710*, BAGD: 106C, CB: 343C

755 Ἀριστόβουλος, *Aristoboulos*, n.pr., "best advisor." *Aristobulus.* S: *711*, BAGD: 106D, CB: –

756 ἄριστον, *ariston*, n. *meal, feast.* S: *712*, BAGD: 106D, CB: –

757 ἀρκετός, *arketos*, a. *enough, sufficient.* S: *713*, BAGD: 107A, CB: 343C

758 ἀρκέω, *arkeō*, v. *(mid./pass.) to be content, satisfied; (act.) to be sufficient.* S: *714*, BAGD: 107A, CB: 343C

759 ἄρκος, *arkos*, n. *bear.* S: *715**, BAGD: 107B, CB: 343C

760 ἄρκτος, *arktos*, n. variant: *bear.* S: *715*, BAGD: 107B, CB: –

761 ἅρμα, *harma*, n. *chariot, carriage.* S: *716*, BAGD: 107B, CB: 355B

762 Ἁρμαγεδών, *Harmagedōn*, n.pr., "Mount Megiddo." *Armageddon.* S: *717*, BAGD: 107C, CB: –

763 Ἀρμίν, *Armin*, n.pr. variant: *Armin.* S: *689**, BAGD: 18C cf. Ἀδμίν, CB: –

764 ἁρμόζω, *harmozō*, v. *to promise for marriage, betroth.* S: *718*, BAGD: 107C, CB: 355B

765 ἁρμός, *harmos*, n. *joint.* S: *719*, BAGD: 107D, CB: 355B

766 ἀρνέομαι, *arneomai*, v. *to deny, disown, renounce, repudiate.* S: *720*, BAGD: 107D, CB: 343C

767 Ἀρνί, *Arni*, n.pr. variant: *Arni.* S: *150*, BAGD: 108B, CB: –

768 ἀρνίον, *arnion*, n. *lamb, sheep; the Lamb.* S: *721*, BAGD: 108B, CB: 343C

769 ἀροτριάω, *arotriaō*, v. *to plow, furrow.* S: *722*, BAGD: 108B, CB: –

770 ἄροτρον, *arotron*, n. *plow.* S: *723*, BAGD: 108B, CB: –

771 ἁρπαγή, *harpagē*, n. *greediness, confiscation, robbery, plunder.* S: *724*, BAGD: 108B, CB: 355B

772 ἁρπαγμός, *harpagmos*, n. *something to hold onto.* S: *725*, BAGD: 108C, CB: 355B

773 ἁρπάζω, *harpazō*, v. *to catch, steal, carry off.* S: *726*, BAGD: 109A, CB: 355B

774 ἅρπαξ, *harpax*, a. *swindling, robbing; ferocious, ravenous.* S: *727*, BAGD: 109B, CB: 355B

775 ἀρραβών, *arrabōn*, n. *deposit which guarantees, downpayment, pledge.* S: *728*, BAGD: 109B, CB: 343C

776 ἄρρην, *arrēn*, n. variant: *male.* S: *730*, BAGD: 109D cf. ἄρσην, CB: 343C

777 ἄρρητος, *arrētos*, a. *inexpressible, not to be spoken.* S: *731*, BAGD: 109C, CB: 343C

778 ἀρρωστέω, *arrōsteō*, v. variant: *to be ill.* S: *732**, BAGD: 109D, CB: 343C

779 ἄρρωστος, *arrōstos*, a. *sick, ill.* S: *732*, BAGD: 109D, CB: –

780 ἀρσενοκοίτης, *arsenokoitēs*, n. *one engaging in homosexual acts, sexual deviant.* S: *733*, BAGD: 109D, CB: 343C

781 ἄρσην, *arsēn*, a. *male.* S: *730*, BAGD: 109D, CB: 343C

782 Ἀρτεμᾶς, *Artemas*, n.pr., "[given by] Artemis." *Artemas.* S: *734*, BAGD: 110A, CB: –

783 Ἄρτεμις, *Artemis*, n.pr. *Artemis.* S: *735*, BAGD: 110A, CB: –

784 ἀρτέμων, *artemōn*, n. *foresail, sail.* S: *736*, BAGD: 110A, CB: –

785 ἄρτι, *arti*, adv. *now, at once, immediately.* S: *737*, BAGD: 110B, CB: 343C

786 ἀρτιγέννητος, *artigennētos*, a. *newborn.* S: *738*, BAGD: 110C, CB: –

787 ἄρτιος, *artios*, a. *thorough, complete, capable, proficient.* S: *739*, BAGD: 110C, CB: 343C

788 ἄρτος, *artos*, n. *(loaf of) bread, food.* S: *740*, BAGD: 110C, CB: 343C

789 ἀρτύω, *artyō*, v. *to make salty, season.* S: *741*, BAGD: 111A, CB: 343C

790 Ἀρφαξάδ, *Arphaxad*, n.pr. *Arphaxad.* S: *742*, BAGD: 111A, CB: –

791 ἀρχάγγελος, *archangelos*, n. *archangel.* S: *743*, BAGD: 111A, CB: 343B

792 ἀρχαῖος, *archaios*, a. *ancient, of old.* S: *744*, BAGD: 111B, CB: 343B

793 Ἀρχέλαος, *Archelaos*, n.pr., "ruler of people." *Archelaus.* S: *745*, BAGD: 111C, CB: –

794 ἀρχή, *archē*, n. *beginning, origin, first; ruler, power, authority; position of authority, domain.* S: *746*, BAGD: 111D, CB: 343B

795 ἀρχηγός, *archēgos*, n. *author, originator, founder; leader, ruler.* S: *747*, BAGD: 112C, CB: 343B

796 ἀρχιερατικός, *archieratikos*, a. *of the high priest.* S: *748*, BAGD: 112D, CB: 343B

797 ἀρχιερεύς, *archiereus*, n. *chief priest, high priest.* S: *749*, BAGD: 112D, CB: 343B

798 ἀρχιληστής, archilēstēs, n. variant: *head of a rebellion.*
S: *3027*,* BAGD: 113A, CB: –

799 ἀρχιποίμην, archipoimēn, n. *chief shepherd.* S: *750,*
BAGD: 113A, CB: 343B

800 Ἄρχιππος, Archippos, n.pr., "master of the horse." *Archippus.*
S: *751,* BAGD: 113A, CB: –

801 ἀρχισυνάγωγος, archisynagōgos, n. *leader of the synagogue.*
S: *752,* BAGD: 113B, CB: –

802 ἀρχιτέκτων, architektōn, n. *expert builder.* S: *753,*
BAGD: 113B, CB: 343B

803 ἀρχιτελώνης, architelōnēs, n. *chief tax collector.* S: *754,*
BAGD: 113B, CB: 343B

804 ἀρχιτρίκλινος, architriklinos, n. *master of the banquet, head
waiter.* S: *755,* BAGD: 113B, CB: –

805 ἀρχοστασία, archostasia, n. variant: *election of magistrates.*
S: *150,* BAGD: –, CB: –

806 ἄρχω, archō, v. *(act.) to rule; (mid.) to begin.* S: *757 & 756,*
BAGD: 113C, CB: 343B

807 ἄρχων, archōn, n. *ruler, leader, official.* S: *758,* BAGD: 113D,
CB: 343B

808 ἄρωμα, arōma, n. *spices, salves, scented oils, perfumes.* S: *759,*
BAGD: 114B, CB: 343C

809 Ἀσά, Asa, n.pr., poss. "healer" BDB; "myrtle" KB. *Asa.*
S: *760,* BAGD: 114B cf. Ἀσάφ, CB: –

810 ἀσάλευτος, asaleutos, a. *unshakable, immovable, fixed.* S: *761,*
BAGD: 114B, CB: 343C

811 Ἀσάφ, Asaph, n.pr., "gatherer." variant: *Asaph.* S: *760*,*
BAGD: 114B, CB: –

812 ἄσβεστος, asbestos, a. *unquenchable, inextinguishable.* S: *762,*
BAGD: 114B, CB: 343C

813 ἀσέβεια, asebeia, n. *ungodliness, godlessness, impiety.* S: *763,*
BAGD: 114C, CB: 344A

814 ἀσεβέω, asebeō, v. *to do ungodly acts, act impiously.* S: *764,*
BAGD: 114C, CB: 344A

815 ἀσεβής, asebēs, a. *ungodly, wicked, impious.* S: *765,*
BAGD: 114C, CB: 344A

816 ἀσέλγεια, aselgeia, n. *debauchery, sensuality, lewdness.*
S: *766,* BAGD: 114D, CB: 344A

817 ἄσημος, asēmos, a. *ordinary, obscure, insignificant.* S: *767,*
BAGD: 115A, CB: –

818 Ἀσήρ, Asēr, n.pr., "happy one." *Asher.* S: *768,* BAGD: 115A,
CB: –

819 ἀσθένεια, astheneia, n. *weakness, illness, infirmity.* S: *769,*
BAGD: 115A, CB: 344A

820 ἀσθενέω, astheneō, v. *to be weak, ill.* S: *770,* BAGD: 115B,
CB: 344A

821 ἀσθένημα, asthenēma, n. *failing, weakness.* S: *771,*
BAGD: 115C, CB: –

822 ἀσθενής, asthenēs, a. *weak, ill.* S: *772,* BAGD: 115C,
CB: 344A

823 Ἀσία, Asia, n.pr. *Asia.* S: *773,* BAGD: 116A, CB: –

824 Ἀσιανός, Asianos, n.pr.g. *one from the Roman province of
Asia.* S: *774,* BAGD: 116A, CB: –

825 Ἀσιάρχης, Asiarchēs, n.pr. *official of the province, Asiarch.*
S: *775,* BAGD: 116A, CB: –

826 ἀσιτία, asitia, n. *going without food.* S: *776,* BAGD: 116B,
CB: –

827 ἄσιτος, asitos, a. *going without food.* S: *777,* BAGD: 116B,
CB: –

828 ἀσκέω, askeō, v. *to strive, do one's best.* S: *778,* BAGD: 116B,
CB: 344A

829 ἀσκός, askos, n. *wineskin, leather bag holding wine.* S: *779,*
BAGD: 116C, CB: –

830 ἀσμένως, asmenōs, adv. *warmly, gladly.* S: *780,*
BAGD: 116C, CB: –

831 ἄσοφος, asophos, a. *unwise, foolish.* S: *781,* BAGD: 116C,
CB: 344A

832 ἀσπάζομαι, aspazomai, v. *to give greetings.* S: *782,*
BAGD: 116C, CB: 344A

833 ἀσπασμός, aspasmos, n. *greeting.* S: *783,* BAGD: 117A,
CB: 344A

834 ἄσπιλος, aspilos, a. *without spot, defect or blemish.* S: *784,*
BAGD: 117A, CB: 344A

835 ἀσπίς, aspis, n. *viper, asp, cobra.* S: *785,* BAGD: 117B,
CB: 344A

836 ἄσπονδος, aspondos, a. *unforgiving, not reconcilable.* S: *786,*
BAGD: 117B, CB: –

837 ἀσσάριον, assarion, n. *assarion (coin worth 1/16 of a day's
wage).* S: *787,* BAGD: 117B, CB: –

838 Ἀσσάρων, Assarōn, n.pr. variant: *Assaron.* S: *4565*,*
BAGD: 117B, CB: –

839 ἆσσον, asson, adv. *nearer.* S: *788,* BAGD: 117B, CB: –

840 Ἄσσος, Assos, n.pr. *Assos.* S: *789*,* BAGD: 117B, CB: –

841 ἀστατέω, astateō, v. *to be homeless, a vagabond.* S: *790,*
BAGD: 117B, CB: –

842 ἀστεῖος, asteios, a. *not ordinary, beautiful, pleasing.* S: *791,*
BAGD: 117C, CB: –

843 ἀστήρ, astēr, n. *star.* S: *792,* BAGD: 117C, CB: 344A

844 ἀστήρικτος, astēriktos, a. *unstable, weak.* S: *793,*
BAGD: 118A, CB: –

845 ἄστοργος, astorgos, a. *without love, heartless.* S: *794,*
BAGD: 118A, CB: 344A

846 ἀστοχέω, astocheō, v. *to wander away, miss the mark; to turn
to, deviate from.* S: *795,* BAGD: 118A, CB: 344A

847 ἀστραπή, astrapē, n. *lightning; light, ray of light.* S: *796,*
BAGD: 118A, CB: 344A

848 ἀστράπτω, astraptō, v. *to flash, gleam like lightning.* S: *797,*
BAGD: 118B, CB: –

849 ἄστρον, astron, n. *star, constellation.* S: *798,* BAGD: 118B,
CB: 344A

850 Ἀσύγκριτος, Asynkritos, n.pr., "incomparable." *Asyncritus.*
S: *799,* BAGD: 118C, CB: –

851 ἀσύμφωνος, asymphōnos, a. *disagreeable, not harmonious.*
S: *800,* BAGD: 118C, CB: –

852 ἀσύνετος, asynetos, a. *senseless, dull, without understanding,
foolish.* S: *801,* BAGD: 118C, CB: 344A

853 ἀσύνθετος, asynthetos, a. *faithless, untrustworthy.* S: *802,*
BAGD: 118D, CB: –

854 ἀσφάλεια, *asphaleia*, n. *security, safety; certainty, truth.*
S: *803*, BAGD: 118D, CB: 344A

855 ἀσφαλής, *asphalēs*, a. *safe, firm, certain; definite; the truth.*
S: *804*, BAGD: 119A, CB: 344A

856 ἀσφαλίζω, *asphalizō*, v. *to make secure; fasten.* S: *805*,
BAGD: 119A, CB: 344A

857 ἀσφαλῶς, *asphalōs*, adv. *carefully, securely; under guard;
assuredly, beyond a doubt.* S: *806*, BAGD: 119A, CB: 344A

858 ἀσχημονέω, *aschēmoneō*, v. *to act improperly, dishonorably,
indecently, rudely.* S: *807*, BAGD: 119B, CB: –

859 ἀσχημοσύνη, *aschēmosynē*, n. *indecent act, shame.* S: *808*,
BAGD: 119B, CB: –

860 ἀσχήμων, *aschēmōn*, a. *unpresentable, shameful, indecent.*
S: *809*, BAGD: 119B, CB: 344A

861 ἀσωτία, *asōtia*, n. *debauchery, dissipation, wildness.* S: *810*,
BAGD: 119C, CB: –

862 ἀσώτως, *asōtōs*, adv. *wildly, in debauchery, in dissipation.*
S: *811*, BAGD: 119C, CB: 344A

863 ἀτακτέω, *atakteō*, v. *to be idle, lazy.* S: *812*, BAGD: 119C,
CB: –

864 ἄτακτος, *ataktos*, a. *idle, lazy.* S: *813*, BAGD: 119C, CB: –

865 ἀτάκτως, *ataktōs*, adv. *idly, irresponsibly.* S: *814*,
BAGD: 119D, CB: –

866 ἄτεκνος, *ateknos*, a. *childless, without children.* S: *815*,
BAGD: 119D, CB: 377B cf. *teknon*

867 ἀτενίζω, *atenizō*, v. *to look intently, gaze, stare.* S: *816*,
BAGD: 119D, CB: 344A

868 ἄτερ, *ater*, pp.*. *without, apart from.* S: *817*, BAGD: 120A,
CB: –

869 ἀτιμάζω, *atimazō*, v. *to dishonor, disgrace, treat shamefully,
insult.* S: *818*, BAGD: 120A, CB: 344A

870 ἀτιμάω, *atimaō*, v. *to treat shamefully, dishonor, disgrace.*
S: *818**, BAGD: 120A, CB: 344A cf. *atimazō*

871 ἀτιμία, *atimia*, n. *dishonor, disgrace, shame; common use.*
S: *819*, BAGD: 120A, CB: 344B

872 ἄτιμος, *atimos*, a. *without honor, dishonored, despised.* S: *820*,
BAGD: 120B, CB: 344B

873 ἀτιμόω, *atimoō*, v. variant: *to disgrace.* S: *821*, BAGD: 120B,
CB: –

874 ἀτμίς, *atmis*, n. *mist, vapor; billows (of smoke).* S: *822*,
BAGD: 120B, CB: –

875 ἄτομος, *atomos*, a. *in a flash, in a moment.* S: *823*,
BAGD: 120B, CB: 344B

876 ἄτοπος, *atopos*, a. *wrong, wicked; unusual, surprising.* S: *824*,
BAGD: 120C, CB: –

877 Ἀττάλεια, *Attaleia*, n.pr. *Attalia.* S: *825*, BAGD: 120C, CB: –

878 αὐγάζω, *augazō*, v. *to see.* S: *826*, BAGD: 120C, CB: 344B

879 αὐγή, *augē*, n. *daylight, dawn.* S: *827*, BAGD: 120D, CB: 344B

880 Αὔγουστος, *Augoustos*, n.pr., *"reverant, holy." Augustus.*
S: *828*, BAGD: 120D, CB: –

881 αὐθάδης, *authadēs*, a. *overbearing, arrogant, stubborn,
self-willed.* S: *829*, BAGD: 120D, CB: –

882 αὐθαίρετος, *authairetos*, a. *on one's own initiative, of one's
own accord.* S: *830*, BAGD: 121A, CB: –

883 αὐθεντέω, *authenteō*, v. *to have authority over.* S: *831*,
BAGD: 121A, CB: 344B cf. -*ein*

884 αὐλέω, *auleō*, v. *to play the flute.* S: *832*, BAGD: 121B,
CB: 344B

885 αὐλή, *aulē*, n. *palace, house; courtyard, sheepfold.* S: *833*,
BAGD: 121B, CB: 344B

886 αὐλητής, *aulētēs*, n. *flute player.* S: *834*, BAGD: 121B, CB: –

887 αὐλίζομαι, *aulizomai*, v. *to spend the night, find lodging.*
S: *835*, BAGD: 121C, CB: –

888 αὐλός, *aulos*, n. *flute.* S: *836*, BAGD: 121C, CB: –

889 αὐξάνω, *auxanō*, v. *to cause to grow; (intr.) grow, increase.*
S: *837*, BAGD: 121C, CB: 344B

890 αὔξησις, *auxēsis*, n. *growth, increase.* S: *838*, BAGD: 122A,
CB: 344B

891 αὔξω, *auxō*, v. variant: *to cause to grow; (intr.) to grow,
increase.* S: *837**, BAGD: 121C, CB: 344B

892 αὔριον, *aurion*, adv. *tomorrow, the next day.* S: *839*,
BAGD: 122A, CB: –

893 αὐστηρός, *austēros*, a. *hard, severe, strict, exacting.* S: *840*,
BAGD: 122B, CB: –

894 αὐτάρκεια, *autarkeia*, n. *contentment, having all of one's
needs, sufficiency.* S: *841*, BAGD: 122B, CB: 344B

895 αὐτάρκης, *autarkēs*, a. *content.* S: *842*, BAGD: 122B,
CB: 344B

896 αὐτοκατάκριτος, *autokatakritos*, a. *self-condemned.* S: *843*,
BAGD: 122C, CB: 344B

897 αὐτόματος, *automatos*, a. *by itself, automatic.* S: *844*,
BAGD: 122C, CB: 344B

898 αὐτόπτης, *autoptēs*, n. *eyewitness.* S: *845*, BAGD: 122C,
CB: –

899 αὐτός, *autos*, p.inten. *he, she, it; the same one.* S: *846* & *847* &
848, BAGD: 122C, CB: 344B

900 αὐτόφωρος, *autophōros*, a. *in the act.* S: *1888**, BAGD: 124A,
CB: –

901 αὐτόχειρ, *autocheir*, a. *or* n. *with one's own hand.* S: *849*,
BAGD: 124A, CB: –

902 αὐχέω, *aucheō*, v. *to boast.* S: *3166**, BAGD: 124A, CB: 344B

903 αὐχμηρός, *auchmēros*, a. *dark.* S: *850*, BAGD: 124B, CB: –

904 ἀφαιρέω, *aphaireō*, v. *to take away from, remove; to cut (off).*
S: *851*, BAGD: 124B, CB: 342B

905 ἀφανής, *aphanēs*, a. *hidden, invisible.* S: *852*, BAGD: 124C,
CB: –

906 ἀφανίζω, *aphanizō*, v. *to destroy, disfigure; to perish, vanish,
disappear.* S: *853*, BAGD: 124C, CB: 342B

907 ἀφανισμός, *aphanismos*, n. *disappearance, destruction.*
S: *854*, BAGD: 124D, CB: –

908 ἄφαντος, *aphantos*, a. *disappearing, invisible.* S: *855*,
BAGD: 124D, CB: –

909 ἀφεδρών, *aphedrōn*, n. *latrine.* S: *856*, BAGD: 124D, CB: –

910 ἀφειδία, *apheidia*, n. *harsh treatment, unsparing.* S: *857*,
BAGD: 124D, CB: –

911 ἀφελότης, *aphelotēs*, n. *sincerity, simplicity.* S: *858*,
BAGD: 124D, CB: –

912 ἄφεσις, *aphesis*, n. *forgiveness, pardon, release.* S: *859*, BAGD: 125A, CB: 342B

913 ἁφή, *haphē*, n. *ligament, joint.* S: *860*, BAGD: 125A, CB: 355B

914 ἀφθαρσία, *aphtharsia*, n. *imperishableness, immortality.* S: *861*, BAGD: 125B, CB: 342C

915 ἄφθαρτος, *aphthartos*, a. *imperishable, immortal, lasting forever.* S: *862*, BAGD: 125B, CB: 342C

916 ἀφθονία, *aphthonia*, n. variant: *willingness.* S: *150*, BAGD: 125C, CB: –

917 ἀφθορία, *aphthoria*, n. *integrity, soundness, purity.* S: *150*, BAGD: 125C, CB: –

918 ἀφίημι, *aphiēmi*, v. *to forgive, pardon, remit, cancel; to leave, abandon.* S: *863*, BAGD: 125C, CB: 342B

919 ἀφικνέομαι, *aphikneomai*, v. *to reach.* S: *864*, BAGD: 126C, CB: –

920 ἀφιλάγαθος, *aphilagathos*, a. *not loving good.* S: *865*, BAGD: 126C, CB: –

921 ἀφιλάργυρος, *aphilargyros*, a. *not loving money, not greedy.* S: *866*, BAGD: 126C, CB: –

922 ἄφιξις, *aphixis*, n. *leaving, departure.* S: *867*, BAGD: 126D, CB: –

923 ἀφίστημι, *aphistēmi*, v. *to leave, withdraw, abandon; to revolt, mislead.* S: *868*, BAGD: 126D, CB: 342B

924 ἄφνω, *aphnō*, adv. *suddenly.* S: *869*, BAGD: 127A, CB: –

925 ἀφόβως, *aphobōs*, adv. *fearlessly, without the slightest qualm, boldly.* S: *870*, BAGD: 127A, CB: 342B

926 ἀφομοιόω, *aphomoioō*, v. *(pass.) to be like, similar.* S: *871*, BAGD: 127B, CB: 342C

927 ἀφοράω, *aphoraō*, v. *to fix one's eyes; look away.* S: *872 & 542*, BAGD: 127B, CB: –

928 ἀφορίζω, *aphorizō*, v. *to separate, set apart, exclude.* S: *873*, BAGD: 127B, CB: 342C

929 ἀφορμή, *aphormē*, n. *opportunity, opening, pretext.* S: *874*, BAGD: 127C, CB: 342C

930 ἀφρίζω, *aphrizō*, v. *to foam at the mouth.* S: *875*, BAGD: 127C, CB: –

931 ἀφρός, *aphros*, n. *foam, froth.* S: *876*, BAGD: 127D, CB: –

932 ἀφροσύνη, *aphrosynē*, n. *foolishness, lack of sense.* S: *877*, BAGD: 127D, CB: 342C

933 ἄφρων, *aphrōn*, a. *foolish, ignorant.* S: *878*, BAGD: 127D, CB: 342C

934 ἀφυπνόω, *aphypnoō*, v. *to fall asleep.* S: *879*, BAGD: 127D, CB: –

935 ἀφυστερέω, *aphystereō*, v. variant: *withhold, keep back.* S: *650**, BAGD: 128A, CB: –

936 ἄφωνος, *aphōnos*, a. *silent, mute, without speech; without meaning.* S: *880*, BAGD: 128A, CB: –

937 Ἀχάζ, *Achaz*, n.pr., "he has grasped." *Ahaz.* S: *881*, BAGD: 128A, CB: –

938 Ἀχαΐα, *Achaia*, n.pr. *Achaia.* S: *882*, BAGD: 128A, CB: –

939 Ἀχαϊκός, *Achaikos*, n.pr., "belonging to Achaia." *Achaicus.* S: *883*, BAGD: 128B, CB: –

940 ἀχάριστος, *acharistos*, a. *ungrateful.* S: *884*, BAGD: 128B, CB: –

941 Ἀχάς, *Achas*, n.pr., "he has grasped." variant: *Ahaz.* S: *881**, BAGD: 128B, CB: –

942 ἀχειροποίητος, *acheiropoiētos*, a. *not made by human hands.* S: *886*, BAGD: 128B, CB: 339A

943 Ἀχίμ, *Achim*, n.pr., "Yahweh is my brother." *Akim.* S: *885**, BAGD: 128B, CB: –

944 ἀχλύς, *achlys*, n. *mistiness, dimness of sight.* S: *887*, BAGD: 128B, CB: –

945 ἀχρεῖος, *achreios*, a. *worthless, useless, unworthy.* S: *888*, BAGD: 128C, CB: –

946 ἀχρειόω, *achreioō*, v. *(pass.) to become worthless, depraved.* S: *889*, BAGD: 128C, CB: –

947 ἄχρηστος, *achrēstos*, a. *useless, worthless.* S: *890*, BAGD: 128C, CB: 339A cf. -on

948 ἄχρι, *achri*, pp.* & c. *until, up to, as far as, as long as.* S: *891*, BAGD: 128D, CB: 339A

949 ἄχυρον, *achyron*, n. *chaff.* S: *892*, BAGD: 129A, CB: –

950 ἀψευδής, *apseudēs*, a. *not a liar, free from deceit, trustworthy.* S: *893*, BAGD: 129C, CB: 343B

951 ἀψίνθιον, *apsinthion*, n. variant: *wormwood.* S: *894**, BAGD: 129C, CB: 343B

952 ἄψινθος, *apsinthos*, n. *Wormwood, bitterness.* S: *894*, BAGD: 129C, CB: 343B

953 ἄψυχος, *apsychos*, a. *lifeless, inanimate.* S: *895*, BAGD: 129C, CB: –

954 β, *b*, letter. *letter of the Greek alphabet.* S: *150*, BAGD: 129B, CB: –

955 Βάαλ, *Baal*, n.pr., "master, owner, lord." *Baal.* S: *896*, BAGD: 129B, CB: –

956 Βαβυλών, *Babylōn*, n.pr., "gate of god[s]." *Babylon.* S: *897*, BAGD: 129B, CB: 344B

957 βαθμός, *bathmos*, n. *standing, rank.* S: *898*, BAGD: 130A, CB: –

958 βάθος, *bathos*, n. *depth, deep thing; extreme.* S: *899*, BAGD: 130A, CB: 344C

959 βαθύνω, *bathynō*, v. *to go down deep, dig deep.* S: *900*, BAGD: 130B, CB: –

960 βαθύς, *bathys*, a. *deep.* S: *901*, BAGD: 130B, CB: 344C

961 βάϊον, *baion*, n. *(palm) branch.* S: *902**, BAGD: 130C, CB: –

962 Βαλαάμ, *Balaam*, n.pr., poss. "Baal [lord] of the people" BDB or "the clan brings forth" IDB. *Balaam.* S: *903*, BAGD: 130C, CB: –

963 Βαλάκ, *Balak*, n.pr., "devastator." *Balak.* S: *904*, BAGD: 130C, CB: –

964 βαλλάντιον, *ballantion*, n. *purse, money-bag.* S: *905**, BAGD: 130D, CB: 344B

965 βάλλω, *ballō*, v. *to throw, pour; to put, set.* S: *906*, BAGD: 130D, CB: 344B

966 βαπτίζω, *baptizō*, v. *to baptize, wash; the baptizer.* S: *907*, BAGD: 131C, CB: 344C

967 βάπτισμα, *baptisma*, n. *baptism.* S: *908*, BAGD: 132C, CB: 344B

968 βαπτισμός, *baptismos*, n. *baptism, ceremonial washing.* S: *909*, BAGD: 132D, CB: 344C

969 βαπτιστής, *baptistēs*, n. *Baptist.* S: *910*, BAGD: 132D, CB: 344C

970 βάπτω, *baptō*, v. *to dip (in).* S: *911*, BAGD: 132D, CB: 344C

971 βαρ, *bar*, l.[n.]. variant: *son.* S: *920**, BAGD: 133A, CB: –

972 Βαραββᾶς, *Barabbas*, n.pr., "son of a father" *poss.* "son of a rabbi." *Barabbas.* S: *912*, BAGD: 133A, CB: –

973 Βαράκ, *Barak*, n.pr., "lightning." *Barak.* S: *913*, BAGD: 133A, CB: –

974 Βαραχίας, *Barachias*, n.pr., "Yahweh blesses." *Berekiah.* S: *914*, BAGD: 133A, CB: –

975 βάρβαρος, *barbaros*, a. *non-Greek, foreign, "barbarian".* S: *915*, BAGD: 133B, CB: 344C

976 βαρέω, *bareō*, v. *(pass.) to be burdened, under pressure.* S: *916*, BAGD: 133C, CB: 344C

977 βαρέως, *bareōs*, adv. *with difficulty.* S: *917*, BAGD: 133C, CB: 344C

978 Βαρθολομαῖος, *Bartholomaios*, n.pr., "son of Talmai." *Bartholomew.* S: *918*, BAGD: 133D, CB: –

979 Βαριησοῦς, *Bariēsous*, n.pr., "son of Jesus [Joshua]." *Bar-Jesus.* S: *919*, BAGD: 133D, CB: –

980 Βαριωνᾶ, *Bariōna*, n.pr., "son of Jonah" *or* "John." *son of Jonah, Bar-Jona.* S: *920*, BAGD: 133D, CB: –

981 Βαριωνᾶς, *Bariōnas*, n.pr., "son of Jonah" *or* "John." variant: *son of Jonah, Bar-Jona.* S: *920*, BAGD: 133D, CB: –

982 Βαρναβᾶς, *Barnabas*, n.pr., "son of comfort." *Barnabas.* S: *921**, BAGD: 133D, CB: –

983 βάρος, *baros*, n. *burden, weight.* S: *922*, BAGD: 133D, CB: 344C

984 Βαρσαββᾶς, *Barsabbas*, n.pr., "son of the Sabbath" *or* "son of Saba." *Barsabbas.* S: *923**, BAGD: 134A, CB: –

985 Βαρτιμαῖος, *Bartimaios*, n.pr., "son of Timai" *or* "son of uncleanness." *Bartimaeus.* S: *924*, BAGD: 134A, CB: –

986 βαρύνω, *barynō*, v. variant: *to burden, grieve.* S: *925*, BAGD: 134B, CB: 344C

987 βαρύς, *barys*, a. *burdensome, heavy, important; savage, fierce.* S: *926*, BAGD: 134B, CB: 344C

988 βαρύτιμος, *barytimos*, a. *very expensive.* S: *927*, BAGD: 134B, CB: 344C

989 βασανίζω, *basanizō*, v. *to torture, torment; (pass.) to be tortured, tormented, in pain.* S: *928*, BAGD: 134C, CB: 344C

990 βασανισμός, *basanismos*, n. *torment, torture, agony.* S: *929*, BAGD: 134C, CB: 344C

991 βασανιστής, *basanistēs*, n. *torturer.* S: *930*, BAGD: 134D, CB: 344C

992 βάσανος, *basanos*, n. *torment, severe pain, torture.* S: *931*, BAGD: 134D, CB: 344C

993 βασιλεία, *basileia*, n. *kingdom, kingship, royal rule.* S: *932*, BAGD: 134D, CB: 344C

994 βασίλειος, *basileios*, a. *royal, royal (palace).* S: *934 & 933*, BAGD: 136A, CB: 344C

995 βασιλεύς, *basileus*, n. *king.* S: *935*, BAGD: 136A, CB: 344C

996 βασιλεύω, *basileuō*, v. *to reign as a king, become king.* S: *936*, BAGD: 136C, CB: 344C

997 βασιλικός, *basilikos*, a. *royal.* S: *937*, BAGD: 136D, CB: 344C

998 βασιλίσκος, *basiliskos*, n. variant: *petty king.* S: *937**, BAGD: 136D, CB: 344C cf. *basilikos*

999 βασίλισσα, *basilissa*, n. *queen.* S: *938*, BAGD: 137A, CB: 344C

1000 βάσις, *basis*, n. *foot.* S: *939*, BAGD: 137A, CB: 344C

1001 βασκαίνω, *baskainō*, v. *to bewitch.* S: *940*, BAGD: 137A, CB: 344C

1002 βαστάζω, *bastazō*, v. *to carry, bear up, carry off; to tolerate, help, support.* S: *941*, BAGD: 137B, CB: 344C

1003 βάτος¹, *batos¹*, n. *bush, brier, thornbush.* S: *942*, BAGD: 137C, CB: –

1004 βάτος², *batos²*, n. *bath (a unit of liquid measure, between eight and nine gallons).* S: *943*, BAGD: 137C, CB: –

1005 βάτραχος, *batrachos*, n. *frog.* S: *944*, BAGD: 137D, CB: –

1006 βατταλογέω, *battalogeō*, v. *to babble, prattle.* S: *945**, BAGD: 137D, CB: 345A

1007 βδέλυγμα, *bdelygma*, n. *abomination, something detestable.* S: *946*, BAGD: 137D, CB: 345A

1008 βδελυκτός, *bdelyktos*, a. *detestable, abominable.* S: *947*, BAGD: 138A, CB: –

1009 βδελύσσομαι, *bdelyssomai*, v. *(mid.) to abhor, detest; (pass.) to be vile, abhorrent.* S: *948**, BAGD: 138A, CB: –

1010 βέβαιος, *bebaios*, a. *firm, sure, certain, binding.* S: *949*, BAGD: 138B, CB: 345A

1011 βεβαιόω, *bebaioō*, v. *to confirm; keep strong.* S: *950*, BAGD: 138C, CB: 345A

1012 βεβαίωσις, *bebaiōsis*, n. *confirmation.* S: *951*, BAGD: 138D, CB: 345A

1013 βέβηλος, *bebēlos*, a. *godless, irreligious, profane, worldly.* S: *952*, BAGD: 138D, CB: –

1014 βεβηλόω, *bebēloō*, v. *to desecrate, profane.* S: *953*, BAGD: 138D, CB: –

1015 Βεελζεβούλ, *Beelzeboul*, n.pr., "lord [baal] of the flies." *Beelzebub.* S: *954*, BAGD: 139A, CB: 345A

1016 Βελιάρ, *Beliar*, n.pr., "wicked, without use." *Belial.* S: *955**, BAGD: 139A, CB: 345A

1017 βελόνη, *belonē*, n. *needle.* S: *4476**, BAGD: 139B, CB: –

1018 βέλος, *belos*, n. *arrow.* S: *956*, BAGD: 139B, CB: 345A

1019 βελτίων, *beltiōn*, a. *better, very well.* S: *957**, BAGD: 139B, CB: –

1020 Βενιαμείν, *Beniamein*, n.pr., "son of the right hand" *or* "Southerner." variant: *Benjamin.* S: *958**, BAGD: 139B, CB: –

1021 Βενιαμίν, *Beniamin*, n.pr., "son of the right hand" *or* "Southerner." *Benjamin.* S: *958*, BAGD: 139B, CB: –

1022 Βερνίκη, *Bernikē*, n.pr., "victorious." *Bernice.* S: *959*, BAGD: 139C, CB: –

1023 Βέροια, *Beroia*, n.pr. *Berea.* S: *960*, BAGD: 139C, CB: –

1024 Βεροιαῖος, *Beroiaios*, a.pr.g. *from Berea, Berean.* S: *961*, BAGD: 139C, CB: –

1025 Βέρος, *Beros*, n.pr. variant: *Beros.* S: *150*, BAGD: 139C cf. Βεροιαι=ος, CB: –

1026 Βεωρσόρ, *Beōorsor*, n.pr. variant: *Bosor.* S: *1007**, BAGD: 139C cf. Βεώρ, CB: –

1027 Βεώρ, *Beōr*, n.pr., *perhaps* "a burning." *Beor.* S: *1007**, BAGD: 139C, CB: –

1028 Βηθαβαρά, *Bēthabara*, n.pr. variant: *Bethabara.* S: *962*, BAGD: 139C, CB: –

1029 Βηθανία, *Bēthania*, n.pr., "House of Ananiah" [*or* "the poor" *or* "unripe figs]." *Bethany.* S: *963*, BAGD: 139D, CB: –

1030 Βηθαραβά, *Bētharaba*, n.pr. variant: *Betharaba.* S: *962**, BAGD: 139D, CB: –

1031 Βηθεσδά, *Bēthesda*, n.pr., "site [house] of mercy." *Bethesda.* S: *964*, BAGD: 139D, CB: –

1032 Βηθζαθά, *Bēthzatha*, n.pr. variant: *Bethzatha.* S: *964**, BAGD: 140A, CB: –

1033 Βηθλέεμ, *Bēthleem*, n.pr., "house of bread" *poss.* "temple of Lakhmu." *Bethlehem.* S: *965**, BAGD: 140A, CB: 345A

1034 Βηθσαϊδά, *Bēthsaida*, n.pr., "site [house] of fishing." *Bethsaida.* S: *966*, BAGD: 140A, CB: –

1035 Βηθσαϊδάν, *Bēthsaidan*, n.pr. variant: *Bethsaida.* S: *966**, BAGD: 140A, CB: –

1036 Βηθφαγή, *Bēthphagē*, n.pr., "house of unripe figs." *Bethphage.* S: *967*, BAGD: 140B, CB: –

1037 βῆμα, *bēma*, n. *judicial court, judge's seat.* S: *968*, BAGD: 140B, CB: 345A

1038 Βηρεύς, *Bēreus*, n.pr. variant: *Bereus.* S: *150*, BAGD: –, CB: –

1039 βήρυλλος, *bēryllos*, n. *beryl.* S: *969*, BAGD: 140B, CB: 345A

1040 βία, *bia*, n. *force, violence, pounding (of surf).* S: *970*, BAGD: 140C, CB: 345A

1041 βιάζω, *biazō*, v. *(mid.) to force one's way.* S: *971*, BAGD: 140C, CB: 345A

1042 βίαιος, *biaios*, a. *violent, strong.* S: *972*, BAGD: 141A, CB: 345A

1043 βιαστής, *biastēs*, n. *forceful one.* S: *973*, BAGD: 141A, CB: 345A

1044 βιβλαρίδιον, *biblaridion*, n. *little scroll.* S: *974*, BAGD: 141A, CB: 345A cf. *biblos*

1045 βιβλιδάριον, *biblidarion*, n. variant: *little scroll.* S: *974*, BAGD: 141A, CB: 345A cf. *biblos*

1046 βιβλίον, *biblion*, n. *scroll, book, certificate.* S: *975*, BAGD: 141B, CB: 345A

1047 βίβλος, *biblos*, n. *book, scroll.* S: *976*, BAGD: 141C, CB: 345A

1048 βιβρώσκω, *bibrōskō*, v. *to eat.* S: *977*, BAGD: 141C, CB: –

1049 Βιθυνία, *Bithynia*, n.pr. *Bithynia.* S: *978*, BAGD: 141D, CB: –

1050 βίος, *bios*, n. *life; what one lives on, property, possessions.* S: *979*, BAGD: 141D, CB: 345A

1051 βιόω, *bioō*, v. *to live.* S: *980*, BAGD: 142A, CB: 345A

1052 βίωσις, *biōsis*, n. *the way one lives.* S: *981*, BAGD: 142A, CB: –

1053 βιωτικός, *biōtikos*, a. *(lesser things) of this life.* S: *982*, BAGD: 142A, CB: 345A

1054 βλαβερός, *blaberos*, a. *harmful.* S: *983*, BAGD: 142B, CB: –

1055 βλάπτω, *blaptō*, v. *to hurt, injure.* S: *984*, BAGD: 142B, CB: 345A

1056 βλαστάνω, *blastanō*, v. *to sprout, bud.* S: *985*, BAGD: 142B, CB: 345A

1057 βλαστάω, *blastaō*, v. variant: *to sprout, bud.* S: *985**, BAGD: 142B, CB: 345A cf. *blastanō*

1058 Βλάστος, *Blastos*, n.pr., "sprout [of a vine or branch]." *Blastus.* S: *986*, BAGD: 142C, CB: –

1059 βλασφημέω, *blasphēmeō*, v. *to blaspheme, insult, slander, curse.* S: *987*, BAGD: 142C, CB: 345A

1060 βλασφημία, *blasphēmia*, n. *blasphemy, slander, malicious talk.* S: *988*, BAGD: 143A, CB: 345A

1061 βλάσφημος, *blasphēmos*, a. *blasphemous, slanderous, abusive.* S: *989*, BAGD: 143A, CB: 345A

1062 βλέμμα, *blemma*, n. *act of seeing.* S: *990*, BAGD: 143B, CB: –

1063 βλέπω, *blepō*, v. *to see, look at; to watch out, beware, pay attention.* S: *991*, BAGD: 143B, CB: 345A

1064 βλητέος, *blēteos*, a. *must be put.* S: *992*, BAGD: 144A, CB: –

1065 Βοανηργές, *Boanērges*, l.[pr.n.]., "sons of thunder." *Boanerges.* S: *993**, BAGD: 144A, CB: 345A

1066 βοάω, *boaō*, v. *to call, cry out, shout.* S: *994*, BAGD: 144B, CB: 345B

1067 Βόες, *Boes*, n.pr., *perhaps* "in him is strength." *Boaz.* S: *1003**, BAGD: 144B, CB: –

1068 βοή, *boē*, n. *cry, shout.* S: *995*, BAGD: 144C, CB: 345B

1069 βοήθεια, *boētheia*, n. *help; support (to hold something together).* S: *996*, BAGD: 144C, CB: –

1070 βοηθέω, *boētheō*, v. *to help, come to the aid of.* S: *997*, BAGD: 144C, CB: –

1071 βοηθός, *boēthos*, a. *helpful (one).* S: *998*, BAGD: 144D, CB: 345B

1072 βόθρος, *bothros*, n. variant: *pit, cistern.* S: *999**, BAGD: 144D, CB: –

1073 βόθυνος, *bothynos*, n. *pit, cistern.* S: *999*, BAGD: 144D, CB: –

1074 βολή, *bolē*, n. *throwing.* S: *1000*, BAGD: 144D, CB: –

1075 βολίζω, *bolizō*, v. *to take a sounding.* S: *1001*, BAGD: 144D, CB: –

1076 βολίς, *bolis*, n. variant: *missile, arrow, javelin.* S: *1002*, BAGD: 144D, CB: –

1077 Βοόζ, *Booz*, n.pr., *perhaps* "in him is strength." variant: *Boaz.* S: *1003*, BAGD: 145A cf. Βόος, CB: –

1078 Βόος, *Boos*, n.pr., *perhaps* "in him is strength." *Boaz.* S: *1003**, BAGD: 145A, CB: –

1079 βόρβορος, *borboros*, n. *mud, filth.* S: *1004*, BAGD: 145A, CB: 345B

1080 βορρᾶς, *borras*, n. *the north.* S: *1005*, BAGD: 145B, CB: –

1081 βόσκω, *boskō*, v. *to feed, tend; (pass.) to eat, graze.* S: *1006*, BAGD: 145B, CB: 345B

1082 Βοσόρ, *Bosor*, n.pr. variant: *Bosor.* S: *1007*, BAGD: 145B, CB: –

1083 βοτάνη, *botanē*, n. *crop.* S: *1008*, BAGD: 145B, CB: 345B

1084 βότρυς, *botrys*, n. *grape cluster, bunch of grapes.* S: *1009*, BAGD: 145C, CB: –

1085 βουλευτής, *bouleutēs*, n. *member of a council.* S: *1010*, BAGD: 145C, CB: –

1086 βουλεύω, *bouleuō*, v. *to make plans, consider, decide, plot.* S: *1011*, BAGD: 145C, CB: 345B cf. *-omai*

1087 βουλή, *boulē*, n. *plan, purpose, will, decision.* S: *1012*, BAGD: 145D, CB: 345B

1088 βούλημα, *boulēma*, n. *plan, will, choice.* S: *1013*, BAGD: 145D, CB: 345B

1089 βούλομαι, *boulomai*, v. *to wish, will, desire; to choose, determine, plan.* S: *1014*, BAGD: 146A, CB: 345B

1090 βουνός, *bounos*, n. *hill.* S: *1015*, BAGD: 146C, CB: –

1091 βοῦς, *bous*, n. *ox, cattle.* S: *1016*, BAGD: 146C, CB: 345B

1092 βραβεῖον, *brabeion*, n. *prize.* S: *1017*, BAGD: 146D, CB: 345B

1093 βραβεύω, *brabeuō*, v. *to rule.* S: *1018*, BAGD: 146D, CB: 345B

1094 βραδύνω, *bradynō*, v. *to delay, hesitate.* S: *1019*, BAGD: 147A, CB: –

1095 βραδυπλοέω, *bradyploeō*, v. *to sail slowly.* S: *1020*, BAGD: 147A, CB: –

1096 βραδύς, *bradys*, a. *slow.* S: *1021*, BAGD: 147A, CB: –

1097 βραδύτης, *bradytēs*, n. *slowness.* S: *1022*, BAGD: 147A, CB: –

1098 βραχίων, *brachiōn*, n. *arm.* S: *1023*, BAGD: 147B, CB: –

1099 βραχύς, *brachys*, a. *little, short.* S: *1024*, BAGD: 147B, CB: 345B

1100 βρέφος, *brephos*, n. *baby, infant.* S: *1025*, BAGD: 147B, CB: 345B

1101 βρέχω, *brechō*, v. *to rain; to make wet.* S: *1026*, BAGD: 147C, CB: 345B

1102 βριμάομαι, *brimaomai*, v. variant: *to be indignant.* S: *1690**, BAGD: 147C, CB: –

1103 βροντή, *brontē*, n. *thunder.* S: *1027*, BAGD: 147D, CB: 345B

1104 βροχή, *brochē*, n. *rain.* S: *1028*, BAGD: 147D, CB: 345B

1105 βρόχος, *brochos*, n. *restriction, restraint.* S: *1029*, BAGD: 147D, CB: –

1106 βρυγμός, *brygmos*, n. *gnashing, grinding.* S: *1030*, BAGD: 147D, CB: 345B

1107 βρύχω, *brychō*, v. *to gnash, grind.* S: *1031*, BAGD: 148A, CB: 345B

1108 βρύω, *bryō*, v. *to flow, pour forth.* S: *1032*, BAGD: 148A, CB: –

1109 βρῶμα, *brōma*, n. *food, what is eaten.* S: *1033*, BAGD: 148A, CB: 345B

1110 βρώσιμος, *brōsimos*, a. *eatable.* S: *1034*, BAGD: 148B, CB: 345B

1111 βρῶσις, *brōsis*, n. *consumable, food, rust, corrosion.* S: *1035*, BAGD: 148B, CB: 345B

1112 βυθίζω, *bythizō*, v. *(act.) to plunge; (pass.) to sink.* S: *1036*, BAGD: 148C, CB: –

1113 βυθός, *bythos*, n. *open sea, the deep.* S: *1037*, BAGD: 148C, CB: –

1114 βυρσεύς, *byrseus*, n. *tanner.* S: *1038*, BAGD: 148D, CB: –

1115 βύσσινος, *byssinos*, a. *made of fine linen.* S: *1039*, BAGD: 148D, CB: –

1116 βύσσος, *byssos*, n. *fine linen.* S: *1040*, BAGD: 148D, CB: –

1117 βωμός, *bōmos*, n. *altar.* S: *1041*, BAGD: 148D, CB: 345B

1118 γ, *g*, letter. *letter of the Greek alphabet.* S: *150*, BAGD: 149A, CB: –

1119 Γαββαθᾶ, *Gabbatha*, n.pr., *possibly* "height, ridge." *Gabbatha.* S: *1042*, BAGD: 149A, CB: –

1120 Γαβριήλ, *Gabriēl*, n.pr., "[strong] man of God [El]." *Gabriel.* S: *1043*, BAGD: 149A, CB: –

1121 γάγγραινα, *gangraina*, n. *gangrene.* S: *1044*, BAGD: 149A, CB: –

1122 Γάδ, *Gad*, n.pr., "fortune." *Gad.* S: *1045*, BAGD: 149A, CB: –

1123 Γαδαρηνός, *Gadarēnos*, a.pr.g., "from Gadara." *Gadarene.* S: *1046*, BAGD: 149A, CB: –

1124 Γάζα¹, *Gaza¹*, n.pr., "strong." *Gaza.* S: *1048*, BAGD: 149B, CB: –

1125 γάζα², *gaza²*, n. *treasury.* S: *1047*, BAGD: 149B, CB: –

1126 γαζοφυλάκιον, *gazophylakion*, n. *treasury, place where offerings are put.* S: *1049*, BAGD: 149B, CB: 354A

1127 Γάϊος, *Gaios*, n.pr. *Gaius.* S: *1050*, BAGD: 149C, CB: 354A

1128 γάλα, *gala*, n. *milk.* S: *1051*, BAGD: 149C, CB: 354A

1129 Γαλάτης, *Galatēs*, n.pr.g., "from Galatia." *Galatian.* S: *1052*, BAGD: 149D, CB: –

1130 Γαλατία, *Galatia*, n.pr. *Galatia.* S: *1053*, BAGD: 149D, CB: –

1131 Γαλατικός, *Galatikos*, a.pr.g., "of Galatia." *Galatian.* S: *1054*, BAGD: 150A, CB: –

1132 γαλήνη, *galēnē*, n. *calm.* S: *1055*, BAGD: 150B, CB: 354A

1133 Γαλιλαία, *Galilaia*, n.pr., "ring, circle," *hence* "region." *Galilee.* S: *1056*, BAGD: 150B, CB: 354A

1134 Γαλιλαῖος, *Galilaios*, a.pr.g., "from Galilee." *Galilean.* S: *1057*, BAGD: 150C, CB: 354A cf. *Galilaia*

1135 Γαλλία, *Gallia*, n.pr. variant: *Gaul.* S: *1053**, BAGD: 150C, CB: –

1136 Γαλλίων, *Galliōn*, n.pr. *Gallio.* S: *1058*, BAGD: 150C, CB: –

1137 Γαμαλιήλ, *Gamaliēl*, n.pr., "recompense of God [El]." *Gamaliel.* S: *1059*, BAGD: 150C, CB: –

1138 γαμέω, *gameō*, v. *to marry.* S: *1060*, BAGD: 150D, CB: 354A

1139 γαμίζω, *gamizō*, v. *to give in marriage, marry.* S: *1061**, BAGD: 151A, CB: 354A

1140 γαμίσκω, *gamiskō*, v. *(pass.) to be given in marriage.* S: *1061*, BAGD: 151B, CB: 354A

1141 γάμος, *gamos*, n. *wedding banquet.* S: *1062*, BAGD: 151B, CB: 354A

1142 γάρ, *gar*, c. *shows inference or continuation: for, because, indeed, but.* S: *1063*, BAGD: 151C, CB: 354A

1143 γαστήρ, *gastēr*, n. *belly, womb, gluttony.* S: *1064*, BAGD: 152C, CB: –

1144 Γαύδη, *Gaudē*, n.pr. variant: *Gauda.* S: *2802**, BAGD: 433B cf. Κλαυ=δα, CB: –

1145 γέ, *ge*, pt.emph. *emphatic particle: indeed, surely.* S: *1065*, BAGD: 152D, CB: –

1146 Γεδεών, *Gedeōn*, n.pr., "one who cuts, hacks." *Gideon.* S: *1066*, BAGD: 153B, CB: –

1147 γέεννα, *geenna*, n., "Valley of Hinnom." *Gehenna, hell.* S: *1067*, BAGD: 153B, CB: 354A cf. *geh-*

1148 Γεθσημανῆ, *Gethsēmanē*, n.pr., "olive oil press." variant: *Gethsemane.* S: *1068*, BAGD: 153B cf. Γεθσημανι, CB: 354B cf. *Gethsēmani*

1149 Γεθσημανί, *Gethsēmani*, n.pr., "olive oil press." *Gethsemane.* S: *1068**, BAGD: 153B, CB: 354B

1150 γείτων, *geitōn*, n. *neighbor.* S: *1069*, BAGD: 153C, CB: –

1151 γελάω, *gelaō*, v. *to laugh.* S: *1070*, BAGD: 153C, CB: 354A

1152 γέλως, *gelōs*, n. *laughter.* S: *1071*, BAGD: 153C, CB: 354A

1153 γεμίζω, *gemizō*, v. *to fill.* S: *1072*, BAGD: 153C, CB: 354A

1154 γέμω, *gemō*, v. *to be full.* S: *1073*, BAGD: 153D, CB: 354A

1155 γενεά, *genea*, n. *generation, one's own kind or race, descendant.* S: *1074*, BAGD: 153D, CB: 354A

1156 γενεαλογέω, *genealogeō*, v. *to trace genealogical descent.* S: *1075*, BAGD: 154B, CB: 354A

1157 γενεαλογία, *genealogia*, n. *genealogy, lineage.* S: *1076*, BAGD: 154B, CB: 354A

1158 γενέθλια, *genethlia*, n. variant: *birthday (celebration).* S: *1077**, BAGD: 154C cf. γενέθλιος, CB: –

1159 γενέθλιος, *genethlios*, a. variant: *pertaining to birth, birthday.* S: *1077**, BAGD: 154C, CB: –

1160 γενέσια, *genesia*, n. *birthday.* S: *1077*, BAGD: 154C, CB: –

1161 γένεσις, *genesis*, n. *birth; genealogy, descent; (course of one's) life.* S: *1078*, BAGD: 154D, CB: 354A

1162 γενετή, *genetē*, n. *birth.* S: *1079*, BAGD: 155A, CB: –

1163 γένημα, *genēma*, n. *fruit, product, yield, harvest.* S: *1081**, BAGD: 155A, CB: 354A

1164 γεννάω, *gennaō*, v. *to become the father of; to bear, give birth to; (pass.) to be conceived, born.* S: *1080*, BAGD: 155B, CB: 354A

1165 γέννημα, *gennēma*, n. *offspring, brood.* S: *1081*, BAGD: 155D, CB: 354A

1166 Γεννησαρέτ, *Gennēsaret*, n.pr. *Gennesaret.* S: *1082*, BAGD: 156A, CB: –

1167 γέννησις, *gennēsis*, n. variant: *birth.* S: *1083*, BAGD: 156A, CB: –

1168 γεννητός, *gennētos*, a. *pertaining to birth.* S: *1084*, BAGD: 156A, CB: –

1169 γένος, *genos*, n. *family, offspring; nation, people, native (of a region); classification or kind.* S: *1085*, BAGD: 156A, CB: 354B

1170 Γερασηνός, *Gerasēnos*, a.pr.g., "from Gerasa." *Gerasene.* S: *1086**, BAGD: 156D, CB: –

1171 Γεργεσηνός, *Gergesēnos*, a.pr.g., "from Gergesa." variant: *Gergesene.* S: *1086*, BAGD: 156D, CB: –

1172 γερουσία, *gerousia*, n. *assembly of the elders.* S: *1087*, BAGD: 156D, CB: 354B

1173 γέρων, *gerōn*, n. *old person.* S: *1088*, BAGD: 157A, CB: 354B

1174 γεύομαι, *geuomai*, v. *to taste, eat, partake of.* S: *1089*, BAGD: 157A, CB: 354B

1175 γεωργέω, *geōrgeō*, v. *to farm, cultivate.* S: *1090*, BAGD: 157B, CB: –

1176 γεώργιον, *geōrgion*, n. *(farmer's) field.* S: *1091*, BAGD: 157B, CB: –

1177 γεωργός, *geōrgos*, n. *farmer, tenant farmer, share-cropper.* S: *1092*, BAGD: 157B, CB: –

1178 γῆ, *gē*, n. *earth, world, country, region; land, ground, soil.* S: *1093*, BAGD: 157C, CB: 354A

1179 γῆρας, *gēras*, n. *old age.* S: *1094*, BAGD: 157D, CB: 354B cf. *gerōn*

1180 γηράσκω, *gēraskō*, v. *to grow old, age.* S: *1095*, BAGD: 158A, CB: 354B

1181 γίνομαι, *ginomai*, v. *to be, become, happen.* S: *1096*, BAGD: 158A, CB: 354B

1182 γινώσκω, *ginōskō*, v. *to know, come to know, recognize, understand; to have sexual relations.* S: *1097*, BAGD: 160D, CB: 354B

1183 γλεῦκος, *gleukos*, n. *(sweet) wine.* S: *1098*, BAGD: 162A, CB: 354B

1184 γλυκύς, *glykys*, a. *sweet, fresh (water).* S: *1099*, BAGD: 162A, CB: 354B

1185 γλῶσσα, *glōssa*, n. *tongue; language.* S: *1100*, BAGD: 162B, CB: 354B

1186 γλωσσόκομον, *glōssokomon*, n. *container for money.* S: *1101*, BAGD: 162D, CB: 354B

1187 γναφεύς, *gnapheus*, n. *bleacher, fuller.* S: *1102*, BAGD: 162D, CB: –

1188 γνήσιος, *gnēsios*, a. *true, loyal, sincere, genuine.* S: *1103*, BAGD: 162D, CB: 354B

1189 γνησίως, *gnēsiōs*, adv. *genuinely, sincerely.* S: *1104*, BAGD: 163A, CB: –

1190 γνόφος, *gnophos*, n. *darkness.* S: *1105*, BAGD: 163A, CB: –

1191 γνώμη, *gnōmē*, n. *purpose, resolve; judgment; consent.* S: *1106*, BAGD: 163A, CB: 354B

1192 γνωρίζω, *gnōrizō*, v. *to make known, tell, reveal.* S: *1107*, BAGD: 163B, CB: 354B

1193 γνώριμος, *gnōrimos*, a. variant: *acquainted with, known to.* S: *1110**, BAGD: 163C, CB: 354B

1194 γνῶσις, *gnōsis*, n. *knowledge, understanding.* S: *1108*, BAGD: 163D, CB: 354B

1195 γνώστης, *gnōstēs*, n. *one well acquainted with, expert in.* S: *1109*, BAGD: 164A, CB: –

1196 γνωστός, *gnōstos*, a. *known.* S: *1110*, BAGD: 164B, CB: 354B

1197 γογγύζω, *gongyzō*, v. *to grumble, complain, mutter.* S: *1111*, BAGD: 164B, CB: –

1198 γογγυσμός, *gongysmos*, n. *complaint, grumbling; whispering, private talk.* S: *1112*, BAGD: 164C, CB: –

1199 γογγυστής, *gongystēs*, n. *grumbler, complainer.* S: *1113*, BAGD: 164C, CB: –

1200 γόης, *goēs*, n. *imposter.* S: *1114*, BAGD: 164D, CB: 354C

1201 Γολγοθᾶ, *Golgotha*, n.pr., "skull." *Golgotha.* S: *1115*, BAGD: 164D, CB: –

1202 Γόμορρα, *Gomorra*, n.pr., "to overwhelm with water." *Gomorrah.* S: *1116*, BAGD: 164D, CB: –

1203 γόμος, *gomos*, n. *cargo, freight.* S: *1117*, BAGD: 164D, CB: –

1204 γονεύς, *goneus*, n. *(pl.) parents.* S: *1118*, BAGD: 165A, CB: –

1205 γόνυ, *gony*, n. *knee.* S: *1119*, BAGD: 165A, CB: 354C

1206 γονυπετέω, *gonypeteō*, v. *to kneel (before).* S: *1120*, BAGD: 165B, CB: 354C

1207 γράμμα, *gramma*, n. *letter (of the alphabet); document, Scriptures, written code; education.* S: *1121*, BAGD: 165B, CB: 354C

1208 γραμματεύς, *grammateus*, n. *teacher of / expert in the law, scholar, scribe, city clerk.* S: *1122*, BAGD: 165D, CB: 354C

1209 γραπτός, *graptos*, a. *written.* S: *1123*, BAGD: 166A, CB: 354C

1210 γραφή, *graphē*, n. *Scripture.* S: *1124*, BAGD: 166A, CB: 354C

1211 γράφω, *graphō*, v. *to write.* S: *1125*, BAGD: 166C, CB: 354C

1212 γραώδης, *graōdēs*, a. *old wives' tale.* S: *1126*, BAGD: 167B, CB: –

1213 γρηγορέω, *grēgoreō*, v. *to keep watch, be on guard.* S: *1127*, BAGD: 167B, CB: 354C

1214 γυμνάζω, *gymnazō*, v. *to train, exercise.* S: *1128*, BAGD: 167C, CB: 354C

1215 γυμνασία, *gymnasia*, n. *training, exercise.* S: *1129*, BAGD: 167D, CB: 354C

1216 γυμνητεύω, *gymnēteuō*, v. variant: *to be poorly dressed.* S: *1130*, BAGD: 167D, CB: –

1217 γυμνιτεύω, *gymniteuō*, v. *to be in ragged clothing, poorly dressed.* S: *1130**, BAGD: 167D, CB: –

1218 γυμνός, *gymnos*, a. *naked, without clothing; needing (more or better) clothing.* S: *1131*, BAGD: 167D, CB: 354C

1219 γυμνότης, *gymnotēs*, n. *nakedness, insufficiently clothed.* S: *1132*, BAGD: 168A, CB: 354C

1220 γυναικάριον, *gynaikarion*, n. *weak-willed woman, "little woman".* S: *1133*, BAGD: 168B, CB: 354C

1221 γυναικεῖος, *gynaikeios*, a. *feminine, weaker.* S: *1134*, BAGD: 168B, CB: 354C

1222 γυνή, *gynē*, n. *woman; wife.* S: *1135*, BAGD: 168B, CB: 354C

1223 Γώγ, *Gōg*, n.pr. *Gog.* S: *1136*, BAGD: 168D, CB: 354C

1224 γωνία, *gōnia*, n. *corner; cornerstone, capstone, keystone.* S: *1137*, BAGD: 168D, CB: 354C

1225 δ, *d*, letter. *letter of the Greek alphabet.* S: *150*, BAGD: 169A, CB: –

1226 Δαβίδ, *Dabid*, n.pr. variant: *David.* S: *1138*, BAGD: 171B cf. Δαυίδ, CB: 346B cf. *Dauid*

1227 δαιμονίζομαι, *daimonizomai*, v. *to be demon-possessed.* S: *1139*, BAGD: 169A, CB: 346B

1228 δαιμόνιον, *daimonion*, n. *demon, (pagan) god.* S: *1140*, BAGD: 169A, CB: 346B

1229 δαιμονιώδης, *daimoniōdēs*, a. *of the devil, demonic.* S: *1141*, BAGD: 169D, CB: –

1230 δαίμων, *daimōn*, n. *demon, evil spirit.* S: *1142*, BAGD: 169D, CB: 346B

1231 δάκνω, *daknō*, v. *to bite.* S: *1143*, BAGD: 169D, CB: –

1232 δάκρυον, *dakryon*, n. *teardrop.* S: *1144*, BAGD: 170A, CB: –

1233 δακρύω, *dakryō*, v. *to weep, shed tears.* S: *1145*, BAGD: 170A, CB: –

1234 δακτύλιος, *daktylios*, n. *(finger) ring.* S: *1146*, BAGD: 170A, CB: 346B

1235 δάκτυλος, *daktylos*, n. *finger.* S: *1147*, BAGD: 170A, CB: 346B

1236 Δαλμανουθά, *Dalmanoutha*, n.pr. *Dalmanutha.* S: *1148*, BAGD: 170B, CB: –

1237 Δαλματία, *Dalmatia*, n.pr., "deceitful." *Dalmatia.* S: *1149*, BAGD: 170B, CB: –

1238 δαμάζω, *damazō*, v. *to tame, subdue, control.* S: *1150*, BAGD: 170B, CB: –

1239 δάμαλις, *damalis*, n. *heifer, young cow.* S: *1151*, BAGD: 170B, CB: 346B

1240 Δάμαρις, *Damaris*, n.pr. *Damaris.* S: *1152*, BAGD: 170C, CB: –

1241 Δαμασκηνός, *Damaskēnos*, a.pr.g., "from Damascus." *Damascene.* S: *1153*, BAGD: 170C, CB: –

1242 Δαμασκός, *Damaskos*, n.pr. *Damascus.* S: *1154*, BAGD: 170C, CB: –

1243 Δάν, *Dan*, n.pr. variant: *Dan.* S: *150*, BAGD: 170D, CB: –

1244 δανείζω, *daneizō*, v. variant: *to lend, (mid.) to borrow.* S: *1155*, BAGD: 170D, CB: –

1245 δάνειον, *daneion*, n. *debt, loan.* S: *1156*, BAGD: 170D, CB: –

1246 δανειστής, *daneistēs*, n. variant: *moneylender, creditor.* S: *1157*, BAGD: 170D, CB: 346B

1247 δανίζω, *danizō*, v. *to lend; (mid.) to borrow.* S: *1155*, BAGD: 170D, CB: –

1248 Δανιήλ, *Daniēl*, n.pr., "God [El] is my judge." *Daniel.* S: *1158*, BAGD: 170D, CB: –

1249 δάνιον, *danion*, n. variant: *debt, loan.* S: *1156**, BAGD: 170D, CB: –

1250 δανιστής, *danistēs*, n. *moneylender, creditor.* S: *1157*, BAGD: 170D, CB: 346B

1251 δαπανάω, *dapanaō*, v. *to spend; to pay expenses.* S: *1159*, BAGD: 171A, CB: –

1252 δαπάνη, *dapanē*, n. *cost, expense.* S: *1160*, BAGD: 171A, CB: –

1253 Δαυίδ, *Dauid*, n.pr., "beloved one." *David.* S: *1138**, BAGD: 171B, CB: 346B

1254 δέ, *de*, pt. & c. *but, and, then, rather.* S: *1161*, BAGD: 171C, CB: –

1255 δέησις, *deēsis*, n. *prayer, request, petition.* S: *1162*, BAGD: 171D, CB: 346B

1256 δεῖ, *dei*, v.imper. *it is a must, it is necessary (one should, ought).* S: *1163*, BAGD: 172A, CB: 346B

1257 δεῖγμα, *deigma*, n. *example.* S: *1164*, BAGD: 172C, CB: 346B

1258 δειγματίζω, *deigmatizō*, v. *to expose to public disgrace; to make a spectacle of.* S: *1165*, BAGD: 172C, CB: 346C

1259 δείκνυμι, *deiknymi*, v. *to show, explain, make known.* S: *1166*, BAGD: 172D, CB: 346C

1260 δείκνύω, *deiknyō*, v. variant: *to show, point out, make known.*
S: *1166*, BAGD: 172D cf. δείκνυμι, CB: 346C cf. *deiknymi*

1261 δειλία, *deilia*, n. *timidity, cowardice.* S: *1167*, BAGD: 173A,
CB: 346C

1262 δειλιάω, *deiliaō*, v. *to be afraid, cowardly, timid.* S: *1168*,
BAGD: 173A, CB: 346C

1263 δειλινός, *deilinos*, a. variant: *in the afternoon, toward
evening.* S: *150*, BAGD: 173A, CB: –

1264 δειλός, *deilos*, a. *afraid, cowardly, timid.* S: *1169*,
BAGD: 173A, CB: –

1265 δεῖνα, *deina*, n. *a certain one.* S: *1170*, BAGD: 173A, CB: –

1266 δεινός, *deinos*, a. variant: *fearful, terrible.* S: *150*,
BAGD: 173A, CB: 346C

1267 δεινῶς, *deinōs*, adv. *terribly, fiercely.* S: *1171*, BAGD: 173B,
CB: –

1268 δειπνέω, *deipneō*, v. *to eat supper, dine.* S: *1172*,
BAGD: 173B, CB: 346C

1269 δειπνοκλήτωρ, *deipnoklētōr*, n. variant: *host.* S: *150*,
BAGD: 173B, CB: –

1270 δεῖπνον, *deipnon*, n. *banquet, supper, evening meal.* S: *1173*,
BAGD: 173B, CB: 346C

1271 δεῖπνος, *deipnos*, n. variant: *banquet, supper, evening meal.*
S: *1173**, BAGD: 173C, CB: 346C cf. *-on*

1272 δεισιδαιμονία, *deisidaimonia*, n. *religion.* S: *1175*,
BAGD: 173C, CB: 346C

1273 δεισιδαίμων, *deisidaimōn*, a. *(very) religious.* S: *1174**,
BAGD: 173D, CB: 346C

1274 δέκα, *deka*, n.num. *ten.* S: *1176*, BAGD: 173D, CB: 346C

1275 δεκαδύο, *dekadyo*, n.num. variant: *twelve.* S: *1177*,
BAGD: 173D cf. δέκα, CB: –

1276 δεκαέξ, *dekaex*, n.num. variant: *sixteen.* S: *1176 + 1803**,
BAGD: 173D cf. δέκα, CB: –

1277 δεκαοκτώ, *dekaoktō*, n.num. *eighteen.* S: *1176 + 2532 +
3638*, BAGD: 173D cf. δέκα, CB: –

1278 δεκαπέντε, *dekapente*, n.num. *fifteen.* S: *1178*,
BAGD: 173D cf. δέκα, CB: –

1279 Δεκάπολις, *Dekapolis*, n.pr., "[league of] ten cities."
Decapolis. S: *1179*, BAGD: 174A, CB: –

1280 δεκατέσσαρες, *dekatessares*, n.num. *fourteen.* S: *1180*,
BAGD: 173D cf. δέκα, CB: –

1281 δέκατος, *dekatos*, a.num. *tenth, tithe.* S: *1182 & 1181*,
BAGD: 174A, CB: 346C

1282 δεκατόω, *dekatoō*, v. *to collect a tenth; (pass.) to pay a tenth.*
S: *1183*, BAGD: 174B, CB: 346C

1283 δεκτός, *dektos*, a. *acceptable, favorable.* S: *1184*,
BAGD: 174B, CB: 346C

1284 δελεάζω, *deleazō*, v. *to entice, seduce, lure.* S: *1185*,
BAGD: 174B, CB: –

1285 δένδρον, *dendron*, n. *tree.* S: *1186*, BAGD: 174C, CB: 346C

1286 δεξιοβόλος, *dexiobolos*, n. variant: *spearman [?].* S: *1187**,
BAGD: 174C, CB: –

1287 δεξιολάβος, *dexiolabos*, n. *spearman.* S: *1187*,
BAGD: 174C, CB: –

1288 δεξιός, *dexios*, a. *right, right-handed, right-sided.* S: *1188*,
BAGD: 174C, CB: 347A

1289 δέομαι, *deomai*, v. *to pray; ask, beg, plead.* S: *1189*,
BAGD: 175A, CB: 346C

1290 δέος, *deos*, n. *awe, fear, reverence.* S: *127**, BAGD: 172A
cf. δει=, CB: –

1291 Δερβαῖος, *Derbaios*, a.pr.g., "from Derbe." *from Derbe.*
S: *1190*, BAGD: 175C, CB: –

1292 Δέρβη, *Derbē*, n.pr. *Derbe.* S: *1191*, BAGD: 175C, CB: –

1293 δέρμα, *derma*, n. *skin, leather.* S: *1192*, BAGD: 175C,
CB: 346C

1294 δερμάτινος, *dermatinos*, a. *made of leather.* S: *1193*,
BAGD: 175C, CB: –

1295 δέρρις, *derris*, n. variant: *skin.* S: *2359**, BAGD: 175C, CB: –

1296 δέρω, *derō*, v. *to beat up, strike, flog, slap.* S: *1194*,
BAGD: 175D, CB: 346C

1297 δεσμεύω, *desmeuō*, v. *to tie up, bind; to arrest.* S: *1195*,
BAGD: 175D, CB: 346C

1298 δεσμέω, *desmeō*, v. variant: *to tie, bind.* S: *1196*,
BAGD: 175D, CB: 346C cf. *-euō*

1299 δέσμη, *desmē*, n. *bundle.* S: *1197*, BAGD: 176A, CB: 346C

1300 δέσμιος, *desmios*, n. *prisoner, one under arrest.* S: *1198*,
BAGD: 176A, CB: 346C

1301 δεσμός, *desmos*, n. *chain, fetter, imprisonment.* S: *1199*,
BAGD: 176A, CB: 346C

1302 δεσμοφύλαξ, *desmophylax*, n. *jailer, warden.* S: *1200*,
BAGD: 176B, CB: 346C

1303 δεσμωτήριον, *desmōtērion*, n. *prison, jail.* S: *1201*,
BAGD: 176B, CB: 346C

1304 δεσμώτης, *desmōtēs*, n. *prisoner.* S: *1202*, BAGD: 176B,
CB: 346C

1305 δεσπότης, *despotēs*, n. *master; Sovereign Lord.* S: *1203*,
BAGD: 176C, CB: 346C

1306 δεῦρο, *deuro*, adv.pl. *come, come here.* S: *1204*,
BAGD: 176C, CB: 347A

1307 δεῦτε, *deute*, adv. *come, come here.* S: *1205*, BAGD: 176D,
CB: 347A

1308 δευτεραῖος, *deuteraios*, a. *on the following day, on the
second day.* S: *1206*, BAGD: 177A, CB: –

1309 δεύτερον, *deuteron*, a. [used as adv.]. *for the second time,
secondly.* S: *1208**, BAGD: 177A cf. -ος, CB: 347A cf. -os

1310 δευτερόπρωτος, *deuteroprōtos*, a. variant: *lit: "second-first".*
S: *1207*, BAGD: 177A, CB: –

1311 δεύτερος, *deuteros*, a. *second.* S: *1208*, BAGD: 177A,
CB: 347A

1312 δέχομαι, *dechomai*, v. *to welcome, receive, accept.* S: *1209*,
BAGD: 177B, CB: 346B

1313 δέω, *deō*, v. *to tie, bind, imprison.* S: *1210*, BAGD: 177D,
CB: 346C

1314 δή, *dē*, pt.emph. *indeed, therefore.* S: *1211*, BAGD: 178B,
CB: –

1315 δηλαυγῶς, *dēlaugōs*, adv. variant: *very clearly.* S: *5081**,
BAGD: 178B, CB: –

1316 δῆλος, *dēlos*, a. *clear, plain, evident.* S: *1212*, BAGD: 178B, CB: 346C

1317 δηλόω, *dēloō*, v. *to make clear, bring to light, show, point.* S: *1213*, BAGD: 178C, CB: 346C

1318 Δημᾶς, *Dēmas*, n.pr., "common folks." *Demas.* S: *1214*, BAGD: 178D, CB: –

1319 δημηγορέω, *dēmēgoreō*, v. *to deliver a public address.* S: *1215*, BAGD: 178D, CB: –

1320 Δημήτριος, *Dēmētrios*, n.pr., "of Demeter." *Demetrius.* S: *1216*, BAGD: 178D, CB: –

1321 δημιουργός, *dēmiourgos*, n. *builder, craftsman, maker.* S: *1217*, BAGD: 178D, CB: 346C

1322 δῆμος, *dēmos*, n. *people, crowd.* S: *1218*, BAGD: 179A, CB: 346C

1323 δημόσιος, *dēmosios*, a. *public, publicly.* S: *1219*, BAGD: 179B, CB: 346C

1324 δηνάριον, *dēnarion*, n. *denarius [a day's wage].* S: *1220*, BAGD: 179B, CB: –

1325 δήποτε, *dēpote*, adv. variant: *whatever.* S: *1221*, BAGD: 179B, CB: –

1326 δηποτοῦν, *dēpotoun*, adv. variant: *no matter.* S: *150*, BAGD: 179B cf. δήπου, CB: –

1327 δήπου, *dēpou*, adv. *surely, of course.* S: *1222*, BAGD: 179B, CB: –

1328 διά, *dia*, pp. (gen.) *through, by means of;* (acc.) *because of, for the sake of, therefore.* S: *1223*, BAGD: 179B, CB: 347A

1329 διαβαίνω, *diabainō*, v. *to pass through, come over, cross.* S: *1224*, BAGD: 181C, CB: –

1330 διαβάλλω, *diaballō*, v. (pass.) *to have accusations brought upon someone.* S: *1225*, BAGD: 181D, CB: 347A

1331 διαβεβαιόομαι, *diabebaioomai*, v. *to confidently affirm, stress, insist on.* S: *1226*, BAGD: 181D, CB: 345A cf. *bebioō*

1332 διαβλέπω, *diablepō*, v. *to see clearly; to open eyes wide.* S: *1227*, BAGD: 181D, CB: 345A cf. *blepō*

1333 διάβολος, *diabolos*, a. [used as n.]. *devilish, malicious, slanderous; (as noun) devil.* S: *1228*, BAGD: 182A, CB: 347A

1334 διαγγέλλω, *diangellō*, v. *to proclaim (throughout); to give notice.* S: *1229*, BAGD: 182B, CB: 347B

1335 διαγίνομαι, *diaginomai*, v. *to pass, elapse (of time).* S: *1230*, BAGD: 182B, CB: –

1336 διαγινώσκω, *diaginōskō*, v. *to determine, decide.* S: *1231*, BAGD: 182B, CB: –

1337 διαγνωρίζω, *diagnōrizō*, v. variant: *to give an exact report.* S: *1232*, BAGD: 182B, CB: –

1338 διάγνωσις, *diagnōsis*, n. *decision.* S: *1233*, BAGD: 182C, CB: –

1339 διαγογγύζω, *diagongyzō*, v. *to mutter, grumble, complain.* S: *1234*, BAGD: 182C, CB: –

1340 διαγρηγορέω, *diagrēgoreō*, v. *to become fully awake.* S: *1235*, BAGD: 182C, CB: –

1341 διάγω, *diagō*, v. *to live, conduct one's life.* S: *1236*, BAGD: 182C, CB: –

1342 διαδέχομαι, *diadechomai*, v. *to receive (in turn).* S: *1237*, BAGD: 182C, CB: –

1343 διάδημα, *diadēma*, n. *crown, diadem.* S: *1238*, BAGD: 182D, CB: 347A

1344 διαδίδωμι, *diadidōmi*, v. *to distribute, divide up.* S: *1239*, BAGD: 182D, CB: –

1345 διάδοχος, *diadochos*, n. *successor.* S: *1240*, BAGD: 182D, CB: –

1346 διαζώννυμι, *diazōnnymi*, v. *to wrap around, tie around, put on.* S: *1241*, BAGD: 182D, CB: 347B

1347 διαθήκη, *diathēkē*, n. *covenant; will, testament.* S: *1242*, BAGD: 183A, CB: 347B

1348 διαίρεσις, *diairesis*, n. *difference, variety.* S: *1243*, BAGD: 183C, CB: 347A

1349 διαιρέω, *diaireō*, v. *to divide, distribute, apportion.* S: *1244*, BAGD: 183D, CB: –

1350 διακαθαίρω, *diakathairō*, v. *to clear out, clean out.* S: *1245**, BAGD: 183D, CB: –

1351 διακαθαρίζω, *diakatharizō*, v. *to clear out, clean out.* S: *1245*, BAGD: 183D, CB: 360B cf. *katharizō*

1352 διακατελέγχομαι, *diakatelenchomai*, v. *to refute (thoroughly).* S: *1246*, BAGD: 184A, CB: –

1353 διακελεύω, *diakeleuō*, v. variant: *to order.* S: *1781**, BAGD: 184A, CB: –

1354 διακονέω, *diakoneō*, v. *to serve, wait on, help, attend to.* S: *1247*, BAGD: 184A, CB: 347A

1355 διακονία, *diakonia*, n. *ministry, service.* S: *1248*, BAGD: 184B, CB: 347A

1356 διάκονος, *diakonos*, n. *servant, minister, deacon.* S: *1249*, BAGD: 184C, CB: 347A

1357 διακόσιοι, *diakosioi*, a.num. *two hundred.* S: *1250*, BAGD: 185A, CB: –

1358 διακούω, *diakouō*, v. *to give a (legal) hearing.* S: *1251**, BAGD: 185A, CB: –

1359 διακρίνω, *diakrinō*, v. *to make a distinction, judge a dispute;* (mid./pass.) *to doubt, hesitate, waver.* S: *1252*, BAGD: 185A, CB: 347A

1360 διάκρισις, *diakrisis*, n. *distinguishing, differentiation; passing judgment.* S: *1253*, BAGD: 185B, CB: 347A

1361 διακωλύω, *diakōlyō*, v. *to deter, prevent.* S: *1254*, BAGD: 185C, CB: –

1362 διαλαλέω, *dialaleō*, v. *to talk about, discuss.* S: *1255*, BAGD: 185C, CB: –

1363 διαλέγομαι, *dialegomai*, v. *to reason, discuss, discourse; to argue, dispute.* S: *1256*, BAGD: 185C, CB: 347A

1364 διαλείπω, *dialeipō*, v. *to stop, cease.* S: *1257*, BAGD: 185D, CB: 347A

1365 διάλεκτος, *dialektos*, n. *language.* S: *1258*, BAGD: 185D, CB: 347A

1366 διαλιμπάνω, *dialimpanō*, v. variant: *to stop, cease.* S: *150*, BAGD: 185D, CB: –

1367 διαλλάσσομαι, *diallassomai*, v. *to become reconciled.* S: *1259**, BAGD: 186A, CB: 347A

1368 διαλογίζομαι, *dialogizomai*, v. *to think, wonder about; to talk, discuss, argue.* S: *1260*, BAGD: 186A, CB: 347B

1369 διαλογισμός, *dialogismos*, n. *thought, doubt; argument, dispute.* S: *1261*, BAGD: 186A, CB: 347B

1370 διαλύω, *dialyō*, v. *to disperse, break up.* S: *1262*, BAGD: 186B, CB: 347B

1371 διαμαρτύρομαι, *diamartyromai*, v. *to (solemnly) warn or charge; to (solemnly) testify about.* S: *1263*, BAGD: 186C, CB: 347B

1372 διαμάχομαι, *diamachomai*, v. *to argue vigorously, contend sharply.* S: *1264*, BAGD: 186C, CB: –

1373 διαμένω, *diamenō*, v. *to remain (constantly).* S: *1265*, BAGD: 186C, CB: 364B cf. *menō*

1374 διαμερίζω, *diamerizō*, v. *to divide, distribute.* S: *1266*, BAGD: 186D, CB: –

1375 διαμερισμός, *diamerismos*, n. *division.* S: *1267*, BAGD: 186D, CB: 347B

1376 διανέμω, *dianemō*, v. *(pass.) to be spread.* S: *1268*, BAGD: 186D, CB: –

1377 διανεύω, *dianeuō*, v. *to make signs, nod, beckon.* S: *1269*, BAGD: 187A, CB: –

1378 διανόημα, *dianoēma*, n. *thought.* S: *1270*, BAGD: 187A, CB: 347B

1379 διάνοια, *dianoia*, n. *mind, thinking, understanding.* S: *1271*, BAGD: 187A, CB: 347B

1380 διανοίγω, *dianoigō*, v. *to open; (pass.) to be opened; to explain.* S: *1272*, BAGD: 187B, CB: 347B

1381 διανυκτερεύω, *dianyktereuō*, v. *to spend the (entire) night.* S: *1273*, BAGD: 187B, CB: 347B

1382 διανύω, *dianyō*, v. *to continue.* S: *1274*, BAGD: 187B, CB: –

1383 διαπαντός, *diapantos*, adv. variant: *always, continually, constantly.* S: *1275*, BAGD: 179B cf. διά A.II.1a., CB: 368C cf. *pas*

1384 διαπαρατριβή, *diaparatribē*, n. *constant friction.* S: *3859*, BAGD: 187C, CB: –

1385 διαπεράω, *diaperaō*, v. *to cross over.* S: *1276*, BAGD: 187C, CB: –

1386 διαπλέω, *diapleō*, v. *to sail across, sail through.* S: *1277*, BAGD: 187C, CB: –

1387 διαπονέομαι, *diaponeomai*, v. *to be greatly disturbed, troubled, annoyed.* S: *1278**, BAGD: 187C, CB: –

1388 διαπορεύομαι, *diaporeuomai*, v. *to go through, travel through.* S: *1279*, BAGD: 187D, CB: –

1389 διαπορέω, *diaporeō*, v. *to be perplexed, puzzled, in wonder.* S: *1280*, BAGD: 187D, CB: –

1390 διαπραγματεύομαι, *diapragmateuomai*, v. *to gain, earn.* S: *1281*, BAGD: 187D, CB: 347B

1391 διαπρίω, *diapriō*, v. *(pass.) to be furious.* S: *1282*, BAGD: 187D, CB: –

1392 διαρήγνυμι, *diarēgnymi*, v. variant: *to tear, break.* S: *1284**, BAGD: 188A, CB: 347B

1393 διαρήσσω, *diarēssō*, v. variant: *to tear, break.* S: *1284**, BAGD: 188A, CB: –

1394 διαρθρόω, *diarthroō*, v. variant: *(pass.) to be able to speak.* S: *150*, BAGD: 187D, CB: –

1395 διαρπάζω, *diarpazō*, v. *to rob, carry off (possessions).* S: *1283*, BAGD: 188A, CB: –

1396 διαρρήγνυμι, *diarrēgnymi*, v. *to tear (clothes), break (chains).* S: *1284*, BAGD: 188A, CB: 347B

1397 διασαφέω, *diasapheō*, v. *to tell, explain.* S: *1285*, BAGD: 188B, CB: –

1398 διασείω, *diaseiō*, v. *to extort money.* S: *1286*, BAGD: 188B, CB: 347B

1399 διασκορπίζω, *diaskorpizō*, v. *to scatter.* S: *1287*, BAGD: 188B, CB: 347B

1400 διασπάω, *diaspaō*, v. *(pass.) to be torn to pieces.* S: *1288*, BAGD: 188C, CB: –

1401 διασπείρω, *diaspeirō*, v. *(pass.) to be scattered.* S: *1289*, BAGD: 188C, CB: 347B

1402 διασπορά, *diaspora*, n. *scattering, dispersion, Diaspora.* S: *1290*, BAGD: 188C, CB: 347B

1403 διαστέλλω, *diastellō*, v. *(mid.) to give orders, command, authorize; (pass.) what was commanded.* S: *1291**, BAGD: 188D, CB: 347B

1404 διάστημα, *diastēma*, n. *later time, interval.* S: *1292*, BAGD: 188D, CB: –

1405 διαστολή, *diastolē*, n. *difference, distinction.* S: *1293*, BAGD: 188D, CB: –

1406 διαστρέφω, *diastrephō*, v. *(act.) to subvert, pervert, make turn away; (pass.) to be perverted, depraved, turned from the truth.* S: *1294*, BAGD: 189A, CB: –

1407 διασῴζω, *diasōzō*, v. *to heal, save, spare, bring safely through.* S: *1295**, BAGD: 189A, CB: 347B

1408 διαταγή, *diatagē*, n. *putting into effect, institution.* S: *1296*, BAGD: 189B, CB: –

1409 διάταγμα, *diatagma*, n. *edict, command.* S: *1297*, BAGD: 189B, CB: 347B

1410 διαταράσσω, *diatarassō*, v. *(pass.) to be greatly troubled, perplexed, confused.* S: *1298*, BAGD: 189B, CB: –

1411 διατάσσω, *diatassō*, v. *(act./mid.) to command, order, direct; (pass.) to be required, ordered, put into effect.* S: *1299*, BAGD: 189C, CB: 347B

1412 διατελέω, *diateleō*, v. *to continue, remain.* S: *1300*, BAGD: 189C, CB: 377B cf. *teleō*

1413 διατηρέω, *diatēreō*, v. *to keep, treasure.* S: *1301*, BAGD: 189D, CB: 347B

1414 διατί, *diati*, pt.inter. variant: *why?.* S: *1302*, BAGD: 179B cf. διά B.II.2., CB: –

1415 διατίθεμαι, *diatithemai*, v. variant: *to decree, ordain.* S: *1303*, BAGD: 189D, CB: 347B

1416 διατίθημι, *diatithēmi*, v. *to make a covenant or a will; to confer, assign.* S: *1303*, BAGD: 189D, CB: 347B

1417 διατρίβω, *diatribō*, v. *to stay, remain, spend some time.* S: *1304*, BAGD: 190A, CB: –

1418 διατροφή, *diatrophē*, n. *food, sustenance.* S: *1305*, BAGD: 190A, CB: –

1419 διαυγάζω, *diaugazō*, v. *to dawn, shine through.* S: *1306*, BAGD: 190A, CB: 347B

1420 διαυγής, *diaugēs*, a. *transparent.* S: *1307**, BAGD: 190B, CB: –

1421 διαφανής, *diaphanēs*, a. variant: *transparent.* S: *1307*, BAGD: 190B, CB: –

1422 διαφέρω, *diapherō*, v. *(tr.) to carry, spread out; (intr.) to differ; to be more valuable than.* S: *1308*, BAGD: 190B, CB: 370A cf. *pherō*

1423 διαφεύγω, *diapheugō*, v. *to escape, flee.* S: *1309*, BAGD: 190C, CB: –

1424 διαφημίζω, *diaphēmizō*, v. *to spread news about, circulate.* S: *1310*, BAGD: 190C, CB: –

1425 διαφθείρω, *diaphtheirō*, v. *to destroy, corrupt.* S: *1311*, BAGD: 190C, CB: 347B

1426 διαφθορά, *diaphthora*, n. *decay.* S: *1312*, BAGD: 190D, CB: 347B

1427 διάφορος, *diaphoros*, a. *different; superior, outstanding, excellent.* S: *1313*, BAGD: 190D, CB: –

1428 διαφυλάσσω, *diaphylassō*, v. *to guard carefully.* S: *1314*, BAGD: 191A, CB: –

1429 διαχειρίζω, *diacheirizō*, v. *(mid.) to kill, murder.* S: *1315**, BAGD: 191A, CB: –

1430 διαχλευάζω, *diachleuazō*, v. *to make fun of, scoff at, sneer at.* S: *5512**, BAGD: 191A, CB: –

1431 διαχωρίζω, *diachōrizō*, v. *(pass.) to be separated.* S: *1316**, BAGD: 191A, CB: 347A cf. *-esthai*

1432 διγαμία, *digamia*, n. variant: *second marriage.* S: *150*, BAGD: 191A, CB: –

1433 δίγαμος, *digamos*, a. variant: *pertaining to a second marriage.* S: *150*, BAGD: 191A, CB: –

1434 διδακτικός, *didaktikos*, a. *able to teach, skillful at instructing.* S: *1317*, BAGD: 191B, CB: 347B

1435 διδακτός, *didaktos*, a. *taught, instructed.* S: *1318*, BAGD: 191B, CB: 347B

1436 διδασκαλία, *didaskalia*, n. *teaching, doctrine.* S: *1319*, BAGD: 191C, CB: 347B

1437 διδάσκαλος, *didaskalos*, n. *teacher.* S: *1320*, BAGD: 191C, CB: 347B

1438 διδάσκω, *didaskō*, v. *to teach, instruct.* S: *1321*, BAGD: 192A, CB: 347C

1439 διδαχή, *didachē*, n. *teaching, instruction.* S: *1322*, BAGD: 192B, CB: 347B

1440 δίδραχμον, *didrachmon*, n. *two-drachma (temple tax).* S: *1323*, BAGD: 192C, CB: 347C

1441 Δίδυμος, *Didymos*, n.pr., "twin." *Didymus.* S: *1324*, BAGD: 192C, CB: 347C

1442 διδῶ, *didō*, v. *I give.* S: *1325**, BAGD: 192C cf. δίδωμι, CB: 347C cf. *didōmi*

1443 δίδωμι, *didōmi*, v. *to give.* S: *1325*, BAGD: 192C, CB: 347C

1444 διεγείρω, *diegeirō*, v. *to get up, arouse, stimulate.* S: *1326*, BAGD: 193D, CB: 348C cf. *egeirō*

1445 διενθυμέομαι, *dienthymeomai*, v. *to think, ponder, reflect.* S: *1760**, BAGD: 194A, CB: –

1446 διεξέρχομαι, *diexerchomai*, v. variant: *to come out.* S: *1831**, BAGD: 194A, CB: –

1447 διέξοδος, *diexodos*, n. *(street) corner.* S: *1327*, BAGD: 194A, CB: 347C

1448 διερμηνεία, *diermēneia*, n. variant: *explanation, interpretation, translation.* S: *2058**, BAGD: 194B, CB: 347C

1449 διερμηνευτής, *diermēneutēs*, n. *interpreter, translator.* S: *1328*, BAGD: 194B, CB: 347C

1450 διερμηνεύω, *diermēneuō*, v. *to interpret, translate, explain.* S: *1329*, BAGD: 194B, CB: 347C

1451 διέρχομαι, *dierchomai*, v. *to go through, travel throughout.* S: *1330*, BAGD: 194C, CB: 347C

1452 διερωτάω, *dierōtaō*, v. *to find out, ask.* S: *1331*, BAGD: 194D, CB: –

1453 διετής, *dietēs*, a. *two years old.* S: *1332*, BAGD: 194D, CB: –

1454 διετία, *dietia*, n. *two years.* S: *1333*, BAGD: 194D, CB: –

1455 διηγέομαι, *diēgeomai*, v. *to tell, report, describe.* S: *1334*, BAGD: 195A, CB: 347C

1456 διήγησις, *diēgēsis*, n. *account, narrative.* S: *1335*, BAGD: 195A, CB: 347C

1457 διηνεκής, *diēnekēs*, a. *forever, endless, for all time.* S: *1336**, BAGD: 195A, CB: –

1458 διθάλασσος, *dithalassos*, a. *sandbar, sandbank.* S: *1337*, BAGD: 195A, CB: –

1459 διϊκνέομαι, *diikneomai*, v. *to penetrate, pierce.* S: *1338*, BAGD: 195B, CB: –

1460 διΐστημι, *diistēmi*, v. *to leave, pass.* S: *1339*, BAGD: 195B, CB: –

1461 διϊστορέω, *diistoreō*, v. variant: *to examine carefully.* S: *333**, BAGD: 195B, CB: –

1462 διϊσχυρίζομαι, *diischyrizomai*, v. *to assert, insist, maintain firmly.* S: *1340*, BAGD: 195B, CB: –

1463 δικάζω, *dikazō*, v. variant: *to judge, condemn.* S: *2613**, BAGD: 195B, CB: –

1464 δικαιοκρισία, *dikaiokrisia*, n. *righteous judgment.* S: *1341*, BAGD: 195C, CB: 347C

1465 δίκαιος, *dikaios*, a. *right, righteous, upright.* S: *1342*, BAGD: 195C, CB: 347C

1466 δικαιοσύνη, *dikaiosynē*, n. *righteousness, what is right, justice.* S: *1343*, BAGD: 196B, CB: 347C

1467 δικαιόω, *dikaioō*, v. *to justify, vindicate, declare righteous.* S: *1344*, BAGD: 197C, CB: 347C

1468 δικαίωμα, *dikaiōma*, n. *regulation, requirement, commandment; act of righteousness.* S: *1345*, BAGD: 198A, CB: 347C

1469 δικαίως, *dikaiōs*, adv. *justly, uprightly, righteously.* S: *1346*, BAGD: 198B, CB: 347C

1470 δικαίωσις, *dikaiōsis*, n. *justification.* S: *1347*, BAGD: 198B, CB: 347C

1471 δικαστής, *dikastēs*, n. *judge.* S: *1348*, BAGD: 198B, CB: –

1472 δίκη, *dikē*, n. *justice, punishment.* S: *1349*, BAGD: 198C, CB: 348A

1473 δίκτυον, *diktyon*, n. *(fish) net.* S: *1350*, BAGD: 198C, CB: –

1474 δίλογος, *dilogos*, a. *insincere, double-tongued.* S: *1351*, BAGD: 198D, CB: –

1475 διό, *dio*, c.infer. *therefore, that is why, for this reason.* S: *1352*, BAGD: 198D, CB: 348A

1476 διοδεύω, *diodeuō*, v. *to go through, travel through.* S: *1353*, BAGD: 198D, CB: –

1477 Διονύσιος, *Dionysios*, n.pr., "belonging to Dionysus." *Dionysius*. S: *1354*, BAGD: 199A, CB: –

1478 διόπερ, *dioper*, c.infer. *therefore, for this reason.* S: *1355*, BAGD: 199A, CB: –

1479 διοπετής, *diopetēs*, a. *(the image) fallen from heaven.* S: *1356*, BAGD: 199A, CB: –

1480 διόρθωμα, *diorthōma*, n. *reform.* S: *2735**, BAGD: 199A, CB: –

1481 διόρθωσις, *diorthōsis*, n. *a new order.* S: *1357*, BAGD: 199A, CB: 348A

1482 διορύσσω, *dioryssō*, v. *to break in.* S: *1358*, BAGD: 199B, CB: 348A

1483 Διόσκουροι, *Dioskouroi*, n.pr., "sons of Zeus." *the twin gods Castor and Pollux, the Dioscuri.* S: *1359*, BAGD: 199B, CB: –

1484 διότι, *dioti*, c. *therefore, because.* S: *1360*, BAGD: 199B, CB: –

1485 Διοτρέφης, *Diotrephēs*, n.pr., "nurtured by Zeus." *Diotrephes*. S: *1361**, BAGD: 199C, CB: 348A

1486 διπλόος, *diploos*, a. *double, twice as much.* S: *1362**, BAGD: 199C cf. διπλοῦς, CB: 348A cf. *diplous*

1487 διπλοῦς, *diplous*, a. *double, twice as much.* S: *1362*, BAGD: 199C, CB: 348A

1488 διπλόω, *diploō*, v. *to double, pay back double.* S: *1363*, BAGD: 199D, CB: –

1489 δίς, *dis*, adv. *twice, again.* S: *1364*, BAGD: 199D, CB: –

1490 δισμυριάς, *dismyrias*, n. *twenty thousand.* S: *1417 + 3461*, BAGD: 199D, CB: –

1491 διστάζω, *distazō*, v. *to doubt.* S: *1365*, BAGD: 200A, CB: 348A

1492 δίστομος, *distomos*, a. *double-edged.* S: *1366*, BAGD: 200A, CB: 348A

1493 δισχίλιοι, *dischilioi*, a.num. *two thousand.* S: *1367*, BAGD: 200A, CB: 348A

1494 διϋλίζω, *diylizō*, v. *to strain out, filter out.* S: *1368**, BAGD: 200B, CB: –

1495 διχάζω, *dichazō*, v. *to turn (one against another), cause a separation.* S: *1369*, BAGD: 200B, CB: –

1496 διχοστασία, *dichostasia*, n. *division, dissension.* S: *1370*, BAGD: 200B, CB: 347B

1497 διχοτομέω, *dichotomeō*, v. *to cut to pieces.* S: *1371*, BAGD: 200C, CB: –

1498 διψάω, *dipsaō*, v. *to be thirsty.* S: *1372*, BAGD: 200C, CB: 348A

1499 δίψος, *dipsos*, n. *thirst.* S: *1373*, BAGD: 200D, CB: 348A

1500 δίψυχος, *dipsychos*, a. *double-minded.* S: *1374*, BAGD: 201A, CB: 348A

1501 διωγμός, *diōgmos*, n. *persecution.* S: *1375*, BAGD: 201A, CB: 348A

1502 διώκτης, *diōktēs*, n. *persecutor.* S: *1376*, BAGD: 201B, CB: 348A

1503 διώκω, *diōkō*, v. *to persecute; to pursue, press on.* S: *1377*, BAGD: 201B, CB: 348A

1504 δόγμα, *dogma*, n. *decree, regulation.* S: *1378*, BAGD: 201C, CB: 348A

1505 δογματίζω, *dogmatizō*, v. *(pass.) to submit to a rule, regulation.* S: *1379*, BAGD: 201D, CB: 348A

1506 δοκέω, *dokeō*, v. *to think, consider, regard; to seem good.* S: *1380*, BAGD: 201D, CB: 348A

1507 δοκιμάζω, *dokimazō*, v. *to test, try, examine; interpret.* S: *1381*, BAGD: 202C, CB: 348A

1508 δοκιμασία, *dokimasia*, n. *testing, trying, examination.* S: *1381**, BAGD: 202D, CB: 348A

1509 δοκιμή, *dokimē*, n. *character, test, proof.* S: *1382*, BAGD: 202D, CB: 348A

1510 δοκίμιον, *dokimion*, n. *testing, proved genuineness.* S: *1383*, BAGD: 203A, CB: 348A

1511 δόκιμος, *dokimos*, a. *approved by testing, genuine.* S: *1384*, BAGD: 203A, CB: 348A

1512 δοκός, *dokos*, n. *plank, beam of wood.* S: *1385*, BAGD: 203A, CB: –

1513 δόλιος, *dolios*, a. *deceitful, dishonest, tricky.* S: *1386*, BAGD: 203B, CB: –

1514 δολιόω, *dolioō*, v. *to practice deceit, deceive.* S: *1387*, BAGD: 203B, CB: –

1515 δόλος, *dolos*, n. *deceit, slyness, trickery.* S: *1388*, BAGD: 203B, CB: –

1516 δολόω, *doloō*, v. *to distort, falsify.* S: *1389*, BAGD: 203B, CB: 348A

1517 δόμα, *doma*, n. *gift.* S: *1390*, BAGD: 203C, CB: –

1518 δόξα, *doxa*, n. *glory, splendor, brilliance; honor, praise.* S: *1391*, BAGD: 203C, CB: 348B

1519 δοξάζω, *doxazō*, v. *to glorify, give praise, honor.* S: *1392*, BAGD: 204C, CB: 348B

1520 Δορκάς, *Dorkas*, n.pr., "gazelle." *Dorcas*. S: *1393*, BAGD: 204D, CB: –

1521 δόσις, *dosis*, n. *gift, act of giving.* S: *1394*, BAGD: 204D, CB: 348A

1522 δότης, *dotēs*, n. *giver.* S: *1395*, BAGD: 205A, CB: 348A

1523 Δουβέριος, *Douberios*, a.pr.g., "from Doberus." variant: *Doberian*. S: *1190**, BAGD: 205A, CB: –

1524 δουλαγωγέω, *doulagōgeō*, v. *to enslave, bring to subjection.* S: *1396*, BAGD: 205A, CB: 348A cf. *-ōgō*

1525 δουλεία, *douleia*, n. *slavery, bondage.* S: *1397*, BAGD: 205A, CB: 348B

1526 δουλεύω, *douleuō*, v. *to serve (as a slave).* S: *1398*, BAGD: 205A, CB: 348B

1527 δούλη, *doulē*, n. *female servant.* S: *1399*, BAGD: 205C, CB: –

1528 δοῦλος[1], *doulos*[1], n. *servant, slave.* S: *1401 & 1400*, BAGD: 205C, CB: 348B

1529 δοῦλος[2], *doulos*[2], a. *slavish, servile.* S: *1401*, BAGD: 205C, CB: 348B

1530 δουλόω, *douloō*, v. *to enslave.* S: *1402*, BAGD: 206A, CB: –

1531 δοχή, *dochē*, n. *banquet.* S: *1403*, BAGD: 206B, CB: 348A

1532 δράκων, *drakōn*, n. *dragon.* S: *1404*, BAGD: 206B, CB: 348B

1533 δράσσομαι, *drassomai*, v. *to catch, seize.* S: *1405*, BAGD: 206C, CB: –

1534 δραχμή, *drachmē*, n. *silver coin, drachma.* S: *1406*, BAGD: 206C, CB: –

1535 δρέπανον, *drepanon*, n. *sickle.* S: *1407*, BAGD: 206D, CB: 348B

1536 δρόμος, *dromos*, n. *race, course; course (in life), career.* S: *1408*, BAGD: 206D, CB: 348B

1537 Δρούσιλλα, *Drousilla*, n.pr. *Drusilla.* S: *1409*, BAGD: 207A, CB: –

1538 δύναμαι, *dynamai*, v. *to be able, have ability.* S: *1410*, BAGD: 207A, CB: 348B

1539 δύναμις, *dynamis*, n. *power, ability; miracle.* S: *1411*, BAGD: 207B, CB: 348B

1540 δυναμόω, *dynamoō*, v. *(pass.) to be strengthened.* S: *1412*, BAGD: 208C, CB: 348B

1541 δυνάστης, *dynastēs*, n. *ruler, sovereign, (court) official.* S: *1413*, BAGD: 208C, CB: 348B

1542 δυνατέω, *dynateō*, v. *to be able, powerful, strong.* S: *1414*, BAGD: 208C, CB: 348B

1543 δυνατός, *dynatos*, a. *possible (based on power); powerful, able, the Mighty One.* S: *1415*, BAGD: 208C, CB: 348B

1544 δύνω, *dynō*, v. *to set (of the sun).* S: *1416*, BAGD: 209A, CB: 348B

1545 δύο, *dyo*, n.num. *two.* S: *1417*, BAGD: 209A, CB: 348B

1546 δυσβάστακτος, *dysbastaktos*, a. *hard to carry.* S: *1419*, BAGD: 209B, CB: –

1547 δυσεντερία, *dysenteria*, n. variant: *dysentery.* S: *1420*, BAGD: 209C, CB: –

1548 δυσεντέριον, *dysenterion*, n. *dysentery.* S: *1420**, BAGD: 209C, CB: –

1549 δυσερμήνευτος, *dysermēneutos*, a. *hard to explain.* S: *1421*, BAGD: 209C, CB: –

1550 δύσις, *dysis*, n. variant: *west.* S: *150*, BAGD: 209C, CB: –

1551 δύσκολος, *dyskolos*, a. *hard, difficult.* S: *1422*, BAGD: 209C, CB: –

1552 δυσκόλως, *dyskolōs*, adv. *hard, with difficulty.* S: *1423*, BAGD: 209D, CB: –

1553 δυσμή, *dysmē*, n. *west (setting of the sun).* S: *1424*, BAGD: 209D, CB: –

1554 δυσνόητος, *dysnoētos*, a. *hard to understand.* S: *1425*, BAGD: 209D, CB: 348C

1555 δυσφημέω, *dysphēmeō*, v. *(pass.) to be slandered.* S: *987**, BAGD: 209D, CB: –

1556 δυσφημία, *dysphēmia*, n. *bad report, slander.* S: *1426*, BAGD: 209D, CB: –

1557 δώδεκα, *dōdeka*, n.num. *twelve.* S: *1427*, BAGD: 210A, CB: 348A

1558 δωδέκατος, *dōdekatos*, a. *twelfth.* S: *1428*, BAGD: 210B, CB: –

1559 δωδεκάφυλον, *dōdekaphylon*, n. *twelve tribes.* S: *1429*, BAGD: 210B, CB: 348A cf. *-on*

1560 δῶμα, *dōma*, n. *roof, housetop.* S: *1430*, BAGD: 210B, CB: 348A

1561 δωρεά, *dōrea*, n. *gift.* S: *1431*, BAGD: 210B, CB: 348A

1562 δωρεάν, *dōrean*, adv. *freely, free of charge, without payment.* S: *1432*, BAGD: 210C, CB: 348A

1563 δωρέομαι, *dōreomai*, v. *to give, confer, bestow.* S: *1433*, BAGD: 210C, CB: 348A

1564 δώρημα, *dōrēma*, n. *gift.* S: *1434*, BAGD: 210D, CB: 348A

1565 δῶρον, *dōron*, n. *gift, offering.* S: *1435*, BAGD: 210D, CB: 348A

1566 δωροφορία, *dōrophoria*, n. variant: *the bringing of a gift.* S: *1248*, BAGD: 211C, CB: –

1567 ε, *e*, letter. *letter of the Greek alphabet.* S: *150*, BAGD: 211A, CB: –

1568 ἔα, *ea*, pt.excl. *ha!, aha!.* S: *1436*, BAGD: 211A, CB: –

1569 ἐάν, *ean*, c. *if.* S: *1437*, BAGD: 211A, CB: 348C

1570 ἐάνπερ, *eanper*, c. *if, if indeed.* S: *1437 + 4007*, BAGD: 211D, CB: 348C cf. *ean*

1571 ἑαυτοῦ, *heautou*, p.reflex. *himself, herself, itself, themselves.* S: *1438*, BAGD: 211D, CB: 355B cf. *-os*

1572 ἐάω, *eaō*, v. *to let, allow, permit.* S: *1439*, BAGD: 212C, CB: –

1573 ἑβδομήκοντα, *hebdomēkonta*, n.num. *seventy.* S: *1440*, BAGD: 212D, CB: 355B

1574 ἑβδομηκοντάκις, *hebdomēkontakis*, adv. *seventy times.* S: *1441*, BAGD: 213A, CB: 355B cf. *-ta*

1575 ἕβδομος, *hebdomos*, a. *seventh.* S: *1442*, BAGD: 213A, CB: –

1576 Ἔβερ, *Eber*, n.pr., "[regions] beyond [the river]" *or* source of the word "Hebrew." *Eber.* S: *1443**, BAGD: 213A, CB: –

1577 Ἑβραϊκός, *Hebraikos*, a.pr. variant: *Hebrew.* S: *1444*, BAGD: 213A, CB: –

1578 Ἑβραῖος, *Hebraios*, n.pr.g. *a Hebrew; a Hebraic Jew.* S: *1445*, BAGD: 213B, CB: –

1579 Ἑβραΐς, *Hebrais*, n.pr. *Aramaic, Hebrew dialect.* S: *1446*, BAGD: 213B, CB: –

1580 Ἑβραϊστί, *Hebraisti*, adv.pr. *in Aramaic, in the Hebrew dialect.* S: *1447*, BAGD: 213C, CB: 355C

1581 ἐγγίζω, *engizō*, v. *come near, draw near.* S: *1448*, BAGD: 213C, CB: 351A

1582 ἐγγράφω, *engraphō*, v. *to write in, write on, record.* S: *1449*, BAGD: 213D, CB: 351A

1583 ἔγγυος, *engyos*, a. *(as noun) guarantee, guarantor.* S: *1450*, BAGD: 214A, CB: 351A

1584 ἐγγύς, *engys*, adv. *near, close.* S: *1451*, BAGD: 214A, CB: 351A

1585 ἐγγύτερον, *engyteron*, adv.comp. variant: *nearer, closer.* S: *1452*, BAGD: 214A cf. ἐγγύς, CB: –

1586 ἐγείρω, *egeirō*, v. *to wake, raise (the dead), arise.* S: *1453*, BAGD: 214C, CB: 348C

1587 ἔγερσις, *egersis*, n. *resurrection.* S: *1454*, BAGD: 215B, CB: 348C

1588 ἐγκάθετος, *enkathetos*, a. *(as noun) spy.* S: *1455*, BAGD: 215B, CB: –

1589 ἐγκαίνια, *enkainia*, n. *Feast of Dedication (Hanukkah).* S: *1456*, BAGD: 215B, CB: –

1590 ἐγκαινίζω, *enkainizō*, v. *(pass.) to be put into effect, inaugurate; (act.) to open.* S: *1457*, BAGD: 215B, CB: 351A

1591 ἐγκακέω, *enkakeō*, v. *to give up, become discouraged, lose heart.* S: *1573**, BAGD: 215C, CB: 351A

1592 ἐγκαλέω, *enkaleō*, v. *to bring charges, accuse; (pass.) to be charged with, have an accusation brought to.* S: *1458*, BAGD: 215C, CB: 351A

1593 ἐγκαταλείπω, *enkataleipō*, v. *to forsake, leave, abandon.* S: *1459*, BAGD: 215D, CB: –

1594 ἐγκατοικέω, *enkatoikeō*, v. *to live among.* S: *1460*, BAGD: 216A, CB: –

1595 ἐγκαυχάομαι, *enkauchaomai*, v. *to boast.* S: *2620*, BAGD: 216A, CB: 351A

1596 ἐγκεντρίζω, *enkentrizō*, v. *to graft into.* S: *1461*, BAGD: 216A, CB: 351A

1597 ἐγκλείω, *enkleiō*, v. variant: *to lock up.* S: *2623**, BAGD: 216B, CB: –

1598 ἔγκλημα, *enklēma*, n. *charge, accusation.* S: *1462*, BAGD: 216B, CB: 351A

1599 ἐγκομβόομαι, *enkomboomai*, v. *to clothe (oneself) with, put on.* S: *1463*, BAGD: 216B, CB: –

1600 ἐγκοπή, *enkopē*, n. *hinderance, restraint.* S: *1464*, BAGD: 216B, CB: 351A

1601 ἐγκόπτω, *enkoptō*, v. *to hinder, stop, impede progress.* S: *1465*, BAGD: 216C, CB: 351A

1602 ἐγκράτεια, *enkrateia*, n. *self-control.* S: *1466*, BAGD: 216C, CB: 351A

1603 ἐγκρατεύομαι, *enkrateuomai*, v. *to have control (of oneself).* S: *1467*, BAGD: 216C, CB: 351A

1604 ἐγκρατής, *enkratēs*, a. *disciplined, self-controlled.* S: *1468*, BAGD: 216D, CB: 351A

1605 ἐγκρίνω, *enkrinō*, v. *to classify.* S: *1469*, BAGD: 216D, CB: –

1606 ἐγκρύπτω, *enkryptō*, v. *to mix, put into.* S: *1470*, BAGD: 216D, CB: 351B

1607 ἔγκυος, *enkyos*, a. *pregnant.* S: *1471*, BAGD: 216D, CB: –

1608 ἐγχρίω, *enchriō*, v. *to put on, rub on, anoint.* S: *1472*, BAGD: 217A, CB: 346A cf. *chriō*

1609 ἐγώ, *egō*, p.pers. *I, me, my; we, us, our.* S: *1473 & 1691 & 1698 & 170*, BAGD: 217A, CB: 348C

1610 ἐδαφίζω, *edaphizō*, v. *to dash to the ground, raze.* S: *1474*, BAGD: 217C, CB: –

1611 ἔδαφος, *edaphos*, n. *ground.* S: *1475*, BAGD: 217D, CB: –

1612 ἑδραῖος, *hedraios*, a. *firm, steadfast.* S: *1476*, BAGD: 217D, CB: 355C

1613 ἑδραίωμα, *hedraiōma*, n. *foundation.* S: *1477*, BAGD: 218A, CB: 355C

1614 Ἐζεκίας, *Hezekias*, n.pr., "God [El] strengthens." *Hezekiah.* S: *1478**, BAGD: 218A, CB: –

1615 ἐθελοθρησκία, *ethelothrēskia*, n. *self-imposed religion.* S: *1479**, BAGD: 218A, CB: –

1616 ἐθίζω, *ethizō*, v. *(pass.) to be accustomed, required.* S: *1480*, BAGD: 218B, CB: –

1617 ἐθνάρχης, *ethnarchēs*, n. *governor.* S: *1481*, BAGD: 218B, CB: –

1618 ἐθνικός, *ethnikos*, a. *pagan, Gentile.* S: *1482*, BAGD: 218B, CB: 352C

1619 ἐθνικῶς, *ethnikōs*, adv. *like a Gentile, like a pagan.* S: *1483*, BAGD: 218B, CB: 352C

1620 ἔθνος, *ethnos*, n. *Gentile, pagan; (foreign) nation, a people.* S: *1484*, BAGD: 218B, CB: 352C

1621 ἔθος, *ethos*, n. *custom, practice, habit.* S: *1485*, BAGD: 218D, CB: 353A

1622 ἔθω, *ethō*, v. variant: *to be accustomed.* S: *1486*, BAGD: 234A cf. εἴωθα, CB: 349A

1623 εἰ, *ei*, pt.cond. *if, since.* S: *1487*, BAGD: 219A, CB: 348C

1624 εἰδέα, *eidea*, n. *appearance.* S: *2397**, BAGD: 220C, CB: –

1625 εἶδον, *eidon*, v. *to see, watch; realize.* S: *3708**, BAGD: 220C, CB: 349A

1626 εἶδος, *eidos*, n. *form, appearance, sight.* S: *1491*, BAGD: 221B, CB: 349A

1627 εἰδωλεῖον, *eidōleion*, n. *temple of an idol.* S: *1493*, BAGD: 221B, CB: 349A

1628 εἰδωλόθυτος, *eidōlothytos*, a. *(food) sacrificed to idols.* S: *1494*, BAGD: 221B, CB: 349A

1629 εἰδωλολάτρης, *eidōlolatrēs*, n. *idolater.* S: *1496*, BAGD: 221C, CB: 349A

1630 εἰδωλολατρία, *eidōlolatria*, n. *idolatry.* S: *1495**, BAGD: 221C, CB: 349A

1631 εἴδωλον, *eidōlon*, n. *idol.* S: *1497*, BAGD: 221C, CB: 349A

1632 εἰκῇ, *eikē*, adv. *in vain, for nothing, to no purpose.* S: *1500**, BAGD: 221D, CB: –

1633 εἴκοσι, *eikosi*, n.num. *twenty.* S: *1501*, BAGD: 222A, CB: 349A

1634 εἴκω, *eikō*, v. *to give in, yield.* S: *1502*, BAGD: 222A, CB: 349A

1635 εἰκών, *eikōn*, n. *image, likeness, portrait.* S: *1504*, BAGD: 222B, CB: 349A

1636 εἰλικρίνεια, *eilikrineia*, n. *sincerity.* S: *1505*, BAGD: 222D, CB: –

1637 εἰλικρινής, *eilikrinēs*, a. *pure, wholesome.* S: *1506*, BAGD: 222D, CB: –

1638 εἰ μήν, *ei mēn*, adv. variant: *surely, certainly.* S: *2229 + 3375*, BAGD: 220B, CB: –

1639 εἰμί, *eimi*, v. *to be, exist, be present.* S: *1510 & 1488 & 1498 & 151*, BAGD: 222D, CB: 349A

1640 εἶμι, *eimi*, v. variant: *to go.* S: *150*, BAGD: 226A, CB: 349A

1641 εἵνεκεν, *heineken*, pp.*. *because of, on account of.* S: *1752*, BAGD: 226A, CB: 356A cf. *heneken*

1642 εἴπερ, *eiper*, pt.cond. *if indeed, if in fact, since.* S: *1512**, BAGD: 219A cf. εἰ VI.11., CB: –

1643 εἴπως, *eipōs*, pt. variant: *if perhaps, if somehow.* S: *1513**, BAGD: 219A cf. εἰ VI.12., CB: –

1644 εἰρηνεύω, *eirēneuō*, v. *to live in peace, be at peace.* S: *1514*, BAGD: 227A, CB: 349A

1645 εἰρήνη, *eirēnē*, n. *peace, harmony, tranquility; safety, welfare, health.* S: *1515*, BAGD: 227B, CB: 349A

1646 εἰρηνικός, *eirēnikos*, a. *peace-loving, peaceable, peaceful.* S: *1516*, BAGD: 228A, CB: 349A

1647 εἰρηνοποιέω, *eirēnopoieō*, v. *to make peace.* S: *1517*, BAGD: 228A, CB: 349A

1648 εἰρηνοποιός, eirēnopoios, a. *making peace.* S: *1518*, BAGD: 228A, CB: 349A

1649 εἴρω, eirō, v. variant: *to say, speak.* S: *3004**, BAGD: 468A cf. λέγω, CB: –

1650 εἰς, eis, pp. *to, toward, into; for.* S: *1519*, BAGD: 228A, CB: 349A

1651 εἷς, heis, n.num. *one, single.* S: *1520 & 3391*, BAGD: 230D, CB: 355C

1652 εἰσάγω, eisagō, v. *to bring in, take in.* S: *1521*, BAGD: 232B, CB: 339C cf. *agō*

1653 εἰσακούω, eisakouō, v. *(pass.) to be heard, listened to.* S: *1522*, BAGD: 232B, CB: 349B

1654 εἰσδέχομαι, eisdechomai, v. *to receive, welcome.* S: *1523*, BAGD: 232C, CB: 349B

1655 εἴσειμι, eiseimi, v. *to go in, enter.* S: *1524*, BAGD: 232C, CB: –

1656 εἰσέρχομαι, eiserchomai, v. *to go in, enter.* S: *1525*, BAGD: 232C, CB: 349B

1657 εἰσκαλέομαι, eiskaleomai, v. *to invite into.* S: *1528**, BAGD: 233B, CB: 349B

1658 εἴσοδος, eisodos, n. *entering, entrance; reception, welcome.* S: *1529*, BAGD: 233B, CB: 349B

1659 εἰσπηδάω, eispēdaō, v. *to rush in.* S: *1530*, BAGD: 233C, CB: –

1660 εἰσπορεύομαι, eisporeuomai, v. *to go in, enter.* S: *1531*, BAGD: 233C, CB: 372A cf. *poreuomai*

1661 εἰστρέχω, eistrechō, v. *to run in.* S: *1532*, BAGD: 233D, CB: –

1662 εἰσφέρω, eispherō, v. *to bring in, lead in.* S: *1533*, BAGD: 233D, CB: 349B

1663 εἶτα, eita, adv. *then, after that, next.* S: *1534*, BAGD: 233D, CB: 349B

1664 εἴτε, eite, pt. *if, whether .. or.* S: *1535*, BAGD: 219A cf. εἰ VI.13., CB: 349B

1665 εἴωθα, eiōtha, v. *to have a custom.* S: *1486**, BAGD: 234A, CB: –

1666 ἐκ, ek, pp. *of, out of; from, away from.* S: *1537*, BAGD: 234A, CB: 349B

1667 ἕκαστος, hekastos, a. *each, every.* S: *1538*, BAGD: 236C, CB: 355C

1668 ἑκάστοτε, hekastote, adv. *always, at any time.* S: *1539*, BAGD: 236D, CB: –

1669 ἑκατόν, hekaton, n.num. *hundred.* S: *1540*, BAGD: 236D, CB: –

1670 ἑκατονταετής, hekatontaetēs, a. *a hundred years old.* S: *1541**, BAGD: 236D, CB: –

1671 ἑκατονταπλασίων, hekatontaplasiōn, a. *a hundred times.* S: *1542*, BAGD: 237A, CB: –

1672 ἑκατοντάρχης, hekatontarchēs, n. *centurion, officer.* S: *1543*, BAGD: 237A, CB: 355C

1673 ἑκατόνταρχος, hekatontarchos, n. variant: *centurion, officer.* S: *1543**, BAGD: 237A, CB: 355C

1674 ἐκβαίνω, ekbainō, v. *to leave, go out.* S: *1831**, BAGD: 237B, CB: –

1675 ἐκβάλλω, ekballō, v. *to take out, remove; to drive out, expel; bring out, send out.* S: *1544*, BAGD: 237B, CB: 349B

1676 ἔκβασις, ekbasis, n. *way out; outcome, end, result.* S: *1545*, BAGD: 237D, CB: –

1677 ἐκβλαστάνω, ekblastanō, v. variant: *to sprout up.* S: *1816**, BAGD: 238A, CB: –

1678 ἐκβολή, ekbolē, n. *throwing out (a ship's cargo), jettisoning.* S: *1546*, BAGD: 238A, CB: –

1679 ἐκγαμίζω, ekgamizō, v. variant: *to marry, give in marriage.* S: *1547*, BAGD: 238A, CB: –

1680 ἐκγαμίσκω, ekgamiskō, v. variant: *to give in marriage.* S: *1548*, BAGD: 238A cf. ἐκγαμίζω, CB: –

1681 ἔκγονος, ekgonos, a. *(as noun) grandchild.* S: *1549*, BAGD: 238A, CB: –

1682 ἐκδαπανάω, ekdapanaō, v. *(pass.) to be completely expended, exhausted.* S: *1550*, BAGD: 238B, CB: –

1683 ἐκδέχομαι, ekdechomai, v. *to wait for, expect, look forward to.* S: *1551*, BAGD: 238B, CB: 349C

1684 ἔκδηλος, ekdēlos, a. *clear, very evident, plain.* S: *1552*, BAGD: 238B, CB: –

1685 ἐκδημέω, ekdēmeō, v. *to be away, absent.* S: *1553*, BAGD: 238B, CB: 349C

1686 ἐκδίδωμι, ekdidōmi, v. *(mid.) to rent, lease.* S: *1554*, BAGD: 238C, CB: –

1687 ἐκδιηγέομαι, ekdiēgeomai, v. *to tell.* S: *1555*, BAGD: 238C, CB: 349C

1688 ἐκδικέω, ekdikeō, v. *to avenge, take revenge; to grant justice, get justice.* S: *1556*, BAGD: 238C, CB: 349C

1689 ἐκδίκησις, ekdikēsis, n. *justice; vengeance; punishment.* S: *1557*, BAGD: 238D, CB: 349C

1690 ἔκδικος, ekdikos, a. *punishing, avenging.* S: *1558*, BAGD: 238D, CB: 349C

1691 ἐκδιώκω, ekdiōkō, v. *to drive out, persecute.* S: *1559*, BAGD: 239A, CB: 349C

1692 ἔκδοτος, ekdotos, a. *handed over, given up, delivered up.* S: *1560*, BAGD: 239A, CB: 349C

1693 ἐκδοχή, ekdochē, n. *expectation.* S: *1561*, BAGD: 239A, CB: 349C

1694 ἐκδύω, ekdyō, v. *to strip off clothing, unclothe.* S: *1562*, BAGD: 239A, CB: 349C

1695 ἐκεῖ, ekei, adv. *there, in a place where.* S: *1563*, BAGD: 239A, CB: 349C

1696 ἐκεῖθεν, ekeithen, adv. *from there, from that place.* S: *1564*, BAGD: 239B, CB: –

1697 ἐκεῖνος, ekeinos, p.demo. *that, those; he, she, it.* S: *1565*, BAGD: 239B, CB: 349C

1698 ἐκεῖσε, ekeise, adv. *there, a place where.* S: *1566*, BAGD: 240A, CB: –

1699 ἐκζητέω, ekzēteō, v. *to seek out, seek earnestly; (pass.) to be held responsible.* S: *1567*, BAGD: 240A, CB: 350A

1700 ἐκζήτησις, ekzētēsis, n. *controversy, useless speculation.* S: *2214**, BAGD: 240B, CB: 350A

1701 ἐκθαμβέω, ekthambeō, v. *(pass.) to be overwhelmed with wonder, distressed, alarmed.* S: *1568*, BAGD: 240B, CB: 350A

1702 ἔκθαμβος, *ekthambos*, a. *(utterly) astonished.* S: *1569*, BAGD: 240B, CB: 350A

1703 ἐκθαυμάζω, *ekthaumazō*, v. *to wonder, be amazed.* S: *2296**, BAGD: 240B, CB: 350A

1704 ἔκθετος, *ekthetos*, a. *thrown out, exposed (to elements), abandoned.* S: *1570*, BAGD: 240B, CB: –

1705 ἐκκαθαίρω, *ekkathairō*, v. *to cleanse, clean out, get rid of.* S: *1571*, BAGD: 240B, CB: 349C

1706 ἐκκαίω, *ekkaiō*, v. *(pass.) to be inflamed, have a strong desire.* S: *1572*, BAGD: 240C, CB: –

1707 ἐκκακέω, *ekkakeō*, v. variant: *to lose heart.* S: *1573*, BAGD: 240C, CB: 351A

1708 ἐκκεντέω, *ekkenteō*, v. *to pierce.* S: *1574*, BAGD: 240C, CB: –

1709 ἐκκλάω, *ekklaō*, v. *(pass.) to be broken off.* S: *1575*, BAGD: 240C, CB: 349C

1710 ἐκκλείω, *ekkleiō*, v. *to alienate, shut out, exclude.* S: *1576*, BAGD: 240C, CB: –

1711 ἐκκλησία, *ekklēsia*, n. *church, congregation, assembly.* S: *1577*, BAGD: 240D, CB: 349C

1712 ἐκκλίνω, *ekklinō*, v. *to turn away, turn aside.* S: *1578*, BAGD: 241C, CB: –

1713 ἐκκολυμβάω, *ekkolymbaō*, v. *to swim away.* S: *1579*, BAGD: 241D, CB: –

1714 ἐκκομίζω, *ekkomizō*, v. *to carry out.* S: *1580*, BAGD: 241D, CB: –

1715 ἐκκοπή, *ekkopē*, n. variant: *hindrance.* S: *1464**, BAGD: 216B cf. ἐγκοπή, CB: –

1716 ἐκκόπτω, *ekkoptō*, v. *to cut off, cut down.* S: *1581*, BAGD: 241D, CB: 349C

1717 ἐκκρεμάννυμι, *ekkremannymi*, v. *(mid.) to hang upon (words).* S: *1582**, BAGD: 242A, CB: –

1718 ἐκλαλέω, *eklaleō*, v. *to tell.* S: *1583*, BAGD: 242A, CB: –

1719 ἐκλάμπω, *eklampō*, v. *to shine.* S: *1584*, BAGD: 242A, CB: 349C

1720 ἐκλανθάνομαι, *eklanthanomai*, v. *to forget.* S: *1585*, BAGD: 242B, CB: –

1721 ἐκλέγομαι, *eklegomai*, v. *to chose, pick, select.* S: *1586*, BAGD: 242B, CB: 349C

1722 ἐκλείπω, *ekleipō*, v. *to fail, end, stop.* S: *1587*, BAGD: 242C, CB: 349C

1723 ἐκλεκτός, *eklektos*, a. *elect, chosen, the Chosen One.* S: *1588*, BAGD: 242D, CB: 349C

1724 ἐκλογή, *eklogē*, n. *election, choice, selection.* S: *1589*, BAGD: 243A, CB: 349C

1725 ἐκλύω, *eklyō*, v. *(pass.) to lose heart; give up; collapse in weariness.* S: *1590*, BAGD: 243A, CB: 349C

1726 ἐκμάσσω, *ekmassō*, v. *to wipe off, dry off.* S: *1591*, BAGD: 243B, CB: –

1727 ἐκμυκτηρίζω, *ekmyktērizō*, v. *to sneer at, ridicule.* S: *1592*, BAGD: 243B, CB: 349C

1728 ἐκνεύω, *ekneuō*, v. *to slip away, withdraw.* S: *1593*, BAGD: 243B, CB: –

1729 ἐκνήφω, *eknēphō*, v. *to come to one's sense, become sober.* S: *1594*, BAGD: 243B, CB: 349C

1730 ἑκούσιος, *hekousios*, a. *spontaneous, willing.* S: *1595*, BAGD: 243B, CB: –

1731 ἑκουσίως, *hekousiōs*, adv. *willingly; deliberately, intentionally.* S: *1596*, BAGD: 243C, CB: –

1732 ἔκπαλαι, *ekpalai*, adv. *for a long time, long ago.* S: *1597*, BAGD: 243C, CB: –

1733 ἐκπειράζω, *ekpeirazō*, v. *to test, put to a test, try, tempt.* S: *1598*, BAGD: 243C, CB: 349C

1734 ἐκπέμπω, *ekpempō*, v. *to send away, send out.* S: *1599*, BAGD: 243C, CB: –

1735 ἐκπερισσῶς, *ekperissōs*, adv. *emphatically.* S: *1537 + 4053*, BAGD: 243C, CB: –

1736 ἐκπετάννυμι, *ekpetannymi*, v. *to hold out, spread out.* S: *1600*, BAGD: 243D, CB: –

1737 ἐκπηδάω, *ekpēdaō*, v. *to rush out.* S: *1530**, BAGD: 243D, CB: –

1738 ἐκπίπτω, *ekpiptō*, v. *to fall off; to fail; to run aground, be dashed to pieces.* S: *1601*, BAGD: 243D, CB: 349C

1739 ἐκπλέω, *ekpleō*, v. *to sail (from).* S: *1602*, BAGD: 244A, CB: –

1740 ἐκπληρόω, *ekplēroō*, v. *to fulfill.* S: *1603*, BAGD: 244A, CB: 349C

1741 ἐκπλήρωσις, *ekplērōsis*, n. *end, completion.* S: *1604*, BAGD: 244B, CB: –

1742 ἐκπλήσσω, *ekplēssō*, v. *(pass.) to be amazed, astonished.* S: *1605*, BAGD: 244B, CB: 349C

1743 ἐκπνέω, *ekpneō*, v. *to breathe one's last breath, die.* S: *1606*, BAGD: 244B, CB: 349C

1744 ἐκπορεύομαι, *ekporeuomai*, v. *to go out, come out, leave.* S: *1607*, BAGD: 244B, CB: 350A

1745 ἐκπορνεύω, *ekporneuō*, v. *to engage in sexual immorality.* S: *1608*, BAGD: 244D, CB: –

1746 ἐκπτύω, *ekptyō*, v. *to scorn, spit out.* S: *1609*, BAGD: 244D, CB: 350A

1747 ἐκπυρόω, *ekpyroō*, v. variant: *to set on fire, destroy by fire.* S: *150*, BAGD: 244D, CB: –

1748 ἐκριζόω, *ekrizoō*, v. *to uproot.* S: *1610*, BAGD: 244D, CB: 350A

1749 ἔκστασις, *ekstasis*, n. *amazement, astonishment, bewilderment; a trance.* S: *1611*, BAGD: 245A, CB: 350A

1750 ἐκστρέφω, *ekstrephō*, v. *(pass.) to be warped, perverted.* S: *1612*, BAGD: 245B, CB: –

1751 ἐκσῴζω, *eksōzō*, v. variant: *to bring safely.* S: *4982**, BAGD: 245B, CB: –

1752 ἐκταράσσω, *ektarassō*, v. *to throw into an uproar, into confusion.* S: *1613*, BAGD: 245B, CB: –

1753 ἐκτείνω, *ekteinō*, v. *to stretch out, reach out; point, motion.* S: *1614*, BAGD: 245B, CB: 350A

1754 ἐκτελέω, *ekteleō*, v. *to finish, bring to a conclusion.* S: *1615*, BAGD: 245C, CB: –

1755 ἐκτένεια, *ekteneia*, n. *earnestness.* S: *1616*, BAGD: 245C, CB: –

1756 ἐκτενής, *ektenēs*, a. *deep, earnest.* S: *1618*, BAGD: 245C, CB: –

1757 ἐκτενῶς, ektenōs, adv. *deeply, earnestly.* S: *1619 & 1617,* BAGD: 245D, CB: 350A

1758 ἐκτίθημι, ektithēmi, v. *(mid.) to explain; (pass.) to be placed out in the elements, exposed, abandoned.* S: *1620,* BAGD: 245D, CB: –

1759 ἐκτινάσσω, ektinassō, v. *to shake off, shake out.* S: *1621,* BAGD: 245D, CB: 350A

1760 ἐκτός, ektos, adv. *outside, beyond, except.* S: *1622,* BAGD: 246A, CB: –

1761 ἕκτος, hektos, a. *sixth, noon (the sixth hour).* S: *1623,* BAGD: 246A, CB: –

1762 ἐκτρέπω, ektrepō, v. *to turn away, wander away from; be disabled.* S: *1624,* BAGD: 246B, CB: 350A

1763 ἐκτρέφω, ektrephō, v. *to feed, nourish; to bring up, rear (children).* S: *1625,* BAGD: 246C, CB: 350A

1764 ἔκτρομος, ektromos, a. variant: *trembling.* S: *1790*,* BAGD: 246C, CB: –

1765 ἔκτρωμα, ektrōma, n. *abnormal or untimely birth.* S: *1626,* BAGD: 246C, CB: 350A

1766 ἐκφέρω, ekpherō, v. *to bring out, carry out; to produce.* S: *1627,* BAGD: 246D, CB: 370A cf. *pherō*

1767 ἐκφεύγω, ekpheugō, v. *to escape.* S: *1628,* BAGD: 246D, CB: 349C

1768 ἐκφοβέω, ekphobeō, v. *to frighten, terrify.* S: *1629,* BAGD: 247A, CB: –

1769 ἔκφοβος, ekphobos, a. *frightened, terrified.* S: *1630,* BAGD: 247A, CB: –

1770 ἐκφύω, ekphyō, v. *to come out, put forth.* S: *1631,* BAGD: 247A, CB: –

1771 ἐκφωνέω, ekphōneō, v. variant: *cry out.* S: *1537 + 5455,* BAGD: 247A, CB: –

1772 ἐκχέω, ekcheō, v. *to pour out, shed, scatter; (pass.) to be poured out, shed; to rush (for profit).* S: *1632,* BAGD: 247B, CB: 349B

1773 ἐκχύννομαι, ekchynnomai, v. variant: *to be poured out, shed, spilled.* S: *1632*,* BAGD: 247B cf. -έω, CB: 349B cf. *-eō*

1774 ἐκχωρέω, ekchōreō, v. *to go out, go away.* S: *1633,* BAGD: 247C, CB: –

1775 ἐκψύχω, ekpsychō, v. *to die, expire.* S: *1634,* BAGD: 247C, CB: –

1776 ἑκών, hekōn, a. *voluntarily, by one's own choice.* S: *1635,* BAGD: 247D, CB: –

1777 ἐλαία, elaia, n. *olive, olive tree.* S: *1636,* BAGD: 247D, CB: 350A

1778 ἔλαιον, elaion, n. *olive oil.* S: *1637,* BAGD: 247D, CB: 350A

1779 ἐλαιών, elaiōn, n. *Mount of Olives, olive grove.* S: *1638,* BAGD: 248A, CB: 350A

1780 Ἐλαμίτης, Elamitēs, n.pr.g., "highland." *Elamite.* S: *1639,* BAGD: 248A, CB: –

1781 ἐλάσσων, elassōn, a. [also used as adv.]. *lesser, cheaper, younger.* S: *1640,* BAGD: 248A, CB: 350A

1782 ἐλαττονέω, elattoneō, v. *to have too little.* S: *1641,* BAGD: 248B, CB: –

1783 ἐλαττόω, elattoō, v. *to make lower than; (pass.) to be made lower than, become lesser, diminish.* S: *1642,* BAGD: 248B, CB: –

1784 ἐλάττων, elattōn, a. variant: *lesser, cheaper, younger.* S: *1640,* BAGD: 248A cf. ἐλάσσων, CB: 350A cf. *elassōn*

1785 ἐλαύνω, elaunō, v. *to row (with oars); (pass.) to be driven.* S: *1643,* BAGD: 248C, CB: –

1786 ἐλαφρία, elaphria, n. *lightness, levity.* S: *1644,* BAGD: 248C, CB: –

1787 ἐλαφρός, elaphros, a. *light, not burdensome.* S: *1645,* BAGD: 248C, CB: –

1788 ἐλάχιστος, elachistos, a. *least, very small, trivial.* S: *1646 & 1647,* BAGD: 248D, CB: 350A

1789 Ἐλεάζαρ, Eleazar, n.pr., "God [El] is a help." *Eleazar.* S: *1648,* BAGD: 249A, CB: –

1790 ἐλεάω, eleaō, v. *to show mercy, be merciful.* S: *1653*,* BAGD: 249A, CB: 350A

1791 ἐλεγμός, elegmos, n. *rebuke, reproof.* S: *1650*,* BAGD: 249A, CB: 350A

1792 ἔλεγξις, elenxis, n. *rebuke, reproof.* S: *1649,* BAGD: 249A, CB: 350A

1793 ἔλεγχος, elenchos, n. *certainty, proof.* S: *1650,* BAGD: 249A, CB: 350A

1794 ἐλέγχω, elenchō, v. *to expose; to rebuke, refute, show fault; to convince, convict.* S: *1651,* BAGD: 249B, CB: 350A

1795 ἐλεεινός, eleeinos, a. *pitiful.* S: *1652,* BAGD: 249C, CB: 350A

1796 ἐλεέω, eleeō, v. *to have mercy on, pity; to show mercy to, show pity to.* S: *1653,* BAGD: 249C, CB: 350A

1797 ἐλεημοσύνη, eleēmosynē, n. *gift to the poor, alms, charitable gift.* S: *1654,* BAGD: 249D, CB: 350A

1798 ἐλεήμων, eleēmōn, a. *merciful.* S: *1655,* BAGD: 250A, CB: 350A

1799 ἔλεος, eleos, n. *mercy, pity.* S: *1656,* BAGD: 250A, CB: 350A

1800 ἐλευθερία, eleutheria, n. *freedom, liberty.* S: *1657,* BAGD: 250C, CB: 350B

1801 ἐλεύθερος, eleutheros, a. *free, released.* S: *1658,* BAGD: 250D, CB: 350B

1802 ἐλευθερόω, eleutheroō, v. *to set free, liberate.* S: *1659,* BAGD: 250D, CB: 350B

1803 ἔλευσις, eleusis, n. *coming, advent.* S: *1660,* BAGD: 251A, CB: 350B

1804 ἐλεφάντινος, elephantinos, a. *made of ivory.* S: *1661,* BAGD: 251A, CB: –

1805 Ἐλιακείμ, Eliakeim, n.pr., "God [El] establishes." variant: *Eliakim.* S: *1662,* BAGD: 251B, CB: –

1806 Ἐλιακίμ, Eliakim, n.pr., "God [El] establishes." *Eliakim.* S: *1662*,* BAGD: 251B, CB: –

1807 ἕλιγμα, heligma, n. variant: *package, roll.* S: *3395*,* BAGD: 251B, CB: –

1808 Ἐλιέζερ, Eliezer, n.pr., "God [El] is [my] help." *Eliezer.* S: *1663,* BAGD: 251B, CB: –

1809 Ἐλιούδ, Elioud, n.pr., "God [El] is [my] grandeur." *Eliud.* S: *1664,* BAGD: 251B, CB: –

1810 Ἐλισάβετ, *Elisabet*, n.pr., "God [El] is [my] oath." *Elizabeth.* S: *1665*, BAGD: 251B, CB: –

1811 Ἐλισαῖος, *Elisaios*, n.pr., "God [El] is [my] salvation." *Elisha.* S: *1666**, BAGD: 251B, CB: –

1812 Ἐλισσαῖος, *Elissaios*, n.pr., "God [El] is [my] salvation." variant: *Elisha.* S: *1666*, BAGD: 251B cf. Ἐλισαι=ος, CB: –

1813 ἑλίσσω, *helissō*, v. *to roll up.* S: *1667 & 1507*, BAGD: 251B, CB: –

1814 ἕλκος, *helkos*, n. *sore, abscess.* S: *1668*, BAGD: 251C, CB: –

1815 ἑλκόω, *helkoō*, v. *(pass.) to be covered with sores.* S: *1669*, BAGD: 251C, CB: –

1816 ἑλκύω, *helkyō*, v. *to drag, draw, pull in.* S: *1670*, BAGD: 251C, CB: –

1817 Ἑλλάς, *Hellas*, n.pr. *Greece.* S: *1671*, BAGD: 251D, CB: 355C

1818 Ἕλλην, *Hellēn*, n.pr. *Greek, Gentile.* S: *1672*, BAGD: 251D, CB: 355C

1819 Ἑλληνικός, *Hellēnikos*, a.pr. *Greek (language).* S: *1673*, BAGD: 252A, CB: 355C

1820 Ἑλληνίς, *Hellēnis*, n.pr. *Greek.* S: *1674*, BAGD: 252A, CB: 355C

1821 Ἑλληνιστής, *Hellēnistēs*, n.pr.g. *Grecian Jew, Hellenist.* S: *1675*, BAGD: 252B, CB: 355C

1822 Ἑλληνιστί, *Hellēnisti*, adv.pr. *in Greek (language).* S: *1676*, BAGD: 252B, CB: 355C

1823 ἐλλογάω, *ellogaō*, v. *to charge (to one's account).* S: *1677**, BAGD: 252B cf. ἐλλογέω, CB: 350B cf. *ellogeō*

1824 ἐλλογέω, *ellogeō*, v. *(pass.) to be charged to one's account.* S: *1677*, BAGD: 252B, CB: 350B

1825 Ἐλμαδάμ, *Elmadam*, n.pr. *Elmadam.* S: *1678**, BAGD: 252C, CB: –

1826 Ἐλμωδάμ, *Elmōdam*, n.pr. variant: *Elmodam.* S: *1678*, BAGD: 252C cf. Ἐλμαδάμ, CB: –

1827 ἐλπίζω, *elpizō*, v. *to hope, hope for, put hope in, expect.* S: *1679*, BAGD: 252C, CB: 350B

1828 ἐλπίς, *elpis*, n. *hope, expectation.* S: *1680*, BAGD: 252D, CB: 350B

1829 Ἐλύμας, *Elymas*, n.pr., *poss.* "wise one" hence "magician." *Elymas.* S: *1681*, BAGD: 253C, CB: –

1830 ἐλωΐ, *elōi*, l.[n.+p.]. *Eloi [Aramaic: my God].* S: *1682*, BAGD: 253D, CB: 350B cf. *ēli ēli lema*

1831 ἐμαυτοῦ, *emautou*, p.reflex. *myself, my own, of my own accord.* S: *1683*, BAGD: 253D, CB: –

1832 ἐμβαίνω, *embainō*, v. *to get into, step into, embark.* S: *1684*, BAGD: 254A, CB: –

1833 ἐμβάλλω, *emballō*, v. *to throw into.* S: *1685*, BAGD: 254A, CB: 350B

1834 ἐμβαπτίζω, *embaptizō*, v. variant: *to dip into.* S: *1686**, BAGD: 254A, CB: –

1835 ἐμβάπτω, *embaptō*, v. *to dip into.* S: *1686*, BAGD: 254B, CB: 344C cf. *baptō*

1836 ἐμβατεύω, *embateuō*, v. *to go into great detail about.* S: *1687*, BAGD: 254B, CB: –

1837 ἐμβιβάζω, *embibazō*, v. *to put on board (a vessel).* S: *1688*, BAGD: 254C, CB: –

1838 ἐμβλέπω, *emblepō*, v. *to look (closely, directly) at, gaze at.* S: *1689*, BAGD: 254C, CB: 350B

1839 ἐμβριμάομαι, *embrimaomai*, v. *to warn sternly, rebuke harshly; to be deeply moved.* S: *1690*, BAGD: 254D, CB: 350B

1840 ἐμέω, *emeō*, v. *to spit out.* S: *1692*, BAGD: 254D, CB: 350B

1841 ἐμμαίνομαι, *emmainomai*, v. *to be enraged.* S: *1693*, BAGD: 255A, CB: –

1842 Ἐμμανουήλ, *Emmanouēl*, n.pr., "God with us." *Immanuel.* S: *1694*, BAGD: 255A, CB: 350B

1843 Ἐμμαοῦς, *Emmaous*, n.pr., "hot springs." *Emmaus.* S: *1695**, BAGD: 255A, CB: –

1844 ἐμμένω, *emmenō*, v. *to remain in, stay in; remain faithful, continue in.* S: *1696*, BAGD: 255B, CB: 350B

1845 ἐμμέσῳ, *emmesō*, v. variant: *among.* S: *1722 + 3319*, BAGD: 255B, CB: –

1846 Ἐμμώρ, *Hemmōr*, n.pr., "male donkey." *Hamor.* S: *1697**, BAGD: 255B, CB: –

1847 ἐμός, *emos*, a.poss. *my, mine.* S: *1699*, BAGD: 255C, CB: 350B

1848 ἐμπαιγμονή, *empaigmonē*, n. *scoffing, mocking.* S: *150*, BAGD: 255D, CB: 350B

1849 ἐμπαιγμός, *empaigmos*, n. *jeering, scoffing, mocking.* S: *1701*, BAGD: 255D, CB: –

1850 ἐμπαίζω, *empaizō*, v. *to mock, ridicule.* S: *1702*, BAGD: 255D, CB: 350B

1851 ἐμπαίκτης, *empaiktēs*, n. *scoffer, mocker.* S: *1703*, BAGD: 255D, CB: –

1852 ἐμπέμπω, *empempō*, v. variant: *to send in.* S: *649**, BAGD: 255D, CB: –

1853 ἐμπεριπατέω, *emperipateō*, v. *to walk among.* S: *1704*, BAGD: 256A, CB: 350B

1854 ἐμπιμπλάω, *empimplaō*, v. variant: *to provide, fill, satisfy.* S: *1705**, BAGD: 256A cf. ἐμπίμπλημι, CB: –

1855 ἐμπίμπλημι, *empimplēmi*, v. *(act.) to provide, fill, satisfy; (pass.) to be filled to satisfaction; to enjoy one's company.* S: *1705*, BAGD: 256A, CB: 350B

1856 ἐμπίμπρημι, *empimprēmi*, v. *to burn, set on fire.* S: *1714**, BAGD: 256B, CB: –

1857 ἐμπιπλάω, *empiplaō*, v. variant: *to provide, fill, satisfy.* S: *1705**, BAGD: 256A cf. ἐμπίμπλημι, CB: –

1858 ἐμπίπλημι, *empiplēmi*, v. variant: *to provide, fill, satisfy.* S: *1705*, BAGD: 256A cf. ἐμπίμπλημι, CB: –

1859 ἐμπίπρημι, *empiprēmi*, v. variant: *to burn, set on fire.* S: *1714**, BAGD: 256B, CB: –

1860 ἐμπίπτω, *empiptō*, v. *to fall into.* S: *1706*, BAGD: 256B, CB: –

1861 ἐμπλέκω, *emplekō*, v. *(mid./pass.) to be involved in, become entangled.* S: *1707*, BAGD: 256C, CB: –

1862 ἐμπλοκή, *emplokē*, n. *braiding.* S: *1708*, BAGD: 256C, CB: –

1863 ἐμπνέω, *empneō*, v. *to breath.* S: *1709*, BAGD: 256C, CB: 350B

1864 ἐμπορεύομαι, *emporeuomai*, v. *to carry on business; exploit.* S: *1710*, BAGD: 256D, CB: 350B

1865 ἐμπορία, *emporia*, n. *business, trade.* S: *1711*, BAGD: 256D, CB: –

1866 ἐμπόριον, *emporion*, n. *market, marketplace.* S: *1712*, BAGD: 257A, CB: –

1867 ἔμπορος, *emporos*, n. *merchant.* S: *1713*, BAGD: 257A, CB: –

1868 ἐμπρήθω, *emprēthō*, v. variant: *to burn, set on fire.* S: *1714*, BAGD: 256B cf. ἐμπίμπρημι, CB: –

1869 ἔμπροσθεν, *emprosthen*, adv. & pp.*. *before, in front of, in the presence of.* S: *1715*, BAGD: 257A, CB: 350B

1870 ἐμπτύω, *emptyō*, v. *to spit on, spit at.* S: *1716*, BAGD: 257C, CB: –

1871 ἐμφανής, *emphanēs*, a. *seen, revealed, visible.* S: *1717*, BAGD: 257C, CB: 350B

1872 ἐμφανίζω, *emphanizō*, v. *to show; report; to present (legal) charges; petition; (pass.) to appear.* S: *1718*, BAGD: 257D, CB: 350B

1873 ἔμφοβος, *emphobos*, a. *afraid, terrified.* S: *1719*, BAGD: 257D, CB: –

1874 ἐμφυσάω, *emphysaō*, v. *to breathe on.* S: *1720*, BAGD: 258A, CB: 350B

1875 ἔμφυτος, *emphytos*, a. *implanted.* S: *1721*, BAGD: 258A, CB: 350B

1876 ἐμφωνέω, *emphōneō*, v. variant: *to call.* S: *5455*, BAGD: 258B, CB: –

1877 ἐν, *en*, pp. *of place: in, at, among, with; of time: during, while; causal: by means of, with, because of.* S: *1722*, BAGD: 258B, CB: 350B

1878 ἐναγκαλίζομαι, *enankalizomai*, v. *to take in one's arms.* S: *1723*, BAGD: 261D, CB: 350C

1879 ἐνάλιος, *enalios*, a. *creatures pertaining to the sea.* S: *1724*, BAGD: 261D, CB: –

1880 ἐνάλλομαι, *enallomai*, v. variant: *leap upon.* S: *2177*, BAGD: 261D, CB: –

1881 ἐνανθρωπέω, *enanthrōpeō*, v. variant: *to take on human form.* S: *150*, BAGD: 261D, CB: 350C

1882 ἔναντι, *enanti*, adv. [used as pp.*]. *before.* S: *1725*, BAGD: 261D, CB: 350C

1883 ἐναντίον, *enantion*, adv. [used as pp.*]. *before, in the sight of.* S: *1726*, BAGD: 261D, CB: 350C

1884 ἐναντιόομαι, *enantioomai*, v. variant: *to oppose.* S: *150*, BAGD: 262A, CB: –

1885 ἐναντίος, *enantios*, a. *against, opposite, in hostility.* S: *1727*, BAGD: 262A, CB: 350C cf. -*on*

1886 ἐναργής, *enargēs*, a. variant: *clear, evident, visible.* S: *1756*, BAGD: 262B, CB: –

1887 ἐνάρχομαι, *enarchomai*, v. *to begin.* S: *1728*, BAGD: 262B, CB: 343B cf. *archō*

1888 ἔνατος, *enatos*, a. *ninth (ninth hour = three p.m.).* S: *1766*, BAGD: 262B, CB: –

1889 ἐναφίημι, *enaphiēmi*, v. variant: *to let, permit.* S: *863*, BAGD: 262C, CB: –

1890 ἐνδεής, *endeēs*, a. *needy, poor, impoverished.* S: *1729*, BAGD: 262C, CB: –

1891 ἔνδειγμα, *endeigma*, n. *evidence, plain indication.* S: *1730*, BAGD: 262C, CB: –

1892 ἐνδείκνυμι, *endeiknymi*, v. *to show, display.* S: *1731*, BAGD: 262C, CB: –

1893 ἔνδειξις, *endeixis*, n. *demonstration, proof, sign.* S: *1732*, BAGD: 262D, CB: 350C

1894 ἔνδεκα, *hendeka*, n.num. *eleven.* S: *1733*, BAGD: 262D, CB: –

1895 ἑνδέκατος, *hendekatos*, a. *eleventh.* S: *1734*, BAGD: 262D, CB: –

1896 ἐνδέχομαι, *endechomai*, v.imper. *it is possible.* S: *1735*, BAGD: 262D, CB: –

1897 ἐνδημέω, *endēmeō*, v. *to be at home.* S: *1736*, BAGD: 263A, CB: 350C

1898 ἐνδιδύσκω, *endidyskō*, v. *to put on, dress (another); (mid.) dress oneself.* S: *1737*, BAGD: 263A, CB: –

1899 ἔνδικος, *endikos*, a. *just, deserved.* S: *1738*, BAGD: 263B, CB: –

1900 ἐνδόμησις, *endomēsis*, n. variant: *construction, material.* S: *1739*, BAGD: 263B, CB: –

1901 ἐνδοξάζομαι, *endoxazomai*, v. *to be glorified.* S: *1740*, BAGD: 263B, CB: 351A

1902 ἔνδοξος, *endoxos*, a. *honored; wonderful; radiant; expensive.* S: *1741*, BAGD: 263B, CB: 351A

1903 ἔνδυμα, *endyma*, n. *clothing, garment.* S: *1742*, BAGD: 263C, CB: 351A

1904 ἐνδυναμόω, *endynamoō*, v. *to give strength, strengthen; (mid./pass.) to be strong, strengthened.* S: *1743*, BAGD: 263D, CB: 351A

1905 ἐνδύνω, *endynō*, v. *to worm one's way, creep in.* S: *1744*, BAGD: 263D, CB: –

1906 ἔνδυσις, *endysis*, n. *putting on.* S: *1745*, BAGD: 263D, CB: –

1907 ἐνδύω, *endyō*, v. *to clothe, dress; (mid.) clothe oneself.* S: *1746*, BAGD: 264A, CB: 351A

1908 ἐνδώμησις, *endōmēsis*, n. *what something is made of, material.* S: *1739*, BAGD: 264B, CB: –

1909 ἐνέδρα, *enedra*, n. *plot, ambush.* S: *1747*, BAGD: 264C, CB: 351A

1910 ἐνεδρεύω, *enedreuō*, v. *to wait in ambush, lie in wait for.* S: *1748*, BAGD: 264C, CB: –

1911 ἔνεδρον, *enedron*, n. variant: *plot, ambush.* S: *1749*, BAGD: 264C, CB: –

1912 ἐνειλέω, *eneileō*, v. *to wrap in.* S: *1750*, BAGD: 264C, CB: –

1913 ἔνειμι, *eneimi*, v. *to be inside; contents.* S: *1751*, BAGD: 264C, CB: –

1914 ἕνεκα, *heneka*, pp.*. variant: *for the sake of; for this reason, because.* S: *1752*, BAGD: 264D, CB: 356A

1915 ἕνεκεν, *heneken*, pp.*. *for, for the sake of, for this reason, because.* S: *1752*, BAGD: 264D, CB: 356A

1916 ἐνενήκοντα, *enenēkonta*, n.num. *ninety.* S: *1768*, BAGD: 265A, CB: –

1917 ἐνεός, *eneos*, a. *speechless.* S: *1769*, BAGD: 265A, CB: –

1918 ἐνέργεια, *energeia*, n. *working, power, energy.* S: *1753*, BAGD: 265A, CB: 351A

1919 ἐνεργέω, energeō, v. *to be at work in; to produce.* S: *1754,* BAGD: 265B, CB: 351A

1920 ἐνέργημα, energēma, n. *working, activity.* S: *1755,* BAGD: 265C, CB: 351A

1921 ἐνεργής, energēs, a. *active, effective.* S: *1756,* BAGD: 265D, CB: 351A

1922 ἐνευλογέω, eneulogeō, v. *(pass.) to be blessed.* S: *1757,* BAGD: 265D, CB: 351A

1923 ἐνέχω, enechō, v. *to oppose, be hostile toward, bear a grudge against; (pass.) to be burdened.* S: *1758,* BAGD: 265D, CB: 351A

1924 ἐνθάδε, enthade, adv. *here, in this place, to this place.* S: *1759,* BAGD: 266A, CB: –

1925 ἔνθεν, enthen, adv. *from here.* S: *1782*,* BAGD: 266A, CB: –

1926 ἐνθυμέομαι, enthymeomai, v. *to consider, reflect on.* S: *1760,* BAGD: 266A, CB: 351B

1927 ἐνθύμησις, enthymēsis, n. *thought, reflection; design, idea.* S: *1761,* BAGD: 266B, CB: 351B

1928 ἔνι, eni, v. *there is.* S: *1762,* BAGD: 266B, CB: –

1929 ἐνιαυτός, eniautos, n. *year.* S: *1763,* BAGD: 266B, CB: 351A

1930 ἐνίοτε, eniote, adv. variant: *sometimes.* S: *4178*,* BAGD: 266D, CB: –

1931 ἐνίστημι, enistēmi, v. *to be present, (as ptc.) the present.* S: *1764,* BAGD: 266D, CB: –

1932 ἐνισχύω, enischyō, v. *to strengthen (another); to regain (one's own) strength.* S: *1765,* BAGD: 266D, CB: 351A

1933 ἐννέα, ennea, n.num. *nine.* S: *1767,* BAGD: 267A, CB: –

1934 ἐννεός, enneos, a. variant: *speechless.* S: *1769,* BAGD: 265A cf. ἐνεός, CB: –

1935 ἐννεύω, enneuō, v. *to make a sign, nod.* S: *1770,* BAGD: 267A, CB: –

1936 ἔννοια, ennoia, n. *attitude, thought.* S: *1771,* BAGD: 267A, CB: 351B

1937 ἔννομος, ennomos, a. *under law, subject to the law; legal (assembly).* S: *1772,* BAGD: 267B, CB: 351B

1938 ἐννόμως, ennomōs, adv. variant: *subject to the law, in possession of the law.* S: *1722 + 3551,* BAGD: 267B, CB: –

1939 ἔννυχος, ennychos, a. [used as adv.]. *while it was still dark, at night.* S: *1773*,* BAGD: 267B, CB: –

1940 ἐνοικέω, enoikeō, v. *to live in, live with.* S: *1774,* BAGD: 267B, CB: 351B

1941 ἐνορκίζω, enorkizō, v. *to charge by oath, adjure.* S: *3726*,* BAGD: 267C, CB: –

1942 ἑνότης, henotēs, n. *unity.* S: *1775,* BAGD: 267C, CB: 356A

1943 ἐνοχλέω, enochleō, v. *(act.) to cause trouble; (pass.) to be troubled.* S: *1776,* BAGD: 267D, CB: 351B

1944 ἔνοχος, enochos, a. *subject to; guilty, liable for.* S: *1777,* BAGD: 267D, CB: 351B

1945 ἔνταλμα, entalma, n. *rule, commandment, precept.* S: *1778,* BAGD: 268B, CB: –

1946 ἐνταφιάζω, entaphiazō, v. *to prepare (a corpse) for burial, bury.* S: *1779,* BAGD: 268B, CB: 351B

1947 ἐνταφιασμός, entaphiasmos, n. *preparation for burial, burial.* S: *1780,* BAGD: 268B, CB: 351B

1948 ἐντέλλω, entellō, v. *(mid.) to command, give orders, give instructions.* S: *1781*,* BAGD: 268B, CB: 351B

1949 ἐντεῦθεν, enteuthen, adv. *from here, from this place.* S: *1782,* BAGD: 268C, CB: –

1950 ἔντευξις, enteuxis, n. *prayer, intercession.* S: *1783,* BAGD: 268D, CB: 351B

1951 ἐντίθημι, entithēmi, v. variant: *to put in, implant.* S: *150,* BAGD: 268D, CB: –

1952 ἔντιμος, entimos, a. *highly valued, honored, precious.* S: *1784,* BAGD: 268D, CB: 351B

1953 ἐντολή, entolē, n. *command, commandment, regulation.* S: *1785,* BAGD: 269A, CB: 351B

1954 ἐντόπιος, entopios, a. *resident, local.* S: *1786,* BAGD: 269B, CB: –

1955 ἐντός, entos, adv. *inside, within.* S: *1787,* BAGD: 269B, CB: 351B

1956 ἐντρέπω, entrepō, v. *to cause shame; (pass.) to be ashamed; (mid.) to care about, respect.* S: *1788,* BAGD: 269D, CB: –

1957 ἐντρέφω, entrephō, v. *(pass.) to be brought up, reared, trained.* S: *1789,* BAGD: 269D, CB: –

1958 ἔντρομος, entromos, a. *trembling.* S: *1790,* BAGD: 269D, CB: –

1959 ἐντροπή, entropē, n. *shame, humiliation.* S: *1791,* BAGD: 269D, CB: –

1960 ἐντρυφάω, entryphaō, v. *to revel, carouse.* S: *1792,* BAGD: 270A, CB: –

1961 ἐντυγχάνω, entynchanō, v. *to intercede, appeal, petition.* S: *1793,* BAGD: 270A, CB: 351B

1962 ἐντυλίσσω, entylissō, v. *to wrap up (a body); (pass.) to be folded.* S: *1794,* BAGD: 270B, CB: –

1963 ἐντυπόω, entypoō, v. *(pass.) to be engraved, carved.* S: *1795,* BAGD: 270B, CB: –

1964 ἐνυβρίζω, enybrizō, v. *to insult.* S: *1796,* BAGD: 270B, CB: –

1965 ἐνυπνιάζομαι, enypniazomai, v. *to dream.* S: *1797,* BAGD: 270B, CB: 351B

1966 ἐνύπνιον, enypnion, n. *dream.* S: *1798,* BAGD: 270C, CB: 351B

1967 ἐνώπιον, enōpion, pp.*. *before, in the presence of; in behalf of, by authority of.* S: *1799,* BAGD: 270C, CB: 351B

1968 Ἐνώς, Enōs, n.pr., "[mortal] man." *Enosh.* S: *1800,* BAGD: 271A, CB: –

1969 ἐνωτίζομαι, enōtizomai, v. *to listen carefully, pay attention to.* S: *1801,* BAGD: 271A, CB: 351B

1970 Ἐνώχ, Henōch, n.pr., "initiated" ISBE; "follower" BDB. *Enoch.* S: *1802*,* BAGD: 271B, CB: 351B

1971 ἕξ, hex, n.num. *six.* S: *1803*,* BAGD: 271B, CB: 356B

1972 ἐξαγγέλλω, exangellō, v. *to declare, proclaim.* S: *1804,* BAGD: 271B, CB: 353C

1973 ἐξαγοράζω, exagorazō, v. *(act.) to redeem; (mid.) to make the most (of the time).* S: *1805,* BAGD: 271B, CB: 353B

1974 ἐξάγω, exagō, v. *to lead out, bring out, escort.* S: *1806,* BAGD: 271C, CB: 339C cf. agō

1975 ἐξαιρέω, exaireō, v. *(act.) to gouge, take out, tear out; (mid.) to rescue, set free.* S: *1807,* BAGD: 271D, CB: –

1976 ἐξαίρω, *exairō*, v. *to expel, remove, drive away.* S: *1808*, BAGD: 272A, CB: –

1977 ἐξαιτέω, *exaiteō*, v. *(mid.) to ask for.* S: *1809**, BAGD: 272A, CB: 353B cf. *-omai*

1978 ἐξαίφνης, *exaiphnēs*, adv. *suddenly, unexpectedly.* S: *1810*, BAGD: 272B, CB: –

1979 ἐξακολουθέω, *exakoloutheō*, v. *to follow, obey.* S: *1811*, BAGD: 272B, CB: 353B

1980 ἐξακόσιοι, *hexakosioi*, a.num. *six hundred.* S: *1812*, BAGD: 272B, CB: –

1981 ἐξαλείφω, *exaleiphō*, v. *to wipe away, blot out, cancel.* S: *1813*, BAGD: 272C, CB: 353B

1982 ἐξάλλομαι, *exallomai*, v. *to jump up.* S: *1814*, BAGD: 272C, CB: –

1983 ἐξανάστασις, *exanastasis*, n. *resurrection.* S: *1815*, BAGD: 272D, CB: 353C

1984 ἐξανατέλλω, *exanatellō*, v. *to spring up.* S: *1816*, BAGD: 272D, CB: –

1985 ἐξανίστημι, *exanistēmi*, v. *to raise up (seed) = have children; (intr.) to stand up.* S: *1817*, BAGD: 272D, CB: 353C

1986 ἐξανοίγω, *exanoigō*, v. variant: *to open fully.* S: *455*, BAGD: 272D, CB: –

1987 ἐξαπατάω, *exapataō*, v. *to deceive, cheat.* S: *1818*, BAGD: 273A, CB: 353C

1988 ἐξάπινα, *exapina*, adv. *suddenly.* S: *1819*, BAGD: 273A, CB: –

1989 ἐξαπορέω, *exaporeō*, v. *(mid.) to despair; (pass.) to be in despair.* S: *1820**, BAGD: 273A, CB: –

1990 ἐξαποστέλλω, *exapostellō*, v. *to send out, send away.* S: *1821*, BAGD: 273A, CB: 353C

1991 ἐξαρτάω, *exartaō*, v. variant: *to be attached to, an adherent.* S: *150*, BAGD: 273C, CB: –

1992 ἐξαρτίζω, *exartizō*, v. *to finish, complete; (pass.) to be equipped, furnished.* S: *1822*, BAGD: 273C, CB: 353C

1993 ἐξαστράπτω, *exastraptō*, v. *to flash like lightning.* S: *1823*, BAGD: 273D, CB: –

1994 ἐξαυτῆς, *exautēs*, adv. *immediately, at once, right now.* S: *1824*, BAGD: 273D, CB: –

1995 ἐξεγείρω, *exegeirō*, v. *to raise.* S: *1825*, BAGD: 273D, CB: –

1996 ἔξειμι[1], *exeimi*[1], v. *to leave, go out, go away.* S: *1826*, BAGD: 273D, CB: 353C

1997 ἔξειμι[2], *exeimi*[2], v. variant: *it is permitted, lawful (see 2003).* S: *1832**, BAGD: 275B cf. ἔξεστι, CB: 353C

1998 ἐξελέγχω, *exelenchō*, v. variant: *to convict.* S: *1827*, BAGD: 274A, CB: 350A cf. *elegchō*

1999 ἐξέλκω, *exelkō*, v. *(pass.) to be dragged away.* S: *1828*, BAGD: 274A, CB: –

2000 ἐξέραμα, *exerama*, n. *vomit, what is disgorged.* S: *1829*, BAGD: 274B, CB: –

2001 ἐξεραυνάω, *exeraunaō*, v. *to search intently, inquire carefully.* S: *1830*, BAGD: 274B, CB: 353C cf. *-aunō*

2002 ἐξέρχομαι, *exerchomai*, v. *to go out, leave.* S: *1831*, BAGD: 274B, CB: 353C

2003 ἔξεστι, *exesti*, v.imper. *it is legal, it is proper, it is permitted.* S: *1832*, BAGD: 275B, CB: 353C

2004 ἐξετάζω, *exetazō*, v. *to make a search; to ask, inquire, question.* S: *1833*, BAGD: 275C, CB: –

2005 ἐξέφνης, *exephnēs*, adv. variant: *suddenly, unexpectedly.* S: *1810**, BAGD: 272B cf. ἐξαίφνης, CB: –

2006 ἐξέχω, *exechō*, v. variant: *to stand out, be prominent.* S: *150*, BAGD: 275D, CB: –

2007 ἐξηγέομαι, *exēgeomai*, v. *to tell, make known, describe, report.* S: *1834*, BAGD: 275D, CB: 353C

2008 ἐξήκοντα, *hexēkonta*, n.num. *sixty.* S: *1835*, BAGD: 276A, CB: –

2009 ἑξῆς, *hexēs*, adv. *next, afterward.* S: *1836*, BAGD: 276A, CB: –

2010 ἐξηχέω, *exēcheō*, v. *(pass.) to ring out, be caused to sound out.* S: *1837**, BAGD: 276A, CB: –

2011 ἕξις, *hexis*, n. *constant use, practice.* S: *1838*, BAGD: 276B, CB: 356B

2012 ἐξιστάνω, *existanō*, v. variant: *to confuse, amaze; (intr.) to be out of one's senses, amazed.* S: *1839**, BAGD: 276B, CB: 356C cf. *existēmi*

2013 ἐξιστάω, *existaō*, v. variant: *to confuse, amaze; (intr.) to be out of one's senses, amazed.* S: *1839**, BAGD: 276B cf. ἐξίστημι, CB: 356C cf. *existēmi*

2014 ἐξίστημι, *existēmi*, v. *to amaze, astound; (intr.) to be amazed, out of one's senses.* S: *1839*, BAGD: 276B, CB: 353C

2015 ἐξισχύω, *exischyō*, v. *to have power, be strong enough.* S: *1840*, BAGD: 276C, CB: –

2016 ἔξοδος, *exodos*, n. *exodus, departure.* S: *1841*, BAGD: 276D, CB: 353C

2017 ἐξολεθρεύω, *exolethreuō*, v. *(pass.) to be completely cut off from.* S: *1842**, BAGD: 276D, CB: 353C

2018 ἐξομολογέω, *exomologeō*, v. *(act.) to consent; (mid.) to openly confess, admit, praise.* S: *1843*, BAGD: 277A, CB: 353C

2019 ἐξορκίζω, *exorkizō*, v. *to charge under oath, adjure.* S: *1844*, BAGD: 277B, CB: 353C

2020 ἐξορκιστής, *exorkistēs*, n. *one driving out evil spirits, exorcist.* S: *1845*, BAGD: 277B, CB: 353C

2021 ἐξορύσσω, *exoryssō*, v. *to dig through, tear out.* S: *1846*, BAGD: 277C, CB: –

2022 ἐξουδενέω, *exoudeneō*, v. *(pass.) to be rejected, treated with contempt.* S: *1847*, BAGD: 277C, CB: 353C

2023 ἐξουδενόω, *exoudenoō*, v. variant: *(pass.) to be rejected, treated with contempt.* S: *1847*, BAGD: 277C, CB: 353C cf. *-eō*

2024 ἐξουθενέω, *exoutheneō*, v. *to treat with contempt, look down on, ridicule; (pass.) to be rejected, despised.* S: *1848*, BAGD: 277C, CB: 353C

2025 ἐξουθενόω, *exouthenoō*, v. variant: *despise, disdain.* S: *1848**, BAGD: 277C, CB: 353C cf. *-eō*

2026 ἐξουσία, *exousia*, n. *authority, power, right, dominion.* S: *1849*, BAGD: 277D, CB: 353C

2027 ἐξουσιάζω, *exousiazō*, v. *to have power over; (pass.) to be mastered.* S: *1850*, BAGD: 279A, CB: 353C

2028 ἐξουσιαστικός, *exousiastikos*, a. variant: *authoritative.* S: *150*, BAGD: 279A, CB: –

2029 ἐξοχή, *exochē*, n. *leading, prominent.* S: *1851*, BAGD: 279A, CB: –

2030 ἐξυπνίζω, *exypnizō*, v. *to wake up, arouse.* S: *1852*, BAGD: 279B, CB: –

2031 ἔξυπνος, *exypnos*, a. *awake, aroused.* S: *1853*, BAGD: 279B, CB: –

2032 ἔξω, *exō*, adv. *out, outside.* S: *1854*, BAGD: 279B, CB: 353C

2033 ἔξωθεν, *exōthen*, adv. *from the outside.* S: *1855*, BAGD: 279D, CB: –

2034 ἐξωθέω, *exōtheō*, v. *to drive out, expel; to run aground.* S: *1856*, BAGD: 280A, CB: –

2035 ἐξώτερος, *exōteros*, a. *outside, farthest out.* S: *1857*, BAGD: 280A, CB: –

2036 ἔοικα, *eoika*, v. *to be like, resemble.* S: *1503**, BAGD: 280A, CB: 351B

2037 ἑορτάζω, *heortazō*, v. *to celebrate a festival.* S: *1858*, BAGD: 280A, CB: 356A

2038 ἑορτή, *heortē*, n. *feast, festival.* S: *1859*, BAGD: 280B, CB: 356A

2039 ἐπαγγελία, *epangelia*, n. *promise.* S: *1860*, BAGD: 280C, CB: 351B

2040 ἐπαγγέλλομαι, *epangellomai*, v. *to promise; to profess, lay claim to.* S: *1861**, BAGD: 280D, CB: 351B

2041 ἐπάγγελμα, *epangelma*, n. *promise.* S: *1862*, BAGD: 281A, CB: 351B

2042 ἐπάγω, *epagō*, v. *to bring upon; to make guilty.* S: *1863*, BAGD: 281B, CB: 339C cf. *agō*

2043 ἐπαγωνίζομαι, *epagōnizomai*, v. *to contend, fight.* S: *1864*, BAGD: 281B, CB: 351B

2044 ἐπαθροίζω, *epathroizō*, v. *(pass.) to increase; to be collected.* S: *1865*, BAGD: 281B, CB: –

2045 Ἐπαίνετος, *Epainetos*, n.pr., "praised." *Epenetus.* S: *1866*, BAGD: 281C, CB: –

2046 ἐπαινέω, *epaineō*, v. *to praise, commend.* S: *1867*, BAGD: 281C, CB: 351B

2047 ἔπαινος, *epainos*, n. *praise, commendation.* S: *1868*, BAGD: 281C, CB: 351B

2048 ἐπαίρω, *epairō*, v. *to lift up; to look up.* S: *1869*, BAGD: 281D, CB: –

2049 ἐπαισχύνομαι, *epaischynomai*, v. *to be ashamed of.* S: *1870*, BAGD: 282A, CB: 351B

2050 ἐπαιτέω, *epaiteō*, v. *to beg.* S: *1871*, BAGD: 282B, CB: 340A cf. *aiteō*

2051 ἐπακολουθέω, *epakoloutheō*, v. *to follow after, accompany; be devoted to.* S: *1872*, BAGD: 282B, CB: 351B

2052 ἐπακούω, *epakouō*, v. *to hear, listen to.* S: *1873*, BAGD: 282C, CB: 351B

2053 ἐπακροάομαι, *epakroaomai*, v. *to listen to.* S: *1874*, BAGD: 282C, CB: 351B

2054 ἐπάν, *epan*, c.temp. *when, as soon as.* S: *1875*, BAGD: 282C, CB: –

2055 ἐπάναγκες, *epanankes*, adv. *necessarily.* S: *1876*, BAGD: 282D, CB: –

2056 ἐπανάγω, *epanagō*, v. *to put out (to sea); to return.* S: *1877*, BAGD: 282D, CB: –

2057 ἐπαναμιμνήσκω, *epanamimnēskō*, v. *to remind again.* S: *1878**, BAGD: 282D, CB: –

2058 ἐπαναπαύομαι, *epanapauomai*, v. *to rest on, rely on.* S: *1879*, BAGD: 282D, CB: 351B

2059 ἐπανέρχομαι, *epanerchomai*, v. *to return (home).* S: *1880*, BAGD: 283A, CB: 352B cf. *erchomai*

2060 ἐπανίστημι, *epanistēmi*, v. *to rebel against, rise up (in rebellion).* S: *1881**, BAGD: 283A, CB: –

2061 ἐπανόρθωσις, *epanorthōsis*, n. *correcting.* S: *1882*, BAGD: 283A, CB: 351C

2062 ἐπάνω, *epanō*, adv. *above, on, upon; more than.* S: *1883*, BAGD: 283B, CB: –

2063 ἐπάρατος, *eparatos*, a. *accursed.* S: *1944**, BAGD: 283C, CB: –

2064 ἐπαρκέω, *eparkeō*, v. *to help, aid.* S: *1884*, BAGD: 283C, CB: –

2065 ἐπαρχεία, *eparcheia*, n. *province.* S: *1885**, BAGD: 283C, CB: –

2066 ἐπάρχειος, *eparcheios*, a. variant: *belonging to an eparch.* S: *1885**, BAGD: 283C, CB: –

2067 ἐπαρχικός, *eparchikos*, a. variant: *pertaining to the eparch.* S: *150*, BAGD: 283C, CB: –

2068 ἔπαυλις, *epaulis*, n. *place to live, residence.* S: *1886*, BAGD: 283D, CB: –

2069 ἐπαύριον, *epaurion*, adv. *the next day, tomorrow.* S: *1887*, BAGD: 283D, CB: –

2070 ἐπαυτοφώρῳ, *epautophōrō*, a. variant: *pertaining to being caught in the act.* S: *1888*, BAGD: 125A cf. αὐτόφωρος, CB: –

2071 Ἐπαφρᾶς, *Epaphras*, n.pr., "handsome." *Epaphras.* S: *1889*, BAGD: 283D, CB: –

2072 ἐπαφρίζω, *epaphrizō*, v. *to foam up.* S: *1890*, BAGD: 283D, CB: –

2073 Ἐπαφρόδιτος, *Epaphroditos*, n.pr., "handsome." *Epaphroditus.* S: *1891*, BAGD: 284A, CB: –

2074 ἐπεγείρω, *epegeirō*, v. *to stir up, arouse, excite.* S: *1892*, BAGD: 284A, CB: –

2075 ἐπεί, *epei*, c. *since, because, for otherwise.* S: *1893*, BAGD: 284A, CB: –

2076 ἐπειδή, *epeidē*, c. *when; since, because.* S: *1894*, BAGD: 284B, CB: –

2077 ἐπειδήπερ, *epeidēper*, c. *inasmuch as, since, whereas.* S: *1895*, BAGD: 284B, CB: –

2078 ἐπεῖδον, *epeidon*, v. *to show favor, concern; to consider, look at.* S: *1896*, BAGD: 284B, CB: –

2079 ἔπειμι, *epeimi*, v. *to follow, approach.* S: *1966**, BAGD: 284C, CB: 351C

2080 ἐπείπερ, *epeiper*, c. variant: *since, indeed.* S: *1897*, BAGD: 284C, CB: –

2081 ἐπεισαγωγή, *epeisagōgē*, n. *introduction, bringing in.* S: *1898*, BAGD: 284C, CB: –

2082 ἐπεισέρχομαι, *epeiserchomai*, v. *to come in, happen.* S: *1904**, BAGD: 284C, CB: –

2083 ἔπειτα, epeita, adv. *then, later, afterward.* S: *1899*, BAGD: 284C, CB: –

2084 ἐπέκεινα, epekeina, adv. *beyond, farther on.* S: *1900*, BAGD: 284D, CB: –

2085 ἐπεκτείνομαι, epekteinomai, v. *to strain toward, stretch out.* S: *1901*, BAGD: 284D, CB: 351C

2086 ἐπενδύομαι, ependyomai, v. *to be clothed with.* S: *1902*, BAGD: 284D, CB: 351C

2087 ἐπενδύτης, ependytēs, n. *outer garment, coat.* S: *1903*, BAGD: 285A, CB: –

2088 ἐπέρχομαι, eperchomai, v. *to come, come upon, happen to.* S: *1904*, BAGD: 285A, CB: 351C

2089 ἐπερωτάω, eperotaō, v. *to ask, question.* S: *1905*, BAGD: 285B, CB: 351C

2090 ἐπερώτημα, eperōtēma, n. *pledge.* S: *1906*, BAGD: 285C, CB: 351C

2091 ἐπέχω, epechō, v. *(tr.) hold out, hold fast; (intr.) to give attention, watch, notice; to stay, stop.* S: *1907*, BAGD: 285C, CB: –

2092 ἐπηρεάζω, epēreazō, v. *to mistreat, speak maliciously against.* S: *1908*, BAGD: 285D, CB: –

2093 ἐπί, epi, pp. *(gen.) on, over, when; (dat.) on, at, in, while; (acc.) across, over, on, to, for, while.* S: *1909*, BAGD: 285D, CB: 351C

2094 ἐπιβαίνω, epibainō, v. *to go up, go upon, ride upon, board (a vessel).* S: *1910*, BAGD: 289D, CB: –

2095 ἐπιβάλλω, epiballō, v. *(tr.) to throw over; to place; lay hold of, seize, arrest; to sew on; (intr.) to break over.* S: *1911*, BAGD: 289D, CB: –

2096 ἐπιβαρέω, epibareō, v. *to burden, weigh down excessively.* S: *1912*, BAGD: 290B, CB: 351C

2097 ἐπιβιβάζω, epibibazō, v. *to put (someone) on (a mount).* S: *1913*, BAGD: 290B, CB: –

2098 ἐπιβλέπω, epiblepō, v. *to look at, show special attention, consider, care about.* S: *1914*, BAGD: 290B, CB: 345A cf. *blepō*

2099 ἐπίβλημα, epiblēma, n. *patch.* S: *1915*, BAGD: 290C, CB: –

2100 ἐπιβοάω, epiboaō, v. variant: *to cry out loudly.* S: *1916*, BAGD: 290C, CB: –

2101 ἐπιβουλή, epiboulē, n. *plan, plot.* S: *1917*, BAGD: 290C, CB: –

2102 ἐπιγαμβρεύω, epigambreuō, v. *to marry (as next of kin).* S: *1918*, BAGD: 290C, CB: –

2103 ἐπίγειος, epigeios, a. *earthly.* S: *1919*, BAGD: 290C, CB: 351C

2104 ἐπιγίνομαι, epiginomai, v. *to come up, occur, happen.* S: *1920*, BAGD: 290D, CB: –

2105 ἐπιγινώσκω, epiginōskō, v. *to know (fully), recognize, realize, come to understand.* S: *1921*, BAGD: 291A, CB: 351C

2106 ἐπίγνωσις, epignōsis, n. *knowledge, understanding, insight.* S: *1922*, BAGD: 291B, CB: 351C

2107 ἐπιγραφή, epigraphē, n. *inscription, superscription, written notice.* S: *1923*, BAGD: 291C, CB: 351C

2108 ἐπιγράφω, epigraphō, v. *(act.) to write; (pass.) to be written (upon), inscribed.* S: *1924*, BAGD: 291C, CB: 351C

2109 ἐπιδείκνυμι, epideiknymi, v. *to show, call attention to; to prove, point out.* S: *1925*, BAGD: 291D, CB: –

2110 ἐπιδέχομαι, epidechomai, v. *to welcome, receive as a guest; to have to do with, accept, recognize.* S: *1926*, BAGD: 292A, CB: –

2111 ἐπιδημέω, epidēmeō, v. *to live as a visitor, foreigner.* S: *1927*, BAGD: 292A, CB: –

2112 ἐπιδιατάσσομαι, epidiatassomai, v. *to add to (a covenant).* S: *1928*, BAGD: 292B, CB: –

2113 ἐπιδίδωμι, epididōmi, v. *to give, deliver, hand over to.* S: *1929*, BAGD: 292B, CB: –

2114 ἐπιδιορθόω, epidiorthoō, v. *to straighten out, correct (in addition).* S: *1930*, BAGD: 292B, CB: –

2115 ἐπιδύω, epidyō, v. *to go down, set (of the sun).* S: *1931*, BAGD: 292C, CB: –

2116 ἐπιείκεια, epieikeia, n. *gentleness.* S: *1932*, BAGD: 292C, CB: 351C

2117 ἐπιεικής, epieikēs, a. *gentle, considerate.* S: *1933*, BAGD: 292C, CB: 351C

2118 ἐπιζητέω, epizēteō, v. *to look for, run after, seek earnestly.* S: *1934*, BAGD: 292D, CB: 352B

2119 ἐπιθανάτιος, epithanatios, a. *condemned to die.* S: *1935*, BAGD: 292D, CB: –

2120 ἐπίθεσις, epithesis, n. *laying on.* S: *1936*, BAGD: 293A, CB: 352B

2121 ἐπιθυμέω, epithymeō, v. *to long for, desire; covet, lust.* S: *1937*, BAGD: 293A, CB: 352B

2122 ἐπιθυμητής, epithymētēs, n. *one who desires, sets heart on (evil).* S: *1938*, BAGD: 293B, CB: –

2123 ἐπιθυμία, epithymia, n. *desire, longing; coveting, craving, lusting.* S: *1939*, BAGD: 293B, CB: 352B

2124 ἐπιθύω, epithyō, v. variant: *to offer a sacrifice.* S: *2380**, BAGD: 293D, CB: –

2125 ἐπικαθίζω, epikathizō, v. *to sit down (upon).* S: *1940*, BAGD: 293D, CB: –

2126 ἐπικαλέω, epikaleō, v. *(act./pass.) to call (upon), name, be named; (mid.) appeal to, call upon for aid.* S: *1941**, BAGD: 294A, CB: 351C cf. *-omai*

2127 ἐπικάλυμμα, epikalymma, n. *cover-up, covering, veil.* S: *1942*, BAGD: 294B, CB: –

2128 ἐπικαλύπτω, epikalyptō, v. *(pass.) to be covered.* S: *1943*, BAGD: 294C, CB: 359B cf. *kalyptō*

2129 ἐπικατάρατος, epikataratos, a. *cursed.* S: *1944*, BAGD: 294C, CB: 351C

2130 ἐπίκειμαι, epikeimai, v. *to lay upon; to press, crowd upon, demand insistently.* S: *1945*, BAGD: 294C, CB: 360C cf. *keimai*

2131 ἐπικέλλω, epikellō, v. *to run aground.* S: *2027**, BAGD: 294D, CB: –

2132 ἐπικερδαίνω, epikerdainō, v. variant: *to gain in addition.* S: *2770**, BAGD: 294D, CB: –

2133 ἐπικεφάλαιον, epikephalaion, n. variant: *(poll) tax.* S: *2778**, BAGD: 294D, CB: –

2134 Ἐπικούρειος, Epikoureios, a.pr. *or* n.pr., "of Epicurus." *Epicurean.* S: *1946*, BAGD: 294D, CB: –

2135 ἐπικουρία, epikouria, n. *help.* S: *1947*, BAGD: 294D, CB: –

2136 ἐπικράζω, epikrazō, v. variant: *to shout threats.* S: *150*, BAGD: 295A, CB: –

2137 ἐπικρίνω, epikrinō, v. *to decide, determine.* S: *1948*, BAGD: 295A, CB: –

2138 ἐπιλαμβάνομαι, epilambanomai, v. *to take hold, catch, trap, seize.* S: *1949*, BAGD: 295A, CB: 352A

2139 ἐπιλάμπω, epilampō, v. variant: *to shine out, shine forth.* S: *2989*, BAGD: 295B, CB: 352A

2140 ἐπιλανθάνομαι, epilanthanomai, v. *to forget.* S: *1950*, BAGD: 295B, CB: –

2141 ἐπιλέγω, epilegō, v. *(pass.) to be called; (mid.) to choose.* S: *1951**, BAGD: 295C, CB: 352A

2142 ἐπιλείπω, epileipō, v. *to not have (time); to fail to have.* S: *1952*, BAGD: 295C, CB: –

2143 ἐπιλείχω, epileichō, v. *to lick.* S: *621**, BAGD: 295D, CB: –

2144 ἐπιλησμονή, epilēsmonē, n. *forgetfulness.* S: *1953*, BAGD: 295D, CB: –

2145 ἐπίλοιπος, epiloipos, a. *remaining, the rest.* S: *1954*, BAGD: 295D, CB: –

2146 ἐπίλυσις, epilysis, n. *interpretation, explanation.* S: *1955*, BAGD: 295D, CB: 352A

2147 ἐπιλύω, epilyō, v. *to explain; (pass.) to be settled, decided.* S: *1956*, BAGD: 295D, CB: 352A

2148 ἐπιμαρτυρέω, epimartyreō, v. *to testify that, bear witness about.* S: *1957*, BAGD: 296A, CB: 352A

2149 ἐπιμέλεια, epimeleia, n. *needs, care, attention.* S: *1958*, BAGD: 296A, CB:

2150 ἐπιμελέομαι, epimeleomai, v. *to take care of, look after.* S: *1959*, BAGD: 296A, CB: –

2151 ἐπιμελῶς, epimelōs, adv. *carefully, diligently.* S: *1960*, BAGD: 296A, CB: –

2152 ἐπιμένω, epimenō, v. *to stay, remain; to continue in, keep on, persevere.* S: *1961*, BAGD: 296B, CB: 352A

2153 ἐπινεύω, epineuō, v. *to accept, give consent.* S: *1962*, BAGD: 296C, CB: –

2154 ἐπίνοια, epinoia, n. *thought, intention.* S: *1963*, BAGD: 296C, CB: 352A

2155 ἐπιορκέω, epiorkeō, v. *to break an oath, swear falsely.* S: *1964*, BAGD: 296D, CB: –

2156 ἐπίορκος, epiorkos, a. *perjured.* S: *1965*, BAGD: 296D, CB: –

2157 ἐπιούσιος, epiousios, a. *daily.* S: *1967*, BAGD: 296D, CB: 352A

2158 ἐπιπίπτω, epipiptō, v. *to fall upon, come eagerly, embrace; to come on.* S: *1968*, BAGD: 297C, CB: –

2159 ἐπιπλήσσω, epiplēssō, v. *to rebuke, strike at.* S: *1969*, BAGD: 297D, CB: –

2160 ἐπιποθέω, epipotheō, v. *to long for, crave, desire.* S: *1971*, BAGD: 297D, CB: 352A

2161 ἐπιπόθησις, epipothēsis, n. *longing (for).* S: *1972*, BAGD: 298A, CB: 352A

2162 ἐπιπόθητος, epipothētos, a. *longed for.* S: *1973*, BAGD: 298A, CB: –

2163 ἐπιποθία, epipothia, n. *longing, desire.* S: *1974*, BAGD: 298A, CB: 352A

2164 ἐπιπορεύομαι, epiporeuomai, v. *to come to, go to.* S: *1975*, BAGD: 298A, CB: 372A cf. *poreuomai*

2165 ἐπιράπτω, epiraptō, v. *to sew on.* S: *1976*, BAGD: 298A, CB: –

2166 ἐπιρίπτω, epiriptō, v. *to throw on.* S: *1977*, BAGD: 298B, CB: –

2167 ἐπισείω, episeiō, v. variant: *to urge on, incite.* S: *3982**, BAGD: 298B, CB: 352A

2168 ἐπίσημος, episēmos, a. *notorious, prominent, outstanding.* S: *1978*, BAGD: 298B, CB: –

2169 ἐπισιτισμός, episitismos, n. *food, something to eat.* S: *1979*, BAGD: 298C, CB: –

2170 ἐπισκέπτομαι, episkeptomai, v. *to visit, show concern, care for, come to help.* S: *1980*, BAGD: 298C, CB: 352A

2171 ἐπισκευάζομαι, episkeuazomai, v. *to get ready, make preparations.* S: *643**, BAGD: 298C, CB: 352A cf. *episkiazo*

2172 ἐπισκηνόω, episkēnoō, v. *to rest upon, take up residence.* S: *1981*, BAGD: 298D, CB: 352A

2173 ἐπισκιάζω, episkiazō, v. *to cast a shadow, overshadow; to envelope with a cloud.* S: *1982*, BAGD: 298D, CB: 352A

2174 ἐπισκοπέω, episkopeō, v. *to see to, care for; to serve as an overseer.* S: *1983*, BAGD: 298D, CB: 352A

2175 ἐπισκοπή, episkopē, n. *coming, visitation; place of leadership, office of overseer.* S: *1984*, BAGD: 299A, CB: 352A

2176 ἐπίσκοπος, episkopos, n. *overseer, guardian, supervisor.* S: *1985*, BAGD: 299B, CB: 352A

2177 ἐπισπάομαι, epispaomai, v. *to (attempt to) conceal circumcision.* S: *1986*, BAGD: 299D, CB: –

2178 ἐπισπείρω, epispeirō, v. *to sow afterward.* S: *4687**, BAGD: 300A, CB: –

2179 ἐπίσταμαι, epistamai, v. *to understand, know, be aware.* S: *1987*, BAGD: 300A, CB: 352A

2180 ἐπίστασις, epistasis, n. *stirring up, rebellion; pressure.* S: *1999*, BAGD: 300B, CB: –

2181 ἐπιστάτης, epistatēs, n. *master.* S: *1988*, BAGD: 300B, CB: 352A

2182 ἐπιστέλλω, epistellō, v. *to write a letter.* S: *1989*, BAGD: 300C, CB: 352A

2183 ἐπιστήμη, epistēmē, n. variant: *understanding, knowledge.* S: *150*, BAGD: 300C, CB: 352A

2184 ἐπιστήμων, epistēmōn, a. *understanding, expert, learned.* S: *1990*, BAGD: 300C, CB: –

2185 ἐπιστηρίζω, epistērizō, v. *to strengthen.* S: *1991*, BAGD: 300D, CB: 352A

2186 ἐπιστολή, epistolē, n. *letter, epistle.* S: *1992*, BAGD: 300D, CB: 352A

2187 ἐπιστομίζω, epistomizō, v. *to silence.* S: *1993*, BAGD: 301A, CB: –

2188 ἐπιστρέφω, epistrephō, v. *to turn (around, back, from), return.* S: *1994*, BAGD: 301A, CB: 352A

2189 ἐπιστροφή, *epistrophē*, n. *conversion.* S: *1995*, BAGD: 301C, CB: 352A

2190 ἐπισυνάγω, *episynagō*, v. *to gather together.* S: *1996*, BAGD: 301D, CB: 352A

2191 ἐπισυναγωγή, *episynagōgē*, n. *gathering, meeting, assembling.* S: *1997*, BAGD: 301D, CB: 352A

2192 ἐπισυντρέχω, *episyntrechō*, v. *to run together to.* S: *1998*, BAGD: 301D, CB: –

2193 ἐπισυρράπτω, *episyrraptō*, v. variant: *to sew on.* S: *1976*, BAGD: 301D, CB: –

2194 ἐπισύστασις, *episystasis*, n. variant: *uprising, disturbance, insurrection.* S: *1999*, BAGD: 301D, CB: 352A

2195 ἐπισφαλής, *episphalēs*, a. *dangerous, unsafe.* S: *2000*, BAGD: 302A, CB: –

2196 ἐπισχύω, *epischyō*, v. *to insist.* S: *2001*, BAGD: 302A, CB: –

2197 ἐπισωρεύω, *episōreuō*, v. *to gather a great number, accumulate.* S: *2002*, BAGD: 302A, CB: –

2198 ἐπιταγή, *epitagē*, n. *command, order; authority.* S: *2003*, BAGD: 302A, CB: –

2199 ἐπιτάσσω, *epitassō*, v. *to command, order.* S: *2004*, BAGD: 302B, CB: 352A

2200 ἐπιτελέω, *epiteleō*, v. *to finish, complete, end; to perfect, attain a goal; (mid.) to undergo.* S: *2005*, BAGD: 302B, CB: 352A cf. *-eisthai*

2201 ἐπιτήδειος, *epitēdeios*, a. *needful, necessary, suitable.* S: *2006*, BAGD: 302D, CB: –

2202 ἐπιτίθημι, *epitithēmi*, v. *to place, lay upon, put on.* S: *2007*, BAGD: 302D, CB: 352B

2203 ἐπιτιμάω, *epitimaō*, v. *to rebuke, warn.* S: *2008*, BAGD: 303B, CB: 352B

2204 ἐπιτιμία, *epitimia*, n. *punishment.* S: *2009*, BAGD: 303C, CB: 352B

2205 ἐπιτρέπω, *epitrepō*, v. *to let, allow, permit, give permission.* S: *2010*, BAGD: 303C, CB: –

2206 ἐπιτροπεύω, *epitropeuō*, v. variant: *to be governor, procurator.* S: *2233**, BAGD: 303D, CB: –

2207 ἐπιτροπή, *epitropē*, n. *commission, permission.* S: *2011*, BAGD: 303D, CB: –

2208 ἐπίτροπος, *epitropos*, n. *foreman, manager, guardian.* S: *2012*, BAGD: 303D, CB: 352B

2209 ἐπιτυγχάνω, *epitynchanō*, v. *to obtain, receive, gain.* S: *2013*, BAGD: 303D, CB: –

2210 ἐπιφαίνω, *epiphainō*, v. *(act.) to appear, make an appearance, show oneself; (pass.) shine.* S: *2014*, BAGD: 304A, CB: 352A

2211 ἐπιφάνεια, *epiphaneia*, n. *appearing, splendor, appearance.* S: *2015*, BAGD: 304A, CB: 352A

2212 ἐπιφανής, *epiphanēs*, a. *glorious, splendid.* S: *2016*, BAGD: 304B, CB: 352A

2213 ἐπιφαύσκω, *epiphauskō*, v. *to shine on.* S: *2017*, BAGD: 304C, CB: –

2214 ἐπιφέρω, *epipherō*, v. *to bring upon, inflict.* S: *2018*, BAGD: 304C, CB: 352A

2215 ἐπιφωνέω, *epiphōneō*, v. *to shout, cry out loudly.* S: *2019*, BAGD: 304D, CB: 352A

2216 ἐπιφώσκω, *epiphōskō*, v. *to dawn, begin, shine forth.* S: *2020*, BAGD: 304D, CB: –

2217 ἐπιχειρέω, *epicheireō*, v. *to attempt, try to.* S: *2021*, BAGD: 304D, CB: –

2218 ἐπιχείρησις, *epicheirēsis*, n. variant: *attempt, attack.* S: *150*, BAGD: 305A, CB: –

2219 ἐπιχέω, *epicheō*, v. *to pour on, pour over.* S: *2022*, BAGD: 305A, CB: –

2220 ἐπιχορηγέω, *epichorēgeō*, v. *to support, supply; (pass.) to be supported, receive.* S: *2023*, BAGD: 305A, CB: –

2221 ἐπιχορηγία, *epichorēgia*, n. *support, help.* S: *2024*, BAGD: 305B, CB: –

2222 ἐπιχρίω, *epichriō*, v. *to put on, anoint on, spread on.* S: *2025*, BAGD: 305B, CB: 346A cf. *chriō*

2223 ἐπιψαύω, *epipsauō*, v. variant: *to touch, grasp, attain.* S: *2017**, BAGD: 305B, CB: –

2224 ἐποικοδομέω, *epoikodomeō*, v. *to build up, build on.* S: *2026*, BAGD: 305B, CB: 352B

2225 ἐποκέλλω, *epokellō*, v. variant: *to run aground.* S: *2027*, BAGD: 294D cf. ἐπικέλλω, CB: –

2226 ἐπονομάζω, *eponomazō*, v. *(pass.) to be called, named.* S: *2028*, BAGD: 305C, CB: 352B

2227 ἐποπτεύω, *epopteuō*, v. *to see, observe.* S: *2029*, BAGD: 305C, CB: 352B

2228 ἐπόπτης, *epoptēs*, n. *eyewitness.* S: *2030*, BAGD: 305D, CB: 352B

2229 ἔπος, *epos*, n. *word.* S: *2031*, BAGD: 305D, CB: 352B

2230 ἐπουράνιος, *epouranios*, a. *heavenly, celestial; heavenly realms.* S: *2032*, BAGD: 305D, CB: 352B

2231 ἑπτά, *hepta*, n.num. *seven.* S: *2033*, BAGD: 306B, CB: 356A

2232 ἑπτάκις, *heptakis*, adv. *seven times.* S: *2034*, BAGD: 306B, CB: 356A

2233 ἑπτακισχίλιοι, *heptakischilioi*, a.num. *seven thousand.* S: *2035*, BAGD: 306C, CB: –

2234 ἑπταπλασίων, *heptaplasiōn*, a. variant: *sevenfold.* S: *4179*, BAGD: 306C, CB: –

2235 Ἔραστος, *Erastos*, n.pr., "beloved." *Erastus.* S: *2037*, BAGD: 306C, CB: –

2236 ἐραυνάω, *eraunaō*, v. *to search, look into, try to find out.* S: *2045**, BAGD: 306C, CB: 352C

2237 ἐργάζομαι, *ergazomai*, v. *to work, be active, accomplish (something).* S: *2038*, BAGD: 306D, CB: 352C

2238 ἐργασία, *ergasia*, n. *trade, business, making money; indulgence.* S: *2039*, BAGD: 307C, CB: 352B

2239 ἐργάτης, *ergatēs*, n. *worker, laborer, one who does (something).* S: *2040*, BAGD: 307C, CB: 352B

2240 ἔργον, *ergon*, n. *work, deed, activity, task, job.* S: *2041*, BAGD: 307D, CB: 352C

2241 ἐρεθίζω, *erethizō*, v. *to stir up, provoke, arouse; embitter, provoke, irritate.* S: *2042*, BAGD: 308D, CB: –

2242 ἐρείδω, *ereidō*, v. *to stick fast, make immovable, jam.* S: *2043*, BAGD: 308D, CB: –

2243 ἐρεύγομαι, *ereugomai*, v. *to utter, proclaim.* S: *2044*, BAGD: 308D, CB: –

2244 ἐρημία, *erēmia*, n. *remote place, desert, countryside.* S: *2047*, BAGD: 308D, CB: 352B

2245 ἔρημος, *erēmos*, a. *deserted, remote, solitary.* S: *2048*, BAGD: 309A, CB: 352B

2246 ἐρημόω, *erēmoō*, v. *(pass.) to be brought to ruin, laid waste.* S: *2049*, BAGD: 309B, CB: 352B

2247 ἐρήμωσις, *erēmōsis*, n. *desolation, devastation, destruction.* S: *2050*, BAGD: 309B, CB: 352B

2248 ἐρίζω, *erizō*, v. *to quarrel.* S: *2051*, BAGD: 309B, CB: –

2249 ἐριθεία, *eritheia*, n. *selfish ambition, faction, strife.* S: *2052*, BAGD: 309B, CB: 352C

2250 ἔριον, *erion*, n. *wool.* S: *2053*, BAGD: 309C, CB: –

2251 ἔρις, *eris*, n. *quarrel, strife, dissension, discord.* S: *2054*, BAGD: 309C, CB: 352C

2252 ἐρίφιον, *eriphion*, n. *goat.* S: *2055*, BAGD: 309D, CB: 352C

2253 ἔριφος, *eriphos*, n. *(young) goat.* S: *2056*, BAGD: 309D, CB: 352C

2254 Ἑρμᾶς, *Hermas*, n.pr. *Hermas.* S: *2057*, BAGD: 309D, CB: –

2255 ἑρμηνεία, *hermēneia*, n. *interpretation, translation.* S: *2058*, BAGD: 310A, CB: 356A

2256 ἑρμηνευτής, *hermēneutēs*, n. variant: *translator.* S: *1328**, BAGD: 310A, CB: 356A

2257 ἑρμηνεύω, *hermēneuō*, v. *to translate, give the meaning, interpret, explain.* S: *2059*, BAGD: 310A, CB: 356A

2258 Ἑρμῆς, *Hermēs*, n.pr., *possibly* "rock, cairn." *Hermes.* S: *2060*, BAGD: 310A, CB: –

2259 Ἑρμογένης, *Hermogenēs*, n.pr., "born of Hermes." *Hermogenes.* S: *2061*, BAGD: 310A, CB: –

2260 ἑρπετόν, *herpeton*, n. *reptile.* S: *2062*, BAGD: 310B, CB: –

2261 ἐρυθρός, *erythros*, a. *red.* S: *2063*, BAGD: 310B, CB: –

2262 ἔρχομαι, *erchomai*, v. *to come, go.* S: *2064*, BAGD: 310B, CB: 352B

2263 ἐρωτάω, *erōtaō*, v. *to ask; beg, urge; pray.* S: *2065*, BAGD: 311D, CB: 352C

2264 ἐσθής, *esthēs*, n. *clothing, robe.* S: *2066*, BAGD: 312B, CB: 352C

2265 ἔσθησις, *esthēsis*, n. variant: *government.* S: *2067*, BAGD: 312B cf. ἐσθής, CB: –

2266 ἐσθίω, *esthiō*, v. *to eat, consume, devour.* S: *2068 & 5315*, BAGD: 312B, CB: 352C

2267 ἔσθω, *esthō*, v. variant: *to eat, consume, devour.* S: *2068**, BAGD: 312B, CB: 352C cf. *esthiō*

2268 Ἑσλί, *Hesli*, n.pr., "Yahweh sets apart." *Esli.* S: *2069**, BAGD: 313B, CB: –

2269 ἔσοπτρον, *esoptron*, n. *mirror.* S: *2072*, BAGD: 313B, CB: 352C

2270 ἑσπέρα, *hespera*, n. *evening.* S: *2073*, BAGD: 313C, CB: –

2271 ἑσπερινός, *hesperinos*, a. variant: *pertaining to the evening.* S: *150*, BAGD: 313C, CB: –

2272 Ἑσρώμ, *Hesrōm*, n.pr., "enclosure." *Hezron.* S: *2074**, BAGD: 313C, CB: –

2273 ἑσσόομαι, *hessoomai*, v. *to be inferior, lesser, worse off.* S: *2274**, BAGD: 313C, CB: –

2274 ἔσχατος, *eschatos*, a. *last (of a series), least, final.* S: *2078*, BAGD: 313D, CB: 352C

2275 ἐσχάτως, *eschatōs*, adv. *finally; at the point of death.* S: *2079*, BAGD: 314B, CB: 352C

2276 ἔσω, *esō*, adv. *in, inner, inside, inwardly.* S: *2080*, BAGD: 314B, CB: 352C

2277 ἔσωθεν, *esōthen*, adv. *from within, from inside, inwardly.* S: *2081*, BAGD: 314B, CB: –

2278 ἐσώτερος, *esōteros*, a. *inner.* S: *2082*, BAGD: 314C, CB: 352C

2279 ἑταῖρος, *hetairos*, n. *friend, comrade, companion.* S: *2083*, BAGD: 314C, CB: 356A

2280 ἑτερόγλωσσος, *heteroglōssos*, a. *speaking in a foreign language.* S: *2084*, BAGD: 314D, CB: 356A

2281 ἑτεροδιδασκαλέω, *heterodidaskaleō*, v. *to teach false doctrine, teach heresy.* S: *2085*, BAGD: 314D, CB: 356A

2282 ἑτεροζυγέω, *heterozygeō*, v. *to yoke together in a mismatch.* S: *2086*, BAGD: 314D, CB: 356A

2283 ἕτερος, *heteros*, a. *other, different.* S: *2087*, BAGD: 315A, CB: 356A

2284 ἑτέρως, *heterōs*, adv. *differently, other, otherwise.* S: *2088*, BAGD: 315C, CB: 356A

2285 ἔτι, *eti*, adv. *still, yet, again.* S: *2089*, BAGD: 315C, CB: 353A

2286 ἑτοιμάζω, *hetoimazō*, v. *to prepare, be ready.* S: *2090*, BAGD: 316A, CB: 356B

2287 Ἕτοιμας, *Hetoimas*, n.pr. *Hetoimas.* S: *1681**, BAGD: 316C, CB: –

2288 ἑτοιμασία, *hetoimasia*, n. *readiness, preparation.* S: *2091*, BAGD: 316C, CB: 356B

2289 ἕτοιμος, *hetoimos*, a. *ready, prepared.* S: *2092*, BAGD: 316C, CB: 356B

2290 ἑτοίμως, *hetoimōs*, adv. *readily.* S: *2093*, BAGD: 316D, CB: –

2291 ἔτος, *etos*, n. *year.* S: *2094*, BAGD: 316D, CB: –

2292 εὖ, *eu*, adv. *well; well done!.* S: *2095*, BAGD: 317B, CB: 353A

2293 Εὕα, *Heua*, n.pr., "life." *Eve.* S: *2096**, BAGD: 317B, CB: –

2294 εὐαγγελίζω, *euangelizō*, v. *to preach (bring) the good news (gospel).* S: *2097*, BAGD: 317B, CB: 353A

2295 εὐαγγέλιον, *euangelion*, n. *gospel, good news.* S: *2098*, BAGD: 317D, CB: 353A

2296 εὐαγγελιστής, *euangelistēs*, n. *evangelist, preacher of the gospel.* S: *2099*, BAGD: 318C, CB: 353A

2297 εὐαρεστέω, *euaresteō*, v. *to please.* S: *2100*, BAGD: 318C, CB: 353A

2298 εὐάρεστος, *euarestos*, a. *pleasing.* S: *2101*, BAGD: 318D, CB: 353A

2299 εὐαρέστως, *euarestōs*, adv. *in an acceptable or pleasing manner.* S: *2102*, BAGD: 318D, CB: –

2300 Εὔβουλος, *Euboulos*, n.pr., "good counsel." *Eubulus.* S: *2103*, BAGD: 319A, CB: –

2301 εὖγε, *euge*, adv. *well done!, excellent!.* S: *2095**, BAGD: 319A, CB: –

2302 εὐγενής, eugenēs, a. *of noble birth, of noble character.* S: *2104*, BAGD: 319A, CB: 353B

2303 εὐγλωττία, euglōttia, n. variant: *glibness, fluency of speech.* S: *2129**, BAGD: 319A, CB: –

2304 εὐδία, eudia, n. *fair weather.* S: *2105*, BAGD: 319A, CB: 353A

2305 εὐδοκέω, eudokeō, v. *to be well pleased, delight.* S: *2106*, BAGD: 319B, CB: 353A

2306 εὐδοκία, eudokia, n. *goodwill, good purpose, favor, pleasure, desire.* S: *2107*, BAGD: 319C, CB: 353A

2307 εὐεργεσία, euergesia, n. *act of kindness, good deed.* S: *2108*, BAGD: 319D, CB: 353A

2308 εὐεργετέω, euergeteō, v. *to do good to.* S: *2109*, BAGD: 320A, CB: 353A

2309 εὐεργέτης, euergetēs, n. *benefactor.* S: *2110*, BAGD: 320A, CB: 353A

2310 εὔθετος, euthetos, a. *fit, fit for service, useable, suitable.* S: *2111*, BAGD: 320B, CB: –

2311 εὐθέως, eutheōs, adv. *immediately, at once.* S: *2112*, BAGD: 320B, CB: 353B

2312 εὐθυδρομέω, euthydromeō, v. *to sail straight, run a straight course.* S: *2113*, BAGD: 320D, CB: –

2313 εὐθυμέω, euthymeō, v. *to keep up one's courage; to be happy, cheerful.* S: *2114*, BAGD: 320D, CB: –

2314 εὔθυμος, euthymos, a. *encouraged, cheerful, in good spirits.* S: *2115*, BAGD: 320D, CB: –

2315 εὐθύμως, euthymōs, adv. *gladly, cheerfully.* S: *2115**, BAGD: 320D, CB: –

2316 εὐθύνω, euthynō, v. *to make straight, straighten; to go straight.* S: *2116*, BAGD: 320D, CB: –

2317 εὐθύς[1], euthys[1], adv. *immediately, at once, as soon as.* S: *2117*, BAGD: 321A, CB: 353B

2318 εὐθύς[2], euthys[2], a. *straight; right, upright.* S: *2117*, BAGD: 321A, CB: 353B

2319 εὐθύτης, euthytēs, n. *righteousness, uprightness.* S: *2118*, BAGD: 321B, CB: –

2320 εὐκαιρέω, eukaireō, v. *to have a chance to, have the opportunity to; to spend one's time.* S: *2119*, BAGD: 321B, CB: 353B

2321 εὐκαιρία, eukairia, n. *opportunity, the right moment.* S: *2120*, BAGD: 321B, CB: 353B

2322 εὔκαιρος, eukairos, a. *opportune, well timed, suitable; time of need.* S: *2121*, BAGD: 321C, CB: 353B

2323 εὐκαίρως, eukairōs, adv. *opportunely, in season.* S: *2122*, BAGD: 321C, CB: 353B

2324 εὔκοπος, eukopos, a. *easy, easier.* S: *2123**, BAGD: 321D, CB: –

2325 εὐλάβεια, eulabeia, n. *reverence, reverent submission.* S: *2124*, BAGD: 321D, CB: 353B

2326 εὐλαβέομαι, eulabeomai, v. *to have holy fear, reverence.* S: *2125*, BAGD: 321D, CB: 353B

2327 εὐλαβής, eulabēs, a. *devout, godly, God-fearing.* S: *2126*, BAGD: 322A, CB: 353B

2328 εὐλογέω, eulogeō, v. *to praise, give thanks to, speak well of, extol; (pass.) to be blessed, receive blessing.* S: *2127*, BAGD: 322B, CB: 353B

2329 εὐλογητός, eulogētos, a. *praised, blessed.* S: *2128*, BAGD: 322C, CB: 353B

2330 εὐλογία, eulogia, n. *blessing, praise, thanksgiving; flattery; generosity.* S: *2129*, BAGD: 322D, CB: 353B

2331 εὐμετάδοτος, eumetadotos, a. *generous.* S: *2130*, BAGD: 323A, CB: –

2332 Εὐνίκη, Eunikē, n.pr., "good victory." *Eunice.* S: *2131*, BAGD: 323B, CB: –

2333 εὐνοέω, eunoeō, v. *to settle matters by coming to terms.* S: *2132*, BAGD: 323B, CB: –

2334 εὔνοια, eunoia, n. *wholeheartedness, enthusiasm, eagerness.* S: *2133*, BAGD: 323B, CB: –

2335 εὐνουχίζω, eunouchizō, v. *to emasculate, make (oneself) a eunuch; to be celibate, renounce marraige.* S: *2134*, BAGD: 323C, CB: 353B

2336 εὐνοῦχος, eunouchos, n. *eunuch, court official.* S: *2135*, BAGD: 323C, CB: 353B

2337 Εὐοδία, Euodia, n.pr., "good way" poss. "good fragrance." *Euodia.* S: *2136*, BAGD: 323D, CB: 353B

2338 εὐοδόω, euodoō, v. *(pass.) to get along with; to have a way opened; to prosper, get along well.* S: *2137*, BAGD: 323D, CB: –

2339 εὐπάρεδρος, euparedros, a. *devoted.* S: *2145**, BAGD: 324A, CB: –

2340 εὐπειθής, eupeithēs, a. *submissive, obedient, compliant.* S: *2138*, BAGD: 324A, CB: –

2341 εὐπερίσπαστος, euperispastos, a. variant: *easily distracting.* S: *2139**, BAGD: 324A, CB: –

2342 εὐπερίστατος, euperistatos, a. *easily entangling, constricting, obstructing.* S: *2139*, BAGD: 324A, CB: –

2343 εὐποιΐα, eupoiia, n. *doing good.* S: *2140*, BAGD: 324A, CB: –

2344 εὐπορέω, euporeō, v. *to have (financial) ability, have plenty, be well off.* S: *2141*, BAGD: 324B, CB: –

2345 εὐπορία, euporia, n. *prosperity, prosperous income.* S: *2142*, BAGD: 324B, CB: –

2346 εὐπρέπεια, euprepeia, n. *beauty.* S: *2143*, BAGD: 324B, CB: –

2347 εὐπρόσδεκτος, euprosdektos, a. *acceptable, favorable.* S: *2144*, BAGD: 324C, CB: 353B

2348 εὐπρόσεδρος, euprosedros, a. variant: *constant.* S: *2145*, BAGD: 324D, CB: –

2349 εὐπροσωπέω, euprosōpeō, v. *to make a good impression, make a good showing.* S: *2146*, BAGD: 324D, CB: –

2350 εὐρακύλων, eurakylōn, n. *northeast wind, Euraquilo.* S: *2148**, BAGD: 324D, CB: –

2351 εὑρίσκω, heuriskō, v. *(act.) to find, discover, meet; (mid.) to obtain; (pass.) to be found.* S: *2147*, BAGD: 324D, CB: 356B

2352 εὐροκλύδων, euroklydōn, n. variant: *southeast wind, Euroclydon.* S: *2148*, BAGD: 325D, CB: –

2353 εὐρύχωρος, eurychōros, a. *broad, spacious.* S: *2149*, BAGD: 326A, CB: –

2354 εὐσέβεια, *eusebeia*, n. *godliness, piety.* S: *2150*, BAGD: 326A, CB: 353B

2355 εὐσεβέω, *eusebeō*, v. *to worship; to put religion into practice, show piety toward.* S: *2151*, BAGD: 326B, CB: 353B

2356 εὐσεβής, *eusebēs*, a. *devout, godly, pious, reverent.* S: *2152*, BAGD: 326B, CB: 353B

2357 εὐσεβῶς, *eusebōs*, adv. *in a godly manner.* S: *2153*, BAGD: 326C, CB: 353B

2358 εὔσημος, *eusēmos*, a. *intelligible, clear, distinct.* S: *2154*, BAGD: 326C, CB: –

2359 εὔσπλαγχνος, *eusplanchnos*, a. *compassionate, tenderhearted.* S: *2155*, BAGD: 326C, CB: 353B

2360 εὐσχημονέω, *euschēmoneō*, v. variant: *to behave in an affected manner.* S: *807**, BAGD: 327A, CB: –

2361 εὐσχημόνως, *euschēmonōs*, adv. *decently, fittingly, becomingly, properly.* S: *2156*, BAGD: 327A, CB: –

2362 εὐσχημοσύνη, *euschēmosynē*, n. *modesty, presentability.* S: *2157*, BAGD: 327A, CB: 353B

2363 εὐσχήμων, *euschēmōn*, a. *presentable, proper, right; prominent, of high standing.* S: *2158*, BAGD: 327A, CB: –

2364 εὐτόνως, *eutonōs*, adv. *vehemently, vigorously.* S: *2159*, BAGD: 327B, CB: –

2365 εὐτραπελία, *eutrapelia*, n. *coarse joking, vulgar jesting.* S: *2160*, BAGD: 327C, CB: –

2366 Εὔτυχος, *Eutychos*, n.pr., "fortunate." *Eutychus.* S: *2161*, BAGD: 327C, CB: –

2367 εὐφημία, *euphēmia*, n. *good report.* S: *2162*, BAGD: 327C, CB: –

2368 εὔφημος, *euphēmos*, a. *admirable, appealing, praiseworthy.* S: *2163*, BAGD: 327C, CB: –

2369 εὐφορέω, *euphoreō*, v. *to produce a good crop, be fruitful.* S: *2164*, BAGD: 327C, CB: –

2370 εὐφραίνω, *euphrainō*, v. *(act.) to cause celebration, make glad; (mid./pass.) to celebrate, rejoice, be glad.* S: *2165*, BAGD: 327C, CB: 353B

2371 Εὐφράτης, *Euphratēs*, n.pr. *Euphrates.* S: *2166*, BAGD: 328A, CB: –

2372 εὐφροσύνη, *euphrosynē*, n. *joy, gladness, cheerfulness.* S: *2167*, BAGD: 328A, CB: 353B

2373 εὐχαριστέω, *eucharisteō*, v. *to thank, give thanks, render gratitude.* S: *2168*, BAGD: 328A, CB: 353A

2374 εὐχαριστία, *eucharistia*, n. *expression of thanks, thanksgiving, gratitude.* S: *2169*, BAGD: 328C, CB: 353A

2375 εὐχάριστος, *eucharistos*, a. *thankful.* S: *2170*, BAGD: 329A, CB: 353A

2376 εὐχή, *euchē*, n. *vow, oath; prayer.* S: *2171*, BAGD: 329B, CB: 353A

2377 εὔχομαι, *euchomai*, v. *to pray for; wish for.* S: *2172*, BAGD: 329B, CB: 353A

2378 εὔχρηστος, *euchrēstos*, a. *useful, helpful, serviceable.* S: *2173*, BAGD: 329C, CB: –

2379 εὐψυχέω, *eupsycheō*, v. *to be cheerful, glad.* S: *2174*, BAGD: 329D, CB: –

2380 εὐωδία, *euōdia*, n. *aroma, fragrance.* S: *2175*, BAGD: 329D, CB: 353B

2381 εὐώνυμος, *euōnymos*, a. *left (direction), south.* S: *2176*, BAGD: 329D, CB: 353B

2382 εὐωχία, *euōchia*, n. variant: *banquet, feasting.* S: *150*, BAGD: 330A, CB: –

2383 ἐφάλλομαι, *ephallomai*, v. *to jump on, leap upon.* S: *2177*, BAGD: 330A, CB: –

2384 ἐφάπαξ, *ephapax*, adv. *once for all; at the same time.* S: *2178*, BAGD: 330A, CB: 351C

2385 Ἐφεσῖνος, *Ephesinos*, a.pr.g., "of Ephesus." variant: *Ephesian.* S: *2179*, BAGD: 330A cf. Ἐφέσιος, CB: –

2386 Ἐφέσιος, *Ephesios*, a.pr.g., "of Ephesus." *Ephesian.* S: *2180*, BAGD: 330A, CB: –

2387 Ἔφεσος, *Ephesos*, n.pr. *Ephesus.* S: *2181*, BAGD: 330B, CB: –

2388 ἐφευρετής, *epheuretēs*, n. *inventor, contriver.* S: *2182*, BAGD: 330B, CB: –

2389 ἐφημερία, *ephēmeria*, n. *(priestly) division, group, class.* S: *2183*, BAGD: 330C, CB: –

2390 ἐφήμερος, *ephēmeros*, a. *daily, for the day.* S: *2184*, BAGD: 330C, CB: –

2391 ἐφικνέομαι, *ephikneomai*, v. *to come (to), reach (to).* S: *2185*, BAGD: 330C, CB: –

2392 ἐφίστημι, *ephistēmi*, v. *to approach, come near, stand beside, stop; to be imminent, at hand.* S: *2186*, BAGD: 330D, CB: 356C cf. histēmi

2393 ἐφοράω, *ephoraō*, v. variant: *to gaze upon.* S: *1896**, BAGD: 331A, CB: –

2394 Ἐφραίμ, *Ephraim*, n.pr., "doubly fruitful." *Ephraim.* S: *2187**, BAGD: 331A, CB: –

2395 ἐφφαθά, *ephphatha*, l.[v.]. *ephphatha!, be opened!.* S: *2188*, BAGD: 331B, CB: 351C

2396 ἐχθές, *echthes*, adv. *yesterday.* S: *5504**, BAGD: 331B, CB: –

2397 ἔχθρα, *echthra*, n. *hostility, hatred, antagonism.* S: *2189*, BAGD: 331B, CB: 348C

2398 ἐχθρός, *echthros*, a. *(as noun) enemy.* S: *2190*, BAGD: 331B, CB: 348C

2399 ἔχιδνα, *echidna*, n. *viper, snake.* S: *2191*, BAGD: 331D, CB: –

2400 ἔχω, *echō*, v. *(tr.) to have, hold, keep; (intr.) to be.* S: *2192*, BAGD: 331D, CB: 348C

2401 ἕως, *heōs*, c. & pp.*. *up to, until.* S: *2193*, BAGD: 334B, CB: 356A

2402 ς, [*stigma*], letter. variant: *an obsolete letter (stigma or vau), used as the numeral "six".* S: *150*, BAGD: 335B, CB: –

2403 ζ, *z*, letter. *letter of the Greek alphabet.* S: *150*, BAGD: 335B, CB: –

2404 Ζαβουλών, *Zaboulōn*, n.pr., "honor." *Zebulun.* S: *2194*, BAGD: 335B, CB: –

2405 Ζακχαῖος, *Zakchaios*, n.pr., "righteous one, pure one." *Zacchaeus.* S: *2195*, BAGD: 335B, CB: –

2406 Ζάρα, *Zara*, n.pr., "dawning, shining" *or* "flashing [red or scarlet] light." *Zerah.* S: *2196**, BAGD: 335D, CB: –

2407 ζαφθάνι, *zaphthani*, l.[v.+p.]. variant: *sabachthani.* S: *4518**, BAGD: 335D, CB: –

2408 Ζαχαρίας, *Zacharias*, n.pr., "Yahweh remembers." *Zechariah.* S: *2197*, BAGD: 335D, CB: –

2409 ζάω, *zaō*, v. *to live, Living One.* S: *2198*, BAGD: 336A, CB: 379B

2410 ζβέννυμι, *zbennymi*, v. variant: *to extinguish, put out.* S: *4570**, BAGD: 337B, CB: –

2411 Ζεβεδαῖος, *Zebedaios*, n.pr., "Yahweh bestows." *Zebedee.* S: *2199*, BAGD: 337B, CB: –

2412 ζεστός, *zestos*, a. *hot.* S: *2200*, BAGD: 337B, CB: 379C

2413 ζεύγνυμι, *zeugnymi*, v. variant: *to connect, join.* S: *4801**, BAGD: 337B, CB: 379C

2414 ζεῦγος, *zeugos*, n. *yoke; pair.* S: *2201*, BAGD: 337B, CB: 379C

2415 ζευκτηρία, *zeuktēria*, n. *rope, band.* S: *2202*, BAGD: 337B, CB: –

2416 Ζεύς, *Zeus*, n.pr., "shine, bright." *Zeus.* S: *2203*, BAGD: 337C, CB: 379C

2417 ζέω, *zeō*, v. *to have great fervor.* S: *2204*, BAGD: 337C, CB: 379C

2418 ζηλεύω, *zēleuō*, v. *to be earnest, eager.* S: *2206**, BAGD: 337C, CB: –

2419 ζῆλος, *zēlos*, n. *zeal, ardent concern, enthusiasm; jealousy, envy, rage.* S: *2205*, BAGD: 337D, CB: 379B

2420 ζηλόω, *zēloō*, v. *to desire, eagerly desire, show zeal; to be jealous, envious, covet.* S: *2206*, BAGD: 338A, CB: 379B

2421 ζηλωτής, *zēlōtēs*, n. *zealot, enthusiast, adherent.* S: *2207 & 2208*, BAGD: 338A, CB: 379B

2422 ζημία, *zēmia*, n. *loss, damage.* S: *2209*, BAGD: 338C, CB: 379C

2423 ζημιόω, *zēmioō*, v. *(pass.) to forfeit, suffer loss or damage.* S: *2210*, BAGD: 338C, CB: 379C cf. *-omai*

2424 Ζηνᾶς, *Zēnas*, n.pr., "gift of Zeus." *Zenas.* S: *2211*, BAGD: 338C, CB: –

2425 Ζήνων, *Zēnōn*, n.pr. variant: *Zeno.* S: *150*, BAGD: 338D, CB: –

2426 ζητέω, *zēteō*, v. *to look for, seek out; to try to obtain, desire to possess, strive for.* S: *2212*, BAGD: 338D, CB: 379C

2427 ζήτημα, *zētēma*, n. *question for discussion, point of dispute, controversy.* S: *2213*, BAGD: 339B, CB: –

2428 ζήτησις, *zētēsis*, n. *argument, debate, controversy, discussion.* S: *2214*, BAGD: 339B, CB: 379C

2429 ζιζάνιον, *zizanion*, n. *weed, darnel.* S: *2215*, BAGD: 339C, CB: 379C

2430 Ζμύρνα, *Zmyrna*, n.pr. variant: *Smyrna.* S: *4667**, BAGD: 339C, CB: –

2431 Ζοροβαβέλ, *Zorobabel*, n.pr., "offspring of Babylon." *Zerubbabel.* S: *2216**, BAGD: 339C, CB: –

2432 ζόφος, *zophos*, n. *blackness, darkness, gloom.* S: *2217*, BAGD: 339D, CB: –

2433 ζυγός, *zygos*, n. *yoke, pair of scales.* S: *2218*, BAGD: 339D, CB: 379C

2434 ζύμη, *zymē*, n. *yeast, leaven.* S: *2219*, BAGD: 340A, CB: 379C

2435 ζυμόω, *zymoō*, v. *to leaven, ferment, work as yeast.* S: *2220*, BAGD: 340A, CB: 379C

2436 ζωγρέω, *zōgreō*, v. *to capture (alive).* S: *2221*, BAGD: 340A, CB: –

2437 ζωή, *zōē*, n. *life.* S: *2222*, BAGD: 340B, CB: 379C

2438 ζώνη, *zōnē*, n. *belt, sash.* S: *2223*, BAGD: 341B, CB: 379C

2439 ζώννυμι, *zōnnymi*, v. *to dress, clothe oneself, put on a belt or sash.* S: *2224*, BAGD: 341C, CB: 379C

2440 ζωννύω, *zōnnyō*, v. variant: *to dress, clothe oneself, put on a belt or sash.* S: *2224*, BAGD: 341C, CB: 379C cf. *zōnnymi*

2441 ζωογονέω, *zōogoneō*, v. *to give life, make alive; to preserve life, keep alive.* S: *2225**, BAGD: 341C, CB: 379C

2442 ζῷον, *zōon*, n. *living creature, animal.* S: *2226**, BAGD: 341C, CB: 379C

2443 ζωοποιέω, *zōopoieō*, v. *to make alive, give life to.* S: *2227**, BAGD: 341D, CB: 379C

2444 η, *ē*, letter. *letter of the Greek alphabet.* S: *150*, BAGD: 342A, CB: –

2445 ἤ, *ē*, pt.disj. or comp. *or; (in a series) either .. or; (in comparison) than.* S: *2228*, BAGD: 342A, CB: –

2446 ἦ, *ē*, adv. variant: *truly.* S: *2229*, BAGD: 343A, CB: –

2447 ἦ μήν, *ē mēn*, adv. variant: *surely.* S: *2229 + 3375*, BAGD: 343A cf. ἦ, CB: –

2448 ἡγεμονεύω, *hēgemoneuō*, v. *to govern, lead, rule.* S: *2230*, BAGD: 343A, CB: –

2449 ἡγεμονία, *hēgemonia*, n. *reign, leadership, rulership.* S: *2231*, BAGD: 343A, CB: 355C

2450 ἡγενδεμ, *hēgemōn*, n. *ruler, prince, governor, prefect, procurator.* S: *2232*, BAGD: 343B, CB: 355C

2451 ἡγέομαι, *hēgeomai*, v. *to lead, rule, guide; to consider, think, regard.* S: *2233*, BAGD: 343C, CB: 355C

2452 ἡδέως, *hēdeōs*, adv. *gladly, with delight.* S: *2234 & 2236*, BAGD: 343D, CB: 355C

2453 ἤδη, *ēdē*, adv. *already, by this time, even now.* S: *2235*, BAGD: 344A, CB: 348C

2454 ἡδονή, *hēdonē*, n. *pleasure, desire, enjoyment.* S: *2237*, BAGD: 344B, CB: 355C

2455 ἡδύοσμον, *hēdyosmon*, n. *mint.* S: *2238*, BAGD: 344B, CB: 355C

2456 ἦθος, *ēthos*, n. *character, i.e., habit and custom.* S: *2239*, BAGD: 344C, CB: 353A

2457 ἥκω, *hēkō*, v. *to come, to have come, be present.* S: *2240*, BAGD: 344C, CB: 355C

2458 ἠλί[1], *ēli[1]*, l.[n.+p.]. variant: *Eli [Hebrew: my God].* S: *2241*, BAGD: 345A, CB: 350B

Ē Ἠλί[2], *li[2]*, n.pr., "ascent [to God]." *Heli.* S: *2242*, BAGD: 345A, CB: –

2460 Ἠλίας, *lias*, n.pr., "Yahweh is [my] God." *Elijah.* S: *2243*, BAGD: 345A, CB: –

2461 ἡλικία, *hēlikia*, n. *life, time in life, age; stature, height.* S: *2244*, BAGD: 345A, CB: 355C

2462 ἡλίκος, *hēlikos*, a. *how much, how great, how large.* S: *2245*, BAGD: 345C, CB: –

2463 ἥλιος, *hēlios*, n. *sun.* S: *2246*, BAGD: 345C, CB: 355C

2464 ἧλος, *hēlos*, n. *nail (used in crucifixion)*. S: *2247*, BAGD: 345D, CB: –

2465 ἡμέρα, *hēmera*, n. *day, time of the day, time, period of time.* S: *2250*, BAGD: 345D, CB: 355C

2466 ἡμέτερος, *hēmeteros*, a. *our, our own.* S: *2251*, BAGD: 347D, CB: 356A

2467 ἡμιθανής, *hēmithanēs*, a. *half dead.* S: *2253*, BAGD: 348A, CB: –

2468 ἥμισυς, *hēmisys*, a. *half (temporal and spacial).* S: *2255*, BAGD: 348A, CB: –

2469 ἡμιώριον, *hēmiōrion*, n. *half an hour.* S: *2256*, BAGD: 348A, CB: –

2470 ἡμίωρον, *hēmiōron*, n. variant: *half an hour.* S: *2256**, BAGD: 348A cf. ἡμίωρον, CB: –

2471 ἡνίκα, *hēnika*, pt. *when, whenever, at the time when.* S: *2259*, BAGD: 348B, CB: –

2472 ἤπερ, *ēper*, pt.comp. *than.* S: *2260**, BAGD: 342A cf. ἤ 2.e. β., CB: –

2473 ἤπιος, *ēpios*, a. *gentle, kind.* S: *2261*, BAGD: 348B, CB: 352A

2474 Ἤρ, *r*, n.pr., *"watcher, watchful." Er.* S: *2262*, BAGD: 348B, CB: –

2475 ἤρεμος, *ēremos*, a. *peaceful, quiet, tranquil.* S: *2263*, BAGD: 348B, CB: –

2476 Ἡρώδης, *Hērōdēs*, n.pr. *Herod.* S: *2264**, BAGD: 348C, CB: 356A cf. -os

2477 Ἡρωδιανοί, *Hērōdianoi*, n.pr.g. *Herodians.* S: *2265**, BAGD: 348D, CB: –

2478 Ἡρωδιάς, *Hērōdias*, n.pr. *Herodias.* S: *2266**, BAGD: 348D, CB: 356A cf. -eios

2479 Ἡρωδίων, *Hērōdiōn*, n.pr. *Herodion.* S: *2267**, BAGD: 348D, CB: –

2480 Ἡσαΐας, *saias*, n.pr., *"Yahweh saves." Isaiah.* S: *2268**, BAGD: 348D, CB: –

2481 Ἡσαῦ, *sau*, n.pr., *"hairy." Esau.* S: *2269*, BAGD: 349A, CB: –

2482 ἥσσων, *hēssōn*, a. *for the worse; (as adv.) less.* S: *2276**, BAGD: 349A, CB: –

2483 ἡσυχάζω, *hēsychazō*, v. *to be silent, have no objection; to rest; to lead a quiet life; to give up.* S: *2270*, BAGD: 349A, CB: 356A

2484 ἡσυχία, *hēsychia*, n. *quietness, silence; settling down, lack of disturbance.* S: *2271*, BAGD: 349B, CB: 356A

2485 ἡσύχιος, *hēsychios*, a. *quiet.* S: *2272*, BAGD: 349C, CB: 356A

2486 ἤτοι, *ētoi*, pt.disj. *(in a series) whether .. or.* S: *2273*, BAGD: 342A cf. ἤ 1.b., CB: –

2487 ἡττάομαι, *hēttaomai*, v. *to be mastered, overcome.* S: *2274**, BAGD: 349C, CB: –

2488 ἥττημα, *hēttēma*, n. *loss, defeat.* S: *2275*, BAGD: 349C, CB: 356B

2489 ἥττων, *hēttōn*, a. variant: *for the worse; (as adv.) less.* S: *2276**, BAGD: 349A cf. ἥσσων, CB: –

2490 ἠχέω, *ēcheō*, v. *to resound, ring out.* S: *2278*, BAGD: 349C, CB: 348C

2491 ἦχος[1], *ēchos*[1], n. *sound, tone, blast (of a trumpet); news, report.* S: *2279*, BAGD: 349D, CB: 348C

2492 ἦχος[2], *ēchos*[2], n. *roar, sound, noise.* S: *2279**, BAGD: 349D, CB: 348C

2493 ἠχώ, *ēchō*, n. variant: *sound.* S: *2279**, BAGD: 349D, CB: –

2494 θ, *th*, letter. *letter of the Greek alphabet.* S: *150*, BAGD: 350A, CB: –

2495 θά, *tha*, l.[v.]. *come!.* S: *3134**, BAGD: 491B cf. μαρὰν ἀθα, CB: –

2496 θάβιτα, *thabita*, l.[n.]. variant: *girl.* S: *5008**, BAGD: 350A, CB: –

2497 Θαδδαῖος, *Thaddaios*, n.pr., *poss.* "nipple." *Thaddaeus.* S: *2280*, BAGD: 350A, CB: –

2498 θάλασσα, *thalassa*, n. *sea, lake.* S: *2281*, BAGD: 350A, CB: 377C

2499 θάλπω, *thalpō*, v. *to care for, cherish, comfort.* S: *2282*, BAGD: 350B, CB: –

2500 Θαμάρ, *Thamar*, n.pr., *"date palm." Tamar.* S: *2283**, BAGD: 350C, CB: –

2501 θαμβέω, *thambeō*, v. *(pass.) to be amazed, astounded.* S: *2284*, BAGD: 350C, CB: 377C

2502 θάμβος, *thambos*, n. *amazement, astonishment, wonder.* S: *2285*, BAGD: 350C, CB: 377C

2503 θανάσιμος, *thanasimos*, a. *deadly.* S: *2286*, BAGD: 350D, CB: –

2504 θανατηφόρος, *thanatēphoros*, a. *deadly.* S: *2287*, BAGD: 350D, CB: –

2505 θάνατος, *thanatos*, n. *death.* S: *2288*, BAGD: 350D, CB: 377C

2506 θανατόω, *thanatoō*, v. *to put to death, kill.* S: *2289*, BAGD: 351C, CB: 377C

2507 θάπτω, *thaptō*, v. *to bury, entomb.* S: *2290*, BAGD: 351D, CB: 377C

2508 Θάρα, *Thara*, n.pr. *Terah.* S: *2291*, BAGD: 351D, CB: –

2509 θαρρέω, *tharreō*, v. *to have confidence, be bold.* S: *2292*, BAGD: 352A, CB: 377C

2510 θαρσέω, *tharseō*, v. *take heart!, take courage!, cheer up!.* S: *2293*, BAGD: 352A, CB: 377C

2511 θάρσος, *tharsos*, n. *encouragement, courage.* S: *2294*, BAGD: 352A, CB: –

2512 θαῦμα, *thauma*, n. *wonder, marvel, astonishment.* S: *2295*, BAGD: 352A, CB: 377C

2513 θαυμάζω, *thaumazō*, v. *to be amazed (at), in wonder, astonished, surprised.* S: *2296*, BAGD: 352B, CB: 377C

2514 θαυμάσιος, *thaumasios*, a. *wonderful, remarkable.* S: *2297*, BAGD: 352D, CB: 377C

2515 θαυμαστός, *thaumastos*, a. *wonderful, marvelous, remarkable.* S: *2298*, BAGD: 352D, CB: 377C

2516 θεά, *thea*, n. *goddess.* S: *2299*, BAGD: 353A, CB: 377C

2517 θεάομαι, *theaomai*, v. *to see, look at; visit.* S: *2300*, BAGD: 353A, CB: 377C

2518 θεατρίζω, *theatrizō*, v. *to publicly expose.* S: *2301*, BAGD: 353C, CB: 377C cf. -omai

2519 θέατρον, *theatron*, n. *theatre, spectacle, theatrical play.* S: *2302*, BAGD: 353C, CB: 377C

2520 θεῖον, *theion*, n. *sulfur.* S: *2303*, BAGD: 353D, CB: 377C

2521 θεῖος, *theios*, a. *divine.* S: *2304*, BAGD: 353D, CB: 377C

2522 θειότης, *theiotēs*, n. *divine nature, divinity.* S: *2305*, BAGD: 354A, CB: 377C

2523 θειώδης, *theiōdēs*, a. *(yellow) as sulfur.* S: *2306*, BAGD: 354A, CB: –

2524 Θέκλα, *Thekla*, n.pr. variant: *Thecla.* S: *150*, BAGD: 354B, CB: –

2525 θέλημα, *thelēma*, n. *will, decision, desire.* S: *2307*, BAGD: 354B, CB: 377C

2526 θέλησις, *thelēsis*, n. *will, decision.* S: *2308*, BAGD: 354C, CB: 377C

2527 θέλω, *thelō*, v. *to will, decide, want to; wish, desire.* S: *2309*, BAGD: 354D, CB: 377C

2528 θεμέλιον, *themelion*, n. *foundation.* S: *2310**, BAGD: 355D, CB: –

2529 θεμέλιος, *themelios*, n. *foundation.* S: *2310*, BAGD: 355D, CB: 378A

2530 θεμελιόω, *themelioō*, v. *to lay a foundation; to make steadfast.* S: *2311*, BAGD: 356A, CB: 378A

2531 θεοδίδακτος, *theodidaktos*, a. *taught by God.* S: *2312*, BAGD: 356B, CB: –

2532 θεολόγος, *theologos*, n. variant: *one who speaks of God or divine things.* S: *2312'*, BAGD: 356B, CB: –

2533 θεομαχέω, *theomacheō*, v. variant: *to fight against God.* S: *2313*, BAGD: 356C, CB: –

2534 θεομάχος, *theomachos*, a. *fighting against God.* S: *2314*, BAGD: 356C, CB: 378A

2535 θεόπνευστος, *theopneustos*, a. *God-breathed, inspired by God.* S: *2315*, BAGD: 356C, CB: 378A

2536 θεός, *theos*, n. *God; (pagan) god, goddess.* S: *2316*, BAGD: 356D, CB: 378A

2537 θεοσέβεια, *theosebeia*, n. *worship of God, reverence for God.* S: *2317*, BAGD: 358B, CB: 378A

2538 θεοσεβής, *theosebēs*, a. *godly, God-fearing, devout.* S: *2318*, BAGD: 358B, CB: 378B

2539 θεοστυγής, *theostygēs*, a. *God-hating.* S: *2319*, BAGD: 358C, CB: 378B

2540 θεότης, *theotēs*, n. *Deity, Divinity.* S: *2320*, BAGD: 358C, CB: 378B

2541 Θεόφιλος, *Theophilos*, n.pr., "friend of God." *Theophilus.* S: *2321*, BAGD: 358D, CB: 378A

2542 θεραπεία, *therapeia*, n. *service, care; (hence) healing.* S: *2322*, BAGD: 358D, CB: 378B

2543 θεραπεύω, *therapeuō*, v. *to heal, cure; (pass.) to be healed; to serve.* S: *2323*, BAGD: 359A, CB: 378B

2544 θεράπων, *therapōn*, n. *servant.* S: *2324*, BAGD: 359B, CB: 378B

2545 θερίζω, *therizō*, v. *to reap, harvest.* S: *2325*, BAGD: 359B, CB: 378B

2546 θερισμός, *therismos*, n. *harvest.* S: *2326*, BAGD: 359C, CB: 378B

2547 θεριστής, *theristēs*, n. *harvester, reaper.* S: *2327*, BAGD: 359C, CB: 378B

2548 θερμαίνω, *thermainō*, v. *(mid.) to keep warm, warm (oneself).* S: *2328*, BAGD: 359C, CB: 378B

2549 θέρμη, *thermē*, n. *heat.* S: *2329*, BAGD: 359C, CB: 378B

2550 θέρος, *theros*, n. *summer.* S: *2330*, BAGD: 359D, CB: 378B

2551 Θεσσαλία, *Thessalia*, n.pr. variant: *Thessaly.* S: *150*, BAGD: 359D, CB: –

2552 Θεσσαλονικεύς, *Thessalonikeus*, n.pr.g., "from Thessalonica." *Thessalonian.* S: *2331*, BAGD: 359D, CB: 378B

2553 Θεσσαλονίκη, *Thessalonikē*, n.pr. *Thessalonica.* S: *2332*, BAGD: 359D, CB: –

2554 Θευδᾶς, *Theudas*, n.pr., "gift of God." *Theudas.* S: *2333*, BAGD: 359D, CB: –

2555 θεωρέω, *theōreō*, v. *to see, look at, watch closely; perceive, experience.* S: *2334*, BAGD: 360A, CB: 378A

2556 θεωρία, *theōria*, n. *sight, spectacle.* S: *2335*, BAGD: 360B, CB: 378A

2557 θήκη, *thēkē*, n. *sheath, scabbard.* S: *2336*, BAGD: 360B, CB: 377C

2558 θηλάζω, *thēlazō*, v. *to nurse a baby; (as noun) nursing infant.* S: *2337*, BAGD: 360C, CB: –

2559 θῆλυς, *thēlys*, a. *female, pertaining to women.* S: *2338*, BAGD: 360C, CB: 377C

2560 θήρα, *thēra*, n. *trap, net.* S: *2339*, BAGD: 360D, CB: –

2561 θηρεύω, *thēreuō*, v. *to catch in a mistake.* S: *2340*, BAGD: 360D, CB: –

2562 θηριομαχέω, *thēriomacheō*, v. *to fight wild animals.* S: *2341*, BAGD: 360D, CB: –

2563 θηρίον, *thērion*, n. *(wild) animal, (fiendish) beast, snake.* S: *2342*, BAGD: 361A, CB: 378B

2564 θησαυρίζω, *thēsaurizō*, v. *to store up, gather, reserve.* S: *2343*, BAGD: 361B, CB: 378B

2565 θησαυρός, *thēsauros*, n. *treasure, what is stored up; storeroom.* S: *2344*, BAGD: 361C, CB: 378B

2566 θιγγάνω, *thinganō*, v. *to touch.* S: *2345*, BAGD: 361D, CB: –

2567 θλίβω, *thlibō*, v. *(act.) to press upon, crowd up to; cause trouble; (pass.) to be narrow; to be pressed, troubled, persecuted.* S: *2346*, BAGD: 362A, CB: 378B

2568 θλῖψις, *thlipsis*, n. *trouble, distress, oppression, tribulation.* S: *2347**, BAGD: 362B, CB: 378B

2569 θνήσκω, *thnēskō*, v. *(perf.) to have died, be dead.* S: *2348**, BAGD: 362C, CB: 378B

2570 θνητός, *thnētos*, a. *mortal.* S: *2349*, BAGD: 362D, CB: 378B

2571 θορυβάζω, *thorybazō*, v. *(pass.) to be upset, distracted.* S: *5182**, BAGD: 362D, CB: 378B

2572 θορυβέω, *thorybeō*, v. *to start a riot, throw into disorder; (pass.) to be alarmed, in commotion, distressed.* S: *2350*, BAGD: 362D, CB: 378B

2573 θόρυβος, *thorybos*, n. *uproar, riot, commotion, disturbance.* S: *2351*, BAGD: 363A, CB: 378B

2574 θραυματίζω, *thraumatizō*, v. variant: *to break.* S: *2352**, BAGD: 363A, CB: –

2575 θραύω, *thrauō*, v. *(pass.) to be oppressed, downtrodden.* S: *2352*, BAGD: 363B, CB: –

2576 θρέμμα, *thremma*, n. *livestock, domestic animal.* S: *2353*, BAGD: 363B, CB: 378B

2577 θρηνέω, *thrēneō*, v. *to sing a funeral dirge, lament, mourn.* S: *2354*, BAGD: 363B, CB: 378B

2578 θρῆνος, *thrēnos*, n. variant: *dirge, funeral song.* S: *2355*, BAGD: 363B, CB: 378B

2579 θρησκεία, *thrēskeia*, n. *religion, worship.* S: *2356*, BAGD: 363B, CB: 378B

2580 θρῆσκος, *thrēskos*, a. *religious.* S: *2357*, BAGD: 363D, CB: 378B

2581 θριαμβεύω, *thriambeuō*, v. *to lead in a triumphal procession.* S: *2358*, BAGD: 363D, CB: 378B

2582 θρίξ, *thrix*, n. *hair, a hair.* S: *2359*, BAGD: 363D, CB: 378B

2583 θροέω, *throeō*, v. *(pass.) to be alarmed, disturbed.* S: *2360*, BAGD: 364A, CB: –

2584 θρόμβος, *thrombos*, n. *drop.* S: *2361*, BAGD: 364B, CB: –

2585 θρόνος, *thronos*, n. *throne.* S: *2362*, BAGD: 364B, CB: 378B

2586 θρύπτω, *thryptō*, v. variant: *to break in pieces.* S: *150*, BAGD: 364C, CB: –

2587 Θυάτειρα, *Thyateira*, n.pr. *Thyatira.* S: *2363*, BAGD: 364C, CB: –

2588 θυγάτηρ, *thygatēr*, n. *daughter.* S: *2364*, BAGD: 364D, CB: 378C

2589 θυγάτριον, *thygatrion*, n. *little daughter.* S: *2365*, BAGD: 365A, CB: –

2590 θύελλα, *thyella*, n. *storm.* S: *2366*, BAGD: 365A, CB: –

2591 θύϊνος, *thyinos*, a. *citron, from the citron tree.* S: *2367*, BAGD: 365A, CB: –

2592 θυμίαμα, *thymiama*, n. *incense; burning incense, offering of incense.* S: *2368*, BAGD: 365A, CB: 378C

2593 θυμιατήριον, *thymiatērion*, n. *incense altar.* S: *2369*, BAGD: 365B, CB: 378C

2594 θυμιάω, *thymiaō*, v. *to burn incense, offer incense.* S: *2370*, BAGD: 365B, CB: 378C

2595 θυμομαχέω, *thymomacheō*, v. *to quarrel, be fighting mad.* S: *2371*, BAGD: 365B, CB: –

2596 θυμός, *thymos*, n. *wrath, fury, anger, rage.* S: *2372*, BAGD: 365B, CB: 378C

2597 θυμόω, *thymoō*, v. *(pass.) to become angry.* S: *2373*, BAGD: 365C, CB: 378C

2598 θύρα, *thyra*, n. *door, gate, entrance.* S: *2374*, BAGD: 365D, CB: 378C

2599 θυρεός, *thyreos*, n. *shield.* S: *2375*, BAGD: 366A, CB: 378C

2600 θυρίς, *thyris*, n. *window.* S: *2376*, BAGD: 366A, CB: –

2601 θυρωρός, *thyrōros*, n. *doorkeeper, watcher (at door or gate).* S: *2377*, BAGD: 366A, CB: –

2602 θυσία, *thysia*, n. *sacrifice, offering.* S: *2378*, BAGD: 366B, CB: 378C

2603 θυσιαστήριον, *thysiastērion*, n. *altar.* S: *2379*, BAGD: 366D, CB: 378C

2604 θύω, *thyō*, v. *to kill, butcher; to offer sacrifice.* S: *2380*, BAGD: 367A, CB: 378C

2605 Θωμᾶς, *Thōmas*, n.pr., "twin." *Thomas.* S: *2381*, BAGD: 367C, CB: –

2606 θώραξ, *thōrax*, n. *breastplate.* S: *2382*, BAGD: 367C, CB: 378B

2607 ι, *i*, letter. *letter of the Greek alphabet.* S: *150*, BAGD: 367B, CB: –

2608 Ἰάϊρος, *Iairos*, n.pr., "he gives light." *Jairus.* S: *2383**, BAGD: 367B, CB: –

2609 Ἰακώβ, *Iakōb*, n.pr., "follower, replacer, one who follows the heel." *Jacob.* S: *2384*, BAGD: 367B, CB: 358C

2610 Ἰάκωβος, *Iakōbos*, n.pr., "follower, replacer, one who follows the heel." *James.* S: *2385*, BAGD: 367D, CB: 358C

2611 ἴαμα, *iama*, n. *healing.* S: *2386*, BAGD: 368A, CB: 358C

2612 Ἰαμβρῆς, *Iambrēs*, n.pr. *Jambres.* S: *2387*, BAGD: 368B, CB: –

2613 Ἰανναί, *Iannai*, n.pr. *Jannai.* S: *2388**, BAGD: 368B, CB: –

2614 Ἰάννης, *Iannēs*, n.pr. *Jannes.* S: *2389**, BAGD: 368B, CB: –

2615 ἰάομαι, *iaomai*, v. *(mid.) to heal; (pass.) to be healed, freed.* S: *2390*, BAGD: 368B, CB: 358C

2616 Ἰάρετ, *Iaret*, n.pr., "servant" KB *Jared.* S: *2391**, BAGD: 368C, CB: –

2617 ἴασις, *iasis*, n. *healing, cure.* S: *2392*, BAGD: 368C, CB: 358C

2618 ἴασπις, *iaspis*, n. *jasper.* S: *2393*, BAGD: 368D, CB: 358C

2619 Ἰάσων, *Iasōn*, n.pr., "to heal." *Jason.* S: *2394*, BAGD: 368D, CB: 358C

2620 ἰατρός, *iatros*, n. *doctor, physician.* S: *2395*, BAGD: 368D, CB: 358C

2621 Ἰαχίν, *Iachin*, n.pr. variant: *Jachin.* S: *150*, BAGD: 369A, CB: –

2622 ιβ, *ib*, n.num. variant: *two letters representing the number twelve.* S: *150*, BAGD: 369B, CB: –

2623 ἴδε, *ide*, pt. *see!, look!; here, there.* S: *2396*, BAGD: 369B, CB: 358C

2624 ἰδέα, *idea*, n. variant: *appearance.* S: *2397*, BAGD: 369C, CB: –

2625 ἴδιος, *idios*, a. *one's own, private.* S: *2398*, BAGD: 369C, CB: 358C

2626 ἰδιώτης, *idiōtēs*, n. *ordinary, untrained person, one who does not understand, an inquirer.* S: *2399*, BAGD: 370C, CB: 358C

2627 ἰδού, *idou*, pt. *look!, suddenly, now; here, there.* S: *2400*, BAGD: 370D, CB: 358C

2628 Ἰδουμαία, *Idoumaia*, n.pr., "[land of] Edom." *Idumea.* S: *2401*, BAGD: 371B, CB: –

2629 ἱδρώς, *hidrōs*, n. *sweat, perspiration.* S: *2402*, BAGD: 371C, CB: –

2630 Ἰεζάβελ, *Iezabel*, n.pr., poss. "unexalted, without a husband" BDB. *Jezebel.* S: *2403**, BAGD: 371C, CB: –

2631 Ἱεράπολις, *Hierapolis*, n.pr., "[pagan] sacred city." *Hierapolis.* S: *2404*, BAGD: 371C, CB: 356B

2632 ἱερατεία, *hierateia*, n. *priestly office, priesthood.* S: *2405*, BAGD: 371D, CB: 356B

2633 ἱεράτευμα, *hierateuma,* n. *priesthood.* S: *2406,* BAGD: 371D, CB: 356B

2634 ἱερατεύω, *hierateuō,* v. *to serve as a priest.* S: *2407,* BAGD: 371D, CB: 356B

2635 Ἱερεμίας, *Ieremias,* n.pr., "Yahweh loosens [the womb]" BDB; "Yahweh lifts up" IDB; "Yahweh establishes" KB. *Jeremiah.* S: *2408*,* BAGD: 371D, CB: –

2636 ἱερεύς, *hiereus,* n. *priest.* S: *2409,* BAGD: 372A, CB: 356B

2637 Ἱεριχώ, *Ierichō,* n.pr., "moon city." *Jericho.* S: *2410*,* BAGD: 372B, CB: –

2638 ἱερόθυτος, *hierothytos,* a. *sacrificed to pagan gods.* S: *1494*,* BAGD: 372B, CB: –

2639 ἱερόν, *hieron,* n. *temple, sanctuary.* S: *2411,* BAGD: 372B, CB: 356B

2640 ἱεροπρεπής, *hieroprepēs,* a. *reverent, pertaining to proper reverence, worthy of reverence.* S: *2412,* BAGD: 372D, CB: 356B

2641 ἱερός, *hieros,* a. *sacred, holy, set apart for God.* S: *2413,* BAGD: 372D, CB: 356B

2642 Ἱεροσόλυμα, *Hierosolyma,* n.pr. variant: *Jerusalem.* S: *2414,* BAGD: 372D, CB: 358C

2643 Ἱεροσολυμίτης, *Hierosolymitēs,* n.pr.g., "of Jerusalem." *inhabitant of Jerusalem.* S: *2415,* BAGD: 373B, CB: –

2644 ἱεροσυλέω, *hierosyleō,* v. *to rob temples.* S: *2416,* BAGD: 373C, CB: 356B

2645 ἱερόσυλος, *hierosylos,* a. *temple robber.* S: *2417,* BAGD: 373C, CB: 356C

2646 ἱερουργέω, *hierourgeō,* v. *to perform priestly duty, serve as a priest.* S: *2418,* BAGD: 373C, CB: 356C

2647 Ἱερουσαλήμ, *Ierousalēm,* n.pr., "foundation of Shalem [peace]." *Jerusalem.* S: *2419*,* BAGD: 372D, CB: 358C

2648 ἱερωσύνη, *hierōsynē,* n. *priesthood.* S: *2420,* BAGD: 373C, CB: 356C

2649 Ἰεσσαί, *Iessai,* n.pr. *Jesse.* S: *2421,* BAGD: 373D, CB: –

2650 Ἰεφθάε, *Iephthae,* n.pr., "Yahweh opens, frees." *Jephthah.* S: *2422,* BAGD: 373D, CB: –

2651 Ἰεχονίας, *Iechonias,* n.pr., "Yahweh supports." *Jeconiah.* S: *2423,* BAGD: 373D, CB: –

2652 Ἰησοῦς, *Iēsous,* n.pr., "Yahweh saves." *Jesus, Joshua.* S: *2424,* BAGD: 373D, CB: 358C

2653 ἱκανός, *hikanos,* a. *sufficient, considerable, much; appropriate, competent, worthy, deserving.* S: *2425,* BAGD: 374B, CB: 356C

2654 ἱκανότης, *hikanotēs,* n. *competence, fitness, capability.* S: *2426,* BAGD: 374D, CB: 356C

2655 ἱκανόω, *hikanoō,* v. *to make competent, qualify one for, authorize.* S: *2427,* BAGD: 374D, CB: 356C

2656 ἱκετηρία, *hiketēria,* n. *petition, supplication.* S: *2428,* BAGD: 375A, CB: 356C

2657 ἰκμάς, *ikmas,* n. *moisture.* S: *2429,* BAGD: 375A, CB: –

2658 Ἰκόνιον, *Ikonion,* n.pr. *Iconium.* S: *2430,* BAGD: 375B, CB: –

2659 ἱλαρός, *hilaros,* a. *cheerful, without grudging.* S: *2431,* BAGD: 375B, CB: 356C

2660 ἱλαρότης, *hilarotēs,* n. *cheerfully, not grudgingly.* S: *2432,* BAGD: 375B, CB: –

2661 ἱλάσκομαι, *hilaskomai,* v. *(mid.) to make atonement for; (pass.) to have mercy on, be merciful to.* S: *2433,* BAGD: 375C, CB: 356C

2662 ἱλασμός, *hilasmos,* n. *atoning sacrifice.* S: *2434,* BAGD: 375C, CB: 356C

2663 ἱλαστήριον, *hilastērion,* n. *atoning sacrifice; atonement cover.* S: *2435,* BAGD: 375D, CB: 356C

2664 ἵλεως, *hileōs,* a. *forgiving, gracious; (may God be) gracious!, God forbid!.* S: *2436,* BAGD: 376A, CB: 356C

2665 Ἰλλυρικόν, *Illyrikon,* n.pr. *Illyricum.* S: *2437,* BAGD: 376A, CB: –

2666 ἱμάς, *himas,* n. *(leather) thong, strap.* S: *2438,* BAGD: 376B, CB: –

2667 ἱματίζω, *himatizō,* v. *(pass.) to be dressed, clothed.* S: *2439,* BAGD: 376B, CB: –

2668 ἱμάτιον, *himation,* n. *clothing, cloak, robe.* S: *2440,* BAGD: 376B, CB: 356C

2669 ἱματισμός, *himatismos,* n. *clothing.* S: *2441,* BAGD: 376D, CB: –

2670 ἱμείρομαι, *himeiromai,* v. variant: *to desire, long for.* S: *2442,* BAGD: 565B cf. ὁμείρομαι, CB: –

2671 ἵνα, *hina,* c. *shows prupose or result: in order that, in order to, so that, then.* S: *2443,* BAGD: 376D, CB: 356C

2672 ἱνατί, *hinati,* pt.inter. *why?.* S: *2444,* BAGD: 378C, CB: 356C cf. *hina*

2673 Ἰόππη, *Ioppē,* n.pr., "beautiful." *Joppa.* S: *2445,* BAGD: 378D, CB: –

2674 Ἰορδάνης, *Iordanēs,* n.pr., "descending." *Jordan.* S: *2446,* BAGD: 378D, CB: 358C

2675 ἰός, *ios,* n. *poison, venom; corrosion, rust.* S: *2447,* BAGD: 378D, CB: 358C

2676 Ἰουδά, *Iouda,* n.pr., "praised." variant: *Judah.* S: *2448,* BAGD: 379D cf. Ἰούδας, CB: 358C

2677 Ἰουδαία, *Ioudaia,* n.pr., "land of the Judahites." *Judea.* S: *2449,* BAGD: 379A, CB: 358C

2678 ἰουδαΐζω, *ioudaizō,* v. *to follow Jewish customs, live as a Jew.* S: *2450*,* BAGD: 379B, CB: 358C

2679 Ἰουδαϊκός, *Ioudaikos,* a.pr., "Jewish." *Jewish.* S: *2451,* BAGD: 379B, CB: 358C

2680 Ἰουδαϊκῶς, *Ioudaikōs,* adv.pr., "Jewish." *like a Jew, in a Jewish manner.* S: *2452,* BAGD: 379B, CB: 358C

2681 Ἰουδαῖος, *Ioudaios,* a.pr.g., "Jewish." *Jewish (people).* S: *2453,* BAGD: 379B, CB: 358C

2682 Ἰουδαϊσμός, *Ioudaismos,* n.pr., "Judaism." *Judaism.* S: *2454,* BAGD: 379D, CB: 358C

2683 Ἰούδας, *Ioudas,* n.pr., "praised." *Judah, Judas, Jude.* S: *2455,* BAGD: 379D, CB: 359A

2684 Ἰουλία, *Ioulia,* n.pr., "of Julian [the family of Julius Caesar]." *Julia.* S: *2456,* BAGD: 380B, CB: –

2685 Ἰούλιος, *Ioulios,* n.pr., "of Julian [the family of Julius Caesar]." *Julius.* S: *2457,* BAGD: 380B, CB: –

2686 Ἰουνία, *Iounia,* n.pr. variant: *Junia.* S: *2456*,* BAGD: 380B cf. Ἰουνιᾶς, CB: –

2687 Ἰουνιᾶς, *Iounias*, n.pr. *Junias.* S: *2458**, BAGD: 380B, CB: –

2688 Ἰοῦστος, *Ioustos*, n.pr., "just." *Justus.* S: *200*, BAGD: 380B, CB: –

2689 ἱππεύς, *hippeus*, n. *horseman, cavalryman.* S: *2460*, BAGD: 380C, CB: –

2690 ἱππικός, *hippikos*, a. *mounted (troops), pertaining to a horseman.* S: *2461**, BAGD: 380C, CB: 356C

2691 ἵππος, *hippos*, n. *horse.* S: *2462*, BAGD: 380C, CB: 356C

2692 ἶρις, *iris*, n. *rainbow.* S: *2463*, BAGD: 380C, CB: 359A

2693 Ἰσαάκ, *Isaak*, n.pr., "he [God] laughs." *Isaac.* S: *2464*, BAGD: 380D, CB: 359A

2694 ἰσάγγελος, *isangelos*, a. *like an angel.* S: *2465*, BAGD: 380D, CB: 359A

2695 Ἰσαχάρ, *Isachar*, n.pr., "there is a reward" [Ge. 30:18]; "may [God] show mercy" IDB; "hired hand" KB. variant: *Issachar.* S: *2466*, BAGD: 381D cf. Ἰσσαχάρ, CB: –

2696 Ἰσκαριώθ, *Iskariōth*, n.pr.[g.?]., "man of Kerioth *or* of the assassins." variant: *Iscariot.* S: *2469**, BAGD: 380D, CB: –

2697 Ἰσκαριώτης, *Iskariōtēs*, n.pr.[g.?]., "man of Kerioth *or* of the assassins." *Iscariot.* S: *2469*, BAGD: 380D, CB: –

2698 ἴσος, *isos*, a. *equal, same; agreeable.* S: *2470*, BAGD: 381A, CB: 359A

2699 ἰσότης, *isotēs*, n. *equality, fairness.* S: *2471*, BAGD: 381B, CB: 359A

2700 ἰσότιμος, *isotimos*, a. *as precious as, of equal value.* S: *2472*, BAGD: 381B, CB: 359A

2701 ἰσόψυχος, *isopsychos*, a. *like, of like soul, heart or mind.* S: *2473*, BAGD: 381B, CB: 359A

2702 Ἰσραήλ, *Israēl*, n.pr., "he struggles with God [El]." *Israel.* S: *2474*, BAGD: 381C, CB: 359A

2703 Ἰσραηλίτης, *Israēlitēs*, n.pr.g., "of Israel." *Israelite, (one) of Israel.* S: *2475*, BAGD: 381D, CB: 359A

2704 Ἰσσαχάρ, *Issachar*, n.pr., "there is a reward" [Ge. 30:18]; "may [God] show mercy" IDB; "hired hand" KB. *Issachar.* S: *2466**, BAGD: 381D, CB: –

2705 ἵστημι, *histēmi*, v. *(intr.) to stand (firm), be present; to stop; (tr.) to make stand, place, put, establish.* S: *2476*, BAGD: 381D, CB: 356C

2706 ἱστίον, *histion*, n. variant: *sail.* S: *150*, BAGD: 382D, CB: –

2707 ἱστορέω, *historeō*, v. *to get acquainted with, visit.* S: *2477*, BAGD: 383A, CB: 357A

2708 ἰσχυρός, *ischyros*, a. *powerful, strong, forceful.* S: *2478*, BAGD: 383A, CB: 359A

2709 ἰσχύς, *ischys*, n. *strength, power.* S: *2479*, BAGD: 383C, CB: 359A

2710 ἰσχύω, *ischyō*, v. *to be strong, powerful, able.* S: *2480*, BAGD: 383D, CB: 359A

2711 ἴσως, *isōs*, adv. *perhaps.* S: *2481*, BAGD: 384A, CB: –

2712 Ἰταλία, *Italia*, n.pr. *Italy.* S: *2482*, BAGD: 384A, CB: –

2713 Ἰταλικός, *Italikos*, a.pr.g., "of Italy." *Italian.* S: *2483*, BAGD: 384A, CB: –

2714 Ἰτουραῖος, *Itouraios*, a.pr., "pertaining to Jetur." *Iturea.* S: *2484**, BAGD: 384A, CB: –

2715 ἰχθύδιον, *ichthydion*, n. *little fish.* S: *2485*, BAGD: 384B, CB: 358C

2716 ἰχθύς, *ichthys*, n. *fish.* S: *2486*, BAGD: 384B, CB: 358C

2717 ἴχνος, *ichnos*, n. *step, footstep; course of action.* S: *2487*, BAGD: 384B, CB: –

2718 Ἰωαθάμ, *Iōatham*, n.pr., "Yahweh will complete." *Jotham.* S: *2488**, BAGD: 384C, CB: –

2719 Ἰωακίμ, *Iōakim*, n.pr., "Yahweh lifts up, establishes." variant: *Jehoiakim.* S: *150*, BAGD: 384C, CB: –

2720 Ἰωανάν, *Iōanan*, n.pr., prob. "Yahweh is gracious." *Joanan.* S: *2489**, BAGD: 384C, CB: –

2721 Ἰωάννα, *Iōanna*, n.pr., prob. "Yahweh is gracious." *Joanna.* S: *2489 & 2490*, BAGD: 384C, CB: –

2722 Ἰωάννης, *Iōannēs*, n.pr., "Yahweh is gracious." *John.* S: *2491*, BAGD: 384C, CB: –

2723 Ἰωάς, *Iōas*, n.pr., "Yahweh bestows" ISBE, "man of Yahweh" KB. variant: *Joash.* S: *150*, BAGD: 385A, CB: –

2724 Ἰώβ, *Iōb*, n.pr., "where is my father *poss.* where is my father, O God?." *Job.* S: *2492*, BAGD: 385A, CB: –

2725 Ἰωβήδ, *Iōbēd*, n.pr., "servant *or* worshiper." *Obed.* S: *5601**, BAGD: 385B, CB: –

2726 Ἰωδά, *Iōda*, n.pr. *Joda.* S: *2455**, BAGD: 385B, CB: 358C cf. *Ioda*

2727 Ἰωήλ, *Iōēl*, n.pr., "Yahweh is God." *Joel.* S: *2493*, BAGD: 385B, CB: –

2728 Ἰωνάθας, *Iōnathas*, n.pr., "Yahweh has given." variant: *Jonathas.* S: *2491**, BAGD: 385B, CB: –

2729 Ἰωνάμ, *Iōnam*, n.pr., "Yahweh is gracious." *Jonam.* S: *2494**, BAGD: 385B, CB: –

2730 Ἰωνάν, *Iōnan*, n.pr. variant: *Jonan.* S: *2494*, BAGD: 385B cf. Ἰωνάμ, CB: –

2731 Ἰωνᾶς, *Iōnas*, n.pr., "dove." *Jonah.* S: *2495*, BAGD: 385B, CB: –

2732 Ἰωράμ, *Iōram*, n.pr., "Yahweh exalts." *Jehoram.* S: *2496*, BAGD: 385C, CB: –

2733 Ἰωρίμ, *Iōrim*, n.pr. *Jorim.* S: *2497**, BAGD: 385C, CB: –

2734 Ἰωσαφάτ, *Iōsaphat*, n.pr., "Yahweh has judged." *Jehoshaphat.* S: *2498*, BAGD: 385C, CB: –

2735 Ἰωσή, *Iōsē*, n.pr., "he will add." variant: *Jose.* S: *2499*, BAGD: 385C cf. Ἰωσῆς, CB: –

2736 Ἰωσῆς, *Iōsēs*, n.pr., "he will add." *Joses, Joseph.* S: *2500*, BAGD: 385C, CB: –

2737 Ἰωσήφ, *Iōsēph*, n.pr., "he will add." *Joseph.* S: *2501*, BAGD: 385C, CB: –

2738 Ἰωσήχ, *Iōsēch*, n.pr. *Josech.* S: *2501**, BAGD: 385D, CB: –

2739 Ἰωσίας, *Iōsias*, n.pr., "let *or* may Yahweh give." *Josiah.* S: *2502*, BAGD: 386A, CB: –

2740 ἰῶτα, *iōta*, n. *smallest letter (of the Greek alphabet).* S: *2503*, BAGD: 386A, CB: 358C

2741 κ, *k*, letter. *letter of the Greek alphabet.* S: *150*, BAGD: –, CB: –

2742 κάβος, *kabos*, n. variant: *cab.* S: *943**, BAGD: 386A, CB: –

2743 κἀγώ, *kagō*, contr. [c.+p.]. *and I, I also, but I.* S: *2504*, BAGD: 386A, CB: –

2744 κάδος, *kados*, n. variant: *jar, container.* S: *943*,* BAGD: 386B, CB: –

2745 καθά, *katha*, c. *or* adv. *(just) as.* S: *2505,* BAGD: 386B, CB: –

2746 καθαίρεσις, *kathairesis*, n. *tearing down, demolishment, destruction.* S: *2506,* BAGD: 386B, CB: –

2747 καθαιρέω, *kathaireō*, v. *to take down, demolish, overthrow; (pass.) to be robbed of, suffer the loss of.* S: *2507,* BAGD: 386C, CB: –

2748 καθαίρω, *kathairō*, v. *to prune, clear unproductive wood, cleanse.* S: *2508,* BAGD: 386D, CB: 360B

2749 καθάπερ, *kathaper*, c. *or* adv. *as, just as, like.* S: *2509,* BAGD: 387A, CB: –

2750 καθάπτω, *kathaptō*, v. *to fasten, attach, take hold of, seize.* S: *2510,* BAGD: 387A, CB: –

2751 καθαρίζω, *katharizō*, v. *to make clean, cleanse, purify.* S: *2511,* BAGD: 387B, CB: 360B

2752 καθαρισμός, *katharismos*, n. *cleansing, purification, washing.* S: *2512,* BAGD: 387D, CB: 360B

2753 κάθαρμα, *katharma*, n. variant: *scapegoat.* S: *4027*,* BAGD: 387D, CB: 360B

2754 καθαρός, *katharos*, a. *clean, pure, clear of responsibility, innocent.* S: *2513,* BAGD: 388A, CB: 360B

2755 καθαρότης, *katharotēs*, n. *cleanness, purity.* S: *2514,* BAGD: 388B, CB: 360B

2756 καθέδρα, *kathedra*, n. *seat, bench.* S: *2515,* BAGD: 388B, CB: 360C

2757 καθέζομαι, *kathezomai*, v. *to sit down, be seated.* S: *2516,* BAGD: 388C, CB: 360C

2758 καθείς, *katheis*, contr. [pp.+n.]. variant: *individually.* S: *2596 + 1520,* BAGD: 230D cf. εἷς 5.e., CB: –

2759 καθεξῆς, *kathexēs*, adv. *in order, in a sequence.* S: *2517,* BAGD: 388D, CB: –

2760 καθερίζω, *katherizō*, v. variant: *to make clean, cleanse, purify.* S: *2511*,* BAGD: 387B cf. καθαρίζω, CB: –

2761 καθεύδω, *katheudō*, v. *to sleep, fall asleep.* S: *2518,* BAGD: 388D, CB: 360C

2762 καθηγητής, *kathēgētēs*, n. *teacher.* S: *2519,* BAGD: 388D, CB: –

2763 καθήκω, *kathēkō*, v. *to be fitting; (pcpl.) things that ought to be, that are proper.* S: *2520,* BAGD: 389A, CB: 360C

2764 κάθημαι, *kathēmai*, v. *to sit, seat, ride; to live, stay, reside.* S: *2521,* BAGD: 389B, CB: 360C

2765 καθημέραν, *kathēmeran*, contr. [pp.+n.]. variant: *every day, daily, day after day.* S: *2596 + 2250,* BAGD: 345D cf. ἡμέρα 2., CB: –

2766 καθημερινός, *kathēmerinos*, a. *daily.* S: *2522,* BAGD: 389D, CB: –

2767 καθίζω, *kathizō*, v. *(tr.) to place, seat (someone), appoint; (intr.) to sit down, come to rest upon; stay, live.* S: *2523,* BAGD: 389D, CB: 360C

2768 καθίημι, *kathiēmi*, v. *to let down, lower.* S: *2524,* BAGD: 390B, CB: –

2769 καθιστάνω, *kathistanō*, v. variant: *see 2770.* S: *2525*,* BAGD: 390B, CB: 360C cf. *kathistēmi*

2770 καθίστημι, *kathistēmi*, v. *to put in charge, appoint; to escort, bring, take; (pass.) to be made, become, be appointed.* S: *2525,* BAGD: 390B, CB: 360C

2771 καθό, *katho*, adv. variant: *insofar as, to the degree that.* S: *2526,* BAGD: 390D, CB: –

2772 καθολικός, *katholikos*, a. variant: *general, universal.* S: *2526',* BAGD: 390D, CB: –

2773 καθόλου, *katholou*, adv. *at all, entirely, completely.* S: *2527,* BAGD: 391A, CB: –

2774 καθοπλίζω, *kathoplizō*, v. *(mid.) to fully arm or equip (oneself).* S: *2528,* BAGD: 391A, CB: 357A cf. *hoplizō*

2775 καθοράω, *kathoraō*, v. *(pass.) to be clearly seen, perceived.* S: *2529,* BAGD: 391A, CB: 360C

2776 καθότι, *kathoti*, c. *as, to the degree that; because.* S: *2530,* BAGD: 391B, CB: –

2777 καθώς, *kathōs*, adv. *as, just as, even as; in accordance with.* S: *2531,* BAGD: 391B, CB: 360C

2778 καθώσπερ, *kathōsper*, adv. *just as.* S: *2509*,* BAGD: 391D, CB: –

2779 καί, *kai*, c. *and, but, yet, even.* S: *2532,* BAGD: 391D, CB: 359A

2780 Καϊάφας, *Kaiaphas*, n.pr. *Caiaphas.* S: *2533,* BAGD: 393D, CB: –

2781 καίγε, *kaige*, pt. variant: *even, even though.* S: *2534,* BAGD: 152D cf. γέ 3.c., CB: –

2782 Κάϊν, *Kain*, n.pr., "metal worker" BDB KB; "brought forth, acquired" [Ge. 4:1]. *Cain.* S: *2535,* BAGD: 394A, CB: –

2783 Καϊνάμ, *Kainam*, n.pr., "worker in iron, metal worker." *Cainan, Kenan.* S: *2536*,* BAGD: 394A, CB: –

2784 Καϊνάν, *Kainan*, n.pr., "worker in iron, metal worker." variant: *Cainan.* S: *2536,* BAGD: 394A cf. Καϊνάμ, CB: –

2785 καινός, *kainos*, a. *new, latest, anew.* S: *2537,* BAGD: 394A, CB: 359A

2786 καινότης, *kainotēs*, n. *newness.* S: *2538,* BAGD: 394C, CB: 359A

2787 καινοφωνία, *kainophōnia*, n. variant: *chatter, empty talk.* S: *2757*,* BAGD: 428A cf. κενοφωνία, CB: –

2788 καίπερ, *kaiper*, c. *though, even though, although.* S: *2539,* BAGD: 394C, CB: –

2789 καιρός, *kairos*, n. *time (particular and general); right time, opportune time, proper time, appointed time.* S: *2540,* BAGD: 394D, CB: 359A

2790 Καῖσαρ, *Kaisar*, n.pr. *Caesar.* S: *2541,* BAGD: 395D, CB: 359A

2791 Καισάρεια, *Kaisareia*, n.pr. *Caesarea.* S: *2542,* BAGD: 396A, CB: –

2792 καίτοι, *kaitoi*, pt. *and yet.* S: *2543,* BAGD: 396A, CB: –

2793 καίτοιγε, *kaitoige*, pt. *although, and yet.* S: *2544,* BAGD: 396B, CB: –

2794 καίω, *kaiō*, v. *to light (a wick), keep burning.* S: *2545,* BAGD: 396B, CB: 359A

2795 κἀκεῖ, *kakei*, contr. [c.+adv.]. *and there, and where.* S: *2546,* BAGD: 396C, CB: –

2796 κἀκεῖθεν, *kakeithen*, contr. [c.+adv.]. *and from there.* S: *2547,* BAGD: 396D, CB: –

2797 κἀκεῖνος, *kakeinos*, contr. [c.+p.demo.]. *and that one.* S: *2548*, BAGD: 396D, CB: –

2798 κακία, *kakia*, n. *evil, wickedness, depravity, malice.* S: *2549*, BAGD: 397A, CB: 359A

2799 κακοήθεια, *kakoētheia*, n. *malice.* S: *2550*, BAGD: 397B, CB: –

2800 κακολογέω, *kakologeō*, v. *to curse, malign, speak evil of.* S: *2551*, BAGD: 397B, CB: 359B

2801 κακοπάθεια, *kakopatheia*, n. *suffering.* S: *2552*, BAGD: 397B, CB: 359B

2802 κακοπαθέω, *kakopatheō*, v. *to suffer trouble, endure hardship.* S: *2553*, BAGD: 397C, CB: 359B

2803 κακοποιέω, *kakopoieō*, v. *to do evil, do what is wrong.* S: *2554*, BAGD: 397C, CB: 359B

2804 κακοποιός, *kakopoios*, a. *wrongdoing.* S: *2555*, BAGD: 397C, CB: 359B

2805 κακός, *kakos*, a. *evil, wicked, wrong, bad.* S: *2556*, BAGD: 397D, CB: 359B

2806 κακοῦργος, *kakourgos*, a. *criminal, evildoer.* S: *2557*, BAGD: 398B, CB: 359B

2807 κακουχέω, *kakoucheō*, v. *(pass.) to be mistreated, maltreated, tormented.* S: *2558*, BAGD: 398B, CB: –

2808 κακόω, *kakoō*, v. *to harm, mistreat, oppress, persecute; poison, embitter.* S: *2559*, BAGD: 398B, CB: 359B

2809 κακῶς, *kakōs*, adv. *badly, wrongly, terribly; (with 2400) to be ill.* S: *2560*, BAGD: 398C, CB: 359B

2810 κάκωσις, *kakōsis*, n. *oppression, mistreatment.* S: *2561*, BAGD: 398C, CB: 359B

2811 καλάμη, *kalamē*, n. *straw.* S: *2562*, BAGD: 398C, CB:

2812 κάλαμος, *kalamos*, n. *reed, staff, stick, measuring rod, pen.* S: *2563*, BAGD: 398D, CB: 359B

2813 καλέω, *kaleō*, v. *to call, invite, summon.* S: *2564*, BAGD: 398D, CB: 359B

2814 καλλιέλαιος, *kallielaios*, n. *cultivated olive tree.* S: *2565*, BAGD: 400A, CB: 359B

2815 καλοδιδάσκαλος, *kalodidaskalos*, a. *teaching what is good.* S: *2567*, BAGD: 400A, CB: 359B

2816 Καλοὶ λιμένες, *Kaloi limenes*, n.pr., "fair havens." *Fair Havens.* S: *2568**, BAGD: 400A, CB: –

2817 καλοκαγαθία, *kalokagathia*, n. variant: *nobility of character, excellence.* S: *2552**, BAGD: 400B, CB: –

2818 καλοποιέω, *kalopoieō*, v. *to do what is right or good.* S: *2569*, BAGD: 400B, CB: 359B

2819 καλός, *kalos*, a. *good, right; beautiful, fine, excellent.* S: *2570 & 2566*, BAGD: 400B, CB: 359B

2820 κάλυμμα, *kalymma*, n. *veil, covering.* S: *2571*, BAGD: 400D, CB: 359B

2821 καλύπτω, *kalyptō*, v. *cover, veil, hide.* S: *2572*, BAGD: 401A, CB: 359B

2822 καλῶς, *kalōs*, adv. *rightly, well.* S: *2573*, BAGD: 401B, CB: 359B

2823 κάμηλος, *kamēlos*, n. *camel.* S: *2574*, BAGD: 401C, CB: 359B

2824 κάμιλος, *kamilos*, n. variant: *rope, ship's cable.* S: *2574**, BAGD: 401D, CB: –

2825 κάμινος, *kaminos*, n. *furnace, oven.* S: *2575*, BAGD: 401D, CB: –

2826 καμμύω, *kammyō*, v. *close, shut (the eyes).* S: *2576*, BAGD: 402A, CB: –

2827 κάμνω, *kamnō*, v. *to grow weary; be sick.* S: *2577*, BAGD: 402A, CB: –

2828 κάμπτω, *kamptō*, v. *to bend, bow (on a knee).* S: *2578*, BAGD: 402B, CB: 359B

2829 κἄν, *kan*, contr. [c.+pt.]. *and if, even if.* S: *2579*, BAGD: 402C, CB: –

2830 Κανά, *Kana*, n.pr., "reed." *Cana.* S: *2580**, BAGD: 402C, CB: –

2831 Καναναῖος, *Kananaios*, n.pr., "zealot or of Cana." *Zealot, Cananaean.* S: *2581**, BAGD: 402D, CB: 359B

2832 Κανανίτης, *Kananitēs*, n.pr.g., "of Canaan or of Cana." variant: *Canaanite, from Cana.* S: *2581*, BAGD: 402D, CB: –

2833 Κανδάκη, *Kandakē*, n.pr., *title?* "queen." *Candace.* S: *2582*, BAGD: 402D, CB: –

2834 κανών, *kanōn*, n. *rule, standard; sphere of activity, limit.* S: *2583*, BAGD: 403A, CB: 359B

2835 Καπερναούμ, *Kapernaoum*, n.pr., "village of Nahum." variant: *Capernaum.* S: *2584*, BAGD: 426B cf. Καφαρναούμ, CB: –

2836 καπηλεύω, *kapēleuō*, v. *to act as a peddler, trade in for profit.* S: *2585*, BAGD: 403A, CB: 359B

2837 καπνός, *kapnos*, n. *smoke.* S: *2586*, BAGD: 403B, CB: –

2838 Καππαδοκία, *Kappadokia*, n.pr. *Cappadocia.* S: *2587*, BAGD: 403B, CB: –

2839 καραδοκία, *karadokia*, n. variant: *eager expectation.* S: *603**, BAGD: 403B, CB: –

2840 καρδία, *kardia*, n. *heart, mind (seat of thought and emotion).* S: *2588*, BAGD: 403B, CB: 359B

2841 καρδιογνώστης, *kardiognōstēs*, n. *knower of the heart.* S: *2589*, BAGD: 404C, CB: 359B

2842 Κάρπος, *Karpos*, n.pr., "fruit(ful)." *Carpus.* S: *2591*, BAGD: 404C, CB: 359B

2843 καρπός, *karpos*, n. *fruit, crop, harvest.* S: *2590*, BAGD: 404C, CB: 359B

2844 καρποφορέω, *karpophoreō*, v. *to produce a crop, bear fruit.* S: *2592*, BAGD: 405A, CB: 359B

2845 καρποφόρος, *karpophoros*, a. *crop, fruitbearing.* S: *2593*, BAGD: 405B, CB: –

2846 καρτερέω, *kartereō*, v. *to persevere, endure.* S: *2594*, BAGD: 405B, CB: 359C

2847 κάρφος, *karphos*, n. *speck, chip, particle.* S: *2595*, BAGD: 405C, CB: –

2848 κατά, *kata*, pp. *(gen.) against, contrary to, opposed; down, throughout; (acc.) in, by, with, in accordance with, for.* S: *2596*, BAGD: 405C, CB: 359C

2849 καταβαίνω, *katabainō*, v. *to go down, descend.* S: *2597*, BAGD: 408B, CB: 359C

2850 καταβάλλω, *kataballō*, v. *(pass.) to be struck down; (mid.) to lay (a foundation).* S: *2598*, BAGD: 408D, CB: 359C

2851 καταβαρέω, *katabareō*, v. *to burden, be a burden.* S: *2599*, BAGD: 408D, CB: 360A

2852 καταβαρύνω, *katabarynō*, v. *(pass.) to become heavy, burdened.* S: *925**, BAGD: 408D, CB: –

2853 κατάβασις, *katabasis*, n. *place that goes down, slope, down-grade.* S: *2600*, BAGD: 409A, CB: –

2854 καταβιβάζω, *katabibazō*, v. variant: *to bring down.* S: *2601*, BAGD: 409A, CB: –

2855 καταβοάω, *kataboaō*, v. variant: *to cry out, bring charges, complain.* S: *150*, BAGD: 409A, CB: –

2856 καταβολή, *katabolē*, n. *creation (of the world), beginning, foundation.* S: *2602*, BAGD: 409A, CB: 360A

2857 καταβραβεύω, *katabrabeuō*, v. *to disqualify for a prize, decide against.* S: *2603*, BAGD: 409B, CB: 360A

2858 καταγγελεύς, *katangeleus*, n. *advocate, proclaimer.* S: *2604*, BAGD: 409B, CB: 360A

2859 καταγγέλλω, *katangellō*, v. *to preach, proclaim, advocate, report.* S: *2605*, BAGD: 409B, CB: 360A

2860 καταγελάω, *katagelaō*, v. *to laugh at, mock.* S: *2606*, BAGD: 409C, CB: 360A

2861 καταγινώσκω, *kataginōskō*, v. *to condemn, convict; (pass.) to be in the wrong, condemned.* S: *2607*, BAGD: 409D, CB: 360A

2862 κατάγνυμι, *katagnymi*, v. *to break.* S: *2608*, BAGD: 409D, CB: –

2863 καταγράφω, *katagraphō*, v. *to write.* S: *1125**, BAGD: 410A, CB: –

2864 κατάγω, *katagō*, v. *to bring, bring down, land (on shore).* S: *2609*, BAGD: 410A, CB: 339C cf. *agō*

2865 καταγωνίζομαι, *katagōnizomai*, v. *(mid.) to conquer, defeat, overcome.* S: *2610*, BAGD: 410A, CB: 360A

2866 καταδέω, *katadeō*, v. *to bandage, bind up.* S: *2611*, BAGD: 410B, CB: 346C cf. *deō*

2867 κατάδηλος, *katadēlos*, a. *clear, quite plain.* S: *2612*, BAGD: 410B, CB: –

2868 καταδικάζω, *katadikazō*, v. *to condemn.* S: *2613*, BAGD: 410B, CB: 360A

2869 καταδίκη, *katadikē*, n. *condemnation.* S: *1349**, BAGD: 410B, CB: 360A

2870 καταδιώκω, *katadiōkō*, v. *to look for, search for.* S: *2614*, BAGD: 410C, CB: 360A

2871 καταδουλόω, *katadouloō*, v. *to make a slave, enslave.* S: *2615*, BAGD: 410C, CB: –

2872 καταδυναστεύω, *katadynasteuō*, v. *(act.) to exploit, oppress, dominate; (pass.) to be under the power of, oppressed by.* S: *2616*, BAGD: 410C, CB: –

2873 κατάθεμα, *katathema*, n. *cursed thing.* S: *2652**, BAGD: 410C, CB: 360B

2874 καταθεματίζω, *katathematizō*, v. *to (call down a) curse.* S: *2653**, BAGD: 410D, CB: 360B

2875 καταισχύνω, *kataischynō*, v. *to dishonor, humiliate, shame, disappoint.* S: *2617*, BAGD: 410D, CB: 360A

2876 κατακαίω, *katakaiō*, v. *to burn up, consume.* S: *2618*, BAGD: 411A, CB: –

2877 κατακαλύπτω, *katakalyptō*, v. *(mid.) to cover (the head).* S: *2619*, BAGD: 411A, CB: 360A cf. *-omai*

2878 κατακαυχάομαι, *katakauchaomai*, v. *to boast about; to triumph over.* S: *2620*, BAGD: 411B, CB: 360A

2879 κατάκειμαι, *katakeimai*, v. *to lie down (in bed); to recline (at dinner).* S: *2621*, BAGD: 411C, CB: 360C cf. *keimai*

2880 κατακλάω, *kataklaō*, v. *to break in pieces.* S: *2622*, BAGD: 411C, CB: 361A cf. *klaō*

2881 κατακλείω, *katakleiō*, v. *to lock up.* S: *2623*, BAGD: 411C, CB: –

2882 κατακληροδοτέω, *kataklērodoteō*, v. variant: *to parcel out by lot.* S: *2624*, BAGD: 411D, CB: –

2883 κατακληρονομέω, *kataklēronomeō*, v. *to give as an inheritance.* S: *2624**, BAGD: 411D, CB: –

2884 κατακλίνω, *kataklinō*, v. *(act.) to cause to sit; (pass.) to recline (at a table).* S: *2625*, BAGD: 411D, CB: –

2885 κατακλύζω, *kataklyzō*, v. *(pass.) to be deluged, flooded.* S: *2626*, BAGD: 411D, CB: –

2886 κατακλυσμός, *kataklysmos*, n. *flood, deluge.* S: *2627*, BAGD: 411D, CB: 360A

2887 κατακολουθέω, *katakoloutheō*, v. *to follow.* S: *2628*, BAGD: 412A, CB: 340B cf. *akoloutheō*

2888 κατακόπτω, *katakoptō*, v. *to cut.* S: *2629*, BAGD: 412A, CB: 343A cf. *apokoptō*

2889 κατακρημνίζω, *katakrēmnizō*, v. *to throw down a cliff.* S: *2630*, BAGD: 412A, CB: –

2890 κατάκριμα, *katakrima*, n. *condemnation.* S: *2631*, BAGD: 412A, CB: 360A

2891 κατακρίνω, *katakrinō*, v. *to condemn.* S: *2632*, BAGD: 412A, CB: 360A

2892 κατάκρισις, *katakrisis*, n. *condemnation.* S: *2633*, BAGD: 412B, CB: 360A

2893 κατακύπτω, *katakyptō*, v. *to stoop down, bend down.* S: *2596 + 2955*, BAGD: 412C, CB: –

2894 κατακυριεύω, *katakyrieuō*, v. *to lord it over, gain dominion over, subdue.* S: *2634*, BAGD: 412C, CB: 360A

2895 καταλαλέω, *katalaleō*, v. *to speak against, slander, accuse.* S: *2635*, BAGD: 412C, CB: 360A

2896 καταλαλιά, *katalalia*, n. *slander, defamation, evil speech.* S: *2636*, BAGD: 412D, CB: 360A

2897 κατάλαλος, *katalalos*, a. *slanderous, defamatory.* S: *2637*, BAGD: 412D, CB: 360A

2898 καταλαμβάνω, *katalambanō*, v. *to obtain, attain, take hold of; seize, overtake; (mid.) to grasp, understand, realize, find out.* S: *2638*, BAGD: 412D, CB: 360A cf. *-omai*

2899 καταλέγω, *katalegō*, v. *to put on a list, enroll, select.* S: *2639*, BAGD: 413B, CB: –

2900 κατάλειμμα, *kataleimma*, n. variant: *remnant.* S: *2640*, BAGD: 413C, CB: 360A

2901 καταλείπω, *kataleipō*, v. *to leave (behind), neglect; (pass.) remain (behind).* S: *2641*, BAGD: 413C, CB: 360A

2902 καταλιθάζω, *katalithazō*, v. *to stone to death.* S: *2642*, BAGD: 413D, CB: –

2903 καταλλαγή, *katallagē*, n. *reconciliation.* S: *2643*, BAGD: 414A, CB: 360A

2904 καταλλάσσω, *katallassō*, v. *to reconcile.* S: *2644*, BAGD: 414A, CB: 360A

2905 κατάλοιπος, *kataloipos*, a. *remaining, left over; (as noun) remnant, the rest.* S: *2645*, BAGD: 414B, CB: 360A

2906 κατάλυμα, *katalyma*, n. *guest room; inn.* S: *2646*, BAGD: 414B, CB: 360A

2907 καταλύω, *katalyō*, v. *(tr.) throw down, abolish, destroy; (intr.) to be a guest, rest, find lodging.* S: *2647*, BAGD: 414B, CB: 360A

2908 καταμανθάνω, *katamanthanō*, v. *notice carefully, consider closely.* S: *2648*, BAGD: 414C, CB: –

2909 καταμαρτυρέω, *katamartyreō*, v. *to bring testimony against, bear testimony against.* S: *2649*, BAGD: 414D, CB: 360A

2910 καταμένω, *katamenō*, v. *to stay, live.* S: *2650*, BAGD: 414D, CB: –

2911 καταμόνας, *katamonas*, a. variant: *in private, alone.* S: *2651*, BAGD: 527C cf. μόνος 3., CB: 359C

2912 κατανάθεμα, *katanathema*, n. variant: *curse.* S: *2652*, BAGD: 414D, CB: 360B

2913 καταναθεματίζω, *katanathematizō*, v. variant: *to curse.* S: *2653*, BAGD: 414D, CB: 360B

2914 καταναλίσκω, *katanaliskō*, v. *to consume.* S: *2654*, BAGD: 414D, CB: –

2915 καταναρκάω, *katanarkaō*, v. *to burden, be a burden.* S: *2655*, BAGD: 414D, CB: –

2916 κατανεύω, *kataneuō*, v. *to signal, nod.* S: *2656*, BAGD: 415A, CB: –

2917 κατανοέω, *katanoeō*, v. *to pay attention, notice, observe; consider, contemplate.* S: *2657*, BAGD: 415A, CB: 360A

2918 κατανтάω, *katantaō*, v. *to come to, arrive at; attain, reach.* S: *2658*, BAGD: 415B, CB: 360A

2919 κατάνυξις, *katanyxis*, n. *stupor, bewilderment.* S: *2659*, BAGD: 415C, CB: –

2920 κατανύσσομαι, *katanyssomai*, v. *to be pierced, stabbed.* S: *2660**, BAGD: 415C, CB: –

2921 καταξιόω, *kataxioō*, v. *(pass.) to be counted worthy, considered worthy.* S: *2661*, BAGD: 415C, CB: 360B

2922 καταπατέω, *katapateō*, v. *to trample.* S: *2662*, BAGD: 415D, CB: 360A

2923 κατάπαυσις, *katapausis*, n. *rest.* S: *2663*, BAGD: 415D, CB: 360A

2924 καταπαύω, *katapauō*, v. *to keep from, restrain; to give rest; to rest, cease.* S: *2664*, BAGD: 415D, CB: 360A

2925 καταπέτασμα, *katapetasma*, n. *curtain.* S: *2665*, BAGD: 416A, CB: 360A

2926 καταπίμπρημι, *katapimprēmi*, v. variant: *to burn to ashes.* S: *150*, BAGD: 416B, CB: –

2927 καταπίνω, *katapinō*, v. *to swallow, devour; (pass.) to be swallowed up, overwhelmed, drowned.* S: *2666*, BAGD: 416B, CB: 360B

2928 καταπίπτω, *katapiptō*, v. *to fall down.* S: *2667*, BAGD: 416C, CB: 360B

2929 καταπλέω, *katapleō*, v. *to sail to.* S: *2668*, BAGD: 416D, CB: –

2930 καταπονέω, *kataponeō*, v. *(pass.) to be oppressed, distressed.* S: *2669*, BAGD: 416D, CB: –

2931 καταποντίζω, *katapontizō*, v. *(pass.) to be drowned; to sink.* S: *2670*, BAGD: 417A, CB: –

2932 κατάρα, *katara*, n. *curse, imprecation.* S: *2671*, BAGD: 417A, CB: 360B

2933 καταράομαι, *kataraomai*, v. *(mid.) to curse.* S: *2672*, BAGD: 417A, CB: 360B

2934 καταργέω, *katargeō*, v. *to nullify, abolish, make ineffective; (pass.) cease, pass away.* S: *2673*, BAGD: 417B, CB: 360B

2935 καταριθμέω, *katarithmeō*, v. *(pass.) to be numbered among, belong to.* S: *2674*, BAGD: 417C, CB: –

2936 καταρτίζω, *katartizō*, v. *to restore, put in order, mend; to make complete, equip, train; to prepare, ordain.* S: *2675*, BAGD: 417D, CB: 360B

2937 κατάρτισις, *katartisis*, n. *perfection, completion.* S: *2676*, BAGD: 418A, CB: 360B

2938 καταρτισμός, *katartismos*, n. *preparation, training, equipping.* S: *2677*, BAGD: 418A, CB: 360B

2939 κατασείω, *kataseiō*, v. *to motion, signal.* S: *2678*, BAGD: 418A, CB: 360B

2940 κατασκάπτω, *kataskaptō*, v. *(act.) to tear down; (pass.) to be ruined.* S: *2679*, BAGD: 418B, CB: –

2941 κατασκευάζω, *kataskeuazō*, v. *to prepare, make ready; to build, construct; to set up, arrange, furnish.* S: *2680*, BAGD: 418B, CB: 360B

2942 κατασκηνόω, *kataskēnoō*, v. *to perch, nest; to live, dwell.* S: *2681*, BAGD: 418C, CB: 360B

2943 κατασκήνωσις, *kataskēnōsis*, n. *nest.* S: *2682*, BAGD: 418C, CB: 360B

2944 κατασκιάζω, *kataskiazō*, v. *to overshadow.* S: *2683*, BAGD: 418D, CB: –

2945 κατασκοπέω, *kataskopeō*, v. *to spy on, lie in wait for.* S: *2684*, BAGD: 418D, CB: –

2946 κατάσκοπος, *kataskopos*, n. *spy.* S: *2685*, BAGD: 418D, CB: 360B

2947 κατασοφίζομαι, *katasophizomai*, v. *to deal treacherously with.* S: *2686*, BAGD: 418D, CB: –

2948 καταστέλλω, *katastellō*, v. *(act.) to quiet, restrain.* S: *2687*, BAGD: 419A, CB: –

2949 κατάστημα, *katastēma*, n. *the way one lives, behavior.* S: *2688*, BAGD: 419A, CB: –

2950 καταστολή, *katastolē*, n. *appearance, behavior.* S: *2689*, BAGD: 419A, CB: –

2951 καταστρέφω, *katastrephō*, v. *to overturn, upset.* S: *2690*, BAGD: 419A, CB: –

2952 καταστρηνιάω, *katastrēniaō*, v. *to be filled with desires that conflict with dedication to someone.* S: *2691*, BAGD: 419B, CB: –

2953 καταστροφή, *katastrophē*, n. *ruin, destruction.* S: *2692*, BAGD: 419B, CB: –

2954 καταστρώννυμι, *katastrōnnymi*, v. *(pass.) to be scattered.* S: *2693*, BAGD: 419B, CB: –

2955 κατασύρω, *katasyrō*, v. *to drag away.* S: *2694*, BAGD: 419B, CB: –

2956 κατασφάζω, *katasphazō*, v. *to kill, slaughter, strike down.* S: *2695*, BAGD: 419C, CB: –

2957 κατασφάττω, *katasphattō*, v. variant: *to kill, slaughter, strike down.* S: *2695,* BAGD: 419C, CB: –

2958 κατασφραγίζω, *katasphragizō*, v. *(pass.) to be sealed up.* S: *2696,* BAGD: 419C, CB: 360B

2959 κατάσχεσις, *kataschesis*, n. *possession, taking into possession.* S: *2697,* BAGD: 419C, CB: –

2960 κατατίθημι, *katatithēmi*, v. *(mid.) to grant a favor, do a favor.* S: *2698,* BAGD: 419C, CB: –

2961 κατατομή, *katatomē*, n. *mutilation, cutting away.* S: *2699,* BAGD: 419D, CB: 360B

2962 κατατοξεύω, *katatoxeuō*, v. variant: *to shoot down.* S: *2700,* BAGD: 419D, CB: –

2963 κατατρέχω, *katatrechō*, v. *to run down.* S: *2701,* BAGD: 419D, CB: –

2964 καταυγάζω, *kataugazō*, v. variant: *to shine upon, illuminate.* S: *826*,* BAGD: 419D, CB: –

2965 καταφέρω, *katapherō*, v. *to cast (a vote) against; to bring (charges); (pass.) to be overwhelmed (by sleep).* S: *2702,* BAGD: 419D, CB: –

2966 καταφεύγω, *katapheugō*, v. *to flee, take refuge.* S: *2703,* BAGD: 420A, CB: 360B

2967 καταφθείρω, *kataphtheirō*, v. *(pass.) to be depraved, corrupt.* S: *2704,* BAGD: 420A, CB: 370C cf. *phtheirō*

2968 καταφιλέω, *kataphileō*, v. *to kiss.* S: *2705,* BAGD: 420B, CB: 360B

2969 καταφρονέω, *kataphroneō*, v. *to despise, look down on, scorn, show contempt.* S: *2706,* BAGD: 420B, CB: 360B

2970 καταφροιητής, *kataphronētēs*, n. *scoffer, despiser.* S: *2707,* BAGD: 420C, CB: 360B

2971 καταφωνέω, *kataphōneō*, v. variant: *to shout at.* S: *2019*,* BAGD: 420C, CB: –

2972 καταχέω, *katacheō*, v. *to pour out, pour down.* S: *2708,* BAGD: 420C, CB: –

2973 καταχθόνιος, *katachthonios*, a. *under the earth, subterranean.* S: *2709,* BAGD: 420D, CB: 360A

2974 καταχράομαι, *katachraomai*, v. *to make full use of; to be engrossed in.* S: *2710,* BAGD: 420D, CB: –

2975 καταψηφίζομαι, *katapsēphizomai*, v. variant: *to be enrolled.* S: *4785*,* BAGD: 421A, CB: –

2976 καταψύχω, *katapsychō*, v. *to cool off, refresh with.* S: *2711,* BAGD: 421A, CB: –

2977 κατείδωλος, *kateidōlos*, a. *full of idols / images.* S: *2712,* BAGD: 421A, CB: 360B

2978 κατέναντι, *katenanti*, adv. *ahead, before, in the sight of; opposite of.* S: *2713,* BAGD: 421B, CB: –

2979 κατενώπιον, *katenōpion*, adv. & pp.*. *in the sight of, in the presence of; before.* S: *2714,* BAGD: 421B, CB: 360B

2980 κατεξουσιάζω, *katexousiazō*, v. *to exercise authority over.* S: *2715,* BAGD: 421C, CB: 360B

2981 κατεργάζομαι, *katergazomai*, v. *to produce, accomplish, bring about, do.* S: *2716,* BAGD: 421C, CB: –

2982 κατέρχομαι, *katerchomai*, v. *to go down, come down.* S: *2718,* BAGD: 422A, CB: 352B cf. *erchomai*

2983 κατεσθίω, *katesthiō*, v. *to eat up, consume.* S: *2719,* BAGD: 422A, CB: –

2984 κατέσθω, *katesthō*, v. variant: *to eat up, consume.* S: *2719*,* BAGD: 422A, CB: –

2985 κατευθύνω, *kateuthynō*, v. *to guide, direct, lead.* S: *2720,* BAGD: 422B, CB: –

2986 κατευλογέω, *kateulogeō*, v. *to bless.* S: *2127*,* BAGD: 422C, CB: 360B

2987 κατεφίσταμαι, *katephistamai*, v. *to make an attack upon, rise up against.* S: *2721*,* BAGD: 422C, CB: –

2988 κατέχω, *katechō*, v. *to hold back, suppress, restrain; hold fast, possess; (pass.) to be bound.* S: *2722,* BAGD: 422C, CB: 360B

2989 κατηγορέω, *katēgoreō*, v. *to accuse, bring charges against.* S: *2723,* BAGD: 423A, CB: 360B

2990 κατηγορία, *katēgoria*, n. *(legal) charge, accusation.* S: *2724,* BAGD: 423C, CB: 360B

2991 κατήγορος, *katēgoros*, n. *accuser.* S: *2725,* BAGD: 423C, CB: 360B

2992 κατήγωρ, *katēgōr*, n. *accuser.* S: *2725*,* BAGD: 423C, CB: –

2993 κατήφεια, *katēpheia*, n. *gloominess.* S: *2726,* BAGD: 423C, CB: –

2994 κατηχέω, *katēcheō*, v. *(act.) to instruct; (pass.) to be instructed, informed.* S: *2727,* BAGD: 423D, CB: 360B

2995 κατιόω, *katioō*, v. *(pass.) to become corroded, tarnished.* S: *2728,* BAGD: 424A, CB: –

2996 κατισχύω, *katischyō*, v. *to overcome, prevail; to be able.* S: *2729,* BAGD: 424A, CB: 360C

2997 κατοικέω, *katoikeō*, v. *to live in, reside in, settle.* S: *2730,* BAGD: 424A, CB: 360C

2998 κατοίκησις, *katoikēsis*, n. *where one lives, residence.* S: *2731,* BAGD: 424C, CB: –

2999 κατοικητήριον, *katoikētērion*, n. *dwelling place, home.* S: *2732,* BAGD: 424C, CB: 360C

3000 κατοικία, *katoikia*, n. *where one lives, dwelling place.* S: *2733,* BAGD: 424C, CB: –

3001 κατοικίζω, *katoikizō*, v. *to cause to live in.* S: *2730*,* BAGD: 424C, CB: –

3002 κατοπτρίζω, *katoptrizō*, v. *(mid.) to reflect or to look at, contemplate.* S: *2734*,* BAGD: 424D, CB: –

3003 κατόρθωμα, *katorthōma*, n. variant: *success, prosperity, good order.* S: *2735,* BAGD: 424D, CB: –

3004 κάτω, *katō*, adv. *below; down, downward; bottom.* S: *2736,* BAGD: 425A, CB: 360C

3005 κατώτερος, *katōteros*, a. *lower.* S: *2737,* BAGD: 425A, CB: 360C

3006 κατωτέρω, *katōterō*, adv. *under, lower.* S: *2736,* BAGD: 425A, CB: –

3007 Καῦδα, *Kauda*, n.pr. *Cauda.* S: *2802*,* BAGD: 433B cf. Κλαυ=δα, CB: –

3008 καῦμα, *kauma*, n. *(scorching) heat.* S: *2738,* BAGD: 425B, CB: 360C

3009 καυματίζω, *kaumatizō*, v. *(act.) to scorch, burn; (pass.) to be scorched, seared.* S: *2739,* BAGD: 425B, CB: 360C

3010 καυματόω, *kaumatoō*, v. variant: *to be scorched by the heat.* S: *2739*,* BAGD: 425B, CB: –

3011 καῦσις, *kausis*, n. *burning.* S: *2740,* BAGD: 425B, CB: –

3012 καυσόω, *kausoō*, v. *(pass.) to be consumed by fire, burned up.* S: *2741*, BAGD: 425B, CB: –

3013 καυστηριάζω, *kaustēriazō*, v. *(pass.) to be seared as with a hot iron.* S: *2743**, BAGD: 425C, CB: 360C cf. *-omai*

3014 καύσων, *kausōn*, n. *(scorching) heat, hot day.* S: *2742*, BAGD: 425C, CB: –

3015 καυτηριάζω, *kautēriazō*, v. variant: *(pass.) to be seared with a hot iron.* S: *2743*, BAGD: 425C, CB: 360C

3016 καυχάομαι, *kauchaomai*, v. *to boast, brag about; to rejoice in, glory in.* S: *2744*, BAGD: 425C, CB: 360C

3017 καύχημα, *kauchēma*, n. *something to boast about, boasting; pride, joy.* S: *2745*, BAGD: 426A, CB: 360C

3018 καύχησις, *kauchēsis*, n. *boasting, pride; glorying in.* S: *2746*, BAGD: 426B, CB: 360C

3019 Καφαρναούμ, *Kapharnaoum*, n.pr., "village of Nahum." *Capernaum.* S: *2584**, BAGD: 426B, CB: –

3020 Κεγχρεαί, *Kenchreai*, n.pr. *Cenchrea.* S: *2747*, BAGD: 426C, CB: –

3021 κέδρος, *kedros*, n. variant: *cedar tree.* S: *2748**, BAGD: 426C, CB: –

3022 Κεδρών, *Kedrōn*, n.pr. *Kidron.* S: *2748*, BAGD: 426C, CB: –

3023 κεῖμαι, *keimai*, v. *to lay, lie, be laid, laid out; be destined, appointed.* S: *2749*, BAGD: 426C, CB: 360C

3024 κειρία, *keiria*, n. *strip of linen, bandage, graveclothes.* S: *2750*, BAGD: 427A, CB: –

3025 κείρω, *keirō*, v. *(act.) to shear (another); (mid.) to have one's hair cut.* S: *2751*, BAGD: 427A, CB: –

3026 κέλευσμα, *keleusma*, n. *loud command, signal.* S: *2752*, BAGD: 427B, CB: 360C

3027 κελεύω, *keleuō*, v. *to order, direct, command.* S: *2753*, BAGD: 427B, CB: 360C

3028 κενεμβατεύω, *kenembateuō*, v. variant: *to step on emptiness, make a misstep.* S: *150*, BAGD: 427C, CB: –

3029 κενοδοξία, *kenodoxia*, n. *vain conceit, empty conceit.* S: *2754*, BAGD: 427C, CB: 361A

3030 κενόδοξος, *kenodoxos*, a. *conceited.* S: *2755*, BAGD: 427D, CB: 361A

3031 κενός, *kenos*, a. *empty, empty-handed; vain, ineffective, useless; foolish.* S: *2756*, BAGD: 427D, CB: 361A

3032 κενοφωνία, *kenophōnia*, n. *chatter, empty talk.* S: *2757*, BAGD: 428A, CB: –

3033 κενόω, *kenoō*, v. *to empty, deprive; (pass.) to be hollow, emptied, of no value.* S: *2758*, BAGD: 428A, CB: 361A

3034 κέντρον, *kentron*, n. *sting, goad.* S: *2759*, BAGD: 428B, CB: 361A

3035 κεντυρίων, *kentyriōn*, n. *centurion.* S: *2760*, BAGD: 428C, CB: 361A

3036 κενῶς, *kenōs*, adv. *without reason, in vain, to no purpose.* S: *2761*, BAGD: 428C, CB: –

3037 κεραία, *keraia*, n. *least stroke of a pen, projection [a portion of a letter of the alphabet].* S: *2762*, BAGD: 428D, CB: 361A

3038 κεραμεύς, *kerameus*, n. *potter.* S: *2763*, BAGD: 428D, CB: 361A

3039 κεραμικός, *keramikos*, a. *pertaining to a potter.* S: *2764*, BAGD: 428D, CB: 361A

3040 κεράμιον, *keramion*, n. *clay jar.* S: *2765*, BAGD: 428D, CB: 361A

3041 κέραμος, *keramos*, n. *clay roof tile.* S: *2766*, BAGD: 429A, CB: 361A

3042 κεράννυμι, *kerannymi*, v. *to mix; (pass.) to be poured.* S: *2767*, BAGD: 429A, CB: 361A

3043 κέρας, *keras*, n. *horn.* S: *2768*, BAGD: 429B, CB: 361A

3044 κεράτιον, *keration*, n. *carob pod.* S: *2769*, BAGD: 429B, CB: –

3045 κερδαίνω, *kerdainō*, v. *to gain; make money; win over; spare.* S: *2770*, BAGD: 429C, CB: 361A

3046 κέρδος, *kerdos*, n. *gain, profit.* S: *2771*, BAGD: 429C, CB: 361A

3047 κέρμα, *kerma*, n. *coin.* S: *2772*, BAGD: 429D, CB: –

3048 κερματιστής, *kermatistēs*, n. *money exchanger.* S: *2773*, BAGD: 429D, CB: –

3049 κεφάλαιον, *kephalaion*, n. *the (main) point; price, sum of money.* S: *2774*, BAGD: 429D, CB: 361A

3050 κεφαλαιόω, *kephalaioō*, v. variant: *to strike on the head.* S: *2775*, BAGD: 430A, CB: 361A

3051 κεφαλή, *kephalē*, n. *head.* S: *2776*, BAGD: 430A, CB: 361A

3052 κεφαλιόω, *kephalioō*, v. *to strike on the head.* S: *2775*, BAGD: 430C, CB: 361A

3053 κεφαλίς, *kephalis*, n. *section of a scroll.* S: *2777*, BAGD: 430C, CB: 361A

3054 κηδεύω, *kēdeuō*, v. variant: *to take care of, bury.* S: *150*, BAGD: 430D, CB: –

3055 κημόω, *kēmoō*, v. *to muzzle.* S: *5392**, BAGD: 430D, CB: –

3056 κῆνσος, *kēnsos*, n. *(poll) tax.* S: *2778*, BAGD: 430D, CB: 361A

3057 κῆπος, *kēpos*, n. *garden, grove.* S: *2779*, BAGD: 430D, CB: –

3058 κηπουρός, *kēpouros*, n. *gardener.* S: *2780*, BAGD: 430D, CB: –

3059 κηρίον, *kērion*, n. variant: *wax, honeycomb.* S: *2781*, BAGD: 430D, CB: –

3060 κήρυγμα, *kērygma*, n. *preaching, proclamation, message.* S: *2782*, BAGD: 430D, CB: 361A

3061 κῆρυξ, *kēryx*, n. *herald, preacher, proclaimer.* S: *2783**, BAGD: 431A, CB: 361A

3062 κηρύσσω, *kēryssō*, v. *to preach, proclaim, tell.* S: *2784*, BAGD: 431B, CB: 361A

3063 κῆτος, *kētos*, n. *huge fish.* S: *2785*, BAGD: 431D, CB: 361A

3064 Κηφᾶς, *Kēphas*, n.pr., "rock." *Cephas (Aramaic for Peter).* S: *2786*, BAGD: 431D, CB: 361A

3065 κιβώριον, *kibōrion*, n. *ciborium.* S: *150*, BAGD: 431D, CB: –

3066 κιβωτός, *kibōtos*, n. *ark, box, chest.* S: *2787*, BAGD: 431D, CB: 361A

3067 κιθάρα, *kithara*, n. *harp, lyre.* S: *2788*, BAGD: 432A, CB: –

3068 κιθαρίζω, *kitharizō*, v. *to play the harp or lyre.* S: *2789*, BAGD: 432A, CB: –

3069 κιθαρῳδός, *kitharōdos*, n. *harpist, lyre player.* S: *2790*, BAGD: 432A, CB: –

3070 Κιλικία, *Kilikia*, n.pr. *Cilicia.* S: *2791*, BAGD: 432A, CB: –

3071 Κίλιξ, *Kilix*, n.pr.g., "of Cilicia." variant: *Cilician.* S: *2791*, BAGD: 432B, CB: –

3072 κινάμωμον, *kinamōmon*, n. variant: *cinnamon.* S: *2792*, BAGD: 432D cf. κιννάμωμον, CB: –

3073 κινδυνεύω, *kindyneuō*, v. *to be in danger.* S: *2793*, BAGD: 432B, CB: 361A

3074 κίνδυνος, *kindynos*, n. *danger, risk.* S: *2794*, BAGD: 432B, CB: 361A

3075 κινέω, *kineō*, v. *to move, remove; to shake, stir up; (pass.) to be moved, removed; be aroused.* S: *2795*, BAGD: 432C, CB: –

3076 κίνησις, *kinēsis*, n. variant: *motion.* S: *2796*, BAGD: 432D, CB: –

3077 κιννάμωμον, *kinnamōmon*, n. *cinnamon.* S: *2792**, BAGD: 432D, CB: –

3078 Κίς, *Kis*, n.pr., "bow, power." *Kish.* S: *2797*, BAGD: 432D, CB: –

3079 κίχρημι, *kichrēmi*, v. *to lend.* S: *5531**, BAGD: 433A, CB: –

3080 κλάδος, *klados*, n. *branch, twig.* S: *2798*, BAGD: 433A, CB: 361A

3081 κλαίω, *klaiō*, v. *to weep, cry, wail, mourn.* S: *2799*, BAGD: 433A, CB: 361A

3082 κλάσις, *klasis*, n. *breaking.* S: *2800*, BAGD: 433B, CB: 361A

3083 κλάσμα, *klasma*, n. *broken piece, fragment.* S: *2801*, BAGD: 433B, CB: 361B

3084 Κλαῦδα, *Klauda*, n.pr. variant: *Clauda.* S: *2802**, BAGD: 433B, CB: –

3085 Κλαύδη, *Klaudē*, n.pr. variant: *Clauda.* S: *2802*, BAGD: 433B cf. Κλαυ=δα, CB: –

3086 Κλαυδία, *Klaudia*, n.pr., *poss.* "lame." *Claudia.* S: *2803*, BAGD: 433C, CB: –

3087 Κλαύδιος, *Klaudios*, n.pr. *Claudius.* S: *2804*, BAGD: 433C, CB: –

3088 κλαυθμός, *klauthmos*, n. *weeping, crying.* S: *2805*, BAGD: 433C, CB: 361B

3089 κλάω, *klaō*, v. *to break.* S: *2806*, BAGD: 433D, CB: 361A

3090 κλείς, *kleis*, n. *key.* S: *2807*, BAGD: 433D, CB: 361B

3091 κλείω, *kleiō*, v. *to close, shut, lock.* S: *2808*, BAGD: 434A, CB: 361B

3092 κλέμμα, *klemma*, n. *theft, stealing.* S: *2809*, BAGD: 434B, CB: –

3093 Κλεοπᾶς, *Kleopas*, n.pr., "renowned father." *Cleopas.* S: *2810**, BAGD: 434B, CB: –

3094 κλέος, *kleos*, n. *credit, honor.* S: *2811*, BAGD: 434B, CB: 361B

3095 κλέπτης, *kleptēs*, n. *thief.* S: *2812*, BAGD: 434B, CB: 361B

3096 κλέπτω, *kleptō*, v. *steal.* S: *2813*, BAGD: 434C, CB: 361B

3097 κλῆμα, *klēma*, n. *branch.* S: *2814*, BAGD: 434C, CB: 361B

3098 Κλήμης, *Klēmēs*, n.pr., "mild." *Clement.* S: *2815*, BAGD: 434C, CB: –

3099 κληρονομέω, *klēronomeō*, v. *to inherit, acquire.* S: *2816*, BAGD: 434D, CB: 361B

3100 κληρονομία, *klēronomia*, n. *inheritance.* S: *2817*, BAGD: 435A, CB: 361B

3101 κληρονόμος, *klēronomos*, n. *heir, one who inherits.* S: *2818*, BAGD: 435B, CB: 361B

3102 κλῆρος, *klēros*, n. *(casting) lots; share, place, inheritance.* S: *2819*, BAGD: 435B, CB: 361B

3103 κληρόω, *klēroō*, v. *(pass.) to be chosen, appointed.* S: *2820*, BAGD: 435D, CB: 361B

3104 κλῆσις, *klēsis*, n. *call, calling; situation, station in life.* S: *2821*, BAGD: 435D, CB: 361B

3105 κλητός, *klētos*, a. *called, invited.* S: *2822*, BAGD: 436A, CB: 361B

3106 κλίβανος, *klibanos*, n. *(fire of a) furnace, oven.* S: *2823*, BAGD: 436B, CB: –

3107 κλίμα, *klima*, n. *region.* S: *2824*, BAGD: 436B, CB: –

3108 κλινάριον, *klinarion*, n. *bed, stretcher.* S: *2825**, BAGD: 436B, CB: –

3109 κλίνη, *klinē*, n. *bed, mat, stretcher.* S: *2825*, BAGD: 436B, CB: –

3110 κλινίδιον, *klinidion*, n. *bed, mat, stretcher.* S: *2826*, BAGD: 436C, CB: –

3111 κλίνω, *klinō*, v. *to bow down, lay down; to be over (late in the day).* S: *2827*, BAGD: 436C, CB: –

3112 κλισία, *klisia*, n. *group reclining for a meal.* S: *2828*, BAGD: 436D, CB: –

3113 κλοπή, *klopē*, n. *theft, stealing.* S: *2829*, BAGD: 436D, CB: –

3114 κλύδων, *klydōn*, n. *raging waters, waves.* S: *2830*, BAGD: 436D, CB: –

3115 κλυδωνίζομαι, *klydōnizomai*, v. *to be tossed back and forth by waves.* S: *2831*, BAGD: 436D, CB: –

3116 Κλωπᾶς, *Klōpas*, n.pr. *Clopas.* S: *2832*, BAGD: 436D, CB: –

3117 κνήθω, *knēthō*, v. *(pass.) to feel an itch.* S: *2833*, BAGD: 437A, CB: –

3118 Κνίδος, *Knidos*, n.pr., "age." *Cnidus.* S: *2834*, BAGD: 437A, CB: –

3119 κοδράντης, *kodrantēs*, n. *penny, smallest Roman coin.* S: *2835*, BAGD: 437A, CB: –

3120 κοιλία, *koilia*, n. *belly, stomach, womb.* S: *2836*, BAGD: 437B, CB: 361B

3121 κοιμάω, *koimaō*, v. *(pass.) to fall asleep, sleep; die.* S: *2837*, BAGD: 437C, CB: 361B

3122 κοίμησις, *koimēsis*, n. *(noun) sleep.* S: *2838*, BAGD: 437D, CB: –

3123 κοινός, *koinos*, a. *common; (ceremonially) unclean, impure, unholy.* S: *2839*, BAGD: 438A, CB: 361B

3124 κοινόω, *koinoō*, v. *to make (ceremonially) unclean, impure; to defile.* S: *2840*, BAGD: 438B, CB: 361B

3125 κοινωνέω, *koinōneō*, v. *to share in, participate in.* S: *2841*, BAGD: 438C, CB: 361B

3126 κοινωνία, *koinōnia*, n. *fellowship, participation, sharing, contribution.* S: *2842*, BAGD: 438D, CB: 361B

3127 κοινωνικός, *koinōnikos*, a. *willing to share, generous.* S: *2843*, BAGD: 439C, CB: 361B

3128 κοινωνός, *koinōnos*, n. *partner, participant.* S: *2844*, BAGD: 439C, CB: 361B

3129 κοινῶς, *koinōs*, adv. variant: *in the common language or dialect.* S: *150*, BAGD: 440A, CB: –

3130 κοίτη, *koitē*, n. *(marriage) bed; conception; sexual immorality.* S: *2845*, BAGD: 440A, CB: 361B

3131 κοιτών, *koitōn*, n. *bedroom; trusted personal servant, chamberlain.* S: *2846*, BAGD: 440B, CB: –

3132 κόκκινος, *kokkinos*, a. *scarlet, (bright) red.* S: *2847*, BAGD: 440B, CB: 361B

3133 κόκκος, *kokkos*, n. *seed, kernel of grain.* S: *2848*, BAGD: 440C, CB: –

3134 κολάζω, *kolazō*, v. *to punish.* S: *2849*, BAGD: 440C, CB: 361C

3135 κολακεία, *kolakeia*, n. *flattery.* S: *2850*, BAGD: 440D, CB: –

3136 κόλασις, *kolasis*, n. *punishment.* S: *2851*, BAGD: 440D, CB: 361B

3137 Κολασσαεύς, *Kolassaeus*, n.pr.g., "of Colosse." variant: *Colossian.* S: *2858**, BAGD: 441A, CB: –

3138 Κολασσαί, *Kolassai*, n.pr. variant: *Colosse.* S: *2857**, BAGD: 441A, CB: –

3139 κολαφίζω, *kolaphizō*, v. *to strike with the fists, beat, torment; (pass.) receive a beating, be brutally treated.* S: *2852*, BAGD: 441A, CB: 361B

3140 κολλάω, *kollaō*, v. *(mid.) to join, associate with, cling to; (pass.) to be united, stuck to, piled up; to stay near, follow; to be hired out.* S: *2853*, BAGD: 441C, CB: 361C

3141 κολλούριον, *kollourion*, n. *eye salve.* S: *2854*, BAGD: 441D, CB: 361C

3142 κολλυβιστής, *kollybistēs*, n. *money exchanger.* S: *2855*, BAGD: 442A, CB: –

3143 κολοβόω, *koloboō*, v. *to cut short, shorten.* S: *2856*, BAGD: 442A, CB: 361C

3144 Κολοσσαεύς, *Kolossaeus*, n.pr.g., "of Colosse." variant: *Colossian.* S: *2858*, BAGD: 441A cf. Κολασσαεύς, CB: –

3145 Κολοσσαί, *Kolossai*, n.pr., "punishment." *Colosse.* S: *2857*, BAGD: 441A, CB: –

3146 κόλπος, *kolpos*, n. *lap area: side, bosom, chest; bay.* S: *2859*, BAGD: 442B, CB: 361C

3147 κολυμβάω, *kolymbaō*, v. *to swim.* S: *2860*, BAGD: 442C, CB: –

3148 κολυμβήθρα, *kolymbēthra*, n. *pool.* S: *2861*, BAGD: 442C, CB: –

3149 κολωνία, *kolōnia*, n. *Roman colony.* S: *2862*, BAGD: 442C, CB: –

3150 κομάω, *komaō*, v. *to have long hair.* S: *2863*, BAGD: 442D, CB: –

3151 κόμη, *komē*, n. *(long) hair.* S: *2864*, BAGD: 442D, CB: –

3152 κομίζω, *komizō*, v. *(act.) to bring; (mid.) to receive (what is due), reward, be repaid.* S: *2865*, BAGD: 442D, CB: 361C cf. -omai

3153 κομψότερον, *kompsoteron*, adv.comp. *better.* S: *2866*, BAGD: 443A, CB: –

3154 κονιάω, *koniaō*, v. *(pass.) to be whitewashed.* S: *2867*, BAGD: 443A, CB: 361C

3155 κονιορτός, *koniortos*, n. *dust.* S: *2868*, BAGD: 443B, CB: –

3156 κοπάζω, *kopazō*, v. *to die down, abate.* S: *2869*, BAGD: 443B, CB: –

3157 κοπετός, *kopetos*, n. *mourning, sorrowing, lamentation.* S: *2870*, BAGD: 443B, CB: 361C

3158 κοπή, *kopē*, n. *defeat, cutting down.* S: *2871*, BAGD: 443C, CB: –

3159 κοπιάω, *kopiaō*, v. *to work, labor, give effort; to become tired, grow weary.* S: *2872*, BAGD: 443C, CB: 361C

3160 κόπος, *kopos*, n. *labor, work; bother, trouble, difficulty.* S: *2873*, BAGD: 443C, CB: 361C

3161 κοπρία, *kopria*, n. *manure pile, rubbish pile.* S: *2874*, BAGD: 443D, CB: 361C

3162 κόπριον, *koprion*, n. *fertilizer, manure.* S: *2874**, BAGD: 443D, CB: 361C

3163 κόπρος, *kopros*, n. variant: *dung, manure.* S: *2874**, BAGD: 444A, CB: 361C

3164 κόπτω, *koptō*, v. *to cut; (mid.) to mourn, beat one's breast.* S: *2875*, BAGD: 444A, CB: 361C

3165 κόραξ, *korax*, n. *raven, crow.* S: *2876*, BAGD: 444B, CB: –

3166 κοράσιον, *korasion*, n. *(little) girl.* S: *2877*, BAGD: 444B, CB: 361C

3167 κορβᾶν, *korban*, l.[n.]. *Corban.* S: *2878*, BAGD: 444B, CB: 361C

3168 κορβανᾶς, *korbanas*, n. *temple treasury.* S: *2878*, BAGD: 444C, CB: 361C

3169 Κόρε, *Kore*, n.pr., "shaven, bald." *Korah.* S: *2879**, BAGD: 444C, CB: –

3170 κορέννυμι, *korennymi*, v. *(pass.) to be filled to the full, have enough.* S: *2880*, BAGD: 444C, CB: –

3171 Κορίνθιος, *Korinthios*, n.pr.g., "of Corinth." *Corinthian.* S: *2881*, BAGD: 444D, CB: –

3172 Κόρινθος, *Korinthos*, n.pr., "decoration." *Corinth.* S: *2882*, BAGD: 444D, CB: 361C

3173 Κορνήλιος, *Kornēlios*, n.pr., "of a horn." *Cornelius.* S: *2883*, BAGD: 444D, CB: –

3174 κόρος, *koros*, n. *cor (dry measure between ten and twelve bushels).* S: *2884*, BAGD: 444D, CB: 361C

3175 κοσμέω, *kosmeō*, v. *to make beautiful, decorate, dress; trim (a lamp); (pass.) to put in order; be adorned, decorated, beautifully dressed.* S: *2885*, BAGD: 445A, CB: 361C

3176 κοσμικός, *kosmikos*, a. *earthly, worldly.* S: *2886*, BAGD: 445B, CB: 361C

3177 κόσμιος, *kosmios*, a. *respectable, honorable.* S: *2887*, BAGD: 445C, CB: 361C

3178 κοσμίως, *kosmiōs*, adv. variant: *modestly.* S: *2887**, BAGD: 445C, CB: 361C

3179 κοσμοκράτωρ, *kosmokratōr*, n. *(pl.) powers of the world.* S: *2888*, BAGD: 445C, CB: 361C

3180 κόσμος, *kosmos*, n. *world: earth, world system, whole universe; adornment.* S: *2889*, BAGD: 445D, CB: 361C

3181 Κούαρτος, *Kouartos*, n.pr., "fourth [born]." *Quartus.* S: *2890*, BAGD: 447B, CB: –

3182 κοῦμ, *koum*, l.[v.]. *koum (Aramaic: stand up!).* S: *2891**, BAGD: 447B, CB: –

3183 κοῦμι, *koumi*, l.[v.]. variant: *koumi (Aramaic: stand up!)*. S: *2891*, BAGD: 447B, CB: –

3184 κουστωδία, *koustōdia*, n. *guard*. S: *2892*, BAGD: 447B, CB: –

3185 κουφίζω, *kouphizō*, v. *to lighten, make lighter*. S: *2893*, BAGD: 447B, CB: –

3186 κόφινος, *kophinos*, n. *(large) basket*. S: *2894*, BAGD: 447C, CB: –

3187 κράβαττος, *krabattos*, n. *bed, (sleeping) mat*. S: *2895**, BAGD: 447C, CB: –

3188 κράββατος, *krabbatos*, n. variant: *bed, (sleeping) mat*. S: *2895*, BAGD: 447C cf. κράβαττος, CB: –

3189 κράζω, *krazō*, v. *call out, cry out, shout, exclaim*. S: *2896*, BAGD: 447C, CB: 362A

3190 κραιπάλη, *kraipalē*, n. *dissipation*. S: *2897*, BAGD: 448A, CB: 361C

3191 κρανίον, *kranion*, n. *skull*. S: *2898*, BAGD: 448A, CB: –

3192 κράσπεδον, *kraspedon*, n. *edge, border, hem; tassel*. S: *2899*, BAGD: 448B, CB: –

3193 κραταιός, *krataios*, a. *mighty, powerful*. S: *2900*, BAGD: 448B, CB: 362A

3194 κραταιόω, *krataioō*, v. *(pass.) to be strong, become strong*. S: *2901*, BAGD: 448B, CB: 362A

3195 κρατέω, *krateō*, v. *to arrest, seize into custody; to take, grab, hold onto, obtain; (pass.) to be kept from, held*. S: *2902*, BAGD: 448C, CB: 362A

3196 κράτιστος, *kratistos*, a. *most excellent, "your Excellency"*. S: *2903*, BAGD: 449A, CB: 362A

3197 κράτος, *kratos*, n. *power, strength*. S: *2904*, BAGD: 449A, CB: 362A

3198 κραυγάζω, *kraugazō*, v. *to shout, cry out*. S: *2905*, BAGD: 449B, CB: 362A

3199 κραυγή, *kraugē*, n. *crying out, shouting, verbal brawling*. S: *2906*, BAGD: 449C, CB: –

3200 κρέας, *kreas*, n. *meat*. S: *2907*, BAGD: 449C, CB: 362A

3201 κρείσσων, *kreissōn*, a. variant: *better, superior, greater*. S: *2908**, BAGD: 449D, CB: 362A

3202 κρείττων, *kreittōn*, a. *better, superior, greater*. S: *2909 & 2908*, BAGD: 449D, CB: 362A

3203 κρεμάννυμι, *kremannymi*, v. *to hang on, hang upon*. S: *2910*, BAGD: 450A, CB: 362A

3204 κρημνός, *krēmnos*, n. *steep bank, cliff*. S: *2911*, BAGD: 450B, CB: –

3205 Κρής, *Krēs*, n.pr.g., "of Crete." *Cretan*. S: *2912*, BAGD: 450B, CB: –

3206 Κρήσκης, *Krēskēs*, n.pr., "increasing." *Crescens*. S: *2913*, BAGD: 450B, CB: –

3207 Κρήτη, *Krētē*, n.pr. *Crete*. S: *2914*, BAGD: 450C, CB: –

3208 κριθή, *krithē*, n. *barley*. S: *2915*, BAGD: 450C, CB: –

3209 κρίθινος, *krithinos*, a. *made of barley (flour)*. S: *2916*, BAGD: 450C, CB: –

3210 κρίμα, *krima*, n. *judgment, condemnation; sentence, punishment*. S: *2917*, BAGD: 450C, CB: 362A

3211 κρίνον, *krinon*, n. *lily*. S: *2918*, BAGD: 451A, CB: –

3212 κρίνω, *krinō*, v. *to decide, consider; to judge, pass judgment on, condemn*. S: *2919*, BAGD: 451B, CB: 362A

3213 κρίσις, *krisis*, n. *judgment, condemnation, justice*. S: *2920*, BAGD: 452C, CB: 362A

3214 Κρίσπος, *Krispos*, n.pr., "curled." *Crispus*. S: *2921*, BAGD: 453B, CB: –

3215 κριτήριον, *kritērion*, n. *court of law; legal dispute, lawsuit*. S: *2922*, BAGD: 453B, CB: –

3216 κριτής, *kritēs*, n. *judge*. S: *2923*, BAGD: 453C, CB: 362A

3217 κριτικός, *kritikos*, a. *able to discern or judge*. S: *2924*, BAGD: 453D, CB: 362A

3218 κρούω, *krouō*, v. *to knock (on a gate or door)*. S: *2925*, BAGD: 453D, CB: 362A

3219 κρύπτη, *kryptē*, n. *hidden place*. S: *2926**, BAGD: 454A, CB: 362A

3220 κρυπτός, *kryptos*, a. *hidden, unseen, secret*. S: *2927*, BAGD: 454A, CB: 362A

3221 κρύπτω, *kryptō*, v. *to hide*. S: *2928*, BAGD: 454B, CB: 362A

3222 κρυσταλλίζω, *krystallizō*, v. *to be clear as crystal*. S: *2929*, BAGD: 454D, CB: 362A

3223 κρύσταλλος, *krystallos*, n. *rock crystal*. S: *2930*, BAGD: 454D, CB: 362A

3224 κρυφαῖος, *kryphaios*, a. *hidden, unseen, secret*. S: *2927**, BAGD: 454D, CB: 362A

3225 κρυφῇ, *kryphē*, adv. *in secret*. S: *2931**, BAGD: 454D, CB: 362A

3226 κρύφιος, *kryphios*, a. variant: *hidden, secret*. S: *2927**, BAGD: 455A, CB: 362A

3227 κτάομαι, *ktaomai*, v. *to get, gain, buy; take along; to control*. S: *2932*, BAGD: 455A, CB: 362A

3228 κτῆμα, *ktēma*, n. *wealth, possessions; piece of property, field*. S: *2933*, BAGD: 455B, CB: 362A

3229 κτῆνος, *ktēnos*, n. *(domestic) animal: donkey, horse, cattle*. S: *2934*, BAGD: 455B, CB: 362A

3230 κτήτωρ, *ktētōr*, n. *(land) owner*. S: *2935*, BAGD: 455C, CB: –

3231 κτίζω, *ktizō*, v. *to create; (as noun) Creator*. S: *2936*, BAGD: 455C, CB: 362B

3232 κτίσις, *ktisis*, n. *creation, creature; governmental institution*. S: *2937*, BAGD: 455D, CB: 362A

3233 κτίσμα, *ktisma*, n. *creature, created thing*. S: *2938*, BAGD: 456B, CB: 362A

3234 κτίστης, *ktistēs*, n. *Creator*. S: *2939*, BAGD: 456B, CB: 362B

3235 κυβεία, *kybeia*, n. *cunning, craftiness, trickery*. S: *2940*, BAGD: 456C, CB: –

3236 κυβέρνησις, *kybernēsis*, n. *administration*. S: *2941*, BAGD: 456C, CB: 362B

3237 κυβερνήτης, *kybernētēs*, n. *sea captain, pilot*. S: *2942*, BAGD: 456C, CB: 362B

3238 κυκλεύω, *kykleuō*, v. *to surround*. S: *2944**, BAGD: 456D, CB: –

3239 κυκλόθεν, *kyklothen*, adv. *(all) around; from all sides*. S: *2943*, BAGD: 456D, CB: –

3240 κυκλόω, *kykloō*, v. *to surround: gather around, march around*. S: *2944*, BAGD: 456D, CB: 362B cf. *-los*

3241 κύκλῳ, kyklō, adv. *all around, in a circle, surrounding.* S: *2945*, BAGD: 456D, CB: –

3242 κύλισμα, kylisma, n. variant: *wallowing, rolling.* S: *2946*, BAGD: 457B, CB: –

3243 κυλισμός, kylismos, n. *wallowing, rolling around.* S: *2946**, BAGD: 457B, CB: –

3244 κυλίω, kyliō, v. *(mid.) to roll around.* S: *2947*, BAGD: 457B, CB: –

3245 κυλλός, kyllos, a. *crippled, maimed.* S: *2948*, BAGD: 457B, CB: 362B

3246 κῦμα, kyma, n. *waves, surf.* S: *2949*, BAGD: 457C, CB: –

3247 κύμβαλον, kymbalon, n. *cymbal.* S: *2950*, BAGD: 457C, CB: –

3248 κύμινον, kyminon, n. *cummin.* S: *2951*, BAGD: 457C, CB: 362B

3249 κυνάριον, kynarion, n. *(little or domesticated) dog.* S: *2952*, BAGD: 457D, CB: 362B

3250 Κύπριος, Kyprios, n.pr.g., "*of Cyprus.*" *from Cyprus.* S: *2953*, BAGD: 457D, CB: –

3251 Κύπρος, Kypros, n.pr., "*copper.*" *Cyprus.* S: *2954*, BAGD: 457D, CB: –

3252 κύπτω, kyptō, v. *to stoop down, bend down.* S: *2955*, BAGD: 458A, CB: –

3253 Κυρεῖνος, Kyreinos, n.pr. variant: *Quirinius.* S: *2956**, BAGD: 458A, CB: –

3254 Κυρηναῖος, Kyrēnaios, n.pr.g., "*of Cyrene.*" *from Cyrene.* S: *2956*, BAGD: 458A, CB: –

3255 Κυρήνη, Kyrēnē, n.pr., "*wall.*" *Cyrene.* S: *2957*, BAGD: 458A, CB: –

3256 Κυρήνιος, Kyrēnios, n.pr. *Quirinius.* S: *2958*, BAGD: 458B, CB: –

3257 κυρία, kyria, n. *lady (female "lord").* S: *2959**, BAGD: 458B, CB: 362B

3258 κυριακός, kyriakos, a. *pertaining to the Lord, the Lord's.* S: *2960*, BAGD: 458C, CB: 362B

3259 κυριεύω, kyrieuō, v. *to lord over, be master of, have authority over.* S: *2961*, BAGD: 458D, CB: 362B

3260 Κυρίνιος, Kyrinios, n.pr. variant: *Quirinius.* S: *2958**, BAGD: 458B, CB: –

3261 κύριος, kyrios, n. *lord, master, owner, sir; (of God) Lord, Master.* S: *2962*, BAGD: 458D, CB: 362B

3262 κυριότης, kyriotēs, n. *authority, dominion, power, lordship.* S: *2963*, BAGD: 460D, CB: 362B

3263 κυρόω, kyroō, v. *to reaffirm; to establish a covenant, ratify, validate.* S: *2964*, BAGD: 461A, CB: 362B

3264 κύων, kyōn, n. *dog.* S: *2965*, BAGD: 461B, CB: 362B

3265 κῶλον, kōlon, n. *dead body, corpse.* S: *2966*, BAGD: 461B, CB: –

3266 κωλύω, kōlyō, v. *to hinder, stop, restrain, forbid; oppress; (pass.) to be prevented, kept from.* S: *2967*, BAGD: 461B, CB: 361C

3267 κώμη, kōmē, n. *village, town.* S: *2968*, BAGD: 461D, CB: 361C

3268 κωμόπολις, kōmopolis, n. *village, market town.* S: *2969*, BAGD: 461D, CB: –

3269 κῶμος, kōmos, n. *orgy, revelry, carousing.* S: *2970*, BAGD: 461D, CB: 361C

3270 κώνωψ, kōnōps, n. *gnat, mosquito.* S: *2971*, BAGD: 462A, CB: 361C

3271 Κῶς, Kōs, n.pr., "*summit.*" *Cos.* S: *2972*, BAGD: 462A, CB: –

3272 Κωσάμ, Kōsam, n.pr., "*diviner.*" *Cosam.* S: *2973*, BAGD: 462A, CB: –

3273 κωφός, kōphos, a. *unable to talk or speak, mute; deaf.* S: *2974*, BAGD: 462A, CB: 361C

3274 λ, l, letter. *letter of the Greek alphabet.* S: *150*, BAGD: 462A, CB: –

3275 λαγχάνω, lanchanō, v. *to choose by lot, decide by lot; receive (by lot or divine will).* S: *2975*, BAGD: 462B, CB: 362C

3276 Λάζαρος, Lazaros, n.pr., "*one whom God helps.*" *Lazarus.* S: *2976*, BAGD: 462B, CB: –

3277 λάθρᾳ, lathra, adv. *secretly, quietly.* S: *2977**, BAGD: 462C, CB: –

3278 λαῖλαψ, lailaps, n. *storm, hurricane, whirlwind.* S: *2978*, BAGD: 462D, CB: 362B

3279 λακάω, lakaō, v. *to burst open.* S: *2997**, BAGD: 463A, CB: 362B

3280 λακτίζω, laktizō, v. *to kick.* S: *2979*, BAGD: 463A, CB: –

3281 λαλέω, laleō, v. *to speak, talk.* S: *2980*, BAGD: 463A, CB: 362B

3282 λαλιά, lalia, n. *speech, a way of speaking, i.e., language.* S: *2981*, BAGD: 464A, CB: 362C

3283 λαμά, lama, l.[pp.+p.inter.]. variant: *lama (Hebrew: why?).* S: *2982*, BAGD: 464A, CB: –

3284 λαμβάνω, lambanō, v. *to take, receive; (pass.) to be received, selected.* S: *2983*, BAGD: 464A, CB: 362C

3285 Λάμεχ, Lamech, n.pr. *Lamech.* S: *2984*, BAGD: 465C, CB: –

3286 λαμπάς, lampas, n. *lamp, lantern, torch.* S: *2985*, BAGD: 465C, CB: 362C

3287 λαμπρός, lampros, a. *bright, shining, splendorous, elegant.* S: *2986*, BAGD: 465D, CB: 362C

3288 λαμπρότης, lamprotēs, n. *brightness.* S: *2987*, BAGD: 466A, CB: 362C

3289 λαμπρῶς, lamprōs, adv. *in luxury, splendidly.* S: *2988*, BAGD: 466A, CB: 362C

3290 λάμπω, lampō, v. *to give light, shine.* S: *2989*, BAGD: 466A, CB: 362C

3291 λανθάνω, lanthanō, v. *to keep secret, escape notice, be hidden.* S: *2990*, BAGD: 466B, CB: 362C

3292 λαξευτός, laxeutos, a. *cut in rock.* S: *2991*, BAGD: 466C, CB: –

3293 Λαοδίκεια, Laodikeia, n.pr. *Laodicea.* S: *2993*, BAGD: 466C, CB: –

3294 Λαοδικεύς, Laodikeus, n.pr.g., "*of Laodicea.*" *Laodicean.* S: *2994*, BAGD: 466C, CB: –

3295 λαός, laos, n. *people, crowd.* S: *2992*, BAGD: 466C, CB: 362C

3296 λάρυγξ, larynx, n. *throat.* S: *2995*, BAGD: 467B, CB: –

3297 Λασαία, Lasaia, n.pr. *Lasea.* S: *2996*, BAGD: 467B, CB: –

3298 Λασέα, *Lasea*, n.pr. variant: *Lasea*. S: *2996**, BAGD: 467B, CB: –

3299 λάσκω, *laskō*, v. variant: *to burst open*. S: *2997*, BAGD: 467B, CB: 362C

3300 λατομέω, *latomeō*, v. *to cut, hew (rock)*. S: *2998*, BAGD: 467B, CB: –

3301 λατρεία, *latreia*, n. *worship, ministry, service (to God)*. S: *2999*, BAGD: 467B, CB: 362C

3302 λατρεύω, *latreuō*, v. *to serve, minister (in religious duties)*. S: *3000*, BAGD: 467C, CB: 362C

3303 λάχανον, *lachanon*, n. *plant, herb, vegetable*. S: *3001*, BAGD: 467D, CB: 362B

3304 Λεββαῖος, *Lebbaios*, n.pr., "[one near to] my heart." variant: *Lebbaeus*. S: *3002*, BAGD: 467D, CB: –

3305 λεγιών, *legiōn*, n. *legion*. S: *3003**, BAGD: 467D, CB: –

3306 λέγω, *legō*, v. *to say, tell; ask, answer*. S: *3004 & 2036 & 2046 & 448*, BAGD: 468A, CB: 362C

3307 λεῖμμα, *leimma*, n. *remnant*. S: *3005*, BAGD: 470B, CB: 362C

3308 λεῖος, *leios*, a. *smooth, level*. S: *3006*, BAGD: 470B, CB: –

3309 λείπω, *leipō*, v. *to lack, fall short*. S: *3007*, BAGD: 470B, CB: 362C

3310 λειτουργέω, *leitourgeō*, v. *to perform religious duties; serve*. S: *3008*, BAGD: 470C, CB: 362C

3311 λειτουργία, *leitourgia*, n. *religious service, ceremony; service, ministry, help*. S: *3009*, BAGD: 471A, CB: 362C

3312 λειτουργικός, *leitourgikos*, a. *ministering, engaged in holy service*. S: *3010*, BAGD: 471B, CB: 362C

3313 λειτουργός, *leitourgos*, n. *servant, minister, one who cares for (another)*. S: *3011*, BAGD: 471B, CB: 362C

3314 λείχω, *leichō*, v. variant: *to lick*. S: *621**, BAGD: 471C, CB: –

3315 Λέκτρα, *Lektra*, n.pr. variant: *Lectra*. S: *150*, BAGD: 471C, CB: –

3316 λεμά, *lema*, l.[pp.+p.inter.]. *lama (Aramaic: why?)*. S: *2982**, BAGD: 464A cf. λαμά, CB: –

3317 λέντιον, *lention*, n. *towel*. S: *3012*, BAGD: 471C, CB: –

3318 λεπίς, *lepis*, n. *scale, flake*. S: *3013*, BAGD: 471C, CB: –

3319 λέπρα, *lepra*, n. *leprosy*. S: *3014*, BAGD: 471D, CB: 362C

3320 λεπρός, *lepros*, a. *leprous; (as noun) leper*. S: *3015*, BAGD: 472A, CB: 362C

3321 λεπτός, *leptos*, a. *small copper coin*. S: *3016**, BAGD: 472A, CB: 362C

3322 Λευί, *Leui*, n.pr., *perhaps* "wild cow" *or* "person pledged for a debt or vow." *Levi*. S: *3017*, BAGD: 472A, CB: 362C

3323 Λευίς, *Leuis*, n.pr., *perhaps* "wild cow" *or* "person pledged for a debt or vow." variant: *Levi*. S: *3018**, BAGD: 472A cf. Λευί, CB: 362C cf. *Leui*

3324 Λευίτης, *Leuitēs*, n.pr.g., "of Levi." *Levite*. S: *3019**, BAGD: 472B, CB: 363A

3325 Λευιτικός, *Leuitikos*, a.pr.g., "pertaining to Levi." *Levitical*. S: *3020**, BAGD: 472B, CB: 362C

3326 λευκαίνω, *leukainō*, v. *to bleach, whiten*. S: *3021*, BAGD: 472B, CB: –

3327 λευκοβύσσινος, *leukobyssinos*, a. variant: *white linen*. S: *1039**, BAGD: 472B, CB: –

3328 λευκός, *leukos*, a. *white; bright, gleaming*. S: *3022*, BAGD: 472B, CB: 363A

3329 λέων, *leōn*, n. *lion*. S: *3023*, BAGD: 472D, CB: 362C

3330 λήθη, *lēthē*, n. *forgetfulness*. S: *3024*, BAGD: 472D, CB: 362C

3331 λῆμψις, *lēmpsis*, n. *receiving*. S: *3028**, BAGD: 473A, CB: 362C

3332 ληνός, *lēnos*, n. *winepress*. S: *3025*, BAGD: 473A, CB: –

3333 λῆρος, *lēros*, n. *nonsense, idle talk*. S: *3026*, BAGD: 473A, CB: –

3334 λῃστής, *lēstēs*, n. *robber, bandit; rebel, revolutionary*. S: *3027*, BAGD: 473A, CB: 362C

3335 λῆψις, *lēpsis*, n. variant: *receiving*. S: *3028*, BAGD: 473A, CB: 362C

3336 λίαν, *lian*, adv. *very much, greatly, completely*. S: *3029*, BAGD: 473B, CB: 363A

3337 λίβανος, *libanos*, n. *frankincense, incense*. S: *3030*, BAGD: 473C, CB: 363A

3338 λιβανωτός, *libanōtos*, n. *censer (bowl for burning incense)*. S: *3031*, BAGD: 473D, CB: 363A

3339 Λιβερτῖνος, *Libertinos*, n.pr., "Freedman." *Freedman*. S: *3032*, BAGD: 473D, CB: 363A

3340 Λιβύη, *Libyē*, n.pr. *Libya*. S: *3033*, BAGD: 473D, CB: –

3341 Λιβυστῖνος, *Libystinos*, n.pr.g., "of Libya." variant: *Libyan*. S: *3032**, BAGD: 473D, CB: –

3342 λιθάζω, *lithazō*, v. *to stone*. S: *3034*, BAGD: 473D, CB: –

3343 λίθινος, *lithinos*, a. *made of stone*. S: *3035*, BAGD: 474A, CB: 363A

3344 λιθοβολέω, *lithoboleō*, v. *to throw stones*. S: *3036*, BAGD: 474A, CB: –

3345 λίθος, *lithos*, n. *stone, boulder*. S: *3037*, BAGD: 474B, CB: 363A

3346 λιθόστρωτος, *lithostrōtos*, a. *(as noun) stone pavement*. S: *3038*, BAGD: 474D, CB: –

3347 λικμάω, *likmaō*, v. *to crush*. S: *3039*, BAGD: 474D, CB: –

3348 λιμήν, *limēn*, n. *harbor*. S: *3040*, BAGD: 475A, CB: –

3349 λίμνη, *limnē*, n. *lake*. S: *3041*, BAGD: 475A, CB: 363A

3350 λιμός, *limos*, n. *hunger, famine, starvation*. S: *3042*, BAGD: 475A, CB: 363A

3351 λίνον, *linon*, n. *linen (garment); wick of a lamp*. S: *3043*, BAGD: 475B, CB: –

3352 Λίνος, *Linos*, n.pr. *Linus*. S: *3044**, BAGD: 475C, CB: –

3353 λιπαρός, *liparos*, a. *costly, rich; (as noun) riches*. S: *3045*, BAGD: 475C, CB: –

3354 λίτρα, *litra*, n. *(Roman) pound (about 12 oz. or 327 gr.)*. S: *3046*, BAGD: 475D, CB: –

3355 λίψ, *lips*, n. *southwest*. S: *3047*, BAGD: 475D, CB: –

3356 λογεία, *logeia*, n. *collection*. S: *3048**, BAGD: 475D, CB: 363A

3357 λογίζομαι, *logizomai*, v. *to credit, count, reckon; regard, think, consider*. S: *3049*, BAGD: 475D, CB: 363A

3358 λογικός, *logikos*, a. *spiritual, logical.* S: *3050*, BAGD: 476C, CB: 363A

3359 λόγιον, *logion*, n. *(pl.) words, sayings, oracles.* S: *3051*, BAGD: 476C, CB: 363A

3360 λόγιος, *logios*, a. *learned, eloquent.* S: *3052*, BAGD: 476D, CB: 363A

3361 λογισμός, *logismos*, n. *thought; argument, reasoning.* S: *3053*, BAGD: 476D, CB: 363A

3362 λογομαχέω, *logomacheō*, v. *to quarrel about words.* S: *3054*, BAGD: 477A, CB: 363A

3363 λογομαχία, *logomachia*, n. *quarrel about words.* S: *3055*, BAGD: 477A, CB: 363A

3364 λόγος, *logos*, n. *word, matter, thing; the Word.* S: *3056*, BAGD: 477A, CB: 363A

3365 λόγχη, *lonchē*, n. *spear, lance.* S: *3057*, BAGD: 479B, CB: –

3366 λοιδορέω, *loidoreō*, v. *to insult, curse.* S: *3058*, BAGD: 479C, CB: 363A

3367 λοιδορία, *loidoria*, n. *insult, slander, verbal abuse.* S: *3059*, BAGD: 479C, CB: 363A

3368 λοίδορος, *loidoros*, n. *slanderer, verbal abuser.* S: *3060*, BAGD: 479C, CB: 363B

3369 λοιμός, *loimos*, n. & a. *pestilence; troublemaker, public menace.* S: *3061*, BAGD: 479D, CB: –

3370 λοιπός, *loipos*, a. *remaining, left over, rest.* S: *3063* & 3062 & 3064*, BAGD: 479D, CB: 363B

3371 Λουκᾶς, *Loukas*, n.pr. *Luke.* S: *3065*, BAGD: 480B, CB: –

3372 Λούκιος, *Loukios*, n.pr. *Lucius.* S: *3066*, BAGD: 480C, CB: –

3373 λουτρόν, *loutron*, n. *washing, bath.* S: *3067*, BAGD: 480C, CB: 363B

3374 λούω, *louō*, v. *to wash, have a bath.* S: *3068*, BAGD: 480D, CB: 363B

3375 Λύδδα, *Lydda*, n.pr. *Lydda.* S: *3069*, BAGD: 481A, CB: –

3376 Λυδία, *Lydia*, n.pr. *Lydia.* S: *3070*, BAGD: 481B, CB: 363B

3377 Λυκαονία, *Lykaonia*, n.pr. *Lycaonia.* S: *3071*, BAGD: 481B, CB: –

3378 Λυκαονιστί, *Lykaonisti*, adv.pr. *in (the) Lycaonian (language).* S: *3072*, BAGD: 481B, CB: –

3379 Λυκία, *Lykia*, n.pr. *Lycia.* S: *3073*, BAGD: 481B, CB: –

3380 λύκος, *lykos*, n. *wolf.* S: *3074*, BAGD: 481B, CB: 363B

3381 λυμαίνω, *lymainō*, v. *to destroy, damage, ruin.* S: *3075**, BAGD: 481C, CB: –

3382 λυπέω, *lypeō*, v. *(act.) to cause sorrow, grief; (pass.) to be sorrowful, sad, distressed.* S: *3076*, BAGD: 481C, CB: 363B

3383 λύπη, *lypē*, n. *sorrow, grief, pain.* S: *3077*, BAGD: 482A, CB: 363B

3384 Λυσανίας, *Lysanias*, n.pr. *Lysanias.* S: *3078*, BAGD: 482B, CB: –

3385 Λυσίας, *Lysias*, n.pr. *Lysias.* S: *3079*, BAGD: 482B, CB: –

3386 λύσις, *lysis*, n. *divorce.* S: *3080*, BAGD: 482B, CB: 363B

3387 λυσιτελέω, *lysiteleō*, v. *to be advantageous, (imper. form) it is better.* S: *3081*, BAGD: 482B, CB: –

3388 Λύστρα, *Lystra*, n.pr. *Lystra.* S: *3082*, BAGD: 482C, CB: –

3389 λύτρον, *lytron*, n. *ransom, price of release.* S: *3083*, BAGD: 482C, CB: 363B

3390 λυτρόω, *lytroō*, v. *to redeem, free someone by paying a ransom.* S: *3084*, BAGD: 482D, CB: 363B

3391 λύτρωσις, *lytrōsis*, n. *redemption, ransoming, releasing.* S: *3085*, BAGD: 483A, CB: 363B

3392 λυτρωτής, *lytrōtēs*, n. *deliverer, redeemer.* S: *3086*, BAGD: 483A, CB: 363B

3393 λυχνία, *lychnia*, n. *lampstand.* S: *3087*, BAGD: 483A, CB: 363B

3394 λύχνος, *lychnos*, n. *lamp.* S: *3088*, BAGD: 483B, CB: 363B

3395 λύω, *lyō*, v. *to loose, release, untie; to break, destroy.* S: *3089*, BAGD: 483C, CB: 363B

3396 Λωΐς, *Lōis*, n.pr., *perhaps* "more desirable, better." *Lois.* S: *3090*, BAGD: 484C, CB: –

3397 Λώτ, *Lōt*, n.pr. *Lot.* S: *3091*, BAGD: 484C, CB: –

3398 μ, *m*, letter. *letter of the Greek alphabet.* S: *150*, BAGD: 484B, CB: –

3399 Μάαθ, *Maath*, n.pr., "to be small." *Maath.* S: *3092**, BAGD: 484B, CB: –

3400 Μαγαδάν, *Magadan*, n.pr. *Magadan.* S: *3093**, BAGD: 484B, CB: –

3401 Μαγδαλά, *Magdala*, n.pr. variant: *Magdala.* S: *3093*, BAGD: 484B cf. Μαγαδάν, CB: –

3402 Μαγδαληνή, *Magdalēnē*, n.pr.g., "from Magdala." *Magdalene.* S: *3094*, BAGD: 484B, CB: –

3403 Μαγεδών, *Magedōn*, n.pr. variant: *Megiddo.* S: *717**, BAGD: 107C cf. Ἁρμαγεδδών, CB: –

3404 μαγεία, *mageia*, n. *magic.* S: *3095*, BAGD: 484B, CB: 363B

3405 μαγεύω, *mageuō*, v. *to practice sorcery, magic.* S: *3096*, BAGD: 484D, CB: 363B

3406 μαγία, *magia*, n. variant: *magic.* S: *3095*, BAGD: 484B cf. μαγεία, CB: –

3407 μάγος, *magos*, n. *sorcerer; (pl.) Magi.* S: *3097*, BAGD: 484D, CB: 363B

3408 Μαγώγ, *Magōg*, n.pr., *perhaps* "land of Gog." *Magog.* S: *3098*, BAGD: 485B, CB: 363B

3409 Μαδιάμ, *Madiam*, n.pr. *Midian.* S: *3099*, BAGD: 485B, CB: –

3410 μαζός, *mazos*, n. variant: *breast.* S: *3149**, BAGD: 485B, CB: 364A

3411 μαθητεύω, *mathēteuō*, v. *(act./tr.) to teach; to make a disciple; (pass./intr.) to become a disciple.* S: *3100*, BAGD: 485C, CB: 364A

3412 μαθητής, *mathētēs*, n. *disciple, student, follower.* S: *3101*, BAGD: 485C, CB: 364A

3413 μαθήτρια, *mathētria*, n. *(female) disciple, student, follower.* S: *3102*, BAGD: 486A, CB: 364A cf. -tēs

3414 Μαθθαῖος, *Maththaios*, n.pr., "gift of Yahweh." *Matthew.* S: *3156**, BAGD: 496A cf. Ματθαι=ος, CB: –

3415 Μαθθάτ, *Maththat*, n.pr., "gift of God." *Matthat.* S: *3158**, BAGD: 496A cf. Ματθάτ, CB: –

3416 Μαθθίας, *Maththias*, n.pr., "gift of Yahweh." *Matthias.* S: *3159**, BAGD: 496A cf. Ματθίας, CB: –

3417 Μαθουσαλά, *Mathousala,* n.pr., "man of the javelin." *Methuselah.* S: *3103**, BAGD: 486B, CB: −

3418 Μαϊνάν, *Mainan,* n.pr. variant: *Mainan.* S: *3104,* BAGD: 503C cf. Μεννά, CB: −

3419 μαίνομαι, *mainomai,* v. *to rave, be insane, out of one's mind.* S: *3105,* BAGD: 486B, CB: 363B

3420 μακαρίζω, *makarizō,* v. *to call blessed; to consider blessed.* S: *3106,* BAGD: 486C, CB: 363C

3421 μακάριος, *makarios,* a. *blessed, fortunate, happy, good.* S: *3107,* BAGD: 486C, CB: 363C

3422 μακαρισμός, *makarismos,* n. *blessedness, joy.* S: *3108,* BAGD: 487A, CB: 363C

3423 Μακεδονία, *Makedonia,* n.pr. *Macedonia.* S: *3109,* BAGD: 487B, CB: −

3424 Μακεδών, *Makedōn,* n.pr.g., "from Macedonia." *Macedonian.* S: *3110,* BAGD: 487B, CB: −

3425 μάκελλον, *makellon,* n. *meat market, food market.* S: *3111,* BAGD: 487B, CB: −

3426 μακράν, *makran,* adv. & pp.*. *far away, distant, long way off.* S: *3112,* BAGD: 487C, CB: 363C

3427 μακρόθεν, *makrothen,* adv. *from a distance, from far away.* S: *3113,* BAGD: 487D, CB: 363C

3428 μακροθυμέω, *makrothymeō,* v. *to have patience; to be patient.* S: *3114,* BAGD: 488A, CB: 363C

3429 μακροθυμία, *makrothymia,* n. *patience, forbearance.* S: *3115,* BAGD: 488B, CB: 363C

3430 μακροθύμως, *makrothymōs,* adv. *patiently.* S: *3116,* BAGD: 488C, CB: 363C

3431 μακρός, *makros,* a. *lengthy, long; distant, far away.* S: *3117,* BAGD: 488C, CB: 363C cf. *makran*

3432 μακροχρόνιος, *makrochronios,* a. *pertaining to having a long life.* S: *3118,* BAGD: 488C, CB: −

3433 μαλακία, *malakia,* n. *sickness, ailment.* S: *3119,* BAGD: 488C, CB: 363C

3434 μαλακός, *malakos,* a. *fine, soft; (as noun) male prostitute.* S: *3120,* BAGD: 488D, CB: 363C cf. *-kia*

3435 Μαλελεήλ, *Maleleēl,* n.pr., "praise of God [El]." *Mahalalel.* S: *3121,* BAGD: 488D, CB: −

3436 μάλιστα, *malista,* adv.super. *especially.* S: *3122,* BAGD: 488D, CB: −

3437 μᾶλλον, *mallon,* adv.comp. *more, more than; rather, instead.* S: *3123,* BAGD: 489A, CB: 363C

3438 Μάλχος, *Malchos,* n.pr., "king." *Malchus.* S: *3124,* BAGD: 489D, CB: −

3439 μάμμη, *mammē,* n. *grandmother.* S: *3125,* BAGD: 490A, CB: −

3440 μαμωνᾶς, *mamōnas,* n. *wealth, assets.* S: *3126,* BAGD: 490A, CB: 363C

3441 Μαναήν, *Manaēn,* n.pr., "comforter." *Manaen.* S: *3127,* BAGD: 490A, CB: −

3442 Μανασσῆς, *Manassēs,* n.pr., "one that makes to forget." *Manasseh.* S: *3128,* BAGD: 490B, CB: −

3443 μανθάνω, *manthanō,* v. *to learn, study, be instructed.* S: *3129,* BAGD: 490B, CB: 363C

3444 μανία, *mania,* n. *insanity, madness.* S: *3130,* BAGD: 490D, CB: 363C

3445 μάννα, *manna,* n. *manna.* S: *3131,* BAGD: 490D, CB: 363C

3446 μαντεύομαι, *manteuomai,* v. *to fortune-tell, divine.* S: *3132,* BAGD: 491A, CB: 363C

3447 μαραίνω, *marainō,* v. *(pass.) to fade away, disappear.* S: *3133,* BAGD: 491B, CB: −

3448 μαράνα θά, *marana tha,* l.[n.+v.]. *maranatha (Aramaic: "Come, Lord!").* S: *3134**, BAGD: 491B, CB: 363C

3449 μαργαρίτης, *margaritēs,* n. *pearl.* S: *3135,* BAGD: 491C, CB: 363C

3450 Μάρθα, *Martha,* n.pr., "lady [female lord]." *Martha.* S: *3136,* BAGD: 491C, CB: −

3451 Μαρία, *Maria,* n.pr., *perhaps* "beloved" *or* "plump." *Mary.* S: *3137,* BAGD: 491C, CB: −

3452 Μαριάμ, *Mariam,* n.pr., *perhaps* "beloved" *or* "plump." variant: *Mary.* S: *3137**, BAGD: 492B, CB: −

3453 Μᾶρκος, *Markos,* n.pr., [Latin] "large hammer." *Mark.* S: *3138**, BAGD: 492B, CB: −

3454 μάρμαρος, *marmaros,* n. *marble.* S: *3139,* BAGD: 492C, CB: −

3455 μαρτυρέω, *martyreō,* v. *to testify, give testimony; commend, speak well of, vouch for.* S: *3140,* BAGD: 492C, CB: 363C

3456 μαρτυρία, *martyria,* n. *testimony, evidence; (good) reputation.* S: *3141,* BAGD: 493C, CB: 363C

3457 μαρτύριον, *martyrion,* n. *testimony, proof.* S: *3142,* BAGD: 493D, CB: 363C

3458 μαρτύρομαι, *martyromai,* v. *to testify, declare; to insist on, urge.* S: *3143,* BAGD: 494A, CB: 363C

3459 μάρτυς, *martys,* n. *witness, testimony; martyr.* S: *3144,* BAGD: 494B, CB: 363C

3460 μασάομαι, *masaomai,* v. *to gnaw, bite.* S: *3145,* BAGD: 495A, CB: −

3461 μασθός, *masthos,* n. variant: *breast.* S: *3149**, BAGD: 495B cf. μαστός, CB: −

3462 μασσάομαι, *massaomai,* v. variant: *to gnaw.* S: *3145,* BAGD: 495A cf. μασάομαι, CB: −

3463 μαστιγόω, *mastigoō,* v. *to flog, whip, scourge; to punish, chastise.* S: *3146,* BAGD: 495A, CB: 363C

3464 μαστίζω, *mastizō,* v. *to flog, scourge.* S: *3147,* BAGD: 495A, CB: 363C

3465 μάστιξ, *mastix,* n. *flogging device, whip; suffering; disease, sickness.* S: *3148,* BAGD: 495B, CB: 363C

3466 μαστός, *mastos,* n. *breast, chest.* S: *3149,* BAGD: 495B, CB: 364A

3467 ματαιολογία, *mataiologia,* n. *meaningless talk, empty talk.* S: *3150,* BAGD: 495C, CB: 364A

3468 ματαιολόγος, *mataiologos,* a. *(as noun) idle talker.* S: *3151,* BAGD: 495C, CB: 364A

3469 μάταιος, *mataios,* a. *worthless, futile, useless, empty.* S: *3152,* BAGD: 495C, CB: 364A

3470 ματαιότης, *mataiotēs,* n. *emptiness, futility, frustration.* S: *3153,* BAGD: 495D, CB: 364A

3471 ματαιόω, mataioō, v. (pass.) to become futile, given over to worthlessness. S: 3154, BAGD: 495D, CB: 364A

3472 μάτην, matēn, adv. in vain, to no end. S: 3155, BAGD: 495D, CB: 364A

3473 Ματθαῖος, Matthaios, n.pr., "gift of Yahweh." variant: Matthew. S: 3156, BAGD: 496A, CB: –

3474 Ματθάν, Matthan, n.pr., "gift." Matthan. S: 3157, BAGD: 496A, CB: –

3475 Ματθάτ, Matthat, n.pr., "gift." variant: Mathat. S: 3158, BAGD: 496A, CB: –

3476 Ματθίας, Matthias, n.pr., "gift of Yahweh." variant: Matthias. S: 3159, BAGD: 496A, CB: –

3477 Ματταθά, Mattatha, n.pr., "gift." Mattatha. S: 3160, BAGD: 496A, CB: –

3478 Ματταθίας, Mattathias, n.pr., "gift of Yahweh." Mattathias. S: 3161, BAGD: 496B, CB: –

3479 μάχαιρα, machaira, n. sword. S: 3162, BAGD: 496B, CB: 363B

3480 μάχη, machē, n. quarrel, conflict, fighting. S: 3163, BAGD: 496C, CB: 363B

3481 μάχομαι, machomai, v. to fight, quarrel, argue. S: 3164, BAGD: 496C, CB: 363B

3482 μεγαλαυχέω, megalaucheō, v. variant: to become proud, boast. S: 3166, BAGD: 496D, CB: –

3483 μεγαλεῖος, megaleios, a. (as pl. noun) wonders, mighty deeds. S: 3167, BAGD: 496D, CB: 364A

3484 μεγαλειότης, megaleiotēs, n. majesty, greatness, grandeur. S: 3168, BAGD: 496D, CB: 364A

3485 μεγαλοπρεπής, megaloprepēs, a. majestic, magnificent. S: 3169, BAGD: 497A, CB: –

3486 μεγαλύνω, megalynō, v. to glorify, regard hgihly, praise, exalt; to lengthen, expand. S: 3170, BAGD: 497A, CB: 364A

3487 μεγάλως, megalōs, adv. greatly. S: 3171, BAGD: 497B, CB: –

3488 μεγαλωσύνη, megalōsynē, n. majesty. S: 3172, BAGD: 497B, CB: 364A

3489 μέγας, megas, a. great, large; loud, intense; violent. S: 3173, BAGD: 497C, CB: 364A

3490 μέγεθος, megethos, n. greatness. S: 3174, BAGD: 498C, CB: –

3491 μεγιστάν, megistan, n. great man, prince, high official. S: 3175*, BAGD: 498C, CB: 364A cf. -es

3492 μέγιστος, megistos, a.super. very great. S: 3176, BAGD: 497C cf. μέγας 2.b. β., CB: 364A

3493 μεθερμηνεύω, methermēneuō, v. to translate, give the meaning. S: 3177, BAGD: 498D, CB: 364C

3494 μέθη, methē, n. drunkenness. S: 3178, BAGD: 498D, CB: 364C

3495 μεθιστάνω, methistanō, v. variant: to move, remove; bring, lead astray; (pass.) to lose, be discharged. S: 3179, BAGD: 498D, CB: –

3496 μεθίστημι, methistēmi, v. to move, remove; bring, lead astray; (pass.) to lose, be discharged. S: 3179, BAGD: 498D, CB: –

3497 μεθοδεία, methodeia, n. scheming, craftiness, strategy. S: 3180, BAGD: 499A, CB: 364C

3498 μεθόριον, methorion, n. variant: boundary; (pl.) region. S: 3181*, BAGD: 499B, CB: –

3499 μεθύσκω, methyskō, v. (pass.) to be or become drunk, intoxicated. S: 3182, BAGD: 499B, CB: 364C

3500 μέθυσος, methysos, n. drunkard. S: 3183, BAGD: 499B, CB: 364C

3501 μεθύω, methyō, v. to get drunk. S: 3184, BAGD: 499C, CB: 364C

3502 μείγνυμι, meignymi, v. to mix, mingle. S: 3396*, BAGD: 499C, CB: –

3503 μειγνύω, meignyō, v. variant: to mix, mingle. S: 3396*, BAGD: 499C, CB: –

3504 μειζότερος, meizoteros, a.comp. variant: greater. S: 3186, BAGD: 497C cf. μέγας, CB: 364A cf. meizōn

3505 μείζων, meizōn, a.comp. greater, larger; older; louder; more. S: 3187 & 3185, BAGD: 497C cf. μέγας, CB: 364A

3506 μέλας, melas, a. black; ink. S: 3189 & 3188, BAGD: 499D, CB: 364A

3507 Μελεά, Melea, n.pr. Melea. S: 3190*, BAGD: 500A, CB: –

3508 μέλει, melei, v. (imper.) it is a care, it is a concern; (pers.) to trouble; to concern. S: 3199*, BAGD: 500A, CB: 364B cf. melō

3509 μελετάω, meletaō, v. to plot, think about, meditate on; to give oneself wholly to, practice, cultivate. S: 3191, BAGD: 500B, CB: –

3510 μέλι, meli, n. honey. S: 3192, BAGD: 500C, CB: –

3511 μελισσεῖον, melisseion, n. variant: beehive. S: 3193*, BAGD: 500D, CB: –

3512 μελισσῖον, melission, n. variant: beehive. S: 3193*, BAGD: 500D, CB: –

3513 μελίσσιος, melissios, a. variant: pertaining to the bee, honeycomb. S: 3193, BAGD: 500D, CB: –

3514 Μελίτη, Melitē, n.pr. Malta. S: 3194, BAGD: 500D, CB: –

3515 Μελιτήνη, Melitēnē, n.pr. variant: Malta. S: 3194*, BAGD: 500D, CB: –

3516 μέλλω, mellō, v. to be about to, on the point of; to be destined, must; to intend to; (what is) to come, the future. S: 3195, BAGD: 500D, CB: 364A

3517 μέλος, melos, n. part, member, limb. S: 3196, BAGD: 501D, CB: 364B

3518 Μελχί, Melchi, n.pr., "my king." Melki. S: 3197, BAGD: 502A, CB: –

3519 Μελχισέδεκ, Melchisedek, n.pr., "[my] king is Zedek [just]." Melchizedek. S: 3198*, BAGD: 502A, CB: 364A

3520 μέλω, melō, v. variant: to care, be concerned. S: 3199, BAGD: 500A cf. μέλει, CB: 364B

3521 μεμβράνα, membrana, n. parchment. S: 3200, BAGD: 502A, CB: –

3522 μέμφομαι, memphomai, v. to find fault with, blame. S: 3201, BAGD: 502B, CB: 364B

3523 μεμψίμοιρος, mempsimoiros, a. fault-finding, complaining. S: 3202, BAGD: 502C, CB: 364B

3524 μέμψις, *mempsis*, n. variant: *a reason for complaint.*
S: *3437**, BAGD: 502C, CB: 364B

3525 μέν, *men*, pt.aff. *often untranslated; used with other particles to show contrast: on the one hand, one .. or the other.*
S: *3303*, BAGD: 502C, CB: 364B

3526 Μενάμ, *Menam*, n.pr. variant: *Menam.* S: *3104**,
BAGD: 503C cf. Μεννά, CB: –

3527 Μεννά, *Menna*, n.pr. *Menna.* S: *150*, BAGD: 503C, CB: –

3528 μενοῦν, *menoun*, pt. *rather, on the contrary.* S: *3304**,
BAGD: 503C, CB: –

3529 μενοῦνγε, *menounge*, pt. *rather, on the contrary, indeed.*
S: *3304*, BAGD: 503C, CB: –

3530 μέντοι, *mentoi*, pt. *but, yet, nevertheless, really.* S: *3305*,
BAGD: 503C, CB: –

3531 μένω, *menō*, v. *to stay, remain, live, dwell, abide.* S: *3306*,
BAGD: 503C, CB: 364B

3532 μερίζω, *merizō*, v. *to give, assign; (mid.) to divide, share; (pass.) to be divided.* S: *3307*, BAGD: 504C, CB: 364B

3533 μέριμνα, *merimna*, n. *worry, concern, anxiety.* S: *3308*,
BAGD: 504D, CB: 364B

3534 μεριμνάω, *merimnaō*, v. *to worry, have anxiety, be concerned.* S: *3309*, BAGD: 505A, CB: 364B

3535 μερίς, *meris*, n. *district; part, share, what is common between.* S: *3310*, BAGD: 505A, CB: 364B

3536 μερισμός, *merismos*, n. *dividing, separation; distribution, apportionment.* S: *3311*, BAGD: 505C, CB: –

3537 μεριστής, *meristēs*, n. *arbiter.* S: *3312*, BAGD: 505D, CB: –

3538 μέρος, *meros*, n. *part, share, portion; (pl.) district, region.*
S: *3313*, BAGD: 505D, CB: 364B

3539 μεσάζω, *mesazō*, v. variant: *to be in the middle.* S: *3322**,
BAGD: 506C, CB: –

3540 μεσημβρία, *mesēmbria*, n. *(of time) noon, midday; (of place) south.* S: *3314*, BAGD: 506D, CB: –

3541 μεσιτεύω, *mesiteuō*, v. *to confirm, guarantee.* S: *3315*,
BAGD: 506D, CB: 364B

3542 μεσίτης, *mesitēs*, n. *mediator.* S: *3316*, BAGD: 506D,
CB: 364B

3543 μεσονύκτιον, *mesonyktion*, n. *midnight.* S: *3317*,
BAGD: 507A, CB: 364B

3544 Μεσοποταμία, *Mesopotamia*, n.pr., "[land] between rivers."
Mesopotamia. S: *3318*, BAGD: 507A, CB: –

3545 μέσος, *mesos*, a. *middle, center, among; between; in front of, before.* S: *3319*, BAGD: 507B, CB: 364B

3546 μεσότοιχον, *mesotoichon*, n. *dividing wall.* S: *3320*,
BAGD: 508A, CB: 364B

3547 μεσουράνημα, *mesouranēma*, n. *midair.* S: *3321*,
BAGD: 508A, CB: –

3548 μεσόω, *mesoō*, v. *to be halfway through, at midpoint.*
S: *3322*, BAGD: 508B, CB: –

3549 Μεσσίας, *Messias*, n.pr., "anointed." *Messiah, Anointed One.*
S: *3323*, BAGD: 508B, CB: 364B

3550 μεστός, *mestos*, a. *full.* S: *3324*, BAGD: 508B, CB: 364B

3551 μεστόω, *mestoō*, v. *(pass.) to be filled.* S: *3325*,
BAGD: 508C, CB: –

3552 μετά, *meta*, pp. *(gen.) with, among; (acc.) after, later.*
S: *3326*, BAGD: 508C, CB: 364B

3553 μεταβαίνω, *metabainō*, v. *to go on, leave, move from.*
S: *3327*, BAGD: 510C, CB: 364B

3554 μεταβάλλω, *metaballō*, v. *(mid.) to change one's mind.*
S: *3328*, BAGD: 510D, CB: –

3555 μετάγω, *metagō*, v. *to turn, steer.* S: *3329*, BAGD: 510D,
CB: –

3556 μεταδίδωμι, *metadidōmi*, v. *to impart, share, contribute to needs.* S: *3330*, BAGD: 510D, CB: 364B

3557 μετάθεσις, *metathesis*, n. *removal, taking up; change, transformation.* S: *3331*, BAGD: 511A, CB: 364C

3558 μεταίρω, *metairō*, v. *to move on, leave.* S: *3332*,
BAGD: 511A, CB: –

3559 μετακαλέω, *metakaleō*, v. *(mid.) to send for, summon, call to oneself.* S: *3333*, BAGD: 511A, CB: 364B cf. -omai

3560 μετακινέω, *metakineō*, v. *(pass.) to be moved, removed, shifted from.* S: *3334*, BAGD: 511B, CB: –

3561 μεταλαμβάνω, *metalambanō*, v. *to share in, receive a share.*
S: *3335*, BAGD: 511B, CB: 364B

3562 μετάλημψις, *metalēmpsis*, n. *receiving, sharing with.*
S: *3336**, BAGD: 511C, CB: 364B

3563 μεταλλάσσω, *metallassō*, v. *to exchange.* S: *3337*,
BAGD: 511C, CB: 364C

3564 μεταμέλομαι, *metamelomai*, v. *(mid.) to regret, repent; (pass.) to be repentant, changed of mind, remorseful.*
S: *3338*, BAGD: 511C, CB: 364C

3565 μεταμορφόω, *metamorphoō*, v. *(pass.) to be transformed, transfigured, changed in form.* S: *3339*, BAGD: 511D,
CB: 364C

3566 μετανοέω, *metanoeō*, v. *to repent.* S: *3340*, BAGD: 511D,
CB: 364C

3567 μετάνοια, *metanoia*, n. *repentance, change of mind.* S: *3341*,
BAGD: 512C, CB: 364C

3568 μεταξύ, *metaxy*, adv. *(spacial) between; (temporal) meanwhile, next.* S: *3342*, BAGD: 512D, CB: –

3569 μεταπέμπω, *metapempō*, v. *to summon, send for.* S: *3343*,
BAGD: 513B, CB: –

3570 μεταστρέφω, *metastrephō*, v. *to pervert; to turn into, change.* S: *3344*, BAGD: 513B, CB: –

3571 μετασχηματίζω, *metaschēmatizō*, v. *(act.) to transform, change (the form); (mid.) to masquerade, disguise (oneself).*
S: *3345*, BAGD: 513B, CB: 364C

3572 μετατίθημι, *metatithēmi*, v. *to change (from one place or position to another); to bring back; to take away.* S: *3346*,
BAGD: 513C, CB: 364C

3573 μετατρέπω, *metatrepō*, v. *(pass.) to be changed, turned.*
S: *3344**, BAGD: 513D, CB: –

3574 μεταφυτεύω, *metaphyteuō*, v. variant: *to transplant.* S: *150*,
BAGD: 513D, CB: –

3575 μετέπειτα, *metepeita*, adv. *afterward.* S: *3347*,
BAGD: 514A, CB: –

3576 μετέχω, *metechō*, v. *to share in, partake in, take part in.*
S: *3348*, BAGD: 514A, CB: 364C

3577 μετεωρίζομαι, *meteōrizomai*, v. *to worry about, be anxious.*
S: *3349**, BAGD: 514A, CB: –

3578 μετοικεσία, *metoikesia*, n. *exile, deportation.* S: *3350*, BAGD: 514B, CB: 364C

3579 μετοικίζω, *metoikizō*, v. *to send to another place, exile, deport.* S: *3351*, BAGD: 514B, CB: –

3580 μετοχή, *metochē*, n. *something in common, sharing, participation.* S: *3352*, BAGD: 514C, CB: 364C

3581 μέτοχος, *metochos*, a. *sharing in, partners with.* S: *3353*, BAGD: 514C, CB: 364C

3582 μετρέω, *metreō*, v. *to measure.* S: *3354*, BAGD: 514C, CB: 364C

3583 μετρητής, *metrētēs*, n. *measure (about nine or ten gallons).* S: *3355*, BAGD: 514D, CB: 364C

3584 μετριοπαθέω, *metriopatheō*, v. *to deal gently.* S: *3356*, BAGD: 514D, CB: –

3585 μετρίως, *metriōs*, adv. *not greatly, moderately.* S: *3357*, BAGD: 515A, CB: –

3586 μέτρον, *metron*, n. *measure, limit, what is apportioned.* S: *3358*, BAGD: 515A, CB: 364C

3587 μέτωπον, *metōpon*, n. *forehead.* S: *3359*, BAGD: 515B, CB: –

3588 μέχρι, *mechri*, pp.* & c. *until, to the point of.* S: *3360*, BAGD: 515B, CB: 364A

3589 μέχρις, *mechris*, c. & pp.*. variant: *until, to the point of.* S: *3360**, BAGD: 515C, CB: 364A cf. *mechri*

3590 μή, *mē*, pt.neg. *no, not, (with 4024) absolutely not.* S: *3361*, BAGD: 515D, CB: 364A

3591 μήγε, *mēge*, pt.neg. *not.* S: *3361 + 1065*, BAGD: 152D cf. γέ 3.b., CB: –

3592 μηδαμῶς, *mēdamōs*, adv. *surely not, by no means, certainly not.* S: *3365*, BAGD: 517D, CB: –

3593 μηδέ, *mēde*, pt.neg.disj. *nor, or not, and not, but not.* S: *3366*, BAGD: 517D, CB: –

3594 μηδείς, *mēdeis*, a. *no one, not anyone, nobody, nothing.* S: *3367*, BAGD: 518A, CB: 364A

3595 μηδέποτε, *mēdepote*, adv. *never.* S: *3368*, BAGD: 518B, CB: –

3596 μηδέπω, *mēdepō*, adv. *not yet.* S: *3369*, BAGD: 518B, CB: –

3597 Μῆδος, *Mēdos*, n.pr.g., "of Media." *Mede.* S: *3370*, BAGD: 518B, CB: –

3598 μηθαμῶς, *mēthamōs*, adv. variant: *by no means, certainly not.* S: *3365**, BAGD: 517D cf. μηδαμῶς, CB: –

3599 μηθείς, *mētheis*, a. variant: *no one, nothing.* S: *3367**, BAGD: 518A cf. μηδείς, CB: –

3600 μηκέτι, *mēketi*, adv. *no longer, never again.* S: *3371*, BAGD: 518C, CB: –

3601 μῆκος, *mēkos*, n. *length.* S: *3372*, BAGD: 518C, CB: –

3602 μηκύνω, *mēkynō*, v. *(pass.) to grow (long), become long.* S: *3373*, BAGD: 518D, CB: –

3603 μηλωτή, *mēlōtē*, n. *sheepskin.* S: *3374*, BAGD: 518D, CB: –

3604 μήν[1], *mēn[1]*, n. *month.* S: *3375*, BAGD: 518D, CB: 364B

3605 μήν[2], *mēn[2]*, pt. *(with 1623) surely.* S: *3376*, BAGD: 518D, CB: 364B

3606 μηνύω, *mēnyō*, v. *to inform, report, tell.* S: *3377*, BAGD: 519A, CB: –

3607 μήποτε, *mēpote*, pt. & c. *never, otherwise, that .. not.* S: *3379*, BAGD: 519B, CB: 364B

3608 μήπου, *mēpou*, c. variant: *lest, that .. somewhere.* S: *3361 + 4225*, BAGD: 519C, CB: –

3609 μήπω, *mēpō*, adv. *not yet.* S: *3380*, BAGD: 519C, CB: –

3610 μήπως, *mēpōs*, adv. variant: *so that .. somehow, lest.* S: *3381*, BAGD: 519C, CB: –

3611 μηρός, *mēros*, n. *thigh.* S: *3382*, BAGD: 519D, CB: –

3612 μήτε, *mēte*, c.neg. *and not, neither, nor.* S: *3383*, BAGD: 519D, CB: –

3613 μήτηρ, *mētēr*, n. *mother.* S: *3384*, BAGD: 520A, CB: 364C

3614 μήτι, *mēti*, pt.inter. *often not translated; expects a no answer to a question: surely not, unless.* S: *3385 & 3387*, BAGD: 520B, CB: –

3615 μήτιγε, *mētige*, pt.inter. *how much more, not to speak of.* S: *3386*, BAGD: 520B, CB: –

3616 μήτρα, *mētra*, n. *womb.* S: *3388*, BAGD: 520B, CB: 364C

3617 μητραλῴας, *mētralōas*, n. variant: *one who kills a mother.* S: *3389*, BAGD: 520C, CB: –

3618 μητρολῴας, *mētrolōas*, n. *one who kills a mother.* S: *3389*, BAGD: 520C, CB: –

3619 μητρόπολις, *mētropolis*, n. variant: *capital city.* S: *3390*, BAGD: 520C, CB: 364C

3620 μιαίνω, *miainō*, v. *to pollute, stain, defile; (pass.) to be defiled, corrupted, become ceremonially unclean.* S: *3392*, BAGD: 520D, CB: 364C

3621 μίασμα, *miasma*, n. *corruption, defilement.* S: *3393*, BAGD: 521A, CB: 364C

3622 μιασμός, *miasmos*, n. *corruption, pollution, defilement.* S: *3394*, BAGD: 521A, CB: 364C

3623 μίγμα, *migma*, n. *mixture, compound.* S: *3395*, BAGD: 521A, CB: –

3624 μίγνυμι, *mignymi*, v. variant: *to mix, mingle.* S: *3396*, BAGD: 499C cf. μείγνυμι, CB: –

3625 μικρός, *mikros*, a. *little, small, short, lesser.* S: *3398 & 3397*, BAGD: 521A, CB: 364C

3626 Μίλητος, *Milētos*, n.pr. *Miletus.* S: *3399*, BAGD: 521D, CB: –

3627 μίλιον, *milion*, n. *(Roman) mile (about 4,854 feet).* S: *3400*, BAGD: 521D, CB: –

3628 μιμέομαι, *mimeomai*, v. *to imitate, follow an example, use as a model.* S: *3401*, BAGD: 521D, CB: 365A

3629 μιμητής, *mimētēs*, n. *imitator, an example.* S: *3402*, BAGD: 522A, CB: 365A

3630 μιμνῄσκομαι, *mimnēskomai*, v. *to remember, recall, bring to remembrance.* S: *3403**, BAGD: 522B, CB: 365A

3631 μισέω, *miseō*, v. *to hate; (pass.) to be hated, detestable.* S: *3404*, BAGD: 522C, CB: 365A

3632 μισθαποδοσία, *misthapodosia*, n. *reward; punishment.* S: *3405*, BAGD: 523A, CB: 365A

3633 μισθαποδότης, *misthapodotēs*, n. *rewarder.* S: *3406*, BAGD: 523A, CB: 365A

3634 μίσθιος, *misthios*, n. *hired worker.* S: *3407*, BAGD: 523A, CB: 365A

3635 μισθός, *misthos*, n. *wage; reward; what is paid back.*
S: *3408*, BAGD: 523B, CB: 365A

3636 μισθόω, *misthoō*, v. *to hire.* S: *3409*, BAGD: 523D, CB: 365A

3637 μίσθωμα, *misthōma*, n. *rented house, rented lodging.*
S: *3410*, BAGD: 523D, CB: 365A

3638 μισθωτός, *misthōtos*, n. *hired worker.* S: *3411*,
BAGD: 523D, CB: 365A

3639 Μιτυλήνη, *Mitylēnē*, n.pr. *Mitylene.* S: *3412*, BAGD: 524A,
CB: –

3640 Μιχαήλ, *Michaēl*, n.pr., "Who is like God [El]?." *Michael.*
S: *3413*, BAGD: 524A, CB: 364C

3641 μνᾶ, *mna*, n. *mina (100 drachmas).* S: *3414*, BAGD: 524A,
CB: –

3642 μνάομαι, *mnaomai*, v. variant: *be engaged, betrothed.*
S: *3415*, BAGD: 524B, CB: –

3643 Μνάσων, *Mnasōn*, n.pr. *Mnason.* S: *3416*, BAGD: 524B,
CB: –

3644 μνεία, *mneia*, n. *remembrance, mention.* S: *3417*,
BAGD: 524B, CB: 365A

3645 μνῆμα, *mnēma*, n. *(burial) tomb.* S: *3418*, BAGD: 524C,
CB: 365A

3646 μνημεῖον, *mnēmeion*, n. *tomb, grave.* S: *3419*,
BAGD: 524C, CB: 365A

3647 μνήμη, *mnēmē*, n. *remembrance, recalling, memory.* S: *3420*,
BAGD: 524D, CB: 365A

3648 μνημονεύω, *mnēmoneuō*, v. *to remember; to think of.*
S: *3421*, BAGD: 525A, CB: 365A

3649 μνημόσυνον, *mnēmosynon*, n. *memory, remembrance;
memorial offering.* S: *3422*, BAGD: 525B, CB: 365A

3650 μνηστεύω, *mnēsteuō*, v. *(pass.) to be pledged to marriage,
betrothed, become engaged.* S: *3423*, BAGD: 525C, CB: –

3651 μογγιλάλος, *mongilalos*, a. variant: *pertaining to speaking in
a hoarse or weak voice.* S: *3424**, BAGD: 525C, CB: 365A
cf. *mogilalos*

3652 μογιλάλος, *mogilalos*, a. *hardly able to talk, speaking with
difficulty.* S: *3424*, BAGD: 525D, CB: 365A

3653 μόγις, *mogis*, adv. *scarcely ever.* S: *3425*, BAGD: 525D,
CB: –

3654 μόδιος, *modios*, n. *large bowl (holds about eight dry quarts).*
S: *3426*, BAGD: 525D, CB: –

3655 μοιχαλίς, *moichalis*, n. *adulteress; (as adj.) adulterous.*
S: *3428*, BAGD: 526A, CB: 365A

3656 μοιχάω, *moichaō*, v. *to commit adultery.* S: *3429*,
BAGD: 526A, CB: 365A

3657 μοιχεία, *moicheia*, n. *adultery.* S: *3430*, BAGD: 526B,
CB: 365A

3658 μοιχεύω, *moicheuō*, v. *(act.) to commit adultery; (pass.) to
become an adulterer.* S: *3431*, BAGD: 526B, CB: 365A

3659 μοιχός, *moichos*, n. *adulterer.* S: *3432*, BAGD: 526C,
CB: 365A

3660 μόλις, *molis*, adv. *with difficulty, hardly; very rarely.* S: *3433*,
BAGD: 526D, CB: –

3661 Μολόχ, *Moloch*, n.pr., "[shameful] king." *Molech.* S: *3434*,
BAGD: 526D, CB: –

3662 μολύνω, *molynō*, v. *to defile, soil, stain, make impure.*
S: *3435*, BAGD: 526D, CB: 365A

3663 μολυσμός, *molysmos*, n. *contamination, defilement.* S: *3436*,
BAGD: 527A, CB: 365A

3664 μομφή, *momphē*, n. *grievance, cause for complaint.* S: *3437*,
BAGD: 527A, CB: –

3665 μονή, *monē*, n. *room; dwelling place, abode.* S: *3438*,
BAGD: 527A, CB: 365B

3666 μονογενής, *monogenēs*, a. *one and only, unique.* S: *3439*,
BAGD: 527B, CB: 365B

3667 μόνον, *monon*, adv. *only, alone; just, even, simply.* S: *3440*,
BAGD: 527C cf. μόνος, CB: 365B cf. *monos*

3668 μόνος, *monos*, a. *only, alone, by oneself.* S: *3441*,
BAGD: 527C, CB: 365B

3669 μονόφθαλμος, *monophthalmos*, a. *one-eyed.* S: *3442*,
BAGD: 528B, CB: 367A cf. *ophthalmos*

3670 μονόω, *monoō*, v. *(pass.) to be left alone.* S: *3443*,
BAGD: 528B, CB: –

3671 μορφή, *morphē*, n. *form, outward appearance; nature,
character.* S: *3444*, BAGD: 528B, CB: 365B

3672 μορφόω, *morphoō*, v. *(pass.) to be formed, take on a form.*
S: *3445*, BAGD: 528C, CB: 365B

3673 μόρφωσις, *morphōsis*, n. *embodiment, formulation;
(outward) form, appearance.* S: *3446*, BAGD: 528C,
CB: 365B

3674 μοσχοποιέω, *moschopoieō*, v. *to make an idol in the shape
of a calf.* S: *3447*, BAGD: 528C, CB: –

3675 μόσχος, *moschos*, n. *calf, ox.* S: *3448*, BAGD: 528C,
CB: 365B

3676 μουσικός, *mousikos*, a. *(as noun) musician.* S: *3451*,
BAGD: 528D, CB: 365B

3677 μόχθος, *mochthos*, n. *toil, hardship, exertion.* S: *3449*,
BAGD: 528D, CB: 365A

3678 μυελός, *myelos*, n. *marrow.* S: *3452*, BAGD: 528D, CB: –

3679 μυέω, *myeō*, v. *(pass.) to learn a secret.* S: *3453*,
BAGD: 529A, CB: 365B

3680 μῦθος, *mythos*, n. *myth, story, tale.* S: *3454*, BAGD: 529A,
CB: 365B

3681 μυκάομαι, *mykaomai*, v. *to roar.* S: *3455*, BAGD: 529B,
CB: –

3682 μυκτηρίζω, *myktērizō*, v. *(pass.) to be mocked, treated with
contempt.* S: *3456*, BAGD: 529B, CB: 365B

3683 μυλικός, *mylikos*, a. *pertaining to a grinding mill.* S: *3457*,
BAGD: 529B, CB: 365B

3684 μύλινος, *mylinos*, a. *pertaining to a grinding mill.* S: *3458**,
BAGD: 529B, CB: 365B

3685 μύλος, *mylos*, n. *hand mill or millstone for grinding.* S: *3458*,
BAGD: 529B, CB: 365B

3686 μυλών, *mylōn*, n. variant: *millhouse.* S: *3459*, BAGD: 529C,
CB: –

3687 μυλωνικός, *mylōnikos*, a. variant: *pertaining to the millhouse.*
S: *150*, BAGD: 529C, CB: –

3688 Μύρα, *Myra*, n.pr. *Myra.* S: *3460*, BAGD: 529C, CB: –

3689 μυριάς, *myrias*, n. *myriad, ten thousand; thousands upon
thousands.* S: *3461*, BAGD: 529C, CB: –

3690 μυρίζω, myrizō, v. *to pour perfume, anoint.* S: *3462*, BAGD: 529D, CB: –

3691 μύριοι, myrioi, a.num. *ten thousand.* S: *3463*, BAGD: 529D, CB: –

3692 μυρίος, myrios, a. *pertaining to the number ten thousand.* S: *3463**, BAGD: 529D, CB: –

3693 μύρον, myron, n. *perfume, myrrh, ointment.* S: *3464*, BAGD: 529D, CB: 365B

3694 Μύρρα, Myrra, n.pr. variant: *Myra.* S: *3460**, BAGD: 529C cf. Μύρα, CB: –

3695 Μυσία, Mysia, n.pr. *Mysia.* S: *3465*, BAGD: 530A, CB: –

3696 μυστήριον, mystērion, n. *mystery, secret.* S: *3466*, BAGD: 530A, CB: 365B

3697 μυωπάζω, myōpazō, v. *to be nearsighted.* S: *3467*, BAGD: 531A, CB: –

3698 μώλωψ, mōlōps, n. *wound, welt, bruise.* S: *3468*, BAGD: 531A, CB: 365A

3699 μωμάομαι, mōmaomai, v. *(mid.) to criticize, find fault, blame; (pass.) to be discredited, have fault found with.* S: *3469*, BAGD: 531A, CB: –

3700 μῶμος, mōmos, n. *blemish.* S: *3470*, BAGD: 531A, CB: –

3701 μωραίνω, mōrainō, v. *(act.) to make foolish, show one foolish; (pass.) to become a fool, be made a fool; (pass.) to become saltless, tasteless, inert.* S: *3471*, BAGD: 531B, CB: 365B

3702 μωρία, mōria, n. *foolishness.* S: *3472*, BAGD: 531B, CB: 365B

3703 μωρολογία, mōrologia, n. *foolish talk.* S: *3473*, BAGD: 531B, CB: 365B

3704 μωρός, mōros, a. *foolish.* S: *3474*, BAGD: 531C, CB: 365B

3705 Μωσεύς, Mōseus, n.pr., "drawn out" [Ex. 2:10]; *Egyptian* "son." variant: *Moses.* S: *3475*, BAGD: 531D cf. Μωϋσῆς, CB: –

3706 Μωσῆς, Mōsēs, n.pr., "drawn out" [Ex. 2:10]; *Egyptian* "son." variant: *Moses.* S: *3475*, BAGD: 531D cf. Μωϋσῆς, CB: –

3707 Μωϋσῆς, Mōysēs, n.pr., "drawn out [Ex. 2:10]; *Egyptian* son." *Moses.* S: *3475*, BAGD: 531D, CB: 365B

3708 ν, n, letter. *letter of the Greek alphabet.* S: *150*, BAGD: –, CB: –

3709 Ναασσών, Naassōn, n.pr., "small viper." *Nahshon.* S: *3476*, BAGD: 532A, CB: –

3710 Ναγγαί, Nangai, n.pr. *Naggai.* S: *3477*, BAGD: 532A, CB: –

3711 Ναζαρά, Nazara, n.pr., *poss.* "sprout, branch" *or* "watchtower." variant: *Nazareth.* S: *3478**, BAGD: 532A, CB: –

3712 Ναζαράθ, Nazarath, n.pr., *poss.* "sprout, branch" *or* "watchtower." variant: *Nazareth.* S: *3478**, BAGD: 532A, CB: –

3713 Ναζαράτ, Nazarat, n.pr., *poss.* "sprout, branch" *or* "watchtower." variant: *Nazareth.* S: *3478**, BAGD: 532A, CB: –

3714 Ναζαρέθ, Nazareth, n.pr., *poss.* "sprout, branch" *or* "watchtower." *Nazareth.* S: *3478*, BAGD: 532A, CB: –

3715 Ναζαρέτ, Nazaret, n.pr. variant: *Nazareth.* S: *3478*, BAGD: 532A, CB: 365C

3716 Ναζαρηνός, Nazarēnos, a.pr.g., "of Nazareth." *of Nazareth; (as noun) Nazarene.* S: *3479*, BAGD: 532B, CB: –

3717 Ναζωραῖος, Nazōraios, n.pr.g., "of Nazareth." *Nazarene, of Nazareth.* S: *3480*, BAGD: 532B, CB: 365C

3718 Ναθάμ, Natham, n.pr., "gift." *Nathan.* S: *3481**, BAGD: 532D, CB: –

3719 Ναθάν, Nathan, n.pr., "gift." variant: *Nathan.* S: *3481*, BAGD: 532D cf. Ναθάμ, CB: –

3720 Ναθαναήλ, Nathanaēl, n.pr., "gift of God [El]." *Nathanael.* S: *3482*, BAGD: 532D, CB: –

3721 ναί, nai, pt.aff. *or* emph. *yes, indeed.* S: *3483*, BAGD: 532D, CB: –

3722 Ναιμάν, Naiman, n.pr., "pleasantness." *Naaman.* S: *3497**, BAGD: 533B, CB: –

3723 Ναΐν, Nain, n.pr., "pleasant, delightful." *Nain.* S: *3484*, BAGD: 533B, CB: –

3724 ναός, naos, n. *temple.* S: *3485*, BAGD: 533B, CB: 365B

3725 Ναούμ, Naoum, n.pr., "comfort." *Nahum.* S: *3486*, BAGD: 534A, CB: –

3726 νάρδος, nardos, n. *nard.* S: *3487*, BAGD: 534A, CB: –

3727 Νάρκισσος, Narkissos, n.pr. *Narcissus.* S: *3488*, BAGD: 534B, CB: –

3728 ναυαγέω, nauageō, v. *to be shipwrecked, have a shipwreck.* S: *3489*, BAGD: 534B, CB: 365B

3729 ναύκληρος, nauklēros, n. *ship owner or captain.* S: *3490*, BAGD: 534B, CB: –

3730 ναῦς, naus, n. *ship.* S: *3491*, BAGD: 534C, CB: –

3731 ναύτης, nautēs, n. *sailor.* S: *3492*, BAGD: 534C, CB: –

3732 Ναχώρ, Nachōr, n.pr. *Nahor.* S: *3493*, BAGD: 534C, CB: –

3733 νεανίας, neanias, n. *young man.* S: *3494*, BAGD: 534C, CB: –

3734 νεανίσκος, neaniskos, n. *young man.* S: *3495*, BAGD: 534C, CB: 365C

3735 Νεά πολις, Nea polis, n.pr., "new city." *Neapolis.* S: *3496**, BAGD: 535D cf. νέος 3., CB: 365C cf. nea/

3736 Νεάπολις, Neapolis, n.pr., "new city." variant: *Neapolis.* S: *3496*, BAGD: 535D cf. νέος 3., CB: 365C cf. nea/

3737 Νεεμάν, Neeman, n.pr., "pleasantness." variant: *Naaman.* S: *3497*, BAGD: 533B cf. Ναιμάν, CB: –

3738 νεκρός, nekros, a. *dead; (as noun) dead person, corpse.* S: *3498*, BAGD: 534D, CB: 365C

3739 νεκρόω, nekroō, v. *(act.) to put to death; (pass.) to be as good as dead.* S: *3499*, BAGD: 535C, CB: 365C

3740 νέκρωσις, nekrōsis, n. *death, deadness.* S: *3500*, BAGD: 535C, CB: 365C

3741 νεομηνία, neomēnia, n. *New Moon Celebration.* S: *3561**, BAGD: 535D, CB: 365C

3742 νέος, neos, a. *new, fresh, young, younger.* S: *3501*, BAGD: 535D, CB: 365C

3743 νεοσσός, neossos, n. variant: *the young (of a bird).* S: *3502*, BAGD: 543D cf. νόσος, CB: –

3744 νεότης, neotēs, n. *youth, childhood.* S: *3503*, BAGD: 536C, CB: 365C

3745 νεόφυτος, neophytos, a. newly converted. S: 3504, BAGD: 536C, CB: 365C

3746 Νέρων, Nerōn, n.pr., "[family name]." variant: Nero. S: 3505, BAGD: 536D, CB: –

3747 Νεύης, Neuēs, n.pr. variant: Neues. S: 150, BAGD: 536D, CB: –

3748 νεύω, neuō, v. to motion, nod (as a signal). S: 3506, BAGD: 536D, CB: –

3749 νεφέλη, nephelē, n. cloud. S: 3507, BAGD: 536D, CB: 365C

3750 Νεφθαλίμ, Nephthalim, n.pr. Naphtali. S: 3508*, BAGD: 537A, CB: –

3751 νέφος, nephos, n. cloud. S: 3509, BAGD: 537A, CB: 365C

3752 νεφρός, nephros, n. mind (lit. "kidney"). S: 3510, BAGD: 537A, CB: 365C

3753 νεωκόρος, neōkoros, n. guardian of the temple. S: 3511, BAGD: 537B, CB: 365C

3754 νεωτερικός, neōterikos, a. pertaining to youth, youthful. S: 3512, BAGD: 537B, CB: –

3755 νή, nē, pt.aff. as surely as. S: 3513, BAGD: 537B, CB: 365C

3756 νήθω, nēthō, v. to spin (yarn). S: 3514, BAGD: 537C, CB: –

3757 νηπιάζω, nēpiazō, v. to be (like) a child. S: 3515, BAGD: 537C, CB: –

3758 νήπιος, nēpios, a. child, infant; childlike, childish. S: 3516, BAGD: 537C, CB: 365C

3759 Νηρεύς, Nēreus, n.pr. Nereus. S: 3517, BAGD: 538A, CB: –

3760 Νηρί, Nēri, n.pr., "lamp of Yahweh." Neri. S: 3518, BAGD: 538A, CB: –

3761 νησίον, nēsion, n. small island. S: 3519, BAGD: 538A, CB: –

3762 νῆσος, nēsos, n. island. S: 3520, BAGD: 538A, CB: –

3763 νηστεία, nēsteia, n. fasting, going without food. S: 3521, BAGD: 538A, CB: 365C

3764 νηστεύω, nēsteuō, v. to fast, go without food. S: 3522, BAGD: 538B, CB: 365C

3765 νῆστις, nēstis, n. hungry, without food. S: 3523, BAGD: 538C, CB: 365C

3766 νηφαλέος, nēphaleos, a. variant: temperate (in the use of alcohol). S: 3524*, BAGD: 538D, CB: –

3767 νηφάλιος, nēphalios, a. temperate (in the use of alcohol). S: 3524, BAGD: 538D, CB: 365C

3768 νήφω, nēphō, v. to be self-controlled, clear-headed. S: 3525, BAGD: 538D, CB: 365C

3769 Νίγερ, Niger, n.pr., "black." Niger. S: 3526, BAGD: 539A, CB: –

3770 Νικάνωρ, Nikanōr, n.pr., "victor." Nicanor. S: 3527, BAGD: 539A, CB: –

3771 νικάω, nikaō, v. to overcome, overpower; to conquer, triumph. S: 3528, BAGD: 539A, CB: 365C

3772 νίκη, nikē, n. victory. S: 3529, BAGD: 539C, CB: 365C

3773 Νικόδημος, Nikodēmos, n.pr., "victor over people." Nicodemus. S: 3530, BAGD: 539C, CB: –

3774 Νικολαΐτης, Nikolaitēs, n.pr.g., "follower of Nicolas." Nicolaitan. S: 3531, BAGD: 539D, CB: 365C

3775 Νικόλαος, Nikolaos, n.pr., "victor over people." Nicolas. S: 3532, BAGD: 539D, CB: 365C

3776 Νικόπολις, Nikopolis, n.pr., "victory city." Nicopolis. S: 3533, BAGD: 539D, CB: –

3777 νῖκος, nikos, n. victory. S: 3534, BAGD: 539D, CB: 365C

3778 Νινευή, Nineuē, n.pr. variant: Nineveh. S: 3535*, BAGD: 540A, CB: 365C

3779 Νινευΐ, Nineui, n.pr. variant: Nineveh. S: 3535, BAGD: 540A cf. Νινευή, CB: 365C

3780 Νινευΐτης, Nineuitēs, n.pr.g., "of Nineveh." Ninevite. S: 3536*, BAGD: 540A, CB: 365C

3781 νιπτήρ, niptēr, n. basin for washing. S: 3537, BAGD: 540A, CB: –

3782 νίπτω, niptō, v. to wash; bathe. S: 3538, BAGD: 540B, CB: 365C

3783 νοέω, noeō, v. to understand, see with insight, reflect. S: 3539, BAGD: 540B, CB: 365C

3784 νόημα, noēma, n. thought, mind; scheme, design, plot. S: 3540, BAGD: 540D, CB: 365C

3785 νόθος, nothos, a. illegitimate, born out of wedlock. S: 3541, BAGD: 540D, CB: 366A

3786 νομή, nomē, n. pasture. S: 3542, BAGD: 541A, CB: 366A

3787 νομίζω, nomizō, v. to think, suppose, expect, consider. S: 3543, BAGD: 541A, CB: 366A

3788 νομικός, nomikos, a. pertaining to the law; (as noun) expert in the law, lawyer. S: 3544, BAGD: 541B, CB: 366A

3789 νομίμως, nomimōs, adv. properly, in accordance to the rules. S: 3545, BAGD: 541C, CB: 366A

3790 νόμισμα, nomisma, n. coin. S: 3546, BAGD: 541D, CB: –

3791 νομοδιδάσκαλος, nomodidaskalos, n. teacher of the law. S: 3547, BAGD: 541D, CB: 366A

3792 νομοθεσία, nomothesia, n. law, legislation. S: 3548, BAGD: 541D, CB: 366A

3793 νομοθετέω, nomotheteō, v. (pass.) to be given law; to be founded, enacted. S: 3549, BAGD: 541D, CB: 366A

3794 νομοθέτης, nomothetēs, n. lawgiver. S: 3550, BAGD: 542A, CB: 366A

3795 νόμος, nomos, n. law, regulation, principle. S: 3551, BAGD: 542A, CB: 366A

3796 νοσέω, noseō, v. to be unhealthy, ill. S: 3552, BAGD: 543C, CB: 366A

3797 νόσημα, nosēma, n. variant: disease. S: 3553, BAGD: 543C, CB: 366A

3798 νόσος, nosos, n. disease, illness. S: 3554, BAGD: 543C, CB: 366A

3799 νοσσιά, nossia, n. chick, young (of a bird). S: 3555, BAGD: 543D, CB: 366A

3800 νοσσίον, nossion, n. young (of a bird). S: 3556, BAGD: 543D, CB: –

3801 νοσσός, nossos, n. young (of a bird). S: 3502*, BAGD: 543D, CB: –

3802 νοσφίζω, nosphizō, v. (mid.) to hold back for oneself, steal by misappropriating. S: 3557*, BAGD: 543D, CB: –

3803 νότος, *notos*, n. *south, south wind.* S: *3558*, BAGD: 544A, CB: 366A

3804 νουθεσία, *nouthesia*, n. *warning, admonition; instruction.* S: *3559*, BAGD: 544A, CB: 366A

3805 νουθετέω, *noutheteō*, v. *to warn, admonish; instruct.* S: *3560*, BAGD: 544B, CB: 366A

3806 νουμηνία, *noumēnia*, n. variant: *New Moon Celebration.* S: *3561*, BAGD: 535D cf. νεομηνία, CB: 365C

3807 νουνεχῶς, *nounechōs*, adv. *wisely, thoughtfully.* S: *3562*, BAGD: 544B, CB: –

3808 νοῦς, *nous*, n. *mind, thinking; understanding, insight.* S: *3563*, BAGD: 544C, CB: 366A

3809 Νύμφαν, *Nymphan*, n.pr. *Nympha.* S: *3564**, BAGD: 545A, CB: –

3810 Νυμφᾶς, *Nymphas*, n.pr. variant: *Nymphas.* S: *3564*, BAGD: 545A cf. Νυμφαν, CB: –

3811 νύμφη, *nymphē*, n. *bride; daughter-in-law.* S: *3565**, BAGD: 545B, CB: 366A

3812 νυμφίος, *nymphios*, n. *bridegroom.* S: *3566*, BAGD: 545B, CB: 366A

3813 νυμφών, *nymphōn*, n. *bridegroom.* S: *3567*, BAGD: 545B, CB: 366A

3814 νῦν, *nyn*, adv. *now, as it is; (with the article [3836]) the present (time).* S: *3568*, BAGD: 545C, CB: 366A

3815 νυνί, *nyni*, adv. *now, as it is; indeed, in fact.* S: *3570*, BAGD: 546B, CB: 366B

3816 νύξ, *nyx*, n. *night, evening.* S: *3571*, BAGD: 546B, CB: 366B

3817 νύσσω, *nyssō*, v. *to pierce, stab.* S: *3572*, BAGD: 547A, CB: –

3818 νυστάζω, *nystazō*, v. *to become drowsy; to sleep, be idle.* S: *3573*, BAGD: 547A, CB: –

3819 νυχθήμερον, *nychthēmeron*, n. *a night and a day.* S: *3574*, BAGD: 547A, CB: –

3820 Νῶε, *Nōe*, n.pr., "rest, comfort." *Noah.* S: *3575*, BAGD: 547C, CB: 365C

3821 νωθρός, *nōthros*, a. *slow to learn; lazy, sluggish.* S: *3576*, BAGD: 547C, CB: –

3822 νῶτος, *nōtos*, n. *back (of a human body).* S: *3577*, BAGD: 547C, CB: –

3823 ξ, *x*, letter. *letter of the Greek alphabet.* S: *150*, BAGD: –, CB: –

3824 ξαίνω, *xainō*, v. variant: *to comb (wool).* S: *837**, BAGD: 547B, CB: –

3825 ξενία, *xenia*, n. *place to stay, guest room.* S: *3578*, BAGD: 547B, CB: 379B

3826 ξενίζω, *xenizō*, v. *to receive a guest, entertain; (pass.) to stay as a guest; to think of something as strange, be surprised, astonished.* S: *3579*, BAGD: 547D, CB: 379B

3827 ξενοδοχέω, *xenodocheō*, v. *to show hospitality.* S: *3580*, BAGD: 548A, CB: 379B

3828 ξένος, *xenos*, a. *strange, foreign, alien; (as noun) foreigner, stranger, alien; host, one who shows hospitality.* S: *3581*, BAGD: 548A, CB: 379B

3829 ξέστης, *xestēs*, n. *pitcher, jug.* S: *3582*, BAGD: 548B, CB: –

3830 ξηραίνω, *xērainō*, v. *to wither, shrivel; become rigid.* S: *3583*, BAGD: 548C, CB: 379B

3831 ξηρός, *xēros*, a. *dried up, shriveled, withered; paralyzed.* S: *3584*, BAGD: 548C, CB: 379B

3832 ξύλινος, *xylinos*, a. *made of wood, wooden.* S: *3585*, BAGD: 549A, CB: –

3833 ξύλον, *xylon*, n. *wood; tree; wooden club, stocks.* S: *3586*, BAGD: 549A, CB: 379B

3834 ξυράω, *xyraō*, v. *to have one's hair shaved.* S: *3587*, BAGD: 549C, CB: –

3835 ο, *o*, letter. *letter of the Greek alphabet.* S: *150*, BAGD: –, CB: –

3836 ὁ, *ho*, art. *(often not translated) the, this, that, who.* S: *3588 & 5120*, BAGD: 549B, CB: –

3837 ὀγδοήκοντα, *ogdoēkonta*, n.num. *eighty.* S: *3589*, BAGD: 552D, CB: –

3838 ὄγδοος, *ogdoos*, a. *eighth.* S: *3590*, BAGD: 552D, CB: 366B

3839 ὄγκος, *onkos*, n. *hinderance, impediment.* S: *3591*, BAGD: 553A, CB: 366C

3840 ὅδε, *hode*, p.demo. *this (one); thus.* S: *3592*, BAGD: 553A, CB: –

3841 ὁδεύω, *hodeuō*, v. *to travel.* S: *3593*, BAGD: 553B, CB: –

3842 ὁδηγέω, *hodēgeō*, v. *to lead, guide; explain, instruct.* S: *3594*, BAGD: 553B, CB: 357A

3843 ὁδηγός, *hodēgos*, n. *guide, leader.* S: *3595*, BAGD: 553C, CB: 357A

3844 ὁδοιπορέω, *hodoiporeō*, v. *to be on a journey, travel.* S: *3596*, BAGD: 553D, CB: 357A

3845 ὁδοιπορία, *hodoiporia*, n. *journey.* S: *3597*, BAGD: 553D, CB: –

3846 ὁδοποιέω, *hodopoieō*, v. variant: *to make a path.* S: *3598 + 4160*, BAGD: 553D, CB: –

3847 ὁδός, *hodos*, n. *road, path, way.* S: *3598*, BAGD: 553D, CB: 357A

3848 ὀδούς, *odous*, n. *tooth.* S: *3599*, BAGD: 555A, CB: 366B

3849 ὀδυνάω, *odynaō*, v. *to grieve, be anxious, in agony.* S: *3600*, BAGD: 555A, CB: –

3850 ὀδύνη, *odynē*, n. *anguish, grief, pain.* S: *3601*, BAGD: 555B, CB: 366B

3851 ὀδυρμός, *odyrmos*, n. *deep sorrow, mourning, lamentation.* S: *3602*, BAGD: 555B, CB: 366B

3852 Ὀζίας, *Ozias*, n.pr., "Yahweh is [my] strength." *Uzziah.* S: *3604**, BAGD: 555B, CB: –

3853 ὄζω, *ozō*, v. *to give off a bad odor, stink, smell.* S: *3605*, BAGD: 555C, CB: –

3854 ὅθεν, *hothen*, adv. *from where, from there; therefore, this is why.* S: *3606*, BAGD: 555C, CB: –

3855 ὀθόνη, *othonē*, n. *linen sheet.* S: *3607*, BAGD: 555C, CB: –

3856 ὀθόνιον, *othonion*, n. *(pl.) strips of linen, bandages.* S: *3608*, BAGD: 555C, CB: –

3857 οἶδα, *oida*, v. *to know, understand, recognize, realize.* S: *1492**, BAGD: 555D, CB: 366B

3858 οἰκεῖος, *oikeios*, a. *belonging to the household, of the immediate family.* S: *3609*, BAGD: 556D, CB: 366B

3859 οἰκετεία, *oiketeia*, n. *servant in a household.* S: *2322**, BAGD: 556D, CB: –

3860 οἰκέτης, *oiketēs*, n. *house servant, domestic slave.* S: *3610*, BAGD: 557A, CB: 366B

3861 οἰκέω, *oikeō*, v. *to live, dwell.* S: *3611*, BAGD: 557A, CB: 366B

3862 οἴκημα, *oikēma*, n. *cell, room in a prison.* S: *3612*, BAGD: 557A, CB: –

3863 οἰκητήριον, *oikētērion*, n. *dwelling, home.* S: *3613*, BAGD: 557B, CB: 366B

3864 οἰκία, *oikia*, n. *house, home; family.* S: *3614*, BAGD: 557B, CB: 366B

3865 οἰκιακός, *oikiakos*, n. *member of a household.* S: *3615*, BAGD: 557D, CB: –

3866 οἰκοδεσποτέω, *oikodespoteō*, v. *to manage one's home.* S: *3616*, BAGD: 558A, CB: 366B

3867 οἰκοδεσπότης, *oikodespotēs*, n. *head or owner of the house, landowner.* S: *3617*, BAGD: 558A, CB: 366B

3868 οἰκοδομέω, *oikodomeō*, v. *to build, build up, rebuild; to edify, strengthen, benefit.* S: *3618*, BAGD: 558A, CB: 366B

3869 οἰκοδομή, *oikodomē*, n. *building, construction; building up, edification, strengthening.* S: *3619*, BAGD: 558D, CB: 366B

3870 οἰκοδομία, *oikodomia*, n. variant: *edification.* S: *3620*, BAGD: 559C, CB: –

3871 οἰκοδόμος, *oikodomos*, n. *builder.* S: *3618**, BAGD: 559C, CB: –

3872 οἰκονομέω, *oikonomeō*, v. *to manage.* S: *3621*, BAGD: 559C, CB: 366B

3873 οἰκονομία, *oikonomia*, n. *management, administration, job of administration; what is put into effect, plan.* S: *3622*, BAGD: 559C, CB: 366B

3874 οἰκονόμος, *oikonomos*, n. *manager, administrator, director, trustee.* S: *3623*, BAGD: 560A, CB: 366B

3875 οἶκος, *oikos*, n. *house, home; family, lineage.* S: *3624*, BAGD: 560B, CB: 366B

3876 οἰκουμένη, *oikoumenē*, n. *the (inhabited) world, (Roman) world; humankind.* S: *3625*, BAGD: 561B, CB: 366C

3877 οἰκουργός, *oikourgos*, a. *busy at home, domestic.* S: *3626**, BAGD: 561C, CB: –

3878 οἰκουρός, *oikouros*, a. variant: *staying at home, domestic.* S: *3626*, BAGD: 561C, CB: –

3879 οἰκτείρω, *oikteirō*, v. variant: *to have compassion on.* S: *3627*, BAGD: 561D, CB: –

3880 οἰκτιρμός, *oiktirmos*, n. *compassion, mercy, pity.* S: *3628*, BAGD: 561D, CB: 366C

3881 οἰκτίρμων, *oiktirmōn*, a. *merciful, compassionate.* S: *3629*, BAGD: 561D, CB: 366C

3882 οἰκτίρω, *oiktirō*, v. *to have compassion on.* S: *3627*, BAGD: 561D, CB: 366C

3883 οἶμαι, *oimai*, v. variant: *to think, suppose, expect.* S: *3633*, BAGD: 562C cf. οἴομαι, CB: –

3884 οἰνοπότης, *oinopotēs*, n. *drunkard, wine-drinker.* S: *3630*, BAGD: 562A, CB: 366C

3885 οἶνος, *oinos*, n. *wine.* S: *3631*, BAGD: 562A, CB: 366C

3886 οἰνοφλυγία, *oinophlygia*, n. *drunkenness.* S: *3632*, BAGD: 562C, CB: 366C

3887 οἴομαι, *oiomai*, v. *to suppose, think, expect.* S: *3633*, BAGD: 562C, CB: –

3888 οἷος, *hoios*, p.rel. *what sort of, what kind of.* S: *3634*, BAGD: 562C, CB: 357A

3889 οἱοσδηποτοῦν, *hoiosdēpotoun*, adv. variant: *no matter what.* S: *150*, BAGD: 562D, CB: –

3890 ὀκνέω, *okneō*, v. *to delay, hesitate.* S: *3635*, BAGD: 563A, CB: –

3891 ὀκνηρός, *oknēros*, a. *lazy, idle, not active; troublesome.* S: *3636*, BAGD: 563A, CB: –

3892 ὀκταήμερος, *oktaēmeros*, a. *eighth day.* S: *3637*, BAGD: 563A, CB: –

3893 ὀκτώ, *oktō*, n.num. *eight.* S: *3638*, BAGD: 563A, CB: 366C

3894 ὀλεθρευτής, *olethreutēs*, n. variant: *destroyer.* S: *3644**, BAGD: 564B cf. ὀλοθρευτής, CB: –

3895 ὀλεθρεύω, *olethreuō*, v. variant: *to destroy.* S: *3645**, BAGD: 564B cf. ὀλοθρεύω, CB: 366C

3896 ὀλέθριος, *olethrios*, a. variant: *deadly, destructive.* S: *3639**, BAGD: 563C, CB: –

3897 ὄλεθρος, *olethros*, n. *destruction, ruin.* S: *3639*, BAGD: 563B, CB: 366C

3898 ὀλιγοπιστία, *oligopistia*, n. *littleness of faith.* S: *570**, BAGD: 563B, CB: –

3899 ὀλιγόπιστος, *oligopistos*, a. *of little faith.* S: *3640*, BAGD: 563B, CB: –

3900 ὀλίγος, *oligos*, a. *little, small, short; (pl.) few.* S: *3641*, BAGD: 563C, CB: 366C

3901 ὀλιγόψυχος, *oligopsychos*, a. *timid, fainthearted.* S: *3642*, BAGD: 564A, CB: 366C

3902 ὀλιγωρέω, *oligōreō*, v. *to make light of, despise.* S: *3643*, BAGD: 564A, CB: 366C

3903 ὀλίγως, *oligōs*, adv. *scarcely, barely, hardly.* S: *3689**, BAGD: 564B, CB: –

3904 ὀλοθρευτής, *olothreutēs*, n. *destroyer.* S: *3644*, BAGD: 564B, CB: 366C

3905 ὀλοθρεύω, *olothreuō*, v. *to destroy.* S: *3645*, BAGD: 564B, CB: 366C

3906 ὁλοκαύτωμα, *holokautōma*, n. *burnt offering.* S: *3646*, BAGD: 564B, CB: 357A

3907 ὁλοκληρία, *holoklēria*, n. *completeness, wholeness (in healing).* S: *3647*, BAGD: 564C, CB: –

3908 ὁλόκληρος, *holoklēros*, a. *whole, complete.* S: *3648*, BAGD: 564C, CB: –

3909 ὀλολύζω, *ololyzō*, v. *to wail, cry out.* S: *3649*, BAGD: 564C, CB: –

3910 ὅλος, *holos*, a. *all, whole, entire; throughout.* S: *3650*, BAGD: 564D, CB: 357A

3911 ὁλοτελής, *holotelēs*, a. *through and through, wholly, completely.* S: *3651*, BAGD: 565A, CB: –

3912 Ὀλυμπᾶς, *Olympas*, n.pr. *Olympas.* S: *3652*, BAGD: 565A, CB: –

3913 ὄλυνθος, *olynthos*, n. *late fig.* S: *3653*, BAGD: 565A, CB: –

3914 ὅλως, *holōs*, adv. *completely, (not) at all; actually.* S: *3654*, BAGD: 565B, CB: 357A

3915 ὄμβρος, ombros, n. rainstorm. S: 3655, BAGD: 565B, CB: 366C

3916 ὁμείρομαι, homeiromai, v. to love, long for. S: 2442*, BAGD: 565B, CB: –

3917 ὁμιλέω, homileō, v. to talk, converse. S: 3656, BAGD: 565C, CB: –

3918 ὁμιλία, homilia, n. company, associations. S: 3657, BAGD: 565C, CB: –

3919 ὅμιλος, homilos, n. variant: crowd, throng. S: 3658, BAGD: 565D, CB: –

3920 ὁμίχλη, homichlē, n. mist, fog. S: 150, BAGD: 565D, CB: –

3921 ὄμμα, omma, n. eye. S: 3659, BAGD: 565D, CB: 366C

3922 ὄμνυμι, omnymi, v. variant: to swear, take an oath. S: 3660*, BAGD: 565D, CB: 366C

3923 ὀμνύω, omnyō, v. to declare an oath, swear an oath, promise with an oath. S: 3660, BAGD: 565D, CB: 366C

3924 ὁμοθυμαδόν, homothymadon, adv. united, in togetherness, as one. S: 3661, BAGD: 566C, CB: 357A

3925 ὁμοιάζω, homoiazō, v. variant: to be like, resemble. S: 3662, BAGD: 566C, CB: –

3926 ὁμοιοπαθής, homoiopathēs, a. like, of the same quality or kind of desires. S: 3663, BAGD: 566C, CB: 357A

3927 ὅμοιος, homoios, a. like, similar, of a same or similar nature or quality. S: 3664, BAGD: 566D, CB: 357A

3928 ὁμοιότης, homoiotēs, n. similarity, likeness. S: 3665, BAGD: 567A, CB: 357A

3929 ὁμοιόω, homoioō, v. to make like, compare; (pass.) to be like, become like. S: 3666, BAGD: 567B, CB: 357A

3930 ὁμοίωμα, homoiōma, n. likeness; looking like, image; form, appearance. S: 3667, BAGD: 567C, CB: 357A

3931 ὁμοίως, homoiōs, adv. likewise, in the same way, similarly. S: 3668, BAGD: 567D, CB: 357A

3932 ὁμοίωσις, homoiōsis, n. likeness. S: 3669, BAGD: 568A, CB: 357A

3933 ὁμολογέω, homologeō, v. to confess, acknowledge, agree, admit, declare. S: 3670, BAGD: 568A, CB: 357A

3934 ὁμολογία, homologia, n. confession, profession, acknowledgment. S: 3671, BAGD: 568D, CB: 357A

3935 ὁμολογουμένως, homologoumenōs, adv. beyond all question, most certainly. S: 3672, BAGD: 569A, CB: –

3936 ὁμόσε, homose, adv. variant: together. S: 150, BAGD: 569B, CB: –

3937 ὁμότεχνος, homotechnos, a. of the same trade. S: 3673, BAGD: 569B, CB: –

3938 ὁμοῦ, homou, adv. together. S: 3674, BAGD: 569B, CB: –

3939 ὁμόφρων, homophrōn, a. living in harmony with, like-minded. S: 3675, BAGD: 569C, CB: –

3940 ὅμως, homōs, adv. just as; at the same time. S: 3676, BAGD: 569C, CB: –

3941 ὄναρ, onar, n. dream. S: 3677, BAGD: 569D, CB: 366C

3942 ὀνάριον, onarion, n. young donkey. S: 3678, BAGD: 570A, CB: 366C

3943 ὀνειδίζω, oneidizō, v. to heap insults on, denounce, find fault, rebuke. S: 3679, BAGD: 570A, CB: 366C

3944 ὀνειδισμός, oneidismos, n. disgrace, insult. S: 3680, BAGD: 570B, CB: 366C

3945 ὄνειδος, oneidos, n. disgrace. S: 3681, BAGD: 570B, CB: 366C

3946 Ὀνήσιμος, Onēsimos, n.pr., "useful." Onesimus. S: 3682, BAGD: 570C, CB: 366C

3947 Ὀνησίφορος, Onēsiphoros, n.pr., "one bringing usefulness." Onesiphorus. S: 3683, BAGD: 570C, CB: –

3948 ὀνικός, onikos, a. pertaining to a donkey, millstone worked by a donkey. S: 3684, BAGD: 570C, CB: 366C

3949 ὀνίνημι, oninēmi, v. to have benefit or joy. S: 3685, BAGD: 570D, CB: 366C

3950 ὄνομα, onoma, n. name; title; reputation. S: 3686, BAGD: 570D, CB: 366C

3951 ὀνομάζω, onomazō, v. to give a name, designate a name; to confess; (mid.) to call oneself; (pass.) to be named; be known. S: 3687, BAGD: 573D, CB: 367A

3952 ὄνος, onos, n. donkey (female or male). S: 3688, BAGD: 574A, CB: 367A

3953 ὄντως, ontōs, adv. really, certainly, surely. S: 3689, BAGD: 574A, CB: –

3954 ὄξος, oxos, n. wine vinegar. S: 3690, BAGD: 574B, CB: 367B

3955 ὀξύς, oxys, a. sharp; swift, quick. S: 3691, BAGD: 574C, CB: –

3956 ὀπή, opē, n. hole, opening. S: 3692, BAGD: 574D, CB: –

3957 ὄπισθεν, opisthen, adv. from behind; after. S: 3693, BAGD: 574D, CB: 367A

3958 ὀπίσω, opisō, adv. behind, after, following. S: 3694, BAGD: 575A, CB: 367A

3959 ὁπλίζω, hoplizō, v. (mid.) to arm oneself with. S: 3695, BAGD: 575C, CB: 357A

3960 ὅπλον, hoplon, n. instrument, weapon, armor. S: 3696, BAGD: 575C, CB: 357A

3961 ὁποῖος, hopoios, a. what kind of, what sort of. S: 3697, BAGD: 575D, CB: –

3962 ὁπότε, hopote, pt.temp. variant: when. S: 3698, BAGD: 576A, CB: –

3963 ὅπου, hopou, pt.pl. where, wherever; whenever. S: 3699, BAGD: 576A, CB: –

3964 ὀπτάνομαι, optanomai, v. (mid.) to appear. S: 3700, BAGD: 576C, CB: 367A

3965 ὀπτασία, optasia, n. (supernatural) vision. S: 3701, BAGD: 576C, CB: 367A

3966 ὀπτός, optos, a. broiled. S: 3702, BAGD: 576C, CB: –

3967 ὀπώρα, opōra, n. fruit. S: 3703, BAGD: 576D, CB: –

3968 ὅπως, hopōs, c. & adv. that, so that, (in order) to. S: 3704, BAGD: 576D, CB: 357A

3969 ὅραμα, horama, n. (supernatural) vision; sight (from God). S: 3705, BAGD: 577B, CB: 357A

3970 ὅρασις, horasis, n. appearance; vision. S: 3706, BAGD: 577C, CB: 357A

3971 ὁρατός, horatos, a. pertaining things visible, things seen. S: 3707, BAGD: 577C, CB: 357A

3972 ὁράω, *horaō*, v. *to see, notice; perceive; (pass.) to appear, be seen.* S: *3708*, BAGD: 577D, CB: 357A

3973 ὀργή, *orgē*, n. *wrath, anger; punishment.* S: *3709*, BAGD: 578D, CB: 367A

3974 ὀργίζω, *orgizō*, v. *(mid./pass.) to be angry, enraged.* S: *3710*, BAGD: 579C, CB: 367A

3975 ὀργίλος, *orgilos*, a. *quick-tempered, inclined to anger.* S: *3711*, BAGD: 579D, CB: 367A

3976 ὀργυιά, *orgyia*, n. *fathom (about six feet).* S: *3712*, BAGD: 579D, CB: –

3977 ὀρέγω, *oregō*, v. *(mid.) to set one's heart on, strive for, aspire to, desire.* S: *3713**, BAGD: 579D, CB: 367A cf. *-omai*

3978 ὀρεινός, *oreinos*, a. *hilly, (as noun) hill country.* S: *3714*, BAGD: 580A, CB: 367A

3979 ὄρεξις, *orexis*, n. *lust, desire.* S: *3715*, BAGD: 580A, CB: 367A

3980 ὀρθοποδέω, *orthopodeō*, v. *to act in line with (the truth), act rightly.* S: *3716*, BAGD: 580A, CB: 367B

3981 ὀρθός, *orthos*, a. *straight, level.* S: *3717*, BAGD: 580B, CB: 367B

3982 ὀρθοτομέω, *orthotomeō*, v. *to handle correctly, guide on a straight path.* S: *3718*, BAGD: 580B, CB: 367B

3983 ὀρθρίζω, *orthrizō*, v. *to get up early in the morning.* S: *3719*, BAGD: 580C, CB: –

3984 ὀρθρινός, *orthrinos*, a. *early in the morning.* S: *3720*, BAGD: 580C, CB: –

3985 ὄρθριος, *orthrios*, a. variant: *early in the morning.* S: *3721*, BAGD: 580C, CB: –

3986 ὄρθρος, *orthros*, n. *dawn, daybreak, early in the morning.* S: *3722*, BAGD: 580C, CB: –

3987 ὀρθῶς, *orthōs*, adv. *correctly, rightly, plainly.* S: *3723*, BAGD: 580D, CB: 367B

3988 ὁρίζω, *horizō*, v. *to determine, set, appoint, decree.* S: *3724*, BAGD: 580D, CB: 357A

3989 ὄρνιξ, *ornix*, n. variant: *bird, hen.* S: *3733**, BAGD: 582A, CB: –

3990 ὅριον, *horion*, n. *region, area, vicinity.* S: *3725*, BAGD: 581B, CB: 357A

3991 ὁρκίζω, *horkizō*, v. *to command; implore, adjure.* S: *3726*, BAGD: 581B, CB: 357A

3992 ὅρκος, *horkos*, n. *oath.* S: *3727*, BAGD: 581C, CB: 357B

3993 ὁρκωμοσία, *horkōmosia*, n. *oath, taking of an oath.* S: *3728*, BAGD: 581D, CB: 357B

3994 ὁρμάω, *hormaō*, v. *to rush (as in a stampede).* S: *3729*, BAGD: 581D, CB: –

3995 ὁρμή, *hormē*, n. *plot, decision; impulse, desire.* S: *3730*, BAGD: 581D, CB: 357B

3996 ὅρμημα, *hormēma*, n. *sudden violence.* S: *3731*, BAGD: 581D, CB: –

3997 ὄρνεον, *orneon*, n. *bird.* S: *3732*, BAGD: 581D, CB: –

3998 ὄρνις, *ornis*, n. *hen, bird.* S: *3733*, BAGD: 582A, CB: 367B

3999 ὁροθεσία, *horothesia*, n. *exact place, fixed boundary.* S: *3734*, BAGD: 582A, CB: –

4000 ὅρος, *horos*, n. variant: *limit.* S: *150*, BAGD: 582B, CB: 357B

4001 ὄρος, *oros*, n. *hill, hillside, mountain, mountainside.* S: *3735*, BAGD: 582B, CB: 367B

4002 ὀρύσσω, *oryssō*, v. *to dig up, dig out.* S: *3736*, BAGD: 582D, CB: –

4003 ὀρφανός, *orphanos*, a. *(as noun) an orphan.* S: *3737*, BAGD: 583A, CB: 367B

4004 ὀρχέομαι, *orcheomai*, v. *to dance.* S: *3738*, BAGD: 583B, CB: 367A

4005 ὅς, *hos*, p.rel. *who, which, what, that; anyone, someone, a certain one.* S: *3739*, BAGD: 583B, CB: –

4006 ὁσάκις, *hosakis*, adv. *as often as, whenever.* S: *3740*, BAGD: 585B, CB: 357B

4007 ὅσγε, *hosge*, p.rel. & pt. variant: *who.* S: *3739 + 1065*, BAGD: 583B cf. ὅς I.10.b., CB: –

4008 ὅσιος, *hosios*, a. *holy; (as noun) Holy One.* S: *3741*, BAGD: 585C, CB: 357B

4009 ὁσιότης, *hosiotēs*, n. *holiness.* S: *3742*, BAGD: 585D, CB: 357B

4010 ὁσίως, *hosiōs*, adv. *holy, in a devout manner.* S: *3743*, BAGD: 585D, CB: –

4011 ὀσμή, *osmē*, n. *fragrance, odor.* S: *3744*, BAGD: 586A, CB: 367B

4012 ὅσος, *hosos*, a. *how great, how much, how far; as, just as.* S: *3745*, BAGD: 586B, CB: 357B

4013 ὅσπερ, *hosper*, p.rel. & pt. variant: *whosoever.* S: *3746*, BAGD: 583B cf. ὅς I.10.e., CB: –

4014 ὀστέον, *osteon*, n. *bone.* S: *3747*, BAGD: 586C, CB: 367B

4015 ὅστις, *hostis*, p.rel. & indef. *who, whoever, whatever; someone, anyone, everyone.* S: *3748 & 3755*, BAGD: 586D, CB: –

4016 ὀστοῦν, *ostoun*, n. variant: *bone.* S: *3747*, BAGD: 586C cf. ὀστέον, CB: 367B cf. *osteon*

4017 ὀστράκινος, *ostrakinos*, a. *made of clay.* S: *3749*, BAGD: 587C, CB: 367B

4018 ὄσφρησις, *osphrēsis*, n. *sense of smell.* S: *3750*, BAGD: 587C, CB: –

4019 ὀσφῦς, *osphys*, n. *waist, loins, body; belt.* S: *3751**, BAGD: 587D, CB: 367B

4020 ὅταν, *hotan*, pt.temp. *when, whenever; at once; as soon as.* S: *3752*, BAGD: 587D, CB: –

4021 ὅτε, *hote*, pt.temp. *when, while, after; as, as soon as.* S: *3753*, BAGD: 588B, CB: 357B

4022 ὅτι, *hoti*, c. *that; because, since; for.* S: *3754*, BAGD: 588C, CB: 357B

4023 οὗ, *hou*, adv.pl. *where; to which.* S: *3757*, BAGD: 589D, CB: –

4024 οὐ, *ou*, adv.neg. *no, not, not at all, in no way, (with 3590) absolutely not.* S: *3756*, BAGD: 590A, CB: –

4025 οὐά, *oua*, pt.interj. *so!, aha!.* S: *3758*, BAGD: 591A, CB: –

4026 οὐαί, *ouai*, pt.interj. *woe!, how dreadful!.* S: *3759*, BAGD: 591A, CB: 367B

4027 οὐδαμῶς, *oudamōs*, adv. *by no means.* S: *3760*, BAGD: 591B, CB: –

4028 οὐδέ, *oude*, c.neg. *and not, nor, neither, not either, not even.* S: *3761*, BAGD: 591C, CB: –

4029 οὐδείς, *oudeis*, a. *no one, not anyone, nothing.* S: *3762*, BAGD: 591D, CB: 367B

4030 οὐδέποτε, *oudepote*, adv. *never.* S: *3763*, BAGD: 592B, CB: –

4031 οὐδέπω, *oudepō*, adv. *not yet, not ever.* S: *3764*, BAGD: 592C, CB: –

4032 οὐθείς, *outheis*, a. variant: *no one, nobody, not anyone, nothing.* S: *3762**, BAGD: 591D cf. οὐδείς, CB: 367B cf. *oudeis*

4033 οὐκέτι, *ouketi*, adv. *no longer, not again, not any more, no further.* S: *3765*, BAGD: 592C, CB: –

4034 οὐκοῦν, *oukoun*, adv. *so, then (to introduce a question).* S: *3766*, BAGD: 592D, CB: –

4035 Οὐλαμμαούς, *Oulammaous*, n.pr. variant: *Oulammaous.* S: *1695**, BAGD: 592D, CB: –

4036 οὖν, *oun*, pt.infer. & trans. *therefore, then, so then.* S: *3767*, BAGD: 592D, CB: –

4037 οὔπω, *oupō*, adv. *not yet, still not; not ever.* S: *3768*, BAGD: 593C, CB: 367B

4038 οὐρά, *oura*, n. *tail.* S: *3769*, BAGD: 593C, CB: –

4039 οὐράνιος, *ouranios*, a. *heavenly, in heaven, from heaven.* S: *3770*, BAGD: 593C, CB: 367B

4040 οὐρανόθεν, *ouranothen*, adv. *from heaven.* S: *3771*, BAGD: 593D, CB: 367B

4041 οὐρανός, *ouranos*, n. *heaven; sky, air.* S: *3772*, BAGD: 593D, CB: 367B

4042 Οὐρβανός, *Ourbanos*, n.pr., "refined, elegant." *Urbanus.* S: *3773*, BAGD: 595C, CB: –

4043 Οὐρίας, *Ourias*, n.pr., "Yahweh is [my] flame, light." *Uriah.* S: *3774*, BAGD: 595C, CB: –

4044 οὖς, *ous*, n. *ear; listening, responding.* S: *3775*, BAGD: 595C, CB: 367B

4045 οὐσία, *ousia*, n. *wealth; estate, property.* S: *3776*, BAGD: 596A, CB: 367B

4046 οὔτε, *oute*, adv. [used as neg.]. *and not, neither, nor.* S: *3777*, BAGD: 596A, CB: –

4047 οὗτος, *houtos*, p.demo. *this, this one, these; (as object) him, her, it, them.* S: *3778* & *5023* & *5025* & *502*, BAGD: 596B, CB: 357B

4048 οὕτως, *houtōs*, adv. *in this manner, thus, in the same way, likewise.* S: *3779*, BAGD: 597C, CB: –

4049 οὐχί, *ouchi*, adv.neg. *not, no!.* S: *3780*, BAGD: 598B, CB: –

4050 ὀφειλέτης, *opheiletēs*, n. *debtor, one who owes, is obligated, guilty.* S: *3781*, BAGD: 598B, CB: 367A

4051 ὀφειλή, *opheilē*, n. *debt; marital duty; (pl.) taxes.* S: *3782*, BAGD: 598C, CB: 367A

4052 ὀφείλημα, *opheilēma*, n. *debt, obligation.* S: *3783*, BAGD: 598C, CB: 367A

4053 ὀφείλω, *opheilō*, v. *to owe, be in debt; be bound by oath; be obligated, ought, must.* S: *3784*, BAGD: 598D, CB: 367A

4054 ὄφελον, *ophelon*, pt. *How I wish! How I hope!.* S: *3785*, BAGD: 599A, CB: 367A

4055 ὄφελος, *ophelos*, n. *good, gain, benefit.* S: *3786*, BAGD: 599B, CB: –

4056 ὀφθαλμοδουλία, *ophthalmodoulia*, n. *eye-service, service performed to attract attention.* S: *3787**, BAGD: 599B, CB: –

4057 ὀφθαλμός, *ophthalmos*, n. *eye.* S: *3788*, BAGD: 599B, CB: 367A

4058 ὄφις, *ophis*, n. *snake, serpent.* S: *3789*, BAGD: 600A, CB: 367A

4059 ὀφρῦς, *ophrys*, n. *eyebrow, brow (of a hill).* S: *3790**, BAGD: 600B, CB: –

4060 ὀχετός, *ochetos*, n. variant: *drain, sewer.* S: *856**, BAGD: 600C, CB: –

4061 ὀχλέω, *ochleō*, v. *(pass.) to be tormented, disturbed.* S: *3791**, BAGD: 600C, CB: –

4062 ὀχλοποιέω, *ochlopoieō*, v. *to form a mob.* S: *3792*, BAGD: 600C, CB: –

4063 ὄχλος, *ochlos*, n. *crowd, people, multitude, mob.* S: *3793*, BAGD: 600C, CB: 366B

4064 Ὀχοζίας, *Ochozias*, n.pr., "Yahweh has upheld." variant: *Ahaziah.* S: *150*, BAGD: 601A, CB: –

4065 ὀχύρωμα, *ochyrōma*, n. *stronghold, fortress.* S: *3794*, BAGD: 601A, CB: 366B

4066 ὀψάριον, *opsarion*, n. *(small) fish.* S: *3795*, BAGD: 601B, CB: 367A

4067 ὀψέ, *opse*, adv. *in the evening, late in the day; (as prep.) after.* S: *3796*, BAGD: 601B, CB: 367A

4068 ὀψία, *opsia*, n. variant: *evening.* S: *3798**, BAGD: 601C, CB: –

4069 ὄψιμος, *opsimos*, a. *late (in the season), spring.* S: *3797*, BAGD: 601C, CB: 367A

4070 ὄψιος, *opsios*, a. *late; (as noun) evening.* S: *3798*, BAGD: 601C, CB: –

4071 ὄψις, *opsis*, n. *face; appearance.* S: *3799*, BAGD: 601D, CB: 367A

4072 ὀψώνιον, *opsōnion*, n. *pay, wage; support, compensation.* S: *3800*, BAGD: 602A, CB: 367A

4073 π, *p*, letter. *letter of the Greek alphabet.* S: *150*, BAGD: –, CB: –

4074 παγιδεύω, *pagideuō*, v. *to trap, entrap.* S: *3802*, BAGD: 602A, CB: –

4075 παγίς, *pagis*, n. *trap, snare.* S: *3803*, BAGD: 602A, CB: 367B

4076 πάγος, *pagos*, n. variant: *hill.* S: *697**, BAGD: 105B cf. Ἄρειος πάγος, CB: 367B

4077 πάθημα, *pathēma*, n. *suffering, misfortune; passion.* S: *3804*, BAGD: 602B, CB: 368C

4078 παθητός, *pathētos*, a. *subject to suffering.* S: *3805*, BAGD: 602D, CB: 368C

4079 πάθος, *pathos*, n. *lust, sexual passion.* S: *3806*, BAGD: 602D, CB: 368C

4080 παιδαγωγός, *paidagōgos*, n. *guardian, custodian, supervisor.* S: *3807*, BAGD: 603A, CB: 367B

4081 παιδάριον, *paidarion*, n. *little boy, child.* S: *3808*, BAGD: 603B, CB: 367B

4082 παιδεία, *paideia*, n. *discipline, training.* S: *3809*, BAGD: 603B, CB: 367B

4083 παιδευτής, *paideutēs*, n. *instructor, teacher; discipliner, corrector.* S: *3810*, BAGD: 603D, CB: 367C

4084 παιδεύω, *paideuō*, v. *instruct, train, educate; discipline, punish.* S: *3811*, BAGD: 603D, CB: 367C

4085 παιδιόθεν, *paidiothen*, adv. *from childhood.* S: *3812*, BAGD: 604A, CB: –

4086 παιδίον, *paidion*, n. *child.* S: *3813*, BAGD: 604A, CB: 367C

4087 παιδίσκη, *paidiskē*, n. *female servant, female slave, maidservant.* S: *3814*, BAGD: 604B, CB: 367C

4088 παιδόθεν, *paidothen*, adv. variant: *from childhood.* S: *3812**, BAGD: 604C, CB: –

4089 παίζω, *paizō*, v. *to indulge in revelry, play, amuse oneself, dance.* S: *3815*, BAGD: 604C, CB: 367C

4090 παῖς, *pais*, n. *boy, child, youth; servant, slave, attendant.* S: *3816*, BAGD: 604C, CB: 367C

4091 παίω, *paiō*, v. *to strike, hit.* S: *3817*, BAGD: 605B, CB: –

4092 Πακατιανός, *Pakatianos*, a.pr.g., "in Pacatia." variant: *Pacatian.* S: *3818**, BAGD: 605C, CB: –

4093 πάλαι, *palai*, adv. *long ago, in the past, already.* S: *3819*, BAGD: 605C, CB: 367C

4094 παλαιός, *palaios*, a. *old.* S: *3820*, BAGD: 605D, CB: 367C

4095 παλαιότης, *palaiotēs*, n. *the old way, obsoleteness, age.* S: *3821*, BAGD: 606A, CB: 367C

4096 παλαιόω, *palaioō*, v. *(act.) to make obsolete; (pass.) to wear out, become obsolete, become old.* S: *3822*, BAGD: 606A, CB: 367C

4097 πάλη, *palē*, n. *struggle.* S: *3823*, BAGD: 606A, CB: –

4098 παλιγγενεσία, *palingenesia*, n. *renewal; rebirth.* S: *3824*, BAGD: 606A, CB: 367C

4099 πάλιν, *palin*, adv. *again, once more; furthermore; on the other hand.* S: *3825*, BAGD: 606C, CB: 367C

4100 παλινγενεσία, *palingenesia*, n. variant: *rebirth, regeneration.* S: *3824**, BAGD: 606A cf. παλιγγενεσία, CB: 367C

4101 παμπληθεί, *pamplēthei*, adv. *with one voice, all together.* S: *3826*, BAGD: 607B, CB: –

4102 πάμπολυς, *pampolys*, a. variant: *very great.* S: *3827*, BAGD: 607B, CB: –

4103 Παμφυλία, *Pamphylia*, n.pr. *Pamphylia.* S: *3828*, BAGD: 607B, CB: –

4104 πανδοκεῖον, *pandokeion*, n. variant: *inn.* S: *3829**, BAGD: 607C, CB: –

4105 πανδοκεύς, *pandokeus*, n. variant: *innkeeper.* S: *3830**, BAGD: 607D cf. πανδοχεύς, CB: –

4106 πανδοχεῖον, *pandocheion*, n. *inn.* S: *3829*, BAGD: 607C, CB: –

4107 πανδοχεύς, *pandocheus*, n. *innkeeper.* S: *3830*, BAGD: 607D, CB: –

4108 πανήγυρις, *panēgyris*, n. *joyful assembly, festal gathering.* S: *3831*, BAGD: 607D, CB: 367C

4109 πανοικεί, *panoikei*, adv. *with one's whole family.* S: *3832*, BAGD: 607D, CB: –

4110 πανοπλία, *panoplia*, n. *full armor.* S: *3833*, BAGD: 607D, CB: 367C

4111 πανουργία, *panourgia*, n. *cunning, craftiness, deception, duplicity.* S: *3834*, BAGD: 608A, CB: 367C

4112 πανοῦργος, *panourgos*, a. *crafty, clever, sly.* S: *3835*, BAGD: 608A, CB: 367C

4113 πανπληθεί, *panplēthei*, adv. variant: *all together.* S: *3826**, BAGD: 607B cf. παμπληθεί, CB: –

4114 πανταχῇ, *pantachē*, adv. *everywhere.* S: *3837**, BAGD: 608B, CB: –

4115 πανταχόθεν, *pantachothen*, adv. variant: *from every direction.* S: *3836*, BAGD: 608B, CB: –

4116 πανταχοῦ, *pantachou*, adv. *everywhere; in all directions.* S: *3837*, BAGD: 608B, CB: –

4117 παντελής, *pantelēs*, a. *complete, perfect, absolute; at all.* S: *3838*, BAGD: 608C, CB: 367C

4118 πάντη, *pantē*, adv. *in every way.* S: *3839**, BAGD: 608D, CB: –

4119 πάντοθεν, *pantothen*, adv. *from all directions; completely, entirely.* S: *3840*, BAGD: 608D, CB: –

4120 παντοκράτωρ, *pantokratōr*, n. *Almighty.* S: *3841*, BAGD: 608D, CB: 367C

4121 πάντοτε, *pantote*, adv. *always, at all times, forever.* S: *3842*, BAGD: 609B, CB: 367C

4122 πάντως, *pantōs*, adv. *surely, certainly, by all possible means, quite.* S: *3843*, BAGD: 609B, CB: –

4123 παρά, *para*, pp. *(gen.) from; (dat.) with, before, among, in the sight of; (acc.) beside, along side, by, at.* S: *3844*, BAGD: 609C, CB: 367C

4124 παραβαίνω, *parabainō*, v. *to break, transgress; to leave, turn aside.* S: *3845*, BAGD: 611C, CB: 368A

4125 παραβάλλω, *paraballō*, v. *to come near (by ship); compare.* S: *3846*, BAGD: 611D, CB: 368A

4126 παράβασις, *parabasis*, n. *transgression, breaking, violation.* S: *3847*, BAGD: 611D, CB: 368A

4127 παραβάτης, *parabatēs*, n. *lawbreaker, transgressor.* S: *3848*, BAGD: 612A, CB: 368A

4128 παραβιάζομαι, *parabiazomai*, v. *to urge strongly, persuade.* S: *3849*, BAGD: 612A, CB: –

4129 παραβολεύομαι, *paraboleuomai*, v. *to risk, expose to danger.* S: *3851**, BAGD: 612A, CB: –

4130 παραβολή, *parabolē*, n. *parable, illustration, proverb.* S: *3850*, BAGD: 612B, CB: 368A

4131 παραβουλεύομαι, *parabouleuomai*, v. variant: *to be careless, have no concern.* S: *3851*, BAGD: 612B, CB: –

4132 παραγγελία, *parangelia*, n. *order, command; instruction.* S: *3852*, BAGD: 613A, CB: 368B

4133 παραγγέλλω, *parangellō*, v. *to order, command, direct; to give instruction.* S: *3853*, BAGD: 613B, CB: 368B

4134 παραγίνομαι, *paraginomai*, v. *to come, arrive, be present; to appear.* S: *3854*, BAGD: 613C, CB: 354B cf. ginomai

4135 παράγω, *paragō*, v. *to pass by, go on, walk beside; to pass away.* S: *3855*, BAGD: 613D, CB: –

4136 παραδειγματίζω, *paradeigmatizō*, v. *to subject to public disgrace, hold up to contempt.* S: *3856*, BAGD: 614A, CB: 368A

4137 παράδεισος, *paradeisos*, n. *paradise.* S: *3857*, BAGD: 614A, CB: 368A

4138 παραδέχομαι, *paradechomai*, v. *to accept, welcome, receive.* S: *3858*, BAGD: 614B, CB: –

4139 παραδιατριβή, *paradiatribē*, n. variant: *useless occupation.* S: *3859*, BAGD: 614B, CB: –

4140 παραδίδωμι, *paradidōmi*, v. *to hand over, betray, deliver to prison; to entrust, commit.* S: *3860*, BAGD: 614B, CB: 368A

4141 παράδοξος, *paradoxos*, a. *remarkable, wonderful.* S: *3861*, BAGD: 615D, CB: –

4142 παράδοσις, *paradosis*, n. *tradition; teachings.* S: *3862*, BAGD: 615D, CB: 368A

4143 παραζηλόω, *parazēloō*, v. *to make envious, arouse jealousy.* S: *3863*, BAGD: 616A, CB: –

4144 παραθαλάσσιος, *parathalassios*, a. *by the lake, by the sea.* S: *3864*, BAGD: 616A, CB: –

4145 παραθεωρέω, *paratheōreō*, v. *(pass.) to be overlooked, neglected.* S: *3865*, BAGD: 616B, CB: –

4146 παραθήκη, *parathēkē*, n. *deposit, thing entrusted to.* S: *3866*, BAGD: 616B, CB: 368B

4147 παραινέω, *paraineō*, v. *to warn, urge.* S: *3867*, BAGD: 616B, CB: 368A

4148 παραιτέομαι, *paraiteomai*, v. *to request, beg; to make excuses; to refuse, reject.* S: *3868*, BAGD: 616C, CB: 368A

4149 παρακαθέζομαι, *parakathezomai*, v. *to sit beside.* S: *3869**, BAGD: 616D, CB: –

4150 παρακαθίζω, *parakathizō*, v. variant: *to sit down beside.* S: *3869*, BAGD: 616D, CB: –

4151 παρακαλέω, *parakaleō*, v. *to ask, beg, plead; to comfort, encourage, exhort, urge; to call, invite.* S: *3870*, BAGD: 617A, CB: 368A

4152 παρακαλύπτω, *parakalyptō*, v. *(pass.) to be hidden.* S: *3871*, BAGD: 617D, CB: 359B cf. *kalyptō*

4153 παρακαταθήκη, *parakatathēkē*, n. variant: *deposit.* S: *3872*, BAGD: 617D, CB: 368B cf. *parathēkē*

4154 παράκειμαι, *parakeimai*, v. *to be present, ready.* S: *3873*, BAGD: 617D, CB: –

4155 παράκλησις, *paraklēsis*, n. *encouragement, comfort, consolation, appeal.* S: *3874*, BAGD: 618A, CB: 368A

4156 παράκλητος, *paraklētos*, n. *counselor, intercessor, helper.* S: *3875*, BAGD: 618B, CB: 368A

4157 παρακοή, *parakoē*, n. *disobedience, unwillingness to hear.* S: *3876*, BAGD: 618D, CB: 368A

4158 παρακολουθέω, *parakoloutheō*, v. *to follow, accompany; to know all about; to investigate.* S: *3877*, BAGD: 618D, CB: 368A

4159 παρακούω, *parakouō*, v. *to refuse to listen, ignore.* S: *3878*, BAGD: 619A, CB: 368A

4160 παρακύπτω, *parakyptō*, v. *to bend over; to look (intently).* S: *3879*, BAGD: 619B, CB: –

4161 παραλαμβάνω, *paralambanō*, v. *to take with; take charge of; to receive, accept.* S: *3880*, BAGD: 619B, CB: 368A

4162 παραλέγομαι, *paralegomai*, v. *to sail past, move along.* S: *3881*, BAGD: 619D, CB: –

4163 παράλιος, *paralios*, a. *(located) by the sea; (as noun) seacoast.* S: *3882*, BAGD: 620A, CB: –

4164 παραλλαγή, *parallagē*, n. *change, variation.* S: *3883*, BAGD: 620A, CB: –

4165 παραλογίζομαι, *paralogizomai*, v. *to deceive, delude.* S: *3884*, BAGD: 620B, CB: 368A

4166 παραλυτικός, *paralytikos*, a. *(as noun) paralytic, lame person.* S: *3885*, BAGD: 620B, CB: 368A

4167 παράλυτος, *paralytos*, a. variant: *(as noun) paralytic.* S: *3885**, BAGD: 620B, CB: 368A

4168 παραλύω, *paralyō*, v. *(pass.) to be paralyzed, disabled; (as noun) paralytic.* S: *3886*, BAGD: 620B, CB: 368A

4169 παραμένω, *paramenō*, v. *to continue; to remain with.* S: *3887*, BAGD: 620C, CB: 368A

4170 παραμυθέομαι, *paramytheomai*, v. *to comfort, encourage, console.* S: *3888*, BAGD: 620D, CB: 368B

4171 παραμυθία, *paramythia*, n. *comfort, consolation.* S: *3889*, BAGD: 620D, CB: 368B

4172 παραμύθιον, *paramythion*, n. *comfort, consolation, encouragement.* S: *3890*, BAGD: 620D, CB: 368B

4173 παράνοια, *paranoia*, n. variant: *madness, foolishness.* S: *3913**, BAGD: 621A, CB: –

4174 παρανομέω, *paranomeō*, v. *to violate the law, act contrary to the law.* S: *3891*, BAGD: 621A, CB: 368B

4175 παρανομία, *paranomia*, n. *wrongdoing, lawlessness.* S: *3892*, BAGD: 621A, CB: –

4176 παραπικραίνω, *parapikrainō*, v. *to rebel, disobey.* S: *3893*, BAGD: 621A, CB: 368B

4177 παραπικρασμός, *parapikrasmos*, n. *rebellion, revolt.* S: *3894*, BAGD: 621B, CB: 368B

4178 παραπίπτω, *parapiptō*, v. *to fall away, commit apostasy.* S: *3895*, BAGD: 621B, CB: 368B

4179 παραπλέω, *parapleō*, v. *to sail past.* S: *3896*, BAGD: 621B, CB: –

4180 παραπλήσιος, *paraplēsios*, a. *(as adv.) almost, nearly.* S: *3897**, BAGD: 621C, CB: 368B

4181 παραπλησίως, *paraplēsiōs*, adv. *in just the same way.* S: *3898*, BAGD: 621C, CB: –

4182 παραπορεύομαι, *paraporeuomai*, v. *to pass by, go through.* S: *3899*, BAGD: 621D, CB: –

4183 παράπτωμα, *paraptōma*, n. *trespass, transgression, sin against.* S: *3900*, BAGD: 621D, CB: 368B

4184 παραρρέω, *pararreō*, v. *to drift away, flow past, slip away.* S: *3901*, BAGD: 621D, CB: 368B

4185 παράσημος, *parasēmos*, a. *distinguished, marked; (as noun) figurehead (on a ship).* S: *3902*, BAGD: 622A, CB: –

4186 παρασκευάζω, *paraskeuazō*, v. *(act.) to prepare; (mid.) to get ready; (mid./pass.) to be ready.* S: *3903*, BAGD: 622A, CB: 368B

4187 παρασκευή, *paraskeuē*, n. *Preparation Day.* S: *3904*, BAGD: 622B, CB: 368B

4188 παραστάτις, *parastatis*, n. variant: *supporter.* S: *4368**, BAGD: 622B, CB: –

4189 παρατείνω, *parateinō*, v. *to keep on, prolong, extend.* S: *3905*, BAGD: 622C, CB: –

4190 παρατηρέω, *paratēreō*, v. *to watch closely, observe.* S: *3906*, BAGD: 622C, CB: 368B

4191 παρατήρησις, *paratērēsis*, n. *careful observation.* S: *3907*, BAGD: 622D, CB: 368B

4192 παρατίθημι, *paratithēmi*, v. *(act.) to set before; (mid.) to entrust, commit.* S: *3908*, BAGD: 622D, CB: –

4193 παρατυγχάνω, *paratynchanō*, v. *to happen to be there.* S: *3909*, BAGD: 623A, CB: –

4194 παραυτίκα, *parautika*, adv. *(as adj.) momentary.* S: *3910*, BAGD: 623B, CB: –

4195 παραφέρω, *parapherō*, v. *to take away, remove; (pass.) to be carried away.* S: *3911*, BAGD: 623B, CB: –

4196 παραφρονέω, *paraphroneō*, v. *to be out of one's mind, insane.* S: *3912*, BAGD: 623C, CB: 370C cf. *phroneō*

4197 παραφρονία, *paraphronia*, n. *madness, insanity.* S: *3913*, BAGD: 623C, CB: –

4198 παραφροσύνη, *paraphrosynē*, n. variant: *madness, insanity.* S: *3913**, BAGD: 623C, CB: –

4199 παραχειμάζω, *paracheimazō*, v. *to spend the winter.* S: *3914*, BAGD: 623D, CB: –

4200 παραχειμασία, *paracheimasia*, n. *spending the winter.* S: *3915*, BAGD: 623D, CB: –

4201 παραχράομαι, *parachraomai*, v. variant: *to misuse.* S: *2710**, BAGD: 623D, CB: –

4202 παραχρῆμα, *parachrēma*, adv. *immediately, instantly, at once.* S: *3916*, BAGD: 623D, CB: –

4203 πάρδαλις, *pardalis*, n. *leopard.* S: *3917*, BAGD: 623D, CB: 368B

4204 παρεδρεύω, *paredreuō*, v. *to serve regularly, sit beside.* S: *4332**, BAGD: 624A, CB: –

4205 πάρειμι, *pareimi*, v. *to be present, here; to have come.* S: *3918*, BAGD: 624A, CB: 368B

4206 παρεισάγω, *pareisagō*, v. *to bring in secretly.* S: *3919*, BAGD: 624C, CB: –

4207 παρείσακτος, *pareisaktos*, a. *brought in secretly, infiltrated.* S: *3920*, BAGD: 624C, CB: –

4208 παρεισδύω, *pareisdyō*, v. *to slip in secretly.* S: *3921*, BAGD: 624D, CB: –

4209 παρεισέρχομαι, *pareiserchomai*, v. *to come in, sneak in; to add to.* S: *3922*, BAGD: 624D, CB: 368B

4210 παρεισφέρω, *pareispherō*, v. *to do one's best.* S: *3923*, BAGD: 625A, CB: –

4211 παρεκτός, *parektos*, adv. & pp.*. *(as adv.) besides; (as prep.) except for, apart from.* S: *3924*, BAGD: 625A, CB: 368B

4212 παρεμβάλλω, *paremballō*, v. *to build, erect.* S: *4016**, BAGD: 625B, CB: 368B

4213 παρεμβολή, *parembolē*, n. *camp, barracks; army.* S: *3925*, BAGD: 625B, CB: 368B

4214 παρενοχλέω, *parenochleō*, v. *to make difficult, trouble.* S: *3926*, BAGD: 625C, CB: –

4215 παρεπίδημος, *parepidēmos*, a. *(as noun) stranger.* S: *3927*, BAGD: 625D, CB: 368B

4216 παρέρχομαι, *parerchomai*, v. *to go by, pass by; (pass.) to pass away, come to an end, disappear; be taken away.* S: *3928*, BAGD: 625D, CB: 368B

4217 πάρεσις, *paresis*, n. *leaving unpunished, passing over.* S: *3929*, BAGD: 626B, CB: 368B

4218 παρέχω, *parechō*, v. *to present, give; to show, give proof; to cause, bring about, promote; (mid.) to set (an example); to provide; to get for oneself.* S: *3930*, BAGD: 626B, CB: 348C cf. *echō*

4219 παρηγορία, *parēgoria*, n. *comfort.* S: *3931*, BAGD: 626D, CB: –

4220 παρθενία, *parthenia*, n. *virginity.* S: *3932*, BAGD: 626D, CB: 368C

4221 παρθένος, *parthenos*, n. *virgin (male and female).* S: *3933*, BAGD: 627A, CB: 368C

4222 Πάρθοι, *Parthoi*, n.pr.g., "of Partia." *Parthian.* S: *3934**, BAGD: 627B, CB: –

4223 παρίημι, *pariēmi*, v. *to leave undone, neglect; (pass.) to be feeble, weakened, listless.* S: *3935*, BAGD: 627C, CB: 368B

4224 παριστάνω, *paristanō*, v. variant: *see 4225.* S: *3936**, BAGD: 627C, CB: 368B

4225 παρίστημι, *paristēmi*, v. *to place beside, put at disposal; to present, make an offering; (intr.) to stand before, provide, come to aid.* S: *3936*, BAGD: 627C, CB: 368B

4226 Παρμενᾶς, *Parmenas*, n.pr., "steady, reliable." *Parmenas.* S: *3937*, BAGD: 628C, CB: –

4227 πάροδος, *parodos*, n. *passing by.* S: *3938*, BAGD: 628D, CB: –

4228 παροικέω, *paroikeō*, v. *to live as a stranger, visit; to migrate.* S: *3939*, BAGD: 628D, CB: 368B

4229 παροικία, *paroikia*, n. *residence as a stranger.* S: *3940*, BAGD: 629A, CB: 368B

4230 πάροικος, *paroikos*, a. *strange; (as noun) alien, foreigner, stranger.* S: *3941*, BAGD: 629A, CB: 368B

4231 παροιμία, *paroimia*, n. *figure of speech, proverb, maxim.* S: *3942*, BAGD: 629B, CB: 368B

4232 πάροινος, *paroinos*, a. *drunken, given to drunkenness.* S: *3943*, BAGD: 629B, CB: 368C

4233 παροίχομαι, *paroichomai*, v. *to pass by.* S: *3944*, BAGD: 629B, CB: –

4234 παρομοιάζω, *paromoiazō*, v. *to be like.* S: *3945*, BAGD: 629B, CB: 368C

4235 παρόμοιος, *paromoios*, a. *like, similar.* S: *3946*, BAGD: 629B, CB: 368C

4236 παροξύνω, *paroxynō*, v. *(intr.) to be greatly distressed; to be angered, irritated.* S: *3947*, BAGD: 629C, CB: 368C

4237 παροξυσμός, *paroxysmos*, n. *sharp disagreement; spurring on, encouraging.* S: *3948*, BAGD: 629C, CB: 368C

4238 παροράω, *pororaō*, v. variant: *to overlook, take no notice of.* S: *5237**, BAGD: 629C, CB: –

4239 παροργίζω, *parorgizō*, v. *to anger, exasperate.* S: *3949*, BAGD: 629D, CB: 368C

4240 παροργισμός, *parorgismos*, n. *anger.* S: *3950*, BAGD: 629D, CB: 368C

4241 παροτρύνω, *parotrynō*, v. *to incite, arouse.* S: *3951*, BAGD: 629D, CB: –

4242 παρουσία, *parousia*, n. *presence; coming, advent.* S: *3952*, BAGD: 629D, CB: 368C

4243 παροψίς, *paropsis*, n. *dish.* S: *3953*, BAGD: 630B, CB: –

4244 παρρησία, *parrēsia*, n. *boldness, confidence, frankness; public, openness (of speech).* S: *3954*, BAGD: 630C, CB: 368C

4245 παρρησιάζομαι, *parrēsiazomai*, v. *to speak boldly, preach fearlessly.* S: *3955*, BAGD: 631A, CB: 368C

4246 πᾶς, *pas*, a. *all, every (thing, one), whole; always.* S: *3956*, BAGD: 631A, CB: 368C

4247 πάσχα, *pascha*, n. *Passover, Passover week; Passover meal; Passover lamb.* S: *3957*, BAGD: 633B, CB: 368C

4248 πάσχω, *paschō*, v. *to suffer.* S: *3958*, BAGD: 633D, CB: 368C

4249 Πάταρα, *Patara*, n.pr. *Patara.* S: *3959*, BAGD: 634C, CB: –

4250 πατάσσω, *patassō*, v. *to hit, strike; kill.* S: *3960*, BAGD: 634D, CB: 368C

4251 πατέω, *pateō*, v. *to trample on, tread on.* S: *3961*, BAGD: 634D, CB: 368C

4252 πατήρ, *patēr*, n. *father; (pl.) parents, ancestors.* S: *3962*, BAGD: 635A, CB: 368C

4253 Πάτμος, *Patmos*, n.pr. *Patmos.* S: *3963*, BAGD: 636C, CB: –

4254 πατραλῴας, *patralōas*, n. variant: *one who kills one's father.* S: *3964*, BAGD: 636D, CB: –

4255 πατριά, *patria*, n. *family, family line, clan; people, nation.* S: *3965*, BAGD: 636D, CB: 369A

4256 πατριάρχης, *patriarchēs*, n. *patriarch, father of a nation.* S: *3966*, BAGD: 636D, CB: –

4257 πατρικός, *patrikos*, a. *paternal, from one's ancestors.* S: *3967*, BAGD: 636D, CB: 369A

4258 πατρίς, *patris*, n. *hometown, homeland.* S: *3968*, BAGD: 636D, CB: 369A

4259 Πατροβᾶς, *Patrobas*, n.pr., "father of existence." *Patrobas.* S: *3969**, BAGD: 637A, CB: –

4260 πατρολῴας, *patrolōas*, n. *one who kills one's father.* S: *3964**, BAGD: 637A, CB: –

4261 πατροπαράδοτος, *patroparadotos*, a. *handed down from forefathers.* S: *3970*, BAGD: 637A, CB: –

4262 πατρῷος, *patrōos*, a. *ancestral, from forefathers.* S: *3971*, BAGD: 637B, CB: –

4263 Παῦλος, *Paulos*, n.pr., "little." *Paul, Paulus.* S: *3972*, BAGD: 637B, CB: 369A

4264 παύω, *pauō*, v. *(act.) to cause to stop; (mid.) to stop, cease, finish.* S: *3973*, BAGD: 638A, CB: –

4265 Πάφος, *Paphos*, n.pr. *Paphos.* S: *3974*, BAGD: 638B, CB: –

4266 παχύνω, *pachynō*, v. *to become calloused of heart, make fat.* S: *3975*, BAGD: 638B, CB: 367B

4267 πέδη, *pedē*, n. *foot shackle, fetter.* S: *3976*, BAGD: 638C, CB: –

4268 πεδινός, *pedinos*, a. *level, flat.* S: *3977*, BAGD: 638C, CB: 369A

4269 πεζεύω, *pezeuō*, v. *to go on foot, travel by walking.* S: *3978*, BAGD: 638D, CB: –

4270 πεζῇ, *pezē*, adv. *on foot.* S: *3979*, BAGD: 638D, CB: –

4271 πεζός, *pezos*, a. variant: *on foot.* S: *3979**, BAGD: 638D, CB: –

4272 πειθαρχέω, *peitharcheō*, v. *to obey; to take advice.* S: *3980*, BAGD: 638D, CB: 369A

4273 πειθός, *peithos*, a. *persuasive.* S: *3981*, BAGD: 639A, CB: 369A

4274 πειθώ, *peithō*, n. variant: *persuasiveness.* S: *3981**, BAGD: 639A, CB: 369A

4275 πείθω, *peithō*, v. *to convince, persuade; to trust in, have confidence in, be persuaded.* S: *3982*, BAGD: 639A, CB: 369A

4276 Πειλᾶτος, *Peilatos*, n.pr. variant: *Pilate.* S: *4091**, BAGD: 657D cf. Πιλα=τος, CB: –

4277 πεινάω, *peinaō*, v. *to be hungry.* S: *3983*, BAGD: 640A, CB: 369A

4278 πεῖρα, *peira*, n. *to try to do, attempt; to face, experience.* S: *3984*, BAGD: 640A, CB: 369A

4279 πειράζω, *peirazō*, v. *to test, tempt; to try to trap; to examine (oneself).* S: *3985*, BAGD: 640B, CB: 369A

4280 πειρασμός, *peirasmos*, n. *test; trial; temptation.* S: *3986*, BAGD: 640D, CB: 369A

4281 πειράω, *peiraō*, v. *to try, attempt.* S: *3987*, BAGD: 641A, CB: 369A

4282 πεισμονή, *peismonē*, n. *persuasion.* S: *3988*, BAGD: 641B, CB: 369A

4283 πέλαγος, *pelagos*, n. *open sea; depths.* S: *3989*, BAGD: 641B, CB: –

4284 πελεκίζω, *pelekizō*, v. *to behead.* S: *3990*, BAGD: 641C, CB: –

4285 πεμπταῖος, *pemptaios*, a. variant: *on the fifth day.* S: *150*, BAGD: 641C, CB: –

4286 πέμπτος, *pemptos*, a. *fifth.* S: *3991*, BAGD: 641C, CB: –

4287 πέμπω, *pempō*, v. *to send.* S: *3992*, BAGD: 641D, CB: 369A

4288 πένης, *penēs*, a. *poor.* S: *3993*, BAGD: 642C, CB: 369A

4289 πενθερά, *penthera*, n. *mother-in-law.* S: *3994*, BAGD: 642C, CB: –

4290 πενθερός, *pentheros*, n. *father-in-law.* S: *3995*, BAGD: 642C, CB: –

4291 πενθέω, *pentheō*, v. *to mourn, grieve (over).* S: *3996*, BAGD: 642C, CB: 369A

4292 πένθος, *penthos*, n. *mourning, grief, sadness.* S: *3997*, BAGD: 642D, CB: 369A

4293 πενιχρός, *penichros*, a. *poor, needy.* S: *3998*, BAGD: 642D, CB: 369A

4294 πεντάκις, *pentakis*, adv. *five times.* S: *3999*, BAGD: 643A, CB: –

4295 πεντακισχίλιοι, *pentakischilioi*, a.num. *five thousand.* S: *4000*, BAGD: 643A, CB: 369A

4296 πεντακόσιοι, *pentakosioi*, a.num. *five hundred.* S: *4001*, BAGD: 643A, CB: –

4297 πέντε, *pente*, n.num. *five.* S: *4002*, BAGD: 643A, CB: 369A

4298 πεντεκαιδέκατος, *pentekaidekatos*, a. *fifteenth.* S: *4003*, BAGD: 643A, CB: –

4299 πεντήκοντα, *pentēkonta*, n.num. *fifty.* S: *4004*, BAGD: 643A, CB: –

4300 πεντηκοστή, pentēkostē, n. *Pentecost, fiftieth (day after Passover)*. S: *4005*, BAGD: 643A, CB: 369A

4301 πεποίθησις, pepoithēsis, n. *confidence, trust*. S: *4006*, BAGD: 643B, CB: 369B

4302 -περ, -per, pt.emph. variant: *an affix for various kinds of emphasis*. S: *4007*, BAGD: 643C, CB: –

4303 Πέραια, Peraia, n.pr. variant: *Peraea*. S: *150*, BAGD: 643D cf. πέραν 2., CB: –

4304 περαιτέρω, peraiterō, adv. *further, beyond*. S: *4012 + 2087*, BAGD: 643D, CB: –

4305 πέραν, peran, adv. *on the other side; (as noun) opposite side, region across*. S: *4008*, BAGD: 643D, CB: –

4306 πέρας, peras, n. *end, limit*. S: *4009*, BAGD: 644A, CB: 369B

4307 Πέργαμος, Pergamos, n.pr. *Pergamum*. S: *4010*, BAGD: 644B, CB: –

4308 Πέργη, Pergē, n.pr. *Perga*. S: *4011*, BAGD: 644B, CB: –

4309 περί, peri, pp. *(gen.) about, concerning, in regard to; (acc.) around, about, nearby*. S: *4012*, BAGD: 644B, CB: 369B

4310 περιάγω, periagō, v. *(tr.) to take (a wife); (intr.) to go about, travel about*. S: *4013*, BAGD: 645C, CB: –

4311 περιαιρέω, periaireō, v. *to take away; (pass.) to be taken away; to cut loose, set sail; to be given up, abandoned*. S: *4014*, BAGD: 645D, CB: –

4312 περιάπτω, periaptō, v. *to kindle (a fire)*. S: *681**, BAGD: 645D, CB: –

4313 περιαστράπτω, periastraptō, v. *to flash around, shine around*. S: *4015*, BAGD: 645D, CB: –

4314 περιβάλλω, periballō, v. *to dress, clothe, wrap around*. S: *4016*, BAGD: 646A, CB: –

4315 περιβλέπω, periblepō, v. *to look around at*. S: *4017*, BAGD: 646B, CB: 345A cf. blepō

4316 περιβόλαιον, peribolaion, n. *covering, robe*. S: *4018*, BAGD: 646C, CB: 369B

4317 περιδέω, perideō, v. *to wrap around*. S: *4019*, BAGD: 646C, CB: 346C cf. deō

4318 περιεργάζομαι, periergazomai, v. *to be a busybody*. S: *4020*, BAGD: 646D, CB: 369B

4319 περίεργος, periergos, a. *meddlesome, curious; (as noun) busybody; (pl.) sorcery, magical arts*. S: *4021*, BAGD: 646D, CB: 369B

4320 περιέρχομαι, perierchomai, v. *to go around*. S: *4022*, BAGD: 646D, CB: 369B

4321 περιέχω, periechō, v. *to seize, encircle; to contain, to say*. S: *4023*, BAGD: 647A, CB: 369B

4322 περιζώννυμι, perizōnnymi, v. *to buckle a belt around, gird, dress for service*. S: *4024*, BAGD: 647B, CB: 369C

4323 περιζωννύω, perizōnnyō, v. variant: *to buckle a belt around, dress for service, gird*. S: *4024**, BAGD: 647B, CB: 369C cf. perizōnnymi

4324 περίθεσις, perithesis, n. *wearing, putting on*. S: *4025*, BAGD: 647C, CB: –

4325 περιΐστημι, periistēmi, v. *to stand around; avoid, shun*. S: *4026*, BAGD: 647C, CB: –

4326 περικάθαρμα, perikatharma, n. *scum, refuse*. S: *4027*, BAGD: 647D, CB: 369B

4327 περικαθίζω, perikathizō, v. variant: *to sit around*. S: *4776**, BAGD: 647D, CB: –

4328 περικαλύπτω, perikalyptō, v. *to blindfold, cover the face or eyes; to cover (with gold)*. S: *4028*, BAGD: 647D, CB: 359B cf. kalyptō

4329 περίκειμαι, perikeimai, v. *to surround, place or tie around; to be subject to*. S: *4029*, BAGD: 647D, CB: –

4330 περικεφαλαία, perikephalaia, n. *helmet*. S: *4030*, BAGD: 648A, CB: 369B

4331 περικρατής, perikratēs, a. *secure, having power, being in command of, getting under control*. S: *4031*, BAGD: 648B, CB: –

4332 περικρύβω, perikrybō, v. *to seclude oneself, hide, conceal oneself*. S: *4032**, BAGD: 648B, CB: –

4333 περικυκλόω, perikykloō, v. *to encircle, surround*. S: *4033*, BAGD: 648B, CB: –

4334 περιλάμπω, perilampō, v. *to shine around, blaze around*. S: *4034*, BAGD: 648C, CB: 369B

4335 περιλείπομαι, perileipomai, v. *to be left, remain*. S: *4035**, BAGD: 648C, CB: 369B

4336 περιλείχω, perileichō, v. variant: *to lick all around, lick off*. S: *621**, BAGD: 648C, CB: –

4337 περίλυπος, perilypos, a. *overwhelmingly sorrowful; greatly distressing*. S: *4036*, BAGD: 648C, CB: –

4338 περιμένω, perimenō, v. *to wait for*. S: *4037*, BAGD: 648C, CB: 369B

4339 πέριξ, perix, adv. *around*. S: *4038*, BAGD: 648D, CB: –

4340 περιοικέω, perioikeō, v. *to live in a neighborhood; (as noun) neighbor*. S: *4039*, BAGD: 648D, CB: –

4341 περίοικος, perioikos, a. *neighboring; (as noun) neighbor*. S: *4040*, BAGD: 648D, CB: –

4342 περιούσιος, periousios, a. *one's very own, special*. S: *4041*, BAGD: 648D, CB: 369B

4343 περιοχή, periochē, n. *passage (of Scripture), portion*. S: *4042*, BAGD: 648D, CB: –

4344 περιπατέω, peripateō, v. *to walk (around); to live, conduct one's life*. S: *4043*, BAGD: 649A, CB: 369B

4345 περιπείρω, peripeirō, v. *to pierce*. S: *4044*, BAGD: 649D, CB: –

4346 περιπίπτω, peripiptō, v. *to fall into the hands of; to strike; to face, be involved in*. S: *4045*, BAGD: 649D, CB: 369B

4347 περιποιέω, peripoieō, v. *(mid.) to keep, save; to gain for oneself; to buy, acquire*. S: *4046**, BAGD: 650A, CB: 369B cf. -omai

4348 περιποίησις, peripoiēsis, n. *possession, property; sharing in, gaining; saving*. S: *4047*, BAGD: 650A, CB: 369B

4349 περιραίνω, perirainō, v. variant: *to sprinkle all around*. S: *150*, BAGD: 650B, CB: –

4350 περιραντίζω, perirantizō, v. variant: *to sprinkle all around*. S: *150*, BAGD: 650B cf. περιρρήγνυμι, CB: –

4351 περιρήγνυμι, perirēgnymi, v. *to strip off, tear off*. S: *4048*, BAGD: 650B, CB: –

4352 περισπάω, perispaō, v. *(pass.) to be distracted*. S: *4049*, BAGD: 650B, CB: –

4353 περισσεία, *perisseia*, n. *abundance, prevalence.* S: *4050*, BAGD: 650C, CB: 369C

4354 περίσσευμα, *perisseuma*, n. *overflow, plenty; what is left over, scraps.* S: *4051*, BAGD: 650C, CB: 369C

4355 περισσεύω, *perisseuō*, v. *to have abundance, more than enough, overflow.* S: *4052*, BAGD: 650C, CB: 369C

4356 περισσός, *perissos*, a. *exceeding, going beyond; full, abundant; (compar.) more than; (as noun) advantage.* S: *4053*, BAGD: 651B, CB: 369C

4357 περισσότερον, *perissoteron*, adv. variant: *even more, so much more.* S: *4054*, BAGD: 651C, CB: 369C

4358 περισσότερος, *perissoteros*, a. *more than, even more; greater than; with special honor.* S: *4055*, BAGD: 651C, CB: 369C

4359 περισσοτέρως, *perissoterōs*, adv. *to a much greater degree; especially, frequently, extremely.* S: *4056*, BAGD: 651D, CB: 369C

4360 περισσῶς, *perissōs*, adv. *even more, all the more.* S: *4057*, BAGD: 651D, CB: 369C

4361 περιστερά, *peristera*, n. *dove, pigeon.* S: *4058*, BAGD: 651D, CB: 369C

4362 περιτέμνω, *peritemnō*, v. *to circumcise.* S: *4059*, BAGD: 652B, CB: 369C

4363 περιτίθημι, *peritithēmi*, v. *to put on, set on; to treat with.* S: *4060*, BAGD: 652C, CB: 378C cf. *tithēmi*

4364 περιτομή, *peritomē*, n. *circumcision; the Jews.* S: *4061*, BAGD: 652D, CB: 369C

4365 περιτρέπω, *peritrepō*, v. *to drive (to insanity).* S: *4062*, BAGD: 653A, CB: –

4366 περιτρέχω, *peritrechō*, v. *to run throughout, run about.* S: *4063*, BAGD: 653A, CB: –

4367 περιφέρω, *peripherō*, v. *to carry, carry around; (pass.) to be blown about, carried here and there.* S: *4064*, BAGD: 653B, CB: 369B

4368 περιφρονέω, *periphroneō*, v. *to despise, look down on.* S: *4065*, BAGD: 653B, CB: 369B

4369 περίχωρος, *perichōros*, a. *neighboring; (as noun) surrounding country.* S: *4066*, BAGD: 653C, CB: –

4370 περίψημα, *peripsēma*, n. *refuse, garbage.* S: *4067*, BAGD: 653C, CB: 369C

4371 περπερεύομαι, *perpereuomai*, v. *to boast, brag.* S: *4068*, BAGD: 653D, CB: –

4372 Περσίς, *Persis*, n.pr., "female Persian." *Persis.* S: *4069*, BAGD: 653D, CB: –

4373 πέρυσι, *perysi*, adv. *from last year, since last year.* S: *4070*, BAGD: 653D, CB: 369C

4374 πετεινόν, *peteinon*, n. *bird.* S: *4071*, BAGD: 654A, CB: 369C

4375 πέτομαι, *petomai*, v. *to fly.* S: *4072*, BAGD: 654A, CB: –

4376 πέτρα, *petra*, n. *rock.* S: *4073*, BAGD: 654A, CB: 369C

4377 Πέτρος, *Petros*, n.pr., "rock, stone." *Peter.* S: *4074*, BAGD: 654D, CB: 369C

4378 πετρώδης, *petrōdēs*, a. *rocky, stony; (as noun) rocky place.* S: *4075*, BAGD: 655C, CB: 369C

4379 πήγανον, *pēganon*, n. *rue (a garden herb).* S: *4076*, BAGD: 655D, CB: 369A

4380 πηγή, *pēgē*, n. *spring, well (of water); flow (of blood).* S: *4077*, BAGD: 655D, CB: 369A

4381 πήγνυμι, *pēgnymi*, v. *to set up.* S: *4078*, BAGD: 656A, CB: 369A

4382 πηδάλιον, *pēdalion*, n. *rudder, steering paddle.* S: *4079*, BAGD: 656A, CB: –

4383 πηλίκος, *pēlikos*, a. *how great, how large.* S: *4080*, BAGD: 656B, CB: –

4384 πηλός, *pēlos*, n. *mud, lump of clay.* S: *4081*, BAGD: 656B, CB: 369A

4385 πήρα, *pēra*, n. *traveler's bag.* S: *4082*, BAGD: 656C, CB: 369B

4386 πηρόω, *pēroō*, v. variant: *to disable, maim.* S: *4456**, BAGD: 656D, CB: 369C

4387 πήρωσις, *pērōsis*, n. variant: *nearsightedness, blindness.* S: *4457**, BAGD: 656D, CB: 369C

4388 πῆχυς, *pēchys*, n. *measure of length: cubit, or time: hour.* S: *4083*, BAGD: 656D, CB: –

4389 πιάζω, *piazō*, v. *to seize, arrest, capture.* S: *4084*, BAGD: 657A, CB: –

4390 πιέζω, *piezō*, v. *(pass.) to be pressed down.* S: *4085*, BAGD: 657B, CB: –

4391 πιθανολογία, *pithanologia*, n. *fine-sounding arguments, persuasive speech.* S: *4086*, BAGD: 657B, CB: 371A

4392 πιθός, *pithos*, a. variant: *persuasive.* S: *3981**, BAGD: 639A cf. πειθός, CB: –

4393 πικραίνω, *pikrainō*, v. *to turn sour, make bitter; to become sour, embittered.* S: *4087*, BAGD: 657B, CB: 371A

4394 πικρία, *pikria*, n. *bitterness.* S: *4088*, BAGD: 657C, CB: 371A

4395 πικρός, *pikros*, a. *bitter, salty.* S: *4089*, BAGD: 657C, CB: 371A

4396 πικρῶς, *pikrōs*, adv. *bitterly.* S: *4090*, BAGD: 657D, CB: 371A

4397 Πιλᾶτος, *Pilatos*, n.pr., "[family name]." *Pilate.* S: *4091**, BAGD: 657D, CB: –

4398 πίμπλημι, *pimplēmi*, v. *to fill; (pass.) to be filled, completed.* S: *4130*, BAGD: 658A, CB: 371A

4399 πίμπρημι, *pimprēmi*, v. *to swell.* S: *4092*, BAGD: 658B, CB: 371A

4400 πινακίδιον, *pinakidion*, n. *(small) writing tablet.* S: *4093*, BAGD: 658B, CB: –

4401 πινακίς, *pinakis*, n. variant: *(small) writing tablet.* S: *4093**, BAGD: 658C, CB: –

4402 πίναξ, *pinax*, n. *platter, dish.* S: *4094*, BAGD: 658C, CB: –

4403 πίνω, *pinō*, v. *to drink.* S: *4095*, BAGD: 658C, CB: 371A

4404 πιότης, *piotēs*, n. *richness, nourishing sap.* S: *4096*, BAGD: 659A, CB: 371A

4405 πιπράσκω, *pipraskō*, v. *to sell.* S: *4097*, BAGD: 659A, CB: 371A

4406 πίπτω, *piptō*, v. *to fall, collapse; to bow down; to die.* S: *4098*, BAGD: 659B, CB: 371A

4407 Πισιδία, *Pisidia*, n.pr. *Pisidia.* S: *4099*, BAGD: 660B, CB: –

4408 Πισίδιος, *Pisidios*, a.pr., "of Pisidia." *Pisidian.* S: *4099**, BAGD: 660B, CB: –

4409 πιστεύω, *pisteuō*, v. *to believe, put one's faith in, trust; (pass.) entrust.* S: *4100*, BAGD: 660B, CB: 371A

4410 πιστικός, *pistikos*, a. *pure.* S: *4101*, BAGD: 662B, CB: –

4411 πίστις, *pistis*, n. *faith, faithfulness, belief.* S: *4102*, BAGD: 662B, CB: 371A

4412 πιστός, *pistos*, a. *faithful, trustworthy, reliable, believing.* S: *4103*, BAGD: 664C, CB: 371A

4413 πιστόω, *pistoō*, v. *(pass.) to be convinced of.* S: *4104*, BAGD: 665B, CB: 371A

4414 πλανάω, *planaō*, v. *to lead astray, cause to wander, deceive; (mid./pass.) to be deceived, deluded.* S: *4105*, BAGD: 665B, CB: 371A

4415 πλάνη, *planē*, n. *error, delusion, deception.* S: *4106*, BAGD: 665D, CB: 371A

4416 πλάνης, *planēs*, n. variant: *wanderer.* S: *4107**, BAGD: 666A, CB: 371A

4417 πλανήτης, *planētēs*, n. *wanderer; (as adj.) wandering.* S: *4107*, BAGD: 666A, CB: 371A

4418 πλάνος, *planos*, a. *deceiving, leading astray; (as noun) deceiver, imposter.* S: *4108*, BAGD: 666A, CB: 371A

4419 πλάξ, *plax*, n. *stone tablet.* S: *4109*, BAGD: 666A, CB: 371A

4420 πλάσμα, *plasma*, n. *what is formed, molded.* S: *4110*, BAGD: 666B, CB: –

4421 πλάσσω, *plassō*, v. *to form, mold.* S: *4111*, BAGD: 666C, CB: 371A

4422 πλαστός, *plastos*, a. *made up, fabricated, false.* S: *4112*, BAGD: 666C, CB: –

4423 πλατεῖα, *plateia*, n. *(great) street.* S: *4113*, BAGD: 666D, CB: 371A

4424 πλάτος, *platos*, n. *width, breadth.* S: *4114*, BAGD: 666D, CB: 371A

4425 πλατύνω, *platynō*, v. *to open wide, make wide.* S: *4115*, BAGD: 667A, CB: 371A

4426 πλατύς, *platys*, a. *wide, broad.* S: *4116*, BAGD: 667A, CB: 371A

4427 πλέγμα, *plegma*, n. *something braided or woven.* S: *4117*, BAGD: 667A, CB: –

4428 πλέκω, *plekō*, v. *to twist together, weave, braid.* S: *4120*, BAGD: 667B, CB: –

4429 πλεονάζω, *pleonazō*, v. *to make increase; (intr.) to grow, increase, have abundance.* S: *4121*, BAGD: 667B, CB: 371B

4430 πλεονεκτέω, *pleonekteō*, v. *to exploit, take advantage of, outwit.* S: *4122*, BAGD: 667C, CB: 371B

4431 πλεονέκτης, *pleonektēs*, n. *greedy person.* S: *4123*, BAGD: 667C, CB: 371B

4432 πλεονεξία, *pleonexia*, n. *greediness, avarice.* S: *4124*, BAGD: 667D, CB: 371B

4433 πλευρά, *pleura*, n. *side (of the body).* S: *4125*, BAGD: 668A, CB: –

4434 πλέω, *pleō*, v. *to travel by ship, sail.* S: *4126*, BAGD: 668A, CB: –

4435 πληγή, *plēgē*, n. *plague; punishment: beating, flogging, wounding.* S: *4127*, BAGD: 668A, CB: 371A

4436 πλῆθος, *plēthos*, n. *large number, crowd, multitude, assembly.* S: *4128*, BAGD: 668B, CB: 371B

4437 πληθύνω, *plēthynō*, v. *to increase, grow in numbers, abound.* S: *4129*, BAGD: 669A, CB: 371B

4438 πλήκτης, *plēktēs*, n. *violent man, bully.* S: *4131*, BAGD: 669B, CB: –

4439 πλήμμυρα, *plēmmyra*, n. *flood, high water.* S: *4132**, BAGD: 669B, CB: –

4440 πλήν, *plēn*, c. & pp.*. *but, however, only, yet.* S: *4133*, BAGD: 669B, CB: 371B

4441 πλήρης, *plērēs*, a. *full.* S: *4134*, BAGD: 669D, CB: 371B

4442 πληροφορέω, *plērophoreō*, v. *to fulfill (completely); (pass.) to be fully assured, convinced, persuaded.* S: *4135*, BAGD: 670B, CB: 371B

4443 πληροφορία, *plērophoria*, n. *full assurance, certainty, conviction.* S: *4136*, BAGD: 670C, CB: 371B

4444 πληρόω, *plēroō*, v. *to fulfill, make full; (pass.) to be filled, full, complete.* S: *4137*, BAGD: 670C, CB: 371B

4445 πλήρωμα, *plērōma*, n. *fullness, fulfillment.* S: *4138*, BAGD: 672A, CB: 371B

4446 πλησίον, *plēsion*, adv. & pp.* & n. *near, close by; (as noun) neighbor; (as prep.) near.* S: *4139*, BAGD: 672C, CB: 371B

4447 πλησμονή, *plēsmonē*, n. *indulgence, gratification.* S: *4140*, BAGD: 673A, CB: –

4448 πλήσσω, *plēssō*, v. *(pass.) to be struck.* S: *4141*, BAGD: 673A, CB: –

4449 πλοιάριον, *ploiarion*, n. *(small) boat.* S: *4142*, BAGD: 673B, CB: –

4450 πλοῖον, *ploion*, n. *boat, ship.* S: *4143*, BAGD: 673B, CB: –

4451 πλοκή, *plokē*, n. variant: *braiding, braid.* S: *1708**, BAGD: 673C, CB: –

4452 πλόος, *ploos*, n. *voyage, navigation.* S: *4144*, BAGD: 673C, CB: –

4453 πλοῦς, *plous*, n. *voyage, navigation.* S: *4144**, BAGD: 673C cf. πλόος, CB: –

4454 πλούσιος, *plousios*, a. *rich, wealthy; (as noun) rich person.* S: *4145*, BAGD: 673C, CB: 371B

4455 πλουσίως, *plousiōs*, adv. *richly, generously, abundantly.* S: *4146*, BAGD: 673D, CB: 371B

4456 πλουτέω, *plouteō*, v. *to be rich; (pf.) to have acquired wealth.* S: *4147*, BAGD: 673D, CB: 371B

4457 πλουτίζω, *ploutizō*, v. *to make rich; (pass.) to be enriched.* S: *4148*, BAGD: 674A, CB: 371B

4458 πλοῦτος, *ploutos*, n. *riches, wealth.* S: *4149*, BAGD: 674B, CB: 371B

4459 πλύνω, *plynō*, v. *to wash (things).* S: *4150*, BAGD: 674C, CB: 371B

4460 πνεῦμα, *pneuma*, n. *spirit, heart, mind; (Holy) Spirit, spirit, ghost; wind, breath.* S: *4151*, BAGD: 674C, CB: 371B

4461 πνευματικός, *pneumatikos*, a. *spiritual, pertaining to the Spirit.* S: *4152*, BAGD: 678D, CB: 371C

4462 πνευματικῶς, *pneumatikōs*, adv. *spiritually; figuratively.* S: *4153*, BAGD: 679B, CB: 371C

4463 πνέω, *pneō*, v. *to blow (of wind).* S: *4154*, BAGD: 679C, CB: 371B

4464 πνίγω, *pnigō*, v. *to choke, drown.* S: *4155*, BAGD: 679D, CB: 371C

4465 πνικτός, pniktos, a. *strangled, choked; (as noun) meat of strangled animals.* S: *4156*, BAGD: 679D, CB: 371C

4466 πνοή, pnoē, n. *wind, breath.* S: *4157*, BAGD: 680B, CB: 371C

4467 ποδαπός, podapos, a. variant: *what kind of; how great!, how magnificent!.* S: *4217**, BAGD: 694D cf. ποταπός, CB: –

4468 ποδήρης, podērēs, a. *reaching to the feet; (as noun) robe reaching to the feet.* S: *4158*, BAGD: 680B, CB: –

4469 ποδονιπτήρ, podoniptēr, n. variant: *basin for washing feet.* S: *3537**, BAGD: 680B, CB: –

4470 πόθεν, pothen, adv. *from where, from which.* S: *4159*, BAGD: 680B, CB: –

4471 ποία, poia, n. variant: *grass, herb.* S: *4169**, BAGD: 680D, CB: –

4472 ποιέω, poieō, v. *to do, make, practice, produce.* S: *4160*, BAGD: 680D, CB: 371C

4473 ποίημα, poiēma, n. *what is made, workmanship, creation.* S: *4161*, BAGD: 683B, CB: 371C

4474 ποίησις, poiēsis, n. *doing, working.* S: *4162*, BAGD: 683B, CB: 371C

4475 ποιητής, poiētēs, n. *doer, keeper, obeyer; poet.* S: *4163*, BAGD: 683B, CB: 371C

4476 ποικίλος, poikilos, a. *of various kinds, of all kinds.* S: *4164*, BAGD: 683C, CB: –

4477 ποιμαίνω, poimainō, v. *to shepherd, take care of sheep; to rule, lead.* S: *4165*, BAGD: 683D, CB: 371C

4478 ποιμήν, poimēn, n. *shepherd; pastor.* S: *4166*, BAGD: 684A, CB: 371C

4479 ποίμνη, poimnē, n. *flock.* S: *4167*, BAGD: 684C, CB: 371C

4480 ποίμνιον, poimnion, n. *flock.* S: *4168*, BAGD: 684C, CB: 371C

4481 ποῖος, poios, a. *what?, which?, of what kind?.* S: *4169*, BAGD: 684C, CB: –

4482 πολεμέω, polemeō, v. *to fight, make war.* S: *4170*, BAGD: 685A, CB: 371C

4483 πόλεμος, polemos, n. *war, battle, fight.* S: *4171*, BAGD: 685A, CB: 371C

4484 πόλις, polis, n. *city, town, village.* S: *4172*, BAGD: 685B, CB: 371C

4485 πολιτάρχης, politarchēs, n. *city official.* S: *4173*, BAGD: 686A, CB: 371C

4486 πολιτεία, politeia, n. *citizenship.* S: *4174*, BAGD: 686A, CB: 371C

4487 πολίτευμα, politeuma, n. *citizenship.* S: *4175*, BAGD: 686B, CB: 371C

4488 πολιτεύομαι, politeuomai, v. *to fulfill one's duty; to conduct oneself, lead one's life.* S: *4176*, BAGD: 686C, CB: 372A

4489 πολίτης, politēs, n. *citizen, subjects of a kingdom; neighbor.* S: *4177*, BAGD: 686D, CB: 371C

4490 πολλάκις, pollakis, adv. *many times, again and again, often, constantly.* S: *4178*, BAGD: 686D, CB: –

4491 πολλαπλασίων, pollaplasiōn, a. *many times as much.* S: *4179*, BAGD: 686D, CB: –

4492 πολυεύσπλαγχνος, polyeusplanchnos, a. variant: *rich in compassion.* S: *4184**, BAGD: 687A, CB: –

4493 πολύλαλος, polylalos, a. variant: *talkative, garrulous.* S: *150*, BAGD: 687B, CB: –

4494 πολυλογία, polylogia, n. *speaking many words, wordiness.* S: *4180*, BAGD: 687B, CB: –

4495 πολυμερῶς, polymerōs, adv. *at many times, in many ways.* S: *4181*, BAGD: 687B, CB: –

4496 πολυπλήθεια, polyplētheia, n. variant: *large crowd.* S: *150*, BAGD: 687B, CB: –

4497 πολυποίκιλος, polypoikilos, a. *manifold, (very) many sided.* S: *4182*, BAGD: 687B, CB: –

4498 πολύς, polys, a. *many, great, large; (compar.) more than, greater than; (super.) the most; very large.* S: *4183 & 4118 & 4119*, BAGD: 687C, CB: 372A

4499 πολύσπλαγχνος, polysplanchnos, a. *full of compassion, full of mercy.* S: *4184*, BAGD: 689D, CB: 372A

4500 πολυτελής, polytelēs, a. *expensive, of great worth, costly.* S: *4185*, BAGD: 690A, CB: 372A

4501 πολύτιμος, polytimos, a. *expensive, of great worth, valuable.* S: *4186*, BAGD: 690A, CB: –

4502 πολυτρόπως, polytropōs, adv. *in various ways.* S: *4187*, BAGD: 690A, CB: –

4503 πόμα, poma, n. *drink.* S: *4188*, BAGD: 690B, CB: 372A

4504 πονηρία, ponēria, n. *evil, wickedness, malice.* S: *4189*, BAGD: 690C, CB: 372A

4505 πονηρός, ponēros, a. *evil, wicked, bad; crime.* S: *4190 & 4191*, BAGD: 690D, CB: 372A

4506 πόνος, ponos, n. *pain, agony; hard work, toil.* S: *4192*, BAGD: 691C, CB: 372A

4507 Ποντικός, Pontikos, a.pr.g., "of Pontus." *from Pontus.* S: *4193*, BAGD: 691D, CB: –

4508 Πόντιος, Pontios, n.pr., "[tribal name]." *Pontius.* S: *4194*, BAGD: 691D, CB: –

4509 πόντος, pontos, n. variant: *open sea.* S: *5117**, BAGD: 691D, CB: –

4510 Πόντος, Pontos, n.pr., "sea." *Pontus.* S: *4195*, BAGD: 691D, CB: –

4511 Πόπλιος, Poplios, n.pr., "first." *Publius.* S: *4196*, BAGD: 692A, CB: –

4512 πορεία, poreia, n. *journey, trip; going about one's business, way of life, conduct.* S: *4197*, BAGD: 692A, CB: –

4513 πορεύομαι, poreuomai, v. *to come, go, travel.* S: *4198*, BAGD: 692B, CB: 372A

4514 πορθέω, portheō, v. *to destroy, annihilate; to raise havoc, pillage.* S: *4199*, BAGD: 693A, CB: –

4515 πορία, poria, n. variant: *journey, trip; conduct, way of life.* S: *4197**, BAGD: 692A cf. πορεία, CB: –

4516 πορισμός, porismos, n. *means of gain.* S: *4200*, BAGD: 693A, CB: –

4517 Πόρκιος, Porkios, n.pr., "[tribal name]." *Porcius.* S: *4201*, BAGD: 693A, CB: –

4518 πορνεία, porneia, n. *sexual immorality, sexual sin, marital unfaithfulness, adultery.* S: *4202*, BAGD: 693B, CB: 372A

4519 πορνεύω, porneuō, v. *to commit sexual immorality, adultery.* S: *4203*, BAGD: 693C, CB: 372A

4520 πόρνη, pornē, n. *prostitute.* S: *4204*, BAGD: 693C, CB: 372A

4521 πόρνος, pornos, n. one who is sexually immoral. S: 4205, BAGD: 693D, CB: 372A

4522 πόρρω, porrō, adv. far, a long way off; (compar.) farther. S: 4206, BAGD: 693D, CB: 372A

4523 πόρρωθεν, porrōthen, adv. from a distance, at a distance. S: 4207, BAGD: 693D, CB: 372A cf. porrō

4524 πορρωτέρω, porrōterō, adv. variant: farther. S: 4208, BAGD: 693D cf. πόρρω, CB: –

4525 πορφύρα, porphyra, n. purple (cloth or robe). S: 4209, BAGD: 694A, CB: 372A

4526 πορφύρεος, porphyreos, a. purple. S: 4210*, BAGD: 694A cf. -οῦς, CB: –

4527 πορφυρόπωλις, porphyropōlis, n. dealer in purple cloth. S: 4211, BAGD: 694A, CB: –

4528 πορφυροῦς, porphyrous, a. purple. S: 4210, BAGD: 694A, CB: –

4529 ποσάκις, posakis, adv. how many times?; how often!. S: 4212, BAGD: 694B, CB: –

4530 πόσις, posis, n. drinking; a drink. S: 4213, BAGD: 694B, CB: 372A

4531 πόσος, posos, a. how great?, how much?, how many?; how great!, how many!, how much!. S: 4214, BAGD: 694B, CB: –

4532 ποταμός, potamos, n. river, stream, torrent. S: 4215, BAGD: 694D, CB: 372A

4533 ποταμοφόρητος, potamophorētos, a. swept away by a torrential flow of a river. S: 4216, BAGD: 694D, CB: 372A

4534 ποταπός, potapos, a. of what kind?; how great!. S: 4217, BAGD: 694D, CB: –

4535 ποταπῶς, potapōs, adv. variant: in what way, how. S: 4458*, BAGD: 695A, CB: –

4536 πότε, pote, adv.inter. when? how long?. S: 4219, BAGD: 695A, CB: 372B

4537 ποτέ, pote, pt. once, at one time, formerly; now, now at last. S: 4218, BAGD: 695A, CB: 372B

4538 πότερον, poteron, a. or pt. whether. S: 4220, BAGD: 695B, CB: –

4539 ποτήριον, potērion, n. cup. S: 4221, BAGD: 695B, CB: 372B

4540 ποτίζω, potizō, v. to give or offer a drink; to water. S: 4222, BAGD: 695D, CB: 372B

4541 Ποτίολοι, Potioloi, n.pr., "rotten [sulphur] smell" or "well, spring." Puteoli. S: 4223, BAGD: 696A, CB: –

4542 πότος, potos, n. carousing, drinking party. S: 4224, BAGD: 696A, CB: 372B

4543 πού, pou, adv. somewhere, a place where; about, approximately. S: 4225, BAGD: 696B, CB: 372B

4544 ποῦ, pou, adv.inter.pl. where?, at what place?. S: 4226, BAGD: 696A, CB: 372B

4545 Πούδης, Poudēs, n.pr., "modest." Pudens. S: 4227, BAGD: 696C, CB: –

4546 πούς, pous, n. foot; leg. S: 4228, BAGD: 696C, CB: 372B

4547 πρᾶγμα, pragma, n. thing, matter, practice. S: 4229, BAGD: 697A, CB: 372B

4548 πραγματεία, pragmateia, n. (pl.) affairs, concerns. S: 4230, BAGD: 697B, CB: 372B

4549 πραγματεύομαι, pragmateuomai, v. to put capital to work, do business. S: 4231, BAGD: 697B, CB: 372B

4550 πραιτώριον, praitōrion, n. Praetorium; palace (of the governor); palace guard. S: 4232, BAGD: 697C, CB: –

4551 πράκτωρ, praktōr, n. officer. S: 4233, BAGD: 697D, CB: 372B

4552 πρᾶξις, praxis, n. deed, action, practice; function. S: 4234, BAGD: 697D, CB: 372B

4553 πρᾶος, praos, a. variant: gentle, humble, considerate. S: 4235*, BAGD: 698D cf. πραΰς, CB: –

4554 πραότης, praotēs, n. variant: gentleness, humility, courtesy, considerateness. S: 4236*, BAGD: 699A cf. πραΰτης, CB: –

4555 πρασιά, prasia, n. group. S: 4237, BAGD: 698B, CB: –

4556 πράσσω, prassō, v. to do, act, practice. S: 4238, BAGD: 698B, CB: 372B

4557 πραϋπαθία, praupathia, n. gentleness. S: 4236, BAGD: 698D, CB: 372B

4558 πραΰς, praus, a. gentle, meek. S: 4239, BAGD: 698D, CB: 372B

4559 πραΰτης, prautēs, n. gentleness, meekness, humility. S: 4240, BAGD: 699A, CB: 372B

4560 πρέπω, prepō, v. to be proper, appropriate, fitting. S: 4241, BAGD: 699B, CB: 372B

4561 πρεσβεία, presbeia, n. delegation, ambassador. S: 4242, BAGD: 699B, CB: 372B

4562 πρεσβευτής, presbeutēs, n. variant: old man. S: 4246, BAGD: 699C, CB: 372B

4563 πρεσβεύω, presbeuō, v. to be an ambassador. S: 4243, BAGD: 699C, CB: 372B

4564 πρεσβυτέριον, presbyterion, n. body or council of the elders, Sanhedrin. S: 4244, BAGD: 699C, CB: 372B

4565 πρεσβύτερος, presbyteros, a. older; ancestral; (as noun) elder. S: 4245, BAGD: 699D, CB: 372B

4566 πρεσβύτης, presbytēs, n. elderly man. S: 4246, BAGD: 700D, CB: 372B

4567 πρεσβῦτις, presbytis, n. elderly woman. S: 4247, BAGD: 700D, CB: 372B

4568 πρηνής, prēnēs, a. headlong, headfirst in prone position. S: 4248, BAGD: 700D, CB: 372B

4569 πρίζω, prizō, v. (pass.) to be sawn in two. S: 4249, BAGD: 701A, CB: –

4570 πρίν, prin, adv. before. S: 4250, BAGD: 701A, CB: –

4571 Πρίσκα, Priska, n.pr. Prisca, Priscilla. S: 4251, BAGD: 701B, CB: –

4572 Πρίσκιλλα, Priskilla, n.pr. variant: Priscilla, Prisca. S: 4252, BAGD: 701B, CB: –

4573 πρίω, priō, v. variant: (pass.) to be sawn in two. S: 4249*, BAGD: 701A cf. πρίζω, CB: –

4574 πρό, pro, pp. (of place) before, at; (of time) before, some time ago. S: 4253, BAGD: 701C, CB: 372C

4575 προάγω, proagō, v. to go on ahead, lead the way; to bring out, bring to trial. S: 4254, BAGD: 702A, CB: 339C cf. agō

4576 προαιρέω, proaireō, v. (mid.) to decide, determine. S: 4255*, BAGD: 702B, CB: –

4577 προαιτιάομαι, *proaitiaomai*, v. *to make a charge beforehand.*
S: *4256*, BAGD: 702C, CB: –

4578 προακούω, *proakouō*, v. *to hear about beforehand.* S: *4257*,
BAGD: 702C, CB: –

4579 προαμαρτάνω, *proamartanō*, v. *to sin earlier, to have sinned
beforehand.* S: *4258*, BAGD: 702C, CB: –

4580 προαύλιον, *proaulion*, n. *entryway, gateway.* S: *4259*,
BAGD: 702D, CB: –

4581 προβαίνω, *probainō*, v. *(spacial) to go on, go on farther;
(temporal) to be well along (in years), advanced (in age).*
S: *4260*, BAGD: 702D, CB: 372C

4582 προβάλλω, *proballō*, v. *to push to the front, cause to come to
the front; to sprout, put forth.* S: *4261*, BAGD: 702D, CB: –

4583 προβατικός, *probatikos*, a. *pertaining to sheep; (as noun) the
Sheep (Gate).* S: *4262*, BAGD: 703A, CB: –

4584 προβάτιον, *probation*, n. variant: *lamb.* S: *4263**,
BAGD: 703A, CB: 372C

4585 πρόβατον, *probaton*, n. *sheep.* S: *4263*, BAGD: 703C,
CB: 372C

4586 προβιβάζω, *probibazō*, v. *(pass.) to be prompted, caused to
come forward.* S: *4264*, BAGD: 703C, CB: –

4587 προβλέπω, *problepō*, v. *(mid.) to plan, select, provide.*
S: *4265*, BAGD: 703C, CB: –

4588 προγίνομαι, *proginomai*, v. *to commit beforehand, happen
previously.* S: *4266*, BAGD: 703C, CB: 372C

4589 προγινώσκω, *proginōskō*, v. *to know beforehand, foreknow;
(mid.) to choose beforehand.* S: *4267*, BAGD: 703D,
CB: 372C

4590 πρόγνωσις, *prognōsis*, n. *foreknowledge.* S: *4268*,
BAGD: 703D, CB: 372C

4591 πρόγονος, *progonos*, a. *parents, forefathers, ancestors.*
S: *4269*, BAGD: 704A, CB: –

4592 προγράφω, *prographō*, v. *to write beforehand; to show
clearly, advertise, proclaim.* S: *4270*, BAGD: 704A,
CB: 372C

4593 πρόδηλος, *prodēlos*, a. *obvious, clear, evident.* S: *4271*,
BAGD: 704B, CB: –

4594 προδίδωμι, *prodidōmi*, v. *to give beforehand.* S: *4272*,
BAGD: 704C, CB: –

4595 προδότης, *prodotēs*, n. *traitor, betrayer, treacherous one.*
S: *4273*, BAGD: 704C, CB: –

4596 πρόδρομος, *prodromos*, a. *going before, forerunner.* S: *4274*,
BAGD: 704C, CB: 372C

4597 προεῖπον, *proeipon*, v. variant: *to foretell, tell beforehand.*
S: *4302**, BAGD: 704D, CB: 372C cf. *prolegō*

4598 προελπίζω, *proelpizō*, v. *to be the first to hope, hope
beforehand.* S: *4276*, BAGD: 705A, CB: 372C

4599 προενάρχομαι, *proenarchomai*, v. *to begin beforehand,
begin previously.* S: *4278*, BAGD: 705A, CB: 343B cf. *archō*

4600 προεπαγγέλλω, *proepangellō*, v. *(mid.) to promise
beforehand; (pass.) to be promised previously.* S: *4279**,
BAGD: 705B, CB: 372C

4601 προέρχομαι, *proerchomai*, v. *to go on ahead; to lead; to visit
in advance.* S: *4281*, BAGD: 705B, CB: 372C

4602 προετοιμάζω, *proetoimazō*, v. *to prepare in advance.*
S: *4282*, BAGD: 705D, CB: 372C

4603 προευαγγελίζομαι, *proeuangelizomai*, v. *to announce the
gospel in advance.* S: *4283*, BAGD: 705D, CB: 372C

4604 προέχω, *proechō*, v. *(mid.) to be better off, have an
advantage.* S: *4284**, BAGD: 705D, CB: 348C cf. *echō*

4605 προηγέομαι, *proēgeomai*, v. *to put above, go before.*
S: *4285*, BAGD: 706A, CB: –

4606 πρόθεσις, *prothesis*, n. *setting forth: plan, purpose, will; (as
adj.) consecrated (bread).* S: *4286*, BAGD: 706A, CB: 373B

4607 προθεσμία, *prothesmia*, n. *set time, fixed or limited time.*
S: *4287**, BAGD: 706B, CB: –

4608 προθυμία, *prothymia*, n. *eagerness, willingness, readiness.*
S: *4288*, BAGD: 706C, CB: 373B

4609 πρόθυμος, *prothymos*, a. *willing, eager.* S: *4289*,
BAGD: 706C, CB: –

4610 προθύμως, *prothymōs*, adv. *eagerly, willingly.* S: *4290*,
BAGD: 706D, CB: –

4611 πρόϊμος, *proimos*, a. *early; (as noun) autumn rains.*
S: *4406**, BAGD: 706D, CB: 372C

4612 προϊνός, *proinos*, a. variant: *early, belonging to the morning.*
S: *4407**, BAGD: 707A, CB: 372C

4613 προΐστημι, *proistēmi*, v. *(act/mid) to manage, direct, lead;
(mid.) to devote oneself, busy oneself to.* S: *4291*,
BAGD: 707A, CB: –

4614 προκαλέω, *prokaleō*, v. *(mid.) to provoke, challenge.*
S: *4292**, BAGD: 707B, CB: –

4615 προκαταγγέλλω, *prokatangellō*, v. *to foretell, predict,
announce beforehand.* S: *4293*, BAGD: 707B, CB: 372C

4616 προκαταρτίζω, *prokatartizō*, v. *to arrange for in advance,
get ready beforehand.* S: *4294*, BAGD: 707C, CB: 372C

4617 προκατέχω, *prokatechō*, v. variant: *to gain possession of or
occupy previously.* S: *4284**, BAGD: 707C, CB: –

4618 πρόκειμαι, *prokeimai*, v. *(pass.) to be set before, present.*
S: *4295*, BAGD: 707C, CB: 372C

4619 προκηρύσσω, *prokēryssō*, v. *to preach beforehand.* S: *4296*,
BAGD: 707D, CB: –

4620 προκοπή, *prokopē*, n. *progress, advancement.* S: *4297*,
BAGD: 707D, CB: 372C

4621 προκόπτω, *prokoptō*, v. *to go ahead, go forward, advance.*
S: *4298*, BAGD: 707D, CB: 372C

4622 πρόκριμα, *prokrima*, n. *partiality, discrimination, prejudice.*
S: *4299*, BAGD: 708A, CB: 372C

4623 προκυρόω, *prokyroō*, v. *to establish previously, ratify
beforehand.* S: *4300*, BAGD: 708B, CB: 372C

4624 προλαμβάνω, *prolambanō*, v. *to take beforehand; to go on
ahead; (pass.) to be caught, detected.* S: *4301*,
BAGD: 708B, CB: 372C

4625 προλέγω, *prolegō*, v. *to tell beforehand; to speak in the past.*
S: *4302 & 4277 & 4280*, BAGD: 708B, CB: 372C

4626 προμαρτύρομαι, *promartyromai*, v. *to predict, bear witness
to beforehand.* S: *4303*, BAGD: 708C, CB: –

4627 προμελετάω, *promeletaō*, v. *to worry beforehand.* S: *4304*,
BAGD: 708C, CB: –

4628 προμεριμνάω, *promerimnaō*, v. *to worry or be anxious
beforehand.* S: *4305*, BAGD: 708C, CB: 372C

4629 προνοέω, *pronoeō*, v. *to provide for, care for; to consider, have regard for.* S: *4306*, BAGD: 708C, CB: 372C

4630 πρόνοια, *pronoia*, n. *foresight, provision, care.* S: *4307*, BAGD: 708D, CB: 372C

4631 πρόοιδα, *prooida*, v. variant: *to know beforehand, know previously.* S: *4308*, BAGD: 709A, CB: –

4632 προοράω, *prooraō*, v. *to see previously; to see ahead, foresee; (mid.) to see in front of.* S: *4308 & 4275*, BAGD: 709A, CB: –

4633 προορίζω, *proorizō*, v. *to predestine, decide beforehand.* S: *4309*, BAGD: 709B, CB: –

4634 προπάσχω, *propaschō*, v. *to suffer previously.* S: *4310*, BAGD: 709B, CB: –

4635 προπάτωρ, *propatōr*, n. *forefather, ancestor.* S: *3962**, BAGD: 709B, CB: 372C

4636 προπέμπω, *propempō*, v. *to accompany, escort; to send on one's way, help on one's journey.* S: *4311*, BAGD: 709B, CB: –

4637 προπετής, *propetēs*, a. *rash, reckless, thoughtless.* S: *4312*, BAGD: 709C, CB: –

4638 προπορεύομαι, *proporeuomai*, v. *to go before.* S: *4313*, BAGD: 709C, CB: –

4639 πρός, *pros*, pp. *(gen.) to, for; (dat.) on, at, near, by; (acc.) to, toward; with; in order to; against.* S: *4314*, BAGD: 709C, CB: 373A

4640 προσάββατον, *prosabbaton*, n. *day before the Sabbath.* S: *4315*, BAGD: 711A, CB: –

4641 προσαγορεύω, *prosagoreuō*, v. *to designate.* S: *4316*, BAGD: 711B, CB: –

4642 προσάγω, *prosagō*, v. *to bring to; to approach, come near.* S: *4317*, BAGD: 711B, CB: 339C cf. *agō*

4643 προσαγωγή, *prosagōgē*, n. *access; approach.* S: *4318*, BAGD: 711C, CB: 373A

4644 προσαιτέω, *prosaiteō*, v. *to beg.* S: *4319*, BAGD: 711C, CB: –

4645 προσαίτης, *prosaitēs*, n. *beggar.* S: *4319**, BAGD: 711C, CB: –

4646 προσαναβαίνω, *prosanabainō*, v. *to move up, go up.* S: *4320*, BAGD: 711C, CB: –

4647 προσαναλαμβάνω, *prosanalambanō*, v. variant: *to take in besides, welcome.* S: *4355**, BAGD: 711C, CB: –

4648 προσαναλίσκω, *prosanaliskō*, v. variant: *to spend lavishly or in addition.* S: *4321*, BAGD: 711C, CB: –

4649 προσαναλόω, *prosanaloō*, v. variant: *to spend lavishly or in addition.* S: *4321*, BAGD: 711C, CB: –

4650 προσαναπληρόω, *prosanaplēroō*, v. *to supply, fill up.* S: *4322*, BAGD: 711D, CB: 373A

4651 προσανατίθημι, *prosanatithēmi*, v. *to add; to consult, ask advice.* S: *4323*, BAGD: 711D, CB: –

4652 προσανέχω, *prosanechō*, v. variant: *to rise up toward.* S: *4317**, BAGD: 711D, CB: –

4653 προσαπειλέω, *prosapeileō*, v. *to threaten further.* S: *4324*, BAGD: 711D, CB: –

4654 προσαχέω, *prosacheō*, v. variant: *to resound.* S: *4317**, BAGD: 711D, CB: –

4655 προσδαπανάω, *prosdapanaō*, v. *to spend extra.* S: *4325*, BAGD: 712A, CB: –

4656 προσδέομαι, *prosdeomai*, v. *to need.* S: *4326*, BAGD: 712A, CB: 373A

4657 προσδέχομαι, *prosdechomai*, v. *to receive, welcome, accept; to wait for, anticipate.* S: *4327*, BAGD: 712B, CB: 373A

4658 προσδίδωμι, *prosdidōmi*, v. variant: *to give (over).* S: *1929**, BAGD: 712C, CB: –

4659 προσδοκάω, *prosdokaō*, v. *to look forward to, expect, wait for.* S: *4328*, BAGD: 712C, CB: 373A

4660 προσδοκία, *prosdokia*, n. *anticipation, expectation; apprehension.* S: *4329*, BAGD: 712C, CB: –

4661 προσεάω, *proseaō*, v. *to allow to go farther.* S: *4330*, BAGD: 712D, CB: –

4662 προσεγγίζω, *prosengizō*, v. variant: *to approach, come near.* S: *4331*, BAGD: 712D, CB: 351A cf. *engizō*

4663 προσεδρεύω, *prosedreuō*, v. variant: *to serve, wait upon.* S: *4332*, BAGD: 712D, CB: –

4664 προσεργάζομαι, *prosergazomai*, v. *to earn more.* S: *4333*, BAGD: 713A, CB: –

4665 προσέρχομαι, *proserchomai*, v. *to come to, approach, draw near; to agree to.* S: *4334*, BAGD: 713A, CB: 373A

4666 προσευχή, *proseuchē*, n. *prayer; place of prayer.* S: *4335*, BAGD: 713B, CB: 373A

4667 προσεύχομαι, *proseuchomai*, v. *to pray.* S: *4336*, BAGD: 713D, CB: 373A

4668 προσέχω, *prosechō*, v. *to watch out, be on guard, beware; to pay attention, devote, apply oneself.* S: *4337*, BAGD: 714B, CB: 373A

4669 προσηλόω, *prosēloō*, v. *to nail to.* S: *4338*, BAGD: 714D, CB: –

4670 προσήλυτος, *prosēlytos*, n. *convert (to Judaism).* S: *4339*, BAGD: 715A, CB: 373A

4671 πρόσθεσις, *prosthesis*, n. variant: *presentation, setting forth.* S: *4286**, BAGD: 715B, CB: 373B

4672 πρόσκαιρος, *proskairos*, a. *lasting only for a short time, temporary.* S: *4340*, BAGD: 715B, CB: 373A

4673 προσκαλέω, *proskaleō*, v. *(mid.) to call, summon, send for; gather together.* S: *4341**, BAGD: 715C, CB: 373A

4674 προσκαρτερέω, *proskartereō*, v. *to join, adhere to; to be ready; to give attention, be faithful; to spend much time together.* S: *4342*, BAGD: 715C, CB: 373A

4675 προσκαρτέρησις, *proskarterēsis*, n. *perseverance, patience.* S: *4343*, BAGD: 715D, CB: 373A

4676 προσκεφάλαιον, *proskephalaion*, n. *cushion.* S: *4344*, BAGD: 715D, CB: –

4677 προσκληρόω, *prosklēroō*, v. *(pass.) to be joined with, associated with.* S: *4345*, BAGD: 716A, CB: 373A

4678 πρόσκλησις, *prosklēsis*, n. variant: *summons, invitation.* S: *4346**, BAGD: 716A, CB: 373A

4679 προσκλίνω, *prosklinō*, v. *(pass.) to be rallied to, associated with.* S: *4347**, BAGD: 716A, CB: –

4680 πρόσκλισις, *prosklisis*, n. *favoritism, partiality.* S: *4346*, BAGD: 716A, CB: 373A

4681 προσκολλάω, *proskollaō*, v. *(pass.) to be united to.* S: *4347*, BAGD: 716A, CB: 373A

4682 πρόσκομμα, *proskomma*, n. *stumbling block, something that causes one to stumble.* S: *4348*, BAGD: 716B, CB: 373A

4683 προσκοπή, *proskopē*, n. *stumbling block, occasion for stumbling.* S: *4349*, BAGD: 716B, CB: 373B

4684 προσκόπτω, *proskoptō*, v. *to strike, beat; (intr.) to stumble, fall.* S: *4350*, BAGD: 716B, CB: 373B

4685 προσκυλίω, *proskyliō*, v. *to roll in front of, roll up to.* S: *4351*, BAGD: 716C, CB: –

4686 προσκυνέω, *proskyneō*, v. *to worship, pay homage, show reverence; to kneel down (before).* S: *4352*, BAGD: 716C, CB: 373B

4687 προσκυνητής, *proskynētēs*, n. *worshiper.* S: *4353*, BAGD: 717B, CB: 373B

4688 προσλαλέω, *proslaleō*, v. *to talk with.* S: *4354*, BAGD: 717B, CB: –

4689 προσλαμβάνω, *proslambanō*, v. *to take aside, take along; to partake; to welcome, accept.* S: *4355*, BAGD: 717B, CB: 373B

4690 προσλέγω, *proslegō*, v. variant: *to answer.* S: *150*, BAGD: 717C, CB: 372C

4691 πρόσλημψις, *proslēmpsis*, n. *acceptance.* S: *4356*, BAGD: 717C, CB: 373B

4692 πρόσληψις, *proslēpsis*, n. variant: *acceptance.* S: *4356*, BAGD: 717C, CB: 373B cf. *proslēmpsis*

4693 προσμένω, *prosmenō*, v. *to be with, continue in, remain, stay.* S: *4357*, BAGD: 717C, CB: 373B

4694 προσορμίζω, *prosormizō*, v. *(pass.) to be anchored, come into harbor.* S: *4358*, BAGD: 717D, CB: –

4695 προσοφείλω, *prosopheilō*, v. *to owe (in addition).* S: *4359*, BAGD: 717D, CB: 367A cf. *opheilō*

4696 προσοχθίζω, *prosochthizō*, v. *to be angry, provoked.* S: *4360*, BAGD: 717D, CB: –

4697 προσπαίω, *prospaiō*, v. variant: *to strike against, beat against.* S: *150*, BAGD: 717D, CB: –

4698 πρόσπεινος, *prospeinos*, a. *hungry.* S: *4361*, BAGD: 718A, CB: –

4699 προσπήγνυμι, *prospēgnymi*, v. *to nail to (the cross).* S: *4362*, BAGD: 718A, CB: –

4700 προσπίπτω, *prospiptō*, v. *to fall down before; to beat against, strike against.* S: *4363*, BAGD: 718A, CB: –

4701 προσποιέω, *prospoieō*, v. *to act as if, pretend.* S: *4364**, BAGD: 718B, CB: –

4702 προσπορεύομαι, *prosporeuomai*, v. *to come to, approach.* S: *4365*, BAGD: 718B, CB: 372A cf. *poreuomai*

4703 προσρήγνυμι, *prosrēgnymi*, v. *to strike upon.* S: *4366*, BAGD: 718B cf. προσρήσσω, CB: –

4704 προσρήσσω, *prosrēssō*, v. variant: *to strike upon.* S: *4366**, BAGD: 718B, CB: –

4705 προστάσσω, *prostassō*, v. *(act./mid.) to command, order; (pass.) to be set, prescribed.* S: *4367*, BAGD: 718C, CB: 373B

4706 προστάτις, *prostatis*, n. *helper.* S: *4368*, BAGD: 718D, CB: –

4707 προστίθημι, *prostithēmi*, v. *to add to, increase ; (pass.) to be brought to, given.* S: *4369*, BAGD: 718D, CB: 373B

4708 προστρέχω, *prostrechō*, v. *to run up to.* S: *4370*, BAGD: 719B, CB: –

4709 προσφάγιον, *prosphagion*, n. *(little) fish.* S: *4371*, BAGD: 719C, CB: –

4710 πρόσφατος, *prosphatos*, a. *new.* S: *4372*, BAGD: 719C, CB: 373B

4711 προσφάτως, *prosphatōs*, adv. *recently.* S: *4373*, BAGD: 719C, CB: –

4712 προσφέρω, *prospherō*, v. *to bring to, present, offer; to treat as, deal with.* S: *4374*, BAGD: 719C, CB: 373B

4713 προσφιλής, *prosphilēs*, a. *lovely, pleasing.* S: *4375*, BAGD: 720B, CB: –

4714 προσφορά, *prosphora*, n. *offering, presentation.* S: *4376*, BAGD: 720B, CB: 373B

4715 προσφωνέω, *prosphōneō*, v. *to call out; speak to, address.* S: *4377*, BAGD: 720C, CB: –

4716 προσχαίρω, *proschairō*, v. variant: *to be glad.* S: *4370**, BAGD: 720C, CB: –

4717 πρόσχυσις, *proschysis*, n. *sprinkling.* S: *4378*, BAGD: 720C, CB: 373A

4718 προσψαύω, *prospsauō*, v. *to touch.* S: *4379*, BAGD: 720C, CB: –

4719 προσωπολημπτέω, *prosōpolēmpteō*, v. *to show favoritism, partiality.* S: *4380*, BAGD: 720C, CB: 373B

4720 προσωπολήμπτης, *prosōpolēmptēs*, n. *one who shows favoritism, partiality.* S: *4381*, BAGD: 720D, CB: 373B

4721 προσωπολημψία, *prosōpolēmpsia*, n. *favoritism, partiality.* S: *4382*, BAGD: 720D, CB: 373B

4722 προσωπολημπτέω, *prosōpolēpteō*, v. variant: *to show favoritism, partiality.* S: *4380*, BAGD: 720C cf. προσωπολημπτέω, CB: 373B cf. *-mpteō*

4723 προσωπολήπτης, *prosōpolēptēs*, n. variant: *one who shows favoritism, partiality.* S: *4381*, BAGD: 720D, CB: 373B cf. *-mptēs*

4724 προσωποληψία, *prosōpolēpsia*, n. variant: *favoritism, partiality.* S: *4382*, BAGD: 720D, CB: 373B cf. *-mpsia*

4725 πρόσωπον, *prosōpon*, n. *face; presence, sight; (with various pp.) before, in front of.* S: *4383*, BAGD: 720D, CB: 373B

4726 προτάσσω, *protassō*, v. variant: *to determine beforehand, allot beforehand.* S: *4384*, BAGD: 721D, CB: 373B

4727 προτείνω, *proteinō*, v. *to stretch out.* S: *4385*, BAGD: 721D, CB: –

4728 πρότερος, *proteros*, a. *before; (as adv.) before, formerly.* S: *4387 & 4386*, BAGD: 721D, CB: 373B

4729 προτίθημι, *protithēmi*, v. *(mid.) to plan, purpose; to present, bring forth.* S: *4388**, BAGD: 722B, CB: 373B

4730 προτρέπω, *protrepō*, v. *to encourage, urge on.* S: *4389**, BAGD: 722B, CB: –

4731 προτρέχω, *protrechō*, v. *to run ahead.* S: *4390*, BAGD: 722B, CB: –

4732 προϋπάρχω, *prouparchō*, v. *to exist formerly.* S: *4391*, BAGD: 722C, CB: –

4733 πρόφασις, *prophasis*, n. *excuse; pretense, show, cover.*
S: *4392*, BAGD: 722C, CB: –

4734 προφέρω, *propherō*, v. *to bring out.* S: *4393*, BAGD: 722D,
CB: 370A cf. *pherō*

4735 προφητεία, *prophēteia*, n. *prophecy.* S: *4394*, BAGD: 722D,
CB: 373A

4736 προφητεύω, *prophēteuō*, v. *to prophesy.* S: *4395*,
BAGD: 723A, CB: 373A

4737 προφήτης, *prophētēs*, n. *prophet.* S: *4396*, BAGD: 723B,
CB: 373A

4738 προφητικός, *prophētikos*, a. *prophetic.* S: *4397*,
BAGD: 724B, CB: 373A

4739 προφῆτις, *prophētis*, n. *prophetess.* S: *4398*, BAGD: 724B,
CB: 373C

4740 προφθάνω, *prophthanō*, v. *to anticipate, come before.*
S: *4399*, BAGD: 724B, CB: –

4741 προχειρίζω, *procheirizō*, v. *(mid.) to choose, appoint.*
S: *4400**, BAGD: 724C, CB: 372C

4742 προχειροτονέω, *procheirotoneō*, v. *to choose beforehand,
appoint beforehand.* S: *4401*, BAGD: 724C, CB: 372C

4743 Πρόχορος, *Prochoros*, n.pr. *Procorus.* S: *4402*,
BAGD: 724C, CB: –

4744 πρύμνα, *prymna*, n. *stern (of a vessel).* S: *4403*,
BAGD: 724D, CB: –

4745 πρωΐ, *prōi*, adv. *early in the morning.* S: *4404*, BAGD: 724D,
CB: 372C

4746 πρωΐα, *prōia*, n. *early morning.* S: *4405*, BAGD: 724D, CB: –

4747 πρώϊμος, *prōimos*, a. variant: *early; (as noun) autumn rains.*
S: *4406*, BAGD: 706D cf. πρόϊμος, CB: 372C

4748 πρωϊνός, *prōinos*, a. *early, pertaining to the morning.*
S: *4407*, BAGD: 725A, CB: 372C

4749 πρῷρα, *prōra*, n. *bow (of a vessel).* S: *4408**, BAGD: 725A,
CB: –

4750 πρωτεύω, *prōteuō*, v. *to be supreme, first, have first place.*
S: *4409*, BAGD: 725A, CB: –

4751 πρωτοκαθεδρία, *prōtokathedria*, n. *most important seat, seat
of honor.* S: *4410*, BAGD: 725B, CB: 373B

4752 πρωτοκλισία, *prōtoklisia*, n. *place of honor.* S: *4411*,
BAGD: 725B, CB: 373B

4753 πρωτόμαρτυς, *prōtomartys*, n. variant: *first martyr.* S: *3144**,
BAGD: 725B, CB: –

4754 πρῶτον, *prōton*, adv. *first; earlier; above all.* S: *4412*,
BAGD: 725B cf. -ος, CB: 373B

4755 πρῶτος, *prōtos*, a. *first.* S: *4413*, BAGD: 725B, CB: 373B

4756 πρωτοστάτης, *prōtostatēs*, n. *ringleader, leader.* S: *4414*,
BAGD: 726C, CB: 373B

4757 πρωτοτόκια, *prōtotokia*, n. *inheritance rights (of the
firstborn).* S: *4415*, BAGD: 726C, CB: 373B cf. -kos

4758 πρωτότοκος, *prōtotokos*, a. *firstborn.* S: *4416*, BAGD: 726C,
CB: 373B

4759 πρώτως, *prōtōs*, adv. *for the first time.* S: *4412**,
BAGD: 727A, CB: –

4760 πταίω, *ptaiō*, v. *to stumble, fall, trip.* S: *4417*, BAGD: 727A,
CB: 373C

4761 πτέρνα, *pterna*, n. *heel.* S: *4418*, BAGD: 727B, CB: 373C

4762 πτερύγιον, *pterygion*, n. *highest point.* S: *4419*,
BAGD: 727B, CB: 373C

4763 πτέρυξ, *pteryx*, n. *wing.* S: *4420*, BAGD: 727B, CB: 373C

4764 πτηνός, *ptēnos*, a. *winged; (as noun) bird.* S: *4421*,
BAGD: 727C, CB: –

4765 πτοέω, *ptoeō*, v. *(pass.) to be startled, frightened.* S: *4422*,
BAGD: 727C, CB: –

4766 πτόησις, *ptoēsis*, n. *something alarming.* S: *4423*,
BAGD: 727C, CB: –

4767 Πτολεμαΐς, *Ptolemais*, n.pr. *Ptolemais.* S: *4424*,
BAGD: 727C, CB: –

4768 πτύον, *ptyon*, n. *winnowing fork.* S: *4425*, BAGD: 727C,
CB: 374A

4769 πτύρω, *ptyrō*, v. *(pass.) to be frightened.* S: *4426*,
BAGD: 727D, CB: –

4770 πτύσμα, *ptysma*, n. *saliva, spit.* S: *4427*, BAGD: 727D, CB: –

4771 πτύσσω, *ptyssō*, v. *to roll up.* S: *4428*, BAGD: 727D, CB: –

4772 πτύω, *ptyō*, v. *to spit (saliva).* S: *4429*, BAGD: 727D, CB: –

4773 πτῶμα, *ptōma*, n. *dead body, carcass, corpse.* S: *4430*,
BAGD: 727D, CB: 374A

4774 πτῶσις, *ptōsis*, n. *falling, crash.* S: *4431*, BAGD: 728A,
CB: 374A

4775 πτωχεία, *ptōcheia*, n. *poverty.* S: *4432*, BAGD: 728A,
CB: 374A

4776 πτωχεύω, *ptōcheuō*, v. *to be or become poor.* S: *4433*,
BAGD: 728A, CB: 374A

4777 πτωχός, *ptōchos*, a. *poor; (as noun) poor, beggar.* S: *4434*,
BAGD: 728B, CB: 374A

4778 πυγμή, *pygmē*, n. *fist; with a fist = NIV "ceremonial".*
S: *4435*, BAGD: 728C, CB: 374A

4779 Πύθιος, *Pythios*, n.pr. variant: *Pythian.* S: *150*, BAGD: –,
CB: –

4780 πύθων, *pythōn*, n. *spirit of divination.* S: *4436**,
BAGD: 728D, CB: 374A

4781 πυκνός, *pyknos*, a. *often, frequent, numerous.* S: *4437*,
BAGD: 729A, CB: –

4782 πυκτεύω, *pykteuō*, v. *to fight with the fist, box.* S: *4438*,
BAGD: 729A, CB: –

4783 πύλη, *pylē*, n. *(city) gate.* S: *4439*, BAGD: 729B, CB: 374A

4784 πυλών, *pylōn*, n. *gate, door, entryway.* S: *4440*,
BAGD: 729C, CB: 374A

4785 πυνθάνομαι, *pynthanomai*, v. *to ask, inquire, question.*
S: *4441*, BAGD: 729C, CB: –

4786 πῦρ, *pyr*, n. *fire, flames.* S: *4442*, BAGD: 729D, CB: 374A

4787 πυρά, *pyra*, n. *fire.* S: *4443*, BAGD: 730C, CB: 374A

4788 πύργος, *pyrgos*, n. *tower, watchtower.* S: *4444*,
BAGD: 730D, CB: –

4789 πυρέσσω, *pyressō*, v. *to burn with a fever.* S: *4445*,
BAGD: 730D, CB: 374A

4790 πυρετός, *pyretos*, n. *fever.* S: *4446*, BAGD: 730D, CB: 374A

4791 πύρινος, *pyrinos*, a. *fiery red, the color of fire.* S: *4447*,
BAGD: 731A, CB: 374A

4792 πυρόω, *pyroō*, v. *to burn; to burn inwardly.* S: *4448*,
BAGD: 731A, CB: 374A

4793 πυρράζω, *pyrrazō*, v. *to be red, the color of fire.* S: *4449*,
BAGD: 731B, CB: 374A

4794 πυρρός, *pyrros*, a. *fiery red, the color of fire.* S: *4450*,
BAGD: 731C, CB: 374A

4795 Πύρρος, *Pyrros*, n.pr., "fiery red." *Pyrrhus.* S: *150*,
BAGD: 731C, CB: 374A

4796 πύρωσις, *pyrōsis*, n. *burning, painful.* S: *4451*, BAGD: 731C,
CB: 374A

4797 πωλέω, *pōleō*, v. *to sell.* S: *4453*, BAGD: 731C, CB: 371C

4798 πῶλος, *pōlos*, n. *colt.* S: *4454*, BAGD: 731D, CB: 372A

4799 πώποτε, *pōpote*, adv. *ever, at any time.* S: *4455*,
BAGD: 732A, CB: 372A

4800 πωρόω, *pōroō*, v. *to harden, deaden, make dull.* S: *4456*,
BAGD: 732A, CB: 372A

4801 πώρωσις, *pōrōsis*, n. *hardening, stubbornness.* S: *4457*,
BAGD: 732A, CB: 372A

4802 πῶς, *pōs*, pt.inter. *how? in what way?; how!.* S: *4459*,
BAGD: 732D, CB: –

4803 πώς, *pōs*, pt. *somehow, in some way.* S: *4458* & *4452*,
BAGD: 732B, CB: –

4804 ρ, *r*, letter. *letter of the Greek alphabet.* S: *150*, BAGD: 733A,
CB: –

4805 'Ραάβ, *Rhaab*, n.pr., "spacious, broad." *Rahab.* S: *4460*,
BAGD: 733A, CB: –

4806 ραββί, *rhabbi*, l.[n.]. *Rabbi.* S: *4461*, BAGD: 733A, CB: 374A

4807 ραββονί, *rhabboni*, l.[n.]. variant: *Rabboni.* S: *4462*,
BAGD: 733A cf. ραββουνί, CB: 374A cf. *rhabhouni*

4808 ραββουνί, *rhabbouni*, l.[n.]. *Rabboni.* S: *4462*, BAGD: 733A,
CB: 374A

4809 ραββωνί, *rhabbōni*, l.[n.]. variant: *Rabboni.* S: *4462**,
BAGD: 733A cf. ραββουνί, CB: 374A cf. *rhabbouni*

4810 ραβδίζω, *rhabdizō*, v. *to beat with a rod.* S: *4463*,
BAGD: 733B, CB: 374A

4811 ράβδος, *rhabdos*, n. *rod, staff, stick; measuring rod; scepter.*
S: *4464*, BAGD: 733B, CB: 374A

4812 ραβδοῦχος, *rhabdouchos*, n. *officer.* S: *4465*, BAGD: 733C,
CB: 374A

4813 ραβιθά, *rhabitha*, l.[n.]. variant: *(Aramaic) little girl.* S: *150*,
BAGD: 733C, CB: –

4814 'Ραγαύ, *Rhagau*, n.pr., "friend [of God]." *Reu.* S: *4466**,
BAGD: 733C, CB: –

4815 ραδιούργημα, *rhadiourgēma*, n. *crime, legal infraction.*
S: *4467*, BAGD: 733C, CB: –

4816 ραδιουργία, *rhadiourgia*, n. *trickery.* S: *4468*, BAGD: 733C,
CB: –

4817 ραίνω, *rhainō*, v. variant: *(pass.) to be sprinkled.* S: *911**,
BAGD: 733D, CB: 374A

4818 'Ραιφάν, *Rhaiphan*, n.pr. *Rephan.* S: *4481**, BAGD: 737A
cf. 'Ρομφά, CB: –

4819 ρακά, *rhaka*, l.[a.]., "empty-headed [?]." *Raca.* S: *4469*,
BAGD: 733D, CB: 374A

4820 ράκος, *rhakos*, n. *piece of cloth.* S: *4470*, BAGD: 734A, CB: –

4821 'Ραμά, *Rhama*, n.pr., "elevated spot." *Ramah.* S: *4471**,
BAGD: 734A, CB: –

4822 ραντίζω, *rhantizō*, v. *to sprinkle.* S: *4472*, BAGD: 734B,
CB: 374A

4823 ραντισμός, *rhantismos*, n. *sprinkling.* S: *4473*, BAGD: 734B,
CB: 374A

4824 ραπίζω, *rhapizō*, v. *to strike, slap.* S: *4474*, BAGD: 734B,
CB: 374A

4825 ράπισμα, *rhapisma*, n. *slap, strike.* S: *4475*, BAGD: 734C,
CB: 374A

4826 ράσσω, *rhassō*, v. variant: *to strike, dash, throw down.*
S: *4486*, BAGD: 734C, CB: –

4827 ραφίς, *rhaphis*, n. *needle.* S: *4476*, BAGD: 734C, CB: –

4828 ραχά, *rhacha*, l.[a.]., "empty-headed [?]." variant: *Raca.*
S: *4469**, BAGD: 733D cf. ρακά, CB: 374A

4829 'Ραχάβ, *Rhachab*, n.pr., "spacious, broad." *Rahab.* S: *4477*,
BAGD: 734D, CB: –

4830 'Ραχήλ, *Rhachēl*, n.pr., "ewe." *Rachel.* S: *4478*,
BAGD: 734D, CB: –

4831 'Ρεβέκκα, *Rhebekka*, n.pr., *poss.* "choice calf." *Rebekah.*
S: *4479*, BAGD: 734D, CB: –

4832 ρέδη, *rhedē*, n. *carriage.* S: *4480**, BAGD: 734D, CB: –

4833 'Ρεμφάν, *Rhemphan*, n.pr. variant: *Remphan.* S: *4481*,
BAGD: 737A cf. 'Ρομφά, CB: –

4834 'Ρεφάν, *Rhephan*, n.pr. variant: *Rephan.* S: *4481**,
BAGD: 737A cf. 'Ρομφά, CB: –

4835 ρέω, *rheō*, v. *to flow.* S: *4482*, BAGD: 735A, CB: 374A

4836 'Ρήγιον, *Rhēgion*, n.pr. *Rhegium.* S: *4484*, BAGD: 735A,
CB: –

4837 ρῆγμα, *rhēgma*, n. *destruction, ruin.* S: *4485*, BAGD: 735A,
CB: –

4838 ρήγνυμι, *rhēgnymi*, v. *to burst, break forth; to tear to pieces;
to throw violently.* S: *4486*, BAGD: 735A, CB: –

4839 ρῆμα, *rhēma*, n. *word, saying; matter; thing.* S: *4487*,
BAGD: 735B, CB: 374A

4840 'Ρησά, *Rhēsa*, n.pr. *Rhesa.* S: *4488*, BAGD: 735D, CB: –

4841 ρήσσω, *rhēssō*, v. variant: *to throw violently.* S: *4486*,
BAGD: 735D, CB: –

4842 ρήτωρ, *rhētōr*, n. *lawyer.* S: *4489*, BAGD: 735D, CB: 374B

4843 ρητῶς, *rhētōs*, adv. *clearly, exactly.* S: *4490*, BAGD: 736A,
CB: –

4844 ρίζα, *rhiza*, n. *root.* S: *4491*, BAGD: 736A, CB: 374B

4845 ριζόω, *rhizoō*, v. *(pass.) to be rooted.* S: *4492*, BAGD: 736B,
CB: 374B cf. -omai

4846 ριπή, *rhipē*, n. *twinkling, rapid movement (of the eye).*
S: *4493*, BAGD: 736B, CB: 374B

4847 ριπίζω, *rhipizō*, v. *(pass.) to be tossed about.* S: *4494*,
BAGD: 736B, CB: 374B

4848 ριπτέω, *rhipteō*, v. *to throw off.* S: *4495*, BAGD: 736C, CB: –

4849 ρίπτω, *rhiptō*, v. *to throw, drop; to lay; (pass.) to be helpless,
laid out.* S: *4496*, BAGD: 736C, CB: –

4850 'Ροβοάμ, *Rhoboam*, n.pr., "[my] people will enlarge,
expand." *Rehoboam.* S: *4497*, BAGD: 736D, CB: –

4851 Ῥόδη, *Rhodē*, n.pr., "rose." *Rhoda*. S: *4498*, BAGD: 736D, CB: –

4852 Ῥόδος, *Rhodos*, n.pr., "rose." *Rhodes*. S: *4499*, BAGD: 737A, CB: –

4853 ῥοιζηδόν, *rhoizēdon*, adv. *with a roar*. S: *4500*, BAGD: 737A, CB: –

4854 Ῥομφά, *Rhompha*, n.pr. variant: *Rompha*. S: *4481**, BAGD: 737A, CB: –

4855 ῥομφαία, *rhomphaia*, n. *sword*. S: *4501*, BAGD: 737A, CB: 374B

4856 ῥοπή, *rhopē*, n. variant: *downward movement, twinkling*. S: *4493**, BAGD: 737B, CB: –

4857 Ῥουβήν, *Rhoubēn*, n.pr., "See, a son!" [Ge. 29:32]; "substitute a son" IDB. *Reuben*. S: *4502*, BAGD: 737B, CB: –

4858 Ῥούθ, *Rhouth*, n.pr., "friendship" BDB, *poss.* "comrade, companion" ISBE; "refreshed" IDB. *Ruth*. S: *4503*, BAGD: 737B, CB: –

4859 Ῥοῦφος, *Rhouphos*, n.pr., "red-haired." *Rufus*. S: *4504*, BAGD: 737B, CB: –

4860 ῥύμη, *rhymē*, n. *street, alley, lane*. S: *4505*, BAGD: 737C, CB: –

4861 ῥύομαι, *rhyomai*, v. *to rescue, deliver*. S: *4506*, BAGD: 737C, CB: 374B

4862 ῥυπαίνω, *rhypainō*, v. *to be vile*. S: *4510**, BAGD: 737D, CB: 374B

4863 ῥυπαρεύω, *rhypareuō*, v. variant: *(pass.) to be fouled, defiled*. S: *4510**, BAGD: 738A, CB: 374B

4864 ῥυπαρία, *rhyparia*, n. *(moral) filth*. S: *4507*, BAGD: 738A, CB: 374B

4865 ῥυπαρός, *rhyparos*, a. *shabby, dirty; moral vileness, filthiness*. S: *4508*, BAGD: 738A, CB: 374B

4866 ῥύπος, *rhypos*, n. *dirt*. S: *4509*, BAGD: 738A, CB: 374B

4867 ῥυπόω, *rhypoō*, v. variant: *to defile, pollute*. S: *4510*, BAGD: 738B, CB: 374B cf. -eō

4868 ῥύσις, *rhysis*, n. *flow (of blood), bleeding*. S: *4511*, BAGD: 738B, CB: 374B

4869 ῥυτίς, *rhytis*, n. *wrinkle*. S: *4512*, BAGD: 738B, CB: –

4870 Ῥωμαϊκός, *Rhōmaikos*, a.pr. variant: *Roman, Latin*. S: *4513*, BAGD: 738C, CB: –

4871 Ῥωμαῖος, *Rhōmaios*, a.pr.g., "of Rome." *Roman, from Rome; (as noun) Roman citizen*. S: *4514*, BAGD: 738C, CB: –

4872 Ῥωμαϊστί, *Rhōmaisti*, adv.pr. *in Latin (language)*. S: *4515*, BAGD: 738C, CB: –

4873 Ῥώμη, *Rhōmē*, n.pr. *Rome*. S: *4516*, BAGD: 738C, CB: –

4874 ῥώννυμι, *rhōnnymi*, v. *to be strong; (pass.) farewell, goodbye*. S: *4517*, BAGD: 738D, CB: –

4875 σ, *s*, letter. *letter of the Greek alphabet*. S: *150*, BAGD: –, CB: –

4876 σαβαχθάνι, *sabachthani*, l.[v.+p.]. *sabachthani (Aramaic: "you have forsaken me")*. S: *4518**, BAGD: 738B, CB: –

4877 Σαβαώθ, *Sabaōth*, l.[pr.n.]. *Almighty ["of Hosts"]*. S: *4519*, BAGD: 738B, CB: 374B

4878 σαββατισμός, *sabbatismos*, n. *Sabbath-rest, Sabbath observance*. S: *4520*, BAGD: 739A, CB: 374B

4879 σάββατον, *sabbaton*, n. *Sabbath*. S: *4521*, BAGD: 739A, CB: 374B

4880 σαγήνη, *sagēnē*, n. *(large) dragnet*. S: *4522*, BAGD: 739C, CB: –

4881 Σαδδουκαῖος, *Saddoukaios*, n.pr., *poss.* "followers of Zadok; righteous." *Sadducee*. S: *4523*, BAGD: 739D, CB: 374B

4882 Σαδώκ, *Sadōk*, n.pr., "righteous one." *Zadok*. S: *4524*, BAGD: 739D, CB: –

4883 σαίνω, *sainō*, v. *(pass.) to be unsettled, disturbed*. S: *4525*, BAGD: 740A, CB: –

4884 σάκκος, *sakkos*, n. *sackcloth*. S: *4526*, BAGD: 740A, CB: –

4885 Σαλά, *Sala*, n.pr., "missile [a weapon], sprout" ISBE. variant: *Sala*. S: *4527*, BAGD: 740B, CB: –

4886 Σαλαθιήλ, *Salathiēl*, n.pr., "I have asked [him] of God [El]" BDB ISBE KB; *poss.* "God [El] is a shield" IDB. *Shealtiel*. S: *4528*, BAGD: 740B, CB: –

4887 Σαλαμίς, *Salamis*, n.pr., "peace." *Salamis*. S: *4529*, BAGD: 740B, CB: –

4888 σαλεύω, *saleuō*, v. *to shake up; agitate; (pass.) to be shaken, swayed, unsettled*. S: *4531*, BAGD: 740C, CB: 374B

4889 Σαλήμ, *Salēm*, n.pr., "peace." *Salem*. S: *4532*, BAGD: 740D, CB: 374B

4890 Σαλίμ, *Salim*, n.pr. *Salim*. S: *4530**, BAGD: 740D, CB: –

4891 Σαλμών, *Salmōn*, n.pr., "little spark" KB. *Salmon*. S: *4533*, BAGD: 740D, CB: –

4892 Σαλμώνη, *Salmōnē*, n.pr. *Salmone*. S: *4534*, BAGD: 740D, CB: –

4893 σάλος, *salos*, n. *tossing motion, rolling motion (of the surging waves)*. S: *4535*, BAGD: 741A, CB: 374B

4894 σάλπιγξ, *salpinx*, n. *trumpet*. S: *4536*, BAGD: 741A, CB: 374B

4895 σαλπίζω, *salpizō*, v. *to sound a trumpet, announce with a trumpet*. S: *4537*, BAGD: 741A, CB: 374B

4896 σαλπιστής, *salpistēs*, n. *trumpeter*. S: *4538*, BAGD: 741B, CB: 374B

4897 Σαλώμη, *Salōmē*, n.pr., "peaceful, prosperous one." *Salome*. S: *4539*, BAGD: 741B, CB: –

4898 Σαλωμών, *Salōmōn*, n.pr. variant: *Solomon*. S: *4672**, BAGD: 741B, CB: 374B

4899 Σαμάρεια, *Samareia*, n.pr., "belonging to the clan of Shemer" [1Ki 16:24] BDB. *Samaria*. S: *4540*, BAGD: 741B, CB: 374B

4900 Σαμαρία, *Samaria*, n.pr., "belonging to the clan of Shemer" [1Ki 16:24] BDB. variant: *Samaria*. S: *4540**, BAGD: 741B cf. Σαμάρεια, CB: 374B

4901 Σαμαρίτης, *Samaritēs*, n.pr.g., "of Samaria." *Samaritan*. S: *4541**, BAGD: 741C, CB: 374B

4902 Σαμαρῖτις, *Samaritis*, n.pr.g. & a., "of Samaria." *Samaritan*. S: *4542**, BAGD: 741D, CB: 374B

4903 Σαμοθράκη, *Samothrakē*, n.pr., "Thracian Samos." *Samothrace*. S: *4543*, BAGD: 741D, CB: –

4904 Σάμος, *Samos*, n.pr., "heights, lofty place." *Samos*. S: *4544*, BAGD: 741D, CB: –

4905 Σαμουήλ, Samouēl, n.pr., "his name is God [El]" BDB IDB ISBE; "heard of God [El]" KD; "the unnamed god is El" KB. *Samuel.* S: *4545*, BAGD: 741D, CB: –

4906 Σαμφουρειν, Samphourein, n.pr. variant: *Sepphoris.* S: *150*, BAGD: 742A, CB: –

4907 Σαμψών, Sampsōn, n.pr., "little one of Shemesh [pagan sun god]" *or* "sunny" BDB IDB KB. *Samson.* S: *4546*, BAGD: 742A, CB: –

4908 σανδάλιον, sandalion, n. *sandal.* S: *4547*, BAGD: 742A, CB: –

4909 σανίς, sanis, n. *plank, board.* S: *4548*, BAGD: 742A, CB: –

4910 Σαούλ, Saoul, n.pr., "asked of God" *or poss.* "dedicated to God." *Saul.* S: *4549*, BAGD: 742A, CB: –

4911 σαπρός, sapros, a. *bad, rotten, decayed; unwholesome.* S: *4550*, BAGD: 742B, CB: 374B

4912 Σάπφιρα, Sapphira, n.pr., "beautiful." *Sapphira.* S: *4551**, BAGD: 742B, CB: –

4913 σάπφιρος, sapphiros, n. *sapphire stone.* S: *4552**, BAGD: 742C, CB: 374B

4914 σαργάνη, sarganē, n. *(large flexible) basket.* S: *4553*, BAGD: 742C, CB: –

4915 Σάρδεις, Sardeis, n.pr. *Sardis.* S: *4554*, BAGD: 742C, CB: –

4916 σάρδινος, sardinos, n. variant: *carnelian, sard.* S: *4555*, BAGD: 742C, CB: –

4917 σάρδιον, sardion, n. *carnelian.* S: *4556**, BAGD: 742D, CB: 374B

4918 σαρδόνυξ, sardonyx, n. *sardonyx.* S: *4557*, BAGD: 742D, CB: 374B

4919 Σάρεπτα, Sarepta, n.pr., *poss.* "smelting place" BDB; "place of pigmenting, staining" KB. *Zarephath.* S: *4558*, BAGD: 742D, CB: –

4920 σαρκικός, sarkikos, a. *material; worldly, sinful; pertaining to the flesh.* S: *4559*, BAGD: 742D, CB: 374B

4921 σάρκινος, sarkinos, a. *fleshly, made of flesh; human; worldly, unspiritual.* S: *4560*, BAGD: 743A, CB: 374C

4922 σάρξ, sarx, n. *flesh, body; human, humankind; sinful nature.* S: *4561*, BAGD: 743B, CB: 374C

4923 Σαρούχ, Sarouch, n.pr., "descendant, i.e., younger branch" BDB. variant: *Serug.* S: *4562*, BAGD: 747C cf. Σερούχ, CB: –

4924 σαρόω, saroō, v. *to sweep, sweep clean.* S: *4563*, BAGD: 744D, CB: –

4925 Σάρρα, Sarra, n.pr., "princess." *Sarah.* S: *4564*, BAGD: 744D, CB: 374C

4926 Σαρών, Sarōn, n.pr., "plain, level country." *Sharon.* S: *4565**, BAGD: 744D, CB: –

4927 Σατάν, Satan, n.pr., "hostile opponent." variant: *Satan.* S: *4566**, BAGD: 744D, CB: 374C

4928 Σατανᾶς, Satanas, n.pr., "hostile opponent." *Satan.* S: *4567*, BAGD: 744D, CB: 374C

4929 σάτον, saton, n. *seah (dry measure of about 12 quarts).* S: *4568*, BAGD: 745B, CB: –

4930 Σαῦλος, Saulos, n.pr., "asked for" *poss.* "dedicated to God." *Saul.* S: *4569*, BAGD: 745B, CB: –

4931 σβέννυμι, sbennymi, v. *to extinguish, quench, snuff out.* S: *4570*, BAGD: 745B, CB: 374C

4932 σεαυτοῦ, seautou, p.reflex. *yourself.* S: *4572*, BAGD: 745C, CB: –

4933 σεβάζομαι, sebazomai, v. *to worship.* S: *4573*, BAGD: 745C, CB: 374C

4934 σέβασμα, sebasma, n. *object of worship.* S: *4574*, BAGD: 745D, CB: 374C

4935 σεβαστός, sebastos, a. *(as adj.) revered, worthy of reverence, imperial; (as noun) Emperor.* S: *4575*, BAGD: 745D, CB: 374C

4936 σέβω, sebō, v. *(mid.) to worship, be devout, God-fearing.* S: *4576**, BAGD: 746A, CB: 374C

4937 σειρά, seira, n. variant: *chain.* S: *4577*, BAGD: 746B, CB: –

4938 σειρός, seiros, n. variant: *pit, cave.* S: *4577**, BAGD: 746B, CB: –

4939 σεισμός, seismos, n. *earthquake; storm.* S: *4578*, BAGD: 746B, CB: 374C

4940 σείω, seiō, v. *to cause to shake; (pass.) to be shaken, stirred up.* S: *4579*, BAGD: 746C, CB: 374C

4941 Σεκοῦνδος, Sekoundos, n.pr., "second." *Secundus.* S: *4580*, BAGD: 746C, CB: –

4942 Σελεύκεια, Seleukeia, n.pr. *Seleucia.* S: *4581*, BAGD: 746C, CB: –

4943 σελήνη, selēnē, n. *moon.* S: *4582*, BAGD: 746D, CB: 374C

4944 σεληνιάζομαι, selēniazomai, v. *(pass.) to have a seizure.* S: *4583*, BAGD: 746D, CB: 374C

4945 Σεμεΐ, Semei, n.pr., "Yahweh has heard." variant: *Semei.* S: *4584*, BAGD: 746D cf. Σεμεῖν, CB: –

4946 Σεμεΐν, Semein, n.pr., "Yahweh has heard." *Semein.* S: *4584**, BAGD: 746D, CB: –

4947 σεμίδαλις, semidalis, n. *finely ground flour.* S: *4585*, BAGD: 746D, CB: –

4948 σεμνός, semnos, a. *worthy of respect, noble.* S: *4586*, BAGD: 746D, CB: 375A

4949 σεμνότης, semnotēs, n. *holiness, seriousness, respect.* S: *4587*, BAGD: 747A, CB: 375A

4950 Σέργιος, Sergios, n.pr. *Sergius.* S: *4588*, BAGD: 747B, CB: –

4951 Σερούκ, Serouk, n.pr., "descendant, i.e., younger branch" BDB. variant: *Serug.* S: *4562**, BAGD: 747C cf. Σερούχ, CB: –

4952 Σερούχ, Serouch, n.pr., "descendant, i.e., younger branch" BDB. *Serug.* S: *4562**, BAGD: 747C, CB: –

4953 Σήθ, Sēth, n.pr., "determined, granted" [Ge 4:25]; "restitution" KB. *Seth.* S: *4589*, BAGD: 747C, CB: –

4954 Σήμ, Sēm, n.pr., "name, fame." *Shem.* S: *4590*, BAGD: 747C, CB: –

4955 σημαίνω, sēmainō, v. *to make known; to indicate (beforehand), predict, foretell.* S: *4591*, BAGD: 747C, CB: 374C

4956 σημεῖον, sēmeion, n. *(miraculous) sign, signal, mark.* S: *4592*, BAGD: 747D, CB: 374C

4957 σημειόω, sēmeioō, v. *(mid.) to take special note of.* S: *4593*, BAGD: 748D, CB: –

4958 σήμερον, *sēmeron*, adv. *today, this day.* S: *4594*, BAGD: 749A, CB: 374A

4959 σημικίνθιον, *sēmikinthion*, n. variant: *apron.* S: *4612**, BAGD: 751A cf. σιμικίνθιον, CB: –

4960 σήπω, *sēpō*, v. *to rot, decay.* S: *4595*, BAGD: 749B, CB: –

4961 σηρικός, *sērikos*, a. variant: *silken; (as noun) silk (cloth).* S: *4596*, BAGD: 751D cf. σίρος, CB: –

4962 σής, *sēs*, n. *moth.* S: *4597*, BAGD: 749B, CB: 375A

4963 σητόβρωτος, *sētobrōtos*, a. *moth-eaten.* S: *4598*, BAGD: 749C, CB: –

4964 σθενόω, *sthenoō*, v. *to strengthen, make strong.* S: *4599*, BAGD: 749C, CB: –

4965 σιαγών, *siagōn*, n. *cheek.* S: *4600*, BAGD: 749C, CB: –

4966 σιαίνομαι, *siainomai*, v. variant: *to be disturbed, annoyed.* S: *4525**, BAGD: 749C, CB: –

4967 σιγάω, *sigaō*, v. *to be or become silent; (pass.) to be hidden, concealed.* S: *4601*, BAGD: 749C, CB: –

4968 σιγή, *sigē*, n. *silence.* S: *4602*, BAGD: 749D, CB: –

4969 σιδήρεος, *sidēreos*, a. *made of iron.* S: *4603*, BAGD: 750A cf. -οῦς, CB: 375A cf. -ous

4970 σίδηρος, *sidēros*, n. *iron.* S: *4604*, BAGD: 750A, CB: 375A

4971 σιδηροῦς, *sidērous*, a. *made of iron.* S: *4603**, BAGD: 750A, CB: 375A

4972 Σιδών, *Sidōn*, n.pr., "fishery." *Sidon.* S: *4605*, BAGD: 750A, CB: –

4973 Σιδώνιος, *Sidōnios*, a.pr.g., "of Sidon." *Sidonian.* S: *4606*, BAGD: 750B, CB: 375A

4974 σικάριος, *sikarios*, n. *terrorist, assassin.* S: *4607*, BAGD: 750B, CB: –

4975 σίκερα, *sikera*, l.[n.]. *fermented drink, beer.* S: *4608*, BAGD: 750B, CB: –

4976 Σίλας, *Silas*, n.pr., "asked for" *poss.* "dedicated to God." *Silas.* S: *4609*, BAGD: 750C, CB: –

4977 Σιλουανός, *Silouanos*, n.pr., "asked for" *poss.* "dedicated to God." *Silas, Silvanus.* S: *4610*, BAGD: 750C, CB: –

4978 Σιλωάμ, *Silōam*, n.pr., "sent." *Siloam.* S: *4611*, BAGD: 750D, CB: –

4979 Σιμαίας, *Simaias*, n.pr. variant: *Simaias.* S: *150*, BAGD: 750D, CB: –

4980 σιμικίνθιον, *simikinthion*, n. *apron.* S: *4612*, BAGD: 751A, CB: –

4981 Σίμων, *Simōn*, n.pr., "he has heard" *or* "obedient one." *Simon.* S: *4613*, BAGD: 751A, CB: –

4982 Σινά, *Sina*, n.pr., "Sin" [pagan moon god]; "glare" [from white chalk] ISBE. *Sinai.* S: *4614**, BAGD: 751C, CB: 375A

4983 σίναπι, *sinapi*, n. *mustard plant.* S: *4615*, BAGD: 751C, CB: 375A

4984 σινδών, *sindōn*, n. *linen (cloth or garment).* S: *4616*, BAGD: 751C, CB: 375A

4985 σινιάζω, *siniazō*, v. *to sift.* S: *4617*, BAGD: 751D, CB: 375A

4986 σιρικός, *sirikos*, a. *silken; (as noun) silk (cloth).* S: *4596**, BAGD: 751D, CB: –

4987 σιρός, *siros*, n. *dungeon, pit, cave.* S: *4577**, BAGD: 751D, CB: –

4988 σιτευτός, *siteutos*, a. *fattened.* S: *4618*, BAGD: 752A, CB: 375A

4989 σιτίον, *sition*, n. *(food made from) grain.* S: *4621**, BAGD: 752A, CB: –

4990 σιτιστός, *sitistos*, a. *fattened; (as noun) fattened cattle.* S: *4619*, BAGD: 752A, CB: –

4991 σιτομέτριον, *sitometrion*, n. *measured allowance of food, ration of grain.* S: *4620*, BAGD: 752A, CB: –

4992 σῖτος, *sitos*, n. *wheat, grain.* S: *4621*, BAGD: 752B, CB: 375A

4993 Σιχάρ, *Sichar*, n.pr. variant: *Sychar.* S: *4965**, BAGD: 795D cf. Συχάρ, CB: –

4994 Σιών, *Siōn*, n.pr., "citadel." *Zion.* S: *4622*, BAGD: 752B, CB: 375A

4995 σιωπάω, *siōpaō*, v. *to be quiet, remain silent.* S: *4623*, BAGD: 752C, CB: –

4996 σιωπῇ, *siōpē*, adv. variant: *quietly, privately.* S: *2977**, BAGD: 752C, CB: –

4997 σκανδαλίζω, *skandalizō*, v. *to cause to sin, cause to fall (into sin), offend; to fall away (from the faith), go astray; to take offense.* S: *4624*, BAGD: 752D, CB: 375A

4998 σκάνδαλον, *skandalon*, n. *stumbling block, obstacle, offense; something that causes sin.* S: *4625*, BAGD: 753A, CB: 375A

4999 σκάπτω, *skaptō*, v. *to dig.* S: *4626*, BAGD: 753B, CB: –

5000 Σκαριώθ, *Skariōth*, n.pr.[g.?]. variant: *Scarioth.* S: *2469**, BAGD: 753C, CB: –

5001 Σκαριώτης, *Skariōtēs*, n.pr.[g.?]. variant: *Scariot.* S: *2469**, BAGD: 753C, CB: –

5002 σκάφη, *skaphē*, n. *lifeboat, (small) boat.* S: *4627*, BAGD: 753C, CB: –

5003 σκέλος, *skelos*, n. *leg.* S: *4628*, BAGD: 753C, CB: –

5004 σκέπασμα, *skepasma*, n. *clothing, covering.* S: *4629*, BAGD: 753D, CB: –

5005 Σκευᾶς, *Skeuas*, n.pr. *Sceva.* S: *4630*, BAGD: 753D, CB: –

5006 σκευή, *skeuē*, n. *(ship's) tackle, gear.* S: *4631*, BAGD: 754A, CB: –

5007 σκεῦος, *skeuos*, n. *possession, merchandise, object, thing; jar, vessel, dish.* S: *4632*, BAGD: 754A, CB: 375A

5008 σκηνή, *skēnē*, n. *tabernacle; tent, shelter, dwelling.* S: *4633*, BAGD: 754C, CB: 375A

5009 σκηνοπηγία, *skēnopēgia*, n. *(Feast of) Tabernacles.* S: *4634*, BAGD: 754D, CB: 375A

5010 σκηνοποιός, *skēnopoios*, n. *tentmaker.* S: *4635*, BAGD: 755A, CB: 375A

5011 σκῆνος, *skēnos*, n. *tent.* S: *4636*, BAGD: 755B, CB: 375A

5012 σκηνόω, *skēnoō*, v. *to live, dwell; to spread a tent.* S: *4637*, BAGD: 755C, CB: 375A

5013 σκήνωμα, *skēnōma*, n. *tent, dwelling place, lodging place.* S: *4638*, BAGD: 755C, CB: 375A

5014 σκιά, *skia*, n. *shadow, shade.* S: *4639*, BAGD: 755D, CB: 375A

5015 σκιρτάω, *skirtaō*, v. *to leap.* S: *4640*, BAGD: 755D, CB: –

5016 σκληροκαρδία, *sklērokardia*, n. *hardness of heart, stubbornness, obstinacy.* S: *4641*, BAGD: 756A, CB: 375A

5017 σκληρός, *sklēros*, a. *hard, harsh.* S: *4642*, BAGD: 756A, CB: 375A

5018 σκληρότης, *sklērotēs*, n. *hardness, stubbornness.* S: *4643*, BAGD: 756B, CB: 375A

5019 σκληροτράχηλος, *sklērotrachēlos*, a. *stiff-necked, stubborn.* S: *4644*, BAGD: 756B, CB: 375A

5020 σκληρύνω, *sklērynō*, v. *to harden (the heart), make obstinate, make stubborn; (pass.) to be hardened, become obstinate.* S: *4645*, BAGD: 756B, CB: 375A

5021 σκολιός, *skolios*, a. *crooked; corrupt.* S: *4646*, BAGD: 756B, CB: –

5022 σκόλοψ, *skolops*, n. *thorn.* S: *4647*, BAGD: 756C, CB: 375B

5023 σκοπέω, *skopeō*, v. *to watch out for, take notice of, look to.* S: *4648*, BAGD: 756D, CB: 375B

5024 σκοπός, *skopos*, n. *goal.* S: *4649*, BAGD: 756D, CB: 375B

5025 σκορπίζω, *skorpizō*, v. *to scatter, disperse.* S: *4650*, BAGD: 757A, CB: 375B

5026 σκορπίος, *skorpios*, n. *scorpion.* S: *4651*, BAGD: 757A, CB: 375B

5027 σκοτεινός, *skoteinos*, a. *dark.* S: *4652*, BAGD: 757B, CB: 375B

5028 σκοτία, *skotia*, n. *darkness, the dark.* S: *4653*, BAGD: 757B, CB: 375B

5029 σκοτίζομαι, *skotizomai*, v. *(pass.) to be or become dark, be darkened.* S: *4654**, BAGD: 757C, CB: 375B

5030 σκότος, *skotos*, n. *darkness, the dark.* S: *4655*, BAGD: 757C, CB: 375B

5031 σκοτόω, *skotoō*, v. *(pass.) to be or become darkened.* S: *4656*, BAGD: 758A, CB: 375B

5032 σκύβαλον, *skybalon*, n. *rubbish, refuse.* S: *4657*, BAGD: 758A, CB: 375B

5033 Σκύθης, *Skythēs*, n.pr.g. *Scythian.* S: *4658*, BAGD: 758B, CB: –

5034 σκυθρωπός, *skythrōpos*, a. *to look somber, appear downcast.* S: *4659*, BAGD: 758B, CB: –

5035 σκύλλω, *skyllō*, v. *to bother, annoy; (pass.) to be harassed; (mid.) to trouble oneself.* S: *4660*, BAGD: 758B, CB: –

5036 σκῦλον, *skylon*, n. *(pl.) spoils, booty.* S: *4661*, BAGD: 758B, CB: –

5037 σκωληκόβρωτος, *skōlēkobrōtos*, a. *eaten by worms.* S: *4662*, BAGD: 758C, CB: –

5038 σκώληξ, *skōlēx*, n. *worm.* S: *4663*, BAGD: 758C, CB: –

5039 σμαράγδινος, *smaragdinos*, a. *(of) emerald.* S: *4664*, BAGD: 758C, CB: 375B

5040 σμάραγδος, *smaragdos*, n. *emerald.* S: *4665*, BAGD: 758C, CB: 375B

5041 σμῆγμα, *smēgma*, n. variant: *ointment, salve.* S: *3395**, BAGD: 758D, CB: –

5042 σμίγμα, *smigma*, n. variant: *mixture, compound.* S: *3395**, BAGD: 758D, CB: –

5043 σμύρνα[1], *smyrna*[1], n. *myrrh.* S: *4666*, BAGD: 758D, CB: 375B

5044 Σμύρνα[2], *Smyrna*[2], n.pr. *Smyrna.* S: *4667*, BAGD: 759A, CB: 375B

5045 Σμυρναῖος, *Smyrnaios*, a.pr.g., "of Smyrna." variant: *Smyrnaean.* S: *4668*, BAGD: 759A, CB: –

5046 σμυρνίζω, *smyrnizō*, v. *to mix with myrrh.* S: *4669*, BAGD: 759A, CB: 375B

5047 Σόδομα, *Sodoma*, n.pr. *Sodom.* S: *4670*, BAGD: 759A, CB: –

5048 Σολομών, *Solomōn*, n.pr., "peace, well being." *Solomon.* S: *4672*, BAGD: 759B, CB: 375B

5049 σορός, *soros*, n. *coffin, bier.* S: *4673*, BAGD: 759B, CB: –

5050 σός, *sos*, a.poss. *your, yours.* S: *4674*, BAGD: 759B, CB: –

5051 σουδάριον, *soudarion*, n. *piece of cloth, burial cloth, handkerchief.* S: *4676*, BAGD: 759C, CB: –

5052 Σουσάννα, *Sousanna*, n.pr., "lily." *Susanna.* S: *4677*, BAGD: 759C, CB: –

5053 σοφία, *sophia*, n. *wisdom.* S: *4678*, BAGD: 759C, CB: 375B

5054 σοφίζω, *sophizō*, v. *to make wise; (pass.) to be cleverly invented.* S: *4679*, BAGD: 760B, CB: 375B

5055 σοφός, *sophos*, a. *wise; expert, skilled.* S: *4680*, BAGD: 760B, CB: 375B

5056 Σπανία, *Spania*, n.pr. *Spain.* S: *4681*, BAGD: 760C, CB: –

5057 σπαράσσω, *sparassō*, v. *to convulse, shake violently.* S: *4682*, BAGD: 760D, CB: –

5058 σπαργανόω, *sparganoō*, v. *to wrap (in cloth).* S: *4683*, BAGD: 760D, CB: –

5059 σπαταλάω, *spatalaō*, v. *to live in pleasure, in self-indulgence.* S: *4684*, BAGD: 761A, CB: –

5060 σπάω, *spaō*, v. *(mid.) to draw (a sword).* S: *4685*, BAGD: 761A, CB: –

5061 σπεῖρα, *speira*, n. *company of soldiers, cohort.* S: *4686*, BAGD: 761A, CB: –

5062 σπείρω, *speirō*, v. *to sow seed, scatter seed.* S: *4687*, BAGD: 761B, CB: 375C

5063 σπεκουλάτωρ, *spekoulatōr*, n. *executioner.* S: *4688*, BAGD: 761C, CB: –

5064 σπένδω, *spendō*, v. *(pass.) to be poured out like a drink offering.* S: *4689*, BAGD: 761C, CB: 375C

5065 σπέρμα, *sperma*, n. *seed; children, offspring, descendants.* S: *4690*, BAGD: 761D, CB: 375C

5066 σπερμολόγος, *spermologos*, a. *babbler, chatterer.* S: *4691*, BAGD: 762B, CB: 375C

5067 σπεύδω, *speudō*, v. *to hurry, hasten.* S: *4692*, BAGD: 762B, CB: 375C

5068 σπήλαιον, *spēlaion*, n. *den, cave, hideout.* S: *4693*, BAGD: 762B, CB: 375C

5069 σπιλάς, *spilas*, n. *blemish, spot.* S: *4694*, BAGD: 762C, CB: –

5070 σπίλος, *spilos*, n. *stain, blot.* S: *4696*, BAGD: 762D, CB: –

5071 σπιλόω, *spiloō*, v. *to corrupt; (pass.) to be stained, defiled.* S: *4695*, BAGD: 762D, CB: –

5072 σπλαγχνίζομαι, *splanchnizomai*, v. *to have compassion on, have pity on.* S: *4697*, BAGD: 762D, CB: 375C

5073 σπλάγχνον, *splanchnon*, n. *inward parts of body: intestines; of emotions: heart, affection, tenderness, compassion.* S: *4698*, BAGD: 763A, CB: 375C

5074 σπόγγος, *spongos*, n. *sponge.* S: *4699*, BAGD: 763B, CB: –

5075 σποδός, *spodos*, n. *ashes.* S: *4700*, BAGD: 763B, CB: –

5076 σπορά, *spora*, n. *seed.* S: *4701*, BAGD: 763B, CB: 375C

5077 σπόριμος, *sporimos*, a. *what is sown; (as noun) grainfield.* S: *4702*, BAGD: 763B, CB: 375C cf. *-ros*

5078 σπόρος, *sporos*, n. *seed.* S: *4703*, BAGD: 763B, CB: 375C

5079 σπουδάζω, *spoudazō*, v. *to be eager, make every effort, do one's best.* S: *4704*, BAGD: 763C, CB: 375C

5080 σπουδαῖος, *spoudaios*, a. *zealous, eager, earnest; (compar.) more enthusiastic, very earnest.* S: *4705 & 4706 & 4707*, BAGD: 763C, CB: 375C

5081 σπουδαίως, *spoudaiōs*, adv. *earnestly, zealously, with vigor; (compar.) all the more eager, with special urgency.* S: *4709 & 4708*, BAGD: 763D, CB: 375C

5082 σπουδή, *spoudē*, n. *hurry, haste; earnestness, diligence, zeal, eagerness.* S: *4710*, BAGD: 763D, CB: 375C

5083 σπυρίς, *spyris*, n. *basket.* S: *4711*, BAGD: 764A, CB: –

5084 στάδιον, *stadion*, n. *stadium, race course; stade (about 200 yards).* S: *4712*, BAGD: 764A, CB: –

5085 στάμνος, *stamnos*, n. *jar.* S: *4713*, BAGD: 764B, CB: –

5086 στασιαστής, *stasiastēs*, n. *insurrectionist, revolutionary.* S: *4955**, BAGD: 764B, CB: –

5087 στάσις, *stasis*, n. *continuance, state of existence; uprising, insurrection, riot; dispute, discord.* S: *4714*, BAGD: 764C, CB: 376A

5088 στατήρ, *statēr*, n. *four-drachma coin, stater (four days' wages).* S: *4715*, BAGD: 764C, CB: 376A

5089 σταυρός, *stauros*, n. *cross.* S: *4716*, BAGD: 764D, CB: 376A

5090 σταυρόω, *stauroō*, v. *to crucify.* S: *4717*, BAGD: 765B, CB: 376A

5091 σταφυλή, *staphylē*, n. *(bunch of) grapes.* S: *4718*, BAGD: 765C, CB: –

5092 στάχυς[1], *stachys[1]*, n. *head of grain.* S: *4719*, BAGD: 765D, CB: 375C

5093 Στάχυς[2], *Stachys[2]*, n.pr., "head of grain." *Stachys.* S: *4720*, BAGD: 765D, CB: –

5094 στέγη, *stegē*, n. *roof.* S: *4721*, BAGD: 765D, CB: –

5095 στέγω, *stegō*, v. *to put up with, stand, endure; to protect, cover.* S: *4722*, BAGD: 765D, CB: 376A

5096 στεῖρα, *steira*, n. *(state of) barrenness, infertility.* S: *4723**, BAGD: 766A, CB: –

5097 στέλλω, *stellō*, v. *(mid.) to avoid, keep away from.* S: *4724*, BAGD: 766A, CB: 376A

5098 στέμμα, *stemma*, n. *wreath.* S: *4725*, BAGD: 766A, CB: 376A

5099 στεναγμός, *stenagmos*, n. *groan, sigh.* S: *4726*, BAGD: 766B, CB: 376A

5100 στενάζω, *stenazō*, v. *to groan, sigh; to grumble.* S: *4727*, BAGD: 766B, CB: 376A

5101 στενός, *stenos*, a. *narrow.* S: *4728*, BAGD: 766B, CB: 376A

5102 στενοχωρέω, *stenochōreō*, v. *(pass.) to be crushed; to withhold, be restricted.* S: *4729*, BAGD: 766C, CB: 376A

5103 στενοχωρία, *stenochōria*, n. *distress, hardship, difficulty.* S: *4730*, BAGD: 766C, CB: 376A

5104 στερεός, *stereos*, a. *solid, strong; standing firm, steadfast.* S: *4731*, BAGD: 766D, CB: 376A

5105 στερεόω, *stereoō*, v. *to make strong; (pass.) to become strong, be strengthened.* S: *4732*, BAGD: 766D, CB: –

5106 στερέωμα, *stereōma*, n. *firmness, steadfastness.* S: *4733*, BAGD: 766D, CB: –

5107 Στεφανᾶς, *Stephanas*, n.pr., "victor's wreath." *Stephanas.* S: *4734*, BAGD: 767A, CB: –

5108 Στέφανος[1], *Stephanos[1]*, n.pr., "victor's wreath." *Stephen.* S: *4736**, BAGD: 767A, CB: 376A

5109 στέφανος[2], *stephanos[2]*, n. *woven crown, wreath, victory garland.* S: *4735*, BAGD: 767A, CB: 376A

5110 στεφανόω, *stephanoō*, v. *to crown, present a wreath.* S: *4737*, BAGD: 767C, CB: 376A

5111 στῆθος, *stēthos*, n. *chest, breast.* S: *4738*, BAGD: 767D, CB: –

5112 στήκω, *stēkō*, v. *to stand, stand firm, be steadfast.* S: *4739*, BAGD: 767D, CB: 376A

5113 στηριγμός, *stērigmos*, n. *security, firmness.* S: *4740*, BAGD: 768A, CB: –

5114 στηρίζω, *stērizō*, v. *to strengthen, establish, stand firm; to be resolute.* S: *4741*, BAGD: 768A, CB: 376A

5115 στιβάς, *stibas*, n. *leafy branch.* S: *4746**, BAGD: 768B, CB: –

5116 στίγμα, *stigma*, n. *mark, scar.* S: *4742*, BAGD: 768C, CB: 376A

5117 στιγμή, *stigmē*, n. *instant, moment.* S: *4743*, BAGD: 768C, CB: –

5118 στίλβω, *stilbō*, v. *to dazzle, be radiant.* S: *4744*, BAGD: 768D, CB: –

5119 στοά, *stoa*, n. *covered colonnade, portico.* S: *4745*, BAGD: 768D, CB: 376A

5120 στοιβάς, *stoibas*, n. variant: *leafy branch.* S: *4746*, BAGD: 768B cf. στιβάς, CB: –

5121 Στοϊκός, *Stoikos*, a.pr. *Stoic.* S: *4770**, BAGD: 768D, CB: –

5122 στοιχεῖον, *stoicheion*, n. *principle, basic principle; element (of nature); elementary truths.* S: *4747*, BAGD: 768D, CB: 376A

5123 στοιχέω, *stoicheō*, v. *to follow, walk in, adhere to.* S: *4748*, BAGD: 769C, CB: 376A

5124 στολή, *stolē*, n. *(flowing) robe.* S: *4749*, BAGD: 769C, CB: 376A

5125 στόμα, *stoma*, n. *mouth; edge (of a sword).* S: *4750*, BAGD: 769D, CB: 376A

5126 στόμαχος, *stomachos*, n. *stomach.* S: *4751*, BAGD: 770B, CB: –

5127 στρατεία, *strateia*, n. *warfare; fight.* S: *4752*, BAGD: 770B, CB: 376A

5128 στράτευμα, *strateuma*, n. *army, troops, soldiers.* S: *4753*, BAGD: 770B, CB: 376A

5129 στρατεύομαι, *strateuomai*, v. *(mid.) to serve as a soldier; to wage war, fight, battle.* S: *4754*, BAGD: 770B, CB: 376A

5130 στρατηγός, *stratēgos*, n. *magistrate, praetor; captain, officer.* S: *4755*, BAGD: 770C, CB: 376A

5131 στρατιά, *stratia*, n. *host, army (of heaven), (celestial) bodies.* S: *4756*, BAGD: 770D, CB: 376A

5132 στρατιώτης, *stratiōtēs*, n. *soldier*. S: *4757*, BAGD: 770D, CB: 376A

5133 στρατολογέω, *stratologeō*, v. *commanding officer*. S: *4758*, BAGD: 770D, CB: 376A

5134 στρατοπεδάρχης, *stratopedarchēs*, n. variant: *military commander, commander of a camp*. S: *4759*, BAGD: 771A, CB: 376B

5135 στρατοπέδαρχος, *stratopedarchos*, n. variant: *military commander, commander of a camp*. S: *4759**, BAGD: 771A, CB: 376B cf. *-ēs*

5136 στρατόπεδον, *stratopedon*, n. *army*. S: *4760*, BAGD: 771A, CB: 376B

5137 στρεβλόω, *strebloō*, v. *to distort, twist*. S: *4761*, BAGD: 771A, CB: –

5138 στρέφω, *strephō*, v. *to turn, turn away, return; to change, repent, turn one's life*. S: *4762*, BAGD: 771A, CB: 376B

5139 στρηνιάω, *strēniaō*, v. *to live in luxury*. S: *4763*, BAGD: 771C, CB: –

5140 στρῆνος, *strēnos*, n. *luxury*. S: *4764*, BAGD: 771C, CB: –

5141 στρουθίον, *strouthion*, n. *sparrow*. S: *4765*, BAGD: 771C, CB: 376B

5142 στρώννυμι, *strōnnymi*, v. variant: *to spread out; (pass.) to be furnished*. S: *4766*, BAGD: 771C, CB: –

5143 στρωννύω, *strōnnyō*, v. *to spread out; (pass.) to be furnished*. S: *4766*, BAGD: 771C, CB: –

5144 στυγητός, *stygētos*, a. *hated*. S: *4767*, BAGD: 771D, CB: –

5145 στυγνάζω, *stygnazō*, v. *to be gloomy, sad; (of weather) to be overcast, gloomy*. S: *4768*, BAGD: 771D, CB: –

5146 στῦλος, *stylos*, n. *pillar, column; (fig.) leader*. S: *4769**, BAGD: 772A, CB: 376B

5147 Στωϊκός, *Stoikos*, a.pr. variant: *Stoic*. S: *4770*, BAGD: 768D cf. Στοϊκός, CB: –

5148 σύ, *sy*, p.pers. *you, your*. S: *4771 & 4571 & 4671 & 467*, BAGD: 772A, CB: –

5149 συγγένεια, *syngeneia*, n. *family, relative, one's own people*. S: *4772*, BAGD: 772C, CB: 376C

5150 συγγενής, *syngenēs*, a. *family, relative, one's own race or people*. S: *4773*, BAGD: 772C, CB: 376C

5151 συγγενίς, *syngenis*, n. *(female) relative*. S: *4773**, BAGD: 772D, CB: –

5152 συγγνώμη, *syngnōmē*, n. *concession*. S: *4774*, BAGD: 773A, CB: –

5153 συγκάθημαι, *synkathēmai*, v. *to sit with*. S: *4775*, BAGD: 773A, CB: –

5154 συγκαθίζω, *synkathizō*, v. *to sit down together; to be seated together*. S: *4776*, BAGD: 773B, CB: –

5155 συγκακοπαθέω, *synkakopatheō*, v. *to suffer together with, endure hardship with*. S: *4777*, BAGD: 773B, CB: 376C

5156 συγκακουχέομαι, *synkakoucheomai*, v. *(pass.) to be mistreated with*. S: *4778**, BAGD: 773B, CB: –

5157 συγκαλέω, *synkaleō*, v. *(act.) to call together; (mid.) to call to one's side, summon*. S: *4779*, BAGD: 773B, CB: 359B cf. *kaleō*

5158 συγκαλύπτω, *synkalyptō*, v. *to conceal*. S: *4780*, BAGD: 773B, CB: 376C

5159 συγκάμπτω, *synkamptō*, v. *(pass.) to be bent over*. S: *4781*, BAGD: 773B, CB: –

5160 συγκαταβαίνω, *synkatabainō*, v. *to come, go down with*. S: *4782*, BAGD: 773C, CB: –

5161 συγκατάθεσις, *synkatathesis*, n. *agreement*. S: *4783*, BAGD: 773C, CB: –

5162 συγκατανεύω, *synkataneuō*, v. variant: *to agree, consent*. S: *150*, BAGD: 773C, CB: –

5163 συγκατατίθημι, *synkatatithēmi*, v. *(mid.) to consent, agree with*. S: *4784**, BAGD: 773C, CB: –

5164 συγκαταψηφίζομαι, *synkatapsēphizomai*, v. *(pass.) to be added, chosen together with*. S: *4785**, BAGD: 773C, CB: –

5165 σύγκειμαι, *synkeimai*, v. variant: *to recline together*. S: *4873**, BAGD: 773D, CB: –

5166 συγκεράννυμι, *synkerannymi*, v. *to combine, unite*. S: *4786*, BAGD: 773D, CB: 376C

5167 συγκινέω, *synkineō*, v. *to stir up, arouse*. S: *4787*, BAGD: 773D, CB: –

5168 συγκλείω, *synkleiō*, v. *to catch (fish hemmed up in a net); to confine, imprison, lock up*. S: *4788*, BAGD: 774A, CB: 376C

5169 συγκληρονόμος, *synklēronomos*, a. *inheriting together; (as noun) co-heir*. S: *4789*, BAGD: 774A, CB: 376C

5170 συγκοινωνέω, *synkoinōneō*, v. *to share with, be connected with*. S: *4790*, BAGD: 774B, CB: 376C

5171 συγκοινωνός, *synkoinōnos*, n. *sharer, companion, participant, partner*. S: *4791*, BAGD: 774B, CB: 376C

5172 συγκομίζω, *synkomizō*, v. *to bury, entomb*. S: *4792*, BAGD: 774C, CB: –

5173 συγκρίνω, *synkrinō*, v. *to express, explain; to compare*. S: *4793*, BAGD: 774D, CB: 376C

5174 συγκύπτω, *synkyptō*, v. *to bend over, be crippled*. S: *4794*, BAGD: 775A, CB: –

5175 συγκυρία, *synkyria*, n. *event that just happens, coincidence*. S: *4795*, BAGD: 775A, CB: –

5176 συγχαίρω, *synchairō*, v. *to rejoice with*. S: *4796*, BAGD: 775A, CB: 376C

5177 συγχέω, *syncheō*, v. *to baffle, confuse; to stir up, cause trouble; (pass.) to be bewildered, confused; to be in an uproar, stirred up*. S: *4797*, BAGD: 775A, CB: –

5178 συγχράομαι, *synchraomai*, v. *to associate with, have dealings with*. S: *4798*, BAGD: 775B, CB: –

5179 συγχύνω, *synchynō*, v. variant: *to baffle, confuse; to stir up, cause trouble; (pass.) to be confused; to be in an uproar, stirred up*. S: *4797*, BAGD: 775A cf. συγχέω, CB: –

5180 σύγχυσις, *synchysis*, n. *uproar, confusion*. S: *4799*, BAGD: 775C, CB: –

5181 συγχωρέω, *synchōreō*, v. variant: *to permit*. S: *2010**, BAGD: 775C, CB: –

5182 συζάω, *syzaō*, v. *to live with*. S: *4800*, BAGD: 775C, CB: 377A

5183 συζεύγνυμι, *syzeugnymi*, v. *to join together*. S: *4801*, BAGD: 775C, CB: 377A

5184 συζητέω, *syzēteō*, v. *to discuss; to debate, argue*. S: *4802*, BAGD: 775D, CB: –

5185 συζήτησις, *syzētēsis*, n. variant: *dispute, discussion.* S: *4803*, BAGD: 775D, CB: –

5186 συζητητής, *syzētētēs*, n. *philosopher, debater.* S: *4804*, BAGD: 775D, CB: –

5187 σύζυγος, *syzygos*, a. *yokefellow, comrade.* S: *4805*, BAGD: 775D, CB: 377A

5188 συζωοποιέω, *syzōopoieō*, v. *to make alive with (someone).* S: *4806*, BAGD: 776A, CB: 377A

5189 συκάμινος, *sykaminos*, n. *mulberry tree.* S: *4807*, BAGD: 776A, CB: –

5190 συκῆ, *sykē*, n. *fig tree.* S: *4808*, BAGD: 776B, CB: 376B

5191 συκομορέα, *sykomorea*, n. *sycamore-fig tree.* S: *4809**, BAGD: 776B, CB: –

5192 σῦκον, *sykon*, n. *fig.* S: *4810*, BAGD: 776B, CB: –

5193 συκοφαντέω, *sykophanteō*, v. *to accuse falsely, oppress; to cheat, extort.* S: *4811*, BAGD: 776C, CB: –

5194 συλαγωγέω, *sylagōgeō*, v. *to take captive.* S: *4812*, BAGD: 776C, CB: 376B

5195 συλάω, *sylaō*, v. *to rob.* S: *4813*, BAGD: 776C, CB: 376B

5196 συλλαλέω, *syllaleō*, v. *to talk with, discuss with, confer with.* S: *4814*, BAGD: 776C, CB: –

5197 συλλαμβάνω, *syllambanō*, v. *to seize, arrest, capture; to become pregnant, conceive; to help, come to the aid of.* S: *4815*, BAGD: 776D, CB: 376B

5198 συλλέγω, *syllegō*, v. *to pick, pull up, collect.* S: *4816*, BAGD: 777A, CB: 376B

5199 συλλογίζομαι, *syllogizomai*, v. *to discuss together.* S: *4817*, BAGD: 777A, CB: –

5200 συλλυπέω, *syllypeō*, v. *(pass.) to be deeply distressed, grieved with.* S: *4818*, BAGD: 777A, CB: –

5201 συμβαίνω, *symbainō*, v. *to happen; to come about.* S: *4819*, BAGD: 777B, CB: –

5202 συμβάλλω, *symballō*, v. *to dispute with; to confer with, meet with; to ponder; to engage in (war); (mid.) to help, assist.* S: *4820*, BAGD: 777B, CB: –

5203 συμβασιλεύω, *symbasileuō*, v. *to reign with, be king with.* S: *4821*, BAGD: 777C, CB: 376B

5204 συμβιβάζω, *symbibazō*, v. *(pass.) to be held together; to be united; (act.) to conclude; to prove; to instruct, teach, advise.* S: *4822*, BAGD: 777D, CB: –

5205 συμβουλεύω, *symbouleuō*, v. *to advise, counsel; (mid.) to plot, conspire, consult.* S: *4823*, BAGD: 777D, CB: 376B

5206 συμβούλιον, *symboulion*, n. *plan, plot; decision; council.* S: *4824*, BAGD: 778A, CB: 376B

5207 σύμβουλος, *symboulos*, n. *counselor, advisor.* S: *4825*, BAGD: 778B, CB: 376B

5208 Συμεών, *Symeōn*, n.pr., "he has heard" *or* "obedient one." *Simeon, Simon.* S: *4826*, BAGD: 778B, CB: –

5209 συμμαθητής, *symmathētēs*, n. *fellow disciple.* S: *4827*, BAGD: 778B, CB: 364A cf. *mathētēs*

5210 συμμαρτυρέω, *symmartyreō*, v. *to testify with; to confirm.* S: *4828*, BAGD: 778B, CB: 376B

5211 συμμερίζομαι, *symmerizomai*, v. *to share with.* S: *4829*, BAGD: 778C, CB: –

5212 συμμέτοχος, *symmetochos*, a. *sharing with, being partner with.* S: *4830*, BAGD: 778C, CB: –

5213 συμμιμητής, *symmimētēs*, n. *fellow imitator.* S: *4831*, BAGD: 778C, CB: 376B

5214 συμμορφίζω, *symmorphizō*, v. *(pass.) to become like, be conformed to.* S: *4833**, BAGD: 778D, CB: 376B cf. *-omai*

5215 σύμμορφος, *symmorphos*, a. *conformed, being like.* S: *4832*, BAGD: 778D, CB: 376B

5216 συμμορφόω, *symmorphoō*, v. variant: *to give the same form.* S: *4833*, BAGD: 778D, CB: 376B cf. *-omai*

5217 συμπαθέω, *sympatheō*, v. *to sympathize with.* S: *4834*, BAGD: 778D, CB: 376B

5218 συμπαθής, *sympathēs*, a. *sympathetic.* S: *4835*, BAGD: 779A, CB: –

5219 συμπαραγίνομαι, *symparaginomai*, v. *(mid.) to come together.* S: *4836*, BAGD: 779A, CB: –

5220 συμπαρακαλέω, *symparakaleō*, v. *(pass.) to be mutually encouraged.* S: *4837*, BAGD: 779A, CB: 368A cf. *parakaleō*

5221 συμπαραλαμβάνω, *symparalambanō*, v. *to take along with.* S: *4838*, BAGD: 779A, CB: –

5222 συμπαραμένω, *symparamenō*, v. variant: *to stay with (someone) to help.* S: *4839*, BAGD: 779A, CB: 364B cf. *menō*

5223 συμπάρειμι, *sympareimi*, v. *to be present with.* S: *4840*, BAGD: 779A, CB: –

5224 συμπάσχω, *sympaschō*, v. *to suffer with, share in suffering.* S: *4841*, BAGD: 779B, CB: 376B

5225 συμπέμπω, *sympempō*, v. *to send with.* S: *4842*, BAGD: 779B, CB: –

5226 συμπεριέχω, *symperiechō*, v. variant: *to surround, stand around together.* S: *150*, BAGD: 779C, CB: –

5227 συμπεριλαμβάνω, *symperilambanō*, v. *to put one's arms around, embrace.* S: *4843*, BAGD: 779C, CB: –

5228 συμπίνω, *sympinō*, v. *to drink with.* S: *4844*, BAGD: 779C, CB: –

5229 συμπίπτω, *sympiptō*, v. *to collapse.* S: *4098**, BAGD: 779C, CB: –

5230 συμπληρόω, *symplēroō*, v. *(pass.) to be swamped, become full; to be fulfilled, come to an end.* S: *4845*, BAGD: 779C, CB: 376B

5231 συμπνίγω, *sympnigō*, v. *to choke; to crush.* S: *4846*, BAGD: 779D, CB: 376B

5232 συμπολίτης, *sympolitēs*, n. *fellow citizen.* S: *4847*, BAGD: 780A, CB: 376B

5233 συμπορεύομαι, *symporeuomai*, v. *to go with, come together.* S: *4848*, BAGD: 780A, CB: –

5234 συμποσία, *symposia*, n. variant: *common meal.* S: *4849**, BAGD: 780A, CB: –

5235 συμπόσιον, *symposion*, n. *group.* S: *4849*, BAGD: 780A, CB: –

5236 συμπρεσβύτερος, *sympresbyteros*, n. *fellow elder.* S: *4850*, BAGD: 780A, CB: –

5237 συμφέρω, *sympherō*, v. *to bring together; to be helpful, be gained; (as noun) common good; (as imper. verb) it is good, better, beneficial.* S: *4851*, BAGD: 780B, CB: 370A cf. *pherō*

5238 σύμφημι, *symphēmi*, v. *to agree with.* S: *4852*,
BAGD: 780C, CB: –

5239 σύμφορος, *symphoros*, a. *beneficial, advantageous; (as noun) good, benefit, advantage.* S: *4851**, BAGD: 780C, CB: –

5240 συμφορτίζω, *symphortizō*, v. variant: *to burden together with others.* S: *4833**, BAGD: 780C, CB: –

5241 συμφυλέτης, *symphyletēs*, n. *(pl.) one's own countrymen, people.* S: *4853*, BAGD: 780C, CB: –

5242 σύμφυτος, *symphytos*, a. *united, being one with.* S: *4854*, BAGD: 780D, CB: 376B

5243 συμφύω, *symphyō*, v. *to grow up with.* S: *4855*, BAGD: 780D, CB: –

5244 συμφωνέω, *symphōneō*, v. *to agree with; to match, fit in with.* S: *4856*, BAGD: 780D, CB: –

5245 συμφώνησις, *symphōnēsis*, n. *harmony, agreement.* S: *4857*, BAGD: 781A, CB: –

5246 συμφωνία, *symphōnia*, n. *music.* S: *4858*, BAGD: 781A, CB: 376B

5247 σύμφωνος, *symphōnos*, a. *mutually consenting, agreeing.* S: *4859*, BAGD: 781B, CB: –

5248 συμψηφίζω, *sympsēphizō*, v. *to calculate, compute.* S: *4860*, BAGD: 781B, CB: –

5249 σύμψυχος, *sympsychos*, a. *united in spirit, harmonious.* S: *4861*, BAGD: 781B, CB: 376B

5250 σύν, *syn*, pp. *with; as, besides.* S: *4862*, BAGD: 781C, CB: 376B

5251 συνάγω, *synagō*, v. *to gather together, assemble; invite, call together.* S: *4863*, BAGD: 782A, CB: 376B

5252 συναγωγή, *synagōgē*, n. *synagogue; congregation, meeting.* S: *4864*, BAGD: 782D, CB: 376B

5253 συναγωνίζομαι, *synagōnizomai*, v. *to join in a struggle, help, assist.* S: *4865*, BAGD: 783B, CB: 376B

5254 συναθλέω, *synathleō*, v. *to contend at one's side, together.* S: *4866*, BAGD: 783B, CB: 376C

5255 συναθροίζω, *synathroizō*, v. *to bring together; (pass.) to be gathered.* S: *4867*, BAGD: 783B, CB: 376C

5256 συναίρω, *synairō*, v. *to settle (monetary accounts).* S: *4868*, BAGD: 783C, CB: –

5257 συναιχμάλωτος, *synaichmalōtos*, n. *fellow prisoner.* S: *4869*, BAGD: 783C, CB: 376B

5258 συνακολουθέω, *synakoloutheō*, v. *to follow, accompany.* S: *4870*, BAGD: 783D, CB: 376B

5259 συναλίζω, *synalizō*, v. *to eat with.* S: *4871*, BAGD: 783D, CB: 376B

5260 συναλίσκομαι, *synaliskomai*, v. variant: *to be made captive together with.* S: *4871**, BAGD: 784A, CB: 376B

5261 συναλλάσσω, *synallassō*, v. *to reconcile.* S: *4900**, BAGD: 784B, CB: –

5262 συναναβαίνω, *synanabainō*, v. *to come with, travel with.* S: *4872*, BAGD: 784B, CB: 341A cf. *anabainō*

5263 συνανάκειμαι, *synanakeimai*, v. *to eat with, have dinner with.* S: *4873*, BAGD: 784B, CB: –

5264 συναναμείγνυμι, *synanameignymi*, v. *to associate with.* S: *4874**, BAGD: 784B, CB: –

5265 συναναπαύομαι, *synanapauomai*, v. *to find rest together, be refreshed together.* S: *4875*, BAGD: 784B, CB: –

5266 συναναστρέφομαι, *synanastrephomai*, v. variant: *to associate with, go about with.* S: *150*, BAGD: 784B, CB: –

5267 συναντάω, *synantaō*, v. *to meet; to happen to.* S: *4876*, BAGD: 784C, CB: 376C

5268 συνάντησις, *synantēsis*, n. variant: *meeting.* S: *4877*, BAGD: 784C, CB: –

5269 συναντιλαμβάνομαι, *synantilambanomai*, v. *to help, come to the aid of.* S: *4878*, BAGD: 784C, CB: –

5270 συναπάγω, *synapagō*, v. *(pass.) to be led away, carried off; to associate with (the lowly).* S: *4879*, BAGD: 784D, CB: –

5271 συναποθνήσκω, *synapothnēskō*, v. *to die with.* S: *4880**, BAGD: 784D, CB: 376C

5272 συναπόλλυμι, *synapollymi*, v. *(mid.) to die with, perish with.* S: *4881*, BAGD: 785A, CB: –

5273 συναποστέλλω, *synapostellō*, v. *to send with.* S: *4882*, BAGD: 785A, CB: –

5274 συναρμολογέω, *synarmologeō*, v. *(pass.) to be joined together, fit together.* S: *4883*, BAGD: 785B, CB: –

5275 συναρπάζω, *synarpazō*, v. *to seize; (pass.) to be caught, seized.* S: *4884*, BAGD: 785B, CB: –

5276 συναυλίζομαι, *synaulizomai*, v. variant: *(mid.) to spend the night with.* S: *4871**, BAGD: 783D cf. συναλίζω, CB: –

5277 συναυξάνω, *synauxanō*, v. *to grow together.* S: *4885*, BAGD: 785B, CB: –

5278 σύνδεσμος, *syndesmos*, n. *bond; sinew; captive.* S: *4886*, BAGD: 785B, CB: 376C

5279 συνδέω, *syndeō*, v. *(pass.) to be imprisoned with, bound with.* S: *4887*, BAGD: 785C, CB: 346C cf. *deō*

5280 συνδοξάζω, *syndoxazō*, v. *(pass.) to be glorified with, share glory with.* S: *4888*, BAGD: 785D, CB: 376C

5281 σύνδουλος, *syndoulos*, n. *fellow servant.* S: *4889*, BAGD: 785D, CB: 376C

5282 συνδρομή, *syndromē*, n. *running together.* S: *4890*, BAGD: 785D, CB: –

5283 συνεγείρω, *synegeirō*, v. *to raise up with.* S: *4891*, BAGD: 785D, CB: –

5284 συνέδριον, *synedrion*, n. *Sanhedrin; (local) council.* S: *4892*, BAGD: 786A, CB: 376C

5285 συνέδριος, *synedrios*, n. variant: *member of the council.* S: *150*, BAGD: 786B, CB: 376C cf. *-on*

5286 σύνεδρος, *synedros*, n. variant: *member of the council.* S: *150*, BAGD: 786C, CB: 376C

5287 συνείδησις, *syneidēsis*, n. *conscience.* S: *4893*, BAGD: 786C, CB: 376C

5288 συνείδω, *syneidō*, v. variant: *to consider, know.* S: *4894*, BAGD: 791B cf. σύνοιδα, CB: 376C

5289 σύνειμι[1], *syneimi*[1], v. *to be with; (as noun) companion.* S: *4895*, BAGD: 787A, CB: –

5290 σύνειμι[2], *syneimi*[2], v. *to gather together, come together.* S: *4896*, BAGD: 787A, CB: –

5291 συνεισέρχομαι, *syneiserchomai*, v. *to enter together with.* S: *4897*, BAGD: 787A, CB: 376C

5292 συνέκδημος, synekdēmos, n. *traveling companion.* S: *4898*, BAGD: 787A, CB: –

5293 συνεκλεκτός, syneklektos, a. *chosen together with.* S: *4899*, BAGD: 787B, CB: –

5294 συνεκπορεύομαι, synekporeuomai, v. variant: *to go out with.* S: *150*, BAGD: 787B, CB: –

5295 συνελαύνω, synelaunō, v. variant: *to drive, force, bring.* S: *4900*, BAGD: 787B, CB: –

5296 συνεπιμαρτυρέω, synepimartyreō, v. *to testify at the same time.* S: *4901*, BAGD: 787B, CB: –

5297 συνεπίσκοπος, synepiskopos, n. variant: *fellow overseer.* S: *4862 + 1985*, BAGD: 787B, CB: –

5298 συνεπιτίθημι, synepitithēmi, v. *(mid.) to join in an accusation, join in an attack.* S: *4934**, BAGD: 787B, CB: –

5299 συνέπομαι, synepomai, v. *to accompany.* S: *4902*, BAGD: 787C, CB: –

5300 συνεργέω, synergeō, v. *to work together, work with; (as noun) fellow worker.* S: *4903*, BAGD: 787C, CB: 376C

5301 συνεργός, synergos, a. *fellow worker.* S: *4904*, BAGD: 787D, CB: 376C

5302 συνέρχομαι, synerchomai, v. *to come together, gather, assemble; to go along with, accompany.* S: *4905*, BAGD: 788A, CB: 376C

5303 συνεσθίω, synesthiō, v. *to eat with.* S: *4906*, BAGD: 788B, CB: –

5304 σύνεσις, synesis, n. *understanding, insight; intelligence.* S: *4907*, BAGD: 788C, CB: 376C

5305 συνετός, synetos, a. *intelligent, learned.* S: *4908*, BAGD: 788D, CB: 376C

5306 συνευδοκέω, syneudokeō, v. *to approve of, give approval; to be willing.* S: *4909*, BAGD: 788D, CB: –

5307 συνευωχέομαι, syneuōcheomai, v. *to partake in a feast together.* S: *4910**, BAGD: 789A, CB: –

5308 συνεφίστημι, synephistēmi, v. *to join in an attack.* S: *4911*, BAGD: 789A, CB: –

5309 συνέχω, synechō, v. *to cover (ears); to crowd (against); to guard, hold in custody; to compel, urge on; (pass.) to suffer, be distressed; to be devoted to.* S: *4912*, BAGD: 789A, CB: 376C

5310 συνήδομαι, synēdomai, v. *to delight in agreement.* S: *4913*, BAGD: 789C, CB: –

5311 συνήθεια, synētheia, n. *custom, practice.* S: *4914*, BAGD: 789C, CB: –

5312 συνηλικιώτης, synēlikiōtēs, n. *person of one's own age, contemporary.* S: *4915*, BAGD: 789D, CB: –

5313 συνθάπτω, synthaptō, v. *(pass.) to be buried with.* S: *4916*, BAGD: 789D, CB: 377A

5314 συνθλάω, synthlaō, v. *(pass.) to be broken to pieces.* S: *4917*, BAGD: 790A, CB: –

5315 συνθλίβω, synthlibō, v. *to press around, crowd against.* S: *4918*, BAGD: 790A, CB: –

5316 συνθρύπτω, synthryptō, v. *to break.* S: *4919*, BAGD: 790A, CB: –

5317 συνίημι, syniēmi, v. *to understand, realize.* S: *4920*, BAGD: 790A, CB: 376C

5318 συνιστάω, synistaō, v. variant: *see 5319.* S: *4921*, BAGD: 790C, CB: 376C

5319 συνίστημι, synistēmi, v. *to commend, recommend; to demonstrate, bring out, prove to be; (intr.) to stand with; to hold together; to be formed.* S: *4921*, BAGD: 790C, CB: 376C

5320 συνίω, syniō, v. variant: *to understand, realize.* S: *4920**, BAGD: 790A, CB: –

5321 συνοδεύω, synodeuō, v. *to travel with.* S: *4922*, BAGD: 791A, CB: –

5322 συνοδία, synodia, n. *company of travelers, caravan.* S: *4923*, BAGD: 791A, CB: –

5323 σύνοιδα, synoida, v. *to share knowledge with; to be conscious (of oneself).* S: *4894**, BAGD: 791B, CB: 376C

5324 συνοικέω, synoikeō, v. *to live with.* S: *4924*, BAGD: 791C, CB: –

5325 συνοικοδομέω, synoikodomeō, v. *(pass.) to be built up together.* S: *4925*, BAGD: 791C, CB: 376C

5326 συνομιλέω, synomileō, v. *to talk with, converse with.* S: *4926*, BAGD: 791C, CB: –

5327 συνομορέω, synomoreō, v. *to be next door to.* S: *4927*, BAGD: 791C, CB: –

5328 συνοράω, synoraō, v. *to realize, become aware.* S: *4894**, BAGD: 791C, CB: –

5329 συνορία, synoria, n. variant: *neighboring country.* S: *150*, BAGD: 791D, CB: –

5330 συνοχή, synochē, n. *anguish, distress.* S: *4928*, BAGD: 791D, CB: –

5331 συνταράσσω, syntarassō, v. variant: *to throw into confusion, disturb.* S: *4952**, BAGD: 791D, CB: –

5332 συντάσσω, syntassō, v. *to command, direct, instruct.* S: *4929*, BAGD: 791D, CB: –

5333 συντέλεια, synteleia, n. *end, close, completion.* S: *4930*, BAGD: 792A, CB: 377A

5334 συντελέω, synteleō, v. *to finish, accomplish; (pass.) to be fulfilled, be over, accomplished.* S: *4931*, BAGD: 792A, CB: 377A

5335 συντέμνω, syntemnō, v. *to cut short, speed up.* S: *4932*, BAGD: 792B, CB: –

5336 συντεχνίτης, syntechnitēs, n. variant: *one who follows the same trade.* S: *150*, BAGD: 792C, CB: –

5337 συντηρέω, syntēreō, v. *to protect, defend; to treasure, preserve in memory; (pass.) to be preserved.* S: *4933*, BAGD: 792C, CB: –

5338 συντίθημι, syntithēmi, v. *(mid.) to agree, decide.* S: *4934**, BAGD: 792D, CB: –

5339 συντόμως, syntomōs, adv. *briefly.* S: *4935*, BAGD: 793A, CB: –

5340 συντρέχω, syntrechō, v. *to run together, go together.* S: *4936*, BAGD: 793A, CB: 377A

5341 συντρίβω, syntribō, v. *to break, destroy; (pass.) to be broken, bruised, dashed to pieces.* S: *4937*, BAGD: 793B, CB: –

5342 σύντριμμα, syntrimma, n. *ruin, destruction.* S: *4938*, BAGD: 793C, CB: –

5343 σύντροφος, syntrophos, a. *brought up with (in a family).* S: *4939*, BAGD: 793C, CB: –

5344 συντυγχάνω, syntynchanō, v. *to come together with, meet.* S: *4940*, BAGD: 793C, CB: −

5345 Συντύχη, Syntychē, n.pr., "coincidence, success." *Syntyche.* S: *4941*, BAGD: 793D, CB: −

5346 συντυχία, syntychia, n. variant: *occurrence, incident.* S: *4795**, BAGD: 793D, CB: −

5347 συνυποκρίνομαι, synypokrinomai, v. *to join in one's hypocrisy.* S: *4942*, BAGD: 793D, CB: −

5348 συνυπουργέω, synypourgeō, v. *to join to help.* S: *4943*, BAGD: 793D, CB: −

5349 συνωδίνω, synōdinō, v. *to join in the pains of childbirth, suffer agony together.* S: *4944*, BAGD: 793D, CB: −

5350 συνωμοσία, synōmosia, n. *plot, conspiracy.* S: *4945*, BAGD: 793D, CB: −

5351 Σύρα, Syra, n.pr. variant: *Syrian woman.* S: *4949**, BAGD: 794A, CB: −

5352 Συράκουσαι, Syrakousai, n.pr. *Syracuse.* S: *4946*, BAGD: 794A, CB: −

5353 Συρία, Syria, n.pr. *Syria.* S: *4947*, BAGD: 794A, CB: −

5354 Σύρος, Syros, n.pr.g., "of Syria." *Syrian.* S: *4948*, BAGD: 794B, CB: −

5355 Συροφοινίκισσα, Syrophoinikissa, n.pr.g. *woman of Syrian Phoenicia.* S: *4949**, BAGD: 794B, CB: −

5356 Συροφοίνισσα, Syrophoinissa, n.pr.g. variant: *Syrophoenician.* S: *4949*, BAGD: 794B, CB: −

5357 συρρήγνυμι, syrrēgnymi, v. variant: *to dash together.* S: *150*, BAGD: 794B, CB: −

5358 Σύρτις, Syrtis, n.pr. *Syrtis.* S: *4950**, BAGD: 794C, CB: −

5359 σύρω, syrō, v. *to drag, tow; to sweep.* S: *4951*, BAGD: 794C, CB: −

5360 συσπαράσσω, sysparassō, v. *to cause to convulse.* S: *4952*, BAGD: 794C, CB: −

5361 σύσσημον, syssēmon, n. *signal.* S: *4953*, BAGD: 794D, CB: −

5362 σύσσωμος, syssōmos, a. *co-member of a body.* S: *4954*, BAGD: 794D, CB: −

5363 συστασιαστής, systasiastēs, n. variant: *fellow insurrectionist.* S: *4955*, BAGD: 794D, CB: −

5364 συστατικός, systatikos, a. *commendatory, recommended.* S: *4956*, BAGD: 795A, CB: −

5365 συσταυρόω, systauroō, v. *(pass.) to be crucified with.* S: *4957*, BAGD: 795A, CB: 377A

5366 συστέλλω, systellō, v. *to wrap up, cover up; (pass.) to be shortened, limited.* S: *4958*, BAGD: 795A, CB: −

5367 συστενάζω, systenazō, v. *to join in groaning, groan together.* S: *4959*, BAGD: 795B, CB: 376A cf. *stenazō*

5368 συστοιχέω, systoicheō, v. *to correspond.* S: *4960*, BAGD: 795B, CB: 377A

5369 συστρατιώτης, systratiōtēs, n. *fellow soldier.* S: *4961*, BAGD: 795B, CB: −

5370 συστρέφω, systrephō, v. *to gather up, bring together.* S: *4962*, BAGD: 795C, CB: 377A

5371 συστροφή, systrophē, n. *commotion, disorderly gathering; conspiracy, plot.* S: *4963*, BAGD: 795C, CB: −

5372 συσχηματίζω, syschēmatizō, v. *(mid.) to conform to a pattern or mold; (pass.) to be conformed to a pattern or mold.* S: *4964*, BAGD: 795C, CB: 377A

5373 Συχάρ, Sychar, n.pr. *Sychar.* S: *4965*, BAGD: 795D, CB: 376B

5374 Συχέμ, Sychem, n.pr., poss. "shoulder [saddle of a hill]" BDB; "shoulders [and upper back]" KB. *Shechem.* S: *4966*, BAGD: 795D, CB: −

5375 σφαγή, sphagē, n. *slaughter.* S: *4967*, BAGD: 795D, CB: −

5376 σφάγιον, sphagion, n. *offering for slaughter.* S: *4968*, BAGD: 796A, CB: −

5377 σφάζω, sphazō, v. *to kill, slay, murder.* S: *4969*, BAGD: 796A, CB: 375C

5378 σφάλλω, sphallō, v. variant: *(pass.) to slip, stumble, fall.* S: *150*, BAGD: 796A, CB: −

5379 σφόδρα, sphodra, adv. *very, greatly, exceedingly.* S: *4970*, BAGD: 796A, CB: 375C

5380 σφοδρῶς, sphodrōs, adv. *violently.* S: *4971*, BAGD: 796B, CB: −

5381 σφραγίζω, sphragizō, v. *to seal.* S: *4972*, BAGD: 796B, CB: 375C

5382 σφραγίς, sphragis, n. *seal.* S: *4973*, BAGD: 796C, CB: 375C

5383 σφυδρόν, sphydron, n. *ankle.* S: *4974**, BAGD: 797A, CB: −

5384 σφυρόν, sphyron, n. variant: *ankle or heel.* S: *4974*, BAGD: 797A, CB: −

5385 σχεδόν, schedon, adv. *nearly, almost.* S: *4975*, BAGD: 797A, CB: −

5386 σχῆμα, schēma, n. *form, outward appearance.* S: *4976*, BAGD: 797B, CB: 374C

5387 σχίζω, schizō, v. *to tear, divide; (pass.) to be torn, divided, split (in opinion).* S: *4977*, BAGD: 797B, CB: 374C

5388 σχίσμα, schisma, n. *tear, split; division, dissension.* S: *4978*, BAGD: 797C, CB: 374C

5389 σχοινίον, schoinion, n. *(pl.) cords, ropes.* S: *4979*, BAGD: 797D, CB: −

5390 σχολάζω, scholazō, v. *to devote oneself to; to be unoccupied, stand empty.* S: *4980*, BAGD: 797D, CB: −

5391 σχολή, scholē, n. *lecture hall.* S: *4981*, BAGD: 798A, CB: −

5392 σώζω, sōzō, v. *to save, rescue, deliver; to heal.* S: *4982**, BAGD: 798A, CB: 375C

5393 σῶμα, sōma, n. *body (living or dead).* S: *4983*, BAGD: 799A, CB: 375B

5394 σωματικός, sōmatikos, a. *bodily, physical.* S: *4984*, BAGD: 800B, CB: 375B

5395 σωματικῶς, sōmatikōs, adv. *in bodily form, corporeally.* S: *4985*, BAGD: 800B, CB: 375B

5396 Σώπατρος, Sōpatros, n.pr., "saving one's father." *Sopater.* S: *4986*, BAGD: 800B, CB: −

5397 σωρεύω, sōreuō, v. *to heap up, pile up; (pass.) to be loaded down.* S: *4987*, BAGD: 800C, CB: −

5398 Σωσθένης, Sōsthenēs, n.pr. *Sosthenes.* S: *4988*, BAGD: 800C, CB: −

5399 Σωσίπατρος, Sōsipatros, n.pr., "saving one's father." *Sosipater.* S: *4989*, BAGD: 800C, CB: −

5400 σωτήρ, sōtēr, n. *Savior.* S: *4990*, BAGD: 800D, CB: 375C

5401 σωτηρία, sōtēria, n. *salvation, rescue, deliverance.* S: *4991*, BAGD: 801B, CB: 375C

5402 σωτήριον, sōtērion, n. *salvation.* S: *4992*, BAGD: 801D cf. -ιος, CB: 375C

5403 σωτήριος, sōtērios, a. *bringing salvation, saving, delivering.* S: *4992**, BAGD: 801D, CB: 375C

5404 σωφρονέω, sōphroneō, v. *to be in a right state of mind, have sober judgment; to be self-controlled.* S: *4993*, BAGD: 802A, CB: 375B

5405 σωφρονίζω, sōphronizō, v. *to train, encourage, advise.* S: *4994*, BAGD: 802A, CB: –

5406 σωφρονισμός, sōphronismos, n. *self-discipline.* S: *4995*, BAGD: 802B, CB: –

5407 σωφρόνως, sōphronōs, adv. *in self-control.* S: *4996*, BAGD: 802C, CB: 375B

5408 σωφροσύνη, sōphrosynē, n. *propriety, appropriateness; reasonableness, mental soundness.* S: *4997*, BAGD: 802C, CB: 375B

5409 σώφρων, sōphrōn, a. *self-controlled.* S: *4998*, BAGD: 802C, CB: 375B

5410 τ, t, letter. *letter of the Greek alphabet.* S: *150*, BAGD: 802B, CB: –

5411 ταβέρναι, tabernai, n. variant: *tavern, shop, store.* S: *4999**, BAGD: 802B, CB: –

5412 Ταβιθά, Tabitha, n.pr., "gazelle." *Tabitha.* S: *5000*, BAGD: 802B, CB: –

5413 τάγμα, tagma, n. *turn, order.* S: *5001*, BAGD: 802D, CB: –

5414 τακτός, taktos, a. *appointed, fixed.* S: *5002*, BAGD: 803A, CB: –

5415 ταλαιπωρέω, talaipōreō, v. *to grieve, lament.* S: *5003*, BAGD: 803A, CB: 377A

5416 ταλαιπωρία, talaipōria, n. *misery, distress.* S: *5004*, BAGD: 803B, CB: 377A

5417 ταλαίπωρος, talaipōros, a. *wretched, miserable.* S: *5005*, BAGD: 803B, CB: 377A

5418 ταλαντιαῖος, talantiaios, a. *weighing a talent (about 57 to 80 lbs.).* S: *5006*, BAGD: 803B, CB: –

5419 τάλαντον, talanton, n. *talent (weight and monetary unit; about 57 to 80 lbs.).* S: *5007*, BAGD: 803C, CB: –

5420 ταλιθά, talitha, l.[n]. *talitha (Aramaic: "little girl").* S: *5008*, BAGD: 803C, CB: 377A

5421 ταμεῖον, tameion, n. *room, inner room, storeroom.* S: *5009*, BAGD: 803C, CB: –

5422 τανῦν, tanyn, contr. [art.+adv.]. variant: *concerning the present, now.* S: *3569*, BAGD: 545C cf. νυ=ν 3.c., CB: –

5423 τάξις, taxis, n. *order, succession; kind, nature.* S: *5010*, BAGD: 803D, CB: 377A

5424 ταπεινός, tapeinos, a. *humble, lowly, downcast, timid.* S: *5011*, BAGD: 804A, CB: 377A

5425 ταπεινοφροσύνη, tapeinophrosynē, n. *humility, humbleness, modesty.* S: *5012*, BAGD: 804C, CB: 377A

5426 ταπεινόφρων, tapeinophrōn, a. *humble.* S: *5391**, BAGD: 804C, CB: 377A

5427 ταπεινόω, tapeinoō, v. *(act.) to humble (oneself), lower (oneself); (pass.) to be humbled, brought low, in need.* S: *5013*, BAGD: 804C, CB: 377A

5428 ταπείνωσις, tapeinōsis, n. *humbleness, lowliness, humiliation.* S: *5014*, BAGD: 805A, CB: 377A

5429 ταράσσω, tarassō, v. *to trouble, disturb, throw into confusion; (pass.) to be disturbed, terrified, confused; to be stirred up.* S: *5015*, BAGD: 805B, CB: 377A

5430 ταραχή, tarachē, n. variant: *disturbance.* S: *5016*, BAGD: 805C, CB: 377A

5431 τάραχος, tarachos, n. *commotion; disturbance.* S: *5017*, BAGD: 805C, CB: 377A

5432 Ταρσεύς, Tarseus, n.pr.g. *Tarsus.* S: *5018*, BAGD: 805C, CB: –

5433 Ταρσός, Tarsos, n.pr. *Tarsus.* S: *5019*, BAGD: 805D, CB: –

5434 ταρταρόω, tartaroō, v. *to send to hell, hold captive in Tartarus.* S: *5020*, BAGD: 805D, CB: –

5435 τάσσω, tassō, v. *(act./mid.) to appoint, determine, arrange; devote; (pass.) to be established, appointed, assigned.* S: *5021*, BAGD: 805D, CB: 377A

5436 ταῦρος, tauros, n. *bull, ox.* S: *5022*, BAGD: 806B, CB: 377A

5437 ταὐτά, tauta, contr. [art.+p.]. variant: *the same things.* S: *5024*, BAGD: 806B, CB: 377A

5438 ταφή, taphē, n. *burial place.* S: *5027*, BAGD: 806B, CB: 377A

5439 τάφος, taphos, n. *tomb, grave.* S: *5028*, BAGD: 806B, CB: 377A

5440 τάχα, tacha, adv. *perhaps, possibly.* S: *5029*, BAGD: 806C, CB: –

5441 ταχέως, tacheōs, adv. *quickly, in haste; very soon.* S: *5030 & 5032 & 5033*, BAGD: 806D, CB: –

5442 ταχινός, tachinos, a. *swift; soon, imminent.* S: *5031*, BAGD: 807A, CB: 377A

5443 τάχος, tachos, n. *quickness, immediateness; (in pp. phrase) quickly, immediately, soon.* S: *5034*, BAGD: 806D cf. ταχέως, CB: –

5444 ταχύς, tachys, a. *quick, swift; (as adv.) quickly, momentarily, soon.* S: *5036 & 5035*, BAGD: 807B, CB: 377A

5445 τέ, te, pt. *and, but (often not translated).* S: *5037*, BAGD: 807B, CB: –

5446 τεῖχος, teichos, n. *wall.* S: *5038*, BAGD: 808A, CB: 377B

5447 τεκμήριον, tekmērion, n. *convincing proof.* S: *5039*, BAGD: 808A, CB: 377B

5448 τεκνίον, teknion, n. *dear children, little children.* S: *5040*, BAGD: 808A, CB: 377B

5449 τεκνογονέω, teknogoneō, v. *to have children, bear a child.* S: *5041*, BAGD: 808A, CB: 377B

5450 τεκνογονία, teknogonia, n. *childbearing.* S: *5042*, BAGD: 808B, CB: 377B

5451 τέκνον, teknon, n. *child, son, daughter, offspring, descendant.* S: *5043*, BAGD: 808B, CB: 377B

5452 τεκνοτροφέω, teknotropheō, v. *to bring up children.* S: *5044*, BAGD: 808D, CB: 377B

5453 τεκνόω, teknoō, v. variant: *to bear (a child).* S: *150*, BAGD: 809A, CB: 377B

5454 τέκτων, tektōn, n. *carpenter, woodworker.* S: *5045*, BAGD: 809A, CB: 377B

5455 τέλειος, teleios, a. *perfect, mature, finished.* S: *5046*, BAGD: 809A, CB: 377B

5456 τελειότης, teleiotēs, n. *perfection, maturity, completeness.* S: *5047*, BAGD: 809C, CB: 377B

5457 τελειόω, teleioō, v. *to perfect, complete, finish; (pass.) to reach a goal, be fulfilled, completed, made perfect.* S: *5048*, BAGD: 809D, CB: 377B

5458 τελείως, teleiōs, adv. *fully, completely, perfectly.* S: *5049*, BAGD: 810B, CB: 377B

5459 τελείωσις, teleiōsis, n. *perfection, accomplishment, fulfillment.* S: *5050*, BAGD: 810B, CB: 377B

5460 τελειωτής, teleiōtēs, n. *perfecter.* S: *5051*, BAGD: 810C, CB: 377B

5461 τελεσφορέω, telesphoreō, v. *to mature (to fruitfulness).* S: *5052*, BAGD: 810C, CB: –

5462 τελευτάω, teleutaō, v. *to die.* S: *5053*, BAGD: 810C, CB: 377B

5463 τελευτή, teleutē, n. *death.* S: *5054*, BAGD: 810C, CB: 377B

5464 τελέω, teleō, v. *to finish, complete, fulfill; (pass.) to be finished, be completed, fulfilled, perfected.* S: *5055*, BAGD: 810D, CB: 377B

5465 τέλος, telos, n. *end, result, outcome, finish, goal; revenue, tax, duty.* S: *5056*, BAGD: 811B, CB: 377B

5466 τελωνεῖον, telōneion, n. variant: *revenue or tax office.* S: *5058**, BAGD: 812C cf. -ιον, CB: 377B cf. -ion

5467 τελώνης, telōnēs, n. *tax collector.* S: *5057*, BAGD: 812B, CB: 377B

5468 τελώνιον, telōnion, n. *tax collector's booth.* S: *5058*, BAGD: 812C, CB: 377B

5469 τέρας, teras, n. *wonder, miracle.* S: *5059*, BAGD: 812C, CB: 377B

5470 Τέρτιος, Tertios, n.pr., "third." *Tertius.* S: *5060*, BAGD: 812D, CB: –

5471 Τέρτουλλος, Tertoullos, n.pr., "third." variant: *Tertullus.* S: *150*, BAGD: 813A, CB: –

5472 Τέρτυλλος, Tertyllos, n.pr., "third." *Tertullus.* S: *5061*, BAGD: 813A, CB: –

5473 τεσσαράκοντα, tessarakonta, n.num. variant: *forty.* S: *5062*, BAGD: 813A, CB: 377B

5474 τεσσαρακονταετής, tessarakontaetēs, a.num. *(of) forty years.* S: *5063*, BAGD: 813B, CB: –

5475 τέσσαρες, tessares, n.num. *four.* S: *5064*, BAGD: 813B, CB: 377B

5476 τεσσαρεσκαιδέκατος, tessareskaidekatos, a.num. *fourteenth.* S: *5065*, BAGD: 813B, CB: –

5477 τεσσεράκοντα, tesserakonta, n.num. *forty.* S: *5062**, BAGD: 813A cf. τεσσαράκοντα, CB: 377B

5478 τεσσερακονταετής, tesserakontaetēs, a.num. *(of) forty years.* S: *5063**, BAGD: 813B, CB: –

5479 τεταρταῖος, tetartaios, a. *fourth (day).* S: *5066*, BAGD: 813C, CB: –

5480 τέταρτος, tetartos, a. *fourth.* S: *5067*, BAGD: 813C, CB: –

5481 τετράγωνος, tetragōnos, a. *square, cubical.* S: *5068*, BAGD: 813C, CB: –

5482 τετράδιον, tetradion, n. *squad of four soldiers.* S: *5069*, BAGD: 813D, CB: 377C

5483 τετρακισχίλιοι, tetrakischilioi, a.num. *four thousand.* S: *5070*, BAGD: 813D, CB: 377C

5484 τετρακόσιοι, tetrakosioi, a.num. *four hundred.* S: *5071*, BAGD: 813D, CB: –

5485 τετράμηνος, tetramēnos, a. *(for) four months.* S: *5072*, BAGD: 813D, CB: –

5486 τετραπλόος, tetraploos, a. [used as adv.]. *four times (as much).* S: *5073*, BAGD: 813D cf. -οῦς, CB: –

5487 τετραπλοῦς, tetraplous, a. [used as adv.]. *four times (as much).* S: *5073**, BAGD: 813D, CB: –

5488 τετράπους, tetrapous, a. *four-footed; (as noun) four-footed animal.* S: *5074*, BAGD: 814A, CB: –

5489 τετραρχέω, tetrarcheō, v. *to be a tetrarch.* S: *5075*, BAGD: 814A, CB: –

5490 τετράρχης, tetrarchēs, n. *tetrarch.* S: *5076*, BAGD: 814A, CB: –

5491 τεφρόω, tephroō, v. *to reduce to ashes by fire.* S: *5077*, BAGD: 814B, CB: –

5492 τέχνη, technē, n. *skill, trade, craft.* S: *5078*, BAGD: 814B, CB: 377A

5493 τεχνίτης, technitēs, n. *craftsman, skilled worker, architect, designer.* S: *5079*, BAGD: 814B, CB: 377B

5494 τήκομαι, tēkomai, v. *(pass.) to be melted.* S: *5080**, BAGD: 814B, CB: 377B

5495 τηλαυγῶς, tēlaugōs, adv. *clearly, plainly.* S: *5081*, BAGD: 814C, CB: –

5496 τηλικοῦτος, tēlikoutos, p.demo. *so great, so large.* S: *5082*, BAGD: 814C, CB: –

5497 τηνικαῦτα, tēnikauta, adv. variant: *at that time, then.* S: *150*, BAGD: 814D, CB: –

5498 τηρέω, tēreō, v. *to keep, guard, obey, observe.* S: *5083*, BAGD: 814D, CB: 377B

5499 τήρησις, tērēsis, n. *jail, prison, custody; keeping, observance.* S: *5084*, BAGD: 815C, CB: 377B

5500 Τιβεριάς, Tiberias, n.pr. *Tiberias.* S: *5085*, BAGD: 815C, CB: –

5501 Τιβέριος, Tiberios, n.pr. *Tiberius.* S: *5086*, BAGD: 815C, CB: –

5502 τίθημι, tithēmi, v. *(act.) to place, put; (pass.) to be placed or put; (mid.) to set, appoint, decide, arrange.* S: *5087*, BAGD: 815D, CB: 378C

5503 τίκτω, tiktō, v. *to give birth to; bear, produce.* S: *5088*, BAGD: 816D, CB: 378C

5504 τίλλω, tillō, v. *to pick (heads of grain).* S: *5089*, BAGD: 817A, CB: –

5505 Τιμαῖος, Timaios, n.pr., "precious, valuable." *Timaeus.* S: *5090*, BAGD: 817A, CB: –

5506 τιμάω, timaō, v. *to honor, show respect, give recognition.* S: *5091*, BAGD: 817A, CB: 378C

5507 τιμή, timē, n. *honor, value, respect; nobility, specialness; money, cost.* S: *5092*, BAGD: 817B, CB: 378C

5508 τίμιος, timios, a. *precious, valuable, honored; costly.*
S: *5093*, BAGD: 818A, CB: 378C

5509 τιμιότης, timiotēs, n. *wealth.* S: *5094*, BAGD: 818B, CB: –

5510 Τιμόθεος, Timotheos, n.pr., "precious one of God." *Timothy.*
S: *5095*, BAGD: 818B, CB: –

5511 Τίμων, Timōn, n.pr., "precious, valuable." *Timon.* S: *5096*,
BAGD: 818C, CB: –

5512 τιμωρέω, timōreō, v. *to punish.* S: *5097*, BAGD: 818C, CB: –

5513 τιμωρία, timōria, n. *punishment.* S: *5098*, BAGD: 818D,
CB: –

5514 τίνω, tinō, v. *to pay (a price or penalty).* S: *5099*,
BAGD: 818D, CB: –

5515 τίς, tis, p.inter. *who?, what?, which?, why?.* S: *5101*,
BAGD: 818D, CB: 378C

5516 τὶς, tis, p.indef. *one, anyone, anything; some, someone,
something.* S: *5100*, BAGD: 819D, CB: 378C

5517 Τίτιος, Titios, n.pr. *Titius.* S: *200@*, BAGD: 820D, CB: –

5518 τίτλος, titlos, n. *sign, prepared notice, inscription.* S: *5102*,
BAGD: 820D, CB: 378C

5519 Τίτος, Titos, n.pr. *Titus.* S: *5103*, BAGD: 820D, CB: –

5520 τοί, toi, pt. variant: *surely (emphasizing reliability).* S: *5104*,
BAGD: 821A, CB: –

5521 τοιγαροῦν, toigaroun, pt. *therefore, then.* S: *5105*,
BAGD: 821A, CB: –

5522 τοίγε, toige, pt. variant: *indeed.* S: *5105*, BAGD: 821A
cf. τοί, CB: –

5523 τοίνυν, toinyn, pt.infer. *then, therefore.* S: *5106*,
BAGD: 821A, CB: –

5524 τοιόσδε, toiosde, a. *such as this, of this kind.* S: *5107*,
BAGD: 821B, CB: –

5525 τοιοῦτος, toioutos, a. *such, such as this, of such a kind.*
S: *5108*, BAGD: 821B, CB: 378C

5526 τοῖχος, toichos, n. *wall.* S: *5109*, BAGD: 821C, CB: 378C

5527 τόκος, tokos, n. *interest (on a monetary loan).* S: *5110*,
BAGD: 821D, CB: 378C

5528 τολμάω, tolmaō, v. *to dare, be bold, courageous.* S: *5111*,
BAGD: 821D, CB: 378C

5529 τολμηρός, tolmēros, a. *bold, daring, audacious; (as comp.
adv.) quite boldly.* S: *5112**, BAGD: 822A, CB: 378C

5530 τολμηρότερον, tolmēroteron, adv.comp. variant: *rather
boldly.* S: *5112*, BAGD: 822A, CB: 378C cf. -toron

5531 τολμηροτέρως, tolmēroterōs, adv. variant: *rather boldly.*
S: *5112**, BAGD: 822A, CB: –

5532 τολμητής, tolmētēs, n. *bold man, daring man.* S: *5113*,
BAGD: 822A, CB: 378C

5533 τομός, tomos, a. *cutting, sharp; (compar.) sharper.* S: *5114**,
BAGD: 822A, CB: –

5534 τόξον, toxon, n. *bow (weapon).* S: *5115*, BAGD: 822B,
CB: 379A

5535 τοπάζιον, topazion, n. *topaz.* S: *5116*, BAGD: 822B,
CB: 379A

5536 τόπος, topos, n. *place, location.* S: *5117*, BAGD: 822B,
CB: 379A

5537 τοσοῦτος, tosoutos, a. *so great, so many, so large, so long.*
S: *5118*, BAGD: 823B, CB: –

5538 τότε, tote, adv. *then, when, at that time.* S: *5119*,
BAGD: 823D, CB: 379A

5539 τοὐναντίον, tounantion, contr. [art.+pp.*]. variant: *but, on
the contrary.* S: *5121*, BAGD: 261D cf. ἐναντίον 2., CB: –

5540 τοὔνομα, tounoma, contr. [art.+n.]. variant: *named, by name.*
S: *5122*, BAGD: 570D cf. ὄνομα I.1., CB: –

5541 τοὐπίσω, toupisō, contr. [art.+adv.]. variant: *back, behind.*
S: *3694**, BAGD: 575A cf. ὀπίσω 1., CB: –

5542 τουτέστιν, toutestin, contr. [art.+v.]. variant: *that is to say,
by this we mean.* S: *5123**, BAGD: 222D cf. εἰμί II.3., CB: –

5543 τράγος, tragos, n. *male goat.* S: *5131*, BAGD: 824B,
CB: 379A

5544 τράπεζα, trapeza, n. *table.* S: *5132*, BAGD: 824B, CB: 379A

5545 τραπεζίτης, trapezitēs, n. *banker.* S: *5133*, BAGD: 824D,
CB: –

5546 τραῦμα, trauma, n. *(pl.) wounds.* S: *5134*, BAGD: 824D,
CB: –

5547 τραυματίζω, traumatizō, v. *to wound.* S: *5135*,
BAGD: 824D, CB: –

5548 τραχηλίζω, trachēlizō, v. *(pass.) to be laid bare.* S: *5136*,
BAGD: 824D, CB: –

5549 τράχηλος, trachēlos, n. *neck, throat.* S: *5137*, BAGD: 825A,
CB: 379A

5550 τραχύς, trachys, a. *rough, uneven.* S: *5138*, BAGD: 825A,
CB: 379A

5551 Τραχωνῖτις, Trachōnitis, n.pr., "rough, stony district."
Traconitis. S: *5139*, BAGD: 825A, CB: –

5552 τρεῖς, treis, n.num. *three.* S: *5140*, BAGD: 825B, CB: 379A

5553 Τρεῖς ταβέρναι, Treis tabernai, n.pr., "three taverns." *Three
Taverns.* S: *5140 + 4999*, BAGD: 802B cf. ταβέρναι,
CB: 379A cf. treis

5554 τρέμω, tremō, v. *to tremble, fear.* S: *5141*, BAGD: 825B,
CB: –

5555 τρέφω, trephō, v. *to care for, feed, nurse; (pass.) to be
nurtured, cared for.* S: *5142*, BAGD: 825C, CB: –

5556 τρέχω, trechō, v. *to run; to strive, give effort.* S: *5143*,
BAGD: 825D, CB: 379A

5557 τρῆμα, trēma, n. *eye (of a needle).* S: *5169**, BAGD: 826A,
CB: –

5558 τριάκοντα, triakonta, n.num. *thirty.* S: *5144*, BAGD: 826A,
CB: –

5559 τριακόσιοι, triakosioi, a.num. *three hundred.* S: *5145*,
BAGD: 826A, CB: –

5560 τρίβολος, tribolos, n. *thistle.* S: *5146*, BAGD: 826A,
CB: 379A

5561 τρίβος, tribos, n. *path.* S: *5147*, BAGD: 826B, CB: –

5562 τριετία, trietia, n. *(for) three years.* S: *5148*, BAGD: 826B,
CB: –

5563 τρίζω, trizō, v. *to gnash, grind.* S: *5149*, BAGD: 826B, CB: –

5564 τρίμηνος, trimēnos, a. *(as noun) (for) three months.* S: *5150*,
BAGD: 826B, CB: –

5565 τρίς, tris, adv. *three times.* S: *5151*, BAGD: 826B, CB: 379A

5566 τρίστεγον, tristegon, n. *third story (of a building).* S: *5152,* BAGD: 826C, CB: –

5567 τρισχίλιοι, trischilioi, a.num. *three thousand.* S: *5153,* BAGD: 826C, CB: 379A

5568 τρίτον, triton, adv. *third, for the third time.* S: *5154*,* BAGD: 826C cf. τρίτος, CB: 379A cf. *-os*

5569 τρίτος, tritos, a. *third.* S: *5154,* BAGD: 826C, CB: 379A

5570 τρίχινος, trichinos, a. *made of hair, hairy.* S: *5155,* BAGD: 827A, CB: –

5571 τρόμος, tromos, n. *trembling, fear.* S: *5156,* BAGD: 827A, CB: 379A

5572 τροπή, tropē, n. *shifting, turning, variation, change.* S: *5157,* BAGD: 827A, CB: –

5573 τρόπος, tropos, n. *manner, way, kind; way of life.* S: *5158,* BAGD: 827B, CB: 379A

5574 τροποφορέω, tropophoreō, v. *to endure, put up with.* S: *5159,* BAGD: 827C, CB: –

5575 τροφή, trophē, n. *food, nourishment.* S: *5160,* BAGD: 827D, CB: –

5576 Τρόφιμος, Trophimos, n.pr., "nourished [child]." *Trophimus.* S: *5161,* BAGD: 827D, CB: –

5577 τροφός, trophos, n. *mother, nurse.* S: *5162,* BAGD: 827D, CB: 379A

5578 τροφοφορέω, trophophoreō, v. variant: *to care for (as a nurse).* S: *5159*,* BAGD: 828A, CB: –

5579 τροχιά, trochia, n. *path, course.* S: *5163,* BAGD: 828A, CB: –

5580 τροχός, trochos, n. *wheel; (fig.) whole course (of life).* S: *5164,* BAGD: 828A, CB: 379A

5581 τρύβλιον, tryblion, n. *bowl.* S: *5165,* BAGD: 828B, CB: –

5582 τρυγάω, trygaō, v. *to gather or pick (grapes).* S: *5166,* BAGD: 828B, CB: 379A

5583 τρυγών, trygōn, n. *(pl.) doves, turtledoves.* S: *5167,* BAGD: 828B, CB: –

5584 τρυμαλιά, trymalia, n. *eye (of a needle).* S: *5168,* BAGD: 828B, CB: –

5585 τρύπημα, trypēma, n. *eye (of a needle).* S: *5169,* BAGD: 828C, CB: –

5586 Τρύφαινα, Tryphaina, n.pr., "dainty." *Tryphena.* S: *5170,* BAGD: 828C, CB: –

5587 τρυφάω, tryphaō, v. *to live in luxury, lead a life of self-indulgence.* S: *5171,* BAGD: 828C, CB: –

5588 τρυφή, tryphē, n. *luxury, splendor; carousal, indulgence, reveling.* S: *5172,* BAGD: 828D, CB: –

5589 Τρυφῶσα, Tryphōsa, n.pr., "delicate." *Tryphosa.* S: *5173,* BAGD: 828D, CB: –

5590 Τρῳάς, Trōas, n.pr. *Troas.* S: *5174*,* BAGD: 829A, CB: –

5591 Τρωγύλλιον, Trōgyllion, n.pr. variant: *Trogyllium.* S: *5175,* BAGD: 829A, CB: –

5592 τρώγω, trōgō, v. *to eat, feed on.* S: *5176,* BAGD: 829B, CB: 379A

5593 τυγχάνω, tynchanō, v. *to take part in; to obtain, provide; (intr.) to happen a certain way, to be extraordinary; perhaps.* S: *5177,* BAGD: 829B, CB: –

5594 τυμπανίζω, tympanizō, v. *(pass.) to be tortured, tormented.* S: *5178,* BAGD: 829D, CB: –

5595 τυπικῶς, typikōs, adv. *as an example.* S: *5179*,* BAGD: 829D, CB: 379A

5596 τύπος, typos, n. *pattern, model, example, type; idol.* S: *5179,* BAGD: 829D, CB: 379B

5597 τύπτω, typtō, v. *to strike, beat, wound.* S: *5180,* BAGD: 830B, CB: 379B

5598 Τύραννος[1], Tyrannos[1], n.pr., "ruler." *Tyrannus.* S: *5181,* BAGD: 830C, CB: 379B

5599 τύραννος[2], tyrannos[2], n. variant: *despotic ruler, tyrant.* S: *150,* BAGD: 830C, CB: 379B

5600 τυρβάζω, tyrbazō, v. variant: *(mid.) trouble oneself; (pass.) to be troubled.* S: *5182,* BAGD: 830D, CB: –

5601 Τύριος, Tyrios, n.pr.g., "of Tyre." *Tyrian.* S: *5183,* BAGD: 830D, CB: –

5602 Τύρος, Tyros, n.pr., "rocky place." *Tyre.* S: *5184,* BAGD: 830D, CB: –

5603 τυφλός, typhlos, a. *blind; (as noun) blind person.* S: *5185,* BAGD: 830D, CB: 379A

5604 τυφλόω, typhloō, v. *to cause blindness, deprive of sight.* S: *5186,* BAGD: 831A, CB: –

5605 τυφόομαι, typhoomai, v. *(pass.) to be or become conceited.* S: *5187*,* BAGD: 831A, CB: –

5606 τύφω, typhō, v. *(pass.) to smolder, smoke.* S: *5188,* BAGD: 831C, CB: –

5607 τυφωνικός, typhōnikos, a. *of hurricane force.* S: *5189,* BAGD: 831C, CB: –

5608 Τυχικός, Tychikos, n.pr., "good fortune." *Tychicus.* S: *5190,* BAGD: 831C, CB: –

5609 υ, y, letter. *letter of the Greek alphabet.* S: *150,* BAGD: –, CB: –

5610 ὑακίνθινος, hyakinthinos, a. *dark blue,* poss. *dark red.* S: *5191,* BAGD: 831B, CB: –

5611 ὑάκινθος, hyakinthos, n. *jacinth.* S: *5192,* BAGD: 831B, CB: 357B

5612 ὑάλινος, hyalinos, a. *of glass.* S: *5193,* BAGD: 831D, CB: 357B

5613 ὕαλος, hyalos, n. *glass.* S: *5194,* BAGD: 831D, CB: –

5614 ὑβρίζω, hybrizō, v. *to insult, mistreat.* S: *5195,* BAGD: 831D, CB: 357C

5615 ὕβρις, hybris, n. *insult, mistreatment; disaster, damage.* S: *5196,* BAGD: 832A, CB: 357B

5616 ὑβριστής, hybristēs, n. *insolent man, violent man.* S: *5197,* BAGD: 832A, CB: 357C

5617 ὑγιαίνω, hygiainō, v. *to be healthy, sound.* S: *5198,* BAGD: 832B, CB: 357C

5618 ὑγιής, hygiēs, a. *healthy, sound, well.* S: *5199,* BAGD: 832C, CB: 357C

5619 ὑγρός, hygros, a. *moist, green.* S: *5200,* BAGD: 832C, CB: 357C

5620 ὑδρία, hydria, n. *water jar.* S: *5201,* BAGD: 832C, CB: –

5621 ὑδροποτέω, hydropoteō, v. *to drink water (exclusively).* S: *5202,* BAGD: 832D, CB: –

5622 ὑδρωπικός, *hydrōpikos*, a. *suffering from dropsy (edema)*. S: *5203*, BAGD: 832D, CB: –

5623 ὕδωρ, *hydōr*, n. *water*. S: *5204*, BAGD: 832D, CB: 357C

5624 ὑετός, *hyetos*, n. *rain*. S: *5205*, BAGD: 833B, CB: 357C

5625 υἱοθεσία, *huiothesia*, n. *adoption as sons, sonship*. S: *5206*, BAGD: 833B, CB: 357C

5626 υἱός, *huios*, n. *son, child, descendant; one of a class or kind*. S: *5207*, BAGD: 833C, CB: 357C

5627 ὕλη, *hylē*, n. *forest, wood*. S: *5208*, BAGD: 836A, CB: 357C

5628 Ὑμέναιος, *Hymenaios*, n.pr., "of [pagan god] Hymen." *Hymenaeus*. S: *5211*, BAGD: 836A, CB: –

5629 ὑμέτερος, *hymeteros*, a. *your, your own*. S: *5212*, BAGD: 836A, CB: –

5630 ὑμνέω, *hymneō*, v. *to sing hymns, sing praises*. S: *5214*, BAGD: 836B, CB: 357C

5631 ὕμνος, *hymnos*, n. *hymn, song of praise*. S: *5215*, BAGD: 836B, CB: 357C

5632 ὑπάγω, *hypagō*, v. *to go (away)*. S: *5217*, BAGD: 836C, CB: –

5633 ὑπακοή, *hypakoē*, n. *obedience*. S: *5218*, BAGD: 837A, CB: 357C

5634 ὑπακούω, *hypakouō*, v. *to obey, be obedient; to answer (the door)*. S: *5219*, BAGD: 837B, CB: 357C

5635 ὕπανδρος, *hypandros*, a. *married*. S: *5220*, BAGD: 837C, CB: –

5636 ὑπαντάω, *hypantaō*, v. *to go out to meet; to oppose*. S: *5221*, BAGD: 837D, CB: 358A

5637 ὑπάντησις, *hypantēsis*, n. *meeting*. S: *5222*, BAGD: 837D, CB: 358A

5638 ὕπαρξις, *hyparxis*, n. *property, goods, possessions*. S: *5223*, BAGD: 837D, CB: 358A

5639 ὑπάρχω, *hyparchō*, v. *to have, possess; (as noun) possessions; to be, exist*. S: *5225 & 5224*, BAGD: 838A, CB: –

5640 ὑπείκω, *hypeikō*, v. *to submit, yield*. S: *5226*, BAGD: 838B, CB: –

5641 ὑπεναντίος, *hypenantios*, a. *opposing, being against; (as noun) enemy*. S: *5227*, BAGD: 838B, CB: 358A cf. *-ion*

5642 ὑπέρ, *hyper*, pp. *(acc.) above, beyond, more than; (gen.) for, in behalf of, for the sake of; in place of*. S: *5228*, BAGD: 838B, CB: 358A

5643 ὑπεραίρομαι, *hyperairomai*, v. *to become conceited, exalt oneself*. S: *5229*, BAGD: 839D, CB: –

5644 ὑπέρακμος, *hyperakmos*, a. *past one's prime, getting along in years*. S: *5230*, BAGD: 839D, CB: 358A

5645 ὑπεράνω, *hyperanō*, adv. *far above, high above*. S: *5231*, BAGD: 840A, CB: –

5646 ὑπερασπίζω, *hyperaspizō*, v. variant: *to shield, protect*. S: *784**, BAGD: 840A, CB: 358A

5647 ὑπεραυξάνω, *hyperauxanō*, v. *to grow more and more, increase abundantly*. S: *5232*, BAGD: 840A, CB: 358A

5648 ὑπερβαίνω, *hyperbainō*, v. *to wrong, transgress against, sin against*. S: *5233*, BAGD: 840A, CB: 358A

5649 ὑπερβαλλόντως, *hyperballontōs*, adv. *more severely, to a much greater degree*. S: *5234*, BAGD: 840A, CB: –

5650 ὑπερβάλλω, *hyperballō*, v. *to go beyond, surpass, be incomparable*. S: *5235*, BAGD: 840B, CB: –

5651 ὑπερβολή, *hyperbolē*, n. *all-surpassing, surpassingly great, most excellent, beyond measure*. S: *5236*, BAGD: 840B, CB: –

5652 ὑπερεγώ, *hyperegō*, adv. [pp.+p.]. variant: *(as adv.) even more*. S: *5228 + 1473*, BAGD: 840C, CB: –

5653 ὑπερείδω, *hypereidō*, v. variant: *to overlook, i.e., not punish*. S: *5237*, BAGD: 841D cf. ὑπεροράω, CB: –

5654 ὑπερέκεινα, *hyperekeina*, adv. *beyond; (as noun) regions beyond*. S: *5238*, BAGD: 840C, CB: –

5655 ὑπερεκπερισσοῦ, *hyperekperissou*, adv. *immeasurably; most earnestly; in the highest regard*. S: *5240*, BAGD: 840C, CB: –

5656 ὑπερεκπερισσῶς, *hyperekperissōs*, adv. variant: *beyond all measure, most highly*. S: *5240**, BAGD: 840C, CB: 358A

5657 ὑπερεκτείνω, *hyperekteinō*, v. *to go too far, overextend, stretch out beyond*. S: *5239*, BAGD: 840D, CB: –

5658 ὑπερεκχύννω, *hyperekchynnō*, v. *(pass.) to be running over, overflowing*. S: *5240**, BAGD: 840D, CB: –

5659 ὑπερεντυγχάνω, *hyperentynchanō*, v. *to intercede*. S: *5241*, BAGD: 840D, CB: 358A

5660 ὑπερέχω, *hyperechō*, v. *to govern, have authority; to be better than, transcend; (as noun) surpassing greatness*. S: *5242*, BAGD: 840D, CB: 358A

5661 ὑπερηφανία, *hyperēphania*, n. *arrogance, pride*. S: *5243*, BAGD: 841A, CB: 358A

5662 ὑπερήφανος, *hyperēphanos*, a. *proud, arrogant*. S: *5244*, BAGD: 841B, CB: 358A

5663 ὑπερλίαν, *hyperlian*, adv. *exceedingly, beyond measure; (with 693) super-apostles*. S: *5244*, BAGD: 841B, CB: –

5664 ὑπερνικάω, *hypernikaō*, v. *to thoroughly conquer, go beyond conquest*. S: *5245*, BAGD: 841C, CB: 358A

5665 ὑπέρογκος, *hyperonkos*, a. *boastful*. S: *5246*, BAGD: 841C, CB: –

5666 ὑπεροράω, *hyperoraō*, v. *to overlook, disregard*. S: *5237**, BAGD: 841D, CB: –

5667 ὑπεροχή, *hyperochē*, n. *authority, superiority*. S: *5247*, BAGD: 841D, CB: –

5668 ὑπερπερισσεύω, *hyperperisseuō*, v. *to increase all the more, exceed bounds, overflow*. S: *5248*, BAGD: 841D, CB: 358A

5669 ὑπερπερισσῶς, *hyperperissōs*, adv. *beyond all measure, exceedingly*. S: *5249*, BAGD: 842A, CB: 358A

5670 ὑπερπλεονάζω, *hyperpleonazō*, v. *to be (greatly) abundant*. S: *5250*, BAGD: 842A, CB: 358A

5671 ὑπερυψόω, *hyperypsoō*, v. *to exalt to the highest place*. S: *5251*, BAGD: 842A, CB: –

5672 ὑπερφρονέω, *hyperphroneō*, v. *to think too highly of oneself*. S: *5252*, BAGD: 842A, CB: 358A

5673 ὑπερῷον, *hyperōon*, n. *upstairs room, upper story*. S: *5253*, BAGD: 842B, CB: –

5674 ὑπέχω, *hypechō*, v. *to experience*. S: *5254*, BAGD: 842B, CB: –

5675 ὑπήκοος, *hypēkoos*, a. *obedient*. S: *5255*, BAGD: 842B, CB: 358A

5676 ὑπηρετέω, hypēreteō, v. *to serve, care for needs.* S: *5256,* BAGD: 842C, CB: 358A

5677 ὑπηρέτης, hypēretēs, n. *servant, attendant, helper.* S: *5257,* BAGD: 842C, CB: 358A

5678 ὕπνος, hypnos, n. *sleep, slumber.* S: *5258,* BAGD: 843A, CB: 358A

5679 ὑπό, hypo, pp. *(gen.) by, by means of; (acc.) under; at (a time of day).* S: *5259,* BAGD: 843A, CB: 358A

5680 ὑποβάλλω, hypoballō, v. *to secretly persuade, instigate secretly.* S: *5260,* BAGD: 843D, CB: –

5681 ὑπογραμμός, hypogrammos, n. *example, model.* S: *5261,* BAGD: 843D, CB: 358B

5682 ὑπόδειγμα, hypodeigma, n. *example, model, pattern, copy.* S: *5262,* BAGD: 844A, CB: 358B

5683 ὑποδείκνυμι, hypodeiknymi, v. *to show; to warn.* S: *5263,* BAGD: 844B, CB: –

5684 ὑποδεικνύω, hypodeiknyō, v. variant: *to show; to warn.* S: *5263*,* BAGD: 844B, CB: –

5685 ὑποδέχομαι, hypodechomai, v. *to welcome, receive as a guest.* S: *5264,* BAGD: 844B, CB: –

5686 ὑποδέω, hypodeō, v. *(mid.) to put on (sandals).* S: *5265,* BAGD: 844B, CB: 346C cf. *deō*

5687 ὑπόδημα, hypodēma, n. *sandal.* S: *5266,* BAGD: 844C, CB: –

5688 ὑπόδικος, hypodikos, a. *accountable, answerable.* S: *5267,* BAGD: 844C, CB: –

5689 ὑποζύγιον, hypozygion, n. *donkey.* S: *5268,* BAGD: 844C, CB: –

5690 ὑποζώννυμι, hypozōnnymi, v. *to undergird, brace.* S: *5269,* BAGD: 844D, CB: –

5691 ὑποκάτω, hypokatō, adv. *(us pp.*) under.* S: *5270,* BAGD: 844D, CB: –

5692 ὑπόκειμαι, hypokeimai, v. variant: *to lie below, be found.* S: *150,* BAGD: 845A, CB: 358B cf. *-menon*

5693 ὑποκρίνομαι, hypokrinomai, v. *to pretend.* S: *5271,* BAGD: 845A, CB: 358B

5694 ὑπόκρισις, hypokrisis, n. *hypocrisy.* S: *5272,* BAGD: 845A, CB: 358B

5695 ὑποκριτής, hypokritēs, n. *hypocrite.* S: *5273,* BAGD: 845B, CB: 358B

5696 ὑπολαμβάνω, hypolambanō, v. *to take up; to show hospitality; to reply; to suppose, think, believe.* S: *5274,* BAGD: 845B, CB: 358B

5697 ὑπολαμπάς, hypolampas, n. variant: *window, opening.* S: *2985*,* BAGD: 845C, CB: 358B

5698 ὑπόλειμμα, hypoleimma, n. *remnant.* S: *2640*,* BAGD: 845C, CB: 358B

5699 ὑπολείπω, hypoleipō, v. *(pass.) to be left, remaining.* S: *5275,* BAGD: 845C, CB: 358B

5700 ὑπολήνιον, hypolēnion, n. *pit for a winepress.* S: *5276,* BAGD: 845C, CB: –

5701 ὑπολιμπάνω, hypolimpanō, v. *to leave behind.* S: *5277,* BAGD: 845D, CB: –

5702 ὑπομένω, hypomenō, v. *to stay behind; to stand firm, endure, persevere.* S: *5278,* BAGD: 845D, CB: 358B

5703 ὑπομιμνήσκω, hypomimnēskō, v. *to remind, call to mind; (pass.) to remember.* S: *5279*,* BAGD: 846A, CB: 358B

5704 ὑπόμνησις, hypomnēsis, n. *reminder, memory, remembrance.* S: *5280,* BAGD: 846B, CB: 358B

5705 ὑπομονή, hypomonē, n. *perseverance, endurance, patience.* S: *5281,* BAGD: 846B, CB: 358B

5706 ὑπονοέω, hyponoeō, v. *to think, suppose; expect; to sense, suspect.* S: *5282,* BAGD: 846D, CB: –

5707 ὑπόνοια, hyponoia, n. *suspicion.* S: *5283,* BAGD: 846D, CB: –

5708 ὑποπιάζω, hypopiazō, v. variant: *to wear out, weaken; to beat up, treat roughly.* S: *5299*,* BAGD: 848D cf. ὑπωπιάζω, CB: –

5709 ὑποπλέω, hypopleō, v. *to sail to the lee of.* S: *5284,* BAGD: 846D, CB: –

5710 ὑποπνέω, hypopneō, v. *to blow gently (of wind).* S: *5285,* BAGD: 846D, CB: –

5711 ὑποπόδιον, hypopodion, n. *footstool.* S: *5286,* BAGD: 846D, CB: –

5712 ὑπόστασις, hypostasis, n. *confidence, trust, being sure; being, essence.* S: *5287,* BAGD: 847A, CB: 358B

5713 ὑποστέλλω, hypostellō, v. *(act.) to draw back, withdraw; (mid.) to hesitate, shrink back.* S: *5288,* BAGD: 847B, CB: –

5714 ὑποστολή, hypostolē, n. *shrinking back.* S: *5289,* BAGD: 847C, CB: 358B

5715 ὑποστρέφω, hypostrephō, v. *to turn back toward, return; to turn one's back on, turn away.* S: *5290,* BAGD: 847C, CB: –

5716 ὑποστρωννύω, hypostrōnnyō, v. *to spread out.* S: *5291*,* BAGD: 847C, CB: –

5717 ὑποταγή, hypotagē, n. *obedience, submission.* S: *5292,* BAGD: 847D, CB: 358B

5718 ὑποτάσσω, hypotassō, v. *to put in subjection, subject, subordinate; (pass.) to submit, be subject to.* S: *5293,* BAGD: 847D, CB: 358B cf. *-omai*

5719 ὑποτίθημι, hypotithēmi, v. *(act.) to risk, lay down (a life); (mid.) to point out, teach.* S: *5294,* BAGD: 848B, CB: –

5720 ὑποτρέχω, hypotrechō, v. *to sail to the lee of.* S: *5295,* BAGD: 848B, CB: –

5721 ὑποτύπωσις, hypotypōsis, n. *example, pattern.* S: *5296,* BAGD: 848C, CB: 358B

5722 ὑποφέρω, hypopherō, v. *to endure, bear up under, stand up under.* S: *5297,* BAGD: 848C, CB: 370A cf. *pherō*

5723 ὑποχωρέω, hypochōreō, v. *to withdraw, retreat.* S: *5298,* BAGD: 848C, CB: –

5724 ὑπωπιάζω, hypōpiazō, v. *to wear out, weaken; to beat up, treat roughly.* S: *5299,* BAGD: 848D, CB: 358B

5725 ὗς, hys, n. *female pig, sow.* S: *5300,* BAGD: 848D, CB: 358B

5726 ὑσσός, hyssos, n. variant: *javelin.* S: *150,* BAGD: 848D, CB: –

5727 ὕσσωπος, hyssōpos, n. *hyssop.* S: *5301,* BAGD: 849A, CB: –

5728 ὑστερέω, hystereō, v. *to lack, be in need, destitute; to be inferior; to fall short.* S: *5302,* BAGD: 849A, CB: 358B

5729 ὑστέρημα, hysterēma, n. *what is lacking; poverty; what is needed.* S: *5303,* BAGD: 849B, CB: 358B

5730 ὑστέρησις, *hysterēsis*, n. *need, poverty, lack.* S: *5304*, BAGD: 849C, CB: 358B

5731 ὕστερος, *hysteros*, a. *(compar.) later, second; (neuter) finally, last of all.* S: *5306 & 5305*, BAGD: 849C, CB: 358B

5732 ὑφαίνω, *hyphainō*, v. variant: *to weave.* S: *150*, BAGD: 849D, CB: –

5733 ὑφαντός, *hyphantos*, a. *woven.* S: *5307*, BAGD: 849D, CB: –

5734 ὑψηλός, *hypsēlos*, a. *high, mighty; proud, arrogant; highly valued; (compar.) more exalted.* S: *5308*, BAGD: 849D, CB: 358B

5735 ὑψηλοφρονέω, *hypsēlophroneō*, v. *to be arrogant, proud.* S: *5309*, BAGD: 850A, CB: 358B

5736 ὕψιστος, *hypsistos*, a. *highest, most exalted; (as a title of God) the Most High.* S: *5310*, BAGD: 850B, CB: 358B

5737 ὕψος, *hypsos*, n. *height, high position, heaven.* S: *5311*, BAGD: 850C, CB: 358B

5738 ὑψόω, *hypsoō*, v. *to lift up, elevate, exalt.* S: *5312*, BAGD: 850D, CB: 358B

5739 ὕψωμα, *hypsōma*, n. *height; pretension.* S: *5313*, BAGD: 851C, CB: 358B

5740 φ, *ph*, letter. *letter of the Greek alphabet.* S: *150*, BAGD: –, CB: –

5741 φάγος, *phagos*, n. *glutton.* S: *5314*, BAGD: 851A, CB: –

5742 φαιλόνης, *phailonēs*, n. *cloak.* S: *5341**, BAGD: 851A, CB: –

5743 φαίνω, *phainō*, v. *(act.) to shine, give light; (mid./pass.) to appear, be visible;.* S: *5316*, BAGD: 851B, CB: 369C

5744 Φάλεκ, *Phalek*, n.pr., "water canal." *Peleg.* S: *5317*, BAGD: 852B, CB: –

5745 φανερός, *phaneros*, a. *visible, clear, plain, known.* S: *5318*, BAGD: 852B, CB: 369C

5746 φανερόω, *phaneroō*, v. *(act.) to reveal, make known, show; (pass.) to appear, be disclosed, displayed, revealed.* S: *5319*, BAGD: 852D, CB: 369C

5747 φανερῶς, *phanerōs*, adv. *openly, publicly.* S: *5320*, BAGD: 853A, CB: 369C

5748 φανέρωσις, *phanerōsis*, n. *manifestation, disclosure, revelation.* S: *5321*, BAGD: 853B, CB: 369C

5749 φανός, *phanos*, n. *torch, lantern.* S: *5322*, BAGD: 853B, CB: –

5750 Φανουήλ, *Phanouēl*, n.pr., "face of God [El]." *Phanuel.* S: *5323*, BAGD: 853B, CB: –

5751 φαντάζω, *phantazō*, v. *(pass.) to become visible; (as noun) a sight.* S: *5324*, BAGD: 853B, CB: 369C

5752 φαντασία, *phantasia*, n. *pomp, pageantry.* S: *5325*, BAGD: 853B, CB: 369C

5753 φάντασμα, *phantasma*, n. *ghost.* S: *5326*, BAGD: 853C, CB: 369C

5754 φάραγξ, *pharanx*, n. *valley, ravine.* S: *5327*, BAGD: 853C, CB: –

5755 Φαραώ, *Pharaō*, n.pr., "the great house." *Pharaoh.* S: *5328*, BAGD: 853C, CB: –

5756 Φαρές, *Phares*, n.pr., "breaking out." *Perez.* S: *5329*, BAGD: 853C, CB: –

5757 Φαρισαῖος, *Pharisaios*, n.pr., "separate ones." *Pharisee.* S: *5330*, BAGD: 853C, CB: 369C

5758 φαρμακεία, *pharmakeia*, n. *witchcraft, magic.* S: *5331*, BAGD: 854A, CB: 369C

5759 φαρμακεύς, *pharmakeus*, n. variant: *magician, sorcerer.* S: *5332*, BAGD: 854A, CB: –

5760 φάρμακον, *pharmakon*, n. *magic potion, charm; (pl.) magic arts.* S: *5331**, BAGD: 854A, CB: 369C cf. *-os*

5761 φάρμακος, *pharmakos*, n. *one who practices magical arts, magician.* S: *5333**, BAGD: 854B, CB: 369C

5762 φάσις, *phasis*, n. *news, report.* S: *5334*, BAGD: 854B, CB: –

5763 φάσκω, *phaskō*, v. *to claim, assert.* S: *5335*, BAGD: 854B, CB: –

5764 φάτνη, *phatnē*, n. *manger, stall.* S: *5336*, BAGD: 854B, CB: –

5765 φαῦλος, *phaulos*, a. *evil, bad.* S: *5337*, BAGD: 854C, CB: 370A

5766 φέγγος, *phengos*, n. *light, radiance.* S: *5338*, BAGD: 854C, CB: 370A

5767 φείδομαι, *pheidomai*, v. *to spare, refrain from.* S: *5339*, BAGD: 854D, CB: –

5768 φειδομένως, *pheidomenōs*, adv. *sparingly.* S: *5340*, BAGD: 854D, CB: 370A

5769 φελόνης, *phelonēs*, n. variant: *cloak.* S: *5341*, BAGD: 851A cf. φαιλόνης, CB: –

5770 φέρω, *pherō*, v. *to bring, bear, carry; lead.* S: *5342*, BAGD: 854D, CB: 370A

5771 φεύγω, *pheugō*, v. *flee, escape, elude.* S: *5343*, BAGD: 855D, CB: 370A

5772 Φῆλιξ, *Phēlix*, n.pr., "fortunate, lucky." *Felix.* S: *5344*, BAGD: 856A, CB: –

5773 φήμη, *phēmē*, n. *news, report.* S: *5345*, BAGD: 856B, CB: –

5774 φημί, *phēmi*, v. *to say, declare, affirm.* S: *5346*, BAGD: 856B, CB: 370A

5775 φημίζω, *phēmizō*, v. variant: *to spread (news) by saying.* S: *1310**, BAGD: 856C, CB: –

5776 Φῆστος, *Phēstos*, n.pr., "festal, joyful." *Festus.* S: *5347*, BAGD: 856C, CB: –

5777 φθάνω, *phthanō*, v. *to precede; to arrive, attain, come.* S: *5348*, BAGD: 856D, CB: 370C

5778 φθαρτός, *phthartos*, a. *perishable, not lasting, mortal.* S: *5349*, BAGD: 857A, CB: 370C

5779 φθέγγομαι, *phthengomai*, v. *to speak, proclaim.* S: *5350*, BAGD: 857A, CB: –

5780 φθείρω, *phtheirō*, v. *to destroy, corrupt; (pass.) to be corrupted, destroyed, perish; to be led astray.* S: *5351*, BAGD: 857B, CB: 370C

5781 φθινοπωρινός, *phthinopōrinos*, a. *pertaining to the (late) autumn.* S: *5352*, BAGD: 857C, CB: –

5782 φθόγγος, *phthongos*, n. *voice, sound; note, musical tone.* S: *5353*, BAGD: 857C, CB: –

5783 φθονέω, *phthoneō*, v. *to envy, be jealous of.* S: *5354*, BAGD: 857C, CB: 370C

5784 φθόνος, *phthonos*, n. *envy.* S: *5355*, BAGD: 857D, CB: 370C

5785 φθορά, *phthora*, n. *perishableness, destruction, corruption; depravity.* S: *5356*, BAGD: 858A, CB: 370C

5786 φιάλη, *phialē*, n. *bowl.* S: *5357*, BAGD: 858B, CB: –

5787 φιλάγαθος, philagathos, a. *loving what is good.* S: *5358*, BAGD: 858B, CB: 370A

5788 Φιλαδέλφεια, Philadelpheia, n.pr., "love of brother/sister." *Philadelphia.* S: *5359*, BAGD: 858B, CB: 370A

5789 φιλαδελφία, philadelphia, n. *brotherly love; brotherly kindness.* S: *5360*, BAGD: 858C, CB: 370A

5790 φιλάδελφος, philadelphos, a. *loving as brothers.* S: *5361*, BAGD: 858C, CB: 370A

5791 φίλανδρος, philandros, a. *loving one's husband.* S: *5362*, BAGD: 858C, CB: 370A

5792 φιλανθρωπία, philanthrōpia, n. *love, kindness.* S: *5363*, BAGD: 858D, CB: 370A

5793 φιλανθρώπως, philanthrōpōs, adv. *in kindness, kindly.* S: *5364*, BAGD: 858D, CB: 370A

5794 φιλαργυρία, philargyria, n. *love of money, avarice, greed.* S: *5365*, BAGD: 859A, CB: 370A

5795 φιλάργυρος, philargyros, a. *money-loving, avaricious, greedy.* S: *5366*, BAGD: 859A, CB: 370A

5796 φίλαυτος, philautos, a. *loving oneself, selfish.* S: *5367*, BAGD: 859A, CB: 370A

5797 φιλέω, phileō, v. *to love; to kiss.* S: *5368*, BAGD: 859B, CB: 370A

5798 φιλήδονος, philēdonos, a. *loving pleasure.* S: *5369*, BAGD: 859C, CB: 370A

5799 φίλημα, philēma, n. *kiss.* S: *5370*, BAGD: 859C, CB: 370A

5800 Φιλήμων, Philēmōn, n.pr., "beloved." *Philemon.* S: *5371*, BAGD: 859D, CB: 370A

5801 Φίλητος, Philētos, n.pr., "beloved." *Philetus.* S: *5372**, BAGD: 859D, CB: 370A

5802 φιλία, philia, n. *friendship, love.* S: *5373*, BAGD: 859D, CB: 370A

5803 Φιλιππήσιος, Philippēsios, n.pr.g., "of Philippi." *Philippian.* S: *5374*, BAGD: 859D, CB: 370A

5804 Φίλιπποι, Philippoi, n.pr. *Philippi.* S: *5375*, BAGD: 860A, CB: 370A

5805 Φίλιππος, Philippos, n.pr., "horse lover." *Philip.* S: *5376*, BAGD: 860A, CB: 370A

5806 φιλόθεος, philotheos, a. *loving God.* S: *5377*, BAGD: 860C, CB: 370B

5807 Φιλόλογος, Philologos, n.pr., "lover of words [education]." *Philologus.* S: *5378*, BAGD: 860C, CB: 370A

5808 φιλονεικία, philoneikia, n. *dispute, strife.* S: *5379*, BAGD: 860D, CB: 370A

5809 φιλόνεικος, philoneikos, a. *contentious, quarrelsome.* S: *5380*, BAGD: 860D, CB: 370A

5810 φιλοξενία, philoxenia, n. *hospitality, entertainment of strangers.* S: *5381*, BAGD: 860D, CB: 370B

5811 φιλόξενος, philoxenos, a. *hospitable.* S: *5382*, BAGD: 860D, CB: 370B

5812 φιλοπρωτεύω, philoprōteuō, v. *to love to be first.* S: *5383*, BAGD: 860D, CB: 370A

5813 φίλος, philos, a. *friendly; (as noun) friend.* S: *5384*, BAGD: 861A, CB: 370A

5814 φιλοσοφία, philosophia, n. *philosophy, human wisdom.* S: *5385*, BAGD: 861B, CB: 370A

5815 φιλόσοφος, philosophos, n. *philosopher.* S: *5386*, BAGD: 861B, CB: 370B

5816 φιλόστοργος, philostorgos, a. *devoted, loving dearly.* S: *5387*, BAGD: 861C, CB: 370B

5817 φιλότεκνος, philoteknos, a. *loving one's children.* S: *5388*, BAGD: 861C, CB: 370B

5818 φιλοτιμέομαι, philotimeomai, v. *to have an ambition, aspire to a goal.* S: *5389*, BAGD: 861C, CB: 370B

5819 φιλοφρόνως, philophronōs, adv. *hospitably, in a friendly manner.* S: *5390*, BAGD: 861D, CB: 370A

5820 φιλόφρων, philophrōn, a. variant: *well disposed, friendly, kind.* S: *5391*, BAGD: 861D, CB: 370A

5821 φιμόω, phimoō, v. *to muzzle; to silence; (pass.) to be quiet.* S: *5392*, BAGD: 861D, CB: –

5822 φλαγελλόω, phlagelloō, v. variant: *to flog.* S: *5417**, BAGD: 862A, CB: –

5823 Φλέγων, Phlegōn, n.pr., "burning." *Phlegon.* S: *5393*, BAGD: 862A, CB: –

5824 φλογίζω, phlogizō, v. *to set on fire.* S: *5394*, BAGD: 862A, CB: –

5825 φλόξ, phlox, n. *flame, blaze.* S: *5395*, BAGD: 862A, CB: –

5826 φλυαρέω, phlyareō, v. *to gossip, talk nonsense.* S: *5396*, BAGD: 862B, CB: –

5827 φλύαρος, phlyaros, a. *gossipy.* S: *5397*, BAGD: 862B, CB: –

5828 φοβέομαι, phobeomai, v. *to fear, be afraid, alarmed; to reverence, respect, worship.* S: *5399*, BAGD: 862B, CB: 370B

5829 φοβερός, phoberos, a. *fearful, dreadful, terrible.* S: *5398*, BAGD: 862B, CB: 370B

5830 φοβέω, phobeō, v. variant: *to fear, be afraid, alarmed; to reverence, respect, worship.* S: *5399*, BAGD: 862B, CB: 370B

5831 φόβητρον, phobētron, n. *fearful event.* S: *5400*, BAGD: 863C, CB: 370B

5832 φόβος, phobos, n. *fear, terror; respect, reverence.* S: *5401*, BAGD: 863C, CB: 370B

5833 Φοίβη, Phoibē, n.pr., "radiant." *Phoebe.* S: *5402*, BAGD: 864A, CB: –

5834 Φοινίκη, Phoinikē, n.pr., "land of purple [dye]; *poss.* land of date palms." *Phoenicia.* S: *5403*, BAGD: 864A, CB: –

5835 Φοινίκισσα, Phoinikissa, n.pr., "of Phoenicia." variant: *Phoenician.* S: *4949**, BAGD: 794B cf. Συροφοινίκισσα, CB: –

5836 φοῖνιξ[1], phoinix[1], n. *palm tree, palm branch.* S: *5404*, BAGD: 864B, CB: 370B

5837 Φοῖνιξ[2], Phoinix[2], n.pr. *Phoenix.* S: *5405*, BAGD: 864B, CB: 370B

5838 φονεύς, phoneus, n. *murderer.* S: *5406*, BAGD: 864C, CB: –

5839 φονεύω, phoneuō, v. *to commit murder, kill.* S: *5407*, BAGD: 864C, CB: –

5840 φόνος, phonos, n. *murder, killing.* S: *5408*, BAGD: 864D, CB: 370B

5841 φορέω, phoreō, v. *to wear, bear.* S: *5409*, BAGD: 864D, CB: –

5842 φόρον, *phoron*, n. *forum.* S: *5410**, BAGD: 102B cf. 'Απ(πίου φόρον, CB: 370B cf. *-os*

5843 φόρος, *phoros*, n. *tax.* S: *5411*, BAGD: 865A, CB: 370B

5844 φορτίζω, *phortizō*, v. *to load down (with a burden); (pass.) to be burdened.* S: *5412*, BAGD: 865A, CB: 370B

5845 φορτίον, *phortion*, n. *burden, load, cargo.* S: *5413*, BAGD: 865A, CB: 370B

5846 φόρτος, *phortos*, n. variant: *cargo.* S: *5414*, BAGD: 865B, CB: 370B

5847 Φορτουνᾶτος, *Phortounatos*, n.pr., "fortunate." *Fortunatus.* S: *5415**, BAGD: 865B, CB: –

5848 φραγέλλιον, *phragellion*, n. *whip.* S: *5416*, BAGD: 865B, CB: 370B

5849 φραγελλόω, *phragelloō*, v. *to flog.* S: *5417*, BAGD: 865B, CB: 370B

5850 φραγμός, *phragmos*, n. *barrier, wall, country lane.* S: *5418*, BAGD: 865C, CB: 370B

5851 φράζω, *phrazō*, v. *to explain, interpret.* S: *5419*, BAGD: 865C, CB: –

5852 φράσσω, *phrassō*, v. *to shut; (pass.) to be stopped, silenced.* S: *5420*, BAGD: 865C, CB: 370B

5853 φρέαρ, *phrear*, n. *well, shaft, Abyss.* S: *5421*, BAGD: 865D, CB: 370C

5854 φρεναπατάω, *phrenapataō*, v. *to deceive.* S: *5422*, BAGD: 865D, CB: –

5855 φρεναπάτης, *phrenapatēs*, n. *deceiver.* S: *5423*, BAGD: 865D, CB: –

5856 φρήν, *phrēn*, n. *(pl.) thinking, understanding.* S: *5424*, BAGD: 865D, CB: 370C

5857 φρίσσω, *phrissō*, v. *to shudder.* S: *5425*, BAGD: 866A, CB: –

5858 φρονέω, *phroneō*, v. *to think, regard, hold an opinion; to set one's mind on; to have a (certain) attitude.* S: *5426*, BAGD: 866A, CB: 370C

5859 φρόνημα, *phronēma*, n. *mind.* S: *5427*, BAGD: 866C, CB: 370C

5860 φρόνησις, *phronēsis*, n. *wisdom, understanding.* S: *5428*, BAGD: 866C, CB: 370C

5861 φρόνιμος, *phronimos*, a. *wise, sensible, shrewd; (with 4123 + 4932) conceited.* S: *5429*, BAGD: 866D, CB: 370C

5862 φρονίμως, *phronimōs*, adv. *shrewdly, wisely.* S: *5430*, BAGD: 866D, CB: 370C

5863 φροντίζω, *phrontizō*, v. *to be careful, concerned.* S: *5431*, BAGD: 866D, CB: 370C

5864 φρουρέω, *phroureō*, v. *to guard; (pass.) to be held prisoner; to be shielded.* S: *5432*, BAGD: 867B, CB: 370C

5865 φρυάσσω, *phryassō*, v. *to rage, rave.* S: *5433*, BAGD: 867B, CB: –

5866 φρύγανον, *phryganon*, n. *brushwood, firewood.* S: *5434*, BAGD: 867B, CB: –

5867 Φρυγία, *Phrygia*, n.pr. *Phrygia.* S: *5435*, BAGD: 867C, CB: –

5868 φυγαδεύω, *phygadeuō*, v. variant: *(tr.) to cause to become a fugitive; (intr.) to be a fugitive, live in exile.* S: *150*, BAGD: 867C, CB: –

5869 Φύγελος, *Phygelos*, n.pr., "fugitive." *Phygelus.* S: *5436**, BAGD: 867C, CB: –

5870 φυγή, *phygē*, n. *flight, fleeing.* S: *5437*, BAGD: 867C, CB: 370C

5871 φυλακή, *phylakē*, n. *prison, jail, haunt; guard; watch (of the night).* S: *5438*, BAGD: 867D, CB: 370C

5872 φυλακίζω, *phylakizō*, v. *to imprison.* S: *5439*, BAGD: 868A, CB: 370C

5873 φυλακτήριον, *phylaktērion*, n. *phylactery.* S: *5440*, BAGD: 868A, CB: 370C

5874 φύλαξ, *phylax*, n. *guard, sentry.* S: *5441*, BAGD: 868B, CB: 370C

5875 φυλάσσω, *phylassō*, v. *to obey, keep; to guard, watch; to keep away from, abstain.* S: *5442*, BAGD: 868B, CB: 370C

5876 φυλή, *phylē*, n. *tribe; people, nation.* S: *5443*, BAGD: 868D, CB: 370C

5877 φύλλον, *phyllon*, n. *leaf.* S: *5444*, BAGD: 869A, CB: 370C

5878 φύραμα, *phyrama*, n. *lump (of clay), batch (of dough).* S: *5445*, BAGD: 869A, CB: 370C

5879 φυσικός, *physikos*, a. *pertaining to things of nature: natural, instinctive; (as noun) creatures of instinct.* S: *5446*, BAGD: 869B, CB: 370C

5880 φυσικῶς, *physikōs*, adv. *by instinct, naturally.* S: *5447*, BAGD: 869B, CB: 370C

5881 φυσιόω, *physioō*, v. *to puff up, inflate; (pass.) to be proud, arrogant.* S: *5448*, BAGD: 869B, CB: 370C

5882 φύσις, *physis*, n. *nature; natural state of being or characterists.* S: *5449*, BAGD: 869B, CB: 370C

5883 φυσίωσις, *physiōsis*, n. *arrogance, pride.* S: *5450*, BAGD: 870A, CB: –

5884 φυτεία, *phyteia*, n. *plant.* S: *5451*, BAGD: 870A, CB: 370C

5885 φυτεύω, *phyteuō*, v. *to plant.* S: *5452*, BAGD: 870A, CB: 370C

5886 φύω, *phyō*, v. *to grow up, come up.* S: *5453*, BAGD: 870B, CB: 370C

5887 φωλεός, *phōleos*, n. *hole (in the ground), den.* S: *5454*, BAGD: 870B, CB: –

5888 φωνέω, *phōneō*, v. *to call (out), summon.* S: *5455*, BAGD: 870B, CB: 370B

5889 φωνή, *phōnē*, n. *voice, sound, tone.* S: *5456*, BAGD: 870C, CB: 370B

5890 φῶς, *phōs*, n. *light; daylight; firelight.* S: *5457*, BAGD: 871D, CB: 370B

5891 φωστήρ, *phōstēr*, n. *star; brilliance, splendor.* S: *5458*, BAGD: 872C, CB: 370B

5892 φωσφόρος, *phōsphoros*, a. *light-bearing; (as noun) morning star.* S: *5459*, BAGD: 872D, CB: 370B

5893 φωτεινός, *phōteinos*, a. *full of light; bright.* S: *5460*, BAGD: 872D, CB: 370B

5894 φωτίζω, *phōtizō*, v. *to give light, shine; (pass.) to be enlightened, illuminated.* S: *5461*, BAGD: 872D, CB: 370B

5895 φωτισμός, *phōtismos*, n. *light, illumination.* S: *5462*, BAGD: 873C, CB: 370B

5896 χ, *ch*, letter. *letter of the Greek alphabet.* S: *150*, BAGD: –, CB: –

5897 χαίρω, *chairō*, v. *to rejoice, be glad, delighted; (as a greeting) Hail!, Greetings!*. S: *5463*, BAGD: 873B, CB: 345B

5898 χάλαζα, *chalaza*, n. *hail, hailstorm, hailstone*. S: *5464*, BAGD: 874B, CB: 345B

5899 χαλάω, *chalaō*, v. *to lower, let down*. S: *5465*, BAGD: 874B, CB: –

5900 Χαλδαῖος, *Chaldaios*, n.pr.g., "of Chaldea." *Chaldean*. S: *5466*, BAGD: 874C, CB: –

5901 χαλεπός, *chalepos*, a. *difficult, harsh; violent*. S: *5467*, BAGD: 874C, CB: 345B

5902 χαλιναγωγέω, *chalinagōgeō*, v. *to keep in check, keep a rein on one's mouth*. S: *5468*, BAGD: 874C, CB: –

5903 χαλινός, *chalinos*, n. *bit, bridle*. S: *5469*, BAGD: 874C, CB: –

5904 χαλινόω, *chalinoō*, v. variant: *to bridle, hold in check*. S: *5468**, BAGD: 874D, CB: –

5905 χάλκεος, *chalkeos*, a. *made of bronze*. S: *5470*, BAGD: 875B cf. -οῦς, CB: –

5906 χαλκεύς, *chalkeus*, n. *metalworker*. S: *5471*, BAGD: 874D, CB: 345B

5907 χαλκηδών, *chalkēdōn*, n. *chalcedony*. S: *5472*, BAGD: 874D, CB: 345B

5908 χαλκίον, *chalkion*, n. *kettle*. S: *5473*, BAGD: 874D, CB: 345B

5909 χαλκολίβανον, *chalkolibanon*, n. *burnished bronze, fine bronze*. S: *5474*, BAGD: 875A, CB: 345B

5910 χαλκός, *chalkos*, n. *copper, bronze; objects of copper*. S: *5475*, BAGD: 875A, CB: 345B

5911 χαλκοῦς, *chalkous*, a. *made of bronze*. S: *5470**, BAGD: 875B, CB: –

5912 χαμαί, *chamai*, adv. *to the ground, on the ground*. S: *5476*, BAGD: 875B, CB: –

5913 Χανάαν, *Chanaan*, n.pr., "land of purple *hence* merchant trader." *Canaan*. S: *5477**, BAGD: 875B, CB: –

5914 Χαναναῖος, *Chananaios*, a.pr.g., "of Canaan." *Canaanite*. S: *5478*, BAGD: 875B, CB: –

5915 χαρά, *chara*, n. *joy, rejoicing, happiness, gladness*. S: *5479*, BAGD: 875C, CB: 345B

5916 χάραγμα, *charagma*, n. *mark, stamp; image, idol*. S: *5480*, BAGD: 876A, CB: 345B

5917 χαρακτήρ, *charaktēr*, n. *exact representation, reproduction*. S: *5481*, BAGD: 876B, CB: 345C

5918 χάραξ, *charax*, n. *barricade, palisade*. S: *5482*, BAGD: 876B, CB: 345C

5919 χαρίζομαι, *charizomai*, v. *to give grace; to forgive, cancel (a debt); to grant; to hand over into custody*. S: *5483*, BAGD: 876C, CB: 345C

5920 χάριν, *charin*, c. or pp.*. *therefore, because of this, for this reason*. S: *5484*, BAGD: 877A, CB: 345C cf. -is

5921 χάρις, *charis*, n. *grace, favor, gift, benefit; credit; thanks, blessing*. S: *5485*, BAGD: 877B, CB: 345C

5922 χάρισμα, *charisma*, n. *gracious gift*. S: *5486*, BAGD: 878D, CB: 345C

5923 χαριτόω, *charitoō*, v. *to give graciously; (as noun) one highly favored*. S: *5487*, BAGD: 879A, CB: 345C

5924 Χαρράν, *Charran*, n.pr., *earlier* "mountaineer;" *perhaps* "sanctuary" IDB. *Haran*. S: *5488*, BAGD: 879A, CB: –

5925 χάρτης, *chartēs*, n. *(papyrus) paper*. S: *5489*, BAGD: 879B, CB: –

5926 χάσμα, *chasma*, n. *chasm*. S: *5490*, BAGD: 879B, CB: –

5927 χεῖλος, *cheilos*, n. *lip; edge (of a shoreline)*. S: *5491*, BAGD: 879C, CB: 345C

5928 χειμάζω, *cheimazō*, v. *(pass.) to be a battered in a storm*. S: *5492*, BAGD: 879C, CB: –

5929 χείμαρρος, *cheimarros*, n. *valley*. S: *5493*, BAGD: 879C, CB: –

5930 χειμών, *cheimōn*, n. *winter; stormy weather*. S: *5494*, BAGD: 879D, CB: –

5931 χείρ, *cheir*, n. *hand, area or portion of the hand; power, control*. S: *5495*, BAGD: 879D, CB: 345C

5932 χειραγωγέω, *cheiragōgeō*, v. *to lead by the hand*. S: *5496*, BAGD: 880D, CB: –

5933 χειραγωγός, *cheiragōgos*, n. *someone who leads by the hand, leader*. S: *5497*, BAGD: 880D, CB: –

5934 χειρόγραφον, *cheirographon*, n. *written code, record of debt*. S: *5498*, BAGD: 880D, CB: 345C

5935 χειροποίητος, *cheiropoiētos*, a. *hand-made, man-made*. S: *5499*, BAGD: 880D, CB: 345C

5936 χειροτονέω, *cheirotoneō*, v. *to appoint, choose*. S: *5500*, BAGD: 881A, CB: 345C

5937 χείρων, *cheirōn*, a. *worse (than); more severe than*. S: *5501*, BAGD: 881B, CB: –

5938 Χερούβ, *Cheroub*, n.pr. *(pl.) cherubim*. S: *5502**, BAGD: 881B, CB: 345C

5939 χήρα, *chēra*, n. *widow*. S: *5503*, BAGD: 881C, CB: 345C

5940 χθές, *chthes*, adv. variant: *yesterday*. S: *5504*, BAGD: 881D, CB: –

5941 χιλίαρχος, *chiliarchos*, n. *military officer, commander*. S: *5506*, BAGD: 881D, CB: 345C

5942 χιλιάς, *chilias*, n. *thousand*. S: *5505*, BAGD: 882A, CB: 345C

5943 χίλιοι, *chilioi*, a.num. *thousand*. S: *5507*, BAGD: 882A, CB: 345C

5944 Χίος, *Chios*, n.pr. *Kios*. S: *5508*, BAGD: 882B, CB: –

5945 χιτών, *chitōn*, n. *tunic, robe, clothing, undergarment*. S: *5509*, BAGD: 882B, CB: –

5946 χιών, *chiōn*, n. *snow*. S: *5510*, BAGD: 882B, CB: 345C

5947 χι''', *chi^'*, n.num. variant: *616*. S: *5516**, BAGD: 882D, CB: –

5948 χλαμύς, *chlamys*, n. *robe, cloak*. S: *5511*, BAGD: 882B, CB: –

5949 χλευάζω, *chleuazō*, v. *to sneer, mock, scoff*. S: *5512*, BAGD: 882C, CB: –

5950 χλιαρός, *chliaros*, a. *lukewarm*. S: *5513*, BAGD: 882C, CB: 345C

5951 Χλόη, *Chloē*, n.pr., "tender shoot." *Chloe*. S: *5514*, BAGD: 882C, CB: 346A

5952 χλωρός, *chlōros*, a. *light green; pale*. S: *5515*, BAGD: 882D, CB: 346A

5953 χξς, *chs*, n.num. variant: *666.* S: *5516**, BAGD: 882D, CB: –

5954 χοϊκός, *choikos*, a. *made of dust, of the earth.* S: *5517,* BAGD: 883A, CB: 346A

5955 χοῖνιξ, *choinix*, n. *(almost one liter or) quart.* S: *5518,* BAGD: 883B, CB: –

5956 χοῖρος, *choiros*, n. *pig.* S: *5519,* BAGD: 883B, CB: 346A

5957 χολάω, *cholaō*, v. *to be angry.* S: *5520,* BAGD: 883B, CB: –

5958 χολή, *cholē*, n. *gall, bile.* S: *5521,* BAGD: 883B, CB: 346A

5959 χόος, *choos*, n. *dust.* S: *5522,* BAGD: 884B, CB: 346A

5960 Χοραζίν, *Chorazin*, n.pr. *Korazin.* S: *5523,* BAGD: 883C, CB: –

5961 χορηγέω, *chorēgeō*, v. *to supply, provide.* S: *5524,* BAGD: 883D, CB: –

5962 χορός, *choros*, n. *dance; (pl.) dancing.* S: *5525,* BAGD: 883D, CB: –

5963 χορτάζω, *chortazō*, v. *to feed; (pass.) to be filled to satisfaction, eat one's fill.* S: *5526,* BAGD: 883D, CB: 346A

5964 χόρτασμα, *chortasma*, n. *food.* S: *5527,* BAGD: 884A, CB: 346A

5965 χόρτος, *chortos*, n. *grass, plant.* S: *5528,* BAGD: 884A, CB: 346A

5966 Χουζᾶς, *Chouzas*, n.pr., "little judge." *Cuza.* S: *5529,* BAGD: 884B, CB: –

5967 χοῦς, *chous*, n. *dust.* S: *5522**, BAGD: 884B, CB: 346A

5968 χράομαι, *chraomai*, v. *to make use of, use; to do, act, proceed.* S: *5530,* BAGD: 884B, CB: 346A

5969 χράω, *chraō*, v. variant: *to lend.* S: *5531,* BAGD: 433A cf. κίχρημι, CB: 346A cf. *-omai*

5970 χρεία, *chreia*, n. *need, necessity.* S: *5532,* BAGD: 884D, CB: 346A

5971 χρεοφειλέτης, *chreopheiletēs*, n. *debtor.* S: *5533,* BAGD: 885B, CB: –

5972 χρεωφειλέτης, *chreōpheiletēs*, n. variant: *debtor.* S: *5533,* BAGD: 885B, CB: –

5973 χρή, *chrē*, pt. or v.imper. *it should, it is necessary.* S: *5534,* BAGD: 885B, CB: 346A

5974 χρήζω, *chrēzō*, v. *to need, have need of.* S: *5535,* BAGD: 885B, CB: 346A

5975 χρῆμα, *chrēma*, n. *money; (pl.) the rich.* S: *5536,* BAGD: 885C, CB: 346A

5976 χρηματίζω, *chrēmatizō*, v. *to warn; (pass.) to bear a name; to be warned, told about, revealed to.* S: *5537,* BAGD: 885C, CB: 346A

5977 χρηματισμός, *chrēmatismos*, n. *proclamation or answer from God.* S: *5538,* BAGD: 885D, CB: 346A

5978 χρήσιμος, *chrēsimos*, n. *pertaining to value, usefulness, advantage.* S: *5539,* BAGD: 885D, CB: –

5979 χρῆσις, *chrēsis*, n. *relations, functions.* S: *5540,* BAGD: 885D, CB: –

5980 χρηστεύομαι, *chrēsteuomai*, v. *to be kind.* S: *5541,* BAGD: 886A, CB: 346A

5981 χρηστολογία, *chrēstologia*, n. *smooth talk, attractive speech.* S: *5542,* BAGD: 886A, CB: 346A

5982 χρηστός, *chrēstos*, a. *easy, good; kind, loving, benevolent.* S: *5543,* BAGD: 886A, CB: 346A

5983 χρηστότης, *chrēstotēs*, n. *kindness, goodness.* S: *5544,* BAGD: 886B, CB: 346A

5984 χρῖσμα, *chrisma*, n. *anointing.* S: *5545**, BAGD: 886C, CB: 346A

5985 Χριστιανός, *Christianos*, n.pr.g., "of Christ." *Christian.* S: *5546,* BAGD: 886C, CB: 346A

5986 Χριστός, *Christos*, n.pr. *Christ, Anointed One, Messiah.* S: *5547,* BAGD: 886D, CB: 346A

5987 χρίω, *chriō*, v. *to anoint.* S: *5548,* BAGD: 887C, CB: 346A

5988 χρονίζω, *chronizō*, v. *to take a long time, delay; to stay a long time.* S: *5549,* BAGD: 887D, CB: 346B

5989 χρόνος, *chronos*, n. *time, period of time.* S: *5550,* BAGD: 887D, CB: 346B

5990 χρονοτριβέω, *chronotribeō*, v. *to spend time.* S: *5551,* BAGD: 888C, CB: 346B

5991 χρύσεος, *chryseos*, a. *made of gold.* S: *5552,* BAGD: 888D cf. -οῦς, CB: 346B cf. *-ous*

5992 χρυσίον, *chrysion*, n. *gold; gold jewelry or coins.* S: *5553,* BAGD: 888C, CB: 346B

5993 χρυσοδακτύλιος, *chrysodaktylios*, a. *having or wearing a gold ring.* S: *5554,* BAGD: 888C, CB: –

5994 χρυσόλιθος, *chrysolithos*, n. *chrysolite.* S: *5555,* BAGD: 888C, CB: 346B

5995 χρυσόπρασος, *chrysoprasos*, n. *chrysoprase.* S: *5556,* BAGD: 888D, CB: 346B

5996 χρυσός, *chrysos*, n. *gold.* S: *5557,* BAGD: 888D, CB: 346B

5997 χρυσοῦς, *chrysous*, a. *made of gold.* S: *5552**, BAGD: 888D, CB: 346B

5998 χρυσόω, *chrysoō*, v. *(pass.) to be adorned with gold.* S: *5558,* BAGD: 889A, CB: 346B

5999 χρώς, *chrōs*, n. *skin, surface of the body.* S: *5559,* BAGD: 889A, CB: –

6000 χωλός, *chōlos*, a. *lame, crippled.* S: *5560,* BAGD: 889A, CB: 346A

6001 χώρα, *chōra*, n. *country, land, region; countryside, field.* S: *5561,* BAGD: 889B, CB: 346A

6002 Χωραζίν, *Chōrazin*, n.pr. variant: *Korazin.* S: *5523**, BAGD: 883C cf. Χοραζίν, CB: –

6003 χωρέω, *chōreō*, v. *to go, come; to accept; to make room, have room.* S: *5562,* BAGD: 889C, CB: 346A

6004 χωρίζω, *chōrizō*, v. *to divide, separate, leave; (pass.) to be separated from, set apart.* S: *5563,* BAGD: 890A, CB: 346A

6005 χωρίον, *chōrion*, n. *place, parcel of land, field.* S: *5564,* BAGD: 890B, CB: 346A

6006 χωρίς, *chōris*, adv. *(as adv.) by itself, separately; (as pp.*) without, besides, apart from, independent from.* S: *5565,* BAGD: 890C, CB: 346A

6007 χωρισμός, *chōrismos*, n. variant: *division.* S: *150,* BAGD: 891A, CB: –

6008 χῶρος, *chōros*, n. *northwest.* S: *5566,* BAGD: 891C, CB: 346A

6009 ψ, *ps*, letter. *letter of the Greek alphabet.* S: *150,* BAGD: –, CB: –

6010 ψάλλω, *psallō*, v. *to sing hymns, sing songs of praise.* S: 5567, BAGD: 891A, CB: 373B

6011 ψαλμός, *psalmos*, n. *Psalms (book of or section of OT); psalm, hymn of praise.* S: 5568, BAGD: 891B, CB: 373C

6012 ψευδάδελφος, *pseudadelphos*, n. *false brother.* S: 5569, BAGD: 891B, CB: 373C

6013 ψευδαπόστολος, *pseudapostolos*, n. *false apostle.* S: 5570, BAGD: 891B, CB: 373C

6014 ψευδής, *pseudēs*, a. *false, lying; (as noun) liar.* S: 5571, BAGD: 891C, CB: 373C

6015 ψευδοδιδάσκαλος, *pseudodidaskalos*, n. *false teacher.* S: 5572, BAGD: 891C, CB: 373C

6016 ψευδολόγος, *pseudologos*, a. *false of speech; (as noun) liar.* S: 5573, BAGD: 891D, CB: 373C

6017 ψεύδομαι, *pseudomai*, v. *to lie, speak untruths.* S: 5574, BAGD: 891D, CB: 373C

6018 ψευδομαρτυρέω, *pseudomartyreō*, v. *to give false testimony.* S: 5576, BAGD: 891D, CB: 373C

6019 ψευδομαρτυρία, *pseudomartyria*, n. *false testimony.* S: 5577, BAGD: 892A, CB: 373C

6020 ψευδόμαρτυς, *pseudomartys*, n. *false witness, one who gives false testimony.* S: 5575*, BAGD: 892A, CB: 373C

6021 ψευδοπροφήτης, *pseudoprophētēs*, n. *false prophet.* S: 5578, BAGD: 892A, CB: 373C

6022 ψεῦδος, *pseudos*, n. *lie, falsehood, deception.* S: 5579, BAGD: 892B, CB: 373C

6023 ψευδόχριστος, *pseudochristos*, n. *(pl.) false Christs.* S: 5580, BAGD: 892B, CB: 373C

6024 ψευδώνυμος, *pseudōnymos*, a. *falsely called or identified.* S: 5581, BAGD: 892C, CB: 373C

6025 ψεῦσμα, *pseusma*, n. *falsehood, untruth.* S: 5582, BAGD: 892C, CB: –

6026 ψεύστης, *pseustēs*, n. *liar.* S: 5583, BAGD: 892C, CB: 373C

6027 ψηλαφάω, *psēlaphaō*, v. *to touch, handle.* S: 5584, BAGD: 892C, CB: –

6028 ψηφίζω, *psēphizō*, v. *to calculate; to estimate.* S: 5585, BAGD: 892D, CB: –

6029 ψῆφος, *psēphos*, n. *stone, vote (cast by stones).* S: 5586, BAGD: 892D, CB: 373C

6030 ψιθυρισμός, *psithyrismos*, n. *whispering gossip.* S: 5587, BAGD: 892D, CB: 373C

6031 ψιθυριστής, *psithyristēs*, n. *gossip, whisperer.* S: 5588, BAGD: 893A, CB: 373C

6032 ψίξ, *psix*, n. variant: *bit, crumb.* S: 5589*, BAGD: 893A, CB: –

6033 ψιχίον, *psichion*, n. *crumb, very small piece.* S: 5589, BAGD: 893A, CB: –

6034 ψυχή, *psychē*, n. *life, soul; heart, mind; a person.* S: 5590, BAGD: 893B, CB: 373C

6035 ψυχικός, *psychikos*, a. *pertaining to the natural state: physical, unspiritual, without the Spirit.* S: 5591, BAGD: 894B, CB: 373C

6036 ψῦχος, *psychos*, n. *cold.* S: 5592*, BAGD: 894C, CB: 373C

6037 ψυχρός, *psychros*, a. *cold.* S: 5593, BAGD: 894C, CB: 373C

6038 ψύχω, *psychō*, v. *(pass.) to grow cold.* S: 5594, BAGD: 894D, CB: 373C

6039 ψωμίζω, *psōmizō*, v. *to feed; to give to the poor.* S: 5595, BAGD: 894D, CB: –

6040 ψωμίον, *psōmion*, n. *piece of bread.* S: 5596, BAGD: 894D, CB: –

6041 ψώχω, *psōchō*, v. *to rub.* S: 5597, BAGD: 894D, CB: –

6042 Ὦ¹, *Ō¹*, letter; n.pr. *letter of the Greek alphabet; Omega.* S: 5598, BAGD: 895A, CB: –

6043 ὦ², *ō²*, pt.interj. *O!, Oh!.* S: 5599, BAGD: 895A, CB: –

6044 Ὠβήδ, *Ōbēd*, n.pr., "servant" *or* "worshiper." variant: *Obed.* S: 5601, BAGD: 385B cf. Ἰωβήδ, CB: –

6045 ὧδε, *hōde*, adv. *here.* S: 5602, BAGD: 895B, CB: –

6046 ᾠδή, *ōdē*, n. *song.* S: 5603, BAGD: 895C, CB: 366B

6047 ὠδίν, *ōdin*, n. *labor, birth pain; agony (of death).* S: 5604, BAGD: 895C, CB: 366B

6048 ὠδίνω, *ōdinō*, v. *to suffer the pains of childbirth.* S: 5605, BAGD: 895D, CB: 366B

6049 ὦμος, *ōmos*, n. *(pl.) shoulders.* S: 5606, BAGD: 895D, CB: –

6050 ὠνέομαι, *ōneomai*, v. *to buy.* S: 5608, BAGD: 895D, CB: 366C

6051 ᾠόν, *ōon*, n. *egg.* S: 5609*, BAGD: 896A, CB: –

6052 ὥρα, *hōra*, n. *hour, portion of time, while, moment.* S: 5610, BAGD: 896A, CB: 357A

6053 ὡραῖος, *hōraios*, a. *beautiful.* S: 5611, BAGD: 896D, CB: 357A

6054 ὠρύομαι, *ōryomai*, v. *to roar.* S: 5612, BAGD: 897A, CB: –

6055 ὡς, *hōs*, pt. & c. *as, that, how, about, when; like, as.* S: 5613, BAGD: 897A, CB: 357B

6056 ὡσάν, *hōsan*, rel.adv. + pt. variant: *as if, as it were, so to speak.* S: 5613 + 302, BAGD: 899A, CB: –

6057 ὡσαννά, *hōsanna*, I.[v.+pt.]. *Hosanna! (exclamation of praise, originally "Save [us]!").* S: 5614, BAGD: 899A, CB: 357B

6058 ὡσαύτως, *hōsautōs*, adv. *in the same way, so also, likewise, similarly.* S: 5615, BAGD: 899B, CB: –

6059 ὡσεί, *hōsei*, pt.comp. *like, as; about (an approximation).* S: 5616, BAGD: 899B, CB: –

6060 Ὠσηέ, *Hōsēe*, n.pr., "salvation." *Hosea.* S: 5617, BAGD: 899C, CB: –

6061 ὥσπερ, *hōsper*, pt.comp. *as, just as; like.* S: 5618, BAGD: 899C, CB: 357B

6062 ὡσπερεί, *hōsperei*, pt.comp. *like, as though, as it were.* S: 5619, BAGD: 899D, CB: –

6063 ὥστε, *hōste*, pt. *for this reason, therefore, so; so that, resulting in; to, for the purpose of.* S: 5620, BAGD: 899D, CB: –

6064 ὠτάριον, *ōtarion*, n. *ear.* S: 5621*, BAGD: 900B, CB: –

6065 ὠτίον, *ōtion*, n. *ear.* S: 5621, BAGD: 900B, CB: –

6066 ὠφέλεια, *ōpheleia*, n. *value, advantage.* S: 5622, BAGD: 900B, CB: 367A

6067 ὠφελέω, *ōpheleō*, v. *to be of good use; to have value; to help; to devote (as a gift) to God.* S: 5623, BAGD: 900C, CB: 367A

6068 ὠφέλιμος, *ōphelimos*, a. *valuable, useful, profitable.* S: 5624, BAGD: 900D, CB: –

We want to hear from you. Please send your comments about this book to us in care of the address below. Thank you.

GRAND RAPIDS, MICHIGAN 49530

w w w . z o n d e r v a n . c o m